WINE ENTHUSIAST
MAGAZINE

Essential BUYING GUIDE 2009

RUNNING PRESS
PHILADELPHIA • LONDON

9 8 7 6 5 4 3 2 1
Digit on the right indicates the number of this printing

Library of Congress Control Number: 2008933723

ISBN: 978-0-7624-3283-7

Cover design by Bill Jones
Interior design by Jan Greenberg, Bill Jones, and Anita Gross
Edited by Diana von Glahn
Typography: Adobe Garamond and Helvetica Neue

Running Press Book Publishers
2300 Chestnut Street
Philadelphia, Pennsylvania 19103-4371

Visit us on the web!
www.runningpresscooks.com
www.wineenthusiast.com/magazine

PHOTOGRAPHY CREDITS

Cover photo: © Japack Company/CORBIS
p.1: © Susie M. Eising Food Photography/Stockfood America
p.3 top: © Ted Stefanski/Cephas, bottom: © Kevin Judd/Cephas
p.4: © Nigel Blythe/Cephas
p.5: Courtesy of *Wine Enthusiast Magazine*
p.7: © Mick Rock/Cephas
p.8: © Mick Rock/Cephas
pp.10-11 all: Courtesy of *Wine Enthusiast Magazine*
p.12: © Louis de Rohan/Cephas
p.43: © Kevin Judd/Cephas
p.121: © Walter Geiersperger/Cephas
p.140: © Steven Morris/Cephas
p.179: © Mick Rock/Cephas
p.266: © Mick Rock/Cephas
p.288: © Mike Newton/Cephas
p.391: © Kevin Judd/Cephas
p.417: © Mick Rock/Cephas
p.440: © Juan Espi/Cephas
p.466: © Mick Rock/Cephas
p.537: © Ted Stefanski/Cephas
p.539: © Mick Rock/Cephas
p.540: © Clay McLachlan/Cephas

Contents

Foreword

It sounds like a dream come true for many wine enthusiasts: making a living by sipping and evaluating the greatest wines from all over the world. Yes, it's true that members of our tasting panel sample thousands of wines every year. But of course, there is a great deal of work involved in actually tasting wine for review purposes (see How We Taste and Rate on page 8). But even given all the procedures and pressures, there is sublime pleasure to be had in trying new wines, whether the wine is a new grape variety, was produced in an unfamiliar region, or is just a new vintage of an old favorite. Every time we uncork, there is a new experience to be had. It's almost always pleasurable at some level; sometimes, it's simply sublime. And that brings us to this book.

The *Wine Enthusiast Essential Buying Guide 2009* includes more than 40,000 ratings and reviews of wines, the best that our tasting panel has sampled since we established the tasting and review program in 1999. We've arranged the reviews so that the book is as easy to use as possible—divided according to countries and alphabetized by producer name. Three other crucial bits of information are presented as prominently as possible: the quality score (based on the *Wine Enthusiast* 100-point scale), the vintage, and the grape variety, wherever possible. Experienced wine enthusiasts can go straight to the producing countries and producers whose wines they've enjoyed in the past or have currently cellared to check scores. Novices will find this guide an indispensable tool to peruse before treks to the retail store. The *Wine Enthusiast Essential Buying Guide 2009* makes it easy to find values, track the performance of certain producers' wines over time, and get an idea of the general characteristics of wines from a certain region.

It's all about enjoyment: drinking what you like while continuing to experiment, trying some new wines, and taking advantage of the charm and power of wine. It's mind-boggling, the diversity that variables of grape variety, climate, soil, vineyard technique, and winemaking skill can produce.

We also encourage you to check us out online at www.wineenthusiast.com/magazine for our continually updated wine database, as well as the world's best vintage chart. It is the ideal companion to this book, providing you with everything you need to make wise buying decisions when at the retail store or restaurant.

Cheers,

Adam Strum
Publisher and Editor-in-Chief
Wine Enthusiast Magazine

Wine-Buying Strategies

SMART WINE BUYING TAKES PLANNING

In America, most wine is consumed the night it is bought. Whether it is a bottle of Opus One for a dinner party or a box of Franzia White Zin to improve Tuesday-night leftovers, it's often opened immediately with little thought.

Unfortunately, buying wine that way sacrifices a great deal of the pleasure of wine, and rarely provides the best deal. Pretentious though it may seem, it's worthwhile to develop a strategy for acquiring wine. It's both fun and rewarding.

There are a number of reasons for planning your purchases, but they almost all lead to having a supply on hand, ideally in a wine cellar or refrigerated storage cabinet. The most obvious advantage is that some wines improve with age, and even if you can afford to buy properly aged vintages, they may be very difficult to find. Buying young saves money, but also means that you'll be able to enjoy the wine when it's at its peak.

Of course, most wine doesn't improve with age, but if you're reading this, you most likely appreciate the wine that does. Most better reds certainly improve with a few years, and though many of today's wines are made to reach their peaks within a decade, most are released when they're only two or three years old. Hold them for even three or four years and they will improve tremendously. But if you buy wines at that peak stage, you will have to pay a premium.

Serious collectors, of course, often see wine as an investment that can be sold at an appreciated value in the future. Others see the real value in having far better wines to drink themselves.

Of course, some wines just keep on improving for decades: top Bordeaux, Burgundies, Napa Cabs, Barolos, and many Spanish wines fall in this category. It's not wise to drink them when they're only a few years old; if you do, they probably won't be much better than ordinary wines. Some people even develop a taste for old wines that many would consider past their prime, while others enjoy learning what happens to wines as they age.

You can obviously save a great deal when you cellar wines yourself, but even cursory planning can also save a lot of money. Buying wine on sale can be very rewarding. Almost every retailer offers at least 10 percent off for full cases, sometimes mixed cases, and that's like getting more than a bottle free with each case.

Some wines are even sold as futures. This primarily applies to top labels, but even some relatively modest wineries sell wine this way if it's in short supply. For example, after disastrous fires and earthquakes in wine warehouses, some producers in California offered attractive futures for their wines to maintain cash flow.

When all is said and done, however, perhaps the best reason for planning ahead is to have the right wine on hand when you want it. It's awful nice to be able to go into your cellar and grab a perfectly aged bottle that's the perfect match for dinner, or to take a special treat to a celebration without a trip to the wine store. In many areas, finding a special bottle could require ordering ahead, or a long drive to a state-controlled liquor store that is open during limited hours.

The only downside to having good wines on hand is a mixed one: You're more likely to enjoy it!

WHAT DO YOU LIKE?

Of course, it doesn't make much sense to have a cellar full of wine you don't like. Wine-buying guides provide good reference points for wines you've never tasted, but you'll probably want to buy only one bottle of a wine you haven't tasted instead of many, even if the producer has a good reputation or a well-known reviewer has awarded it a high score. Reputation and wine scores should be starting points, since people's tastes differ widely. Fortunately, there are a lot of ways to help guide your purchases.

One way to improve your odds is to learn which reviewers have tastes that mirror yours. For example, if you love massive Cabernets, which are extremely full bodied and high in alcohol, find which critics rave over them. Also learn which reviewers prefer more restrained wines that might be more suitable for enjoying with food.

All that said, the best way to learn what you like is by tasting wine. Take wine-tasting classes at wine stores or local colleges and adult schools. Attend wine events where you can taste a wide variety of wines. Try wines by the glass when available at restaurants and bars. Wine clubs and tasting parties with friends can be both great fun and very informative. Take recommendations from friends, but be sure to consider whether their tastes are similar to yours. Whatever you do, pay attention and take notes. And don't forget to spit (when you're at a tasting, not at a restaurant!)—otherwise, all the wine will taste great!

You'll almost always find some surprises, particularly with some inexpensive wines. Most important, accept your own tastes. Drinking wine isn't about forcing yourself to learn to like wines that don't suit you. Remember, above all of the terminology and technicality, the most important thing about wine should be the ability to get the most out of every glass, so that you actually enjoy what you're drinking. Drink—and buy—what you like and don't apologize or try to impress others.

MAKING THE PURCHASE

Once you've decided what wine you like, buy more of it. Although wine choices were once very limited, and still are in some states, in most areas, choices have multiplied, and expand daily as restrictive laws fall to lawsuits or change to reflect today's attitudes and to increase tax revenues.

The old-time wine store—and its modern counterpart—remains one of the best places to buy wines. Clerks in these stores tend to be knowledgeable about wine, and if you become a regular, they can learn more about your tastes and steer you toward wines you'll likely enjoy. Many shops now offer classes, wine tastings, and other events, and some will even order special wines and ship or deliver them to your home.

In many states, you can buy wine in supermarkets, giant discounters, club stores, discount wine and liquor outlets, and even convenience stores. And they're not just selling basic wine, either. Costco has emerged as one of the nation's largest retailers of fine wines including some that cost hundreds of dollars a bottle.

With barriers to interstate shipping of wine falling, direct purchases from wineries are making more and more sense. While it hardly pays to buy widely distributed wines direct from the wineries and pay shipping when you can buy the same wine at a neighborhood store many times for less, often the only place to get some wines is from the winery. This includes special bottles from big producers, including limited production bottlings and library wines.

For these wines, the most fun of all is to visit the winery, where you can taste before buying. As wineries spring up all over the country, that may not require a trip to Napa Valley. Many wineries also sell directly over the Internet, by brochure or mail, or by phone, and many independent firms sell wines from many producers as well.

If you're especially fond of certain wineries' wines, it can be fun to sign up for their wine clubs. They typically send a few bottles to members a few times a year, generally at a discount, often including wines not available except to club members or at the winery. Most wine clubs have special events, too, often at the wineries but some in other locations.

Whatever you do, don't forget the wine once it's in your cellar. While some wines improve with age, most don't.

How We Taste and Rate

Although *Wine Enthusiast* was first published in 1988, the magazine didn't regularly publish its own wine reviews until 1999. Beginning that year, the magazine's *Buying Guide* began to include the reviews of its own editors and other qualified tasters. The *Wine Enthusiast Essential Buying Guide 2009* focuses on new releases and selected older wines.

Today, approximately 500 wine reviews are included in each issue of *Wine Enthusiast Magazine.* Each review contains a score on the 100-point scale, the full name of the wine, its suggested national retail price, and a tasting note. If a price cannot be confirmed, $NA (not available) will be printed. Prices are for 750 ml bottles unless otherwise indicated.

This compilation contains all of the wines formally reviewed by the *Wine Enthusiast* tasting panel from its inception through the final issue of 2006.

Regular contributors to our Buying Guide include Tasting Director/Senior Editor Joe Czerwinski, Senior Editor Susan Kostrzewa, and Contributing Editor Michael Schachner in New York; European Editor Roger Voss in Bordeaux; Italian Editor Monica Larner in Rome; West Coast Editor Steve Heimoff in California; and Contributing Editor Paul Gregutt in Seattle. Past contributors whose initials may appear in this guide include former Tasting Directors Mark Mazur and Chuck Simeone, former Senior Editor Daryna Tobey, former Tasting Coordinator Kristen Fogg, Contributing Editor Jeff Morgan, and former contributing tasters Martin Neschis and Larry Walker.

If a wine was evaluated by a single reviewer, that taster's initials appear following the note. When no initials appear, the wine was evaluated by two or more reviewers and the score and tasting note reflect the input of all tasters.

TASTING METHODOLOGY AND GOALS

Tastings are conducted individually or in a group setting and performed blind or in accordance with accepted industry practices (it is not possible to taste the wines blind when visiting producers, for example). When wines are tasted in our offices or for specific tasting features, they are tasted blind, in flights defined by grape variety, place of origin, and vintage.

We assess quality by examining five distinct characteristics: appearance, bouquet, flavor, mouthfeel, and finish. Above all, our tasters are looking for balance and harmony, with additional consideration given for ability to improve with age. Price is not a factor in assigning scores to wines. When possible, wines considered flawed or uncustomary are retasted.

ABOUT THE SCORES

Ratings reflect what our editors felt about a particular wine. Beyond the rating, we encourage you to read the accompanying tasting note to learn about a wine's special characteristics.

Classic 98–100:	The pinnacle of quality.
Superb 94–97:	A great achievement.
Excellent 90–93:	Highly recommended.
Very Good 87–89:	Often good value; well recommended.
Good 83–86:	Suitable for everyday consumption; often good value.
Acceptable 80–82:	Can be employed in casual, less-critical circumstances.

Wines receiving a rating below 80 are not reviewed.

SPECIAL DESIGNATIONS

Best Buys are wines that offer a high level of quality in relation to price. There are no specific guidelines or formulae for determining Best Buys, but they are generally priced below $15.

Editors' Choice wines are those that offer excellent quality at a price above our Best Buy range, or a wine at any price with unique qualities that merit special attention.

Cellar Selections are wines deemed highly collectible and/or requiring time in a temperature-controlled wine cellar to reach their maximum potential. A Cellar Selection designation does not mean that a wine must be stored to be enjoyed, but that cellaring will probably result in a more enjoyable bottle. In general, an optimum time for cellaring will be indicated.

Contributors

Tasting Director and Senior Editor Joe Czerwinski joined *Wine Enthusiast Magazine* in 1999 as an associate editor. In addition to managing the entire tasting and review program, he reviews wines from France, Germany, Australia, and New Zealand.

West Coast Editor Steve Heimoff was born in New York City and moved to California to attend grad school. He quickly discovered wine, which became his passion. He has been with *Wine Enthusiast Magazine* for 14 years and reviews virtually all of the California wines. His book, *A Wine Journey along the Russian River*, was published in 2005 by University of California Press. His most recent book was published in Fall 2007.

Susan Kostrzewa is a senior editor and Web editor for *Wine Enthusiast magazine* and *Wine Enthusiast* online. Kostrzewa has written and edited wine, food and travel stories for the past 11 years, and in addition to editing *Wine Enthusiast*'s print magazine and online publication, currently reviews wines from South Africa, Greece, Hungary, Israel, and all the U.S., except California and Washington.

European Editor Roger Voss is a wine and food author and journalist. He has been writing on wine and food for the past 26 years. His books include *France: A Feast of Food and Wine*; *The Wines of the Loire*; *Pocket Guide to the Wines of the Loire, Alsace, and the Rhône;* and *Fortified Wines.* He is based in Bordeaux, France, from where he reviews the wines of Austria, France, and Portugal.

Monica Larner has lived in Italy on and off for the past 16 years and is *Wine Enthusiast Magazine*'s Italian Editor. Based in Rome, she is a member of the Italian Association of Sommeliers and has published three books on her adopted home. When not in Europe, she can be found with pruning shears in hand on the family-run Larner Vineyard in Santa Barbara Country, California.

In addition to reviewing Pacific Northwest wines for *Wine Enthusiast Magazine*, Seattle-based **Contributing Editor Paul Gregutt** writes on wine for the *Seattle Times*, the *Yakima Herald-Republic*, the *Walla Walla Union-Bulletin*, and *Pacific Northwest* magazine. He has written two editions of *Northwest Wines*, and his book, *Washington Wines and Wineries*, was published by the University of California Press in 2007.

Michael Schachner is a New York-based journalist specializing in wine, food, and travel. His articles appear regularly in *Wine Enthusiast Magazine*, for which he is a contributing editor and a member of the magazine's tasting panel. In addition, he is a wine consultant and professional speaker. His areas of wine expertise include Spain, Italy, and South America.

Argentina

Argentina features a vaunted winemaking history that began some five hundred years ago when Spanish missionaries first arrived and planted vines. But it wasn't until about two hundred years ago that Argentina developed a commercial wine industry, largely centered in the province of Mendoza, located about four hundred miles directly west of Buenos Aires.

For all intents and purposes, Argentina's wine industry was until fairly recently geared toward domestic consumption. Nineteenth and early twentieth-century immigrants from Spain and Italy had a huge thirst for wine, and the vineyards that they planted along the western edge of the country, where the climate is dry, the temperatures are warm, and there's plenty of water available from the mighty Andes, produced copious amounts of varietal and blended reds that the Argentine population drank with nary a complaint.

Harvesting grapes in a vineyard of Peñaflor, Mendoza, Argentina

To a large extent, that's still the case. Argentineans remain the primary consumers of their own wines. But as the global wine market began to take shape in the latter half of the twentieth century, Argentina refocused its winemaking and marketing efforts to highlight exports. Today, there are approximately one hundred wineries throughout Argentina that are sending their wines overseas. Mendoza, with its numerous subzones, remains front and center among wine regions, with areas like San Rafael, La Rioja, San Juan, Salta, and Cafayate vying for second chair.

Due to a pervasive hot, dry climate, it's safe to say that red wines outperform white wines in almost all parts of Argentina; although the higher one goes into the Andes, the cooler it gets and the crisper the white wines become. And with such deep Italian and Spanish roots running through the country's people, that makes sense.

Malbec, which was brought to Argentina from France some 150 years ago, has emerged as Argentina's signature grape. It is grown throughout the country, and while it varies in style, one can safely call it fruity, aromatic, and lush. In flatter, warmer vineyards, Malbec can be soft and simple, an easy wine for everyday drinking and blending. But if taken into the foothills of the mountains or grown in old vineyards, it can be a wine of immense character.

Joining Malbec on the red roster is Cabernet Sauvignon, which is flavorful and serious when coming from top wineries like Terrazas de Los Andes, Catena Zapata, Norton, Cobos, or Chakana, to name several. Picked ripe, like in California and aged mostly in French oak barrels, Argentinean Cabernet has what it takes.

Other red grapes one frequently encounters are Bonarda and Sangiovese, both of which were brought over from Italy, as well as Merlot, Syrah, Tempranillo, and even some Pinot Noir.

Among white wines, one of Argentina's best and most distinctive offerings is Torrontès, an import from Galicia in Spain. Floral and occasionally exotic in scent and taste, Torrontès seems to do best in the more northern Salta region, where there's higher humidity and more rain than in Mendoza.

And as stated before, the Andean foothills are proving to be the prime spot for Chardonnay. At elevations of more than 3,000 feet above sea level, warm days and cool nights yield naturally fresh and properly acidic wines. Flavors of pineapple, green banana, and other tropical fruits are common among Argentina's modern-day Chardonnays.

[Ñ]

[ñ] 2003 Malbec (Uco Valley) $30. 86 —*M.S. (12/1/2006)*

1919

1919 2004 Cabernet Sauvignon (Mendoza) $10. 83 —*M.S. (8/1/2006)*

1919 2004 Malbec (Mendoza) $10. 85 Best Buy —*M.S. (8/1/2006)*

1919 2004 Syrah (Mendoza) $10. 81 —*M.S. (11/1/2006)*

ACHÁVAL-FERRER

Achaval-Ferrer 2004 Finca Altamira Malbec (La Consulta) $112. Violet in color and broad as the Argentinean pampas, this single-vineyard Malbec is a powder keg of power. The nose oozes dark fruity and fancy new oak,while the palate is loaded with boysenberry, cassis and black olive. It's a little linear and tight, but its purity is beyond reproach. 92 —*M.S. (2/1/2007)*

Achával-Ferrer 2002 Finca Altamira Malbec (Mendoza) $85. 88 —*M.S. (7/1/2005)*

Achával-Ferrer 2000 Finca Altamira Malbec (Mendoza) $85. 86 —*M.S. (5/1/2003)*

Achaval-Ferrer 2004 Finca Bella Vista Malbec (Perdriel) $112. Like its cousins, the Bella Vista vineyard bottling is dark as night. But this wine shows more blueberry and sage on the nose, while the palate is a touch funky as it unloads black fruit infused with the essence of smoked meat and fennel. Very acidic and tannic, but with food it will show nicely. 90 —*M.S. (2/1/2007)*

Achaval-Ferrer 2004 Finca Mirador Malbec (Medrano) $112. Lush up front and full of cinnamon, sandalwood and blackberry aromas. The palate offers up plum, cassis and blackberry, and overall this wine seems to be the most fruit-forward and intense of Achaval Ferrer's three single-vineyard ultrapremium Malbecs. It's literally a bonanza of dark fruit and flesh. 90 —*M.S. (2/1/2007)*

Achaval-Ferrer 2005 Malbec (Mendoza) $26. This reviewer's most vexing Argentine property strikes again with its first-ever appellation-style Mendoza Malbec. To me the wine is mildly bretty and staunch, with unrefined, bulky flavors, tartness at the core, and a strangely salty finish. Just this side of acceptable is the only way I can describe it. 6,500 cases produced. 81 —*M.S. (5/1/2007)*

Achaval-Ferrer 2004 Quimera Red Blend (Mendoza) $48. Fairly granular and pruney, this wine based on Malbec, Merlot, Cabernet Sauvignon and Cab Franc is scattered like buck shot. There's color, body and acidity but the fruit is hard to identify and the overall feel is rather soft and chunky. At this price it could use more finesse and balance. 85 —*M.S. (2/1/2007)*

Achával-Ferrer 2001 Quimera Red Blend (Mendoza) $55. 85 —*M.S. (5/1/2003)*

ACORDEÓN

Acordeón 2004 Malbec (Mendoza) $10. A big, plump Malbec with 14.5% alcohol but also attractive plum, marzipan and earth notes. The palate is nice and fruity as it delivers solid plum and cherry flavors, while the finish is warm and cuddly. More size than style, but it handles its weight well. 86 Best Buy —*M.S. (2/1/2007)*

Acordeón 2004 Syrah (Mendoza) $10. 81 —*M.S. (11/1/2006)*

AITOR IDER BALBO

Aitor Ider Balbo 2006 El Encanto Cabernet Sauvignon-Malbec (Mendoza) $8. A dose of cherry cough drop adds sweetness to what is otherwise a tart, simple, steely version of Cabernet Sauvignon blended with Malbec. The mouthfeel is sheering and lean, while the finish offers some out of place butter to fatten up the astringent red fruit. 82 —*M.S. (12/1/2007)*

ALAMOS

Alamos 2003 Bonarda (Mendoza) $10. 81 —*M.S. (11/15/2005)*

Alamos 2002 Bonarda (Mendoza) $10. 86 —*M.S. (7/1/2004)*

Alamos 2000 Bonarda (Mendoza) $13. 84 —*M.S. (11/1/2002)*

Alamos 2002 Cabernet Sauvignon (Mendoza) $10. 84 —*M.S. (7/1/2004)*

Alamos 2001 Cabernet Sauvignon (Mendoza) $10. 86 —*M.S. (5/1/2003)*

Alamos 1999 Cabernet Sauvignon (Mendoza) $13. 84 —*M.S. (11/1/2002)*

Alamos 2004 Chardonnay (Mendoza) $10. 85 Best Buy —*M.S. (11/15/2005)*

Alamos 2003 Chardonnay (Mendoza) $10. 87 —*M.S. (7/1/2004)*

Alamos 2002 Chardonnay (Mendoza) $10. 86 —*M.S. (5/1/2003)*

Alamos 2001 Chardonnay (Mendoza) $13. 83 —*M.S. (7/1/2002)*

Alamos 2004 Malbec (Mendoza) $10. 87 Best Buy —*M.S. (11/15/2005)*

Alamos 2003 Malbec (Mendoza) $10. 88 Best Buy —*M.S. (3/1/2005)*

Alamos 2002 Malbec (Mendoza) $11. 86 —*M.S. (12/1/2003)*

Alamos 2001 Malbec (Mendoza) $11. 86 —*M.S. (5/1/2003)*

Alamos 2000 Malbec (Mendoza) $13. 83 —*M.S. (11/1/2002)*

Alamos 2002 Pinot Noir (Mendoza) $10. 85 —*M.S. (7/1/2004)*

Alamos 2004 Viognier (Mendoza) $10. 87 Best Buy —*M.S. (11/15/2005)*

Alamos 2003 Viognier (Mendoza) $10. 86 —*M.S. (7/1/2004)*

ALBERTI 154

Alberti 154 2003 Cabernet Sauvignon (Mendoza) $10. 86 Best Buy —*M.S. (11/15/2005)*

Alberti 154 2002 Cabernet Sauvignon (Mendoza) $10. 86 Best Buy —*M.S. (7/1/2004)*

Alberti 154 2003 Merlot (Mendoza) $10. 83 —*M.S. (11/15/2005)*

Alberti 154 2002 Merlot (Mendoza) $10. 83 —*M.S. (7/1/2004)*

ALEPH

Aleph 2003 Cabernet Sauvignon (Mendoza) $25. Quite earthy and ripe, as tree bark, leather and prune make up the bouquet. The mouth is lively and snappy, with red fruit taking over and holding reign. Sheer, zesty and juicy describes the mouthfeel, while overall the wine delivers depth and integrity. Not overly complex but very good and straightforward. 88 —*M.S. (8/1/2007)*

Aleph 2004 Malbec (Mendoza) $25. A steady-as-she-goes type of Malbec with dark, heavy aromas and ripe berry and black cherry flavors. It's a good wine with heft, ripeness and solidity, but it doesn't sway much from the basic blueprint of average Mendocino Malbec. Expect size and extract more than refinement. 85 —*M.S. (5/1/2007)*

ALESSANDRO SPERI

Alessandro Speri 2004 Prodigo Malbec (Mendoza) $15. Black fruit and a hint of tire rubber work the nose, and that's backed up by raspberry and sweet vanilla flavors. This wine is pretty good overall, with depth and push, but it's also a bit starchy and slightly green at its core. 85 —*M.S. (8/1/2007)*

Alessandro Speri 2004 Prodigo Reserva Malbec (Mendoza) $30. Full and inviting up front, with hickory and leather in addition to dark-fruit aromas. This is a collaboration between two Italian buddies and the wine features black cherry and plum flavors but also rather grabby, heavy tannins. It's ultimately chewy and a bit hard, but still it's eminently satisfying. 87 —*M.S. (8/1/2007)*

ALFREDO ROCA

Alfredo Roca 2004 Cabernet Sauvignon (San Rafael) $11. Herbal aromas infiltrate the nose, and the palate features midlevel red fruit with a strong herbal edge. The finish shows saline, chocolate and pepper, and never does it rise much above struggling. 82 —*M.S. (12/31/2007)*

Alfredo Roca 2002 Cabernet Sauvignon (San Rafael) $12. 85 —*M.S. (11/15/2005)*

Alfredo Roca 2006 Chardonnay (San Rafael) $10. Way too much banana, mango and sugar. Not a prime-time player. 80 —*M.S. (12/1/2007)*

Alfredo Roca 2004 Chardonnay (San Rafael) $12. 82 —*M.S. (11/15/2005)*

Alfredo Roca 2004 Malbec (San Rafael) $11. Big and spicy at first, and then vegetal, lesser characteristics seep in and take over. The palate has baked black fruit and a finish of bitter chocolate and pepper, but also some rooty, bark-like issues. There's no point of focus to this wine. 82 —*M.S. (12/31/2007)*

Alfredo Roca 2003 Malbec (San Rafael) $11. 85 —*M.S. (12/1/2006)*

Alfredo Roca 2002 Malbec (San Rafael) $12. 86 —*M.S. (12/31/2005)*

Alfredo Roca 2004 Tocai Friulano (San Rafael) $12. 81 —*M.S. (12/31/2005)*

ALMA DE LOS ANDES

Alma de los Andes 2005 Bonarda (Mendoza) $10. Like most of Alma's wines, this Bonarda is smooth, fruity and approachable. The nose is simple and offers some spice, licorice and herb notes, while the berry flavors are just as they should be: easy and jammy. There's nothing challenging about this red; just pour it with pizza or burgers and enjoy. 86 Best Buy —*M.S. (8/1/2007)*

Alma de los Andes 2005 Malbec (Mendoza) $10. Dark and ripe on the nose, with a touch of class that distinguishes it from the many that inhabit this range of wine. Aromas of black fruits, black olives and herbs are pretty and set the stage for full black cherry and chocolate flavors. For $10 you're getting a lot of quality juice. 89 Best Buy —*M.S. (5/1/2007)*

Alma de los Andes 2004 Gran Reserva Malbec (Mendoza) $25. Cinnamon and other sultry, exotic aromas envelop the heavy, saturated bouquet, while plum flavors veer a bit toward prune as the palate yields to a rich, almost liqueur-like finish. May be a case of more ripeness working against the wine, because Alma's less-ripe, less-extracted Malbecs seem even better. 87 —*M.S. (5/1/2007)*

Alma de los Andes 2004 Reserva Malbec (Mendoza) $14. Guillermo Banfi is making some take-notice wines, not the least of which is this smooth, supple Malbec. The nose hits firmly but not hard, with blueberry, licorice and cassis. The palate is medium in size and length, with fully ripe black cherry, plum and black currant flavors. All the right things are front and center. 91 Best Buy —*M.S. (5/1/2007)*

Alma de los Andes 2005 Malbec-Cabernet Sauvignon (Mendoza) $10. Not entirely sure what the difference is between the Alma de los Andes and Sur de los Andes lines (because they come from the same winery), but this 50-50 blend, while needing a little time to find its stride, provides ample fruit, peppery spice and good mouthfeel. It's not a thriller but it more than makes the grade in this price category. 85 Best Buy —*M.S. (5/1/2007)*

ALTA VISTA

Alta Vista 2002 Premium Bonarda (Mendoza) $10. 86 Best Buy —*M.S. (10/1/2004)*

Alta Vista 2003 Premium Cabernet Sauvignon (Mendoza) $13. 87 —*M.S. (11/1/2006)*

Alta Vista 2006 Premium Chardonnay (Mendoza) $14. Melon, lemon and other white-fruit aromas and flavors define this mediocre, somewhat blanched-out wine. Compared to so many other Chardonnays from around the world, this one doesn't really stack up. 83 —*M.S. (5/1/2007)*

Alta Vista 2005 Premium Chardonnay (Mendoza) $13. 85 —*M.S. (11/1/2006)*

Alta Vista 2002 Premium Chardonnay (Mendoza) $10. 84 —*M.S. (5/1/2003)*

Alta Vista 2001 Premium Chardonnay (Mendoza) $10. 85 —*M.S. (5/1/2003)*

Alta Vista 1999 Malbec (Mendoza) $12. 82 —*M.S. (11/1/2002)*

Alta Vista 2002 Alto Malbec (Mendoza) $60. 91 —*M.S. (7/1/2005)*

Alta Vista 1998 Alto Malbec (Mendoza) $60. 84 —*M.S. (11/1/2002)*

Alta Vista 2004 Grande Reserve Malbec (Mendoza) $23. Alta Vista is one of several Mendoza Malbecs from 2004 that pales next to that winery's basic bottling. Yes, there's heft, cassis and sweetness, but overall the wine doesn't have the focus, purity and density to rank higher. It's a good wine but it's also slightly candied, medicinal and fleshy. 400 cases produced. 86 —*M.S. (5/1/2007)*

Alta Vista 2000 Grand Reserve Malbec (Mendoza) $20. 87 —*M.S. (5/1/2003)*

Alta Vista 2002 Grande Reserve Malbec (Mendoza) $20. 89 —*M.S. (7/1/2005)*

Alta Vista 2004 Premium Malbec (Mendoza) $13. 88 Best Buy —*M.S. (11/1/2006)*

Alta Vista 2002 Premium Malbec (Mendoza) $10. 89 Best Buy —*M.S. (10/1/2004)*

Alta Vista 2001 Premium Malbec (Mendoza) $10. 83 —*M.S. (1/1/2004)*

Alta Vista 2000 Premium Malbec (Mendoza) $10. 82 —*M.S. (5/1/2003)*

Alta Vista 2003 Alto Malbec-Cabernet Sauvignon (Mendoza) $60. 88 —*M.S. (8/1/2006)*

Alta Vista 2000 Red Blend (Mendoza) $8. 82 —*M.S. (5/1/2003)*

Alta Vista 2000 Cosecha Tempranillo Blend (Mendoza) $8. 84 —*M.S. (11/1/2002)*

Alta Vista 2002 Malbec-Tempranillo Tempranillo Blend (Mendoza) $8. 82 —*M.S. (10/1/2004)*

Alta Vista 2006 Premium Torrontes (Salta) $14. Very fragrant and rich, especially when measured against the rest of the Argentine Torrontes field. This version has ethereal floral aromas backed by melon and tropical fruit flavors. It's round, rich and attractive. 87 —*M.S. (5/1/2007)*

Alta Vista 2005 Premium Torrontès (Salta) $13. 85 —*M.S. (11/1/2006)*

Alta Vista 2003 Premium Torrontès (Mendoza) $10. 86 —*M.S. (7/1/2004)*

Alta Vista 2002 Premium Torrontès (Mendoza) $10. 83 —*M.S. (5/1/2003)*

Alta Vista 2003 Chardonnay-Torrontès White Blend (Mendoza) $8. 84 —*M.S. (10/1/2004)*

Alta Vista 2000 Cosecha White Blend (Mendoza) $8. 80 —*M.S. (5/1/2003)*

ALTAS CUMBRES

Altas Cumbres 2002 Cabernet Sauvignon (Mendoza) $9. 88 Best Buy —*M.S. (11/15/2004)*

Altas Cumbres 2002 Cabernet Sauvignon-Malbec (Mendoza) $9. 88 Best Buy —*M.S. (11/15/2004)*

Altas Cumbres 2002 Malbec (Mendoza) $9. 87 Best Buy —*M.S. (11/15/2004)*

Altas Cumbres 2003 Viognier (Mendoza) $9. 84 —*M.S. (11/15/2004)*

ALTOCEDRO

Altocedro 2004 Año Cero Malbec (Mendoza) $12. 87 Best Buy —*M.S. (12/1/2006)*

Altocedro 2001 Año Cero Malbec (Mendoza) $12. 83 —*M.S. (11/15/2005)*

Altocedro 2003 Reserva Malbec (Mendoza) $16. Aromas of beef bouillon, leather and earth hide most of the fruit that's on the bouquet, while the palate runs a bit soft and toward the Porty, liqueur side of the fence. Seems like a wine that's a bit too hunky; it's got some qualities but is starving for balance. 84 —*M.S. (5/1/2007)*

Altocedro 2001 Reserva Malbec (Mendoza) $17. 85 —*M.S. (11/15/2005)*

ALTO SALVADOR

Alto Salvador 2005 Cabernet Sauvignon (Mendoza) $9. Spearmint and dry red fruit carry the nose. The palate shows basic sweet cherry and strawberry flavors but not much Cabernet character. All in all it's a stripped-back wine that offers rudimentary red-fruit character. 82 —*M.S. (8/1/2007)*

Alto Salvador 2005 Malbec (Mendoza) $9. Sort of soupy and stewy to begin with. The palate is stocky and forward, with short black plum and berry flavors. Quite ripe on the back end as it finishes chewy and soft. Organic. 83 —*M.S. (8/1/2007)*

ALTOS DE MEDRANO

Altos de Medrano 2001 Reserva Viña Hormigas Malbec (Mendoza) $24. 92 —*M.S. (12/1/2003)*

ALTOS LAS HORMIGAS

Altos Las Hormigas 2005 Malbec (Mendoza) $11. Always a good deal, the 2005 offers mocha, coffee and lemon peel aromas on what can only be called an oaky bouquet. The palate is fairly ripe, a touch hard and tannic, and ultimately not too complicated or heavy. Drink now to experience Malbec's easygoing charms. 87 Best Buy —*M.S. (2/1/2007)*

Altos Las Hormigas 2003 Malbec (Mendoza) $12. 89 Best Buy —*M.S. (7/1/2005)*

Altos Las Hormigas 2001 Malbec (Mendoza) $9. 88 Best Buy —*M.S. (11/15/2003)*

Altos Las Hormigas 2004 Reserva Viña Hormigas Malbec (Mendoza) $23. 91 —*M.S. (12/31/2005)*

Altos Las Hormigas 2002 Reserva Viña Hormigas Malbec (Mendoza) $25. 92 Editors' Choice —*M.S. (7/1/2005)*

ALTOSUR

Altosur 2002 Estate Bottled Cabernet Sauvignon (Mendoza) $10. 81 —*M.S. (7/1/2005)*

Altosur 2002 Chardonnay (Mendoza) $10. 83 —*M.S. (7/1/2005)*

Altosur 2002 Merlot (Mendoza) $10. Quite jumbled and big at 14.2% alcohol. 85 Best Buy —*M.S. (7/1/2005)*

ALTURA

Altura 1,024 2005 Cabernet Sauvignon (Mendoza) $10. Leather and cassis aromas greet you, but airing turns them toward leafy and green. Flavors of cherry, raspberry and red currants are also a touch lean and green, but for the most part the wine shows verve and a good mouthfeel even if the flavors aren't perfect. 84 —*M.S. (12/1/2007)*

Altura 1,024 2004 Cabernet Sauvignon (Mendoza) $10. Initial aromas are like a maple-covered doughnut meeting raspberry jam, while the palate deals straight-ahead berry flavors with little to nothing in the way of accents. It's a touch starchy and tannic, but overall it's perfectly good if measured conservatively. 84 —*M.S. (2/1/2007)*

AMBIENTE

Ambiente 2004 Malbec (Mendoza) $12. 81 —*M.S. (12/1/2006)*

Ambiente 2003 Tempranillo (Mendoza) $12. 84 —*M.S. (12/1/2006)*

AMOR DE LOS ANDES

Amor de los Andes 2002 Malbec (Mendoza) $15. 84 —*M.S. (3/1/2005)*

Amor de los Andes 2002 Syrah (La Rioja) $11. 83 —*M.S. (3/1/2005)*

Amor de los Andes 2002 Tempranillo (Mendoza) $15. 83 —*M.S. (3/1/2005)*

ANASTASIA

Anastasia 2001 Chardonnay (Mendoza) $10. 88 Best Buy —*M.S. (5/1/2003)*

ANDALHUE

Andalhue 2004 Organico Malbec (Mendoza) $12. 84 —*M.S. (11/15/2005)*

ANDEAN

Andean 2004 Finca La Escondida Reserva Chardonnay (San Juan) $16. 90 Editors' Choice —*M.S. (11/1/2006)*

ANDELUNA

Andeluna 2003 Grand Reserve Pasionado Bordeaux Blend (Mendoza) $50. 91 —*M.S. (6/1/2006)*

Andeluna 2003 Limited Release Cabernet Franc (Mendoza) $50. 86 —*M.S. (8/1/2006)*

Andeluna 2004 Reserve Cabernet Sauvignon (Tupungato) $23. Big and bulky, with a mixed bag of aromas that includes field scents, rubber and baked fruit. The palate deals berry and plum flavors, while the finish tilts toward heavy and medicinal. Seems like this one got a bit overripe and sticky. The 2003 was better. 85 —*M.S. (10/1/2007)*

Andeluna 2003 Reserve Cabernet Sauvignon (Mendoza) $23. 90 —*M.S. (6/1/2006)*

Andeluna 2004 Winemaker's Selection Cabernet Sauvignon (Mendoza) $13. Mocha, coffee and other oak-based aromas are front and center on the nose. The palate is quite sweet and rich, with cola and dark fruit flavors. Generally speaking this wine has the right qualifications to make a positive impression; it is, however, oaky and on the stewy side. Imported by Kysela Pere et Fils, Ltd. 85 —*M.S. (10/1/2007)*

Andeluna 2003 Winemaker's Selection Cabernet Sauvignon (Mendoza) $13. 88 Best Buy —*M.S. (8/1/2006)*

Andeluna 2003 Reserve Chardonnay (Mendoza) $23. 88 —*M.S. (6/1/2006)*

Andeluna 2004 Winemaker's Selection Chardonnay (Mendoza) $13. 81 —*M.S. (4/1/2006)*

Andeluna 2004 Reserve Malbec (Tupungato) $23. At 15% alcohol and with a nose full of prune, blazing oak and simmering blackberry jam, this is not for the weak. In fact, it may not be for the strong, because while we like the wine's sun-baked, ultraripe personality, we also acknowledge that it's teetering on the brink and probably won't age for very long. 88 —*M.S. (10/1/2007)*

Andeluna 2003 Reserve Malbec (Mendoza) $23. 92 Editors' Choice —*M.S. (6/1/2006)*

Andeluna 2004 Winemaker's Selection Malbec (Mendoza) $13. Full, serious and ripe, with leather, animal and an underside of savory oak and bacon. Typical of the house style, the wine is lush and jammy, with syrupy black-fruit flavors setting up a composed, rich finish. Best for fans of hefty, New World reds. 88 Best Buy —*M.S. (10/1/2007)*

Andeluna 2003 Winemaker's Selection Malbec (Mendoza) $13. 89 Best Buy —*M.S. (8/1/2006)*

Andeluna 2004 Reserve Merlot (Tupungato) $23. Plenty of patience is required with this wine, because at first it's rough and stewy, with herb and tomato aromas. Airing reveals a blackberry core and tannin-infused oak notes, while the finish features mostly char and vanilla. Has its merits but also some weaknesses. 84 —*M.S. (10/1/2007)*

Andeluna 2003 Reserve Merlot (Mendoza) $23. 88 —*M.S. (6/1/2006)*

Andeluna 2003 Winemaker's Selection Merlot (Mendoza) $13. 86 —*M.S. (6/1/2006)*

Andeluna 2006 Winemaker's Selection Torrontes (Mendoza) $13. White peach and a bit of sweat accent the expiring bouquet, while the flavors are of dull, heavy apples dotted with sauerkraut and pickle accents. Imported by Kysela Pere et Fils, Ltd. 82 —*M.S. (12/1/2007)*

ANDES GRAPES

Andes Grapes 2002 Maia Cabernet Sauvignon (Mendoza) $8. 81 —*M.S. (10/1/2004)*

Andes Grapes 2002 Maia Malbec (Mendoza) $8. 84 —*M.S. (10/1/2004)*

Andes Grapes 2002 Maia Merlot (Mendoza) $8. 82 —*M.S. (10/1/2004)*

Andes Grapes 2002 Maia Syrah (Mendoza) $8. 81 —*M.S. (10/1/2004)*

Andes Grapes 2002 Maia Tempranillo (Mendoza) $8. 83 —*M.S. (10/1/2004)*

ANGARO

Angaro 2002 Finca la Celia Cabernet Sauvignon-Tempranillo (Uco Valley) $6. 83 —*M.S. (5/1/2003)*

Angaro 2001 Finca la Celia Cabernet Sauvignon-Tempranillo (Uco Valley) $6. 86 —*M.S. (11/1/2002)*

Angaro 2002 Finca la Celia Chardonnay (Uco Valley) $6. 83 —*M.S. (5/1/2003)*

Angaro 2002 Finca la Celia Merlot (Uco Valley) $6. 84 —*M.S. (5/1/2003)*

Angaro 2002 Finca la Celia Red Blend (Uco Valley) $6. 81 —*M.S. (5/1/2003)*

Angaro 2000 Finca la Celia Red Blend (Uco Valley) $6. 81 —*M.S. (11/1/2002)*

Angaro 2002 Finca la Celia Sauvignon Blanc (Uco Valley) $6. 82 —*M.S. (5/1/2003)*

ANTIS

Antis 2004 Cabernet Sauvignon (Mendoza) $12. 80 —*M.S. (8/1/2006)*

Antis 2003 Malbec (Mendoza) $12. 88 Best Buy —*M.S. (4/1/2006)*

Antis 2004 Reserve Malbec (Mendoza) $17. 86 —*M.S. (8/1/2006)*

Antis 2004 Reserve Merlot (Mendoza) $14. Cherry aromas are brought down a notch by grassy notes that signal questionable ripeness, while the palate runs more earthy and muddled than bright and fruity. Still, along the way you get chocolate and plum flavors along with hard, jagged tannins. 83 —*M.S. (2/1/2007)*

Antis 2003 Cuvee Celebration Reserve Red Blend (Mendoza) $24. 88 —*M.S. (8/1/2006)*

ANTONIO CESAR CAVALLI

Antonio Cesar Cavalli 2005 White Pearl Cabernet Sauvignon (Mendoza) $14. Better than jug wine even if it comes in a big bottle, with clean, lightly expressive cherry, raspberry and plum flavors. There's a little heat and roughness to the finish, but given the league that it's playing in you can't complain about the overall quality of this Mendoza Cabernet. A big-time barbecue or party wine. 84 Best Buy —*M.S. (10/1/2007)*

Antonio Cesar Cavalli 2006 White Pearl Torrontes (Salta) $13. Of all the large-format White Pearl varietals, this Torrontes tastes and feels the best. It has the grape's pungent aromas of acacia and talc, and the flavors are solid and persistent as the palate yields green melon and honey. Finishes tangy and fresh, meaning it hasn't yet started to fade. 85 Best Buy —*M.S. (12/1/2007)*

ANTONIO NERVIANI

Antonio Nerviani 2001 Reserve Cabernet Sauvignon (Mendoza) $16. 86 —*M.S. (11/15/2005)*

Antonio Nerviani 2001 Reserve Malbec (Mendoza) $16. 81 —*M.S. (11/15/2005)*

Antonio Nerviani 2001 Reserve Meritage (Mendoza) $16. 85 —*M.S. (7/1/2005)*

ANTUCURA

Antucura 2004 Cabernet Sauvignon-Merlot (Uco Valley) $50. This vintage seems more medicinal and overtly ripe than the more balanced 2003. It has high alcohol (15.2%) and medium acidity, thus it's a touch gummy and syrupy. But if you like power at the core of your Cabernet-Merlot blends and you don't mind a little fire in the hole after drinking, then we recommend this chewy, ripe, very modern offering. 87 —*M.S. (12/31/2007)*

Antucura 2003 Cabernet Sauvignon-Merlot (Uco Valley) $45. Like its little brother Calvulcura, this wine is Cabernet Sauvignon mixed with Merlot. It's a big boy with stewed berries, prune and licorice on the bouquet. Below that heavy nose is a palate that's sweet and ripe, and arguably too much so. If chocolate, richness and heft are your thing, this is a winner; purists, however, may wish for more tannin, structure and nuance. 89 —*M.S. (10/1/2007)*

Antucura 2003 Calvulcura Merlot-Cabernet Sauvignon (Uco Valley) $25. After you chop your way through the black forest of char, roasted berry and coffee aromas, you'll encounter a pretty large mass of flavors that include blackberry, cola, root beer and cinnamon. It's a fairly packed and saturated wine at 14.9%, and the finish of mocha and chocolate accentuates the wine's oak elevage. Best for those who like ripeness and size. The blend is 60% Merlot and 40% Cab Sauvignon. 88 —*M.S. (10/1/2007)*

ARGENTINE BEEF

Argentine Beef 2003 Cabernet Sauvignon (Cafayate) $10. 81 —*M.S. (12/31/2005)*

ATILIO AVENA

Atilio Avena 2002 Roble Malbec (Mendoza) $13. 84 —*M.S. (4/1/2006)*

ATILIO AVENA

Atilio Avena 2004 Torrontès (Mendoza) $10. 80 —*M.S. (4/1/2006)*

BALBI

Balbi 1997 Reserve Cabernet Sauvignon (Mendoza) $13. 87 Best Buy (8/1/2000)

Balbi 2002 Malbec (Mendoza) $8. 83 —*M.S. (12/1/2003)*

Balbi 1999 Malbec (Mendoza) $8. 82 —*D.T. (5/1/2002)*

Balbi 1998 Malbec (Mendoza) $8. 80 *—M.S. (11/15/2001)*

Balbi 1998 Red Blend (Mendoza) $7. 85 Best Buy *(8/1/2000)*

Balbi 2002 Syrah (Mendoza) $8. 81 *—M.S. (2/1/2004)*

Balbi 1999 Syrah (Mendoza) $8. 85 *—S.H. (11/1/2002)*

Balbi 1998 Syrah (Mendoza) $8. 86 Best Buy *(10/1/2001)*

Balbi 1998 Syrah (Mendoza) $10. 83 *(8/1/2000)*

Balbi 1997 White Blend (Mendoza) $7. 83 *(8/1/2000)*

BAUDRON

Baudron 1999 Malbec (Mendoza) $8. 85 Best Buy *—C.S. (5/1/2002)*

BEC

BEC 2005 Nuevo Malbec (Mendoza) $12. 84 *—M.S. (8/1/2006)*

BENEGRAS

Benegas 2006 Clara Benegas Chardonnay (Mendoza) $11. The bouquet hits with reduced aromas of children's vitamin and pineapple, while the palate goes straight to hard cider and orange peel. It's a firm, acidic style that finishes citric and a touch bitter. Doesn't really smell or taste much like Chardonnay. 82 *—M.S. (8/1/2007)*

Benegas 2005 Malbec (Mendoza) $22. Raring to go is this huge, forward Malbec made by Federico Benegas (with consultant Michel Rolland). If you know the rep of the latter, then it's not surprising that this bomber weighs in at 15% alcohol. Ripeness is evident at all turns as the wine shows monstrous black-fruit aromas and flavors, all supported by potent oak that results in strong nuances of chocolate mint chip and mocha. 91 *—M.S. (5/1/2007)*

Benegas 2005 Libertad Vineyard Syrah (Mendoza) $22. Wines can be big and loaded with everything, yet still be hard to enjoy. This is a case in point: It weighs in at 15% and brings searing aromas of tree bark, char and shoe polish. The palate is a saturated fusing of berry syrup, chocolate and alcohol. Almost Port-like in weight and style, but also very aggressive. 82 *—M.S. (8/1/2007)*

BENMARCO

BenMarco 2004 Cabernet Sauvignon (Mendoza) $20. 88 *—M.S. (12/1/2006)*

BenMarco 2002 Malbec (Mendoza) $20. 90 *—M.S. (12/1/2003)*

BERNARD MAGREZ

Bernard Magrez 2003 La Bienvenida Malbec (Mendoza) $39. Frenchman Bernard Magrez is building a global brand via high-quality, smartly named wines such as this (La Bienvenida means The Welcoming in Spanish). But the cuteness ends there; this is serious Malbec with maple, leather and coffee aromas in addition to rich berry scents. The palate is integrated and deep, with lively acidity and tannins but enough cuddly fruit to ensure balance. An excellent Argentinean debut for Monsieur Magrez. Imported by Bernard Magrez USA. 92 *—M.S. (8/1/2007)*

BIG DADDY VINEYARDS

Big Daddy Vineyards 2003 Bodega Polo Gran Reserva Bordeaux Blend (Carodilla) $8. 82 *—M.S. (7/1/2004)*

Big Daddy Vineyards 2002 Bodega Polo Cabernet Sauvignon (La Consulta) $8. 82 *—M.S. (5/1/2003)*

Big Daddy Vineyards 2002 Bodega Polo Cabernet Sauvignon (San Martin) $8. 81 *—M.S. (5/1/2003)*

Big Daddy Vineyards 2003 Chardonnay (Mendoza) $9. 82 *—M.S. (6/1/2006)*

Big Daddy Vineyards 2003 Bodega Polo Chardonnay (San Martin) $8. 80 *—M.S. (2/1/2004)*

Big Daddy Vineyards 2003 Malbec (Mendoza) $9. 84 *—M.S. (8/1/2006)*

Big Daddy Vineyards 2003 Bodega Polo Malbec (Carodilla) $8. 81 *—M.S. (7/1/2004)*

Big Daddy Vineyards 2002 Bodega Polo Malbec (San Martin) $8. 85 *—M.S. (5/1/2003)*

Big Daddy Vineyards 2002 Bodega Polo Malbec (Maipú) $8. 82 *—M.S. (5/1/2003)*

Big Daddy Vineyards 2002 Sanes SA Malbec (Mendoza) $8. 86 Best Buy *—M.S. (5/1/2003)*

Big Daddy Vineyards 2001 Tawert SA Malbec (Tupungato) $8. 84 *—M.S. (5/1/2003)*

Big Daddy Vineyards 2003 Merlot (Mendoza) $9. 82 *—M.S. (8/1/2006)*

Big Daddy Vineyards 2003 Bodega Polo Merlot (Carodilla) $8. *—M.S. (7/1/2004)*

Big Daddy Vineyards 2002 Bodega Polo Merlot (Carodilla) $8. 85 *—M.S. (5/1/2003)*

Big Daddy Vineyards 2002 Bodega Polo Merlot (Uco Valley) $8. 87 Best Buy *—M.S. (5/1/2003)*

Big Daddy Vineyards 2001 Tawert SA Merlot (Mendoza) $8. 85 *—M.S. (5/1/2003)*

Big Daddy Vineyards 2002 Sanes SA Red Blend (Mendoza) $8. 83 *—M.S. (5/1/2003)*

Big Daddy Vineyards 2001 Tawert SA Red Blend (Mendoza) $8. 80 *—M.S. (5/1/2003)*

Big Daddy Vineyards 2003 Syrah (Mendoza) $9. 88 Best Buy *—M.S. (8/1/2006)*

Big Daddy Vineyards 2002 Sanes SA Syrah (Mendoza) $8. 86 Best Buy *—M.S. (5/1/2003)*

Big Daddy Vineyards 2001 Tawert SA Syrah (Mendoza) $8. 83 *—M.S. (5/1/2003)*

Big Daddy Vineyards 2002 Sanes SA Tempranillo (Mendoza) $8. 84 *—M.S. (5/1/2003)*

BLASON

Blason 2002 Chardonnay (Mendoza) $10. 85 *—M.S. (5/1/2003)*

BODEGA CATENA ZAPATA

Bodega Catena Zapata 1999 Nicolas Catena Zapata Cabernet Blend (Mendoza) $90. 92 Cellar Selection *—M.S. (5/1/2003)*

Bodega Catena Zapata 2001 Cabernet Sauvignon (Mendoza) $60. 87 *—M.S. (7/1/2004)*

Bodega Catena Zapata 2002 Nicolas Catena Zapata Cabernet Sauvignon-Malbec (Mendoza) $95. 92 Editors' Choice *—M.S. (11/1/2006)*

Bodega Catena Zapata 2002 Chardonnay (Mendoza) $30. 89 *—M.S. (7/1/2004)*

Bodega Catena Zapata 2001 Malbec (Mendoza) $50. 90 *—M.S. (12/1/2003)*

Bodega Catena Zapata 2001 Nicolas Catena Zapata Red Blend (Mendoza) $90. 90 *—M.S. (11/15/2005)*

BODEGA CECCHIN

Bodega Cecchin 2006 Esencias de la Tierra Cabernet Sauvignon (Mendoza) $15. Turning toward brick in color, with leaner aromas that offer dry fruit and equally dry spice notes. The palate deals mild blackberry flavors before a scratchy finish, while the feel is suspect. It seems to be fast approaching its end, meaning drink now. Made from organic grapes. 84 *—M.S. (12/1/2007)*

BODEGA CHACRA

Bodega Chacra 2006 No. 32 Pinot Noir (Río Negro Valley) $120. From vines planted in 1932, this Pinot Noir is simply beautiful. It's bigger and more dense than its younger brother, No. 55, but maybe a tad less elegant and a bit more cellar worthy. The aromas are a blend of fine French oak and natural Pinot aromas of tea, cherry and raspberry. Mineral and coffee appear late on the finish. Unlike any other Pinot from the continent and much more like Burgundy or Oregon than most neophyte New Worlders. 93 Cellar Selection *—M.S. (10/1/2007)*

Bodega Chacra 2006 No. 55 Pinot Noir (Río Negro Valley) $100. Hands down, this is the finest Pinot Noir from South America that I've ever tasted, and that includes Chile, Argentina and anyplace else. Italy's Piero Incisa della Rocchetta of Sassicaia fame started this project in 2004, and it's now finding a groove. This wine is as elegant as Burgundy but as full of flavor as something from California. The color is rosy, the aromas beguiling, and the meeting of oak and fruit just perfect. Terrific for contemplating on its own or with food. Versatility should be its middle name. 94 Editors' Choice *—M.S. (10/1/2007)*

BODEGA ELVIRA CALLE

Bodega Elvira Calle 2003 Alberti 154 Malbec (Mendoza) $10. 84 *—M.S. (11/15/2004)*

BODEGA FAMILIA BARBERIS

Bodega Familia Barberis 2004 Antigua Cava Cabernet Sauvignon (Mendoza) $6. Flat and soupy, as if the life had been drained out of it. Barely acceptable, even with a big production of 40,000 cases. 80 *—M.S. (10/1/2007)*

Bodega Familia Barberis 2005 Finca la Daniela Chardonnay (Mendoza) $10. Honeysuckle and other sweet aromas greet you. In back of that there are flavors of pineapple, mango and apple. This runs crisp and tangy with more lemon-drop character than butter or vanilla. 84 *—M.S. (8/1/2007)*

Bodega Familia Barberis 2002 Blason Malbec (Mendoza) $10. 81 *—M.S. (5/1/2003)*

Bodega Familia Barberis 2006 Cava Negra Malbec (Mendoza) $8. Light and spicy, with snappy, lean flavors of cherry and cranberry. This is more tart and underwhelming than most Malbec fans probably want, but it's not bad if you crave a lip-smacking red with zest. 83 *—M.S. (8/1/2007)*

Bodega Familia Barberis 2004 Cava Negra Malbec (Mendoza) $8. A little rough and rugged at first, but it eventually finds a groove that includes cherry and blackberry flavors backed by reasonable tannins and structure. A good jammy wine with no real frills or thrills but also no disappointments. 85 Best Buy *—M.S. (2/1/2007)*

Bodega Familia Barberis 2003 Cava Negra Malbec (Mendoza) $8. 84 Best Buy *—M.S. (11/15/2005)*

Bodega Familia Barberis 2004 Finca la Daniela Malbec (Mendoza) $10. Candied fruit aromas lead to a hard, underdeveloped palate that houses tannin and oddly flavored raspberry notes. Not a lot else to say about it. 81*—M.S. (10/1/2007)*

Bodega Familia Barberis 2003 Finca La Daniela Malbec (Mendoza) $10. 84 *—M.S. (7/1/2005)*

Bodega Familia Barberis 2004 Humberto Barberis Gran Reserva Malbec (Mendoza) $30. Quite piercing and fiery at first, which announces that it is fully oaked. Along the way there's savory notes, saucy leather and flashes of dark fruit. This would be a better wine with more fruit and flesh, and less barrel. The dill, vanilla and spice flavors are a bit too dominant. 85 *—M.S. (12/31/2007)*

Bodega Familia Barberis 2004 La Daniela Malbec (Mendoza) $10. Chunky and awkward, with odd aromas that lead into a syrupy, weird palate that's full of medicinal flavors and other interferences. Lacks discipline and focus; doesn't hit the proper flavor profile for good Malbec. 80 *—M.S. (2/1/2007)*

Bodega Familia Barberis 1999 Malbec (Mendoza) $15. Seems a little weedy and green, but it's not overly "old" in nature despite having a number of years' worth of bottle age. That said, those greenish notes are confirmed on the palate, while raisin pokes its way through late. 82 *—M.S. (2/1/2007)*

Bodega Familia Barberis 2002 Blason Tempranillo (Mendoza) $10. 81 *—M.S. (5/1/2003)*

Bodega Familia Barberis 2004 Finca la Daniela Tempranillo (Mendoza) $10. Big and colorful, with soupy aromas blended with a waft of heavy berries. The palate is packed with anonymous red fruits, but the mouthfeel is pretty hard and miserly. Tastes reasonably good but has little in common with Spanish Tempranillo. 83 *—M.S. (10/1/2007)*

BODEGA FILIPPO FIGARI

Bodega Filippo Figari 2003 Single Vineyard Reserve Malbec (Mendoza) $26. 88 *—M.S. (12/1/2006)*

BODEGA JOSÉ QUATTROCCHI

Bodega José Quattrocchi 2005 Valle Huarpe Syrah (Mendoza) $14. Hot and earthy up front, with mocha-like aromas. The palate and finish are syrupy, and the wine ends in a pool of chocolate and berry extract. This is an example of why Argentine Syrah has not found its groove. 81 *—M.S. (10/1/2007)*

Bodega José Quattrocchi 2002 Nino Franco Torrontès (Mendoza) $13. 80 *—M.S. (5/1/2003)*

BODEGA LA RURAL

Bodega La Rural 2000 Felipe Rutini Chardonnay (Tupungato) $17. 82 *—M.S. (5/1/2003)*

BODEGA LOPEZ

Bodega Lopez 2002 Cabernet Xero Cabernet Sauvignon (Mendoza) $9. 83 *—M.S. (11/15/2004)*

Bodega Lopez 2002 Malbec Xero Malbec (Mendoza) $9. 84 *—M.S. (11/15/2004)*

BODEGA LURTON

Bodega Lurton 2003 Bonarda (Uco Valley) $7. 82 *—M.S. (11/15/2004)*

Bodega Lurton 2005 Cabernet Sauvignon (Uco Valley) $9. 84 *—M.S. (11/1/2006)*

Bodega Lurton 2003 Cabernet Sauvignon (Uco Valley) $9. 84 *—M.S. (11/15/2004)*

Bodega Lurton 2004 Gran Lurton Cabernet Sauvignon (Mendoza) $18. 87 *—M.S. (12/1/2006)*

Bodega Lurton 2004 Reserva Cabernet Sauvignon (Mendoza) $13. Drinkability combined with power, and for $13: Alert the authorities! This is a textbook everyday Cabernet Sauvignon, the antithesis of a stripped-down, mass-market plonkster. The cola, berry and cherry flavors are pure as can be while the chocolaty, modestly tannic finish is lasting and secure. 89 Best Buy *—M.S. (2/1/2007)*

Bodega Lurton 2002 Reserva Cabernet Sauvignon (Uco Valley) $12. 89 Best Buy *—M.S. (11/15/2004)*

Bodega Lurton 2005 Reserva Chardonnay (Mendoza) $13. 81 *—M.S. (11/1/2006)*

Bodega Lurton 2005 Malbec (Uco Valley) $9. 84 *—M.S. (12/1/2006)*

Bodega Lurton 2003 Malbec (Uco Valley) $9. 86 Best Buy *—M.S. (11/15/2004)*

Bodega Lurton 2004 Reserva Malbec (Mendoza) $13. 86 *—M.S. (12/1/2006)*

Bodega Lurton 2005 Pinot Gris (Uco Valley) $8. 83 *—M.S. (2/1/2006)*

Bodega Lurton 2005 Rosé Blend (Mendoza) $8. 83 *—M.S. (12/1/2006)*

Bodega Lurton 2005 Torrontès (Mendoza) $9. 85 Best Buy *—M.S. (12/1/2006)*

Bodega Lurton 2004 Torrontès (Uco Valley) $7. 83 *—M.S. (11/15/2004)*

Bodega Lurton 2003 Torrontès (Mendoza) $7. 90 Best Buy *—P.G. (11/15/2004)*

Bodega Lurton 2005 Flor de Torrontès Reserva Torrontès (Uco Valley) $13. 80 *—M.S. (12/1/2006)*

BODEGA NANNI

Bodega Nanni 2001 Single Estate Vineyard Cabernet Sauvignon (Cafayate) $11. 84 *—M.S. (2/1/2004)*

Bodega Nanni 2001 Single Estate Vineyard Malbec (Cafayate) $11. 84 *—M.S. (12/1/2003)*

Bodega Nanni 2001 Tannat (Cafayate) $11. 85 *—M.S. (2/1/2004)*

BODEGA NOEMÍA DE PATAGONIA

Bodega Noemía de Patagonia 2005 A Lisa Malbec (Río Negro Valley) $24. 90 *—M.S. (12/15/2006)*

Bodega Noemía de Patagonia 2004 J. Alberto Malbec (Río Negro Valley) $38. 91 *—M.S. (12/15/2006)*

Bodega Noemía de Patagonia 2004 Noemía Malbec (Río Negro Valley) $110. 92 *—M.S. (12/15/2006)*

Bodega Noemía de Patagonia 2003 Noemía Malbec (Río Negro Valley) $152. 93 Editors' Choice *—M.S. (4/1/2006)*

Bodega Noemía de Patagonia 2002 Noemía Malbec (Río Negro Valley) $140. 92 *—M.S. (7/1/2005)*

BODEGA NORTON

Bodega Norton 2002 Barbera (Mendoza) $8. 85 *—M.S. (7/1/2004)*

Bodega Norton 2003 Perdriel Single Vineyard Bordeaux Blend (Mendoza) $64. As good as it gets from Argentina. Winemaker Jorge Riccitelli has artfully crafted a bruising but lovable modern Bordeaux blend that hits every note on the head. The nose offers black olive, berry essence and a ton of chocolate, while the tannic but balanced palate sports luscious black cherry, cassis and more. For a stud of a wine, it has nuance and character—meaning it's not just a fat fruitball. At 70% Malbec with Merlot and Cabernet, this is the ideal wine for a great steak. Just 250 cases produced. 94 Editors' Choice *—M.S. (8/1/2007)*

Bodega Norton 2006 Cabernet Sauvignon (Mendoza) $10. A little charred and bulky, but pretty good for a basic New World Cabernet. The nose is a mix of ripe fruit, licorice and herbs, while the palate is tame and veers to strawberry. Simple and a touch herbal. 84 *—M.S. (8/1/2007)*

Bodega Norton 2002 Cabernet Sauvignon (Mendoza) $8. 84 *—M.S. (7/1/2004)*

Bodega Norton 1999 Cabernet Sauvignon (Mendoza) $8. 84 *—M.S. (11/1/2002)*

Bodega Norton 2004 Reserva Cabernet Sauvignon (Luján de Cuyo) $18. Not nearly as intense and Cab-like as the 2003. For whatever reason, this vintage is bouncy and light, with a touch of smoked meat and rubber but mostly simple raspberry and cherry flavors. The feel borders on jammy, and it finishes with a touch of chocolate but also kind of herbal. 85 *—M.S. (12/31/2007)*

Bodega Norton 2003 Reserva Cabernet Sauvignon (Luján de Cuyo) $18. Here's another success from Bodega Norton. The nose is rich and big, with crusty chocolate and coconut aromas. More chocolate blends with blackberry and pepper in the mouth, while on the finish there's sexy layered darkness. It's New World pomp and pleasantness in all its glory. 90 *—M.S. (8/1/2007)*

Bodega Norton 2006 Rosado Cabernet Sauvignon (Mendoza) $10. Very few of Argentina's rosés make the grade, and this stange Cabernet-based brew from Norton smells like orange marmalade and tastes much the same.

Having never seen a Norton rosé before, it makes us wonder why now? 80 —*M.S. (7/1/2007)*

Bodega Norton 2006 Chardonnay (Mendoza) $10. This is probably the best varietal-level Chardonnay Norton has produced. It's oak-tipped, with butterscotch and spice aromas offering some character to the nose. The melon, pineapple and pear flavors are sweet, but enough acidity creeps into the game to keep things balanced. Might we even suggest some elegance appears on this full-fruited Best Buy? 88 Best Buy —*M.S. (12/1/2007)*

Bodega Norton 1999 Chardonnay (Mendoza) $8. 80 —*M.S. (7/1/2002)*

Bodega Norton 2002 Reserve Chardonnay (Mendoza) $14. 86 —*M.S. (7/1/2004)*

Bodega Norton 2006 Malbec (Mendoza) $10. Simple red-fruit aromas, sweetness and balance come right away on the bouquet, and the palate is basically the same thing: pleasant strawberry and raspberry flavors and a good feel. Nothing fancy but smooth and fun to drink. Commendable given that production is 50,000 cases. 86 Best Buy —*M.S. (8/1/2007)*

Bodega Norton 2002 Malbec (Mendoza) $8. 86 —*M.S. (7/1/2004)*

Bodega Norton 1999 Malbec (Mendoza) $8. 85 Best Buy —*M.S. (11/1/2002)*

Bodega Norton 1998 Malbec (Mendoza) $9. 80 *(5/1/2002)*

Bodega Norton 2005 Reserva Malbec (Luján de Cuyo) $18. Jammy red-fruit aromas mixed with buttery oak make for a simple, sappy nose. There's more butter on the palate in addition to solid blackberry flavors. It finishes round but short, with yet another wave of barrel. A very good wine but not one that wows. 87 —*M.S. (10/1/2007)*

Bodega Norton 2004 Reserva Malbec (Luján de Cuyo) $18. Young, rambunctious and rather carbonic on the nose, with candied, fleshy fruit dosed with a lot of new-oak butter on the palate. Maybe this wine will knit together with a few more months in bottle, but now it's wayward, sweet and chunky and requires more effort to like than it should. 84 —*M.S. (5/1/2007)*

Bodega Norton 2003 Reserve Malbec (Mendoza) $21. 89 —*M.S. (11/15/2005)*

Bodega Norton 2002 Reserve Malbec (Mendoza) $16. 90 —*M.S. (7/1/2004)*

Bodega Norton 1999 Reserve Malbec (Mendoza) $14. 87 Best Buy —*M.S. (11/1/2002)*

Bodega Norton 2006 Merlot (Mendoza) $10. Simple jammy aromas lead to a hard, acidic palate offers some red fruit flavor but also an undercurrent of field greens. A lasting streak of bell pepper on the finish doesn't help bring it around. 82 —*M.S. (10/1/2007)*

Bodega Norton 1999 Merlot (Mendoza) $8. 85 Best Buy —*M.S. (11/1/2002)*

Bodega Norton 2002 Reserve Merlot (Mendoza) $16. 87 —*M.S. (7/1/2004)*

Bodega Norton 2002 La Privada Red Blend (Mendoza) $20. 91 Editors' Choice —*M.S. (7/1/2004)*

Bodega Norton 1999 Privada Red Blend (Mendoza) $21. 83 —*M.S. (11/1/2002)*

Bodega Norton 1998 Privada Red Blend (Mendoza) $14. 83 —*M.S. (11/15/2001)*

Bodega Norton 2002 Sangiovese (Mendoza) $8. 85 —*M.S. (7/1/2004)*

Bodega Norton 1998 Sangiovese (Mendoza) $9. 81 *(5/1/2002)*

Bodega Norton 2006 Sauvignon Blanc (Mendoza) $10. Sauvignon Blanc is not Norton's strong point. This is heavy and dull on the nose, with equally heavy melon and peach flavors. Deep in its core you see what it may want to be, but still this vintage doesn't shine. 80 —*M.S. (8/1/2007)*

Bodega Norton 2003 Sauvignon Blanc (Mendoza) $8. 85 —*M.S. (7/1/2004)*

Bodega Norton 2002 Sauvignon Blanc (Mendoza) $8. 85 —*M.S. (5/1/2003)*

Bodega Norton 2000 Sauvignon Blanc (Mendoza) $8. 83 —*M.S. (11/15/2001)*

Bodega Norton 2006 Torrontes (Mendoza) $10. In a nutshell, this wine is focused in the right direction. Round up front, with melon, papaya and floral aromas. A creamy texture holds flavors of papaya, peach and melon. Solid on the finish and pleasant as Torrontes goes. A fine apéritif when served properly chilled. 86 Best Buy —*M.S. (5/1/2007)*

Bodega Norton 2003 Torrontès (Mendoza) $8. 85 —*M.S. (7/1/2004)*

BODEGA NQN

Bodega NQN 2004 Patagonia Universe Bordeaux Blend (Neuquén) $45. Also called Classico, this prestige blend of Malbec, Merlot and Cabernet Sauvignon hits like a hammer on the nose and then flows into a semi syrupy palate that offers ripeness but not as much harmony as the winery's more modest Malma. Maybe it's the Merlot and Cab, but the wine seems a bit short and solitary given its high aspirations. 87 —*M.S. (2/1/2007)*

Bodega NQN 2004 Malma Malbec (Neuquén) $10. 87 Best Buy —*M.S. (12/15/2006)*

Bodega NQN 2004 Malma Reserva Malbec (Neuquén) $20. 88 —*M.S. (12/15/2006)*

Bodega NQN 2005 Picada 15 Red Blend (Neuquén) $8. 87 Best Buy —*M.S. (12/15/2006)*

Bodega NQN 2005 Malma Sauvignon Blanc (Neuquén) $10. 84 —*M.S. (12/15/2006)*

BODEGA PRIVADA

Bodega Privada 2002 Cabernet Sauvignon (Mendoza) $8. 81 —*M.S. (7/1/2004)*

Bodega Privada 2003 Chardonnay (Mendoza) $8. 84 —*M.S. (7/1/2004)*

Bodega Privada 2005 Malbec (Mendoza) $8. Full-bodied and round, with a hint of raisiny ultraripeness on the nose. The fruit flavors rund tangy and a bit rubbery, but the feel is juicy and the finish is healthy and tight. A bit more crisp and lean than one might expect but good nonetheless. 85 Best Buy —*M.S. (2/1/2007)*

Bodega Privada 2002 Malbec (Mendoza) $8. 84 —*M.S. (7/1/2004)*

Bodega Privada 2002 Merlot (Mendoza) $8. 84 —*M.S. (7/1/2004)*

Bodega Privada 2003 Sauvignon Blanc (Mendoza) $8. 81 —*M.S. (7/1/2004)*

Bodega Privada 2002 Syrah (Mendoza) $8. 85 Best Buy —*M.S. (7/1/2004)*

Bodega Privada 2002 Torrontès (Salta) $8. 83 —*M.S. (7/1/2004)*

BODEGA Y CAVAS DE WEINERT

Bodega Y Cavas De Weinert 2000 Gran Vino Bordeaux Blend (Luján de Cuyo) $26. 90 Editors' Choice —*M.S. (7/1/2005)*

BODEGAS CARO

Bodegas Caro 2004 Caro Bordeaux Blend (Mendoza) $42. This Rothschild-Catena blend is dark as night on the nose, with a strong blast of freshly laid pavement. The palate is a little more acidic and snappy than expected, and as the wine unfolds it offers clean and persistent red-fruit flavors but nothing extraordinary. 88 —*M.S. (12/1/2007)*

Bodegas Caro 2003 Caro Cabernet Sauvignon-Malbec (Mendoza) $42. Lively is one way to describe this Cabernet-Malbec blend. The bouquet is full of smoky balsam wood, leather and solid berry fruit, while the palate is both juicy and plentiful as it pushes equal amounts of bold black fruit and warming oak. A very solid Argentinean icon wine with impeccable structure and liveliness. Better in 2008. 91 Editors' Choice —*M.S. (5/1/2007)*

Bodegas Caro 2002 Cabernet Sauvignon-Malbec (Mendoza) $45. 90 —*M.S. (6/1/2006)*

Bodegas Caro 2001 Cabernet Sauvignon-Malbec (Mendoza) $40. 90 —*M.S. (2/1/2004)*

Bodegas Caro 2003 Amancaya Cabernet Sauvignon-Malbec (Mendoza) $15. 92 Editors' Choice —*M.S. (3/1/2005)*

Bodegas Caro 2006 Amancaya Malbec-Cabernet Sauvignon (Mendoza) $19. Amancaya, a blend of Malbec and Cabernet Sauvignon, never fails to impress. This wine is rich and controlled but also alert and upright. It is juicy and succulent, with ripe blackberry and cassis at its base. Finishes tight and long, and sports a fine structure throughout. 90 Editors' Choice —*M.S. (12/1/2007)*

Bodegas Caro 2005 Amancaya Malbec-Cabernet Sauvignon (Mendoza) $20. From the Catena-Rothschild partnership that is Bodegas Caro, Amancaya blends Malbec and Cabernet Sauvignon in an appealing way. The nose is a touch bretty and rustic, but airing reveals stout fruit and structure. The flavor profile revolves around ripe plum and berry, while coffee and a touch of heat and alcohol work the finish. Another year in bottle would not hurt this wine. 88 —*M.S. (5/1/2007)*

Bodegas Caro 2004 Amancaya Malbec-Cabernet Sauvignon (Mendoza) $18. 91 Editors' Choice —*M.S. (12/31/2005)*

BODEGAS DEL TUPUN

Bodegas del Tupun 2005 Marlena Cabernet Sauvignon (Mendoza) $10. 84 *(11/15/2006)*

Bodegas del Tupun 2006 Marlena Chardonnay-Viognier (Mendoza) $10. 83 *(11/15/2006)*

Bodegas del Tupun 2005 Marlena Malbec (Mendoza) $10. 84 *(11/15/2006)*

BODEGAS EL POR VENIR DE LOS ANDES

Bodegas El Por Venir de los Andes 2004 Laborum Limited Edition Malbec (Cafayate) $49. For an average vintage this is an average wine. It has some bramble, leather and mild green notes to the nose, which are backed by red-fruit and brambly flavors. The feel is fresh and racy due to firm acids. Not the most expressive wine going, but nobody is going to call it flat or flabby. 85 —*M.S. (8/1/2007)*

Bodegas El Por Venir de los Andes 2005 Amauta Red Blend (Salta) $20. An improvement over the previous vintage, this blend of Malbec, Cabernet and Syrah from Cafayate is earthy and baked, with savory leather and spice aromas laid over dark berry notes. It's a ripe, rich wine with meaty plum, berry and cherry flavors. And the mouthfeel is quite good. 89 —*M.S. (12/1/2007)*

Bodegas El Por Venir de los Andes 2004 Amauta Red Blend (Cafayate) $20. Opens with a smoke shack full of hickory and jerky before settling in a dark mass. The palate is sweet and a touch awkward, with heavy Port-like weight and strange but provoking berry flavors. An odd blend of Malbec, Cab and Syrah that needs fine tuning. 84 —*M.S. (10/1/2007)*

BODEGAS ESCORIHUELA

Bodegas Escorihuela 2005 Cruz Alta Reserve Cabernet Sauvignon (Mendoza) $13. If you'd like a little character, bramble and spice to your Cab, then this is where you should go. Yes, it starts out with leather, pickle barrel and a lot of bramble bush, but every time you go back to it there's more fruit, polish, complexity and style. It's interesting, ripe and a step up from your basic street-level Cabernet. 88 Best Buy —*M.S. (10/1/2007)*

Bodegas Escorihuela 2003 High Altitude Cabernet Sauvignon-Malbec (Agrelo) $10. 86 Best Buy —*M.S. (11/15/2004)*

Bodegas Escorihuela 2002 High Altitude Cabernet Sauvignon-Malbec (Mendoza) $10. 90 Best Buy —*P.G. (11/15/2004)*

Bodegas Escorihuela 2006 Cruz Alta Reserve Chardonnay (Mendoza) $13. Pineapple and apple aromas are fairly attractive and fresh, as is the light, wet and zippy palate, which shows mostly citrus and apple flavors. The finish is mild and clean, and overall the wine delivers clarity and a dominant citrus profile. 86 —*M.S. (12/1/2007)*

Bodegas Escorihuela 2006 La Vuelta Unoaked Chardonnay (Mendoza) $8. The style is obtuse and the wine is sweet as sin and unctuous. Aromas of canned pear and peach suggest a lot of residual sugar. 82 —*M.S. (12/1/2007)*

Bodegas Escorihuela 2005 Cruz Alta Malbec (Mendoza) $10. Burnt coffee, mocha, and ultimately an eerie pepper quality take the nose in an unfortunate direction, while the fruit is more in the tart, underdeveloped berry vein than it is ripe and boistrous. Finishes with thin tannins and a scratchy feel. 82 —*M.S. (12/1/2007)*

Bodegas Escorihuela 2004 Cruz Alta President's Reserve Malbec (Mendoza) $20. Cruz Alta is a new, higher-end label from Escorihuela, the long-time maker of value-priced Don Gascón. This is indeed a reserve-level wine (with 15% Cabernet and Syrah), and it's ripe, forward, powerful and mildly tannic. And there's lots of oak to offset the dark berry flavors. Finishes toasty and firm, with mocha. 90 —*M.S. (10/1/2007)*

Bodegas Escorihuela 2005 Cruz Alta Reserve Malbec (Mendoza) $13. Starts with roasted coffee, berry liqueur and toast, while the palate is pretty dense and loaded with boysenberry and cherry. The feel is solid and juicy, with firm acids and tannins supporting a peppery finish. Saturated and staunch, but ordinary. 86 —*M.S. (12/1/2007)*

Bodegas Escorihuela 2006 La Vuelta Malbec (Mendoza) $8. La Vuelta means "the return," and after a glass or two of this, and with modest expectations, you may want to return to this lighter-styled Malbec. Flavorwise, we're talking strawberry-, cherry- and raspberry-infused tea, while light but noticeable oaking yields finishing notes of mocha. 85 Best Buy —*M.S. (10/1/2007)*

Bodegas Escorihuela 2002 High Altitude Red Blend (Mendoza) $10. 88 Best Buy —*M.S. (2/1/2004)*

Bodegas Escorihuela 2005 Cruz Alta Reserve Syrah (Mendoza) $13. Mocha and chocolate welcome you in, but once you get in there isn't much to taste. There's generic red fruit, spice and leather, but the wine seems acidified and on the razor's edge. Not overly generous and the mouthfeel is sheering. 84 —*M.S. (12/1/2007)*

Bodegas Escorihuela 2002 High Altitude White Blend (Mendoza) $10. 86 —*M.S. (7/1/2004)*

BODEGAS HISPANO ARGENTINAS

Bodegas Hispano Argentinas 2002 Martins Malbec (Mendoza) $9. 86 Best Buy —*M.S. (12/1/2003)*

BODEGA SOTTANO

Bodega Sottano 2004 Sottano Cabernet Sauvignon (Luján de Cuyo) $12. Minty and borderline volatile, with candied cherry and raisin flavors. A generic wine with grabby tannins and grit but little to no elegance. 80 —*M.S. (8/1/2007)*

Bodega Sottano 2004 Sottano Malbec (Luján de Cuyo) $12. A lot of oak has been piled onto this wine and it doesn't seem to be sinking in. The nose is awkward and the palate delivers nothing more than candied cherry. A very simple specimen that's not too bad but offers almost nothing in the way of complexity or character. 82 —*M.S. (5/1/2007)*

BODEGA SUR

Bodega Sur 2003 Infinito Malbec (Mendoza) $30. Forward and nicely oaked, with spearmint, cinnamon and green wood aromas courtesy of serious barreling. With racy acidity and full tannins, this wine hits the palate hard but with tasty cherry and raspberry flavors. A touch sheer and thus best with meat, this wine has many attributes but could stand more finesse. 88 —*M.S. (5/1/2007)*

BODEGAS Y VINEDOS SANTA SOFIA

Bodegas y Vinedos Santa Sofia 2002 Urban Oak Red Blend (Uco Valley) $9. 88 Best Buy —*M.S. (2/1/2004)*

BROQUEL

Broquel 2002 Cabernet Sauvignon (Mendoza) $15. 86 —*M.S. (10/1/2004)*

Broquel 2000 Cabernet Sauvignon (Mendoza) $15. 87 —*M.S. (5/1/2003)*

Broquel 2003 Chardonnay (Argentina) $15. 85 —*M.S. (10/1/2004)*

Broquel 2002 Chardonnay (Mendoza) $15. 88 —*M.S. (7/1/2004)*

Broquel 2001 Chardonnay (Mendoza) $15. 86 —*M.S. (5/1/2003)*

Broquel 2002 Malbec (Argentina) $15. 89 —*M.S. (10/1/2004)*

Broquel 2001 Malbec (Mendoza) $15. 88 —*M.S. (12/1/2003)*

Broquel 2000 Malbec (Mendoza) $15. 88 —*M.S. (5/1/2003)*

BUDINI

Budini 2004 Cabernet Sauvignon (Mendoza) $11. 85 —*M.S. (12/1/2006)*

Budini 2005 Chardonnay (Mendoza) $11. 81 —*M.S. (11/1/2006)*

Budini 2004 Malbec (Mendoza) $11. Bacon, tire rubber, pine tar and black cherry aromas set the stage for heady black plum, smoked meat and spice flavors. This is a stylish, serious red for the price; it has balance and structure as well as integrity and personality. 88 Best Buy —*M.S. (2/1/2007)*

BYBLOS

Byblos 2004 Bonarda (Mendoza) $8. 83 —*M.S. (11/15/2005)*

Byblos 2004 Semi-Sweet Bonarda (Mendoza) $8. 82 —*M.S. (11/15/2005)*

CABRA MONTES

Cabra Montes 2004 Cabernet Sauvignon (Agrelo) $9. 82 —*M.S. (8/1/2006)*

Cabra Montes 2004 Chardonnay (Uco Valley) $9. 86 Best Buy —*M.S. (8/1/2006)*

Cabra Montes 2004 Merlot (Agrelo) $9. 85 Best Buy —*M.S. (8/1/2006)*

CABRINI

Cabrini 2000 Cabernet Sauvignon (Mendoza) $11. 88 Best Buy —*M.S. (11/1/2002)*

Cabrini 2000 Malbec (Mendoza) $11. 86 Best Buy —*M.S. (11/1/2002)*

CALIGIORE

Caligiore 2005 Staccato Organic Cabernet Sauvignon-Malbec (Mendoza) $9. Dormant and a bit chemical on the nose, with rubbery fruit and a lean body. Woody and borderline hot on the finish. 81 —*M.S. (10/1/2007)*

Caligiore 2005 Reserve Organic Malbec (Mendoza) $15. Here's a nice wine that pushes the right buttons while not raising any red flags. Raspberry and vanilla flavors are solid and pleasing, while the medium-weight palate features depth and balance. This is not the richest, most overpowering Malbec you'll find, but it comes from 75-year-old vines and its virtues far outdistance its faults. 88 —*M.S. (8/1/2007)*

Caligiore 2005 Reserve Organic Syrah (Mendoza) $15. Nail polish on the nose along with clay will have you wondering. The palate on this organic wine is also a bit shaky; rubbery cherry and raspberry flavors are lean and the aftertaste is fiery. Too unusual and challenging. 81 —*M.S. (8/1/2007)*

CAOBA

Caoba 2004 Reserve Chardonnay (Mendoza) $13. 83 —*M.S. (11/1/2006)*

Caoba 2005 Malbec (Mendoza) $10. 86 Best Buy —*M.S. (11/1/2006)*

CARINAE

Carinae 2004 Malbec (Mendoza) $11. 81 —*M.S. (11/1/2006)*

Carinae 2004 Reserva Malbec (Mendoza) $15. 82 —*M.S. (11/1/2006)*

Carinae 2004 Prestige Red Blend (Mendoza) $26. Here's a fiery, bolstered blend of Malbec, Cabernet and Syrah that burns the nostrils with berry, herb and minty oak aromas. The palate gets some major points for its sweet, pure black-fruit flavors but there always seems to be some protruding alcohol that makes you question the label's stated 14%. One one hand it's handsome and just right; on the other it seems overdone. 89 *—M.S. (2/1/2007)*

CARLOS BASSO

Carlos Basso 2006 Cabernet Sauvignon (San Carlos) $13. Root beer and tree bark aromas give this a rooty, savory, almost baked quality. But the palate is ripe and pure, with cassis, black cherry and fresh prune flavors. Finishing fudge and coffee notes amid strong but respectable tannins make this a worthy value. 88 Best Buy *—M.S. (12/1/2007)*

Carlos Basso 2004 Cabernet Sauvignon (San Carlos) $13. Slightly rubbery and chemical at first, although time allows cherry and tobacco to take over. The palate is sweet and loaded with generic red-fruit flavors that touch on cherry and strawberry. Finishes full but a little creamy and candied. Not complex but tastes good once it hits its stride. 86 *—M.S. (2/1/2007)*

Carlos Basso 2000 Cabernet Sauvignon (San Carlos) $12. 85 *—M.S. (11/1/2002)*

Carlos Basso 2006 Dos Fincas Cabernet Sauvignon-Malbec (Uco Valley) $10. Snappier and more crisp than in the past; this blend of Cabernet and Malbec hits with red-fruit aromas and a touch of vanilla. Next comes raspberry flavors mixed with cola, vanilla and a dollop of butter. Has staying power and depth, but is a little short on core fruit. 85 Best Buy *—M.S. (12/1/2007)*

Carlos Basso 2005 Dos Fincas Cabernet Sauvignon-Malbec (Mendoza) $10. A little loose on the bouquet, with a whiff of sulfur and leather to go with wild berry aromas. In the mouth, it's got an Old World coarseness that turns the flavor profile to pepper and espresso. At 60% Cabernet and 40% Malbec, it's worth the price. 86 Best Buy *—M.S. (10/1/2007)*

Carlos Basso 2004 Dos Fincas Cabernet Sauvignon-Malbec (Uco Valley) $10. 90 Best Buy *—M.S. (12/1/2006)*

Carlos Basso 2005 Dos Fincas Cabernet Sauvignon-Merlot (Mendoza) $10. Soft, easy and totally ripe, this easygoing blend of Cabernet and Merlot should win over most consumers because it's a friendly sort that's endowed with cola, plum and abundant richness. Opponents may find it soft and mealy, but no matter where you stand it should be drunk as soon as possible. Imported by SWG Imports. 88 Best Buy *—M.S. (10/1/2007)*

Carlos Basso 2004 Dos Fincas Cabernet Sauvignon-Merlot (Uco Valley) $10. 91 Best Buy *—M.S. (12/1/2006)*

Carlos Basso 2006 Malbec (San Carlos) $13. Basso makes good wines year in and year out. This Malbec is saturated and potent. It needs time to air out or it could be intimidating. Once open, look for cassis and blackberry flavors in front of a dessert-worthy finish. Tastes a touch hot despite only 13.5% posted alcohol. 88 Best Buy *—M.S. (12/1/2007)*

Carlos Basso 2004 Malbec (Luján de Cuyo) $13. 90 Best Buy *—M.S. (12/1/2006)*

Carlos Basso 2000 Malbec (Mendoza) $12. 83 *—M.S. (11/1/2002)*

Carlos Basso 2005 San Carlos Malbec (Mendoza) $13. Too funky, animal and vegetal to recommend. The wine has color and size but the aromas and flavors just aren't that pleasant. Tastes more like rhubarb and carob than fresh berries. 80 *—M.S. (10/1/2007)*

Carlos Basso 2006 Tunuyan Sauvignon Blanc (Mendoza) $10. Tan in color, with musky aromas. Flavors of cucumber and citrus alert you to the fact that this is Sauvignon Blanc; because nothing else really does. Overall it's a foxy, musky wine without much SB character. 80 *—M.S. (10/1/2007)*

CARMELO PATTI

Carmelo Patti 2002 Gran Assemblage Bordeaux Blend (Mendoza) $55. Weak and hazy to the eye, with a slightly stewy "old-wine" character. But it's only from 2002, so it's not exactly ancient. So why the color? Maybe it's already on its way to full maturity, and if that's the case that means the vegetal notes that are currently dominating the fading fruit are here to stay. 85 *—M.S. (2/1/2007)*

Carmelo Patti 2003 Extra Brut Sparkling Blend (Mendoza) $17. 85 *—M.S. (12/31/2005)*

Carmelo Patti 2002 Extra Brut Sparkling Blend (Mendoza) $19. 87 *—M.S. (12/31/2004)*

CASA BOHER

Casa Boher 2003 Cabernet Sauvignon (Mendoza) $11. 83 *—M.S. (11/15/2005)*

Casa Boher 2003 Malbec (Mendoza) $11. 87 Best Buy *—M.S. (7/1/2005)*

Casa Boher 2003 Merlot (Mendoza) $11. 83 *—M.S. (11/15/2005)*

Casa Boher 2003 Sauvignon Blanc (Mendoza) $11. 83 *—M.S. (7/1/2005)*

CASA DE TANGO

Casa de Tango 1998 Reserve Syrah (Mendoza) $12. 83 *(10/1/2001)*

CASA MONTES

Casa Montes 2001 Alzamora Grand Reserve Oak Malbec (San Juan) $14. 87 *—M.S. (11/1/2006)*

Casa Montes 2001 Alzamora Grand Reserve Oak Syrah (San Juan) $14. 83 *—M.S. (11/1/2006)*

CASATERRA

Casaterra 2002 Cabernet Sauvignon (Mendoza) $7. 80 *—M.S. (7/1/2004)*

Casaterra 2003 Chardonnay (Mendoza) $8. 86 Best Buy *—M.S. (7/1/2004)*

Casaterra 2002 Malbec (Mendoza) $8. 84 *—M.S. (10/1/2004)*

Casaterra 2002 Merlot (Mendoza) $7. 84 *—M.S. (2/1/2004)*

CASTLE VIEW

Castle View 2004 Cabernet Sauvignon (Mendoza) $6. 83 Best Buy *—M.S. (11/15/2005)*

Castle View 2004 Chardonnay (Mendoza) $6. 82 *—M.S. (11/15/2005)*

Castle View 2004 Malbec (Mendoza) $6. 82 *—M.S. (12/31/2005)*

Castle View 2004 Merlot (Mendoza) $6. 84 Best Buy *—M.S. (12/31/2005)*

CATENA

Catena 2002 Cabernet Sauvignon (Mendoza) $20. 87 *—M.S. (11/15/2005)*

Catena 1999 Agrelo Cabernet Sauvignon (Mendoza) $20. 87 *—J.C. (5/1/2002)*

Catena 2001 Agrelo Vineyard Cabernet Sauvignon (Mendoza) $23. 84 *—M.S. (5/1/2003)*

Catena 2000 Alta Cabernet Sauvignon (Mendoza) $60. 87 *—M.S. (7/1/2004)*

Catena 2004 Chardonnay (Mendoza) $18. 86 *—M.S. (6/1/2006)*

Catena 2003 Chardonnay (Mendoza) $18. 90 Editors' Choice *—M.S. (3/1/2005)*

Catena 2001 Agrelo Vineyards Chardonnay (Mendoza) $20. 87 *—M.S. (5/1/2003)*

Catena 2000 Agrelo Vineyards Chardonnay (Mendoza) $15. 85 *—M.S. (7/1/2002)*

Catena 2002 Alta Chardonnay (Mendoza) $30. 88 *—M.S. (3/1/2005)*

Catena 2002 Alta Chardonnay (Mendoza) $30. 88 *—M.S. (11/15/2005)*

Catena 2001 Alta Chardonnay (Mendoza) $33. 90 *—M.S. (7/1/2004)*

Catena 2000 Alta Chardonnay (Mendoza) $32. 84 *—M.S. (5/1/2003)*

Catena 1999 Alta Adrianna Vineyard Chardonnay (Mendoza) $30. 88 *—M.S. (7/1/2002)*

Catena 2003 Malbec (Mendoza) $20. 88 *—M.S. (11/15/2005)*

Catena 2002 Malbec (Mendoza) $22. 88 *—M.S. (3/1/2005)*

Catena 1999 Alta Malbec (Mendoza) $55. 86 *—D.T. (5/1/2002)*

Catena 2000 Alta Angelica Vineyard Malbec (Mendoza) $55. 90 *—M.S. (5/1/2003)*

Catena 2001 Bodega Catena Zapata Malbec (Mendoza) $25. 88 *—M.S. (12/1/2003)*

CATENA ALTA

Catena Alta 2002 Malbec (Mendoza) $45. 89 *—M.S. (4/1/2006)*

CAVA NEGRA

Cava Negra 2002 Malbec (Mendoza) $8. 85 Best Buy *—M.S. (3/1/2005)*

CAVAS DE CHACRAS

Cavas de Chacras 1999 Reserve Malbec (Mendoza) $13. 85 *—M.S. (8/1/2006)*

Cavas de Chacras 2004 Rosé Reserve Rosé Blend (Mendoza) $10. 80 *—M.S. (8/1/2006)*

CAVAS DE SANTOS

Cavas de Santos 2002 Cabernet Sauvignon (Mendoza) $11. 83 *—M.S. (11/15/2005)*

Cavas de Santos 2002 Gran Malbec (Mendoza) $17. 85 *—M.S. (11/15/2005)*

CAVAS DEL CONDE

Cavas del Conde 2002 Cabernet Sauvignon (Mendoza) $9. 80 *—M.S. (11/15/2005)*

Cavas del Conde 2002 Malbec (Mendoza) $9. 83 *—M.S. (11/15/2005)*

Cavas del Conde 2004 Primacia Merlot (Mendoza) $7. 81 *—M.S. (6/1/2006)*

Cavas del Conde 2002 Piedra del Molino Syrah (Mendoza) $7. 80 *—M.S. (4/1/2006)*

Cavas del Conde 2004 Primacia Syrah (Mendoza) $7. 83 *—M.S. (4/1/2006)*

CAVAS DEL VALLE

Cavas del Valle 2000 Malbec (Tupungato) $15. 85 *—M.S. (11/1/2002)*

CHAKANA

Chakana 2005 Bonarda (Mendoza) $11. If you've never tried Argentine Bonarda, Chakana is a good place to start. The nose offers the varietal's typical vulcanized rubber and dark-fruit aromas, while the palate is smooth and full of straightforward blackberry. Complicated it's not, but it is pleasant. 87 Best Buy *—M.S. (8/1/2007)*

Chakana 2004 Bonarda (Mendoza) $12. 87 Best Buy *—M.S. (11/15/2005)*

Chakana 2005 Cabernet Sauvignon (Mendoza) $11. Few Argentinean wineries are doing everyday red wines better than Chakana. A case in point is this excellent, superbly balanced, easy-drinking Cab. The nose is meaty, earthy and magnetic, while the palate is ripe, harmonious and full of cassis and raspberry. It's fruity more than complex, with stature and style. 90 Best Buy *—M.S. (8/1/2007)*

Chakana 2004 Cabernet Sauvignon (Mendoza) $12. 87 Best Buy *—M.S. (11/15/2005)*

Chakana 2003 Reserve Cabernet Sauvignon (Mendoza) $23. 82 *—M.S. (11/15/2005)*

Chakana 2005 Malbec (Mendoza) $11. The 2005 starts with smoke, heft and dark fruit, while the reasonably rich palate boasts black cherry and plum flavors. This is a solid, value-priced Malbec, as it delivers the grape's weight and fruit but in a well-balanced way. 87 Best Buy *—M.S. (5/1/2007)*

Chakana 2004 Malbec (Mendoza) $12. 88 Best Buy *—M.S. (11/15/2005)*

Chakana 2003 Malbec (Mendoza) $11. 89 Best Buy *—M.S. (3/1/2005)*

Chakana 2005 Reserve Malbec (Luján de Cuyo) $20. The nose is like a convention of all the food groups: there's bold fruit, grilled meat, cola and even some yeasty toast. The palate is juicy and hits with firm, lively blackberry and boysenberry flavors. And the finish offers continuity between the midpalate and end game. A very nice wine from a consistent winery. 89 *—M.S. (12/1/2007)*

Chakana 2004 Reserve Malbec (Luján de Cuyo) $20. Chakana is not the first winery whose basic Malbec comes across cleaner and more approachable than its reserve, which isn't to say we don't like this deeper, more brooding style. It's just that it doesn't have the length or depth to match the extract. So in the final analysis it's fine but soft and bit lacking. 86 *—M.S. (5/1/2007)*

Chakana 2003 Reserve Malbec (Mendoza) $23. 90 *—M.S. (11/15/2005)*

Chakana 2006 Rosé Malbec (Luján de Cuyo) $10. Chakana is earning a reputation for value and consistency. Even in a tough category like Argentine rosado this winery has crafted a tasty, rewarding, fairly fresh wine that features sweet, bouncy cherry and raspberry fruit and a full, round finish. Will go great with summer barbecues and picnics. 87 Best Buy *—M.S. (7/1/2007)*

Chakana 2005 Rosé Malbec (Mendoza) $12. 83 *—M.S. (4/1/2006)*

Chakana 2004 Estate Selection Red Blend (Luján de Cuyo) $25. 91 *—M.S. (12/1/2007)*

Chakana 2003 Estate Selection Red Blend (Mendoza) $30. Chakana makes some good wines, and the pack is led by this prestige-level blend of Cab Sauvignon, Malbec and Bonarda. It's plenty racy and forward, with plum and berry flavors that ring the bell. Toward the end some oak-based vanilla enters the game to applause. A yummy, well-made wine. 90 *—M.S. (10/1/2007)*

Chakana 2006 Sauvignon Blanc (Luján de Cuyo) $10. Very rough and salty, with oversized, aggressive Sauv-like aromas and flavors that are well within the realm of varietal correctness but just not very pleasant. There's a lot of sweat, pungency and salinity to this one. 80 *—M.S. (8/1/2007)*

Chakana 2004 Shiraz (Mendoza) $12. 90 Best Buy *—M.S. (10/1/2005)*

CHATEAU CHANTAL

Chateau Chantal 2005 Reserve Malbec (Luján de Cuyo) $14. A hard, rough, unfocused type of Malbec. It's all over the map and it just doesn't come together in a way that makes you want to spend much time with it. 80 *—M.S. (5/1/2007)*

CHEVAL DES ANDES

Cheval des Andes 2002 Cabernet Sauvignon-Malbec (Mendoza) $75. 93 Cellar Selection *—M.S. (7/1/2005)*

CHILCAS

Chilcas 2006 Piedra Feliz Pinot Noir (San Rafael) $15. From first sniff to last, the nose never makes much of an impression; the wine has funk and generic chemical aromas but also your basic red apple and char. Pretty big and aggressive in the mouth, with snaggy acids and rough tannins. 81 *—M.S. (10/1/2007)*

CHILENSIS

Chilensis 2005 Reserva Merlot (San Rafael) $8. Mature-smelling, with earth and bramble vying with berry aromas. The palate is firm and feels solid, while the flavors of mixed berries are offset by some herbal action. Feels and tastes good enough, with no overt flaws. 84 Best Buy *—M.S. (8/1/2007)*

CINCO TIERRAS

Cinco Tierras 2003 Malbec (Mendoza) $10. 85 Best Buy *—M.S. (12/31/2005)*

Cinco Tierras 2003 Reserve Malbec (Mendoza) $14. 84 *—M.S. (12/31/2005)*

CLOS DE LOS SIETE

Clos de los Siete 2003 Malbec (Mendoza) $16. 91 Editors' Choice *—M.S. (7/1/2005)*

Clos de los Siete 2002 7 Red Blend (Mendoza) $15. 90 Best Buy *—M.S. (10/1/2004)*

Clos de los Siete 2004 Red Wine Red Blend (Mendoza) $17. 89 *—M.S. (6/1/2006)*

COIRON

Coiron 2003 Malbec (Mendoza) $9. 81 *—M.S. (12/1/2006)*

COLOMÉ

Colomé 2005 Estate Malbec (Calchaqui Valley) $25. This high-altitude wine shows a cool, rubbery essence but also warmth, animal notes and rusticity. It's polished to a point, but also a wild ride. The palate is lightly saucy and spicy, and the fruit isn't overly defined or welcoming. But in between the folds there's power and bite. 88 *—M.S. (12/1/2007)*

Colomé 2004 Estate Red Blend (Calchaqui Valley) $25. 91 Editors' Choice *—M.S. (12/1/2006)*

Colomé 2003 Reserva Red Blend (Calchaqui Valley) $90. 92 *—M.S. (12/1/2006)*

Colomé 2006 Torrontès (Calchaqui Valley) $13. 90 Editors' Choice *—M.S. (12/1/2006)*

COLONIA LAS LIEBRES

Colonia Las Liebres 2005 Bonarda (Mendoza) $9. 87 Best Buy *—M.S. (11/1/2006)*

CONCHA Y TORO

Concha y Toro 2002 Xplorador Malbec (Mendoza) $7. 86 Best Buy *—M.S. (11/15/2005)*

Concha y Toro 2001 Xplorador Malbec (Mendoza) $7. 86 Best Buy *—M.S. (10/1/2004)*

Concha y Toro 2000 Xplorador Malbec (Mendoza) $8. 85 Best Buy *—M.S. (11/1/2002)*

CONQUISTA

Conquista 2005 Malbec (Mendoza) $9. Clean and smooth, with plenty of unadulterated red-fruit aromas. The palate is plump, with ripe plum and berry flavors. Finishes with crisp tannins, raspberry flavors and some style. It's the type of wine that has made Malbec's value-worthy reputation what it is today. 89 Best Buy *—M.S. (2/1/2007)*

Conquista 2004 Malbec (Mendoza) $8. 84 Best Buy *—M.S. (11/15/2005)*

CRISTOBAL 1492

Cristobal 1492 2003 Bonarda (Mendoza) $10. 87 Best Buy *—M.S. (11/15/2005)*

Cristobal 1492 2003 Cabernet Sauvignon (Mendoza) $10. 85 Best Buy *—M.S. (11/15/2005)*

Cristobal 1492 2003 Malbec (Mendoza) $10. 80 *—M.S. (12/31/2005)*

Cristobal 1492 2003 Oak Reserve Malbec (Mendoza) $15. 87 *—M.S. (11/15/2005)*

Cristobal 1492 2003 Oak Reserve Shiraz (Mendoza) $19. 83 *—M.S. (11/15/2005)*

Cristobal 1492 2004 Verdelho (Mendoza) $10. 84 *—M.S. (11/15/2005)*

CROTTA

Crotta 2001 Tempranillo (Mendoza) $8. 84 *—M.S. (5/1/2003)*

CUQ

CUQ 2004 Merlot-Bonarda Red Blend (Mendoza) $15. 81 —*M.S. (12/31/2005)*

DAVIS FAMILY

Davis Family 2000 Gusto Vita Malbec (Mendoza) $30. 90 —*M.S. (5/1/2003)*

DIABLO DE UCO

Diablo de Uco 2002 Cabernet Sauvignon (Mendoza) $13. 86 —*M.S. (11/15/2004)*

Diablo de Uco 2003 Malbec (Mendoza) $13. 85 —*M.S. (12/31/2005)*

Diablo de Uco 2002 Malbec (Mendoza) $13. 87 —*M.S. (11/15/2004)*

Diablo de Uco 2002 Merlot (Mendoza) $13. 82 —*M.S. (11/15/2004)*

DOMAINE CHANDON

Domaine Chandon NV Fresco Brut Champagne Blend (Mendoza) $11. 85 Best Buy —*D.T. (11/15/2002)*

DOMAINE JEAN BOUSQUET

Domaine Jean Bousquet 2006 Cabernet Sauvignon (Tupungato) $12. Most of Bousquet's wines are enigmatic. They show some good qualities but also signs of overcropping and underripeness. That said, this wine is typical: it's scattershot in its delivery of green-infused berry fruit, tannins and wood. It's okay but never settles down. Imported by North American Beverage Group. 83 —*M.S. (10/1/2007)*

Domaine Jean Bousquet 2003 Cabernet Sauvignon (Mendoza) $12. 87 Best Buy —*M.S. (11/15/2005)*

Domaine Jean Bousquet 2006 Chardonnay (Tupungato) $12. Toasty but also pickled, with a lot of wood spice and other oak-based aromas and flavors. At one moment the wine seems to have the right stuff: citrus and some length. But upon further inspection the fruit turns foxy and shows itself to be overripe. Loses steam as it unfolds. Imported by North American Beverage Group. 83 —*M.S. (12/1/2007)*

Domaine Jean Bousquet 2004 Chardonnay (Tupungato) $11. 86 Best Buy —*M.S. (7/1/2005)*

Domaine Jean Bousquet 2005 Organic Chardonnay (Tupungato) $13. 84 —*M.S. (8/1/2006)*

Domaine Jean Bousquet 2006 Malbec (Tupungato) $12. This is Bousquet's better 2006 Malbec because it doesn't have the heavy-handed oak of the Reserva. Here you get a ton of ripe, clean fruit with secondary leather and earth aromas. The palate is lively as it hits with firm blackberry and plum flavors. Not complex but good in its simplicity. Imported by North American Beverage Group. 87 Best Buy —*M.S. (10/1/2007)*

Domaine Jean Bousquet 2004 Malbec (Mendoza) $11. 89 Best Buy —*M.S. (11/15/2005)*

Domaine Jean Bousquet 2005 Organic Malbec (Tupungato) $13. 84 —*M.S. (8/1/2006)*

Domaine Jean Bousquet 2006 Reserva Malbec (Tupungato) $18. Rubbery and overly woody, and the palate really burns along with high acidity and short, staccato fruit flavors. Zesty and challenging throughout; it just doesn't push the right buttons given its reserve status and price. 82 —*M.S. (10/1/2007)*

Domaine Jean Bousquet 2005 Rosé Malbec-Cabernet Sauvignon (Tupungato) $10. 84 —*M.S. (4/1/2006)*

Domaine Jean Bousquet 2006 Merlot (Tupungato) $12. Sweet berry aromas are also noticeably green and medicinal, while the palate offers raspberry flavors with a giant supplement of leafy, weedy flavors. On one hand the wine has some class and style; on the other hand questionable purity and ripeness stand out. Imported by North American Beverage Group. 81 —*M.S. (10/1/2007)*

Domaine Jean Bousquet 2004 Merlot (Mendoza) $11. 86 Best Buy —*M.S. (11/15/2005)*

Domaine Jean Bousquet 2005 Organic Merlot (Tupungato) $13. 84 —*M.S. (8/1/2006)*

DOMINGO HERMANOS

Domingo Hermanos 2001 Palo Domingo Red Blend (Salta) $49. 87 —*M.S. (7/1/2004)*

DOMINGO MOLINA

Domingo Molina 2000 Malbec (Argentina) $15. 86 —*M.S. (5/1/2003)*

DON MIGUEL GASCÓN

Don Miguel Gascón 2005 Malbec (Mendoza) $14. This wine seems less intense and extracted than in past years. The nose begins with some rough-riding sulfur and then basic but nondescript berry aromas and flavors. Feels good on the tongue and finishes fairly long. Still solid for everyday and by-the-glass drinking. 20,000 cases made. 85 —*M.S. (5/1/2007)*

Don Miguel Gascón 2004 Malbec (Mendoza) $13. 87 —*M.S. (11/15/2005)*

Don Miguel Gascón 2003 Malbec (Mendoza) $12. 87 Best Buy —*M.S. (10/1/2004)*

Don Miguel Gascón 2002 Malbec (Mendoza) $12. 87 —*M.S. (12/1/2003)*

Don Miguel Gascón 2000 Malbec (Mendoza) $10. 88 *(11/15/2001)*

Don Miguel Gascón 2006 Gascón Malbec (Mendoza) $12. Getting past the giant blast of oak that dominates the bouquet is not an easy task, but the intrepid wood chopper will find another side to this wine, one that's full of bright, juicy black fruit and syrupy core sweetness. Of course, the oak is always present and with that comes mocha, coffee and vanilla notes. Imported by Gascon USA. 86 —*M.S. (12/31/2007)*

Don Miguel Gascón 2003 President's Blend Malbec (Mendoza) $22. 91 Editors' Choice —*M.S. (6/1/2006)*

Don Miguel Gascón 2000 President's Blend Malbec (Mendoza) $20. 86 —*M.S. (11/1/2002)*

Don Miguel Gascón 2004 Syrah (Mendoza) $14. Brutally charred and saturated with leather and mushroom but no discernible fruit. The palate is a heavy mass of wayward oak and black nothing. Syrah in Argentina is a shaky endeavor, and this one doesn't help the cause. 82 —*M.S. (2/1/2007)*

Don Miguel Gascón 2003 Syrah (Mendoza) $12. 87 Best Buy —*M.S. (10/1/2004)*

Don Miguel Gascón 2002 Syrah (Mendoza) $12. 84 —*M.S. (2/1/2004)*

Don Miguel Gascón 2000 Syrah (Mendoza) $12. 85 —*M.S. (11/1/2002)*

Don Miguel Gascón 2005 Viognier (Mendoza) $13. 88 Best Buy —*M.S. (6/1/2006)*

Don Miguel Gascón 2004 Viognier (Mendoza) $12. 86 —*M.S. (11/15/2004)*

Don Miguel Gascón 2003 Viognier (Mendoza) $12. 85 —*M.S. (7/1/2004)*

Don Miguel Gascón 2002 Viognier (Mendoza) $12. 83 —*M.S. (2/1/2004)*

DON RODOLFO

Don Rodolfo 2003 High Altitude Vineyards Cabernet Sauvignon (Cafayate) $10. 82 —*M.S. (11/15/2004)*

Don Rodolfo 2004 High Altitude Vineyards Malbec (Cafayate) $10. 84 —*M.S. (12/1/2006)*

Don Rodolfo 2003 High Altitude Vineyards Malbec (Cafayate) $10. 82 —*M.S. (11/15/2004)*

Don Rodolfo 2003 High Altitude Vineyards Shiraz (Cafayate) $10. 87 Best Buy —*M.S. (11/15/2004)*

Don Rodolfo 2004 High Altitude Vineyards Tannat (Cafayate) $10. 86 Best Buy —*M.S. (12/1/2006)*

Don Rodolfo 2002 High Altitude Vineyards Tannat (Cafayate) $10. 81 —*M.S. (3/1/2005)*

Don Rodolfo 2005 High Altitude Vineyards Torrontès (Cafayate) $10. 83 —*M.S. (11/1/2006)*

Don Rodolfo 2003 High Altitude Vineyards Torrontès (Cafayate) $10. 85 Best Buy —*M.S. (11/15/2004)*

DOÑA CRISTINA

Doña Cristina 2001 Red Blend (Mendoza) $14. 82 —*M.S. (11/15/2005)*

DOÑA PAULA

Doña Paula 2004 Estate Cabernet Sauvignon (Mendoza) $16. Warm and oaky up front, with menthol. The palate is short and feels kind of flat as it offers up standard raspberry and other red-fruit flavors. Finishes with milk chocolate notes but overall it doesn't have much texture or personality. 83 —*M.S. (8/1/2007)*

Doña Paula 2003 Estate Cabernet Sauvignon (Luján de Cuyo) $15. 89 *(12/31/2004)*

Doña Paula 2002 Estate Cabernet Sauvignon (Luján de Cuyo) $15. 86 —*M.S. (2/1/2004)*

Doña Paula 2006 Los Cardos Cabernet Sauvignon (Luján de Cuyo) $10. A little bit of leather and smoke meat give the blackberry bouquet something different, while the palate is round, forward and shows good plum and berry flavors. Some heat and spice on the finish do not detract from the overall package, which makes the grade if it doesn't blow you away. 86 Best Buy —*M.S. (12/1/2007)*

Doña Paula 2005 Los Cardos Cabernet Sauvignon (Luján de Cuyo) $10. 83 —*M.S. (11/1/2006)*

Doña Paula 2003 Los Cardos Cabernet Sauvignon (Luján de Cuyo) $10. 85 —*M.S. (10/1/2004)*

Doña Paula 2002 Los Cardos Cabernet Sauvignon (Luján de Cuyo) $8. 85 Best Buy —*M.S. (2/1/2004)*

Doña Paula 2005 Estate Chardonnay (Luján de Cuyo) $16. Fading fast; this plump, hot-climate Chard is pretty much as expected: there's lots of oak covering peach, butterscotch and apple cider aromas and flavors. Borderline cloying. 83 —*M.S. (8/1/2007)*

Doña Paula 2003 Estate Chardonnay (Luján de Cuyo) $15. 86 *(12/31/2004)*

Doña Paula 2002 Estate Chardonnay (Luján de Cuyo) $15. 86 —*M.S. (10/1/2004)*

Doña Paula 2005 Los Cardos Chardonnay (Mendoza) $10. 82 —*M.S. (11/1/2006)*

Doña Paula 2004 Los Cardos Chardonnay (Mendoza) $9. 86 Best Buy —*M.S. (11/15/2005)*

Doña Paula 2004 Los Cardos Chardonnay (Luján de Cuyo) $9. 85 *(12/31/2004)*

Doña Paula 2003 Los Cardos Chardonnay (Luján de Cuyo) $10. 86 Best Buy —*M.S. (10/1/2004)*

Doña Paula 2002 Los Cardos Chardonnay (Luján de Cuyo) $8. 85 Best Buy —*M.S. (2/1/2004)*

Doña Paula 2002 Séleccion de Bodega Single Vineyard Chardonnay (Luján de Cuyo) $29. 89 *(12/31/2004)*

Doña Paula 1999 Malbec (Mendoza) $12. 83 —*M.S. (12/1/2003)*

Doña Paula 2006 Estate Malbec (Luján de Cuyo) $16. A veneer of oak and aromas of root beer greet you, while cherry and raspberry flavors work the palate. It's a lively, tannic wine with a candied, slightly resiny/minty flavor profile and finish. Best with food. 85 —*M.S. (10/1/2007)*

Doña Paula 2003 Estate Malbec (Luján de Cuyo) $15. 87 *(12/31/2004)*

Doña Paula 2006 Los Cardos Malbec (Luján de Cuyo) $10. Big and fruity, and for the most part holds together and exhibits more good qualities than its faults. The flavor profile drives full-bodied black fruit and a finish that cuts out quietly. Not over the top in any way. 85 Best Buy —*M.S. (12/1/2007)*

Doña Paula 2003 Los Cardos Malbec (Luján de Cuyo) $10. 84 —*M.S. (11/15/2004)*

Doña Paula 1999 Los Cardos Malbec (Mendoza) $8. 84 —*M.S. (12/1/2003)*

Doña Paula 2005 Los Cardos Rosé Malbec (Mendoza) $10. 80 —*M.S. (12/1/2006)*

Doña Paula 2004 Selección de Bodega Single Vineyard Malbec (Luján de Cuyo) $35. Pronounced oak is the opening blast, and amid the shy red berry and tomato leaf aromas there are hints of leather, mint and coconut. All these scents indicate that heavy wood was thrown at the wine, so while the power and goals of the wine are admirable, it's weighed down presently by a touch too much resin. Maybe that'll drift with time but that's not for sure. 88 —*M.S. (10/1/2007)*

Doña Paula 1999 Séleccion de Bodega Single Vineyard Malbec (Luján de Cuyo) $12. 84 —*M.S. (12/1/2003)*

Doña Paula 2004 Estate Merlot (Tupungato) $NA. This wine kicks off in spicy, almost saucy fashion, but airing reveals plum and cherry aromas and flavors that are backed by moderately spiky tannins and some chocolate flavor. Hits the spot with its forward attitude and healthy fruit, but lacks the complexity of a higher-tier red. 85 —*M.S. (2/1/2007)*

Doña Paula 2003 Estate Merlot (Tupungato) $15. 85 *(12/31/2004)*

Doña Paula 2002 Estate Merlot (Tupungato) $15. 85 —*M.S. (10/1/2004)*

Doña Paula 2003 Los Cardos Merlot (Tupungato) $10. 80 —*M.S. (10/1/2004)*

Doña Paula 2002 Los Cardos Merlot (Tupungato) $8. 85 Best Buy —*M.S. (2/1/2004)*

Doña Paula 2002 Estate Red Blend (Luján de Cuyo) $15. 84 —*M.S. (2/1/2004)*

Doña Paula 2005 Los Cardos Sauvignon Blanc (Mendoza) $10. 82 —*M.S. (12/1/2006)*

Doña Paula 2004 Los Cardos Sauvignon Blanc (Tupungato) $9. 85 Best Buy *(12/31/2004)*

Doña Paula 2005 Shiraz-Malbec (Mendoza) $16. Big and ripe, with hefty aromas of stewed fruit, cola and mint. The palate is broad but drying, with average plum and blackberry flavors. It lacks some vitality and doesn't hit the high notes, but it's wholesome and qualifies as big-boned and ready. 86 —*M.S. (12/1/2007)*

Doña Paula 2003 Estate Shiraz-Malbec (Luján de Cuyo) $15. 88 *(12/31/2004)*

Doña Paula 2003 Los Cardos Syrah (Luján de Cuyo) $10. 82 —*M.S. (10/1/2004)*

Doña Paula 2002 Los Cardos Syrah (Luján de Cuyo) $8. 85 Best Buy —*M.S. (2/1/2004)*

DURIGUTTI

Durigutti 2004 Bonarda (Mendoza) $10. As Bonarda goes, this wine is one of the best I've tried. From the onset there's pure fruit on the nose along with hints of mint and vanilla. The palate beams with red cherry, plum and chocolate. It's a statuesque red with the price of a thousand inferior wines. Highly recommended should you come across it. 89 Best Buy —*M.S. (2/1/2007)*

Durigutti 2004 Malbec (Mendoza) $12. Quite unusual in its aromas; there's a funky but not offputting mix of saucy fruit, aged cheese and green olive. The palate is also aloof, as obtuse berry flavors blend with savory notes and a bit more olive. Good mouthfeel and finishing length help it along. 85 —*M.S. (2/1/2007)*

Durigutti 2003 Malbec (Mendoza) $12. 88 Best Buy —*M.S. (12/31/2005)*

Durigutti 2003 Reserva Malbec (Mendoza) $29. 90 —*M.S. (12/1/2006)*

ECOS

Ecos 2002 Malbec (Mendoza) $12. 85 —*M.S. (10/1/2004)*

Ecos 2003 Syrah (Mendoza) $12. 87 Best Buy —*M.S. (10/1/2004)*

EL CIPRES

El Cipres 2003 Malbec (Mendoza) $10. Fairly piercing and hot, with sweet, gratuitious red-fruit flavors and little semblance of a purpose. Generic red wine on its best day. 80 —*M.S. (5/1/2007)*

EL NIÑO

El Niño 2003 Malbec (Mendoza) $19. 88 —*M.S. (7/1/2005)*

EL ROSAL

El Rosal 2005 Reserve Cabernet Sauvignon (San Rafael) $17. From San Rafael in southern Mendoza, this Cab Sauvignon picks up a little more steam and complexity every time you go back to it. The nose is your basic cassis and raspberry, while the medium-weight palate features ripe fruit finishing in a sweet cascade of milk chocolate and burnt brown sugar. Satisfying, especially if you like a hint of sweetness to your Cab. 87 —*M.S. (10/1/2007)*

El Rosal 2005 Reserve Malbec (San Rafael) $17. Touches of tree bark, nutmeg and aged cheese give the nose diversity compared to the standard blackberry and vanilla, and in the mouth the wine is full of cola, root beer and other savory flavors in addition to berry fruit. It's a bit grabby and tannic, but overall it is quite good. 88 —*M.S. (10/1/2007)*

ENRIQUE FOSTER

Enrique Foster 2004 Firmado Malbec (Luján de Cuyo) $90. Purple as can be, with a loaded bouquet of black fruit and oak. This is your classic heavyweight, and while 2004 was not a great vintage in Mendoza, this wine still shows excellent depth, weight and balance. Firm on the finish, with big tannins and grab. Production was only 175 cases; drink now–2009. Imported by Southern Wine Group. 91 —*M.S. (8/1/2007)*

Enrique Foster 2006 Ique Malbec (Mendoza) $11. Spunky and funky on the nose, with some heat and bramble. There's definitely a gamy side to this wine, but as it airs it picks up more of Malbec's trademark feel and fruit. Not as forward and clean as it should be; but has its benefits. Imported by Southern Wine Group. 85 —*M.S. (8/1/2007)*

Enrique Foster 2006 IQUE Malbec (Mendoza) $11. A draft of menthol and aromas of chocolate and mossy fruit work pretty nicely on the nose, while the palate is superripe, a bit candied and accented by spice and coffee. This is a strong starter, though it falls off a little on the finish. 86 Best Buy —*M.S. (12/1/2007)*

Enrique Foster 2004 Ique Malbec (Mendoza) $11. 84 —*M.S. (12/1/2006)*

Enrique Foster 2003 Ique Malbec (Mendoza) $12. 88 Best Buy —*M.S. (11/15/2004)*

Enrique Foster 2003 Edicion Limitada Malbec (Luján de Cuyo) $45. The bouquet is fairly tight, with aromas of coffee, crushed minerals, crude oil and fine herbs. The palate runs snappier than most high-end Malbecs, but it also delivers on the promise of ripeness and black-fruit flavors. Finishes in healthy fashion, with some slickness and speed. Very nice and likely even better with food. 1,000 cases made. Imported by Slocum & Sons. 88 —*M.S. (8/1/2007)*

Enrique Foster 2002 Limited Edition Malbec (Luján de Cuyo) $36. 87 —*M.S. (11/15/2004)*

Enrique Foster 2003 Reserva Malbec (Luján de Cuyo) $23. A good finisher, with early minty, resiny aromas giving way to broader, more typical ripe aromas and flavors. The mouthfeel is lively courtesy of vivid core acidity, while the berry and cherry flavors come across ripe and grabby. The more air you give it the better it'll perform. Imported by Slocum & Sons. 88 —*M.S. (10/1/2007)*

Enrique Foster 2002 Reserva Malbec (Luján de Cuyo) $23. 87 —*M.S. (11/15/2004)*

Enrique Foster 2003 Reserva Finca Castro Barros Malbec (Luján de Cuyo) $25. This wine seems mulchy and warm; it comes out of the bottle with attitude and some fire. As it settles, you get berry, bramble and leather, and always does it seem a little "traditional" in style rather than modern and polished up. Definitely a full-bodied, oily wine that could use more flavor and fruit. 86 —*M.S. (12/31/2007)*

Enrique Foster 2004 Terruño Lunlunta Malbec (Mendoza) $20. A little damp and heavy, with molasses, stewed berry and char on the nose. The palate, however, is fairly jumpy and alert; fiery berry flavors hit with force and some heat. On the finish you'll find berry essence and some bramble. Is it slightly green at its core? We think so. Imported by Southern Wine Group. 85 —*M.S. (8/1/2007)*

Enrique Foster 2004 Terruño Vistalba Malbec (Mendoza) $20. A blasting bouquet of oak and affiliated cinnamon and spice are wave one, while next up there's dark fruit and a wealth of vanilla. This is one saturated Malbec, with menthol and tannins in spades. Only medium follow-through on the finish tempers the final grade. Imported by Southern Wine Group. 89 —*M.S. (10/1/2007)*

ESCALERA AL SOL

Escalera al Sol 1999 Syrah (Mendoza) $6. 83 *(10/1/2001)*

ESTANCIA

Estancia 2000 Ancon Malbec (Mendoza) $25. 88 —*C.S. (5/1/2002)*

ESTEPA

Estepa 2003 Mística Malbec (Río Negro Valley) $22. This Patagonian Malbec requires patience and forgiveness. The nose is milky and green at first, but airing paroles riper, redder aromas and flavors. Ultimately there's decent berry character and plumpness but not a lot of follow through or finish. 84 —*M.S. (10/1/2007)*

ETCHART

Etchart 1999 Chardonnay (Cafayate) $NA. 83 —*M.S. (9/1/2001)*

Etchart 1999 Rio de Plata Malbec (Mendoza) $7. 81 —*J.C. (5/1/2002)*

Etchart 1999 Torrontès (Cafayate) $NA. 84 —*M.S. (9/1/2001)*

EZIO

Ezio 2004 Merlot (Famatina Valley) $6. 85 Best Buy —*M.S. (6/1/2006)*

Ezio 2004 Pinot Grigio (Famatina Valley) $6. 82 —*M.S. (2/1/2006)*

FABRE MONTMAYOU

Fabre Montmayou 2005 Malbec (Luján de Cuyo) $10. 89 Best Buy —*M.S. (12/1/2006)*

Fabre Montmayou 2002 Malbec (Mendoza) $10. 87 Best Buy —*M.S. (7/1/2005)*

Fabre Montmayou 2002 Gran Reserva Malbec (Mendoza) $15. 90 Best Buy —*M.S. (7/1/2005)*

Fabre Montmayou 2006 Rosé Malbec (Luján de Cuyo) $9. Dry, peppery and lacking in elegance, this Malbec is herbal and dilute on the nose, with sweet and candied raspberry flavors. While this winery's red wines are usually very good, this isn't likely to do much for you. 81 —*M.S. (7/1/2007)*

FALLING STAR

Falling Star 2004 Cabernet Sauvignon (Cuyo) $5. 82 —*M.S. (7/1/2005)*

Falling Star 2002 Cabernet Sauvignon (Mendoza) $6. 84 Best Buy —*M.S. (2/1/2004)*

Falling Star 2004 Chardonnay (Cuyo) $5. 83 Best Buy —*M.S. (3/1/2005)*

Falling Star 2002 Chardonnay (Mendoza) $5. 84 Best Buy —*M.S. (2/1/2004)*

Falling Star 2001 Chardonnay (Mendoza) $5. 85 Best Buy —*M.S. (5/1/2003)*

Falling Star 2000 Chardonnay (Mendoza) $5. 80 —*M.S. (11/15/2001)*

Falling Star 2004 Merlot-Malbec (Cuyo) $5. 84 Best Buy —*M.S. (3/1/2005)*

Falling Star 2001 Merlot-Malbec (Mendoza) $6. 80 —*M.S. (5/1/2003)*

Falling Star 2004 Sauvignon Blanc-Semillon (Cuyo) $5. 84 Best Buy —*M.S. (7/1/2005)*

FAMILIA CASSONE

Familia Cassone 2001 Malbec (Luján de Cuyo) $9. 84 —*M.S. (12/1/2003)*

Familia Cassone 1999 Reserva Malbec (Mendoza) $13. 88 Best Buy —*M.S. (11/1/2002)*

FAMILIA LLAVER ORO

Familia Llaver Oro 2001 Sauvignon Blanc (Mendoza) $16. 82 —*M.S. (2/1/2004)*

Familia Llaver Oro 1999 Syrah (Mendoza) $18. 83 —*M.S. (2/1/2004)*

FAMILIA SCHROEDER

Familia Schroeder 2005 Saurus Patagonia Cabernet Sauvignon (Neuquén) $9. Cabernet may always struggle to achieve ripeness in Patagonia, but Schroeder is getting pretty decent plum and blackberry character out of this wine. The mouthfeel, however, runs kind of hard and sheer. May get better in future vintages. 84 —*M.S. (10/1/2007)*

Familia Schroeder 2004 Saurus Patagonia Cabernet Sauvignon (Argentina) $9. 82 —*M.S. (6/1/2006)*

Familia Schroeder 2005 Saurus Patagonia Select Cabernet Sauvignon (Neuquén) $14. Plum, blackberry and other fruit aromas work the nose, which is light and airy more than deep and concentrated. The palate is also a touch thin for a reserve-level wine, but the fruit is clean and the finish offers both chocolate and black pepper. 85 —*M.S. (10/1/2007)*

Familia Schroeder NV Saurus Extra Brut Champagne Blend (Neuquén) $10. Popcorn, green-apple and scallion aromas precede crisp, tart flavors of barely ripe peach and grapefruit. The finish is short and citrusy, boosted by choppy acids. Racy but not rich. 83 —*M.S. (12/31/2007)*

Familia Schroeder 2006 Saurus Patagonia Chardonnay (Neuquén) $9. Clean but weightless, with little substance or stuffing to it. This is a cool-climate, Patagonian Chard from young vines, hence it is reticent and watery. The winery's pricier Patagonian Select is a better option. 81 —*M.S. (10/1/2007)*

Familia Schroeder 2006 Saurus Patagonia Select Chardonnay (Neuquén) $14. Movie popcorn, baked fruits and plenty of toast and vanilla work the entry, while forward flavors of apple and pear are kicked up a notch by full acidity. And what that all means is that fruit pierces the fairly heavy oak on this wine, leaving you with a lot of the positives of New World Chardonnay. Nice in this price range. 89 Best Buy —*M.S. (10/1/2007)*

Familia Schroeder 2005 Saurus Patagonia Select Chardonnay (Argentina) $13. 83 —*M.S. (6/1/2006)*

Familia Schroeder 2005 Saurus Patagonia Malbec (Neuquén) $9. Sweet plum, raisin and chocolate work the welcoming nose, and on the palate the wine is generous but easy to understand; the flavors are flush and ripe but none too complicated. Simply stated, this wine is healthy and well made. 87 Best Buy —*M.S. (10/1/2007)*

Familia Schroeder 2004 Saurus Patagonia Malbec (Argentina) $9. 85 Best Buy —*M.S. (4/1/2006)*

Familia Schroeder 2005 Saurus Patagonia Select Malbec (Neuquén) $14. Nice on the nose. The palate is steady but on the leaner side, with prickly tannins joining berry fruit, chocolate and toast. A tighter, Patagonian style of Malbec, meaning it's firm as opposed to lush. 85 —*M.S. (10/1/2007)*

Familia Schroeder 2004 Saurus Patagonia Select Malbec (Argentina) $13. 89 Best Buy —*M.S. (4/1/2006)*

Familia Schroeder 2005 Saurus Patagonia Merlot (Neuquén) $9. Familia Schroeder is making good, restrained wines in Neuquén. This Merlot won't rock your world but it will deliver firm, fresh raspberry flavors, food-friendly acidity and solid tannins. And it's even got some chewy sweetness. 86 Best Buy —*M.S. (10/1/2007)*

Familia Schroeder 2004 Saurus Patagonia Merlot (Argentina) $9. 83 —*M.S. (6/1/2006)*

Familia Schroeder 2005 Saurus Patagonia Select Merlot (Neuquén) $14. Open and rewarding, with strawberry and raspberry aromas followed by ripe, clean cherry and raspberry flavors. Don't expect a ton of depth or richness, but do expect a food-friendly wine that's convincing and well made. 88 —*M.S. (10/1/2007)*

Familia Schroeder 2004 Saurus Patagonia Select Merlot (Argentina) $13. 84 —*M.S. (6/1/2006)*

Familia Schroeder 2004 Saurus Patagonia Select Pinot Noir (Argentina) $13. 81 —*M.S. (6/1/2006)*

Familia Schroeder 2003 Red Blend (Neuquén) $42. Congratulations go to Schroeder for having the guts to blend Pinot Noir and Malbec, and to get a great wine out of it. The mix is pure Patagonia, and after some fiery, dark aromas the palate takes over with a mix of bright fruit and chocolate. Round, large and full to the last drop, this is well worth a go should you come across it. 1,000 cases made. 91 —*M.S. (10/1/2007)*

Familia Schroeder 2006 Saurus Patagonia Select Sauvignon Blanc (Neuquén) $14. This variety doesn't seem to have adapted well to Patagonia. For starters, it has virtually no inherent Sauvignon Blanc character: it's oaky, sour and scratchy, with a lean and watery finish. It's not a foul or dirty wine; but it isn't what we've come to expect from SB. 81 —*M.S. (10/1/2007)*

Familia Schroeder 2005 Saurus Patagonia Select Sauvignon Blanc (Argentina) $13. 85 *—M.S. (4/1/2006)*

Familia Schroeder 2006 Deseado Torrontes (Neuquén) $13. Sweet and frothy, and made quite close to the Moscato style, meaning the nose is full of flowers and lime. The palate is a mix of crushed children's vitamins, mango and ripe melon. 85 *—M.S. (12/31/2007)*

FANTELLI

Fantelli 2005 Cabernet Sauvignon (Mendoza) $9. Pencil eraser, tomato leaf and sweet fruit aromas are the appropriate set up to a candied palate that's sweet with cherry and strawberry essence. It's a wine with kick but it has also has chunky side. 83 *—M.S. (8/1/2007)*

Fantelli 2002 Cabernet Sauvignon (Mendoza) $8. 81 *—M.S. (10/1/2004)*

Fantelli 2004 Serie Magno Cabernet Sauvignon (Mendoza) $19. A little choppy and tannic, with thin red-fruit aromas. The palate is of medium depth, with a bit of tannin-driven rawness to make things a little harder than ideal. Otherwise it's steady and warming. 84 *—M.S. (10/1/2007)*

Fantelli 2006 Chardonnay (Mendoza) $9. Holds it together for the most part, but this isn't what you'd call a focused or interesting wine. The nose is mildly fruity, while the palate is shapeless and doesn't deliver recognizable Chard flavors. It rates as a generic dry white wine with hints of melon and peach. 83 *—M.S. (10/1/2007)*

Fantelli 2003 Chardonnay (Mendoza) $8. 84 *—M.S. (10/1/2004)*

Fantelli 2001 Chardonnay (Mendoza) $9. 83 *—M.S. (2/1/2004)*

Fantelli 2000 Chardonnay (Mendoza) $9. 82 *—M.S. (7/1/2002)*

Fantelli 2005 Malbec (Mendoza) $9. Leather, mint and a touch of raisin make for a fairly ripe and mature bouquet. The palate follows with reasonably vibrant berry flavors and a little chocolaty heft. If it falls a bit flat on the tail that only means that it's not for aging and is meant to drink now. 86 Best Buy *—M.S. (8/1/2007)*

Fantelli 2004 Malbec (Mendoza) $9. 83 *—M.S. (6/1/2006)*

Fantelli 2002 Malbec (Mendoza) $8. 86 Best Buy *—M.S. (10/1/2004)*

Fantelli 2001 Malbec (Mendoza) $9. 84 *—M.S. (12/1/2003)*

Fantelli 1999 Malbec (Mendoza) $10. 83 *(5/1/2002)*

Fantelli 2004 Serie Magno Malbec (Mendoza) $18. Mildly sweet and easy on the nose, while the palate offers berry and cherry flavors that are not too complicated. A touch of new oak produces some char and pepper on the back palate and finish, while overall it has a nice personality. The best so far from this winery. 87 *—M.S. (2/1/2007)*

Fantelli 2002 Merlot (Mendoza) $8. 86 Best Buy *—M.S. (10/1/2004)*

Fantelli 1999 Merlot (Mendoza) $10. 83 *—C.S. (5/1/2002)*

Fantelli 1999 Sangiovese (Mendoza) $10. 84 *—C.S. (5/1/2002)*

Fantelli 2004 Syrah (Mendoza) $9. 85 Best Buy *—M.S. (6/1/2006)*

Fantelli 2002 Syrah (Mendoza) $8. 86 Best Buy *—M.S. (10/1/2004)*

Fantelli 2001 Syrah (Mendoza) $9. 85 *—M.S. (2/1/2004)*

Fantelli 2006 Torrontes (Mendoza) $9. Over the years the Fantelli wines have not impressed, but this Torrontes works nicely, especially if you like some weight and sweetness to your white wine. The nose offers apple blossoms and honey, while the peach, pear and applesauce flavors are round and sweet. Seems to have some residual sugar. 85 Best Buy *—M.S. (12/1/2007)*

Fantelli 2005 Torrontès (Mendoza) $9. 83 *—M.S. (8/1/2006)*

Fantelli 2004 Torrontès (Mendoza) $8. 83 *—M.S. (12/31/2005)*

Fantelli 2003 Torrontès (Mendoza) $8. 85 Best Buy *—M.S. (10/1/2004)*

FELIPE RUTINI

Felipe Rutini 2004 Chardonnay (Tupungato) $18. 85 *—M.S. (6/1/2006)*

Felipe Rutini 2002 Chardonnay (Mendoza) $19. 88 *—M.S. (7/1/2004)*

Felipe Rutini 1999 Reserve Chardonnay (Mendoza) $19. 83 *—M.S. (7/1/2002)*

Felipe Rutini 2003 Malbec (La Consulta) $18. 89 *—M.S. (4/1/2006)*

Felipe Rutini 2005 Malbec (Mendoza) $18. Staunch cherry and grape aromas are indicative of what the wine will give. The palate pushes ahead with plum and cherry flavors, but the fruit isn't overly developed and the mouthfeel is more tight and sheer than cushioned and rich. Zesty and firm on the finish, which is par for this course. 86 *—M.S. (12/1/2007)*

Felipe Rutini 2002 Malbec (Mendoza) $19. 90 *—M.S. (7/1/2004)*

Felipe Rutini 2001 Malbec (Mendoza) $20. 89 *—M.S. (12/1/2003)*

Felipe Rutini 2000 Malbec (Tupungato) $18. 91 Editors' Choice *—M.S. (5/1/2003)*

Felipe Rutini 2003 Encuentro Malbec-Merlot (Tupungato) $25. 90 Editors' Choice *—M.S. (6/1/2006)*

Felipe Rutini 2003 Merlot (Tupungato) $18. 85 *—M.S. (6/1/2006)*

Felipe Rutini 2002 Merlot (Mendoza) $20. 82 *—M.S. (3/1/2005)*

Felipe Rutini 2002 Merlot (Mendoza) $19. 87 *—M.S. (7/1/2004)*

Felipe Rutini 2000 Merlot (Tupungato) $18. 86 *—M.S. (5/1/2003)*

Felipe Rutini 1999 Apartado Red Blend (Mendoza) $60. 90 *—M.S. (5/1/2003)*

FILLIPO FIGAR

Fillipo Figar 2000 Anastasia Cabernet Sauvignon (Mendoza) $10. 84 *—M.S. (11/1/2002)*

Fillipo Figar 2001 Anastasia Malbec (Mendoza) $10. 85 Best Buy *—M.S. (11/1/2002)*

FILUS

Filus 2004 Alto Medrano Cabernet Sauvignon (Mendoza) $9. Rather raw and weak for Argentinean Cab, with reedy, brambly aromas. The palate is tangy and short, which again isn't what one is generally looking for from Cabernet. Adequate mouthfeel is this wine's lone savior. 80 *—M.S. (2/1/2007)*

Filus 2005 Reserve Malbec (Mendoza) $18. A full and pulsing wine, with leather and other animal notes to make things more interesting. The mouth is like a black-fruit explosion: muscular berry and tannins fly all over the place, ending in a lively, almost fiery finish. A bit grabby and overexcited, but good with grilled meats. 87 *—M.S. (10/1/2007)*

Filus 2003 Reserve Malbec (Mendoza) $16. 85 *—M.S. (12/31/2005)*

Filus 2005 Alto Medrano Merlot (Mendoza) $9. Despite a young, jumpy and jammy beginning, this wine soon finds a groove that includes ripe cherry and berry flavors backed by a nice mouthfeel and a full finish that keeps its form. If there's the smallest bit of green on the nose and flavor it's forgiven by overall good quality. 86 Best Buy *—M.S. (5/1/2007)*

Filus 2004 Alto Medrano Syrah (Mendoza) $9. A bushel of punched-up red fruit carries the nose, but there's not much oak, character or nuance to hang your hat on. The palate is equally red-fruit dominated, but the mouthfeel is hard and stingy and the wine stumbles to a rubbery, grabby finish. 84 *—M.S. (2/1/2007)*

FINCA DE DOMINGO

Finca de Domingo 1999 Malbec (Argentina) $12. 85 *—M.S. (5/1/2003)*

Finca de Domingo 2003 Torrontès (Argentina) $8. 82 *—M.S. (7/1/2004)*

Finca de Domingo 2001 Torrontès (Cafayate) $7. 82 *—M.S. (5/1/2003)*

FINCA DEL VALLE

Finca del Valle 2001 Cabernet Sauvignon (Mendoza) $8. 83 *—M.S. (2/1/2004)*

Finca del Valle 2000 Lazzaro Coleccion Familia Cabernet Sauvignon (Mendoza) $12. 88 Best Buy *—M.S. (11/1/2002)*

Finca del Valle 2001 Chardonnay (Mendoza) $7. 81 *—M.S. (2/1/2004)*

Finca del Valle 2001 Malbec (Mendoza) $7. 82 *—M.S. (12/1/2003)*

Finca del Valle 2001 Merlot (Mendoza) $7. 82 *—M.S. (2/1/2004)*

Finca del Valle 2003 Lazzaro Coleccion Familia Merlot (Mendoza) $9. 81 *—M.S. (10/1/2004)*

Finca del Valle 2002 Trinomium Red Blend (Mendoza) $10. 86 Best Buy *—M.S. (2/1/2004)*

FINCA EL PERAL

Finca El Peral 2005 Malbec (Tupungato) $11. Aromas of red clay and spice are at the center of the nose on this lighter-styled wine. In the mouth, there's sappy raspberry fruit and a finish that's both drying and a touch cloying. Still, for the most part this wine keeps it together. 84 *—M.S. (5/1/2007)*

FINCA EL PORTILLO

Finca El Portillo 2005 Cabernet Sauvignon (Mendoza) $10. Roasted and toasted, this heavily charred wine doesn't have the pedigree to take on such oak; what you get is a big ball of coffee, mocha and medicinal flavors but very little definition. 82 *—M.S. (5/1/2007)*

Finca El Portillo 2004 Cabernet Sauvignon (Mendoza) $9. 84 *—M.S. (11/15/2005)*

Finca El Portillo 2005 Chardonnay (Uco Valley) $9. 87 Best Buy *—M.S. (8/1/2006)*

Finca El Portillo 2004 Chardonnay (Mendoza) $9. 85 Best Buy *—M.S. (11/15/2005)*

Finca El Portillo 2006 Estate Bottled Chardonnay (Uco Valley) $11. Slightly floral, with some toast and vanilla. But from there it doesn't do much to impress. The palate is jumpy and wacky with tangy, tart lemony flavors. Very aggressive on the palate and tough to embrace. 81 *—M.S. (8/1/2007)*

Finca El Portillo 2006 Malbec (Uco Valley) $12. Solid, ripe and smooth on the nose, then red cherry and raspberry come forward on the zesty, tangy palate. The finish is long and healthy, but a bit monotone in its delivery. Freshness and pop are not lacking in this young Malbec. 86 —*M.S. (10/1/2007)*

Finca El Portillo 2005 Malbec (Mendoza) $10. As this winery's young vines take on some age, the wines are getting better. This Malbec shows graham cracker and plum aromas on a ready-to-go bouquet, while the palate is almost lush as it delivers tasty strawberry, raspberry and chocolate flavors. Simple enough for novices but also interesting enough to satisfy more savvy imbibers. 88 Best Buy —*M.S. (2/1/2007)*

Finca El Portillo 2004 Malbec (Mendoza) $9. 86 Best Buy —*M.S. (11/15/2005)*

Finca El Portillo 2006 Rosé Malbec (Uco Valley) $11. Clean but lean, with tart, tangy flavors of cherries and citrus. This wine offers freshness but little in the way of fruit or folly. It's adequate as crisp quaffers go but does nothing to stir the beast. 83 —*M.S. (7/1/2007)*

Finca El Portillo 2004 Merlot (Alto Valle de Uco) $9. 83 —*M.S. (12/31/2005)*

Finca El Portillo 2006 Estate Bottled Pinot Noir (Uco Valley) $12. Smells like cherry juice and offers reserved but basic candied fruit flavors. There are touches of cherry and raspberry in front of caramel and vanilla on the finish. The feel is crisp and there's a core quality to the wine that may show brighter in future vintages. 83 —*M.S. (12/1/2007)*

Finca El Portillo 2005 Sauvignon Blanc (Uco Valley) $9. 84 —*M.S. (8/1/2006)*

Finca El Portillo 2004 Sauvignon Blanc (Alto Valle de Uco) $9. 83 —*M.S. (7/1/2005)*

Finca El Portillo 2006 Estate Bottled Sauvignon Blanc (Uco Valley) $11. The nose kicks off with ripe apple and zest and draws you in. The palate is live-wire pineapple and green apple with plenty of tang and a worthy mouthfeel. Even on the finish it holds the line. 84 —*M.S. (8/1/2007)*

Finca El Portillo 2005 Syrah (Mendoza) $10. 87 Best Buy —*M.S. (12/1/2006)*

FINCA EL RETIRO

Finca El Retiro 2003 Cabernet Sauvignon (Mendoza) $11. 82 —*M.S. (8/1/2006)*

Finca El Retiro 2004 Malbec (Mendoza) $11. Fairly deep and dense, with graphite, crude oil and leather aromas that muscle up the black-fruit foundation. The palate runs a bit short and hot, with compact berry flavors and pointed acidity. Lacks mouthfeel and complexity when put to the test. 85 —*M.S. (2/1/2007)*

Finca El Retiro 2003 Malbec (Mendoza) $11. 86 Best Buy —*M.S. (8/1/2006)*

Finca El Retiro 2004 Reserva Especial Malbec (Mendoza) $17. Solid and dark, but with a pasty, mildly green nose. Frankly, this wine isn't up to the winery's regular Malbec, as heavier oak takes on a lemony character. In addition, an attempt at greater ripeness has left a wine that's reduced and lacks cushion. 83 —*M.S. (2/1/2007)*

Finca El Retiro 2003 Reserva Especial Malbec (Mendoza) $17. 88 —*M.S. (6/1/2006)*

Finca El Retiro 2003 Syrah (Mendoza) $11. 83 —*M.S. (8/1/2006)*

Finca El Retiro 2003 Reserva Especial Tempranillo (Mendoza) $17. 85 —*M.S. (6/1/2006)*

FINCA FLICHMAN

Finca Flichman 2006 Misterio Rosé Shiraz-Malbec (Mendoza) $8. Sweet fruit and cinnamon notes open the nose before it turns funky and less than pure. In the mouth, there's heavy plum and blueberry flavors. Overall it's too clumsy and heavy to rate better. The blend is 50/50 Malbec and Shiraz. 83 —*M.S. (7/1/2007)*

Finca Flichman 1999 Syrah (Mendoza) $10. 83 —*M.S. (11/15/2001)*

Finca Flichman 1998 Reserva Syrah (Mendoza) $13. 86 *(10/1/2001)*

FINCA KOCH

Finca Koch 2003 Cabernet Sauvignon (Tupungato) $15. 83 —*M.S. (12/1/2006)*

Finca Koch 2001 Cabernet Sauvignon (Mendoza) $19. 89 Editors' Choice —*M.S. (7/1/2004)*

Finca Koch 2001 Cabernet Sauvignon (Tupungato) $17. 88 —*M.S. (5/1/2003)*

Finca Koch 2003 Martin Koch Thirteen Months Cabernet Sauvignon (Tupungato) $14. 87 —*M.S. (12/1/2006)*

Finca Koch 2004 Martin Koch Six Months Malbec (Luján de Cuyo) $14. 88 —*M.S. (12/1/2006)*

Finca Koch 2004 Torrontès (Cafayate) $9. 83 —*M.S. (12/1/2006)*

FINCA LA ANITA

Finca La Anita 1999 Linea Tonel Red Blend (Mendoza) $NA. This old-timer proves that Argentinean Malbec is not a great cellar dweller. This smells, tastes and feels much older than its eight years. It's full of tobacco, dried spices and a dominating leafiness. The blend is 70% Syrah and 30% Malbec. 82 —*M.S. (10/1/2007)*

Finca La Anita 1996 Syrah (Mendoza) $50. 85 *(11/1/2001)*

FINCA LA DANIELA

Finca La Daniela 2002 Malbec (Mendoza) $11. 86 Best Buy —*M.S. (5/1/2005)*

FINCA LA NINA

Finca La Nina 2003 Cabernet Sauvignon (Mendoza) $9. 87 Best Buy —*M.S. (11/15/2005)*

FINCA SIMONASSI

Finca Simonassi 2003 Reserve Malbec (Mendoza) $10. 84 —*M.S. (12/1/2006)*

FINCA SOPHENIA

Finca Sophenia 2004 Synthesis The Blend Bordeaux Blend (Tupungato) $37. Broad and bullish is this blend of Merlot, Malbec and Cabernet Sauvignon. The nose is rich and granular, with hints of plum, raisin and iodine. It airs out nicely, exposing boysenberry and cassis flavors. And it finishes rock solid, with depth. It's all here; excellent wine from a mediocre vintage. 91 —*M.S. (12/1/2007)*

Finca Sophenia 2003 Synthesis Bordeaux Blend (Tupungato) $40. 90 —*M.S. (6/1/2006)*

Finca Sophenia 2004 Cabernet Sauvignon (Tupungato) $17. Interesting Argentine Cabernet, with rooty, baked aromas that settle in and impress if given time. The palate is balanced by subtle red-fruit and earthy flavors, while the feel is stocky and grabby courtesy of strong tannins. A good wine with a lot of positives. 88 —*M.S. (10/1/2007)*

Finca Sophenia 2003 Estate Cabernet Sauvignon (Tupungato) $18. 90 Editors' Choice —*M.S. (11/15/2005)*

Finca Sophenia 2003 Chardonnay (Mendoza) $15. 84 —*M.S. (3/1/2005)*

Finca Sophenia 2005 Altosur Chardonnay (Tupungato) $11. 86 Best Buy —*M.S. (6/1/2006)*

Finca Sophenia 2006 Malbec (Tupungato) $17. This wine needs time to get its legs underneath it. It comes on young and rugged and gamy, but if you let it sit and air out for 20 minutes it turns deeper, riper and much more fruity. And by the time it settles you're smack dab in the middle of mountain berry and other natural flavors. Will get better with some bottle time. 90 —*M.S. (8/1/2007)*

Finca Sophenia 2003 Malbec (Mendoza) $17. 87 —*M.S. (3/1/2005)*

Finca Sophenia 2006 Altosur Malbec (Tupungato) $11. Fast becoming one of Argentina's most reliable value brands, Altosur got it right in 2006 with its basic Malbec. The wine is full, chewy, healthy and bright. It has all the attributes of good, young Malbec: plums, berries and chocolate, with lushness and some style. 88 Best Buy —*M.S. (8/1/2007)*

Finca Sophenia 2005 Altosur Malbec (Tupungato) $18. 87 —*M.S. (8/1/2006)*

Finca Sophenia 2002 Altosur Malbec (Mendoza) $10. 88 Best Buy —*M.S. (3/1/2005)*

Finca Sophenia 2005 Synthesis Malbec (Tupungato) $25. In the past this was a Bordeaux blend but now it's all or almost all Malbec. And because it hails from cooler Tupungato it features floral aromas more than heavy berry scents, and in the mouth it's all about red fruit as opposed to beefy black fruit. If it's a bit short on the finish, chalk that up to its racier, more streamlined frame. 89 —*M.S. (8/1/2007)*

Finca Sophenia 2006 Altosur Rosé Malbec (Tupungato) $11. Finca Sophenia's bargain label is Altosur, and this pink wine is actually more murky red than true rose in color. And the flavors are of baked strawberry mixed with rhubarb. As a whole it does little to propel the reputation of Argentine rosé. 80 —*M.S. (7/1/2007)*

Finca Sophenia 2005 Altosur Rosé Malbec (Tupungato) $10. 86 Best Buy —*M.S. (6/21/2006)*

Finca Sophenia 2002 Merlot (Mendoza) $17. 84 —*M.S. (3/1/2005)*

Finca Sophenia 2006 Altosur Merlot (Tupungato) $11. Don't let the bright purple color and plum/prune aromas fool you: the wine looks deeper and fleshier than it is. In fact, while the palate deals heft and tannin, the depth of fruit is modest and the final package winds up being uncomplicated, but in a good way. 85 —*M.S. (10/1/2007)*

Finca Sophenia 2003 Estate Merlot (Tupungato) $18. 85 —*M.S. (11/15/2005)*

Finca Sophenia 2004 Altosur Rose Merlot-Malbec (Tupungato) $10. 83 —*M.S. (4/1/2006)*

Finca Sophenia 2004 Altosur Sauvignon Blanc (Mendoza) $10. 86 Best Buy —*M.S. (11/15/2005)*

FINCA URQUIZA

Finca Urquiza 2001 Cabernet Sauvignon (Mendoza) $12. 85 —*M.S. (3/1/2005)*

Finca Urquiza 2001 Malbec (Mendoza) $12. 83 —*M.S. (3/1/2005)*

FINCAS DON MARTINO

Fincas Don Martino 2003 Violetas Malbec (Luján de Cuyo) $20. If you don't mind a little overt wood on your Malbec, then this will certainly do the trick and more. The nose offers some maple and mature berry aromas, while the palate pumps oak-infused black cherry fruit. Lengthy on the finish, with mocha and vanilla. Like we said, it's a bit toasty and woody, but overall it works like a charm. 90 —*M.S. (8/1/2007)*

Fincas Don Martino 2002 Violetas Reserve Malbec (Luján de Cuyo) $40. Starts out good, with menthol and wintergreen dominating the nose. The palate is forward and endowed with a lot of red-fruit flavors, but the mouthfeel lets it down. There's too much bounding acidity and not nearly enough lushness. 85 —*M.S. (10/1/2007)*

FLOURISH

Flourish 2004 Malbec (Mendoza) $11. 85 —*M.S. (11/15/2005)*

FUNDACION DE MENDOZA

Fundacion de Mendoza 1999 Prestigio Cabernet Blend (Mendoza) $15. 83 —*M.S. (11/1/2002)*

FUNKY LLAMA

Funky Llama 2005 Cabernet Sauvignon (Mendoza) $6. Every llama has its day, and for Funky Llama this is one to take to the bank. The olive, leather and dry oaky aromas set the stage for solid cassis, raspberry and herb flavors. The body, feel and finish seem right, so for the money it's a blue chip special. 87 Best Buy —*M.S. (10/1/2007)*

Funky Llama 2004 Cabernet Sauvignon (Mendoza) $6. 81 —*M.S. (8/1/2006)*

Funky Llama 2003 Cabernet Sauvignon (Mendoza) $6. 80 —*M.S. (7/1/2005)*

Funky Llama 2006 Chardonnay (Mendoza) $6. All in all this isn't a bad little wine for the price. It is a touch musky and heavy on the nose, but the palate holds form as it delivers round banana and melon flavors along with some vanilla and sponge cake on the finish. 83 —*M.S. (8/1/2007)*

Funky Llama 2004 Chardonnay (Mendoza) $6. 84 Best Buy —*M.S. (6/1/2006)*

Funky Llama 2003 Chardonnay (Mendoza) $6. 84 Best Buy —*M.S. (3/1/2005)*

Funky Llama 2005 Malbec (Mendoza) $6. Jumbled and rubbery, as you might expect given the price. The palate is sketchy with its lean cherry and raspberry flavors, but overall it's an acceptable effort that won't have you dumping the bottle out. 50,000 cases made. 81 —*M.S. (5/1/2007)*

Funky Llama 2004 Malbec (Mendoza) $6. 85 Best Buy —*M.S. (4/1/2006)*

Funky Llama 2003 Malbec (Mendoza) $6. 82 —*M.S. (3/1/2005)*

Funky Llama 2004 Rosé Malbec (Mendoza) $6. 85 Best Buy —*M.S. (4/1/2006)*

Funky Llama 2004 Merlot (Mendoza) $6. 82 —*M.S. (6/1/2006)*

Funky Llama 2004 Shiraz (Mendoza) $6. 83 —*M.S. (6/1/2006)*

Funky Llama 2004 Tempranillo (Mendoza) $6. 80 —*M.S. (6/1/2006)*

Funky Llama 2003 Tempranillo (Mendoza) $6. 84 Best Buy —*M.S. (3/1/2005)*

GENTILE COLLINS

Gentile Collins 2001 Chardonnay (Mendoza) $8. 86 Best Buy —*M.S. (5/1/2003)*

Gentile Collins 2001 Malbec (Mendoza) $8. 86 —*M.S. (5/1/2003)*

Gentile Collins 2002 Gran Syrah (Mendoza) $15. 87 —*M.S. (11/1/2006)*

Gentile Collins 2002 Tempranillo (Mendoza) $8. 80 —*M.S. (5/1/2003)*

GOUGUENHEIM WINERY

Gouguenheim Winery 2004 Cabernet Sauvignon (Mendoza) $10. 84 —*M.S. (8/1/2006)*

Gouguenheim Winery 2004 Malbec (Mendoza) $10. 83 —*M.S. (8/1/2006)*

Gouguenheim Winery 2003 Flores de Valle Melosa Azul Malbec (Mendoza) $26. 87 —*M.S. (11/1/2006)*

Gouguenheim Winery 2003 Otoño Malbec (Mendoza) $10. 86 Best Buy —*M.S. (7/1/2005)*

Gouguenheim Winery 2004 Verano Merlot (Mendoza) $10. 88 Best Buy —*M.S. (8/1/2006)*

Gouguenheim Winery 2003 Verano Merlot (Mendoza) $10. 83 —*M.S. (7/1/2005)*

Gouguenheim Winery 1999 Silvestre Red Blend (Tupungato) $15. 80 —*M.S. (3/1/2005)*

Gouguenheim Winery 2004 Primavera Syrah (Mendoza) $10. 82 —*M.S. (8/1/2006)*

GRAFFIGNA

Graffigna 2004 Grand Reserve Cabernet Sauvignon (San Juan) $20. Graffigna has shown improvement with its current set of releases. This Cab starts out dark, charred and full of blackberry aromas and flavors. It initially seems flashy and ready for anything. But the more you run it across your palate, the more the acidity rises up. And before long it almost seems scouring and jumpy. Imported by Pernod Ricard USA. 86 —*M.S. (12/31/2007)*

Graffigna 1998 Selección Especial Cabernet Sauvignon (Tulum Valley) $10. 81 —*M.S. (11/15/2001)*

Graffigna 1999 Selección Especial Cabernet Sauvignon (Tulum Valley) $10. 82 —*C.S. (5/1/2002)*

Graffigna 2004 Malbec (San Juan) $11. 82 —*M.S. (11/15/2005)*

Graffigna 2001 Don Santiago Malbec (San Juan) $20. 81 —*M.S. (3/1/2005)*

Graffigna 2000 Don Santiago Malbec (San Juan) $11. 82 —*M.S. (12/1/2003)*

Graffigna 2004 Grand Reserve Malbec (San Juan) $20. Olive, blackberry and toasty oak all give hope, but when this wine crosses the palate the acidity is so intense that it causes you to take count of your cheeks, tongue and teeth. On one hand, there's blackberry and cassis flavors to enjoy; on the other, the mouthfeel leaves you roughed up. Imported by Pernod Ricard USA. 84 —*M.S. (12/31/2007)*

Graffigna 2003 G Malbec (Pedernal Valley) $18. 85 —*M.S. (12/31/2005)*

Graffigna 2001 Selección Especial Estate Bottled Malbec (Tulum Valley) $10. 81 —*M.S. (12/1/2003)*

Graffigna 1999 Selección Especial Malbec (Tulum Valley) $10. 85 Best Buy —*C.S. (5/1/2002)*

Graffigna 2005 Pinot Grigio (San Juan) $10. 80 —*M.S. (2/1/2006)*

Graffigna 2000 Selección Especial Estate Bottled Red Blend (San Juan) $10. 80 —*M.S. (5/1/2003)*

Graffigna 2004 Shiraz (San Juan) $11. 83 —*M.S. (6/1/2006)*

Graffigna 2003 G Shiraz (Pedernal Valley) $18. 83 —*M.S. (4/1/2006)*

Graffigna 1999 Syrah (Tulum Valley) $18. 81 *(1/1/2004)*

Graffigna 2001 Don Santiago Syrah (San Juan) $18. 86 —*M.S. (11/15/2004)*

Graffigna 2000 Don Santiago Syrah (Tulum Valley) $18. 80 —*M.S. (2/1/2004)*

Graffigna 1999 Selección Especial Syrah (Tulum Valley) $10. 82 *(10/1/2001)*

Graffigna 2001 Selección Especial Syrah-Cabernet (Tulum Valley) $10. 80 —*M.S. (2/1/2004)*

HACIENDA DEL PLATA

Hacienda del Plata 2002 Reserve Cabernet Sauvignon (Mendoza) $24. 82 —*M.S. (8/1/2006)*

Hacienda del Plata 2003 Zagal Cabernet Sauvignon (Mendoza) $15. 83 —*M.S. (6/1/2006)*

Hacienda del Plata 2002 Zagal Malbec (Mendoza) $15. 80 —*M.S. (6/1/2006)*

Hacienda del Plata 2005 Sauvignon Blanc (Mendoza) $15. 82 —*M.S. (8/1/2006)*

HAT IN THE RING

Hat in the Ring 2006 Master Cabernet Sauvignon (Mendoza) $10. Very sweet at first, with aromas of cherry cough drop and crème de cassis. Turns cheesy with air, and once the palate arrives be prepared for tangy pie cherry flavors in front of a starchy, lean finish. Offers the basics but nothing more. 82 —*M.S. (12/1/2007)*

HÉLÉNE GARCIN

Hélène Garcin 2005 Clos des Andes Malbec (Mendoza) $20. Peppery red fruit and a strong whiff of a wet dog make this a leap of faith. The palate holds that peppery element while also showing raspberry and cassis notes. Vanilla and wood spice are front and center on the finish, and while it gets better with time, it never quite reaches fifth gear. 86 *—M.S. (12/1/2007)*

Hélène Garcin 2005 Paso Doble Red Blend (Mendoza) $17. Tomato leaf, baked beans and burnt leather challenge the wine's purity, but patience is rewarded with dry, herbal flavors and spicy wood notes. Mouthfeel and body are the wine's attributes; otherwise it's fairly wedded to the saucy, stewy style that can be Argentina. One-third each of Cabernet Sauvignon, Malbec and Syrah. 84 *—M.S. (12/1/2007)*

HENRY LAGARDE

Henry Lagarde 1999 Estate Bottled Cabernet Sauvignon (Luján de Cuyo) $10. 85 *—M.S. (5/1/2003)*

Henry Lagarde 2005 Reserve Cabernet Sauvignon (Mendoza) $11. This is your quintessential New World Best Buy. The bouquet is full, slightly oaky and a touch burnt, and overall it's very nice. Same goes for the mouth, full of ripe berry and cassis flavors. It's medium to full in terms of weight and intensity, while the tannins create a chewy, masculine sensation. 89 Best Buy *—M.S. (12/1/2007)*

Henry Lagarde 2003 Vino de Guarda Cabernet Sauvignon (Mendoza) $50. A hulk of a wine with forced oak that results in aromas of mint, char, citrus peel and smoke. The palate is endowed with ample black cherry, raspberry and mocha flavors, while the finish mixes orange peel, chocolate and a lot of leftover wood resin. Interesting but very oaked up and not quite in perfect balance. 88 *—M.S. (12/31/2007)*

Henry Lagarde 2000 Malbec (Luján de Cuyo) $12. 86 *—M.S. (12/1/2003)*

Henry Lagarde 1999 Malbec (Luján de Cuyo) $10. 86 *—M.S. (5/1/2003)*

Henry Lagarde 2006 Altas Cumbres Malbec (Mendoza) $9. Mildly dusty on the surface, but for the most part Lagarde's entry-level Malbec is jammy and tart, with lean plum and berry flavors. The finish shows a light touch of oak and vanilla, but the feel is rather crisp and hard. Not a lot of flesh or cushion here. 83 *—M.S. (12/1/2007)*

Henry Lagarde 2005 Reserve Malbec (Mendoza) $11. Spice, rose hips and raspberry make for an open and welcoming nose. The palate delivers generic berry flavors, size, tannins and spice. It finishes a little harsh, with pepper and burnt notes. But mostly it's a solid everyday Malbec. 85 *—M.S. (12/1/2007)*

Henry Lagarde 2000 Merlot (Luján de Cuyo) $10. 87 *—M.S. (5/1/2003)*

Henry Lagarde 2002 Viognier (Luján de Cuyo) $10. 83 *—M.S. (5/1/2003)*

HIGH ALTITUDE

High Altitude 2005 Chardonnay-Viognier (Agrelo) $12. 84 *—M.S. (6/1/2006)*

High Altitude 2005 Malbec-Cabernet Sauvignon (Agrelo) $12. 86 *—M.S. (12/1/2006)*

High Altitude 2004 Malbec-Cabernet Sauvignon (Mendoza) $10. 88 Best Buy *—M.S. (11/15/2005)*

HUMBERTO BARBERIS

Humberto Barberis 1999 Malbec (Mendoza) $13. 83 *—M.S. (5/1/2003)*

HUMBERTO CANALE

Humberto Canale 2005 Patagonia Classic Malbec (Alto Valle del Río Negro) $10. Simple aromas may lack vibrancy but aren't offputting. And frankly speaking, it's nice to smell soft berry fruit and not much else (namely burnt or buttery oak). The palate, meanwhile, is plump, bright and full of clean but basic boysenberry fruit. Finishes thin but sturdy. 86 Best Buy *—M.S. (12/1/2007)*

ICHANKA

Ichanka 2005 Syrah (La Rioja) $10. 85 Best Buy *—M.S. (12/1/2006)*

Ichanka 2005 Torrontès (La Rioja) $10. 83 *—M.S. (12/1/2006)*

INCA

Inca 2002 Barbera-Merlot Barbera (Salta) $NA. 84 *—M.S. (7/1/2004)*

Inca 2004 Cabernet Sauvignon-Malbec (Calchaqui Valley) $9. 86 Best Buy *—M.S. (12/1/2006)*

Inca 2002 Cabernet Sauvignon-Malbec (Salta) $NA. 81 *—M.S. (7/1/2004)*

Inca 2003 Barbera-Merlot Red Blend (Calchaqui Valley) $9. 87 Best Buy *—M.S. (12/1/2006)*

Inca 2002 Tannat (Salta) $NA. 83 *—M.S. (7/1/2004)*

Inca 2003 Torrontès (Salta) $NA. 86 *—M.S. (7/1/2004)*

Inca 2005 Torrontès-Chardonnay White Blend (Calchaqui Valley) $9. 86 Best Buy *—M.S. (11/1/2006)*

INFINITUS

Infinitus 2004 Malbec (Río Negro Valley) $13. 86 *—M.S. (12/15/2006)*

Infinitus 2005 Gran Reserva Merlot (Río Negro Valley) $25. 86 *—M.S. (12/15/2006)*

J. & F. LURTON

J. & F. Lurton 2001 Gran Lurton Reserve Cabernet Blend (Uco Valley) $18. 86 *—M.S. (11/15/2004)*

J. & F. Lurton 2002 Gran Lurton Cabernet Sauvignon (Mendoza) $18. 87 *—M.S. (7/1/2005)*

J. & F. Lurton 2004 Reserva Chardonnay (Mendoza) $12. 85 *—M.S. (7/1/2005)*

J. & F. Lurton 2003 Chacayes Malbec (Mendoza) $75. 92 Cellar Selection *—M.S. (12/1/2006)*

J. & F. Lurton 2002 Chacayes Malbec (Mendoza) $75. 92 *—M.S. (11/15/2004)*

J. & F. Lurton 2003 Piedra Negra Malbec (Uco Valley) $28. 90 *—M.S. (12/1/2006)*

J. & F. Lurton 2002 Piedra Negra Malbec (Uco Valley) $30. 90 *—M.S. (11/15/2004)*

J. & F. Lurton 2002 Reserva Malbec (Mendoza) $13. 86 *—M.S. (7/1/2005)*

J. & F. Lurton 2004 Bodega Lurton Pinot Gris (Uco Valley) $7. 84 Best Buy *—M.S. (7/1/2005)*

J. & F. Lurton 2003 Tierra del Fuego Red Blend (Mendoza) $6. 85 Best Buy *—M.S. (11/15/2004)*

J. & F. Lurton 2004 Tierra del Fuego White Blend (Mendoza) $6. 85 Best Buy *—M.S. (11/15/2004)*

J. ALBERTO

J. Alberto 2004 Malbec (Río Negro Valley) $40. 90 *—M.S. (4/1/2006)*

JOFFRÉ E HIJAS

Joffré e Hijas 2004 Grand Cabernet Sauvignon (Uco Valley) $21. 82 *—M.S. (11/1/2006)*

Joffré e Hijas 2004 Grand Chardonnay (Mendoza) $21. 85 *—M.S. (4/1/2006)*

Joffré e Hijas 2004 Grand Malbec (Uco Valley) $19. 87 *—M.S. (12/1/2006)*

Joffré e Hijas 2003 Grand Malbec (Mendoza) $21. 86 *—M.S. (6/1/2006)*

Joffré e Hijas 2003 Reserve Malbec (Uco Valley) $40. 82 *—M.S. (4/1/2006)*

Joffré e Hijas 2003 Grand Merlot (Mendoza) $21. 82 *—M.S. (6/1/2006)*

Joffré e Hijas 2003 Reserva Merlot (Uco Valley) $40. 83 *—M.S. (8/1/2006)*

KAIKEN

Kaiken 2005 Cabernet Sauvignon (Mendoza) $14. A little big and heavy, but that's the style that Kaiken has pushed since arriving on the market a few years ago. This version has baked-fruit aromas backed by lemon peel and espresso, while the palate is rich, dark and syrupy, but also oaky and tannic. Seems to want to offer more than it can deliver. The 14.5% alcohol level tells you that it's a big boy. 86 *—M.S. (12/1/2007)*

Kaiken 2004 Cabernet Sauvignon (Mendoza) $14. For two years running this basic Cabernet has been the laggard among the Kaiken wines, which are made by Montes S.A. of Chile. The '04 offers alcohol, rubbery black fruit and creamy oak and chocolate. What it doesn't have is finesse, complexity or style. Good as a simple quaffer but that's as far as it goes. 84 *—M.S. (2/1/2007)*

Kaiken 2003 Cabernet Sauvignon (Mendoza) $13. 86 *—M.S. (7/1/2005)*

Kaiken 2002 Cabernet Sauvignon (Mendoza) $13. 90 Editors' Choice *—M.S. (11/15/2004)*

Kaiken 2004 Ultra Cabernet Sauvignon (Mendoza) $25. Right off the bat you can tell this is a smooth, balanced, modern Cabernet because the bouquet pushes fruit, richness and spice in equal amounts. Alluring and dark on the palate, with cassis, olive and chocolate flavors. A masculine wine that doesn't tread lightly. From Montes out of Chile. 90 *—M.S. (2/1/2007)*

Kaiken 2003 Ultra Cabernet Sauvignon (Mendoza) $23. 90 Editors' Choice *—M.S. (7/1/2005)*

Kaiken 2005 Malbec (Mendoza) $14. A big and mauling version of Malbec. The nose is minty and dark, while the palate runs syrupy and full, with heavy black-fruit flavors darkened even more by a persistent peppery streak. Much less restrained and elegant than the Kaiken Ultra. 85 *—M.S. (12/1/2007)*

Kaiken 2004 Malbec (Mendoza) $14. Wavy and earthy, but with plenty of oak and stout black fruit. This is a stocky Malbec with a ton of oak-based chocolate, mocha and mint surrounding intense but not overly complex berry flavors. It's a mouthful for sure, with all the heft and richness Argentina has to offer. 90 Best Buy *—M.S. (2/1/2007)*

Kaiken 2003 Malbec (Mendoza) $13. 89 Best Buy *—M.S. (7/1/2005)*

Kaiken 2002 Malbec (Mendoza) $13. 91 Best Buy *—M.S. (3/1/2005)*

Kaiken 2005 Ultra Malbec (Mendoza) $25. Since coming onto the scene with the 2002 vintage, this Chilean-run venture (Montes S.A.) has hit the right notes time after time. The 2005 Ultra is exactly as we've come to expect: It's saturated, dark, meaty and ripe, with huge blackberry flavors and lavish creamy oak. Very modern, but done in the right way. 91 *—M.S. (10/1/2007)*

Kaiken 2004 Ultra Malbec (Mendoza) $25. Fairly well roasted and beefy, with dark-fruit aromas and a strong hint of chocolate on the nose. The palate is international in personality, meaning developed berry flavors are blended with oak-based toast and chocolate. It really spreads its wings on the finish, and should drink nicely for another three years. 91 *—M.S. (2/1/2007)*

Kaiken 2003 Ultra Malbec (Mendoza) $23. 91 *—M.S. (7/1/2005)*

KONO BARU

Kono Barú 2006 Malbec (Mendoza) $16. Mildly grassy and dilute on the nose, with sweet, candied berry flavors and a sticky, woody finish. It's fairly full in the mouth, but it lacks the precision, darkness and focus of a top-flight Malbec. 83 *—M.S. (10/1/2007)*

LA POSTA

La Posta 2004 Estela Armando Vineyard Bonarda (Mendoza) $17. Peppery is the first thing that comes to mind, while the palate seems gooey and sweet. More jammy, creamy and borderline sticky than balanced. Like a spoonful of straberry jam. 82 *—M.S. (2/1/2007)*

LA PUERTA

La Puerta 2005 Reserva Bonarda (Famatina Valley) $15. Granular and syrupy on the nose, and that same thickness of fruit is resurrected on the palate. Gritty on the finish, and sweet and lifeless as a whole. 81 *—M.S. (8/1/2007)*

La Puerta 2004 Cabernet Sauvignon (La Rioja) $8. 84 Best Buy *—M.S. (8/1/2006)*

La Puerta 2005 Chardonnay (La Rioja) $8. 80 *—M.S. (6/1/2006)*

La Puerta 2006 Malbec (Famatina Valley) $9. Quite syrupy and stewy, with chunky fruit flavors and a lot of wayward heft. On the plus side there's coffee and bitter chocolate, but overall there's just not much elegance or lightness. 83 *—M.S. (8/1/2007)*

La Puerta 2005 Malbec (La Rioja) $8. 86 Best Buy *—M.S. (4/1/2006)*

La Puerta 2005 Merlot (La Rioja) $8. 80 *—M.S. (6/1/2006)*

La Puerta 2005 Shiraz (La Rioja) $8. 84 Best Buy *—M.S. (8/1/2006)*

La Puerta 2005 Reserva Syrah (Famatina Valley) $15. Fairly sweet on the nose, with plum and a touch of spice. Things get more rugged in the mouth, where cherry and blackberry flavors carry a medicinal edge. A big Syrah but also a clumsy, heavy-handed one. Proceed with caution. 83 *—M.S. (8/1/2007)*

La Puerta 2005 Torrontès (La Rioja) $8. 86 Best Buy *—M.S. (4/1/2006)*

La Puerta 2006 Torrontes (Famatina Valley) $9. A bit heavy and bitter, but otherwise this is pretty decent. Not much can be said about the mild nose: it's typical but not that expressive. The palate, meanwhile, has a lot of weight and peach-pit bitterness, while the finish is a bit sluggish. 83 *—M.S. (8/1/2007)*

LA YUNTA

La Yunta 2005 Tinto Red Blend (Mendoza) $10. This colorful, clumsy wine shows glaring powdered-drink and candied cherry aromas and flavors, and while it's kind of scouring and rough it manages to make its mark via its juicy ripeness. Not a stellar wine but has its merits; the blend is Cabernet Sauvignon, Malbec and Bonarda. 83 *—M.S. (10/1/2007)*

La Yunta 2006 Torrontes (La Rioja) $10. Aromas of lychee fruit, pineapple, nectarine and baby powder are fairly typical and welcoming. The palate offers bright but somewhat nondescript flavors that ultimately tilt toward melon. The finish hangs in there, showing moderate grace and length. All in all this is decent Torrontes from La Rioja, a province to the north of Mendoza. 84 *—M.S. (10/1/2007)*

La Yunta 2005 Torrontès (La Rioja) $10. 85 Best Buy *—M.S. (11/1/2006)*

La Yunta 2002 Torrontès (Famatina Valley) $9. 80 *—M.S. (7/1/2004)*

La Yunta 2001 Torrontès (Argentina) $9. 84 *—M.S. (5/1/2003)*

LAS MORAS

Las Moras 2006 Bonarda (San Juan) $9. Jammy on the nose, with a touch of hard cheese backing that up. The mouth is jumpy and rustic, with raspberry and cherry skin flavors. Finishes lean, scouring and a bit hard. 83 *—M.S. (8/1/2007)*

Las Moras 2005 Bonarda (San Juan) $9. 82 *—M.S. (11/1/2006)*

Las Moras 2004 Bonarda (San Juan) $8. 85 Best Buy *—M.S. (11/15/2005)*

Las Moras 2005 Reserve Cabernet Sauvignon-Shiraz (San Juan) $12. Start off with aromas of rubber band and buttery oak. In the mouth, there's sweet red fruit and chocolate, while the finish is long and once again buttery. Adequate, but scratchy and grabby as a whole. 83 *—M.S. (5/1/2007)*

Las Moras 2004 Reserva Cabernet Sauvignon-Shiraz (San Juan) $13. 88 Best Buy *—M.S. (12/1/2006)*

Las Moras 2006 Chardonnay (San Juan) $9. Chardonnay is not Argentina's calling card, but this basic version issues apple, butter cup and mineral aromas backed by zesty, sheer citrus and pineapple flavors. Expect no heft or oak on this. It's straightforward warm-climate Chard, nothing more or less. 84 *—M.S. (5/1/2007)*

Las Moras 2006 Reserve Chardonnay (San Juan) $12. This is a heavy wine with banana, oak and other sweet, cloying flavors. The feel seems too extracted and resiny to match the quality of the fruit, which just isn't that great. 83 *—M.S. (5/1/2007)*

Las Moras 2005 Reserva Chardonnay (San Juan) $13. 84 *—M.S. (11/1/2006)*

Las Moras 2004 Reserva Chardonnay (San Juan) $12. 85 *—M.S. (11/15/2005)*

Las Moras 2006 Malbec (San Juan) $9. Some dry oak and smoke frames simple earth and berry aromas, but the mouth is condensed and flat. There isn't much bounce to this overripe red; it's heavy and seems to have caught a lot of sun in the vineyard. 83 *—M.S. (8/1/2007)*

Las Moras 2005 Malbec (San Juan) $9. 84 *—M.S. (12/1/2006)*

Las Moras 2005 Reserve Malbec (San Juan) $12. Fairly good as a whole, but generic with no one thing sticking out. Yes, it's a good middleweight that should draw more smiles than frowns, but in the end it's simply a nice red with simple raspberry flavors and a bouncy personality. 84 *—M.S. (5/1/2007)*

Las Moras 2004 Reserva Malbec (San Juan) $12. Plenty of oak, vanilla and creamy notes on the nose of this base-level Malbec. A rather acid-driven palate delivers raw but clean red-fruit flavors, but not much charm or body. Tangy and mildly sharp in the long run. 83 *—M.S. (5/1/2007)*

Las Moras 2004 Mora Negra Red Blend (Tulum Valley) $38. Finca Las Moras is getting fancy with this proprietary blend of Malbec and Bonarda, and with good results. The wine offers earthy, heavily wooded aromas in front of generous black cherry and chocolate flavors. It's a saturated, superripe wine that may miss a beat or two along the tour but has its positives. 88 *—M.S. (10/1/2007)*

Las Moras 2002 Mora Negra Red Blend (Tulum Valley) $36. 90 *—M.S. (4/1/2006)*

Las Moras 2006 Sauvignon Blanc (San Juan) $9. Sauvignon Blanc is far from being Argentina's signature grape, so the fact that this one from San Juan province is legitimate, crisp and varietally correct is impressive. Beyond that, the wine delivers true lime, passion fruit and citrus aromas and flavors. Fresh and easy to like. 87 Best Buy *—M.S. (8/1/2007)*

Las Moras 2005 Sauvignon Blanc (San Juan) $9. 81 *—M.S. (12/1/2006)*

Las Moras 2005 Shiraz (San Juan) $9. 86 Best Buy *—M.S. (12/1/2006)*

Las Moras 2004 Shiraz (San Juan) $8. 87 Best Buy *—M.S. (10/1/2005)*

Las Moras 2004 Reserva Tannat (San Juan) $13. 86 *—M.S. (12/1/2006)*

Las Moras 2003 Reserva Tannat (San Juan) $10. 85 Best Buy *—M.S. (8/1/2006)*

Las Moras 2006 Viognier (San Juan) $9. With varietally correct aromas and nice overall balance, this ranks as a solid, fairly legitimate Argentine Viognier. Hailing from warmer San Juan province, this is a citrus- and honey-based white with size, spice and mouthfeel. For the most part it gets things right. 85 Best Buy *—M.S. (10/1/2007)*

Las Moras 2005 Viognier (San Juan) $8. 84 Best Buy *—M.S. (6/1/2006)*

Las Moras 2004 Viognier (San Juan) $8. 84 Best Buy *—M.S. (11/15/2005)*

LAUREL GLEN

Laurel Glen 2003 Terra Rosa Malbec (Mendoza) $14. 87 *—M.S. (7/1/2005)*

Laurel Glen 2002 Vale La Pena Malbec (Mendoza) $34. 87 *—M.S. (7/1/2005)*

Laurel Glen 2001 Vale La Pena Malbec (Mendoza) $30. 91 *—M.S. (12/1/2003)*

Laurel Glen 2001 Vale La Pena Malbec (Mendoza) $30. 91 *—M.S. (12/1/2003)*

LLAMA

Llama 2004 Roble Malbec (Mendoza) $10. Among the myriad critter wines that are coming out of South America, this Malbec is a serious offering with a balanced, broad set of fruity aromas and a plump, berry driven palate. Has the right amount of acidity and tannins to create a good mouthfeel, and the finish remains soft enough to enjoy. 87 Best Buy —*M.S. (2/1/2007)*

LOS CIELOS

Los Cielos 2005 Cabernet Sauvignon-Malbec (Mendoza) $9. 83 —*M.S. (11/1/2006)*

Los Cielos 2005 Trebbiano-Chardonnay White Blend (Mendoza) $9. 84 —*M.S. (11/1/2006)*

LUCA

Luca 2000 Chardonnay (Mendoza) $32. 89 —*M.S. (7/1/2002)*

Luca 2000 Malbec (Altos de Mendoza) $37. 90 —*M.S. (12/1/2003)*

LUIGI BOSCA

Luigi Bosca 2003 Gala 2 Bordeaux Blend (Mendoza) $37. 85 —*M.S. (8/1/2006)*

Luigi Bosca 2002 Gala 2 Bordeaux Blend (Mendoza) $33. 90 Editors' Choice —*M.S. (3/1/2005)*

Luigi Bosca 2004 Gala 2 Cabernet Blend (Mendoza) $35. Butter and dill are the first aromas to make themselves noticed, and below that there's raw oak and lighter-weight fruit notes. The palate shows ample resin and wood notes along with pepper and spice. It's a good wine with serious intent, but it seems a little overwooded and a tiny bit green. Cabernet Sauvignon leads the blend, with Merlot and Cab Franc filling it out. 87 —*M.S. (12/1/2007)*

Luigi Bosca 2002 Finca La Linda Cabernet Sauvignon (Mendoza) $10. 86 Best Buy —*M.S. (3/1/2005)*

Luigi Bosca 2004 Reserva Cabernet Sauvignon (Mendoza) $18. Starts out sort of soft and shy, with modest red-fruit aromas. In the mouth, raspberry and cherry flavors get a quick lift from grabby, firm tannins. And by the time this baby hits its groove you're onto a finish defined by a starchy feel and long-lasting Cabernet essence. Airing is this wine's best friend; decant or drink over time. 88 —*M.S. (8/1/2007)*

Luigi Bosca 2003 Reserva Cabernet Sauvignon (Mendoza) $18. 81 —*M.S. (12/1/2006)*

Luigi Bosca 2004 Finca La Linda Chardonnay (Mendoza) $10. 86 Best Buy —*M.S. (3/1/2005)*

Luigi Bosca 2005 Reserva Chardonnay (Mendoza) $18. 88 —*M.S. (11/1/2006)*

Luigi Bosca 2004 Reserva Chardonnay (Mendoza) $15. 86 —*M.S. (3/1/2005)*

Luigi Bosca 2003 Malbec (Luján de Cuyo) $20. 90 —*M.S. (8/1/2006)*

Luigi Bosca 2005 Finca La Linda Malbec (Mendoza) $11. Hard black fruit and notes of tire rubber and tar indicate that this is a dark, masculine wine. And while it does offer power, it's actually quite racy and balanced in the mouth. Flavorwise, expect black raspberry and some bitter cocoa. Overall, there's nothing unripe about it. 88 Best Buy —*M.S. (10/1/2007)*

Luigi Bosca 2003 Finca La Linda Malbec (Mendoza) $10. 84 —*M.S. (7/1/2005)*

Luigi Bosca 2002 Finca La Linda Malbec (Mendoza) $10. 87 Best Buy —*M.S. (3/1/2005)*

Luigi Bosca 2004 Reserva Malbec (Mendoza) $18. Pure, jammy and heady: voilà, it's modern Malbec. The palate here is inviting, with decadent plum and blackberry flavors working in tandem. The finish is plush at first, with chocolate and espresso notes coming later. With plenty of virtues, this is a very nice wine from an average vintage. 89 —*M.S. (8/1/2007)*

Luigi Bosca 2003 Reserva Malbec (Mendoza) $18. 89 —*M.S. (12/1/2006)*

Luigi Bosca 2001 Reserva Malbec (Mendoza) $16. 84 —*M.S. (3/1/2005)*

Luigi Bosca 2001 Reserva Merlot (Mendoza) $16. 82 —*M.S. (3/1/2005)*

Luigi Bosca 2004 Single Vineyard D.O.C Malbec (Luján de Cuyo) $22. Full, chewy, doughy, spicy and intensely fruity. This single-vineyard Malbec offers a little bit of everything, and all in balanced, measured doses. The cherry and blackberry fruit is bold but pure, while chocolate comes in to darken things up. A textbook steak and potatoes wine with a bit of complexity, but mostly it's about easygoing fun. 92 —*M.S. (10/1/2007)*

Luigi Bosca 1997 Finca Los Nobles Cabernet Bouchet Red Blend (Argentina) $70. 89 —*M.S. (7/1/2005)*

Luigi Bosca 1997 Finca Los Nobles Malbec Verdot Red Blend (Mendoza) $58. 91 —*M.S. (7/1/2005)*

Luigi Bosca 2005 Reserva Pinot Noir (Maipú) $18. Mendoza Pinot Noir is not what you'd call typical or world class. This wine hints at baked beans and sweet oak, with roasted fruit flavors supported by a lot of vanilla and resin. Too heavyhanded. 82 —*M.S. (12/1/2007)*

Luigi Bosca 2002 Gala 1 Red Blend (Mendoza) $33. 86 —*M.S. (3/1/2005)*

Luigi Bosca 2006 Riesling (Mendoza) $18. Argentinean Rieslings come along as often as Haley's comet. But this clean, round wine is pretty good in its own right. It features dry almond, white pepper and apple flavors, with additional almond skins on the mineral, lean finish. Not entirely a novelty with 1,550 cases total production. 85 —*M.S. (10/1/2007)*

Luigi Bosca 2006 Reserva Sauvignon Blanc (Mendoza) $18. Quite tropical on the nose, with aromas of pineapple and passion fruit. The palate is a soft, honeyed bowl of kiwi, melon, cucumber and white pepper, while the finish is dry and gets more hollow as the wine warms up. Not a classic Sauvignon, but it has its virtues. 84 —*M.S. (10/1/2007)*

Luigi Bosca 2004 Reserva Sauvignon Blanc (Maipú) $15. 81 —*M.S. (7/1/2005)*

Luigi Bosca 2002 Reserva Syrah (Mendoza) $16. 89 Editors' Choice —*M.S. (3/1/2005)*

Luigi Bosca 2004 Finca La Linda Tempranillo (Mendoza) $10. 88 Best Buy —*M.S. (12/1/2006)*

Luigi Bosca 2003 Finca La Linda Tempranillo (Mendoza) $10. 87 Best Buy —*M.S. (3/1/2005)*

Luigi Bosca 2006 Finca La Linda Viognier (Mendoza) $11. Here and there you'll find a very well-made Argentine Viognier because the country's warmth and the grape can go together. A case in point is this plump, lush specimen that sports developed lemon and orange flavors and a long, acid-propelled finish. 88 Best Buy —*M.S. (10/1/2007)*

Luigi Bosca 2004 Finca La Linda Viognier (Luján de Cuyo) $10. 80 —*M.S. (7/1/2005)*

Luigi Bosca 2005 Gala 3 White Blend (Mendoza) $30. 86 —*M.S. (11/1/2006)*

LUIS CORREAS

Luis Correas 1997 Malbec (Mendoza) $9. 82 —*C.S. (5/1/2002)*

MAIPE

Maipe 2006 Cabernet Sauvignon (Mendoza) $10. Both the Maipe Malbec and this Cabernet Sauvignon show very good purity of fruit and skillful winemaking. This wine is full of black-fruit aromas, depth and style. The palate pushes ripe plum and berry fruit along with chocolate, and the finish is chewy and correct in terms of tannins and structure. 88 Best Buy —*M.S. (12/1/2007)*

Maipe 2006 Malbec (Mendoza) $10. Sweet aromas that verge on syrupy set up a sweet and easy palate of black cherry and cassis. This has a nice texture as it shows good body, feel and fruit quality. Maipe means "lord of the winds" in a native language, and while this Malbec won't transport you anywhere, it's good for the price. 86 Best Buy —*M.S. (12/1/2007)*

MAPEMA

Mapema 2002 Primera Zona Bordeaux Blend (Mendoza) $31. This Bordeaux-style blend is rather heavy, and from the bouquet you can tell that it carries a strong level of oak. The palate is full of red fruit and spunk, but as you let it sit on the palate the acidity comes on aggressively before finishing a bit rough. 86 —*M.S. (2/1/2007)*

MARCUS JAMES

Marcus James 2000 Chardonnay (Mendoza) $11. 80 —*M.S. (7/1/2002)*

MARTINO

Martino 2003 Malbec (Mendoza) $19. Heavier than in the past, with foresty aromas offset by oak-based bacon and vanilla notes. This ranks as a medium to big effort, and it comes with black cherry and dark plum flavors. But on the mid and back palate the wine falls off quickly, leaving little finish and some raisin. 83 —*M.S. (5/1/2007)*

Martino 2002 Malbec (Luján de Cuyo) $19. 87 —*M.S. (12/31/2005)*

Martino 2002 Old Vines Malbec (Mendoza) $55. 90 —*M.S. (11/15/2004)*

MAURICIO LORCA

Mauricio Lorca 2005 Opalo Cabernet Sauvignon (Vista Flores) $18. Even if this full-bodied Cab starts with some eggy, pastry-like aromas, it soon finds its form. The nose brings char and baked black fruit, while the palate is full of creamy blackberry and brown sugar flavors. Rather rich and ripe, with medium tannins and mild acidity. Drink sooner than later. 89 —*M.S. (8/1/2007)*

Mauricio Lorca 2003 Poetico Cabernet Sauvignon (Vista Flores) $21. Attractive and well put together from start to finish. This Cab (with 15% Malbec) is jammed with cassis, raspberry and other juicy berry flavors, while the lushness of the wine rolls over your palate with ease. It's not easy to find Cabernet this good in the $20 range, so get after this one while it's under the radar. 91 Editors' Choice —*M.S. (8/1/2007)*

Mauricio Lorca 2005 Opalo Malbec (Vista Flores) $18. This is a delicious and somewhat rare style of Malbec: it has none of the usual oak. What you wind up with is fruity, clean and pure. The body is maybe a touch leaner without the oak; the flavor profile is brighter and more linear. 90 —*M.S. (8/1/2007)*

Mauricio Lorca 2004 Poetico Malbec (Vista Flores) $21. Mauricio Lorca makes wine for Enrique Foster but his private label is something to keep an eye on. Poetico is potent and fairly pure; and it contains 10% Cabernet and 5% Syrah in addition to 85% Malbec. The palate delivers hearty blackberry, plum and vanilla flavors, while the finish is sturdy as a statue, with length and firm tannins. 89 —*M.S. (8/1/2007)*

Mauricio Lorca 2005 Opalo Syrah (Vista Flores) $18. Starts out all rowdy and sweaty, with animal hide and warm earth. And that all makes sense: this is unoaked, unmolested Syrah and thus it has its funky side. Along the roadside there's blackberry and pepper flavors and peppy acids and tannins. An interesting ride that's not without its ups and downs. 86 —*M.S. (8/1/2007)*

MAYOL

Mayol 2003 Pircas Vineyard Bonarda (Mendoza) $15. 87 —*M.S. (11/15/2004)*

Mayol 2002 Pircas Vineyard Bonarda (Vista Flores) $15. 85 —*M.S. (7/1/2004)*

Mayol 2003 Sebastian Vineyard Cabernet Sauvignon (Tupungato) $15. 84 —*M.S. (12/31/2005)*

Mayol 2003 Montuiri Vineyard Malbec (Luján de Cuyo) $15. 84 —*M.S. (12/31/2005)*

Mayol 2002 Montuiri Vineyard Malbec (Luján de Cuyo) $15. 88 —*M.S. (7/1/2004)*

Mayol 2002 Pircas Vineyard Syrah (Vista Flores) $15. 87 —*M.S. (7/1/2004)*

MAYU

Mayu 2004 Malbec (San Juan) $11. We haven't seen much improvement in this wine since the 2003 vintage. It's still lacking forward, ripe fruit and instead shows more leather and drying, firm tannins. Shows glimpses of higher quality but can't support them. 83 —*M.S. (12/31/2007)*

Mayu 2003 Malbec (San Juan) $11. 82 —*M.S. (11/15/2005)*

MEDANOS

Medanos 2004 Cabernet Sauvignon (Mendoza) $13. 80 —*M.S. (11/15/2005)*

Medanos 2006 Malbec (Mendoza) $14. Malbec seems like the best bet for this organic label, which has shown some shaky wines alongside this. Even this one has a mild lactic, pasty streak to the nose along with raspberry and peppery spice. Lacks the cuddle and depth of the better Argentine Malbecs. 83 —*M.S. (12/31/2007)*

MEDRANO

Medrano 2001 Cabernet Sauvignon (Maipú) $9. 84 —*M.S. (7/1/2004)*

Medrano 2002 Chardonnay (Tupungato) $9. 84 —*M.S. (2/1/2004)*

Medrano 2001 Malbec (Luján de Cuyo) $9. 86 —*M.S. (2/1/2004)*

Medrano 2001 Merlot (Luján de Cuyo) $9. 82 —*M.S. (7/1/2004)*

Medrano 2001 Syrah (Mendoza) $9. 84 —*M.S. (7/1/2004)*

MELIPAL

Melipal 2004 Malbec (Mendoza) $20. 88 —*M.S. (11/1/2006)*

Melipal 2003 Malbec (Mendoza) $20. 89 —*M.S. (11/15/2005)*

Melipal 2006 Ikella Malbec (Mendoza) $15. Short on berries and jam and heavily oaked, thus fruit plays second fiddle to oak spice, spearmint and hard cinnamon on the nose. The palate is on the brambly side, while the finish is fairly long and a bit leathery. Has body and size but lacks the fine points. 83 —*M.S. (12/31/2007)*

Melipal 2005 Malbec Rosé Malbec (Mendoza) $14. 84 —*M.S. (11/1/2006)*

Melipal 2004 Reserve Malbec (Mendoza) $42. 90 —*M.S. (11/1/2006)*

Melipal 2003 Reserve Malbec (Mendoza) $40. 91 —*M.S. (11/15/2005)*

MICHEL LAROCHE/JORGE CODERCH

Michel Laroche/Jorge Coderch 2002 Colina Negra Cabernet Sauvignon (San Rafael) $15. 88 *(2/1/2004)*

MICHEL TORINO

Michel Torino 2001 Cabernet Sauvignon (Cafayate) $14. 82 —*M.S. (7/1/2004)*

Michel Torino 2006 Coleccion Cabernet Sauvignon (Calchaqui Valley) $12. A fleshy wine with aromas of wet clay and earth. It seems a little hot and herbal at its foundation, but around the edges there are flavors of cherry and raspberry. The feel is chunky and innocuous, with mild tannins. 83 —*M.S. (12/1/2007)*

Michel Torino 2007 Cuma Organic Cabernet Sauvignon (Cafayate) $13. Bubble gum on the nose makes you wonder about carbonic maceration, but that technique wasn't used to make this fruity, simple and generally nice little Cabernet. Don't expect complexity from it, or much varietal character; this is your basic red wine with adequate sweetness and some chocolate. 84 —*M.S. (12/1/2007)*

Michel Torino 2005 Don David Cabernet Sauvignon (Cafayate) $15. Coconut, green herbs and fresh-cut wood work the nose, followed by fairly herbal berry flavors. There is oak throughout, and mildly coarse tannins, thus the structure is solid. 84—*M.S. (10/1/2007)*

Michel Torino 2003 Don David Cabernet Sauvignon (Cafayate) $15. 87 —*M.S. (6/1/2006)*

Michel Torino 2002 Don David Cabernet Sauvignon (Cafayate) $14. 87 —*M.S. (10/1/2004)*

Michel Torino 1999 Don David Cabernet Sauvignon (Cafayate) $14. 83 —*M.S. (5/1/2002)*

Michel Torino 2002 Don David Chardonnay (Cafayate) $14. 83 —*M.S. (7/1/2004)*

Michel Torino 2006 Don David Chardonnay (Cafayate) $15. Chardonnay in sunny, high-altitude Cafayate will always prove challenging, but this wine gets it right. There's a lot of spicy forward oak, and thus the palate is expectedly creamy and tinged with vanilla, cinnamon and white pepper notes along with pineapple and mango fruit. The feel and body are both correct and textured. It's sweet and oaky but well made. 87 —*M.S. (12/1/2007)*

Michel Torino 2006 Ciclos Fumé Blanc (Cafayate) $27. 86 —*M.S. (12/15/2006)*

Michel Torino 2000 Malbec (Cafayate) $10. 81 —*D.T. (5/1/2002)*

Michel Torino 2006 Coleccion Malbec (Calchaqui Valley) $12. Earthy and mildly lactic on the nose, with tight, lean, herbal flavors. Doesn't rise above mediocre. 83 —*M.S. (10/1/2007)*

Michel Torino 2001 Colección Malbec (Cafayate) $10. 84 —*M.S. (12/1/2003)*

Michel Torino 2007 Cuma Organic Malbec (Cafayate) $13. This marks the U.S. debut of Torino's organic line called Cuma, which means clean and pure in a native language. The wine is indeed that; it's a grapy, fun wine with ribald boysenberry fruit. And with air it shows some softness that makes it go down easy. 85 —*M.S. (12/1/2007)*

Michel Torino 2005 Don David Malbec (Cafayate) $15. Smooth and consistent Malbec from Cafayate is what Michel Torino is all about. Don David is a higher-aiming effort, and while it shows a touch of northern Argentina's herbal, sun-affected characteristics, it's also a well-balanced, formulaic Malbec that hits all the markers: good color, nice body, friendly tannins and plenty of oak. 88 —*M.S. (10/1/2007)*

Michel Torino 2003 Don David Malbec (Cafayate) $15. 90 Best Buy —*M.S. (4/1/2006)*

Michel Torino 2002 Don David Malbec (Cafayate) $14. 87 —*M.S. (10/1/2004)*

Michel Torino 2001 Don David Malbec (Cafayate) $14. 83 —*M.S. (7/1/2004)*

Michel Torino 2001 Don David Malbec (Cafayate) $14. 85 —*M.S. (12/1/2003)*

Michel Torino 2004 Don David Malbec (Cafayate) $15. 88 —*M.S. (12/15/2006)*

Michel Torino 2004 Ciclos Malbec-Merlot (Cafayate) $25. 92 Editors' Choice —*M.S. (12/1/2006)*

Michel Torino 2006 Coleccion Pinot Noir (Calchaqui Valley) $12. Light and tea-like, with sour berry flavors and a hint of pickle; the feel is lean and scratchy. 80 —*M.S. (12/1/2007)*

Michel Torino 2003 Altimus Red Blend (Cafayate) $50. 91 —*M.S. (6/1/2006)*

Michel Torino 2000 Altimus Red Blend (Cafayate) $45. 82 —*M.S. (5/1/2003)*

Michel Torino 2004 Ciclos Sauvignon Blanc (Cafayate) $25. 85 —*M.S. (8/1/2006)*

Michel Torino 2007 Cuma Organic Torrontes (Cafayate) $13. Dynamic aromas of honeysuckle and mint gumdrop precede intense honey, orange, tangerine and marmalade flavors. This is a thicker, more oily style of Torrontes than the commonly seen watery ones, and it makes a statement via its viscosity and power. 87 —*M.S. (12/1/2007)*

Michel Torino 2006 Don David Torrontes (Cafayate) $15. A touch of oak on this wine leads to a kiss of vanilla and wax on the nose alongside melon and peach scents. The palate is full of zing and lemon, and underneath there's more in the way of orange marmalade. Finishes long and lemony, with some natural heat. 87 —*M.S. (12/1/2007)*

Michel Torino 2004 Don David Torrontès (Cafayate) $15. 84 —*M.S. (4/1/2006)*

Michel Torino 2003 Don David Torrontès (Cafayate) $14. 86 —*M.S. (10/1/2004)*

Michel Torino 2002 Don David Torrontès (Cafayate) $14. 85 —*M.S. (7/1/2004)*

Michel Torino 2000 Don David Torrontès (Cafayate) $14. 84 —*M.S. (5/1/2003)*

Michel Torino 2005 Don David Reserve Torrontès (Cafayate) $15. 84 —*M.S. (11/1/2006)*

MIL PIEDRAS

Mil Piedras 2004 Cabernet Sauvignon (Mendoza) $15. Basic but flat, with red-fruit aromas that stir little excitement. Early on, the flavor profile yields youthful cassis and plum notes, but with time it turns more tart and unforgiving. Finishes with slight fruit and hints of rubber. 83 —*M.S. (2/1/2007)*

Mil Piedras 2003 Cabernet Sauvignon (Mendoza) $12. 84 —*M.S. (11/15/2005)*

Mil Piedras 2005 Malbec (Mendoza) $11. A touch of coconut and cream accents the dark-fruited bouquet, while the palate is less overtly oaky and more emphatic with its plum and berry flavors. No doubt this is a chewy, ripe, fruit-forward style. It's not for aging nor contemplating; best to just drink it down with meats and pastas. 87 Best Buy —*M.S. (12/1/2007)*

Mil Piedras 2004 Malbec (Mendoza) $15. A bit burnt and toasty early, with mild blackberry aromas forming a good backdrop. The palate is soft and ripe, with textbook burly but lovable black-fruit flavors. Has some juiciness as a result of solid but balancing acidity. A much better wine than the previous vintage. 86 —*M.S. (2/1/2007)*

Mil Piedras 2003 Malbec (Mendoza) $12. 80 —*M.S. (11/15/2005)*

Mil Piedras 2003 Tempranillo (Mendoza) $12. 84 —*M.S. (11/15/2005)*

MJ GALLIARD

MJ Galliard 2004 Cabernet Sauvignon (Mendoza) $16. 81 —*M.S. (12/1/2006)*

MJ Galliard 2003 Malbec (Mendoza) $20. 82 —*M.S. (7/1/2004)*

MJ Galliard 2003 Merlot (Mendoza) $20. 85 —*M.S. (7/1/2004)*

MJ Galliard 2003 Sauvignon Blanc (Mendoza) $20. 83 —*M.S. (7/1/2004)*

MJ Galliard 2004 Syrah (Mendoza) $26. A strong whiff of minty green runs through the bouquet, while the fruit aromas are prickly and lean toward rhubarb and red cherry. The palate is darker, but rather nondescript, while the finish is a black hole of rubbery tannins and coffee. 83 —*M.S. (2/1/2007)*

MONTE CINCO

Monte Cinco 2003 Oak Malbec (Mendoza) $42. 91 —*M.S. (11/15/2004)*

MURVILLE

Murville NV Brut Nature Champagne Blend (San Rafael) $14. 83 —*M.S. (1/1/2004)*

ÑANDÚ

Ñandú 2004 Malbec (Mendoza) $12. 81 —*M.S. (11/15/2005)*

Ñandú 2003 Malbec (San Rafael) $12. 86 —*M.S. (7/1/2005)*

NATIVO

Nativo 2002 El Felino Malbec (Mendoza) $16. 88 —*M.S. (12/1/2003)*

NAVARRO CORREAS

Navarro Correas 2001 Ultra Bordeaux Blend (Mendoza) $27. 87 —*M.S. (2/1/2004)*

Navarro Correas 2002 Colección Privada Cabernet Sauvignon (Mendoza) $11. 87 Best Buy —*M.S. (11/15/2005)*

Navarro Correas 2000 Colección Privada Cabernet Sauvignon (Mendoza) $16. 82 —*M.S. (11/1/2002)*

Navarro Correas 2002 Gran Reserva Cabernet Sauvignon (Mendoza) $19. 84 —*M.S. (11/15/2005)*

Navarro Correas 2001 Gran Reserva Altos del Rio Cabernet Sauvignon (Mendoza) $23. 89 —*M.S. (2/1/2004)*

Navarro Correas 2001 Colección Privada Chardonnay (Mendoza) $16. 84 —*M.S. (11/1/2002)*

Navarro Correas 2003 Colección Privada Chardonnay (Mendoza) $11. 85 —*M.S. (11/15/2005)*

Navarro Correas 2003 Colección Privada Malbec (Mendoza) $10. 89 Best Buy —*M.S. (3/1/2005)*

Navarro Correas 2000 Colección Privada Malbec (Mendoza) $16. 85 —*M.S. (11/1/2002)*

Navarro Correas 2001 Gran Reserva Altos del Rio Malbec (Mendoza) $23. 89 —*M.S. (12/1/2003)*

Navarro Correas 2003 Colección Privada Merlot (Mendoza) $11. 86 Best Buy —*M.S. (11/15/2005)*

Navarro Correas 2000 Colección Privada Merlot (Mendoza) $16. 86 —*M.S. (11/1/2002)*

Navarro Correas 2003 Colección Privada Syrah (Mendoza) $11. 85 —*M.S. (4/1/2006)*

Navarro Correas 2000 Colección Privada Syrah (Mendoza) $16. 87 —*M.S. (11/1/2002)*

NIETO SENETINER

Nieto Senetiner 2004 Limited Edition Bonarda (Mendoza) $25. Black as night, with aromas of leather, wild berries and wet dog. It is salty and oaky in the mouth, with vanilla and tannin but not a whole lot of ripe, lovable dark fruit. Gets better as it evolves, but where's the dark, sweet fruit to match the oak, tannins and tightness? 85 —*M.S. (12/31/2007)*

Nieto Senetiner 2003 Limited Edition Bonarda (Mendoza) $22. If you like a burly, colorful red with a ton of fruit, oak and power, then give this Argentinean bruiser a try. The nose exudes warm aromas of tight-grained oak and berry compote, while the massive palate hits like a ton of bricks on the way to a chocolaty, tannic tail. Some may say it's overdone, but if you've tried more than a few Bonarda you'll peg this as the real deal. 90 Editors' Choice —*M.S. (2/1/2007)*

Nieto Senetiner 2002 Limited Edition Bonarda (Luján de Cuyo) $30. 84 —*M.S. (10/1/2004)*

Nieto Senetiner 2003 Don Nicanor Bordeaux Blend (Mendoza) $12. 86 —*M.S. (11/1/2006)*

Nieto Senetiner 2001 Don Nicanor Bordeaux Blend (Luján de Cuyo) $15. 85 —*M.S. (10/1/2004)*

Nieto Senetiner 2003 Cadus Cabernet Sauvignon (Mendoza) $40. Nothing is hidden in this bruising, forward Cab. The nose is oaky as can be, but also endowed with intense black fruit. The palate might register as soft to some, but there's still a tannic foundation that bolsters blackberry, spice cake and molasses flavors. Not super long on the finish but intense in a lumbering sort of way. Drink now–2011. 90 —*M.S. (8/1/2007)*

Nieto Senetiner 2000 Cadus Cabernet Sauvignon (Luján de Cuyo) $40. 85 —*M.S. (10/1/2004)*

Nieto Senetiner 2005 Reserva Cabernet Sauvignon (Mendoza) $9. The wood is a bit forced, and overall this wine has a heavy, full-fruited personality. But the depth and ripeness are pretty nice and the blackberry, dark plum and cassis flavors are earnest. A bit tannic and not all that varietal. 85 —*M.S. (8/1/2007)*

Nieto Senetiner 2004 Reserva Cabernet Sauvignon (Mendoza) $9. Bacon, toast and some herbal aromas come up from the dark nose, while the oak-driven palate deals cassis, blackberry and mint. With stark tannins, body weight and lots of color, this wine does not play the part of the wallflower. It's pretty rugged stuff. 86 Best Buy —*M.S. (2/1/2007)*

Nieto Senetiner 2001 Reserva Nieto Cabernet Sauvignon-Shiraz (Luján de Cuyo) $10. 82 —*M.S. (10/1/2004)*

Nieto Senetiner 2006 Santa Isabel Cabernet Sauvignon (Mendoza) $7. Touches of smoke and leather mix with dill and nondescript berry aromas on the nose. The palate offers modest cherry and raspberry flavors but also a heavier and more driving buttery oak character. A little awkward and could benefit from less heavyhanded oak. 83 —*M.S. (12/1/2007)*

Nieto Senetiner 2005 Santa Isabel Cabernet Sauvignon (Mendoza) $6. A stewy Cabernet; the nose mixes cola with Fernet Branca and never does the wine approach anything we might label charming. It's linear and tight, with narrow flavors of cranberry and cherry. Short on texture and never shows much variation. 82 —*M.S. (8/1/2007)*

Nieto Senetiner 2006 Reserva Chardonnay (Mendoza) $9. Young and sturdy, with pear and apple aromas enveloped in popcorn and wood. The palate offers standard New World weight and sweetness along with flavors of pear, vanilla and oak. More on the full-bodied, oaky side, but generally it's balanced and approachable. 85 Best Buy —*M.S. (8/1/2007)*

Nieto Senetiner 2005 Reserva Chardonnay (Mendoza) $10. 83 —*M.S. (12/1/2006)*

Nieto Senetiner 2004 Reserva Chardonnay (Mendoza) $10. 86 Best Buy —*M.S. (7/1/2005)*

Nieto Senetiner 2006 Don Nicanor Chardonnay-Viognier (Mendoza) $17. Can't say that the heavy dose of oak on this wine is helping the cause. The nose is quite resiny and cloying, while the palate is creamy and full, but loaded with wood chip and vanilla flavors. As might be expected, even more oak flavor dominates the finish. 83 —*M.S. (10/1/2007)*

Nieto Senetiner 2006 Santa Isabel Chardonnay-Viognier (Mendoza) $7. Light fragrances of talcum powder and apricots lead off this mild-mannered blend, which runs easy and smooth before thinning out on the back palate and finish. But along the way there's good citrus and green-fruit flavors backed by adequate acidity. A good quaff for the price. 85 Best Buy *—M.S. (10/1/2007)*

Nieto Senetiner 2001 Cadus Malbec (Mendoza) $37. 81 *—M.S. (11/15/2005)*

Nieto Senetiner 2000 Cadus Malbec (Luján de Cuyo) $40. 88 *—M.S. (10/1/2004)*

Nieto Senetiner 2000 Cadus Estiba 39 Malbec (Mendoza) $60. 92 Editors' Choice *—M.S. (12/31/2005)*

Nieto Senetiner 2002 Cadus Single Vineyard Malbec (Mendoza) $45. 92 Editors' Choice *—M.S. (12/31/2005)*

Nieto Senetiner 2004 Don Nicanor Malbec (Luján de Cuyo) $17. Starts out a bit woody and toasted, but time allows dark and burly fruit to enter the fray—and the end result is alluring. On the palate, it's nice and plummy, with chocolate as well. Full-bodied and ripe, this is Mendoza Malbec as we've come to know and like it. 89 *—M.S. (5/1/2007)*

Nieto Senetiner 2005 Reserva Malbec (Mendoza) $9. Quite charred and burnt on the nose, which may have resulted from the wine getting more oak treatment than it deserved. The palate is weakly strung together, and it shows flavors of black olive, cooked berries and mocha. A step up from basic, but not a big one. 83 *—M.S. (12/1/2007)*

Nieto Senetiner 2004 Reserva Malbec (Mendoza) $10. 87 Best Buy *—M.S. (11/1/2006)*

Nieto Senetiner 2003 Reserva Malbec (Mendoza) $10. 89 Best Buy *—M.S. (7/1/2005)*

Nieto Senetiner 2002 Reserva Nieto Malbec (Luján de Cuyo) $10. 88 Best Buy *—M.S. (10/1/2004)*

Nieto Senetiner 2006 Santa Isabel Malbec (Mendoza) $7. In a shrinking domain (wines for under $10), this junior-league Malbec shows sweet, jammy aromas and legitimate berry flavors. And that alone puts it ahead of the game. The palate is basically a mish-mash of berry flavors and raw tannins, but with food, preferably hamburgers or ribs, it will do the trick. 86 Best Buy *—M.S. (10/1/2007)*

Nieto Senetiner 2005 Santa Isabel Malbec (Mendoza) $7. For an everyday red that won't wreck the wallet, this juicy, fresh Malbec qualifies. It offers sweet aromas of plum and berry, and the palate follows suit with blueberry and blackberry. The depth and complexity are limited but the fundamentals and enjoyment factor are measurable. 85 Best Buy *—M.S. (10/1/2007)*

Nieto Senetiner 2004 Reserva Merlot (Mendoza) $9. Surprise! Here's a Merlot from Mendoza that shows good fruit, a touch of leather and some herbal essence on the bouquet. The palate is more or less on the money, and it wraps sweet black cherry and plum flavors in a blanket of correct acids and legitimate tannins. Nice overall, with finishing cola and blackberry flavors. 86 Best Buy *—M.S. (2/1/2007)*

Nieto Senetiner 2003 Reserva Merlot (Mendoza) $10. 84 *—M.S. (11/15/2005)*

Nieto Senetiner 2002 Cadus Syrah (Mendoza) $37. 91 Editors' Choice *—M.S. (12/31/2005)*

NOVUS

Novus 2006 Cabernet Sauvignon (Mendoza) $10. Simple but nice in its class. The nose offers bulky but clean fruit and a touch of saddle, while the palate is ample, fruity and round. It flairs out on the finish but keeps rolling in the right direction. Good for the price. 85 Best Buy *—M.S. (8/1/2007)*

Novus 2005 Cabernet Sauvignon (Mendoza) $10. 83 *—M.S. (11/1/2006)*

Novus 2003 Cabernet Sauvignon (Mendoza) $10. 83 *—M.S. (8/1/2006)*

Novus 2006 Reserve Cabernet Sauvignon (Uco Valley) $15. Novus' basic Cab is probably a better wine for the money. This one seems to want to justify its reserve status by offering more oak. But that oak carries that creamy vanilla and carob flavor, making the wine sticky. And maybe the raw material is a bit overripe as well. 83 *—M.S. (8/1/2007)*

Novus 2006 Chardonnay (Alto Valle de Uco) $10. Canned pear aromas carry the nose toward a dead-weight palate that shows touches of passion fruit and melon but no clarity or purpose. No need to bother with this. 80 *—M.S. (5/1/2007)*

Novus 2004 Chardonnay (Mendoza) $11. 85 *—M.S. (6/1/2006)*

Novus 2005 Malbec (Mendoza) $10. 89 Best Buy *—M.S. (12/1/2006)*

Novus 2003 Malbec (Mendoza) $11. 87 Best Buy *—M.S. (4/1/2006)*

Novus 2006 Reserve Malbec (Uco Valley) $15. Good wine, especially if you like some new oak that brings a lot of cream, vanilla and chocolate to the game. Along the way there's plenty of boysenberry, blueberry and other sweet dark-fruit flavors. A winner that should meet the expectations of many. 88 *—M.S. (8/1/2007)*

Novus 2005 Limited Edition Malbec-Cabernet Sauvignon (Uco Valley) $20. Good out of the blocks, with full and creamy berry aromas. The palate doesn't exactly follow that lead as it shows slightly tart red cherry and cranberry flavors. And by the finish there's even a lemony tingle. Best if you like a juicy style. 85 *—M.S. (10/1/2007)*

Novus 2005 Syrah (Mendoza) $10. 88 Best Buy *—M.S. (12/1/2006)*

Novus 2003 Syrah (Mendoza) $11. 85 *—M.S. (6/1/2006)*

Novus 2005 Reserve Syrah (Alto Valle de Uco) $13. Good but sort of generic. The nose exudes strawberry and milk chocolate, and the palate features blueberry fruit and some citrus-like acidity. The mouthfeel is a bit raw and tangy, but overall it is clean and presents itself well. 84 *—M.S. (8/1/2007)*

O. FOURNIER

O. Fournier 2001 A Crux Red Blend (Mendoza) $42. 89 *—M.S. (7/1/2005)*

O. Fournier 2002 B Crux Red Blend (Mendoza) $21. 89 *—M.S. (7/1/2005)*

ORIGIN

Origin 2005 Malbec (Mendoza) $7. Malbec from Argentina is supposed to be ripe and easy to drink. This one is green, sharp and weighted down by rhubarb aromas and flavors as well as a rough mouthfeel. 81 *—M.S. (5/1/2007)*

Origin 2004 Reserve Series Malbec (Mendoza) $18. Classic dark-cherry aromas start it out. Next up comes a ripe, snappy, zesty palate defined by pulsating raspberry accented with touches of milk chocolate and a blast of smoke. A serious wine with integrity. 88 *—M.S. (2/1/2007)*

PALO ALTO

Palo Alto 2004 Amadores Cabernet Sauvignon (Argentina) $21. Earthy and leathery initially, but airing reveals dark plum and violet-like aromas. The palate is sturdy and healthy, with nice acidity and tannins propelling ripe berry and cassis. The finish is fudgy and round, with vanilla shadings. Shows only the slightest hint of green tobacco at its core. 87 *—M.S. (2/1/2007)*

Palo Alto 2003 Amadores Cabernet Sauvignon-Merlot (Argentina) $20. A bit jumbled and certainly it goes heavy on the oak. But as things settle you'll find buttery vanilla notes accenting relatively solid berry fruit. The end result is pretty good. Give it some air. 85 *—M.S. (10/1/2007)*

Palo Alto 2004 Amadores Malbec (Argentina) $21. 86 *—M.S. (12/1/2006)*

Palo Alto 2005 Amadores Limited Edition Pinot Noir (Mendoza) $16. 82 *—M.S. (12/1/2006)*

PANNOTIA VINEYARDS

Pannotia Vineyards 2004 Malbec (Luján de Cuyo) $13. The new Malbecs keep pouring in from Argentina, among them this heavy, damp example that's unfocused and raisiny. Very much at the base level of what is acceptable. 80 *—M.S. (5/1/2007)*

PARIS GOULART

Paris Goulart 2005 Reserva Malbec-Cabernet Sauvignon (Mendoza) $15. This wine shows molasses and Boston baked beans on the nose along with peppery spice. The bouquet is a touch stewy, but the palate delivers core black cherry and cola along with tight, ripe tannins. The wine takes a little while to warm up and it remains saucy, but that's not uncommon for Mendoza. 86 *—M.S. (12/1/2007)*

PASCUAL TOSO

Pascual Toso 2004 Maipo Vineyards Cabernet Sauvignon (Mendoza) $11. A bit stemmy and brambly, so right from the first sniff you know that it's not a lush, berry filled Cab. And the palate confirms the nose, offering baked fruit with green, herbal overtones. Finishes with a blast of coconut and mint courtesy of whatever barrels it rested in. 84 *—M.S. (2/1/2007)*

Pascual Toso 2006 Maipu Vineyards Cabernet Sauvignon (Mendoza) $12. A little more complexity than normal, as the nose offers dry spices like nutmeg and cinnamon. The palate deals your typical mix of cassis and black cherry, while the structure is defined by balanced tannins. A little weak in the middle and short on the finish, but at this price that's being picky. 87 Best Buy *—M.S. (12/1/2007)*

Pascual Toso 2002 Reserve Cabernet Sauvignon (Mendoza) $18. 87 *—M.S. (7/1/2004)*

Pascual Toso 2005 Maipo Vineyards Chardonnay (Mendoza) $11. 87 Best Buy *—M.S. (12/1/2006)*

Pascual Toso 2004 Maipo Vineyards Malbec (Mendoza) $11. 87 Best Buy *—M.S. (12/1/2006)*

Pascual Toso 2006 Maipu Vineyards Malbec (Mendoza) $12. A year or two ago when Paul Hobbs began consulting for Toso things changed for the better. This is the rare Best Buy that can swim with the big fish and give them a run for the money. Pop the cork and enjoy lusty dark aromas of Turkish tobacco and berry compote. In the mouth, there's a riot of fruit flavors to ponder followed by a smooth, lusty finish. 91 Best Buy *—M.S. (12/1/2007)*

Pascual Toso 2002 Reserve Malbec (Mendoza) $18. 86 *—M.S. (7/1/2004)*

Pascual Toso 2003 Estate Bottled Merlot (Maipú) $NA. 80 *—M.S. (7/1/2005)*

Pascual Toso 2005 Maipo Vineyards Sauvignon Blanc (Mendoza) $11. 86 Best Buy *—M.S. (12/1/2006)*

Pascual Toso NV Toso Brut Sparkling Blend (Mendoza) $10. Burnt popcorn and some ammonia make the nose fairly harsh. Time softens it a bit as it yields to green-fruit flavors. Finishes dry as a soda cracker, with some Old World touches. Not an easy wine to enjoy; it's very lean and underdeveloped. 82 *—M.S. (12/31/2007)*

PIATTELLI

Piattelli 2003 Cabernet Sauvignon (Tupungato) $14. 86 *—M.S. (12/1/2006)*

Piattelli 2001 Cabernet Sauvignon (Mendoza) $15. 87 *—M.S. (7/1/2004)*

Piattelli 2004 Malbec (Luján de Cuyo) $14. A sweet cherry essence characterizes the playful bouquet, while plenty of new oak adds mint and coconut. The palate is juicy, and a starburst of rugged, young fruit is prominently on display. Maybe it could use a bit more weight and darkness to rate excellent; but what's here is more than casual and well worth a go. 88 *—M.S. (2/1/2007)*

PIRCAS NEGRAS

Pircas Negras 2005 Organic Torrontès (Famatina Valley) $10. 85 Best Buy *—M.S. (8/1/2006)*

PLAZA DE MULAS

Plaza de Mulas 2005 Chardonnay (Mendoza) $8. 84 Best Buy *—M.S. (8/1/2006)*

PRELUDIO

Preludio 2004 Malbec (Mendoza) $18. 89 *—M.S. (12/1/2006)*

Preludio 2003 Malbec (Mendoza) $16. 87 *—M.S. (12/31/2005)*

Preludio 2003 Acorde #1 Reserve Malbec-Cabernet Sauvignon (Mendoza) $36. 85 *—M.S. (6/1/2006)*

Preludio 2004 Syrah (Mendoza) $18. Whereas Preludio's Malbecs impressed, this Syrah is more of a murky, amorphous red wine that's neither here nor there. The nose is a touch lactic, while the palate is roasted and heavy, with a carob flavor making itself a bit too noticed. 83 *—M.S. (2/1/2007)*

Preludio 2004 Tempranillo (Mendoza) $16. 86 *—M.S. (12/1/2006)*

Preludio 2003 Tempranillo (Mendoza) $14. 85 *—M.S. (11/15/2005)*

PROEMIO

Proemio 2003 Reserve Malbec (Mendoza) $22. Regal and ready, and showing equal amounts of early maturity along with youthful fruit and menthol aromas. The palate is saturated with raspberry and black cherry, while the lengthy finish offers coffee and chocolate. Drive and power are not in short supply, so take this one with fatty foods like ribs or steak. 90 *—M.S. (8/1/2007)*

PULMARY

Pulmary 2004 Donaria Bonarda (Mendoza) $20. 83 *—M.S. (12/31/2005)*

Pulmary 2004 Donaria Malbec (Mendoza) $20. 83 *—M.S. (12/31/2005)*

QUARA

Quara 2004 Cabernet Sauvignon (Cafayate) $9. 84 *—M.S. (11/15/2005)*

Quara 2004 Malbec (Cafayate) $9. 82 *—M.S. (11/15/2005)*

Quara 2004 Merlot (Cafayate) $9. 84 *—M.S. (11/15/2005)*

Quara 2004 Tannat (Cafayate) $9. 83 *—M.S. (8/1/2006)*

Quara 2004 Torrontès (Cafayate) $9. 85 Best Buy *—M.S. (12/31/2005)*

RAZA

Raza 2003 Limited Edition Malbec (Famatina Valley) $40. 89 *—M.S. (11/1/2006)*

Raza 2004 Silver Reserve Malbec (Famatina Valley) $13. 86 *—M.S. (11/1/2006)*

Raza 2003 Limited Edition Syrah (Famatina Valley) $40. 83 *—M.S. (11/1/2006)*

Raza 2004 Silver Reserve Syrah (Famatina Valley) $13. 84 *—M.S. (8/1/2006)*

Raza 2004 Silver Reserve Torrontès (Famatina Valley) $13. 86 *—M.S. (8/1/2006)*

RELINCHO

Relincho 2002 Cabernet Sauvignon-Merlot (Mendoza) $7. 82 *—M.S. (3/1/2005)*

RENACER

Renacer 2006 Punto Final Malbec (Perdriel) $11. Color, power, flavor and commendable balance; that's pretty much the format for Punto Final, one of Argentina's go-to brands for Malbec. This youngster is ripe and ready, and it holds form onto a long finish. If it seems a little young and clumsy upon pouring, air it out and it'll improve. 90 Best Buy *—M.S. (8/1/2007)*

Renacer 2005 Punto Final Reserva Malbec (Perdriel) $18. Is there a better, more consistent Malbec on the market today than Punto Final? The 2005 is typically rich and dense, with saturated berry aromas and a strong but balanced oak element. The palate is a potpourri of berries, chocolate and vanilla, while the mouthfeel is juicy and stacked. Quite delicious; this is the type of wine that gives Argentine Malbec its good name. 91 Editors' Choice *—M.S. (8/1/2007)*

Renacer 2004 Punto Final Malbec (Perdriel) $11. 91 Best Buy *—M.S. (11/1/2006)*

Renacer 2004 Punto Final Reserva Malbec (Perdriel) $18. 92 Editors' Choice *—M.S. (12/1/2006)*

Renacer 2003 Renacer R Malbec (Perdriel) $48. Dynamite Malbec from the Renacer family that's behind the emerging Punto Final label. This is a monumental effort with 24 months of French oak aging. What you get is quality from head to toe, with pure and unyielding flavors backed by a big wave of tannins. Will age for several more years, and by then this rock's power may have settled down a little. 275 cases produced. 93 *—M.S. (5/1/2007)*

RICARDO SANTOS

Ricardo Santos 2005 La Madras Vineyard Malbec (Mendoza) $18. 89 *—M.S. (12/1/2006)*

Ricardo Santos 2004 La Madras Vineyard Malbec (Mendoza) $17. 88 *—M.S. (6/1/2006)*

Ricardo Santos 2003 La Madras Vineyard Malbec (Mendoza) $18. 84 *—M.S. (12/31/2005)*

Ricardo Santos 2002 La Madras Vineyard Malbec (Maipú) $17. 90 Editors' Choice *—M.S. (7/1/2004)*

RINCON PRIVADO

Rincon Privado 1996 Special Reserve Cabernet Sauvignon (San Rafael) $20. 83 *—M.S. (5/1/2003)*

Rincon Privado 1999 Malbec (San Rafael) $11. 84 *—M.S. (5/1/2003)*

Rincon Privado 1999 Merlot (San Rafael) $11. 84 *—M.S. (5/1/2003)*

Rincon Privado 1999 Pinot Noir (San Rafael) $11. 84 *—M.S. (5/1/2003)*

ROMANCE

Romance 2002 Red Blend (Mendoza) $8. 82 *—M.S. (7/1/2004)*

ROSELL BOHER

Rosell Boher NV Brut Champagne Blend (Argentina) $27. 85 *—M.S. (12/31/2004)*

Rosell Boher 1999 Grande Cuvée Champagne Blend (Argentina) $40. 89 Editors' Choice *—M.S. (12/31/2004)*

RUTINI

Rutini 2006 Trumpeter Cabernet Sauvignon (Mendoza) $11. Rutini's value brand exhibits a lot of forced toast, popcorn and burnt notes, all of which tells us that they want us to smell and taste oak. Supporting the wood brigade is syrupy cola and ripe black cherry flavors as well as creamy chocolate finishing notes. Candied but pleasant. 85 *—M.S. (12/1/2007)*

Rutini 2006 Trumpeter Chardonnay (Mendoza) $11. A heavy Chardonnay with corn and nut aromas. Mango, honey and syrupy pear flavors are just too heavy and flat to really enjoy. Has its flashes but they are brief and get wiped out by the wine's clumsy overall character. 83 *—M.S. (12/1/2007)*

SALENTEIN

Salentein 2003 Cabernet Sauvignon (Uco Valley) $19. 89 Cellar Selection *—M.S. (12/1/2006)*

Salentein 2002 Cabernet Sauvignon (Mendoza) $18. 90 *—M.S. (3/1/2005)*

Salentein 2001 Cabernet Sauvignon (Mendoza) $18. 91 *—S.H. (1/1/2002)*

Salentein 2002 El Portillo Cabernet Sauvignon (Mendoza) $9. 81 *—M.S. (7/1/2004)*

Salentein 2003 El Portillo Chardonnay (Mendoza) $9. 84 *—M.S. (7/1/2004)*

Salentein 2004 Malbec (Uco Valley) $19. 90 *—M.S. (12/1/2006)*

Salentein 2003 Malbec (Mendoza) $18. 88 *—M.S. (12/31/2005)*

Salentein 2002 Malbec (Mendoza) $18. 86 *—M.S. (7/1/2004)*

Salentein 2001 Malbec (Mendoza) $9. 84 *—M.S. (7/1/2004)*

Salentein 2001 Malbec (Mendoza) $18. 91 *—S.H. (1/1/2002)*

Salentein 2002 El Portillo Malbec (Mendoza) $9. 84 *—M.S. (7/1/2004)*

Salentein 2001 Finca el Portillo Malbec (Uco Valley) $9. 87 Best Buy *—M.S. (12/1/2003)*

Salentein 2003 Reserve Malbec (Uco Valley) $62. This is the best and most expensive wine ever released by Dutch-owned Salentein, and it proves that this winery has finally mastered Mendoza. The color is excellent and the nose is full of bold fruit, leather, mint and more. It's a huge Malbec with saturated cassis and black cherry flavors, and the feel and lushness are just right. For a ripe mini monster that's sure to please, drink this now and over the next three years, preferably with grilled beef. 93 Editors' Choice *—M.S. (10/1/2007)*

Salentein 2002 Merlot (Mendoza) $18. 83 *—M.S. (11/15/2005)*

Salentein 2001 Merlot (Mendoza) $19. 88 *—M.S. (7/1/2004)*

Salentein 2002 El Portillo Merlot (Mendoza) $9. 82 *—M.S. (7/1/2004)*

Salentein 2003 Pinot Noir (Uco Valley) $19. 86 *—M.S. (12/1/2006)*

Salentein 2003 Finca el Portillo Sauvignon Blanc (Mendoza) $9. 85 *—M.S. (7/1/2004)*

Salentein 2001 Shiraz (Mendoza) $18. 90 *—S.H. (1/1/2002)*

Salentein 2002 Syrah (Mendoza) $18. 88 *—M.S. (3/1/2005)*

Salentein 2003 Syrah (Uco Valley) $19. 90 *—M.S. (12/1/2006)*

Salentein 2004 Finca El Portillo Syrah (Alto Valle de Uco) $9. 82 *—M.S. (4/1/2006)*

Salentein 2002 El Portillo Tempranillo (Mendoza) $9. 82 *—M.S. (7/1/2004)*

SAN HUBERTO

San Huberto 2005 Bonarda (Aminga Valley) $9. 84 *—M.S. (12/1/2006)*

San Huberto 2002 Bonarda (Aminga Valley) $7. 82 *—M.S. (10/1/2004)*

San Huberto 2002 Cabernet Sauvignon (Aminga Valley) $8. 83 *—M.S. (10/1/2004)*

San Huberto 2003 Crianza Cabernet Sauvignon (Argentina) $10. 85 Best Buy *—M.S. (6/1/2006)*

San Huberto 2005 Chardonnay (Aminga Valley) $10. 80 *—M.S. (6/1/2006)*

San Huberto 2002 Chardonnay (Aminga Valley) $8. 83 *—M.S. (10/1/2004)*

San Huberto 2005 Malbec (Aminga Valley) $10. 83 *—M.S. (4/1/2006)*

San Huberto 2002 Malbec (La Rioja) $8. 83 *—M.S. (10/1/2004)*

San Huberto 1997 Malbec (Argentina) $9. 82 *—J.C. (5/1/2002)*

San Huberto 2003 Crianza Malbec (Argentina) $10. 85 Best Buy *—M.S. (4/1/2006)*

San Huberto 2002 Medalla d'Oro Crianza Malbec (Aminga Valley) $10. 81 *—M.S. (10/1/2004)*

San Huberto 2005 Torrontès (Aminga Valley) $9. 86 Best Buy *—M.S. (4/1/2006)*

San Huberto 2002 Torrontès (Aminga Valley) $7. 84 *—M.S. (10/1/2004)*

SAN POLO

San Polo 2005 Auka Malbec (Mendoza) $32. A difficult wine to assess. For starters, it's heavily oaked and very dark in aromas; think tar, char and espresso. The palate is narrowly focused and tannic, with dark fruit peeking thru here and there. Finishes sheer, with coffee and bitter chocolate. Could get better with time, or it might never really open up. Needs at least another year in bottle to show its true colors. 86 *—M.S. (12/1/2007)*

San Polo 2003 Auka Malbec (San Carlos) $15. 88 *—M.S. (7/1/2005)*

San Polo 2004 Auka Merlot (San Carlos) $15. 84 *—M.S. (12/31/2005)*

San Polo 2003 Auka Merlot (San Carlos) $15. 83 *—M.S. (7/1/2005)*

SAN TELMO

San Telmo 2000 Cabernet Sauvignon (Mendoza) $10. 82 *—C.S. (5/1/2002)*

San Telmo 2003 Chardonnay (Mendoza) $7. 82 *—M.S. (7/1/2005)*

San Telmo 2000 Chardonnay (Mendoza) $10. 82 *—M.S. (11/15/2001)*

San Telmo 2005 Malbec (Mendoza) $8. Brambly and aggressive, with rubbery aromas that aren't what you'd call "inviting." There's some cherry and raspberry on the palate, but also a lot of uncomplimentary raspy notes as well as an overriding burnt, grassy flavor. 82 *—M.S. (2/1/2007)*

San Telmo 2004 Malbec (Mendoza) $7. 83 *—M.S. (11/15/2005)*

San Telmo 2003 Malbec (Mendoza) $7. 84 Best Buy *—M.S. (3/1/2005)*

San Telmo 2003 Merlot (Mendoza) $7. 80 *—M.S. (7/1/2005)*

San Telmo 2003 Shiraz (Mendoza) $7. 86 Best Buy *—M.S. (3/1/2005)*

SANTA EUGENIA

Santa Eugenia 1999 Malbec (Mendoza) $7. 82 *—C.S. (5/1/2002)*

SANTA FAUSTINA

Santa Faustina 2002 Alto Lunlunta Vineyard Malbec (Mendoza) $20. Ripe, with leather, balsamic, and prune aromas. Saturated in the mouth, but ultimately it's narrow in scope. On the finish, creamy oak rises up to leave butter and resin flavors. A fairly big wine with ample barrel influence. 85 *—M.S. (11/1/2006)*

Santa Faustina 2005 Finca Los Lirios Malbec (Mendoza) $10. Dry and lean up front, but clean. It's fast and tart in the mouth, with a finish that borders on sour. A lot more acidity and snap than substance. 81 *—M.S. (8/1/2007)*

Santa Faustina 2004 Finca Los Lirios de los Andes Malbec (Mendoza) $15. Intense on the nose and colorful, but in the end this wine shows little character, complexity or style. It's all about color and extract but you don't get much richness, charm or ripeness. And it's almost sassy and tangy on the palate and finish. 83 *—M.S. (8/1/2007)*

Santa Faustina 2002 Medrano Vineyard Syrah (Mendoza) $20. 80 *—M.S. (11/1/2006)*

SANTA JULIA

Santa Julia 2001 Cabernet Sauvignon (Mendoza) $8. 84 *—M.S. (5/1/2003)*

Santa Julia 2000 Cabernet Sauvignon (Mendoza) $8. 84 *(12/15/2001)*

Santa Julia 1996 Oak Reserva Malbec Cabernet Sauvignon (Mendoza) $10. 87 Best Buy *(5/1/2000)*

Santa Julia 2006 Organica Cabernet Sauvignon (Mendoza) $9. A really nice and lighter-styled Cabernet with bright fruit and spicy oak crawling on the bouquet. The palate is full of friendly raspberry, strawberry and plum, while the finish is round and chocolaty. For the money, this is an extremely complete little wine that offers just-right balance throughout. 88 Best Buy *—M.S. (5/1/2007)*

Santa Julia 2005 Organica Cabernet Sauvignon (Mendoza) $9. 86 Best Buy *—M.S. (8/1/2006)*

Santa Julia 2006 Reserva Cabernet Sauvignon (Mendoza) $11. Finding affordable but good Cab is not an easy chore, so let this solid, smoky wine fit that bill. The nose is like a cowboy campfire, complete with hickory, leather and cured meat. The palate is full-force and tannic, with plum and berry fruit. It may be slightly cooked and not for the long haul; so drink now. 86 Best Buy *—M.S. (10/1/2007)*

Santa Julia 2005 Reserva Cabernet Sauvignon (Mendoza) $12. Robust and with a touch of raisin, this full-bodied Cab hits many correct notes. The oak may be a bit buttery and the tannins fairly full, but overall this does a good job of impersonating a much pricier wine; it's big, liberally oaked, ripe and quite good as a whole. 88 Best Buy *—M.S. (8/1/2007)*

Santa Julia 2004 Reserva Cabernet Sauvignon (Mendoza) $12. 85 *—M.S. (11/1/2006)*

Santa Julia 2002 Reserva Cabernet Sauvignon (Mendoza) $10. 87 Best Buy *—M.S. (10/1/2004)*

Santa Julia 2000 Reserva Cabernet Sauvignon (Mendoza) $11. 86 *(12/15/2001)*

Santa Julia 1999 Reserva Cabernet Sauvignon (Mendoza) $10. 84 *—M.S. (11/15/2001)*

Santa Julia 2005 Chardonnay (Mendoza) $8. 81 *—M.S. (6/1/2006)*

Santa Julia 2002 Chardonnay (Mendoza) $9. 85 *—M.S. (2/1/2004)*

Santa Julia 2001 Chardonnay (Mendoza) $7. 83 *—M.S. (7/1/2002)*

Santa Julia 2000 Chardonnay (Mendoza) $7. 84 Best Buy *—M.S. (11/15/2001)*

Santa Julia 2006 Organica Chardonnay (Mendoza) $9. Toasty aromas precede heavy, edgeless flavors, and in the end there's not much body or substance to the wine. It's just a sweet, simple white. 82 *—M.S. (5/1/2007)*

Santa Julia 2005 Organica Chardonnay (Mendoza) $9. 83 *—M.S. (6/1/2006)*

Santa Julia 2005 Reserva Chardonnay (Mendoza) $12. This reserve-level Chardonnay isn't that expensive yet it shows considerably more balance and complexity than the winery's regular Chard. This version offers peach and other stone-fruit aromas, while the palate presents smooth white fruit and toast flavors. Fairly long, with a healthy feel throughout. 87 Best Buy *—M.S. (8/1/2007)*

Santa Julia 2004 Reserva Chardonnay (Mendoza) $12. 87 Best Buy *—M.S. (6/1/2006)*

Santa Julia 2002 Reserva Chardonnay (Mendoza) $10. 85 *—M.S. (10/1/2004)*

Santa Julia 2000 Reserva Chardonnay (Mendoza) $9. 85 *(12/15/2001)*

Santa Julia 2006 Malbec (Mendoza) $8. Santa Julia doesn't try to trick you with its wines. They are what they are, and for under $10 this creamy, berry-packed wine should please the masses. The fruit is plump and ripe, while the mouthfeel is round and healthy. A great model for quality, affordable Malbec. 87 Best Buy *—M.S. (8/1/2007)*

Santa Julia 2003 Malbec (Mendoza) $9. 84 *—M.S. (10/1/2004)*

Santa Julia 2001 Malbec (Mendoza) $9. 87 Best Buy *—M.S. (5/1/2003)*

Santa Julia 2000 Malbec (Mendoza) $7. 86 *(12/15/2001)*

Santa Julia 2006 Reserva Malbec (Mendoza) $11. Big and jammy, and all in all it's a solid, good Malbec. Aromas of tar and prune give way to plum and blackberry flavors. On the finish, it's a touch salty and drying, but with food it will be smoother. Good for the money, although limited in depth and complexity. 86 Best Buy *—M.S. (10/1/2007)*

Santa Julia 2005 Reserva Malbec (Mendoza) $11. A rambunctious young buck of a wine, with untamed aromas and plenty of aggressiveness from front to back. It clamps with firm tannins while delivering dark plum and other black-fruit flavors. Gets better with airing and may improve in the bottle. Now, it needs food to tame the beast. 86 Best Buy *—M.S. (10/1/2007)*

Santa Julia 2004 Reserva Malbec (Mendoza) $12. 87 Best Buy *—M.S. (11/1/2006)*

Santa Julia 2002 Reserva Malbec (Mendoza) $10. 86 *—M.S. (12/1/2003)*

Santa Julia 2000 Reserva Malbec (Mendoza) $11. 88 Best Buy *(12/15/2001)*

Santa Julia 1999 Reserva Malbec (Mendoza) $10. 84 *—M.S. (11/15/2001)*

Santa Julia 2000 Merlot (Mendoza) $8. 85 Best Buy *(12/15/2001)*

Santa Julia 2001 Merlot (Mendoza) $8. 85 *—M.S. (5/1/2003)*

Santa Julia 2005 Pinot Grigio (Mendoza) $8. 80 *—M.S. (11/1/2006)*

Santa Julia 2000 Malbec-Cab Sauv Red Blend (Mendoza) $7. 86 *(12/15/2001)*

Santa Julia 2006 Pinot Grigio (Mendoza) $8. It's hard to understand why Santa Julia would want to make an oaked Pinot Grigio in Mendoza, but they did. And we find it as odd and difficult to get through as you might expect. The nose is nutty and full of popcorn, while the palate offers heady, honeyed apricot and peach flavors. 80 *—M.S. (10/1/2007)*

Santa Julia 2001 Red Blend (Mendoza) $9. 83 *—M.S. (5/1/2003)*

Santa Julia NV Extra Brut Sparkling Blend (Mendoza) $13. 85 *—M.S. (6/1/2006)*

Santa Julia 2005 Reserva Tempranillo (Mendoza) $12. Opens with brambly, leathery aromas; later shows some true Tempranillo character, namely body, tannin and dark-fruit flavors. This is not flawed, but it is rather oaky and demanding. 84 *—M.S. (10/1/2007)*

Santa Julia 2006 Torrontes (Mendoza) $8. Light and generally fresh, but turns dull and distant on the palate and finish. Dig as you might, you still won't find much flesh on the bones of this medium-weight, mildly floral white. 82 *—M.S. (5/1/2007)*

Santa Julia 2005 Torrontès (Mendoza) $8. 84 Best Buy *—M.S. (8/1/2006)*

Santa Julia 2003 Torrontès (Mendoza) $7. 83 *—M.S. (2/1/2004)*

Santa Julia 2002 Torrontès (Argentina) $8. 85 *—M.S. (11/15/2003)*

Santa Julia 2001 Torrontès (Mendoza) $7. 87 Best Buy *(12/15/2001)*

Santa Julia 2000 Torrontès (Mendoza) $7. 87 Best Buy *(12/15/2001)*

Santa Julia 2000 Torrontès (Mendoza) $7. 86 Best Buy *—M.S. (11/15/2001)*

Santa Julia 2006 Tardío Torrontes (Mendoza) $12. As always, this late-harvest white delivers peach and lychee aromas, and it's even better in the mouth, where intense lychee and pineapple flavors rise up and steal the show. 87 *—M.S. (8/1/2007)*

Santa Julia 2004 Tardío Torrontès (Mendoza) $13. 86 *—M.S. (8/1/2006)*

Santa Julia 2000 Tardio Torrontès (Mendoza) $10. 85 Best Buy *—M.S. (11/15/2001)*

Santa Julia 2001 Tardio Late Harvest Torrontès (Mendoza) $12. 86 *—M.S. (5/1/2003)*

Santa Julia 2005 Viognier (Mendoza) $8. Round, simple and easy to enjoy if you don't mind a lack of Viognier typicity replaced by chunky apple aromas and flavors. There's also some citrus and apricot to bulk up the flavor profile. Overall it's a full-bodied but indifferent white. Drink right away for best results. 84 *—M.S. (10/1/2007)*

Santa Julia 2005 Viognier (Mendoza) $9. 82 *—M.S. (11/1/2006)*

Santa Julia 2002 Viognier (Mendoza) $12. 83 *—M.S. (2/1/2004)*

Santa Julia 2002 Viognier (Mendoza) $8. 85 *—M.S. (5/1/2003)*

SEPTIMA

Septima 2005 Cabernet Sauvignon (Mendoza) $12. The only thing holding this value-priced Cab back is that it seems slightly overripe, which results in a bouquet that's mildly cooked and grainy and a palate that's rooty and sweet. But if you like softer tannins and flavors of root beer, chocolate and spice, this has plenty of that. 86 *—M.S. (12/1/2007)*

Septima 2003 Cabernet Sauvignon (Mendoza) $8. 81 *—M.S. (3/1/2005)*

Septima 2001 Cabernet Sauvignon (Mendoza) $9. 84 *—M.S. (2/1/2004)*

Septima 2002 Reserva Cabernet Sauvignon-Malbec (Mendoza) $14. 88 *—M.S. (11/15/2004)*

Septima 2006 Chardonnay (Mendoza) $12. Value-level Chardonnay has never really been Argentina's strong suit, but this fuller-bodied version is pretty good. It starts with citrus, orange peel and some dusty scents, which are backed by melon, apple and citrus flavors. It finishes with some pithy bitterness but overall it's nice for Mendoza Chardonnay. 86 *—M.S. (12/1/2007)*

Septima 2006 Malbec (Mendoza) $12. Septima is owned by Codorníu of Spain, and it hit the market solidly in 2002, disappeared for a couple of years, and now is back with a great Best Buy. The 2006 Malbec is a rock star wine in sheep's clothing. Shows size and power along with pure fruit, texture and balance. Lush and fruity until the end. 90 Best Buy *—M.S. (12/1/2007)*

Septima 2003 Malbec (Mendoza) $8. 87 Best Buy *—M.S. (11/15/2004)*

Septima 2002 Malbec (Mendoza) $9. 88 Best Buy *—M.S. (12/1/2003)*

Septima 2001 Red Blend (Mendoza) $8. 81 *—M.S. (5/1/2003)*

Septima 2005 Syrah (Mendoza) $12. A giant smack of coffee and earth rip at you from the glass, while the palate starts out medicinally sweet before folding in chocolate and leather. The feel settles at soft, but it's not flabby. And the finishing notes of mocha-covered strawberry are pleasant. 85 *—M.S. (12/1/2007)*

SILVERTOP DE ARGENTINA

Silvertop de Argentina 2005 Malbec (Mendoza) $9. Here's a warm, round, ripe Malbec with a lot of standard, good qualities. The raspberry, plum and cherry flavors are solid and steady, while the feel and finish are satisfying and generally quite sound. A perfectly good wine for the price. 86 Best Buy *—M.S. (5/1/2007)*

SIMONASSI

Simonassi 2004 Premium Cabernet Sauvignon (Mendoza) $12. Earthy and less than fruity on the nose, then short and sour in the mouth. A clipped, abrupt wine that is too tart for its own good. 80 *—M.S. (2/1/2007)*

Simonassi 2003 Estate Malbec (San Rafael) $10. 87 Best Buy *—M.S. (12/1/2006)*

Simonassi 2004 Premium Malbec (Mendoza) $12. 81 *—M.S. (12/1/2006)*

SOLALTO

SolAlto 2005 Chardonnay (San Juan) $8. 85 Best Buy *—M.S. (6/1/2006)*

SolAlto 2004 Malbec (San Juan) $8. 81 *—M.S. (6/1/2006)*

SolAlto 2004 Pinot Grigio (San Juan) $8. 84 Best Buy *—M.S. (2/1/2006)*

SORBUS

Sorbus 2004 Malbec (Mendoza) $8. 86 Best Buy *—M.S. (12/31/2005)*

SOUTHERN WILLOWS

Southern Willows 2002 Merlot (Mendoza) $9. 81 *—M.S. (3/1/2005)*

SUBLIMIS

Sublimis 2004 Limited Edition Cabernet Sauvignon (Mendoza) $12. 81 *—M.S. (12/1/2006)*

SUR DE LOS ANDES

Sur de los Andes 2006 Bonarda (Mendoza) $10. Concentrated and intense, but typical of Bonarda this is a fierce wine with a rock-hard mouthfeel and slightly tart, limited raspberry flavors. Not exactly sour but it makes your mouth seize up and take notice. 83 *—M.S. (12/31/2007)*

Sur de los Andes 2005 Bonarda (Mendoza) $9. Still not sure what the difference is between Sur de los Andes and Alma de los Andes (they're from the same winery), but this wine seems a tiny bit more open and friendly than the Alma. It's evolved, sweet and full of blackberry and blueberry flavors. And the finish carries some warm baked notes that anchor the deal. 87 Best Buy *—M.S. (8/1/2007)*

Sur de los Andes 2005 Reserva Bonarda (Mendoza) $15. Heavily coated with coconut and oiled leather aromas, however, the palate recedes to Bonarda's typical angularity. The flavors of blackberry and cherry are solid, but the mouthfeel runs rough and sheer. And it finishes with some saltiness and leather. A good wine, not without its fault. 87 *—M.S. (12/31/2007)*

Sur de los Andes 2006 Cabernet Sauvignon (Mendoza) $13. Dense, rich and encouraging on the nose, with full blackberry flavors and a flush mouthfeel. For Argentine Cab this gets it right much more than wrong. The flavors are fairly well developed and the finish has length. 86 *—M.S. (10/1/2007)*

Sur de los Andes 2006 Malbec (Mendoza) $13. Rowdy and aggressive stuff; where's the charm and poise, even in a value-priced wine? The nose is rambling and penetrating, while the palate is tart like sucking candy. A raw wine that should be better. 80 *—M.S. (10/1/2007)*

Sur de los Andes 2005 Malbec (Mendoza) $9. Everything you want in a value Malbec is on display here. The nose is big and muscular, with ripe fruit aromas and touch of earth and mushroom. Meanwhile, the palate is all black fruit all the time; it shows girth and chocolate in front of a finish that lasts a good while. 89 Best Buy *—M.S. (5/1/2007)*

Sur de los Andes 2005 Gran Reserva Malbec (Mendoza) $25. Something seems afoot with Sur de los Andes' so-called Gran Reserva Malbecs. Both the 2004 and epecially this '05 are wines that don't handle their oak well. This wine has an aromatic package of green tobacco and ash, while the wood burns its way through the palate. A rough ride that gets marginally better with a lot of swirling and patience. 81 *—M.S. (10/1/2007)*

Sur de los Andes 2004 Gran Reserva Malbec (Mendoza) $21. Personally, I liked Sur de los Andes' basic Malbec more than this oakier, heavier Gran Reserva. This wine is a bit odd, with nutmeg-infused flavors that run toward fruit cake. In addition, there's heat on the finish despite a stated 13.6% alcohol, which is reasonable. Seems like a case of trying to do more with less. 84 *—M.S. (5/1/2007)*

Sur de los Andes 2005 Reserva Malbec (Mendoza) $15. Stick with Sur's basic 2005 Malbec because it's fresher and cleaner than this raisiny, tannic brooder that tastes a little too much of stewy fruit and liqueur. 84 *—M.S. (10/1/2007)*

Sur de los Andes 2004 Reserve Malbec (Mendoza) $13. Guillermo Banfi's Sur de los Andes and Alma de los Andes wines are excellent across the board. This reserve-level holdover from 2004 offers mint, chocolate and leather aromas in front of ripe cherry and raspberry flavors. Almost crisp and choppy, but on the other hand precise and zesty. Not unlike a very good Dolcetto from Italy. 89 Best Buy *—M.S. (5/1/2007)*

Sur de los Andes 2006 Malbec-Cabernet Sauvignon (Mendoza) $13. Almost sugar-beet sweet on the nose, with a good dose of oak and size. The palate is expectedly big, but with fairly hard tannins and limited depth of fruit. Ultimately there's not much cushion, so it seems hard. 84 *—M.S. (10/1/2007)*

Sur de los Andes 2005 Malbec-Cabernet Sauvignon (Mendoza) $9. There doesn't seem to be a bad wine in the Sur de los Andes portfolio. This Malbec-Cabernet blend deals black cherry on the nose and behind that there's alert, focused cherry and raspberry flavors. Overall it's a basic red that's a touch tight and grabby, but in general it's enjoyable. 86 Best Buy *—M.S. (5/1/2007)*

Sur de los Andes 2006 Torrontes (Cafayate) $10. One whiff of this wine tells you why we say Torrontes is aromatic. The bouquet is generous as it delivers butter cup, acacia and mango aromas. The palate, meanwhile, is ripe and hefty. Maybe it's a touch creamy and soft, but overall the wine is flavorful, pleasant and offers more than enough size. 85 Best Buy *— M.S. (5/1/2007)*

SUSANA BALBO

Susana Balbo 2003 Cabernet Sauvignon (Mendoza) $27. Rich, warm and possessing a ton of dry oak, this is one serious Argentine Cabernet. The palate is grippy as a rubber glove, with snappy berry flavors and pointed acidity. It's ripe, racy and edgy, with substance to the fruit, feel and finish. Drink now through 2010. 90 *—M.S. (8/1/2007)*

Susana Balbo 2001 Malbec (Mendoza) $27. 89 *—M.S. (12/1/2003)*

Susana Balbo 2006 Crios Rose of Malbec Malbec (Mendoza) $11. Love the big handprint on the label as well as the burgundy color of this Malbec rosé, which ranks as one of the most consistent pink wines from a country (Argentina) that doesn't do rosé all that well. Winemaker Susana Balbo gets the size and tint from her Malbec fruit but manages to corral the bubble-gum sweetness and cloying weight that can afflict Argentine rosados. Crios is the right call for an Argentinean-style barbecue featuring empanadas, lots of salads and plenty of meat. 88 Best Buy *—M.S. (7/1/2007)*

Susana Balbo 2005 Crios Malbec (Mendoza) $15. 90 Best Buy *—M.S. (12/1/2006)*

TAMARÍ

Tamarí 2006 Reserva Malbec (Mendoza) $13. Chunky, big and forward, with some fiery horseradish and spent campfire on the nose. Blackberry, wild raspberry and leather work the demanding, starchy palate, and the finish is short and generally clean and healthy. 85 *—M.S. (12/31/2007)*

Tamarí 2005 Reserva Malbec (Mendoza) $13. Rather beefy and stout on the bouquet, although there's some decent fruit lurking below. The palate is easygoing and medium in intensity, with normal plum and cherry flavors. Unexpressive but good enough as a whole. 10,000 cases made. Imported by Paterno Wines International. 84 *—M.S. (5/1/2007)*

Tamarí 2004 Reserva Malbec (Mendoza) $12. 85 *—M.S. (8/1/2006)*

Tamarí 2003 Reserva Malbec (Mendoza) $10. 80 *—M.S. (11/15/2005)*

TANGO

Tango 2002 Cabernet Sauvignon (Mendoza) $9. 84 *—M.S. (11/15/2004)*

Tango 2002 Reserve Cabernet Sauvignon (Mendoza) $12. 89 Best Buy *— M.S. (11/15/2004)*

Tango 2002 Chardonnay (Mendoza) $9. 84 *—M.S. (3/1/2005)*

Tango 2002 Malbec (Mendoza) $9. 83 *—M.S. (11/15/2004)*

Tango 2001 Malbec (Mendoza) $10. 83 *—M.S. (12/1/2003)*

Tango 2002 Reserve Malbec (Mendoza) $12. 85 *—M.S. (11/15/2004)*

Tango 2002 Merlot (Mendoza) $9. 85 Best Buy *—M.S. (11/15/2004)*

Tango 2002 Syrah (Mendoza) $9. 84 *—M.S. (11/15/2004)*

TANGO SUR

Tango Sur 2004 Cabernet Sauvignon (Mendoza) $9. 82 *—M.S. (8/1/2006)*

Tango Sur 2003 Cabernet Sauvignon (Mendoza) $8. 80 *—M.S. (3/1/2005)*

Tango Sur 2004 Chardonnay (Mendoza) $9. 83 *—M.S. (4/1/2006)*

Tango Sur 2003 Chardonnay (Mendoza) $8. 85 Best Buy *—M.S. (3/1/2005)*

Tango Sur 2004 Malbec (Mendoza) $9. 86 Best Buy *—M.S. (4/1/2006)*

Tango Sur 2003 Malbec (Mendoza) $8. 83 *—M.S. (3/1/2005)*

Tango Sur 2005 Rosé Malbec (Mendoza) $9. Strange, rubbery and a little funky as well. At least in the mouth the feel is solid and the acidity up where it should be. Just a weird wine that proves that Argentina is not really rosé country. 81 *—M.S. (7/1/2007)*

Tango Sur 2004 Rosé Malbec (Mendoza) $9. 84 *—M.S. (4/1/2006)*

Tango Sur 2004 Merlot (Mendoza) $9. 87 Best Buy *—M.S. (6/1/2006)*

Tango Sur 2004 Shiraz (Mendoza) $9. 84 *—M.S. (6/1/2006)*

Tango Sur 2003 Shiraz (Mendoza) $8. 85 Best Buy *—M.S. (3/1/2005)*

Tango Sur 2005 Tempranillo (Mendoza) $8. This Tempranillo is leafy and leathery, with light raspberry aromas backed by thin plum and berry flavors. It's an aggressive, standard red wine that's neither here nor there. 82 *—M.S. (10/1/2007)*

Tango Sur 2003 Tempranillo (Mendoza) $8. 85 Best Buy *—M.S. (3/1/2005)*

TAPIZ

Tapiz 2000 Cabernet Sauvignon (Mendoza) $8. 85 *—M.S. (11/1/2002)*

Tapiz 1999 Cabernet Sauvignon (Mendoza) $8. 85 Best Buy *—M.S. (11/15/2001)*

Tapiz 2001 Chardonnay (Mendoza) $8. 85 *—M.S. (5/1/2003)*

Tapiz 2000 Chardonnay (Mendoza) $8. 84 *—S.H. (7/1/2002)*

Tapiz 1999 Chardonnay (Mendoza) $8. 83 *—M.S. (11/15/2001)*

Tapiz 2002 Malbec (Mendoza) $8. 87 Best Buy *—M.S. (2/1/2004)*

Tapiz 2001 Malbec (Mendoza) $8. 87 Best Buy *—M.S. (5/1/2003)*

Tapiz 2000 Malbec (Mendoza) $8. 85 *—M.S. (11/1/2002)*

Tapiz 1999 Malbec (Mendoza) $8. 83 *—M.S. (11/15/2001)*

Tapiz 2001 Merlot (Mendoza) $8. 84 *—S.H. (1/1/2002)*

Tapiz 2000 Merlot (Mendoza) $8. 86 Best Buy *—M.S. (11/1/2002)*

TAWERT S.A.

Tawert S.A. 2005 Solo Tango Cabernet Sauvignon (Mendoza) $6. This Cab is sheer and tannic, with red plums and stern berry flavors. Adequate initially but the heat and tannins soon cover the palate. 81 *—M.S. (10/1/2007)*

Tawert S.A. 2005 Solo Tango Reserva Cabernet Sauvignon (Mendoza) $9. Spearmint and sawdust announce oak, but the wine isn't up to much after that. It's vegetal and settles on bland berry and plum flavors. 80 *—M.S. (8/1/2007)*

Tawert S.A. 2005 Solo Tango Chardonnay (Mendoza) $6. Ripe to overripe apple grips the nose, while the palate deals one-note citrus flavors. It's a flush, fat Chardonnay that's losing balance with each passing day. Finishes with an avalanche of orange character. 81 *—M.S. (8/1/2007)*

Tawert S.A. 2005 Solo Tango Malbec (Mendoza) $6. Rather raisiny and herbal, with deep plum and blackberry flavors. It's a weighty wine with a finish that runs straight to prune and chocolate. A bit heavy and dull even at this everyday price point. 83 *—M.S. (8/1/2007)*

TEKIAH

Tekiah 2003 Syrah (Argentina) $11. 84 *—J.C. (4/1/2005)*

TELTECA

Telteca 2005 Oak Cabernet Sauvignon (Mendoza) $8. Strawberry jam and green herbs on the nose, with milk chocolate and carob blended with vegetables and berry fruit on the palate. Too stalky and green, with a ragged mouthfeel. 80 *—M.S. (8/1/2007)*

Telteca 2006 Oak Chardonnay (Mendoza) $8. A little buttery and wayward, but not without its good points, which include ripe apple, melon, citrus and papaya flavors. The body is fairly hefty and the finish carries heat, but overall offers decent fruit-salad flavors and pretty good balance. 84 *—M.S. (10/1/2007)*

Telteca 2006 Uma Chardonnay (Mendoza) $6. This Chardonnay-Semillon blend is not normal. It tempts you early with fresh, lightly floral aromas. But once it gets to your taste buds you quickly realize that something's up. In this case, we're talking sweet, sticky flavors that aren't textbook and don't really stir much interest. Weird and cloying. 81 *—M.S. (8/1/2007)*

Telteca 2004 Antá Reserve Malbec (Mendoza) $13. Warm, earthy, leathery and grapy, with a mildly tart, underdeveloped palate that offsets any roughness with a blanket of creamy oak resulting in flavors of berries and milk chocolate. With more focus, riper fruit and less oak, this wine could better. 84 *—M.S. (10/1/2007)*

Telteca 2005 Oak Malbec (Mendoza) $8. Not a bad value. The wine is a touch reduced and short on mouthfeel and aromatics, but it still delivers creamy vanilla flavors, raspberry essence and decent density. The sum of all its parts is better than the individual components. Best now, and in casual settings. 84 Best Buy *—M.S. (10/1/2007)*

Telteca 2005 Oak Merlot (Mendoza) $8. Bold berry aromas turn a little sweet and simple with airing, while the palate deals plum and berry flavors on a tight, tannic frame. Bright and colorful but fairly rough and basic in what it has to offer. 83 *—M.S. (10/1/2007)*

Telteca 2005 Gran Reserva Red Blend (Mendoza) $20. What else can you say about this three-grape blend other than it's heavily oaked and doesn't have the fruit or complexity to handle it? The bouquet is like a trip through the sawmill, and the palate is akin to biting into a log. 81 *—M.S. (10/1/2007)*

Telteca 2006 Antá Sauvignon Blanc (Mendoza) $13. Punchbowl melon and tropical fruit aromas are the lead act. Next up is a zesty palate of green apple, melon and citrus. The body is a bit plump and round, while the finish shows orange peel and lime zest. Good for Mendoza Sauv Blanc. 86 *—M.S. (8/1/2007)*

Telteca 2006 Uma Shiraz (Mendoza) $6. For the price, this is pretty good. Not very Syrah-like, but if you enjoy plum, cherry and currant flavors along with pretty good mouthfeel and balance, you'll get it here. 84 Best Buy *—M.S. (10/1/2007)*

Telteca 2006 Uma Torrontes (Mendoza) $6. Soft, lightly fragrant and peachy, with a hint of talcum powder to the nose. The palate offers your basic mix of melon and lychee, while the feel is good and there's a persistent finish. Straightforward stuff. 84 Best Buy *—M.S. (8/1/2007)*

TEMPUS ALBA

Tempus Alba 2003 Preludio Syrah (Mendoza) $15. 85 *—M.S. (10/1/2005)*

TERRA BUENA

Terra Buena 2006 Chardonnay (Mendoza) $9. California winemaker Patrick Campbell makes this perfumed, unusual Chardonnay, which is challenged but ultimately proves its worth. While it's nothing like Burgundy or other varietally correct Chards, it does show sweet melon, mango and other candied flavors. More for those wanting a simple, sweeter style. 84 *—M.S. (10/1/2007)*

Terra Buena 2004 Tempranillo (Mendoza) $9. Round, pretty and ripe; a dead knock-off for modern-style Rioja. There are sun-baked aromas but not the cooked type, with a palate that pushes dark berry flavors and chocolate. A rich, almost medicinal wine, the type that can often cost $50. And here it's $9. Weighs in at 14.6%, so it should have its fans. 89 Best Buy *—M.S. (10/1/2007)*

TERRA ROSA

Terra Rosa 2002 Cabernet Sauvignon (Mendoza) $10. 85 *—M.S. (10/1/2004)*

TERRAZAS

Terrazas 1999 Alto Cabernet Sauvignon (Mendoza) $9. 83 *(5/1/2002)*

Terrazas 1999 Reserva Cabernet Sauvignon (Mendoza) $17. 87 *—C.S. (5/1/2002)*

Terrazas 1999 Reserva Malbec (Mendoza) $17. 83 *(5/1/2002)*

TERRAZAS DE LOS ANDES

Terrazas de Los Andes 2005 Cabernet Sauvignon (Mendoza) $12. Warm earth and other dark, leathery aromas dominate. In the mouth, there's black cherry and raspberry flavors supported by scratchy tannins. Despite some grab and clumsiness, this is a good Cabernet with ripeness and a forward personality. 86 *—M.S. (8/1/2007)*

Terrazas de Los Andes 2004 Cabernet Sauvignon (Mendoza) $12. 86 *(5/1/2005)*

Terrazas de Los Andes 2001 Afincado Los Aromos Vineyard Cabernet Sauvignon (Mendoza) $38. 87 *—M.S. (3/1/2005)*

Terrazas de Los Andes 2002 Alto Cabernet Sauvignon (Mendoza) $9. 85 *—M.S. (2/1/2004)*

Terrazas de Los Andes 1999 Gran Cabernet Sauvignon, Vineyard los Aromos Cabernet Sauvignon (Mendoza) $38. 88 *—M.S. (7/1/2004)*

Terrazas de Los Andes 2004 Reserva Cabernet Sauvignon (Mendoza) $NA. Very dark in color and concentrated on the nose, with pencil lead and leather accenting black-fruit aromas. The palate is moderately complex as it pushes blackberry, black cherry and cola. Nice in flavors and good in the mouth. It's everything you'd expect from a standard Cab but it doesn't go beyond the call. 87 *—M.S. (2/1/2007)*

Terrazas de Los Andes 2003 Reserva Cabernet Sauvignon (Mendoza) $16. 90 *(5/1/2005)*

Terrazas de Los Andes 2002 Reserva Cabernet Sauvignon (Mendoza) $16. 88 *(5/1/2005)*

Terrazas de Los Andes 2001 Reserva Cabernet Sauvignon (Mendoza) $15. 87 *—M.S. (7/1/2004)*

Terrazas de Los Andes 2000 Reserva Cabernet Sauvignon (Mendoza) $17. 85 *—M.S. (5/1/2003)*

Terrazas de Los Andes 2006 Chardonnay (Mendoza) $10. For an affordable Argentine Chardonnay, this is not a bad effort. But it is a little oily and loaded down with movie popcorn and buttery aromas. Medium in depth, with candied flavors and a peppery bitterness to the finish. 84 *—M.S. (8/1/2007)*

Terrazas de Los Andes 2004 Chardonnay (Mendoza) $12. 85 *(5/1/2005)*

Terrazas de Los Andes 2002 Alto Chardonnay (Mendoza) $8. 86 Best Buy *—M.S. (7/1/2004)*

Terrazas de Los Andes 2000 Alto Chardonnay (Mendoza) $8. 83 *—M.S. (7/1/2002)*

Terrazas de Los Andes 2006 Reserva Chardonnay (Mendoza) $16. Getting pricey as Argentine Chard goes, this moderately rich wine has true aromas and flavors, meaning there's some apple, pear and butter to sniff and vanilla-tinged peach and melon to taste. Not as complex or complicated as maybe it should be, but easy to like. 85 *—M.S. (8/1/2007)*

Terrazas de Los Andes 2004 Reserva Chardonnay (Mendoza) $16. 88 *(5/1/2005)*

Terrazas de Los Andes 2002 Reserva Chardonnay (Mendoza) $15. 89 *—M.S. (7/1/2004)*

Terrazas de Los Andes 2001 Reserva Chardonnay (Mendoza) $17. 85 *—M.S. (5/1/2003)*

Terrazas de Los Andes 2005 Malbec (Mendoza) $10. 86 Best Buy *—M.S. (11/1/2006)*

Terrazas de Los Andes 2004 Malbec (Mendoza) $12. 86 *(5/1/2005)*

Terrazas de Los Andes 2003 Afincado Las Compuertas Vineyard Malbec (Mendoza) $45. 88 *—M.S. (11/1/2006)*

Terrazas de Los Andes 2001 Afincado Las Compuertas Vineyard Malbec (Mendoza) $38. 86 *—M.S. (3/1/2005)*

Terrazas de Los Andes 2002 Alto Malbec (Mendoza) $8. 85 Best Buy *—M.S. (12/1/2003)*

Terrazas de Los Andes 1999 Gran Malbec Vineyard las Compuertas Malbec (Mendoza) $38. 91 *—M.S. (12/1/2003)*

Terrazas de Los Andes 2004 Reserva Malbec (Mendoza) $16. 88 *—M.S. (11/1/2006)*

Terrazas de Los Andes 2003 Reserva Malbec (Mendoza) $16. 89 *(5/1/2005)*

Terrazas de Los Andes 2001 Reserva Malbec (Mendoza) $17. 87 *—M.S. (12/1/2003)*

Terrazas de Los Andes 2000 Reserva Malbec (Mendoza) $17. 87 *—M.S. (5/1/2003)*

TERZA

Terza 2005 Volta Rosé Malbec (Mendoza) $10. 85 *—M.S. (12/1/2006)*

TIKAL

Tikal 2001 Amorío Malbec (Mendoza) $30. 89 *—M.S. (12/1/2003)*

TITTARELLI

Tittarelli 2004 Bonarda (Mendoza) $10. 85 Best Buy *—M.S. (11/1/2006)*

Tittarelli 2004 Reserva Bonarda (Mendoza) $13. 82 *—M.S. (12/1/2006)*

Tittarelli 2004 Reserva de Familia Bonarda (Mendoza) $20. 81 *—M.S. (11/1/2006)*

Tittarelli 2004 Cabernet Sauvignon (Mendoza) $10. It's not nice to pile on, but in tasting this producer's wines over the past couple of years it makes you wonder. This Cabernet is light as strawberry water, with as much peach and citrus flavor as berry. It's barely worth a sniff and a sip. 80 *—M.S. (2/1/2007)*

Tittarelli 2004 Chardonnay (Mendoza) $10. 84 *—M.S. (11/1/2006)*

Tittarelli 2004 Reserva Malbec (Mendoza) $13. 83 *—M.S. (12/1/2006)*

Tittarelli 2004 Reserva de Familia Malbec (Mendoza) $20. Coconut and maple on the nose indicate heavy new oak, and you therefore expect richness and weight. But the palate is nails as far as acidity goes; no matter how much patience you show it, this wine lacks mouthfeel and balance. 83 *—M.S. (2/1/2007)*

Tittarelli 2004 Reserva Tempranillo (Mendoza) $13. The nose is a dark, clumsy confluence of rubber, stewed cherry and horseradish, and the palate is both tangy and bouncy, with a hard feel and plenty of acidic kick. Misses too many marks to rate better. 81 *—M.S. (10/1/2007)*

Tittarelli 2003 Reserva de Familia Tempranillo (Mendoza) $20. 80 *—M.S. (12/1/2006)*

TRAPICHE

Trapiche 2005 Broquel Bonarda (Mendoza) $15. Rustic yet complete, with dark, sweet aromas of toasted coconut, mint and berry syrup. The palate is juicy and balanced, and that's really the key in distinguishing the top Bonardas from the more frequently found hard and scouring ones. In our book, Broquel is a Bonarda you can count on. 89 *—M.S. (12/31/2007)*

Trapiche 2004 Broquel Bonarda (Mendoza) $15. 90 Best Buy *—M.S. (11/1/2006)*

Trapiche 2005 Cabernet Sauvignon (Mendoza) $8. 85 Best Buy *—M.S. (8/1/2006)*

Trapiche 2003 Cabernet Sauvignon (Mendoza) $7. 82 *—M.S. (7/1/2004)*

Trapiche 1999 Cabernet Sauvignon (Mendoza) $10. 83 *(5/1/2002)*

Trapiche 2005 Broquel Cabernet Sauvignon (Mendoza) $15. This '05 Cab, shows berry aromas and some herbal essence, followed by flavors of boysenberry, blackberry, plum and coffee. It's well-oaked and solid, with tannic bite and good texture. A serious and real wine for a good price. 88 *—M.S. (12/1/2007)*

Trapiche 2004 Broquel Cabernet Sauvignon (Mendoza) $14. 89 Best Buy *—M.S. (6/1/2006)*

Trapiche 2004 Medalla Cabernet Sauvignon (Mendoza) $35. 89 *(12/1/2006)*

Trapiche 2003 Medalla Cabernet Sauvignon (Mendoza) $25. 84 *—M.S. (12/31/2005)*

Trapiche 2002 Medalla Cabernet Sauvignon (Mendoza) $25. 83 *—M.S. (11/15/2005)*

Trapiche 2005 Oak Cask Cabernet Sauvignon (Mendoza) $11. Not a bad steak or burger wine given that it offers some kicking acidity to go with sassy cherry and oak-based flavors. This is more of a forward, racy Cabernet. It doesn't lay heavily on the palate; in fact, it's a touch jumpy and staunch despite its oak cask moniker. 86 Best Buy *—M.S. (10/1/2007)*

Trapiche 2004 Oak Cask Cabernet Sauvignon (Mendoza) $10. 87 Best Buy *—M.S. (6/1/2006)*

Trapiche 2003 Oak Cask Cabernet Sauvignon (Mendoza) $10. 86 Best Buy *—M.S. (12/31/2005)*

Trapiche 2002 Oak Cask Cabernet Sauvignon (Mendoza) $10. 85 *—M.S. (7/1/2004)*

Trapiche 2000 Oak Cask Cabernet Sauvignon (Mendoza) $9. 87 Best Buy *—M.S. (5/1/2003)*

Trapiche 2005 Chardonnay (Mendoza) $7. 84 Best Buy *—M.S. (6/1/2006)*

Trapiche 2004 Chardonnay (Mendoza) $8. 84 Best Buy *—M.S. (6/1/2006)*

Trapiche 2005 Broquel Chardonnay (Mendoza) $14. 88 *—M.S. (6/1/2006)*

Trapiche 2004 Broquel Chardonnay (Mendoza) $14. 87 *—M.S. (4/1/2006)*

Trapiche 2006 Oak Cask Chardonnay (Mendoza) $11. Toasty but dull, with oily walnut aromas matched by stale fruit. This is heavy and baked out; sweet and flat as a board. 81 *—M.S. (12/1/2007)*

Trapiche 2005 Oak Cask Chardonnay (Mendoza) $10. 85 Best Buy *—M.S. (6/1/2006)*

Trapiche 2004 Oak Cask Chardonnay (Mendoza) $10. 84 *—M.S. (4/1/2006)*

Trapiche 2002 Oak Cask Chardonnay (Mendoza) $10. 83 *—M.S. (2/1/2004)*

Trapiche 2001 Oak Cask Chardonnay (Mendoza) $9. 84 *—M.S. (5/1/2003)*

Trapiche 2005 Malbec (Mendoza) $8. 86 Best Buy *—M.S. (4/1/2006)*

Trapiche 2003 Malbec (Mendoza) $7. 86 Best Buy *—M.S. (7/1/2004)*

Trapiche 1999 Malbec (Mendoza) $10. 83 *—D.T. (5/1/2002)*

Trapiche 2005 Broquel Malbec (Mendoza) $15. Broquel always offers a little more elegance and pedigree than most value Malbecs, and the 2005 has body, a silky feel and aromas and flavors of tobacco, baked blackberries and leather. It's a ripe, moderately tannic wine that's best for near-term drinking. 88 *—M.S. (12/1/2007)*

Trapiche 2004 Broquel Malbec (Mendoza) $15. 87 *—M.S. (6/1/2006)*

Trapiche 2005 Oak Cask Malbec (Mendoza) $11. If you want ripe-fruit aromas and flavors along with spice, pepper and coffee accents, this well-oaked but reasonably restrained Malbec is your ticket. The flavors run closer to raspberry and strawberry than many big Malbecs, and the texture and balance are just right. This wine delivers the maximum given its price and pedigree. 89 Best Buy *—M.S. (10/1/2007)*

Trapiche 2004 Oak Cask Malbec (Mendoza) $10. 88 Best Buy *—M.S. (8/1/2006)*

Trapiche 2003 Oak Cask Malbec (Mendoza) $10. 88 Best Buy *—M.S. (6/1/2006)*

Trapiche 2002 Oak Cask Malbec (Mendoza) $10. 86 Best Buy *—M.S. (7/1/2004)*

Trapiche 2001 Oak Cask Malbec (Mendoza) $10. 87 *—M.S. (12/1/2003)*

Trapiche 2000 Oak Cask Malbec (Mendoza) $9. 86 *—M.S. (5/1/2003)*

Trapiche 2004 Viña Carlos Gei Berra Malbec (Mendoza) $50. 90 *(12/1/2006)*

Trapiche 2003 Viña Felipe Villafañe Malbec (La Consulta) $35. 90 *—M.S. (6/1/2006)*

Trapiche 2003 Viña José Blanco Malbec (Mendoza) $34. 91 Cellar Selection *—M.S. (6/1/2006)*

Trapiche 2004 Viña Pedro Gonzalez Malbec (Mendoza) $50. 91 *(12/1/2006)*

Trapiche 2003 Viña Pedro Gonzalez Malbec (Mendoza) $35. 91 Editors' Choice *—M.S. (4/1/2006)*

Trapiche 2004 Viña Victorio Coletto Malbec (Mendoza) $50. 93 Editors' Choice *(12/1/2006)*

Trapiche 2005 Merlot (Mendoza) $7. 81 *—M.S. (6/1/2006)*

Trapiche 2002 Merlot (Mendoza) $7. 84 *—M.S. (5/1/2003)*

Trapiche 2004 Iscay Merlot-Malbec (Mendoza) $55. 90 *(12/1/2006)*

Trapiche 2003 Iscay Merlot-Malbec (Mendoza) $48. 85 *—M.S. (8/1/2006)*

Trapiche 2005 Oak Cask Pinot Noir (Mendoza) $9. 80 *—M.S. (6/1/2006)*

Trapiche 2000 Falling Star Red Blend (Mendoza) $5. 80 *(5/1/2002)*

Trapiche 1999 Iscay Red Blend (Mendoza) $50. 87 *—C.S. (5/1/2002)*

Trapiche 2005 Oak Cask Syrah (Mendoza) $11. Big and boisterous, as if you're sniffing a bed of coal, menthol and macerated black fruit. The palate is sun-drenched and juicy, but not what you'd call elevated. And the finish mixes savory flavors with tight tannins. A good red wine that bears little semblance to Old World Syrah. 86 Best Buy *—M.S. (12/1/2007)*

Trapiche 2004 Oak Cask Shiraz (Mendoza) $9. 83 *—M.S. (8/1/2006)*

Trapiche 2006 Torrontès (Mendoza) $8. 86 Best Buy *(12/1/2006)*

TRIVENTO

Trivento 2005 Select Cabernet Sauvignon (Mendoza) $12. Dark fruit and plenty of oak on the nose, with a creamy vanilla-based palate that's sporting plenty of new wood to match the bouquet. The barrel is front and center here, but there's also solid Cab texture and power. Imported by Excelsior Wine & Spirits. 86 *—M.S. (10/1/2007)*

Trivento 2004 Select Chardonnay (Mendoza) $15. 84 *—M.S. (11/15/2005)*

Trivento 2004 Golden Reserve Malbec (Mendoza) $20. Full, dark and minty, with aromatic notes of coconut and ink. One look, sniff and sip tells you this is a dark, ripe wine with extract. It's fairly lush but still tannic and balanced, with black coffee and other dark flavors on the somewhat narrow palate and finish. Imported by Excelsior Wine & Spirits. 89 *—M.S. (10/1/2007)*

Trivento 2003 Golden Reserve Malbec (Mendoza) $20. 91 *—M.S. (12/1/2006)*

Trivento 2002 Golden Reserve Malbec (Mendoza) $20. 87 *—M.S. (3/1/2005)*

Trivento 2005 Select Malbec (Mendoza) $12. Concha Y Toro's Argentine property seems to be getting it right with Malbec. This affordable number is dark and dense, with plum and prune on the nose and concentrated berry flavors on the palate. For a meaty, structured, fully oaked Malbec,

Trivento is the call. Imported by Excelsior Wine & Spirits. 88 Best Buy —*M.S. (10/1/2007)*

Trivento 2005 Select Syrah (Mendoza) $12. Once you cut through the heavy, minty oak, there's a decent wine hiding in the folds. The body carries reasonably ripe black cherry and raspberry flavors as well as plenty of wood-generated tannin, but does it taste much like Syrah? I find it more generic and woody than varietal. Imported by Excelsior Wine & Spirits. 83 —*M.S. (10/1/2007)*

TRUMPETER

Trumpeter 2003 Cabernet Sauvignon (Mendoza) $9. 84 —*M.S. (3/1/2005)*

Trumpeter 2002 Cabernet Sauvignon (Mendoza) $9. 84 —*M.S. (7/1/2004)*

Trumpeter 1999 Maipú Cabernet Sauvignon (Argentina) $12. 85 —*M.S. (11/1/2002)*

Trumpeter 2004 Chardonnay (Tupungato) $9. 85 Best Buy —*M.S. (6/1/2006)*

Trumpeter 2002 Chardonnay (Mendoza) $9. 85 —*M.S. (7/1/2004)*

Trumpeter 2001 Chardonnay (Argentina) $9. 85 —*M.S. (7/1/2002)*

Trumpeter 2000 Tupungato Chardonnay (Argentina) $12. 85 —*M.S. (7/1/2002)*

Trumpeter 2004 Malbec (Tupungato) $9. 83 —*M.S. (6/1/2006)*

Trumpeter 2003 Malbec (Mendoza) $9. 87 Best Buy —*M.S. (3/1/2005)*

Trumpeter 2002 Malbec (Mendoza) $9. 87 Best Buy —*M.S. (7/1/2004)*

Trumpeter 2000 Malbec (Argentina) $12. 86 Best Buy —*M.S. (11/1/2002)*

Trumpeter 2004 Malbec-Syrah (Tupungato) $9. 86 Best Buy —*M.S. (6/1/2006)*

Trumpeter 2003 Malbec-Syrah (Mendoza) $9. 85 Best Buy —*M.S. (3/1/2005)*

Trumpeter 2002 Malbec-Syrah (Mendoza) $9. 86 —*M.S. (7/1/2004)*

Trumpeter 2004 Merlot (Tupungato) $9. 85 Best Buy —*M.S. (6/1/2006)*

Trumpeter 2003 Merlot (Mendoza) $9. 84 —*M.S. (3/1/2005)*

Trumpeter 2002 Merlot (Tupungato) $9. 85 —*M.S. (7/1/2004)*

Trumpeter 2000 Merlot (Tupungato) $12. 86 Best Buy —*M.S. (11/1/2002)*

Trumpeter 2002 Syrah (Mendoza) $9. 85 —*M.S. (7/1/2004)*

Trumpeter 2000 Syrah (Luján de Cuyo) $12. 85 —*M.S. (11/1/2002)*

VALENTIN BIANCHI

Valentin Bianchi 2002 Elsa Barbera (San Rafael) $9. 83 —*M.S. (7/1/2004)*

Valentin Bianchi 2001 Elsa Barbera (San Rafael) $8. 82 —*M.S. (5/1/2003)*

Valentin Bianchi 2000 Elsa Barbera (San Rafael) $8. 80 *(5/1/2002)*

Valentin Bianchi 2002 Cabernet Sauvignon (San Rafael) $18. 87 —*M.S. (7/1/2004)*

Valentin Bianchi 2002 Cabernet Sauvignon (San Rafael) $18. 84 —*M.S. (7/1/2004)*

Valentin Bianchi 1999 Cabernet Sauvignon (Mendoza) $14. 87 —*M.S. (11/1/2002)*

Valentin Bianchi 2005 Elsa Cabernet Sauvignon (San Rafael) $9. 83 —*M.S. (11/1/2006)*

Valentin Bianchi 2004 Elsa Cabernet Sauvignon (San Rafael) $9. 85 Best Buy —*M.S. (12/31/2005)*

Valentin Bianchi 2001 Elsa Cabernet Sauvignon (San Rafael) $8. 85 —*M.S. (5/1/2003)*

Valentin Bianchi 2000 Enzo Bianchi Gran Cru Cabernet Sauvignon (San Rafael) $53. 89 —*M.S. (7/1/2004)*

Valentin Bianchi 2005 Famiglia Bianchi Cabernet Sauvignon (San Rafael) $18. Not sure exactly what's happening at Bianchi in San Rafael. A few years back Bianchi's wines were almost all exemplary but lately they've been all over the map. This overoaked, charred Cabernet is a perfect example of a wine without a cause. It's burnt, herbal and while it has mouthfeel, nothing seems to be working in tandem. 83 —*M.S. (8/1/2007)*

Valentin Bianchi 2004 Famiglia Bianchi Cabernet Sauvignon (San Rafael) $18. 89 —*M.S. (8/1/2006)*

Valentin Bianchi 2003 Famiglia Bianchi Cabernet Sauvignon (Argentina) $18. 84 —*M.S. (11/15/2005)*

Valentin Bianchi 2002 Famiglia Bianchi Cabernet Sauvignon (San Rafael) $18. 88 *(10/1/2004)*

Valentin Bianchi 2004 Particular Cabernet Sauvignon (San Rafael) $30. We've been watching this wine for several years and it doesn't seem to be on the upswing. This vintage is good as Cabernet goes, but it comes across a little racy and jumpy. The mouthfeel runs tight and the tannins are spunky and on the border of being rough. Maybe another year will settle it down. 86 —*M.S. (8/1/2007)*

Valentin Bianchi 2003 Particular Cabernet Sauvignon (Mendoza) $30. 90 —*M.S. (11/15/2005)*

Valentin Bianchi 1997 Particular Proprietor's Reserve Cabernet Sauvignon (San Rafael) $28. 84 —*M.S. (5/1/2003)*

Valentin Bianchi 2003 Chardonnay (San Rafael) $18. 86 —*M.S. (7/1/2004)*

Valentin Bianchi 2000 Chardonnay (San Rafael) $15. 87 —*M.S. (7/1/2002)*

Valentin Bianchi 2001 Elsa Chardonnay (San Rafael) $11. 80 —*M.S. (7/1/2002)*

Valentin Bianchi 2006 Famiglia Bianchi Chardonnay (San Rafael) $18. Vanilla and floral aromas have a suspicious artificiality to them, and in the mouth it's a sweet, sugary ride toward a cloying finish. 82 —*M.S. (8/1/2007)*

Valentin Bianchi 2005 Famiglia Bianchi Chardonnay (San Rafael) $18. Sweet pear and powdered sugar carry the confected nose, while the palate is also on the sweet side, with sugared citrus and banana flavors. Feelwise, there's adequate acidity to keep it wet and juicy, while the finish is candied but not what you'd call sticky. Imported by Quintessential Family of Wines, LLC. 84 —*M.S. (8/1/2007)*

Valentin Bianchi 2004 Famiglia Bianchi Chardonnay (Argentina) $18. 83 —*M.S. (11/15/2005)*

Valentin Bianchi 2003 Famiglia Bianchi Chardonnay (San Rafael) $18. 85 *(10/1/2004)*

Valentin Bianchi 2002 Malbec (San Rafael) $18. 88 —*M.S. (7/1/2004)*

Valentin Bianchi 2002 Malbec (San Rafael) $18. 84 —*M.S. (7/1/2004)*

Valentin Bianchi 2001 Malbec (Mendoza) $16. 88 —*M.S. (12/1/2003)*

Valentin Bianchi 1999 Malbec (Mendoza) $13. 89 Best Buy —*M.S. (11/1/2002)*

Valentin Bianchi 2005 Elsa Malbec (San Rafael) $9. 85 Best Buy —*M.S. (12/1/2006)*

Valentin Bianchi 2004 Elsa Malbec (Mendoza) $9. 84 —*M.S. (12/31/2005)*

Valentin Bianchi 2003 Elsa Malbec (San Rafael) $9. 84 *(10/1/2004)*

Valentin Bianchi 2001 Elsa Malbec (San Rafael) $8. 86 Best Buy —*M.S. (5/1/2003)*

Valentin Bianchi 1999 Elsa Malbec (San Rafael) $7. 86 Best Buy —*M.S. (11/1/2002)*

Valentin Bianchi 2005 Famiglia Bianchi Malbec (San Rafael) $18. Dark to the eye and nose, with aromas of rubber, black fruit and lots of sharp-edged oak. Wood more than fruit controls the front of the palate and the finish, but inbetween the folds you'll find plump berry and black pepper flavors. A nice Malbec but arguably a little heavy on the oak. 87 —*M.S. (8/1/2007)*

Valentin Bianchi 2004 Famiglia Bianchi Malbec (San Rafael) $18. In no way is this Malbec standard. The nose puts out leather, smoked meat and no small amount of funk, and at first the palate seems extra earthy and raisiny. But with time and air the wine gains its legs and exhibits character, herbal notes, pure fruit and length on the finish. Unconventional but intriguing. Imported by Quintessential Family of Wines, LLC. 88 —*M.S. (5/1/2007)*

Valentin Bianchi 2003 Famiglia Bianchi Malbec (San Rafael) $18. 83 —*M.S. (11/15/2005)*

Valentin Bianchi 2002 Famiglia Bianchi Malbec (San Rafael) $18. 87 *(10/1/2004)*

Valentin Bianchi 2004 Particular Malbec (San Rafael) $30. In previous vintages this was a favorite, but the '04 vintage, while ripe and manly, seems a little commonplace by comparison. The nose is mostly a mixing of oak and heavy fruit scents, while the palate is your standard trio of black cherry, raspberry and chocolate. Finishes tight, with some creamy wood notes. Imported by Quintessential Wines, LLC. 87 —*M.S. (5/1/2007)*

Valentin Bianchi 2003 Particular Malbec (San Rafael) $30. 91 Editors' Choice —*M.S. (7/1/2005)*

Valentin Bianchi 2002 Particular Malbec (San Rafael) $30. 90 —*M.S. (3/1/2005)*

Valentin Bianchi 2003 Particular Merlot (Mendoza) $30. 88 —*M.S. (11/15/2005)*

Valentin Bianchi 2005 Don Valentin Lacrado Red Blend (San Rafael) $12. This is a blend of Cab Sauvignon, Malbec and Merlot that's agile, fresh and offers good mouthfeel. The nose deals crushed brick, leather, spice and light red fruit, while the flavors run toward red cherry and red currants. Uncomplicated; drink now. Imported by Quintessential Wines, LLC. 87 Best Buy —*M.S. (10/1/2007)*

Valentin Bianchi 2002 Enzo Bianchi Red Blend (San Rafael) $53. Having always liked this wine, which is 86% Cab and the rest Malbec and Merlot, the 2002 seems a touch bland and underwhelming. The color is dense and the nose muscular and herbal, but it peters out quickly and shows no signs that it will get better with age. Imported by Quintessential Wines, LLC. 86 *—M.S. (10/1/2007)*

Valentin Bianchi 2001 Enzo Bianchi Red Blend (San Rafael) $53. 89 *(10/1/2004)*

Valentin Bianchi 2003 Sauvignon Blanc (San Rafael) $18. 85 *—M.S. (7/1/2004)*

Valentin Bianchi 2002 Sauvignon Blanc (San Rafael) $12. 88 *—M.S. (5/1/2003)*

Valentin Bianchi 2006 Famiglia Bianchi Sauvignon Blanc (San Rafael) $15. Mildly fragrant but then overly sweet and candied on the palate. This is very syrupy stuff, with sugary mango and pear flavors. It isn't interesting in a fine-wine kind of way but fans of sweet, simple whites may like it because it's not poorly made. 81 *—M.S. (8/1/2007)*

Valentin Bianchi 2005 Famiglia Bianchi Sauvignon Blanc (San Rafael) $15. 83 *—M.S. (8/1/2006)*

Valentin Bianchi 2004 Famiglia Bianchi Sauvignon Blanc (San Rafael) $15. 84 *—M.S. (11/15/2005)*

Valentin Bianchi 2002 Elsa Semillon-Chardonnay (San Rafael) $8. 83 *—M.S. (5/1/2003)*

Valentin Bianchi 2003 Famiglia Bianchi Late Harvest Semillon-Sauvignon Blanc (San Rafael) $23. With little to compare it to, it's hard to evaluate the correctness of this Semillon sweetie from Argentina. Let's just say that it's a weird wine that carries a vivid yellow color and aromas and flavors of honey, corn syrup and hominy. 82 *—M.S. (10/1/2007)*

Valentin Bianchi 2003 Elsa Syrah (San Rafael) $9. 84 *(10/1/2004)*

Valentin Bianchi 2003 Elsa White Blend (San Rafael) $9. 83 *—M.S. (7/1/2004)*

VALERO

Valero 2003 Especial Syrah (Mendoza) $10. 83 *—J.C. (4/1/2005)*

VIEJA BODEGA

Vieja Bodega 2003 Reserve Malbec (Mendoza) $9. 86 Best Buy *—M.S. (6/1/2006)*

Vieja Bodega 2003 Reserve Syrah (Mendoza) $9. 87 Best Buy *—M.S. (8/1/2006)*

VIENTO SUR

Viento Sur 2003 Cabernet Sauvignon (Mendoza) $9. 87 Best Buy *—M.S. (6/1/2006)*

Viento Sur 2003 Malbec (Mendoza) $9. 87 Best Buy *—M.S. (4/1/2006)*

Viento Sur 2003 Syrah (Mendoza) $9. 83 *—M.S. (8/1/2006)*

Viento Sur 2005 Torrontès (Mendoza) $9. 85 Best Buy *—M.S. (4/1/2006)*

VILA

Vila 2005 Bonarda (Mendoza) $9. Despite some warm earth and compost on the nose, this shows positives such as solid cherry, plum and blackberry flavors. It opens on the midpalate but then thins out rather drastically on the finish. Like most in its class, it's hard Bonarda; but it has its merits, too. 85 Best Buy *—M.S. (12/31/2007)*

Vila 2005 Malbec (Mendoza) $9. Pretty good wine with only the mildest weedy, herbal notes. For the most part this is full, sunny Malbec; only a hint of green and finishing black pepper vies with the dark berry and plum flavors that one should expect. Decent balance; ordinary as a whole. 84 *—M.S. (12/1/2007)*

VIMINI

Vimini 2005 Chardonnay (Uco Valley) $13. 82 *—M.S. (12/1/2006)*

VIÑA AMALIA

Viña Amalia 2004 Reservado Cabernet Sauvignon (Mendoza) $25. The opening of floral and plum aromas is nice, and that's followed by some earth and heft. The palate is fleshy and tannic, with deep raspberry and plum flavors. The depth on this wine is pretty good, yet it finishes sort of short. 87 *—M.S. (10/1/2007)*

Viña Amalia 2004 Reservado Malbec (Mendoza) $25. Leather, dark fruit and citrus peel make for a good nose, while the palate is meaty and a bit heavy as it pours on those classic dark-fruit flavors that Malbec is known for. Best to get at this one now because neither the palate nor the finish shows much acidity. A touch hollow. 86 *—M.S. (10/1/2007)*

VIÑA ANTIGUA

Viña Antigua 2005 Sangiovese-Bonarda Red Blend (Maipú) $7. A firm blast of alcohol mixed with hot raspberry defines the nose, while the acidic palate is zesty and finishes with a rush of red apple skin. Airing settles it somewhat but it stays kind of raw. 82 *—M.S. (2/1/2007)*

Viña Antigua 2004 Sangiovese-Bonarda Red Blend (Maipú) $7. 83 *—M.S. (12/1/2006)*

VINA COBOS

Vina Cobos 1999 Malbec (Mendoza) $65. 92 Cellar Selection *—M.S. (11/1/2002)*

Vina Cobos 1999 Bramare Malbec (Mendoza) $37. 90 *—M.S. (11/1/2002)*

Viña Cobos 2002 Cobos Malbec (Mendoza) $60. 93 Editors' Choice *—M.S. (3/1/2005)*

VIÑA CORNEJO COSTAS

Viña Cornejo Costas 2004 Don Rodolfo Cabernet Sauvignon (Cafayate) $10. Quite green and on the verge of deserving the dreaded weedy designation, this Cab fails to show much ripe fruit character even if the mouthfeel is decent. It's like a wet-vintage cru bourgeois Bordeaux. 80 *—M.S. (10/1/2007)*

VIÑA MAIPÚ

Viña Maipú 2003 Malbec (Maipú) $8. 83 *—M.S. (12/1/2006)*

VINECOL

VinEcol 2006 Organic Cabernet Sauvignon (Mendoza) $12. An organic wine that is rough and oily on the nose and tannic and choppy in the mouth. It's a hard, wine with sweaty, sharp scents and too much black olive and funk. Not a disaster but it requires an awful lot from the buyer. 81 *—M.S. (12/1/2007)*

VinEcol 2006 Organic Malbec (Mendoza) $12. Sweet and reduced aromas of red licorice and prune lead to sketchy red cherry flavors and not much body. The wine is closed, hard and chewy, but with a lot of fruit-forward potency. 82 *—M.S. (12/31/2007)*

VINITERRA

Viniterra 1999 Lujan de Cuyo Malbec (Mendoza) $15. 90 Best Buy *—M.S. (5/1/2003)*

Viniterra 1999 Syrah (Mendoza) $10. 90 Best Buy *—M.S. (5/1/2003)*

VISTALBA

Vistalba 2004 Corte A Red Blend (Mendoza) $60. Carlos Pulenta used to run Trapiche and now that he's on his own, we should keep on the lookout for his rich, ripe Malbecs and red blends from the Vistalba zone of Mendoza. This heavyweight contains Malbec, Cabernet and Bonarda, and it's a brawny, ripe, creamy sort of wine with plenty of berry and dark plum character. Very nice now but not quite spectacular; our bet is that it will get better in future vintages. 89 *—M.S. (5/1/2007)*

Vistalba 2004 Corte B Red Blend (Mendoza) $25. Clove and other challenging aromas greet you, and never does this blend of Malbec, Cabernet, Bonarda and Merlot get it fully together. The palate seems a little reduced and short on feel, and while it widens and softens on the finish, the ride to get there is bumpy. Expect better in 2005. 86 *—M.S. (10/1/2007)*

WEINERT

Weinert 2004 Carrascal Bordeaux Blend (Mendoza) $13. Smoke, rubber and a touch of herbs and leaves make this more traditional in style, meaning it offers Old World Bordeaux notes of earth, mineral and subdued fruit as opposed to ripe, jammy berry notes. It's not a big, aggressive wine but it does have tannic strength and intensity. Malbec, Merlot and Cab Sauvignon make up the blend. 86 *—M.S. (10/1/2007)*

Weinert 2003 Carrascal Bordeaux Blend (Mendoza) $13. 87 *—M.S. (6/1/2006)*

Weinert 2002 Weinert Carrascal Bordeaux Blend (Mendoza) $13. 87 *—M.S. (7/1/2005)*

Weinert 2000 Cavas de Weinert Bordeaux Blend (Mendoza) $26. This wine is only going to appeal to the consumer who likes older, funkier wines and thinks anything modern stinks. This is a reedy, herbal, earthy wine that is probably past its prime. It has some leftover raspberry and red plum, but the more air it sees the less it has to offer. 83 *—M.S. (12/1/2007)*

Weinert 2000 Cabernet Sauvignon (Mendoza) $22. 84 *—M.S. (8/1/2006)*

Weinert 2003 Malbec (Mendoza) $23. A good effort by Cavas Weinert. The wine is starting to mature, and along the road you get ripe berry aromas that broaden and improve with time. The plum, blackberry and red apple flavors are right, as is the tannin-to-acid balance. The only complaint is a mild chemical-paint thinner note at the base of the bouquet. 88 *—M.S. (10/1/2007)*

Weinert 2002 Malbec (Mendoza) $23. Cavas Weinert is an old-school Mendoza winery and it holds its wines longer than most, which is why this 2002 is just now a new release. Thank Weinert for the bottle age and give this wine plenty of air. What you'll get is earth, leather, complexity, depth and ample berry fruit and chocolate. Decant for best results. 90 —*M.S. (10/1/2007)*

Weinert 2000 Malbec (Mendoza) $23. 86 —*M.S. (11/15/2005)*

Weinert 2005 Montfleury Gran Rosé Rosé Blend (Mendoza) $12. 83 —*M.S. (8/1/2006)*

Weinert 2006 Carrascal Sauvignon Blanc (Mendoza) $13. If this isn't one of the strangest, most unique Sauvignon Blancs on the market, then please tell us what is. With a tan/peach color, this wine has its own agenda. The palate pushes peach, cantaloupe and floral notes, but where's the acidity and where's the grassiness? 83 —*M.S. (10/1/2007)*

Weinert 2003 Cosecha de Otoño Sauvignon Blanc (Mendoza) $72. 80 —*M.S. (8/1/2006)*

Weinert 2005 Carrascal White Blend (Mendoza) $13. 83 —*M.S. (4/1/2006)*

XUMEK

Xumek 2005 Sol Huarpe Malbec (Zonda Valley) $15. Sol Huarpe's top wine, Xumek, has style and saucy sass. It's not just cookie-cutter ripe and rich, but instead shows herbs, mushroom and also ample black plum and berry flavors. In general it's nice for those seeking a touch more from their Argentinean Malbec. And it hails from lesser-known San Juan and not Mendoza, which may explain its unusual characteristics. 88 —*M.S. (12/1/2007)*

Xumek 2003 Sol Huarpe Malbec (San Juan) $18. 90 Editors' Choice —*M.S. (12/31/2005)*

Xumek 2004 Sol Huarpe Syrah (Zonda Valley) $14. Sweet on the bouquet, although there's a bit of a lactic note. The palate is bright and fruity, but the feel is narrow and goes hard with the tannins. Finishes mildly grabby but it's fruity throughout. A good effort but a little challenging. Can you tell that it has its contradictions? 85 —*M.S. (12/1/2007)*

Xumek 2003 Sol Huarpe Syrah (Zonda Valley) $14. 88 —*M.S. (10/1/2005)*

YACOCHUYA

Yacochuya 2000 Malbec (Cafayate) $48. 93 —*M.S. (12/1/2003)*

ZOLO

Zolo 2004 Cabernet Sauvignon (Mendoza) $14. 85 —*M.S. (6/1/2006)*

Zolo 2003 Cabernet Sauvignon (Mendoza) $14. 85 —*M.S. (11/15/2005)*

Zolo 2004 Reserve Cabernet Sauvignon (Mendoza) $19. Apparently heavily charred is what constitutes a reserve bottling at Zolo, because the wine smells like a cup of java along with leather and melted rubber. Eventually fruit emerges, and it's in the dark and stormy category, meaning it's big, bold and peppery but not too suave or defined. 83 —*M.S. (2/1/2007)*

Zolo 2005 Chardonnay (Mendoza) $11. 84 —*M.S. (11/1/2006)*

Zolo 2004 Chardonnay (Mendoza) $14. 82 —*M.S. (6/1/2006)*

Zolo 2003 Chardonnay (Mendoza) $14. 82 —*M.S. (11/15/2005)*

Zolo 2004 Reserve Chardonnay (Mendoza) $19. 83 —*M.S. (12/1/2006)*

Zolo 2004 Malbec (Mendoza) $14. Early Middle Eastern aromas of cumin and the like yield to burnt toast and charred hamburger. The palate is perfectly juicy and for the most part balanced, with berry and plum flavors. With pop and ripping acidity, this is a lively number that should go well with burgers, pizza and similar finger foods. 85 —*M.S. (2/1/2007)*

Zolo 2003 Malbec (Mendoza) $14. 86 —*M.S. (12/31/2005)*

Zolo 2004 Reserve Malbec (Mendoza) $19. Big, dark and smoky, with leather and basic fruit aromas. The palate is bold and generically fruity, with coffee and chocolate notes on the back end. The finish seems a bit sheer and limited as the fruit disappears quickly on an outgoing wave of outsized acidity. 85 —*M.S. (2/1/2007)*

Zolo 2004 Merlot (Mendoza) $11. Gets out of the blocks with an almost nutty, leathery character, while the palate pushes heavy licorice and meaty fruit. Not a refined wine, with tannins that are grabby and aggressive. 83 —*M.S. (2/1/2007)*

Zolo 2003 Merlot (Mendoza) $14. 84 —*M.S. (11/15/2005)*

Zolo 2006 Sauvignon Blanc (Mendoza) $14. The citrus and grapefruit aromas come across a little mealy and the wine never really rises above its candied citrus and apple cider qualities. It is pretty good on the tongue, however, and feels juicy. If chilled down it won't be a bad quaff. 83 —*M.S. (8/1/2007)*

Zolo 2005 Sauvignon Blanc (Mendoza) $13. 84 —*M.S. (4/1/2006)*

Zolo 2004 Sauvignon Blanc (Mendoza) $13. 83 —*M.S. (11/15/2005)*

Zolo 2006 Torrontes (Mendoza) $14. Cloying and spritzy with sweet, sugary aromas. It doesn't really offer much reason to come back to it after the first nosing and sip. 80 —*M.S. (5/1/2007)*

Zolo 2005 Torrontès (Mendoza) $14. 83 —*M.S. (4/1/2006)*

ZUCCARDI

Zuccardi 2000 Q Cabernet Sauvignon (Mendoza) $20. 87 —*M.S. (2/1/2004)*

Zuccardi 1999 Q Cabernet Sauvignon (Mendoza) $22. 89 *(5/1/2002)*

Zuccardi 2000 Q Chardonnay (Mendoza) $20. 81 —*M.S. (2/1/2004)*

Zuccardi 1999 Q Chardonnay (Mendoza) $22. 89 *(12/15/2001)*

Zuccardi 2004 Q Malbec (Mendoza) $20. Overt oak is the first thing you encounter on the nose, but underneath the heavy wood covering is a polished and sincere wine. The mouth is lively and juicy, with commendable plum and raspberry flavors. And while the finish is sort of basic in its vanilla and chocolate character, it has a nice feel to it. A wine with virtues but maybe a touch too much new oak. 88 —*M.S. (8/1/2007)*

Zuccardi 2002 Q Malbec (Mendoza) $20. 90 Editors' Choice —*M.S. (6/1/2006)*

Zuccardi 2000 Q Malbec (Mendoza) $20. 88 —*M.S. (12/1/2003)*

Zuccardi 1999 Q Malbec (Mendoza) $22. 90 Editors' Choice *(12/15/2001)*

Zuccardi 1998 Q Malbec (Mendoza) $22. 84 —*M.S. (11/15/2001)*

Zuccardi 2000 Q Merlot (Mendoza) $20. 83 —*M.S. (2/1/2004)*

Zuccardi 1999 Q Merlot (Mendoza) $22. 90 —*C.S. (5/1/2002)*

Zuccardi 2002 Zeta Red Blend (Argentina) $45. 86 —*M.S. (6/1/2006)*

Zuccardi 2003 Q Tempranillo (Mendoza) $20. 84 —*M.S. (12/1/2006)*

Zuccardi 2002 Q Tempranillo (Mendoza) $20. 86 —*M.S. (6/1/2006)*

Zuccardi 2001 Q Tempranillo (Mendoza) $20. 84 —*M.S. (10/1/2004)*

Zuccardi 2000 Q Tempranillo (Mendoza) $20. 82 —*M.S. (2/1/2004)*

Australia

Although Philip Schaffer was the first to plant a successful vineyard in Australia in 1791, it was not until the mid-nineteenth century that grape growing and viticulture was more widespread throughout South Australia, Victoria, and New South Wales. In the 1880s, however, phylloxera (see Glossary) spread through Victoria and New South Wales. South Australia's very stringent (and still existent) quarantine policy spared its vines from the louse and, to this day, the state is the seat of Australia's wine production.

It's only been during the past twenty or so years that Australia has become known on the world stage as a premium wine-producing nation. It is now home to about 1,800 wineries and is the fourth-largest wine-exporting country (behind France, Italy, and Spain), with export sales topping $2.7 billion in 2004. The country's biggest export markets are the United States and the United Kingdom, though Australian wine is exported to over one hundred countries.

Australia is vast; at over 7.6 million square kilometers, it is roughly the size of the continental United States, but is home to only about 15 percent of America's population. In spite of its size, many wine drinkers outside Australia have it in their heads that Oz wines all taste the same. To characterize them all as broad-shouldered, plum- and berry-flavored, well-oaked wines that are high in alcohol is as short-sighted as saying that all Americans—from the Bronx to Alabama—have the same accent. With that in mind, here's a broad overview of some of the country's best-known winemaking regions, or Geographical Indications (GIs), and the wines for which each region is best known.

Zinfandel vines of Cape Mentelle, Margaret River, Western Australia.

The general area around Perth, in the southwestern corner of Western Australia, is home to some of the country's most coveted, premium-quality wines. The Margaret River GI is the most renowned of the GIs in Western Australia. The region's maritime climate yields structured, age-worthy Cabernet Sauvignons, and some of the country's best Chardonnays. Semillon and Sauvignon Blanc blends are successful here, too.

In South Australia, where most of Australia's wine is produced, most GIs are located within a drive of the port city of Adelaide. It is in this state that Shiraz flourishes—just about every winery makes one.

Clare Valley, home to some of Australia's best Riesling (all of which is sealed with a screwcap), is located about eighty-five miles north of Adelaide. It has an altitude of 400 to 500 meters above sea level, and benefits from cool evening breezes and warm summers. Barossa Valley, just southwest of Clare, is hot, dry, and flat, with summertime temperatures that can top 100 degrees Fahrenheit. Most of Australia's flagship Shirazes come from Barossa Valley. The wines are generally big and broad, with luscious, extracted plum and berry fruit. Grenache and Cabernet Sauvignon, too, are very good here. Eden Valley, just south of Barossa, succeeds with both reds and whites, but you'll find that its Rieslings, Chardonnays, and Viogniers are among the country's best.

Directly south of Adelaide are McLaren Vale and, to its east, the Adelaide Hills. Like Barossa Valley, McLaren Vale also specializes in Shiraz and Grenache (and to a lesser degree, Cabernet). The Vale's microclimates are varied—some areas are flat and hot, others cooler, yielding wines from one GI that can taste very different. Most McLaren Vale reds, though, are lush in the midpalate, often with a silky, chalky feel. The Adelaide Hills, at an altitude of about 400 meters above sea level, specializes in wines that thrive in cooler climates: Sauvignon Blanc, Chardonnay, Pinot Noir, Riesling, and other aromatic whites. Other reds can thrive in the region's warmest sites. Coonawarra, even farther south from Adelaide, is famed for its terra rossa soils, from which yield long-lived Cabernet Sauvignon.

Though there are a number of winegrowing regions in the state of Victoria, the best known is the Yarra Valley, from whence come some very good Chardonnays and Pinot Noirs. Wines from this region are often delicate and understated, rather than powerful, which again proves just how broad the spectrum is on Australia's wine styles. Rutherglen, in northeastern Victoria, is home to the country's (and really, some of the world's) most renowned fortified Muscats. Tasmania, the island just south of Victoria, is home to some of Australia's coolest grape-growing sites. As such, Riesling, Chardonnay, and Pinot Noir thrive here; production of sparkling wines containing the latter two grapes is also a specialty.

Just north of Sydney in New South Wales lies the Hunter Valley, an area with hot temperatures moderated by mild maritime breezes, and rain in the months leading up to harvest. This is Semillon country; the region's famed white wine is known for its long aging potential. Shiraz and Chardonnay are also very good here.

AUSTRALIA

2 UP

2 Up 2006 Shiraz (South Australia) $14. A warm, inviting wine, with scents of brown sugar, plum and baking spices. The tannins are creamy-soft, imparting a lush texture, balanced by just enough acidity to keep it from being thick or cloying. Finishes with plenty of fruit, plus a dash of chocolate. 88 *—J.C. (11/15/2007)*

2 Up 2005 Shiraz (South Australia) $14. From the makers of Kangarilla Road but from purchased McLaren Vale and Fleurieu Peninsula fruit, this is an outstanding value. It's a high-intensity Aussie Shiraz, powerful but not without nuance, combining smoky, meaty scents with blackberry and spice, even some white pepper on the finish. Tannins are creamy-smooth, so there's no need for further aging. 90 Best Buy *—J.C. (6/1/2007)*

2 Up 2004 Shiraz (South Australia) $14. 83 *—D.T. (6/1/2006)*

3 HILLS HIGH

3 Hills High 2001 Cabernet Sauvignon (South Australia) $20. 87 *—D.T. (12/31/2005)*

3 Hills High 2002 Sangiovese-Shiraz Red Blend (South Australia) $20. 89 *—D.T. (4/1/2006)*

3 Hills High 2005 Watervale Riesling (South Australia) $20. 87 *—D.T. (12/1/2005)*

3 Hills High 2004 Sauvignon Blanc (Adelaide Hills) $18. 86 *—D.T. (12/1/2005)*

3 Hills High 2001 Shiraz (South Australia) $20. 86 *—D.T. (12/31/2005)*

42°S

42°S 2005 Pinot Noir (Tasmania) $13. A pretty good value, this Pinot clocks in at a relatively modest 12.6% alcohol level, yet still manages to show good ripe fruit. The texture is round, the tannins supple, while the flavors featue black cherries, earth and cola. Finishes crisp. 86 *—J.C. (6/1/2007)*

9 MILE ROAD

9 Mile Road 2004 Cabernet Sauvignon (South Australia) $15. A debut release from American importer George Galey, this is a creamy-textured Cabernet that's not a blockbuster but rather an elegant, balanced rendition of the variety. Cassis, vanilla and cedar are the main players, with subtle herbal notes adding complexity. Drink now–2012. 89 *—J.C. (2/1/2007)*

9 Mile Road 2004 Shiraz (South Australia) $15. 83 *—D.T. (10/1/2006)*

A.T. RICHARDSON

A.T. Richardson 2006 Chockstone Riesling (Grampians) $20. From a hilly portion of Western Victoria, this wine is a little softer in style than many other Aussie Rieslings. It still has plenty of lime and wet stone scents, but there's also a slightly confected, bubble-gum-like quality. Drink now. 86 *—J.C. (9/1/2007)*

ABBEY ROCK

Abbey Rock 2000 Cabernet Sauvignon-Merlot (South Eastern Australia) $10. 86 Best Buy *—M.S. (12/15/2002)*

Abbey Rock 2001 Chardonnay (South Eastern Australia) $10. 86 *—D.T. (6/1/2003)*

Abbey Rock 2001 Shiraz (South Eastern Australia) $10. 85 *—K.F. (3/1/2003)*

ABBEY VALE

Abbey Vale 1999 Chardonnay (Margaret River) $14. 85 *—M.N. (6/1/2001)*

Abbey Vale 2004 Vat 351 Chardonnay (Margaret River) $9. 87 Best Buy *—D.T. (5/1/2005)*

Abbey Vale 1999 Verdelho (Margaret River) $16. 86 *—M.M. (10/1/2000)*

Abbey Vale 2000 Verdelho (Margaret River) $14. 83 *—D.T. (9/1/2001)*

ADAMS BROTHERS

Adams Brothers 2001 Reserve Selection Shiraz (Clare Valley) $28. 89 *—D.T. (2/1/2004)*

ALDINGA BAY

Aldinga Bay 2001 Sangiovese (McLaren Vale) $19. 85 *—D.T. (5/1/2004)*

ALICE WHITE

Alice White 2006 Cabernet Sauvignon (South Eastern Australia) $7. Light in body, but fresh and clean, this was a surprise performer in our last round of tastings. Herbal overtones to the cedar, cherry and tobacco notes are correct from a flavor standpoint, but note that this wine doesn't have the stuffing to pair with hearty, traditional Cabernet pairings. 85 Best Buy *—J.C. (11/15/2007)*

Alice White 2005 Cabernet Sauvignon (South Eastern Australia) $7. This modest Cabernet Sauvignon displays scents of cooked berries and slighted stewed fruit flavors. It's moderately full-bodied, but lacks vibrance. 82 *—J.C. (2/1/2007)*

Alice White 2003 Cabernet Sauvignon (South Eastern Australia) $7. 86 Best Buy *—D.T. (11/15/2004)*

Alice White 2001 Cabernet Sauvignon (South Eastern Australia) $8. 84 *—C.S. (6/1/2002)*

Alice White 2000 Cabernet Sauvignon (South Eastern Australia) $8. 83 *—D.T. (9/1/2001)*

Alice White 1999 Cabernet Sauvignon (South Eastern Australia) $7. 84 *(6/1/2001)*

Alice White 2006 Cabernet Sauvignon-Shiraz (South Eastern Australia) $7. This medium-bodied red blends 60% Cabernet Sauvignon with 40% Shiraz in a wine that balances simple, jammy fruit with a touch of spice. 83 *—J.C. (11/15/2007)*

Alice White 2005 Cabernet Sauvignon-Shiraz (South Eastern Australia) $7. 83 *—D.T. (11/15/2006)*

Alice White 2004 Cabernet Sauvignon-Shiraz (South Eastern Australia) $7. 81 *—D.T. (10/1/2005)*

Alice White 2000 Cabernet Sauvignon-Shiraz (South Eastern Australia) $7. 87 Best Buy *—M.N. (6/1/2001)*

Alice White 2006 Chardonnay (South Eastern Australia) $7. An entry-level wine, pleasingly round and soft, with enough vanilla, melon and tropical fruit flavors to merit commendation. Could use a touch more crispness, but at this price, who's complaining? 84 Best Buy *—J.C. (8/1/2007)*

Alice White 2005 Chardonnay (South Eastern Australia) $7. 83 *—D.T. (6/1/2006)*

Alice White 2003 Chardonnay (South Eastern Australia) $7. 86 *—S.H. (9/1/2004)*

Alice White 2002 Chardonnay (South Eastern Australia) $8. 86 Best Buy *—D.T. (8/1/2003)*

Alice White 2004 Merlot (South Eastern Australia) $7. 82 *—D.T. (10/1/2005)*

Alice White 2003 Merlot (South Eastern Australia) $7. 85 *—S.H. (9/1/2004)*

Alice White 2002 Merlot (South Eastern Australia) $8. 84 *—D.T. (6/1/2003)*

Alice White 2005 Lexia Muscat of Alexandria Muscat (South Eastern Australia) $7. 84 Best Buy *—D.T. (11/15/2006)*

Alice White 2006 Pinot Noir (South Eastern Australia) $7. A soft, earthy red powered by modest cherry fruit and ending on a chocolaty note. 82 *—J.C. (11/15/2007)*

Alice White 2006 Riesling (South Eastern Australia) $7. Muted apple and melon flavors are a touch heavy and sweet in this atypically styled Australian Riesling. 81 *—J.C. (9/1/2007)*

Alice White 2005 Semillon-Chardonnay (South Eastern Australia) $7. 83 *—D.T. (4/1/2006)*

Alice White 2004 Semillon-Chardonnay (South Eastern Australia) $7. 82 *—D.T. (3/1/2005)*

Alice White 2005 Shiraz (South Eastern Australia) $7. 82 *—D.T. (6/1/2006)*

Alice White 2003 Shiraz (South Eastern Australia) $7. 87 *—S.H. (9/1/2004)*

Alice White 2001 Shiraz (South Eastern Australia) $8. 86 Best Buy *—K.F. (3/1/2003)*

Alice White 2000 Shiraz (South Eastern Australia) $8. 86 Best Buy *(10/1/2001)*

Alice White 1999 Shiraz (South Eastern Australia) $8. 83 *—M.N. (6/1/2001)*

ALKOOMI

Alkoomi 2001 Cabernet Sauvignon (Frankland River) $25. 91 Editors' Choice *—D.T. (5/1/2004)*

Alkoomi 2000 Southlands Red Blend (Western Australia) $11. 84 *(9/1/2001)*

Alkoomi 2006 Riesling (Frankland River) $18. Seems to be built for aging, with its incipient petrol character waiting to emerge even more in time, and a sharp, citrusy tang to its flavors. Long and tart; try after 2010. 87 *—J.C. (8/1/2007)*

Alkoomi 2002 Riesling (Frankland River) $17. 88 *—D.T. (8/1/2003)*

Alkoomi 2004 Sauvignon Blanc (Frankland River) $20. 88 *(7/1/2005)*

Alkoomi 2002 Sauvignon Blanc (Frankland River) $17. 91 Editors' Choice *—D.T. (10/1/2003)*

Alkoomi 2001 Sauvignon Blanc (Frankland River) $17. 87 *(8/1/2002)*

Alkoomi 2000 Sauvignon Blanc (Frankland River) $15. 85 *—J.F. (9/1/2001)*

Alkoomi 2001 Shiraz (Frankland River) $22. 88 *—D.T. (5/1/2004)*

Alkoomi 1999 Shiraz (Frankland River) $20. 89 *(10/1/2001)*

Alkoomi 2004 White Label Shiraz (Western Australia) $14. On the light side, with herbal, tea-like notes accenting tart cherry fruit. 82 *—J.C. (11/15/2007)*

Alkoomi 2000 Southlands White Blend (Western Australia) $11. 86 Best Buy *—D.T. (9/1/2001)*

Alkoomi 2001 Southlands Frankland River White Blend (Western Australia) $11. 89 Best Buy *—C.S. (11/15/2002)*

ALL SAINTS

All Saints 1999 Cabernet Sauvignon (Rutherglen) $30. 92 *—S.H. (1/1/2002)*

All Saints 1998 Shiraz (Rutherglen) $28. 86 *—M.S. (3/1/2003)*

All Saints 1999 Carlyle Reserve Shiraz (Rutherglen) $40. 90 Cellar Selection *—M.S. (3/1/2003)*

ALLANDALE

Allandale 2001 Cabernet Sauvignon (Mudgee) $23. 87 *—D.T. (12/31/2004)*

Allandale 2003 Chardonnay (Hunter Valley) $15. 90 Best Buy *—D.T. (4/1/2006)*

Allandale 2002 Chardonnay (Hunter Valley) $18. 86 *(7/2/2004)*

Allandale 2000 Chardonnay (Hunter Valley) $13. 84 *—J.C. (7/1/2002)*

Allandale 2002 Semillon (Hunter Valley) $15. 88 *—D.T. (4/1/2006)*

Allandale 2002 Matthew Shiraz (Hunter Valley) $20. 91 *—D.T. (4/1/2006)*

AMADIO

Amadio 2004 Shiraz (Adelaide Hills) $16. Despite this wine's elevated alcohol content (15.5%), it doesn't come across as hot, just as full-bodied, a testament to its admirable concentration. Plum, dred spices and meaty, earthy notes all build on the palate, finishing with supple tannins. Drink now. 90 Editors' Choice *—J.C. (5/1/2007)*

AMAROO

Amaroo 2005 Merlot (New South Wales) $8. Overly green, with herbal flavors that overpower the mocha, cherry and vanilla notes. Decent texture and a dusty, clean finish. 82 *—J.C. (6/1/2007)*

AMBERLEY

Amberley 1997 Reserve Cabernet Sauvignon (Margaret River) $45. 82 *—D.T. (8/1/2005)*

Amberley 2001 Cabernet Sauvignon-Merlot (Margaret River) $24. 87 *—D.T. (12/31/2004)*

Amberley 2002 Charlotte Street Chardonnay (Western Australia) $11. 84 *(7/2/2004)*

Amberley 2004 Chenin Blanc (Margaret River) $12. 87 Best Buy *—D.T. (5/1/2005)*

Amberley 2003 Proprietary Chenin Blanc (Margaret River) $13. 86 *—D.T. (11/15/2004)*

Amberley 2003 Semillon-Sauvignon Blanc (Margaret River) $17. 87 *—D.T. (11/15/2004)*

Amberley 2001 Proprietary Semillon-Sauvignon Blanc (Margaret River) $15. 83 *—D.T. (5/1/2004)*

ANDREW GARRETT ESTATES

Andrew Garrett Estates 2001 Kelly's Promise Cabernet Sauvignon-Merlot (South Eastern Australia) $9. 84 *—D.T. (9/1/2004)*

Andrew Garrett Estates 2002 Kelly's Promise Chardonnay (South Eastern Australia) $9. 86 *(7/1/2004)*

ANDREW HARRIS

Andrew Harris 1999 Premium Chardonnay (Mudgee) $13. 87 *—J.C. (7/1/2002)*

Andrew Harris 2000 Reserve Chardonnay (Mudgee) $23. 89 *—J.C. (7/1/2002)*

ANDREW PEACE

Andrew Peace 2004 Masterpeace Cabernet Sauvignon-Merlot (South Eastern Australia) $9. 84 *—D.T. (12/31/2005)*

Andrew Peace 2006 MasterPeace Big Tail Red Cabernet Sauvignon-Merlot (South Eastern Australia) $12. Supple and rather soft for a blend that favors Cabernet over Merlot by 80-20. Simple cherry fruit is accented by mint and cinnamon notes, finishing soft. 84 *—J.C. (11/15/2007)*

Andrew Peace 2002 Chardonnay (South Eastern Australia) $8. 80 *(7/2/2004)*

Andrew Peace 2004 Masterpeace Chardonnay (South Eastern Australia) $9. 84 *—D.T. (10/1/2005)*

Andrew Peace 2005 Peace Family Vineyard Chardonnay (South Eastern Australia) $8. A top value in Australian Chardonnay, this wine features bold mango, peach and melon scents capped off by smoky oak notes that suggest grilled fruit. It's plump and soft, with a smoky—maybe slightly too smoky—and toasty finish. Drink now. 86 Best Buy *—J.C. (6/1/2007)*

Andrew Peace 2002 Red Blend (South Eastern Australia) $8. 86 Best Buy *—D.T. (5/1/2004)*

Andrew Peace 2004 Masterpeace Red Blend (South Eastern Australia) $9. 85 Best Buy *—D.T. (8/1/2005)*

Andrew Peace 2006 Masterpeace Red Willie Blend Red Blend (South Eastern Australia) $12. Round and ample in the mouth, this blend of Shiraz, Cabernet Sauvignon, Grenache and Mataro (Mourvèdre) features plenty of fruit for the money. Red berries on the nose and black cherries and a hint of stone fruit on the palate are all tied up by a finish that's clean and crisp without being excessively tart. Drink now. 87 Best Buy *—J.C. (11/15/2007)*

Andrew Peace 2006 Peace Family Vineyard Red Blend (South Eastern Australia) $8. With a blend that includes Shiraz, Cabernet, Grenache and Mataro, there's a certain amount of generic red designed into this wine. It's slightly earthy, with some cherry fruit and a bit of spice on the finish. 83 *—J.C. (11/15/2007)*

Andrew Peace 2005 Peace Family Vineyard Red Blend (South Eastern Australia) $8. Basic Australian red wine done well, this blend of 44% Shiraz, 29% Cabernet Sauvignon, 17% Grenache and 10% Mataro is medium-bodied, with jammy cherry fruit and touches of graham crackers and Nilla wafers. Creamy in texture, with a slightly sticky quality to the finish. 85 Best Buy *—J.C. (11/15/2007)*

Andrew Peace 2002 Shiraz (South Eastern Australia) $8. 85 *—D.T. (12/31/2003)*

Andrew Peace 2004 Masterpeace Shiraz (South Eastern Australia) $9. A bit warm and raisiny, with aromas and flavors of cooked, jammy fruit, soft tannins and a short finish. 82 *—J.C. (11/15/2007)*

Andrew Peace 2005 Peace Family Vineyard Shiraz (South Eastern Australia) $8. The aromas present an interesting mix of fruity, bubble-gum notes and deeper, earthy, leathery tones. Flavors are seemingly a bit sweet and tart, with little texture. 82 *—J.C. (7/1/2007)*

Andrew Peace 2005 Masterpeace Shiraz-Cabernet Sauvignon-Grenache-Mataro Red Blend (South Eastern Australia) $9. With so many blended reds, one wonders why Andrew Peace doesn't just throw them all together and realize some economies of scale and easier branding. This particular blend offers slightly confected cherry flavors and a touch of dusty wood, finished with some warmth and spice. 83 *—J.C. (11/15/2007)*

Andrew Peace 2005 Masterpeace Shiraz-Sangiovese Rosé Rosé Blend (South Eastern Australia) $9. Seems a bit tired already, with a heaviness in the mouth and dulled fruit flavors. There's stone and spice remaining, but where's the fruit? 81 *—J.C. (4/1/2007)*

ANGOVE'S

Angove's 2000 Classic Reserve Cabernet Sauvignon (South Australia) $10. 85 *—D.T. (6/1/2003)*

Angove's 1999 Classic Reserve Cabernet Sauvignon (South Eastern Australia) $10. 86 Best Buy *(9/1/2001)*

Angove's 1997 Classic Reserve Cabernet Sauvignon (South Eastern Australia) $12. 85 *(4/1/2000)*

Angove's 2002 Long Row Cabernet Sauvignon (South Australia) $10. 84 *—D.T. (11/15/2004)*

Angove's 1999 Sarnia Farm Cabernet Sauvignon (Padthaway) $9. 82 *—D.T. (1/1/2002)*

Angove's 2005 Vineyard Select Cabernet Sauvignon (Coonawarra) $21. From a very late vintage that suffered from low yields, this 2,000-case cuvée of Cabernet Sauvignon offers plenty of Coonawarra character: dried herbs, mint and a bit of green pepper add a slightly medicinal edge to the cassis flavors. Finishes dusty, dry and herbal; try in 2009. 87 *—J.C. (4/1/2007)*

Angove's 2003 Vineyard Select Cabernet Sauvignon (Coonawarra) $20. 87 *—D.T. (12/31/2005)*

Angove's 2002 Vineyard Select Cabernet Sauvignon (Coonawarra) $20. 87 *—D.T. (12/31/2004)*

Angove's 2003 Bear Crossing Cabernet Sauvignon-Merlot (South Australia) $7. 84 Best Buy *—D.T. (2/1/2006)*

Angove's 2002 Bear Crossing Cabernet Sauvignon-Merlot (South Australia) $7. 84 *—D.T. (6/1/2003)*

Angove's 2000 Bear Crossing Cabernet Sauvignon-Merlot (South Australia) $7. 86 Best Buy *—J.C. (6/1/2002)*

Angove's 2003 Bear Crossing Chardonnay (South Australia) $7. 82 —*D.T. (11/15/2004)*

Angove's 2002 Bear Crossing Chardonnay (South Australia) $7. 85 —*D.T. (8/1/2003)*

Angove's 2001 Bear Crossing Chardonnay (South Australia) $7. 85 Best Buy —*J.C. (7/1/2002)*

Angove's 2002 Classic Reserve Chardonnay (South Australia) $9. 87 Best Buy —*D.T. (6/1/2003)*

Angove's 2000 Classic Reserve Chardonnay (South Australia) $9. 86 —*M.N. (6/1/2001)*

Angove's 2004 Long Row Chardonnay (South Australia) $10. 84 —*D.T. (10/1/2005)*

Angove's 2003 Long Row Chardonnay (South Australia) $10. 84 —*D.T. (12/31/2004)*

Angove's 2003 Sarnia Farm Chardonnay (Padthaway) $14. 84 —*D.T. (12/31/2004)*

Angove's 2005 Red Belly Black Chardonnay (South Eastern Australia) $12. A multi-region blend with a striking label, this Chardonnay features stone fruit and sweet corn flavors touched with vanilla. It's a bit simple and almost sweet-tasting, with a sharp tartness to the finish. 83 —*J.C. (4/1/2007)*

Angove's 2006 Vineyard Select Chardonnay (Limestone Coast) $19. A blend of wines from two separate vineyards, this Chardonnay features nutty, toasty oak, buttery notes from malolactic fermentation and plenty of tropical and citrus fruit. It's crisp for an Australian Chardonnay, with a buttery reprise on the long finish. 87 —*J.C. (4/1/2007)*

Angove's 2006 Nine Vines Rosé Grenache-Shiraz (South Australia) $11. This rosé is a gorgeous deep rose color—almost a light red. Modest raspberry fruit mingles with a minerally note that's akin to crushed vitamin tablets, then finishes crisp, with mouthwatering acidity. A refreshing summer quaff. 84 —*J.C. (7/1/2007)*

Angove's 2005 Nine Vines Rosé Grenache-Syrah (South Australia) $10. 86 Best Buy —*D.T. (11/15/2005)*

Angove's 2002 Long Row Merlot (South Australia) $10. 84 —*D.T. (12/31/2004)*

Angove's 2001 Classic Reserve Pinot Noir (South Australia) $10. 84 —*D.T. (6/1/2003)*

Angove's 2006 Vineyard Select Riesling (Clare Valley) $19. The 900 cases produced of this wine are all destined for the U.S., as consumer acceptance of Australian Riesling seems to be expanding. It's an intensely citrusy wine, dominated by limes and oranges, filled with bold, crisp flavors. Medium-bodied, with a clean finish, this would go well with many fish preparations. 88 —*J.C. (4/1/2007)*

Angove's 2003 Vineyard Select Riesling (Clare Valley) $19. 86 —*D.T. (3/1/2005)*

Angove's 2005 Rosé Rosé Blend (South Eastern Australia) $11. Slightly soft, this really needs to be well chilled to give it additional refreshment value. Raspberry and mulberry flavors are simple and fruity, finishing a bit short. The blend is 70% Grenache, 30% Shiraz. 84 —*J.C. (4/1/2007)*

Angove's 2001 Classic Reserve Sauvignon Blanc (South Australia) $10. 84 *(1/1/2004)*

Angove's 2004 Long Row Sauvignon Blanc (South Australia) $10. 83 —*D.T. (11/15/2004)*

Angove's 2004 Vineyard Select Sauvignon Blanc (Adelaide Hills) $19. 87 —*D.T. (12/1/2005)*

Angove's 2002 Bear Crossing Semillon-Chardonnay (South Australia) $7. 86 Best Buy —*D.T. (12/31/2003)*

Angove's 2002 Bear Crossing Shiraz (South Australia) $7. 86 Best Buy —*D.T. (11/15/2003)*

Angove's 2000 Classic Reserve Shiraz (South Australia) $10. 85 —*M.S. (3/1/2003)*

Angove's 1999 Classic Reserve Shiraz (South Australia) $9. 83 *(10/1/2001)*

Angove's 2003 Long Row Shiraz (South Australia) $10. 84 —*D.T. (2/1/2006)*

Angove's 2004 Red Belly Black Shiraz (South Eastern Australia) $12. Named for a common snake, this is a pleasant commercial Shiraz, marrying blackberry fruit with plenty of vanilla from American oak. Then it adds spice and meaty notes to give it enough complexity to hang at the dinner table, finishing with crisp acidity. 85 —*J.C. (4/1/2007)*

Angove's 2002 Red Belly Black Shiraz (Limestone Coast) $13. 84 —*D.T. (11/15/2004)*

Angove's 2002 Sarnia Farm Shiraz (Padthaway) $14. 88 —*D.T. (12/31/2004)*

Angove's 2005 Vineyard Select Shiraz (McLaren Vale) $21. From a single McLaren Vale vineyard, this is fermented in old-fashioned open-top cement vats, then aged 18 months in American oak. It's a spicy Shiraz, filled with clove, star anise and meaty notes, but backed by plum and cassis flavors that roll out luxuriously across the palate. 88 —*J.C. (4/1/2007)*

Angove's 2003 Vineyard Select Shiraz (McLaren Vale) $20. 89 —*D.T. (12/31/2005)*

Angove's 2002 Vineyard Select Shiraz (McLaren Vale) $20. 89 —*D.T. (3/1/2005)*

Angove's 2006 Nine Vines Viognier (South Eastern Australia) $11. Victoria Angove credits Yalumba with doing much of the pioneering work with this variety in Australia; this is Angove's first commercial release, coming in at 3,000 cases. It's a full, buxom version of Viognier, with full-blown stone fruit flavors bolstered by ample alcohol and touches of spice and honeysuckle. Good value. 85 —*J.C. (4/1/2007)*

ANGUS THE BULL

Angus The Bull 2004 Cabernet Sauvignon (South Eastern Australia) $19. This is pretty ripe stuff, with scents of coffee, chocolate and fruitcake that give way to flavors of cassis, tobacco and vanilla on the palate. Shows decent complexity and some youthful tannins; try now with rare beef or lamb or hold another 2–3 years. 88 —*J.C. (2/1/2007)*

ANNIE'S LANE

Annie's Lane 2002 Cabernet Sauvignon-Merlot (Clare Valley) $13. 88 Best Buy —*D.T. (12/31/2004)*

Annie's Lane 2003 Chardonnay (Clare Valley) $13. 85 *(7/2/2004)*

Annie's Lane 2003 Chardonnay (Clare Valley) $NA. 86 —*D.T. (1/1/2002)*

Annie's Lane 2002 Chardonnay (Clare Valley) $13. 88 —*D.T. (8/1/2003)*

Annie's Lane 2006 Riesling (Clare Valley) $15. Medium-bodied, with what appears to be a touch of residual sugar to help round it out, this fresh, apple-y Riesling also features hints of orange blossom and florists' greens. 86 —*J.C. (8/1/2007)*

Annie's Lane 2004 Riesling (Clare Valley) $14. 87 —*D.T. (8/1/2006)*

Annie's Lane 2003 Riesling (Clare Valley) $14. 88 Best Buy —*D.T. (5/1/2004)*

Annie's Lane 2002 Riesling (Clare Valley) $14. 86 —*D.T. (8/1/2003)*

Annie's Lane 2004 Coppertrail Riesling (Clare Valley) $14. 87 —*D.T. (10/1/2005)*

Annie's Lane 2002 Semillon (Clare Valley) $NA. 88 —*D.T. (2/1/2004)*

Annie's Lane 2004 Shiraz (Clare Valley) $13. Medium- to full-bodied, this richly earthy Shiraz also brings along plenty of complexity in its aromas and flavors of smoke, tobacco, cola and blackberry. There's some oak, but this bargain-priced beauty is more about displaying the Clare Valley terroir than simple fruit or oak, unusual in this price range. Drink now–2012. 88 Best Buy —*J.C. (11/15/2007)*

Annie's Lane 1999 Copper Trail Shiraz (Clare Valley) $32. 86 —*D.T. (12/31/2003)*

Annie's Lane 2001 Coppertrail Shiraz (Clare Valley) $30. 89 —*D.T. (12/1/2005)*

Annie's Lane 2000 Coppertrail Shiraz-Grenache-Mourvedre Red Blend (Clare Valley) $20. 84 —*D.T. (9/1/2004)*

ANNVERS

Annvers 2001 Cabernet Sauvignon (Langhorne Creek) $28. 87 —*D.T. (5/1/2004)*

Annvers 2001 Shiraz (McLaren Vale) $30. 85 —*D.T. (5/1/2004)*

ANTIPODEAN

Antipodean 1999 Chardonnay (Eden Valley) $NA. 83 —*D.T. (8/1/2003)*

AQUILA

Aquila 2001 Cabernet Sauvignon (Margaret River) $15. 86 —*D.T. (10/1/2003)*

Aquila 2000 Cabernet Sauvignon (Margaret River) $15. 84 —*D.T. (10/1/2003)*

Aquila 1999 Shiraz (Blackwood Valley) $17. 83 *(10/1/2001)*

ARAMIS

Aramis 2003 Shiraz (McLaren Vale) $21. 87 —*J.C. (12/15/2006)*

Aramis 2003 The Governor Shiraz (McLaren Vale) $32. Smoky and bacony, with complex meat and spice elements balancing bold blackberry fruit. Long and tannic on the finish. 91 —*J.C. (6/1/2007)*

AUSTRALIA

ARCHETYPE

Archetype 2005 Cabernet Sauvignon-Shiraz (Barossa) $14. This virtually 50-50 blend comes across as a bit simple and chunky, but well made. It's sturdy enough to stand up to burgers and the like, offering modest cassis and berry fruit and a dusty finish. 84 *—J.C. (6/1/2007)*

Archetype 2005 Shiraz (Barossa) $14. Barossa doesn't yield many Best Buys, but this one features aromatically complex notes of pepper and spice atop stylish blackberry and blueberry fruit. There's some warmth, but also a pleasantly expansive mouthfeel. Drink now. 89 Best Buy *—J.C. (11/1/2007)*

Archetype 2005 Old Vine Reserve Shiraz (Barossa Valley) $20. This wine poses an interesting contrast to the regular bottling, as it's lower in alcohol and also tighter and more structured. Meat and savory notes are layered over tart berry flavors, finishing on a crisp note. This may age longer than Archetype's regular 2005 Shiraz, but will it ever provide as much pleasure? 87 *—J.C. (11/1/2007)*

Archetype 2004 Old Vine Reserve Shiraz (Barossa Valley) $35. 91 *—D.T. (8/1/2006)*

ARMSTRONG

Armstrong 1999 Shiraz (Victoria) $54. 88 *(11/1/2001)*

ARTHUR'S CREEK

Arthur's Creek 1996 Estate Cabernet Sauvignon (Yarra Valley) $40. 84 *—J.C. (6/1/2002)*

Arthur's Creek 1995 Estate Cabernet Sauvignon (Yarra Valley) $40. 84 *(9/1/2001)*

Arthur's Creek 1999 Chardonnay (Yarra Valley) $25. 85 *—J.C. (7/1/2002)*

ARUNDA

Arunda 1999 Cabernet Sauvignon-Merlot (South Eastern Australia) $9. 85 *—S.H. (6/1/2002)*

Arunda 2000 Chardonnay (South Eastern Australia) $9. 87 Best Buy *—S.H. (9/1/2002)*

Arunda 2001 Shiraz-Cabernet Sauvignon (South Eastern Australia) $9. 86 *—S.H. (1/1/2002)*

AUSTRALIAN DOMAINE WINES

Australian Domaine Wines 1999 Alliance Shiraz (South Eastern Australia) $18. 86 *(10/1/2001)*

AUSVETIA

AusVetia 1997 Shiraz (South Australia) $60. 89 *(11/1/2001)*

BALGOWNIE ESTATE

Balgownie Estate 2000 Cabernet Sauvignon (Bendigo) $25. 91 *—M.S. (12/15/2002)*

Balgownie Estate 2002 Shiraz (Bendigo) $30. 89 *—D.T. (10/1/2005)*

Balgownie Estate 2000 Shiraz (Bendigo) $25. 86 *—D.T. (3/1/2003)*

BALLANDEAN

Ballandean 2002 Cabernet Sauvignon (Granite Belt) $13. 82 *—D.T. (12/31/2005)*

Ballandean 2004 Semillon-Sauvignon Blanc (Granite Belt) $13. 85 *—D.T. (12/1/2005)*

Ballandean 2002 Shiraz (Granite Belt) $13. 83 *—D.T. (12/1/2005)*

BALLAST STONE ESTATE WINES

Ballast Stone Estate Wines 2004 Cabernet Sauvignon (South Eastern Australia) $15. A blend of estate-grown fruit from Currency Creek and McLaren Vale, the flagship label of the Ballast Stone line represents a solid value. Cassis fruit is showcased admirably by hints of eucalyptus and wood-derived accents of toasted coconut and vanilla, while the texture is surprisingly lush and the finish velvety. 89 *—J.C. (3/1/2007)*

Ballast Stone Estate Wines 2004 Stonemason Cabernet Sauvignon (Currency Creek) $10. Loaded with chocolate and cassis aromas and flavors, this medium-bodied Cabernet Sauvignon has just enough herbal nuance to be identifiable as Cabernet without going to excess. With time, the fruit takes on a slightly cooked character similar to molasses, but the soft tannins provide adequate structure for near-term drinking. 85 Best Buy *—J.C. (3/1/2007)*

Ballast Stone Estate Wines 2004 Stonemason Cabernet Sauvignon-Shiraz (Currency Creek) $10. Roughly two-thirds Cab, one-third Shiraz, this is a bulky, brawny wine at the price point, offering intense flavors of dried fruit, cassis and chocolate delivered assertively, without much complexity or finesse. It's the kind of rough and ready wine to pair with grilled burgers or sausages. 86 Best Buy *—J.C. (6/1/2007)*

Ballast Stone Estate Wines 2005 Stonemason Unwooded Chardonnay (Currency Creek) $10. This decidedly thick, syrupy-textured Chardonnay displays hints of tropical fruit, but also features some offputting lactic and asphalt notes. 80 *—J.C. (3/1/2007)*

Ballast Stone Estate Wines 2004 Steeple Jack Merlot (South Australia) $7. Consumers looking for a soft, fleshy Merlot at a bargain price need look no further than this bottling. It's plummy and a bit herbal, but loaded with attractive vanilla notes. Easy to drink; a good by-the-glass pour. 85 Best Buy *—J.C. (6/1/2007)*

Ballast Stone Estate Wines 2005 Stonemason Semillon-Sauvignon Blanc (South Australia) $10. A nearly 50-50 blend, this effort is lean and green, with hints of quince, passion fruit and underripe plum that give it a strident character. Finishes with some chalky, minerally notes, making it worth a try with raw shellfish. 84 *—J.C. (2/1/2007)*

Ballast Stone Estate Wines 2004 Stonemason Shiraz (Currency Creek) $10. A distinctly different take on $10 Australian Shiraz, this wine offers up perfumey scents of anise and a bit of stone fruit—perhaps apricot? In the mouth, spicedrop flavors ride easily over a foundation of earth, coffee and leather. If you're tired of jammy Shirazes, this might be just the ticket. 86 Best Buy *—J.C. (3/1/2007)*

Ballast Stone Estate Wines NV Sparkling Blend (Currency Creek) $17. 84 *—D.T. (12/31/2003)*

BALNAVES OF COONAWARRA

Balnaves of Coonawarra 2004 The Blend Bordeaux Blend (Coonawarra) $20. Mainly Cabernet Sauvignon and Merlot, The Blend combines cassis and blackberry fruit, adds vanilla and cinnamon touches from barrel aging and just a slight herbal note. It's crisp and youthfully tannic, with hints of coffee and a dustiness to the finish. Should be better in another couple of years. 90 Editors' Choice *—J.C. (6/1/2007)*

Balnaves of Coonawarra 1998 The Blend Bordeaux Blend (Coonawarra) $15. 85 *—M.S. (12/15/2002)*

Balnaves of Coonawarra 1997 The Blend Bordeaux Blend (Coonawarra) $26. 87 *—J.F. (9/1/2001)*

Balnaves of Coonawarra 2002 Cabernet Sauvignon (Coonawarra) $35. This has dark chocolate and cassis flavors similar to those found in Balnaves' 2002 Cabernet-Merlot, but adds some medicinal herbal notes as well. Crisply focused, with a slightly lean personality and a finish dusty with tannin. Drink 2008–2015. 88 *—J.C. (6/1/2007)*

Balnaves of Coonawarra 1998 Cabernet Sauvignon (Coonawarra) $30. 85 *—M.S. (12/15/2002)*

Balnaves of Coonawarra 1997 Cabernet Sauvignon (Coonawarra) $37. 82 *—D.T. (9/1/2001)*

Balnaves of Coonawarra 1998 The Tally Reserve Cabernet Sauvignon (Coonawarra) $75. 87 *—D.T. (12/31/2003)*

Balnaves of Coonawarra 2002 Cabernet Sauvignon-Merlot (Coonawarra) $28. It's labeled Cabernet-Merlot, but the reality is that the Merlot content is less than 10%. Still, it must bring something positive to the blend, as this is more richly textured and lush than Balnaves' straight Cabernet Sauvignon. Dark aromas and flavors sing gracefully, offering hints of chocolate, anise, cassis, coffee and spice. Finishes long, with velvety tannins; drink now–2015, possibly longer. 91 Editors' Choice *—J.C. (6/1/2007)*

Balnaves of Coonawarra 1998 Cabernet Sauvignon-Merlot (Coonawarra) $20. 86 *—M.S. (12/15/2002)*

Balnaves of Coonawarra 1997 Cabernet Sauvignon-Merlot (Coonawarra) $30. 89 *—J.F. (9/1/2001)*

Balnaves of Coonawarra 2005 Chardonnay (Coonawarra) $32. This upscale Australian Chard shows excellent clarity and perfume on the nose, mixing tropical fruit with hints of toast and vanilla. On the palate, there's a patina of dry woodiness, but that's backed by plenty of bright fruit flavors and a plump mouthfeel. Mouthwatering on the finish. If the wood integrates over the next few months, this has potential to score 90 points. 89 *—J.C. (3/1/2007)*

Balnaves of Coonawarra 1999 Chardonnay (Coonawarra) $30. 84 *—D.T. (8/1/2003)*

Balnaves of Coonawarra 2004 Shiraz (Coonawarra) $28. Balnaves is a reliable source for well-balanced red wines that never seem to go over the top. This shows cinnamon and clove notes and a certain dried-fruit character on the nose, followed by flavors of coffee, prune and spice. It's full-bodied, yet firm, with crisp acids and firm tannins that promise a long life. Drink 2010–2020. 90 *—J.C. (5/1/2007)*

Balnaves of Coonawarra 1998 Shiraz (Coonawarra) $30. 88 *—K.F. (3/1/2003)*

BALTHASAR RESS

Balthazar of the Barossa 2003 Shiraz (Barossa Valley) $35. A slightly syrupy-textured Shiraz that seems destined for early drinking. Winemaker and grapegrower Anita Bowen has turned out a solid effort from a challenging vintage. White pepper accents ripe blackberries, finishing with hints of cooked fruit and lingering spice. Drink now–2013. 88 *—J.C. (11/1/2007)*

Balthasar Ress 2001 Balthazar of the Barossa Shiraz (Barossa Valley) $35. 89 *—D.T. (9/1/2004)*

BANNOCKBURN VINEYARDS

Bannockburn Vineyards 2001 Chardonnay (Geelong) $38. 87 *(7/2/2004)*

Bannockburn Vineyards 2001 Chardonnay by Farr Chardonnay (Geelong) $39. 86 *(7/2/2004)*

BANROCK STATION

Banrock Station 2006 Cabernet Sauvignon (South Eastern Australia) $5. A bit chunky and lacking in elegance, but offers an assertive mouthful of cassis and vanilla flavors that would capably partner weeknight steaks or burgers. Imported by Pacific Wine Partners. 84 Best Buy *—J.C. (11/15/2007)*

Banrock Station 2005 Cabernet Sauvignon (South Eastern Australia) $5. Light in weight, what impresses about this wine is that it doesn't try too hard. The cherry-berry fruit is modest, there are some herbal overtones and peppery accents, but it's crisp and clean; an easy quaff for a busy weeknight. 84 Best Buy *—J.C. (2/1/2007)*

Banrock Station 2004 Cabernet Sauvignon (South Eastern Australia) $7. 82 *—D.T. (12/31/2005)*

Banrock Station 2005 Chardonnay (South Eastern Australia) $5. 84 Best Buy *—D.T. (4/1/2006)*

Banrock Station 2004 Chardonnay (South Eastern Australia) $7. 83 *—D.T. (10/1/2005)*

Banrock Station 2003 Chardonnay (South Eastern Australia) $7. 84 *(7/2/2004)*

Banrock Station 2001 Chardonnay (South Eastern Australia) $6. 83 *—J.C. (7/1/2002)*

Banrock Station 2005 Merlot (South Eastern Australia) $5. 84 Best Buy *—D.T. (11/15/2006)*

Banrock Station 2001 Merlot (South Eastern Australia) $6. 82 *—C.S. (6/1/2002)*

Banrock Station 2000 Merlot (South Eastern Australia) $6. 82 *—J.F. (9/1/2001)*

Banrock Station 2005 Riesling (South Eastern Australia) $5. 85 Best Buy *—D.T. (8/1/2006)*

Banrock Station 2004 Riesling (South Eastern Australia) $7. 84 Best Buy *—D.T. (10/1/2005)*

Banrock Station 2005 Semillon-Chardonnay (South Eastern Australia) $5. This blend of 75% Semillon and 25% Chardonnay boasts rather subdued flavors, but works in just enough ripe pear and melon flavors to satisfy. It's medium-bodied, with hints of dried spices for complexity and a mouthwatering finish. It's a great value at this rock-bottom price. 85 Best Buy *—J.C. (2/1/2007)*

Banrock Station 2004 Semillon-Chardonnay (South Eastern Australia) $5. 83 Best Buy *—D.T. (4/1/2006)*

Banrock Station 2003 Semillon-Chardonnay (South Eastern Australia) $6. 84 Best Buy *—D.T. (3/1/2005)*

Banrock Station 2000 Semillon-Chardonnay (South Eastern Australia) $6. 88 Best Buy *—D.T. (9/1/2001)*

Banrock Station 2005 Shiraz (South Eastern Australia) $5. The raspberry and vanilla flavors are a bit simple but tasty, and the texture is slightly creamy, smoothed along by supple tannins. Ends with a modest burst of berry zinger tea, just enough to help this otherwise soft wine pair with food. Drink now. 84 Best Buy *—J.C. (3/1/2007)*

Banrock Station 2003 Shiraz (South Eastern Australia) $7. 84 Best Buy *—D.T. (12/31/2005)*

Banrock Station 2000 Shiraz (South Eastern Australia) $8. 87 Best Buy *(10/1/2001)*

Banrock Station 1999 Shiraz (South Eastern Australia) $7. 88 Best Buy *—M.M. (10/1/2000)*

Banrock Station 2004 White Shiraz (South Eastern Australia) $5. 84 Best Buy *—D.T. (4/1/2006)*

Banrock Station 2004 Shiraz-Cabernet Sauvignon (South Eastern Australia) $5. A blend of 78% Shiraz and 22% Cabernet, this would be a solid choice for such large parties as weddings and anniversaries. The cherry fruit flavors are tinged with hints of herbs that take on a slightly medicinal character, but the mouthfeel is smooth and the finish supple and easy. Drink now. 84 Best Buy *—J.C. (2/1/2007)*

Banrock Station 2003 Shiraz-Cabernet Sauvignon (South Eastern Australia) $6. 86 Best Buy *—D.T. (8/1/2005)*

Banrock Station 2000 Shiraz-Cabernet Sauvignon (South Eastern Australia) $6. 87 Best Buy *(9/1/2001)*

BARNADOWN RUN

Barnadown Run 1999 Heathcote Cabernet Sauvignon (Victoria) $28. 87 *—J.C. (6/1/2002)*

Barnadown Run 1999 Shiraz (Victoria) $25. 85 *(11/1/2001)*

Barnadown Run 2000 Heathcote/Bendigo Winery Shiraz (Victoria) $30. 84 *—D.T. (1/28/2003)*

BAROSSA OLD VINE COMPANY

Barossa Old Vine Company 2004 Shiraz (Barossa) $105. A blend of several extremely old vineyard parcels, this features deep, intoxicating blackberry flavors offset by hints of toast and dried spices. Thick and rich, it rolls easily across the palate, yet remains surprisingly balanced and structured, not heavy or soft. From Carl Lindner, winemaker for Langmeil. Drink 2010–2020, possibly longer. 93 *—J.C. (11/1/2007)*

BAROSSA VALLEY ESTATE

Barossa Valley Estate 2000 Ebenezer Cabernet Sauvignon-Merlot (Barossa Valley) $30. 86 *—D.T. (12/31/2003)*

Barossa Valley Estate 1999 Chardonnay (Barossa Valley) $10. 87 Best Buy *—M.M. (10/1/2000)*

Barossa Valley Estate 2000 Chardonnay (South Australia) $10. 85 *(6/1/2001)*

Barossa Valley Estate 2004 Spires Chardonnay (Barossa Valley) $12. 86 *—D.T. (12/1/2005)*

Barossa Valley Estate 2003 Spires Chardonnay (Barossa Valley) $12. 84 *(3/1/2005)*

Barossa Valley Estate 2003 Spires Chardonnay (Barossa Valley) $12. 83 *(7/2/2004)*

Barossa Valley Estate 2002 Spires Chardonnay (Barossa Valley) $10. 86 *—D.T. (8/1/2003)*

Barossa Valley Estate 1998 Shiraz (Barossa Valley) $10. 89 Best Buy *(10/1/2000)*

Barossa Valley Estate 2000 Shiraz (South Australia) $10. 86 *(10/1/2001)*

Barossa Valley Estate 1999 Black Pepper Sparkling Shiraz (Barossa Valley) $NA. 90 *(3/1/2005)*

Barossa Valley Estate 2004 E&E Black Pepper Shiraz (Barossa) $90. Lush and chocolaty, yet also filled with layers of cherry fruit. Winemaker Stuart Bourne compares it to Cherry Ripe, an Australian candy bar similar to Mounds with cherry mixed into the coconut filling, and he's spot on. This starts off creamy-smooth, then develops a velvety edge of tannin on the long finish. Close in quality to the still-stunning 1998; drink now–2020. Imported by Pacific Wine Partners. 93 Cellar Selection *—J.C. (11/1/2007)*

Barossa Valley Estate 2003 E&E Black Pepper Shiraz (Barossa Valley) $85. Winemaker Stuart Bourne calls 2003 a thinking man's vintage, and he was clearly on form, crafting a delicious wine filled with blackberry tea aromas and flavors. It's just slightly creamy on the palate, but still firm, turning a bit crisp at the end. Drink 2008–2013. Imported by Pacific Wine Partners. 90 *—J.C. (11/1/2007)*

Barossa Valley Estate 2002 E&E Black Pepper Shiraz (Barossa Valley) $85. 90 *(6/1/2006)*

Barossa Valley Estate 2001 E&E Black Pepper Shiraz (Barossa Valley) $85. 92 *—D.T. (12/31/2004)*

Barossa Valley Estate 2000 E&E Black Pepper Shiraz (Barossa Valley) $NA. 90 *(3/1/2005)*

Barossa Valley Estate 1999 E&E Black Pepper Shiraz (Barossa Valley) $NA. 92 *(3/1/2005)*

Barossa Valley Estate 1998 E&E Black Pepper Shiraz (Barossa Valley) $NA. 93 *(3/1/2005)*

Barossa Valley Estate 1997 E&E Black Pepper Shiraz (Barossa Valley) $65. 90 *(10/1/2000)*

Barossa Valley Estate 1996 E&E Black Pepper Shiraz (Barossa Valley) $NA. 94 *(3/1/2005)*

Barossa Valley Estate 1994 E&E Black Pepper Shiraz (Barossa Valley) $NA. 92 *(3/1/2005)*

Barossa Valley Estate 1991 E&E Black Pepper Shiraz (Barossa Valley) $NA. 93 *(3/1/2005)*

Barossa Valley Estate 2003 E&E Sparkling Shiraz (Barossa) $70. This is one of Australia's top sparkling Shirazes, and this will be the first vintage it's being imported to the U.S. in commercial quantity (150 cases). It's chocolaty and rich, with flavors of brandied cherries and brown sugar.

Drink now–2010. Imported by Pacific Wine Partners. 90 —*J.C.* *(11/1/2007)*

Barossa Valley Estate 2001 E&E Sparkling Shiraz (South Australia) $70. The famous E&E Shiraz also comes in a sparkling version. There's no denying the quality of the 2001, which boasts bold aromas of toast, cedar, vanilla and blackberries. The mouthfeel is full, creamy and lush, and while it finishes a touch sweet, there's just enough tannin and acid to keep it balanced. Delicious now, but these wines can age 10 or more years from the vintage. 90 —*J.C. (12/31/2007)*

Barossa Valley Estate 1998 E&E Sparkling Shiraz (Barossa Valley) $NA. 88 —*D.T. (2/1/2004)*

Barossa Valley Estate 2002 Ebenezer Shiraz (Barossa Valley) $35. 87 —*D.T. (8/1/2006)*

Barossa Valley Estate 2003 Ebenezer Shiraz (Barossa) $35. A slightly roasted quality permeates this wine, lending hints of coffee and asphalt to the sturdy black olive flavors. Turns a bit crisp and tart on the finish; drink now–2010. Imported by Pacific Wine Partners. 88 —*J.C. (11/1/2007)*

Barossa Valley Estate 2001 Ebenezer Shiraz (Barossa Valley) $30. 88 *(3/1/2005)*

Barossa Valley Estate 2000 Ebenezer Shiraz (Barossa Valley) $28. 90 —*D.T. (2/1/2004)*

Barossa Valley Estate 1999 Ebenezer Shiraz (Barossa Valley) $30. 90 —*D.T. (3/1/2003)*

Barossa Valley Estate 1998 Ebenezer Shiraz (Barossa Valley) $32. 89 —*J.C. (9/1/2002)*

Barossa Valley Estate 1997 Ebenezer Shiraz (Barossa Valley) $29. 90 *(10/1/2000)*

Barossa Valley Estate 1996 Ebenezer Shiraz (Barossa Valley) $25. 91 *(4/1/2000)*

Barossa Valley Estate 2003 Spires Shiraz (Barossa Valley) $12. 85 —*D.T. (12/1/2005)*

Barossa Valley Estate 2002 Spires Shiraz (Barossa Valley) $12. 84 —*D.T. (11/15/2004)*

Barossa Valley Estate 2001 Spires Shiraz (Barossa Valley) $10. 84 —*D.T. (12/31/2003)*

BARRATT

Barratt 2001 Chardonnay (Piccadilly Valley) $40. 88 —*D.T. (8/1/2003)*

Barratt 2001 The Reserve Pinot Noir (Piccadilly Valley) $50. 84 —*D.T. (12/31/2003)*

BARWANG

Barwang 1997 Regional Selection Cabernet Sauvignon (Coonawarra) $18. 90 *(12/1/1999)*

Barwang 1997 Vintage Select Cabernet Sauvignon (South Eastern Australia) $10. 86 *(12/1/1999)*

Barwang 1996 Winemaker's Reserve Cabernet Sauvignon (New South Wales) $25. 93 *(12/1/1999)*

Barwang 1998 Regional Selection Chardonnay (Yarra Valley) $14. 84 —*S.H. (9/1/2001)*

Barwang 1997 Regional Selection Chardonnay (South Eastern Australia) $16. 88 *(12/1/1999)*

Barwang 1997 Vintage Select Chardonnay (South Eastern Australia) $10. 87 Best Buy *(12/1/1999)*

Barwang 1999 Merlot (South Eastern Australia) $9. 83 —*M.M. (9/1/2001)*

Barwang 1998 Regional Selection Merlot (Coonawarra) $14. 87 —*J.F. (9/1/2001)*

Barwang 1997 Regional Selection Merlot (Coonawarra) $20. 81 —*S.H. (10/1/2000)*

Barwang 1999 Shiraz (South Eastern Australia) $9. 83 *(10/1/2001)*

Barwang 1997 Regional Selection Shiraz (South Eastern Australia) $18. 90 *(12/1/1999)*

Barwang 1997 Vintage Select Shiraz (South Eastern Australia) $10. 87 Best Buy *(12/1/1999)*

Barwang 1997 Winemaker's Reserve Shiraz (Coonawarra) $20. 88 —*S.H. (10/1/2000)*

Barwang 1996 Winemaker's Reserve Shiraz (Coonawarra) $25. 91 *(12/1/1999)*

Barwang 1996 Winemaker's Reserve Shiraz (New South Wales) $25. 91 *(12/1/1999)*

BASEDOW

Basedow 1999 Chardonnay (Barossa Valley) $18. 84 —*J.C. (7/1/2002)*

Basedow 1998 Shiraz (Barossa Valley) $20. 85 *(10/1/2001)*

Basedow 1996 Johannes Shiraz (Barossa Valley) $60. 83 —*D.T. (1/28/2003)*

BATTLE OF BOSWORTH

Battle of Bosworth 2002 Cabernet Sauvignon (McLaren Vale) $28. 90 —*D.T. (3/1/2005)*

Battle of Bosworth 2005 Shiraz (McLaren Vale) $30. This is a creamy-textured Shiraz with mouthfilling flavors of brown sugar, blackberries, vanilla and a hint of peppery spice. It falls off a bit on the finish and doesn't seem to offer much in terms of ageability, but it tastes pretty darn good right now. 88 —*J.C. (12/31/2007)*

Battle of Bosworth 2003 Shiraz (McLaren Vale) $28. 92 —*D.T. (2/1/2006)*

BECKETT'S FLAT

Beckett's Flat 2002 Cabernet Sauvignon-Shiraz (Margaret River) $22. 86 —*J.M. (4/3/2004)*

Beckett's Flat 2004 Kosher Cabernet Sauvignon-Shiraz (Margaret River) $19. This producer can be a bit inconsistent (the 2004 Shiraz was marred by a vinegary note), but his Cab-Shiraz blend offers coffee and red berry flavors, a smooth mouthfeel and a dusty, crisp finish. 85 —*J.C. (4/1/2007)*

Beckett's Flat 2006 Kosher Chardonnay (Margaret River) $16. Starts with mainly melon aromas, but there's also some peach and a hint of smokiness to add a bit of nuance. Round and soft in the mouth, with melon and citrus flavors. A slight nuttiness acts to diminish the overt fruit while adding a deeper bass note. Drink now. 83 —*J.C. (4/1/2007)*

Beckett's Flat 2002 Reserve Chardonnay (Margaret River) $22. 87 —*D.T. (10/1/2003)*

Beckett's Flat 2004 Reserve Kosher Chardonnay (Margaret River) $20. 84 —*D.T. (4/1/2006)*

Beckett's Flat 2003 Reserve Kosher Chardonnay (Margaret River) $18. 82 —*D.T. (12/1/2005)*

Beckett's Flat 2006 Cerise Kosher Rosé Blend (Margaret River) $16. Sweet and weighty, this marries cherry, strawberry and watermelon rind aromas with somewhat honeyed flavors. 82 —*J.C. (4/1/2007)*

Beckett's Flat 2004 Cerise Kosher Rosé Blend (Margaret River) $17. 86 —*D.T. (4/1/2006)*

Beckett's Flat 2002 Sauvignon Blanc-Semillon (Margaret River) $20. 80 —*J.M. (4/3/2004)*

Beckett's Flat 2006 Kosher Sauvignon Blanc-Semillon (Margaret River) $16. This 60-40 blend features bold scents of passion fruit and a hint of red berries on the nose, then tropical fruit and citrus flavors on the palate. It's a bit plump and soft, but attractive nonetheless. 85 —*J.C. (4/1/2007)*

Beckett's Flat 2003 Kosher Late Harvest Semillon (Margaret River) $16. 83 —*D.T. (8/1/2006)*

Beckett's Flat 2002 Late Harvest Semillon (Margaret River) $18. 83 —*D.T. (10/1/2003)*

Beckett's Flat 2001 Semillon-Sauvignon Blanc (Margaret River) $15. 84 —*D.T. (10/1/2003)*

Beckett's Flat 2004 Kosher Semillon-Sauvignon Blanc (Margaret River) $17. 86 —*D.T. (4/1/2006)*

Beckett's Flat 2002 Shiraz (Margaret River) $22. 87 —*J.M. (4/3/2004)*

Beckett's Flat 2001 Shiraz (Margaret River) $18. 87 —*M.S. (3/1/2003)*

Beckett's Flat 2000 Shiraz (Margaret River) $17. 86 *(10/1/2001)*

Beckett's Flat 2003 Kosher Shiraz (Margaret River) $20. 81 —*D.T. (4/1/2006)*

BELLARINE ESTATE

Bellarine Estate 2000 James Paddock Chardonnay (South Eastern Australia) $15. 88 —*J.C. (7/1/2002)*

Bellarine Estate 2000 Portarlington Ridge Merlot (South Eastern Australia) $14. 83 —*D.T. (1/1/2002)*

Bellarine Estate 1999 Shiraz (Bellarine Peninsula) $15. 81 *(10/1/2001)*

BELLVALE

Bellvale 2004 Pinot Noir (Gippsland) $30. Shows a bit of bricking to its color, along with woodsy aromas of sassafras and root beer. Seems prematurely mature, with dried fruit flavors and hints of earthy decay, but a silky-textured finish. Drink now. 83 —*J.C. (5/1/2007)*

BENJAMIN

Benjamin NV Museum Reserve Muscat (Victoria) $16. 95 —*S.H. (9/1/2002)*

Benjamin NV Museum Reserve Muscat (Victoria) $16. 91 —*L.W. (3/1/2000)*

Benjamin NV Tawny Port (South Eastern Australia) $10. 88 Best Buy *—L.W. (3/1/2000)*

Benjamin NV Museum Reserve Tokay (Victoria) $16. 92 *—L.W. (3/1/2000)*

BERRY'S BRIDGE

Berry's Bridge 2004 Shiraz (Pyrenees) $47. Successfully marries the lushly ripe character found on the nose—brandied black cherries and chocolate—with firm structure and brighter notes of juicy red raspberries, all framed by oak shadings of vanilla and toasted coconut. The long finish is mouthwatering, with just enough dusty tannin to suggest cellaring 3–4 years. Drink 2010–2020. 93 Cellar Selection *(11/15/2007)*

BETHANY

Bethany 2003 Chardonnay (Barossa) $23. 84 *—D.T. (4/1/2006)*

Bethany 2002 Chardonnay (Barossa) $26. 84 *—D.T. (10/1/2005)*

Bethany 2004 Riesling (Barossa) $25. 88 *—D.T. (4/1/2006)*

Bethany 2002 Shiraz (Barossa) $37. 81 *—D.T. (10/1/2005)*

BILLABONG

Billabong 1999 Merlot (South Eastern Australia) $8.81 *—J.F. (9/1/2001)*

Billabong 1999 Shiraz (South Eastern Australia) $8. 85 Best Buy *(10/1/2001)*

BIMBADGEN

Bimbadgen 2001 Proprietary Estate Chardonnay (Hunter Valley) $11. 83 *(7/2/2004)*

Bimbadgen 2001 Proprietary Grand Ridge Chardonnay (Hunter Valley) $10. 85 *(7/2/2004)*

Bimbadgen 2002 Grand Ridge Verdelho (Hunter Valley) $10. 85 *—D.T. (5/1/2004)*

BIRD IN HAND

Bird in Hand 2001 Cabernet Sauvignon (Adelaide Hills) $28. 88 *—D.T. (5/1/2004)*

Bird in Hand 2001 Nest Egg Cabernet Sauvignon (Adelaide Hills) $40. 89 *—D.T. (5/1/2004)*

Bird in Hand 2005 Merlot (Adelaide Hills) $26. If more Merlot tasted like this, maybe winegeeks would stop looking down their noses at it. This is a creamy, lush wine, filled with hints of mocha, vanilla, black cherry and plum that swirl together into a long, fruit-filled finish. Drink now. 90 Editors' Choice *—J.C. (5/1/2007)*

Bird in Hand 2001 Merlot (Adelaide Hills) $28. 83 *—D.T. (1/1/2002)*

Bird in Hand 2001 Two in the Bush Merlot-Cabernet Sauvignon (Adelaide Hills) $16. 88 *—D.T. (9/1/2004)*

Bird in Hand NV Joy Pinot Noir (Adelaide Hills) $70. 88 *—D.T. (12/31/2004)*

Bird in Hand NV Sparkling Pinot Noir (Adelaide Hills) $25. 84 *—D.T. (12/31/2004)*

Bird in Hand 2001 Sparkling Pinot Noir (Adelaide Hills) $22. 87 *—C.S. (12/1/2002)*

Bird in Hand 2006 Sauvignon Blanc (Adelaide Hills) $20. Difficult to warm up to, this wine starts off on the wrong foot by offering up onion or garlic aromas, then compounds that with ungiving flavors of hard melon. It's too bad, because the mouthfeel is suitably rich and oily in the style of an Austrian or Collio Sauvignon. 82 *—J.C. (6/1/2007)*

Bird in Hand 2006 Two in the Bush Semillon-Sauvignon Blanc (Adelaide Hills) $16. This blend of Semillon and Sauvignon Blanc is a clean, refreshing quaff. Filled with passion fruit and gooseberry notes, it's simple, fruity and goes down easy. 84 *—J.C. (3/1/2007)*

Bird in Hand 2000 Shiraz (Fleurieu Peninsula) $26. 87 *—M.S. (3/1/2003)*

BLACK CREEK

Black Creek 1998 Verdelho (Hunter Valley) $10. 82 *—M.M. (10/1/2000)*

BLACK OPAL

Black Opal 2000 Cabernet Sauvignon (South Eastern Australia) $11. 85 *—M.S. (12/15/2002)*

Black Opal 1999 Cabernet Sauvignon (South Eastern Australia) $11. 84 *—R.V. (11/15/2001)*

Black Opal 2005 Cabernet Sauvignon-Merlot (South Eastern Australia) $8. Light in body but with a slightly syrupy mouthfeel, this wine features modest cherry-berry flavors and a powerful herbal streak. Finishes tart and short. 81 *—J.C. (7/1/2007)*

Black Opal 2004 Cabernet Sauvignon-Merlot (South Eastern Australia) $8. Shows some rather rustic notes of coffee and leather, which serve to give it a bit of individuality at the price point. Almost sweet-seeming cassis fruit dominates, turning slightly herbal on the finish. 84 Best Buy *—J.C. (5/1/2007)*

Black Opal 2002 Cabernet Sauvignon-Merlot (South Eastern Australia) $8. 85 Best Buy *—D.T. (12/31/2004)*

Black Opal 2000 Cabernet Sauvignon-Merlot (South Eastern Australia) $11. 84 *—D.T. (6/1/2003)*

Black Opal 1998 Cabernet Sauvignon-Merlot (Barossa Valley) $16. 83 *—M.N. (6/1/2001)*

Black Opal 2005 Chardonnay (South Eastern Australia) $8. Plump and mouthfilling, this offering boasts slightly honeyed scents and broad, understated tropical fruit flavors. A bit soft and simple, but ably fills a useful commercial niche. Drink now. 84 Best Buy *—J.C. (3/1/2007)*

Black Opal 2004 Chardonnay (South Eastern Australia) $10. 85 Best Buy *—D.T. (5/1/2005)*

Black Opal 2003 Chardonnay (South Eastern Australia) $8. 83 *—D.T. (11/15/2004)*

Black Opal 2002 Chardonnay (South Eastern Australia) $14. 83 *(7/2/2004)*

Black Opal 2001 Chardonnay (South Eastern Australia) $11. 83 *—J.C. (7/1/2002)*

Black Opal 1998 Chardonnay (South Australia) $11. 83 *—L.W. (12/31/1999)*

Black Opal 2004 Shiraz (South Eastern Australia) $8. A surprisingly strong effort from this Foster's-stable value brand, this ultrasoft, creamy-textured Shiraz combines scents of cassis with flavors that gradually turn redder and slightly rhubarby, moving through cherry to end crisp and cranberryish. Dustings of spice and cocoa keep it from being too simply fruity. Drink now. 86 Best Buy *—J.C. (2/1/2007)*

Black Opal 2003 Shiraz (South Eastern Australia) $10. 82 *—D.T. (12/31/2005)*

Black Opal 2001 Shiraz (South Eastern Australia) $12. 84 *—D.T. (12/31/2003)*

Black Opal 2000 Shiraz (South Eastern Australia) $11. 87 Best Buy *—M.S. (3/1/2003)*

Black Opal 1999 Shiraz (South Eastern Australia) $11. 83 *(10/1/2001)*

Black Opal 1996 Shiraz (Barossa Valley) $16. 84 *—L.W. (12/31/1999)*

Black Opal 2005 Shiraz-Cabernet Sauvignon (South Eastern Australia) $8. 83 *—D.T. (11/15/2006)*

Black Opal 2001 Shiraz-Cabernet Sauvignon (South Eastern Australia) $12. 82 *—D.T. (1/1/2002)*

BLACK SWAN

Black Swan 2002 Cabernet Sauvignon (South Eastern Australia) $8. 82 *—D.T. (1/1/2002)*

Black Swan 2006 Chardonnay (South Eastern Australia) $8. Smells better than it tastes, with attractive scents of grilled peaches and buttered tropical fruit. But the flavors are of scorched popcorn, finishing short and slightly acrid. 81 *—J.C. (8/1/2007)*

Black Swan 2003 Chardonnay (South Eastern Australia) $8. 84 *(7/2/2004)*

Black Swan 2003 Chardonnay (South Eastern Australia) $8. 83 *—D.T. (11/15/2004)*

Black Swan 2002 Chardonnay (South Eastern Australia) $8. 85 *—D.T. (8/1/2003)*

Black Swan 2003 Merlot (South Eastern Australia) $8. 85 Best Buy *—D.T. (12/31/2004)*

Black Swan 2004 Shiraz-Merlot Red Blend (South Eastern Australia) $9. 82 *—D.T. (10/1/2005)*

Black Swan 2002 Shiraz (South Eastern Australia) $8. 83 *—D.T. (1/1/2002)*

Black Swan 2004 Shiraz-Cabernet Sauvignon (South Eastern Australia) $9. 83 *—D.T. (10/1/2005)*

Black Swan 2003 Chardonnay & Semillon White Blend (South Eastern Australia) $9. 84 *—D.T. (11/15/2004)*

BLACKBILLY

Blackbilly 2006 Pinot Gris (Fleurieu Peninsula) $15. Features melon and red berry fruit, touched by a hint of herbaceousness. Weighty, but balanced by tart, citrusy acids. 88 *—J.C. (6/1/2007)*

BLEASDALE

Bleasdale 2003 Mulberry Tree Cabernet Sauvignon (Langhorne Creek) $19. Smoky and caramelly at first, but there are also plenty of tart cherries and some herbal notes. Smooth enough in the mouth, this medium-bodied Cab finishes with dark chocolate flavors framing tangy cherry fruit. Drink now–2012. 85 *—J.C. (2/1/2007)*

Bleasdale 2000 Mulberry Tree Cabernet Sauvignon (Langhorne Creek) $16. 87 *—J.C. (6/1/2002)*

Bleasdale 1999 Cabernet Sauvignon-Shiraz (Langhorne Creek) $12. 86 *—J.C. (9/1/2002)*

Bleasdale 1999 Bremerview Shiraz (Langhorne Creek) $15. 89 Best Buy *(10/1/2001)*

Bleasdale 2003 Shiraz-Cabernet Sauvignon (Langhorne Creek) $16. This 50-50 blend—actuallly it's 51-49—features crisp berry fruit and modest cedar accents. Medium-bodied with a creamy texture, it finishes tart and cranberryish. Drink now. 85 *—J.C. (2/1/2007)*

BLUE MARLIN

Blue Marlin 2004 Chardonnay (South Eastern Australia) $10. 83 *—D.T. (10/1/2005)*

BLUE PYRENEES

Blue Pyrenees 1999 Cabernet Sauvignon (Victoria) $15. 82 *—M.S. (12/15/2002)*

Blue Pyrenees 2004 Chardonnay (Pyrenees) $16. 88 *—D.T. (6/1/2006)*

Blue Pyrenees 2001 Chardonnay (Victoria) $NA. 81 *—D.T. (8/1/2003)*

Blue Pyrenees 1999 Estate Reserve Chardonnay (Victoria) $20. 87 *—J.C. (7/1/2002)*

Blue Pyrenees 2000 Shiraz (Pyrenees) $16. 89 *—D.T. (6/1/2006)*

Blue Pyrenees 1999 Shiraz (Victoria) $15. 87 Editors' Choice *(10/1/2001)*

Blue Pyrenees 1999 Estate Reserve Shiraz (Victoria) $20. 85 *—J.C. (9/1/2002)*

BLUE TONGUE

Blue Tongue 2004 Chardonnay (South Eastern Australia) $10. 83 *—D.T. (8/1/2006)*

Blue Tongue 2002 Chardonnay (South Eastern Australia) $7. 84 *—D.T. (8/1/2003)*

Blue Tongue 2004 Shiraz (South Eastern Australia) $9. 83 *—D.T. (6/1/2006)*

Blue Tongue 2002 Shiraz (South Eastern Australia) $7. 83 *—D.T. (1/1/2002)*

BOGGY CREEK

Boggy Creek 2003 Cabernet Sauvignon (King Valley) $15. 87 *—D.T. (6/1/2006)*

Boggy Creek 2004 Chardonnay (King Valley) $19. 86 *—D.T. (4/1/2006)*

Boggy Creek 2004 Unwooded Chardonnay (King Valley) $15. 88 *—D.T. (4/1/2006)*

Boggy Creek 2003 Shiraz (King Valley) $21. 87 *—D.T. (4/1/2006)*

BOOKPURNONG HILL

Bookpurnong Hill 1999 Cabernet Sauvignon (Riverland) $40. 87 *—D.T. (9/1/2001)*

Bookpurnong Hill 1999 Petite Verdot (South Eastern Australia) $40. 85 *—D.T. (9/1/2001)*

Bookpurnong Hill 1999 Block 267 Rhône Red Blend (Riverland) $40. 84 *—D.T. (9/1/2001)*

Bookpurnong Hill 1999 Shiraz (Riverland) $43. 87 *(11/1/2001)*

BOOLAROO

Boolaroo 2003 Chardonnay (Victoria) $14. 86 *—D.T. (8/1/2005)*

BOUTÍQUE WILDFLOWER

Boutíque Wildflower 2003 Chardonnay (South Eastern Australia) $11. 84 *—D.T. (6/1/2006)*

BOUTIQUE WINES

Boutique Wines 1998 The Region Chardonnay (Adelaide Hills) $22. 88 *(6/1/2001)*

BOWEN ESTATE

Bowen Estate 2003 Shiraz (Coonawarra) $27. 89 *—D.T. (6/1/2006)*

BOX STALLION

Box Stallion 2001 Red Barn Chardonnay (Mornington Peninsula) $20. 84 *—D.T. (5/1/2005)*

Box Stallion 2001 The Enclosure Chardonnay (Mornington Peninsula) $30. 82 *—D.T. (5/1/2005)*

BRANSON COACH HOUSE

Branson Coach House 2004 Greenock Coach House Block Cabernet Sauvignon (Barossa Valley) $105. 91 *—D.T. (11/15/2006)*

Branson Coach House 2002 Rare Single Vineyard Coach House Block Shiraz (Barossa Valley) $75. 93 *—D.T. (12/31/2004)*

Branson Coach House 2002 Single Vineyard Greenock Block Shiraz (Barossa Valley) $45. 91 *—D.T. (12/31/2004)*

BREMERTON

Bremerton 1999 Tamblyn Rhône Red Blend (Langhorne Creek) $20. 84 *—D.T. (6/1/2002)*

Bremerton 2000 Sauvignon Blanc (Langhorne Creek) $17. 81 *—J.F. (9/1/2001)*

Bremerton 2006 Matilda Plains Sauvignon Blanc (Langhorne Creek) $14. This light- to medium-bodied wine avoids the vegetal side of Sauvignon Blanc, instead offering scents of green apple and lime, maybe a hint of pineapple. The texture is crystalline and hard, adding bright passion fruit flavors and a tart, citrusy finish. Drink now. 86 *—J.C. (6/1/2007)*

Bremerton 2000 Selkirk Shiraz (Langhorne Creek) $18. 85 *—K.F. (3/1/2003)*

Bremerton 1999 Young Vine Shiraz (Langhorne Creek) $20. 86 *(10/1/2001)*

BRICK ROAD

Brick Road 2004 Shiraz (McLaren Vale) $20. An excellent wine at an excellent price, this Shiraz combines complex scents of underbrush and spice with bright cherry aromas, then adds richness and weight on the palate. The long, concentrated finish picks up hints of warm dark chocolate. 90 Editors' Choice *—J.C. (2/1/2007)*

BROKEN EARTH

Broken Earth 2004 Chardonnay (South Eastern Australia) $8. 84 Best Buy *—D.T. (8/1/2006)*

Broken Earth 2004 Shiraz (South Eastern Australia) $8. 81 *—D.T. (10/1/2006)*

BROKENWOOD

Brokenwood 2002 Cricket Pitch Cabernet Blend (McLaren Vale & Padthaway) $17. 90 *—D.T. (8/1/2005)*

Brokenwood 2004 Cricket Pitch Sauvignon Blanc-Semillon (South Eastern Australia) $16. A portion of this wine was fermented in barrel, and it shows, but what also shows is the high level of ripeness attained by at least some of the grapes. The aromas highlight exotic scents of honey and apricots, marked by traces of smoke and toast. It's surprisingly full-bodied for an Australian blend of these two grape varieties, but could use a touch more length on the finish to really shine. 86 *—J.C. (3/1/2007)*

Brokenwood 2004 Semillon (Hunter Valley) $22. 87 *—D.T. (8/1/2005)*

Brokenwood 2001 Semillon (Hunter Valley) $17. 87 *—J.C. (2/1/2002)*

Brokenwood 2002 Graveyard Vineyard Shiraz (Hunter Valley) $100. 95 *—D.T. (8/1/2005)*

Brokenwood 1999 Graveyard Vineyard Shiraz (Hunter Valley) $69. 88 *(11/1/2001)*

Brokenwood 2002 Rayner Vineyard Shiraz (McLaren Vale) $70. 88 *—D.T. (10/1/2005)*

Brokenwood 2002 Wade Block 2 Shiraz (McLaren Vale) $46. 89 *—D.T. (10/1/2005)*

Brokenwood 2001 Wade Block 2 Vineyard Selection Shiraz (McLaren Vale) $37. 86 *—D.T. (5/1/2004)*

BROOKLAND VALLEY

Brookland Valley 1999 Cabernet Sauvignon-Merlot (Margaret River) $27. 87 *—D.T. (10/1/2003)*

Brookland Valley 2000 Estate Cabernet Sauvignon-Merlot (Margaret River) $33. 90 *—D.T. (9/1/2004)*

Brookland Valley 2002 Verse 1 Cabernet Sauvignon-Merlot (Margaret River) $15. 85 *—D.T. (12/1/2005)*

Brookland Valley 2002 Verse 1 Cabernet Sauvignon-Merlot (Margaret River) $15. 87 *—D.T. (6/1/2006)*

Brookland Valley 2002 Chardonnay (Margaret River) $27. 86 *—D.T. (5/1/2005)*

Brookland Valley 2001 Estate Chardonnay (Margaret River) $27. 88 *(7/2/2004)*

Brookland Valley 2002 Verse 1 Chardonnay (Margaret River) $16. 84 *(1/1/2004)*

Brookland Valley 2001 Verse 1 Chardonnay (Margaret River) $20. 84 *—D.T. (10/1/2003)*

Brookland Valley 2004 Verse 1 Semillon-Sauvignon Blanc (Margaret River) $16. 88 *—D.T. (10/1/2005)*

Brookland Valley 2002 Verse 1 Semillon-Sauvignon Blanc (Margaret River) $16. 85 *—D.T. (10/1/2003)*

Brookland Valley 2001 Verse 1 Shiraz (Margaret River) $18. 87 *—M.S. (3/1/2003)*

BROWN BROTHERS

Brown Brothers 2001 Estate Bottled Cabernet Sauvignon (Victoria) $13. 84 *—D.T. (12/31/2003)*

Brown Brothers 2000 Patricia Reserve Cabernet Sauvignon (Victoria) $30. 88 *(8/1/2004)*

Brown Brothers 2003 Chardonnay (Victoria) $13. 86 *—D.T. (10/1/2005)*

Brown Brothers 2001 Estate Bottled Chardonnay (Victoria) $11. 84 *—D.T. (12/31/2003)*

Brown Brothers 2001 Patricia Reserve Chardonnay (Victoria) $28. 88 *(8/1/2004)*

Brown Brothers 2000 Patricia Reserve Merlot (Victoria) $30. 87 *(8/1/2004)*

Brown Brothers 1999 Patricia Late Harvested Noble Riesling (Australia) $33. 91 *(8/1/2004)*

Brown Brothers 2000 Patricia Reserve Shiraz (Victoria) $33. 88 *(8/1/2004)*

BROWNS OF PADTHAWAY

Browns of Padthaway 2002 Estate Grown Verdelho (Padthaway) $13. 86 *—D.T. (11/15/2004)*

BRUMBY CANYON

Brumby Canyon 2002 Jillaroo Red Red Blend (South Australia) $14. 87 *—D.T. (12/31/2004)*

BUCKELEY'S

Buckeley's 2002 Cabernet Sauvignon-Shiraz (South Australia) $10. 88 Best Buy *—S.H. (10/1/2003)*

Buckeley's 1999 Chardonnay (South Australia) $10. 84 *—M.S. (10/1/2000)*

Buckeley's 2002 Chardonnay (South Australia) $10. 89 Best Buy *—S.H. (10/1/2003)*

Buckeley's 2001 Chardonnay (South Australia) $10. 85 *—J.C. (7/1/2002)*

Buckeley's 2000 Chardonnay (South Australia) $10. 84 *—J.C. (1/1/2004)*

Buckeley's 2002 Merlot (South Australia) $10. 85 *—S.H. (10/1/2003)*

Buckeley's 2002 Sauvignon Blanc (Currency Creek) $10. 84 *—D.T. (11/15/2004)*

Buckeley's 2001 Shiraz (South Australia) $12. 85 *—S.H. (10/1/2003)*

Buckeley's 2000 Shiraz (South Australia) $10. 81 *(10/1/2001)*

BULLETIN PLACE

Bulletin Place 2006 Cabernet Sauvignon (South Eastern Australia) $8. The Bulletin Place reds tend to be on the lighter-bodied side of things, and this Cabernet is clean, crisp and cool, with herbal and eucalyptus shadings to its cherry fruit. 83 *—J.C. (11/15/2007)*

Bulletin Place 2005 Cabernet Sauvignon (South Eastern Australia) $8. Starts off a bit brambly and herbal, but the fruit is spicy and fresh, showing some supple tannins on the midpalate. Cherry flavors pick up a minty herbaceousness on the finish that would make this wine work well with lamb. Drink now. 85 Best Buy *—J.C. (2/1/2007)*

Bulletin Place 2004 Cabernet Sauvignon (South Eastern Australia) $9. 85 Best Buy *—D.T. (11/15/2006)*

Bulletin Place 1999 Cabernet Sauvignon (South Eastern Australia) $10. 83 *—C.S. (6/1/2002)*

Bulletin Place 2005 Chardonnay (South Eastern Australia) $8. 84 Best Buy *—D.T. (11/15/2006)*

Bulletin Place 2004 Chardonnay (South Eastern Australia) $8. 87 Best Buy *—D.T. (12/31/2004)*

Bulletin Place 2001 Chardonnay (South Eastern Australia) $8. 85 *—D.T. (11/15/2003)*

Bulletin Place 1999 Chardonnay (South Eastern Australia) $8. 85 *—M.N. (6/1/2001)*

Bulletin Place 2002 Merlot (South Eastern Australia) $10. 83 *—D.T. (1/1/2002)*

Bulletin Place 2005 Shiraz (South Eastern Australia) $8. Rather light in body for Shiraz, with clean cherry-berry flavors that turn crisp and fresh on the finish. 83 *—J.C. (3/1/2007)*

Bulletin Place 2003 Shiraz (South Eastern Australia) $8. 84 Best Buy *—D.T. (5/1/2005)*

Bulletin Place 2000 Shiraz (South Eastern Australia) $10. 86 *—K.F. (3/1/2003)*

Bulletin Place 1999 Shiraz (South Eastern Australia) $10. 84 *—M.N. (10/1/2001)*

Bulletin Place 1998 Shiraz (South Australia) $10. 85 *(10/1/2000)*

BUNDALEER

Bundaleer 2002 Shiraz (Heathcote) $40. 91 *—D.T. (12/31/2004)*

BURTON

Burton 1999 Cabernet Sauvignon (Coonawarra) $27. 85 *—D.T. (6/1/2003)*

Burton 1998 Reserve Cabernet Sauvignon (Coonawarra) $40. 86 *—D.T. (6/1/2003)*

Burton 2000 Cabernet Sauvignon-Merlot (South Eastern Australia) $16. 88 *—D.T. (8/1/2003)*

BUSH BIKE

Bush Bike 2004 Chardonnay (Western Australia) $14. 86 *—D.T. (12/1/2005)*

Bush Bike 2003 Merlot-Shiraz (Western Australia) $14. 87 *—D.T. (2/1/2006)*

Bush Bike 2004 Riesling (Western Australia) $14. 83 *—D.T. (12/1/2005)*

Bush Bike 2003 Shiraz (Western Australia) $14. 83 *—D.T. (12/31/2005)*

CALEDONIA AUSTRALIS

Caledonia Australis 2001 Chardonnay (Gippsland) $30. 85 *—D.T. (8/1/2005)*

Caledonia Australis 2003 Mount Macleod Chardonnay (Gippsland) $17. 88 *—D.T. (8/1/2005)*

Caledonia Australis 2003 Pinot Noir (Gippsland) $26. 86 *—D.T. (10/1/2005)*

Caledonia Australis 2003 Mount Macleod Pinot Noir (Gippsland) $17. 89 Editors' Choice *—D.T. (12/31/2005)*

CALLAHAN

Callahan 1998 Shiraz (South Eastern Australia) $11. 88 Best Buy *(10/1/2001)*

Callahan Hill 2000 Shiraz (South Eastern Australia) $9. 87 Best Buy *(10/1/2001)*

CALLARA ESTATE

Callara Estate 2000 Reserve Bin Shiraz (South Eastern Australia) $8. 86 Best Buy *(10/1/2001)*

CAMELBACK

Camelback 2003 Rockbank Vineyard Cabernet Sauvignon-Merlot (Victoria) $19. Creamy and soft, this blend of 795 Cabernet and 21% Merlot boasts cherry and cassis aromas and flavors that feature hints of eucalyptus and coffee. Drink now. 87 *—J.C. (2/1/2007)*

Camelback 2005 Rockbank Vineyard Chardonnay (Victoria) $17. Smoky and nutty on the nose, this will hook fans of oaky Chardonnay. Citrus and acacia blossom notes add nuance to this medium-bodied Chardonnay; it's a bit dominated by oak but seems to have the material to support it—at least in the short term. Drink now. 87 *—J.C. (3/1/2007)*

CAMPBELLS

Campbells 1995 The Barkly Durif (Rutherglen) $30. 86 *—D.T. (6/1/2003)*

Campbells 1993 The Barkly Durif (Rutherglen) $30. 84 *—J.C. (9/1/2002)*

Campbells NV Muscat (Rutherglen) $19. Delicately floral on the nose, this sweet but wonderfully balanced Muscat offers a fine introduction to the Rutherglen Muscat style. Pineapple, raisin and spice flavors persist a good long time, trailing elegantly away on the finish. 91 Editors' Choice *—J.C. (12/15/2007)*

Campbells NV Muscat (Rutherglen) $17. 87 *—D.T. (12/31/2004)*

Campbells NV Merchant Prince Rare Muscat (Rutherglen) $85. This wine has the rich hue of dark coffee in the glass, greening a bit at the rim. Aromas and flavors of Guinness stout, raisin and coffee fully saturate the senses, picking up hints of spicecake on the enormously long finish. Incredibly sweet, yet it's still drinkable. 97 Editors' Choice *—J.C. (12/15/2007)*

Campbells NV Rutherglen Muscat (Rutherglen) $10. 94 Editors' Choice *—J.M. (12/1/2002)*

Campbells 1998 Bobbie Burns Shiraz (Rutherglen) $20. 83 *—J.C. (9/1/2002)*

Campbells NV Tokay (Rutherglen) $19. For a fortified wine with a light amber hue, this is wonderfully fresh and citrusy, with aromas and flavors of marmalade and bergamot. Honeyed, toffee-like notes add depth, with the richness of the wine brought home by the slightly viscous finish. 89 *—J.C. (12/15/2007)*

Campbells NV Tokay (Rutherglen) $17. 88 *—D.T. (12/31/2004)*

Campbells NV Isabella Rare Tokay (Rutherglen) $85. Campbells utilizes a modified solera system, so small portions of this blend are 60 or more years of age, imparting an incredibly elegant note of rancio. Luscious raisins and toffee bring intensely concentrated, sweet flavors, impeccably balanced. This is not in the immense blockbuster style, instead showing great harmony and purity, with all its pieces in nearly perfect proportion. 97 Editors' Choice *—J.C. (12/15/2007)*

CANONBAH BRIDGE

Canonbah Bridge 1999 Vintage Reserve Champagne Blend (Victoria) $20. 85 *—D.T. (12/31/2004)*

Canonbah Bridge 2002 Rams Leap Chardonnay (New South Wales) $12. 83 *(7/2/2004)*

Canonbah Bridge 2002 Ram's Leap Merlot (Western Plains) $12. 86 *—D.T. (9/1/2004)*

Canonbah Bridge 2000 Ram's Leap Semillon-Sauvignon Blanc (New South Wales) $10. 84 *—D.T. (12/31/2003)*

Canonbah Bridge 2002 Drought Reserve Shiraz (Western Plains) $30. 84 *—D.T. (10/1/2006)*

Canonbah Bridge 2000 Ram's Leap Shiraz (New South Wales) $10. 84 *—D.T. (12/31/2003)*

Canonbah Bridge 2002 Rams Leap Shiraz (Mudgee) $12. 81 *—D.T. (11/15/2004)*

CAPE CLAIRAULT

Cape Clairault 1996 The Clairault Reserve Red Bordeaux Blend (Margaret River) $35. 92 *—M.S. (10/1/2000)*

CAPE JAFFA

Cape Jaffa 1999 Shiraz (Limestone Coast) $18. 84 *(10/1/2001)*

CAPE MENTELLE

Cape Mentelle 1999 Cabernet Sauvignon (Margaret River) $42. 88 *—D.T. (10/1/2003)*

Cape Mentelle 2001 Cabernet Sauvignon (Margaret River) $40. 91 *(12/15/2005)*

Cape Mentelle 2002 Cabernet Sauvignon-Merlot (Margaret River) $19. 86 *—D.T. (12/31/2004)*

Cape Mentelle 2003 Trinders Cabernet Sauvignon-Merlot (Margaret River) $16. 87 *(12/15/2005)*

Cape Mentelle 2001 Trinders Cabernet Sauvignon-Merlot (Margaret River) $18. 90 Editors' Choice *—D.T. (10/1/2003)*

Cape Mentelle 2003 Chardonnay (Margaret River) $26. 90 Editors' Choice *(12/15/2005)*

Cape Mentelle 2002 Chardonnay (Margaret River) $25. 87 *(7/2/2004)*

Cape Mentelle 2001 Chardonnay (Margaret River) $25. 86 *—D.T. (10/1/2003)*

Cape Mentelle 2006 Sauvignon Blanc-Semillon (Margaret River) $16. This 60-40 blend reveals a bit of herbal grassiness and yellow plum in its bouquet, then adds melon flavors that flesh out the palate. It's an attractive, medium-weight wine that finishes a little short and soft. Drink now. 85 *—J.C. (5/1/2007)*

Cape Mentelle 2005 Sauvignon Blanc-Semillon (Margaret River) $13. 88 Best Buy *(12/15/2005)*

Cape Mentelle 2003 Sauvignon Blanc-Semillon (Margaret River) $19. 89 *—D.T. (9/1/2004)*

Cape Mentelle 2004 Shiraz (Margaret River) $24. This is a complex, dark-fruited wine that merits serious attention from consumers looking for a slightly different style of Australian Shiraz. Cedar and dark chocolate scents frame slightly herbal nuances, blackberry fruit and hints of leather and tree bark. The texture is ultrasmooth and silky, leading easily into a long, earthy finish. Drink now–2015. 90 *—J.C. (4/1/2007)*

Cape Mentelle 2003 Shiraz (Western Australia) $23. 90 Editors' Choice *(12/15/2005)*

Cape Mentelle 2002 Shiraz (Margaret River) $19. 89 *—D.T. (11/15/2004)*

Cape Mentelle 2001 Shiraz (Margaret River) $19. 88 *—D.T. (10/1/2003)*

Cape Mentelle 1999 Shiraz (Margaret River) $19. 88 *(10/1/2001)*

CARLEI

Carlei 2002 Green Vineyards Shiraz (Heathcote) $31. 87 *—D.T. (12/31/2005)*

CARRAMAR ESTATE

Carramar Estate 1999 Chardonnay (South Eastern Australia) $9. 82 *—J.C. (9/10/2002)*

Carramar Estate 1999 Merlot (South Eastern Australia) $9. 83 *—D.T. (6/1/2002)*

Carramar Estate 2000 Shiraz (South Eastern Australia) $9. 83 *(10/1/2001)*

CASCABEL

Cascabel 1999 Shiraz (Fleurieu Peninsula) $19. 84 *(10/1/2001)*

CEDAR CREEK

Cedar Creek 1999 Shiraz (South Eastern Australia) $13. 81 *(10/1/2001)*

CHAIN OF PONDS

Chain of Ponds 1998 Ledge Shiraz (Adelaide Hills) $36. 88 *(11/1/2001)*

CHALICE BRIDGE

Chalice Bridge 1999 Cabernet Sauvignon (Margaret River) $20. 89 *—M.S. (12/15/2002)*

Chalice Bridge 2003 Cabernet Sauvignon-Shiraz (Margaret River) $16. 87 *—D.T. (8/1/2005)*

Chalice Bridge 2003 Chardonnay (Margaret River) $16. 81 *—D.T. (10/1/2005)*

Chalice Bridge 2001 Chardonnay (Western Australia) $16. 85 *—D.T. (8/1/2003)*

CHAMBERS ROSEWOOD VINEYARDS

Chambers Rosewood Vineyards NV Muscat (Rutherglen) $15. Medium amber in color, this Muscat boasts scents of berries, pineapple and raisin to go with flavors of honey and spice. It's a lush, sweet style, with less complexity than some, but great texture and length. 89 *—J.C. (12/15/2007)*

Chambers Rosewood Vineyards NV Grand Muscat (Rutherglen) $100. Coffee-colored, with enticing scents of orange drizzled with dark maple syrup, coffee and raisins. Sweet, upfront and lushly textured, this is an easy-to-appreciate Muscat with great length. 92 *—J.C. (12/15/2007)*

Chambers Rosewood Vineyards NV Rare Muscat (Rutherglen) $300. This Muscat is the color of dark coffee, with a greenish inflection at the rim, showing the high average age of the blend. It is incredibly rich and sweet—it pretty much oozes across the palate with intense flavors of molasses and dried dates before finishing long, long, long. A wine you can still taste minutes after spitting or swallowing. 95 *—J.C. (12/15/2007)*

Chambers Rosewood Vineyards NV Grand Muscadelle Tokay (Rutherglen) $140. Dark amber in color, with some greening evident at the rim, this Tokay features aromas of scorched coffee and Guinness stout-like flavors, but is also sweet, with hints of molasses and raisins. It's a solid effort, representative of its classification. 91 *—J.C. (12/15/2007)*

Chambers Rosewood Vineyards NV Muscadelle Tokay (Rutherglen) $15. Made mistelle fashion, with fortification taking place prior to fermentation to help preserve the variety's citrus and tea-leaf aromas and flavors. Honeyed orange and lemon flavors take on a leafy edge, showing a hint of bitterness on the finish. 86 *—J.C. (12/15/2007)*

Chambers Rosewood Vineyards NV Rare Muscadelle Tokay (Rutherglen) $300. Befitting its age, this wine is dark coffee in color, changing to greenish at the rim. Flavors are malty and molasses-like, accented by scents of burnt coffee and sugar. This is broad, mouthcoating and sweet—an authoritative expression of Rutherglen Rare Tokay. 93 *—J.C. (12/15/2007)*

CHAPEL HILL

Chapel Hill 2005 Cabernet Sauvignon (McLaren Vale) $18. A well-made, well-balanced Cabernet Sauvignon, with smoke and vanilla notes that play up the jammy blackberry fruit. Finishes with hints of dried spices and coffee, as well as some furry-textured tannins. This wine starts off with some tarry aromas that seem to dissapate with airing, so a quick decanting may help this wine at the table. Drink now–2015. 88 *—J.C. (5/1/2007)*

Chapel Hill 2000 Cabernet Sauvignon (South Eastern Australia) $25. 82 *—D.T. (9/1/2004)*

Chapel Hill 2005 Unwooded Chardonnay (McLaren Vale) $15. Frankly fruit-driven, with bold aromas of melon and pear tinged with butter. Slightly honeyed fruit is gradually overtaken by spicy, peppery elements on the finish, but this is plump and fresh, a reasonably fair value in Australian Chardonnay. 87 *—J.C. (2/1/2007)*

Chapel Hill 2002 Unwooded Chardonnay (South Australia) $15. 85 *(7/2/2004)*

Chapel Hill 2004 Shiraz (McLaren Vale) $18. An interesting contrast to the majority of Australian Shiraz, Chapel Hill's 2004 boasts crisp acidity and a juicy, lipsmacking finish. Dollops of vanilla and caramel highlight bright berry flavors. Drink now–2012. 88 *—J.C. (2/1/2007)*

Chapel Hill 2005 The Prophet Shiraz (McLaren Vale) $30. This is a big, loud Shiraz, bursting with blackberry fruit and scents of cola, vanilla and toast. The flavors favor blackberries but also blend in hints of fruitcake and spice that easily conceal its 14.9% alcohol. Long and lush on the finish, this is delicious now but should also hold at least five years. 91 Editors' Choice —*J.C. (12/31/2007)*

Chapel Hill 2004 Shiraz-Grenache (McLaren Vale) $15. At 85% Shiraz, why not just call it that? Marketing aside, this is a good, workaday wine, with somewhat generic cherry-berry flavors and helpings of coffee and tobacco. The texture in the mouth is smooth and creamy, while the finish turns crisp and mouthwatering. Drink now. 86 —*J.C. (2/1/2007)*

CHARLES CIMICKY

Charles Cimicky 1997 The Red Blend Bordeaux Blend (Barossa Valley) $30. 91 —*M.S. (3/1/2000)*

Charles Cimicky 2005 Trumps Grenache-Shiraz (Barossa Valley) $18. A blend of 65% Grenache and 35% Shiraz, this is a lush, easy-to-drink wine meant for early consumption. The blend brings stone fruit and cherries, underscored by spice cake and chocolate, with hints of espresso and cola on the finish. 89 —*J.C. (11/1/2007)*

Charles Cimicky 2005 The Autograph Shiraz (Barossa) $NA. With its bright acidity, Cimicky's 2005 Autograph stands out a bit from the pack of Barossa Shiraz. Blueberry-blackberry fruit and peppery spice is underlined by vibrant acids, which give this wine a more reined-in feel than many of its counterparts. Despite supple tannins, it comes across as firm on the finish, where it picks up hints of caramel or maple syrup. 90 —*J.C. (11/1/2007)*

Charles Cimicky 2004 The Autograph Shiraz (Barossa Valley) $45. Gorgeously expressive, with mixed berry fruit that runs the gamut from mulberries to blueberries and blackberries, but also hints of coffee, black olive and a big whack of vanilla-scented oak. Full-bodied, lush and creamy, with a velvety finish, this should drink well now and over the next 10 years or more. 92 —*J.C. (11/1/2007)*

Charles Cimicky 1999 Daylight Chamber Shiraz (Barossa Valley) $19. 88 *(10/1/2001)*

Charles Cimicky 1998 Reserve Shiraz (Barossa Valley) $40. 90 *(6/1/2001)*

Charles Cimicky 1998 Signature Shiraz (Barossa Valley) $30. 89 *(11/1/2001)*

Charles Cimicky 1997 Signature Shiraz (Barossa Valley) $30. 92 *(3/1/2000)*

CHARLES MELTON

Charles Melton 2002 Cabernet Sauvignon (Barossa Valley) $35. 90 —*D.T. (4/1/2006)*

Charles Melton 2001 Cabernet Sauvignon (Barossa Valley) $44. 91 —*D.T. (2/1/2004)*

Charles Melton 2000 Cabernet Sauvignon-Shiraz (Barossa Valley) $44. 84 —*D.T. (12/31/2003)*

Charles Melton 2000 Grenache (Barossa Valley) $37. 87 —*D.T. (9/1/2004)*

Charles Melton 2004 Nine Popes Rhône Red Blend (Barossa Valley) $50. Shows the wonderfully silky side of Grenache—the main part of the blend—in its diaphanous, delicate texture that manages to be soft but not too soft, beautifully framing flavors of cherries, spice and cola. Long on the finish, trailing away slowly and elegantly. Drink now–2015. 93 —*J.C. (11/1/2007)*

Charles Melton 2002 Nine Popes Red Blend (Barossa Valley) $37. 85 —*D.T. (10/1/2005)*

Charles Melton 2001 Nine Popes Red Blend (Barossa Valley) $39. 90 —*D.T. (2/1/2004)*

Charles Melton 1999 Nine Popes Red Blend (Barossa Valley) $39. 89 —*D.T. (2/1/2004)*

Charles Melton 2005 Rosé Blend (Barossa Valley) $15. 91 Best Buy —*D.T. (6/21/2006)*

Charles Melton 2004 Rosé Blend (Barossa Valley) $16. 89 —*D.T. (12/31/2004)*

Charles Melton 2003 Rosé Blend (Barossa Valley) $18. 90 Editors' Choice —*D.T. (9/1/2004)*

Charles Melton 2007 Rosé of Virginia Rosé Blend (Barossa Valley) $23. Bold strawberry and cherry flavors come across as just a tiny bit sweet—and there is 8 g/L of residual sugar in this wine. But despite a slightly confected quality, this effusive, berry-flavored blend of Grenache, Cabernet Sauvignon, Shiraz and Pinot Meunier finishes clean and refreshing. Not meant for aging; drink until the next vintage becomes available. 89 —*J.C. (12/31/2007)*

Charles Melton 2003 Rose of Virginia Rosé Blend (Barossa Valley) $15. 88 —*D.T. (2/1/2004)*

Charles Melton 2004 Shiraz (Barossa Valley) $40. Rich and chocolaty, yet also bursting with berry fruit. There's plenty of spice, too, making this a complete package. Supple tannins impart a creamy texture, while the finish picks up a hint of tea leaf. Drink now–2015. 91 —*J.C. (11/1/2007)*

Charles Melton 2002 Shiraz (Barossa Valley) $35. 87 —*D.T. (4/1/2006)*

Charles Melton 2001 Shiraz (Barossa Valley) $39. 90 —*D.T. (2/1/2004)*

Charles Melton 2000 Shiraz (Barossa Valley) $39. 91 —*D.T. (2/1/2004)*

Charles Melton 2000 Laura Shiraz (Barossa Valley) $39. 89 —*D.T. (5/1/2004)*

Charles Melton 2003 The Father in Law Shiraz (South Australia) $18. 89 —*D.T. (8/1/2006)*

Charles Melton NV Sparkling Red Sparkling Blend (Barossa) $60. 88 —*J.C. (12/31/2006)*

CHATEAU REYNELLA

Chateau Reynella 2002 Cabernet Sauvignon (McLaren Vale) $NA. 88 —*D.T. (3/1/2005)*

Chateau Reynella 1996 Basket Pressed Cabernet Sauvignon-Merlot (McLaren Vale) $24. 88 —*M.S. (4/1/2000)*

Chateau Reynella 2002 Chardonnay (McLaren Vale) $14. 87 —*D.T. (12/1/2005)*

Chateau Reynella 2001 Chardonnay (McLaren Vale) $15. 84 —*D.T. (8/1/2003)*

Chateau Reynella 1999 Chardonnay (McLaren Vale) $11. 90 Best Buy —*M.N. (6/1/2001)*

Chateau Reynella 1998 Chardonnay (McLaren Vale) $11. 90 Best Buy *(3/1/2000)*

Chateau Reynella 2002 Basket Pressed Grenache (McLaren Vale) $24. 87 —*D.T. (3/1/2005)*

Chateau Reynella 2002 Basket Pressed Shiraz (McLaren Vale) $28. 88 —*D.T. (3/1/2005)*

Chateau Reynella 2000 Basket Pressed Shiraz (McLaren Vale) $28. 87 —*C.S. (3/1/2003)*

Chateau Reynella 1999 Basket Pressed Shiraz (McLaren Vale) $30. 87 *(11/1/2001)*

Chateau Reynella 1996 Basket Pressed Shiraz (McLaren Vale) $24. 90 —*M.S. (4/1/2000)*

CHECKERED CAB

Checkered Cab 2003 Cabernet Sauvignon (South Australia) $10. 86 Best Buy —*D.T. (6/1/2006)*

CHEEKY CHICK

Cheeky Chick 2005 Peeper's Blend Red Blend (South Australia) $10. Name aside, the wine in the bottle is a solid effort, blending a variety of grapes from McLaren Vale and Coonawarra into a medium-bodied, softly textured wine with scents of leather and cranberry and flavors that turn darker, toward cola and blackberry. 84 —*J.C. (11/15/2007)*

CHEVIOT BRIDGE

Cheviot Bridge 2000 Cabernet Sauvignon-Merlot (South Eastern Australia) $16. 85 —*M.M. (12/15/2002)*

Cheviot Bridge 1999 Cabernet Sauvignon-Merlot (Yea Valley) $16. 87 —*M.M. (12/15/2002)*

Cheviot Bridge 2001 Chardonnay (South Eastern Australia) $16. 83 —*J.C. (7/1/2002)*

Cheviot Bridge 2000 Chardonnay (Victoria) $16. 90 —*J.C. (7/1/2002)*

Cheviot Bridge 2001 Merlot (Yea Valley) $17. 85 —*D.T. (6/1/2003)*

Cheviot Bridge 2001 Pinot Noir (Yea Valley) $17. 87 —*D.T. (10/1/2003)*

Cheviot Bridge 2000 Shiraz (South Eastern Australia) $16. 84 —*M.M. (12/15/2002)*

CIGALE

Cigale 2005 Grenache-Mourvèdre-Shiraz Rhône Red Blend (Barossa Valley) $23. This is an attractive Rhône-style blend of 40% Grenache, 32% Mourvèdre and 28% Shiraz, showing facets of each variety. There's a bit of cola or chocolate from the Mourvèdre, blackberry and spice from the Shiraz and superripe stone fruit from the Grenache, which also contributes a lovely textural component. This is intense without being weighty or heavy, lingering elegantly on the finish. 90 Editors' Choice —*J.C. (6/1/2007)*

Cigale 2005 Shiraz (Barossa Valley) $24. Starts off with lovely blueberry, smoke and spice aromas, but adds hints of raisiny flavors that aren't as likable. It's a medium-bodied Shiraz with more focus than many others; one that has some impressive attributes, but a persistent note of dried fruit brings down the score. 87 —*J.C. (6/1/2007)*

Cigale 2004 Shiraz (Barossa Valley) $25. 88 —*D.T. (8/1/2006)*

AUSTRALIA

CLARENDON HILLS

Clarendon Hills 2004 Brookman Cabernet Sauvignon (Clarendon) $65. 91 *—D.T. (10/1/2006)*

Clarendon Hills 2003 Brookman Cabernet Sauvignon (Clarendon) $75. 92 *—D.T. (8/1/2005)*

Clarendon Hills 2004 Hickinbotham Cabernet Sauvignon (Clarendon) $70. 91 *—D.T. (10/1/2006)*

Clarendon Hills 2003 Hickinbotham Cabernet Sauvignon (Clarendon) $75. 90 *—D.T. (8/1/2005)*

Clarendon Hills 2004 Sandown Cabernet Sauvignon (Clarendon) $65. 92 Cellar Selection *—D.T. (10/1/2006)*

Clarendon Hills 2003 Sandown Cabernet Sauvignon (Clarendon) $70. 91 *—D.T. (8/1/2005)*

Clarendon Hills 2004 Blewitt Springs Grenache (Clarendon) $70. 93 *—J.C. (12/15/2006)*

Clarendon Hills 2003 Blewitt Springs Grenache (Clarendon) $80. 95 Cellar Selection *—D.T. (3/1/2005)*

Clarendon Hills 2004 Clarendon Grenache (Clarendon) $61. 90 *—J.C. (12/15/2006)*

Clarendon Hills 2003 Clarendon Grenache (Clarendon) $73. 93 *—D.T. (8/1/2005)*

Clarendon Hills 2003 Hickinbotham Grenache (Clarendon) $73. 90 *—D.T. (8/1/2005)*

Clarendon Hills 2004 Kangarilla Grenache (Clarendon) $70. 92 *—J.C. (12/15/2006)*

Clarendon Hills 2003 Kangarilla Grenache (Clarendon) $80. 92 *—D.T. (3/1/2005)*

Clarendon Hills 2004 Romas Grenache (Clarendon) $100. 95 Cellar Selection *—J.C. (12/15/2006)*

Clarendon Hills 2003 Romas Grenache (Clarendon) $115. 91 *—D.T. (8/1/2005)*

Clarendon Hills 2004 Brookman Merlot (Clarendon) $60. 90 *—J.C. (12/15/2006)*

Clarendon Hills 2003 Brookman Merlot (Clarendon) $65. 90 *—D.T. (3/1/2005)*

Clarendon Hills 1999 Moritz Shiraz (Clarendon) $49. 87 *(11/1/2001)*

Clarendon Hills 2004 Astralis Syrah (Clarendon) $325. 98 Cellar Selection *—J.C. (12/15/2006)*

Clarendon Hills 2003 Astralis Syrah (Clarendon) $375. 95 Cellar Selection *—D.T. (3/1/2005)*

Clarendon Hills 2004 Bakers Gully Syrah (Clarendon) $65. 89 *—J.C. (12/15/2006)*

Clarendon Hills 2003 Bakers Gully Syrah (Clarendon) $75. 89 *—D.T. (8/1/2005)*

Clarendon Hills 2004 Brookman Syrah (Clarendon) $100. 95 *—J.C. (12/15/2006)*

Clarendon Hills 2003 Brookman Syrah (Clarendon) $75. 95 Cellar Selection *—D.T. (8/1/2005)*

Clarendon Hills 2004 Hickinbotham Syrah (Clarendon) $100. 96 Cellar Selection *—J.C. (12/15/2006)*

Clarendon Hills 2003 Hickinbotham Syrah (Clarendon) $115. 94 *—D.T. (3/1/2005)*

Clarendon Hills 2004 Liandra Syrah (Clarendon) $78. 94 Editors' Choice *—J.C. (12/15/2006)*

Clarendon Hills 2003 Liandra Syrah (Clarendon) $90. 90 *—D.T. (8/1/2005)*

Clarendon Hills 2004 Moritz Syrah (Clarendon) $78. 93 *—J.C. (12/15/2006)*

Clarendon Hills 2003 Moritz Syrah (Clarendon) $90. 93 *—D.T. (3/1/2005)*

Clarendon Hills 2004 Piggott Range Syrah (Clarendon) $150. 94 *—J.C. (12/15/2006)*

Clarendon Hills 2003 Piggott Range Syrah (Clarendon) $175. 92 *—D.T. (8/1/2005)*

CLASSIC MCLAREN

Classic McLaren 2000 La Testa Cabernet Sauvignon (McLaren Vale) $41. 88 *—D.T. (12/31/2003)*

Classic McLaren 2000 Cabernet Sauvignon-Merlot (McLaren Vale) $19. 86 *—D.T. (12/31/2003)*

Classic McLaren 2000 La Testa Merlot (McLaren Vale) $41. 85 *—D.T. (6/1/2003)*

Classic McLaren 2000 La Testa Shiraz (McLaren Vale) $78. 89 *—D.T. (6/1/2003)*

CLIMBING

Climbing 2005 Cabernet Sauvignon (Orange) $14. With its slightly herbal overtones of oregano, this is a Bordeaux-like rendition of Cabernet Sauvignon; it's also got the acid and tannic structure to set it apart from stereotypical New World Cabernets. It is firm and slightly drying on the finish, so pair it with rare roast beef or lamb for best effect. 87 *(9/1/2007)*

Climbing 2004 Cabernet Sauvignon (Orange) $17. 84 *—D.T. (8/1/2006)*

Climbing 2006 Chardonnay (Orange) $14. Starts off with smoke and apple scents, then adds flavors that are crisp and citrusy, with a touch of pineapple. It's a clean, refreshing style of Chardonnay without too much vanilla or toast. 86 *(9/1/2007)*

Climbing 2005 Chardonnay (Orange) $17. 87 *—D.T. (8/1/2006)*

Climbing 2005 Merlot (Orange) $14. This Merlot shows its cool-region influence in its olivaceous flavors tinged with coffee, roasted bell pepper and eucalyptus. It's firmly built and will ably partner burgers or roasts, but will never be charming. 84 *—J.C. (11/15/2007)*

Climbing 2004 Merlot (Orange) $17. 86 *—D.T. (6/1/2006)*

Climbing 2006 Pinot Grigio (Orange) $14. There's a light salmon hue to this wine, but along with that lovely color has come some slightly bitter notes from skin contact. Red apple, melon and pear flavors are carried by a plump-textured wine with a touch of tannin. Drink now. 84 *(9/1/2007)*

Climbing 2005 Shiraz (Orange) $14. Starts off smoky, with meat-like notes, then adds cola, blackberries and spice on the palate. It's round in the mouth, with some dusty tannins and crisp acids on the finish, suggesting a pairing with richer cuts of beef or lamb. Drink now–2012. 87 *—J.C. (11/15/2007)*

CLONAKILLA

Clonakilla 1999 Shiraz (Langhorne Creek) $19. 85 *(10/1/2001)*

Clonakilla 2002 Command Shiraz (Barossa Valley) $77. Creamy and intense, with layers of smoke and vanilla over blackberry fruit. Long, with soft tannins. 92 *—J.C. (6/1/2007)*

Clonakilla 2003 Hilltops Shiraz (New South Wales) $25. 88 *—D.T. (12/1/2005)*

Clonakilla 2005 Shiraz-Viognier (Canberra District) $61. Wonderfully fruity, complex and elegant, with red berries and stone fruits underscored by peppery, herbal notes. Firmly structured, this should age up to 10 years. 93 Cellar Selection *—J.C. (6/1/2007)*

Clonakilla 2005 Shiraz-Viognier (Canberra District) $61. Wonderfully fruity, complex and elegant, with red berries and stone fruits underscored by peppery, herbal notes. Firmly structured, this should age up to 10 years. 93 Cellar Selection *—J.C. (6/1/2007)*

CLOVER HILL

Clover Hill 2003 Brut Champagne Blend (Tasmania) $32. In a recent lineup of Australian sparklers, Clover Hill's 2003 Brut was a standout, showing convincing toasty, autolytic notes layered over crisp apple and citrus flavors. It's medium-bodied and slightly creamy in texture, with a long, crisp finish. 89 *—J.C. (12/31/2007)*

Clover Hill 2001 Brut Champagne Blend (Tasmania) $30. 88 *—J.C. (12/31/2006)*

Clover Hill 2000 Brut Champagne Blend (Tasmania) $30. 87 *—D.T. (12/31/2005)*

Clover Hill 1998 Brut Champagne Blend (Tasmania) $29. 85 *—D.T. (12/31/2003)*

Clover Hill 1996 Brut Champagne Blend (Tasmania) $29. 80 *—J.M. (1/1/2003)*

COATES

Coates 2004 Shiraz (McLaren Vale) $37. A new producer to Larchet's lineup, this starts off with smoky, cola-like aromas, then adds cooler-climate cherry and berry flavors. Mouthwatering and long on the finish. 89 *—J.C. (6/1/2007)*

COCKATOO RIDGE

Cockatoo Ridge 2002 Cabernet Sauvignon-Merlot (South Australia) $7. 83 *—D.T. (9/1/2004)*

Cockatoo Ridge 2002 The Real Taste of Australia Cabernet Sauvignon-Merlot (South Australia) $7. 83 *—D.T. (9/1/2004)*

Cockatoo Ridge 2000 The Real Taste of Australia Cabernet Sauvignon-Merlot (South Australia) $7. 84 *—M.S. (12/15/2002)*

Cockatoo Ridge NV Brut Champagne Blend (South Australia) $10. 81 *— (12/1/2002)*

Cockatoo Ridge NV Brut Champagne Blend (South Eastern Australia) $7. 85 Best Buy —*D.T. (12/31/2004)*

Cockatoo Ridge 2003 Chardonnay (South Australia) $7. 84 *(7/2/2004)*

Cockatoo Ridge 2001 Chardonnay (South Australia) $7. 83 —*D.T. (8/1/2003)*

Cockatoo Ridge 2000 Chardonnay (Australia) $7. 83 —*J.C. (7/1/2002)*

Cockatoo Ridge 2004 Sauvignon Blanc (South Eastern Australia) $7. 84 Best Buy —*D.T. (12/1/2005)*

Cockatoo Ridge 2002 Shiraz (South Australia) $7. 83 —*D.T. (11/15/2004)*

Cockatoo Ridge 2000 Shiraz (South Australia) $7. 86 Best Buy —*K.F. (3/1/2003)*

Cockatoo Ridge NV Brut Sparkling Blend (South Eastern Australia) $10. Broad in the mouth and lacking overall freshness, this Australian sparkler offers modest citrus, earth and apple aromas and flavors. 81 —*J.C. (12/31/2007)*

COCKFIGHTER'S GHOST

Cockfighter's Ghost 2001 Cabernet Sauvignon (Langhorne Creek) $19. 84 —*D.T. (5/1/2004)*

Cockfighter's Ghost 1998 Premium Reserve Cabernet Sauvignon (Coonawarra) $35. 84 —*D.T. (6/1/2002)*

Cockfighter's Ghost 2004 Chardonnay (Hunter Valley) $19. 87 —*D.T. (4/1/2006)*

Cockfighter's Ghost 2001 Chardonnay (Hunter Valley) $18. 87 *(7/2/2004)*

Cockfighter's Ghost 2004 Semillon (Hunter Valley) $17. 86 —*D.T. (4/1/2006)*

Cockfighter's Ghost 2001 Shiraz (McLaren Vale) $23. 87 —*D.T. (9/1/2004)*

Cockfighter's Ghost 2004 Verdelho (Hunter Valley) $17. 88 —*D.T. (4/1/2006)*

COLDSTREAM HILLS

Coldstream Hills 2003 Chardonnay (Yarra Valley) $17. This is a nicely balanced Chardonnay, one in which no single element dominates. The fruit is mellow, tending toward the soft flavors of melon and pear, while the oak is deftly handled, imparting smoky notes that frame, not overwhelm. A harmonious, medium-bodied wine that could pair easily with various chicken dishes. 87 —*J.C. (2/1/2007)*

Coldstream Hills 2002 Chardonnay (Yarra Valley) $18. 85 *(7/2/2004)*

Coldstream Hills 2000 Chardonnay (Yarra Valley) $18. 81 —*J.C. (9/10/2002)*

Coldstream Hills 1998 Chardonnay (Yarra Valley) $22. 91 —*J.M. (1/1/2003)*

Coldstream Hills 2003 Reserve Chardonnay (Yarra Valley) $20. Bold scents of smoke and grilled peaches seem a bit obvious and simple, and those notes continue on the palate, overriding any other nuance there might be, then pick up a hint of bitterness on the finish. 84 —*J.C. (2/1/2007)*

Coldstream Hills 2005 Pinot Noir (Yarra Valley) $17. A strong showing for coldstream Hills, with herb and sous bois shadings that give the cherry fruit further depth and dimension. It's medium-bodied and creamy-textured, with a finish that turns darker, adding chocolate notes. Drink now. 88 —*J.C. (2/1/2007)*

Coldstream Hills 2002 Pinot Noir (Yarra Valley) $18. 87 —*D.T. (10/1/2003)*

Coldstream Hills 1998 Sauvignon Blanc (Yarra Valley) $17. 88 —*S.H. (10/1/2000)*

Coldstream Hills 2005 Sauvignon Blanc (Yarra Valley) $17. 86 —*D.T. (4/1/2006)*

Coldstream Hills 2002 Sauvignon Blanc (Victoria) $18. 86 —*D.T. (5/1/2004)*

Coldstream Hills 2001 Sauvignon Blanc (Yarra Valley) $NA. 86 *(2/1/2002)*

COOKOOTHAMA

Cookoothama 2001 Chardonnay (South Eastern Australia) $11.83 —*J.C. (1/1/2004)*

Cookoothama 2000 Pigeage Limited Release Merlot (Darlington Point) $25. 85 —*C.S. (6/1/2002)*

Cookoothama 2002 Sauvignon Blanc (King Valley) $10. 84 —*D.T. (1/1/2002)*

Cookoothama 2001 Botrytis Semillon (South Eastern Australia) $18. 87 —*D.T. (9/1/2004)*

COORALOOK

Cooralook 2002 Cabernet Sauvignon (Strathbogie Range) $20. 86 —*D.T. (4/1/2006)*

Cooralook 2004 Pinot Gris (Mornington Peninsula) $16. 84 —*D.T. (2/1/2006)*

Cooralook 2003 Pinot Noir (Mornington Peninsula) $20. 87 —*D.T. (4/1/2006)*

CORIOLE

Coriole 2004 Cabernet Sauvignon (McLaren Vale) $30. 86 —*D.T. (12/31/2005)*

Coriole 2001 Cabernet Sauvignon (McLaren Vale) $29. 87 —*D.T. (12/31/2004)*

Coriole 2003 Mary Kathleen Reserve Cabernet Sauvignon-Merlot (McLaren Vale) $45. The 2003 vintage wasn't an easy one in McLaren Vale, and this wine reflects the coolness of the year, with minty, herbal notes that edge out the chocolate and cassis flavors. Structured and framed by dusty tannins, without the lushness required to pull it through in the end. Drink now-2010. 87 —*J.C. (2/1/2007)*

Coriole 2001 Mary Kathleen Reserve Cabernet Sauvignon-Merlot (McLaren Vale) $45. 89 —*D.T. (3/1/2005)*

Coriole 2006 Chenin Blanc (McLaren Vale) $15. Australian Chenin Blanc may not be grabbing the headlines here in the States, but this is a fresh, crisp white that strikes a fine balance between fruit and austerity: The lime and stone fruit flavors are matched by chalky notes and a minerally finish. Worth a try with shellfish or lean, white-fleshed fish. 87 —*J.C. (2/1/2007)*

Coriole 2004 Chenin Blanc (McLaren Vale) $16. 87 —*D.T. (3/1/2005)*

Coriole 2003 Chenin Blanc (McLaren Vale) $15. 86 —*D.T. (5/1/2004)*

Coriole 2006 Rosé Nebbiolo (McLaren Vale) $19. 87 —*D.T. (11/15/2006)*

Coriole 2003 Contour 4 Sangiovese-Shiraz Red Blend (McLaren Vale) $16. 88 —*D.T. (4/1/2006)*

Coriole 2001 Lalla Rookh Old Vines Red Blend (McLaren Vale) $29. 89 —*D.T. (9/1/2004)*

Coriole 2003 Sangiovese (McLaren Vale) $NA. 87 —*D.T. (3/1/2005)*

Coriole 2003 Semillon-Sauvignon Blanc (South Eastern Australia) $15. 85 —*D.T. (9/1/2004)*

Coriole 2004 (McLaren Vale-Adelaide Hills) Semillon-Sauvignon Blanc (McLaren Vale) $16. 86 —*D.T. (3/1/2005)*

Coriole 2004 Shiraz (McLaren Vale) $25. This impressively dark, full-bodied Shiraz appears to be in a bit of a closed phase, to judge by its present muted aromatics. Firm and shut down on the finish, this should reveal more blackberry and coffee flavors after 2008. 89 —*J.C. (2/1/2007)*

Coriole 2003 Shiraz (McLaren Vale) $27. 87 —*D.T. (12/31/2005)*

Coriole 2004 Lloyd Reserve Shiraz (McLaren Vale) $65. This masterful Shiraz is lush and velvety yet not overly soft—there's a backbone underneath that should allow this wine to age easily through 2015 at least. Heady, concentrated scents of cassis mingle easily with smoke and vanilla, adding dense layers of chocolate and cinnamon on the palate. A long, mouthcoating finish confirms the wine's quality. 93 —*J.C. (2/1/2007)*

Coriole 2001 Lloyd Reserve Shiraz (McLaren Vale) $65. 91 —*D.T. (3/1/2005)*

Coriole 2000 Lloyd Reserve Shiraz (McLaren Vale) $NA. 88 —*D.T. (5/1/2004)*

Coriole 2004 The Soloist Shiraz (McLaren Vale) $40. 91 —*D.T. (11/15/2006)*

Coriole 2003 Redstone Shiraz-Cabernet Sauvignon (McLaren Vale) $20. Coriole's basic Shiraz-Cab blend is a solid wine, one that offers graham cracker and blueberry aromas and similar flavors, picking up hints of blackberry, coffee and pepper. It's crisp and firm without being particularly tannic. Drink now. 86 —*J.C. (2/1/2007)*

Coriole 2001 Redstone Shiraz-Cabernet Sauvignon (McLaren Vale) $20. 87 —*D.T. (9/1/2004)*

Coriole 2003 The Old Barn Shiraz-Cabernet Sauvignon (McLaren Vale) $NA. This blend offers an intriguing array of scents and flavors, ranging from dried spices, mint and blueberries to raspberry and citrus. This complexity is underscored by the long finish and fine tannins. Very good wine, it's just missing a bit of depth on the midpalate. Not presently imported, but may be available later in 2007. 87 —*J.C. (2/1/2007)*

CRABTREE

Crabtree 1999 Watervale Riesling (Clare Valley) $16. 86 —*M.M. (9/1/2001)*

CRAGG'S CREEK

Cragg's Creek 2003 Unwooded Chardonnay (Riverland) $15. 80 —*D.T. (10/1/2005)*

CRANEFORD

Craneford NV Champagne Blend (Barossa Valley) $30. 85 *—C.S. (12/1/2002)*

Craneford 2000 Chardonnay (Barossa Valley) $12. 85 *—J.C. (7/1/2002)*

Craneford 2005 John Zilm Grenache (Barossa Valley) $27. Exceptional ripeness has brought soft tannins and high alcohol, but the acids are bright enough to point up the cherry fruit. Some peppery, savory, meaty overtones add complexity. Drink now and over the next few years. 88 *—J.C. (11/1/2007)*

Craneford 2002 97 Year Old Single Vineyard Grenache (Barossa Valley) $28. 88 *—D.T. (9/1/2004)*

Craneford 2003 John Zilm Merlot (Barossa Valley) $30. 87 *—D.T. (4/1/2006)*

Craneford 2003 John Zilm Petite Verdot (Barossa Valley) $33. 86 *—D.T. (6/1/2006)*

Craneford 2000 Quartet Red Blend (Barossa Valley) $24. 87 *—J.C. (9/1/2002)*

Craneford 2000 Riesling (Eden Valley) $12. 90 Editors' Choice *—M.M. (2/1/2002)*

Craneford 2000 Semillon (Barossa Valley) $12. 90 Best Buy *—J.C. (2/1/2002)*

Craneford 2006 Shiraz (Barossa Valley) $33. Recently bottled, Craneford's 2006 Shiraz is very youthful and primary, with cherry-berry aromas and flavors completely dominating at this stage. It's almost confected in its fruity forwardness, yet shows enough structure to mostly rein in its ebullience. Drink 2009–2015. 88 *—J.C. (11/1/2007)*

Craneford 2005 Shiraz (Barossa Valley) $33. Soft tannins make this easy to drink, with a structure built upon crisp acids. Ripe black cherry flavors also feature hints of licorice and dill, so there's more to it than simple fruit. Drink now–2010. 87 *—J.C. (11/1/2007)*

Craneford 2004 Allyson Parsons Shiraz (Barossa Valley) $19. A dark, earthy style, laden with cassis, tobacco and shadings of vanilla. This is medium-bodied, with surprisingly crisp acids for the Barossa that give it an almost claret-like feel. Drink now–2012. 89 *—J.C. (3/1/2007)*

Craneford 2005 Fire Station Shiraz (Barossa Valley) $NA. A step up in seriousness from Craneford's easy-drinking regular Shiraz, the Fire Station bottling is sourced from 80-year-old vines from the northern Barossa. Cola, spice and meat notes mark the aromas, while the blackberry fruit on the palate is very juicy and fresh. A touch of cedar on the finish brings the fruit back into focus. Drink now–2015. 90 *—J.C. (11/1/2007)*

Craneford 2004 John Zilm Shiraz (Barossa Valley) $35. Although the winery bills this as a step up from its Allyson Parsons Shiraz—and maybe it will improve with cellaring—right now it's a bit disjointed, with powerful chocolate fudge vying with tart plum flavors that turn lemony on the finish. Try after 2010. 86 *—J.C. (3/1/2007)*

Craneford 2000 Shiraz (Barossa Valley) $28. 85 *—D.T. (3/1/2003)*

Craneford 2004 Viognier (Adelaide Hills) $17. 88 *—D.T. (12/31/2005)*

CREED OF BAROSSA

Creed of Barossa 2004 The Pretty Miss Shiraz-Cabernet Franc-Viognier Red Blend (Barossa) $21. Shows off the soft, supple mouthfeel that Barossa Shiraz is capable of achieving, anchoring it with bold flavors of black cherries, dried spices and hints of cracked pepper. Lingering notes of spice and warmth mark the finish. So creamy in texture, it begs to be consumed now. 89 *—J.C. (3/1/2007)*

CULLEN

Cullen 2002 Diana Madeline Bordeaux Blend (Margaret River) $75. 88 *—D.T. (10/1/2006)*

Cullen 2000 Diana Madeline Bordeaux Blend (Margaret River) $50. 90 *—D.T. (10/1/2003)*

Cullen 2003 Mangan Bordeaux Blend (Margaret River) $40. 88 *(4/1/2005)*

Cullen 2001 Diana Madeline Cabernet Sauvignon-Merlot (Margaret River) $75. 92 Cellar Selection *—R.V. (4/1/2005)*

Cullen 2002 Chardonnay (Margaret River) $55. 89 *(4/1/2005)*

Cullen 2003 Ephraim Clarke Semillon-Sauvignon Blanc (Margaret River) $30. 87 *(4/1/2005)*

Cullen 2001 Ephraim Clarke Semillon-Sauvignon Blanc (Margaret River) $30. 89 *—D.T. (10/1/2003)*

CURLY FLAT

Curly Flat 1999 Pinot Noir (Victoria) $30. 86 *—D.T. (9/1/2004)*

CURRENCY CREEK ESTATE

Currency Creek Estate 2003 The Black Swamp Cabernet Sauvignon (Currency Creek) $17. 83 *—D.T. (12/31/2005)*

Currency Creek Estate 2004 The Viaduct Unwooded Chardonnay (Currency Creek) $14. 84 *—D.T. (12/1/2005)*

Currency Creek Estate 2005 Sedgeland Sauvignon Blanc (Currency Creek) $14. 83 *—D.T. (6/1/2006)*

Currency Creek Estate 2003 Ostrich Hill Shiraz (Currency Creek) $17. 86 *—D.T. (12/31/2005)*

CUTTAWAY HILL ESTATE

Cuttaway Hill Estate 2005 Merlot (Southern Highlands) $13. This doesn't measure up to the winery's surprisingly good Pinot Noir, but still offers enough sour plum, pie cherry and mocha notes to warrant commendation. It's rather light in body, with a tart edge to the finish. 83 *—J.C. (11/15/2007)*

Cuttaway Hill Estate 2003 Merlot (Southern Highlands) $13. 87 Best Buy *—D.T. (12/1/2005)*

Cuttaway Hill Estate 2006 Pinot Noir (Southern Highlands) $13. For the realistic price, this does offer surprisingly authentic Pinot Noir character, blending cinnamon and mushroom notes with cherry fruit. It's lightweight but pretty—a charming, elegant red that would pair well with salmon or chicken dishes. 86 *—J.C. (11/15/2007)*

Cuttaway Hill Estate 2004 Southern Highlands Pinot Gris (Australia) $16. 86 *—D.T. (12/1/2005)*

Cuttaway Hill Estate 2004 Sauvignon Blanc (Australia) $13. 84 *—D.T. (12/1/2005)*

D'ARENBERG

D'Arenberg 2001 The Galvo Garage Bordeaux Blend (South Australia) $35. 87 *—D.T. (12/31/2003)*

D'Arenberg 2003 The Coppermine Road Cabernet Sauvignon (McLaren Vale) $65. 86 *—D.T. (8/1/2006)*

D'Arenberg 2002 The Coppermine Road Cabernet Sauvignon (McLaren Vale) $65. 89 *—D.T. (3/1/2005)*

D'Arenberg 1999 The Coppermine Road Cabernet Sauvignon (McLaren Vale) $65. 90 *—M.S. (12/15/2002)*

D'Arenberg 2002 The High Trellis Cabernet Sauvignon (McLaren Vale) $19. 87 *—D.T. (3/1/2005)*

D'Arenberg 2001 The High Trellis Cabernet Sauvignon (McLaren Vale) $18. 85 *—D.T. (5/1/2004)*

D'Arenberg 2000 The High Trellis Cabernet Sauvignon (McLaren Vale) $18. 89 *—M.S. (12/15/2002)*

D'Arenberg 2004 The Olive Grove Chardonnay (McLaren Vale) $16. 89 *—D.T. (8/1/2006)*

D'Arenberg 2003 The Olive Grove Chardonnay (McLaren Vale) $16. 89 *—D.T. (3/1/2005)*

D'Arenberg 2002 The Olive Grove Chardonnay (McLaren Vale) $15. 85 *(7/2/2004)*

D'Arenberg 2001 The Olive Grove Chardonnay (McLaren Vale) $15. 83 *—J.C. (7/1/2002)*

D'Arenberg 2001 The Custodian Grenache (McLaren Vale) $19. 88 *—D.T. (3/1/2005)*

D'Arenberg 1999 The Custodian Grenache (McLaren Vale) $23. 85 *—D.T. (12/31/2003)*

D'Arenberg 2002 The Derelict Vineyard Grenache (McLaren Vale) $35. 86 *—D.T. (3/1/2005)*

D'Arenberg 2004 The Stump Jump G-S-M (McLaren Vale) $10. 88 Best Buy *—D.T. (8/1/2006)*

D'Arenberg 2002 The Twentyeight Road Mourvèdre (McLaren Vale) $35. 90 *—D.T. (3/1/2005)*

D'Arenberg 1999 The Twentyeight Road Mourvèdre (McLaren Vale) $30. 85 *—D.T. (12/31/2003)*

D'Arenberg 2001 d'Arry's Original Shiraz Grenache Red Blend (McLaren Vale) $18. 88 *—D.T. (5/1/2004)*

D'Arenberg 2002 The Galvo Garage Red Blend (McLaren Vale) $35. 86 *—D.T. (3/1/2005)*

D'Arenberg 2002 The Ironstone Pressings Red Blend (McLaren Vale) $65. 89 *—D.T. (3/1/2005)*

D'Arenberg 2000 The Ironstone Pressings Red Blend (McLaren Vale) $65. 84 *—D.T. (12/31/2003)*

D'Arenberg 2003 The Laughing Magpie Shiraz Viognier Red Blend (McLaren Vale) $35. 88 *—D.T. (3/1/2005)*

D'Arenberg 2002 The Sticks & Stones Red Blend (McLaren Vale) $40. 88 —*D.T. (3/1/2005)*

D'Arenberg 2003 The Stump Jump Red Blend (McLaren Vale) $10. 85 Best Buy —*D.T. (3/1/2005)*

D'Arenberg 2001 The Stump Jump Red Blend (McLaren Vale) $11. 86 —*D.T. (12/31/2003)*

D'Arenberg 2003 The Cadenzia Rhône Red Blend (McLaren Vale) $NA. 89 —*D.T. (8/1/2005)*

D'Arenberg 2005 The Dry Dam Riesling (McLaren Vale) $16. This light to medium-bodied wine is crisp and refreshing. It may lack some of the power of other Australian Rieslings, but it does offer zesty lime and green apple flavors and a touch of mineral dustiness on the finish. Drink now–2010. 86 —*J.C. (9/1/2007)*

D'Arenberg 2003 The Money Spider Roussanne (McLaren Vale) $22. 87 —*D.T. (3/1/2005)*

D'Arenberg 2001 The Broken Fishplate Sauvignon Blanc (Adelaide Hills) $15. 82 *(8/1/2002)*

D'Arenberg 2005 The Dead Arm Shiraz (McLaren Vale) $65. The Dead Arm frequently seems to have a tough edge to it, packing in plenty of intensity but not being particularly lush or inviting. The 2005 is driven by powerful blackberry and blueberry fruit, finishing on notes of pepper and spice. Give it 3–4 years to soften. 88 —*J.C. (12/31/2007)*

D'Arenberg 2003 The Dead Arm Shiraz (McLaren Vale) $65. 90 —*J.C. (12/15/2006)*

D'Arenberg 2002 The Dead Arm Shiraz (McLaren Vale) $65. 91 —*D.T. (3/1/2005)*

D'Arenberg 2000 The Dead Arm Shiraz (McLaren Vale) $65. 90 —*C.S. (3/1/2003)*

D'Arenberg 1998 The Dead Arm Shiraz (McLaren Vale) $60. 87 *(11/1/2001)*

D'Arenberg 2002 The Footbolt Shiraz (McLaren Vale) $19. 86 —*D.T. (3/1/2005)*

D'Arenberg 2000 The Footbolt Shiraz (McLaren Vale) $18. 86 —*D.T. (3/1/2003)*

D'Arenberg 1999 The Footbolt Shiraz (McLaren Vale) $17. 85 *(10/1/2001)*

D'Arenberg 1997 The Footbolt Shiraz (McLaren Vale) $15. 91 *(11/15/1999)*

D'Arenberg 2002 The Laughing Magpie Shiraz (McLaren Vale) $35. 88 —*D.T. (5/1/2004)*

D'Arenberg 2002 d'Arry's Original Shiraz-Grenache (McLaren Vale) $19. 87 —*D.T. (3/1/2005)*

D'Arenberg 2004 The Hermit Crab White Blend (McLaren Vale) $16. 86 —*D.T. (10/1/2006)*

D'Arenberg 2002 The Hermit Crab White Blend (McLaren Vale) $15. 85 —*D.T. (5/1/2004)*

D'Arenberg 2005 The Stump Jump White Blend (McLaren Vale) $10. 84 —*D.T. (10/1/2006)*

D'Arenberg 2003 The Stump Jump White Blend (McLaren Vale) $10. 85 Best Buy —*D.T. (3/1/2005)*

D'Arenberg 2002 The Stump Jump White Blend (McLaren Vale) $10. 87 —*D.T. (11/15/2003)*

DALWHINNIE

Dalwhinnie 2002 Moonambel Cabernet Sauvignon (Victoria) $50. 88 —*D.T. (10/1/2006)*

Dalwhinnie 2000 Chardonnay (Australia) $54. 82 *(7/2/2004)*

Dalwhinnie 2001 Pyrenees Chardonnay (Australia) $40. 87 —*D.T. (5/1/2005)*

Dalwhinnie 2001 Pyrenees Shiraz (Australia) $49. 90 —*D.T. (8/1/2005)*

DAVID FRANZ

David Franz 2000 Georgie's Walk Cabernet Sauvignon (Barossa) $40. 92 —*D.T. (10/1/2006)*

David Franz 1999 Georgie's Walk Cabernet Sauvignon-Shiraz (Barossa-Langhorne Creek) $40. 86 —*D.T. (11/15/2004)*

David Franz 2000 Benjamin's Promise Shiraz (Barossa) $40. 87 —*J.C. (12/15/2006)*

David Franz 1999 Benjamin's Promise Shiraz (Barossa Valley) $40. 88 *(11/15/2004)*

DAVID HOOK WINES

David Hook Wines 2002 The Gorge Shiraz (Hunter Valley) $17. 87 —*D.T. (4/1/2006)*

DAVID TRAEGER

David Traeger 1998 Shiraz (Victoria) $24. 83 *(11/1/2001)*

DAVID WYNN

David Wynn 1996 Cabernet Sauvignon (Eden Valley) $15. 80 *(3/1/2000)*

David Wynn 1999 Chardonnay (Barossa Valley) $11. 82 —*M.N. (6/1/2001)*

David Wynn 1995 Patriarch Shiraz (Eden Valley) $30. 92 —*M.G. (11/15/1999)*

DE BORTOLI

De Bortoli 2001 Cabernet Sauvignon (Yarra Valley) $35. 85 —*D.T. (10/1/2005)*

De Bortoli 2000 Cabernet Sauvignon (Yarra Valley) $34. 86 *(11/1/2004)*

De Bortoli 1999 Melba Reserve Cabernet Sauvignon (Yarra Valley) $59. 84 *(11/1/2004)*

De Bortoli 1998 Melba Reserve Cabernet Sauvignon (Yarra Valley) $60. 85 —*D.T. (12/31/2003)*

De Bortoli 2004 Willowglen Cabernet Sauvignon-Merlot (South Eastern Australia) $9. 86 Best Buy —*D.T. (2/1/2006)*

De Bortoli 2003 Chardonnay (Yarra Valley) $27. 87 *(11/1/2004)*

De Bortoli 2001 Chardonnay (Yarra Valley) $30. 82 *(7/2/2004)*

De Bortoli 2003 dB Chardonnay (Big Rivers) $9. 83 —*D.T. (12/31/2004)*

De Bortoli 2002 dB Chardonnay (Riverina) $6. 84 *(7/2/2004)*

De Bortoli 2001 Deen Vat 7 Chardonnay (South Eastern Australia) $10. 84 —*D.T. (12/31/2003)*

De Bortoli 2003 Gulf Station Chardonnay (Yarra Valley) $20. 85 *(11/1/2004)*

De Bortoli 2003 Hunter Valley Chardonnay (Hunter Valley) $20. 87 —*D.T. (11/15/2004)*

De Bortoli 2003 dB Merlot (South Eastern Australia) $8. 84 Best Buy —*D.T. (10/1/2005)*

De Bortoli 2005 dB Selection Petite Sirah (South Eastern Australia) $9. 87 Best Buy —*D.T. (8/1/2006)*

De Bortoli 2003 dB Selection Petite Sirah (Big Rivers) $8. 85 —*D.T. (11/15/2005)*

De Bortoli 2004 Deen Vat 1 Petite Sirah (South Eastern Australia) $13. 86 —*D.T. (11/15/2006)*

De Bortoli 2004 Deen Vat 4 Petite Verdot (South Eastern Australia) $13. 83 —*D.T. (11/15/2006)*

De Bortoli 2002 Deen Vat 4 Petite Verdot (South Eastern Australia) $10. 88 Best Buy —*D.T. (5/1/2004)*

De Bortoli 2005 Windy Peak Pinot Grigio (Victoria) $17. 84 —*D.T. (2/1/2006)*

De Bortoli 2002 Pinot Noir (Yarra Valley) $34. 86 *(11/1/2004)*

De Bortoli 2002 Gulf Station Pinot Noir (Yarra Valley) $20. 86 *(11/1/2004)*

De Bortoli 2003 Windy Peak Pinot Noir (Victoria) $15. 85 —*D.T. (12/31/2004)*

De Bortoli 2004 Gulf Station Riesling (Yarra Valley) $20. 85 —*D.T. (12/31/2004)*

De Bortoli 2003 Windy Peak Cabernet Rosé Blend (Yarra Valley) $15. 82 —*D.T. (10/1/2005)*

De Bortoli 2002 Windy Peak Sangiovese (King Valley) $15. 86 —*D.T. (12/31/2004)*

De Bortoli 2005 Deen De Bortoli Vat 2 Sauvignon Blanc (South Eastern Australia) $12. 86 —*D.T. (6/1/2006)*

De Bortoli 2004 Deen Vat 2 Sauvignon Blanc (South Eastern Australia) $11. 86 Best Buy —*D.T. (10/1/2005)*

De Bortoli 2003 Noble One Botrytis Semillon (New South Wales) $29. 91 —*D.T. (8/1/2006)*

De Bortoli 2002 Noble One Botrytis Semillon (New South Wales) $29. 88 *(11/1/2004)*

De Bortoli 2002 Shiraz (Yarra Valley) $34. 87 *(11/1/2004)*

De Bortoli 1998 Shiraz (Yarra Valley) $28. 85 *(11/1/2001)*

De Bortoli 1999 GS Reserve Shiraz (Yarra Valley) $59. 84 *(11/1/2004)*

De Bortoli 1997 GS Reserve Shiraz (Yarra Valley) $60. 87 —*D.T. (12/31/2003)*

De Bortoli 2002 Gulf Station Shiraz (Yarra Valley) $20. 85 *(11/1/2004)*

De Bortoli 2004 Willowglen Shiraz (South Eastern Australia) $9. 83 —*D.T. (10/1/2005)*

AUSTRALIA

De Bortoli 2005 dB Selection Shiraz-Cabernet Sauvignon (South Eastern Australia) $9. 83 *—D.T. (11/15/2006)*

De Bortoli 2004 Willowglen Shiraz-Cabernet Sauvignon (South Eastern Australia) $9. 82 *—D.T. (10/1/2005)*

De Bortoli NV dB Brut Sparkling Blend (South Eastern Australia) $10. 83 *—D.T. (12/31/2005)*

DAVID HOOK WINES

David Hook Wines 2005 The Gorge Shiraz (Hunter Valley) $15. For a Shiraz from a warmer growing region, this shows admirable nuance and spice, blending hints of cracked pepper with raspberry and blackberry fruit. It's perfumed on the nose, boasts a slightly creamy texture in the mouth and finishes long—it's everything you could ask for, at a realistic price. 90 Best Buy *—J.C. (11/15/2007)*

David Hook Wines 2004 The Gorge Shiraz (Hunter Valley) $15. Cherry, berry and stone fruit aromas and flavors mark this fruity, not particularly complex quaff that would do well washing down barbecue and the like. Ultrasoft, with a very supple finish. Drink now. 87 *—J.C. (5/1/2007)*

DE BORTOLI

De Bortoli 2006 dB Selection Cabernet-Petit Verdot-Merlot Bordeaux Blend (South Eastern Australia) $9. A wine of contradictions, with notes of candied cherries but also dark cassis, and a sweet-tasting finish that features some drying, leafy tannins. 82 *—J.C. (11/15/2007)*

De Bortoli 2004 Deen Vat 9 Cabernet Sauvignon (South Eastern Australia) $13. A successful bottling from De Bortoli, this Cabernet does have some slightly herbal notes, but they accent the tart cherry, cedar and chocolate flavors that lie at this wine's core. The tannins are supple, with structure provided by crisp acidity that gives the fruit a cranberry twist on the finish. 86 *—J.C. (2/1/2007)*

De Bortoli 2006 dB Selection Chardonnay (South Eastern Australia) $9. A bit angular and tart, but this is a suitable starter-type Chardonnay—crisp and clean, with a focus on citrus. There's kiwi, lemon, kumquat and tangerine flavors, finishing briskly. 84 *—J.C. (6/1/2007)*

De Bortoli 2005 Deen Vat 7 Chardonnay (South Eastern Australia) $13. This wine starts off rather toasty and woody-smelling, but the wood is much less noticeable on the palate, where pear and peach flavors take over, given focus by crisp, citrusy notes on the finish. 86 *—J.C. (2/1/2007)*

De Bortoli 2005 Estate Grown Chardonnay (Yarra Valley) $25. De Bortoli's top wines come off their estate vineyards in the Yarra Valley, and this Chardonnay is a hit, balancing the lead-pencil scents of French oak barrels against layers of honeyed apple and pear fruit and a zippy note of citrus. It's round in the mouth without being fat, crisp on the finish while showing a touch of buttery richness. Drink now. 90 Editors' Choice *—J.C. (5/1/2007)*

De Bortoli 2005 Reserve Release Chardonnay (Yarra Valley) $40. Shows subtle oaking in its hints of toast and vanilla, but the standout facet of this wine is its ripe melon fruit, which gives it size and roundness but lacks a little touch of richness. The result is an easy-to-drink wine that's clean and refreshing on the palate. 87 *—J.C. (5/1/2007)*

De Bortoli NV Show Liqueur Muscat Hamburg (New South Wales) $22. This wine shows its age in the dark coffee color rimmed with green. Dates and raisins provide the foundation for complex molasses and rancio notes that build on the finish, where enough citrusy notes provide balance to the syrupy-sweet flavors. 90 Editors' Choice *—J.C. (12/15/2007)*

De Bortoli 2005 Deen Vat 10 Pinot Noir (South Eastern Australia) $15. With its supple, silky texture, this herb-inflected Pinot Noir is surprisingly easy to drink. Red cherry fruit carries hints of vanilla, turning herbal and slightly drying on the finish. 85 *—J.C. (2/1/2007)*

De Bortoli 2005 Estate Grown Pinot Noir (Yarra Valley) $30. Like De Bortoli's Estate Grown Pinot Noir, this Reserve Release (also estate grown), is firmly built. Crisp acids and a big, burly mouthfeel accent sour cherry and cranberry fruit and an increased dose of new oak. It's plenty muscular, but could use a touch more finesse. 87 *—J.C. (5/1/2007)*

De Bortoli 2005 Reserve Release Pinot Noir (Yarra Valley) $40. Like De Bortoli's Estate Grown Pinot Noir, this Reserve Release (also estate grown), is firmly built. Crisp acids and a big, burly mouthfeel accent sour cherry and cranberry fruit and an increased dose of new oak. It's plenty muscular, but could use a touch more finesse. 86 *—J.C. (5/1/2007)*

De Bortoli 2005 Deen De Bortoli Vat 5 Botrytis Sémillon (Riverina) $14. It's not easy to find bargain-priced stickies, but this offering from De Bortoli is a solid attempt. It's like their Noble One Botrytis Sémillon, just dialed back a notch, with less oak and concentration, but still boasting dried apricot and candied pineapple flavors that end with a hint of orange rind. 86 *—J.C. (12/15/2007)*

De Bortoli 2005 Noble One Botrytis Sémillon (New South Wales) $29. De Bortoli has made Noble One into one of Austrlia's benchmark dessert wines through consistently strong efforts like the 2005. Scents of vanilla and cinnamon add layers of complexity to the dried apricot and orange marmalade flavors. Medium-bodied and sweet, with a long finish, pair it like you would any fine Sauternes. 90 *—J.C. (12/15/2007)*

De Bortoli 2005 Deen De Bortoli Vat 8 Shiraz (South Eastern Australia) $12. A lightweight Shiraz with minimal tannin but a wealth of assertively tart blackberry flavors. Crisp and tangy on the finish. 83 *—J.C. (7/1/2007)*

De Bortoli 2004 Deen De Bortoli Vat 8 Shiraz (South Eastern Australia) $13. A very good wine at a fair price, De Bortoli's Vat 8 features just enough leather and spice layered over blackberry, blueberry and vanilla flavors to impart complexity without overshadowing the fruit. Finishes a bit crisp, with the emphasis on tart berry flavors. 87 *—J.C. (6/1/2007)*

De Bortoli 2006 dB Selection Shiraz-Cabernet Shiraz-Cabernet Sauvignon (South Eastern Australia) $9. A slightly burnt or roasted character to this wine's simple berry fruit knock it down a point or two, as it does offer decent weight and texture in the mouth. 82 *—J.C. (11/15/2007)*

DE IULIIS

De Iuliis 1999 Show Reserve Verdelho (Hunter Valley) $9. 83 *—J.C. (2/1/2002)*

DEAKIN ESTATE

Deakin Estate 2004 Cabernet Sauvignon (Victoria) $9. 85 Best Buy *—D.T. (11/15/2006)*

Deakin Estate 2001 Cabernet Sauvignon (Victoria) $9. 84 *—D.T. (6/1/2003)*

Deakin Estate 2005 Chardonnay (Victoria) $9. 85 Best Buy *—D.T. (8/1/2006)*

Deakin Estate 2004 Chardonnay (Victoria) $9. 85 Best Buy *—D.T. (5/1/2005)*

Deakin Estate 2003 Chardonnay (Victoria) $9. 84 *—D.T. (12/31/2004)*

Deakin Estate 2002 Chardonnay (Victoria) $8. 85 Best Buy *(7/2/2004)*

Deakin Estate 2004 Sauvignon Blanc (Victoria) $9. 85 Best Buy *—D.T. (8/1/2005)*

Deakin Estate 2002 Shiraz (Victoria) $9. 84 *—D.T. (5/1/2005)*

Deakin Estate 2000 Shiraz (Australia) $11. 86 *(10/1/2001)*

Deakin Estate 1998 Shiraz (Victoria) $12. 89 *(11/15/1999)*

DEEN DE BORTOLI

Deen De Bortoli 2000 Vat 5 Botrytis Semillon (South Eastern Australia) $10. 84 *—D.T. (9/1/2004)*

Deen De Bortoli 1999 Vat 8 Shiraz (South Eastern Australia) $10. 86 *(10/1/2001)*

DELATITE

Delatite 2000 Devil's River Mansfield Cabernet Sauvignon-Merlot (Victoria) $18. 84 *—D.T. (12/31/2003)*

Delatite 1999 Mansfield Chardonnay (Victoria) $16. 83 *—D.T. (8/1/2003)*

Delatite 2004 Dead Man's Hill Gewürztraminer (Victoria) $19. 85 *—D.T. (5/1/2005)*

Delatite 2004 Sauvignon Blanc (Victoria) $19. 82 *—D.T. (8/1/2005)*

Delatite 1998 Mansfield Limited Release Shiraz (Victoria) $17. 87 *—K.F. (12/31/2003)*

DE LISIO WINES

De Lisio Wines 2005 Catalyst Red Blend (McLaren Vale) $44. This spicy blend of Shiraz and Grenache doesn't have the opulence of De Lisio's Quarterback blend, but boasts more complexity. Cinnamon, pepper, coffee and anise notes embellish the wine's crisp, red-fruit flavors without overwhelming them, leaving behind a lingering sense of balance. Drink now–2015. 89 *(11/15/2007)*

De Lisio Wines 2005 Quarterback Red Blend (McLaren Vale) $24. This wine seamlessly blends four varieties—Shiraz, Grenache, Cabernet Sauvignon and Merlot—into an elegant mix of chocolate, cassis and plum flavor. It's wonderfully supple and rounded in the mouth, finishing with lingering notes of smoke and cassis. 90 Editors' Choice *(11/15/2007)*

DEVIL'S LAIR

Devil's Lair 2001 Bordeaux Blend (Margaret River) $23. 87 *—D.T. (10/1/2005)*

Devil's Lair 2003 Red Wine Bordeaux Blend (Margaret River) $23. A surprisingly strong effort from a Foster's label that's languished a bit in recent years, this is an intense, moderately ageworthy red that's two-thirds Cabernet Sauvignon, the rest is a blend of Merlot and Cabernet Franc. Scents of dark chocolate and mint add cassis, finishing with firm dusty-textured tannins. Drink 2008–2015. 90 *—J.C. (6/1/2007)*

Devil's Lair 2000 Cabernet Sauvignon (Margaret River) $23. 84 *—D.T. (10/1/2003)*

Devil's Lair 2002 Cabernet Sauvignon-Merlot (Margaret River) $23. 87 —*D.T. (6/1/2006)*

Devil's Lair 1999 Fifth Leg Cabernet Sauvignon-Merlot (Margaret River) $22. 86 —*M.S. (12/15/2002)*

Devil's Lair 2003 Chardonnay (Margaret River) $23. 86 —*D.T. (10/1/2005)*

Devil's Lair 2002 Chardonnay (Margaret River) $23. 87 *(7/2/2004)*

Devil's Lair 2001 Chardonnay (Margaret River) $23. 83 —*D.T. (8/1/2003)*

Devil's Lair 2004 Fifth Leg Red Blend (Western Australia) $12. 86 —*D.T. (8/1/2006)*

Devil's Lair 2003 Fifth Leg Red Blend (Western Australia) $12. 83 —*D.T. (8/1/2005)*

Devil's Lair 2001 Fifth Leg Red Red Blend (Margaret River) $12. 87 —*D.T. (10/1/2003)*

Devil's Lair 2004 Fifth Leg White Blend (Western Australia) $12. 86 —*D.T. (8/1/2005)*

Devil's Lair 2003 Fifth Leg White Blend (Margaret River) $12. 86 —*D.T. (12/31/2004)*

Devil's Lair 1999 Fifth Leg White White Blend (Margaret River) $11. 87 Best Buy —*D.T. (10/1/2003)*

DEVIL'S MARBLES

Devil's Marbles 2003 Shiraz (Limestone Coast) $10. 85 Best Buy —*D.T. (6/1/2006)*

Devil's Marbles 2004 Chardonnay/Verdelho White Blend (Limestone Coast) $10. 87 Best Buy —*D.T. (4/1/2006)*

DI GIORGIO FAMILY WINES

Di Giorgio Family Wines 2000 Lucindale Cabernet Sauvignon (Limestone Coast) $22. 86 —*D.T. (9/1/2004)*

Di Giorgio Family Wines 2001 Lucindale Merlot (Limestone Coast) $22. 86 —*D.T. (12/31/2003)*

Di Giorgio Family Wines NV Lucindale Sparkling Blend (Coonawarra) $18. 84 —*D.T. (12/31/2003)*

DIAMOND RIDGE

Diamond Ridge 2000 Shiraz (South Eastern Australia) $8. 81 —*J.C. (9/1/2002)*

DINGO'S DESIRE

Dingo's Desire 2003 Chardonnay (South Eastern Australia) $8. 86 Best Buy *(7/2/2004)*

DOMINIQUE PORTET

Dominique Portet 2002 Cabernet Sauvignon (Heathcote) $35. 87 —*D.T. (10/1/2005)*

Dominique Portet 2000 Cabernet Sauvignon (Yarra Valley) $30. 84 —*D.T. (12/31/2003)*

Dominique Portet 2004 Fontaine Rosé Blend (Yarra Valley) $18. 87 —*D.T. (12/31/2005)*

Dominique Portet 2004 Sauvignon Blanc (Yarra Valley) $20. 89 *(7/1/2005)*

Dominique Portet 2004 Handpicked Sauvignon Blanc (South Eastern Australia) $13. 84 —*D.T. (10/1/2005)*

Dominique Portet 2002 Shiraz (Heathcote) $35. 89 —*D.T. (12/1/2005)*

DONNELLY RIVER

Donnelly River 1997 Shiraz (Currency Creek) $16. 87 *(10/1/2001)*

DOWNING ESTATE

Downing Estate 2002 Cabernet Sauvignon (Heathcote) $35. 89 —*D.T. (10/1/2006)*

DUTSCHKE

Dutschke 2005 WillowBend Single Vineyard Merlot-Shiraz-Cabernet Sauvignon Red Blend (Barossa Valley) $20. A luscious Merlot-based blend, this is full-bodied, soft and rounded. Flavors build upon a base of coffee and black cherry or plum, then add hints of musk and cinnamon. Long and silky-textured on the finish; best enjoyed over the next five or six years. 92 Editors' Choice —*J.C. (11/1/2007)*

Dutschke 2005 Oscar Semmler Single Vineyard Reserve Shiraz (Barossa Valley) $60. This is terrifically lush and easy to drink now, but don't be fooled into thinking this won't age—there's plenty of structure lurking underneath the layers of blackberry and blueberry fruit and veneer of toasty, vanilla-marked oak. Plus, there's spicy complexity as well, lending savory, meaty notes to the compelling mix. Drink now–2020. 94 Editors' Choice —*J.C. (11/1/2007)*

Dutschke 2005 St. Jakobi Single Vineyard Shiraz (Barossa Valley) $40. Compared to Dutschke's top-of-line Oscar Semmler Reserve, this is a softer, almost pillowy style of Shiraz, luxurious in the way the tannins caress the palate. Complex flavors of cola, mint, pepper, blackberries, vanilla and dried spices finish long, showing a hint of warmth but also lingering fruit and licorice flavors. Drink now–2015. 93 Editors' Choice —*J.C. (11/1/2007)*

EARTHWORKS

Earthworks 2004 Shiraz (Barossa Valley) $15. 83 —*D.T. (12/31/2005)*

EDEN SPRINGS

Eden Springs 1999 High-Eden Shiraz (Eden Valley) $25. 87 *(11/1/2001)*

ELDER VINE

Elder Vine 2002 Shiraz (Barossa Valley) $13. 88 Best Buy —*D.T. (11/15/2005)*

ELDERTON

Elderton 2004 Cabernet Sauvignon (Barossa) $26. From vines approximately 40 years of age, this is quintessential Barossa Shiraz, offering hints of mint and chocolate layered over a base of ripe cassis. It's approachable now, thanks to the soft tannins on the lush finish. 90 —*J.C. (11/1/2007)*

Elderton 2004 Ashmead Single Vineyard Cabernet Sauvignon (Barossa) $79. Past vintages of Elderton wines have been heavily oaked, and this wine is no exception—plenty of cedary, vanilla-laden aromas burst from the glass. But they're well balanced by crisp cassis flavors that turn chocolaty on the finish, where they also pick up a hint of tobacco. Delicious now, but it should drink well until at least 2014. 92 —*J.C. (11/1/2007)*

Elderton 2001 Ashmead Single Vineyard Cabernet Sauvignon (Barossa) $73. 88 —*D.T. (10/1/2006)*

Elderton 1999 Ashmead Single Vineyard Cabernet Sauvignon (Barossa Valley) $33. 86 —*D.T. (5/1/2004)*

Elderton 2000 Exclusive Estate Wine Cabernet Sauvignon (Barossa Valley) $27. 89 —*D.T. (5/1/2004)*

Elderton 2004 Ode to Lorraine Cabernet Sauvignon-Shiraz-Merlot (Barossa) $44. This blend of 57% Cabernet, 27% Shiraz and 16% Merlot is a barrel selection, named for the family matriarch. It's amply oaked, roaring forth with smoke, toast and vanilla, but there's also a tight core of mixed berry fruit and a long finish. Give it 2–3 years. 91 —*J.C. (11/1/2007)*

Elderton 2004 Unwooded Chardonnay (South Australia) $14. 83 —*D.T. (10/1/2005)*

Elderton 2000 Merlot (Barossa Valley) $30. 88 —*D.T. (9/1/2004)*

Elderton 2002 Riverina Botrytis Semillon (Barossa Valley) $17. 86 —*D.T. (9/1/2004)*

Elderton 2005 Tantalus Shiraz-Cabernet-Malbec-Merlot Red Blend (South Australia) $14. The real performers in the Elderton stable are at the top end, but this blended red is still a decent effort. It's full-bodied and flavorful but a bit warm, with the black cherry fruit struggling to hide the alcohol. Drink now. 84 —*J.C. (11/15/2007)*

Elderton 2004 Shiraz (Barossa) $29. Starts off with abundant savory notes of leather and hints of rhubarb and sour cherries. The tannins are ripe, giving the wine a creamy texture, but without a great deal of expansiveness in the midpalate. Finishes well, with lingering spice notes. 89 —*J.C. (11/1/2007)*

Elderton 2004 Command Shiraz (Barossa) $83. The current release, 2003, is an excellent wine, but this vintage kicks it up a notch. It's brighter, fresher and more vibrant than its amply endowed precursor, bursting with peppery raspberries. Creamy and rich, yet wonderfully balanced, and while you could drink it now, it will also cellar well for 10-plus years. 95 Cellar Selection —*J.C. (11/1/2007)*

Elderton 2003 Command Shiraz (Barossa) $83. Despite a tough vintage, this is a lush, complete wine. Vanilla and cedar notes on the nose serve to accent the layers of intense—verging on syrupy—blackberry fruit. It's easy enough to drink now, but rich enough that you may want to hold it another couple of years. Just don't expect this one to age more than a decade. 93 —*J.C. (11/1/2007)*

Elderton 1997 Command Shiraz (Barossa Valley) $62. 93 *(11/1/2001)*

Elderton 2003 The Ashmead Family Shiraz (Barossa) $30. 87 —*D.T. (12/1/2005)*

ELDREDGE VINEYARDS

Eldredge Vineyards 2000 MSG Red Blend (Clare Valley) $19. 87 —*D.T. (5/1/2004)*

Eldredge Vineyards 2002 Semillon-Sauvignon Blanc (Clare Valley) $14. 88 —*D.T. (12/31/2003)*

ELEMENT

Element 2001 Chardonnay (Western Australia) $14. 85 *(7/1/2002)*

Element 2001 Shiraz-Cabernet Sauvignon (Western Australia) $14. 88 *(7/1/2002)*

Element 2001 Chenin/Verdelho White Blend (Western Australia) $8. 85 *(7/1/2002)*

ELLEN LANDING

Ellen Landing 1999 Cabernet Sauvignon (Riverland) $19. 86 *—D.T. (9/1/2001)*

Ellen Landing 1999 Petite Verdot (Riverland) $19. 82 *—D.T. (9/1/2001)*

Ellen Landing 2000 Shiraz (Riverland) $19. 85 *(3/1/2003)*

Ellen Landing 1999 Shiraz (Riverland) $16. 83 *(10/1/2001)*

ELYSIAN FIELDS

Elysian Fields 2000 Chardonnay (Adelaide Hills) $23. 84 *—D.T. (8/1/2003)*

Elysian Fields 2001 Riesling (Clare Valley) $20. 86 *—D.T. (8/1/2003)*

EPPALOCK RIDGE

Eppalock Ridge 2000 Shiraz (Victoria) $25. 88 *(11/1/2001)*

Eppalock Ridge 1999 Heathcote Shiraz (Heathcote) $25. 85 *—D.T. (3/1/2003)*

EPSILON

Epsilon 2004 Coalsack Shiraz (Barossa Valley) $23. 85 *—D.T. (12/1/2005)*

EUROA CREEKS

Euroa Creeks 2002 Shiraz (Victoria) $60. 92 *—D.T. (5/1/2004)*

EVANS & TATE

Evans & Tate 2002 Gnangara Cabernet Sauvignon (Western Australia) $11. 88 Best Buy *—D.T. (5/1/2004)*

Evans & Tate 2001 Redbrook Cabernet Sauvignon (Margaret River) $49. 87 *—D.T. (10/1/2005)*

Evans & Tate 1999 Redbrook Cabernet Sauvignon (Margaret River) $49. 91 *(12/15/2002)*

Evans & Tate 2003 Underground Series Cabernet Sauvignon (Western Australia) $11. 85 *—D.T. (12/31/2005)*

Evans & Tate 2005 Chardonnay (Margaret River) $18. The company may be going through a troubled time, but based on this showing, the winemaking seems as sound as ever. Vanilla and toast elements are nicely integrated with the pear fruit, which adds a fresh, citrusy note on the finish. Medium-bodied, this seems nicely suited as a partner to mild chicken dishes where the subtle nutmeg and cinnamon spice notes will come to the fore. Drink now. 89 *—J.C. (2/1/2007)*

Evans & Tate 2004 Chardonnay (Margaret River) $16. 85 *—D.T. (12/1/2005)*

Evans & Tate 2002 Chardonnay (Margaret River) $15. 89 *(7/2/2004)*

Evans & Tate 2001 Chardonnay (Margaret River) $15. 86 *(12/15/2002)*

Evans & Tate 2003 Gnangara Unwooded Chardonnay (Western Australia) $11. 87 *—D.T. (11/15/2003)*

Evans & Tate 2002 Gnangara Unwooded Chardonnay (Western Australia) $11. 85 *(12/15/2002)*

Evans & Tate 2001 Redbrook Chardonnay (Margaret River) $39. 90 *(7/2/2004)*

Evans & Tate 2000 Redbrook Chardonnay (Margaret River) $39. 87 *(12/15/2002)*

Evans & Tate 2004 Underground Series Unwooded Chardonnay (Western Australia) $11. 87 Best Buy *—D.T. (12/1/2005)*

Evans & Tate 2003 Classic Red Red Blend (Margaret River) $15. 86 *—D.T. (10/1/2005)*

Evans & Tate 2001 Classic Red Red Blend (Margaret River) $14. 88 *(12/15/2002)*

Evans & Tate 2005 Underground Series Sauvignon Blanc (Western Australia) $11. 86 Best Buy *—D.T. (11/15/2005)*

Evans & Tate 2003 Margaret River Classic White Semillon-Sauvignon Blanc (Margaret River) $15. 82 *—D.T. (9/1/2004)*

Evans & Tate 2003 Shiraz (Margaret River) $18. Shows more structure than most Australian Shiraz at this price point, its firm acidity and ample tannins framing plum and vanilla flavors. Hints of eucalyptus, chocolate and coffee add complexity on the nose and finish. Drink now–2012. 89 *—J.C. (2/1/2007)*

Evans & Tate 2001 Shiraz (Margaret River) $18. 89 *(12/15/2002)*

Evans & Tate 2001 Gnangara Shiraz (Western Australia) $11. 85 *(12/15/2002)*

Evans & Tate 2004 Underground Series Shiraz (Western Australia) $11 83 *—D.T. (12/31/2005)*

Evans & Tate 2002 Classic White White Blend (Margaret River) $14. 86 *(12/15/2002)*

EVANS FAMILY

Evans Family 1998 Howard Shiraz (Hunter Valley) $20. 83 *(10/1/2001)*

EVANS WINE COMPANY

Evans Wine Company 1998 Cabernet Sauvignon (King Valley) $12. 87 Best Buy *—M.S. (10/1/2000)*

FAT CROC

Fat Croc 2002 Chardonnay (South Eastern Australia) $8. 88 Best Buy *—P.G. (11/15/2004)*

FEATHERTOP

Feathertop 2002 Merlot (Alpine Valleys) $16. 85 *—D.T. (8/1/2005)*

Feathertop 2004 Sauvignon Blanc (Alpine Valleys) $16. 90 *—D.T. (8/1/2005)*

FERN HILL

Fern Hill 1999 Shiraz (McLaren Vale) $22. 90 *(11/1/2001)*

FERNGROVE

Ferngrove 2004 Majestic Cabernet Sauvignon (Frankland River) $24. For a winery in only its fifth vintage, Ferngrove's 2004 Majestic Cabernet is a solid effort. Scents of toast, eucayptus and cherries turn slightly darker and take on a vanillin quality on the palate, married to a soft, velvety mouthfeel. Finishes soft and easy, enlivened by just a squirt of acidity. Drink now–2010. 88 *—J.C. (2/1/2007)*

Ferngrove 2003 Cabernet Sauvignon-Merlot (Frankland River) $13. 86 *—D.T. (8/1/2006)*

Ferngrove 2003 The Stirlings Cabernet Sauvignon-Shiraz (Frankland River) $30. Cabernet Sauvignon dominates the blend, at 71%, and as you might expect, the aromas contain a bit of green and herbal that gives a slightly medicinal edge to the cherry and cedar flavors. It's medium-bodied, with a slightly creamy texture and some dry, dusty tannins on the finish. Drink it now with a rare steak, or hold it a few years until it smooths out and turns more cedary. 87 *—J.C. (4/1/2007)*

Ferngrove 2006 Chardonnay (Frankland River) $15. With its bold aromas of melon, peach and pear, this is a fruit-driven wine of modest appeal. Simple fruit-cocktail flavors add a blast of citrus on the finish. 84 *—J.C. (4/1/2007)*

Ferngrove 2004 Chardonnay (Frankland River) $13. 84 *—D.T. (4/1/2006)*

Ferngrove 2006 Cossack Riesling (Frankland River) $22. Frankland River is turning out to be a fine source for Australian Rieslings, like this offering from Ferngrove. Honey, baked apple and wet stone aromas and flavors are intense and pure, while the wine is weighty with concentration to the point of a slight oiliness to its texture. Finishes long. 91 Editors' Choice *—J.C. (8/1/2007)*

Ferngrove 2005 Cossack Riesling (Frankland River) $18. 88 *—D.T. (4/1/2006)*

Ferngrove 2006 Symbols Sauvignon Blanc-Semillon (Frankland River) $12. Grassy and herbal, this is a slightly pungent rendition of the classic white Bordeaux grapes. It's simultaneously herbaceous and stony, lacking a bit of flesh in the midpalate, but would serve well to wash down raw oysters. 83 *—J.C. (3/1/2007)*

Ferngrove 2005 Sauvignon Blanc-Semillon (Frankland River) $13. 86 *—D.T. (4/1/2006)*

Ferngrove 2004 Dragon Shiraz (Frankland River) $24. This full-bodied, mouthfilling Shiraz isn't as dense or rich as it could be, but is still a hedonistic wine that avoids going over the top. Subtle smoke, vanilla and spice notes mark the blueberry and blackberry fruit flavors, which linger elegantly on the finish. 90 *—J.C. (4/1/2007)*

Ferngrove 2004 Estate Shiraz (Frankland River) $15. 86 *—D.T. (11/15/2006)*

Ferngrove 2005 Symbols Shiraz-Viognier (Frankland River) $12. Ferngrove's entry-level Shiraz includes 5% Viognier, but it avoids any Viognier-derived stone-fruit character, instead yielding up savory spice scents, a hint of mint and ripe blackberry and plum flavors. Tannins are soft, with acid providing the needed structure. Pepper and clove on the finish bring this bargain to a satisfying close. Drink now. 87 Best Buy *—J.C. (11/15/2007)*

Fetish 2005 The Watcher Shiraz (Barossa Valley) $20. This is a dark, earthier style of Barossa Shiraz, with savory notes of coffee and black olive

AUSTRALIA

versus the bold fruit found in other wines. There's still plenty of blackberry and plum fruit, it's just not as obvious and upfront. Turns slightly dusty on the finish, suggesting that this may be better with a year or two in the cellar. 89 —*J.C. (11/1/2007)*

Fetish 2004 The Watcher Shiraz (Barossa Valley) $20. This is an intriguing wine that underscores some of the overgeneralizations paid to Barossa Shiraz. Rather than making a big, fudgy, monolithic style, winemaker Rolf Binder has crafted a wine that's complex and surprisingly light on its feet, marrying cherries with hints of wintergreen, spice and dried mushroom that linger elegantly on the finish. 88 —*J.C. (3/1/2007)*

FIDDLERS CREEK

Fiddlers Creek 1999 Cabernet Sauvignon-Merlot (South Eastern Australia) $10. 84 —*M.S. (12/15/2002)*

Fiddlers Creek 2000 Chardonnay (South Eastern Australia) $7. 83 —*D.T. (6/1/2003)*

FINAL CUT

Final Cut 2005 Shiraz (McLaren Vale) $15. Stock up on this beauty, which marries smoke and vanilla notes from toasty oak with blackberry and blueberry fruit. But there's more to it than berries and oak, as it develops further complexity with air, culminating in a rush of black olive, coffee and a hint of peppery spice. The mouthwatering finish features just the right amount of dusty tannin to pair effectively with any red meats, and suggests that this is one bargain wine that won't be over the hill in a year or two. 90 Best Buy —*J.C. (11/15/2007)*

FIRE BLOCK

Fire Block 2005 Dry Rosé Grenache (Clare Valley) $14. 87 —*D.T. (4/1/2006)*

Fire Block 2003 Old Vine Grenache (Clare Valley) $19. Simple tart-cherry flavors finish crisp. This is on the light and lean side, but mouthwatering on the finish. 86 —*J.C. (6/1/2007)*

Fire Block 2002 Old Vine Grenache (Clare Valley) $19. 87 —*D.T. (10/1/2005)*

FIRE GULLY

Fire Gully 2000 Cabernet Sauvignon (Margaret River) $24. 90 —*D.T. (10/1/2003)*

Fire Gully 1999 Cabernet Sauvignon-Merlot (Margaret River) $23. 89 *(10/1/2003)*

Fire Gully 1999 Merlot (Margaret River) $24. 86 —*D.T. (10/1/2003)*

Fire Gully 2002 White Blend (Margaret River) $19. 82 —*D.T. (5/1/2004)*

FISHBONE

Fishbone 2003 Cabernet Sauvignon-Shiraz (Western Australia) $15. 87 —*D.T. (8/1/2006)*

Fishbone 2005 Unwooded Chardonnay (Western Australia) $15. 83 —*D.T. (11/15/2006)*

Fishbone 2005 Merlot (Western Australia) $15. With its mocha and herb aromas, this is recognizably Merlot, albeit one with slightly candied cherry fruit and a medicinal edge. Crisp on the finish. 83 —*J.C. (6/1/2007)*

Fishbone 2004 Merlot (Western Australia) $15. 88 —*D.T. (6/1/2006)*

Fishbone 2005 Classic White White Blend (Western Australia) $15. 85 —*D.T. (8/1/2006)*

FIVE GEESE

Five Geese 2004 Grenache-Shiraz (McLaren Vale) $23. 84 —*D.T. (11/15/2006)*

FLINDER'S BAY

Flinder's Bay 2003 Mayflower Malbec-Merlot (Margaret River) $19. An unusual blend of Malbec and Merlot, with crunchy, fresh cherry-berry flavors and hints of earth and vanilla. 87 —*J.C. (6/1/2007)*

Flinder's Bay 2001 Shiraz (Margaret River) $18. 90 —*D.T. (9/1/2004)*

Flinder's Bay 1999 Shiraz (Margaret River) $18. 86 *(10/1/2001)*

FONTHILL

Fonthill 2002 Dust of Ages Grenache (McLaren Vale) $30. 89 —*D.T. (5/1/2004)*

Fonthill 2001 Silk Shiraz (McLaren Vale) $32. 90 —*D.T. (5/1/2004)*

Fonthill 1999 Silk Shiraz (McLaren Vale) $23. 92 Editors' Choice —*D.T. (12/31/2003)*

FONTY'S POOL

Fonty's Pool 2003 Chardonnay (Pemberton) $18. 88 —*D.T. (4/1/2006)*

Fonty's Pool 2003 Pinot Noir (Pemberton) $18. 85 —*D.T. (4/1/2006)*

Fonty's Pool 2003 Shiraz (Pemberton) $18. 86 —*D.T. (6/1/2006)*

FOREFATHERS

Forefathers 2004 Shiraz (McLaren Vale) $25. Veteran winemaker Nick Goldschmidt is based in Healdsburg, California, as head of winemaking for Allied Domecq, but manages to find enough time to turn out this fine example of McLaren Vale Shiraz. The texture is lush and creamy, while the flavors run the gamut from dark mixed fruit to chocolate and spice. It firms up a bit on the finish, so while this is approachable now, it should easily age through 2015. 90 —*J.C. (2/1/2007)*

Forefathers 2001 Shiraz (McLaren Vale) $18. 89 —*J.M. (1/1/2003)*

FOUR EMUS

Four Emus 2004 Cabernet Sauvignon Shiraz Merlot Cabernet Blend (Western Australia) $11. 80 —*D.T. (12/31/2005)*

Four Emus 2005 Chardonnay (Western Australia) $11. 84 —*D.T. (6/1/2006)*

Four Emus 2005 Sauvignon Blanc-Semillon (Western Australia) $11. 86 Best Buy —*D.T. (11/15/2005)*

FOUR SISTERS

Four Sisters 2004 Chardonnay (South Eastern Australia) $13. 85 —*D.T. (6/1/2006)*

Four Sisters 2002 Chardonnay (Goulburn Valley) $12. 86 *(7/2/2004)*

Four Sisters 2005 Sauvignon Blanc (South Eastern Australia) $13. This is a simple, crisp seafood-ready white, lean without being angular. Green apple, honey and clover-blossom aromas yield to grassy, field-fresh flavors backed by pervasive notes of white grapefruit. 86 —*J.C. (2/1/2007)*

Four Sisters 2002 Trevor Mast 2002 Four Sisters Shiraz (South Eastern Australia) $12. 84 —*D.T. (5/1/2005)*

FOX CREEK

Fox Creek 2002 Reserve Cabernet Sauvignon (McLaren Vale) $30. 91 —*D.T. (3/1/2005)*

Fox Creek 2001 Duet Cabernet Sauvignon-Merlot (McLaren Vale) $22. 89 —*D.T. (12/31/2003)*

Fox Creek 2000 Duet Cabernet Sauvignon-Merlot (McLaren Vale) $15. 87 —*M.S. (12/15/2002)*

Fox Creek 2005 Chardonnay (McLaren Vale) $13. 87 —*D.T. (10/1/2006)*

Fox Creek 2004 Chardonnay (McLaren Vale) $13. 87 —*D.T. (3/1/2005)*

Fox Creek 2002 Chardonnay (South Australia) $15. 87 —*D.T. (8/1/2003)*

Fox Creek 2002 Chardonnay (South Australia) $15. 87 *(7/2/2004)*

Fox Creek 2001 Reserve Merlot (McLaren Vale) $27. 89 —*D.T. (9/1/2004)*

Fox Creek 2001 Red Blend (McLaren Vale) $20. 87 —*D.T. (12/31/2003)*

Fox Creek 2002 JSM Red Blend (McLaren Vale) $20. 90 —*D.T. (3/1/2005)*

Fox Creek 2005 Sauvignon Blanc (McLaren Vale) $13. 87 —*D.T. (10/1/2006)*

Fox Creek 2004 Sauvignon Blanc (South Australia) $13. 87 —*D.T. (3/1/2005)*

Fox Creek 2002 Sauvignon Blanc (South Australia) $15. 87 —*D.T. (11/15/2004)*

Fox Creek 2001 Sauvignon Blanc (South Australia) $15. 86 *(8/1/2002)*

Fox Creek 2002 Semillon-Sauvignon Blanc (South Australia) $15. 88 —*D.T. (11/15/2004)*

Fox Creek 2004 Reserve Shiraz (McLaren Vale) $73. Epitomizes the lush, immediately approachable style, with a mouthfeel so creamy it almost seems liquorous or syrupy. The flavors are ultraclean and precise, marrying crème de cassis with vanilla and hints of coconut. Soft tannins cushion the long finish. Drink now–2012. 92 —*J.C. (2/1/2007)*

Fox Creek 2002 Reserve Shiraz (McLaren Vale) $74. 91 —*D.T. (3/1/2005)*

Fox Creek 2004 Short Row Shiraz (McLaren Vale) $27. 90 —*D.T. (11/15/2006)*

Fox Creek 2003 Short Row Shiraz (McLaren Vale) $27. 90 —*D.T. (3/1/2005)*

Fox Creek 2001 Short Row Shiraz (McLaren Vale) $30. 89 —*D.T. (6/1/2003)*

Fox Creek 2000 Short Row Shiraz (McLaren Vale) $31. 91 —*D.T. (3/1/2003)*

Fox Creek 2001 JSM Shiraz-Cabernet Sauvignon (McLaren Vale) $19. 87 —*D.T. (11/15/2004)*

Fox Creek 2000 JSM Shiraz-Cabernet Sauvignon (McLaren Vale) $27. 90 —*D.T. (12/31/2003)*

Fox Creek 2004 Shiraz-Grenache (McLaren Vale) $17. This lush, full-bodied Shiraz-Grenache features ripe blackberry and black cherry flavors, framed by plenty of vanilla, cedar and spice. It's opulent and rich without being too heavy, with a long finish that adds hints of cinnamon, clove and mocha. The blend is 65% Shiraz, 35% Grenache. Drink now–2010. 91 Editors' Choice —*J.C. (2/1/2007)*

Fox Creek 2001 Shiraz-Grenache (McLaren Vale) $17. 88 —*D.T. (12/31/2004)*

Fox Creek NV Vixen Sparkling Blend (McLaren Vale) $15. 86 —*C.S. (12/1/2002)*

Fox Creek NV Vixen Sparkling Blend (South Australia) $17. 88 —*D.T. (3/1/2005)*

Fox Creek NV Vixen Sparkling Shiraz-Cabernet Franc-Cabernet Sauvignon Sparkling Blend (McLaren Vale) $19. 88 —*J.C. (12/31/2006)*

Fox Creek 2005 Verdelho (McLaren Vale) $13. Fox Creek's 2005 Verdelho has turned out to be a very enjoyable Chardonnay alternative, matching barrel fermentation and buttery, toasty notes with pear, melon and citrus flavors. It's a plump, succulent wine that goes down easy, filling the niche for a medium-bodied, oaked white at a very reasonable price. 89 Best Buy —*J.C. (2/1/2007)*

Fox Creek 2003 Verdelho (McLaren Vale) $13. 88 Best Buy —*D.T. (11/15/2004)*

Fox Creek 2002 Verdelho (South Australia) $15. 88 Editors' Choice —*D.T. (12/31/2003)*

Fox Creek 2004 Shadow's Run White Blend (South Australia) $10. 86 Best Buy —*D.T. (3/1/2005)*

FRANKLAND ESTATE

Frankland Estate 2004 Isolation Ridge Vineyard Chardonnay (Frankland River) $21. 88 —*D.T. (6/1/2006)*

Frankland Estate 2001 Isolation Ridge Vineyard Chardonnay (Western Australia) $20. 84 *(7/2/2004)*

Frankland Estate 2000 Isolation Ridge Vineyard Chardonnay (Western Australia) $20. 90 Editors' Choice —*J.C. (7/1/2002)*

Frankland Estate 2002 Olmo's Reward Merlot-Cabernet Franc (Frankland River) $29. A blend of Merlot and Cabernet Franc, this is a creamy, dense wine filled with black cherry, tobacco and mocha flavors. Soft enough to drink now. 90 —*J.C. (6/1/2007)*

Frankland Estate 2000 Olmo's Reward Red Blend (Western Australia) $26. 86 —*D.T. (9/1/2004)*

Frankland Estate 2002 Cooladerra Vineyard Riesling (Western Australia) $18. 89 —*D.T. (8/1/2003)*

Frankland Estate 2006 Isolation Ridge Vineyard Riesling (Frankland River) $19. Perennially one of Western Australia's best Rieslings, this is a medium-bodied effort that's deceptively light on its feet for having 13.5% alcohol. Aromas of flowers, wet stone and live ferns meld easily into hard-to-pin-down flavors that finish crisp and refreshing. Imported by USA Wine West. 89 —*J.C. (8/1/2007)*

Frankland Estate 2004 Isolation Ridge Vineyard Riesling (Frankland River) $20. 88 —*D.T. (10/1/2005)*

Frankland Estate 2001 Isolation Ridge Vineyard Riesling (Western Australia) $18. 87 —*D.T. (8/1/2003)*

Frankland Estate 2002 Poison Hill Vineyard Riesling (Western Australia) $18. 85 —*D.T. (8/1/2003)*

Frankland Estate 1999 Isolation Ridge Vineyard Shiraz (Western Australia) $20. 87 *(10/1/2001)*

FROGMORE CREEK

Frogmore Creek 2005 Estate Bottled Chardonnay (Tasmania) $17. This wine comes across as strongly citrusy at first, then picks up more nuanced scents of pineapple and corn silk. It's round and amply endowed on the palate, with a lot of sweet corn character, but otherwise well done. 86 —*J.C. (6/1/2007)*

Frogmore Creek 2005 Estate Bottled Pinot Noir (Tasmania) $20. Starts off herbal and perfumed, then adds root beer, earth and cherry notes. It's distinctly Pinot Noir in style, with relatively light body and delicate structure finishing crisp. Flavors are savory, earthy and mushroomy, but with a top note of red cherries. A pretty, lightweight wine that would pair well with salmon. 87 —*J.C. (6/1/2007)*

FROG ROCK

Frog Rock 2003 Chardonnay (Mudgee) $24. 84 —*D.T. (4/1/2006)*

Frog Rock 1999 Chardonnay (Mudgee) $20. 86 —*M.S. (3/1/2003)*

Frog Rock 1999 Shiraz (Mudgee) $24. 86 —*M.S. (3/1/2003)*

Frog Rock 1998 Shiraz (Mudgee) $25. 91 *(11/1/2001)*

GEMTREE

Gemtree 2002 Chardonnay (McLaren Vale) $17. 85 *(7/2/2004)*

Gemtree 2003 Citrine Chardonnay (McLaren Vale) $15. 88 —*D.T. (3/1/2005)*

Gemtree 2003 Cinnabar Grenache-Tempranillo-Shiraz Red Blend (McLaren Vale) $25. 88 —*D.T. (3/1/2005)*

Gemtree 2003 Tatty Road CS-PV-MER Red Blend (McLaren Vale) $25. 87 —*D.T. (3/1/2005)*

Gemtree 2002 Obsidian Shiraz (McLaren Vale) $40. 89 —*D.T. (3/1/2005)*

Gemtree 2003 Uncut Shiraz (McLaren Vale) $28. 89 —*D.T. (3/1/2005)*

GEOFF MERRILL

Geoff Merrill 2001 Cabernet Sauvignon (South Australia) $23. 87 —*D.T. (3/1/2005)*

Geoff Merrill 1990 Cabernet Sauvignon (South Australia) $50. 89 *(2/1/2002)*

Geoff Merrill 1985 Cabernet Sauvignon (South Australia) $60. 85 *(2/1/2002)*

Geoff Merrill 1980 Cabernet Sauvignon (South Australia) $55. 89 *(2/1/2002)*

Geoff Merrill 1998 Reserve Cabernet Sauvignon (Coonawarra) $35. 89 —*D.T. (3/1/2005)*

Geoff Merrill 1997 Reserve Cabernet Sauvignon (South Australia) $30. 82 —*S.H. (1/1/2002)*

Geoff Merrill 1996 Reserve Cabernet Sauvignon (South Australia) $40. 88 *(2/1/2002)*

Geoff Merrill 1995 Reserve Cabernet Sauvignon (South Australia) $35. 91 Cellar Selection *(2/1/2002)*

Geoff Merrill 2003 Cabernet Sauvignon-Merlot (South Australia) $15. 85 —*D.T. (3/1/2005)*

Geoff Merrill 2000 Pimpala Vineyard Estate Grown Cabernet Sauvignon-Merlot (McLaren Vale) $33. 91 —*D.T. (3/1/2005)*

Geoff Merrill 2002 Cabernet Sauvignon-Shiraz (South Australia) $20. 87 —*D.T. (3/1/2005)*

Geoff Merrill 2002 Chardonnay (McLaren Vale) $20. 86 —*D.T. (3/1/2005)*

Geoff Merrill 1999 Reserve Chardonnay (McLaren Vale) $26. 87 —*D.T. (3/1/2005)*

Geoff Merrill 1996 Reserve Chardonnay (South Eastern Australia) $25. 90 Editors' Choice *(2/1/2002)*

Geoff Merrill 1995 Reserve Chardonnay (South Eastern Australia) $22. 88 *(2/1/2002)*

Geoff Merrill 2004 Grenache Rose Grenache (McLaren Vale) $15. 88 —*D.T. (3/1/2005)*

Geoff Merrill 2001 Merlot (South Australia) $23. 88 —*D.T. (3/1/2005)*

Geoff Merrill 2003 Liquid Asset SZ-Gren-Vio Red Blend (McLaren Vale) $19. 86 —*D.T. (3/1/2005)*

Geoff Merrill 2001 Sz-Gren-M Rhône Red Blend (South Australia) $20. 87 —*D.T. (3/1/2005)*

Geoff Merrill 2004 Sauvignon Blanc (McLaren Vale) $20. 86 —*D.T. (3/1/2005)*

Geoff Merrill 2004 Sauvignon Blanc-Semillon (South Australia) $15. 88 —*D.T. (3/1/2005)*

Geoff Merrill 2001 Shiraz (McLaren Vale) $23. 90 —*D.T. (3/1/2005)*

Geoff Merrill 1998 Henley Shiraz (McLaren Vale) $145. 91 —*D.T. (3/1/2005)*

Geoff Merrill 1996 Henley Shiraz (Australia) $100. 93 Cellar Selection *(2/1/2002)*

Geoff Merrill 1998 Reserve Shiraz (McLaren Vale) $40. 90 —*D.T. (3/1/2005)*

Geoff Merrill 1998 Reserve Shiraz (McLaren Vale) $30. 89 —*S.H. (1/1/2002)*

Geoff Merrill 1997 Reserve Shiraz (McLaren Vale) $45. 89 *(2/1/2002)*

Geoff Merrill 1996 Reserve Shiraz (McLaren Vale) $32. 90 *(11/1/2001)*

Geoff Merrill 1995 Reserve Shiraz (South Australia) $40. 91 Cellar Selection *(2/1/2002)*

Geoff Merrill 1994 Reserve Shiraz (South Eastern Australia) $40. 90 Editors' Choice *(2/1/2002)*

GHOST GUM

Ghost Gum 2000 Cabernet Sauvignon (South Eastern Australia) $9. 83 —*D.T. (6/1/2002)*

Ghost Gum 2003 Chardonnay (South Eastern Australia) $9. 82 —*D.T. (6/1/2006)*

Ghost Gum 2000 Chardonnay (South Eastern Australia) $9. 84 —*J.C. (7/1/2002)*

Ghost Gum 2002 Shiraz (South Eastern Australia) $9. 86 Best Buy —*D.T. (6/1/2006)*

Ghost Gum 2000 Shiraz (South Eastern Australia) $9. 84 —*K.F. (1/28/2003)*

Ghost Gum 1998 Shiraz (South Eastern Australia) $9. 87 Best Buy *(10/1/2001)*

GIACONDA

Giaconda 2001 Chardonnay (Victoria) $125. 86 *(7/2/2004)*

Giaconda 2005 Nantua Vineyard Chardonnay (Victoria) $50. 92 —*D.T. (11/15/2006)*

Giaconda 2004 Nantua Vineyard Pinot Noir (Victoria) $100. 90 —*D.T. (11/15/2006)*

Giaconda 2005 Aeolia Roussanne (Victoria) $100. 90 —*D.T. (11/15/2006)*

Giaconda 2002 Aeolia Roussanne (Victoria) $75. 89 —*D.T. (11/15/2004)*

Giaconda 2001 Aeolia Roussanne (Victoria) $75. 93 *(6/1/2003)*

Giaconda 2002 Nantua Les Deux White Blend (Victoria) $45. 88 *(7/2/2004)*

Giaconda 2001 Nantua Les Deux White Blend (Victoria) $45. 90 *(6/1/2003)*

Giaconda 2004 Warner Vineyard Shiraz (Victoria) $100. Maybe the closest thing to French Syrah you'll find coming out of Australia, this Shiraz defies the Oz stereotype, offering up elegant perfumes of hickory smoke, black pepper and herbs that bear a striking resemblance to top-notch Côte-Rôtie. Layers of blackberry and blueberry fruit provide a solid foundation for the smoky, meaty complexity that emerges on the palate. This is not an overweight, overly tannic wine, but a supremely balanced rendition of Shiraz that should age gracefully for up to 15 years. 94 Cellar Selection —*J.C. (4/1/2007)*

GIANT STEPS

Giant Steps 2002 Merlot (Yarra Valley) $35. 86 —*D.T. (5/1/2005)*

Giant Steps 2002 Pinot Noir (Yarra Valley) $35. 86 —*D.T. (8/1/2005)*

GIBSON'S BAROSSAVALE

Gibson's BarossaVale 2005 Australian Old Vine Collection Grenache (McLaren Vale) $100. A tiny bottling (220 cases) of old-vine Grenache, this wine features lovely aromas of cinnamon, clove and ripe cherries. In the mouth it's surprisingly elegant, delivering cherry and spice flavors without excessive weight, ending on a slightly tart note. Drink now and over the next 4–5 years. 90 —*J.C. (12/31/2007)*

Gibson's BarossaVale 1999 Merlot (South Australia) $28. 83 —*C.S. (6/1/2002)*

Gibson's BarossaVale 2000 Sparkling Merlot (South Australia) $26. 88 —*M.S. (6/1/2003)*

Gibson's BarossaVale 2005 Wilfreda Blend Rhône Red Blend (Barossa) $40. A blend of 50% Shiraz, 38% Mourvèdre—often called Mataro in Australia—and 12% Grenache, this lush, rounded wine is all too easy to drink. Cola and plum aromas and flavors capture the essence of sun-warmed fruit, yet despite the ample ripeness there's no heaviness or alcoholic heat. Drink now and over the next few years. 90 —*J.C. (11/1/2007)*

Gibson's BarossaVale 2004 Shiraz (Barossa) $50. This is a spice-driven Shiraz, powered by peppery, savory notes that keep the rich blueberry fruit flavors moving across the palate. Tannins are ripe, imparting a creamy texture in the mouth, while the finish shows flourishes of dusty earth and spice. Drink now–2014 or beyond. 91 —*J.C. (11/1/2007)*

Gibson's BarossaVale 2000 Shiraz (South Australia) $40. 89 —*K.F. (3/1/2003)*

Gibson's BarossaVale 1999 Shiraz (Barossa Valley) $35. 90 *(11/1/2001)*

Gibson's BarossaVale 2005 Australian Old Vine Collection Shiraz (Barossa) $105. Incredibly perfumed, with peppery spice, vanilla, anise and blackberries all forming a wonderful whirlwind of aromas. Yet despite the complexity and obvious concentration, it's not heavy at all, delivering masses of flavor without excessive weight or obtrusive tannin. Mouthfeel is slightly creamy, the finish is long and spicy; in short, it's the complete package. Drink now–2017. 93 —*J.C. (11/1/2007)*

Gibson's BarossaVale 2005 Australian Old Vine Collection Shiraz (Eden Valley) $105. Even more spicy and meaty in nature than Gibson's Barossa bottling, this microcuvée—only 160 cases were bottled—highlights the savory side of Eden Valley Shiraz. Cola and blackberry flavors help round it out, but this is a slightly leaner style, albeit one that's complex and elegant. Drink 2009–2020. 92 —*J.C. (11/1/2007)*

Gibson's BarossaVale 2000 Australian Old Vine Collection Shiraz (Barossa Valley) $75. 87 —*K.F. (3/1/2003)*

GLAETZER

Glaetzer 2006 Amon Ra Shiraz (Barossa Valley) $90. Shows a slightly lifted, peppery character on the nose, but also plenty of toasty oak and bold fruit. Loads of blackberries, blueberries and chocolate cascade over the palate, accented with enough spice and warmth to leave a fleeting impression of fruitcake. Lush and long on the finish. Drink now–2020 or beyond. 95 —*J.C. (11/1/2007)*

Glaetzer 2005 Amon-Ra Unfiltered Shiraz (Barossa Valley) $80. From a single vineyard in the Ebenezer region, this is simply stupendous stuff. It is a bit Port-like in its rich layers of blackberry fruit, but it also displays great freshness and drive, giving it a juicy, fresh fruit character that's accented even more by dustings of pepper and dried spices. A beautiful marriage of drinkability and ageability; drink now–2020. 95 —*J.C. (11/1/2007)*

Glaetzer 2006 Bishop Shiraz (Barossa Valley) $45. This could use a year or two in the cellar, as right now the wine is a little toughly textured, despite showing ample body and weight. Green peppercorn notes accent cherry fruit, picking up a hint of tea leaves on the finish. 89 —*J.C. (11/1/2007)*

Glaetzer 2006 Anaperenna Shiraz-Cabernet Sauvignon (Barossa Valley) $NA. A blend of 75% Shiraz and 25% Cabernet Sauvignon, this is the rechristened Godolphin, renamed because of a trademark conflict. Mint and tobacco notes frame the lush chocolaty layers of dark fruit—mainly cassis. Long and wonderfully supple on the finish. Drink now–2020. 94 —*J.C. (11/1/2007)*

Glaetzer 2005 Godolphin Shiraz-Cabernet Sauvignon (Barossa Valley) $60. A blend of 80% Shiraz and 20% Cabernet, this rich, almost Port-like wine also shows a slight herbal note—enough to give it some lift and complexity. It's inky black in color, imbued with layers of dark fruit so deep they threaten to suck you in before being lightened ever so slightly by hints of vanilla and spice. Long and lush on the finish. Drink now–2015. 94 —*J.C. (11/1/2007)*

Glaetzer 2006 Wallace Shiraz-Grenache (Barossa Valley) $25. Sweetly fragrant, with hints of white pepper and stone fruit that veer toward cherries and spice on the palate. The silky texture is a treat, with just enough tart acidity on the finish for balance. Drink now–2010. 90 —*J.C. (11/1/2007)*

GLEN ELDON

Glen Eldon 2005 Riesling (Eden Valley) $17. Contrasts seductive aromas of fresh flowers, apples, pears and citrus with a firm, unyielding array of stony, minerally flavors. Medium-bodied and a bit viscous, yet finishes clean and refreshing. 86 —*J.C. (8/1/2007)*

Glen Eldon 2003 Riesling (Eden Valley) $18. 86 —*D.T. (11/15/2004)*

Glen Eldon 2004 Dry Bore Shiraz (Barossa) $27. A terrific value, this boasts knockout aromas of blueberry pie and cracked pepper, followed by a velvety, rich texture and flavors that pick up hints of additional spice, grilled meat and black olive. It juxtaposes ripeness, texture and complexity to make a complete package worth cellaring until 2010 and drinking over the following 10 years. 93 Editors' Choice —*J.C. (11/1/2007)*

Glen Eldon 2001 Dry Bore Shiraz (Barossa Valley) $25. 89 —*D.T. (12/31/2004)*

GLENDONBROOK

Glendonbrook 2001 Shiraz, Cabernet, Merlot Red Blend (Hunter Valley) $17. 84 —*M.S. (12/15/2002)*

GOLD

Gold 2006 White Wine with 24k Gold Leaf Added Chardonnay (Australia) $20. To distinguish this from the oceans of Chards out there, this doesn't say "Chardonnay" anywhere on the label, instead opting for flecks of gold leaf in a clear bottle. At least the wine is pretty good, making it a harmless marketing gimmick. It's round and ample, with flavors of honeyed melon and pear that finish fruity, clean and fresh. 86 —*J.C. (4/1/2007)*

GOLDING

Golding 2004 Billy Goat Hill Chardonnay (Lenswood) $22. 85 —*D.T. (6/1/2006)*

Golding 2004 Sauvignon Blanc (Adelaide Hills) $15. 88 —*D.T. (8/1/2005)*

Golding 2002 Lenswood Sauvignon Blanc (Adelaide Hills) $17. 90 Editors' Choice —*D.T. (5/1/2004)*

Golding 2005 Western Branch Sauvignon Blanc (Lenswood) $20. 85 —*D.T. (8/1/2006)*

GORGE

Gorge 2004 Pinot Grigio (Hunter Valley) $15. 85 —*D.T. (12/1/2005)*

AUSTRALIA

GOTHAM

Gotham 2004 Shiraz (Langhorne Creek) $19. 82 *—D.T. (6/1/2006)*

GOUNDREY

Goundrey 2003 Offspring Cabernet Sauvignon (Western Australia) $16. 86 *—D.T. (12/31/2005)*

Goundrey 2002 Offspring Cabernet Sauvignon (Western Australia) $15. 88 *—D.T. (12/31/2004)*

Goundrey 2003 Offspring Chardonnay (Western Australia) $16. 85 *—D.T. (10/1/2005)*

Goundrey 2002 Offspring Chardonnay (Western Australia) $15. 85 *—D.T. (12/31/2004)*

Goundrey 1999 Shiraz-Grenache Red Blend (South Eastern Australia) $13. 85 *—J.C. (9/1/2002)*

Goundrey 2005 Offspring Riesling (Western Australia) $13. 86 *—D.T. (10/1/2006)*

Goundrey 2002 Offspring Shiraz (Western Australia) $15. 87 *—D.T. (5/1/2005)*

GRANDIS

Grandis 2000 Merlot (South Australia) $14. 84 *—D.T. (1/1/2002)*

GRANT BURGE

Grant Burge 2004 Cameron Vale Cabernet Sauvignon (Barossa) $NA. A lean, restrained style of Barossa Cabernet, with minty, herbal aromas and crisp cassis fruit. Nicely balanced, and it should drink well over the next several years. 87 *—J.C. (11/1/2007)*

Grant Burge 2002 Cameron Vale Cabernet Sauvignon (Barossa) $19. 88 *—D.T. (4/1/2006)*

Grant Burge 2001 Cameron Vale Cabernet Sauvignon (Barossa Valley) $20. 87 *—D.T. (2/1/2004)*

Grant Burge 2000 Shadrach Cabernet Sauvignon (South Australia) $50. 93 *—D.T. (10/1/2006)*

Grant Burge 1999 Shadrach Cabernet Sauvignon (Coonawarra) $70. 91 *—D.T. (2/1/2004)*

Grant Burge 2002 Barossa Vines Cabernet Sauvignon-Merlot (Barossa Valley) $12. 85 *—D.T. (12/1/2005)*

Grant Burge 2005 Barossa Vines Chardonnay (Barossa) $14. This fat, rather anonymous Chardonnay exhibits adequate tropical and citrus fruit but also a sour edge to its flavors. 82 *—J.C. (3/1/2007)*

Grant Burge 2003 Barossa Vines Chardonnay (Barossa Valley) $11. 85 *—D.T. (2/1/2004)*

Grant Burge 2002 Barossa Vines Chardonnay (Barossa Valley) $11. 86 *—D.T. (2/1/2004)*

Grant Burge 2001 Barossa Vines Chardonnay (Barossa Valley) $13. 83 *—J.C. (7/1/2002)*

Grant Burge 2006 Barossa Wines Unoaked Chardonnay (Barossa) $14. A solid, well-made offering, Grant Burge's unoaked Chardonnay offers a medium-bodied mouthful of authoritative flavor at a reasonable price. Baked apple and poached pear aromas and flavors intensify rather than fall off on the finish, unusual at this price point. Drink now. 87 *—J.C. (8/1/2007)*

Grant Burge 2003 Barossa Vines Unwooded Chardonnay (Barossa Valley) $11. 83 *(5/1/2004)*

Grant Burge 2003 Summers Chardonnay (South Australia) $19. 89 *—D.T. (8/1/2005)*

Grant Burge 2002 Summers Chardonnay (Eden Valley) $17. 87 *(7/2/2004)*

Grant Burge 2000 Summers Chardonnay (Eden Valley) $18. 87 *—D.T. (8/1/2003)*

Grant Burge 2003 Summers Eden Valley Chardonnay (Barossa Valley) $18. 87 *—D.T. (2/1/2004)*

Grant Burge 2004 Hillcot Merlot (Barossa) $19. Herbal, briary and peppery, with hints of rhubarb and cherry providing a semblance of fruitiness. A bit tough and hard on the finish. 82 *—J.C. (2/1/2007)*

Grant Burge 2003 Abednego Rhône Red Blend (Barossa) $NA. Only the second vintage of this wine, which sits above The Holy Trinity in the Grant Burge hierarchy. The 2003 is a blend of 36% Mataro, 33% Grenache and 31% Shiraz, showing hints of tea and cola on the nose to go with dark blackberry and coffee flavors. This is crisp and well-structured, with some drying tannins on the finish that suggest short-term cellaring. Drink 2010–2018. 91 *—J.C. (11/1/2007)*

Grant Burge 2003 Hillcot Merlot (Barossa Valley) $19. 88 *—D.T. (4/1/2006)*

Grant Burge 2000 The Holy Trinity Red Blend (Barossa Valley) $33. 88 *—D.T. (2/1/2004)*

Grant Burge 2001 The Holy Trinity Rhône Red Blend (Barossa Valley) $33. 88 *—D.T. (5/1/2004)*

Grant Burge 2003 The Holy Trinity Rhône Red Blend (Barossa) $NA. The 2003 Holy Trinity is slightly bigger and riper than the extremely stylish 2002, but also a touch less complex. Cedar and dried spice notes frame cherry and raspberry fruit, which turns crisp and shows some firm tannins on the finish. A blend of Grenache, Shiraz and Mourvèdre. Drink now–2012. 89 *—J.C. (11/1/2007)*

Grant Burge 2002 The Holy Trinity Rhône Red Blend (Barossa) $34. 87 *—D.T. (8/1/2006)*

Grant Burge 1999 The Holy Trinity Rhône Red Blend (Barossa Valley) $33. 88 *—D.T. (6/1/2003)*

Grant Burge 1998 The Holy Trinity Rhône Red Blend (Barossa Valley) $35. 89 *—J.C. (9/1/2002)*

Grant Burge 1997 The Holy Trinity Rhône Red Blend (Barossa Valley) $33. 88 *—J.C. (9/1/2001)*

Grant Burge 2005 Thorn Riesling (Eden Valley) $19. 89 *—D.T. (8/1/2006)*

Grant Burge 2004 Thorn Riesling (Eden Valley) $19. 88 *—D.T. (4/1/2006)*

Grant Burge 2002 Thorn Riesling (Eden Valley) $19. 90 *—D.T. (8/1/2005)*

Grant Burge 2005 Kraft Sauvignon Blanc (South Australia) $19. 88 *—D.T. (6/1/2006)*

Grant Burge 2004 Kraft Sauvignon Blanc (South Australia) $19. 88 *—D.T. (8/1/2005)*

Grant Burge 2003 Kraft Sauvignon Blanc (Barossa Valley) $16. 87 *—D.T. (2/1/2004)*

Grant Burge 1998 Kraft Sauvignon Blanc (Barossa Valley) $16. 84 *(4/1/2000)*

Grant Burge 2005 Barossa Vines Shiraz (Barossa) $15. Simple and fruity, with bright cherries and blackberries that carry right through the palate and onto the finish. Slightly creamy in texture, with just a hint of tea leaf to keep things interesting. Drink now. 86 *—J.C. (11/1/2007)*

Grant Burge 2003 Barossa Vines Shiraz (Barossa) $15. 86 *—D.T. (10/1/2005)*

Grant Burge 2002 Barossa Vines Shiraz (Barossa Valley) $11. 85 *—D.T. (2/1/2004)*

Grant Burge 2000 Barossa Vines Shiraz (Barossa Valley) $11. 85 *—J.C. (9/1/2002)*

Grant Burge 1999 Barossa Vines Shiraz (Barossa Valley) $11. 86 *(10/1/2001)*

Grant Burge 2004 Filsell Shiraz (Barossa) $31. From a vineyard planted in 1927, this is aged in a blend of French and American oak. Subtle dill notes mark the nose, but there's more vanilla and even more blackberry and blueberry fruit. It's not as soft or lush as some Barossa Shirazes, finishing with a dusty, satiny texture. Drink now–2014. 89 *—J.C. (11/1/2007)*

Grant Burge 2003 Filsell Shiraz (Barossa) $30. 90 *—D.T. (2/1/2006)*

Grant Burge 2002 Filsell Shiraz (Barossa Valley) $30. 91 *—D.T. (10/1/2005)*

Grant Burge 2000 Filsell Shiraz (Barossa Valley) $25. 87 *—K.F. (1/1/2004)*

Grant Burge 1998 Filsell Shiraz (Barossa Valley) $25. 87 *—M.M. (6/1/2001)*

Grant Burge 2005 Filsell Old Vine Shiraz (Barossa) $NA. This has more red-fruit character than most Barossa Shirazes, with cherry and raspberry flavors mingling with vanilla and carried by an almost syrupy mouthfeel—almost like a berry-vanilla compote. Sure, it could use bit a more spice and complexity, but that would be quibbling; this is luscious stuff to drink now through 2015. 90 *—J.C. (11/1/2007)*

Grant Burge 1999 Meshach Shiraz (Barossa Valley) $145. 91 Cellar Selection *—D.T. (2/1/2004)*

Grant Burge 2005 Meshach Shiraz (Barossa) $NA. As might be expected from a wine not to be released until 2010, this is showing little development or complexity at this stage. What it does have is bountiful raspberry and blueberry fruit and lashings of vanilla, caramel and cedar. Should be a good one down the road. 91 *—J.C. (11/1/2007)*

Grant Burge 2002 Meshach Shiraz (Barossa) $95. This is the current release of Grant Burge's Meshach, which is typically held back for additional bottle age—the already bottled 2005 will be released in 2010. It displays extraordinary complexity in its scents of tea, coffee, spice and marinated beef, but the primary focus remains on its elegant blackberry fruit. Try around 2010. 90 *—J.C. (11/1/2007)*

Grant Burge 2001 Meshach Shiraz (Barossa) $82. 92 *—D.T. (2/1/2006)*

Grant Burge 2000 Meshach Shiraz (Barossa Valley) $82. 91 *—D.T. (8/1/2005)*

Grant Burge 1998 Meshach Shiraz (Barossa) $150. Elegantly combines plenty of spicy, meaty notes with round, ripe cherry-berry fruit. Dark flavors of soy or oyster sauce impart a savory element, adding a bass note to the finely tuned chorus of flavors. Finishes long and velvety. Drink now–2016. 92 *—J.C. (11/1/2007)*

Grant Burge 1996 Meshach Shiraz (Barossa Valley) $145. 94 Cellar Selection *(11/1/2001)*

Grant Burge 2005 Miamba Shiraz (Barossa) $19. Soft and fleshy in texture, with slightly pruny dark plum fruit and a charming hint of black licorice. Supple tannins frame the crisp finish. Seems a bit shy aromatically; try checking it again in 2008, as it should evolve relatively rapidly. 88 *—J.C. (11/1/2007)*

Grant Burge 2004 Miamba Shiraz (Barossa) $19. This is rather big and burly, powered by rich blackberry fruit, spice and earthy notes that are highlighted by brighter raspberry tones. It could use a more polished mouthfeel and greater length on the finish, but its muscular nature would do well paired with grilled steak. Drink now–2012. 88 *—J.C. (3/1/2007)*

Grant Burge 2003 Miamba Shiraz (Barossa) $19. 85 *—D.T. (6/1/2006)*

Grant Burge 2002 Miamba Shiraz (Barossa Valley) $15. 88 *—D.T. (5/1/2004)*

Grant Burge 2001 Miamba Shiraz (Barossa Valley) $15. 87 *—D.T. (2/1/2004)*

Grant Burge 2000 Miamba Shiraz (Barossa Valley) $15. 89 *—S.H. (1/1/2002)*

Grant Burge 1999 Miamba Shiraz (Barossa Valley) $15. 87 *—S.H. (9/1/2002)*

Grant Burge 2002 Filsell Shiraz-Cabernet Sauvignon (Barossa Valley) $25. 90 *—D.T. (5/1/2004)*

Grant Burge 2001 Filsell Shiraz-Cabernet Sauvignon (Barossa Valley) $25. 88 *—D.T. (2/1/2004)*

Grant Burge 2003 Nebuchadnezzar Shiraz-Cabernet Sauvignon (Barossa) $34. 88 *—D.T. (2/1/2006)*

Grant Burge 2003 Balthasar Shiraz-Viognier (Barossa) $33. 88 *—D.T. (6/1/2006)*

Grant Burge 2002 Balthasar Shiraz-Viognier (Barossa Valley) $32. 88 *—D.T. (10/1/2005)*

GREEN POINT

Green Point 2004 Cabernet Sauvignon-Shiraz (Victoria) $18. 88 *—D.T. (8/1/2006)*

Green Point 2004 Chardonnay (Victoria) $16. There's an intriguing hint of graphite to this wine, but otherwise it's pretty straightforward, with simple apple, pear and citrus flavors. Slightly viscous in the mouth, finishing slightly warm. Drink now. 85 *—J.C. (8/1/2007)*

Green Point 2003 Chardonnay (Yarra Valley) $16. 87 *(12/15/2005)*

Green Point 2002 Chardonnay (Yarra Valley) $16. 86 *—D.T. (12/31/2004)*

Green Point 2004 Reserve Chardonnay (Yarra Valley) $27. 88 *—D.T. (11/15/2006)*

Green Point 2003 Reserve Chardonnay (Yarra Valley) $24. 89 *(12/15/2005)*

Green Point 2002 Reserve Chardonnay (Yarra Valley) $25. 90 *—D.T. (12/31/2004)*

Green Point 2006 Rosé Pinot Noir (Victoria) $18. A dry rosé of Pinot Noir made in a truly savory style, this wine features touches of peach, melon and citrus, but comes across as unusually stony and minerally. The crisp, dry finish will offer plenty of summer refreshment. 86 *—J.C. (7/1/2007)*

Green Point 2003 Shiraz (Victoria) $18. 89 *(12/15/2005)*

Green Point 2002 Shiraz (Victoria) $18. 89 *—D.T. (12/31/2004)*

Green Point 2004 Reserve Shiraz (Yarra Valley) $25. Shows good complexity in its spice-driven aromas and earthy flavors, but also the slightest hint of raisining to the brambly, blackberry-inflected fruit. Has plenty of size and structure, ending with dusty tannins on the long finish. Try 2008–2015. 89 *—J.C. (5/1/2007)*

Green Point 2003 Reserve Shiraz (Yarra Valley) $24. 90 Editors' Choice *(12/15/2005)*

Green Point 2002 Reserve Shiraz (Yarra Valley) $25. 88 *—D.T. (5/1/2005)*

GREENOCK CREEK

Greenock Creek 2003 Cabernet Sauvignon (Barossa Valley) $125. 88 *—D.T. (10/1/2006)*

Greenock Creek 2004 Alices Shiraz (Barossa Valley) $50. Heady and superripe, this is a huge, mouthfilling wine that fits the ooze monster moniker, yet it finishes with structure and elegance. Camphor and cracked pepper scents accent the blackberry, dark chocolate and mint flavors that finish long, framed by dusty tannins. Drink now–2025. 95 Editors' Choice *—J.C. (11/1/2007)*

Greenock Creek 2004 Apricot Block Shiraz (Barossa Valley) $55. Smells almost Port-like, with expansive aromas of fruit cake, maple syrup and chocolate, then delivers a similar array of flavors, although completely dry. Full-bodied, lush and richly textured, this is almost too much, although the intriguing spice notes of cinnamon, clove and allspice help rein in the waves of chocolate and dried fruit. Long, velvety and slightly warm on the finish. Drink now–2015. 93 Editors' Choice *—J.C. (11/1/2007)*

Greenock Creek 2004 Seven Acre Shiraz (Barossa Valley) $75. An immensely aromatic expression of Barossa Shiraz, with bold notes of menthol, raspberries, chocolate and spice all bursting forth. The flavors are similar, and similarly expressive, although this wine lacks some of the richness of texture found in Greenock Creek's 2004 Alices or Apricot Block Shirazes. Finishes long, with a touch of warmth. Drink now–2015. 91 *—J.C. (11/1/2007)*

GREG NORMAN ESTATES

Greg Norman Estates 2003 Cabernet-Merlot Cabernet Sauvignon-Merlot (Limestone Coast) $15. The first golfer brand rolls right along, churning out thousands of cases of supple, user-friendly wines at affordable price points. This blend of 83% Cabernet Sauvignon and 17% Merlot offers cherry and tobacco flavors and a tart, crisp finish. 84 *—J.C. (2/1/2007)*

Greg Norman Estates 2002 Cabernet Sauvignon-Merlot (Limestone Coast) $17. 84 *—D.T. (12/31/2004)*

Greg Norman Estates NV Champagne Blend (Australia) $19. 91 *—K.F. (12/1/2002)*

Greg Norman Estates NV Australian Sparkling Champagne Blend (South Eastern Australia) $19. 87 *—M.M. (12/1/2001)*

Greg Norman Estates 2004 Chardonnay (Victoria) $14. 85 *—D.T. (12/1/2005)*

Greg Norman Estates 2003 Chardonnay (Victoria) $14. 87 *—D.T. (10/1/2005)*

Greg Norman Estates 2002 Chardonnay (Victoria) $14. 88 *(7/2/2004)*

Greg Norman Estates 2001 Chardonnay (Yarra Valley) $17. 81 *—D.T. (8/1/2003)*

Greg Norman Estates 2000 Chardonnay (Yarra Valley) $17. 84 *—J.C. (7/1/2002)*

Greg Norman Estates 1998 Chardonnay (Yarra Valley) $15. 88 *(12/31/1999)*

Greg Norman Estates 2005 Shiraz (Limestone Coast) $15. Next time you drop a six-stroke lead on the last day of the country club tournament, head for the dining room and order a bottle of this mainstream Shiraz. It goes down easy, thanks to its roundness and supple tannins, yet still offers enough complexity and tannin to stand up to simply grilled steaks. 87 *—J.C. (11/15/2007)*

Greg Norman Estates 2003 Shiraz (Limestone Coast) $16. 86 *—D.T. (2/1/2006)*

Greg Norman Estates 1999 Shiraz (Limestone Coast) $17. 83 *—J.C. (9/1/2002)*

Greg Norman Estates 1998 Shiraz (Limestone Coast) $17. 87 *(6/1/2001)*

Greg Norman Estates 2000 Padthaway Reserve Shiraz (South Australia) $40. 88 *—D.T. (12/1/2005)*

Greg Norman Estates 1999 Reserve Shiraz (South Eastern Australia) $40. 90 *—D.T. (9/1/2004)*

Greg Norman Estates 1998 Reserve Shiraz (McLaren Vale) $40. 92 *(10/1/2003)*

Greg Norman Estates 2002 Shiraz-Cabernet Sauvignon (Limestone Coast) $16. 88 *—D.T. (10/1/2005)*

Greg Norman Estates NV Sparkling Blend (Australia) $19. 85 *—D.T. (12/31/2003)*

Greg Norman Estates NV Sparkling Blend (South Eastern Australia) $19. 85 *—D.T. (12/31/2003)*

Greg Norman Estates NV Sparkling Blend (South Eastern Australia) $16. 88 *—D.T. (12/31/2004)*

GROOM

Groom 2006 Sauvignon Blanc (Adelaide Hills) $18. Although Daryl Groom is now a senior VP at Beam Wine Estates in California, his deal allows him time to do a small amount of his own wines, like this 100% stainless Sauvignon Blanc. It's not overly ripe, but it's not overly green either—meaning that it strikes just the right balance. Hints of ripe peach and melon are matched with vibrant acidity and a slightly creamy texture, all at a reasonably low alcohol reading of 12.8%. 89 *—J.C. (6/1/2007)*

Groom 2005 Sauvignon Blanc (Adelaide Hills) $17. 89 —*D.T. (6/1/2006)*

Groom 2004 Sauvignon Blanc (Adelaide Hills) $16. 89 —*D.T. (8/1/2005)*

Groom 2003 Sauvignon Blanc (Adelaide Hills) $16. 90 Editors' Choice —*D.T. (5/1/2004)*

Groom 2002 Sauvignon Blanc (Adelaide Hills) $16. 91 —*J.M. (6/1/2003)*

Groom 2001 Shiraz (Barossa Valley) $40. 94 —*J.M. (6/1/2003)*

GROSSET

Grosset 2001 Gaia Cabernet Blend (Clare Valley) $40. 91 Cellar Selection —*D.T. (2/1/2004)*

Grosset 2000 Picadilly Chardonnay (Adelaide Hills) $31. 91 —*J.C. (7/1/2002)*

Grosset 2003 Piccadilly Chardonnay (Adelaide Hills) $37. 91 —*D.T. (8/1/2005)*

Grosset 2002 Piccadilly Chardonnay (Clare Valley) $39. 93 —*D.T. (9/1/2004)*

Grosset 2006 Polish Hill Riesling (Clare Valley) $33. In blind tastings of young wines such as we do for these reviews, the ultimate heights certain wines may achieve can be hard to discern. Such is the case for Grosset's Polish Hill Riesling, a wine that impresses for its power and clarity at this age, but clearly has much more to give. Floral and mineral notes open, followed by strident apple and lime flavors. It's zingy, bold and intense—impressive now, but try to give it at least five years to see how badly this rating underestimates its apogee. 90 Cellar Selection —*J.C. (6/1/2007)*

Grosset 2004 Polish Hill Riesling (Clare Valley) $34. 90 —*D.T. (10/1/2005)*

Grosset 2003 Polish Hill Riesling (Clare Valley) $29. 91 —*D.T. (2/1/2004)*

Grosset 2002 Polish Hill Riesling (Clare Valley) $30. 91 Editors' Choice —*D.T. (8/1/2003)*

Grosset 2001 Polish Hill Riesling (Clare Valley) $29. 92 —*J.C. (2/1/2002)*

Grosset 2006 Watervale Riesling (Clare Valley) $29. There's a greenish tinge to this wine's fruit, but it also features complex minerally elements, so the end result is something like fresh ferns, crushed stone and fresh-squeezed limes. It's plump in the mouth, yet sharply focused, finishing crisp and refreshing. Imported by USA Wine West. 90 —*J.C. (9/1/2007)*

Grosset 2003 Watervale Riesling (Clare Valley) $24. 88 —*D.T. (9/1/2004)*

Grosset 2002 Watervale Riesling (Clare Valley) $25. 87 —*D.T. (8/1/2003)*

GULLIN LANDSCAPE

Gullin Landscape 1999 Red Earth Cabernet Cabernet Sauvignon (Coonawarra) $11. 84 —*M.S. (12/15/2002)*

Gullin Landscape 2000 Chardonnay (South Eastern Australia) $8. 83 —*D.T. (8/1/2003)*

Gullin Landscape 1999 Red Earth Shiraz (McLaren Vale) $16. 88 —*D.T. (3/1/2003)*

HAAN

Haan 2004 Hanenhof Merlot-Cabernet Sauvignon-Cabernet Franc Bordeaux Blend (Barossa Valley) $20. A potentially polarizing wine, with enough black cherry and cassis fruit and a creamy, supple texture, but also with strong greenish overtones of eucalyptus or mint, even a touch of green pea. Picks up cedar, vanilla and coffee shadings on the finish. Drink now. 89 —*J.C. (6/1/2007)*

Haan 2004 Wilhelmus Bordeaux Blend (Barossa Valley) $48. The five classic Bordeaux varieties find new expression in this Barossan blend. It's cherry-scented and cheerful, with hints of raspberry and vanilla to keep it interesting. With its creamy, supple tannins and mouthwatering finish, this seems likely to be best now through 2012. 90 —*J.C. (11/1/2007)*

Haan 2002 Hanenhof Bordeaux Blend (Barossa Valley) $20. 90 —*D.T. (5/1/2005)*

Haan 2004 Prestige Merlot (Barossa Valley) $48. Merlot in the Barossa can be a tricky proposition, but this bottling successfully juxtaposes superripe, chocolate fudge notes with surprisingly tart acids. Hints of licorice, vanilla and black cherries impart complexity, while creamy tannins and crisp acids mark the finish. Drink now–2012. 88 —*J.C. (11/1/2007)*

Haan 2005 Hanenhof Merlot-Cabernet Franc (Barossa Valley) $22. This comes out of the bottle a bit tarry and rubbery, so splash it around in a decanter a bit if you get the chance. You'll be rewarded by Cabernet Franc's trademark leafy aromas set off by Merlot's background of plum and chocolate. Tannins are ultrasmooth, so there's no need to age this; drink now–2010. 87 —*J.C. (11/1/2007)*

Haan 2004 Hanenhof Shiraz (Barossa Valley) $20. An outstanding value, this wine bursts from the glass with spice, herb and brambly shadings that are nicely complex and true to the grape variety. It's not just a fruit-filled wine, but one that offers a panopoly of briary, brambly fruit alongside plenty of spice and a meaty, sauvage component. It's round and lush in the mouth, finishing spicy and long, with mouthwatering persistence. Drink now–2012. 92 Editors' Choice —*J.C. (4/25/2007)*

Haan 2003 Estate Wine Viognier (Barossa Valley) $30. 80 —*D.T. (11/15/2004)*

HAHNDORF HILL WINERY

Hahndorf Hill Winery 2006 Sauvignon Blanc (Adelaide Hills) $19. Partners Larry Jacobs and Marc Dobson evidently brought a knack for growing Sauvignon Blanc with them from their former winery in South Africa—Mulderbosch. This is a plump, rather full-bodied Sauvignon with an almost smoky, Fumé character to go with flavors of underripe peach and melon. Drink now. 87 —*J.C. (6/1/2007)*

HAMELIN BAY

Hamelin Bay 1999 Cabernet Sauvignon (Margaret River) $29. 88 —*C.S. (6/1/2002)*

Hamelin Bay 2001 Chardonnay (Margaret River) $22. 85 *(7/2/2004)*

Hamelin Bay 2000 Chardonnay (Margaret River) $28. 84 —*J.C. (7/1/2002)*

Hamelin Bay 2001 Sauvignon Blanc (Margaret River) $22. 87 *(8/1/2002)*

Hamelin Bay 2000 Sauvignon Blanc (Margaret River) $22. 82 —*J.C. (2/1/2002)*

Hamelin Bay 1999 Semillon-Sauvignon Blanc (Margaret River) $19. 90 —*S.H. (2/1/2002)*

Hamelin Bay 2004 Five Ashes Vineyard Semillon-Sauvignon Blanc (Margaret River) $19. 85 —*D.T. (10/1/2005)*

HAMILTON'S BLUFF

Hamilton's Bluff 1999 Cowra Chardonnay (South Eastern Australia) $10. 82 —*D.T. (9/1/2001)*

HAMILTON'S EWELL VINEYARD

Hamilton's Ewell Vineyard 2000 Ewell Vineyard Cabernet Sauvignon (Barossa Valley) $18. 90 Editors' Choice —*M.S. (12/15/2002)*

Hamilton's Ewell Vineyard 2002 Sturt River Cabernet Sauvignon-Shiraz (South Australia) $14. 83 —*D.T. (8/1/2005)*

Hamilton's Ewell Vineyard 2000 Railway Chardonnay (Barossa Valley) $13. 83 —*J.C. (7/1/2002)*

Hamilton's Ewell Vineyard 2004 Sturt River Chardonnay (South Australia) $14. 83 —*D.T. (10/1/2005)*

Hamilton's Ewell Vineyard 1999 Fuller's Barn Shiraz (Barossa Valley) $30. 88 —*K.F. (3/1/2003)*

Hamilton's Ewell Vineyard 2002 Railway Shiraz (Barossa Valley) $25. 87 —*D.T. (10/1/2005)*

HANDPICKED

Handpicked 2004 Chardonnay (South Eastern Australia) $13. 84 —*D.T. (5/1/2005)*

HANGING ROCK

Hanging Rock 2002 Strathbogie Chardonnay (Victoria) $16. 85 *(7/2/2004)*

HARDYS

Hardys 2001 Stamp of Australia Cabernet Sauvignon (South Eastern Australia) $6. 82 —*D.T. (1/1/2002)*

Hardys 1994 Thomas Hardy Cabernet Sauvignon (Coonawarra) $50. 90 *(3/1/2000)*

Hardys 1999 Tintara Cabernet Sauvignon (South Australia) $18. 83 —*J.C. (6/1/2002)*

Hardys 2002 Nottage Hill Cabernet Sauvignon-Shiraz (South Eastern Australia) $8. 86 Best Buy —*D.T. (11/15/2004)*

Hardys 2000 Nottage Hill Cabernet Sauvignon-Shiraz (South Eastern Australia) $8. 84 —*M.S. (12/15/2002)*

Hardys 2005 Nottage Hill Chardonnay (South Eastern Australia) $8. 85 Best Buy —*D.T. (6/1/2006)*

Hardys 2004 Nottage Hill Chardonnay (South Eastern Australia) $8. 84 Best Buy —*D.T. (10/1/2005)*

Hardys 2003 Nottage Hill Chardonnay (South Eastern Australia) $8. 85 Best Buy *(7/2/2004)*

Hardys 2002 Nottage Hill Chardonnay (South Eastern Australia) $8. 87 Best Buy —*D.T. (8/1/2003)*

Hardys 2001 Nottage Hill Chardonnay (South Eastern Australia) $7. 85 Best Buy —*J.C. (7/1/2002)*

Hardys 2000 Nottage Hill Chardonnay (South Eastern Australia) $7. 83 —*M.N. (6/1/2001)*

AUSTRALIA

Hardys 2005 Oomoo Unwooded Chardonnay (McLaren Vale) $15. 84 —*D.T. (4/1/2006)*

Hardys 2005 Stamp of Australia Chardonnay (South Eastern Australia) $6. 82 —*D.T. (11/15/2006)*

Hardys 2002 Stamp of Australia Chardonnay (South Eastern Australia) $6. 85 —*D.T. (8/1/2003)*

Hardys 2001 Tintara Chardonnay (Adelaide Hills) $15. 86 —*D.T. (8/1/2003)*

Hardys 2000 Tintara Chardonnay (South Australia) $15. 87 —*J.C. (7/1/2002)*

Hardys 2005 Nottage Hill Merlot (South Eastern Australia) $9. It's supple and round, but the flavors of mint and stewed prunes aren't entirely complementary, marrying into something akin to black cherry cough syrup. Imported by International Cellars. 82 —*J.C. (11/15/2007)*

Hardys 2003 Nottage Hill Merlot (South Eastern Australia) $8. 85 Best Buy —*D.T. (4/1/2006)*

Hardys 2002 Nottage Hill Merlot (South Eastern Australia) $8. 83 —*D.T. (8/1/2005)*

Hardys 2000 Nottage Hill Merlot (South Eastern Australia) $7. 84 —*D.T. (6/1/2002)*

Hardys 2006 Stamp of Australia Merlot (South Eastern Australia) $7. Light in body almost to the point of why bother, with confected cherry and anise flavors. Imported by International Cellars. 80 —*J.C. (11/15/2007)*

Hardys 2006 Nottage Hill Pinot Noir (South Eastern Australia) $9. Light and insubstantial in the mouth, with flavors of cooked strawberries and leather. Imported by International Cellars. 80 —*J.C. (11/15/2007)*

Hardys 2005 Nottage Hill Pinot Noir (South Eastern Australia) $9. 85 Best Buy —*D.T. (11/15/2006)*

Hardys NV Whiskers Blake Classic Tawny Port (South Eastern Australia) $13. This widely available, bargain-priced tawny remains an Australian classic, offering toffee and walnut aromas and flavors along with dust-covered leather and just a hint of fresh fruit. It's lighter in weight than you might expect from a Port-inspired New World wine, but offers a tasty drop on a wintry evening. Imported by Pacific Wine Partners. 88 Best Buy —*J.C. (12/15/2007)*

Hardys 2005 Stamp of Australia Riesling (South Eastern Australia) $6. 84 Best Buy —*D.T. (4/1/2006)*

Hardys 2002 Botrytis Semillon (South Eastern Australia) $15. 90 Best Buy —*D.T. (8/1/2006)*

Hardys 2000 Tintara Botrytis Semillon (South Eastern Australia) $17. 90 —*J.M. (12/1/2002)*

Hardys 2001 Eileen Hardy Shiraz (McLaren Vale) $90. 88 —*D.T. (4/1/2006)*

Hardys 2000 Eileen Hardy Shiraz (South Australia) $90. 88 —*D.T. (5/1/2004)*

Hardys 1999 Eileen Hardy Shiraz (South Australia) $85. 86 —*D.T. (3/1/2003)*

Hardys 1998 Eileen Hardy Shiraz (McLaren Vale & Padthaway) $70. 89 *(11/1/2001)*

Hardys 1996 Eileen Hardy Shiraz (McLaren Vale & Padthaway) $62. 93 *(3/1/2000)*

Hardys 2005 Nottage Hill Shiraz (South Eastern Australia) $9. A pleasant surprise, Hardys' 2005 Nottage Hill Shiraz offers plum, blackberry and blueberry fruit flavors and touches of vanilla. There are even some coffee, meat and spice nuances on the finish, unusual for a wine in this price range. Drink now. Imported by International Cellars. 86 Best Buy —*J.C. (11/15/2007)*

Hardys 2004 Nottage Hill Shiraz (South Eastern Australia) $9. 85 Best Buy —*D.T. (11/15/2006)*

Hardys 2001 Nottage Hill Shiraz (South Eastern Australia) $8. 86 Best Buy —*D.T. (5/1/2004)*

Hardys 2000 Nottage Hill Shiraz (South Eastern Australia) $8. 88 Best Buy —*M.S. (3/1/2003)*

Hardys 2001 Oomoo Shiraz (McLaren Vale) $12. 86 —*D.T. (12/31/2005)*

Hardys NV Sparkling Shiraz (South Australia) $20. Smells and tastes heavily oaked, with vanilla, smoke and toast layered over notes of blackberry and chocolate. Still, the texture is nice and the wood—if you like that sort of thing—is tasty. Finishes with a slightly drying edge. Imported by Pacific Wine Partners. 86 —*J.C. (12/31/2007)*

Hardys NV Sparkling Shiraz (South Australia) $20. 89 —*D.T. (12/31/2005)*

Hardys 2004 Stamp of Australia Shiraz (South Eastern Australia) $6. 84 Best Buy —*D.T. (12/31/2005)*

Hardys 2002 Stamp of Australia Shiraz (South Eastern Australia) $6. 83 —*D.T. (1/1/2002)*

Hardys 2001 Stamp of Australia Shiraz (South Eastern Australia) $6. 83 —*D.T. (1/1/2002)*

Hardys 1999 Tintara Shiraz (South Australia) $18. 87 *(10/1/2001)*

Hardys 2005 Stamp of Australia Shiraz-Grenache (South Eastern Australia) $6. 83 —*D.T. (4/1/2006)*

HARTZ BARN WINES

Hartz Barn Wines 2001 Mail Box Merlot (Barossa Valley) $30. 83 —*D.T. (1/1/2002)*

Hartz Barn Wines 2001 General Store Shiraz (Barossa Valley) $30. 84 —*D.T. (5/1/2004)*

HASTWELL & LIGHTFOOT

Hastwell & Lightfoot 2000 Shiraz (McLaren Vale) $28. 87 —*D.T. (9/1/2004)*

Hastwell & Lightfoot 2002 Viognier (McLaren Vale) $22. 86 —*D.T. (5/1/2004)*

HAWKERS GATE

Hawkers Gate 2000 Shiraz (McLaren Vale) $21. 85 —*D.T. (5/1/2004)*

HEARTLAND

Heartland 2005 Cabernet Sauvignon (Langhorne Creek-Limestone Creek) $17. A step up from the basic Stickleback Red, the 2005 Cabernet Sauvignon offers flavors of chocolate and cassis, with just a touch of roasted bell pepper for varietal character. The texture is creamy-smooth, yet the wine ends crisp, with a mouthwatering finish. Drink now. 88 *(11/15/2007)*

Heartland 2005 Stickleback Red Red Blend (South Australia) $12. Made by Ben Glaetzer, the Heartland wines are meant to offer an affordable entry to the Epicurean portfolio. The Stickleback Red blends Cabernet Sauvignon with Shiraz and Grenache to make an attractive wine for everyday drinking. Some smoky notes frame black cherry and black olive fruit, while the texture is creamy on the midpalate, fading a bit on the finish. 85 *(11/15/2007)*

Heartland 2003 Director's Cut Shiraz (Langhorne Creek-Limestone Creek) $24. 88 —*D.T. (12/1/2005)*

Heartland 2006 Stickleback White White Blend (South Australia) $12. This blend of Chardonnay, Sémillon and Verdelho is fleshy and round, with aromas and flavors of peach pit, melon and spice and a tart finish. It's a friendly little white for everyday drinking. 86 *(11/15/2007)*

Heartland 2004 Stickleback White Blend (South Australia) $11. 88 Best Buy —*D.T. (8/1/2005)*

Heartland 2006 Viognier-Pinot Gris White Blend (Langhorne Creek-Limestone Creek) $17. A plump, well-endowed white that tames Viognier's exuberance with Pinot Gris's restrained aromas. Peach, melon and spice flavors do show some exotic honeysuckle notes that fade quickly on the finish. 87 *(11/15/2007)*

Heartland 2004 Viognier-Pinot Gris White Blend (Langhorne Creek) $12. 89 Best Buy —*D.T. (8/1/2005)*

HEATH WINES

Heath Wines 2003 100-Year Old Vine Cabernet Sauvignon (Barossa Valley) $60. A somewhat disjointed effort that features dried fruit—date and prune—and molasses flavors but also citrusy acids and smoky, herbal, peppery scents. Shows plenty of concentration and intensity, but not all parts are working in harmony. 84 —*J.C. (5/1/2007)*

Heath Wines 2003 Southern Sisters Reserve Cabernet Sauvignon-Merlot (Barossa Valley) $20. Already shows some slight bricking at the rim, with herbal, leathery overtones and chocolate and molasses bass notes. The texture is soft and creamy, but the finish is tangy and crisp. Pleasant enough, but its future is uncertain; drink now. 85 —*J.C. (2/1/2007)*

Heath Wines 2002 Southern Roo Cabernet Sauvignon-Shiraz (South Australia) $14. 83 —*D.T. (5/1/2005)*

Heath Wines 2003 Southern Sisters Reserve Pinot Noir (Adelaide Hills) $20. Leafy and tea-like, with hints of cherry and leather. This is restrained in its fruitiness, ending dry and leafy. 82 —*J.C. (2/1/2007)*

Heath Wines 2004 Southern Sisters Reserve Riesling (Clare Valley) $20. Slightly brassy in color, this Riesling is already showing a touch of age to its aromas and flavors as well. There's hints of smoke and petrol to go with flavors of orange marmalade and honey. Finishes with orange and spice notes. Drink now. 86 —*J.C. (5/1/2007)*

Heath Wines 2003 100 Year Old Vine Shiraz (Barossa Valley) $60. 86 —*J.C. (12/15/2006)*

AUSTRALIA

HEATHCOTE ESTATE

Heathcote Estate 2004 II Shiraz (Heathcote) $48. Full-bodied and tannic, with dried-fruit notes of cherries and dates, old cheese and spice. Complex and old-school. 90 —*J.C. (6/1/2007)*

Heathcote Estate 2003 Shiraz (Heathcote) $48. 92 —*D.T. (4/1/2006)*

HEATHFIELD RIDGE

Heathfield Ridge 1998 Cabernet Sauvignon (Limestone Coast) $15. 83 *(10/1/2000)*

Heathfield Ridge 1999 Cabernet Sauvignon (Limestone Coast) $16. 84 —*M.S. (12/15/2002)*

Heathfield Ridge 1997 Patrick Cabernet Sauvignon (Coonawarra) $40. 85 —*M.S. (12/15/2002)*

Heathfield Ridge 2000 Reserve Chardonnay (Limestone Coast) $16. 83 —*D.T. (8/1/2003)*

Heathfield Ridge 1999 Merlot (Limestone Coast) $16. 85 —*D.T. (6/1/2003)*

Heathfield Ridge 1999 Shiraz (Limestone Coast) $16. 84 —*M.S. (1/28/2003)*

Heathfield Ridge 1998 Jennifer Shiraz (Padthaway) $34. 87 —*M.S. (3/1/2003)*

HEATHVALE

Heathvale 2004 Shiraz (Eden Valley) $23. Eden Valley fruit is rarely left to stand on its own, often lending a bit of spice to larger Barossa blends, but this is a single-vineyard bottling from former viticulture teacher Trevor March. It's savory and supple, with a slightly meaty character, vanilla and spice notes all wrapped around a core of lush raspberry fruit. Drink now–2012. 89 —*J.C. (11/1/2007)*

HEAVEN'S GATE

Heaven's Gate 2001 Shiraz (Barossa Valley) $15. 86 —*D.T. (12/31/2003)*

HEGGIE'S VINEYARD

Heggie's Vineyard 1998 Chardonnay (Eden Valley) $20. 85 —*D.T. (9/1/2001)*

Heggie's Vineyard 1996 Merlot (Eden Valley) $22. 82 —*M.M. (9/1/2001)*

Heggie's Vineyard 1998 Viognier (Eden Valley) $22. 82 *(10/1/2000)*

Heggie's Vineyard 1999 Viognier (Eden Valley) $22. 85 Best Buy —*D.T. (2/1/2002)*

Heggie's Vineyard 2004 Chardonnay (Eden Valley) $20. 88 —*D.T. (12/1/2005)*

Heggie's Vineyard 2001 Chardonnay (Eden Valley) $20. 92 —*S.H. (1/1/2002)*

Heggie's Vineyard 2000 Chardonnay (Eden Valley) $20. 84 —*D.T. (8/1/2003)*

Heggie's Vineyard 1998 Merlot (Eden Valley) $22. 84 —*S.H. (12/15/2002)*

Heggie's Vineyard 2004 Viognier (Eden Valley) $20. 87 —*D.T. (12/1/2005)*

HENSCHKE

Henschke 2002 Cyril Henschke Bordeaux Blend (Eden Valley) $100. 90 —*D.T. (10/1/2006)*

Henschke 2000 Cyril Henschke Cabernet Sauvignon-Merlot-Cabernet Franc Bordeaux Blend (Eden Valley) $100. 92 —*D.T. (5/1/2004)*

Henschke 2000 Lenswood Abbott's Prayer Bordeaux Blend (Adelaide Hills) $60. 90 —*D.T. (2/1/2004)*

Henschke 2002 Lenswood Abbotts Prayer Bordeaux Blend (Adelaide Hills) $70. 87 —*D.T. (8/1/2005)*

Henschke 1996 Lenswood Abbotts Prayer Bordeaux Blend (Adelaide Hills) $55. 88 —*M.S. (4/1/2000)*

Henschke 2002 Cranes Chardonnay (Eden Valley) $38. 87 *(7/2/2004)*

Henschke 2000 Cranes Chardonnay (Eden Valley) $36. 87 —*J.C. (7/1/2002)*

Henschke 2005 Croft Chardonnay (Lenswood) $45. Effusively smoky and toasty, this flamboyant, full-bodied Chardonnay bursts with scents and flavors of grilled nuts and grilled peaches. It's lavishly oaked, but it works, coming together in a rush of nutty, fruity flavors that linger on the finish. 91 —*J.C. (8/1/2007)*

Henschke 2003 Lenswood Croft Chardonnay (Adelaide Hills) $45. 89 —*D.T. (8/1/2005)*

Henschke 2002 Lenswood Croft Chardonnay (Adelaide Hills) $40. 93 Editors' Choice —*D.T. (2/1/2004)*

Henschke 1998 Lenswood Croft Chardonnay (Adelaide Hills) $40. 88 *(3/1/2000)*

Henschke 2003 Abbotts Prayer Vineyard Merlot (Lenswood) $70. Fans of ultrasoft, creamy-oaky wines will find a lot to like in this. Scents of toast, cedar and caramel lead the way, backed up by plum and herb flavors and lashings of oak. Worth holding 1–2 years to see if it integrates. 87 —*J.C. (5/1/2007)*

Henschke 2001 Lenswood Abbotts Prayer Merlot (Adelaide Hills) $70. 89 —*D.T. (8/1/2005)*

Henschke 2005 Little Hampton Innes Vineyard Pinot Gris (Adelaide Hills) $30. 89 —*D.T. (11/15/2006)*

Henschke 2003 Little Hampton Innes Vineyard Pinot Gris (Adelaide Hills) $30. 87 —*D.T. (8/1/2005)*

Henschke 2002 Little Hampton Innes Vineyard Pinot Gris (Adelaide Hills) $28. 89 —*D.T. (2/1/2004)*

Henschke 2004 Little Hampton Innes Vineyard Pinot Gris (Adelaide Hills) $30. 89 —*D.T. (8/1/2005)*

Henschke 2004 Henry's Seven Red Blend (Barossa) $32. Wonderfully spicy and complex on the nose, with scents of smoke, spice, mulled blackberries and a hint of caramel. This is round and full in the mouth without being heavy, with spice-driven flavors but also dark fruit flavors that finish firm, crisp and long. A blend of 60% Syrah, 30% Grenache and 5% each Mourvèdre and Viognier. 90 —*J.C. (7/1/2007)*

Henschke 2002 Henry's Seven Red Blend (Barossa Valley) $30. 89 —*D.T. (5/1/2004)*

Henschke 2001 Henry's Seven Red Blend (Barossa Valley) $25. 82 —*D.T. (1/1/2002)*

Henschke 2003 Keyneton Estate Euphonium Red Blend (Barossa) $45. This is primarily (70%) Shiraz, with a blend of Cab Sauvignon, Merlot and Cab Franc, but it comes across more like a Bordeaux blend. Vanilla and cedar notes from oak aging accent cassis fruit—and there's a hint of mint as well. Medium-bodied, with a long, dusty yet mouthwatering finish. Drink now–2015. 89 —*J.C. (6/1/2007)*

Henschke 2000 Keyneton Estate Red Blend (Eden Valley) $40. 89 —*D.T. (2/1/2004)*

Henschke 2004 Johann's Garden Rhône Red Blend (Barossa Valley) $38. Despite weighing in at 15.5% alcohol, this wine carries it well, coming across as satisfyingly ample; zaftig without being heavy. The mouthfilling flavors of boysenberry and black cherry carry hints of vanilla and spice, with enough length on the finish to confirm the wine's quality. The blend is 69% Grenache, 19% Mourvèdre and 12% Shiraz. 88 —*J.C. (6/1/2007)*

Henschke 2002 Johann's Garden Rhône Red Blend (Eden Valley) $30. 87 —*D.T. (5/1/2004)*

Henschke 2005 Julius Riesling (Eden Valley) $30. 90 —*D.T. (11/15/2006)*

Henschke 2003 Julius Riesling (Eden Valley) $23. 88 —*D.T. (2/1/2004)*

Henschke 2001 Julius Riesling (Eden Valley) $25. 89 —*D.T. (8/1/2003)*

Henschke 2003 Lenswood Green's Hill Riesling (Adelaide Hills) $NA. 92 —*D.T. (1/1/2002)*

Henschke 2005 Coralinga Sauvignon Blanc (Adelaide Hills) $27. 90 —*D.T. (11/15/2006)*

Henschke 2004 Lenswood Coralinga Sauvignon Blanc (Adelaide Hills) $27. 85 *(7/1/2005)*

Henschke 2003 Lenswood Coralinga Sauvignon Blanc (Adelaide Hills) $23. 89 —*D.T. (2/1/2004)*

Henschke 2005 Louis Semillon (Eden Valley) $27. 88 —*D.T. (11/15/2006)*

Henschke 2002 Louis Semillon (Eden Valley) $25. 89 —*D.T. (2/1/2004)*

Henschke 2002 Hill of Grace Vineyard Shiraz (Eden Valley) $550. This is a bold, full-flavored, authoritative example of Eden Valley Shiraz. Cool-climate notes of cracked pepper elegantly frame waves of blackberry fruit that are fresh and zingy, not cooked or confected. This is firmly structured and built for the cellar, yet the tannins are ripe, forming a silky web that supports the fruit on the prolonged finish. Drink 2012–2035. 96 Cellar Selection —*J.C. (11/1/2007)*

Henschke 2001 Hill of Grace Vineyard Shiraz (Eden Valley) $400. Readers fortunate enough to latch onto a bottle of the fewer than 300 imported to the U.S. will find themselves with a super bottle of Shiraz that manages to deliver great flavor intensity without relying on excessive weight. Notes of cracked black pepper and herbal nuances add complexity to the liquorous blackberry aromas, building in spicy intensity through the anise-inflected finish. Approachable now, but should drink well through at least 2015. 93 Cellar Selection —*J.C. (5/1/2007)*

Henschke 1999 Hill of Grace Shiraz (Eden Valley) $350. 96 Cellar Selection —*D.T. (5/1/2004)*

Henschke 1998 Hill of Grace Shiraz (Eden Valley) $300. 94 Cellar Selection —*D.T. (2/1/2004)*

Henschke 2004 Mount Edelstone Vineyard Shiraz (Eden Valley) $100. In the cool 2004 vintage, the nearly 100-year-old vines of Henschke's Mount Edelstone Vineyard have yielded a tart, crisp wine of considerable cellaring potential. The scents of pepper, blackberries and potpourri and flavors of vanilla and raspberries are buoyed by velvety tannins and a creamy mouthfeel, tightening up on the long finish. May not be as flashy as the 2003, but it may live longer. Drink 2012–2030. 92 *—J.C. (11/1/2007)*

Henschke 2003 Mount Edelstone Vineyard Shiraz (Eden Valley) $100. A marvelous effort, this features a gorgeously seductive bouquet of herbs, spice, blueberries and stone fruit, all framed by a touch of cedary oak. In the mouth, it's creamy and lush, but well-structured, ending with a dose of dusty tannins and an extra blast of fruit. Has it all: ample complexity, intensity and length, with its components in finely judged balance for aging through 2015. 93 *—J.C. (4/25/2007)*

Henschke 2001 Mt. Edelstone Shiraz (Eden Valley) $70. 94 Editors' Choice *—D.T. (5/1/2004)*

Henschke 2004 Tappa Pass Shiraz (Barossa) $NA. The first vintage of this wine was only in 2002, but already this bottling is proving to be excellent. Floral elements mark the nose, along with spice and blackberries, while the tannins are wonderfully soft, imparting a deliciously lush mouthfeel. Firms up a bit on the finish, suggesting that it should age well through at least 2014. 91 *—J.C. (11/1/2007)*

Henschke 2003 Tilly's Vineyard White Blend (Eden Valley) $NA. 87 *—D.T. (1/1/2002)*

HENTLEY FARM

Hentley Farm 2006 Fools Bay Dirty Bliss Grenache-Shiraz (Barossa Valley) $15. Nicely complex, with peppery aromas setting the stage for notes of maraschino cherries and a hint of orange peel. Cherries and other stone fruits provide plenty of supple roundness on the palate, finishing with a touch of spice. Drink now–2010. 88 *—J.C. (11/1/2007)*

Hentley Farm 2005 Shiraz (Barossa Valley) $25. Inky and tarry, with a distinct black fruit character. There's licorice and plum, elegantly framed by 30% new French oak. The round, supple mouthfeel turns velvety on the long finish, suggesting at least 5–7 years of positive evolution. 90 *—J.C. (11/1/2007)*

Hentley Farm 2002 Shiraz (Barossa Valley) $27. 84 *—D.T. (10/1/2005)*

Hentley Farm 2006 Fools Bay Dusty's Desire Shiraz (Barossa Valley) $15. Slightly tarry and earthy, with briary, blackberry fruit at the core. Shows plenty of complexity and structure to go with fine balance. Nicely done for a wine at this price point, with the ability to age through 2015. 88 *—J.C. (11/1/2007)*

Hentley Farm 2004 The Beast Shiraz (Barossa Valley) $90. The Beast seems to be in a bit of an awkward stage right now, showing a touch of alcohol atop its cedar, blackberries, vanilla and chocolate. It's full-bodied, firmly structured by dusty tannins, and shows good drive and freshness, although there's a slightly raisiny edge to the finish. Give it another few years to pull itself together. Drink 2010–2020. 90 *—J.C. (11/1/2007)*

Hentley Farm 2005 The Beauty Shiraz (Barossa Valley) $55. Despite the name—this does exhibit gorgeous complexity and perfume—don't be fooled into thinking this shy or delicate. At 15% alcohol, it fills the mouth with layers of chocolate sauce and ripe berries, with hints of vanilla, cinnamon, stone fruit and violets. Finishes with silky tannins and lingering notes of fresh fruit and dried spices. Drink now–2020. 94 Editors' Choice *—J.C. (11/1/2007)*

HERITAGE ROAD

Heritage Road 1999 Bethany Creek Vineyard Limited Reserve Cabernet Sauvignon (Barossa Valley) $30. 93 *—S.H. (6/1/2002)*

Heritage Road 2000 Old Saxonvale Vineyard Reserve Cabernet Sauvignon (Hunter Valley) $18. 82 *—D.T. (6/1/2002)*

Heritage Road 1998 Reserve Cabernet Sauvignon (Limestone Coast) $16. 89 *(12/1/2000)*

Heritage Road 1999 Reserve Old Mundulla Vineyard Cabernet Sauvignon (Limestone Coast) $18. 90 Editors' Choice *—S.H. (9/1/2001)*

Heritage Road 1999 Chardonnay (Hunter Valley) $13. 87 *—S.H. (6/1/2001)*

Heritage Road 1998 Chardonnay (Hunter Valley) $13. 87 *(12/1/2000)*

Heritage Road 2001 Sandy Hollow Vineyard Chardonnay (Hunter Valley) $12. 88 *—S.H. (1/1/2002)*

Heritage Road 2000 Merlot (South Australia) $12. 82 *—S.H. (9/1/2001)*

Heritage Road 2001 Shiraz (South Australia) $12. 85 *—S.H. (12/15/2002)*

Heritage Road 2000 Shiraz (South Australia) $12. 83 *(10/1/2001)*

Heritage Road 1998 Shiraz (South Australia) $10. 88 Best Buy *(12/1/2000)*

Heritage Road 2000 Mundulla Vineyard Reserve Shiraz (Limestone Coast) $18. 85 *(1/1/2004)*

Heritage Road 1998 Reserve Shiraz (Limestone Coast) $16. 91 *(12/1/2000)*

Heritage Road 1999 Vine Vale Vineyard Limited Release Reserve Shiraz (Barossa Valley) $30. 91 *—S.H. (1/1/2002)*

Heritage Road 1998 Chardonnay (Hunter Valley) $9. 85 *(10/1/1999)*

HEWITSON

Hewitson 2005 Miss Harry G-S-M (Barossa Valley) $22. An appealing blend of 55% Grenache, 33% Shiraz and 12% Mourvèdre, this offering from Hewitson boasts upfront scents of cherries, caramel and vanilla, then adds a hint of dark coffee or tree bark on the palate. The creamy texture and the lush fruit make this easy to drink now and over the next few years. 88 *—J.C. (11/1/2007)*

Hewitson 2004 Miss Harry Dry Grown & Ancient G-S-M (Barossa Valley) $20. 87 *—D.T. (4/1/2006)*

Hewitson 2005 Old Garden Mourvèdre (Barossa Valley) $41. From vines more than 150 years old, this shows an unusually lush texture for Mourvèdre. Starts with a potpourri of spices, like cinnamon, clove and cola, then adds vanilla and black cherry flavors before ending with a flourish of coffee and tree bark. Long and velvety on the finish. Drink now–2015 or beyond. 92 *—J.C. (11/1/2007)*

Hewitson 2004 Old Garden Mourvèdre (Barossa Valley) $36. 88 *—D.T. (8/1/2006)*

Hewitson 1999 Shiraz (Barossa Valley) $27. 88 *(11/1/2001)*

Hewitson 2001 L'Oizeau Shiraz (McLaren Vale) $27. 87 *—D.T. (9/1/2004)*

Hewitson 2005 Ned & Henry's Shiraz (Barossa Valley) $22. Hewitson's best Shiraz to date is this lush, creamy-textured offering, filled with dense chocolate and blackberry aromas and flavors. Hints of coffee linger on the long, velvety finish. The price is fair, too. Drink now–2015. 90 Editors' Choice *—J.C. (11/1/2007)*

Hewitson 2003 Ned & Henry's Shiraz (Barossa Valley) $20. 89 *—D.T. (10/1/2005)*

HILL OF CONTENT

Hill of Content 2003 Grenache-Shiraz (Clare Valley) $14. The Grenache gives bright cherry flavors, while the Shiraz component is darker and tarry. Dusty tannins impart a muscular finish. 87 Best Buy *—J.C. (6/1/2007)*

Hill of Content 2001 Grenache Shiraz Grenache-Syrah (Clare-McClaren Vale) $13. 89 *—D.T. (9/1/2004)*

Hill of Content 2002 Pinot Noir (Victoria) $15. 89 *—D.T. (9/1/2004)*

Hill of Content 2004 Benjamin's Blend White Blend (Western Australia) $14. 82 *—D.T. (10/1/2005)*

Hill of Content 2002 Benjamin's Blend White Blend (Western Australia) $12. 89 *—D.T. (9/1/2004)*

HILLSVIEW VINEYARDS

Hillsview Vineyards 1999 Blewitt Springs Cabernet Sauvignon (Fleurieu Peninsula) $15. 88 *—D.T. (6/1/2003)*

HOFFMANN'S

Hoffmann's 2002 Shiraz (McLaren Vale) $24. 90 *—D.T. (2/1/2006)*

HOLLICK

Hollick 1997 Bordeaux Blend (Coonawarra) $20. 87 *—M.S. (10/1/2000)*

Hollick 1998 Cabernet Sauvignon-Merlot (Coonawarra) $20. 83 *—J.C. (6/1/2002)*

Hollick 2001 Chardonnay (Coonawarra) $15. 87 *(7/2/2004)*

Hollick 1999 Chardonnay (Coonawarra) $17. 83 *—J.C. (7/1/2002)*

Hollick 1998 Reserve Chardonnay (Coonawarra) $17. 91 *—M.M. (10/1/2000)*

Hollick 1998 Wilgha Shiraz (Coonawarra) $34. 87 *—J.C. (9/1/2002)*

Hollick 1999 Shiraz-Cabernet Sauvignon (Limestone Coast) $17. 87 *—J.C. (9/1/2002)*

HOPE ESTATE

Hope Estate 1999 Cabernet Sauvignon (Hunter Valley) $13. 86 *(7/1/2001)*

Hope Estate 1999 Cabernet Sauvignon-Merlot (Hunter Valley) $13. 85 *—J.F. (9/1/2001)*

Hope Estate 2005 Chardonnay (Hunter Valley) $10. 86 Best Buy *(6/1/2006)*

Hope Estate 2003 Chardonnay (Hunter Valley) $11. 86 Best Buy *—D.T. (5/1/2005)*

Hope Estate 2002 Chardonnay (Hunter Valley) $10. 88 Best Buy *(7/2/2004)*

Hope Estate 2000 Chardonnay (Hunter Valley) $10. 87 *—J.C. (7/1/2002)*

Hope Estate 1999 Chardonnay (Hunter Valley) $10. 86 *(7/1/2001)*

Hope Estate 2006 Merlot (Hunter Valley) $12. Leathery and meaty, with dark plum and lightly raisined flavors. This is fairly full for an inexpensive Merlot, with soft, silky tannins on the finish. 83 *—J.C. (11/15/2007)*

Hope Estate 2005 Merlot (Hunter Valley) $10. 86 Best Buy *(6/1/2006)*

Hope Estate 2003 Merlot (Hunter Valley) $11. 86 Best Buy *—D.T. (4/1/2006)*

Hope Estate 1999 Merlot (Hunter Valley) $13. 85 *(7/1/2001)*

Hope Estate 2002 Estate Merlot (Hunter Valley) $15. 83 *—D.T. (12/1/2005)*

Hope Estate 2006 Shiraz (Hunter Valley) $12. Dense and blackberryish on the nose, this medium- to full-bodied Shiraz offers plenty of fruit in soft, easy-to-drink package. Hints of dried spices give it more interest than your average $12 Shiraz. 87 Best Buy *—J.C. (11/15/2007)*

Hope Estate 2005 Shiraz (Hunter Valley) $10. 87 Best Buy *(6/1/2006)*

Hope Estate 2003 Shiraz (Hunter Valley) $10. 85 Best Buy *(6/1/2006)*

Hope Estate 2000 Shiraz (Hunter Valley) $14. 85 *(10/1/2001)*

Hope Estate 1999 Shiraz (Hunter Valley) $13. 89 Best Buy *(7/1/2001)*

Hope Estate 1998 Shiraz (Hunter Valley) $13. 83 *(4/1/2000)*

Hope Estate 2005 The Ripper! Shiraz (Western Australia) $15. A nicely balanced red. It's not the richest, deepest wine out there, but it does offer plenty of red plum and raspberry flavors, framed by vanilla-scented oak. It's reasonably long on the finish, too, where the wine picks up attractive cedary accents. 87 *—J.C. (11/15/2007)*

Hope Estate 2003 The Ripper! Shiraz (Western Australia) $16. 90 *—D.T. (2/1/2006)*

Hope Estate 2004 The Ripper! Shiraz (Western Australia) $15. 89 *(6/1/2006)*

Hope Estate 2004 Verdelho (Hunter Valley) $9. 85 Best Buy *—D.T. (8/1/2005)*

Hope Estate 2002 Verdelho (Hunter Valley) $8. 84 *—D.T. (12/31/2003)*

Hope Estate 2000 Verdelho (Hunter Valley) $9. 84 *—M.M. (2/1/2002)*

Hope Estate 1998 Verdelho (Hunter Valley) $9. 87 Best Buy *(7/1/2001)*

Hope Estate 2005 Estate Verdelho (Hunter Valley) $10. 86 Best Buy *—D.T. (11/15/2005)*

HOUGHTON

Houghton 2005 Chardonnay (Western Australia) $15. 86 *—D.T. (4/1/2006)*

Houghton 2004 Red Blend (Western Australia) $15. 86 *—D.T. (8/1/2006)*

Houghton 2005 Semillon-Sauvignon Blanc (Western Australia) $15. 84 *—D.T. (8/1/2006)*

Houghton 2005 Shiraz (Western Australia) $15. 89 *—D.T. (8/1/2006)*

Houghton 2005 White Blend (Western Australia) $15. 87 *—D.T. (8/1/2006)*

HOWARD PARK

Howard Park 2001 Mad Fish Bordeaux Blend (Western Australia) $16. 89 *—D.T. (9/1/2004)*

Howard Park 2002 Cabernet Sauvignon (Western Australia) $37. 88 *—D.T. (4/1/2006)*

Howard Park 2001 Cabernet Sauvignon (Western Australia) $37. 87 *—D.T. (8/1/2005)*

Howard Park 2003 Leston Cabernet Sauvignon (Margaret River) $21. 89 *—D.T. (8/1/2006)*

Howard Park 2002 Leston Cabernet Sauvignon (Margaret River) $21. 90 *—D.T. (12/1/2005)*

Howard Park 2001 Leston Cabernet Sauvignon (Margaret River) $30. 91 *—D.T. (5/1/2004)*

Howard Park 2004 Scotsdale Cabernet Sauvignon (Great Southern) $20. Rather lean, with a slight hint of eucalyptus to the tart plum flavors. Picks up some cedary notes on the finish, but although this medium-bodied, smooth-textured wine is pleasant enough, it could use more complexity and lushness. 85 *—J.C. (2/1/2007)*

Howard Park 2003 Scotsdale Cabernet Sauvignon (Great Southern) $21. 91 *—D.T. (8/1/2006)*

Howard Park 2002 Scotsdale Cabernet Sauvignon (Great Southern) $21. 86 *—D.T. (10/1/2005)*

Howard Park 2001 Scotsdale Cabernet Sauvignon (Great Southern) $30. 87 *—D.T. (5/1/2004)*

Howard Park 1999 Cabernet Sauvignon-Merlot (Western Australia) $48. 88 *(10/1/2003)*

Howard Park 2004 Chardonnay (Great Southern) $26. 88 *—D.T. (10/1/2006)*

Howard Park 2001 Chardonnay (Western Australia) $25. 88 *(10/1/2003)*

Howard Park 2003 Mad Fish Chardonnay (Western Australia) $18. 88 *(7/2/2004)*

Howard Park 2002 Mad Fish Chardonnay (Western Australia) $16. 89 *—D.T. (10/1/2003)*

Howard Park 2005 Riesling (Western Australia) $20. 89 *—D.T. (10/1/2006)*

Howard Park 2004 Leston Shiraz (Margaret River) $20. A gorgeous example of Shiraz from Margaret River, the 2004 Leston bottling is big without being bulky, soft without being flabby. It's generously endowed with cassis and cherry fruit, seamlessly integrated with notes of vanilla, tobacco and dried spices. Drink now–2015. 91 Editors' Choice *—J.C. (4/1/2007)*

Howard Park 2003 Leston Shiraz (Margaret River) $21. 90 *—D.T. (8/1/2006)*

Howard Park 2002 Leston Shiraz (Margaret River) $21. 89 *—D.T. (10/1/2005)*

Howard Park 2001 Leston Shiraz (Margaret River) $30. 90 *—D.T. (11/15/2004)*

Howard Park 2000 Leston Shiraz (Margaret River) $30. 89 *(10/1/2003)*

Howard Park 2002 Mad Fish Shiraz (Western Australia) $18. 89 *—D.T. (11/15/2004)*

Howard Park 2001 Mad Fish Shiraz (Western Australia) $16. 85 *—D.T. (10/1/2003)*

Howard Park 2004 Scotsdale Shiraz (Great Western) $20. 89 *—D.T. (11/15/2006)*

Howard Park 2003 Scotsdale Shiraz (Great Southern) $21. 92 Editors' Choice *—D.T. (8/1/2006)*

Howard Park 2002 Scotsdale Shiraz (Great Southern) $21. 90 *—D.T. (12/1/2005)*

Howard Park 2001 Scotsdale Shiraz (Margaret River) $30. 86 *—D.T. (11/15/2004)*

Howard Park 2000 Scottsdale Shiraz (Margaret River) $30. 86 *—D.T. (10/1/2003)*

HUGH HAMILTON

Hugh Hamilton 2005 The Villain Cabernet Sauvignon (McLaren Vale) $24. Cassis and chocolate notes dominate, but there's enough minty, eucalypt character to impart complexity, all framed by some firm, dusty tannins. Finishes long and mouthwatering; drink now–2015. Multiple U.S. importers. 89 *—J.C. (12/1/2007)*

Hugh Hamilton 2006 Jim Jim Unoaked Chardonnay (McLaren Vale) $10. This is surprisingly textured for an entry-level Chard, with a slightly viscous mouthfeel and straightforward flavors of apple, pear, citrus and spice. Drink now. Multiple U.S. importers. 85 Best Buy *—J.C. (8/1/2007)*

Hugh Hamilton 2006 The Scallywag Unwooded Chardonnay (McLaren Vale) $16. You won't mistake this for Chablis anytme soon, but it is a solid expression of unwooded Chardonnay. Buttery, it features pineapple and spice flavors and a lush, rounded palate. Easy to drink, with citrus and spice on the finish. Multiple U.S. importers. 88 *—J.C. (8/1/2007)*

Hugh Hamilton 2004 The Madam Sparkling Merlot (McLaren Vale) $15. Produced by the transfer method, with gas levels adjusted and a dosage the results in approximately 14g/L of sugar, this is a slightly mint and eucalypt-scented sparkler dominated by black cherries and coffee. Ends on a slightly dusty note. Multipe U.S. Importers. 86 *—J.C. (12/1/2007)*

Hugh Hamilton 2004 The Ratbag Merlot (McLaren Vale) $20. Plump and creamy in texture, this is a very good Australian Merlot, marrying black cherry fruit with hints of mocha and mint, and retaining a sense of firmness to the finish. 87 *—J.C. (12/1/2007)*

Hugh Hamilton 2005 The Mongrel Sangiovese (McLaren Vale) $20. Inspired by a trip to Tuscany, Hamilton planted Sangiovese in the mid-1990s, and while this wouldn't be mistaken for Chianti, it does have Sangiovese's classic cherry and tobacco flavors. It's less full-bodied than the other Hamilton offerings, making it more of a picnic red, or one to pair with chicken rather than steak. Multiple U.S. importers. 87 *—J.C. (12/1/2007)*

Hugh Hamilton 2005 Jim Jim Shiraz (McLaren Vale) $12. A good wine at a good price, the 2006 Jim-Jim Shiraz offers bouncy raspberry fruit, hints of cracked pepper and vanilla and a medium-bodied, reasonably lush mouthfeel. Multiple U.S. importers. 86 *—J.C. (12/1/2007)*

Hugh Hamilton 2005 The Rascal Shiraz (McLaren Vale) $24. This full-bodied wine could use a touch more lushness in the midpalate to help carry its assertive flavors of blackberries and chocolate. Mouthwatering fruit on the finish is backed by firm tannins, suggesting at least a few years of cellaring potential. Would go nicely with grilled steak. Multiple U.S. Importers. 88 *—J.C. (8/1/2007)*

Hugh Hamilton 1998 Shiraz (McLaren Vale) $16. 86 *(10/1/2001)*

Hugh Hamilton 2005 Jekyll & Hyde Shiraz-Viognier (McLaren Vale) $45. The Viognier component adds a wonderfully creamy, fat texture to this wine, but doesn't impose on the Shiraz aromatics of blueberries and blackberries. It's lush and fruit-filled, finishing with a touch of licorice. Drink now–2015. Multiple U.S. Importers. 91 *—J.C. (12/1/2007)*

Hugh Hamilton 2005 The Scoundrel Tempranillo (McLaren Vale) $24. Only the third vintage of Tempranillo for Hamilton, it's rather crisp and firm, with fresh blackberry fruit framed by vanilla and tobacco. It's nicely complex, adding hints of dried spices, eucalyptus and pepper on the finish, but could use a touch more lushness to make it really sing. Multiple U.S. Importers. 87 *—J.C. (12/1/2007)*

Hugh Hamilton 2006 The Trickster Verdelho (McLaren Vale) $16. Reasonably thick and viscous on the palate, this is a slightly honey-scented wine with dominant flavors of pear and melon. Finishes long, with peppery spice notes that linger. Multiple U.S. importers. 88 *—J.C. (12/1/2007)*

Hugh Hamilton 2006 The Loose Cannon Viognier (McLaren Vale) $16. Hamilton calls Viognier, "the most difficult grape to grow," but this is a very good New World version. It's floral and citric upfront, with hints of peppery spice, then builds on the palate to add flavors of peach and melon. Drink now. Multiple U.S. importers. 88 *—J.C. (12/1/2007)*

HUNDRED ACRE

Hundred Acre 2004 Ancient Way Vineyard Summer's Blocks Shiraz (Barossa Valley) $200. Incredibly dark in color but light on its feet, this wine somehow manages to hide its 15.5% alcohol under fruit that's neither overblown or jammy. Spice- and herb-driven complexity is the order of the day, with scents of violets lending an exotic note to the aromas. It's mouthfilling and palate-coating but wonderfully balanced, picking up hints of black olive and espresso on the lingering finish. Good now, but appears to have the stuff to evolve over at least 10–15 years. 94 *—J.C. (11/1/2007)*

HUNGERFORD HILL

Hungerford Hill 2004 Fishcage Cabernet Sauvignon-Merlot (South Eastern Australia) $13. A second label from Hungerford Hill, Fishcage features cassis and vanilla aromas and flavors, with a hint of mint that intensifies on the finish. Creamy-textured, the wine finishes with surprisingly good length and a touch of chocolate. Drink now. 86 *—J.C. (5/1/2007)*

Hungerford Hill 2005 Tumbarumba Chardonnay (New South Wales) $25. The notes here are somewhat discordant—like two parts of an orchestra a touch out of sync. First up are some lovely aromas of smoke, grilled nuts, pear and citrus. Then there's a bit of overly sweet fruit on the palate, and a tart, chalky finish that brings things to a close. It's not clear where this is headed, although it does give some pleasure now. 85 *—J.C. (5/1/2007)*

Hungerford Hill 2005 Tumbarumba Pinot Noir (New South Wales) $20. A crisp, light-bodied Pinot Noir that shows decent varietal character but only modest intensity, Hungerford Hill's 2005 bottling features hints of chocolate and cedar layered over delicate cherry fruit. 83 *—J.C. (6/1/2007)*

Hungerford Hill 2005 Riesling (Clare Valley) $20. A fruit-driven style, Hungerford Hill's 2005 Riesling features lime and peach on the nose, augmenting those with a hint of honey on the palate. A burst of citrus on the finish caps off this medium-bodied wine. Drink over the next couple of years for its youthful vivacity. 89 *—J.C. (5/1/2007)*

Hungerford Hill 2004 Shiraz (Hunter Valley) $20. With its aromas and flavors of toast, cedar and vanilla, this is a bit woody, but there's still plenty of fresh cherries and berries to help support the 15 months of aging in French oak. Medium-bodied, with a juicy, mouthwatering quality to the fruit that helps balance the dry oaky notes. 87 *—J.C. (5/1/2007)*

Hungerford Hill 2005 Fishcage Shiraz-Viognier (South Eastern Australia) $13. A creamy-textured, medium-bodied wine, this entry-level offering from Hungerford Hill offers scents of coffee and mixed spices alongside earthier notes. Blackberry and pepper flavors fade slowly on the finish, revealing slightly dusty tannins—just enough to cut through the fat of a juicy hamburger. 87 *—J.C. (11/15/2007)*

HUNTER VALLEY ELEMENTS

Hunter Valley Elements 1999 Shiraz (Hunter Valley) $20. 86 *(10/1/2001)*

INDIS

Indis 2004 Chardonnay (Western Australia) $15. 87 *—D.T. (12/1/2005)*

INKWELL

Inkwell 2005 Shiraz (McLaren Vale) $25. Despite carrying a lofty 16% alcohol level, this wine doesn't seem the least bit hot. Instead it's creamy-smooth and full-bodied, with aromas and flavors of brown sugar, blackberries, vanilla and some savory, peppery notes for added complexity. Then it finishes long as well, folding in hints of spice cake. Drink now. 92 Editors' Choice *—J.C. (12/31/2007)*

INNOCENT BYSTANDER

Innocent Bystander 2007 Moscato (Victoria) $10. This attractively colored sparkler is a light peachy-pink hue, with fragrant aromas of oranges, lemons and tropical fruit. It's light in weight (only 5.5% alcohol) but also rather sweet, and could use just a little zip to help balance out the sugar. 85 *—J.C. (12/31/2007)*

Innocent Bystander 2004 Pinot Gris (Yarra Valley) $20. 88 *—D.T. (5/1/2005)*

Innocent Bystander 2004 Rose Pinot Noir (Yarra Valley) $16. 87 *—D.T. (10/1/2005)*

Innocent Bystander 2002 Sangiovese Merlot Red Blend (South Eastern Australia) $20. 87 *—D.T. (8/1/2005)*

IRONBERRY

Ironberry 2006 Cabernet Shiraz Merlot Red Blend (Western Australia) $10. Not quite as strong an effort as the 2005, Ironberry's 2006 is distinctly herbal, with greenish notes imparting a medicinal quality to the wine's black cherry flavors. Still, the alcohol and acids are relatively restrained and in reasonable balance, with some pretty tea-like notes on the finish. 84 *—J.C. (11/15/2007)*

Ironberry 2005 Cabernet Shiraz Merlot Red Blend (Western Australia) $9. Comes out of the chute showing a funky, rubbery edge, but that blows off with a little time to reveal dark, somewhat earthy notes of cola and blackberry. It's medium-bodied, with good length to the finish, where it picks up enough dusty tannins to give it backbone. 87 Best Buy *—J.C. (11/15/2007)*

IRONWOOD

Ironwood 2003 Chardonnay (South Eastern Australia) $6. 85 Best Buy *—D.T. (12/31/2004)*

Ironwood 2002 Shiraz (South Eastern Australia) $6. 84 Best Buy *—D.T. (5/1/2005)*

IRVINE

Irvine 2002 Unoaked Chardonnay (Eden Valley) $16. 84 *(7/2/2004)*

JACKAROO

JackaRoo 2003 Chardonnay (South Eastern Australia) $9. 83 *(7/2/2004)*

Jackaroo 2001 Big Red Red Blend (South Eastern Australia) $7. 86 Best Buy *—D.T. (12/31/2004)*

Jackaroo 2001 Shiraz (South Eastern Australia) $7. 86 *—D.T. (11/15/2004)*

JACOB'S CREEK

Jacob's Creek 2003 Cabernet Sauvignon (South Eastern Australia) $9. 83 *—D.T. (12/31/2005)*

Jacob's Creek 2002 Cabernet Sauvignon (South Eastern Australia) $9. 83 *—D.T. (11/15/2004)*

Jacob's Creek 2001 Cabernet Sauvignon (South Eastern Australia) $10. 84 *—D.T. (6/1/2003)*

Jacob's Creek 1998 Cabernet Sauvignon (Barossa Valley) $11. 88 Best Buy *(2/1/2001)*

Jacob's Creek 2002 Reserve Cabernet Sauvignon (South Australia) $13. 88 Best Buy *—D.T. (12/31/2005)*

Jacob's Creek 2001 Reserve Cabernet Sauvignon (South Australia) $13. 88 Best Buy *—D.T. (2/1/2004)*

Jacob's Creek 2003 Cabernet Sauvignon-Merlot (South Eastern Australia) $9. 82 *—D.T. (8/1/2005)*

Jacob's Creek 2002 Cabernet Sauvignon-Merlot (South Australia) $9. 86 Best Buy *—D.T. (2/1/2004)*

Jacob's Creek NV Sparkling Rosé Champagne Blend (South Eastern Australia) $12. This soft, creamy rosé sparkler is cleanly made, but also rather sweet, with citrus and raspberry fruit. Imported by Pernod Ricard USA. 82 *—J.C. (12/31/2007)*

Jacob's Creek NV Brut Cuvee Champagne Blend (South Eastern Australia) $12. 85 Best Buy *—D.T. (2/1/2004)*

Jacob's Creek NV Brut Cuvée Chardonnay-Pinot Noir Champagne Blend (South Eastern Australia) $12. Shows some positive character on the nose in its hints of ginger and citrus, but seems bland and flavorless on the palate. Imported by Pernod Ricard USA. 81 *—J.C. (8/1/2007)*

Jacob's Creek 2004 Reserve Chardonnay-Pinot Noir Champagne Blend (South Australia) $12. A step up from the Jacob's Creek NV Brut Cuvée, this sparkler comes across as soft and fruity, with abundant apple, melon and citrus flavors that finish clean, if somewhat lacking for crispness and length. Imported by Pernod Ricard USA. 83 *—J.C. (8/1/2007)*

Jacob's Creek 2006 Chardonnay (South Eastern Australia) $9. This starts off a bit slow, without much in the way of aromas, but it fleshes out on the palate to offer ample apple, citrus and melon flavors. Soft, lacks cut to the finish. Imported by Pernod Ricard USA. 83 —*J.C. (8/1/2007)*

Jacob's Creek 2005 Chardonnay (South Eastern Australia) $8. 84 Best Buy —*D.T. (8/1/2006)*

Jacob's Creek 2004 Chardonnay (South Eastern Australia) $8. 81 —*D.T. (5/1/2005)*

Jacob's Creek 2003 Chardonnay (South Eastern Australia) $8. 84 *(7/2/2004)*

Jacob's Creek 2002 Chardonnay (South Eastern Australia) $9. 84 —*D.T. (6/1/2003)*

Jacob's Creek 2001 Chardonnay (South Eastern Australia) $8. 84 —*J.C. (7/1/2002)*

Jacob's Creek 2000 Chardonnay (Barossa Valley) $10. 87 Best Buy *(2/1/2001)*

Jacob's Creek 1999 Chardonnay (South Eastern Australia) $9. 85 —*J.C. (5/1/2000)*

Jacob's Creek 2002 Limited Release Chardonnay (Barossa Valley) $33. 89 —*D.T. (11/15/2004)*

Jacob's Creek 2000 Limited Release Chardonnay (Padthaway) $33. 89 *(6/1/2003)*

Jacob's Creek 1997 Limited Release Chardonnay (Padthaway) $38. 90 *(2/1/2001)*

Jacob's Creek 2004 Reserve Chardonnay (South Australia) $13. 83 —*D.T. (8/1/2006)*

Jacob's Creek 2003 Reserve Chardonnay (South Eastern Australia) $13. 86 —*D.T. (10/1/2005)*

Jacob's Creek 2002 Reserve Chardonnay (South Australia) $13. 88 Best Buy —*D.T. (2/1/2004)*

Jacob's Creek 2001 Reserve Chardonnay (South Australia) $13. 84 —*D.T. (6/1/2003)*

Jacob's Creek 2000 Reserve Chardonnay (South Australia) $14. 85 —*J.C. (7/1/2002)*

Jacob's Creek 1999 Reserve Chardonnay (Barossa Valley) $16. 88 *(2/1/2001)*

Jacob's Creek 1998 Reserve Chardonnay (Padthaway) $16. 88 *(5/1/2000)*

Jacob's Creek 1997 Reserve Chardonnay (Padthaway) $14. 85 *(10/1/1999)*

Jacob's Creek 2004 Merlot (South Eastern Australia) $9. 83 —*D.T. (10/1/2005)*

Jacob's Creek 2003 Merlot (South Eastern Australia) $9. 83 —*D.T. (3/1/2005)*

Jacob's Creek 2002 Merlot (South Eastern Australia) $9. 84 —*D.T. (9/1/2004)*

Jacob's Creek 2001 Merlot (South Eastern Australia) $10. 84 —*D.T. (6/1/2003)*

Jacob's Creek 2000 Merlot (South Eastern Australia) $10. 82 —*J.C. (6/1/2002)*

Jacob's Creek 1998 Merlot (South Eastern Australia) $10. 84 *(5/1/2000)*

Jacob's Creek 2002 Red Blend (South Eastern Australia) $9. 83 —*M.S. (12/15/2002)*

Jacob's Creek 2006 Riesling (South Eastern Australia) $9. Simple apple and lime flavors are citrusy and fresh, finishing crisp and dry. There's not much concentration, but it's still a zesty, refreshing drink. Drink now. Imported by Pernod Ricard USA. 84 —*J.C. (9/1/2007)*

Jacob's Creek 2005 Riesling (South Eastern Australia) $9. 84 —*D.T. (4/1/2006)*

Jacob's Creek 2004 Riesling (South Eastern Australia) $9. 82 —*D.T. (12/1/2005)*

Jacob's Creek 2002 Riesling (Barossa Valley) $9. 84 —*D.T. (2/1/2004)*

Jacob's Creek 2004 Reserve Riesling (South Australia) $13. 84 —*D.T. (8/1/2006)*

Jacob's Creek 2006 Reserve Riesling (South Australia) $15. Plunk down the extra coin for the JC Reserve Riesling. The aromas are exactly what you'd expect in a Riesling—floral, citrusy and minerally all at once—while the flavors of green apple and lime are stony without being hard. A lean, surprisingly elegant wine that delicately fades on the finish. Imported by Pernod Ricard USA. 90 Best Buy —*J.C. (9/1/2007)*

Jacob's Creek 2003 Reserve Riesling (Clare Valley) $13. 88 Best Buy —*D.T. (2/1/2004)*

Jacob's Creek 2002 Reserve Riesling (South Australia) $14. 87 —*D.T. (8/1/2003)*

Jacob's Creek 2003 Steingarten Riesling (Barossa) $28. Not quite as powerful or intense as the 2002, but still a good drop, the 2003 Steingarten features straightforward lime and wet stone aromas backed by a long, zesty finish. Drink now, or hold and see if more complexity develops with another five years in a cool cellar. Imported by Pernod Ricard USA. 86 —*J.C. (9/1/2007)*

Jacob's Creek 2002 Steingarten Riesling (Barossa) $25. The idea behind the delayed release of the Steingarten Riesling is that the wine needs time to show its best. This is a broad-shouldered, muscular Riesling even five years after the vintage, showing off smoky, dieselly notes to go with hints of honey and citrus. Spicy and minerally on the finish. Imported by Pernod Ricard USA. 88 —*J.C. (9/1/2007)*

Jacob's Creek 2004 Semillon-Chardonnay (South Eastern Australia) $8. 83 —*D.T. (4/1/2006)*

Jacob's Creek 2003 Semillon-Chardonnay (South Eastern Australia) $8. 84 Best Buy —*D.T. (11/15/2004)*

Jacob's Creek 2000 Semillon-Chardonnay (Barossa Valley) $8. 85 *(2/1/2001)*

Jacob's Creek 2005 Semillon-Sauvignon Blanc (South Eastern Australia) $8. 84 Best Buy —*D.T. (8/1/2006)*

Jacob's Creek 2005 Shiraz (South Eastern Australia) $9. Delivers what you might expect from an entry-level Shiraz produced in voluminous quantities. Blackberry preserves aromas and flavors, adequate weight and a slightly syrupy texture. Imported by Pernod Ricard USA. 83 —*J.C. (7/1/2007)*

Jacob's Creek 2000 Shiraz (South Eastern Australia) $10. 87 Best Buy —*M.S. (3/1/2003)*

Jacob's Creek 1999 Shiraz (South Eastern Australia) $11. 84 —*J.C. (9/1/2002)*

Jacob's Creek 1998 Shiraz (South Eastern Australia) $9. 87 Best Buy *(3/1/2000)*

Jacob's Creek 1998 Shiraz (South Eastern Australia) $10. 88 Best Buy *(5/1/2000)*

Jacob's Creek 2005 Centenary Hill Shiraz (Barossa Valley) $33. The qualitative equal of the excellent 2002, the 2005 Centenary Hill is a big, rich wine that shows just a bit of warmth to its ripe black cherry flavors. Pepper and spice notes add interest, while the soft, dusty-textured tannins give this wine an easy approachability not seen in older vintages. Drink now–2018. Imported by Pernod Ricard USA. 91 —*J.C. (11/1/2007)*

Jacob's Creek 2004 Centenary Hilll Shiraz (Barossa Valley) $33. Not quite as impressive as the 2002, but this is still an excellent wine. It's dark in color, a dense purple hue that presages its black cherry and chocolate aromas and flavors. Accented by spice notes and chewy tannins on the finish, this appears to need time in the cellar. Drink 2010–2018. Imported by Pernod Ricard USA. 90 —*J.C. (11/1/2007)*

Jacob's Creek 2003 Centenary Hill Shiraz (Barossa Valley) $33. Starts off rather spicy and peppery, fills the midpalate with modest blackberry fruit, then closes with a blast of vanilla-laden oak. This is a medium-bodied, savory offering that blends of a couple of old-vine parcels from Barossa's Tanunda subregion. Drink now-2012. Imported by Pernod Ricard USA. 89 —*J.C. (11/1/2007)*

Jacob's Creek 2002 Centenary Hill Shiraz (Barossa Valley) $33. For years this was Orlando's top Shiraz, but it has been rebranded Jacob's Creek for its greater name recognition. It's still a very fine wine, a big step up from what you might expect under the JC label, featuring oaky notes of toasted coconut, caramel and vanilla layered over blueberry and plum fruit. It's mouthfilling, with velvety-textured tannins and mouthwatering acids. Drink now–2015. Imported by Pernod Ricard USA. 91 —*J.C. (6/1/2007)*

Jacob's Creek 1998 Centenary Hill Shiraz (Barossa Valley) $33. Seemingly fully mature, this still shows a dark, saturated color, but the flavors are moving from sour plum fruit to more meaty, savory flavors with plenty of pepper and spice. Some chewy tannins remain, but as the clock is ticking on the fruit, this would be better consumed in the short term. Imported by Pernod Ricard USA. 91 —*J.C. (11/1/2007)*

Jacob's Creek 1995 Centenary Hill Shiraz (Barossa Valley) $33. Still a dark wine, with a little bricking. Minty on the nose, which also hints at leather and vanilla. Brown sugar, leather and meat flavors seem mature, carried along on a creamy-syrupy mouthfeel. Turns a bit drying on the finish. Probably time to drink up. Note: This was bottled under the Orlando label, but we've cataloged it as Jacob's Creek so that all of the vintages of the wine will be under the same lookup. Not imported. 89 —*J.C. (11/1/2007)*

Jacob's Creek 2004 Reserve Shiraz (South Australia) $12. Reminiscent of some Paso Robles red wines, this superripe Shiraz has some sweetly grassy or alfalfa-like aromas to go alongside blackberry and chocolate flavors that lean toward coffee and caramel on the finish. It's round in the mouth, the tannins ultrasoft; drink now. Imported by Pernod Ricard USA. 85 —*J.C. (11/15/2007)*

Jacob's Creek 2001 Reserve Shiraz (South Australia) $13. 88 Best Buy —*D.T. (2/1/2004)*

Jacob's Creek 1999 Reserve Shiraz (South Australia) $18. 87 *(9/1/2002)*

Jacob's Creek 1998 Reserve Shiraz (Barossa Valley) $18. 91 *(2/1/2001)*

Jacob's Creek 1997 Reserve Shiraz (Barossa Valley) $15. 89 *(5/1/2000)*

Jacob's Creek 2006 Rosé Shiraz (South Eastern Australia) $8. This plump, soft rosé would be ideal for uncritical quaffing by the pool this summer. Herbal, strawberry and citrus notes go down easy, the softness on the mid-palate balanced by mouthwatering acidity on the finish. Imported by Pernod Ricard USA. 84 Best Buy —*J.C. (7/1/2007)*

Jacob's Creek 2004 Shiraz-Cabernet Sauvignon (South Eastern Australia) $8. 83 —*D.T. (11/15/2006)*

Jacob's Creek 2002 Shiraz-Cabernet Sauvignon (South Eastern Australia) $8. 84 Best Buy —*D.T. (12/31/2004)*

Jacob's Creek 2001 Shiraz-Cabernet Sauvignon (South Eastern Australia) $9. 83 —*D.T. (1/1/2002)*

Jacob's Creek 2000 Shiraz-Cabernet Sauvignon (South Eastern Australia) $10. 83 —*J.C. (9/1/2002)*

Jacob's Creek 1998 Shiraz-Cabernet Sauvignon (South Eastern Australia) $9. 87 Best Buy *(5/1/2000)*

Jacob's Creek 1999 Limited Release Shiraz-Cabernet Sauvignon (South Eastern Australia) $50. 89 —*D.T. (12/31/2004)*

Jacob's Creek 1998 Limited Release Shiraz-Cabernet Sauvignon (South Australia) $50. 92 Cellar Selection *(2/1/2001)*

Jacob's Creek 1997 Limited Release Shiraz-Cabernet Sauvignon (South Australia) $50. 90 —*D.T. (12/15/2002)*

Jacob's Creek 1994 Limited Release 150th Annivers Shiraz-Cabernet Sauvignon (South Eastern Australia) $65. 91 *(5/1/2000)*

Jacob's Creek 2003 Syrah-Grenache (South Eastern Australia) $8. 83 —*D.T. (9/1/2004)*

Jacob's Creek 1999 White Blend (South Eastern Australia) $8. 87 Best Buy *(5/1/2000)*

JAMES ESTATE

James Estate 2000 Cabernet Sauvignon (McLaren Vale) $13. 86 Best Buy *(11/1/2002)*

James Estate 1999 Cabernet Sauvignon (McLaren Vale) $13. 82 —*S.H. (6/1/2002)*

James Estate 2001 Sundara Cabernet Sauvignon-Merlot (South Eastern Australia) $9. 82 *(11/1/2002)*

James Estate 2000 Sundara Cabernet Sauvignon-Merlot (Hunter Valley) $9. 85 —*S.H. (6/1/2002)*

James Estate 2000 Compass Chardonnay (Hunter Valley) $13. 90 Best Buy —*S.H. (6/1/2002)*

James Estate 2001 Reserve Chardonnay (Hunter Valley) $20. 84 *(11/1/2002)*

James Estate 2001 Sundara Chardonnay (South Eastern Australia) $9. 84 *(11/1/2002)*

James Estate 2000 Merlot (South Eastern Australia) $13. 84 *(11/1/2002)*

James Estate 2000 Reserve Merlot (Hunter Valley) $20. 87 *(11/1/2002)*

James Estate 1995 Botrytis Semillon (Australia) $25. 92 —*J.M. (12/1/2002)*

James Estate 2000 Sundara Semillon-Chardonnay (Hunter Valley) $9. 88 Best Buy —*S.H. (6/1/2002)*

James Estate 2000 Shiraz (South Eastern Australia) $13. 85 Best Buy *(11/1/2002)*

James Estate 1999 Shiraz (Hunter Valley) $13. 84 —*S.H. (6/1/2002)*

James Estate 2000 Reserve Shiraz (Frankland River) $20. 89 *(11/1/2002)*

James Estate 2000 Reserve Shiraz (McLaren Vale & Langhorne Creek) $20. 88 *(11/1/2002)*

James Estate 2000 Sundara Shiraz-Cabernet Sauvignon (Hunter Valley) $9. 84 —*S.H. (6/1/2002)*

James Estate 2001 Verdelho (Hunter Valley) $13. 85 *(11/1/2002)*

JANSZ

Jansz NV Premium Cuvée Champagne Blend (Tasmania) $20. A well-made sparkler, Jansz's Premium Cuvée shows lovely nuances of toast and super-fresh lemon zest layered over ripe apple scents. It's light and fresh, with a slight creaminess to the texture, with flavors that lean toward apple and citrus, but with some savory undercurrents of toast and mushrooms. Drink now. 90 Editors' Choice —*J.C. (6/1/2007)*

Jansz NV Premium Non Vintage Cuvée Brut Chardonnay (Australia) $19. 84 —*D.T. (12/31/2005)*

Jansz NV Premium Rosé Pinot Noir (Tasmania) $20. Jansz's rosé shows slightly less toasty, autolytic character than its Premium Cuvée, instead showcasing more fruit. Aromas suggest peach or berry, with hints of red apples and citrus as well, with a medium-weight, creamy mouthfeel. Fresh and fruit-driven on the finish. Drink now. 89 —*J.C. (6/1/2007)*

JCP MALTUS

JCP Maltus 2003 The Colonial Estate L'Étranger Cabernet Sauvignon (Barossa Valley) $27. 84 —*D.T. (8/1/2005)*

JCP Maltus 2003 ÉMIGRÉ Red Blend (Barossa Valley) $100. 87 —*D.T. (4/1/2006)*

JCP Maltus 2003 EXILE Red Blend (Barossa Valley) $200. 90 —*D.T. (4/1/2006)*

JCP Maltus 2002 EXILE Red Blend (Barossa Valley) $200. 86 —*D.T. (8/1/2005)*

JIM BARRY

Jim Barry 1997 McCrae Wood Bordeaux Blend (Clare & Eden Valleys) $30. 82 —*D.T. (9/1/2001)*

Jim Barry 2000 First Eleven XI Cabernet Sauvignon (Coonawarra) $17. 91 —*D.T. (3/1/2005)*

Jim Barry 2004 The Cover Drive Cabernet Sauvignon (South Australia) $17. 88 —*D.T. (8/1/2006)*

Jim Barry 2003 The Cover Drive Cabernet Sauvignon (South Australia) $17. 88 —*D.T. (12/31/2005)*

Jim Barry 2002 The Cover Drive Cabernet Sauvignon (South Australia) $17. 89 —*D.T. (5/1/2005)*

Jim Barry 2002 The Cover Drive Cabernet Sauvignon (Clare Valley-Coonawarra) $15. 90 Editors' Choice —*D.T. (11/15/2004)*

Jim Barry 2001 The Cover Drive Cabernet Sauvignon (Coonawarra) $15. 90 Editors' Choice —*D.T. (5/1/2004)*

Jim Barry 2003 Lodge Hill Riesling (Clare Valley) $15. 89 Editors' Choice —*D.T. (2/1/2004)*

Jim Barry 2005 The Florita Riesling (Clare Valley) $30. 92 —*D.T. (11/15/2006)*

Jim Barry 2004 The Florita Riesling (Clare Valley) $30. 93 Cellar Selection —*D.T. (4/1/2006)*

Jim Barry 2004 The Lodge Hill Riesling (Clare Valley) $17. 85 —*D.T. (10/1/2005)*

Jim Barry 2002 The Lodge Hill Riesling (Clare Valley) $15. 90 Best Buy —*D.T. (8/1/2003)*

Jim Barry 2002 Armagh Shiraz (Clare Valley) $100. 94 —*D.T. (6/1/2006)*

Jim Barry 2001 Armagh Shiraz (Clare Valley) $100. 92 —*D.T. (5/1/2004)*

Jim Barry 1996 The Armagh Shiraz (Clare Valley) $75. 97 *(11/15/1999)*

Jim Barry 2001 Lodge Hill Shiraz (Clare Valley) $15. 87 *(12/1/2003)*

Jim Barry 2002 McRae Wood Shiraz (Clare Valley) $35. 92 —*D.T. (1/1/2002)*

Jim Barry 2001 McRae Wood Shiraz (Clare Valley) $35. 90 —*D.T. (5/1/2004)*

Jim Barry 2000 McRae Wood Shiraz (Clare Valley) $35. 89 *(12/1/2003)*

Jim Barry 2000 The Armagh Shiraz (Clare Valley) $100. 94 *(12/1/2003)*

Jim Barry 1999 The Armagh Shiraz (Clare Valley) $100. 95 Cellar Selection —*S.H. (12/15/2002)*

Jim Barry 1997 The Armagh Shiraz (Clare Valley) $100. 93 Cellar Selection *(11/1/2001)*

Jim Barry 2004 The Lodge Hill Shiraz (Clare Valley) $17. 88 —*D.T. (8/1/2006)*

Jim Barry 2003 The Lodge Hill Shiraz (Clare Valley) $17. 85 —*D.T. (12/1/2005)*

Jim Barry 2002 The Lodge Hill Shiraz (Clare Valley) $15. 89 Editors' Choice —*D.T. (9/1/2004)*

Jim Barry 1999 The Mcrae Wood Shiraz (Clare Valley) $35. 92 Editors' Choice —*S.H. (12/15/2002)*

JINDALEE

Jindalee 2004 Cabernet Sauvignon (South Eastern Australia) $9. 83 —*D.T. (12/31/2005)*

Jindalee 2004 Chardonnay (South Eastern Australia) $8. 84 Best Buy —*D.T. (6/1/2006)*

Jindalee 2005 Sauvignon Blanc (South Eastern Australia) $8. 84 Best Buy —*D.T. (6/1/2006)*

JINKS CREEK

Jinks Creek 2002 Pinot Noir (Gippsland) $30. 88 —*D.T. (9/1/2004)*

Jinks Creek 2004 Sauvignon Blanc (Gippsland) $25. 87 *(7/1/2005)*

Jinks Creek 2002 Sauvignon Blanc (Gippsland) $20. 84 —*D.T. (5/1/2004)*

Jinks Creek 2002 Shiraz (Yarra Valley) $30. 85 —*D.T. (9/1/2004)*

JJ HAHN

JJ Hahn 2002 1928 Shiraz (Barossa Valley) $40. Complex and supple, but lacks just a bit of energy and vigor; the fruit comes across as a bit dried rather than pristinely fresh, with hints of molasses and brown sugar. Still, there's plenty of it, matched by hints of pepper, grilled meat, coffee and vanilla. Drink now and over the next few years. 88 —*J.C. (11/1/2007)*

JOHN DUVAL WINES

John Duval Wines 2005 Plexus S-G-M Rhône Red Blend (Barossa Valley) $35. With only 10% new oak used for this cuvée, there's just a hint of vanilla here; the aromas are dominated by black cherries and dusty spice notes. The flavors follow suit, picking up a bit of blueberry as well, delivered via a silky-textured palate. Finishes crisp, making it a good candidate with burgers or chops. Drink now–2015. 90 —*J.C. (11/1/2007)*

John Duval Wines 2004 Plexus S-G-M Rhône Red Blend (Barossa Valley) $35. Roughly half Shiraz, with the balance divided between Grenache and Mourvèdre, former Penfolds winemaker John Duval's second vintage on his own features lots of dusty earth and spice, sprinkled over cherry fruit. Tannins are soft, the mouthfeel lush, with the cherries turning tart on the finish. Drink now–2014. 90 —*J.C. (11/1/2007)*

John Duval Wines 2003 Plexus S-G-M Red Blend (Barossa Valley) $35. 90 —*D.T. (8/1/2005)*

John Duval Wines 2005 "Reserve" Shiraz (Barossa Valley) $NA. The wine is in the bottle, but hasn't been named yet, hence the "Reserve" designation. Underneath a slightly smoky, toasty exterior lies an explosion of cherry, raspberry and black cherry fruit that's wonderfully pure without being simple. The texture is creamy and lush without being unstructured or jammy, while the finish goes on and on. Drink now–2020. 96 Cellar Selection —*J.C. (11/1/2007)*

John Duval Wines 2005 Entity Shiraz (Barossa Valley) $40. Tight and oaky at first, but this gradually opens with air to reveal copious blueberry and blackberry aromas and flavors. Vanilla and spice accent the primary fruit, while the tannins are supple, imparting a creamy mouthfeel. Long on the finish. Despite its youthful drinkability, this wine should age through at least 2015. 92 —*J.C. (11/1/2007)*

John Duval Wines 2004 Entity Shiraz (Barossa Valley) $40. On the elegant side for Barossa, with polished textures and a long finish. The 2004 Entity is dark in nature, carrying ample blueberry and blackberry fruit that's highlighted by peppery spice. Drink now–2014, maybe longer. 92 —*J.C. (11/1/2007)*

JOHN HONGELL

John Hongell 2001 Biscay Vineyard Shiraz (Barossa Valley) $25. 90 —*D.T. (8/1/2005)*

JOSEPH

Joseph 2003 Moda Cabernet Sauvignon-Merlot (McLaren Vale) $48. Made from partially dried grapes—"moda amarone"—this is a lush, creamy Cabernet (85%) with bold chocolate and cassis flavors. Soft and elegant on the finish. 91 —*J.C. (6/1/2007)*

Joseph 2002 Moda Cabernet Sauvignon-Merlot (McLaren Vale) $48. 90 —*D.T. (6/1/2006)*

Joseph 2005 D'Elena Pinot Grigio (McLaren Vale) $21. 86 —*D.T. (10/1/2006)*

KAESLER

Kaesler 2001 Cabernet Sauvignon (Barossa Valley) $22. 92 Editors' Choice —*D.T. (2/1/2004)*

Kaesler 2001 Stonehorse Chardonnay (Geelong) $NA. 87 —*D.T. (2/1/2004)*

Kaesler 2005 Avignon Rhône Red Blend (Barossa Valley) $30. A blend of approximately 40% each Grenache and Shiraz with 20% Mataro, Kaelser's 2005 Avignon offers up explosive notes of licorice and plum, hints of lighter stone fruits, like peach or apricot, then finishes with blackberries, cola and vanilla. Lush and smooth, an opulent mouthful for near-term consumption. 92 —*J.C. (11/1/2007)*

Kaesler 2002 Avignon Red Blend (Barossa Valley) $24. 90 —*D.T. (2/1/2004)*

Kaesler 2003 Stonehorse Red Blend (Barossa Valley) $19. 86 —*D.T. (5/1/2005)*

Kaesler 2002 Stonehorse Red Blend (Barossa Valley) $18. 86 —*D.T. (2/1/2004)*

Kaesler 2003 Old Vine Semillon (Barossa Valley) $17. 87 —*D.T. (2/1/2004)*

Kaesler 2005 Old Bastard Shiraz (Barossa Valley) $140. From vines planted in 1893, this wine combines spicy complexity with size and ultraconcentrated fruit. It tips the scales at 16% alcohol, but wears it well, hiding it under hints of licorice and subtle wood spice and layers of blackberry and blueberry fruit. Yes, it's big, but it's not inelegant, finishing lush, long and spicy. Terrific stuff that should drink well from 2010–2020. 95 —*J.C. (11/1/2007)*

Kaesler 2001 Old Bastard Shiraz (Barossa Valley) $110. 92 —*D.T. (2/1/2004)*

Kaesler 2005 Old Vine Shiraz (Barossa Valley) $56. This comes out of the blocks at full speed, delivering a huge hit of licorice, blackberry and plum on the nose, then follows that up with deep mouthfilling flavors. Yet it's surprisingly elegant and silky on the extended finish. Lovely; drink now–2015. 92 —*J.C. (11/1/2007)*

Kaesler 2001 Old Vine Shiraz (Barossa Valley) $45. 93 Editors' Choice —*D.T. (2/1/2004)*

Kaesler 2000 Old Vine Shiraz (Barossa Valley) $NA. 89 —*D.T. (2/1/2004)*

Kaesler 2002 Stonehorse Shiraz (Barossa Valley) $28. 88 —*D.T. (2/1/2004)*

Kaesler 2005 The Bogan Shiraz (Barossa Valley) $65. Big and bold, like the excellent '04 version. If anything, it emphasizes the fruit even a bit more, with less spicy complexity, but it's a black hole of plum and blackberry fruit that explodes in the mouth, staining the palate with fruity intensity. The alcohol level must be elevated, but it's well concealed by supple tannins. Drink now–2015. 93 —*J.C. (11/1/2007)*

Kaesler 2004 The Bogan Shiraz (Barossa Valley) $65. Big and bold, with an unmistakable hit of American oak—vanilla and dill—on the nose, but also huge levels of fruit concentration. Creamy, thick and mouthfilling, loaded with blackberries and spice. The long, robust finish suggests a certain amount of ageability, although this is certainly enjoyable now. Drink now–2015. 93 —*J.C. (11/1/2007)*

KALBARRI

Kalbarri 2003 Bin Select 667 Shiraz (South Eastern Australia) $7. 83 —*D.T. (6/1/2006)*

KALLESKE

Kalleske 2006 Clarry's Grenache-Shiraz (Barossa Valley) $30. Showing a flashy, extroverted personality, Kalleske's blend of 80% Grenache and 20% Shiraz shows hints of coffee and toast, but the focus here is on forward fruit. Lush cherry, peach and apricot flavors end on notes of white pepper and spice. Drink now–2010. 91 —*J.C. (11/1/2007)*

Kalleske 2005 Greenock Shiraz (Barossa Valley) $40. A bit closed and brooding on the nose, showing merely traces of dark chocolate and espresso. Despite its sullen state, this wine's potential is clear from its ample weight and structure, dark chocolate and plum flavors and promising finish, which brightens to add raspberries and a hint of black pepper. Drink 2010–2020. 92 —*J.C. (11/1/2007)*

KANGA RESERVE

Kanga Reserve 2004 Chardonnay (South Eastern Australia) $6. 84 Best Buy —*D.T. (6/1/2006)*

KANGARILLA ROAD

Kangarilla Road 1997 Bordeaux Blend (McLaren Vale) $20. 86 —*M.S. (12/15/2002)*

Kangarilla Road 2004 Cabernet Sauvignon (McLaren Vale) $22. It's round and full-bodied in the mouth, but this wine isn't just another jammy Australian Cabernet—there's some structure here, giving a sense of size without excess weight and defining the finish with dusty, fine-textured tannins. The fruit is dense, though, and dark, running the fine line between chocolaty cassis and prune before picking up hints of dates and dried spices. Drink now–2010. 88 —*J.C. (3/1/2007)*

Kangarilla Road 2000 Cabernet Sauvignon (McLaren Vale) $23. 82 —*D.T. (6/1/2002)*

Kangarilla Road 1999 Cabernet Sauvignon (McLaren Vale) $23. 90 —*C.S. (6/1/2002)*

Kangarilla Road 1998 Cabernet Sauvignon (McLaren Vale) $23. 83 —*M.S. (10/1/2000)*

Kangarilla Road 2005 Chardonnay (McLaren Vale) $18. This is a broad, mouthfilling Chardonnay that gets a lot of things right. The aromas are citrusy and tropical, kept in check by hints of pith. The oak is nicely judged, with spice and nutty, cereal-like notes adding complexity to the bold fruit.

A minor quibble is the warmth and slightly elevated alcohol on the finish. Drink now. 86 —*J.C. (3/1/2007)*

Kangarilla Road 2004 Shiraz (McLaren Vale) $22. Kangarilla Road has become a reliable source of high-quality Shiraz, sold at reasonable prices. The 2004 is a soft, full-bodied wine filled with aromas and flavors of chocolate fudge, plums, dried cherries and spice, with a long, lively finish. Drink now. 89 —*J.C. (2/1/2007)*

Kangarilla Road 2002 Shiraz (McLaren Vale) $21. 89 —*D.T. (3/1/2005)*

Kangarilla Road 2001 Shiraz (McLaren Vale) $21. 86 —*S.H. (10/1/2003)*

Kangarilla Road 2000 Shiraz (McLaren Vale) $21. 87 —*J.C. (9/1/2002)*

Kangarilla Road 1999 Shiraz (McLaren Vale) $19. 85 *(10/1/2001)*

Kangarilla Road 2003 Shiraz-Viognier (McLaren Vale) $21. 90 —*D.T. (3/1/2005)*

Kangarilla Road 2002 Zinfandel (McLaren Vale) $33. 88 —*D.T. (3/1/2005)*

Kangarilla Road 2001 Zinfandel (McLaren Vale) $33. 85 —*S.H. (12/31/2003)*

KANGAROO RIDGE

Kangaroo Ridge 2002 Cabernet Sauvignon (South Eastern Australia) $6. 82 —*D.T. (5/1/2004)*

Kangaroo Ridge 2002 Chardonnay (South Eastern Australia) $8. 87 Best Buy *(7/2/2004)*

Kangaroo Ridge 2002 Merlot (South Eastern Australia) $8. 83 —*D.T. (9/1/2004)*

Kangaroo Ridge 2002 Shiraz (South Eastern Australia) $8. 83 —*D.T. (9/1/2004)*

KATHERINE HILLS

Katherine Hills 2000 Cabernet Sauvignon (South Australia) $10. 85 —*D.T. (12/31/2003)*

KATNOOK ESTATE

Katnook Estate 2000 Cabernet Sauvignon (Coonawarra) $22. 90 —*D.T. (12/31/2004)*

Katnook Estate 1999 Cabernet Sauvignon (Coonawarra) $22. 85 —*D.T. (6/1/2003)*

Katnook Estate 2000 Odyssey Cabernet Sauvignon (Coonawarra) $50. 91 Cellar Selection —*D.T. (10/1/2005)*

Katnook Estate 2002 Chardonnay (Coonawarra) $17. 84 —*D.T. (5/1/2005)*

Katnook Estate 2001 Chardonnay (Coonawarra) $20. 85 *(7/2/2004)*

Katnook Estate 2000 Chardonnay (Coonawarra) $17. 84 —*D.T. (8/1/2003)*

Katnook Estate 1999 Merlot (Coonawarra) $22. 83 —*D.T. (1/1/2002)*

Katnook Estate 2004 Sauvignon Blanc (Coonawarra) $15. 87—*D.T. (8/1/2005)*

Katnook Estate 2002 Shiraz (Coonawarra) $22. 85 —*D.T. (12/1/2005)*

Katnook Estate 2000 Shiraz (Coonawarra) $22. 89 —*K.F. (3/1/2003)*

Katnook Estate 2002 Prodigy Shiraz (Coonawarra) $50. 90 —*D.T. (6/1/2006)*

Katnook Estate 1999 Prodigy Shiraz (Coonawarra) $50. 90 —*K.F. (3/1/2003)*

KELLY'S PROMISE

Kelly's Promise 2002 Cabernet Sauvignon-Merlot (South Eastern Australia) $8. 84 Best Buy —*D.T. (8/1/2005)*

Kelly's Promise 2000 Cabernet Sauvignon-Merlot (South Eastern Australia) $9. 87 Best Buy —*M.S. (12/15/2002)*

Kelly's Promise 2003 Chardonnay (South Eastern Australia) $8. 86 Best Buy *(7/2/2004)*

Kelly's Promise 2002 Shiraz (South Eastern Australia) $8. 83 —*D.T. (11/15/2004)*

KELLY'S REVENGE

Kelly's Revenge 2004 Chardonnay (South Eastern Australia) $6. 84 Best Buy—*D.T. (11/15/2005)*

Kelly's Revenge 2005 Shiraz (South Eastern Australia) $5. Light in body, with modest cherry and vanilla aromas and flavors. The finish is slightly syrupy, verging on cloying. Imported by North Lake Wines. 82 —*J.C. (11/15/2007)*

Kelly's Revenge 2003 Shiraz (South Eastern Australia) $6. 83 Best Buy —*D.T. (12/31/2005)*

KILDA

Kilda 2005 Chardonnay (South Eastern Australia) $7. 86 Best Buy —*D.T. (8/1/2006)*

KILIKANOON

Kilikanoon 2004 R Reserve Shiraz (Barossa Valley) $60. A terrific effort from two Barossa vineyards, one in Greenock and the other in Vinevale, this is wonderfully perfumed and floral on the nose, yet also peppery and fruity—in a word, complex. Ditto the flavors, which range from coffee to olive, chocolate to vanilla and berries to spice. All of these elements are tied together by a creamy, lush texture and a long, elegant and refined finish. Drink now–2020. 95 Editors' Choice —*J.C. (11/1/2007)*

Kilikanoon 2004 Testament Shiraz (Barossa Valley) $40. Not far behind Kilikanoon's R Reserve—and, indeed, it comes from the same vineyards—the 2004 Testament is also a tour de force. There's a hint of rhubarb and spicy cinnamon that lends intrigue to the aromas of rich blackberry fruit, while the flavors seamlessly blend in hints of red raspberries and cracked pepper. Finishes long, crisp and mouthwatering. Drink now–2020. 94 Editors' Choice —*J.C. (11/1/2007)*

Kilikanoon 2005 Killerman's Run Shiraz-Grenache (South Australia) $20. Lush and creamy on the palate, this is wonderfully soft and enveloping, offering a hedonistic mouthful of black cherry fruit, yet not without ample complexity. The ripe cherry core is surrounded by flashes of vanilla, hints of peppery spice and cola, and finishes with a touch of licorice. Drink now–2012. 91 Editors' Choice —*J.C. (12/31/2007)*

KILLERBY

Killerby 2000 Cabernet Sauvignon (Western Australia) $30. 88 —*D.T. (5/1/2004)*

Killerby 1999 Cabernet Sauvignon (Western Australia) $30. 88 *(6/1/2001)*

Killerby 2000 Chardonnay (Western Australia) $45. 87 —*J.C. (7/1/2002)*

Killerby 2002 Sauvignon Blanc (Margaret River) $15. 83 —*D.T. (5/1/2004)*

Killerby 1999 Semillon-Sauvignon Blanc (Western Australia) $15. 86 —*J.C. (9/1/2001)*

Killerby 1999 Shiraz (Western Australia) $30. 87 *(11/1/2001)*

KISSING BRIDGE

Kissing Bridge 2002 Chardonnay (South Eastern Australia) $6. 83 *(7/2/2004)*

Kissing Bridge 2001 Chardonnay (South Eastern Australia) $8. 83 —*D.T. (6/1/2003)*

Kissing Bridge 2002 Merlot (South Eastern Australia) $10. 81 —*D.T. (12/1/2005)*

Kissing Bridge 2001 Shiraz (South Eastern Australia) $6. 84 —*D.T. (9/1/2004)*

Kissing Bridge 2000 Shiraz (South Eastern Australia) $8. 83 —*D.T. (10/1/2003)*

KNAPPSTEIN

Knappstein 2004 Enterprise Vineyard Cabernet Sauvignon (Clare Valley) $40. Heavily extracted and heavily oaked, this Cabernet starts with a rush of vanilla and cedar, then backs that up with tobacco and cassis. It's practically chewy in the mouth, ending with coffee and additional cedar flavors. 88 —*J.C. (6/1/2007)*

Knappstein 2006 Hand Picked Riesling (Clare Valley) $15. This is a sturdy, muscular Riesling. Although it starts off with some deceptive floral—lilac—aromas, its assertive apple and lime flavors flow relentlessly over the palate. Powerful and intense, it nevertheless finishes clean and refreshing, making it a solid counterpoint to richly sauced fish dishes. 88 —*J.C. (6/1/2007)*

KNAPPSTEIN LENSWOOD VINEYARDS

Knappstein Lenswood Vineyards 2002 Lenswood Sauvignon Blanc (Adelaide Hills) $NA. 84 —*D.T. (5/1/2004)*

KOALA VALLEY

Koala Valley 2003 Chardonnay (Riverland) $8. 85 Best Buy *(7/2/2004)*

KONO BARÚ

Kono Barú 2005 Shiraz (South Eastern Australia) $13. This is a clean and fruity Shiraz—and one that fits the Australian success formula almost predictably. Jammy blackberry and cassis fruit is framed by touches of oak-derived vanilla and spice, tannins are soft and the mouthfeel supple. It's well done, even if it lacks a certain degree of individuality. 85 —*J.C. (11/15/2007)*

KOONOWLA

Koonowla 2006 Riesling (Clare Valley) $19. Starts with a hint of honey to go with Asian pear and dried spices, developing into a medium-bodied, round Riesling with strong apple, pear, spice and tangerine flavors. It could be a touch longer on the finish, but it does have a pleasant tactile quality that gives it added refreshment. 89 —*J.C. (8/1/2007)*

Koonowla 2000 Shiraz (Clare Valley) $20. 87 *—D.T. (3/1/2003)*

KOOYONG

Kooyong 2000 Pinot Noir (Mornington Peninsula) $28. 85 *—D.T. (9/1/2004)*

Kooyong 2001 Estate Pinot Noir (Mornington Peninsula) $31. 90 *—D.T. (10/1/2005)*

KOPPAMURRA

Koppamurra 1998 Cabernet Blend (South Australia) $20. 83 *—J.C. (6/1/2002)*

Koppamurra 1999 Red Blend (Limestone Coast) $20. 85 *—M.S. (12/15/2002)*

KOPPAROSSA

Kopparossa 1999 Shiraz (Coonawarra) $24. 89 *—K.F. (3/1/2003)*

KURTZ FAMILY

Kurtz Family 2000 Boundary Row Grenache (Barossa Valley) $18. 88 *—J.C. (9/1/2002)*

Kurtz Family 2005 Boundary Row Grenache-Shiraz-Mataro G-S-M (Barossa Valley) $20. The base of this is 60% Grenache from an 85-year-old vineyard near Kalimna, which provides lush black cherry fruit. That's dressed up with hints of cola, tree bark, licorice and chocolate from the 25% Shiraz and 15% Mataro. Tasty now, but should continue to drink well over the next 3–4 years or more. 90 Editors' Choice *—J.C. (11/1/2007)*

Kurtz Family 2005 Seven Sleepers Red Blend (Barossa Valley) $17. This is primarily Cabernet Sauvignon and Shiraz, but there are bits and pieces of Petit Verdot, Grenache, Merlot and Malbec included as well. So while it doesn't show a lot of distinctly varietal character, what it does have is plenty of round, lush fruit, with hints of cedar and dried herbs and a silky finish. Drink now–2012. 88 *—J.C. (11/1/2007)*

Kurtz Family 2005 Boundary Row Shiraz (Barossa Valley) $27. Full-throttle, obvious Barossa-style Shiraz, loaded with vanilla-scented oak, but also with blackberry fruit. The tannins are soft, imparting a wonderfully creamy texture and completely filling the mouth. Lush and oaky—this may not be for the intellectual wine drinker—but it's definitely hedonistic. Drink now–2012. 92 *—J.C. (11/1/2007)*

Kurtz Family 1998 Boundary Row Shiraz (Barossa Valley) $25. 90 *(6/1/2001)*

LABYRINTH

Labyrinth 2004 Valley Farm Vineyard Pinot Noir (Yarra Valley) $30. It's light in body—rather delicate, really—but does boast harmonious flavors of dried spices, cherries and mushrooms. A pretty style of Pinot destined to be consumed young. 85 *—J.C. (6/1/2007)*

Labyrinth 2003 Valley Farm Vineyard Pinot Noir (Yarra Valley) $35. 85 *—D.T. (12/1/2005)*

Labyrinth 2002 Valley Farm Vineyard Pinot Noir (Yarra Valley) $38. 92 Editors' Choice *—D.T. (8/1/2005)*

Labyrinth 2004 Viggers Vineyard Pinot Noir (Yarra Valley) $39. Shows slightly better length than the 2004 Valley Farm Vineyard Pinot from winemaker Ariki Hill, but this bottling is still a delicate, lighter-bodied style. Black cherry, cola and savory, mushroomy notes give it a dark flavor profile, while supple tannins impart a dusty mouthfeel. Drink now–2010. 86 *—J.C. (6/1/2007)*

Labyrinth 2003 Viggers Vineyard Pinot Noir (Yarra Valley) $42. 89 *—D.T. (12/1/2005)*

Labyrinth 2002 Viggers Vineyard Pinot Noir (Yarra Valley) $45. 89 *—D.T. (10/1/2005)*

LAKE BREEZE

Lake Breeze 2002 Cabernet Sauvignon (Langhorne Creek) $22. This is well-priced for the quality in the bottle. Aromas of thoroughly ripe black currant carry a whiff of shoe polish, picking up hints of dried herbs and coffee on the palate. Muscular and large-framed, with crisp acids to support the alcohol and a long, mouthwatering finish. 91 Editors' Choice *—J.C. (6/1/2007)*

Lake Breeze 2002 Bernoota Shiraz-Cabernet Sauvignon (Langhorne Creek) $20. The Langhorne Creek region is becoming an interesting source for high-quality wines at reasonable prices. This 60-40 Shiraz-Cab blend features dark plum and cassis fruit flavors framed by oaky notes of toasted coconut and vanilla. It's lush and ultrasoft in the mouth, making it immediately accessible. Drink now–2008. 90 *—J.C. (4/1/2007)*

Lake Breeze 2002 Winemaker's Reserve Shiraz (Langhorne Creek) $36. 89 *—D.T. (10/1/2006)*

LALLA GULLY

Lalla Gully 2005 Riesling (Tasmania) $20. Shows promise, exhibiting classic petrol, apple and citrus aromas and flavors, but wraps up with a tart finish that resembles tinned citrus. It's plump in the mouth, long but a bit metallic on the finish. 85 *—J.C. (2/1/2007)*

LANGHORNE CROSSING

Langhorne Crossing 2003 Red Blend (Langhorne Creek) $11. 82 *—D.T. (12/1/2005)*

Langhorne Crossing 2004 Shiraz-Cabernet Sauvignon (Langhorne Creek) $10. There's a slightly herbal streak to this wine's cherry-berry aromas, which translates into a medicinal edge to the cherry-berry flavors. It's a bit syrupy in texture, but finishes minty fresh. 84 *—J.C. (11/15/2007)*

LANGMEIL

Langmeil 2005 Blacksmith Cabernet Sauvignon (Barossa Valley) $23. Wonderfully varietal Cab Sauvignon from a region that can sometimes lose some of the variety's characteristic herbal notes. Mint and dried herbs on the nose give way to classic cassis fruit. It's nicely rounded yet still firm enough in structure, picking up subtle vanilla shadings on the finish. Drink now–2015. 88 *—J.C. (11/1/2007)*

Langmeil 2002 The Blacksmith Cabernet Sauvignon (Barossa Valley) $20. 93 Editors' Choice *—D.T. (3/1/2005)*

Langmeil 1985 Liqueur Shiraz Tawny Shiraz (Barossa Valley) $56. 92 *—D.T. (3/1/2005)*

Langmeil 2002 The Freedom Shiraz (Barossa Valley) $60. 93 *—D.T. (3/1/2005)*

Langmeil 2005 Valley Floor Shiraz (Barossa Valley) $23. Langmeil's entry-level Shiraz is an impressive effort, combining bright aromatics and bold flavors of mulberries, blackberries and raspberries, then framing them with subtle undertones of vanilla. The texture is creamy and ultrasmooth, turning crisp and a bit tart on the finish. Drink now–2012. 88 *—J.C. (4/1/2007)*

Langmeil 2002 Valley Floor Shiraz (Barossa Valley) $23. 90 *—D.T. (12/31/2004)*

Langmeil 2005 Three Gardens Shiraz-Grenache-Mourvèdre Rhône Red Blend (Barossa Valley) $17. Filled with complex aromas and flavors, this only just lacks a touch of weight and presence on the palate. Tea leaves, cherries and a hint of apricot swirl together elegantly, leaving a lasting impression on the finish. Drink now–2010. 87 *—J.C. (11/1/2007)*

Langmeil 2004 Three Gardens Shiraz-Grenache-Mourvèdre Rhône Red Blend (Barossa) $17. Combines bright red cherry-berry flavors with hints of meatiness, cinnamon and some peppery-herbal notes. It's full-bodied, with a lush, creamy texture and a finish that shows a bit of alcoholic warmth, yet remains spicy and fresh. Ready to drink. 86 *—J.C. (6/1/2007)*

Langmeil 2003 Three Gardens SGM Shiraz-Grenache (Barossa Valley) $16. 87 *—D.T. (3/1/2005)*

Langmeil 2006 Hangin' Snakes Shiraz-Viognier (Barossa Valley) $22. Despite containing only 5% Viognier, this smells a bit floral and apricot-like, and some may take it to task for that, but it does serve to distinguish this silky, easy-drinking wine from Langmeil's Valley Floor Shiraz. It does have a sensational, glycerol-laden texture, and finishes with lingering spice notes, so there's more to it than stone fruit and flowers. Drink now–2010. 90 *—J.C. (11/1/2007)*

LARK HILL

Lark Hill 1999 Canberra Yass Valley Cabernet Sauvignon-Merlot (New South Wales) $35. 83 *—D.T. (9/1/2004)*

Lark Hill 2001 Canberra Yass Valley Chardonnay (New South Wales) $35. 85 *(7/2/2004)*

LARRIKIN

Larrikin 2002 Shiraz (Barossa Valley) $28. 89 *—D.T. (12/31/2004)*

LAUGHING JACK

Laughing Jack 2003 Shiraz (Barossa Valley) $28. Laughing Jack is a nickname for the Kookaburra, so this is a critter wine of a sort. But the resemblance ends there; this is a very good wine, layered with the complex scents and flavors of cracked green and black peppercorns, chocolate, black olive, roasted coffee beans and caramelized plums. Firm on the finish, so give it another six months or so to loosen up. 88 *—J.C. (2/1/2007)*

LAWRENCE VICTOR ESTATE

Lawrence Victor Estate 1999 Shiraz (Coonawarra) $25. 89 *—D.T. (9/1/2004)*

LEASINGHAM

Leasingham 1999 Bin 56 Cabernet Sauvignon (Clare Valley) $19. 88 *—D.T. (6/1/2003)*

Leasingham 1998 Classic Clare Cabernet Sauvignon (Clare Valley) $35. 90 —*C.S. (6/1/2002)*

Leasingham 1997 Classic Clare Cabernet Sauvignon (Clare Valley) $35. 90 —*D.T. (9/1/2001)*

Leasingham 1996 Classic Clare Cabernet Sauvignon (Clare Valley) $28. 91 —*M.S. (4/1/2000)*

Leasingham 2001 Bin 56 Cabernet Sauvignon-Malbec (Clare Valley) $19. 88 —*D.T. (2/1/2004)*

Leasingham 2005 Bin 7 Riesling (Clare Valley) $15. Sorry to steal the moniker from the company's Shiraz, but this is Classic Clare too, offering bold flavors of honey-coated minerals perked up by curls of lime zest. Firmly built and close to dry, you can drink it now for its power and fruit, or hold it up to 10 years or more, if you like your Australian Rieslings with more age on them. 91 Best Buy —*J.C. (5/1/2007)*

Leasingham 2004 Bin 7 Riesling (Clare Valley) $15. 86 —*D.T. (5/1/2005)*

Leasingham 2003 Bin 7 Riesling (Clare Valley) $16. 89 —*D.T. (2/1/2004)*

Leasingham 2002 Bin 7 Riesling (Clare Valley) $16. 90 Editors' Choice —*D.T. (8/1/2003)*

Leasingham 2001 Bin 7 Riesling (Clare Valley) $9. 87 Best Buy —*M.M. (2/1/2002)*

Leasingham 2000 Bin 7 Riesling (Clare Valley) $8. 88 Best Buy —*M.M. (9/1/2001)*

Leasingham 2003 Classic Clare Riesling (Clare Valley) $NA. 92 —*D.T. (2/1/2004)*

Leasingham 2004 Magnus Riesling (Clare Valley) $12. 86 —*D.T. (5/1/2005)*

Leasingham 2003 Magnus Riesling (Clare Valley) $12. 87 Best Buy —*D.T. (11/15/2004)*

Leasingham 2001 Bin 61 Shiraz (Clare Valley) $21. 90 Editors' Choice *(11/15/2003)*

Leasingham 2000 Bin 61 Shiraz (Clare Valley) $21. 83 —*D.T. (2/1/2003)*

Leasingham 1999 Bin 61 Shiraz (Clare Valley) $17. 90 Editors' Choice —*J.C. (9/1/2002)*

Leasingham 1998 Bin 61 Shiraz (Clare Valley) $17. 85 *(10/1/2001)*

Leasingham 1997 Bin 61 Shiraz (Clare Valley) $15. 88 *(3/1/2000)*

Leasingham 2001 Classic Clare Shiraz (Clare Valley) $45. 92 —*D.T. (8/1/2005)*

Leasingham 1999 Classic Clare Shiraz (Clare Valley) $45. 91 *(11/15/2003)*

Leasingham 1998 Classic Clare Shiraz (Clare Valley) $35. 88 *(11/1/2001)*

Leasingham 1997 Classic Clare Shiraz (Clare Valley) $28. 87 *(10/1/2000)*

Leasingham 1994 Classic Clare Shiraz (Clare Valley) $NA. 91 —*D.T. (2/1/2004)*

Leasingham 1995 Show Reserve Shiraz (Clare Valley) $NA. 91—*D.T. (2/1/2004)*

Leasingham 1994 Sparkling Shiraz (Clare Valley) $NA. 89 —*D.T. (2/1/2004)*

Leasingham 2003 Magnus Shiraz-Cabernet Sauvignon (Clare Valley) $12. This 60-40 blend of Shiraz and Cabernet Sauvignon delivers plenty of bang for the buck, accenting blackberry and fudge flavors with hints of coffee and roasted meat. The long, mouthwatering finish rests on supple tannins that should give this wine life through 2010. 87 Best Buy —*J.C. (2/1/2007)*

Leasingham 2002 Magnus Shiraz-Cabernet Sauvignon (Clare Valley) $12. 84 —*D.T. (8/1/2005)*

Leasingham 2001 Magnus Shiraz-Cabernet Sauvignon (Clare Valley) $10. 85 *(12/31/2003)*

LEEUWIN ESTATE

Leeuwin Estate 1999 Art Series Cabernet Sauvignon (Margaret River) $45. 89 —*D.T. (10/1/2003)*

Leeuwin Estate 1998 Art Series Cabernet Sauvignon (Margaret River) $NA. 92 *(10/1/2002)*

Leeuwin Estate 1997 Art Series Cabernet Sauvignon (Margaret River) $NA. 88 *(10/1/2002)*

Leeuwin Estate 1996 Art Series Cabernet Sauvignon (Margaret River) $NA. 89 *(10/1/2002)*

Leeuwin Estate 1995 Art Series Cabernet Sauvignon (Margaret River) $NA. 87 *(10/1/2002)*

Leeuwin Estate 1994 Art Series Cabernet Sauvignon (Margaret River) $NA. 88 *(10/1/2002)*

Leeuwin Estate 1993 Art Series Cabernet Sauvignon (Margaret River) $NA. 87 *(10/1/2002)*

Leeuwin Estate 1999 Prelude Cabernet Sauvignon-Merlot (Margaret River) $29. 85 —*D.T. (10/1/2003)*

Leeuwin Estate 1998 Prelude Vineyards Cabernet Sauvignon-Merlot (Margaret River) $NA. 87 *(10/1/2002)*

Leeuwin Estate 2001 Art Series Chardonnay (Margaret River) $65. 87 —*D.T. (5/1/2005)*

Leeuwin Estate 2000 Art Series Chardonnay (Margaret River) $65. 91 —*D.T. (10/1/2003)*

Leeuwin Estate 1999 Art Series Chardonnay (Margaret River) $65. 90 Cellar Selection *(10/1/2002)*

Leeuwin Estate 2004 Prelude Vineyards Chardonnay (Margaret River) $29. 87 —*D.T. (8/1/2006)*

Leeuwin Estate 2002 Prelude Vineyards Chardonnay (Margaret River) $29. 87 —*D.T. (3/1/2005)*

Leeuwin Estate 2001 Prelude Vineyards Chardonnay (Margaret River) $29. 89 *(7/2/2004)*

Leeuwin Estate 2000 Prelude Vineyards Chardonnay (Margaret River) $29. 90 —*D.T. (10/1/2003)*

Leeuwin Estate 1999 Prelude Vineyards Chardonnay (Margaret River) $29. 89 —*J.C. (9/10/2002)*

Leeuwin Estate 2005 Art Series Riesling (Margaret River) $22. Nicely complex, with touches of home heating oil that impart a welcome minerality. Honey and apple scents pick up riper, more stone-fruity notes on the lush, soothing palate, then finish in a rush of crisp green-apple tartness. Drink 2008–2018. 89 —*J.C. (9/1/2007)*

Leeuwin Estate 2004 Art Series Riesling (Margaret River) $22. 91 Editors' Choice —*D.T. (8/1/2006)*

Leeuwin Estate 2003 Art Series Riesling (Margaret River) $22. 89 —*D.T. (5/1/2005)*

Leeuwin Estate 2002 Art Series Riesling (Margaret River) $22. 88 —*D.T. (8/1/2003)*

Leeuwin Estate 2001 Art Series Riesling (Margaret River) $NA. 88 *(10/1/2002)*

Leeuwin Estate 2004 Siblings Sauvignon Blanc-Semillon (Margaret River) $20. 86 —*D.T. (8/1/2006)*

Leeuwin Estate 2001 Siblings Semillon-Sauvignon Blanc (Western Australia) $20. 86 *(10/1/2002)*

Leeuwin Estate 2001 Art Series Shiraz (Margaret River) $30. 86 —*D.T. (11/15/2006)*

Leeuwin Estate 2000 Art Series Shiraz (Margaret River) $30. 87 —*D.T. (12/31/2003)*

Leeuwin Estate 1999 Art Series Shiraz (Margaret River) $NA. 89 *(10/1/2002)*

Leeuwin Estate 2002 Siblings Shiraz (Margaret River) $20. 84 —*D.T. (10/1/2006)*

Leeuwin Estate 2002 Siblings White Blend (Margaret River) $20. 87 —*D.T. (10/1/2003)*

LEN EVANS

Len Evans 1999 Shiraz (McLaren Vale) $30. 89 *(11/1/2001)*

LEWINSBROOK CREEK

Lewinsbrook Creek 2000 Shiraz (South Eastern Australia) $8. 85 Best Buy *(10/1/2001)*

LIMB

Limb 2001 Patterson Hill Cabernet Sauvignon (Barossa Valley) $40. 87 —*D.T. (11/15/2004)*

Limb 2000 Patterson Hill Cabernet Sauvignon (Barossa Valley) $38. 86 —*C.S. (6/1/2002)*

Limb 2001 Three Pillars Reds Red Blend (Barossa Valley) $20. 86 —*D.T. (12/31/2004)*

Limb 2000 Patterson Hill Shiraz (Barossa Valley) $42. 88 —*K.F. (3/1/2003)*

LIMELIGHT

Limelight 1999 Syrah (McLaren Vale) $50. 90 *(11/1/2001)*

LINDEMANS

Lindemans 1999 Pyrus Bordeaux Blend (Coonawarra) $30. 89 —*D.T. (11/15/2004)*

Lindemans 1998 Pyrus Cabernet Blend (Coonawarra) $27. 90 —*M.S. (12/15/2002)*

Lindemans 2006 Bin 45 Cabernet Sauvignon (South Eastern Australia) $8. A bold, fruity wine without much nuance, this offers blackberry and chocolate flavors, a creamy texture and some dusty tannins on the finish. Sturdy enough to stand up to steak. 84 Best Buy —*J.C. (11/15/2007)*

Lindemans 2005 Bin 45 Cabernet Sauvignon (South Eastern Australia) $8. Jammy and grapy, this is a fruity, cleanly made wine, but it lacks much in the way of structure and complexity. Drink now. 83 —*J.C. (2/1/2007)*

Lindemans 2003 Bin 45 Cabernet Sauvignon (South Eastern Australia) $8. 82 —*D.T. (11/15/2004)*

Lindemans 2002 Bin 45 Cabernet Sauvignon (South Eastern Australia) $8. 85 —*D.T. (12/31/2003)*

Lindemans 2000 Bin 45 Cabernet Sauvignon (South Eastern Australia) $8. 86 Best Buy —*J.M. (12/15/2002)*

Lindemans 2003 Reserve Cabernet Sauvignon (South Australia) $10. For a $10 wine, this offers plenty of flavor, ranging from touches of cedar and brown sugar to dried fruit compote. There's decent richness, and genuine Cabernet character comes through on the finish, which features an herbal note, a touch of chocolate and moderate tannins. Drink now. 85 Best Buy —*J.C. (5/1/2007)*

Lindemans 2000 St. George Cabernet Sauvignon (Coonawarra) $30. 90 —*D.T. (11/15/2004)*

Lindemans 1998 St. George Cabernet Sauvignon (Coonawarra) $27. 88 —*M.S. (12/15/2002)*

Lindemans 1998 Cabernet Sauvignon-Merlot (Padthaway) $15. 88 Best Buy —*M.S. (12/15/2002)*

Lindemans 2005 Bin 80 Cabernet Sauvignon-Merlot (South Eastern Australia) $8. Simple and grapy, with touches of confected fruit and just a hint of chocolate on the slightly angular finish. 83 —*J.C. (11/15/2007)*

Lindemans 2004 Bin 80 Cabernet Sauvignon-Merlot (South Eastern Australia) $8. 82 —*D.T. (12/31/2005)*

Lindemans 2001 Chardonnay (Padthaway) $13. 84 —*J.C. (7/1/2002)*

Lindemans 1998 Chardonnay (Padthaway) $15. 85 —*S.H. (10/1/2000)*

Lindemans 1997 Chardonnay (Padthaway) $13. 87 *(11/15/1999)*

Lindemans 2006 Bin 65 Chardonnay (South Eastern Australia) $8. Early vintages of this were great values, and the 2006 version is a solid effort as well, offering up aromas of smoky, grilled fruit and toasted marshmallow. It's medium-bodied, with spicy, orangey flavors that fall away quickly on the finish. Drink now. 84 Best Buy —*J.C. (8/1/2007)*

Lindemans 2005 Bin 65 Chardonnay (South Eastern Australia) $8. 84 Best Buy —*D.T. (8/1/2006)*

Lindemans 2003 Bin 65 Chardonnay (South Eastern Australia) $8. 82 *(7/2/2004)*

Lindemans 2002 Bin 65 Chardonnay (South Eastern Australia) $8. 87 Best Buy —*D.T. (11/15/2003)*

Lindemans 2001 Bin 65 Chardonnay (South Eastern Australia) $9. 84 —*J.C. (7/1/2002)*

Lindemans 1999 Bin 65 Chardonnay (South Australia) $10. 86 *(10/1/2000)*

Lindemans 2004 Reserve Chardonnay (South Eastern Australia) $11. This is a simple, fruity quaff, full of tangerine and melon flavors. There's ample weight, but a somewhat abbreviated finish. 84 —*J.C. (2/1/2007)*

Lindemans 2003 Reserve Chardonnay (South Australia) $10. 82 —*D.T. (5/1/2005)*

Lindemans 2002 Reserve Chardonnay (South Australia) $10. 83 —*D.T. (8/1/2003)*

Lindemans 2005 Bin 40 Merlot (South Eastern Australia) $8. 81 —*D.T. (11/15/2006)*

Lindemans 2001 Bin 40 Merlot (Riverland) $8. 80 —*J.M. (12/15/2002)*

Lindemans 2003 Reserve Merlot (South Australia) $10. This is a relatively small-lot wine (under 10,000 cases were imported), and maybe the extra attention it received helped, because this is a decent value. Black cherry and cassis notes show nice purity, while hints of mint and vanilla add dimension and some dusty tannins on the finish give it a modicum of structure. Drink now. 85 Best Buy —*J.C. (2/1/2007)*

Lindemans 2002 Reserve Merlot (South Australia) $10. 84 —*D.T. (8/1/2005)*

Lindemans 2005 Bin 85 Pinot Grigio (South Eastern Australia) $8. Although it's labeled Pinot Grigio, this is thousands of miles away from northeastern Italy in style. It's broad in the mouth, marked by pear, melon and spice notes, without the citrusy balance of Italian versions, yet it all works together, with the spice—crushed pepper and ground cinnamon—providing a sense of focus. Lacks a bit of depth, but at this price, who's complaining? 85 Best Buy —*J.C. (2/1/2007)*

Lindemans 2004 Bin 85 Pinot Grigio (South Eastern Australia) $8. 81 —*D.T. (12/1/2005)*

Lindemans 2005 Bin 99 Pinot Noir (South Eastern Australia) $8. 85 Best Buy —*D.T. (11/15/2006)*

Lindemans 2001 Bin 99 Pinot Noir (South Australia) $9. 84 —*J.C. (9/1/2002)*

Lindemans 2005 Bin 75 Riesling (South Eastern Australia) $8. Pronounced floral notes give way with air to baked apple and citrus aromas. Those flavors dominate the palate, widening out to become a bit broad and unfocused. This wine comes out of the chute fast, then fades on the finish, where it lacks the acidic zip to impart length. 85 Best Buy —*J.C. (2/1/2007)*

Lindemans 2004 Bin 75 Riesling (South Eastern Australia) $8. 84 Best Buy —*D.T. (8/1/2006)*

Lindemans 2002 Bin 75 Riesling (South Eastern Australia) $8. 87 Best Buy —*D.T. (11/15/2004)*

Lindemans 2003 Bin 75 Riesling (South Eastern Australia) $8. 83 —*D.T. (12/1/2005)*

Lindemans 2005 Bin 95 Sauvignon Blanc (South Eastern Australia) $8. This basic fig- and melon-flavored Sauvignon lacks depth and richness, but still makes for an easy quaff. 83 —*J.C. (2/1/2007)*

Lindemans 2004 Bin 95 Sauvignon Blanc (South Eastern Australia) $8. 84 Best Buy —*D.T. (10/1/2005)*

Lindemans 2003 Bin 95 Sauvignon Blanc (South Eastern Australia) $8. 86 Best Buy —*D.T. (11/15/2004)*

Lindemans 2001 Bin 95 Sauvignon Blanc (South Eastern Australia) $8. 81 —*J.M. (12/15/2002)*

Lindemans 2000 Bin 95 Sauvignon Blanc (South Australia) $9. 84 —*J.C. (2/1/2002)*

Lindemans 1998 Bin 9255 Semillon (Hunter Valley) $16. 91 Best Buy —*J.C. (2/1/2002)*

Lindemans 2005 Bin 77 Semillon-Chardonnay (South Eastern Australia) $8. A nearly 50-50 blend, Lindemands Bin 77 Semillon-Chardonnay represents a solid value. Verging on full-bodied, it starts with scents of cantaloupe, then adds in notes of cinnamon and clove on the palate. The spice notes linger on the finish, surprising in a wine this inexpensive. 84 Best Buy —*J.C. (2/1/2007)*

Lindemans 2002 Bin 77 Semillon-Chardonnay (South Eastern Australia) $8. 82 —*D.T. (1/1/2002)*

Lindemans 2001 Bin 77 Semillon-Chardonnay (South Australia) $9. 80 —*J.M. (12/15/2002)*

Lindemans 2000 Cawarra Semillon-Chardonnay (South Eastern Australia) $NA. 84 —*D.T. (2/1/2002)*

Lindemans 1998 Shiraz (Padthaway) $16. 87 *(10/1/2001)*

Lindemans 2005 Bin 50 Shiraz (South Eastern Australia) $8. Round and grapy, with simple dark fruit flavors that hint at coffee or chocolate. Shows a little more tannin on the finish than some others in this price range, all the better to pair with steaks or burgers. Drink now. 84 Best Buy —*J.C. (3/1/2007)*

Lindemans 2001 Bin 50 Shiraz (South Eastern Australia) $9. 84 —*J.C. (9/1/2002)*

Lindemans 2004 Reserve Shiraz (Padthaway) $10. As the Lindemans Bin series has slipped a bit, the Reserve tier has taken over the spot in the line-up, offering solid value. This is well-made, commercially styled Shiraz, offering all of what consumers have come to expect: jammy berry flavors framed by vanilla and chocolate. Turns fresh on the finish. Drink now. 86 Best Buy —*J.C. (6/1/2007)*

Lindemans 2003 Reserve Shiraz (South Australia) $10. 84 —*D.T. (12/31/2005)*

Lindemans 2002 Reserve Shiraz (South Australia) $10. 86 Best Buy —*D.T. (5/1/2005)*

Lindemans 1999 Reserve Shiraz (Padthaway) $15. 89 Best Buy —*M.S. (3/1/2003)*

Lindemans 2005 Bin 55 Shiraz-Cabernet Sauvignon (South Eastern Australia) $8. 84 Best Buy —*D.T. (11/15/2006)*

Lindemans 2000 Cawarra Shiraz-Cabernet Sauvignon (South Eastern Australia) $6. 83 —*M.S. (12/15/2002)*

Lindemans 1999 Limestone Ridge Shiraz-Cabernet Sauvignon (Coonawarra) $30. 90 Cellar Selection —*D.T. (11/15/2004)*

Lindemans 2004 Bin 70 White Blend (South Eastern Australia) $8. 84 Best Buy —*D.T. (12/1/2005)*

LITTLE BOOMEY

Little Boomey 2004 Cabernet Sauvignon-Merlot (South Australia) $7. 83 —*D.T. (12/31/2005)*

Little Boomey 2004 Shiraz (South Australia) $7. 83 —*D.T. (10/1/2005)*

Little Boomey 2004 Shiraz-Cabernet Sauvignon (South Australia) $7. 82 —*D.T. (10/1/2005)*

LITTLE PENGUIN

Little Penguin 2005 Cabernet Sauvignon (South Eastern Australia) $8. Bold and grapy on the nose, this wine delivers plenty of blackberry and grape flavors, just touched with vanilla. It's jammy and almost sweet-tasting, but satisfies the fruit itch. Drink now. 84 Best Buy —*J.C. (2/1/2007)*

Little Penguin 2003 Cabernet Sauvignon (South Eastern Australia) $7. 82 —*D.T. (11/15/2004)*

Little Penguin 2005 Chardonnay (South Eastern Australia) $8. 81 —*D.T. (11/15/2006)*

Little Penguin 2004 Chardonnay (South Eastern Australia) $8. 84 Best Buy —*D.T. (10/1/2005)*

Little Penguin 2003 Chardonnay (South Eastern Australia) $7. 85 Best Buy —*D.T. (11/15/2004)*

Little Penguin 2005 Merlot (South Eastern Australia) $8. 83 —*D.T. (11/15/2006)*

Little Penguin 2004 Merlot (South Eastern Australia) $8. 83 —*D.T. (10/1/2005)*

Little Penguin 2003 Merlot (South Eastern Australia) $7. 82 —*D.T. (3/1/2005)*

Little Penguin 2006 Pinot Noir (South Eastern Australia) $8. Herbal, leafy aromas and flavors call to mind tomatoes and beet greens despite a pleasantly round, supple mouthfeel. 81 —*J.C. (11/15/2007)*

Little Penguin 2005 Pinot Noir (South Eastern Australia) $8. 83 —*D.T. (11/15/2006)*

Little Penguin 2005 Shiraz (South Eastern Australia) $8. It's a bit simple, but cleanly made and fruit-forward, with plum and berry flavors that steam right on through from start to finish. Will easily wash down a variety of midweek dishes. 84 Best Buy —*J.C. (3/1/2007)*

Little Penguin 2003 Shiraz (South Eastern Australia) $7. 84 Best Buy —*D.T. (12/31/2004)*

Little Penguin 2005 White Shiraz (South Eastern Australia) $8. 84 Best Buy —*D.T. (12/1/2005)*

LITTLE REBEL

Little Rebel 2004 Cabernet Sauvignon-Merlot (Yarra Valley) $15. This is a classically proportioned Bordeaux blend, featuring 70% Cabernet Sauvignon and 30% Merlot. Mint and cassis aromas pick up shadings of dried herbs and tobacco on the palate, ending with good persistence and a certain degree of elegance. Because of that, serve this wine alongside a roast rather than a big, beefy steak. 87 —*J.C. (11/15/2007)*

LITTLE'S

Little's 2000 Green Label Semillon-Chardonnay (Hunter Valley) $12. 87 —*D.T. (12/31/2003)*

LOGAN AUSTRALIA

Logan Australia 1999 Chardonnay (Orange) $17. 84 —*J.C. (7/1/2002)*

Logan Australia 1999 Reserve Chardonnay (Orange) $21. 86 —*D.T. (8/1/2003)*

Logan Australia 2000 Ripe Chardonnay (Hunter Valley) $10. 82 —*D.T. (8/1/2003)*

Logan Australia 1998 Ripe Red Blend (Orange) $10. 84 —*M.S. (12/15/2002)*

Logan Australia 2001 Logan Sauvignon Blanc (Orange) $13. 84 —*D.T. (5/1/2004)*

LONG FLAT

Long Flat 2003 Cabernet Sauvignon (Coonawarra) $14. 87 *(12/1/2005)*

Long Flat 2004 Cabernet Sauvignon-Merlot (South Eastern Australia) $9. A light, crisp Cabernet-Merlot blend, with slightly weedy flavors of red cherries that seem to darken and deepen slightly from sip to sip. Finishes tart. Comes in a one-liter Prisma Pak. 83 —*J.C. (5/1/2007)*

Long Flat 2004 Chardonnay (Yarra Valley) $14. 86 *(12/1/2005)*

Long Flat 2002 Chardonnay (South Eastern Australia) $8. 85 *(7/2/2004)*

Long Flat 2002 Merlot (South Eastern Australia) $8. 84 —*D.T. (9/1/2004)*

Long Flat 2004 Pinot Noir (Yarra Valley) $14. 85 *(12/1/2005)*

Long Flat 2002 Cabernet-Shiraz-Malbec Red Blend (South Eastern Australia) $8. 84 —*D.T. (11/15/2005)*

Long Flat 2004 Riesling (Eden Valley) $14. 86 *(12/1/2005)*

Long Flat 2004 Sauvignon Blanc (Adelaide Hills) $14. 85 *(12/1/2005)*

Long Flat 2004 Semillon-Sauvignon Blanc (South Eastern Australia) $7. 83 *(12/1/2005)*

Long Flat 2002 Semillon-Sauvignon Blanc (South Eastern Australia) $7. 84 —*D.T. (5/1/2004)*

Long Flat 2004 Shiraz (Barossa) $14. 87 *(12/1/2005)*

LONGVIEW

Longview 2003 Devil's Elbow Cabernet Sauvignon (Adelaide Hills) $19. 90 Editors' Choice —*D.T. (8/1/2005)*

Longview 2005 Red Bucket Cabernet Sauvignon-Shiraz (Adelaide Hills) $14. An earthy style, with tobacco, black olive and coffee flavors that accurately reflect the 75% Cabernet Sauvignon-25% Shiraz blend. 83 —*J.C. (11/15/2007)*

Longview 2005 Blue Cow Chardonnay (Adelaide Hills) $18. 89 —*D.T. (10/1/2006)*

Longview 2004 Blue Cow Chardonnay (Adelaide Hills) $16. 89 —*D.T. (8/1/2005)*

Longview 2004 Black Crow Nebbiolo (Adelaide Hills) $21. 86 —*D.T. (8/1/2006)*

Longview 2003 Black Crow Nebbiolo (Adelaide Hills) $20. 86 —*D.T. (8/1/2005)*

Longview 2005 Iron Knob Riesling (Adelaide Hills) $16. 87 —*D.T. (8/1/2006)*

Longview 2005 Whippet Sauvignon Blanc (Adelaide Hills) $16. 88 —*D.T. (8/1/2006)*

Longview 2004 Whippet Sauvignon Blanc (Adelaide Hills) $16. 86 —*D.T. (8/1/2005)*

Longview 2004 Yakka Shiraz (Adelaide Hills) $20. 87 —*D.T. (8/1/2006)*

Longview 2003 Yakka Shiraz-Viognier (Adelaide Hills) $19. 90 —*D.T. (8/1/2005)*

Longview 2005 Beau Sea Viognier (Adelaide Hills) $20. 87 —*D.T. (10/1/2006)*

Longview 2004 Beau Sea Viognier (Adelaide Hills) $18. 87 —*D.T. (8/1/2005)*

LONGWOOD

Longwood 2005 The Shearer Shiraz (McLaren Vale) $20. Round and plush, this is immediately accessible, and should be consumed over the near term. Vanilla, cedar and a hint of caramel accent the blackberry jam flavors. The fruit is a bit cooked, but it picks up a nice peppery edge and some coffee notes on the finish. 90 Editors' Choice —*J.C. (4/1/2007)*

Longwood 1999 Shiraz (McLaren Vale) $28. 89 —*M.M. (6/1/2001)*

LONSDALE RIDGE

Lonsdale Ridge 2002 Chardonnay (Victoria) $8. 85 Best Buy *(7/2/2004)*

Lonsdale Ridge 2002 Merlot (Victoria) $8. 85 Best Buy —*D.T. (9/1/2004)*

Lonsdale Ridge 2002 Shiraz (Victoria) $8. 83 —*D.T. (12/31/2004)*

LOOSE END

Loose End 2006 Rosé Grenache (Barossa) $20. Smells enticing, offering up hints of plums and dusty red fruit, but the flavors are candied and simple, like maraschino cherries. 80 —*J.C. (7/1/2007)*

Loose End 2005 Rosé Grenache (Barossa) $15. 85 —*D.T. (11/15/2006)*

Loose End 2005 G-S-M (Barossa) $17. Nicely aromatic and complex, this blend of Grenache, Shiraz and Merlot is a cheery, unpretentious bistro red. Mint, anise and black cherry flavors all swirl together, unfettered by much oak. An easy-drinking wine, suitable for varied dishes. 87 —*J.C. (11/1/2007)*

Loose End 2004 G-S-M (Barossa) $17. 89 —*D.T. (8/1/2006)*

Loose End NV Sparkling MSM Red Blend (Barossa) $20. 87 —*J.C. (12/31/2006)*

Loose End 2005 Shiraz (Barossa) $21. A plump, soft Shiraz that shows hints of surmaturité in its stone-fruit aromas that edge toward raisin with extended airing. Pepper, licorice and blackberry flavors go down easily. Drink now. 88 —*J.C. (11/1/2007)*

Loose End 2004 Shiraz-Viognier (Barossa) $18. 84 —*D.T. (6/1/2006)*

LORIKEET

Lorikeet NV Brut Champagne Blend (South Eastern Australia) $10. 86 Best Buy —*D.T. (12/31/2005)*

Lorikeet NV Extra Dry Champagne Blend (South Eastern Australia) $10. 86 Best Buy —*D.T. (12/31/2005)*

Lorikeet NV Sparkling Shiraz (South Eastern Australia) $10. 84 —*D.T. (12/31/2005)*

Lorikeet NV Sparkling Shiraz (South Eastern Australia) $9. 84 Best Buy —*D.T. (12/31/2004)*

Lorikeet NV Brut Sparkling Blend (South Eastern Australia) $9. 85 Best Buy —*D.T. (12/31/2004)*

Lorikeet NV Extra Dry Sparkling Blend (South Eastern Australia) $9. 84 Best Buy —*D.T. (12/31/2004)*

LOWE

Lowe 1997 Ashbourne Vineyard Chardonnay (Hunter Valley) $18. 81 —*J.C. (9/10/2002)*

LUNAR WINES

Lunar Wines 2004 Cabernet Sauvignon (Barossa Valley) $47. Superripe cherry and cassis fruit is framed by vanilla and caramel oak. Although this seems a bit confected at first, give it a bit of air and the wine comes together, shedding its sugary overcoat and showing greater depth and balance. Drink now–2012. 90 —*J.C. (11/1/2007)*

M. CHAPOUTIER AUSTRALIA

M. Chapoutier Australia 2000 Mount Benson Shiraz (Australia) $30. $30. 88 *(11/1/2001)*

M.BROWN

M.Brown 1998 Shiraz (Barossa Valley) $20. 85 *(10/1/2001)*

MACAW CREEK

Macaw Creek 2003 Grenache-Shiraz (South Australia) $17. 86 —*D.T. (5/1/2005)*

MACQUARIEDALE

Macquariedale 1999 Four Winds Vineyard Chardonnay (Hunter Valley) $17. 85 —*J.C. (7/1/2002)*

Macquariedale 1999 Old Vine Semillon (Hunter Valley) $18. 87 —*J.C. (2/1/2002)*

Macquariedale 1999 Thomas Shiraz (Hunter Valley) $22. 83 —*J.C. (9/1/2002)*

MAD FISH

Mad Fish 2005 Rosé Cabernet Sauvignon (Western Australia) $14. 86 —*D.T. (4/1/2006)*

Mad Fish 2003 Cabernet Sauvignon-Shiraz (Western Australia) $15. 87 —*D.T. (12/1/2005)*

Mad Fish 2004 Chardonnay (Western Australia) $15. 85 —*D.T. (12/1/2005)*

Mad Fish 2005 Riesling (Western Australia) $14. 88 —*D.T. (4/1/2006)*

Mad Fish 2005 Sauvignon Blanc (Western Australia) $15. Tastes like it's trying to be New Zealand Sauvignon Blanc, boasting a plump, almost sweet-tasting mouthfeel and tropical-tinged flavors that veer into the realm of green peas. short and honeyed on the finish—is this fully dry? 85 —*J.C. (2/1/2007)*

Mad Fish 2004 Sauvignon Blanc (Western Australia) $15. 87 —*D.T. (12/1/2005)*

Mad Fish 2004 Shiraz (Western Australia) $14. 87 —*D.T. (4/1/2006)*

MAGPIE ESTATE

Magpie Estate 2004 The Schnell Shiraz-Grenache (Barossa Valley) $17. Another in the long list of well-priced wines from Rolf Binder, this blend of 60% Shiraz and 40% Grenache boasts aromas of smoked meats, cola and spice, maybe even a touch of lavender. It's not terribly rich or concentrated, but makes up for that with complexity and charming spice-box, meat and black olive flavors. Best now–2012. 90 Editors' Choice —*J.C. (11/1/2007)*

MAK

Mak 2003 Chardonnay (Adelaide Hills) $16. 89 Editors' Choice *(7/2/2004)*

Mak 2001 Chardonnay (Adelaide Hills) $16. 87 —*J.C. (7/1/2002)*

Mak 2000 Cabernet, Shiraz, Merlot Red Blend (Coonawarra) $18. 84 —*M.S. (12/15/2002)*

Mak 2002 Shiraz (Clare Valley) $18. 87 —*D.T. (10/1/2006)*

MANDU

Mandu 2004 Cabernet Sauvignon (Margaret River) $12. This is a big, full-bodied, highly extracted wine, with some chewy tannins and slightly elevated alcohol on the finish. Flavors are oaky and dark, with chocolate and cassis joined by a hint of roasted pepper. A bit of a bruiser; drink it now with rare beef or lamb to help mellow its tannins, or age it several years and see if it develops more finesse. 87 Best Buy —*J.C. (2/1/2007)*

Mandu 2003 Cabernet Sauvignon (Margaret River) $12. 84 —*D.T. (8/1/2006)*

MARCUS JAMES

Marcus James 2000 Shiraz (South Eastern Australia) $6. 84 *(10/1/2001)*

MARGAN

Margan 2003 Limited Release Single Vineyard Ceres Hill Barbera (Hunter Valley) $15. 86 —*D.T. (4/1/2006)*

Margan 2002 Cabernet Sauvignon (Hunter Valley) $17. 90 —*D.T. (4/1/2006)*

Margan 2000 Cabernet Sauvignon (Hunter Valley) $15. 82 —*D.T. (6/1/2002)*

Margan 2000 Chardonnay (Hunter Valley) $12. 87 —*J.C. (7/1/2002)*

Margan 2003 Merlot (Hunter Valley) $17. 88 —*D.T. (4/1/2006)*

Margan 2000 Semillon (Hunter Valley) $12. 88 Best Buy —*J.C. (2/1/2002)*

Margan 1999 Semillon (Hunter Valley) $13. 81 —*J.C. (9/1/2001)*

Margan 2004 Botrytis Semillon (Hunter Valley) $25. 87 —*D.T. (8/1/2006)*

Margan 2003 Shiraz (Hunter Valley) $19. Clove, peppermint and chocolate constitute the bouquet of this medium-bodied Shiraz. Plum, chocolate and spice flavors finish with slightly chalky tannins, but there's enough fruit for balance. Drink now with rare beef, or hold 2-3 years. 87 —*J.C. (2/1/2007)*

Margan 2000 Shiraz (Hunter Valley) $16. 85 *(10/1/2001)*

Margan 2006 Shiraz Saignée Rosé (Hunter Valley) $17. A bit earthy and leathery, with a hint of sweetness balanced by crisp acidity. This is intriguing for its complexity rather than its purity of fruit. 83 —*J.C. (7/1/2007)*

Margan 2005 Shiraz Saignée Rosé (Hunter Valley) $15. 89 —*D.T. (4/1/2006)*

Margan 2001 Verdelho (Hunter Valley) $13. 89 *(2/1/2002)*

Margan 1999 Verdelho (Hunter Valley) $13. 89 —*M.M. (1/1/2004)*

MARIENBERG

Marienberg 1997 Reserve Shiraz (South Australia) $20. 86 *(10/1/2001)*

MARINDA PARK

Marinda Park 2001 Chardonnay (Mornington Peninsula) $19. 81 —*D.T. (8/1/2003)*

Marinda Park 2001 Pinot Noir (Mornington Peninsula) $26. 85 —*D.T. (10/1/2003)*

MARKTREE

Marktree 1999 Soldier's Block Vineyard Chardonnay (Australia) $9. 83 —*J.C. (7/1/2002)*

Marktree 1999 Soldier's Block Vineyard Shiraz (New South Wales) $9. 85 *(10/1/2001)*

Marktree 1999 White Blend (Australia) $7. 83 —*D.T. (2/1/2002)*

MARQUEE

Marquee 2001 Selections Chain of Ponds Cabernet Sauvignon-Cabernet Franc-Merlot Cabernet Blend (Kangaroo Island) $30. 88 —*D.T. (8/1/2005)*

Marquee 2001 Selections Cabernet Sauvignon (Adelaide Hills) $28. 89 —*D.T. (12/31/2004)*

Marquee 2001 Selections Classic Cabernet Sauvignon (South Eastern Australia) $10. 85 Best Buy —*D.T. (11/15/2004)*

Marquee 2000 Selections Saddler's Creek Cabernet Sauvignon (South Eastern Australia) $20. 87 —*D.T. (12/31/2004)*

Marquee 2003 Signature Cabernet Sauvignon (Langhorne Creek) $20. 89 —*D.T. (8/1/2006)*

Marquee 2004 Artisan Wines Classic Cabernet Sauvignon-Merlot (Victoria) $10. 83 —*D.T. (12/31/2005)*

Marquee 2003 Classic Cabernet Sauvignon-Merlot (Victoria) $10. 85 Best Buy —*D.T. (8/1/2005)*

Marquee 2002 Chardonnay (South Eastern Australia) $12. 88 Best Buy *(7/2/2004)*

Marquee 2001 Adelaide Hills Chardonnay (Adelaide Hills) $27. 86 *(7/2/2004)*

Marquee 2004 Artisan Wines Classic Chardonnay (Victoria) $10. 85 Best Buy —*D.T. (12/1/2005)*

Marquee 2003 Artisan Wines Classic Chardonnay (Victoria) $10. 83 —*D.T. (5/1/2005)*

Marquee 2006 Classic Chardonnay (South Eastern Australia) $10. Starts off with understated apple and pear aromas, then adds some peach flavors to the mix. It's medium-bodied, with a touch of canned fruit flavors on the finish. 83 —*J.C. (8/1/2007)*

Marquee 2001 Macedon Ranges Chardonnay (Victoria) $27. 83 *(7/2/2004)*

Marquee 2001 Selections Chardonnay (Mornington Peninsula) $20. 85 —*D.T. (11/15/2004)*

Marquee 1999 Shoalhaven Coast Chardonnay (New South Wales) $17. 85 *(7/2/2004)*

Marquee 2004 Signature Chardonnay (Yarra Valley) $15. 84 —*D.T. (4/1/2006)*

Marquee 1999 Selections Pfeiffer Wines Marsanne (Victoria) $15. 83 —*D.T. (12/31/2004)*

Marquee 1999 Selections Pfeiffer Wines Merlot (South Eastern Australia) $25. 83 —*D.T. (5/1/2005)*

Marquee 2003 Signature Merlot (Rutherglen) $20. 84 —*D.T. (4/1/2006)*

Marquee NV Selections Classic Muscat (Rutherglen) $25. 89 —*D.T. (12/31/2004)*

Marquee 2000 Selections Pinot Noir (Macedon Ranges) $27. 81 —*D.T. (12/31/2004)*

Marquee 2001 Selections Port Phillip Estate Pinot Noir (Mornington Peninsula) $27. 89 —*D.T. (8/1/2005)*

Marquee 2004 Signature Pinot Noir (Mornington Peninsula) $20. 88 —*D.T. (4/1/2006)*

Marquee NV Tawny Port (Rutherglen) $25. 87 —*D.T. (12/31/2004)*

Marquee 2006 Artisan Wines Classic Riesling (Victoria) $10. An off-dry style, marked by residual sugar, which gives it a sweetly fruity profile. Obvious honey and peach notes verge on simple, but don't lack elegance. Drink now. 87 Best Buy —*J.C. (9/1/2007)*

Marquee 2004 Artisan Wines Classic Riesling (Victoria) $10. 82 —*D.T. (12/1/2005)*

Marquee 2002 Selections Chain of Ponds Sauvignon Blanc (Adelaide Hills) $15. 86 —*D.T. (11/15/2004)*

Marquee 2002 Hunter Valley Semillon-Chardonnay (New South Wales) $17. 83 —*D.T. (11/15/2004)*

Marquee 2004 Signature Semillon-Chardonnay (Hunter Valley) $15. 84 —*D.T. (4/1/2006)*

Marquee 2001 Selections Chain of Ponds Shiraz (McLaren Vale) $25. 87 —*D.T. (3/1/2005)*

Marquee 2005 Artisan Wines Classic Shiraz (Victoria) $10. Light to medium in body, this red-fruited Shiraz is a bit simple, but offers extremely fruity, cherry-berry flavors. It verges on confected, then turns crisp on the finish. 83 —*J.C. (11/15/2007)*

Marquee 2004 Signature Shiraz (McLaren Vale) $20. 88 —*D.T. (6/1/2006)*

Marquee 2005 Seduction Red Wine Shiraz-Cabernet Sauvignon (Victoria) $20. This 75-25 Shiraz-Cab blend features modest aromas of dried dates, brightening into raspberry scents with time in the glass. On the light side, thinning out a bit on the finish, but features plenty of bright raspberry flavors. A bit simple, but tasty. Drink now. 85 —*J.C. (4/1/2007)*

Marquee NV Selections Selections Cleveland Winery Brut Sparkling Blend (Macedon Ranges) $27. 86 —*D.T. (12/31/2004)*

Marquee NV Selections Classic Tokay (Rutherglen) $25. 90 —*D.T. (12/31/2004)*

Marquee 2001 Selections Shoalhaven Coast Verdelho (New South Wales) $15. 83 —*D.T. (11/15/2004)*

MARQUIS PHILIPS

Marquis Philips 2000 Cabernet Sauvignon (South Eastern Australia) $15. 92 —*S.H. (6/1/2002)*

Marquis Philips 2000 Merlot (South Eastern Australia) $15. 87 —*S.H. (6/1/2002)*

Marquis Philips 2000 Sarah's Blend Red Blend (South Eastern Australia) $15. 93 Best Buy —*S.H. (6/1/2002)*

Marquis Philips 2000 Shiraz (South Eastern Australia) $15. 88 —*S.H. (6/1/2002)*

MASSENA

Massena 2005 The Howling Dog Petite Sirah (Barossa Valley) $32. This could easily stand alongside the best Petite Sirahs from California. It's perfumed and floral on the nose, then adds palate-staining blueberries and hints of cedar, licorice and chocolate. The silky tannins on the finish are firm enough to suggest cellaring through 2010, and optimum drinking through 2020, possibly longer. 93 Editors' Choice —*J.C. (11/1/2007)*

Massena 2005 The Moonlight Run Red Blend (Barossa Valley) $30. Wonderfully fragrant and complex on the nose, with bright cherry fruit but also beguiling hints of cinnamon, herbes de Provençe, tea and white pepper. If this didn't show its alcohol a bit on the finish it would have scored at least a couple of points higher. Drink now–2012. 89 —*J.C. (11/1/2007)*

Massena 2005 The Eleventh Hour Shiraz (Barossa Valley) $42. Lush and creamy-textured, but not without structure. Although its blackberry and vanilla flavors are immediately approachable, this is worth decanting or aging several years, as it develops additional complexity over time, offering up hints of pepper, cinnamon and briary spice. Mouthwatering and long on the finish; drink now–2020. 93 —*J.C. (11/1/2007)*

MATILDA PLAINS

Matilda Plains 2001 Red Blend (Langhorne Creek) $12. 82 —*D.T. (9/1/2004)*

MCGUIGAN

McGuigan 2005 Bin 4000 Cabernet Sauvignon (Limestone Coast) $10. A simple, fruity Cabernet that adds hints of smoke and peppery spice to blackberry fruit. It's smooth in texture, if somewhat light in body, picking up some chocolaty notes on the finish. Drink now. 84 —*J.C. (5/1/2007)*

McGuigan 1999 Genus 4 Cabernet Sauvignon (Hunter Valley) $20. 91 Editors' Choice —*M.S. (12/15/2002)*

McGuigan 2001 Bin 7000 Chardonnay (Hunter Valley) $10. 88 Best Buy —*J.C. (7/1/2002)*

McGuigan 2000 Black Label Chardonnay (South Eastern Australia) $8. 86 Best Buy —*J.C. (7/1/2002)*

McGuigan 2000 Genus 4 Chardonnay (Hunter Valley) $20. 86 —*D.T. (8/1/2003)*

McGuigan 2005 Bin 3000 Merlot (Limestone Coast) $10. Smoke and herb aromas meet caramel and cherry flavors in this unassuming little Merlot. It's nicely creamy on the palate, and you could do a lot worse than if your local restaurant was offering this as its house pour for $6 per glass. 84 —*J.C. (6/1/2007)*

McGuigan 2001 Bin 3000 Merlot (Murray River Valley) $10. 84 —*D.T. (6/1/2003)*

McGuigan 1998 Bin 3000 Merlot (South Eastern Australia) $9. 89 Best Buy *(11/15/1999)*

McGuigan 2000 Black Label Merlot (South Eastern Australia) $8. 80 —*J.C. (6/1/2002)*

McGuigan 2005 Bin 2000 Shiraz (Limestone Coast) $10. Relatively light in weight, this Shiraz nonetheless features an attractive array of aromas and flavors, ranging from cola and blackberry to earth and spice. It could use more depth and does turn a bit tart on the finish, but it's still a solid burger wine. 83 —*J.C. (11/15/2007)*

McGuigan 2000 Bin 2000 Shiraz (Murray River Valley) $10. 86 —*P.G. (10/1/2001)*

McGuigan 1999 Bin 2000 Shiraz (South Eastern Australia) $10. 86 *(6/1/2001)*

McGuigan 2000 Black Label Shiraz (South Eastern Australia) $8. 86 Best Buy —*C.S. (3/1/2003)*

McGuigan 1999 Genus 4 Shiraz (Hunter Valley) $20. 91 Editors' Choice —*M.S. (3/1/2003)*

McGuigan 2001 The Black Label Shiraz (South Eastern Australia) $10. 86 —*M.S. (6/1/2003)*

MCLAREN VALE PREMIUM WINES

McLaren Vale Premium Wines 2004 III Associates Renaissance Bordeaux Blend (McLaren Vale) $20. 88 —*D.T. (8/1/2006)*

McLaren Vale Premium Wines 2002 Associates Chardonnay (McLaren Vale) $13. 85 *(7/2/2004)*

McLaren Vale Premium Wines 2003 III Associates Three Score & 10 Grenache (McLaren Vale) $20. 87 —*J.C. (12/15/2006)*

McLaren Vale Premium Wines 2000 III Associates The Third Degree Red Blend (McLaren Vale) $17. 85 —*D.T. (5/1/2004)*

McLaren Vale Premium Wines 2005 III Associates Sabbatical Sauvignon Blanc (McLaren Vale) $20. 87 —*D.T. (8/1/2006)*

MCLAREN WINES

McLaren Wines 2001 Linchpin Shiraz (McLaren Vale) $45. 90 *—D.T. (3/1/2005)*

MCPHERSON

McPherson 2001 Cabernet Sauvignon (Murray-Darling) $8. 85 *—D.T. (10/1/2003)*

McPherson 2000 Cabernet Sauvignon (South Eastern Australia) $8. 85 Best Buy *—D.T. (6/1/2002)*

McPherson 1999 Cabernet Sauvignon (South Eastern Australia) $8. 83 *—M.N. (6/1/2001)*

McPherson 1999 Cabernet Sauvignon-Shiraz (South Eastern Australia) $8. 87 Best Buy *—S.H. (10/1/2000)*

McPherson 2002 Chardonnay (Australia) $8. 85 Best Buy *(7/2/2004)*

McPherson 2001 Chardonnay (Murray-Darling) $8. 82 *—D.T. (8/1/2003)*

McPherson 1999 Chardonnay (South Eastern Australia) $7. 85 *—S.H. (10/1/2000)*

McPherson 2000 Murray-Darling Chardonnay (Australia) $7. 87 Best Buy *—J.C. (7/1/2002)*

McPherson 2001 Merlot (South Eastern Australia) $8. 85 *—D.T. (11/15/2003)*

McPherson 2000 Merlot (South Eastern Australia) $8. 84 *—S.H. (6/1/2002)*

McPherson 2002 Shiraz (Australia) $8. 84 *—D.T. (9/1/2004)*

McPherson 2001 Shiraz (Murray-Darling) $8. 87 *—M.S. (3/1/2003)*

McPherson 2000 Shiraz (South Eastern Australia) $8. 88 Best Buy *(10/1/2001)*

McPherson 1999 Shiraz (South Eastern Australia) $8. 86 Best Buy *—S.H. (11/1/2000)*

McPherson 2000 Reserve Shiraz (Goulburn Valley) $19. 89 *—M.S. (3/1/2003)*

McPherson 1999 White Blend (South Eastern Australia) $7. 85 *—M.S. (10/1/2000)*

MCWILLIAM'S HANWOOD ESTATE

McWilliam's Hanwood Estate 2005 Cabernet Sauvignon (South Eastern Australia) $12. The citrusy streak that marks this at times becomes too much, giving the wine some angles it doesn't need, but does have some pleasing brown sugar and plum aromas and offers a reasonably full mouthfeel. 84 *—J.C. (11/15/2007)*

McWilliam's Hanwood Estate 2004 Cabernet Sauvignon (South Eastern Australia) $12. 86 *—D.T. (12/31/2005)*

McWilliam's Hanwood Estate 2003 Cabernet Sauvignon (South Eastern Australia) $11. 87 Best Buy *—D.T. (12/31/2004)*

McWilliam's Hanwood Estate 2002 Cabernet Sauvignon (South Eastern Australia) $12. 87 Best Buy *(10/1/2003)*

McWilliam's Hanwood Estate 1998 1877 Cabernet Sauvignon-Shiraz (South Eastern Australia) $85. 92 *(10/1/2003)*

McWilliam's Hanwood Estate 2004 Chardonnay (South Eastern Australia) $12. 87 Best Buy *—D.T. (12/1/2005)*

McWilliam's Hanwood Estate 2003 Chardonnay (South Eastern Australia) $11. 86 Best Buy *—D.T. (12/31/2004)*

McWilliam's Hanwood Estate 2001 Chardonnay (South Eastern Australia) $11. 82 *—D.T. (1/1/2002)*

McWilliam's Hanwood Estate 2002 Hanwood Estate Chardonnay (South Eastern Australia) $12. 88 Best Buy *(10/1/2003)*

McWilliam's Hanwood Estate 2005 Merlot (South Eastern Australia) $12. In a flight of inexpensive Australian Merlot, this wine stood out for its density and concentration. Which is not to say it's a big wine, but it does offer plenty of mixed berry fruit and hints of chocolate in a medium-bodied wine. Picks up some savory olive and coffee notes on the mouthwatering finish. 85 *—J.C. (11/15/2007)*

McWilliam's Hanwood Estate 2004 Merlot (South Eastern Australia) $12. 85 *—D.T. (6/1/2006)*

McWilliam's Hanwood Estate 2003 Merlot (South Eastern Australia) $12. 84 *—D.T. (5/1/2005)*

McWilliam's Hanwood Estate 2002 Merlot (South Eastern Australia) $12. 85 *(10/1/2003)*

McWilliam's Hanwood Estate 2005 Shiraz (South Eastern Australia) $12. Fruit-forward and a bit simple, with blackberry flavors that seem to lack nuance and show a touch of warmth on the finish. Tannins are hardly evident, making this an easy quaff without food. 83 *—J.C. (11/15/2007)*

McWilliam's Hanwood Estate 2004 Shiraz (South Eastern Australia) $12. 84 *—D.T. (6/1/2006)*

McWilliam's Hanwood Estate 2002 Shiraz (South Eastern Australia) $12. 86 *(10/1/2003)*

McWilliam's Hanwood Estate 2001 Shiraz (South Eastern Australia) $11. 85 *—M.S. (12/15/2002)*

MCWILLIAM'S OF COONAWARRA

McWilliam's of Coonawarra 2000 Cabernet Sauvignon (Coonawarra) $25. 88 *—D.T. (11/15/2004)*

McWilliam's of Coonawarra 1999 Cabernet Sauvignon (Coonawarra) $25. 89 *(10/1/2003)*

McWilliam's of Coonawarra 2001 Brand's Laira Vineyards Cabernet Sauvignon (Coonawarra) $28. 89 *—D.T. (6/1/2006)*

McWilliam's of Coonawarra 2000 Shiraz (Coonawarra) $25. 88 *—D.T. (9/1/2004)*

McWilliam's of Coonawarra 2000 Brand's Laira Vineyards Shiraz (Coonawarra) $28. 90 *—D.T. (12/31/2004)*

McWilliam's of Coonawarra 1999 Laira Vineyard Shiraz (Coonawarra) $25. 89 *(10/1/2003)*

McWilliam's of Coonawarra 2000 Stentiford's Reserve Old Vines Shiraz (Coonawarra) $55. 89 *—D.T. (4/1/2006)*

McWilliam's of Coonawarra 1999 Stentiford's Reserve Old Vines Shiraz Shiraz (Coonawarra) $49. 90 *(10/1/2003)*

MEEREA PARK

Meerea Park 1999 Alexander Munro Shiraz (Hunter Valley) $38. 89 *—M.S. (3/1/2003)*

Meerea Park 2001 The Aunts Shiraz (Hunter Valley) $24. 83 *—D.T. (11/15/2004)*

Meerea Park 2000 The Aunts Shiraz (Hunter Valley) $24. 88 *—M.S. (3/1/2003)*

Meerea Park 1999 The Aunts Shiraz (Hunter Valley) $24. 84 *(11/1/2001)*

MERMAID RIDGE

Mermaid Ridge 2004 Chardonnay (Great Southern) $15. 87 *—D.T. (6/1/2006)*

Mermaid Ridge 2002 Shiraz (Great Southern) $15. 87 *—D.T. (6/1/2006)*

MESH

Mesh 2006 Riesling (Eden Valley) $25. This is deceptive, alternating between soft and hard, seductive and prickly. Honey and poached pear aromas vie with firm lime and mineral notes, while the flavors contrast lime sherbet with crushed stone. Long and intense on the finish. 90 *—J.C. (8/1/2007)*

Mesh 2004 Riesling (Eden Valley) $25. 87 *—D.T. (10/1/2005)*

MITCHELL

Mitchell 2002 Sevenhill Vineyard Cabernet Sauvignon (Clare Valley) $24. 89 *—D.T. (12/31/2005)*

Mitchell 2001 Sevenhill Vineyard Cabernet Sauvignon (Clare Valley) $25. 90 *—D.T. (2/1/2004)*

Mitchell 1999 Sevenhill Vineyard Cabernet Sauvignon (Clare Valley) $28. 93 Editors' Choice *—M.S. (12/15/2002)*

Mitchell 2001 Grenache (Clare Valley) $18. 88 *—D.T. (2/1/2004)*

Mitchell 2002 GSM Red Blend (Clare Valley) $15. 91 Best Buy *—D.T. (2/1/2006)*

Mitchell 2004 Watervale Riesling (Clare Valley) $16. 90 Editors' Choice *—D.T. (4/1/2006)*

Mitchell 2003 Watervale Riesling (Clare Valley) $18. 90 Editors' Choice *—D.T. (2/1/2004)*

Mitchell 2001 Watervale Riesling (Clare Valley) $19. 90 *—D.T. (8/1/2003)*

Mitchell 2000 Watervale Riesling (Clare Valley) $NA. 89 *—D.T. (2/1/2004)*

Mitchell 1992 Watervale Riesling (Clare Valley) $NA. 91 *—D.T. (2/1/2004)*

Mitchell 2004 Semillon (Clare Valley) $16. 84 *—D.T. (4/1/2006)*

Mitchell 2002 Semillon (Clare Valley) $18. 89 *—D.T. (2/1/2004)*

Mitchell 2001 The Growers Semillon (Clare Valley) $18. 85 *—D.T. (12/31/2003)*

Mitchell 2002 Peppertree Vineyard Shiraz (Clare Valley) $26. 91 *—D.T. (2/1/2004)*

Mitchell 2001 Peppertree Vineyard Shiraz (Clare Valley) $26. 90 Editors' Choice *—D.T. (2/1/2004)*

Mitchell 2000 Peppertree Vineyard Shiraz (Clare Valley) $26. 82 *—D.T. (1/28/2003)*

Mitchell 1999 Peppertree Vineyard Shiraz (Clare Valley) $26. 85 *—J.C. (9/1/2002)*

Mitchell 1998 Peppertree Vineyard Shiraz (Clare Valley) $NA. 89 *—D.T. (2/1/2004)*

Mitchell 1997 Peppertree Vineyard Shiraz (Clare Valley) $NA. 87 *—D.T. (2/1/2004)*

MITCHELTON

Mitchelton 1998 Marsanne (Goulburn Valley) $18. 90 *—S.H. (10/1/2000)*

Mitchelton 2001 Crescent Red Blend (Central Victoria) $21. 90 *—D.T. (5/1/2005)*

Mitchelton 2000 Airstrip Rhône White Blend (Central Victoria) $20. 91 Editors' Choice *(2/1/2002)*

Mitchelton 2002 Airstrip Marsanne Roussanne Viognier Rhône White Blend (South Australia/Victoria) $20. 87 *—D.T. (5/1/2004)*

Mitchelton 1996 Print Shiraz (Victoria) $45. 92 *(10/1/2000)*

Mitchelton 1999 Print Shiraz (Central Victoria) $42. 90 *—D.T. (12/31/2004)*

Mitchelton 1999 Thomas Mitchell Shiraz (Victoria) $11. 83 *(10/1/2001)*

MITOLO

Mitolo 2005 Jester Cabernet Sauvignon (McLaren Vale) $19. A surprising misstep from this fine winery and consulting winemaker Ben Glaetzer. The characteristic Mitolo/Glaetzer creamy-textured tannins are there, but the flavors are a bit simple and grapy, marked by peppery, leafy notes. It is awfully young, so maybe it will pull together in a another few months. 85 *—J.C. (5/1/2007)*

Mitolo 2004 Serpico Cabernet Sauvignon (McLaren Vale) $57. 90 *—D.T. (10/1/2006)*

Mitolo 2005 G.A.M. Shiraz (McLaren Vale) $47. Winemaker Ben Glaetzer has crafted yet another excellent wine for the Mitolo family, and even though the Reiver Shiraz seems a touch better this vintage, the G.A.M. is no slouch. Its bouquet of vanilla, spice and plum pudding even smells rich, and that's followed by a medium- to full-bodied wine with a creamy texture and authoritative fruit flavors. Shows a touch of warmth on the finish, but also spice notes and some dusty tannins. Drink 2008–2015. 90 *—J.C. (4/1/2007)*

Mitolo 2004 G. A. M. Shiraz (McLaren Vale) $45. 92 *—J.C. (12/15/2006)*

Mitolo 2005 Jester Shiraz (McLaren Vale) $20. Although a very good wine, this is a bit disappointing coming from winemaker Ben Glaetzer. Blackberry preserve flavors are soft and full-bodied without being especially rich or deep, with hints of vanilla and fresh grasses. Finishes fresh, with tart berry flavors. 87 *—J.C. (8/1/2007)*

Mitolo 2002 Jester Shiraz (McLaren Vale) $20. 90 Editors' Choice *—D.T. (12/31/2004)*

Mitolo 2006 Reiver Shiraz (Barossa Valley) $50. Boasts a dense, inky color, but at this tender age the flavors lack the weight and opulence of the 2005 version. Coffee and cedar notes frame tart blackberries, finishing long and elegantly. It's juicy and fresh, with plenty of appeal now, yet should age well for up to 10 years. 90 *—J.C. (11/1/2007)*

Mitolo 2005 Reiver Shiraz (Barossa Valley) $47. This brooding beast starts with scents of dark chocolate and coffee, then adds plenty of fruit in the form of blueberries and blackberries on the rich, chewy palate. Despite the wine's considerable heft and density of fruit, there's enough spicy complexity and a surprising degree of elegance to the long, tongue-tingling finish. Drink now–2015. 94 Editors' Choice *—J.C. (4/1/2007)*

Mitolo 2005 Savitar Shiraz (McLaren Vale) $59. Nitpicking Europhiles might find this a touch warm on the palate, but it's a full-bodied, lusty expression of Australian Shiraz, with fruit that kaleidoscopically moves from raspberries to black cherries and on to blackberries, all the while graced with hints of peppery spice that echo elegantly on the long finish. Drink 2010–2020. 93 *—J.C. (12/31/2007)*

MONDAVI/ROSEMOUNT

Mondavi/Rosemount 2002 Kirralaa Cabernet Sauvignon (South Eastern Australia) $15. 88 *—D.T. (12/31/2004)*

Mondavi/Rosemount 2001 Kirralaa Cabernet Sauvignon (South Eastern Australia) $15. 87 *—D.T. (10/1/2003)*

Mondavi/Rosemount 2003 Kirralaa Chardonnay (South Eastern Australia) $14. 86 *(7/2/2004)*

Mondavi/Rosemount 2002 Kirralaa Chardonnay (South Eastern Australia) $14. 87 *—S.H. (12/31/2003)*

Mondavi/Rosemount 2001 Kirralaa Merlot (South Eastern Australia) $15. 87 *—D.T. (10/1/2003)*

Mondavi/Rosemount 2002 Kirralaa Bushvine Shiraz (South Eastern Australia) $15. 86 *—D.T. (11/15/2004)*

Mondavi/Rosemount 2001 Kirralaa Bushvine Shiraz (South Eastern Australia) $15. 86 *—D.T. (10/1/2003)*

Mondavi/Rosemount 2001 Kirralaa Indelible Reserve Shiraz (Victoria) $50. 88 *—D.T. (5/1/2004)*

MOON DOG ACRE

Moon Dog Acre 2004 Shiraz (South Eastern Australia) $8. 83 *—D.T. (4/1/2006)*

MOONDARRA

Moondarra 2001 Conception Unfiltered Pinot Noir (Victoria) $50. 91 *—D.T. (10/1/2003)*

MOORILLA

Moorilla 2003 Black Label Unwooded Chardonnay (Tasmania) $20. Fully mature and ready to drink, Moorilla's unwooded Chardonnay is a big, mouthfilling, powerful wine, featuring aromas and flavors of buttered stones, with touches of honey, spice (anise) and citrus embellishment. A Wine Angel Selection, imported by USA Wine Imports, Inc. 88 *—J.C. (6/1/2007)*

Moorilla 2005 Estate Pinot Noir (Tasmania) $35. A top-notch offering, Moorilla's 2005 Pinot Noir shows the potential of this variety in cool-climate Tasmania. Cola and black cherry scnets ride easily above a vaguely mushroomy backdrop, and although the flavors are earthy and feature plenty of sous-bois notes, they're balanced by ripe black cherry fruit. It's round and soft, with a silky lingering finish and framed by well-judged oak that never intrudes on the overall picture. Imported by USA Wine Imports, Inc. 90 Editors' Choice *—J.C. (6/1/2007)*

Moorilla 2003 Estate Pinot Noir (Tasmania) $35. Both this wine and the 2005 showed good "Pinosity," blending mushroomy, earthy complexity with velvety tannins. Black cherry and plum flavors provide enough fruit for balance, while the finish is long. Imported by USA Wine Imports, Inc. 90 Editors' Choice *—J.C. (6/1/2007)*

MOOROOROO

Moorooroo 2001 Limited Release Shiraz (Barossa Valley) $78. 85 *—D.T. (4/1/2006)*

MORGAN SIMPSON

Morgan Simpson 2000 Cabernet Sauvignon (McLaren Vale) $17. 82 *—M.S. (12/15/2002)*

Morgan Simpson 2002 Row 42 Cabernet Sauvignon (McLaren Vale) $25. 87 *—D.T. (5/1/2005)*

Morgan Simpson 2000 Chardonnay (McLaren Vale) $13. 87 *—D.T. (8/1/2003)*

Morgan Simpson 2002 Shiraz (McLaren Vale) $25. 89 *—D.T. (12/31/2005)*

Morgan Simpson 2000 Stone Hill Shiraz (McLaren Vale) $17. 90 Editors' Choice *—D.T. (3/1/2003)*

MOSS WOOD

Moss Wood 2001 Cabernet Sauvignon (Margaret River) $60. 90 *—D.T. (12/31/2004)*

Moss Wood 2000 Glenmore Vineyard Cabernet Sauvignon (Margaret River) $31. 89 *—D.T. (10/1/2003)*

Moss Wood 2003 The Amy's Blend Cabernet Sauvignon (Margaret River) $26. 89 *—D.T. (5/1/2005)*

Moss Wood 2002 Ribbon Vale Vineyard Cabernet Sauvignon-Merlot (Margaret River) $33. 85 *—D.T. (5/1/2005)*

Moss Wood 2003 Chardonnay (Margaret River) $40. 87 *—D.T. (3/1/2005)*

Moss Wood 2002 Chardonnay (Margaret River) $48. 88 *(7/2/2004)*

Moss Wood 2001 Chardonnay (Margaret River) $45. 87 *—D.T. (10/1/2003)*

Moss Wood 2001 Pinot Noir (Margaret River) $35. 87 *—D.T. (12/31/2004)*

Moss Wood 1999 Pinot Noir (Margaret River) $36. 87 *—D.T. (10/1/2003)*

Moss Wood 2002 Semillon (Margaret River) $24. 86 *—D.T. (11/15/2004)*

Moss Wood 2000 Semillon (Margaret River) $20. 89 *(10/1/2003)*

MOUNT HORROCKS

Mount Horrocks 2004 Riesling (Clare Valley) $25. 88 *—D.T. (10/1/2005)*

Mount Horrocks 2002 Riesling (Clare Valley) $21. 88 *—D.T. (8/1/2003)*

Mount Horrocks 2006 Cordon Cut Riesling (Clare Valley) $31. A medium-bodied dessert wine, with intense pineapple and citrus flavors that echo through the long, balanced finish. 91 *—J.C. (6/1/2007)*

Mount Horrocks 2006 Cordon Cut Riesling (Clare Valley) $31. The grapes are partially severed from the vine, then left to dry prior to harvest. The result is a medium-bodied dessert wine that has become an Australian classic, with intense pineapple and citrus flavors that echo through the long, balanced finish. Imported by USA Wine West. 91 *—J.C. (12/15/2007)*

Mount Horrocks 2002 Cordon Cut Riesling (Clare Valley) $26. 91 *—D.T. (9/1/2004)*

Mount Horrocks 2001 Cordon Cut Riesling (Clare Valley) $27. 92 *—D.T. (2/1/2004)*

Mount Horrocks 2006 Watervale Riesling (Clare Valley) $25. Smells ripe, with scents of honey, baked apples and spice, but also a refreshing lime zest top note. It's medium-bodied, with flavors that mirror the aromas, with the lime intensifying on the fresh, minerally finish. Imported by USA Wine West. 87 *—J.C. (8/1/2007)*

Mount Horrocks 2003 Watervale Riesling (Clare Valley) $20. 91 Editors' Choice *—D.T. (2/1/2004)*

Mount Horrocks 1999 Shiraz (Clare Valley) $28. 89 *—D.T. (5/1/2004)*

MOUNT LANGI GHIRAN

Mount Langi Ghiran 2004 Pinot Gris (Victoria) $20. 84 *—D.T. (10/1/2006)*

Mount Langi Ghiran 2003 Pinot Gris (Victoria) $18. 85 *—D.T. (8/1/2005)*

Mount Langi Ghiran 2005 Riesling (Victoria) $20. Nicely balanced and harmonious, this is elegantly wrought, blended from cool portions of Victoria. Floral notes serve to accent the apple, melon and mineral aromas and flavors, finishing with good length. Drink now–2015. 90 Editors' Choice *—J.C. (2/1/2007)*

Mount Langi Ghiran 2004 Riesling (Victoria) $18. 89 *—D.T. (10/1/2005)*

Mount Langi Ghiran 2003 Riesling (Victoria) $17. 85 *—D.T. (5/1/2004)*

Mount Langi Ghiran 1999 Shiraz (Victoria) $36. 88 *—D.T. (9/1/2004)*

Mount Langi Ghiran 2004 Billi Billi Shiraz (Victoria) $14. The price is right for this lush, immediately attractive Shiraz from Victoria. Smoky, vanilla-scented oak frames black currant and tobacco flavors that finish soft and velvety. Lacks the depth to age past 2010, but very flattering now. Imported by Epic Wines. 88 *—J.C. (11/15/2007)*

Mount Langi Ghiran 2003 Billi Billi Shiraz (Victoria) $15. 90 Best Buy *—J.C. (12/15/2006)*

Mount Langi Ghiran 2002 Billi Billi Shiraz (Victoria) $15. 88 *—D.T. (2/1/2006)*

Mount Langi Ghiran 2000 Langi Shiraz (Victoria) $35. 90 *—D.T. (8/1/2005)*

MOUNT MARY

Mount Mary 2001 Quintet Bordeaux Blend (Yarra Valley) $120. 90 *(8/1/2005)*

Mount Mary 2001 Chardonnay (Yarra Valley) $90. 90 *—D.T. (12/1/2005)*

MOUNTADAM

Mountadam 1997 Chardonnay (Eden Valley) $15. 89 *(10/1/1999)*

Mountadam 1996 Pinot Noir (Eden Valley) $16. 81 *(10/1/1999)*

MR. RIGGS

Mr. Riggs 2006 Watervale Riesling (Clare Valley) $25. Racy and tart, this is more acid than fruit, with modest apple and citrus flavors and a bouquet of lime and wet stones. Try with oysters or other fresh shellfish. 85 *—J.C. (8/1/2007)*

Mr. Riggs 2005 Shiraz (Adelaide) $18. Ben Riggs is the winemaker for Penny's Hill, but this Shiraz sources fruit from Langhorne Creek as well as McLaren Vale to help keep the price under $20. It's a lush, chocolaty Shiraz, with notes of superripe fruit—plums and blackberries—and a rich, fudge-like character that's balanced by dusty tannins on the finish. 91 Editors' Choice *(11/15/2007)*

Mr. Riggs 2005 The Gaffer Shiraz (McLaren Vale) $20. Looking for a stereotypically rich, dense Australian Shiraz? Look no further. This is tooth-staining and palate-coating, yet doesn't seem overdone at all, blending leather, coffee, blackberry and plum flavors into a creamy, rich concoction with a long, fruit-filled finish. Only 20% new oak, so the fruit dominates. Drink now–2012. 91 Editors' Choice *—J.C. (4/1/2007)*

MT. BILLY

Mt. Billy 2003 Harmony Rhône Red Blend (Barossa Valley) $33. The dominant note is sour plum. Grace notes of mint, chocolate and leather give it a modicum of complexity, but this blend of 50% Shiraz, 25% Mourvèdre and 25% Grenache is tart and a bit clipped on the finish. It's medium-bodied, with a slightly creamy texture, but lacks the richness and expansiveness of the best Australian blends. 86 *—J.C. (6/1/2007)*

Mt. Billy 2002 Harmony Rhône Red Blend (Barossa Valley) $36. 88 *—D.T. (12/31/2005)*

Mt. Billy 2003 Antiquity Shiraz (Barossa Valley) $49. Consumers who like French-inspired Australian Shiraz should buy as much of this wine as they can find. The grapes are from 80–110-year-old vineyards, the winemaking is by Dan Standish (formerly at Torbreck) and the results are heavenly. Aromas are floral—verging on herbal in the way of the northern Rhône—backed by blueberries. It's creamy and lush, mouthcoating, while the complex flavors range from blueberry to raspberry and black olive to spice. Finishes long and peppery, with a dusting of fine tannins and uplifted fruit. Delicious now, but it should evolve through 2015. 94 Editors' Choice *—J.C. (6/1/2007)*

Mt. Billy 2001 Antiquity Shiraz (Barossa Valley) $49. 90 *—D.T. (8/1/2005)*

Mt. Billy 2002 Liqueur Shiraz (Barossa Valley) $26. 94 *—D.T. (12/31/2005)*

MT. JAGGED

Mt. Jagged 2003 Chardonnay (Southern Fleurieu) $15. 85 *—D.T. (10/1/2005)*

Mt. Jagged 2001 Lightly Wooded Chardonnay (Southern Fleurieu) $18. 82 *—D.T. (8/1/2003)*

Mt. Jagged 2001 Merlot-Cabernet Sauvignon (McLaren Vale) $15. 87 *—D.T. (9/1/2004)*

Mt. Jagged NV Sparkling Red Red Blend (South Australia) $18. 86 *—D.T. (12/31/2005)*

MURDOCK

Murdock 1999 Cabernet Sauvignon (Coonawarra) $50. 90 *—D.T. (12/31/2004)*

Murdock 2003 Riesling (Coonawarra) $22. 87 *—D.T. (12/31/2004)*

NARDONE BAKER

Nardone Baker 2000 Cabernet Sauvignon (South Eastern Australia) $10. 81 *—M.S. (12/15/2002)*

Nardone Baker 2001 Cabernet Sauvignon-Merlot (South Eastern Australia) $10. 86 *—M.S. (12/15/2002)*

Nardone Baker 2001 Chardonnay (South Eastern Australia) $10. 87 *—D.T. (8/1/2003)*

NEIGHBOURS

Neighbours 1999 Shiraz (McLaren Vale) $20. 87 *—D.T. (3/1/2003)*

NELWOOD WINES

Nelwood Wines 2004 Nelwood Station Bulldozer Red Blend (South Australia) $12. You might not know it from the name, but this is a bit of a critter wine, as Bulldozer is a nickname for the hairy-nosed wombat. In any event, it's a step up from much of the competition, offering sturdy cassis flavors tinged with pepper and herbs and a clean, mouthwatering finish. Imported by MHW, Ltd. 86 *—J.C. (11/15/2007)*

NEPENTHE

Nepenthe 2000 The Fugue Bordeaux Blend (Adelaide Hills) $27. 88 *—D.T. (12/31/2003)*

Nepenthe 2003 Tryst Cabernet Blend (Adelaide Hills) $14. 86 *—D.T. (8/1/2005)*

Nepenthe 1998 The Fugue Cabernet Sauvignon (Adelaide Hills) $27. 87 *—J.C. (6/1/2002)*

Nepenthe 2001 The Fugue Cabernet Sauvignon-Merlot (Adelaide Hills) $20. 91 Editors' Choice *—D.T. (8/1/2005)*

Nepenthe 2000 Zoes Chardonnay (Adelaide Hills) $15. 86 *—J.C. (7/1/2002)*

Nepenthe 1999 Pinot Noir (South Australia) $25. 85 *—J.C. (9/1/2002)*

Nepenthe 2002 Charleston Pinot Noir (Adelaide Hills) $20. 87 *—D.T. (8/1/2005)*

Nepenthe 2002 Tryst Red Blend (Adelaide Hills) $14. 86 *—D.T. (12/31/2004)*

Nepenthe 2004 Sauvignon Blanc (Adelaide Hills) $14. 87 *—D.T. (8/1/2005)*

Nepenthe 2001 Sauvignon Blanc (Adelaide Hills) $17. 86 *—J.C. (2/1/2002)*

Nepenthe 2004 Tryst White Blend (Adelaide Hills) $14. 87 *—D.T. (8/1/2005)*

Nepenthe 1999 Zinfandel (South Australia) $36. 87 *—D.T. (6/1/2003)*

Nepenthe 2001 Charleston Zinfandel (Adelaide Hills) $39. 86 *—D.T. (12/31/2004)*

NEXT GENERATION

Next Generation 2004 NXG Cabernet-Merlot Cabernet Sauvignon-Merlot (South Eastern Australia) $9. Medium- to full-bodied, this is a broad, mouthfilling Cab-Merlot that comes across just this side of overripe, with plum and prune notes both apparent. Earthy notes provide a bass, while cedary oak sets the treble. Finishes with a touch of warmth and a hint of medicinal herbs. Drink now. 85 Best Buy *—J.C. (5/1/2007)*

Next Generation 2005 NXG Chardonnay (South Eastern Australia) $9. A new line of wines, the NXG Chardonnay represents a solid value, with abundant aromatics of citrus, flowers and anise and reasonably complex flavors to match. It's medium- to full-bodied, but kept in balance by decent acidity and hints at minerality on the finish. 86 Best Buy *—J.C. (3/1/2007)*

Next Generation 2004 NXG Shiraz (South Eastern Australia) $9. Seems a bit grapy to judge by the nose, but the flavors run toward blackberries, with hints of earth and hickory smoke. It's a medium-bodied wine, with smoke, spice and meat overtones to the finish. 83 *—J.C. (11/15/2007)*

NICK FALDO

Nick Faldo 2004 Sauvignon Blanc (Coonawarra) $14. This vinous effort ranks on a par with golfer namesake Nick's recent results, which is to say, acceptable. Grassy, green bean aromas and flavors are weighty and rich enough, but lack fruit and energy. 81 *—J.C. (2/1/2007)*

Nick Faldo 2003 Shiraz (Coonawarra) $15. A stronger effort than the golfer's white wine, this Shiraz slips down as easily as an uphill 10-foot putt. Subtle vanilla and cedar shadings frame dried cherries and plums, while the mouthful is smooth, with a silky touch to the finish. Drink now. 87 *—J.C. (2/1/2007)*

NINE STONES

Nine Stones 2005 Shiraz (McLaren Vale) $11. With its supple tannins and expansive mouthfeel, this wine has some real positives working for it, but there's also a definite clove and rubber edge to the aromas and the flavors show more leather and spice than fresh fruit. Turns crisp on the finish. 85 *—J.C. (11/15/2007)*

Nine Stones 2003 Shiraz (McLaren Vale) $12. 88 Best Buy *—D.T. (3/1/2005)*

Nine Stones 2005 Shiraz (Barossa) $11. A top-flight value, this bargain Shiraz features briary, savory notes layered over a base of tart blackberries. Hints of grilled meat and spice bring added complexity, while the tannins are supple. If anything, it's a bit too easy to drink—but at the price, who's complaining? 87 Best Buy *—J.C. (11/1/2007)*

Nine Stones 2003 Shiraz (Barossa) $12. 86 *—D.T. (5/1/2005)*

Nine Stones 2005 Hilltops Shiraz (New South Wales) $11. Here's a solid effort from a little-known growing region near Canberra. It's peppery and herbal, showing its relatively cool-climate origins, but also shows enough mixed berry fruit for balance. Savory spice notes on the finish impart complexity. Drink now–2012. 88 Best Buy *—J.C. (11/15/2007)*

NINTH ISLAND

Ninth Island 2005 Pinot Noir (Tasmania) $19. 88 *—D.T. (11/15/2006)*

Ninth Island 2005 Riesling (Tasmania) $14. Fat and a bit oily in texture, this is neither as floral or expressive as Riesling can be, but it still makes for a goodd drop. Scents and flavors of peach, superripe apples and a touch of melon finish dry, with a slight hint of bitterness. 85 *—J.C. (6/1/2007)*

Ninth Island 2001 Riesling (Tasmania) $16. 87 *—D.T. (8/1/2003)*

NIRVANA

Nirvana 2000 White Blend (Margaret River) $10. 80 *(9/1/2001)*

NOON

Noon 2004 Reserve Cabernet Sauvignon (South Australia) $120. 90 *—D.T. (10/1/2006)*

Noon 2003 Reserve Cabernet Sauvignon (McLaren Vale) $55. 92 *—D.T. (3/1/2005)*

Noon 2002 Reserve Cabernet Sauvignon (McLaren Vale) $55. 94 *—D.T. (5/1/2004)*

Noon 2003 Eclipse Grenache (McLaren Vale) $55. 91 *—D.T. (3/1/2005)*

Noon 2002 Eclipse Grenache-Shiraz (McLaren Vale) $55. 90 *—D.T. (5/1/2004)*

Noon 2003 Reserve Shiraz (McLaren Vale) $55. 91 *—D.T. (3/1/2005)*

Noon 2002 Reserve Shiraz (McLaren Vale) $55. 92 *—D.T. (5/1/2004)*

NORFOLK RISE

Norfolk Rise 2005 Noolook Pinot Gris (Mount Benson) $16. 86 *—D.T. (2/1/2006)*

NORMAN WINES, LTD.

Norman Wines, Ltd. 2001 Teal Lake Cabernet Sauvignon-Merlot (South Eastern Australia) $13. 86 Best Buy *—M.S. (12/15/2002)*

Norman Wines, Ltd. 2001 Teal Lake Chardonnay (South Eastern Australia) $13. 83 *—D.T. (6/1/2003)*

Norman Wines, Ltd. 2001 Teal Lake Pinot Noir (South Eastern Australia) $16. 82 *—D.T. (6/1/2003)*

NORMANS

Normans 2002 Chais Clarendon Cabernet Sauvignon (South Australia) $30. 88 *—D.T. (10/1/2005)*

Normans 1999 Chais Clarendon Cabernet Sauvignon (Adelaide Hills) $30. 92 *—D.T. (12/31/2004)*

Normans 2001 Encounter Bay Cabernet Sauvignon (South Australia) $10. 86 Best Buy *—D.T. (3/1/2005)*

Normans 2002 Old Vine Cabernet Sauvignon (South Australia) $15. 86 *—D.T. (12/31/2005)*

Normans 2003 Encounter Bay Chardonnay (South Eastern Australia) $10. 86 Best Buy *—D.T. (3/1/2005)*

Normans 2002 Old Vine Grenache (McLaren Vale) $15. 87 *—D.T. (3/1/2005)*

Normans 2001 Chais Clarendon Shiraz (McLaren Vale) $30. 90 *—D.T. (12/31/2004)*

Normans 2001 Encounter Bay Shiraz (South Australia) $10. 86 Best Buy *—D.T. (3/1/2005)*

Normans 2003 Old Vine Shiraz (South Australia) $15. 86 *—D.T. (2/1/2006)*

Normans 2002 Old Vine Shiraz (South Australia) $15. 87 *—D.T. (3/1/2005)*

NUGAN FAMILY ESTATES

Nugan Family Estates 2002 Alcira Vineyard Cabernet Sauvignon (Coonawarra) $23. 89 *—D.T. (6/1/2006)*

Nugan Family Estates 2004 Chardonnay (South Eastern Australia) $12. 84 *—D.T. (6/1/2006)*

Nugan Family Estates 2002 3rd Generation Chardonnay (South Eastern Australia) $12. 82 *(7/2/2004)*

Nugan Family Estates 2002 Alcira Vineyard Chardonnay (Coonawarra) $18. 84 *(7/2/2004)*

Nugan Family Estates 2004 Frasca's Lane Vineyard Chardonnay (King Valley) $22. 88 *—D.T. (6/1/2006)*

Nugan Family Estates 2001 Third Generation Chardonnay (South Eastern Australia) $11. 82 *—J.C. (7/1/2002)*

Nugan Family Estates 2004 Manuka Grove Durif (South Eastern Australia) $23. 89 *—D.T. (8/1/2006)*

Nugan Family Estates 2002 Frasca's Lane Vineyard Sauvignon Blanc (King Valley) $16. 86 *—D.T. (11/15/2004)*

Nugan Family Estates 2002 KLN Vineyard Botrytis Semillon (Riverina) $22. 84 *—D.T. (9/1/2004)*

Nugan Family Estates 2005 Shiraz (South Eastern Australia) $14. Starts with aromas of clove, coffee and black olive, then adds brighter flavors of red berries on the palate before picking up some tea-like notes and a hint of chocolate on the finish. This medium-bodied Shiraz should prove versatile at the table. 85 *—J.C. (11/15/2007)*

Nugan Family Estates 2004 Shiraz (South Eastern Australia) $12. 82 *—D.T. (6/1/2006)*

Nugan Family Estates 2004 McLaren Parish Vineyard Shiraz (McLaren Vale) $23. 87 *—D.T. (6/1/2006)*

Nugan Family Estates 2002 Third Generation Shiraz (South Eastern Australia) $12. 86 *—D.T. (11/15/2004)*

O'LEARY WALKER

O'Leary Walker 2002 Cabernet Sauvignon-Merlot (Clare-Adelaide Hills) $15. 87 *—D.T. (2/1/2004)*

O'Leary Walker 2001 Chardonnay (Adelaide Hills) $20. 86 *(7/2/2004)*

O'Leary Walker 2003 Watervale Riesling (Clare Valley) $15. 87 *—D.T. (2/1/2004)*

O'Leary Walker 2002 Watervale Semillon (Clare Valley) $20. 87 *—D.T. (9/1/2004)*

O'Leary Walker 2002 Shiraz (Clare-McClaren Vale) $15. 86 *—D.T. (2/1/2004)*

OAKLEY ADAMS

Oakley Adams 1999 Merlot (South Eastern Australia) $10. 83 *—C.S. (6/1/2002)*

OAKRIDGE

Oakridge 2003 Pinot Noir (Yarra Valley) $21. 86 *—D.T. (12/1/2005)*

OCCAM'S RAZOR

Occam's Razor 2001 Shiraz (Heathcote) $26. 90 *—D.T. (12/31/2003)*

OFF THE LEASH.

Off the Leash 2006 Max Shiraz-Viognier (Adelaide Hills) $23. From a relatively cool growing region, this Shiraz-Viognier is appropriately peppery and bright, with a hint of violets and crisp blueberry and blackberry fruit. The tannins are soft, making this wine instantly accessible, and it finishes peppery and fresh. Drink now–2012. Imported by Tom Eddy Wines. 89 *—J.C. (12/31/2007)*

OLD SCHOOL

Old School 2002 Cabernet Sauvignon (Barossa Valley) $34. 90 *—D.T. (10/1/2006)*

Old School 2002 Shiraz (Barossa Valley) $34. 90 *—D.T. (6/1/2006)*

OLIVERHILL

Oliverhill 2000 Bradey Block Grenache (McLaren Vale) $20. 87 *—J.C. (9/1/2002)*

Oliverhill 2003 Jimmy Section Shiraz (McLaren Vale) $33. 92 *—D.T. (3/1/2005)*

Oliverhill 2000 Jimmy Section Shiraz (McLaren Vale) $33. 92 Editors' Choice *(11/1/2001)*

ONE LEGGED DUCK

One Legged Duck 2000 Redhouse Red Blend (South Australia) $14. 89 Editors' Choice *—D.T. (12/31/2003)*

ORIGIN

Origin 2002 Reserve Series Shiraz (Barossa Valley) $19. 87 *—D.T. (10/1/2005)*

ORMON HILL

Ormon Hill 2001 Shiraz (Heathcote) $20. 89 *—D.T. (12/31/2004)*

OUTBACK CHASE

Outback Chase 2003 Chardonnay (South Eastern Australia) $7. 84 Best Buy *—D.T. (5/1/2005)*

Outback Chase 2003 Wobbly White White Blend (South Eastern Australia) $7. 83 *—D.T. (5/1/2005)*

OWEN'S ESTATE

Owen's Estate 1999 Cabernet Sauvignon-Shiraz (South Eastern Australia) $13. 86 *—S.H. (9/1/2001)*

Owen's Estate 1999 Chardonnay (South Eastern Australia) $15. 84 *—J.C. (7/1/2002)*

Owen's Estate 1999 Merlot (South Eastern Australia) $15. 84 *—S.H. (9/1/2001)*

Owen's Estate 1999 Sauvignon Blanc (McLaren Vale) $13. 90 Best Buy *—S.H. (9/1/2001)*

Owen's Estate 1998 Shiraz (South Australia) $15. 85 *(4/1/2000)*

Owen's Estate 1999 Shiraz (South Australia/Victoria) $14. 82 *(10/1/2001)*

OXFORD LANDING

Oxford Landing 2006 Cabernet Rosé Cabernet Sauvignon (South Australia) $9. A touch of herbaceousness speaks to this wine's Cabernet Sauvignon origins, adding a bit of spice to its otherwise ordinary strawberry-fruity flavors. Finishes soft, without much length or intensity. 83 *—J.C. (7/1/2007)*

Oxford Landing 1999 Limited Release Cabernet Sauvignon (South Australia) $10. 84 *—D.T. (9/1/2001)*

Oxford Landing 1999 Cabernet Sauvignon-Shiraz (South Australia) $8. 86 Best Buy *—D.T. (9/1/2001)*

Oxford Landing 2005 Chardonnay (South Australia) $9. 85 Best Buy *—D.T. (6/1/2006)*

Oxford Landing 2004 Chardonnay (South Australia) $9. 86 Best Buy *—D.T. (8/1/2005)*

Oxford Landing 2002 Chardonnay (Eden Valley) $7. 85 *(7/1/2004)*

Oxford Landing 2000 Chardonnay (South Australia) $8. 83 *—D.T. (9/1/2001)*

Oxford Landing 1998 Limited Release Grenache (South Australia) $10. 86 Best Buy *—J.C. (9/1/2001)*

Oxford Landing 2003 Merlot (South Australia) $9. 86 Best Buy *—D.T. (5/1/2005)*

Oxford Landing 1999 Merlot (South Australia) $8. 84 Best Buy *(9/1/2001)*

Oxford Landing 2002 Shiraz (South Australia) $9. 83 *—D.T. (5/1/2005)*

Oxford Landing 1999 Limited Release Shiraz (South Australia) $10. 84 *(10/1/2001)*

Oxford Landing 2005 Viognier (South Australia) $9. 86 Best Buy *—D.T. (10/1/2006)*

Oxford Landing 2004 Viognier (South Australia) $9. 86 Best Buy *—D.T. (8/1/2005)*

Oxford Landing 1998 Limited Release Viognier (South Australia) $10. 85 *(10/1/2000)*

OZ ROZ

Oz Roz 2004 Rosé of Shiraz (South Eastern Australia) $7. 83 *—D.T. (12/1/2005)*

PAIKO

Paiko 2003 Regent Reserve Cabernet Sauvignon-Petit Verdot Cabernet Blend (Murray-Darling) $14. Some producers are promoting Petit Verdot as a top performer in Australia's warm inland regions, but there have been mixed results. This blend is almost half PV, presumably the source of its bold black-olive aromas and crisp mouthfeel, partially balanced by the cassis and plum of warm-climate Cabernet. 84 *—J.C. (6/1/2007)*

Paiko 2005 Chardonnay (Alpine Valleys) $10. 82 *—D.T. (11/15/2006)*

Paiko 2004 Chardonnay (Alpine Valleys) $10. 82 *—D.T. (5/1/2005)*

Paiko 2002 Merlot (Murray-Darling) $10. 86 Best Buy *—D.T. (8/1/2005)*

Paiko 2004 Shiraz (Murray-Darling) $11. Clean and fresh, with crisp black currant flavors and a tobacco-leaf edge. Earth and herb elements give it enough interest to warrant a second sip, while the refreshing acidity suggests reasonable versatility at the table; try with roast or grilled chicken. 86 Best Buy *—J.C. (11/15/2007)*

Paiko 2002 Shiraz (Murray-Darling) $10. 85 Best Buy *—D.T. (5/1/2005)*

Paiko 2004 Viognier (Murray-Darling) $10. 84 *—D.T. (12/1/2005)*

PALANDRI

Palandri 2002 Cabernet Sauvignon (Western Australia) $15. 85 *—D.T. (12/31/2005)*

Palandri 2001 Cabernet Sauvignon (Western Australia) $16. 87 *(8/1/2003)*

Palandri 2002 Cabernet Sauvignon-Merlot (Western Australia) $16. 88 *—D.T. (9/1/2004)*

Palandri 2001 Cabernet Sauvignon-Merlot (Western Australia) $16. 87 *(8/1/2003)*

Palandri 2004 Chardonnay (Western Australia) $12. 86 *—D.T. (12/1/2005)*

Palandri 2002 Merlot (Western Australia) $15. 87 *—D.T. (8/1/2005)*

Palandri 2001 Merlot (Western Australia) $16. 86 *(8/1/2003)*

Palandri 2006 Riesling (Western Australia) $NA. It's the anti-Australian Riesling, with a light, fresh feel, and ripe fruit flavors that verge on the tropical. Pineapple and mango are possibilities, as are other more common fruits: apples, pears, limes and peaches. A simple, fruity quaff that satisfies. 86 *—J.C. (8/1/2007)*

Palandri 2004 Boundary Road Sauvignon Blanc (Western Australia) $11. 84 *—D.T. (10/1/2005)*

Palandri 2001 Shiraz (Western Australia) $16. 88 *(8/1/2003)*

PARACOMBE

Paracombe 2002 Cabernet Franc (Adelaide Hills) $30. 83 *—D.T. (8/1/2005)*

Paracombe 2002 Cabernet Sauvignon (Adelaide Hills) $35. 84 *—D.T. (8/1/2005)*

Paracombe 2002 The Reuben Red Blend (Adelaide Hills) $30. 85 *—D.T. (8/1/2005)*

Paracombe 2001 The Reuben Red Blend (Adelaide Hills) $30. 89 *—D.T. (5/1/2005)*

Paracombe 2004 Sauvignon Blanc (Adelaide Hills) $23. 87 *(7/1/2005)*

Paracombe 2002 Shiraz (Adelaide Hills) $35. 87 *—D.T. (8/1/2005)*

Paracombe 1999 Shiraz (Adelaide Hills) $28. 86 *—K.F. (3/1/2003)*

Paracombe 1998 Shiraz (Adelaide Hills) $28. 91 *(11/1/2001)*

Paracombe 2001 Somerville Shiraz (Adelaide Hills) $80. 90 *—D.T. (8/1/2005)*

Paracombe 1997 Somerville Shiraz (Adelaide Hills) $70. 86 *—K.F. (3/1/2003)*

PARINGA

Paringa 2001 Individual Vineyard Shiraz (South Australia) $10. 90 Best Buy *—J.C. (11/15/2002)*

Paringa 2000 Individual Vineyard Shiraz (South Australia) $10. 89 Best Buy *(10/1/2001)*

PARKER

Parker 2003 Coonawarra Estate Terra Rossa Cabernet Sauvignon (Coonawarra) $30. Smoky and cedary, this wine's bouquet also carries with it that herbal edge so typical of Coonawarra. Dried-fruit flavors lack a touch of freshness, but the mouthfeel is creamy, the tannins supple. Turns a bit drying on the finish, so try it with rare beef in the near term. 86 *—J.C. (5/1/2007)*

Parker 2001 Terra Rosa Cabernet Sauvignon (Coonawarra) $30. 90 *—D.T. (12/31/2004)*

Parker 2000 Terra Rosa First Growth Cabernet Sauvignon-Merlot (Coonawarra) $70. 87 *—D.T. (12/31/2004)*

Parker 2001 Terra Rossa First Growth Cabernet Sauvignon-Merlot (Coonawarra) $70. 90 *—D.T. (10/1/2006)*

PASSING CLOUDS

Passing Clouds 2003 Reserve Shiraz (Bendigo) $27. A bold, fruit-driven style of Shiraz, but one that doesn't sacrifice complexity, as it retains hints of earth and spice that give its brambly blackberry flavors even greater appeal. At over 15% alcohol, it's a big wine, but there's no detectable heat, and the coffee-tinged finish is long and dusty. Drink now–2015. 92 Editors' Choice *—J.C. (2/1/2007)*

Passing Clouds 1998 Shiraz (Bendigo) $25. 85 *(11/1/2001)*

Passing Clouds 1997 Shiraz (Bendigo) $28. 86 *—M.N. (6/1/2001)*

Passing Clouds 1998 Graeme's Blend Shiraz-Cabernet Sauvignon (Bendigo) $25. 86 *—J.C. (9/1/2002)*

PATRITTI

Patritti NV Shargren Sparkling Red Wine Shiraz-Grenache (South Australia) $11. 85 *—J.C. (12/31/2006)*

Patritti NV Shargren Sparkling Blend (South Australia) $12. 82 *—D.T. (12/31/2003)*

PEARSON VINEYARDS

Pearson Vineyards 1999 Cabernet Franc (Clare Valley) $30. 87 *—D.T. (2/1/2004)*

Pearson Vineyards 2002 Cabernet Sauvignon (Clare Valley) $39. 88 *—D.T. (5/1/2005)*

Pearson Vineyards 1999 Cabernet Sauvignon (Clare Valley) $39. 88 *—D.T. (2/1/2004)*

Pearson Vineyards 2003 Riesling (Clare Valley) $NA. 87 *—D.T. (2/1/2004)*

PENFOLDS

Penfolds 1998 Bin 389 Cabernet Sauvignon (Australia) $19. 89 *(3/1/2001)*

Penfolds 2004 Bin 407 Cabernet Sauvignon (South Australia) $26. Starts off with herbal aromatics that come surprisingly close to vegetal, but seems to gather itself with some time in the glass, adding rich chocolate and cassis aromas and flavors to the mix. Dusty tannins and a balanced but tight feel suggest a few years in the cellar. Drink 2010–2020. 88 *—J.C. (12/31/2007)*

Penfolds 2003 Bin 407 Cabernet Sauvignon (South Australia) $25. Fresh herbal notes add a cool-climate touch to this wine's cherry aromas, while on the palate chocolaty oak frames the cherry and cassis flavors. It's silky in texture, with a finish that's filled with soft but persistent tannins. Drink now through 2012. 89 *—J.C. (2/1/2007)*

Penfolds 2002 Bin 407 Cabernet Sauvignon (South Australia) $25. 84 *—D.T. (10/1/2005)*

Penfolds 2001 Bin 407 Cabernet Sauvignon (South Eastern Australia) $26. 89 *—D.T. (5/1/2004)*

Penfolds 1998 Bin 407 Cabernet Sauvignon (South Australia) $19. 90 Editors' Choice *(3/1/2001)*

Penfolds 1996 Bin 407 Cabernet Sauvignon (South Australia) $25. 86 *(12/31/1999)*

Penfolds 2004 Bin 707 Cabernet Sauvignon (South Australia) $88. Behind some mint, eucalyptus and cedar aromas, this is a big, meaty Cabernet, with lots of flesh and power. The tight cassis fruit needs some time to unfold and the mouthdrying tannins need some time to resolve, but all the ingredients for future excellence are in place. Drink 2012–2020. A blend of Coonawarra and Barossa fruit, with just a smidgen from McLaren Vale. 92 Cellar Selection *—J.C. (11/1/2007)*

Penfolds 2002 Bin 707 Cabernet Sauvignon (South Australia) $80. 90 *—D.T. (10/1/2005)*

Penfolds 2001 Bin 707 Cabernet Sauvignon (South Australia) $80. 90 *—D.T. (11/15/2004)*

Penfolds 1999 Bin 707 Cabernet Sauvignon (South Australia) $80. 93 Cellar Selection *—M.S. (12/15/2002)*

Penfolds 1998 Bin 707 Cabernet Sauvignon (South Australia) $90. 93 *(3/1/2001)*

Penfolds 2004 Block 42 Kalimna Cabernet Sauvignon (Barossa Valley) $225. This is incredibly dark, concentrated stuff from what may be the oldest (planted in 1886) continuously producing Cabernet vineyard in the world. Minty, herbal notes combine with chocolate and cassis to yield a complex, balanced whole. Despite the density of the fruit, there's absolutely no sense of heaviness or excessive weight, and while the tannins appear creamy on the midpalate, they fan out into a silky sheen on the lingering finish. About 500 cases produced. Drink 2012–2030. 97 Cellar Selection *—J.C. (11/1/2007)*

Penfolds 2003 Thomas Hyland Cabernet Sauvignon (South Australia) $15. 84 *—D.T. (8/1/2006)*

Penfolds 2002 Thomas Hyland Cabernet Sauvignon (South Australia) $15. 85 *—D.T. (12/31/2005)*

Penfolds 2001 Thomas Hyland Cabernet Sauvignon (South Australia) $15. 87 *—D.T. (12/31/2003)*

Penfolds 2004 Koonunga Hill Cabernet Sauvignon (South Eastern Australia) $11. The 2004 vintage favored Cabernet, and that quality has evidently trickled down to this bargain from Penfolds. Hints of brown sugar and raisin on the nose give an impression of great ripeness, but that's balanced by fresh black currant, coffee and black olive flavors. Tannins are supple, but finish on a slightly dusty note, giving the wine enough backbone to pair with steak. 87 Best Buy *—J.C. (11/15/2007)*

Penfolds 2003 Koonunga Hill Cabernet Sauvignon (South Eastern Australia) $12. Adds a touch more oak influence to the basic Penfolds entry-level formula of smooth, supple tannins and dark fruit, offering vanilla and cassis notes on the nose and some dried fruit flavors on the palate. Fine with a midweek burger or steak. 85 *—J.C. (5/1/2007)*

Penfolds 2005 Rawson's Retreat Cabernet Sauvignon (South Eastern Australia) $9. This nails the bargain Cab formula: take some dark plum and cassis fruit, imbue it with decent length and balance and make sure the tannins are soft, creamy and immediately accessible. It's not a profound wine, but it will do a good job washing down grilled fare. 85 Best Buy *—J.C. (5/1/2007)*

Penfolds 2004 Koonunga Hill Cabernet Sauvignon-Merlot (South Eastern Australia) $12. Slightly weedy and herbal, but this wine also boasts plenty of chocolate and cassis to help balance the score. The finish features soft tannins, crisp acids and a slightly charred, coffee-like component. Drink now. 85 *—J.C. (2/1/2007)*

Penfolds 2003 Koonunga Hill Cabernet Sauvignon-Merlot (South Eastern Australia) $12. 83 *—D.T. (12/31/2005)*

Penfolds 2001 Koonunga Hill Cabernet Sauvignon-Merlot (South Eastern Australia) $9. 88 Best Buy *—M.S. (12/15/2002)*

Penfolds 2004 Bin 389 Cabernet Sauvignon-Shiraz (South Australia) $28. Sometimes referred to as a "Baby Grange," Penfolds has made Bin 389 in 47 consecutive vintages. The 2004—a blend of 53% Cabernet Sauvignon and 47% Shiraz—is rich and full-bodied, with vanilla and spice framing cassis fruit. Picks up hints of chocolate, cinnamon and clove on the dusty, firm finish. Drink 2010–2020. 89 *—J.C. (12/31/2007)*

Penfolds 2003 Bin 389 Cabernet Sauvignon-Shiraz (South Australia) $25. Dense and slightly pruny, with scents of overripe or baked plum and flavors that include black olive and earth. It's weighty and rich enough to get the job done with a fatty steak. 86 *—J.C. (2/1/2007)*

Penfolds 2000 Bin 389 Cabernet Sauvignon-Shiraz (South Eastern Australia) $26. 89 *—D.T. (10/1/2003)*

Penfolds 1999 Bin 389 Cabernet Sauvignon-Shiraz (South Australia) $26. 87 *—M.S. (12/15/2002)*

Penfolds 2004 Bin 60A Cabernet Sauvignon-Shiraz (South Australia) $225. There are approximately 1,000 cases of this wine, which blends 56% Coonawarra Cabernet Sauvignon with 44% Barossa Shiraz into a stunning combination of cassis and blackberries. Lifted bits of flowers on the nose resemble fine teas and dried herbs, adding the requisite complexity, while the mouthfeel artfully balances the weight of Shiraz with the structure of Cabernet. Mouthwatering and long, with fine, dusty tannins that bode well for aging. Drink 2014–2030. 96 Cellar Selection *—J.C. (11/1/2007)*

Penfolds 1997 Adelaide Hills Chardonnay (Adelaide Hills) $27. 86 *(12/31/1999)*

Penfolds 2003 Koonunga Hill Chardonnay (South Eastern Australia) $11. 83 *—D.T. (12/1/2005)*

Penfolds 2002 Koonunga Hill Chardonnay (South Eastern Australia) $10. 84 *—D.T. (10/1/2003)*

Penfolds 2001 Koonunga Hill Chardonnay (South Eastern Australia) $10. 82 *—J.C. (7/1/2002)*

Penfolds 1998 Koonunga Hill Chardonnay (South Australia) $10. 86 *(12/31/1999)*

Penfolds 2005 Rawson's Retreat Chardonnay (South Eastern Australia) $9. With its slightly buttery flavors, hints of pear and citrus and plump mouthfeel, this is mainstream Australian Chardonnay in all of its market-share gobbling typicalness. Ends with a slightly soft, dusty feel to the finish. 84 *—J.C. (2/1/2007)*

Penfolds 2003 Rawson's Retreat Chardonnay (South Eastern Australia) $9. 83 *(7/2/2004)*

Penfolds 2002 Rawson's Retreat Chardonnay (South Australia) $9. 86 Best Buy *—D.T. (10/1/2003)*

Penfolds 2001 Rawson's Retreat Chardonnay (South Eastern Australia) $11. 83 *—J.C. (7/1/2002)*

Penfolds 1998 The Valleys Chardonnay (Clare & Eden Valleys) $12. 83 *(3/1/2000)*

Penfolds 2004 Thomas Hyland Chardonnay (South Australia) $14. Penfolds white wine program is making strides—although one wonders if it is at the expense of sister brand such as Lindemans and Rosemount. This is a nicely balanced, elegant Chardonnay that blends toasty, mealy notes with layered pear, peach and citrus fruit. Drink it over the next 6–9 months. 87 *—J.C. (2/1/2007)*

Penfolds 2003 Thomas Hyland Chardonnay (South Australia) $14. 85 *(7/2/2004)*

Penfolds 2002 Thomas Hyland Chardonnay (South Australia) $14. 84 *—D.T. (6/1/2003)*

Penfolds 2001 Thomas Hyland Chardonnay (Adelaide Hills) $18. 87 *—J.C. (7/1/2002)*

Penfolds 2003 Yattarna Chardonnay (Adelaide Hills) $65. Penfolds high-end Chardonnay seems to be settling into stride, less marked by oak than in its earliest incarnations and showing more restrained fruit as well. Melon and citrus flavors are accented by hints of pencilly oak on the long finish. Good now, but should also be capable of aging a few years. 90 *J.C. (2/1/2007)*

Penfolds 2001 Yattarna Chardonnay (South Eastern Australia) $65. 91 *—D.T. (11/15/2004)*

Penfolds 2000 Yattarna Chardonnay (Adelaide Hills) $65. 89 *—D.T. (10/1/2003)*

Penfolds 1999 Yattarna Chardonnay (South Australia) $65. 92 *(6/1/2003)*

Penfolds 1998 Yattarna Chardonnay (South Eastern Australia) $65. 92 Cellar Selection *(3/1/2001)*

Penfolds 2005 Bin 138 G-S-M (Barossa Valley) $23. Mainly Grenache (approximately 70%), with the balance Syrah and Mataro, this is a forward, soft, easy-to-drink wine that doesn't appear to have the same ageability as so many of the other Penfolds Bin wines. Cherries and berries play on the palate, accented by spice and a bright burst of acidity on the finish. Drink now–2012. 87 *—J.C. (11/1/2007)*

Penfolds 2004 Bin 138 Old Vine G-S-M (Barossa Valley) $22. 88 *—D.T. (8/1/2006)*

Penfolds 2005 Rawson's Retreat Merlot (South Eastern Australia) $9. 81 *—D.T. (11/15/2006)*

Penfolds 2001 Rawson's Retreat Merlot (South Eastern Australia) $11. 82 *—J.C. (6/1/2002)*

Penfolds 2002 Cellar Reserve Pinot Noir (Adelaide Hills) $35. 88 *—D.T. (8/1/2005)*

Penfolds 2003 Bin 138 Old Vine GSM Red Blend (Barossa Valley) $22. 86 *—D.T. (10/1/2005)*

Penfolds 2000 Bin 2 Shiraz/Mourvedre Red Blend (South Eastern Australia) $11. 90 *—J.C. (9/1/2002)*

Penfolds 2003 Bin 2 Shiraz-Mourvedre Red Blend (South Eastern Australia) $12. 83 *—D.T. (12/1/2005)*

Penfolds 1996 Bin 389 Rhône Red Blend (South Australia) $25. 88 *(12/31/1999)*

Penfolds NV Great Grandfather Rare Old Liqueur Tawny Rhône Red Blend (Barossa Valley) $70. Thought to be a blend of Shiraz, Grenache and Mourvèdre, although some of the older components could conceivably contain traces of other varieties. The average age of the components is 40 or 45 years, and the wine's color reflects that age, being amber at the center and fading to a greenish tinge at the rim. Toffee and coffee notes permeate the wine, which boasts lovely rounded edges, honey and a bit of dried apricot. Rich, with a long finish ending on lingering rancio notes. 95 *—J.C. (11/1/2007)*

Penfolds 2006 Bin 51 Riesling (Eden Valley) $19. Smells like baked apples drizzled with honey, served on a bed of crushed stone. It's a wine of contradictions that blends warm, inviting notes with harder, harsher ones. Quite lean in the mouth, with a dry finish and mouthtingling acids. 89 *—J.C. (9/1/2007)*

Penfolds 2000 Reserve Riesling (Eden Valley) $18. 88 *(3/1/2001)*

Penfolds 1999 Reserve Riesling (Eden Valley) $15. 87 *—M.M. (2/1/2002)*

Penfolds 2003 Reserve Bin Riesling (Eden Valley) $16. 87 *—D.T. (8/1/2005)*

Penfolds 2002 Reserve Bin Riesling (Eden Valley) $19. 87 *—D.T. (8/1/2003)*

Penfolds 1998 Adelaide Hills Semillon (South Australia) $16. 82 *—J.C. (2/1/2002)*

Penfolds 1997 Adelaide Hills Semillon (Adelaide Hills) $27. 89 *—M.S. (4/1/2000)*

Penfolds 2003 Koonunga Hill Semillon-Chardonnay (South Eastern Australia) $11. 82 *—D.T. (12/1/2005)*

Penfolds 2001 Koonunga Hill Semillon-Chardonnay (South Australia) $9. 82 *—D.T. (2/1/2002)*

Penfolds 2005 Rawson's Retreat Semillon-Chardonnay (South Eastern Australia) $9. This blend features the exact same percentages of Semillon (57%) and Chardonnay (43%) as Lindemans Bin 77 Sem-Chard from the same corporate winemaking stable, but tastes distinctly different. It's less weighty and fruity, with more emphasis on minerality and spice, even hints of pepper. Could use more length on the finish. 84 *—J.C. (2/1/2007)*

Penfolds 2001 Rawson's Retreat Semillon-Chardonnay (South Eastern Australia) $11. 83 *—J.C. (7/1/2002)*

Penfolds 2001 Bin 128 Shiraz (Coonawarra) $24. 87 *—D.T. (11/15/2004)*

Penfolds 2000 Bin 128 Shiraz (Coonawarra) $24. 88 *—D.T. (12/31/2003)*

Penfolds 1999 Bin 128 Shiraz (Coonawarra) $24. 88 *—J.C. (9/1/2002)*

Penfolds 1998 Bin 128 Shiraz (Coonawarra) $22. 90 *(3/1/2001)*

Penfolds 1996 Bin 128 Shiraz (Coonawarra) $22. 89 *(10/1/1999)*

Penfolds 2000 Bin 28 Kalimna Shiraz (South Australia) $24. 87 *—D.T. (6/1/2003)*

Penfolds 2003 Bin 28 Kalimna Shiraz (South Eastern Australia) $22. This is a throwback to the Penfolds style of the past, with plenty of stuffing and tannin packed into a dark red wine. Chocolate and plum flavors pick up hints of eucalyptus and leathery notes on the firm finish. Drink 2008–2015. 89 *—J.C. (2/1/2007)*

Penfolds 1999 Bin 28 Kalimna Shiraz (South Australia) $24. 89 *—J.C. (9/1/2002)*

Penfolds 2002 Grange Shiraz (South Australia) $250. The bulk of this year's Grange (77.5%) is from Barossa, with the remainder coming from McLaren Vale. It starts off with scents of maple syrup and lightly caramelized blackberries, plums and a hint of mocha, while on the palate it turns rich and creamy in texture with the bold fruit underscored by vanilla. There's plenty of power here, but it's restrained and tight. Give it until 2015 or so, after which it should last two decades or more. 95 Cellar Selection *—J.C. (11/1/2007)*

Penfolds 2001 Grange Shiraz (South Australia) $225. 93 *—J.C. (12/15/2006)*

Penfolds 2000 Grange Shiraz (South Australia) $225. 90 *(10/1/2005)*

Penfolds 1999 Grange Shiraz (South Australia) $225. 93 Cellar Selection *—D.T. (11/15/2004)*

Penfolds 1997 Grange Shiraz (South Australia) $195. 90 *(9/1/2002)*

Penfolds 1996 Grange Shiraz (South Australia) $185. 96 Cellar Selection *(3/1/2001)*

Penfolds 1994 Grange Shiraz (South Australia) $163. 96 *(10/1/1999)*

Penfolds 2004 Kalimna Bin 28 Shiraz (South Australia) $23. Aged in 100% American oak, of all the Penfolds wines it still probably best epitomizes the traditional Barossa style, marrying vanilla and dill with dark cherries, blackberries and chocolate. Mouthfilling and creamy in texture, with a touch of tartness to the finish. Drink now–2020. 88 *—J.C. (11/1/2007)*

Penfolds 2001 Kalimna Bin 28 Shiraz (South Eastern Australia) $24. 89 *—D.T. (11/15/2004)*

Penfolds 1996 Kalimna Bin 28 Shiraz (South Australia) $25. 90 *(10/1/1999)*

Penfolds 1996 Kalimna Bin 285 Shiraz (South Australia) $25. 86 *(12/31/1999)*

Penfolds 2005 Koonunga Hill Shiraz (South Eastern Australia) $11. Comes out of the chute with a blast of almost grapy black cherry fruit, accented by smoke and vanilla. It's full-bodied, with clear flavors and decent intensity, but lacks depth and falls off a bit on the finish, costing it a point or two. It's still a good, serviceable Shiraz for everyday drinking. 84 *—J.C. (11/15/2007)*

Penfolds 2004 Koonunga Hill Shiraz (South Eastern Australia) $12. 85 —*D.T. (11/15/2006)*

Penfolds 2003 Koonunga Hill Shiraz (South Eastern Australia) $12. 84 —*D.T. (6/1/2006)*

Penfolds 2000 Magill Estate Shiraz (Adelaide Hills) $50. 92 —*D.T. (10/1/2003)*

Penfolds 1999 Magill Estate Shiraz (South Australia) $50. 91 *(9/1/2002)*

Penfolds 1996 Magill Estate Shiraz (South Australia) $47. 91 *(10/1/1999)*

Penfolds 2001 Magill Estate Shiraz Shiraz (South Australia) $50. 91 —*D.T. (11/15/2004)*

Penfolds 2004 RWT Shiraz (Barossa) $82. Practically roars from the glass with vanilla and spice, yet despite aging in mainly new French oak, the fruit flows forth in waves, adding cherries and blackberries to the mix. Creamy, lush and mouthfilling, this is a top-notch effort that may be drunk now and over the next 15 or more years. 93 —*J.C. (11/1/2007)*

Penfolds 2003 RWT Shiraz (Barossa Valley) $75. 90 —*J.C. (12/15/2006)*

Penfolds 2002 RWT Shiraz (Barossa Valley) $70. 90 *(10/1/2005)*

Penfolds 2001 RWT Shiraz (Barossa Valley) $80. 91 Cellar Selection —*D.T. (11/15/2004)*

Penfolds 2000 RWT Shiraz (Barossa Valley) $69. 93 —*D.T. (10/1/2003)*

Penfolds 1999 RWT Shiraz (Barossa Valley) $70. 93 *(9/1/2002)*

Penfolds 1998 RWT Shiraz (Barossa Valley) $70. 95 Editors' Choice *(3/1/2001)*

Penfolds 2003 St. Henri Shiraz (South Australia) $42. A blend of Barossa and Clare fruit, St. Henri is aged in large old oak vats, giving a very different result from the typical Australian Shiraz. With no oak overlay, it's chocolaty and tarry, with plummy fruit. The 2003 is full-bodied, with mildly coarse, chewy tannins, yet may not turn out to be as long-lived as the best St. Henri vintages. Drink 2010–2018. 89 —*J.C. (11/1/2007)*

Penfolds 2002 St. Henri Shiraz (South Australia) $40. 89 —*D.T. (11/15/2006)*

Penfolds 2001 St. Henri Shiraz (South Australia) $40. 87 —*D.T. (10/1/2005)*

Penfolds 2000 St. Henri Shiraz (South Australia) $40. 89 —*D.T. (11/15/2004)*

Penfolds 1999 St. Henri Shiraz (South Australia) $39. 91 —*D.T. (10/1/2003)*

Penfolds 1998 St. Henri Shiraz (South Australia) $40. 90 *(9/1/2002)*

Penfolds 2003 Thomas Hyland Shiraz (South Australia) $15. 84 —*D.T. (12/31/2005)*

Penfolds 2000 Thomas Hyland Shiraz (South Eastern Australia) $18. 85 —*M.S. (3/1/2003)*

Penfolds 1998 Grange Shiraz-Cabernet Sauvignon (South Australia) $205. 95 —*D.T. (10/1/2003)*

Penfolds 2004 Koonunga Hill Shiraz-Cabernet Sauvignon (South Eastern Australia) $12. Grapy and simple, with a slight herbal edge to the fruity aromas and flavors. Seems a bit soft and unstructured, then picks up a tart, citrusy edge on the finish. 83 —*J.C. (2/1/2007)*

Penfolds 2003 Koonunga Hill Shiraz-Cabernet Sauvignon (South Eastern Australia) $12. 84 —*D.T. (12/1/2005)*

Penfolds 2002 Koonunga Hill Shiraz-Cabernet Sauvignon (South Eastern Australia) $12. 84 —*D.T. (10/1/2005)*

Penfolds 2000 Koonunga Hill Shiraz-Cabernet Sauvignon (South Eastern Australia) $11. 87 Best Buy —*M.S. (12/15/2002)*

Penfolds 1999 Koonunga Hill Shiraz-Cabernet Sauvignon (South Eastern Australia) $15. 87 *(3/1/2001)*

Penfolds 1997 Koonunga Hill Shiraz-Cabernet Sauvignon (South Australia) $11. 88 Best Buy *(10/1/1999)*

Penfolds 2005 Rawson's Retreat Shiraz-Cabernet Sauvignon (South Eastern Australia) $9. 82 —*D.T. (11/15/2006)*

Penfolds 1998 Koonunga Hill White Blend (South Australia) $8. 85 *(12/31/1999)*

PENLEY ESTATE

Penley Estate 2003 Phoenix Cabernet Sauvignon (Coonawarra) $20. With its extremely supple texture, this is Cabernet you could drink tonight alongside filet mignon. The creaminess will complement the silkiness of the meat, while hints of green peppercorn serve to accent the ripe cherry and chocolate flavors. Drink now–2010. 89 —*J.C. (2/1/2007)*

Penley Estate 2002 Phoenix Cabernet Sauvignon (Coonawarra) $25. 89 —*D.T. (5/1/2005)*

Penley Estate 2001 Phoenix Cabernet Sauvignon (Coonawarra) $25. 86 —*D.T. (5/1/2004)*

Penley Estate 2000 Phoenix Cabernet Sauvignon (Coonawarra) $25. 85 —*M.S. (12/15/2002)*

Penley Estate 2002 Reserve Cabernet Sauvignon (Coonawarra) $65. 91 —*D.T. (10/1/2006)*

Penley Estate 1999 Reserve Cabernet Sauvignon (Coonawarra) $58. 88 —*D.T. (6/1/2003)*

Penley Estate 1998 Vintage Blend Cabernet Sauvignon-Shiraz (South Australia) $30. 89 —*D.T. (12/15/2002)*

Penley Estate 1994 Pinot Noir-Chardonnay Sparkling Wine Champagne Blend (Coonawarra) $30. 82 —*M.S. (1/1/2004)*

Penley Estate 2001 Chardonnay (Coonawarra) $25. 85 *(7/2/2004)*

Penley Estate 2003 Hyland Shiraz (Coonawarra) $20. Peppery and herbal, with tart cherry flavors that veer almost into lemon. Crisp on the finish. 83 —*J.C. (2/1/2007)*

Penley Estate 2002 Hyland Shiraz (Coonawarra) $25. 90 —*D.T. (10/1/2005)*

Penley Estate 2001 Hyland Shiraz (Coonawarra) $25. 86 —*D.T. (9/1/2004)*

Penley Estate 1999 Hyland Shiraz (Coonawarra) $25. 91 Editors' Choice —*K.F. (3/1/2003)*

Penley Estate 1998 Hyland Shiraz (Coonawarra) $25. 87 *(11/1/2001)*

Penley Estate 2000 Special Select Shiraz (Coonawarra) $65. 88 —*D.T. (10/1/2005)*

Penley Estate 2003 Condor Shiraz-Cabernet Sauvignon (Coonawarra) $20. Features heady scents of dried fruit, anise and pepper, but this big wine never really spreads its wings. The mouthfeel isn't especially rich or layered, while the flavors lean heavily toward dried fruit compote with hints of honey and spice—sort of like Amarone lite. Drink now. 85 —*J.C. (2/1/2007)*

PENMARA

Penmara 2000 Chardonnay (New South Wales) $8. 84 —*J.C. (7/1/2002)*

Penmara 2000 Reserve Chardonnay (New South Wales) $13. 88 —*J.C. (7/1/2002)*

Penmara 2000 Five Families Shiraz (New South Wales) $9. 85 *(10/1/2001)*

PENNA LANE

Penna Lane 2001 Cabernet Sauvignon (Clare Valley) $25. 86 —*D.T. (2/1/2004)*

Penna Lane 2003 Riesling (Clare Valley) $21 85 —*D.T. (2/1/2004)*

Penna Lane 2001 Shiraz (Clare Valley) $25. 86 —*D.T. (2/1/2004)*

Penna Lane 2000 Shiraz (Clare Valley) $20. 85 —*D.T. (3/1/2003)*

PENNY'S HILL

Penny's Hill 2002 Chardonnay (McLaren Vale) $18. 87 *(7/2/2004)*

Penny's Hill 2004 Red Dot Chardonnay-Viognier (McLaren Vale) $20. 87 —*D.T. (12/31/2005)*

Penny's Hill 2003 Cadenzia Grenache (McLaren Vale) $30. 88 —*D.T. (8/1/2005)*

Penny's Hill 2005 Shiraz (McLaren Vale) $35. More classically structured than the wine Ben Riggs makes under the Mr Riggs label, this is more savory and spicy, with blueberry fruit marked by hints of cinnamon, clove and cracked pepper. Long and mouthwatering on the finish. 91 *(11/15/2007)*

Penny's Hill 2003 Shiraz (McLaren Vale) $33. 90 —*D.T. (12/1/2005)*

Penny's Hill 1999 Shiraz (McLaren Vale) $33. 89 *(11/1/2001)*

Penny's Hill 2003 Red Dot Shiraz (McLaren Vale & Langhorne Creek) $18. 87 —*D.T. (3/1/2005)*

PENNYFIELD WINES

Pennyfield Wines 2002 Basket Pressed Petite Verdot (Riverland) $19. 86 —*D.T. (6/1/2006)*

Pennyfield Wines 2002 Basket Pressed Shiraz (Riverland) $22. 86 —*D.T. (10/1/2005)*

PEPPER TREE

Pepper Tree 2000 Grand Reserve Cabernet Sauvignon (Coonawarra) $100. 91 —*D.T. (8/1/2006)*

Penny's Hill 2005 Shiraz (McLaren Vale) $35. More classically structured than the wine Ben Riggs makes under the Mr Riggs label, this is more savory and spicy, with blueberry fruit marked by hints of cinnamon, clove and cracked pepper. Long and mouthwatering on the finish. 91 *(11/15/2007)*

Pepper Tree 2003 Grand Reserve Chardonnay (Wrattonbully) $34. 93 Editors' Choice *—D.T. (6/1/2006)*

Pepper Tree 2004 Grand Reserve Merlot (Wrattonbully) $41. Features some herbal overtones to the plummy fruit, also some leather nuances to the bouquet, but offers up a soft, creamy mouthful of plum and chocolate-like fruit. The leathery notes and a metallic hint on the finish may put off fans of squeaky-clean wines, but this still has plenty to commend it. Drink now. 87 *—J.C. (5/1/2007)*

Pepper Tree 2004 Reserve Merlot (Wrattonbully) $25. Shows some vegetal notes of tomato and cherry peppers, but despite that indication of under-ripeness the tannins are supple enough, ending soft and dusty on the tongue. 85 *—J.C. (5/1/2007)*

Pepper Tree 2003 Grand Reserve Shiraz (Wrattonbully) $55. 90 *—D.T. (6/1/2006)*

Pepper Tree 2004 Reserve Shiraz (Wrattonbully) $25. From the relatively new growing region of Wrattonbully, this Shiraz features exotic peach and apricot-like aromas and flavors, backed by some herbal notes and a pinch of peppery spice. Picks up additional spice and even some tea nuances on the finish. It's a bit out of the ordinary, but tasty and unique. 88 *—J.C. (5/1/2007)*

Pepper Tree 2004 Grand Reserve Tannat (Wrattonbully) $58. 90 *—D.T. (8/1/2006)*

PERRINI

Perrini 1999 Meadows Shiraz (McLaren Vale) $18. 88 *(10/1/2001)*

PETALUMA

Petaluma 2002 Cabernet Sauvignon-Merlot (Coonawarra) $35. This is a straightforward blend of Cabernet Sauvignon (51%) and Merlot (49%) with plenty of toasty oak. It starts with scents of cassis and vanilla, then adds a hint of mint on the palate. It's all delivered in a restrained style—medium-bodied, with charred oak on the finish. 85 *—J.C. (7/1/2007)*

Petaluma 2001 Cabernet Sauvignon-Merlot (Coonawarra) $35. 90 *—D.T. (8/1/2005)*

Petaluma 2000 Unfiltered Cabernet Sauvignon-Merlot (Coonawarra) $36. 87 *—D.T. (9/1/2004)*

Petaluma 2004 Croser Pinot Noir-Chardonnay Champagne Blend (Piccadilly Valley) $30. A blend of 68% Pinot Noir and 32% Chardonnay, this is one of the lighter-bodied Australian sparklers, featuring fruit-forward aromas of pineapple, vanilla and coconut. Flavors of citrus and toast are more standard fare; the wine finishes with good length, suggesting a few years of cellaring will do it no harm. 87 *—J.C. (8/1/2007)*

Petaluma 2004 Chardonnay (Piccadilly Valley) $30. Nicely integrated oak saturates the bouquet with suggestions of toast and spice without being overt, alongside custard and melon aromas. Flavors of buttered cashews, melon and citrus are round and soft in the mouth. This is a big, buxom Chardonnay, full-bodied, with a slightly warm, nutty finish. Drink now. 89 *—J.C. (8/1/2007)*

Petaluma 2001 Chardonnay (Piccadilly Valley) $28. 90 Editors' Choice *(7/2/2004)*

Petaluma 1999 Chardonnay (Piccadilly Valley) $32. 82 *—J.C. (7/1/2002)*

Petaluma 2001 Tiers Chardonnay (Piccadilly Valley) $64. 85 *(7/2/2004)*

Petaluma 1999 Tiers Vineyard Chardonnay (Piccadilly Valley) $120. 89 *—J.C. (7/1/2002)*

Petaluma 2000 Riesling (Australia) $14. 88 *(2/1/2002)*

Petaluma 2006 Hanlin Hill Riesling (Clare Valley) $20. Simultaneously floral and minerally on the nose, the 2006 Hanlin Hill Riesling is an all-around delight. Filled with apple, nectarine, melon and lime fruit, it manages to conceal the Clare Valley's sometimes hard edges with ripe fruit. Finishes dusty, minerally and long; this should have a long, positive evolution. 90 *—J.C. (6/1/2007)*

Petaluma 2003 Hanlin Hill Vineyard Riesling (Clare Valley) $16. 89 Best Buy *—D.T. (5/1/2004)*

Petaluma 2002 Shiraz (Adelaide Hills) $30. 89 *—D.T. (3/1/2005)*

Petaluma 1999 Shiraz (Adelaide Hills) $36. 85 *—K.F. (3/1/2003)*

Petaluma 1999 Bridgewater Mill Shiraz (Australia) $15. 88 Best Buy *—J.C. (9/1/2002)*

PETER HOWLAND

Peter Howland 2004 Maxwell Vineyard Chardonnay (Hunter Valley) $25. Winemaker Peter Howland is making a name for himself by sourcing grapes from all over Australia. From his home base in the Hunter Valley, this Chardonnay deftly balances oaky notes of allspice and brown sugar with elements of Asian pear, melon and citrus. It's medium- to full-bodied, but held in check by zesty acidity. Long and nuanced on the finish. Drink now–2010, maybe longer. 90 *—J.C. (8/1/2007)*

Peter Howland 2004 Langley Vineyard Shiraz (Western Australia) $35. Not as impressive as Howland's Parsons Vineyard bottling, this is still a very good Shiraz. Cedar and vanilla notes layer atop dark fruit flavors, ending dry and softly tannic. A touch of alcoholic warmth lingers on the finish. Drink now–2012. 87 *—J.C. (4/1/2007)*

Peter Howland 2004 Parsons Vineyard Shiraz (Frankland River) $35. The 2004 Parsons Vineyard Shiraz starts off a bit unflattering, but with vigorous decanting a swan emerges. Subtle toasted oak and vanilla notes, complex floral scents and bold blackberry fruit all combine in a creamy, rich, dense wine with plenty of character. Picks up more complexity on the finish, adding hints of chocolate, coffee and spice. Drink now–2015. 92 Editors' Choice *—J.C. (4/1/2007)*

Peter Howland 2004 Pine Lodge Vineyard Shiraz (Mount Barker) $35. This wine shows an interesting blend of leathery, meaty, clove aromas with creamy raspberry, strawberry and blueberry fruit flavors. It's medium- to full-bodied, ending on a slightly metallic note. Although the tannins suggest further development, the wine's aromatic evolution may not be as predictable as its textural development; the safer bet is to drink now. 89 *—J.C. (6/1/2007)*

PETER LEHMANN

Peter Lehmann 1999 The Mentor Cabernet Blend (Barossa Valley) $50. 90 *—D.T. (2/1/2004)*

Peter Lehmann 2002 Cabernet Sauvignon (Barossa) $16. 86 *—D.T. (12/31/2005)*

Peter Lehmann 2001 The Barossa Cabernet Sauvignon (Barossa Valley) $16. 88 *—D.T. (12/31/2004)*

Peter Lehmann 2005 Chardonnay (Barossa) $12. 83 *—D.T. (11/15/2006)*

Peter Lehmann 2002 Chardonnay (Barossa Valley) $12. 85 *—D.T. (12/31/2004)*

Peter Lehmann 2003 G-S-M (Barossa) $18. 84 *—D.T. (4/1/2006)*

Peter Lehmann 2003 Clancy's Red Blend (Barossa) $16. 85 *—D.T. (2/1/2006)*

Peter Lehmann 2002 Clancy's Red Blend (Barossa Valley) $16. 84 *—D.T. (12/31/2004)*

Peter Lehmann 2002 Mentor Red Blend (Barossa) $38. A Cabernet-based blend, Lehmann's Mentor features a slightly herbaceous note, but one that's amply balanced by dark cassis fruit. It's fresh and appealing, with enough firm tannins on the finish to make it pair wonderfully with rare beef now, or worth holding a few years to soften. 89 *—J.C. (11/1/2007)*

Peter Lehmann 1998 Mentor Red Blend (Barossa Valley) $50. 84 *—D.T. (8/1/2005)*

Peter Lehmann 2005 Riesling (Eden Valley) $15. Lean and a bit austere in texture, this is a crisp, citrusy Riesling that hints at crushed stone on the nose. Citrus and pineapple aromas turn to white grapefruit by the finish, then linger elegantly. 88 *—J.C. (2/1/2007)*

Peter Lehmann 2004 Riesling (Eden Valley) $16. 87 *—D.T. (8/1/2005)*

Peter Lehmann 2003 Riesling (Eden Valley) $16. 88 *—D.T. (12/31/2004)*

Peter Lehmann 1998 Reserve Riesling (Eden Valley) $NA. 90 *—D.T. (2/1/2004)*

Peter Lehmann 2003 Semillon (Barossa Valley) $11. 89 Best Buy *—D.T. (8/1/2005)*

Peter Lehmann 2002 Semillon (Barossa Valley) $11. 87 Best Buy *—D.T. (2/1/2004)*

Peter Lehmann 2004 Shiraz (Barossa) $16. Despite having the best lots skimmed off into various different cuvées, Lehmann's regular Shiraz remains pleasant and easy drinking. Cinnamon and clove scents accent red fruit flavors, while hints of pie crust and vanilla add grace notes. Drink now. 85 *—J.C. (3/1/2007)*

Peter Lehmann 2002 Eight Songs Shiraz (Barossa) $38. A lush, supple Shiraz with cassis and blackberry fruit wrapped in a soft coat of caramel, coffee and vanilla oak. Nicely complex, yet at the same time this is easy to drink. Finishes long, framed by dusty tannins, suggesting at least 5–7 years of future drinkability. 90 *—J.C. (11/1/2007)*

Peter Lehmann 1999 Eight Songs Shiraz (Barossa Valley) $45. 90 *—D.T. (8/1/2005)*

Peter Lehmann 1999 Eight Songs Shiraz (Barossa Valley) $55. 89 *—D.T. (2/1/2004)*

Peter Lehmann 2003 Stonewell Shiraz (Barossa) $NA. The 2003 vintage wasn't an easy one in Barossa, and Lehmann's Stonewell bottling is one of its weaker efforts in recent years. That said, it's still an attractive, open-knit Shiraz with plenty of berry and chocolate flavors and some slightly drying tannins on the finish. Drink now–2012. To be released February 2008. 88 *—J.C. (11/1/2007)*

Peter Lehmann 2002 Stonewell Shiraz (Barossa) $95. More lifted and aromatic than some other vintages of the Stonewell Shiraz, the 2002 features red fruit flavors and a slightly herbal tinge. Tannins are creamy-smooth, yet the acids are a bit hard-edged at this stage. Give it another few years to round into form; drink from 2010–2015. 90 *—J.C. (11/1/2007)*

Peter Lehmann 2001 Stonewell Shiraz (Barossa) $90. A great vintage for Lehmann's top Shiraz, the 2001 Stonewell boasts incredibly dense, rich, chocolate-fudge-like aromas. This is extremely ripe and opulent without ever going over the edge. Balanced, lush and complete. Drink now–2015. 93 Editors' Choice *—J.C. (11/1/2007)*

Peter Lehmann 2000 Stonewell Shiraz (Barossa) $90. Complex and a bit feral on the nose, offering up clove and cured meat aromas and flavors wrapped around a core of creamy blackberry fruit. Soft and supple on the finish, suggesting early drinkability; try now–2010. 88 *—J.C. (11/1/2007)*

Peter Lehmann 1999 Stonewell Shiraz (Barossa) $75. A nicely balanced Shiraz, with restrained mint, chocolate and cedar aromas layered over dark, plummy fruit. Turns a bit tart and tangy on the finish, but overall shows a solid degree of elegance and finesse. Evolving much as predicted in our earlier review (12/15/06). Drink now–2015. 89 *—J.C. (11/1/2007)*

Peter Lehmann 1999 Stonewell Shiraz (Barossa) $75. 90 *—J.C. (12/15/2006)*

Peter Lehmann 1998 Stonewell Shiraz (Barossa) $75. Shows the warmth of the vintage in its slightly elevated alcohol levels and flavors of brandied black cherries. It's big, a bit bulky and lacking elegance, but still a chunky, flavorful mouthful of Shiraz. As predicted in our last review of this wine (8/1/05), it should drink well through 2010. 90 *—J.C. (11/1/2007)*

Peter Lehmann 1998 Stonewell Shiraz (Barossa Valley) $75. 91 *—D.T. (8/1/2005)*

Peter Lehmann 1996 Stonewell Shiraz (Barossa) $75. A standout Stonewell, the 1996 still appears to have a decade or more of life still ahead of it. Smoke and mint notes mark the slightly closed nose, then layers of wonderfully creamy black cherry fruit flow across the palate. Yet despite the lush mouthfeel, the wine still comes across as structured on the long finish. Drink now–2020. 93 *—J.C. (11/1/2007)*

Peter Lehmann 1994 Stonewell Shiraz (Barossa) $60. Filled with aromas of smoke, scorched earth and even a bit of soy sauce, this is a big, beefy Shiraz with a lush midpalate. Turns a bit tighter and a bit rubbery on the finish, making its future evolution uncertain; drink up. 90 *—J.C. (11/1/2007)*

Peter Lehmann 1991 Stonewell Shiraz (Barossa) $36. This vintage of Lehmann's top Shiraz seems to be at or close to peak, with creamy tannins framing slightly stewed blackberry and plum fruit. Spicy-savory notes add complexity, while vanilla and dark chocolate flavors finish. Supple and soft; drink now and over the next few years. 90 *—J.C. (11/1/2007)*

Peter Lehmann 1989 Stonewell Shiraz (Barossa) $36. The American oak still clearly shows in this wine, which features vanilla and a touch of dill on the nose, but also blackberry and cherry fruit and a hint of milk chocolate. It's become creamy and soft with age, adding tobacco notes to vanilla and crisp berry flavors on the finish. Drink up. 88 *—J.C. (11/1/2007)*

Peter Lehmann 1999 The Barossa Shiraz (Barossa Valley) $17. 88 Editors' Choice *(10/1/2001)*

Peter Lehmann 1997 The Barossa Shiraz (Barossa Valley) $15. 89 *(11/15/1999)*

Peter Lehmann 2001 The Futures Shiraz (Barossa Valley) $NA. 89 *—D.T. (2/1/2004)*

Peter Lehmann 2004 Clancy's Shiraz-Cabernet Sauvignon-Merlot Red Blend (Barossa) $16. A good value, Lehmann's 2004 Clancy's easily blends cherry, blackberry, vanilla, smoke, spice, coffee and maple syrup aromas and flavors into a harmonious, integrated whole. The texture is creamy-soft, showing just a dusting of tannins on the finish. Drink now. 88 *—J.C. (3/1/2007)*

PETERSONS

Petersons 1999 Shiraz (Mudgee) $20. 84 *(10/1/2001)*

PETTAVEL

Pettavel 2001 Platina Cabernet Sauvignon-Cabernet Franc (Geelong) $25. 84 *—D.T. (8/1/2005)*

Pettavel 2003 Evening Star Chardonnay (Geelong) $17. 87 *—D.T. (8/1/2005)*

Pettavel 2002 Platina Chardonnay (Geelong) $25. 83 *—D.T. (12/31/2005)*

Pettavel 2004 Evening Star Riesling (Geelong) $17. 88 *—D.T. (8/1/2005)*

Pettavel 2004 Evening Star Sauvignon Blanc-Semillon (Geelong) $17. 88 *—D.T. (8/1/2005)*

PEWSEY VALE

Pewsey Vale 2006 Individual Vineyard Selection Riesling (Eden Valley) $16. This is a reasonably full-bodied, rounded example of Australian Riesling that smells of honey and peaches, but with a sense of underlying stony bedrock. It's minerally on the palate, with just enough frills to dress it up, turning lusher on the finish. Good price, too. 89 Editors' Choice *—J.C. (8/1/2007)*

Pewsey Vale 2003 Riesling (Eden Valley) $15. 90 Best Buy *—D.T. (2/1/2004)*

PFEIFFER

Pfeiffer NV Muscat (Rutherglen) $18. The Pfeiffer style emphasizes freshness, and this wine reflects that in its floral and ripe berry aromas. Hints of raisin, honey and pineapple add richness and sweetness, balanced by peppery spice notes on the finish. 90 Editors' Choice *—J.C. (12/15/2007)*

PHILIP SHAW

Philip Shaw 2005 No. 11 Chardonnay (Orange) $30. Mostly barrel-fermented in French oak, this is a smoky, nutty Chardonnay that successfully integrates the wood with pear and honey notes. The texture in the mouth is rich and layered, ending long and tinged with roasted nuts. Drink now–2010. 90 *(9/1/2007)*

Philip Shaw 2004 No 11 Chardonnay (Orange) $30. 90 *—D.T. (6/1/2006)*

Philip Shaw 2005 No. 17 Merlot-Cabernet Franc-Cabernet Sauvignon Bordeaux Blend (Orange) $25. This shows a bit of Graves-like character, blending tobacco-leaf and smoky-cedary hints with black cherry and cassis fruit. Medium-bodied, this doesn't have the lushness of many Australian wines from warmer regions, yet isn't overly hard. Try in 2010. The blend is 43% Merlot, 34% Cabernet Franc, 23% Cabernet Sauvignon. 88 *(9/1/2007)*

Philip Shaw 2005 No. 8 Pinot Noir (Orange) $40. A bit on the lean side, and with some drying tannins on the finish, this is one wine in the Philip Shaw lineup that's less than impressive. Cola and earth notes overshadow the black cherry fruit, and there's a slight menthol edge to the flavors. 85 *(9/1/2007)*

Philip Shaw 2006 No. 19 Sauvignon Blanc (Orange) $20. A ripe style of Sauvignon Blanc, with bold melon and fig flavors that blend in hints of nectarine as well. Not a herbal, grassy style, but one that shows plenty of ripeness and weight yet finishes with some chalky, minerally notes. Drink now. 88 *(9/1/2007)*

Philip Shaw 2005 No 19 Sauvignon Blanc (Orange) $25. 87 *—D.T. (6/1/2006)*

Philip Shaw 2005 No, 89 Shiraz-Viognier (Orange) $45. Only contains 1% Viognier, so maybe the impression is subliminal, but there does seem to be a hint of apricot to this wine's raspberry-blueberry fruit and cracked pepper. It's medium-bodied, with firm acids but soft tannins on the finish. Drink now and over the next 8 years. 90 *(9/1/2007)*

PICARDY

Picardy 2002 Merlot-Cabernet Sauvignon-Cabernet Franc Bordeaux Blend (Pemberton) $18. 87 *—D.T. (6/1/2006)*

Picardy 2004 Chardonnay (Pemberton) $27. 87 *—D.T. (8/1/2006)*

Picardy 2004 Pinot Noir (Pemberton) $27. 84 *—D.T. (11/15/2006)*

Picardy 1999 Shiraz (Western Australia) $28. 84 *(11/1/2001)*

PIERRO

Pierro 2000 Red Table Wine Cabernet Sauvignon (Margaret River) $45. 88 *—D.T. (10/1/2003)*

Pierro 2001 Chardonnay (Margaret River) $45. 90 *(10/1/2003)*

Pierro 2001 Semillon-Sauvignon Blanc (Margaret River) $25. 86 *—D.T. (10/1/2003)*

PIKE & JOYCE

Pike & Joyce 2003 Lenswood Chardonnay (Adelaide Hills) $27. 87 *—D.T. (8/1/2005)*

Pike & Joyce 2004 Lenswood Pinot Gris (Adelaide Hills) $21. 87 *—D.T. (8/1/2005)*

Pike & Joyce 2002 Lenswood Pinot Noir (Adelaide Hills) $27. 89 *—D.T. (8/1/2005)*

Pike & Joyce 2002 Sauvignon Blanc (Adelaide Hills) $20. 87 *—D.T. (5/1/2004)*

Pike & Joyce 2005 Lenswood Sauvignon Blanc (Adelaide Hills) $20. Green pea, lime and quince aromas set the stage for a medium-bodied, slightly creamy wine. Citrus, fig and melon flavors finish long and crisp. 88 *—J.C. (6/1/2007)*

Pike & Joyce 2004 Lenswood Sauvignon Blanc (Adelaide Hills) $21. 88 *—D.T. (8/1/2005)*

AUSTRALIA

PIKES

Pikes 2000 Shiraz-Grenache-Mourvedre Red Blend (Clare Valley) $20. 90 *—D.T. (5/1/2004)*

Pikes 2003 Riesling (Clare Valley) $19. 87 *—D.T. (5/1/2004)*

Pikes 2002 Riesling (Clare Valley) $18. 89 *—D.T. (8/1/2003)*

Pikes 2005 Dry Riesling (Clare Valley) $19. Scents of green apple, lime and wet stones set the stage for the appealing, mouthwatering flavors of green apple and lime that follow. Has nicely delineated flavors, just falls a tiny bit short on the finish. Imported by USA Wine West. 87 *—J.C. (9/1/2007)*

Pikes 2004 Dry Riesling (Clare Valley) $19. 91 *—D.T. (8/1/2005)*

Pikes 2001 Reserve Riesling (Clare Valley) $23. 88 *—D.T. (8/1/2003)*

Pikes 2004 The Merle Reserve Riesling (Clare Valley) $38. 91 Editors' Choice *—D.T. (4/1/2006)*

Pikes 2002 Luccio Sangiovese (Clare Valley) $15. 86 *—D.T. (12/1/2005)*

Pikes 1999 Shiraz (Clare Valley) $19. 84 *(10/1/2001)*

Pikes 1998 Reserve Shiraz (Clare Valley) $48. 89 *(11/1/2001)*

Pikes 2006 Gill's Farm Viognier (Clare Valley) $22. Floral on the nose, this captures Viognier's elusive fragrance in a peachy, spiced wine that's plump but not overly heavy. 90 Editors' Choice *—J.C. (6/1/2007)*

PINK BY YELLOWGLEN

Pink by Yellowglen NV Champagne Blend (South Eastern Australia) $12. 84 *—J.C. (12/31/2006)*

PINK KNOT

Pink Knot 2005 Rosé Blend (McLaren Vale) $12. 83 *—D.T. (12/1/2005)*

PIPERS BROOK VINEYARD ESTATE

Pipers Brook Vineyard Estate 2003 Estate Pinot Noir (Tasmania) $35. At four years past vintage, the oak overlay on this wine is still strong, giving rise to doubt about whether it will ever properly integrate. As a result, this wine isn't very Pinot Noir-ish, although it's still very good. Toast and vanilla notes are backed by tart red berries and a hint of orange zest on the crisp finish. 87 *—J.C. (6/1/2007)*

Pipers Brook Vineyard Estate 2003 Reserve Pinot Noir (Tasmania) $63. Overwooded and overpriced, that's the verdict on this Tasmanian Pinot Noir. Toast and vanilla notes dominate, while the cherry fruit's acids remain angular, finishing crisp and tangy. It's a good wine, just not very Pinot, unless being Pinot is just a question of having high acids and soft tannins. 85 *—J.C. (6/1/2007)*

Pipers Brook Vineyard Estate 2002 Riesling (Tasmania) $19. 87 *—D.T. (8/1/2003)*

PIPING SHRIKE

Piping Shrike 2005 Shiraz (Barossa Valley) $19. A super value from Charles Cimicky, the 2005 Piping Shrike is a dense, full-bodied example of Barossa Shiraz. Deep blueberry and plum fruit is accented by hints of vanilla, chocolate and coffee that linger on the long, drawn-out finish. Drink now–2012. 90 Editors' Choice *—J.C. (4/1/2007)*

Piping Shrike 2004 Shiraz (Barossa Valley) $14. 84 *—D.T. (10/1/2005)*

Piping Shrike 2003 Shiraz (Barossa Valley) $14. 87 *—D.T. (5/1/2005)*

PIRATHON

Pirathon 2005 Shiraz (Barossa Valley) $30. There's no doubt this is done in what some critics might call a fruit-bomb style. But boy is it gorgeously made. The creamy-smooth mouthfeel and lush layers of flavors effortlessly carry palate-saturating notes of licorice and plum. Long on the finish, with a surprising degree of elegance. A blend of various growers' fruit vinified by winemaker Troy Kalleske. Drink now–2015. 93 *—J.C. (11/1/2007)*

PIRRAMIMMA

Pirramimma 1998 Shiraz (McLaren Vale) $20. 87 *(10/1/2001)*

PLANTAGENET

Plantagenet 1999 Mount Barker Chardonnay (Western Australia) $21. 85 *—J.C. (7/1/2002)*

Plantagenet 2006 Omrah Unoaked Chardonnay (Western Australia) $15. A fruit-driven wine, with apricot and peach scents dominating the bouquet. The mouthfeel is rather plump and pulpy in texture, carrying the flavors of peach and pineapple easily over the palate. Ends with a slightly tinned-fruit character. 84 *—J.C. (4/1/2007)*

Plantagenet 2003 OMRAH unoaked Chardonnay (Western Australia) $15. 85 *(7/2/2004)*

Plantagenet 2000 Unoaked Chardonnay (Western Australia) $14. 84 *—J.C. (7/1/2002)*

Plantagenet 2006 Off The Rack Chenin Blanc (Western Australia) $25. Off the rack refers to the fact that the grapes for this dessert wine have been partially dried to concentrate the sugars, resulting in a moderately sweet (80g/L) wine with flavors of golden raisin and mango, a hint of sweet corn and a trace of bitterness on the finish. 85 *—J.C. (12/15/2007)*

Plantagenet 2005 Omrah Pinot Noir (Western Australia) $15. A decent effort at a fair price, Plantagenet's attempt to jump on the Pinot Noir bandwagon is a medium-bodied wine featuring cherry and chocolate aromas and flavors. There's some delicate dried grass or hay notes as well, while the flavors darken on the finish. 84 *—J.C. (6/1/2007)*

Plantagenet 2005 Riesling (Great Southern) $15. Nicely blends ripe peaches with wet stones to give a wine that has something for fruit- and rock-lovers alike. It's medium- to full-bodied, finishing with accents of dried spices. Drink now–2010. 88 *—J.C. (9/1/2007)*

Plantagenet 2006 Hazard Hill Rosé Wine Rosé Blend (Western Australia) $12. There's an herbaceous note to this wine's bouquet suggestive of bell pepper, but thankfully, it's not a dominant aroma—there's also plenty of cherry fruit. It's predominantly Merlot, with some Grenache blended in, and the result marries cherries with leafy, tobacco-like flavors. 86 *—J.C. (7/1/2007)*

Plantagenet 2006 Omrah Sauvignon Blanc (Western Australia) $15. This wine's bouquet of pineapple, passion fruit and pink grapefruit is immediately attractive, leading easily into a palate of mixed citrus. A little leaner than the winery's Hazard Hill Semillon-Sauvignon Blanc, but probably better suited to raw shellfish. Clean and refreshing on the finish. Drink now. 87 *—J.C. (5/1/2007)*

Plantagenet 2005 Hazard Hill Semillon-Sauvignon Blanc (Western Australia) $12. This blend of 75% Semillon and 25% Sauvignon Blanc seems a bit simple at first, offering scents only of citrus and chalk. But it opens up a bit more on the palate, featuring some plump stone fruit flavors before ending on zippy lime and grapefruit notes. Drink now, preferably with seafood. 87 Best Buy *—J.C. (5/1/2007)*

Plantagenet 2001 Estate Shiraz (Mount Barker) $25. 85 *—D.T. (5/1/2004)*

Plantagenet 2004 Hazard Hill Shiraz (Western Australia) $12. A decent value, Plantagenet's 2004 Hazard Hill Shiraz is a round, soft wine, perhaps in part because of the 10% Grenache that was included in the blend. Black tea and berry scents pick up coffee and anise on the finish. Drink now. 86 *—J.C. (4/1/2007)*

Plantagenet 1998 Mount Barker Shiraz (Western Australia) $28. 88 *(11/1/2001)*

Plantagenet 2004 Omrah Shiraz (Western Australia) $15. Seems a bit overdone, with blackberry flavors that head toward jam and cooked fruit rather than fresh berries. Graham cracker and chocolate notes add complexity to this reasonably rich wine that just needs a little more vitality to bring it to the next level of quality. 86 *—J.C. (4/1/2007)*

Plantagenet 2001 Omrah Shiraz (Western Australia) $15. 87 *—D.T. (5/1/2004)*

Plantagenet 2000 Omrah Shiraz (Western Australia) $17. 84 *—D.T. (2/1/2003)*

Plantagenet 1998 Omrah Shiraz (Western Australia) $18. 88 *—M.S. (10/1/2000)*

Plantagenet 1997 Omrah Shiraz (Mount Barker) $17. 88 *—M.S. (4/1/2000)*

POOLES ROCK WINES

Pooles Rock Wines 2001 Chardonnay (Hunter Valley) $24. 87 *—D.T. (8/1/2003)*

Pooles Rock Wines 2001 Firestick Chardonnay (Adelaide Hills) $14. 85 *—D.T. (8/1/2003)*

POONAWATTA ESTATE

Poonawatta Estate 2006 The Eden Riesling (Eden Valley) $35. Incredibly powerful, with bold lime sherbet aromas that are nearly overwhelming in their intensity. Flavors are strident and linear at this young stage, underscored by vibrant acidity and fantastic length. You can enjoy it now for its brute force, but will be better rewarded by cellaring it for 5–10 years. 91 Cellar Selection *—J.C. (8/1/2007)*

Poonawatta Estate 2005 The 1880 Shiraz (Eden Valley) $95. Named after the date it was planted, this wine comes from a two-acre block that's said to be the seventh-oldest Shiraz vineyard in Australia. Perhaps this is at a closed phase in its evolution, as both samples tasted showed only modest weight and clipped finishes, despite boasting crisp blueberry, vanilla, cinnamon and toasty oak flavors. 88 *—J.C. (11/1/2007)*

POTHANA VINEYARDS

Pothana Vineyards 2004 Big Mouth Red Shiraz-Viognier (New South Wales) $15. From winemaker David Hook, who previously worked for Tyrrell's and Lakes Folly, this is an outstanding bargain. A blend of 95% Shiraz and 5% Viognier, it offers loads of cola, chocolate, plum and blueberry, framed with just enough structuring acid and tannin to give it balance. Try this with grilled steak or lamb over the next few years. 90 Best Buy *—J.C. (5/1/2007)*

PREECE

Preece 1998 Sauvignon Blanc (Victoria) $15. 87 *—S.H. (10/1/2000)*

PRETTY SALLY

Pretty Sally 2003 Single Vineyard Estate Cabernet Sauvignon (Victoria) $25. 88 *—D.T. (10/1/2006)*

Pretty Sally 2006 Estate Rosé (Victoria) $15. Full-bodied and distressingly soft, this orangey-pink rosé is broad and mouthfilling, while the modest peach and chocolate flavors finish short. 81 *—J.C. (7/1/2007)*

PRIMO ESTATE

Primo Estate 2006 La Biondina Columbard (Adelaide Hills) $15. Thickly textured and pulpy, this wine features citrus and melon flavors, then finishes on a tangy, grapefruity note. 85 *—J.C. (6/1/2007)*

Primo Estate 1999 Il Briccone Red Blend (Adelaide Hills) $18. 84 *—J.C. (9/1/2002)*

Primo Estate 2005 Joseph La Magia Botrytis Riesling-Traminer White Blend (Eden Valley) $24. A soft and fruity dessert wine, not overly sweet, but overflowing with peach and apricot flavors, underscored by orange and lime zest. Imported by USA Wine West. 87 *—J.C. (12/15/2007)*

Primo Estate 2003 La Biondina White Blend (Adelaide Hills) $NA. 85 *—D.T. (5/1/2004)*

Primo Estate 2005 La Biondina White Blend (Adelaide) $15. 84 *—D.T. (8/1/2006)*

Primo Estate 2004 La Biondina (Adelaide, not Adelaide Hills) White Blend (Adelaide Hills) $16. 87 *—D.T. (8/1/2005)*

PUNT ROAD

Punt Road 2003 Cabernet Sauvignon (Yarra Valley) $22. 90 *—D.T. (10/1/2006)*

Punt Road 2004 Chardonnay (Yarra Valley) $18. 84 *—D.T. (4/1/2006)*

Punt Road 2004 Pinot Gris (Yarra Valley) $20. 83 *—D.T. (2/1/2006)*

Punt Road 2003 Pinot Noir (Yarra Valley) $22. 84 *—D.T. (4/1/2006)*

Punt Road 2003 Shiraz (Yarra Valley) $22. 86 *—D.T. (4/1/2006)*

PUNTERS CORNER

Punters Corner 1999 Cabernet Sauvignon (Coonawarra) $25. 88 *—M.S. (12/15/2002)*

Punters Corner 1998 Cabernet Sauvignon (Coonawarra) $27. 89 *(9/1/2001)*

Punters Corner 1999 Cabernet Sauvignon-Merlot (Coonawarra) $27. 89 *(9/1/2001)*

Punters Corner 2000 Chardonnay (Coonawarra) $19. 87 *—D.T. (8/1/2003)*

Punters Corner 2002 Triple Crown Red Blend (Coonawarra) $20. 84 *—D.T. (5/1/2005)*

Punters Corner 2001 Triple Crown Red Blend (Coonawarra) $20. 88 *—D.T. (5/1/2004)*

Punters Corner 2002 Shiraz (Coonawarra) $28. 86 *—D.T. (10/1/2005)*

Punters Corner 1998 Shiraz (Coonawarra) $26. 87 *—J.C. (9/1/2002)*

Punters Corner 2000 Spartacus Reserve Shiraz (Coonawarra) $62. 84 *—D.T. (9/1/2004)*

Punters Corner 1999 Spartacus Reserve Shiraz (Coonawarra) $60. 91 *—J.C. (9/1/2002)*

Punters Corner 1998 Spartacus Reserve Shiraz (Coonawarra) $46. 85 *(11/1/2001)*

PURE LOVE WINES

Pure Love Wines 2005 Layer Cake Shiraz (Barossa Valley) $15. A new project from Jayson Woodbridge (the owner of Napa's Hundred Acre label), Layer Cake refers to the soils of his Barossa Vineyard, but it could equally apply to the richness and density of the wine. It's creamy in texture, and filled with blueberries, spice and everything nice, finally ending with hints of coffee and chocolate. 90 Best Buy *—J.C. (4/1/2007)*

QUARTETTO

Quartetto 2000 Shiraz (McLaren Vale) $20. 84 *—D.T. (1/28/2003)*

R.L. BULLER & SON

R.L. Buller & Son NV Calliope Rare Muscat (Rutherglen) $86. This is dark, almost black in color at the center, with greening evident at the rim. Syrupy, intense aromas of coffee and dark chocolate make an immediate impact on the nose, followed by syrupy, intense flavors of coffee and molasses. There's mind-boggling concentration here, but just enough acidity to provide a sense of balance. Still, it's hard to imagine drinking more than a couple of ounces of this at a time. 94 *—J.C. (12/15/2007)*

R.L. Buller & Son NV Premium Fine Muscat (Victoria) $16. Fragrant with berries and citrus, this Muscat is also syrupy sweet without being cloying. Hints of coffee and caramel provide a deeper, darker foundation on the palate, with bits of candied orange peel and chocolate on the finish. 91 Editors' Choice *—J.C. (12/15/2007)*

R.L. Buller & Son NV Premium Fine Tawny (Victoria) $16. Dark amber in color, this still shows its red-grape origins in vaguely berrylike scents and flavors. Hints of chocolate and caramel provide a sweet touch to this supple, medium-bodied fortified. Finishes peppery and warm. 86 *—J.C. (12/15/2007)*

R.L. Buller & Son NV Tawny (Victoria) $13. More of a murky garnet than truly tawny, this inexpensive Port-style wine features chocolate, plum and prune flavors and a supple, silky mouthfeel. 85 *—J.C. (12/15/2007)*

R.L. Buller & Son NV Calliope Rare Tokay (Rutherglen) $86. Just a tiny serving of this dark nectar will last a long time. The malty, porter-ish aromas intrigue, followed by incredibly rich and syrupy flavors accompanied by mouthwatering acids and enormous peristence. Layers of complexity gradually unfold in the glass, revealing hints of honey, caramel and beguiling rancio notes. 98 Editors' Choice *—J.C. (12/15/2007)*

R.L. Buller & Son NV Premium Fine Tokay (Victoria) $16. Buller's top wines are from Rutherglen, but this entry-level Tokay carries the broader Victoria GI. There's a blast of bergamot upfront, the penetrating citrus notes layered over tea leaves and caramel flavors. Viscous and mouthcoating, it finishes long and citrusy-sweet. 90 *—J.C. (12/15/2007)*

RAFFERTY'S RULES

Rafferty's Rules 2002 Fat Chance Cabernet Sauvignon-Merlot (South Eastern Australia) $19. This blend of roughly two-thirds Cabernet and one-third Merlot offers scents of dried herbs, cedar and raisined cassis, then turns rather crisp on the palate. Although the wine lacks a bit of flesh and richness, the tannins are supple and the flavors are totally correct: cassis, cedar and dried herbs. 84 *—J.C. (7/1/2007)*

Rafferty's Rules 2002 Angels' Share Shiraz (South Eastern Australia) $17. Don't be fooled into thinking this is your typical fruit-driven South Eastern Australia blend from mediocre growing regions. Instead, the bulk of the wine (70%) comes from McLaren Vale, with 15% each from Langhorne Creek and Heathcote, blended into a dark, meaty wine filled with notes of cola, coffee, soy and tapenade. Spicy and complex on the finish. 89 Editors' Choice *—J.C. (11/15/2007)*

Rafferty's Rules 2002 The Ringer Shiraz-Cabernet Sauvignon (South Eastern Australia) $19. Creamy and lush, seemingly destined for immediate consumption. Eucalyptus marks the nose, giving it a lifted quality, but the main flavors are of plum and cassis, wrapped in a soft cocoon of caramel and cedar. Drink now. 89 *—J.C. (4/1/2007)*

RAINMAKERS

RainMakers 2004 Shiraz-Grenache (McLaren Vale) $24. This is pretty oaky, but features enough fruit to support the wood. There's cedar, vanilla and a bit of coconut, but also some slightly stewed cassis. It's creamy and thickly textured, with plush tannins and masses of vanilla-laden flavor. Drink now. 88 *—J.C. (7/1/2007)*

RainMakers 2003 Shiraz-Grenache (McLaren Vale) $23. 84 *—D.T. (4/1/2006)*

RAM'S LEAP

Ram's Leap 2004 Merlot (Western Plains) $11. Displays some pretty aromas and flavors of white pepper, mint and mixed cherries and berries, but the tannins are firm and drying, the mouthfeel hard and ungenerous. 84 *—J.C. (2/1/2007)*

Ram's Leap 2005 Shiraz (Western Plains) $12. This is a rustic style of Shiraz, with hints of beef bouillon and cola layered over earth and plum notes. Chewy tannins bring it home, suggesting a pairing with rare roasts. 85 *—J.C. (11/15/2007)*

Ram's Leap 2004 Shiraz (Western Plains) $11. 85 *—D.T. (11/15/2006)*

RANFURLYS WAY

Ranfurlys Way 2003 Cabernet Sauvignon (Clare Valley) $29. 86 *—D.T. (10/1/2006)*

Ranfurlys Way 2004 Chardonnay (Adelaide Hills) $25. 85 *—D.T. (12/1/2005)*

Ranfurlys Way 2005 Riesling (Clare Valley) $29. 88 *—D.T. (12/1/2005)*

Ranfurlys Way 2001 Shiraz (Clare Valley) $29. 88 *—D.T. (12/31/2005)*

RAZOR'S EDGE

Razor's Edge 2006 Unwooded Chardonnay (South Australia) $12. For an unwooded Chardonnay, this is unusually plump and pillowy in texture, with layers of tropical fruit given shape on the finish by a squirt of citrus.

A hint of spice adds extra nuance to this crowd-pleasing wine. 87 Best Buy —*J.C. (8/1/2007)*

RBJ

RBJ 2001 Vox Populi Grenache (Barossa Valley) $10. 87 Best Buy —*D.T. (11/15/2004)*

RED BUCKET

Red Bucket 2005 Semillon-Sauvignon Blanc (Adelaide Hills) $13. 85 —*D.T. (8/1/2006)*

RED HILL ESTATE

Red Hill Estate 2001 Penguin's Kiss Chardonnay (Mornington Peninsula) $10. 83 —*D.T. (8/1/2003)*

RED KNOT

Red Knot 2006 Cabernet Sauvignon (McLaren Vale) $12. Earth and wet clay notes dampen this wine's medicinal black cherry flavors. Tasted twice, with consistent notes. 82 —*J.C. (11/15/2007)*

Red Knot 2005 Cabernet Sauvignon (McLaren Vale) $12. Smooth, with absolutely no rough edges—or even much texture at all—this grapy, juicy Cabernet goes down easy enough, it just doesn't leave much of a lasting impression. Quaffable. 83 —*J.C. (5/1/2007)*

Red Knot 2003 Cabernet Sauvignon (Fleurieu Peninsula) $12. 87 Best Buy —*D.T. (11/15/2004)*

Red Knot 2005 Shiraz (McLaren Vale) $12. At its suggested retail price of $12, this is a great value in Aussie Shiraz. It's not the biggest or most muscular, but it does offer authoritative flavors of blackberries, pepper, leather and spice, a creamy texture and a crisp, fresh finish. And the Zork closure gives it additional appeal. 88 Best Buy —*J.C. (4/1/2007)*

Red Knot 2004 Shiraz (McLaren Vale) $12. 86 —*D.T. (10/1/2005)*

Red Knot 2003 Shiraz (McLaren Vale) $12. 87 Best Buy —*D.T. (11/15/2004)*

REDBANK

Redbank 2002 The Fugitive Cabernet Sauvignon (Victoria) $15. 89 —*D.T. (5/1/2005)*

Redbank 2000 Percydale Cabernet Sauvignon-Merlot (King Valley) $16. 91 Editors' Choice —*S.H. (12/15/2002)*

Redbank 1999 Percydale Cabernet Sauvignon-Merlot (King Valley) $15. 84 —*D.T. (9/1/2001)*

Redbank 1998 Long Paddock Cabernet Sauvignon-Shiraz (Victoria) $14. 88 —*M.M. (10/1/2000)*

Redbank 1998 Long Paddock Chardonnay (Victoria) $11. 85 —*M.M. (10/1/2000)*

Redbank 2003 The Long Paddock Chardonnay (Victoria) $10. 87 Best Buy —*D.T. (5/1/2005)*

Redbank 2002 The Long Paddock Chardonnay (Victoria) $10. 87 —*D.T. (8/1/2003)*

Redbank 2001 The Long Paddock Chardonnay (Victoria) $10. 190 —*S.H. (1/1/2002)*

Redbank 2003 The Long Paddock Merlot (Victoria) $10. 86 Best Buy —*D.T. (10/1/2005)*

Redbank 2004 Goldmine Series Sunday Morning Pinot Gris (King Valley) $16. 89 —*D.T. (8/1/2005)*

Redbank 2001 Sunday Morning Pinot Gris (King Valley) $16. 87 —*S.H. (1/1/2002)*

Redbank 2000 Sunday Morning Pinot Gris (King Valley) $15. 87 —*M.M. (9/1/2001)*

Redbank 2002 The Long Paddock Sauvignon Blanc (Victoria) $10. 85 —*D.T. (12/31/2003)*

Redbank 1999 Fighting Flat Shiraz (King Valley) $15. 82 *(10/1/2001)*

Redbank 2001 The Anvil Shiraz (Heathcote) $50. 91 —*D.T. (8/1/2005)*

Redbank 2000 The Fighting Flat Shiraz (King Valley) $16. 86 —*S.H. (12/15/2002)*

Redbank 2004 The Long Paddock Shiraz (Victoria) $11. It's not that expressive on the nose, but this wine offers lipsmacking berry and cassis flavors framed by extremely supple tannins and sound acidity, then picks up a hint of mint on the finish. 85 —*J.C. (11/15/2007)*

Redbank 2000 The Long Paddock Shiraz-Cabernet Sauvignon (Victoria) $10. 90 Best Buy —*S.H. (12/15/2002)*

Redbank 2004 The Widow Jones Viognier (King Valley) $16. 87 —*D.T. (8/1/2005)*

REDHOUSE

Redhouse 2004 Shiraz-Grenache (South Australia) $17. A 60-40 blend of Shiraz and Grenache that also blends fruit from Barossa and McLaren Vale, this medium-bodied wine features scents of cedar, vanilla and mocha. The flavors are of tart cherries coated in chocolate, while the finish is crisp and clean. 85 —*J.C. (2/1/2007)*

Redhouse 2001 Shiraz-Grenache (McLaren Vale) $15. 87 —*D.T. (12/31/2004)*

REILLY'S

Reilly's 2002 Dry Land Cabernet Sauvignon (Clare Valley) $27. 89 —*D.T. (12/31/2005)*

Reilly's 2004 Old Bushvine Grenache (Clare Valley) $19. Reilly's Clare Valley location tends to give its wines a little more focus than some of the wines coming out of nearby Barossa, like in this fine example of old vine Grenache. Aromas of brandied cherries sprinkled with star anise add touches of chocolate and earth on the palate. It's full, round and generous, yet finishes firm and focused. Drink now and over the next few years. 91 Editors' Choice —*J.C. (6/1/2007)*

Reilly's 2003 Old Bushvine Grenache-Shiraz (Clare Valley) $17. 92 Editors' Choice —*J.C. (12/15/2006)*

Reilly's 2006 Barking Mad Riesling (Clare Valley) $15. Light and fresh, with only 12% alcohol, this Riesling from reliable producer Reilly's features scents of limes, wet stone and cinnamon, but doesn't show enough intensity of flavor to merit a higher rating. It's clean and refreshing, a light summertime sipper for pool or patio. 86 —*J.C. (8/1/2007)*

Reilly's 2004 Barking Mad Riesling (Clare Valley) $13. 84 —*D.T. (10/1/2005)*

Reilly's 2004 Watervale Riesling (Clare Valley) $15. 85 —*D.T. (10/1/2005)*

Reilly's 1999 Watervale Riesling (Clare Valley) $12. 87 —*M.M. (2/1/2002)*

Reilly's 2004 Barking Mad Shiraz (Clare Valley) $17. Reilly's entry-level Shiraz is a bold wine loaded with brandied fruitcake scents and layered with Christmas pudding and chocolate. It's close to being over the top, with plenty of late-harvest, dried-fruit character, yet stays lively thanks to heaps of invigorating spice. Drink now. 88 —*J.C. (3/1/2007)*

Reilly's 2002 Dry Land Shiraz (Clare Valley) $25. 85 —*D.T. (12/1/2005)*

Reilly's 1999 Dry Land Shiraz (Clare Valley) $25. 90 *(11/1/2001)*

Reilly's 2002 Stolen Block Shiraz (Clare Valley) $38. Although this is very good, it's a bit of a disappointment compared to what this fine producer is capable of achieving. The bouquet is dark in overall tone and nearly impenetrable—with aeration the toasted, charcoal-like scents give way to hints of vanilla—while the flavors are surprisingly tart. Simple blackberry and boysenberry fruit flavors turn crisp and spicy on the finish. 88 —*J.C. (6/1/2007)*

RESCHKE

Reschke 2002 Bos Cabernet Sauvignon (Coonawarra) $30. 88 —*D.T. (5/1/2005)*

Reschke 2002 Bos Cabernet Sauvignon (Coonawarra) $35. 90 —*D.T. (5/1/2004)*

Reschke 2002 Vitulus Cabernet Sauvignon (Coonawarra) $20. 88 —*D.T. (5/1/2005)*

Reschke 2002 Vitulus Cabernet Sauvignon (Coonawarra) $26. 89 —*D.T. (5/1/2004)*

REVOLUTION

Revolution 2006 Shiraz (McLaren Vale) $21. Comes out of the chute a bit tarry and rubbery, but seems to come around with some time in the glass, offering a lush, dense texture and flavors of coffee and black olive that finally show some berry shadings on the finish. 88 *(11/15/2007)*

REYNOLDS

Reynolds 2002 Cabernet Sauvignon (New South Wales) $8. 85 Best Buy —*S.H. (11/15/2004)*

Reynolds 2001 Cabernet Sauvignon (New South Wales) $10. 83 —*S.H. (12/15/2002)*

Reynolds 2001 Reserve Cabernet Sauvignon (Orange) $15. 86 *(9/1/2003)*

Reynolds 2002 Chardonnay (New South Wales) $10. 86 —*D.T. (12/31/2003)*

Reynolds 2001 Chardonnay (New South Wales) $10. 88 Best Buy —*J.C. (7/1/2002)*

Reynolds 2002 Reserve Chardonnay (Orange) $15. 87 *(9/1/2003)*

Reynolds 2001 Merlot (New South Wales) $10. 85 —*S.H. (12/15/2002)*

Reynolds 2001 Reserve Merlot (Orange) $15. 85 *(9/1/2003)*

Reynolds 2002 Sauvignon Blanc (New South Wales) $10. 87 Best Buy —*S.H. (3/1/2003)*

Reynolds 2002 Reserve Sauvignon Blanc (Orange) $15. 84 *(9/1/2003)*

Reynolds 2001 Shiraz (New South Wales) $10. 85 Best Buy —*S.H. (12/15/2002)*

Reynolds 2001 Reserve Shiraz (Orange) $15. 87 *(9/1/2003)*

RIBBONVALE

Ribbonvale 1998 Cabernet Sauvignon-Merlot (Margaret River) $18. 90 —*D.T. (10/1/2003)*

RICHARD HAMILTON

Richard Hamilton 2004 Colton's GSM Rhône Red Blend (McLaren Vale) $18. This wine shows the same intensity as the Gumprs' Shiraz but with a softer, more approachable structure, making it a great value for consumers who don't wish to delay their gratification. Notes of chocolate, blueberry, leather, black pepper and licorice are mouthfilling without being either heavy or overly soft, while the finish is long and lush. It's layered, balanced and complex—all for under $20. 91 Editors' Choice —*J.C. (6/1/2007)*

Richard Hamilton 2006 Slate Quarry Riesling (McLaren Vale) $16. An expressive Riesling, starting with its assertively floral aromas and backed by bold flavors of peaches, apples and mixed citrus fruits. It's a bit plumper than many Australian Rieslings, with an appealingly wooly texture to the lengthy finish. 89 —*J.C. (6/1/2007)*

Richard Hamilton 2005 Gumprs' Shiraz (McLaren Vale) $18. Full-bodied and lushly textured, this is a bold, lusty Shiraz that has been heavily dosed with oak, yet features fruit intensity to match. Toasted coconut and vanilla notes frame the nose, picking up hints of smoke and leather, but the fruit pours through on the palate, adding flavors of crushed blueberries. Has enough structure to suggesting aging another few years, although tannin pigs may want to slurp it down now. 91 Editors' Choice —*J.C. (6/1/2007)*

RIDDOCH ESTATE

Riddoch Estate 2002 Katnook Estate Cabernet Sauvignon-Merlot (Coonawarra) $45. 88 —*D.T. (5/1/2005)*

Riddoch Estate 2000 Katnook Estate Cabernet Sauvignon-Merlot (Coonawarra) $11. 87 —*D.T. (6/1/2003)*

Riddoch Estate 2001 Cabernet Sauvignon-Shiraz (Coonawarra) $11. 87 Best Buy —*D.T. (12/31/2004)*

Riddoch Estate 2000 Katnook Estate Cabernet Sauvignon-Shiraz (Coonawarra) $11. 88 Best Buy —*D.T. (12/31/2003)*

Riddoch Estate 1996 Shiraz (Coonawarra) $18. 88 *(10/1/2000)*

RINGBOLT

Ringbolt 2002 Cabernet Sauvignon (Margaret River) $15. 87 —*D.T. (5/1/2005)*

Ringbolt 2001 Cabernet Sauvignon (Margaret River) $14. 89 Best Buy —*D.T. (2/1/2004)*

Ringbolt 2001 Cabernet Sauvignon (Margaret River) $15. 88 —*D.T. (10/1/2003)*

RIPE

Ripe 1999 Chardonnay (Hunter Valley) $10. 85 —*J.C. (7/1/2002)*

RIVERINA ESTATES

Riverina Estates 2002 Kanga's Leap Cabernet Sauvignon (South Eastern Australia) $8. 82 —*D.T. (8/1/2003)*

Riverina Estates 2002 Bushman's Gully Chardonnay (South Eastern Australia) $7. 83 *(7/2/2004)*

Riverina Estates 2001 Lizard Ridge Chardonnay (South Eastern Australia) $7. 84 *(7/2/2004)*

Riverina Estates 2001 Lombard Station Premium Selection Chardonnay (South Eastern Australia) $10. 84 *(7/2/2004)*

Riverina Estates 2001 Warburn Chardonnay (New South Wales) $10. 86 —*D.T. (8/1/2003)*

Riverina Estates 2001 Lombard Station Premium Selection Merlot (South Eastern Australia) $9. 85 —*D.T. (10/1/2003)*

Riverina Estates 2001 Warburn Semillon (South Eastern Australia) $10. 83 —*D.T. (9/1/2004)*

Riverina Estates 2001 Warburn Semillon (New South Wales) $10. 86 Best Buy —*D.T. (11/15/2004)*

Riverina Estates 2003 Bushman's Gully Semillon-Chardonnay (South Eastern Australia) $7. 86 Best Buy —*D.T. (11/15/2004)*

Riverina Estates 2001 Lombard Station Premium Selection Semillon-Chardonnay (South Eastern Australia) $9. 85 —*D.T. (11/15/2003)*

Riverina Estates 2000 1164 Family Reserve Shiraz (South Eastern Australia) $30. 87 —*D.T. (12/31/2003)*

Riverina Estates 1998 1164 Family Reserve Shiraz (Riverina) $29. 88 —*M.S. (3/1/2003)*

Riverina Estates 2002 Bushman's Gully Shiraz (South Eastern Australia) $7. 84 Best Buy —*D.T. (12/31/2004)*

Riverina Estates 2002 Kanga's Leap Shiraz (South Eastern Australia) $7. 83 —*D.T. (9/1/2004)*

Riverina Estates 2001 Warburn Shiraz (New South Wales) $10. 84 —*D.T. (5/1/2005)*

Riverina Estates 2000 Warburn Show Reserve Shiraz (Riverina) $15. 81 —*D.T. (1/28/2003)*

Riverina Estates 2001 Bushman's Gully Shiraz-Cabernet Sauvignon (South Eastern Australia) $6. 85 —*D.T. (10/1/2003)*

ROBINVALE

Robinvale 2003 Shiraz-Cabernet Sauvignon-Merlot Red Blend (Victoria) $20. 85 —*D.T. (12/31/2005)*

ROCKBARE

RockBare 2005 Chardonnay (McLaren Vale) $16. A broad, weighty wine, marked by toasty, cereal-grain aromas and flavors. The fruit is relatively modest, but tends toward melon and fig, with vanilla and spice notes filling in the holes. A bit short on the finish. 85 —*J.C. (2/1/2007)*

RockBare 2003 Chardonnay (McLaren Vale) $13. 86 *(7/2/2004)*

RockBare 2002 Chardonnay (McLaren Vale) $12. 85 —*S.H. (10/1/2003)*

RockBare 2001 Chardonnay (McLaren Vale) $12. 85 —*J.C. (9/10/2002)*

RockBare 2004 Shiraz (McLaren Vale) $17. A fine example of the style that has come to typify Australian Shiraz, this is a round, lush wine, bursting with ripe berry and plum fruit and lashings of vanilla. There's not a huge amount of complexity or structure, just mouthfilling fruit and oak. Drink now. 87 —*J.C. (2/1/2007)*

RockBare 2002 Shiraz (McLaren Vale) $15. 85 —*S.H. (10/1/2003)*

ROCKFORD

Rockford 2004 Alicante Bouschet (Barossa Valley) $NA. 89 —*D.T. (3/1/2005)*

Rockford 2001 Rod & Spur Cabernet Blend (Barossa Valley) $NA. 93 —*D.T. (2/1/2004)*

Rockford 2003 Rifle Range Cabernet Sauvignon (Barossa Valley) $NA. Despite a challenging year in the Barossa, especially for Cabernet, this is a charming, medium-bodied wine that should drink well for the next 8 years or so. Aromas are slightly leafy and herbal, but also feature plenty of red currant fruit, while the tannins are well-ripened but still show typical Cab structure. Long on the finish. 92 —*J.C. (11/1/2007)*

Rockford 2001 Rifle Ranch Cabernet Sauvignon (Barossa Valley) $40. 94 Editors' Choice —*D.T. (2/1/2004)*

Rockford 2002 Rifle Range Cabernet Sauvignon (Barossa Valley) $53. 93 —*D.T. (8/1/2005)*

Rockford 2000 Moppa Springs GSM Grenache-Shiraz (Barossa Valley) $40. 90 —*D.T. (3/1/2005)*

Rockford 2003 Moppa Springs G-M-S Rhône Red Blend (Barossa Valley) $NA. In contrast to many of the Barossa's Grenache-dominant blends, this is not a punchy, fruity, glug-it-down style. In fact, the operative word here is delicate, referring to the intricate interplay of spice, tea, herbs, rose petals and red cherries on the nose and the silky tannins on the palate. Drink now–2015, and serve it with some of the same dishes you might pair with Pinot Noir, such as veal or poultry. 92 —*J.C. (11/1/2007)*

Rockford 1999 Moppa Springs Red Blend (Barossa Valley) $30. 92 —*D.T. (2/1/2004)*

Rockford 2001 Hand Picked Riesling (Eden Valley) $25. 92 Editors' Choice —*D.T. (2/1/2004)*

Rockford 2000 Semillon (Barossa Valley) $25. 90 —*D.T. (2/1/2004)*

Rockford 2004 Basket Press Shiraz (Barossa Valley) $NA. This superb wine features elements of cola, smoke and earth, but rising above all is the wonderfully pure raspberry fruit. Delicate in texture, with a long, silky finish, this is almost Burgundian in style, not a huge blockbuster, but a model of elegance and finesse. Drinks well now, but as a recent taste of the '96 showed, these are wines that can age 10 years past the vintage with ease. 94 —*J.C. (11/1/2007)*

Rockford 2001 Basket Press Shiraz (Barossa Valley) $55. 93 —*D.T. (2/1/2004)*

Rockford NV Black Shiraz (Barossa Valley) $NA. 92 —*D.T. (2/1/2004)*

Rockford 2004 Rod & Spur Shiraz-Cabernet Sauvignon (Barossa Valley) $NA. The blend is 55-45 in favor of the Shiraz, but the Cabernet imparts a dusty, minty note to the aromas that extends right through the lingering finish, buffered by plenty of ripe cherry flavors from the Shiraz. Like all of the Rockford wines, there's a delicacy to the style, with no excessive extraction, alcohol or harsh tannins. Drink now–2015. 90 —*J.C.* *(11/1/2007)*

ROCKY GULLY

Rocky Gully 2005 Riesling (Frankland River) $14. Produced by Frankland Estate, this is a full-bodied, richly textured Riesling with aromas and flavors of honey, crushed stone and citrus. It's surprisingly long on the finish. Imported by USA Wine West. 90 Best Buy —*J.C. (8/1/2007)*

Rocky Gully 2004 Dry Riesling (Frankland River) $14. 88 —*D.T. (10/1/2005)*

Rocky Gully 2004 Shiraz (Frankland River) $14. 85 —*D.T. (12/1/2005)*

Rocky Gully 2005 Shiraz-Viognier (Frankland River) $15. It may be a bit chunky and lacking grace, but this wine still offers a mouthful of authoritative flavors, ranging from blackberry to prune and from chocolate to black olive, ending on a note of scorched coffee or chocolate. 84 —*J.C. (11/15/2007)*

Rocky Gully 2004 Shiraz-Viognier (Frankland River) $14. A bit floral and peppery, with meat and mixed berry flavors as well. Easy quaffing, and nicely complex at this price point. 87 —*J.C. (6/1/2007)*

ROLF BINDER

Rolf Binder 2004 Heinrich Shiraz-Grenache-Mataro Rhône Red Blend (Barossa Valley) $14. Winemaker Rolf Binder's tribute to his father is this blend of 45% Shiraz, 35% Grenache and 20% Mataro, a Côtes du Rhône-style offering. For the price, it's a worthy effort, featuring scents and flavors of blackberry and cherry liqueur, vanilla and a hint of green peppercorn. The texture is creamy-smooth, and the only quibble is the touch of alcoholic warmth that shows through on the finish. Drink now. 87 —*J.C. (3/1/2007)*

Rolf Binder 2005 Heinrich Shiraz-Mataro-Grenache Rhône Red Blend (Barossa Valley) $28. A blend of 55% Shiraz, 30% Mataro and 15% Grenache, the 2005 Heinrich is a hauntingly complex wine, featuring cedar and floral notes on the nose, followed up on the palate by flavors reminiscent of sandalwood, Asian spices and dusty earth, with just enough cherry fruit to pull it all together. Tannins are soft, the finish long and supple. Drink now–2015. 92 Editors' Choice —*J.C. (11/1/2007)*

Rolf Binder 2003 Hales Shiraz (Barossa Valley) $20. This is from Barossa, but the bouquet is more like that of a cool-climate Shiraz, packed with pepper and herbs that accent red berries. Flavors are meaty and spice-driven, backed by ample berry fruit and wrapped in a creamy cloak of soft tannins. Nicely complex, especially at the realistic price point. Drink now–2012. 90 Editors' Choice —*J.C. (2/1/2007)*

Rolf Binder 2005 Heysen Shiraz (Barossa Valley) $45. Somehow winemaker Rolf Binder manages to combine cool, savory aspects with bold, ripe-fruit flavors. The 2005 Heysen marries cinnamon, clove and peppery spice with blackberries and plums, tying it all together with a robe of vanilla and chocolaty oak and finishing with a hint of espresso. This is a creamy, full-bodied wine whose fruit conceals considerable tannin; drink 2010–2020. 93 Editors' Choice —*J.C. (11/1/2007)*

Rolf Binder 2005 Halliwell Shiraz-Grenache (Barossa Valley) $22. This is 60% Shiraz and 40% Grenache, with the Grenache providing some volume and roundness while the Shiraz provides the more assertive flavor notes. It's a heady blend of sweet—cola—and savory—black olive and coffee—notes, with a long, supple finish. Drink now–2015. 91 Editors' Choice —*J.C. (11/1/2007)*

Rolf Binder 2004 Halliwell Shiraz-Grenache (Barossa Valley) $14. Rolf Binder's eponymous wines used to be sold under the Veritas label, but now his name is front and center. This entry-level Shiraz-Grenache offers a great introduction to the Binder style, combining a velvety mouthfeel with elegant notes of spice and earth. There's black and plum fruit, but uncommon complexity for an Australian wine in this price range. 88 —*J.C. (2/1/2007)*

ROLLING

Rolling 2006 Chardonnay (Central Ranges) $10. Light and fresh, with simple but clean and well-crafted apple and citrus flavors. It's a good picnic or lunch wine, paired with chicken salad or grilled chicken breast. 85 Best Buy *(9/1/2007)*

Rolling 2005 Chardonnay (Central Ranges) $13. 86 —*D.T. (8/1/2006)*

Rolling 2005 Sauvignon Blanc-Semillon (Central Ranges) $13. 87 —*D.T. (8/1/2006)*

Rolling 2005 Shiraz (Central Ranges) $10. An easy-drinking Shiraz, with crisp, well-defined blueberry fruit, a smear of chocolate and a twist of cracked pepper. Not much in the way of tannin, so drink now. 86 Best Buy *(9/1/2007)*

Rolling 2004 Shiraz (Central Ranges) $13. 84 —*D.T. (11/15/2006)*

ROSEMOUNT

Rosemount 1996 Traditional Bordeaux Blend (McLaren Vale) $21. 89 *(11/15/1999)*

Rosemount 2001 Traditional Cabernet Blend (McLaren Vale & Langhorne Creek) $30. 89 —*D.T. (5/1/2004)*

Rosemount 1999 Traditional Cabernet Blend (McLaren Vale & Langhorne Creek) $7. 88 —*C.S. (12/15/2002)*

Rosemount 2005 Cabernet Sauvignon (South Eastern Australia) $12. Plump, soft and friendly, this is a prime example of the easy-drinking wines that Rosemount is turning out. There's plenty of cassis fruit, along with hints of chocolate, plum and a hint of mint. 86 *(8/1/2007)*

Rosemount 2002 Cabernet Sauvignon (South Eastern Australia) $12. 84 —*D.T. (3/1/2005)*

Rosemount 1996 Cabernet Sauvignon (South Eastern Australia) $11. 87 *(11/15/1999)*

Rosemount 2001 Diamond Label Cabernet Sauvignon (South Eastern Australia) $11. 86 —*D.T. (12/31/2003)*

Rosemount 2003 Hill of Gold Cabernet Sauvignon (Mudgee) $17. Unlike some other vintages of this wine, which have seemed a bit hard, this effort is full-bodied and lush, albeit a bit unstructured. The result is a softly tannic mouthful of cola, black currant and dried-spice flavors that would be a fine companion to tonight's grilled steak. Good now. 87 —*J.C. (2/1/2007)*

Rosemount 2002 Hill of Gold Cabernet Sauvignon (Mudgee) $17. 88 —*D.T. (9/1/2004)*

Rosemount 2000 Hill of Gold Cabernet Sauvignon (Mudgee) $19. 89 —*M.S. (12/15/2002)*

Rosemount 1999 Hill of Gold Cabernet Sauvignon (Mudgee) $19. 85 —*D.T. (9/1/2001)*

Rosemount 1999 Orange Vineyard Cabernet Sauvignon (McLaren Vale & Langhorne Creek) $30. 82 —*M.S. (12/15/2002)*

Rosemount 2002 Show Reserve Cabernet Sauvignon (Coonawarra) $24. 87 —*D.T. (12/1/2005)*

Rosemount 2001 Show Reserve Cabernet Sauvignon (Coonawarra) $24. 90 —*D.T. (8/1/2005)*

Rosemount 2000 Show Reserve Cabernet Sauvignon (Coonawarra) $24. 90 Editors' Choice —*D.T. (10/1/2003)*

Rosemount 1998 Show Reserve Cabernet Sauvignon (Coonawarra) $24. 90 —*S.H. (6/1/2001)*

Rosemount 2000 Cabernet Sauvignon-Merlot (South Eastern Australia) $8. 86 —*S.H. (6/1/2001)*

Rosemount 2001 Estate Bottled Cabernet Sauvignon-Merlot (South Eastern Australia) $9. 86 Best Buy —*M.S. (12/15/2002)*

Rosemount 1997 Mountain Blue Cabernet Sauvignon-Shiraz (Mudgee) $40. 89 —*M.S. (10/1/2000)*

Rosemount 2006 Chardonnay (South Eastern Australia) $12. Broad and mouthcoating, this wine displays ample weight and texture and bold, authoritative flavors. Melon, pear and dried spices mingle easily on the palate. 86 *(8/1/2007)*

Rosemount 2003 Chardonnay (South Eastern Australia) $10. 84 —*D.T. (12/31/2004)*

Rosemount 1999 Chardonnay (South Eastern Australia) $12. 85 —*M.M. (10/1/2000)*

Rosemount 2004 Diamond Label Chardonnay (South Eastern Australia) $10. 84 —*D.T. (10/1/2005)*

Rosemount 2003 Diamond Label Chardonnay (South Eastern Australia) $10. 86 Best Buy *(7/2/2004)*

Rosemount 2002 Diamond Label Chardonnay (South Eastern Australia) $10. 86 —*D.T. (8/1/2003)*

Rosemount 2000 Diamond Label Chardonnay (South Eastern Australia) $10. 88 Best Buy —*S.H. (9/1/2001)*

Rosemount 2000 Estate Bottled Chardonnay (South Eastern Australia) $10. 86 —*M.M. (6/1/2001)*

Rosemount 1998 Giant's Creek Chardonnay (Hunter Valley) $17. 87 —*S.H. (6/1/2001)*

Rosemount 2002 Giants Creek Chardonnay (Hunter Valley) $17. 85 *(7/2/2004)*

Rosemount 2001 Giants Creek Chardonnay (Hunter Valley) $17. 88 *(2/1/2003)*

Rosemount 1999 Giants Creek Chardonnay (Hunter Valley) $17. 84 —*J.C. (7/1/2002)*

Rosemount 2004 Hill of Gold Chardonnay (Mudgee) $13. 86 —*D.T. (8/1/2006)*

Rosemount 2002 Hill of Gold Chardonnay (Mudgee) $17. 87 *—D.T. (10/1/2003)*

Rosemount 2001 Hill of Gold Chardonnay (Mudgee) $17. 85 *—J.C. (7/1/2002)*

Rosemount 2000 Hill of Gold Chardonnay (Mudgee) $17. 82 *—D.T. (9/1/2001)*

Rosemount 2002 Orange Vineyard Chardonnay (Orange) $23. 85 *(7/2/2004)*

Rosemount 2001 Orange Vineyard Chardonnay (Orange) $22. 88 *(2/1/2003)*

Rosemount 1998 Orange Vineyard Chardonnay (Hunter Valley) $22. 91 *(11/15/1999)*

Rosemount 1999 Rose Label Orange Vineyard Chardonnay (Orange) $23. 91 Editors' Choice *—S.H. (9/1/2001)*

Rosemount 2002 Roxburgh Chardonnay (Hunter Valley) $25. 89 *—D.T. (4/1/2006)*

Rosemount 2001 Roxburgh Chardonnay (Hunter Valley) $30. 89 *(2/1/2003)*

Rosemount 1998 Roxburgh Chardonnay (Hunter Valley) $30. 86 *—S.H. (9/1/2001)*

Rosemount 2005 Show Reserve Chardonnay (Hunter Valley) $20. A disappointing effort, this is a rather simple, one-dimensional wine this vintage, with buttered pear and peach flavors and hints of smoke that are pleasant enough but lack depth and richness. 84 *—J.C. (2/1/2007)*

Rosemount 2004 Show Reserve Chardonnay (Hunter Valley) $20. 87 *—D.T. (4/1/2006)*

Rosemount 2003 Show Reserve Chardonnay (Hunter Valley) $20. 87 *—D.T. (10/1/2005)*

Rosemount 2002 Show Reserve Chardonnay (Hunter Valley) $15. 85 *(7/2/2004)*

Rosemount 2001 Show Reserve Chardonnay (Hunter Valley) $18. 86 *(2/1/2003)*

Rosemount 1999 Show Reserve Chardonnay (Hunter Valley) $18. 92 Editors' Choice *—S.H. (6/1/2001)*

Rosemount 2002 Giants Creek Chardonnay-Viognier (Hunter Valley) $17. 88 *—D.T. (4/1/2006)*

Rosemount 2002 Merlot (South Eastern Australia) $12. 84 *—D.T. (3/1/2005)*

Rosemount 2003 Diamond Label Merlot (South Eastern Australia) $12. 83 *—D.T. (12/31/2005)*

Rosemount 2000 Diamond Label Merlot (South Eastern Australia) $11. 86 *—D.T. (6/1/2003)*

Rosemount 1999 Diamond Label Merlot (South Eastern Australia) $11. 87 Best Buy *—S.H. (9/1/2001)*

Rosemount 1999 Orange Vineyard Merlot (Orange) $26. 86 *—D.T. (6/1/2003)*

Rosemount 1998 Orange Vineyard Merlot (Orange) $26. 89 *(9/1/2001)*

Rosemount 2006 Pinot Grigio (South Eastern Australia) $12. A wine that's been under development at Rosemount for three years, this is the variety's debut under the Rosemount label. It's plump and round in the mouth, featuring honey and peach notes that turn crisper on the finish. 86 *(8/1/2007)*

Rosemount 2004 Pinot Noir (South Eastern Australia) $12. 84 *—D.T. (12/1/2005)*

Rosemount 2003 Pinot Noir (South Eastern Australia) $12. 84 *—D.T. (12/31/2004)*

Rosemount 2005 Diamond Label Pinot Noir (South Eastern Australia) $12. 84 *—D.T. (11/15/2006)*

Rosemount 2001 Diamond Label Pinot Noir (South Eastern Australia) $12. 83 *—J.C. (9/1/2002)*

Rosemount 1999 Diamond Label Pinot Noir (South Eastern Australia) $12. 87 Best Buy *—S.H. (9/1/2001)*

Rosemount 2001 Grenache-Shiraz Red Blend (Australia) $9. 83 *—J.C. (9/1/2002)*

Rosemount 2000 Grenache-Shiraz Rhône Red Blend (South Eastern Australia) $8. 87 Best Buy *—J.C. (9/1/2001)*

Rosemount 2003 GSM (McLaren Vale) $22. The star of the Rosemount lineup for its excellent quality-price ratio, this is a spicy, peppery wine that's infinitely more complex than the diamond-label offerings. The mouthfeel is creamy smooth, while dark flavors of plum and cola are framed by touches of tree bark. Drink now–2010. 90 Editors' Choice *(8/1/2007)*

Rosemount 2001 GSM Rhône Red Blend (McLaren Vale & Langhorne Creek) $30. 89 *—D.T. (5/1/2004)*

Rosemount 2000 GSM Grenache Syrah Mouvedre Red Blend (Barossa Valley) $30. 89 *(2/1/2003)*

Rosemount 1999 GSM Grenache Syrah Mourvedre Red Blend (McLaren Vale) $30. 90 *—J.C. (9/1/2002)*

Rosemount 2003 Riesling (South Eastern Australia) $10. 87 Best Buy *—D.T. (3/1/2005)*

Rosemount 2005 Diamond Label Riesling (South Eastern Australia) $10. 85 Best Buy *—D.T. (4/1/2006)*

Rosemount 2004 Diamond Label Riesling (South Eastern Australia) $10. 85 Best Buy *—D.T. (12/1/2005)*

Rosemount 2001 Estate Bottled Riesling (South Eastern Australia) $9. 86 *—D.T. (8/1/2003)*

Rosemount 2005 Sauvignon Blanc (South Eastern Australia) $12. Fairly weighty, but with typical gooseberry and pink grapefruit aromas and flavors. A full-flavored style, but one that seems a touch simple and maybe even a bit high in alcohol as well. 85 *(8/1/2007)*

Rosemount 2002 Sauvignon Blanc (South Eastern Australia) $10. 85 *—D.T. (10/1/2003)*

Rosemount 2001 Sauvignon Blanc (South Eastern Australia) $10. 84 *—D.T. (2/1/2002)*

Rosemount 2000 Estate Bottled Sauvignon Blanc (South Eastern Australia) $10. 85 *—J.F. (9/1/2001)*

Rosemount 2003 Semillon (South Eastern Australia) $10. 85 Best Buy *—D.T. (8/1/2005)*

Rosemount 2000 Semillon (South Eastern Australia) $NA. 82 *—D.T. (2/1/2002)*

Rosemount 2000 Diamond Label Bottled Semillon (South Eastern Australia) $10. 85 *—J.C. (9/1/2001)*

Rosemount 2002 Semillon-Chardonnay (South Eastern Australia) $8. 86 Best Buy *—D.T. (10/1/2003)*

Rosemount 2005 Shiraz (South Eastern Australia) $12. Round and accessible, this is another easy-drinking wine from Rosemount. Blackberry, plum and dried spice flavors are varietally correct and displayed on a couch of soft tannins. 85 *(8/1/2007)*

Rosemount 2003 Shiraz (South Eastern Australia) $12. 87 Best Buy *—D.T. (3/1/2005)*

Rosemount 2004 Diamond Label Shiraz (South Eastern Australia) $12. 82 *—D.T. (10/1/2006)*

Rosemount 2002 Diamond Label Shiraz (South Eastern Australia) $12. 85 *—D.T. (10/1/2003)*

Rosemount 2001 Diamond Label Shiraz (South Eastern Australia) $12. 87 *—J.C. (9/1/2002)*

Rosemount 1999 Diamond Label Shiraz (South Eastern Australia) $11. 87 Best Buy *—M.S. (10/1/2000)*

Rosemount 2001 Estate Bottled Shiraz (South Eastern Australia) $10. 86 *—M.S. (3/1/2003)*

Rosemount 2003 Hill of Gold Shiraz (Mudgee) $17. 85 *—D.T. (10/1/2005)*

Rosemount 2002 Hill of Gold Shiraz (Mudgee) $17. 86 *—D.T. (11/15/2004)*

Rosemount 2000 Hill of Gold Shiraz (Mudgee) $19. 86 *(2/1/2003)*

Rosemount 1999 Hill of Gold Shiraz (Mudgee) $18. 89 Editors' Choice *(10/1/2001)*

Rosemount 1999 Orange Vineyard Shiraz (Orange) $26. 87 *—J.M. (12/15/2002)*

Rosemount 2001 Show Reserve Shiraz (South Australia) $24. 86 *—D.T. (12/31/2005)*

Rosemount 2000 Show Reserve Shiraz (McLaren Vale & Langhorne Creek) $24. 88 *—D.T. (6/1/2003)*

Rosemount 1999 Show Reserve Shiraz (McLaren Vale & Langhorne Creek) $24. 86 *(2/1/2003)*

Rosemount 2001 Estate Bottled Shiraz-Cabernet Sauvignon (South Australia/Victoria) $8. 87 Best Buy *—S.H. (11/15/2002)*

Rosemount 1999 Mountain Blue Shiraz-Cabernet Sauvignon (Mudgee) $50. 91 *(2/1/2003)*

Rosemount 2002 Balmoral Shiraz (McLaren Vale) $45. An interesting wine, in that it doesn't fit the current rage for blockbuster Shiraz. As winemaker Charles Whish says, "It doesn't have to be huge and rich and jammy—it needs to have finesse and length." This vintage does show a slightly lifted, vinyl-like note on the nose, but then settles down to offer elegant flavors of plum, spice and vanilla. Finishes long. Drink now–2015. 91 *(8/1/2007)*

Rosemount 2001 Balmoral Syrah (McLaren Vale) $50. 89 *—D.T. (11/15/2006)*

Rosemount 2000 Balmoral Syrah (McLaren Vale) $50. 90 *—D.T. (12/31/2003)*

Rosemount 1999 Balmoral Syrah (McLaren Vale) $50. 92 *(2/1/2003)*

Rosemount 1998 Balmoral Syrah (McLaren Vale) $50. 90 *(11/1/2001)*

Rosemount 1997 Balmoral Syrah (McLaren Vale) $50. 93 *—M.S. (10/1/2000)*

Rosemount 2005 Shiraz-Grenache (South Eastern Australia) $12. The Grenache gives this a slightly softer, rounder profile than the straight Shiraz, while the flavors lean toward plum and cherry. Silky on the finish, but a bit warm from alcohol, also. 85 *(8/1/2007)*

Rosemount 2001 Chardonnay-Semillon White Blend (South Eastern Australia) $8. 85 Best Buy *—D.T. (2/1/2002)*

Rosemount 2002 Diamond Label White Blend (South Eastern Australia) $9. 86 *—D.T. (10/1/2003)*

Rosemount 2002 Diamond Label Chardonnay-Semillon White Blend (South Eastern Australia) $10. 86 *—D.T. (10/1/2003)*

Rosemount 2005 Diamond Label Traminer Riesling White Blend (South Eastern Australia) $10. 81 *—D.T. (8/1/2006)*

Rosemount 2004 Diamond Label Traminer Riesling White Blend (South Eastern Australia) $8. 80 *—D.T. (12/1/2005)*

Rosemount 2002 Estate Bottled Traminer-Riesling White Blend (South Eastern Australia) $9. 83 *—D.T. (10/1/2003)*

Rosemount 2001 Traminer-Riesling White Blend (South Eastern Australia) $8. 83 *—D.T. (2/1/2002)*

ROSENBLUM

Rosenblum 2001 Feather Foot Man Jingalu Special Artist Series Shiraz (McLaren Vale) $31. 90 *—S.H. (1/1/2002)*

ROSS ESTATE

Ross Estate 1999 Bordeaux Blend (Barossa Valley) $20. 85 *—J.C. (6/1/2002)*

Ross Estate 2005 Lynedoch Bordeaux Blend (Barossa Valley) $27. A blend of 40% Cab Sauvignon, 40% Cab Franc and 20% Merlot, this is slightly floral on the nose, but also a touch herbal and exhibits a bit of ash-like Cab Franc character. It does boast a creamy mouthfeel and plenty of ripe cherry fruit, so if you're not averse to some green notes you may like this even more. Drink now–2015. 87 *—J.C. (11/1/2007)*

Ross Estate 2005 Cabernet Sauvignon (Barossa Valley) $27. There's an earthy, dark-humus character that comes through in many of the Ross Estate wines, and this Cabernet shows it as well, blending that with hints of green herbs, chocolate and cassis. It's a bit coarse in texture at this young age; give it another year or two to settle down, then drink it over the next five to six. 86 *—J.C. (11/1/2007)*

Ross Estate 1999 Cabernet Sauvignon (Barossa Valley) $20. 89 *—C.S. (6/1/2002)*

Ross Estate 2001 Chardonnay (Barossa Valley) $12. 87 *—J.C. (7/1/2002)*

Ross Estate 2003 Old Vine Grenache (Barossa Valley) $20. 91 Editors' Choice *—J.C. (12/15/2006)*

Ross Estate 1999 Old Vine Grenache (Barossa Valley) $18. 89 *—J.C. (9/1/2002)*

Ross Estate 2000 Semillon (Barossa Valley) $12. 87 *—J.C. (2/1/2002)*

Ross Estate 2005 Shiraz (Barossa Valley) $27. Displays plenty of cola and earth aromas upfront, balanced by hints of pepper and a core of blackberry fruit. A solid, medium-bodied effort that's not overweight or overripe, just a nice, easy-drinking Shiraz with some earthy character. Drink now–2015. 87 *—J.C. (11/1/2007)*

Ross Estate 2000 Shiraz (Barossa Valley) $20. 87 *—D.T. (3/1/2003)*

Ross Estate 2005 Lights Out Shiraz (Barossa Valley) $17. Expertly combines flavors of licorice, pepper and cherries in a surprisingly elegant format. The ripe tannins impart a silky texture to the wine in the mouth, and the cherries really expand on the finish. Drink now–2012. 88 *—J.C. (11/1/2007)*

Ross Estate 2002 North Ridge Shiraz (Barossa Valley) $18. 91 Editors' Choice *—J.C. (12/15/2006)*

ROTHBURY ESTATE

Rothbury Estate 2001 Cabernet Sauvignon (South Eastern Australia) $7. 87 Best Buy *—D.T. (10/1/2003)*

Rothbury Estate 2002 Chardonnay (South Eastern Australia) $8. 85 *—D.T. (8/1/2003)*

Rothbury Estate 2001 Chardonnay (South Eastern Australia) $8. 90 Best Buy *—J.C. (7/1/2002)*

Rothbury Estate 1998 Chardonnay (South Eastern Australia) $8. 86 Best Buy *—M.S. (10/1/2000)*

Rothbury Estate 2002 Brokenback Chardonnay (Hunter Valley) $30. 84 *(7/2/2004)*

Rothbury Estate 2001 Brokenback Chardonnay (Hunter Valley) $30. 84 *(7/2/2004)*

Rothbury Estate 2001 Shiraz (South Eastern Australia) $7. 85 Best Buy *—S.H. (12/15/2002)*

Rothbury Estate 1999 Brokenback Shiraz (Hunter Valley) $34. 89 *—D.T. (12/31/2003)*

RUFUS STONE

Rufus Stone 1998 Shiraz (McLaren Vale) $30. 88 *(11/1/2001)*

RUMBALL

Rumball NV M3 Coonawarra Cuvée Sparkling Merlot (Coonawarra) $28. 85 *—J.C. (12/31/2006)*

Rumball NV SB13 Sparkling Shiraz (South Eastern Australia) $26. 90 Editors' Choice *—M.M. (12/1/2001)*

Rumball NV SB16 Coonawarra Cuvée Sparkling Shiraz (Coonawarra) $26. 84 *—D.T. (12/31/2004)*

Rumball NV SB17 Coonawarra Cuvée Sparkling Shiraz (Coonawarra) $27. 86 *—J.C. (12/31/2006)*

RUSDEN

Rusden 2005 Chookshed Zinfandel (Barossa Valley) $85. A briary, open-knit Zinfandel with hints of strawberries on the vanilla-scented nose. Juicy and berry-filled on the palate, with ample varietal character, accentuated by zesty acidity on the finish. Drink now–2010. 88 *—J.C. (11/1/2007)*

RUTHERGLEN ESTATES

Rutherglen Estates 2004 Red Red Blend (Rutherglen) $12. 82 *—D.T. (11/15/2006)*

Rutherglen Estates 2004 The Reunion Red Blend (Rutherglen) $15. 87 *—D.T. (4/1/2006)*

Rutherglen Estates 2004 The Alliance White Blend (Rutherglen) $14. 86 *—D.T. (10/1/2006)*

RYMILL

Rymill 1996 Shiraz (Coonawarra) $17. 90 *(4/1/2000)*

SAINT JOHN'S ROAD

Saint John's Road 2003 Old Vine Semillon (Barossa Valley) $20. 84 *—D.T. (3/1/2005)*

SALENA ESTATE

Salena Estate 2001 Cabernet Sauvignon Cabernet Blend (South Australia) $10. 84 *(9/2/2004)*

Salena Estate 2000 Ellen Landing Cabernet Sauvignon (Riverland) $18. 83 *—M.S. (12/15/2002)*

Salena Estate 1999 Ellen Landing Cabernet Sauvignon (South Eastern Australia) $18. 84 *—D.T. (6/1/2002)*

Salena Estate 2003 Chardonnay (Riverland) $10. 86 Best Buy *(7/2/2004)*

Salena Estate 2001 Chardonnay (Riverland) $11. 85 *—J.C. (7/1/2002)*

Salena Estate 2002 Merlot (South Australia) $10. 84 *(9/2/2004)*

Salena Estate 2000 Merlot (Riverland) $11. 86 *—C.S. (6/1/2002)*

Salena Estate 2001 Petite Verdot (South Australia) $10. 86 Best Buy *(9/2/2004)*

Salena Estate 2001 Shiraz (South Australia) $10. 85 *(9/2/2004)*

Salena Estate 1999 Shiraz (Riverland) $12. 89 Best Buy *(10/1/2001)*

SALISBURY

Salisbury 1999 Shiraz (South Eastern Australia) $8. 87 Best Buy *(10/1/2001)*

SANDALFORD

Sandalford 1999 Cabernet Sauvignon (Mount Barker & Margaret River) $22. 90 Editors' Choice *(7/1/2002)*

Sandalford 1998 Cabernet Sauvignon (Western Australia) $24. 88 *(1/1/2004)*

Sandalford 2001 Chardonnay (Western Australia) $21. 88 *(7/1/2002)*

Sandalford 2000 Merlot (Western Australia) $24. 86 *(7/1/2002)*

Sandalford 2001 Riesling (Western Australia) $17. 87 *(7/1/2002)*

Sandalford 2001 Semillon-Sauvignon Blanc (Western Australia) $16. 85 *(7/1/2002)*

Sandalford 1997 Shiraz (Mount Barker & Margaret River) $23. 85 *(4/1/2000)*

Sandalford 1998 Shiraz (Western Australia) $24. 90 *(7/1/2002)*

SANDHURST RIDGE

Sandhurst Ridge 2001 Cabernet Sauvignon (Bendigo) $50. 87 *—D.T. (8/1/2005)*

S.C. PANNELL

S.C. Pannell 2006 Rosé Grenache (McLaren Vale) $17. This is a vibrant wine in every way, from its bright pink color to its bold stone fruit aromas and its tart, mouthwatering finish. Sourced from bushvine Grenache more than 30 years old, there's a touch of minerality to help balance the berry and peach flavors. Drink now. 88 *—J.C. (7/1/2007)*

S.C. Pannell 2005 Shiraz (McLaren Vale) $55. Stephen Pannell's family founded Moss Wood in Western Australia back in 1967, and he's a former chief red winemaker at BRL Hardy. So it's no surprise that his Shiraz is excellent, in a firmly structured, restrained style. Mixed berry fruit is accented by hints of spice and chocolate in this wine that shows more textural interest than overall volume. Best from 2009. 90 *(11/15/2007)*

SCHILD ESTATE

Schild Estate 2004 Cabernet Sauvignon (Barossa) $24. A consistent performer in recent vintages, Schild Estate should be turning heads with values like this. The bouquet is intoxicatingly rich and dense, filled with cassis and chocolate fudge, while the texture in the mouth is supple and creamy. Yet the flavors are surprisingly fresh, offering cassis flavors enlivened with dashes of mint and rhubarb. It's a drink-now style, but a delicious one. 90 Editors' Choice *—J.C. (6/1/2007)*

Schild Estate 2002 Cabernet Sauvignon (Barossa Valley) $24. 84 *—D.T. (5/1/2005)*

Schild Estate 2001 Cabernet Sauvignon (Barossa Valley) $19. 83 *—D.T. (1/1/2002)*

Schild Estate 2002 Merlot (Barossa) $23. A solid effort for an Australian Merlot—not, seemingly, a grape variety that performs its best Down Under. This is leathery and meaty, with hints of Worcestershire layered over slightly pruny fruit. Ultrasupple and creamy, with a coffee-tinged, mouthwatering finish. Drink now. 88 *—J.C. (2/1/2007)*

Schild Estate 2004 Frontignac Muscat Blanc à Petit Grain (Barossa) $14. 84 *—D.T. (11/15/2006)*

Schild Estate 2004 GMS Red Blend (Barossa Valley) $22. 88 *—D.T. (2/1/2006)*

Schild Estate 2006 Old Bush Vine Grenache-Mataro-Shiraz GMS Rhône Red Blend (Barossa) $17. A bargain by Barossa pricing standards—or any standards for that matter—Schild Estate's 2006 GMS combines a slightly herbal note with full-on black cherry flavors, enhanced by hints of licorice and plum. Ample and round, this blend of 50% Grenache, 30% Mataro and 20% Shiraz offers attractive early drinking. 90 Editors' Choice *—J.C. (11/1/2007)*

Schild Estate 2006 Riesling (Barossa) $15. In recent years, Schild Estate is making a slew of tasty wines at consumer-friendly prices. Its 2006 Riesling is cut from similar cloth, offering obvious peach and tropical fruit notes that coat the palate. It's a complex mélange of fruit that finishes with dry, mouthwatering flavors but without any strong sense of minerality. 89 *—J.C. (9/1/2007)*

Schild Estate 2005 Riesling (Barossa) $13. Schild Estate is turning out a bevy of likeable, well-priced wines from the Barossa, including this lime- and mineral-scented Riesling. It adds honey and ripe citrus notes on the palate, then ends crisp, clean and refreshing. Drink over the next few years for its unabashed joyfulness. 88 Best Buy *—J.C. (5/1/2007)*

Schild Estate 2003 Riesling (Barossa Valley) $15. 86 *—D.T. (12/31/2004)*

Schild Estate 2004 Semillon (Barossa Valley) $18. 85 *—D.T. (10/1/2005)*

Schild Estate 2002 Shiraz (Barossa) $24. 88 *—D.T. (12/1/2005)*

Schild Estate 2005 Ben Schild Reserve Shiraz (Barossa) $48. Not quite up to the standards set by the 2004, this is nevertheless an excellent Shiraz, full-bodied and lush. Blackberry fruit dominates the aromas, framed by vanilla and just a touch of dill. Folds in plenty of earthy complexity on the palate, plus hints of cola and coffee, making this more than a simple fruit-and-oak confection. Drink now–2015. 90 *—J.C. (11/1/2007)*

Schild Estate 2004 Ben Schild Reserve Shiraz (Barossa) $48. 94 Editors' Choice *—J.C. (12/15/2006)*

Schild Estate 2003 Ben Schild Reserve Shiraz (Barossa Valley) $65. 86 *—D.T. (12/1/2005)*

Schild Estate 2003 Moorooroo Limited Release Shiraz (Barossa Valley) $85. Creamy-textured, full-bodied and showing a bit of warmth, this is lush and lavishly oaked. Chocolate, vanilla and plum flavors play major roles, with earthier notes, hints of spice and tobacco in support. Likely to mature quickly; drink now–2012. 92 *—J.C. (11/1/2007)*

Schild Estate 2002 Moorooroo Limited Release Shiraz (Barossa Valley) $78. This is a lavishly oaked wine, filled with scents of caramel, nuts, chocolate, toasted coconut, vanilla and coffee. It completely fills the mouth with creamy, lush flavor—a combination of vanilla and fruit syrup, with complexity added by touches of cracked pepper and meat. So easy to drink now; the only question is its future evolution. 92 *—J.C. (6/1/2007)*

Schild Estate 2005 Sparkling Shiraz (Barossa) $24. A soft, easy-drinking sparkling Shiraz, much like Schild's still versions. Toast, vanilla and blackberry aromas and flavors are creamy-textured in the mouth and surprisingly elegant on the finish. 88 *—J.C. (12/31/2007)*

Schild Estate 2004 Sparkling Shiraz (Barossa) $24. 90 Editors' Choice *J.C. (12/31/2006)*

SCREWED

Screwed 2005 Pink Red Blend (McLaren Vale) $10. 82 *—D.T. (11/15/2006)*

Screwed 2004 Red Red Blend (McLaren Vale) $10. 85 Best Buy *—D.T. (11/15/2006)*

Screwed 2005 White Semillon-Chardonnay (McLaren Vale) $10. 85 Best Buy *—D.T. (8/1/2006)*

SEAVIEW

Seaview 1997 Champagne Blend (South Eastern Australia) $10. 87 *(11/15/1999)*

Seaview 2000 Brut Champagne Blend (South Eastern Australia) $9. 85 Best Buy *—S.H. (12/1/2002)*

Seaview 1999 Brut Champagne Blend (South Eastern Australia) $10. 88 Best Buy *(12/1/2001)*

Seaview 1997 Chardonnay (McLaren Vale) $10. 83 *(12/31/1999)*

Seaview NV Brut Sparkling Blend (South Eastern Australia) $10. 84 *—D.T. (12/31/2004)*

SERAFINO

Serafino 2001 Shiraz (McLaren Vale) $20. 89 Editors' Choice *—D.T. (3/1/2005)*

SEXTON

Sexton 2003 Giant Steps Vineyard Chardonnay (Yarra Valley) $25. Smoky oak plays a prominent role in this wine's flavor profile, so if you are oak averse, be warned. There's even some pronounced notes reminiscent of buttered popcorn. But the restrained melon and pear fruit gives the oaky coat some structure, imbuing it with a crisp, tart finish and bringing it to life. 86 *—J.C. (2/1/2007)*

Sexton 2002 Giant Steps Vineyard Chardonnay (Yarra Valley) $35. 86 *(7/2/2004)*

Sexton 2003 Giant Steps Vineyard, Bernard Clones Chardonnay (Yarra Valley) $40. 87 *—D.T. (5/1/2005)*

SHADOWFAX WINES

Shadowfax Wines 2001 Chardonnay (Victoria) $9. 83 *—D.T. (8/1/2003)*

SHALLOW CREEK

Shallow Creek 2002 Shiraz (Victoria) $24. 84 *—D.T. (5/1/2004)*

SHAW AND SMITH

Shaw and Smith 2004 M3 Vineyard Chardonnay (Adelaide Hills) $29. 90 *—D.T. (11/15/2006)*

Shaw and Smith 2003 M3 Vineyard Chardonnay (Adelaide Hills) $29. 90 *—D.T. (8/1/2005)*

Shaw and Smith 2004 Sauvignon Blanc (Adelaide Hills) $19. 90 Editors' Choice *—D.T. (8/1/2005)*

Shaw and Smith 2004 Shiraz (Adelaide Hills) $29. 88 *—D.T. (11/15/2006)*

Shaw and Smith 2003 Shiraz (Adelaide Hills) $29. 88 *—D.T. (8/1/2005)*

SHEEP'S BACK

Sheep's Back 2002 Old Vine Shiraz (Barossa Valley) $20. The best vintage yet for this full-bodied Shiraz boasts complex, pungent aromas of hickory smoke, black pepper, filled out by ripe blackberries. In the mouth it's not quite as complex, but delivers plenty of intensity and a potent dose of supple tannins, ending crisp and clean. 89 *—J.C. (6/1/2007)*

Sheep's Back 2001 Old Vine Shiraz (Barossa Valley) $23. 88 *—D.T. (12/31/2004)*

Sheep's Back 2000 Old Vine Shiraz (Barossa Valley) $23. 86 *—D.T. (12/31/2003)*

SHINGLEBACK

Shingleback 2004 Cabernet Sauvignon (McLaren Vale) $22. This lizard-labeled wine puts other critter wines to shame, offering a complex bouquet of coffee, leather, spice cake and dried fruit. Mouthcoating flavors of dried cherries and plums are framed by coffee, spice and leather and carried across the palate by a lush, softly tannic texture. Drink now–2012. 92 Editors' Choice *—J.C. (2/1/2007)*

Shingleback 2002 Cabernet Sauvignon (McLaren Vale) $19. 89 *—D.T. (12/31/2004)*

Shingleback 2005 Chardonnay (McLaren Vale) $18. 87 *—D.T. (10/1/2006)*

Shingleback 2005 Grenache (McLaren Vale) $22. 87 *—D.T. (11/15/2006)*

Shingleback 2005 Rosé Grenache (McLaren Vale) $17. 87 *—D.T. (6/21/2006)*

Shingleback 2004 Shiraz (McLaren Vale) $22. An excellent value, Shingleback's 2004 Shiraz boasts attractive aromas of mulberries and boysenberries, then follows that up with bold, forward, berry-fruit flavors. But it has nuance, showing deft oaking and hints of spice to balance the fruit's intensity. Long, mouthwatering and complex on the finish, picking up notes of chocolate, coffee and vanilla. Drink now–2012. 91 Editors' Choice *—J.C. (2/1/2007)*

Shingleback 2003 Shiraz (McLaren Vale) $20. 88 *—D.T. (10/1/2005)*

Shingleback 2002 Shiraz (McLaren Vale) $19. 89 *(11/15/2004)*

Shingleback NV Black Bubbles Sparkling Shiraz (McLaren Vale) $20. 86 *—D.T. (12/31/2005)*

Shingleback NV Black Bubbles Sparkling Shiraz (McLaren Vale) $22. 84 *—J.C. (12/31/2006)*

Shingleback 2002 D Block Reserve Shiraz (McLaren Vale) $50. 88 *—D.T. (10/1/2005)*

Shingleback 2001 D Block Reserve Shiraz (McLaren Vale) $40. 90 *(11/15/2004)*

SHOOFLY

Shoofly 2004 Buzz Cut White Blend (South Eastern Australia) $14. 84 *—D.T. (10/1/2006)*

SHOTTESBROOKE

Shottesbrooke 2005 Shiraz (McLaren Vale) $23. Slightly higher-toned than many McLaren Vale Shirazes, with fruit that veers toward raspberry combining with hints of brown sugar, spice and fresh meat. It's medium-bodied but potent, picking up nutty, chocolaty notes on the finsh. Drink now–2013. 89 *—J.C. (8/1/2007)*

Shottesbrooke 2000 Shiraz (South Australia) $17. 88 *—C.S. (3/1/2003)*

Shottesbrooke 2005 Eliza Shiraz (McLaren Vale) $39. Not the biggest, blackest or most extracted Shiraz, this is a more elegant, complex example, boasting hints of violets and espresso on the nose, alongside smoky, meaty notes and plenty of berry fruit. It's fresh and not overly weighty, managing to seem light in weight without being light on flavor. 91 *—J.C. (12/31/2007)*

Shottesbrooke 1998 Eliza Shiraz (McLaren Vale) $30. 90 *(11/1/2001)*

Shottesbrooke 2000 Eliza Reserve Shiraz (McLaren Vale) $30. 91 *—C.S. (3/1/2003)*

SIDESHOW

Sideshow 2004 The Contortionist Red Blend (South Eastern Australia) $9. 86 Best Buy *—D.T. (2/1/2006)*

Sideshow 2004 Queen Roma Riesling (South Eastern Australia) $9. 84 *—D.T. (4/1/2006)*

SILVERWING

Silverwing 2005 Cabernet Sauvignon-Shiraz (Margaret River) $10. 86 Best Buy *—D.T. (8/1/2006)*

Silverwing NV Brut Champagne Blend (Australia) $11. Broad in the mouth and on the sweet side, this Chardonnay-Pinot Noir blend does offer some attractive gingery notes on the nose, while the flavors favor baked apples. 82 *—J.C. (12/31/2007)*

Silverwing 2005 Chardonnay (Yarra Valley) $10. 84 *—D.T. (8/1/2006)*

Silverwing 2004 Pinot Noir (Yarra Valley) $10. 85 Best Buy *—D.T. (11/15/2006)*

Silverwing 2004 Riesling (Adelaide Hills) $13. 87 *—D.T. (8/1/2006)*

SIMON GILBERT

Simon Gilbert 2000 Semillon-Sauvignon Blanc (Hunter Valley) $10. 85 *—J.C. (9/1/2001)*

Simon Gilbert 2004 Central Ranges Semillon-Sauvignon Blanc (New South Wales) $15. 85 *—D.T. (8/1/2006)*

Simon Gilbert 1999 Shiraz (Mudgee) $10. 83 *(10/1/2001)*

Simon Gilbert 1998 Wongalere Shiraz (McLaren Vale) $35. 89 *(11/1/2001)*

Simon Gilbert 2004 Central Ranges Verdelho (New South Wales) $14. 88 *—D.T. (10/1/2006)*

SIMON HACKETT

Simon Hackett 2000 Cabernet Sauvignon (McLaren Vale) $18. 89 *—M.S. (12/15/2002)*

Simon Hackett 1999 Cabernet Sauvignon (McLaren Vale) $18. 90 *(6/1/2001)*

Simon Hackett 1997 Foggo Road Cabernet Sauvignon (McLaren Vale) $38. 92 *(6/1/2001)*

Simon Hackett 1999 Foggo Road Limited Release Cabernet Sauvignon (McLaren Vale) $38. 87 *—D.T. (6/1/2003)*

Simon Hackett 2001 Chardonnay (Barossa Valley) $18. 85 *—D.T. (8/1/2003)*

Simon Hackett 1999 Chardonnay (Barossa Valley) $15. 91 Best Buy *—S.H. (6/1/2001)*

Simon Hackett 2005 Brightview Chardonnay (Barossa Valley) $15. An overt, tropical Chardonnay with oodles of fruit. This is a bit broad and lacking focus despite having hints of quince and a trace of minerality that lend som semblance of structure. Turns a bit sour-citrusy on the finish. 85 *—J.C. (2/1/2007)*

Simon Hackett 2004 Brightview Chardonnay (Barossa Valley) $15. 87 *—D.T. (3/1/2005)*

Simon Hackett 2002 Brightview Chardonnay (Barossa Valley) $15. 85 *(7/2/2004)*

Simon Hackett 2005 Old Vine Grenache (McLaren Vale) $15. A top-notch offering for current consumption, this wine boasts a complex bouquet of black cherries, cinnamon, clove, coffee, vanilla, herbal notes and hints of green peppercorns—it's a wine you can sit and sniff almost endlessly. The flavors are more straightforward—black cherry and spice—while the texture is delicate, almost soft. Drink now. 90 Best Buy *—J.C. (6/1/2007)*

Simon Hackett 2002 Old Vine Grenache (McLaren Vale) $18. 87 *—D.T. (3/1/2005)*

Simon Hackett 2001 Old Vine Grenache (McLaren Vale) $18. 89 *—D.T. (9/1/2004)*

Simon Hackett 2000 Old Vine Grenache (McLaren Vale) $18. 84 *—J.C. (9/1/2002)*

Simon Hackett 2006 Brightview Sémillon (Barossa Valley) $17. Although some Australian Semillons are built to age, this one is immediately accessible, offering stony, minerally scents and flavors that hint of petrol, wet stones and green apples. It's medium-bodied, with a bright finish that manages to be crisp without being sharp or angular. Drink it over the next 2–3 years. 87 *—J.C. (2/1/2007)*

Simon Hackett 2004 Brightview Semillon (Barossa Valley) $15. 88 Editors' Choice *—D.T. (3/1/2005)*

Simon Hackett 2000 Brightview Semillon (Barossa Valley) $15. 90 *—J.C. (2/1/2002)*

Simon Hackett 2002 Shiraz (McLaren Vale) $18. 87 *—D.T. (3/1/2005)*

Simon Hackett 2001 Shiraz (McLaren Vale) $18. 85 *—D.T. (3/1/2003)*

Simon Hackett 2000 Shiraz (McLaren Vale) $18. 85 *(10/1/2001)*

Simon Hackett 1999 Shiraz (McLaren Vale) $18. 89 *(6/1/2001)*

Simon Hackett 1998 Anthony's Reserve Shiraz (McLaren Vale) $38. 92 *(6/1/2001)*

SIMPLICITY

Simplicity 2004 Red Wine Red Blend (McLaren Vale) $10. This unspecified blend of varieties from McLaren Vale is rather crisp, lacking the usual lush mouthfeel of South Australian red wines. There's a bit of a smoky, tarry note on the nose, then high-toned cherry and cranberry fruit, maybe even a touch of rhubarb. Drink now. 84 *—J.C. (3/1/2007)*

Simplicity 2005 Pink Rosé Blend (McLaren Vale) $10. 82 *—D.T. (11/15/2006)*

Simplicity 2005 White Blend (McLaren Vale) $10. 82 *—D.T. (11/15/2006)*

SIRROMET

Sirromet 2002 Seven Scenes Chardonnay (Queensland) $30. 87 *—D.T. (11/15/2006)*

SKILLOGALEE

Skillogalee 2003 Riesling (Clare Valley) $18. 85 *—D.T. (5/1/2004)*

Skillogalee 2001 Shiraz (Clare Valley) $25. 89 *—D.T. (9/1/2004)*

SLIPSTREAM

Slipstream 2005 Fastback Shiraz (McLaren Vale) $30. Crafted by winemaker by Reid Bosward (of Kaesler) and sourced from importer This well-endowed Shiraz should impress novices and connoisseurs alike. Despite 15% alcohol, there's no sensation of untoward heat, just waves of amazingly pure blueberry and blackberry fruit, capably framed by vanilla and baking spices. It's creamy and lush in the mouth, and finishes long, echoing with fruit and spice. Drink now–2013. 93 Editors' Choice —*J.C. (4/1/2007)*

Slipstream 2005 Shiraz-Grenache (McLaren Vale) $18. A blend of 72% Shiraz and 28% Grenache, this wine is full-bodied and creamy, yet has some dusty tannins on the finish. Take scents of prune and anise, add flavors of coffee and vanilla to make a reasonable complex, satisfying blend. Drink now, with rare beef or lamb. 89 —*J.C. (7/1/2007)*

SMITH & HOOPER

Smith & Hooper 2000 Wrattonbully-Limited Edition Merlot (South Australia) $30. 87 —*D.T. (6/1/2003)*

SONS OF EDEN

Sons of Eden 2001 Kennedy Grenache-Syrah (Barossa Valley) $20. 87 —*D.T. (9/1/2004)*

Sons of Eden 2003 Kennedy G-S-M Rhône Red Blend (Barossa Valley) $23. 86 —*D.T. (5/1/2005)*

Sons of Eden 2000 Remus Old Vine Shiraz (Barossa Valley) $40. 88 —*D.T. (6/1/2003)*

SOUTHERN TRACKS

Southern Tracks 2001 Chardonnay (South Eastern Australia) $10. 84 —*D.T. (6/1/2003)*

Southern Tracks 2000 Red Blend (South Eastern Australia) $10. 81 —*M.S. (12/15/2002)*

SPRING VALE

Spring Vale 2005 Gewürztraminer (Tasmania) $35. Plump and a bit sweet, this is a rare example of Australian Gewürztraminer. Smells honeyed yet floral, boasting scents of apples and orange blossom, then offers flavors of ripe apples and a touch of peach, underscored by intense citrus. Long and crisp on the finish. Drink now. 89 —*J.C. (6/1/2007)*

Spring Vale 2005 Pinot Noir (Tasmania) $55. A relatively lush, fruit-forward, modern-style wine that wouldn't be out of place in a lineup of California Pinots. There are hints of graham cracker or pastry crust on the nose to go with oodles of blueberry fruit, and the creamy mouthfeel and supple tannins are just right. Not that complex, but definitely satisfying. 88 —*J.C. (6/1/2007)*

SPRINGWOOD PARK

Springwood Park 1998 Nicholas Shiraz (McLaren Vale) $35. 89 —*D.T. (12/31/2003)*

ST. ANDREWS ESTATE

St. Andrews Estate 2000 Ceravolo Chardonnay (Adelaide Hills) $12. 83 —*J.C. (7/1/2002)*

St. Andrews Estate 2000 Adelaide Plains Shiraz (Adelaide Hills) $22. 89 *(11/1/2001)*

St. Andrews Estate 2000 Ceravolo Shiraz-Cabernet Sauvignon (Adelaide Hills) $20. 88 —*M.S. (3/1/2003)*

ST. HALLETT

St. Hallett 1999 Cabernet Sauvignon (Barossa Valley) $21. 85 —*D.T. (6/1/2002)*

St. Hallett 2005 Gamekeeper's Reserve Shiraz-Grenache Red Blend (Barossa) $12. Only 6% Grenache, so labeling it as a blend seems as much marketing as reality. Seems like a lightweight Shiraz, offering up blueberry and blackberry fruit, a creamy, lush texture but not much depth. Finishes with a touch of spice and mouthwaterng acids. Drink now. 86 —*J.C. (7/1/2007)*

St. Hallett 2002 Gamekeepers Reserve Red Blend (Barossa Valley) $NA. 90 Editors' Choice —*D.T. (2/1/2004)*

St. Hallett 1999 Gamekeeper's Reserve Rhône Red Blend (Barossa Valley) $10. 88 Best Buy —*M.M. (10/1/2000)*

St. Hallett 2006 GST Red Blend (Barossa) $NA. Wine takes its moniker from the blend: Grenache, Shiraz and Touriga Nacional. Lovely aromas of blueberries, flowers and spice lead into a medium-bodied wine that marries a slightly creamy texture with peppery notes. Turns a bit dry and tea-like or herbal on the finish. Drink now–2012. 89 —*J.C. (11/1/2007)*

St. Hallett 2005 Blackwell Shiraz (Barossa) $35. Aged entirely in American oak, and it shows a bit on the nose, where hints of dill and menthol give a greenish tinge to the vanilla and blackberry aromas. Crisp and juicy, with some powdery-textured tannins on the finish that should resolve rapidly over the next few years. 88 —*J.C. (11/1/2007)*

St. Hallett 2004 Blackwell Shiraz (Barossa) $35. At first sniff, this seems overly oaky, stuffed with vanilla, cedar and wood spice, but give it a chance. As it sits in the glass, the fruit begins to emerge, and on the palate, there's ample berry fruit to complement the lavish oak. It's creamy and richly textured, with a layered, vanilla-like finish. Drink now–2012. 91 —*J.C. (5/1/2007)*

St. Hallett 2002 Blackwell Shiraz (Barossa Valley) $39. 91 —*D.T. (3/1/2005)*

St. Hallett 2001 Blackwell Shiraz (Barossa Valley) $30. 90 —*D.T. (2/1/2004)*

St. Hallett 2000 Blackwell Shiraz (Barossa Valley) $30. 90 —*D.T. (5/1/2004)*

St. Hallett 1997 Blackwell Shiraz (Barossa Valley) $25. 90 Cellar Selection —*J.C. (9/1/2002)*

St. Hallett 1998 Blackwell Shiraz (Barossa Valley) $25. 91 —*S.H. (12/15/2002)*

St. Hallett 2005 Faith Shiraz (Barossa) $16. A nicely balanced entry-level Shiraz, this features flavors of blackberries and plums, licorice and spice, yet manages to remain fresh and fruity. Easy to drink now and over the next year or two. 88 —*J.C. (11/1/2007)*

St. Hallett 2004 Faith Shiraz (Barossa) $20. 88 —*D.T. (6/1/2006)*

St. Hallett 2002 Faith Shiraz (Barossa Valley) $20. 88 —*D.T. (2/1/2004)*

St. Hallett 2000 Faith Shiraz (Barossa Valley) $19. 87 —*S.H. (12/15/2002)*

St. Hallett 1999 Faith Shiraz (Barossa Valley) $18. 88 *(10/1/2001)*

St. Hallett 2001 Gamekeepers Shiraz (South Australia) $11. 85 —*S.H. (12/15/2002)*

St. Hallett 2001 Gamekeepers Reserve Shiraz (Barossa Valley) $NA. 88 —*D.T. (2/1/2004)*

St. Hallett 2003 Old Block Shiraz (Barossa) $70. This is not an obviously fruity Shiraz, but it is rich, creamy-textured and individualistic. Scents of café au lait, toffee and milk chocolate add hints of date on the palate, then linger elegantly on the finish. Drink now–2012. 91 —*J.C. (5/1/2007)*

St. Hallett 2002 Old Block Shiraz (Barossa) $64. 92 —*D.T. (6/1/2006)*

St. Hallett 2001 Old Block Shiraz (Barossa Valley) $52. 91 —*D.T. (2/1/2004)*

St. Hallett 2000 Old Block Shiraz (Barossa Valley) $54. 93 —*D.T. (5/1/2004)*

St. Hallett 1997 Old Block Shiraz (Barossa Valley) $40. 92 Editors' Choice *(11/1/2001)*

St. Hallett 1998 Old Block Shiraz (Barossa Valley) $40. 95 Editors' Choice —*S.H. (12/15/2002)*

St. Hallett 2006 Poacher's Blend Semillon-Sauvignon Blanc White Blend (Barossa) $12. There is 8g/L of residual sugar, so some tasters might object to a hint of sweetness, but others will just find it helps to accentuate the wine's fruit-forward nature. Pear and fig flavors pick up some honeyed stone fruit notes on the palate but this is nicely balanced and easy to drink. 87 Best Buy —*J.C. (11/15/2007)*

St. Hallett 2003 Poacher's Blend White Blend (Barossa Valley) $NA. 88 —*D.T. (2/1/2004)*

St. Hallett 2001 Poachers Blend White Blend (South Australia) $10. 88 —*S.H. (1/1/2002)*

ST. MARYS

St. Marys 1999 House Block Cabernet Sauvignon (Coonawarra) $20. 85 —*C.S. (6/1/2002)*

St. Marys 2004 Bells & Whistles Red Blend (Limestone Coast) $19. This blend of Cabernet Sauvignon (55%), Shiraz (20%), Cabernet Franc (15%) and Merlot (10%) features inviting aromas of cherries, cola, dried spices and vanilla. The flavors are similar, but with more accent on strident red cherries and cranberries, finishing crisp and firm. Drink now–2010. 86 —*J.C. (3/1/2007)*

St. Marys 1999 Shiraz (Coonawarra) $19. 87 *(10/1/2001)*

St. Marys 2000 Shiraz (Limestone Coast) $20. 88 —*M.S. (3/1/2003)*

STANLEY BROTHERS

Stanley Brothers 1998 Thoroughbred Cabernet Sauvignon (Barossa Valley) $22. 87 —*C.S. (6/1/2002)*

Stanley Brothers 1999 Pristine Chardonnay (Barossa Valley) $16. 85 —*J.C. (7/1/2002)*

Stanley Brothers 1998 Pristine Chardonnay (Barossa Valley) $15. 86 —*M.M. (10/1/2000)*

Stanley Brothers 1999 Black Sheep Red Blend (Barossa Valley) $18. 85 —*M.S. (12/15/2002)*

Stanley Brothers 1998 Black Sheep Red Blend (Barossa Valley) $16. 86 —*M.S. (10/1/2000)*

Stanley Brothers 1999 John Hancock Shiraz (Barossa Valley) $24. 88 —*D.T. (3/1/2003)*

STANLEY LAMBERT

Stanley Lambert 2002 Mustang Sally Shiraz (South Australia) $13. Brown sugar and cherry flavors also boast a notable tomato-herbal tinge. Creamy and supple on the palate, this wine's texture is almost slightly syrupy, picking up a dry, peppery edge on the finish. Imported by AUSA Pacific, LLC. 84 *—J.C. (11/15/2007)*

Stanley Lambert 2004 The Family Tree Individual Vineyard Shiraz (Barossa Valley) $80. This is traditional Barossa Shiraz, aged in new American oak hogsheads, which have imparted a thick layer of vanilla and dill over the top of some lovely blackberry-tinged fruit. The texture is creamy, the tannins, supple, the finish infused with notes of coffee, spun sugar and spice. Drink now–2014, possibly longer. Imported by AUSA Pacific, LLC. 90 *—J.C. (11/1/2007)*

STANTON & KILLEEN

Stanton & Killeen NV Classic Muscat (Rutherglen) $35. Dark amber in color, this example of classic Muscat is wonderfully balanced between the freshness of youth and the power and complexity of age. Raisin, malt and Guinness stout-like notes meet vibrant orange-zest and honey characters in a sweet, harmonious whole. 92 *—J.C. (12/15/2007)*

Stanton & Killeen NV Classic Tokay (Rutherglen) $35. Powerful tea and bergamot notes are fresh and orangey, balancing deeper, richer notes of toffee and honey. Long on the finish, and not overly sweet. 89 *—J.C. (12/15/2007)*

STARVEDOG LANE

Starvedog Lane 1999 Cabernet Sauvignon (Adelaide Hills) $23. 84 *—D.T. (6/1/2003)*

Starvedog Lane 2001 Chardonnay (Adelaide Hills) $17. 86 *(7/2/2004)*

Starvedog Lane 2000 Chardonnay (Adelaide Hills) $19. 84 *—D.T. (8/1/2003)*

Starvedog Lane 2004 No Oak Chardonnay (Adelaide Hills) $15. 85 *—D.T. (8/1/2005)*

Starvedog Lane 2003 Shiraz-Viognier Rhône Red Blend (Adelaide Hills) $15. 86 *—D.T. (8/1/2005)*

Starvedog Lane 2004 Sauvignon Blanc (Adelaide Hills) $15. 86 *—D.T. (8/1/2005)*

Starvedog Lane 2003 Sauvignon Blanc (Adelaide Hills) $15. 87 *—D.T. (9/1/2004)*

Starvedog Lane 1999 Shiraz (Adelaide Hills) $23. 85 *—K.F. (3/1/2003)*

STEFANO LUBIANA

Stefano Lubiana NV Brut Champagne Blend (Tasmania) $34. 84 *—M.M. (12/1/2001)*

Stefano Lubiana 2003 Chardonnay (Tasmania) $NA. Mature and ready to drink, this is a light to medium-bodied Chardonnay with a slightly buttery, pear-scented bouquet and flavors of buttered toast and citrus marmalade. More toast and butter on the finish, so drink up before the fruit totally fades. 87 *—J.C. (6/1/2007)*

Stefano Lubiana 2005 Pinot Noir (Tasmania) $NA. This medium-bodied, nicely structured Pinot Noir is impeccably made, it just could use a touch more flesh to round it out and give it a more seductive nature. Toast and black cherry aromas carry a slight briary or herbal nuance, while the flavors at this early juncture favor toasted marshmallow and caramel, followed by notes of chocolate and coffee. Giuve it a couple of years for the oak to integrate. 87 *—J.C. (6/1/2007)*

Stefano Lubiana 1999 Pinot Noir (Tasmania) $39. 87 *—J.C. (9/1/2002)*

Stefano Lubiana 1999 Riesling (Tasmania) $27. 84 *—M.M. (2/1/2002)*

Stefano Lubiana NV Brut Sparkling Blend (Tasmania) $NA. Smells attractive, with hints of vanilla and cocnut layered over toast and apple, and the flavors are in the same vein—apples and citrus, with a bit of an earthy, mushroomy note underneath—but this sample lacked the zip and crispness of a really top-flight sparkler. 84 *—J.C. (6/1/2007)*

STEVE HOFF

Steve Hoff 2005 Cabernet Sauvignon (Barossa Valley) $28. With its mint and cassis on the nose, this wine is clearly identifiable as Cabernet despite its easy drinkability. Tannins are supple, the mouthfeel nicely round, with a long, fruit-driven finish that develops some lovely black tea and tobacco notes. Drink now–2015. 89 *—J.C. (11/1/2007)*

Steve Hoff 2002 Cabernet Sauvignon (Barossa) $25. 83 *—D.T. (10/1/2005)*

Steve Hoff 1999 Cabernet Sauvignon (Barossa Valley) $18. 83 *—J.C. (6/1/2002)*

Steve Hoff 2004 Shiraz (Barossa) $29. Starts off a bit tarry and meaty, but those elements are balanced by baking spices and blackberry pie. This is medium-bodied on the palate, where the flavors run more toward blueberries. Lovely expression of fruit, with just a bit of spice on the finish. Drink now–2012. 88 *—J.C. (11/1/2007)*

Steve Hoff 2000 Shiraz (Barossa Valley) $20. 86 *—D.T. (3/1/2003)*

Steve Hoff 2004 Rossco's Shiraz (Barossa Valley) $47. This is prototypical Barossa Valley Shiraz, boasting a big, lush mouthfeel and great depth of ripe fruit. Vanilla and dill notes from 18 months in oak add another layer of decadence to the blackberry and plum flavors. Finishes long, buffered by a creamy texture and soft tannins. Drink now–2015. 92 *—J.C. (11/1/2007)*

Steve Hoff 2002 Rossco's Shiraz (Barossa) $40. 87 *—D.T. (10/1/2005)*

STICKS

Sticks 2002 Cabernet Sauvignon (Yarra Valley) $15. 84 *—D.T. (5/1/2005)*

Sticks 2003 Chardonnay (Yarra Valley) $16. 85 *(7/2/2004)*

Sticks 2002 Chardonnay (Yarra Valley) $15. 91 Best Buy *—S.H. (10/1/2003)*

Sticks 2004 Pinot Noir (Yarra Valley) $17. Light to medium in body, this has the silky mouthfeel of Pinot Noir to go with its crisp cherry-cranberry flavors. Hints of tomato leaf and tea start off engaging and herbal, but turn a bit drying and tannic on the finish. 86 *—J.C. (2/1/2007)*

Sticks 2002 Pinot Noir (Yarra Valley) $15. 86 *—S.H. (10/1/2003)*

Sticks 2004 Shiraz (Yarra Valley) $17. Yarra Valley is perhaps best known as Pinot Noir country, and this wine reflects the cool climate in its layers of peppery spice that gently frame black cherry and cola flavors. Peppery and clean on the finish. Drink now–2010. 87 *—J.C. (3/1/2007)*

STONEHAVEN

Stonehaven 1999 Cabernet Sauvignon (Limestone Coast) $14. 86 *—D.T. (6/1/2003)*

Stonehaven 1997 Cabernet Sauvignon (Limestone Coast) $18. 88 *(11/1/2000)*

Stonehaven 1998 Reserve Cabernet Sauvignon (Coonawarra) $46. 91 *—D.T. (12/15/2002)*

Stonehaven 1996 Reserve Cabernet Sauvignon (McLaren Vale) $40. 88 *(11/1/2000)*

Stonehaven 2003 Winemaker's Selection Cabernet Sauvignon (South Australia) $12. 85 *(11/1/2005)*

Stonehaven 2001 Chardonnay (Limestone Coast) $13. 83 *(7/2/2004)*

Stonehaven 2001 Chardonnay (South Eastern Australia) $8. 86 *—J.C. (7/1/2002)*

Stonehaven 2000 Chardonnay (Limestone Coast) $16. 87 *—J.C. (7/1/2002)*

Stonehaven 1999 Chardonnay (Limestone Coast) $17. 89 *(11/1/2000)*

Stonehaven 1999 Chardonnay (South Eastern Australia) $9. 86 *(11/1/2000)*

Stonehaven 2003 Premium Chardonnay (South Eastern Australia) $6. 83 *(7/2/2004)*

Stonehaven 1999 Reserve Chardonnay (Padthaway) $29. 87 *—J.C. (7/1/2002)*

Stonehaven 1997 Reserve Chardonnay (Australia) $29. 87 *(11/1/2000)*

Stonehaven 2004 Winemaker's Selection Chardonnay (South Australia) $12. 85 *(11/1/2005)*

Stonehaven 2003 Merlot (South Eastern Australia) $6. 81 *—D.T. (12/1/2005)*

Stonehaven 2000 Merlot (Padthaway) $9. 85 Best Buy *—D.T. (6/1/2002)*

Stonehaven 1999 Merlot (South Eastern Australia) $9. 87 *(11/1/2000)*

Stonehaven 2005 Winemaker's Selection Riesling (South Australia) $10. This medium-bodied Riesling may have just a touch of residual sugar to help bulk it up, but it stays true to the variety's floral, spice-scented nature. Green apple and lime flavors are crisply defined, finishing with contrasting sensations of chalky minerality and fruit syrup. 85 Best Buy *—J.C. (8/1/2007)*

Stonehaven 2004 Winemaker's Selection Riesling (South Australia) $12. 86 *(11/1/2005)*

Stonehaven 2004 Shiraz (South Eastern Australia) $6. 84 Best Buy *—D.T. (10/1/2005)*

Stonehaven 1999 Shiraz (South Eastern Australia) $9. 83 *(10/1/2001)*

Stonehaven 1999 Shiraz (Limestone Coast) $16. 88 *—M.S. (3/1/2003)*

Stonehaven 1998 Shiraz (Limestone Coast) $17. 87 *(11/1/2000)*

Stonehaven 1998 Shiraz (South Eastern Australia) $9. 88 Best Buy *(11/1/2000)*

Stonehaven 1997 Reserve Shiraz (Padthaway) $46. 86 *(11/1/2001)*

Stonehaven 1996 Reserve Shiraz (Padthaway) $46. 88 *(11/1/2000)*

Stonehaven 2003 Winemaker's Selection Shiraz (South Australia) $12. 85 *(11/1/2005)*

Stonehaven 1999 Shiraz-Cabernet Sauvignon (South Eastern Australia) $9. 86 *(11/1/2000)*

STONEY RISE

Stoney Rise 2002 Shiraz (Limestone Coast) $19. 87 *—D.T. (12/31/2004)*

STONIER

Stonier 2005 Chardonnay (Mornington Peninsula) $20. Like Stonier's Pinot Noirs, the Chardonnay is amply oaked, although the Chardonnay seems to be able to handle it better. Movie popcorn scents waft from the glass, but there's also plenty of peach and tangerine fruit to support the oak. Long and citrusy on the finish, picking up hints of butter. This is good now, but may be slightly better next year. 88 *—J.C. (6/1/2007)*

Stonier 2004 Reserve Chardonnay (Mornington Peninsula) $35. A top-notch effort, Stonier's Reserve Chardonnay boasts layers of richly textured fruit and oak hung on a frame of citrusy acidity. Scents of baked apple and toasted nuts are balanced by lemon custard, while the toasted hazelnut and grilled peach flavors feel round in the mouth. Drink now–2010. 91 *—J.C. (8/1/2007)*

Stonier 2005 Pinot Noir (Mornington Peninsula) $25. Lacks fruit intensity and weight, instead offering up rather earthy, root beer-like scents and only modest cherry flavor. 82 *—J.C. (6/1/2007)*

Stonier 2004 Reserve Pinot Noir (Mornington Peninsula) $40. Creamy in texture, but the flavors contain a plethora of mushroom and decay notes that overwhelm the modest cherry fruit. There's a slightly aldehydic note, and the wine finishes short. 83 *—J.C. (5/1/2007)*

STORM BAY

Storm Bay 2005 Chardonnay (Tasmania) $17. A well-made, mainstream Chardonnay aged in French oak, but with no malolactic fermentation to retain its zesty freshness. It's broad and mouthcoating, with flavors of ripe stone fruits and melon but also a bright, refreshing undercurrant of citrus and spice. Good value. 89 *—J.C. (6/1/2007)*

Storm Bay 2005 Pinot Noir (Tasmania) $20. One of three labels from Hood Wines, Storm Bay is perhaps the most modern, featuring bright cherry and sassafras aromas and herb and cherry flavors. The texture is soft and pillowy, while the finish is crisp and lingering. Not as complex as some of the other Tasmanian Pinots, but still well crafted. 86 *—J.C. (6/1/2007)*

STRINGY BRAE

Stringy Brae 1998 Cabernet Sauvignon (Clare Valley) $33. 84 *—D.T. (6/1/2002)*

Stringy Brae 1999 Shiraz (Clare Valley) $30. 83 *—D.T. (1/28/2003)*

SYLVAN SPRINGS

Sylvan Springs 1999 Cabernet Sauvignon (McLaren Vale) $18. 84 *—D.T. (6/1/2002)*

Sylvan Springs 2000 Shiraz (McLaren Vale) $20. 84 *—D.T. (1/28/2003)*

Sylvan Springs 2005 Hard Yards Shiraz (McLaren Vale) $19. Nicely concentrated, with layers of chocolate and potent cassis flavors that are tinged with hints of peppery spice. Medium-bodied, with enough structure to make it capable of lasting several years in the cellar. 89 *—J.C. (8/1/2007)*

Sylvan Springs 2004 Hard Yards Shiraz (McLaren Vale) $19. Starts off with some mildly lactic notes on the nose, but also plenty of plum, herb and cola scents. Similar flavors dominate the palate, which is nicely creamy, buoyed by soft tannins, then finishes a little short and herbal. A decent effort. 84 *—J.C. (2/1/2007)*

T'GALLANT

T'Gallant 2000 Chardonnay (Mornington Peninsula) $18. 87 *—J.C. (7/1/2002)*

T'Gallant 2000 Imogen Pinot Gris (Mornington Peninsula) $18. 86 *—M.M. (2/1/2002)*

T'Gallant 2000 Tribute Pinot Gris (Mornington Peninsula) $20. 88 *—M.M. (2/1/2002)*

T'Gallant 2000 Pinot Noir (Mornington Peninsula) $25. 85 *—J.C. (9/1/2002)*

TAHBILK

Tahbilk 2002 Cabernet Sauvignon (Nagambie Lakes) $25. 88 *—D.T. (12/31/2005)*

Tahbilk 1999 Cabernet Sauvignon (Nagambie Lakes) $20. 84 *—D.T. (5/1/2005)*

Tahbilk 1998 Cabernet Sauvignon (Australia) $18. 92 *—S.H. (6/1/2002)*

Tahbilk 2000 Reserve Cabernet Sauvignon (Nagambie Lakes) $59. 91 *—D.T. (6/1/2006)*

Tahbilk 1994 Reserve Cabernet Sauvignon (Goulburn Valley) $35. 93 *(6/1/2001)*

Tahbilk 2003 Chardonnay (Nagambie Lakes) $NA. 84 *—D.T. (4/1/2006)*

Tahbilk 2005 Marsanne (Nagambie Lakes) $18. 89 *—D.T. (10/1/2006)*

Tahbilk 1999 Marsanne (Victoria) $12. 88 *(2/1/2002)*

Tahbilk 2002 Shiraz (Nagambie Lakes) $25. 87 *—D.T. (6/1/2006)*

Tahbilk 1998 Shiraz (Victoria) $18. 85 *(10/1/2001)*

Tahbilk 1997 Shiraz (Goulburn Valley) $18. 89 *—S.H. (10/1/2000)*

Tahbilk 2000 1860 Vines Shiraz (Nagambie Lakes) $125. 92 *—D.T. (4/1/2006)*

Tahbilk 1996 1860 Vines Shiraz (Nagambie Lakes) $125. 92 Cellar Selection *—D.T. (8/1/2005)*

Tahbilk 1994 1860 Vines Shiraz (Goulburn Valley) $60. 92 *(10/1/2000)*

Tahbilk 2000 Reserve Shiraz (Nagambie Lakes) $59. 88 *—D.T. (4/1/2006)*

Tahbilk 2005 Viognier (Nagambie Lakes) $19. 88 *—D.T. (10/1/2006)*

TAIT WINES

Tait Wines 2005 Basket Pressed Cabernet Sauvignon (Barossa Valley) $30. Mint and cassis aromas and flavors also pick up a slightly pruny or raisiny edge, and this wine does show some alcoholic warmth in the finish, evidence of superripe—maybe even overripe—fruit. It is dark and lush, with supple tannins and a full mouthfeel so on balance it's a very good wine, just be aware that it may be overdone for some tastes. 88 *—J.C. (11/1/2007)*

Tait Wines 2002 Basket Pressed Cabernet Sauvignon (Barossa Valley) $30. 91 *—D.T. (2/1/2004)*

Tait Wines 2002 The Ball Buster Red Blend (Barossa Valley) $17. 89 *—D.T. (2/1/2004)*

Tait Wines 2005 The Ball Buster Shiraz (Barossa Valley) $17. This is 80% Shiraz, with the remainder split evenly between Cabernet Sauvignon and Merlot. It's a touch cedary on the nose, with forceful plum and prune flavors and a hint of licorice on the finish. It's not that complex, but dark, full and satisfying. Drink now–2012. 87 *—J.C. (11/1/2007)*

Tait Wines 2005 Basket Pressed Shiraz (Barossa Valley) $40. Like all of the 2005 offerings from Tait, this flirts with overripeness, hinting at alcoholic heat and raisiny fruit. The payoff is in the lush mouthfeel and supple tannins, dark plum-prune flavors and immensely likeable hints of licorice on the powerful finish. Drink now–2012. 89 *—J.C. (11/1/2007)*

Tait Wines 2000 Basket Press Shiraz (Barossa Valley) $25. 84 *—D.T. (1/28/2003)*

Tait Wines 2002 Basket Pressed Shiraz (Barossa Valley) $33. 92 *—D.T. (2/1/2004)*

TALL POPPY

Tall Poppy 2005 Cabernet Sauvignon (Murray-Darling) $13. Starts off a bit stinky and rubbery, but rights itself in a few minutes to show coffee and cola flavors, a supple texture and a soft finish. 83 *—J.C. (11/15/2007)*

Tall Poppy 2005 Select Cabernet Sauvignon (South Eastern Australia) $9. With its upfront vanilla, cinnamon and cherry aromas and flavors, this is likely to be a crowdpleaser. It's supple and easy to drink, with lingering oaky notes on the finish. 85 Best Buy *—J.C. (11/15/2007)*

Tall Poppy 2005 Merlot (Murray-Darling) $13. The plum and blackberry fruit is a touch stewed and the wood treatment not totally integrated, resulting in a drying, cedary finish. 80 *—J.C. (11/15/2007)*

Tall Poppy 2005 Select Merlot (South Eastern Australia) $9. A soft, supple, medium-bodied wine that would be right at home being poured by the glass in a family-style restaurant, the Tall Poppy Select Merlot features lightly stewed plum and berry fruit and hints of dried spices. 83 *—J.C. (11/15/2007)*

Tall Poppy 2005 Shiraz (Murray-Darling) $13. An earthy style, with coffee, cola and spice notes leading the way past some vaguely blackberryish fruit. 82 *—J.C. (11/15/2007)*

Tall Poppy 2005 Select Shiraz (South Eastern Australia) $9. Straightforward cherry, vanilla and spice flavors mark this medium-bodied red. It's a cheerful, easy-drinking wine with no pretensions that will pair well with casual foods from burgers to pizza. 85 Best Buy *—J.C. (11/15/2007)*

TALAGANDRA

Talagandra 2001 Chardonnay (Australia) $17. 85 *—J.C. (9/10/2002)*

Talagandra 2000 Canberra District Shiraz (Australia) $19. 83 *—M.S. (2/1/2003)*

TALTARNI

Taltarni 1995 Cabernet Sauvignon (Victoria) $16. 88 *(12/31/1999)*

Taltarni 2000 Cabernet Sauvignon-Merlot (Victoria) $14. 87 *—D.T. (12/31/2003)*

Taltarni 2004 Three Monks Cabernet Sauvignon-Merlot (Victoria) $16. A relatively simple, fruity wine, with cassis fruit accented by hints of bright cherries and rhubarb. It's medium-bodied, maybe even a little light in substance, with dried herb and chocolate making an appearance on the finish. Drink now. 85 *—J.C. (6/1/2007)*

Taltarni 2003 Three Monks Cabernet Sauvignon-Merlot (Victoria) $16. 89 *—D.T. (8/1/2006)*

Taltarni 2005 Sauvignon Blanc (Victoria) $16. 87 *—D.T. (4/1/2006)*

Taltarni 2004 Sauvignon Blanc (Victoria) $16. 88 *—D.T. (12/1/2005)*

Taltarni 2000 Sauvignon Blanc (Victoria) $13. 82 *—J.F. (9/1/2001)*

Taltarni 2004 Shiraz (Heathcote) $35. 85 *—D.T. (8/1/2006)*

Taltarni 2003 Shiraz (Heathcote) $35. 87 *—D.T. (12/1/2005)*

Taltarni 2002 Shiraz (Pyrenees) $20. 89 *—D.T. (6/1/2006)*

Taltarni 1997 Estate Grown Shiraz (Victoria) $16. 89 *(12/31/1999)*

Taltarni 2000 Cephas Shiraz-Cabernet Sauvignon (Victoria) $30. 88 *—D.T. (12/31/2003)*

Taltarni NV Brut Tache Sparkling Blend (Australia) $22. 88 *—D.T. (12/31/2003)*

Taltarni NV Brut Tache Sparkling Blend (Victoria) $20. 89 *—D.T. (12/31/2005)*

Taltarni 2003 Brut Taché Sparkling Blend (Victoria) $20. 86 *—J.C. (12/31/2006)*

TAMAR RIDGE

Tamar Ridge 2005 Pinot Gris (Tasmania) $20. A full, plump style with 14% alcohol, but one that carries it well, balanced by spicy, peppery flavors and perhaps even a touch of residual sugar. Aromas of wet stones, peach blossom and apple-pear-lime fruit presage the ripely fruity flavors of apples, pears and melon. Finishes long. Drinkable now, although might develop more interesting spice nuances in another few years. 88 *—J.C. (6/1/2007)*

Tamar Ridge 2003 Pinot Noir (Tasmania) $25. Tamar Ridge's 2003 Pinot Noir is on the oaky side, with aromas of toast and caramel overshadowing the slightly mushroomy black-cherry fruit. The mouthfeel is round and the tannins soft, this just needs slightly more concentrated fruit and a lighter hand with the oak. 86 *—J.C. (6/1/2007)*

Tamar Ridge 2005 Devil's Corner Pinot Noir (Tasmania) $15. Shows a much lighter touch with the oak than Tamar Ridge's 2003 Pinot Noir, and to the wine's benefit. Dusty plum scents are touched with slightly floral, herbal notes, while the texture is properly Pinot—silky and lingering on the finish. Good value. 88 *—J.C. (6/1/2007)*

Tamar Ridge 2004 Riesling (Tasmania) $20. A classically-styled Australian Riesling, Tamar Ridge's 2004 offers plenty of mineral and lime scents, wrapped around a lean, crisp, racy structure and steely flavors of green apples and lime. Long and piquant on the finish, yet surprisingly elegant at the same time. Drink now, although it should easily hold another five years or so. 90 *—J.C. (6/1/2007)*

Tamar Ridge 2005 Limited Release Botrytis Riesling (Tasmania) $25. Wonderfully botrytized dessert wine, with dried apricot and orange marmalade scents and grace notes of dried spices. It's moderately rich and viscous, perhaps just a bit low in acidity but delicious just the same, combining flavors of honey, apricots and citrus on a finish that's not overly sweet. Drink now. 90 *—J.C. (6/1/2007)*

Tamar Ridge 2005 Sauvignon Blanc (Tasmania) $20. Similar to some New Zealand versions of Sauvignon BLanc, this wine features a powerful scent of sweet green peas alongside riper notes of passion fruit and stone fruit. It's on the full side, with 14% alcohol, but carries it well. The veggie note isn't a favorite here, but the wine comes together nicely, finishing with lingering honey and citrus flavors. Drink now. 87 *—J.C. (6/1/2007)*

Tamar Ridge 2004 Sauvignon Blanc (Tasmania) $20. 89 *(7/1/2005)*

TAPANAPPA

TapaNappa 2003 Whalebone Vineyard Cabernet Sauvignon-Shiraz-Cabernet Franc Cabernet Blend (Wrattonbully) $63. This is a joint venture between some awfully big names in wine—Croser, Cazes and Bollinger—and the wine is very good. The bouquet shows off the expensive French oak barrels (smoke and cedar), while the palate impresses with its creamy texture and supple tannins. At this stage, though, the flavors lack complexity and nuance, blending black cherry and plum with smoke and vanilla. A good first vintage—let's hope subsequent releases are even better. 89 *—J.C. (5/1/2007)*

TAPESTRY

Tapestry 2004 Cabernet Sauvignon (McLaren Vale) $22. This great value turns the neat trick of boasting an almost molasses-like density of fruit without seeming overly heavy. It's full-bodied, with hints of smoke, vanilla and herbs that add complexity to the cherry fruit, while on the finish, the tannins are soft and the flavors linger elegantly. Drink now through 2012. 91 Editors' Choice *—J.C. (2/1/2007)*

Tapestry 2003 Cabernet Sauvignon (McLaren Vale) $22. 89 *—D.T. (6/1/2006)*

Tapestry 2002 Cabernet Sauvignon (McLaren Vale) $21. 86 *—D.T. (10/1/2005)*

Tapestry 2001 Cabernet Sauvignon (McLaren Vale) $20. 89 *—D.T. (5/1/2004)*

Tapestry 1999 Bin 388 Cabernet Sauvignon (McLaren Vale) $25. 83 *—D.T. (6/1/2002)*

Tapestry 2003 Fifteen Barrels Cabernet Sauvignon (McLaren Vale) $40. Despite the name, only 10 barrels of this wine were made in the difficult 2003 vintage. It's round and full, soft but not completely lacking structure. Lush cassis and chocolate flavors firm up a bit on the finish, adding hints of dried spices and cedar. Drink now–2015. 90 *—J.C. (2/1/2007)*

Tapestry 2001 Fifteen Barrels Cabernet Sauvignon (McLaren Vale) $36. 86 *—D.T. (5/1/2004)*

Tapestry 2005 Chardonnay (McLaren Vale) $15. This is a lush, richly textured Chardonnay that showcases ripe peach and melon wrapped in a soft cocoon of vanilla and buttered toast. Yes, the wine is woody, but the fruit matches the oak's intensity. Ends long, marked by dried spice nuances. 90 Best Buy *—J.C. (2/1/2007)*

Tapestry 2004 Chardonnay (McLaren Vale) $16. 86 *—D.T. (4/1/2006)*

Tapestry 2002 Chardonnay (McLaren Vale) $15. 85 *(7/2/2004)*

Tapestry 2006 Riesling (McLaren Vale) $15. McLaren Vale isn't known for Riesling the same way as the Clare or Eden Valleys are, but this effort is a strong one, showing hints of nectarine and tangerine alongside slatey, minerally components. Finishes long and steely, but cushioned just the right amount by ripe fruit. Drink now, although this might age for a few years. 90 Best Buy *—J.C. (2/1/2007)*

Tapestry 2005 Riesling (McLaren Vale) $16. 85 *—D.T. (4/1/2006)*

Tapestry 2005 Shiraz (McLaren Vale) $22. This impeccably made wine boasts a rich, almost unctuous mouthfeel that beautifully complements its flavors of blackberries, dried spices, toast and vanilla. It's delicious now, but the flavors are so young and primary it's hard to imagine it not being even better in another year or two. Long on the finish, with echoes of oak and fruit lingering elegantly. 91 Editors' Choice *—J.C. (8/1/2007)*

Tapestry 2004 Shiraz (McLaren Vale) $22. Full-bodied and creamy in texture, this wine comes dangerously close to being heavy and lacking freshness. Thankfully, it stays just this side of that line, balancing rich chocolate fudge flavors with savory notes of cedar and smoke and mixed berries that turn tart on the finish. 86 *—J.C. (2/1/2007)*

Tapestry 2002 Shiraz (McLaren Vale) $21. 87 *—D.T. (2/1/2006)*

Tapestry 2001 Shiraz (McLaren Vale) $19. 87 *—D.T. (3/1/2005)*

Tapestry 2006 Bakers Gully Vineyard Shiraz (McLaren Vale) $15. From a well-known vineyard source, this is certainly dark in color, but the aromatics are a bit muted. Tannins are soft, imparting a creamy texture, but the flavors of blackberries and plum lean toward prune before picking up a tangy note on the finish. It's maybe just too young at this stage, but it seems a bit disjointed. 86 *—J.C. (11/15/2007)*

Tapestry 1999 Bin 338 Shiraz (McLaren Vale) $25. 87 *(11/1/2001)*

Tapestry 2004 The Vincent Shiraz (McLaren Vale) $41. A relative bargain in the scheme of South Australian Shiraz, this is a cherry-picked selection from the Baker's Gully Vineyard. It smells like mint, vanilla and chocolate at first, then unfolds on the palate into something akin to thin mints with vanilla and blackberry sauces, topped with black olives and coffee—yet all in one harmonious, savory whole. Long, silky and mouthwatering on the finish, this is enjoyable now, but with the stuffing to last through 2020. 93 Editors' Choice *—J.C. (12/31/2007)*

Tapestry 2003 The Vincent Shiraz (McLaren Vale) $40. 89 *—J.C. (12/15/2006)*

Tapestry 2002 The Vincent Shiraz (McLaren Vale) $39. 87 *—D.T. (3/1/2005)*

Tapestry 2001 The Vincent Shiraz (McLaren Vale) $36. 88 *—D.T. (11/15/2004)*

TATACHILLA

Tatachilla 2000 Cabernet Sauvignon (McLaren Vale) $20. 81 *—D.T. (6/1/2002)*

Tatachilla 1999 Cabernet Sauvignon (Padthaway) $20. 81 *—D.T. (6/1/2002)*

Tatachilla 1998 Cabernet Sauvignon (McLaren Vale) $20. 86 *—M.M. (9/1/2001)*

Tatachilla 2000 Breakneck Creek Cabernet Sauvignon (South Australia) $12. 83 *—J.C. (6/1/2002)*

Tatachilla 1999 Wattle Park Cabernet Sauvignon (South Australia) $10. 87 *(6/1/2001)*

Tatachilla 2000 Chardonnay (Padthaway) $15. 84 *—J.C. (7/1/2002)*

Tatachilla 2000 Chardonnay (McLaren Vale) $14. 86 *—D.T. (8/1/2003)*

Tatachilla 2000 Chardonnay (Adelaide Hills) $25. 83 *—D.T. (8/1/2003)*

Tatachilla 1999 Chardonnay (Padthaway) $16. 84 *—D.T. (9/1/2001)*

Tatachilla 1999 Chardonnay (McLaren Vale) $14. 80 *—J.C. (9/10/2002)*

Tatachilla 1998 Chardonnay (McLaren Vale) $12. 84 *(6/1/2001)*

Tatachilla 2001 Breakneck Creek Chardonnay (South Australia) $9. 82 *(7/2/2004)*

Tatachilla 1999 Wattle Park Chardonnay (South Australia) $10. 88 Best Buy *—M.M. (9/1/2001)*

Tatachilla 1998 Grenache-Shiraz (McLaren Vale) $14. 84 *—J.C. (9/1/2001)*

Tatachilla 1999 Clarendon Vineyards Merlot (McLaren Vale) $35. 87 *—J.C. (6/1/2002)*

Tatachilla 2000 Wattle Park Merlot (South Australia) $12. 86 *—J.C. (6/1/2002)*

Tatachilla 1999 Wattle Park Merlot (South Australia) $10. 87 Best Buy *—M.M. (9/1/2001)*

Tatachilla 2000 Grenache/Shiraz Red Blend (McLaren Vale) $15. 84 *—J.C. (9/1/2002)*

Tatachilla 1999 Grenache-Mourvedre Rhône Red Blend (South Australia) $9. 86 *—J.C. (9/1/2002)*

Tatachilla 2000 Shiraz (McLaren Vale) $20. 87 *—D.T. (5/1/2004)*

Tatachilla 1999 Shiraz (McLaren Vale) $22. 87 *—J.C. (9/1/2002)*

Tatachilla 2002 Breakneck Creek Shiraz (South Australia) $9. 85 *—D.T. (9/1/2004)*

Tatachilla 2000 Breakneck Creek Shiraz (South Australia) $9. 88 Best Buy *—J.C. (9/1/2002)*

Tatachilla 2001 Foundation Shiraz (McLaren Vale) $35. Dense, rich and chewy, this is a relative bargain in the rapidly escalating world of Australian Shiraz. Pungent espresso, black pepper and blackberry aromas are backed by flavors that veer ever so slightly toward dried fruits and earth. Long and supple on the finish, filled with dusty tannins, exotic spice and echoes of fruit. Drink now–2012. 92 Editors' Choice *—J.C. (4/25/2007)*

Tatachilla 1998 Foundation Shiraz (McLaren Vale) $45. 88 *—D.T. (3/1/2003)*

Tatachilla 1996 Foundation Shiraz (McLaren Vale) $40. 91 Editors' Choice *(11/1/2001)*

Tatachilla 2000 Chenin Blanc-Semillon-Sauvignon Blanc White Blend (South Australia) $9. 80 *—D.T. (2/1/2002)*

Tatachilla 1999 Chenin Blanc-Semillon-Sauvignon Blanc White Blend (South Australia) $10. 84 *—D.T. (2/1/2002)*

TATIARRA

Tatiarra 2005 Cambrian Shiraz (Heathcote) $56. A big but balanced Shiraz, Tatiarra's Cambrian Shiraz takes its name from the ancient rocks that underlie the vineyards. Black cherries, licorice and mineral notes finish long, picking up nuances of black olives. Drink now–2015, possibly longer. 92 *(11/15/2007)*

Tatiarra 2003 Cambrian Shiraz (Heathcote) $58. 90 *—D.T. (12/1/2005)*

TEAL LAKE

Teal Lake 2002 Private Reserve Cabernet Sauvignon (South Eastern Australia) $19. 83 *—J.M. (4/3/2004)*

Teal Lake 2002 Cabernet Sauvignon-Merlot (South Eastern Australia) $13. 83 *—J.C. (4/1/2005)*

Teal Lake 2003 Chardonnay (South Eastern Australia) $13. 84 *—J.C. (4/1/2005)*

Teal Lake 1999 Herzog Selection Chardonnay (South Eastern Australia) $12. 85 *(4/1/2001)*

Teal Lake 2002 Petit Verdot-Cabernet Red Blend (South Eastern Australia) $13. 85 *—J.C. (4/1/2005)*

Teal Lake 2001 Shiraz (South Eastern Australia) $13. 87 *—K.F. (3/1/2003)*

Teal Lake 2000 Shiraz (South Eastern Australia) $12. 85 *(4/1/2001)*

Teal Lake 2002 Shiraz-Cabernet Sauvignon (South Eastern Australia) $12. 84 *—J.C. (4/1/2005)*

TEMPLE BRUER

Temple Bruer 1999 Cabernet Blend (Langhorne Creek) $20. 82 *—J.C. (6/1/2002)*

Temple Bruer 2001 Reserve Cabernet Blend (Langhorne Creek) $22. 89 *—D.T. (5/1/2005)*

Temple Bruer 1998 Reserve Cabernet Sauvignon (Langhorne Creek) $16. 93 Editors' Choice *—J.F. (9/1/2001)*

Temple Bruer 2002 Cabernet-Merlot Cabernet Sauvignon-Merlot (Langhorne Creek) $16. Potentially interesting blackberry fruit from the blend of 61% Cab Sauvignon, 28% Merlot and 11% Cab Franc is hidden under a pile of lumber. Cedar, vanilla and heaps of sawdust are the dominant flavors. 80 *—J.C. (7/1/2007)*

Temple Bruer 2001 Cabernet Sauvignon-Merlot (McLaren Vale & Langhorne Creek) $16. 88 *—D.T. (12/31/2003)*

Temple Bruer 1999 Cabernet Sauvignon-Merlot (Langhorne Creek) $16. 81 *—D.T. (6/1/2002)*

Temple Bruer 2003 Chenin Blanc (Langhorne Creek) $15. 84 *—D.T. (5/1/2005)*

Temple Bruer 1998 Cornucopia Grenache (Langhorne Creek) $13. 85 *—J.C. (9/1/2002)*

Temple Bruer 1998 Reserve Merlot (Langhorne Creek) $20. 84 *—D.T. (6/1/2002)*

Temple Bruer 2000 Shiraz-Malbec (Langhorne Creek) $16. 88 *—D.T. (5/1/2004)*

TEMPUS TWO

Tempus Two 2005 Vine Vale Shiraz (Barossa Valley) $25. This is a big, robust Shiraz that manages to be all that without being angular. Some leather and spice notes lead the way on the nose, while the flavors lean toward blackberry, coffee and cola. Soft tannins and tart berries mark the close. 88 *—J.C. (11/1/2007)*

TEUSNER

Teusner 2005 Avatar Rhône Red Blend (Barossa Valley) $40. An oak-aged blend of Grenache (55%), Shiraz (25%) and Mataro (20%), this is a lush, black-cherry-scented wine framed by cedary notes. The mouthfeel is pillowy-soft and caressing yet not devoid of structure, while a complex mélange of spices adds depth and nuance. Drink now–2012. 92 *—J.C. (11/1/2007)*

Teusner 2006 Joshua Rhône Red Blend (Barossa Valley) $30. A blend of 65% Grenache with the rest Mataro (Mourvèdre) and Shiraz, this sees no oak, so the fruit's bold character shines. Black cherries lead the way, accented by a hint of almond. The texture is smooth; there's a sense of delicacy here, despite the authoritative flavors. Drink now–2010. 89 *—J.C. (11/1/2007)*

Teusner 2005 Albert Shiraz (Barossa Valley) $60. Although it's not indicated on the front label, this is 100% Shiraz, sourced from 60-year-old vines in the Ebenezer district and 90-year-old vines near Gomersal. It's Teusner's best wine, loaded with spice and savory notes that perfectly highlight the rich blackberry fruit. Not jammy or overblown, it has enough structure to suggest a drinking window from 2010–2020. 92 *—J.C. (11/1/2007)*

Teusner 2005 The Riebke Ebenezer Road Shiraz (Barossa Valley) $25. From the northern section of Barossa Valley off relatively young vines, this is dark-fruited, filled with scents and flavors of cola, spice, loam, blackberries and plums. Turns a bit crisp on the finish. Drink 2008–2015. 89 *—J.C. (11/1/2007)*

THE BLACK CHOOK

The Black Chook 2004 Shiraz-Viognier (South Australia) $18. 84 *—D.T. (12/31/2005)*

THE COLONIAL ESTATE

The Colonial Estate 2004 Etranger Cabernet Sauvignon-Shiraz (Barossa Valley) $30. 85 *—D.T. (10/1/2006)*

The Colonial Estate 2004 Évangéliste Reserve Chardonnay (Adelaide Hills) $30. 90 *—D.T. (6/1/2006)*

The Colonial Estate 2005 Enchanteur Rosé Grenache (Barossa Valley) $20. 83 *—D.T. (4/1/2006)*

The Colonial Estate 2004 L'Eclaireur Sauvignon Blanc (Adelaide Hills) $25. 89 *(7/1/2005)*

The Colonial Estate 2004 Explorateur Shiraz (Barossa Valley) $30. 86 *—D.T. (6/1/2006)*

The Black Chook 2006 Shiraz-Viognier (McLaren Vale & Langhorne Creek) $18. Winemaker Ben Riggs coferments the Shiraz with Viognier skins in an attempt to build in additional complexity at a reasonable price, and this wine delivers lovely blackberry, licorice, stone fruit and black tea-leaf notes as a result, ending with a touch of coffee. Drink now. 89 *(11/15/2007)*

The Black Chook 2006 VMR White Blend (South Australia) $18. VMR stands for Viognier, Marsanne and Roussanne, which are blended together in this flamboyantly floral version of a Rhône-style white. Apricot, melon and citrus flavors strike the palate with a lush, almost oily impression, yet finish long and crisp. Drink now. 90 Editors' Choice *(11/15/2007)*

THE COLONIAL ESTATE

The Colonial Estate 2005 Etranger Cabernet Sauvignon (Barossa Valley) $35. A dialed-up Cabernet, but one that shows a nod to the Old World in its dried herb and black olive shadings. There's ripe cassis and lush chocolate as well, with maybe a touch of fruitcake. Ends with soft tannins. Drink now–2015. 89 *—J.C. (11/1/2007)*

The Colonial Estate 2004 Etranger Cabernet Sauvignon (Barossa Valley) $33. Dense, richly fruited and superripe, this is a chewy wine filled with chocolate and spice flavors. 92 Editors' Choice *—J.C. (6/1/2007)*

The Colonial Estate 2006 Evangeliste Reserve Chardonnay (Adelaide Hills) $30. This wine delivers plenty of honey and peach notes upfront, then closes with lime and mineral notes from the tiny proportion of Eden Valley Riesling that's been blended in. Crisp and steely. 88 *—J.C. (12/31/2007)*

The Colonial Estate 2005 Exodus Chardonnay (Piccadilly Valley) $58. A round, corpulent style of Chardonnay, nutty and rich but balanced by crisp apple and citrus notes. A bit of Eden Valley Riesling provides the wine's freshness. 88 *—J.C. (12/31/2007)*

The Colonial Estate 2005 Alexander Laing Single Vineyard Old Vine Grenache (Barossa Valley) $NA. Like a couple of other Colonial Estate 2005s, this has a lifted nose that flirts with volatile vinyl and acetone scents, then settles down to deliver spice and chocolate. This is really fudge-like and dense, picking up hints of pepper on the finish along with some dusty tannins. Should be long-lived for Australian Grenache; drink now–2015. 90 *—J.C. (11/1/2007)*

The Colonial Estate 2006 Enchanteur Rosé Grenache (Barossa Valley) $25. This broad, mouthfilling Grenache rosé features hints of berries, chocolate and some herbaceous notes. It's more like a light red than a true rosé, showing considerable weight and body, then finishes dry, with a hint of minerality. 89 *—J.C. (12/31/2007)*

The Colonial Estate 2005 Envoy G-S-M (Barossa Valley) $35. Dense and rich, with a resemblance to chocolate fudge. A blend of 60% Grenache, 30% Shiraz and 10% Mataro, this is a touch raisiny but clearly very concentrated and intense. Drink now. 87 *—J.C. (11/1/2007)*

The Colonial Estate 2005 John Speke Single Vineyard G-S-M (Barossa Valley) $60. From the same vineyard that provides fruit for John Duval's Plexus, this is a blend of approximately 50% Grenache, 30% Shiraz and 20% Mourvèdre. There's a slightly lifted, vinyl quality to the aromas on first nosing, but once accustomed to it, it's no longer bothersome, leaving the way open for chocolate, cherry and cola flavors. Coffee and spice notes mark the supple finish. Drink now–2012. 89 *—J.C. (11/1/2007)*

The Colonial Estate 2005 Émigré Red Blend (Barossa Valley) $80. A blend of Shiraz, Grenache, Cabernet Sauvignon, Mourvèdre and even a tiny bit of Muscadelle, this is perfumed and floral on the nose, but it also boasts scents of cinnamon, coffee, chocolate and earth. It's lush and dense on the palate, rich and creamy in weight and texture, ending with hints of vanilla and spice. Approachable now, but should drink well for up to 10 years. 91 *—J.C. (11/1/2007)*

The Colonial Estate 2006 Expatrié Reserve Sémillon (Barossa) $30. Like the other white wines in Malthus's Australian portfolio, this blends in a touch of Eden Valley Riesling to add acidity rather than simply adding tartaric. The result in this case is a broad, plump wine with hints of pear and clove, finishing with additional spice on the finish. 88 *—J.C. (12/31/2007)*

The Colonial Estate 2005 Exile Shiraz (Barossa Valley) $160. A single-vineyard wine that contains about 85% Shiraz, 10% Mourvèdre and 5% Grenache, this is an incredibly concentrated wine. Slightly lifted aromas keep it from seeming heavy, but the flavors are dense and fudge-like, chocolaty and superripe. Dusty tannins on the finish suggest cellaring through 2010, and it should age well through at least 2020. 92 Cellar Selection *—J.C. (11/1/2007)*

The Colonial Estate 2005 Explorateur Old Vine Shiraz (Barossa Valley) $35. A blend of fruit from the northern end of the Barossa, this is dark and loamy, filled with earth, spice and tobacco, but also featuring hints of meat, black olive and blueberries. The mouthfeel is lush and soft, and despite some slightly cooked fruit there's surprising freshness on the dusty finish. Drink now–2015. 90 *—J.C. (11/1/2007)*

The Colonial Estate 2005 Mungo Park Single Vineyard Shiraz (Barossa Valley) $65. Perfumed and floral at first, but this wine also features some deeper, darker notes of black pepper and black olive. It's plenty rich on the palate, oozing with earth and cola flavors that stay lively through the finish. Drink now–2015. 91 *—J.C. (11/1/2007)*

THE EDGE

The Edge 2002 Sauvignon Blanc (King Valley) $16. 86 *—D.T. (11/15/2004)*

The Edge 2001 Sauvignon Blanc (King Valley) $15. 87 *(1/1/2004)*

THE GATE

The Gate 2003 Shiraz (McLaren Vale) $32. 87 *—D.T. (6/1/2006)*

The Gate 2003 Shiraz (McLaren Vale) $32. 89 *—D.T. (12/31/2005)*

The Gate 2002 Shiraz (McLaren Vale) $32. 86 *—D.T. (12/31/2004)*

THE GREEN VINEYARDS

The Green Vineyards 1999 The Forties Old Block Shiraz (Victoria) $30. 86 *(11/1/2001)*

THE LANE

The Lane 2001 19th Meeting Cabernet Sauvignon (Adelaide Hills) $44. 88 *—D.T. (5/1/2004)*

The Lane 2002 Beginning Chardonnay (Adelaide Hills) $38. 89 *(7/2/2004)*

The Lane 2002 Gathering Semillon-Sauvignon Blanc (Adelaide Hills) $30. 90 *—D.T. (5/1/2004)*

The Lane 2001 Reunion Shiraz (Adelaide Hills) $44. 87 *—D.T. (9/1/2004)*

THE LUCKY COUNTRY

The Lucky Country 2003 Grenache- Syrah- Mourvedre Grenache (Barossa Valley) $13. 86 *—D.T. (3/1/2005)*

THE MUTTS NUTS

The Mutts Nuts 2004 Shiraz (Wrattonbully) $10. Herbal—but in a good way—showing off some cool-climate spice and cherry aromas. It's light in body, with peppery, herbal and red fruit flavors that finish fresh. Drink now. 85 Best Buy *—J.C. (3/1/2007)*

THE WILLOWS

The Willows 2004 Shiraz (Barossa Valley) $30. Aging in small American oak has given this a bold sheen of vanilla and dill to go with its fruit-derived flavors of chocolate and blackberries. Creamy and ripe, with a supple texture and slightly crisp finish. Drink now–2012. 88 *—J.C. (11/1/2007)*

The Willows 2004 Bonesetter Shiraz (Barossa) $64. The fruit for this cuvée comes from an older block of vines, then goes into French oak for aging, so it's substantially different from The Willows' regular Shiraz bottling. Cinnamon, pepper, cherry and vanilla notes intermingle on the nose, imparting a distinct cinnamon-red hot character that's balanced on the palate by creamy layers of cherry and raspberry fruit. Supple and elegant on the finish. Drink now–2014. 90 *—J.C. (11/1/2007)*

THE WINNER'S TANK

The Winner's Tank 2004 Shiraz (Langhorne Creek) $16. 86 *—D.T. (12/1/2005)*

THE WISHING TREE

The Wishing Tree 2006 Unoaked Chardonnay (Western Australia) $10. One of Larchet's own brands, this wine is soft and broad in texture, with pear and citrus flavors that finish apple-y fresh. 86 Best Buy *—J.C. (6/1/2007)*

The Wishing Tree 2005 Unoaked Chardonnay (Western Australia) $10. 87 Best Buy *—D.T. (4/1/2006)*

The Wishing Tree 2004 Unoaked Chardonnay (Western Australia) $11. 86 Best Buy *—D.T. (11/15/2005)*

The Wishing Tree 2005 Shiraz (Western Australia) $10. A medium-bodied Shiraz that shows ample freshness and spice, not the jammy character often associated with this price point. 86 Best Buy *—J.C. (6/1/2007)*

THIRSTY LIZARD

Thirsty Lizard 2002 Chardonnay (South Eastern Australia) $8. 83 *—D.T. (1/1/2002)*

Thirsty Lizard 2005 Shiraz (South Eastern Australia) $9. Light and a bit lemony, this bargain-priced Shiraz features plenty of the jammy blackberry flavors that consumers have come to identify with the genre. It's a simple, fruity quaff in a convenient Tetra Prisma container. 83 *—J.C. (7/1/2007)*

Thirsty Lizard 2002 Shiraz (South Eastern Australia) $8. 81 *—D.T. (1/1/2002)*

Thirsty Lizard 2000 Shiraz (South Eastern Australia) $8. 81 *—D.T. (12/31/2003)*

Thirsty Lizard 2004 White Shiraz (South Eastern Australia) $8. 82 *—D.T. (12/1/2005)*

THOMAS MITCHELL

Thomas Mitchell 1998 Marsanne (South Eastern Australia) $14. 86 Best Buy *—S.H. (10/1/2000)*

THORNY DEVIL

Thorny Devil 2003 Shiraz (Gundagai) $11. 86 *—D.T. (12/1/2005)*

THREE BRIDGES

Three Bridges 1999 Golden Mist Boytrytis Semillon (Riverina) $18. 91 *—J.M. (12/1/2002)*

TIM ADAMS

Tim Adams 2002 Cabernet Sauvignon (Clare Valley) $33. A reliable source for Australian Cab Sauvignon, Tim Adams' 2002 effort features scents of sun-dried blackberries, leather and a touch of herbaceousness. It's large-scaled and full-bodied, picking up hints of raisined fruit on the finish. 88 *—J.C. (6/1/2007)*

Tim Adams 2001 Cabernet Sauvignon (Clare Valley) $21. 88 *—D.T. (2/1/2004)*

Tim Adams 2000 Cabernet Sauvignon (Clare Valley) $23. 89 *—D.T. (12/31/2003)*

Tim Adams 2003 The Benefit Cabernet Sauvignon (Clare Valley) $15. 87 *—D.T. (8/1/2006)*

Tim Adams 2004 The Fergus Grenache (Clare Valley) $18. 87 *—D.T. (11/15/2006)*

Tim Adams 2001 The Fergus Grenache (Clare Valley) $20. 88 *—D.T. (2/1/2004)*

Tim Adams 2006 Pinot Gris (Clare Valley) $18. 90 Editors' Choice *—D.T. (10/1/2006)*

Tim Adams 2005 Riesling (Clare Valley) $18. 88 *—D.T. (10/1/2006)*

Tim Adams 2003 Riesling (Clare Valley) $15. 87 *—D.T. (2/1/2004)*

Tim Adams 1999 Riesling (Clare Valley) $NA. 90 *—D.T. (2/1/2004)*

Tim Adams 1994 Botrytis Riesling (Clare Valley) $NA. 90 *—D.T. (2/1/2004)*

Tim Adams 2005 The Benefit Riesling (Clare Valley) $15. 85 *—D.T. (10/1/2006)*

Tim Adams 2004 Sémillon (Clare Valley) $18. There's a pronounced lemony streak that runs through this wine, from the bouquet to the flavors and onto the slightly puckery finish. A touch of spice adds interest, but this is still pretty one-dimensional. Drink now, or try cellaring and see if it develops additional complexity in 5–10 years. 84 *—J.C. (2/1/2007)*

Tim Adams 2002 Semillon (Clare Valley) $15. 86 *—D.T. (2/1/2004)*

Tim Adams 2002 Shiraz (Clare Valley) $21. 90 Editors' Choice *—D.T. (2/1/2004)*

Tim Adams 2002 The Aberfeldy Shiraz (Clare Valley) $50. 89 *—D.T. (11/15/2006)*

Tim Adams 2001 The Aberfeldy Shiraz (Clare Valley) $45. 92 *—D.T. (2/1/2004)*

Tim Adams 2004 The Benefit Shiraz (Southern Flinders Ranges) $NA. 86 *—D.T. (8/1/2006)*

TIMBUKTU

Timbuktu 2004 Big Block Red Red Blend (South Australia) $10. Despite being only medium-bodied and featuring some tart, lemony notes on the finish, this seems a touch ponderous, with earthy flavors dominating blackberry fruit. 82 *—J.C. (11/15/2007)*

Timbuktu 2005 Deluxe Shiraz (Fleurieu Peninsula) $8. Winemaker Ben Riggs's attempt at bargain-priced Shiraz is a solid effort, offering hints of smoke and dried fruit, but also decent depth and blackberry-black cherry flavors. It lacks the weight and richness of a big boy, finishing slightly peppery and warm (it is labeled at 15% alcohol). Drink now. 84 Best Buy *—J.C. (7/1/2007)*

TIM GRAMP

Tim Gramp 2001 Proprietary Grenache (Clare Valley) $17. 88 *—D.T. (9/1/2004)*

Tim Gramp 2002 Watervale Riesling (Clare Valley) $18. 83 *—D.T. (5/1/2005)*

Tim Gramp 2000 Proprietary Shiraz (Clare Valley) $29. 87 *—D.T. (9/1/2004)*

TIN COWS

Tin Cows 2001 Chardonnay (Yarra Valley) $13. 88 *—S.H. (1/1/2002)*

Tin Cows 2000 Merlot (Yarra Valley) $13. 90 *—S.H. (1/1/2002)*

Tin Cows 2001 Pinot Noir (Yarra Valley) $13. 89 *—S.H. (1/1/2002)*

Tin Cows 2001 Shiraz (Yarra Valley) $13. 90 *—S.H. (1/1/2002)*

TIN SHED

Tin Shed 2004 Melting Pot Shiraz (Eden Valley) $29. A spicy, savory rendition of Shiraz reflective of a slightly cooler climate, with peppery notes accenting bright cherry-berry fruit. Cinnamon and clove mark the crisp finish. Drink now–2012. 89 *—J.C. (11/1/2007)*

Tin Shed 2003 Single Wire Shiraz (Eden Valley) $51. Almost Rhône-ish in its spicy, savory notes and sour plum flavors. It's meaty and peppery, with sausage-like notes. Only medium-bodied, this is not a typical Barossa heavyweight, but a wine that relies on aromatics and complexity for its charm. Drink now–2012. 90 *—J.C. (11/1/2007)*

TINTARA

Tintara 2004 Cabernet Sauvignon (McLaren Vale) $17. This is a big, slightly alcoholic Cabernet, but one that seems to lack a bit for structure and definition. The tannins are soft and the acidity seems low, giving this wine a creamy texture to go along with flavors of cassis and dried spices. Drink now. 85 *—J.C. (2/1/2007)*

Tintara 2003 Cabernet Sauvignon (McLaren Vale) $18. 87 *—D.T. (3/1/2005)*

Tintara 2004 Reserve Grenache (McLaren Vale) $50. 88 *—D.T. (11/15/2006)*

Tintara 2003 Reserve Grenache (McLaren Vale) $49. 90 *—D.T. (3/1/2005)*

Tintara 2004 Shiraz (McLaren Vale) $17. This is a joy to smell, filled with expansive notes of toasted coconut, ripe berries and vanilla, but also some darker, meatier scents. Unfortunately, the palate can't quite match the excitement level—the flavors are a bit simple and fruit-driven, while the mouthfeel could use more lushness and depth. It's still a good effort and a worthy companion to steak or roasts. 86 *—J.C. (2/1/2007)*

Tintara 2003 Shiraz (McLaren Vale) $18. 88 *—D.T. (3/1/2005)*

Tintara 2003 Reserve Shiraz (McLaren Vale) $40. Sturdily built on a chewy bed of tannins, but this impressively dark, full-bodied wine struggles to express its fruit. Plum, dark chocolate and earth flavors pick up a hint of black pepper on the finish. 86 *—J.C. (2/1/2007)*

Tintara 2002 Reserve Shiraz (McLaren Vale) $49. 90 *—D.T. (3/1/2005)*

TOA

Toa 2004 Cabernet Sauvignon (McLaren Vale) $25. Starts with barrel-derived scents of coffee, maple syrup and smoke, but also exhibits aromas of cassis and just the merest hint of herbal complexity. The cassis flavors take over the palate, where the mouthfeel is creamy-smooth, buffered by soft tannins. Turns a little dusty and dry on the finish, sufficient to suggest 2–3 years of cellaring. Try in 2010. 89 *—J.C. (3/1/2007)*

Toa 2004 Shiraz (McLaren Vale) $25. A subsidiary label from Coriole, the Toa Shiraz is a sturdy, seemingly ageable red filled with plum and cassis fruit and garnished by a hint of vanilla. It's earthy and solid, with a layered finish. Drink 2008–2012. 89 *—J.C. (2/1/2007)*

TORBRECK

Torbreck 2005 Les Amis Grenache (Barossa Valley) $145. Winemaker David Powell gets this Grenache from vines planted in 1901 in Seppeltsfield. Their concentrated fruit yields a black-cherry-scented wine that's broad and mouthfilling, yet kept focused by flavors of earth and spice. Picks up a touch of vanilla from the new French oak on the finish, but also ends with a luscious, velvety texture. Drink now–2012. 93 *—J.C. (11/1/2007)*

Torbreck 2005 The Pict Mataro (Barossa Valley) $145. From an 85-year-old Mourvèdre vineyard in the Moppa subregion. The two years spent in new French oak is noticeable at this young stage, it should merge seamlessly with the dark fruit given a few years' time. Toast and cedar frame cola and earth, while the wine finishes with dark Asian spices. Unusually lush and rounded for the variety; drink 2008–2020. 94 *—J.C. (11/1/2007)*

Torbreck 2002 The Bothie Muscat (Barossa Valley) $NA. 88 *—D.T. (2/1/2004)*

Torbreck 2006 Juveniles Rhône Red Blend (Barossa Valley) $19. The price is right for this tank-aged blend of 60% Grenache, 20% Shiraz and 20% Mourvèdre. Ripe stone fruit flavors—is that a hint of apricot amid the cherries?—dominate, with a bit of spice creeping in on the silky finish. But what really sets this wine apart is its caressing, soft, delicate texture. Drink now–2010. 91 Editors' Choice *—J.C. (11/1/2007)*

Torbreck 2002 Juveniles Red Blend (Barossa Valley) $25. 90 Editors' Choice *—D.T. (2/1/2004)*

Torbreck 2005 The Steading Rhône Red Blend (Barossa Valley) $35. Different in style from the equally good 2004, the 2005 Steading is a bigger, richer, warmer wine, with brandied cherry fruit flavors and a rather fat, almost oily mouthfeel. More fruit and feel, less earth and spice. Drink it up over the next few years. 92 *—J.C. (11/1/2007)*

Torbreck 2004 The Steading Rhône Red Blend (Barossa Valley) $35. This is a wonderfully lush blend. Dark earth and cola notes come from the Mourvèdre, spice from the Syrah and cherry and almond components from the Grenache. Long on the finish, where the earth and spice notes really come through. Drink now–2010. 92 —*J.C. (11/1/2007)*

Torbreck 2001 The Steading Red Blend (Barossa Valley) $35. 89 —*D.T. (2/1/2004)*

Torbreck 2002 Woodcutter's Red (Barossa Valley) $20. 88 —*D.T. (2/1/2004)*

Torbreck 2006 Saignée Rosé Blend (Barossa Valley) $20. Although not indicated on the label, this is 100% Mourvèdre, bone dry and barrel fermented. As a result, it's not your typical fresh and fruity rosé, showing instead dark, complex flavors of cola, chocolate tree bark and earth. Hints of strawberry lighten it somewhat, but this is almost more red than rosé. Drink now–2008. 90 —*J.C. (12/31/2007)*

Torbreck 2001 Run Rig Shiraz (Barossa Valley) $145. 92 —*D.T. (2/1/2004)*

Torbreck 2001 Descendant Shiraz (Barossa Valley) $85. 90 —*D.T. (2/1/2004)*

Torbreck 2005 The Factor Shiraz (Barossa Valley) $105. Tarry and peppery, dark and meaty, it's difficult to describe how a wine that is so packed with lush blackberry and plum fruit can remain complex. The fruit completely fills the mouth, yet nuances of spicy, meaty complexity somehow permeate, building in intensity on the long finish. Supple enough to drink now, but should evolve positively through at least 2015 and last another 5–10 years beyond that. 97 Cellar Selection —*J.C. (11/1/2007)*

Torbreck 2004 The Factor Shiraz (Barossa Valley) $105. Perfumed on the nose, with hints of roses, pepper and game all adding complexity atop the base of berries and earth. This is wonderfully creamy in texture and crammed with lush fruit, but by no means is it what you'd dismissively call a fruit bomb, as there is considerable nuance to the flavors, ending on notes of pepper, meat and dried spices. Drink now–2020. 94 —*J.C. (11/1/2007)*

Torbreck 2001 The Factor Shiraz (Barossa Valley) $85. 89 —*D.T. (2/1/2004)*

Torbreck 2005 The Struie Shiraz (Barossa) $50. This has a distinctly spicy, savory, meaty quality to its aromas, possibly due to the one-third of the blend that comes from Eden Valley. Those elements impart great complexity to this wine, building on its core of blackberry fruit. Like all the Torbreck wines, this shows a rich, layered texture and a long finish. Drink now–2020. 93 —*J.C. (11/1/2007)*

Torbreck 2006 Woodcutter's Shiraz (Barossa Valley) $20. Tobreck's entry-level Shiraz boasts lovely aromas of blueberries and spice, with a hint of pepper. On the palate, blueberries and blackberries shine, and the texture is lush, tightening up just enough on the finish. This is a blend of 78 different lots, according to winemaker David Powell, mainly matured in old, large wood. Drink now–2014. 91 Editors' Choice —*J.C. (11/1/2007)*

Torbreck 2005 Descendant Shiraz-Viognier (Barossa Valley) $105. Unlike most of the Torbreck wines, this is single-vineyard Shiraz, cofermented with a small proportion of Viognier, then aged in barrels previously used for RunRig. Hints of apricot and bacon fat impart beautiful nuance to the blackberry fruit. This is slightly firmer than Torbreck's other reds, worth cellaring for five years or so, then drinking over the next 15. 95 Cellar Selection —*J.C. (11/1/2007)*

Torbreck 2004 RunRig Shiraz-Viognier (Barossa Valley) $220. Despite being loaded with complexity—spicy, meaty, savory and vanilla notes all feature in this wine—there's also explosive fruit. Swirls of blueberry and blackberry flavors are head-spinning and the texture is compellingly rich and velvety. If that isn't enough, the finish lasts for minutes. A blend of Shiraz from eight vineyards, all at least 90 years old, plus a tiny proportion (3%) of Viognier. Drink now–2024. 98 Cellar Selection —*J.C. (11/1/2007)*

Torbreck 2001 The Struie Shiraz (Barossa Valley) $50. 89 —*D.T. (2/1/2004)*

Torbreck 2002 White Blend (Barossa Valley) $35. 88 —*D.T. (2/1/2004)*

Torbreck 2002 Woodcutter's White Blend (Barossa Valley) $16. 85 —*D.T. (2/1/2004)*

TOWER ESTATE

Tower Estate 2002 Riesling (Clare Valley) $24. 88 —*D.T. (8/1/2003)*

TRENTHAM

Trentham 2000 Big Rivers Shiraz (Australia) $11. 88 Best Buy —*D.T. (12/31/2003)*

Trentham 2000 Murphy's Lore Big Rivers Shiraz-Cabernet Sauvignon (Australia) $8. 84 —*D.T. (12/31/2003)*

TREVOR MAST

Trevor Mast 2001 Four Sisters Merlot (South Eastern Australia) $12. 83 —*D.T. (1/1/2002)*

Trevor Mast 2000 Four Sisters Shiraz (South Eastern Australia) $15. 81 —*D.T. (1/1/2002)*

TURKEY FLAT

Turkey Flat 2001 Cabernet Sauvignon (Barossa Valley) $36. 87 —*D.T. (2/1/2004)*

Turkey Flat 2006 Grenache (Barossa Valley) $29. From a vineyard planted in 1920, this is a rather structured Barossa Valley Grenache. Spicy and herbal on the nose, fleshed out with black cherry fruit, but turning crisp and firm on the finish. 87 —*J.C. (11/1/2007)*

Turkey Flat 2002 Grenache (Barossa Valley) $15. 88 —*D.T. (2/1/2004)*

Turkey Flat 2002 Marsanne-Semillon (Barossa Valley) $17. 87 —*D.T. (2/1/2004)*

Turkey Flat 2005 Mourvèdre (Barossa Valley) $38. A slightly fruitier style of Mourvèdre than most Barossa offerings, with plum and blackberry fruit leading the way, backed by cola and hints of tree bark and dusty leather. Crisp, tart berries come through on the finish. 87 —*J.C. (11/1/2007)*

Turkey Flat 2002 The Turk Red Blend (Barossa Valley) $16. 85 —*D.T. (2/1/2004)*

Turkey Flat 2005 Butchers Block S-G-M Rhône Red Blend (Barossa Valley) $24. This blend of Shiraz, Grenache and Mataro is meaty and savory, with spice and leather notes that impart a dark, mysterious character. Sour plum and cola flavors continue the dark theme, buffered by soft tannins. Finishes long. Drink now–2012. 89 —*J.C. (11/1/2007)*

Turkey Flat 2001 Butchers Block Rhône Red Blend (Barossa Valley) $25. 87 —*D.T. (2/1/2004)*

Turkey Flat 2006 Rosé (Barossa Valley) $19. This is a bright red rosé—more like a tranlucent red than a pink wine—and it even acts a little like a red wine, offering ample palate weight and grip to go with its summery flavors of fresh berries. So ripely fruity that it almost tastes a bit sweet on the finish, but it stays this side of balanced. Drink now. 88 —*J.C. (7/1/2007)*

Turkey Flat 2003 Rosé (Barossa Valley) $16. 87 —*D.T. (2/1/2004)*

Turkey Flat 2005 Shiraz (Barossa Valley) $48. Owner/winemaker Peter Schulz has taken a little-known page from Hermitage, using a small amount of Marsanne to add a rich, glyceric mouthfeel to this impressively endowed wine. Savory, spicy notes give complexity to the ripe blackberry fruit flavors, which linger elegantly on the finish, couched in soft tannins. Drink now–2020. 94 —*J.C. (11/1/2007)*

Turkey Flat 2001 Shiraz (Barossa Valley) $36. 90 —*D.T. (2/1/2004)*

TURRAMURRA ESTATE

Turramurra Estate 1999 Proprietary Chardonnay (Mornington Peninsula) $23. 85 *(7/2/2004)*

TWELVE STAVES

Twelve Staves 2000 Grenache (McLaren Vale) $18. 86 —*J.C. (9/1/2002)*

Twelve Staves 1999 Grenache (McLaren Vale) $20. 85 —*J.C. (9/1/2001)*

Twelve Staves 2004 Shiraz-Grenache (McLaren Vale) $18. A 60-40 blend, this wine starts off with scents of vanilla, coffee and cinnamon, but backs that up with plenty of blackberry and plum fruit. It's big and full-bodied, but firm, defined by structure rather than lushness. Drink now-2012. 90 Editors' Choice —*J.C. (2/1/2007)*

TWIN BEAKS

Twin Beaks 2002 Chardonnay (South Eastern Australia) $10. 85 Best Buy —*D.T. (12/31/2004)*

Twin Beaks 2002 Merlot (South Eastern Australia) $10. 84 —*D.T. (12/31/2004)*

TWO HANDS

Two Hands 2004 Aphrodite Cabernet Sauvignon (Barossa Valley) $159. 89 —*D.T. (10/1/2006)*

Two Hands 2004 Aerope Grenache (Barossa Valley) $102. 90 —*J.C. (12/15/2006)*

Two Hands 2005 Yesterday's Hero Grenache (Barossa Valley) $45. A forward, fruit-driven Grenache that seems destined for early consumption, Yesterday's Hero features scents of dust-covered, sun-warmed cherries and hints of carob and leather. The flavors are bright and bouncy—cherry and vanilla—with a creamy texture and a tart, fresh finish. It's easy to like and easy to drink. 88—*J.C. (6/1/2007)*

Two Hands 2006 Brilliant Disguise 500ML Moscato (Barossa Valley) $19. 89 —*D.T. (11/15/2006)*

AUSTRALIA

Two Hands 2002 Brave Faces Red Blend (Barossa Valley) $27. 86 —*D.T. (12/31/2003)*

Two Hands 2004 The Wolf Riesling (Clare Valley) $24. 89 —*D.T. (3/1/2005)*

Two Hands 2003 The Wolf Riesling (Clare Valley) $19. 90 Editors' Choice —*D.T. (2/1/2004)*

Two Hands 2005 Angel's Share Shiraz (McLaren Vale) $30. 87 —*D.T. (10/1/2006)*

Two Hands 2002 Angel's Share Shiraz (McLaren Vale) $20. 86 —*D.T. (12/31/2003)*

Two Hands 2005 Ares Shiraz (Barossa Valley) $150. Two Hands' top-of-the-line Shiraz is a selection of the best barrels, boasting luscious vanilla and cedar from the oak, but also layers of raspberry and blackberry fruit. It's creamy, lush and vanilla-laden but elegant at the same time, with a long, slightly tart finish. Delicious now, but should age well through 2015. 93 —*J.C. (11/1/2007)*

Two Hands 2005 Bad Impersonator Single Vineyard Shiraz (Barossa Valley) $54. An elegant, medium-bodied Shiraz, with aromas and flavors of red berries and a hint of red peppercorn. Peppery in flavor, yet with smooth, supple tannins. Drink now. 87 —*J.C. (11/1/2007)*

Two Hands 2005 Bella's Garden Shiraz (Barossa Valley) $60. Nicely balanced, with subtle suede, cinnamon, plum and berry aromas and flavors. This is supple just to the point of being a bit creamy in the mouth, with a long, velvety finish. Approachable now, but should improve through at least 2012. 92 —*J.C. (11/1/2007)*

Two Hands 2005 Gnarly Dudes Shiraz (Barossa Valley) $30. A pleasant, well-made Shiraz, featuring mixed berry fruit and just a modicum of spice. Slightly richer and deeper than Two Hands' Bad Impersonator, but still not a heavyweight. Turns bright and crisp, with some raspberry flavors on the finish. Drink now. 89 —*J.C. (11/1/2007)*

Two Hands 2003 Lily's Garden Shiraz (McLaren Vale) $60. 90 —*D.T. (3/1/2005)*

Two Hands 2004 The Bull and the Bear Shiraz-Cabernet Sauvignon (Barossa Valley) $55. Defines the modern Oz fruit-bomb style, offering scents of blueberry liqueur alongside hints of vanilla and smoke before exploding on the palate with incredibly luscious, ripe fruit. Full-bodied and creamy-textured, this is a big wine at 15% alcohol, but it shows no sign of heat. Drink now-2012. 91 —*J.C. (2/1/2007)*

Two Hands 2004 The Bull and the Bear Shiraz-Cabernet Sauvignon (Barossa Valley) $59. 86 —*D.T. (10/1/2006)*

Two Hands 2005 Brave Faces Shiraz-Grenache (Barossa Valley) $36. 89 —*J.C. (12/15/2006)*

TYRRELL'S

Tyrrell's 2001 Moore's Creek Cabernet Sauvignon (South Eastern Australia) $9. 86 Best Buy —*D.T. (6/1/2003)*

Tyrrell's 2002 Old Winery Cabernet Sauvignon-Merlot (New South Wales) $10. 88 Best Buy —*D.T. (12/31/2003)*

Tyrrell's 2001 Old Winery Cabernet Sauvignon-Merlot (New South Wales) $15. 83 —*D.T. (1/1/2002)*

Tyrrell's 2003 Lost Block Chardonnay (South Eastern Australia) $14. 88 —*D.T. (5/1/2005)*

Tyrrell's 1999 Moon Mountain Chardonnay (Hunter Valley) $21. 88 —*J.C. (7/1/2002)*

Tyrrell's 2005 Moore's Creek Chardonnay (South Eastern Australia) $10. 87 Best Buy —*D.T. (8/1/2006)*

Tyrrell's 2002 Moore's Creek Chardonnay (South Eastern Australia) $9. 87 Best Buy —*D.T. (6/1/2003)*

Tyrrell's 2003 Old Winery Chardonnay (New South Wales) $12. 86 *(7/2/2004)*

Tyrrell's 2002 Old Winery Chardonnay (Hunter Valley) $14. 88 —*D.T. (8/1/2003)*

Tyrrell's 2001 Old Winery Hunter Valley/McLaren Vale Chardonnay (Hunter Valley) $14. 87 —*J.C. (7/1/2002)*

Tyrrell's 2005 Reserve Chardonnay (Hunter Valley) $17. This comes across as a bit restrained on the nose, showing only hints of lemon curd and vanilla wafers, then ratchets up the intensity on the palate, where it displays bold citrusy flavors limned with a touch of vanilla. Medium-bodied, it finishes fresh and vibrant, with enough crispness to pair with shellfish. 86 —*J.C. (2/1/2007)*

Tyrrell's 2003 Reserve Chardonnay (Hunter Valley) $25. 88 *(7/2/2004)*

Tyrrell's 2000 Reserve Chardonnay (Hunter Valley) $37. 88 —*M.M. (6/1/2001)*

Tyrrell's 2003 Vat 47 Chardonnay (Hunter Valley) $40. 89 —*D.T. (4/1/2006)*

Tyrrell's 2004 Vat 47 Chardonnay (Hunter Valley) $40. Fits the Chardonnay image to a T, with descriptors like smoke, clove, cinnamon, apple and citrus all coming readily to mind. It's fuller-bodied than some past vintages, with pineapple and vanilla flavors on the palate, and a long, crisp finish. 88 —*J.C. (8/1/2007)*

Tyrrell's 2001 Vat 47 Chardonnay (Hunter Valley) $60. 84 *(7/2/2004)*

Tyrrell's 2000 Vat 47 Chardonnay (Hunter Valley) $50. 89 *(8/1/2003)*

Tyrrell's 1999 Reserve Merlot (McLaren Vale) $37. 89 —*C.S. (6/1/2002)*

Tyrrell's 2003 Lost Block Pinot Noir (South Eastern Australia) $14. 85 —*D.T. (11/15/2005)*

Tyrrell's 2000 Old Winery Pinot Noir (South Eastern Australia) $15. 82 —*J.C. (9/1/2002)*

Tyrrell's 2000 Vat 6 Pinot Noir (Hunter Valley) $40. 85 —*D.T. (10/1/2005)*

Tyrrell's 1999 Vat 6 Hunter Pinot Noir (Hunter Valley) $50. 90 —*D.T. (5/1/2004)*

Tyrrell's 2003 Lost Block Semillon (Hunter Valley) $18. 86 —*D.T. (9/1/2004)*

Tyrrell's 1994 Vat 1 Semillon (Hunter Valley) $50. 87 —*J.C. (2/1/2002)*

Tyrrell's 2004 Moore's Creek Semillon-Sauvignon Blanc (South Eastern Australia) $9. 86 Best Buy —*D.T. (3/1/2005)*

Tyrrell's 2003 Moore's Creek Semillon-Sauvignon Blanc (New South Wales) $9. 86 —*D.T. (9/1/2004)*

Tyrrell's 2002 Moore's Creek Semillon-Sauvignon Blanc (Hunter Valley) $9. 85 —*D.T. (11/15/2003)*

Tyrrell's 2003 Old Winery Semillon-Sauvignon Blanc (Western Australia) $7. 85 —*D.T. (5/1/2004)*

Tyrrell's 2002 The Long Flat Semillon-Sauvignon Blanc (South Eastern Australia) $7. 84 Best Buy —*D.T. (5/1/2004)*

Tyrrell's 1999 Brokenback Shiraz (Hunter Valley) $24. 85 —*M.S. (3/1/2003)*

Tyrrell's 2003 DB24 Shiraz (McLaren Vale) $80. 92 Cellar Selection —*J.C. (12/15/2006)*

Tyrrell's 2004 Moore's Creek Shiraz (South Eastern Australia) $10. 82 —*D.T. (10/1/2006)*

Tyrrell's 2001 Moore's Creek Shiraz (South Eastern Australia) $9. 86 Best Buy —*K.F. (3/1/2003)*

Tyrrell's 2001 Old Winery Shiraz (Hunter Valley) $10. 85 —*K.F. (3/1/2003)*

Tyrrell's 2001 Reserve Shiraz (McLaren Vale) $12. 87 Best Buy —*D.T. (11/15/2004)*

Tyrrell's 1999 Reserve Shiraz (McLaren Vale) $37. 88 *(11/1/2001)*

Tyrrell's 2002 Rufus Stone Shiraz (McLaren Vale) $30. 87 —*D.T. (3/1/2005)*

Tyrrell's 2000 The Long Flat Vineyard Shiraz (South Australia) $9. 87 Best Buy *(10/1/2001)*

Tyrrell's 2002 Vat 8 Shiraz (Hunter Valley) $40. 86 —*D.T. (10/1/2006)*

Tyrrell's 1998 Vat 9 Shiraz (Hunter Valley) $50. 88 *(12/31/2003)*

Tyrrell's 1997 Vat 9 Shiraz (Hunter Valley) $40. 88 —*D.T. (4/1/2006)*

Tyrrell's 2001 The Long Flat Vineyard White Blend (South Eastern Australia) $7. 85 Best Buy —*D.T. (2/1/2002)*

TYRRELL'S OLD WINERY

Tyrrell's Old Winery 2003 Chardonnay (Hunter Valley & McLaren Vale) $11. 86 Best Buy —*D.T. (12/31/2004)*

UBET

UBET 2001 Chardonnay (South Eastern Australia) $10. 84 —*D.T. (6/1/2003)*

UBET 2001 Shiraz (South Eastern Australia) $10. 86 —*M.S. (3/1/2003)*

VASSE FELIX

Vasse Felix 2003 Heytesbury Bordeaux Blend (Margaret River) $50. 93 Cellar Selection —*D.T. (10/1/2006)*

Vasse Felix 2001 Heytesbury Bordeaux Blend (Margaret River) $40. 91 —*D.T. (5/1/2005)*

Vasse Felix 2001 Cabernet Sauvignon (Margaret River) $30. 90 —*D.T. (10/1/2003)*

Vasse Felix 2000 Cabernet Sauvignon (Margaret River) $30. 92 Editors' Choice —*M.S. (12/15/2002)*

Vasse Felix 2000 Cabernet Sauvignon (Margaret River) $30. 89 *—D.T. (11/15/2004)*

Vasse Felix 1999 Cabernet Sauvignon (Western Australia) $30. 84 *—D.T. (9/1/2001)*

Vasse Felix 1998 Cabernet Sauvignon (Western Australia) $29. 92 *—M.S. (10/1/2000)*

Vasse Felix 2001 Cabernet Sauvignon-Merlot (Margaret River) $20. 88 *—D.T. (10/1/2003)*

Vasse Felix 2002 Adam's Road Cabernet Sauvignon-Merlot (Margaret River) $15. 87 *—D.T. (9/1/2004)*

Vasse Felix 2003 Adams Road Cabernet Sauvignon-Merlot (Margaret River) $15. 84 *—D.T. (12/31/2005)*

Vasse Felix 2002 Chardonnay (Margaret River) $20. 87 *(7/2/2004)*

Vasse Felix 2001 Chardonnay (Margaret River) $24. 88 *—D.T. (10/1/2003)*

Vasse Felix 1998 Chardonnay (Western Australia) $19. 90 *(10/1/2000)*

Vasse Felix 2004 Adams Road Chardonnay (Margaret River) $15. 86 *—D.T. (10/1/2005)*

Vasse Felix 2003 Adams Road Chardonnay (Margaret River) $15. 85 *—D.T. (12/31/2004)*

Vasse Felix 2001 Heytesbury Chardonnay (Margaret River) $30. 92 *—D.T. (10/1/2003)*

Vasse Felix 2001 Heytesbury Chardonnay (Western Australia) $30. 88 *(7/2/2004)*

Vasse Felix 2000 Heytesbury Chardonnay (Western Australia) $30. 87 *—J.C. (7/1/2002)*

Vasse Felix 2000 Heytesbury Red Blend (Margaret River) $40. 91 *—D.T. (10/1/2003)*

Vasse Felix 1999 Heytesbury Red Blend (Western Australia) $40. 93 Editors' Choice *—S.H. (12/15/2002)*

Vasse Felix 2001 Shiraz (Margaret River) $30. 90 *—D.T. (11/15/2004)*

Vasse Felix 2001 Shiraz (Margaret River) $30. 91 *—S.H. (10/1/2003)*

Vasse Felix 2000 Shiraz (Margaret River) $30. 91 Editors' Choice *—S.H. (12/15/2002)*

Vasse Felix 1999 Shiraz (Margaret River) $30. 89 *(11/1/2001)*

Vasse Felix 1998 Shiraz (Margaret River) $27. 91 *—M.S. (10/1/2000)*

Vasse Felix 2002 Adam's Road Shiraz (Margaret River) $15. 89 Editors' Choice *—D.T. (5/1/2004)*

VIRGIN HILLS

Virgin Hills 1998 Red Blend (Victoria) $30. 86 *—J.C. (9/1/2002)Í*

VOYAGER ESTATE

Voyager Estate 2000 Chardonnay (Margaret River) $20. 84 *—J.C. (7/1/2002)*

Voyager Estate 1999 Shiraz (Margaret River) $19. 85 *(10/1/2001)*

WAGTAIL

Wagtail 2006 Riesling (Adelaide Hills) $10. Surprisingly complete and harmonious for a Riesling in this price range, Wagtail's 2006 boasts opening scents of honey, ripe apples, citrus and crushed stone. Peach and citrus flavors dominate the palate, ending dry and stony. Drink now. 87 Best Buy *—J.C. (9/1/2007)*

Wagtail 2005 Shiraz (Barossa) $10. Blackberry fruit is framed in chocolate, cedar and cola nuances, while the texture is creamy, the tannins supple and the finish long. Drink now. 87 Best Buy *—J.C. (11/1/2007)*

Wagtail 2005 Shiraz-Grenache (McLaren Vale) $10. A bargain blend (62% Shiraz, 38% Grenache) that offers a mouthful of warm cherry-berry fruit and hints of vanilla and pastry crust. Finishes crisp and tart. Drink now. 85 Best Buy *—J.C. (7/1/2007)*

WAKEFIELD ESTATE

Wakefield Estate 2002 Cabernet Sauvignon (Clare Valley) $16. 86 *—D.T. (2/1/2004)*

Wakefield Estate 2001 Cabernet Sauvignon (Clare Valley) $15. 87 *—D.T. (5/1/2004)*

Wakefield Estate 1998 St. Andrews Cabernet Sauvignon (Clare Valley) $60. 89 *—D.T. (2/1/2004)*

Wakefield Estate 2002 Promised Land Cabernet Sauvignon-Merlot (South Australia) $13. 87 *—D.T. (11/15/2003)*

Wakefield Estate 2004 Chardonnay (Clare Valley) $17. 87 *—D.T. (10/1/2006)*

Wakefield Estate 2003 Chardonnay (South Australia) $18. 86 *(7/2/2004)*

Wakefield Estate 2003 Promised Land Chardonnay (South Australia) $13. 85 *(7/2/2004)*

Wakefield Estate 2002 Promised Land Unwooded Chardonnay (South Australia) $10. 82 *—D.T. (8/1/2003)*

Wakefield Estate 2005 Promised Land Unwooded Chardonnay (South Australia) $13. 86 *—D.T. (11/15/2006)*

Wakefield Estate 2000 St. Andrews Chardonnay (Clare Valley) $17. 84 *(7/2/2004)*

Wakefield Estate 2005 Riesling (Clare Valley) $17. 86 *—D.T. (10/1/2006)*

Wakefield Estate 2005 Promised Land Riesling (South Australia) $13. With its pronounced weight, bit of residual sugar and slightly oily texture, this is not a prototypical Australian Riesling. But it is well made, with flavors of baked apple and citrus that last on the finish. 85 *—J.C. (2/1/2007)*

Wakefield Estate 2004 Shiraz (Clare Valley) $17. This wine takes some time in the glass to fully open up and express itself, but when it does, it's a beauty. Hints of menthol and toast frame blackberry and blueberry fruit, while subtle notes of vanilla and coffee surround an earthy core. It's full-bodied and viscous, with an almost Port-like texture and dry, dusty tannins on the finish. Hold 3–5 years. 90 Editors' Choice *—J.C. (3/1/2007)*

Wakefield Estate 2002 Shiraz (Clare Valley) $16. 86 *—D.T. (2/1/2004)*

Wakefield Estate 1999 St. Andrews Shiraz (Clare Valley) $60. 90 *—D.T. (2/1/2004)*

Wakefield Estate 2004 Promised Land Shiraz-Cabernet Sauvignon (South Australia) $13. Full-bodied and richly textured, it delivers a big mouthful of wine for the price. The flavors are dark, leaning toward the coffee, tobacco and cassis range, with hints of vanilla and mint. Reasonably long on the finish, picking up a slightly tart edge to the flavors. Drink now–2010. 88 Best Buy *—J.C. (2/1/2007)*

Wakefield Estate 2001 Promised Land Shiraz-Cabernet Sauvignon (South Australia) $13. 83 *—D.T. (1/1/2002)*

WALLABY CREEK

Wallaby Creek 2000 Chardonnay (South Eastern Australia) $7. 82 *—D.T. (1/1/2002)*

Wallaby Creek 2001 Merlot (Big Rivers) $6. 81 *—D.T. (1/1/2002)*

Wallaby Creek 2000 Shiraz (South Eastern Australia) $7. 82 *—M.S. (1/28/2003)*

WANDIN VALLEY

Wandin Valley 2000 Riley's Reserve Cabernet Sauvignon (Hunter Valley) $20. 86 *—D.T. (9/1/2004)*

Wandin Valley 2002 Chardonnay (Hunter Valley) $13. 85 *(7/2/2004)*

Wandin Valley NV Muscat (South Eastern Australia) $15. 84 *—D.T. (12/31/2004)*

Wandin Valley 2002 Verdelho (Hunter Valley) $13. 87 *—D.T. (11/15/2004)*

WARBURN

Warburn 2000 Show Reserve Cabernet Sauvignon-Merlot (Riverina) $15. 85 *—M.S. (12/15/2002)*

Warburn 2000 Show Reserve Durif (Riverina) $15. 88 *—D.T. (6/1/2003)*

WARRABILLA

Warrabilla 2004 Parola's Limited Release Cabernet Sauvignon (Rutherglen) $60. 90 *—D.T. (10/1/2006)*

Warrabilla 2004 Reserve Cabernet Sauvignon (Rutherglen) $45. 91 *—D.T. (10/1/2006)*

Warrabilla 1998 Chardonnay (Rutherglen) $18. 85 *—S.H. (10/1/2000)*

Warrabilla 2004 Parola's Limited Release Durif (Rutherglen) $55. 88 *—D.T. (6/1/2006)*

Warrabilla 2004 Reserve Durif (Rutherglen) $40. 88 *—D.T. (6/1/2006)*

Warrabilla 2000 Petite Sirah (Rutherglen) $27. 88 *—J.C. (9/1/2002)*

Warrabilla 1999 Petite Sirah (Victoria) $29. 83 *—D.T. (9/1/2001)*

Warrabilla 2000 Shiraz (Rutherglen) $27. 87 *—J.C. (9/1/2002)*

WARREN MANG VINEYARDS

Warren Mang Vineyards 2002 Vinello Red Blend (King Valley) $20. 85 *—D.T. (1/1/2002)*

WARRENMANG

Warrenmang 1999 Estate Shiraz (Victoria) $45. 89 *—D.T. (8/1/2005)*

WATER WHEEL

Water Wheel 1999 Cabernet Sauvignon (Bendigo) $15. 82 *—J.C. (6/1/2002)*

Water Wheel 2000 Chardonnay (Bendigo) $12. 84 *—D.T. (6/1/2003)*

Water Wheel 2005 Memsie Sauvignon Blanc-Semillon-Roussanne White Blend (Bendigo) $16. When a reviewer's notes on a wine include the sentence, "What is this?" you know it's a wine struggling for identity. So it is with this mutt-ly blend. It's flinty and not terribly expressive at first, then adds hints of honey and pears, while the texture is oddly thick and pulpy. Turns tangy on the finish. A different breed, especially considering it's 80% Sauvignon Blanc. 82 *—J.C. (3/1/2007)*

WAYNE THOMAS

Wayne Thomas 2004 Cabernet Sauvignon (McLaren Vale) $22. Veteran winemaker Wayne Thomas has crafted a prototypical Australian Cabernet, mingling mint and eucalyptus notes with cassis fruit and a touch of chocolaty oak. The texture is creamy enough to suggest early drinkability, yet there are also velvety-dusty tannins that should enable the wine to develop over the next several years. 90 *—J.C. (6/1/2007)*

Wayne Thomas 2005 Elevenses Chardonnay (McLaren Vale) $20. Fresh and gingery on the nose, this an attractive 100% Chardonnay sparkler with assertive flavors of green apple, lime and toast. It's slightly creamy in the mouth, yet finishes long and crisp, with plenty of refreshing zest. 89 *—J.C. (8/1/2007)*

Wayne Thomas 2004 Petite Verdot (McLaren Vale) $24. 89 *—D.T. (8/1/2006)*

Wayne Thomas 2005 Shiraz (McLaren Vale) $22. The bouquet is complex—mixing black cherries and plums, vanilla and spice—the flavors dark and chocolaty, the mouthfeel creamy and dense. Impressively rich, just lacks a spark, finishing a bit heavy. With its high alcohol (15.5%) and concentration, this is probably best paired with the cheese course. 89 *—J.C. (6/1/2007)*

Wayne Thomas 2003 Shiraz (McLaren Vale) $21. 89 *—J.C. (12/15/2006)*

WEDGETAIL-ROSSETTO WINES

Wedgetail-Rossetto Wines 2001 Shiraz-Cabernet Sauvignon (Riverina) $8. 82 *—D.T. (12/31/2003)*

WEST CAPE HOWE

West Cape Howe 2003 Cabernet Sauvignon (Western Australia) $19. 87 *—D.T. (8/1/2006)*

West Cape Howe 2004 Book Ends Cabernet Sauvignon (Great Southern) $20. This is a medium-bodied, well structured Cabernet that looks set to reward at least 3–4 years of cellaring. It already shows a complex array of flavors, ranging from coffee, leather and earth to plum, blackberry and dried spices. It just needs some time for the firm tannins to soften. 90 Editors' Choice *—J.C. (2/1/2007)*

West Cape Howe 2004 Chardonnay (Western Australia) $18. This deeply golden wine is heavily marked by its time in oak, filled with smoky, toasted aromas and flavors of grilled peaches. Ultimately, the wood dominates the flavor profile. For fans of oaky Chardonnay; drink now. 84 *—J.C. (4/1/2007)*

West Cape Howe 2003 Chardonnay (Western Australia) $18. 86 *—D.T. (8/1/2006)*

West Cape Howe 2005 Unwooded Chardonnay (Western Australia) $15. 83 *—D.T. (11/15/2006)*

West Cape Howe 2006 Riesling (Western Australia) $17. Starts with scents of lime sherbet, but also hints of herbs, kerosene and stone fruits. Citrus and underripe peaches are the main flavors. This wine is clean and fresh, but seems to lack a little flesh in the midpalate. Drink now. 85 *—J.C. (9/1/2007)*

West Cape Howe 2004 Riesling (Western Australia) $17. 86 *—D.T. (8/1/2006)*

West Cape Howe 2004 Semillon-Sauvignon Blanc (Western Australia) $15. 83 *—D.T. (8/1/2006)*

WHISTLER

Whistler 2005 The Reserve Shiraz (Barossa) $NA. Even though the vines were only planted in 1994, this is top-shelf stuff, dry grown, concentrated and intense. Bits of mint and licorice give dimension to the ripe blackberry and blueberry flavors, the mouthfeel is full and creamy and the finish turns dry and firm, showing solid structure. Approachable now, but probably best from 2010 to 2020. 93 *—J.C. (11/1/2007)*

WHITE KNOT

White Knot 2005 Chardonnay (McLaren Vale) $12. 84 *—D.T. (8/1/2006)*

WHITSEND ESTATE

Whitsend Estate 2002 Cabernet Sauvignon (Yarra Valley) $20. 87 *—D.T. (12/31/2004)*

WILDBERRY ESTATE

Wildberry Estate 2004 Cabernet Sauvignon-Merlot (Margaret River) $19. Shows something of a Graves-like flavor profile, with dark coffee, earth and tobacco notes arrayed alongside cedar, cola and black cherry. It's a complex, medium-weight wine with enough soft tannin to stand up to rare beef or lamb, but enough elegance to please. Drink now–2010. 89 *—J.C. (5/1/2007)*

Wildberry Estate 2006 Chardonnay (Margaret River) $19. Wildberry Estate's 2006 Chardonnay deftly juxtaposes a soft, plump midpalate with a firm, crisp backbone. The structure gives added zip to the lime and honeydew flavors, which finish fresh and clean. Drink now. 87 *—J.C. (8/1/2007)*

Wildberry Estate 2004 Shiraz (Margaret River) $19. Starts off rather dark and brooding, with scents of coffee, dark chocolate and saddle leather, but despite the almost scorched aromas, there's also a bright beam of red fruit. Medium-weight and supple in the mouth, finishing crisp. 85 *—J.C. (4/1/2007)*

WILLOW BRIDGE

Willow Bridge 2001 Estate Cabernet Sauvignon (Western Australia) $13. 87 *—D.T. (5/1/2004)*

Willow Bridge 2001 Winemaker's Reserve Cabernet Sauvignon-Merlot (Western Australia) $13. 87 *—D.T. (9/1/2004)*

WILLOW CREEK

Willow Creek 1998 Cabernet Sauvignon (Mornington Peninsula) $21. 87 *—S.H. (9/1/2001)*

Willow Creek 1999 Tulum Reserve Chardonnay (Mornington Peninsula) $26. 86 *—S.H. (9/1/2001)*

Willow Creek 2001 Unoaked Chardonnay (Mornington Peninsula) $18. 85 *—J.C. (7/1/2002)*

Willow Creek 2000 Unoaked Chardonnay (Mornington Peninsula) $18. 85 *—S.H. (9/1/2001)*

Willow Creek 2000 Sauvignon Blanc (Mornington Peninsula) $18. 86 *—S.H. (9/1/2001)*

WILLOWGLEN

Willowglen 2001 Shiraz (South Eastern Australia) $6. 84 Best Buy *—D.T. (12/31/2003)*

Willowglen 2003 De Bortoli Wines Shiraz-Cabernet Sauvignon (South Eastern Australia) $9. 84 *—D.T. (12/31/2004)*

WILSON VINEYARD (AUS)

Wilson Vineyard (AUS) 2000 Gallery Series Cabernet Sauvignon (Clare Valley) $22. 89 *—D.T. (5/1/2004)*

Wilson Vineyard (AUS) 2002 Proprietary Riesling (Clare Valley) $18. 90 Editors' Choice *—D.T. (5/1/2004)*

WINDSHAKER RIDGE

Windshaker Ridge 2004 Carnelian (Western Australia) $14. 87 *—D.T. (8/1/2006)*

WINDSHAKER RIDGE

Windshaker Ridge 2003 Carnelian (Western Australia) $13. 86 *—D.T. (8/1/2005)*

Windshaker Ridge 2003 Chardonnay (Western Australia) $13. 84 *—D.T. (10/1/2005)*

Windshaker Ridge 2003 Shiraz (Western Australia) $13. 86 *—D.T. (12/1/2005)*

Windshaker Ridge 2005 Verdelho (Western Australia) $14. 87 *—D.T. (10/1/2006)*

Windshaker Ridge 2003 Verdelho (Western Australia) $13. 87 Best Buy *—D.T. (8/1/2005)*

WINDY PEAK

Windy Peak 2002 Chardonnay (Victoria) $13. 86 *(7/2/2004)*

Windy Peak 2001 Pinot Noir (Victoria) $13. 85 *—D.T. (10/1/2003)*

Windy Peak 2000 Shiraz (Victoria) $13. 81 *(10/1/2001)*

WINNER'S TANK

Winner's Tank 2006 Shiraz (Langhorne Creek) $16. Barossa-based winemaker Reid Bosward crafts this lush, opulent Shiraz from Langhorne Creek. Bold blueberry and blackberry flavors are soft and pillowy in texture, picking up brushes of chocolate and asphalt on the finish. 89 *(11/15/2007)*

WINTER CREEK

Winter Creek 2005 The Old Barossa Blend Grenache-Shiraz (Barossa) $25. This 75-25 Grenache-Shiraz blend features complex aromas of pepper, dusty earth, leather and black cherries. The tannins are ripe, the mouthfeel round and the fruit surges forward on the palate, picking up a touch of licorice on the finish. Drink now–2012. 89 *—J.C. (11/1/2007)*

Winter Creek 2004 The Old Barossa Blend Grenache-Shiraz (Barossa Valley) $27. The blend is 75-25 in favor of Grenache, yielding a slightly warm yet only medium-bodied wine with strong black cherry overtones. But there's also a sense of dusty, sun-baked earth and hints of spice to add complexity. Drink now. 87 *—J.C. (6/1/2007)*

Winter Creek 2004 Shiraz (Barossa Valley) $30. A fresh, easy-drinking Shiraz, brimming with blackberries. No, there's not a ton of complexity, but this wine delivers a mouthful of pure, slightly jammy fruit that should prove versatile at the table. Drink now–2012. 87 *—J.C. (11/1/2007)*

Winter Creek 2000 Shiraz (Barossa Valley) $20. 89 *—M.S. (3/1/2003)*

WIRRA WIRRA

Wirra Wirra 2003 Scrubby Rise Chardonnay (McLaren Vale) $11. 84 *—D.T. (3/1/2005)*

Wirra Wirra 2003 Scrubby Rise Chardonnay (South Australia) $13. 87 Best Buy *(7/2/2004)*

Wirra Wirra 2004 Sexton's Acre Unwooded Chardonnay (McLaren Vale) $NA. 84 *—D.T. (3/1/2005)*

Wirra Wirra 2002 Grenache (McLaren Vale) $27. 89 *—D.T. (3/1/2005)*

Wirra Wirra 2002 Church Block Red Blend (McLaren Vale) $17. 88 *—D.T. (3/1/2005)*

Wirra Wirra 1999 Church Block Red Blend (McLaren Vale) $20. 81 *—J.C. (9/1/2002)*

Wirra Wirra 2000 Scrubby Rise Red Blend (Fleurieu Peninsula) $10. 87 Best Buy *—J.C. (9/1/2002)*

Wirra Wirra 2002 Scrubby Rise SZ-CS-PV Red Blend (McLaren Vale) $11. 87 Best Buy *—D.T. (3/1/2005)*

Wirra Wirra 2001 Hand Picked Riesling (Fleurieu Peninsula) $13. 86 *—M.M. (2/1/2002)*

Wirra Wirra 2000 Hand Picked Riesling (McLaren Vale) $13. 87 *—M.M. (1/1/2004)*

Wirra Wirra 2004 Mrs. Wigley Rosé Blend (South Australia) $19. 88 *—D.T. (2/1/2006)*

Wirra Wirra 2002 Shiraz (McLaren Vale) $27. 89 *—D.T. (3/1/2005)*

Wirra Wirra 2001 Shiraz (McLaren Vale) $26. 88 *—D.T. (12/31/2003)*

Wirra Wirra 1999 Shiraz (McLaren Vale) $28. 86 *—J.C. (9/1/2002)*

Wirra Wirra 1998 Chook Block Shiraz (McLaren Vale) $75. 89 *(11/1/2001)*

Wirra Wirra 1998 R.S.W. Shiraz (McLaren Vale) $67. 92 *—D.T. (12/31/2003)*

Wirra Wirra 1997 R.S.W. Shiraz (McLaren Vale) $35. 90 *(10/1/2000)*

Wirra Wirra 2002 RSW Shiraz (McLaren Vale) $54. 91 Cellar Selection *—D.T. (3/1/2005)*

Wirra Wirra 2003 Scrubby Rise Shiraz (South Australia) $12. 86 *—D.T. (12/1/2005)*

Wirra Wirra 2002 Scrubby Rise Shiraz (South Australia) $10. 86 *—D.T. (9/1/2004)*

Wirra Wirra 2001 Scrubby Rise White Blend (Fleurieu Peninsula) $10. 81 *—D.T. (2/1/2002)*

Wirra Wirra 2000 Scrubby Rise White Blend (McLaren Vale) $13. 82 *—D.T. (1/1/2002)*

Wirra Wirra 1999 Scrubby Rise White Blend (McLaren Vale) $13. 90 Best Buy *—M.S. (10/1/2000)*

WISE

Wise 1997 Cabernet Sauvignon (Margaret River) $17. 86 *—M.S. (10/1/2000)*

Wise 1999 Aquercus Unwooded Chardonnay (Margaret River) $10. 85 *(10/1/2000)*

Wise 2003 Reserve Chardonnay (Pemberton) $35. 89 *—D.T. (12/1/2005)*

Wise 2003 Single Vineyard Chardonnay (Western Australia) $25. 84 *—D.T. (12/1/2005)*

Wise 2005 Unwooded Chardonnay (Pemberton) $15. This weighty blend of mixed tropical fruit and citrus ably answers the call for fresh fruit, unadorned by oak. Balanced and fresh, this would be a nice wine to sip on its own at the start of a meal. 87 *—J.C. (3/1/2007)*

Wise 2004 Unwooded Chardonnay (Pemberton) $15. 86 *—D.T. (12/1/2005)*

Wise 2001 Unwooded Chardonnay (Western Australia) $13. 83 *—J.C. (7/1/2002)*

Wise 2005 Classic White Semillon-Sauvignon Blanc (Western Australia) $16. Herbal almost to the point of vegetal, with aromas of tobacco or tomato leaf backed by citrusy flavors and a crisp, grapefruity finish. This is a distinctive wine, one that may have its fans, but I suspect they'll be in the minority. 82 *—J.C. (3/1/2007)*

Wise 2004 Classic White Semillon-Sauvignon Blanc (Western Australia) $16. 86 *—D.T. (12/1/2005)*

Wise 2002 Eagle Bay Shiraz (Margaret River) $28. 88 *—D.T. (12/1/2005)*

Wise 1998 Eagle Bay Shiraz (Western Australia) $20. 85 *(10/1/2001)*

Wise 2002 Shiraz-Cabernet Sauvignon (Margaret River) $12. 82 *—D.T. (8/1/2006)*

WIT'S END

Wit's End 2002 Shiraz (McLaren Vale) $NA. 88 *—D.T. (5/1/2005)*

WOLF BLASS

Wolf Blass 2001 Gold Label Cabernet Sauvignon-Cabernet Franc Cabernet Blend (Adelaide Hills) $NA. 89 *—D.T. (2/1/2004)*

Wolf Blass 2002 Gold Label Cabernet Sauvignon (Coonawarra) $24. 90 *—D.T. (12/31/2004)*

Wolf Blass 2000 Gold Label Cabernet Sauvignon (Coonawarra) $NA. 88 *—D.T. (5/1/2004)*

Wolf Blass 2004 Grey Label Cabernet Sauvignon (Langhorne Creek) $32. This is a big, dense, dark-fruited wine, but also one that is surprisingly tart. Cedary, meaty and minty notes lead the way on the nose, while the flavors are of coffee, mint, cedar and cassis. Tannins are drying on the finish, so serve with rare beef or lamb to help tame them. 86 *—J.C. (6/1/2007)*

Wolf Blass 2003 Grey Label Cabernet Sauvignon (Langhorne Creek) $32. 88 *—D.T. (8/1/2006)*

Wolf Blass 2002 Grey Label Cabernet Sauvignon (Langhorne Creek) $32. 90 *—D.T. (11/15/2004)*

Wolf Blass 1998 Jimmy Watson Trophy Black Label` Cabernet Sauvignon (Barossa Valley) $50. 93 Cellar Selection *—S.H. (12/15/2002)*

Wolf Blass 1998 Platinum Label Cabernet Sauvignon (Barossa Valley) $34. 90 *—D.T. (12/31/2003)*

Wolf Blass 2001 Presidents Selection Cabernet Sauvignon (South Australia) $19. 85 *—D.T. (8/1/2005)*

Wolf Blass 2000 Presidents Selection Cabernet Sauvignon (South Australia) $20. 87 *—D.T. (6/1/2003)*

Wolf Blass 2005 Yellow Label Cabernet Sauvignon (South Australia) $12. Surprisingly herbal and coarsely textured for a Wolf Blass effort, with cherry, tobacco and tomato notes running together on the palate. Finishes a bit better, with coffee and chocolate notes that provide a sense of richness. 83 *—J.C. (11/15/2007)*

Wolf Blass 2004 Yellow Label Cabernet Sauvignon (South Australia) $12. This rather lightweight Cabernet features cherry-scented fruit and hints of mint to go along with herb-inflected cherry flavors. Tannins are slightly drying, just enough to help cut through the grease of a weeknight burger. A solid commercial effort; drink now. 84 *—J.C. (3/1/2007)*

Wolf Blass 2002 Yellow Label Cabernet Sauvignon (South Australia) $12. 88 Best Buy *—D.T. (11/15/2004)*

Wolf Blass 2001 Yellow Label Cabernet Sauvignon (South Australia) $14. 87 *—D.T. (12/31/2003)*

Wolf Blass 2000 Yellow Label Cabernet Sauvignon (South Australia) $12. 87 Best Buy *—M.S. (12/15/2002)*

Wolf Blass 1999 Yellow Label Cabernet Sauvignon (South Australia) $12. 86 *(6/1/2001)*

Wolf Blass 1997 Yellow Label Cabernet Sauvignon (South Australia) $12. 87 Best Buy *(3/1/2000)*

Wolf Blass 2000 Black Label Cabernet Sauvignon-Shiraz (Barossa-Langhorne Creek) $60. 89 *—D.T. (5/1/2004)*

Wolf Blass 2001 Chardonnay (South Australia) $12. 84 *—D.T. (8/1/2003)*

Wolf Blass 1999 Chardonnay (South Australia) $12. 86 *—L.W. (3/1/2000)*

Wolf Blass 2000 Barrel Fermented Chardonnay (South Australia) $12. 86 *(6/1/2001)*

Wolf Blass 2004 Gold Label Chardonnay (Adelaide Hills) $21. 88 *—D.T. (8/1/2005)*

Wolf Blass 2003 Gold Label Chardonnay (Adelaide Hills) $20. 88 *—D.T. (11/15/2004)*

Wolf Blass 2004 Presidents Selection Chardonnay (South Australia) $17. A no-apologies, New World style of Chardonnay, with plenty of toasty oak framing lush buttered and grilled peaches. Big-fruited, this has the richness to pair with Dungeness crab, and a long, relatively harmonious finish as well. 89 *—J.C. (2/1/2007)*

Wolf Blass 2003 Presidents Selection Chardonnay (South Australia) $14. 84 *(7/2/2004)*

Wolf Blass 2002 Presidents Selection Chardonnay (South Australia) $15. 87 *(7/2/2004)*

Wolf Blass 2001 Presidents Selection Chardonnay (South Australia) $15. 84 *—D.T. (6/1/2003)*

Wolf Blass 2005 Yellow Label Chardonnay (South Australia) $12. 86 *—D.T. (8/1/2006)*

Wolf Blass 2004 Yellow Label Chardonnay (South Australia) $12. 83 *—D.T. (10/1/2005)*

Wolf Blass 2003 Yellow Label Chardonnay (South Australia) $12. 84 *—D.T. (11/15/2004)*

Wolf Blass 2001 Merlot (South Australia) $14. 85 *(6/1/2003)*

Wolf Blass 2004 Yellow Label Merlot (South Australia) $12. 84 *—D.T. (6/1/2006)*

Wolf Blass 2003 Yellow Label Merlot (South Australia) $12. 84 *—D.T. (10/1/2005)*

Wolf Blass 2005 Gold Label Riesling (Adelaide) $14. Pretty straightforward stuff, with green apple and citrus aromas and just hints of honey and petrol. It's medium-bodied, with a touch of residual sugar, but ends with mouthwatering acids. Drink now–2010. 86 *—J.C. (9/1/2007)*

Wolf Blass 2003 Gold Label Riesling (Clare & Eden Valleys) $14. 87 *—D.T. (2/1/2004)*

Wolf Blass 2001 Gold Label Riesling (Eden Valley) $12. 89 *—M.M. (2/1/2002)*

Wolf Blass 2000 Gold Label Riesling (South Australia) $12. 89 Editors' Choice *—M.M. (9/1/2001)*

Wolf Blass 1999 Gold Label Riesling (South Australia) $12. 86 *—M.S. (10/1/2000)*

Wolf Blass 2006 Yellow Label Riesling (South Australia) $12. This bargain-priced Riesling from Wolf Blass features aromas of lime sherbet alongside hints of quince and floral elements. On the palate, it's intense and zippy, filled with loads of apple and lime flavor. It's not especially complex, but bold and strident. 87 Best Buy *—J.C. (6/1/2007)*

Wolf Blass 2003 Gold Label Sauvignon Blanc (Adelaide Hills) $NA. 87 *—D.T. (2/1/2004)*

Wolf Blass 2000 Shiraz (South Australia) $12. 85 *—M.S. (3/1/2003)*

Wolf Blass 2005 Gold Label Shiraz (Barossa) $25. With its soft tannins, this is a drink-me-now style of Shiraz, but one that shows a little extra depth and complexity. Floral notes perk up the aromas while cherries and berries flavor the palate, turning a bit crisp on the finish. Drink now–2011. 88 *—J.C. (11/1/2007)*

Wolf Blass 2004 Gold Label Shiraz (Barossa Valley) $25. Shows distinctive Barossa style, with a touch of alcoholic warmth to the superripe blackberry liqueur flavors. Ample oak imparts toast, vanilla, mint and chocolate complexity. It's a big, full-bodied wine, but because of its ripeness is approachable now. 90 *—J.C. (4/1/2007)*

Wolf Blass 2001 Gold Label Shiraz (Barossa Valley) $24. 87 *—D.T. (2/1/2004)*

Wolf Blass 2002 Gold Label Shiraz-Viognier Shiraz (Barossa Valley) $NA. 90 Editors' Choice *—D.T. (5/1/2004)*

Wolf Blass 2005 Platinum Label Shiraz (Barossa) $85. At this young age and only a couple of months after bottling, the French oak is showing a bit in the smoky, toasty aromas. But there's plenty of fruit to balance out the wood—plummy, fruitcake-like flavors that wash over the palate in creamy, lush waves. Mouthfilling and rich, with a supple, long finish; if it's a trifle less complex and structured than the 2004, it makes up for it in sheer lusciousness. Drink now–2015. 93 *—J.C. (11/1/2007)*

Wolf Blass 2004 Platinum Label Shiraz (Barossa) $85. The inclusion of a large proportion of Eden Valley fruit gives this wonderfully complex aromas of cracked peppers and dried spices, which build upon a solid core of ripe blackberry fruit. Creamy and lush on the midpalate, it firms up considerably by the finish. This stays true to Wolf Blass's approachable style while layering on additional depth and potential longevity. Drink now–2016 and possibly beyond. 92 *—J.C. (11/1/2007)*

Wolf Blass 2003 Platinum Label Shiraz (Barossa) $85. The bouquet of this wine—like the color—is dense and impenetrable, a brooding inky purpleness that's almost overwhelming. Flavors are embryonic and unevolved, but lean toward blackberry, blueberry and spice, with an almost chewy texture in the mouth. This is closed in and not very flashy right now, but it shows all the material for the cellar. 92 *—J.C. (5/1/2007)*

Wolf Blass 2002 Platinum Label Shiraz (Barossa) $72. 90 *—D.T. (4/1/2006)*

Wolf Blass 2001 Platinum Label Shiraz (Adelaide Hills) $72. 90 *—D.T. (5/1/2004)*

Wolf Blass 1999 Platinum Label Shiraz (Barossa Valley) $72. 87 *—D.T. (5/1/2004)*

Wolf Blass 2005 Presidents Selection Shiraz (South Australia) $19. Full-bodied, with soft tannins and plenty of oak, this easy-to-drink Shiraz fits perfectly in the Wolf Blass idiom of accessibility. Caramel and dark plum flavors add hints of vanilla and toast, finishing long. A perfect steakhouse choice when you want to keep the wine tab reasonable. 88 *—J.C. (11/15/2007)*

Wolf Blass 2004 Presidents Selection Shiraz (South Australia) $19. A solid Shiraz, Wolf Blass's Presidents Selection offers refined scents of pencil shavings, black currants and caramel. It's a wine with admirable purity of flavor, the blackberry and cassis fruit cleanly framed by vanilla-laden oak. Picks up a slightly brambly, briary edge on the finish. Drink now–2012. 89 *—J.C. (2/1/2007)*

Wolf Blass 2003 Presidents Selection Shiraz (South Australia) $17. 88 *—D.T. (2/1/2006)*

Wolf Blass 2001 Presidents Selection Shiraz (South Australia) $19. 88 *—D.T. (5/1/2004)*

Wolf Blass 2000 Presidents Selection Shiraz (South Australia) $20. 87 *—M.S. (3/1/2003)*

Wolf Blass 2005 Yellow Label Shiraz (South Australia) $12. The warm 2005 growing season worked well with Blass's approachable style, resulting in a full-bodied but soft Shiraz loaded with plummy fruit. Hints of cedar, leather and earth impart remarkable complexity to an entry-level wine, finishing with a touch of coffee. 87 Best Buy *—J.C. (11/15/2007)*

Wolf Blass 2004 Yellow Label Shiraz (South Australia) $12. A medium-bodied, smoothly textured Shiraz, Wolf Blass's 2004 Yellow Label skillfully blends hints of cracked pepper, black tea and dried spices with fresh berry fruit. Dry and clean on the finish, with enough dusty tannins to pair with grilled burgers or sausages. 86 *—J.C. (11/15/2007)*

Wolf Blass 2003 Yellow Label Shiraz (South Australia) $12. 86 *—D.T. (12/31/2005)*

Wolf Blass 2002 Yellow Label Shiraz (South Australia) $12. 87 Best Buy *—D.T. (5/1/2005)*

Wolf Blass 2001 Black Label Shiraz-Cabernet Sauvignon (South Australia) $62. 88 *—D.T. (4/1/2006)*

Wolf Blass 2002 Red Label Shiraz-Cabernet Sauvignon (South Australia) $12. 88 *—D.T. (11/15/2003)*

Wolf Blass 2001 Red Label Shiraz-Cabernet Sauvignon (South Australia) $12. 87 *—D.T. (12/31/2003)*

Wolf Blass 2000 Red Label Shiraz-Cabernet Sauvignon (South Australia) $12. 84 *—M.S. (12/15/2002)*

Wolf Blass 1999 Red Label Shiraz-Cabernet Sauvignon (South Australia) $12. 87 *—D.T. (9/1/2001)*

Wolf Blass 2004 Yellow Label Shiraz-Cabernet Sauvignon (South Australia) $12. Boasts some snappy scents of fresh herbs and cherries, but the flavors are a bit simple and the wine lacks texture, turning tart on the finish. Good, but just that. 83 *—J.C. (2/1/2007)*

Wolf Blass NV Brut NV Sparkling Blend (Australia) $10. 87 Best Buy *—D.T. (12/31/2004)*

Wolf Blass NV Traditional Method Brut Sparkling Blend (South Australia) $11. 86 Best Buy *—D.T. (12/31/2003)*

WOMBAT GULLY

Wombat Gully 2000 Cabernet Sauvignon (South Eastern Australia) $10. 80 *—M.S. (12/15/2002)*

Wombat Gully 2001 Shiraz (South Eastern Australia) $10. 84 *—M.S. (1/28/2003)*

WOOD PARK

Wood Park 1999 Cabernet Sauvignon-Shiraz (King Valley) $25. 88 *(9/1/2001)*

Wood Park 1998 Cabernet Sauvignon-Shiraz (King Valley) $22. 84 *—D.T. (9/1/2001)*

Wood Park 1999 Meadow Creek Chardonnay (Victoria) $25. 82 *—D.T. (9/1/2001)*

WOOP WOOP

Woop Woop 2006 Chardonnay (South Eastern Australia) $11. A great value in unoaked Chardonnay, the 2006 Woop Woop features understated peach and pineapple aromas but really roars to life on the palate. It's broad and mouthfilling but not overly fat, firming up and gaining focus on the finish, where it effortlessly blends peach, melon and pineapple flavors. Drink now. 87 Best Buy —*J.C. (6/1/2007)*

Woop Woop 2004 Chardonnay (South Eastern Australia) $11. 87 Best Buy —*D.T. (12/31/2004)*

WYNDHAM ESTATE

Wyndham Estate 2002 Bin 444 Cabernet Sauvignon (South Eastern Australia) $10. 86 Best Buy —*D.T. (5/1/2005)*

Wyndham Estate 2001 Bin 444 Cabernet Sauvignon (South Eastern Australia) $10. 85 —*D.T. (10/1/2003)*

Wyndham Estate 2000 Bin 444 Cabernet Sauvignon (South Eastern Australia) $10. 84 —*M.S. (12/15/2002)*

Wyndham Estate 1998 Bin 444 Cabernet Sauvignon (South Eastern Australia) $12. 84 *(9/1/2001)*

Wyndham Estate 1997 Bin 444 Cabernet Sauvignon (South Eastern Australia) $12. 83 *(6/1/2001)*

Wyndham Estate 2002 Bin 888 Cabernet Sauvignon-Merlot (South Eastern Australia) $10. 87 Best Buy —*D.T. (11/15/2004)*

Wyndham Estate 2000 Bin 888 Cabernet Sauvignon-Merlot (South Eastern Australia) $10. 84 —*D.T. (12/31/2003)*

Wyndham Estate 1999 Bin 888 Cabernet Sauvignon-Merlot (South Eastern Australia) $10. 86 Best Buy —*J.C. (6/1/2002)*

Wyndham Estate 1997 Show Reserve Cabernet Sauvignon-Merlot (Hunter Valley) $25. 90 *(9/1/2001)*

Wyndham Estate 2005 Bin 222 Chardonnay (South Eastern Australia) $9. 83 —*D.T. (8/1/2006)*

Wyndham Estate 2004 Bin 222 Chardonnay (South Eastern Australia) $9. 83 —*D.T. (12/1/2005)*

Wyndham Estate 2003 Bin 222 Chardonnay (New South Wales) $9. 85 *(7/2/2004)*

Wyndham Estate 2002 Bin 222 Chardonnay (South Eastern Australia) $9. 83 —*D.T. (6/1/2003)*

Wyndham Estate 2000 Bin 222 Chardonnay (South Eastern Australia) $9. 87 Best Buy —*J.C. (7/1/2002)*

Wyndham Estate 2001 Show Reserve Chardonnay (South Eastern Australia) $19. 85 *(7/2/2004)*

Wyndham Estate 2004 Bin 999 Merlot (South Eastern Australia) $10. 83 —*D.T. (6/1/2006)*

Wyndham Estate 2002 Bin 999 Merlot (South Eastern Australia) $10. 84 —*D.T. (9/1/2004)*

Wyndham Estate 2001 Bin 999 Merlot (South Eastern Australia) $10. 85 —*D.T. (6/1/2003)*

Wyndham Estate 2000 Bin 999 Merlot (South Eastern Australia) $10. 82 —*J.F. (9/1/2001)*

Wyndham Estate 2006 Bin 333 Pinot Noir (South Eastern Australia) $10. Simple, fruity and clean, with strawberry and cherry flavors that pick up nuances of tea leaf on the dry, silky finish. Imported by Pernod Ricard USA. 84 —*J.C. (11/15/2007)*

Wyndham Estate 2004 Bin 333 Pinot Noir (South Eastern Australia) $10. 83 —*D.T. (12/1/2005)*

Wyndham Estate 1999 Bin 333 Pinot Noir (South Eastern Australia) $10. 86 Best Buy —*M.S. (10/1/2000)*

Wyndham Estate 2006 Bin 505 Rosé Shiraz (South Eastern Australia) $9. Full soft and a little sweet, this is a well-made, fruit-driven rosé loaded with watermelon and strawberry flavors. Not the most complex wine ever, but fine for poolside sipping. Imported by Pernod Ricard USA. 84 —*J.C. (7/1/2007)*

Wyndham Estate 2002 Bin 777 Semillon (South Eastern Australia) $9. 84 —*D.T. (12/31/2003)*

Wyndham Estate 1999 Bin 777 Semillon (South Eastern Australia) $10. 85 —*J.C. (9/1/2001)*

Wyndham Estate 2005 Bin 777 Semillon-Sauvignon Blanc (South Eastern Australia) $9. 85 Best Buy —*D.T. (11/15/2006)*

Wyndham Estate 2004 Bin 777 Semillon-Sauvignon Blanc (South Eastern Australia) $9. 82 —*D.T. (12/1/2005)*

Wyndham Estate NV Bin 555 Shiraz (South Eastern Australia) $17. This is a jammy, fruit-forward rendition of sparkling Shiraz, with plenty of blueberry and blackberry flavors and a touch of sugar on the finish. Imported by Pernod Ricard USA. 85 —*J.C. (12/31/2007)*

Wyndham Estate 2002 Bin 555 Shiraz (South Eastern Australia) $10. 86 Best Buy —*D.T. (12/31/2004)*

Wyndham Estate 2001 Bin 555 Shiraz (South Eastern Australia) $10. 84 —*D.T. (10/1/2003)*

Wyndham Estate 2000 Bin 555 Shiraz (South Eastern Australia) $10. 81 —*M.S. (1/28/2003)*

Wyndham Estate 1998 Bin 555 Shiraz (South Eastern Australia) $12. 88 —*M.M. (6/1/2001)*

WYNNS COONAWARRA ESTATE

Wynns Coonawarra Estate 1956 Claret Bordeaux Blend (Coonawarra) $NA. 88 —*D.T. (2/1/2005)*

Wynns Coonawarra Estate 2000 Cabernet Blend (Coonawarra) $13. 85 —*D.T. (12/31/2003)*

Wynns Coonawarra Estate 1999 Cabernet Blend (Coonawarra) $13. 86 Best Buy —*J.M. (12/15/2002)*

Wynns Coonawarra Estate 1998 Cabernet Blend (Coonawarra) $13. 87 *(11/1/2001)*

Wynns Coonawarra Estate 2003 Cabernet-Shiraz-Merlot Cabernet Sauvignon-Shiraz (Coonawarra) $16. A solid example of the benefits of blending Shiraz and Cabernet, with enough spicy, briary blackberry fruit to counter the touch of herbaceousness in the Cabernet. It's medium-bodied and a touch creamy on the palate, a nicely complex and satisfying wine at a reasonable price. 88 —*J.C. (6/1/2007)*

Wynns Coonawarra Estate 2001 Cabernet Shiraz Merlot Cabernet Blend (Coonawarra) $11. 86 Best Buy —*D.T. (12/1/2005)*

Wynns Coonawarra Estate 2001 Cabernet Sauvignon (Coonawarra) $11. 87 Best Buy —*D.T. (11/15/2004)*

Wynns Coonawarra Estate 2000 Cabernet Sauvignon (Coonawarra) $15. 85 —*D.T. (12/31/2003)*

Wynns Coonawarra Estate 1999 Cabernet Sauvignon (Coonawarra) $14. 88 —*J.M. (12/15/2002)*

Wynns Coonawarra Estate 1998 Cabernet Sauvignon (Coonawarra) $NA. 90 —*D.T. (2/1/2005)*

Wynns Coonawarra Estate 1998 Cabernet Sauvignon (Coonawarra) $15. 91 Best Buy *(11/1/2001)*

Wynns Coonawarra Estate 1996 Cabernet Sauvignon (Coonawarra) $NA. 89 —*D.T. (2/1/2005)*

Wynns Coonawarra Estate 1991 Cabernet Sauvignon (Coonawarra) $NA. 91 *(11/1/2001)*

Wynns Coonawarra Estate 1991 Cabernet Sauvignon (Coonawarra) $NA. 91 —*D.T. (2/1/2005)*

Wynns Coonawarra Estate 1990 Cabernet Sauvignon (Coonawarra) $NA. 90 —*D.T. (2/1/2005)*

Wynns Coonawarra Estate 1988 Cabernet Sauvignon (Coonawarra) $NA. 86 *(11/1/2001)*

Wynns Coonawarra Estate 1986 Cabernet Sauvignon (Coonawarra) $NA. 91 —*D.T. (2/1/2005)*

Wynns Coonawarra Estate 1965 Cabernet Sauvignon (Coonawarra) $NA. 90 —*D.T. (2/1/2005)*

Wynns Coonawarra Estate 1962 Cabernet Sauvignon (Coonawarra) $NA. 89 —*D.T. (2/1/2005)*

Wynns Coonawarra Estate 2003 John Riddoch Cabernet Sauvignon (Coonawarra) $45. 90 —*D.T. (10/1/2006)*

Wynns Coonawarra Estate 1994 John Riddoch Cabernet Sauvignon (Coonawarra) $NA. 93 Cellar Selection *(11/1/2001)*

Wynns Coonawarra Estate 1990 John Riddoch Cabernet Sauvignon (Coonawarra) $NA. 92 *(11/1/2001)*

Wynns Coonawarra Estate 1988 John Riddoch Cabernet Sauvignon (Coonawarra) $NA. 88 *(11/1/2001)*

Wynns Coonawarra Estate 1998 John Riddoch Limited Release Cabernet Sauvignon (Coonawarra) $35. 90 —*J.M. (12/15/2002)*

Wynns Coonawarra Estate 2003 Chardonnay (Coonawarra) $11. 85 *(7/2/2004)*

Wynns Coonawarra Estate 2002 Chardonnay (Coonawarra) $13. 88 —*D.T. (8/1/2003)*

Wynns Coonawarra Estate 2001 Chardonnay (Coonawarra) $9. 84 —*J.C. (7/1/2002)*

Wynns Coonawarra Estate 2000 Chardonnay (Coonawarra) $13. 88 *(11/1/2001)*

Wynns Coonawarra Estate 1997 Chardonnay (Coonawarra) $13. 83 —*M.M. (10/1/2000)*

Wynns Coonawarra Estate 2002 Red Blend (Coonawarra) $11. 87 Best Buy —*D.T. (10/1/2005)*

Wynns Coonawarra Estate 2005 Riesling (Coonawarra) $14. 85 —*D.T. (10/1/2006)*

Wynns Coonawarra Estate 2004 Riesling (Coonawarra) $15. 88 *—D.T. (4/1/2006)*

Wynns Coonawarra Estate 2003 Riesling (Coonawarra) $11. 86 Best Buy *—D.T. (11/15/2004)*

Wynns Coonawarra Estate 2002 Riesling (Coonawarra) $12. 90 Best Buy *—D.T. (11/15/2003)*

Wynns Coonawarra Estate 2004 Shiraz (Coonawarra) $16. 85 *—D.T. (6/1/2006)*

Wynns Coonawarra Estate 2003 Shiraz (Coonawarra) $12. 85 *—D.T. (12/1/2005)*

Wynns Coonawarra Estate 2001 Shiraz (Coonawarra) $14. 86 *—D.T. (12/31/2003)*

Wynns Coonawarra Estate 2000 Shiraz (Coonawarra) $15. 87 *—J.C. (9/1/2002)*

Wynns Coonawarra Estate 1999 Shiraz (Coonawarra) $15. 85 *(10/1/2001)*

Wynns Coonawarra Estate 1998 Michael Shiraz (Coonawarra) $49. 90 *(9/1/2002)*

Wynns Coonawarra Estate 1997 Michael Shiraz (Coonawarra) $49. 91 Cellar Selection *(11/1/2001)*

XANADU

Xanadu 1999 Cabernet Sauvignon (Margaret River) $18. 87 *(10/1/2003)*

Xanadu 2005 Dragon Cabernet Sauvignon-Merlot (Western Australia) $14. Varietally correct Cabernet from a coolish climate, with mint and tobacco shadings to the cassis fruit, medium body and some dusty tannins on the firm finish. 84 *—J.C. (11/15/2007)*

Xanadu 1998 Lagan Estate Reserve Cabernet Sauvignon (Margaret River) $32. 89 *(10/1/2003)*

Xanadu 2002 Chardonnay (Margaret River) $15. 86 *(10/1/2003)*

Xanadu 2000 Chardonnay (Margaret River) $15. 90 Best Buy *—J.C. (7/1/2002)*

Xanadu 2002 Merlot (Frankland River) $10. 87 Best Buy *(10/1/2003)*

Xanadu 2000 Merlot (Margaret River) $22. 88 *—C.S. (6/1/2002)*

Xanadu 2002 Sauvignon Blanc (Margaret River) $10. 85 *(10/1/2003)*

Xanadu 2001 Shiraz (Frankland River) $18. 85 *(10/1/2003)*

Xanadu 2000 Shiraz (Frankland River) $17. 89 *—M.S. (3/1/2003)*

Xanadu 2005 Dragon Shiraz (Western Australia) $14. Epitomizes the fruit-forward, confected style of inexpensive Shiraz, with berry-punch aromas, tart berry flavors and a finish that falls off quickly. 82 *—J.C. (11/15/2007)*

Xanadu 2002 Shiraz-Cabernet Sauvignon (Frankland River) $10. 86 Best Buy *(10/1/2003)*

YABBY LAKE VINEYARD

Yabby Lake Vineyard 2004 Chardonnay (Mornington Peninsula) $38. 87 *—D.T. (11/15/2006)*

Yabby Lake Vineyard 2004 Pinot Noir (Mornington Peninsula) $58. 90 *—D.T. (11/15/2006)*

YACCA PADDOCK

Yacca Paddock 2002 Dolcetto (Adelaide Hills) $42. 88 *—D.T. (8/1/2005)*

Yacca Paddock 2003 Red Blend (Adelaide Hills) $65. 90 *—D.T. (8/1/2005)*

YALUMBA

Yalumba 2000 Cabernet Sauvignon (Barossa Valley) $17. 87 *—D.T. (12/31/2003)*

Yalumba 1999 Cabernet Sauvignon (Barossa Valley) $17. 87 *—J.C. (6/1/2002)*

Yalumba 1997 Cabernet Sauvignon (Clare Valley) $25. 91 Editors' Choice *(6/1/2001)*

Yalumba 2002 The Menzies Cabernet Sauvignon (Coonawarra) $45. 89 *—D.T. (6/1/2006)*

Yalumba 2000 The Menzies Cabernet Sauvignon (Coonawarra) $45. 90 *—D.T. (5/1/2005)*

Yalumba 1999 The Menzies Cabernet Sauvignon (Coonawarra) $40. 90 *—D.T. (12/31/2003)*

Yalumba 1997 The Menzies Cabernet Sauvignon (Coonawarra) $30. 83 *—D.T. (9/1/2001)*

Yalumba 1996 The Menzies Cabernet Sauvignon (Coonawarra) $28. 86 *(4/1/2000)*

Yalumba 2001 Y Series Cabernet Sauvignon (South Australia) $10. 84 *—D.T. (6/1/2003)*

Yalumba 2001 Cabernet Sauvignon-Shiraz (Barossa Valley) $17. 85 *—D.T. (5/1/2005)*

Yalumba 2004 The Signature Cabernet Sauvignon-Shiraz (Barossa) $NA. A lifted hint of mint on the nose comes from the Cabernet, while raspberry and spice come from the Shiraz. Both contribute to the full, complete mouthfeel and lush, creamy texture. The long finish displays some smoky barrel notes, but overall the wood here is well integrated. Should be a classic when it's released in 2008. Drink 2010–2020 or beyond. 93 *—J.C. (11/1/2007)*

Yalumba 2003 The Signature Cabernet Sauvignon-Shiraz (Barossa) $50. Yalumba's proprietary blend of Cabernet and Shiraz is aged in new oak, showing plenty of toast and vanilla at this early stage. But this also boasts enough blackberry and cassis fruit to balance the wood, at least for now. Lightens up on the finish, suggesting short-term consumption. Drink 2008–2013. 90 *—J.C. (11/1/2007)*

Yalumba 2000 The Signature Cabernet Sauvignon-Shiraz (Barossa Valley) $45. 87 *—D.T. (5/1/2005)*

Yalumba 1998 The Signature Cabernet Sauvignon-Shiraz (Barossa Valley) $40. 89 Cellar Selection *(5/1/2003)*

Yalumba 1997 The Signature Cabernet Sauvignon-Shiraz (Barossa Valley) $44. 88 *—D.T. (12/15/2002)*

Yalumba 1996 The Signature Cabernet Sauvignon-Shiraz (Barossa Valley) $40. 91 *—M.M. (1/1/2004)*

Yalumba 2002 Chardonnay (Barossa Valley) $15. 85 *(7/2/2004)*

Yalumba 2000 Chardonnay (Barossa Valley) $16. 85 *—J.C. (7/1/2002)*

Yalumba 2002 Heggies Vineyard Chardonnay (Eden Valley) $20. 85 *(7/2/2004)*

Yalumba 1997 Reserve Chardonnay (Eden Valley) $15. 84 *(3/1/2000)*

Yalumba 2005 Wild Ferment Chardonnay (Eden Valley) $17. 88 *—D.T. (10/1/2006)*

Yalumba 2003 Wild Ferment Chardonnay (Eden Valley) $17. 87 *(7/2/2004)*

Yalumba 2006 Y Series Unwooded Chardonnay (South Australia) $11. A well-made, satisfying Chardonnay at a bargain price, this features adequate complexity and mouthfilling flavors of pear, melon and cinnamon. Clean and crisp on the finish. Drink now. 86 Best Buy *—J.C. (8/1/2007)*

Yalumba 2002 Y Series Unwooded Chardonnay (South Australia) $10. 86 *—D.T. (6/1/2003)*

Yalumba 2003 Y series Unwooded Chardonnay (Eden Valley) $9. 86 Best Buy *(7/2/2004)*

Yalumba 2006 Bush Vine Grenache (Barossa) $16. The variety's raspberry and cherry fruit also features a helping of peppery spice and a hint of green leafiness in this attractive example. The mouthfeel is ample and round, the flavors fresh and fruity, turning a bit peppery on the finish. Drink now–2012. 88 *—J.C. (11/1/2007)*

Yalumba 2004 Bush Vine Grenache (Barossa) $17. 84 *—D.T. (11/15/2006)*

Yalumba 2002 Bush Vine Grenache (Barossa Valley) $15. 87 *—D.T. (2/1/2004)*

Yalumba 2001 Bush Vine Grenache (Barossa Valley) $15. 84 *(5/1/2003)*

Yalumba 2000 Bush Vine Grenache (Barossa Valley) $16. 87 *—M.S. (12/15/2002)*

Yalumba 2005 Hand Picked Tricentenary Vines Grenache (Barossa) $30. Much more intense than Yalumba's Bush Vine bottling, this is almost resiny at times, with a sinewy, herbal note imparting strength and complexity to the lush raspberry-vanilla flavors. From vines planted in 1889, this finishes long, peppery and herbal, a fitting counterpoint to the creamy texture and soft tannins. Drink now–2012. 92 *—J.C. (11/1/2007)*

Yalumba 2001 Tricentenary Grenache (Barossa Valley) $15. 87 *—D.T. (12/31/2003)*

Yalumba 2000 Tricentenary Grenache (Barossa Valley) $30. 87 *—S.H. (12/15/2002)*

Yalumba 2003 Tricentenary Vines Grenache (Barossa Valley) $32. 87 *—D.T. (3/1/2005)*

Yalumba 2001 Y Series Merlot (South Australia) $10. 82 *—D.T. (1/1/2002)*

Yalumba 2000 Y Series Merlot (South Australia) $10. 82 *—S.H. (6/1/2002)*

Yalumba 2005 Y Series Pinot Grigio (South Australia) $11. 87 Best Buy *—D.T. (10/1/2006)*

Yalumba NV Antique Tawny Port (Barossa Valley) $17. 89 *—D.T. (11/15/2003)*

Yalumba NV Antique Tawny Port (Barossa Valley) $17. 89 *(5/1/2003)*

Yalumba 2004 Hand Picked t/g/v Tempranillo-Grenache-Viog Red Blend (Barossa) $32. 88 *—D.T. (2/1/2006)*

Yalumba 2003 m/g/s Red Blend (Barossa Valley) $32. 89 *—D.T. (5/1/2005)*

Yalumba 2000 Mawsons Red Blend (Limestone Coast) $20. 87 —*D.T. (5/1/2004)*

Yalumba 1999 Shiraz-Viognier Red Blend (Barossa Valley) $30. 85 —*S.H. (1/1/2002)*

Yalumba 2002 Rhône Red Blend (Barossa Valley) $30. 91 Editors' Choice —*D.T. (2/1/2004)*

Yalumba 2004 Hand Picked m/g/s Rhône Red Blend (Barossa) $32. 90 —*D.T. (2/1/2006)*

Yalumba 2003 Riesling (South Eastern Australia) $11. 88 Best Buy —*D.T. (3/1/2005)*

Yalumba 2002 Mesh Riesling (Eden Valley) $25. 89 *(8/1/2003)*

Yalumba 2001 Pewsey Vale Riesling (Eden Valley) $18. 88 *(5/1/2003)*

Yalumba 2006 Y Series Riesling (South Australia) $11. Nicely complex on the nose, offering up dusty, minerally notes alongside baked apple. Flavors feature some petrol notes, but also honey and preserved citrus, ending a little short. Drink now. 87 Best Buy —*J.C. (9/1/2007)*

Yalumba 2002 Y Series Riesling (South Australia) $10. 85 *(5/1/2003)*

Yalumba 2001 Y Series Riesling (South Australia) $10. 85 —*S.H. (9/1/2002)*

Yalumba 2006 Y Series Rosé Sangiovese (South Australia) $11. A disappointing effort that's perfumed and herbal on the nose, then shows plenty of weight on the palate, but not much intensity of flavor. 82 —*J.C. (7/1/2007)*

Yalumba 2005 Y Series Rosé Sangiovese (South Australia) $11. 87 Best Buy —*D.T. (6/21/2006)*

Yalumba 2005 Y Series Sauvignon Blanc (South Australia) $11. 86 Best Buy —*D.T. (8/1/2006)*

Yalumba 2001 Shiraz (Barossa Valley) $17. 85 —*D.T. (2/1/2004)*

Yalumba 2000 Shiraz (Barossa Valley) $17. 86 *(5/1/2003)*

Yalumba 1999 Shiraz (Barossa Valley) $16. 87 *(10/1/2001)*

Yalumba 2000 Handpicked Shiraz (Barossa Valley) $30. 89 *(5/1/2003)*

Yalumba 2004 The Octavius Shiraz (Barossa) $NA. Quite possibly the best Octavius yet; features explosive Shiraz aromas of raspberries and peppery spice. Is the usual intense barrel treatment more restrained, or the fruit just that much more expressive? The texture is wonderfully lush and creamy, with an expansive mouthfeel and complex flavors of berries and spice that linger elegantly on the finish. Probably best from 2010–2020. 94 Cellar Selection —*J.C. (11/1/2007)*

Yalumba 2003 The Octavius Shiraz (Barossa) $110. Caught between the outstanding '02 and '04 vintages, this is still an excellent vintage of The Octavius, but one to drink before the other two. The wine is open-knit, less structured and slightly lighter in body, with approachable spice, meat and blackberry flavors. Drink now–2013. 90 —*J.C. (11/1/2007)*

Yalumba 2002 The Octavius Shiraz (Barossa) $100. Smoky and cedary on the nose, with hints of cured meat that accent the explosive red fruit flavors. The mouthfeel is creamy smooth, the tannins wonderfully supple but undeniably present, elegantly framing the lingering, spicy finish. Drink now–2020. 93 Cellar Selection —*J.C. (11/1/2007)*

Yalumba 2000 The Octavius Shiraz (Barossa Valley) $85. 91 —*D.T. (8/1/2005)*

Yalumba 1999 The Octavius Shiraz (Barossa Valley) $80. 92 Cellar Selection —*D.T. (2/1/2004)*

Yalumba 1995 The Octavius Shiraz (Barossa Valley) $80. 88 *(4/1/2000)*

Yalumba 1997 The Octavius Old Vine Shiraz (Barossa Valley) $80. 92 Cellar Selection *(11/1/2001)*

Yalumba 2001 Y Series Shiraz (South Australia) $10. 82 —*D.T. (1/28/2003)*

Yalumba 2000 Y Series Shiraz (South Australia) $10. 84 —*S.H. (1/1/2002)*

Yalumba 2005 Shiraz-Viognier (Barossa) $16. Yalumba is Australia's champion of Viognier, and in this case it's cofermented with Shiraz to make a wonderfully savory, spicy wine that marries raspberry aromas with just a hint of apricot. Tart berry fruit serves as a counterpoint to the soft tannins and creamy texture. Drink now–2010. 88 —*J.C. (11/1/2007)*

Yalumba 2001 Shiraz-Viognier (Barossa Valley) $30. 90 —*D.T. (2/1/2004)*

Yalumba 2005 Hand Picked Shiraz-Viognier (Barossa) $30. Still an attractive value, Yalumba's top Shiraz-Viognier features classic scents of raspberries and apricot, framed by oak from the winery's own cooperage. The flavors are darker and richer, heading toward blackberries and blueberries, the wine's soft, voluminous texture accented by a healthy amount of spice on the long, silky finish. Drink now–2015. 92 Editors' Choice —*J.C. (11/1/2007)*

Yalumba 2003 Hand Picked Shiraz-Viognier (Barossa) $32. 91 —*D.T. (2/1/2006)*

Yalumba 2006 Y Series Shiraz-Viognier (South Australia) $11. With its attractive scents of ripe raspberries and apricot, this is an unusually aromatic wine for the price. Lacks a bit of weight and richness on the palate, but this is a pretty wine that should charm most consumers. Drink now. 86 Best Buy —*J.C. (11/1/2007)*

Yalumba 2004 Viognier (Eden Valley) $17. 88 —*D.T. (10/1/2006)*

Yalumba 2004 Viognier (South Australia) $11. 87 Best Buy —*D.T. (3/1/2005)*

Yalumba 2003 Viognier (Eden Valley) $17. 87 —*D.T. (12/31/2004)*

Yalumba 2001 Viognier (Eden Valley) $18. 88 *(5/1/2003)*

Yalumba 2000 Viognier (Eden Valley) $17. 88 —*R.V. (11/15/2001)*

Yalumba 1999 Viognier (Eden Valley) $16. 85 —*M.M. (9/1/2001)*

Yalumba 2002 Heggies Vineyard Viognier (Eden Valley) $20. 87 —*D.T. (5/1/2004)*

Yalumba 1998 Limited Release Viognier (Barossa Valley) $14. 86 *(10/1/2000)*

Yalumba 2003 The Virgilius Viognier (Eden Valley) $40. 92 —*D.T. (3/1/2005)*

Yalumba 2002 The Virgilius Viognier (Eden Valley) $36. 91 —*D.T. (2/1/2004)*

Yalumba 2004 Virgilius Viognier (Eden Valley) $40. 93 Editors' Choice —*D.T. (6/1/2006)*

Yalumba 2005 Y Series Viognier (South Australia) $11. 88 Best Buy —*D.T. (8/1/2006)*

Yalumba 2003 Y Series Viognier (Eden Valley) $9. 87 Best Buy —*D.T. (2/1/2004)*

Yalumba 2002 Y Series Viognier (South Australia) $10. 84 —*D.T. (12/31/2003)*

Yalumba 2000 Y Series Viognier (South Australia) $10. 84 —*S.H. (9/1/2002)*

Yalumba 2000 Y Series Viognier (South Australia) $10. 89 Best Buy —*D.T. (2/1/2002)*

YANGARRA ESTATE VINEYARD

Yangarra Estate Vineyard 2005 Single Vineyard Old Vine Grenache (McLaren Vale) $25. A consistent performer over the years, Yangarra's Grenache is one of the rare examples that appears to have the stuff to improve for two or three years. Aromas are dominated by oak at this young age—cedar, vanilla and coffee—but there's plenty of dense, plummy fruit that comes through on the palate and a firmly tannic finish that promises better things ahead. Imported by Sovereign Wine Imports. 90 —*J.C. (6/1/2007)*

Yangarra Estate Vineyard 2004 Old Vine Grenache (McLaren Vale) $25. 90 —*(8/1/2005)*

Yangarra Estate Vineyard 2003 Old Vine Grenache (McLaren Vale) $20. 91 —*D.T. (3/1/2005)*

Yangarra Estate Vineyard 2002 Old Vine Grenache (McLaren Vale) $20. 89 Editors' Choice —*D.T. (9/1/2004)*

Yangarra Estate Vineyard 2005 Cadenzia Grenache-Shiraz-Mourvèdre Rhône Red Blend (McLaren Vale) $25. Cadenzia is a term the McLaren Vale producers have agreed to use on their top Grenache-based blends; in this instance it's 47% Grenache, 41% Shiraz and only 12% Mourvèdre. Like Yangarra's other wines, this one is heavily extracted, with dark flavors of chocolate, cassis and coffee. There's intense fruit, backed by firm structure and some spice; hold 1–2 years, then drink it over the next 5–8. Imported by Sovereign Wine Imports. 89 —*J.C. (6/1/2007)*

Yangarra Estate Vineyard 2002 Grenache Shiraz Mourvedre Rhône Red Blend (McLaren Vale) $20. 90 —*D.T. (12/31/2004)*

Yangarra Estate Vineyard 2003 GSM Rhône Red Blend (McLaren Vale) $20. 92 —*D.T. (3/1/2005)*

Yangarra Estate Vineyard 2005 Rosé Grenache-Shiraz (McLaren Vale) $12. 89 Best Buy —*D.T. (6/21/2006)*

Yangarra Estate Vineyard 2006 Single Vineyard Rosé Shiraz-Grenache (McLaren Vale) $15. This 60-40 blend is oddly perfumed, almost like a hand lotion or petroleum jelly, but its bouquet also features likeable hints of melon and citrus. It's truly dry and more Provençal in style than most Australian rosés, finishing with some chalky minerality. 85 —*J.C. (7/1/2007)*

Yangarra Estate Vineyard 2004 Shiraz (McLaren Vale) $25. 92 —*D.T. (8/1/2006)*

Yangarra Estate Vineyard 2003 Shiraz (McLaren Vale) $20. 90 —*D.T. (3/1/2005)*

Yangarra Estate Vineyard 2002 Shiraz (McLaren Vale) $20. 90 Editors' Choice *(11/15/2004)*

Yangarra Estate Vineyard 2005 Single Vineyard Shiraz (McLaren Vale) $20. An impressively endowed effort, this features a slightly lifted, floral component to its bouquet that adds to its complexity, blending seamlessly with scents of dark plum, vanilla, smoke, coffee and spice. The mouthfilling flavors frame bold fruit in firm spice, giving this wine ample structure and length. Drink now–2015. Imported by Sovereign Wine Imports. 93 Editors' Choice *—J.C. (6/1/2007)*

YANGARRA PARK

Yangarra Park 2001 Cabernet Sauvignon (South Eastern Australia) $10. 84 *—S.H. (6/1/2002)*

Yangarra Park 2000 Cabernet Sauvignon (South Eastern Australia) $10. 84 *—D.T. (6/1/2002)*

Yangarra Park 2001 Appelation Series Cabernet Sauvignon (Coonawarra) $17. 88 *—S.H. (1/1/2002)*

Yangarra Park 2001 Chardonnay (South Eastern Australia) $10. 87 Best Buy *—S.H. (7/1/2002)*

Yangarra Park 2000 Chardonnay (South Eastern Australia) $10. 87 Best Buy *—J.C. (7/1/2002)*

Yangarra Park 2001 Merlot (South Eastern Australia) $10. 87 Best Buy *—S.H. (6/1/2002)*

Yangarra Park 2001 Appelation Series Merlot (McLaren Vale) $17. 90 *—S.H. (1/1/2002)*

Yangarra Park 2001 Shiraz (South Eastern Australia) $10. 87 Best Buy *—S.H. (9/1/2002)*

Yangarra Park 2001 Appellation Series Shiraz (McLaren Vale) $NA. 89 *—S.H. (1/1/2002)*

YARRA BURN

Yarra Burn 2000 Cabernet Sauvignon (Yarra Valley) $21. 89 *—D.T. (6/1/2003)*

Yarra Burn 2003 Chardonnay (Yarra Valley) $15. 85 *—D.T. (5/1/2005)*

Yarra Burn 2002 Chardonnay (Yarra Valley) $15. 86 *(7/2/2004)*

Yarra Burn 2000 Chardonnay (Yarra Valley) $16. 84 *—D.T. (8/1/2003)*

Yarra Burn 1997 Bastard Hill Chardonnay (Yarra Valley) $27. 86 *(6/1/2003)*

Yarra Burn 2001 Pinot Noir (Yarra Valley) $19. 86 *—D.T. (9/1/2004)*

Yarra Burn 2000 Pinot Noir (Yarra Valley) $19. 82 *(1/1/2004)*

Yarra Burn 2000 Shiraz (Victoria) $21. 84 *—D.T. (12/31/2003)*

YARRA YERING

Yarra Yering 2003 Dry Red Wine No.1 Cabernet Blend (Yarra Valley) $75. 89 *—D.T. (10/1/2006)*

YARRABANK

Yarrabank 1996 Cuvée Brut Champagne Blend (Australia) $32. 90 *—M.M. (12/1/2001)*

Yarrabank 1999 Yering Station Cuvee Sparkling Blend (Victoria) $22. 88 *—D.T. (12/31/2005)*

YARRAMAN

Yarraman 2004 Hell Raiser Cabernet Sauvignon-Merlot (South Eastern Australia) $10. This 50-50 blend features bright, strident notes of crisp, red plums and slightly medicinal herbs, then adds a layer of coffee-laden oak. Tobacco and vanilla scents provide touches of nuance to this medium-weight wine. Drink now. 86 Best Buy *—J.C. (5/1/2007)*

Yarraman 2005 Hay Burner Chardonnay (South Eastern Australia) $10. Another bargain-priced Australian Chardonnay, Hay Burner starts off with buttered toast and popcorn aromas, then backs them up with flavors of citrus custard and some riper melon and peach notes. Surprisingly rich and intense for the price point, a reflection of the soft market for Chardonnay grapes in Australia. Drink now. 86 Best Buy *—J.C. (6/1/2007)*

Yarraman 2004 Rip Snorter Shiraz-Cabernet Sauvignon (South Eastern Australia) $10. At $10 suggested retail, this is a solid bargain that should please anyone looking for a plump, ready-to-drink red. It has a slightly syrupy texture and soft tannins balanced by a tart edge on the finish, while the bold flavors of cherries round out the midpalate. Drink now. 87 Best Buy *—J.C. (4/1/2007)*

YELLOW BY YELLOWGLEN

Yellow by Yellowglen NV Chardonnay (South Eastern Australia) $12. 82 *—J.C. (12/31/2006)*

YELLOW TAIL

Yellow Tail 2003 Cabernet Sauvignon (South Eastern Australia) $7. 82 *—D.T. (11/15/2004)*

Yellow Tail 2003 Cabernet Sauvignon-Merlot (South Eastern Australia) $7. 82 *—D.T. (9/1/2004)*

Yellow Tail 2003 Cabernet Sauvignon-Shiraz (South Eastern Australia) $7. 83 *—D.T. (12/31/2004)*

Yellow Tail 2003 Chardonnay (South Eastern Australia) $7. 84 *(7/2/2004)*

Yellow Tail 2002 Chardonnay (South Eastern Australia) $7. 84 *—D.T. (6/1/2003)*

Yellow Tail 2000 Chardonnay (South Eastern Australia) $7. 88 Best Buy *—M.M. (6/1/2001)*

Yellow Tail 2003 Merlot (South Eastern Australia) $7. 84 Best Buy *—D.T. (12/31/2004)*

Yellow Tail 2001 Merlot (Australia) $7. 82 *—D.T. (6/1/2003)*

Yellow Tail 2004 Pinot Grigio (South Eastern Australia) $7. 83 *—D.T. (2/1/2006)*

Yellow Tail 2004 The Reserve Pinot Grigio (South Eastern Australia) $11. 82 *—D.T. (2/1/2006)*

Yellow Tail 2002 Shiraz (South Eastern Australia) $7. 86 Best Buy *—K.F. (3/1/2003)*

Yellow Tail 2001 Shiraz (South Eastern Australia) $7. 86 Best Buy *—J.C. (9/1/2002)*

Yellow Tail 2000 Shiraz (South Eastern Australia) $7. 85 Best Buy *—M.N. (6/1/2001)*

Yellow Tail NV Sparkling White Wine Sparkling Blend (South Eastern Australia) $11. Clean, fruity and frankly sweet, this would be an ideal sparkler to use in making Bellinis or similar cocktails, or as an ingredient in holiday punches. 83 *—J.C. (12/31/2007)*

YERING STATION

Yering Station 2001 Cabernet Sauvignon (Yarra Valley) $17. 88 *—D.T. (8/1/2005)*

Yering Station 2000 Cabernet Sauvignon (Yarra Valley) $17. 88 *—D.T. (12/31/2004)*

Yering Station 1999 Reserve Cabernet Sauvignon (Yarra Valley) $43. 90 *—D.T. (11/15/2004)*

Yering Station 2004 Chardonnay (Yarra Valley) $18. 88 *—D.T. (8/1/2006)*

Yering Station 2003 Chardonnay (Yarra Valley) $17. 86 *—D.T. (12/1/2005)*

Yering Station 2002 Chardonnay (Yarra Valley) $17. 86 *—D.T. (12/31/2004)*

Yering Station 2001 Chardonnay (Yarra Valley) $20. 85 *(7/2/2004)*

Yering Station 2000 Chardonnay (Yarra Valley) $20. 85 *—D.T. (8/1/2003)*

Yering Station 1999 Chardonnay (Yarra Valley) $20. 90 *—S.H. (6/1/2001)*

Yering Station 2001 Reserve Chardonnay (Yarra Valley) $39. 87 *(7/2/2004)*

Yering Station 2004 Pinot Noir (Yarra Valley) $18. This Pinot shows some attractive black cherry fruit, but also a charred, roasted-beet edge to its aromas and flavors. It's medium-bodied, with a tart finish and slightly dry, leafy tannins. 84 *—J.C. (2/1/2007)*

Yering Station 2001 Pinot Noir (Yarra Valley) $17. 89 *—D.T. (12/31/2004)*

Yering Station 2000 Pinot Noir (Yarra Valley) $28. 83 *(6/1/2003)*

Yering Station 1999 Pinot Noir (Yarra Valley) $22. 88 *(6/1/2001)*

Yering Station 2004 Extra Dry Rosé Pinot Noir (Yarra Valley) $13. 89 *—D.T. (8/1/2005)*

Yering Station 2003 Reserve Pinot Noir (Yarra Valley) $36. 88 *—D.T. (12/1/2005)*

Yering Station 2002 Reserve Pinot Noir (Yarra Valley) $36. 90 *—D.T. (10/1/2005)*

Yering Station 2000 Reserve Pinot Noir (Yarra Valley) $36. 86 *(6/1/2003)*

Yering Station 1998 Reserve Pinot Noir (Yarra Valley) $36. 91 *(6/1/2001)*

Yering Station 2006 Late Harvest Riesling (Yarra Valley) $18. An intriguing but offbeat wine, with some of the traditional character of Australian dry Riesling—austere, minerally aromatics and screeching acid levels—but also sweet flavors of peach and lime. Imported by Epic Wines. 84 *—J.C. (12/15/2007)*

Yering Station 2001 Shiraz (Yarra Valley) $17. 85 *—D.T. (12/31/2004)*

Yering Station 1999 Shiraz (Yarra Valley) $22. 86 *—J.C. (9/1/2002)*

Yering Station 2001 Reserve Shiraz (Yarra Valley) $36. 91 *—D.T. (9/1/2004)*

Yering Station 1998 Reserve Shiraz (Yarra Valley) $36. 93 Editors' Choice *—J.C. (9/1/2002)*

Yering Station 2002 Shiraz-Viognier (Yarra Valley) $17. 85 *—D.T. (12/1/2005)*

Yering Station 2003 Reserve Shiraz-Viognier (Yarra Valley) $36. 89 *—D.T. (4/1/2006)*

Yering Station 2004 M.V.R. White Blend (Yarra Valley) $17. 86 *—D.T. (8/1/2005)*

Yering Station 2003 M.V.R. White Blend (Yarra Valley) $17. 86 *—D.T. (12/31/2004)*

YERINGBERG

Yeringberg 2002 Bordeaux Blend (Yarra Valley) $65. 90 *—D.T. (10/1/2006)*

YOU BET

You Bet 2002 Shiraz (South Eastern Australia) $10. 82 *—D.T. (12/31/2004)*

YUNBAR

Yunbar 2000 Craig's Cabernet Sauvignon (Barossa Valley) $23. 89 *—C.S. (6/1/2002)*

Yunbar 2000 Chaste Chardonnay (Barossa Valley) $15. 82 *—J.C. (7/1/2002)*

Yunbar 2000 Miracle Merlot (Barossa Valley) $23. 86 *—C.S. (6/1/2002)*

Yunbar 2000 Eden Riesling (Barossa Valley) $15. 86 *—M.M. (2/1/2002)*

Yunbar 2000 Sinner's Shiraz (Barossa Valley) $23. 82 *—J.C. (9/1/2002)*

ZEEPAARD

Zeepaard 2005 Sauvignon Blanc (Western Australia) $10. 84 *—D.T. (8/1/2006)*

ZEMA ESTATE

Zema Estate 2001 Cluny Bordeaux Blend (Coonawarra) $25. 90 *—D.T. (6/1/2006)*

Zema Estate 2001 Cabernet Sauvignon (Coonawarra) $25. 89 *—D.T. (6/1/2006)*

ZILZIE

Zilzie 2002 Selection 23 Cabernet Sauvignon-Merlot (Victoria) $10. 83 *—D.T. (9/1/2004)*

Zilzie 2002 Selection 23 Chardonnay (Victoria) $10. 85 *(7/2/2004)*

Zilzie 2003 Viognier (Victoria) $14. 87 *—D.T. (5/1/2004)*

ZONTE'S FOOTSTEP

Zonte's Footstep 2003 Cabernet Sauvignon-Malbec (Langhorne Creek) $15. 82 *—D.T. (5/1/2005)*

Austria

Thanks to two grapes and two wine styles, Austrian wine has an important presence on the international wine-making stage. One of these grapes is Riesling, of which Austrian wine producers are some of the greatest exponents. The other is Grüner Veltliner, of which Austrian wine producers have a virtual monopoly, but one they exploit with panache and stunning results.

The wine styles are both white, but otherwise completely different. There are beautifully crisp, balanced, dry whites; and there are some of the most impressive sweet, botrytis wines, rich, unctuous, and intense.

These are the traditional Austrian wine styles. In recent years, red wines have become increasingly important and of better quality. Using local as well as international grape varieties, Austrian reds now cover one third of the country's vineyards.

Austrian vineyards at Retz, Niederösterreich.

Austria's wine-making history goes back to ancient Roman days, with some of today's best vineyards planted at that time, Grape varieties—red and white—are found on Austrian labels, along with the geographic origin. Today's Austrian vineyards are found in the east of country, whereas classic areas are along the Danube Valley, north-west of Vienna, and in the far east in the province of Burgenland.

The Danube Valley offers superlatives, both in wine and in wine country. The beautiful Wachau vineyards, best known but also one of the smallest wine regions, are caught between steep mountain slopes and the wide Danube River. The purest, most elegant Rieslings and Grüner Veltliners are made by a succession of some of the best producers in Austria. Quality levels are specific to the region: the lightest style is Steinfeder, next is Federspiel, and the richest style is Smaragd.

Other Danube districts include the Kremstal and Kamptal. Both make great white wines: the Kamptal produces some of the most characteristic Grüner Veltliner, crisp, dry, and peppery, from vineyards that are generally cooler than those of Kremstal. One of Austria's most famed vineyard sites, Heiligenstein (rock of saints), is in Kremstal.

North of the Danube, stretching away to the north-east corner of the country, is the Weinviertel, the largest Austrian wine area. Great value wines come from here, mainly made with Grüner Veltliner. A new wine designation is DAC, modeled on the French AC or the Italian DOC: stressing geographic origin rather than grape variety, DAC wines are some of the best everyday dry white wines coming out of Austria.

The Burgenland is where the great dessert wines, and—increasingly—red wines come from. This is the hottest region of Austria, dominated by the marshy, shallow Neusiedlersee lake. Great sweet wines come from the villages all around the lake, while reds come from here as well as hillier vineyards further south.

Wines from Styria, a smaller area in the south east, are worth seeking out. The region has astonished the world with the quality of its Sauvignon Blanc and Chardonnay, and some great white wine makers are based there, as well.

ADOLF & HEINRICH FUCHS

Adolf & Heinrich Fuchs 2003 Chardonnay (Südsteiermark) $16. 84 *—R.V. (5/1/2005)*

Adolf & Heinrich Fuchs 2001 Classik Trocken Chardonnay (Südsteiermark) $13. 86 *—R.V. (11/1/2002)*

Adolf & Heinrich Fuchs 2003 Classic Gelber Muskateller (Südsteiermark) $NA. 85 *—R.V. (5/1/2005)*

Adolf & Heinrich Fuchs 2003 Classic Halbtrocken Gewürztraminer (Burgenland) $NA. 84 *—R.V. (5/1/2005)*

Adolf & Heinrich Fuchs 2003 Libelich Gewürztraminer (Südsteiermark) $NA. 83 *—R.V. (5/1/2005)*

Adolf & Heinrich Fuchs 2003 Classic Grüner Veltliner (Neusiedlersee) $NA. 83 *—R.V. (5/1/2005)*

Adolf & Heinrich Fuchs 2001 Classik Trocken Grüner Veltliner (Burgenland) $13. 87 *—R.V. (11/1/2002)*

Adolf & Heinrich Fuchs 2003 Reserve Grüner Veltliner (Burgenland) $NA. 86 *—R.V. (5/1/2005)*

Adolf & Heinrich Fuchs NV Landwein Muskat Ottonel (Burgenland) $NA. 83 *—R.V. (5/1/2005)*

Adolf & Heinrich Fuchs 2003 Sauvignon Blanc (South Styria) $20. 87 *(7/1/2005)*

Adolf & Heinrich Fuchs 2001 Classik Trocken Sauvignon Blanc (Südsteiermark) $13. 86 *—R.V. (11/1/2002)*

Adolf & Heinrich Fuchs 2003 Classic Weissburgunder (Südsteiermark) $NA. 83 *—R.V. (5/1/2005)*

Adolf & Heinrich Fuchs 2003 Classic Welschriesling (Südsteiermark) $NA. 85 *—R.V. (5/1/2005)*

ALLRAM

Allram 2003 Gaisberg Grüner Veltliner (Kamptal) $25. 90 *—J.C. (5/1/2005)*

Allram 2003 Strassertal Grüner Veltliner (Kamptal) $14. 87 *—J.C. (5/1/2005)*

ANTON BAUER

Anton Bauer 2001 Wagram Reserve Cabernet Blend (Donauland) $28. 84 *—J.C. (5/1/2005)*

Anton Bauer 2003 Wagram Reserve Grüner Veltliner (Donauland) $20. 87 *—J.C. (5/1/2005)*

Anton Bauer 2003 Wagram Cuvée No. 9 Red Blend (Donauland) $20. 86 *—J.C. (3/1/2006)*

Anton Bauer 2002 Reserve Riesling (Donauland) $18. 88 *—J.C. (12/15/2004)*

Anton Bauer 2005 Rosé Trocken Rosé Blend (Donauland) $12. Having tasted the 2006 informally, go for that vintage if it's available in your market. The 2005 is still hanging in there, but its strawberry flavors are starting to fade. Remains dry and clean on the finish. 83 *—J.C. (7/1/2007)*

ARACHON

Arachon 2005 A Kira Blaufränkisch (Burgenland) $NA. The second wine from the Arachon winery, this is soft and perfumed, with flavors of quince jelly, and candy. Touches of wood just edge in some structure. 85 *—R.V. (10/1/2007)*

Arachon 2005 Evolution Red Blend (Burgenland) $NA. This 2005 vintage has highly spicy, new wood aromas, but on the palate, the fresh red berry fruits, citrus and lively acidity assert themselves. Age for two years. 88 *—R.V. (10/1/2007)*

BERNHARD OTT

Bernhard Ott 2005 Am Berg Grüner Veltliner (Donauland) $18. A single vineyard bottling from master Grüner Veltliner producer, Bernhard Ott. It is fresh, crisp, flowery, light and clean. A great aperitif wine. 88 *—R.V. (2/1/2007)*

Bernhard Ott 2005 Rosenberg Grüner Veltliner (Donauland) $15. Bernhard Ott is a Grüner Veltliner specialist, with 90% of his vineyard planted to Austria's national white varietal. This single vineyard wine is a lilting, dancing wine, with delicious green apple flavors layered with spice. Drink now, or age for 2-3 years. 90 Best Buy *—R.V. (2/1/2007)*

BOCKFLIESS

Bockfliess 1999 Pinot Blanc (Weinviertel) $14. 86 *—J.C. (3/1/2002)*

BRAUNSTEIN

Braunstein 2003 Oxhoft Chardonnay (Burgenland) $18. 83 *—J.C. (11/15/2005)*

Braunstein 2002 Oxhoft Chardonnay (Burgenland) $18. 85 *—J.C. (11/15/2005)*

Braunstein 2003 Mitterjoch Zweigelt (Burgenland) $14. 82 *—J.C. (3/1/2006)*

BRÜNDLMAYER

Bründlmayer 2005 Eiswein Gelber Muskateller (Kamptal) $NA. The exotic flavors of Gelber Muskateller, all the spice and fresh acidity lychees, make this an immediately enticing wine. With its vibrant, primary flavors, it is hugely enjoyable. 91 *—R.V. (2/1/2007)*

Bründlmayer 2002 Gelber Muskateller Beerenauslese Gelber Muskateller (Kamptal) $NA. This is as much about spice and fresh sweet apple flavors as it is about actual botrytis sweetness. The Gelber Muskateller gives tastes of cinnamon, pepper and nutmeg as well as fruit, while preserving the raciness of the grape variety. 90 *—R.V. (2/1/2007)*

Bründlmayer 2002 Gelber Muskateller Trockenbeerenauslese Gelber Muskateller (Kamptal) $NA. As Gelber Muskateller ages, it loses spice and gains flavors of caramel and vanilla, and crystallized cherries. The acidity is still there, giving it delicious freshness that just jumps from the glass. 92 *—R.V. (2/1/2007)*

Bründlmayer 2000 Kamptaler Terrasssen Grüner Veltliner (Kamptal) $18. 87 *—J.C. (3/1/2002)*

Bründlmayer 2004 Ried Käferberg Beerenauslese Grüner Veltliner (Kamptal) $NA. Grüner Veltliner's pepper is just below the surface of this fresh, but concentrated wine. It has lovely crispness, a burst of pear and orange peel flavors, and almost ethereal lightness. Ried Käferberg is a single vineyard just outside Langenlois. 92 *—R.V. (2/1/2007)*

Bründlmayer 2000 Ried Loiser Berg Trockenbeerenauslese Grüner Veltliner (Kamptal) $NA. Loiser Berg is a cool vineyard, facing south, to the west of Langenlois. Grüner Veltliner and Riesling grow well. This TBA is now maturing well, as its gold color proves. While the primary fruit flavors have gone, there is still great freshness, with honey and spices the main tastes. Judging by that freshness, it still has many years to go. 93 *—R.V. (2/1/2007)*

Bründlmayer 2003 Langenloiser Spiegel Grau und Weissburgunder Pinot Gris (Kamptal) $NA. 91 *—R.V. (2/1/2006)*

Bründlmayer 2002 Langenloiser Spiegel Grau und Weissburgunder Pinot Gris (Kamptal) $NA. 92 *—R.V. (2/1/2006)*

Bründlmayer 2004 Cécile Pinot Noir (Kamptal) $62. A firmly tannic, young Pinot Noir with red berry fruits under this strong surface dryness. As it develops over the next year, it will become a more elegant, balanced wine, but never one with great power. Cécile is Willi Bründlmayer's daughter. 89 *—R.V. (10/1/2007)*

Bründlmayer 2003 Langenloiser Dechant Pinot Noir (Kamptal) $40. An elegant Blauburgunder (Pinot Noir) that has fresh, juicy fruit, some warmth of spices and almonds, but mainly great purity of red cherry flavors. Tannins give a good shape to this attractive wine. 88 *—R.V. (10/1/2007)*

Bründlmayer 2006 Kamptaler Terrassen Riesling (Kamptal) $24. A crisp apples-and-spice Riesling, packed with crisp fresh acidity, which has deceptive layers of concentration. There's a great vibrant lift of fresh fruit to finish. 88 *—R.V. (12/31/2007)*

Bründlmayer 2005 Kamptaler Terrassen Riesling (Kamptal) $23. 88 *—R.V. (10/1/2006)*

Bründlmayer 2006 Langenloiser Steinmassel Riesling (Kamptal) $30. Soft and finely perfumed, this is full-bodied Riesling, adding just a touch of sweetness to the pear and white currant fruit flavors. This is a great vintage of this wine, probably the best since 2002. 91 *—R.V. (12/31/2007)*

Bründlmayer 2004 Langenloiser Kamptaler Terrassen Riesling (Kamptal) $25. 90 *—R.V. (8/1/2005)*

Bründlmayer 2003 Langenloiser Kamptaler Terrassen Riesling (Kamptal) $25. 89 *—R.V. (8/1/2005)*

Bründlmayer 2005 Langenloiser Steinmassel Riesling (Kamptal) $30. 90 *—R.V. (10/1/2006)*

Bründlmayer 2003 Langenloiser Steinmassel Riesling (Kamptal) $34. 93 *—R.V. (8/1/2005)*

Bründlmayer 2000 Langenloiser Steinmassel Riesling (Kamptal) $25. 90 *—J.C. (3/1/2002)*

Bründlmayer 2006 Zöbinger Heiligenstein Riesling (Kamptal) $62. The Heiligenstein vineyard is a great one, and from this Willi Bründlmayer produces three great wines. Of the three, this is the most accessible when young, already a complete wine, with minerality and also warmth from the very ripe, rounded fruits, just edged with crispness. 93 *—R.V. (12/31/2007)*

Bründlmayer 2005 Zöbinger Heiligenstein Riesling (Kamptal) $36. 93 Editors' Choice *—R.V. (10/1/2006)*

Bründlmayer 2003 Zöbinger Heiligenstein Riesling (Kamptal) $39. 91 *—R.V. (8/1/2005)*

Bründlmayer 2006 Zöbinger Heiligenstein Alte Reben Riesling (Kamptal) $62. The old vines on the steep slopes of the Heiligenstein vineyard give one of Austria's greatest wines. This is one of those Rieslings that will last indefinitely, a powerful, concentrated blend of white fruits, perfumes, peaches, very tight and closed now. Racy acidity and minerality shoot through the richness. Give this 10 years at least. 96 Cellar Selection *—R.V. (12/31/2007)*

Bründlmayer 2005 Zöbinger Heiligenstein Alte Reben Riesling (Kamptal) $NA. 95 Editors' Choice *—R.V. (10/1/2006)*

Bründlmayer 2001 Zöbinger Heiligenstein Alte Reben Riesling (Kamptal) $49. 95 Cellar Selection *—R.V. (8/1/2005)*

Bründlmayer 2000 Zöbinger Heiligenstein Beerenauslese 375ml Riesling (Kamptal) $95. 92 Cellar Selection *—R.V. (10/1/2006)*

Bründlmayer 2006 Zöbinger Heiligenstein Lyra Riesling (Kamptal) $58. One of Bründlmayer's specialities is the lyre training system, which opens out the canopy to get the maximum exposure. It gives a wine that has extra intensity, flavors of white currants vying with lychees, almonds, a perfumed aura. The end is satisfying, with acidity adding a lift. 94 *—R.V. (12/31/2007)*

Bründlmayer 2005 Zöbinger Heiligenstein Lyra Riesling (Kamptal) $60. 94 Cellar Selection *—R.V. (10/1/2006)*

Bründlmayer 2002 Zöbinger Heiligenstein Lyra Riesling (Kamptal) $66. 93 Editors' Choice *—R.V. (8/1/2005)*

Bründlmayer 2000 Zöbinger Heiligenstein Riesling Beerenauslese Riesling (Kamptal) $NA. The Riesling, in all its noble glory, can make some of the greatest sweet wines, and Bründlmayer shows how with this delicate, but finely balanced wine. Unlike some of his TBA offerings, this is light, as much to do with freshness as sweetness. Delicious and now ready to drink. 93 *—R.V. (2/1/2007)*

Bründlmayer 2003 Ried Ladner St. Laurent (Kamptal) $24. All the juiciness of the St. Laurent is in this fruity wine: great red berries, the flesh of red plums, touches of blueberry tannins. This is all about vivid colors and flavors. A delicious summer wine. 87 *—R.V. (10/1/2007)*

CHRISTIAN FISCHER

Christian Fischer 2004 Premium Merlot Merlot (Thermenregion) $50. There's considerable richness in this broad, generous, velvet- textured wine that brings out the red fruit and ripeness. The 18-months barrel aging have not dampened the fruit, but have certainly contributed to the power of this impressive wine. 90 *—R.V. (10/1/2007)*

Christian Fischer 2004 Classic Pinot Noir (Thermenregion) $24. Thermenregion, just west of Vienna, is getting a reputation for its international varietal red wines. This Pinot Noir shows how, even at a good, value-drinking level, the wines have good intensity and complex flavors. This has black cherry flavors, along with a touch of wood. A delicious ready-to-drink wine. 88 *—R.V. (10/1/2007)*

Christian Fischer 2004 Premium Pinot Noir (Thermenregion) $37. The clay slopes around the village of Soss have produced an impressively dense Pinot Noir, rich, with evidence of wood aging and soft opulence. The black fruits are dominant, but this is superripe, powerful and dense. 89 *—R.V. (10/1/2007)*

Christian Fischer 2004 Premium Gradenthal Red Blend (Thermenregion) $35. Any thought that Austria cannot produce world-class reds would disappear with this wine. A blend of Zweigelt, Cabernet Sauvignon and Merlot, it is powerful, rich and spicy, with dense black cherry and new wood flavors. The touch of nutmeg sprinkled over the juicy fruit adds an exotic touch. 91 Cellar Selection *—R.V. (10/1/2007)*

Christian Fischer 2004 Classic St. Laurent (Thermenregion) $23. A big, hearty wine, packed with dense fruit, blackberry jelly flavors, ripe, earthy and generous. There is some wood here, and the juicy full fruits. A delicious wine for stews, hearty meats. 87 *—R.V. (10/1/2007)*

Christian Fischer 2005 Fasangarten Classic Zweigelt (Thermenregion) $17. This is an easy, juicy wine, entry-level wine in Christian Fischer's impressive range of reds. It has delicious strawberry and berry fruits, an open softness, balanced with acidity and a friendly, earthy feel. 87 *—R.V. (10/1/2007)*

DINSTLGUT LOIBEN

Dinstlgut Loiben 2005 Loibenberg Grüner Veltliner (Wachau) $NA. 88 *—R.V. (10/1/2006)*

Dinstlgut Loiben 2005 Loibenberg Riesling (Wachau) $NA. 88 *—R.V. (10/1/2006)*

Dinstlgut Loiben 2003 Loibenberg Trockenbeerenaulese Riesling (Wachau) $NA. 93 *—R.V. (10/1/2006)*

Dinstlgut Loiben 2005 Pfaffenberg Riesling (Kremstal) $NA. 89 *—R.V. (10/1/2006)*

DOMAINE WACHAU

Domaine Wachau 2005 Achleiten Smaragd Grüner Veltliner (Wachau) $27. 90 *—R.V. (10/1/2006)*

Domaine Wachau 2003 Dürnsteiner Kellerberg Smaragd Grüner Veltliner (Wachau) $23. 88 *—R.V. (5/1/2005)*

Domaine Wachau 2002 Federspiel Terrassen Grüner Veltliner (Wachau) $13. 87 Best Buy *—R.V. (11/15/2004)*

Domaine Wachau 2003 Loibner Loibenberg Federspiel Grüner Veltliner (Wachau) $11. 87 Best Buy *—R.V. (5/1/2005)*

Domaine Wachau 2005 Achleiten Smaragd Riesling (Wachau) $33. 89 *—R.V. (10/1/2006)*

Domaine Wachau 2003 Dürnsteiner Kellerberg Smaragd Riesling (Wachau) $30. 90 *—R.V. (5/1/2005)*

Domaine Wachau 2005 Loibenberg Smaragd Riesling (Wachau) $33. 91 *—R.V. (10/1/2006)*

Domaine Wachau 2003 Terrassen Federspiel Riesling (Wachau) $12. 90 Best Buy *—J.C. (5/1/2005)*

DOMAINES SCHLUMBERGER

Domaines Schlumberger NV Cuvée Klimt Brut Welschriesling (Weinviertel) $18. 84 *—J.C. (12/31/2001)*

Domaines Schlumberger NV Cuvée Klimt Brut Welschriesling (Osterreichischer Sekt) $20. 85 *—J.C. (12/31/2003)*

DOMÄNE MÜLLER

Domäne Müller 1997 Ried Burgegg Fürstenstück Der Pinot Gris (Weststeiermark) $16. 90 *—R.V. (2/1/2006)*

E. & M. BERGER

E. & M. Berger 2002 Grüner Veltliner (Kremstal) $11. 85 *—M.S. (11/15/2003)*

E. & M. Berger 2000 Zehetnerin Grüner Veltliner (Kremstal) $14. 84 *—J.C. (3/1/2002)*

EICHINGER

Eichinger 2002 Strasser Gaisberg Grüner Veltliner (Kamptal) $25. 89 *—J.C. (5/1/2005)*

Eichinger 2002 Strasser Gaisberg Riesling (Kamptal) $25. 90 *—J.C. (5/1/2005)*

Elfenhof 1999 Beerenauslese Chardonnay (Burgenland) $NA. 87 *—R.V. (5/1/2004)*

ELFENHOF

Elfenhof 2001 Spatlese Lieblich Chardonnay (Burgenland) $NA. 85 *—R.V. (5/1/2004)*

Elfenhof 1999 Eiswein Nebbiolo (Neusiedlersee-Hügelland) $NA. 89 Editors' Choice *—R.V. (5/1/2004)*

EMMERICH KNOLL

Emmerich Knoll 2005 Loibenberg Smaragd Grüner Veltliner (Wachau) $46. 89 *—R.V. (10/1/2006)*

Emmerich Knoll 2004 Loibner Federspiel Grüner Veltliner (Wachau) $22. 85 *—J.C. (8/1/2006)*

Emmerich Knoll 2003 Loibner Federspiel Trocken Grüner Veltliner (Wachau) $22. 88 *—J.C. (11/15/2005)*

Emmerich Knoll 2004 Loibner Ried Kreutles Federspiel Grüner Veltliner (Wachau) $26. 90 Editors' Choice *—J.C. (8/1/2006)*

Emmerich Knoll 2004 Ried Kreutles Loibner Smaragd Grüner Veltliner (Wachau) $35. 89 *—J.C. (3/1/2006)*

Emmerich Knoll 2002 Ried Kreutles Smaragd Grüner Veltliner (Wachau) $33. 90 *—J.C. (5/1/2005)*

Emmerich Knoll 2005 Loibenberg Smaragd Riesling (Wachau) $50. 91 *—R.V. (10/1/2006)*

Emmerich Knoll 2004 Loibner Federspiel Riesling (Wachau) $28. 86 *—J.C. (8/1/2006)*

Emmerich Knoll 2002 Loibner Ried Loibenberg Riesling Smaragd Riesling (Wachau) $45. 92 *—J.C. (12/15/2004)*

ERIC & WALTER POLZ

Eric & Walter Polz 2001 Grassnitzberg Grauburgunder (Südsteiermark) $NA. 90 *—R.V. (2/1/2006)*

Eric & Walter Polz 2005 Hochgrassnitzberg Sauvignon Blanc (Südsteiermark) $47. 90 *—R.V. (10/1/2006)*

Eric & Walter Polz 2003 Hochgrassnitzberg Reserve Sauvignon Blanc (Südsteiermark) $60. 91 Cellar Selection *—R.V. (10/1/2006)*

Eric & Walter Polz 2000 Steirische Klassik Sauvignon Blanc (Südsteiermark) $27. 85 *—J.C. (3/1/2002)*

Eric & Walter Polz 2005 Therese Sauvignon Blanc (Südsteiermark) $29. 89 *—R.V. (10/1/2006)*

ERICH SALOMON

Erich Salomon 2000 Hochterrassen Grüner Veltliner (Kremstal) $11. 83 *—J.C. (3/1/2002)*

ERNST TRIEBAUMER

Ernst Triebaumer 2004 Blaufränkisch (Neusiedlersee-Hügelland) $NA. 85 *—R.V. (10/1/2006)*

Ernst Triebaumer 2004 Gmärk Blaufränkisch (Neusiedlersee-Hügelland) $24. 89 *—R.V. (10/1/2006)*

Ernst Triebaumer 2003 Mariental Blaufränkisch (Neusiedlersee-Hügelland) $NA. 93 Editors' Choice *—R.V. (10/1/2006)*

Ernst Triebaumer 2003 Oberer Wald Blaufränkisch (Neusiedlersee-Hügelland) $43. 91 *—R.V. (10/1/2006)*

Ernst Triebaumer 2004 Ried Mariental Blaufränkisch (Burgenland) $117. 93 Cellar Selection *—R.V. (10/1/2007)*

Ernst Triebaumer 2004 Ried Oberer Wald Blaufränkisch (Burgenland) $43. Red plums and black cherries dominate this ripe, fruity wine, which brings in plenty of fresh acidity to balance the dry underlying tannins. The Oberer Wald vineyard, on the eastern shores of the Neusiedlersee, gives uncomplicated wines that are great partners with hearty food. 90 *—R.V. (10/1/2007)*

Ernst Triebaumer 2003 Cabernet Sauvignon-Merlot (Burgenland) $63. Velvet and smooth black fruits are on the surface of this Bordeaux blend. But underneath this softness is a dense, concentrated tannic wine, with wood flavors, dry layers and the power to age for several years. While this may not be a Burgenland blend, it has some of the herbal, spice character of the reds from this region. 91 *—R.V. (10/1/2007)*

Ernst Triebaumer 2001 Sauvignon Blanc (Burgenland) $10. 90 *—S.H. (10/1/2004)*

Ernst Triebaumer 2001 Auslese Sauvignon Blanc (Burgenland) $32. 86 *—R.V. (5/1/2004)*

Ernst Triebaumer 2001 Beerenauslese Traminer (Burgenland) $32. 87 *—R.V. (5/1/2004)*

Ernst Triebaumer 1998 Ausbruch Essenz Weissburgunder (Burgenland) $81. 90 *—R.V. (5/1/2004)*

Ernst Triebaumer 1999 Ausbruch Essenz White Blend (Burgenland) $135. 91 *—R.V. (5/1/2004)*

Ernst Triebaumer 2004 Ruster Ausbruch White Blend (Neusiedlersee-Hügelland) $69. A blend of Chardonnay, Weissburgunder and Welschriesling, this is one of the top vintages from Ernst Triebaumer. A huge weight botrytis, though fresh with Asian spice and lychee flavors. Orange peel adds to the rich complexity of this wine. 93 *—R.V. (2/1/2007)*

Ernst Triebaumer 2002 Ruster Ausbruch White Blend (Neusiedlersee-Hügelland) $69. In their youth—and this is still young—the wines of Ernst Triebaumer show great freshness and almond flavors as much as the hugely rich sweetness and botrytis. There is some delicacy here, leaving a fresh, light taste in the mouth. But just watch this wine develop—over 10 years or more. 91 *—R.V. (2/1/2007)*

Ernst Triebaumer 1999 Ruster Ausbruch Essenz White Blend (Neusiedlersee-Hügelland) $167. This is just liquid honey, with a touch of lemon. It is so smooth and with nuts and lemon peel. Sweet, rich and balanced. Delicious, with a crisp aftertaste. 95 *—R.V. (2/1/2007)*

ERWIN SABATHI

Erwin Sabathi 2002 Mervielleux Morillon Chardonnay (Styria) $45. 89 *—J.C. (12/15/2004)*

Erwin Sabathi 2005 Klassic Sauvignon Blanc (Styria) $16. 85 *—J.C. (12/1/2006)*

Erwin Sabathi 2003 Klassik Sauvignon Blanc (Styria) $15. 84 *—J.C. (12/15/2004)*

Erwin Sabathi 2002 Merviellieux Sauvignon Blanc (Styria) $50. 86 *—J.C. (12/15/2004)*

Erwin Sabathi 2005 Poharnig Sauvignon Blanc (Styria) $32. 88 *—J.C. (12/1/2006)*

Erwin Sabathi 2004 Poharnig Sauvignon Blanc (Südsteiermark) $30. 87 *—J.C. (8/1/2006)*

Erwin Sabathi 2003 Poharnig Sauvignon Blanc (Styria) $30. 87 *(7/1/2005)*

Erwin Sabathi 2003 Possnitzberg Sauvignon Blanc (Styria) $35. 90 *—J.C. (12/15/2004)*

Erwin Sabathi 2005 Pössnitzberg Sauvignon Blanc (Styria) $37. 86 *—J.C. (12/1/2006)*

Erwin Sabathi 2004 Pössnitzberg Sauvignon Blanc (South Styria) $35. 88 *—J.C. (8/1/2006)*

F X PICHLER

F X Pichler 2001 Dürnsteiner Kellerberg Smaragd Grüner Veltliner (Wachau) $NA. 92 *—R.V. (5/1/2005)*

FAMILIE ZULL

Familie Zull 2003 DAC Grüner Veltliner (Weinviertel) $23. 86 *—R.V. (5/1/2005)*

FEILER-ARTINGER

Feiler-Artinger 2005 Blaufränkisch (Burgenland) $12. Fresh, lively and spicy, with great ripe, red fruit and light tannins. The acidity highlights the vibrant fruit character. Drink now. Bottled in screwcap. 87 Best Buy *—R.V. (10/1/2007)*

Feiler-Artinger 2005 Umriss Blaufränkisch (Burgenland) $20. Smooth wine, with softened fruit and ripe red-berry flavors. There is some good depth of flavor, coming from the wood and spicy edge, as well as the herbal, juicy nature of the fruit. Screwcap. 89 *—R.V. (10/1/2007)*

Feiler-Artinger 2000 Umriss Blaufränkisch (Burgenland) $25. 85 *—R.V. (11/1/2002)*

Feiler-Artinger 2002 Umriss Trocken Blaufränkisch (Burgenland) $20. 87 *—J.C. (5/1/2005)*

Feiler-Artinger 2004 1010 Cabernet Blend (Burgenland) $54. First created in 1992, this international blend is a fine contribution to Bordeaux-style wines around the world. Cabs and Merlot are the basis, and the relatively cool conditions of 2004 have given a delicate, elegant wine, with fresh black berry fruits. 91 Editors' Choice *—R.V. (10/1/2007)*

Feiler-Artinger 2005 1011 Cabernet Blend (Burgenland) $52. Since 1992, Hans and Kurt Feiler have produced what they call the 1000 Series, a blend of Cabernet Franc and Merlot. This 2005 vintage follows the same theme, keeping close to a Bordeaux model, while adding extra sweetness and ripeness to the fruit. Wood aging helps soften the wine, but it is also a question of soft tannins and richness. 90 *—R.V. (10/1/2007)*

Feiler-Artinger 2005 Cabernet Sauvignon (Burgenland) $20. This Cabernet Sauvignon is rare for the Feilers. Normally the fruit goes into a blend. But in 2005, they have chosen to release a varietal Cabernet, a lean, somewhat austere wine, showing the aging potential, but also just showing some green character. Tough, with high acidity. 86 *—R.V. (10/1/2007)*

Feiler-Artinger 2000 1006 Cabernet Sauvignon-Merlot (Burgenland) $60. 90 *—R.V. (11/1/2002)*

Feiler-Artinger 2004 Muskat Ottonel Ruster Ausbruch Muskat Ottonel (Neusiedlersee-Hügelland) $48. This spicy version of the Muscat family is only found in Austria in the area around Lake Neusiedl. This wine shows great varietal character, with nutmeg flavors dominating; relatively dry to taste. The sweetness is there, but what is so delicious about this wine is its balance. 94 *—R.V. (5/1/2007*

Feiler-Artinger 2005 Solitaire Red Blend (Burgenland) $50. This is the Feilers' flagship red, a blend of Blaufränkisch, Merlot and Cabernet Sauvignon, smooth, ripe and velvety. The tannins seem soft initially because of the new French wood flavors, but to finish, they become firm, dry and tough, promising some good aging. For now, enjoy the sweet blackberry fruits. 91 *—R.V. (10/1/2007)*

Feiler-Artinger 2004 Solitaire Red Blend (Burgenland) $50. A finely structured wine, packed with ripe fruit, dense tannins and sweet plum juice flavors. Elegant, this wears its alcohol well, showing good structure and the potential for aging. 90 *—R.V. (10/1/2007)*

Feiler-Artinger 2002 Solitaire Red Blend (Burgenland) $50. 88 *—J.C. (3/1/2006)*

Feiler-Artinger 2000 Solitaire Red Blend (Burgenland) $60. 91 *—R.V. (11/1/2002)*

Feiler-Artinger 2004 Zweigelt & More Red Blend (Burgenland) $36. The "more" is Cabernet Franc, added, according to Hans Feiler, "in just a tiny touch." And, although the French wood caramel and vanilla flavors are powerful, there's just enough to catch the perfume of the Cab. But, with its dark fruits, this is much more about long-lived Zweigelt. 89 *—R.V. (10/1/2007)*

Feiler-Artinger 2003 Zweigelt & More Red Blend (Burgenland) $36. The addition of Cabernet Sauvignon, despite the warm year, leaves the Zweigelt tasting green. There is a distinct vegetal character here, which also comes through in dry tannins. Maybe 2–3 years will help. 84 *—R.V. (10/1/2007)*

Feiler-Artinger 2002 Beerenauslese Traminer (Burgenland) $NA. 88 *—R.V. (5/1/2004)*

Feiler-Artinger 1999 Ruster Ausbruch Welschriesling (Burgenland) $50. 88 —*R.V. (11/1/2002)*

Feiler-Artinger 1998 Ruster Ausbruch Welschriesling (Burgenland) $50. 93 Editors' Choice —*R.V. (11/1/2002)*

Feiler-Artinger 2000 White Blend (Burgenland) $NA. 90 —*R.V. (5/1/2004)*

Feiler-Artinger 2001 Ausbruch White Blend (Burgenland) $40. 93 Cellar Selection —*R.V. (5/1/2004)*

Feiler-Artinger 2002 Auslese White Blend (Burgenland) $25. 87 —*R.V. (5/1/2004)*

Feiler-Artinger 2002 Beerenauslese White Blend (Burgenland) $27. 89 —*R.V. (5/1/2004)*

Feiler-Artinger 2001 Ruster Ausbruch White Blend (Neusiedlersee-Hügelland) $45. With their generic Ruster Ausbruch, Kurt and Hans Feiler are able to make fascinating blends, such as this combination of Chardonnay, Neuburger, Weissburgunder and Welschriesling. With this mix, and after more than 5 years, this is a wine that doesn't show fruit as much as richness. It is creamy and opulent, showing some spice; still young at heart, with dry botrytis and honey on the finish. 94 —*R.V. (5/1/2007)*

Feiler-Artinger 2004 Ruster Ausbruch Essenz White Blend (Neusiedlersee-Hügelland) $58 375 ml. This is the pinnacle of sweet wines at Feiler -Artinger. The name is right—it is the essence of all great sweet wines in one bottle. It is one of those wines whose taste lingers, but along the way, there is the most delicious wild flower honey, figs, pineapple, peach and nuts. They are beautifully woven together into a very complete wine, which needs only one thing: aging. 96 Cellar Selection —*R.V. (5/1/2007)*

Feiler-Artinger 1999 Ruster Ausbruch Essenz White Blend (Burgenland) $60. 92 —*R.V. (11/1/2002)*

Feiler-Artinger 2004 Ruster Ausbruch Essenz 375ml White Blend (Burgenland) $50. 92 Editors' Choice —*J.C. (12/1/2006)*

Feiler-Artinger 2004 Pinot Cuvée Ruster Ausbruch White Blend (Neusiedlersee-Hügelland) $40 375 ml. There's great depth to this wine. It is sweet, yes, but the range of fruits—from apricot to white pears to orange peel—and the weight and richness give it great intensity of flavor. In 10 years, this will be even better. 93 —*R.V. (5/1/2007)*

Feiler-Artinger 2004 Ruster Ausbruch Pinot Cuvée 375ml White Blend (Burgenland) $38. 90 —*J.C. (12/1/2006)*

Feiler-Artinger 2001 Ruster Ausbruch Pinot Cuvée White Blend (Neusiedlersee-Hügelland) $37 375 ml. Made from Grauburgunder and Weissburgunder, this is an intensely ripe wine, with aromas from the Pinot Gris and weight from the Pinot Blanc. There's an edge of pepper alongside fresh acidity. Ripe oranges give a lift to the aftertaste. 93 —*R.V. (2/1/2007)*

Feiler-Artinger 1998 Pinot Cuvée Ruster Ausbruch White Blend (Neusiedlersee-Hügelland) $48 375 ml. The acidity is still here in this now-mature wine, keeping it lively while all the flavors swirl around. Pepper and richness combine, while the sweetness has given way to intense power and concentration. Flavors of toast and dark toffee leave a rich, almost dry aftertaste. 93 —*R.V. (5/1/2007)*

Feiler-Artinger 1998 Ruster Ausbruch Pinot Cuvée White Blend (Burgenland) $60. 92 —*R.V. (11/1/2002)*

Feiler-Artinger 2001 Ruster Ausbruch Pinot Cuvée White Riesling (Burgenland) $37. 94 —*R.V. (2/1/2006)*

Feiler-Artinger 2006 Zweigelt (Burgenland) $12. Very pure varietal flavors, with firm tannins under a burst of vivid raspberries and red currant fruits. The freshness is all there still. Drink now for its fruit, or hold for 2 years for complexity. 87 Best Buy —*R.V. (10/1/2007)*

Feiler-Artinger 2005 Zweigelt Beerenauslese (Burgenland) $NA. With its reputation for sweet wines, and its big range of reds, it's not surprising that Feiler-Artinger should come up with this wine. It is a curiosity, vaguely like a young tawny Port in its flavors, the tannins of the grapes clashing with the sweetness of the botrytis fruit. The acidity, though, helps, along with the apricot and plum compote flavors. 85 —*R.V. (12/31/2007)*

FELSNER

Felsner 2006 Gedersdorf Moosburgerin Grüner Veltliner (Kremstal) $16. Ripe, creamy style of Grüner Veltliner, with green plums, fresh acidity and just a touch of textured spice. This is a delicious wine, lively but rich, finishing with a great, vibrant aftertaste. 88 —*R.V. (12/31/2007)*

Felsner 2005 Gedersdorfer Moosburgerin Grüner Veltliner (Kremstal) $20. 88 —*J.C. (12/1/2006)*

Felsner 2004 Gedersdorfer Moosburgerin Grüner Veltliner (Kremstal) $15. 87 —*J.C. (11/15/2005)*

Felsner 2005 Gedersdorfer Vordernberg Grüner Veltliner (Kremstal) $26. 88 —*J.C. (12/1/2006)*

Felsner 2004 Gedersdorfer Vordernberg Grüner Veltliner (Kremstal) $19. 86 —*J.C. (11/15/2005)*

Felsner 1999 Icon Eiswein 375 ml Grüner Veltliner (Kremstal) $35. 87 —*J.C. (3/1/2006)*

Felsner 2004 Lössterrassen Grüner Veltliner (Kremstal) $10. 87 Best Buy —*J.C. (8/1/2006)*

Felsner 2004 Rohrendorfer Leithen Alte Reben Trocken Grüner Veltliner (Kremstal) $20. 85 —*J.C. (11/15/2005)*

Felsner 2006 Rohrendorfer Gebling Riesling (Kremstal) $19. Although Manfred Felsner is better known as a Grüner Veltliner producer, he makes Rieslings from his Rohrendorfer vineyard. This 2006 is fresh, lightly aromatic, with good green acidity and some crisp, green apple flavors. Screwcap. 87 —*R.V. (12/31/2007)*

Felsner 2005 Rohrendorfer Gebling Riesling (Kremstal) $23. 87 —*J.C. (12/1/2006)*

Felsner 2004 Rohrendorfer Gebling Riesling (Kremstal) $18. 87 —*J.C. (3/1/2006)*

Felsner 2002 Gedersdorfer Weitgasse Zweigelt (Kremstal) $19. 88 —*J.C. (5/1/2005)*

FISCHER

Fischer 2003 Pinot Noir (Thermenregion) $38. 84 —*J.C. (8/1/2006)*

Fischer 2004 Fasangarten Classic Zweigelt (Thermenregion) $17. 87 —*J.C. (8/1/2006)*

FORSTREITER

Forstreiter 2003 Exclusiv Grüner Veltliner (Kremstal) $15. 88 —*R.V. (5/1/2005)*

Forstreiter 2003 Kremser Kogl Bergwein Grüner Veltliner (Kremstal) $11. 89 —*R.V. (5/1/2005)*

Forstreiter 2003 Schiefer Grüner Veltliner (Kremstal) $18. 90 —*R.V. (5/1/2005)*

FRANZ HIRTZBERGER

Franz Hirtzberger 1997 Grauburgunder (Austria) $37. 84 *(5/1/2004)*

Franz Hirtzberger 2003 Honivogl Smaragd Grüner Veltliner (Wachau) $70. 91 —*J.C. (5/1/2005)*

Franz Hirtzberger 2003 Rotes Tor Federspiel Grüner Veltliner (Wachau) $25. 87 —*J.C. (11/15/2005)*

Franz Hirtzberger 2004 Rotes Tor Smaragd Grüner Veltliner (Wachau) $46. 90 —*J.C. (3/1/2006)*

Franz Hirtzberger 2003 Singerriedal Smaragd Riesling (Wachau) $80. 88 —*J.C. (5/1/2005)*

Franz Hirtzberger 2004 Spitzer Hochrain Smaragd Riesling (Wachau) $66. 90 —*J.C. (8/1/2006)*

Franz Hirtzberger 2004 Spitzer Singerriedel Smaragd Riesling (Wachau) $80. 91 Cellar Selection —*J.C. (8/1/2006)*

Franz Hirtzberger 2001 Steinterrassen Federspiel Riesling (Wachau) $24. 93 —*R.V. (8/1/2003)*

FRANZ LETH

Franz Leth 2005 Scheiben Grüner Veltliner (Donauland) $35. 90 Cellar Selection —*R.V. (10/1/2006)*

Franz Leth 2005 Scheiben Roter Veltliner (Donauland) $26. 89 —*R.V. (10/1/2006)*

Franz Leth 2003 Selection Roter Veltliner (Donauland) $28. 89 —*R.V. (5/1/2005)*

FRANZ MITTELBACH

Franz Mittelbach 2002 Tegernseerhof Bergdistel Dürnsteiner Grüner Veltliner (Wachau) $24. 86 —*J.C. (12/15/2004)*

FREIE WEINGÄRTNER WACHAU

Freie Weingärtner Wachau 2004 Grüner Veltliner (Wachau) $9. 88 Best Buy —*J.C. (8/1/2006)*

Freie Weingärtner Wachau 2001 Domaine Wachau Achleiten Smaragd Grüner Veltliner (Wachau) $27. 88 —*R.V. (11/1/2002)*

Freie Weingärtner Wachau 2001 Domaine Wachau Terrassen Federspeil Grüner Veltliner (Wachau) $11. 86 *(11/1/2002)*

Freie Weingärtner Wachau 2004 Riesling (Wachau) $11. 85 —*J.C. (3/1/2006)*

Freie Weingärtner Wachau 2001 Domäne Wachau Achleiten Smaragd Riesling (Wachau) $30. 88 —*R.V. (8/1/2003)*

Freie Weingärtner Wachau 1995 Exceptional Reserve Riesling (Wachau) $35. 86 —*M.S. (5/1/2000)*

GERHARD PITTNAUER

Gerhard Pittnauer 2004 Pannobile Red Blend (Neusiedlersee) $38. A blend of Zweigelt, Blaufränkisch and Merlot, this is Pittnauer's top wine, a smooth and ripe, with a brushed velvet texture. The surface softness only masks the power underneath. The tannins are dusty, but dense; the black jelly-flavored fruits power through the wood and tannins. It's big, but balanced. 91 *—R.V. (10/1/2007)*

Gerhard Pittnauer 2005 Red Pitt Red Blend (Neusiedlersee) $25. This is Gerhard Pittnauer's entry-level wine, and delicious it is, all juicy fruit with just a modicum of wood. The red fruits are vibrant, ripe, open and friendly. Great barbecue material. 87 *—R.V. (10/1/2007)*

Gerhard Pittnauer 2005 Classic St. Laurent (Neusiedlersee) $19. This goes for the earthy side of St. Laurent, especially the aroma. None the worse for that, because the wine is very drinkable, a powerball of juicy fruit, of fresh berries and delicious acidity. 87 *—R.V. (10/1/2007)*

Gerhard Pittnauer 2004 St Laurent Alte Reben St. Laurent (Neusiedlersee) $47. Impressive, what a master winemaker can do with St. Laurent grapes. Retains the typical fresh, juicy character, but plumbs depths of flavor and richness that are not often found. The finishing acidity gives freshness. 90 *—R.V. (10/1/2007)*

Gerhard Pittnauer 2005 Weisse Reben White Blend (Neusiedlersee) $18. Pittnauer's white blend of Chard, Grüner Veltliner and Sauvignon Blanc. Fresh and lightly citric with a touch of fresh white currants. It's soft and easy, with a crisp aftertaste. 85 *—R.V. (8/1/2007)*

Gerhard Pittnauer 2005 Classic Zweigelt (Neusiedlersee) $18. Classic in Austrian terms means no, or very little wood, leaving the fruit to speak for itself. Black cherry fruits, pure and refreshing, suggest this could even be a summer red served chilled. 86 *—R.V. (10/1/2007)*

GERNOT AND HEIKE HEINRICH

Gernot and Heike Heinrich 2004 Gabarinza Red Blend (Burgenland) $60. A beautifully elegant wine, blending three Austrian varieties with Merlot. Gernot Heinrich regards this as his flagship wine, and he has managed to make an impressive wine that keeps its richness and opulence well under control. The overall impression is of fresh cherries, plum skins, some toast flavors and a background of herbs and spice. A wine that should age 3–4 years. 92 Cellar Selection *—R.V. (10/1/2007)*

Gernot and Heike Heinrich 2003 Salzberg Red Blend (Burgenland) $88. This 2003, with its hot year provenance, shows lush fruit, chocolate flavors, and a long, superrich spicy aftertaste. What it does miss is acidity, suggesting it is a wine that will age relatively fast. But for those who like denseness and power, this is one to go for. 89 *—R.V. (10/1/2007)*

GESELLMANN

Gesellmann 2004 Creitzer Reserve Blaufränkisch (Burgenland) $25. The Mittelburgenland, south of the Neusiedlersee, is also known as Blaufränkisch land, so here is one of Albert Gesellmann's interpretations. He emphasizes the spice, the red berry fruits and the soft, silky tannins in a wine that has depth and weight, without losing freshness. 90 *—R.V. (10/1/2007)*

Gesellmann 2004 Siglos Pinot Noir (Burgenland) $30. A single-vineyard Pinot Noir, full of ripe, juicy, fresh fruit that is rounded and filled out with wood aging and flavors of vanilla. But at the heart this remains a red berry and cherry fruit-flavored wine. Screwcap. 89 *—R.V. (10/1/2007)*

Gesellmann 2004 Op Eximium Cuvée 17 Red Blend (Burgenland) $34. Dominated by Blaufränkisch, with St. Laurent and Zweigelt, Op (or Opus) Eximium was first made in 1988 (hence cuvée 17 for the 2004). This particular vintage is one of the finest, a suave, velour-like wine, with black plums, figs and dark, firm tannins all working together. The acidity that spears through the wine keeps it fresh, but there's more in the way of concentration. Screwcap. 92 Editors' Choice *—R.V. (10/1/2007)*

Gesellmann 2006 ZB Red Blend (Burgenland) $16. The Zweigelt's juiciness seems to go so well with the more intense character of the Blauburgunder. There's not much complexity in this deliciously fresh, red-fruited wine. Screwcap. 87 *—R.V. (10/1/2007)*

Gesellmann 2004 Beerenauslese Scheurebe (Burgenland) $30. Made from the Sämling grape (also known as the Scheurebe), this is a wonderfully intense wine, balancing sweetness with crisp white pear acidity. It layers botrytis dryness with sweet hedgerow honey and a pure fruit character. 90 *—R.V. (12/31/2007)*

Gesellmann 2004 Beerenauslese Scheurebe (Mittelburgenland) $NA. The fruit and the richness are all Austrian, with the weight of the Scheurebe giving both richness and power to the wine. 90 *—R.V. (2/1/2007)*

Gesellmann 2005 Sämling Eiswein Scheurebe (Mittelburgenland) $NA. Although Albert Gesellmann is better known for his reds, he certainly knows how to make this dessert style of wine. This eiswein is pierced through with citrus acidity shining through the intense honeyed sweetness and syrupy texture. Should age well. 92 *—R.V. (2/1/2007)*

AUSTRIA

GIEFING

Giefing 2005 Ruster Ausbruch Furmint Furmint (Neusiedlersee-Hügelland) $60. A seriously rich wine from restaurant owner Erich Giefing. Sweetness dominates, with a touch of pepper, a characteristic of the Furmint grape. It is perhaps not the most subtle of wines, but the botrytis is all there, giving enough dryness to suggest it's a wine for aging. 88 *—R.V. (5/1/2007)*

Giefing 2004 Ruster Ausbruch White Blend (Neusiedlersee-Hügelland) $65. Made from Chard and Neuberger, this is a fresh wine, with honey and yeast aromas, and delicious bitter marmalade flavors that float over the rich texture of the wine. 91 *—R.V. (2/1/2007)*

GRAF KOENIGSEGG

Graf Hardegg 2004 Reserve Vom Schloss Grüner Veltliner (Niederösterreich) $27. A rich wine, with some wood flavors, and intense ripe, creamy fruit. Flavors of baked apples, of pears and ripe acidity give this wine both structure and density. 90 *—R.V. (8/1/2007)*

Graf Hardegg 2005 Veltlinsky Grüner Veltliner (Niederösterreich) $10. Very soft, very light, pleasantly acidic and fresh. This wine is designed to show how easy and drinkable Grüner Veltliner is (as if we needed any persuading). It's certainly attractive, but lacks real varietal focus. Screwcap. 86 Best Buy *—R.V. (8/1/2007)*

Graf Hardegg 2005 Vom Schloss Grüner Veltliner (Niederösterreich) $18. A crisp, austere wine; it is a little lean, but does show fine varietal character. Treat this as a good food wine, rather than as an apéritif. 87 *—R.V. (8/1/2007)*

Graf Hardegg 2005 Vom Schloss Riesling (Niederösterreich) $18. This wine is gently perfumed, soft, with delicious citrus and grapefruit flavors along with white berries. The acidity adds to the freshness. 90 *—R.V. (8/1/2007)*

Graf Hardegg NV V Viognier (Austria) $54. A rare find in Austria, this shows the potential of Viognier. Flavors of apricot liqueur, summer flower aromas, and concentration come together to make a rich, powerful wine. Because Viognier is not approved as a varietal in Austria, this is sold as a non-vintage table wine, but in fact this wine is from the 2004 vintage. 90 *—R.V. (8/1/2007)*

Graf Hardegg 2004 Weisse Reserve Vom Schloss White Blend (Niederösterreich) $30. An unusual blend of Chardonnay, Grüner Veltliner and Riesling that works so well, it's not possible to detect which varietal gives which characteristic to this richly layered wine. Aged in wood, this is ripe and concentrated with flavors of spring herbs along side firm minerality. 91 Editors' Choice *—R.V. (8/1/2007)*

GRAF KOENIGSEGG

Graf Koenigsegg 2005 Velt 1 Grüner Veltliner (Burgenland) $11. 87 Best Buy *—J.C. (12/1/2006)*

GRITSCH MAURITIUSHOF

Gritsch Mauritiushof 2003 Singerriedel Grüner Veltliner (Wachau) $27. 87 *—J.C. (12/15/2004)*

Gritsch Mauritiushof 2003 1000 Eimerberg Select Neuburger (Wachau) $19. 88 *—J.C. (11/15/2005)*

Gritsch Mauritiushof 2003 1000 Eimerberg Smaragd Riesling (Wachau) $25. 92 Editors' Choice *—J.C. (11/15/2005)*

Gritsch Mauritiushof 2005 Spitzer 1000 Eimerberg Smaragd Riesling (Wachau) $28. 92 Editors' Choice *—J.C. (12/1/2006)*

GROSS

Gross 1997 Grauburgunder (Austria) $20. 84 *(5/1/2004)*

Gross 1998 Sauvignon Blanc (Styria) $37. 88 *—M.S. (5/1/2000)*

GSELLMANN & GSELLMANN

Gsellmann & Gsellmann 2000 Gelber Muskateller Trockenbeerenauslese Muskateller (Burgenland) $35. 87 *—J.C. (12/15/2004)*

Gsellmann & Gsellmann 2001 Blauburgunder Pinot Noir (Burgenland) $26. 81 *—J.C. (5/1/2005)*

Gsellmann & Gsellmann 2001 Pannobile Red Blend (Burgenland) $20. 86 *—J.C. (5/1/2005)*

Gsellmann & Gsellmann 2001 Eiswein White Blend (Burgenland) $25. 88 *—J.C. (12/15/2004)*

Gsellmann & Gsellmann 1998 Vom Goldberg Chardonnay-Weissburgunder Trockenbeerenauslese 375 ml White Blend (Burgenland) $25. 85 *—J.C. (12/15/2004)*

Gsellmann & Gsellmann 1999 Von Golser Goldberg Beerenauslese White Blend (Burgenland) $20. 87 *—J.C. (12/15/2004)*

GSELLMANN & HANS

Gsellmann & Hans 2003 Scheurebe Eiswein Scheurebe (Neusiedlersee) $27. A delicate but intense wine, with ripe apricot flavors. Liquid honey and just a hint of spice add an intriguing element to a delicious wine. 92 —*R.V. (2/1/2007)*

GUNTER TRIEBAUMER

Gunter Triebaumer 2005 Blaufränkisch (Neusiedlersee-Hügelland) $16. Günter Triebaumer's family winery has seen many changes since he took over in 2003, not least of which is this easy, fruity red, with its spice, cassis and oak flavors, and fresh red currant acidity. Screwcap. 86 —*R.V. (10/1/2007)*

Gunter Triebaumer 2004 Blaufränkisch Reserve Blaufränkisch (Neusiedlersee-Hügelland) $35. Fine perfumes, some toast along with vanilla, and sweet, rich ripe fruit. Together, these attributes make a finely structured wine, packed with black fruits and soft tannins, with just a core of dryness. Screwcap. 89 —*R.V. (10/1/2007)*

Gunter Triebaumer 2006 Blaufränkisch Rosé Blaufränkisch (Neusiedlersee-Hügelland) $13. A medium dry style, with an onion skin color and a palate that is fresh, very fragrant and crisp under the soft aftertaste. 85 —*R.V. (7/1/2007)*

Gunter Triebaumer 2004 Blaufränkisch-Cabernet Red Blend (Neusiedlersee-Hügelland) $21. The aroma is all spice. To taste, there's plenty of spice as well, but the fruit is almost extravagant in its sweetness, vibrancy and very forward character. Too much? No, it all works, and it's totally drinkable. 88 —*R.V. (10/1/2007)*

Gunter Triebaumer 2005 Trie Red Blend (Neusiedlersee-Hügelland) $14. "Trie" is a play on Gunter Triebaumer's red blend (Zweigelt, St Laurent, Cab Sauvignon); a deliciously fresh wine, spicy, peppery and very food friendly. 86 —*R.V. (10/1/2007)*

H. & M. HOFER

H. & M. Hofer 2005 Grüner Veltliner Kirchlissen Grüner Veltliner (Weinviertel) $17. Organic wine from this family winery in Auersthal. It has deliciously fresh fruit, flavors of white plums and just a touch of grapefruit. Concentrated, with a delicious finish. 89 —*R.V. (8/1/2007)*

H. & C. NITTNAUS

H.& C. Nittnaus 2001 Beerenauslese Riesling Riesling (Neusiedlersee) $29. Ripe nuts and white fruits give a fresh, light, almost dancing character to this wine. It is still young to taste, with the fruits and acidity still developing, but there is also some mature Riesling character just creeping in. Plenty of time for more aging, though. 91 —*R.V. (5/1/2007)*

H.& C. Nittnaus 2003 Premium Beerenauslese White Blend (Neusiedlersee) $NA. Hans and Christine Nittnaus' range of Premium sweet wines is delicious, but also quite delicate, tinged with freshness and crispness as well as the proper botrytis. An enjoyable wine. 89 —*R.V. (2/1/2007)*

H.& C. Nittnaus 2003 Premium Beerenauslese White Blend (Neusiedlersee) $26. Smooth and velvety, this wine has richness and weight to go with its honey and syrup flavors. It also has a good, dry botrytis layer that balances, along with good acidity. A finely poised wine. 90 —*R.V. (5/1/2007)*

H.& C. Nittnaus 2005 Zweigelt Beerenauslese Zweigelt (Neusiedlersee) $29. A sweet wine from red grapes, but with a deliciously enticing pink/gold color. The flavor is pure strawberries; not much botrytis, and very apparent acidity. 88 —*R.V. (5/1/2007)*

HAFNER KOSHER

Hafner Kosher 2002 Pinot Gris (Burgenland) $8. 83 —*R.V. (2/1/2006)*

HANS IGLER

Hans Igler 2004 Hochberg Blaufränkisch (Mittelburgenland) $22. An excellent example of the Blaufränkisch grape, Wolfgang Reisner's 2004 from the Hochberg vineyard shows all the right soft tannins, rich juicy fruit, with a touch of earthiness along with the black cherry and wood flavors. 89 —*R.V. (10/1/2007)*

Hans Igler 2003 Pinot Blanc (Burgenland) $15. 85 —*J.C. (11/15/2005)*

Hans Igler 2003 Ab Ericio Red Blend (Mittelburgenland) $60. A blend of half Merlot with Blaufränkisch and Zweigelt; 21 months in wood give serious toasty, nutmeg flavors. They work, although more fruit would help. This is a cult wine in Austria, but there is a risk that it does go over the top. 89 —*R.V. (10/1/2007)*

Hans Igler 2002 Ab Ericio Red Blend (Burgenland) $62. 89 —*J.C. (3/1/2006)*

Hans Igler 2004 Vulcano Red Blend (Mittelburgenland) $35. Vulcano is the German spelling. Quite a mix of grapes, here: Blaufränkisch, Cabernet Sauvignon, Zweigelt and Merlot. One of Austria's top red winemakers, Hans Igler revels in the power of this wine, taming it with smooth tannins, new wood and rich density. The one downside is that it needs to be drunk fast, falling apart in the bottle after 30 minutes. 90 —*R.V. (10/1/2007)*

Hans Igler 2002 Vulcano Red Blend (Burgenland) $35. 88 —*J.C. (5/1/2005)*

Hans Igler 2003 Classic Zweigelt (Burgenland) $17. 85 —*J.C. (3/1/2006)*

HANS PITNAUER

Hans Pitnauer 2003 Franz-Josef Cabernet Blend (Carnuntum) $39. 91 —*R.V. (10/1/2006)*

Hans Pitnauer 2004 Quo Vadis Merlot-Cabernet Sauvignon (Carnuntum) $37. 90 —*R.V. (10/1/2006)*

Hans Pitnauer 2005 Ried Bildenspitz Sauvignon Blanc (Carnuntum) $18. 86 —*R.V. (10/1/2006)*

Hans Pitnauer 2004 Bienenfresser Zweigelt Bärnreiser Zweigelt (Carnuntum) $23. 89 —*R.V. (10/1/2006)*

HEIDI SCHROCK

Heidi Schrock 2004 Turner Ruster Ausbruch Furmint (Neusiedlersee-Hügelland) $NA. A single vineyard wine (Turner is the name of the vineyard). Based on 100% Furmint, a Hungarian grape, there is freshness that floats over the richness and sweetness, giving a lift of citrus to go with the orange marmalade flavors. 90—*R.V. (2/1/2007)*

Heidi Schrock 1999 Ausbruch Pinot Blanc (Burgenland) $78. 91 Cellar Selection —*R.V. (5/1/2004)*

Heidi Schrock 2002 Ruster Ausbruch White Blend (Burgenland) $65. 91 —*R.V. (5/1/2004)*

Heidi Schrock 2001 Ruster Ausbruch White Blend (Burgenland) $67. 90 —*R.V. (5/1/2004)*

Heidi Schrock 2004 Aus den Flügeln der Morgenrote Ruster Ausbruch White Blend (Neusiedlersee-Hügelland) $NA. "On the wings of dawn," a quote from Psalm 139, is the name of this wine from Heidi Schröck. It's a blend of five different grapes, fermented and aged in wood. The result is a wine that, while still young, shows enormous richness, along with apricot jelly flavors and great sweetness balanced with a dry layer of botrytis. 92 —*R.V. (2/1/2007)*

Heidi Schrock 2005 Beerenauslese White Blend (Neusiedlersee-Hügelland) $NA. Attractive and fresh, with peaches and apricots mingling with honey and lemon. Despite its relatively high alcohol, this feels and tastes light; food-friendly. 89 —*R.V. (2/1/2007)*

HEINRICH

Heinrich 2004 Blaufränkisch (Burgenland) $19. 86 —*J.C. (3/1/2006)*

Heinrich 2001 Pannobile Red Blend (Neusiedlersee) $34. 83 —*J.C. (5/1/2005)*

Heinrich 1997 Red Red Blend (Burgenland) $16. 82 —*J.C. (5/1/2000)*

Heinrich 2004 Zweigelt (Burgenland) $19. 83 —*J.C. (8/1/2006)*

Heinrich 2003 Zweigelt (Burgenland) $19. 89 —*J.C. (5/1/2005)*

HEISS

Heiss 1999 Trockenbeerenauslese Riesling (Burgenland) $50. 86 —*J.C. (12/15/2004)*

Heiss 2001 Barrique Beerenauslese Sauvignon Blanc (Neusiedlersee) $35. 90 Editors' Choice —*J.C. (12/15/2004)*

Heiss 2001 Eiswein 375 ml Traminer (Neusiedlersee) $45. 91 —*J.C. (12/15/2004)*

Heiss 1998 Weissburgunder-Sauvignon Blanc Trockenbeerenauslese 375 ml White Blend (Neusiedlersee) $45. 90 —*J.C. (12/15/2004)*

HELMUT LANG

Helmut Lang 1999 TBA Chardonnay (Neusiedlersee) $35. 89 —*R.V. (11/1/2002)*

Helmut Lang 1997 TBA Chardonnay (Neusiedlersee) $35. 85 —*R.V. (11/1/2002)*

Helmut Lang 1999 Beerenauslese Gewürztraminer (Neusiedlersee) $35. 90 —*R.V. (11/1/2002)*

Helmut Lang 1998 TBA Rheinriesling Riesling (Neusiedlersee) $35. 84 —*R.V. (11/1/2002)*

Helmut Lang 2000 Beerenauslese Sauvignon Blanc (Neusiedlersee) $NA. 83 —*R.V. (11/1/2002)*

Helmut Lang 1999 Beerenauslese Samling 88 White Blend (Neusiedlersee) $35. 88 —*R.V. (11/1/2002)*

Helmut Lang 1997 Eiswein Cuvée White Blend (Neusiedlersee) $38. 81 —*R.V. (11/1/2002)*

Helmut Lang 1999 TBA Samling 88 White Blend (Neusiedlersee) $NA. 86 —*R.V. (11/1/2002)*

HIEDLER

Hiedler 2003 Heiligenstein Riesling (Kamptal) $49. 91 —*R.V. (8/1/2005)*

Hiedler 2003 Maximum Riesling (Kamptal) $59. 89 —*R.V. (8/1/2005)*

Hiedler 2003 Steinhaus Riesling (Kamptal) $34. 87 —*R.V. (8/1/2005)*

Hiedler 2005 Zöbinger Heiligenstein Riesling (Kamptal) $45. 91 —*R.V. (10/1/2006)*

HILLINGER

Hillinger 2005 Secco Rosé Pinot Noir (Burgenland) $15. The name is derived from the intended style of the wine—Prosecco-like—although the grape variety is Pinot Noir. It's pale salmon in color, with delicate scents of strawberry, citrus and fresh herbs, and the texture is creamy. Finishes a bit sweet and soft, befitting the style. 83 —*J.C. (7/1/2007)*

Hillinger 2003 St. Laurent (Burgenland) $27. 90 Editors' Choice —*J.C. (3/1/2006)*

Hillinger 2004 Welschriesling (Burgenland) $9. 88 Best Buy —*J.C. (8/1/2006)*

Hillinger 2002 White Blend (Neusiedlersee) $55. 88 —*R.V. (5/1/2004)*

Hillinger 2004 Zweigelt (Burgenland) $18. 90 Editors' Choice —*J.C. (8/1/2006)*

Hillinger 2003 Trocken Zweigelt (Burgenland) $17. 87 —*J.C. (5/1/2005)*

HIRSCH

Hirsch 2000 Kammerner Heiligenstein Grüner Veltliner (Kamptal) $20. 88 —*J.C. (3/1/2002)*

Hirsch 2005 Zöbinger Heiligenstein Grüner Veltliner (Kamptal) $22. 89 —*R.V. (10/1/2006)*

Hirsch 2005 Zöbinger Heiligenstein Riesling (Kamptal) $40. 90 —*R.V. (10/1/2006)*

HOCHRIEGL

Hochriegl NV Extra Trocken Sekt Sparkling Blend (Austria) $19. 83 —*J.C. (6/1/2006)*

HOGL

Hogl 2003 Grüner Veltliner (Wachau) $10. 88 Best Buy —*J.C. (3/1/2006)*

Hogl 2003 Ried Schon Smaragd Grüner Veltliner (Wachau) $22. 91 Editors' Choice —*J.C. (5/1/2005)*

Hogl 2003 Stammliegenschaften Schön Smaragd Grüner Veltliner (Wachau) $24. 87 —*J.C. (11/15/2005)*

Hogl 2003 Terrassen-Spitzergraben Federspiel Grüner Veltliner (Wachau) $15.90 Best Buy —*J.C. (8/1/2006)*

Hogl 2005 Loibner Vision Smaragd Riesling (Wachau) $30. 93 Cellar Selection —*J.C. (12/1/2006)*

Hogl 2003 Loibner Vision Smaragd Riesling (Wachau) $25. 88 —*J.C. (11/15/2005)*

Hogl 2005 Ried Bruck Viessling Smaragd Riesling (Wachau) $38. 92 —*J.C. (12/1/2006)*

Hogl 2003 Terrassen Spitzergraben Federspiel Riesling (Wachau) $12. 85 —*J.C. (8/1/2005)*

HÖPLER

Höpler 2006 Grüner Veltliner (Neusiedlersee-Hügelland) $12. Almost like drinking in a heurige, those Austrian taverns where you can sample the new wine, as this is so fresh, crisp and vividly fruity. A perfect summer wine. 86 —*R.V. (8/1/2007)*

Höpler 2004 Eiswein Grüner Veltliner (Neusiedlersee-Hügelland) $45. A gentle expression of eiswein, with more richness and less acidity than some. There is toffee and orange marmalade, and a soft aftertaste. 88 —*R.V. (8/1/2007)*

Höpler 2006 Pinot Blanc (Neusiedlersee-Hügelland) $14. A smooth, young, fresh wine with soft acidity. No marks for complexity, but plenty of pleasure here. Designed for drinking within the year. 85 —*R.V. (8/1/2007)*

Höpler 1999 Privat Reserve Pinot Blanc Pinot Blanc (Neusiedlersee) $21. For a five-year-old wine, this is still very fresh, with a soft, off-dry character, flavors of spices and almonds, and soft acidity. An excellent apéritif wine. 86 —*R.V. (5/1/2007)*

Höpler 2004 Rosenberg Pinot Noir (Burgenland) $29. Somewhat rustic initially, then shows very pure red cherry flavors along with fresh acidity. The structure is light and fresh rather than tannic, leaning towards sweetness and ripeness. Not a wine for aging, but enjoyable now. 87 —*R.V. (10/1/2007)*

Höpler 2006 Riesling (Neusiedlersee-Hügelland) $17. Very young for a Riesling, this has a freshness that is deliciously drinkable. However, it's youth seems to lend a sharp citric character and a metallic edge. Drink near the end of 2007. 84 —*R.V. (8/1/2007)*

Höpler 2001 Noble Reserve Trockenbeerenauslese White Blend (Neusiedlersee-Hügelland) $41. This is densely rich, but well balanced between honey, acidity and botrytis. A wine that should age well for many years. 92 —*R.V. (2/1/2007)*

Höpler 2001 Trockenbeerenauslese White Blend (Neusiedlersee-Hügelland) $45. Rich and dense, this wine is all sweetness. There is nutmeg, along with ripe apricots and lashings of honey. Mild acidity makes this full and on the fat side. 89 —*R.V. (2/1/2007)*

Höpler 2004 Zweigelt (Neusiedlersee-Hügelland) $17. Fresh, juicy Zweigelt, full of spice, red berry fruits, light acidity and vibrant flavors. Great for barbecues or grilled meats. 86 —*R.V. (10/1/2007)*

IBY

Iby 2005 Classic Blaufränkisch (Mittelburgenland) $14. Classic in Austrian terms means a wine that has no wood aging. So this wine from the red wine heartland of Austria is all about fruit. It is herbal, layered with acidity on top of flavors of redcurrants and cranberries. The tannins offer a firm support to the ripe fruit. Drink now. 85 —*R.V. (2/1/2007)*

Iby 2004 Hochäcker Blaufränkisch (Mittelburgenland) $18. A dry, firmly tannic wine that needs time to develop. Then those delicious herbal, red berry and elegant fruits will break out of the box of dry tannins and wood flavors. The Iby family's cellar in Horitschon in Burgenland, old on the outside, modern inside, is an increasingly fine source of solid red wines. 89 —*R.V. (2/1/2007)*

Iby 2005 Classic Zweigelt (Mittelburgenland) $14. 86 Best Buy —*R.V. (11/15/2006)*

ILSE MAZZA

Ilse Mazza 2002 Achleiten Smaragd Riesling (Wachau) $40. 87 —*J.C. (5/1/2005)*

JAUNEGG

Jaunegg 2002 Muri Chardonnay (Styria) $23. 87 —*J.C. (12/15/2004)*

Jaunegg 2003 Knily Pinot Gris (Styria) $18. 88 *(2/1/2006)*

Jaunegg 2002 Knily Pinot Gris (Styria) $20. 83 *(2/1/2006)*

Jaunegg 2005 Klassik Sauvignon Blanc (Styria) $16. 89 Editors' Choice —*J.C. (12/1/2006)*

Jaunegg 2004 Klassik Sauvignon Blanc (Styria) $15. 86 —*J.C. (11/15/2005)*

Jaunegg 2003 Klassik Sauvignon Blanc (Styria) $15. 84 —*J.C. (11/15/2005)*

Jaunegg 2005 Knily Sauvignon Blanc (Styria) $26. 85 —*J.C. (12/1/2006)*

Jaunegg 2003 Knily Sauvignon Blanc (Styria) $25. 87 *(7/1/2005)*

Jaunegg 2005 Daniel's White Blend (Styria) $11. 87 Best Buy —*J.C. (12/1/2006)*

JOHANN DONABAUM

Johann Donabaum 2003 Berglage Loiben Smaragd Grüner Veltliner (Wachau) $27. 88 —*J.C. (8/1/2006)*

Johann Donabaum 2002 Loibner Garten Grüner Veltliner Smaragd Grüner Veltliner (Wachau) $19. 87 —*J.C. (12/15/2004)*

Johann Donabaum 2003 Loibner Garten Smaragd Grüner Veltliner (Wachau) $19. 91 —*J.C. (8/1/2006)*

Johann Donabaum 2002 Spitzer Point Grüner Veltliner (Wachau) $22. 87 —*J.C. (12/15/2004)*

Johann Donabaum 2003 Spitzer Point Federspiel Grüner Veltliner (Wachau) $13. 86 —*J.C. (3/1/2006)*

Johann Donabaum 2001 Spitzer Point Reserve Grüner Veltliner (Wachau) $25. 90 —*J.C. (12/15/2004)*

Johann Donabaum 2003 Bergterrassen Smaragd Riesling (Wachau) $25. 91 Editors' Choice —*J.C. (11/15/2005)*

Johann Donabaum 2005 Spitzer Setzberg Smaragd Riesling (Wachau) $36. 91 —*J.C. (12/1/2006)*

JOHANN HEINRICH

Johann Heinrich 2006 Blaufränkisch (Burgenland) $15. Classic spice and red fruits from this attractive, generous Blanfränkisch. Made to be drunk young, it is already soft, juicy and fruity, with great freshness from acidity. 86 —*R.V. (10/1/2007)*

Johann Heinrich 2003 Cupido Péché Mignon Blaufränkisch (Burgenland) $69. When Silvia Heinrich, Johann Heinrich's daughter (whose name is on this bottle) pushes the alcohol up to 14%, she somehow loses the intense varietal character. What we find instead is a powerful wine, with layers of wood, big spice and pepper and rounded black fruits, but one with no sense of place. 88 *—R.V. (10/1/2007)*

Johann Heinrich 2005 Goldberg Reserve Blaufränkisch (Burgenland) $38. The Goldberg is an 8-acre vineyard, which produces dense and concentrated fruit from old vines. The wine has ripe, juicy fruit, intense tannins and a strong mineral character from the terroir. Barrique aging has added spice and vanilla and some smokiness, but the wood does not dominate the powerful fruit flavors. 90 *—R.V. (10/1/2007)*

Johann Heinrich 2004 Vitikult Blaufränkisch (Burgenland) $24. For Johann Heinrich, this wine is a celebration of Blaufränkisch. It goes back to a more rustic era in one sense, losing freshness, but gaining in depth of flavor, in structure and light wood flavors. It's worth aging for 2–3 years. 88 *—R.V. (10/1/2007)*

Johann Heinrich 2003 Elegy Merlot-Cabernet Sauvignon (Burgenland) $NA. With Elegy, Johann Heinrich strays away from Austria to produce his interpretation of a Merlot and Cabernet Sauvignon blend. It is a finely structured wine, the oak flavors and the tannins holding well together to give elegance, pointed up by the black currant fruits and a touch of citrus. 89 *—R.V. (10/1/2007)*

Johann Heinrich 2006 Siglos Red Blend (Burgenland) $18. A blend of Zweigelt and Blaufränkisch, very round, soft and perfumed. Blackberries, currants and gingerbread are all there, as well as light acidity plus balancing juicy sweetness. 87 *—R.V. (10/1/2007)*

Johann Heinrich 2005 Terra O. Red Blend (Burgenland) $48. A blend with local and international grapes all piled together. It works, because this has delicious black fruits, taut tannins, layers of spice and herbs and a backbone of refreshing acidity. The tannins suggests aging potential—perhaps four years. 91 *—R.V. (10/1/2007)*

JOHANN SCHWARZ

Johann Schwarz 2004 White White Blend (Neusiedlersee) $45. 89 *—R.V. (10/1/2006)*

JOHANN TOPF

Johann Topf 2003 Strassertal Grüner Veltliner (Kamptal) $14. 88 Editors' Choice *—J.C. (5/1/2005)*

JOHANNESHOF REINISCH

Johanneshof Reinisch 2002 Grande Reserve Pinot Noir (Thermenregion) $60. A big, bold wine, now getting mature. Solidly full of ripe berry fruits, wood and soft tannins, it also has a complexity of other flavors: spice, thyme, smokiness. Impressive for its density and power. 90 Editors' Choice *—R.V. (10/1/2007)*

Johanneshof Reinisch 2004 Grillenhügel Pinot Noir (Thermenregion) $26. As with so many red wine producers in Thermenregion, Pinot Noir and its local derivatives (Blauer Burgunder and Blaufränkisch) do very well at Johann Reinisch's estate. This full-blown wine, earthy, ripe and with great balancing acidity, is packed with red plum and strawberry flavors. Screwcap. 90 *—R.V. (10/1/2007)*

Johanneshof Reinisch 2005 Reserve Rotgipfler (Thermenregion) $NA. This cross between Traminer and Roter Veltliner is found mainly in the Thermenregion in Austria. This example is rich and perfumed, with some hint of lychees but low acidity. Wood aging does little for it. Screwcap. 87 *—R.V. (8/1/2007)*

Johanneshof Reinisch 2005 Tradition Rotgipfler (Thermenregion) $15. The Rotgipfler is a rare grape, found almost entirely in the Thermenregion south of Vienna. It produces a crisp, dry, elegant wine, with some structure and flavors of green grape skins. Fresh and crisp aftertaste. 88 *—R.V. (5/1/2007)*

Johanneshof Reinisch 2004 Frauenfeld St. Laurent (Thermenregion) $26. St. Laurent is a speciality at Johanneshof Reinisch (they make 4 different wines from this varietal). From the Frauenfeld vineyard, this particular interpretation of the grape is packed with berry fruits, a juicy, lightly acidic structure and just hints in the form of spice of the 16 months of barrel aging. 88 *—R.V. (10/1/2007)*

Johanneshof Reinisch 2000 Grande Reserve St. Laurent (Thermenregion) $60. A ripe, fruity wine, with a strong element of new wood, giving spice and bitter chocolate The fruit is equally big and vibrant, with fresh flavors of blueberries. The wine is aged for 22 months in wood. 88 *—R.V. (10/1/2007)*

JOSEF EHMOSER

Josef Ehmoser 2006 Aurum Grüner Veltliner (Wagram-Donauland) $38. Despite its high alcohol, this wine manages to preserve its balance. That's because the Grüner acidity creeps through the weight. With his top wine, Ehmoser goes for a tropical fruit profile here, with mangos on top of vanilla and spice. There's structure too, which suggests this powerful wine could age for 2–3 years. 91 Cellar Selection *—R.V. (12/31/2007)*

Josef Ehmoser 2004 Aurum Grüner Veltliner (Donauland) $32. 91 Editors' Choice *—J.C. (3/1/2006)*

Josef Ehmoser 2006 Hohenberg Grüner Veltliner (Wagram-Donauland) $23. The loess slopes of the Wagram give typically full-bodied Grüner Veltliner. This rich wine, from the Hohenberg vineyard, is ripe, certainly full, with a classic edge of pepper and coriander. But the apple fruit freshness is also there. Screwcap. 89 *—R.V. (12/31/2007)*

Josef Ehmoser 2005 Hohenberg Grüner Veltliner (Donauland) $23. 2 Editors' Choice *—J.C. (12/1/2006)*

Josef Ehmoser 2004 Hohenberg Grüner Veltliner (Donauland) $22. 86 *—J.C. (11/15/2005)*

Josef Ehmoser 2003 Hohenberg Grüner Veltliner (Donauland) $22. 86 *—R.V. (5/1/2005)*

Josef Ehmoser 2003 Hohenberg Grüner Veltliner (Donauland) $22. 88 *—J.C. (12/15/2004)*

Josef Ehmoser 2006 Von den Terrassen Grüner Veltliner (Donauland) $14. The long slope of the Wagram, a relic of the ice age, gives its name to the Terrassen (Terraces) vineyard. This is classic, peppery Grüner, raised to a higher quality by the intensity of the pear flavors and the exotic spicy touch. Screwcap. 89 Best Buy *—R.V. (8/1/2007)*

Josef Ehmoser 2005 Von Den Terrassen Grüner Veltliner (Donauland) $15. 88 *—J.C. (8/1/2006)*

Josef Ehmoser 2004 Von Den Terrassen Grüner Veltliner (Donauland) $15. 85 *—J.C. (3/1/2006)*

Josef Ehmoser 2003 Von Den Terrassen Grüner Veltliner (Donauland) $15. 84 *—J.C. (12/15/2004)*

Josef Ehmoser 2003 Pinot Blanc (Donauland) $20. 86 *—J.C. (5/1/2005)*

Josef Ehmoser 2006 Vom Gelben Löss Riesling (Donauland) $22. Loess soil, fine silt derived from glacial deposits, is the core characteristic of the Wagram vineyards. With Riesling's ability to take its varietal flavor from the soil, this wine shows richness and opulence, while still keeping close to fresh apples and spice flavors. It's young, but already drinkable. 88 *—R.V. (8/1/2007)*

Josef Ehmoser 2005 Vom Gelben Löss Riesling (Donauland) $22. 86 *—J.C. (8/1/2006)*

Josef Ehmoser 2004 Vom Gelben Löss Riesling (Donauland) $22. 89 *—J.C. (3/1/2006)*

Josef Ehmoser 2003 Vom Gelben Löss Riesling (Donauland) $22. 85 *—J.C. (12/15/2004)*

Josef Ehmoser 2006 Weissburgunder (Wagram-Donauland) $19. Ehmoser is a young grower going places. This Weissburgunder (aka Pinot Blanc) is full-bodied, but with an emphasis of green, fresh fruits. There is acidity in spadesful, giving a crisp aftertaste. Screwcap. 87 *—R.V. (12/31/2007)*

JOSEF HIRSCH

Josef Hirsch 2003 Gaisberg Zöbing Riesling (Kamptal) $45. 87 *—R.V. (8/1/2005)*

JOSEF JAMEK

Josef Jamek 2000 Smaragd Ried Achleiten Grüner Veltliner (Wachau) $40. 86 *—J.C. (3/1/2002)*

Josef Jamek 2003 Ried Klaus Smaragd Riesling (Wachau) $70. 88 *—R.V. (5/1/2005)*

JOSEF SCHMID

Josef Schmid 2002 Alte Reben Priorissa Grüner Veltliner (Kremstal) $30. 92 Editors' Choice *—J.C. (5/1/2005)*

Josef Schmid 2002 Urgestein Bergterrassen Riesling (Kremstal) $23. 90 Editors' Choice *—J.C. (5/1/2005)*

JURIS

Juris 2001 Altenberg Chardonnay (Burgenland) $13. 87 *—S.H. (10/1/2004)*

Juris 2000 Reserve Chardonnay (Burgenland) $25. 85 *—S.H. (10/1/2004)*

Juris 2001 TBA Chardonnay (Burgenland) $45. 90 *—R.V. (5/1/2004)*

Juris 2004 Reserve Pinot Noir (Burgenland) $42. A solidly structured wine, with a chalky mineral character that promises some good aging potential. This wood-aged Reserve is one of the stars of the Juris winery, a Burgundian Pinot Noir in its richness with elegance, and its tannins. Fruit is there, all red cherries, but is well integrated. 90 Editors' Choice *—R.V. (10/1/2007)*

Juris 2005 Selection Pinot Noir (Burgenland) $24. Georg Stiegelmar was one of the pioneers of red wines in Austria, and the family continues the tradition with this fresh Pinot Noir. Surprises with its depth of flavor, complex tannins and sense of structure and shape. Just a little earthiness says this is still young. 88 *—R.V. (10/1/2007)*

Juris 2001 TBA Welschriesling (Burgenland) $45. 92 *—R.V. (5/1/2004)*

Juris 2001 Ausbruch White Blend (Burgenland) $40. 89 *—R.V. (5/1/2004)*

JURTSCHITSCH SONNHOF

Jurtschitsch Sonnhof 2006 Dechant Alte Reben Grüner Veltliner (Kamptal) $39. Power and rich, spicy creaminess are the hallmarks of this full-bodied wine. Tropical fruit flavors of mango and lychee are spiced up with nutmeg. There is a fresh tingle on the palate, intriguing and leaving a positive question over its ageworthiness— 2–4 years. 90 —*R.V. (12/31/2007)*

Jurtschitsch Sonnhof 2004 Loiserberg Grüner Veltliner Trockenbeerenauslese Grüner Veltliner (Kamptal) $60. Almost nectar, this wine is supremely rich and concentrated, with toffee and honey flavors combining with apricots, orange peel and refreshing acidity. This is a great example of a TBA because of its richness, silky texture and balance. 94 —*R.V. (5/1/2007)*

Jurtschitsch Sonnhof 2006 Schenkenbichl Grüner Veltliner (Kamptal) $48. Big, bold and soft, this is way too heavy. Sure, the Grüner spice is all there, but it is at the expense of a fresh, racy character. The toast character doesn't quite work either. 85 —*R.V. (12/31/2007)*

Jurtschitsch Sonnhof 2001 Schenkenbichl Grüner Veltliner Langenlois Grüner Veltliner (Kamptal) $21. 90 —*R.V. (11/1/2002)*

Jurtschitsch Sonnhof 2006 Schenkenbichl Auslese Grüner Veltliner (Kamptal) $34. A lively, fresh wine that only just borders on sweetness, reserving some the botrytised fruit for richness instead. There are fine flavors of lychees, crispened up with white currants, while spice comes through but well in balance. 88 —*R.V. (12/31/2007)*

Jurtschitsch Sonnhof 2001 Spiegel Reserve Grüner Veltliner Langenlois Grüner Veltliner (Kamptal) $55. 94 Editors' Choice —*R.V. (11/1/2002)*

Jurtschitsch Sonnhof 2001 Steinhaus Grüner Veltliner Langenlois Grüner Veltliner (Kamptal) $21. 89 —*R.V. (11/1/2002)*

Jurtschitsch Sonnhof 2001 Troken Gruve Grüner Veltliner (Kamptal) $16. 85 —*R.V. (11/1/2002)*

Jurtschitsch Sonnhof 2000 Rotspon Red Blend (Kamptal) $28. 86 —*R.V. (11/1/2002)*

Jurtschitsch Sonnhof 2006 Heiligenstein Alte Reben Riesling (Kamptal) $48. Smooth and rich, this is a big wine, initially almost Chardonnay-like in its creamy richness. But then the Riesling's fresh perfumes and intense acidity kick in. White berries follow, while there are hints of white pear. Age this wine for five years. 90 —*R.V. (12/31/2007)*

Jurtschitsch Sonnhof 2006 Zöbinger Heiligenstein Riesling (Kamptal) $32. This great vineyard shows through in the quality of this intensely perfumed wine, all white fruits, just a hint vegetal, with green peas. The structure is all here, as is the citrus fresh aftertaste. 89 —*R.V. (12/31/2007)*

Jurtschitsch Sonnhof 2005 Zöbinger Heiligenstein Alte Reben Riesling (Kamptal) $59. 90 —*R.V. (10/1/2006)*

Jurtschitsch Sonnhof 2005 Zöbinger Heiligenstein Reserve Riesling (Kamptal) $83. 92 —*R.V. (10/1/2006)*

Jurtschitsch Sonnhof 2001 Zoebinger Heiligenstein Riesling Riesling (Kamptal) $NA. 90 —*R.V. (11/1/2002)*

Jurtschitsch Sonnhof 2004 Tanzer Reserve Zweigelt (Kamptal) $59. This very spicy, new wood dominated wine, tastes initially only of toast. It's hard to find the fruit, but underneath all that wood is a lively, berry fruited wine waiting to get out. The acidity is the key—and this wine needs 2 years. 89 —*R.V. (10/1/2007)*

KALMUCK

Kalmuck 2004 Grüner Veltliner (Wachau) $13. 88 Best Buy —*J.C. (3/1/2006)*

KOLLWENTZ

Kollwentz 1996 Chardonnay Welschriesling Trockenbeerenauslese White Blend (Neusiedlersee-Hügelland) $83. Ten years of aging lends great maturity and authority to this impressive wine. The honey stays and toffee flavors arrive as the fruit disappears. This is all about richness and concentration, a syrupy smoothness and softness, but still sustained by some acidity. 93 —*R.V. (5/1/2007)*

Kollwentz 2002 Sauvignon Blanc Beerenauslese Sauvignon Blanc (Burgenland) $74. 92 —*R.V. (5/1/2004)*

Kollwentz 1999 TBA Sauvignon Blanc (Burgenland) $121. 92 Editors' Choice —*R.V. (5/1/2004)*

Kollwentz 2002 TBA Scheurebe (Burgenland) $121. 86 —*R.V. (5/1/2004)*

Kollwentz 2002 Beerenauslese Welschriesling (Burgenland) $74. 88 —*R.V. (5/1/2004)*

Kollwentz 1999 TBA Welschriesling (Burgenland) $121. 92 Cellar Selection —*R.V. (5/1/2004)*

KRACHER

Kracher 2004 Nouvelle Vague Trockenbeerenauslese Nummer 9 Chardonnay (Neusiedlersee) $87. The Chardonnay came in at number 9 with the 2002 vintage, the last time Kracher released a full range of TBAs (2003 was too dry for botrytis). So it's fascinating to see how the acidity of great sweet 2004s is present in a wine that is beautifully balanced. It has vanilla, caramel and ripe peach flavors; beautifully fresh and very pure. 94 —*R.V. (2/1/2007)*

Kracher 2001 Nummer 3 TBA Chardonnay (Burgenland) $74. 88 —*R.V. (5/2/2004)*

Kracher 2001 Nummer 7 TBA Chardonnay (Burgenland) $84. 94 —*R.V. (5/2/2004)*

Kracher 2001 Nummer 2 TBA Muskat Ottonel (Burgenland) $74. 90 —*R.V. (5/2/2004)*

Kracher 2004 Zwischen den Seen Trockenbeerenauslese Nummer 5 Muskat Ottonel (Neusiedlersee) $77. For a grape that is naturally honeyed and sweet, Kracher has come up with a surprise. This is more about freshness and delicious acidity than about sweetness, which is almost a background to this smooth, intense, delicious wine. 93 —*R.V. (2/1/2007)*

Kracher 2005 Pinot Gris (Neusiedlersee) $14. 87 —*R.V. (10/1/2006)*

Kracher 2003 Pinot Gris (Burgenland) $16. 88 —*J.C. (5/1/2005)*

Kracher 2003 Blend One Red Blend (Neusiedlersee) $NA. 89 —*R.V. (10/1/2006)*

Kracher 2001 Nummer 4 TBA Scheurebe (Burgenland) $74. 92 Cellar Selection —*R.V. (5/2/2004)*

Kracher 2001 Nummer 9 TBA Scheurebe (Burgenland) $91. 91 —*R.V. (5/2/2004)*

Kracher 2004 Zwischen den Seen Trockenbeerenauslese Nummer 10 Scheurebe (Neusiedlersee) $90. The most complex of Kracher's 2004 TBAs, as well as the richest in residual sugar. It has mandarin orange, peaches and crystallized fruits. There is freshness, despite its sweetness. It should age magnificently. 97 Cellar Selection —*R.V. (2/1/2007)*

Kracher 2004 Zwischen den Seen Trockenbeerenauslese Nummer 4 Scheurebe (Neusiedlersee) $72. When Kracher gets his hands on Scheurebe, the results are brilliant. This wine has structure, weight, great acidity and intense flavors. If the alcohol is high, that certainly doesn't show on this well balanced wine, with its fresh aftertaste. 92 —*R.V. (2/1/2007)*

Kracher 2001 Nummer 1 TBA Traminer (Burgenland) $69. 89 —*R.V. (5/2/2004)*

Kracher 2004 Nouvelle Vague Trockenbeerenauslese Nummer 3 Traminer (Neusiedlersee) $72. As befits the Traminer grape, this wine is packed with spice as well as richness. The sweetness is less apparent; great almond and lychee flavors give this wine plenty of character. 89 —*R.V. (2/1/2007)*

Kracher 2004 Nouvelle Vague Trockenbeerenauslese Nummer 8 Traminer (Neusiedlersee) $87. Like his earlier Traminer (Nummer 3), this wine is layered with dryness as well as richness. It is intense and very concentrated, a great combination of spice, acidity and syrup. There is a touch of vanilla and coconut as well as flavors of ripe pears. 93 —*R.V. (2/1/2007)*

Kracher 2001 Nummer 5 TBA Welschriesling (Burgenland) $74. 94 Editors' Choice —*R.V. (5/2/2004)*

Kracher 2001 Nummer 8 TBA Welschriesling (Burgenland) $91. 95 Cellar Selection —*R.V. (5/2/2004)*

Kracher 2004 Zwischen den Seen Trockenbeerenauslese Nummer 2 Welschriesling (Neusiedlersee) $67. Very aromatic, this wine revels in its layers of fresh tropical fruits, acidity and botrytis. It is rich but at the same time fresh and crisp. 90 —*R.V. (2/1/2007)*

Kracher 2004 Zwischen den Seen Trockenbeerenauslese Nummer 7 Welschriesling (Neusiedlersee) $83. So maybe Welschriesling is not the same as real Riesling, but this wine certainly has all the pure acidity and freshly perfumed character of one. It is a wine for the purist: refined and elegant, with white fruits giving a lift to the finish. 95 —*R.V. (2/1/2007)*

Kracher 2005 Beerenauslese Cuvée 375ml White Blend (Neusiedlersee) $29. 90 —*R.V. (10/1/2006)*

Kracher 2004 Nouvelle Vague Trockenbeerenauslese Grande Cuvée Nummer 6 White Blend (Neusiedlersee) $80. This 2004, matured in small French oak (hence Nouvelle Vague) is a smooth, sensational blend of grape varieties, rich and at the same time structured, and quite likely to be the wine out of the 10 TBAs Kracher has produced in 2004 that will age beautifully. But enjoy it now for the honey, the dry botrytis and the sweet orange peel and apricot flavors. 96 Editors' Choice —*R.V. (2/1/2007)*

Kracher 2003 Cuvée No 1. Nouvelle Vague Trockenbeerenauslese 375 ml White Blend (Neusiedlersee) $72. 92 —*R.V. (10/1/2006)*

Kracher 2001 Eiswein Cuvée 375 ml White Blend (Burgenland) $38. 93 Editors' Choice —*J.C. (3/1/2006)*

Kracher 2002 Kracher No. 12 375ml White Blend (Neusiedlersee) $110. 94 Editors' Choice —*R.V. (10/1/2006)*

Kracher 2001 Nummer 6 Grande Cuvée TBA White Blend (Burgenland) $81. 93 Editors' Choice —*R.V. (5/2/2004)*

Kracher 2004 Nouvelle Vague Trockenbeerenauslese Nummer 1 Zweigelt (Neusiedlersee) $67. A pale rose-colored wine, made from the red grape Zwiegelt. Intriguing sweetness along with some tannins add to the freshness of the prune and citrus flavors. Delicious. 88 —*R.V. (2/1/2007)*

KRUTZLER

Krutzler 2004 Blaufränkisch (Burgenland) $23. 83 —*J.C. (3/1/2006)*

Krutzler 2003 Perwolff Red Blend (Burgenland) $93. 85 —*J.C. (3/1/2006)*

LAURENZ AND SOPHIE

Laurenz and Sophie 2004 Singing Grüner Veltliner (Austria) $13. 86 —*J.C. (8/1/2006)*

LAURENZ V.

Laurenz V. 2004 Charming Grüner Veltliner (Kamptal) $25. 89 —*J.C. (8/1/2006)*

LEITNER

Leitner 2005 Weisser Riesling Beerenauslese Riesling (Neusiedlersee) $29. "Weisser Riesling" is Burgenland's name for Riesling, and this Beerenauslese has much of the intense but delicate flavors of this great grape. There is tons of acidity, and the botrytis and sweetness play only a part of the fine shape and taste of this fresh wine. 90 —*R.V. (2/1/2007)*

Leitner 2002 Weisser Riesling Trockenbeerenauslese White Riesling (Neusiedlersee) $39. The botrytis texture of this wine—the dryness underlying the sweetness—is delicious. There is balance, allowing the acidity to join the honeyed sweetness. Pepper adds a touch of seasoning to this unctuous wine. 92 —*R.V. (2/1/2007)*

LENZ MOSER

Lenz Moser 2005 Klosterkeller Siegendorf Cabernet Sauvignon-Merlot (Burgenland) $8. An easy blend of Cabernet Sauvignon and Merlot, with fresh acidity and soft tannins. Flavors of red plums and black currants dominate, with a light hint of spice to finish. 85 Best Buy —*R.V. (10/1/2007)*

Lenz Moser 2006 Selection Red Blend (Burgenland) $NA. A very open, soft wine that shows lightweight, attractive red fruits. Its softness makes it drinkable now, with fresh acidity dominating the lower layer of dry tannins. 86 —*R.V. (10/1/2007)*

Lenz Moser 2005 Beerenauslese Prestige White Blend (Burgenland) $15. A fresh, clean wine, with attractive acidity. From the merchant house of Lenz Moser, here is a wine that has sweet apple and cream flavors, some white fruits, and light acidity. 87 —*R.V. (5/1/2007)*

LEO ALZINGER

Leo Alzinger 2005 Loibenberg Grüner Veltliner Smaragd Grüner Veltliner (Wachau) $55. 92 —*R.V. (10/1/2006)*

Leo Alzinger 2003 Loibner Loibenberg Smaragd Grüner Veltliner (Wachau) $NA. 89 —*R.V. (5/1/2005)*

Leo Alzinger 2005 Loibenberg Smaragd Riesling (Wachau) $60. 90 —*R.V. (10/1/2006)*

LEOPLOLD & SILVANE SOMMER

Leoplold & Silvane Sommer 2003 Spätlese Gewürztraminer (Neusiedlersee-Hügelland) $15. 88 —*R.V. (5/1/2005)*

Leoplold & Silvane Sommer 2001 M Grüner Veltliner Grüner Veltliner (Neusiedlersee) $13. 91 —*R.V. (11/1/2002)*

Leoplold & Silvane Sommer 2003 M Grüner Veltliner (Neusiedlersee-Hügelland) $15. 87 —*R.V. (5/1/2005)*

Leoplold & Silvane Sommer 2003 Premium Reserve Grüner Veltliner (Neusiedlersee-Hügelland) $19. 86 —*R.V. (5/1/2005)*

Leoplold & Silvane Sommer 2001 Premium Reserve Trocken Grüner Ventliner Grüner Veltliner (Neusiedlersee) $18. 88 —*R.V. (11/1/2002)*

LETH

Leth 2006 Scheiben Grüner Veltliner (Wagram-Donauland) $40. Pears and honey go together in this rich wine. Perhaps the power is too much, but it certainly impresses with its mineral structure, green spices and complex mix of exotic fruits and reined-in intensity. Screwcap. 90 —*R.V. (12/31/2007)*

Leth 2006 Steinagrund Grüner Veltliner (Wagram-Donauland) $16. A smooth, creamy single-vineyard wine, with white fruits and delicious balancing acidity. There is some crispness as well as richness, and an edge of spice. Acidity dominates on the finish. Screwcap. 88 —*R.V. (12/31/2007)*

Leth 2004 Reserve Pinot Noir (Donauland) $30. Deliciously soft, red-fruited wine that has very fresh acidity, red cherry flavors, lightly supported by the flavors from barrique aging. There's some citrus as well as the red currants, very vivid fruit. 88 —*R.V. (10/1/2007)*

Leth 2006 Felser Weinberge Riesling (Wagram-Donauland) $18. A lively, light, dancing wine that is lifted by acidity, white fruits, crisp currants and a touch of pepper. Enjoyable, fresh, vibrant and great as an apéritif. Screwcap. 87 —*R.V. (12/31/2007)*

Leth 2006 Wagramterrassen Riesling (Wagram-Donauland) $34. The epitome of aristocratic, full-bodied Riesling. This wine has all the rosehip and white flower aromas, followed by structured, fresh, crisp green pear and white currant fruits. There is a great purity of line here, directed by the acidity and the cutting crispness of the aftertaste. Screwcap. 91 Editors' Choice —*R.V. (12/31/2007)*

Leth 2006 Scheiben Roter Veltliner (Wagram-Donauland) $30. The rare Roter Veltliner is almost entirely confined to the slopes of the Wagram. Here it gives a style that is fragrant, with aromas of hedgerow flowers and delicate roses. Here these characters are combined with a full, tropical fruit character, touches of mango along with intense spice and acidity. Screwcap. 91 —*R.V. (12/31/2007)*

Leth 2005 Scheiben Trockenbeerenauslese Weissburgunder (Wagram-Donauland) $50. From the Scheiben vineyard, this Weissburgunder-(Pinot Blanc) based wine is dominated by its nutmeg spice even before the sweetness arrives. It is elegant, not hugely intense, but obviously very sweet. However, there is also a fine freshness here. 90 —*R.V. (12/31/2007)*

Leth 2003 Gigama Reserve Zweigelt (Donauland) $48. Made from Zweigelt, this is Franz Leth's flagship red. It shows a much more serious, austere side to Zweigelt, one which needs aging. The blueberry flavors and dark plum skins are one aspect, the other is the spice from wood aging. Keep for 2–3 years. 90 —*R.V. (10/1/2007)*

LOIMER

Loimer 2003 Grüner Veltliner (Langenlois) $17. 88 —*J.C. (5/1/2005)*

Loimer 2003 Käferberg Grüner Veltliner (Kamptal) $25. 88 —*J.C. (5/1/2005)*

Loimer 2002 Lois Grüner Veltliner (Langenlois) $11. 86 —*M.S. (11/15/2003)*

Loimer 2003 Riesling (Langenlois) $17. 84 —*J.C. (8/1/2005)*

Loimer 2003 Seeberg Trocken Riesling (Kamptal) $25. 85 —*J.C. (8/1/2005)*

Loimer 2003 Steinmassl Riesling (Kamptal) $40. 88 —*J.C. (8/1/2005)*

LUDWIG EHN

Ludwig Ehn 2005 Zöbinger Heiligenstein Riesling (Kamptal) $22. 89 —*R.V. (10/1/2006)*

MACHHERNDL

Machherndl 2006 Kollmütz Federspiel Grüner Veltliner (Wachau) $15. The rock soils of the Kollmütz vineyard give a very lean, mineral, almost austere character to this wine, in its early development. This is going to broaden out—there are already the green plum, intense flavors and a bright, crisp acidity. Screwcap. 88 —*R.V. (12/31/2007)*

Machherndl 2003 Kollmütz Federspiel Grüner Veltliner (Wachau) $15. 85 —*J.C. (8/1/2006)*

Machherndl 2003 Kollmütz Federspiel Grüner Veltliner (Wachau) $15. 86 —*J.C. (11/15/2005)*

Machherndl 2006 Smaragd Kollmitz Grüner Veltliner (Wachau) $25. Big spice is proper for a Grüner Veltliner Smaragd wine, the richest category in the Wachau. But Machherndl also manages not to forget white fruits, a layer of acidity, and a full, but crisp varietal character. 89 —*R.V. (12/31/2007)*

Machherndl 2005 Smaragd Kollmitz Grüner Veltliner (Wachau) $22. The Kollmitz's Joching vineyard is at the heart of Erich Machherndl's wines, producing both Riesling and Grüner Veltliner. This Grüner is impressively rich in a smooth, creamy style, with fresh green apples and white currant flavors. It should age well, its richness giving it the right structure. 90 Cellar Selection —*R.V. (8/1/2007)*

Machherndl 2003 Smaragd Kollmitz Grüner Veltliner (Wachau) $25. 90 Editors' Choice —*J.C. (3/1/2006)*

Machherndl 2006 Smaragd Steinwand Grüner Veltliner (Wachau) $20. Very pure, crisp fruit, flavored with green plums, fresh acidity and intense minerality. Delicious, if just on the wrong side of plump. 87 —*R.V. (12/31/2007)*

Machherndl 2006 Hochrain Old Vines Pinot Blanc (Wachau) $20. It is odd to find a Pinot Blanc in the land of Grüner Veltliner and Riesling. But a block of loam soil, planted with old vines gave Erich Machherndl the idea for this wine. The concentration of the old vines produces a full, creamy wine, green-plum flavored, with some cinnamon and weight. 87 —*R.V. (12/31/2007)*

Machherndl 2006 Kollmitz Federspiel Riesling (Wachau) $20. A smooth, soft, rich wine, with ripe, intensely aromatic fruit. This tastes of mineral, but with an overlay of tropical fruits, lychees and spice. A touch of toastiness gives complexity and extra interest to this fresh wine. Screwcap. 89 —*R.V. (12/31/2007)*

Machherndl 2006 Smaragd Steinterrassen Riesling (Wachau) $30. Full and rich, maybe missing some acidity, but replacing that with powered white nectarines. The pepper, though, causes the wine to fall short, giving it an edge. It needs time to develop properly—give it 2–3 years at least. 88 —*R.V. (12/31/2007)*

MALAT

Malat 2005 Reserve Cabernet Sauvignon (Kremstal) $48. You can tell this is Gerald Malat's flagship red by the weight of the bottle. And, yes, it is a fine wine. The Cabernet structure and dry tannins are all here, as part of a firm, blackberry fruit-flavored wine, that shows some herbal character as well as wood. Age for three years. 90 —*R.V. (10/1/2007)*

Malat 2003 Dreigarten Grüner Veltliner (Kremstal) $29. 90 —*R.V. (5/1/2005)*

Malat 2004 Höhlgraben Grüner Veltliner (Kremstal) $22. 87 —*J.C. (8/1/2006)*

Malat 2004 Zistel Reserve Pinot Gris (Kremstal) $39. 89 —*R.V. (2/1/2006)*

Malat 2005 Reserve Pinot Noir (Kremstal) $40. A very direct wine, which just shouts Pinot Noir. There's no mistaking the ripe cherry aromas and fresh fruit, packed with acidity, just edged by some rustic character. The tannins are here, but the fruit is overwhelming. 89 —*R.V. (10/1/2007)*

Malat 2002 Das Beste Von Riesling Auslese Riesling (Kremstal) $60. 89 —*J.C. (8/1/2006)*

Malat 2004 Silberbühel Riesling (Kremstal) $38. 91 —*R.V. (8/1/2005)*

Malat 2003 Silberbühel Riesling (Kremstal) $36. 89 —*R.V. (5/1/2005)*

Malat 2004 Steinbühel Riesling (Kremstal) $27. 89 —*R.V. (8/1/2005)*

Malat 2003 Brunnkreuz Reserve Sauvignon Blanc (Kremstal) $39. 88 —*J.C. (8/1/2006)*

Malat 2004 Reserve Sauvignon Blanc (Austria) $36. 86 *(7/1/2005)*

Malat 2005 Reserve St. Laurent (Kremstal) $35. Pure strawberry aromas lead in to delicious, ripe, sweet fruits. It shows the highly drinkable nature of the St. Laurent grape, with red cherry fruits and light touch of tannin. It could age over the next two years, but drink it now with pleasure. 89 —*R.V. (10/1/2007)*

MANFRED TEMENT

Manfred Tement 2001 Zieregg Sauvignon Blanc (Südsteiermark) $25. 91 —*R.V. (11/1/2002)*

MANFRED WEISS

Manfred Weiss 2004 Bouvier Trockenbeerenauslese Bouvier (Neusiedlersee) $29. There is not much Bouvier in Austria, but what there is seems to lend itself to sweet wines. This wine is fat, with low acidity, but has fine richness, a touch of spice and lychee flavors. Not a wine for aging, but enjoyable now. 89 —*R.V. (5/1/2007)*

Manfred Weiss 2005 Grüner Veltliner Eiswein Grüner Veltliner (Neusiedlersee) $20. Ice wines from Grüner Veltliner are not often found in Burgenland, but with the fresh ripeness and poise of this wine, you wonder why. It has a great lift to it from the fresh acidity and the green pear fruit flavors. 88 —*R.V. (5/1/2007)*

Manfred Weiss 1999 Eiswein 375 ml Grüner Veltliner (Burgenland) $19. 91 Editors' Choice —*J.C. (3/1/2006)*

MANTLERHOF

Mantlerhof 2005 Grüner Veltliner Eiswein Grüner Veltliner (Kremstal) $38. A very light, fresh, delicate wine, that shows crispness, flavors of sweet apples and just a touch of pepper. Picked on December 13, 2005, at a temperature of 17 degrees, according to Sepp Mantler. 87 —*R.V. (5/1/2007)*

Mantlerhof 2003 Wieland Riesling (Kremstal) $45. 87 —*R.V. (8/1/2005)*

Mantlerhof 2001 Wieland Riesling (Kremstal) $28. 89 —*R.V. (8/1/2003)*

Mantlerhof 2004 Zehetnerin Riesling (Kremstal) $25. 90 —*R.V. (8/1/2005)*

Mantlerhof 2003 Zehetnerin Riesling (Kremstal) $25. 89 —*R.V. (8/1/2005)*

Mantlerhof 2000 Roter Veltliner (Kremser) $18. 87 —*J.C. (3/1/2002)*

MARKOWITSCH

Markowitsch 2006 Blaufränkisch (Carnuntum) $NA. Fresh mulberry and blueberry fruits with a mineral edge give this structure and freshness; layered with firm, dry tannins. The acidity accentuates the juicy, chewy flavors. It could be drunk now, but 2–3 years aging will soften those tannins. 88 —*R.V. (10/1/2007)*

Markowitsch 2004 Reserve Chardonnay (Carnuntum) $NA. 90 —*R.V. (10/1/2006)*

Markowitsch 2005 Alte Reben Grüner Veltliner (Carnuntum) $NA. 90 —*R.V. (10/1/2006)*

Markowitsch 2005 Schanzäcker Grüner Veltliner (Carnuntum) $13. 88 Best Buy —*R.V. (10/1/2006)*

Markowitsch 2004 Schanzäcker Grüner Veltliner (Carnuntum) $13. 89 Best Buy —*R.V. (11/15/2005)*

Markowitsch 2005 Pinot Noir (Carnuntum) $NA. This is the second level wine made from Pinot Noir by Gerhard Markowitsch. But it still exhibits great varietal flavor, with those piercing acid edges balanced with delicious red cherry fruits. Great freshness. 88 —*R.V. (10/1/2007)*

Markowitsch 2004 Reserve Pinot Noir (Carnuntum) $NA. With its 18 months wood aging, this is a velvety smooth wine, layering its fruits easily and with plenty of ripeness. The tannins and fresh, red-fruit acidity all fit into the roundness of this generous wine. Only the dry, spicy aftertaste suggests aging potential. 91 Editors' Choice —*R.V. (10/1/2007)*

Markowitsch 2005 Rosenberg Red Blend (Carnuntum) $NA. The flagship wine, from Gerhard Markowitsch's best vineyard site, is as impressive as usual. It piles dark berries on to spice from both fruit and wood. The tannins are ripe, with hints of toast from the wood lying alongside the firmly structured fruit. Age this wine for at least five years. 93 —*R.V. (10/1/2007)*

Markowitsch 2003 Rosenberg Red Blend (Carnuntum) $NA. 93 Cellar Selection —*R.V. (10/1/2006)*

Markowitsch 2006 Rubin Red Blend (Carnuntum) $NA. This blend of Zweigelt and Blaunfränkisch is a trade mark of the Carnuntum region, giving a delicious, fruity wine brimming with young red fruits, only lightly touched by tannins. The same exuberant fruit as a good Beaujolais. 89 —*R.V. (10/1/2007)*

Markowitsch 2004 Rothenberg St. Laurent (Carnuntum) $31. 89 —*R.V. (10/1/2006)*

MARTIN NIGL

Martin Nigl 2001 Privat Grüner Veltliner Grüner Veltliner (Kremstal) $39. 90 —*R.V. (11/1/2002)*

MARTIN PASLER

Martin Pasler 2001 Trockenbeerenauslese C Chardonnay (Burgenland) $35. 90 —*J.C. (12/15/2004)*

Martin Pasler 2001 Trockenbeerenauslese 375 ml Muskat Ottonel (Burgenland) $30. 93 Editors' Choice —*J.C. (12/15/2004)*

Martin Pasler 2001 Beerenauslese Welschriesling (Burgenland) $15. 84 —*J.C. (12/15/2004)*

MEINKLANG

Meinklang 2004 Pinot Gris (Burgenland) $15. 86 —*R.V. (2/1/2006)*

MELITTA & MATTHIAS LEITNER

Melitta & Matthias Leitner 2000 TBA Riesling (Neusiedlersee) $39. 87 —*R.V. (5/1/2004)*

Melitta & Matthias Leitner 1999 TBA Riesling (Neusiedlersee) $39. 89 —*R.V. (5/1/2004)*

Melitta & Matthias Leitner 2000 Eiswein White Blend (Neusiedlersee) $NA. 90 —*R.V. (5/1/2004)*

METTERNICH-SALOMON

Metternich-Salomon 2005 Pfaffenberg Riesling (Kremstal) $NA. 92 Editors' Choice —*R.V. (10/1/2006)*

Metternich-Salomon 2006 Pfaffenberg Reserve Riesling (Kremstal) $NA. This is an impressive, very rich, just off-dry wine, floral and flinty, with spice and green plum flavors. It needs at least 3 years to develop its full potential. Glass stopper. 92 —*R.V. (12/31/2007)*

MICHLITS

Michlits 2005 Frizzante Rosé Pinot Noir (Burgenland) $15. This medium-salmon-hued rosé does show some earthy, sous-bois Pinot Noir character on the nose, then adds savory, meaty flavors. The mouthfeel is creamy, the end result not terribly refreshing but complex and worth a try. 84 —*J.C. (7/1/2007)*

MICHLITS-STADLMANN

Michlits-Stadlmann 1999 Auslese Traminer (Neusiedlersee) $16. 85 —*J.C. (3/1/2002)*

MÜNZENRIEDER

Münzenrieder 2002 Sämling Trockenbeerenauslese Scheurebe (Neusiedlersee) $NA. Sämling (also known as Scheurebe) makes quite weighty sweet wines. This wine is all power, and also all about toffee. It is liquid syrup, with a texture to match. There may well be acidity there, but to taste this is more to do with sweetness. 87 —*R.V. (2/1/2007)*

Münzenrieder 1999 Sämling Trockenbeerenauslese Scheurebe (Neusiedlersee) $NA. This shows great intensity of fruit, of honey and of orange marmalade flavors. It has weight, great richness and, with those few extra years to mature, is a delicious, if intensely rich, wine. 90 —*R.V. (2/1/2007)*

Münzenrieder 1998 Welschriesling Trockenbeerenauslese Welschriesling (Neusiedlersee) $NA. A lean wine, which is now certainly mature. There is certainly sweetness there, with some good perfumed fruit flavors, but it is lighter than the normal wines in the Münzenrieder offering, making it probably more food friendly. The acidity at the end is welcome. 87 —*R.V. (2/1/2007)*

Münzenrieder 2002 Welschriesling Chardonnay Trockenbeerenauslese White Blend (Neusiedlersee) $NA. With its relatively low alcohol, this wine is rich in texture and powered by intense sweetness. There is honey and ripe fruit flavors and acidity under the sweetness. Mature; drink now. 89 —*R.V. (2/1/2007)*

NECKENMARKT

Neckenmarkt 2004 Blaufränkisch Classic Blaufränkisch (Burgenland) $12. 87 Best Buy —*J.C. (3/1/2006)*

Neckenmarkt 2004 Classic Zweigelt (Burgenland) $12. 85 —*J.C. (8/1/2006)*

NEUMEISTER WINERY

Neumeister Winery 2002 Grauburgunder Saziani Pinot Gris (Südsteiermark) $30. 91 —*R.V. (2/1/2006)*

Neumeister Winery 2004 Grauburgunder Steirische Klassik Pinot Gris (Südsteiermark) $19. 89 —*R.V. (2/1/2006)*

Neumeister Winery 2003 Moarfeitl Sauvignon Blanc (Styria) $37. 86 *(7/1/2005)*

Neumeister Winery 2003 Steirische Klassik Sauvignon Blanc (Styria) $31. 86 *(7/1/2005)*

NIGL

Nigl 2002 Privat Grüner Veltliner (Kremstal) $50. 91 —*R.V. (5/1/2005)*

Nigl 2003 Kremsleiten Riesling (Kremstal) $44. 89 —*R.V. (8/1/2005)*

Nigl 2003 Privat Riesling (Kremstal) $71. 91 —*R.V. (8/1/2005)*

Nigl 2003 Senftenberger Piri Riesling (Kremstal) $47. 90 —*R.V. (8/1/2005)*

NIKOLAIHOF

Nikolaihof 1990 Smaragd Grüner Veltliner (Wachau) $NA. 89 —*R.V. (4/1/2005)*

Nikolaihof 2000 Im Weingebirge Smaragd Riesling (Wachau) $35. 91 —*R.V. (8/1/2003)*

Nikolaihof 2000 Steiner Hund Premium Riesling (Wachau) $51. 90 —*R.V. (4/1/2005)*

Nikolaihof 2000 Vom Stein Federspiel Riesling (Wachau) $24. 90 —*J.C. (3/1/2002)*

Nikolaihof 2001 Nikolauswein Trockenbeerenauslese White Blend (Wachau) $NA. The biodynamic estate of Nikolaihof is one of the oldest in the Wachau. The tradition is upheld by the Saahs family, who make wonderfully intense wines. This TBA is so fresh and lively that the sweetness only forms a part of the beautiful citrus and apricot fruits. 92 —*R.V. (2/1/2007)*

NITTNAUS

Nittnaus 1999 Cabernet Sauvignon (Burgenland) $29. 83 —*J.C. (3/1/2002)*

Nittnaus 1999 Von den Hugeln Red Blend (Burgenland) $21. 83 —*J.C. (3/1/2002)*

Nittnaus 1999 Selection St. Laurent (Burgenland) $25. 84 —*J.C. (3/1/2002)*

Nittnaus 2001 TBA White Blend (Burgenland) $47. 89 —*R.V. (5/1/2004)*

Nittnaus 2000 Traminer White Blend (Burgenland) $NA. 89 —*R.V. (5/1/2004)*

NITTNAUS ANITA UND HANS

Nittnaus Anita und Hans 2004 Trockenbeerenauslese Chardonnay-Pinot Blanc (Neusiedlersee) $49. This is impressive. It has huge intensity of flavor, a wine that shows wall-to-wall botrytis, along with honey. It isn't so much obviously sweet as rich and concentrated. It will age for many years. 93 Cellar Selection —*R.V. (12/31/2007)*

Nittnaus Anita und Hans 2004 Kurzberg Pinot Noir (Burgenland) $30. A fresh, fruity wine, full of wild strawberry flavors, with cranberry tannins. The acidity is full on, but the ripe tannins edging through give structure and the promise of 2–3 years aging. 89 —*R.V. (10/1/2007)*

Nittnaus Anita und Hans 2005 Heideboden Red Blend (Burgenland) $24. Dense, with rustic aromas, a little barnyard. The fruit is smooth in texture, touched by new wood and 14 months barrique aging. The tannins need time to settle down, with acidity shooting through the fruit. 87 —*R.V. (10/1/2007)*

Nittnaus Anita und Hans 2004 Heideboden Red Blend (Burgenland) $24. On the eastern slopes of the Neusiedlersee, the Heideboden vineyard produces this finely melded Zweigelt and Blaufränkisch blend. With red berry fruits, herbs and spice, it brings together fresh juicy fruits, with a subtle, rounding element of wood. Acidity keeps the whole lively. 89 —*R.V. (10/1/2007)*

Nittnaus Anita und Hans 2004 Pannobile Red Blend (Burgenland) $36. The Pannobile name is used by a group of producers in Gols on the north-east corner of Neusiedl to describe Zweigelt and Blaufränkisch blends. This version of the style is rich and soft, with a dense texture, touches of spice, flavors of black cherries, finishing with crisp, young acidity. 89 —*R.V. (10/1/2007)*

Nittnaus Anita und Hans 2006 Blauer Zweigelt Zweigelt (Burgenland) $16. This is in the fresh, fruity style of Zweigelt, with red berry flavors. The acidity, certainly at this stage, is high, almost too fresh, but there is also a good touch of spice. 85 —*R.V. (10/1/2007)*

NITTNAUS HANS UND CHRISTINE

Nittnaus Hans und Christine 2006 Edelgrund Blaufränkisch (Burgenland) $16. Hugely dry, tannic wine that is going to need several years aging. But the structure and balance are there, along with dark berry flavors, mixed with a firm, mineral character. This is powerful stuff. 89 —*R.V. (10/1/2007)*

Nittnaus Hans und Christine 2004 Nit'ana Red Blend (Burgenland) $24. This is Hans Nittnaus's international wine, with Cab Sauvignon and Merlot in the blend along with St. Laurent and Zweigelt. It offers complex flavors, mixing black fruits with smooth toast from barrique aging. There's a vegetal edge to it, which detracts from the overall impression. 87 —*R.V. (10/1/2007)*

Nittnaus Hans und Christine 2003 Nit'ana Red Blend (Burgenland) $24. An open, generous, ripe wine, with fresh red plum fruit flavors, layered with acidity. The barrique aging is still apparent, leaving high toast. Despite the addition of Cabernet Sauvignon and Syrah, this still tastes very Austrian and spicy, the Zweigelt and Blaufränkisch dominating. 88 —*R.V. (10/1/2007)*

Nittnaus Hans und Christine 2003 Vigor Rubens Red Blend (Burgenland) $29. This is the Nittnaus' flagship red, a powerful, rounded wine, expressing soft Merlot, along with juicy Zweigelt and St. Laurent. There are delicious black plum, tobacco and spice aromas, while the black fruit flavors are spiked with sage, green herbs and black berries. Barrel aging adds complexity, but does not dominate. 90 Editors' Choice —*R.V. (10/1/2007)*

Nittnaus Hans und Christine 2003 Selection St. Laurent (Burgenland) $20. Barrique aged wine, with toasty flavors, tobacco and blueberry, finished with smooth vanilla and morello cherries. There is an edge of acidity, maybe almost tartness which gives it a very vibrant aftertaste. 86 —*R.V. (10/1/2007)*

Nittnaus Hans und Christine 2003 Golser Luckenwald Zweigelt (Burgenland) $24. Soft, unfocused wine that shows attractive, easy fruits, but not much sense of structure. The fruit is sweet, light and touched with tannins. Drink now. 85 —*R.V. (10/1/2007)*

Nittnaus Hans und Christine 2005 Turn Me Red Zweigelt (Burgenland) $14. With its pretty girl label, this is not intended to be serious. The Zweigelt is attractive, soft, with good berry flavors. It does finish too soft, indicative of residual sugar, but that's what happens when a wine is created specially for the U.S. Screwcap. 83 —*R.V. (10/1/2007)*

Nittnaus Hans und Christine 2006 Vom Heideboden Zweigelt (Burgenland) $16. A firmly tannic wine, solid and concentrated, which shows great spicy Zweigelt varietal flavor, as well as dense black cherries and toast. This is a wine that needs some aging, maybe over three years. 88 —*R.V. (10/1/2007)*

Nittnaus Hans und Christine 2004 Zweigelt von den Hügeln Zweigelt (Burgenland) $20. Pleasing, fresh fruit flavors of dark berries, plum skins and black figs. The spice of the fruit dominates this lively, juicy wine. Great barbecue wine. 87 —*R.V. (10/1/2007)*

OCHS

Ochs 1999 Eiswein Blaufränkisch (Weiden am See) $30. 85 —*J.C. (3/1/2002)*

Ochs 1998 Ungerberg & Zeiselberg & Satz Welschriesling (Weiden am See) $29. 86 —*J.C. (3/1/2002)*

ORIEL

Oriel 2004 Ortolan Falkenstein Grüner Veltliner (Weinviertel) $20. 84 —*J.C. (3/1/2006)*

PAUL ACHS

Paul Achs 2004 Blaufränkisch (Burgenland) $19. 87 *—J.C. (3/1/2006)*

Paul Achs 2004 Zweigelt (Burgenland) $19. Friendly and fruity, made for everyday consumption, showing spice, red cherries and a flavor of minerality that manifests itself in the acidity. Partial aging in older barrels has softened the pure intensity of the fruit, but without adding wood flavors. 88 *—R.V. (10/1/2007)*

PITNAUER

Pitnauer 2004 Hagelsberg Grüner Veltliner (Carnuntum) $16. 85 *—J.C. (11/15/2005)*

Pitnauer 2002 Hagelsberg Ernte Pinot Blanc (Carnuntum) $20. 87 *—J.C. (12/15/2004)*

Pitnauer 2003 Hagelsberg St. Laurent (Carnuntum) $19. 85 *—J.C. (3/1/2006)*

Pitnauer 2003 Classic Zweigelt (Carnuntum) $17. 84 *—J.C. (3/1/2006)*

Pitnauer 2004 Klassik Blaufränkisch (Neusiedlersee) $22. 88 *—J.C. (3/1/2006)*

Pitnauer 2003 Klassik Blaufränkisch (Neusiedlersee) $23. 88 *—J.C. (5/1/2005)*

Pitnauer 2003 Klassik Zweigelt (Burgenland) $18. 89 *—J.C. (3/1/2006)*

PLODER-ROSENBERG

Ploder-Rosenberg 2003 Sauvignon Blanc (Styria) $8. 84 Best Buy *—J.C. (11/15/2005)*

Ploder-Rosenberg 2002 Linea Sauvignon Blanc (Styria) $15. 88 *—J.C. (11/15/2005)*

PÖCKL

Pöckl 2004 Solo Rosso Red Blend (Burgenland) $22. 87 *—J.C. (3/1/2006)*

Pöckl 2003 Zweigelt (Burgenland) $15. 84 *—J.C. (5/1/2005)*

Pöckl 2004 Classique Zweigelt (Burgenland) $22. 82 *—J.C. (8/1/2006)*

AUSTRIA

PRAGER

Prager 2005 Achleiten Smaragd Grüner Veltliner (Wachau) $45. 95 Editors' Choice *—R.V. (10/1/2006)*

Prager 2004 Achleiten Smaragd Grüner Veltliner (Wachau) $39. 92 Editors' Choice *—J.C. (8/1/2006)*

Prager 2004 Hinter Der Burg Federspiel Grüner Veltliner (Wachau) $22. 86 *—J.C. (8/1/2006)*

Prager 2003 Hinter Der Burg Federspiel Grüner Veltliner (Wachau) $22. 87 *—J.C. (5/1/2005)*

Prager 2004 Weitenberg Smaragd Grüner Veltliner (Wachau) $36. 86 *—J.C. (8/1/2006)*

Prager 2004 Zwerithaler Smaragd Grüner Veltliner (Wachau) $39. 82 *—J.C. (3/1/2006)*

Prager 2005 Achleiten Smaragd Riesling (Wachau) $48. 95 Cellar Selection *—R.V. (10/1/2006)*

Prager 2004 Achleiten Smaragd Riesling (Wachau) $48. 93 *—J.C. (3/1/2006)*

Prager 2003 Durnstein Kaiserberg Smaragd Riesling (Wachau) $42. 89 *—J.C. (11/15/2005)*

Prager 2004 Hollerin Smaragd Riesling (Wachau) $42. 89 *—J.C. (8/1/2006)*

Prager 2004 Kaiserberg Smaragd Riesling (Wachau) $42. 88 *—J.C. (8/1/2006)*

Prager 2004 Klaus Smaragd Riesling (Wachau) $48. 89 *—J.C. (8/1/2006)*

Prager 2004 Steinriegl Federspiel Riesling (Wachau) $28. 87 *—J.C. (8/1/2006)*

Prager 2003 Steinriegl Federspiel Riesling (Wachau) $28. 88 *—J.C. (5/1/2005)*

Prager 2003 Steinriegl Smaragd Riesling (Wachau) $56. 92 *—R.V. (5/1/2005)*

Prager 2004 Wachstum Bodenstein Smaragd Riesling (Wachau) $48. 89 *—J.C. (8/1/2006)*

Prager 2003 Weissenkirchen Klaus Smaragd Riesling (Wachau) $47. 90 *J.C. (11/15/2005)*

Prager 2003 Weissenkirchen Smaragd Wachstum Bodenstein Riesling (Wachau) $47. 91 *—J.C. (5/1/2005)*

PRIELER

Prieler 2005 Johanneshöhe Blaufränkisch (Burgenland) $24. Aged in large wooden casks, this is a supple, fresh style of wine, beautifully crafted from Blaufränkisch, showing the varietal's blueberry and cranberry flavors, along with a firm, tannic and mineral note. 90 *—R.V. (10/1/2007)*

Prieler 2005 Pinot Noir (Burgenland) $66. A sensuously Burgundian style of Pinot Noir, the tannins and wood aging a mere seasoning for the rich, but round, soft fruits. Great red berries, along with cherries, leave a layer of acidity. 89 *—R.V. (10/1/2007)*

Prieler 2004 Schützner Stein Red Blend (Burgenland) $52. The 600-foot Schützner Stein broods over the Neusiedlersee, a great place to grow Blaufränkisch. Blended with Merlot, this is impressive, a powerhouse of dense tannins and black fruit. The acidity shows through, but the wine is as much about extreme concentration. It needs aging, over five years and more. 92 Cellar Selection *—R.V. (10/1/2007)*

PROIDL

Proidl 2003 Senftenberg Grüner Veltliner (Kremstal) $29. 89 *—R.V. (5/1/2005)*

Proidl 2004 Senftenberg Müller-Thurgau Trockenbeerenauslese Müller-Thurgau (Kremstal) $NA. A ripe, peppery wine, which has rich sweetness, but also a structured nature. It is fresh, but the alcohol is noticeable and takes away from the honeyed, dry botrytis character. 88 *—R.V. (2/1/2007)*

Proidl 1999 Eiswein White Blend (Neusiedlersee-Hügelland) $NA. Astonishingly young. There is a freshness and lift to it that shows the impressive ageability of an eiswein. Clean honey and orange peel flavors blend well with the sweetness. 90 *—R.V. (2/1/2007)*

R&A PFAFFL

R&A Pfaffl 2005 Exclusiv Chardonnay (Niederösterreich) $NA. 89 *—R.V. (10/1/2006)*

R&A Pfaffl 2000 Exclusiv Trocken Chardonnay (Weinviertel) $18. 87 *—R.V. (11/1/2002)*

R&A Pfaffl 2002 Rossern Chardonnay (Weinviertel) $45. 90 *—R.V. (5/1/2005)*

R&A Pfaffl 2005 Goldjoch Grüner Veltliner (Niederösterreich) $NA. This powerful, intense, wood-aged Grüner Veltliner is Pfaffl's finest expression of the grape. It is opulent, rich, powerful, but intensely structured, the wood lending a counterpoint to the fresh acidity and pepper characters of the grape. 93 *—R.V. (8/1/2007)*

R&A Pfaffl 2001 Goldjoch Grüner Veltliner (Weinviertel) $18. 93 *—R.V. (11/1/2002)*

R&A Pfaffl 2003 Haidviertel DAC Grüner Veltliner (Weinviertel) $19. 88 *—R.V. (5/1/2005)*

R&A Pfaffl 2001 Hundsleien/Sandtal Trocken Grüner Ventliner Grüner Veltliner (Weinviertel) $18. 90 *—R.V. (11/1/2002)*

R&A Pfaffl 2005 Hundsleiten Grüner Veltliner (Niederösterreich) $NA. 92 *—R.V. (10/1/2006)*

R&A Pfaffl 2004 Hundsleiten Grüner Veltliner (Niederösterreich) $NA. 89 *—R.V. (10/1/2006)*

R&A Pfaffl 2003 Hundsleiten/Sandtal Grüner Veltliner (Weinviertel) $21. 89 *—R.V. (5/1/2005)*

R&A Pfaffl 2000 Hundsleiten/Sandtal Grüner Veltliner (Weinviertel) $18. 92 *—R.V. (11/1/2002)*

R&A Pfaffl 2005 Zeisneck Grüner Veltliner (Weinviertel) $13. 88 *—R.V. (10/1/2006)*

R&A Pfaffl 2004 Pinot Noir (Vienna) $NA. This is the first vintage from vineyards the Pfaffl family bought in the northern suburbs of Vienna. Aged in wood, it is smooth, still young, with some good earthy characters along with round, red cherry flavors. There's a dollop of spice to help it along. 90 *—R.V. (10/1/2007)*

R&A Pfaffl 1999 Excellant Reserve Red Blend (Weinviertel) $23. 87 *—R.V. (11/1/2002)*

R&A Pfaffl 2003 Heidrom Red Blend (Niederösterreich) $NA. A blend of Merlot, Cab Sauvignon and Blauer Zweigelt, aged for two years in wood. The wood only underlines the richness of the black plum, bitter cherry and cocoa flavors. It is elegant, understated, wearing its power well. Age for 5–6 years. 92 Cellar Selection *—R.V. (10/1/2007)*

R&A Pfaffl 2005 Riesling am Berg Riesling (Niederösterreich) $NA. This is a gently medium-sweet wine, but that hardly does justice to the beautiful balance between the acidity, sweetness, freshness and lightness. It just floats, only given a slight pull earthwards by the mineral aftertaste. 91 Editors' Choice *—R.V. (8/1/2007)*

R&A Pfaffl 2005 Terrassen Sonnleiten Riesling (Neusiedlersee-Hügelland) $NA. The steep terraced vineyard of the Sonnleiten, perfectly exposed, has produced a tense, vibrant Riesling, showing the mineral side of the grape, along with pink grapefruit and white currant flavors. It will age over many years. 90 *—R.V. (8/1/2007)*

R&A Pfaffl 2001 Terrasen Sonnleiten Riesling (Weinviertel) $18. 94 Editors' Choice *—R.V. (11/1/2002)*

R&A Pfaffl 2005 Terrassen Sonnleiten Riesling (Niederösterreich) $NA. 92 *—R.V. (10/1/2006)*

R&A Pfaffl 2004 Terrassen Sonnleiten Riesling (Niederösterreich) $NA. 92 *—R.V. (10/1/2006)*

R&A Pfaffl 2004 St. Laurent (Niederösterreich) $NA. Smooth, wood aged wine, rich and packed with soft tannins and dense black cherries and black berries. Hints of smoke from the wood, and powered through with acidity. 89 *—R.V. (10/1/2007)*

R&A Pfaffl 2005 Altenberg Saint Laurent St. Laurent (Niederösterreich) $NA. 90 *—R.V. (10/1/2006)*

R&A Pfaffl 2005 Saint Laurent St. Laurent (Niederösterreich) $NA. 87 *—R.V. (10/1/2006)*

R&A Pfaffl 2005 Nussern Weissburgunder (Niederösterreich) $NA. 88 *—R.V. (10/1/2006)*

RAINER WESS

Rainer Wess 2005 Loibenberg Grüner Veltliner (Wachau) $32. 90 *—R.V. (10/1/2006)*

Rainer Wess 2004 Loibenberg Grüner Veltliner (Wachau) $33. 89 *—R.V. (10/1/2006)*

Rainer Wess 2005 Pfaffenberg Grüner Veltliner (Kremstal) $33. 88 *—R.V. (10/1/2006)*

Rainer Wess 2004 Pfaffenberg Grüner Veltliner (Wachau) $33. 90 *—J.C. (3/1/2006)*

Rainer Wess 2004 Terrassen Grüner Veltliner (Wachau) $21. 90 Editors' Choice *—J.C. (8/1/2006)*

Rainer Wess 2004 Wachauer Grüner Veltliner (Wachau) $17. 87 *—J.C. (8/1/2006)*

Rainer Wess 2003 Wachauer Trocken Grüner Veltliner (Wachau) $17. 85 *—J.C. (11/15/2005)*

Rainer Wess 2005 Loibenberg Riesling (Wachau) $32. 89 *—R.V. (10/1/2006)*

Rainer Wess 2004 Loibenberg Riesling (Wachau) $33. 91 *—J.C. (3/1/2006)*

Rainer Wess 2005 Pfaffenberg Riesling (Kremstal) $32. 90 *—R.V. (10/1/2006)*

Rainer Wess 2004 Pfaffenberg Riesling (Wachau) $33. 88 *—J.C. (8/1/2006)*

Rainer Wess 2004 Trocken Riesling (Wachau) $17. 88 *—J.C. (8/1/2006)*

Rainer Wess 2003 Trocken Riesling (Wachau) $26. 89 *—J.C. (5/1/2005)*

REITERER

Reiterer 2006 Schilcher Classic Blauer Wildbacher (Weststeiermark) $15. The classic, highly crisp (call it acid) rosé of Weststeiermark is an acquired taste, currently a cult in Vienna. Think of its cassis and piercing redcurrant flavors with food (perhaps fish or seafood) and this style makes perfect sense. To drink young, but not too chilled or the acidity kills the fruit. Screwcap. 85 *—R.V. (7/1/2007)*

Reiterer 2006 Schilcher Engelgarten Blauer Wildbacher (Weststeiermark) $11. Made from the local Blauer Wildbacher grape (as with all Schilcher wines), this is a relatively rich, cranberry and citrus flavored rosé, with tannins and forest berry fruits. It's delicious, just don't be shocked by the typical acidity. 88 Best Buy *—R.V. (7/1/2007)*

REPOLUSK

Repolusk 2000 Morillon Chardonnay (Austria) $25. 84 *—S.H. (9/1/2002)*

Repolusk 2000 Gelber Muskateller (Austria) $23. 86 *—S.H. (9/1/2002)*

Repolusk 2000 Schilcher Red Blend (Austria) $22. 86 *—S.H. (9/1/2002)*

Repolusk 1999 Sweigelt Red Blend (Austria) $24. 86 *—S.H. (9/1/2002)*

Repolusk 2000 Sauvignon Blanc (Austria) $26. 88 *—S.H. (9/1/2002)*

Repolusk 2000 Roter Traminer Spatlese Traminer (Austria) $28. 86 *—S.H. (9/1/2002)*

Repolusk 2000 Welschriesling (Austria) $21. 85 *—S.H. (9/1/2002)*

Repolusk 2000 Weissburgunder White Blend (Austria) $23. 83 *—S.H. (9/1/2002)*

RUDI PICHLER

Rudi Pichler 2004 Federspiel Grüner Veltliner (Wachau) $25. 88 *—J.C. (8/1/2006)*

Rudi Pichler 2003 Federspiel Grüner Veltliner (Wachau) $24. 86 *—J.C. (5/1/2005)*

Rudi Pichler 2003 Hochrain Smaragd Grüner Veltliner (Wachau) $57. 88 *—R.V. (5/1/2005)*

Rudi Pichler 2004 Terrassen Smaragd Grüner Veltliner (Wachau) $38. 87 *—J.C. (3/1/2006)*

Rudi Pichler 2003 Wösendorfer Kollmütz Smaragd Grüner Veltliner (Wachau) $47. 90 *—J.C. (5/1/2005)*

Rudi Pichler 2005 Achleiten Smaragd Riesling (Wachau) $62. 90 *—R.V. (10/1/2006)*

Rudi Pichler 2003 Weissenkirchner Achleiten Smaragd Riesling (Wachau) $63. 93 *—J.C. (5/1/2005)*

SALOMON-UNDHOF

Salomon-Undhof 2005 Noble Reserve Gelber Traminer (Kremstal) $NA. Produced from a relation of the Gewürztraminer grape, this Gelber Traminer is sweet, not excessively so, more dominated by allspice, lychees and touched with botrytis. 90 *—R.V. (12/31/2007)*

Salomon-Undhof 2006 Hochterrassen Grüner Veltliner (Kremstal) $18. A simple but delicious Grüner Veltliner from terraced vineyards above the city of Stein. It's very fresh, but has a full-textured character, with kiwis and some spice. The finish is delicious clear and green. Glass stopper. 87 *—R.V. (12/31/2007)*

Salomon-Undhof 2006 Lindberg Reserve Grüner Veltliner (Kremstal) $34. A wonderfully pure, fresh and natural wine, limpid with minerality, green fruits, concentrated pepper and spice. This is a powerful expression of Grüner Veltliner, a rich, but freshly green wine. Glass stopper. 91 Editors' Choice *—R.V. (12/31/2007)*

Salomon-Undhof 2003 Lindberg Reserve Grüner Veltliner (Kremstal) $35. 89 *—R.V. (5/1/2005)*

Salomon-Undhof 2006 Von Stein Reserve Grüner Veltliner (Kremstal) $42. A ripe, creamy wine, full and with a pepper edge. The wine has structure, richness and flavors of quince, green plum and green beans and a likely ability to age. Glass stopper. 89 *—R.V. (12/31/2007)*

Salomon-Undhof 2006 Wachtberg Grüner Veltliner (Kremstal) $18. A creamy, smooth wine, flavored with pears, even lychees and full, ripe Grüner Veltliner. This shows the rich side of the grape, while still keeping its essential freshness. Typical pepper flavors come to finish. Glass stopper. 90 *—R.V. (12/31/2007)*

Salomon-Undhof 2006 Wieden Tradition Grüner Veltliner (Kremstal) $22. From a vineyard right in the city of Krems, this Grüner is all spice and mineral; very fresh, elegant, green and crisp. It's probably an early drinking wine, delicious now and for the next 3–4 years. Glass stopper. 88 *—R.V. (12/31/2007)*

Salomon-Undhof 2001 Kremser Koegl Riesling (Kremstal) $23. 90 *—R.V. (11/1/2002)*

Salomon-Undhof 2001 Kremser Pfaffenberg Riesling (Kremstal) $18. 91 Editors' Choice *—R.V. (11/1/2002)*

Salomon-Undhof 2006 Pfaffenberg Riesling (Kremstal) $26. This is a steely, crisp, mineral wine, with lemon and orange zest flavors, piercingly fresh acidity and a touch of cinnamon. Glass stopper. 90 *—R.V. (12/31/2007)*

Salomon-Undhof 2005 Pfaffenberg Riesling (Kremstal) $27. 90 *—R.V. (10/1/2006)*

Salomon-Undhof 2003 Pfaffenberg Riesling (Kremstal) $27. 89 *—R.V. (8/1/2005)*

Salomon-Undhof 2004 Steinterrassen Riesling (Kremstal) $18. 87 *—R.V. (8/1/2005)*

Salomon-Undhof 2003 Steinterrassen Riesling (Kremstal) $18. 86 *—R.V. (8/1/2005)*

Salomon-Undhof 2006 Undhof Kögl Riesling (Kremstal) $22. Poised, elegant, light and fresh, this is delicate Riesling, with an edge of minerality, steel and green fruits. This comes from the Kögl, at the heart of the Salomon Undhof vineyard holdings. Glass stopper. 89 *—R.V. (12/31/2007)*

Salomon-Undhof 2003 Undhof Kögl Riesling (Kremstal) $24. 89 *—R.V. (8/1/2005)*

Salomon-Undhof 2006 Undhof Kögl Reserve Riesling (Kremstal) $42. The Kögl vineyard is right behind the city of Krems, a steep schist slope facing the Danube river, perfect for Riesling. This is a hugely rich wine, its richness giving a creamy, full-bodied character, intense with its flavors of white pears, tropical fruits and spice. It should age well over the next 10 years. Glass stopper. 93 Cellar Selection *—R.V. (12/31/2007)*

Salomon-Undhof 2003 Undhof Kögl Reserve Riesling (Kremstal) $42. 93 Cellar Selection *—R.V. (8/1/2005)*

SCHINDLER

Schindler 2004 Sauvignon Blanc (Burgenland) $7. 85 Best Buy *—J.C. (11/15/2005)*

SCHLOSS GOBELSBURG

Schloss Gobelsburg 2001 Altheiligenstiftung Grüner Ventliner Grüner Veltliner (Kamptal) $17. 88 *—R.V. (11/1/2002)*

Schloss Gobelsburg 2000 Vom Urgestein Riesling (Kamptal) $19. 87 *—J.C. (3/1/2002)*

Schloss Gobelsburg 2005 Zöbinger Heiligenstein Riesling (Kamptal) $36. 93 *—R.V. (10/1/2006)*

SCHLOSSWEINGUT GRAF HARDEGG

Schlossweingut Graf Hardegg 2003 Tethys Austrian White Blend (Weinviertel) $25. 90 *—R.V. (5/1/2005)*

Schlossweingut Graf Hardegg 2003 Drei Kruezen Grüner Veltliner (Weinviertel) $15. 86 *—R.V. (5/1/2005)*

Schlossweingut Graf Hardegg 2003 Veltlinsky Grüner Veltliner (Weinviertel) $11. 84 *—R.V. (5/1/2005)*

SCHLUMBERGER

Schlumberger NV Cuvée Klimt Brut White Blend (Osterreichischer Sekt) $19. 83 *—J.C. (6/1/2006)*

SCHUBERTH

Schuberth 2003 Hintaus Kabinett Grüner Veltliner (Kamptal) $16. 86 *—J.C. (8/1/2006)*

SEPP MOSER

Sepp Moser 2003 Breiter Rain Grüner Veltliner (Kremstal) $NA. 87 *—R.V. (5/1/2005)*

Sepp Moser 2002 Riesling Gebling Riesling (Kremstal) $30. 89 *—R.V. (8/1/2005)*

Sepp Moser 2003 Schnabel Sauvignon Blanc (Kremstal) $25. 84 *(7/1/2005)*

SETZER

Setzer 2005 1 Lage Grüner Veltliner (Niederösterreich) $21. This is in the middle range from Hans Setzer's impressive collection of Grüner Veltliner. Fresh, but with good weight and intensity. Flavors of dry grapefruit and citrus fruits, along with some light spice and pepper give a delicious, properly varietal character. 89 *—R.V. (8/1/2007)*

Setzer 2005 8000 Grüner Veltliner (Niederösterreich) $33. From densely planted vines, this is a ripe, very fruity wine, with low acidity, emphasizing the cream and pepper character of the grape. It is not the style of Grüner that can be drunk too young—give it another year to be at its optimum. 89 *—R.V. (8/1/2007)*

Setzer 2004 Grüner Veltliner 8000 Grüner Veltliner (Niederösterreich) $37. The 8000 in the wine's name refers to the number of vines per hectare (the acre equivalent would be around 3,200); the very dense planting is to stress the vines and cut yields from individual plants. The result is a wine that is richly concentrated, smooth and dense, with the classic Grüner pepper, but powerful and creamy. 90 Editors' Choice *—R.V. (8/1/2007)*

Setzer 2002 Ried Eichholz Grüner Veltliner (Weinviertel) $NA. From the first vintage of Grüner Veltliner wines under the Weinviertel DAC, this offering from Hans Setzer is crisp, fresh and light, showing a little softness from age, but still full of vibrant white currants and pepper. 88 *—R.V. (8/1/2007)*

Setzer 2005 Riesling (Niederösterreich) $20. 84 *—R.V. (8/1/2007)*

Setzer 2005 Kreimelberg Roter Veltliner (Niederösterreich) $21. A relatively rare varietal that is believed to originate in the Krems region. This example shows the varietal's high acidity that needs an off-dry flavor to compensate. It has a nice caramel layer which helps in the balance. 88 *—R.V. (8/1/2007)*

SONNHOF

Sonnhof 2000 Grüve Grüner Veltliner (Kamptal) $15. 83 *—J.C. (3/1/2002)*

Sonnhof 2000 Schenkenbichl Trocken Grüner Veltliner (Kamptal) $37. 91 *—J.C. (3/1/2002)*

Sonnhof 2000 Steinhaus Trocken Grüner Veltliner (Kamptal) $19. 86 *—J.C. (3/1/2002)*

Sonnhof 2000 Zobinger Heiligenstein Trocken Riesling (Kamptal) $28. 88 *—J.C. (3/1/2002)*

SPAETROT GEBESHUBER

Spaetrot Gebeshuber 2001 Beerenauslese Pinot Gris (Thermenregion) $27. 87 *—R.V. (2/1/2006)*

STADT KREMS

Stadt Krems 2004 Sandgrube Grüner Veltliner (Kremstal) $14. 89 Best Buy *—J.C. (8/1/2006)*88 *—J.C. (3/1/2006)*

Stadt Krems 2004 Weinzierlberg Grüner Veltliner (Kremstal) $17. 87 *—J.C. (3/1/2006)*

Stadt Krems 2004 Grillenparz Riesling (Kremstal) $27. 89 *—J.C. (3/1/2006)*

Stadt Krems 2003 Grillenparz Riesling (Kremstal) $27. 89 *—J.C. (8/1/2005)* 87 *—J.C. (8/1/2006)*

STEFAN HOFFMAN

Stefan Hoffman 1999 Ausbruch Chardonnay (Neusiedlersee) $38. 88 *—R.V. (11/1/2002)*

Stefan Hoffman 2001 Ausbruch Traminer Gewürztraminer (Neusiedlersee) $28. 90 *—R.V. (11/1/2002)*

STEINDORFER

Steindorfer 2001 Cuvée Klaus Eiswein 375 ml White Blend (Neusiedlersee) $30. 90 *—J.C. (12/15/2004)*

STEININGER

Steininger 2000 Beerenauslese Grüner Veltliner (Kamptal) $35. Sweet quince jelly flavors, along with a touch of toffee, suggest a wine that is sweeter than it is. It finishes rich, but also with a layer of dryness. Seems to lack acidity. 87 *—R.V. (5/1/2007)*

Steininger 2004 Grand Grüner Veltliner (Kamptal) $22. 90 Editors' Choice *—J.C. (3/1/2006)*

Steininger 2000 Beerenauslese Riesling (Kamptal) $40. The Steiningers are known as sparkling wine producers. Sweet wines, though, come out in suitable years. This Riesling still has lovely currant and white fruit freshness, and looks set for a good period of aging. 90 *—R.V. (5/1/2007)*

Steininger 2003 Kabinett Riesling (Kamptal) $NA. 85 *—R.V. (8/1/2005)*

STIFT KLOSTERNEUBURG

Stift Klosterneuburg 2001 Ried Wiegen Trocken Grüner Veltliner (Donauland) $NA. 87 *—R.V. (11/1/2002)*

Stift Klosterneuburg 2000 Ried Stiftsbreite, St. Laurent Ausstich Red Blend (Thermenregion) $NA. 86 *—R.V. (11/1/2002)*

Stift Klosterneuburg 2001 Ried Franzhauser Riesling (Donauland) $11. 86 *—R.V. (11/1/2002)*

Stift Klosterneuburg 2000 Ried Stiftsbreite Ausstich Sankt Laurent Riesling (Thermenregion) $NA. 86 *—R.V. (11/1/2002)*

STRAUSS

Strauss 2003 Gamlitzberg Pinot Blanc Classic Pinot Blanc (Steiermark) $12. 86 Best Buy *—J.C. (12/15/2004)*

Strauss 2004 Classic Sauvignon Blanc (Steiermark) $16. 86 *—J.C. (8/1/2006)*

TEGERNSEERHOF

Tegernseerhof 2003 Bergdistel Grüner Veltliner (Wachau) $20. 90 Editors' Choice *—J.C. (3/1/2006)*

Tegernseerhof 2006 Dürnsteiner Rosé Zweigelt (Wachau) $12. This is a lovely pale pink rosé with aromas of strawberries and rose petals. Despite being labeled at a modest 12% alcohol, there's plenty of weight, and the flavors are bold: strawberries balanced by citrus and a touch of mineral. Finishes dry, with a rich texture. Delicious on its own, but should be versatile at the table as well. 90 Best Buy *—J.C. (7/1/2007)*

TERRA GOMELIZ

Terra Gomeliz 2003 Sauvignon Blanc (Südsteiermark) $17. 87 *—R.V. (5/1/2005)*

Terra Gomeliz 2003 Welschriesling (Südsteiermark) $NA. 84 *—R.V. (5/1/2005)*

TSCHEPPE

Tscheppe 2002 Czamillonberg Chardonnay (Styria) $22. 86 *—J.C. (12/15/2004)*

Tscheppe 2002 Possnitzberg Pinot Gris (Styria) $18. 87 *—J.C. (5/1/2005)*

Tscheppe 2004 Pössnitzberg Pinot Gris (Südsteiermark) $19. 88 *—R.V. (2/1/2006)*

Tscheppe 2001 Possnitzberg Reserve Pinot Gris (Styria) $33. 87 *—J.C. (5/1/2005)*

Tscheppe 2003 Pössnitzberg Reserve Pinot Gris (Südsteiermark) $33. 90 *—R.V. (2/1/2006)*

Tscheppe 2003 Czamillonberg Sauvignon Blanc (Styria) $25. 84 *—J.C. (12/15/2004)*

TSCHERMONEGG

Tschermonegg 2002 Grauburgunder (Styria) $15. 87 *—J.C. (11/15/2005)*

Tschermonegg 2004 Grauburgunder Pinot Gris (Südsteiermark) $15. 87 *—R.V. (2/1/2006)*

Tschermonegg 2002 Oberglanzberg Sauvignon Blanc (Styria) $29. 87 *(7/1/2005)*

Tschermonegg 2003 Weissburgunder (Styria) $10. 84 *—J.C. (11/15/2005)*

TÜRK

Türk 2005 Eiswein Vom Grüner Veltliner (Kremstal) $NA. From botrytized grapes picked at the first frost on November 25, 2005, this is intensely sweet. But—as with all good Eiswein—it is poised on a knife-edge with acidity as intense as the sweetness. This is a fine, elegant wine, which will repay cellaring for at least three years. 90 *—R.V. (2/1/2007)*

Türk 2005 Frechau Grüner Veltliner (Kremstal) $NA. Hugely rich, this powerful wine is very ripe, packed with lychees and spicy fruit flavors. The super-ripe fruit, selectively picked on November 30 in 2005, is dense, concentrated, medium sweet, but pierced through with fine, fresh acidity. 89 *—R.V. (2/1/2007)*

Türk 2005 Vom Urgestein Grüner Veltliner (Kremstal) $13. 88 Best Buy *—R.V. (11/15/2006)*

Türk 2004 Vom Urgestein Grüner Veltliner (Kremstal) $NA. From the slopes of the Krems vineyards, above the Danube, this lively, fresh spicy Grüner has just the right mineral crispness along with some of the weight that comes from the Kremstal. At two years old, this wine is ready to drink, a great food accompaniment, ripeness balancing the poised acidity. 87 *—R.V. (2/1/2007)*

UMATHUM

Umathum 2004 Joiser Kirschgarten Blaufränkisch (Burgenland) $60. This comes from a terraced vineyard that Josef Umathum revived in 2001. Here is an already impressive testament to the quality of the vineyard. With its aromas of cedar and pine cones, the palate is densely packed with black fruits, dark tannins, red berries and a chocolate finish. 91 Editors' Choice *—R.V. (12/31/2007)*

Umathum 2006 Grauburgunder (Burgenland) $25. Whites from red wine specialist Umathum are rare, but then so is Pinot Gris in Austria. This wine has a racy quality, topped with spice that sets it apart from its nearest comparison, Alsace. There is a touch of wood as well as the spice, lively and fresh to finish. 88 *—R.V. (12/31/2007)*

Umathum 2004 Hallebühl Red Blend (Burgenland) $60. Made from 40-year-old vines, this blend, dominated by Zweigelt, but also with some Blaufränkisch and Cabernet Sauvignon, is concentrated and intensely fruity, with an elegant, smooth texture that only hints at the concentrated tannic structure underneath. It's not hugely powerful; it's more sensuous and deliciously long-lasting. 91 *—R.V. (10/1/2007)*

Umathum 2001 Frauenkirchner Vom Stein St. Laurent (Burgenland) $67. 88 *—J.C. (3/1/2006)*

Umathum 2006 Beerenauslese White Blend (Burgenland) $19. Richness in a glass, this flows around the mouth, unctuous, velvety, a mouthful of honey. If the acidity is only just a hint, it doesn't matter, this is delicious now, and a seductive treat. 90 *—R.V. (12/31/2007)*

Umathum 2006 Zweigelt (Burgenland) $19. In the young, fresh, fruity style of Zweigelt, this is packed with juicy, peppery black cherry flavors, lightened with crisp acidity and lively tannins. It's ready to drink now, no aging needed. Glass stopper. 86 *—R.V. (12/31/2007)*

Umathum 2003 Zweigelt (Burgenland) $20. 88 *—J.C. (3/1/2006)*

VELICH

Velich 2002 Darscho Chardonnay (Burgenland) $25. 82 *—J.C. (11/15/2005)*

Velich 2001 Darscho Chardonnay (Burgenland) $25. 85 *—J.C. (12/15/2004)*

Velich 2002 Tiglat Chardonnay (Burgenland) $55. 84 *—J.C. (11/15/2005)*

Velich 2001 Tiglat Chardonnay (Burgenland) $55. 89 *—J.C. (11/15/2005)*

Velich 2001 Beerenauslese 375 ml Muskat Ottonel (Neusiedlersee) $30. 93 Editors' Choice *—J.C. (12/15/2004)*

Velich 1999 Trockenbeerenauslese Welschriesling (Burgenland) $75. 92 *—J.C. (12/15/2004)*

Velich 2001 Trockenbeerenauslese 375 ml Welschriesling (Burgenland) $70. 94 *—J.C. (3/1/2006)*

Velich 2000 Seewinkel Beerenauslese White Riesling (Burgenland) $21. 86 *—J.C. (12/15/2004)*

WALTER GLATZER

Walter Glatzer 2000 Kabinett Grüner Veltliner (Carnuntum) $11. 82 *—J.C. (3/1/2002)*

WEINBAU SCHANDL

Weinbau Schandl 2002 Ruster Ausbruch Pinot Blanc (Burgenland) $55. 88 *—R.V. (3/1/2006)*

WEINBAU ZAHEL

Weinbau Zahel 2001 Trocken Pinot Grigio (Weinviertel) $13. 85 *—R.V. (11/1/2002)*

WEINBERGHOF FRITSCH

Weinberghof Fritsch 2003 Steinberg Grüner Veltliner (Donauland) $17. 90 *—R.V. (5/1/2005)*

WEINGUT ALLRAM

Weingut Allram 2005 Zöbinger Heiligenstein Riesling (Kamptal) $38. 90 *—R.V. (10/1/2006)*

Weingut Allram 2004 Zöbinger Heiligenstein Riesling (Kamptal) $38. 89 *—R.V. (10/1/2006)*

WEINGUT RICHARD ZAHEL

Weingut Richard Zahel 2005 Nussberg Riesling (Vienna) $NA. 88 *—R.V. (10/1/2006)*

Weingut Richard Zahel 2004 Nussberg Gemischter Satz Grande Reserve White Blend (Vienna) $NA. 90 Editors' Choice *—R.V. (10/1/2006)*

WEINGUT TFXT

Weingut TFXT 2000 Arachon Red Blend (Mittelburgenland) $32. 90 *—R.V. (11/1/2002)*

WEINKELLEREI TIEDL

Weinkellerei Tiedl 1999 Barrique Blaufränkisch (Neusiedlersee) $15. 88 *—R.V. (11/1/2002)*

Weinkellerei Tiedl 2001 Trocken Pinot Blanc (Neusiedlersee) $13. 90 *—R.V. (11/1/2002)*

Weinkellerei Tiedl 2000 Blauer Zweigelt Red Blend (Neusiedlersee) $15. 85 *—R.V. (11/1/2002)*

WEINRIEDER

Weinrieder 2005 Grüner Veltliner (Weinviertel) $12. 87 Best Buy *—R.V. (10/1/2006)*

Weinrieder 2004 Alte Reben Grüner Veltliner (Niederösterreich) $24. 93 Editors' Choice *—R.V. (10/1/2006)*

Weinrieder 2005 Schneiderberg Grüner Veltliner (Niederösterreich) $15. 90 Best Buy *—R.V. (10/1/2006)*

Weinrieder 2001 Schneiderberg Grüner Veltliner (Austria) $12. 91 *—S.H. (10/1/2004)*

Weinrieder 2003 Schneidersberg DAC Grüner Veltliner (Weinviertel) $12. 89 Best Buy *—R.V. (5/1/2005)*

Weinrieder 2001 Bockgarten II Riesling (Austria) $25. 90 *—S.H. (10/1/2004)*

Weinrieder 2004 Bockgärten II Riesling (Niederösterreich) $29. 92 *—R.V. (10/1/2006)*

Weinrieder 2005 Kugler Riesling (Niederösterreich) $19. 91 Editors' Choice *—R.V. (10/1/2006)*

Weinrieder 2003 Schneiderberg Eiswein 375mL Riesling (Niederösterreich) $70. 95 Cellar Selection *—R.V. (10/1/2006)*

Weinrieder 2004 Hohenleiten Welschriesling Auslese Welschriesling (Niederösterreich) $38. 90 *—R.V. (10/1/2006)*

Weinrieder 2005 Hohenleiten Welschriesling Eiswein 375mL Welschriesling (Niederösterreich) $40. 92 *—R.V. (10/1/2006)*

Weinrieder 2005 Hölzler Welschriesling Eiswein 375mL Welschriesling (Niederösterreich) $35. 93 *—R.V. (10/1/2006)*

WENINGER

Weninger 2004 Dürrau Blaufränkisch (Burgenland) $129. Made from a single vineyard, this is Franz Weninger's flagship wine. Pure Blaufränkisch, it shows all the exotic flavors of the grape—mineral, spices, black cherries—packaged with dark tannins and smoky, toasty wood. To finish, there is cocoa along with a touch of sweet citrus. Great aging potential. 93 Cellar Selection *—R.V. (10/1/2007)*

WENZEL

Wenzel 2001 Bandkraften Blaufränkisch (Burgenland) $25. 88 *—J.C. (5/1/2005)*

Wenzel 2003 Noble Selection 375ml Gelber Muskateller (Burgenland) $22. 88 *—J.C. (12/1/2006)*

Wenzel 2003 Pinot Gris (Burgenland) $19. 87 *—R.V. (2/1/2006)*

Wenzel 2001 Pinot Gris (Burgenland) $19. 92 Editors' Choice *—J.C. (5/1/2005)*

Wenzel 2002 Beerenauslese Riesling (Burgenland) $40. 91 Editors' Choice *—J.C. (12/15/2004)*

Wenzel 2004 Sauvignon Blanc Ruster Ausbruch Sauvignon Blanc (Neusiedlersee-Hügelland) $NA. The Wenzel family continue to make small quantities of finely crafted wines, like this intensely flavored Sauvignon Blanc. The sweetness is well controlled by fresh acidity and lemon curd flavors, while the honey gives the right amount of dryness. Age it for another five years. 91 *—R.V. (5/1/2007)*

Wenzel 2004 Am Fusse des Berges Ruster Ausbruch White Blend (Neusiedlersee-Hügelland) $52. This exotic blend of Sauvignon Blanc, Pinot Gris, Welschriesling and Gelber Muskateller hangs together well. There's plenty of aromatic grapes here to give spice and character to the wine, while the S.B. lends rich botrytis and body. A well-balanced wine with fresh acidity on the finish. 90 *—R.V. (5/1/2007)*

Wenzel 2002 Am Fusse des Berges Ruster Ausbruch 375 ml White Blend (Burgenland) $52. 86 *—J.C. (3/1/2006)*

Wenzel 2001 Am Fusse Des Berges Ruster Ausbruch 375 ml White Blend (Burgenland) $60. 90 *—J.C. (12/15/2004)*

Wenzel 2003 Noble Selection 375ml White Blend (Burgenland) $20. 86 *—J.C. (12/1/2006)*

Wenzel 2004 Saz Ruster Ausbruch White Blend (Neusiedlersee-Hügelland) $87. This blend of Furmint and Gelber Muskateller—the traditional blend for Ruster Ausbruch—is a refreshingly delicate wine, showing delicious apricot freshness as well as the proper honeyed touch. The acidity powers through the wine, promising great aging potential as well as making it delicious to drink now. 94 *—R.V. (5/1/2007)*

Wenzel 2001 Saz Ruster Ausbruch White Blend (Burgenland) $120. 95 *—J.C. (12/15/2004)*

Wenzel 2002 Saz Ruster Ausbruch 375 ml White Blend (Burgenland) $120. 94 *—J.C. (12/1/2006)*

WERNER DUSCHANEK

Werner Duschanek 2000 Image Barrique Cabernet Sauvignon (Mittelburgenland) $NA. 90 *—R.V. (11/1/2002)*

Werner Duschanek 2000 Spatlese Pinot Noir (Mittelburgenland) $NA. 86 *—R.V. (11/1/2002)*

Werner Duschanek 2000 Zweigelt Red Blend (Mittelburgenland) $NA. 84 *—R.V. (11/1/2002)*

WIENINGER

Wieninger 2005 Herrenholz Grüner Veltliner (Vienna) $14. 89 Best Buy *—R.V. (10/1/2006)*

Wieninger 2004 Herrenholz Grüner Veltliner (Vienna) $15. 88 Editors' Choice *—J.C. (8/1/2006)*

Wieninger 2003 Herrenholz Grüner Veltliner (Vienna) $17. 90 Editors' Choice *—J.C. (5/1/2005)*

Wieninger 2005 Kaasgraben Grüner Veltliner (Vienna) $23. 91 *—R.V. (10/1/2006)*

Wieninger 2004 Leicht & Trocken Grüner Veltliner (Vienna) $12. 84 *—J.C. (3/1/2006)*

Wieninger 2003 Leicht & Trocken Grüner Veltliner (Vienna) $12. 89 Best Buy *—J.C. (5/1/2005)*

Wieninger 2005 Nussberg Grüner Veltliner (Vienna) $15. 90 Best Buy *—R.V. (10/1/2006)*

Wieninger 2005 Preussen Grüner Veltliner (Vienna) $32. 92 Cellar Selection *—R.V. (10/1/2006)*

Wieninger 2004 Grand Select Pinot Noir (Vienna) $30. A big, wood-aged wine, which at this stage shows considerable flavors from the Burgundy barrel aging. But then there's the fruit—red berries, cherries and sweetness—merging into what will be a soft, velvet wine. Give it 2–3 years. 91 *—R.V. (10/1/2007)*

Wieninger 2005 Wiener Trilogie Red Blend (Vienna) $20. This is Fritz Wieninger's "everyday" red, a blend of Zweigelt, Merlot and Cab Sauvignon. A ripe, fruity wine, with great juicy flavors from the Zweigelt, packed with red berries, just touched by wood, spice and open, friendly acidity. 88 *—R.V. (10/1/2007)*

Wieninger 2004 Wiener Trilogie Red Blend (Vienna) $19. 86 *—R.V. (10/1/2006)*

Wieninger 2003 Wiener Trilogie Red Blend (Austria) $19. 85 *—J.C. (3/1/2006)*

Wieninger 2005 Nussberg Riesling (Vienna) $25. 91 *—R.V. (10/1/2006)*

Wieninger 2005 Preussen Riesling (Vienna) $32. 89 *—R.V. (10/1/2006)*

Wieninger 2003 Riedencuvée Riesling (Vienna) $15. 89 *—J.C. (5/1/2005)*

Wieninger 2004 Riedencuvée Riesling (Vienna) $14. 87 *—J.C. (8/1/2006)*

Wieninger 2001 Riedencuvée Vienna Riesling (Austria) $NA. 86 *—R.V. (8/1/2003)*

Wieninger 2004 Nussberg Alte Reben White Blend (Vienna) $25. 92 Editors' Choice *—R.V. (10/1/2006)*

Wieninger 2001 Nussberg Alte Reben White Blend (Vienna) $26. 90 Editors' Choice *—J.C. (12/15/2004)*

Wieninger 2003 Nußberg Alte Reben White Blend (Vienna) $25. 86 *—J.C. (8/1/2006)*

Wieninger 2005 Rosengartl Alte Reben White Blend (Vienna) $32. Described by Fritz Wieninger as the most expensive vineyard land in Austria—because of the demand for high-end housing in this district of Vienna—Rosengartl is at the heart of the Nussberg. This blend of Grüner Veltliner, Weissburgunder and Traminer is concentrated, high in alcohol (14.5%) but still shows considerable refinement, acidity as well as spice and pepper flavors. 92 *—R.V. (2/1/2007)*

Wieninger 2005 WB Wieninger Blend White Blend (Vienna) $11. 85 *—R.V. (10/1/2006)*

WILLI BRUNDLMAYER

Willi Brundlmayer 2001 Langenloiser Steinmassel Riesling (Kamptal) $25. 93 Editors' Choice *—R.V. (11/1/2002)*

Willi Brundlmayer 2001 Lyra Zöbinger Heiligenstein Riesling (Kamptal) $48. 93 *—R.V. (8/1/2003)*

WILLI OPITZ

Willi Opitz 1998 Weisser Schilfmandl Muskat Ottonel Muscat (Burgenland) $50. 90 *—R.V. (11/1/2002)*

Willi Opitz 2001 White Blend (Neusiedlersee) $18. 88 *—R.V. (5/1/2004)*

Willi Opitz 2002 Goldackerl White Blend (Neusiedlersee) $18. 89 *—R.V. (5/1/2004)*

Willi Opitz 2001 Schilfwein Zweigelt (Neusiedlersee) $46. 87 *—R.V. (5/1/2004)*

WIMMER-CZERNY

Wimmer-Czerny 2000 Grüner Veltliner Beerenauslese (Donauland) $54. For sheer alcoholic power, there's not much to beat this wine. For the pleasure it gives, well that's harder. This is more about richness, with high levels of pepper, new wood and structure. An acquired taste. 85 *—R.V. (2/1/2007)*

Wimmer-Czerny 2003 Fumberg Grüner Veltliner (Donauland) $16. 87 *—R.V. (5/1/2005)*

WINZER KREMS

Winzer Krems 2006 Kellermeister Privat Goldberg Grüner Veltliner (Kremstal) $NA. This is from the premium range produced by the Winzer Krems cooperative. It is a freshly fruity, bramble-flavored wine, lifted with acidity, light flavors of wood and a good, fresh, juicy, spicy aftertaste. 89 *—R.V. (8/1/2007)*

Winzer Krems 2005 Kremser Goldberg Grüner Veltliner (Kremstal) $16. 88 *—R.V. (10/1/2006)*

Winzer Krems 2006 Kremser Wachtberg Grüner Veltliner (Kremstal) $22. A bone-dry, crisp wine, with green pears and only a hint of Grüner's pepper character. Attractive, creamy and fresh. 87 *—R.V. (12/31/2007)*

Winzer Krems 2005 Kremser Wachtberg Grüner Veltliner (Kremstal) $22. 87 *—R.V. (10/1/2006)*

Winzer Krems 2006 Ried Sandgrube Grüner Veltliner (Kremstal) $NA. The Sandgrube vineyard is at the historic heart of the Kremstal appellation. This is soft, but with a mineral edge that gives it cool structure and fresh green pear flavors. There's a nice lightness to the aftertaste. 88 *—R.V. (8/1/2007)*

Winzer Krems 2005 Kellermeister Privat Eiswein Riesling (Niederösterreich) $35. While this wine has the right piercing, shattering acidity of an eiswein, there's a toffee/caramel element that takes away from its purity. Perfumes are good, and there's a lively touch of white fruit. 87 *—R.V. (12/31/2007)*

Winzer Krems 2003 Kellermeister Privat Kremser Kremsleiten Riesling (Kremstal) $15. 88 *—R.V. (8/1/2005)*

Winzer Krems 2005 Kremser Pfaffenberg Riesling (Kremstal) $24. 89 *—R.V. (10/1/2006)*

Winzer Krems 2003 Kremser Pfaffenberg Riesling (Kremstal) $17. 87 *—R.V. (5/1/2005)*

Winzer Krems 2006 Kremser Pfaffenberg Hauerinnung Riesling (Kremstal) $25. Here is a contradiction that works, a wine that is both rich and delicate. The light, dancing touch of the Riesling is fleshed out with delicious perfumed acidity, but always the crispness and flavors of white currants are here. 90 *—R.V. (12/31/2007)*

Winzer Krems 2005 Kremser Pfaffenberg Hauerinnung Riesling (Kremstal) $NA. A full, young-tasting Riesling, from one of the great Krems vineyards, Pfaffenberg. Its elegance and perfumed character are enhanced by the flavor of white fruits and currants. With its structure, this is a wine that needs aging. 89 *—R.V. (8/1/2007)*

Winzer Krems 2006 Privat Kremser Kremsleiten Riesling (Kremstal) $NA. Intense and full-bodied, with green pear and kiwi flavors. Acidity dominates from start to finish, powered by pure fruit flavors, enhanced by enticing perfumes. 86 *—R.V. (8/1/2007)*

Winzer Krems 2004 Riesling von den Terrassen Riesling (Kremstal) $10. 86 *—R.V. (8/1/2005)*

Winzer Krems 2005 Kellermeister Privat Kremser Zweigelt (Kremstal) $14. This is from the premium range produced by the Winzer Krems cooperative. It is a freshly fruity, bramble-flavored wine, lifted with acidity. Has light flavors of wood, and a fresh, juicy, spicy aftertaste. 87 *—R.V. (10/1/2007)*

WOHLMUTH

Wohlmuth 1999 Summus Cabernet Blend (South Styria) $25. 85 *—J.C. (3/1/2002)*

Wohlmuth 2001 Summus Chardonnay (Südsteiermark) $18. 87 *—R.V. (11/1/2002)*

Wohlmuth 2000 Summus Gewürztraminer (South Styria) $16. 86 *—J.C. (3/1/2002)*

Wohlmuth 2000 Summus Muskateller (South Styria) $16. 84 *—J.C. (3/1/2002)*

Wohlmuth 2000 Summus Pinot Blanc (South Styria) $15. 83 *—J.C. (3/1/2002)*

Wohlmuth 2004 Pinot Gris (Südsteiermark) $12. 88 *—R.V. (2/1/2006)*

Wohlmuth 2000 Summus Pinot Gris (South Styria) $16. 84 *—J.C. (3/1/2002)*

Wohlmuth 2003 Sauvignon Blanc (South Styria) $27. 86 *(7/1/2005)*

Wohlmuth 2001 Summus Sauvignon Blanc (Südsteiermark) $20. 88 *—R.V. (11/1/2002)*

Wohlmuth 2000 Summus Sauvignon Blanc (South Styria) $18. 83 *—J.C. (3/1/2002)*

ZANTHO

Zantho 2006 Blaufränkisch Blaufränkisch (Burgenland) $15. Zantho is the ancient name of Andau, home to the winery. It specializes in wines from the local grapes, and this Blaufränkisch is a good example. The wine has some black fruit flavors, spice, hints of wood aging and a ripe, herbal, earthy aftertaste. Drink now. Glass stopper. 87 *—R.V. (10/1/2007)*

Zantho 2006 Muskat Ottonel (Burgenland) $13. Very Muscat, very aromatic, this is a light, crowd-pleasing apéritif wine that dances on the palate. It's dry, but the lychee-like perfumed flavor and the spice make it softer and easier. Glass stopper. 87 *—R.V. (12/31/2007)*

Zantho 2006 St. Laurent (Burgenland) $15. Lively, perfumed, properly fresh and fruity as befits a juicy, ripe St. Laurent. There are no pretensions here, just pleasurable strawberry-and citrus-edged wine. 88 *—R.V. (10/1/2007)*

Zantho 2003 St. Laurent (Burgenland) $13. 84 *—J.C. (3/1/2006)*

Zantho 2002 St. Laurent (Burgenland) $13. 87 *—J.C. (5/1/2005)*

Zantho 2006 Beerenauslese White Blend (Burgenland) $19. A blend of Welschriesling and Scheurebe, this is a fresh and delicate wine that wears its sweetness easily. Some botrytis, some honey, but the acidity comes into play as does the pineapple flavor. Glass stopper. 86 *—R.V. (12/31/2007)*

Zantho 2006 Zweigelt (Burgenland) $15. Juicy red cherries and raspberries, plus a good line of citrus offer freshness and lively, vibrant flavors. The tannin is present, but really only as a support, not to suggest aging. Glass stopper. 87 *—R.V. (10/1/2007)*

Zantho 2002 Zweigelt (Burgenland) $13. 87 *—J.C. (5/1/2005)*

Zantho 2004 Reserve Zweigelt (Burgenland) $25. Zantho is a joint venture between winemakers Josef Umathum and Wolfgang Peck, who buy grapes from selected members of the local cooperative of Andau. This Reserve is certainly the best wine in the range, a sophisticated wine that has seen new wood aging; this has highlighted the sweet red fruits, given point to the acidity and spice, as well as adding complexity to the black plum flavors. 90 *—R.V. (10/1/2007)*

ZIMMERMAN

Zimmermann 2006 Kapuzinerberg Riesling (Kremstal) $18. Classic Riesling, all fresh currants and stone fruits with a touch of spice, finishing full and rich. This wine comes from the Kapuzinerberg vineyard on the southern slopes of the Krems hills. Screwcap. 88 *—R.V. (8/1/2007)*

Zimmermann 2006 Kremser Kraxn Riesling (Kremstal) $20. The Kraxn (pronounced "KRAX-en") is well-placed for Riesling, with its southern exposure close to the Danube river. The richness of the fruit shows through in this soft, open, opulent wine, with its pepper and white fruit flavors. 87 *—R.V. (8/1/2007)*

Zimmermann 2006 Rosshimmel Riesling Riesling (Kremstal) $20. Alois Zimmermann's top Rieslings come from the Rosshimmel vineyard. A concentrated wine, still with youthful structure and closed white fruits. The acidity and intensity of flavor all point to long-term potential—give it 5 years at least. 90 Cellar Selection *—R.V. (8/1/2007)*

ZULL

Zull 2006 Lust & Laune Blauer Portugieser (Niederösterreich) $15. Made from Blauer Portugieser, this is a fresh, red fruit-flavored wine, all light acidity and soft strawberry jam flavors. Drink lightly chilled like a Beaujolais. In the dictionary, the name means "joy and humor": that sums up the wine pretty well. Screwcap. 85 *—R.V. (10/1/2007)*

Zull 2005 Chardonnay Trockenbeerenauslese Chardonnay (Weinviertel) $NA. An intensely rich wine balanced with delicious, refreshing acidity. Honey and lemon are the main thread of flavors, weaving through the soft, rich fruit. With all that acidity, the likelihood is that this wine will age well. 90 *—R.V. (5/1/2007)*

Zull 2000 Odfeld Grüner Veltliner (Weinviertel) $17. 90 *—J.C. (3/1/2002)*

Zull 2004 Pinot Noir (Niederösterreich) $41. Light and fresh, this relies on its clean lines, even with that slightly funky edge of Pinot Noir. It has its pure red fruit flavors and acidity; the tannins suggest structure, offering some firm, food-friendly tastes. 88 *—R.V. (10/1/2007)*

Zull 2003 Pinot Noir (Niederösterreich) $41. A limited-production wine that shows the fruity side of Pinot Noir, delicious raspberry and strawberry flavors, with soft tannins and light acidity. There is some softness, almost sweetness, to finish. 87 *—R.V. (10/1/2007)*

Zull 2004 Schrattenthal 9 Red Blend (Niederösterreich) $30. Special selection of Zweigelt, Cabernet Sauvignon and Merlot from the top sites in the Schrattenthal vineyard. This is well structured, the fine tannins weaving through the black currant and cranberry flavors, a lightning bolt of acidity coming through to finish. Age for two years. 90 *—R.V. (10/1/2007)*

Zull 2006 Zweigelt (Niederösterreich) $17. A fine performance with this lively wine, which shows all the juicy, fruity character of Zweigelt, just touched by spice, and with some solid tannins playing through. There's good acidity, fresh red currant flavor and a finely balanced aftertaste. 89 *—R.V. (10/1/2007)*

Chile

Chile saw its original grapevines arrive with sixteenth-century Spanish missionaries, but the first semblance of a modern winemaking industry dates back to the early part of the nineteenth century, when a naturalist by the name of Claudio Gay imported about sixty varieties of grapes from France. In turn, some of these grapes were planted in the Maipo Valley, which encompasses the city of Santiago, and by the 1850s commercial wine existed.

From an American's perspective, Chilean wine started to make its mark in the 1970s, when protectionist restrictions were lifted by the military dictatorship headed by Augusto Pinochet. Almost immediately, exports spiked, with value-priced wines pouring into America as well as other countries. Some thirty years later, Chile is one of the world's most aggressive exporters; its wines make it to nearly one hundred countries around the globe, with shipments to the United States leading the way.

Wine barrels in the cellars of Viña Luis Felipe Edwards, Chile.

In many ways, the climate, geology, and geography of Chile are like that of western North America, but turned upside-down. Chile's north is a bone-dry desert, roughly equal to Baja California, only drier. The middle of the country is verdant and river-fed, with soils perfect for all sorts of agriculture, not the least of which is grapes. So in that sense it's like California, Oregon, and Washington. And as one goes south it quickly gets colder and more rugged, not unlike British Columbia and eventually Alaska.

In the midsection of this 4,000-mile-long sliver of a country, there's a 500-mile chunk called the Central Valley, and within this valley there are a number of prime wine-growing regions. The most historic is Maipo, in which just about all grapes are grown. But it's Cabernet Sauvignon that has always been king in Maipo. Whether it's a simple everyday Maipo Cabernet like Cousiño-Macul's Antiguas Reservas or one of the country's best premium offerings like Concha y Toro's Don Melchor, a Maipo Cabernet is well worth hailing.

Other prominent wine regions include Aconcagua and Limari, the two northern frontiers of premium grape growing. There aren't many wineries there, but the wines are solid and true. Bordering Maipo to the west is the Casablanca Valley, first planted by Pablo Morandé and his family in the early 1990s. Cool and coastal, Casablanca and neighboring Leyda and San Antonio are prime spots for Chardonnay and Sauvignon Blanc but have trouble when it comes to producing ripe red wines.

South of Maipo is Rapel and its two parallel valleys: Cachapoal and Colchagua. Here the weather is warm, and the majority of grapes are red. Colchagua is arguably the leading region in Chile for red wines, and there's a plethora of big, burly wines based on Syrah, Cabernet Sauvignon, Merlot, Malbec, and Carmenère coming from Colchagua wineries including Montes, Casa Lapostolle, Viu Manent, MontGras, and Los Vascos.

Further south are the regions of Curicó and Maule. It was in Curicó that Miguel Torres of Spain set up shop in 1979 and introduced the then-revolutionary concept of steel-tank fermentation to Chile. To borrow a well-used phrase and apply it to how wine is now being made throughout the country: the rest is history.

2 BROTHERS

2 Brothers 2003 Big Tattoo Syrah (Colchagua Valley) $9. 82 —*M.S. (11/1/2005)*

AGUSTINOS

Agustinos 2000 Estate Cabernet Sauvignon (Cachapoal Valley) $8. 83 —*D.T. (1/1/2002)*

Agustinos 2000 Reserve Cabernet Sauvignon (Cachapoal Valley) $13. 85 —*D.T. (7/1/2002)*

Agustinos 2001 Reserve Carmenère (Maipo Valley) $9. 82 —*D.T. (7/1/2002)*

Agustinos 2000 Reserve Carmenère (Maipo Valley) $13. 83 —*D.T. (7/1/2002)*

Agustinos 2001 Estate Chardonnay (Cachapoal Valley) $8. 85 —*J.C. (7/1/2002)*

Agustinos 2000 Estate Chardonnay (Cachapoal Valley) $8. 84 —*M.S. (7/1/2002)*

Agustinos 2000 Reserve Chardonnay (Cachapoal Valley) $13. 85 —*M.S. (7/1/2002)*

Agustinos 2000 Reserve Merlot (Cachapoal Valley) $13. 85 —*C.S. (12/1/2002)*

ALFASI

Alfasi 1998 Cabernet Sauvignon (Maule Valley) $8. 82 —*J.C. (2/1/2001)*

Alfasi 2000 Reserve Cabernet Sauvignon (Maule Valley) $10. 87 Best Buy —*J.M. (4/3/2004)*

Alfasi 1998 Reserve Cabernet Sauvignon (Maule Valley) $8. 80 —*M.S. (7/1/2003)*

Alfasi 1999 Chardonnay (Maule Valley) $8. 84 *(4/1/2001)*

Alfasi 2002 Reserve Chardonnay-Sauvignon (Maule Valley) $8. 82 —*J.C. (4/1/2005)*

Alfasi 2002 Reserve Malbec-Syrah (Central Valley) $10. 81 —*J.M. (4/3/2004)*

Alfasi 1998 Merlot (Maule Valley) $7. 85 *(4/1/2001)*

Alfasi 2001 Estate Bottled Merlot (Maule Valley) $6. 80 —*M.S. (7/1/2003)*

Alfasi 2001 Reserve Merlot (Maule Valley) $10. 82 —*J.C. (4/1/2005)*

Alfasi 1998 Reserve Merlot (Maule Valley) $10. 80 *(4/1/2001)*

Alfasi 1998 Flora Semi Dry Red Blend (Maule Valley) $10. 82 —*D.T. (7/1/2002)*

Alfasi 1999 Sauvignon Blanc (Maule Valley) $8. 86 *(4/1/2001)*

Alfasi 2001 Late Harvest Sauvignon Blanc (Maule Valley) $15. 82 —*J.C. (4/1/2005)*

ALMAVIVA

Almaviva 1998 Bordeaux Blend (Puente Alto) $87. 93 Cellar Selection —*M.M. (2/1/2001)*

Almaviva 2003 Cabernet Blend (Puente Alto) $75. 94 Editors' Choice —*M.S. (10/1/2006)*

Almaviva 2000 Cabernet Blend (Puente Alto) $91. 92 Cellar Selection —*M.S. (12/1/2002)*

Almaviva 1999 Red Blend (Maipo Valley) $91. 92 Cellar Selection —*J.C. (3/1/2002)*

ALTA CIMA

Alta Cima 2003 6.330 Premium Reserve Red Blend (Lontué Valley) $18. Sauvignon is the leader in this four-grape blend that starts out with aged barnyard aromas before revealing raspberry and rhubarb flavors. And on the back end there's some green character some might call weedy. 82 —*M.S. (11/15/2007)*

ALTAÏR

Altaïr 2002 Sideral Cabernet Blend (Rapel Valley) $25. 89 —*M.S. (11/1/2005)*

Altaïr 2002 Altair Cabernet Sauvignon (Cachapoal Valley) $55. 88 —*M.S. (11/1/2005)*

Altaïr 2003 Red Blend (Cachapoal Valley) $59. 94 Editors' Choice —*M.S. (11/1/2005)*

Altaïr 2003 Sideral Red Blend (Rapel Valley) $29. 91 —*M.S. (11/1/2005)*

ANTINORI-MATTE

Antinori-Matte 2001 Albis Cabernet Sauvignon (Maipo Valley) $53. 92 —*M.S. (8/1/2004)*

Antinori-Matte 2002 Albis Cabernet Sauvignon-Carmenère (Maipo Valley) $55. 87 —*M.S. (7/1/2006)*

ANTIYAL

Antiyal 2003 Red Blend (Maipo Valley) $50. 86 —*M.S. (3/1/2006)*

Antiyal 1999 Red Blend (Maipo Valley) $30. 89 —*S.H. (12/1/2002)*

Antiyal 2004 Sons of the Sun Red Blend (Maipo Valley) $50. 91 Editors' Choice —*M.S. (11/15/2006)*

Antiyal 2000 Super Chilean Blend Red Blend (Maipo Valley) $32. 90 *C.S. (2/1/2003)*

APALTAGUA

Apaltagua 2003 Cabernet Sauvignon (Colchagua Valley) $10. 85 Best Buy —*M.S. (11/1/2005)*

Apaltagua 2001 Cabernet Sauvignon (Colchagua Valley) $10. 87 —*S.H. (1/1/2002)*

Apaltagua 2005 Estate Cabernet Sauvignon (Colchagua Valley) $10. 85 Best Buy —*M.S. (11/15/2006)*

Apaltagua 2003 Carmenère (Colchagua Valley) $10. 85 Best Buy —*M.S. (11/1/2005)*

Apaltagua 2001 Carmenère (Colchagua Valley) $10. 88 Best Buy —*S.H. (11/15/2002)*

Apaltagua 2005 Envero Carmenère (Colchagua Valley) $15. Only 2,000 cases of this well-constructed Carmenère exist, and it succeeds from start to finish while never trying to do too much. The fruit is pure and ripe, showing Carmenère's rarely seen bright and forward side. And the finish seeps with spice and chocolate. With this wine there's way more fruit than herbal character. 89 Best Buy —*M.S. (11/15/2007)*

Apaltagua 2000 Envero Carmenère (Colchagua Valley) $15. 91 Best Buy —*S.H. (12/1/2002)*

Apaltagua 2005 Estate Carmenère (Colchagua Valley) $10. Fiery and generic at first, and only later does the wine start to show some of the olive and oily black fruit that defines this variety. The palate is fairly smooth and round-edged, with mouthfeel ranking ahead of complexity and flavor in terms of what's best. 84 —*M.S. (11/15/2007)*

Apaltagua 2004 Estate Carmenère (Colchagua Valley) $10. 86 —*M.S. (12/31/2006)*

Apaltagua 2002 Estate Bottled Carmenère (Colchagua Valley) $10. 85 Best Buy —*M.S. (2/1/2005)*

Apaltagua 2003 Grial Carmenère (Colchagua Valley) $40. Tasted blind, this is the third straight vintage Grial has pulled a 91. That tells you that winemaker Alvaro Espinoza is as consistent as they come and that Carmenère is capable of excellence. This wine offers lovely aromas and racy berry and plum flavors. And along the way there's enrichening pulp, oak and tannins. Drink now into 2009. 91 —*M.S. (11/15/2007)*

Apaltagua 2002 Grial Carmenère (Colchagua Valley) $40. 91 Editors' Choice —*M.S. (2/1/2005)*

Apaltagua 2000 Grial Carmenère (Colchagua Valley) $30. 91 —*S.H. (12/1/2002)*

Apaltagua 2003 Vineyard Selection Envero Carmenère (Colchagua Valley) $15. 88 —*M.S. (11/1/2005)*

ARAUCO

Arauco 2004 Reserve Cabernet Sauvignon (Maule Valley) $16. 86 —*M.S. (7/1/2006)*

Arauco 2004 Reserve Carmenère (Maule Valley) $16. 87 —*M.S. (3/1/2006)*

Arauco 2003 Lagrimas de Luna Red Blend (Maule Valley) $55. 81 —*M.S. (5/1/2006)*

Arauco 2004 Reserve Shiraz (Maule Valley) $16. 83—*M.S. (3/1/2006)*

ARBOLEDA

Arboleda 2003 Cabernet Sauvignon (Maipo Valley) $15. Full and lively, but also a touch leafy, green and oaky. The barrel element remains staunch despite the fact that this is an '03 (meaning an older year). Along the way the fruit is sweet, almost sticky. And the finish is creamy and persistent. Drink now; it's not about to improve. 86 —*M.S. (11/15/2007)*

Arboleda 2001 Cabernet Sauvignon (Maipo Valley) $15. 86 —*M.S. (7/1/2005)*

Arboleda 1999 Cabernet Sauvignon (Maipo Valley) $20. 86 —*M.S. (3/1/2002)*

Arboleda 1998 Cabernet Sauvignon (Maipo Valley) $20. 88 *(10/1/2001)*

Arboleda 2003 Carmenère (Colchagua Valley) $15. 87 —*M.S. (12/15/2005)*

Arboleda 2002 Carmenère (Colchagua Valley) $15. 82 —*M.S. (7/1/2005)*

Arboleda 2000 Carmenère (Colchagua Valley) $20. 85 —*S.H. (12/1/2002)*

Arboleda 1999 Carmenère (Maipo Valley) $20. 88 *—M.S. (3/1/2002)*

Arboleda 2006 Chardonnay (Casablanca Valley) $15. Among Chilean Chardonnays, this one gets it more right than wrong. The nose deals apple pie and mineral, while the palate shows mostly apple, pear and butterscotch flavors. Not complex or stately, but round, fresh and generally on target. 87 *—M.S. (11/15/2007)*

Arboleda 2005 Chardonnay (Casablanca Valley) $15. 90 Best Buy *—M.S. (10/1/2006)*

Arboleda 2003 Chardonnay (Casablanca Valley) $15. 83 *—M.S. (12/15/2005)*

Arboleda 2000 Chardonnay (Central Valley) $8. 86 *—M.S. (3/1/2002)*

Arboleda 2003 Merlot (Colchagua Valley) $15. 87 *—M.S. (7/1/2006)*

Arboleda 2002 Merlot (Colchagua Valley) $15. 86 *—M.S. (5/1/2006)*

Arboleda 2001 Merlot (Colchagua Valley) $15. 86 *—M.S. (3/1/2004)*

Arboleda 2000 Merlot (Colchagua Valley) $20. 88 *—M.S. (3/1/2002)*

Arboleda 1999 Merlot (Colchagua Valley) $20. 87 *(10/1/2001)*

Arboleda 2006 Sauvignon Blanc (Leyda Valley) $15. More than a touch of the vegetal aromas mars the simple, quiet bouquet, while the palate delivers standard green berry and grass flavors along with some herbaceous accents. This wine has bite and style, but it's a little too vegetal for its own good. 84 *—M.S. (11/15/2007)*

Arboleda 2005 Sauvignon Blanc (Leyda Valley) $15. 86 *—M.S. (7/1/2006)*

Arboleda 2004 Shiraz (Colchagua Valley) $15. Dusty and a touch herbal; this wine struggles for total purity of flavors and aromas, but it gets it partially right, especially with its mouthfeel. Flavors of black cherry and raspberry are a little bit green and pasty, while the oak bites more than it should. Good up to a certain level, but with issues. 85 *—M.S. (11/15/2007)*

Arboleda 2002 Syrah (Colchagua Valley) $15. 86 *—M.S. (2/1/2005)*

Arboleda 2001 Syrah (Colchagua Valley) $15. 88 *—M.S. (6/1/2004)*

Arboleda 2000 Syrah (Colchagua Valley) $20. 84 *—S.H. (12/1/2002)*

Arboleda 1999 Syrah (Colchagua Valley) $20. 88 Editors' Choice *(10/1/2001)*

ARESTI

Aresti 2005 Cabernet Sauvignon (Central Valley) $9. As Aresti's vines get older its wines appear to be getting better. A case in point is this Cab, which shows nice plum and berry aromas followed by forward red plum and raspberry flavors. It's medium bodied and solid, with a touch of woodiness expressed through lingering vanilla and chocolate flavors. 87 Best Buy *—M.S. (3/1/2007)*

Aresti 2004 Cabernet Sauvignon (Curicó Valley) $9. 86 Best Buy *—M.S. (7/1/2006)*

Aresti 2003 Cabernet Sauvignon (Chile) $8. 80 *—M.S. (7/1/2005)*

Aresti 1999 Family Collection Cabernet Sauvignon (Curicó Valley) $30. 81 *—M.S. (7/1/2005)*

Aresti 1999 Family Collection Cabernet Sauvignon (Rio Claro) $26. 88 *—M.S. (3/1/2002)*

Aresti 2002 Montemar Cabernet Sauvignon (Curicó Valley) $8. 82 *—M.S. (8/1/2004)*

Aresti 2001 Montemar Cabernet Sauvignon (Curicó Valley) $8. 85 Best Buy *—M.S. (7/1/2003)*

Aresti 1999 Montemar Cabernet Sauvignon (Curicó Valley) $8. 87 Best Buy *(9/1/2000)*

Aresti 1999 Reserva Cabernet Sauvignon (Rio Claro) $11. 89 Best Buy *(9/1/2000)*

Aresti 2004 Reserve Cabernet Sauvignon (Rio Claro) $13. 83 *—M.S. (7/1/2006)*

Aresti 2000 Reserve Cabernet Sauvignon (Rio Claro) $11. 85 *—M.S. (7/1/2003)*

Aresti 2006 A Rosé Cabernet Sauvignon (Curicó Valley) $9. There's very little to latch onto with this tart, pickly pink wine from Chile. It has kick but no cushion, and it deals only acidic apple and grapefruit flavors. 80 *—M.S. (7/1/2007)*

Aresti 2005 Carmenère (Curicó Valley) $9. Early aromas of balsam wood, green herbs and olive are backed by dark fruit notes, while the palate delivers playful raspberry flavors alongside olive. It's a bit acidic but short on the finish. Typical and pretty good as a whole. 84 *—M.S. (5/1/2007)*

Aresti 2003 Carmenère (Curicó Valley) $8. 83 *—M.S. (11/1/2005)*

Aresti 2004 Reserve Carmenère (Curicó Valley) $13. 83 *—M.S. (7/1/2006)*

Aresti 2001 Reserve Carmenère (Rio Claro) $11. 85 *—M.S. (7/1/2003)*

Aresti 2005 Chardonnay (Curicó Valley) $9. 84 *—M.S. (7/1/2006)*

Aresti 2004 Chardonnay (Curicó Valley) $8. 84 Best Buy *—M.S. (11/1/2005)*

Aresti 1999 Chardonnay (Curicó Valley) $8. 84 *(9/1/2000)*

Aresti 2005 Gewürztraminer (Curicó Valley) $9. 83 *—M.S. (7/1/2006)*

Aresti 2002 Montemar Gewürztraminer (Curicó Valley) $8. 82 *—M.S. (7/1/2003)*

Aresti 2005 Merlot (Curicó Valley) $9. Perfectly nice and approachable; this slightly sweet and easy Merlot has just enough depth and heft to satisfy serious wine drinkers but also a cheerful, simple presentation that will satiate novices. Good feel, healthy and dripping with raspberry and plum flavors. 87*—M.S. (5/1/2007)*

Aresti 2004 Merlot (Curicó Valley) $9. 82 *—M.S. (7/1/2006)*

Aresti 2003 Merlot (Chile) $8. 82 *—M.S. (11/1/2005)*

Aresti 2000 Montemar Merlot (Curicó Valley) $8. 81 *—D.T. (7/1/2002)*

Aresti 1999 Montemar Merlot (Curicó Valley) $8. 85 Best Buy *(9/1/2000)*

Aresti 1999 Reserva Merlot (Rio Claro) $11. 87 Best Buy *(9/1/2000)*

Aresti 2004 Reserve Merlot (Rio Claro) $13. 83 *—M.S. (7/1/2006)*

Aresti 2001 Reserve Merlot (Rio Claro) $11. 82 *—M.S. (7/1/2003)*

Aresti 2000 Reserve Merlot (Rio Claro) $11. 86 *—M.S. (3/1/2002)*

Aresti 2005 Estate Selection Pinot Noir (Curicó Valley) $11. Light in color, with dry, simple aromas of cherries and cinnamon. This is a pretty nice effort given the wine's price. It has some sweet, chocolaty side notes to go with finishing toast and pepper. 85 *—M.S. (5/1/2007)*

Aresti 2006 Sauvignon Blanc (Curicó Valley) $9. 84 *—M.S. (11/15/2006)*

Aresti 2005 Sauvignon Blanc (Curicó Valley) $9. 84 *—M.S. (7/1/2006)*

Aresti 2004 Sauvignon Blanc (Curicó Valley) $8. 84 Best Buy *—M.S. (11/1/2005)*

Aresti 2002 Montemar Sauvignon Blanc (Curicó Valley) $8. 83 *—M.S. (7/1/2003)*

Aresti 2000 Montemar Sauvignon Blanc (Curicó Valley) $8. 86 Best Buy *—M.M. (8/1/2001)*

Aresti 1999 Reserva Sauvignon Blanc (Rio Claro) $11. 87 *(9/1/2000)*

Aresti 2001 Reserve Sauvignon Blanc (Rio Claro) $11. 82 *—M.S. (7/1/2003)*

Aresti 2005 Winemakers' Sauvignon Blanc (Leyda Valley) $17. 82 *—M.S. (7/1/2006)*

BALDUZZI

Balduzzi 1999 Reserva Cabernet Sauvignon (Maule Valley) $11. 81 *—M.S. (7/1/2003)*

Balduzzi 2001 Reserva Chardonnay (Maule Valley) $9. 80 *—M.S. (7/1/2003)*

BARON PHILIPPE DE ROTHSCHILD

Baron Philippe de Rothschild 2000 Escudo Rojo Bordeaux Blend (Chile) $15. 88 Best Buy *—D.T. (7/1/2002)*

Baron Philippe de Rothschild 2001 Reserva Cabernet Sauvignon (Maipo Valley) $10. 86 Best Buy *—M.S. (3/1/2004)*

Baron Philippe de Rothschild 2000 Reserva Cabernet Sauvignon (Maipo Valley) $10. 85 *—P.G. (12/1/2002)*

Baron Philippe de Rothschild 2001 Reserva Carmenère (Rapel Valley) $10. 87 Best Buy *—P.G. (12/1/2002)*

Baron Philippe de Rothschild 2001 Reserva Chardonnay (Casablanca Valley) $10. 85 *—P.G. (12/1/2002)*

Baron Philippe de Rothschild 2004 Escudo Rojo Red Blend (Maipo Valley) $15. Early aromas are earthy, sort of like coffee grinds mixed with baked fruit. The palate hits with a dose of creamy milk chocolate, while later on berries and vanilla rise up. More of a plump, sweet and unctuous wine made from Cabernet Sauvignon, Carmenère, Syrah and Cabernet Franc. Imported by North Lake Wines. 85 *—M.S. (11/15/2007)*

Baron Philippe de Rothschild 2003 Escudo Rojo Red Blend (Maipo Valley) $15. 87 *—M.S. (5/1/2006)*

Baron Philippe de Rothschild 2001 Escudo Rojo Red Blend (Maipo Valley) $15. 86 *—S.H. (1/1/2002)*

Baron Philippe de Rothschild 1999 Escudo Rojo Red Blend (Maipo Valley) $15. 81 *—S.H. (11/20/2002)*

BIG FAT LLAMA

Big Fat Llama 2005 Cabernet Sauvignon (Chile) $8. 83 *—M.S. (11/15/2006)*

Big Fat Llama 2005 Chardonnay (Chile) $8. 83 *—M.S. (7/1/2006)*

BOTALCURA

Botalcura 2003 La Porfia Grand Reserve Cabernet Sauvignon (Rapel Valley) $20. 86 *(10/1/2006)*

Botalcura 2002 La Porfia Grand Reserve Cabernet Sauvignon (Maule Valley) $18. 84 *—M.S. (2/1/2005)*

Botalcura 2003 Reserve El Delirio Cabernet Sauvignon (Maule Valley) $11. 87 Best Buy *—M.S. (7/1/2006)*

Botalcura 2003 La Porfia Grand Reserve Carmenère (Curicó Valley) $20. 85 *(10/1/2006)*

Botalcura 2002 La Porfia Grand Reserve Carmenère (Central Valley) $18. 83 *—M.S. (7/1/2005)*

Botalcura 2004 La Porfia Grand Reserve Chardonnay (Casablanca Valley) $20. 84 *(10/1/2006)*

Botalcura 2005 El Delirio Chardonnay-Viognier (Central Valley) $12. 87 Best Buy *(10/1/2006)*

Botalcura 2003 La Porfia Grand Reserve Malbec (Maipo Valley) $20. 85 *(10/1/2006)*

Botalcura 2004 El Delirio Merlot (Central Valley) $12. 84 *(10/1/2006)*

Botalcura 2003 El Delirio Merlot (Central Valley) $13. 86 *—M.S. (2/1/2005)*

Botalcura 2004 Reserve El Delirio Syrah-Malbec Red Blend (Central Valley) $11. 84 *—M.S. (7/1/2006)*

Botalcura 2005 El Delirio Sauvignon Blanc (Casablanca Valley) $12. 85 *(10/1/2006)*

CALAMA

Calama 2001 Cabernet Sauvignon (Central Valley) $6. 83 *—M.S. (7/1/2003)*

Calama 2002 Chardonnay (Casablanca Valley) $9. 86 *—M.S. (7/1/2003)*

Calama 2001 Merlot (Casablanca Valley) $9. 83 *—M.S. (7/1/2003)*

Calama 2002 Sauvignon Blanc (Curicó Valley) $6. 82 *—M.S. (7/1/2003)*

CALCU

Calcu 2005 Red Blend (Colchagua Valley) $12. A new brand out of Colchagua. The wine is rather herbal and gamy, with mildly green strawberry and raspberry flavors. A final wave of dill and tomato leaf on the finish pretty much seals it away as a greener wine. The blend is Cabernet Sauvignon, Cab Franc and Carmenère. Imported by Global Vineyard Importers. 82 *—M.S. (11/15/2007)*

CALIBORO ESTATE

Caliboro Estate 2004 Erasmo Bordeaux Blend (Maule Valley) $27. Three years into this upper-level project from Francesco Marone of Italy and we're still waiting for that blockbuster success. The 2004 is a very good wine with darkness, licorice and coffee aromas backed by red berry and plum flavors. It has a ripped mouthfeel and structure, but it's also a touch tart at its core. Will 2005 offer more? 88 *—M.S. (9/1/2007)*

Caliboro Estate 2002 Erasmo Bordeaux Blend (Maule Valley) $30. 87 *—M.S. (3/1/2006)*

Caliboro Estate 2001 Erasmo Bordeaux Blend (Maule Valley) $30. 88 *—M.S. (11/1/2005)*

CALINA

Calina 2001 Cabernet-Carmenere Cabernet Blend (Maule Valley) $14. 90 Best Buy *—S.H. (12/1/2002)*

Calina 2000 Reserve-Cabernet Sauvignon/Carmenere Cabernet Blend (Maule Valley) $13. 86 *—D.T. (7/1/2002)*

Calina 1999 Bravura Cabernet Sauvignon (Colchagua Valley) $50. 89 *—M.S. (7/1/2003)*

Calina 2005 Reserva Cabernet Sauvignon (Rapel Valley) $8. On the whole, Calina is a solid, textbook Chilean Cabernet, meaning it's endowed with blackberry, plum, tobacco and cola aromas and flavors. The finish shows a little oak in the form of mocha, while the feel is pleasant. Nothing earth-shaking, but perfectly good. Imported by Sovereign Wine Imports. 86 Best Buy *—M.S. (5/1/2007)*

Calina 2004 Reserva Cabernet Sauvignon (Colchagua Valley) $8. Slightly prickly from the start, but snappy throughout. Raspberry, cherry and red plum flavors are short and mildly pickled; however, the zest and mouthfeel of the wine are more than adequate. 83 *—M.S. (3/1/2007)*

Calina 2002 Reserva Cabernet Sauvignon (Colchagua Valley) $9. 84 *—M.S. (10/1/2006)*

Calina 2000 Reserve Cabernet Sauvignon (Colchagua Valley) $8. 84 *—S.H. (6/1/2001)*

Calina 2001 Bravura Cabernet Sauvignon-Merlot (Maule Valley) $40. 88 *—M.S. (7/1/2006)*

Calina 1999 Carmenère (Maule Valley) $7. 88 Best Buy *—M.M. (1/1/2004)*

Calina 2005 Alcance Carmenère (Maule Valley) $15. The Calina label seems to have hit its stride; this Carmenère opens with scents of black fruit, dill sprigs and chocolate. The palate broadens with olive, plum, blackberry and coffee flavors, and as a whole it comes together with a certain ease that announces it's on the money. 90 Best Buy *—M.S. (11/15/2007)*

Calina 2004 Alcance Carmenère (Maule Valley) $15. 85 *—M.S. (7/1/2006)*

Calina 2005 Reserva Carmenère (Maule Valley) $8. Granted, the nose deals a full blast of Carmenère's typical tomato, olive and peppery aromas, but the body is just right and the palate features some core fruit that's dark, ripe and rippled with proper tannins and acidity. Anyone curious about Carmenère will be well served starting here. 87 Best Buy *—M.S. (5/1/2007)*

Calina 2004 Reserva Carmenère (Maule Valley) $9. 84 *—M.S. (7/1/2006)*

Calina 2002 Reserve Carmenère (Maule Valley) $8. 85 Best Buy *—M.S. (6/1/2004)*

Calina 2001 Reserve Carmenère (Maule Valley) $8. 85 *—S.H. (12/1/2002)*

Calina 2000 Reserve Carmenère (Maule Valley) $8. 90 *—S.H. (11/15/2001)*

Calina 2001 Chardonnay (Casablanca Valley) $8. 86 Best Buy *—S.H. (1/1/2002)*

Calina 2005 Reserva Chardonnay (Casablanca Valley) $8. Every Calina 2005 wine we tried was rock-solid and deserving of Best Buy notoriety. This one delivers ripe pear and melon aromas in front of apple and nectarine flavors. All in all it's a full-bodied, plump Chard with good enough balance and acidity that it seems entirely fresh. Imported by Sovereign Wine Imports. 87 Best Buy *—M.S. (5/1/2007)*

Calina 2003 Reserva Chardonnay (Casablanca Valley) $9. 88 Best Buy *—M.S. (7/1/2006)*

Calina 2002 Reserve Chardonnay (Casablanca Valley) $8. 85 Best Buy *—M.S. (8/1/2004)*

Calina 2000 Reserve Chardonnay (Casablanca Valley) $8. 86 Best Buy *—M.S. (7/1/2002)*

Calina 1996 Merlot (Maule Valley) $16. 90 *(11/15/1999)*

Calina 2005 Alcance Merlot (Maule Valley) $15. Menthol, cola and pepper are just some of the deep aromas that work the nose on this heavyweight Merlot (14.5%). The flavors of black currants, plum and oak are good up front but fall off somewhat on the midpalate and finish. Structured, firm and tannic, especially for Chilean Merlot. 87 *—M.S. (11/15/2007)*

Calina 2005 Reserva Merlot (Maule Valley) $8. If you don't mind some sweetness on both the nose and palate, then you'll be thrilled with this affordable Merlot that pulses with plum and berry flavors in front of a sculpted, perfectly clean finish. Nothing complicated, yet for clarity, fullness and energy it's a high scorer. 87 Best Buy *—M.S. (5/1/2007)*

Calina 2003 Reserva Merlot (Maule Valley) $9. 84 *—M.S. (7/1/2006)*

Calina 2002 Reserve Merlot (Maule Valley) $8. 87 Best Buy *—M.S. (8/1/2004)*

Calina 2001 Reserve Merlot (Maule Valley) $8. 86 *—M.S. (7/1/2003)*

Calina 2000 Reserve Merlot (Maule Valley) $8. 85 *—S.H. (6/1/2001)*

CALITERRA

Caliterra 1998 Cabernet Sauvignon (Central Valley) $8. 84 *—M.S. (12/1/1999)*

Caliterra 2002 Cabernet Sauvignon (Central Valley) $8. 87 Best Buy *—M.S. (6/1/2004)*

Caliterra 2000 Cabernet Sauvignon (Colchagua Valley) $9. 87 *—M.S. (3/1/2002)*

Caliterra 1999 Cabernet Sauvignon (Central Valley) $8. 87 Best Buy *—S.H. (2/1/2001)*

Caliterra 1998 Arboleda Cabernet Sauvignon (Maipo Valley) $20. 85 *—S.H. (2/1/2003)*

Caliterra 2005 Reserva Cabernet Sauvignon (Colchagua Valley) $11. Plenty of barrel-driven coffee and mocha aromas set the stage for cassis, black cherry and vanilla flavors. Feelwise, this is a moderately tight, structured wine with persistence and power. The finish, meanwhile, is chocolaty and stout. It's yet another well-priced '05 Cabernet out of Chile. 89 Best Buy *—M.S. (3/1/2007)*

Caliterra 2002 Reserva Cabernet Sauvignon (Colchagua Valley) $15. 84 *—M.S. (11/1/2005)*

Caliterra 1997 Reserve Cabernet Sauvignon (Maipo Valley) $13. 88 Best Buy *—M.S. (12/1/1999)*

Caliterra 2005 Tribute Cabernet Sauvignon (Colchagua Valley) $17. Aromas of tree bark, cola, mushroom and black olive get this Cab going, while on the palate it keeps that savory-over-fruity character by showing meaty, mildly herbal flavors. It's full, a bit tannic and grabby, but overall it has an honest feel and integrity. 87 —*M.S. (11/15/2007)*

Caliterra 2004 Tribute Cabernet Sauvignon (Colchagua Valley) $17. 86 —*M.S. (11/15/2006)*

Caliterra 2001 Carmenère (Colchagua Valley) $20. 86 —*M.S. (3/1/2002)*

Caliterra 1999 Arboleda Carmenère (Maipo Valley) $20. 85 —*S.H. (2/1/2003)*

Caliterra 2005 Tribute Carmenère (Colchagua Valley) $17. Caliterra's Tribute series, if this is any example, features pretty heavy oak treatment. Here we're talking sawmill style, meaning the nose is buxom and burnt. In the mouth, wood overshadows fruit. And even when you get to the heart of it, the wine's kind of acidic and sharp. 83 —*M.S. (9/1/2007)*

Caliterra 2003 Chardonnay (Central Valley) $8. 86 Best Buy —*M.S. (2/1/2005)*

Caliterra 2001 Chardonnay (Central Valley) $8. 88 Best Buy —*S.H. (12/1/2002)*

Caliterra 2000 Chardonnay (Central Valley) $10. 85 *(10/1/2001)*

Caliterra 1999 Chardonnay (Central Valley) $8. 86 —*S.H. (2/1/2001)*

Caliterra 2005 Reserva Chardonnay (Curicó Valley) $11. 86 Best Buy —*M.S. (10/1/2006)*

Caliterra 2003 Reserva Chardonnay (Casablanca Valley) $13. 87 —*M.S. (7/1/2005)*

Caliterra 2005 Tribute Chardonnay (Casablanca Valley) $17. 85 —*M.S. (10/1/2006)*

Caliterra 2005 Tribute Malbec (Colchagua Valley) $17. Not really sure what happened here. The 2004 Caliterra Tribute Malbec was a solid, ripe wine. This one, to the contrary, is decidedly foxy, with tangy fruit and herbal edges. And it's chalky and grabby on the finish, which sort of eliminates Malbec's natural friendliness. 83 —*M.S. (11/15/2007)*

Caliterra 2004 Tribute Malbec (Colchagua Valley) $17. 88 —*M.S. (10/1/2006)*

Caliterra 2003 Merlot (Rapel Valley) $7. 83 —*M.S. (7/1/2005)*

Caliterra 2002 Merlot (Central Valley) $8. 83 —*M.S. (3/1/2004)*

Caliterra 2001 Merlot (Central Valley) $8. 83 —*D.T. (7/1/2002)*

Caliterra 2000 Merlot (Rapel Valley) $8. 84 —*S.H. (6/1/2001)*

Caliterra 1999 Merlot (Central Valley) $10. 85 *(10/1/2001)*

Caliterra 1998 Merlot (Central Valley) $8. 83 —*S.H. (2/1/2001)*

Caliterra 1999 Arboleda Merlot (Colchagua Valley) $20. 84 —*S.H. (5/1/2001)*

Caliterra 2005 Reserva Merlot (Colchagua Valley) $11. Slightly roasted and rubbery, with basic Merlot aromas of plums, berries and bramble bush. The palate runs sort of sweet, with round plum and blackberry flavors. And on the finish you may find some licorice and chocolate to make things more complex. 86 Best Buy —*M.S. (3/1/2007)*

Caliterra 2004 Sauvignon Blanc (Central Valley) $7. 84 Best Buy —*M.S. (7/1/2005)*

Caliterra 2003 Sauvignon Blanc (Central Valley) $8. 85 Best Buy —*M.S. (6/1/2004)*

Caliterra 2001 Sauvignon Blanc (Central Valley) $7.86 —*M.S. (3/1/2002)*

Caliterra 2000 Sauvignon Blanc (Central Valley) $9. 86 Best Buy *(10/1/2001)*

Caliterra 1999 Sauvignon Blanc (Central Valley) $8. 84 —*S.H. (2/1/2001)*

Caliterra 2006 Reserva Sauvignon Blanc (Curicó Valley) $11. This Sauvignon Blanc shows some true Chilean character; there's pungency and snap to it. The palate hits with solid citrus and then pineapple and green apple notes take over on the finish. Shows balance at all checkpoints. 86 Best Buy —*M.S. (9/1/2007)*

Caliterra 2005 Tribute Shiraz (Colchagua Valley) $17. Heavy aromas of horse stable and compost give this wine a classic "barnyard" nose, and while it does settle somewhat it always maintains its bramble and tomato flavor profile. This is herbal, rough Shiraz and no matter the size or oak it's a tough trek. 81 —*M.S. (9/1/2007)*

Caliterra 2004 Tribute Shiraz (Colchagua Valley) $17. 88 —*M.S. (10/1/2006)*

Caliterra 2001 Syrah (Central Valley) $NA. 83 —*M.S. (6/1/2004)*

Caliterra 2000 Syrah (Central Valley) $8. 84 —*D.T. (7/1/2002)*

Caliterra 1999 Arboleda Syrah (Colchagua Valley) $20. 83 —*S.H. (2/1/2003)*

CANEPA

Canepa 1997 Private Reserve Cabernet Sauvignon (Curicó Valley) $12. 85 —*M.S. (11/15/1999)*

Canepa 1998 Chardonnay (Rancagua) $10. 80 —*M.S. (11/15/1999)*

Canepa 1999 Sauvignon Blanc (Cachapoal Valley) $8. 84 —*M.S. (11/15/1999)*

CARMEN

Carmen 1999 Reserve Cabernet Blend (Maipo Valley) $15. 89 Best Buy —*S.H. (12/1/2002)*

Carmen 2002 Cabernet Sauvignon (Maipo Valley) $7. 83 —*M.S. (3/1/2004)*

Carmen 1999 Cabernet Sauvignon (Central Valley) $8. 84 —*D.T. (8/1/2001)*

Carmen 1998 Cabernet Sauvignon (Central Valley) $8. 84 —*M.M. (1/1/2004)*

Carmen 2003 Classic Cabernet Sauvignon (Maipo Valley) $7. 84 *(12/15/2004)*

Carmen 2003 Estate Grown Reserve Cabernet Sauvignon (Maipo Valley) $13. 88 Best Buy —*M.S. (7/1/2006)*

Carmen 2000 Estate Grown Reserve Cabernet Sauvignon (Maipo Valley) $15. 88 —*M.S. (7/1/2003)*

Carmen 2002 Gold Reserve Cabernet Sauvignon (Maipo Valley) $50. 86 —*M.S. (12/31/2006)*

Carmen 2001 Gold Reserve Cabernet Sauvignon (Maipo Valley) $70. 88 —*M.S. (7/1/2005)*

Carmen 1997 Gold Reserve Cabernet Sauvignon (Maipo Valley) $65. 88 *(2/1/2001)*

Carmen 1999 Gold reserve Estate Bottled Single Vineyard Cabernet Sauvignon (Maipo Valley) $65. 88 —*C.S. (12/1/2002)*

Carmen 2003 Nativa Cabernet Sauvignon (Maipo Valley) $16. 83 —*M.S. (12/15/2005)*

Carmen 2002 Nativa Cabernet Sauvignon (Maipo Valley) $16. 86 —*M.S. (7/1/2005)*

Carmen 2001 Nativa Cabernet Sauvignon (Maipo Valley) $16. 84 —*M.S. (7/1/2005)*

Carmen 1999 Nativa Cabernet Sauvignon (Maipo Valley) $15. 85 —*M.S. (3/1/2002)*

Carmen 2000 Nativa Organic Wine Cabernet Sauvignon (Maipo Valley) $15. 87 —*M.S. (12/1/2002)*

Carmen 2004 Reserve Cabernet Sauvignon (Maipo Valley) $15. 84 —*M.S. (11/15/2006)*

Carmen 2002 Reserve Cabernet Sauvignon (Maipo Valley) $14. 87 *(12/15/2004)*

Carmen 2001 Reserve Cabernet Sauvignon (Maipo Valley) $15. 85 —*M.S. (3/1/2004)*

Carmen 1999 Reserve Cabernet Sauvignon (Maipo Valley) $15. 87 —*M.S. (3/1/2002)*

Carmen 1998 Reserve Cabernet Sauvignon (Maipo Valley) $17. 88 *(2/1/2001)*

Carmen 2004 Carmenère (Rapel Valley) $7. 85 Best Buy —*M.S. (3/1/2006)*

Carmen 2003 Carmenère (Rapel Valley) $7. 82 —*M.S. (11/1/2005)*

Carmen 2001 Carmenère (Rapel Valley) $7. 85 Best Buy —*M.S. (7/1/2003)*

Carmen 2004 Reserve Carmenère-Cabernet Sauvignon (Maipo Valley) $15. 89 —*M.S. (12/31/2006)*

Carmen 2002 Reserve Carmenère-Cabernet Sauvignon (Maipo Valley) $16. 86 —*M.S. (11/1/2005)*

Carmen 1999 Chardonnay (Central Valley) $8. 84 —*M.S. (8/1/2000)*

Carmen 2004 Chardonnay (Casablanca Valley) $7. 84 Best Buy —*M.S. (5/1/2006)*

Carmen 2001 Chardonnay (Central Valley) $8. 85 —*M.S. (3/1/2002)*

Carmen 2004 Classic Chardonnay (Casablanca Valley) $7. 85 Best Buy *(12/15/2004)*

Carmen 2002 Classic Chardonnay (Central Valley) $8. 85 Best Buy —*M.S. (7/1/2003)*

Carmen 2003 Nativa Chardonnay (Maipo Valley) $14. 86 —*M.S. (7/1/2005)*

Carmen 2000 Nativa Chardonnay (Maipo Valley) $13. 87 —*M.S. (3/1/2002)*

Carmen 1999 Nativa Chardonnay (Maipo Valley) $15. 82 *(8/1/2001)*

Carmen 1997 Reserva Chardonnay (Maipo Valley) $11. 85 —*M.N. (2/1/2001)*

Carmen 2005 Reserve Chardonnay (Casablanca Valley) $12. 88 Best Buy —*M.S. (10/1/2006)*

Carmen 2004 Reserve Chardonnay (Casablanca Valley) $12. 86 —*M.S. (7/1/2006)*

Carmen 2003 Reserve Chardonnay (Casablanca Valley) $13. 85 —*M.S. (11/1/2005)*

Carmen 2001 Reserve Chardonnay (Maipo Valley) $13. 87 —*M.S. (3/1/2002)*

Carmen 2000 Reserve Chardonnay (Maipo Valley) $17. 84 —*M.M. (8/1/2001)*

Carmen 2004 Wine Maker's Reserve Chardonnay (Casablanca Valley) $25. Not so sure about the freshness and lasting power of this 2004 white, but at this point in time it's holding the line. The nose offers oak and roasted nuts, with lemon curd and butterscotch backing things up. Meanwhile, the mouth deals tangy melon and peanut brittle. At its peak now. 86 —*M.S. (11/15/2007)*

Carmen 2002 Winemaker's Reserve Chardonnay (Casablanca Valley) $45. 83 —*M.S. (7/1/2005)*

Carmen 1999 Winemaker's Reserve Chardonnay (Casablanca Valley) $40. 85 —*J.C. (3/1/2002)*

Carmen 1997 Winemaker's Reserve Chardonnay (Casablanca Valley) $25. 89 —*M.M. (1/1/2004)*

Carmen 2005 Gewürztraminer (Curicó Valley) $7. 85 Best Buy —*M.S. (7/1/2006)*

Carmen 2004 Merlot (Rapel Valley) $7. 83 —*M.S. (3/1/2006)*

Carmen 2002 Merlot (Rapel Valley) $7. 85 Best Buy —*M.S. (8/1/2004)*

Carmen 2003 Classic Merlot (Rapel Valley) $7. 85 Best Buy *(12/15/2004)*

Carmen 2004 Reserve Merlot (Casablanca Valley) $13. 86 —*M.S. (10/1/2006)*

Carmen 2003 Reserve Merlot (Casablanca Valley) $13. 86 —*M.S. (12/15/2005)*

Carmen 2002 Reserve Merlot (Rapel Valley) $14. 87 *(12/15/2004)*

Carmen 2001 Reserve Merlot (Rapel Valley) $15. 87 —*M.S. (3/1/2004)*

Carmen 1999 Reserve Merlot (Rapel Valley) $15. 85 —*J.C. (3/1/2002)*

Carmen 1998 Reserve Merlot (Rapel Valley) $15. 89 —*M.N. (2/1/2001)*

Carmen 2000 Reserve Estate Grown Merlot (Rapel Valley) $15. 85 —*S.H. (12/1/2002)*

Carmen 2003 Reserve Petite Sirah (Maipo Valley) $15. 88 —*M.S. (5/1/2006)*

Carmen 1997 Reserve Petite Sirah (Chile) $14. 84 —*M.S. (11/15/1999)*

Carmen 1999 Reserve Pinot Noir (Maipo Valley) $17. 83 —*J.C. (3/1/2002)*

Carmen 1999 Reserve Carmenère/Cabernet Sauvignon Red Blend (Maipo Valley) $17. 84 —*D.T. (7/1/2002)*

Carmen 2001 Wine Maker's Reserve Red Blend (Maipo Valley) $40. 88 —*M.S. (10/1/2006)*

Carmen 1999 Winemaker's Reserve Red Blend (Maipo Valley) $40. 90 Editors' Choice —*C.S. (12/1/2002)*

Carmen 1997 Winemaker's Reserve Red Blend (Maipo Valley) $40. 91 Editors' Choice —*M.N. (2/1/2001)*

Carmen 2000 Winemaker's Reserve Red Red Blend (Maipo Valley) $40. 91 Editors' Choice —*M.S. (11/1/2005)*

Carmen 2005 Sauvignon Blanc (Curicó Valley) $7. 86 Best Buy —*M.S. (3/1/2006)*

Carmen 2004 Classic Sauvignon Blanc (Curicó Valley) $7. 83 *(12/15/2004)*

Carmen 2002 Classic Sauvignon Blanc (Central Valley) $7. 85 Best Buy —*M.S. (7/1/2003)*

Carmen 2005 Reserve Sauvignon Blanc (Casablanca Valley) $12. 81 —*M.S. (7/1/2006)*

Carmen 2004 Reserve Sauvignon Blanc (Casablanca Valley) $12. 86 —*M.S. (11/1/2005)*

Carmen 2003 Reserve Sauvignon Blanc (Casablanca Valley) $14. 84 *(12/15/2004)*

Carmen 2002 Reserve Sauvignon Blanc (Casablanca Valley) $13. 87 —*M.S. (6/1/2004)*

Carmen 2001 Reserve Sauvignon Blanc (Casablanca Valley) $13. 86 —*M.S. (3/1/2002)*

Carmen 2004 Shiraz (Maipo Valley) $7. 85 Best Buy —*M.S. (3/1/2006)*

Carmen 2003 Reserve Shiraz (Maipo Valley) $14. 87 —*M.S. (11/1/2005)*

Carmen 2002 Reserve Shiraz (Maipo Valley) $17. 85 —*M.S. (2/1/2005)*

Carmen 2003 Reserve Shiraz-Cabernet Sauvignon (Maipo Valley) $15. 87 —*M.S. (3/1/2006)*

Carmen 1999 Reserve Syrah-Cabernet (Maipo Valley) $17. 85 —*D.T. (7/1/2002)*

Carmen 2005 Rosé Syrah-Cabernet (Maipo Valley) $10. 84 —*M.S. (11/15/2006)*

CARTA VIEJA

Carta Vieja 2003 Chardonnay (Maule Valley) $8. 81 —*M.S. (7/1/2005)*

Carta Vieja 2001 Estate Bottled Chardonnay (Maule Valley) $6. 84 Best Buy —*M.S. (7/1/2003)*

Carta Vieja 2003 Sauvignon Blanc (Maule Valley) $8. 83 —*M.S. (7/1/2005)*

CASA JULIA

Casa Julia 2002 Cabernet Sauvignon (Maipo Valley) $8. 86 Best Buy —*M.S. (7/1/2003)*

Casa Julia 2000 Cabernet Sauvignon (Maipo Valley) $9. 82 *(7/1/2002)*

Casa Julia 2002 Reserve Cabernet Sauvignon (Maipo Valley) $15. 87 —*M.S. (2/1/2005)*

Casa Julia 2001 Reserve Cabernet Sauvignon (Maipo Valley) $12. 88 Best Buy —*M.S. (7/1/2003)*

Casa Julia 2003 Merlot (Rapel Valley) $10. 85 Best Buy —*M.S. (2/1/2005)*

Casa Julia 2002 Merlot (Rapel Valley) $8. 85 Best Buy —*M.S. (7/1/2003)*

Casa Julia 2001 Merlot (Chile) $9. 89 Best Buy —*C.S. (11/15/2002)*

Casa Julia 2000 Merlot (Rapel Valley) $9. 85 —*D.T. (7/1/2002)*

Casa Julia 2000 Reserve Merlot (Maipo Valley) $12. 85 —*D.T. (7/1/2002)*

Casa Julia 2003 Sauvignon Blanc (Maule Valley) $10. 82 —*M.S. (7/1/2005)*

Casa Julia 2001 Sauvignon Blanc (Maule Valley) $8. 87 Best Buy —*M.S. (7/1/2003)*

Casa Julia 2001 Syrah (Maipo Valley) $8. 84 —*M.S. (7/1/2003)*

CASA LAPOSTOLLE

Casa Lapostolle 2005 Cabernet Sauvignon (Rapel Valley) $12. Bargain hunters should stalk this toasty, firm, well-made Cab because there aren't many better in the price range. The palate features pure dark cherry and cassis flavors, while the structure is tight but not hard. Finishes with coffee and sweet, ripe tannins. Drink now and all the way through 2008. 89 Best Buy —*M.S. (9/1/2007)*

Casa Lapostolle 2004 Cabernet Sauvignon (Rapel Valley) $10. 86 Best Buy —*M.S. (7/1/2006)*

Casa Lapostolle 2003 Cabernet Sauvignon (Rapel Valley) $10. 90 Best Buy —*M.S. (11/1/2005)*

Casa Lapostolle 2002 Cabernet Sauvignon (Rapel Valley) $10. 88 Best Buy *(3/1/2005)*

Casa Lapostolle 1999 Cabernet Sauvignon (Rapel Valley) $10. 81 —*J.C. (3/1/2002)*

Casa Lapostolle 1997 Cabernet Sauvignon (Rapel Valley) $12. 91 Best Buy —*M.S. (11/15/1999)*

Casa Lapostolle 1999 Cuvée Alexandre Cabernet Sauvignon (Colchagua Valley) $20. 90 —*M.S. (3/1/2002)*

Casa Lapostolle 1998 Cuvée Alexandre Cabernet Sauvignon (Colchagua Valley) $25. 85 —*D.T. (8/1/2001)*

Casa Lapostolle 2005 Cuvée Alexandre Apalta Vineyard Cabernet Sauvignon (Colchagua Valley) $23. It doesn't take an expert to quickly realize that this is a fine Cabernet. The nose deals potent black cherry and char, while airing unleashes a subtle perfume and floral notes. In the mouth, there's ripe berry flavors and chocolate, while late in the game the tannins stay smooth but tight. A congruent wine with no flaws. Ready now or ageable for a couple of years. 91 —*M.S. (9/1/2007)*

Casa Lapostolle 2004 Cuvée Alexandre Apalta Vineyard Cabernet Sauvignon (Colchagua Valley) $22. 90 —*M.S. (5/1/2006)*

Casa Lapostolle 2003 Cuvée Alexandre Apalta Vineyard Cabernet Sauvignon (Colchagua Valley) $21. 91 Editors' Choice —*M.S. (11/1/2005)*

Casa Lapostolle 2001 Cuvée Alexandre Apalta Vineyard Cabernet Sauvignon (Colchagua Valley) $22. 92 Editors' Choice *(3/1/2005)*

Casa Lapostolle 2001 Estate Bottled Cabernet Sauvignon (Rapel Valley) $12. 90 Editors' Choice —*M.S. (7/1/2003)*

Casa Lapostolle 2006 Chardonnay (Casablanca Valley) $11. Basic pear, apple and melon—your so-called usual suspects—work the bouquet, while on the palate it's largely about oak-infused candied fruit. Overall the wine comes across confected and sugary, and the finish is resiny. Soft in acidity thus soft in mouthfeel. 83 —*M.S. (9/1/2007)*

Casa Lapostolle 2005 Chardonnay (Casablanca Valley) $12. A little bit of out-of-place oak guards the nose, making you think that it's just popcorn, peanuts and Cracker Jack. But beyond the sweet, toasty character there's tropical fruit, solid acidity and good overall balance. 85 —*M.S. (5/1/2007)*

Casa Lapostolle 2003 Chardonnay (Casablanca Valley) $10. 87 Best Buy *(3/1/2005)*

Casa Lapostolle 2002 Chardonnay (Casablanca Valley) $12. 86 —*M.S. (6/1/2004)*

Casa Lapostolle 2001 Chardonnay (Casablanca Valley) $10. 88 Best Buy —*M.S. (11/15/2003)*

Casa Lapostolle 2000 Chardonnay (Casablanca Valley) $10. 85 —*M.S. (3/1/2002)*

Casa Lapostolle 2002 Cuvée Alexandre Chardonnay (Casablanca Valley) $17. 89 —*M.S. (6/1/2004)*

Casa Lapostolle 2000 Cuvée Alexandre Chardonnay (Casablanca Valley) $18. 87 —*M.S. (3/1/2002)*

Casa Lapostolle 2005 Cuvée Alexandre Atalayas Vineyard Chardonnay (Casablanca Valley) $20. 89 —*M.S. (12/31/2006)*

Casa Lapostolle 2004 Cuvée Alexandre Atalayas Vineyard Chardonnay (Casablanca Valley) $18. 89 —*M.S. (3/1/2006)*

Casa Lapostolle 2003 Cuvée Alexandre Atalayas Vineyard Chardonnay (Casablanca Valley) $18. 90 Editors' Choice *(3/1/2005)*

Casa Lapostolle 2005 Merlot (Rapel Valley) $13. An early blast of green bean and bell pepper soon subsides, leaving black currant, cherry and black pepper in its wake. The palate is healthy and sturdy, with cherry and cassis flavors mingling with mildly persistent green notes. While not vegetal, this Merlot does show some classic large-production characteristics: namely, dilution of fruit and a light herbaceousness. 86 —*M.S. (3/1/2007)*

Casa Lapostolle 2003 Merlot (Rapel Valley) $10. 86 Best Buy *(3/1/2005)*

Casa Lapostolle 2000 Merlot (Rapel Valley) $11. 81 —*J.C. (3/1/2002)*

Casa Lapostolle 1999 Merlot (Rapel Valley) $14. 88 —*J.C. (2/1/2001)*

Casa Lapostolle 2001 Cuvée Alexandre Merlot (Colchagua Valley) $20. 88 —*M.S. (6/1/2004)*

Casa Lapostolle 1999 Cuvée Alexandre Merlot (Colchagua Valley) $25. 89 —*M.S. (3/1/2002)*

Casa Lapostolle 1998 Cuvée Alexandre Merlot (Rapel Valley) $22. 85 —*J.F. (8/1/2001)*

Casa Lapostolle 2005 Cuvée Alexandre Apalta Vineyard Merlot (Colchagua Valley) $23. Dense and solid, this is top-flight Chilean Merlot without any hints of green to drag it down. The nose deals polished oak and bright berry aromas; the palate offers a perfect feel and impressive plum, berry, chocolate and vanilla flavors. Properly tannic and balanced. 91 Editors' Choice —*M.S. (9/1/2007)*

Casa Lapostolle 2004 Cuvée Alexandre Apalta Vineyard Merlot (Colchagua Valley) $20. 87 —*M.S. (7/1/2006)*

Casa Lapostolle 2003 Cuvée Alexandre Apalta Vineyard Merlot (Colchagua Valley) $21. 90 Editors' Choice —*M.S. (12/15/2005)*

Casa Lapostolle 2002 Cuvée Alexandre Apalta Vineyard Merlot (Colchagua Valley) $19. 91 Editors' Choice *(3/1/2005)*

Casa Lapostolle 2004 Estate Bottled Merlot (Rapel Valley) $12. 88 Best Buy —*M.S. (3/1/2006)*

Casa Lapostolle 2002 Estate Bottled Merlot (Rapel Valley) $12. 88 Best Buy —*M.S. (7/1/2003)*

Casa Lapostolle 2001 Apalta Red Blend (Colchagua Valley) $55. 88 —*M.S. (6/1/2004)*

Casa Lapostolle 2003 Borobo Red Blend (Rapel Valley-Casablanca Valley) $70. Ripe and full on both the bouquet and palate. It's a rich wine from a good year, and thus the prune, licorice and chocolate aromas take center stage. In the mouth, this multigrape blend that ranges from Bordeaux varieties to Pinot Noir is on the money. It's round, rewarding and full of deep black fruit and sweet, balancing fudge and candy. Better sooner than later, seeing that the perceptible acidity is minor. 92 —*M.S. (9/1/2007)*

Casa Lapostolle 2001 Borobo Red Blend (Rapel Valley-Casablanca Valley) $65. 90 —*M.S. (3/1/2006)*

Casa Lapostolle 2004 Clos Apalta Red Blend (Colchagua Valley) $70. Attractive mint and spice aromas play with herbal black fruit on the firm bouquet, and after that there's plenty of blackberry and plum to propel the palate. As always, this is a premier Chilean red blend that grafts pure power to elegance. It may not have the potency and density of fruit of the 2003, but it isn't lacking. 91 —*M.S. (9/1/2007)*

Casa Lapostolle 2003 Clos Apalta Red Blend (Colchagua Valley) $65. 94 Editors' Choice —*M.S. (5/1/2006)*

Casa Lapostolle 2002 Clos Apalta Red Blend (Colchagua Valley) $65. 92 Editors' Choice *(3/1/2005)*

Casa Lapostolle 1999 Clos Apalta Red Blend (Chile) $60. 94 Editors' Choice —*M.S. (3/1/2002)*

Casa Lapostolle 2006 Sauvignon Blanc (Rapel Valley) $11. Every year the price on this wine creeps up and yet the quality falls. The 2006 is a load and a half at 14.5%, and it has virtually no zest or acidity to keep it balanced. It's full of banana and mealy pear flavors, and the pleasure quotient is close to zero. 81 —*M.S. (9/1/2007)*

Casa Lapostolle 2005 Sauvignon Blanc (Rapel Valley) $10. 83 —*M.S. (3/1/2006)*

Casa Lapostolle 2004 Sauvignon Blanc (Rapel Valley) $8. 86 Best Buy *(3/1/2005)*

Casa Lapostolle 2001 Sauvignon Blanc (Casablanca Valley) $8. 85 —*M.S. (3/1/2002)*

Casa Lapostolle 2000 Sauvignon Blanc (Rapel Valley) $9. 86 —*M.M. (2/1/2001)*

Casa Lapostolle 2003 Estate Bottled Sauvignon Blanc (Rapel Valley) $9. 85 —*M.S. (6/1/2004)*

Casa Lapostolle 2004 Cuvée Alexandre Syrah (Cachapoal Valley) $26. Immediately pleasurable, with luscious aromas of ripe fruits and savory oak. This winery is getting very good results from its high-end Syrah, as evidenced by this jammy, dark wine that's charred, toasty and loaded with the essentials. Drink now or hold for a couple of years. 90 —*M.S. (5/1/2007)*

Casa Lapostolle 2002 Cuvée Alexandre Syrah (Rapel Valley) $22. 91 Editors' Choice *(3/1/2005)*

Casa Lapostolle 2001 Cuvée Alexandre Syrah (Rapel Valley) $20. 88 —*M.S. (7/1/2003)*

Casa Lapostolle 2003 Cuvée Alexandre Requinoa Vineyard Syrah (Rapel Valley) $23. 89 —*M.S. (11/1/2005)*

CASA RIVAS

Casa Rivas 2001 Reserva Estate Bottled Cabernet Sauvignon (Maipo Valley) $10. 84 —*M.S. (12/1/2002)*

Casa Rivas 2003 Carmenère (Maipo Valley) $7. 81 —*M.S. (11/1/2005)*

Casa Rivas 2002 Carmenère (Maipo Valley) $7. 83 —*M.S. (6/1/2004)*

Casa Rivas 2001 Estate Bottled Carmenère (Maipo Valley) $6. 83 —*M.S. (7/1/2003)*

Casa Rivas 2002 Gran Reserva Carmenère (Maipo Valley) $22. 86 —*M.S. (6/1/2004)*

Casa Rivas 2003 Chardonnay (Maipo Valley) $7. 81 —*M.S. (6/1/2004)*

Casa Rivas 2002 Estate Bottled Chardonnay (Maipo Valley) $6. 84 —*M.S. (7/1/2003)*

Casa Rivas 2001 Reserva Estate Bottled Chardonnay (Maipo Valley) $10. 85 —*M.S. (7/1/2003)*

Casa Rivas 2003 Merlot (Maipo Valley) $7. 82 —*M.S. (7/1/2005)*

Casa Rivas 2002 Merlot (Maipo Valley) $7. 85 —*M.S. (6/1/2004)*

Casa Rivas 2001 Estate Bottled Merlot (Maipo Valley) $6. 86 —*K.F. (12/1/2002)*

Casa Rivas 2002 Reserva Merlot (Maipo Valley) $11. 85 —*M.S. (7/1/2005)*

Casa Rivas 2003 Sauvignon Blanc (Maipo Valley) $7. 86 Best Buy —*M.S. (6/1/2004)*

CASA SILVA

Casa Silva 1999 Altura Cabernet Blend (Colchagua Valley) $90. 91 Cellar Selection —*M.S. (3/1/2002)*

Casa Silva 2000 Quinta Generacion Cabernet Blend (Colchagua Valley) $25. 88 —*M.S. (7/1/2003)*

Casa Silva 1999 Quinta Generacion Cabernet Blend (Colchagua Valley) $20. 89 —*M.S. (3/1/2002)*

Casa Silva 2003 Los Lingues Gran Reserva Cabernet Sauvignon (Colchagua Valley) $17. 89 —*M.S. (5/1/2006)*

Casa Silva 2004 Reserva Cabernet Sauvignon (Colchagua Valley) $10. 88 Best Buy —*M.S. (5/1/2006)*

Casa Silva 2000 Classic Carmenère (Colchagua Valley) $10. 88 Best Buy —*M.S. (3/1/2002)*

Casa Silva 2003 Los Lingues Gran Reserva Carmenère (Colchagua Valley) $17. 88 —*M.S. (3/1/2006)*

Casa Silva 2002 Los Lingues Gran Reserva Carmenère (Colchagua Valley) $17. 88 —*M.S. (3/1/2006)*

Casa Silva 2004 Reserva Carmenère (Colchagua Valley) $10. 86 Best Buy —*M.S. (3/1/2006)*

Casa Silva 2000 Reserve Carmenère (Colchagua Valley) $15. 89 —*M.S. (3/1/2002)*

Casa Silva 2001 Reserve Est Bottled Carmenère (Colchagua Valley) $15. 88 —*M.S. (7/1/2003)*

Casa Silva 2001 Classic Chardonnay (Colchagua Valley) $10. 87 Best Buy —*M.S. (3/1/2002)*

Casa Silva 2003 Angostura Gran Reserva Merlot (Colchagua Valley) $17. 87 —*M.S. (5/1/2006)*

Casa Silva 2000 Reserve Merlot (Colchagua Valley) $15. 88 —*M.S. (3/1/2002)*

Casa Silva 2002 Quinta Generacion Red Blend (Colchagua Valley) $22. 88 —*M.S. (5/1/2006)*

Casa Silva 2003 Lolol Gran Reserva Shiraz (Colchagua Valley) $17. 88 —*M.S. (3/1/2006)*

Casa Silva 2003 Reserva Shiraz (Colchagua Valley) $10. 85 Best Buy —*M.S. (3/1/2006)*

Casa Silva 2001 Quinta Generacion White Blend (Colchagua Valley) $23. 82 —*M.S. (7/1/2003)*

Casa Silva 2000 Quinta Generacion White Blend (Colchagua Valley) $20. 86 —*M.S. (3/1/2002)*

Casa Silva 2003 Quinta Generación White Blend (Colchagua Valley) $17. 86 —*M.S. (7/1/2006)*

CASA VERDI

Casa Verdi 2004 Aniceto Reserve Cabernet Sauvignon (Aconcagua Valley) $13. 86 —*M.S. (5/1/2006)*

CHÂTEAU LA JOYA

Château La Joya 2000 Gran Reserva Cabernet Sauvignon (Colchagua Valley) $16. 86 —*M.S. (3/1/2002)*

Château La Joya 1998 Gran Reserva Cabernet Sauvignon (Colchagua Valley) $15. 87 *(6/1/2001)*

Château La Joya 2000 Reserva Cabernet Sauvignon (Colchagua Valley) $12. 85 —*M.S. (3/1/2002)*

Château La Joya 1999 Reserva Cabernet Sauvignon (Colchagua Valley) $10. 87 Best Buy *(6/1/2001)*

Château La Joya 1998 Cuvée Premium Carmenère (Colchagua Valley) $28. 90 Editors' Choice *(6/1/2001)*

Château La Joya 2000 Gran Reserva Carmenère (Colchagua Valley) $20. 88 —*M.S. (3/1/2002)*

Château La Joya 2001 Estate Bottled Reserve Chardonnay (Colchagua Valley) $12. 87 Best Buy —*M.S. (7/1/2003)*

Château La Joya 1999 Gran Reserva Chardonnay (Colchagua Valley) $10. 86 *(6/1/2001)*

Château La Joya 1998 Gran Reserva Chardonnay (Colchagua Valley) $15. 84 —*M.N. (2/1/2001)*

Château La Joya 2000 Reserva Chardonnay (Colchagua Valley) $10. 84 *(6/1/2001)*

Château La Joya 1999 Selection Chardonnay (Colchagua Valley) $11. 83 —*M.N. (2/1/2001)*

Château La Joya 2001 Estate Bottled Reserve Malbec (Colchagua Valley) $12. 84 —*M.S. (7/1/2003)*

Château La Joya 2000 Reserva Malbec (Colchagua Valley) $NA. 84 —*M.S. (3/1/2002)*

Château La Joya 1999 Estate Bottled Gran Reserve Merlot (Colchagua Valley) $15. 87 —*C.S. (2/1/2003)*

Château La Joya 2000 Estate Bottled Reserve Merlot (Colchagua Valley) $12. 87 Best Buy —*K.F. (7/1/2003)*

Château La Joya 2000 Gran Reserva Merlot (Colchagua Valley) $16. 87 —*M.S. (3/1/2002)*

Château La Joya 1998 Gran Reserva Merlot (Colchagua Valley) $15. 89 Best Buy *(6/1/2001)*

Château La Joya 1999 Reserva Merlot (Colchagua Valley) $10. 84 *(6/1/2001)*

Château La Joya 2000 Reserva Sauvignon Blanc (Colchagua Valley) $10. 85 *(6/1/2001)*

CHÂTEAU LOS BOLDOS

Château Los Boldos 1998 Grand Cru Cabernet Sauvignon (Requinoa) $45. 89 —*C.S. (12/1/2002)*

Château Los Boldos 2003 Grand Reserve Cabernet Sauvignon (Requinoa) $11. 86 —*M.S. (5/1/2006)*

Château Los Boldos 2003 Tradition Cabernet Sauvignon (Requinoa) $8. 84 Best Buy —*M.S. (7/1/2006)*

Château Los Boldos 2000 Vieilles Vignes Cabernet Sauvignon (Requinoa) $20. 89 —*M.S. (5/1/2006)*

Château Los Boldos 1999 Vielles Vignes Cabernet Sauvignon (Requinoa) $20. 87 —*C.S. (12/1/2002)*

Château Los Boldos 1997 Grand Cru Cabernet Sauvignon-Merlot (Requinoa) $40. 87 —*D.T. (7/1/2002)*

Château Los Boldos 2005 Grand Reserve Carmenère (Requinoa) $11. 83 —*M.S. (3/1/2006)*

Château Los Boldos 2005 Tradition Carmenère (Requinoa) $8. 83 —*M.S. (3/1/2006)*

Château Los Boldos 1999 CLB Reserve Chardonnay (Rapel Valley) $14. 82 —*M.S. (7/1/2003)*

Château Los Boldos 2001 Vielles Vignes Chardonnay (Requinoa) $16. 86 —*M.S. (7/1/2003)*

Château Los Boldos 2003 Grand Reserve Merlot (Requinoa) $11. 83 —*M.S. (7/1/2006)*

Château Los Boldos 2004 Altitude Red Blend (Requinoa) $11. 86 —*M.S. (3/1/2006)*

Château Los Boldos 2005 Tradition Shiraz (Requinoa) $8. 82 —*M.S. (3/1/2006)*

CHILCAS

Chilcas 2005 Cabernet Sauvignon (Central Valley) $7. A little bit of oak and forest gives this basic Cab some early complexity, and in the mouth it doesn't disappoint. There's nice red fruit and some grabby tannins and acids. It's a true everyday performer that should please most red-wine drinkers. 86 Best Buy —*M.S. (9/1/2007)*

Chilcas 2005 Colina Negra Cabernet Sauvignon (Maule Valley) $15. A full and solid wine with some leather and robust oak on the nose backed by racier cherry and plum flavors. The mnouthfeel and balance are both good, and overall the wine is packed to its core with berry boldness and choppy, serious tannins. 87 —*M.S. (11/15/2007)*

Chilcas 2005 Reserva Cabernet Sauvignon (Maule Valley) $9. Nice cherry and raspberry aromas work the front end, while the palate is defined by simple but ripe berry and red plum flavors. This easy-going Cab works the red-fruit end of the spectrum, and there's just enough complexity throughout to push it to the next level. 87 Best Buy —*M.S. (9/1/2007)*

Chilcas 2005 Reserva Carmenère (Rapel Valley) $9. Cola, coffee and leathery dark-fruit aromas carry the bouquet. Next comes a palate of snappy cherry and raspberry fruit that's neither flat nor flabby. Call it a little racy and rambunctious if you will, but better that it dances on your tongue rather than falling asleep. 87 Best Buy —*M.S. (9/1/2007)*

Chilcas 2006 Chardonnay (Central Valley) $7. A light coating of toasty, buttery oak creates just the right woodiness, while the pear, honey and quince flavors are entirely inviting and pleasant. There's even some warm nuttiness on the delicate finish. A go-for-it Chard at this price. 87 Best Buy —*M.S. (9/1/2007)*

Chilcas 2006 Reserva Chardonnay (Maule Valley) $9. In this case "reserva" equals heavily oaked, and the nose exhibits a bit too much toast and popcorn. The palate is also pretty woody but it's salvaged by baked apple, lemon and pecan flavors. Finishes slightly grabby, with some peach flavor and a hint of resin. 84 —*M.S. (9/1/2007)*

Chilcas 2006 Rio Azul Chardonnay (Casablanca Valley) $15. Soft and simple on the nose, with bulk. Size more than substance seems to be the theme here. The palate is a wide load of apple cider and nondescript citrus, while the back end and finish are chunky and lose focus as they rumble along. A forward wine but what's it really aiming to be? 84 —*M.S. (9/1/2007)*

Chilcas 2005 Merlot (Central Valley) $7. After an early blast of mint and menthol, the nose works its way toward solid berry, spice and vanilla flavors. The finish is round and moderately long, with no sharp angles or jagged edges. Good yet standard Merlot at a welcome price point. 85 Best Buy —*M.S. (11/15/2007)*

Chilcas 2005 Red One Red Blend (Maule Valley) $15. A blend of five red grapes, and it's neither here nor there. The nose is mildly jammy and plenty oaky, while the red-fruit palate is tangy and sharp. At the scale this one comes up short; there's hardly any mouthfeel to it. 82 —*M.S. (11/15/2007)*

Chilcas 2006 Sauvignon Blanc (Central Valley) $7. Punchbowl aromas carry some sweetness, but the flavor package is pure green fruit and citrus, with maybe a touch of pink grapefruit. It's wet, refreshing and pretty good in terms of balance and feel. 85 Best Buy *—M.S. (9/1/2007)*

Chilcas 2006 Aguas Frescas Sauvignon Blanc (Casablanca Valley) $15. A standout Casablanca Valley Sauvignon for $15? Yes. Right from the start the pure, defined citrus and grass aromas draw you in. After that, the grapefruit on the palate is clean and quenching, while on the fringe there's a hint of pickle and green apple. Overall it's a wine that pushes the right buttons. 90 Best Buy *—M.S. (9/1/2007)*

Chilcas 2006 Reserva Sauvignon Blanc (Colchagua Valley) $9. Chilcas is a new-to-us label that seems to be on the right path. This Sauvignon is round and melony, with fresh aromas and zesty flavors of grapefruit, kiwi and tangerine. There's even elevated finishing notes of grass and green herbs. Tasty Chilean white for under $10. Grab it and drink that night. 88 Best Buy *—M.S. (9/1/2007)*

Chilcas 2005 Reserva Syrah (Rapel Valley) $9. The bouquet blends barnyard and black currants, so in that way it's classic and pretty good. The palate, however, is tangy, short and more "red" in style than the nose leads you to expect. Good freshness and aromas but maybe more tangy and tight than Chilean Syrah should be. 84 *—M.S. (9/1/2007)*

CHILENSIS

Chilensis 2005 Cabernet Sauvignon (Central Valley) $7. Perfectly good Cab is what you get here. The nose deals some char and leather, but largely it features clean fruit scents. The palate may be a bit short, but along the way the flavors of cassis and berries are commendable. Well done for a value wine. 86 Best Buy *—M.S. (9/1/2007)*

Chilensis 2005 Reserva Cabernet Sauvignon (Central Valley) $9. A bit rubbery and earthy at first, and then it steps it up to deliver generic but good sweet-and-sour red fruit along with lean, easy tannins. There's nothing complicated or special about this; it's basic Cabernet done decently. 84 Best Buy *—M.S. (11/15/2007)*

Chilensis 2005 Carmenère (Central Valley) $7. Warm and chunky, with a fair amount of compost and mushroom to the bouquet. Flavors of lean raspberries and green herbs are less than stunning, while the mouthfeel seems a bit crisp and tight. Adequate but not very generous or ripe. 83 *—M.S. (9/1/2007)*

Chilensis 2005 Reserva Carmenère (Rapel Valley) $9. Plenty of barrel char and spice get it going, and behind those aromas there's leather and meaty fruit aromas. Flavors of plum, blackberry and chocolate work the palate, while the finish is easy going and smooth but fairly innocuous in its feel and lasting impression. 85 Best Buy *—M.S. (9/1/2007)*

Chilensis 2005 Chardonnay (Central Valley) $7. Mealy and flat, with oily flavors of baked apples and bitter walnuts. Not a disaster but devoid of personality and pulse. 81 *—M.S. (11/15/2007)*

Chilensis 2005 Reserva Chardonnay (Casablanca Valley) $9. A step up from the regular Chardonnay but still a wine with issues. In this case, we're talking about lack of excitement and style. The wine has body, citrus, tropical fruit and a bit of nuttiness, but it falls short of crossing the line that separates the better wines from the average ones. 84 *—M.S. (11/15/2007)*

Chilensis 2005 Merlot (Central Valley) $7. Sweet and spicy up front, but also sort of foxy and herbal. The palate pushes plum, berry and vanilla, while the finish is short, mildly bitter and seemingly a bit burnt. 83 *—M.S. (11/15/2007)*

Chilensis 2005 Reserva Sauvignon Blanc (Casablanca Valley) $9. Light and airy, with floral apple and cleanser aromas. The palate is sweet and melony, but is it Sauvignon Blanc? Hard to tell, really; this tastes as much like your average jug white as it does Sauvignon Blanc. 81 *—M.S. (9/1/2007)*

Chilensis 2004 Syrah (Central Valley) $7. Leather and spice are the more appealing aromas, while the palate features tightly wound but limited raspberry and red berry flavors. A narrow wine with snap, acidity and tartness but not much wealth or richness. 82 *—M.S. (9/1/2007)*

Chilensis 2005 Reserva Syrah (Central Valley) $9. Heavy and mossy, with foresty aromas that transition toward burnt. The palate runs scratchy and sharp, with red plum and cherry skin flavors. Has its qualities but in general it runs with too much heat and friction. 82 *—M.S. (9/1/2007)*

CONCHA Y TORO

Concha y Toro 2004 Casillero del Diablo Cabernet Sauvignon (Central Valley) $9. 87 Best Buy *—M.S. (11/1/2005)*

Concha y Toro 2003 Casillero del Diablo Cabernet Sauvignon (Central Valley) $9. 86 Best Buy *—M.S. (8/1/2004)*

Concha y Toro 2001 Casillero del Diablo Cabernet Sauvignon (Central Valley) $10. 85 *—M.S. (12/1/2002)*

Concha y Toro 2000 Casillero del Diablo Cabernet Sauvignon (Maipo Valley) $10. 85 *(12/31/2001)*

Concha y Toro 1999 Casillero del Diablo Cabernet Sauvignon (Maipo Valley) $11. 84 *(1/1/2004)*

Concha y Toro 1998 Casillero del Diablo Cabernet Sauvignon (Maipo Valley) $10. 85 *—M.S. (12/1/1999)*

Concha y Toro 2005 Casillero del Diablo Reserve Cabernet Sauvignon (Central Valley) $9. Here's proof that Chile and Cabernet go together like birds of a feather. The wine is full of black cherry and cassis flavors, and the mouthfeel is exceedingly fresh and proper. And the vanilla and chocolate-covered espresso beans on the finish are a classy ending touch. 87 Best Buy *—M.S. (3/1/2007)*

Concha y Toro 2004 Don Melchor Cabernet Sauvignon (Puente Alto) $50. In recent years, with winemaker Enrique Tirado firmly at the helm, Don Melchor has gotten better and better. And while 2004 was an average year in Chile, this ranks as the best Melchor we've sampled. The wine has beautiful blackberry, cola and pepper aromas in front of cassis, cherry, plum, nutmeg and cinnamon flavors. It's brawny but balanced, with excellent natural acidity. Best from 2008–2012. 92 *—M.S. (11/15/2007)*

Concha y Toro 2002 Don Melchor Cabernet Sauvignon (Puente Alto) $47. 91 *—M.S. (5/1/2006)*

Concha y Toro 1999 Don Melchor Cabernet Sauvignon (Puente Alto) $40. 91 *—M.S. (6/1/2004)*

Concha y Toro 1998 Don Melchor Cabernet Sauvignon (Maipo Valley) $40. 87 *—M.S. (3/1/2002)*

Concha y Toro 2003 Don Melchor Vintage 17 Cabernet Sauvignon (Puente Alto) $47. 90 Cellar Selection *—M.S. (10/1/2006)*

Concha y Toro 2002 Marques de Casa Concha Cabernet Sauvignon (Puente Alto) $14. 89 Best Buy *—M.S. (8/1/2004)*

Concha y Toro 2001 Marques de Casa Concha Cabernet Sauvignon (Rapel Valley) $16. 91 Editors' Choice *—M.S. (3/1/2004)*

Concha y Toro 2000 Marques de Casa Concha Cabernet Sauvignon (Maipo Valley) $14. 89 Best Buy *—M.S. (12/1/2002)*

Concha y Toro 1999 Marques de Casa Concha Cabernet Sauvignon (Puente Alto) $15. 87 *(12/31/2001)*

Concha y Toro 1997 Marques de Casa Concha Cabernet Sauvignon (Maipo Valley) $14. 86 *—M.S. (12/1/1999)*

Concha y Toro 1997 Private Reserve Don Melchor Cabernet Sauvignon (Maipo Valley) $40. 88 *—M.S. (2/1/2001)*

Concha y Toro 2003 Terrunyo Cabernet Sauvignon (Pirque) $28. 91 Editors' Choice *—M.S. (7/1/2006)*

Concha y Toro 2002 Terrunyo Cabernet Sauvignon (Pirque) $28. 88 *—M.S. (11/1/2005)*

Concha y Toro 2001 Terrunyo Cabernet Sauvignon (Maipo Valley) $29. 92 Cellar Selection *—M.S. (3/1/2004)*

Concha y Toro 1999 Terrunyo Cabernet Sauvignon (Pirque) $29. 90 *—M.S. (3/1/2002)*

Concha y Toro 1997 Terrunyo Cabernet Sauvignon (Maipo Valley) $29. 87 *—J.C. (2/1/2001)*

Concha y Toro 1997 Trio Cabernet Sauvignon (Maipo Valley) $9. 84 *—M.S. (12/1/1999)*

Concha y Toro 2004 Xplorador Cabernet Sauvignon (Central Valley) $7. 86 Best Buy *—M.S. (11/1/2005)*

Concha y Toro 2003 Xplorador Cabernet Sauvignon (Central Valley) $7. 87 Best Buy *—M.S. (12/1/2004)*

Concha y Toro 2001 Xplorador Cabernet Sauvignon (Maipo Valley) $8. 85 Best Buy *—M.S. (7/1/2003)*

Concha y Toro 1999 Xplorador Cabernet Sauvignon (Maipo Valley) $8. 83 *—J.C. (2/1/2001)*

Concha y Toro 2003 Carmín de Peumo Carmenère (Peumo) $74. Setting a new high bar for Carmenère is this luxury version from Concha y Toro's Cachapoal vineyard. And while it deserves to be drunk sooner than later, we recommend it for the best steak you grill this year. It's a strapped, juicy wine with tons of coffee, chocolate and berry essence. It's too hard or layered, so get at it soon for its upfront fruit and character. 92 *—M.S. (11/15/2007)*

Concha y Toro 2004 Casillero del Diablo Carmenère (Central Valley) $9. 88 Best Buy *—M.S. (3/1/2006)*

Concha y Toro 2003 Casillero del Diablo Carmenère (Rapel Valley) $10. 87 Best Buy *—M.S. (5/30/2005)*

Concha y Toro 2001 Casillero Del Diablo Carmenère (Rapel Valley) $10. 84 *—M.S. (12/1/2002)*

Concha y Toro 2005 Casillero del Diablo Reserve Carmenère (Central Valley) $9. A plump, round, mostly welcoming bouquet sets you up for full cherry, strawberry, plum and sucking candy flavors. Feels good across the palate and finishes sturdy, with a touch of overt vanilla oak. Like always, this represents everyday Carmenère in fine form. 86 Best Buy —*M.S. (5/1/2007)*

Concha y Toro 2003 Frontera Carmenère (Central Valley) $11. 84 Best Buy —*R.V. (11/15/2004)*

Concha y Toro 2003 Terrunyo Carmenère (Cachapoal Valley) $28. 90 —*M.S. (3/1/2006)*

Concha y Toro 2002 Terrunyo Carmenère (Cachapoal Valley) $28. 90 —*M.S. (7/1/2005)*

Concha y Toro 2001 Terrunyo Carmenère (Cachapoal Valley) $28. 89 —*M.S. (8/1/2004)*

Concha y Toro 2000 Terrunyo Carmenère (Peumo) $29. 91 —*M.S. (7/1/2003)*

Concha y Toro 1999 Terrunyo Carmenère (Peumo) $29. 91 —*M.S. (3/1/2002)*

Concha y Toro 2004 Terrunyo Block 27 Carmenère (Peumo) $28. Every year one of Chile's most earnestly made Carmenères is Terrunyo, and the 2004, while a touch softer and less focused than the '03, is still a very nice wine that offers the best this grape can deliver. It's a plump internationally-styled red with berry syrup and chocolate flavors, while the finish is rich, chewy and smooth. Drink now through 2008. 89 —*M.S. (11/15/2007)*

Concha y Toro 2005 Amelia Chardonnay (Casablanca Valley) $35. Sort of heavy, with touches of baked corn and hay. But it also has nice baked apple flavors and pretty good oak. On the finish, there's vanilla, almond, citrus and apple, and then very late comes hazelnut and even more vanilla. Drink now; it's not going to last much longer. 88 —*M.S. (11/15/2007)*

Concha y Toro 2004 Amelia Chardonnay (Casablanca Valley) $35. 88 —*M.S. (7/1/2006)*

Concha y Toro 2003 Amelia Chardonnay (Casablanca Valley) $34. 88 —*M.S. (7/1/2005)*

Concha y Toro 2002 Amelia Chardonnay (Casablanca Valley) $33. 90 —*M.S. (3/1/2004)*

Concha y Toro 1997 Amelia Chardonnay (Casablanca Valley) $18. 88 —*M.S. (12/1/1999)*

Concha y Toro 2001 Amelia Limited Release Chardonnay (Casablanca Valley) $33. 88 —*M.S. (7/1/2003)*

Concha y Toro 2001 Block 25 Terrunyo Chardonnay (Casablanca Valley) $25. 91 —*M.S. (7/1/2003)*

Concha y Toro 2005 Casillero del Diablo Chardonnay (Casablanca Valley) $9. One of the best under-$10 Chardonnays anywhere is Casillero del Diablo, made by Marcelo Papa of Concha y Toro. The wine overdelivers on the nose, where custard, lemon blossom and buttered popcorn work in tandem to set up eye-opening apple, melon and light mineral flavors. Not heavy but still full and toasty. A rewarding and generous wine; get it while you can. 88 Best Buy —*M.S. (5/1/2007)*

Concha y Toro 2004 Casillero del Diablo Chardonnay (Central Valley) $9. 87 Best Buy —*M.S. (11/1/2005)*

Concha y Toro 2003 Casillero del Diablo Chardonnay (Casablanca Valley) $10. 87 Best Buy —*M.S. (3/1/2004)*

Concha y Toro 2001 Casillero del Diablo Chardonnay (Casablanca Valley) $10. 86 Best Buy —*M.S. (7/1/2003)*

Concha y Toro 2000 Casillero del Diablo Chardonnay (Casablanca Valley) $10. 86 Best Buy *(12/31/2001)*

Concha y Toro 1998 Casillero del Diablo Chardonnay (Casablanca Valley) $10. 85 —*M.S. (12/1/1999)*

Concha y Toro 2005 Marques de Casa Concha Chardonnay (Pirque) $19. If oak is your thing, this has plenty of it. The nose is heavily toasted and the palate is loaded with cinnamon, nuts and wood spice. But in between the layers of oak there's nectarine, peach and tropical fruit flavors that are of high quality. Drink as soon as possible; the wine is beginning to soften and lose its snap. 88 —*M.S. (9/1/2007)*

Concha y Toro 2004 Marques de Casa Concha Chardonnay (Pirque) $16. 87 —*M.S. (5/1/2006)*

Concha y Toro 2002 Marques de Casa Concha Chardonnay (Casablanca Valley) $15. 88 —*M.S. (3/1/2004)*

Concha y Toro 2000 Marques de Casa Concha Chardonnay (Pirque) $15. 90 Editors' Choice *(12/31/2001)*

Concha y Toro 1997 Marques de Casa Concha Chardonnay (Maipo Valley) $14. 87 —*M.S. (12/1/1999)*

Concha y Toro 2002 Terrunyo Chardonnay (Casablanca Valley) $25. 89 —*M.S. (3/1/2004)*

Concha y Toro 2000 Terrunyo Chardonnay (Casablanca Valley) $25. 88 —*M.S. (3/1/2002)*

Concha y Toro 1998 Trio Chardonnay (Casablanca Valley) $9. 84 —*M.S. (12/1/1999)*

Concha y Toro 2004 Xplorador Chardonnay (Central Valley) $7. 86 Best Buy —*M.S. (11/1/2005)*

Concha y Toro 2003 Xplorador Chardonnay (Central Valley) $7. 86 Best Buy —*M.S. (6/1/2004)*

Concha y Toro 2002 Xplorador Chardonnay (Casablanca Valley) $7. 84 —*M.S. (3/1/2004)*

Concha y Toro 2001 Xplorador Chardonnay (Casablanca Valley) $7. 86 Best Buy —*M.S. (7/1/2003)*

Concha y Toro 2000 Xplorador Chardonnay (Casablanca Valley) $8. 88 Best Buy —*M.M. (8/1/2001)*

Concha y Toro 1999 Xplorador Chardonnay (Casablanca Valley) $8. 84 —*J.C. (2/1/2001)*

Concha y Toro 2004 Casillero del Diablo Merlot (Central Valley) $9. 85 Best Buy —*M.S. (11/1/2005)*

Concha y Toro 2003 Casillero del Diablo Merlot (Central Valley) $10. 88 Best Buy —*M.S. (3/1/2004)*

Concha y Toro 2001 Casillero del Diablo Merlot (Rapel Valley) $10. 83 —*C.S. (12/1/2002)*

Concha y Toro 2000 Casillero del Diablo Merlot (Rapel Valley) $10. 86 *(12/31/2001)*

Concha y Toro 2005 Marques de Casa Concha Merlot (Peumo) $19. The first thing you take from this wine is that it has a strong herbal/green element to the nose. Now that could be Chilean Merlot in its most natural form or it could indicate some ripeness issues. Regardless, the wine shows a full body and power but also olive flavors and rock-hard tannins. Imported by Excelsior Wine & Spirits. 86 —*M.S. (11/15/2007)*

Concha y Toro 2002 Marques de Casa Concha Merlot (Peumo) $14. 89 Best Buy —*M.S. (6/1/2004)*

Concha y Toro 2001 Marques de Casa Concha Merlot (Peumo) $14. 87 —*M.S. (7/1/2003)*

Concha y Toro 2000 Marques de Casa Concha Merlot (Rapel Valley) $14. 88 Best Buy —*M.S. (12/1/2002)*

Concha y Toro 1999 Marques de Casa Concha Merlot (Peumo) $15. 88 —*J.C. (12/31/2001)*

Concha y Toro 1997 Marques de Casa Concha Merlot (Rapel Valley) $14. 84—*M.S. (12/1/1999)*

Concha y Toro 2004 Marqués de Casa Concha Merlot (Peumo) $19. 90 Editors' Choice —*M.S. (10/1/2006)*

Concha y Toro 2003 Marqués de Casa Concha Merlot (Peumo) $14. 89 Best Buy —*M.S. (11/1/2005)*

Concha y Toro 1998 Trio Merlot (Rapel Valley) $9. 80 —*M.S. (12/1/1999)*

Concha y Toro 2004 Xplorador Merlot (Central Valley) $7. 83 —*M.S. (11/1/2005)*

Concha y Toro 2003 Xplorador Merlot (Central Valley) $7. 85 Best Buy —*M.S. (8/1/2004)*

Concha y Toro 2002 Xplorador Merlot (Rapel Valley) $7. 87 Best Buy —*M.S. (7/1/2003)*

Concha y Toro 2000 Xplorador Merlot (Rapel Valley) $8. 85 Best Buy *(12/31/2001)*

Concha y Toro 1999 Xplorador Merlot (Rapel Valley) $8. 85 —*J.C. (2/1/2001)*

Concha y Toro 2002 Block 30 Terrunyo Sauvignon Blanc (Casablanca Valley) $20. 89 —*M.S. (7/1/2003)*

Concha y Toro 2007 Casillero del Diablo Sauvignon Blanc (Central Valley) $10. Simple and spry, with pulsating citrus aromas and flavors that convey a sense of purity and purpose. This boasts lively grapefruit, lime and stone-fruit notes in front of a clean, alert finish. Versatile enough to serve with oysters or mussels, or as an apéritif. 87 Best Buy —*M.S. (11/15/2007)*

Concha y Toro 2005 Casillero del Diablo Sauvignon Blanc (Central Valley) $9. 84 —*M.S. (5/1/2006)*

Concha y Toro 2004 Casillero del Diablo Sauvignon Blanc (Central Valley) $10. 85 Best Buy —*M.S. (7/1/2005)*

Concha y Toro 2003 Casillero del Diablo Sauvignon Blanc (Central Valley) $10. 86 Best Buy —*M.S. (3/1/2004)*

Concha y Toro 1998 Casillero del Diablo Sauvignon Blanc (Maipo Valley) $10. 86 —*M.S. (12/1/1999)*

Concha y Toro 1999 Late Harvest Sauvignon Blanc (Maule Valley) $15. 89 —*J.M. (12/1/2002)*

Concha y Toro 2001 Late Harvest Private Reserve Sauvignon Blanc (Maule Valley) $14. 88 *—M.S. (5/1/2006)*

Concha y Toro 2006 Terrunyo Sauvignon Blanc (Casablanca Valley) $25. Meticulous winemaker Ignacio Recabarren has been working and working the Terrunyo Sauvignon Blanc for the past five years and in 2006 he seems to have nailed it. You can smell and taste its purity and style. The citrus and minerality are unparalleled in Chile, while the finish is as long as the country it comes from. 91 Editors' Choice *—M.S. (5/1/2007)*

Concha y Toro 2005 Terrunyo Sauvignon Blanc (Casablanca Valley) $25. 89 *—M.S. (10/1/2006)*

Concha y Toro 2004 Terrunyo Sauvignon Blanc (Casablanca Valley) $21. 90 Editors' Choice *(7/1/2005)*

Concha y Toro 2003 Terrunyo Sauvignon Blanc (Casablanca Valley) $20. 90 *—M.S. (3/1/2004)*

Concha y Toro 2001 Terrunyo Sauvignon Blanc (Casablanca Valley) $20. 88 *—M.S. (3/1/2002)*

Concha y Toro 1999 Terrunyo Sauvignon Blanc (Casablanca Valley) $29. 88 *—J.C. (2/1/2001)*

Concha y Toro 2004 Terrunyo Block 34 Shiraz (Cachapoal Valley) $28. 92 Editors' Choice *—M.S. (7/1/2006)*

Concha y Toro 2003 Marques de Casa Concha Syrah (Peumo) $16. 89 Editors' Choice *—M.S. (11/1/2005)*

Concha y Toro 2004 Marqués de Casa Concha Syrah (Peumo) $19. 91 Editors' Choice *—M.S. (10/1/2006)*

CONDE DE VELÀZQUEZ

Conde de Velàzquez 2001 El Conde Gran Reserva Cabernet Sauvignon (Aconcagua Valley) $10. 84 *—M.S. (7/1/2005)*

Conde de Velázquez 2004 Estate Vintage Cabernet Sauvignon (Aconcagua Valley) $15. As good a wine from Conde de Velázquez as we've come across. This reserve-level Cab starts with tight cherry aromas but evolves on the palate with plum, berry and cough drop flavors. Sizable, thorough and well balanced, with body and structure. 88 *—M.S. (9/1/2007)*

Conde de Velàzquez 2001 Estate Vintage Cabernet Sauvignon (Aconcagua Valley) $13. 85 *—M.S. (7/1/2005)*

Conde de Velázquez 2003 Reserva Cabernet Sauvignon (Aconcagua Valley) $8. Rubbery and drying, with aromas of barrel char and butter that overpower any fruit that might want to escape. Simple plum and cherry flavors work the palate, but they're fading. And the finish is drying and lightly tannic. 83 *—M.S. (9/1/2007)*

Conde de Velàzquez 2001 Reserva Cabernet Sauvignon (Aconcagua Valley) $7. 81 *—M.S. (7/1/2005)*

Conde de Velàzquez 2002 Reserva Cabernet Sauvignon-Carmenère (Aconcagua Valley) $7. 80 *—M.S. (7/1/2005)*

Conde de Velázquez 2005 El Conde Gran Reserva Chardonnay (Aconcagua Valley) $11. Soft and supple aromas of baked peach and squash register sort of mushy, while the palate is plump and sweet, with cantaloupe the overriding flavor. This is a heavy, grabby wine that won't last too long, so get at it soon. 83 *—M.S. (5/1/2007)*

Conde de Velàzquez 2003 El Conde Gran Reserva Chardonnay (Aconcagua Valley) $11. 84 *—M.S. (11/1/2005)*

Conde de Velázquez 2005 Reserva Chardonnay (Aconcagua Valley) $8. An innocuous Chardonnay that stays basic and largely expressionless from start to finish. Along the way are spots of melon, stone fruits and vanilla. All in all, it's an acceptable wine with a round, smooth mouthfeel but simple flavors. 83 *—M.S. (5/1/2007)*

Conde de Velàzquez 2003 Reserva Merlot (Aconcagua Valley) $7. 83 *—M.S. (11/1/2005)*

Conde de Velázquez 2004 Don Raphael Reserva Merlot (Aconcagua Valley) $9. A little weak in color and density, this lightweight Merlot offers dry, peppery aromas in front of modest wild berry flavors. It's a touch choppy and woody. 83 *—M.S. (11/15/2007)*

Conde de Velázquez 2005 El Conde Gran Reserva Merlot (Aconcagua Valley) $12. There's a weighty overlay of oak, but the fruit is here and it's fairly balanced and reserved in nature. This is in a softer style with black cherry and sweet plum flavors, and not too much acidity. Drink now. 86 *—M.S. (9/1/2007)*

Conde de Velázquez 2003 El Conde Gran Reserva Merlot (Aconcagua Valley) $11. Early aromas are like a pile of pencil shavings, and later some herbal fruit enters the frame. Raspberry and bramble are the lead flavors, while the mouthfeel and balance are solid and push the wine to a reasonable finish. Not a head-turner but it gets the job done. 84 *—M.S. (11/15/2007)*

Conde de Velázquez 2005 Condesa Real Premium Blend Red Blend (Aconcagua Valley) $24. There is absolutely nothing wrong with this lighter-styled version of Cabernet Sauvingon, Syrah and Merlot. It opens with weightless flower petal and red-fruit aromas, and the palate meets the challenge with clean plum and berry flavors supported by an undercurrent of creamy oak. At just over 400 cases, it's definitely a success for this winery. 89 *—M.S. (9/1/2007)*

Conde de Velàzquez 2003 Sauvignon Blanc (Aconcagua Valley) $7. 84 Best Buy *—M.S. (2/1/2005)*

Conde de Velázquez 2006 Don Raphael Single Vineyard Sauvignon Blanc (Aconcagua Valley) $9. Apple and even some hazelnut create a sweet nose, then comes a soda-like palate that houses lime and orange flavors. It's a fairly intense, live-wire sort of wine, but it's also a touch candied and drab. 84 *—M.S. (9/1/2007)*

Conde de Velàzquez 2003 Syrah (Aconcagua Valley) $6. 80 *—M.S. (12/15/2005)*

Conde de Velázquez 2004 Reserva Syrah (Aconcagua Valley) $8. A lot of oak covers herbal, black-olive aromas, but only for so long. Once the wine airs out, what's left is an acceptable but olive-ridden red that's leathery, drying and generally devoid of any ripe characteristics. 81 *—M.S. (5/1/2007)*

Conde de Velàzquez 2002 Reserva Syrah (Aconcagua Valley) $7. 81 *—M.S. (2/1/2005)*

CONFIN

Confin 2004 Cabernet Sauvignon (Rapel Valley) $11. 85 *—M.S. (10/1/2006)*

Confin 2004 Winemaker Reserve Cabernet Sauvignon (Rapel Valley) $14. 86 *—M.S. (10/1/2006)*

Confin 2005 Carmenère (Rapel Valley) $12. 85 *—M.S. (11/15/2006)*

Confin 2005 Chardonnay (Rapel Valley) $11. 84 *—M.S. (10/1/2006)*

Confin 2004 Merlot (Rapel Valley) $11. 83 *—M.S. (10/1/2006)*

Confin 2004 Winemaker Reserve Merlot (Rapel Valley) $14. 86 *—M.S. (10/1/2006)*

Confin 2004 Premium Reserve Red Blend (Rapel Valley) $20. 88 *—M.S. (11/15/2006)*

CONO SUR

Cono Sur 2005 20 Barrels Limited Edition Cabernet Sauvignon (Maipo Valley) $25. Quite woodsy and mossy on the nose. The palate is actually pretty juicy and fresh by comparison, with plum and cherry flavors. The mouthfeel and tannins, however, are a bit raw and firm, so to avoid the evil clamp down we strongly suggest drinking this wine with food. 87 *—M.S. (11/15/2007)*

Cono Sur 2004 20 Barrels Limited Edition Cabernet Sauvignon (Maipo Valley) $25. 88 *—M.S. (11/15/2006)*

Cono Sur 2005 The Southern Cone Cabernet Sauvignon (Central Valley) $10. 87 Best Buy *—M.S. (11/15/2006)*

Cono Sur 2005 Visión Cabernet Sauvignon (Maipo Valley) $15. A nicely made Chilean Cabernet that delivers ripe, toasty fruit-based aromas in front of tasty cassis and blackberry flavors. As for mouthfeel, it's full and layered as it pours on the toast and vanilla shadings. Simply stated, it's a clean, easy, fresh red wine with a bit of character. 88 *—M.S. (3/1/2007)*

Cono Sur 2005 The Southern Cone Carmenère (Colchagua Valley) $10. 87 Best Buy *—M.S. (11/15/2006)*

Cono Sur 2006 20 Barrels Limited Edition Chardonnay (Casablanca Valley) $20. Fleshy and sweet, with white corn on the nose. Flavors of Juicy Fruit gum, lime and mango push it even further into the sweet and tropical category. There's just not much body, structure or point to this wine; it's yet another pricey but underwhelming Chilean Chardonnay. 84 *—M.S. (11/15/2007)*

Cono Sur 2005 20 Barrels Limited Edition Chardonnay (Casablanca Valley) $25. 85 *—M.S. (12/31/2006)*

Cono Sur 2006 Visión Chardonnay (Casablanca Valley) $14. This is solid Chardonnay even if it's a touch sweet and aggressive. The nose is sulfuric early on, but cleaner if given time. The palate is all about candied melon and guava, while the finish is tight and narrow. With good acidity, it's lively on the tongue. Best if you like some sweetness in your white wines. 86 *—M.S. (11/15/2007)*

Cono Sur 2005 Single Vineyard Visión Chardonnay (Casablanca Valley) $14. 84 *—M.S. (12/31/2006)*

Cono Sur 2006 Sustainable Agriculture Chardonnay (Colchagua Valley) $13. Tan in color and fairly sharp stuff, with a prickly feel and piercing flavors of melon and peaches. At 14% alcohol it seems over the edge. 82 *—M.S. (11/15/2007)*

Cono Sur 2004 20 Barrels Limited Edition Merlot (Colchagua Valley) $25. Aromatically, this wine is sound. Scents of blackberry, dark plum, smoke and molasses are convincing. But it's rather snappy and electric in the mouth, with piercing acidity that creates a sharp mouthfeel. On the finish, there are lasting flavors courtesy of medium tannins and that aforementioned pulsing acidity. 85 *—M.S. (3/1/2007)*

Cono Sur 2001 20 Barrels Merlot (Colchagua Valley) $22. 83 *—M.S. (6/1/2004)*

Cono Sur 2001 Reserve Merlot (Rapel Valley) $12. 85 *—M.S. (7/1/2003)*

Cono Sur 2005 The Southern Cone Merlot (Central Valley) $10. 87 Best Buy *—M.S. (11/15/2006)*

Cono Sur 2005 Visión Merlot (Colchagua Valley) $15. Early on, this wine seems a touch grassy and green, but time permits the darker fruit characteristics to come out. In the mouth, expect berry and plum flavors mixed with a hint of herbal green, while the finish is oaky, minty and a bit hot. Robust and grabby, but a healthy specimen. 86 *—M.S. (3/1/2007)*

Cono Sur 2005 20 Barrels Limited Edition Pinot Noir (Casablanca Valley) $25. True, spicy and dark on the nose; the bouquet is on the money and doesn't make you question the wine's pedigree. In the mouth, bright red fruit is almosty citrusy, while the finish offers laser-like cherry and raspberry notes with the essence of cola and pepper. A nice example of serious Chilean Pinot. 87 *—M.S. (5/1/2007)*

Cono Sur 2001 20 Barrels Pinot Noir (Casablanca Valley) $22. 86 *—M.S. (8/1/2004)*

Cono Sur 2005 Ocio Pinot Noir (Casablanca Valley) $50. Dark and jammy, this wine delivers a charred nose along with rhubarb and prickle. It's quite tangy and stand-up, with racy cherry and berry flavors. Does it ever really find a groove that makes it worth twice as much as the 20 Barrels bottling? We don't think so. It's modern but undistinguished. 85 *—M.S. (5/1/2007)*

Cono Sur 2001 Reserve Pinot Noir (Casablanca Valley) $12. 82 *—M.S. (7/1/2003)*

Cono Sur 2006 The Southern Cone Riesling (Bío Bío Valley) $10. If you like the Australian Rieslings, which often push petrol, mineral and shy fruit, than this is for you. It hails from cool and southerly Bío Bío, and it's an honest Riesling with lemony freshness and grapefruit on the palate, followed by a juicy finish. A potential by-the-glass favorite. 87 Best Buy *—M.S. (11/15/2007)*

Cono Sur 2006 20 Barrels Limited Edition Sauvignon Blanc (Casablanca Valley) $20. Like its predecessor, the 2005, this wine has strong jalapeño, bell pepper and tomato leaf aromas. In fact, for a time it smells like salsa. The palate offers slap-you-in-the-face fruit and zest, while the finish is racy due to young, jumpy acidity. A nice wine with seafood appetizers. 87 *—M.S. (5/1/2007)*

Cono Sur 2005 20 Barrels Limited Edition Sauvignon Blanc (Casablanca Valley) $25. Praise goes to the integrity of this wine. It's true Sauvignon Blanc, with prickly green aromas along with cucumber, citrus and green apple flavors. Up to that point it's got all that you want, but the mouthfeel seems sort of spritzy and in the end it doesn't seem to be in total unison. Drink now or wait for the 2006. 86 *—M.S. (5/1/2007)*

Cono Sur 2005 Single Vineyard Visión Sauvignon Blanc (Casablanca Valley) $14. Disjointed in many ways, but there's also some genuine intent to this wine. The nose is fairly true to the varietal: it delivers tropical fruit plus salad greens. But the palate is wavy, glossy and too tangy with citrus. The wine seems to be grasping for a guide map but to no avail. 84 *—M.S. (9/1/2007)*

Cono Sur 2006 Visión Sauvignon Blanc (Casablanca Valley) $14. There's no escaping the asparagus and canned bean aromas that consume the bouquet, but those scents do fade after a while and the nose eventually leads to flavors of lime, white peach and citrus. The zest and balance are good, and the vegetal character becomes less austere with time; but all along the way the wine carries that love-it-or-hate-it snap of green. 86 *—M.S. (11/15/2007)*

Cono Sur 2005 The Southern Cone Syrah (Rapel Valley) $10. Boysenberry and raspberry aromas carry the fresh, snappy nose toward a tart but generally precise palate that really pours on the red fruit flavors. The feel is a touch jagged and sharp, but the wine's core clarity and uncomplicated focus make it worthwhile. 84 *—M.S. (5/1/2007)*

Cono Sur 2006 The Southern Cone Viognier (Colchagua Valley) $10. A touch rough and oily initially, but later on you get punchbowl aromas followed by banana, lemon and melon flavors. There's both weight and acidity to the palate, but also some flatness and a lack of focus. Not a commonplace wine. 84 *—M.S. (11/15/2007)*

COUSIÑO-MACUL

Cousiño-Macul 1998 Cabernet Sauvignon (Maipo Valley) $11. 82 *(2/1/2001)*

Cousiño-Macul 2004 Antiguas Reservas Cabernet Sauvignon (Maipo Valley) $14. 86 *—M.S. (12/31/2006)*

Cousiño-Macul 2002 Antiguas Reservas Cabernet Sauvignon (Maipo Valley) $13. 83 *—M.S. (7/1/2005)*

Cousiño-Macul 2001 Antiguas Reservas Cabernet Sauvignon (Maipo Valley) $13. 89 Best Buy *—M.S. (3/1/2004)*

Cousiño-Macul 1997 Antiguas Reservas Cabernet Sauvignon (Maipo Valley) $13. 83 *(2/1/2001)*

Cousiño-Macul 1999 Antiguas Reservas Estate Bottled Cabernet Sauvignon (Maipo Valley) $14. 87 *—C.S. (2/1/2003)*

Cousiño-Macul 2002 Finis Terrae Cabernet Sauvignon-Merlot (Maipo Valley) $30. 88 *—M.S. (3/1/2004)*

Cousiño-Macul 1997 Finis Terrae Cabernet Sauvignon-Merlot (Maipo Valley) $32. 83 *(2/1/2001)*

Cousiño-Macul 2004 Lota Cabernet Sauvignon-Merlot (Maipo Valley) $60. 90 *—M.S. (12/31/2006)*

Cousiño-Macul 2004 Chardonnay (Maipo Valley) $9. 80 *—M.S. (7/1/2005)*

Cousiño-Macul 2001 Chardonnay (Maipo Valley) $9. 83 *—M.S. (7/1/2002)*

Cousiño-Macul 2005 Antiguas Reservas Chardonnay (Maipo Valley) $14. This wine shows a tad too much canned fruit, saccharine and wayward flesh for my liking. It smells slightly tropical but totally common, while the melon and citrus flavors come with a syrupy mouthfeel. Overall it's bland and won't improve. Better in previous years. 25,000 cases produced. 83 *—M.S. (5/1/2007)*

Cousiño-Macul 2004 Antiguas Reservas Chardonnay (Maipo Valley) $14. 87 *—M.S. (3/1/2006)*

Cousiño-Macul 2003 Antiguas Reservas Chardonnay (Maipo Valley) $13. 87 *—M.S. (3/1/2004)*

Cousiño-Macul 2004 Merlot (Maipo Valley) $9. 84 *—M.S. (3/1/2006)*

Cousiño-Macul 2002 Merlot (Maipo Valley) $9. 87 *—K.F. (2/1/2003)*

Cousiño-Macul 2001 Merlot (Maipo Valley) $9. 84 *—M.S. (7/1/2003)*

Cousiño-Macul 2000 Merlot (Maipo Valley) $9. 82 *—C.S. (12/1/2002)*

Cousiño-Macul 1998 Reserva Merlot (Maipo Valley) $15. 86 *(2/1/2001)*

Cousiño-Macul 2001 Finis Terrae Merlot-Cabernet Sauvignon (Maipo Valley) $20. 90 Editors' Choice *—M.S. (3/1/2004)*

Cousiño-Macul 2006 Doña Isidora Riesling (Maipo Valley) $10. A full-bodied, Southern Hemisphere style of Riesling with a touch of petrol on the nose but mostly bigger tropical aromas. The palate is loaded with ripe grapefruit, citrus pith and good acidity. Heavy yet balanced for a warm-climate Riesling, with a long finish of citrus. 86 Best Buy *—M.S. (11/15/2007)*

Cousiño-Macul 2003 Doña Isadora Riesling (Maipo Valley) $9. 88 Best Buy *—M.S. (3/1/2004)*

Cousiño-Macul 2000 Dona Isidora Riesling (Maipo Valley) $8. 85 *—M.S. (8/1/2003)*

Cousiño-Macul 1999 Doña Isidora Riesling (Maipo Valley) $14. 82 *(2/1/2001)*

Cousiño-Macul 2006 Sauvignon Gris (Maipo Valley) $12. 87 *—M.S. (12/31/2006)*

CRUCERO

Crucero 2000 Syrah (Colchagua Valley) $8. 85 Best Buy *(10/1/2001)*

D. BOSLER

D. Bosler 2002 Birdsnest Pinot Noir (Casablanca Valley) $10. 87 Best Buy *—M.S. (7/1/2005)*

D. Bosler 2000 Birdsnest Pinot Noir (Casablanca Valley) $12. 86 *—D.T. (7/1/2002)*

DALLAS CONTÉ

Dallas Conté 2003 Cabernet Sauvignon (Maipo Valley) $10. 83 *—M.S. (5/1/2006)*

Dallas Conté 2000 Cabernet Sauvignon (Rapel Valley) $10. 85 *—M.S. (7/1/2003)*

Dallas Conté 1999 Cabernet Sauvignon (Colchagua Valley) $9. 86 *—J.C. (2/1/2001)*

Dallas Conté 1997 Cabernet Sauvignon (Colchagua Valley) $10. 88 Best Buy *—M.S. (8/1/2000)*

Dallas Conté 1999 Reserve Cabernet Sauvignon-Merlot (Rapel Valley) $15. 85 *—M.S. (7/1/2003)*

Dallas Conté 2002 Chardonnay (Casablanca Valley) $10. 84 *—M.S. (7/1/2003)*

Dallas Conté 1998 Chardonnay (Colchagua Valley) $10. 89 Best Buy *—M.M. (2/1/2001)*

Dallas Conté 2001 Merlot (Rapel Valley) $10. 84 *—M.S. (8/1/2004)*

Dallas Conté 2000 Merlot (Rapel Valley) $10. 85 *—M.S. (7/1/2003)*

Dallas Conté 1997 Merlot (Colchagua Valley) $10. 87 Best Buy —*M.S. (5/1/2000)*

DE MARTINO

De Martino 1999 Cabernet Sauvignon (Maipo Valley) $10. 81 —*J.C. (2/1/2001)*

De Martino 1999 Estate Bottled Prima Reserva Cabernet Sauvignon (Maipo Valley) $13. 84 —*M.S. (12/1/2002)*

De Martino 2002 Estate Bottled Gran Familia Cabernet Sauvignon (Maipo Valley) $45. 85 —*M.S. (5/1/2006)*

De Martino 2004 Legado Reserva Cabernet Sauvignon (Maipo Valley) $15. With this wine, De Martino has again proved that it is very capable of producing quality wines at all price points. This Cab features attractive cedar and earth notes along with brooding fruit, while the palate is all about controlled generosity: It shows tannins, black cherry and active acidity. 88 —*M.S. (3/1/2007)*

De Martino 2005 Organic Cabernet Sauvignon (Maipo Valley) $15. Potent, granular aromas of berries and earth precede a juicy, condensed palate that is overflowing with ripe, robust blackberry and cassis flavors. This is a rich, silky wine with touches of tobacco and espresso on the finish. It shows all the characteristics of a fine Chilean Cabernet. 90 Best Buy —*M.S. (3/1/2007)*

De Martino 1998 Prima Reserva Cabernet Sauvignon (Maipo Valley) $13. 81 —*J.C. (2/1/2001)*

De Martino 1997 Reserva de Familia Cabernet Sauvignon (Maipo Valley) $35. 85 —*D.T. (8/1/2001)*

De Martino 2003 Legada Reserva Carmenère (Maipo Valley) $15. 85 —*M.S. (1/1/2005)*

De Martino 2005 Legado Reserva Carmenère (Maipo Valley) $15. 87 —*M.S. (10/1/2006)*

De Martino 1999 Prima Reserva Carmenère (Maipo Valley) $12. 89 —*M.S. (7/1/2003)*

De Martino 1999 Reserva de la Familia Carmenère (Maipo Valley) $10. 88 —*M.S. (7/1/2003)*

De Martino 2005 Single Vineyard Carmenère (Maipo Valley) $25. Everything about this select-level Carmenère is impressive. It's colorful and wrapped in a cloak of classy oak. The palate is juicy and balanced to a tee, with dark berry flavors busting free. A little young oak emerges on the finish, but it vanishes in short order once you air things out. A wonderful red wine regardless of variety. 300 cases made. 92 Editors' Choice —*M.S. (5/1/2007)*

De Martino 1999 Estate Bottled Chardonnay (Maipo Valley) $10. 81 *(2/1/2001)*

De Martino 2000 Estate Bottled Prima Reserva Chardonnay (Maipo Valley) $10. 89 —*M.S. (7/1/2003)*

De Martino 2004 Legada Reserva Chardonnay (Limarí Valley) $15. 87 —*M.S. (3/1/2006)*

De Martino 2005 Legado Reserva Chardonnay (Limarí Valley) $15. 87 —*M.S. (10/1/2006)*

De Martino 1999 Prima Reserva Chardonnay (Maipo Valley) $13. 82 *(2/1/2001)*

De Martino 1999 Reserva de Familia Chardonnay (Casablanca Valley) $35. 84 —*M.S. (7/1/2003)*

De Martino 2005 Single Vineyard Chardonnay (Limarí Valley) $25. A little more floral and waxy than some, but also a touch more complex and interesting than most. The nose is exotic, while the palate runs more tangy and slick than might be expected. The finish is warm and loaded with apple, while depth is pretty good, too. 88 —*M.S. (5/1/2007)*

De Martino 2000 Estate Bottled - Prima Reserva Merlot (Maipo Valley) $13. 90 Editors' Choice —*M.S. (12/1/2002)*

De Martino 1999 Prima Reserva Merlot (Maipo Valley) $13. 80 —*J.C. (2/1/2001)*

De Martino 1998 Reserva de Familia Red Blend (Maipo Valley) $35. 85 —*J.C. (8/1/2001)*

De Martino 2001 Estate Bottled - Prima Reserva Sauvignon Blanc (Maipo Valley) $10. 84 —*M.S. (7/1/2003)*

De Martino 2004 Legado Reserva Sauvignon Blanc (Maipo Valley) $15. 87 —*M.S. (7/1/2005)*

De Martino 2004 Legado Reserva Syrah (Maipo Valley) $15. Violets coat the primary nose, while lilac and pencil-lead aromas come in later. A juicy palate of black raspberry and zesty plum skins is both racy yet satisfying as it suggests grilled meats as a pairing. A bit of fresh raisin on the finish confirms the wine's ripeness. 88 —*M.S. (2/1/2007)*

De Martino 2003 Legada Reserva Syrah (Colchagua Valley) $15. 86 —*M.S. (11/1/2005)*

DOMAINES BARONS DE ROTHSCHILD (LAFITE)

Domaines Barons de Rothschild (Lafite) 2000 Le Dix de Los Vascos Cabernet Sauvignon (Colchagua Valley) $40. 89 —*M.S. (3/1/2004)*

Domaines Barons de Rothschild (Lafite) 2005 Los Vascos Cabernet Sauvignon (Colchagua Valley) $12. Punchy and fruity up front, this Cab doesn't seem to be trying to do too much and thus it succeeds on many fronts. The cherry and plum flavors are clean if unspectacular, while the finish shows full tannins, some bitter chocolate and pretty good feel. Nothing out of the ordinary but perfectly fine. 86 —*M.S. (5/1/2007)*

Domaines Barons de Rothschild (Lafite) 2003 Los Vascos Cabernet Sauvignon (Colchagua Valley) $11. 88 Best Buy —*M.S. (12/1/2004)*

Domaines Barons de Rothschild (Lafite) 2002 Los Vascos Cabernet Sauvignon (Colchagua Valley) $10. 86 —*M.S. (3/1/2004)*

Domaines Barons de Rothschild (Lafite) 2001 Los Vascos Grande Reserve Cabernet Sauvignon (Colchagua Valley) $17. 87 —*M.S. (3/1/2004)*

Domaines Barons de Rothschild (Lafite) 2004 Los Vascos Reserve Cabernet Sauvignon (Colchagua Valley) $21. 90 —*M.S. (11/15/2006)*

Domaines Barons de Rothschild (Lafite) 2006 Los Vascos Chardonnay (Colchagua Valley) $12. Unlike just about any other Chardonnay out there, this hugely tropical and grassy wine is much like Sauvignon Blanc. It's all citrus and acids, with only a streak of melony sweetness to soften it up. Still, it's clean and laser-beam crisp, and if you like Sauvignon Blanc or Spanish Verdejo you'll probably like this, too. 85 —*M.S. (3/1/2007)*

Domaines Barons de Rothschild (Lafite) 2005 Los Vascos Chardonnay (Colchagua Valley) $12. 88 Best Buy —*M.S. (5/1/2006)*

Domaines Barons de Rothschild (Lafite) 2003 Los Vascos Chardonnay (Colchagua Valley) $10. 86 Best Buy —*M.S. (3/1/2004)*

Domaines Barons de Rothschild (Lafite) 2005 Los Vascos Sauvignon Blanc (Casablanca Valley) $12. 88 Best Buy —*M.S. (7/1/2006)*

Domaines Barons de Rothschild (Lafite) 2004 Los Vascos Sauvignon Blanc (Central Valley) $11. 85 —*M.S. (2/1/2005)*

Domaines Barons de Rothschild (Lafite) 2003 Los Vascos Sauvignon Blanc (Colchagua Valley) $10. 87 Best Buy —*M.S. (3/1/2004)*

DOMUS AUREA

Domus Aurea 2003 Cabernet Sauvignon (Maipo Valley) $50. Five years ago we said Domus Aurea could become one of Chile's very best Cabernets. But then focus, winemakers and other things changed and the quality slipped. But Domus seems to be back with a vengeance in 2003. A nosing yields a lot of earth, tobacco and leather, while the sly but sure flavor profile is centered on baked plum and cassis along with some herbal, terroir-ish shadings. Still not for everyone, but very, very interesting and not generic. 92 —*M.S. (9/1/2007)*

Domus Aurea 2002 Cabernet Sauvignon (Maipo Valley) $45. 89 —*M.S. (10/1/2006)*

Domus Aurea 2001 Cabernet Sauvignon (Maipo Valley) $45. 84 —*M.S. (12/15/2005)*

Domus Aurea 2001 Cabernet Sauvignon (Maipo Valley) $45. 87 —*M.S. (5/1/2006)*

Domus Aurea 1999 Cabernet Sauvignon (Maipo Valley) $42. 85 —*M.S. (11/1/2005)*

DON OSVALDO

Don Osvaldo 2004 Carmenère (Colchagua Valley) $10. 82 —*M.S. (7/1/2006)*

Don Osvaldo 2003 Vina Bisquertt Reserve Carmenère (Colchagua Valley) $15. 81 —*M.S. (7/1/2006)*

DUO

Duo 2003 Cabernet Sauvignon-Merlot (Maipo Valley) $14. 88 —*M.S. (5/1/2006)*

Duo 2005 Sauvignon Blanc (Casablanca Valley) $14. 85 —*M.S. (5/1/2006)*

ECHEVERRIA

Echeverria 2004 Cabernet Sauvignon (Molina) $12. Solid and fresh, with full, generally clean berry aromas that are backed up by praiseworthy plum and berry flavors. It's a juicy wine with good tannic structure, and the finish is dry, toasty and a little fiery. Nice for a moderately oaked, medium-bodied red. 86 —*M.S. (3/1/2007)*

Echeverria 2002 Cabernet Sauvignon (Molina) $16. 84 —*M.S. (2/1/2005)*

Echeverria 1999 Family Reserve Cabernet Sauvignon (Molina) $29. 90 —*M.S. (2/1/2005)*

Echeverria 2003 Limited Edition Cabernet Sauvignon (Central Valley) $28. 91 —*M.S. (12/31/2006)*

Echeverria 2000 Molina Cabernet Sauvignon (Chile) $8. 87 Best Buy —*C.S. (12/1/2002)*

Echeverria 2004 Reserva Cabernet Sauvignon (Molina) $18. 88 —*M.S. (11/15/2006)*

Echeverria 2001 Reserva Cabernet Sauvignon-Merlot (Curicó Valley) $18. 88 —*M.S. (12/1/2004)*

Echeverria 2006 Carmenère (Molina) $9. From the full-bodied, full-color school comes this ripe, willing red. It's heady and loaded with black cherry and chocolate flavors, while the succulent finish is bold, chewy and laden with fudge. Not intellectual but big in fruit and flavor. 87 Best Buy —*M.S. (5/1/2007)*

Echeverria 2005 Carmenère (Central Valley) $12. 81 —*M.S. (11/15/2006)*

Echeverria 2002 Molina Carmenère (Curicó Valley) $9. 83 —*M.S. (6/1/2004)*

Echeverria 2004 Reserva Carmenère (Central Valley) $18. 88 —*M.S. (12/31/2006)*

Echeverria 2005 Reserva Chardonnay (Molina) $18. 85 —*M.S. (11/15/2006)*

Echeverria 2004 Reserva Chardonnay (Molina) $18. 82 —*M.S. (3/1/2006)*

Echeverria 2006 Unwooded Chardonnay (Molina) $9. Yellow Delicious apple and melon aromas start it off in a fruity direction, and the palate shows peach and pear flavors. With no oak, there's no butter, toast or resin to speak of. There is, however, a sugary almost Riesling-esque quality to the wine. All in all, it's unconventional but pretty good, with a nice bolt of acidity keeping it wide awake. Imported by T. Edward Wines. 85 Best Buy —*M.S. (9/1/2007)*

Echeverria 2005 Unwooded Chardonnay (Molina) $13. 82 —*M.S. (3/1/2006)*

Echeverria 2003 Unwooded Chardonnay (Molina) $9. 82 —*M.S. (2/1/2005)*

Echeverria 2000 Merlot (Maule Valley) $12. 88 Best Buy —*C.S. (12/1/2002)*

Echeverria 2004 Reserva Merlot (Molina) $13. Full and dark, with meaty aromas that can't be overlooked. The palate is rich and round, teetering on lush but with enough acidity to keep it on an even keel. And the flavors of wild berries and cassis are chewy and satisfying. Starts off stronger than it finishes, but still quite good as a whole. 87 —*M.S. (3/1/2007)*

Echeverria 1999 Reserva Merlot (Chile) $16. 84 —*D.T. (7/1/2002)*

Echeverria 2002 Reserva Red Blend (Central Valley) $18. 86 —*M.S. (12/31/2006)*

Echeverria 2006 Sauvignon Blanc (Molina) $9. Opens with inviting green apple aromas before delivering citric, lemony flavors on a surprisingly soft frame that isn't overloaded with scouring acidity. All this means the wine is ready to drink now; it has decent fruit with hints of lime and mineral. 85 Best Buy —*M.S. (3/1/2007)*

Echeverria 2003 Sauvignon Blanc (Molina) $9. 82 —*M.S. (2/1/2005)*

Echeverria 2006 Reserva Sauvignon Blanc (Molina) $13. Seems as though Echeverria's idea of reserve Sauvignon is to let the grapes stay on the vines for too long. The wine lacks expression and a pulse. It's borderline DOA, in fact; the regular 2006 Sauvignon Blanc is livelier. 80 —*M.S. (5/1/2007)*

Echeverria 2004 Reserva Syrah (Colchagua Valley) $18. 88 —*M.S. (11/15/2006)*

EL GRANO

El Grano 2001 Carmenère (Rapel Valley) $10. 87 —*M.S. (11/15/2003)*

EL HUIQUE

El Huique 2002 Cabernet Sauvignon (Colchagua Valley) $8. 82 —*M.S. (7/1/2005)*

El Huique 2002 Reserva Carmenère (Colchagua Valley) $12. 83 —*M.S. (2/1/2005)*

El Huique 2001 Chardonnay (Colchagua Valley) $9. 80 —*M.S. (2/1/2005)*

EL TOQUI

El Toqui 2002 Prestige Cabernet Sauvignon (Cachapoal Valley) $13. 82 —*M.S. (10/1/2006)*

ENCIERRA

Encierra 2002 Vineyard Reserve Red Blend (Colchagua Valley) $25. 87 —*M.S. (12/1/2004)*

ERRAZURIZ

Errazuriz 1998 Don Maximiano Founder's Reserve Cabernet Blend (Aconcagua Valley) $30. 86 —*S.H. (2/1/2001)*

Errazuriz 2003 Viñedo Chadwick Cabernet Blend (Maipo Valley) $100. 93 Editors' Choice —*M.S. (10/1/2006)*

Errazuriz 2001 Cabernet Sauvignon (Aconcagua Valley) $12. 87 Best Buy —*M.S. (7/1/2003)*

Errazuriz 2004 Don Maximiano Founder's Reserve Cabernet Sauvignon (Aconcagua Valley) $50. Errazuriz continues to work on its Don Max prestige wine, and while this version has fine feel, weight and ripeness, there are some slight stewy notes and a lot of oak-based spice flavors that don't quite ring this taster's bell. Expect notes of molasses, tobacco and clove as you delve into this layered, rather uncommon Cabernet-based blend. 88 —*M.S. (3/1/2007)*

Errazuriz 2003 Don Maximiano Founder's Reserve Cabernet Sauvignon (Aconcagua Valley) $50. 87 —*M.S. (7/1/2006)*

Errazuriz 2002 Don Maximiano Founder's Reserve Cabernet Sauvignon (Aconcagua Valley) $49. 88 —*M.S. (11/1/2005)*

Errazuriz 2000 Don Maximiano Founder's Reserve Cabernet Sauvignon (Aconcagua Valley) $60. 88 —*M.S. (3/1/2004)*

Errazuriz 1999 Don Maximo Estate Reserva Cabernet Sauvignon (Aconcagua Valley) $25. 82 —*D.T. (7/1/2002)*

Errazuriz 1997 El Ceibo Estate Cabernet Sauvignon (Aconcagua Valley) $8. 88 *(11/15/1999)*

Errazuriz 2000 El Ceibo Estate Estate Cabernet Sauvignon (Aconcagua Valley) $10. 87 Best Buy —*S.H. (12/1/2002)*

Errazuriz 1999 El Ceibo Estate Estate Cabernet Sauvignon (Aconcagua Valley) $10. 85 —*S.H. (6/1/2001)*

Errazuriz 2005 Estate Cabernet Sauvignon (Aconcagua Valley) $11. Full and chewy, as it should be. The nose is earthy and solid, while the palate veers toward red berries, primarily strawberries and plums. In the mouth, the wine comes across a touch hot, but overall its lively, ripe and medium in weight and complexity. In its class it's exactly what you'd expect. 86 Best Buy —*M.S. (3/1/2007)*

Errazuriz 2004 Estate Cabernet Sauvignon (Aconcagua Valley) $11. 88 Best Buy —*M.S. (11/1/2005)*

Errazuriz 2002 Estate Cabernet Sauvignon (Aconcagua Valley) $10. 88 Best Buy —*M.S. (6/1/2004)*

Errazuriz 2005 Max Reserva Cabernet Sauvignon (Aconcagua Valley) $21. Once past the oak-driven aromas of coconut and mint you'll find a lusty bouquet full of cherry and cassis. The palate deals sweet and dried spices (cinnamon and clove) along with medium-strength but clean berry flavors. And the finish is toasty and warming. A very nice wine, but quite woody in its present state. 88 —*M.S. (3/1/2007)*

Errazuriz 2003 Max Reserva Cabernet Sauvignon (Aconcagua Valley) $21. 91 Editors' Choice —*M.S. (11/1/2005)*

Errazuriz 2002 Max Reserva Cabernet Sauvignon (Aconcagua Valley) $19. 85 —*M.S. (7/1/2005)*

Errazuriz 2000 Max Reserva Cabernet Sauvignon (Aconcagua Valley) $60. 85 —*M.S. (3/1/2004)*

Errazuriz 1999 Reserva Cabernet Sauvignon (Aconcagua Valley) $25. 87 —*S.H. (12/1/2002)*

Errazuriz 2002 Viñedo Chadwick Cabernet Sauvignon (Maipo Valley) $64. 87 —*M.S. (11/1/2005)*

Errazuriz 2000 Viñedo Chadwick Cabernet Sauvignon (Maipo Valley) $70. 91 —*M.S. (3/1/2004)*

Errazuriz 1999 Don Maximaino's Founder's Reserve Cabernet Sauvignon-Merlot (Aconcagua Valley) $60. 87 —*S.H. (12/1/2002)*

Errazuriz 2005 Single Vineyard Don Maximiano Estate Carmenère (Aconcagua Valley) $25. A whole lot of heavy oak is weighing this wine down. Aromas of smoked meat and mint are minor compared to the charcoal, vanilla and seared wood that dominate. And in the mouth, it's clumsy; heat, heft and vanilla complete this mission gone astray. 81 —*M.S. (5/1/2007)*

Errazuriz 2003 Don Maximiano Estate Single Vineyard Carmenère (Aconcagua Valley) $25. 85 —*M.S. (11/1/2005)*

Errazuriz 2004 Single Vineyard Carmenère (Aconcagua Valley) $25. 89 —*M.S. (3/1/2006)*

Errazuriz 2002 Chardonnay (Casablanca Valley) $10. 86 Best Buy —*M.S. (6/1/2004)*

Errazuriz 2005 Estate Chardonnay (Casablanca Valley) $11. 86 Best Buy —*M.S. (10/1/2006)*

Errazuriz 2004 Estate Chardonnay (Casablanca Valley) $11. 85 —*M.S. (7/1/2005)*

Errazuriz 2004 Estate Chardonnay (Casablanca Valley) $11. 87 Best Buy —*M.S. (11/1/2005)*

Errazuriz 2000 Estate Chardonnay (Casablanca Valley) $10. 84 —*M.S. (7/1/2002)*

Errazuriz 1999 La Escultura Estate Chardonnay (Casablanca Valley) $10. 87 Best Buy —*S.H. (2/1/2001)*

Errazuriz 2000 La Escultura Estate Reserva Chardonnay (Casablanca Valley) $10. 86 Best Buy —*M.S. (7/1/2002)*

Errazuriz 2005 Wild Ferment Chardonnay (Casablanca Valley) $21. The number of $20 Chards that rate this high are few and far between. We like this natural-yeast wine from a great vintage because it shows ripeness, balance and complexity. The nose is both toasty and sweet, while the melon, apple and mango flavors are ripe but not over the top. A big wine with New World kick; drink soon to appreciate its fruit quality. 90 —*M.S. (5/1/2007)*

Errazuriz 2004 Wild Ferment Chardonnay (Casablanca Valley) $21. 87 —*M.S. (7/1/2006)*

Errazuriz 2002 Wild Ferment Chardonnay (Casablanca Valley) $19. 86 —*M.S. (11/1/2005)*

Errazuriz 2001 Wild Ferment Chardonnay (Casablanca Valley) $NA. 85 —*M.S. (6/1/2004)*

Errazuriz 1999 Wild Ferment La Escultura Estate Chardonnay (Casablanca Valley) $22. 90 —*S.H. (2/1/2001)*

Errazuriz 2000 Fumé Blanc (Casablanca Valley) $10. 85 —*S.H. (5/1/2001)*

Errazuriz 2001 Merlot (Curicó Valley) $10. 84 —*S.H. (1/1/2002)*

Errazuriz 1999 Don Maximiano Estate Reserva Merlot (Aconcagua Valley) $25. 82 —*D.T. (7/1/2002)*

Errazuriz 1999 El Decanso Estate Merlot (Curicó Valley) $10. 87 Best Buy —*S.H. (2/1/2001)*

Errazuriz 2006 Estate Merlot (Aconcagua Valley) $11. Nice Merlot, a bit generic, but very forward and full of bold berry fruit, spicy oak and vanilla. It shows a sassy, rugged side but also a simple, pleasant, fruity side. Gets better with some airing, which is proof that it's got the right wiring to satisfy. 86 Best Buy —*M.S. (11/15/2007)*

Errazuriz 2005 Estate Merlot (Curicó Valley) $11. 86 Best Buy —*M.S. (11/15/2006)*

Errazuriz 2004 Estate Merlot (Curicó Valley) $11. 86 Best Buy —*M.S. (11/1/2005)*

Errazuriz 2003 Estate Merlot (Curicó Valley) $11. 84 —*M.S. (2/1/2005)*

Errazuriz 2000 Max Reserva Merlot (Aconcagua Valley) $25. 83 —*M.N. (3/1/2004)*

Errazuriz 2005 Wild Ferment Pinot Noir (Casablanca Valley) $30. Holding this up to some high standards, given that it's $30 and only 200 cases were made, Wild Ferment more than makes the grade and ranks as one of Chile's best Pinots to date. There's guarded oak along with dried cherry and leather aromas. That's followed by ripe black cherry, spicy plum and chocolate flavors. Fine in a California sort of way. 90 Editors' Choice —*M.S. (5/1/2007)*

Errazuriz 2004 The Blend Limited Edition Red Blend (Aconcagua Valley) $40. A nonconformist blend of Cabernet Sauvignon, Syrah, Carmenère, Petit Verdot and Sangiovese that starts with hard mint and oak aromas that are echoed on the palate, which is foresty and slightly herbal. As it opens, however, richness, sweetness and harmony emerge. It's maybe not a star but it has its virtues. 88 —*M.S. (5/1/2007)*

Errazuriz 2000 Viñedo Chadwick Red Blend (Maipo Valley) $65. 87 —*M.S. (3/1/2004)*

Errazuriz 2005 Estate Sauvignon Blanc (Casablanca Valley) $11. 87 Best Buy —*M.S. (10/1/2006)*

Errazuriz 2004 Estate Sauvignon Blanc (Casablanca Valley) $11. 87 Best Buy —*M.S. (2/1/2005)*

Errazuriz 2000 Estate Sauvignon Blanc (Casablanca Valley) $10. 80 —*M.S. (7/1/2003)*

Errazuriz 1999 La Escultura Sauvignon Blanc (Casablanca Valley) $10. 87 —*S.H. (2/1/2001)*

Errazuriz 2005 Late Harvest Sauvignon Blanc (Casablanca Valley) $13. 87 —*M.S. (10/1/2006)*

Errazuriz 1999 Late Harvest Sauvignon Blanc (Casablanca Valley) $11. 86 —*J.M. (12/1/2002)*

Errazuriz 2006 Single Vineyard Sauvignon Blanc (Casablanca Valley) $20. 89 —*M.S. (12/31/2006)*

Errazuriz 2004 La Cumbre Shiraz (Aconcagua Valley) $50. 88 —*M.S. (12/31/2006)*

Errazuriz 2003 La Cumbre Shiraz (Aconcagua Valley) $39. 88 —*M.S. (11/1/2005)*

Errazuriz 2005 Max Reserva Shiraz (Aconcagua Valley) $21. Here is another case where an Errazuriz wine has color and size but not so much balance and harmony. As with several others, it's woody to the point of searing, with vanilla and resin running on top of medium-depth plum and blackberry flavors. Lacks the complexity and density to match the wood. 83 —*M.S. (5/1/2007)*

Errazuriz 2003 Max Reserva Shiraz (Aconcagua Valley) $19. 85 —*M.S. (11/1/2005)*

Errazuriz 1999 Don Maximiano Estate - Reserva Syrah (Aconcagua Valley) $25. 86 —*D.T. (7/1/2002)*

Errazuriz 2000 Max Reserva Syrah (Aconcagua Valley) $25. 83 —*S.H. (1/1/2002)*

Errazuriz Ovalle 2004 Veo Grande Cabernet Sauvignon (Colchagua Valley) $8. 83 —*M.S. (11/15/2006)*

ESTAMPA

Estampa 2005 Estate Bottled Red Blend (Colchagua Valley) $8. More ripe and round than herbal or earthy, and right there you're ahead of the game. This wine has live-wire cassis and cherry flavors; has swagger and gritty, solid flavors. 86 Best Buy —*M.S. (11/15/2007)*

Estampa 2003 Gold Assemblage Carmenère Red Blend (Colchagua Valley) $18. 86 —*M.S. (10/1/2006)*

Estampa 2005 Reserve Assemblage Cabernet Sauvignon Carménère Petit Verdot Red Blend (Colchagua Valley) $12. Blending Cabernet, Carmenère and Petit Verdot could only happen in Chile, and here it takes on a candied, simple personality that will please undemanding palates but may bore those seeking more. If you're after red-berry flavors, body and alcohol, this wine fits the bill. 85 —*M.S. (11/15/2007)*

Estampa 2004 Reserve Assemblage Cabernet Sauvignon Carménère Petit Verdot Red Blend (Colchagua Valley) $12. 89 Best Buy —*M.S. (11/15/2006)*

Estampa 2005 Reserve Assemblage Carménère Cabernet Sauvignon Cabernet Franc Red Blend (Colchagua Valley) $12. This three-grape blend runs heavy on the Carmenère, and overall it's got more color and aromatic promise than results. The nose is round and sweet but the palate doesn't match it; it tastes tangy and short, and there's a raw feel coming courtesy of jagged tannins. 86 —*M.S. (11/15/2007)*

Estampa 2004 Reserve Assemblage Carmenère-Cabernet Sauvignon-Cabernet Franc Red Blend (Colchagua Valley) $12. 86 —*M.S. (10/1/2006)*

Estampa 2004 Reserve Assemblage Syrah Red Blend (Colchagua Valley) $12. Dark and just a touch herbal and green on the nose, but overall it's a pretty, beefy blend of Syrah (60%), Cabernet and Merlot that should win over even the most discerning of critics. The palate is balanced and features a rich, comfortable feel. And the finish is crisp but also long and rewarding. For $12 there's not much you can gripe about. 88 Best Buy —*M.S. (9/1/2007)*

Estampa 2005 Reserve Assemblage Syrah-Cabernet Sauvignon-Merlot Red Blend (Colchagua Valley) $12. Estampa's new crop of wines seem to be hit-and-miss. This blend of Syrah and 35% Cabernet and Merlot is a bit herbal and heavy. The palate shows prune flavors along with more generic red-fruit notes; finishes coarse. Not terrible but not interesting either. 85 —*M.S. (11/15/2007)*

Estampa 2005 Syrah-Cabernet (Colchagua Valley) $8. A rewarding mix of sweet red fruits and earthy chocolate is what this Syrah-Cabernet blend holds in store. The nose deals cola and coffee with some syrupy berry aromas, while the palate is grabby and a touch rough but also endowed with a ripe, forward fruit character. 85 Best Buy —*M.S. (9/1/2007)*

Estampa 2004 Estate Syrah-Cabernet (Colchagua Valley) $8. This is a hulking berry-driven wine with big, jammy aromas. And ultimately it is nothing more than an average Chilean red, meaning it has bulk and color but not much individuality or character. The 2005 version of this wine has more bounce and personality. We say stick to that. 83 —*M.S. (9/1/2007)*

Estampa 2005 Estate White Blend (Colchagua Valley) $9. Not a bad wine, with its almond skin and light pear character. But it's also starting to fade, and soon it'll be in flat-line status because the acidity is low and the remaining voltage minimal. Best immediately, or wait for the fresher 2006. It's 51% Viognier and 49% Chard. 84 —*M.S. (11/15/2007)*

Estampa 2006 Reserve Assemblage White Blend (Casablanca Valley) $12. It takes some getting used to if you're going to like this wine. First off, there's a wicked cat pee and green shot to the nose, both of which are classic Casablanca Sauvignon smells. But the citrus and other fruits that are there to offset the pungency don't really step up and do the job. So ultimately the wine has an awful lot of pickle, tart passion fruit and celery. 83 —*M.S. (11/15/2007)*

Estampa 2005 Reserve Assemblage White Blend (Central Valley) $12. 88 Best Buy —*M.S. (11/15/2006)*

Estampa 2006 Viognier Chardonnay White Blend (Colchagua Valley) $8. The bouquet smells like spiked fruit cocktail, and in the long run what's wrong with that? The palate is open and fairly easy, with a touch of kick pushing citrus, tropical fruit and even some mineral notes. A more citrusy and fresh style of Viognier, with 15% Chardonnay. 87 Best Buy *—M.S. (11/15/2007)*

FRANCISCO GILLMORE

Francisco Gillmore 1998 Cabernet Franc (Maule Valley) $27. 83 *—D.T. (7/1/2002)*

Francisco Gillmore 2000 Concepcion Cabernet Sauvignon (Maule Valley) $7. 81 *—M.S. (7/1/2003)*

Francisco Gillmore 1998 Concepcion Gran Reserva Cabernet Sauvignon (Maule Valley) $11. 86 *—C.S. (2/1/2003)*

Francisco Gillmore 1998 Concepcion Reserva Cabernet Sauvignon (Maule Valley) $11. 86 *—K.F. (7/1/2003)*

Francisco Gillmore 2001 Concepcion Chardonnay (Maule Valley) $7. 83 *—M.S. (7/1/2003)*

Francisco Gillmore 1999 Concepcion Gran Reserva Chardonnay (Maule Valley) $19. 85 *—M.S. (7/1/2003)*

Francisco Gillmore 1999 Concepcion Reserva Chardonnay (Maule Valley) $11. 83 *—M.S. (7/1/2003)*

Francisco Gillmore 2000 Concepcion Merlot (Maule Valley) $7. 81 *—M.S. (7/1/2003)*

Francisco Gillmore 1999 Concepcion Reserva Merlot (Maule Valley) $11. 80 *—M.S. (7/1/2003)*

Francisco Gillmore 2000 Concepcion Gran Reserva Syrah (Maule Valley) $16. 88 *—K.F. (2/1/2003)*

GRAN DOMINIO

Gracia de Chile 2006 Reserva Estate Vineyard Carmenère (Curicó Valley) $12. Ripe and pure with blackberry and olive aromas, and the flavors of black fruits mixed with some meatiness and cola are true and tasty. The feel is a touch racy and acidic, but that's working to keep this balanced. 87 Best Buy *—M.S. (9/1/2007)*

Gracia de Chile 2006 Reserve Pinot Noir (Bío Bío Valley) $11. Surprise! This is a legitimate, true to the variety Pinot Noir from southerly Bío Bío Valley. The wine has dryness and balance, a little wood, and pure aromas and flavors of raspberry, cherry ice tea and chocolate. It's lively and streamlined on the palate, so it will work with food. A definite winner in an emerging category that is Chilean Pinot. 87 Best Buy *—M.S. (11/15/2007)*

Gracia de Chile 2006 Reserve Syrah (Aconcagua Valley) $10. A little grapy and heavy, but overall this purple-colored Syrah is good. The bouquet is sweet with plum and prune, and the palate, while a little tangy and young, has vibrant if generic plum and berry flavors. Best if youthful, fruity New World reds are your thing. 84 *—M.S. (9/1/2007)*

GRAN DOMINIO

Gran Dominio 1999 San Cayetano Vineyards Gran Reserva Cabernet Franc (Maule Valley) $19. 85 *—S.H. (1/1/2002)*

Gran Dominio 1999 Nueva Aldea Vineyard Gran Reserva Cabernet Sauvignon (Iata Valley) $17. 84 *—S.H. (1/1/2002)*

Gran Dominio 1999 Nueva Aldea Vineyard Chardonnay (Iata Valley) $14. 85 *—S.H. (1/1/2002)*

GRAN ROBLE

Gran Roble 2003 Cabernet Sauvignon (Curicó Valley) $11. 82 *—M.S. (11/1/2005)*

Gran Roble 2003 Carmenère (Curicó Valley) $11. 84 *—M.S. (11/1/2005)*

Gran Roble 2003 Chardonnay (Curicó Valley) $11. 80 *—M.S. (7/1/2005)*

GUELBENZU

Guelbenzu 2002 Jardin Cabernet Blend (Colchagua Valley) $9. 85 *—M.S. (7/1/2003)*

Guelbenzu 2003 Hoppe Cabernet Sauvignon-Carmenère (Colchagua Valley) $15. 84 *—M.S. (3/1/2006)*

Guelbenzu 2003 Jardin Cabernet Sauvignon-Carmenère (Colchagua Valley) $8. 85 Best Buy *—M.S. (7/1/2006)*

Guelbenzu 2002 Jardin Chardonnay (Colchagua Valley) $9. 83 *—M.S. (7/1/2003)*

Guelbenzu 2004 Küme Red Blend (Colchagua Valley) $15. This Spanish producer's Chilean label relies on Cabernet and Carmenère for this blend, and it's a little vegetal and murky at first. Airing frees oak and creamy red-fruit flavors, while the chocolaty finish is of medium length. 85 *—M.S. (9/1/2007)*

HARAS

Haras 2001 Elegance Cabernet Sauvignon (Maipo Valley) $40. 89 *—M.S. (5/1/2006)*

Haras 2003 Chardonnay (Maipo Valley) $11. 86 Best Buy *—M.S. (2/1/2005)*

Haras 2003 Character Chardonnay (Maipo Valley) $14. 85 *—M.S. (5/1/2006)*

Haras 2004 Elegance Chardonnay (Maipo Valley) $20. 84 *—M.S. (5/1/2006)*

HARAS DE PIRQUE

Haras de Pirque 2002 Character Cabernet Sauvignon (Maipo Valley) $14. 85 *—M.S. (7/1/2006)*

Haras de Pirque 2001 Character Cabernet Sauvignon (Maipo Valley) $20. 89 *—M.S. (3/1/2004)*

Haras de Pirque 2001 Elegance Cabernet Sauvignon (Maipo Valley) $40. 91 *—M.S. (3/1/2004)*

Haras de Pirque 2004 Estate Cabernet Sauvignon (Maipo Valley) $10. This Maipo estate is now aligned with Chateau Ste. Michelle of Washington, which doesn't exactly impact this nice everyday Cabernet. Bramble and fresh berry aromas offer an entry, then there's chewy raspberry on the palate along with a grace of vanilla and some warmth. A bone-warming wine for fall and winter. 87 Best Buy *—M.S. (11/15/2007)*

Haras de Pirque 2002 Estate Cabernet Sauvignon (Maipo Valley) $10. 87 Best Buy *—M.S. (7/1/2006)*

Haras de Pirque 2001 Estate Cabernet Sauvignon (Maipo Valley) $11. 88 *—M.S. (3/1/2004)*

Haras de Pirque 2002 Estate Carmenère (Maipo Valley) $11. 87 *—M.S. (3/1/2004)*

Haras de Pirque 2002 Character Chardonnay (Maipo Valley) $15. 87 *—M.S. (3/1/2004)*

Haras de Pirque 2003 Elegance Chardonnay (Maipo Valley) $25. 85 *—M.S. (2/1/2005)*

Haras de Pirque 2002 Elegance Chardonnay (Maipo Valley) $25. 88 *—M.S. (3/1/2004)*

Haras de Pirque 2006 Estate Chardonnay (Maipo Valley) $10. Hard, dry and minerally on the bouquet, with cider and pineapple as the main flavors. Zesty, lively and racy for sure, but also loaded down with juice-like flavors of apples and oranges. Big on kick but short on balance and elegance. Isn't 14.8% is just too much for what should be an easygoing Chardonnay? 84 *—M.S. (11/15/2007)*

Haras de Pirque 2005 Estate Chardonnay (Maipo Valley) $10. 84 *—M.S. (7/1/2006)*

Haras de Pirque 2002 Estate Chardonnay (Maipo Valley) $11. 86 *—M.S. (3/1/2004)*

Haras de Pirque 2004 Character Sauvignon Blanc (Maipo Valley) $14. 84 *—M.S. (3/1/2006)*

Haras de Pirque 2002 Character Sauvignon Blanc (Maipo Valley) $15. 86 *—M.S. (3/1/2004)*

Haras de Pirque 2006 Estate Sauvignon Blanc (Maipo Valley) $10. Normally the Maipo Valley produces warm, dull Sauvignon Blancs. But this one has more kick and purity of fruit than most. The nose delivers tropical and melon aromas, while the palate is packed with lime, citrus and grapefruit flavors. It's on the big side and a little clingy on the finish, but mostly it gets things right. 87 *—M.S. (11/15/2007)*

Haras de Pirque 2005 Estate Sauvignon Blanc (Maipo Valley) $10. 84 *—M.S. (7/1/2006)*

Haras de Pirque 2002 Estate Sauvignon Blanc (Maipo Valley) $11. 85 *—M.S. (3/1/2004)*

Haras de Pirque 2003 Character Syrah (Maipo Valley) $14. 88 *—M.S. (7/1/2006)*

IN SITU

In Situ 2003 Gran Reserva Cabernet Sauvignon (Aconcagua Valley) $20. 83 *—M.S. (11/1/2005)*

J. & F. LURTON

J. & F. Lurton 2003 Gran Araucano Cabernet Sauvignon (Colchagua Valley) $35. Nice pepper and cola aromas on this small-production Cabernet from the Lurton brothers. It has stylish fruit but also some leather and depth. The palate is brighter than expected, with lively cherry and plum flavors. Just flashy enough, with cheek-popping acidity. 88 *—M.S. (9/1/2007)*

J. & F. Lurton 2002 Gran Araucano Cabernet Sauvignon (Colchagua Valley) $35. 85 *—M.S. (5/1/2006)*

J. & F. Lurton 2005 Hacienda Araucano Cabernet Sauvignon (Central Valley) $11. 84 *—M.S. (11/15/2006)*

J. & F. Lurton 2004 Hacienda Araucano Cabernet Sauvignon (Central Valley) $11. 85 *—M.S. (5/1/2006)*

J. & F. Lurton 2003 Hacienda Araucano Cabernet Sauvignon (Colchagua Valley) $10. 87 Best Buy *—M.S. (11/1/2005)*

J. & F. Lurton 2003 Araucano Clos de Lolol Cabernet Sauvignon-Carmenère (Colchagua Valley) $20. Razor-sharp acidity and zest is the thing that overrides this blend of Cabernet Sauvignon and Carmenère. At first the zip almost cuts through the palate, and only airing and patience brings it back to ground level. As it opens some cherry and raspberry enters the scene. Arguably too sharp for a blend of these two friendly grapes. 84 *—M.S. (11/15/2007)*

J. & F. Lurton 2002 Araucano Clos de Lolol Cabernet Sauvignon-Carmenère (Colchagua Valley) $25. 87 *—M.S. (3/1/2006)*

J. & F. Lurton 2003 Alka Carmenère (Colchagua Valley) $65. 87 *—M.S. (3/1/2006)*

J. & F. Lurton 2002 Alka Carmenère (Colchagua Valley) $55. 87 *—M.S. (2/1/2005)*

J. & F. Lurton 2005 Hacienda Araucano Carmenère (Central Valley) $11. Somewhat leafy and green, with dry aromas of spice and red fruit doing what they can to boost the wine. The palate offers raspberry and apple skin flavors along with scratchy, drying tannins. Not a lush wine but not bad in its weight and delivery. 84 *—M.S. (5/1/2007)*

J. & F. Lurton 2004 Hacienda Araucano Carmenère (Colchagua Valley) $11. 85 *—M.S. (3/1/2006)*

J. & F. Lurton 2003 Hacienda Araucano Carmenère (Colchagua Valley) $10. 87 Best Buy *—M.S. (12/1/2004)*

J. & F. Lurton 2002 Hacienda Araucano Carmenère (Colchagua Valley) $10. 84 *—M.S. (8/1/2004)*

J. & F. Lurton 2006 Hacienda Araucano Carmenere Rosado Carmenère (Central Valley) $11. Everyone appreciates a pioneer, although not necessarily when that winery is pioneering rosé from Carmenère. This is a classic "what were they thinking?" wine; it is flat, murky and heavy as cream. It barely passes for acceptable. 80 *—M.S. (7/1/2007)*

J. & F. Lurton 2003 Gran Araucano Chardonnay (Colchagua Valley) $19. 89 *—M.S. (2/1/2005)*

J. & F. Lurton 2002 Gran Araucano Chardonnay (Colchagua Valley) $18. 86 *—M.S. (6/1/2004)*

J. & F. Lurton 2006 Hacienda Araucano Chardonnay (Colchagua Valley) $11. The nose is more or less a junction of toasted corn and nuts, while the sweet palate deals pear, quince jelly, buttered nuts and vanilla. Quite sugary and basic in its approach. 83 *—M.S. (5/1/2007)*

J. & F. Lurton 2005 Hacienda Araucano Chardonnay (Colchagua Valley) $11. 84 *—M.S. (5/1/2006)*

J. & F. Lurton 2004 Hacienda Araucano Chardonnay (Colchagua Valley) $10. 86 Best Buy *—M.S. (11/1/2005)*

J. & F. Lurton 2006 Hacienda Araucano Pinot Noir (Central Valley) $14. This is a new wine from the Lurton brothers, and it's got good weight, color and integrity. It also shows a lot of hickory and pickle from the oak and some wayward vanilla on the juicy, jumpy palate. Not a refined wine but pretty good for size and zip. 86 *—M.S. (11/15/2007)*

J. & F. Lurton 2006 Gran Araucano Sauvignon Blanc (Casablanca Valley) $20. A heavier, fuller more complex style of Sauvignon, reflected in the high price tag. The nose offers ripe pineapple, passion fruit and touches of green bean and canned peas. In the mouth, there's more of that varietal, green character resulting in fresh lettuce flavors to complement more standard tropical fruit. Drink as soon as possible; it's not getting any fresher or more interesting. 86 *—M.S. (9/1/2007)*

J. & F. Lurton 2005 Gran Araucano Sauvignon Blanc (Casablanca Valley) $20. 82 *—M.S. (3/1/2006)*

J. & F. Lurton 2004 Gran Araucano Sauvignon Blanc (Casablanca Valley) $19. 85 *—M.S. (7/1/2005)*

J. & F. Lurton 2002 Gran Araucano Sauvignon Blanc (Casablanca Valley) $18. 80 *—M.S. (6/1/2004)*

J. & F. Lurton 2007 Hacienda Araucano Sauvignon Blanc (Central Valley) $11. Pungent and a touch sweaty and pickled, with lemon zest, citrus and celery notes from start to finish. The wine has fairly true flavors, but it also shows a touch of weightiness on the palate. Not a bad wine but it doesn't show much character. 84 *—M.S. (11/15/2007)*

J. & F. Lurton 2006 Hacienda Araucano Sauvignon Blanc (Central Valley) $11. 84 *—M.S. (12/31/2006)*

J. & F. Lurton 2005 Hacienda Araucano Sauvignon Blanc (Central Valley) $11. 84 *—M.S. (7/1/2006)*

J. & F. Lurton 2004 Hacienda Araucano Sauvignon Blanc (Central Valley) $9. 85 Best Buy *—M.S. (7/1/2005)*

J. & F. Lurton 2003 Hacienda Araucano Sauvignon Blanc (Central Valley) $10. 88 Best Buy *—M.S. (6/1/2004)*

J. BOUCHON

J. Bouchon 2003 Reserva Especial Cabernet Sauvignon (Maule Valley) $14. 84 *—M.S. (7/1/2006)*

J. Bouchon 2004 Reserva Especial Carmenère (Maule Valley) $14. 84 *—M.S. (7/1/2006)*

J. Bouchon 2004 Reserva Especial Malbec (Maule Valley) $14. 81 *—M.S. (5/1/2006)*

J. Bouchon 2004 Merlot (Maule Valley) $9. 82 *—M.S. (5/1/2006)*

J. Bouchon 2003 Premium Assemblage Red Blend (Maule Valley) $27. Bouchon's top-shelf red begins leathery and minty, with background red-fruit aromas poking through. The palate is lively and juicy, with slightly sheer and grabby tannins creating some jaggedness. Finishes in solid fashion, with weight and clarity. 86 *—M.S. (5/1/2007)*

KINGSTON FAMILY

Kingston Family 2004 Alazan Pinot Noir (Casablanca Valley) $28. 89 *—M.S. (11/1/2005)*

Kingston Family 2005 Tobiano Pinot Noir (Casablanca Valley) $18. Light in color, and with alluring true-Pinot aromas of brewed tea, cherry jam and cigar box. The approach Kingston takes is to make something in the California style, and this has the size and richness of fruit to qualify as such. A really nice wine that's far from ordinary and shows what Casablanca can do when it's on the right path. 89 *—M.S. (9/1/2007)*

Kingston Family 2004 Tobiano Pinot Noir (Casablanca Valley) $18. 87 *—M.S. (11/1/2005)*

Kingston Family 2006 Cariblanco Sauvignon Blanc (Casablanca Valley) $16. Light in color but lively in its aromas of lettuce, half-sour pickle, fresh asparagus and passion fruit. The palate is zesty and jumpy, with lemon-lime flavors, passion fruit and a touch of minerality. And the finish is quite long for Sauvignon, a direct reflection of the wine's heft and 14.5% alcohol. 88 *—M.S. (9/1/2007)*

Kingston Family 2004 Cariblanco Sauvignon Blanc (Casablanca Valley) $15. 90 *—M.S. (11/1/2005)*

Kingston Family 2004 Bayo Oscuro Syrah (Casablanca Valley) $28. It takes a while for the oak and leather elements to lessen on the nose, and by then the wine has taken on a meaty, reserved, mildly burnt character. It's a woody number with some complexity, namely bitter chocolate that envelops the back palate and finish. Throughout it shows size and intent but never does it fully pull it off. 550 cases made. 85 *—M.S. (9/1/2007)*

Kingston Family 2003 Bayo Oscuro Syrah (Casablanca Valley) $28. 85 *—M.S. (11/1/2005)*

Kingston Family 2005 Tobiano Syrah (Casablanca Valley) $18. Tobiano in 2005 is preferable to Kingston's 2004 Bayo Oscuro Syrah. This wine has more lift, fruit and balance. The nose is lightly fruity and rubbery, while the palate issues snappy boysenberry and controlled herb notes. Not your average New World Syrah; it'll make you think. 88 *—M.S. (9/1/2007)*

KONO BARÚ

Kono Barú 2005 Cabernet Sauvignon (Central Valley) $13. A little char and herbal lift accent the confected nose on this Central Valley wine. The palate is jammy sweet with raspberry and cherry flavors, while the finish shows a dose of Cabernet character but mostly just pleasant, innocuous sweetness. 84 *—M.S. (11/15/2007)*

Kono Barú 2006 Unwooded Chardonnay (Central Valley) $13. Racy and loaded with apricot, melon, apple and corn aromas and flavors. It's sweet and sticky on the palate, while the finish is ponderous. 82 *—M.S. (11/15/2007)*

Kono Barú 2006 Sauvignon Blanc (Central Valley) $13. Peaches and cream on the nose? And this is supposed to be Sauvignon Blanc, a wine known for its piquant pungency? Guess not, because it's full of soft, flabby peach and papaya flavors rather than citrus and snap. Get it while it still has a pulse. 82 *—M.S. (11/15/2007)*

KUYEN

Kuyen 2004 Syrah-Cabernet (Maipo Valley) $25. As in the past, this blend of 51% Syrah and 49% Cab is rock-solid, with tight, tough herbal-olive undertones supporting spicy dark fruit and road tar aromas. The palate has pepper, blackberry and roasted plum flavors, while chocolate and espresso notes gather on the finish. Just 400 cases made by talented winemaker Alvaro Espinoza. 88 *—M.S. (9/1/2007)*

Kuyen 2003 Syrah-Cabernet (Maipo Valley) $23. 89 *—M.S. (3/1/2006)*

Kuyen 2002 Red Wine Syrah-Cabernet (Maipo Valley) $22. 88 *—M.S. (2/1/2005)*

LA CAPITANA

La Capitana 2002 Cabernet Sauvignon (Cachapoal Valley) $12. 84 —*M.S. (3/1/2004)*

La Capitana 2002 Carmenère (Cachapoal Valley) $12. 87 —*M.S. (3/1/2004)*

La Capitana 2003 Chardonnay (Cachapoal Valley) $12. 85 —*M.S. (3/1/2004)*

LA PALMA

La Palma 2003 Cabernet Sauvignon (Cachapoal Valley) $7. 83 —*M.S. (3/1/2004)*

La Palma 2002 Cabernet Sauvignon (Cachapoal Valley) $7. 85 Best Buy —*M.S. (7/1/2003)*

La Palma 2001 Cabernet Sauvignon (Rapel Valley) $10. 87 Best Buy —*D.T. (7/1/2002)*

La Palma 2000 Reserve Cabernet Sauvignon (Rapel Valley) $12. 83 —*D.T. (7/1/2002)*

La Palma 1999 Reserve Cabernet Sauvignon (Rapel Valley) $10. 89 Best Buy —*J.C. (3/1/2002)*

La Palma 1998 Reserve Cabernet Sauvignon (Rapel Valley) $10. 81 —*M.N. (1/1/2004)*

La Palma 2001 Cabernet Sauvignon-Merlot (Rapel Valley) $10. 83 —*D.T. (7/1/2002)*

La Palma 2002 Estate Bottled Cabernet Sauvignon-Merlot (Cachapoal Valley) $10. 86 —*M.S. (7/1/2003)*

La Palma 1999 Reserve Cabernet Sauvignon-Merlot (Rapel Valley) $10. 85 —*D.T. (7/1/2002)*

La Palma 2001 Reserve Est Bottled Est Grown Carmenère (Cachapoal Valley) $10. 82 —*M.S. (7/1/2003)*

La Palma 2003 Chardonnay (Cachapoal Valley) $8. 86 Best Buy —*M.S. (3/1/2004)*

La Palma 2001 Chardonnay (Rapel Valley) $10. 83 —*M.S. (7/1/2002)*

La Palma 2000 Chardonnay (Rapel Valley) $6. 82 —*J.C. (3/1/2002)*

La Palma 1999 Chardonnay (Rapel Valley) $7. 82 —*M.M. (1/1/2004)*

La Palma 2002 Estate Bottled Chardonnay (Cachapoal Valley) $8. 83 —*M.S. (7/1/2003)*

La Palma 2000 Reserve Chardonnay (Rapel Valley) $12. 83 —*M.S. (7/1/2002)*

La Palma 1999 Reserve Chardonnay (Rapel Valley) $10. 85 —*J.F. (8/1/2001)*

La Palma 2003 Merlot (Cachapoal Valley) $7. 82 —*M.S. (3/1/2004)*

La Palma 2002 Merlot (Cachapoal Valley) $7. 84 —*M.S. (7/1/2003)*

La Palma 2001 Merlot (Rapel Valley) $10. 84 —*D.T. (7/1/2002)*

La Palma 2000 Merlot (Rapel Valley) $6. 84 Best Buy —*J.C. (3/1/2002)*

La Palma 1999 Merlot (Rapel Valley) $8. 85 —*M.M. (2/1/2001)*

La Palma 2000 Reserve Merlot (Rapel Valley) $12. 83 —*D.T. (7/1/2002)*

La Palma 2003 Merlot-Cabernet Sauvignon (Rapel Valley) $8. 83 —*M.S. (3/1/2004)*

La Palma 2003 Sauvignon Blanc (Rapel Valley) $8. 85 —*M.S. (3/1/2004)*

La Palma 2002 Estate Bottled Sauvignon Blanc (Cachapoal Valley) $8. 86 Best Buy —*M.S. (7/1/2003)*

LA PLAYA

La Playa 1994 Maxima Claret Bordeaux Blend (Maipo Valley) $21. 85 *(2/1/2001)*

La Playa 2002 Axel Primero Cabernet Blend (Colchagua Valley) $30. 88 —*M.S. (7/1/2006)*

La Playa 1996 Claret Maxima Cabernet Blend (Maipo Valley) $23. 85 —*D.T. (7/1/2002)*

La Playa 2003 Axel Cabernet Sauvignon (Colchagua Valley) $20. 92 Cellar Selection —*M.S. (7/1/2006)*

La Playa 2003 Block Selection Cabernet Sauvignon (Colchagua Valley) $11. 88 Best Buy —*M.S. (11/1/2005)*

La Playa 2004 Block Selection Estate Reserve Cabernet Sauvignon (Colchagua Valley) $10. Possibly too oaky at first blush, as coconut and sawmill shavings are the initial aromas. But as it settles, brighter red fruit emerges, and on the back end there's proper acidity and balance that keeps the whole deal well framed. 86 Best Buy —*M.S. (3/1/2007)*

La Playa 2003 Estate Cabernet Sauvignon (Colchagua Valley) $8. 83 —*M.S. (7/1/2006)*

La Playa 2004 Estate Rose Cabernet Sauvignon (Colchagua Valley) $8. 81 —*M.S. (5/1/2006)*

La Playa 2005 Rosé Cabernet Sauvignon (Colchagua Valley) $7. 83 —*M.S. (10/1/2006)*

La Playa 2004 Block Selection Esate Reserve Carmenère (Colchagua Valley) $10. Starts off with some forest floor, moss, leather and olive notes, all typical aromas for Carmenère. The palate on this middleweight is chunky and easy, maybe a touch flat, with flavors of baked plum, black olive and soy. Finishes chewy, soft and quiet. Drink now. 85 Best Buy —*M.S. (3/1/2007)*

La Playa 2001 Estate Reserve Carmenère (Colchagua Valley) $10. 87 Best Buy —*M.S. (7/1/2003)*

La Playa 2005 Block Selection Estate Reserve Chardonnay (Casablanca Valley) $10. 85 Best Buy —*M.S. (11/15/2006)*

La Playa 2000 Estate Bottled Chardonnay (Maipo Valley) $7. 85 —*M.M. (1/1/2004)*

La Playa 2002 Estate Reserve Chardonnay (Colchagua Valley) $10. 87 Best Buy —*M.S. (7/1/2003)*

La Playa 1999 Estate Reserve Chardonnay (Maipo Valley) $11. 84 —*J.F. (8/1/2001)*

La Playa 2003 Reserve Chardonnay (Colchagua Valley) $10. 85 Best Buy —*M.S. (2/1/2005)*

La Playa 2004 Merlot (Colchagua Valley) $8. 85 Best Buy —*M.S. (11/1/2005)*

La Playa 2001 Estate Reserve Merlot (Colchagua Valley) $10. 81 —*M.S. (7/1/2005)*

La Playa 1999 Estate Reserve Merlot (Colchagua Valley) $10. 87 Best Buy —*M.S. (7/1/2003)*

La Playa 1998 Claret Red Blend (Maipo Valley) $10. 83 —*M.M. (2/1/2001)*

La Playa 2006 Estate Sauvignon Blanc (Colchagua Valley) $7. In its price range you can't beat this for freshness and flavor. The nose is a touch floral and sweet, while the palate is forward and flush with mild gooseberry and citrus flavors. Finishes clean and short, with a certain slickness that seems appropriate. 85 Best Buy—*M.S. (3/1/2007)*

La Playa 2003 Estate Sauvignon Blanc (Colchagua Valley) $7. 82 —*M.S. (8/1/2004)*

La Playa 2000 Estate Bottled Sauvignon Blanc (Maipo Valley) $8. 83 —*J.C. (3/1/2002)*

La Playa 2003 Axel Syrah (Colchagua Valley) $20. 87 —*M.S. (7/1/2006)*

LAURA HARTWIG

Laura Hartwig 1999 Gran Reserva Cabernet Blend (Colchagua Valley) $23. 90 —*M.S. (3/1/2002)*

Laura Hartwig 2001 Cabernet Sauvignon (Colchagua Valley) $12. 87 —*M.S. (6/1/2004)*

Laura Hartwig 2002 Carmenère (Colchagua Valley) $12. 86 —*M.S. (6/1/2004)*

Laura Hartwig 1999 Carmenère (Colchagua Valley) $12. 87 Best Buy —*M.S. (3/1/2002)*

Laura Hartwig 2000 Chardonnay (Colchagua Valley) $11. 87 Best Buy —*M.S. (2/1/2002)*

Laura Hartwig 1999 Merlot (Colchagua Valley) $12. 88 Best Buy —*M.S. (3/1/2002)*

Laura Hartwig 2000 Gran Reserva Red Blend (Colchagua Valley) $20. 87 —*M.S. (6/1/2004)*

LAUREL GLEN

Laurel Glen 2001 Terra Rosa Cabernet Sauvignon (Central Valley) $10. 83 —*S.H. (1/1/2002)*

Laurel Glen 2000 Terra Rosa Cabernet Sauvignon (Central Valley) $10. 86 —*S.H. (2/1/2003)*

LAYLA

Layla 2000 Malbec (Maule Valley) $9. 81 —*M.S. (7/1/2003)*

LEYDA

Leyda 2003 Estación Reserve Carmenère (Colchagua Valley) $12. 86 —*M.S. (12/1/2004)*

Leyda 2006 Classic Chardonnay (San Antonio) $11. From as close to the Pacific coast as one can get in Chile, this Chardonnay has fresh, secure aromas of pear, wild flowers and buttercup. The mouth is full of vibrant acids that release tangy flavors of orange, lemon and mango. That tang is preserved on the finish, which isn't that dissimilar to certain dry Rieslings. Good as goes value-priced Chilean Chadonnay. 86 Best Buy —*M.S. (11/15/2007)*

Leyda 2005 Falaris Hill Vineyard Chardonnay (San Antonio) $17. Pickled and funky, this wine seems to be at the end of its road. The nose has a bit of burnt hay, while the mouth is still juicy but also rustic, green and herbal. For whatever reason, this doesn't have much freshness or purity of flavor. 83 —*M.S. (11/15/2007)*

Leyda 2003 Falaris Hill Vineyard Reserve Chardonnay (Leyda Valley) $18. 86 —*M.S. (7/1/2005)*

Leyda 2006 Lot 5 - Wild Yeasts Chardonnay (San Antonio) $26. A floral specimen with buttercup, apple, pear and pie crust on the nose. But in the mouth the wine is juicy and monotone, with apple and orange flavors that are tangy, thin and racy. This wine moves fast but doesn't impress like a top Chardonnay should. 84 —*M.S. (11/15/2007)*

Leyda 2006 Las Brisas Vineyard Pinot Noir (San Antonio) $20. From very close to the Pacific coast comes this full, funky Pinot that begins with aromas of burnt compost and leaves and then segues to caramel. It's better in the mouth, where bramble, plum and cumin flavors are exotic and don't pound you over the head. Not for everyone; it's a touch earthy and mulchy. 85 —*M.S. (11/15/2007)*

Leyda 2006 Lot 21 Pinot Noir (San Antonio) $36. Tea, raspberry and tree bark aromas are interesting and inviting, while the strawberry and cherry flavors are a little gritty and reduced but true to the blueprint in terms of taste. On the finish, chocolate, vanilla and other oak-based flavors do their thing. Not a perfect New World Pinot but it's on the right path. 88 —*M.S. (11/15/2007)*

Leyda 2006 Classic Sauvignon Blanc (San Antonio) $11. Pungent and green on the nose, which makes it 100% varietally correct. It smells and tastes of cool-climate terroir, and if you enjoy simple but likable citrus, melon, snap pea and bell pepper characteristics, this has it. Good by the glass or by the bottle. 87 Best Buy —*M.S. (11/15/2007)*

Leyda 2006 Garuma Vineyard Sauvignon Blanc (San Antonio) $17. Leyda is known for wines of character; the problem is that sometimes the character isn't very appealing. This is a case in point; the wine has a lot of pickle, canned pea and other vegetal traits, with a flat feel. 82 —*M.S. (11/15/2007)*

LEYENDA DEL TOQUI

Leyenda del Toqui 2001 Bordeaux Blend (Cachapoal Valley) $45. 85 —*M.S. (12/31/2006)*

LOICA

Loica 2004 Carmenère (Maipo Valley) $12. 84 —*M.S. (3/1/2006)*

Loica 2004 Sauvignon Blanc (Maule Valley) $12. 82 —*M.S. (12/15/2005)*

LOS VASCOS

Los Vascos 2004 Cabernet Sauvignon (Colchagua Valley) $11. 89 Best Buy —*M.S. (5/1/2006)*

Los Vascos 2001 Cabernet Sauvignon (Colchagua Valley) $10. 83 —*M.S. (7/1/2003)*

Los Vascos 2000 Cabernet Sauvignon (Colchagua Valley) $10. 84 —*J.C. (3/1/2002)*

Los Vascos 1999 Cabernet Sauvignon (Colchagua Valley) $11. 86 *(2/1/2001)*

Los Vascos 1999 Le Dix Cabernet Sauvignon (Colchagua Valley) $40. 88 —*M.S. (7/1/2003)*

Los Vascos 2003 Reserve Cabernet Sauvignon (Colchagua Valley) $20. 89 —*M.S. (5/1/2006)*

Los Vascos 2002 Reserve Cabernet Sauvignon (Colchagua Valley) $20. 87 —*M.S. (11/1/2005)*

Los Vascos 2000 Reserve Cabernet Sauvignon (Colchagua Valley) $18. 80 —*M.S. (12/1/2002)*

Los Vascos 1999 Reserve Cabernet Sauvignon (Colchagua Valley) $15. 86 —*J.C. (3/1/2002)*

Los Vascos 1998 Reserve Cabernet Sauvignon (Colchagua Valley) $18. 87 *(2/1/2001)*

Los Vascos 1997 Reserve Cabernet Sauvignon (Colchagua Valley) $15. 85 —*M.S. (5/1/2000)*

Los Vascos 2004 Chardonnay (Colchagua Valley) $10. 82 —*M.S. (2/1/2005)*

Los Vascos 2002 Chardonnay (Colchagua Valley) $10. 85 —*M.S. (7/1/2003)*

Los Vascos 2000 Chardonnay (Colchagua Valley) $11. 86 *(2/1/2001)*

Los Vascos 1997 Le Dix de Los Vascos Red Blend (Colchagua Valley) $40. 88 —*M.S. (5/1/2000)*

Los Vascos 1996 Le Dix de Los Vascos Red Blend (Colchagua Valley) $40. 91 —*M.S. (5/1/2000)*

Los Vascos 2006 Sauvignon Blanc (Casablanca Valley) $12. A wonderfully made varietal white that's just what Chilean SB should be. A blend of sweet pears and snappy grassy scents work the nose, while lime and grapefruit are at the head of the palate. A lasting finish confirms this wine's quality and character. 89 Best Buy —*M.S. (3/1/2007)*

LUIS FELIPE EDWARDS

Luis Felipe Edwards 2002 Doña Bernarda Bordeaux Blend (Colchagua Valley) $22. 88 —*M.S. (3/1/2006)*

Luis Felipe Edwards 1997 Cabernet Sauvignon (Colchagua Valley) $10. 82 —*M.S. (11/15/1999)*

Luis Felipe Edwards 2001 Doña Bernarda Cabernet Sauvignon (Colchagua Valley) $24. 85 —*M.S. (7/1/2005)*

Luis Felipe Edwards 1999 Doña Bernarda Cabernet Sauvignon (Colchagua Valley) $26. 87 —*M.S. (3/1/2002)*

Luis Felipe Edwards 2000 Estate Bottled Cabernet Sauvignon (Colchagua Valley) $8. 84 —*M.S. (12/1/2002)*

Luis Felipe Edwards 2004 Family Selection Gran Reserva Cabernet Sauvignon (Colchagua Valley) $15. New packaging on LFE's wines make them appear more modern, and certainly the cedar and balsam aromas that override the cherry and berry notes are indicative of a so-called modern wine. Otherwise, look for buttery red-fruit flavors with vanilla on the finish. 85 —*M.S. (3/1/2007)*

Luis Felipe Edwards 2002 Gran Reserva Cabernet Sauvignon (Colchagua Valley) $13. 82 —*M.S. (7/1/2005)*

Luis Felipe Edwards 2001 Gran Reserva Cabernet Sauvignon (Colchagua Valley) $13. 87 —*M.S. (8/1/2004)*

Luis Felipe Edwards 2000 Gran Reserva - Estate Bottled Cabernet Sauvignon (Colchagua Valley) $13. 87 —*M.S. (12/1/2002)*

Luis Felipe Edwards 2003 Pupilla Cabernet Sauvignon (Colchagua Valley) $8. 83 —*M.S. (8/1/2004)*

Luis Felipe Edwards 1999 Pupilla Cabernet Sauvignon (Colchagua Valley) $8. 85 —*M.S. (11/15/1999)*

Luis Felipe Edwards 1999 Reserva Cabernet Sauvignon (Colchagua Valley) $12. 85 —*M.S. (3/1/2002)*

Luis Felipe Edwards 1997 Reserva Cabernet Sauvignon (Colchagua Valley) $13. 86 —*M.S. (11/15/1999)*

Luis Felipe Edwards 2003 Carmenère (Colchagua Valley) $8. 86 Best Buy —*M.S. (3/1/2006)*

Luis Felipe Edwards 2001 Carmenère (Colchagua Valley) $8. 86 —*M.S. (8/1/2004)*

Luis Felipe Edwards 2002 Estate Carmenère (Colchagua Valley) $8. 84 —*M.S. (8/1/2004)*

Luis Felipe Edwards 1999 Estate Bottled Carmenère (Colchagua Valley) $11. 84 —*J.C. (8/1/2001)*

Luis Felipe Edwards 2004 Family Selection Gran Reserva Carmenère (Colchagua Valley) $15. A heavy wine with savory aromas of leather, animal fur, soy and baked plums. The palate is noticeably salty and dull, while the finish offers some tannic grab along with a touch of chocolate. Limited in its virtues but not offensive. 83 —*M.S. (3/1/2007)*

Luis Felipe Edwards 2003 Gran Reserva Carmenère (Colchagua Valley) $13. 85 —*M.S. (3/1/2006)*

Luis Felipe Edwards 2001 Gran Reserva Carmenère (Colchagua Valley) $13. 86 —*M.S. (3/1/2004)*

Luis Felipe Edwards 1999 Chardonnay (Colchagua Valley) $10. 88 Best Buy —*M.S. (11/15/1999)*

Luis Felipe Edwards 2004 Chardonnay (Colchagua Valley) $8. 84 Best Buy —*M.S. (11/1/2005)*

Luis Felipe Edwards 2003 Chardonnay (Colchagua Valley) $8. 85 Best Buy —*M.S. (6/1/2004)*

Luis Felipe Edwards 2001 Chardonnay (Colchagua Valley) $8. 85 —*M.S. (3/1/2002)*

Luis Felipe Edwards 2005 Estate Chardonnay (Colchagua Valley) $8. 81 —*M.S. (12/31/2006)*

Luis Felipe Edwards 2002 Malbec (Colchagua Valley) $8. 86 Best Buy —*M.S. (12/1/2003)*

Luis Felipe Edwards 2002 Gran Reserva Malbec (Colchagua Valley) $13. 85 —*M.S. (8/1/2004)*

Luis Felipe Edwards 2001 Gran Reserva Malbec (Colchagua Valley) $13. 86 —*M.S. (12/1/2003)*

Luis Felipe Edwards 2002 Merlot (Colchagua Valley) $8. 84 —*M.S. (8/1/2004)*

Luis Felipe Edwards 2001 Merlot (Colchagua Valley) $8. 85 Best Buy —*C.S. (12/1/2002)*

Luis Felipe Edwards 1999 Estate Bottled Merlot (Colchagua Valley) $10. 83 —*J.F. (8/1/2001)*

Luis Felipe Edwards 2001 Gran Reserva Merlot (Colchagua Valley) $13. 86 —*M.S. (3/1/2004)*

Luis Felipe Edwards 2000 Gran Reserva Estate Bottled Merlot (Colchagua Valley) $13. 85 —*C.S. (12/1/2002)*

Luis Felipe Edwards 2005 Estate Sauvignon Blanc (Central Valley) $8. Baked and heavy, with corn and hay aromas. The palate is one part banana and one part orange peel. Quite heavy for Sauvignon Blanc and without much varietal character. Imported by William Grant & Sons. 80 —*M.S. (9/1/2007)*

Luis Felipe Edwards 2002 Shiraz (Colchagua Valley) $7. 84 —*M.S. (8/1/2004)*

Luis Felipe Edwards 2005 Estate Shiraz (Colchagua Valley) $8. This little Shiraz has a good foundation to it. The nose is round and warm, with simple fruit and earth aromas. The palate is a touch tannic and rubbery, but it's holding solid raspberry and red plum flavors. Somewhat on the sheer side, with enough character that it deserves a look. 84 Best Buy —*M.S. (5/1/2007)*

Luis Felipe Edwards 2004 Family Selection Gran Reserva Shiraz (Colchagua Valley) $NA. Full and chunky on the nose, with some wood shavings, spice and fairly smooth red fruit. The palate is zesty and bright; the cherry and plum flavors are a touch tart and lean, but they are tasty. Finishes racy and a little gritty courtesy of hard tannins. 84 —*M.S. (5/1/2007)*

Luis Felipe Edwards 2002 Gran Reserva Shiraz (Colchagua Valley) $13. 88 —*M.S. (8/1/2004)*

MANTA

Manta 2003 Sauvignon Blanc (Central Valley) $6. 86 Best Buy —*M.S. (2/1/2005)*

MAQUIS

Maquis 2004 Lien Red Blend (Colchagua Valley) $18. 88 —*M.S. (10/1/2006)*

Maquis 2003 Lien Red Blend (Colchagua Valley) $15. 85 —*M.S. (3/1/2006)*

MARQUÉS DE CASA CONCHA

Marqués de Casa Concha 2003 Chardonnay (Pirque) $15. 87 —*M.S. (7/1/2005)*

MATETIC

Matetic 2003 EQ Pinot Noir (San Antonio) $25. 86 —*M.S. (11/1/2005)*

Matetic 2004 EQ Sauvignon Blanc (San Antonio) $15. 88 —*M.S. (11/1/2005)*

Matetic 2003 EQ Syrah (San Antonio) $25. 90 —*M.S. (11/1/2005)*

MCMANIS

McManis 2002 River Junction Chardonnay (Central Valley) $10. 82 —*S.H. (1/1/2002)*

McManis 2002 River Junction Pinot Grigio (Central Valley) $10. 86 —*S.H. (1/1/2002)*

MELANIA

Melania 2006 Chardonnay (Maule Valley) $8. Ripe to the point that it's soft and flat. Big apple and banana flavors run the palate, while the finish is so low in acid that it takes on extra weight. Inoffensive but devoid of a measurable pulse. 82 —*M.S. (9/1/2007)*

Melania 2006 Colección Especial Sauvignon Blanc (Maule Valley) $10. Quite sweet to the nose, and then strapping and aggressive on the palate. The flavors of gooseberry and sweet bell peppers are not easy to wrap yourself around, and it finishes kind of clunky. 82 —*M.S. (9/1/2007)*

Melania 2004 Colección Especial Chardonnay (Maule Valley) $11. 83 —*M.S. (11/1/2005)*

Melania 2004 Colección Especial Merlot (Maule Valley) $11. 83 —*M.S. (11/1/2005)*

MICHEL LAROCHE/JORGE CODERCH

Michel Laroche/Jorge Coderch 2002 Rio Azul Chardonnay (Casablanca Valley) $13. 87 *(2/1/2004)*

Michel Laroche/Jorge Coderch 2002 Piedra Feliz Pinot Noir (Casablanca Valley) $NA. 83 *(2/1/2004)*

MIGUEL TORRES

Miguel Torres 2001 Manso de Velasco Cabernet Sauvignon (Curicó Valley) $37. 91 —*M.S. (7/1/2005)*

Miguel Torres 2000 Manso de Velasco Cabernet Sauvignon (Curicó Valley) $35. 90 —*M.S. (7/1/2003)*

Miguel Torres 1999 Manso de Velasco Cabernet Sauvignon (Curicó Valley) $33. 90 —*M.S. (3/1/2002)*

Miguel Torres 2004 Manso de Velasco Viejas Viñas Cabernet Sauvignon (Curicó Valley) $32. Manso ranks among the biggest, most historic and most consistent Chilean Cabernets going. The 2004 isn't perfect but it exhibits classic old-vines blueberry and cassis aromas and flavors. There's not too much obvious oak and the tannins seem a little soft. Which means it's more or less ready to drink now (ahead of the '03). 90 —*M.S. (9/1/2007)*

Miguel Torres 2003 Manso de Velasco Viejas Viñas Cabernet Sauvignon (Curicó Valley) $32. 92 Editors' Choice —*M.S. (7/1/2006)*

Miguel Torres 2003 Santa Digna Cabernet Sauvignon (Curicó Valley) $12. 86 —*M.S. (11/1/2005)*

Miguel Torres 2002 Santa Digna Cabernet Sauvignon (Curicó Valley) $13. 85 —*M.S. (7/1/2003)*

Miguel Torres 2000 Santa Digna Cabernet Sauvignon (Curicó Valley) $13. 86 —*M.S. (3/1/2002)*

Miguel Torres 1999 Santa Digna Cabernet Sauvignon (Curicó Valley) $12. 88 Best Buy —*J.C. (2/1/2001)*

Miguel Torres 2004 Santa Digna Reserve Cabernet Sauvignon (Central Valley) $10. Here's a value-priced Cab with enough black-fruit aromas and depth to bring it to the next level. The palate is a bit charred and chocolaty, with blackberry as the lead flavor. Almost heavy and meaty, but not at all overstuffed and clumsy. What affordable Chilean Cab is all about. 87 Best Buy —*M.S. (3/1/2007)*

Miguel Torres 2006 Santa Digna Selection Rosé Cabernet Sauvignon (Central Valley) $9. Red like a ruby and broad as can be, there's nothing here but clumsy, juicy flavors of red sucking candy and Kool-Aid. With an almost inperceptible touch of spritz the wine brings to the table its own persona...which isn't all that appealing. Definitely not one of the winery's gems. 81 —*M.S. (7/1/2007)*

Miguel Torres 2006 Santa Digna Reserve Rosé Cabernet Sauvignon (Curicó Valley) $10. 80 —*M.S. (11/15/2006)*

Miguel Torres 2003 Santa Digna Rose Cabernet Sauvignon (Curicó Valley) $9. 84 —*M.S. (8/1/2004)*

Miguel Torres 2005 Tormenta Cabernet Sauvignon (Central Valley) $13. 84 —*M.S. (11/15/2006)*

Miguel Torres 2004 Tormenta Cabernet Sauvignon (Central Valley) $11. 83 —*M.S. (5/1/2006)*

Miguel Torres 2003 Santa Digna Reserva Carmenère (Curicó Valley) $16. 85 —*M.S. (11/1/2005)*

Miguel Torres 2005 Santa Digna Reserve Carmenère (Central Valley) $12. 88 Best Buy —*M.S. (11/15/2006)*

Miguel Torres 2004 Santa Digna Reserve Carmenère (Curicó Valley) $12. 85 —*M.S. (7/1/2006)*

Miguel Torres 2002 Santa Digna Carmenère-Cabernet Sauvignon (Curicó Valley) $25.88 —*M.S. (12/1/2004)*

Miguel Torres 2004 Maquehua Chardonnay (Curicó Valley) $18. 87 —*M.S. (7/1/2006)*

Miguel Torres 2003 Maquehua Chardonnay (Curicó Valley) $16. 89 —*M.S. (2/1/2005)*

Miguel Torres 2002 Maquehua Chardonnay (Curicó Valley) $19. 88 —*M.S. (7/1/2003)*

Miguel Torres 2000 Maquehua Chardonnay (Curicó Valley) $19. 85 —*M.M. (8/1/2001)*

Miguel Torres 1999 Maquehua Chardonnay (Curicó Valley) $19. 90 Editors' Choice —*J.C. (2/1/2001)*

Miguel Torres 2002 Santa Digna Chardonnay (Curicó Valley) $10. 86 —*M.S. (7/1/2003)*

Miguel Torres 2006 Santa Digna Reserve Chardonnay (Curicó Valley) $11. Very offbeat, with aromas of passion fruit gone wrong. The palate is full of mealy citrus flavors and overripe grapefruit. A weird and not too appealing take on Chardonnay. It's more like Sauvignon Blanc. 80 —*M.S. (5/1/2007)*

Miguel Torres 2005 Santa Digna Selection Chardonnay (Curicó Valley) $11. 84 —*M.S. (3/1/2006)*

Miguel Torres 2000 Don Miguel Gewürztraminer-Riesling (Curicó Valley) $11. 88 Best Buy —*J.C. (2/1/2001)*

Miguel Torres 2004 Santa Digna Merlot (Curicó Valley) $12. 86 —*M.S. (11/1/2005)*

Miguel Torres 2003 Santa Digna Merlot (Curicó Valley) $10. 83 *—M.S. (2/1/2005)*

Miguel Torres 2002 Santa Digna Merlot (Curicó Valley) $10. 83 *—M.S. (7/1/2003)*

Miguel Torres 2005 Santa Digna Reserve Merlot (Curicó Valley) $12. A very good Merlot with positive red fruit aromas graced by some penetrating spiciness. The palate is almost creamy as it delivers red fruit flavors and mouthfilling tannins. The finish, however, is short on definition and length. Best to drink now in uncomplicated settings. 87 Best Buy *—M.S. (3/1/2007)*

Miguel Torres 2000 Conde de Superunda Red Blend (Curicó Valley) $70. 90 *(11/15/2005)*

Miguel Torres 2001 Cordillera Red Blend (Curicó Valley) $27. 88 *—M.S. (11/1/2005)*

Miguel Torres 2000 Cordillera Red Blend (Curicó Valley) $26. 90 *—M.S. (3/1/2002)*

Miguel Torres 1999 Cordillera Red Blend (Curicó Valley) $26. 91 Editors' Choice *—J.C. (2/1/2001)*

Miguel Torres 2000 Rosé Blend (Curicó Valley) $8. 82 *—J.C. (2/1/2001)*

Miguel Torres 2004 Late Harvest Riesling (Curicó Valley) $22. With its heavy orange and amber tint and giant apricot, leather and Madeira aromas, this is an interesting sweet Riesling that isn't made year in and year out. The wine delivers beerenauslese-style orange and honey flavors, with milk chocolate, rum and raisin on the finish. It's not quite perfect or world class, but it's very nice for Chilean dessert wine. 89 *—M.S. (11/15/2007)*

Miguel Torres 2000 Copihue Sauvignon Blanc (Curicó Valley) $15. 85 *—M.S. (3/1/2002)*

Miguel Torres 2003 Santa Digna Sauvignon Blanc (Curicó Valley) $10. 81 *—M.S. (2/1/2005)*

Miguel Torres 2000 Santa Digna Sauvignon Blanc (Curicó Valley) $12. 85 *—J.C. (2/1/2001)*

Miguel Torres 2006 Santa Digna Selection Sauvignon Blanc (Central Valley) $10. Be it whites or reds, the Santa Digna line from Miguel Torres is proving itself to offer clean, true flavors that anyone can appreciate. The SB gives off scallion and citrus aromas in front of a full palate defined by body weight and flavors of capsicum, pickle and melon rind. It's a steady, honest varietal wine. 87 Best Buy *—M.S. (3/1/2007)*

Miguel Torres 2005 Santa Digna Selection Sauvignon Blanc (Curicó Valley) $11. 82 *—M.S. (5/1/2006)*

Miguel Torres 2004 Santa Digna Reserve Shiraz (Curicó Valley) $12. 87 Best Buy *—M.S. (10/1/2006)*

MILLAMAN

Millaman 2000 Cabernet Sauvignon (Curicó Valley) $8. 86 Best Buy *—M.S. (12/1/2002)*

Millaman 2004 Old Vines Reserva Cabernet Sauvignon-Malbec (Curicó Valley) $NA. 85 *—M.S. (12/15/2005)*

Millaman 2000 Chardonnay (Curicó Valley) $8. 80 *—M.S. (7/1/2002)*

Millaman 2000 Red Blend (Curicó Valley) $8. 85 Best Buy *—C.S. (12/1/2002)*

Millaman 2000 Sauvignon Blanc (Curicó Valley) $8. 85 *—M.S. (7/1/2003)*

Millaman 2002 Reserva Zinfandel (Central Valley) $NA. 85 *—M.S. (7/1/2006)*

MONTES

Montes 2004 Montes Alpha M Bordeaux Blend (Colchagua Valley) $93. A world-class wine from Chile? It has been for almost a decade, but now that it's pushing $100 we are looking at it quite critically. In 2004 the wine shows strong oak and some sweet creaminess, and in the mouth it's loaded with black plum and blackberry pie flavors. Finishes layered and deep, with chocolate and mocha. 92 *—M.S. (9/1/2007)*

Montes 2000 Montes Alpha M Bordeaux Blend (Colchagua Valley) $72. 89 *—M.S. (3/1/2004)*

Montes 1999 Montes Alpha M Bordeaux Blend (Colchagua Valley) $72. 88 *—D.T. (7/1/2002)*

Montes 2000 Ltd. Selection-Apalta Vnyd-Carmenere/Cab Sauv Cabernet Blend (Colchagua Valley) $16. 82 *—D.T. (7/1/2002)*

Montes 1996 Cabernet Sauvignon (Curicó Valley) $7. 89 *(11/15/1999)*

Montes 2006 Classic Series Cabernet Sauvignon (Colchagua Valley) $12. The fact that the wine's bouquet is subdued and gentle is a bonus. This version offers some creamy oak character and smooth but simple berry flavors. Not stellar but not bad, either. 85 *—M.S. (11/15/2007)*

Montes 2005 Classic Series Cabernet Sauvignon (Colchagua Valley) $12. Smells nice, with notes of leather and earth accenting the deep fruit that drives the bouquet. The palate is perfectly ripe and full of cassis and berry flavors, while the finish is jazzed up by touches of coffee, char and baked fruit. Shows a fine texture and grip that goes beyond what you normally get in a wine of this price. 89 Best Buy *—M.S. (3/1/2007)*

Montes 2005 Montes Alpha Cabernet Sauvignon (Colchagua Valley) $25. Starts out with subdued aromas of forest floor, black olive and pine needles before it bursts with black-fruit aromas. The palate is a bit heavy and sticky, but it houses legitimate cassis, black plum and berry flavors. A pure, serious Cabernet from a good vintage and a good region. 89 *—M.S. (11/15/2007)*

Montes 2004 Montes Alpha Cabernet Sauvignon (Colchagua Valley) $25. 86 *—M.S. (12/31/2006)*

Montes 2003 Montes Alpha Cabernet Sauvignon (Colchagua Valley) $23. 90 Editors' Choice *—M.S. (11/1/2005)*

Montes 2002 Montes Alpha Cabernet Sauvignon (Colchagua Valley) $22. 88 *—M.S. (3/1/2004)*

Montes 2001 Montes Alpha Cabernet Sauvignon (Curicó Valley) $20. 88 *—M.S. (3/1/2004)*

Montes 2000 Montes Alpha Cabernet Sauvignon (Curicó Valley) $20. 86 *—M.S. (7/1/2003)*

Montes 1999 Montes Alpha Cabernet Sauvignon (Colchagua Valley) $22. 90 *—M.S. (3/1/2002)*

Montes 2005 Reserve Cabernet Sauvignon (Colchagua Valley) $12. Smells nice, with notes of leather and earth accenting the deep fruit that drives the bouquet. The palate is perfectly ripe and full of cassis and berry flavors, while the finish is jazzed up by touches of coffee, char and baked fruit. Shows a fine texture and grip that goes beyond what you normally get in a wine of this price. 90 Best Buy *—M.S. (3/1/2007)*

Montes 2004 Reserve Cabernet Sauvignon (Colchagua Valley) $10. 87 Best Buy *—M.S. (11/1/2005)*

Montes 2002 Reserve Cabernet Sauvignon (Colchagua Valley) $10. 87 Best Buy *—M.S. (3/1/2004)*

Montes 2001 Reserve Cabernet Sauvignon (Curicó Valley) $10. 86 Best Buy *—M.S. (7/1/2003)*

Montes 1999 Reserve Cabernet Sauvignon (Colchagua Valley) $10. 85 *—J.C. (7/1/2002)*

Montes 2000 Reserve Oak Aged Cabernet Sauvignon (Colchagua Valley) $10. 84 *—M.S. (7/1/2003)*

Montes 2002 Cabernet Sauvignon-Carmenère (Colchagua Valley) $16. 88 *—M.S. (3/1/2004)*

Montes 2004 Limited Selection Cabernet Sauvignon-Carmenère (Leyda Valley) $16. 86 *—M.S. (11/1/2005)*

Montes 2004 Purple Angel Carmenère (Colchagua Valley) $57. Bold and serious Carmenère at the highest level of extraction and price is what Purple Angel from Montes is all about. The nose has earth, tobacco and plenty of oak, while the raspberry, red plum and licorice flavors that characterize the palate make themselves noticed. A tiny bit of green pepper and vanilla on the finish sing to the varietal and the barrel. With 8% Petit Verdot. 89 *—M.S. (9/1/2007)*

Montes 2006 Classic Series Chardonnay (Curicó Valley) $12. Apple and melon aromas are soft and easy, while the palate shows okay pear flavors that are heavily touched up by resiny, vanilla-tinged oak. There's a lot of wood character and not much vitality or spirit. A candied, basic wine made in fairly large quantity (25,000 cases). 83 *—M.S. (11/15/2007)*

Montes 2005 Classic Series Chardonnay (Curicó Valley) $12. With a bouquet of pears and baked fruits, this medium-weight, mildly oaked Chard has what it takes to reel you in. The palate answers the bell with sweet peach and pear flavors, and the finish holds its course. Overall it's a simple, tasty fruitball of a Chard. 86 *—M.S. (9/1/2007)*

Montes 2005 Montes Alpha Chardonnay (Casablanca Valley) $25. 87 *—M.S. (12/31/2006)*

Montes 2004 Montes Alpha Chardonnay (Casablanca Valley) $23. 88 *—M.S. (7/1/2006)*

Montes 2003 Montes Alpha Chardonnay (Casablanca Valley) $23. 89 *—M.S. (11/1/2005)*

Montes 2003 Montes Alpha Chardonnay (Casablanca Valley) $23. 89 Editors' Choice *—M.S. (2/1/2005)*

Montes 2002 Montes Alpha Chardonnay (Casablanca Valley) $20. 88 *—M.S. (3/1/2004)*

Montes 2001 Montes Alpha Chardonnay (Casablanca Valley) $20. 90 Editors' Choice *—M.S. (7/1/2003)*

Montes 2000 Montes Alpha Chardonnay (Curicó Valley) $20. 90 *—M.S. (2/1/2002)*

Montes 1998 Montes Alpha Special Cuvée Chardonnay (Curicó Valley) $20. 91 *—M.S. (5/1/2000)*

Montes 2005 Reserve Chardonnay (Colchagua Valley) $12. This medium-bodied Chard leads with healthy oak-based aromas of toast and vanilla, and there's also some warm radiator dust along with baked apple and pear scents. It's a round-styled wine with apple and melon flavors, and the finish yields mostly toast and vanilla. Still alive and kicking courtesy of core acidity. 86 *—M.S. (9/1/2007)*

Montes 2004 Reserve Chardonnay (Curicó Valley) $10. 86 Best Buy *—M.S. (11/1/2005)*

Montes 2003 Reserve Chardonnay (Curicó Valley) $10. 86 Best Buy *—M.S. (2/1/2005)*

Montes 2001 Reserve Chardonnay (Curicó Valley) $10. 89 Best Buy *—M.S. (3/1/2002)*

Montes 1999 Reserve Chardonnay (Curicó Valley) $NA. 84 *(1/1/2004)*

Montes 2002 Reserve Barrel Fermented Chardonnay (Curicó Valley) $10. 88 Best Buy *—M.S. (7/1/2003)*

Montes 2002 Fumé Blanc (Curicó Valley) $10. 87 *—M.S. (11/15/2003)*

Montes 2001 Reserve Fumé Blanc (Curicó Valley) $10. 90 Best Buy *—M.S. (3/1/2002)*

Montes 2004 Late Harvest Botrytised Gewürztraminer-Riesling (Curicó Valley) $24. 92 *—M.S. (5/1/2006)*

Montes 2000 Malbec (Colchagua Valley) $10. 89 Best Buy *—M.S. (3/1/2002)*

Montes 2005 Classic Series Malbec (Colchagua Valley) $12. Licorice, mint and black plum aromas foreshadow somewhat tart, snappy fruit flavors. The wine has a good mouthfeel but registers a little short on depth of fruit and the sweetness that usually defines South American Malbec. Finishes with some vanilla but also acidic crispness. With 15% Cabernet Sauvignon. 86 *—M.S. (9/1/2007)*

Montes 2001 Oak Aged Reserve Malbec (Colchagua Valley) $10. 86 Best Buy *—M.S. (7/1/2003)*

Montes 2005 Reserve Malbec (Colchagua Valley) $12. Floral and dark, with char and tar adding masculinity to the bouquet. The palate is juicy and balanced, with blackberry as the prime flavor and tobacco and pepper adding nuance. Finishes with a cushy feel and warmth, and overall it sings a nice tune. 88 Best Buy *—M.S. (9/1/2007)*

Montes 2004 Reserve Malbec (Colchagua Valley) $10. 88 Best Buy *—M.S. (11/1/2005)*

Montes 1999 Reserve Malbec (Colchagua Valley) $10. 87 Best Buy *(8/1/2001)*

Montes 2002 Reserve Oak Aged Malbec (Colchagua Valley) $10. 83 *—M.S. (12/1/2003)*

Montes 2005 Alpha Merlot (Colchagua Valley) $25. In general we're fans of Montes, so it was with disappointment that we found soupy aromas and a hard, hot feel on this Merlot. Yes, there's black cherry and plum flavors, but also in the mix are olive, green pepper and bitter tannins. This wine sticks out for its hard mouthfeel and pitch-black finishing notes. 84 *—M.S. (11/15/2007)*

Montes 2005 Classic Series Merlot (Colchagua Valley) $12. Here's a nice, well-made wine that reaches a bit farther than many in its class. You get some oak, cinnamon and cocoa on the nose, while the palate runs more toward herbal and natural than polished and sweet. A little warm and rugged but good in an unadulterated sense. 86 *—M.S. (5/1/2007)*

Montes 2004 Montes Alpha Merlot (Colchagua Valley) $25. A nosing reveals dark berry aromas along with tomato and a strong licorice character that's reminiscent of gumdrops. The palate shows slightly drying tannins and oak, which results in mocha accents on a plum and berry foundation. Very nice overall, with a good mouthfeel. 88 *—M.S. (3/1/2007)*

Montes 2000 Montes Alpha Merlot (Curicó Valley) $20. 88 *—M.S. (7/1/2003)*

Montes 1999 Montes Alpha Apalta Vineyard Merlot (Colchagua Valley) $22. 85 *—D.T. (7/1/2002)*

Montes 2004 Reserve Merlot (Colchagua Valley) $10. 87 Best Buy *—M.S. (11/1/2005)*

Montes 2003 Reserve Merlot (Colchagua Valley) $10. 83 *—M.S. (2/1/2005)*

Montes 2001 Reserve Special Cuvée Merlot (Colchagua Valley) $10. 84 *—M.S. (7/1/2003)*

Montes 2002 Reserve Special Cuvée Merlot (Colchagua Valley) $10. 86 *—M.S. (3/1/2004)*

Montes 2000 Special Cuvée Merlot (Colchagua Valley) $10. 88 Best Buy *—M.S. (3/1/2002)*

Montes 2002 Montes Alpha Merlot-Cabernet Franc (Colchagua Valley) $20. 88 *—M.S. (3/1/2004)*

Montes 2006 Limited Selection Pinot Noir (Casablanca & Leyda Valleys) $16. Like many Chilean Pinots, this starts out funky as a three-legged llama. The bouquet pumps bramble, dusty country road and roasted berry fruit. But with time it settles and unfolds, and in the end there are sweet herbal fruit flavors along with spice and vanilla. Voilà! It's honest PN from Chile. 87 *—M.S. (11/15/2007)*

Montes 2004 Limited Selection Pinot Noir (Casablanca Valley) $16. 82 *—M.S. (11/1/2005)*

Montes 2003 Limited Selection Pinot Noir (Casablanca Valley) $16. 85 *—M.S. (7/1/2005)*

Montes 2000 Oak Aged Pinot Noir (Casablanca Valley) $16. 87 *—D.T. (7/1/2002)*

Montes 2002 Oak Aged Limited Selection Pinot Noir (Casablanca Valley) $16. 85 *—M.S. (8/1/2004)*

Montes 2002 Reserve Pinot Noir (Casablanca Valley) $10. 84 *—M.S. (3/1/2004)*

Montes 2003 Purple Angel Red Blend (Colchagua Valley) $48. 90 *—M.S. (11/1/2005)*

Montes 2006 Classic Series Sauvignon Blanc (Casablanca Valley) $12. Fresh and snappy, with aromas of pine, citrus and tropical fruits. Montes usually shows a good hand with Sauvignon, and they have in this case. The wine is full and melony but also racy and touched by a little green bean and aparagus. And that's as complex as it gets. 87 Best Buy *—M.S. (3/1/2007)*

Montes 2006 Limited Selection Leyda Vineyard Sauvignon Blanc (Leyda Valley) $16. A good but hardly outstanding wine. It offers mineral and citrus aromas but also some funk (think a European train during the summer). Passion fruit, orange and grapefruit flavors control the palate, which is spritzy and soda-like. Best by the glass, with cod or conch fritters. 86 *—M.S. (5/1/2007)*

Montes 2004 Limited Selection Leyda Vineyard Sauvignon Blanc (Leyda Valley) $16. 87 *—M.S. (11/1/2005)*

Montes 2001 Reserva Sauvignon Blanc (Curicó Valley) $10. 89 Best Buy *—M.S. (3/1/2002)*

Montes 2004 Reserve Sauvignon Blanc (Casablanca Valley) $10. 86 Best Buy *—M.S. (2/1/2005)*

Montes 2003 Reserve Sauvignon Blanc (Casablanca Valley) $10. 88 *—M.S. (3/1/2004)*

Montes 2002 Reserve Sauvignon Blanc (Casablanca Valley) $10. 89 Best Buy *—M.S. (7/1/2003)*

Montes 2005 Alpha Syrah (Colchagua Valley) $25. Montes Alpha always ranks as one of Chile's most honest Syrahs. It starts out big, bruising and foward before transitioning to something more spicy, leathery and complex. It is always a bold wine, but with finishing accents of espresso and crude oil, it takes on a special, proprietary darkness that is eminently likable. 90 *—M.S. (11/15/2007)*

Montes 2006 Cherub Rose of Syrah (Colchagua Valley) $17. Out of the ordinary projects such as Cherub are what we've come to expect from Montes, but how quickly winemaker Aurelio Montes has figured out the nuances of rosé from Syrah. In just its second year, this wine has found its groove. More elegant than the inaugural 2005, this vintage is quite Mediterranean in style, with a vivid pink/red color and the freshest, purest fruit flavors. Who would have thought that a Chilean rosé could be this nicely put together? 90 *—M.S. (7/1/2007)*

Montes 2005 Cherub Rosé of Syrah (Colchagua Valley) $16. 89 *—M.S. (11/15/2006)*

Montes 2003 Folly Syrah (Colchagua Valley) $NA. 92 *—M.S. (3/1/2006)*

Montes 2001 Folly Syrah (Colchagua Valley) $70. 92 *—M.S. (3/1/2004)*

Montes 2004 Montes Alpha Syrah (Colchagua Valley) $25. 91 Editors' Choice *—M.S. (11/15/2006)*

Montes 2003 Montes Alpha Syrah (Colchagua Valley) $23. 91 Editors' Choice *—M.S. (11/1/2005)*

Montes 2002 Montes Alpha Syrah (Colchagua Valley) $22. 86 *—M.S. (3/1/2004)*

Montes 2001 Montes Alpha Syrah (Curicó Valley) $20. 87 *—M.S. (7/1/2003)*

Montes 2000 Montes Alpha-Viñedo Apalta Syrah (Colchagua Valley) $22. 87 *(11/1/2001)*

Montes 2004 Montes Folly Syrah (Apalta) $93. Opens with tobacco, leather and prune, and two sniffs is all you need to determine that this is something special. The '04 Folly seems more subdued and maybe a bit more balanced than previous efforts, which stressed power and extract. This wine has some snap to go with the expected black fruit, chocolate and black olive flavors and accents. 91 *—M.S. (5/1/2007)*

Montes 2000 Montes Folly Syrah (Colchagua Valley) $70. 91 Cellar Selection *—S.H. (12/1/2002)*

Montes 2000 Late Harvest White Blend (Curicó Valley) $18. 88 *—M.S. (3/1/2004)*

MONTGRAS

MontGras 2002 Antu Cabernet Sauvignon (Colchagua Valley) $19. 86 *M.S. (12/15/2005)*

MontGras 2003 Antu Ninquén Cabernet Sauvignon (Colchagua Valley) $19. 87 *—M.S. (3/1/2006)*

MontGras 2002 Ninquén Mountain Vineyard Cabernet Sauvignon (Colchagua Valley) $31. 87 *—M.S. (5/1/2006)*

MontGras 2000 Ninquén Mountain Vineyard Cabernet Sauvignon (Colchagua Valley) $30. 90 *(3/1/2003)*

MontGras 2004 Reserva Cabernet Sauvignon (Colchagua Valley) $11. 89 Best Buy *—M.S. (5/1/2006)*

MontGras 2003 Reserva Cabernet Sauvignon (Colchagua Valley) $12. 90 Best Buy *—M.S. (11/1/2005)*

MontGras 2001 Reserva Cabernet Sauvignon (Colchagua Valley) $10. 90 Best Buy *—M.S. (6/1/2004)*

MontGras 1999 Reserve Cabernet Sauvignon (Colchagua Valley) $9. 87 Best Buy *—M.S. (3/1/2002)*

MontGras 2004 Reserva Cabernet Sauvignon-Syrah (Colchagua Valley) $10. 87 Best Buy *—M.S. (3/1/2006)*

MontGras 2003 Reserva Cabernet Sauvignon-Syrah (Colchagua Valley) $12. 88 Best Buy *—M.S. (12/15/2005)*

MontGras 2000 Reserva Estate Bottled Cabernet Sauvignon-Syrah (Colchagua Valley) $10. 87 Best Buy *(3/1/2003)*

MontGras 2004 Reserva Carmenère (Colchagua Valley) $11. 86 Best Buy *—M.S. (3/1/2006)*

MontGras 2000 Reserva Estate Bottled Carmenère (Colchagua Valley) $10. 84 *(3/1/2003)*

MontGras 2005 Reserva Chardonnay (Colchagua Valley) $10. 87 Best Buy *—M.S. (5/1/2006)*

MontGras 2003 Reserva Chardonnay (Colchagua Valley) $11. 85 *—M.S. (12/15/2005)*

MontGras 2000 Reserve Chardonnay (Colchagua Valley) $9. 86 *—M.S. (3/1/2002)*

MontGras 2000 Merlot (Colchagua Valley) $6. 85 Best Buy *—M.S. (3/1/2002)*

MontGras 2004 Reserva Merlot (Colchagua Valley) $11. 87 Best Buy *—M.S. (5/1/2006)*

MontGras 2003 Reserva Merlot (Colchagua Valley) $11. 87 Best Buy *—M.S. (11/1/2005)*

MontGras 1999 Reserva Estate Bottled Merlot (Colchagua Valley) $10. 86 *(3/1/2003)*

MontGras 1999 Ninquén Red Blend (Colchagua Valley) $30. 89 *—M.S. (3/1/2002)*

MontGras 2004 Quatro Reserva Red Blend (Colchagua Valley) $15. 90 Best Buy *—M.S. (12/15/2005)*

MontGras 2003 Quatro Reserva Red Blend (Colchagua Valley) $16. 88 *—M.S. (11/1/2005)*

MontGras 1999 Quatro Reserva Estate Bottled Red Blend (Colchagua Valley) $13. 86 *(3/1/2003)*

MontGras 2001 Sauvignon Blanc (Colchagua Valley) $6. 86 Best Buy *—M.S. (3/1/2002)*

MontGras 2002 Estate Sauvignon Blanc (Central Valley) $7. 86 Best Buy *(3/1/2003)*

MontGras 2005 Reserva Sauvignon Blanc (Casablanca Valley) $10. 85 Best Buy *—M.S. (3/1/2006)*

MontGras 2002 Reserve Sauvignon Blanc (Casablanca Valley) $10. 86 *(3/1/2003)*

MontGras 2003 Limited Edition Syrah (Colchagua Valley) $15. 89 *—M.S. (11/1/2005)*

MontGras 2002 Limited Edition Syrah (Colchagua Valley) $16. 86 *—M.S. (6/1/2004)*

MontGras 2004 Ninquén Antu Mountain Vineyard Syrah (Colchagua Valley) $19. 88 *—M.S. (3/1/2006)*

MontGras 2001 Limited Edition Zinfandel (Colchagua Valley) $15. 88 *(3/1/2003)*

MORANDÉ

Morandé 2001 Edicion Limitada 66 Barricas Cabernet Franc (Maipo Valley) 87 *—M.S. (7/1/2003)*

Morandé 2002 Edicion Limitada 66 Barricas Cabernet Franc (Maipo Valley) $20. 88 *—M.S. (8/1/2004)*

Morandé 2004 Cabernet Sauvignon (Maipo Valley) $8. 86 Best Buy *—M.S. (5/1/2006)*

Morandé 2002 Cabernet Sauvignon (Central Valley) $7. 87 Best Buy *—M.S. (7/1/2003)*

Morandé 1999 Cabernet Sauvignon (Maipo Valley) $30. 89 *(8/1/2002)*

Morandé 2001 Grand Reserve Vitisterra Cabernet Sauvignon (Maipo Valley) $13. 88 Best Buy *—M.S. (7/1/2003)*

Morandé 2000 Grand Reserve Vitisterra Cabernet Sauvignon (Maipo Valley) $14. 89 Best Buy *—C.S. (12/1/2002)*

Morandé 2000 House of Morande Cabernet Sauvignon (Maipo Valley) $30. 84 *—M.S. (7/1/2003)*

Morandé 2001 House of Morandé Cabernet Sauvignon (Maipo Valley) $35. 90 *—M.S. (3/1/2004)*

Morandé 2002 Reserve Terrarum Cabernet Sauvignon (Maipo Valley) $10. 86 Best Buy *—M.S. (7/1/2003)*

Morandé 1999 Terrarum Cabernet Sauvignon (Maipo Valley) $9. 88 Best Buy *(8/1/2001)*

Morandé 2002 Vitisterra Grand Reserve Cabernet Sauvignon (Maipo Valley) $15. 88 *—M.S. (2/1/2005)*

Morandé 1999 Edicion Limitada Cabernet Sauvignon-Merlot (Cachapoal Valley) $18. 87 *(8/1/2002)*

Morandé 2001 Golden Reserve Carignane (Loncomilla Valley) $25. 82 *—M.S. (3/1/2004)*

Morandé 2002 Edicion Limitada Carmenère (Maipo Valley) $20. 85 *—M.S. (3/1/2004)*

Morandé 2002 Reserve Terrarum Carmenère (Maipo Valley) $9. 84 *—M.S. (7/1/2003)*

Morandé 2001 Terrarum Carmenère (Maipo Valley) $9. 87 Best Buy *(8/1/2002)*

Morandé 2003 Terrarum Reserva Carmenère (Maipo Valley) $11. 82 *—M.S. (3/1/2004)*

Morandé 2004 Terrarum Reserve Carmenère (Maipo Valley) $11. 84 *—M.S. (3/1/2006)*

Morandé 2005 Chardonnay (Maipo Valley) $8. 85 Best Buy *—M.S. (5/1/2006)*

Morandé 2003 Chardonnay (Maipo Valley) $8. 84 *—M.S. (3/1/2004)*

Morandé 2006 Gran Reserva Chardonnay (Casablanca Valley) $16. This is like a bowl of fruit salad. The nose is fresh but the palate runs sweet with mango, papaya and other tropical flavors. It's neither heavy nor light on the palate, and overall it doesn't bear much resemblance to what most Chardonnays smell and taste like. 83 *—M.S. (11/15/2007)*

Morandé 2002 Grand Reserve Vitisterra Chardonnay (Casablanca Valley) $15. 87 *—M.S. (12/1/2004)*

Morandé 2001 Morande Pionero Chardonnay (Central Valley) $7. 84 *—M.S. (7/1/2003)*

Morandé 2006 Reserva Chardonnay (Casablanca Valley) $10. Better than the winery's oakier, heavier Gran Reserva. This version has floral, light aromas and then a sweet, almost candied palate of crystallized mango and pineapple. It may be too sweet for some, but if you like a blend of sugary, oily, pulpy fruit along with decent acidity, this has it. 85 Best Buy *—M.S. (11/15/2007)*

Morandé 2003 Reserva Chardonnay (Casablanca Valley) $11. 86 *—M.S. (3/1/2004)*

Morandé 2001 Terrarum Chardonnay (Maipo Valley) $10. 84 *(8/1/2002)*

Morandé 2002 Terrarum Reserve Chardonnay (Maipo Valley) $10. 85 *—M.S. (6/1/2004)*

Morandé 2001 Visiterra Chardonnay (Casablanca Valley) $15. 86 *(8/1/2002)*

Morandé 2002 Vitisterra Grand Reserve Chardonnay (Casablanca Valley) $15. 86 *—M.S. (7/1/2003)*

Morandé 2005 Terrarum Reserve Gewürztraminer (Casablanca Valley) $11. 86 Best Buy *—M.S. (7/1/2006)*

Morandé 2002 Edición Limitada 88 Barricas Malbec (Maipo Valley) $17. 84 *—M.S. (12/1/2003)*

Morandé 2004 Edición Limitada Malbec (Maipo Valley) $21. Morandé likes to dabble in Malbec, and we haven't been big fans in the past. This wine is much better; it is still a bit saucy on the nose, and there's a touch of that herbal essence that gets into so many Chilean reds. But overall it has fast-hitting black fruit, soy, spice and mocha notes that serve it well. 87—*M.S. (11/15/2007)*

Morandé 1999 Morande Edicion Limitada Malbec 1999 Malbec (Maipo Valley) $17. 82 —*M.S. (7/1/2003)*

Morandé 2003 Merlot (Central Valley) $8. 83 —*M.S. (8/1/2004)*

Morandé 2002 Grand Reserve Vitisterra Merlot (Maipo Valley) $15. 88 —*M.S. (8/1/2004)*

Morandé 2001 Grand Reserve Vitisterra Merlot (Maipo Valley) $13. 85 —*M.S. (7/1/2003)*

Morandé 2000 Pionero Merlot (Central Valley) $7. 86 Best Buy —*J.F. (8/1/2001)*

Morandé 2003 Terrarum Reserva Merlot (Maipo Valley) $11. 85 —*M.S. (3/1/2004)*

Morandé 2003 Pinot Noir (Casablanca Valley) $8. 86 Best Buy —*M.S. (7/1/2005)*

Morandé 2002 Pinot Noir (Casablanca Valley) $7. 81 —*M.S. (7/1/2003)*

Morandé 2001 Pinot Noir (Casablanca Valley) $11. 85 *(8/1/2002)*

Morandé 2001 Edicion Limitada Rosé de Pinot Noir Pinot Noir (Casablanca Valley) $13. 85 *(8/1/2002)*

Morandé 2001 Pionero Pinot Noir (Casablanca Valley) $7. 84 Best Buy *(8/1/2002)*

Morandé 2006 Reserva Pinot Noir (Casablanca Valley) $10. Orange rind and pineapple/passion fruit aromas announce this wine as less than serious. And the palate confirms the suspicions raised up front: it's jumbled, hot and acidic. Pablo Morandé may be a pioneer with Casablanca Pinot, but this wine doesn't really impress. 82 —*M.S. (11/15/2007)*

Morandé 2003 Reserva Organico Pinot Noir (Casablanca Valley) $11. 85 —*M.S. (3/1/2004)*

Morandé 2003 Terrarum Reserve Pinot Noir (Casablanca Valley) $10. 87 Best Buy —*M.S. (7/1/2005)*

Morandé 2000 Late Harvest Riesling (Casablanca Valley) $13. 87 —*M.S. (3/1/2004)*

Morandé 2005 Sauvignon Blanc (Curicó Valley) $8. 82 —*M.S. (7/1/2006)*

Morandé 2004 Sauvignon Blanc (Curicó Valley) $8. 83 —*M.S. (7/1/2005)*

Morandé 2003 Sauvignon Blanc (Central Valley) $20. 84 —*M.S. (3/1/2004)*

Morandé 2002 Sauvignon Blanc (Central Valley) $7. 83 —*M.S. (7/1/2003)*

Morandé 2001 Sauvignon Blanc (Casablanca Valley) $11. 87 *(8/1/2002)*

Morandé 2000 Edicion Limitada Golden Harvest Sauvignon Blanc (Casablanca Valley) $25. 90 *(8/1/2002)*

Morandé 2000 Pionero Sauvignon Blanc (Central Valley) $7. 83 —*M.S. (7/1/2003)*

Morandé 2005 Terrarum Reserve Sauvignon Blanc (Casablanca Valley) $11. 83 —*M.S. (5/1/2006)*

Morandé 2003 Terrarum Reserve Sauvignon Blanc (Casablanca Valley) $10. 86 Best Buy —*M.S. (6/1/2004)*

Morandé 2003 Syrah (Maipo Valley) $8. 84 —*M.S. (3/1/2004)*

Morandé 2002 Syrah (Central Valley) $7. 86 Best Buy —*M.S. (7/1/2003)*

Morandé 2005 Gran Reserva Syrah (Maipo Valley) $16. Chocolate, a hint of mint, spice and black fruit make this a true-smelling Syrah. The flavors run a little bit red, i.e. raspberry and red plum, and the finish offers a smack of oak along with dried fruit flavors. More of an acid-based, lively style. 87 —*M.S. (11/15/2007)*

Morandé 2002 Grand Reserve Vitisterra Syrah (Maipo Valley) $15. 82 —*M.S. (8/1/2004)*

Morandé 2001 Pionero Syrah (Central Valley) $7. 82 *(8/1/2002)*

Morandé 2001 Vitisterra Grand Reserve Syrah (Maipo Valley) $15. 86 —*M.S. (7/1/2003)*

Morandé 2002 Edicion Limitada Syrah-Cabernet (Maipo Valley) $20. 87 —*M.S. (6/1/2004)*

Morandé 1999 Edicion Limitada Syrah-Cabernet (Maipo Valley) $18. 88 *(8/1/2002)*

Morandé 2001 Edición Limitada 22 Barricas Syrah-Cabernet (Maipo Valley) $18. 89 —*M.S. (7/1/2003)*

NIDO DE AGUILA

Nido de Aguila 2002 Armonía Bordeaux Blend (Maipo Valley) $20. 91 Editors' Choice —*M.S. (2/1/2005)*

Nido de Aguila 2003 Armonía Reserva Bordeaux Blend (Maipo Valley) $15. 89 —*M.S. (5/1/2006)*

Nido de Aguila 2003 Reserva Cabernet Sauvignon (Maipo Valley) $15. 83 —*M.S. (12/15/2005)*

Nido de Aguila 2003 Reserva Merlot (Maipo Valley) $15. 81 —*M.S. (12/15/2005)*

Nido de Aguila 2002 Reserva Merlot-Cabernet Sauvignon (Maipo Valley) $18. 89 —*M.S. (2/1/2005)*

Nido de Aguila 2005 Reserva Syrah (Maipo Valley) $16. A little murky and rubbery, but not so much so that the wine completely suffers. It does have solid dark-fruit flavors and the mouthfeel is stout and sturdy, with proper tannins. Common stuff; no drama. Pretty good but nothing more. 84 —*M.S. (5/1/2007)*

NUEVOMUNDO

Nuevomundo 2004 Cabernet Sauvignon-Malbec (Maipo Valley) $15. 87 —*M.S. (12/15/2005)*

Nuevomundo 2005 Reserva Sauvignon Blanc (Maipo Valley) $15. 81 —*M.S. (3/1/2006)*

ODFJELL

Odfjell 2003 Orzada Cabernet Franc (Maule Valley) $18. 88 —*M.S. (11/1/2005)*

Odfjell 2005 Armador Cabernet Sauvignon (Maipo Valley) $12. Slightly granular and brambly on the nose, which never really opens up. The palate is round, sweet, a bit medicinal and healthy due to snappy acidity, firm tannins and decent overall structure. Truthfully, it's a straight-down-the-middle wine from a producer that always does this well or better. 85 —*M.S. (11/15/2007)*

Odfjell 2004 Armador Cabernet Sauvignon (Maipo Valley) $10. 87 Best Buy —*M.S. (10/1/2006)*

Odfjell 2003 Armador Cabernet Sauvignon (Maipo Valley) $12. 85 —*M.S. (11/1/2005)*

Odfjell 2002 Armador Cabernet Sauvignon (Central Valley) $10. 88 Best Buy —*M.S. (8/1/2004)*

Odfjell 2003 Orzada Cabernet Sauvignon (Colchagua Valley) $18. 89 —*M.S. (11/1/2005)*

Odfjell 2002 Rojo Cabernet Sauvignon (Chile) $8. 87 Best Buy —*M.S. (8/1/2004)*

Odfjell 2003 Orzada Carignan (Maule Valley) $18. 87 —*M.S. (11/1/2005)*

Odfjell 2001 Orzada Carineña (Chile) $15. 87 —*M.S. (8/1/2004)*

Odfjell 2004 Armador Carmenère (Maule Valley) $12. 87 Best Buy —*M.S. (10/1/2006)*

Odfjell 2003 Armador Carmenère (Maule Valley) $12. 90 Best Buy —*M.S. (11/15/2005)*

Odfjell 2002 Armador Carmenère (Central Valley) $12. 87 —*M.S. (8/1/2004)*

Odfjell 2004 Orzada Carmenère (Maule Valley) $18. 89 —*M.S. (10/1/2006)*

Odfjell 2003 Orzada Carmenère (Central Valley) $18. 90 —*M.S. (11/1/2005)*

Odfjell 2004 Orzada Malbec (Lontué Valley) $18. One big step up from the value level is this classy, succulent Malbec from Odfjell, a winery whose successes far outnumber its duds. Expect opening aromas of toasted coconut, black cherry, mocha and even fresh mushroom. The palate is blazing with sweet berry and plum flavors, and then chocolate and coffee take over on the finish. It's the full package in terms of Chilean Malbec; about as good as it gets. Only 254 cases made. 90 —*M.S. (9/1/2007)*

Odfjell 2003 Orzada Malbec (Curicó Valley) $18. 91 Editors' Choice —*M.S. (11/1/2005)*

Odfjell 2005 Armador Merlot (Maipo Valley) $12. Spicy and woody to begin with, but time unveils strawberry jam aromas. There's not a ton of definition to the palate, but it's reasonably fruity and smooth, with ample vanilla flavors to the creamy finish. If you prefer a broad, softer Merlot with some buttery oak, this is for you. 86 Best Buy —*M.S. (11/15/2007)*

Odfjell 2004 Armador Merlot (Central Valley) $12. 87 Best Buy —*M.S. (10/1/2006)*

Odfjell 2003 Armador Merlot (Maipo Valley) $12. 87 Best Buy —*M.S. (11/1/2005)*

Odfjell 2002 Armador Merlot (Central Valley) $12. 87 —*M.S. (8/1/2004)*

Odfjell 2003 Aliara Red Blend (Central Valley) $25. It took a few years for Odfjell to get its Aliara blend right. For starters, it's not an easy wine, as it's based on Carmenère and has Cabernet Sauvignon, Franc, Carignan and Malbec in the mix. But the 2003 is excellent in how it delivers coffee and other roasted aromas in front of ripe cassis, berry and chocolate flavors. It's one part savory and one part sweet; overall it's 100% impressive. 368 cases made. 91 —*M.S. (5/1/2007)*

Odfjell 2002 Aliara Red Blend (Chile) $26. 84 —*M.S. (11/1/2005)*

Odfjell 2000 Aliara Red Blend (Chile) $25. 88 —*M.S. (8/1/2004)*

Odfjell 2005 Armador Syrah (Maipo Valley) $12. A little bit funky, especially at first, but if you give it time the early Syrah-based animal and sweat aromas give way to purer black fruit, bramble and plenty of oak-driven warmth. It has its merits such as color and mouthfeel, but all in all it doesn't quite get it rolling in exactly the right direction. 86 —*M.S. (11/15/2007)*

Odfjell 2004 Armador Syrah (Maipo Valley) $12. 86 —*M.S. (10/1/2006)*

Odfjell 2003 Armador Syrah (Maipo Valley) $12. 86 —*M.S. (11/1/2005)*

OOPS

Oops 2005 Cabernet Sauvignon (Central Valley) $12. A bit wanting as Cabernet goes, with cherry and tea aromas. The palate is richer than the nose, offering big, ripe fruit that's generic in style but generally clean and pleasant. Mild chocolate and brown sugar notes on the finish ensure its friendliness. Imported by Schwartz-Olcott Importers. 85 —*M.S. (11/15/2007)*

Oops 2005 Carmenère (Central Valley) $12. Like with the Oops Carmenère/Merlot blend, this varietal bottling tells the story of how Carmenère was discovered in Chile. The wine, however, doesn't offer a whole lot. It's hard, rubbery and lightly baked, with grabby tannins supporting midland berry flavors. 83 —*M.S. (5/1/2007)*

Oops 2005 Carmenère Merlot Red Blend (Central Valley) $12. The good side of this concept wine is that it tells the story of Carmenère, the so-called lost Bordeaux variety. Unfortunately, not as much attention was paid to the wine itself, which includes 30% Merlot and tastes mildly of raspberry and herbs but also shows a hard, grating mouthfeel. 82—*M.S. (5/1/2007)*

Oops 2006 Sauvignon Blanc (Central Valley) $12. The Oops concept is to blend Carmenère, the so-called lost variety, into everything, including Sauvignon Blanc. And while you don't really taste the red in this, you do get bell pepper, melon and citrus. A little watery and dilute in the long run. Imported by Schwartz-Olcott Importers. 83 —*M.S. (11/15/2007)*

ORIEL

Oriel 2000 VQM Cabernet Sauvignon (Maipo Valley) $17. 82 —*M.S. (11/1/2005)*

ORIGIN

Origin 2004 Chardonnay (Central Valley) $10. 88 Best Buy —*M.S. (7/1/2006)*

Origin 2004 Merlot (Central Valley) $10. 85 Best Buy —*M.S. (5/1/2006)*

Origin 2005 Rosé Blend (Rapel Valley) $10. 85 —*M.S. (5/1/2006)*

OVEJA NEGRA

Oveja Negra 2005 Cabernet Sauvignon-Syrah (Central Valley) $8. The start is a bit foresty but under the microscope this blend has the chops to deserve a Best Buy call out. The palate is perfectly ripe and loaded with plum, berry and vanilla from the oak. It is easy to take and finishes in clean, medium-length fashion. Nothing complicated; just a good-drinking red wine for not much cash. 87 Best Buy —*M.S. (9/1/2007)*

Oveja Negra 2006 Chardonnay-Viognier (Central Valley) $8. Interesting and not that far off the mark. Normally Chardonnay and Viognier make for clumsy partners, but not so in this case. The nose has sweet acacia blossom aromas, and that's followed by a plump but largely anonymous palate that turns to apricots and honey on the finish. A little cloying but good in small doses. 84 —*M.S. (9/1/2007)*

Oveja Negra 2005 Cabernet Franc-Carménère Red Blend (Central Valley) $8. Mossy on the nose, teetering on overripe and heavy. The palate throws out black olive, mulchy blackberry and earthy plum flavors, and then there's coffee and ultimately burnt toast on the finish. 83 —*M.S. (11/15/2007)*

Oveja Negra 2006 Rosé Rosé Blend (Central Valley) $8. This little rosado blend has some appealing characteristics, namely its spice- and melon-tinged nose and its guava, mango and raspberry flavors. But it's also rather sweet and simple in feel and finish. Best as a quick refresher. 83 —*M.S. (7/1/2007)*

PANGEA

Pangea 2004 Apalta Vineyards Syrah (Colchagua Valley) $50. An impressive debut for this flagship wine from Ventiquero's portion of the Apalta vineyards. Australian John Duval consults (ex-Penfolds), and his influence is reflected in the careful tannin management and smooth texture. Opens with considerable coffee and toast from the oak, but also shows blackberry and boysenberry fruit balanced by crisp acidity. Seems to have the basic ingredients, just lacks a bit of richness and length. 89 *(7/1/2007)*

PASO DEL SOL

Paso del Sol 2001 Cabernet Sauvignon (Central Valley) $6. 85 Best Buy *M.S. (12/1/2002)*

Paso del Sol 2004 Carmenère (Central Valley) $6. 81 —*M.S. (7/1/2005)*

Paso del Sol 2004 Chardonnay (Central Valley) $6. 81 —*M.S. (2/1/2005)*

Paso del Sol 2001 Chardonnay (Central Valley) $6. 83 —*M.S. (7/1/2003)*

Paso del Sol 2003 Merlot (Central Valley) $6. 82 —*M.S. (7/1/2005)*

Paso del Sol 2004 Sauvignon Blanc (Central Valley) $6. 83 Best Buy —*M.S. (7/1/2005)*

PEÑALOLEN

Peñalolen 2004 Cabernet Sauvignon (Maipo Valley) $18. 89 —*M.S. (11/15/2006)*

Peñalolen 2003 Cabernet Sauvignon (Maipo Valley) $18. 88 —*M.S. (12/15/2005)*

Peñalolen 2002 Cabernet Sauvignon (Maipo Valley) $17. 87 —*M.S. (2/1/2005)*

Peñalolen 2001 Cabernet Sauvignon (Maipo Valley) $16. 86 —*S.H. (11/1/2004)*

Peñalolen 2000 Cabernet Sauvignon (Maipo Valley) $15. 84 —*M.S. (8/1/2004)*

Peñalolen 2000 Cabernet Sauvignon (Maipo Valley) $15. 84 —*M.S. (11/1/2005)*

Peñalolen 1999 Cabernet Sauvignon (Maipo Valley) $15. 84 —*M.S. (7/1/2003)*

Peñalolen 2006 Sauvignon Blanc (Limarí Valley) $12. There's a movement in Chile toward the Limari Valley for cooler-climate grapes like Sauvignon Blanc, yet this one hasn't really found its groove. The wine seems a bit soft and distant, with dilute aromas and flavors of peach, melon and apple. Yet the body is moderate to heavy, and the finish is sort of mealy. 83 —*M.S. (9/1/2007)*

Peñalolen 2005 Sauvignon Blanc (Limarí Valley) $12. 82 —*M.S. (3/1/2006)*

Peñalolen 2004 Sauvignon Blanc (Limarí Valley) $12. 85 —*M.S. (11/1/2005)*

Peñalolen 2003 Sauvignon Blanc (Limarí Valley) $12. 84 —*S.H. (12/1/2004)*

Peñalolen 2002 Sauvignon Blanc (Casablanca Valley) $12. 87 —*S.H. (8/1/2004)*

PENGWINE

Pengwine 2003 Cabernet Sauvignon-Carmenère Cabernet Blend (Maipo Valley) $10. 83 —*M.S. (11/1/2005)*

Pengwine 2003 Humboldt Reserve Cabernet Sauvignon (Maipo Valley) $16. 84 —*M.S. (11/1/2005)*

Pengwine 2003 Rockhopper Reserve Cabernet Sauvignon-Carmenère (Maipo Valley) $15. A little herbal and olive-filled from front to back, but with offsetting berry and sweet spice characteristics. The wine features decent dark-fruit flavors and milk chocolate on the finish, but along the way a strong and persistent shock of green drives the wine into a corner it can't escape from. Cabernet with 15% Carmenère. 84 —*M.S. (5/1/2007)*

Pengwine 2005 Magellan Reserve Chardonnay (Maipo Valley) $14. 82 —*M.S. (10/1/2006)*

Pengwine 2004 King Special Selection Red Blend (Maipo Valley) $30. 85 —*M.S. (10/1/2006)*

PETEROA

Peteroa 2003 Reserve Cabernet Sauvignon (Central Valley) $12. Not what you'd call a clean, direct wine. The nose is nutty and dirty, while the flavors are underdeveloped, vegetal and tart. Barely worth a look. 80 —*M.S. (9/1/2007)*

Peteroa 2004 Reserve Carmenère (Central Valley) $12. Immediately this wine hits you with everything that has given Carmenère its shaky reputation; meaning vegetal/herbal aromas and flavors along with hints of saddle leather and the ol' horse stable. The mouthfeel is a savior because it's smooth and healthy, but the aromas and flavors barely cut it. 82 —*M.S. (11/15/2007)*

Peteroa 2004 Reserve Chardonnay (Central Valley) $12. This turned out to be the best of the Peteroa current line, and it's an '04 Chardonnay, which tells you that new releases are not this winery's bag. Still, this is okay if you like marmalade flavors and size, with some peach strudel on the finish. Drink yesterday; it's losing steam fast. 84 —*M.S. (11/15/2007)*

Peteroa 2003 Reserve Merlot (Central Valley) $12. This is the first year we've reviewed this winery's range of wines, and so far the results are not that good. Like other Peteroa wines, this has a lot of funk, bramble and other unfocused aromas and flavors. It's okay on a good day but devoid of the cleanliness and charms we desire. 81 —*M.S. (11/15/2007)*

Peteroa 2003 Reserve Pinot Noir (Central Valley) $12. An earthy, rubbery Pinot that's not likely to sway the drinker of Burgundy any closer to Chile. This is tart, bulky stuff with size and zero subtlety. 80 —*M.S. (11/15/2007)*

PORTA

Porta 2000 Estates Cabernet Sauvignon (Aconcagua Valley) $10. 86 Best Buy —*M.S. (12/1/2002)*

Porta 2000 Grand Reserve Cabernet Sauvignon (Aconcagua Valley) $21. 87 —*C.S. (12/1/2002)*

Porta 2006 Reserva Cabernet Sauvignon (Aconcagua Valley) $11. Bramble, leather and red fruit make for a decent nose, while the palate is basically deep and fruity, with an emphasis on blackberry and cherry flavors. For the most part the wine has structure and feel, although there's a spot of bitterness on the finish. 85 —*M.S. (11/15/2007)*

Porta 1999 Reserve Cabernet Sauvignon (Aconcagua Valley) $14. 83 —*M.S. (12/1/2002)*

Porta 2006 Reserva Cabernet Sauvignon-Carmenère (Chile) $12. Peppery dark-cherry aromas are a decent opening, but after that settles quickly into a nebulous realm of bland raspberry and milk chocolate. More generic than interesting, with an acceptable finish and mouthfeel. 83 —*M.S. (9/1/2007)*

Porta 2000 Reserve Cabernet Sauvignon/Carmenere Cabernet Blend (Chile) $14. 84 —*D.T. (7/1/2002)*

Porta 1999 Estates Carmenère (Maipo Valley) $10. 81 —*J.C. (8/1/2001)*

Porta 2006 Reserva Carmenère (Maipo Valley) $11. Woodsy berry aromas keep the nose upright and welcoming, but the palate doesn't do much other than push generic raspberry and cherry skin flavors. It's a forward, rather acidic wine that's simple and straightforward. 83 —*M.S. (9/1/2007)*

Porta 2000 Chardonnay (Cachapoal Valley) $9. 86 —*M.S. (7/1/2002)*

Porta 2000 Grand Reserve Chardonnay (Cachapoal Valley) $21. 82 —*M.S. (7/1/2002)*

Porta 2006 Reserva Chardonnay (Central Valley) $11. Heavy and unfocused, with a lot of oak and overripe melon. Not much precision here; it's more about weight and size, not finesse or style. 80 —*M.S. (9/1/2007)*

Porta 2000 Reserve Chardonnay (Cachapoal Valley) $13. 83 —*M.S. (7/1/2002)*

Porta 1999 Select Reserve Chardonnay (Cachapoal Valley) $13. 86 —*J.F. (8/1/2001)*

Porta 2000 Estates Merlot (Aconcagua Valley) $9. 86 Best Buy —*M.S. (12/1/2002)*

Porta 2006 Reserva Merlot (Maipo Valley) $11. Dark in color and a little soft in body, but overall this broad and beefy wine works. The nose is meaty and ripe, while the palate carries softly baked black-fruit flavors. It's nothing out of the ordinary but it scores points for its density and intensity. 86 Best Buy —*M.S. (11/15/2007)*

Porta 2000 Grand Reserve Pinot Noir (Bío Bío Valley) $22. 87 —*D.T. (7/1/2002)*

Porta 1999 Grand Reserve Pinot Noir (Bío Bío Valley) $22. 85 *(8/1/2001)*

Porta 2006 Reserva Pinot Noir (Bío Bío Valley) $12. Wood spice and the wine's secondary fruit aromas are acceptable, as is the tart, linear palate. But as a whole there's just not enough going on for it to rank better. Better when newly opened; it doesn't show a lot as it breathes. 83 —*M.S. (11/15/2007)*

Porta 2005 Reserva Syrah (Aconcagua Valley) $12. More from the big, friendly school of Syrahs, although a little generic in the final analysis. The bouquet is rich and a touch syrupy, but the palate features a solid core of ripe, deep black fruits. Not perfect but shows plenty of flavor, width, weight and fruit. 86 —*M.S. (9/1/2007)*

PORTAL DEL ALTO

Portal Del Alto 1999 Cabernet Sauvignon (Maule Valley) $7. 84 —*J.C. (2/1/2001)*

Portal Del Alto 1999 Gran Reserva Cabernet Sauvignon (Maipo Valley) $12. 87 Best Buy —*C.S. (12/1/2002)*

Portal Del Alto 1998 Gran Reserva Alejandro Hernández Cabernet Sauvignon (Maipo Valley) $15. 84 —*M.M. (1/1/2004)*

Portal Del Alto 2000 Hand Picked Selection Cabernet Sauvignon (Central Valley) $7. 86 Best Buy —*M.S. (12/1/2002)*

Portal Del Alto 2000 Reserva Cabernet Sauvignon (Maule Valley) $10. 82 —*M.S. (12/1/2002)*

Portal Del Alto 1998 Reserva Cabernet Sauvignon (Maipo Valley) $12. 85 —*M.N. (2/1/2001)*

Portal Del Alto 2000 Gran Reserva Carmenère (Maule Valley) $12. 84 —*D.T. (7/1/2002)*

Portal Del Alto 2000 Chardonnay (Maule Valley) $7. 87 Best Buy —*M.M. (2/1/2001)*

Portal Del Alto 2000 Gran Reserva Chardonnay (Maipo Valley) $12. 80 —*M.S. (7/1/2002)*

Portal Del Alto 1999 Reserva Chardonnay (Central Valley) $12. 87 —*M.N. (2/1/2001)*

Portal Del Alto 1999 Pinot Noir (San Fernando) $7. 83 —*M.M. (1/1/2004)*

PRIMUS

Primus 1998 Veramonte Red Blend (Casablanca Valley) $20. 83 —*M.M. (1/1/2004)*

RIO ALTO

Rio Alto 2002 Syrah (Aconcagua Valley) $8. 81 —*M.S. (6/1/2004)*

ROOT:1

Root:1 2005 Cabernet Sauvignon (Colchagua Valley) $12. A bit of burning bush and pepper work the nose along with plum and cotton candy. This is a simple but well-made Chilean Cab that offers mildly candied flavors along with some spice. It's the standard stuff: color, body, warmth, sizzle and sweetness. 85 —*M.S. (11/15/2007)*

Root:1 2003 Cabernet Sauvignon (Maipo Valley) $12. 83 —*M.S. (5/1/2006)*

Root:1 2006 The Original Ungrafted Sauvignon Blanc (Casablanca Valley) $12. Tropical fruit, gooseberry and green apple make for a nice nose, while the palate is solid and crisp as it emphasizes apple, citrus and green melon flavors. A touch of pepper on the finish seals the deal on this light and friendly wine. 86 —*M.S. (11/15/2007)*

SAN NICOLAS

San Nicolas 2005 Cabernet Sauvignon (Curicó Valley) $8. Quite a bit of bramble and horsehide on the nose leads to a sketchy whole, while a palate that's dominated by red berries is muddled by mild herbal notes and a touch of peppery bitterness. Has commendable balance and weight but doesn't register as entirely clean and ripe. 83 —*M.S. (3/1/2007)*

San Nicolas 2003 Cabernet Sauvignon (Curicó Valley) $8. 85 Best Buy —*M.S. (11/1/2005)*

San Nicolas 2003 Sophia Gran Reserva Cabernet Sauvignon (Curicó Valley) $15. 84 —*M.S. (10/1/2006)*

San Nicolas 2001 Sophia Gran Reserva Cabernet Sauvignon (Curicó Valley) $14. 84 —*M.S. (8/1/2005)*

San Nicolas 2004 Chardonnay (Curicó Valley) $8. 84 Best Buy —*M.S. (11/1/2005)*

San Nicolas 2003 Chardonnay (Curicó Valley) $8. 81 —*M.S. (11/1/2005)*

San Nicolas 2004 Sabrina Reserve Chardonnay (Curicó Valley) $11. 86 Best Buy —*M.S. (11/1/2005)*

San Nicolas 2005 Merlot (Curicó Valley) $8. 82 —*M.S. (11/15/2006)*

San Nicolas 2003 Maigo Reserve Merlot (Curicó Valley) $11. 85 —*M.S. (10/1/2006)*

San Nicolas 2005 Sauvignon Blanc (Curicó Valley) $8. 83 —*M.S. (10/1/2006)*

San Nicolas 2003 Sauvignon Blanc (Curicó Valley) $8. 80 —*M.S. (7/1/2005)*

SAN PEDRO

San Pedro 2003 1865 Reserva Cabernet Sauvignon (Maipo Valley) $18. Less dark than most, which indicates that the wine is well into its aging process. On the nose, you'll find buttery dill aromas, while on the palate there's some leafy berry, tomato and cola flavors. Decent but unspectacular, and it seems as though it's beginning to fade away. 84 —*M.S. (9/1/2007)*

San Pedro 2001 1865 Reserva Cabernet Sauvignon (Maipo Valley) $19. 87 *(11/1/2005)*

San Pedro 2002 Cabo de Hornos Cabernet Sauvignon (Lontué Valley) $35. 90 *(11/1/2005)*

San Pedro 2001 Cabo de Hornos Cabernet Sauvignon (Lontué Valley) $35. 91 Editors' Choice *(11/1/2005)*

San Pedro 2000 Cabo de Hornos Cabernet Sauvignon (Lontué Valley) $35. 85 *(11/1/2005)*

San Pedro 1999 Cabo de Hornos Cabernet Sauvignon (Lontué Valley) $35. 91 Editors' Choice *(11/1/2005)*

San Pedro 1998 Cabo de Hornos Cabernet Sauvignon (Lontué Valley) $45. 86 —*M.S. (3/1/2002)*

San Pedro 2005 Castillo de Molina Reserva Cabernet Sauvignon (Lontué Valley) $10. 87 Best Buy *—M.S. (11/15/2006)*

San Pedro 2004 Castillo de Molina Reserva Cabernet Sauvignon (Lontué Valley) $11. 86 Best Buy *(11/1/2005)*

San Pedro 2003 Castillo de Molina Reserva Cabernet Sauvignon (Lontué Valley) $11. 86 Best Buy *—M.S. (11/1/2005)*

San Pedro 2002 Castillo De Molina Reserva Cabernet Sauvignon (Lontué Valley) $10. 84 *—M.S. (2/1/2005)*

San Pedro 2001 Castillo de Molina Reserva Cabernet Sauvignon (Lontué Valley) $11. 86 *—M.S. (7/1/2003)*

San Pedro 2005 Gato Negro Cabernet Sauvignon (Central Valley) $5. 83 Best Buy *(11/1/2005)*

San Pedro 2002 Gato Negro Cabernet Sauvignon (Central Valley) $5. 83 *—M.S. (7/1/2003)*

San Pedro 2000 Reserva 1865 Cabernet Sauvignon (Maipo Valley) $20. 85 *—M.S. (7/1/2003)*

San Pedro 2002 San Andrés Cabernet Sauvignon (Lontué Valley) 82 *—M.S. (7/1/2003)*

San Pedro 2004 1865 Reserva Carmenère (Maule Valley) $18. High priced for Carmenère, especially one of this marginal quality. The nose is all olives and herbal essence, while the palate shows a coating of cinnamon oak on top of midland red cherry and raspberry flavors. Not that impressive given that it's a reserve-level effort. 82 *—M.S. (3/1/2007)*

San Pedro 2002 1865 Reserva Carmenère (Maule Valley) $19. 85 *(11/1/2005)*

San Pedro 2006 Gato Negro Chardonnay (Central Valley) $5. Almost gray-green in color, with rudimentary apple and pear aromas. The wine is basically an amorphous, anonymous concoction that runs sweet, simple and inoffensive. It even shows some cinnamon and baked apple on the finish that leaves an apple pie/strudel sensation. 82 *—M.S. (5/1/2007)*

San Pedro 2002 Gato Negro Carmenère (Lontué Valley) $5. 81 *—M.S. (1/1/2004)*

San Pedro 2005 Castillo de Molina Reserva Chardonnay (Casablanca Valley) $10. 87 Best Buy *—M.S. (11/15/2006)*

San Pedro 2004 Castillo de Molina Reserva Chardonnay (Casablanca Valley) $11. 84 *(11/1/2005)*

San Pedro 2003 Castillo De Molina Reserva Chardonnay (Casablanca Valley) $10. 86 Best Buy *—M.S. (7/1/2005)*

San Pedro 2002 Castillo de Molina Reserva Chardonnay (Lontué Valley) $11. 87 *—M.S. (7/1/2003)*

San Pedro 2003 Gato Blanco Chardonnay (Central Valley) $5. 83 Best Buy *—M.S. (2/1/2005)*

San Pedro 2002 San Andrés Chardonnay (Lontué Valley) $NA. 84 *—M.S. (7/1/2003)*

San Pedro 2002 1865 Reserva Malbec (Curicó Valley) $19. 87 *(11/1/2005)*

San Pedro 2002 35 South Land of Passion and Fantasy Merlot (Lontué Valley) $8. 84 *—M.S. (7/1/2003)*

San Pedro 2003 Castillo de Molina Reserva Merlot (Lontué Valley) $11. 83 *—M.S. (11/1/2005)*

San Pedro 2002 Gato Negro Merlot (Lontué Valley) $5. 82 *—M.S. (7/1/2003)*

San Pedro 2002 San Andrés Merlot (Lontué Valley) 82 *—M.S. (7/1/2003)*

San Pedro 2003 Gato Blanco Sauvignon Blanc (Central Valley) $5. 82 *—M.S. (2/1/2005)*

San Pedro 2006 Gato Negro Sauvignon Blanc (Central Valley) $5. 85 Best Buy *—M.S. (11/15/2006)*

San Pedro 2005 Gato Negro Sauvignon Blanc (Central Valley) $5. 83 Best Buy *—M.S. (12/15/2005)*

San Pedro 2002 San Andrés Sauvignon Blanc (Lontué Valley) 85 *—M.S. (7/1/2003)*

San Pedro 2005 Castillo de Molina Reserva Shiraz (Lontué Valley) $10. 88 Best Buy *—M.S. (11/15/2006)*

San Pedro 2004 Castillo de Molina Reserva Shiraz (Lontué Valley) $11. 84 *(11/1/2005)*

San Pedro 2003 Castillo de Molina Reserva Shiraz (Lontué Valley) $11. 86 Best Buy *—M.S. (11/1/2005)*

SANTA ALICIA

Santa Alicia 2003 Gran Reserva Cabernet Sauvignon (Maipo Valley) $13. For full-bodied, true Cabernet at a reasonable price, Santa Alicia's 2003 Gran Reserva is a winner. The plum and berry flavors are clean and supported by proper creamy oak, and the tannins are pliable and add backbone. Drink now. 88 Best Buy *—M.S. (11/15/2007)*

Santa Alicia 2002 Gran Reserva Cabernet Sauvignon (Maipo Valley) $13. 84 *—M.S. (7/1/2006)*

Santa Alicia 2001 Gran Reserva Cabernet Sauvignon (Maipo Valley) $13. 85 *—M.S. (3/1/2004)*

Santa Alicia 1998 Gran Reserva Cabernet Sauvignon (Maipo Valley) $14. 82 *—D.T. (7/1/2002)*

Santa Alicia 2005 Reserve Cabernet Sauvignon (Maipo Valley) $9. Made in the heavier, denser style. That means the aromas are rich and jammy, while the wine has a soft, doughy texture supplemented by pruny berry flavors. Texture is the wine's focal point; it finishes with some spicy heat and stickiness. 85 Best Buy *—M.S. (11/15/2007)*

Santa Alicia 2003 Reserve Cabernet Sauvignon (Maipo Valley) $9. 88 Best Buy *—M.S. (7/1/2006)*

Santa Alicia 2001 Reserve Cabernet Sauvignon (Maipo Valley) $8. 81 *—M.S. (3/1/2004)*

Santa Alicia 2001 Estate Bottled Reserve Carmenère (Maipo Valley) $8. 85 Best Buy *—M.S. (7/1/2003)*

Santa Alicia 2005 Reserve Carmenère (Maipo Valley) $9. Round and warm on the nose, with turned earth, baked tomato and red plum aromas. The palate follows the nose by dealing baked plum and earthy/herbal accents, while the finish is harmonious. With a good mouthfeel, the wine comes across fairly generous. 86 Best Buy *—M.S. (11/15/2007)*

Santa Alicia 2002 Reserve Carmenère (Maipo Valley) $8. 87 Best Buy *—M.S. (8/1/2004)*

Santa Alicia 2001 Estate Chardonnay (Maipo Valley) $6. 80 *—M.S. (7/1/2002)*

Santa Alicia 2006 Reserve Chardonnay (Maipo Valley) $9. Peach, apricot, apple and butterscotch aromas lead toward an acidic palate that shows apple, melon, pineapple and other citrus fruit flavors. The wine has kick and acid-propelled drive but little elegance as it exhibits almost nothing in common with the Chardonnay of Burgundy or California. 83 *—M.S. (11/15/2007)*

Santa Alicia 2004 Reserve Chardonnay (Maipo Valley) $9. 86 Best Buy *—M.S. (7/1/2006)*

Santa Alicia 2003 Reserve Chardonnay (Maipo Valley) $8. 85 *—M.S. (8/1/2004)*

Santa Alicia 2006 Reserve Malbec (Maipo Valley) $9. Malbec from Chile may not seem as natural as from Argentina, but you will not go wrong with this stocky, soft, lightly baked offering. The palate has a touch of herbal lift to accent the black fruit, while the finish is firm, comfortable and consistent. 86 Best Buy *—M.S. (11/15/2007)*

Santa Alicia 2003 Reserve Malbec (Maipo Valley) $9. 81 *—M.S. (10/1/2006)*

Santa Alicia 2001 Reserve Malbec (Maipo Valley) $8. 86 *—M.S. (8/1/2004)*

Santa Alicia 2000 Reserve Malbec (Maipo Valley) $8. 87 Best Buy *—D.T. (7/1/2002)*

Santa Alicia 2000 Estate Bottled Reserve Merlot (Maipo Valley) $6. 88 Best Buy *—M.S. (12/1/2002)*

Santa Alicia 2003 Gran Reserva Merlot (Maipo Valley) $13. Very dark and chunky, but also loud and aggressive. This is simply a big, purple wine with mid-level ripeness and only modest depth of flavor. It's grabby and tannic, and if that's all you're after it's serviceable. 82 *—M.S. (11/15/2007)*

Santa Alicia 2002 Gran Reserva Merlot (Maipo Valley) $13. 84 *—M.S. (7/1/2006)*

Santa Alicia 2001 Gran Reserva Merlot (Maipo Valley) $13. 83 *—M.S. (8/1/2004)*

Santa Alicia 1999 Gran Reserva Merlot (Maipo Valley) $14. 84 *—D.T. (7/1/2002)*

Santa Alicia 2005 Reserve Merlot (Maipo Valley) $9. Leafy and dry at first, and then more lively and bruising as it opens. The palate shows herbal plum and berry flavors along with spiky tannins and plenty of acidic snap. Not a dull wine, but it rates as rugged and demanding. 84 Best Buy *—M.S. (11/15/2007)*

Santa Alicia 2002 Estate Bottled Reserve Sauvignon Blanc (Maipo Valley) $8. 84 *—M.S. (7/1/2003)*

Santa Alicia 2006 Reserve Sauvignon Blanc (Maipo Valley) $9. Tan in color, with flat, mildly sweaty aromas. The palate is also kind of flat and without zing, while the flavors of cucumber, passion fruit and gooseberry are distant at best. Not difficult or flawed, but not the best example of Chilean SB. 83 *—M.S. (11/15/2007)*

Santa Alicia 2004 Reserve Sauvignon Blanc (Maipo Valley) $9. 80 *—M.S. (7/1/2006)*

Santa Alicia 2003 Reserve Sauvignon Blanc (Maipo Valley) $8. 85 Best Buy *—M.S. (3/1/2004)*

Santa Alicia 2005 Reserve Shiraz (Maipo Valley) $9. Big and burly, with aromas of ground spices, leather, roasted meat and blackberry. The flavors of plum, wild berry and espresso draw no complaints, and overall this is one good, ripe, big-boned wine with texture and body. Best if you like saturated but balanced modern reds. 88 Best Buy *—M.S. (11/15/2007)*

Santa Alicia 2001 Reserve Syrah (Maipo Valley) $8. 86 Best Buy *—M.S. (8/1/2004)*

Santa Alicia 2004 Late Harvest Muscatel White Blend (Limarí Valley) $10. 84 *—M.S. (5/1/2006)*

SANTA AMELIA

Santa Amelia 1997 Reserve Selection Cabernet Sauvignon (Maule Valley) $8. 83 *—M.S. (11/15/1999)*

SANTA CAROLINA

Santa Carolina 2001 VSC Bordeaux Blend (Maipo Valley) $35. 85 *—M.S. (11/1/2005)*

Santa Carolina 2003 Barrica Selection Cabernet Sauvignon (Maipo Valley) $13. 86 *—M.S. (12/15/2005)*

Santa Carolina 2001 Barrica Selection Cabernet Sauvignon (Maipo Valley) $13. 84 *(11/15/2003)*

Santa Carolina 2003 Colección Especial Cabernet Sauvignon (Rapel Valley) $7. 85 Best Buy *—M.S. (11/15/2005)*

Santa Carolina 2004 Reserva Cabernet Sauvignon (Colchagua Valley) $10. 84 *—M.S. (10/1/2006)*

Santa Carolina 1999 Reserva Cabernet Sauvignon (Colchagua Valley) $9. 84 *—D.T. (7/1/2002)*

Santa Carolina 1998 Reserva Cabernet Sauvignon (Colchagua Valley) $9. 82 *—D.T. (7/1/2002)*

Santa Carolina 1997 Reserva Cabernet Sauvignon (Maipo Valley) $9. 82 *—M.S. (11/15/1999)*

Santa Carolina 1997 Reserva de Familia Cabernet Sauvignon (Maipo Valley) $15. 88 Best Buy *(8/1/2000)*

Santa Carolina 2004 Barrica Selection Carmenère (Rapel Valley) $15. 81 *—M.S. (10/1/2006)*

Santa Carolina 2003 Barrica Selection Carmenère (Rapel Valley) $13. 84 *—M.S. (12/15/2005)*

Santa Carolina 2001 Barrica Selection Carmenère (Rapel Valley) $13. 84 *(11/15/2003)*

Santa Carolina 2003 Barrica Selection Chardonnay (Maipo Valley) $13. 84 *—M.S. (12/15/2005)*

Santa Carolina 2002 Barrica Selection Chardonnay (Casablanca Valley) $13. 84 *(11/15/2003)*

Santa Carolina 1998 Reserva de la Familia Chardonnay (Maipo Valley) $15. 90 Best Buy *—M.N. (2/1/2001)*

Santa Carolina 1999 Merlot (Maule Valley) $9. 83 *—D.T. (7/1/2002)*

Santa Carolina 2002 Coleccion Especial Merlot (Rapel Valley) $7. 84 *(11/15/2003)*

Santa Carolina 1999 VSC Red Blend (Chile) $35. 86 *(11/15/2003)*

Santa Carolina 2002 Coleccion Especial Sauvignon Blanc (Rapel Valley) $7. 84 *(11/15/2003)*

Santa Carolina 2005 Reserva Sauvignon Blanc (Rapel Valley) $10. Wet and citrusy is the most generous way to describe this one. It's foxy and round but going nowhere. Best to wait for 2006. 80 *—M.S. (9/1/2007)*

Santa Carolina 2005 Barrica Selection Syrah (Maipo Valley) $15. 85 *—M.S. (10/1/2006)*

Santa Carolina 2003 Barrica Selection Syrah (Maipo Valley) $13. 86 *—M.S. (12/15/2005)*

Santa Carolina 2002 Barrica Selection Syrah (Maule Valley) $13. 84 *(11/15/2003)*

SANTA EMA

Santa Ema 1996 Catalina Bordeaux Blend (Rapel Valley) $28. 85 *(8/1/2001)*

Santa Ema 2005 Cabernet Sauvignon (Maipo Valley) $12. Dark and dense, but also a touch warm and soupy. Air allows it to unfold and show boysenberry and plum flavors, while the feel is creamy, syrupy and flush. Overall it's tasty enough and reasonably well made, although there are some herbal flavors that rise up on the midpalate and finish. A big-production wine at 45,000 cases. 85 *—M.S. (9/1/2007)*

Santa Ema 2004 Amplus Cabernet Sauvignon (Cachapoal Valley) $19. 82 *—M.S. (11/15/2006)*

Santa Ema 2000 Estate Bottled Cabernet Sauvignon (Maipo Valley) $9. 85 *—M.S. (7/1/2003)*

Santa Ema 1998 Estate Bottled Cabernet Sauvignon (Maipo Valley) $9. 86 *—J.C. (2/1/2001)*

Santa Ema 2004 Reserve Cabernet Sauvignon (Maipo Valley) $14. Respectably deep, but strong wintergreen, olive and leather aromas cloud the fruit quotient. A nice feel to the palate but the fruit is not what you'd call pure; funky rhubarb and black olive accents are just too prominent. 83 *—M.S. (3/1/2007)*

Santa Ema 2002 Reserve Cabernet Sauvignon (Maipo Valley) $14. 87 *—M.S. (7/1/2005)*

Santa Ema 2001 Reserve Cabernet Sauvignon (Maipo Valley) $14. 87 *—M.S. (7/1/2003)*

Santa Ema 1999 Reserve Cabernet Sauvignon (Maipo Valley) $14. 86 *—M.S. (12/1/2002)*

Santa Ema 2003 60/40 Barrel Select Cabernet Sauvignon-Merlot (Maipo Valley) $11. 89 Best Buy *—M.S. (12/15/2005)*

Santa Ema 2002 60/40 Barrel Select Cabernet Sauvignon-Merlot (Maipo Valley) $10. 86 Best Buy *—M.S. (2/1/2005)*

Santa Ema 2001 Barrel Select Cabernet Sauvignon-Merlot (Maipo Valley) $12. 87 *—M.S. (7/1/2003)*

Santa Ema 1999 Barrel Select Cabernet Sauvignon-Merlot (Maipo Valley) $10. 87 *—D.T. (7/1/2002)*

Santa Ema 2003 Carmenère (Cachapoal Valley) $10. 80 *—M.S. (2/1/2005)*

Santa Ema 2001 Carmenère (Rapel Valley) $10. 83 *—M.S. (3/1/2004)*

Santa Ema 2004 Barrel Select Carmenère (Cachapoal Valley) $11. Adequate but uninspiring is this rooty, savory wine that comes on too sweet and soft. It's all about baked fruit with cola and vanilla accents, and while those flavors are good for a parfait or ice cream sundae, they're too soft and gooey for a dry red wine. 83 *—M.S. (3/1/2007)*

Santa Ema 2000 Estate Carmenère (Rapel Valley) $9. 87 Best Buy *—D.T. (7/1/2002)*

Santa Ema 2002 Gran Reserva Carmenère (Cachapoal Valley) $17. 85 *—M.S. (2/1/2005)*

Santa Ema 2001 Reserve Carmenère (Maipo Valley) $16. 82 *—M.S. (3/1/2004)*

Santa Ema 2000 Reserve Carmenère (Rapel Valley) $16. 86 *—D.T. (7/1/2002)*

Santa Ema 2006 Chardonnay (Casablanca Valley) $9. Clean and fresh, but devoid of character and excitement. This is a rudimentary wine with apple and citrus flavors and some grapefruit on the finish. It is weightless and generally tropical in personality. 83 *—M.S. (3/1/2007)*

Santa Ema 2004 Chardonnay (Casablanca Valley) $9. 85 Best Buy *—M.S. (11/1/2005)*

Santa Ema 2003 Chardonnay (Casablanca Valley) $9. 84 *—M.S. (6/1/2004)*

Santa Ema 2001 Estate Chardonnay (Maipo Valley) $9. 83 *—M.S. (7/1/2002)*

Santa Ema 2003 Reserve Chardonnay (Casablanca Valley) $14. 86 *—M.S. (2/1/2005)*

Santa Ema 1999 Reserve Chardonnay (Maipo Valley) $14. 83 *(2/1/2001)*

Santa Ema 2005 Merlot (Cachapoal Valley) $12. Aromas of bramble and berries are sweetened by hints of cocoa and mocha, while the palate pushes prime cherry and plum flavors. The feel is lively and healthy, while the finish is good and whole. A satisfying mid-level red in every way. 86 *—M.S. (5/1/2007)*

Santa Ema 2003 Merlot (Cachapoal Valley) $9. 86 Best Buy *—M.S. (2/1/2005)*

Santa Ema 2001 Merlot (Rapel Valley) $9. 81 *—M.S. (7/1/2003)*

Santa Ema 1998 Merlot (Maipo Valley) $9. 83 *—J.C. (2/1/2001)*

Santa Ema 2004 Reserve Merlot (Maipo Valley) $14. A heavy offering with overbearing oak that results in aromas of coconut, chocolate mint and tire rubber. The palate is just as thick and cumbersome as the bouquet, with chocolate mint riding on a base of cherry and berry. Seems overripe and too coated with cloying, minty wood notes. It's like a box of Junior Mints. 83 *—M.S. (3/1/2007)*

Santa Ema 2003 Reserve Merlot (Maipo Valley) $14. 81 *—M.S. (5/1/2006)*

Santa Ema 2001 Reserve Merlot (Maipo Valley) $14. 80 *—M.S. (7/1/2003)*

Santa Ema 1999 Reserve Merlot (Maipo Valley) $14. 82 *—D.T. (7/1/2002)*

Santa Ema 1998 Reserve Merlot (Maipo Valley) $14. 87 *—J.C. (2/1/2001)*84 *—M.S. (11/15/2006)*

Santa Ema 2003 Catalina Red Blend (Cachapoal Valley) $37. Catalina is Santa Ema's top Cabernet-based blend, yet it shows a lot of leafiness and bell pepper. Yes, it has a good feel and the longer you work with it the more you'll like it. But for me it has a bit too much olive and green to rate higher. 86 *—M.S. (5/1/2007)*

Santa Ema 2002 Catalina Red Blend (Cachapoal Valley) $38. 91 *—M.S. (3/1/2006)*

Santa Ema 2001 Catalina Red Blend (Rapel Valley) $28. 90 *—M.S. (2/1/2005)*

Santa Ema 1998 Catalina Red Blend (Rapel Valley) $28. 85 *—M.S. (7/1/2003)*

Santa Ema 2003 Rivalta Red Blend (Cachapoal Valley) $72. 88 *—M.S. (11/15/2006)*

Santa Ema 2006 Sauvignon Blanc (Maipo Valley) $12. Ultimately this would make for a good bistro or patio white. The bouquet is light and sweet, as is the palate. Baked apple and ripe citrus lead the flavor profile on this clean, mildly sweet Sauvignon. More than decent as a whole. 85 *—M.S. (3/1/2007)*

Santa Ema 2004 Sauvignon Blanc (Maipo Valley) $8. 84 Best Buy *—M.S. (7/1/2005)*

Santa Ema 2002 Estate Bottled Sauvignon Blanc (Maipo Valley) $8. 86 Best Buy *—M.S. (7/1/2003)*

Santa Ema 2004 Barrel Select Syrah (Cachapoal Valley) $11. Black in color, with heavy menthol and licorice aromas. The palate is lean, hard and stretched thin. You get some generic berry flavors and maybe some raisin on the finish. Just doesn't feel comfortable on the palate. 82 *—M.S. (5/1/2007)*

SANTA EMILIANA

Santa Emiliana 2002 Sincerity Merlot-Cabernet Sauvignon (Rapel Valley) $15. 88 *—R.V. (4/1/2005)*

SANTA HELENA

Santa Helena 2002 Notas De Guarda Cabernet Sauvignon (Colchagua Valley) $18. 89 *—M.S. (2/1/2005)*

Santa Helena 2001 Seleccion del Directorio Reserva Cabernet Sauvignon (Central Valley) $11. 89 *—M.S. (8/1/2004)*

Santa Helena 2002 Siglo de oro Cabernet Sauvignon (Central Valley) $9. 88 Best Buy *—M.S. (8/1/2004)*

Santa Helena 2002 Vernus Cabernet Sauvignon (Colchagua Valley) $18. 88 *—M.S. (2/1/2005)*

Santa Helena 2002 Seleccion del Directorio Reserva Carmenère (Central Valley) $11. 84 *—M.S. (8/1/2004)*

Santa Helena 2002 Siglo de Oro Carmenère (Central Valley) $9. 83 *—M.S. (8/1/2004)*

Santa Helena 2003 Seleccion del Directorio Reserva Chardonnay (Casablanca Valley) $11. 85 *—M.S. (2/1/2005)*

Santa Helena 2002 Seleccion del Directorio Reserva Chardonnay (Casablanca Valley) $11. 81 *—M.S. (8/1/2004)*

Santa Helena 2003 Siglo de Oro Chardonnay (Casablanca Valley) $9. 83 *—M.S. (8/1/2004)*

Santa Helena 2001 Seleccion del Directorio Reserva Merlot (Central Valley) $11. 86 *—M.S. (8/1/2004)*

Santa Helena 2002 Siglo de Oro Merlot (Central Valley) $9. 83 *—M.S. (8/1/2004)*

Santa Helena 2001 Late Harvest Riesling (Curicó Valley) $11. 83 *—M.S. (8/1/2004)*

Santa Helena 2002 Seleccion del Dierctorio Reserva Sauvignon Blanc (Central Valley) $11. 84 *—M.S. (8/1/2004)*

Santa Helena 2003 Siglo de Oro Sauvignon Blanc (Curicó Valley) $9. 85 *—M.S. (8/1/2004)*

SANTA INES

Santa Ines 1998 Enigma Reserva Cabernet Sauvignon (Maipo Valley) $20. 85 *—M.S. (12/1/2002)*

Santa Ines 2001 Estate Bottled Cabernet Sauvignon (Maipo Valley) $11. 85 *—M.S. (12/1/2002)*

Santa Ines 2004 Reserva Cabernet Sauvignon (Maipo Valley) $14. Some mint and chocolate notes blend with aromas of dark fruit, followed up by slightly warm berry and plum flavors. What's rather unusual here is that the mouthfeel is feisty and almost sheer, courtesy of racy acids. There's no doubt this comes across a touch sharp. 84 *—M.S. (3/1/2007)*

Santa Ines 2002 Chardonnay (Central Valley) $7. 83 *—M.S. (7/1/2003)*

Santa Ines 1999 Enigma Reserva Chardonnay (Maipo Valley) $15. 85 *—M.S. (7/1/2003)*

Santa Ines 2000 Legado de Armida Reserva Chardonnay (Maipo Valley) $6. 88 Best Buy *—M.S. (7/1/2003)*

Santa Ines 2005 Reserva Chardonnay (Maipo Valley) $14. Starts with mild butterscotch and some apple before merging into a palate of spiced apple and melon. Seems a touch dilute and watery when put on the scale, so the score suffers a bit. Overall it's pretty good but weak in the middle. 84 *—M.S. (5/1/2007)*

Santa Ines 2001 Estate Bottled Merlot (Maipo Valley) $8. 86 *—K.F. (12/1/2002)*

Santa Ines 1998 Legado de Armida Reserva Merlot (Maipo Valley) $6. 86 Best Buy *—M.S. (5/1/2000)*

Santa Ines 2006 Estate Sauvignon Blanc (Maipo Valley) $10. A chalky lightness is the starting point for this soda-like quaffer. On the palate, there's lemon-lime and Fresca flavors followed by a finish of chunky grapefruit. Totally decent if this you know what to expect. 83 *—M.S. (3/1/2007)*

Santa Ines 2001 Legado de Armida Reserva Sauvignon Blanc (Maipo Valley) $10. 87 *—M.S. (7/1/2003)*

Santa Ines 2004 Reserva Syrah (Colchagua Valley) $14. A bit toasty and minty, but you also get some black truffle and blackberry on the nose. The palate offers solid cassis and black-fruit flavors, and overall it seems ripe to the core. Jumpy acidity gives the wine a forward personality. 86 *—M.S. (5/1/2007)*

SANTA MARVISTA

Santa Marvista 2003 Reserva Chardonnay (Central Valley) $6. 82 *—M.S. (6/1/2004)*

Santa Marvista 2003 Reserva Merlot (Central Valley) $6. 83 *—M.S. (3/1/2004)*

SANTA MONICA

Santa Monica 2000 Chardonnay (Rapel Valley) $8. 82 *—J.F. (8/1/2001)*

SANTA RITA

Santa Rita 2000 Cabernet Sauvignon (Rapel Valley) $7. 83 *—D.T. (7/1/2002)*

Santa Rita 2005 120 Cabernet Sauvignon (Rapel Valley) $8. This perennial Best Buy shines in 2005. It's clean, inviting and ready to go as piercing cherry, plum and cola flavors make a stand. Flush, warm and fairly full-bodied, 120 is one of those bargain lines that satisfies. More than 300,000 cases made, so it's good stuff made on a grand scale. 86 Best Buy *—M.S. (5/1/2007)*

Santa Rita 2002 120 Cabernet Sauvignon (Rapel Valley) $8. 83 *—M.S. (3/1/2004)*

Santa Rita 2001 120 Cabernet Sauvignon (Rapel Valley) $8. 84 *(8/1/2003)*

Santa Rita 1999 120 Cabernet Sauvignon (Rapel Valley) $7. 81 *—M.M. (2/1/2001)*

Santa Rita 2005 120 Rosé Cabernet Sauvignon (Maipo Valley) $8. 87 Best Buy *—M.S. (5/1/2006)*

Santa Rita 2002 Casa Real Cabernet Sauvignon (Maipo Valley) $50. 91 *—M.S. (5/1/2006)*

Santa Rita 2001 Casa Real Cabernet Sauvignon (Maipo Valley) $65. 93 Editors' Choice *—M.S. (11/15/2004)*

Santa Rita 1999 Casa Real Cabernet Sauvignon (Maipo Valley) $65. 94 *—M.S. (3/1/2002)*

Santa Rita 1997 Casa Real Cabernet Sauvignon (Maipo Valley) $40. 92 *—M.S. (5/1/2000)*

Santa Rita 1999 Casa Real Old Vines Cabernet Sauvignon (Maipo Valley) $65. 92 *(8/1/2003)*

Santa Rita 1999 Floresta Apalta Estate Cabernet Sauvignon (Colchagua Valley) $30. 91 Editors' Choice *(8/1/2003)*

Santa Rita 2002 Floresta Apalta Vineyard Cabernet Sauvignon (Apalta) $28. 89 *—M.S. (11/15/2004)*

Santa Rita 2004 Medalla Real Cabernet Sauvignon (Maipo Valley) $19. Aromas of roasted coffee, asphalt and pepper give the black cherry, olive and bell pepper scents some character. In the mouth, we find leafy red fruit along with olive flavors, while the texture is juicy and lively. No dead weight or balance issues; but it is a bit green. 86 *—M.S. (9/1/2007)*

Santa Rita 2003 Medalla Real Cabernet Sauvignon (Maipo Valley) $18. 87 *—M.S. (5/1/2006)*

Santa Rita 2000 Medalla Real Cabernet Sauvignon (Maipo Valley) $18. 88 *(8/1/2003)*

Santa Rita 1999 Medalla Real Cabernet Sauvignon (Maipo Valley) $18. 89 *—M.S. (3/1/2002)*

Santa Rita 2002 Medalla Real Special Reserve Cabernet Sauvignon (Maipo Valley) $18. 88 *—M.S. (11/15/2004)*

Santa Rita 1998 Medalla Real Special Reserve Cabernet Sauvignon (Maipo Valley) $15. 82 *—M.N. (2/1/2001)*

Santa Rita 2005 Reserva Cabernet Sauvignon (Maipo Valley) $11. Give Santa Rita a good Cabernet vintage like 2005 and they will make good wines from the top down to the everyday level. The latter category is well represented with this exuberant, balanced wine. The nose is ripe but natural, while the cherry and berry flavors rush over the palate and roll along the finish. Very nice in this price range. 89 Best Buy *—M.S. (11/15/2007)*

Santa Rita 2004 Reserva Cabernet Sauvignon (Maipo Valley) $11. If you can handle the large-quantity characteristics that govern this wine, particularly olive, herbal notes and vegetal aromas and flavors, then it's pretty nice. For those opposed to traditional Bordeaux-style green notes, it's probably better to upgrade to Santa Rita's richer, riper Medalla Real. Good on the whole but not great; yet at 150,000 cases it's hard to expect better. 85 *—M.S. (9/1/2007)*

Santa Rita 2002 Reserva Cabernet Sauvignon (Maipo Valley) $12.86 *—M.S. (11/15/2004)*

Santa Rita 2001 Reserva Cabernet Sauvignon (Maipo Valley) $12. 87 *(8/1/2003)*

Santa Rita 2000 Reserva Cabernet Sauvignon (Maipo Valley) $8. 84 *—M.S. (12/1/2002)*

Santa Rita 1999 Reserva Cabernet Sauvignon (Maipo Valley) $11. 82 *—D.T. (8/1/2001)*

Santa Rita 1998 Reserve Cabernet Sauvignon (Maipo Valley) $13. 83 *—M.N. (2/1/2001)*

Santa Rita 2004 120 Carmenère (Rapel Valley) $8. 84 *—M.S. (3/1/2006)*

Santa Rita 2002 120 Carmenère (Colchagua Valley) $8. 86 Best Buy *(8/1/2003)*

Santa Rita 2000 120 Carmenère (Rapel Valley) $7. 85 Editors' Choice *—J.C. (8/1/2001)*

Santa Rita 2005 Reserva Carmenère (Rapel Valley) $11. Carmenère isn't an easy grape to get right, and that's evidenced here. The nose encourages with darkness and apparent density, but it quickly turns to oak. The palate veers straight to black plum and oily herbal notes, but doesn't back it up with much. 83 *—M.S. (11/15/2007)*

Santa Rita 1999 Reserva Carmenère (Rapel Valley) $11. 83 *—J.C. (8/1/2001)*

Santa Rita 2005 120 Chardonnay (Maipo Valley) $8. 85 Best Buy *—M.S. (7/1/2006)*

Santa Rita 2003 120 Chardonnay (Aconcagua Valley) $NA. 83 *—M.S. (6/1/2004)*

Santa Rita 2002 120 Chardonnay (Maipo Valley) $8. 85 Best Buy *(8/1/2003)*

Santa Rita 2001 120 Chardonnay (Lontué Valley) $NA. 83 *—M.S. (7/1/2002)*

Santa Rita 2000 120 Chardonnay (Lontué Valley) $7. 84 *(2/1/2001)*

Santa Rita 2005 Medalla Real Chardonnay (Casablanca Valley) $19. Over time Santa Rita's Medalla Chardonnay has gotten better, but it's still a wine with some holes to fill. For starters, 14.5% alcohol equates to heft and heat, while the mouthfeel comes across grabby and resiny. And while it's not overoaked, the tangerine and pineapple flavors seem more melony and soft than crisp. 86 *—M.S. (5/1/2007)*

Santa Rita 2001 Medalla Real Chardonnay (Casablanca Valley) $15. 85 *—M.S. (3/1/2002)*

Santa Rita 1999 Medalla Real Special Reserve Chardonnay (Casablanca Valley) $13. 81 *—M.M. (8/1/2001)*

Santa Rita 2005 Reserva Chardonnay (Casablanca Valley) $12. 84 *—M.S. (7/1/2006)*

Santa Rita 2003 Reserva Chardonnay (Casablanca Valley) $12. 85 *—M.S. (11/15/2004)*

Santa Rita 2002 Reserva Chardonnay (Casablanca Valley) $12. 87 *(8/1/2003)*

Santa Rita 2001 Reserva Chardonnay (Casablanca Valley) $11. 85 *—M.S. (7/1/2003)*

Santa Rita 2000 Reserva Chardonnay (Casablanca Valley) $11. 85 *—M.M. (8/1/2001)*

Santa Rita 1999 Reserva Chardonnay (Maipo Valley) $13. 84 *—M.N. (2/1/2001)*

Santa Rita 2002 120 Merlot (Rapel Valley) $8. 84 *—M.S. (3/1/2004)*

Santa Rita 2001 120 Merlot (Lontué Valley) $9. 85 *—K.F. (12/1/2002)*

Santa Rita 2000 120 Merlot (Lontué Valley) $7. 86 Best Buy *—J.C. (3/1/2002)*

Santa Rita 2005 Reserva Merlot (Maipo Valley) $11. Dark and peppery up front, and also fairly green. This is classic herbal Merlot from Chile, which doesn't mean that it's bad. Just expect olive flavors with your black cherry and peppery notes from front to back. Full and grabby on the palate. 84 *—M.S. (11/15/2007)*

Santa Rita 2004 Reserva Merlot (Maipo Valley) $12. 82 *—M.S. (7/1/2006)*

Santa Rita 2003 Reserva Merlot (Maipo Valley) $12. 84 *—M.S. (11/15/2004)*

Santa Rita 2002 Reserva Merlot (Maipo Valley) $12. 86 *—M.S. (3/1/2004)*

Santa Rita 2001 Reserva Merlot (Maipo Valley) $13. 84 *—K.F. (12/1/2002)*

Santa Rita 2000 Floresta Red Blend (Maipo Valley) $30. 89 *—M.S. (12/1/2004)*

Santa Rita 1999 Floresta Red Blend (Maipo Valley) $30. 89 *(8/1/2003)*

Santa Rita 1999 Floresta Apalta Estate Red Blend (Colchagua Valley) $30. 92 Editors' Choice *—M.S. (3/1/2002)*

Santa Rita 1999 Triple C Red Blend (Maipo Valley) $45. 91 *—M.S. (3/1/2002)*

Santa Rita 2006 120 Sauvignon Blanc (Lontué Valley) $8. Chill it and kill it, and you probably won't be disappointed. There isn't a lot of character to the nose, but the palate offers round melon and citrus flavors supported by pretty good acidity. It's a little sugary but sound and tropical. More than 200,000 cases produced, so it should be widely available. 84 Best Buy *—M.S. (9/1/2007)*

Santa Rita 2005 120 Sauvignon Blanc (Lontué Valley) $8. 81 *—M.S. (7/1/2006)*

Santa Rita 2003 120 Sauvignon Blanc (Lontué Valley) $8. 85 Best Buy *—M.S. (6/1/2004)*

Santa Rita 2000 120 Sauvignon Blanc (Curicó Valley) $8. 84 *(8/1/2003)*

Santa Rita 2006 Floresta Sauvignon Blanc (Leyda Valley) $23. This is the first Sauvignon Blanc Santa Rita has done under its higher-end Floresta label. This has its share of qualities, namely lemon-lime and grapefruit aromas, body weight that separates it from the simple-but-zesty category, and depth of fruit. Drink as soon as possible. 88 *—M.S. (11/15/2007)*

Santa Rita 2001 Medalla Real Sauvignon Blanc (Rapel Valley) $18. 85 *—M.S. (3/1/2002)*

Santa Rita 2006 Reserva Sauvignon Blanc (Casablanca Valley) $11. Fairly intense celery, asparagus and capsicum-based aromas could be described as vegetal or just green; you be the judge. In the mouth, the flavors of passion fruit and tangerine are solid while the finish shields bell pepper and grapefruit. 84 *—M.S. (9/1/2007)*

Santa Rita 2005 Reserva Sauvignon Blanc (Casablanca Valley) $12. 85 *—M.S. (10/1/2006)*

Santa Rita 2004 Reserva Sauvignon Blanc (Casablanca Valley) $12. 87 Best Buy *—M.S. (11/15/2004)*

Santa Rita 2003 Reserva Sauvignon Blanc (Casablanca Valley) $12. 83 *—M.S. (3/1/2004)*

Santa Rita 2002 Reserva Sauvignon Blanc (Casablanca Valley) $12. 86 *(8/1/2003)*

Santa Rita 2003 120 Shiraz (Maipo Valley) $8. 85 Best Buy *—M.S. (11/15/2004)*

Santa Rita 2002 Reserva Shiraz (Maipo Valley) $12. 85 *—M.S. (11/15/2004)*

SEÑA

Seña 2003 Bordeaux Blend (Aconcagua Valley) $70. 87 *—M.S. (12/31/2006)*

Seña 2002 Bordeaux Blend (Aconcagua Valley) $70. 91 *—M.S. (10/1/2006)*

Seña 2001 Bordeaux Blend (Aconcagua Valley) $70. 91 *—M.S. (2/1/2005)*

Seña 2000 Bordeaux Blend (Aconcagua Valley) $70. 88 *—M.S. (6/1/2004)*

Seña 1999 Bordeaux Blend (Aconcagua Valley) $70. 88 *—S.H. (12/1/2002)*

Seña 1998 Bordeaux Blend (Aconcagua Valley) $66. 89 *(10/1/2001)*

Seña 1997 Bordeaux Blend (Aconcagua Valley) $60. 92 *—S.H. (2/1/2001)*

SIEGEL

Siegel 2001 Crucero Cabernet Sauvignon (Colchagua Valley) $9. 87 *—M.S. (12/1/2002)*

Siegel 2000 El Crucero Reserva Cabernet Sauvignon (Colchagua Valley) $13. 89 *—M.S. (12/1/2002)*

SIMONE

Simone 2004 Grand Reserve Cabernet Blend (Maule Valley) $15. Quite smooth and polished. It's a blend of Cabernet Sauvignon with Carmenère and Petit Verdot adding something of value. The wine is snappy, healthy and well balanced. The flavors don't veer far from the comfortable middle of the road; there's a tilt toward red berries and plums, with some cassis to sweeten the load. 89 *—M.S. (11/15/2007)*

Simone 2005 Special Reserve Cabernet Sauvignon (Maule Valley) $10. If it weren't for the slight lettuce-like aromas and flavors that snake through the wine's nose and palate, this would be ideal. And even with those hints of green it has good red fruit and vanilla flavors backed by chewy tannins. 85 Best Buy *—M.S. (9/1/2007)*

SINCERITY

Sincerity 2004 Chardonnay (Casablanca Valley) $17. 90 Editors' Choice *—M.S. (11/1/2005)*

Sincerity 2003 Merlot-Cabernet Sauvignon (Colchagua Valley) $17. 90 *—M.S. (12/15/2005)*

SOUTHERN WIND

Southern Wind 2002 Chardonnay (Rapel Valley) $6. 83 *—M.S. (3/1/2004)*

ST. EMILIANA

St. Emiliana 2002 Sincerity Organically Grown Merlot-Cabernet Sauvignon (Colchagua Valley) $15. 91 Editors' Choice *—M.S. (8/1/2004)*

STERLING

Sterling 2002 Vintner's Collection Chardonnay (Central Valley) $13. 84 *—S.H. (9/1/2004)*

TARAPACA

Tarapaca 1997 Zavala Bordeaux Blend (Maipo Valley) $25. 87 *(8/1/2000)*

Tarapaca 1999 Cabernet Sauvignon (Maipo Valley) $9. 87 Best Buy *(8/1/2001)*

Tarapaca 1999 Gran Reserva Cabernet Sauvignon (Maipo Valley) $15. 82 *—M.S. (3/1/2004)*

Tarapaca 2002 Reserva Cabernet Sauvignon (Maipo Valley) $10. 84 *—M.S. (5/1/2006)*

Tarapaca 1999 Reserva Cabernet Sauvignon (Maipo Valley) $12. 84 *—J.C. (7/1/2002)*

Tarapaca 2003 Reserva Carmenère (Maipo Valley) $10. 82 *—M.S. (3/1/2006)*

Tarapaca 2003 Chardonnay (Maipo Valley) $8. 83 *—M.S. (2/1/2005)*

Tarapaca 2000 Chardonnay (Maipo Valley) $9. 85 *—S.H. (2/1/2003)*

Tarapaca 2001 Reserva Chardonnay (Casablanca Valley) $11. 84 *—M.S. (6/1/2004)*

Tarapaca 2001 Merlot (Maipo Valley) $8. 85 Best Buy *—M.S. (3/1/2004)*

Tarapaca 2002 Estate Bottled Merlot (Maipo Valley) $8. 84 *—M.S. (8/1/2004)*

Tarapaca 2001 Reserva Merlot (Casablanca Valley) $11. 82 *—M.S. (3/1/2004)*

Tarapaca 1999 Reserva Merlot (Maipo Valley) $12. 82 *—D.T. (7/1/2002)*

Tarapaca 2000 Sauvignon Blanc (Maipo Valley) $14. 82 *—M.M. (8/1/2001)*

Tarapaca 2000 La Isla Vineyard Sauvignon Blanc (Maipo Valley) $14. 86 *—M.S. (7/1/2003)*

Tarapaca 2004 Reserva Sauvignon Blanc (Maipo Valley) $10. 87 Best Buy *—M.S. (3/1/2006)*

TERRA ANDINA

Terra Andina 2001 Reserve Cabernet Blend (Rapel Valley) $15. 89 *—M.S. (8/1/2004)*

Terra Andina 2004 Cabernet Sauvignon (Central Valley) $8. 85 Best Buy *—M.S. (5/1/2006)*

Terra Andina 2002 Cabernet Sauvignon (Central Valley) $8. 85 Best Buy *—M.S. (12/1/2004)*

Terra Andina 2003 Alto Reserve Cabernet Sauvignon (Maipo Valley) $13. 88 Best Buy *—M.S. (5/1/2006)*

Terra Andina 2002 Reserve Cabernet Sauvignon (Maipo Valley) $13. 90 Best Buy *—M.S. (8/1/2004)*

Terra Andina 2003 Carmenère (Central Valley) $8. 88 Best Buy *—M.S. (11/1/2005)*

Terra Andina 2001 Carmenère (Central Valley) $8. 85 Best Buy *—M.S. (12/1/2004)*

Terra Andina 2004 Chardonnay (Central Valley) $8. 82 *—M.S. (11/1/2005)*

Terra Andina 2003 Chardonnay (Central Valley) $8. 86 Best Buy *—M.S. (2/1/2005)*

Terra Andina 2003 Alto Reserve Chardonnay (Casablanca Valley) $13. 84 *—M.S. (5/1/2006)*

Terra Andina 2002 Reserve Chardonnay (Casablanca Valley) $13. 85 *—M.S. (8/1/2004)*

Terra Andina 2004 Merlot (Central Valley) $8. 86 Best Buy *—M.S. (11/1/2005)*

Terra Andina 2003 Merlot (Central Valley) $8. 86 Best Buy *—M.S. (2/1/2005)*

Terra Andina 2004 Sauvignon Blanc (Central Valley) $8. 85 Best Buy *—M.S. (11/1/2005)*

Terra Andina 2003 Sauvignon Blanc (Central Valley) $8. 85 Best Buy *—M.S. (8/1/2004)*

Terra Andina 2003 Shiraz (Central Valley) $8. 84 Best Buy *—M.S. (12/15/2005)*

Terra Andina 2002 Shiraz (Central Valley) $8. 84 Best Buy *—M.S. (2/1/2005)*

Terra Andina 2002 Reserve Shiraz-Cabernet Sauvignon (Maipo Valley) $15. 86 *—M.S. (8/1/2004)*

TERRA NOVA

Terra Nova 2003 Chardonnay (Curicó Valley) $7. 83 *—M.S. (7/1/2005)*

Terra Nova 2003 Sauvignon Blanc (Curicó Valley) $7. 80 *—M.S. (7/1/2005)*

TERRAMATER

TerraMater 2001 Altum Reserve Cabernet Sauvignon (Curicó Valley) $17. 87 *—M.S. (7/1/2005)*

TerraMater 2002 Reserva Cabernet Sauvignon (Central Valley) $12. 84 *—M.S. (7/1/2005)*

TerraMater 2001 Single Vineyard Cabernet Sauvignon (Maipo Valley) $8. 85 *—M.S. (12/1/2002)*

TerraMater 2003 Merlot (Maipo Valley) $9. 88 Best Buy *—M.S. (7/1/2005)*

TerraMater 1999 Altum Reserve Single Vineyard Merlot (Maipo Valley) $20. 83 *—M.S. (1/28/2004)*

TerraMater 1999 Altum Single Vineyard Reserve San Clemente Merlot (Maule Valley) $17. 83 *—M.S. (7/1/2005)*

TerraMater 2003 Reserva Merlot (Central Valley) $12. 87 Best Buy *—M.S. (7/1/2005)*

TerraMater 2001 Single Vineyard Zinfandel-Shiraz Red Blend (Central Valley) $8. 80 *—M.S. (7/1/2003)*

TerraMater 2001 Unusual Cabernet, Zinfandel, Shiraz Red Blend (Maipo Valley) $22. 81 *—M.S. (2/1/2005)*

TerraMater 2000 Unusual Carmenère-Shiraz Red Blend (Central Valley) $22. 84 *—M.S. (11/1/2005)*

TerraMater 2004 Sauvignon Blanc (Maipo Valley) $9. 86 Best Buy *—M.S. (7/1/2005)*

TERRANOBLE

TerraNoble 2006 Cabernet Sauvignon (Central Valley) $7. Makes the grade among bargain-priced wines. The nose is a bit leafy and green, but the palate offers enough chunky red-fruit flavors to offset any lingering green flavor elements. Finishes peppery, with some chalky grab. 84 Best Buy *—M.S. (11/15/2007)*

TerraNoble 2005 Gran Reserva Cabernet Sauvignon (Colchagua Valley) $14. Copious oak is mostly unabsorbed, thus the nose breathes mocha and burnt coffee aromas. The fruit is big and oily, and there's a lot of olive on the finish. Funky and herbal as a whole. 82 *—M.S. (11/15/2007)*

TerraNoble 2004 Gran Reserva Cabernet Sauvignon (Colchagua Valley) $14. 90 Best Buy *—M.S. (11/15/2006)*

TerraNoble 2003 Gran Reserva Cabernet Sauvignon (Colchagua Valley) $17. 86 *—M.S. (10/1/2006)*

TerraNoble 2002 Gran Reserva Cabernet Sauvignon (Colchagua Valley) $13. 82 *—M.S. (11/1/2005)*

TerraNoble 2001 Gran Reserva Cabernet Sauvignon (Maule Valley) $20. 88 *—M.S. (3/1/2004)*

TerraNoble 1999 Gran Reserva Cabernet Sauvignon (Colchagua Valley) $14. 86 *(8/1/2001)*

TerraNoble 2005 Reserva Cabernet Sauvignon (Colchagua Valley) $12. Like most TerraNoble 2005 and 2006 reds, this has a burnt, scattershot nose along with animal and leather notes. The label boasts fresh fruit, but the wine itself has a roasted profile and doesn't manage to rise above decent. 83 *—M.S. (11/15/2007)*

TerraNoble 2004 Reserva Cabernet Sauvignon (Colchagua Valley) $11. 87 Best Buy *—M.S. (11/15/2006)*

TerraNoble 2003 Reserva Cabernet Sauvignon (Colchagua Valley) $11. 85 *—M.S. (12/15/2005)*

TerraNoble 2006 Vineyard Selection Cabernet Sauvignon (Colchagua Valley) $8. Quite hard-cooked on the bouquet, but the berry and cassis flavors are ripe and juicy. If you can ignore the wine's persistent burnt oak character, clearly an attempt to elevate the wine to its Vineyard Selection name, it has pretty good feel, heft and integrity. 85 Best Buy *—M.S. (11/15/2007)*

TerraNoble 2005 Vineyard Selection Cabernet Sauvignon (Colchagua Valley) $8. TerraNoble certainly hits you with some major oak character, but still the wine works in its price range. The nose is woody while the palate is plump and full of berry flavors along with some buttery character. Shows spice and a hint of green on the finish. 85 Best Buy *—M.S. (9/1/2007)*

TerraNoble 2006 Gran Reserva Carmenère (Maule Valley) $14. Every time this wine hits the palate it registers as sheer and aggressive. And that's unfortunate because in past years TerraNoble had a way with Carmenère. This wine, however, is stark and acidic in the mouth even if it does have true flavors and aromas of herbs, olives and berries. Just not well balanced. 82 *—M.S. (11/15/2007)*

TerraNoble 2005 Gran Reserva Carmenère (Maule Valley) $14. A touch of vanilla cream mixes with a strong hit of bell pepper on the nose, and behind that there's red fruit that's pure and simple but very high in acid. In fact, this is an unusual Carmenère in that it's jousty and almost sour when most are heavier and softer. 83 *—M.S. (5/1/2007)*

TerraNoble 2003 Gran Reserva Carmenère (Maule Valley) $13. 90 Best Buy *—M.S. (12/15/2005)*

TerraNoble 1999 Gran Reserva Carmenère (Maule Valley) $24. 86 *—J.C. (8/1/2001)*

TerraNoble 2005 Reserva Carmenère (Maule Valley) $12. This is one aggressive varietal wine. The nose is packed with sweaty leather and olive notes, while the palate is rough and tart at the edges. There are notes of cola and burnt coffee on the finish, but by then you may just grow tired of wrestling with it. 85 *—M.S. (11/15/2007)*

TerraNoble 2004 Reserva Carmenère (Maule Valley) $11. TerraNoble is fast becoming one of our favorite across-the-board producers in Chile. Hardly anything this winery is making disappoints. And that goes for this powerful red that boasts rubber, leather and herbal aromas in front of sassy dark plum and black cherry flavors. Fresh and puckery now; this wine will drink well for a couple of years to come. 87 Best Buy *—M.S. (3/1/2007)*

TerraNoble 2003 Reserva Carmenère (Maule Valley) $12. 89 Best Buy *—M.S. (2/1/2005)*

TerraNoble 2001 Reserva Carmenère (Chile) $12. 89 Best Buy *—M.S. (3/1/2004)*

TerraNoble 2005 Vineyard Selection Carmenère (Colchagua Valley) $8. One of the most consistent value Carmenères from Chile is always TerraNoble's, and this '05 doesn't disappoint. The bouquet oozes black fruit, coffee and spice notes, while the palate is poised and tasty: the blackberry, plum and cola flavors are rock solid. Finishes warm and plush, with just a mild herbal edge. 88 Best Buy *—M.S. (9/1/2007)*

TerraNoble 2006 Chardonnay (Central Valley) $7. Citrus is the overriding component, but there are touches of apple and apricot on the nose. In the mouth, it's all about orange and tangerine and really not much else. A citrus ball if ever there was one. 83 *—M.S. (9/1/2007)*

TerraNoble 2005 Chardonnay (Casablanca Valley) $7. 86 Best Buy *—M.S. (3/1/2006)*

TerraNoble 2004 Chardonnay (Casablanca Valley) $8. 87 Best Buy *—M.S. (7/1/2005)*

TerraNoble 2003 Chardonnay (Casablanca Valley) $8. 86 Best Buy *—M.S. (3/1/2004)*

TerraNoble 2000 Chardonnay (Maule Valley) $9. 82 *—M.M. (8/1/2001)*

TerraNoble 2006 Vineyard Selection Chardonnay (Casablanca Valley) $8. In the lower depths of the value zone you'll find this respectable Chard that offers light melon and tropical fruit aromas in front of lemon-lime flavors. This is a more acidic, citrusy style of wine, yet it's flush and not at all sour. 84 Best Buy *—M.S. (5/1/2007)*

TerraNoble 2005 Vineyard Selection Chardonnay (Casablanca Valley) $9. 86 Best Buy *—M.S. (10/1/2006)*

TerraNoble 2005 Merlot (Central Valley) $7. Dark cherry and toast mix with some herbal character on the bouquet, while the medium-sized palate offers raspberry, blackberry and black olive flavors. It's a touch drying as a whole but it won't go badly with basic foods. 84 Best Buy *—M.S. (11/15/2007)*

TerraNoble 2000 Merlot (Maule Valley) $9. 81 *—J.F. (8/1/2001)*

TerraNoble 2004 Gran Reserva Merlot (Maule Valley) $16. 89 *—M.S. (10/1/2006)*

TerraNoble 2003 Gran Reserva Merlot (Maule Valley) $13. 88 Best Buy *—M.S. (11/1/2005)*

TerraNoble 2002 Gran Reserva Merlot (Maule Valley) $14. 83 *—M.S. (7/1/2005)*

TerraNoble 2005 Reserva Merlot (Maule Valley) $11. Fairly potent and full-bodied, with dark fruit aromas made interesting by hints of leather and earth. The acidity on this wine is up there, so the fruit takes on a zesty red-berry quality as it crosses your palate. And on the finish there's light vanilla and a slight sense of creaminess. 87 Best Buy *—M.S. (3/1/2007)*

TerraNoble 2002 Reserva Merlot (Maule Valley) $12. 84 *—M.S. (7/1/2005)*

TerraNoble 2005 Vineyard Selection Merlot (Maule Valley) $8. A lot of color but short in the finesse department. What you have here is a big, buxom, young Merlot with aggressive aromas and tart, underdeveloped raspberry and plum flavors. Has looks but no polish. 83 *—M.S. (9/1/2007)*

TerraNoble 2006 Sauvignon Blanc (Central Valley) $7. Haven't tasted Sauvignon Blanc from TerraNoble before, and that's a good thing. This is a heavy, nutty, oily wine that's a touch caustic and tough to wrestle with. If this winery's going to continue with SB it should be better than this. 80 *—M.S. (9/1/2007)*

TerraNoble 2007 Vineyard Selection Sauvignon Blanc (Maule Valley) $8. Light floral and vanilla notes accent citrus and typical varietal grassiness on both the nose and palate, which makes this a pleasant wine. This is a nice quaffer at a good price, and novices may like it as well because it carries a little residual sweetness on the finish. 86 Best Buy *—M.S. (11/15/2007)*

TerraNoble 2006 Vineyard Selection Sauvignon Blanc (Maule Valley) $8. 87 Best Buy *—M.S. (11/15/2006)*

TerraNoble 2004 Vineyard Selection Syrah (Maule Valley) $8. No matter how much color this has, the basics are at once aggressive and boring. The nose is brambly and lean, a sure indication of limited, tangy flavors that carry some serious herbal character. There's little to this Syrah. 81 *—M.S. (9/1/2007)*

TRINCAO

Trincao 2001 Reserva Carmenère (Maipo Valley) $11. 85 *—M.S. (8/1/2004)*

Trincao 2001 Reserva Syrah (Maipo Valley) $11. 87 Best Buy *—M.S. (8/1/2004)*

TWO BROTHERS

Two Brothers 2001 Big Tattoo Red Red Blend (Colchagua Valley) $9. 87 Best Buy *—M.S. (7/1/2003)*

UNDURRAGA

Undurraga 2001 Cabernet Sauvignon (Colchagua Valley) $7. 86 Best Buy *—M.S. (3/1/2002)*

Undurraga 2000 Cabernet Sauvignon (Colchagua Valley) $7. 85 Best Buy *—M.M. (2/1/2001)*

Undurraga 2002 Altazor Cabernet Sauvignon (Maipo Valley) $42. 88 *—M.S. (5/1/2006)*

Undurraga 1999 Altazor Cabernet Sauvignon (Maipo Valley) $46. 90 Cellar Selection *(2/1/2004)*

Undurraga 2004 Founder's Collection Cabernet Sauvignon (Maipo Valley) $22. 84 *—M.S. (12/31/2006)*

Undurraga 2002 Founder's Collection Cabernet Sauvignon (Maipo Valley) $21. 88 *—M.S. (5/1/2006)*

Undurraga 1999 Founder's Collection Cabernet Sauvignon (Maipo Valley) $25. 86 *—M.S. (7/1/2003)*

Undurraga 1997 Founder's Collection Cabernet Sauvignon (Maipo Valley) $25. 85 *(8/1/2001)*

Undurraga 2003 Reserva Cabernet Sauvignon (Maipo Valley) $11. 87 Best Buy *—M.S. (5/1/2006)*

Undurraga 2001 Reserva Cabernet Sauvignon (Maipo Valley) $14. 87 *(2/1/2004)*

Undurraga 1998 Reserva Cabernet Sauvignon (Maipo Valley) $12. 82 *—M.M. (2/1/2001)*

Undurraga 2004 Aliwen Reserva Cabernet Sauvignon-Carmenère (Central Valley) $10. 85 Best Buy *—M.S. (12/31/2006)*

Undurraga 2006 Aliwen Cabernet Sauvignon-Syrah (Colchagua Valley) $10. Raw and spicy aromas greet you, with floral, more rosy scents offering backup. The palate is fresh to the point of crisp, but not very detailed or stylish. And the finish is like hitting a cement pad without padding. Seems a little rough and tumble, and not very detailed. 84 *—M.S. (11/15/2007)*

Undurraga 2004 Reserva Carmenère (Colchagua Valley) $12. 87 Best Buy —*M.S. (12/31/2006)*

Undurraga 2003 Reserva Carmenère (Colchagua Valley) $11. 85 —*M.S. (12/15/2005)*

Undurraga 2002 Reserva Carmenère (Colchagua Valley) $14. 87 *(2/1/2004)*

Undurraga 2001 Reserva Carmenère (Colchagua Valley) $11. 87 —*M.S. (7/1/2003)*

Undurraga 1998 Reserva Carmenère (Colchagua Valley) $12. 84 *(2/1/2001)*

Undurraga 1999 Reserve Carmenère (Colchagua Valley) $11. 84 —*M.S. (3/1/2002)*

Undurraga 2006 Chardonnay (Central Valley) $7. Undurraga is on a bit of a roll when it comes to its value-priced Chardonnays. This '06 is clean and aromatic, with zero funk and no overoaking. The apple and melon flavors are easy and clean, while the finish is round and moderately deep. For $7 you can't ask for much more. 85 Best Buy —*M.S. (5/1/2007)*

Undurraga 2001 Chardonnay (Maipo Valley) $7. 86 Best Buy —*M.S. (3/1/2002)*

Undurraga 2000 Chardonnay (Maipo Valley) $7. 85 —*M.M. (1/1/2004)*

Undurraga 2005 Aliwen Reserva Chardonnay (Central Valley) $10. 90 Best Buy —*M.S. (11/15/2006)*

Undurraga 2006 Reserva Chardonnay (Maipo Valley) $12. Peach, vanilla and match stick notes work the nose, followed by flavors of banana, citrus and vanilla. The wine has full-blast acidity working in its favor, thus it's sort of racy and driving even if the oak is unabsorbed and the finish rather hollow. Totally New World in style, feel and flavor. 84 —*M.S. (11/15/2007)*

Undurraga 2005 Reserva Chardonnay (Maipo Valley) $12. 89 Best Buy —*M.S. (11/15/2006)*

Undurraga 2002 Reserva Chardonnay (Maipo Valley) $14. 86 *(2/1/2004)*

Undurraga 2001 Reserva Chardonnay (Maipo Valley) $12. 85 —*M.S. (7/1/2003)*

Undurraga 1998 Reserva Chardonnay (Maipo Valley) $12. 82 —*M.M. (2/1/2001)*

Undurraga 2002 Gewürztraminer (Maipo Valley) $9. 84 —*M.S. (7/1/2003)*

Undurraga 2000 Merlot (Maipo Valley) $7. 83 *(2/1/2001)*

Undurraga 2006 Reserva Merlot (Maipo Valley) $12. Starts with plain and simple sweet fruit then offers lean red-fruit flavors slathered with a blanket's worth of buttery oak, and thus the feel is creamy and lactic. Maybe this will improve with some bottle age, but not guarantees. 84 —*M.S. (11/15/2007)*

Undurraga 2003 Reserva Merlot (Maipo Valley) $11. 84 —*M.S. (5/1/2006)*

Undurraga 2001 Reserva Merlot (Maipo Valley) $12. 87 —*M.S. (7/1/2003)*

Undurraga 1999 Reserva Merlot (Maipo Valley) $12. 81 *(2/1/2001)*

Undurraga 2001 Pinot Noir (Maipo Valley) $7. 86 Best Buy —*M.S. (3/1/2002)*

Undurraga 2000 Pinot Noir (Maipo Valley) $7. 82 —*M.S. (2/1/2001)*

Undurraga 2002 Reserva Pinot Noir (Maipo Valley) $14. 84 *(2/1/2004)*

Undurraga 2001 Reserva Pinot Noir (Maipo Valley) $12. 84 —*M.S. (7/1/2003)*

Undurraga 1999 Reserva Pinot Noir (Maipo Valley) $12. 84 —*M.M. (2/1/2001)*

Undurraga 2006 Sauvignon Blanc (Central Valley) $7. 82 —*M.S. (11/15/2006)*

Undurraga 2005 Sauvignon Blanc (Central Valley) $7. 84 Best Buy —*M.S. (11/15/2005)*

Undurraga 2003 Sauvignon Blanc (Lontué Valley) $10. 85 *(12/31/2003)*

Undurraga 2001 Sauvignon Blanc (Lontué Valley) $7. 86 Best Buy —*M.S. (3/1/2002)*

Undurraga 2007 Aliwen Sauvignon Blanc (Maipo Valley) $10. Piercing grapefruit and passion fruit aromas stir interest, but the palate leaves you wanting more than just sheer lime and tangerine. The wine is a little too citric and sharp. 83 —*M.S. (11/15/2007)*

Undurraga 2006 Aliwen Reserva Sauvignon Blanc (Central Valley) $10. 87 Best Buy —*M.S. (12/31/2006)*

Undurraga 2004 Reserva Syrah (Colchagua Valley) $12. 86 —*M.S. (12/31/2006)*

ÚNICO

Único Luis Miguel 2003 Gran Reserva Cabernet Sauvignon (Maipo Valley) $15. From Ventisquero and the Mexican crooner Luis Miguel, this wine has color, heft and size but not a whole lot of finesse or elegance. What it does deliver is rich, basic Cabernet flavors of black cherry and cassis and some toast on the finish. Good but rather regular stuff. 85 —*M.S. (9/1/2007)*

VALDIVIESO

Valdivieso 2004 Single Vineyard Reserve Cabernet Sauvignon (Maipo Valley) $17. A little heavier and more savory than some, as it lacks that in-your-face zap that some Chilean Cabs possess. Still, it's a very nice rendition with cassis, blackberry and some green herbs on the palate. Along the way you may encounter interesting notes of salami, black olive and fennel. 87 —*M.S. (3/1/2007)*

Valdivieso 2004 Single Vineyard Reserve Cabernet Franc (Colchagua Valley) $17. 87 —*M.S. (12/31/2006)*

Valdivieso 2003 Single Vineyard Reserve Cabernet Franc (Central Valley) $17. 90 —*M.S. (5/1/2006)*

Valdivieso 2001 Single Vineyard Reserve Cabernet Franc (Lontué Valley) $17. 89 —*M.S. (8/1/2004)*

Valdivieso 2000 Single Vineyard Reserve Cabernet Franc (Lontué Valley) $17. 88 Best Buy —*M.S. (7/1/2003)*

Valdivieso 2004 Cabernet Sauvignon (Central Valley) $7. 84 Best Buy —*M.S. (7/1/2006)*

Valdivieso 2001 Cabernet Sauvignon (Central Valley) $8. 85 Best Buy —*M.S. (7/1/2003)*

Valdivieso 2002 Barrel Selection Reserve Cabernet Sauvignon (Central Valley) $10. 88 Best Buy —*M.S. (7/1/2005)*

Valdivieso 2003 Reserve Cabernet Sauvignon (Central Valley) $13. 88 Best Buy —*M.S. (7/1/2006)*

Valdivieso 2000 Reserve Cabernet Sauvignon (Central Valley) $13. 88 —*M.S. (2/1/2005)*

Valdivieso 2000 Reserve Cabernet Sauvignon (Central Valley) $20. 89 —*C.S. (2/1/2003)*

Valdivieso 1998 Reserve Cabernet Sauvignon (Central Valley) $20. 87 —*J.C. (3/1/2002)*

Valdivieso 2002 Rosé Cabernet Sauvignon (Central Valley) $8. 82 —*M.S. (7/1/2003)*

Valdivieso 2004 Chardonnay (Central Valley) $7. 83 —*M.S. (5/1/2006)*

Valdivieso 2003 Chardonnay (Central Valley) $7. 87 Best Buy —*M.S. (6/1/2004)*

Valdivieso 2000 Barrel Selection Chardonnay (Central Valley) $12. 86 —*M.S. (3/1/2002)*

Valdivieso 2003 Reserve Chardonnay (Casablanca Valley) $13. 86 —*M.S. (12/15/2005)*

Valdivieso 2001 Reserve Chardonnay (Central Valley) $14. 88 —*M.S. (7/1/2003)*

Valdivieso 2001 Reserve Chardonnay (Casablanca Valley) $13. 81 —*M.S. (2/1/2005)*

Valdivieso 1999 Reserve Chardonnay (Central Valley) $20. 90 Editors' Choice —*J.C. (3/1/2002)*

Valdivieso 2004 Malbec (Central Valley) $7. 83 —*M.S. (5/1/2006)*

Valdivieso 2003 Malbec (Rapel Valley) $7. 87 Best Buy —*M.S. (12/1/2004)*

Valdivieso 2001 Malbec (Central Valley) $17. 82 —*M.S. (12/1/2003)*

Valdivieso 2004 Single Vineyard Reserve Malbec (Lontué Valley) $17. A full nose of charred oak and smoky black cherry is phase one. The next level consists of dark fruit flavors and pulsing acidity, while the final act (the finish) is moderately complex, with nice chocolate and mushroom notes. Satisfying and sort of snappy. 87 —*M.S. (9/1/2007)*

Valdivieso 2003 Single Vineyard Reserve Malbec (Maule Valley) $17. 85 —*M.S. (5/1/2006)*

Valdivieso 2000 Single Vineyard Reserve Malbec (Maule Valley) $17. 87 —*M.S. (12/1/2004)*

Valdivieso 2000 Single Vineyard Reserve Malbec (Lontué Valley) $17. 85 —*M.S. (7/1/2003)*

Valdivieso 1999 Single Vineyard Reserve Malbec (Curicó Valley) $23. 88 —*M.S. (3/1/2002)*

Valdivieso 2005 Merlot (Central Valley) $6. 83 Best Buy —*M.S. (11/15/2006)*

Valdivieso 2004 Merlot (Central Valley) $7. 86 Best Buy —*M.S. (5/1/2006)*

Valdivieso 2003 Merlot (Central Valley) $7. 85 Best Buy —*M.S. (2/1/2005)*

Valdivieso 2002 Merlot (Central Valley) $7. 86 —*M.S. (3/1/2004)*

Valdivieso 2004 Single Vineyard Reserve Merlot (Lontué Valley) $17. Basic red-fruit aromas feature accents of tobacco and green herbs, while the palate is fresh and zesty due to strong natural acidity. Overall it's a solid wine but in the final analysis it shows a bit more green character than is desirable. 85 —*M.S. (3/1/2007)*

Valdivieso 2002 Single Vineyard Reserve Merlot (Curicó Valley) $17. 87 —*M.S. (5/1/2006)*

Valdivieso 2000 Single Vineyard Reserve Merlot (Central Valley) $17. 85 —*M.S. (7/1/2003)*

Valdivieso 2000 Single Vineyard Reserve Merlot (Lontué Valley) $17. 87 —*M.S. (7/1/2005)*

Valdivieso 1999 Single Vineyard Reserve Merlot (Central Valley) $19. 89 —*R.V. (9/1/2001)*

Valdivieso 2005 Reserve Pinot Noir (Casablanca Valley) $13. 84 —*M.S. (12/31/2006)*

Valdivieso 2002 Reserve Pinot Noir (Lontué Valley) $13. 86 —*M.S. (8/1/2004)*

Valdivieso 1999 Reserve Pinot Noir (Maule Valley) $23. 88 —*M.S. (3/1/2002)*

Valdivieso NV Caballo Loco - No. 4 Red Blend (Lontué Valley) $35. 91 —*M.S. (3/1/2002)*

Valdivieso NV Caballo Loco No 6 Red Blend (Central Valley) $35. 89 —*C.S. (2/1/2003)*

Valdivieso NV Caballo Loco No. 5 Red Blend (Lontué Valley) $40. 91 —*M.S. (1/1/2004)*

Valdivieso NV Caballo Loco Number 8 Red Blend (Central Valley) $35. 90 —*M.S. (12/31/2006)*

Valdivieso NV Caballo Loco Number Seven Red Blend (Lontué Valley) $35. 91 Editors' Choice —*M.S. (3/1/2006)*

Valdivieso 2004 Eclat Red Blend (Maule Valley) $26. Here's an unusual mix of Syrah and Carignan that runs lean and racy. The nose offers more spice and leather than ripeness, while the palate is downright tangy and teetering on sharp. Freshness and power are not issues; but it might be too tangy and citrusy for anyone expecting a beefy, extracted wine. 86 —*M.S. (9/1/2007)*

Valdivieso 2002 Eclat Red Blend (Maule Valley) $25. 89 —*M.S. (3/1/2006)*

Valdivieso 2005 Sauvignon Blanc (Central Valley) $6. 84 Best Buy —*M.S. (7/1/2006)*

Valdivieso 2004 Sauvignon Blanc (Central Valley) $7. 83 —*M.S. (12/15/2005)*

Valdivieso 2002 Sauvignon Blanc (Central Valley) $8. 84 —*M.S. (7/1/2003)*

Valdivieso 2004 Reserve Sauvignon Blanc (Casablanca Valley) $13. 85 —*M.S. (3/1/2006)*

Valdivieso 2003 Reserve Shiraz (Lontué Valley) $13. 85 —*M.S. (11/1/2005)*

Valdivieso 2000 Barrel Selection Reserve Syrah (Central Valley) $12. 84 *(10/1/2001)*

Valdivieso 2004 Reserva Syrah (Central Valley) $13. 85 —*M.S. (12/31/2006)*

Valdivieso 2003 Reserve Viognier (Maule Valley) $13. 82 —*M.S. (11/1/2005)*

VALENTINO

Valentino NV Red Blend (Maipo Valley) $11. From the Nido de Aguila winery, this is a non-vintage blend of Cabernet, Merlot and Syrah that weighs in light and herbal. The nose is kind of saucy and sulfuric, and the palate is lean and racy. Flavorwise, it's more or less harmonious but nondescript, with light but short vanilla shadings on the finish. 84 —*M.S. (9/1/2007)*

VALLETE FONTAINE

Vallete Fontaine 1999 Memorias Cabernet Sauvignon (Maipo Valley) $NA. 81 —*D.T. (11/15/2002)*

VENTISQUERO

Ventisquero 2003 Gran Reserva Cabernet Sauvignon (Maipo Valley) $16. 88 —*M.S. (5/1/2006)*

Ventisquero 2003 Grey Cabernet Sauvignon (Maipo Valley) $30. Smoke, mint, cassis and blackberry all show themselves on the nose of this solid wine. It's a good representation of the variety, despite having 15% Syrah blended in, marked by a touch of herb and also some noteworthy structure. Starts out thick and lush, then firms up on the finish, suggesting a positive evolution through at least 2012. 88 *(7/1/2007)*

Ventisquero 2003 Grey Cabernet Sauvignon (Maipo Valley) $27. 88 *(2/1/2006)*

Ventisquero 2004 Grey Carmenère (Maipo Valley) $30. Shows plenty of leafy character on the nose, although our reviewers disagreed over whether it was overly green. Flavors are deeply chocolaty and plum-like, with a round mouthfeel and creamy tannins. Soft and plush on the finish, with a balanced blend of spice and fruit. Drink now–2012. 88 *(7/1/2007)*

Ventisquero 2003 Grey Carmenère (Maipo Valley) $27. 89 *(2/1/2006)*

Ventisquero 2003 Gran Reserva Merlot (Maipo Valley) $19. 87 *(2/1/2006)*

Ventisquero 2004 Reserva Pinot Noir (Casablanca Valley) $13. Smoky and earthy, with overtones of beet, cola and chocolate. This is light in body, with supple tannins and crisp acids that say Pinot Noir, even if the fruit is a bit muddled. Turns peppery on the finish. 83 *(7/1/2007)*

Ventisquero 2006 Reserva Sauvignon Blanc (Casablanca Valley) $13. Starts with a blast of peach and passion fruit alongside slightly grassy elements, then adds melon and grapefruit flavors. Finishes clean and fresh; easy-drinking. Drink now. 87 *(7/1/2007)*

Ventisquero 2003 Gran Reserva Syrah (Maipo Valley) $19. 88 *(2/1/2006)*

VERAMONTE

Veramonte 2004 Primus Bordeaux Blend (Casablanca Valley) $17. 88 *M.S. (12/31/2006)*

Veramonte 2002 Primus Bordeaux Blend (Casablanca Valley) $16. 88 *(2/1/2005)*

Veramonte 2002 Cabernet Sauvignon (Maipo Valley) $10. 86 Best Buy *(2/1/2005)*

Veramonte 2000 Cabernet Sauvignon (Maipo Valley) $10. 91 Best Buy —*S.H. (12/1/2002)*

Veramonte 2005 Reserva Cabernet Sauvignon (Colchagua Valley) $10. Veramonte is now turning to warmer Colchagua for its Cabernet. That's a good idea, which is reflected in this standard-fare wine that hits with lively cassis and blackberry aromas and flavors before fading away on a firm, tannic finish. Imported by Franciscan Estate Selections, Ltd. 85 Best Buy —*M.S. (11/15/2007)*

Veramonte 2004 Reserva Cabernet Sauvignon (Maipo Valley) $10. 87 Best Buy —*M.S. (10/1/2006)*

Veramonte 2002 Single Vineyard Cabernet Sauvignon (Maipo Valley) $35. 89 *(2/1/2005)*

Veramonte 2003 Chardonnay (Casablanca Valley) $10. 85 Best Buy *(2/1/2005)*

Veramonte 2000 Chardonnay (Casablanca Valley) $10. 85 —*J.M. (11/15/2001)*

Veramonte 2006 Reserva Chardonnay (Casablanca Valley) $10. Veramonte is one of the early proponents of Casablanca, and this wine sings a pretty tune. The bouquet offers apple, melon, pear and a kiss of solid oak, while the palate shows vanilla along with soft pear and apple flavors. Balanced and a touch sweet, but not too oaky or resiny. Imported by Huneeus Vintners, LLC. 87 Best Buy —*M.S. (11/15/2007)*

Veramonte 2003 Single Vineyard Chardonnay (Casablanca Valley) $35. 88 *(2/1/2005)*

Veramonte 2002 Merlot (Casablanca Valley) $10. 84 *(2/1/2005)*

Veramonte 2002 Merlot (Casablanca Valley) $10. 86 Best Buy —*M.S. (3/1/2004)*

Veramonte 2000 Merlot (Maipo Valley) $10. 90 Best Buy —*S.H. (12/1/2002)*

Veramonte 1999 Merlot (Casablanca Valley) $10. 82 —*J.C. (2/1/2001)*

Veramonte 2005 Reserva Merlot (Casablanca Valley) $10. A little olive and stewed berry on the nose is followed by black cherry and blackberry flavors that are propped up by leggy core acidity. Gets better with time in the glass and has its strong suits, namely honest fruit and not much oak. Imported by Franciscan Estate Selections, Ltd. 86 Best Buy —*M.S. (11/15/2007)*

Veramonte 2004 Reserva Merlot (Casablanca Valley) $10. 88 Best Buy —*M.S. (10/1/2006)*

Veramonte 2002 Single Vineyard Merlot (Casablanca Valley) $35. 90 *(2/1/2005)*

Veramonte 2002 Pinot Noir (Casablanca Valley) $10. 86 —*M.S. (3/1/2004)*

Veramonte 2001 Primus Red Blend (Casablanca Valley) $20. 89 —*M.S. (3/1/2004)*

Veramonte 2000 Primus Red Blend (Casablanca Valley) $20. 82 —*M.S. (7/1/2003)*

Veramonte 1999 Primus Red Blend (Casablanca Valley) $20. 86 —*D.T. (7/1/2002)*

Veramonte 1998 Primus Red Blend (Casablanca Valley) $20. 83 —*M.M. (2/1/2001)*

Veramonte 2004 Sauvignon Blanc (Casablanca Valley) $10. 88 Best Buy *(2/1/2005)*

Veramonte 2003 Sauvignon Blanc (Casablanca Valley) $10. 87 Best Buy —*M.S. (3/1/2004)*

Veramonte 2001 Sauvignon Blanc (Casablanca Valley) $10. 85 —*S.H. (12/1/2002)*

VERANDA

Veranda 2002 Reserve Pinot Noir (Casablanca Valley) $15. 86 —*M.S. (8/1/2004)*

Veranda 2002 Founder's Reserve Red Blend (Aconcagua Valley) $50. 87 —*M.S. (3/1/2004)*

Veranda 2002 Reserve Red Blend (Maipo Valley) $20. 85 —*M.S. (3/1/2004)*

VIÑA AQUITANIA

Viña Aquitania 2003 Agapanto Cabernet Sauvignon (Maipo Valley) $12. 84 —*M.S. (7/1/2006)*

Viña Aquitania 2002 Agapanto Cabernet Sauvignon (Maipo Valley) $10. 87 Best Buy —*M.S. (3/1/2004)*

Viña Aquitania 2002 Lazuli Cabernet Sauvignon (Maipo Valley) $32. 90 —*M.S. (3/1/2004)*

Viña Aquitania 2003 Sol de Sol Chardonnay (Malleco) $30. 88 —*M.S. (5/1/2006)*

Viña Aquitania 2002 Sol de Sol Chardonnay (Malleco) $32. 89 —*M.S. (3/1/2004)*

VIÑA BISQUERTT

Viña Bisquertt 2003 Casa La Joya Gran Reserva Cabernet Sauvignon (Colchagua Valley) $14. This wine is already at peak maturity and isn't showing the brightness and spunk that Colchagua Cabernet does when it's young. That said, the wine's cola, dill and butter aromas are reasonably attractive, and the berry and plum flavors, while covered in buttery oak, are round and smooth. Drink now for best results. 85 —*M.S. (9/1/2007)*

Viña Bisquertt 2002 Casa La Joya Gran Reserve Cabernet Sauvignon (Colchagua Valley) $13. 85 —*M.S. (12/15/2005)*

Viña Bisquertt 2004 Casa La Joya Reserve Cabernet Sauvignon (Colchagua Valley) $9. 89 Best Buy —*M.S. (5/1/2006)*

Viña Bisquertt 2003 Casa La Joya Reserve Cabernet Sauvignon (Colchagua Valley) $9. 87 Best Buy —*M.S. (12/15/2005)*

Viña Bisquertt 2003 Casa La Joya Gran Reserve Carmenère (Colchagua Valley) $13. 89 Best Buy —*M.S. (3/1/2006)*

Viña Bisquertt 2002 Casa La Joya Gran Reserve Carmenère (Colchagua Valley) $13. 88 Best Buy —*M.S. (12/15/2005)*

Viña Bisquertt 2004 Casa La Joya Reserve Carmenère (Colchagua Valley) $10. 87 Best Buy —*M.S. (3/1/2006)*

Viña Bisquertt 2004 Casa La Joya Gran Reserve Chardonnay (Colchagua Valley) $14. 87 —*M.S. (12/31/2006)*

Viña Bisquertt 2003 Casa La Joya Gran Reserve Chardonnay (Colchagua Valley) $13. 85 —*M.S. (12/15/2005)*

Viña Bisquertt 2006 Casa La Joya Reserve Chardonnay (Colchagua Valley) $10. A come-down from previous vintages, this wine is lacking in precision and character. The nose is nothing more than talcum powder and canned pears, while the palate is a clumsy gathering of mealy apple and baked peaches. 81 —*M.S. (3/1/2007)*

Viña Bisquertt 2004 Casa La Joya Reserve Malbec (Colchagua Valley) $9. 85 Best Buy —*M.S. (5/1/2006)*

Viña Bisquertt 2003 Casa La Joya Gran Reserve Merlot (Colchagua Valley) $14. Dark plum and chocolaty, round aromas are standard but nice, while the blackberry flavors and soft texture make for an easy-to-like palate. This wine is mature now and drinking quite well; it's simple, solid and shouldn't disappoint. 86 —*M.S. (11/15/2007)*

Viña Bisquertt 2002 Casa La Joya Gran Reserve Merlot (Colchagua Valley) $13. 86 —*M.S. (5/1/2006)*

Viña Bisquertt 2004 Casa La Joya Reserve Merlot (Colchagua Valley) $10. Solid red cherry, plum and a touch of citrus peel define the nose, while prime berry and black cherry are the lead flavors on the palate. As for finishing notes, look for spice and a slight bit of herbal green character. All in all it's a good Merlot that should satisfy. 86 Best Buy —*M.S. (3/1/2007)*

Viña Bisquertt 2003 Casa La Joya Reserve Merlot (Colchagua Valley) $9. 88 Best Buy —*M.S. (12/15/2005)*

Viña Bisquertt 2006 Casa La Joya Reserve Sauvignon Blanc (Colchagua Valley) $10. Fairly pungent on the nose as it offers gooseberry, citrus and other typical grassy, green aromas. The palate provides mostly citrus flavors, particularly tangerine and grapefruit. A minor amount of character and complexity make it worth a go. 84 —*M.S. (3/1/2007)*

Viña Bisquertt 2004 Casa La Joya Reserve Sauvignon Blanc (Colchagua Valley) $9. 84 —*M.S. (3/1/2006)*

Viña Bisquertt 2004 Casa La Joya Reserve Shiraz (Colchagua Valley) $9. 86 Best Buy —*M.S. (3/1/2006)*

Viña Bisquertt 2003 Casa La Joya Reserve Shiraz (Colchagua Valley) $9. 82 —*M.S. (12/15/2005)*

VIÑA CANTERA

Viña Cantera 2006 Cantaluna Pinot Noir (Casablanca Valley) $11. Pinot Noir from Chile is still a new entity, and this one doesn't do much to further the cause. It's lemony and lacking in pure fruit, with a flat mouthfeel and a weedy bite to the finish. 81 —*M.S. (11/15/2007)*

Viña Cantera 2005 Cantaluna Sauvignon Blanc (Casablanca Valley) $11. This wine is past its prime. It's dilute and probably always was, but now it has lost its pulse and is fast approaching flat-line status. Along the way there's some leftover citric burn and a hint of green pea and bell pepper. 81 —*M.S. (11/15/2007)*

VIÑA CASA TAMAYA

Viña Casa Tamaya 2002 Estate Bottled Reserve Chardonnay (Limarí Valley) $15. 82 —*M.S. (8/1/2004)*

Viña Casa Tamaya 2001 Estate Bottled Reserve Red Blend (Limarí Valley) $15. 82 —*M.S. (8/1/2004)*

Viña Casa Tamaya 2001 Reserve Viognier-Chardonnay White Blend (Chile) $15. 83 —*M.S. (6/1/2004)*

VIÑA CASAS DEL BOSQUE

Viña Casas del Bosque 2001 Cabernet Sauvignon (Rapel Valley) $11. 84 —*M.S. (7/1/2003)*

Viña Casas del Bosque 2000 Cabernet Sauvignon (Rapel Valley) $10. 84 —*D.T. (7/1/2002)*

Viña Casas del Bosque 2000 Gran Bosque Cabernet Sauvignon (Rapel Valley) $17. 86 —*M.S. (3/1/2004)*

Viña Casas del Bosque 2002 Gran Bosque Family Reserve Cabernet Sauvignon (Rapel Valley) $35. 85 —*M.S. (11/1/2005)*

Viña Casas del Bosque 2002 Reserve Cabernet Sauvignon (Rapel Valley) $12. 84 —*M.S. (3/1/2004)*

Viña Casas del Bosque 2001 Reserve Cabernet Sauvignon (Rapel Valley) $16. 87 —*M.S. (7/1/2003)*

Viña Casas del Bosque 2000 Reserve Cabernet Sauvignon (Rapel Valley) $17. 88 —*C.S. (12/1/2002)*

Viña Casas del Bosque 2002 Chardonnay (Casablanca Valley) $10. 85 —*M.S. (7/1/2003)*

Viña Casas del Bosque 2000 Chardonnay (Rapel Valley) $9. 82 —*J.C. (7/1/2002)*

Viña Casas del Bosque 1999 Gredas Negras Chardonnay (Casablanca Valley) $15. 80 —*M.S. (7/1/2002)*

Viña Casas del Bosque 2001 Reserve Chardonnay (Casablanca Valley) $15. 82 —*M.S. (7/1/2003)*

Viña Casas del Bosque 2000 Reserve Chardonnay (Casablanca Valley) $NA. 81 —*J.C. (7/1/2002)*

Viña Casas del Bosque 2003 Reserva Merlot (Casablanca Valley) $12. 80 —*M.S. (11/1/2005)*

Viña Casas del Bosque 2000 Reserva Merlot (Casablanca Valley) $10. 86 —*D.T. (7/1/2002)*

Viña Casas del Bosque 2002 Reserve Merlot (Casablanca Valley) $12. 85 —*M.S. (3/1/2004)*

Viña Casas del Bosque 2004 Reserva Pinot Noir (Casablanca Valley) $12. 87 Best Buy —*M.S. (11/1/2005)*

Viña Casas del Bosque 2002 Reserve Pinot Noir (Casablanca Valley) $12. 85 —*M.S. (3/1/2004)*

Viña Casas del Bosque 2001 Reserve Pinot Noir (Casablanca Valley) $16. 85 —*M.S. (7/1/2003)*

Viña Casas del Bosque 2004 Sauvignon Blanc (Casablanca Valley) $10. 83 —*M.S. (11/1/2005)*

Viña Casas del Bosque 2003 Sauvignon Blanc (Casablanca Valley) $9. 86 —*M.S. (3/1/2004)*

Viña Casas del Bosque 2002 Sauvignon Blanc (Casablanca Valley) $10. 85 —*M.S. (7/1/2003)*

Viña Casas del Bosque 2000 Sauvignon Blanc (Casablanca Valley) $9. 80 —*M.S. (7/1/2003)*

Viña Casas del Bosque 2003 Casa Viva Sauvignon Blanc (Casablanca Valley) $7. 85 Best Buy —*M.S. (3/1/2004)*

Viña Casas del Bosque 2004 Reserva Sauvignon Blanc (Casablanca Valley) $12. 87 Best Buy *—M.S. (11/1/2005)*

Viña Casas del Bosque 2002 Reserve Sauvignon Blanc (Casablanca Valley) $15. 83 *—M.S. (7/1/2003)*

Viña Casas del Bosque 2001 Reserve Sauvignon Blanc (Casablanca Valley) $15. 84 *—M.S. (7/1/2003)*

Viña Casas del Bosque 2003 Reserva Syrah (Casablanca Valley) $12. 80 *—M.S. (11/1/2005)*

Viña Casas del Bosque 2002 Reserve Syrah (Casablanca Valley) $12. 83 *—M.S. (3/1/2004)*

VIÑA CASAS PATRONALES

Viña Casas Patronales 2005 Casas Patronales Cabernet Sauvignon (Maule Valley) $9. This is the first we've seen of this brand, and frankly the wine is overdone with toast to the point that char functions as a blanket over underripe, mildly vegetal fruit. It's roasted, herbal and a little hot. 83 *—M.S. (9/1/2007)*

Viña Casas Patronales 2005 Casas Patronales Cabernet Sauvignon-Carmenère (Maule Valley) $9. Herbal, medicinal and olive aromas start this in the wrong direction, and even patient airing can't bring it around. There is never much freshness, although the mouthfeel is sassy and acidic. 82 *—M.S. (9/1/2007)*

Viña Casas Patronales 2005 Casas Patronales Carmenère (Maule Valley) $9. Quite murky and overoaked. The nose drips root beer and tree bark, while the palate is a jumble of wood spice, beefy fruit and heat. Balance and freshness are fleeting in this wine. 81 *—M.S. (9/1/2007)*

Viña Casas Patronales 2005 Casas Patronales Merlot (Maule Valley) $9. Sort of earthy and heavy, with oak and forest aromas settling onto the nose. The cherry and plum flavors are a touch warm but still satisfying, while the finish is a little choppy but generally pleasant. 84 *—M.S. (9/1/2007)*

Viña Casas Patronales 2006 Casas Patronales Sauvignon Blanc (Maule Valley) $9. Light and citrusy, and also fairly green. This is your standard stripped down model that pushes green apple, green melon and lime. Get the picture? It's a green wine that has freshness but not much depth. 83 *—M.S. (9/1/2007)*

VIÑA EL AROMO

Viña el Aromo 2001 Private Reserve Cabernet Sauvignon (Maule Valley) $10. 87 *—M.S. (6/1/2004)*

Viña el Aromo 2002 Private Reserve Carmenère (Maule Valley) $10. 84 *—M.S. (6/1/2004)*

Viña el Aromo 2003 Chardonnay (Maule Valley) $10. 83 *—M.S. (6/1/2004)*

VIÑA LA ROSA

Viña La Rosa 2005 Don Reca Limited Release Cabernet Sauvignon (Cachapoal Valley) $20. Purple in hue, with big, toasty aromas of baked fruit, marshmallow, vanilla and mint. If you hadn't guessed by now, it's a fairly oaky wine that's grounded by sweet cassis, cherry and tobacco flavors. It's ripe throughout, with some hard finishing tannins that result in a clamped-down mouthfeel. 86 *—M.S. (5/1/2007)*

Viña La Rosa 2002 Don Reca Cabernet Sauvignon (Cachapoal Valley) $30. 85 *—M.S. (3/1/2004)*

Viña La Rosa 2005 La Capitana Barrel Reserve Cabernet Sauvignon (Cachapoal Valley) $15. Ripe and rich, with a lot of dark fruit on the nose. The palate is a bit more snappy than the bouquet as it deals upright black cherry flavors resting on a bed of detectable acidity. There's ample oak late in the game, but the fruit and overall quality of the wine can handle it. This is one of La Rosa's better efforts in recent years. 89 *—M.S. (3/1/2007)*

Viña La Rosa 2004 La Capitana Barrel Reserve Cabernet Sauvignon (Cachapoal Valley) $14. 85 *—M.S. (10/1/2006)*

Viña La Rosa 2005 La Palma Reserva Cabernet Sauvignon (Cachapoal Valley) $10. A darker wine with char, tar, hard spice and black fruit aromas leading to cherry, cola and blackberry flavors. This is a flush, generous Cabernet with bold, tannic fruit flowing all the way to the finish. It's not a complex, ethereal type of wine but it has its good points. 85 *—M.S. (5/1/2007)*

Viña La Rosa 2004 La Palma Cabernet Sauvignon (Cachapoal Valley) $7. 86 Best Buy *—M.S. (11/1/2005)*

Viña La Rosa 2003 La Capitana Carmenère (Cachapoal Valley) $12. 87 Best Buy *—M.S. (2/1/2005)*

Viña La Rosa 2004 La Capitana Barrel Reserve Carmenère (Cachapoal Valley) $14. 82 *—M.S. (3/1/2006)*

Viña La Rosa 2002 La Palma Reserve Carmenère (Cachapoal Valley) $12. 82 *—M.S. (6/1/2004)*

Viña La Rosa NV Brut Chardonnay (Cachapoal Valley) $12. Powdered sugar and other lightly confected aromas set up more steely apple and pineapple flavors. Finishes pithy, with grapefruit. Drying and short, but still a reasonable facsimile of Champagne. 83 *—M.S. (12/31/2007)*

Viña La Rosa 2003 Don Reca Chardonnay (Cachapoal Valley) $30. 85 *—M.S. (3/1/2004)*

Viña La Rosa 2006 La Capitana Barrel Reserve Chardonnay (Cachapoal Valley) $15. Given that this wine comes from the Cachapoal Valley, which is warm and normally puts out red wines, this is quite a success. The bouquet is vanilla-tinged and full of apple and nut oil, while the palate blends fresh pear and buttered toast flavors. It's smooth but still fairly fresh, with a richer, somewhat oily mouthfeel that is likely the result of its hotter terroir. 87 *—M.S. (9/1/2007)*

Viña La Rosa 2004 La Capitana Chardonnay (Cachapoal Valley) $15. 85 *—M.S. (11/1/2005)*

Viña La Rosa 2006 La Palma Chardonnay (Cachapoal Valley) $9. Light, powdery aromas don't have a whole lot to say, while the dry, waxy palate features mild but solid apple and white pepper flavors. Finishes with some pear-like sweetness but also the bite of bitter almonds. 84 *—M.S. (3/1/2007)*

Viña La Rosa 2005 La Palma Chardonnay (Cachapoal Valley) $8. 85 Best Buy *—M.S. (3/1/2006)*

Viña La Rosa 2005 La Palma Reserva Chardonnay (Cachapoal Valley) $10. Quite fruity and soothing as Chilean Chardonnay goes. The nose is stocked with swaying peach, apple and pear aromas, while the rich palate features much of the same, with a dusting of cinnamon. Round and ready to drink right away. 87 Best Buy *—M.S. (9/1/2007)*

Viña La Rosa 2001 Sparkling Chardonnay (Cachapoal Valley) $15. 80 *—M.S. (12/31/2004)*

Viña La Rosa 2002 Don Reca Merlot (Cachapoal Valley) $30. 86 *—M.S. (3/1/2004)*

Viña La Rosa 2003 La Capitana Merlot (Cachapoal Valley) $12. 85 *—M.S. (11/1/2005)*

Viña La Rosa 2004 La Capitana Barrel Reserve Merlot (Cachapoal Valley) $14. 86 *—M.S. (3/1/2006)*

Viña La Rosa 2004 La Palma Merlot (Cachapoal Valley) $7. 82 *—M.S. (11/1/2005)*

Viña La Rosa 2003 La Palma Merlot (Cachapoal Valley) $7. 83 *—M.S. (2/1/2005)*

Viña La Rosa 2005 La Palma Reserva Merlot (Cachapoal Valley) $10. If you like an easy-drinking but serious red wine, you'll fall for this full, meaty Merlot that offers nice red and black fruit notes and also a fair share of young, tolerable oak. Slightly more upscale than your average Chilean value Merlot, with a nice foundation of core fruit. 87 Best Buy *—M.S. (5/1/2007)*

Viña La Rosa 2002 Don Reca Merlot-Cabernet Sauvignon (Cachapoal Valley) $30. 85 *—M.S. (3/1/2004)*

Viña La Rosa 2004 Don Reca Limited Release Merlot-Cabernet Sauvignon (Cachapoal Valley) $20. 87 *—M.S. (10/1/2006)*

Viña La Rosa 2006 La Palma Rosé Merlot-Cabernet Sauvignon (Cachapoal Valley) $8. 83 *—M.S. (11/15/2006)*

Viña La Rosa 2005 La Palma Rosé Merlot-Cabernet Sauvignon (Cachapoal Valley) $9. 85 Best Buy *—M.S. (5/1/2006)*

Viña La Rosa 2006 La Palma Sauvignon Blanc (Cachapoal Valley) $8. 84 Best Buy *—M.S. (11/15/2006)*

Viña La Rosa 2005 La Palma Sauvignon Blanc (Cachapoal Valley) $9. 85 Best Buy *—M.S. (12/15/2005)*

Viña La Rosa 2004 La Palma Sauvignon Blanc (Cachapoal Valley) $7. 86 Best Buy *—M.S. (2/1/2005)*

Viña La Rosa 2004 La Capitana Shiraz (Cachapoal Valley) $17. 87 *—M.S. (3/1/2006)*

VIÑA LEYDA

Viña Leyda 2001 Vintage Selection Bordeaux Blend (Chile) $20. 88 *—M.S. (3/1/2004)*

Viña Leyda 2002 Estación Cabernet Sauvignon (Maipo Valley) $NA. 83 *—M.S. (3/1/2004)*

Viña Leyda 2001 Reserve Cabernet Sauvignon (Maipo Valley) $17. 87 *—M.S. (3/1/2004)*

Viña Leyda 2002 Reserve Carmenère (Colchagua Valley) $18. 83 *—M.S. (11/1/2005)*

Viña Leyda 2001 Reserve Carmenère (Colchagua Valley) $17. 88 *—M.S. (3/1/2004)*

Viña Leyda 2003 Estación Chardonnay (Chile) $NA. 85 *—M.S. (3/1/2004)*

Viña Leyda 2002 Falaris Hill Vineyard Reserve Chardonnay (Chile) $17. 87 *—M.S. (3/1/2004)*

Viña Leyda 2001 Falaris Hill Vineyard Reserve Chardonnay (Leyda Valley) $17. 85 *—M.S. (3/1/2004)*

Viña Leyda 2002 Estación Merlot (Maipo Valley) $NA. 82 *—M.S. (3/1/2004)*

Viña Leyda 2003 Cahuil Vineyard Reserve Pinot Noir (Leyda Valley) $22. 84 *—M.S. (11/1/2005)*

Viña Leyda 2002 Cahuil Vineyard Reserve Pinot Noir (Leyda Valley) $20. 86 *—M.S. (3/1/2004)*

Viña Leyda 2002 Las Brisas Vineyard Reserve Pinot Noir (Chile) $NA. 87 *—M.S. (3/1/2004)*

Viña Leyda 2003 Las Brisas Vineyars Reserve Pinot Noir (Leyda Valley) $15. 80 *—M.S. (7/1/2005)*

Viña Leyda 2003 Lot 21 Pinot Noir (Leyda Valley) $32. 86 *—M.S. (11/1/2005)*

Viña Leyda 2002 Lot 21 Pinot Noir (Chile) $NA. 89 *—M.S. (3/1/2004)*

Viña Leyda 2002 Vintage Selection Red Blend (Central Valley) $22. 83 *—M.S. (11/1/2005)*

Viña Leyda 2003 Estación Sauvignon Blanc (Chile) $NA. 86 *—M.S. (3/1/2004)*

Viña Leyda 2004 Estación Reserve Sauvignon Blanc (Leyda Valley) $12. 86 *—M.S. (11/1/2005)*

VIÑA MORANDE

Viña Morande 2000 Morande Terrarum 2000 Cabernet Sauvignon (Maipo Valley) $9. 86 Best Buy *—M.S. (12/1/2002)*

Viña Morande 2000 Pionero Cabernet Sauvignon (Central Valley) $7. 85 Best Buy *—M.S. (12/1/2002)*

Viña Morande 2000 Terrarum Cabernet Sauvignon (Maipo Valley) $9. 86 Best Buy *—M.S. (12/1/2002)*

Viña Morande 2001 Edicion Limitada Golden Reserve Red Blend (Loncomilla Valley) $80. 90 *(11/1/2005)*

VIÑA PÉREZ CRUZ

Viña Pérez Cruz 2005 Reserva Cabernet Sauvignon (Maipo Valley) $11. 88 Best Buy *—M.S. (12/31/2006)*

Viña Pérez Cruz 2004 Reserva Cabernet Sauvignon (Maipo Valley) $13. Strong on the bouquet, which opens with a blast of oak, berries and black licorice. The palate features bold plum and cherry, and it is ripe enough to suggest raisins. Finishes smooth, with another shot of anise. Enjoyable, with soft tannins. 87 *—M.S. (11/15/2007)*

Viña Pérez Cruz 2004 Reserva Limited Edition Carmenère (Maipo Valley) $19. 91 Editors' Choice *—M.S. (12/31/2006)*

Viña Pérez Cruz 2004 Cot Reserva Limited Edition Malbec (Maipo Valley) $19. The color and mouthfeel is fine. But the aromas and flavors offer more bramble and vegetal characteristics than is ideal. So while it flows nicely, the flavor profile gets stuck on jalapeño, tomato leaf and green tobacco. But mouthfeel is not an issue; it's a chewy, statuesque sort of red. 1,100 cases made. 86 *—M.S. (9/1/2007)*

Viña Pérez Cruz 2003 Liguai Red Blend (Maipo Valley) $35. 91 Editors' Choice *—M.S. (12/31/2006)*

Viña Pérez Cruz 2004 Reserva Limited Edition Syrah (Maipo Valley) $19. 92 Editors' Choice *—M.S. (12/31/2006)*

VIÑA REQUINGUA

Viña Requingua 2002 Potro de Piedra Family Reserve Bordeaux Blend (Curicó Valley) $20. 86 *—M.S. (11/1/2005)*

Viña Requingua 2001 Potro de Piedra Family Reserve Cabernet Blend (Curicó Valley) $18. 88 *—M.S. (6/1/2004)*

Viña Requingua 2002 Puerto Viejo Cabernet Sauvignon (Curicó Valley) $10. 86 Best Buy *—M.S. (8/1/2004)*

Viña Requingua 2005 Puerto Viejo Reserve Cabernet Sauvignon (Curicó Valley) $9. Heavy and furry smelling, but soon it opens to show floral red fruit and root beer aromas. The palate is snappy but tasty, with plum and berry flavors coming with some lactic grab. Requires some leniency but generally speaking it's pretty decent wine. Imported by Wineco Corp. 84 *—M.S. (11/15/2007)*

Viña Requingua 2005 Toro de Piedra Reserva Cabernet Sauvignon (Curicó Valley) $14. Full and meaty, but kind of awkward and earthy. The nose has leather and stewed blackberry while the palate shows black fruit, cassis, chocolate and even some nutmeg. The feel is tannic and fiery, and overall the wine is sort of saucy and big-boned. Imported by Wineco Corp. 84 *—M.S. (11/15/2007)*

Viña Requingua 2003 Toro de Piedra Reserva Cabernet Sauvignon (Curicó Valley) $14. 88 *—M.S. (11/1/2005)*

Viña Requingua 2001 Toro de Pierdra Reserve Cabernet Sauvignon (Curicó Valley) $13. 88 Best Buy *—M.S. (8/1/2004)*

Viña Requingua 2003 Potro de Piedra Family Reserve Cabernet Sauvignon-Cabernet Franc (Curicó Valley) $25. 89 *—M.S. (7/1/2006)*

Viña Requingua 2003 Puerto Viejo Carmenère (Curicó Valley) $9. 81 *—M.S. (11/1/2005)*

Viña Requingua 2005 Puerto Viejo Reserve Carmenère (Curicó Valley) $9. The bouquet is redolent of air freshener and light spices but not much else. The palate, meanwhile, is candied and short on substance; it's sweet yet hollow, and the finish is drying and peppery. Imported by Wineco Corp. 83 *—M.S. (11/15/2007)*

Viña Requingua 2005 Toro de Piedra Reserva Carmenère-Cabernet Sauvignon (Curicó Valley) $14. This Carmenère blend starts with piercing oak notes manifested in scents of butter and lactic paint, while the palate is equally infused with wood grain that lends a bitter spiciness to the basic fruit. Imported by Wineco Corp. 82 *—M.S. (11/15/2007)*

Viña Requingua 2004 Puerto Viejo Chardonnay (Curicó Valley) $9. 82 *—M.S. (7/1/2005)*

Viña Requingua 2003 Puerto Viejo Chardonnay (Curicó Valley) $10. 86 Best Buy *—M.S. (6/1/2004)*

Viña Requingua 2006 Puerto Viejo Reserve Chardonnay (Curicó Valley) $9. Yellowish in color, with round, vanilla-based aromas. The palate is slightly resiny, but there's also some nice white pepper and apple flavors. Yes, it's probably too woody for its own good, but overall the wine has a balanced mouthfeel and isn't yet slipping to the soft and spineless zone where most Chilean Chards go to die. Imported by Wineco Corp. 84 Best Buy *—M.S. (11/15/2007)*

Viña Requingua 2003 Puerto Viejo Merlot (Curicó Valley) $9. 80 *—M.S. (7/1/2005)*

Viña Requingua 2002 Puerto Viejo Merlot (Curicó Valley) $10. 84 *—M.S. (6/1/2004)*

Viña Requingua 2005 Puerto Viejo Reserve Merlot (Curicó Valley) $9. This is a complete and pleasant red. The nose has a bit of wood, some cured meat and ripe fruit aromas, while the mouth delivers juicy red-berry flavors along with a touch of apple skin. One of this brand's better efforts; it tastes like a real and true Merlot. Imported by Wineco Corp. 86 Best Buy *—M.S. (11/15/2007)*

Viña Requingua 2006 Puerto Viejo Reserve Sauvignon Blanc (Curicó Valley) $9. Aromas of melon, tropical fruit and apple get it going. The next step is a round apple-n-melon palate with some citrus at the base. For the most part it reflects the fact that it comes from the warm Curicó Valley, which by all accounts is not Sauvignon Blanc country. It's a heavy-handed example of S.B. Imported by Wineco Corp. 83 *—M.S. (11/15/2007)*

VIÑA SAN ESTEBAN

Viña San Esteban 2003 President's Select Cabernet Sauvignon (Aconcagua Valley) $13. 84 *—M.S. (11/1/2005)*

Viña San Esteban 2002 Reserva Carmenère (Aconcagua Valley) $8. 82 *—M.S. (6/1/2004)*

Viña San Esteban 2003 Reserva Merlot (Aconcagua Valley) $10. 83 *—M.S. (11/1/2005)*

Viña San Esteban 2001 Reserva Merlot (Aconcagua Valley) $8. 85 Best Buy *—M.S. (3/1/2004)*

Viña San Esteban 2003 Reserva Shiraz (Aconcagua Valley) $10. 83 *—M.S. (11/1/2005)*

VIÑA SANTA MONICA

Viña Santa Monica 1999 Cabernet Sauvignon (Rapel Valley) $8. 83 *—M.S. (7/1/2003)*

Viña Santa Monica 2001 Chardonnay (Rapel Valley) $8. 87 Best Buy *—M.S. (7/1/2003)*

Viña Santa Monica 2001 Riesling (Rapel Valley) $8. 84 *—M.S. (8/1/2003)*

Viña Santa Monica 2002 Sauvignon Blanc (Rapel Valley) $8. 84 *—M.S. (7/1/2003)*

VIÑA TABALÍ

Viña Tabalí 2003 Reserva Cabernet Sauvignon (Limarí Valley) $14. 83 *—M.S. (5/1/2006)*

Viña Tabalí 2003 Reserva Carmenère (Limarí Valley) $14. 84 *—M.S. (3/1/2006)*

Viña Tabalí 2004 Reserva Especial Chardonnay (Limarí Valley) $17. 88 *—M.S. (7/1/2006)*

Viña Tabalí 2003 Reserva Merlot (Limarí Valley) $14. 82 *—M.S. (3/1/2006)*

Viña Tabalí 2004 Reserva Pinot Noir (Limarí Valley) $18. 81 *—M.S. (7/1/2006)*

Viña Tabalí 2003 Reserva Especial Red Blend (Limarí Valley) $19. 85 *—M.S. (3/1/2006)*

Viña Tabalí 2005 Sauvignon Blanc (Limarí Valley) $10. 84 *—M.S. (5/1/2006)*

Viña Tabalí 2004 Reserva Shiraz (Limarí Valley) $15. 84 *—M.S. (3/1/2006)*

VIÑEDOS DE CANATA

Viñedos de Canata 2001 Paso Hondo Reserva Cabernet Sauvignon (Bío Bío Valley) $12. 80 *—M.S. (11/1/2005)*

Viñedos de Canata 2002 Carmenère (Bío Bío Valley) $9. 85 Best Buy *—M.S. (3/1/2006)*

Viñedos de Canata 2001 Paso Hondo Reserva Carmenère (Bío Bío Valley) $12. 83 *—M.S. (3/1/2006)*

Viñedos de Canata 2004 Chardonnay (Bío Bío Valley) $9. 84 *—M.S. (11/1/2005)*

Viñedos de Canata 2003 Paso Hondo Reserva Chardonnay (Bío Bío Valley) $12. 86 *—M.S. (11/1/2005)*

Viñedos de Canata 2003 Paso Hondo Alto Selección Malbec (Bío Bío Valley) $16. 84 *—M.S. (11/1/2005)*

Viñedos de Canata 2003 Merlot (Curicó Valley) $9. 81 *—M.S. (11/1/2005)*

Viñedos de Canata 2003 Paso Hondo Alta Selección Merlot (Bío Bío Valley) $16. 84 *—M.S. (11/1/2005)*

Viñedos de Canata 2003 Paso Hondo Alta Seleccion Winemaker's Cuvée Red Blend (Bío Bío Valley) $16. 83 *—M.S. (11/1/2005)*

Viñedos de Canata 2004 Sauvignon Blanc (Bío Bío Valley) $9. 82 *—M.S. (11/1/2005)*

VIÑEDOS ORGANICOS EMILIANA

Viñedos Organicos Emiliana 2004 Adobe Carmenère (Colchagua Valley) $NA. 87 *—M.S. (3/1/2006)*

Viñedos Organicos Emiliana 2007 Natura Chardonnay (Casablanca Valley) $10. This is a fulfilling unoaked, organic wine from Chile's cool Casablanca Valley. This quaffable Chard focuses on pure citrus, grapefruit and peach flavors. There's a touch of natural sweetness but with no oak there's no butter, fat or flab. Breaks the mold and opens the door to a whole other style of Chardonnay. 88 Best Buy *—M.S. (11/15/2007)*

Viñedos Organicos Emiliana 2004 Adobe Syrah (Colchagua Valley) $NA. 88 *—M.S. (3/1/2006)*

VIÑEDOS TORREÓN

Viñedos Torreón 2003 Torreon de Paredes Sauvignon Blanc (Chile) $11. 83 *—M.S. (6/1/2004)*

VINO DE EYZAGUIRRE

Vino de Eyzaguirre 2001 Cabernet Sauvignon (Colchagua Valley) $8. 85 Best Buy *—M.S. (8/1/2004)*

Vino de Eyzaguirre 2001 San Francisco de Mostazal Reserva Especial Merlot (Colchagua Valley) $8. 84 *—M.S. (8/1/2004)*

Vino de Eyzaguirre 2002 Shiraz (Colchagua Valley) $8. 82 *—M.S. (2/1/2005)*

Vino de Eyzaguirre 2001 San Francisco de Mostazal Reserva Especial Syrah (Colchagua Valley) $8. 82 *—M.S. (7/1/2003)*

VIRGINIA LOUISE

Virginia Louise 2005 Pinot Noir (Central Valley) $12. A rusty, bronzing specimen with super dry and fading tomato aromas and not too much fruit to speak of. More unruly than anything, with barely adequate Pinot character. 81 *—M.S. (3/1/2007)*

VIU MANENT

Viu Manent 2005 Cabernet Sauvignon (Colchagua Valley) $8. 84 Best Buy *—M.S. (7/1/2006)*

Viu Manent 2002 Cabernet Sauvignon (Colchagua Valley) $8. 85 Best Buy *—M.S. (3/1/2004)*

Viu Manent 2004 Estate Cabernet Sauvignon (Colchagua Valley) $8. 86 Best Buy *—M.S. (5/1/2006)*

Viu Manent 2003 Estate Bottled Cabernet Sauvignon (Colchagua Valley) $8. 87 Best Buy *—M.S. (11/1/2005)*

Viu Manent 2004 La Capilla Estate Single Vineyard Cabernet Sauvignon (Colchagua Valley) $19. 89 *—M.S. (10/1/2006)*

Viu Manent 2004 Oak Aged Reserve Cabernet Sauvignon (Colchagua Valley) $13. 86 *—M.S. (10/1/2006)*

Viu Manent 2003 Oak Aged Reserve Cabernet Sauvignon (Colchagua Valley) $12. 86 *—M.S. (7/1/2006)*

Viu Manent 2001 Oak Aged Reserve Cabernet Sauvignon (Colchagua Valley) $12. 85 *—M.S. (3/1/2004)*

Viu Manent 2002 Reserve Cabernet Sauvignon (Colchagua Valley) $12. 85 *—M.S. (2/1/2005)*

Viu Manent 1999 Reserve Cabernet Sauvignon (Colchagua Valley) $12. 87 Best Buy *—M.S. (3/1/2002)*

Viu Manent 2005 Single Vineyard La Capilla Estate Cabernet Sauvignon (Colchagua Valley) $22. Fairly woody at first, with cassis, berry and lemon rind on the nose. The palate is chunky and round, with flavors of black currant, blackberry and spice. Toward the end hickory and sap come up, which brings you back to that woodiness of the bouquet. Imported by Atlanta Improvement Co. 88 *—M.S. (11/15/2007)*

Viu Manent 2000 Special Selection Cabernet Sauvignon (Colchagua Valley) $20. 85 *—M.S. (3/1/2004)*

Viu Manent 1998 Special Selection Cabernet Sauvignon (Colchagua Valley) $20. 85 *—J.C. (7/1/2002)*

Viu Manent 2001 Special Selection La Capilla Vineyard Cabernet Sauvignon (Colchagua Valley) $20. 89 *—M.S. (7/1/2005)*

Viu Manent 2002 Carmenère (Colchagua Valley) $8. 87 Best Buy *—M.S. (8/1/2004)*

Viu Manent 2005 Estate Carmenère (Colchagua Valley) $8. 84 Best Buy *—M.S. (11/15/2006)*

Viu Manent 2004 Estate Carmenère (Colchagua Valley) $8. 87 Best Buy *—M.S. (3/1/2006)*

Viu Manent 2003 Estate Bottled Carmenère (Colchagua Valley) $8. 82 *—M.S. (2/1/2005)*

Viu Manent 2003 Oak Aged Reserve Carmenère (Colchagua Valley) $12. 83 *—M.S. (12/15/2005)*

Viu Manent 2002 Oak Aged Reserve Carmenère (Colchagua Valley) $12. 88 Best Buy *—M.S. (6/1/2004)*

Viu Manent 2005 Reserva Carmenère (Colchagua Valley) $13. Blistering oak is the welcome mat, then the nose morphs from hickory to mint to olive. The palate is chewy, even burly, and the finish runs dark and syrupy but also medicinal. For sure this wine has power and ripeness, yet it rates as untamed and badly needs food to settle it down. Imported by Atlanta Improvement Co. 85 *—M.S. (11/15/2007)*

Viu Manent 2004 Reserva Carmenère (Colchagua Valley) $12. 88 Best Buy *—M.S. (3/1/2006)*

Viu Manent 2006 Secreto Carmenère (Colchagua Valley) $13. Initially it smells like clay, but that soon yields. The palate is bold and loaded with oozing black fruit, while the wine finishes with flesh and warmth. It's a big, lumbering specimen that isn't elegant in the least, but it's good in the so-called ripe and ready style. Imported by Atlanta Improvement Co. 86 *—M.S. (11/15/2007)*

Viu Manent 2005 Secreto Carmenère (Colchagua Valley) $13. 87 *—M.S. (10/1/2006)*

Viu Manent 2004 Secreto Carmenère (Colchagua Valley) $12. 85 *—M.S. (3/1/2006)*

Viu Manent 2003 Secreto Carmenère (Colchagua Valley) $12. 86 *—M.S. (11/1/2005)*

Viu Manent 2006 Chardonnay (Colchagua Valley) $8. Chardonnay is not this winery's strong suit, so it's no shock to find this wine awkward, yet it's tolerable. The nose sort of sweet and skunky. The flavors work toward banana and melon, and overall it's not bad but not that great either. 83 *—M.S. (3/1/2007)*

Viu Manent 2004 Barrel Fermented Reserve Chardonnay (Casablanca Valley) $12. 81 *—M.S. (3/1/2006)*

Viu Manent 2003 Barrel Fermented Reserve Chardonnay (Colchagua Valley) $12. 88 Best Buy *—M.S. (2/1/2005)*

Viu Manent 2004 Estate Bottled Chardonnay (Colchagua Valley) $8. 86 Best Buy *—M.S. (7/1/2005)*

Viu Manent 1999 Reserve Chardonnay (Colchagua Valley) $12. 83 *—M.S. (7/1/2003)*

Viu Manent 2004 Malbec (Colchagua Valley) $8. 87 Best Buy *—M.S. (11/1/2005)*

Viu Manent 2002 Malbec (Colchagua Valley) $8. 85 Best Buy *—M.S. (12/1/2003)*

Viu Manent 2000 Malbec (Colchagua Valley) $8. 87 Best Buy *—M.S. (3/1/2002)*

Viu Manent 2003 Los Carlos Estate Single Vineyard Malbec (Colchagua Valley) $18. 91 Editors' Choice *—M.S. (11/1/2005)*

Viu Manent 2004 Oak Aged Reserve Malbec (Colchagua Valley) $13. 89 Best Buy *—M.S. (10/1/2006)*

Viu Manent 2003 Oak Aged Reserve Malbec (Colchagua Valley) $12. 87 Best Buy *—M.S. (12/15/2005)*

Viu Manent 2001 Oak Aged Reserve Malbec (Colchagua Valley) $12. 84 *—P.G. (12/1/2003)*

Viu Manent 2005 Single Vineyard San Carlos Estate Malbec (Colchagua Valley) $22. This score for a $22 Chilean Malbec may cause you to do a double-take, but this is really a great wine. The nose is chock full of berry aromas with earth and leather riding shotgun. Flavors and finishing notes of chocolate truffles, espresso, berry syrup and mocha sum it up. The structure is here, as is the core acidity. This wine has everything. Imported by Atlanta Improvement Co. 92 Editors' Choice *—M.S. (11/15/2007)*

Viu Manent 2004 San Carlos Estate Single Vineyard Malbec (Colchagua Valley) $19. 90 Editors' Choice *—M.S. (10/1/2006)*

Viu Manent 2005 Secreto Malbec (Colchagua Valley) $13. 87 *—M.S. (10/1/2006)*

Viu Manent 2004 Secreto Malbec (Colchagua Valley) $12. 86 *—M.S. (11/1/2005)*

Viu Manent 2001 Special Selection Malbec (Colchagua Valley) $16. 88 *—M.S. (12/1/2003)*

Viu Manent 2000 Special Selection Malbec (Colchagua Valley) $16. 89 *—M.S. (3/1/2002)*

Viu Manent 2004 Viu 1 Malbec (Colchagua Valley) $50. Typically this ranks as the best Malbec in Chile, and the 2004 keeps things going in the right direction. The bouquet is manly, tight, oaky and full of monstrous black fruit. Licorice, blackberry pie and espresso are your key flavors, while the feel is dense but assuringly friendly. Drink from 2008 through 2012. Imported by Atlanta Improvement Co. 92 *—M.S. (11/15/2007)*

Viu Manent 2001 Viu 1 Malbec (Colchagua Valley) $50. 92 *—M.S. (12/1/2003)*

Viu Manent 1999 Viu I Malbec (Colchagua Valley) $39. 93 Editors' Choice *—M.S. (3/1/2002)*

Viu Manent 2004 Merlot (Colchagua Valley) $8. 80 *—M.S. (11/1/2005)*

Viu Manent 2002 Merlot (Colchagua Valley) $8. 86 Best Buy *—M.S. (3/1/2004)*

Viu Manent 1999 Merlot (Colchagua Valley) $8. 83 *—D.T. (7/1/2002)*

Viu Manent 2005 Estate Merlot (Colchagua Valley) $8. 85 Best Buy *—M.S. (11/15/2006)*

Viu Manent 2003 Estate Bottled Merlot (Colchagua Valley) $8. 84 Best Buy *—M.S. (11/1/2005)*

Viu Manent 2003 Oak Aged Reserve Merlot (Colchagua Valley) $12. 83 *—M.S. (12/15/2005)*

Viu Manent 2002 Oak Aged Reserve Merlot (Colchagua Valley) $12. 89 Best Buy *—M.S. (8/1/2004)*

Viu Manent 2005 Reserva Merlot (Colchagua Valley) $13. Good color and grip, but also quite herbal and green, with bell pepper and lettuce appearing on the bouquet. The palate has a correct feel but at all points the wine hits with an unmistakable green pepper and olive character. It's almost there, and it has its good points, but it's just a bit too green. Imported by Atlanta Improvement Co. 84 *—M.S. (11/15/2007)*

Viu Manent 1999 Reserve Merlot (Colchagua Valley) $13. 83 *—D.T. (7/1/2002)*

Viu Manent 2003 Viu 1 Red Blend (Colchagua Valley) $50. 92 Editors' Choice *—M.S. (7/1/2006)*

Viu Manent 2006 Sauvignon Blanc (Colchagua Valley) $8. If you like your white wines charged up and dripping with acidity, then take a look at this ultra-fresh and exceedingly zesty SB. The nose and palate exude sharpness, so much so that the flavor profile is on the edge of being sour. A razor-sharp style of Sauvignon. 83 *—M.S. (3/1/2007)*

Viu Manent 2003 Sauvignon Blanc (Colchagua Valley) $8. 86 Best Buy *—M.S. (3/1/2004)*

Viu Manent 2001 Sauvignon Blanc (Colchagua Valley) $8. 87 *—M.S. (3/1/2002)*

Viu Manent 2004 Estate Bottled Sauvignon Blanc (Colchagua Valley) $8. 88 Best Buy *—M.S. (7/1/2005)*

Viu Manent 2006 Reserve Sauvignon Blanc (Colchagua Valley) $12. Viu's 2006 SBs are not clicking. This wine, while round and seemingly honeyed on the nose, is sharp as razors in the mouth. The entry to the palate is clipped and tart, and there just isn't much flow to the wine. Very high in acids but with a certain purity of fruit. 83 *—M.S. (3/1/2007)*

Viu Manent 2004 Reserve Sauvignon Blanc (Colchagua Valley) $12. 86 *—M.S. (2/1/2005)*

Viu Manent 2006 Secreto Sauvignon Blanc (Colchagua Valley) $13. 88 *—M.S. (12/31/2006)*

Viu Manent 2004 Secreto Sauvignon Blanc (Colchagua Valley) $12. 84 *—M.S. (12/15/2005)*

Viu Manent 2003 Secreto Sauvignon Blanc (Colchagua Valley) $12. 87 Best Buy *—M.S. (7/1/2005)*

Viu Manent 2003 Semillon (Colchagua Valley) $8. 83 *—M.S. (6/1/2004)*

Viu Manent 2005 Secreto Syrah (Colchagua Valley) $13. 87 *—M.S. (11/15/2006)*

Viu Manent 2004 Secreto Syrah (Colchagua Valley) $12. 88 Best Buy *—M.S. (11/1/2005)*

Viu Manent 2006 Secreto Viognier (Colchagua Valley) $13. Very melony and full of pineapple: ripe is the main word used to describe this full-bodied, weighty rendition of Viognier and whatever else makes the blend. Overall it has bold, fat apricot and peach flavors along with a lip-smacking, somewhat cumbersome finish. Drink as soon as possible to preserve maximum stone-fruit character. 85 *—M.S. (11/15/2007)*

Viu Manent 2004 Secreto Viognier (Colchagua Valley) $12. 82 *—M.S. (7/1/2006)*

Viu Manent 2003 Secreto Viognier (Colchagua Valley) $12. 85 *—M.S. (11/1/2005)*

WALNUT CREST

Walnut Crest 2003 Cabernet Sauvignon (Rapel Valley) $5. 86 Best Buy *—M.S. (11/1/2005)*

Walnut Crest 2001 Cabernet Sauvignon (Rapel Valley) $6. 85 Best Buy *—M.S. (12/1/2002)*

Walnut Crest 2003 Chardonnay (Casablanca Valley) $5. 84 Best Buy *—M.S. (6/1/2004)*

Walnut Crest 2001 Chardonnay (Casablanca Valley) $6. 86 Best Buy *—M.S. (7/1/2003)*

Walnut Crest 2003 Merlot (Rapel Valley) $5. 83 *—M.S. (8/1/2004)*

Walnut Crest 2004 Sauvignon Blanc (Central Valley) $5. 84 Best Buy *—M.S. (11/1/2005)*

Walnut Crest 2001 Shiraz (Rapel Valley) $6. 83 *—M.S. (7/1/2003)*

WILLIAM COLE

William Cole 2004 Alto Vuelo Cabernet Sauvignon-Carmenère (Casablanca Valley) $13. 83 *—M.S. (10/1/2006)*

YALI

Yali 2001 Cabernet Sauvignon (Maipo Valley) $6. 86 Best Buy *—M.S. (3/1/2004)*

Yali 2002 Chardonnay (Rapel Valley) $6. 85 Best Buy *—M.S. (3/1/2004)*

Yali 2001 Merlot (Maipo Valley) $6. 84 *—M.S. (8/1/2004)*

Yali 2001 Syrah (Maipo Valley) $6. 84 *—M.S. (8/1/2004)*

YELCHO

Yelcho 2003 Reserva Carmenère (Maipo Valley) $12. 85 *(2/1/2006)*

Yelcho 2005 Chardonnay (Rapel Valley) $7. 81 *—M.S. (10/1/2006)*

Yelcho 2003 Reserva Merlot (Maipo Valley) $11. 81 *—M.S. (7/1/2006)*

Yelcho 2005 Reserva Sauvignon Blanc (Casablanca Valley) $12. 87 *(2/1/2006)*

France

France is the source of some of the greatest wines in the world, but has also been the source of some of the worst. Despite a labeling system that is often confusing to many outside of France, French wine still gives the greatest pleasure of any wine-producing region. The style of French wine echoes that of the French themselves—elegant, well-dressed, showing an appreciation for the good things of life but never to excess. French wines go best with food, never overpowering either in flavor or in alcohol, always well-mannered, often beautiful.

The fact that, today, the quality of even the least-expensive French wine has improved impressively, means that there is a whole new range of wines open to wine drinkers.

Cabernet Sauvignon grapes in a vineyard at Château Pichon-Longueville-Baron, Pauillac, Gironde, France.

All these qualities make it worthwhile to spend some time to get to know French wine and to appreciate its many facets. The country produces all styles of wine, from the cool wines of the Loire Valley, to the stylish whites of Alsace, through the classics of Bordeaux and Burgundy, to the more powerful, muscular offerings of the Rhône, to the warm wines of Languedoc and Roussillon, suffused with sun. And, of course, there are the great Champagnes.

In a world of international brands, where origin doesn't matter, France offers an alternative ethos. There is much talk of terroir, of the place and the culture from which a wine comes. It makes every wine different, makes many of them special. There is no homogeneity here.

France is an ordered country, and despite the seeming chaos of French wine, there is order in the system. Wines come from places, and these places are designated appellations. An appellation—*appellation contrôlée* on a wine label—is not a guarantee of quality. It is a guarantee of origin, and a guarantee that the wine has been made following certain rules specifying grape varieties, soil, planting, yields, and winemaking. The wine has also passed a sensory test which approves its style and its typicity for the appellation.

There are nearly 280 appellations in France, ranging from the huge—Bordeaux appellation, or Champagne—to the tiny, single-vineyard appellations of Coulée de Serrant in the Loire Valley and Romanée-Conti in Burgundy. There are regional appellations, there are district appellations, and there are appellations which cover only one commune.

A good example of this hierarchy is in Burgundy. The main appellation of the region is plain and simple: red and white, Bourgogne Rouge or Bourgogne Blanc. Climbing up the hierarchy are district appellations such as Chablis, for white wines, Mâcon for white and red wines, Côte de Beaune for reds, and so on.

Rising again in quality while the area of the appellation gets smaller are village appellations: Vougeot, Auxey-Duresse, Pommard, Nuits-St-Georges. In these villages, certain superior vineyards are designated premier cru—and you will find the name of the vineyard on the label. At the top of the quality heap are the single-vineyard appellations, the Grand Cru: Clos de Vougeot being perhaps the most famous.

There is one other category of wine which is in some ways the most interesting and exciting: Vin de Pays. These are everyday, ready-to-drink wines that offer some of the best values in the world. The labels, unlike appellation wines, will show grape varieties. Coming generally from the warm south of France, the wines will be warm, ripe, and fruity. The best-known example is Vin de Pays d'Oc.

Having established some of the ground rules for French wine, let's examine the fascinations of the different regions in more detail.

By far the largest, the most important, and one of the best regions, both for great wines and for bargains, is Bordeaux. Great reds from the great chateaus are what make the headlines, but Bordeaux is so big, that there is plenty of choice. Appellations with the name Côtes in the title are always worth seeking out, as are the white wines (yes, Bordeaux makes whites, both dry and sweet). And the general level of quality has improved dramatically. The reds are fruity, but never over-alcoholic, always with a layer of tannin that makes them great food wines. The whites are fresh, the best with wood flavors to give complexity. They may all be called "chateau this," "chateau that," but that's simply a way of saying that many Bordeaux wines come from one individual property.

Cabernet Sauvignon, Merlot, and Cabernet Franc are the main red grapes; Sauvignon Blanc and Sémillon are the main whites. But most Bordeaux is not a single varietal wine—it is more often a blend, which makes these wines more than the sum of their individual parts.

Burgundy is the other big French wine. It is a fifth the size of the Bordeaux region, and produces correspondingly more expensive wines, with fewer bargains, and more disappointments. The best way to buy Burgundy is to follow the best producers, and reliable reviews from buying guides or wine magazines. If you take that advice, the most seductive wines (red from Pinot Noir, white from Chardonnay, always 100 percent) are in your glass. It's not just chance that the Burgundy bottle has rounded sides, the Bordeaux bottle has straight: Burgundy appeals to the senses, Bordeaux to the intellect.

Much larger in scale than Burgundy is the Rhône valley. From the alcoholic and powerful highs of Châteauneuf-du-Pape, through the dense elegance of the Syrah wines of appellations like Côte-Rôtie and Hermitage, this is red wine country. Rich and generous, these wines appeal to wine drinkers used to California reds. And, just like Bordeaux, there is also great value to be found in this region: wines labeled Côtes du Rhône. If they have a village name attached (Rasteau and Seguret are among the best), they will be that much better, even if more expensive.

Bordeaux, Burgundy, and the Rhône are the best-known wine regions of France except for Champagne. This sparkling wine from the chalk slopes east of Paris is France's best answer to a global brand. It is the drink of celebration, of success, and the best way to drown sorrows. And, unlike the still French wines, which have been successfully copied around the world, Champagne remains inimitable, despite thousands of attempts. The combination of cool climate, chalk soil and—there's no other word for it—terroir are just so special.

As a complete contrast, there are the hot, sun-drenched vineyards of the south. Languedoc and Roussillon don't just produce tanker loads of inexpensive wine. Some areas such as Corbières, Minervois, Coteaux du Languedoc, and Côtes de Roussillon offer a magic mix of great value, history, and some fascinating herbal and fruity flavors.

After these greats, come the Loire and Alsace regions, which produce some of the greatest and most fascinating wines in France. Bordeaux and the Rhône are known for reds, Burgundy for reds and whites. The two cool-climate areas of Loire and Alsace are where the whites shine.

Alsace is unique in France in that producers are allowed to put the grape variety on the label of an appellation wine. It is also unique in that the grapes are a mix of German and French: Riesling and Gewürztraminer, Muscat and Pinot Gris. These are not light wines, but they have a fruitiness and a richness that is quite different from the German models just across the Rhine river. At the top of this list are the Alsace Grand Cru vineyards, single vineyards that can produce astonishing quality and longevity.

The Loire Valley is a complete mix. Every style of wine can be found along its six-hundred-mile length. The greatest styles are the Sauvignon Blanc of Sancerre and Pouilly-Fumé, the models for Sauvignon Blanc around the world. And the Chenin Blancs of the central Loire—the sweet wines of Vouvray and Anjou—have a poise and acidity which allows them to age for decades, yet be fresh when young. The dry Chenins of Savennières are the purest expression of their granite soil to be found. Finally, to complete the mix are the reds of Chinon and Bourgueil and the fresh, easy whites of Muscadet.

It's obvious from this brief list that France has variety, in profusion perhaps, but it does mean that there is never a dull moment when reaching for a bottle of French wine. If your wish is to have the same, safe bottle of wine every day, then non-European brands are the better option.

A. SOUTIRAN

A. Soutiran NV Grande Cru Blanc de Blancs Champagne Blend (Champagne) $45. 91 *—P.G. (12/1/2000)*

A. Soutiran 1995 Grande Cru Brut Champagne Blend (Champagne) $60. 90 *(12/1/2000)*

ABARBANEL

Abarbanel 2001 Estate Bottled Chardonnay (Vin de Pays de L'Aude) $14. 81 *—M.S. (9/1/2003)*

Abarbanel 2005 Château de la Salle Old Vines Kosher Gamay (Beaujolais-Villages) $12. Basic Beaujolais, light in body, with grapy, black cherry-ish aromas and flavors and a hint of fresh greens. Ends on a note of bitter chocolate. 83 *—J.C. (4/1/2007)*

Abarbanel 2004 Estate Bottled Kosher Gewürztraminer (Alsace) $18. The Abarbanel family has been making wine in the Alsace since the 15th century, and this delicate, spicy Gewurtztraminer hits the mark on most counts. A perfumed, floral nose leads to a clean, slightly racy array of peaches, spice and sugar, and the finish is subtle but not weak. 85 *—S.K. (4/1/2007)*

Abarbanel 1999 Estate Bottled Merlot (Languedoc) $10. 84 *(4/1/2001)*

Abarbanel 2005 Estate Bottled Kosher Pinot Noir (Alsace) $18. Light in color and intensity, this delicate Pinot Noir features herbal, tomato-like aromas and flavors and modest cherry fruit. Drink now. 82 *—J.C. (4/1/2007)*

Abarbanel 2002 Old Vines Red Blend (Beaujolais-Villages) $12. 87 *—J.M. (4/3/2004)*

Abarbanel 2004 Estate Bottled Kosher Riesling (Alsace) $18. Dry and clean but with a good balance of fruit and tang, this Riesling is enjoyable but leans toward the watery side and has little finish. Flavors of apple and citrus are present, but the wine lacks complexity. 82 *—S.K. (4/1/2007)*

Abarbanel 2002 White Shiraz Shiraz (Vin de Pays de L'Aude) $9. 86 *—J.M. (4/3/2004)*

Abarbanel 2002 Syrah (Vin de Pays de L'Aude) $13. 84 *—J.M. (4/3/2004)*

Abarbanel 2001 Estate Bottled Syrah (Vin de Pays de L'Aude) $13. 83 *—M.S. (9/1/2003)*

Abarbanel 2003 Kosher Syrah Syrah (Vin de Pays de L'Aude) $14. 83 *—J.C. (4/1/2006)*

ABBOTTS

Abbotts 2002 Zephyr Chardonnay (Limoux) $36. 86 *—R.V. (12/31/2006)*

Abbotts 2000 Boreas Rhône Red Blend (Coteaux du Languedoc) $27. 91 Editors' Choice *—R.V. (12/31/2006)*

Abbotts 1999 Cumulo Nimbus Rhône Red Blend (Minervois) $36. 91 *—R.V. (12/31/2006)*

Abbotts 2004 Trigonia Rhône Red Blend (Corbières) $13. This wine is all about minerality. It is dark, with a powerful tannic structure that dominates the spices and red fruits. Strong acidity and a layer of cool freshness mark this wine. A blend of Syrah, Grenache, Carignan and Mourvèdre, it has aging potential for a couple more years. 89 Best Buy *—R.V. (2/1/2007)*

Abbotts 2005 Orthis Rhône White Blend (Coteaux du Languedoc) $13. 86 *—R.V. (12/31/2006)*

Abbotts 1998 Cumulo Nimbus Shiraz (Minervois) $35. 91 *—M.M. (11/1/2000)*

Abbotts 2000 Cumulus Syrah (Minervois) $17. 85 *—J.C. (11/15/2005)*

Abbotts 2001 Notus Syrah (Minervois) $67. It is rich, black and chocolaty, with new French oak flavors layering the power-packed fruit. For those who like big, brawny wines, this is a must-have. 88 *—R.V. (2/1/2007)*

AGRAPART & FILS

Agrapart & Fils NV Blanc de Blancs Brut Champagne Blend (Champagne) $23. 88 *—R.V. (12/1/2002)*

Agrapart & Fils 1995 L'Avizoise Blanc de Blancs Brut Champagne Blend (Champagne) $53. 92 *—R.V. (12/1/2002)*

Agrapart & Fils 2002 L'Avizoise Grand Cru Blanc de Blancs Extra Brut Chardonnay (Champagne) $90. Wood maturation gives this wine roundness, despite its dryness. At the moment, it is too young, very vigorous, and touched by caramel. The feeling is of a weighty, structured wine, even though the aftertaste is fresh. 90 *—R.V. (12/31/2007)*

Agrapart & Fils NV Les Demoiselles Rosé Brut Champagne Blend (Champagne) $60. The lightest pink in color, this delicacy translates into the pure Chardonnay of the Champagne itself which has Pinot Noir added to give color and just a touch of red-fruit flavors. 88 *—R.V. (12/31/2007)*

Agrapart & Fils NV Les Sept Crus Blanc de Blancs Brut Chardonnay (Champagne) $45. This is a blend from seven of Pascal Agrapart's less important vineyards. It tastes as young as many of the vines are crisp with some citrus and fennel, but there is some softness. Not for aging. 87 *—R.V. (12/31/2007)*

Agrapart & Fils 2000 Minéral Blanc de Blancs Brut Chardonnay (Champagne) $50. 90 *—R.V. (11/1/2006)*

Agrapart & Fils 2000 Minéral Extra Brut Chardonnay (Champagne) $60. The fact that this wine comes from the chalkiest of soils and is bone dry gives it considerable austerity. It is definitely mineral in taste and texture, with a touch of salt and grapefruit flavors; very structured and tight. It needs to age. 91 Cellar Selection *—R.V. (12/31/2007)*

Agrapart & Fils NV Terroirs Blanc de Blancs Brut Chardonnay (Champagne) $50. From grand cru vines in Avize, Oger, Cramant and Oiry, this is full and intensely flavored, with very crisp apple and white pear flavors. To finish, the wine rounds out with vanilla and smooth textures. 90 *—R.V. (12/31/2007)*

Agrapart & Fils 2001 Vénus Grand Cru Brut Nature Chardonnay (Champagne) $120. Named not after the goddess of love, but the horse that Agrapart uses to plough the vines, this superb wine comes from 50-year-old vines, the clay element in the soil giving richness, the minerality giving balance, lifting up the yellow fruit flavors with excellent acidity. 93 *—R.V. (12/31/2007)*

AILE D'ARGENT

Aile d'Argent 2005 Barrel Sample Bordeaux White Blend (Bordeaux Blanc) $NA. 87 *—R.V. (6/21/2006)*

ALAIN GRAILLOT

Alain Graillot 1999 La Guiraude Syrah (Crozes-Hermitage) $NA. 92 *—R.V. (6/1/2002)*

ALAIN POULET

Alain Poulet NV Sparkling Blend (Clairette de Die Méthode Dioise Ancestrale) $12. 84 *—S.H. (12/15/2000)*

ALAIN VOGE

Alain Voge 2004 Fleur du Crussol Marsanne (Saint-Péray) $52. This ratchets up the intensity from Voge's other Saint-Pérays, bringing waves of toasty, mealy and citrusy aromas and flavors. It seems almost floral on the nose, yet is authoritatively weighty on the palate. It's powerful, yet crisp, with a long, velvety-textured finish. Delicious now, but should hold well. 93 Editors' Choice *—J.C. (9/1/2007)*

Alain Voge 2004 Cuvée Boisée Rhône White Blend (Saint-Péray) $32. A barrel-fermented blend of Marsanne and Roussanne, this toasty, leesy, custardy wine is rather rich on the palate, with honeyed cereal flavors and peach overtones that linger on the finish. 90 *—J.C. (9/1/2007)*

Alain Voge 2003 Fleur de Crussol Rhône White Blend (Saint-Péray) $51. 84 *—J.C. (11/15/2006)*

Alain Voge 2005 Harmonie Rhône White Blend (Saint-Péray) $28. Fresh, almost floral, with a touch of almonds as well. This is a nicely balanced blend of the richness and weight of Marsanne and its honeyed stone-fruit flavors, with the freshness retained by fermenting in stainless steel. Drink now. 89 *—J.C. (9/1/2007)*

Alain Voge 2005 Syrah (Saint-Joseph) $NA. The first vintage for Voge in Saint-Joseph, this is an attractive, peppery wine bursting with bold red fruit flavors that finish cool and spicy. Drink now–2015. 89 *—J.C. (9/1/2007)*

Alain Voge 2005 Les Peyrouses Syrah (Côtes-du-Rhône) $17. This 100% Syrah is filled with effusive bright berry fruit, liberally seasoned with a dusting of cracked pepper. It's a little light, but offers an easy-to-drink authentic taste of the northern Rhône at a realistic price. 87 *—J.C. (9/1/2007)*

Alain Voge 2004 Les Vieilles Fontaines Syrah (Cornas) $100. A selection of Voge's oldest vines from an especially granitic southeastern exposure, this is more of everything than the Vieilles Vignes bottling—more intense, smoky, dense and dark. The mouthfeel is rich and nearly syrupy, while the flavors burst with cherries and spice that linger on the finish. 91 *—J.C. (9/1/2007)*

Alain Voge 2003 Les Vieilles Fontaines Syrah (Cornas) $NA. From miniscule yields and the product of an outrageously hot, dry summer, this wine still shows some spice, but also jammier cherry and raspberry notes. Syrupy, jammy fruit dominates, but this wine doesn't lack for structure. Give it another 10 years in the cellar and its terroir will be more obvious. 92 *—J.C. (9/1/2007)*

Alain Voge 2004 Vieilles Vignes Syrah (Cornas) $67. Elegant and lighter, in the style of the vintage, with peppery and dried spice notes accenting fresh cherries. Nicely smooth, balanced and easy to drink. Drink–2015. 88 *—J.C. (9/1/2007)*

ALBERT BICHOT

Albert Bichot 2002 Chardonnay (Criots-Bâtard-Montrachet) $250. 92 —*R.V. (9/1/2004)*

Albert Bichot 2003 Domaine du Pavillon Les Charmes Premier Cru Chardonnay (Meursault) $76. 92 —*R.V. (9/1/2005)*

Albert Bichot 2003 Domaine Long-Depaquit Grand Cru Les Vaudésirs Chardonnay (Chablis) $NA. 90 —*R.V. (12/31/2006)*

Albert Bichot 2003 Domaine Long-Depaquit Les Vaucopins Premier Cru Chardonnay (Chablis) $NA. 88 —*R.V. (12/31/2006)*

Albert Bichot 2003 Domaine du Clos Frantin Pinot Noir (Clos Vougeot) $NA. 90 —*R.V. (12/31/2006)*

Albert Bichot 2003 Domaine du Clos Frantin Pinot Noir (Echezeaux) $130. 93 —*R.V. (9/1/2005)*

Albert Bichot 2004 Domaine du Clos Frantin Clos de Vougeot Pinot Noir (Clos Vougeot) $160. A dry, tannin-driven wine, though, underneath, there is fine fruit. The wine is layered, structured with plum skin, leather and herbal flavors, along with pure fruit acidity. It should develop well. **92** —*R.V. (3/1/2007)*

Albert Bichot 2002 Domaine du Clos Frantin Echézeaux Pinot Noir (Echezeaux) $125. 84 —*R.V. (9/1/2004)*

Albert Bichot 2004 Domaine du Clos Frantin Les Malconsorts Premier Cru Pinot Noir (Vosne-Romanée) $122. Ripe, soft, sweet fruit gives this wine great charm. There are some tannins, but in the big picture, they disappear behind the ripe strawberries and the touches of wood. Acidity is there, but more in the feel than in taste. **88** —*R.V. (3/1/2007)*

Albert Bichot 2004 Domaine du Clos Frantin Les Murots Pinot Noir (Gevrey-Chambertin) $60. Dark and tannic, this is a wine that has power and a dense structure. Put this dry, firm character down to youth, because there is clean, ripe red berry fruit there that needs 2–3 years to tame the tannins. The finish is dry, but there is a good lift of acidity. **90** —*R.V. (3/1/2007)*

Albert Bichot 2002 Domaine du Pavillon Aloxe-Corton Clos des Maréchaudes Premier Cru Pinot Noir (Aloxe-Corton) $52. 84 —*R.V. (9/1/2004)*

Albert Bichot 2003 Domaine du Pavillon Clos des Maréchaudes Pinot Noir (Corton) $100. 92 —*R.V. (9/1/2005)*

Albert Bichot 1996 Millennium Cuvée Pinot Noir (Gevrey-Chambertin) $29. 93 *(11/15/1999)*

ALBERT MANN

Albert Mann NV Brut Sparkling Blend (Crémant d'Alsace) $22. 90 —*R.V. (6/1/2006)*

ALBERT PIC

Albert Pic 1997 Montmains Premier Cru White Blend (Chablis) $33. 87 —*M.S. (10/1/1999)*

ALFRED GRATIEN

Alfred Gratien NV Brut Champagne Blend (Champagne) $50. 88 —*R.V. (12/1/2005)*

Alfred Gratien NV Cuvée Paradis Brut Rosé Champagne Blend (Champagne) $110. 90 Cellar Selection —*R.V. (12/1/2005)*

ALPHONSE MELLOT

Alphonse Mellot 2005 En Grands Champs Pinot Noir (Sancerre) $115. While Alphonse Mellot's La Demoiselle shows the weight of Pinot Noir, this En Grands Champs, grown on chalk soil, shows purity of fruit. There may be some leanness to it, but that is balanced by the red berry flavor, and the fresh, vital acidity. The wood element shows through, but it's the fruit that dominates. **91** —*R.V. (10/1/2007)*

Alphonse Mellot 2005 Génération XIX Pinot Noir (Sancerre) $130. There have been 19 generations of Mellots, all called Alphonse, in charge of the family estate in Sancerre. This wine celebrates that fact in dense fruits and dry tannins, a wine that has weight, and certainly needs to age. At this stage, the wood is showing dominance, but there's plenty of fruit here. **92 Cellar Selection** —*R.V. (10/1/2007)*

Alphonse Mellot 2005 La Demoiselle Pinot Noir (Sancerre) $100. Grown on clay soils, this Pinot-Noir based wine has weight and power. Shows some velvet ripeness, but also boasts dense tannins and black plum flavors. Balanced wood is a fine and firm counterweight to the opulent fruit. **92** —*R.V. (10/1/2007)*

Alphonse Mellot 2005 La Moussière Pinot Noir (Sancerre) $65. For a red Sancerre, this is rich, with ripe cherries and black plum skin flavors, reinforced by well-judged wood. The acidity is also well in balance, a layer that lifts the denseness of the fruit and dry tannins. **90** —*R.V. (10/1/2007)*

Alphonse Mellot 2002 Edmond Sauvignon Blanc (Sancerre) $61. Named after Alphonse Jr's father (Edmond Alphonse), this is the top wine from the Mellot estate. With its extra bottle age and wood flavors this is not typical Sancerre. But it is a great wine, packed with ripe, mature fruits, with honey and pistachio flavors and a round, smooth, creamy, caramel character. **94** —*R.V. (9/1/2007)*

Alphonse Mellot 2005 Génération XIX Sauvignon Blanc (Sancerre) $61. Alphonse Mellot Jr, the 19th generation of Alphonses to make wine at La Moussière, has raised his family's domaine to a new height. This is so evident in this super-rich, concentrated wine, but one that doesn't lose sight of its cool climate, chalk soil origins. So there's great opulence, but also a vivid green acidity that strikes right through the wine. **93 Editors' Choice** —*R.V. (9/1/2007)*

Alphonse Mellot 2006 La Moussière Sauvignon Blanc (Sancerre) $30. This is one of Alphonse Mellot's simpler wines, a deliciously fresh, summer meadow wine, with herbs and perfumed flowers and a stream of acidity running through. **88** —*R.V. (9/1/2007)*

ALTER EGO DE PALMER

Alter Ego de Palmer 2005 Barrel Sample Bordeaux Blend (Margaux) $NA. 91 —*R.V. (6/1/2006)*

ANDRÉ ET EDMOND FIGEAT

André et Edmond Figeat 2005 Les Chaumiennes Sauvignon Blanc (Pouilly-Fumé) $18. 90 —*R.V. (8/1/2006)*

ANDRE ET MIREILLE TISSOT

Andre et Mireille Tissot 1995 Brut Sparkling Blend (Crémant de Jura) $24. 89 —*R.V. (6/1/2006)*

Andre et Mireille Tissot 1996 Extra Brut Sparkling Blend (Crémant de Jura) $NA. 87 —*R.V. (6/1/2006)*

ANDRE LORENTZ

Andre Lorentz 2005 Cuvée Particulière Riesling (Alsace) $15. Muted flavors of green apple and lime pith are the only expressions of fruit in this medium-weight selection. Riding on the aromas of petrol and earthy minerality with a short fleeting finish, you're left with a desire for more. **84** *(9/1/2007)*

Andre Lorentz 2003 Cuvée Particuliere Riesling (Alsace) $11. 87 Best Buy —*J.C. (11/1/2005)*

ANTONIN RODET

Antonin Rodet 2004 Chardonnay (Meursault) $43. 88 —*R.V. (12/1/2006)*

Antonin Rodet 2001 Chardonnay (Bourgogne) $11. 84 —*J.C. (10/1/2003)*

Antonin Rodet 1999 Chardonnay (Chassagne-Montrachet) $40. 87 *(12/31/2001)*

Antonin Rodet 1999 Pinot Noir (Gevrey-Chambertin) $34. 89 *(1/1/2004)*

Antonin Rodet 1999 Pinot Noir (Nuits-St.-Georges) $37. 88 *(12/31/2001)*

Antonin Rodet 1998 Pinot Noir (Nuits-St.-Georges) $37. 88 —*P.G. (11/1/2002)*

Antonin Rodet 2002 Les Porêts Pinot Noir (Nuits-St.-Georges) $44. 89 —*R.V. (9/1/2004)*

Antonin Rodet 2002 Rue de Chaux Premier Cru Pinot Noir (Nuits-St. Georges) $57. 88 —*R.V. (9/1/2004)*

ARNOUX & FILS

Arnoux & Fils 2003 1717 Grenache-Syrah (Vacqueyras) $39. 87 —*J.C. (11/15/2006)*

Arnoux & Fils 2003 Seigneur de Lauris Rhône Red Blend (Côtes-du-Rhône) $10. 83 —*J.C. (11/15/2006)*

Arnoux & Fils 2003 Vieux Clocher Rhône Red Blend (Vacqueyras) $NA. 85 —*J.C. (11/15/2006)*

Arnoux & Fils 2005 Vieux Clocher Rhône White Blend (Vacqueyras) $17. 87 —*J.C. (11/15/2006)*

ARTHUR METZ

Arthur Metz 2003 Cuvée Anne-Laure Gewürztraminer (Alsace) $11. 86 Best Buy —*J.C. (11/1/2005)*

Arthur Metz 2005 Cuvée Anne-Laure Pinot Blanc (Alsace) $12. Easy-drinking, this plump wine offers scents of apple, citrus, honey and similar flavors. It's a cleanly made, fruity quaffer that finishes with a touch of anise. Drink now. **86** —*J.C. (7/1/2007)*

Arthur Metz 2004 Cuvée Anne-Laure Riesling (Alsace) $12. Despite being rather full-bodied, this isn't soft at all, instead offering up scents of lime and lemon and firm, assertive flavors of apple and citrus. Finishes crisp and long. This could work as a mouthwatering apéritif or perhaps with raw shellfish. **87 Best Buy** —*J.C. (7/1/2007)*

AUGUSTE ET PIERRE-MARIE CLAPE

Auguste et Pierre-Marie Clape 2004 Syrah (Cornas) $82. Seems to have almost a hint of acetate on the nose, but there's no evidence of volatility on the mildly creamy palate, where bright cherry fruit is accented by cracked peppercorns. Turns a bit chewier on the finish, but remains balanced. Drink 2008–2014. **90** *—J.C. (9/1/2007)*

Auguste et Pierre-Marie Clape 2003 Syrah (Cornas) $82. Rich, creamy and lush, this is like no other Clape Cornas before or since. Jammy raspberry fruit coats the palate, yet without seeming simple or heavy because there's also a remarkable sense of minerality and balance. Long on the finish, buffered by soft tannins. As this ages, expect to see some of the jamminess recede and more of the minerality emerge. Drink 2010–2025, possibly longer. **94 Cellar Selection** *—J.C. (9/1/2007)*

Auguste et Pierre-Marie Clape 2004 Renaissance Syrah (Cornas) $57. Intended to offer a taste of Cornas at an earlier age, the 2004 Renaissance features bright strawberry fruit. It's a bit peppery and herbal, with a light, less tannic structure. Approachable now. **87** *—J.C. (9/1/2007)*

Auguste et Pierre-Marie Clape 2003 Renaissance Syrah (Cornas) $57. For a cuvée intended to be drunk young, this is packed with material. It's thick and dense with jammy raspberry fruit, a product of the hot vintage and tiny yields. Still slightly tannic, so hold off another couple of years. Drink 2010–2020. **90** *—J.C. (9/1/2007)*

AUGUSTIN FLORENT

Augustin Florent NV Syrah (Vin de Pays d'Oc) $9. 82 *(10/1/2001)*

AYALA

Ayala NV Brut Majeur Champagne Blend (Champagne) $NA. A beautifully balanced non-vintage, in the lighter style that is Ayala's hallmark. It is fresh, but shows a good amount of blend with older wines to give weight and complexity. The green fruit flavors are well balanced with secondary aromas of almonds, green berries and lively, but not dominant acidity. **91 Editors' Choice** *—R.V. (12/1/2007)*

Ayala NV Rosé Majeur Brut Champagne Blend (Champagne) $NA. Onion skin veering to pink color for this stylishly presented wine from Ayala, now owned by Bollinger. It has some fresh raspberry fruits, but goes further with its seriously crisp, dry acidity and delicate, elegant balance with structure and mature flavors. **91** *—R.V. (12/1/2007)*

Ayala NV Zéro Dosage Champagne Blend (Champagne) $NA. "Zéro Dosage" means just that; the resulting wine is very dry. It has great crisp, piercing grapefruit freshness, with hints of nuttiness and a lively final acidity. Some bottle age should help tame it. **88** *—R.V. (12/1/2007)*

BAILLY-LAPIERRE

Bailly-Lapierre 2004 Chardonnay Brut Chardonnay (Crémant de Bourgogne) $19. 90 *—R.V. (6/1/2006)*

Bailly-Lapierre 2004 Blanc de Blancs Brut Sparkling Blend (Crémant de Bourgogne) $20. 88 *—R.V. (6/1/2006)*

Bailly-Lapierre NV Rosé Brut Sparkling Blend (Crémant de Bourgogne) $20. 86 *—R.V. (6/1/2006)*

BALLOT MILLOT ET FILS

Ballot Millot et Fils 2004 Les Criots Chardonnay (Meursault) $49. 88 *—R.V. (12/1/2006)*

BALMA VENITIA

Balma Venitia 2005 Des Toques Rhône Red Blend (Côtes-du-Rhône) $NA. 83 *—J.C. (11/15/2006)*

Balma Venitia 2005 Terre des Farisiens Rhône Red Blend (Beaumes-de-Venise) $NA. 83 *—J.C. (11/15/2006)*

Balma Venitia 2004 Terres du Trias Rhône Red Blend (Beaumes-de-Venise) $NA. 84 *—J.C. (11/15/2006)*

BARNAUT

Barnaut 1998 Champagne Blend (Champagne) $58. 86 *—R.V. (11/1/2006)*

BARON DE BRANE

Baron de Brane 2004 Bordeaux Blend (Margaux) $NA. The second wine of Château Brane Cantenac, just released. This shows the the stalky side of Margaux, although the fruit is fresh, with dry tannins and black fruit flavors. Drink this for its ease and delicacy. **87** *—R.V. (2/1/2007)*

BARON GASSIER

Baron Gassier 2003 Rosé Blend (Côtes de Provence) $9. 84 *—J.C. (12/1/2004)*

BARON PHILIPPE DE ROTHSCHILD

Baron Philippe de Rothschild 2000 Baron'arques Bordeaux Blend (Vin de Pays de L'Aude) $40. 89 *—M.S. (1/1/2004)*

Baron Philippe de Rothschild 2006 Le Rosé de Mouton Cadet Bordeaux Blend (Bordeaux Rosé) $9. The first vintage of this wine from the familiar Mouton Cadet brand. The mainly Merlot blend is soft, lightly fruity, not quite sweet, with gentle crushed strawberry flavors. A delicate aftertaste. **84** *—R.V. (7/1/2007)*

Baron Philippe de Rothschild 2002 Mouton Cadet Rouge Bordeaux Blend (Bordeaux) $8. 86 Best Buy *—J.C. (6/1/2005)*

Baron Philippe de Rothschild 2003 Mouton Cadet Bordeaux White Blend (Bordeaux) $8. 84 Best Buy *—J.C. (6/1/2005)*

Baron Philippe de Rothschild 1999 Merlot (Vin de Pays d'Oc) $10. 85 *—D.T. (2/1/2002)*

Baron Philippe de Rothschild 1998 Baron'Arques Rhône Red Blend (Vin de Pays d'Oc) $45. 88 *—M.M. (2/1/2002)*

Baron Philippe de Rothschild 2000 Viognier (Vin de Pays d'Oc) $10. 85 *—S.H. (10/1/2001)*

Baron Philippe de Rothschild 1999 Mouton Cadet White Blend (Bordeaux) $11. 81 *—J.C. (3/1/2001)*

BARONS EDMUND BENJAMIN DE ROTHSCHILD

Barons Edmund Benjamin de Rothschild 1998 Haut-Medoc Bordeaux Blend (Haut-Médoc) $27. 88 *—J.C. (4/1/2001)*

BARTH RENÉ

Barth René 2002 Vignoble de Bennwihr Pinot Blanc (Alsace) $13. 88 Best Buy *—J.C. (8/1/2006)*

Barth René 2003 Vignoble de Bennwihr Pinot Gris (Alsace) $17. 85 *(2/1/2006)*

Barth René 2003 Rebgarten Riesling (Alsace) $19. 83 *—J.C. (8/1/2006)*

Barth René 2004 Vignoble de Bennwihr Riesling (Alsace) $13. A dry, petrolly Riesling, this boasts classic green-apple and lime aromas and flavors and a long, crisply acidic finish. A solid effort that avoids residual sugar but also excessive leanness. **86** *—J.C. (7/1/2007)*

BARTON & GUESTIER

Barton & Guestier 2000 Bordeaux Blend (Médoc) $10. 87 *—R.V. (12/1/2004)*

Barton & Guestier 2004 Thomas Barton Reserve Bordeaux Blend (Bordeaux) $NA. This is the simplest wine in a large range from different Bordeaux appellations. It's simple, with fresh slightly green fruit flavors, dry tannins and a touch of blackcurrants. **83** *—R.V. (2/1/2007)*

Barton & Guestier 2004 Thomas Barton Reserve Bordeaux Blend (Margaux) $NA. An attractive, smoky wine, with soft fruits and some firm tannins. It has some of the right charm for a Margaux, with fresh red fruits and light acidity. **85** *—R.V. (6/1/2007)*

Barton & Guestier 2004 Thomas Barton Reserve Bordeaux Blend (Médoc) $NA. Well-structured, with plenty of cassis and fruit cake flavors, this is a solid, quite dense wine that shows dry tannins, with good ripe fruit as part of the mix. **85** *—R.V. (6/1/2007)*

Barton & Guestier 2004 Thomas Barton Reserve Privée Bordeaux Blend (Médoc) $NA. Private Reserve, it is called, and this full-bodied, well-wooded wine is a definite cut above the other Médoc in the Thomas Barton range. It is has structure, density, well-defined black fruits and a dry, tannic core, which could even promise some aging. This nudges up to a decent château wine. **87** *—R.V. (6/1/2007)*

Barton & Guestier 2004 Thomasm Barton Reserve Bordeaux Blend (Saint-Emilion) $NA. A ripe, full, fruity wine, showing Merlot softness and some attractive red berry and fruit cake flavors. This has a light sense of structure, but needs no aging. **85** *—R.V. (2/1/2007)*

Barton & Guestier 2005 Thomas Barton Reserve Bordeaux White Blend (Sauternes) $NA. Pleasantly sweet, this wine has all the right characteristics of Sauternes—even a touch of dry botrytis flavor—in miniature. There's not much depth of flavor, but it is certainly a good drink for desserts – or as the French would do it, with blue cheese. **85** *—R.V. (11/1/2007)*

Barton & Guestier 2005 Thomas Barton Reserve Bordeaux White Blend (Graves) $NA. A white Graves, part of the Thomas Barton range, this has good, soft, creamy fresh fruit and flavors of green plums, some spice and a fresh, full character. **86** *—R.V. (11/1/2007)*

Barton & Guestier 2002 Cabernet Sauvignon (Vin de Pays d'Oc) $6. 83 *—R.V. (12/1/2004)*

Barton & Guestier 2006 Bistro Wine Cabernet Sauvignon (Vin de Pays d'Oc) $9. With grapes from the Limoux region, the coolest in Languedoc, this wine goes for structure, with stalky, dry tannins. Those flavors, and the black currant fruits, are offset by considerable soft finishing sweetness 82 —*R.V. (12/15/2007)*

Barton & Guestier 2000 French Tom Private Collection Cabernet Sauvignon (Vin de Pays d'Oc) $14. 85 —*S.H. (1/1/2002)*

Barton & Guestier 2002 Chardonnay (Vin de Pays d'Oc) $6. 82 —*R.V. (12/1/2004)*

Barton & Guestier 2002 Chardonnay (Mâcon-Villages) $9. 84 —*R.V. (12/1/2004)*

Barton & Guestier 2000 Chardonnay Saint-Louis Tradition 2000 Chardonnay (Mâcon-Villages) $13. 86 —*S.H. (1/1/2002)*

Barton & Guestier 2006 Bistro Wine Chardonnay (Vin de Pays d'Oc) $10. A simple, clean and fresh Chardonnay, round and fruity, with some vanilla, spice and white peach fruit flavors. The aftertaste is soft, slightly sweet. 83 —*R.V. (12/15/2007)*

Barton & Guestier 1998 Reserve Chardonnay (Vin de Pays d'Oc) $10. 86 Best Buy *(5/1/2000)*

Barton & Guestier 2001 Tradition Chardonnay (Pouilly-Fuissé) $9. 85 Best Buy —*S.H. (12/1/2004)*

Barton & Guestier 1999 Tradition Saint-Louis Chardonnay (Mâcon-Villages) $8. 82 —*D.T. (2/1/2002)*

Barton & Guestier 2001 Tradition Chenin Blanc (Vouvray) $NA. 84 *(11/15/2002)*

Barton & Guestier 2001 Tradition Gamay (Beaujolais-Villages) $8. 83 —*J.C. (11/15/2003)*

Barton & Guestier 2002 Gamay Noir (Beaujolais) $9. 82 —*R.V. (12/1/2004)*

Barton & Guestier 2002 Melon (Muscadet Sèvre Et Maine) $9. 81 —*R.V. (12/1/2004)*

Barton & Guestier 2002 Merlot (Vin de Pays d'Oc) $7. 82 —*S.H. (9/1/2004)*

Barton & Guestier 1999 Merlot (Vin de Pays d'Oc) $7. 82 —*D.T. (2/1/2002)*

Barton & Guestier 2000 French Tom Private Collection Merlot (Vin de Pays d'Oc) $14. 83 —*S.H. (1/1/2002)*

Barton & Guestier 1998 Reserve Merlot (Vin de Pays d'Oc) $10. 86 *(5/1/2000)*

Barton & Guestier 2005 Bistro Wine Pinot Noir (Vin de Pays d'Oc) $10. Lively and juicy, this is packed with fresh red cherry fruits, red currants and some wood. It's round, soft, only lightly tannic. 84 —*R.V. (12/15/2007)*

Barton & Guestier 2000 Saint-Louis Beaujolais Tradition Red Blend (Beaujolais) $13. 84 —*S.H. (1/1/2002)*

Barton & Guestier 2001 Rhône Red Blend (Côtes-du-Rhône) $9. 84 —*R.V. (12/1/2004)*

Barton & Guestier 2001 Tradition Rhône Red Blend (Châteauneuf-du-Pape) $9. 83 —*R.V. (3/1/2004)*

Barton & Guestier 2000 Tradition Rhône Red Blend (Côtes-du-Rhône) $NA. 85 *(11/15/2002)*

Barton & Guestier 2001 Founder's Collection Sauvignon Blanc (Bordeaux) $10. 84 *(11/15/2002)*

Barton & Guestier 2002 Shiraz (Vin de Pays d'Oc) $6. 82 —*R.V. (12/1/2004)*

Barton & Guestier 2001 Syrah (Vin de Pays d'Oc) $7. 83 *(11/15/2002)*

Barton & Guestier 1998 Tradition White Blend (Pouilly-Fuissé) $17. 86 *(5/1/2000)*

BAUCHET PÈRE ET FILS

Bauchet Père et Fils NV Brut Sélection Champagne Blend (Champagne) $NA. 81 —*M.S. (12/15/2003)*

Bauchet Père et Fils NV Premier Cru Brut Sélection Champagne Blend (Champagne) $35. 89 —*M.S. (12/15/2003)*

Bauchet Père et Fils NV Premier Cru Reserve Brut Champagne Blend (Champagne) $40. 85 —*J.C. (12/1/2004)*

Bauchet Père et Fils NV Sélection Roland Bouchet Champagne Blend (Champagne) $33. 83 —*M.S. (12/15/2003)*

BEAUMONT DES CRAYÈRES

Beaumont des Crayères 1997 Fleur de Prestige Champagne Blend (Champagne) $45. 90 —*R.V. (12/1/2004)*

Beaumont des Crayères 1998 Nostalgie Brut Champagne Blend (Champagne) $NA. 90 —*R.V. (11/1/2006)*

BELLEFONTAINE

Bellefontaine 1999 Cabernet Sauvignon (Vin de Pays d'Oc) $7. 83 —*D.T. (2/1/2002)*

BERNARD BAUDRY

Bernard Baudry 2005 Le Clos Guillot Cabernet Franc (Chinon) $NA. One of Baudry's top wines, Le Clos Guillot is made from ungrafted vines, which seems to give an extra intensity to the fruit, as well as power to the tannins. The fruit and the tannins are dense, solid, intense and complex. This is a ripe, spice- and red fruit-flavored wine, certainly a wine for aging—up to 10 years, maybe more. 93 —*R.V. (4/1/2007)*

Bernard Baudry 2005 Les Grézeaux Cabernet Franc (Chinon) $NA. Bernard Baudry is among the very best producers in Chinon, conjuring rich wines from his vineyards at Sonnay, just east of Chinon. Les Grézeaux is testimony to the power of his wines: full of intensely rich, smoky fruits and dark plums, the tannins are solid, promising at least 3–4 years'aging. 92 Editors' Choice —*R.V. (4/1/2007)*

BERNARD CHAVE

Bernard Chave 1999 Tête de Cuvée Syrah (Crozes-Hermitage) $21. 88 *(11/1/2001)*

BERNARD MAGREZ

Bernard Magrez 2004 Château Bois Pertuis Bordeaux Blend (Bordeaux) $24. Magrez calls wines like this 75% Merlot, "the future of midpriced Bordeaux." It's lush and ripe, with black cherry and mocha shadings, and only a hint of herbaceousness. Not overly rich or tannic, it should drink well for the next 5–8 years. Imported by Bernard Magrez. 87 *(11/1/2007)*

Bernard Magrez 2004 Château Haut Mouleyre Bordeaux White Blend (Bordeaux Blanc) $20. Magrez purchased this estate in 2003, so this is the first vintage he's had complete control. Primarily a blend of Sémillon and Sauvignon Gris, it's fresh and apple-y, with hints of grapefruit and lime. Finishes long and crisp. Imported by Bernard Magrez. 86 *(11/1/2007)*

Bernard Magrez 2004 Château La Tour Carnet Bordeaux White Blend (Bordeaux Blanc) $65. From young vines (planted in 2001), this is a blend of Sauvignon Blanc, Sauvignon Gris, Sémillon and a small amount of Muscadelle. Marked by toast and vanilla, it's plump and round on the palate, finishing with some oaky spice. Imported by Bernard Magrez. 90 *(11/1/2007)*

Bernard Magrez 2004 Si Mon Père Savait Red Blend (Côtes du Roussillon) $50. Named in reference to the fact that his father kicked him out of the house at 12 years of age, this superripe cuvée of 46% Carignan, 30% Syrah, 19% Grenache and 5% Mourvèdre seems almost slightly nutty at first, then shows prune and chocolate notes that persist through the extended finish. It's a bit alcoholic, but richly textured and velvety. Imported by Bernard Magrez. 91 *(11/1/2007)*

Bernard Magrez 2003 Château Guerry Rhône Red Blend (Côtes de Bourg) $32. Unusual for Bordeaux, this chateau's plantings contain 20% Malbec, imparting a strong blackberry character to the wine. There's smoky oak, too, and intriguing spice and juiciness on the finish. Imported by Bernard Magrez. 89 *(11/1/2007)*

BESSERAT DE BELLEFON

Besserat de Bellefon NV Cuvée des Moines Blanc de Blancs Brut Champagne Blend (Champagne) $NA. 83 *(1/1/2004)*

Besserat de Bellefon NV Cuvée des Moines Brut Champagne Blend (Champagne) $32. 82 *(1/1/2004)*

Besserat de Bellefon NV Cuvée des Moines Brut Rosé Champagne Blend (Champagne) $45. 84 *(1/1/2004)*

BIELER PÈRE ET FILS

Bieler Père et Fils 2006 Sabine Rosé Blend (Coteaux d'Aix en Provence) $10. A much better effort than the previous vintage, with a plump, easygoing mouthfeel and bright, fruit-forward flavors. It's a bit obvious, but friendly and fresh. Drink now. 86 Best Buy —*J.C. (7/1/2007)*

BILLECART-SALMON

Billecart-Salmon NV Brut Rosé Champagne Blend (Champagne) $68. 92 Editors' Choice —*R.V. (12/1/2005)*

Billecart-Salmon NV Réserve Brut Champagne Blend (Champagne) $45. 92 —*R.V. (12/1/2005)*

Billecart-Salmon 1998 Blanc de Blancs Brut Chardonnay (Champagne) $NA. From a relatively open vintage, this is a wine that is generous, rounded, full of green fruits, and balanced with a ripe texture. It has weight, but has more to do with sheer pleasure. It could age, maybe over five years, but its nutty hints show it is ready to drink. 94 —*R.V. (12/1/2007)*

Billecart-Salmon NV Grand Cru Blanc de Blancs Brut Chardonnay (Champagne) $NA. Crisply dry, and very fresh, this is dominated by green, tangy fruits, pink grapefruit and a core of minerality. It has a lightness, but it does need to age, for its acidity is still massive. 93 —*R.V. (12/1/2007)*

BLANC DE LYNCH-BAGES

Blanc de Lynch-Bages 2003 Bordeaux White Blend (Bordeaux) $35. 92 —*R.V. (6/1/2005)*

BLASON DE BOURGOGNE

Blason de Bourgogne NV Cuvée Brut Champagne Blend (Crémant de Bourgogne) $10. 87 —*R.V. (6/1/2006)*

BOIZEL

Boizel 1998 Brut Champagne Blend (Champagne) $85. 89 —*R.V. (11/1/2006)*

Boizel 1995 Joyau de France Champagne Blend (Champagne) $140. 88 —*R.V. (11/1/2006)*

BOLLINGER

Bollinger 1996 La Grande Année Brut Champagne Blend (Champagne) $90. 93 —*J.C. (12/15/2003)*

Bollinger 1992 La Grande Année Brut Champagne Blend (Champagne) $90. 89 *(12/15/2001)*

Bollinger 1996 R.D. Extra Brut Champagne Blend (Champagne) $190. 97 Cellar Selection —*R.V. (11/1/2006)*

Bollinger 1990 R.D. Extra Brut Champagne Blend (Champagne) $150. 90 *(12/15/2002)*

Bollinger 1988 R.D. Extra Brut Champagne Blend (Champagne) $150. 89 *(12/15/2001)*

Bollinger NV Special Cuvée Brut Champagne Blend (Champagne) $45. 90 Editors' Choice —*J.C. (12/1/2004)*

Bollinger NV Special Cuvée Brut Champagne Blend (Champagne) $45. 92 Editors' Choice —*P.G. (12/15/2002)*

Bollinger NV Special Cuvée Brut Champagne Blend (Champagne) $50. 94 Editors' Choice —*R.V. (12/1/2005)*

BONNAIRE

Bonnaire 1997 Blanc de Blancs Brut Champagne Blend (Champagne) $48. 93 Cellar Selection —*R.V. (12/1/2002)*

BONNY DOON

Bonny Doon 2001 Heart of Darkness Red Blend (Madiran) $18. 91 —*S.H. (2/1/2004)*

BORIE LA VITARELLE

Borie la Vitarelle 2004 Les Terres Blanches Grenache-Syrah (Saint-Chinian) $15. 86 —*R.V. (12/31/2006)*

Borie la Vitarelle 2005 Cuvée des Cigales Rhône Red Blend (Saint-Chinian) $11. 87 Best Buy —*R.V. (12/31/2006)*

Borie la Vitarelle 2004 Les Schistes Rhône Red Blend (Saint-Chinian) $16. "Schist" is the soil for this wine. Old vine Syrah, Grenache and Carignan give a dusty, tannic structure to the biodynamically grown fruit, which is packed with pure acidity and flavors of herbs and black plum skins. 90 —*R.V. (2/1/2007)*

BOSQUET DES PAPES

Bosquet des Papes 2003 Chante le Merle Vieilles Vignes Rhône Red Blend (Châteauneuf-du-Pape) $50. 94 —*R.V. (12/31/2005)*

BOUCHARD AÎNÉ & FILS

Bouchard Aîné & Fils 2001 Chardonnay (Pouilly-Fuissé) $18. 86 —*J.C. (10/1/2003)*

Bouchard Aîné & Fils 2000 Chardonnay (Meursault) $35. 85 —*J.C. (10/1/2003)*

Bouchard Aîné & Fils 1999 Chardonnay (Meursault) $35. 89 *(11/15/2001)*

Bouchard Aîné & Fils 2004 Champ Gain Premier Cru Chardonnay (Puligny-Montrachet) $67. 88 —*R.V. (12/1/2006)*

Bouchard Aîné & Fils 2004 Le Porusot Premier Cru Chardonnay (Meursault) $63. 87 —*R.V. (12/1/2006)*

Bouchard Aîné & Fils 2001 Gamay (Beaujolais-Villages) $8. 85 Best Buy —*J.C. (11/15/2003)*

Bouchard Aîné & Fils 2000 Pinot Noir (Bourgogne) $11. 80 —*J.C. (10/1/2003)*

Bouchard Aîné & Fils 2004 Pinot Noir (Clos de la Roche) $93. A wine from the Grand Cru Clos de la Roche in Morey-Saint-Denis, this is big, rounded, packed with cherry and balancing wood flavors. It has power and generosity. It also packs quite a firm tannin edge, which promises some good aging. 91 —*R.V. (3/1/2007)*

Bouchard Aîné & Fils 2004 Pinot Noir (Echezeaux) $113. Powerful and intense, with flavors of licorice, truffle and red fruits, this is a solid, concentrated wine with plenty of potential for aging. It shows the pedigree of its vineyard in the richness of the fruit as well as its structure, which leaves both freshness and dryness on the finish. 92 —*R.V. (3/1/2007)*

Bouchard Aîné & Fils 1999 Pinot Noir (Pommard) $NA. 86 —*P.G. (11/1/2002)*

Bouchard Aîné & Fils 1999 Pinot Noir (Chambolle-Musigny) $45. 88 —*R.V. (11/1/2002)*

Bouchard Aîné & Fils 2002 Clos du Roi Premier Cru Pinot Noir (Beaune) $32. 87 —*R.V. (9/1/2004)*

Bouchard Aîné & Fils 2000 Cuvée Signature Pinot Noir (Savigny-lès-Beaune) $25. 88 —*J.C. (10/1/2003)*

Bouchard Aîné & Fils 2000 Cuvée Signature La Maziere (Fixin) Pinot Noir (Burgundy) $24. 82 —*J.C. (10/1/2003)*

Bouchard Aîné & Fils 2004 En Champs Pinot Noir (Gevrey-Chambertin) $36. Although this is not a premier cru, the 19-acre En Champs vineyard has a reputation for making solid, meaty wines. This fits that bill, with its dark tannins and layers of acidity. It needs 2–3 years at least to mature. 88 —*R.V. (3/1/2007)*

Bouchard Aîné & Fils 2005 La Mazière Pinot Noir (Fixin) $22. Considering its youth, this is already an accessible wine, with the dry tannins well underneath the black plums, acidity and freshness. It won't age much, but it is attractive and drinkable now. 88 —*R.V. (3/1/2007)*

Bouchard Aîné & Fils 2004 Les Chaboeufs Premier Cru Pinot Noir (Nuits-St.-Georges) $58. At the southern end of Nuits-Saint-Georges, almost in Prémeaux, Les Chaboeufs is clay soil with some chalk. This wine is fresh, ready to drink, with plenty of red fruits and light tannins. 88 —*R.V. (3/1/2007)*

Bouchard Aîné & Fils 2004 Les Cras Pinot Noir (Chambolle-Musigny) $47. Les Cras is a tiny, six-acre vineyard in Chambolle-Musigny. This wine from Bouchard Aîné has great fresh fruit flavors, a softness and charm that is all Chambolle. There are tannins, certainly, but they are tucked underneath the dominant fruit. 90 —*R.V. (3/1/2007)*

BOUCHARD PÈRE & FILS

Bouchard Père & Fils 1998 Chardonnay (Chassagne-Montrachet) $39. 87 —*P.G. (7/1/2000)*

Bouchard Père & Fils 2005 Chardonnay (Chassagne-Montrachet) $48. 88 —*R.V. (12/1/2006)*

Bouchard Père & Fils 2004 Chardonnay (Meursault) $30. 88 —*R.V. (12/1/2006)*

Bouchard Père & Fils 2004 Chardonnay (Montrachet) $600. 95 Cellar Selection —*R.V. (12/1/2006)*

Bouchard Père & Fils 2003 Beaune du Château Premier Cru Chardonnay (Beaune) $75. 88 —*R.V. (9/1/2005)*

Bouchard Père & Fils 2003 Charmes Premier Cru Chardonnay (Meursault) $75. 90 —*R.V. (9/1/2005)*

Bouchard Père & Fils 2002 Chevalier Montrachet Chardonnay (Puligny-Montrachet) $165. 89 —*R.V. (9/1/2004)*

Bouchard Père & Fils 2003 Corton-Charlemagne Chardonnay (Corton-Charlemagne) $115. 94 —*R.V. (9/1/2005)*

Bouchard Père & Fils 2004 La Cabotte Chardonnay (Chevalier-Montrachet) $500. 96 —*R.V. (12/1/2006)*

Bouchard Père & Fils 2004 Les Clous Chardonnay (Meursault) $36. 90 Editors' Choice —*R.V. (12/1/2006)*

Bouchard Père & Fils 2004 Les Gouttes d'Or Premier Cru Chardonnay (Meursault) $84. 92 —*R.V. (12/1/2006)*

Bouchard Père & Fils 2004 Perrières Premier Cru Chardonnay (Meursault) $90. 91 —*R.V. (12/1/2006)*

Bouchard Pere & Fils 2004 Pinot Noir (Clos Vougeot) $200. Rich and velvety, this wine is out to seduce. It has delicious sweet strawberry fruits, soft but deceptively powerful tannins and the refreshing acidity and lift of 2004. It will still age—those tannins show that—but it is already enjoyable. 94 —*R.V. (3/1/2007)*

Bouchard Pere & Fils 2004 Pinot Noir (Bonnes-Mares) $235. At the northern limit of Chambolle-Musigny, the wines from Bonnes-Mares often take on the character of the solid, foursquare wines of Morey-Saint-Denis. But, as with this, they also keep some of the sensuousness of Chambolle. There's lovely, sweet fruit nicely restrained by the acidity and soft, dusty tannins. New wood flavors also add to the mix. 94 —*R.V. (3/1/2007)*

Bouchard Père & Fils 2000 Pinot Noir (Bonnes-Mares) $120. 96 Editors' Choice —*R.V. (11/1/2002)*

Bouchard Père & Fils 1998 Pinot Noir (Pommard) $45. 87 —*P.G. (7/1/2000)*

Bouchard Père & Fils 2003 Beaune du Château Premier Cru Pinot Noir (Beaune) $35. 89 —*R.V. (9/1/2005)*

Bouchard Père & Fils 2003 Beaune Marconnets Premier Cru Pinot Noir (Beaune) $50. 91 —*R.V. (9/1/2005)*

Bouchard Père & Fils 2003 Caillerets Ancienne Cuvée Carnot Premier Cru Pinot Noir (Volnay) $70. 91 —*R.V. (9/1/2005)*

Bouchard Pere & Fils 2004 Chambertin-Clos-de-Bèze Pinot Noir (Chambertin Clos de Bèze) $235. Rich, generous, almost opulent, this brings together great layers of black fruits and figs, wood smoothness and dense, sensual ripeness allied to acidity. There's power here, too, but it's a wine to revel in. **95** —*R.V. (3/1/2007)*

Bouchard Père & Fils 2003 Clos des Chenes Premier Cru Pinot Noir (Volnay) $70. 93 —*R.V. (9/1/2005)*

Bouchard Pere & Fils 2004 Echezeaux Pinot Noir (Echezeaux) $195. All the dark, brooding, intense character of Echezeaux is here. It is a magnificent wine, packed with sweet fruit, bold strokes of flavor, a stream of tannin and red fruit acidity at the end. It should age well, and long. Imported by Henriot, Inc. **95** —*R.V. (3/1/2007)*

Bouchard Père & Fils 2002 Echézeaux Pinot Noir (Echezeaux) $115. 94 —*R.V. (9/1/2004)*

Bouchard Père & Fils 1998 La Vignee Pinot Noir (Bourgogne) $10. 86 Best Buy —*P.G. (7/1/2000)*

Bouchard Père & Fils 2002 Le Corton Pinot Noir (Corton) $67. 94 —*R.V. (9/1/2004)*

Bouchard Père & Fils 2002 Les Cailles Premier Cru Pinot Noir (Nuits-St.-Georges) $60. 88 —*R.V. (9/1/2004)*

Bouchard Pere & Fils 2004 Les Cazetiers Premier Cru Pinot Noir (Gevrey-Chambertin) $110. Deep, intense and rich fruit is the hallmark of this powerful wine. Dark tannins lie under the concentrated juicy black fruits, which have a strong streak of acidity. This is a finely structured wine, offering great enjoyment now, and the promise of five years or more of aging. **91** —*R.V. (3/1/2007)*

Bouchard Père & Fils 2002 Rugiens Premier Cru Pinot Noir (Pommard) $58. 90 —*R.V. (9/1/2004)*

Bouchard Père & Fils 2002 Volnay Clos des Chênes Pinot Noir (Volnay) $46. 91 —*R.V. (9/1/2004)*

BOUVET-LADUBAY

Bouvet-Ladubay NV Trésor Rosé Cabernet Franc (Saumur) $20. 87 —*R.V. (6/1/2006)*

Bouvet-Ladubay NV Signature Brut Champagne Blend (Saumur) $13. 88 Best Buy —*P.G. (12/15/2002)*

Bouvet-Ladubay NV Brut Signature Chenin Blanc (Saumur) $13. 86 —*R.V. (6/1/2006)*

Bouvet-Ladubay NV Excellence Brut Rosé Sparkling Blend (Vin Mousseux) $15. 86 —*M.D. (12/15/2006)*

Bouvet-Ladubay 1998 Saphir Brut Vintage Sparkling Blend (Saumur) $85. 87 —*M.S. (12/15/2003)*

BROTTE

Brotte 2004 La Doucejoie Muscat (Muscat de Beaumes de Venise) $40. The Brotte version of the region's traditional dessert wine is a bit spirity, but fresh, with bold scents of chestnut blossom and orange rind and clean, marmalade-like flavors. Drink now. **88** *(8/1/2007)*

Brotte 2005 *Barrel Sample* Château de Bord Croix de Frégère Laudun Rhône Red Blend (Côtes-du-Rhône Villages) $22. 87 —*J.C. (11/15/2006)*

Brotte 2005 Château de Bord Laudun Rhône Red Blend (Côtes-du-Rhône Villages) $20. From one of the family's own estates, this is a fine effort. Rich flavors of pie cherries and a bit of dried spice glide easily across the palate, cushioned by soft, plush tannins. Drink now–2012. **89** *(8/1/2007)*

Brotte 2003 Château de Bord Laudun Rhône Red Blend (Côtes-du-Rhône Villages) $16. 84 —*J.C. (2/1/2005)*

Brotte 2004 Domaine Barville Rhône Red Blend (Châteauneuf-du-Pape) $40. Produced from a Brotte-owned property, this Châteauneuf is a deliberate counterpoint to the Père Anselme bottling. It sees some new oak, giving it a slightly toasty character to go with dried cherries, prune and baking spices. Firm on the finish; try after 2008. **87** *(8/1/2007)*

Brotte 2003 Domaine Bouvencourt Rhône Red Blend (Vacqueyras) $25. 86 —*J.C. (2/1/2005)*

Brotte 2005 Domaine de la Grivelière Rhône Red Blend (Lirac) $16. Has a touch of roasted character to the black cherry fruit, but the mouthfeel is pleasantly plump and creamy, and hints of black pepper perk up the finish. **85** *(8/1/2007)*

Brotte 2005 Domaine Grosset Cairanne Rhône Red Blend (Côtes-du-Rhône Villages) $20. A Brotte-owned estate, Domaine Grosset shows that when the family puts their heart into doing the best they can, their efforts are rewarded. It's rich and spicy, with cola and plum aromas and flavors that are dense and almost fruitcake-like, finishing with hints of coffee and plum. Drink now-2015. **90** *(8/1/2007)*

Brotte 2005 Domaine Marandy Rhône Red Blend (Saint-Joseph) $25. Lifted cracked pepper and cherry scents on the nose are rounded a bit on the palate by hints of caramelly oak, but this is still a good representation of northern Rhône Syrah, finishing dry and peppery. **87** *(8/1/2007)*

Brotte 2003 Vieilles Vignes Rhône Red Blend (Châteauneuf-du-Pape) $45. 87 —*R.V. (12/31/2005)*

Brotte 2006 Les Eglantiers Rosé Blend (Tavel) $22. This bright, vibrant pink wine ably combines ample fruit with cool, minerally notes to make a complex, tongue-tingling whole. Wet stone aromas accent cherry-berry flavors, and although the wine is round, there's a hint of CO2 to help provide freshness on the finish. **87** —*J.C. (7/1/2007)*

Brotte 2005 Domaine du Versant Doré Viognier (Condrieu) $50. This is half barrel-fermented, and it shows in the wine's scents of toast, but there's plenty of fruit to back that up. Honeysuckle, peach and melon aromas and flavors round out the palate, finishing with hints of peppery spice. Drink now. **90** *(8/1/2007)*

Brotte 2003 Domaine du Versant Doré Viognier (Condrieu) $48. 82 —*J.C. (2/1/2005)*

Brotte 2003 Les Brottiers White Blend (Côtes-du-Rhône) $10. 89 —*J.C. (2/1/2005)*

BRUNO HUNOLD

Bruno Hunold 2004 Gewürztraminer (Alsace) $20. A plump, off-dry style of Gewürztraminer, Hunold's 2004 features a bouquet that could be right out of a textbook: rose petals, lychee and a bit of ginger. This is fresh and spicy, not overblown, and without any bitterness on the finish. **89** —*J.C. (7/1/2007)*

Bruno Hunold 2005 Pinot Gris (Alsace) $20. Weighty and rich, this is a broad Pinot Gris that ideally requires a similarly rich dish as an accompaniment—perhaps a chicken or fish sauced with cream. Hints of almonds accent the melon and peach flavors, while the finish picks up hints of peppery spice and restrained minerality. **87** —*J.C. (7/1/2007)*

Bruno Hunold 2004 Pinot Gris (Alsace) $19. 84 *(2/1/2006)*

Bruno Hunold 2005 Riesling (Alsace) $18. Classically proportioned, with crisp acidity that balances the wine's weight. Lime and green apple aromas set the stage, followed by hints of riper tree fruits and petrol, all the while kept focused by bright citrus flavors. **87** —*J.C. (7/1/2007)*

BRUNO PAILLARD

Bruno Paillard 1995 Brut Champagne Blend (Champagne) $85. 90 *(12/1/2001)*

Bruno Paillard 1990 N.P.U. Champagne Blend (Champagne) $185. 92 —*M.S. (12/31/2005)*

Bruno Paillard NV Première Cuvée Brut Rosé Champagne Blend (Champagne) $56. 90 —*P.G. (12/1/2006)*

Bruno Paillard NV Première Cuvée Brut Champagne Blend (Champagne) $44. 92 —*R.V. (12/1/2005)*

Bruno Paillard NV Premiere Cuvée Brut Rosé Champagne Blend (Champagne) $50. 90 *(12/1/2001)*

Bruno Paillard 1995 Blanc de Blancs Brut Chardonnay (Champagne) $90. Yes, at 12 years this is now mature, but it still has plenty of life. Ripely in balance, this is an impressive, nutty tasting wine that has acidity that acts as a foundation for the ripe structure. It shows how well pure Chardonnay in Champagne can age—and it has more years to come. **94 Editors' Choice** —*R.V. (12/1/2007)*

Bruno Paillard 1995 Blanc de Blancs Brut Chardonnay (Champagne) $66. 89 —*R.V. (11/1/2006)*

Bruno Paillard NV Blanc de Blancs Réserve Privée Brut Chardonnay (Champagne) $59. On the dry side, showing crisp white currants, grapefruit and a chalky structured texture. A delicious wine, firmly in the refreshing apéritif Champagne camp, floating its fruit with considerable delicacy. **91** —*R.V. (12/1/2007)*

Bruno Paillard NV Réserve Privée Brut Chardonnay (Champagne) $60. 91 Editors' Choice *(12/1/2001)*

BRUT DARGENT

Brut Dargent NV Blanc de Blancs Brut Sparkling Blend (Jura) $11. 84 —*M.S. (12/31/2005)*

CALVET

Calvet 1998 Bordeaux Blend (Bordeaux) $7. 84 *(12/1/2000)*

Calvet 1996 Reserve Bordeaux Blend (Bordeaux) $10. 87 *(12/1/2000)*

Calvet 1998 Cabernet Sauvignon (Vin de Pays d'Oc) $7. 85 *(12/1/2000)*

Calvet 1998 Calvet Premiere Chardonnay (Bourgogne) $17. 89 *(12/1/2000)*

Calvet 2002 Calvet Reserve Merlot-Cabernet Sauvignon (Bordeaux) $15. 84 *—J.C. (6/1/2005)*

Calvet 1999 Pinot Noir (Bourgogne) $39. 83 *—P.G. (11/1/2002)*

Calvet 1999 Pinot Noir (Nuits-St.-Georges) $39. 84 *—P.G. (11/1/2002)*

Calvet 1998 Calvet Premiere Pinot Noir (Bourgogne) $17. 85 *(12/1/2000)*

Calvet 2004 Extra Fruit XF Sauvignon Blanc (Bordeaux) $10. 85 Best Buy *(7/1/2005)*

Calvet 1998 Reserve White Blend (Bordeaux) $10. 88 Best Buy *(12/1/2000)*

CAMILLE GIROUD

Camille Giroud 2004 Pinot Noir (Latricières-Chambertin) $195. Big, bold and fruity, this is a wine with all the generosity and power of Grand Cru Gevrey-Chambertin. It is ripe, with forward fruits and a polished texture but there is still a firm bite of tannin underneath. Drinkable now, but it should age. 91 *—R.V. (3/1/2007)*

Camille Giroud 2004 La Richemone Premier Cru Pinot Noir (Nuits-St.-Georges) $NA. From this venerable Beaune négociant, this wine shows more charm than some Nuits St.-Georges, but still has plenty of solid power behind it. There are flavors of dark plums, layers of acidity and perfumed tannin flavors. 89 *—R.V. (3/1/2007)*

Camille Giroud 2004 Lavaut Saint-Jacques Premier Cru Pinot Noir (Gevrey-Chambertin) $98. A rich wine, silky smooth on the surface with some new wood vanilla flavors. It's rich, packed with ripe fruits and relatively lightweight tannins. With its fruitiness, this is the style of wine which would certainly appeal to California Pinot Noir drinkers. 89 *—R.V. (3/1/2007)*

Camille Giroud 2003 Beaune Premier Cru Les Avaux Pinot Noir (Beaune) $51. 89 *—R.V. (9/1/2005)*

CASTEL MONTPLAISIR

Castel Montplaisir 1997 Red Blend (Cahors) $11. 84 *—J.C. (3/1/2001)*

CASTEL ROUBINE

Castel Roubine 1996 Cru Classe Rhône Red Blend (Côtes de Provence) $12. 82 *—J.C. (3/1/2001)*

CATHERINE DE SAINT-JUERY

Catherine de Saint-Juery 1998 Syrah (Coteaux du Languedoc) $8. 84 *(10/1/2001)*

CATTIER

Cattier 1998 Cuvée Renaissance Champagne Blend (Champagne) $NA. 89 *—R.V. (12/1/2004)*

CAVE DE BOURGUEIL

Cave de Bourgueil 2005 Lieu-dit Beauregard Cabernet Franc (Bourgueil) $NA. Supple, with soft, if dry, tannins and a typical Cab Franc smoky flavor. There is just a touch of caramel in the aftertaste. 87 *—R.V. (4/1/2007)*

CAVE DE LUGNY

Cave de Lugny 2001 Les Charmes Chardonnay (Mâcon-Lugny) $9. 82 *—S.H. (1/1/2002)*

CAVE DE RIBEAUVILLÉ

Cave de Ribeauvillé NV Giersberger Brut Pinot Blanc (Crémant d'Alsace) $16. Shows some promise, offering up hints of citrus and toast on the nose, but turns simpler on the palate, where green-apple flavors dominate and the lack of bubbles results in a wine that's duller than it should be. Imported by Global E. Selections, LLC. 81 *—J.C. (12/15/2007)*

Cave de Ribeauvillé 2004 Grand Cru Kirchberg de Ribeauvillé Riesling (Alsace) $22. 88 *—R.V. (2/1/2006)*

Cave de Ribeauvillé 2002 Grand Cru Rosacker Riesling (Alsace) $22. 85 *—J.C. (8/1/2006)*

Cave de Ribeauvillé 2004 Réserve Silberberg Riesling (Alsace) $21. 85 *—R.V. (2/1/2006)*

Cave de Ribeauvillé 2005 Vendages Manuelles Prestige Riesling (Alsace) $14. A solid wine with plenty of lime, grapefruit and dusty mineral notes on both the nose and palate. Medium weight and a clean, fresh finish make this a good choice for lighter fare. 84 *(9/1/2007)*

Cave de Ribeauvillé 2004 Prestige Demi-Sec Tokay Pinot Gris (Alsace) $17. 85 *—R.V. (2/1/2006)*

Cave de Ribeauvillé 2000 Vendanges Tardives Tokay Pinot Gris (Alsace) $40. 89 *—R.V. (2/1/2006)*

CAVE DE SARRAS

Cave de Sarras 1998 Cuvée Champtenaud Syrah (Saint-Joseph) $19. 87 *—M.S. (9/1/2003)*

CAVE DE SAUMUR

Cave de Saumur 2005 Lieu-dit La Croix Verte Cabernet Franc (Saumur) $NA. This single-vineyard wine comes from vines close to the ancient abbey of Fontevraud on the Loire. It is a fresh, black cherry-flavored wine; light, crisp but with some good soft tannins, which open gently and sweetly. There's a good freshness in the aftertaste. 85 *—R.V. (4/1/2007)*

Cave de Saumur 2005 Lieu-dit Les Poyeux Cabernet Franc (Saumur-Champigny) $12. This has a fruity freshness, while keeping quite a severe core of tannins and dryness. That suggests that it could age for two years, although with its fresh aroma it is drinkable now. 87 Best Buy *—R.V. (4/1/2007)*

Cave de Saumur 2005 Lieu-dit Les Vignoles Cabernet Franc (Saumur-Champigny) $NA. The vineyard of Les Vignoles, like so many in this part of the Loire, is planted on soft, chalky soil on a plateau above the river. What gives this wine its attraction is the fine balance between structure and ripe cherry fruits and touches of grilled nuts. At the end, violet perfumes dominate. 86 *—R.V. (4/1/2007)*

Cave de Saumur 2005 Réserve des Vignerons Cabernet Franc (Saumur) $10. Initially quite rustic in character, this wine does open up to give the typical pencil shavings aromas of the Cabernet Franc and sweet, perfumed tannins. A fresh wine, with good black currant flavors. 84 *—R.V. (4/1/2007)*

Cave de Saumur 2005 Réserve des Vignerons Cabernet Franc (Saumur-Champigny) $NA. A fine, minerally wine, with a firm, solid structure giving rich fruits under the tannins. It is fruity, with red cherry flavors and a smoky aftertaste. This could age for a year. 84 *—R.V. (4/1/2007)*

CAVE DE TAIN L'HERMITAGE

Cave de Tain l'Hermitage 2005 Marsanne (Crozes-Hermitage) $15. 83 *—J.C. (11/15/2006)*

Cave de Tain l'Hermitage 2004 Marsanne (Hermitage) $NA. A rich, lushly textured wine made from 100% Marsanne that's barrel fermented, but with the malolactic fermentation blocked. Notes of oranges and apricots lead the way, with an appealing hint of almond. Easy to drink. 88 *—J.C. (9/1/2007)*

Cave de Tain L'Hermitage 2003 Marsanne (Hermitage) $39. 89 *—J.C. (11/15/2006)*

Cave de Tain l'Hermitage 2005 Au Coeur des Siècles Marsanne (Hermitage) $NA. Shows the wood from barrel fermentation and maturation a bit on the nose, but also plenty of citrus. It's broad, yet reined in a bit by oak spice right now, needing time to flesh out. Hard to say it's better than the excellent '04 version, but it's still excellent. 91 *—J.C. (9/1/2007)*

Cave de Tain L'Hermitage 1999 Nobles Rives Marsanne (Hermitage) $NA. 90 *—R.V. (6/1/2002)*

Cave de Tain L'Hermitage 2001 Rhône White Blend (Hermitage) $35. 90 Editors' Choice *—R.V. (2/1/2005)*

Cave de Tain l'Hermitage 2004 Syrah (Cornas) $NA. Starts off with some hints of sour plums and cinnamon, then adds hints of blood and meat. Because of the vintage, it's a bit light, but spicy and complex, with surprising length. Drink now–2015. 88 *—J.C. (9/1/2007)*

Cave de Tain L'Hermitage 2004 Syrah (Saint-Joseph) $18. 86 *—J.C. (11/15/2006)*

Cave de Tain L'Hermitage 2003 Syrah (Hermitage) $52. 88 *—J.C. (11/15/2006)*

Cave de Tain L'Hermitage 2001 Syrah (Cornas) $25. 88 *—R.V. (2/1/2005)*

Cave de Tain l'Hermitage 2005 Arènes Sauvages Syrah (Cornas) $NA. Bottled only two months prior, the co-op's luxury cuvée of Cornas was showing no ill effects. Peppery, herbal and complex on the nose, yet marked by creamy suppleness on the palate, this is blessed with wonderful cherry fruit and a long, lush finish. Drink now–2020. 92 *—J.C. (9/1/2007)*

Cave de Tain L'Hermitage 1999 Cuvée Gambert de Loche Syrah (Hermitage) $70. 90 *—R.V. (6/1/2002)*

Cave de Tain L'Hermitage 2002 Esprit de Granit Syrah (Saint-Joseph) $18. 87 *—R.V. (2/1/2005)*

Cave de Tain l'Hermitage 2004 Gambert de Loche Syrah (Hermitage) $80. A luxury bottling from the local co-op, this is a blend of wines from mainly Le Méal and L'Hermite. It's a touch light in color—because of the vintage—with a spicy, peppery bouquet and flavors of red fruits and spice. Lacks a bit of richness and depth, but shows good complexity. Drink now–2014. 87 *—J.C. (9/1/2007)*

Cave de Tain L'Hermitage 2003 Gambert de Loche Syrah (Hermitage) $85. 90 *—J.C. (11/15/2006)*

Cave de Tain L'Hermitage 2003 Les Hauts du Fief Syrah (Crozes-Hermitage) $20. 88 *—J.C. (11/15/2006)*

Cave de Tain L'Hermitage 1999 Les Hauts du Fief Syrah (Crozes-Hermitage) $15. 88 *—R.V. (6/1/2002)*

CAVE DE VIGNERONS DE BEAUMES-DE-VENISE

Cave de Vignerons de Beaumes-de-Venise 2004 Rosexclusif Muscat (Muscat de Beaumes de Venise) $NA. 88 *—J.C. (11/15/2006)*

Cave de Vignerons de Beaumes-de-Venise 2004 Carte Or Muscat Blanc à Petit Grain (Muscat de Beaumes de Venise) $NA. 84 *—J.C. (11/15/2006)*

CAVE DES VIGNERONS DE MONTFRIN

Cave des Vignerons de Montfrin 2005 Domaine de Barrelle Rhône Red Blend (Côtes-du-Rhône) $NA. 87 *—J.C. (11/15/2006)*

CAVE DES VIGNERONS DE PRISSE

Cave des Vignerons de Prisse 2004 Terres Secrets Chardonnay (Mâcon-Villages) $15. 87 *—R.V. (12/1/2006)*

CAVE FAYOLLE FILS ET FILLE

Cave Fayolle Fils et Fille 2004 Les Pontaix Syrah (Crozes-Hermitage) $NA. 85 *—J.C. (11/15/2006)*

CAVES DES PAPES

Caves des Papes 2001 Les Closiers Red Blend (Châteauneuf-du-Pape) $24. 83 *—J.C. (3/1/2004)*

Caves des Papes 2000 Reserve des Fustiers Red Blend (Gigondas) $18. 83 *—J.C. (3/1/2004)*

Caves des Papes 2005 Heritage Rosé Rhône Red Blend (Côtes-du-Rhône) $11. This dark salmon rosé—a dry blend of Grenache, Syrah, Cinsault and Mourvèdre—charms with its aromas of stone dust and strawberries. It's medium-bodied, not as rich as some southern Rhône rosés, but offers pretty strawberry and peach fruit with touches of herbs and minerals. Drink now. **86 Best Buy** *—J.C. (7/1/2007)*

Caves des Papes 2002 Heritage Rouge Rhône Red Blend (Côtes-du-Rhône) $11. 83 *—J.C. (2/1/2005)*

Caves des Papes 2001 Oratorio Rhône Red Blend (Gigondas) $28. 89 *—J.C. (2/1/2005)*

Caves des Papes 2004 Heritage Rosé Blend (Côtes-du-Rhône) $10. 83 *—J.C. (11/15/2005)*

CAVES FLEURY

Caves Fleury 2006 Sauvignon Blanc Bordeaux White Blend (Bordeaux Blanc) $10. Light, fresh, slightly grassy but more in the white fruit flavor profile. It's soft, with a citrus twang to it, great to drink as an apéritif, leaving a soft, creamy aftertaste. **84** *—R.V. (12/31/2007)*

CELLIER DE SAINT-LOUIS

Cellier de Saint-Louis 2006 La Brasserie Rosé Blend (Vin de Pays Portes de Méditerranée) $8. Yes, you can imagine the scene by the fishing harbor, the small table outside the restaurant. That's the idea: the reality isn't too far off, the wine is light, fresh, dominated by fruit candies and crisp acidity, with a soft aftertaste. **84 Best Buy** *—R.V. (7/1/2007)*

CELLIER DES DAUPHINS

Cellier des Dauphins 2001 Réserve Les Dorinnes Rouge Rhône Red Blend (Côtes-du-Rhône) $14. 83 *—J.C. (2/1/2005)*

Cellier des Dauphins 2003 Prestige Blanc Rhône White Blend (Côtes-du-Rhône) $8. **84 Best Buy** *—J.C. (2/1/2005)*

Cellier des Dauphins 2005 Prestige Rosé Blend (Côtes-du-Rhône) $9. 83 *—J.C. (11/15/2006)*

CHAMARRÉ

Chamarré 2003 Tradition Bordeaux Blend (Bordeaux) $12. Mainly Merlot, this is a dusty, cassis-scented wine that picks up hints of raisin and chocolate. Shows decent length and soft tannins, making it immediately approachable. **85** *(7/1/2007)*

Chamarré NV Grande Reserve Cabernet Sauvignon (Vin de Table Francais) $12. This blend draws from various Bordeaux communes, the French Pyrenees and Languedoc, resulting in a clean, fruity Cabernet Sauvignon that's fairly priced for the quality. There's a bit of dusty wood upfront, but also solid cassis fruit, which never gets overly tannic or severe. Drink now. **86** *(7/1/2007)*

Chamarré NV Grand Reserve Chardonnay (Vin de Table Francais) $12. A blend of lots from Burgundy and the Languedoc, this is a decent little Chardonnay, with pear and melon flavors and hints of honey and cashew. Picks up mild citrusy notes on the abbreviated finish. The fruit is 2005, although it can't say that on the label because of European labeling requirements. **85** *(7/1/2007)*

Chamarré 2005 Selection Chardonnay-Sauvignon (Vin de Pays d'Oc) $10. Simple fruit dominates this blend of 63% Chardonnay and 37% Sauvingon Blanc. Pear and pineapple flavors add hints of grapefruit on the finish, with a slightly syrupy mouthfeel. **84** *(7/1/2007)*

Chamarré 2005 Selection Grenache-Shiraz (Vin de Pays de L'ile de Beaute) $10. From the island of Corsica, this was our pick of the Chamarré wines, combining stony, smoky aromas with flavors of strawberries and herbs. It's a copper-colored rosé that finishes fresh, with a hint of anise. **86 Best Buy** *(7/1/2007)*

Chamarré NV Grande Reserve Pinot Noir (Vin de Table Francais) $12. This has grapes from Pommard, Rully, Nuits-St-Georges and Mercurey in it, as well as a healthy dollop from Corsica, of all places. It's dark in color, with plum and chocolate aromas, but seems a bit tough and lean on the palate, lacking some of Pinot Noir's seductive texture. **84** *(7/1/2007)*

Chamarré 2004 Selection Cabernet Sauvignon-Grenache Red Blend (Vin de Pays d'Oc) $10. This is an unconventional blend that works, with the dark-fruited and firmly structured Cabernet lending depth to the soft, cherry-scented Grenache. It's juicy and lightweight, with a hint of pepper on the finish. **85 Best Buy** *(7/1/2007)*

Chamarré 2004 Selection Shiraz-Merlot (Vin de Pays d'Oc) $10. This blend of 55% Shiraz and 45% Merlot offers smoky, slightly herbal aromas and a large helping of dark fruit. Cooked plums are soft and a bit jammy on the palate, but still offer plenty of flavor, finishing dusty and soft. **84** *(7/1/2007)*

Chamarré 2005 Selection Sauvignon Blanc-Chenin Blanc White Blend (Vin de Pays du Jardin de la France) $10. A nearly 50-50 blend, this starts out with Sauvignon in the lead-grapefruit and melon aromas-then adds typical Chenin notes of apple, pear and citrus on the palate. There's just a hint of sweetness (4g/L residual sugar), which imparts some added weight. **84** *(7/1/2007)*

Chamarré 2003 Tradition White Blend (Jurançon) $14. Not overly sweet, this may be better with cheese or foie gras than with dessert, but it is a pleasant little sweet wine made from both Gros and Petit Manseng. Smells of orange rind and honey swirl from the glass, followed by seductive flavors of papaya and apricot. Crisp and citrusy on the finish-not cloying at all. This is the one wine in the lineup that can probably age beyond a year or two. **87** *(7/1/2007)*

CHAMPAGNE CATTIER

Champagne Cattier NV Chigny-Les-Rosés Premier Cru Champagne Blend (Champagne) $30. 87 *—R.V. (12/15/2003)*

CHANOINE

Chanoine NV Grande Réserve Brut Champagne Blend (Champagne) $24. Very soft, gentle Champagne, showing definite signs of a sweet dosage, with its flavors of brown sugar, baked apples and light acidity. It is full-bodied, which keeps the wine together, but it is too rich. **85** *—R.V. (12/1/2007)*

Chanoine NV Tsarine Cuvée Premium Brut Champagne Blend (Champagne) $46. An enticing, sophisticated wine. While it is fresh, with great floral aromas and flavors, it also shows hints of maturity, with toast just beginning to float over the yeast and grapefruit flavors. The aftertaste is very dry, crisp. **90** *—R.V. (12/31/2007)*

Chanoine NV Tsarine Premier Cru Brut Champagne Blend (Champagne) $46. In a young, fresh style, this is full of white fruits, crisp acidity and pink grapefruit with a sugar touch. The aftertaste, though, is relatively soft, but still in balance with the rest of the flavors. **87** *—R.V. (12/1/2007)*

Chanoine 2002 Tsarine Premier Cru Brut Champagne Blend (Champagne) $54. A deliciously dry wine, evoking flavors of crisp green-apple skins and white currants; this is elegant despite its weight and body. It has freshness, certainly, and needs some bottle age. The style is ripe, but the dryness gives some opening austerity. **90** *—R.V. (12/1/2007)*

Chanoine NV Tsarine Rosé Brut Champagne Blend (Champagne) $40. Crisp, dry but fruity, this has just enough body to support the red currant flavors and crisp red-apple skin texture. A lively, vibrant wine, all freshness and light, just what a rosé should be. **90** *—R.V. (12/31/2007)*

Chanoine 2003 Tsarine Rosé Brut Champagne Blend (Champagne) $57. With this vintage, disgorged in June 2007, there is still great youth. But the fine raspberry and other red fruit flavors make this a well-balanced Champagne, leaning on fruit at this stage, but also showing structure. **88** *—R.V. (12/1/2007)*

Chanoine 2003 Tsarine Grand Cru Blanc de Blancs Chardonnay (Champagne) $75. More toast than fruit even at this young stage, this is a ripe wine, showing big woody, toasty flavors that leave freshness behind. There are flavors of cream, caramel and wood here. Acidity appears on the finish. **87** *—R.V. (12/31/2007)*

CHANSON PÈRE ET FILS

Chanson Père et Fils 2003 Clos des Mouches Premier Cru Chardonnay

FRANCE

(Beaune) $83. 91 *—R.V. (9/1/2005)*

Chanson Père et Fils 2003 Hauts Marconnets Premier Cru Chardonnay (Savigny-lès-Beaune) $34. 89 *—R.V. (9/1/2005)*

Chanson Père et Fils 2002 Vergennes Chardonnay (Corton) $115. 90 *—R.V. (9/1/2004)*

Chanson Père et Fils 2004 Pinot Noir (Gevrey-Chambertin) $45. A dark style of Gevrey, with brooding black fruits and acidity. It has weight, tannins, wood and spices, which hold the wine together in a tight structure. There is power here. **89** *—R.V. (3/1/2007)*

Chanson Père et Fils 2004 Pinot Noir (Nuits-St.-Georges) $55. This wine is in the dry, firm style that is a mark of Nuits-St.-Georges, yet goes beyond that with its concentrated, jammy fruit flavors balanced by dense, dry tannins. It is a good sign of the way Chanson is developing under the control of Bollinger Champagne, and becoming a négociant worth watching. **90** *—R.V. (3/1/2007)*

Chanson Père et Fils 2004 Pinot Noir (Bonnes-Mares) $NA. Rich and spicy, this wine has dense, solid tannins. But they can't hide the deliciously ripe blackberry jelly flavors and the power. It needs time, because the wood and fruit tannins are so dominant at present. Drink 2017. **92** *—R.V. (3/1/2007)*

Chanson Père et Fils 2004 Pinot Noir (Charmes-Chambertin) $NA. It takes charm, as in luck, to find good Charmes-Chambertin. But this is one of the good ones, a big, ripe, dense wine that is just setting out on a slow road of aging. Already, though, the fruit is doing its work, showing black plum skin flavors, while the tannins hold everything together. Give it 5–10 years. **93 Cellar Selection** *—R.V. (3/1/2007)*

Chanson Père et Fils 2003 Pinot Noir (Chambolle-Musigny) $NA. In keeping with the modern, polished style that Chanson seems to have adopted, this is a ripe, new wood-flavored wine. But it doesn't lose the essential charm of Chambolle-Musigny, incorporating the firm tannins into a more sensuous web of fresh fruit. **88** *—R.V. (3/1/2007)*

Chanson Père et Fils 2003 Pinot Noir (Mazis-Chambertin) $NA. This is one of the smaller of the Gevrey-Chambertin Grand Crus. It produces wines of considerable firmness and dryness, at least initially. This wine is certainly quite tough and firm. It is very foursquare and solid, needing time for fruit to emerge. **92** *—R.V. (3/1/2007)*

Chanson Père et Fils 2003 Pinot Noir (Chambertin) $NA. For a 2003, this is surprisingly austere. There is a dark side to the wine, very closed up still, with dry fruits and tannins dominating. It needs time to open up, as befits its exalted status of grand cru in the Burgundy hierarchy. There's great finishing acidity, along with red fruits. **93** *—R.V. (3/1/2007)*

Chanson Père et Fils 2003 Clos de Mouches Premier Cru Pinot Noir (Beaune) $66. 89 *—R.V. (9/1/2005)*

Chanson Père et Fils 2003 Clos des Fêves Premier Cru Pinot Noir (Beaune) $70. 92 *—R.V. (9/1/2005)*

Chanson Père et Fils 2004 Clos de Vougeot Pinot Noir (Clos Vougeot) $147. Although it's crafted in a modern, fruit-forward style, this wine also manages to preserve the proper structure for this grand cru vineyard. The fruits are fresh and delicious, with velvet enveloping the firm tannins. The effect is of a very direct wine, perhaps leaving little for the future, but very good now. **92** *—R.V. (3/1/2007)*

Chanson Père et Fils 2002 Dominode Premier Cru Pinot Noir (Savigny-lès-Beaune) $35. 87 *—R.V. (9/1/2004)*

Chanson Père et Fils 2004 Echezeaux Pinot Noir (Echezeaux) $NA. The class of the grands crus of Vosne-Romanée, such as Echezeaux, is well expressed in this beautifully crafted wine. The hand of master wine consultant, Jean-Pierre Confuron, is obvious in the pure fruits, the ripeness and the richness, along with the proper tannin structure. Another example of the way Chanson has found a new future for itself. **94** *—R.V. (3/1/2007)*

Chanson Père et Fils 2004 Les Suchots Premier Cru Pinot Noir (Vosne-Romanée) $NA. Somewhat dusty in aromas and taste, this wine has plenty of structure. The fruit is harder to find, showing through the wood tannins and the firm, dense texture. Needs 4–5 years to develop. **90** *—R.V. (3/1/2007)*

Chanson Père et Fils 2003 Les Vergelesses Premier Cru Pinot Noir (Pernand-Vergelesses) $36. 88 *—R.V. (9/1/2005)*

Chanson Père et Fils 2002 Premier Cru Les Boudots Pinot Noir (Nuits-St.-Georges) $80. 91 *—R.V. (9/1/2004)*

CHARLES DE CAZANOVE

Charles de Cazanove NV Classique Brut Champagne Blend (Champagne) $26. 87 *—M.S. (6/1/2003)*

CHARLES DE FERE

Charles de Fere NV Grande Cuvée Champagne Blend (Crémant de Bourgogne) $15. 88 *—R.V. (6/1/2006)*

Charles de Fere NV Tradition Brut Chardonnay (France) $10. 87 Best Buy *—P.G. (12/15/2002)*

Charles de Fere NV Tradition Chardonnay Brut Chardonnay (Vin Mousseux) $12. 84 *—R.V. (6/1/2006)*

Charles de Fere NV Réserve French Shiraz Shiraz (Vin Mousseux) $NA. 86 *—R.V. (6/1/2006)*

Charles de Fere NV Brut Tradition Sparkling Blend (France) $12. 87 Best Buy *—M.S. (12/31/2005)*

Charles de Fere NV Cuvée Jean-Louis Blanc de Blancs Brut Sparkling Blend (Vin Mousseux) $10. 83 *—M.D. (12/15/2006)*

Charles de Fere NV Réserve Blanc de Blancs Brut Sparkling Blend (Vin Mousseux) $11. 85 *—R.V. (6/1/2006)*

CHARLES HEIDSIECK

Charles Heidsieck 1982 Blanc de Blancs des Chardonnay Champagne Blend (Champagne) $185. 91 *(12/15/2003)*

Charles Heidsieck 1995 Blanc des Millénaires Champagne Blend (Champagne) $95. 90 *—M.S. (12/31/2005)*

Charles Heidsieck 1983 Blanc des Millénaires Champagne Blend (Champagne) $170. 91 *(12/15/2003)*

Charles Heidsieck 1995 Brut Champagne Blend (Champagne) $65. 90 *(12/15/2003)*

Charles Heidsieck 1995 Brut Champagne Blend (Champagne) $65. 90 *—J.C. (12/1/2005)*

Charles Heidsieck 1999 Millésimé Brut Rosé Champagne Blend (Champagne) $80. Showing signs of toasty maturity. Rosé Champagne does age but it becomes much more like regular (white) Champagne. There are only just hints of red fruits as a reminder of its youthful character. The wine though remains delicious. **89** *—R.V. (12/31/2007)*

Charles Heidsieck 1999 Brut Rosé Champagne Blend (Champagne) $80. 90 *—R.V. (11/1/2006)*

Charles Heidsieck 1996 Brut Rosé Champagne Blend (Champagne) $70. 90 *(12/15/2003)*

Charles Heidsieck 1985 Champagne Charlie Brut Champagne Blend (Champagne) $125. 91 *—R.V. (12/1/2004)*

Charles Heidsieck 1981 Champagne Charlie Brut Champagne Blend (Champagne) $150. 92 *(12/15/2003)*

Charles Heidsieck NV Réserve Brut Champagne Blend (Champagne) $40. 89 *—R.V. (12/1/2005)*

Charles Heidsieck NV Réserve Brut Champagne Blend (Champagne) $35. 89 *(12/15/2003)*

Charles Heidsieck 1995 Blanc des Millénaires Chardonnay (Champagne) $95. This 12-year old shows signs of maturity, but retains freshness and liveliness as well. With its yeasty edge, toasty flavors and wonderful white fruits all in balance, it is finely balanced. The acidity is kept in check by the richness of the mature fruit. A very complete Champagne. **94 Editors' Choice** *—R.V. (12/1/2007)*

Charles Heidsieck 1995 Blanc des Millénaires Chardonnay (Champagne) $95. 89 *—R.V. (11/1/2006)*

CHARLES HOURS

Charles Hours 2001 Cuvée Marie White Blend (Jurançon Sec) $18. 88 *(10/1/2003)*

CHARLES JOGUET

Charles Joguet 2004 Clos de la Dioterie Cabernet Franc (Chinon) $37. One of the top wines from Charles Joguet, this is in the style that has made the reputation of this estate. It is beautifully perfumed, a rich, sweet, densely textured wine that revels in its black fruits, polished by aging in older wood barrels. At the end, the dryness promises several years aging. **91 Editors' Choice** *—R.V. (4/1/2007)*

Charles Joguet 2004 Clos du Chêne Vert Cabernet Franc (Chinon) $37. Jacques Genet, at the head of the Charles Joguet domaine since its eponymous founder retired, can make magnificent Chinon, as this example demonstrates. This is a great, dense and elegant wine. It has an impressive structure, allied to those great red Loire fruit flavors, along with a smoky aftertaste. **92** *—R.V. (4/1/2007)*

Charles Joguet 2005 Cuvée de la Cure Cabernet Franc (Chinon) $22. A single-vineyard wine, this is a dry, firmly tannic wine, with plenty of structure. Having been vinified in stainless steel without any wood, what you are getting is a very pure, fresh fruit character under the tannins. Give it six months. **88** *—R.V. (4/1/2007)*

Charles Joguet 2004 Cuvée de la Cure Cabernet Franc (Chinon) $21. The structure is all here, dark and dry, with plenty of fresh acidity over the red currants. This revels in its fruit flavors, touched with smokiness and dry tannins. To finish, the wine lifts into vibrant ripe fruits. **87** *—R.V. (4/1/2007)*

Charles Joguet 2005 Cuvée Terroir Cabernet Franc (Chinon) $17. This is the lightest wine in the Joguet range. As you would expect from its provenance, it is fresh, fruity, juicy and easy to drink young. With its light tannins, it is great for summer drinking. **86** *—R.V. (4/1/2007)*

Charles Joguet 2005 Les Petites Roches Cabernet Franc (Chinon) $19. A light, fresh wine made from young vines; this has some pleasant red fruits and a touch of dry tannins. The downside is too much acidity. **86** *—R.V. (4/1/2007)*

Charles Joguet 2005 Les Varennes du Grand Clos Cabernet Franc (Chinon) $29. Only just in bottle, this wine needs time—Jacques Genet, the owner, suggest another 9–10 years, but 4–5 would be nearer the mark. A serious wine, as always with this cuvée from Joguet: dense, spicy, black currant flavored, with toast flavors showing to finish. **90** *—R.V. (4/1/2007)*

Charles Joguet 2004 Les Varennes du Grand Clos Cabernet Franc (Chinon) $28. Very fresh, red cherry-flavored wine, more fruit than structure. Some dry tannins show through the fruit on the finish. This is a wine that is about immediate pleasure. **87** *—R.V. (10/1/2007)*

Charles Joguet 2005 Les Varennes du Grand Clos Franc de Pied Cabernet Franc (Chinon) $37. Made from ungrafted vines, this shows its vintage with its rich, smooth, polished fruit over soft, sweet tannins. It has flavors of black plum skins, finishing with red berry acidity and hints of good aging potential. **89** *—R.V. (4/1/2007)*

CHARLES LAFITTE

Charles Lafitte NV Cuvée Spéciale Brut Champagne Blend (Champagne) $37. A fresh, lively Champagne, quite soft with crisp white pears and a light sweetness which integrates well with the fruit. Young, without complexity, a good apéritif Champagne. **87** *—R.V. (12/1/2007)*

Charles Lafitte NV 1834 Cuvée Spéciale Brut Champagne Blend (Champagne) $32. **87** *—P.G. (12/1/2006)*

Charles Lafitte NV Brut Rosé Champagne Blend (Champagne) $43. **88** *—J.C. (12/1/2004)*

Charles Lafitte NV Grand Cuvée Brut Champagne Blend (Champagne) $27. **88** *—M.S. (12/15/2003)*

Charles Lafitte NV Grande Cuvée Brut Champagne Blend (Champagne) $21. **87** *—P.G. (12/15/2002)*

Charles Lafitte NV Grande Cuvée Brut Champagne Blend (Champagne) $27. **85** *—D.T. (12/15/2001)*

Charles Lafitte 1989 Orgueil de France Brut Champagne Blend (Champagne) $100. Heavy-handed Champagne, and rather overblown. The fruit has flavors of ripe apples, with strong hints of sweetness from the dosage. **83** *—R.V. (12/31/2007)*

Charles Lafitte 1989 Orgueil de France Brut Champagne Blend (Champagne) $50. **86** *—P.G. (12/15/2002)*

Charles Lafitte NV Rosé Brut Champagne Blend (Champagne) $47. A full, somewhat sweet wine, fresh with foamy strawberries in the mouth. The acidity is missing somewhere, but this does make for a pleasing wine, certainly a fine partner to fresh fruits. **84** *—R.V. (12/1/2007)*

CHARLES MIGNON & FILS

Charles Mignon & Fils 2003 Rhône Red Blend (Côtes-du-Rhône) $8. **84 Best Buy** *—J.C. (11/15/2006)*

CHARLES VIENOT

Charles Vienot 1996 Pinot Noir (Burgundy) $11. **82** *(5/1/2000)*

CHARTOGNE-TAILLET

Chartogne-Taillet NV Cuvée Sainte-Anne Blanc de Blancs Brut Champagne Blend (Champagne) $41. **90** *—R.V. (12/1/2002)*

Chartogne-Taillet 1996 Cuvée Sainte-Anne Brut Champagne Blend (Champagne) $44. **91 Editors' Choice** *—R.V. (12/1/2002)*

CHARTRON ET TRÉBUCHET

Chartron et Trébuchet 2004 Chardonnay (Chablis) $20. **88** *—J.C. (11/15/2005)*

Chartron et Trébuchet 2003 Chardonnay (Meursault) $38. **87** *—J.C. (11/15/2005)*

Chartron et Trébuchet 2001 White Blend (Mâcon-Villages) $11. **86** *—R.V. (11/15/2003)*

Château Angelus 2005 Barrel Sample Bordeaux Blend (Saint-Emilion Grand Cru) $NA. **94** *—R.V. (6/20/2006)*

CHÂTEAU AME DE MUSSET

Château Ame de Musset 2005 Bordeaux Blend (Lalande de Pomerol) $NA. With Pascal Dalbeck, owner of Classed Growth Saint-Emilion property Château Belair, at the helm, this wine promises good things. It's meaty, well-rounded, but still with good chewy tannins. And there are great fresh red fruits and lively acidity to lift up the richness. Only bottled in 50 cl and in magnums. **90** *—R.V. (11/1/2007)*

CHÂTEAU ANDRON BLANQUET

Château Andron Blanquet 2004 Bordeaux Blend (Saint-Estèphe) $NA. An easy, soft wine, surprisingly so for a Saint-Estèphe; the tannins are dusty rather than dry. It makes it enjoyable now, but probably not for aging. **86** *—R.V. (6/1/2007)*

CHÂTEAU ANGELUS

Château Angelus 2006 Barrel Sample Bordeaux Blend (Saint-Emilion Grand Cru) $NA. 93-95 Barrel Sample. Very dark in color, almost black, this wine has sweetly ripe fruit, very opulent, chocolaty and with seriously concentrated fruit. It is hugely powerful, very dark. **94** *—R.V. (6/1/2007)*

CHÂTEAU ANTHONIC

Château Anthonic 2003 Bordeaux Blend (Moulis-en-Médoc) $NA. **90** *—R.V. (5/1/2006)*

CHÂTEAU AUSONE

Château Ausone 2006 Barrel Sample Bordeaux Blend (Saint-Emilion Grand Cru) $NA. 95-97 Barrel Sample. A hugely dense wine, all power and dark tannins. Very concentrated, this is dark, a firm, solid structure covering the huge black plum fruit flavors. It's all about power. **96** *—R.V. (6/1/2007)*

Château Ausone 2000 Bordeaux Blend (Saint-Emilion) $600. **98** *—R.V. (6/1/2003)*

CHÂTEAU BALESTARD LA TONNELLE

Château Balestard la Tonnelle 2005 Barrel Sample Bordeaux Blend (Saint-Emilion Grand Cru) $NA. **88** *—R.V. (6/21/2006)*

CHÂTEAU BARREYRES

Château Barreyres 2004 Bordeaux Blend (Haut-Médoc) $19. A firm, structured wine, tempered with some smoky wood flavors. The tannins are dry and dominant, leaving the black cherry fruit element behind. Give it 2–3 years. **87** *—R.V. (11/1/2007)*

CHÂTEAU BASTOR LAMONTAGNE

Château Bastor Lamontagne 2004 Barrel Sample Bordeaux White Blend (Sauternes) $NA. **86** *—R.V. (6/1/2005)*

CHÂTEAU BATAILLEY

Château Batailley 2004 Barrel Sample Bordeaux Blend (Pauillac) $NA. **92** *—R.V. (6/1/2005)*

CHÂTEAU BEAUCHÊNE

Château Beauchêne 2003 Grande Réserve Rhône Red Blend (Côtes-du-Rhône) $NA. **87** *—R.V. (12/31/2006)*

Château Beauchêne 2003 Premier Terroir Rhône Red Blend (Côtes-du-Rhône) $11. **89 Best Buy** *—R.V. (12/31/2006)*

CHÂTEAU BEAUMONT

Château Beaumont 2005 Barrel Sample Bordeaux Blend (Haut-Médoc) $NA. **88** *—R.V. (6/21/2006)*

Château Beaumont 2004 Bordeaux Blend (Haut-Médoc) $NA. Light and lean, showing the downside of 2004, this wine only redeems itself with its fresh fruit and spiciness. **85** *—R.V. (6/1/2007)*

CHÂTEAU BEAUREGARD

Château Beauregard 2005 Barrel Sample Bordeaux Blend (Pomerol) $NA. **86** *—R.V. (6/21/2006)*

CHÂTEAU BEAUSÉJOUR-BECOT

Château Beauséjour-Becot 2005 Barrel Sample Bordeaux Blend (Saint-Emilion Grand Cru) $NA. **93** *—R.V. (6/20/2006)*

Château Beauséjour-Becot 2003 Barrel Sample Bordeaux Blend (Saint-Emilion) $NA. **90** *—R.V. (6/3/2004)*

CHÂTEAU BEL AIR

Château Bel Air 2004 Bordeaux Blend (Saint-Emilion Grand Cru) $NA. A big, ripe, fruity wine, backed up with firm tannins. The structure is impressive, giving smoky flavors and layers of new wood. It is rich and potentially long-lasting. Under the inspired control of Pascal Dalbeck, Bel Air is fully living up to its classed growth status. **92** *—R.V. (6/1/2007)*

Château Bel Air 1999 Perponcher Grande Cuvée Bordeaux Blend (Bordeaux Supérieur) $13. 90 *—R.V. (12/1/2002)*

Château Bel Air 2005 Barrel Sample Bordeaux Blend (Saint-Emilion Grand Cru) $NA. 95 *—R.V. (6/20/2006)*

Château Bel Air 2003 Barrel Sample Bordeaux Blend (Saint-Emilion) $NA. 91 *—R.V. (6/3/2004)*

CHÂTEAU BELGRAVE

Château Belgrave 2004 Barrel Sample Bordeaux Blend (Haut-Médoc) $NA. 89 *—R.V. (6/1/2005)*

CHÂTEAU BELON

Château Belon 2002 Bordeaux White Blend (Graves) $12. 84 *—J.C. (6/1/2005)*

CHÂTEAU BERLIQUET

Château Berliquet 2005 Barrel Sample Bordeaux Blend (Saint-Emilion Grand Cru) $NA. 91 *—R.V. (6/1/2006)*

CHÂTEAU BERTINEAU SAINT-VINCENT

Château Bertineau Saint-Vincent 2004 Bordeaux Blend (Lalande de Pomerol) $NA. From a property run by Michel and Dany Rolland, this is a firm wine; structured, but with a velvet sheen that exudes ripeness and style. The tell-tale 2004 fresh acidity keeps the wine on its toes. 88 *—R.V. (6/1/2007)*

CHÂTEAU BERTINERIE

Château Bertinerie 2004 Bordeaux Blend (Premieres Côtes de Blaye) $NA. A Merlot-dominated wine (with 30% Cabernet Sauvignon), this is the simpler of two reds produced by the dynamic Bantegnies family. It shows good concentration, some firm, dusty tannins and fresh, vibrant red fruits. Acidity is there, but well in balance. 86 *—R.V. (11/1/2007)*

Château Bertinerie 2004 Bordeaux White Blend (Premieres Côtes de Blaye) $12. 88 *—R.V. (6/1/2005)*

CHÂTEAU BEYCHEVELLE

Château Beychevelle 2004 Bordeaux Blend (Saint-Julien) $NA. Yes, there is a huge amount of new wood here. It tastes highly toasty, making wood tannins the only ones at present. But there is something more that comes from the almost hidden layer of perfumed fruit. Give this wine the benefit of the doubt—Beychevelle is performing well at the moment. 90 *—R.V. (6/1/2007)*

Château Beychevelle 2001 Bordeaux Blend (Saint-Julien) $70. A harmonious balanced wine, showing fine, fresh acidity. The tannins have closed in somewhat, but you can taste the chocolate, and the sweet character of the ripe fruit. At the end, the acidity gives a fine lift. 93 *—R.V. (12/16/2007)*

Château Beychevelle 2000 Bordeaux Blend (Saint-Julien) $500. 92 *—R.V. (6/1/2003)*

Château Beychevelle 2004 Barrel Sample Bordeaux Blend (Saint-Julien) $NA. 90 *—R.V. (6/1/2005)*

CHÂTEAU BONALGUE

Château Bonalgue 2004 Bordeaux Blend (Pomerol) $NA. In the Bourotte family since 1926, this ancient property has modernized itself. This 2004 shows dominant new wood and black currant fruit flavors, with a herbal element which comes from the percentage of Cabernet Franc in the blend. With its black tannins, it promises aging potential. 88 *—R.V. (6/1/2007)*

CHÂTEAU BONNET

Château Bonnet 2000 Bordeaux Rouge Bordeaux Blend (Bordeaux) $12. 83 *—R.V. (12/1/2002)*

Château Bonnet 2004 Bordeaux White Blend (Entre-Deux-Mers) $10. 88 Best Buy *—R.V. (6/1/2005)*

Château Bonnet 2001 Vinifie en Futs de Chene Entre deux Mers White Blend (Bordeaux) $14. 90 Best Buy *—R.V. (12/1/2002)*

CHÂTEAU BOUSCAUT

Château Bouscaut 2004 Bordeaux Blend (Pessac-Léognan) $NA. One of those Pessac-Leognan properties whose improvement in wine has not yet been matched by a vertiginous rise in price. So buy this 2004—dark, solid, structured and freshly juicy—and rejoice at its value. 88 *—R.V. (6/1/2007)*

Château Bouscaut 2003 Barrel Sample Bordeaux Blend (Pessac-Léognan) $NA. 88 *—R.V. (6/3/2004)*

CHÂTEAU BRANAIRE-DUCRU

Château Branaire-Ducru 2004 Bordeaux Blend (Saint-Julien) $NA. New wood and high extraction are the dominant characteristics of this wine. That makes it in a modern, polished style, which will certainly evolve well, eventually arriving at something that is big and bold. Give it 4–5 years for that. 91 *—R.V. (6/1/2007)*

Château Branaire-Ducru 2003 Bordeaux Blend (Saint-Julien) $40. 91 *—R.V. (5/1/2006*

Château Branaire-Ducru 2001 Bordeaux Blend (Saint-Julien) $60. This is a marvelously complete wine, with its impressive ripe fruit, shining through the open structure. It is firm, but not too much. Stone black fruits are just perfectly ripe. There is just a core of dryness to compliment the rest of the wine. 95 Editors' Choice *—R.V. (12/16/2007)*

Château Branaire-Ducru 2005 Barrel Sample Bordeaux Blend (Saint-Julien) $NA. 94 *—R.V. (6/20/2006)*

Château Branaire-Ducru 2003 Barrel Sample Bordeaux Blend (Saint-Julien) $NA. 89 *—R.V. (6/3/2004)*

CHÂTEAU BRANE-CANTENAC

Château Brane-Cantenac 2004 Bordeaux Blend (Margaux) $NA. A big, thrusting, modern style of wine, packed with ripe black plum skin and vanilla flavors. To balance this power and fruit forward character, the typical 2004 freshness is very apparent, lifting the wine and giving it a vibrant character. 92 *—R.V. (6/1/2007)*

Château Brane-Cantenac 2001 Bordeaux Blend (Margaux) $40. 92 *—R.V. (6/1/2005)*

Château Brane-Cantenac 2005 Barrel Sample Bordeaux Blend (Margaux) $NA. 95 *—R.V. (6/20/2006)*

Château Brane-Cantenac 2003 Barrel Sample Bordeaux Blend (Margaux) $NA. 93 *—R.V. (6/3/2004)*

CHÂTEAU BRILLETTE

Château Brillette 2004 Bordeaux Blend (Moulis-en-Médoc) $NA. A rich, dense, deep velvet structured wine, layering dusty tannins with ripe sweet black plums and wood flavors. Obviously, to judge by the generosity and body of this wine, it has benefited from the advice of consultant Michel Rolland. 90 *—R.V. (6/1/2007)*

CHÂTEAU BROWN

Château Brown 2004 Bordeaux Blend (Pessac-Léognan) $NA. The aromas are dominated by spicy wood, and at this young stage in the wine's evolution that is the same for the taste. The fruit, juicy black currants, is struggling to come through. Give it 3–4 years. 88 *—R.V. (6/1/2007)*

Château Brown 2004 Bordeaux White Blend (Pessac-Léognan) $NA. An attractive, crisp, citrusy wine, full of herbaceous Sauvignon Blanc flavors. The delicious, full-blown fruit is well balanced with spice from the new wood aging. 89 *—R.V. (6/1/2007)*

Château Brown 2003 Bordeaux White Blend (Pessac-Léognan) $50. 89 *—R.V. (6/1/2005)*

CHÂTEAU CAILLOU

Château Caillou 2004 Barrel Sample Bordeaux White Blend (Sauternes) $NA. 88 *—R.V. (6/1/2005)*

CHÂTEAU CALON-SÉGUR

Château Calon-Ségur 2000 Bordeaux Blend (Saint-Estèphe) $90. 93 *—R.V. (6/1/2003)*

CHÂTEAU CAMENSAC

Château Camensac 2004 Barrel Sample Bordeaux Blend (Haut-Médoc) $NA. 90 *—R.V. (6/1/2005)*

CHÂTEAU CAMPLAZENS

Château Camplazens 1999 La Clape Rhône Red Blend (Coteaux du Languedoc) $17. 83 *—M.S. (2/1/2003)*

Château Camplazens 2001 Viognier (Vin de Pays d'Oc) $22. 84 *—M.S. (9/1/2003)*

CHÂTEAU CANON

Château Canon 2006 Barrel Sample Bordeaux Blend (Saint-Emilion Grand Cru) $NA. 93-95 Barrel Sample. A hugely rich wine, full of sweet chocolate and immensely ripe blackberry flavors. Sweet fruits, balanced by sweet and sour acidity. 94 *—R.V. (6/1/2007)*

Château Canon 2005 Barrel Sample Bordeaux Blend (Saint-Emilion Grand Cru) $NA. 93 *—R.V. (6/20/2006)*

CHÂTEAU CANON LĂ GAFFELIÈRE

Château Canon la Gaffelière 2000 Bordeaux Blend (Saint-Emilion) $50. 93 *—R.V. (6/1/2003)*

Château Canon la Gaffelière 2004 Barrel Sample Bordeaux Blend (Saint-Emilion Grand Cru) $NA. 94 *—R.V. (6/1/2005)*

CHÂTEAU CANTEMERLE

Château Cantemerle 2005 Barrel Sample Bordeaux Blend (Haut-Médoc) $NA. 88 *—R.V. (6/21/2006)*

Château Cantemerle 2003 Barrel Sample Bordeaux Blend (Haut-Médoc) $NA. 89 *—R.V. (6/3/2004)*

CHÂTEAU CANTENAC-BROWN

Château Cantenac-Brown 2004 Bordeaux Blend (Margaux) $NA. This estate has consistently underperformed. It was recently purchased by British businessman Simon Halabi, who plans to put fresh impetus into the property. This wine has plenty of plus points: It is well-balanced, emphasizing elegance rather than weight, but it does lack depth and intensity. **89** *—R.V. (6/1/2007)*

Château Cantenac-Brown 2001 Bordeaux Blend (Margaux) $37. 90 *—R.V. (6/1/2005)*

Château Cantenac-Brown 2005 Barrel Sample Bordeaux Blend (Margaux) $NA. 89 *—R.V. (6/21/2006)*

CHÂTEAU CANUET

Château Canuet 1998 Bordeaux Blend (Margaux) $30. 83 *—M.S. (1/1/2004)*

CHÂTEAU CARBONNIEUX

Château Carbonnieux 2004 Bordeaux Blend (Pessac-Léognan) $NA. With its slightly stalky character, its black currant fruits, and its dry, slightly austere tannins freshened by acidity, this is the wine for those who like truly classic Bordeaux. **89** *—R.V. (6/1/2007)*

Château Carbonnieux 2005 Barrel Sample Bordeaux Blend (Pessac-Léognan) $NA. 93 *—R.V. (6/20/2006)*

Château Carbonnieux 2002 Bordeaux White Blend (Pessac-Léognan) $33. 90 Editors' Choice *—J.C. (6/1/2005)*

CHÂTEAU CARDONNE

Château Cardonne 2004 Bordeaux Blend (Médoc) $NA. One of the most northerly gravel outcrops in the Médoc, Cardonne shows some of the structure and intensity of wines from more superior appellations, but at a good price. This firm 2004 layers dry tannins in the style of Saint-Estèphe, dominating the initially austere fruit. It needs time—probably 3–4 years. **88** *—R.V. (6/1/2007)*

CHÂTEAU CARONNE SAINTE-GEMME

Château Caronne Sainte-Gemme 2003 Bordeaux Blend (Haut-Médoc) $17. 86 *—R.V. (5/1/2006)*

CHÂTEAU CAVALIER

Château Cavalier 2006 Rosé Blend (Côtes de Provence) $11. Full, rather flat, this wine lacks real fresh, Mediterranean character. It's well-made, clean, with good acidity, and would certainly go with seafood. But that's it. **84** *—R.V. (7/1/2007)*

CHÂTEAU CERTAN DE MAY DE CERTAN

Château Certan de May de Certan 2006 Barrel Sample Bordeaux Blend (Pomerol) $NA. 92-94 Barrel Sample. Impressive; the tannins maybe too overwhelming. Look instead for the black plums, the spice and the structure. Needs to come into balance. **93** *—R.V. (6/1/2007)*

CHÂTEAU CERTAN-MARZELLE

Château Certan-Marzelle 2004 Bordeaux Blend (Pomerol) $NA. As is the way in Pomerol, this chateau has had its name changed by the current manager, Christian Moueix, from Certan Guiraud (after the family that owned it) back to its original Certan Marzelle. Whatever the nomenclature, the wine itself is impressive, if tough. It is dense, dominated by black fruits, and a solid structure. Made from 100% Merlot. **91** *—R.V. (6/1/2007)*

CHÂTEAU CHASSE-SPLEEN

Château Chasse-Spleen 2003 Bordeaux Blend (Moulis-en-Médoc) $24. 91 *—R.V. (5/1/2006)*

Château Chasse-Spleen 2000 Bordeaux Blend (Moulis) $35. 91 *—R.V. (6/1/2003)*

Château Chasse-Spleen 2004 Barrel Sample Bordeaux Blend (Haut-Médoc) $NA. 89 *—R.V. (6/1/2005)*

CHÂTEAU CHEVAL BLANC

Château Cheval Blanc 2006 Barrel Sample Bordeaux Blend (Saint-Emilion Grand Cru) $NA. 96-98 Barrel Sample. Dark chocolate and mocha flavors, very dark and intense, this is a big, concentrated wine, flavored with bitter cherries and structured. Certainly a great Cheval Blanc. **97** *—R.V. (6/1/2007)*

Château Cheval Blanc 2005 Barrel Sample Bordeaux Blend (Saint-Emilion Grand Cru) $NA. 96 *—R.V. (6/20/2006)*

Château Cheval Blanc 2003 Barrel Sample Bordeaux Blend (Saint-Emilion) $NA. 93 *—R.V. (6/3/2004)*

CHÂTEAU CITRAN

Château Citran 2004 Bordeaux Blend (Haut-Médoc) $NA. Influence of über-consultant Michel Rolland is evident in this wine; a superripe, dense wine with vibrant juicy fruits, plenty of black currant and eucalyptus flavors and a long, smooth aftertaste. **90** *—R.V. (6/1/2007)*

Château Citran 2002 Bordeaux Blend (Haut-Médoc) $NA. 87 *—R.V. (6/1/2005)*

Château Citran 2004 Barrel Sample Bordeaux Blend (Haut-Médoc) $NA. 88 *—R.V. (6/1/2005)*

CHÂTEAU CLARKE

Château Clarke 2004 Bordeaux Blend (Listrac-Médoc) $NA. With its Rothschild family ownership, Clarke is the superstar of Listrac. This 2004 is a wine that shows great ripe fruit along with new wood, but also the proper structure of Listrac, with dry tannins and a foursquare character. **90** *—R.V. (6/1/2007)*

Château Clarke 2003 Bordeaux Blend (Listrac-Médoc) $30. 90 *—R.V. (5/1/2006)*

Château Clarke 2005 Barrel Sample Bordeaux Blend (Listrac-Médoc) $NA. 90 *—R.V. (6/21/2006)*

CHÂTEAU CLERC-MILON

Château Clerc-Milon 2004 Bordeaux Blend (Pauillac) $NA. This finely structured wine offers good aging possibilities. But, for the moment, it has great acidity, juicy red fruits, solid tannins and a powerful new wood element that has come well into balance. **90** *—R.V. (6/1/2007)*

Château Clerc-Milon 2003 Bordeaux Blend (Pauillac) $55. 89 *—R.V. (5/1/2006)*

Château Clerc-Milon 2003 Barrel Sample Bordeaux Blend (Pauillac) $NA. 88 *—R.V. (6/3/2004)*

Château Clerc-Milon 2005 Barrel Sample Bordeaux Blend (Pauillac) $NA. 91 *—R.V. (6/1/2006)*

CHÂTEAU CLOS HAUT PEYRAGUEY

Château Clos Haut Peyraguey 2005 Barrel Sample Bordeaux White Blend (Sauternes) $NA. 91 *—R.V. (6/1/2006)*

CHÂTEAU CLOS LABORY

Château Clos Labory 2004 Bordeaux Blend (Saint-Estèphe) $NA. There's a core of solid, dry tannins that dominate this wine. But, as with so many 2004s, there is also a delicious, almost ready-to-drink freshness, emphasizing the juicy fruit flavors. **88** *—R.V. (6/1/2007)*

Château Clos Labory 2005 Barrel Sample Bordeaux Blend (Saint-Estèphe) $NA. 87 *—R.V. (6/21/2006)*

CHÂTEAU COMTE SAINT MARTIN

Château Comte Saint Martin 2000 Bordeaux Blend (Bordeaux) $8. 80 *M.S. (6/1/2003)*

CHÂTEAU CORMEIL-FIGEAC

Château Cormeil-Figeac 2003 Bordeaux Blend (Saint-Emilion Grand Cru) $32. This particular estate is small but has produced some good, solidly juicy ripe wine, with big black fruit and mocha flavors. **89** *—R.V. (11/1/2007)*

CHÂTEAU COS D'ESTOURNEL

Château Cos d'Estournel 2000 Bordeaux Blend (Saint-Estèphe) $130. 94 *—R.V. (6/1/2003)*

CHÂTEAU COUFRAN

Château Coufran 2004 Bordeaux Blend (Haut-Médoc) $NA. The Miailhe family, owners of Coufran also have Château Siran in Margaux in their portfolio. Coufran 2004 is structured, with dusty tannins, but over the rounded, smooth, almost jammy fruits, an accessible wine, showing good fresh acidity to finish. **89** *—R.V. (6/1/2007)*

Château Coufran 2005 Barrel Sample Bordeaux Blend (Haut-Médoc) $NA. 92 *—R.V. (6/1/2006)*

CHÂTEAU COUHINS-LURTON

Château Couhins-Lurton 2004 Bordeaux Blend (Pessac-Léognan) $NA. Red wine is new to André Lurton's property, only since 2002. This third vintage is dominated by new wood that works well, giving a smooth, velvet texture and a modern, polished feel. **90** *—R.V. (6/1/2007)*

Château Couhins-Lurton 2002 Bordeaux White Blend (Pessac-Léognan) $32. 90 —*R.V. (6/1/2005)*

CHÂTEAU COUTET

Château Coutet 2005 Barrel Sample Bordeaux White Blend (Barsac) $NA. 91 —*R.V. (6/1/2006)*

CHÂTEAU CROIX DE RAMBEAU

Château Croix de Rambeau 2004 Bordeaux Blend (Lussac Saint-Emilion) $20. A rich, succulent wine, full of ripe black currant and spice flavors, wrapped around a core of dry tannins. This is a wine that needs time to develop, but with its toast and other wood flavors and its weighty fruit, it should show well in five years. **89** —*R.V. (6/1/2007)*

CHÂTEAU CROIZET-BAGES

Château Croizet-Bages 2004 Barrel Sample Bordeaux Blend (Pauillac) $NA. 86 —*R.V. (6/1/2005)*

CHÂTEAU D'AGASSAC

Château d'Agassac 2004 Bordeaux Blend (Haut-Médoc) $NA. From almost nowhere, in 10 years Agassac has shot to stardom, thanks to big investments by insurance company Groupama. Under the management of Jean-Luc Zell, new wood has become a dominant item in vinification. In 2004, this is verging on too much, but ripe blackberry flavors should assert themselves in 2–3 years. A wine for modern Bordeaux lovers. **91** —*R.V. (6/1/2007)*

Château d'Agassac 2003 Bordeaux Blend (Haut-Médoc) $NA. 90 —*R.V. (5/1/2006)*

CHÂTEAU D'ANGLUDET

Château d'Angludet 2004 Bordeaux Blend (Margaux) $NA. It may not have great depths, but this wine is fresh and fruity; the black currant fruit blending well with the tannins and crisp acidity. Owned by the Sichel family, this property gives good value, and plenty of pleasure. **88** —*R.V. (6/1/2007)*

Château d'Angludet 2003 Bordeaux Blend (Margaux) $NA. 89 —*R.V. (5/1/2006)*

Château d'Angludet 2005 Barrel Sample Bordeaux Blend (Margaux) $NA. 88 —*R.V. (6/21/2006)*

CHÂTEAU D'ANTUGNAC

Château d'Antugnac 2005 Les Gravas Chardonnay (Limoux) $21. Ripe Chardonnay, barrel fermentation and aging, stirring of the lees—all these elements make for a powerfully rich wine, in which the wood acts as a carefully judged supporting act to the intense apples and cream fruitiness. There is just a touch of Burgundian minerality to give some structure. **92** —*R.V. (12/15/2007)*

Château d'Antugnac 2005 Aux Bons Hommes Red Blend (Limoux) $13. A big, smooth, ripe wine, with rich raspberry-jam flavors and just gently dry tannins. This blend of Merlot with some Syrah and Cabernet Sauvignon comes from vineyards 1,500 feet in the Limoux hills, yet it has the richness of a wine from warmer climate. Wood and spices add interest and richness. **90 Best Buy** —*R.V. (12/15/2007)*

CHÂTEAU D'AQUERIA

Château d'Aqueria 2003 Rhône Red Blend (Lirac) $19. 88 —*J.C. (11/15/2006)*

Château d'Aqueria 2004 Rosé Blend (Tavel) $16. 90 Editors' Choice —*J.C. (6/21/2006)*

CHÂTEAU D'ARCHE

Château d'Arche 2005 Barrel Sample Bordeaux White Blend (Sauternes) $NA. 91 —*R.V. (6/1/2006)*

CHÂTEAU D'ARCINS

Château d'Arcins 2004 Bordeaux Blend (Haut-Médoc) $19. A hard, very firm, lean wine, showing structure and tannins but little in the way of substance. Old-style winemaking produces an old-style wine. **81** —*R.V. (11/1/2007)*

CHÂTEAU D'ARMAILHAC

Château d'Armailhac 2004 Bordeaux Blend (Pauillac) $NA. A light, fresh, very accessible wine that has good, vibrant fruit and acidity. No great depths, but certainly pleasurable. **87** —*R.V. (6/1/2007)*

Château d'Armailhac 2005 Barrel Sample Bordeaux Blend (Pauillac) $NA. 92 —*R.V. (6/20/2006)*

CHÂTEAU D'ARSAC

Château d'Arsac 2003 Cuvée le Colombier Bordeaux Blend (Margaux) $30. 90 —*R.V. (5/1/2006)*

CHÂTEAU D'ISSAN

Château d'Issan 2003 Candale d'Issan Bordeaux Blend (Haut-Médoc) $NA. A stalky, black currant-infused wine, with just hints of raisins and jammy fruit. The acidity and freshness just appear to finish. **87** —*R.V. (11/1/2007)*

CHÂTEAU D'OR ET DE GUEULES

Château d'Or et de Gueules 1998 Rhône Red Blend (Costières de Nimes) $8. 84 —*J.C. (3/1/2001)*

CHÂTEAU D'YQUEM

Château d'Yquem 2005 Barrel Sample Bordeaux White Blend (Sauternes) $NA. 95 —*R.V. (6/20/2006)*

CHÂTEAU DASSAULT

Château Dassault 2005 Barrel Sample Bordeaux Blend (Saint-Emilion Grand Cru) $NA. 87 —*R.V. (6/21/2006)*

CHÂTEAU DAUZAC

Chateau Dauzac 2004 Bordeaux Blend (Margaux) $NA. Managed by André Lurton, this property has been revitalized in the past decade. The 2004 shows smooth blackberry fruit and ripe tannins, underpinned by the spice of finely balanced new wood. This suggests it is not a wine for long-term aging, but will be ready to drink in five years. **91** —*R.V. (6/1/2007)*

Château Dauzac 2004 Barrel Sample Bordeaux Blend (Margaux) $NA. 91 —*R.V. (6/1/2005)*

CHÂTEAU DE BASTET

Château de Bastet 2003 Cuvée Speciale Rhône Red Blend (Côtes-du-Rhône) $18. 88 —*R.V. (4/1/2005)*

CHÂTEAU DE BEAUCASTEL

Château de Beaucastel 1998 Cuvée Hommage à Jacques Perrin Red Blend (Châteauneuf-du-Pape) $240. 98 *(12/31/2001)*

Château de Beaucastel 1998 Rhône Red Blend (Châteauneuf-du-Pape) $62. 96 *(12/31/2001)*

CHÂTEAU DE BELLES EAUX

Château de Belles Eaux 2006 Rosé Blend (Coteaux du Languedoc) $NA. Bright candy-colored pink, with Syrah and Merlot in the blend, this is full-bodied, fat, but clean and fresh. It is more of an aperitif wine than for food, with its structure and richness. **87** —*R.V. (7/1/2007)*

CHÂTEAU DE BERNE

Château de Berne 2006 Cuvée Spéciale Rosé Blend (Côtes de Provence) $24. Blending Cinsault and Grenache, this comes from one of the showplace estates of Provence. Enjoy the crispness, the lightness, the taste of currants, of white fruits and the touch of tannin to give structure. **90** —*R.V. (7/1/2007)*

CHÂTEAU DE BOUSQUET

Château de Bousquet 2004 Bordeaux Blend (Côtes de Bourg) $13. A simple wine that tastes of black currants, plum stones and throws in very dry tannins. The wood element shows with the smoky, meaty character, but mainly this is about fruit and acidity. **86** —*R.V. (11/1/2007)*

CHÂTEAU DE CAMARSAC

Château de Camarsac 2000 Bordeaux Blend (Bordeaux Supérieur) $8. 86 —*R.V. (12/1/2002)*

CHÂTEAU DE CAMPUGET

Château de Campuget 1998 Cuvée Prestige Rhône Red Blend (Costières de Nimes) $14. 87 —*J.C. (3/1/2001)*

CHÂTEAU DE CAPITANS

Château de Capitans 2004 Gamay (Juliénas) $16. 86 —*J.C. (11/15/2005)*

CHÂTEAU DE CAROLLE

Château de Carolle 2005 Bordeaux Blend (Graves) $12. Firmly structured, full of juicy red fruits and fresh currants. The tannins are dry, but dusty, floating in the blueberry fruity character. Good acidity, structure and smoky elements from the wood. This is well-made Bordeaux at a good price. **87 Best Buy** —*R.V. (11/1/2007)*

Château de Carolle 2006 Bordeaux White Blend (Graves) $9. This is a classic white Bordeaux blend, half Sauvignon Blanc, half Sémillon. It enjoys the freshness of 2006, lifted pink grapefruit and citrus flavors, rounded with some wood, and freshened with delicious kiwi fruits. **88 Best Buy** —*R.V. (12/31/2007)*

CHÂTEAU DE CHAMIREY

Château de Chamirey 2001 La Mission Premier Cru Chardonnay (Mercurey) $24. 88 *—J.C. (10/1/2003)*

Château de Chamirey 1995 Pinot Noir (Rully) $19. 87 *(11/15/1999)*

CHÂTEAU DE CHANTEGRIVE

Château de Chantegrive 2004 Bordeaux Blend (Graves) $24. The aromas and initial taste are all of new wood. Only later does some fresh red fruit appear, giving the wine a lift. There is enough fruit here, but this needs time for the wood to calm down. Then the wine will show the vibrancy the structure suggests. 90 Editors' Choice *—R.V. (11/1/2007)*

Château de Chantegrive 2005 Bordeaux White Blend (Graves) $18. A fresh, grassy, herbal wine, with great crisp acidity and intense Sauvignon Blanc flavors. It floats acidity and green flavors along with full, rich fruit. The Chantegrive estate is one of the most important in the southern Graves, an example of what can be done in the region, given investment. Screwcap. 88 *—R.V. (11/1/2007)*

CHÂTEAU DE COULAINE

Château de Coulaine 2005 Cabernet Franc (Chinon) $17. Château de Coulaine operates biologic viticulture, a superior form of organic. This gives a fresh, vibrant fruit character, with some good dry tannins to balance. This is an easy, red-fruit wine, produced from young vines. 86 *—R.V. (4/1/2007)*

Château de Coulaine 2004 Bonnaventure Cabernet Franc (Chinon) $19. Bonnaventure is the family name of the owners of Coulaine. Aged in big wooden barrels, this finely balanced wine has a fresh, juicy character, the tannins lightly swept with spice, the fruit poised and crisp. 88 *—R.V. (4/1/2007)*

CHÂTEAU DE CRUZEAU

Château de Cruzeau 2000 Bordeaux White Blend (Pessac-Léognan) $17. 90 *—R.V. (6/1/2005)*

CHÂTEAU DE FARGUES

Château de Fargues 2005 Barrel Sample Bordeaux White Blend (Sauternes) $NA. 88 *—R.V. (6/21/2006)*

CHÂTEAU DE FESLES

Château de Fesles 1999 Cabernet Franc (Anjou) $12. 86 *—M.M. (1/1/2004)*

Château de Fesles 2005 Chenin Blanc (Bonnezeaux) $41. Luscious and balanced; a superb dessert wine. Brings in the ripeness and richness of great sweet Chenin wines with the grape's ability to save its enormous reserves of acidity. A wine that will age. 93 Cellar Selection *—R.V. (10/1/2007)*

Château de Fesles 2006 Chenin Sec Chenin Blanc (Anjou) $NA. By contrast with the Chenin Sec from Château de Fesle's La Chapelle vineyard, this is unoaked. That brings out the delicious, but powerful fruitiness: nuts, kiwis, a touch of honey and cantaloupe. Drink now, or keep for 3 years before opening. 88 *—R.V. (10/1/2007)*

Château de Fesles 2004 La Chapelle Chenin Sec Chenin Blanc (Anjou) $NA. Aged for 12 months in wood, this has lost some of the fresh, inimitable Chenin Blanc taste. But it has gained in intensity and ageability, the wood bringing out vanilla and dark toast flavors while still keeping the full, fat fruit. Age for four years and this will round out impressively. 90 *—R.V. (10/1/2007)*

CHÂTEAU DE FIEUZAL

Château de Fieuzal 2004 Bordeaux Blend (Pessac-Léognan) $NA. A dry, rather dark, textured wine, that shows some green pepper character. Not up to the normal standard from Fieuzal. 86 *—R.V. (6/1/2007)*

Château de Fieuzal 2005 Barrel Sample Bordeaux Blend (Pessac-Léognan) $NA. 92 *—R.V. (6/1/2006)*

CHÂTEAU DE FONSALETTE

Château de Fonsalette 1998 Réservé Syrah (Côtes-du-Rhône) $50. 85 *(11/1/2001)*

CHÂTEAU DE FRANCE

Château de France 2003 Bordeaux White Blend (Pessac-Léognan) $24. 92 *—R.V. (6/1/2005)*

CHÂTEAU DE GAUDOU

Château de Gaudou 2003 Red Blend (Cahors) $9. The Durou family has been at Gaudou since the 18th century, and today Fabrice Durou is the latest in the line to make Cahors on the 86-acre property. This blend of Malbec, Merlot and Tannat is initially juicy, until the firm, solid tannins kick in. It's still young with blackberry and bold fruit flavors, and young fruit tannins. 89 Best Buy *—R.V. (4/1/2007)*

CHÂTEAU DE JAU

Château de Jau 2002 Grenache Blanc (Grand Roussillon) $26. Made entirely from Grenache Blanc and fortified to 16% alcohol, this is an intriguing dessert wine. After aging in barrel for three years, it's taken on some nutty overtones, yet still retains a perfumed quality and orange-citrus flavors. Probably best with cheeses or on its own. 87 *—J.C. (12/15/2007)*

Château de Jau 2006 Muscat (Muscat de Rivesaltes) $26. A light, perfumy Muscat, with fresh aromas of pineapple and citrus. Shows a touch of alcohol on the finish, ending with orange and lime flavors and a dash of peppery spice. 85 *—J.C. (12/15/2007)*

Château de Jau 2002 Jaja Red Blend (Vin de Pays d'Oc) $9. 82 *—M.S. (9/1/2003)*

Château de Jau 2001 Talon Rouge Syrah (Côtes du Roussillon) $20. 88 *—M.S. (1/1/2004)*

CHÂTEAU DE L'HOSPITALET

Chateau de l'Hospitalet 2003 Grand Vin La Clape Rhône Red Blend (Coteaux du Languedoc) $20. Under the shadow of the coastal mountain of La Clape, near Narbonne, Gerard Bertrand has produced a highly perfumed wine, with dry tannins and fresh, violet scents. It has delicacy and elegance, making it great to drink with food. 90 *—R.V. (2/1/2007)*

CHÂTEAU DE L'ESCARELLE

Château de l'Escarelle 2006 Les Belles Bastides Rosé Blend (Coteaux Varois) $NA. A great blend of Mourvèdre and Syrah, this is cool climate rosé from a hot land. The inland hills of the Coteaux Varois give a freshness, and a lively currant flavored acidity to this wine, which bursts with crisp red and pink grapefruit fruits. 87 *—R.V. (7/1/2007)*

CHÂTEAU DE LA CHAIZE

Château de la Chaize 2001 Gamay (Brouilly) $12. 85 *—J.C. (11/15/2003)*

CHÂTEAU DE LA DAUPHINE

Château de la Dauphine 2004 Bordeaux Blend (Fronsac) $NA. Jean Halley's investment in this estate is paying off in this impressively ripe wine: big and fruity, with generous and rich black, plummy fruits. 89 *—R.V. (6/1/2007)*

CHÂTEAU DE LA GARDINE

Château de la Gardine 2001 Rhône Red Blend (Châteauneuf-du-Pape) $40. 87 *—J.C. (11/15/2005)*

Château de la Gardine 2003 Cuvée Tradition Rhône Red Blend (Châteauneuf-du-Pape) $40. 93 Cellar Selection *—R.V. (12/31/2005)*

CHÂTEAU DE LA RAGOTIERE

Château de la Ragotiere 2005 Terra Vitis Sur Lie Black Label Muscadet (Muscadet Sèvre Et Maine) $14. 87 Best Buy *—R.V. (11/15/2006)*

CHÂTEAU DE LA RIVIÈRE

Château de la Rivière 2004 Bordeaux Blend (Fronsac) $NA. Grand showplace of Fronsac, the fairytale castle of Rivière is now also a B&B. In terms of wines, this is firm, quite dark in texture, almost austere, with just hints of ripe fruit showing through. 87 *—R.V. (6/1/2007)*

CHÂTEAU DE LA ROCHE-AUX-MOINES

Château de la Roche-Aux-Moines 1996 Clos de la Bergerie Chenin Blanc (Loire) $32. 91 *—L.W. (12/31/1999)*

Château de la Roche-Aux-Moines 1996 Becherelle Coulée de Serrant White Blend (Savennières) $26. 86 *—L.W. (10/1/1999)*

CHÂTEAU DE LA ROULERIE

Château de la Roulerie 2006 Chenin Blanc (Anjou) $13. For the moment, this Chenin is at the young, fresh stage in its evolution. There are green and yellow fruits, a supple structure, and just a touch of vanilla and toast to finish. The acidity is here, so drink this with a great fish dish. 87 *—R.V. (10/1/2007)*

Château de la Roulerie 2005 Les Terrasses Chenin Sec Chenin Blanc (Anjou) $20. A creamy, wood-dominated dry wine; the honey and floral flavors of the Chenin are lost at this stage. But there's a good hint of balance, and the spicy wood tastes will tone down in 18 months. 89 *—R.V. (10/1/2007)*

Château de la Roulerie 2005 Premier Cru Chenin Blanc (Chaume) $45. Aged in wood for 18 months, and made from old vines, this is a rich, botrytised wine, with wild flower honey, perfumed peaches and a deliciously piercing acidity. It needs to age at least five years, when the complexity of the fruit will be enhanced by the wood. **91** —*R.V. (10/1/2007)*

CHÂTEAU DE LA TERRIERE

Château de la Terriere 2002 Vieilles Vignes Gamay (Beaujolais-Villages) $12. 86 —*J.C. (11/15/2003)*

CHÂTEAU DE LAMARQUE

Château de Lamarque 2004 Bordeaux Blend (Haut-Médoc) $NA. The magnificent medieval château at Lamarque has seen a remarkable turnaround in its wine fortunes. This 2004 is less successful than the previous vintages, too dry, too dominated by wood for the fruit. But there is power and structure there, so it may well develop. 86 —*R.V. (6/1/2007)*

Château de Lamarque 2004 Barrel Sample Bordeaux Blend (Haut-Médoc) $NA. 86 —*R.V. (6/1/2005)*

CHÂTEAU DE LANCYRE

Château de Lancyre 2005 Pic Saint-Loup Rosé Blend (Coteaux du Languedoc) $NA. 83 —*J.C. (6/19/2006)*

CHÂTEAU DE LUSSAC

Château de Lussac 2000 Le Libertin de Lussac Bordeaux Blend (Lussac Saint-Emilion) $25. 87 —*J.C. (11/15/2005)*

CHÂTEAU DE MALLE

Château de Malle 2004 Barrel Sample Bordeaux White Blend (Sauternes) $NA. 87 —*R.V. (6/1/2005)*

Château de Malle 2004 Barrel Sample Bordeaux White Blend (Sauternes) $NA. 87 —*R.V. (6/1/2005)*

CHÂTEAU DE MARSANNAY

Château de Marsannay 2003 Chardonnay (Marsannay) $20. 90 —*R.V. (9/1/2005)*

Château de Marsannay 2004 Pinot Noir (Gevrey-Chambertin) $45. Smoky aromas mingle with red berries in this attractive wine, which shows the proper weight for a Gevrey along with good fresh fruits, acidity and an important layer of dryness. Expect this wine to be ready by next fall. 88 —*R.V. (3/1/2007)*

Château de Marsannay 2003 Pinot Noir (Gevrey-Chambertin) $48. Heavily weighted towards tannins, here's a wine that gains its power from the richness of 2003. It is big, densely compacted and firm, a wine that is solidly built around the black plums and berries. 87 —*R.V. (3/1/2007)*

Château de Marsannay 2003 Pinot Noir (Marsannay) $20. 88 —*R.V. (9/1/2005)*

Château de Marsannay 2002 Pinot Noir (Gevrey-Chambertin) $48. The weight and structure of this wine comes from the powerful 2002s, as much as from Gevrey-Chambertin. The wine is still very firm, dominated by dry, leathery tannins. Only when the wine is in the mouth for a while do the full, red fruits come through, although on the finish, the tannins close in again. 88 —*R.V. (3/1/2007)*

Château de Marsannay 2004 Le Clos de Jeu Pinot Noir (Marsannay) $24. Literally, the playing field, Le Clos de Jeu is the best known vineyard in Marsannay. This wine, from the chateau owned by Patriarche Père et Fils of Beaune, is light, easy to drink, but also has attractive ripe plum skin flavors. With its layer of tannin, it could age for a few years. 88 —*R.V. (3/1/2007)*

CHÂTEAU DE MAUVANNE

Château de Mauvanne 1999 Cuvée 1 Red Blend (Côtes de Provence) $14. 87 —*M.S. (1/1/2004)*

CHÂTEAU DE MEURSAULT

Château de Meursault 2003 Chardonnay (Meursault) $42. 87 —*R.V. (9/1/2005)*

Château de Meursault 2002 Clos du Château Chardonnay (Bourgogne) $19. 86 —*J.C. (11/15/2005)*

Château de Meursault 2003 Clos du Château Chardonnay (Bourgogne) $21. 89 —*R.V. (9/1/2005)*

Château de Meursault 2003 Premier Cru Chardonnay (Meursault) $58. 90 —*R.V. (9/1/2005)*

Château de Meursault 2003 Pinot Noir (Bourgogne) $20. 85 —*R.V. (9/1/2005)*

Château de Meursault 2000 Pinot Noir (Bourgogne) $16. 83 *(4/1/2003)*

Château de Meursault 2003 Premier Cru Pinot Noir (Beaune) $32. 88 —*R.V. (9/1/2005)*

Château de Meursault 1999 Cent-Vignes Premier Cru Pinot Noir (Beaune) $31. 87 *(4/1/2003)*

Château de Meursault 2001 Clos de Epenots Premier Cru Pinot Noir (Pommard) $43. 82 —*J.C. (11/15/2005)*

Château de Meursault 2002 Clos des Chênes Premier Cru Pinot Noir (Volnay) $45. 88 —*R.V. (9/1/2004)*

Château de Meursault 1999 Clos des Epenots Premier Cru Pinot Noir (Pommard) $40. 88 *(4/1/2003)*

CHÂTEAU DE MONTFAUCON

Château de Montfaucon 2005 Comtesse Madeleine Rhône White Blend (Côtes-du-Rhône) $15. 87 —*J.C. (11/15/2006)*

CHÂTEAU DE MONTGUÉRET

Château de Montguéret 2003 M de Montguéret Cabernet Franc (Anjou Villages) $15. Despite its provenance from a warm year, this still shows too much stalky character. Wood rounds it, but also dominates. It's dry and firm, with a smoky aftertaste. 84 —*R.V. (10/1/2007)*

Château de Montguéret 2003 Le Petit Saint Louis Chenin Blanc (Coteaux du Layon) $10. The richness of this wine comes through on from the ripe, supersweet fruits. It's beginning to mellow, with honey and sweet nuts showing more than the primary white fruits. The aftertaste gives crispness and a light freshness. 89 Best Buy —*R.V. (10/1/2007)*

Château de Montguéret NV White Blend (Crémant de Loire) $15. Château de Montguéret has made a fresh, piercing, crisp Chenin Blanc-based sparkling wine. Just a touch of almond and a backdrop of honey give roundness to this green wine. 86 —*R.V. (10/1/2007)*

Château de Myrat 2004 Barrel Sample Bordeaux White Blend (Barsac) $NA. 88 —*R.V. (6/1/2005)*

CHÂTEAU DE PAMPELONNE

Château de Pampelonne 2006 Rosé Blend (Côtes de Provence) $NA. With its elegant presentation, this is the perfect bottle for summer white tablecloth dining. Made by the cooperative of Saint-Tropez, the lifestyle and the fruit-driven quality of the wine, with super-ripe raspberry flavors, coincide well. 87 —*R.V. (7/1/2007)*

CHÂTEAU DE PARAZA

Château de Paraza 2002 Red Blend (Minervois) $9. 83 —*R.V. (12/1/2004)*

CHÂTEAU DE PENNAUTIER

Château de Pennautier 2000 Cabernet Sauvignon (Vin de Pays d'Oc) $9. 86 Best Buy —*M.S. (2/1/2003)*

Château de Pennautier 2000 L'Orangerie Rhône Red Blend (Languedoc) $9. 85 —*M.S. (2/1/2003)*

Château de Pennautier 2006 Rosé Blend (Cabardes) $11. A yummy rosé from a little known appellation just north of Carcassonne, Pennautier's 2006 Cabardès features bold scents of watermelon and strawberry. The flavors are a colorful jumble of berries, medium-bodied and mouthfilling, finishing fresh and clean. Pack one in the picnic hamper this summer. 87 Best Buy —*J.C. (7/1/2007)*

Château de Pennautier 2001 Syrah (Vin de Pays d'Oc) $8. 82 —*M.S. (1/1/2004)*

CHÂTEAU DE PEZ

Château de Pez 2004 Bordeaux Blend (Saint-Estèphe) $36. Dark, dry tannins are what good Saint-Estèphe is all about when young, and de Pez doesn't disappoint. But it does more, with refined black plum skin flavors, a rich mix of spices and mint, and a refreshing streak of acidity. In 4–5 years, this will be an outstanding wine. 91 Cellar Selection —*R.V. (6/1/2007)*

Château de Pez 2003 Bordeaux Blend (Saint-Estèphe) $36. Despite the hot 2003, this keeps an impressive sense of balance with dense rather than superripe fruit, herbs, black currant jelly and delicious touches of new wood. Structured to age, with dry tannins and acidity. A great success. 92 —*R.V. (11/1/2007)*

Château de Pez 1995 Bordeaux Blend (Saint-Estèphe) $30. 87 *(5/1/2000)*

Château de Pez 2003 Barrel Sample Bordeaux Blend (Saint-Estèphe) $NA. 88 —*R.V. (6/3/2004)*

CHÂTEAU DE PIBARNON

Château de Pibarnon 2005 Rosé Blend (Bandol) $NA. 87 —*J.C. (6/21/2006)*

CHÂTEAU DE PORTETS

Château de Portets 2005 Bordeaux White Blend (Graves) $14. An elegant, full-bodied wine, showing the richness of 2005, but keeping the tropical fruit element in balance with the light toast and butter flavors. The acidity is harder to find, but it comes through with spice in a soft aftertaste. 88 —*R.V. (12/31/2007)*

CHÂTEAU DE POURCIEUX

Château de Pourcieux 2006 Rosé Blend (Côtes de Provence) $13. The 70 acre vineyard of Michel d'Espagnet was painted by Paul Cézanne. This blend of Syrah, with Grenache and Cinsault is crisp, but full-bodied, true pink grapefruit and with a touch of smooth vanilla. The acidity bursts in the mouth at the end. **90 Best Buy** —*R.V. (7/1/2007)*

Château de Pourcieux 2001 Rosé Blend (Côtes de Provence) $9. 83 —*M.S. (9/1/2003)*

CHÂTEAU DE ROQUES

Château de Roques 2004 Merlot (Premieres Côtes de Bordeaux) $NA. From a parcel of Merlot at Château Lezongars, this is a burly, ripe wine; full and packed with solid fruits and dry tannins. The weight of the fruit should sustain and help soften the dryness. It certainly has the richness. 87 —*R.V. (6/1/2007)*

CHÂTEAU DE ROUANNE

Château de Rouanne 2005 Rhône Red Blend (Vinsobres) $20. 88 —*J.C. (11/15/2006)*

CHÂTEAU DE RULLY

Château de Rully 2003 Pinot Noir (Rully) $NA. 85 —*R.V. (9/1/2005)*

CHÂTEAU DE SAINT-COSME

Château de Saint-Cosme 2004 Hominus Fides Rhône Red Blend (Gigondas) $50. **93 Cellar Selection** —*J.C. (11/15/2006)*

CHÂTEAU DE SAINT-MARTIN

Château de Saint-Martin 2006 Cuvée Grande Réserve Rosé Blend (Côtes de Provence) $NA. Underground, lightly musty aromas harm what is otherwise an attractively warm wine, with flavors of wild strawberries and ripe citrus. The acidity gives extra freshness to the taste. Shame about the aroma. 84 —*R.V. (7/1/2007)*

Château de Saint-Martin 2006 Saint-Lambert Rosé Blend (Côtes de Provence) $NA. This misses the freshness of good Provence rosé. With its petrol aroma and bitter flavors, it doesn't live up to its billing as the lighter of the two rosés from Château de Saint-Martin. 80 —*R.V. (7/1/2007)*

CHÂTEAU DE SAINT-ROCH

Château de Saint-Roch 2004 Brunel Rhône Red Blend (Lirac) $13. 89 —*R.V. (12/31/2006)*

CHÂTEAU DE SANCERRE

Château de Sancerre 1997 Sauvignon Blanc (Sancerre) $18. 87 —*M.S. (10/1/1999)*

CHÂTEAU DE SÉGRIÈS

Château de Ségriès 2004 Rhône Red Blend (Lirac) $14. 89 —*J.C. (11/15/2006)*

Château de Ségriès 1999 Cuvée Reservée Rhône Red Blend (Lirac) $12. 87 —*J.C. (12/31/2000)*

Château de Ségriès 2005 Rosé Blend (Tavel) $15. 88 —*J.C. (11/15/2006)*

CHÂTEAU DE SEGUIN

Château de Seguin 1999 Cuvée Carl Bordeaux Blend (Bordeaux Supérieur) $25. 89 —*R.V. (12/1/2002)*

CHÂTEAU DE SÉRAME

Château de Sérame 2001 Rhône Red Blend (Corbières) $10. **86 Best Buy** —*J.C. (11/15/2004)*

CHÂTEAU DE SOURS

Château de Sours 2000 Bordeaux Blanc White Blend (Bordeaux) $8. 87 —*R.V. (12/1/2002)*

CHÂTEAU DE TARGÉ

Château de Targé 2005 Cabernet Franc (Saumur-Champigny) $NA. Edouard Pisani-Ferry has been one of the great producers of Saumur-Champigny over many years. This is a classic—ripe, but fresh red fruits, some soft tannins, a lightness and elegance. And at the end, there's a wonderful burst of smoky, perfumed flavors. 90 —*R.V. (4/1/2007)*

Château de Targé 2004 Cabernet Franc (Saumur-Champigny) $NA. Targé, with its caves hewn out of the chalk cliffs, makes a classic Saumur-Champigny. This wine reflects the vintage, fresh and fruity, but with a layer of smoky tannins. The aftertaste is of cranberry skins. 87 —*R.V. (4/1/2007)*

CHÂTEAU DE TRACY

Château de Tracy 2004 Sauvignon Blanc (Pouilly-Fumé) $35. 91 —*R.V. (8/1/2006)*

Château de Tracy 2002 Sauvignon Blanc (Pouilly-Fumé) $30. 89 *(7/1/2005)*

CHÂTEAU DE VALCOMB

Château de Valcomb 2001 Prestige Rhône Red Blend (Costières de Nimes) $12. 84 —*J.C. (2/1/2005)*

CHÂTEAU DE VAUX

Château de Vaux 2002 Les Gryphées White Blend (Moselle VDQS) $13. **89 Best Buy** —*J.C. (11/15/2004)*

CHÂTEAU DES VILLENEUVE

Château de Villeneuve 2005 Cabernet Franc (Saumur-Champigny) $NA. This wine, the basic Saumur-Champigny from the estate is rich and velvet smooth; a mix of dense, dusty tannins and ripe black fruits, with a touch of wood. **92 Editors' Choice** —*R.V. (4/1/2007)*

CHÂTEAU DES ALBIÈRES

Château des Albières 2001 Cuvée Georges Dardé Red Blend (Saint-Chinian) $NA. 84 —*R.V. (12/1/2004)*

CHÂTEAU DES KARANTES

Chateau des Karantes 2006 Rosé des Karantes Rosé Blend (Coteaux du Languedoc) $12. Down by the Mediterranean, the vineyard of Domaine des Karantes uses 40-year old vines for this blend dominated by Mourvèdre. It is fresh and refreshing, a deftly structured wine, all dancing fruit and elegance. What rosé should be. **90 Best Buy** —*R.V. (7/1/2007)*

CHÂTEAU DES MILLE ANGES

Château des Mille Anges 1996 Bordeaux Blend (Premieres Côtes de Bordeaux) $13. 80 —*M.S. (7/1/2000)*

CHÂTEAU DES ROQUES

Château des Roques 2003 Rhône Red Blend (Vacqueyras) $8. **85 Best Buy** —*J.C. (11/15/2006)*

CHÂTEAU DES TOURS

Château des Tours 2000 Réserve Red Blend (Côtes-du-Rhône) $14. **90 Best Buy** *(10/1/2003)*

CHÂTEAU DEYREM VALENTIN

Château Deyrem Valentin 2001 Bordeaux Blend (Margaux) $NA. 87 —*R.V. (6/1/2005)*

CHÂTEAU DOISY VÉDRINES

Château Doisy Védrines 2004 Barrel Sample Bordeaux White Blend (Sauternes) $NA. 91 —*R.V. (6/1/2005)*

CHÂTEAU DOISY-DAËNE

Château Doisy-Daëne 2005 Barrel Sample Bordeaux White Blend (Barsac) $NA. 91 —*R.V. (6/1/2006)*

CHÂTEAU DU BASTY

Château du Basty 2001 Lantignié Gamay (Beaujolais-Villages) $13. 83 —*J.C. (11/15/2003)*

CHÂTEAU DU CLUZEAU

Château du Cluzeau 2005 Barrel Sample Bordeaux Blend (Listrac-Médoc) 86 —*R.V. (6/21/2006)*

CHÂTEAU DU COURLAT

Château du Courlat 2004 Cuvée Jean-Baptiste Bordeaux Blend (Lussac Saint-Emilion) $NA. Named after Jean-Baptiste Audy, a wine merchant and the grandfather of the present owner, this is the top wine from Courlat. It's highly polished, the new wood smoothing out the rough edges of the dry fruit tannins. It has good fresh fruit and acidity to finish. 89 —*R.V. (6/1/2007)*

CHÂTEAU DU DONJON

Château du Donjon 2005 Rosé Blend (Minervois) 84 —*J.C. (6/19/2006)*

CHÂTEAU DU GALOUPET

Château du Galoupet 2006 Rosé Blend (Côtes de Provence) $NA. A finely structured wine, more serious than many rosés, but still with all the right fresh, crisp fruits. Blending Grenache, Cinsault and Syrah, it exudes southern warmth, without losing its elegance and fresh red fruit character. 90 —*R.V. (7/1/2007)*

CHÂTEAU DU QUINT

Château du Quint 1999 Red Blend (Pomerol) $25. 80 *—M.S. (1/1/2004)*

CHÂTEAU DU TERTRE

Château du Tertre 2004 Bordeaux Blend (Margaux) $NA. A soft, lively wine, with fresh acidity and easy tannins. It's made especially attractive by the spicy wood flavors, but it's not a wine for long-term aging. 88 *—R.V. (6/1/2007)*

Château du Tertre 2001 Bordeaux Blend (Margaux) $31. 92 *—R.V. (6/1/2005)*

CHÂTEAU DU TRIGNON

Château du Trignon 2000 Sablet Rouge Grenache-Syrah (Côtes-du-Rhône) $15. 91 Best Buy *—S.H. (11/15/2002)*

Château du Trignon 2004 Classic Rhône Red Blend (Côtes-du-Rhône) $15. 85 *—J.C. (11/15/2006)*

CHÂTEAU DUCLA

Château Ducla 2005 Bordeaux Blend (Bordeaux Supérieur) $15. There's a great burst of ripe fruitiness with only a hint of dry Bordeaux tannins. There are great peppery red cherry flavors, berry acidity and spice from wood. 86 *—R.V. (11/1/2007)*

Château Ducla 2002 Bordeaux Blend (Bordeaux Supérieur) $13. 81 *—J.C. (6/1/2005)*

Château Ducla 1998 Bordeaux Blend (Bordeaux) $10. 82 *—J.C. (3/1/2001)*

Château Ducla 2005 Bordeaux White Blend (Entre-Deux-Mers) $12. Owned by the Mau family, this estate situated just above the Garonne river south of Bordeaux, is home to an exciting range of red wines. The white is more standard fare, full, soft, with green plum flavors, but given a lift to finish by a touch of wood. 85 *—R.V. (11/1/2007)*

CHÂTEAU DUCRU BEAUCAILLOU

Château Ducru Beaucaillou 2004 Bordeaux Blend (Saint-Julien) $70. Impressively dense, dark flavored wine, very rich and quite extracted. But it still keeps the elegance and some of the freshness of 2004, and there is plenty of blackberry flavor to push the wine along. Heavier than many 2004s, it still shows that great acidity. 94 *—R.V. (12/16/2007)*

Château Ducru Beaucaillou 2003 Barrel Sample Bordeaux Blend (Saint-Julien) $NA. 91 *—R.V. (6/3/2004)*

CHÂTEAU DUHART-MILON

Château Duhart-Milon 2004 Bordeaux Blend (Pauillac) $NA. Often outshone alongside its stablemate, Lafite, Duhart-Milon seems to be coming into its own. It is rich and polished, dominated by new wood and soft, ripe fruit. The flavors are black currant, more jelly than fruit, but the power is also here, coming with the tannins and the intense, fresh acidity. 91 *—R.V. (6/1/2007)*

Château Duhart-Milon 2003 Bordeaux Blend (Pauillac) $55. 89 *—R.V. (5/1/2006)*

Château Duhart-Milon 2005 Barrel Sample Bordeaux Blend (Pauillac) $NA. 89 *—R.V. (6/21/2006)*

CHÂTEAU DUPLESSIS

Château Duplessis 2003 Bordeaux Blend (Moulis-en-Médoc) $NA. 88 *—R.V. (5/1/2006)*

CHÂTEAU DURFORT-VIVENS

Château Durfort-Vivens 2004 Bordeaux Blend (Margaux) $NA. One of the many properties in Margaux owned by the Lurton family (Bordeaux's largest landowners). Durfort-Vivens is an estate that has improved dramatically, as in this 2004, packed with new wood flavors but with great balancing ripe fruit. 92 *—R.V. (6/1/2007)*

Château Durfort-Vivens 2000 Bordeaux Blend (Margaux) $31. 85 *—R.V. (6/1/2003)*

Château Durfort-Vivens 2006 Barrel Sample Bordeaux Blend (Margaux) $NA. 92-94 Barrel Sample. Intensely structured, balanced with sufficient new wood. This has excellent potential, with some freshness, but more weight from the ripe black fruits. 93 *—R.V. (6/1/2007)*

Château Durfort-Vivens 2004 Barrel Sample Bordeaux Blend (Margaux) $NA. 93 *—R.V. (6/1/2005)*

CHÂTEAU FAUGERES

Château Faugeres 2004 Bordeaux Blend (Saint-Emilion Grand Cru) $NA. A beautifully structured wine, with great ripe dark fruits, but also dense and complex. Faugères is showing great class at the moment, and with its balanced, but ripe fruit, this wine is impressive and well worth aging. 92 *—R.V. (6/1/2007)*

Château Faugeres 2000 Bordeaux Blend (Saint-Emilion) $40. 90 *—R.V. (6/1/2003)*

Château Faugeres 2006 Barrel Sample Bordeaux Blend (Saint-Emilion Grand Cru) $NA. 92-94 Barrel Sample. A dark, meaty wine, very New World in its richness and opulence. It is concentrated, packed with black fruit. 93 *—R.V. (6/1/2007)*

CHÂTEAU FAVRAY

Château Favray 2006 Sauvignon Blanc (Pouilly-Fumé) $NA. This is complex, with ripe, almost tropical fruits vying for prominence with a definite mineral structure, which offers a firm core of flavor. It's fresh and fruity now, but this could age over five years to enhance the complexity. 91 *—R.V. (10/1/2007)*

CHÂTEAU FERRANDE

Château Ferrande 2004 Bordeaux Blend (Graves) $19. A stalky, lean wine with austere fruits. The tannins are dry and washed in acidity. It's firm, structured, hinting at some juicy black currants. There's some spice and smokiness from the wood. 86 *—R.V. (11/1/2007)*

Château Ferrande 2005 Barrel Sample Bordeaux Blend (Graves) 91 *—R.V. (6/1/2006)*

CHÂTEAU FERRIÈRE

Château Ferrière 2004 Bordeaux Blend (Margaux) $NA. Soft, pleasant wine that lacks intensity. There is some good acidity as well as fresh fruit, but there's also an unappealing bitterness. 87 *—R.V. (6/1/2007)*

Château Ferrière 2005 Barrel Sample Bordeaux Blend (Margaux) 91 *—R.V. (6/1/2006)*

CHÂTEAU FEYTIT-CLINET

Château Feytit-Clinet 2005 Barrel Sample Bordeaux Blend (Pomerol) 90 *—R.V. (6/21/2006)*

CHÂTEAU FIGEAC

Château Figeac 2006 Barrel Sample Bordeaux Blend (Saint-Emilion Grand Cru) $NA. 92-94 Barrel Sample A closed wine, all dense tannins. There is fruit there, which weighs in behind the tannins, but it is seriously dense and concentrated. 93 *—R.V. (6/1/2007)*

Château Figeac 2005 Barrel Sample Bordeaux Blend (Saint-Emilion Grand Cru) 92 *—R.V. (6/1/2006)*

CHÂTEAU FILHOT

Château Filhot 2004 Barrel Sample Bordeaux White Blend (Sauternes) 88 *—R.V. (6/1/2005)*

CHÂTEAU FLAUGERGUES

Château Flaugergues 2003 Rosé Blend (Coteaux du Languedoc) $12. 83 *—R.V. (12/1/2004)*

CHÂTEAU FOMBRAUGE

Château Fombrauge 2002 Bordeaux Blend (Saint-Emilion Grand Cru) $NA. 88 *—R.V. (6/1/2005)*

Château Fombrauge 2004 Barrel Sample Bordeaux Blend (Saint-Emilion Grand Cru) $NA. 90 *—R.V. (6/1/2005)*

CHÂTEAU FONBADET

Chateau Fonbadet 2004 Bordeaux Blend (Pauillac) $NA. Owned by the Peyronie family, and run by Pascale, this is one of the few estates in Pauillac not classified as a growth in 1855. That makes it a good value for the appellation, and this 2004, with its dense, solid fruit, packed with cassis and ripeness, is a good buy. 91 *—R.V. (6/1/2007)*

Château Fonbadet 2000 Bordeaux Blend (Pauillac) $50. 89 *—J.M. (4/3/2004)*

CHÂTEAU FONRÉAUD

Château Fonréaud 2000 Bordeaux Blend (Listrac) $15. 88 *—R.V. (6/1/2003)*

Château Fonréaud 1999 Red Blend (Listrac) $17. 88 *—R.V. (11/15/2003)*

CHÂTEAU FONTENIL

Château Fontenil 2004 Bordeaux Blend (Fronsac) $NA. When they are not traveling, this is home to Michel and Dany Rolland. The sense of structure gives this wine its sophistication. Along with the structure are layers of black fruit, cocoa, new wood and a solid core of richness. 90 *—R.V. (6/1/2007)*

CHÂTEAU FORTIA

Château Fortia 2003 Cuvée du Baron Rhône Red Blend (Châteauneuf-du-

Pape) $32. 92 *—R.V. (12/31/2005)*

CHÂTEAU FOURCAS DUPRÉ

Château Fourcas Dupré 2004 Bordeaux Blend (Listrac-Médoc) $NA. Red berry fruits dominate a wine that is solid, foursquare, with dry tannins and acidity. The mix is made more lively with cinnamon spice flavors and vanilla from wood. Enjoy in five years. 89 *—R.V. (6/1/2007)*

Château Fourcas Dupré 2005 Barrel Sample Bordeaux Blend (Listrac-Médoc) $NA. 89 *—R.V. (6/21/2006)*

CHÂTEAU FOURCAS-HOSTEN

Château Fourcas-Hosten 2004 Bordeaux Blend (Listrac-Médoc) $NA. Solid fruits and tannins, a judicious use of new wood and some fresh fruits are all in this easy, attractive wine that is already aging well. Drink now or over five years. 88 *—R.V. (6/1/2007)*

Château Fourcas-Hosten 2002 Bordeaux Blend (Listrac-Médoc) $NA. 88 *—R.V. (6/1/2005)*

Château Fourcas-Hosten 2005 Barrel Sample Bordeaux Blend (Listrac-Médoc) $NA. 90 *—R.V. (6/21/2006)*

CHÂTEAU FRANC LA ROSE

Château Franc la Rose 2004 Bordeaux Blend (Saint-Emilion Grand Cru) $29. A small property bought by Jean-Louis Trocard in 1995. This 2004 is dominated, perhaps too much, by new wood. It is difficult to taste the fruit through the wood, and it tastes too light for the amount of wood present. It could come around, but for now, it is for those who like toast and vanilla flavors. 86 *—R.V. (6/1/2007)*

CHÂTEAU FRANC-MAYNE

Château Franc-Mayne 2005 Barrel Sample Bordeaux Blend (Saint-Emilion Grand Cru) $NA. 91 *—R.V. (6/1/2006)*

CHÂTEAU FRANC-PÉRAT

Château Franc-Pérat 2005 Bordeaux Blend (Premieres Côtes de Bordeaux) $NA. Fresh and fruity, showing ripe, vibrant red fruits and soft tannins. This second wine from the Mont-Pérat estate, is packed with red cherries and lively acidity. 87 *—R.V. (11/1/2007)*

CHÂTEAU FUISSÉ

Château Fuissé 2003 Chardonnay (Pouilly-Fuissé) $35. 87 *—J.C. (11/15/2005)*

Château Fuissé 2003 Les Brûlés Chardonnay (Pouilly-Fuissé) $45. 89 *—J.C. (11/15/2005)*

Château Fuissé 2003 Les Clos Chardonnay (Pouilly-Fuissé) $45. 90 *—J.C. (11/15/2005)*

Château Fuissé 2003 Les Combettes Chardonnay (Pouilly-Fuissé) $NA. 90 Editors' Choice *—J.C. (11/15/2005)*

Château Fuissé 2003 Vieilles Vignes Chardonnay (Pouilly-Fuissé) $50. 92 Cellar Selection *—J.C. (11/15/2005)*

CHÂTEAU GAILLARD

Château Gaillard 2005 Chenin Blanc-Chardonnay (Touraine Mesland) $12. Soft, with fat flavors that fill out in the glass. This has a crisp edge to it, though, hinting at mineral, while keeping the ripe pear flavors. The aftertaste shows some of the characteristic Chenin Blanc nuttiness. 87 Best Buy *—R.V. (10/1/2007)*

Château Gaillard 2005 Red Blend (Touraine Mesland) $12. This Cabernet Franc, Malbec and Gamay blend is not for lovers of full-bodied reds, but it does have plenty of lively, fresh bitter cherry and red currant flavors, and a dry, tannic backbone. A great partner with salmon or cold meats. 86 *—R.V. (10/1/2007)*

Château Gaillard 2006 Sauvignon Blanc (Touraine) $15. A fat, full wine, polished by its fresh herbal flavors. There are clean, lime and citrus tastes, a ripe spice and a crisp, green plum aftertaste. 85 *—R.V. (9/1/2007)*

Château Gaillard NV Les Doucinières Sparkling Blend (Crémant de Loire) $22. The blend—Chenin Blanc, Chardonnay and Cabernet Franc—is typical of Loire sparkling wines. It gives a full mousse in the mouth, herbal and green pea flavors, and a soft, creamy aftertaste, backed up by acidity. 86 *—R.V. (10/1/2007)*

CHÂTEAU GAUDRELLE

Château Gaudrelle 2002 Brut Chenin Blanc (Vouvray) $18. 88 *—R.V. (6/1/2006)*

CHÂTEAU GÉNOT-BOULANGER

Château Génot-Boulanger 2000 Pinot Noir (Chambolle-Musigny) $NA. 86 *—R.V. (11/1/2002)*

Château Génot-Boulanger 2002 Clos Blanc Premier Cru Pinot Noir (Pommard) $30. 88 *—R.V. (9/1/2004)*

Château Génot-Boulanger 2002 Les Aussy Pinot Noir (Volnay) $25. 88 *—R.V. (9/1/2004)*

CHÂTEAU GISCOURS

Château Giscours 2004 Bordeaux Blend (Margaux) $NA. A smooth, delicious wine. The fruit flavors go right through this ripe, complex wine, leaving the tannins and wood as supporting acts. As with so many 2004s, the aftertaste is fresh, with great acidity. 93 *—R.V. (6/1/2007)*

Château Giscours 2003 Bordeaux Blend (Margaux) $42. 90 *—R.V. (5/1/2006)*

Château Giscours 2000 Bordeaux Blend (Margaux) $45. 92 *—R.V. (6/1/2003)*

Château Giscours 2004 Barrel Sample Bordeaux Blend (Margaux) $NA. 93 *—R.V. (6/1/2005)*

CHÂTEAU GLORIA

Château Gloria 2000 Bordeaux Blend (Saint-Julien) $30. 87 *—R.V. (6/1/2003)*

CHÂTEAU GRAND CORBIN-DESPAGNE

Château Grand Corbin-Despagne 2004 Bordeaux Blend (Saint-Emilion Grand Cru) $NA. Demoted in 1996, losing its classed growth status, the Despagne family set to work to get back on top, which was achieved in 2006. By 2004, they were on a roll, making a powerfully rich wine, with a good texture, spice from the Cabernet Franc, and some firm, dark tannins, layered with wood. 92 *—R.V. (6/1/2007)*

Château Grand Corbin-Despagne 2000 Bordeaux Blend (Saint-Emilion) $25. 90 *—R.V. (6/1/2003)*

Château Grand Corbin-Despagne 2004 Barrel Sample Bordeaux Blend (Saint-Emilion Grand Cru) $NA. 90 *—R.V. (6/1/2005)*

CHÂTEAU GRAND DESTIEU

Château Grand Destieu 2004 Bordeaux Blend (Saint-Emilion Grand Cru) $NA. A Merlot-based wine from old vines on the plains at the base of the hill of Saint-Emilion. This is soft and fresh, with an element of wood and smoky tannins to give structure and aging potential. The ripe, jammy fruit flavors are balanced by freshness and vibrant acidity. 89 *—R.V. (6/1/2007)*

CHÂTEAU GRAND MAYNE

Château Grand Mayne 2000 Bordeaux Blend (Saint-Emilion) $59. 91 *—R.V. (6/1/2003)*

CHÂTEAU GRAND MOULINET

Château Grand Moulinet 2004 Bordeaux Blend (Pomerol) $23. A dark, dense wine, still very young, but already supple. Merlot was ripe in 2004 and this wine shows it in its opulence and richness. Yet there are tannins here, so drink now, and age over the next five years. A great value for a Pomerol. 87 *—R.V. (11/1/2007)*

CHÂTEAU GRAND-PUY-DUCASSE

Château Grand-Puy-Ducasse 2003 Bordeaux Blend (Pauillac) $30. 88 *—R.V. (5/1/2006)*

Château Grand-Puy-Ducasse 2005 Barrel Sample Bordeaux Blend (Pauillac) $NA. 86 *—R.V. (6/21/2006)*

CHÂTEAU GRANDE CASSAGNE

Château Grande Cassagne 2006 Rosé Rosé Blend (Costières de Nimes) $10. A modest rosé at a modest tariff, this starts with hints of berries and green onions, then shows flavors of rhubarb and sour cherry. Crisp on the finish. 83 *—J.C. (7/1/2007)*

Château Grande Cassagne 2001 Les Rameaux "S" Syrah (Costières de Nimes) $10. 90 Best Buy *—J.C. (11/15/2002)*

CHÂTEAU GRENOUILLE

Château Grenouille 2003 Grenouille Grand Cru Chardonnay (Chablis) $90. 92 *—J.C. (4/1/2006)*

CHÂTEAU GREYSAC

Château Greysac 2004 Bordeaux Blend (Médoc) $NA. One of the largest Médoc estates, with 230 acres of vines, Greysac is a good, reliable source of classically styled Bordeaux. The style has become more modern in recent years, with an increased use of new wood, as in this 2004, which currently dominates. Enjoy it now for its toasty character, or wait for it to calm down. 90 *—R.V. (6/1/2007)*

Château Greysac 2005 Barrel Sample Bordeaux Blend (Médoc) $NA. 86 *—R.V. (6/21/2006)*

CHÂTEAU GRUAUD-LAROSE

Château Gruaud-Larose 2004 Bordeaux Blend (Saint-Julien) $NA. A solid, firm wine; young and closed up. It has an awkward sharpness to its fruit, maybe a stage in its evolution. It seems to be more focused with its dry tannins, layering these right over the fruit. **89** —*R.V. (6/1/2007)*

Château Gruaud-Larose 2003 Bordeaux Blend (Saint-Julien) $60. 90 —*R.V. (5/1/2006)*

Château Gruaud-Larose 2001 Bordeaux Blend (Saint-Julien) $48. What a perfumed, elegant, structured wine, with all the elements of fruit, wood, tannins just in the right place. It shows great tannins, powerful black and red berry fruits, denseness, and a classic, fresh aftertaste. **94** —*R.V. (12/16/2007)*

Château Gruaud-Larose 2005 Barrel Sample Bordeaux Blend (Saint-Julien) $NA. 95 —*R.V. (6/20/2006)*

Château Gruaud-Larose 2003 Barrel Sample Bordeaux Blend (Saint-Julien) $NA. 88 —*R.V. (6/3/2004)*

CHÂTEAU GUIRAUD

Château Guiraud 2005 Barrel Sample Bordeaux White Blend (Sauternes) $NA. 91 —*R.V. (6/1/2006)*

CHÂTEAU HANTEILLAN

Château Hanteillan 2003 Bordeaux Blend (Haut-Médoc) $NA. 85 —*R.V. (5/1/2006)*

CHÂTEAU HAUT BAGES LIBÉRAL

Château Haut Bages Libéral 2004 Bordeaux Blend (Pauillac) $NA. Solid tannins, black fruits and dark chocolate go into this dense wine. It is a powerful statement of Pauillac; this will develop slowly and take its time to soften out. **90** —*R.V. (6/1/2007)*

Château Haut Bages Libéral 2005 Barrel Sample Bordeaux Blend (Pauillac) $NA. 93 —*R.V. (6/20/2006)*

CHÂTEAU HAUT BAILLY

Château Haut Bailly 2004 Bordeaux Blend (Pessac-Léognan) $NA. A beautifully balanced, harmonious wine—as so often in recent years from Haut-Bailly—this is the epitome of deliciously drinkable Bordeaux. The wild strawberry flavors and the elegant, velvet texture are balanced by firm, structured tannins. Like other vintages from Haut-Bailly, expect this to develop over many years. **93 Cellar Selection** —*R.V. (6/1/2007)*

Château Haut Bailly 2005 Barrel Sample Bordeaux Blend (Pessac-Léognan) $NA. 92 —*R.V. (6/1/2006)*

CHÂTEAU HAUT BATAILLEY

Château Haut Batailley 2003 Bordeaux Blend (Pauillac) $30. 89 —*R.V. (5/1/2006)*

CHÂTEAU HAUT BERTINERIE

Château Haut Bertinerie 2004 Bordeaux Blend (Premieres Côtes de Blaye) $NA. A big wood-aged wine made from old vines at the Bertinerie estate. Certainly, there is plenty of wood aroma; in the mouth, the dry wood tannins are balanced by the rich, concentrated black fruits. Coffee and mocha flavors add complexity to an already impressive wine. **90 Editors' Choice** —*R.V. (11/1/2007)*

Château Haut Bertinerie 2005 Bordeaux White Blend (Premieres Côtes de Blaye) $NA. Made from 100% Sauvignon Blanc old vines, this has been given a heavy dose of wood, including barrel fermentation and lees stirring. The result is a definite hit, rich and almost Burgundian in its wood flavors and concentration, but with just that hint of herbaceousness to remind you it is Sauvignon. **90** —*R.V. (11/1/2007)*

Château Haut Bertinerie 2002 Bordeaux White Blend (Premieres Côtes de Blaye) $20. 90 Editors' Choice —*R.V. (6/1/2005)*

CHÂTEAU HAUT BRETON LARIGAUDIERE

Château Haut Breton Larigaudiere 1999 Bordeaux Blend (Margaux) $45. 86 —*J.C. (6/1/2005)*

CHÂTEAU HAUT PERTHUS

Chateau Haut Perthus 2004 Red Blend (Bergerac) $11. With its pronounced aromas of wet leather and Band-Aid, this runs the risk of immediately turning some people off. Yet the mouthfeel is creamy, the tannins supple, and it picks up an intriguing coffee-like note on the finish. **83** —*J.C. (8/1/2007)*

CHÂTEAU HAUT-BEAUSÉJOUR

Château Haut-Beauséjour 2004 Bordeaux Blend (Saint-Estèphe) $25. A lusciously rich wine whose opulence is tempered by some firm, dry tannins as well as crisp acidity. The superripe plum and blackberry fruits are open, generous and demanding to be drunk in the next 2–3 years. **89** —*R.V. (6/1/2007)*

Château Haut-Beauséjour 2003 Bordeaux Blend (Saint-Estèphe) $25. Boasts layers of wood, with black currant and rich white fig flavors, along with dried fruits. This is a ripe, opulent wine reflecting the heat of 2003 in Bordeaux, but still retaining dry tannins that promise aging. **91** —*R.V. (11/1/2007)*

Château Haut-Beauséjour 1997 Cru Bourgeois Bordeaux Blend (Saint-Estèphe) $23. 85 *(5/1/2000)*

CHÂTEAU HAUT-BERGEY

Château Haut-Bergey 2005 Barrel Sample Bordeaux Blend (Pessac-Léognan) $NA. 89 —*R.V. (6/21/2006)*

CHÂTEAU HAUT-BRION

Château Haut-Brion 2004 Bordeaux Blend (Pessac-Léognan) $NA. Of the pair of châteaux, La Mission Haut-Brion and Haut-Brion (both owned by the Dillon banking family) that face each other across the crowded streets of Pessac, Haut-Brion is the one with the structure, the darkness, the brooding character. This is so true of 2004, with its hugely firm structure underlying the initial supple fruit. At the end, the acidity is an enticing surprise, lifting the aftertaste. **96** —*R.V. (6/1/2007)*

Château Haut-Brion 2000 Pessac-Léognan Bordeaux Blend (Bordeaux) $400. 96 —*R.V. (6/1/2003)*

Château Haut-Brion 2006 Barrel Sample Bordeaux Blend (Pessac-Léognan) $NA. 95-97 Barrel Sample. A structured, powerful wine that shows the firm, tough side of Haut-Brion. The fruit is certainly ripe, but it is the big boned character of the wine that is the most impressive. There is a mineral layer to the flavor of the wine, a fascinating additional complexity. **96** —*R.V. (6/1/2007)*

Château Haut-Brion 2004 Barrel Sample Bordeaux Blend (Pessac-Léognan) 95 —*R.V. (6/1/2005)*

Château Haut-Brion 2006 Barrel Sample Bordeaux White Blend (Pessac-Léognan) $NA. 94-96 Barrel Sample. The white wine from Haut-Brion is always one of the stars of the Pessac-Léognan whites, and this great white year is no exception. It's the fruit that leads, and behind this the structure follows. The wood is an essential adjunct to the fruit, a spice-and-toast touch to the recipe. **95** —*R.V. (6/1/2007)*

Château Haut-Brion 2005 Blanc-Barrel Sample Bordeaux White Blend (Pessac-Léognan) 94 —*R.V. (6/20/2006)*

CHÂTEAU HAUT-CANTELOUP

Château Haut-Canteloup 2004 Bordeaux Blend (Haut-Médoc) $NA. One of the lesser known crus bourgeois, Haut-Canteloup has produced a ripe, smooth 2004, with plenty of black currant fruit flavors, marred by an excess of acidity. **87** —*R.V. (6/1/2007)*

CHÂTEAU HAUT-MARBUZET

Château Haut-Marbuzet 2002 Bordeaux Blend (Saint-Estèphe) $NA. 91 —*R.V. (6/1/2005)*

Château Haut-Marbuzet 2004 Barrel Sample Bordeaux Blend (Saint-Estèphe) $NA. 92 —*R.V. (6/1/2005)*

CHÂTEAU HOSANNA

Château Hosanna 2004 Bordeaux Blend (Pomerol) $NA. Christian Moueix gave the celebratory name Hosanna to Château Certan Guiraud after he purchased it in 1999. He has now made his mark on the property, combining elegance and power. The style of the property seems to hone in on structure and tannins, but the fruit, dense and black, is also there. **93** —*R.V. (6/1/2007)*

Château Hosanna 2000 Bordeaux Blend (Pomerol) $179. 94 —*R.V. (6/1/2003)*

Château Hosanna 2006 Barrel Sample Bordeaux Blend (Pomerol) $NA. 92-94 Barrel Sample. Well balanced wine; its rich dark fruits well in harmony with its freshness and dry tannins. Very juicy aftertaste. **93** —*R.V. (6/1/2007)*

Château Hosanna 2004 Barrel Sample Bordeaux Blend (Pomerol) $NA. 94 —*R.V. (6/1/2005)*

CHÂTEAU KIRWAN

Château Kirwan 2004 Bordeaux Blend (Margaux) $NA. Freshness is the hallmark of this wine. The fruit is dominant, ripe and balanced with blackberry acidity. There is a possible hint of overextraction, but that is only a small failing in such a delicious wine. **93** —*R.V. (6/1/2007)*

Château Kirwan 2001 Bordeaux Blend (Margaux) $40. 94 Editors' Choice —*R.V. (6/1/2005)*

Château Kirwan 2005 Barrel Sample Bordeaux Blend (Margaux) $NA. 93 —

R.V. (6/20/2006)

Château Kirwan 2003 Barrel Sample Bordeaux Blend (Margaux) $NA. 89 —*R.V. (6/3/2004)*

CHÂTEAU L'ANCIEN

Château l'Ancien 2003 Bordeaux Blend (Lalande de Pomerol) $NA. A rich, almost raisiny wine, spiced with a touch of mint. This is smooth, with soft tannins, ripe fruit and an impressive density of texture. 89 —*R.V. (11/1/2007)*

CHÂTEAU L'HOSTE-BLANC

Château l'Hoste-Blanc 1999 Bordeaux Blend (Bordeaux Supérieur) $15. 91 —*R.V. (11/15/2002)*

CHÂTEAU LA BESSANE

Château la Bessane 2001 Bordeaux Blend (Margaux) $NA. 87 —*R.V. (6/1/2005)*

CHÂTEAU LA BOUTIGNANE

Château La Boutignane 2001 Grande Reserve Blanc Red Blend (Corbières) $13. 90 Best Buy —*S.H. (12/31/2002)*

Château La Boutignane 1998 Grande Reserve Rouge Red Blend (Corbières) $18. 94 Editors' Choice —*S.H. (12/31/2002)*

Château La Boutignane 2005 Rosé Blend (Corbières) $12. 85 —*J.C. (6/21/2006)*

Château La Boutignane 2003 Rosé de Saignée Rosé Blend (Corbières) $12. 90 Best Buy —*S.H. (10/1/2004)*

CHÂTEAU LA CANORGUE

Château la Canorgue 2001 Rhône Red Blend (Côtes du Luberon) $15. 83 —*J.C. (2/1/2005)*

CHÂTEAU LA CAUSSADE

Château La Caussade 2002 Sauvignon Blanc (Bordeaux) $10. 86 Best Buy —*J.C. (11/15/2004)*

CHÂTEAU LA CONSEILLANTE

Château La Conseillante 2003 Barrel Sample Bordeaux Blend (Pomerol) $NA. 88 —*R.V. (6/3/2004)*

CHÂTEAU LA CROIX BELLEVUE

Château la Croix Bellevue 2004 Bordeaux Blend (Lalande de Pomerol) $NA. Lalande-de-Pomerol, the village to the northwest of Pomerol proper, often produces wines that are very structured, but lack the velvet fruit of Pomerol itself. Here is a fine example, a wine that is very reticent with its fruit, but that blasts its way through on structure and dense tannins. 86 —*R.V. (6/1/2007)*

CHÂTEAU LA CROIX DE GAY

Château la Croix de Gay 2005 Barrel Sample Bordeaux Blend (Pomerol) $NA. 89 —*R.V. (6/21/2006)*

CHÂTEAU LA CROIX DES MOINES

Château la Croix des Moines 2004 Bordeaux Blend (Lalande de Pomerol) $21. One of the properties owned by Jean-Louis Trocard, former president of the Bordeaux Wine Council. La Croix des Moines is a 29-acre property which, in 2004, produced a finely structured wine, packed with dark tannins, supported by a good weight of blackberry fruits. Wood is not an issue in this wine; the fruit and the fruit tannins tell the story. 88 —*R.V. (6/1/2007)*

CHÂTEAU LA CROIX MARTELLE

Château La Croix Martelle 2001 La Réserve du Sirus Red Blend (Minervois) $16. 87 —*R.V. (12/1/2004)*

CHÂTEAU LA DOMINIQUE

Château la Dominique 2005 Barrel Sample Bordeaux Blend (Saint-Emilion Grand Cru) $NA. 90 —*R.V. (6/21/2006)*

CHÂTEAU LA FLEUR DE GAY

Château La Fleur de Gay 2004 Barrel Sample Bordeaux Blend (Pomerol) $NA. 91 —*R.V. (6/1/2005)*

CHÂTEAU LA FLEUR PEYRABON

Château la Fleur Peyrabon 2003 Bordeaux Blend (Pauillac) $27. 91 Cellar Selection —*R.V. (5/1/2006)*

CHÂTEAU LA FLEUR PTRUS

Château La Fleur Ptrus 2005 Barrel Sample Bordeaux Blend (Pomerol) $NA. 93 —*R.V. (6/20/2006)*

CHÂTEAU LA GAFFELIÈRE

Château la Gaffelière 2000 Bordeaux Blend (Saint-Emilion) $120. 94 —*R.V. (6/1/2003)*

Château la Gaffelière 2004 Barrel Sample Bordeaux Blend (Saint-Emilion Grand Cru) $NA. 95 —*R.V. (6/1/2005)*

CHÂTEAU LA GOMERIE

Château la Gomerie 2006 Barrel Sample Bordeaux Blend (Saint-Emilion Grand Cru) $NA. 92-94 Barrel Sample. A single vineyard parcel, producing a rich wine, powered by blackberry fruits. 93 —*R.V. (6/1/2007)*

CHÂTEAU LA GRANDE CLOTTE

Château la Grande Clotte 2004 Bordeaux White Blend (Bordeaux Blanc) $NA. The vines for this wine are in Lussac St-Emilion, a rare outcrop of white vines among the sea of red, and the first white wine to come from the right bank vineyards. Its blend of Sauvignon Blanc and Sémillon gives a delicious freshness in 2004, touched with wood, vibrant with lemon and cantaloupe flavors. 88 —*R.V. (6/1/2007)*

CHÂTEAU LA GRANGE CLINET

Château La Grange Clinet 2004 Bordeaux Blend (Premieres Côtes de Bordeaux) $11. There's plenty of classic Bordeaux black currant here, freshening up this fruity, fragrantly fresh wine. The tannins are a whisper under all this great fruit. 86 Best Buy —*R.V. (11/1/2007)*

CHÂTEAU LA GRAVE À POMEROL

Château La Grave à Pomerol 2004 Bordeaux Blend (Pomerol) $NA. A chewy wine, which loses something with the somewhat stewed character of the fruit. It is dark, dense and dry, with structure, but the fruit appears almost too ripe. 87 —*R.V. (6/1/2007)*

Château La Grave à Pomerol 2000 Bordeaux Blend (Pomerol) $46. 89 —*R.V. (6/1/2003)*

CHÂTEAU LA GURGUE

Château la Gurgue 2004 Bordeaux Blend (Margaux) $NA. Under the same management as Château Chasse-Spleen in neighboring Moulis, la Gurgue's 2004 is in a bigger, richer style than many Margaux. It is about structure, dense tannins and firm fruits. It's impressive and likely to age well. 91 —*R.V. (6/1/2007)*

Château la Gurgue 2001 Bordeaux Blend (Margaux) $21. 90 —*R.V. (6/1/2005)*

CHÂTEAU LA LAGUNE

Château La Lagune 2004 Barrel Sample Bordeaux Blend (Haut-Médoc) $NA. 90 —*R.V. (6/1/2005)*

CHÂTEAU LA LOUVIÈRE

Château la Louvière 2005 Barrel Sample Bordeaux Blend (Pessac-Léognan) $NA. 90 —*R.V. (6/21/2006)*

Château la Louvière 2002 Bordeaux White Blend (Pessac-Léognan) $34. 93 Cellar Selection —*R.V. (6/1/2005)*

Château la Louvière 2006 Barrel Sample Bordeaux White Blend (Pessac-Léognan) $NA. 91-93 Barrel Sample. A finely balanced wine, bringing green, herbaceous fruits together with spice and wood. Not complex, but delicious. 92 —*R.V. (6/1/2007)*

CHÂTEAU LA MASCARONNE

Château la Mascaronne 2006 La Mascaronne Rosé Blend (Côtes de Provence) $NA. With its classic blend of Cinsault and Grenache, this lively rosé has a dusty, southern warmth. It is just on the heavy side, and there is some pepper from the 13.5% alcohol, which spoils the red berry flavors. 85 —*R.V. (7/1/2007)*

CHÂTEAU LA MISSION HAUT-BRION

Château La Mission Haut-Brion 2004 Bordeaux Blend (Pessac-Léognan) $NA. As so often, La Mission is rich, voluptuous, opulent and always a wine that seduces when it is young. But watch for those firm tannins, pure black plum and chocolate flavors, and wait for the dense texture to open up over the next 10 years—and more. 94 Cellar Selection —*R.V. (6/1/2007)*

Château La Mission Haut-Brion 2006 Barrel Sample Bordeaux Blend (Pessac-Léognan) $NA. 94-96 Barrel Sample. A smooth rich wine, with delicious, opulent soft fruit. Spice and tobacco along with acidity and great freshness. It is dense and concentrated, but like velvet. 95 —*R.V. (6/1/2007)*

Château La Mission Haut-Brion 2005 Barrel Sample Bordeaux Blend (Pessac-Léognan) $NA. 94 —*R.V. (6/20/2006)*

Château La Mission Haut-Brion 2003 Barrel Sample Bordeaux Blend (Pessac-Léognan) $NA. 94 *—R.V. (6/3/2004)*

CHÂTEAU LA MOUTÈTE

Château la Moutète 2004 Rosé Blend (Côtes de Provence) $13. 87 *—J.C. (6/21/2006)*

Château la Moutète 2004 Vieilles Vignes Rosé Blend (Côtes de Provence) $17. 87 *—J.C. (6/21/2006)*

CHÂTEAU LA NERTHE

Château La Nerthe 2000 Rouge Rhône Red Blend (Châteauneuf-du-Pape) $40. 89 *—M.S. (9/1/2003)*

CHÂTEAU LA POINTE

Château la Pointe 2005 Barrel Sample Bordeaux Blend (Pomerol) $NA. 92 *—R.V. (6/20/2006)*

CHÂTEAU LA ROSE BELLEVUE

Château la Rose Bellevue 2000 Cuvée Prestige Bordeaux Blend (Premieres Côtes de Blaye) $13. 87 *—R.V. (4/1/2005)*

Château la Rose Bellevue 2002 Cuvée Prestige Blanc Bordeaux White Blend (Premieres Côtes de Blaye) $12. 88 Best Buy *—R.V. (4/1/2005)*

CHÂTEAU LA ROUVIÈRE

Château la Rouvière 2006 Rosé Blend (Bandol) $24. One of the properties owned by the Bunan family, Rouvière's rosé is awkwardly heavy. What it lacks is fresh fruits, what it does have is richness and weight, making its place at the table rather than on the deck. 85 *—R.V. (7/1/2007)*

CHÂTEAU LA TOUR BLANCHE

Château la Tour Blanche 2004 Barrel Sample Bordeaux White Blend (Sauternes) $NA. 91 *—R.V. (6/1/2005)*

CHÂTEAU LA TOUR CARNET

Château La Tour Carnet 2004 Barrel Sample Bordeaux Blend (Haut-Médoc) $NA. 87 *—R.V. (6/1/2005)*

CHÂTEAU LA TOUR DE BESSAN

Château la Tour de Bessan 2003 Bordeaux Blend (Margaux) $NA. 89 *—R.V. (5/1/2006)*

CHÂTEAU LA TOUR DE PIN FIGEAC MOUEIX

Château la Tour de Pin Figeac Moueix 2005 Barrel Sample Bordeaux Blend (Saint-Emilion Grand Cru) $NA. 86 *—R.V. (6/21/2006)*

CHÂTEAU LA TOUR FIGEAC

Château La Tour Figeac 2002 Bordeaux Blend (Saint-Emilion Grand Cru) $NA. 90 *—R.V. (4/1/2005)*

Château La Tour Figeac 2000 Bordeaux Blend (Saint-Emilion Grand Cru) $NA. 94 Cellar Selection *—R.V. (4/1/2005)***Château La Tour Figeac 2006 Barrel Sample Bordeaux Blend (Saint-Emilion Grand Cru) $NA.** 92-94 Barrel Sample. One of the few biodynamic properties in Bordeaux, this estate makes stunning wine. No exception this year, a powerful, pure fruity wine, stacked with blackberries and dark chocolate oak tannins. 93 *—R.V. (6/1/2007)*

Château La Tour Figeac 2004 Barrel Sample Bordeaux Blend (Saint-Emilion Grand Cru) $NA. 91 *—R.V. (6/1/2005)*

CHÂTEAU LA TOUR HAUT-BRION

Château La Tour Haut-Brion 2004 Bordeaux Blend (Pessac-Léognan) $NA. One of the properties under the same family ownership as Haut-Brion, La Tour Haut-Brion is a tiny 12-acre parcel. The 2004 has a smooth richness, coupled with a restrained delicacy that belies that the power of the dense tannins at the core. The aftertaste, though, is more soft and seductive. 91 *—R.V. (6/1/2007)*

Château La Tour Haut-Brion 2000 Bordeaux Blend (Pessac-Léognan) $60. 89 *—R.V. (6/1/2003)*

Château La Tour Haut-Brion 2004 Barrel Sample Bordeaux Blend (Pessac-Léognan) $NA. 91 *—R.V. (6/1/2005)*

CHÂTEAU LABAT

Château Labat 2003 Bordeaux Blend (Haut-Médoc) $14. 84 *—R.V. (5/1/2006)*

CHÂTEAU LABEGORCE MARGAUX

Château Labegorce Margaux 2004 Bordeaux Blend (Margaux) $NA. This château has seen a big investment in recent years and it has paid off. Despite its modern, polished style evidenced by a generous use of new wood, it retains the proper charm of a Margaux, with the fruit floating elegantly over the wood and the tannins. 92 Editors' Choice *—R.V. (6/1/2007)*

Château Labegorce Margaux 2001 Bordeaux Blend (Margaux) $50. 89 *—R.V. (6/1/2005)*

Château Labegorce Margaux 2005 Barrel Sample Bordeaux Blend (Margaux) $NA. 93 *—R.V. (6/20/2006)*

CHÂTEAU LABEGORCE ZÉDÉ

Château Labegorce Zédé 2001 Bordeaux Blend (Margaux) $NA. 90 *—R.V. (6/1/2005)*

CHÂTEAU LACOMBE NOAILLAC

Château Lacombe Noaillac 2005 Bordeaux Blend (Médoc) $NA. Very classic Bordeaux in the best sense. This shows a structure and tannic content that keeps well in balance with the black currant fruits. With its dry core, it promises well as a food wine, cutting through red meats with ease. 88 *—R.V. (11/1/2007)*

Château Lacombe Noaillac 2004 Bordeaux Blend (Médoc) $NA. Fresh and spicy, this simple wine offers plenty of fresh satisfaction, lightweight and easy, with delicious crisp red berries and some dusty tannins. 87 *—R.V. (6/1/2007)*

Château Lacombe Noaillac 2003 Bordeaux Blend (Listrac-Médoc) $26. 84 *—R.V. (5/1/2006)*

CHÂTEAU LAFAURIE PEYRAGUEY

Château Lafaurie Peyraguey 2004 Barrel Sample Bordeaux White Blend (Sauternes) $NA. 90 *—R.V. (6/1/2005)*

CHÂTEAU LAFITE ROTHSCHILD

Château Lafite Rothschild 2004 Bordeaux Blend (Pauillac) $NA. Yes, there is power to this wine. But more than that, it exudes authority; a dense and solid wine with an impressive presence and texture. It has a velvet mouthfeel: the tannins are dusty and mineral, alongside fruit flavors of ripe black plums and dark figs, leavened with fresh acidity. The potential, of course, is there: 20 years if you can wait. 96 *—R.V. (6/1/2007)*

Château Lafite Rothschild 2000 Bordeaux Blend (Pauillac) $400. 99 *—R.V. (6/1/2003)*

Château Lafite Rothschild 2006 Barrel Sample Bordeaux Blend (Pauillac) $NA. 95-97 Barrel Sample. The fruit here is so rich, so juicy that it seems almost ready to drink now—until the tannins kick in. They power down on those delicious fruits, giving them a burst of structure, new wood and spice. 96 *—R.V. (6/1/2007)*

Château Lafite Rothschild 2004 Barrel Sample Bordeaux Blend (Pauillac) 97 *—R.V. (6/1/2005)*

CHÂTEAU LAFLEUR PÉTRUS

Château Lafleur Pétrus 2004 Bordeaux Blend (Pomerol) $NA. A superb wine this is going to be. It is rich, elegant, poised, with its super-ripe, but still fresh, berry fruit flavors exhibiting much of the richness of Merlot when it has been ripened slowly and surely. While this has less intensity than its neighbor of Château Pétrus, the Cabernet Franc in the blend gives it intriguing perfumes. 93 Editors' Choice *—R.V. (6/1/2007)*

Château Lafleur Pétrus 2003 Barrel Sample Bordeaux Blend (Pomerol) 87 *—R.V. (6/3/2004)*

CHÂTEAU LAFON ROCHET

Château Lafon Rochet 2005 Barrel Sample Bordeaux Blend (Saint-Estèphe) 90 *—R.V. (6/1/2006)*

CHÂTEAU LAFONT MENAUT

Château Lafont Menaut 2003 Bordeaux White Blend (Pessac-Léognan) 86 *—R.V. (6/1/2005)*

CHÂTEAU LAFORGE

Château Laforge 2004 Bordeaux Blend (Saint-Emilion Grand Cru) $NA. A Merlot-dominated Saint-Emilion, this is a big, but balanced wine. New wood is present, but this doesn't diminish the ripe blackberry and cherry fruits. It is firm, dry and tannic at this stage, with a hint of coffee, but the aftertaste is fresh, with red currant flavors and acidity. 90 *—R.V. (6/1/2007)*

CHÂTEAU LAGRANGE

Château Lagrange 2004 Bordeaux Blend (Saint-Julien) $NA. A wine that balances its freshness with deep layers of black fruits. Acidity and black currants work well together. Lagrange is over-performing at the moment: an estate that once made correct wines now offers excitement as well. 92 *—R.V. (6/1/2007)*

Château Lagrange 2003 Bordeaux Blend (Saint-Julien) $30. 92 *—R.V.*

(5/1/2006)

Château Lagrange 2006 Barrel Sample Bordeaux Blend (Saint-Julien) $NA. 92-94 Barrel Sample. A well-balanced, layered wine, bringing together rich fruit, solid tannins and fresh finishing acidity. **93** *—R.V. (6/1/2007)*

Château Lagrange 2004 Barrel Sample Bordeaux Blend (Saint-Julien) 91 *—R.V. (6/1/2005)*

CHÂTEAU LAGREZETTE

Château Lagrezette 1997 Le Pigeonnier Malbec (Cahors) $60. 93 *—J.C. (3/1/2001)*

Château Lagrezette 1996 Red Blend (Cahors) $20. 90 *(11/15/1999)*

CHÂTEAU LALANDE-BORIE

Château Lalande-Borie 2000 Bordeaux Blend (Saint-Julien) $25. 89 *—R.V. (6/1/2003)*

CHÂTEAU LAMOTHE

Château Lamothe 2005 Barrel Sample Bordeaux White Blend (Sauternes) 87 *—R.V. (6/21/2006)*

CHÂTEAU LAMOTHE DE HAUX

Château Lamothe de Haux 2004 Bordeaux Blend (Premieres Côtes de Bordeaux) $13. One of two reds from the Chombart family's 209-acre estate. This simpler one emphasizes fresh black currant fruit flavors rather than complexity. There is a good balance between fruit, acidity and some smooth tannins. It's a wine for a good piece of grilled chicken. **86** *—R.V. (11/1/2007)*

Château Lamothe de Haux 2004 Première Cuvée Bordeaux Blend (Premieres Côtes de Bordeaux) $17. This wood-aged wine from Lamothe de Haux is rich and concentrated. The toasty flavors from oak give a fascinating edge of complexity to the smooth vanilla and black plums of the fruit. It could age over two years. **88** *—R.V. (11/1/2007)*

Château Lamothe de Haux 2006 Bordeaux White Blend (Bordeaux Blanc) $NA. A full style, rounded and soft, with fresh white pear and plum flavors. It has a perfumed character from the 20% Muscadelle in the blend, which gives it ripeness but diminishes the fresh acidity. **86** *—R.V. (12/31/2007)*

Château Lamothe de Haux 2004 Cuvée Valentine Sauvignon Gris (Bordeaux Blanc) $NA. This wine is an original. Made from 100% of the rare Sauvignon Gris, its flavors are reminiscent both of the freshly herbaceous character of Sauvignon Blanc, and the spicy character of Pinot Gris. Add in a touch of new wood, and you have a fascinating and complex wine. **91 Editors' Choice** *—R.V. (11/1/2007)*

CHÂTEAU LAMOTHE GUIGNARD

Château Lamothe Guignard 2005 Barrel Sample Bordeaux White Blend (Sauternes) 91 *—R.V. (6/1/2006)*

CHÂTEAU LANGOA-BARTON

Château Langoa-Barton 2004 Bordeaux Blend (Saint-Julien) $NA. What a big-hearted wine this is. It is generous, smooth and ripe, with lovely fruit. There is more than this immediate pleasure, though, because its dense tannins promise a good evolution. Langoa-Barton is the second estate owned by Anthony Barton of Léoville-Barton, and it offers some of the pleasures of Léoville at a lower price. **90** *—R.V. (6/1/2007)*

Château Langoa-Barton 2003 Bordeaux Blend (Saint-Julien) $65. Sweet, rich, dense, very much of its year. At the same time, there is the Barton touch that leaves some fine elegance, to go with the smoky fruits and richness, while acidity gives it a fine lift. **91** *—R.V. (12/16/2007)*

Château Langoa-Barton 2001 Bordeaux Blend (Saint-Julien) $56. Although it is relatively soft, this wine still has everything about it. There is ripeness, but it is balanced with fresh acidity still with an aura of youth. In the core, there are solid blackcurrants, structure. It will certainly age, but drink over 10 years. **92** *—R.V. (12/16/2007)*

Château Langoa-Barton 2000 Bordeaux Blend (Saint-Julien) 90 *—R.V. (6/1/2003)*

CHÂTEAU LAPELLETRIE

Château Lapelletrie 1997 Bordeaux Blend (Saint-Emilion) $20. 84 *—J.C. (3/1/2001)*

CHÂTEAU LARMANDE

Château Larmande 2000 Bordeaux Blend (Saint-Emilion) $25. 89 *—R.V. (6/1/2003)*

CHÂTEAU LAROQUE

Château Laroque 2000 Bordeaux Blend (Saint-Emilion Grand Cru) $45. 90 *—J.C. (6/1/2005)*

Château Laroque 2002 Grand Cru Classe Bordeaux Blend (Saint-Emilion Grand Cru) $45. 87 *—J.C. (11/15/2005)*

CHÂTEAU LAROZE

Château Laroze 2005 Barrel Sample Bordeaux Blend (Saint-Emilion Grand Cru) $NA. 88 *—R.V. (6/21/2006)*

CHÂTEAU LARRIVET HAUT-BRION

Château Larrivet Haut-Brion 2005 Barrel Sample Bordeaux White Blend (Pessac-Léognan) $NA. 91 *—R.V. (6/1/2006)*

CHÂTEAU LASCOMBES

Château Lascombes 2004 Bordeaux Blend (Margaux) $NA. Sometimes a young Bordeaux can taste as if the winemaker has gone over the top with wood. That's the case with Lascombes 2004. It seems that there aren't enough other elements in the wine to sustain such lavish wood flavors. **88** *—R.V. (6/1/2007)*

Château Lascombes 2003 Bordeaux Blend (Margaux) $50. 90 *—R.V. (5/1/2006)*

Château Lascombes 2003 Barrel Sample Bordeaux Blend (Margaux) $NA. 90 *—R.V. (6/3/2004)*

CHÂTEAU LATOUR

Château Latour 2004 Bordeaux Blend (Pauillac) $NA. There are tannins, structure and power, but also supreme elegance. The 2004 acidity comes through in the sweet cassis flavors, supported at the back by dry tannins. Currently, the wine is closed up, losing some of its fresh fruit, but this is a moment in its slow evolution towards a classic Latour. **97** *—R.V. (6/1/2007)*

Château Latour 2006 Barrel Sample Bordeaux Blend (Pauillac) $NA. 95-97 Barrel Sample A ripe wine, showing some concentration but less than in some years at Latour. The acidity. however, is evident, giving a structured , fresh but powerful wine. There is spice from the new wood, but this certainly does not dominate. **96** *—R.V. (6/1/2007)*

Château Latour 2005 Barrel Sample Bordeaux Blend (Pauillac) $NA. 99 *—R.V. (6/20/2006)*

Château Latour 2003 Barrel Sample Bordeaux Blend (Pauillac) $NA. 97 *—R.V. (6/3/2004)*

CHÂTEAU LATOUR À POMEROL

Château Latour à Pomerol 2004 Bordeaux Blend (Pomerol) $NA. A big, dry wine, firm, and not offering much fruit at this stage. It is obviously concentrated, and as it evolves, the fruit will develop richness. This small, 20-acre property is mainly situated on gravel soils next to Pomerol church, at the heart of the appellation. **91** *—R.V. (6/1/2007)*

Château Latour à Pomerol 2005 Barrel Sample Bordeaux Blend (Pomerol) $NA. 91 *—R.V. (6/1/2006)*

Château Latour à Pomerol 2003 Barrel Sample Bordeaux Blend (Pomerol) $NA. 88 *—R.V. (6/3/2004)*

CHÂTEAU LATOUR-MARTILLAC

Château Latour-Martillac 2004 Bordeaux Blend (Pessac-Léognan) $NA. One of the great values from Pessac-Léognan, Latour-Martillac's 2004 is deeply colored and smooth, with some intensely structured tannins and fresh fruit flavors. **89** *—R.V. (6/1/2007)*

Château Latour-Martillac 2002 Bordeaux White Blend (Pessac-Léognan) $NA. 91 *—R.V. (6/1/2005)*

CHÂTEAU LAVILLE HAUT-BRION

Château Laville Haut-Brion 2006 Barrel Sample Bordeaux White Blend (Pessac-Léognan) $NA. 93-95 Barrel Sample. Beautiful, full of white fruits and citrus, concentrated and structured, fleshed out with spice from the wood. **94** *—R.V. (6/1/2007)*

Château Laville Haut-Brion 2005 Blanc-Barrel Sample Bordeaux White Blend (Pessac-Léognan) $NA. 93 *—R.V. (6/20/2006)*

CHÂTEAU LE BON PASTEUR

Château le Bon Pasteur 2004 Bordeaux Blend (Pomerol) $NA. This is balance among all the ripe fruit flavors, elegance among the power. For a Pomerol, stuffed with ripe Merlot, this is powered as much by its fresh fruit as by its richness. A delicious wine that lingers long in the mouth. **91** *—R.V. (6/1/2007)*

Château le Bon Pasteur 2004 Barrel Sample Bordeaux Blend (Pomerol) $NA. 89 *—R.V. (6/1/2005)*

CHÂTEAU LE BREUIL RENAISSANCE

Château Leboscq 2005 Bordeaux Blend (Médoc) $NA. A Cab-dominated wine that reveals attractive, juicy black fruits, balanced with fresh acidity.

There are tannins, but the fruitiness is what this is all about. Drinkable now. **86** —*R.V. (11/1/2007)*

CHÂTEAU LE BREUIL RENAISSANCE

Château Le Breuil Renaissance 2001 Bordeaux Blend (Médoc) $25. 83 —*J.M. (4/3/2004)*

CHÂTEAU LE DEVOY MARTINE

Château le Devoy Martine 2003 Rhône Red Blend (Lirac) $20. 90 Editors' Choice —*J.C. (11/15/2006)*

Château le Devoy Martine 2004 Rhône White Blend (Lirac) $14. 86 —*J.C. (11/15/2006)*

CHÂTEAU LE DROT

Château Le Drot 1998 Bordeaux Blend (Bordeaux) $6. 85 Best Buy —*D.T. (11/15/2002)*

CHÂTEAU LEBOSCQ

Château Leboscq 2003 Bordeaux Blend (Médoc) $NA. 84 —*R.V. (5/1/2006)*

CHÂTEAU LÉOVILLE LAS CASES

Château Léoville Las Cases 2004 Bordeaux Blend (Saint-Julien) $NA. This "super second" lives up to its billing. It is rich and concentrated with dark tannins that lie over the ripe, jammy fruit and black, rich chocolate flavors. Acidity and wood are there, but only just hints after the richness of the fruit. A real, magnificent aging wine. **95** —*R.V. (6/1/2007)*

Château Léoville Las Cases 2003 Bordeaux Blend (Saint-Julien) $190. This is massive, hugely concentrated, topped with wood and intense tannins. Flavors of bitter chocolate are dominant, heavy fruits, blackberries and texture that fills the mouth with dark, dense flavors. Big in all senses. **94** —*R.V. (12/16/2007)*

Château Léoville Las Cases 2001 Bordeaux Blend (Saint-Julien) $190. A classic in development, a wine that will last for decades. It is certainly powerful, but already the shape is finalized, with its plums and berries settling down with perfumes, acidity, just enough tannins and a warm, welcoming richness. A great argument for the superiority of 2001 over 2000. **97 Cellar Selection** —*R.V. (12/16/2007)*

Château Léoville Las Cases 2006 Barrel Sample Bordeaux Blend (Saint-Julien) $NA. 94-96 Barrel Sample. Exceptionally rich wine, packed with solid Cabernet fruits. Dusty tannins, very sweet blackberries and plum flavors. A dry wine with great elegance. **95** —*R.V. (6/1/2007)*

Château Léoville Las Cases 2004 Barrel Sample Bordeaux Blend (Saint-Julien) $NA. 94 —*R.V. (6/1/2005)*

CHÂTEAU LEOVILLE POYFERRE

Chateau Leoville Poyferre 2004 Bordeaux Blend (Saint-Julien) $NA. A powerfully extracted wine, which almost—but not quite—submerges what is a fresh, fruity layer. The new wood that goes with the extraction is obvious at this stage in the wine's development, but that cassis fruit will bring out the freshness later. **93** —*R.V. (6/1/2007)*

Chateau Leoville Poyferre 2003 Bordeaux Blend (Saint-Julien) $75. 93 —*R.V. (5/1/2006)*

Chateau Leoville Poyferre 2001 Bordeaux Blend (Saint-Julien) $80. The completeness of 2001, with its miraculous balance, is present in this wine. The acidity, ripe blackcurrants sit comfortably on top of dry tannins, the fleshiness of the fruit taking the edge off the tannins. It seems to bring out the structure, the fruit and the refreshing acidity of great Cabernet. **95 Cellar Selection** —*R.V. (12/16/2007)*

Chateau Leoville Poyferre 2006 Barrel Sample Bordeaux Blend (Saint-Julien) $NA. 92-94 Barrel Sample. A big, spicy wood-flavored wine, very modern and smooth with its vanilla character. But there's also some dominant tannin that brings strength and power. **93** —*R.V. (6/1/2007)*

Chateau Leoville Poyferre 2005 Barrel Sample Bordeaux Blend (Saint-Julien) $NA. 93 —*R.V. (6/20/2006)*

Chateau Leoville Poyferre 2003 Barrel Sample Bordeaux Blend (Saint-Julien) $NA. 92 —*R.V. (6/3/2004)*

CHÂTEAU LÉOVILLE-BARTON

Château Léoville-Barton 2004 Bordeaux Blend (Saint-Julien) $NA. As so often, Léoville-Barton stands out for its style and elegance. With fresh fruit and acidity allied to generous tannins, it sums up the character of the 2004 vintage. Very classic in Bordeaux terms: not hugely powerful, but delicious. **94 Editors' Choice** —*R.V. (6/1/2007)*

Château Léoville-Barton 2003 Bordeaux Blend (Saint-Julien) $115. 95 —*R.V. (5/1/2006)*

Château Léoville-Barton 2001 Bordeaux Blend (Saint-Julien) $90. A wonderfully firm, concentrated wine that walks a fine, balanced line between richness and poised structure. It is classic in the best sense, showing all the shape of a fine Bordeaux, while adding the extra dimension of the freshest of black fruits, complexity from a few hints of wood, and a dark, brooding, long-lasting aftertaste. **96 Editors' Choice** —*R.V. (12/16/2007)*

Château Léoville-Barton 2005 Barrel Sample Bordeaux Blend (Saint-Julien) $NA. 96 —*R.V. (6/20/2006)*

Château Léoville-Barton 2003 Barrel Sample Bordeaux Blend (Saint-Julien) $NA. 93 —*R.V. (6/3/2004)*

CHÂTEAU LES CARMES HAUT-BRION

Château Les Carmes Haut-Brion 2005 Barrel Sample Bordeaux Blend (Pessac-Léognan) $NA. 93 —*R.V. (6/20/2006)*

CHÂTEAU LES HAUTS-CONSEILLANTS

Château les Hauts-Conseillants 2004 Bordeaux Blend (Lalande de Pomerol) $NA. A blend of 85% Merlot and 15% Cab Franc, here is a wine that seduces with its spice and fresh, smooth fruits. It is not intensely powerful, relying more on its fruits to attract. The new wood flavors add complexity, although at this stage they are still too dominant. **87** —*R.V. (6/1/2007)*

CHÂTEAU LES ORMES DE PEZ

Château les Ormes de Pez 2002 Bordeaux Blend (Saint-Estèphe) $27. 90 —*R.V. (6/1/2005)*

Château les Ormes de Pez 2005 Barrel Sample Bordeaux Blend (Saint-Estèphe) $NA. 92 —*R.V. (6/20/2006)*

Château les Ormes de Pez 2003 Barrel Sample Bordeaux Blend (Saint-Estèphe) $NA. 88 —*R.V. (6/3/2004)*

CHÂTEAU LES ROCHERS MIRANDE

Château Les Rochers Mirande 2000 Red Blend (Montagne-St.-Èmilion) $18. 83 —*M.S. (9/1/2003)*

CHÂTEAU LES ROCHES BLANCHES

Château les Roches Blanches 2006 Barrel Sample Bordeaux Blend (Saint-Julien) $NA. 93-95 Barrel Sample. A powerfully tannic wine. The blackberry fruit is a great counterbalance to this power, leaving a very complete, but solidly constructed wine. **94** —*R.V. (6/1/2007)*

CHÂTEAU LES VALENTINES

Château les Valentines 2006 Rosé Blend (Côtes de Provence) $20. A wonderful fruit salad of grapes goes into this deliciously, freshly impressive rosé. The red fruits and pink grapefruit burst in the mouth, and the freshness delivers a crisp, delicate aftertaste. **91** —*R.V. (7/1/2007)*

CHÂTEAU LESTRILLE

Château Lestrille 2003 Bordeaux Blend (Bordeaux Supérieur) $10. The younger brother of Château Lestrille Capmartin, this is a lightweight, with good red fruit flavors. Tannins are soft, ripe and sweet with some smooth fruitcake flavors from this Merlot-dominated wine. It's an easy mouthful, ready to drink now. **84** —*R.V. (11/1/2007)*

Château Lestrille 2006 Bordeaux White Blend (Entre-Deux-Mers) $12. Perfumed yet rather rustic, this wine has aromatic white fruit flavors, touched with a yeasty, bready character. It's rounded, but misses on the freshness. **84** —*R.V. (12/31/2007)*

CHÂTEAU LESTRILLE CAPMARTIN

Château Lestrille Capmartin 2003 Bordeaux Blend (Bordeaux Supérieur) $NA. It's obvious that the Roumage family sees their future in quality, even at the basic Bordeaux level. This is a wine that punches way above its station, the fruit ripe and rich enough to sustain a heft of wood, giving spice and blackberries together in a satisfying amalgam. **90 Editors' Choice** —*R.V. (11/1/2007)*

Château Lestrille Capmartin 2000 Prestige Bordeaux Blend (Bordeaux) $17. 84 —*R.V. (12/1/2002)*

CHÂTEAU LIEUJEAN

Château Lieujean 2005 Bordeaux Blend (Haut-Médoc) $NA. The vineyard of Lieujean in the northern Haut-Médoc is dominated by Cabernet, and that shows in this firmly fruity, but also structured wine. It is not the power that works here, but the balance. **87** —*R.V. (11/1/2007)*

Château Lieujean 2004 Bordeaux Blend (Haut-Médoc) $NA. Pure fruits and black currant juice flavor are just lightly layered with some tannins making this wine easy, fresh and refreshing. Enjoy now. **86** —*R.V. (6/1/2007)*

CHÂTEAU LILIAN LADOUYS

Château Lilian Ladouys 2004 Bordeaux Blend (Saint-Estèphe) $NA. With the 2003 vintage, Lilian-Ladouys returned to its previous form after a fallow period. This 2004 is a good follow up. It has ripe black plum and mint flavors, and solid, dense tannins, leavened by juicy acidity. **89** —*R.V. (6/1/2007)*

Château Lilian Ladouys 2003 Bordeaux Blend (Saint-Estèphe) $17. 88 —*R.V. (5/1/2006)*

CHÂTEAU LIVERSAN

Château Liversan 2005 Bordeaux Blend (Haut-Médoc) $NA. A finely structured, densely fruity wine, showing all the richness and vibrant fruits of 2005. Flavors of herbs go with the blackberry jelly fruits, dusty tannins and rich blueberry skin flavors. Should age well; give it 5–8 years before maturity. **90** —*R.V. (11/1/2007)*

Château Liversan 2004 Bordeaux Blend (Haut-Médoc) $NA. This cru bourgeois supérieur is a solid, impressive wine, packed with dense tannins, which march alongside the juicy blackberry fruit and berry jelly flavors. It's finely balanced, ready to drink in three years. **89** —*R.V. (6/1/2007)*

CHÂTEAU LOUDENNE

Château Loudenne 2003 Bordeaux Blend (Médoc) $NA. Attractive and structured, with dry tannins balanced by ripe black currant fruits. It is relatively lightweight, despite the year, and ready to drink now. **86** —*R.V. (11/1/2007)*

Château Loudenne 2005 Bordeaux White Blend (Bordeaux Blanc) $NA. A soft, mango-flavored wine, with just a touch of citrus. There's some good acidity, a nice citrus touch and freshness. Drink now. **85** —*R.V. (11/1/2007)*

Château Loudenne 1995 Bordeaux Blend (Médoc) $15. 86 —*M.S. (12/31/1999)*

CHÂTEAU LYNCH-BAGES

Château Lynch-Bages 2004 Bordeaux Blend (Pauillac) $NA. As always, Lynch-Bages comes in with an impressive performance. It is rich, dense and ripe with black fruit flavors. The texture is solid, the intense fruits complemented by ripe tannins. And, to finish, there is the freshness of currant fruit acidity. A really fine wine. **94 Editors' Choice** —*R.V. (6/1/2007)*

Château Lynch-Bages 2000 Bordeaux Blend (Pauillac) $100. 95 —*R.V. (6/1/2003)*

Château Lynch-Bages 2006 Barrel Sample Bordeaux Blend (Pauillac) $NA. 93-95 Barrel Sample. A big, powered wine, packed with both dense fruit and equally dense tannins. Huge structure, but the ripe fruit and the blackberry richness offer great potential. **94** —*R.V. (6/1/2007)*

Château Lynch-Bages 2004 Barrel Sample Bordeaux Blend (Pauillac) 93 —*R.V. (6/1/2005)*

CHÂTEAU LYNCH-MOUSSAS

Château Lynch-Moussas 2005 Barrel Sample Bordeaux Blend (Pauillac) 90 —*R.V. (6/21/2006)*

CHÂTEAU MAGDELAINE

Château Magdelaine 2004 Bordeaux Blend (Saint-Emilion Grand Cru) $69. A hugely rich, concentrated wine for 2004, packed with ripe black plums and berries. This is a great success, with dry tannins balanced by delicious sweet fruit, finishing with a fresh, currant fruit aftertaste. **92** —*R.V. (6/1/2007)*

Château Magdelaine 2000 Bordeaux Blend (Saint-Emilion) $87. 93 —*R.V. (6/1/2003)*

Château Magdelaine 2003 Barrel Sample Bordeaux Blend (Saint-Emilion) $NA. 89 —*R.V. (6/3/2004)*

CHÂTEAU MAINE-GAZIN

Château Maine-Gazin 1997 Bordeaux Blend (Bordeaux) $17. 81 —*J.C. (4/1/2001)*

CHÂTEAU MALARTIC-LAGRAVIERE

Château Malartic-Lagraviere 2004 Bordeaux Blend (Pessac-Léognan) $NA. Since the Bonnie family took over this property, it has improved enormously, and still represents good value. This is balanced and fresh, with aromas of eucalyptus and mint, finishing with ripe, sweet fruit. **90** —*R.V. (6/1/2007)*

Château Malartic-Lagraviere 2005 Barrel Sample Bordeaux Blend (Pessac-Léognan) 90 —*R.V. (6/21/2006)*

Château Malartic-Lagraviere 2006 Le Rosé de Malartic Bordeaux Blend (Bordeaux Rosé) $NA. Quite an innovation from a major Bordeaux chateau – a rosé bottled with a screw top, albeit a very smart, de luxe design. This is a vivid pink colored wine, a blend of Merlot and Cabernet Sauvignon, crisp, fresh, tasting of wild strawberries, a great summer wine. **86** —*R.V. (7/1/2007)*

Château Malartic-Lagraviere 2002 Bordeaux White Blend (Pessac-Léognan) $37. 90 —*R.V. (6/1/2005)*

Château Malartic-Lagraviere 2006 Barrel Sample Bordeaux White Blend (Pessac-Léognan) $NA. 91-93 Barrel Sample. A classic in a great white year. Even though the wine is full and generous, it also has vibrant green fruits and lively acidity. Already shows a great future. **92** —*R.V. (6/1/2007)*

CHÂTEAU MALESCASSE

Château Malescasse 2005 Barrel Sample Bordeaux Blend (Haut-Médoc) 87 —*R.V. (6/21/2006)*

CHÂTEAU MALESCOT SAINT-EXUPERY

Château Malescot Saint-Exupery 2005 Barrel Sample Bordeaux Blend (Margaux) 92 —*R.V. (6/1/2006)*

Château Malescot Saint-Exupery 2003 Barrel Sample Bordeaux Blend (Margaux) 90 —*R.V. (6/3/2004)*

CHÂTEAU MARBUZET

Château Marbuzet 2004 Bordeaux Blend (Saint-Estèphe) $NA. Formerly owned by the Prats family (who still manage Cos d'Estournel), Marbuzet normally makes impressive wine. Not so the 2004, which seems to have acquired a rustic, earthy character, leaving a bitter taste. **86** —*R.V. (6/1/2007)*

Château Marbuzet 2005 Barrel Sample Bordeaux Blend (Saint-Estèphe) 92 —*R.V. (6/20/2006)*

CHÂTEAU MARGAUX

Château Margaux 2004 Bordeaux Blend (Margaux) $NA. If one of 2004's enduring characteristics is its freshness, then Margaux epitomizes this. It is so deliciously fresh and floating, with great black currant and blueberry fruits, pointed up by spice, mint and a sense of elegance and poise. There's no doubt about its aging potential either: just feel that heart of firm tannins. **96** —*R.V. (6/1/2007)*

Château Margaux 2001 Bordeaux Blend (Margaux) $300. 97 —*R.V. (6/1/2005)*

Château Margaux 2006 Barrel Sample Bordeaux Blend (Margaux) $NA. 94-96 Barrel Sample. A year in which Château Margaux had a much higher percentage (90%) than usual of Cabernet Sauvignon. The result is a wine that is pure fruit, very juicy, packed with black currants. It is surprisingly soft even for the usually elegant Margaux, a vintage that will develop relatively fast over 10 years. **95** —*R.V. (6/1/2007)*

Château Margaux 2004 Barrel Sample Bordeaux Blend (Margaux) 96 —*R.V. (6/1/2005)*

Château Margaux 2002 Pavillon Blanc de Château Margaux Bordeaux White Blend (Bordeaux) $58. 91 —*R.V. (6/1/2005)*

CHÂTEAU MARIS

Château Maris 1999 Rhône Red Blend (Minervois La Liviniere) $16. 86 —*M.M. (2/1/2002)*

CHÂTEAU MAROUÏNE

Château Marouïne 2005 Rosé Blend (Côtes de Provence) $13. 88 Best Buy —*J.C. (6/21/2006)*

CHÂTEAU MARQUIS DE TERME

Château Marquis de Terme 2005 Barrel Sample Bordeaux Blend (Margaux) $NA. 87 —*R.V. (6/21/2006)*

CHÂTEAU MARTINENS

Château Martinens 2004 Bordeaux Blend (Margaux) $NA. A high proportion of Merlot in the blend makes this a soft, rounded wine. It is spoiled by rustic, animal flavors and by a streak of acidity to finish that is out of balance with the rest of the wine. **85** —*R.V. (6/1/2007)*

CHÂTEAU MAS NEUF

Château Mas Neuf 1998 Rhône Red Blend (Costières de Nimes) $9. 84 —*J.C. (12/31/2000)*

Château Mas Neuf 2003 Syrah (Costières de Nimes) $10. 88 Best Buy —*S.H. (11/15/2004)*

CHÂTEAU MASSAMIER LA MIGNARDE

Château Massamier la Mignarde 2004 Domus Maximus Rhône Red Blend (Minervois La Liviniere) $34. 91 Editors' Choice —*R.V. (12/31/2006)*

Château Massamier la Mignarde 2004 Tradition Rhône Red Blend (Minervois) $12. 88 Best Buy —*R.V. (12/31/2006)*

Château Massamier la Mignarde 2006 Rosé Blend (Minervois) $15. A rather too full, peppery wine that has caramel and tannin flavors. The fruit is there, red apples, kiwi acidity and pink grapefruit, but the weight is too much. **85** —*R.V. (7/1/2007)*

CHÂTEAU MAUCOIL

Château Maucoil 2003 Rhône Red Blend (Châteauneuf-du-Pape) $NA. 85 —*R.V. (12/31/2005)*

CHÂTEAU MAZEYRES

Château Mazeyres 2002 Bordeaux Blend (Pomerol) $33. 90 —*R.V. (6/1/2005)*

CHÂTEAU MEYNEY

Château Meyney 2000 Bordeaux Blend (Saint-Estèphe) $30. 89 —*R.V. (6/1/2003)*

CHÂTEAU MEZAIN

Château Mezain 2003 Bordeaux White Blend (Bordeaux) $12. 84 —*J.C. (6/1/2005)*

CHÂTEAU MIRAVAL

Château Miraval 2006 Rosé Blend (Côtes de Provence) $NA. A light, very fresh blend of Cinsault and Grenache, crisp, dry, with delicious acidity. The pale, salmon-pink color sets off the red fruit currant flavors. **90** —*R.V. (7/1/2007)*

CHÂTEAU MONBOUSQUET

Château Monbousquet 2000 Bordeaux Blend (Saint-Emilion) $160. 88 —*R.V. (6/1/2003)*

CHÂTEAU MONBRISON

Château Monbrison 2004 Bordeaux Blend (Margaux) $NA. A dense, satisfying wine that shows some Margaux elegance while at the same time having a dark, dry side of tannins that dominate the ripe fruit. **90** —*R.V. (6/1/2007)*

Château Monbrison 2003 Bordeaux Blend (Margaux) $25. 89 —*R.V. (5/1/2006)*

Château Monbrison 2000 Bordeaux Blend (Margaux) $30. 90 —*R.V. (6/1/2003)*

Château Monbrison 2003 Barrel Sample Bordeaux Blend (Margaux) $NA. 89 —*R.V. (6/3/2004)*

CHÂTEAU MONCONTOUR

Château Moncontour 2003 Cuvée Prédilection Chenin Blanc (Vouvray) $NA. 90 —*R.V. (6/1/2006)*

CHÂTEAU MONGRAVEY

Château Mongravey 2001 Bordeaux Blend (Margaux) $30. 86 —*R.V. (6/1/2005)*

CHÂTEAU MONREGARD

Château Monregard la Croix 2004 Bordeaux Blend (Pomerol) $NA. The Bourotte family, which also owns Clos du Clocher in Pomerol, uses consultant Michel Rolland, and the richness of this wine may well be done to his advice. It is very ripe, packed with smooth, velvet Merlot textures and flavors. The flavors are of cooked fruits, plums and blackberries, taking away some freshness, but substituting a fine intensity of taste. **91** —*R.V. (6/1/2007)*

CHÂTEAU MONT-PÉRAT

Château Mont-Pérat 2004 Bordeaux Blend (Premieres Côtes de Bordeaux) $34. Owned by the Despagne family, who make some of the best whites from the Entre-deux-Mers, Mont-Pérat is one of the family's red wine estates. This is dominated by Merlot, giving great juicy fruit flavors, underpinned by some wood, and a velvet, ripe texture. **89** —*R.V. (6/1/2007)*

Château Mont-Pérat 2003 Bordeaux Blend (Premieres Côtes de Bordeaux) $NA. A concentrated and dense wine. Intense in its wood aging, this is still a young wine. The fruit is certainly rich, with black currants dominant overlain with spice from the wood and with dark tannins. **90** —*R.V. (11/1/2007)*

Château Mont-Pérat 2005 Bordeaux White Blend (Bordeaux Blanc) $NA. A big, hugely rich, wood-dominated wine, oozing power and ripe fruit. This is almost Chard-like in its buttery weight, but is the usual Bordeaux blend of Sémillon and Sauvignon Blanc. Those who like power, line up here. **89** —*R.V. (11/1/2007)*

CHÂTEAU MONT-REDON

Château Mont-Redon 2005 Rhône Red Blend (Côtes-du-Rhône) $15. 88 *J.C. (11/15/2006)*

Château Mont-Redon 2003 Rhône Red Blend (Châteauneuf-du-Pape) $45. 92 —*R.V. (12/31/2005)*

CHÂTEAU MONTNER

Château Montner 2000 Rhône Red Blend (Côtes du Roussillon) $8. 87 Best Buy —*M.S. (2/1/2003)*

CHÂTEAU MOULIN DE TRICOT

Château Moulin de Tricot 2001 Bordeaux Blend (Margaux) $NA. 86 —*R.V. (6/1/2005)*

CHÂTEAU MOURGUES DU GRES

Château Mourgues du Gres 2002 Les Galets Rouges Rhône Red Blend (Costières de Nimes) $12. 89 Best Buy —*J.C. (2/1/2005)*

CHÂTEAU MOUTON ROTHSCHILD

Château Mouton Rothschild 2000 Bordeaux Blend (Pauillac) $450. 97 —*R.V. (6/1/2003)*

Château Mouton Rothschild 2006 Barrel Sample Bordeaux Blend (Pauillac) $NA. 96-98 Barrel Sample. The best Mouton for several years. It has great power, great structured Cabernet fruit, and dense, almost dusty tannins. The flavors are concentrated, dense, dark. Power and style. **97** —*R.V. (6/1/2007)*

Château Mouton Rothschild 2004 Barrel Sample Bordeaux Blend (Pauillac) $NA. 93 —*R.V. (6/1/2005)*

Château Mouton Rothschild 2001 Aile d'Argent Bordeaux White Blend (Bordeaux) $50. 87 —*J.C. (6/1/2005)*

CHÂTEAU NAIRAC

Château Nairac 2005 Barrel Sample Bordeaux White Blend (Barsac) $NA. 91 —*R.V. (6/1/2006)*

CHÂTEAU NENIN

Château Nenin 2004 Bordeaux Blend (Pomerol) $NA. From the Pomerol estate under the same ownership as Léoville-las-Cases in Saint-Julien. A big wine, with generous, opulent fruit. Bitter chocolate as well as ripe black skins and big firm fruits and tannins. To finish, there is a lift of freshness, but this is more about sweet fruits. **92** —*R.V. (6/1/2007)*

Château Nenin 2006 Barrel Sample Bordeaux Blend (Pomerol) $NA. 92-94 Barrel Sample. Initially bitter chocolate and cocoa flavors, followed by hugely ripe fruit. Further tastes come through, fresh acidity, full black fruit flavors and dark tannins. Powerful. **93** —*R.V. (6/1/2007)*

Château Nenin 2005 Barrel Sample Bordeaux Blend (Pomerol) $NA. 91 —*R.V. (6/1/2006)*

CHÂTEAU NOTRE DAME DE SALAGOU

Château Notre Dame de Salagou 2002 Red Blend (Coteaux du Languedoc) $NA. 84 —*R.V. (12/1/2004)*

CHÂTEAU OLIVIER

Château Olivier 2004 Bordeaux Blend (Pessac-Léognan) $NA. How Olivier has progressed. The ancient moated castle property is now making delicious wine. Fresh and balanced, this is sweet, soft, layered with red cherry flavors and structured with dark tannins. **92 Editors' Choice** —*R.V. (6/1/2007)*

Château Olivier 2002 Bordeaux White Blend (Pessac-Léognan) $NA. 87 —*R.V. (6/1/2005)*

CHÂTEAU ORMES DE PEZ

Château Ormes de Pez 2004 Bordeaux Blend (Saint-Estèphe) $NA. A wine that brings out the best of the interaction between tannins and fruit. It is deliciously ripe, powered by cassis and sweet blueberry flavors. Underpinning this fruit are solid, dark and intense tannins. The wine should age well—over 10 years and more. **91** —*R.V. (6/1/2007)*

CHÂTEAU PALMER

Château Palmer 2004 Bordeaux Blend (Margaux) $NA. This wine hits the opulent end of the spectrum, with its dense, velvet structure, and superrich fruit. But it is not weighed down with this richness, because the pure fruit, the fine lines of the tannins and the very precise character of the vanilla from the wood all give liveliness. **93 Editors' Choice** —*R.V. (6/1/2007)*

Château Palmer 2003 Bordeaux Blend (Margaux) $120. 94 —*R.V. (5/1/2006)*

Château Palmer 2000 Bordeaux Blend (Margaux) $120. 94 —*R.V. (6/1/2003)*

Château Palmer 2004 Barrel Sample Bordeaux Blend (Margaux) $NA. 93 —*R.V. (6/1/2005)*

CHÂTEAU PAPE-CLEMENT

Château Pape-Clement 2004 Bordeaux Blend (Pessac-Léognan) $NA. Dark, bitter chocolate flavors come together with dusty tannins, new wood and smoky aromas. Despite a slight vegetal hint, the main effect is elegance, with a smooth aftertaste. **90** —*R.V. (6/1/2007)*

Château Pape-Clement 2004 Barrel Sample Bordeaux Blend (Pessac-Léognan) 93 —*R.V. (6/1/2005)*

Château Pape-Clement 2000 Pessac-Léognan Bordeaux Blend (Bordeaux) $80. 94 —*R.V. (6/1/2003)*

Château Pape-Clement 2005 Barrel Sample Bordeaux White Blend (Pessac-Léognan) $NA. 89 —*R.V. (6/21/2006)*

CHÂTEAU PATACHE D'AUX

Château Patache d'Aux 2005 Bordeaux Blend (Médoc) $NA. Densely rich and tannic for a Médoc, this has firm structure over ripe, black fruits and herbal flavors. This will be one for aging, with its solid dry base of firm fruits and hints of stalkiness. **89** —*R.V. (11/1/2007)*

Château Patache d'Aux 2004 Bordeaux Blend (Médoc) $NA. Named after the coaching stage (Patache d'Aux) which was part of the château, this property is looking good, after investment. The 2004 has good ripe fruits, a very open, polished wine, with intense blackberry and spice flavors. **90** —*R.V. (6/1/2007)*

Château Patache d'Aux 2002 Bordeaux Blend (Médoc) $22. 85 —*J.C. (6/1/2005)*

CHÂTEAU PAVEIL DE LUZE

Château Paveil de Luze 2004 Bordeaux Blend (Margaux) $NA. Fresh and light, this is a wine that should be drunk now. The fruit is soft, juicy and easy. **86** —*R.V. (6/1/2007)*

CHÂTEAU PAVIE

Château Pavie 2000 Bordeaux Blend (Saint-Emilion) $250. 93 —*R.V. (6/1/2003)*

Château Pavie Macquin 2005 Barrel Sample Bordeaux Blend (Saint-Emilion Grand Cru) 92 —*R.V. (6/20/2006)*

Château Pavie-Decesse 2000 Bordeaux Blend (Saint-Emilion) 90 —*R.V. (6/1/2003)*

CHÂTEAU PECH-REDON

Château Pech-Redon 2001 La Centaurée Red Blend (Coteaux du Languedoc) 91 —*R.V. (12/1/2004)*

CHÂTEAU PÉRIER

Château Périer 2003 Bordeaux Blend (Médoc) $17. 87 —*R.V. (5/1/2006)*

CHÂTEAU PERRON

Château Perron 2005 Bordeaux Blend (Graves) $NA. A heavily wood-dominated wine, and firmly tannic. The fruit is almost a component of the wood, which needs two years to calm down. This shows some freshness and acidity however, and that helps it on its way. **86** —*R.V. (11/1/2007)*

Château Perron 2006 Bordeaux White Blend (Graves) $NA. A great value white, with fresh grapefruit and crisp acidity. In a few months, the current raw edge will have softened, as the 60% Sémillon in the blend calms down. But it's still a great summer drink. **86** —*R.V. (12/31/2007)*

CHÂTEAU PETIT VILLAGE

Château Petit Village 2004 Barrel Sample Bordeaux Blend (Pomerol) 92 —*R.V. (6/1/2005)*

CHÂTEAU PÉTRUS

Château Pétrus 2004 Bordeaux Blend (Pomerol) $NA. This is a classic. Vintage 2004 has given beautifully ripe Merlot, perfectly poised, but also showing the dryness and power. It is hugely intense, structured, bringing in blackberry flavors, fresh acidity and complex wood, perfumed and rich, concentrated. The aging potential? At least 20 years. **97 Cellar Selection** —*R.V. (6/1/2007)*

Château Pétrus 2000 Bordeaux Blend (Pomerol) $1500. 98 —*R.V. (6/1/2003)*

Château Pétrus 2006 Barrel Sample Bordeaux Blend (Pomerol) $NA. 95-97 Barrel Sample. The freshness of 2006 is here in abundance. But because it is Pétrus, those deliciously lively black fruits are backed up with a formidable battery of tannins and concentration. But never extracted, always properly restrained. **96** —*R.V. (6/1/2007)*

Château Pétrus 2004 Barrel Sample Bordeaux Blend (Pomerol) $NA. 95 —*R.V. (6/1/2005)*

CHÂTEAU PEYRABON

Château Peyrabon 2003 Bordeaux Blend (Haut-Médoc) $NA. 89 —*R.V. (5/1/2006)*

CHÂTEAU PEYRASSOL

Chateau Peyrassol 2006 Rosé Blend (Côtes de Provence) $24. The palest of pink/grey colors shimmer from the glass. This lightness of touch follows through this blend of Cinsault and Grenache. Flavors of herbs as well as crisp fruit make this a great food wine. **88** —*R.V. (7/1/2007)*

CHÂTEAU PHÉLAN-SÉGUR

Château Phélan-Ségur 2004 Bordeaux Blend (Saint-Estèphe) $NA. For a Saint-Estèphe, normally renowned for their youthful tannins, this is relatively soft, going more for freshness and dark plum fruit flavors. But lovers of those tannins won't be totally disappointed, because they are there, hidden at this stage by the fruit. **89** —*R.V. (6/1/2007)*

Château Phélan-Ségur 2003 Bordeaux Blend (Saint-Estèphe) $38. 93 Cellar Selection —*R.V. (5/1/2006)*

Château Phélan-Ségur 2005 Barrel Sample Bordeaux Blend (Saint-Estèphe) 92 —*R.V. (6/20/2006)*

Château Phélan-Ségur 2003 Barrel Sample Bordeaux Blend (Saint-Estèphe) 90 —*R.V. (6/3/2004)*

Château Phélan-Sègur 2000 Bordeaux Blend (Saint-Estèphe) $35. 92 —*R.V. (6/1/2003)*

CHÂTEAU PIBRAN

Château Pibran 2004 Bordeaux Blend (Pauillac) $NA. One of the properties owned by insurance giant AXA, and under the same management as Château Pichon Longueville, this estate is making some impressive wines. The 2004 is modern, concentrated, polished, and dominated by intense, juicy fruits and new wood. **91** —*R.V. (6/1/2007)*

CHÂTEAU PICHON LONGUEVILLE

Château Pichon Longueville 2004 Bordeaux Blend (Pauillac) $NA. An intensely powerful, smooth wine, in a style that has an instant, sexy appeal. But it's not just surface glamour, there is a solid texture, layering the dusty tannins with rich black plums, red berries and vanilla. **94** —*R.V. (6/1/2007)*

Château Pichon Longueville 2003 Bordeaux Blend (Pauillac) $100. 93 —*R.V. (5/1/2006)*

Château Pichon Longueville 2000 Bordeaux Blend (Pauillac) $100. 92 —*R.V. (6/1/2003)*

Château Pichon Longueville 2006 Barrel Sample Bordeaux Blend (Pauillac) $NA. 92-94 Barrel Sample. Bringing together a complex set of flavors, soft fruit, fruit tannins and layers of acidity. The core of the wine is firmly dry and tannic, the envelope soft and generous. **93** —*R.V. (6/1/2007)*

Château Pichon Longueville 2003 Barrel Sample Bordeaux Blend (Pauillac) 91 —*R.V. (6/3/2004)*

Château Pichon Longueville Comtesse de Lalande 2004 Bordeaux Blend (Pauillac) $NA. There is only one question about what is otherwise a magnificent wine—whether the current dominant wood flavors will soften and blend enough. If they do, then the powerful fruit, spice and freshness will all come together in a stellar wine. **94** —*R.V. (6/1/2007)*

Château Pichon Longueville Comtesse de Lalande 2001 Bordeaux Blend (Pauillac) $NA. The high proportion of Merlot in Pichon Lalande is a good reason why this wine, among the great wines of Pauillac, is always so seductive. This is no exception; it charms as well as excites with vibrant fruits as well as serious, dense tannins and acidity that promise good aging. Give it 7–9 years for full maturity to begin. **95 Cellar Selection** —*R.V. (11/1/2007)*

Château Pichon Longueville Comtesse de Lalande 2006 Barrel Sample Bordeaux Blend (Pauillac) $NA. 93-95 Barrel Sample. The relatively high proportion of Merlot in this blend has given a wine that is ripe, generous in structure, while the Cabernet Sauvignon at 64% offers sweet and juicy fruit and tannins. Very pure, fresh fruit flavors. **94** —*R.V. (6/1/2007)*

Château Pichon Longueville Comtesse de Lalande 2005 Barrel Sample Bordeaux Blend (Pauillac) 95 —*R.V. (6/20/2006)*

Château Pichon Longueville 2006 Rosé des Tourelles Bordeaux Blend (Bordeaux Rosé) $NA. The famed Pauillac chateau also makes this heavy pink colored rosé, dominated by Cabernet Sauvignon. It misses freshness and acidity, but certainly wins out on the weight stakes. **84** —*R.V. (7/1/2007)*

CHÂTEAU PIQUE-CAILLOU

Château Pique-Caillou 2005 Barrel Sample Bordeaux Blend (Pessac-Léognan) $NA. 91 —*R.V. (6/1/2006)*

CHÂTEAU PONTET-CANET

Château Pontet-Canet 2004 Bordeaux Blend (Pauillac) $NA. Foursquare, powerful wine that shows great ripeness, solid, firm red berry fruits, a touch of mint, and black, almost impenetrable tannins. Expect this impressive wine to age for 10–15 years. **93** —*R.V. (6/1/2007)*

Château Pontet-Canet 2003 Bordeaux Blend (Pauillac) $55. 91 —*R.V. (5/1/2006)*

Château Pontet-Canet 2005 Barrel Sample Bordeaux Blend (Pauillac) 93 —*R.V. (6/20/2006)*

Château Pontet-Canet 2002 Kosher Bordeaux Blend (Pauillac) $100. 89 —*J.C. (4/1/2006)*

CHÂTEAU POTENSAC

Château Potensac 2004 Bordeaux Blend (Médoc) $NA. The estate, under the same ownership as Léoville-las-Cases in Saint-Julien, shows what can be achieved in the Médoc when care is taken. It is big, round, solid and structured, with complexity coming from dark, sweet fruits and new wood. It is rich and powerful, the aging potential showing from a core of dry tannin. **91 Editors' Choice** —*R.V. (6/1/2007)*

Château Potensac 2005 Barrel Sample Bordeaux Blend (Médoc) $NA. 92 —*R.V. (6/1/2006)*

CHÂTEAU POUJEAUX

Château Poujeaux 2004 Bordeaux Blend (Moulis-en-Médoc) $NA. This is one of the top two wines of Moulis (the other is Chasse-Spleen), and the 2004 maintains the Poujeaux's reputation for making wines beyond their class. This is a big wine, exuding power and authority, packed with ripe, but firm tannins and peppered black cherry fruits. With its structure, it will definitely age. **92 Cellar Selection** —*R.V. (6/1/2007)*

Château Poujeaux 2003 Bordeaux Blend (Moulis-en-Médoc) $25. 92 Editors' Choice —*R.V. (5/1/2006)*

Château Poujeaux 2000 Bordeaux Blend (Moulis) $34. 87 —*R.V. (6/1/2003)*

Château Poujeaux 2004 Barrel Sample Bordeaux Blend (Haut-Médoc) $NA. 91 —*R.V. (6/1/2005)*

CHÂTEAU PREUILLAC

Château Preuillac 2004 Bordeaux Blend (Médoc) $NA. Château Preuillac, deep in the wilds of the northern Médoc, is making very good wine, to judge by this and other recent vintages, thanks to big investments from the Mau family. It is finely balanced, a combination of a dry, firm, tannic structure and ripe, juicy fruit, underpinned by new wood. **89** —*R.V. (6/1/2007)*

Château Preuillac 2003 Bordeaux Blend (Médoc) $NA. 90 —*R.V. (5/1/2006)*

CHÂTEAU PRIEURÉ-LES-TOURS

Château Prieuré-les-Tours 2000 Cuveé Clara Bordeaux White Blend (Graves) $16. 88 —*R.V. (6/1/2005)*

CHÂTEAU PRIEURÉ-LICHINE

Château Prieuré-Lichine 2004 Bordeaux Blend (Margaux) $NA. Alexis Lichine's old château has been revolutionized in the last decade, producing wines with a diamond-like luster, polished with new wood, squeezed black currant juice fruit flavors and ripe tannins. A shiny, gleaming wine. **91** —*R.V. (6/1/2007)*

Château Prieuré-Lichine 2000 Bordeaux Blend (Margaux) $35. 91 —*R.V. (6/1/2003)*

Château Prieuré-Lichine 2004 Barrel Sample Bordeaux Blend (Margaux) $NA. 92 —*R.V. (6/1/2005)*

CHÂTEAU PUECH-HAUT

Château Puech-Haut 2001 Red Blend (Coteaux du Languedoc) $NA. 88 —*R.V. (12/1/2004)*

Château Puech-Haut 2002 Les Complices de Puech-Haut Red Blend (Coteaux du Languedoc) $NA. 85 —*R.V. (12/1/2004)*

Château Puech-Haut 2003 Rosé Blend (Coteaux du Languedoc) $NA. 90 —*R.V. (12/1/2004)*

CHÂTEAU PUY CASTERA

Château Puy Castera 2004 Bordeaux Blend (Haut-Médoc) $NA. Open, generous and rich, this is a well-balanced wine, layering some dry tannins, but more of the fresh fruit and ripe flavors. It could age over 4–5 years, but is almost ready to drink now. **89** —*R.V. (6/1/2007)*

CHÂTEAU QUINAULT L'ENCLOS

Château Quinault L'Enclos 2004 Bordeaux Blend (Saint-Emilion Grand Cru) $NA. Alain Raynaud's vineyard is situated in the city of Libourne, surrounded by housing. His wines have achieved almost cult status. This 2004, with its beautifully smooth, ripe fruit, is more serious than its surface veneer suggests. The tannins are dry, complex and structured, while the rich, juicy flavors are given an extra dimension by the ripe acidity. **92** —*R.V. (6/1/2007)*

CHÂTEAU RABAUD PROMIS

Château Rabaud Promis 2005 Barrel Sample Bordeaux White Blend (Sauternes) $NA. 91 —*R.V. (6/1/2006)*

CHÂTEAU RAHOUL

Château Rahoul 2005 Barrel Sample Bordeaux Blend (Graves) $NA. 88 —*R.V. (6/21/2006)*

CHÂTEAU RAMAFORT

Château Ramafort 2004 Bordeaux Blend (Médoc) $NA. A rich, generous, relatively soft wine, with immediately attractive open fruit, fresh acidity and ripe black currant, juicy flavors. Delicious now; could age. **89** —*R.V. (6/1/2007)*

CHÂTEAU RAUZAN DESPAGNE

Château Rauzan Despagne 2005 Bordeaux White Blend (Bordeaux Blanc) $NA. This shows considerable wood flavors, giving a smooth, creamy character, spiced with some toast and ripe, dense Sémillon. It's big, a definite food wine, showing great style and quality above its simple Bordeaux appellation station. **90 Editors' Choice** —*R.V. (11/1/2007)*

Château Rauzan Despagne 2004 Cuvée de Landereau Bordeaux White Blend (Bordeaux) $12. 87 —*R.V. (6/1/2005)*

CHÂTEAU RAUZAN-GASSIES

Château Rauzan-Gassies 2005 Barrel Sample Bordeaux Blend (Margaux) $NA. 92 —*R.V. (6/20/2006)*

CHÂTEAU RAUZAN-SÉGLA

Château Rauzan-Ségla 2004 Bordeaux Blend (Margaux) $NA. A powerfully ripe wine, with pure black currant flavors over soft, polished tannins. The wood balance is exemplary, offering just the right lift. Touches of cinnamon and vanilla give an extra dimension. **93 Editors' Choice** —*R.V. (6/1/2007)*

Château Rauzan-Ségla 2001 Bordeaux Blend (Margaux) $57. 94 —*R.V. (6/1/2005)*

Château Rauzan-Ségla 2006 Barrel Sample Bordeaux Blend (Margaux) $NA. 92-94 Barrel Sample. Very juicy, full of ripe black currant fruits and with smoky flavors from new wood. Fresh and intense, excellent potential. **93** —*R.V. (6/1/2007)*

Château Rauzan-Ségla 2005 Barrel Sample Bordeaux Blend (Margaux) $NA. 94 —*R.V. (6/20/2006)*

CHÂTEAU RAYNE VIGNEAU

Château Rayne Vigneau 2005 Barrel Sample Bordeaux White Blend (Sauternes) $NA. 90 —*R.V. (6/1/2006)*

CHÂTEAU RÉAL MARTIN

Château Réal Martin 2004 Rhône Red Blend (Côtes de Provence) $10. 85 Best Buy —*J.C. (11/15/2005)*

Château Réal Martin 2001 Syrah-Grenache (Côtes de Provence) $13. 81 —*J.C. (11/15/2005)*

Château Réal Martin 2006 Grande Cuvée Rosé Blend (Côtes de Provence) $15. This is classic Provence rosé (in the best sense) from one of the oldest estates in the region, once owned by the Counts of Provence. It is elegant, relatively delicate, but is filled with herbs and southern warmth, as well as crisp, red berry aftertaste. **88** —*R.V. (7/1/2007)*

CHÂTEAU REDORTIER

Château Redortier 2004 Rhône Red Blend (Beaumes-de-Venise) $NA. 88 —*J.C. (11/15/2006)*

CHÂTEAU REYNON

Château Reynon 2003 Vieilles Vignes Bordeaux White Blend (Bordeaux) $17. 88 —*R.V. (6/1/2005)*

CHÂTEAU RIEUSSEC

Château Rieussec 2004 Barrel Sample Bordeaux White Blend (Sauternes) $NA. 89 —*R.V. (6/1/2005)*

CHÂTEAU ROBIN

Château Robin 2003 Bordeaux Blend (Côtes de Castillon) $20. Stéphane Asséo, who also owns L'Aventure in Paso Robles, California, runs this estate as one of the star properties in Castillon. The wine is rich and plummy, with dense, soft fruit, dusty tannins, layers of new wood and ripe black fruits. Drink now, or keep for 2–3 years. 90 *—R.V. (11/1/2007)*

CHÂTEAU ROLLAN DE BY

Château Rollan de By 2002 Bordeaux Blend (Médoc) $32. 88 *—J.C. (6/1/2005)*

CHÂTEAU ROLLAND-DAILLET

Château Rolland-Maillet 2004 Bordeaux Blend (Saint-Emilion Grand Cru) $NA. One of the Rolland family properties, Rolland-Maillet is punching well above its station with this 2004. It is dense, dusty, packed with ripe black Merlot and soft, rich tannins. A dense, chocolate wine with fine structure. 89 *—R.V. (6/1/2007)*

CHÂTEAU ROMER DU HAYOT

Château Romer du Hayot 2005 Barrel Sample Bordeaux White Blend (Sauternes) $NA. 89 *—R.V. (6/21/2006)*

CHÂTEAU ROQUEFORT

Château Roquefort 2001 Roquefortissime Bordeaux White Blend (Bordeaux) $26. 82 *(7/1/2005)*

CHÂTEAU ROQUETAILLADE

Château Roquetaillade la Grange 2005 Bordeaux Blend (Graves) $NA. Fresh, toasty and dominated by new wood, this is made with an uncompromising New World approach. It's richly smooth, the edges polished by open tannins and blackberry fruit flavors. It's likely to develop fast, but enjoyably. 89 *—R.V. (11/1/2007)*

Château Roquetaillade la Grange 2006 Bordeaux White Blend (Graves) $12. Good, mineral and grass, fresh wine, full of herbaceous Sauvignon Blanc and young Sémillon. It's deliciously brushed by wood. 88 *—R.V. (12/31/2007)*

CHÂTEAU ROQUETTE

Château Roquette 2002 Bordeaux Blend (Bordeaux Supérieur) $NA. A dry wine, relying on dark tannins to bolster the fruit. The structure is all, leaving some austere black currant flavors. This property, in the eastern Entre-deux-Mers used 55% Cabernet Sauvignon in its 2002 blend. 83 *—R.V. (11/1/2007)*

CHÂTEAU ROUBAUD

Château Roubaud 1998 Tradition Rhône Red Blend (Costières de Nimes) $13. 87 *—M.S. (11/1/2000)*

Château Roubaud 2005 Rosé Blend (Costières de Nimes) $15. This is a 50-50 blend of Grenache and Syrah, a medium- to full-bodied rosé from the southern Rhône that boasts flavors of cherries and wet stone and shows decent length on the finish. 84 *—J.C. (7/1/2007)*

CHÂTEAU ROUBINE

Château Roubine 1998 Merlot (Côtes de Provence) $12. 83 *—D.T. (2/1/2002)*

Château Roubine 2000 Cru Classe Rosé Blend (Côtes de Provence) $12. 85 *—M.M. (2/1/2002)*

CHÂTEAU ROUTAS

Château Routas 2003 Rouviere Rosé Blend (Coteaux Varois) $10. 87 Best Buy *—M.S. (11/15/2004)*

Château Routas 2005 Rouvière Rosé Blend (Coteaux Varois) $10. 85 Best Buy *—J.C. (6/21/2006)*

Château Routas 2000 Coquelicot White Blend (Vin de Pays Var) $16. 87 *—M.M. (2/1/2002)*

CHÂTEAU RUSSOL GARDEY

Château Russol Gardey 1999 Grande Réserve Syrah (Minervois) $20. 87 *(10/1/2001)*

CHÂTEAU SAINT ESTEVE D'UCHAUX

Château Saint Esteve d'Uchaux 2001 Vieilles Vignes Rhône Red Blend (Côtes-du-Rhône Villages) $30. 91 Editors' Choice *—J.C. (11/15/2006)*

Château Saint Esteve d'Uchaux 2005 Jeunes Vignes Viognier (Côtes-du-Rhône) $17. 87 *—J.C. (11/15/2006)*

CHÂTEAU SAINT-COSMÉ

Château Saint-Cosmé 2001 Côtes du Rhône Les Deux Albions Rhône Red Blend (Côtes-du-Rhône) $18. 87 *—R.V. (3/1/2004)*

Château Saint-Cosmé 2001 Cuvée Valbelle Rhône Red Blend (Gigondas) $53. 94 *—R.V. (3/1/2004)*

CHÂTEAU SAINT-LAURENT

Château Saint-Laurent 1999 Cabernet Sauvignon-Merlot (Haut-Médoc) $32. 83 *—M.S. (1/1/2004)*

CHÂTEAU SAINT-ROCH

Château Saint-Roch 2004 Brunel Rhône Red Blend (Lirac) $18. 88 *—J.C. (11/15/2006)*

CHÂTEAU SAINTE ROSELINE

Château Sainte Roseline 2004 Cru Classe Lampe de Meduse Rosé Blend (Côtes de Provence) $20. 85 *—J.C. (6/21/2006)*

CHÂTEAU SANSEY

Château Sansey 2005 Bordeaux Blend (Graves) $NA. Tannins are everything here, dense and dusty, dry but with layers of fine black fruits underneath. This shows great potential, from the black currant fruits and acidity to the dark structure. Age for five years. 89 *—R.V. (11/1/2007)*

Château Sansey 2006 Bordeaux White Blend (Graves) $NA. A soft, unfocused wine with some kiwi flavors, which is out of balance with the high, herbaceous acidity. It has a hard edge that looks likely to stay as it matures. 83 *—R.V. (12/31/2007)*

CHÂTEAU SEGONZAC

Château Segonzac 2003 Heritage Bordeaux Blend (Bordeaux Supérieur) $NA. Segonzac's wines are consistently good, and Heritage, the top label, performed well in 2003. The wine has some of the overt richness of the year, with its chocolate and very ripe fruits. But there is good, tough tannin and just the right amount of balancing finishing acidity. 89 *—R.V. (11/1/2007)*

Château Segonzac 2004 Vieilles Vignes Bordeaux Blend (Premieres Côtes de Blaye) $NA. Eucalyptus aromas are right out of the glass here, segueing into a smooth, herbal, vanilla and black fruit-flavored wine. Wood aging softens the tannins, giving a velvet texture, spiked with a dry layer that promises aging over 3–5 years. The Marmet family property is a leading star of Blaye. 90 *—R.V. (11/1/2007)*

CHÂTEAU SIGALAS RABAUD

Château Sigalas Rabaud 2005 Barrel Sample Bordeaux White Blend (Sauternes) $NA. 87 *—R.V. (6/21/2006)*

CHÂTEAU SIGNAC

Château Signac 2000 Melodie d'Amour Red Blend (Côtes-du-Rhône) $17. 89 *—M.S. (9/1/2003)*

Château Signac 2003 Cuvée Terra Amata Chusclan Rhône Red Blend (Côtes-du-Rhône Villages) $21. 90 Editors' Choice *—J.C. (11/15/2006)*

Château Signac 2004 Tradition Chusclan Rhône Red Blend (Côtes-du-Rhône Villages) $16. 87 *—J.C. (11/15/2006)*

CHÂTEAU SIRAN

Château Siran 2004 Bordeaux Blend (Margaux) $NA. A deliciously attractive wine, perfumed and floral, with an immediately attractive and open structure. This wine will develop relatively fast, but over the next decade will be very enjoyable. 89 *—R.V. (6/1/2007)*

Château Siran 2001 Bordeaux Blend (Margaux) $22. 91 Editors' Choice *—R.V. (6/1/2005)*

Château Siran 2005 Barrel Sample Bordeaux Blend (Margaux) $NA. 93 *—R.V. (6/20/2006)*

CHÂTEAU SMITH HAUT-LAFITTE

Château Smith Haut-Lafitte 2004 Bordeaux Blend (Pessac-Léognan) $NA. The Cathiards have scored with their 2004. It is rich and dense, but keeps a fine sense of structure. While the tannins are dusty, almost sweet, they keep good balance with the elegant fruit and the enticing acidity. Keep for five years plus. 93 *—R.V. (6/1/2007)*

Château Smith Haut-Lafitte 2005 Barrel Sample Bordeaux Blend (Pessac-Léognan) $NA. 88 *—R.V. (6/21/2006)*

Château Smith Haut-Lafitte 2004 Bordeaux White Blend (Pessac-Léognan) $NA. Aromas of white peaches set the scene for a deliciously poised, spice and white currant flavored wine. It is delicate, charged with freshness and acidity; a lively crisp wine. 90 *—R.V. (6/1/2007)*

Château Smith Haut-Lafitte 2005 Barrel Sample Bordeaux White Blend (Pessac-Léognan) $NA. 91 *—R.V. (6/1/2006)*

CHÂTEAU SOCIANDO MALLET

Château Sociando Mallet 2002 Bordeaux Blend (Haut-Médoc) $35. 88 *—R.V. (6/1/2005)*

CHÂTEAU SUAU

Château Suau 2005 Barrel Sample Bordeaux White Blend (Barsac) $NA. 90 —*R.V. (6/21/2006)*

CHÂTEAU SUDUIRAUT

Château Suduiraut 2005 Barrel Sample Bordeaux White Blend (Sauternes) $NA. 91 —*R.V. (6/1/2006)*

CHÂTEAU TALBOT

Château Talbot 2004 Bordeaux Blend (Saint-Julien) $NA. Dense and solid, relying on rich tannins to give it structure and richness. The flavor is deep and concentrated, with dark black fruits piling in under the dry tannins. A wine that will develop slowly. 92 —*R.V. (6/1/2007)*

Château Talbot 2003 Bordeaux Blend (Saint-Julien) $32. 90 —*R.V. (5/1/2006)*

Château Talbot 2001 Bordeaux Blend (Saint-Julien) $54. There is a great link here between the tannins, delicious red berry fruits and blackcurrants and the almost architectural structure. The wine certainly has fine fruit, a great balance, very complete, finishing gently, ripe and soft. 94 —*R.V. (12/16/2007)*

Château Talbot 2005 Barrel Sample Bordeaux Blend (Saint-Julien) $NA. 94 —*R.V. (6/20/2006)*

Château Talbot 2003 Barrel Sample Bordeaux Blend (Saint-Julien) $NA. 91 —*R.V. (6/3/2004)*

CHÂTEAU TAYAC

Château Tayac 1995 Cuvée Prestige Bordeaux Blend (Côtes de Bourg) $30. 87 —*J.C. (5/1/2000)*

CHÂTEAU TEYSSIER

Château Teyssier 2004 Bordeaux Blend (Saint-Emilion Grand Cru) $NA. A rich, fruity example of Saint-Emilion. The wine has a great depth of blackberry fruit flavors, with a touch of cocoa. Richness comes from the spicy wood. 87 —*R.V. (6/1/2007)*

Château Teyssier 2005 Barrel Sample Bordeaux Blend (Saint-Emilion Grand Cru) $NA. 88 —*R.V. (6/21/2006)*

Château Teyssier 2006 Pezat Merlot (Bordeaux Rosé) $NA. This 100% Merlot, is soft, full-bodied, with very ripe strawberry and vanilla flavors, in the heavier Bordeaux Rosé style. For a rosé, it is high in alcohol at 13.5%, giving richness and a soft aftertaste. Screwcap. 85 —*R.V. (7/1/2007)*

CHÂTEAU THIEULEY

Château Thieuley 2004 Bordeaux Blend (Bordeaux) $NA. Bordeaux in the best sense, a firm, slightly dry, but also refreshing cassis flavors, with good fruit tannins and a touch of wood. 87 —*R.V. (6/1/2007)*

Château Thieuley 2004 Réserve Francis Courselle Bordeaux Blend (Bordeaux Supérieur) $NA. This 100% Merlot is named after the patriarch of Château Thieuley, still active, who built the estate into one of the benchmarks of the Entre-deux-Mers region of Bordeaux. Smoky aromas lead to crisply ripe black fruit flavors and some solid, dry tannins. Age this wine for 3–4 years. 90 Editors' Choice —*R.V. (6/1/2007)*

Château Thieuley 2003 Bordeaux White Blend (Bordeaux) $13. 91 Best Buy —*R.V. (6/1/2005)*

Château Thieuley 2004 Cuvée Francis Courselle Bordeaux White Blend (Bordeaux Blanc) $NA. A ripe, wood-aged wine with great freshness, a touch of minerality and citrus on top of green pear and melon flavors. 89 —*R.V. (6/1/2007)*

Château Thieuley 2000 Bordeaux Rouge Bordeaux Blend (Bordeaux) $76. 88 —*R.V. (12/1/2002)*

Château Thieuly 2001 Bordeaux Blanc White Blend (Bordeaux) $6. 87 —*R.V. (12/1/2002)*

CHÂTEAU TOUR DE MIRAMBEAU

Château Tour de Mirambeau 2003 Cuvée Passion Bordeaux Blend (Bordeaux) $NA. For a red from the heart of the white wine country of Entre-deux-Mers, this is powerfully dense. It boasts plenty of wood flavors to go with the black currant and dry tannins. But it also has an underlying richness and fine, firm structure. Hold for at least five years. 90 —*R.V. (11/1/2007)*

Château Tour de Mirambeau 2006 Réserve Bordeaux Blend (Bordeaux Rosé) $15. Nettles and hedgerow aromas on what is a delicious rosé. It talks of Merlot, but the reality is more about fresh, crisp red fruits and light acidity. A big success. 89 —*R.V. (7/1/2007)*

Château Tour de Mirambeau 2005 Réserve Bordeaux Blend (Bordeaux) $15. This is all about great fruit bursting out of the glass. Red fruits dominate, with smooth tannins in support. There is a density at the heart of the wine, layered with fresh acidity. Drink now, but will age over 2–3 years. 88 —*R.V. (11/1/2007)*

Château Tour de Mirambeau 2000 Cuvée Passion Bordeaux Rouge Bordeaux Blend (Bordeaux) $19. 91 —*R.V. (12/1/2002)*

Château Tour de Mirambeau 2002 Cuvée Passion Bordeaux White Blend (Bordeaux) $19. 90 Editors' Choice —*R.V. (6/1/2005)*

Château Tour de Mirambeau 2006 Réserve Bordeaux White Blend (Entre-Deux-Mers) $NA. An intensely herbal, thyme-flavored wine, with a creaminess that enhances the full, but still very fresh character. Sauvignon Blanc's green character dominates, but is tamed by the ripeness of the fruit. 88 —*R.V. (12/31/2007)*

Château Tour de Mirambeau 2003 Semillon Noble Sémillon (Bordeaux Blanc) $NA. A beautifully ripe wine made in tiny quantities (5 barrels) in exceptional years from a small parcel of Sémillon. It's rich and unctuous, filled with flavors of molasses and honey, spiced with dry botrytis. There's an intense, smoky aftertaste. 90 —*R.V. (11/1/2007)*

CHÂTEAU TOUR DE PEZ

Château Tour de Pez 2004 Bordeaux Blend (Saint-Estèphe) $NA. With its typical Saint-Estèphe young tannins, this is going to be quite a hard nut to crack for several years. But it does have structure, black fruits and a hint of fresh acidity. Just sit and wait. 88 —*R.V. (6/1/2007)*

CHÂTEAU TOUR LÉOGNAN

Château Tour Léognan 2003 Bordeaux White Blend (Pessac-Léognan) $NA. 87 —*R.V. (6/1/2005)*

CHÂTEAU TOUR SIMARD

Château Tour Simard 1999 Bordeaux Blend (Saint-Emilion Grand Cru) $40. 86 —*J.C. (6/1/2005)*

CHÂTEAU TREYTINS

Château Treytins 2003 Bordeaux Blend (Montagne-St.-Èmilion) $NA. A smooth, velvet-structured wine, very soft and rich, this is elegance in a bottle. Black plum and berry flavors reign supreme here, supported by supple wood. 88 —*R.V. (11/1/2007)*

Château Treytins 2003 Bordeaux Blend (Lalande de Pomerol) $NA. A fruity, wood-flavored wine that doesn't show the ripeness of some 2003s, but does show attractive red-fruit freshness. Lightweight finish. 84 —*R.V. (11/1/2007)*

CHÂTEAU TRIMOULET

Château Trimoulet 1996 Bordeaux Blend (Saint-Emilion) $35. 86 —*J.C. (3/1/2001)*

CHÂTEAU TROCARD

Château Trocard 2004 Bordeaux Blend (Bordeaux Supérieur) $10. Lean, austere wine, that has dry tannins and flavors of stalky currants. It is pleasant enough, with some freshness, but there is a definite green element to it. 83 —*R.V. (6/1/2007)*

Château Trocard 2004 Monrepos Bordeaux Blend (Bordeaux Supérieur) $15. From a small parcel of 12 acres, this 100% Merlot is soft, elegant, with dusty tannins, and great lifted acidity. The wood element—12 months—is well balanced, doing its proper job of underlying the delicious blackberry fruits. 88 —*R.V. (6/1/2007)*

CHÂTEAU TROPLONG-MONDOT

Château Troplong-Mondot 2000 Bordeaux Blend (Saint-Emilion) $85. 92 —*R.V. (6/1/2003)*

Château Troplong-Mondot 2006 Barrel Sample Bordeaux Blend (Saint-Emilion Grand Cru) $NA. 94-96 Barrel Sample. Perfumed wood aromas, with spicy, dark toast flavors. To taste, it is like peering into a dark tunnel, very heavy, firm and unyielding. The fruit's somewhere there in the darkness. 95 —*R.V. (6/1/2007)*

CHÂTEAU TROTANOY

Château Trotanoy 2004 Bordeaux Blend (Pomerol) $NA. Owned by Jean-Pierre Moueix (and run by Christian Moueix), this 19-acre property is on the highest part of the Pomerol plateau. This is a powerful wine, dense with black fruits, dusty dry tannins, tempered with fresh acidity. A serious, ageworthy wine. 94 —*R.V. (6/1/2007)*

Château Trotanoy 2006 Barrel Sample Bordeaux Blend (Pomerol) $NA. 93-95 Barrel Sample. What a fine wine, elegant, structured, impressively balanced, full of spice, black currants, vibrant acidity. A great year at Trotanoy. 94 —*R.V. (6/1/2007)*

Château Trotanoy 2005 Barrel Sample Bordeaux Blend (Saint-Emilion Grand Cru) $NA. 94 —*R.V. (6/20/2006)*

Château Trotanoy 2003 Barrel Sample Bordeaux Blend (Pomerol) $NA. 92

—*R.V. (6/3/2004)*

CHÂTEAU TROTTEVEILLE

Château Trottevieille 2006 Barrel Sample Bordeaux Blend (Saint-Emilion Grand Cru) $NA. 92-94 Barrel Sample. A big, ripe sweet chocolate- and caramel-flavored wine, power but opulence at the same time. There are firm tannins along with some juicy black currant flavors. **93** —*R.V. (6/1/2007)*

CHÂTEAU VAL JOANIS

Château Val Joanis 1999 Cuvée Reserve Les Griottes Red Blend (Côtes du Luberon) $20. 89 —*M.S. (9/1/2003)*

Château Val Joanis 2001 Rouge Red Blend (Côtes du Luberon) $13. 85 —*J.C. (2/1/2005)*

Château Val Joanis 2001 Vigne du Chanoine Trouillet Red Blend (Côtes du Luberon) $30. 88 —*J.C. (2/1/2005)*

Château Val Joanis 1998 Estate Bottled Rhône Red Blend (Côtes du Luberon) $10. 87 —*J.C. (3/1/2001)*

Château Val Joanis 2004 Rosé Blend (Côtes du Luberon) $12. 84 —*J.C. (11/15/2005)*

Château Val Joanis 2002 Blanc White Blend (Côtes du Luberon) $13. 86 —*J.C. (3/1/2004)*

CHÂTEAU VALANDRAUD

Château Valandraud 2005 Barrel Sample Bordeaux Blend (Saint-Emilion Grand Cru) $NA. 91 —*R.V. (6/1/2006)*

Château Valandraud 2002 Kosher Mevushal Bordeaux Blend (Saint-Emilion) $260. 88 *(4/1/2006)*

CHÂTEAU VERDIGNAN

Château Verdignan 2004 Bordeaux Blend (Haut-Médoc) $NA. In the northern reaches of the Haut-Médoc, Verdignan's place in the world is as classic middle-ranking Bordeaux, with good value. And this 2004 fits the bill very well: ripe, juicy fruit, acidity and freshness, a solid tannic structure, developing over four years. **87** —*R.V. (6/1/2007)*

CHÂTEAU VIGNOT

Château Vignot 2004 Bordeaux Blend (Saint-Emilion Grand Cru) $35. Fresher and more floral than the 2003, with flavors that run toward mulberry while adding hints of vanilla and maple syrup. It's richer, creamier and longer than the 2003, showing the results of Seillan having full control over the property for the entire year. Drink now–2015. **91** —*J.C. (6/1/2007)*

Château Vignot 2003 Bordeaux Blend (Saint-Emilion Grand Cru) $35. Starts off with vanilla and black cherry scents, with just a sprinkling of dried herbs. This blend of 60% Merlot and 40% Cabernet Franc is creamy and supple through the mocha-tinged midpalate, then finishes crisper than expected, with some dusty tannins. Drink 2008–2015. Imported by Acadia Imports. **89** —*J.C. (6/1/2007)*

CHÂTEAU VILLA BEL AIR

Château Villa Bel Air 2003 Bordeaux White Blend (Graves) $20. 89 —*R.V. (6/1/2005)*

CHÂTEAU VILLEGEORGE

Château Villegeorge 2004 Bordeaux Blend (Haut-Médoc) $NA. One of the many Bordeaux properties owned by the Lurton family, Villegeorge's 2004 is light and fresh, delicate almost, with ripe red berry fruits and a modicum of tannins and acidity. Drink now, or age for five years. **86** —*R.V. (6/1/2007)*

CHÂTEAU YON FIGEAC

Château Yon Figeac 1995 Bordeaux Blend (Saint-Emilion) $40. 91 Editors' Choice *(4/1/2001)*

CHEVALIER DE GRUAUD

Chevalier de Gruaud 1999 Bordeaux Blend (Saint-Julien) $45. 84 —*J.C. (6/1/2005)*

CHRISTIAN MOUEIX

Christian Moueix 2005 Merlot Bordeaux Blend (Bordeaux) $11. A young, very fruity wine produced by Christian Moueix. It is structured, firm and juicy, layered with dry tannins, probably needing 6–12 months of aging. A touch of pepper, red currants, toast and acidity complete this good, very Bordeaux, wine. **84** —*R.V. (11/1/2007)*

Christian Moueix 2003 Merlot Bordeaux Blend (Bordeaux) $11. A ripe, smooth, velvet-textured wine with great red berry fruit flavors aided by soft tannins. **86 Best Buy** —*R.V. (11/1/2007)*

CIRCUS BY L'OSTAL CAZES

Circus by L'Ostal Cazes 2004 Viognier (Vin de Pays d'Oc) $13. 86 —*J.C. (11/15/2005)*

CLARENDELLE

Clarendelle 2005 Bordeaux Blend (Bordeaux Rosé) $17. A strawberry-flavored wine, fruity and with a touch of sweetness, typical of the Bordeaux rosé style. This is an already mature wine, with flavors of loganberry and only hints of fresh acidity. **83** —*R.V. (11/1/2007)*

Clarendelle 2003 Bordeaux Blend (Bordeaux) $22. As befits its provenance from the hands of the winemaking team of Château Haut-Brion, this is a solid, finely crafted wine, flavored with mint and layers of wood as well as red plums. With these tannins, it could even age a year or two. **87** —*R.V. (11/1/2007)*

Clarendelle 2005 Bordeaux White Blend (Bordeaux Blanc) $22. The white partner in the quartet of Clarendelle wines from the owners of Château Haut-Brion, this is a freshly perfumed wine, with light acidity and some rich, creamy fruit. There's just a touch of almonds and toastiness to add complexity. **85** —*R.V. (11/1/2007)*

CLAUDE CHEVALIER

Claude Chevalier 2003 Les Gréchons Premier Cru Chardonnay (Ladoix) $45. 86 —*R.V. (9/1/2005)*

CLOS DE L'ORATOIRE DES PAPES

Clos de L'Oratoire des Papes 2000 Red Blend (Châteauneuf-du-Pape) $28. 88 —*J.C. (3/1/2004)*

Clos de L'Oratoire des Papes 2003 Rhône Red Blend (Châteauneuf-du-Pape) $35. 90 —*J.C. (11/15/2005)*

CLOS DE LA BRIDERIE

Clos de la Briderie 2005 Vieilles Vignes Chenin Blanc-Chardonnay (Touraine Mesland) $NA. The honey aromas from the dominant Chenin Blanc are enticing. The palate is fresh and soft, but rounded with melon and kiwi flavors. Delicious and full. Clos de la Briderie runs its vineyard biodynamically. **90 Editors' Choice** —*R.V. (10/1/2007)*

Clos de la Briderie 2005 Gris Gamay (Touraine Mesland) $NA. "Gris" in this case means a pale rosé; this Gamay-based wine has a very fresh, if light, structure. Flavors of wild strawberries are here, but it is mainly dry and crisp. **86** —*R.V. (10/1/2007)*

Clos de la Briderie 2005 Vieilles Vignes Red Blend (Touraine Mesland) $NA. A blend of Cabernet Franc, Malbec and Gamay, this is a firmly dry, tannic wine. Its acidity, black plum skin flavors and smoky, herbal undernote give attractive complexity. A great food wine. **88** —*R.V. (10/1/2007)*

CLOS DE LA COULÉE DE SERRANT

Clos de la Coulée de Serrant 2002 Clos de la Coulée de Serrant Chenin Blanc (Savennières-Coulée de Serrant) $79. 95 Cellar Selection —*R.V. (4/1/2005)*

CLOS DE LA LYSARDIÈRE

Clos de la Lysardière 2005 Cabernet Franc (Chinon) $13. A single-vineyard wine that is commercialized by the cooperative at St-Cyr-en-Bourg in Saumur. Although it has no wood element in its maturation, it is still a smooth, velvety wine with round tannins on top of the perfumed flavors and black fruits. **88 Best Buy** —*R.V. (4/1/2007)*

CLOS DE LA VIEILLE EGLISE

Clos de la Vieille Eglise 2004 Bordeaux Blend (Pomerol) $59. A wine with a great weight of fruit. While there is a good amount of new wood, the ripeness and density of the Merlot copes with the toast well. The tannins, dry as they are, show plenty of richness supporting a great well of fruits. **91** —*R.V. (6/1/2007)*

CLOS DE TART

Clos de Tart 2004 Pinot Noir (Clos de Tart) $350. This grand cru monopole, owned by the Mommessin family, makes wine that charms easily, with its perfumes and berry fruit flavors. But there is a definite tannic character that only appears once the wine has been in your mouth for a few moments. Then it is apparent that it is dry, needing aging. The aftertaste is very fresh. **94** —*R.V. (3/1/2007)*

CLOS DES BRUSQUIÈRES

Clos des Brusquières 2003 Rhône Red Blend (Châteauneuf-du-Pape) $32. 91 —*R.V. (12/31/2005)*

CLOS DU CLOCHER

Clos du Clocher 2004 Bordeaux Blend (Pomerol) $NA. A properly velvet-textured Pomerol, showing some of the richness of the Merlot in 2004.

This is a well-balanced, intensely rich wine, the black plum fruit flavors powering through the tannins, and with a good lift of fresh acidity to finish. **90** *—R.V. (6/1/2007)*

CLOS DU MARQUIS

Clos du Marquis 2004 Bordeaux Blend (Saint-Julien) $NA. This is the second wine of Léoville-las-Cases, big and black, stunningly perfumed with eucalyptus and violets. Herbs and ripe black fruit flavors are given shape by the tannins that go straight through the wine. The aftertaste has great acidity. **90** *—R.V. (6/1/2007)*

CLOS DUBREUIL

Clos Dubreuil 2004 Bordeaux Blend (Saint-Emilion Grand Cru) $NA. With its ultra-low yields, and 20 months aging in new French oak, this is very much in the mold of the "garage wines" of the 1990s. It is superrich, weighed down with luscious fruit, powerful toast and spice wood flavors. At 14% alcohol, it is strong indeed for Bordeaux. **86** *—R.V. (6/1/2007)*

CLOS FOURTET

Clos Fourtet 2004 Bordeaux Blend (Saint-Emilion Grand Cru) $NA. This estate seems to be going places, making in 2004 an impressively balanced wine that seems to walk a fine line just the right side of superripeness with consummate ease. It is elegant, yet powerful, dominated by a seamless combination of blackberry jelly fruits and dark, smoky tannins. **93** *—R.V. (6/1/2007)*

Clos Fourtet 2000 Bordeaux Blend (Saint-Emilion) $51. **90** *—R.V. (6/1/2003)*

Clos Fourtet 2004 Barrel Sample Bordeaux Blend (Saint-Emilion Grand Cru) $NA. **92** *—R.V. (6/1/2005)*

CLOS LA COUTALE

Clos la Coutale 1999 Malbec (Cahors) $12. **86 Best Buy** *—D.T. (11/15/2002)*

CLOS L'EGLISE

Clos l'Eglise 2004 Bordeaux Blend (Pomerol) $NA. As an indication of the ripeness of Merlot in 2004, this is a hugely rich wine, very ripe, almost raisiny in character. The fruit is dark and black, with a texture of jelly and flavors of blackberries. **89** *—R.V. (6/1/2007)*

CLOS NARDIAN

Clos Nardian 2004 Bordeaux White Blend (Bordeaux Blanc) $NA. A low-production, low-yield white from a vineyard in the Entre-deux-Mers region of Bordeaux. The result tastes more like a Pessac-Léognan, with its rich, creamy apple and pear flavors, its new wood and its concentration. Great acidity provides the essential backbone to this rich wine. **90** *—R.V. (6/1/2007)*

COLIN

Colin NV Blanche de Castille Premier Cru Blanc de Blancs Brut Chardonnay (Champagne) $NA. Growers based in Vertus, at the southern end of the Chardonnay-dominated Côte des Blancs, the Colin brothers have made a deliciously balanced wine that is rich, with some age, along with good concentration, weighty green fruits, and a touch of almonds. **90** *—R.V. (12/1/2007)*

Colin 2001 Grand Cru Blanc de Blancs Brut Chardonnay (Champagne) $NA. Mainly from grand cru vineyards in Cramant, this is a ripe, smooth, creamy wine whose minerality is subordinated to rich white fruits and a pure, dense structure. Despite its relative youth, the richness means this wine is ready to drink now. **91** *—R.V. (12/1/2007)*

COLLOVRAY ET TERRIER

Collovray et Terrier 2005 Chardonnay (Mâcon-Villages) $17. Fresh, crisp, green apple and white pear fruit flavors are given extra richness by kiwi. There's structure to this wine, but it's mainly simple, open and generous. **86** *—R.V. (8/1/2007)*

Collovray et Terrier 2005 Domaine des Deux Roches Les Cras Chardonnay (Saint-Véran) $36. A delicious green and white fruit-flavored wine, spiced up by some new wood, rounded out with cream and then sharpened with acidity. Ready to drink, but could age for two years. **88** *—R.V. (8/1/2007)*

Collovray et Terrier 2005 Domaine des Deux Roches Rives de Longsault Chardonnay (Saint-Véran) $20. This comes from the 88-acre Domaine des Deux Roches. Big and rich, but freshened with great acidity. The fruits are green, given a tightness by minerality and wood. Drink this summer with freshly caught trout by the camp fire. **89** *—R.V. (8/1/2007)*

Collovray et Terrier 2005 Domaine des Deux Roches Vieilles Vignes Chardonnay (Saint-Véran) $26. There's good concentration with this wine. It shows green apples, pears and green plum skin flavors. On top, there is wood, well balanced with the fruit; a sumptuous mix that shows the generosity of 2005. **90** *—R.V. (8/1/2007)*

Collovray et Terrier 2005 Plénitude de Bonté Chardonnay (Pouilly-Fuissé) $30. "Fullness and goodness" is a rough translation of the name of this wine. It's an accurate description of its richness. There is great spice, bolstering the full fruit, showing a mineral, chalky structure along with fresh green fruits. **90 Editors' Choice** *—R.V. (8/1/2007)*

Collovray et Terrier 2005 Vieilles Vignes Chardonnay (Pouilly-Fuissé) $25. A tight, very mineral wine, with crisp acidity, firm fruit flavors and just hinting at caramel and vanilla. This is still young, hiding behind its structure. Give it 3–4 years. **88** *—R.V. (8/1/2007)*

COMMANDERIE DE LA BARGEMONE

Commanderie de la Bargemone 2006 Rosé Blend (Coteaux d'Aix en Provence) $14. Salmon grey in color, here's a rosé with structure. With its dusty tannins, flavor of pink grapefruit and young, cranberry flavored fruit, this needs time – put a bottle aside for 2008. **86** *—R.V. (7/1/2007)*

Commanderie de la Bargemone 2005 Rosé Blend (Coteaux d'Aix en Provence) $NA. **86** *—J.C. (6/19/2006)*

COMMANDERIE DE PEYRASSOL

Commanderie de Peyrassol 2006 Rosé Blend (Côtes de Provence) $17. The superior rosé from Peyrassol (the other is Château de Peyrassol), this wine includes Syrah in the blend giving the wine some weight and presence. It is soft, with a light touch of vanilla, fresh crisp apples and a dry, but fresh aftertaste. **90** *—R.V. (7/1/2007)*

COMTE AUDOIN DE DAMPIERRE

Comte Audoin de Dampierre NV Grande Cuvée Brut Champagne Blend (Champagne) $39. **90** *—P.G. (12/1/2006)*

COMTE CATHARE

Comte Cathare 1999 Syrvedre Rhône Red Blend (Vin de Pays d'Oc) $15. **88 Editors' Choice** *—M.M. (2/1/2002)*

COMTE DE LANTAGE

Comte de Lantage 1995 Premier Cru Blanc de Blancs Brut Champagne Blend (Champagne) $40. **84** *—M.S. (6/1/2003)*

COMTE LAFOND

Comte LaFond 2002 Sauvignon Blanc (Sancerre) $32. **84** *(7/1/2005)*

Comte LaFond 2000 Grand Cuvée Sauvignon Blanc (Sancerre) $48. **90** *(7/1/2005)*

COS D'ESTOURNEL

Cos d'Estournel 2006 Barrel Sample Bordeaux Blend (Saint-Estèphe) $NA. 93-95 Barrel Sample. There is a considerable amount of wood here, giving a firm, solid structure, like all good wines from St-Estèphe. But the weight and concentration of the fruit balances well with the tannins. **94** *—R.V. (6/1/2007)*

COUDERT PÈRE ET FILS

Coudert Père et Fils 2002 Clos de la Roilette Gamay (Fleurie) $18. **90 Editors' Choice** *—J.C. (11/15/2003)*

COULY-DUTHEIL

Couly-Dutheil 2006 René Couly Rosé Cabernet Franc (Chinon) $16. This has something of the rich, spicy character of red Chinon, but with a lift of cool Loire freshness. It's a winning combination, spoilt by a touch hint of sweetness to finish. **85** *—R.V. (7/1/2007)*

CROIX DU MAYNE

Croix du Mayne 2004 Malbec-Merlot (Cahors) $16. Toasty, with notes of slightly menthol-like oak layered over ripe blackberry fruit. It's a medium-bodied wine that finishes crisp, tart and mouthwatering. Give it another 6–12 months to better integrate the oak, then drink it over the next five or so years. **87** *—J.C. (8/1/2007)*

CUVÉE MYTHIQUE

Cuvée Mythique 2001 Rhône Red Blend (Vin de Pays d'Oc) $17. **89** *—R.V. (12/1/2004)*

DAMIEN LAUREAU

Damien Laureau 2004 Le Bel Ouvrage Chenin Blanc (Savennières) $30. Richness combined with minerality. Quince, honey and white pears are the dominant characters in this powerful, round wine; however, with its hot pepper element, this tastes of its alcohol. The acidity is here, but lost in the wood. **88** *—R.V. (10/1/2007)*

Damien Laureau 2004 Les Genêts Chenin Blanc (Savennières) $23. Damien Laureau is a new name in Savennières, taking over in 1999 from his uncle. As with all Savennières, this is dry, but the wood aging rounds out the fruit to give a superrich wine. Flavors of mango and pear jam go with the smooth vanilla of the wood. It feels sweet, but tastes dry. The acidity keeps the alcohol at bay. 90 —*R.V. (10/1/2007)*

DANIEL CHOTARD

Daniel Chotard 2003 Sauvignon Blanc (Sancerre) $22. 89 *(7/1/2005)*

DANIEL RION

Daniel Rion 1999 Les Beaux-Monts Pinot Noir (Vosne-Romanée) $52. 92 —*P.G. (1/7/2001)*

DAUVERGNE & RANVIER

Dauvergne & Ranvier 2004 Rhône Red Blend (Côtes-du-Rhône) $13. 84 —*J.C. (11/15/2006)*

Dauvergne & Ranvier 2005 *Barrel Sample* François Arnaud Rhône Red Blend (Côtes-du-Rhône) $NA. 88 Best Buy —*J.C. (11/15/2006)*

DE LADOUCETTE

De Ladoucette 2000 Baron de L Sauvignon Blanc (Pouilly-Fumé) $78. 88 *(7/1/2005)*

DE SAINT GALL

De Saint Gall NV Bouzy Brut Champagne Blend (Champagne) $32. 86 —*M.S. (12/1/2000)*

De Saint Gall 1995 Premier Cru Blanc de Blancs Brut Champagne Blend (Champagne) $48. 89 *(12/1/2000)*

De Saint Gall NV Blanc de Blancs Premier Cru Brut Chardonnay (Champagne) $35. 88 —*M.S. (12/15/2003)*

De Saint Gall 1998 Blanc de Blancs Premier Cru Brut Chardonnay (Champagne) $49. 90 —*M.S. (12/15/2003)*

De Saint Gall 1995 Cuvée Orpale Blanc de Blancs Chardonnay (Champagne) $95. 90 —*M.S. (12/15/2003)*

De Saint Gall NV Grand Cru Blanc de Blancs Extra Brut Chardonnay (Champagne) $65. 89 —*R.V. (12/1/2005)*

De Saint Gall 1995 Premier Cru Blanc de Blancs Brut Chardonnay (Champagne) $48. 92 —*J.C. (12/15/2001)*

DE SOUSA & FILS

De Sousa & Fils NV Brut Rosé Champagne Blend (Champagne) $60. 86 —*R.V. (12/15/2006)*

De Sousa & Fils NV Cuvée des Caudalies Blanc de Blancs Vielles Vignes Brut Champagne Blend (Champagne) $60. 87 —*R.V. (12/1/2002)*

De Sousa & Fils 1996 Extra Brut Champagne Blend (Champagne) $130. I96 —*R.V. (11/1/2006)*

De Sousa & Fils 2000 Cuvée des Caudalies Grand Cru Brut Chardonnay (Champagne) $120. 94 —*R.V. (11/1/2006)*

DE VENOGE

De Venoge 1995 Brut Champagne Blend (Champagne) $NA. 89 —*R.V. (12/1/2004)*

DEHOURS

Dehours 2002 Collection Les Genevraux Pinot Meunier (Champagne) $42. 92 —*R.V. (11/1/2006)*

Dehours 2000 Collection Blanc de Pinot Noir Pinot Noir (Champagne) $NA. 94 Editors' Choice —*R.V. (11/1/2006)*

DELAMOTTE

Delamotte 1992 Blanc de Blancs Brut Champagne Blend (Champagne) $63. 90 *(12/1/2000)*

Delamotte NV Brut Champagne Blend (Champagne) $46. 85 —*S.H. (12/1/1999)*

Delamotte NV Brut Champagne Blend (Champagne) $34. 92 Editors' Choice —*P.G. (12/15/2002)*

Delamotte NV Brut Champagne Blend (Champagne) $44. 93 —*R.V. (12/1/2005)*

Delamotte NV Brut Champagne Blend (Champagne) $42. 88 —*S.H. (12/15/2000)*

Delamotte 1999 Blanc de Blancs Brut Chardonnay (Champagne) $79. 88 —*R.V. (11/1/2006)*

Delamotte 1996 Blanc de Blancs Chardonnay (Champagne) $NA. Disgorged in 2006, this wine (and it is a wine, almost more than a Champagne) is young, dry and touched with green plums, secondary flavors of toast and yeast, as well as an white flower perfume. 93 —*R.V. (12/31/2007)*

Delamotte NV Blanc de Blancs Chardonnay (Champagne) $50. With its highly mineral aroma, this is almost like smelling chalk. It's an austere wine, with high acidity, crystal clear on the palate, full of grapefruit flavors and flint texture. Age this wine at least four years. 91 Cellar Selection —*R.V. (12/31/2007)*

DELAS FRERES

Delas Freres 1999 Haute Pierre Grenache-Syrah (Châteauneuf-du-Pape) $40. 85 —*M.S. (9/1/2003)*

Delas Freres 1998 Les Launes Marsanne (Crozes-Hermitage) $10. 83 —*M.S. (9/1/2003)*

Delas Freres 2001 Les Launes Blanc Marsanne (Crozes-Hermitage) $19. 88 —*S.H. (1/1/2002)*

Delas Freres 2001 Selection Delas Merlot (Vin de Pays d'Oc) $8. 85 —*M.S. (9/1/2003)*

Delas Freres 2002 Red Blend (Côtes-du-Ventoux) $9. 81 —*J.C. (3/1/2004)*

Delas Freres 2003 Rhône Red Blend (Côtes-du-Ventoux) $10. 88 Best Buy —*J.C. (11/15/2004)*

Delas Freres 2000 Domaine des Genets Rhône Red Blend (Vacqueyras) $19. 88 —*R.V. (3/1/2004)*

Delas Freres 1999 La Landonne Rhône Red Blend (Côte Rôtie) $105. 94 —*R.V. (6/1/2002)*

Delas Freres 1998 Les Calcerniers Rhône Red Blend (Châteauneuf-du-Pape) $29. 91 Editors' Choice *(3/1/2002)*

Delas Freres 2002 Saint-Esprit Rhône Red Blend (Côtes-du-Rhône) $13. 84 —*J.C. (2/1/2005)*

Delas Freres 1999 St. Espirit Rhône Red Blend (Côtes-du-Rhône) $10. 85 Best Buy *(3/1/2002)*

Delas Freres 2004 Les Challeys Rhône White Blend (Saint-Joseph) $NA. 87 —*J.C. (11/15/2006)*

Delas Frères 2005 Marquise de la Tourette Rhône White Blend (Hermitage) $50. Powerful and intense without going over the top, this is a fine example of white Hermitage. The golden straw color gives a first indication of its richness, followed by scents of honey, even a hint of butterscotch. It's unctuous in the mouth, boasting flavors of grilled nuts and stone fruits, and finishing with just a touch of warmth. 92 —*J.C. (9/1/2007)*

Delas Freres 2005 Saint-Esprit Rhône White Blend (Côtes-du-Rhône) $13. 85 —*J.C. (11/15/2006)*

Delas Freres 1999 Saint-Esprit Rhône White Blend (Côtes-du-Rhône) $9. 85 *(11/15/2001)*

Delas Frères 2005 Chante-Perdrix Syrah (Cornas) $NA. Comprised of fruit purchased from several growers and matured in only about 20% new oak, this is an authentic expression of Cornas, yet one with a surprising degree of elegance. Meaty, bloody and smoky on the nose, with hints of cedar and cinnamon, but with ample concentration of cassis and mulberry fruit. Complex and long on the finish. Drink now–2020. 91 —*J.C. (9/1/2007)*

Delas Freres 1996 Francois de Tournon Syrah (Saint-Joseph) $21. 87 —*M.S. (5/1/2000)*

Delas Freres 2001 François de Tournon Syrah (Saint-Joseph) $27. 87 *(2/1/2005)*

Delas Frères 2005 La Landonne Syrah (Côte Rôtie) $129. Possessed of a powerful charred, espresso-like character on the nose, this isn't that fruit-expressive at first, but on the palate black olive and black cherry flavors surge forward, framed by layered tannins and showing great persistence. Needs time; try from 2012. 92 Cellar Selection —*J.C. (9/1/2007)*

Delas Frères 2005 Les Bessards Syrah (Hermitage) $128. Delas's cuvée parcellaire is a rich wine that's almost syrupy in its concentration and tannic strength. But this definitely has plenty of fruit for balance, mixing cassis with black olive, espresso, cinnamon and clove. Not quite as rich as the '03, but still a classic, with great persistence on the finish. Best after 2015. 94 Cellar Selection —*J.C. (9/1/2007)*

Delas Freres 2003 Les Bessards Syrah (Hermitage) $146. 95 Cellar Selection —*J.C. (11/15/2006)*

Delas Freres 2000 Les Challeys Syrah (Saint-Joseph) $20. 89 —*R.V. (6/1/2002)*

Delas Freres 2002 Les Launes Syrah (Crozes-Hermitage) $19. 84 —*J.C. (2/1/2005)*

Delas Freres 1998 Les Launes Syrah (Crozes-Hermitage) $15. 88 Editors' Choice *(10/1/2001)*

Delas Frères 2005 Marquise de la Tourette Syrah (Hermitage) $67. Delas's big bottling of Hermitage blends three sites, including Les Bessards and L'Hermite to make a Hermitage that should be relatively easy to find at close to 2,000 cases produced. The 2005 is a muscular wine with dusty tannins that demands cellaring, even though it does show attractive notes

FRANCE

of cassis and a distinctive blood-iron-mineral streak. Try after 2015. **91** —*J.C. (9/1/2007)*

Delas Freres 2001 Marquise de la Tourette Syrah (Hermitage) $71. 90 —*R.V. (2/1/2005)*

Delas Freres 1997 Marquise de la Tourette Syrah (Hermitage) $58. 87 *(11/1/2001)*

Delas Freres 2004 Sainte-Épine Syrah (Saint-Joseph) $64. 92 Editors' Choice —*J.C. (11/15/2006)*

Delas Frères 2005 Seigneur de Maugiron Syrah (Côte Rôtie) $73. Although there's only about 20% new oak used in this cuvée, it is somewhat apparent on the nose and palate, where cedar, cinnamon and clove take the lead. There's some pretty—some might say Burgundian—fruit, but it's a touch light and herbal. **87** —*J.C. (9/1/2007)*

Delas Freres 1998 Seigneur de Maugiron Syrah (Côte Rôtie) $25. 91 —*R.V. (6/1/2002)*

Delas Freres 2002 La Galopine Viognier (Condrieu) $51. 87 *(12/1/2004)*

Delas Freres 2001 La Galopine Blanc White Blend (Condrieu) $47. 89 —*S.H. (1/1/2002)*

Delas Freres 2000 Saint-Espirit Blanc White Blend (Côtes-du-Rhône) $9. 87 —*S.H. (1/1/2002)*

DELBECK

Delbeck 1999 Brut Champagne Blend (Champagne) $60. 92 —*J.C. (12/1/2004)*

Delbeck NV Cramant Brut Champagne Blend (Champagne) $48. 84 *(12/31/2000)*

Delbeck NV Rosé Heritage Brut Champagne Blend (Champagne) $42. 92 —*M.M. (12/15/2000)*

DEUTZ

Deutz 1995 Blanc de Blancs Champagne Blend (France) $72. 94 Editors' Choice —*S.H. (12/15/2002)*

Deutz 2000 Brut Champagne Blend (Champagne) $67. This is certainly rich, packed with youthful green- and white-fruit flavors, but it still has that seductive elegance that is the hallmark of Deutz. Here is a wine that definitely needs aging. It has richness but there is still a raw edge. **92** —*R.V. (12/1/2007)*

Deutz 1999 Brut Champagne Blend (Champagne) $72. 90 —*R.V. (11/1/2006)*

Deutz 1995 Brut Champagne Blend (Champagne) $52. 92 —*P.G. (6/1/2001)*

Deutz NV Brut Classic Champagne Blend (Champagne) $49. A soft, gentle style of non-vintage Champagne, due perhaps to its relatively high dosage. But the whole wine is well in balance, the white fruits themselves giving a fine, elegant roundness. **88** —*R.V. (12/1/2007)*

Deutz NV Brut Classic Champagne Blend (Champagne) $37. 89 —*M.S. (12/15/2003)*

Deutz NV Brut Classic Champagne Blend (Champagne) $51. 90 —*P.G. (12/1/2006)*

Deutz NV Brut Classic Champagne Blend (Champagne) $37. 92 —*S.H. (12/15/2002)*

Deutz 2000 Brut Rosé Champagne Blend (Champagne) $77. 90 —*R.V. (11/1/2006)*

Deutz 1998 Cuvée William Deutz Brut Champagne Blend (Champagne) $166. A top wine in the Deutz range, packed with maturing richness, balancing fresh grapefruits against toasted almonds, an elegant structure, and an impressive power of flavor, leaving a dense mouthful of wine that manages to float at the same time. **94** —*R.V. (12/1/2007)*

Deutz 1998 Cuvée William Deutz Brut Champagne Blend (Champagne) $184. 93 —*R.V. (11/1/2006)*

Deutz 1996 Cuvée William Deutz Brut Champagne Blend (Champagne) $158. 93 —*R.V. (12/1/2004)*

Deutz 1995 Cuvée William Deutz Brut Champagne Blend (Champagne) $115. 93 —*M.M. (12/15/2001)*

Deutz 1997 Cuvée William Deutz Brut Rosé Champagne Blend (Champagne) $115. 92 —*R.V. (12/15/2003)*

Deutz 2003 Rosé Brut Champagne Blend (Champagne) $75. The palest of pinks announces the lightness of touch that makes this wine so attractive. Sure, it has ripe strawberry flavors, but they are delicate, laced with acidity, good freshness. A real apéritif wine. **90** —*R.V. (12/1/2007)*

Deutz 1999 Amour de Deutz Blanc de Blancs Brut Chardonnay (Champagne) $206. 94 —*R.V. (11/1/2006)*

Deutz 1995 Amour de Deutz Blanc de Blancs Brut Chardonnay (Champagne) $149. 91 —*J.C. (12/15/2003)*

Deutz 2002 Blanc de Blancs Brut Chardonnay (Champagne) $88. This vintage blanc de blancs is very much in the relatively rich, but also elegant Deutz style. The almost tropical white fruits are balanced with vibrant, fresh acidity, and topped with a soft aftertaste that lingers with almonds and toast. **93** —*R.V. (12/1/2007)*

Deutz 1996 Blanc de Blancs Brut Chardonnay (Champagne) $78. 93 —*J.C. (12/15/2003)*

Deutz 1997 Brut Rosé Pinot Noir (Champagne) $60. 90 —*R.V. (12/15/2003)*

DEVAUX

Devaux NV Grande Réserve Brut Champagne Blend (Champagne) $35. 87 *(6/1/2001)*

DIDIER DAGUENEAU

Didier Dagueneau 2003 Pur Sang Sauvignon Blanc (Pouilly-Fumé) $60. 92 *(7/1/2005)*

DIDIER MONTCHOVET

Didier Montchovet 2002 Hautes Côtes de Beaune Pinot Noir (Bourgogne) $29. 82 —*J.C. (9/1/2006)*

DIEBOLT VALLOIS

Diebolt Vallois 1999 Fleur de Passion à Cramant Blanc de Blancs Champagne Blend (Champagne) $75. 93 —*R.V. (12/1/2004)*

DOMAINE A. CAILBOURDIN

Domaine A. Cailbourdin 2006 Cuvée de Boisfleury Sauvignon Blanc (Pouilly-Fumé) $NA. From clay and chalk soil, Boisfleury is the finest of Alain Cailbourdin's three cuvées. This 2006 gives ripeness and freshness, but also a firm structure and weight behind the mineral front. This should age well—over five years. **91 Editors' Choice** —*R.V. (9/1/2007)*

Domaine A. Cailbourdin 2005 Cuvée de Boisfleury Sauvignon Blanc (Pouilly-Fumé) $NA. A crisp, steely wine, with piercing fresh pink grapefruit flavors. There is a wonderfully clean, refreshing character to this wine, livened with acidity and green fruits. **90** —*R.V. (9/1/2007)*

Domaine A. Cailbourdin 2005 Les Cornets Sauvignon Blanc (Pouilly-Fumé) $NA. Alain Cailbourdin makes three different wines from his three vineyards. Les Cornets is the softest of the three, a pleasingly ripe wine that offers almonds, green herbs, full quince and kiwi fruits. **88** —*R.V. (9/1/2007)*

Domaine A. Cailbourdin 2006 Les Cris Sauvignon Blanc (Pouilly-Fumé) $NA. This is all rocks and chalk and structure, a wine that is set to be a powerful expression of Sauvignon Blanc, even while it is rather one dimensional. The green plum and grapefruit flavors are there, but the taut mineral character dominates. **89** —*R.V. (9/1/2007)*

Domaine A. Cailbourdin 2005 Les Cris Sauvignon Blanc (Pouilly-Fumé) $22. A rich, but mineral-driven wine, with flavors of quince, citrus and green herbs. This is young but over 2–3 years it will develop into a richer, smoother wine. **88** —*R.V. (9/1/2007)*

Domaine A. Cailbourdin 2005 Triptyque Sauvignon Blanc (Pouilly-Fumé) $NA. A blend from all his vines, this is Alain Cailbourdin's wood aged top wine. This is a fine example of a wooded Sauvignon Blanc, judiciously creamy, but not losing the fresh vitality of the grape, adding richness to the already concentrated fruit. It makes a great food wine; drink now. **90** —*R.V. (9/1/2007)*

Domaine A. Cailbourdin 2000 Les Cris Sauvignon Blanc (Pouilly-Fumé) $20. 87 *(8/1/2002)*

DOMAINE A. MAZURD & FILS

Domaine A. Mazurd & Fils 1995 L'Or du Rhône Cuvée Exceptionnelle Grenache (Côtes-du-Rhône) $23. 88 —*J.C. (11/15/2006)*

Domaine A. Mazurd & Fils 1995 Cuvée Mazurka Rhône Red Blend (Côtes-du-Rhône) $20. 87 —*J.C. (11/15/2006)*

DOMAINE ALAIN DELAYE

Domaine Alain Delaye 2000 Chardonnay (Pouilly-Loche) $15. 87 *(10/1/2003)*

DOMAINE ALBERT MANN

Domaine Albert Mann 2002 Grand Cru Schlossberg Riesling (Alsace) $28. 89 —*R.V. (11/1/2005)*

DOMAINE AMIOT-SERVELLE

Domaine Amiot-Servelle 2000 Pinot Noir (Chambolle-Musigny) $46. 87 —*R.V. (11/1/2002)*

Domaine Amiot-Servelle 2000 Les Amoureuses Premier Cru Pinot Noir (Chambolle-Musigny) $100. 91 —*R.V. (11/1/2002)*

DOMAINE ANDRE BRUNEL

Domaine Andre Brunel 1999 Cuvée Sommelongue Rhône Red Blend (Côtes-du-Rhône) $10. 88 Best Buy *—J.C. (3/1/2001)*

DOMAINE ANNE GROS

Domaine Anne Gros 2004 La Combe d'Orveau Pinot Noir (Chambolle-Musigny) $60. The vineyard of La Combe d'Orveau is situated in the southern end of Chambolle-Musigny, within sight of Clos de Vougeot. This 2004 is quintessential Chambolle—rich, opulent, yet full of sensuous elegance. The wine is vibrantly red, layered with acidity, a delicious mouthful of bright fruit that will certainly age into something splendid. 93 *—R.V. (3/1/2007)*

Domaine Anne Gros 2004 Le Grand Maupertui Pinot Noir (Clos Vougeot) $120. Anne Gros calls her share of this parcel in Clos Vougeot Maupertui—her cousin Michel spells it "Maupertuis." Such are the complications of Burgundy. But this wine is anything but a confusion: It's a powerful, beautifully constructed wine, everything in its place—fruit, tannins and smoky wood. This justifies the sometimes questionable place of Clos Vougeot among the Grand Crus. 95 *—R.V. (3/1/2007)*

DOMAINE ANTONIN GUYON

Domaine Antonin Guyon 2002 Clos du Village Pinot Noir (Chambolle-Musigny) $48. 90 *—R.V. (9/1/2004)*

Domaine Antonin Guyon 2002 Corton Bressandes Pinot Noir (Corton) $60. 93 *—R.V. (9/1/2004)*

DOMAINE AUCHÈRE

Domaine Auchère 2004 Cuvée Calcaire Sauvignon Blanc (Sancerre) $21. 84 *(7/1/2005)*

DOMAINE AUTHER

Domaine Auther 2003 Kirchweg Riesling (Alsace) $NA. 89 *—R.V. (5/1/2005)*

DOMAINE BARRAUD

Domaine Barraud 2003 En Buland Chardonnay (Pouilly-Fuissé) $NA. 88 *—J.C. (11/15/2005)*

DOMAINE BASTIDE SAINT VINCENT

Domaine Bastide Saint Vincent 2004 Cuvée Pavane Rhône Red Blend (Vacqueyras) $18. 83 *—J.C. (11/15/2006)*

DOMAINE BEAUMONT

Domaine Beaumont 2005 Saint Pierre Aux Liens Rhône White Blend (Lirac) $NA. 85 *—J.C. (11/15/2006)*

DOMAINE BEGUDE

Domaine Begude 2000 Chardonnay (Vin de Pays d'Oc) $10. 88 Best Buy *—D.T. (2/1/2002)*

DOMAINE BELLE

Domaine Belle 2004 Rhône White Blend (Crozes-Hermitage) $29. 91 Editors' Choice *—J.C. (11/15/2006)*

Domaine Belle 2004 Les Pierrelles Syrah (Crozes-Hermitage) $27. 87 *—J.C. (11/15/2006)*

DOMAINE BERNARD MOREAU ET FILS

Domaine Bernard Moreau et Fils 2004 Chardonnay (Chassagne-Montrachet) $50. 89 *—R.V. (12/1/2006)*

Domaine Bernard Moreau et Fils 2004 Grandes Ruchottes Premier Cru Chardonnay (Chassagne-Montrachet) $85. 93 Editors' Choice *—R.V. (12/1/2006)*

Domaine Bernard Moreau et Fils 2004 Les Chenevottes Premier Cru Chardonnay (Chassagne-Montrachet) $70. 92 *—R.V. (12/1/2006)*

DOMAINE BERTAGNA

Domaine Bertagna 1998 Clos St. Denis Bordeaux Blend (France) $85. 91 *—P.G. (11/1/2002)*

Domaine Bertagna 2004 Corton-Charlemagne Chardonnay (Corton-Charlemagne) $145. Big, opulent and rich, this is all fruit. While there is a hint of wood, the wine is generous with tropical flavors and ripe white pears. If it wasn't for the acidity, this could be New World. 93 *—R.V. (3/1/2007)*

Domaine Bertagna 2004 Les Cras Premier Cru Chardonnay (Vougeot) $90. This wine was first made in 1988 from a small parcel of Chardonnay. It's big and solid, structurally a white version of a red Vougeot. At this stage, it is not particularly fruity, but the acidity indicates a promising future. 89 *—R.V. (3/1/2007)*

Domaine Bertagna 1998 Premier Cru Chardonnay (Nuits-St.-Georges) $27. 89 *—P.G. (11/1/2002)*

Domaine Bertagna 2004 Pinot Noir (Vougeot) $NA. A village wine, one with rich, spicy fruits and wood flavors. The fruit is intense, juicy and leaves a fresh layer of acidity in the mouth. Good structure, yet fruity and ready to drink. 89 *—R.V. (3/1/2007)*

Domaine Bertagna 2004 Pinot Noir (Clos Saint-Denis) $146. What a powerful wine, full of dark, brooding fruits. It's big and solid, but the edges blur into some delicious rich flavors, with hints of acidity on the finish. Very much in the Bertagna style, this is rich and mouth-filling. 93 *—R.V. (3/1/2007)*

Domaine Bertagna 1998 Pinot Noir (Clos Vougeot) $100. 90 *—P.G. (11/1/2002)*

Domaine Bertagna 1998 Pinot Noir (Marsannay) $17. 87 *—P.G. (11/1/2002)*

Domaine Bertagna 2004 Clos de la Perrière Premier Cru Pinot Noir (Vougeot) $90. This premier cru is entirely owned by Domaine Bertagna, making it the flagship of the domaine. This wine shows mineral character as well as finesse. But it is also structured, with dry tannins through the finish. It's not huge, but it certainly is solid. 92 *—R.V. (3/1/2007)*

Domaine Bertagna 1998 Clos de la Perrière Premier Cru Pinot Noir (Vougeot) $60. 90 *(1/1/2004)*

Domaine Bertagna 1998 Clos St Denis Pinot Noir (Clos Vougeot) $96. 91 *—P.G. (11/1/2002)*

Domaine Bertagna 2004 Les Beaux-Monts Premier Cru Pinot Noir (Vosne-Romanée) $90. Rather dry, this shows power rather than elegance. The fruit flavors are ripe, the tannins are very dense at this stage. It is marred by a hint of hard extraction. 88 *—R.V. (3/1/2007)*

Domaine Bertagna 2004 Les Cras Premier Cru Pinot Noir (Vougeot) $80. An aromatic, enticing wine that is also full-bodied with firm tannins. It's already well integrated, bringing in some wood flavors that go well with the intrinsic power of this wine. 91 *—R.V. (3/1/2007)*

Domaine Bertagna 1998 Les Cras Premier Cru Pinot Noir (Vougeot) $55. 87 *—P.G. (11/1/2002)*

Domaine Bertagna 2004 Les Lolières Corton Grand Cru Pinot Noir (Corton les Lolieres) $129. This is right at the northern end of the Corton grand cru vineyard. First palate impressions of this dark, powerful wine are that the acidity and tannins almost smother the fruit. But those fruits are going to push through, bringing new wood flavors along. The aftertaste is of pepper as well as acidity. 92 *—R.V. (3/1/2007)*

Domaine Bertagna 2004 Les Murgers Premier Cru Pinot Noir (Nuits-St.-Georges) $90. Like so many wines of Nuits-St.-Georges, this shows its tannins first. At the heart of this black-fruited wine, there is a delicious, unctuous velvet spot, which shows ripeness and the promise of richness. 91 *—R.V. (3/1/2007)*

Domaine Bertagna 2004 Les Petits Vougeots Premier Cru Pinot Noir (Vougeot) $80. Right next to Clos de Vougeot, this small vineyard has produced a smoky, rich wine with mouthfilling red fruits and new wood flavors. It should develop well, with its intense but balanced tannins. 90 *—R.V. (3/1/2007)*

Domaine Bertagna 2004 Les Plantes Premier Cru Pinot Noir (Chambolle-Musigny) $90. From a small parcel in one of the lesser-known premier crus of Chambolle-Musigny, this is a generous, rich and rounded wine. Red fruits make it very appealing now, but the tannins suggest aging potential. 91 *—R.V. (3/1/2007)*

Domaine Bertagna 2000 Les Plantes Premier Cru Pinot Noir (Chambolle-Musigny) $75. 94 Editors' Choice *—R.V. (11/1/2002)*

DOMAINE BERTHET-RAYNE

Domaine Berthet-Rayne 2003 Rhône Red Blend (Châteauneuf-du-Pape) $32. 87 *—R.V. (12/31/2005)*

DOMAINE BERTRAND STEHELIN

Domaine Bertrand Stehelin 2004 Rhône Red Blend (Gigondas) $24. 88 *—J.C. (11/15/2006)*

DOMAINE BORIE DE MAUREL

Domaine Borie de Maurel 1999 Syrah (Minervois) $9. 84 *(10/1/2001)*

DOMAINE BOTT-GEYL

Domaine Bott-Geyl 2002 Burgreben de Zellenberg Riesling (Alsace) $20. 88 *—R.V. (11/1/2005)*

DOMAINE BRESSY-MASSON

Domaine Bressy-Masson 2003 A La Gloire de Mon Père Rasteau Rhône Red Blend (Côtes-du-Rhône Villages) $NA. 89 *—J.C. (11/15/2006)*

DOMAINE BRUNO COLIN

Domaine Bruno Colin 2004 Chardonnay (Chassagne-Montrachet) $NA. 87 *—R.V. (12/1/2006)*

Domaine Bruno Colin 2004 Les Chaumées Premier Cru Chardonnay (Chassagne-Montrachet) $NA. 93 *—R.V. (12/1/2006)*

DOMAINE BRUSSET

Domaine Brusset 2005 Laurent B Rhône Red Blend (Côtes-du-Rhône) $16. 88 *—J.C. (11/15/2006)*

Domaine Brusset 2004 Tradition Le Grand Montmirail Rhône Red Blend (Gigondas) $27. 87 *—J.C. (11/15/2006)*

Domaine Brusset 2005 Les Clavelles Viognier (Côtes-du-Rhône) $20. 87 *—J.C. (11/15/2006)*

DOMAINE CADY

Domaine Cady 2006 Chenin Blanc (Anjou) $NA. This shows the deliciously fresh Chenin Blanc acidity, giving lively, vibrant green and white fruits. It's a good match with seafood dishes, and will pierce through any rich sauce. 89 *—R.V. (10/1/2007)*

Domaine Cady 2005 Les Varennes Chenin Blanc (Coteaux du Layon Saint Aubin) $NA. Round, unctuous and honeyed but with dry botrytis, this is a dessert wine with great freshness. In the mouth, it feels smooth and rich, with supersweet pear jam. The aftertaste loses some of the freshness, but this is an impressive wine. 90 Editors' Choice *—R.V. (10/1/2007)*

DOMAINE CALVET-THUNEVIN

Domaine Calvet-Thunevin 2004 Présidial Bordeaux Blend (Bordeaux) $12. 86 Best Buy *—R.V. (11/15/2006)*

DOMAINE CASTEL OUALOU

Domaine Castel Oualou 2005 Rosé Blend (Lirac) $NA. 89 *—J.C. (11/15/2006)*

DOMAINE CAZES

Domaine Cazes 2003 Le Canon du Maréchal Rosé Grenache (Vin de Pays d'Oc) $16. 86 *—R.V. (4/1/2005)*

Domaine Cazes 2003 Le Canon du Maréchal Muscat-Viognier (Vin de Pays d'Oc) $15. 87 *—R.V. (4/1/2005)*

Domaine Cazes 2000 Ego Rhône Red Blend (Côtes du Roussillon Villages) $16. 87 *—R.V. (12/31/2006)*

Domaine Cazes 2005 Le Canon du Maréchal Syrah Merlot (Vin de Pays des Côtes Catalanes) $9. A ripe, juicy, easy-drinking wine, a blend of half and half Syrah and Merlot. Carbonic maceration – as used in Beaujolais Nouveau – has given a soft, freshly acidic red-fruited wine. 86 Best Buy *—R.V. (2/1/2007)*

Domaine Cazes 2003 Le Canon du Maréchal Syrah Merlot (Vin de Pays d'Oc) $13. 87 *—R.V. (4/1/2005)*

DOMAINE CHANTAL LESCURE

Domaine Chantal Lescure 2004 Pinot Noir (Volnay) $NA. Although there is no mention on the label, this wine comes from a vineyard called La Famine. Something of a misnomer, because this wine is more about generosity and plenty than famine. It's soft, ripe, with dusty, easy tannins, but there is a core of dryness. The acidity shows at the end. 90 *—R.V. (3/1/2007)*

Domaine Chantal Lescure 2002 Clos de Vougeot Pinot Noir (Clos Vougeot) $100. 94 *—R.V. (9/1/2004)*

Domaine Chantal Lescure 2004 Les Chouacheux Premier Cru Pinot Noir (Beaune) $NA. From the south end of the Beaune appellation, this premier cru has produced a gentle, soft, balanced wine, with attractive, light acidity. Made from 50-year-old vines, it is well structured, with ripe, almost sweet, strawberry fruit flavors. 89 *—R.V. (3/1/2007)*

Domaine Chantal Lescure 2004 Les Damodes Premier Cru Pinot Noir (Nuits-St.-Georges) $NA. Very firm and foursquare, this is a dry, fairly tough wine. In between are layers of juicy fruit and fresh acidity. Typically for Nuits-Saint-Georges, this will need a few years aging. 89 *—R.V. (3/1/2007)*

Domaine Chantal Lescure 2004 Les Suchots Premier Cru Pinot Noir (Vosne-Romanée) $NA. Like so many wines of Vosne-Romanée, this is very complete. All the elements are in the right place, showing power, structure and delicious ripe fruit. Pure, fresh acidity and black fruits lead to a lifted aftertaste. 93 *—R.V. (3/1/2007)*

DOMAINE CHANTE-PERDRIX

Domaine Chante-Perdrix 2003 Rhône Red Blend (Châteauneuf-du-Pape) $32. 88 *—R.V. (12/31/2005)*

DOMAINE CHARLES THOMAS

Domaine Charles Thomas 2002 Clos du Roi Pinot Noir (Corton) $66. 89 *—R.V. (9/1/2004)*

DOMAINE CHAUME-ARNAUD

Domaine Chaume-Arnaud 2004 Rhône Red Blend (Côtes-du-Rhône) $NA. 86 *—J.C. (11/15/2006)*

Domaine Chaume-Arnaud 2005 Vinsobres Rhône White Blend (Côtes-du-Rhône Villages) $22. 84 *—J.C. (11/15/2006)*

DOMAINE CHEVALIER PÈRE ET FILS

Domaine Chevalier Père et Fils 2003 Pinot Noir (Ladoix) $29. 86 *—R.V. (9/1/2005)*

Domaine Chevalier Père et Fils 2003 Ladoix Premier Cru Les Corvées Pinot Noir (Ladoix) $35. 88 *—R.V. (9/1/2005)*

Domaine Christian Moreau Père et Fils 2000 Les Clos Chardonnay (Chablis) $64. 88 *—J.C. (10/1/2003)*

DOMAINE CLUSEL-ROCH

Domaine Clusel-Roch 2002 Syrah (Côte Rôtie) $52. 90 *—R.V. (2/1/2005)*

DOMAINE COLLIN

Domaine Collin 2000 Sparkling Blend (Blanquette de Limoux) $12. 81 *—J.C. (12/15/2003)*

DOMAINE COMTE DE LAUZE

Domaine Comte de Lauze 2003 Rhône Red Blend (Châteauneuf-du-Pape) $40. 87 *—R.V. (12/31/2005)*

DOMAINE COMTE GEORGES DE VOGUË

Domaine Comte Georges de Voguë 2000 Pinot Noir (Chambolle-Musigny) $100. 90 *—R.V. (11/1/2002)*

Domaine Comte Georges de Voguë 2000 Premier Cru Pinot Noir (Chevalier-Montrachet) 91 *—R.V. (11/1/2002)*

DOMAINE CONFURON-COTETIDOT

Domaine Confuron-Cotetidot 2002 Pinot Noir (Chambolle-Musigny) 88 *—R.V. (9/1/2004)*

Domaine Confuron-Cotetidot 1999 Pinot Noir (Chambolle-Musigny) $35. 88 *—R.V. (11/1/2002)*

Domaine Confuron-Cotetidot 2002 Les Suchots Premier Cru Pinot Noir (Vosne-Romanée) 89 *—R.V. (9/1/2004)*

DOMAINE COURBIS

Domaine Courbis 2004 Marsanne (Saint-Joseph) $23. 88 *—J.C. (11/15/2006)*

Domaine Courbis 2005 Les Royes Marsanne (Saint-Joseph) $30. Bursting with scents of honey and toast, this is a broad, moderately rich example of Marsanne. There's a bit of apricot, and also toasted cereal grains, lingering elegantly on the finish. Drink now. 91 *—J.C. (9/1/2007)*

Domaine Courbis 2005 Syrah (Saint-Joseph) $30. An interesting wine that combines slightly herbal notes with confected, fruity ones in a harmonious way. Pepper and crushed red fruits are carried on a creamy texture, punctuated by crisp acids and firm tannins on the finish. Drink 2008-2015. 89 *—J.C. (9/1/2007)*

Domaine Courbis 2005 Champelrose Syrah (Cornas) $50. Very fruit-forward and lush, especially considering the generally tannic nature of the 2005 vintage in the northern Rhône. Minerally notes accent red cherries and plums, with just a touch of toast and vanilla in the background. Drink now–2015. 90 *—J.C. (9/1/2007)*

Domaine Courbis 2004 Champelrose Syrah (Cornas) $45. 89 *—J.C. (11/15/2006)*

Domaine Courbis 2005 La Sabarotte Syrah (Cornas) $80. Easily marries smoky notes from new oak with minerally aromas, then layers on incredibly creamy-textured red cherry-berry fruit, dense and rich. Supple tannins provide focus on the long finish. Drink 2010–2020. 92 Cellar Selection *—J.C. (9/1/2007)*

Domaine Courbis 2005 Les Eygats Syrah (Cornas) $65. Makes a splashy entrance, flashing hints of smoke, toast and vanilla, but there's a firm core of mineral and spice at the heart of this wine that will need some time to emerge. Right now the texture is rich, the red fruit forward, but the wine finishes a bit tough and crisp. Drink 2010–2018. 90 *—J.C. (9/1/2007)*

Domaine Courbis 2005 Les Royes Syrah (Saint-Joseph) $40. Bottled only a few months prior to this tasting, the wine was still rather closed aromatically, but wonderfully ripe and supple on the palate. Waves of superripe, creamy-textured red fruit and vanilla flavors finish long, bolstered by firm tannins. Drink 2010–2018. 91 —*J.C. (9/1/2007)*

Domaine Courbis 2004 Les Royes Syrah (Saint-Joseph) $35. 84 —*J.C. (11/15/2006)*

DOMAINE COURSODON

Domaine Coursodon 2004 Syrah (Saint-Joseph) $28. 83 —*J.C. (11/15/2006)*

Domaine Coursodon 2004 Le Paradis Saint-Pierre Syrah (Saint-Joseph) $35. 86 —*J.C. (11/15/2006)*

DOMAINE D'ANDEZON

Domaine d'Andezon 2004 Vieilles Vignes Rhône Red Blend (Côtes-du-Rhône) $10. 87 Best Buy —*J.C. (11/15/2006)*

DOMAINE D'ANTUGNAC

Domaine d'Antugnac 2006 Chardonnay (Vin de Pays de la Haute Vallée de l'Aude) $11. Fresh Chardonnay is one of the star grape varieties of the Limoux region in western Languedoc. This is a typical easy, soft wine with flavors of green plums and a touch of lychees. Fresh and ready to drink. 86 Best Buy —*R.V. (12/15/2007)*

Domaine d'Antugnac 2006 Merlot (Vin de Pays d'Oc) $10. Fresh, ripe, with soft but dry tannins, this is a well-balanced, easy-drinking Merlot. The flavors are of red plums, strawberry jelly and some smokiness. Ready to drink now. 85 —*R.V. (12/15/2007)*

Domaine d'Antugnac 2005 Pinot Noir (Vin de Pays de la Haute Vallée de l'Aude) $13. From the cool Limoux region of Languedoc, this is almost Burgundian in its tannins and fresh acidity. Perhaps the juiciness is a little simple, but there are great wild strawberry fruit flavors. 86 —*R.V. (12/15/2007)*

Domaine d'Antugnac 2005 Côté Pierre Lys Pinot Noir (Vin de Pays de la Vallée de l'Aude) $15. This is a rich, complex Pinot Noir, with great ripe red fruits flavored with layers of acidity and wood. Produced by two Burgundian growers, Jean-Luc Terrier and Christian Collovray, it has a good resemblance to Burgundy in its finesse and complexity. 91 Best Buy —*R.V. (12/15/2007)*

DOMAINE D'ARDHUY

Domaine d'Ardhuy 2005 Pinot Noir (Nuits-St.-Georges) $57. A firm, dense wine, with new wood flavors, solid tannins and ripe, clean, rich, red fruit flavors. This is a wine with a good future, showing all the right potential in tannins and fruit. 89 —*R.V. (3/1/2007)*

Domaine d'Ardhuy 2003 Pinot Noir (Gevrey-Chambertin) $46. A perfumed wine, with life and freshness. The flavors of ripe fruit, typical of 2003, are very evident, but so also is a lift of acidity and raspberry fruit flavors. Delicious already. 88 —*R.V. (3/1/2007)*

Domaine d'Ardhuy 2003 Clos de Vougeot Pinot Noir (Clos Vougeot) $140. Superripe, this shows the richness of 2003. The tannins are layered between wood and toast flavors, while the fruit is bright and almost sweet. This is big, concentrated and jammy. 90 —*R.V. (3/1/2007)*

Domaine d'Ardhuy 2003 Clos des Langres Pinot Noir (Côte de Nuits-Villages) $32. Clos des Langres, showpiece estate of the Domaine d'Ardhuy, is situated right at the end of the Côte de Nuits, just before it transitions into the Côte de Beaune. This 2003, weighty for a wine from this estate, is still fresh, with crisp acidity topping the attractive, balanced red fruits. 89 —*R.V. (3/1/2007)*

Domaine d'Ardhuy 2005 Les Chaumes Premier Cru Pinot Noir (Vosne-Romanée) $100. A young wine, but one that is going to develop well, with great ripe fruit, acidity and layers of firm tannins. This solid structure amply supports the fruit. Give this wine perhaps five years, and it will show great class. 90 —*R.V. (3/1/2007)*

DOMAINE D'AUPILHAC

Domaine d'Aupilhac 1996 Montpeyroux Red Blend (Coteaux du Languedoc) $15. 92 —*L.W. (10/1/1999)*

DOMAINE D'EOLE

Domaine d'Eole 2006 Rosé Blend (Coteaux d'Aix en Provence) $NA. Fresh perfumes of rose petals, flavors of white peaches and delicious crisp acidity. A well-balanced, drink me now rosé, which has a touch of density to demand food. 87 —*R.V. (7/1/2007)*

DOMAINE DANIEL ET DENIS ALARY

Domaine Daniel et Denis Alary 2005 La Gerbaude Rhône Red Blend (Côtes-du-Rhône) $NA. 88 —*J.C. (11/15/2006)*

DOMAINE DE BEAURENARD

Domaine de Beaurenard 2004 Rhône Red Blend (Côtes-du-Rhône) $14. 85 —*J.C. (11/15/2006)*

Domaine de Beaurenard 2000 Rhône Red Blend (Châteauneuf-du-Pape) $27. 82 —*S.H. (1/1/2002)*

Domaine de Beaurenard 2003 Rasteau Rhône Red Blend (Côtes-du-Rhône Villages) $23. 91 —*J.C. (11/15/2006)*

DOMAINE DE BRIGÉ

Domaine de Brigé 2006 Chenin Blanc (Anjou) $NA. Fresh, concentrated and with a fine Chenin Blanc structure and firm style, this shows plenty of almonds, pears and red apples. The aftertaste has a great lift of acidity. 89 —*R.V. (10/1/2007)*

DOMAINE DE CASANUEVE

Domaine de Caseneuve 2006 Rosé Blend (Côtes de Provence) $12. Full-bodied in style, this is a definite food rosé. It misses out on acidity and freshness, but gains in richness, with sweet strawberry and vanilla flavors over a dry, lightly tannic structure. 88 Best Buy —*R.V. (7/1/2007)*

DOMAINE DE CASSAN

Domaine de Cassan 2004 Rhône Red Blend (Gigondas) $27. 90 —*J.C. (11/15/2006)*

Domaine de Cassan 2004 Cuvée Tradition Rhône Red Blend (Beaumes-de-Venise) $15. 88 —*J.C. (11/15/2006)*

DOMAINE DE CHAMPAGA

Domaine de Champaga 2000 Cuvée Reserve Rhône Red Blend (Côtes-du-Ventoux) $8. 84 —*M.S. (2/1/2003)*

DOMAINE DE CHAMPAL

Domaine de Champal 2004 Chaubayou Syrah (Crozes-Hermitage) $28. 86 —*J.C. (11/15/2006)*

DOMAINE DE CHATENOY

Domaine de Chatenoy 2006 Sauvignon Blanc (Menetou-Salon) $20. The 15th generation of the Clément family to farm in Menetou-Salon, just to the west of Sancerre, makes an elegant Sauvignon Blanc which in its youth shows signs of lees contact and a lightly nutty character over its green fruits. Drink within the next year. 87 —*R.V. (9/1/2007)*

Domaine de Chatenoy 2005 Sauvignon Blanc (Menetou-Salon) $20. An intensely grassy wine, with green fruit and herb flavors, structured and laced with yeast from the lees. It has a hard edge from its straight-laced structure; it needs food. 85 —*R.V. (9/1/2007)*

DOMAINE DE CHEVALIER

Domaine de Chevalier 2004 Bordeaux Blend (Pessac-Léognan) $NA. This property, run so expertly by Olivier Bernard, is now making reds that almost equal its legendary whites. This 2004 is intensely solid, dominated by black berry fruits, by spice, some smokiness aromas. It is finely balanced, smooth, with wood and tannins well integrated. 93 Editors' Choice —*R.V. (6/1/2007)*

Domaine de Chevalier 2004 Barrel Sample Bordeaux Blend (Pessac-Léognan) 93 —*R.V. (6/1/2005)*

Domaine de Chevalier 2000 Pessac-Léognan Bordeaux Blend (Bordeaux) $60. 94 —*R.V. (6/1/2003)*

Domaine de Chevalier 2001 Bordeaux White Blend (Pessac-Léognan) $100. 97 Cellar Selection —*R.V. (6/1/2005)*

Domaine de Chevalier 2006 Barrel Sample Bordeaux White Blend (Pessac-Léognan) $NA. 93-95 Barrel Sample. Domaine de Chevalier's white has a reputation for long aging, and that's the case with 2006. It is the structure that does it, very firm, almost tannic. But the fruit is also a star, ripe, dense, with green plum flavors and touches of spice. Give this at least 10 years. 94 —*R.V. (6/1/2007)*

DOMAINE DE COSTE CHAUDE

Domaine de Coste Chaude 2005 Les 4 Saisons Rosé Visan Grenache (Côtes-du-Rhône Villages) $NA. 87 —*J.C. (11/15/2006)*

Domaine de Coste Chaude 2003 Jupiter Visan Rhône Red Blend (Côtes-du-Rhône Villages) $NA. 90 —*J.C. (11/15/2006)*

Domaine de Coste Chaude 2004 La Rocaille Visan Rhône Red Blend (Côtes-du-Rhône Villages) $NA. 89 —*J.C. (11/15/2006)*

DOMAINE DE COURON

Domaine de Couron 2003 Cuvée Marie Dubois Syrah (Côtes-du-Rhône) $12. 83 —*J.C. (11/15/2006)*

DOMAINE DE COURTEILLAC

Domaine de Courteillac 2001 Bordeaux Blanc White Blend (Bordeaux) $11. 88 —*R.V. (12/1/2002)*

DOMAINE DE CRISTIA

Domaine de Cristia 2003 Renaissance Rhône Red Blend (Châteauneuf-du-Pape) $70. 95 Editors' Choice *—R.V. (12/31/2005)*

DOMAINE DE DEURRE

Domaine de Deurre 2004 Les Rabasses Grenache (Vinsobres) $22. 87 *—J.C. (11/15/2006)*

DOMAINE DE DURBAN

Domaine de Durban 2004 Rhône Red Blend (Beaumes-de-Venise) $NA. 84 *—J.C. (11/15/2006)*

DOMAINE DE FAUTERIE

Domaine de Fauterie 2004 Les Combaud Syrah (Saint-Joseph) $22. 82 *—J.C. (11/15/2006)*

DOMAINE DE FENOUILLET

Domaine de Fenouillet 2005 Muscat Blanc à Petit Grain (Muscat de Beaumes de Venise) $NA. 84 *—J.C. (11/15/2006)*

DOMAINE DE FONTAVIN

Domaine de Fontavin 2004 Rhône Red Blend (Vacqueyras) $NA. 87 *—J.C. (11/15/2006)*

Domaine de Fontavin 2003 Rhône Red Blend (Côtes-du-Rhône) $NA. 83 *—J.C. (11/15/2006)*

Domaine de Fontavin 1999 Rhône Red Blend (Vacqueyras) $17. 87 *—M.S. (2/1/2003)*

DOMAINE DE FONTENILLE

Domaine de Fontenille 2000 Rhône Red Blend (Côtes du Luberon) $13. 90 Best Buy *—J.C. (2/1/2005)*

DOMAINE DE GOURNIER

Domaine de Gournier 2005 Rosé Blend (Vin de Pays des Cévennes) $9. 88 Best Buy *—J.C. (6/21/2006)*

DOMAINE DE JUCHEPIE

Domaine de Juchepie 2002 La Passion Chenin Blanc (Coteaux du Layon La Faye) $NA. La Passion is a fine name for this wine, made by Eddy Oosterlinck. It is a result of his passion that this is such an impressive wine: liquorous, botrytised, yes, but with a beautiful line of acidity, fresh honey and fine structure. Could age for 10 years, or drink now. 92 Cellar Selection *—R.V. (10/1/2007)*

Domaine de Juchepie 2004 Le Sec de Juchepie Chenin Blanc (Anjou) $NA. A spicy wine, hinting at honey with wood and vanilla flavors. As a dry Chenin Blanc, this doesn't come off well; the fruit is a far distant runner to the other flavors. 84 *—R.V. (10/1/2007)*

DOMAINE DE L'AMEILLAUD

Domaine de L'Ameillaud 2005 Rhône Red Blend (Côtes-du-Rhône) $14. 87 *—J.C. (11/15/2006)*

DOMAINE DE L'ESPIGOUETTE

Domaine de L'Espigouette 2004 Rhône Red Blend (Vacqueyras) $24. 89 *J.C. (11/15/2006)*

DOMAINE DE L'HERMITAGE

Domaine de L'Hermitage 2004 Rosé Blend (Bandol) $20. 87 *—J.C. (6/21/2006)*

DOMAINE DE L'OLIVETTE

Domaine de l'Olivette 2006 Rosé Blend (Bandol) $NA. Roasted almond aromas, with fresh, crisp white fruits. This is a properly refreshing wine, touched by caramel, but finishing with delicious acidity. It has power, too, and could carry its freshness into 2008, but why? 88 *—R.V. (7/1/2007)*

DOMAINE DE L'OLIVIER

Domaine de L'Olivier 2001 Chardonnay (Vin de Pays d'Oc) $6. 87 Best Buy *—D.T. (11/15/2002)*

DOMAINE DE L'ORATOIRE SAINT-MARTIN

Domaine de L'Oratoire Saint-Martin 2004 Cuvée Prestige Cairanne Rhône Red Blend (Côtes-du-Rhône Villages) $27. 90 *—J.C. (11/15/2006)*

Domaine de L'Oratoire Saint-Martin 2004 Haut-Coustias Cairanne Rhône White Blend (Côtes-du-Rhône Villages) $17. 90 *—J.C. (11/15/2006)*

DOMAINE DE LA BOISSIERE

Domaine de la Boissiere 1999 Syrah (Costières de Nimes) $19. 87 *(10/1/2001)*

Domaine de la Bouissiere 2001 Cuvée Classique Rhône Red Blend (Gigondas) $24. 91 Editors' Choice *—R.V. (3/1/2004)*

DOMAINE DE LA BRUNE

Domaine de la Brune 2004 Beaumes-de-Venise Rhône Red Blend (Côtes-du-Rhône Villages) $NA. 86 *—J.C. (11/15/2006)*

DOMAINE DE LA CAVE DU ROCHER

Domaine de la Cave du Rocher 2005 Cabernet Franc (Saumur-Champigny) $15. A fresh, smoky, lightly-acidic Saumur Champigny, maybe without great depth, but with vibrant red fruits. Enjoy this year. 85 *—R.V. (10/1/2007)*

DOMAINE DE LA CHARBONNIÈRE

Domaine de la Charbonnière 2003 Cuvée Mourre de Perdrix Rhône Red Blend (Châteauneuf-du-Pape) $30. 91 *—R.V. (12/31/2005)*

DOMAINE DE LA CHEVALERIE

Domaine de la Chevalerie 2003 19 Heures Cabernet Franc (Bourgueil) $NA. Why 19 heures (7 p.m.)? Because that's apéritif time—why else? Velvet smooth, this is a rich offering from a warm vintage. It is succulent and balanced, with some wood and very ripe, juicy fruit. 91 *—R.V. (4/1/2007)*

Domaine de la Chevalerie 2002 Busardières Cabernet Franc (Bourgueil) $NA. This wine is a reflection of its year. There is fruit, along with an attractive velvet texture, but it also has a lean character that comes from fruit that only just managed to get towards ripeness. 84 *—R.V. (4/1/2007)*

DOMAINE DE LA CHEZATTE

Domaine de la Chezatte 2000 Sauvignon Blanc (Sancerre) $20. 86 *(8/1/2002)*

DOMAINE DE LA CÔTE DE L'ANGE

Domaine de la Côte de l'Ange 2003 Vieilles Vignes Rhône Red Blend (Châteauneuf-du-Pape) $NA. 93 Cellar Selection *—R.V. (12/31/2005)*

DOMAINE DE LA COURTADE

Domaine de la Courtade 2006 L'Alycastre Rosé Blend (Côtes de Provence) $NA. This palest of rosés is as fresh and light as its color. A blend of Mourvèdre, Grenache and Tibouren, it is low in alcohol (12%) and touched with pink grapefruit acidity and caramel. 86 *—R.V. (7/1/2007)*

Domaine de la Courtade 2006 La Courtade Rosé Blend (Côtes de Provence) $NA. This is the top of the two rosés produced at Domaine de la Courtade, a Mourvèdre dominated wine that fills the mouth with fresh raspberries and tense acidity. It leaves a crisp taste of red apples and herbs. 89 *—R.V. (7/1/2007)*

DOMAINE DE LA CROZE

Domaine de la Croze 2004 Bel Air Rhône Red Blend (Lirac) $12. Rather herbal on the nose, with a distinct note of fennel that sets it apart from other 2004 Liracs. Lean and red-fruited, leaning toward raspberry and herb rather than dark fruits and dried spices. 85 *—J.C. (11/15/2006)*

DOMAINE DE LA FERRANDIÈRE

Domaine de la Ferrandière 2006 Rosé de Cabernet Cabernet Sauvignon (Vin de Pays d'Oc) $7. This copper-hued rosé is clean and fresh, offering simple fruity flavors at a wallet-pleasing price. Light and refreshing flavors reminiscent of watermelon should do well as a summertime apéritif. 85 Best Buy *—J.C. (7/1/2007)*

DOMAINE DE LA GASQUI

Domaine de la Gasqui 2000 Le Vallat des Taches Red Blend (Vin de Pays de Vaucluse) $10. 85 *—R.V. (11/15/2003)*

DOMAINE DE LA GENESTIÈRE

Domaine de la Genestière 2005 Cuvée Raphaël Rosé Blend (Tavel) $14. 87 *—J.C. (11/15/2006)*

DOMAINE DE LA GUICHARDE

Domaine de la Guicharde 2003 Cuvée Genest Rhône Red Blend (Côtes-du-Rhône Villages) $14. 91 Best Buy *—J.C. (11/15/2006)*

DOMAINE DE LA JANASSE

Domaine de la Janasse 2001 Les Garrigues Grenache (Côtes-du-Rhône Villages) $30. 88 *—R.V. (3/1/2004)*

Domaine de la Janasse 2000 Terre de Buissière Red Blend (Vin de Pays de la Principauté d'Orange) $12. 86 *—R.V. (11/15/2003)*

Domaine de la Janasse 2003 Rhône Red Blend (Châteauneuf-du-Pape)

$45. 94 Editors' Choice *—R.V. (12/31/2005)*

Domaine de la Janasse 2001 Terre d'Argile Rhône Red Blend (Côtes-du-Rhône Villages) $20. 85 *—R.V. (3/1/2004)*

Domaine de la Janasse 2001 Vieilles Vignes Rhône Red Blend (Châteauneuf-du-Pape) $110. 94 *—R.V. (3/1/2004)*

DOMAINE DE LA LOUVETRIE

Domaine de la Louvetrie 2003 Sur Lie Muscadet (Muscadet Sèvre Et Maine) $11. 89 Best Buy *—R.V. (11/15/2004)*

DOMAINE DE LA MAVETTE

Domaine de la Mavette 2003 Rhône Red Blend (Côtes-du-Rhône) $11. 83 *—J.C. (11/15/2006)*

Domaine de la Mavette 2003 Sablet Rhône Red Blend (Côtes-du-Rhône Villages) $13. 89 Best Buy *—J.C. (11/15/2006)*

DOMAINE DE LA MORDORÉE

Domaine de la Mordorée 2003 La Reine des Bois Rhône Red Blend (Lirac) $39. 93 Editors' Choice *—J.C. (11/15/2006)*

Domaine de la Mordorée 2005 La Reine des Bois Rhône White Blend (Lirac) $30. 88 *—J.C. (11/15/2006)*

DOMAINE DE LA NOBLAIE

Domaine de la Noblaie 2004 Les Chiens-Chiens Cabernet Franc (Chinon) $18. This wine is dense, flavored with black cherries and fresh acidity over a smooth, silky texture. It is not as powerful as the 2003, but is ready to drink; a pleasurable, very food-friendly wine. 88 *—R.V. (4/1/2007)*

Domaine de la Noblaie 2003 Les Chiens-Chiens Cabernet Franc (Chinon) $16. No, there are no dogs involved in this, apart from the label picture. The name comes from the parcel of hillside vines. It's a soft, ripe and rich wine, a veritable velvet parcel, all fine tannins and richness, along with fresh acidity. Give this wine two years before drinking. 91 *—R.V. (4/1/2007)*

Domaine de la Noblaie 2005 Les Chiens-Chiens Chenin Blanc (Chinon) $18. There aren't many white wines made in Chinon. But this, made from Chenin Blanc, suggests there should be some more. It is full of attractive peach flavors, with a young, fresh lift, floating with bitter almonds. The texture is good, round and rich. 87 *—R.V. (4/1/2007)*

DOMAINE DE LA PEPIÈRE

Domaine de la Pepière 2003 Muscadet (Muscadet Sèvre Et Maine) $10. 87 Best Buy *—J.C. (11/15/2004)*

DOMAINE DE LA PETITE CASSAGNE

Domaine de la Petite Cassagne 2006 Rosé Rosé Blend (Costières de Nimes) $10. With its scents of melon rind and wet stones, this is clearly no tutti-frutti rosé. There's a hint of cherry, but the emphasis is on lipsmacking minerality from the start all the way through the long, mouthwatering finish. 88 Best Buy *—J.C. (7/1/2007)*

DOMAINE DE LA POUSSE D'OR

Domaine de la Pousse d'Or 2002 Volnay Premier Cru Clos de la Bousse d'Or Pinot Noir (Volnay) $NA. 93 *—R.V. (9/1/2004)*

DOMAINE DE LA PRÉSIDENTE

Domaine de la Présidente 2004 Grands Classiques Cairanne Rhône Red Blend (Côtes-du-Rhône Villages) $NA. 87 *—J.C. (11/15/2006)*

Domaine de la Présidente 2005 Grands Classiques Rhône White Blend (Côtes-du-Rhône) $NA. 89 *—J.C. (11/15/2006)*

DOMAINE DE LA RENJARDE

Domaine de la Renjarde 2002 Rhône Red Blend (Côtes-du-Rhône Villages) $13. 87 *—J.C. (2/1/2005)*

DOMAINE DE LA RIVAUDIERE

Domaine de la Rivaudiere 2006 Rosé Blend (Touraine Amboise) $NA. A ripe, full-bodied, but still crisply fresh wine, packed with flavors of ripe red currants, raspberries and a touch of vanilla. With its relatively low alcohol of 12%, it is just right for those summer evenings. 88 *—R.V. (7/1/2007)*

DOMAINE DE LA ROMANÉE-CONTI

Domaine de la Romanée-Conti 2004 Le Montrachet Chardonnay (Montrachet) $NA. A great wine from a great vintage for whites, this has vanilla, ripe green fruits and a smoky, mineral character. Ripe and delicious, this brings the richness of honey and the rigor of minerality into balance. 97 *—R.V. (3/1/2007)*

Domaine de la Romanée-Conti 2004 Pinot Noir (Richebourg) $NA. Smoky aromas set the scene for a complex, fascinating wine. Like so many 2004s, it is striking for the purity of its fruit. And if there is a hint of green in the tannins, this certainly doesn't do the wine any harm. It's more that it shows how much time it needs to mature. Aftertaste is fresh. 94 *—R.V. (3/1/2007)*

Domaine de la Romanée-Conti 2004 Pinot Noir (Grands-Echezeaux) $129. Initial animal, rustic aromas blow away after a few minutes. On the palate, pure fruits are dominant, just hinting at some of the typical 2004 pepper character. It's a spicy, complex wine, with excellent acidity right through the finish, and always firm. 92 *—R.V. (3/1/2007)*

Domaine de la Romanée-Conti 2004 Pinot Noir (Romanée-Conti) $NA. This wine's considerable power derives from its a solid texture, its multi-faceted red-berry flavors, juiciness, freshness and perfect balancing acidity. You can, and will want to, hold this in the mouth for many minutes. It is a complete wine. 97 *—R.V. (3/1/2007)*

Domaine de la Romanée-Conti 2004 Pinot Noir (Echezeaux) $NA. Pure, fine fruits along the line of raspberry and dark plums—there's almost a dancing quality to this wine, with its freshness and lightness, with acidity and red currants giving the most delicate of finishing touches. 93 *—R.V. (3/1/2007)*

Domaine de la Romanée-Conti 2004 Pinot Noir (La Tâche) $NA. Although this wine is very firm and closed at the outset, it opens—and keeps opening in the mouth—to offer great fruit flavors. It is finely balanced, very pure, combining an ethereal character with the proper feet-in-the-soil taste of great Pinot Noir. Age for 20 years, if you can bear to wait. 96 Cellar Selection *—R.V. (3/1/2007)*

Domaine de la Romanée-Conti 2004 Pinot Noir (Romanée-St.-Vivant) $NA. A delicious, flowery, aromatic wine. The flavors float around the firm core of fine tannins, plum skin and fig flavors, combining with acidity and leaving an impression of delicacy, yet also great aging potential. 95 *—R.V. (3/1/2007)*

DOMAINE DE LA RONCIÈRE

Domaine de la Roncière 2003 Flor de Ronce Rhône Red Blend (Châteauneuf-du-Pape) $70. 89 *—R.V. (12/31/2005)*

DOMAINE DE LA ROYERE

Domaine de la Royere 1999 Cuvée Speciale L'Oppidum Syrah-Grenache (Côtes du Luberon) $11. 83 *—J.C. (2/1/2005)*

DOMAINE DE LA SAUVEUSE

Domaine de la Sauveuse 2005 Cuvée Carolle Rosé Rhône Red Blend (Côtes de Provence) $10. 82 *—J.C. (6/21/2006)*

DOMAINE DE LA SOLITUDE

Domaine de la Solitude 2003 Rhône Red Blend (Châteauneuf-du-Pape) $33. 85 *—R.V. (12/31/2005)*

Domaine de la Solitude 1998 Rhône Red Blend (Côtes-du-Rhône) $10. 88 *—M.M. (12/31/2000)*

DOMAINE DE LA TOURADE

Domaine de la Tourade 2003 Rhône Red Blend (Vacqueyras) $NA. 84 *—J.C. (11/15/2006)*

DOMAINE DE LA VOUGERAIE

Domaine de la Vougeraie 2003 Chardonnay (Beaune) $50. 88 *—R.V. (9/1/2005)*

Domaine de la Vougeraie 2005 Clos de Prieuré Chardonnay (Vougeot) $69. This white Chardonnay from Vougeot is one of a pair of white vineyards owned by the Boisset family of Domaine de la Vougeraie – the other is Le Clos Blanc. This Clos de Prieuré is light, fresh, with flavors of soft pears, an easy wine ready to drink now. 87 *—R.V. (3/1/2007)*

Domaine de la Vougeraie 2002 Clos du Prieuré Chardonnay (Vougeot) $NA. 90 *—R.V. (9/1/2004)*

Domaine de la Vougeraie 2004 La Corvée des Vignes Chardonnay (Puligny-Montrachet) $NA. 90 *—R.V. (12/1/2006)*

Domaine de la Vougeraie 2004 Le Clos Blanc Premier Cru Chardonnay (Vougeot) $69. A white wine vineyard in the heart of the Pinot Noir kingdom of Vougeot is quite a rarity. Domaine de la Vougeraie owns all of this tiny 5-acre vineyard. The wine has a richness and purity of fruit, with apricot and hints of the tropics over a layer of sweet wood. A smooth, creamy texture adds to the allure of this delicious wine. 92 *—R.V. (3/1/2007)*

Domaine de la Vougeraie 2005 Pinot Noir (Bonnes-Mares) $110. Mostly in Chambolle-Musigny, this Grand Cru has a firmer, more solid character than many of the more refined offerings from this village. This is very evident in this dense wine, with its new wood and the power and intensity of black, very ripe fruits. The tannins are already well integrated with the fruit. No doubt this will age. 94 *—R.V. (3/1/2007)*

Domaine de la Vougeraie 2002 Pinot Noir (Gevrey-Chambertin) $NA. 89 —

R.V. (9/1/2004)

Domaine de la Vougeraie 2003 Clos de Vougeot Pinot Noir (Clos Vougeot) $125. A dark, brooding wine from superripe grapes. There is a lot of structure, though not much fruit at this point. Very dry and firm, with its richness coming from its concentrated tannins. This certainly needs to age, 5–10 years at least. **92** *—R.V. (3/1/2007)*

Domaine de la Vougeraie 2004 Les Cras Premier Cru Pinot Noir (Vougeot) $60. A ripe, open, pure-fruited wine, full of richness. It shows delicious, clean strawberry fruit flavors, mixed comfortably with tannins and freshness. The soft side of Pinot Noir, but with plenty of weight behind it. The premier cru of Les Cras is right next to the grand cru of Clos de Vougeot. **91** *—R.V. (3/1/2007)*

Domaine de la Vougeraie 2003 Les Petits Noizons Pinot Noir (Pommard) $80. 90 *—R.V. (9/1/2005)*

Domaine de la Vougeraie 1999 Le Clos Blanc de Vougeot White Blend (Vougeot) $79. 91 *—R.V. (11/1/2001)*

DOMAINE DE LALANDE

Domaine de Lalande 2000 Les Chevrières Chardonnay (Pouilly-Fuissé) $27. 89 *(10/1/2003)*

DOMAINE DE LONGVAL

Domaine de Longval 2005 Rosé Blend (Tavel) $14. 85 *—J.C. (11/15/2006)*

DOMAINE DE MARCOUX

Domaine de Marcoux 2000 Cuvée Classique Rhône Red Blend (Châteauneuf-du-Pape) $50. 90 *—R.V. (3/1/2004)*

DOMAINE DE MONTVAC

Domaine de Montvac 2001 Cuvée Vincila Grenache-Syrah (Vacqueyras) $20. 84 *—J.C. (11/15/2006)*

Domaine de Montvac 2004 Rhône Red Blend (Vacqueyras) $13. 87 *—J.C. (11/15/2006)*

DOMAINE DE MOURCHON

Domaine de Mourchon 2003 Grande Reserve Séguret Rhône Red Blend (Côtes-du-Rhône Villages) $23. 89 *—J.C. (11/15/2006)*

DOMAINE DE NIZAS

Domaine de Nizas 2003 Carignan (Coteaux du Languedoc) $16. 85 *—R.V. (12/1/2004)*

Domaine de Nizas 2005 Vieilles Vignes Carignan (Vin de Pays de Caux) $16. It's impressive how exciting old vine Carignan can be, and what an underrated grape it is. Here's proof that it makes big, perfumed wines, layered with dark tannins and wild flavors of herbs and dark berries. **89 Editors' Choice** *—R.V. (12/15/2007)*

Domaine de Nizas 2001 Red Blend (Coteaux du Languedoc) $20. 88 *—R.V. (12/1/2004)*

Domaine de Nizas 2002 Le Mas Red Blend (Vin de Pays d'Oc) $13. A ripe, smooth wine, dominated by vanilla from wood and by red berry fruits. The tannic structure is subservient to the rich layers of mint and herbal flavors, while the fruit dominates. Finishes with chocolate and firm tannins. **89** *—R.V. (12/15/2007)*

Domaine de Nizas 2001 Mas Sallèles Red Blend (Vin de Pays d'Oc) $13. 88 Best Buy *—R.V. (12/31/2006)*

Domaine de Nizas 2003 Rhône Red Blend (Coteaux du Languedoc) $17. Fresh and juicily fruity, even after its four years of aging, this wine has a good southern warmth and ripeness, full of blackberry flavors and a subtle touch of tannin and dryness under the sweet fruit. It would benefit from another year's aging. **89** *—R.V. (12/15/2007)*

Domaine de Nizas 2002 Rhône Red Blend (Coteaux du Languedoc) $16. 92 Editors' Choice *—R.V. (12/31/2006)*

Domaine de Nizas 2004 Réserve Rhône Red Blend (Vin de Pays d'Oc) $35. An intense wine, superconcentrated, with very rich fruit, layers of dark tannins and wood, and fruit flavors that concentrate on dark plums, black figs and ripe blackberries. The dryness and the finishing acidity show how this wine needs to age. **91** *—R.V. (12/15/2007)*

Domaine de Nizas 2005 Rosé Rhône Red Blend (Coteaux du Languedoc) $16. A soft, fruity wine with some caramel and vanilla flavors along with fresh loganberries. Thereâ€™s attractive crisp acidity to balance the fruitiness. **84** *—R.V. (2/1/2007)*

Domaine de Nizas 2006 Rosé Blend (Coteaux du Languedoc) $16. The Clos du Val owned Domaine de Nizas goes for a full-bodied style of rosé, but manages to pull it off because the fruit is so vibrant and lively. Wild strawberries dominate, with acidity, a touch of caramel and minerality. **90** *—R.V. (7/1/2007)*

Domaine de Nizas 2005 Sauvignon Blanc (Vin de Pays d'Oc) $13. 85 *—R.V. (12/31/2006)*

DOMAINE DE PIAUGIER

Domaine de Piaugier 2004 Rhône Red Blend (Gigondas) $19. 89 *—J.C. (11/15/2006)*

DOMAINE DE POUY

Domaine de Pouy 2003 White Blend (Vin de Pays des Côtes de Gascogne) $8. 87 Best Buy *—M.S. (11/15/2004)*

DOMAINE DE SERVANS

Domaine de Servans 1999 Cuvée Exceptionnelle Grenache (Côtes-du-Rhône) $16. 91 Editors' Choice *—M.S. (9/1/2003)*

DOMAINE DE SOUVIOU

Domaine de Souviou 2006 Rosé Blend (Bandol) $NA. An enticing floral, scented aroma is a good start. And things get even better, with the crisp, red apple and currant flavors, and the touch of vanilla. This is relatively full-bodied, in alcohol at least, but the fresh acidity acts as a great foil. **90** *—R.V. (7/1/2007)*

DOMAINE DE VAUGONDY

Domaine de Vaugondy NV Ph. Perdriaux Brut Chenin Blanc (Vouvray) $12. 88 Best Buy *—M.D. (12/15/2006)*

DOMAINE DE VERQUIERE

Domaine de Verquiere 2004 Sablet Rhône Red Blend (Côtes-du-Rhône Villages) $11. 86 *—J.C. (11/15/2006)*

DOMAINE DE VIEUX TELEGRAPHE

Domaine de Vieux Telegraphe 1998 Red Blend (Châteauneuf-du-Pape) $42. 94 *—M.M. (12/31/2001)*

DOMAINE DE VILLEMAJOU

Domaine de Villemajou 2004 Rhône Red Blend (Corbières) $19. Produced by Gerard Bertrand, this is a typically perfumed wine, with aromas of wild flowers. There are flavors of dried figs and chocolate, with herbs and a dry aftertaste, leaving tannin and acidity. Decant before serving, it is still young. **89** *—R.V. (2/1/2007)*

DOMAINE DE VILLENEUVE

Domaine de Villeneuve 2001 Vieilles Vignes Rhône Red Blend (Châteauneuf-du-Pape) $32. 93 *—R.V. (3/1/2004)*

DOMAINE DE VRIGNAUD

Domaine de Vrignaud 2005 Fourchaume Premier Cru Chardonnay (Chablis) $NA. From a small Chablis producer, this is very soft, showing some ripe fruit but an amorphous structure; rather unfocused. There are plenty of creamy wood and sweet green-fruit flavors, but they need time to hang together better. **87** *—R.V. (8/1/2007)*

Domaine de Vrignaud 2004 Fourchaume Premier Cru Chardonnay (Chablis) $NA. Very open and ripe, touched with wood and centered around some creamy red apple and green pear flavors. The wood comes through strongly later, leaving a powerful vanilla aftertaste. **88** *—R.V. (8/1/2007)*

DOMAINE DENIS GAUDRY

Domaine Denis Gaudry 2000 Pouilly-Fumé White Blend (Pouilly-Fumé) $20. 84 *(8/1/2002)*

DOMAINE DES BAUMARD

Domaine des Baumard NV Carte Corail Rosé Cabernet Franc (Crémant de Loire) $19. 87 *—R.V. (6/1/2006)*

Domaine des Baumard 2005 Chenin Blanc (Quarts de Chaume) $72. From arguably the finest sweet wine vineyard in the Loire, here is a wine that is deceptively fresh on first taste. Then the huge richness kicks in, balanced with blood oranges, white fig and pear flavors, and a mineral character. Complex, this needs many years to develop; superb. **95** *—R.V. (10/1/2007)*

Domaine des Baumard 2004 Chenin Blanc (Savennières) $22. A beautifully crisp wine, fresh and leaping with green fruits. This wine is characterized by its steely core and great acidity, with green plum skins and a structure that promises a long, slow development. **90** *—R.V. (10/1/2007)*

Domaine des Baumard 2003 Chenin Blanc (Savennières) $22. Maybe this lacks the stylistic minerality of Savennières because of the hot vintage, but it replaces that with richness, creamy opulence and developing flavors of vanilla and almonds, leaving the acidity bringing up the final taste. Screwcap. **89** *—R.V. (10/1/2007)*

Domaine des Baumard 2005 Carte d'Or Chenin Blanc (Coteaux du Layon) $26. Certainly sweet, but a sweetness held in check by layers of dry botrytis. This is an apéritif wine, its flavors of apricots touched with white figs making it seem fruity rather than unctuous. Screwcap. **89** —*R.V. (10/1/2007)*

Domaine des Baumard 2005 Clos de Sainte Catherine Chenin Blanc (Coteaux du Layon) $50. Clos de Sainte-Catherine is at the summit of the sweet wines of Coteaux du Layon. This comes from a great year for sweet wines, and that shows in the impressive balance between intense sweetness and acidity. It's smooth and crisp at the same time, a great combination. Age for 10 years and more. Screwcap. **95 Cellar Selection** —*R.V. (10/1/2007)*

Domaine des Baumard 2005 Clos du Papillon Chenin Blanc (Savennières) $39. A superb wine, fresh and ripe, with a characteristic edge of caramel, opulence and bone-dry acidity. This comes from a great vineyard in a great Loire year, so it's no surprise that, like many great Loire Chenin Blanc, it promises lengthy aging—15–20 years if you can wait. In the meantime, now it has youthful vigor and freshness. Screwcap. Available in the U.S. from January 2008. **95 Editors' Choice** —*R.V. (10/1/2007)*

Domaine des Baumard 2004 Clos du Papillon Chenin Blanc (Savennières) $32. So called because the vineyard resembles the wings of a butterfly (papillon), this is the top Baumard Savennières cru. It has richness, a touch of caramel, but an intense mineral, green plum and citrus character that gives it structure and ageability. Screwcap. **93** —*R.V. (10/1/2007)*

Domaine des Baumard 2005 Cuvée le Paon Chenin Blanc (Coteaux du Layon) $45. Peacock (paon) cuvée is a deliciously showy wine, powered with intense sweetness, almost syrup. The counterbalance to all this sweetness is the pear, apricot and citrus elements, which go with the dry layer of botrytis to leave a wine that it has a crisp, fresh aftertaste. Screwcap. **93** —*R.V. (10/1/2007)*

Domaine des Baumard 2004 Cuvée le Paon Chenin Blanc (Coteaux du Layon) $38. A full-bodied wine, very sweet from botrytised grapes selected from old vines. It fills the mouth while keeping its elegance. Preserving the balance is fresh nectarine acidity. Immensely attractive now, this is likely to age well. **91** —*R.V. (10/1/2007)*

Domaine des Baumard 2003 Trie Spéciale Chenin Blanc (Savennières) $38. From a small south-facing parcel next to the Clos du Papillon vineyard, this is a hugely rich wine, maybe excessively so. It comes from the hot 2003 vintage, and the grapes were obviously superripe. It's round, full-bodied, with ripe quince and white fig flavors. Is there minerality there? It's hard to find, just revel in its opulence. Screwcap. **91** —*R.V. (10/1/2007)*

Domaine des Baumard 2002 Tirage Brut Chenin Blanc-Chardonnay (Crémant de Loire) $20. 89 —*R.V. (6/1/2006)*

Domaine des Baumard NV Turquoise Sparkling Blend (Crémant de Loire) $18. A blend of Chenin Blanc and Cab Franc, this literally bubbles with liveliness and freshness. Rich, but the roundness is held in check by acidity and a touch of tannin. It finishes with elegance and a zest of lemon. **89** —*R.V. (10/1/2007)*

DOMAINE DES BERNARDINS

Domaine des Bernardins 2004 Rhône Red Blend (Beaumes-de-Venise) $NA. 87 —*J.C. (11/15/2006)*

DOMAINE DES BERTHIERS

Domaine des Berthiers 2000 Sauvignon Blanc (Pouilly-Fumé) $24. 85 *(8/1/2002)*

DOMAINE DES BLAGUEURS

Domaine des Blagueurs 2000 Syrah (Vin de Pays d'Oc) $9. 89 Best Buy —*S.H. (2/28/2003)*

DOMAINE DES COCCINELLES

Domaine des Coccinelles 2002 Red Blend (Côtes-du-Rhône) $10. 84 —*J.C. (3/1/2004)*

Domaine des Coccinelles 2005 Rhône White Blend (Côtes-du-Rhône) $11. 86 Best Buy —*J.C. (11/15/2006)*

DOMAINE DES COMTES LAFON

Domaine des Comtes Lafon 2004 Charmes Premier Cru Chardonnay (Meursault) $NA. 93 —*R.V. (12/1/2006)*

Domaine des Comtes Lafon 2004 Les Genevrières Premier Cru Chardonnay (Meursault) $NA. 92 Editors' Choice —*R.V. (12/1/2006)*

DOMAINE DES DEUX ROCHES

Domaine des Deux Roches 2001 Chardonnay (St.-Véran) $19. 86 —*S.H. (1/1/2002)*

DOMAINE DES ENTREFAUX

Domaine des Entrefaux 1999 Syrah (Crozes-Hermitage) $13. 88 —*J.C. (12/31/2000)*

DOMAINE DES ESCARAVAILLES

Domaine des Escaravailles 2003 Vin Doux Natural (Rasteau) Grenache (Côtes-du-Rhône Villages) $44. 92 —*J.C. (11/15/2006)*

Domaine des Escaravailles 2000 Côtes du Rhône Les Antimagne Rhône Red Blend (Côtes-du-Rhône) $NA. 86 —*R.V. (3/1/2004)*

Domaine des Escaravailles 2001 Côtes du Rhône Villages Rasteau La Ponce Rhône Red Blend (Côtes-du-Rhône Villages) $NA. 89 —*R.V. (3/1/2004)*

Domaine des Escaravailles 2002 Rhône White Blend (Côtes-du-Rhône) $NA. 85 —*R.V. (3/1/2004)*

DOMAINE DES GRANDES PERRIÈRES

Domaine des Grandes Perrières 2006 Sauvignon Blanc (Sancerre) $20. A light, very fresh style of Sancerre, with fine flinty, mineral character. Plenty of citrus and fresh pears give this an easy, vibrant style. A wine to drink over the next year. **88** —*R.V. (10/1/2007)*

DOMAINE DES HAUTS CHASSIS

Domaine des Hauts Chassis 2004 Les Chassis Syrah (Crozes-Hermitage) $NA. 87 —*J.C. (11/15/2006)*

DOMAINE DES LAMBRAYS

Domaine des Lambrays 2004 Clos des Lambrays Pinot Noir (Clos de Lambrays) $110. To say this is textbook Pinot Noir is to do this stunning wine an injustice. But it does have everything that should be in a great Pinot Noir—the sumptuousness, the silky tannins, the touch of wood, the red fruits. All of these are enveloped in an elegant structure, leaving freshness and delicious, refreshing acidity at the end. **97** —*R.V. (3/1/2007)*

DOMAINE DES MURETTES

Domaine des Murettes 1998 Le Clos de l'Olivier Syrah (Minervois) $12. 87 Best Buy *(10/1/2001)*

DOMAINE DES OLIVIERS

Domaine des Oliviers 2005 Chardonnay (Vin de Pays d'Oc) $8. 88 Best Buy —*R.V. (12/31/2006)*

DOMAINE DES OUCHES

Domaine des Ouches 2005 Cabernet Franc (Bourgueil) $19. With Thomas and Denise Gambier taking over from father Paul, this Gambier family estate is moving upwards. The style—as with this wine—is firm, tannic, solid and intense. The black fruits are subdued at this stage by the dry tannins and the wine needs at least two years to evolve. **91** —*R.V. (4/1/2007)*

DOMAINE DES PERDRIX

Domaine des Perdrix 2003 Pinot Noir (Vosne-Romanée) $80. 90 —*R.V. (9/1/2005)*

Domaine des Perdrix 2003 Pinot Noir (Echezeaux) $200. 89 —*R.V. (9/1/2005)*

Domaine des Perdrix 2001 Pinot Noir (Nuits-St.-Georges) $51. 90 —*J.C. (10/1/2003)*

Domaine des Perdrix 2001 Pinot Noir (Bourgogne) $16. 85 —*J.C. (10/1/2003)*

Domaine des Perdrix 2002 Aux Perdrix Premier Cru Pinot Noir (Nuits-St.-Georges) $93. 90 —*R.V. (9/1/2004)*

Domaine des Perdrix 1999 aux Perdrix Premier Cru Pinot Noir (Nuits-St.-Georges) $61. 91 Cellar Selection *(1/1/2004)*

DOMAINE DES QUARRES

Domaine des Quarres 2006 Cabernet Franc (Cabernet d'Anjou) $15. Medium sweet in style, typical of this appellation, this is soft, great for an aperitif, flavored with strawberry candies and maraschino cherries. All it needs is a hot fudge sundae. **84** —*R.V. (7/1/2007)*

DOMAINE DES RELAGNES

Domaine des Relagnes 2003 Les Petits Pieds d'Armand Rhône Red Blend (Châteauneuf-du-Pape) $68. 94 —*R.V. (12/31/2005)*

DOMAINE DES REMIZIÈRES

Domaine des Remizières 2000 Cuvée Emilie Rhône Red Blend (Hermitage) $NA. 87 —*R.V. (6/1/2002)*

Domaine des Remizières 2004 Syrah (Saint-Joseph) $NA. 88 —*J.C. (11/15/2006)*

Domaine des Remizières 2000 Cuvée Christophe Syrah (Crozes-Hermitage) $30. 88 —*R.V. (6/1/2002)*

Domaine des Remizières 2000 Cuvée Particulière Syrah (Crozes-Hermitage) $NA. 87 —*R.V. (6/1/2002)*

DOMAINE DES ROCHES NUEVES

Domaine des Roches Neuves 2004 La Marginale Cabernet Franc (Saumur-Champigny) $40. A deliciously fruity wine, packed with red currants. The tannins lend a good texture, finished off with acidity. New wood dominates initially, but then the fruit piles in. 90 —*R.V. (4/1/2007)*

Domaine des Roches Neuves 2005 Terres Chaudes Cabernet Franc (Saumur-Champigny) $28. From one of the hottest (chaudes) parts of the Roches Neuves vineyard, this wine shows great structure and a density of fruit flavors, packed with spice and rich tannins. It is a powerful wine, many miles away from the lightweight Saumur-Champigny of tradition. 92 —*R.V. (4/1/2007)*

Domaine des Roches Neuves 2005 L'Insolite Chenin Blanc (Chinon) $25. A creamy wine with toast and acidity. There is an element of spice and a freshness that comes from some green fruit flavors. Soft, gentle aftertaste. 86 —*R.V. (10/1/2007)*

DOMAINE DES SÉNÉCHAUX

Domaine des Sénéchaux 2003 Rhône Red Blend (Châteauneuf-du-Pape) $37. 88 —*R.V. (12/31/2005)*

DOMAINE DU BERNIER

Domaine du Bernier 2005 Chardonnay (Vin de Pays du Jardin de la France) $8. 87 —*R.V. (12/31/2006)*

DOMAINE DU CAYRON

Domaine du Cayron 2004 Rhône Red Blend (Gigondas) $NA. 88 —*J.C. (11/15/2006)*

DOMAINE DU CHÂTEAU VIEUX

Domaine du Château Vieux 2004 Les Hauts Syrah (Saint-Joseph) $36. 87 —*J.C. (11/15/2006)*

DOMAINE DU CHÊNE

Domaine du Chêne 2003 Anais Syrah (Saint-Joseph) $37. 88 —*J.C. (11/15/2006)*

DOMAINE DU COLOMBIER

Domaine du Colombier 2005 Marsanne (Hermitage) $90. Toasty on the nose, accented by hints of peach, then turning honeyed and rich on the palate, with a slightly oily texture. Layers of velvety richness fill the mouth, with just enough acid to leave a lasting finish. 92 —*J.C. (9/1/2007)*

Domaine du Colombier 2005 Marsanne (Crozes-Hermitage) $20. Made solely of Marsanne, this is a lightly honeyed wine, redolent of almonds and apricots. Fresh, clean and easy, and while it might age, it's probably best consumed young. 88 —*J.C. (9/1/2007)*

Domaine du Colombier 2005 Syrah (Hermitage) $90. Bottled only three weeks prior to review, this wine may have been suffering a little when it was tasted last May. There's a bit of spice, but the wine just isn't that expressive, showing crisp and tight, with some raw tannins on the finish. Seems to have potential, so hold five years or more before trying. 88 —*J.C. (9/1/2007)*

Domaine du Colombier 2005 Syrah (Crozes-Hermitage) $22. Starts off a bit stinky and reductive on the nose, but in the mouth it's fresh and fruity. An easy-drinking Crozes-Hermitage, bursting with cherries, brought into focus by some youthful tannins and crisp acids. Drink now-2012. 87 —*J.C. (9/1/2007)*

Domaine du Colombier 2004 Syrah (Hermitage) $90. Nicely defined on the nose, with precise spice and herbal notes that add complexity to the crunchy red fruit flavors. Ripe tannins and an easy finish make for an approachable Hermitage that should be consumed on the young side. Drink now–2015. 90 —*J.C. (9/1/2007)*

DOMAINE DU CORIANÇON

Domaine du Coriançon 2004 Rhône Red Blend (Vinsobres) $NA. 84 —*J.C. (11/15/2006)*

DOMAINE DU GRAND BOUQUETEAU

Domaine du Grand Bouqueteau 2006 Cabernet Franc (Chinon) $NA. Full and fat, made from Cabernet Franc, this is a somewhat heavy wine, redeemed by the ripe strawberries and touch of caramel. More acidity would be welcome. 83 —*R.V. (7/1/2007)*

Domaine du Grand Bouqueteau 2005 Rosé Cabernet Franc (Chinon) $12. 86 —*J.C. (6/21/2006)*

DOMAINE DU GRAND CROS

Domaine du Grand Cros 2006 Jules Rosé Blend (Côtes de Provence) $15. Named after owner Julian Faulkner, this wine is full, missing zing perhaps but with good ripe strawberry and dusty dryness. With its citrus aftertaste, it works much better with food than as an aperitif. 86 —*R.V. (7/1/2007)*

Domaine du Grand Cros NV Le Grand Cros La Maîtresse Rosé Brut Sparkling Blend (Vin Mousseux) $25. From the Côtes de Provence, this is a lightweight sparkling rosé wine that boasts tasty strawberry and sour-apple flavors. A hint of chocolate creeps in on the finish. 86 —*J.C. (12/15/2007)*

DOMAINE DU GRAND TINEL

Domaine du Grand Tinel 2003 Rhône Red Blend (Châteauneuf-du-Pape) $34. 85 —*R.V. (12/31/2005)*

DOMAINE DU GROS NORE

Domaine du Gros Nore 1999 Rosé Blend (Bandol) $20. 87 —*S.H. (2/1/2003)*

DOMAINE DU JONCIER

Domaine du Joncier 2003 Rhône Red Blend (Lirac) $18. 86 —*J.C. (11/15/2006)*

DOMAINE DU MAS BLANC

Domaine du Mas Blanc 1996 Cuvée La Coume Red Blend (Banyuls) $55. 93 —*(11/15/1999)*

DOMAINE DU MONT SAINT-JEAN

Domaine du Mont Saint-Jean 1999 Merlot (Vin de Pays de L'ile de Beaute) $9. 83 —*D.T. (2/1/2002)*

DOMAINE DU MOULIN

Domaine du Moulin 2004 Vieilles Vignes Rhône Red Blend (Vinsobres) $NA. 87 —*J.C. (11/15/2006)*

DOMAINE DU MURINAIS

Domaine du Murinais 2004 Vieilles Vignes Syrah (Crozes-Hermitage) $22. 84 —*J.C. (11/15/2006)*

DOMAINE DU PESQUIER

Domaine du Pesquier 2004 Rhône Red Blend (Gigondas) $28. 86 —*J.C. (11/15/2006)*

DOMAINE DU ROCHOY

Domaine du Rochoy 2004 Sauvignon Blanc (Sancerre) $25. 88 —*R.V. (8/1/2006)*

DOMAINE DU RONCÉE

Domaine du Roncée 2005 Cabernet Franc (Chinon) $18. Initially, the tannins are very firm, closed, and the wine obviously needs aging or decanting. With time, you get the vibrant red fruits over the taste of young tannins. Better to give it 3–4 years. 90 —*R.V. (4/1/2007)*

Domaine du Roncée 2004 Clos des Marroniers Cabernet Franc (Chinon) $25. A very dense wine, which hints at a future—velvet smooth texture. For the moment, it is concentrated, packed with dark tannins and wood flavors, along with some firm blackberry fruit flavors. Hold for two years. 89 —*R.V. (4/1/2007)*

DOMAINE DU TARIQUET

Domaine du Tariquet 2001 Vinifie Et Eleve En Fut De Chene Chardonnay (Vin de Pays des Côtes de Gascogne) $12. 85 —*M.S. (9/1/2003)*

Domaine du Tariquet 2005 Les Premières Grives Gros Manseng (Vin de Pays des Côtes de Gascogne) $15. 90 Best Buy —*R.V. (12/31/2006)*

Domaine du Tariquet 2005 Sauvignon (Vin de Pays des Côtes de Gascogne) $10. 86 Best Buy —*R.V. (12/31/2006)*

Domaine du Tariquet 2005 Chenin Chardonnay White Blend (Vin de Pays des Côtes de Gascogne) $10. 89 Best Buy —*R.V. (11/15/2006)*

DOMAINE DU TRAPADIS

Domaine du Trapadis 2005 Blovac Grenache (Côtes-du-Rhône) $12. 87 Best Buy —*J.C. (11/15/2006)*

Domaine du Trapadis 2001 Rhône Red Blend (Côtes-du-Rhône) $13. 85 —*R.V. (3/1/2004)*

Domaine du Trapadis 2001 Côtes du Rhône Villages Rasteau Rhône Red Blend (Côtes-du-Rhône Villages) $18. 88 —*R.V. (3/1/2004)*

Domaine du Trapadis 2003 Les Adrès Rasteau Rhône Red Blend (Côtes-du-Rhône Villages) $32. 82 —*J.C. (11/15/2006)*

Domaine du Trapadis 2003 Rasteau Rhône Red Blend (Côtes-du-Rhône Villages) $19. 89 *—J.C. (11/15/2006)*

DOMAINE DU TUNNEL

Domaine du Tunnel 2005 Syrah (Cornas) $NA. Shows superripe, almost jammy aromas of cherries and plums, but those are balanced by sprinklings of minerals and spice. Creamy on the palate, the wine gains focus on the finish, where it leans toward cranberries and dusty tannins. Hold until 2012, at least. **90 Cellar Selection** *—J.C. (9/1/2007)*

Domaine du Tunnel 2004 Syrah (Cornas) $NA. With its scents of cherry preserves, spice and leather, this is a more approachable wine than proprietor Stephane Robert's 2005. The lower acidity gives it a sense of lushness, but it's also slightly less concentrated and intense. Drink now–2014. **88** *—J.C. (9/1/2007)*

DOMAINE DU VIEUX TÉLÉGRAPHE

Domaine du Vieux Télégraphe 2003 La Crau Rhône Red Blend (Châteauneuf-du-Pape) $40. 92 *—R.V. (12/31/2005)*

DOMAINE DROUHIN-LAROZE

Domaine Drouhin-Laroze 2004 Pinot Noir (Bonnes-Mares) $149. This wine is deceptive. Initially it seems full of fresh red fruits and spices. But go deeper and that is just the initial flavor; packed with tannins and a big, powerful core, this is just starting out. In 10 years, this will be a finely balanced, mature wine. **92** *—R.V. (3/1/2007)*

Domaine Drouhin-Laroze 2004 Pinot Noir (Chapelle-Chambertin Grand Cru) $119. This is a big wine, and so young. The fruits are vibrantly fresh, but the tannins are still somewhat set apart. Just wait; this is so intense and concentrated that it will be stunning. For now, admire the structure and the fruit from afar; don't open until 2012. **94 Cellar Selection** *—R.V. (3/1/2007)*

Domaine Drouhin-Laroze 2004 Pinot Noir (Clos Vougeot) $149. Philippe Drouhin has produced a monumental Clos de Vougeot. It has power, intensity and great, solid fruit flavors, particularly black plums. Add spice, some wood, delicious acidity and concentration—this wine will age for years. **95 Cellar Selection** *—R.V. (3/1/2007)*

Domaine Drouhin-Laroze 2004 Pinot Noir (Gevrey-Chambertin) $59. Philippe Drouhin has 30 acres in Gevrey-Chambertin, and the wines of this village are his specialty. This village wine shows just the right power, richness and depth of flavor, topped by delicious fresh, red fruited aromas and flavors. Drink now, or hold for 2–3 years. **90** *—R.V. (3/1/2007)*

Domaine Drouhin-Laroze 2004 Au Closeau Premier Cru Pinot Noir (Gevrey-Chambertin) $89. Au Clouseau is a small (1.3 acres) walled vineyard close to the Grand Crus at the back of the village of Gevrey-Chambertin. The wine is perfumed, structured, still very young. Black fruits, layers of sweet tannins, acidity and some balancing wood flavors—this is a wine with a good future. **92** *—R.V. (3/1/2007)*

Domaine Drouhin-Laroze 2004 Chambertin-Clos-de-Bèze Pinot Noir (Chambertin Clos de Bèze) $169. This wine is all power on a leash. It is a wine that is waiting to escape from its youth, there's that much intensity. It's not huge, but it is concentrated, and the black fruits and acidity are already powering through. It needs 5–6 years. **95 Cellar Selection** *—R.V. (3/1/2007)*

DOMAINE DUJAC

Domaine Dujac 2004 Pinot Noir (Morey Saint-Denis) $75. The Seysses family is widely known outside the region; this wine is from their home village. A firm, but still silky wine, with big fruits and pure, ripe strawberry and red plum flavors. **90** *—R.V. (3/1/2007)*

Domaine Dujac 2004 Pinot Noir (Clos de la Roche) $165. On the northern boundary of Morey Saint-Denis, this vineyard produces wines that show some of the power of neighboring Gevrey-Chambertin. This wine, from the hands of the Seysses family, has all that power; it's packed with very rich red fruits and layers of acidity, sweet tannins and a delicious, lifted finish. Impressive wine, with an obvious ability to age. **94** *—R.V. (3/1/2007)*

Domaine Dujac 2004 Aux Combottes Premier Cru Pinot Noir (Gevrey-Chambertin) $135. A ripe, open, opulent wine, with all the right generous Pinot Noir flavors. But it's also spiced with tannins, flavors of loganberries, pepper, herbs and a healthy layer of acidity. Given its tannic structure, this wine should age well over 10 years. **93** *—R.V. (3/1/2007)*

DOMAINE DUSEIGNEUR

Domaine Duseigneur 2003 Angelique Rhône Red Blend (Lirac) $15. 83 *—J.C. (11/15/2006)*

DOMAINE EHRHART

Domaine Ehrhart 2004 Im Berg Pinot Gris (Alsace) $19. **91 Editors' Choice** *—J.C. (2/1/2006)*

Domaine Ehrhart 2004 Herrenweg Riesling (Alsace) $19. Easy to drink with plenty on offer to keep you interested. The nose suggests essences of beeswax, honeysuckle, pear and citrus with the palate conjuring flavors of ripe red apples and baked peaches. Medium-full body and intensity bring the wine into focus while the delicate fruity finish closes nicely. **88** *(9/1/2007)*

Domaine Ehrhart 2004 Schlosberg Grand Cru Riesling (Alsace) $30. This grand cru selection seems to have a bit of everything. Essences of mint, honeydew and apricot are perfectly integrated with flavors of apple, citrus and honey, creating a broad mouthfeel that's coating without being too heavy. A crisp clean finish cuts through the heft to prevent it from falling flat. **88** *(9/1/2007)*

DOMAINE FAMILLE LIGNÈRES

Domaine Famille Lignères 2002 Pièce de Roche Carignan (Corbières) $30. From a vineyard planted in 1892, this 100% Carignan features exciting spice-driven notes that resemble cinnamon red hots. It's a lighter, more feminine style than the other Lignère wines on the palate, but very flavorful, showing great freshness on the finish. **90** *(9/1/2007)*

Domaine Famille Lignères 2003 Cabanon de Pascal Grenache (Corbières) $22. Pure Grenache, and a wonderful expression of the variety. There's a bit of white pepper upfront, followed by hints of peach or apricot, then rich black cherry fruit framed by silky tannins. Dry and peppery on the finish. **91 Editors' Choice** *(9/1/2007)*

Domaine Famille Lignères 2002 Las Vals Mourvèdre (Corbières) $23. Las Vals is a 600-case bottling of 100% Mourvèdre. It shows plenty of the variety's dark, brooding character, with flavors of chocolate, plum and cola rounded out by a dash of tree bark. Lots of micro-oxygenation has resulted in a creamy, lush mouthfeel, making the wine much more approachable in its youth. **89** *(9/1/2007)*

Domaine Famille Lignères 2003 Aric Rhône Red Blend (Corbières) $20. Perhaps the most complete wine in the current lineup is this blend of one-third each Carignan, Mourvèdre and Syrah, which boasts a delicious combination of Carignan's cinnamon spice, Mourvèdre's dark, plummy fruit and Syrah's savory notes. Picks up hints of smoke and anise on the long finish. **92 Editors' Choice** *(9/1/2007)*

Domaine Famille Lignères 2003 Le Signal Rouge Rhône Red Blend (Corbières) $18. One of the winery's larger cuvées at 5,000 cases, this is a blend of Carignan, Mourvèdre, Syrah and Grenache with wonderfully spice-driven aromatics and a creamy-smooth texture on the palate. Drink now. **88** *(9/1/2007)*

Domaine Famille Lignères 2002 Notre Dame Syrah (Corbières) $30. This is the 100% Syrah cuvée, and it shows powerful varietal character in its smoky, peppery, meaty aromas and flavors. Despite a slightly creamy texture, it doesn't come across as heavy or overbearing. **90** *(9/1/2007)*

DOMAINE FERME SAINT-MARTIN

Domaine Ferme Saint-Martin 2004 Cuvée Saint Martin Rhône Red Blend (Beaumes-de-Venise) $17. 90 *—J.C. (11/15/2006)*

DOMAINE FOND CROZE

Domaine Fond Croze 2004 Cuvée Confidence Rhône Red Blend (Côtes-du-Rhône) $10. 84 *—J.C. (11/15/2006)*

Domaine Fond Croze 2004 Cuvée Vincent de Catari Rhône Red Blend (Côtes-du-Rhône Villages) $12. **88 Best Buy** *—J.C. (11/15/2006)*

DOMAINE FONT DE MICHELLE

Domaine Font de Michelle 2003 Rhône Red Blend (Châteauneuf-du-Pape) $35. 89 *—R.V. (12/31/2005)*

DOMAINE FOUASSIER

Domaine Fouassier 2003 Empreinte Pinot Noir (Sancerre) $NA. Made from 45-year-old Pinot Noir, this intensely perfumed wine is fresh, with bitter cherry and smoky flavors. There is some toast from the 12 months in wood, but the final impression is of red fruits and light acidity. **89** *—R.V. (10/1/2007)*

Domaine Fouassier 2005 Domaine les Grands Groux Sauvignon Blanc (Sancerre) $19. This ripe and creamy wine is full of great flinty and green fruit flavors. It is a pure, fresh expression of the chalk soil Sauvignon, with its crisp aftertaste. **90** *—R.V. (9/1/2007)*

Domaine Fouassier 2004 Domaine les Grands Groux Sauvignon Blanc (Sancerre) $17. 90 *—R.V. (8/1/2006)*

Domaine Fouassier 2005 Le Clos de Bannon Sauvignon Blanc (Sancerre) $22. Made from young vines, giving fresh, but soft flavors. While the concentration may not be there, this makes a delicious light apéritif style, all fruit and crispness. **88** *—R.V. (9/1/2007)*

Domaine Fouassier 2005 Les Chasseignes Sauvignon Blanc (Sancerre) $22. A weighty style of Sancerre, full-bodied and powerful with plenty of big, bold fruit flavors. It's round, ripe and dense, able to hold its own against many spicy food dishes. **89** —*R.V. (9/1/2007)*

Domaine Fouassier 2004 Les Grands Champs Sauvignon Blanc (Sancerre) $NA. 87 —*R.V. (8/1/2006)*

Domaine Fouassier 2005 Les Romains Sauvignon Blanc (Sancerre) $22. Full and ripe, this wine is softly rich rather than mineral, but retains plenty of fresh, crisp green fruit flavors, touched with spice and pepper. **89** —*R.V. (9/1/2007)*

Domaine Fouassier 2003 Mélodie de Guastave Fouassier Sauvignon Blanc (Sancerre) $36. Wood aged, giving a softly smoky and creamy style of wine, the acidity a whisper in the background of green plums and toast. This is smooth, ripe and richly full-bodied, a powerful wine that could still take some aging. **92 Cellar Selection** —*R.V. (9/1/2007)*

DOMAINE FRANÇOIS VILLARD

Domaine François Villard 2005 Fruit d'Avilleran Marsanne (Saint-Joseph) $NA. 84 —*J.C. (11/15/2006)*

Domaine François Villard 2004 Mairlant Syrah (Saint-Joseph) $40. 87 —*J.C. (11/15/2006)*

DOMAINE GALÉVAN

Domaine Galévan 2004 Rhône Red Blend (Côtes-du-Rhône) $NA. 82 —*J.C. (11/15/2006)*

DOMAINE GAVOTY

Domaine Gavoty 2006 Cuvée Clarendon Rosé Blend (Côtes de Provence) $15. All fresh fruits, this top cuvée from Gavoty is a great paean to the perfect rosé character of Grenache. The wine is full of almonds, wild raspberries, white currants and a immensely refreshing acidity. **90 Best Buy** —*R.V. (7/1/2007)*

DOMAINE GEORGES ROUMIER

Domaine Georges Roumier 2000 Pinot Noir (Chambolle-Musigny) $45. 87 —*R.V. (11/1/2002)*

Domaine Georges Roumier 2000 Les Amoureuses Premier Cru Pinot Noir (Chambolle-Musigny) $100. 91 —*R.V. (11/1/2002)*

DOMAINE GEORGES VERNAY

Domaine Georges Vernay 2002 Blonde de Seigneur Syrah (Côte Rôtie) $55. 94 Cellar Selection —*R.V. (2/1/2005)*

Domaine Georges Vernay 1999 Maison Rouge Syrah (Côte Rôtie) $45. 88 —*R.V. (6/1/2002)*

Domaine Georges Vernay 2000 Les Terrasses de l'Empire Viognier (Condrieu) $57. 93 —*R.V. (6/1/2002)*

DOMAINE GERARD TREMBLAY

Domaine Gerard Tremblay 1998 Chardonnay (Chablis) $NA. 84 —*R.V. (6/1/2001)*

DOMAINE GIRARD

Domaine Girard 2003 La Garenne Sauvignon Blanc (Sancerre) $20. 87 *(7/1/2005)*

DOMAINE GRAMENON

Domaine Gramenon 1998 Les Laurentides Rhône Red Blend (Côtes-du-Rhône) $16. 88 —*M.M. (12/31/2000)*

DOMAINE GRAND VENEUR

Domaine Grand Veneur 1998 Rhône Red Blend (Côtes-du-Rhône) $9. 86 —*J.C. (12/31/2000)*

DOMAINE GROS FRÈRE ET SOEUR

Domaine Gros Frère et Soeur 2004 Pinot Noir (Vosne-Romanée) $45. Produced by Bernard Gros, this wine is from the heart of the Gros dynasty's vineyards. It has the elegance of fine village Vosne-Romanée, with just an extra touch of aristocratic structure and impressively fresh fruit. The aftertaste is pure fruit. **90** —*R.V. (3/1/2007)*

Domaine Gros Frère et Soeur 2002 Pinot Noir (Echezeaux) $NA. 91 —*R.V. (9/1/2004)*

Domaine Gros Frère et Soeur 2004 Clos de Vougeot Pinot Noir (Clos Vougeot) $90. A beautiful, velvet-smooth wine, with a structure that shows some tannins. But more important, the wine has an opulence and splendor that go beyond the delicious fruitiness. A fine wine, from one of the best parcels of Clos de Vougeot. **94** —*R.V. (3/1/2007)*

Domaine Gros Frère et Soeur 2002 Premier Cru Pinot Noir (Vosne-Romanée) $NA. 89 —*R.V. (9/1/2004)*

DOMAINE GROSSET

Domaine Grosset 2003 Cairanne Rhône Red Blend (Côtes-du-Rhône Villages) $16. 87 —*J.C. (2/1/2005)*

DOMAINE HENRI PERROT-MINOT

Domaine Henri Perrot-Minot 2000 Vieilles Vignes Pinot Noir (Mazoyeres-Chambertin) $109. 93 Cellar Selection *(10/1/2003)*

DOMAINE HENRY PELLÉ

Domaine Henry Pellé 2003 Morogues Sauvignon Blanc (Menetou-Salon) $23. 86 *(7/1/2005)*

DOMAINE HERING

Domaine Hering 2005 Côtes De Barr Riesling (Alsace) $20. Snappy citrus and a crushed stone minerality complement the light, lean structure of the wine. Definitely designed for easy drinking, this would be a deft pairing with fried seafood, having no problem lifting oily textures off your palate. **85** *(9/1/2007)*

DOMAINE HOUCHART

Domaine Houchart 2000 Red Blend (Côtes de Provence) $11. 83 —*M.S. (9/1/2003)*

DOMAINE HUET L'ECHANSONNE

Domaine Huet l'Echansonne 2003 Le Haut-Lieu Demi-Sec Chenin Blanc (Vouvray) $40. 89 —*R.V. (4/1/2005)*

Domaine Houchart 2006 Cuvée Sainte Victoire Rosé Blend (Côtes de Provence) $15. The vineyard for this wine is in the shadow of the massive Mount Ste Victoire. This is a lively wine, full of strawberries and cream. It has a touch of caramel, but it is more about freshness, acidity and crisp berry fruits. **89** —*R.V. (7/1/2007)*

Domaine Houchart 2006 Rosé Blend (Côtes de Provence) $10. From one of the estates owned by the Quiot family, Domaine Houchart's rosé is a simple wine, touched with caramel, bubble gum and light tannins. Soft and full, this could use a bit more freshness. **84** *(7/1/2007)*

Domaine Houchart 2005 Rosé Blend (Côtes de Provence) $10. This pale rosé features a lovely salmon hue and a light, crisp mouthfeel. Shows some bubble gum aromas and flavors, but also hints of anise, mineral and a dry finish. **84** —*J.C. (7/1/2007)*

Domaine Houchart 2006 Tête de Cuvée Rosé Blend (Côtes de Provence) $15. Should rosé have barrel aging? With 10% of this wine aged in wood, there is definitely a broad palate, a sense of ripeness. But what this wine gains in power, it loses in freshness and fruitiness. It certainly works well with food, less so as an apéritif. **89** —*R.V. (7/1/2007)*

DOMAINE J-F MUGNIER

Domaine J-F Mugnier 1999 Pinot Noir (Musigny) $179. 94 Editors' Choice —*R.V. (11/1/2002)*

Domaine J-F Mugnier 1999 Les Fuées Premier Cru Pinot Noir (Chambolle-Musigny) $NA. 91 —*R.V. (11/1/2002)*

DOMAINE JACQUES PRIEUR

Domaine Jacques Prieur 2004 Clos de Mazeray Chardonnay (Meursault) $69. 90 —*R.V. (12/1/2006)*

Domaine Jacques Prieur 2004 Les Combettes Premier Cru Chardonnay (Puligny-Montrachet) $110. 93 Editors' Choice —*R.V. (12/1/2006)*

Domaine Jacques Prieur 2002 Chambertin Pinot Noir (Gevrey-Chambertin) $192. 93 —*R.V. (9/1/2004)*

Domaine Jacques Prieur 1999 Champs Pimont Premier Cru Pinot Noir (Beaune) $48. 92 *(1/1/2004)*

Domaine Jacques Prieur 2002 Clos Vougeot Pinot Noir (Clos Vougeot) $135. 94 —*R.V. (9/1/2004)*

Domaine Jacques Prieur 2002 Greves Premier Cru Pinot Noir (Beaune) $61. 91 —*R.V. (9/1/2004)*

DOMAINE JACQUES PRIEUR & ANTONIN RODET

Domaine Jacques Prieur & Antonin Rodet 1999 Clos de las Feguine Premier Cru Bordeaux Blend (Beaune) $50. 89 —*P.G. (11/1/2002)*

DOMAINE JAMET

Domaine Jamet 2004 Syrah (Côte Rôtie) $96. Fragrantly herbal and peppery on the nose, even coming a little close to vegetal before pulling back and showing more cherry fruit. This is a lightweight effort, but very pretty and perfumed, ideal for drinking while waiting for the blockbuster 2003 to mature. Drink now–2015. **90** —*J.C. (9/1/2007)*

Domaine Jamet 2003 Syrah (Côte Rôtie) $96. Sure, this wine shows the effects of the hot summer in its slightly jammy raspberry flavors, but there's also incredible complexity to complement the fruit intensity—Asian spices, tea, pepper and meat, to name just a few nuances. It's all wrapped in a blanket of soft tannins, but stays fresh-tasting thanks to great minerality despite low acidity. Drink now–2030 or beyond. **97 Cellar Selection** *—J.C. (9/1/2007)*

Domaine Jamet 2002 Syrah (Côte Rôtie) $88. 90 *—R.V. (2/1/2005)*

DOMAINE JAMMES

Domaine Jammes 2006 Exquisit Rosé Blend (Vin de Pays de L'Aude) $15. If you like elegant, designer labels, then Matthieu Jammes is your man. His whole range would fit into any cool bar in any city. This blend of Cinsualt and Grenache is probably his best wine, vibrant, fruit packed and with great, crisp acidity over ripe strawberries. 89 *—R.V. (7/1/2007)*

Domaine Jammes 2006 G Rosé Blend (Vin de Pays de L'Aude) $10. "G" stands for Grenache, and this 100% Grenache with its orange pink color is quintessential Mediterranean rosé. It is lightly spicy, with crème brulée flavors and fresh wild strawberries. The vibrant acidity gives it a great lift. **90 Best Buy** *—R.V. (7/1/2007)*

Domaine Jammes 2006 Le Rosé du Domaine Rosé Blend (Vin de Pays de L'Aude) $8. Distinctive white currant aromas on this Cabernet Sauvignon rosé. It is full of currants and fresh acidity, but with a typical Cabernet structure of tannins, and a background of dryness. At the end, the acidity is dominant. **86 Best Buy** *—R.V. (7/1/2007)*

Domaine Jammes 2006 Pink Rosé Blend (Vin de Pays de L'Aude) $10. In fact, more like the lightest off white rather than pink. The taste though has a good touch of red cherries and fresh white grapefruit, shot through with acidity. Crisp, clean, light. **86 Best Buy** *—R.V. (7/1/2007)*

Domaine Jammes 2006 Sakurairo Rosé Blend (Vin de Pays de L'Aude) $10. A 100% Cinsualt wine, designed to partner sushi. That explains the extreme lightness, the crispness, the acidity. There is a touch of herbal character, of thyme. It is certainly not for apéritif. **85 Best Buy** *—R.V. (7/1/2007)*

DOMAINE JAUME

Domaine Jaume 2004 Génération Rhône Red Blend (Côtes-du-Rhône) $10. 82 *—J.C. (11/15/2006)*

DOMAINE JEAN GRIVOT

Domaine Jean Grivot 2004 Pinot Noir (Echezeaux) $140. The wine tastes from the center outwards, the reverse of peeling fruit. It leads from the rich fruit that is at the heart and goes outwards towards tannins, new wood and spice. It all comes together on the finish. This is a wine of importance and stature. 93 *—R.V. (3/1/2007)*

Domaine Jean Grivot 2004 Pinot Noir (Vosne-Romanée) $45. This is a very rounded wine, balancing the dusty and dryish tannins against the sweet, fresh, juicy fruit. On the finish is the acidity—a great lift of freshness and lightness. 89 *—R.V. (3/1/2007)*

Domaine Jean Grivot 2004 Pinot Noir (Clos Vougeot) $115. Owner of one of the largest parcels of Clos de Vougeot, Grivot makes one of the benchmark wines from the vineyard. This starts out dry to taste, but then there is an explosion of strawberry and red currant fruits as the tannins fall back to reveal a wine that, while big, is certainly not overwhelming—leave that to more powerful vintages than 2004. 94 *—R.V. (3/1/2007)*

Domaine Jean Grivot 2004 Les Beaux Monts Premier Cru Pinot Noir (Vosne-Romanée) $90. Starts with firm fruits, showing more tannin than fruitiness. Then those fruits begin to shine and glow through the structure, although on the finish the dryness returns along with some new wood flavors. 90 *—R.V. (3/1/2007)*

Domaine Jean Grivot 2004 Les Boudots Premier Cru Pinot Noir (Nuits-St.-Georges) $90. Right at the northern end of Nuits-St.-Georges, this premier cru vineyard combines the elegance of neighboring Vosne-Romanée with the more savage character of Nuits. There is a wild, rustic element, plus rounded black fruits and delicious freshness under the rich tannins. 91 *—R.V. (3/1/2007)*

Domaine Jean Grivot 2004 Les Charmois Pinot Noir (Nuits-St.-Georges) $45. There is dryness at the heart of this wine—it is, after all, a Nuits-Saint-Georges. But it is surrounded with ripe berries, great freshness and pure acidity. Surprisingly, there is some bitter chocolate on the finish. 88 *—R.V. (3/1/2007)*

Domaine Jean Grivot 2004 Pinot Noir (Richebourg) $375. This will need years to develop fully—15–20 years probably. For now, it is firmly tannic, very dry and powerful, with juicy fruit and acidity somewhere in there. The elements are not yet knitted together. When they are, this will be a stupendous wine. **95 Cellar Selection** *—R.V. (3/1/2007)*

Domaine Jean Grivot 2004 Roncière Premier Cru Pinot Noir (Nuits-St.-Georges) $90. Just on the south side of the city of Nuits Saint-Georges, this vineyard seems to produce earthy, dry wines that need years to open up. This wine has those qualities, along with a mineral, herbal character. Don't touch it for at least five years. 89 *—R.V. (3/1/2007)*

DOMAINE JEAN ROYER

Domaine Jean Royer 2003 Cuvée Prestige Rhône Red Blend (Châteauneuf-du-Pape) $70. 91 *—R.V. (12/31/2005)*

DOMAINE JEAN-MICHEL GERIN

Domaine Jean-Michel Gerin 1999 Champin le Seigneur Rhône Red Blend (Côte Rôtie) $27. 92 *—R.V. (6/1/2002)*

Domaine Jean-Michel Gerin 2000 La Loye White Blend (Condrieu) $24. 91 *—R.V. (6/1/2002)*

DOMAINE JO PITHON

Domaine Jo Pithon 2005 Chenin Blanc (Savennières) $35. Savennières is a new vineyard acquisition for Jo Pithon, with vines planted on 2.5 acres in 2000. It is properly steely, but shows also richness and intense concentration; an impressive start for a vineyard that will be worth watching as the vines age. 89 *—R.V. (10/1/2007)*

Domaine Jo Pithon 2005 Les 4 Villages Chenin Blanc (Coteaux du Layon) $31. A blend of wines from four different vineyards to make a wine that is partly botrytised, but has a fresh character, along with raisin flavors. Crisp acidity partners the apricots. Drink with food or as an apéritif. 88 *—R.V. (10/1/2007)*

Domaine Jo Pithon 2004 Les Bergères Chenin Blanc (Anjou) $27. Intensely mineral, this is the finest of Jo Pithon's range of single-vineyard dry Anjou wines. It is packed with powerful green fruits lending acidity; there is a touch of wood, but this is more about fruit. To finish, there is ripe, but very dry, structure. 92 *—R.V. (10/1/2007)*

Domaine Jo Pithon 2005 Les Pépinières Chenin Blanc (Anjou) $37. Smooth and elegant with the right Chenin minerality and acidity. There are flavors of kiwi and white currants laced through with vanilla and an intensely refreshing acidity. 90 *—R.V. (10/1/2007)*

Domaine Jo Pithon 2005 Les Treilles Chenin Blanc (Anjou) $37. One of a range of three single-vineyard dry wines from Jo Pithon, this is the firmest, needing long aging as the Chenin develops its secondary flavors. For the moment, it's very dry and closed down, with green fruits, but dominated by structure. Wait five years. **91 Cellar Selection** *—R.V. (10/1/2007)*

Domaine Jo Pithon 2004 Les Varennes Chenin Blanc (Quarts de Chaume) $152. The Quarts de Chaume, the four fingers of land that rise above the Layon Valley, are one of the pinnacles of sweet wines in the Loire. Showing botrytis and layers of dryness over the honey and peach jelly flavors, but also has great freshness. The aftertaste just lasts. 92 *—R.V. (10/1/2007)*

DOMAINE KLIPFEL

Domaine Klipfel 2004 Kirchberg Grand Cru Riesling (Alsace) $16. Vegetal notes and flinty chalk dominate the nose, while essences of green apple and lemon struggle to overcome the intrinsic greenness. The short finish gives no justice to the lush, creamy texture. 84 *(9/1/2007)*

DOMAINE LA BOUISSIERE

Domaine la Bouissiere 2004 Tradition Rhône Red Blend (Gigondas) $28. 90 *—J.C. (11/15/2006)*

DOMAINE LA CABOTTE

Domaine la Cabotte 2004 Gabriel Rhône Red Blend (Côtes-du-Rhône) $14. 86 *—J.C. (11/15/2006)*

DOMAINE LA CHEVALERIE

Domaine la Chevalerie 2004 Chevalerie Cabernet Franc (Bourgueil) $22. From Pierre Caslot, one of the top traditional winemakers in Bourgueil, comes this firm, quite tannic wine, whose solid structure is compensated by the fresh raspberry flavors. This needs at least three years aging, but it does show the firm, classic side of Bourgueil. 89 *—R.V. (4/1/2007)*

Domaine la Chevalerie 2004 Galichets Cabernet Franc (Bourgueil) $20. From 35-year-old vines, Galichets is a richly dense wine, with big, open, red-fruit flavors balanced by solid tannins and velvet acidity. It is a wine designed to age, firm and dark to finish. 90 *—R.V. (4/1/2007)*

DOMAINE LA COSTE

Domaine la Coste 2000 Ultra Red Blend (Coteaux d'Aix en Provence) $28. 90 *—M.S. (2/1/2003)*

DOMAINE LA GARRIGUE

Domaine la Garrigue 2004 Traditional Reserve Rhône Red Blend (Vacqueyras) $19. 87 *—J.C. (11/15/2006)*

DOMAINE LA GRANDE BLANCHE

Domaine la Grande Blanche 2006 Rosé Blend (Côtes de Provence) $9. In its traditional skittle bottle, this is definitely a wine for the table. It is fresh and clean, full of fresh red fruits, with hints of vanilla and a soft, almost sweet aftertaste. 84 —*R.V. (7/1/2007)*

DOMAINE LA HITAIRE

Domaine la Hitaire 2005 Hors Saison Sémillon-Sauvignon Blanc (Vin de Pays des Côtes de Gascogne) $11. 84 —*R.V. (12/31/2006)*

DOMAINE LA MILLIÈRE

Domaine la Millière 2003 Vieilles Vignes Rhône Red Blend (Côtes-du-Rhône) $NA. 84 —*J.C. (11/15/2006)*

DOMAINE LA MONTAGNETTE

Domaine la Montagnette 2004 Rhône Red Blend (Côtes-du-Rhône Villages) $12. 90 Best Buy —*J.C. (11/15/2006)*

DOMAINE LA REMEJEANNE

Domaine la Remejeanne 2004 Les Arbousiers Rhône Red Blend (Côtes-du-Rhône) $NA. 87 —*J.C. (11/15/2006)*

DOMAINE LA ROQUÈTE

Domaine la Roquète 2003 Rhône Red Blend (Châteauneuf-du-Pape) $40. 93 Cellar Selection —*R.V. (12/31/2005)*

DOMAINE LA ROUBINE

Domaine la Roubine 2004 Rhône Red Blend (Gigondas) $24. 91 —*J.C. (11/15/2006)*

DOMAINE LAFLAIVE

Domaine Laflaive 2001 Chardonnay (Bourgogne) $NA. 88 —*S.H. (1/1/2002)*

Domaine Laflaive 1997 White Blend (Bâtard-Montrachet) $NA. 93 —*S.H. (1/1/2002)*

Domaine Laflaive 1998 Les Pucelles Premier Cru White Blend (Puligny-Montrachet) $NA. 85 —*S.H. (1/1/2002)*

DOMAINE LAFOND

Domaine Lafond 2004 Roc-Epine Rhône Red Blend (Côtes-du-Rhône) $9. 87 Best Buy —*J.C. (11/15/2006)*

Domaine Lafond 2003 Roc-Epine La Ferme Romaine Rhône Red Blend (Lirac) $28. 92 Editors' Choice —*J.C. (11/15/2006)*

Domaine Lafond 2005 Roc-Epine Rosé Rosé Blend (Tavel) $17. 89 —*J.C. (6/21/2006)*

DOMAINE LAMARGUE

Domaine Lamargue 2000 Merlot (Vin de Pays d'Oc) $13. 85 —*D.T. (2/1/2002)*

DOMAINE LAMY-PILLOT

Domaine Lamy-Pillot 2004 Chardonnay (Chassagne-Montrachet) $49. 88 —*R.V. (12/1/2006)*

Domaine Lamy-Pillot 2004 Morgeot Premier Cru Chardonnay (Chassagne-Montrachet) $56. 92 —*R.V. (12/1/2006)*

DOMAINE LANDRAT-GUYOLLOT

Domaine Landrat-Guyollot 2005 La Roselière Chasselas (Pouilly-sur-Loire) $27. The other wine of Pouilly-sur-Loire (way behind Pouilly-Fumé in quantity) is this Chasselas grape-based wine, from a much older tradition. This example shows delicious honeysuckle aromas and flavors of honey, flowers and nuts. A rarity, but a style that shouldn't disappear. 87 —*R.V. (10/1/2007)*

Domaine Landrat-Guyollot 2005 Carte Noire Sauvignon Blanc (Pouilly-Fumé) $33. A selection from old vines and made only in good years, Landrat-Guyollot's Carte Noire is rich and creamy, with concentrated white and yellow fruit flavors, some melon, white currants and pink grapefruit. Weighty, promising aging over five years. 91 Cellar Selection —*R.V. (9/1/2007)*

Domaine Landrat-Guyollot 2005 La Rambarde Sauvignon Blanc (Pouilly-Fumé) $22. Light and fresh, this is elegant with green fruits, yellow peach, a mineral layer and citrus. A rambarde was a flat-bottomed boat which used to transport wine from the Loire to Paris. 87 —*R.V. (9/1/2007)*

DOMAINE LAROCHE

Domaine Laroche 1997 Les Blanchots Chardonnay (Chablis) $85. 92 *(11/15/2000)*

Domaine Laroche 2003 Les Clos Grand Cru Chardonnay (Chablis) $75. 91 —*R.V. (9/1/2005)*

Domaine Laroche 1997 Les Vaillons Viellies Vignes Premier Cru Chardonnay (Chablis) $46. 88 —*J.C. (11/1/2000)*

Domaine Laroche 2003 Premier Cru Les Fourchaumes Chardonnay (Chablis) $40. 90 —*R.V. (9/1/2005)*

Domaine Laroche 2003 Reserve de l'Obédience Grand Cru Chardonnay (Chablis) $100. 92 —*R.V. (9/1/2005)*

Domaine Laroche 2003 St. Martin Chardonnay (Chablis) $25. 86 —*J.C. (9/1/2005)*

DOMAINE LE CLOS DE CAVEAU

Domaine le Clos de Caveau 2003 Clos de Caveau Rhône Red Blend (Vacqueyras) $23. 91 —*J.C. (11/15/2006)*

DOMAINE LE CLOS DU CAILLOU

Domaine le Clos du Caillou 2003 Les Quartz Rhône Red Blend (Châteauneuf-du-Pape) $90. 90 —*R.V. (12/31/2005)*

DOMAINE LE COLOMBIER

Domaine le Colombier 2004 Vieilles Vignes Rhône Red Blend (Vacqueyras) $15. 90 Best Buy —*J.C. (11/15/2006)*

DOMAINE LE COUROULU

Domaine le Couroulu 2003 Vieilles Vignes Grenache-Syrah (Vacqueyras) $30. 90 —*J.C. (11/15/2006)*

Domaine le Couroulu 2000 Rhône Red Blend (Côtes-du-Rhône) $12. 86 —*R.V. (3/1/2004)*

Domaine le Couroulu 2000 Cuvée Classique Rhône Red Blend (Vacqueyras) $13. 87 —*R.V. (3/1/2004)*

Domaine le Couroulu 2002 Rhône White Blend (Vacqueyras) $12. 83 —*R.V. (3/1/2004)*

DOMAINE LEFLAIVE

Domaine Leflaive 2003 Chardonnay (Puligny-Montrachet) $80. 90 —*R.V. (12/1/2006)*

Domaine Leflaive 2003 Les Pucelles Premier Cru Chardonnay (Puligny-Montrachet) $175. 96 Editors' Choice —*R.V. (12/1/2006)*

DOMAINE LES AMOURIERS

Domaine les Amouriers 2004 Signature Rhône Red Blend (Vacqueyras) $25. 91 —*J.C. (11/15/2006)*

DOMAINE LES APHILLANTHES

Domaine les Aphillanthes 2003 Le Cros Rhône Red Blend (Côtes-du-Rhône Villages) $NA. 90 Editors' Choice —*J.C. (11/15/2006)*

DOMAINE LES BRUYERES

Domaine les Bruyeres 2004 Syrah (Crozes-Hermitage) $22. 85 —*J.C. (11/15/2006)*

DOMAINE LES GOUBERT

Domaine les Goubert 2000 Cuvée Florence Grenache-Syrah (Gigondas) $50. 88 —*J.C. (11/15/2005)*

DOMAINE LES HERITIERS DU COMTE LAFON

Domaine les Heritiers du Comte Lafon 2003 Clos de la Crochette Chardonnay (Mâcon-Chardonnay) $29. 86 —*J.C. (11/15/2005)*

DOMAINE LES LOGES DE LA FOLIE

Domaine les Loges de la Folie NV Brut Chenin Blanc (Montlouis-sur-Loire) $NA. Creamy, soft, but pricked with high acidity, this dry sparkling wine from Montlouis is made from Chenin Blanc. In the mouth, there's an herbal element, vivid acidity and a crisp aftertaste. 86 —*R.V. (12/15/2007)*

DOMAINE LIGNÈRES

Domaine Lignères 2005 La Baronne Rosé Blend (Vin de Pays de Hauterive) $10. A wine from the cool vineyards of the Montagne d'Alaric in the Aude, this is a fresh style, geared to summer picnics. With its flavors of vivid red cherries, hints of white chocolate and crisp acidity, this is a perfect, easy rosé. Imported by Acadia Imports. 88 Best Buy *(7/1/2007)*

DOMAINE LES PALLIÈRES

Domaine les Pallières 2003 Rhône Red Blend (Gigondas) $35. 89 —*J.C. (11/15/2006)*

DOMAINE LONG-DEPAQUIT

Domaine Long-Depaquit 1998 Vaudsir Chardonnay (Chablis) $NA. 91 —*R.V. (6/1/2001)*

DOMAINE LOUIS CARILLON

Domaine Louis Carillon 2004 Les Perrières Premier Cru Chardonnay (Puligny-Montrachet) $95. 92 —*R.V. (12/31/2006)*

DOMAINE MACHARD DE GRAMONT

Domaine Machard de Gramont 2000 Les Nazoires Pinot Noir (Chambolle-Musigny) $NA. 91 —*R.V. (11/1/2002)*

DOMAINE MARCEL DEISS

Domaine Marcel Deiss 2002 Altenberg de Bergheim Grand Cru Alsace White Blend (Alsace) $95. 92 —*J.C. (8/1/2006)*

Domaine Marcel Deiss 2001 Grasberg Alsace White Blend (Alsace) $58. 91 —*R.V. (4/1/2005)*

Domaine Marcel Deiss 2000 Huebuhl Alsace White Blend (Alsace) $47. 96 Editors' Choice —*R.V. (4/1/2005)*

Domaine Marcel Deiss 2001 Rotenberg Alsace White Blend (Alsace) $47. 95 —*R.V. (4/1/2005)*

Domaine Marcel Deiss 2002 Schoffweg Alsace White Blend (Alsace) $47. 92 —*R.V. (4/1/2005)*

Domaine Marcel Deiss 2001 Bergheim Gewürztraminer (Alsace) $36. 90 —*R.V. (4/1/2005)*

Domaine Marcel Deiss 2001 Saint Hippolyte Gewürztraminer (Alsace) $30. 87 —*R.V. (4/1/2005)*

Domaine Marcel Deiss 2002 Bennwihr Pinot Blanc (Alsace) $17. 88 —*R.V. (4/1/2005)*

Domaine Marcel Deiss 2002 Bergheim Pinot Blanc (Alsace) $20. 91 Editors' Choice —*R.V. (4/1/2005)*

Domaine Marcel Deiss 2002 Beblenheim Pinot Gris (Alsace) $NA. 90 —*R.V. (2/1/2006)*

Domaine Marcel Deiss 2000 Bergheim Pinot Gris (Alsace) $35. 87 —*R.V. (4/1/2005)*

Domaine Marcel Deiss 2001 Sélection de Grains Nobles Pinot Gris (Alsace) $NA. 95 —*R.V. (2/1/2006)*

Domaine Marcel Deiss 2000 Burlenberg Pinot Noir (Alsace) $34. 89 —*R.V. (4/1/2005)*

Domaine Marcel Deiss 2005 Riesling (Alsace) $27. Minerality, peach, melon and sweet pea give way to a fuller bodied mouthfeel with strong intensity. Tropical and honeyed, the finish falls a little short, needing a tinge more acidity to lift those heavy flavors. 86 *(9/1/2007)*

Domaine Marcel Deiss 2002 Beblenheim Riesling (Alsace) $22. 91 —*R.V. (11/1/2005)*

Domaine Marcel Deiss 2002 Saint-Hippolyte Riesling (Alsace) $25. 88 —*R.V. (11/1/2005)*

DOMAINE MARECHAL-CAILLOT

Domaine Marechal-Caillot 1999 Ladoix Cote de Beaune Bordeaux Blend (France) $18. 88 —*P.G. (11/1/2002)*

DOMAINE MARECHAL-CAILLOT

Domaine Marechal-Caillot 1999 Pinot Noir (Bourgogne) $15. 87 —*P.G. (11/1/2002)*

DOMAINE MASSAMIER LA MIGNARDE

Domaine Massamier la Mignarde 2005 Cuvée des Oliviers Rhône Red Blend (Vin de Pays des Coteaux de Peyriac) $10. 87 Best Buy —*R.V. (12/31/2006)*

Domaine Massamier la Mignarde 2006 Cuvée des Oliviers Rosé Blend (Vin de Pays des Coteaux de Peyriac) $10. A slightly dusty textured wine, suggesting tannins as well as fresh fruit. From the Minervois region, this vin de pays has weight, but carries its power lightly, just hinting at caramel among all the red fruits. 88 Best Buy —*R.V. (7/1/2007)*

DOMAINE MASSON-BLONDELET

Domaine Masson-Blondelet 2004 Les Angelots Sauvignon Blanc (Pouilly-Fumé) $18. 91 —*R.V. (8/1/2006)*

Domaine Masson-Blondelet 2004 Villa Paulus Sauvignon Blanc (Pouilly-Fumé) $18. 92 Editors' Choice —*R.V. (8/1/2006)*

DOMAINE MATHIEU

Domaine Mathieu 2003 Marquis Anselme Mathieu Rhône Red Blend (Châteauneuf-du-Pape) $35. 87 —*R.V. (12/31/2005)*

DOMAINE MICHEL BROCK

Domaine Michel Brock 2003 Le Coteau Sauvignon Blanc (Sancerre) $20. 87 *(7/1/2005)*

DOMAINE MICHEL MAGNIEN ET FILS

Domaine Michel Magnien et Fils 2004 Pinot Noir (Clos de la Roche) $133. Hugely perfumed, this also boasts a big, chewy tannic structure, as befits a wine that should age. The flavors are of dark fruits with a hint at leather. The acidity at least is fresh, although there is bitterness on the finish. 89 —*R.V. (3/1/2007)*

Domaine Michel Magnien et Fils 2004 Pinot Noir (Bourgogne) $17. A very fruity wine, with touches of new wood, this is certainly in a modern style, with spice from the wood and some tastes of extraction. But the juiciness is good and the acidity is fresh, so that the wine ends up pleasantly in balance. 83 —*R.V. (3/1/2007)*

Domaine Michel Magnien et Fils 2004 Le Très Girard Pinot Noir (Morey Saint-Denis) $47. Earthy and initially animal, this wine lacks freshness. The tannins are important here, while the fruit only appears after the wine has been in the mouth for several moments. Being charitable, this is young; being less so, it is badly old-fashioned. 87 —*R.V. (3/1/2007)*

Domaine Michel Magnien et Fils 2004 Les Chaffots Premier Cru Pinot Noir (Morey Saint-Denis) $93. This wine epitomizes the firmness of Morey along with its often exotic spice and black fruit flavors, a warming wine that just keeps to the right side of too much extraction. 91 —*R.V. (3/1/2007)*

Domaine Michel Magnien et Fils 2004 Les Goulots Premier Cru Pinot Noir (Gevrey-Chambertin) $NA. A big, burly wine, full of perfumed fruits and a dry tannins thread that runs right through. Its fruit is ripe and intensely flavored, with some jammy sweetness. Acidity floats in on the finish. 87 —*R.V. (3/1/2007)*

Domaine Michel Magnien et Fils 2004 Les Millandes Premier Cru Pinot Noir (Morey Saint-Denis) $90. Powerful, this is a fine wine with good, firm tannins that just keep the burgeoning fruit in check. It has great balance, with a touch of wood, plenty of fresh acidity and spice. 90 —*R.V. (3/1/2007)*

Domaine Michel Magnien et Fils 2004 Les Sentiers Premier Cru Pinot Noir (Chambolle-Musigny) $93. A big, rounded wine, which still manages to preserve some of the right Chambolle elegance. There are tannins, but they stay discreetly behind the fresh black fruits and the finishing acidity. 89 —*R.V. (3/1/2007)*

DOMAINE MICHEL THOMAS ET FILS

Domaine Michel Thomas et Fils 2005 Sauvignon Blanc (Sancerre) $19. 90 —*R.V. (8/1/2006)*

DOMAINE MICHELAS ST JEMM

Domaine Michelas St Jemm 2003 Syrah (Crozes-Hermitage) $18. 89 —*J.C. (11/15/2006)*

DOMAINE MIQUEL

Domaine Miquel 2000 Merlot (Vin de Pays d'Oc) $9. 83 —*M.S. (9/1/2003)*

DOMAINE MOILLARD

Domaine Moillard 2003 Corton Charlemagne Chardonnay (Corton-Charlemagne) $120. 90 —*R.V. (9/1/2005)*

Domaine Moillard 2004 Pinot Noir (Savigny-lès-Beaune) $29. Soft, gentle, this wine shows the perfumed side of Pinot Noir. Sure, there are some tannins, but that is only a sideshow to the aromatics and flavors of sweet fruit and acidity. 87 —*R.V. (3/1/2007)*

Domaine Moillard 2003 Pinot Noir (Chorey-lès-Beaune) $25. 87 —*R.V. (9/1/2005)*

Domaine Moillard 2003 Pinot Noir (Nuits-St.-Georges) $45. 87 —*R.V. (9/1/2005)*

Domaine Moillard 2002 Pinot Noir (Savigny-lès-Beaune) $25. 82 —*J.C. (11/15/2005)*

Domaine Moillard 2004 Beaune-Epenottes Premier Cru Pinot Noir (Beaune) $35. Lightweight, but with a firm tannic background, this wine doesn't completely hang together. It's rather too dry for the fruit, although the flavors of fresh strawberries are attractive when they do come through. 85 —*R.V. (3/1/2007)*

Domaine Moillard 2004 Beaux-Monts Premier Cru Pinot Noir (Vosne-Romanée) $75. Rather dense, tannic and dusty, this wine shows a harder side of Pinot Noir. Fresh strawberry flavors appear, but the toughness dominates. 87 —*R.V. (3/1/2007)*

Domaine Moillard 2004 Pinot Noir (Clos Vougeot) $110. Dark and hugely tannic, this is a wine that is all about structure—black fruit and wood flavors give it a foursquare shape. At this stage, the dryness dominates, but given 3–4 years, the fruit will develop further. **90** *—R.V. (3/1/2007)*

Domaine Moillard 2003 Clos des Grandes Vignes Premier Cru Pinot Noir (Nuits-St.-Georges) $55. **89** *—R.V. (9/1/2005)*

Domaine Moillard 2003 Epenottes Premier Cru Pinot Noir (Pommard) $65. **90** *—R.V. (9/1/2005)*

Domaine Moillard 2004 Les Malconsorts Premier Cru Pinot Noir (Vosne-Romanée) $80. This dark-hued wine is a black fruit bonanza, concentrated and solid. It also has ripeness, herbal flavors, aromas of leather and packed, tight tannins. Designed for aging—nothing less than five years will do. **90** *—R.V. (3/1/2007)*

Domaine Moillard 2004 Les Thorey Premier Cru Pinot Noir (Nuits-St.-Georges) $55. This Les Thorey, hard by the town of Nuits-St.-Georges, is a vineyard that shows the minerality as well as the firmness of good wines from this commune. It has power rather than charm, a solid, foursquare wine that needs four or five years to develop. **89** *—R.V. (3/1/2007)*

Domaine Moillard 2004 Epenots Premier Cru Pinot Noir (Pommard) $60. Pommard has a reputation for producing wines as full and flavorful as the richness of its name suggests. So it is with this wine from the domaine owned by the Thomas family. It is rich, powerful, packed with firm tannins and flavors of rich red fruits, spice and smoke. There is acidity on the finish. **89** *—R.V. (3/1/2007)*

Domaine Moillard 2003 Pinot Noir (Côte de Nuits-Villages) $28. **88** *—R.V. (9/1/2005)*

DOMAINE MONTHELIE-DOUHAIRET

Domaine Monthelie-Douhairet 1999 Clos Le Meix Garnier Monopole Red Blend (Monthelie) $26. **87** *(10/1/2003)*

DOMAINE MOREY COFFINET

Domaine Morey Coffinet 2000 Les Caillerets Premier Cru Chardonnay (Chassagne-Montrachet) $51. **90** *(10/1/2003)*

DOMAINE OLIVIER MERLIN

Domaine Olivier Merlin 2003 Chardonnay (Saint-Véran) $23. **88** *—J.C. (11/15/2005)*

DOMAINE OSTERTAG

Domaine Ostertag 2002 Fronholz Riesling (Alsace) $35. **89** *—R.V. (11/1/2005)*

Domaine Ostertag 2002 Heissenberg Riesling (Alsace) $39. **89** *—R.V. (11/1/2005)*

DOMAINE PASCAL BOUCHARD

Domaine Pascal Bouchard 2002 Special Reserve Bokobsa Chardonnay (Chablis) $32. **80** *—J.C. (4/1/2005)*

DOMAINE PATRICK JAVILLIER

Domaine Patrick Javillier 2004 Cuvée Tête de Murger Chardonnay (Meursault) $78. **93** *—R.V. (12/1/2006)*

DOMAINE PAUL AUTARD

Domaine Paul Autard 2004 Rhône Red Blend (Côtes-du-Rhône) $14. **85** *—J.C. (11/15/2006)*

DOMAINE PÉLAQUIÉ

Domaine Pélaquié 2005 Rosé Blend (Tavel) $NA. **88** *—J.C. (11/15/2006)*

DOMAINE PHILIPPE FAURY

Domaine Philippe Faury 2004 Syrah (Côte Rôtie) $47. **91** *—J.C. (11/15/2006)*

Domaine Philippe Faury 2004 Vieilles Vignes Syrah (Saint-Joseph) $26. **90** *—J.C. (11/15/2006)*

DOMAINE PIERRE ANDRÉ

Domaine Pierre André 2003 Chardonnay (Corton-Charlemagne) $NA. **86** *—R.V. (9/1/2005)*

Domaine Pierre André 2003 Pinot Noir (Ladoix) $NA. **87** *—R.V. (9/1/2005)*

Domaine Pierre André 2003 Château Corton André Clos du Château Pinot Noir (Corton) $NA. **91** *—R.V. (9/1/2005)*

Domaine Pierre André 2003 Corton-Renardes Pinot Noir (Corton) $NA. **90** *—R.V. (9/1/2005)*

DOMAINE PIERRE USSEGLIO ET FILS

Domaine Pierre Usseglio et Fils 2003 Cuvée de Mon Aïeul Rhône Red Blend (Châteauneuf-du-Pape) $79. **86** *—R.V. (12/31/2005)*

DOMAINE PINSON

Domaine Pinson 1999 Les Clos Chardonnay (Chablis) $NA. **92** *—R.V. (6/1/2001)*

DOMAINE RAOUL GAUTHERIN ET FILS

Domaine Raoul Gautherin et Fils 1998 Grenouilles Chardonnay (Chablis) $NA. **81** *—R.V. (6/1/2001)*

DOMAINE RAYMOND USSEGLIO ET FILS

Domaine Raymond Usseglio et Fils 2003 Cuvée Impériale Rhône Red Blend (Châteauneuf-du-Pape) $56. **93 Cellar Selection** *—R.V. (12/31/2005)*

DOMAINE RENÉ MONNIER

Domaine René Monnier 2004 Chardonnay (Chassagne-Montrachet) $50. **90** *—R.V. (12/1/2006)*

Domaine René Monnier 2004 Les Chevalières Chardonnay (Meursault) $45. **91** *—R.V. (12/1/2006)*

DOMAINE ROBERT-DENOGENT

Domaine Robert-Denogent 2002 Cuvée Claude Denogent Chardonnay (Pouilly-Fuissé) $38. **92 Cellar Selection** *—J.C. (11/15/2005)*

Domaine Robert-Denogent 2002 Les Pommards Chardonnay (Saint-Véran) $28. **89** *—J.C. (11/15/2005)*

Domaine Robert-Denogent 2002 Les Taches Chardonnay (Mâcon-Fuissé) $24. **88** *—J.C. (11/15/2005)*

DOMAINE ROGER SABON

Domaine Roger Sabon 2005 Chapelle de Maillac Rhône Red Blend (Lirac) $20. **90** *—J.C. (11/15/2006)*

DOMAINE ROMANÉE CONTI

Domaine Romanée Conti 2000 Le Montrachet Chardonnay (Burgundy) $1000. **93** *(10/1/2003)*

Domaine Romanée Conti 2000 Grands Echezeaux Pinot Noir (Burgundy) $250. **93** *(10/1/2003)*

Domaine Romanée Conti 2000 Richebourg Pinot Noir (Burgundy) $375. **95** *(10/1/2003)*

Domaine Romanée Conti 2000 Romanee-St.-Vivant Pinot Noir (Burgundy) $350. **90** *(10/1/2003)*

DOMAINE ROSSIGNOL-TRAPET

Domaine Rossignol-Trapet 2004 Pinot Noir (Gevrey-Chambertin) $42. The domaine of Rossignol-Trapet is relatively new, started in 1990 in Gevrey-Chambertin, but both families have been producing wine for generations. Their village Gevrey-Chambertin shows considerable amounts of wood and spice flavors, some acidity and quite tight red fruits. **87** *—R.V. (3/1/2007)*

Domaine Rossignol-Trapet 2004 Pinot Noir (Bourgogne) $20. Dark plums and acidity pair together in this well-made, fresh wine. Rossignol-Trapet owns vines only just the wrong side of the tracks in Gevrey-Chambertin from which this wine is made. It is firm, tannic but with plenty of fruit. **86** *—R.V. (3/1/2007)*

Domaine Rossignol-Trapet 2004 Pinot Noir (Chambertin) $104. Smooth and full-bodied, this wine shows power and tannin under a silky surface. There are rich, ripe flavors of perfumed black fruits, acidity and wood leading to a finish of juicy red fruits and herbs. **93** *—R.V. (3/1/2007)*

Domaine Rossignol-Trapet 2004 Pinot Noir (Latricières-Chambertin) $98. Initially austere, with dry tannins, this wine then opens up spectacularly. There are aromas of new wood and red fruits; the palate is treated to a rich, rolling velvet texture overlain with berry fruits, sweet acidity and a delicious, open, juicy finish. It will be even better in 5–10 years, but works well now. **93** *—R.V. (3/1/2007)*

Domaine Rossignol-Trapet 2004 Petite Chapelle Premier Cru Pinot Noir (Gevrey-Chambertin) $58. Dense structure is the hallmark of this wine from the premier cru, which is downslope from La Chapelle Grand Cru. Despite the weighty tannins, this is delicate, with a silky feel edging its way in. Expect it to mature over the next 3–4 years. **90 Cellar Selection** *—R.V. (3/1/2007)*

DOMAINE SAINT AMANT

Domaine Saint Amant 2004 La Borry Viognier (Côtes-du-Rhône) $12. **84** *—J.C. (11/15/2006)*

DOMAINE SAINT-ANDRÉ DE FIGUIÈRE

Domaine Saint-André de Figuière 2006 Vieilles Vignes Rosé Blend (Côtes de Provence) $22. A deliciously fresh but ripe wine, intense in red fruit flavors, elegantly touched with acidity and flavors of wild strawberries and a light tannic structure. The aftertaste is full, but packed with vibrant acidity. **90** —*R.V. (7/1/2007)*

DOMAINE SAINT GAYAN

Domaine Saint Gayan 2001 Rhône Red Blend (Côtes-du-Rhône) $12. **87** —*R.V. (3/1/2004)*

Domaine Saint Gayan 2000 Rhône Red Blend (Gigondas) $23. **89** —*R.V. (3/1/2004)*

Domaine Saint Gayan 2000 Rhône Red Blend (Châteauneuf-du-Pape) $28. **91** —*R.V. (3/1/2004)*

DOMAINE SAINT SIFFREIN

Domaine Saint Siffrein 2005 Rhône Red Blend (Côtes-du-Rhône Villages) $15. **87** —*J.C. (11/15/2006)*

DOMAINE SAINT-PRÉFERT

Domaine Saint-Préfert 2003 Collection Charles Giraud Rhône Red Blend (Châteauneuf-du-Pape) $52. **93** —*R.V. (12/31/2005)*

DOMAINE SAINTE BARBE

Domaine Sainte Barbe 2003 L'Épinet Chardonnay (Viré-Clessé) $19. **89** —*J.C. (11/15/2005)*

DOMAINE SALVAT

Domaine Salvat 2000 Rhône Red Blend (Vin de Pays des Côtes Catalanes) $8. **84** —*M.S. (2/1/2003)*

DOMAINE SANTA DUC

Domaine Santa Duc 2004 Rhône Red Blend (Gigondas) $37. **91** —*J.C. (11/15/2006)*

DOMAINE SANTA DUC

Domaine Santa Duc 2002 Rhône Red Blend (Gigondas) $33. **86** —*J.C. (11/15/2006)*

Domaine Santa Duc 2003 Prestige des Hautes Garrigues Rhône Red Blend (Gigondas) $54. **92** —*J.C. (11/15/2006)*

DOMAINE SERVIN

Domaine Servin 1998 Les Clos Chardonnay (Chablis) $NA. **89** —*R.V. (6/1/2001)*

DOMAINE SIMONNET

Domaine Simonnet 1999 Les Preuses Chardonnay (Chablis) $NA. **91** —*R.V. (6/1/2001)*

DOMAINE SORIN

Domaine Sorin 2006 Terra Amata Rosé Blend (Côtes de Provence) $10. Luc Sorin, from Chablis, arrived in Provence in 1995, buying vines in Bandol and Côtes de Provence. He seems to have kept a northern freshness in this rosé, a crisp, pink grapefruit and cranberry juice flavored wine, with great, refreshing acidity. **91 Best Buy** —*R.V. (7/1/2007)*

DOMAINE ST. DAMIEN

Domaine St. Damien 2003 Vieilles Vignes Rhône Red Blend (Gigondas) $NA. **82** —*J.C. (11/15/2006)*

DOMAINE TINEL-BLONDELET

Domaine Tinel-Blondelet 2004 Genetin Sauvignon Blanc (Pouilly-Fumé) $22. **89** —*R.V. (8/1/2006)*

DOMAINE TRAPET PERE ET FILS

Domaine Trapet Pere et Fils 2005 Pinot Noir (Bourgogne) $34. Fresh, smoky bacon and red fruit flabors, with some soft, easy tannins. Delicious and juicy, great for a simple Burgundy. **87** —*R.V. (3/1/2007)*

Domaine Trapet Pere et Fils 2004 Pinot Noir (Chambertin) $200. From one of the great Gevrey-Chambertin families comes this hugely authentic, impressive wine. With its solid tannins and ripe strawberry fruits, this is big and intense. It is delicious now and shows potential for excellent aging. The finish has both roundness and power. **93 Cellar Selection** —*R.V. (3/1/2007)*

DOMAINE VACHERON

Domaine Vacheron 2005 Pinot Noir (Sancerre) $40. A freshly perfumed wine, with attractive bright cherry flavors that have a lift and crispness to them. The tannins are persistent and dry, layering with the plum skin acidity. This is not a rich wine, but it makes a fascinating alternative to red Burgundy. Would work well with salmon dishes. **88** —*R.V. (10/1/2007)*

Domaine Vacheron 2005 Belle Dame Pinot Noir (Sancerre) $55. A heavily wooded wine, very juicy with high acidity. At the moment, it is only wood. But given Vacheron's reputation for long-lived reds (20 years or more), this powerful wine could develop slowly and well. Wait for at least two years. **90** —*R.V. (10/1/2007)*

Domaine Vacheron 2006 Sauvignon Blanc (Sancerre) $27. With their biodynamic vineyards, it's no wonder that the Vacherons are able to produce such intense fruit, even in their simplest wines. This is fresh but concentrated, with summer currants and pink grapefruit enriched by a firm structure. **89** —*R.V. (9/1/2007)*

Domaine Vacheron 2004 Sauvignon Blanc (Sancerre) $27. **87** —*R.V. (8/1/2006)*

Domaine Vacheron 2005 Les Romains Sauvignon Blanc (Sancerre) $27. While Vacheron is famed for its reds, the whites are of an equal, if not greater, class. This big, dense, rounded wine is from one of the sunniest vineyards in Sancerre, and that shows in its power and richness. The fruits are tropical, white peach, kiwi and green plums, with just a hint of yeast. Let this age for a year. **92 Editors' Choice** —*R.V. (9/1/2007)*

DOMAINE VALETTE

Domaine Valette 2002 Vieilles Vignes Chardonnay (Mâcon Chaintré) $25. **88** —*J.C. (11/15/2005)*

Domaine Valette 2004 Cuvée des Muletiers Syrah (Saint-Joseph) $28. **84** —*J.C. (11/15/2006)*

DOMAINE VINCENT BOUZEREAU

Domaine Vincent Bouzereau 2004 Chardonnay (Meursault) $49. **87** —*R.V. (12/1/2006)*

DOMAINE VINCENT DANCER

Domaine Vincent Dancer 2004 La Romanée Premier Cru Chardonnay (Chassagne-Montrachet) $85. **93** —*R.V. (12/1/2006)*

DOMAINE VINCENT GIRARDIN

Domaine Vincent Girardin 2004 Abbaye de Morgeot Premier Cru Chardonnay (Chassagne-Montrachet) $60. **89** —*R.V. (12/1/2006)*

Domaine Vincent Girardin 2004 Les Charmes-Dessus Premier Cru Chardonnay (Meursault) $69. **93** —*R.V. (12/1/2006)*

Domaine Vincent Girardin 2001 Les Vermots Dessus Chardonnay (Savigny-lès-Beaune) $23. **86** —*J.C. (10/1/2003)*

Domaine Vincent Girardin 1999 Vieilles Vignes Les Chanlins Premier Cru Pinot Noir (Pommard) $42. **89** —*J.C. (10/1/2003)*

DOMAINE VINCENT PARIS

Domaine Vincent Paris 2005 Granit 30 Syrah (Cornas) $40. Produced from young vines, this is Paris' early-drinking Cornas. It's fresh, fruity and not too tannic, with a dry, cinnamon-like overlay to the superripe blueberry fruit. Finishes crisp. **89** —*J.C. (9/1/2007)*

Domaine Vincent Paris 2005 Granit 60 Syrah (Cornas) $49. From old vines, partially destemmed and aged in old (3–10 years) barrels, this is a wonderfully pure expression of Cornas. Think fresh blueberries with a sprinkling of clove and a dash of black pepper. Firm tannins mark the finish; this needs at least five more years of aging. **91** —*J.C. (9/1/2007)*

DOMAINE VINCENT SAUVESTRE

Domaine Vincent Sauvestre 2003 Chablis Premier Cru Beauroy Chardonnay (Chablis) $23. **87** —*J.C. (11/15/2005)*

Domaine Vincent Sauvestre 2003 Pinot Noir (Bourgogne) $15. **84** —*J.C. (11/15/2005)*

Domaine Vincent Sauvestre 2002 Bourgogne Pinot Noir (Bourgogne) $11. **86 Best Buy** —*J.C. (11/15/2005)*

Domaine Vincent Sauvestre 2002 Pommard Clos de la Platière Pinot Noir (Pommard) $29. **86** —*J.C. (11/15/2005)*

DOMAINE VIRET

Domaine Viret 2003 Emergence Saint-Maurice Rhône Red Blend (Côtes-du-Rhône Villages) $40. **91 Editors' Choice** —*J.C. (11/15/2006)*

Domaine Viret 2004 Maréotis Saint-Maurice Rhône Red Blend (Côtes-du-Rhône Villages) $33. **87** —*J.C. (11/15/2006)*

Domaine Viret 2003 Renaissance Saint-Maurice Rhône Red Blend (Côtes-du-Rhône Villages) $22. **87** —*J.C. (11/15/2006)*

DOMAINE VIRGINIE

Domaine Virginie 2006 Sidewise Pinot Noir Pinot Noir (Vin de Pays d'Oc) $8. A play on the film Sideways, of course, but this Pinot Noir rosé with its raspberry bubble gum flavor would probably not impress Miles. It's clean and crisp, but lacks that spark of freshness a good rosé should have. 83 *—R.V. (7/1/2007)*

DOMAINE WEINBACH

Domaine Weinbach 2002 Grand Cru Cuvée Ste Catherine Riesling (Alsace) $68. 93 *—R.V. (5/1/2005)*

Domaine Weinbach 2001 Reserve Personelle Riesling (Alsace) $18. 89 *—R.V. (8/1/2003)*

DOMAINE WILLIAM FEVRE

Domaine William Fevre 1999 Les Clos Chardonnay (Chablis) 90 *—R.V. (6/1/2001)*

DOMAINE ZIND-HUMBRECHT

Domaine Zind-Humbrecht 2002 Clos Windsbuhl Hunawihr Gewürztraminer (Alsace) $70. 90 *—R.V. (4/1/2005)*

Domaine Zind-Humbrecht 2002 Grand Cru Goldert Gueberschwihr Vendange Tardive Gewürztraminer (Alsace) $123. 93 *—R.V. (4/1/2005)*

Domaine Zind-Humbrecht 2000 Grand Cru Hengst Gewürztraminer (Alsace) $68. 96 *—R.V. (10/1/2002)*

Domaine Zind-Humbrecht 2000 Heimbourg Gewürztraminer (Alsace) $54. 92 *—R.V. (10/1/2002)*

Domaine Zind-Humbrecht 2002 Herrenweg de Turckheim Gewürztraminer (Alsace) $43. 89 *—R.V. (4/1/2005)*

Domaine Zind-Humbrecht 2000 Turckheim Gewürztraminer (Alsace) $320. 88 *—R.V. (10/1/2002)*

Domaine Zind-Humbrecht 2000 Vendange Tardive Grand Cru Clos Saint Urbain Gewürztraminer (Alsace) $NA. 98 *—R.V. (10/1/2002)*

Domaine Zind-Humbrecht 2000 Wintzheim Gewürztraminer (Alsace) $32. 90 *—R.V. (10/1/2002)*

Domaine Zind-Humbrecht 2001 Clos Jebsal Séléction des Grains Nobles Pinot Gris (Alsace) $214. 96 Editors' Choice *—R.V. (4/1/2005)*

Domaine Zind-Humbrecht 2000 Clos Windsbuhl Pinot Gris (Alsace) $58. 94 *—R.V. (10/1/2002)*

Domaine Zind-Humbrecht 2002 Clos Windsbuhl Hunawihr Vendange Tardive Pinot Gris (Alsace) $68. 94 *—R.V. (4/1/2005)*

Domaine Zind-Humbrecht 2002 Grand Cru Clos Saint-Urbain Rangen de Thann Pinot Gris (Alsace) $102. 96 *—R.V. (4/1/2005)*

Domaine Zind-Humbrecht 2002 Heimbourg Turckheim Vendange Tardive Pinot Gris (Alsace) $123. 91 *—R.V. (4/1/2005)*

Domaine Zind-Humbrecht 2001 Rotenberg Pinot Gris (Alsace) $42. 88 *—R.V. (4/1/2005)*

Domaine Zind-Humbrecht 2002 Rotenberg Wintzenheim Vendange Tardive Pinot Gris (Alsace) $123. 90 *—R.V. (4/1/2005)*

Domaine Zind-Humbrecht 2000 Selection des Grains Nobles Heimbourg Pinot Gris (Alsace) 97 *—R.V. (10/1/2002)*

Domaine Zind-Humbrecht 2000 Vendange Tardive Clos Jebsal Pinot Gris (Alsace) $75. 96 *—R.V. (10/1/2002)*

Domaine Zind-Humbrecht 2000 Vendange Tardive Herrenweg de Turckheim Pinot Gris (Alsace) $37. 92 *—R.V. (10/1/2002)*

Domaine Zind-Humbrecht 2000 Clos Hauserer Riesling (Alsace) $44. 93 *—R.V. (10/1/2002)*

Domaine Zind-Humbrecht 2000 Grand Cru Brand Riesling (Alsace) $85. 96 *—R.V. (10/1/2002)*

Domaine Zind-Humbrecht 2000 Grand Cru Brand Vendange Tardive Riesling (Alsace) 95 *—R.V. (10/1/2002)*

Domaine Zind-Humbrecht 2002 Grand Cru Clos Saint Urbain Rangen de Thann Riesling (Alsace) $103. 94 *—R.V. (11/1/2005)*

Domaine Zind-Humbrecht 2002 Heimbourg Riesling (Alsace) $57. 90 *—R.V. (11/1/2005)*

Domaine Zind-Humbrecht 2000 Herrenweg de Turckheim Riesling (Alsace) $37. 92 *—R.V. (10/1/2002)*

Domaine Zind-Humbrecht 2000 Vendange Tardive Clos Windsbuhl Riesling (Alsace) $90. 93 *—R.V. (10/1/2002)*

Domaine Zind-Humbrecht NV Zind White Blend (Vin de Table Francais) $29. 87 *—R.V. (4/1/2005)*

DOMAINES ARNAUD DE RAIGNAC

Domaines Arnaud de Raignac 2003 Château de Launay Bordeaux Blend (Bordeaux) $27. It's smoky, toasty and even a bit bacon-scented from its upbringing in 100% new French oak, but this is also a lush, warm, inviting mouthful of wine, filled with cassis fruit and framed by spicy wood. It's 95% Merlot from a hot vintage, so not likely to age all that long, but it's certainly delicious now. 90 *(9/1/2007)*

Domaines Arnaud de Raignac 2003 L'Abbaye de Saint Ferme Les Vignes du Soir Bordeaux Blend (Bordeaux Supérieur) $11. This is a great example of what more inexpensive Bordeaux could be like with proper care in the vineyards and winery. Scents of chocolate, dried herbs and cassis ease into similar flavors, carried on a medium-weight, slightly creamy palate. Turns spicy and firmer on the finish, suggesting it will last until 2010 or so. 87 Best Buy *(9/1/2007)*

Domaines Arnaud de Raignac 2004 Château de Launay Bordeaux White Blend (Bordeaux) $23. Mainly (85%) Sauvignon Blanc, bolstered by Sémillon, this is rather broad and mouthfilling for a Bordeaux blanc. Ripe flavors of melon, fig and peach turn grassy and crisp on the finish. Drink now. 86 *(9/1/2007)*

Domaines Arnaud de Raignac 2003 Château de Launay Vignes d'Elisa Bordeaux White Blend (Bordeaux) $23. An oddity in the modern world of Bordeaux, this is 100% Muscadelle, a variety normally relegated to a miniscule portion of the blend. Honeyed notes of yellow plums or apricots are plump and waxy-textured in the mouth, finishing long but a touch warm. Drink now. 87 *(9/1/2007)*

DOMAINES BUNAN

Domaines Bunan 2006 Bélouvé Rosé Blend (Côtes de Provence) $14. A full, fruity rosé, flavored with almonds, white currants, lychees. With 30% Cabernet Sauvignon in the blend, this is much more structured than many rosés, making it right with food. 88 *—R.V. (7/1/2007)*

DOMAINES GRASSA

Domaines Grassa 2005 Sauvignon Sauvignon Blanc (Vin de Pays des Côtes de Gascogne) $6. 84 *—R.V. (12/31/2006)*

DOMAINES OTT

Domaines Ott 1997 Château De Selle Rouge Rhône Red Blend (Côtes de Provence) $34. 84 *—M.S. (5/1/2000)*

Domaines Ott 1998 Les Domaniers de Calignade Rhône Red Blend (Côtes de Provence) $11. 84 *—M.S. (5/1/2000)*

Domaines Ott 2005 Château de Selle Clair de Noirs Rosé Blend (Côtes de Provence) $38. One of the world's best-known rosés, Ott's Château de Selle is a clean, refreshing, minerally drink. The flavors are difficult to describe exactly, coming across a little like underripe melon combined with grapefruit, herbs and white chocolate. Tasty enough to satisfy the wine crowd, trendy enough to satisfy everyone else. 88 *—J.C. (7/1/2007)*

Domaines Ott 1998 Château De Selle Clair de Noir Rosé Blend (Côtes de Provence) $29. 89 *—M.S. (5/1/2000)*

Domaines Ott 2005 Les Domaniers de Puits Mouret Rosé Blend (Côtes de Provence) $17. A disappointing effort from Ott, this is a bit austere and not showing much fruit. The pleasant anise and herb notes fade quickly on the finish. 83 *—J.C. (7/1/2007)*

Domaines Ott 2004 Clos Mireille Blanc de Blancs White Blend (Côtes de Provence) $20. 88 *—R.V. (12/31/2006)*

DOMAINES POCHON

Domaines Pochon 2004 Etienne Pochon Syrah (Crozes-Hermitage) $17. 87 *—J.C. (11/15/2006)*

DOMAINES SCHLUMBERGER

Domaines Schlumberger 1998 Cuvée Christine Vendange Tardive Gewürztraminer (Alsace) $72. 91 *—J.C. (1/1/2004)*

Domaines Schlumberger 2003 Fleur Gewürztraminer (Alsace) $28. 83 *—J.C. (11/1/2005)*

Domaines Schlumberger 2001 Fleur Gewürztraminer (Alsace) $22. 85 *—M.S. (12/31/2003)*

Domaines Schlumberger 2002 Grand Cru Kessler Gewürztraminer (Alsace) $40. 90 *—J.C. (11/1/2005)*

Domaines Schlumberger 2001 Grand Cru Kessler Gewürztraminer (Alsace) $32. 89 *(6/1/2004)*

Domaines Schlumberger 2002 Grand Cru Kitterlé Gewürztraminer (Alsace) $54. 87 *—J.C. (8/1/2006)*

Domaines Schlumberger 2000 Grand Cru Saering Gewürztraminer (Alsace) $32. 86 *—M.S. (12/31/2003)*

Domaines Schlumberger 2000 Pinot Blanc (Alsace) $14. 87 *—S.H. (1/1/2002)*

Domaines Schlumberger 2002 Les Princes Abbés Pinot Blanc (Alsace) $14. 86 *(6/1/2004)*

Domaines Schlumberger 1998 Cuvée Clarisse Sélection de Grains Nobles Pinot Gris (Alsace) $72. 87 *—M.S. (10/1/2003)*

Domaines Schlumberger 2002 Grand Cru Kitterlé Pinot Gris (Alsace) $44. 94 *—R.V. (2/1/2006)*

Domaines Schlumberger 2000 Grand Cru Kitterlé Pinot Gris (Alsace) $38. 87 *—J.C. (2/1/2005)*

Domaines Schlumberger 1998 Grand Cru Kitterlé Pinot Gris (Alsace) $37. 90 *—M.S. (10/1/2003)*

Domaines Schlumberger 2002 Grand Cru Spiegel Pinot Gris (Alsace) $26. 91 *—R.V. (2/1/2006)*

Domaines Schlumberger 2002 Les Princes Abbés Pinot Gris (Alsace) $21. 87 *(6/1/2004)*

Domaines Schlumberger 1999 Spiegel Pinot Gris (Alsace) $32. 89 *(6/1/2004)*

Domaines Schlumberger 1998 Vendange Tardive Pinot Gris (Alsace) $52. 89 *—R.V. (2/1/2006)*

Domaines Schlumberger 1999 Cuvée Ernest Sélection de Grains Nobles Riesling (Alsace) $72. 91 Cellar Selection *(6/1/2004)*

Domaines Schlumberger 2005 Grand Cru Kessler Riesling (Alsace) $33. Stone dust and ripe green apple fill the nose and palate of this easygoing quaff. A pleasing lemon finish balances the intensity and medium weight, making this a nice, solid selection. 86 *(9/1/2007)*

Domaines Schlumberger 2005 Grand Cru Kitterlé Riesling (Alsace) $34. This grand cru Riesling screams of terroir. Strong aromas of petrol, pineapple and honey emanate from the glass while flavors of ripe red delicious apple, bergamot and ruby red grapefruit dance on your palate. Medium-full body and a long mineral finish add the finishing touches to this beauty. 90 *(9/1/2007)*

Domaines Schlumberger 1999 Grand Cru Kitterlé Riesling (Alsace) $38. 91 *—R.V. (11/1/2005)*

Domaines Schlumberger 2005 Grand Cru Saering Riesling (Alsace) $27. Lighter texture with a clean, citrusy finish, this is a simple quaff made for easy enjoyment. Full of ripe lemon, Granny Smith apple and stone-dust minerality with just a hint of under ripe nectarine. 87 *(9/1/2007)*

Domaines Schlumberger 2004 Grand Cru Saering Riesling (Alsace) $20. With notes of wet stones, petrol, lime and apple, this plump, medium-intensity wine balances nicely. Hints of mint and pineapple core are also exposed on the palate. A persistent finish with a slightly oily viscosity lingers long after the wine is gone. Imported by Maison Marques et Domaines. 89 *(9/1/2007)*

Domaines Schlumberger 2002 Grand Cru Saering Riesling (Alsace) $23. 91 Editors' Choice *—J.C. (11/1/2005)*

Domaines Schlumberger 2000 Grand Cru Saering Riesling (Alsace) $18. 89 *(6/1/2004)*

Domaines Schlumberger 2005 Les Princes Abbés Riesling (Alsace) $17. Typical flavors of apple, key lime and stony minerality intermingle with hints of dried spice and honey, creating a nicely balanced wine with a clean, dry finish. Solid and remarkably refreshing, this is a great choice for warmer afternoons of light grilling or picnicking. 87 *(9/1/2007)*

Domaines Schlumberger 2004 Les Princes Abbés Riesling (Alsace) $17. Slightly schizophrenic, this wine touts a strange but intriguing gamut of aromas and flavors. The nose presents mild vegetal and ashy powder notes while the palate offers more typical nuances of nectarine and lemon. A tart and fleeting finish counters the somewhat creamy, medium-full body, concluding with a feeling of balance. 87 *(9/1/2007)*

Domaines Schlumberger 2003 Les Princes Abbés Riesling (Alsace) $20. 87 *—J.C. (8/1/2006)*

Domaines Schlumberger 2002 Les Princes Abbés Riesling (Alsace) $20. 88 *—R.V. (11/1/2005)*

Domaines Schlumberger 1998 Princes Abbes Riesling (Alsace) $16. 91 *—S.H. (1/1/2002)*

DOPFF & IRION

Dopff & Irion 2000 Grand Cru Vorbourg Gewürztraminer (Alsace) $32. 88 *—J.C. (2/1/2005)*

Dopff & Irion 1998 Les Tonnelles Pinot Noir (Alsace) $19. 86 *—M.S. (11/1/2000)*

Dopff & Irion 2006 Pinot Noir Rosé Pinot (Alsace) $NA. A delicious, fresh wine, with red cherries and fresh red currant flavors. Its attractive pink-grey color adds to the lift and vibrancy of the wine. It just tempts and demands. 89 *—R.V. (7/1/2007)*

Dopff & Irion 2001 Grand Cru Schoenenbourg Riesling (Alsace) $32. 91 Editors' Choice *—J.C. (2/1/2005)*

Dopff & Irion 1995 Schoenenbourg Riesling (Alsace) $30. 81 *—J.C. (12/31/1999)*

Dopff & Irion 1997 Tokay Pinot Gris (Alsace) $16. 84 *(8/1/1999)*

Dopff & Irion 2002 Les Maquisards Tokay Pinot Gris (Alsace) $25. 85 *—R.V. (2/1/2006)*

Dopff & Irion 2003 Crustaces White Blend (Alsace) $11. 85 *—J.C. (2/1/2005)*

DOPFF AU MOULIN

Dopff Au Moulin 1996 Reserve Tokay Pinot Gris (Alsace) $19. 86 *(8/1/1999)*

DOURTHE

Dourthe 2006 Numéro 1 Bordeaux White Blend (Bordeaux Blanc) $NA. Always one of the most reliable and successful white Bordeaux brands, dominated by Sauvignon Blanc. The 2005 is a rich, tropical fruit and white currant-flavored wine. There is some green plum, fresh acidity and a hint of wood. Great as an apéritif, it also works well with sushi. 87 *—R.V. (12/31/2007)*

Dourthe 2003 Numéro 1 Bordeaux White Blend (Bordeaux) $10. 88 Best Buy *—R.V. (6/1/2005)*

DUJAC FILS & PÈRE

Dujac Fils & Père 2001 Chardonnay (Meursault) $44. 82 *—J.C. (12/1/2005)*

DULONG

Dulong 1999 Merlot (Vin de Pays d'Oc) $8. 84 *—D.T. (2/1/2002)*

DUMIEN-SERRETTE

Dumien-Serrette 2005 Syrah (Cornas) $NA. This won't be released until the end of 2007, and honestly it needs a little time to relax. Right now, it's tight and a bit austere, with crisp red fruit flavors and a firm foundation. Try after 2009. 86 *—J.C. (9/1/2007)*

Dumien-Serrette 2004 Syrah (Cornas) $NA. Approachable now for its juicy red fruit and intense minerality, this is a superb example of Cornas from a challenging vintage. It's not deeply colored, but still boasts plenty of intensity to its aromas and flavors, with supple tannins and a long, spice-driven finish. Drink now–2014. 90 *—J.C. (9/1/2007)*

DUVAL-LEROY

Duval-Leroy 1990 Blanc de Chardonnay Champagne Blend (Champagne) $42. 87 *—R.V. (12/1/2004)*

Duval-Leroy NV Brut Champagne Blend (Champagne) $NA. Much drier than many non-vintage Champagnes, this is full of crisp grapefruit flavors, lively green fruits, and a touch of bready yeast. It is a deliciously fresh wine, dancing across the palate. 88 *—R.V. (12/1/2007)*

Duval-Leroy NV Brut Champagne Blend (Champagne) $24. 88 *—R.V. (12/1/2001)*

Duval-Leroy 1996 Brut Champagne Blend (Champagne) $50. As they begin to mature, it's good to be reminded of the 1996 vintage. The initial austerity is now blossoming into finely balanced wines, even though the acidity is always going to be a dominant factor. This wine is still young, in fact, still with its fresh fruits, only just showing some mineral and toast character. Age for 10 years or more. 94 Cellar Selection *—R.V. (12/1/2007)*

Duval-Leroy 1996 Brut Champagne Blend (Champagne) $48. A Chardonnay-dominated blend, with fine, mature, crisp acidity and some toast. There's a freshness to the wine, but the acidity and the depth of flavor promise the typical long aging of 1996 vintage. 92 *—R.V. (2/1/2007)*

Duval-Leroy 1995 Brut Champagne Blend (Champagne) $42. 90 *—P.G. (12/15/2002)*

Duval-Leroy 1995 Femme Brut Champagne Blend (Champagne) $NA. It is appropriate that Duval-Leroy has Femme as its top wine, since the company is run by one of the legendary "Champagne widows" Carol Duval-Leroy. This wine is an indication of the great quality now coming from this producer. It's an elegant wine, dominated by Chardonnay, with intense green fruits, a fine structure, no sign at all of aging. With the wine this fresh it could probably age another 5–10 years. 93 Cellar Selection *—R.V. (12/1/2007)*

Duval-Leroy 1995 Femme Brut Champagne Blend (Champagne) $120. 95 *—M.S. (12/31/2005)*

Duval-Leroy NV Lady Rose Rosé Sec Champagne Blend (Champagne) $NA. Designed as a dessert Champagne, this is made from 100% Pinot Noir, giving a soft, raspberry-ade style of wine, and soft, ripe red fruits. It has softness, rather than great sweetness, but it certainly works with the berry fruits. 88 *—R.V. (12/1/2007)*

Duval-Leroy NV Paris Brut Champagne Blend (Champagne) $28. 92 Editors' Choice *—P.G. (12/15/2002)*

Duval-Leroy NV Rosé de Saignée Brut Champagne Blend (Champagne) $40. 91 *—P.G. (12/1/2006)*

Duval-Leroy 1998 Blanc de Blancs Chardonnay (Champagne) $48. This wine is beginning to get some age to it, but remains fresh. There is some toast, even coffee, while the aftertaste is soft and slightly candied. **88** —*R.V. (12/31/2007)*

Duval-Leroy 1996 Blanc de Chardonnay Chardonnay (Champagne) $32. 90 —*P.G. (12/15/2002)*

Duval-Leroy 1999 Trépail Authentis Chardonnay (Champagne) $80. This is part of a range which returns to origins, with wood fermentation for the wines. Perfumed, green initially and then showing flavors of lychees and earthiness, this has some oak toast, but more of an open flavor from light (and pleasing) oxidation. **90** —*R.V. (12/31/2007)*

Duval-Leroy NV Brut Rosé Pinot Noir (Champagne) $32. 90 —*P.G. (12/15/2002)*

Duval-Leroy NV Rose de Saignée Brut Pinot Noir (Champagne) $NA. The name indicates that this Champagne gets its delicate onion skin pink from the grape skins and not the addition of red wine, as with most rosé Champagnes. Does this make it any better? It's certainly a well integrated wine, the berry fruits very much part of the overall richness and, the acidity in a great supporting role. **91** —*R.V. (12/1/2007)*

E. BARNAUT

E. Barnaut NV Blanc de Noirs Brut Champagne Blend (Champagne) $27. 86 —*R.V. (12/1/2002)*

E. GUIGAL

E. Guigal 2005 Marsanne (Crozes-Hermitage) $20. 88 —*J.C. (11/15/2006)*

E. Guigal 2001 Marsanne (Saint-Joseph) $28. 85 *(2/1/2005)*

E. Guigal 2000 Lieu-dit Saint-Joseph Marsanne (Saint-Joseph) $28. 90 —*R.V. (6/1/2002)*

E. Guigal 2003 Rhône Red Blend (Gigondas) $25. 90 Editors' Choice —*J.C. (11/15/2006)*

E. Guigal 2001 Rhône Red Blend (Châteauneuf-du-Pape) $45. 86 —*J.C. (2/1/2005)*

E. Guigal 1999 Syrah (Hermitage) $55. 95 —*R.V. (6/1/2002)*

E. Guigal 1999 Brune et Blonde Syrah (Côte Rôtie) $40. 94 —*R.V. (6/1/2002)*

E. Guigal 1998 Château d'Ampuis Syrah (Côte Rôtie) $90. 91 —*R.V. (6/1/2002)*

E. Guigal 1998 La Mouline Syrah (Côte Rôtie) $175. 96 —*R.V. (6/1/2002)*

E. Guigal 2004 Rhône White Blend (Côtes-du-Rhône) $12. 86 —*J.C. (11/15/2006)*

E. Guigal 2003 Rhône White Blend (Hermitage) $50. This is a powerful, rich white Hermitage with overtones of buttered nuts. It's slightly waxy, with hints of stone fruit as well. Already shows some hints of age, so this may be best consumed young. **90** —*J.C. (9/1/2007)*

E. Guigal 2000 Viognier (Condrieu) $35. 90 —*R.V. (6/1/2002)*

E. Guigal 2003 Ex Voto Rhône White Blend (Hermitage) $175. After 30 months in new oak, this needs some time to pull itself together. Right now, it's dominated by oaky notes of vanilla and spice. There does appear to be plenty of old-vine material underneath—you can ferret out hints of apricot and almond skin—so this rating may look stingy in 10 or more years. **90** —*J.C. (9/1/2007)*

E. Guigal 2000 La Doriane Viognier (Condrieu) $60. 92 —*R.V. (6/1/2002)*

E. Guigal 2003 Syrah (Hermitage) $80. A spicy, muscular example of Hermitage, this wine features red currant flavors tinged with darker shades of cassis and chocolate. It's slightly creamy in the mouth, turning dry and tannnic on the finish. Drink 2010–2020. **90** —*J.C. (9/1/2007)*

E. Guigal 2003 Syrah (Crozes-Hermitage) $22. 90 Editors' Choice —*J.C. (11/15/2006)*

E. Guigal 2002 Syrah (Hermitage) $75. 90 —*R.V. (2/1/2005)*

E. Guigal 2001 Syrah (Crozes-Hermitage) $20. 87 *(2/1/2005)*

E. Guigal 1999 Syrah (Crozes-Hermitage) $15. 89 —*R.V. (6/1/2002)*

E. Guigal 2003 Brune et Blonde Syrah (Côte Rôtie) $70. Guigal's entry-level Côte-Rôtie seems rather tannic at this moment, but does have ample spice, cassis and prune flavors. Lacks a bit of richness and flesh; give it a few years' time to come back around. Drink 2009–2015. **88** —*J.C. (9/1/2007)*

E. Guigal 2003 Château d'Ampuis Syrah (Côte Rôtie) $175. A cherry-picked blend of six estate parcels, the 2003 Château d'Ampuis fills the gap in the Guigal hierarchy between the largely négoce Brune et Blonde and the single-vineyard bottlings. Aged 38 months in new French oak, there's an understandable layer of vanilla and spice, but also layers of lush berry fruit. Creamy and rich, with a long, surprisingly elegant finish. Drink now–2020. **92** —*J.C. (9/1/2007)*

E. Guigal 2003 Ex Voto Syrah (Hermitage) $450. This bottling from Guigal's own Hermitage holdings is incredibly rich and ripe (15.5% alcohol). In fact, it comes dangerously close to being overblown before the syrupy cherry fruit is reined back in by underlying spice and minerality. Expect that minerally edge to assert itself more with time in the cellar, making this a wine worth revisiting in 10 years' time. **94** —*J.C. (9/1/2007)*

E. Guigal 2003 La Landonne Syrah (Côte Rôtie) $450. Dense and rich but also incredibly complex, long and elegant, this is a momumental Côte-Rôtie. It's darkly fruited and superripe, yet doesn't lose its essential sense of terroir, remaining marked by scents of pepper and espresso to go with the chocolate and cassis fruit. Velvety in texture, this is the one of Guigal's 2003 Côte-Rôties that demands a few years of cellaring. Drink 2010–2040. **99 Cellar Selection** —*J.C. (9/1/2007)*

E. Guigal 2003 La Mouline Syrah (Côte Rôtie) $450. How can a wine be this hugely concentrated, yet remain supremely elegant? Espresso, black olive and floral notes zoom from the glass, backed by layers of rich, creamy cherry fruit, making this a complex, complete wine. Tannins are amazingly supple, imparting a velvety feel to the long finish. Drink now–2025 and beyond. **96 Cellar Selection** —*J.C. (9/1/2007)*

E. Guigal 2003 La Turque Syrah (Côte Rôtie) $450. This is breathtaking stuff, incredibly complex on the nose, where it features hints of vanilla, clove, cinnamon, cassis, pepper and asphalt. It would be a wine to sit and smell all day if it weren't so delicious to taste. Rich waves of cassis fruit cascade over the palate without losing complexity, buffered by incredibly supple tannins. The virtually endless finish confirms the quality. Drink now–2030+. **98 Cellar Selection** —*J.C. (9/1/2007)*

E. Guigal 1999 Lieu-dit Saint-Joseph Syrah (Saint-Joseph) $28. 93 —*R.V. (6/1/2002)*

E. Guigal 2005 Viognier (Condrieu) $50. Guigal's Condrieu is a blend of oak- and steel-fermented lots to help preserve some of the Viognier's freshness. The 2005 is a success, featuring scents of honeysuckle and apricot and a touch of toast. It's reasonably rich on the palate, coating the mouth with ripe, peachy flavors, finishing with credible length. Drink now. **89** —*J.C. (9/1/2007)*

E. Guigal 2003 Viognier (Condrieu) $45. 90 —*R.V. (2/1/2005)*

ELELPHANT ON A TIGHTROPE

Elephant on a Tightrope 2006 Grenache Rosé Grenache (Vin de Pays d'Oc) $11. Full, rather lifeless wine, pale in color with some easy raspberry flavors. It is soft, just sweetened to finish. **81** —*R.V. (7/1/2007)*

Elephant on a Tightrope 2005 Grenache Rosé Grenache (Vin de Pays d'Oc) $11. Another coppery rosé from the south of France, this one seems more austere than most, nicely packaging delicate cherry and floral notes with anise flavors in a lightweight format. **85** —*J.C. (7/1/2007)*

ELIAN DA ROS

Elian da Ros 2004 Chante Coucou Red Blend (Cotes du Marmandais) $27. This is a blend of Bordeaux grapes with the local Abouriou and Fer, perfumed, with great structure and firm tannins. There are mint flavors, pure fresh fruit and a lively but dry aftertaste. **89** —*R.V. (4/1/2007)*

EMMANUEL DARNAUD

Emmanuel Darnaud 2004 Les Trois Chênes Syrah (Crozes-Hermitage) $25. 90 —*J.C. (11/15/2006)*

ÉRIC & JÖEL DURAND

Eric & Joel Durand 1999 Empreintes Rhône Red Blend (Cornas) $37. 95 —*R.V. (6/1/2002)*

Éric & Jöel Durand 2004 Confidence Syrah (Cornas) $NA. Toasty upfront, with blatant oak and vanilla scents, but the wood is matched by the wine's fruity—raspberry and blackberry—intensity. This is lip-smacking, mouth-watering stuff that can be drunk now and over the next 10 years. **91** —*J.C. (9/1/2007)*

Éric & Jöel Durand 2005 Empreintes Syrah (Cornas) $NA. From vines more than 50 years old, this is a surprisingly lush, forward Cornas from a vintage known at most domaines for its hard tannins. Black cherry fruit surrounds a core of dense mineral flavors, with light touches of wood on the finish. It's approachable now but should easily hold until at least 2015. **90** —*J.C. (9/1/2007)*

Éric & Jöel Durand 2004 Empreintes Syrah (Cornas) $NA. Spicy—this is filled with pepper and clove notes—but there's also lovely raspberry fruit. Fresh, balanced and easy to drink now but it should hold together through 2012. **88** —*J.C. (9/1/2007)*

Eric & Joel Durand 2004 Les Coteaux Syrah (Saint-Joseph) $NA. 90 —*J.C. (11/15/2006)*

Éric & Jöel Durand 2005 Prémice Syrah (Cornas) $NA. Makers of more forward Cornas, the Durand brothers' Prémice bottling is easy to drink right away, even in a tannic vintage like 2005. It's ripely fruity and raspberry-scented, with grace notes of smoke, vanilla and spice. Drink now–2015. **88** —*J.C. (9/1/2007)*

ERIC ROCHER

Eric Rocher 2004 Terroir de Champal Syrah (Saint-Joseph) $28. **84** —*J.C. (11/15/2006)*

ERIC TEXIER

Eric Texier 1999 Syrah (Côtes-du-Rhône) $15. **82** *(1/1/2004)*

ERNST BURN

Ernst Burn 1997 Tokay Pinot Gris (Alsace) $18. **88** *(8/1/1999)*

ESPRIT DE CHEVALIER

Esprit de Chevalier 2000 Bordeaux Blend (Pessac-Léognan) $35. **83** —*J.C. (6/1/2005)*

ETIENNE SAUZET

Etienne Sauzet 2004 Chardonnay (Chassagne-Montrachet) $53. **89** —*R.V. (12/1/2006)*

Etienne Sauzet 2004 Chardonnay (Puligny-Montrachet) $57. **90** —*R.V. (12/1/2006)*

Etienne Sauzet 2004 Chardonnay (Bâtard-Montrachet) $228. **95** —*R.V. (12/1/2006)*

Etienne Sauzet 2004 Les Combettes Premier Cru Chardonnay (Puligny-Montrachet) $119. **94** —*R.V. (12/1/2006)*

Etienne Sauzet 2004 Les Perrières Premier Cru Chardonnay (Puligny-Montrachet) $89. **91** —*R.V. (12/1/2006)*

EUGÈNE KLIPFEL

Eugène Klipfel 2004 Grand Cru Kirchberg Tokay Pinot Gris (Alsace) $NA. **84** —*R.V. (2/1/2006)*

EY

Ey 2003 Vigne Lo Clavell Muscat d'Alexandrie (Muscat de Rivesaltes) $16. Honey and fresh orange zest aromas and flavors drive this nicely balanced fortified Muscat. There's a pleasing weightiness to it on the palate, and a slightly creamy texture to go with the pristine flavors. Try with blue cheeses or foie gras. **88** —*J.C. (12/15/2007)*

F. CHAUVENET

F. Chauvenet 2000 Les Jumelles Chardonnay (Mâcon-Villages) $10. **83** —*J.C. (10/1/2003)*

FAIVELEY

Faiveley 2005 Chardonnay (Chablis) $29. Soft and creamy, structured with some green apple skin flavors, and easy, fresh acidity. It has good weight alongside tannins and ripe fruit. **85**—*R.V. (8/1/2007)*

Faiveley 2004 Chardonnay (Mâcon-Prissé) $15. **86** *(11/1/2006)*

Faiveley 2001 Chardonnay (Puligny-Montrachet) $NA. **87** —*S.H. (1/1/2002)*

Faiveley 2004 Clos Rochette Chardonnay (Mercurey) $24. **88** *(11/1/2006)*

Faiveley 2004 Georges Faiveley Chardonnay (Bourgogne) $17. With its hint of tropical fruits, white pears and spice, this is a delicious, full but fruity wine. It's ripe, but with acidity and toasty wood, it finishes fresh and crisp. **87** —*R.V. (3/1/2007)*

Faiveley 2001 Georges Faiveley Chardonnay (Bourgogne) $NA. **86** —*S.H. (1/1/2002)*

Faiveley 2004 Pinot Noir (Chambertin Clos de Bèze) $170. At this stage in the wine's development, it is virtually all tannin. Old wood flavors layered with dryness and spice do appear, and some fruit is apparent in the acidity. The only thing to do is wait at least 10 years. **90** —*R.V. (3/1/2007)*

Faiveley 2004 Pinot Noir (Nuits-St.-Georges) $41. Faiveley is based in Nuits-Saint-Georges, so its range of wines from the appellation is unrivalled. This village wine is, however, something of a disappointment: very dry and earthy, with dark tannins and an old wood flavor. **85** —*R.V. (3/1/2007)*

Faiveley 2004 Pinot Noir (Latricières-Chambertin) $100. This wine shows the big, bold side of wines from Gevrey-Chambertin. But the star of the show is the big, bold tannins rather than fruit. It will certainly mature, and will, eventually, be an impressive wine. But those dry tannins will always remain. **91** —*R.V. (3/1/2007)*

Faiveley 2004 Pinot Noir (Echezeaux) $100. Quite a stern wine, this reveals big, solid tannins to cover the concentrated black fruit flavors. It is foursquare and chunky, a foil for the blackberry fruits and acidity. Keep this wine for 10 years at least. **91** —*R.V. (3/1/2007)*

Faiveley 2003 Pinot Noir (Nuits-St.-Georges) $53. **86** —*J.C. (9/1/2006)*

Faiveley 2004 Aux Chaignots Premier Cru Pinot Noir (Nuits-St.-Georges) $64. A rich, almost juicy wine, showing great red fruits buttressed by firm tannins. The mouthfilling fruit dominates the initial palate, and the dryness of the tannins and wood only really show through on the finish. **91** —*R.V. (3/1/2007)*

Faiveley 2004 Clos de Vougeot Pinot Noir (Clos Vougeot) $111. The Faiveley style for big, bold statements suits this wine. It's powerful, concentrated, dense and rich. There are intense black plum flavors while the tannins are well in balance with the richness of the wine. **92 Cellar Selection** —*R.V. (3/1/2007)*

Faiveley 2004 Domaine de la Croix Jacquelet Pinot Noir (Mercurey) $21. **84** *(11/1/2006)*

Faiveley 2003 Joseph Faiveley Pinot Noir (Bourgogne) $17. **84** —*J.C. (9/1/2006)*

Faiveley 2004 La Combe aux Moines Premier Cru Pinot Noir (Gevrey-Chambertin) $62. A hugely ripe wine, balancing dense tannins against packed fruits. Initially tough, this does open into a richly flavored wine, boasting real Pinot Noir perfumes and juicy fruit to go with the structure. Keep for 4–5 years at least. **89** —*R.V. (3/1/2007)*

Faiveley 2004 La Combe d'Orveau Premier Cru Pinot Noir (Chambolle-Musigny) $88. A big, bold, gutsy, dry wine, with firm tannins. There are black fruits under all this dryness, but there's also an almost-too-solid texture. Age for 5–10 years, or decant before drinking. **88** —*R.V. (3/1/2007)*

Faiveley 2004 Les Cazetiers Premier Cru Pinot Noir (Gevrey-Chambertin) $69. The line of premier crus, of which Les Cazetiers forms a part, are often picked later than the grand crus, the result of facing due east rather than south-east. But it can result in a beautifully perfumed wine. This is such a one; it has exotic aromas and flavors, along with the firm tannins that suggest good aging. **91** —*R.V. (3/1/2007)*

Faiveley 2004 Les Damodes Premier Cru Pinot Noir (Nuits-St.-Georges) $54. The Faiveley style is for firm, ageworthy wines, and this Damodes fits the bill. It's initially austere, but then the solid tannins allow black fruits and pepper to peek through, and the aftertaste has some fresh acidity. **88** —*R.V. (3/1/2007)*

Faiveley 2004 Les Porets Premier Cru Pinot Noir (Nuits-St.-Georges) $58. Big and grainy, this is a heavily textured wine, somewhat extracted with an edge of bitterness. The fruit, though, redeems the wine: It is concentrated and deeply flavored, with fine, fresh acidity coming through. **89** —*R.V. (3/1/2007)*

Faiveley 2004 Les Saint-Georges Premier Cru Pinot Noir (Nuits-St.-Georges) $72. A dry palate layered with high-toast tannins does mask the fruit to some extent at this early stage, but also gives a fine, big, bold, solid structure. This wine needs to age, probably for 10 years or more. **88** —*R.V. (3/1/2007)*

Faiveley 1996 Red Blend (Vosne-Romanée) $40. **87** —*S.H. (12/31/1999)*

Faiveley 1995 Red Blend (Pommard) $48. **92** —*S.H. (12/31/1999)*

Faiveley 1995 Clos des Myglands Red Blend (Mercurey) $24. **87** —*S.H. (12/31/1999)*

Faiveley 1995 Blanc Clos Rochette White Blend (Mercurey) $24. **86** —*S.H. (12/31/1999)*

FAT BASTARD

Fat Bastard 2004 Limited Release Cabernet Sauvignon (Vin de Pays d'Oc) $12. **85 Best Buy** —*R.V. (11/15/2006)*

Fat Bastard 2005 Merlot (Vin de Pays d'Oc) $12. **84** —*R.V. (12/31/2006)*

Fat Bastard 2006 Blushing Bastard Rosé Blend (Vin de Pays d'Oc) $11. A real pink candy wine, that is soft, just off dry, with freshness and some acidity, but more of the lightly sweet fruit. **84** —*R.V. (7/1/2007)*

Fat Bastard 2005 Shiraz (Vin de Pays d'Oc) $12. **83** —*R.V. (12/31/2006)*

FÉRAUD-BRUNEL

Féraud-Brunel 2003 Rhône Red Blend (Gigondas) $33. **91 Editors' Choice** —*J.C. (11/15/2006)*

FERRATON PÈRE ET FILS

Ferraton Père et Fils 2005 La Source Marsanne (Saint-Joseph) $24. N82 —*J.C. (11/15/2006)*

Ferraton Père et Fils 2003 Les Oliviers Marsanne (Saint-Joseph) $NA. **88** —*R.V. (2/1/2005)*

Ferraton Père et Fils 2004 Samorëns Rhône Red Blend (Côtes-du-Rhône) $12. **83** —*J.C. (11/15/2006)*

Ferraton Père et Fils 2004 La Source Syrah (Saint-Joseph) $24. **83** —*J.C.*

(11/15/2006)

Ferraton Père et Fils 2001 Le Grand Courtil Syrah (Crozes-Hermitage) $23. 89 —*R.V. (2/1/2005)*

Ferraton Père et Fils 2000 Les Dionnières Syrah (Hermitage) $76. 90 —*R.V. (2/1/2005)*

FORTANT

Fortant 2003 Cabernet Sauvignon (Vin de Pays d'Oc) $6. 88 Best Buy —*R.V. (12/1/2004)*

Fortant 2003 Chardonnay (Vin de Pays d'Oc) $6. 85 Best Buy —*R.V. (12/1/2004)*

Fortant 1999 Chardonnay (Vin de Pays d'Oc) $10. 81 —*M.S. (4/1/2002)*

Fortant 2003 Merlot (Vin de Pays d'Oc) $6. 85 Best Buy —*R.V. (12/1/2004)*

Fortant 2003 Sauvignon Blanc (Vin de Pays d'Oc) $6. 82 —*R.V. (12/1/2004)*

FOURNIER PÈRE ET FILS

Fournier Père et Fils 2003 Grand Cuvée Fournier Sauvignon Blanc (Pouilly-Fumé) $25. 89 —*R.V. (8/1/2006)*

Fournier Père et Fils 2004 Grande Cuvée Vieilles Vignes Sauvignon Blanc (Pouilly-Fumé) $23. A powerful, fat, still young wine, full of yeast flavors, green apples, plums and with a fine, tight structure—this is a food wine that could certainly age, maybe over 3–4 years. 90 —*R.V. (9/1/2007)*

Fournier Père et Fils 2004 La Chaudouillonne Sauvignon Blanc (Sancerre) $25. An intense, very pure expression of Sauvignon Blanc, with delicious green fruits, flavors of white peaches, grapefruit and some spice. To taste, the fruit is fresh but concentrated, leaving a big mouthful of green and herbs. 90 Editors' Choice —*R.V. (9/1/2007)*

Fournier Père et Fils 2003 Les Chardouillonne Sauvignon Blanc (Sancerre) $25. 90 —*R.V. (8/1/2006)*

FRANÇOIS CHIDAINE

François Chidaine 2004 Chenin Blanc (Montlouis-sur-Loire) $17. 91 Cellar Selection —*R.V. (6/1/2006)*

FRANÇOIS COTAT

François Cotat 2003 Les Monts Damnés Sauvignon Blanc (Sancerre) $28. 86 *(7/1/2005)*

FRANCOIS LABET

Francois Labet NV Champagne Blend (Crémant de Bourgogne) $19. 90 —*R.V. (6/1/2006)*

Francois Labet 2002 Clos du Domaine Chardonnay (Meursault) $120. 87 —*J.C. (4/1/2005)*

Francois Labet 2002 Les Nosroyes Chardonnay (Puligny-Montrachet) $110. 87 —*J.C. (4/1/2005)*

FRANÇOIS SECONDÉ

François Secondé 2002 Blanc de Blancs Brut Chardonnay (Champagne) $NA. Made from grand cru vineyards in Sillery, this is a well-balanced wine, with a dosage on the high side, but there's richness rather than sweetness. Enjoy the almost tropical fruits here. 88 —*R.V. (12/1/2007)*

FRANÇOISE CHAUVENET

Françoise Chauvenet NV Silver Cap Grande Cuvée Blanc de Blancs Brut Sparkling Blend (Vin Mousseux) $10. Despite some earthy, mushroomy aromas, this lightweight sparkler's flavors veer toward lemon and stones. It's rather tart on the finish, and should pair well with raw shellfish. 83 —*J.C. (12/15/2007)*

Françoise Chauvenet NV Silver Cap Grande Cuvée Blanc de Blancs Brut Sparkling Blend (Vin Moelleux) $10. 83 —*M.S. (12/31/2005)*

FREDERIC MAGNIEN

Frederic Magnien 2005 Chardonnay (Chablis) $30. This is a lively, vibrant, easy wine, with crisp apple flavors, minerality and a light citrus finish. 85 —*R.V. (3/1/2007)*

Frederic Magnien 2005 Montmains Premier Cru Chardonnay (Chablis) $42. An attractive, fresh wine with citrus flavors, a touch of wood and a light, mineral character. It is crisp but offers a rounded, soft finish. 88 —*R.V. (3/1/2007)*

Frederic Magnien 2005 Pinot Noir (Bourgogne) $20. This wine comes from the négociant side of Domaine Michel Magnien, run by son Frédéric. It has big, round spice and new wood flavors, not over extracted but definitely with a dry edge to it. It's ripe, and good quality for a simple Burgundy. 84 —*R.V. (3/1/2007)*

Frederic Magnien 2004 Pinot Noir (Charmes-Chambertin) $123. Densely structured, this wine has rich, polished fruit but rough tannins, a curious combination. The wood element is very obvious here, which spoils the already delicious black fruit flavor. Give it time, perhaps. 89 —*R.V. (3/1/2007)*

Frederic Magnien 2004 Pinot Noir (Chambertin Clos de Bèze) $178. A wine that hints at the power of a Gevrey grand cru vineyard, but mainly exhibits the softer side. But there is an element of solid tannin before you get to the Pinot Noir delicacy that continues on to the finish. 91 —*R.V. (3/1/2007)*

Frederic Magnien 2004 Charmes Premier Cru Pinot Noir (Chambolle-Musigny) $87. Delicious ripe fruit, sweet tannins and light, fresh acidity: All the elements are here for a wine that will be a delight to drink in 3–4 years. There are rounded red fruit flavors, along with a core of dry tannins. 91 —*R.V. (3/1/2007)*

Frederic Magnien 2004 Clos Baulet Premier Cru Pinot Noir (Morey Saint-Denis) $67. With its great black fruits, this is a big wine that shows new wood and an edge of tarry flavors. It's tough now, solid and compacted. The fruits are dark and heavy, brooding, demanding attention and time. 89 —*R.V. (3/1/2007)*

Frederic Magnien 2004 Larrets Pinot Noir (Morey Saint-Denis) $NA. A rare white wine from Morey-Saint-Denis, this is full and rich with lively acidity and green pear flavors. Vanilla and ripeness give it body and complexity, while the crispness gives it a lift. 90 —*R.V. (3/1/2007)*

Frederic Magnien 2004 Les Borniques Premier Cru Pinot Noir (Chambolle-Musigny) $87. Dusty fruit and some bitter, extracted flavors spoil this wine. A shame, because it has the weight of black fruits, but they seem to rest uneasily with the off flavors. It's also rather austere for a Chambolle. 86 —*R.V. (3/1/2007)*

Frederic Magnien 2004 Les Saint-Georges Premier Cru Pinot Noir (Nuits-St.-Georges) $87. Hard and with rustic flavors, here's a wine that certainly doesn't show well in its youth. Will it age? The tannins are certainly there, so it could do so, but don't open it in the next few years. 87 —*R.V. (3/1/2007)*

Frederic Magnien 2004 Longecourts Vieille Vigne Pinot Noir (Nuits-St.-Georges) $40. This wine opens to red fruits and soft tannins in the mouth. It's all about fruit, in fact—a juicy, fresh and mouth-filling fruit salad. 88 —*R.V. (3/1/2007)*

Frederic Magnien 2004 Ruchots Premier Cru Pinot Noir (Morey Saint-Denis) $67. A very complete wine, with all the elements in their right places. Of all the Morey Saint-Denis premier crus that Frédéric Magnien has released in 2004, this seems the most successful, keeping extraction and new wood in their place, emphasizing instead the beautiful fruits and freshness. 92 —*R.V. (3/1/2007)*

FRENCH RABBIT

French Rabbit 2005 Cabernet Sauvignon Cabernet Sauvignon (Vin de Pays d'Oc) $10. 83 —*R.V. (12/31/2006)*

French Rabbit 2005 Merlot (Vin de Pays d'Oc) $10. 82 —*R.V. (12/31/2006)*

FRENCH REVOLUTION

French Revolution 1999 Le Rouge Red Blend (Côtes-du-Ventoux) $9. 85 —*M.M. (2/1/2002)*

G. H. MUMM

G. H. Mumm NV Brut Rosé Champagne Blend (Champagne) $60. A fresh, strawberry-flavored wine, with good red berry and red apple-skin textures. The acidity is initially prominent, but then there is also a burst of candy, leaving softness. 87 —*R.V. (12/31/2007)*

G. H. Mumm NV Brut Rosé Champagne Blend (Champagne) $43. 88 —*R.V. (12/15/2003)*

G. H. Mumm NV Carte Classique Extra Dry Champagne Blend (Champagne) $35. 85 —*S.H. (12/15/2002)*

G. H. Mumm NV Carte Classique Extra Dry Champagne Blend (Champagne) $35. 85 —*J.M. (12/15/2001)*

G. H. Mumm NV Cordon Rouge Brut Champagne Blend (Champagne) $30. 88 *(12/1/2000)*

G. H. Mumm NV Cordon Rouge Brut Champagne Blend (Champagne) $45. 86 —*M.S. (12/15/2003)*

G. H. Mumm NV Cordon Rouge Brut Champagne Blend (Champagne) $30. 84 —*S.H. (12/15/2002)*

G. H. Mumm NV Cordon Rouge Brut Champagne Blend (Champagne) $45. 86 —*J.C. (12/15/2001)*

G. H. Mumm 1998 Cuvée R. Lalou Brut Champagne Blend (Champagne) $140. This new release from Mumm is a selection from 12 of the best vineyards owned or run by the company. It is certainly a complex wine, finely balanced with layers of intense, mature fruits, very mineral in structure, and with the crispness of the acidity acting as a support to the citrus and vanilla flavors. Worth aging for another 4–5 years. **93 Cellar Selection** —*R.V. (12/31/2007)*

G. H. Mumm NV Grand Cru Brut Champagne Blend (Champagne) $60. 93 —*R.V. (12/1/2005)*

G. H. Mumm NV Joyesse Demi-Sec Champagne Blend (Champagne) $41. 85 —*J.C. (12/1/2004)*

G. H. Mumm NV Mumm de Cramant Brut Chardonnay (Champagne) $60. This emblematic cuvée from Mumm (known for many years as Crémant de Cramant because it was bottled at a slightly lower pressure) is a celebration of grand cru Chardonnay in Cramant. It is a finely structured, relatively full-bodied wine, showing toast and butter flavors along with the pink grapefruit and crisp apple tastes. **90** —*R.V. (12/31/2007)*

G. H. Mumm NV Mumm de Cramant Brut Chardonnay (Champagne) $70. 88 —*S.H. (12/15/2003)*

GABRIEL MEFFRE

Gabriel Meffre 2001 Domaine de Longue Toque Rhône Red Blend (Gigondas) $18. 90 —*R.V. (3/1/2004)*

Gabriel Meffre 2005 La Chasse du Pape Prestige Rhône Red Blend (Côtes-du-Rhône) $10. 83 —*J.C. (11/15/2006)*

Gabriel Meffre 2003 La Chasse du Pape Prestige Rhône Red Blend (Côtes-du-Rhône) $10. 84 —*J.C. (11/15/2006)*

Gabriel Meffre 2000 Laurus Rhône Red Blend (Vacqueyras) $17. 86 —*R.V. (3/1/2004)*

Gabriel Meffre 2000 Laurus Rhône Red Blend (Gigondas) $20. 87 —*R.V. (3/1/2004)*

Gabriel Meffre 2003 La Chasse du Pape Prestige Rhône White Blend (Côtes-du-Rhône) $10. 84 —*J.C. (11/15/2006)*

Gabriel Meffre 2002 Laurus Rhône White Blend (Hermitage) $NA. 87 —*R.V. (2/1/2005)*

Gabriel Meffre 2002 Laurus Syrah (Hermitage) $NA. 88 —*R.V. (2/1/2005)*

Gabriel Meffre 2001 Laurus Syrah (Saint-Joseph) $NA. 87 —*R.V. (2/1/2005)*

Gabriel Meffre 2000 Laurus Syrah (Cornas) $NA. 85 —*R.V. (2/1/2005)*

GASTON CHIQUET

Gaston Chiquet 1997 Or Premier Cru Champagne Blend (Champagne) $52. 88 —*R.V. (12/1/2004)*

GEORGES DUBOEUF

Georges Duboeuf 2001 Cuvée Prestige Reserve Cabernet Sauvignon (Vin de Pays d'Oc) $10. 84 —*M.S. (9/1/2003)*

Georges Duboeuf 2001 Prestige Cabernet Sauvignon (Vin de Pays d'Oc) $10. 87 Best Buy —*R.V. (12/1/2004)*

Georges Duboeuf 2004 Chardonnay (Saint-Véran) $11. 87 Best Buy —*R.V. (11/15/2006)*

Georges Duboeuf 2001 Chardonnay (Pouilly-Fuissé) $19. 85 —*J.C. (10/1/2003)*

Georges Duboeuf 1999 Chardonnay (St.-Véran) $11. 86 Best Buy —*M.S. (11/1/2000)*

Georges Duboeuf 2005 Chardonnay Chardonnay (Vin de Pays d'Oc) $7. 84 —*R.V. (12/31/2006)*

Georges Duboeuf 2001 Cuvée Prestige Reserve Chardonnay (Vin de Pays d'Oc) $10. 83 —*M.S. (9/1/2003)*

Georges Duboeuf 1999 Les Mures Chardonnay (Pouilly-Loche) $12. 87 —*M.M. (11/1/2000)*

Georges Duboeuf 1999 Milenage Chardonnay (Vin de Pays d'Oc) $9. 83 —*M.S. (11/1/2000)*

Georges Duboeuf 2002 Reserve Chardonnay (Vin de Pays d'Oc) $8. 85 Best Buy —*R.V. (12/1/2004)*

Georges Duboeuf 2003 Gamay (Juliénas) $12. 90 Best Buy —*P.G. (11/15/2004)*

Georges Duboeuf 2001 Gamay (Régnié) $9. 86 Best Buy —*M.M. (11/15/2002)*

Georges Duboeuf 2001 Gamay (Juliénas) $12. 86 —*M.M. (11/15/2002)*

Georges Duboeuf 2001 Gamay (Chiroubles) $12. 85 —*M.M. (11/15/2002)*

Georges Duboeuf 2000 Château de Nervers Gamay (Brouilly) $12. 85 *(1/1/2004)*

Georges Duboeuf 2001 Domaine des Quatre Vents Gamay (Fleurie) $14. 87 —*J.C. (11/15/2003)*

Georges Duboeuf 2001 Domaine des Rosiers Gamay (Moulin-à-Vent) $14. 83 —*J.C. (11/15/2003)*

Georges Duboeuf 2002 Flower label Gamay (Juliénas) $12. 84 —*J.C. (11/15/2003)*

Georges Duboeuf 2002 Grand Cuvée Flower Label Gamay (Brouilly) $11. 87 Best Buy —*J.C. (11/15/2003)*

Georges Duboeuf 2001 Grande Cuvée Gamay (Brouilly) $11. 84 —*M.M. (11/15/2002)*

Georges Duboeuf 2001 Jean Descombes Gamay (Morgon) $12. 84 —*J.C. (11/15/2003)*

Georges Duboeuf 1997 Pisse Vieille Gamay (Brouilly) $11. 88 —*J.C. (11/15/1999)*

Georges Duboeuf 2000 Prestige Gamay (Moulin-à-Vent) $20. 87 *(1/1/2004)*

Georges Duboeuf 2002 Merlot (Vin de Pays d'Oc) $7. 82 —*R.V. (12/1/2004)*

Georges Duboeuf 1998 Domaine de Bordeneuve Merlot (Vin de Pays d'Oc) $8. 85 —*M.S. (12/31/1999)*

Georges Duboeuf 2001 Prestige Merlot (Vin de Pays d'Oc) $10. 86 Best Buy —*R.V. (12/1/2004)*

Georges Duboeuf 1999 Red Blend (St.-Amour) $14. 86 —*M.M. (11/1/2000)*

Georges Duboeuf NV GD Red Blend (Vin de Pays du Torgan) $5. 84 —*S.H. (1/1/2002)*

Georges Duboeuf 2005 Syrah (Vin de Pays d'Oc) $6. A simple, fresh, attractively perfumed wine, with soft tannins and ripe gentle fruit flavors of plums, blueberries and sweet red fruits. **84 Best Buy** —*R.V. (2/1/2007)*

Georges Duboeuf 2000 Syrah (Vin de Pays d'Oc) $7. 82 *(10/1/2001)*

Georges Duboeuf 1999 Viognier (Vin de Pays d'Oc) $15. 87 —*M.S. (11/1/2000)*

GERARD BERTRAND

Gerard Bertrand 2003 Classic Chardonnay (Vin de Pays d'Oc) $10. 82 —*J.C. (12/1/2004)*

Gerard Bertrand 2005 Collection Pinot Noir (Vin de Pays d'Oc) $14. Raspberry flavors give some varietal character to this wine, allowing the tannins to show through as it opens out. There's a definite earthy character, with some undergrowth flavors, but also good ripe fruit. **87** —*R.V. (2/1/2007)*

Gerard Bertrand 2003 La Forge Rhône Red Blend (Corbières) $NA. 91 —*R.V. (12/31/2006)*

Gerard Bertrand 2004 Tautavel Reserve Rhône Red Blend (Côtes du Roussillon Villages) $15. A youthful wine, the flavors are ripe, raisiny and very soft, with black currant. The aftertaste is dry but fruity. **87** —*R.V. (2/1/2007)*

Gerard Bertrand 2005 Terroir Rhône Red Blend (Minervois) $15. Big, bold and structured, this blend of Syrah and Carignan is a rich characterful, wine from one of the most exciting appellations in Languedoc. It shows plenty of Mediterranean warmth and ripeness, but its spice and sweet tannins give complexity as well as power. **89** —*R.V. (2/1/2007)*

Gerard Bertrand 2005 Collection Sauvignon Blanc (Vin de Pays d'Oc) $14. A delicious, herbaceous, grassy style of Sauvignon, fresh but full-bodied. There are flavors of green plums and a touch of thyme. Fresh and crisp. **86** —*R.V. (2/1/2007)*

Gerard Bertrand 2005 Le Blanc de Villemajou Rhône White Blend (Corbières) 88 —*R.V. (12/31/2006)*

Gerard Bertrand 2003 Syrah (Vin de Pays d'Oc) $10. 86 Best Buy —*J.C. (12/1/2004)*

Gerard Bertrand 2005 Terroir Syrah (Coteaux du Languedoc) $NA. 85 —*R.V. (12/31/2006)*

Gerard Bertrand 2005 Viognier Collection Viognier (Vin de Pays d'Oc) $NA. 86 —*R.V. (12/31/2006)*

GIGONDAS LA CAVE

Gigondas la Cave 2004 Beaumirail Rhône Red Blend (Vacqueyras) $NA. 85 —*J.C. (11/15/2006)*

GILLES ROBIN

Gilles Robin 1999 Cuvée Albéric Bouvet Syrah (Crozes-Hermitage) $20. 89 Cellar Selection *(10/1/2001)*

GINESTET

Ginestet 2004 Bordeaux Bordeaux Blend (Bordeaux) $8. 88 —*R.V. (12/31/2006)*

Ginestet 2005 Marquis de Chasse Bordeaux White Blend (Bordeaux Blanc) $9. 85 Best Buy —*R.V. (12/31/2006)*

Ginestet 2004 Marquis de Chasse Bordeaux Blend (Bordeaux) $NA. A stalky, light, tobacco and red fruit-flavored wine. This is tight, spicy and layered with considerable acidity. Definitely needs food. 83 —*R.V. (6/1/2007)*

Ginestet 2005 French RootsCabernet Sauvignon (Vin de Pays d'Oc) $8. 86 —*R.V. (12/31/2006)*

Ginestet 2004 French Roots Merlot (Vin de Pays d'Oc) $8. 86 —*R.V. (12/31/2006)*

Ginestet 2005 French Roots Sauvignon Blanc (Vin de Pays des Côtes de Gascogne) $8. 82 —*R.V. (12/31/2006)*

Ginestet 2005 French Roots Shiraz (Vin de Pays d'Oc) $8. 84 Best Buy —*R.V. (12/31/2006)*

Ginestet 2005 Bordeaux White Blend (Bordeaux Blanc) $NA. This blend of Sau Blanc and Sémillon is somewhat yeasty, but there's an attractive herbaceous ribbon of flavor that goes through, and light green fruit tastes. The aftertaste is rather bitter, spoiling this simple wine. 82 —*R.V. (11/1/2007)*

GIROLATE

Girolate 2004 Bordeaux Blend (Bordeaux) $120. The Despagne family returned to tradition with the making of Girolate, planting a vineyard to the former high density, keeping winemaking simple. This is the 2004, the latest release. Reflecting the heat of that vintage, it is soft, textured, rich and spicy, with a southern warmth, pure superripe Merlot. 90 —*R.V. (6/1/2007)*

Girolate 2003 Bordeaux Blend (Bordeaux) $90. The Despagne family returned to tradition with the making of Girolate, planting a vineyard to the former high density, keeping winemaking simple. This is the 2003, the latest release. Reflecting the heat of that vintage, it is soft, textured, rich and spicy, with a southern warmth. Pure superripe Merlot. 90 —*R.V. (11/1/2007)*

GOSSET

Gosset NV Brut Excellence Champagne Blend (Champagne) $40. 87 —*P.G. (12/15/2003)*

Gosset NV Brut Grande Rosé Champagne Blend (Champagne) $70. 87 —*P.G. (12/15/2002)*

Gosset 1995 Celebris Brut Champagne Blend (Champagne) $150. 87 —*R.V. (12/1/2004)*

Gosset 1998 Celebris Brut Rosé Champagne Blend (Champagne) $135. 88 —*R.V. (12/1/2004)*

Gosset NV Excellence Brut Champagne Blend (Champagne) $40. 84 —*J.C. (12/1/2005)*

Gosset NV Excéllence Brut Champagne Blend (Champagne) $43. 89 —*P.G. (12/1/2006)*

Gosset 1999 Grand Brut Champagne Blend (Champagne) $85. 94 —*R.V. (11/1/2006)*

Gosset 1996 Grand Brut Champagne Blend (Champagne) $75. 90 —*R.V. (12/1/2004)*

Gosset NV Grand Brut Rosé Champagne Blend (Champagne) $70. 87 —*M.S. (12/15/2005)*

Gosset NV Grand Brut Rosé Champagne Blend (Champagne) $69. 87 —*M.M. (12/15/2001)*

Gosset NV Grande Réserve Brut Champagne Blend (Champagne) $60. 90 —*P.G. (12/1/2006)*

Gosset NV Grande Réserve Brut Champagne Blend (Champagne) $60. 92 —*M.S. (12/15/2005)*

Gosset NV Grande Réserve Brut Champagne Blend (Champagne) $52. 90 *(12/31/2000)*

GOULAINE

Goulaine 2005 Vouvray Chenin Blanc (Vouvray) $NA. A medium-dry wine, from a producer better known for Muscadet. It is clean, fresh, attractively citric, with delicious flavors of almonds and a balanced, easy crisp aftertaste. 85 —*R.V. (2/1/2007)*

GRANDES SERRES

Grandes Serres 2004 La Combe des Marchands Rhône Red Blend (Gigondas) $NA. 86 —*J.C. (11/15/2006)*

GRANDIN

Grandin NV Brut Sparkling Blend (Vin Mousseux) $11. 84 —*M.M. (12/15/2001)*

Grandin NV Brut Sparkling Blend (Vin Mousseux) $11. 83 —*M.M. (12/31/2000)*

GRATIEN ET MEYER

Gratien et Meyer NV Cuvée Flamme Rosé Cabernet Franc (Saumur) $27. 88 —*R.V. (6/1/2006)*

Gratien et Meyer NV Cuvée Flamme Brut White Blend (Saumur) $27. 89 —*R.V. (6/1/2006)*

GUILLEMOT-MICHEL

Guillemot-Michel 2002 Quintaine Chardonnay (Mâcon-Villages) $30. 88 —*J.C. (11/15/2005)*

GUSTAVE LORENTZ

Gustave Lorentz 2005 Pinot Blanc Reserve (Alsace) $NA. A fresh, light, crisp wine, just what an Alsace Pinot Blanc – the perfect aperitif wine – should be. There's a good melon and citrus character, with some spice and weight in the mid-palate. 87 —*R.V. (2/1/2007)*

Gustave Lorentz 2002 Altenberg de Bergheim Grand Cru Pinot Gris (Alsace) $NA. Soft, full, rich and spicy, this is an intense wine, expressing the essence of Pinot Gris. It's ripe, off-dry, but with a core of dry toast and almond flavors which go with the pear and nutmeg tastes. This is still a young wine – Lorentz advises 10-15 years aging: more realistic would be another 3-4. 91 —*R.V. (2/1/2007)*

Gustave Lorentz 2005 Reserve Pinot Gris (Alsace) $NA. The simplest, most approachable of the range of seven Pinot Gris from Lorentz, this Reserve is light, fresh, dry, with a touch of spice and smokiness. There's good acidity as well as a core of more weighty ripe pear flavors. 88 —*R.V. (2/1/2007)*

Gustave Lorentz 2000 Grand Cru Kanzlerberg Riesling (Alsace) $39. 91 —*R.V. (5/1/2005)*

Gustave Lorentz NV Cremant d'Alsace Brut Sparkling Blend (Crémant d'Alsace) $NA. Crisp, fresh, citrus and green apple flavors for a deliciously appealing aperitif style of sparkling wine. A blend of equal parts Chardonnay, Pinot Blanc and Pinot Noir, this has a creamy texture which leaves a light floating aftertaste. 89 —*R.V. (2/1/2007)*

GUY CHARLEMAGNE

Guy Charlemagne NV Blanc de Blancs Réserve Brut Champagne Blend (Champagne) $35. 89 —*R.V. (12/1/2002)*

Guy Charlemagne 1996 Mesnillesimé Brut Champagne Blend (Champagne) $50. 92 Editors' Choice —*R.V. (12/1/2002)*

GUY-PIERRE JEAN & FILS

Guy-Pierre Jean & Fils 2003 Hautes-Côtes de Nuits Les Dames Huguettes Pinot Noir (Bourgogne) $22. 85 —*J.C. (9/1/2006)*

H.GERMAIN

H.Germain NV Cuvée President Champagne Blend (Champagne) $37. 91 *(12/31/2000)*

HEART OF DARKNESS

Heart of Darkness 2001 Tannat (Madiran) $18. 87 —*R.V. (3/1/2006)*

HECHT & BANNIER

Hecht & Bannier 2004 Rhône Red Blend (Minervois) $17. A big, burly rich wine, dominated by Syrah and by wood tannins. It is fruity, full of black plums and boysenberries, low in acidity, but structured with some good tannins. It's a wine to drink now. 88 —*R.V. (12/15/2007)*

Hecht & Bannier 2003 Rhône Red Blend (Faugères) $29. A wine that bursts with aromas and wild flavors. From the raspberry and licorice aromas to the chewy, oaky and cranberry flavors, this is a wine that is a great reflection of the southern warmth and richness. 89 —*R.V. (12/15/2007)*

Hecht & Bannier 2003 Rhône Red Blend (Minervois) $NA. 88 —*R.V. (8/1/2006)*

Hecht & Bannier 2003 Rhône Red Blend (Côtes du Roussillon Villages) $NA. 87 —*R.V. (8/1/2006)*

Hecht & Bannier 2002 Rhône Red Blend (Minervois) $21. 86 —*R.V. (3/1/2006)*

Hecht & Bannier 2002 Rhône Red Blend (Côtes du Roussillon Villages) $22. 87 —*R.V. (3/1/2006)*

Hecht & Bannier 2005 Rosé Syrah (Vin de Pays des Côtes de Thau) $10. 84 —*R.V. (8/1/2006)*

Hecht & Bannier 2006 For Boys and Girls Rosé Syrah (Vin de Pays des Côtes de Thau) $10. The color gives the grape away, that grey pink, very seductive. The wine itself is clean, fresh, promising attractive redcurrant fruit flavors and refreshing acidity. It is just off dry, and finishes softly. 87 Best Buy —*R.V. (7/1/2007)*

HEIDSIECK & CO MONOPOLE

Heidsieck & Co Monopole NV Blue Top Brut Champagne Blend (Champagne) $40. Always an enjoyable non-vintage, Heidsieck Monopole's style has changed little despite all the changes in ownership. It has a soft, open character, but never seems sweet, and is more rounded with creamy apple flavors and well-integrated acidity. **88** —*R.V. (12/1/2007)*

Heidsieck & Co Monopole NV Blue Top Brut Champagne Blend (Champagne) $28. 85 —*J.C. (12/1/2004)*

Heidsieck & Co Monopole NV Blue Top Brut Champagne Blend (Champagne) $32. 86 —*J.C. (12/15/2003)*

Heidsieck & Co Monopole NV Blue Top Premier Cru Champagne Blend (Champagne) $39. 93 —*P.G. (12/1/2006)*

Heidsieck & Co Monopole NV Blue Top Premiers Crus Champagne Blend (Champagne) $40. 88 —*J.C. (12/1/2004)*

Heidsieck & Co Monopole NV Diamant Blanc Champagne Blend (Champagne) $100. 88 —*M.S. (12/31/2005)*

Heidsieck & Co Monopole NV Diamant Blanc de Blancs Champagne Blend (Champagne) $50. 87 —*S.H. (12/15/2000)*

Heidsieck & Co Monopole 1995 Diamant Bleu Champagne Blend (Champagne) $70. 91 —*P.G. (12/15/2002)*

Heidsieck & Co Monopole 1998 Diamant Rosé Champagne Blend (Champagne) $130. 90 —*M.S. (12/15/2005)*

Heidsieck & Co Monopole 1988 Diamant Rosé Champagne Blend (Champagne) $70. 89 —*P.G. (12/15/2002)*

Heidsieck & Co Monopole 1988 Diamant Rosé Champagne Blend (Champagne) $70. 92 —*R.V. (12/15/2003)*

Heidsieck & Co Monopole NV Extra Dry Champagne Blend (Champagne) $37. 87 —*M.S. (12/15/2003)*

Heidsieck & Co Monopole 2002 Gold Top Champagne Blend (Champagne) $45. 86 —*R.V. (11/1/2006)*

Heidsieck & Co Monopole NV Monopole Brut Champagne Blend (Champagne) $30. 85 *(12/15/1999)*

Heidsieck & Co Monopole NV Premier Cru Brut Champagne Blend (Champagne) $40. A full-bodied, rounded, well matured bottle, with plenty of attractive toasty flavors rather than fruit. This is a delicious bottle-aged Champagne in an old style, that will be great with food. **90** —*R.V. (12/1/2007)*

Heidsieck & Co Monopole NV Red Top Champagne Blend (Champagne) $27. 87 —*J.C. (12/1/2004)*

Heidsieck & Co Monopole NV Red Top Champagne Blend (Champagne) $26. 85 —*J.C. (12/15/2003)*

Heidsieck & Co Monopole NV Rosé Top Champagne Blend (Champagne) $45. A lively Champagne, initially all froth and fizz. But get through that and there is a pleasant, slightly sweet wine— perhaps more full-bodied than some. The primary red-fruit flavors have been lessened by some bottle age, leaving a wine which has a hint of maturity. **86** —*R.V. (12/1/2007)*

Heidsieck & Co Monopole NV Rosé Top Champagne Blend (Champagne) $43. 89 —*J.C. (12/1/2004)*

Heidsieck & Co Monopole NV Rosé Top Champagne Blend (Champagne) $36. 85 —*R.V. (12/15/2003)*

Heidsieck & Co Monopole NV Diamant Blanc Grands Crus Chardonnay (Champagne) $65. 87 —*J.C. (12/15/2003)*

Heidsieck & Co Monopole 1995 Diamant Bleu Pinot-Chardonnay (Champagne) $130. 91 —*R.V. (12/1/2004)*

HENRI ABELÉ

Henri Abelé NV 1757 Brut Champagne Blend (Champagne) $28. 89 —*J.C. (12/31/2004)*

Henri Abelé NV Brut Champagne Blend (Champagne) $30. 91 Editors' Choice —*P.G. (12/15/2002)*

HENRI BOURGEOIS

Henri Bourgeois 2005 Sauvignon Blanc (Pouilly-Fumé) $18. 89 —*R.V. (8/1/2006)*

Henri Bourgeois 2005 Le MD de Bourgeois Sauvignon Blanc (Sancerre) $24. 93 —*R.V. (8/1/2006)*

Henri Bourgeois 2005 Les Bonnes Bouches Sauvignon Blanc (Sancerre) $20. 89 —*R.V. (8/1/2006)*

HENRI DE VILLAMONT

Henri de Villamont 2005 Chardonnay (Meursault) $22. Mainly from the lieu dit vineyard of Crotot, this is powerful, rounded in the way that Meursault should be. The fruit is ripe, filling the mouth with apples and cream flavors, topped by understated wood. **89** —*R.V. (8/1/2007)*

Henri de Villamont 2005 Chardonnay (Pouilly-Fuissé) $36. With 25% new wood, this has good roundness, but it has kept a deliciously fresh mineral character. The aftertaste is all almonds, ripeness and vivid fruit flavors. **86** —*R.V. (8/1/2007)*

Henri de Villamont 2005 Clos St-Jean Premier Cru Chardonnay (Chassagne-Montrachet) $50. Super-ripe, and powerful, with an edge of new wood, but mainly dominated by apricots and rich white fruits. It's big and ripe, just keeping on the right side of blowsy. **88** —*R.V. (8/1/2007)*

Henri de Villamont 2005 Les Caillerets Premier Cru Chardonnay (Meursault) $50. Muscular, powering its way with richness and structured tannins. The white pear and almond flavors seem to sit on top of this dense wine, which will need to age. It reflects the super-rich side of white Burgundy in 2005. **89** —*R.V. (8/1/2007)*

Henri de Villamont 2005 Sous le Puits Premier Cru Chardonnay (Puligny-Montrachet) $50. Striking a great balance between elegance and richness, this shows plenty of sweet fruit, white peaches and quince, while also keeping poise with its structure and finishing acidity. This will be a great food Chardonnay. **91** —*R.V. (8/1/2007)*

Henri de Villamont 2003 Clos des Guettes Pinot Noir (Savigny-lès-Beaune) $NA. 89 —*R.V. (9/1/2005)*

Henri de Villamont 2002 Grands Pinot Noir (Echezeaux) $80. 90 —*R.V. (9/1/2004)*

Henri de Villamont 2002 Les Baudes Premier Cru Pinot Noir (Chambolle-Musigny) $45. 88 —*R.V. (9/1/2004)*

Henri de Villamont 2003 Les Groseilles Premier Cru Pinot Noir (Chambolle-Musigny) $NA. 90 —*R.V. (9/1/2005)*

Henri de Villamont 2002 Premier Cru Pinot Noir (Chambolle-Musigny) $40. 88 —*R.V. (9/1/2004)*

HENRIOT

Henriot 1996 Brut Champagne Blend (Champagne) $78. 92 —*R.V. (11/1/2006)*

Henriot NV Brut Rosé Champagne Blend (Champagne) $60. 91 —*P.G. (12/1/2006)*

Henriot NV Brut Souverain Champagne Blend (Champagne) $40. A full wine, soft and creamy, with some toasty, yeast character. There's obvious Pinot Noir character, with flavors of white fruits, pink grapefruit and a ripe structure. **89** —*R.V. (12/1/2007)*

Henriot 1990 Cuvée des Enchanteleurs Brut Champagne Blend (Champagne) $149. 94 —*R.V. (11/1/2006)*

Henriot 2002 Rosé Millésimé Champagne Blend (Champagne) $80. Crisp raspberries and red currants here, with a refreshing, lively acidity. If there is any intensity in this finely balanced wine, it is in the relationship between the fruit and the clean structure. But this is not for aging—drink now. **92** —*R.V. (12/1/2007)*

Henriot NV Blanc Souverain Pur Chardonnay (Champagne) $48. The blanc de blancs from Henriot has some fine, toasty, aged character. This is a rich, but still vibrantly fruity wine that shows some baked apple and pink grapefruit but also some maturity. A finely made wine, illustrating the benefits of some bottle age. **92 Editors' Choice** —*R.V. (12/1/2007)*

Henriot NV Souverain Brut Champagne Blend (Champagne) $40. 92 —*R.V. (12/1/2005)*

HENRY NATTER

Henry Natter 2005 Pinot Noir (Sancerre) $25. Soft and smooth, showing mature red berries and a touch of mushroom. Already very ready to drink: light but also with plenty of ripe fruit. **87** —*R.V. (10/1/2007)*

Henry Natter 2005 Rosé Pinot Noir (Sancerre) $25. A delicate onion skin-colored wine, keeping its freshness after 18 months, just touching on toast and caramel, but principally offering bitter cherries and raspberry flavors. **86** —*R.V. (10/1/2007)*

Henry Natter 2006 Sauvignon Blanc (Sancerre) $24. Ripe, tropical fruit flavors from super-ripe grapes. That seems to be the way Henry Natter works, and the result is a soft, smooth wine, with a touch of caramel, quince and white peach flavors. The acidity is only apparent towards the end. **89** —*R.V. (9/1/2007)*

Henry Natter 2004 Sauvignon Blanc (Sancerre) $23. 88 —*R.V. (8/1/2006)*

Henry Natter 2004 François de la Grange de Montigny Sauvignon Blanc (Sancerre) $32. It's quite a flourish of a name that refers to the vineyard from which this wine comes. This 2004 is now mature, a combination of honey, nuts and a hint of green asparagus and aromas of undergrowth. Go for this wine for its secondary flavors, not the fruit, and then it becomes delicious. **90** —*R.V. (9/1/2007)*

HERON

Heron 1996 Red Blend (Vin de Pays d'Oc) $9. 85 *(11/15/1999)*

HERZOG SELECTION

Herzog Selection 1999 Chardonnay (Vin de Pays du Jardin de la France) $8. 84 *(4/1/2001)*

HIPPOLYTE REVERDY

Hippolyte Reverdy 2003 Sauvignon Blanc (Sancerre) $22. 90 *(7/1/2005)*

HUBERT VENEAU

Hubert Veneau 2006 Sauvignon Blanc (Pouilly-Fumé) $20. Round and full, what this lacks in minerality, it makes up for in richness, its white nectarine and peach flavors and New World fruitiness. For a Pouilly-Fumé it is big, but it's also likely to age quickly. 88 *—R.V. (10/1/2007)*

Hubert Veneau 2005 Cuvée S Sauvignon Blanc (Pouilly-Fumé) $30. A seriously herbaceous wine. Flavors of asparagus and green peas are here, alongside intense acidity. Maybe it will calm down in a year. At the moment it's New Zealand on the Loire. 86 *—R.V. (10/1/2007)*

HUGEL

Hugel 2004 Gewürztraminer (Alsace) $20. A broad, mouthfilling wine that's somehow a bit restrained at the same time, without that over-the-top quality some Gewürzts develop. It does have a slightly oily texture, with flavors of citrus and spice on the finish. Drink now. 85 *—J.C. (7/1/2007)*

Hugel 2002 Gewürztraminer (Alsace) $20. 84 *—J.C. (2/1/2005)*

Hugel 1999 Gewürztraminer (Alsace) $19. 87 *(11/1/2001)*

Hugel 2005 Sélection de Grains Nobles Gewürztraminer (Alsace) $210. Full-bodied, lush and sweet, yet despite the presence of ample botrytis, the wine retains a sense of varietal character in its lychee-scented aromas. Dried apricot and pineapple flavors linger for a long time on the mouthwatering finish. Delicious now, and should age well for at least 10 years. The 2001 and 2002 vintages are also currently available, and not far behind in quality. 94 *—J.C. (12/15/2007)*

Hugel 2002 Sélection de Grains Nobles Gewürztraminer (Alsace) $203. Hugel, a firm known for its dry-styled table wines, can make killer sweet wines as well, deftly illustrated by this example. It's full-bodied, broad in the mouth and rich, with considerable weight to its flavors of roses, dried apricots, marmalade and honey, yet stays fresh on the long, mouthwatering finish. Drink now–2020. 93 *—J.C. (12/15/2007)*

Hugel 2001 Sélection de Grains Nobles Gewürztraminer (Alsace) $197. Just a touch less lively than the 2002 and 2005 versions, Hugel's 2001 Gewürztraminer SGN is still excellent, boasting plenty of weight and richness allied to distinctive varietal aromas of rose petals and cracked white pepper alongside the dried apricot notes of botrytis. 92 *—J.C. (12/15/2007)*

Hugel 1997 Vendange Tardive Gewürztraminer (Alsace) $55. 91 *(11/1/2001)*

Hugel 2004 Cuvée les Amours Pinot Blanc (Alsace) $15. Shows great minerality and intensity for an entry-level wine. Pencilly aromas, with an element akin to graphite, but also citrus and green-apple fruit. The flavors stay focused: green apple and lemon mixed with stony, minerally notes. It's only medium-bodied, but the finish is long and almost painfully intense. 90 Best Buy *—J.C. (7/1/2007)*

Hugel 1999 Cuvée Les Amours Pinot Blanc (Alsace) $12. 86 *(11/1/2001)*

Hugel 2001 Vendange Tardive Pinot Gris (Alsace) $92. 92 *—R.V. (2/1/2006)*

Hugel 2005 Riesling (Alsace) $19. Firmly in the Hugel style, with a certain austerity and steeliness to its character. Modest apple and citrus flavors pick up hints of underripe nectarine, finishing with a burst of citrus. Imported by Frederick Wildman & Sons, LTD. 85 *(9/1/2007)*

Hugel 2004 Riesling (Alsace) $18. Made in the traditional Hugel style, this is a dry, high-acid Riesling. Scents of lime and chalk dust combine with green apple and petrol aromas to make for a classic bouquet. Modernists may find the palate a bit lean, but others will find it sharply focused, with a racy, zesty finish. 87 *—J.C. (7/1/2007)*

Hugel 2000 Riesling (Alsace) $17. 85 *—R.V. (8/1/2003)*

Hugel 1998 Hommage à Jean Hugel Riesling (Alsace) $50. 91 *—R.V. (5/1/2005)*

Hugel 2005 Jubilee Hugel Riesling (Alsace) $60. Starts off with fairly soft aromas of honeydew, petrol and steely minerality. More fruit is showcased on the palate with green apple, lime and pineapple core. Medium weight and appropriately balanced, the finish is fresh and crisp. 87 *(9/1/2007)*

Hugel 2004 Jubilee Hugel Riesling (Alsace) $53. Slightly waxy aromas of paraffin are followed by hints of melon and spice on the nose. The palate is comprised of cinnamon and clove with a secondary burst of citrus shining through. A long and slightly honeyed finish completes this broad and mouthfilling selection. 87 *(9/1/2007)*

Hugel 1998 Jubilee Reserve Personelle Riesling (Alsace) $35. 89 *(11/1/2001)*

Hugel 1995 Vendage Tardive Riesling (Alsace) $65. 93 Cellar Selection *(11/1/2001)*

Hugel 1997 Reserve Personelle Tokay Pinot Gris (Alsace) $35. 85 *— (8/1/1999)*

Hugel 2004 Gentil White Blend (Alsace) $11. Lean, minerally, even a bit austere, this is the sort of crisp, mouthwatering drink that used to be more common in the Alsace section of retail shops. Racy lime flavors pair with riper notes of apples and pears, then finish dry. Best on its own, or perhaps with simply prepared lean-fleshed fish such as flounder or sole. Drink now. 86 Best Buy *—J.C. (7/1/2007)*

Hugel 2003 Gentil White Blend (Alsace) $11. 86 Best Buy *—J.C. (2/1/2005)*

J. & F. LURTON

J. & F. Lurton 2006 Les Bateaux Merlot (Vin de Pays d'Oc) $9. The Lurtons get their fruit for this wine from the Carcassonne region, the coolest part of the Languedoc. That explains the simple freshness of the red fruits, the acidity and the supple but dry tannins. Screwcap. 86 Best Buy *—R.V. (12/15/2007)*

J. & F. Lurton 2005 Les Salices Pinot Noir (Vin de Pays d'Oc) $9. 86 Best Buy *—R.V. (12/31/2006)*

J. & F. Lurton 2004 Château des Erles Rhône Red Blend (Fitou) $15. Fitou, a small region entirely surrounded by Corbières, is very dry in the summer. In 2004, when little rain fell, the grapes became extra concentrated, as shown here. There's a powerful burst of fruit, with black cherries, coffee and plenty of spice from the 50% Syrah. Only to finish are the tannins at all apparent. 91 Best Buy *—R.V. (12/15/2007)*

J. & F. Lurton 2003 Château des Erles Cuvée des Ardoises Rhône Red Blend (Fitou) $12. 89 Best Buy *—R.V. (12/31/2006)*

J. & F. Lurton 2003 Mas Janeil Rhône Red Blend (Côtes du Roussillon Villages) $13. A big wine, that balances its generosity with a sense of structure. Pepper and bold black fruits go along with an herbal character. A blend of Grenache, Carignan and Syrah. 89 Best Buy *—R.V. (2/1/2007)*

J. & F. Lurton 2004 Mas Janeil Le Tiradou Rhône Red Blend (Côtes du Roussillon Villages) $30. An intensely herbal wine, packed with flavors of the dry, wild countryside of Roussillon. Licorice, wild thyme and eucalyptus go with the black plum and dark, heavy tannins. The aftertaste is juicy, with hints of acidity. 88 *—R.V. (12/15/2007)*

J. & F. Lurton 2006 Le Rosé des Erles Rosé Blend (Corbières) $9. Salmon pink in color, this is a ripe, rich wine, with fresh acidity but round from the Grenache, spicy from the Syrah, with ripe raspberry flavors. There is a touch of dry tannin to finish. 87 Best Buy *—R.V. (7/1/2007)*

J. & F. Lurton 2006 Terra Sana Rosé Blend (Vin de Pays d'Oc) $11. A deliciously fresh rosé, blending Syrah, Grenache, Cinsault and Carignan, with crisp acidity, pure red currant and citrus flavors, and a great, refreshing zest of acidity to finish. The Terra Sana vineyard is farmed biologically. 89 Best Buy *—R.V. (7/1/2007)*

J. & F. Lurton 2006 Les Fumées Blanches Sauvignon Blanc (Vin de Pays d'Oc) $9. A smoky, intensely herbaceous wine, with flavors of grapefruit, gooseberries and touched with juicy white pears. Just to complete the medley, the aftertaste has some spice. 86 Best Buy *—R.V. (12/15/2007)*

J. & F. Lurton 2003 Les Fumées Blanches Sauvignon Blanc (Vin de Pays de Côtes du Tarn) $9. 83 *—J.C. (12/1/2004)*

J. & F. Lurton 2006 Les Bateaux Rosé de Syrah (Vin de Pays d'Oc) $10. From vineyards close to the Mediterranean, this crisply-made pure pink colored wine is full of red fruit and berry flavors, tempered with acidity, with dryness and with a hint of structure from the ripe Syrah grapes. 88 Best Buy *—R.V. (7/1/2007)*

J. & F. Lurton 2003 Les Salices Viognier (Vin de Pays d'Oc) $10. 86 Best Buy *—J.C. (12/1/2004)*

J. & F. Lurton 2005 Terra Sana White Blend (Vin de Pays Charentais) $10. 88 Best Buy *—R.V. (12/31/2006)*

J. DE TELMONT

J. de Telmont 1993 Consécration Champagne Blend (Champagne) 83 *—R.V. (12/1/2004)*

J. de Telmont 2000 Grand Champagne Blend (Champagne) $NA. 84 *—R.V. (12/1/2004)*

J. de Telmont 1990 Consécration du Siècle Brut Champagne Blend (Champagne) $80. 89 *(6/1/2001)*

J de Telmont NV Grande Réserve Brut Champagne Blend (Champagne) $52. This has simple, creamy fruit, with a touch of almonds and soft, ripe, flavors. There's pears and fresh fruit salad on the palate, and some sweetness in the aftertaste. 86 —*R.V. (12/1/2007)*

J de Telmont 2003 Insolite Chardonnay (Coteaux Champenois) $80. This still white wine from the Champagne region is produced from one parcel of old Chardonnay vines. With spicy wood aromas, and dominant wood flavors, the actual taste of the fruit is hard to discern. There's intense acidity. A curiosity, and a reminder that Champagne is better sparkling. 84 —*R.V. (12/1/2007)*

J. D. LAURENT

J. D. Laurent 2003 Sauvignon Blanc-Sémillon (Bordeaux) $10. 84 —*J.C. (6/1/2005)*

J. MOREAU & FILS

J. Moreau & Fils 2000 Chardonnay (Chablis) $14. 86 *(11/15/2001)*

J. Moreau & Fils 1999 Bougros Chardonnay (Chablis) $45. 88 *(6/1/2002)*

J. Moreau & Fils 2000 Cuvée Joyau Premier Cru Chardonnay (Chablis) $45. 91 *(6/1/2002)*

J. Moreau & Fils 1997 Cuvée Joyeaux Premier Cru Chardonnay (Chablis) $45. 90 *(6/1/2002)*

J. Moreau & Fils 1999 Les Clos Chardonnay (Chablis) $45. 91 *(6/1/2002)*

J. Moreau & Fils 1999 Vaillon Premier Cru Chardonnay (Chablis) $30. 88 *(11/15/2001)*

J. Moreau & Fils 2001 Vaillons Premier Cru Chardonnay (Chablis) $29. 88 —*J.C. (10/1/2003)*

J. Moreau & Fils 1999 Vaucoupin Chardonnay (Chablis) $28. 88 *(6/1/2002)*

J. Moreau & Fils 2000 Vaucoupin Premier Cru Chardonnay (Chablis) $29. 87 —*J.C. (10/1/2003)*

J. Moreau & Fils 2000 Sauvignon Blanc (Sauvignon de St-Bris) $10. 87 Best Buy *(11/15/2001)*

J. VIDAL FLEURY

J. Vidal Fleury 1999 Red Blend (Vacqueyras) $13. 87 —*M.S. (2/1/2003)*

J. Vidal Fleury 2001 Rhône Red Blend (Vacqueyras) $20. 85 —*J.C. (11/15/2006)*

J. Vidal Fleury 2000 Rhône Red Blend (Côtes-du-Rhône) $10. 88 Best Buy —*M.S. (2/1/2003)*

J. Vidal Fleury 2004 Syrah (Crozes-Hermitage) $20. 84 —*J.C. (11/15/2006)*

J. Vidal Fleury 2000 Syrah (Crozes-Hermitage) $16. 87 —*M.S. (9/1/2003)*

J. Vidal Fleury 2004 Blanc Viognier (Côtes-du-Rhône) $11. 87 Best Buy —*J.C. (11/15/2006)*

J.J. VINCENT

J.J. Vincent 2001 Domaine Le Cotoyon Gamay (Juliénas) $17. 87 —*J.C. (11/15/2003)*

J.L. CHAVE

J.L. Chave 2004 Marsanne (Hermitage) $98. Chave's white Hermitage is even better than his acclaimed red in 2004. It's wonderfully toasty upfront, backed by layer upon layer of honeyed fruit that simply defies description. Yet despite the incredible richness, there's also tremendous focus and minerality, so that the wine never seems overly weighty, and it finishes with great length and intensity. Drink it now, or try it in 15 years; the 1991 is singing now at age 16. 96 Cellar Selection —*J.C. (9/1/2007)*

J.L. Chave 1999 Syrah (Hermitage) $125. 97 —*R.V. (6/1/2002)*

J.L. Chave 2004 Syrah (Hermitage) $98. A top-notch effort from a difficult vintage, Chave's 2004 red Hermitage is a complete wine: complex and balanced. Spice, meat and red fruit aromas and flavors swirl together in a mix of power and elegance. Acids are a touch crisp, but that's the vintage speaking. Drink 2010–2025. 94 —*J.C. (9/1/2007)*

J.L. Chave 1998 Syrah (Hermitage) $100. 95 Cellar Selection *(11/1/2001)*

J.P. CHENET

J.P. Chenet 2000 Founder's Reserve Chardonnay (Vin de Pays d'Oc) $8. 85 Best Buy —*D.T. (2/1/2002)*

JACQUART

Jacquart 1997 Blanc de Blancs Brut Champagne Blend (Champagne) $36. 90 —*R.V. (12/1/2004)*

Jacquart 1992 Blanc de Blancs Brut Mosaïque Champagne Blend (Champagne) $38. 91 —*S.H. (12/31/2000)*

Jacquart NV Brut de Nominée Champagne Blend (Champagne) $57. 88 —*R.V. (12/1/2004)*

Jacquart NV Brut Mosaïque Champagne Blend (Champagne) $30. 90 —*P.G. (12/15/2002)*

Jacquart NV Brut Mosaïque Champagne Blend (Champagne) $35. 88 —*R.V. (12/1/2005)*

Jacquart 1996 Brut Mosaïque Champagne Blend (Champagne) $36. 91 —*R.V. (12/1/2004)*

Jacquart NV Brut Mosaïque Rosé Champagne Blend (Champagne) $40. 86 —*R.V. (12/1/2005)*

Jacquart 1998 Brut Mosaïque Rosé Champagne Blend (Champagne) 88 —*R.V. (12/1/2004)*

Jacquart 1999 Cuvée Allegra Champagne Blend (Champagne) $65. 91 —*R.V. (11/1/2006)*

Jacquart NV Demi-Sec Champagne Blend (Champagne) $30. 91 *(12/31/2000)*

Jacquart 1999 Blanc de Blancs Brut Chardonnay (Champagne) $44. 87 —*R.V. (11/1/2006)*

JACQUES PRIEUR

Jacques Prieur 1999 Clos de la Feguine Pinot Noir (Beaune) $50. 89 —*P.G. (11/1/2002)*

JACQUES RAFFAITIN

Jacques Raffaitin 2006 Domaine André Raffaitin Sauvignon Blanc (Sancerre) $NA. A classic Sancerre, with great mineral character. The structure is all there, the green and white fruits are dominant. There is just a hint of lees and yeast on this young wine. 87 —*R.V. (9/1/2007)*

JACQUESSON ET FILS

Jacquesson et Fils 1996 Champagne Blend (Champagne) $120. While it has very bready and yeasty aromas, you can taste the crisp fruits through this. It's an elegantly dry Champagne, with a pure line of white fruits and acidity that go with the beautiful structure. As befits the 1996 vintage, this will certainly age. 94 Cellar Selection —*R.V. (12/1/2007)*

Jacquesson et Fils 1997 Avize Grand Cru Extra Brut Chardonnay (Champagne) $90. This blanc de blancs certainly shows its dryness, but with the wonderful maturity that it is just beginning to develop, it also has plenty of richness. Almonds are emerging to balance the white, almost tropical, fruits, calming the extreme crispness of the acidity. A great wine, which should develop beautifully over the next 10–15 years. 95 Cellar Selection —*R.V. (12/1/2007)*

Jacquesson et Fils NV Brut Rosé Champagne Blend (Champagne) $51. 86 —*R.V. (12/15/2003)*

Jacquesson et Fils 2000 Dizy Corne Bautray Champagne Blend (Champagne) $125. 93 Editors' Choice —*R.V. (12/31/2006)*

Jacquesson et Fils 1995 Grand Vin Signature Extra Brut Rosé Champagne Blend (Champagne) $110. 89 —*R.V. (12/1/2004)*

Jacquesson et Fils 1995 Signature Extra Brut Champagne Blend (Champagne) $90. 95 —*R.V. (12/1/2005)*

JAILLANCE

Jaillance 1999 Grande Réserve Brut Clairette (Crémant de Die) $20. 87 —*M.D. (12/15/2006)*

Jaillance 2004 Grande Tradition Muscat (Clairette de Die) $21. Not too dissimilar from an Italian Moscato d'Asti, this offers exotic scents of oranges and tropical fruit. It's a bit sweet, but balanced in part by the bubbles. This would be great at brunch, or served on its own. 87 —*J.C. (12/15/2007)*

Jaillance NV Brut Sparkling Blend (Crémant de Bourgogne) $16. 87 —*M.D. (12/15/2006)*

JEAN ASTIER

Jean Astier 2002 Rhône Red Blend (Côtes-du-Rhône) $10. 85 —*J.C. (12/11/2003)*

JEAN PABIOT ET FILS

Jean Pabiot et Fils 2004 Domaine des Fines Caillottes Sauvignon Blanc (Pouilly-Fumé) 92 —*R.V. (8/1/2006)*

JEAN-BAPTISTE ADAM

Jean-Baptiste Adam NV Brut Pinot Blanc (Crémant d'Alsace) $20. 86 —*R.V. (6/1/2006)*

Jean-Baptiste Adam 2002 Grand Cru Wineck-Schlossberg Riesling (Alsace) $40. 89 —*R.V. (11/1/2005)*

Jean-Baptiste Adam 2003 Cuvée Jean-Baptiste Tokay Pinot Gris (Alsace) $23. 88 —*R.V. (2/1/2006)*

Jean-Baptiste Adam 2004 Réserve Tokay Pinot Gris (Alsace) $15. 87 —*R.V. (2/1/2006)*

Jean-Baptiste Adam 2004 Reserve Riesling (Alsace) $13. Aromas of petrol and waxed apple suggest a fairly intense offering, as does the slightly oily mouthfeel. Strongly present flavors of orange pith and citrus zest counter the viscosity and heft, allowing for a crisp and refreshing finish. Imported by Chapin Cellars LLC. 87 *(9/1/2007)*

JEAN-CLAUDE BOISSET

Jean-Claude Boisset 2005 Pinot Noir (Gevrey-Chambertin) $40. This comes from one of the top ranges of wines produced by the giant Boisset family group. It is an attractively scented wine, with spice and smoky aromas. The taste is rich, juicy, but well balanced, with fresh black cherry flavors and a good thread of dry tannins. 89 *—R.V. (3/1/2007)*

Jean-Claude Boisset 2003 Pinot Noir (Bourgogne) $16. 84 *(12/31/2005)*

Jean-Claude Boisset 2003 Pinot Noir (Chambolle-Musigny) $50. 88 *—J.C. (12/31/2005)*

Jean-Claude Boisset 2003 Chaînes Carteaux Premier Cru Pinot Noir (Nuits-St.-Georges) $69. 88 *—J.C. (12/31/2005)*

Jean-Claude Boisset 2002 Clos de Verger Premier cru Pinot Noir (Pommard) $NA. 91 *—R.V. (9/1/2004)*

Jean-Claude Boisset 2003 Grand Cru Pinot Noir (Clos Vougeot) $150. 91 *—J.C. (12/31/2005)*

Jean-Claude Boisset 2002 Les Charmes Premier Cru Pinot Noir (Chambolle-Musigny) $80. 92 *—R.V. (9/1/2004)*

JEAN-LOUIS TROCARD

Jean-Louis Trocard 2001 Clos de la Vieille Eglise Merlot-Cabernet Sauvignon (Pomerol) $55. 85 *—J.C. (11/15/2005)*

JEAN-LUC COLOMBO

Jean-Luc Colombo 1999 Cote Bleue Les Pins Couches Red Blend (Coteaux d'Aix en Provence) $30. 87 *—M.S. (2/1/2003)*

Jean-Luc Colombo 2004 La Louvée Rhône Red Blend (Cornas) $88. Strongly ferrous and minerally, with blackberry and blueberry fruit. There's no evidence of the fragility of some 2004 northern Rhônes. This is rich, concentrated and meaty, yet creamy, with supple tannins. Very flattering, with a long finish. This should age well. 92 *—J.C. (4/1/2007)*

Jean-Luc Colombo 1999 La Louvée Rhône Red Blend (Cornas) $NA. Dark, inky in color. What a wonderful bouquet this has developed, offering floral hints, notes of black olive and bright mulberry and blueberry fruit. This is still very youthful and incredibly packed with flavor. Although it seems creamy at first, it firms up on the finish, showing more iron-like minerality on the finish. Hold. 95 *—J.C. (4/1/2007)*

Jean-Luc Colombo 1996 La Louvée Rhône Red Blend (Cornas) $NA. Out of magum, this wine shows thinning fruit and some elevated acids and tannins. Dried cherries, tobacco and cedar are pleasant, but this wine needs to be consumed soon. 86 *—J.C. (4/1/2007)*

Jean-Luc Colombo 1997 Les Abeilles Rhône Red Blend (Côtes-du-Rhône) $9. 90 *(11/15/1999)*

Jean-Luc Colombo 2004 Les Ruchets Rhône Red Blend (Cornas) $88. Toastier, with cedary components and dark flavors of espresso and black olive. This is very firm, dense and muscular—the essence of concentrated Cornas opening with air to show more floral notes. Hold 10 years or more. 92 *—J.C. (4/1/2007)*

Jean-Luc Colombo 2001 Les Ruchets Rhône Red Blend (Cornas) $83. Meaty and cedary on the nose. This is powerful stuff, packing in plenty of black olive and coffee flavors. Tough, burly and muscular, this is still tannic and seems a bit closed. Hold. 90 *—J.C. (4/1/2007)*

Jean-Luc Colombo 2000 Les Ruchets Rhône Red Blend (Cornas) $83. A more supple, lighter-weight vintage. There's more spice and cedar, less densely packed fruit. Picks up berry tea flavors and some drying astringency on the finish. Drink up. 88 *—J.C. (4/1/2007)*

Jean-Luc Colombo 1998 Les Ruchets Rhône Red Blend (Cornas) $NA. A less successful vintage, the '98 Les Ruchets shows some aged garnet color and more mature aromas of tobacco and dried cherries. Light in weight and cedary, this is ready to drink. 87 *—J.C. (4/1/2007)*

Jean-Luc Colombo 1997 Les Ruchets Rhône Red Blend (Cornas) $65. Maybe the best vintage for current consumption, the '91 Les Ruchets features floral scents accompanied by hints of cherries and pomegranates, even some stone fruit flavors. Lush, supple and long. Drink now. 91 *—J.C. (4/1/2007)*

Jean-Luc Colombo 1991 Les Ruchets Rhône Red Blend (Cornas) $NA. Lots of meatiness and blood here, with tobacco and a strong olive, almost briny, note. Rather firm and austere, this gives the impression it could age further, yet never become lush or seductive, so go ahead and drink up. 90 *—J.C. (4/1/2007)*

Jean-Luc Colombo 2004 Rosé de Cote Bleue Rosé Blend (Coteaux d'Aix en Provence) $10. 84 *—J.C. (11/15/2005)*

Jean-Luc Colombo 2005 Les Abeilles Rhône White Blend (Côtes-du-Rhône) $12. 86 *—R.V. (12/31/2006)*

Jean-Luc Colombo 2004 La Divine Syrah (Côte Rôtie) $70. Made solely from purchased grapes, Colombo's 2004 Côte-Rôtie is a commendable effort that seems a touch delicate. Blueberry fruit fades on the finish, replaced by dustings of wood spice. Drink now. 87 *—J.C. (9/1/2007)*

Jean-Luc Colombo 2005 La Violette Syrah (Vin de Pays d'Oc) $12. 85 *—R.V. (12/31/2006)*

Jean-Luc Colombo 2004 Le Rouet Syrah (Hermitage) $70. Peppery and meaty, with stewed plum flavors, this is much more muscular and tannic than Colombo's Côte-Rôtie, yet still lacks the spark seen in his top Cornas bottlings. A bit rustic and wild, but it doesn't seem to have the concentration of fruit to age long term. Drink–2012, with grilled beef. 88 *—J.C. (9/1/2007)*

Jean-Luc Colombo 2001 Les Lauves Syrah (Saint-Joseph) $25. 91 *—R.V. (2/1/2005)*

Jean-Luc Colombo 2002 Les Ruchets Syrah (Cornas) $64. 86 *—J.C. (11/15/2006)*

Jean-Luc Colombo 2001 Les Ruchets Syrah (Cornas) $80. 90 *—J.C. (11/15/2006)*

Jean-Luc Colombo 2004 Terre Brûlées Syrah (Cornas) $78. In this challenging vintage, Colombo's entry-level Cornas is a bit lean and tart, turning crisp and cranberry-like despite having 14% alcohol. Cherry, sandalwood and vanilla flavors are pleasant enough, just without the warmth and flesh of a warmer year. 86 *—J.C. (9/1/2007)*

Jean-Luc Colombo 2003 La Violette Viognier (Vin de Pays d'Oc) $13. 83 *—J.C. (11/15/2005)*

JEAN-LUC JOILLOT

Jean-Luc Joillot NV Champagne Blend (Crémant de Bourgogne) $24. 91 *—R.V. (6/1/2006)*

JEAN-MARC BROCARD

Jean-Marc Brocard 2002 Domaine Sainte Claire Chardonnay (Petit Chablis) $13. 87 *—J.C. (2/1/2005)*

JEAN-MARIE HAAG

Jean-Marie Haag 2003 Vallée Noble Pinot Gris (Alsace) $24. 86 *(2/1/2006)*

JEAN-MAURICE RAFFAULT

Jean-Maurice Raffault 2004 Les Picasses Cabernet Blend (Chinon) $16. This comes from the plateau above the river Vienne, an area where the soil is a mix of clay and chalk. With its vanilla and toast over red, spicy fruit, with a touch of smokiness, this is smooth, ripe and elegant. 89 *—R.V. (4/1/2007)*

Jean-Maurice Raffault 2006 Cabernet Franc (Chinon) $12. To judge by this fresh, crisply fruity example, 2006 is a great year for rosé on the Loire. It has lively raspberry flavors and a great burst of finishing acidity. Delicious. 85 *—R.V. (4/1/2007)*

Jean-Maurice Raffault 2005 Cabernet Franc (Chinon) $12. This is the lightest of the five reds from Jean-Maurice Raffault, a blend of different parcels and soils. It is fresh, packed with red cherry fruit flavors, and should be enjoyed this summer. 86 *—R.V. (4/1/2007)*

Jean-Maurice Raffault 2004 Clos des Capucins Cabernet Franc (Chinon) $NA. This is a rich fruitcake-flavored wine, with pure fresh fruits over layers of tannins. It is delicious and ready to drink, packed with fruit and tannins. 91 *—R.V. (10/1/2007)*

Jean-Maurice Raffault 2005 Les Galuches Cabernet Franc (Chinon) $15. This is one of Raffault's single-vineyard wines, coming from the first slope above the Loire. It is delicate, with light, fresh red fruits and a good smoky edge. This is ready to drink now; might age for another year. 88 *—R.V. (4/1/2007)*

JEAN-MICHEL SORBE

Jean-Michel Sorbe 2005 Sauvignon Blanc (Quincy) $17. Very soft, very ripe, this is a contrast to the greener wines of Sancerre. Sorbe has long been a leading figure in Quincy, and this rounded, almost tropical wine shows, appropriately, quince and white pear flavors. 89 *—R.V. (10/1/2007)*

Jean-Michel Sorbe 2004 La Commanderie Sauvignon Blanc (Reuilly) $14. Sorbe is one of the leading figures in the two small appellations of Reuilly and Quincy. His Reuilly is honeyed, with fresh mandarin and citrus flavors, leading to a soft, open wine, great as an apéritif. 88 *—R.V. (9/1/2007)*

JEAN-PAUL BRUN

Jean-Paul Brun 2002 Terres Dorees L'Ancien Vieilles Vignes Gamay (Beaujolais) $13. 88 Best Buy *—J.C. (11/15/2003)*

JEAN-PHILIPPE MARCHAND

Jean-Philippe Marchand 2004 Vieilles Vignes Pinot Noir (Gevrey-Chambertin) $30. **87** —*J.C. (11/15/2006)*

JEAN-PIERRE MOUEIX

Jean-Pierre Moueix 2005 Bordeaux Blend (Saint-Emilion) $24. This is young, dominated by some spicy wood and quite densely textured fruit and tannin. Impressive for a branded wine, all vibrant fruit, balanced by a firm, dry structure, and with a rich aftertaste. Age this for at least one year. **87** —*R.V. (11/1/2007)*

Jean-Pierre Moueix 2003 Bordeaux Blend (Saint-Emilion) $18. Ripe, sweet and easy, with dried fruit flavors, some ripe fruit and light tannins. Perfumed and attractive; there's just a touch of bitterness from the wood. **85** —*R.V. (11/1/2007)*

JEANJEAN

Jeanjean 2003 Petit Devois Syrah-Grenache (Coteaux du Languedoc) $13. **84** —*R.V. (12/31/2006)*

JOSEPH BURRIER

Joseph Burrier 2003 Château de Beauregard Gamay (Fleurie) $22. **83** —*J.C. (11/15/2005)*

JOSEPH CATLIN

Joseph Cattin 2005 Rosé Pinot Noir (Alsace) $14. A pale rose color with a coppery tinge, this is a surprisingly complex Pinot Noir-based rosé. Hints of leather and spice impart nuance to the cherry flavors, while the mouthfeel has that silky Pinot Noir quality that lingers on the finish. **87** —*J.C. (7/1/2007)*

Joseph Cattin 2005 Riesling (Alsace) $24. Pale yellow in color, this offers up ripe and savory flavors all at once. Notes of pear, peach pit and minerality intermingle with the mouthcoating flavors of sweet dried spice, melon and lime oil. Broad and full, the finish is appropriately dusty and short. **87** *(9/1/2007)*

JOSEPH DROUHIN

Joseph Drouhin 2005 Chardonnay (Chablis) $20. Quite a firm, concentrated wine, showing structure, some wood flavors, pear skins and a creamy finishing consistency. This has more complexity than its simple Chablis appellation suggests. **86** —*R.V. (8/1/2007)*

Joseph Drouhin 2004 Chardonnay (Chablis) $20. **86** *(3/1/2006)*

Joseph Drouhin 2004 Chardonnay (Puligny-Montrachet) $46. **89** —*R.V. (12/1/2006)*

Joseph Drouhin 2003 Chardonnay (Rully) $18. **86** —*J.C. (11/15/2005)*

Joseph Drouhin 2003 Chardonnay (Chassagne-Montrachet) $38. **86** —*J.C. (4/1/2006)*

Joseph Drouhin 2001 Chardonnay (Chassagne-Montrachet) $41. **85** —*J.C. (10/1/2003)*

Joseph Drouhin 2001 Chardonnay (Meursault) $38. **90** —*J.C. (10/1/2003)*

Joseph Drouhin 2001 Chardonnay (Puligny-Montrachet) $42. **89** —*J.C. (10/1/2003)*

Joseph Drouhin 2002 Clos des Mouches Chardonnay (Beaune) $86. **88** *(3/1/2006)*

Joseph Drouhin 2005 Domaine du Vaudon Chardonnay (Chablis) $23. Full-bodied and ripe, with cool green fruits topping some rich vanilla, cream and white currant flavors. It's certainly very fruity, but there's an extra dimension of a youthful structure that needs another year to develop fully. **87** —*R.V. (8/1/2007)*

Joseph Drouhin 2004 Domaine de Vaudon Chardonnay (Chablis) $23. **88** *(3/1/2006)*

Joseph Drouhin 2004 Folatières Premier Cru Chardonnay (Puligny-Montrachet) $65. **91** —*R.V. (12/1/2006)*

Joseph Drouhin 2003 Laforet Chardonnay (Bourgogne) $12. **84** —*J.C. (11/15/2005)*

Joseph Drouhin 2004 Marquis de Laguiche Chardonnay (Montrachet) $596. **96 Editors' Choice** —*R.V. (12/1/2006)*

Joseph Drouhin 2005 Montmains Premier Cru Chardonnay (Chablis) $33. A piercingly steely wine, all angles and acidity. That said, there's a greater depth of flavor that needs time to come out—the richness of the green fruit is there, as is the hint of wood. The corners need to soften for a year or so. **90** —*R.V. (8/1/2007)*

Joseph Drouhin 2004 Montmains Premier Cru Chardonnay (Chablis) $33. **90** *(3/1/2006)*

Joseph Drouhin 2004 Perrières Premier Cru Chardonnay (Meursault) $68. **93 Cellar Selection** —*R.V. (12/1/2006)*

Joseph Drouhin 2005 Premier Cru Chardonnay (Chablis) $29. Ripe but minerally, all flint and crisp fruit along with the richness from the structure and green plum and wood flavors. This blending of fruit from a number of Chablis Premier Cru vineyards shows the rich, ageworthy nature of 2005. **88** —*R.V. (8/1/2007)*

Joseph Drouhin 2004 Premier Cru Chardonnay (Chablis) $29. **89** *(3/1/2006)*

Joseph Drouhin 2001 Vaudesir Chardonnay (Chablis) $51. **90** —*J.C. (10/1/2003)*

Joseph Drouhin 2003 Véro Chardonnay (Bourgogne) $20. **87** —*J.C. (11/15/2005)*

Joseph Drouhin 2001 Gamay (Morgon) $14. **85** —*J.C. (11/15/2003)*

Joseph Drouhin 2001 Gamay (Brouilly) $15. **83** —*J.C. (11/15/2003)*

Joseph Drouhin 2004 Pinot Noir (Clos de la Roche) $112. Great power, delicious fruit and dusty tannins are all present in an elegant parcel. This is an impressive wine, with a balanced structure and texture. And the fruit is so ripe, so seductive without going over the top. Drink in 2012. **95** —*R.V. (3/1/2007)*

Joseph Drouhin 2004 Pinot Noir (Grands-Echezeaux) $188. Power and spice epitomize this wine, a firm, solid structure that keeps complexity and elegance as part of the package, and that will reward long aging. It may be big, but it keeps a sense of proportion, with dark fruits balanced with fresh acidity. **94** —*R.V. (3/1/2007)*

Joseph Drouhin 2004 Pinot Noir (Echezeaux) $127. Often young Echezeaux can show an earthy character, and this wine is no exception. It also has density of texture: Dark, firm and brooding, this wine demands aging. It has the 2004 freshness and acidity to lighten the finish. **94** —*R.V. (3/1/2007)*

Joseph Drouhin 2004 Pinot Noir (Bourgogne) $16. Fresh, fruity and aromatic, this is a soft wine, with just enough dry tannins to give it shape. Touches of spice and pepper are typical of the vintage. **85** —*R.V. (3/1/2007)*

Joseph Drouhin 2004 Pinot Noir (Griotte-Chambertin) $154. Ripe and fresh, this impresses more by the purity of its fruit than by its structure. This suggests that it will age quickly, confiremd by the soft tannins, strawberry fruit flavors and the balancing acidity. **90** —*R.V. (3/1/2007)*

Joseph Drouhin 2004 Pinot Noir (Gevrey-Chambertin) $39. Big and bold, this perfectly sums up the appellation of Gevrey-Chambertin. It's burly and robust, with an initial earthy character, solid fruits and dense, dusty tannins. There's good acidity on the finish. **90** —*R.V. (3/1/2007)*

Joseph Drouhin 2004 Pinot Noir (Charmes-Chambertin) $114. This is the largest of the Gevrey-Chambertin grand crus, a huge (for Burgundy) 31 acres. Drouhin has made the most of its weight and power, a wine of dark plum flavors surrounding a core that is dense and solid. This is already a drinkable wine, but to get the best out of it, the rich fruit needs time to envelop the firm tannins. **93** —*R.V. (3/1/2007)*

Joseph Drouhin 2004 Pinot Noir (Bonnes-Mares) $163. All the generosity and opulence as well as the intense perfumes of Bonnes-Mares are found in this ripe and open wine. The pure fruit flavors dominate, rolling around the tannins, leaving ripe red fruits and acidity in equal measure. **94** —*R.V. (3/1/2007)*

Joseph Drouhin 2004 Pinot Noir (Chambolle-Musigny) $48. Purity is the star quality of this wine. It stems from berry fruits, juicy acidity and a soft, generous structure, which offers ripeness and a texture that stops only just short of opulence. **89** —*R.V. (3/1/2007)*

Joseph Drouhin 2004 Pinot Noir (Clos de la Roche) $112. Great power, delicious fruit and dusty tannins are all present in an elegant parcel. This is an impressive wine, with a balanced structure and texture. And the fruit is so ripe, so seductive without going over the top. Drink in 2012. **95** —*R.V. (3/1/2007)*

Joseph Drouhin 2003 Pinot Noir (Chorey-lès-Beaune) $21. **87** *(3/1/2006)*

Joseph Drouhin 2003 Pinot Noir (Gevrey-Chambertin) $43. **89** —*R.V. (9/1/2005)*

Joseph Drouhin 2003 Pinot Noir (Chambolle-Musigny) $73. **88** —*R.V. (9/1/2005)*

Joseph Drouhin 2001 Pinot Noir (Nuits-St.-Georges) $45. **85** —*J.C. (10/1/2003)*

Joseph Drouhin 2001 Pinot Noir (Côte de Beaune) $23. **84** —*J.C. (10/1/2003)*

Joseph Drouhin 2001 Pinot Noir (Savigny-lès-Beaune) $20. **84** —*J.C. (10/1/2003)*

Joseph Drouhin 2000 Pinot Noir (Bonnes-Mares) $119. **94 Editors' Choice** —*R.V. (11/1/2002)*

Joseph Drouhin 2000 Pinot Noir (Chambolle-Musigny) $39. **88** —*R.V. (11/1/2002)*

Joseph Drouhin 2002 Pinot Noir Chambertin Clos de Bèze $NA. **92** —*R.V.*

(9/1/2004)

Joseph Drouhin 2001 Pinot Noir Charmes-Chambertin $118. 90 *—J.C. (10/1/2003)*

Joseph Drouhin 2002 Clos des Mouches Pinot Noir (Beaune) $57. 89 *—R.V. (9/1/2004)*

Joseph Drouhin 2002 Clos des Mouches Premier Cru Pinot Noir (Beaune) $91. 93 *(3/1/2006)*

Joseph Drouhin 2004 Clos de Vougeot Pinot Noir (Clos Vougeot) $117. Showing the peppery character of 2004, this wine also showcases black fruits and firm tannins. It's pretty tough at this stage, but the fruit is certainly there; in five years this will be impressively complex. **93** *—R.V. (3/1/2007)*

Joseph Drouhin 2002 Pinot Noir (Grands Echézeaux) $179. 96 *—R.V. (9/1/2004)*

Joseph Drouhin 2002 Les Amoureuses Premier Cru Pinot Noir (Chambolle-Musigny) $139. 93 *—R.V. (9/1/2004)*

Joseph Drouhin 2000 Les Baudes Premier Cru Pinot Noir (Chambolle-Musigny) $53. 92 *—R.V. (11/1/2002)*

Joseph Drouhin 2004 Les Petits Monts Premier Cru Pinot Noir (Vosne-Romanée) $132. Part of the Drouhin family domaine, this parcel of vines belongs to Véronique Drouhin. It's a powerful wine, but also complete. There is good density, richness, black fruits and finishing acidity. **91** *—R.V. (3/1/2007)*

Joseph Drouhin 2004 Les Procès Premier Cru Pinot Noir (Nuits-St.-Georges) $NA. This vineyard belongs to Laurent Drouhin, one of the generation of Drouhins currently in charge. It shows the robustness and the dry core of Nuits-St.-Georges, with great red and black fruits and some tough, dry tannins. A chunky sort of wine. Not imported to the U.S. **90** *—R.V. (3/1/2007)*

Joseph Drouhin 2004 Pinot Noir (Musigny) $242. As befits the most seductive of vineyards, this wine is one that wraps itself around you, a charmer of a wine, but one that still retains some of the elegance of a great Chambolle-Musigny. And just when you think it's all up front, the tannins creep up and promise great aging potential. **95 Cellar Selection** *—R.V. (3/1/2007)*

Joseph Drouhin 2004 Premier Cru Pinot Noir (Chambolle-Musigny) $63. A blend of five premier crus from Chambolle, this wine has full fruit flavors, an open, generous style that is very welcoming, but also an elegant side. Dark plum skins flavors and good acidity keep it fresh. **91** *—R.V. (3/1/2007)*

Joseph Drouhin 2000 Premier Cru Pinot Noir (Chambolle-Musigny) $46. 90 *—R.V. (11/1/2002)*

Joseph Drouhin 2004 Véro Pinot Noir (Bourgogne) $21. Named after Véronique Drouhin, this is a blend of village and premier cru wines designed to give more weight than a basic Burgundy. It certainly has considerable elegance, generosity and a good weight of red fruits. The aftertaste is pure and fresh. **87** *—R.V. (3/1/2007)*

JOSEPH LANDRON

Joseph Landron 2003 Amphibolite Nature Melon (Muscadet Sèvre Et Maine) $NA. 90 *—R.V. (1/1/2004)*

JOSEPH MELLOT

Joseph Mellot 2005 Le Rabault Pinot Noir (Sancerre) $28. A light style of Pinot Noir, with strawberry jam aromas. The delicate fruit is shot through with dry tannins and the aftertaste is definitely on the acidic side. **84** *—R.V. (10/1/2007)*

Joseph Mellot 2006 La Chatellenie Sauvignon Blanc (Sancerre) $26. Soft and grassy, with some asparagus flavors, this is ripe, but still vibrant, adding green apples to grapefruit, with some white pears. Easy and rich in the mouth. **88** *—R.V. (9/1/2007)*

Joseph Mellot 2006 La Rimonet Sauvignon Blanc (Quincy) $18. Candy and fruit drops are the first impression of this young wine. It has some good fruit, more in the honeyed and nut character, but that heavily perfumed candy character doesn't fit well. **83** *—R.V. (10/1/2007)*

Joseph Mellot 2005 Le Chant des Vignes Sauvignon Blanc (Pouilly-Fumé) $26. Big-hearted and round, this is a full wine, with apple pie and cream flavors leading to a crisp, mineral aftertaste. It's delicious, very drinkable now, packed with ripe but refreshing fruit. **89** *—R.V. (9/1/2007)*

Joseph Mellot 2005 Le Troncsec Sauvignon Blanc (Pouilly-Fumé) $26. A flinty, crisp style, with currants, green apples, pink grapefruit. Initially austere, it opens to some richness. The aftertaste, though, is crisp to a fault. **86** *—R.V. (9/1/2007)*

Joseph Mellot 2004 Le Troncsec Sauvignon Blanc (Pouilly-Fumé) $25. 86 *—R.V. (8/1/2006)*

Joseph Mellot 2006 Sincérité Sauvignon Blanc (Vin de Pays du Jardin de la France) $10. From vineyards to the west of Sancerre in the Loire, Sancerrois Alexandre Mellot has produced a classically fresh, simple, very drinkable wine, showing great awareness of the apple and green pear character of Sauvignon Blanc. Drink this year. **87 Best Buy** *—R.V. (9/1/2007)*

JOSEPH PERRIER

Joseph Perrier 1998 Cuvée Royale Champagne Blend (Champagne) $52. 89 *—R.V. (11/1/2006)*

Joseph Perrier 1996 Cuvée Royale Champagne Blend (Champagne) $65. 90 *—R.V. (11/1/2006)*

JOSEPH ROTY

Joseph Roty 2004 Rosé Pinot Noir (Marsannay) $20. Marsannay is the only commune in Burgundy known at all for its rosés, and this example does stand out as being different. Herbal, lavender-like aromas lead off, followed by a wine that features slightly tomatoey flavors. Light in body, it finishes sappy and fresh. **83** *—J.C. (7/1/2007)*

JOSMEYER

Josmeyer 2000 Gewürztraminer (Alsace) $21. 84 *—M.S. (6/1/2003)*

Josmeyer 2004 Les Folastries Gewürztraminer (Alsace) $31. 90 *—J.C. (8/1/2006)*

Josmeyer 2001 Pinot Blanc (Alsace) $15. 87 *—M.S. (10/1/2003)*

Josmeyer 2002 Mise du Printemps Pinot Blanc (Alsace) $28. 87 *—J.C. (2/1/2005)*

Josmeyer 2001 Pinot Gris (Alsace) $21. 83 *—M.S. (1/1/2004)*

Josmeyer 2004 Fondation Vieilles Vignes Pinot Gris (Alsace) $NA. 91 *—R.V. (2/1/2006)*

Josmeyer 2002 Grand Cru Brand Pinot Gris (Alsace) $80. 92 *—R.V. (2/1/2006)*

Josmeyer 2004 Le Fromenteau Pinot Gris (Alsace) $30. 87 *—R.V. (2/1/2006)*

Josmeyer 1996 Cuvée Reservée Alsace Pinot Noir (Alsace) $28. 84 *—M.S. (10/1/1999)*

Josmeyer 2001 Grand Cru Hengst Riesling (Alsace) $67. 89 *—R.V. (2/1/2006)*

Josmeyer 2004 Le Dragon Riesling (Alsace) $38. 88 *—J.C. (8/1/2006)*

Josmeyer 2004 Le Kottabe Riesling (Alsace) $27. 87 *—J.C. (8/1/2006)*

Josmeyer 1996 Tokay Pinot Gris (Alsace) $20. 85 *— (8/1/1999)*

Josmeyer 2001 Collection Rare Tokay Pinot Gris (Alsace) $NA. 90 *—R.V. (2/1/2006)*

Josmeyer 1997 Le Fromenteau Tokay Pinot Gris (Alsace) $18. 88 *(8/1/1999)*

KRITER

Kriter NV Blanc de Blancs Champagne Blend (Côte d'Or) $8. 85 *—M.S. (6/1/2003)*

Kriter NV Brut de Brut Champagne Blend (France) $9. 84 *—M.M. (12/15/2001)*

Kriter 2000 Brut Prestige Chardonnay (Côte d'Or) $9. 86 **Best Buy** *—M.S. (6/1/2003)*

Kriter NV Brut Blanc de Blancs Sparkling Blend (France) $12. Fruit-forward and simple, this wine's pleasant apple and citrus flavors begin to dull as the carbonation rapidly fades in the glass. **83** *—J.C. (12/15/2007)*

Kriter NV Brut Blanc de Blancs Sparkling Blend (Vin Mousseux) $11. 84 *—R.V. (6/1/2006)*

Kriter NV Eclat Carmin Rosé Sparkling Blend (France) $12. Light and refreshing, with hints of berries and citrus alongside some herbal elements. The bead is a little on the large side, making the mouthfeel a bit rustic, but it'll do fine at the season's big holiday gatherings. **84** *—J.C. (12/15/2007)*

Kriter NV Eclat Carmin Rosé Sparkling Blend (Vin Mousseux) $11. 85 *—R.V. (6/1/2006)*

KRUG

Krug 1990 Brut Champagne Blend (Champagne) $224. 95 *—M.S. (12/31/2005)*

Krug 1989 Brut Champagne Blend (Champagne) $500. 95 *—R.V. (11/1/2006)*

Krug 1988 Brut Champagne Blend (Champagne) $210. 93 *(12/15/2001)*

Krug NV Brut Rosé Champagne Blend (Champagne) $293. 93 **Cellar Selection** *—M.S. (12/31/2005)*

Krug 1981 Collection Champagne Blend (Champagne) $500. 98 —*R.V. (11/1/2006)*

Krug NV Grande Cuvée Brut Champagne Blend (Champagne) $150. 91 —*J.C. (12/15/2001)*

Krug NV Grande Cuvée Brut Champagne Blend (Champagne) $172. 94 —*J.C. (12/1/2005)*

KUENTZ-BAS

Kuentz-Bas 2002 Collection Riesling (Alsace) $26. 87 —*R.V. (11/1/2005)*

Kuentz-Bas 2000 Collection Rare Riesling (Alsace) $28. 87 —*R.V. (11/1/2005)*

Kuentz-Bas 2000 Grand Cru Eichberg Riesling (Alsace) $42. 90 —*R.V. (11/1/2005)*

Kuentz-Bas 2000 Grand Cru Rangen Riesling (Alsace) $65. 90 —*R.V. (11/1/2005)*

Kuentz-Bas 2000 Tradition Sylvaner (Alsace) $10. 85 —*R.V. (11/15/2003)*

Kuentz-Bas 2003 Tradition Tokay Pinot Gris (Alsace) $22. 86 —*R.V. (2/1/2006)*

L'ARROSOIR

L'Arrosoir à Rosé 2006 Rosé Blend (Vin de Pays d'Oc) $NA. From the estate of Massamier la Mignarde, this pink colored rosé is all froth and candy. Drink it down as an aperitif, don't think too much about its attractive freshness. An arrosoir, by the way, is a watering can. 84 —*R.V. (7/1/2007)*

L'ESTANDON

L'Estandon 2006 Rosé Blend (Côtes de Provence) $11. Made by the cooperative of Brignoles, this is one of the big brands in Provence rosé. A caramel aroma leads to a fat, but still fruity wine, with flavors of sweet raspberries and light, food friendly acidity. 86 Best Buy —*R.V. (7/1/2007)*

L'Estandon 2005 Rosé Blend (Côtes de Provence) $10. As one might expect from a co-op wine, this pale coppery rosé lacks the concentration necessary for greatness, but it remains a fresh, well-made wine, offering anise, mineral and garrigue notes and a mouthwatering finish. 86 Best Buy —*J.C. (7/1/2007)*

L'ORVAL

L'Orval 1999 Merlot (Vin de Pays d'Oc) $6. 84 Best Buy —*D.T. (2/1/2002)*

L'OSTAL CAZES

L'Ostal Cazes 2003 Circus Shiraz-Cabernet Sauvignon (Vin de Pays d'Oc) $13. 86 —*J.C. (11/15/2005)*

LA BASTIDE SAINT VINCENT

La Bastide Saint Vincent 2004 Rhône Red Blend (Gigondas) $23. 83 —*J.C. (11/15/2006)*

LA BAUME

La Baume 2003 Chardonnay (Vin de Pays d'Oc) $8. 87 Best Buy —*R.V. (12/1/2004)*

La Baume 1999 Merlot (Vin de Pays d'Oc) $7. 82 —*D.T. (2/1/2002)*

La Baume 1998 Syrah (Vin de Pays d'Oc) $7. 82 *(10/1/2001)*

LA CHABLISIENNE

La Chablisienne 2004 Chardonnay (Bourgogne) $14. 83 —*J.C. (11/15/2005)*

La Chablisienne 2001 Chardonnay (Petit Chablis) $13. 84 —*J.C. (10/1/2003)*

La Chablisienne 2003 Côte de Léchet Premier Cru Chardonnay (Chablis) $28. 84 —*J.C. (11/15/2005)*

La Chablisienne 2001 Cuvée LC Chardonnay (Chablis) $16. 85 —*J.C. (10/1/2003)*

La Chablisienne 1999 Grenouille Chardonnay (Chablis) 88 —*R.V. (1/1/2004)*

La Chablisienne 2001 Le Chablis Premier Cru Chardonnay (Chablis) $24. 89 —*J.C. (10/1/2003)*

La Chablisienne 2003 Les Preuses Grand Cru Chardonnay (Chablis) $66. 91 —*J.C. (4/1/2006)*

La Chablisienne 2001 Montmain Premier Cru Chardonnay (Chablis) $27. 87 —*J.C. (10/1/2003)*

La Chablisienne 2003 Vaudesir Grand Cru Chardonnay (Chablis) $66. 90 —*J.C. (4/1/2006)*

La Chablisienne 1997 Cuvée Brut Sparkling Blend (Chablis) $16. 80 —*J.C. (12/15/2003)*

LA CRAU DE MA MÈRE

La Crau de Ma Mère 2004 Grenache (Côtes-du-Rhône) $35. 88 —*J.C. (11/15/2006)*

LA CROIX MARTELLE

La Croix Martelle 2001 Petit Frère Pinot Noir (Vin de Pays d'Oc) $24. 84 —*R.V. (12/1/2004)*

LA FORGE ESTATE

La Forge Estate 1999 Syrah (Vin de Pays d'Oc) $12. 85 *(10/1/2001)*

LA NOBLE

La Noble 2004 Merlot (Vin de Pays d'Oc) $9. 85 Best Buy —*R.V. (11/15/2005)*

LA PATACHE

La Patache 2005 Bordeaux Blend (Médoc) $NA. Patache recalls the stagecoach that ran the length of the Médoc in times past. It's a freshly smooth wine, showing the quality of 2005 in a polished, fruity way, the black plum fruits held together by gentle tannins. 86 —*R.V. (11/1/2007)*

La Patache 2004 Cabernet Sauvignon (Médoc) $NA. Good smoky flavors complement this attractively-made wine. The fruits are lifted, forward and easy, but there is a sense of tannin. Spice from the American oak used in aging adds a piquancy. 85 —*R.V. (6/1/2007)*

LA POUSSIE

La Poussie 2002 Sauvignon Blanc (Sancerre) $30. 83 *(7/1/2005)*

LA SAUVAGEONNE

La Sauvageonne 2003 Les Ruffes Red Blend (Coteaux du Languedoc) $11. 84 —*R.V. (12/1/2004)*

La Sauvageonne 2001 Puech de Glen Red Blend (Coteaux du Languedoc) $40. 90 —*R.V. (12/1/2004)*

LA SOUFRANDIÈRE

La Soufrandière 2003 Climat Les Quarts Chardonnay (Pouilly-Vinzelles) $44. 90 —*J.C. (11/15/2005)*

LA VIEILLE FERME

La Vieille Ferme 2003 Red Blend (Côtes-du-Ventoux) $8. 84 Best Buy —*J.C. (2/1/2005)*

La Vieille Ferme 2001 Rhône Red Blend (Côtes-du-Ventoux) $7. 84 —*J.C. (3/1/2004)*

La Vieille Ferme 1997 Rhône Red Blend (Côtes-du-Ventoux) $8. 85 *(11/15/1999)*

La Vieille Ferme 2006 Rosé Rhône Red Blend (Côtes-du-Ventoux) $8. A simple fruity quaff that will drink well with cold roast chicken at lunch, through a hot afternoon by the pool and into a late dinner off the grill. Strawberry and watermelon flavors predominate, with a bit of citrus adding zip to the finish. 85 Best Buy —*J.C. (7/1/2007)*

La Vieille Ferme 2002 Rosé Blend (Côtes-du-Ventoux) $7. 84 —*J.C. (3/1/2004)*

La Vieille Ferme 2000 Rhône White Blend (Côtes du Luberon) $8. 82 —*M.M. (2/1/2002)*

La Vieille Ferme 2003 White Blend (Côtes du Luberon) $8. 84 Best Buy —*J.C. (2/1/2005)*

LABOURE-ROI

Laboure-Roi 2005 Chablis Premier Cru Chardonnay (Chablis) $20. This has some freshness, with red-apple flavors, light and green. There's a spoiling touch of sulfur, probably the result of recent bottling. 84 —*R.V. (8/1/2007)*

Laboure-Roi 2005 Château Labouré-Roi Chardonnay (Bourgogne) $17. Attractive, ripe and full-bodied, this is touched with spice, vanilla and fresh pear flavors. This is an excellent example of white Burgundy: no complexity, just pleasure. 87 —*R.V. (8/1/2007)*

Laboure-Roi 2005 Château Labouré-Roi Clos de la Baronne Chardonnay (Meursault) $48. A limited production wine from Labouré-Roi's own vineyards, this is powerful and ripe, but tempered with refreshing acidity. With its spice and ginger flavors, it rolls richly around the mouth, and then finishes crisp and fresh. 89 —*R.V. (8/1/2007)*

Laboure-Roi 2005 Château Labouré-Roi Premier Cru Clos des Bouches Chères Chardonnay (Meursault) $64. Rich, full and spiced with generous wood, this is deliciously fat Meursault. Almost honeyed in flavor and given backbone by some minerality; there's good ripeness here. An almost opulent wine. 90 —*R.V. (8/1/2007)*

Laboure-Roi 2003 Fourchaume Premier Cru Chardonnay (Chablis) $25. 84 —*J.C. (11/15/2005)*

Laboure-Roi 2003 Premier Cru Chardonnay (Montagny) $16. 85 *—J.C. (11/15/2005)*

Laboure-Roi 2005 Pinot Noir (Nuits-St.-Georges) $36. Quite lean in texture, this wine shows some freshness, but only moderate density of fruit. There are some plum skin flavors, and the finish is dry, with acidity. 84 *—R.V. (3/1/2007)*

Laboure-Roi 2005 Pinot Noir (Gevrey-Chambertin) $36. This fresh, fruity wine has some attractive blackberry flavors along with considerable acidity. The tannins are soft, and the general impression is of a wine that is enjoyably ready to drink. 85 *—R.V. (3/1/2007)*

Laboure-Roi 2004 Pinot Noir (Charmes-Chambertin) $124. Soft, slightly soapy, this is a wine that remains resolutely out of focus. There is a hint of the proper juicy Pinot Noir flavor, but just a hint. For the rest, the wine is light and fresh. 85 *—R.V. (3/1/2007)*

Laboure-Roi 2002 Pinot Noir (Corton) $52. 87 *—R.V. (9/1/2004)*

Laboure-Roi 1998 Pinot Noir (Gevrey-Chambertin) $28. 87 *(10/1/2001)*

Laboure-Roi 2002 Chassagne Montrachet Pinot Noir (Chassagne-Montrachet) $23. 83 *—J.C. (11/15/2005)*

Laboure-Roi 2004 Clos de Vougeot Grand Cru Pinot Noir (Clos Vougeot) $107. Despite its attractive perfumes, this wine seems light and simple for its Grand Cru status. There are pleasant fresh red fruit flavors and some dry tannins, and the wine finishes with a fresh acid lift. 84 *—R.V. (3/1/2007)*

Laboure-Roi 2002 Echézeaux Pinot Noir (Echezeaux) $65. 82 *—R.V. (9/1/2004)*

Laboure-Roi 2004 Les Damodes Premier Cru Pinot Noir (Nuits-St.-Georges) $67. There are some red berry fruits, along with some firm dry fruit tannins, but it's the smoky wood tastes that seem to dominate. The finish is firm, a touch bitter, but there is also a residual sweetness. 87 *—R.V. (3/1/2007)*

Laboure-Roi 2005 Maximum Pinot Noir Pinot Noir (Bourgogne) $14. Fresh and light, this is a pleasant fruity drink, with some tannins, but mainly with red currants and crisp acidity. The aftertaste is soft, almost sweet. 82 *—R.V. (3/1/2007)*

Laboure-Roi 2002 Pommard Pinot Noir (Pommard) $32. 82 *—J.C. (11/15/2005)*

Laboure-Roi 2004 Premier Cru Pinot Noir (Gevrey-Chambertin) $69. This is a blend from a number of different Premier Cru vineyards in Gevrey. It is attractively aromatic, but the taste is dilute, unfocussed. There are tannins, there is fruit, the aftertaste is clean, but the wine does not hang together. 83 *—R.V. (3/1/2007)*

Laboure-Roi 1998 Red Blend (Pommard) $28. 88 *(10/1/2001)*

Laboure-Roi 1998 Domaine Sirugue Clos La Belle Marguerite Red Blend (Côte de Nuits-Villages) $19. 89 Editors' Choice *(10/1/2001)*

Laboure-Roi 1998 White Blend (Chassagne-Montrachet) $28. 89 *(10/1/2001)*

Laboure-Roi 1999 Domaine Rene Manuel Clos des Bouches Cheres Premier Cru White Blend (Meursault) $43. 90 *(10/1/2001)*

LACHETEAU

Lacheteau 2006 Chenin Blanc (Vouvray) $10. A semisweet Vouvray, with its honey flavors still tasting very young. The acidity is all green apple, with freshness coming from the white currant edge. Lacheteau is a négociant, based in the Muscadet region. 86 Best Buy *—R.V. (10/1/2007)*

Lacheteau 2000 Sauvignon Blanc (Vin de Pays du Jardin de la France) $6. 85 Best Buy *—M.M. (2/1/2002)*

LACOUR PAVILLON

LaCour Pavillon 1996 Bordeaux Blend (Bordeaux) $9. 86 *(11/15/1999)*

LALANDE

Lalande 2005 Chardonnay (Vin de Pays des Côtes de Gascogne) $12. 86 *—R.V. (12/31/2006)*

LAMBLIN & FILS

Lamblin & Fils 2001 Chardonnay (Chablis) $13. 82 *—J.C. (10/1/2003)*

Lamblin & Fils 2001 Fourchaumes Premier Cru Chardonnay (Chablis) $23. 88 *—J.C. (10/1/2003)*

Lamblin & Fils 2001 Vieilles Vignes Chardonnay (Chablis) $14. 85 *—J.C. (10/1/2003)*

LANGLOIS-CHÂTEAU

Langlois-Chateau 2002 Château de Varrains Cabernet Franc (Saumur-Champigny) $30. For this vintage, this is an impressively dense wine, packed with firm, solid fruits and layers of new wood. There are flavors of black currants, a touch of spice, and refreshing acidity. 88 *—R.V. (4/1/2007)*

Langlois-Chateau 2004 La Bretonnière Sec Cabernet Franc (Cabernet de Saumur) $NA. Still drinking well today, this salmon-hued rosé boasts complex aromas of herbs, spice and melon. It's round and slightly creamy-textured in the mouth, where the pepper and clove notes take hold, underscoring ripe melon and peach flavors. Spicy and fresh on the long finish, picking up a minerally note. 89 *—J.C. (7/1/2007)*

Langlois-Chateau 2005 Les Montifault Cabernet Franc (Chinon) $19. Owned by Bollinger Champagne, Langlois-Château is one of the top sparkling wine producers in the Loire. But they also make some attractive still wines. This Chinon, soft, fresh and vibrant with red fruits, is a great quaffing wine, simple, with a delicious smoky aftertaste. Drink now. 84 *—R.V. (4/1/2007)*

Langlois-Château 2001 Vieilles Vignes Chenin Blanc (Saumur) $18. 86 *—J.C. (8/1/2006)*

Langlois-Château 2004 Château de Fontaine-Audon Terroir Silex Sauvignon Blanc (Sancerre) $25. 86 *—R.V. (8/1/2006)*

Langlois-Château NV Brut Sparkling Blend (Crémant de Loire) $17. 83 *—J.C. (12/1/2004)*

Langlois-Château NV Brut Rosé Sparkling Blend (Crémant de Loire) $16. 87 *—M.S. (12/15/2003)*

Langlois-Château 1996 Quadrille Brut Sparkling Blend (Crémant de Loire) $24. 88 *—M.S. (12/15/2003)*

Langlois-Château NV Brut White Blend (Crémant de Loire) $21. 90 Editors' Choice *—R.V. (6/1/2006)*

LANSON

Lanson NV Black Label Brut Champagne Blend (Champagne) $28. 84 *—P.G. (12/15/2003)*

Lanson NV Brut Rosé Champagne Blend (Champagne) $50. 85 *—P.G. (12/15/2003)*

Lanson 1997 Gold Label Brut Champagne Blend (Champagne) $55. Already, this is a mature wine, and it's delicious The aromas of toasted brioches and dry fruits confirm, this. So does the palate, a layered toasty, nutty wine, with mature acidity and vanilla. Drink now, it's ready. 91 *—R.V. (2/1/2007)*

Lanson 1995 Gold Label Brut Champagne Blend (Champagne) $45. 87 *(12/15/2001)*

Lanson 1998 Noble Cuvée Brut Champagne Blend (Champagne) $125. An intense, full-bodied style, which balances the Pinots and Chardonnay well. It is ripe, with toasty undercurrents, balanced by a delicious citrus and grapefruit crispness and a fine, long lingering aftertaste. There is a light, but discernible sweetness to finish, although it is certainly Brut. 92 *—R.V. (2/1/2007)*

Lanson 1995 Noble Cuvée Blanc de Blancs Champagne Blend (Champagne) $110. 90 *—P.G. (12/15/2003)*

Lanson 1997 Noble Cuvée Blanc de Blancs Chardonnay (Champagne) $150. Part of the new Noble Cuvée range from Lanson (which also includes a Pinot Noir/Chardonnay blend and a rosé. This is feather light, floating with its bubbles and zesty, citrus fruit flavors, and a dry, crisp aftertaste. Very much an aperitif Champagne. 92 *—R.V. (2/1/2007)*

LARMANDIER-BERNIER

Larmandier-Bernier NV Blanc de Blancs Premier Cru Brut Champagne Blend (Champagne) $58. 88 *—R.V. (12/1/2002)*

Larmandier-Bernier 1997 Special Club Brut Champagne Blend (Champagne) $51. 91 *—R.V. (12/1/2002)*

Larmandier-Bernier NV Blanc de Blancs Premier Cru Chardonnay (Champagne) $58. With its yeasty aromas and fresh, crisp acidity, this is a young-tasting Champagne. There are flavors of green apples, just a hint of toast and a dry aftertaste from the low dosage. 90 *—R.V. (12/31/2007)*

Larmandier-Bernier NV Blanc de Blancs Premier Cru Brut Chardonnay (Champagne) $48. 89 *—R.V. (4/1/2005)*

Larmandier-Bernier NV Terre de Vertus Premier Cru Chardonnay (Champagne) $62. Although this is marked nonvintage, the fruit all comes from 2004. It is made from old vines, giving richness and ripeness, and a generous white fruit character which fully compensates for the very dry nature of the wine. It's delicious, a complex wine of intense character. 94 Editors' Choice *—R.V. (12/31/2007)*

Larmandier-Bernier NV Terre de Vertus Premier Cru Brut Chardonnay (Champagne) $55. 94 *—R.V. (12/1/2005)*

Larmandier-Bernier NV Vieilles Vignes de Cramant Grand Cru Chardonnay (Champagne) $80. While the Larmandier's main vineyard is in Vertus, they also have a parcel in the grand cru vineyard of Cramant. It is full of beautifully ripe fruit, beginning to round out as it ages. Green fruits and white pears, as well as yeast are still dominant; drink 2010. **95** —*R.V. (12/31/2007)*

Larmandier-Bernier 2002 Vieille Vigne de Cramant Chardonnay (Champagne) $70. 92 —*R.V. (11/1/2006)*

LAROCHE

Laroche 2005 Chardonnay Chardonnay (Vin de Pays d'Oc) $10. 87 Best Buy —*R.V. (12/31/2006)*

Laroche 2005 Merlot (Vin de Pays d'Oc) $10. 86 —*R.V. (12/31/2006)*

Laroche 2003 Mas la Chevalière Red Blend (Vin de Pays d'Oc) $20. 89 —*R.V. (12/31/2006)*

Laroche 2001 La Croix Chevalière Rhône Red Blend (Vin de Pays d'Oc) $30. With some maturity, this wine shows delicious food-friendly levels of black fruits, acidity and a fine balancing tannic structure. From Michel Laroche's Languedoc winery near Beziers, this is a blend of Syrah, Mourvèdre, Grenache and Cabernet Sauvignon. Brambles, black currants and licorice all come together in this dense wine. **91 Editors' Choice** —*R.V. (2/1/2007)*

LASSÈGUE

Lassègue 2004 Bordeaux Blend (Saint-Emilion Grand Cru) $50. Like the 2003, this is creamy and supple, but the fruit is fresher and livelier also. The result is a lovely blend of mocha, raspberry and spice accented by hints of vanilla and crushed herbs that linger elegantly on the finish. Drink now–2020. **92** —*J.C. (6/1/2007)*

LAURENS

Laurens 1996 Clos des Demoiselles Brut Chenin Blanc (Crémant de Limoux) $15. 89 Best Buy —*P.G. (12/15/2000)*

LAURENT CHARLES BROTTE

Laurent Charles Brotte 2001 Bouvencourt Rhône Red Blend (Vacqueyras) $20. 81 —*R.V. (3/1/2004)*

LAURENT MIQUEL

Laurent Miquel 2005 Cabernet-Syrah Cabernet Sauvignon-Syrah (Vin de Pays d'Oc) $10. 86 —*R.V. (12/31/2006)*

Laurent Miquel 2005 Cinsault-Syrah Rosé Blend (Vin de Pays d'Oc) $10. 85 —*R.V. (12/31/2006)*

Laurent Miquel 2004 Nord Sud Syrah (Vin de Pays d'Oc) $13. The cherry fruit of this Syrah is light, fresh and poised. Pair with barbecue. **87** —*R.V. (2/1/2007)*

Laurent Miquel 2005 Nord Sud Viognier (Vin de Pays d'Oc) $13. 87 —*R.V. (12/31/2006)*

LAURENT-PERRIER

Laurent-Perrier 1997 Brut Champagne Blend (Champagne) $60. 90 —*R.V. (11/1/2006)*

Laurent-Perrier 1996 Brut Champagne Blend (Champagne) $60. 90 —*R.V. (11/1/2006)*

Laurent-Perrier 1995 Brut Champagne Blend (Champagne) $53. 91 —*M.S. (12/15/2003)*

Laurent-Perrier 1993 Brut Champagne Blend (Champagne) $50. 90 —*S.H. (12/15/2001)*

Laurent-Perrier NV Cuvée Brut Rosé Champagne Blend (Champagne) $60. 90 —*R.V. (12/1/2005)*

Laurent-Perrier NV Cuvée Brut Rosé Champagne Blend (Champagne) $50. 83 —*J.C. (12/15/2000)*

Laurent-Perrier NV Cuvée Ultra Brut Champagne Blend (Champagne) $65. 91 —*P.G. (12/1/2000)*

Laurent-Perrier NV Cuvée Ultra Brut Champagne Blend (Champagne) $39. 86 —*M.S. (12/15/2003)*

Laurent-Perrier NV Demi-Sec Champagne Blend (Champagne) $30. 87 *(12/31/2002)*

Laurent-Perrier 1997 Grand Siècle Champagne Blend (Champagne) $95. 89 —*J.C. (12/1/2004)*

Laurent-Perrier 1990 Grand Siecle Alexandra Rosé Champagne Blend (Champagne) $260. 94 —*S.H. (12/15/2001)*

Laurent-Perrier NV Grand Siècle Brut Champagne Blend (Champagne) $110. 91 —*P.G. (12/1/2006)*

Laurent-Perrier NV Grand Siècle La Cuvée Brut Champagne Blend (Champagne) $140. 95 —*P.G. (12/15/2000)*

Laurent-Perrier NV Grand Siècle La Cuvée Brut Champagne Blend (Champagne) $75. 94 Editors' Choice —*P.G. (12/15/2002)*

Laurent-Perrier NV Grand Siècle La Cuvée Brut Champagne Blend (Champagne) $90. 90 —*M.S. (12/15/2005)*

Laurent-Perrier NV L-P Brut Champagne Blend (Champagne) $30. 89 Editors' Choice —*J.C. (12/1/2004)*

Laurent-Perrier NV L-P Brut Champagne Blend (Champagne) $30. 91 —*P.G. (12/15/2002)*

Laurent-Perrier NV L-P Brut Champagne Blend (Champagne) $40. 91 Editors' Choice *(4/1/2001)*

Laurent-Perrier NV L-P Brut Champagne Blend (Champagne) $34. 87 —*R.V. (12/1/2005)*

Laurent-Perrier NV Ultra Brut Nature Champagne Blend (Champagne) $49. 89 —*R.V. (12/1/2005)*

Laurent-Perrier NV Cuvée Brut Rosé Pinot Noir (Champagne) $48. 90 —*J.C. (12/1/2004)*

LE CELLIER DE MARRENON

Le Cellier de Marrenon 2001 Grand Luberon Rhône Red Blend (Côtes du Luberon) $10. 86 —*J.C. (3/1/2004)*

Le Cellier de Marrenon 2000 Terre de Levant Rhône Red Blend (Côtes-du-Ventoux) $8. 85 Best Buy —*M.S. (9/1/2003)*

LE CLOS DES CAZAUX

Le Clos des Cazaux 2003 Cuvée Prestige Grenache-Syrah (Vacqueyras) $18. 84 —*J.C. (11/15/2006)*

Le Clos des Cazaux 2004 La Tour Sarrazine Rhône Red Blend (Gigondas) $23. 85 —*J.C. (11/15/2006)*

LE DÔME

Le Dôme 2004 Bordeaux Blend (Saint-Emilion Grand Cru) $NA. The flagship single-vineyard wine from the range of wines made by Jonathan Maltus in Saint-Emilion, this is 70% Cabernet Franc, a great testimony to the quality of the grape in one of its home territories. This 2004 has much of the usual power of this wine, with its great spice and dried fruit flavors, underlined with wood. But, being 2004, it also has a great lift and vitality that stops its power being overwhelming. **93** —*R.V. (6/1/2007)*

Le Dôme 2004 Barrel Sample Bordeaux Blend (Saint-Emilion Grand Cru) $NA. 95 —*R.V. (6/1/2005)*

Le Dôme 2005 Barrel Sample Bordeaux Blend (Saint-Emilion Grand Cru) $NA. 93 —*R.V. (6/20/2006)*

LE FONT DE PAPIER

Le Font de Papier 2001 La Fontaine des Papes Rhône Red Blend (Vacqueyras) $NA. 84 —*J.C. (11/15/2006)*

LE GRAND NOIR

Le Grand Noir 2004 Black Sheep Chardonnay-Viognier (Vin de Pays d'Oc) $10. 85 Best Buy —*J.C. (11/15/2005)*

LE MAS DU CÈDRE

Le Mas du Cèdre 2002 Rhône White Blend (Côtes-du-Rhône Brézème) $14. 85 —*J.C. (3/1/2004)*

LE VIEUX DONJON

Le Vieux Donjon 1998 Rhône Red Blend (Châteauneuf-du-Pape) $30. 94 —*M.M. (12/31/2000)*

LEON BEYER

Leon Beyer 2001 Réserve Pinot Gris (Alsace) $33. 90 —*R.V. (2/1/2006)*

Leon Beyer 2001 Riesling (Alsace) $9. 85 —*R.V. (8/1/2003)*

Leon Beyer 2001 Les Ecaillers Riesling (Alsace) $37. 88 —*R.V. (11/1/2005)*

Leon Beyer 1997 Tokay Pinot Gris (Alsace) $35. 80 *(8/1/1999)*

Leon Beyer 2000 Cuvée des Comtes d'Eguisheim Tokay Pinot Gris (Alsace) $46. 94 —*R.V. (2/1/2006)*

Leon Beyer 1997 Sélection de Grains Nobles Tokay Pinot Gris (Alsace) $52. 86 —*R.V. (2/1/2006)*

LÉONCE BOCQUET

Léonce Bocquet 2003 Brut Champagne Blend (Crémant de Bourgogne) $17. 88 —*R.V. (6/1/2006)*

Léonce Bocquet NV Brut Rosé Champagne Blend (Crémant de Bourgogne) $17. 87 —*R.V. (6/1/2006)*

LES AMANTS

Les Amants 2005 Merlot (Bordeaux) $NA. This 100% Merlot shows richness, but still retains an excellent firm texture. There's a certain minerality as well, lifting the blackberry fruits and giving them structure. **88** —*R.V. (11/1/2007)*

LES AMIS DES HOSPICES DE DIJON

Les Amis des Hospices de Dijon NV Champagne Blend (Crémant de Bourgogne) 87 —*M.S. (6/1/2003)*

LES ASTÉRIES

Les Astéries 2004 Bordeaux Blend (Saint-Emilion Grand Cru) $NA. This wine comes from a privileged 2.5-acre vineyard perched on the edge of the city of Saint-Emilion next to cru classé Clos Fourtet. It is beautifully perfumed, rich, opulent almost, but still with a strong sense of structure and dark, dry fruits. The texture is dense, packed with dusty tannins and black currant jelly flavors. It should age well, over at least 10 years. **91 Editors' Choice** —*R.V. (6/1/2007)*

LES CAVES DE BAILLY

Les Caves de Bailly NV Brut de Charvis Rosé Sparkling Blend (Vin Mousseux) $12. 84 —*R.V. (6/1/2006)*

LES CLOS DE PAULILLES

Les Clos de Paulilles 2005 Rimage Grenache (Banyuls) $26. Superripe Grenache gives this fortified dessert wine (16% alcohol) distinctly chocolaty overtones, but there's also an overripe note of prunes. Despite that, it doesn't pack the alcoholic punch or massive weight of Port, making it relatively easy to drink, with an affinity for chocolate desserts. **86** —*J.C. (12/15/2007)*

Les Clos de Paulilles 2005 Rosé Blend (Collioure) $15. 84 —*J.C. (6/21/2006)*

LES DOMANIERS

Les Domaniers 2003 Rosé Blend (Côtes de Provence) $17. 83 —*J.C. (11/15/2005)*

LES FORTS DE LATOUR

Les Forts de Latour 2005 Barrel Sample Bordeaux Blend (Pauillac) $NA. 92 —*R.V. (6/1/2006)*

Les Forts de Latour 2004 Bordeaux Blend (Pauillac) $NA. Latour's second wine is, as so often, on a level with many classed growths. In 2004, it is also a very faithful reflection of the vintage: fresh, lively and vital, with acidity and vibrant blackberry fruits very much up front. If not big, it is deliciously fresh and will develop well over five years. **91** —*R.V. (6/1/2007)*

LES HERETIQUES

Les Heretiques 2001 Red Blend (Vin de Pays de L'Herault) $8. 87 Best Buy —*J.C. (11/15/2002)*

LES JAMELLES

Les Jamelles 2001 Badet Clement & Cie Cabernet Sauvignon (Vin de Pays d'Oc) $9. 86 Best Buy —*M.S. (9/1/2003)*

Les Jamelles 2005 Cabernet Sauvignon Cabernet Sauvignon (Vin de Pays d'Oc) $9. A rather green wine, herbaceous rather than fruity, this lacks depth of flavor, although it is clean, fresh and perfectly drinkable. The aftertaste shows fresh, dry red berry acidity. **82** —*R.V. (2/1/2007)*

Les Jamelles 2003 Cabernet-Merlot Special Reserve Cabernet Sauvignon-Merlot (Vin de Pays d'Oc) $15. This wine comes from cool climate vineyards near the medieval city of Carcassonne, giving it a Bordeaux feel, with structured tannic fruit, some stalky blackcurrant flavors and a ribbon of wood that gives complexity. **88** —*R.V. (2/1/2007)*

Les Jamelles 2005 Chardonnay (Vin de Pays d'Oc) $8. 84 —*R.V. (12/31/2006)*

Les Jamelles 1997 Chardonnay (Vin de Pays d'Oc) $8. 86 *(11/15/1999)*

Les Jamelles 2005 Cinsault (Vin de Pays d'Oc) $8. 87 Best Buy —*J.C. (6/21/2006)*

Les Jamelles 2006 Rosé Cinsault (Vin de Pays d'Oc) $10. A perennial Best Buy, the Les Jamelles Cinsault is a reliable choice for summer quaffing. It's a little fuller than many rosés, but also a touch more complex, adding hints of minerality to the bold, fruity notes of cherries and watermelon. **87 Best Buy** —*J.C. (7/1/2007)*

Les Jamelles 2000 Rose Cinsault (Vin de Pays d'Oc) $8. 86 —*M.M. (2/1/2002)*

Les Jamelles 2000 Merlot (Vin de Pays d'Oc) $8. 85 —*D.T. (2/1/2002)*

Les Jamelles 2005 Merlot (Vin de Pays d'Oc) $9. 82 —*R.V. (12/31/2006)*

Les Jamelles 2005 Pinot Noir Pinot Noir (Vin de Pays d'Oc) $9. The ripe, generous character is here, with some fresh tannins and red berry flavors. It's open, easy-to-drink and shows good vibrant acidity. **88 Best Buy** —*R.V. (2/1/2007)*

Les Jamelles 2000 Sauvignon Blanc (Vin de Pays d'Oc) $8. 85 —*M.M. (2/1/2002)*

Les Jamelles 2005 Syrah Syrah (Vin de Pays d'Oc) $9. Full and packed with fruit, this has all the generosity of southern Syrah, with plenty of perfumed herbal flavors, and a feeling of warmth. **86** —*R.V. (2/1/2007)*

Les Jamelles 1999 Syrah (Vin de Pays d'Oc) $8. 83 *(10/1/2001)*

Les Jamelles 2003 Special Reserve Viognier-Marsanne White Blend (Vin de Pays d'Oc) $15. 84 —*J.C. (11/15/2005)*

LES MARIONETTES

Les Marionettes 2003 Sauvignon Blanc (Vin de Pays d'Oc) $NA. 85 —*R.V. (12/1/2004)*

LES ROCHETTES

Les Rochettes 2001 Sauvignon Blanc (Sancerre) $16. 85 *(8/1/2002)*

LES VIGNERONS DE CASES DE PÉNE

Les Vignerons de Cases de Péne 2003 Château de Peña Réserve S Rhône Red Blend (Côtes du Roussillon Villages) $20. 87 —*R.V. (12/31/2006)*

Les Vignerons de Cases de Péne 2005 Ninet de Peña Viognier (Vin de Pays d'Oc) $10. 86 Best Buy —*R.V. (12/31/2006)*

LES VIGNERONS DE CHUSCLAN

Les Vignerons de Chusclan 2001 La Ferme de Gicon Rhône Red Blend (Côtes-du-Rhône) $9. 84 —*M.S. (9/1/2003)*

Les Vignerons de Chusclan 2004 Les Genets Chusclan Rhône Red Blend (Côtes-du-Rhône Villages) $15. 86 —*J.C. (11/15/2006)*

Les Vignerons de Chusclan 2000 Les Monticauts Rhône Red Blend (Côtes-du-Rhône) $14. 89 Best Buy —*M.S. (9/1/2003)*

Les Vignerons de Chusclan 2003 Les Ribières Chusclan Rhône Red Blend (Côtes-du-Rhône Villages) $15. 87 —*J.C. (11/15/2006)*

LES VIGNERONS DE LA MÉDITERRANÉE

Les Vignerons de la Méditerranée NV Petit Grain Muscat Blanc à Petit Grain (Muscat de Saint-Jean de Minervois) $NA. All the honey and perfumes of Muscat are in this bottle, which has a ripeness balanced by a freshness which make it irresistible. The texture is properly oily, silky perhaps, with just the right touch of acidity. **89** —*R.V. (2/1/2007)*

LES VIGNERONS DE L'ENCLAVE DES PAPES

Les Vignerons de l'Enclave des Papes 2004 Croix de Chêne Rhône Red Blend (Côtes-du-Rhône) $9. 84 —*J.C. (11/15/2006)*

LES VIGNERONS DE TAVEL

Les Vignerons de Tavel 2003 Richesse des Lauzeraies Rhône Red Blend (Lirac) $14. 88 —*J.C. (11/15/2006)*

Les Vignerons de Tavel 2005 Terre des Lauzeraies Rhône White Blend (Côtes-du-Rhône) $9. 82 —*J.C. (11/15/2006)*

Les Vignerons de Tavel 2005 Cuvée Tableau Rosé Blend (Tavel) $14. 86 —*J.C. (11/15/2006)*

Les Vignerons de Tavel 2005 Les Cigaliérs Rosé Blend (Tavel) $14. 88 —*J.C. (11/15/2006)*

LES VIGNERONS DU MONT-VENTOUX

Les Vignerons du Mont-Ventoux 2001 Grange des Dames Rhône Red Blend (Côtes-du-Ventoux) $10. 88 Best Buy —*J.C. (3/1/2004)*

LES VINS DE VIENNE

Les Vins de Vienne 2000 Les Pimpignoles Rhône Red Blend (Côtes-du-Rhône) $40. 90 —*R.V. (3/1/2004)*

Les Vins de Vienne 2004 L'Arzelle Syrah (Saint-Joseph) $28. 87 —*J.C. (11/15/2006)*

Les Vins de Vienne 2004 Les Escartailles Syrah (Côte Rôtie) $46. 87 —*J.C. (11/15/2006)*

Les Vins de Vienne 2004 La Chambée Viognier (Condrieu) $42. 90 —*J.C. (11/15/2006)*

LES VINS SKALLI

Les Vins Skalli 1998 Edition Limitée Cabernet Sauvignon (Vin de Pays d'Oc) $17. 89 —*R.V. (11/15/2002)*

Les Vins Skalli 2000 Oak Aged Chardonnay (Vin de Pays d'Oc) $10. 87 —*R.V. (11/15/2002)*

Les Vins Skalli 1999 Oak Aged Syrah (Vin de Pays d'Oc) $10. 85 —*R.V.*

(11/15/2002)

LOMBARD ET CIE

Lombard et Cie NV Brut Champagne Blend (Champagne) $NA. 85 —*R.V. (12/1/2005)*

LOUIS BERNARD

Louis Bernard 2001 Grenache-Syrah (Côtes-du-Rhône Villages) $11. 81 —*J.C. (3/1/2004)*

Louis Bernard 1999 Grenache-Syrah (Châteauneuf-du-Pape) $28. 88 *(11/15/2001)*

Louis Bernard 2001 Grande Reserve Grenache-Syrah (Châteauneuf-du-Pape) $37. 88 —*R.V. (3/1/2004)*

Louis Bernard 2004 Rhône Red Blend (Gigondas) 84 —*J.C. (11/15/2006)*

Louis Bernard 2003 Rhône Red Blend (Châteauneuf-du-Pape) $35. 87 —*R.V. (12/31/2005)*

Louis Bernard 2003 Rhône Red Blend (Côtes-du-Rhône Villages) $9. 84 —*J.C. (11/15/2006)*

Louis Bernard 2001 Rhône Red Blend (Gigondas) $18. 86 —*R.V. (3/1/2004)*

Louis Bernard 1999 Rhône Red Blend (Côtes-du-Rhône) $9. 85 *(11/15/2001)*

Louis Bernard 2005 Rouge Rhône Red Blend (Côtes-du-Rhône Villages) $12. 85 —*J.C. (11/15/2006)*

Louis Bernard 2006 Rosé Blend (Côtes-du-Rhône) $11. Light pink in color, this wine has attractive delicate, fresh raspberries, caramel and a touch of spice. Good acidity gives it a great lift. There's a definite southern spice and sunshine to this wine. 87 Best Buy —*R.V. (7/1/2007)*

Louis Bernard 2003 Syrah (Crozes-Hermitage) $20. 89 Editors' Choice —*J.C. (11/15/2005)*

Louis Bernard 1999 Syrah (Crozes-Hermitage) $13. 81 *(10/1/2001)*

LOUIS BOUILLOT

Louis Bouillot NV Grand Reserve Brut Champagne Blend (Bourgogne) $12. 87 —*P.G. (12/15/2002)*

Louis Bouillot NV Grande Réserve Perle de Vigne Brut Champagne Blend (Crémant de Bourgogne) $15. 85 —*R.V. (6/1/2006)*

Louis Bouillot NV Perle de Nuit Blanc de Noirs Brut Champagne Blend (Crémant de Bourgogne) $15. 84 —*J.C. (12/1/2004)*

Louis Bouillot 2003 Perle Rare Brut Champagne Blend (Crémant de Bourgogne) $16. 90 —*R.V. (6/1/2006)*

Louis Bouillot NV Perle d'Aurore Rosé Brut Pinot Noir (Crémant de Bourgogne) $15. 88 —*R.V. (6/1/2006)*

Louis Bouillot NV Perle d'Ivoire Blanc de Blancs Brut Sparkling Blend (Crémant de Bourgogne) $15. 84 —*M.D. (12/15/2006)*

Louis Bouillot NV Perle Noire Blanc de Noirs Sparkling Blend (France) $15. 87 —*M.D. (12/15/2006)*

LOUIS DE SACY

Louis de Sacy NV Brut Rosé Champagne Blend (Champagne) $39. 89 —*P.G. (12/15/2003)*

Louis de Sacy NV Cuvée Brut Champagne Blend (Champagne) $35. 87 *(12/15/2001)*

LOUIS JADOT

Louis Jadot 2004 Chardonnay (Bâtard-Montrachet) $203. 94 —*R.V. (12/1/2006)*

Louis Jadot 2002 Chardonnay (Corton-Charlemagne) $70. 94 —*R.V. (9/1/2004)*

Louis Jadot 2000 Chardonnay (Mâcon-Villages) $12. 82 —*D.T. (2/1/2002)*

Louis Jadot 1998 Chardonnay (Pouilly-Fuissé) $22. 88 —*M.S. (7/1/2000)*

Louis Jadot 2004 Champ Gain Premier Cru Chardonnay (Puligny-Montrachet) $61. 94 Cellar Selection —*R.V. (12/1/2006)*

Louis Jadot 2000 Château des Jacques Grand Clos de Loyse Chardonnay (Beaujolais-Villages) $15. 87 Best Buy —*S.H. (11/15/2002)*

Louis Jadot 2004 Chardonnay (Corton-Charlemagne) $113. An intense, powerful wine, which speaks of the importance of the Corton Charlemagne vineyard and also justifies it. It is smooth and creamy, concentrated white fruits to go with an solid structure that promises great aging. 95 —*R.V. (2/1/2007)*

Louis Jadot 2003 Chardonnay (Corton-Charlemagne) $145. 95 —*R.V. (9/1/2005)*

Louis Jadot 2003 Le Clos Blanc Grèves Premier Cru Chardonnay (Beaune) $65. 90 —*R.V. (9/1/2005)*

Louis Jadot 2003 Gamay (Beaujolais) $10. 85 Best Buy —*R.V. (11/15/2004)*

Louis Jadot 2000 Château de Bellevue Gamay (Morgon) $16. 88 —*S.H. (11/15/2002)*

Louis Jadot 2000 Château des Jacques Gamay (Moulin-à-Vent) $20. 87 —*S.H. (11/15/2002)*

Louis Jadot 2000 Domaine du Monnet Gamay (Brouilly) $16. 86 —*S.H. (11/15/2002)*

Louis Jadot 2004 Pinot Noir (Bonnes-Mares) $128. In keeping with its place on the boundary of Morey Saint-Denis and Chambolle-Musigny, this Bonnes-Mares marries the refinement of great Chambolle with the more tough, powered character of Morey. It's smoky, powerful and solid with an explosion of fruits in the mouth, but leaving mouth-watering freshness to finish. 95 —*R.V. (3/1/2007)*

Louis Jadot 2004 Pinot Noir (Bourgogne) $17. 84 —*J.C. (11/15/2006)*

Louis Jadot 2004 Pinot Noir (Chambolle-Musigny) $42. Jacques Lardière, technical wizard of Jadot (and Wine Enthusiast's 2004 Winemaker of the Year), is able to coax every ounce of opulence out of this village wine. Red, verging on black and ripe, fruits and acidity come after initial dryness. And then there is the richness, tempered with elegance. Some premier cru wine has gone into this blend. 90 —*R.V. (3/1/2007)*

Louis Jadot 2004 Pinot Noir (Clos de la Roche) $NA. A big, concentrated wine, dominated by black fruits, some minerality and a dense, solid structure. Attractive herb and perfumed aromas of violets hint at a future when it will be more seductive. 92 —*R.V. (3/1/2007)*

Louis Jadot 2004 Pinot Noir (Clos Saint-Denis) $121. This is a complete, rounded wine. It has all the right firmness to ensure that it will age, but at the same time, it has great, ripe fruits. An open and powerful wine, keeping an element of elegance that will show much more prominently in the years to come. 94 —*R.V. (3/1/2007)*

Louis Jadot 2004 Pinot Noir (Echezeaux) $110. Great, opulent red fruits dominate both the aromas and flavors of this big-hearted wine. It's rounded, open, waiting to be drunk, with its relatively soft tannins and great, ripe flavors. 94 —*R.V. (3/1/2007)*

Louis Jadot 2004 Pinot Noir (Gevrey-Chambertin) $38. Firm, tannic, this is a big wine dominated by its firm structure, although there are some good, ripe black fruits there as well. The aftertaste is rather hard. 88 —*R.V. (3/1/2007)*

Louis Jadot 2004 Pinot Noir (Vosne-Romanée) $41. This is a complete wine, as are so many from Vosne-Romanée, with delicious, mouthwatering acidity and freshness. At the same time there are tannins, and black grape skin flavors. 89 —*R.V. (3/1/2007)*

Louis Jadot 2003 Pinot Noir (Chambertin Clos de Bèze) $200. 96 —*R.V. (9/1/2005)*

Louis Jadot 1999 Pinot Noir (Chambolle-Musigny) $37. 84 —*R.V. (11/1/2002)*

Louis Jadot 1995 Pinot Noir (Marsannay) $20. 87 *(11/15/1999)*

Louis Jadot 2003 Theurons Premier Cru Pinot Noir (Beaune) $42. 91 —*R.V. (9/1/2005)*

Louis Jadot 2004 Pinot Noir (Chambertin Clos de Bèze) $152. If you ever needed to know why Grand Crus are better vineyards and make better wine than the rest, this wine is the perfect example. It has all the richness and opulence of great Pinot Noir, but at the same time, with its firm structure and plum and damson flavors, it magnifies those qualities into something impressive and long-lasting. 96 Cellar Selection —*R.V. (3/1/2007)*

Louis Jadot 2002 Pinot Noir (Chambertin Clos de Bèze) $140. 97 —*R.V. (9/1/2004)*

Louis Jadot 2004 Clos de la Barre Premier Cru Pinot Noir (Volnay) $50. One of the monopoles (wholly owned vineyards) run entirely by Jadot, this is a velvety, elegant wine. While it is not huge, it more than pulls its weight with its appetizing freshness and ripe tannins. 90 —*R.V. (3/1/2007)*

Louis Jadot 2004 Clos de Malte Pinot Noir (Santenay) $25. Santenay is the southernmost wine village in the Côte d'Or, producing wines that are often good value. This soft, slightly earthy wine comes from a vineyard named after the Knights of Malta. It is fresh and open, with good finishing acidity. 87 —*R.V. (3/1/2007)*

Louis Jadot 2004 Clos de Ursules Premier Cru Pinot Noir (Beaune) $46. One of the flagship wines of Louis Jadot, this wine comes from a seven-acre vineyard that is a Jadot monopoly. This is a delicate wine, very elegant, with roundness and sweetness from ripe fruit. The heart is tannins, suggesting that the wine will age well. 91 —*R.V. (3/1/2007)*

Louis Jadot 2004 Pinot Noir (Clos Vougeot) $92. A real blockbuster, with dark tannins and a firm, tough structure. Only right at the end does tasty, ripe fruit show up, but even this is heavy and brooding. If you want power in a Pinot, look no further. **93** *—R.V. (3/1/2007)*

Louis Jadot 2004 Clos Saint-Jacques Premier Cru Pinot Noir (Gevrey-Chambertin) $87. Part of the Louis Jadot domaine, this great vineyard produced a 2004 with intense structure but also a silky feel, enveloping and powering the black, concentrated fruits. For this vintage, this is big and does need to age. **93 Cellar Selection** *—R.V. (3/1/2007)*

Louis Jadot 2002 Corton Greves Premier Cru Pinot Noir (Aloxe-Corton) $70. 93 *—R.V. (9/1/2004)*

Louis Jadot 2002 Gevrey Chambertin Clos Saint-Jacques Premier cru Pinot Noir (Gevrey-Chambertin) $85. 94 *—R.V. (9/1/2004)*

Louis Jadot 1999 Les Baudes Premier Cru Pinot Noir (Chambolle-Musigny) $61. 92 *—R.V. (11/1/2002)*

Louis Jadot 2004 Les Estournelles Saint-Jacques Premier Cru Pinot Noir (Gevrey-Chambertin) $61. This vineyard has produced a firmly tannic wine, with intense, dark, solid flavors. The dry, woody character surrounds fresh fruit. **89** *—R.V. (3/1/2007)*

Louis Jadot 2004 Les Fuées Premier Cru Pinot Noir (Chambolle-Musigny) $64. With just the right generosity of flavor as well as freshness, this is an appetizing and delicious wine. Red cherries and red berry fruits blend with the round, velvet structure to produce a wine with immediate appeal. **91** *—R.V. (3/1/2007)*

Louis Jadot 1999 Les Fuées Premier Cru Pinot Noir (Chambolle-Musigny) $61. 89 *—R.V. (11/1/2002)*

Louis Jadot 2004 Les Suchots Premier Cru Pinot Noir (Vosne-Romanée) $71. A well-balanced wine with fine tannins inside a big, solid character. The fruit is ripe and smooth on the outside, but inside this velvet glove is an iron fist. New wood flavors are dominant in the aftertaste. **90** *—R.V. (3/1/2007)*

Louis Jadot 2002 Volnay Clos des Chênes Premier Cru Pinot Noir (Volnay) $29. 92 *—R.V. (9/1/2004)*

Louis Jadot 2003 Château des Jacques Gamay (Moulin-à-Vent) $22. 89 *—J.C. (11/15/2005)*

Louis Jadot 2001 Domaine du Monnet Gamay (Brouilly) $16. 83 *—J.C. (11/15/2003)*

Louis Jadot 1998 Les Demoiselles Chardonnay (Chevalier-Montrachet) $NA. 91 *—R.V. (11/1/2001)*

LOUIS LATOUR

Louis Latour 2000 Chardonnay (Bâtard-Montrachet) $220. 92 *(8/1/2002)*

Louis Latour 2004 Chardonnay (Bâtard-Montrachet) $280. 94 *—R.V. (12/1/2006)*

Louis Latour 2004 Chardonnay (Bienvenues Bâtard-Montrachet) $250. 94 *—R.V. (12/1/2006)*

Louis Latour 2000 Chardonnay (Meursault) $34. 87 *(8/1/2002)*

Louis Latour 2000 Chardonnay (Beaune) $26. 86 *(8/1/2002)*

Louis Latour 1998 Chardonnay (Meursault) $34. 87 *—P.G. (11/1/2000)*

Louis Latour 1998 Chardonnay (Chassagne-Montrachet) $40. 88 *—P.G. (11/1/2000)*

Louis Latour 2004 Cailleret Premier Cru Chardonnay (Chassagne-Montrachet) $65. 90 *—R.V. (12/1/2006)*

Louis Latour 1998 Charmes Premier Cru Chardonnay (Meursault) $55. 90 *—P.G. (11/1/2000)*

Louis Latour 2000 Château De Blagny Premier Cru Chardonnay (Meursault) $40. 89 *(8/1/2002)*

Louis Latour 2003 Chardonnay (Corton-Charlemagne) $140. 93 *—R.V. (9/1/2005)*

Louis Latour 2004 En Paradis Chardonnay (Pouilly-Vinzelles) $16. The steely, mineral character of a good Pouilly wine is certainly here, along with a rich, creamy texture and pineapple acidity. It's rich, but there is a good, crisp lift on the finish. **89** *—R.V. (3/1/2007)*

Louis Latour 2004 Goutte d'Or Premier Cru Chardonnay (Meursault) $65. 89 *—R.V. (12/1/2006)*

Louis Latour 1998 La Grande Roche Chardonnay (Montagny) $15. 86 *—J.C. (7/1/2000)*

Louis Latour 2000 Les Chenevottes Chardonnay (Chassagne-Montrachet) $47. 88 *(8/1/2002)*

Louis Latour 2003 Les Demoiselles Chardonnay (Chevalier-Montrachet) $470. 94 *—R.V. (9/1/2005)*

Louis Latour 2004 Les Folatières Premier Cru Chardonnay (Puligny-Montrachet) $79. This wine is soft and ripe, but seems to lack structure. Don't expect it to age. **87** *—R.V. (12/1/2006)*

Louis Latour 1998 Les Referts Premier Cru Chardonnay (Puligny-Montrachet) $55. 92 *—P.G. (11/1/2000)*

Louis Latour 2000 Morgeot Chardonnay (Chassagne-Montrachet) $50. 89 *(8/1/2002)*

Louis Latour 1998 Morgeot Premier Cru Chardonnay (Chassagne-Montrachet) $48. 89 *—P.G. (11/1/2000)*

Louis Latour 2002 Chardonnay (Puligny-Montrachet) $37. 89 *—R.V. (9/1/2004)*

Louis Latour 2004 Sous le Puits Premier Cru Chardonnay (Puligny-Montrachet) $49. 90 *—R.V. (12/1/2006)*

Louis Latour 2003 Pinot Noir (Aloxe-Corton) $45. 87 *—R.V. (9/1/2005)*

Louis Latour 2003 les Heritiers Latour Pinot Noir (Chambertin) $220. 93 *—R.V. (9/1/2005)*

Louis Latour 2002 Corton Grancy Pinot Noir (Corton) $NA. 91 *—R.V. (9/1/2004)*

Louis Latour 1996 Pinot Noir (Aloxe-Corton) $29. 90 *(11/15/1999)*

Louis Latour 2002 Le Chaillots Premier Cru Pinot Noir (Aloxe-Corton) $NA. 89 *—R.V. (9/1/2004)*

Louis Latour 1995 Savigny-les-Beaune Pinot Noir (Burgundy) $20. 88 *(11/15/1999)*

LOUIS MAX

Louis Max 2004 Pinot Noir (Gevrey-Chambertin) $46. A ripe, structured wine with plenty of the robust, generous character of Gevrey-Chambertin. On top of the solid tannins are black plums, some spices and a coating of delicious, juicy acidity. Ready to drink, but it should age well over the next few years. **89** *—R.V. (3/1/2007)*

Louis Max 2001 Les Lièvres Pinot Noir (Nuits-St.-Georges) $46. It's good to see a more mature red Burgundy still available, and the extra maturity has allowed this wine to develop some of the classic gamey character of Pinot Noir. It is in a traditional style, here a positive charactertistic, giving weight but also showing delicious ripeness. **89** *—R.V. (3/1/2007)*

LOUIS MOUSSET

Louis Mousset 1999 Prestige Syrah (Côtes-du-Rhône) $10. 80 *(10/1/2001)*

LOUIS PERDRIER

Louis Perdrier NV Blanc de Blancs Brut Sparkling Blend (Vin Mousseux) $8. A pleasant surprise at such a low pricepoint, Louis Perdrier's Blanc de Blancs Brut features competent winemaking, aromas reminiscent of chalk dust and herbs and a clean, abbreviated finish. **84 Best Buy** *—J.C. (12/15/2007)*

Louis Perdrier NV Rosé Sparkling Blend (France) $8. This wine's berry and apple aromas and flavors are only modest in their intensity, but they're clean, and the steady, fine bead makes for a light, refreshing mouthfeel. **83** *—J.C. (12/15/2007)*

Louis Perdrier NV Brut Rosé Sparkling Blend (Vin Mousseux) $8. 83 *—R.V. (6/1/2006)*

LOUIS ROEDERER

Louis Roederer 1995 Blanc de Blancs Brut Champagne Blend (Champagne) $55. 91 Editors' Choice *—M.M. (12/15/2001)*

Louis Roederer 1993 Blanc de Blancs Brut Champagne Blend (Champagne) $55. 91 *—M.S. (12/1/1999)*

Louis Roederer 1997 Brut Champagne Blend (Champagne) $63. 95 *—R.V. (12/1/2004)*

Louis Roederer 1996 Brut Champagne Blend (Champagne) $63. 93 Editors' Choice *—J.C. (12/1/2004)*

Louis Roederer 2000 Brut Millésimé Champagne Blend (Champagne) $72. While 2000 was not a great vintage, Roederer manages to make a fine wine out of it: dry but ripe, crisp but also full-bodied, a pure line of green fruits open with a burst in the mouth. To finish, there are hints of things to come; age five years and more. **94 Cellar Selection** *—R.V. (12/1/2007)*

Louis Roederer NV Brut Premier Champagne Blend (Champagne) $35. This Roederer nonvintage seems to be getting drier, bringing out more of the green fruits and less creamy character. It works well here because the wine has some bottle age, giving a beautifully balanced wine that has great class and elegance. **92** *—R.V. (12/1/2007)*

Louis Roederer NV Brut Premier Champagne Blend (France) $41. 87 *—S.H. (12/15/2002)*

Louis Roederer 1999 Brut Rosé Champagne Blend (Champagne) $71. 89 *—M.S. (12/31/2005)*

Louis Roederer 1998 Brut Rosé Champagne Blend (Champagne) $63. 92 *—R.V. (12/1/2004)*

Louis Roederer 1994 Brut Rosé Champagne Blend (Champagne) $55. 86

—*J.C. (12/15/2000)*

Louis Roederer 1995 Brut Vintage Champagne Blend (France) $59. 93 Editors' Choice —*S.H. (12/15/2002)*

Louis Roederer 2000 Cristal Brut Champagne Blend (Champagne) $211. This is a lightweight Cristal, floating and fresh, without the punch this great wine can have from Pinot Noir. It is also way too young. To taste, there is good balance, but the persistent grapefruit flavor shows the wine's youth. 92 —*R.V. (12/1/2007)*

Louis Roederer 1999 Cristal Brut Champagne Blend (Champagne) $188. 95 —*R.V. (11/1/2006)*

Louis Roederer 1996 Cristal Brut Champagne Blend (Champagne) $175. 91 —*J.C. (12/15/2003)*

Louis Roederer 1995 Cristal Brut Champagne Blend (Champagne) $180. 92 *(12/15/2001)*

Louis Roederer 1996 Cristal Rosé Champagne Blend (Champagne) $295. 90 —*J.C. (12/1/2004)*

Louis Roederer NV Premier Brut Champagne Blend (Champagne) $52. 92 —*R.V. (12/1/2005)*

Louis Roederer NV Premier Brut Champagne Blend (Champagne) $45. 89 —*J.C. (12/1/2004)*

Louis Roederer NV Premier Brut Champagne Blend (Champagne) $51. 87 *(12/15/2001)*

Louis Roederer 2000 Rosé Millésimé Brut Champagne Blend (Champagne) $72. A wine that manages to straddle the twin peaks of freshness and maturity with ease. There are plenty of crisp pink and white fruits, but also a layer of mature acidity that offers a more complex series of secondary flavors, spice, toast and some tannins. 93 —*R.V. (12/1/2007)*

Louis Roederer 1996 Vintage Rose Champagne Blend (France) $55. 92 —*S.H. (12/15/2002)*

Louis Roederer 2000 Blanc de Blancs Brut Chardonnay (Champagne) $72. A finely structured, delicate, elegant wine, this has a pure white fruit and mineral character that lies easily on the palate. The aftertaste is soft but there is still a steely edge to the wine, which promises long aging. Give it at least five years. 91 Cellar Selection —*R.V. (12/1/2007)*

Louis Roederer 1999 Blanc de Blancs Brut Chardonnay (Champagne) $74. 93 —*R.V. (11/1/2006)*

Louis Roederer 1997 Blanc de Blancs Brut Chardonnay (Champagne) $59. 90 —*P.G. (12/15/2003)*

LOUIS SIPP

Louis Sipp 2001 Grand Cru Kirchberg de Ribeauvillé Riesling (Alsace) $28. 90 —*R.V. (11/1/2005)*

LOUIS TÊTE

Louis Tête 2003 Gamay (Moulin-à-Vent) $18. 86 —*J.C. (11/15/2005)*

LUCIEN ALBRECHT

Lucien Albrecht 2004 Cuvée Marie Gewürztraminer (Alsace) $27. A broad, weighty wine, with the florality and spice of the variety held in check in favor of ripe pear and pineapple aromas and flavors. With its discernible residual sugar and low acid levels, it could use more freshness on the finish. 84 —*J.C. (7/1/2007)*

Lucien Albrecht 2002 Cuvée Marie Gewürztraminer (Alsace) $27. 84 —*J.C. (8/1/2006)*

Lucien Albrecht 2004 Reserve Gewürztraminer (Alsace) $18. 88 —*J.C. (11/1/2005)*

Lucien Albrecht 2001 Sélections de Grains Nobles Gewürztraminer (Alsace) $65. A rare misstep from Albrecht, the 2001 Gewürztraminer SGN seems a touch oxidized and nutty, with a broad, dull texture and a hint of butter on the finish. It's ripe and sweet, but it just doesn't seem quite right. 84 —*J.C. (12/15/2007)*

Lucien Albrecht 2001 Vendanges Tardives Gewürztraminer (Alsace) $45. This late-harvest Gewürztraminer boasts hints of dried apricot on the nose to go along with scents of pineapple and spice. It's a gingery-peppery spice note that persists through the palate and onto the finish, joined by ripe pear flavors. Because it's not that sweet or concentrated, this would be a good candidate to pair with foie gras or cheese rather than a true dessert. 87 —*J.C. (12/15/2007)*

Lucien Albrecht 2000 Vendanges Tardives 375 ml Gewürztraminer (Alsace) $41. 88 —*J.C. (2/1/2005)*

Lucien Albrecht 2005 Cuvée Balthazar Pinot Blanc (Alsace) $14. This seems to have a touch of sweetness to it, but it is well balanced by fresh apple and citrus flavors, while hints of honey and spice show up on the finish. Soft and easy to drink on its own as an apéritif. 87 —*J.C. (7/1/2007)*

Lucien Albrecht 2003 Cuvée Balthazar Pinot Blanc (Alsace) $12. 86 —*J.C. (2/1/2005)*

Lucien Albrecht 2001 Clos des Récollets Pinot Gris (Alsace) $100. This is the current release of this unusual wine. It's barrel-fermented and aged, which gives a huge bouquet of buttered nuts, backed by ample peach and melon fruit, and a long, spice-filled, oily finish. Full-bodied and unctuous in texture, it stretches the boundaries of Pinot Gris, and is sure to be controversial. 91 —*J.C. (7/1/2007)*

Lucien Albrecht 2001 Clos des Récollets Pinot Gris (Alsace) $86. 89 —*J.C. (2/1/2005)*

Lucien Albrecht 2004 Cuvée Cécile Pinot Gris (Alsace) $27. Rather honeyed and sweet, with broad, mouthfilling flavors of peach and melon that finally firm up a bit on the finish, adding crisper, citrusy tones. Try with shrimp or lobster accented by additional hints of sweetness. 87 —*J.C. (7/1/2007)*

Lucien Albrecht 2002 Cuvée Cécile Pinot Gris (Alsace) $42. 89 —*R.V. (2/1/2006)*

Lucien Albrecht 2005 Cuvée Romanus Pinot Gris (Alsace) $19. This medium-bodied, off-dry Pinot Gris features the variety's typically understated aromatics, then delivers an assertive mouthful of honey, peach and buttered stones. Explodes with more varied fruit notes on the finish, suggesting that additional aging may be beneficial. Drink now–2012. 90 —*J.C. (7/1/2007)*

Lucien Albrecht 2003 Cuvée Romanus Pinot Gris (Alsace) $16. 86 —*J.C. (2/1/2005)*

Lucien Albrecht 2001 Grand Cru Pfingstberg Pinot Gris (Alsace) $36. 90 Editors' Choice —*J.C. (2/1/2005)*

Lucien Albrecht 2000 Sélection de Grains Nobles Pinot Gris (Alsace) $65. 92 —*R.V. (2/1/2006)*

Lucien Albrecht 2000 Vendages Tardives 375 ml Pinot Gris (Alsace) $46. 88 —*J.C. (2/1/2005)*

Lucien Albrecht 2001 Amplus Pinot Noir (Alsace) $44. 84 —*J.C. (2/1/2005)*

Lucien Albrecht NV Brut Rosé Pinot Noir (Crémant d'Alsace) $20. A pale, coppery sparkling rosé, Albrecht's Crémant features plenty of frothy bubbles and ripe peach and melon aromas and flavors. Seems a bit soft on the finish, but that's balanced by some chalky, minerally notes. 86 —*J.C. (7/1/2007)*

Lucien Albrecht 2001 Clos Himmelreich Riesling (Alsace) $103. Minerality and spicy smoke paired with soft Bartlett pear are a nice introduction, followed by flavors of limey citrus, honeydew and petrol. A lean and refreshing wine with a clean snappy finish. 87 *(9/1/2007)*

Lucien Albrecht 2002 Clos Himmelreich Riesling (Alsace) $95. 89 —*R.V. (2/1/2006)*

Lucien Albrecht 2004 Cuvée Henri Riesling (Alsace) $25. 85 —*J.C. (8/1/2006)*

Lucien Albrecht 2001 Grand Cru Clos Schild Pfingstberg Riesling (Alsace) $96. 90 Cellar Selection —*J.C. (2/1/2005)*

Lucien Albrecht 2001 Grand Cru Pfingstberg Riesling (Alsace) $35. 87 —*J.C. (2/1/2005)*

Lucien Albrecht 2005 Réserve Riesling (Alsace) $18. Floral notes of rose hips and hibiscus dominate this wine along with essences of petrol and white gumdrop. Off-dry and oily, flavors of sweet stewed peaches and spiced applesauce abound on the palate. Given the weight and viscosity, crisper acidity is needed to liven things up. 84 *(9/1/2007)*

Lucien Albrecht 2003 Reserve Riesling (Alsace) $15. 87 —*J.C. (2/1/2005)*

Lucien Albrecht 2000 Vendanges Tardives 375 ml Riesling (Alsace) $41. 88 —*J.C. (2/1/2005)*

Lucien Albrecht NV Blanc de Blancs Brut Sparkling Blend (Crémant d'Alsace) $20. Light and fresh, this is a crisp, citrusy blanc de blancs that hints at earth and ginger root. Long on the finish. 85 —*J.C. (12/15/2007)*

Lucien Albrecht 1997 Tokay Pinot Gris (Alsace) $19. 88 *(8/1/1999)*

LUCIEN CROCHET

Lucien Crochet 2000 La Croix du Roy Sauvignon Blanc (Sancerre) $20. 90 Editors' Choice *(8/1/2002)*

LUCIEN LE MOINE

Lucien Le Moine 2003 Chardonnay (Corton-Charlemagne) $150. 93 —*J.C. (4/1/2006)*

Lucien Le Moine 2003 Les Folatiéres Premier Cru Chardonnay (Puligny-Montrachet) $100. 92 —*J.C. (4/1/2006)*

Lucien Le Moine 2003 Pinot Noir (Clos Saint-Denis) $130. 92 —*J.C. (4/1/2006)*

Lucien Le Moine 2003 Les Charmes Premier Cru Pinot Noir (Chambolle-Musigny) $150. 93 *—J.C. (4/1/2006)*

Lucien Le Moine 2003 Les Suchots Premier Cru Pinot Noir (Vosne-Romanée) $100. 90 *—J.C. (4/1/2006)*

LULU B.

Lulu B. 2005 Pinot Noir (Vin de Pays d'Oc) $10. 84 *—R.V. (12/31/2006)*

M ET F LAMARIE

M et F Lamarie 1999 Château Aiguilloux Cuvée des Trois Seigneurs Red Blend (Corbières) $11. 87 Best Buy *—M.S. (2/1/2003)*

M. CHAPOUTIER

M. Chapoutier 2000 Beaurevoir Grenache (Tavel) $23. 84 *—M.M. (2/1/2002)*

M. Chapoutier 2003 Vin Doux Naturel Grenache (Banyuls) $NA. Some Banyuls can be pruny, but this version from the Rhône-based firm of Chapoutier is remarkably fresh. The wine's sweet, plummy fruit features herbal touches on the nose, but also enough cocoa-like flavors to pair with chocolate and a softly dusty texture to the finish. 90 *—J.C. (12/15/2007)*

M. Chapoutier 2004 Chante-Alouette Marsanne (Hermitage) $70. 87 *—J.C. (11/15/2006)*

M. Chapoutier 2004 De L'Orée Marsanne (Hermitage) $160. Chapoutier's top white in 2004 is this knockout cuvée parcellaire he calls De L'Orée. Aromas of truffles and honey burst from the glass, while the flavors lean toward peaches and toasted nuts. It's full-bodied and undoubtedly high in alcohol, but there's no trace of heat, and while it's broad and mouthfilling because of its size, it still finishes fresh and minerally. 96 Cellar Selection *—J.C. (9/1/2007)*

M. Chapoutier 2005 Deschant Marsanne (Saint-Joseph) $35. 86 *—J.C. (11/15/2006)*

M. Chapoutier 2004 L'Ermite Marsanne (Hermitage) $260. For white Hermitage, this is tight and minerally, with more structure than Chapoutier's other microcuvées and possibly more aging potential. There's a bit of truffle on the nose, but it's not so exotic as the De L'Orée, nor so rich and fat as Le Méal. Finishes with tremendous length and minerality. 95 Cellar Selection *—J.C. (9/1/2007)*

M. Chapoutier 2004 Le Méal Marsanne (Hermitage) $165. Explosively rich and unctuous, this verges on being fat and overblown, then takes a few mincing steps back from the edge. Grilled apricot and peach flavors coat the palate, coming to a climax on the long, oily, fruit-filled finish. 94 *—J.C. (9/1/2007)*

M. Chapoutier 2001 Le Méal Marsanne (Hermitage) $134. 94 Cellar Selection *—J.C. (11/15/2006)*

M. Chapoutier 2000 Les Granits Blanc Marsanne (Saint-Joseph) $88. 88 *—M.S. (9/1/2003)*

M. Chapoutier 2001 Les Meysonniers Marsanne (Crozes-Hermitage) $26. 86 *—M.S. (9/1/2003)*

M. Chapoutier 1998 Domaine des Béates Red Blend (Coteaux d'Aix en Provence) $29. 84 *—M.M. (2/1/2002)*

M. Chapoutier 2004 Rhône Red Blend (Gigondas) $40. 86 *—J.C. (11/15/2006)*

M. Chapoutier 2000 Rhône Red Blend (Gigondas) $39. 88 *—M.S. (9/1/2003)*

M. Chapoutier 1999 Barbe Rac Récolte Rhône Red Blend (Châteauneuf-du-Pape) $141. 88 *—M.S. (9/1/2003)*

M. Chapoutier 2003 Belleruche Rouge Rhône Red Blend (Côtes-du-Rhône) $14. 84 *—J.C. (11/15/2006)*

M. Chapoutier 2000 Belleruche Rouge Rhône Red Blend (Côtes-du-Rhône) $14. 84 *—R.V. (6/1/2002)*

M. Chapoutier 2001 La Bernardine Rhône Red Blend (Châteauneuf-du-Pape) $37. 90 *—J.C. (2/1/2005)*

M. Chapoutier 1999 Le Méal Ermitage Syrah (Hermitage) $150. 98 *—R.V. (6/1/2002)*

M. Chapoutier 2001 Viognier (Condrieu) $83. 88 *—M.S. (9/1/2003)*

M. Chapoutier 2005 Belleruche Blanc Rhône White Blend (Côtes-du-Rhône) $14. 85 *—J.C. (11/15/2006)*

M. Chapoutier 1998 Belleruche Blanc Rhône White Blend (Côtes-du-Rhône) $11. 84 *—M.M. (11/1/2000)*

M. Chapoutier 2000 Chante-Alouette Marsanne (Hermitage) $84. 91 *—M.S. (9/1/2003)*

M. Chapoutier 1999 De l'Orée Ermitage Marsanne (Hermitage) $253. 93 *—R.V. (6/1/2002)*

M. Chapoutier 2001 La Bernardine (Châteauneuf-du-Pape) $44. 85 *—M.S. (9/1/2003)*

M. Chapoutier 2000 Les Beatines Rosé Blend (Coteaux d'Aix en Provence) $13. 85 *—M.M. (2/1/2002)*

M. Chapoutier 2004 Deschants Syrah (Saint-Joseph) $35. Hints of espresso and black olive on the nose give an earthy cast to the black cherry and berry flavors. A bit rustic and lacking depth, but this is a decent effort from a tough vintage. Drink now. 85 *—J.C. (5/31/2007)*

M. Chapoutier 1999 Deschants Syrah (Saint-Joseph) $34. 91 *—R.V. (6/1/2002)*

M. Chapoutier 2004 L'Ermite Syrah (Hermitage) $250. Wonderfully aromatic and complex, blending floral notes with mineral scents, bold cassis fruit and cracked pepper. This is full-bodied and muscular on the palate, the only one of Chapoutier's 2004s that really demands cellaring. Drink 2010–2020. 95 Cellar Selection *—J.C. (9/1/2007)*

M. Chapoutier 2000 L'Ermite Syrah (Hermitage) $368. 91 *—M.S. (9/1/2003)*

M. Chapoutier 2004 La Mordorée Syrah (Côte Rôtie) $150. Made from 70–80-year-old estate-grown vines, this boasts a tremendously complex and seductive bouquet of smoke, violets, raspberries and blackberries. In the mouth, it's a bit less exciting although still very good; it's juicy and fresh, with some firm tannins that are accentuated by crisp acidity. Give it a few years, then drink up before 2015. 89 *—J.C. (9/1/2007)*

M. Chapoutier 2000 La Sizeranne Syrah (Hermitage) $110. 92 *(9/1/2003)*

M. Chapoutier 2004 Le Méal Syrah (Hermitage) $202. Le Méal is said to be the warmest terroir on the Hermitage hill, and thus it is no surprise that this bottling fared the best in the challenging 2004 vintage. Flamboyant, creamy waves of raspberry fruit flood the palate, bringing hints of meat, smoke and pepper along for the ride and developing lovely soft tannins on the caressing finish. Approachable now, but should age well through 2020. 96 *—J.C. (9/1/2007)*

M. Chapoutier 2000 Le Méal Syrah (Hermitage) $317. 96 Cellar Selection *(9/1/2003)*

M. Chapoutier 2004 Le Pavillon Syrah (Hermitage) $225. This was Chapoutier's initial microcuvée of Hermitage, bottled for the first time in 1989. The 2004 version is smoky and gamey, accented by pepper and a hint of rhubarb, but lush red fruit flavors take over on the palate, gliding easily across in a creamy mass that turns chewy on the finish. Drink 2010–2020. 94 *—J.C. (9/1/2007)*

M. Chapoutier 2004 Les Bécasses Syrah (Côte Rôtie) $85. A wine you could sit and smell for a long time, with classic Côte-Rôtie aromas of smoke, pepper and herb twined around a core of raspberry fruit. But on the palate it comes across as a little light and lacking true depth. A pretty, elegant wine with some tea-like tannins on the finish. Drink now–2015. 87 *—J.C. (9/1/2007)*

M. Chapoutier 1999 Les Bécasses Syrah (Côte Rôtie) $79. 94 Cellar Selection *(11/1/2001)*

M. Chapoutier 2000 Les Granits Syrah (Saint-Joseph) $95. 92 *—J.C. (11/15/2006)*

M. Chapoutier 2004 Les Meysonniers Syrah (Crozes-Hermitage) $25. 89 *—J.C. (11/15/2006)*

M. Chapoutier 1997 Les Meysonniers Syrah (Crozes-Hermitage) $24. 86 *—J.C. (7/1/2000)*

M. Chapoutier 2004 Monier de Sizeranne Syrah (Hermitage) $90. Chapoutier's biggest cuvée of Hermitage is the relatively affordable Monier de Sizeranne, a smoky, spicy rendition that's a pretty classic rendition. Peppery notes accent the raspberry, cherry and red fruit flavors that finish with crisp acids. Nicely done, with silky tannins on the finish. Drink now–2015. 90 *—J.C. (9/1/2007)*

M. Chapoutier 2001 Petite Ruche Syrah (Crozes-Hermitage) $23. 82 *—M.S. (9/1/2003)*

M. Chapoutier 1999 Petite Ruche Syrah (Crozes-Hermitage) $19. 86 *(10/1/2001)*

M. Chapoutier 2005 Invitare Viognier (Condrieu) $68. 87 *—J.C. (11/15/2006)*

MAILLY

Mailly NV Brut Rosé Champagne Blend (Champagne) $46. 87 *—R.V. (12/1/2005)*

Mailly 1997 Grand Cru Champagne Blend (Champagne) $40. 87 *—J.C. (12/1/2004)*

Mailly 1998 Grand Cru Brut Champagne Blend (Champagne) $49. 88 *—R.V. (11/1/2006)*

Mailly NV Grand Cru Réserve Brut Champagne Blend (Champagne) $30. 87 *—J.C. (12/1/2004)*

Mailly 1999 L'Intemporelle Grand Cru Brut Champagne Blend (Champagne)

$69. 89 —*R.V. (11/1/2006)*

Mailly 1996 Les Echansons Champagne Blend (Champagne) $89. 93 —*R.V. (11/1/2006)*

MAISON BOUACHON

Maison Bouachon 2004 Duc de Montfort Rhône Red Blend (Gigondas) $NA. 84 —*J.C. (11/15/2006)*

Maison Bouachon 2004 Les Rabassières Rhône Red Blend (Côtes-du-Rhône) $15. 82 —*J.C. (11/15/2006)*

Maison Bouachon 2003 Pierrelongue Rhône Red Blend (Vacqueyras) $18. 87 —*J.C. (11/15/2006)*

Maison Bouachon 2003 Roguebrussane Syrah (Saint-Joseph) $30. 82 —*J.C. (11/15/2006)*

MAISON CHAMPY

Maison Champy 2005 Chardonnay (Pernand-Vergelesses) $NA. A fresh, modern, creamy wine with an enticing layer of new wood and flavors of vanilla and citrus. It lacks real character, but it is certainly very drinkable, with a crisp aftertaste. 87 —*R.V. (3/1/2007)*

Maison Champy 2005 Chardonnay (St.-Romain) $NA. The village of Saint-Romain is a great source of good value whites, like this fresh, creamy wine, with its new wood flavors and lime acidity. It's rounded, but certainly not heavy, with a caramel aftertaste. 87 Best Buy —*R.V. (3/1/2007)*

Maison Champy 2003 Chardonnay (Corton-Charlemagne) $145. 90 —*R.V. (9/1/2005)*

Maison Champy 2005 Signature Chardonnay Chardonnay (Bourgogne) $NA. Well-crafted, this wine has good, fresh fruit with clean acidity and a well-balanced thread of wood. The whole is poised, crisp and light. 86 —*R.V. (3/1/2007)*

Maison Champy 2003 Pinot Noir (Savigny-lès-Beaune) $32. 87 —*R.V. (9/1/2005)*

Maison Champy 2002 Beaune Premier Cru Aux Cras Pinot Noir (Beaune) $29. 84 —*R.V. (9/1/2004)*

Maison Champy 2004 Clos de Vougeot Pinot Noir (Clos Vougeot) $100. While there is an initial edge of bitter extraction to this wine, once it opens up it shows much richer, sweeter fruit. There are solid tannins, and concentration. This is very much in the power-driven Vougeot style. 90 —*R.V. (3/1/2007)*

Maison Champy 2002 Champs Pimont Premier Cru Pinot Noir (Beaune) $41. 85 —*R.V. (9/1/2004)*

Maison Champy 2004 Les Saint Juliens Pinot Noir (Nuits-St.-Georges) $45. Fresh and juicy, this is a light, raspberry fruit wine, only lightly touched by dry tannins. The acidity is there to give structure. From a single vineyard within the Villages appellation of Nuits-Saint-Georges. 86 —*R.V. (3/1/2007)*

Maison Champy 2004 Les Suchots Premier Cru Pinot Noir (Vosne-Romanée) $85. Toasty new wood aromas set the scene for a smooth, velvety wine that has something of the freshness of 2004, but more of new, quite toasty wood flavors. At this stage, it seems the wood is too much for the fruit. 88 —*R.V. (3/1/2007)*

Maison Champy 2004 Mazis-Chambertin Grand Cru Pinot Noir (Mazis-Chambertin) $120. Classic Gevrey-Chambertin, with all its structure and its velvety, intense fruits, this wine already offers full pleasure. If the tannins promise some aging, they do not detract from the rich, sweet fruits and the light, fresh acidity. 91 —*R.V. (3/1/2007)*

Maison Champy 2002 Pommard Premier Cru Les Charmots Pinot Noir (Pommard) $55. 83 —*R.V. (9/1/2004)*

Maison Champy 2004 Vieilles Vignes Pinot Noir (Gevrey-Chambertin) $42. A great success, this wine combines the structure of Gevrey-Chambertin with some beautiful, deeply flavored fruits. The tannins, too, are well managed, with a dusty, fine feel to them, while the red berry fruits are well in balance. 90 —*R.V. (3/1/2007)*

MAISON JAFFELIN

Maison Jaffelin 2001 Chardonnay (Pouilly-Fuissé) $16. 86 —*J.C. (10/1/2003)*

Maison Jaffelin 2001 Les Villages de Jaffelin Chardonnay (Saint-Véran) $13. 85 —*J.C. (10/1/2003)*

MAISON SICHEL

Maison Sichel 2004 Sirius Bordeaux White Blend (Bordeaux) $NA. 87 —*R.V. (6/1/2005)*

MALESAN

Malesan 1999 Château Prieure Malesan Bordeaux Blend (Premieres Côtes de Blaye) $16. 89 Editors' Choice *(9/1/2002)*

Malesan 1999 Reserve de Malesan Bordeaux Blend (Bordeaux) $15. 87 *(9/1/2002)*

Malesan 2000 Rouge Bordeaux Blend (Bordeaux) $9. 85 Best Buy *(9/1/2002)*

Malesan 1999 Vielles Vignes Bordeaux Blend (Bordeaux) $13. 86 *(9/1/2002)*

MARC BREDIF

Marc Bredif 2005 Cabernet Franc (Chinon) $21. The Vouvray-based négociant, Marc Brédif, has made a ripe, soft Chinon, reveling in the sweet fruit of 2005. It has some good, smoked-meat flavors to go with the black fruits. Drink now. 85 —*R.V. (4/1/2007)*

Marc Bredif 1999 Cabernet Franc (Chinon) $16. 88 Editors' Choice —*M.M. (1/1/2004)*

MARC DESCHAMPS

Marc Deschamps 1999 Les Vignes de Berge / Les Loges Sauvignon Blanc (Pouilly-Fumé) $19. 85 *(8/1/2002)*

MARC KREYDENWEISS

Marc Kreydenweiss 1997 Kritt Gewürztraminer (Alsace) $23. 90 —*S.H. (12/31/1999)*

Marc Kreydenweiss 2001 Les Charmes Pinot Blanc (Alsace) $NA. 90 —*S.H. (1/1/2002)*

Marc Kreydenweiss 1997 Moenchberg Pinot Gris (Alsace) $35. 88 —*S.H. (12/31/1999)*

Marc Kreydenweiss 2003 Andlau Riesling (Alsace) $21. 87 —*R.V. (11/1/2005)*

Marc Kreydenweiss 2003 Clos Rebberg Aux Vignes Riesling (Alsace) $89. 89 —*R.V. (11/1/2005)*

Marc Kreydenweiss 2005 Le Château Kastelberg Grand Cru Riesling (Alsace) $77. Quite funky indeed. Saturated with spice such as anise, clove and rotting apples on the orchard floor, the earthy, full-bodied and slightly viscous nature of this beast is overwhelming. We're not quite sure if this one warrants the hefty price tag attached to it. 85 *(9/1/2007)*

Marc Kreydenweiss 2004 Le Château Kastelberg Grand Cru Riesling (Alsace) $69. With a beautiful polished brass color, this is another typically intense offering from Marc Kreydenweiss. A bouquet full of clove, candied apple and honey lead in to the medium-full mouthfeel saturated with dried apricot and sweet spice. The slightly roasty finish complements the structure. 87 *(9/1/2007)*

Marc Kreydenweiss 2003 Grand Cru Kastelberg Riesling (Alsace) $69. 93 Cellar Selection —*R.V. (11/1/2005)*

Marc Kreydenweiss 2005 La Dame Wiebelsberg Grand Cru Riesling (Alsace) $44. Slightly lighter than the 2004, this is still a serious Riesling. Aromas of petrol, minerality and grapefruit complement flavors of apple skin and muted sweet spice, bringing together a medium-bodied wine with a long minerally finish. Showing nicely now, but also the potential to age. 89 *(9/1/2007)*

Marc Kreydenweiss 2004 La Dame Wiebelsberg Grand Cru Riesling (Alsace) $38. This is a serious selection for those who love a little more weight. Chock full of honey, sweet spice and butterscotch, you know what you're getting into from the first whiff. The palate only further complements the nose with the flavor of ripe, red apples elevating the sweeter aromas. Full- bodied and rich with a long, spicy finish. 89 *(9/1/2007)*

Marc Kreydenweiss 2003 La Dame Wiebelsberg Grand Cru Riesling (Alsace) $38. 85 —*J.C. (8/1/2006)*

Marc Kreydenweiss 2001 Grand Cru Moenchberg Le Moine Tokay Pinot Gris (Alsace) $NA. 93 —*S.H. (1/1/2002)*

Marc Kreydenweiss 2004 Clos du Val d'Eléon Alsace White Blend (Alsace) $31. A 50-50 blend of Pinot Gris and Riesling, this is a large-scale wine with aromas and flavors of nuts, anise and baked apples—maybe even a hint of butterscotch. Yet for all that sweet-sounding stuff, there's nothing soft about the hard, stony finish. A tough wine to really come to grips with. 85 —*J.C. (7/1/2007)*

MARCEL HEMARD

Marcel Hemard NV Premier Cru Brut Champagne Blend (Champagne) $NA. 86 —*R.V. (12/15/2005)*

MARC SORREL

Marc Sorrel 2005 Marsanne (Hermitage) $75. Broad, buttery and rich, this is a powerful, low-acid white Hermitage. It's loaded with nutty elements and body, less so with fruit and finesse. 89 —*J.C. (9/1/2007)*

Marc Sorrel 2004 Marsanne (Hermitage) $75. Like the 2005, this is a nutty wine, but it is also a touch crisper and should prove to be marginally longer-lived. Broad and mouthcoating, with layers of richness. **90** *—J.C. (9/1/2007)*

Marc Sorrel 2005 Les Rocoules Marsanne (Hermitage) $145. Honeyed and nutty on the nose, this appears at first sniff to be very ripe and rich. And the palate follows through, delivering waves of fabulously rich fruit that miraculously don't seem heavy. A marvel. **95** *—J.C. (9/1/2007)*

Marc Sorrel 2004 Les Rocoules Marsanne (Hermitage) $140. From 50-year-old vines, this is Sorrel's top cuvée of white Hermitage, laden with scents of truffled honey and almonds. Yet despite that obvious richness on the nose, it's a bit more restrained on the palate than the 2005, with a more powerful structure and marginally less lushness. Not better, not worse, just different: longer on the finish, more tightly constructed and probably longer-lived. **95 Cellar Selection** *—J.C. (9/1/2007)*

Marc Sorrel 2005 Syrah (Hermitage) $75. Very spicy, but also possessing enough cassis and cherry fruit to make a wonderful marriage. The lovely velvety texture just turns a tad dry on the finish; give it five years in the cellar. **90** *—J.C. (9/1/2007)*

Marc Sorrel 2004 Syrah (Hermitage) $75. A bit light, in the style of the vintage, but with wonderfully intricate spice complexity wrapped around leather and red fruit. The creamy mouthfeel gives this wine a sense of delicacy not often found in Hermitage. Drink this pretty wine over the next 7–10 years. **90** *—J.C. (9/1/2007)*

Marc Sorrel 2005 Le Gréal Syrah (Hermitage) $145. Intoxicatingly fruity and forward on the nose, this wine—a blend of Le Méal and Les Greffieux—follows up with rich layers of black fruit. It may lack a little of the minerality found in other parts of Hermitage, but this is immensely seductive stuff—maybe the Pomerol of Hermitage? **94** *—J.C. (9/1/2007)*

Marc Sorrel 2004 Le Gréal Syrah (Hermitage) $140. In a cool vintage like 2004, Sorrel's parcels in the warmest terroirs of the hill (Le Méal and Les Greffieux) can outperform. This is less rich than the 2005, but still amazingly flattering, filled with spicy complexity and red fruit. Drink now–2020. **92** *—J.C. (9/1/2007)*

MARIE DE BEAUREGARD

Marie de Beauregard 2005 Cabernet Franc (Chinon) $NA. The Guy Saget take on Chinon is big and burly, with dark tannins. Still very young, this needs to soften out from its current dryness. But it's impressive, a new-wood aged wine that shows the intensity possible in a hot year like 2005. **90** *—R.V. (4/1/2007)*

Marie de Beauregard 2003 Cabernet Franc (Saumur-Champigny) $NA. Produced by Guy Saget, one of the leading négociants in the Loire, this is a smooth, soft wine, very approachable, with new wood flavors and a polished, velvet texture. For a Saumur-Champigny, it is dense and not at all like the more familiar fresh style. **89** *—R.V. (4/1/2007)*

MARQUIS DE BELON

Marquis de Belon NV Brut Sémillon (Crémant de Bordeaux) $20. 86 *—M.D. (12/15/2006)*

MARQUIS DE CHASSE

Marquis de Chasse 1999 Reserve White Blend (Bordeaux) $9. 84 *—J.C. (3/1/2001)*

MARQUIS DE GOULAINE

Marquis de Goulaine 2005 La Roseraie Rosé Blend (Rosé d'Anjou) $NA. Easy, medium sweet wine, flavored with strawberries and sugar, light, fresh, with good balancing acidity. Light in body, and great for summer afternoons. **84** *—R.V. (7/1/2007)*

MARQUIS DE LA TOUR

Marquis de la Tour NV Rosé Dry Red Blend (Vin Mousseux) $10. Lightly off-dry, flavored with sweet strawberries, the wine's easy flavors are just what's needed for a casual get-together. **85 Best Buy** *—R.V. (12/15/2007)*

Marquis de la Tour NV Brut Collection Privee Sparkling Blend (France) $8. 85 Best Buy *—J.C. (6/1/2005)*

Marquis de la Tour NV Brut White Blend (Vin Mousseux) $10. Almonds and a strongly yeasty element are the main characters of this sparkling wine. It's full, but the fruit still has a texture to it, leaving good acidity to finish. Good value, enjoyable wine. **86 Best Buy** *—R.V. (12/15/2007)*

MARQUIS DE PERLADE

Marquis de Perlade NV Blanc de Blancs Brut Champagne Blend (France) $11. 83 *—P.G. (12/15/2002)*

MARTIN SCHAETZEL

Martin Schaetzel 2003 Kaefferkopf Ammerschwihr Pinot Gris (Alsace) $NA. 90 *—R.V. (2/1/2006)*

Martin Schaetzel 2003 Grand Cru Marckrain Tokay Pinot Gris (Alsace) $NA. 93 *—R.V. (2/1/2006)*

MAS CARLOT

Mas Carlot 2006 Rosé Rosé Blend (Vin de Pays d'Oc) $10. A solid effort, Mas Carlot's 2006 rosé features scents of mixed red berries and hints of spring flowers on the nose, then delivers slightly candied but assertive notes of strawberries, raspberries and cherries on the palate. Crisp and stony on the finish. **86 Best Buy** *—J.C. (7/1/2007)*

MAS DE DAUMAS GASSAC

Mas de Daumas Gassac 2002 Red Blend (Vin de Pays de L'Herault) $50. 93 *—R.V. (12/1/2004)*

Mas de Daumas Gassac 2004 Rhône Red Blend (Vin de Pays de L'Herault) $38. 92 *—R.V. (12/31/2006)*

Mas de Daumas Gassac 2003 Rhône White Blend (Vin de Pays de L'Herault) $50. 90 *—R.V. (12/1/2004)*

MAS DE GOURGONNIER

Mas de Gourgonnier 2005 Rosé Blend (Les Baux de Provence) $NA. 88 *—J.C. (6/21/2006)*

MAS DE LA BARBEN

Mas de la Barben 1998 Syrah (Coteaux du Languedoc) $12. 85 *(10/1/2001)*

MAS DE LA DAME

Mas de la Dame 2005 Rosé du Mas Rosé Blend (Les Baux de Provence) $14. A light, innocuous blend of 50% Grenache, 30% Syrah and 20% Cinsault. This is clean, with modest melon, peach and herb flavors that finish short. **83** *—J.C. (7/1/2007)*

MAS DE LA ROUVIÈRE

Mas de la Rouvière 2006 Rosé Blend (Bandol) $19. Mas is the Provencal name for a farmhouse, a nice touch for a wine that has a fine rural, lavendar scented aroma, and warm, spicy fruit flavors. The owning Bunan family claim this wine will age, and, yes there is weight and structure there, but most will be drunk this summer. **89** *—R.V. (7/1/2007)*

MAS DES BRESSADES

Mas des Bressades 2006 Rosé Rosé Blend (Costières de Nimes) $12. A strong effort, this iss a gorgeous rosé, loaded with wonderfully intermingled flavors of pears and strawberries and graced by hints of spring flowers and spice. It's lush on the palate, ending harmonious and long. **90 Best Buy** *—J.C. (7/1/2007*

MAS DES CHIMÈRES

Mas des Chimères 2001 Red Blend (Coteaux du Languedoc) $18. 88 *—R.V. (12/1/2004)*

MATHILDE ET YVES GANGLOFF

Mathilde et Yves Gangloff 1999 Rhône White Blend (Condrieu) $65. 90 *—R.V. (6/1/2002)*

Mathilde et Yves Gangloff 2004 La Barbarine Syrah (Côte Rôtie) $79. A lovely, elegant example of Côte-Rôtie, with scents of violets and licorice accenting plum and blackberry fruit. Supple and easygoing, with a hint of tea on the finish. Drink now–2014. **89** *—J.C. (9/1/2007)*

MICHEL & STÉPHANE OGIER

Michel & Stéphane Ogier 2004 Syrah (Côte Rôtie) $91. Slightly herbal on the nose, without the great intensity of some vintages, but still having pretty peppered raspberry aromas. This is a bit light in weight, but wonderfully supple, elegant and well-balanced. Finishes long, with silky tannins and a touch of cranberry. Drink now–2014. **90** *—J.C. (9/1/2007)*

Michel & Stéphane Ogier 2004 Belle Hélène Syrah (Côte Rôtie) $199. The 2004s at Ogier are tremendously successful, none more so than the family's top cuvée. The 2004 Belle Hélène boasts waves of creamy raspberry fruit framed by wonderfully supple tannins. Long-lasting on the finish, it's already delicious but should develop additional complexity through 2015. **93** *—J.C. (9/1/2007)*

Michel & Stéphane Ogier 2005 La Rosine Syrah (Vin de Pays des Collines Rhodaniennes) $35. This is spicy and herbal but also loaded with cherry fruit, made with grapes grown not far from teh family's Côte-Rôtie vineyards. It's a bit light in body, but nicely savory and true to its northern Rhône origins, with enough structure to hold for 2–3 years. **88** *—J.C. (9/1/2007)*

Michel & Stéphane Ogier 2004 Lancement Syrah (Côte Rôtie) $180. Wonderfully floral and spicy on the nose, with hints of anise that add nuance to the layers of raspberry fruit. Stéphane Ogier claims he adores the 2004 vintage, and with wines like this, why shouldn't he? This finishes lush and long, and although already approachable, should age effortlessly through at least 2015. **92** *—J.C. (9/1/2007)*

Michel & Stéphane Ogier 2006 La Rosine Viognier (Vin de Pays des Collines Rhodaniennes) $35. A blend of barrel- and tank-fermented wine, this is an attractively floral and fresh Viognier intended for early drinking. There's a hint of honeyed richness to the apricot and pineapple flavors, but it finishes clean and refreshing. Drink now–2008. 88 *—J.C. (9/1/2007)*

MICHEL GONET

Michel Gonet 1996 Brut Champagne Blend (Champagne) $36. 88 *—R.V. (12/1/2002)*

MICHEL GROS

Michel Gros 2004 Chardonnay (Bourgogne Hautes Côtes de Nuits) $28. Light, fresh and delicate, this is an excellently balanced wine that punches above its station in terms of appellation. There are flavors of lemon zest, new wood and delicate vanilla and walnut tastes. It's a great, ready-to-drink Chardonnay. 89 *—R.V. (3/1/2007)*

Michel Gros 2004 Pinot Noir (Bourgogne Hautes Côtes de Nuits) $28. The Hautes Côtes, over the hill from the main stretch of the Côtes de Nuits vineyards, often produces good value Burgundy, and this wine is one of those. It's rounded, relatively soft and easy, with plenty of attractive red fruits and a great line of acidity. 85 *—R.V. (3/1/2007)*

Michel Gros 2004 Pinot Noir (Chambolle-Musigny) $58. This is a dense wine, solid and foursquare, not typical of Chambolle perhaps. There are plenty of fresh fruit and tannins, but they leave a somewhat one-dimensional taste. Not up to the usual standard of this talented winemaker. 87 *—R.V. (3/1/2007)*

Michel Gros 2004 Pinot Noir (Nuits-St.-Georges) $56. The firm tannins typical of Nuits-Saint-Georges are certainly here, along with some new wood and spice. A foursquare wine, showing some fruit, but more tannin. The aftertaste is dry, but lifted with some acidity. 87 *—R.V. (3/1/2007)*

Michel Gros 2004 Pinot Noir (Vosne-Romanée) $58. A firm, quite extracted style of wine, with dense tannins. The fruit is hiding behind structure and dryness. It is a powerful wine, leaving black fruit acidity and plum skin flavors. 88 *—R.V. (3/1/2007)*

Michel Gros 1999 Pinot Noir (Chambolle-Musigny) $38. 89 *—P.G. (1/7/2001)*

Michel Gros 2004 Aux Brûlées Premier Cru Pinot Noir (Vosne-Romanée) $100. A ripe, fruity wine, full of red fruit and spice flavors. There's the proper finesse of Vosne-Romanée here, a sense of poise that goes well with the toast, the acidity and the intensely juicy richness on the finish. 90 *—R.V. (3/1/2007)*

Michel Gros 2004 Clos des Réas Premier Cru Pinot Noir (Vosne-Romanée) $100. This clos, with its impressive stone gateway, is entirely owned by Michel Gros, and in a sense is his flagship, even though it is not a premier cru. This 2004 is a powerful statement, a richly textured wine layered with spice and tannins, plus a minty, herbal character. Acidity hovers around the young, fresh, red fruits, lingering in the mouth for many minutes. 91 *—R.V. (3/1/2007)*

Michel Gros 1999 Clos des Reas Pinot Noir (Vosne-Romanée) $65. 93 *—P.G. (1/7/2001)*

Michel Gros 2004 En la Rue de Vergy Pinot Noir (Morey Saint-Denis) $56. Although not a premier cru, this comes from a single vineyard which lies, as the name indicates, along the road to Vergy, well placed between the grands crus of Clos de Tart and Clos des Lambrays. It is a richly constructed wine, with powerful but fresh raspberry and red cherry skin flavors spiced with new wood. The tannins are here, but the fruit is more prominent. 90 *—R.V. (3/1/2007)*

Michel Gros 2004 Grand Maupertuis Pinot Noir (Clos Vougeot) $135. The Clos de Vougeot wines of the Gros family holdings, divided between the different branches of the family, often carry the name of the parcel. This, from Grand Maupertuis, at the top end of the vineyard, is a structured but rich wine, with some red jelly flavors and sweetness. The tannins are there, but relatively subdued. 92 *—R.V. (3/1/2007)*

Michel Gros 2004 Les Chaliots Pinot Noir (Nuits-St.-Georges) $56. This is not a premier cru, but a single vineyard within the villages vineyards. Michel Gros has made a modern style, dominated by new wood; it ends up too tannic. It could soften, because there are some layers of red fruits, spice and acidity underneath. But at the moment, it needs long-term aging, or, if drunk young, decanting. 87 *—R.V. (3/1/2007)*

Michel Gros 2004 Premier Cru Pinot Noir (Nuits-St.-Georges) $100. A blend from different premier cru vineyards, this is a freshly perfumed wine, with firm new wood and fruit tannins, but also some good ripe fruits. Give it a couple of years, and it will be well in balance, with its good juicy aftertaste. 89 *—R.V. (3/1/2007)*

MICHEL LAROCHE

Michel Laroche 2002 Chardonnay (Vin de Pays d'Oc) $8. 85 Best Buy *(2/1/2004)*

Michel Laroche 2001 Merlot (Vin de Pays d'Oc) $7. 82 *—M.S. (9/1/2003)*

Michel Laroche 2001 Syrah (Vin de Pays d'Oc) $7. 84 *—M.S. (9/1/2003)*

MICHEL LYNCH

Michel Lynch 2005 Merlot (Bordeaux) $11. From the same stable as Château Lynch-Bages, this is superior branded Bordeaux. It is fruity, ripe, full-bodied with solid dense tannins. An impressively powered wine, with some fresh black currant flavor and acidity. 87 Best Buy *—R.V. (11/1/2007)*

Michel Lynch 2003 Bordeaux White Blend (Bordeaux) $10. 86 Best Buy *—R.V. (6/1/2005)*

Michel Lynch 1998 Sauvignon Blanc (Bordeaux) $9. 85 *—D.T. (11/15/2001)*

MICHEL PICARD

Michel Picard 1997 Chardonnay (Pouilly-Fuissé) $24. 84 *—M.P. (6/1/2000)*

Michel Picard 2001 Chardonnay (Vin de Pays d'Oc) $9. 86 Best Buy *—M.S. (9/1/2003)*

Michel Picard 2001 Chardonnay (Chablis) $20. 84 *—J.C. (10/1/2003)*

Michel Picard 1995 Domaine Champs Perdix Chardonnay (Rully) $16. 84 *(6/1/2000)*

Michel Picard 1997 Vouvray Chenin Blanc (Vouvray) $12. 81 *—M.P. (6/1/2000)*

Michel Picard 1996 Grenache (Châteauneuf-du-Pape) $23. 83 *—M.P. (6/1/2000)*

Michel Picard 1996 Pinot Noir (Bourgogne) $12. 82 *—M.P. (6/1/2000)*

Michel Picard 2000 Pinot Noir (Bourgogne) $12. 82 *—J.C. (10/1/2003)*

Michel Picard 2003 Clos des Fiètres Grand Cru Pinot Noir (Corton) $80. 85 *—J.C. (9/1/2006)*

Michel Picard 2003 Récolte du Château de Chassagne-Montrachet Le Charmois Premier Cru Pinot Noir (St.-Aubin) $30. 89 *—J.C. (9/1/2006)*

Michel Picard 2000 Rhône Red Blend (Côtes-du-Rhône) $10. 88 Best Buy *—M.S. (9/1/2003)*

Michel Picard 2001 Syrah (Languedoc) $9. 84 *—M.S. (1/1/2004)*

MICHEL REDDE

Michel Redde 2001 La Moynerie Sauvignon Blanc (Pouilly-Fumé) $21. 84 *(7/1/2005)*

MICHEL REDDE ET FILS

Michel Redde et Fils 2002 Cuvée Majorum Sauvignon Blanc (Pouilly-Fumé) $NA. Powerful, intense and packed with rich green fruits, this is the top wine from Thierry Redde. There's an attractive smoky character to the ripe fruit, a bloom of summer herbs and some good lively apple flavors. Drink now, or keep for another year. 90 *—R.V. (9/1/2007)*

Michel Redde et Fils 1999 Cuvée Majorum Sauvignon Blanc (Pouilly-Fumé) $35. 86 *(7/1/2005)*

Michel Redde et Fils 2005 La Moynerie Sauvignon Blanc (Pouilly-Fumé) $24. A full, rounded wine, with flavors of asparagus, herbs and ripe quinces. There's acidity, some yeastiness and a taut structure. This probably needs another six months aging—drink over the winter 2007–2008. 87 *—R.V. (9/1/2007)*

Michel Redde et Fils 2005 Les Tuilières Sauvignon Blanc (Sancerre) $25. While Redde is based in Pouilly, across the Loire, the family does have vines in Sancerre. This 2005 is a light, yeasty wine, with grassy, herbal flavors and a crisp, intense acidity to finish. 86 *—R.V. (9/1/2007)*

Michel Redde et Fils 2004 Les Tuilières Sauvignon Blanc (Sancerre) $24. 86 *—R.V. (8/1/2006)*

MOËT & CHANDON

Moët & Chandon 1996 Blanc Brut Champagne Blend (Champagne) $50. 89 *—J.C. (12/15/2003)*

Moët & Chandon 1998 Brut Champagne Blend (Champagne) $52. 90 *—R.V. (11/1/2006)*

Moët & Chandon NV Brut Impérial Champagne Blend (Champagne) $38. 89 *—R.V. (12/1/2005)*

Moët & Chandon NV Brut Impérial Champagne Blend (Champagne) $38. 87 *(12/15/2001)*

Moët & Chandon 1995 Brut Impérial Champagne Blend (Champagne) $55. 90 Editors' Choice *—S.H. (12/15/2001)*

Moët & Chandon NV Brut Impérial Rosé Champagne Blend (Champagne) $40. 90 *—M.S. (12/15/2003)*

Moët & Chandon 1995 Brut Impérial Rosé Champagne Blend (Champagne)

$65. 88 *—P.G. (12/15/2002)*

Moët & Chandon NV Brut Rosé Champagne Blend (Champagne) $44. 88 *(12/1/2000)*

Moët & Chandon 1999 Brut Rosé Champagne Blend (Champagne) $65. 89 *—M.S. (12/15/2005)*

Moët & Chandon 1996 Brut Rosé Champagne Blend (Champagne) $55. 92 *—M.S. (12/15/2003)*

Moët & Chandon 1995 Dom Pérignon Champagne Blend (Champagne) $150. 92 *(12/15/2002)*

Moët & Chandon 1998 Dom Pérignon Champagne Blend (Champagne) $130. 91 *—M.S. (12/31/2005)*

Moët & Chandon 1996 Dom Pérignon Champagne Blend (Champagne) $140. 96 *—R.V. (11/1/2006)*

Moët & Chandon 1996 Dom Pérignon Rosé Champagne Blend (Champagne) $425. 95 Editors' Choice *—R.V. (11/1/2006)*

Moët & Chandon 1995 Dom Pérignon Rosé Champagne Blend (Champagne) $300. 94 *—R.V. (11/1/2006)*

Moët & Chandon 1990 Dom Perignon Rosé Champagne Blend (Champagne) $290. 94 Editors' Choice *(12/15/2001)*

Moët & Chandon NV Les Champs de Romont Sillery Champagne Blend (Champagne) $85. 90 *—M.N. (12/15/2001)*

Moët & Chandon NV Les Vignes de Saran Chouilly Champagne Blend (Champagne) $85. 91 *(12/15/2001)*

Moët & Chandon NV Nectar Impérial Champagne Blend (Champagne) $48. 83 *—J.C. (12/15/2003)*

Moët & Chandon NV White Star Champagne Blend (Champagne) $35. 87 *—R.V. (12/15/2006)*

Moët & Chandon 1995 Dom Pérignon Champagne Blend (Champagne) $150. 93 *—J.C. (12/15/2003)*

MOILLARD

Moillard 2005 Chardonnay (Chassagne-Montrachet) $39. Deliciously fresh and creamy, this wine rolls around the mouth with its smooth, ripe texture. There are flavors of almonds, some toast from wood, and just enough acidity. The aftertaste is soft. 88 *—R.V. (3/1/2007)*

Moillard 2005 Chardonnay (Puligny-Montrachet) $45. Light and fresh, with a good touch of minerality and a chalky texture, this wine is crisp and clean, with some old toast flavors. Very drinkable now. 87 *—R.V. (3/1/2007)*

Moillard 2005 Chardonnay (Saint-Véran) $17. Green apple and pear flavors dominate in this fine, fresh, delicious wine. There's a touch of caramel, but the main feel is clean and delicate, with a some minerality to give structure. 87 *—R.V. (3/1/2007)*

Moillard 2005 Clos du Cromin Chardonnay (Meursault) $36. From a 23-acre vineyard on the north side of the appellation, close to Volnay, this Chard is soft, ripe and easy, with fresh touches of minerality on the light almonds and green pear flavors. A delicious wine for spring and summer drinking. 86 *—R.V. (3/1/2007)*

Moillard 2005 Domaine Greffes Chardonnay (Pouilly-Fuissé) $22. A disappointingly thin wine, very light. It's fresh enough, and there is a pleasing touch of citrus, but its aftertaste is somewhat dilute. 82 *—R.V. (3/1/2007)*

Moillard 2005 Les Vaillons Premier Cru Chardonnay (Chablis) $30. If you want a Chardonnay that just goes down easy, this is it. With its citrus and pear fruits, its vanilla layer and its simple, fresh structure, this is great to drink now. 86 *—R.V. (3/1/2007)*

Moillard 2004 Pinot Noir (Chorey-lès-Beaune) $20. An attractive, fresh, red fruity wine, very much in the easy style of Chorey-lès-Beaune. There's some firmness from tannins, but this wine will develop easily and quickly. 87 *—R.V. (3/1/2007)*

Moillard 2002 Reserve Pinot Noir (Bourgogne) $28. 86 *—J.C. (11/15/2005)*

Moillard 1997 Les Violettes Rhône Red Blend (Côtes-du-Rhône) $7. 83 *—M.S. (10/1/1999)*

MOMMESSIN

Mommessin 2002 Chardonnay (Pouilly-Fuissé) $19. 87 *—J.C. (10/1/2003)*

Mommessin 2001 La Clé Saint Pierre Chardonnay (Bourgogne) $12. 84 *—J.C. (10/1/2003)*

Mommessin 2003 Nid D'Abeille Chardonnay (Vin de Pays d'Oc) $8. 83 *—J.C. (12/1/2004)*

Mommessin 2002 Old Vines Chardonnay (Mâcon-Villages) $10. 86 Best Buy *—J.C. (10/1/2003)*

Mommessin 2003 6 Terroirs Gamay (St.-Amour) $21. 87 *—J.C. (11/15/2005)*

Mommessin 2001 Domaine de Champ de Cour Gamay (Moulin-à-Vent) $13. 83 *—J.C. (11/15/2003)*

Mommessin 2001 Les Grumières Gamay (Brouilly) $12. 86 *—M.S. (11/15/2002)*

Mommessin 2000 Reserve Gamay (Fleurie) $15. 83 *—M.S. (11/15/2002)*

Mommessin 2003 Le Montagne Bleue Gamay Noir (Côte de Brouilly) $19. 87 *—J.C. (11/15/2005)*

Mommessin 2001 Pinot Noir (Clos de Tart) $138. 92 *—J.C. (10/1/2003)*

Mommessin 2001 Charmes-Chambertin Pinot Noir (Burgundy) $90. 92 *—J.C. (10/1/2003)*

Mommessin 2001 Clos Sainte Anne des Teurons Les Grèves Premier Cru Pinot Noir (Beaune) $34. 87 *—J.C. (10/1/2003)*

Mommessin 2001 Les Suchots Premier Cru Pinot Noir (Vosne-Romanée) $67. 83 *—J.C. (10/1/2003)*

Mommessin 2000 Oak Aged Pinot Noir (Bourgogne) $13. 84 *—P.G. (11/1/2002)*

Mommessin 2000 Premier Cru Les Charmes Pinot Noir (Chambolle-Musigny) $57. 86 *—P.G. (11/1/2002)*

Mommessin 2000 Premier Cru Santenots Pinot Noir (Volnay) $65. 87 *—P.G. (11/1/2002)*

Mommessin 2002 Red Blend (Brouilly) $12. 86 *—R.V. (11/15/2003)*

Mommessin 1999 Château De Domazan Rhône Red Blend (Côtes-du-Rhône) $8. 84 *(3/1/2001)*

Mommessin 1998 Les Epices Rhône Red Blend (Châteauneuf-du-Pape) $26. 85 *—D.T. (2/1/2002)*

MONMOUSSEAU

Monmousseau 2005 Domaine du Grand Bréviande Cabernet Franc (Chinon) $12. Négociant firm Monmousseau has produced a delicious, smoky wine, packed full of cranberry flavors, rounded tannins and blackberry jelly texture. It's ripe and full, benefiting from the warm year. 88 Best Buy *—R.V. (4/1/2007)*

Monmousseau NV Chenin Blanc (Vouvray) $12. 85 *—R.V. (6/1/2006)*

Monmousseau NV Clos du Château de Mosny Chenin Blanc (Montlouis-sur-Loire) $NA. 86 *—R.V. (6/1/2006)*

Monmousseau NV White Blend (Crémant de Loire) $NA. 90 Editors' Choice *—R.V. (6/1/2006)*

MONT SAINT-VINCENT

Mont Saint-Vincent 2000 Syrah (Vin de Pays d'Oc) $7. 81 *(10/1/2001)*

MONTAUDON

Montaudon NV Brut Champagne Blend (Champagne) $30. 84 *—P.G. (12/15/2000)*

Montaudon NV Brut Champagne Blend (Champagne) $27. 87 *(12/15/2001)*

Montaudon 1995 Brut Champagne Blend (Champagne) $36. 88 *(12/15/1999)*

Montaudon NV Chardonnay Premier Cru Brut Champagne Blend (Champagne) $34. 85 *—M.S. (12/15/2001)*

Montaudon NV Grande Brut Rosé Champagne Blend (Champagne) $31. 86 *—J.C. (12/15/2001)*

Montaudon NV Grande Brut Rosé Champagne Blend (Champagne) $35. 88 *—P.G. (6/1/2001)*

Montaudon NV Prestige Cuvée Classe M Champagne Blend (Champagne) $50. 82 *—P.G. (12/15/2000)*

MONTIRIUS

Montirius 2004 Grenache-Syrah (Vacqueyras) $20. 85 *—J.C. (11/15/2006)*

Montirius 2000 Grenache-Syrah (Vacqueyras) $23. 90 *—R.V. (3/1/2004)*

Montirius 2003 Clos Montirius Grenache-Syrah (Vacqueyras) $22. 90 *—J.C. (11/15/2006)*

Montirius 2002 Rhône Red Blend (Vin de Pays de Vaucluse) $NA. 85 Best Buy *—R.V. (4/1/2005)*

Montirius 2001 Rhône Red Blend (Vacqueyras) $22. 89 *—R.V. (4/1/2005)*

Montirius 2000 Rhône Red Blend (Gigondas) $28. 91 *—R.V. (3/1/2004)*

Montirius 2002 Rhône White Blend (Vacqueyras) $21. 87 *—R.V. (3/1/2004)*

MOREY BLANC

Morey Blanc 2004 Chardonnay (Meursault) $54. 88 *—R.V. (12/1/2006)*

Morey Blanc 2004 Charmes Premier Cru Chardonnay (Meursault) $92. 93 *—R.V. (12/1/2006)*

Morey Blanc 2004 Gouttes d'Or Premier Cru Chardonnay (Meursault) $120. 92 *—R.V. (12/1/2006)*

Morey-Blanc 2004 Clos du Chapitre Premier Cru Pinot Noir (Aloxe-Corton) $64. Soft and gentle, this wine has fresh red berry fruits along with its tannins. It opens in the mouth to give a ripeness and roundness with those red fruits, and acidity is pronounced on the finish. **89** *—R.V. (3/1/2007)*

Morey Blanc 2002 Clos du Chapitre Premier Cru Pinot Noir (Aloxe-Corton) $77. 90 *—R.V. (9/1/2004)*

Morey-Blanc 2004 Corton les Renardes Grand Cru Pinot Noir (Corton Les Renardes) $80. A velvet-smooth wine, deliciously ripe, with sweetness. Great red berry fruits, a touch of new wood and polished tannins create a properly Pinot Noir seduction. **91** *—R.V. (3/1/2007)*

Morey Blanc 2002 Les Vercots Premier Cru Pinot Noir (Aloxe-Corton) $77. 87 *—R.V. (9/1/2004)*

MOULIN DE GASSAC

Moulin de Gassac 2003 Le Mazet Old World Red Blend (Vin de Pays de L'Herault) $11. 89 *—R.V. (12/1/2004)*

Moulin de Gassac 2005 Le Mazet Old World White Rhône White Blend (Vin de Pays de L'Herault) $10. 86 *—R.V. (12/31/2006)*

Moulin de Gassac 2002 Le Mazet Rosé Blend (Vin de Pays de L'Herault) $10. 84 *—J.C. (12/1/2004)*

Moulin de Gassac 2003 Sauvignon Blanc (Vin de Pays de L'Herault) $11. 87 *—R.V. (12/1/2004)*

Moulin de Gassac 2003 Le Mazet Old World White Blend (Vin de Pays de L'Herault) $11. 89 *—R.V. (12/1/2004)*

MOULIN DE LA GARDETTE

Moulin de la Gardette 2003 La Cuvée Tradition Rhône Red Blend (Gigondas) $19. 87 *—J.C. (11/15/2006)*

MOULIN DES COSTES

Moulin des Costes 2006 Rosé Blend (Bandol) $19. Salmon pink in color, this wine perfumed with herbs and hedgerow fruits is all about crisp currants and fresh acidity. There is a structure, though, which puts it firmly and pleasantly with food. **88** *—R.V. (7/1/2007)*

MOUTARD PÈRE ET FILS

Moutard Père et Fils 1999 Brut Chardonnay (Champagne) $50. 87 *—R.V. (11/1/2006)*

MOUTON-CADET

Mouton-Cadet 2004 Bordeaux Blend (Bordeaux) $9. A lean, somewhat austerely tannic wine, with dry tannins. The fruit is subdued, and there are hints of stalky black currant, disappointing from such a famous name. It could work with steak, when the acidity will cut through the meat. **84** *—R.V. (11/1/2007)*

Mouton-Cadet 2000 Rouge Bordeaux Blend (Bordeaux) $14. 84 *—J.M. (4/3/2004)*

Mouton-Cadet 2006 Bordeaux White Blend (Bordeaux Blanc) $10. Lightly perfumed, this white Bordeaux shows the fresh character of the 2006 vintage. The acidity is poised, lifted and goes well with the pink grapefruit flavors. Drink this summer. **85 Best Buy** *—R.V. (12/31/2007)*

NICOLAS FEUILLATTE

Nicolas Feuillatte NV Blanc de Blancs Premier Cru Brut Chardonnay (Champagne) $43. 88 *—J.C. (12/1/2004)*

Nicolas Feuillatte NV Blue Label Brut Champagne Blend (Champagne) $28. 90 *—P.G. (12/1/2006)*

Nicolas Feuillatte NV Brut Champagne Blend (Champagne) $40. 87 *(4/1/2001)*

Nicolas Feuillatte NV Brut Kosher Champagne Blend (Champagne) $47. 86 *—J.M. (4/3/2004)*

Nicolas Feuillatte NV Brut Kosher Mevushal Champagne Blend (Champagne) $45. 86 *—J.C. (12/1/2004)*

Nicolas Feuillatte NV Brut Rosé Champagne Blend (Champagne) $43. A strawberry-fruited wine, with a pink sunset color and light, very fresh fruit. The aftertaste is soft and gentle. **86** *—R.V. (12/31/2007)*

Nicolas Feuillatte NV Brut Rosé Champagne Blend (Champagne) $40. 85 *—R.V. (12/1/2005)*

Nicolas Feuillatte 1998 Cuvée 225 Brut Champagne Blend (Champagne) $100. Matured in 225-liter barrels (hence the name of the cuvée), this has a depth of flavor and a richness that brings out the ripeness and freshness of the fruit, and a fine, elegant balance. A delicious Champagne that could age well. **92 Cellar Selection** *—R.V. (12/1/2007)*

Nicolas Feuillatte 1996 Cuvée Palmes d'Or Brut Champagne Blend (Champagne) $110. 88 *—M.S. (12/31/2005)*

Nicolas Feuillatte 1992 Cuvée Palmes d'Or Brut Champagne Blend (Champagne) $125. 90 *(12/31/2000)*

Nicolas Feuillatte 1996 Cuvée Palmes d'Or Brut Rosé Champagne Blend (Champagne) $125. 91 *—M.S. (1/1/2004)*

Nicolas Feuillatte 1995 Cuvée Speciale Premier Cru Brut Champagne Blend (Champagne) $65. 90 *(12/1/2004)*

Nicolas Feuillatte 1999 Cuvée Spéciale Brut Champagne Blend (Champagne) $65. On the soft side, this ripe, full wine is typical of the vintage. It has pink grapefruit flavors, lightly touched with fine sugar, alongside a crisp structure that promises 2–3 years aging. The aftertaste is open, balancing acidity and softness. **87** *—R.V. (12/1/2007)*

Nicolas Feuillatte 1999 Cuvée Spéciale Brut Champagne Blend (Champagne) $NA. This is very soft, open and ready to drink. It shows the character of the easy-going 1999 vintage. It will not age, it may not come from the greatest year, but its fresh, white fruit flavors are decidedly attractive and welcoming. **89** *—R.V. (2/1/2007)*

Nicolas Feuillatte 1997 Palmes d'Or Brut Champagne Blend (Champagne) $NA. The prestige cuvee from Nicolas Feuillatte is a 50/50 blend of Chardonnay and Pinot Noir, reveling in its richness, and toast character, ripe flavors with almonds and pears together with soft acidity. This is generous, soft and ready to drink. **91** *—R.V. (2/1/2007)*

Nicolas Feuillatte 1997 Palmes d'Or Champagne Blend (Champagne) $120. Yeasty, fresh-baked bread aromas, followed by an impressively fresh wine full of white fruits; white currants and pink grapefruit follow on the palate. It's well rounded with a soft aftertaste and well-balanced acidity, but there's no sign of maturity yet. **91** *—R.V. (12/1/2007)*

Nicolas Feuillatte NV Premier Cru Brut Champagne Blend (Champagne) $30. 90 *—P.G. (12/15/2000)*

Nicolas Feuillatte NV Premier Cru Brut Champagne Blend (Champagne) $33. 87 *—J.C. (12/1/2004)*

Nicolas Feuillatte NV Premier Cru Brut Rosé Champagne Blend (Champagne) $38. 90 **Editors' Choice** *—M.M. (12/15/2001)*

Nicolas Feuillatte NV Premier Cru Brut Rosé Champagne Blend (Champagne) $43. 90 *—J.C. (12/1/2004)*

Nicolas Feuillatte NV Réserve Particulière Brut Champagne Blend (Champagne) $30. An easy, full-bodied non-vintage Champagne, with soft white and tropical fruits, a full dosage and a well-integrated, balanced aftertaste. **86** *—R.V. (12/1/2007)*

Nicolas Feuillatte NV Réserve Particulière Brut Champagne Blend (Champagne) $28. 88 *—R.V. (12/1/2005)*

Nicolas Feuillatte 1999 Blanc de Blancs Brut Chardonnay (Champagne) $NA. A blend of Chardonnay grapes from Epernay and nearby Chouilly, this is a crisply fresh wine, with good depth of green apple and light, delicate flavors. The nuttiness at the end broadens and deepens the complexity of the wine. **89** *—R.V. (2/1/2007)*

Nicolas Feuillatte 1998 Blanc de Blancs Brut Chardonnay (Champagne) $40. 84 *—M.S. (12/31/2005)*

Nicolas Feuillatte NV Blanc de Blancs Premier Cru Brut Chardonnay (Champagne) $35. 85 *—K.F. (12/15/2002)*

Nicolas Feuillatte 1998 Chardonnay Blanc de Blancs Brut Chardonnay (Champagne) $40. Lively white fruit with a mineral edge. The flavors are just showing some signs of mature toast, but at the moment green, crisp tastes predominate. The sweet dosage —relatively high—seems to need time to integrate. **89** *—R.V. (12/1/2007)*

Nicolas Feuillatte 2000 Cuvée Palmes d'Or Rosé Brut Pinot Noir (Champagne) $175. Ultrasoft, strawberry flavored wine, tasting more of bitter red wine than Champagne. Maybe time will integrate it better. **83** *—R.V. (12/1/2007)*

Nicolas Feuillatte 1996 Cuvée Palmes d'Or Brut Rosé Pinot Noir (Champagne) $175. 88 *—J.C. (12/15/2003)*

NICOLAS JOLY

Nicolas Joly 2003 Coulee de Serrant Chenin Blanc (Savennières-Coulée de Serrant) $79. 93 **Cellar Selection** *—J.C. (11/15/2005)*

Nicolas Joly 2003 Les Clos Sacres Chenin Blanc (Savennières) $29. 91 **Editors' Choice** *—J.C. (11/15/2005)*

NICOLAS POTEL

Nicolas Potel 2005 Pinot Noir (Nuits-St.-Georges) $50. If you want perfumed Pinot Noir, this is the wine for you. It is aromatic, full of that sexy, fresh fruit that appeals to Central Coast California Pinot Noir lovers. Yet the structure and the elegance are all Burgundy. And the aftertaste is packed with red fruits and delicious acidity. **90** *—R.V. (3/1/2007)*

Nicolas Potel 2004 Pinot Noir (Gevrey-Chambertin) $44. Nicolas Potel, whose family was once associated with Domaine de la Pousse d'Or in Volnay, is now in business as a négociant. This wine shows great skill, balancing fresh fruit against some depth of tannic flavor. It is a bright, vivid wine that is easy to drink already. **89** —*R.V. (3/1/2007)*

Nicolas Potel 2003 Pinot Noir (Clos Saint-Denis) $123. Very much in the Nicolas Potel style of fruit-driven wines, this still keeps a firm grip on the structure, which is proper to a wine from Morey Saint-Denis. There's great freshness here, but also the ripe fruits of 2003—blueberries, dark plums—plus just a touch of wood and a flourish of acidity to finish. **94** —*R.V. (3/1/2007)*

Nicolas Potel 2003 Pinot Noir (Charmes-Chambertin) $125. Deliciously perfumed fruit, with new-wood richness topped by solid tannins here. This is a dense, chewy wine but also one that offers plenty of juicy, black fruit flavors. Big and bold, it will also age well. **94** —*R.V. (3/1/2007)*

Nicolas Potel 2003 Pinot Noir (Savigny-lès-Beaune) $32. 86 —*J.C. (11/15/2005)*

Nicolas Potel 2001 Pinot Noir (Vosne-Romanée) $40. 88 —*J.C. (10/1/2003)*

Nicolas Potel 2000 Pinot Noir (Volnay) $30. 87 —*C.S. (11/1/2002)*

Nicolas Potel 2000 Maison Dieu Vielles Vignes Pinot Noir (Bourgogne) $17. 83 —*P.G. (11/1/2002)*

Nicolas Potel 2004 Vieilles Vignes Pinot Noir (Vosne-Romanée) $49. A ripe wine, smooth, but also with a lift, offering vibrant red raspberry and currant flavors as well as a lively texture. The wine is delicious, full of life and freshness. **89** —*R.V. (3/1/2007)*

Nicolas Potel 2001 Vieilles Vignes Pinot Noir (Côte de Nuits-Villages) $18. 86 —*J.C. (10/1/2003)*

Nicolas Potel 2000 Vielles Vignes Pinot Noir (Volnay) $17. 86 —*P.G. (11/1/2002)*

NOTRE DAME DE COUSIGNAC

Notre Dame de Cousignac 2005 Rhône Red Blend (Côtes-du-Rhône) $11. 83—*J.C. (11/15/2006)*

OGIER

Ogier 2001 Les Allegories d'Antoine Rhône Red Blend (Gigondas) $34. 84 —*J.C. (11/15/2005)*

Ogier 2004 Les Chaillés Syrah (Saint-Joseph) $21. 86 —*J.C. (11/15/2006)*

OLIVIER LEFLAIVE

Olivier Leflaive 2004 Chardonnay (Meursault) $40. 90 —*R.V. (12/1/2006)*

Olivier Leflaive 2001 Chardonnay (Puligny-Montrachet) $42. 90 —*J.C. (10/1/2003)*

Olivier Leflaive 2001 Chardonnay (Chablis) $18. 86 —*J.C. (10/1/2003)*

Olivier Leflaive 1998 Chardonnay (Puligny-Montrachet) $39. 88 *(6/1/2001)*

Olivier Leflaive 1998 Les Champs Gains 1er Cru Chardonnay (Puligny-Montrachet) $50. 93 Editors' Choice *(6/1/2001)*

Olivier Leflaive 2004 Champ Gain Premier Cru Chardonnay (Puligny-Montrachet) $62. 90 Cellar Selection —*R.V. (12/1/2006)*

Olivier Leflaive 2003 Clos St. Marc Premier Cru Chardonnay (Chassagne-Montrachet) $58. 93 —*R.V. (9/1/2005)*

Olivier Leflaive 2001 En Remilly Premier Cru Chardonnay (St.-Aubin) $30. 86 —*J.C. (10/1/2003)*

Olivier Leflaive 1999 Les Sétilles Chardonnay (Bourgogne) $15. 86 *(6/1/2001)*

Olivier Leflaive 1998 Pinot Noir (Pommard) $42. 89 *(6/1/2001)*

Olivier Leflaive 1998 White Blend (Criots-Bâtard-Montrachet) $150. 94 Cellar Selection *(12/31/2001)*

ORIGIN

Origin 2003 Collection Series Pinot Noir (Santenay) $38. 84 —*J.C. (9/1/2006)*

PANNIER

Pannier 2000 Brut Champagne Blend (Champagne) $52. 87 —*R.V. (11/1/2006)*

Pannier NV Brut Rosé Champagne Blend (Champagne) $40. 87 —*R.V. (12/1/2005)*

Pannier NV Brut Sélection Champagne Blend (Champagne) $26. 90 *(12/31/2000)*

Pannier 1999 Cuvée Louis Eugène Blanc de Noirs Brut Champagne Blend (Champagne) $56. 89 —*R.V. (11/1/2006)*

Pannier 1999 Egérie de Pannier Brut Champagne Blend (Champagne) $77. 93 Editors' Choice —*R.V. (11/1/2006)*

Pannier 1998 Blanc de Blancs Brut Chardonnay (Champagne) $60. 87 —*R.V. (11/1/2006)*

PASCAL & ALAIN LORIEUX

Pascal & Alain Lorieux 2005 Agnès Sorel Cabernet Franc (Saint-Nicolas-de-Bourgueil) $NA. Agnès Sorel, the 15th-century mistress of King Charles VII of France, is believed to have been born in Touraine on the Loire. This wine, named after her, is fresh and crisp, with red berry fruits and acidity. It's a wine that is ready to drink, although the layers of wood and delicate tannins suggest it could lie down for another year. **88** —*R.V. (4/1/2007)*

Pascal & Alain Lorieux 2005 Expression Cabernet Franc (Saint-Nicolas-de-Bourgueil) $NA. A fresh fruity style of St-Nicolas, with some good, easy juicy red fruit flavors, only lightly underlain by a layer of dry tannins. It is still young, but it should certainly be very drinkable in summer 2007. **86** —*R.V. (4/1/2007)*

Pascal & Alain Lorieux 2005 Expression Cabernet Franc (Chinon) $NA. Dense, but relatively soft tannins are balanced by fresh black fruits. This promises some good development, as well—give it at least two years. **87** —*R.V. (4/1/2007)*

Pascal & Alain Lorieux 2005 Les Maugerets Cabernet Franc (Saint-Nicolas-de-Bourgueil) $NA. Classic, fresh and crisp, with that typical Cabernet Franc smoky bacon flavor, this is a lively wine that floats on red fruits and some dry tannins; well blended. **87** —*R.V. (4/1/2007)*

Pascal & Alain Lorieux 2003 Thélème Cabernet Franc (Chinon) $NA. A vibrant, fresh wine, with bramble fruits and lively tannins. For a 2003, though, a very hot year, this wine is surprisingly lightweight, missing any real depth of flavor. **84** —*R.V. (4/1/2007)*

PASCAL & NICOLAS REVERDY

Pascal & Nicolas Reverdy 2003 Cuvée Les Coûtes Sauvignon Blanc (Sancerre) $21. 88 *(7/1/2005)*

Pascal & Nicolas Reverdy 2004 Vieilles Vignes Sauvignon Blanc (Sancerre) $27. 90 —*R.V. (8/1/2006)*

PASCAL DOQUET

Pascal Doquet NV Grand Cru Blanc de Blancs Brut Chardonnay (Champagne) $61. Based mainly on vines in Le Mesnil-sur-Oger, this impressive wine is superbly rich with just the merest hint of age. With its lively mousse, secondary aromas of mocha and flavors of green apples, it is a wine that should develop magnificently over the next 4–5 years. **94 Editors' Choice** —*R.V. (12/31/2007)*

Pascal Doquet 1997 Grand Cru Le Mesnil-sur-Oger Chardonnay (Champagne) $69. 93 —*R.V. (11/1/2006)*

Pascal Doquet 2001 Premier Cru Brut Chardonnay (Champagne) $NA. Ripe grapefruit, green plums and other green stone fruits all show that this wine has some weight, allied with a steely interior. Still young, it fills the mouth with yeast and some toast, but more of an intense freshness. **91** —*R.V. (12/31/2007)*

PASCAL JOLIVET

Pascal Jolivet 2006 Sauvignon Blanc (Sancerre) $25. A forwardly fruity, lightly mineral wine, all freshness and white berry fruits, elegant and well-balanced with the crisp, apple acidity. A great apéritif style of Sancerre. **87** —*R.V. (9/1/2007)*

Pascal Jolivet 1998 Sauvignon Blanc (Sancerre) $19. 83 —*M.S. (7/1/2000)*

Pascal Jolivet 2003 Sauvignon Blanc (Pouilly-Fumé) $20. 89 *(7/1/2005)*

Pascal Jolivet 2000 Sauvignon Blanc (Sancerre) $19. 86 *(8/1/2002)*

Pascal Jolivet 2006 Attitude Sauvignon Blanc (Vin de Pays du Jardin de la France) $14. With its heavy bottle and designer label and name, this must qualify as the most expensive looking vin de pays from the Loire. Somehow the wine, while a pleasant, ripe Sauvignon, doesn't live up to the package. But the price is fine, so enjoy a lively, lightly toasty but still fresh green-fruited wine. **87** —*R.V. (9/1/2007)*

Pascal Jolivet 2006 Château du Nozay Sauvignon Blanc (Sancerre) $32. Almost tropical in its ripeness, this is exotically rich. It is full-bodied, concentrated, powered by white peaches and spliced with green berry fruits. A touch of smokiness adds complexity. **90** —*R.V. (9/1/2007)*

Pascal Jolivet 2000 Château du Nozay Sauvignon Blanc (Sancerre) $21. 86 *(8/1/2002)*

Pascal Jolivet 2000 Clos Du Roy Sauvignon Blanc (Sancerre) $22. 86 *(8/1/2002)*

Pascal Jolivet 2004 Exception Sauvignon Blanc (Sancerre) $78. The wine is full-bodied, with hints of smoke, and with a deliciously fresh, crisp apple aftertaste. It is powerful and rich while not losing any elegance. **92 Editors' Choice** —*R.V. (9/1/2007)*

Pascal Jolivet 2003 Le Château du Nozay Sauvignon Blanc (Sancerre) $26. 89 *(7/1/2005)*

Pascal Jolivet 2006 Les Caillottes Sauvignon Blanc (Sancerre) $30. From old vines on chalky soil, this wine minerality as well as concentration. It is crisp but full, ripe but fresh. There's a touch of spiciness to complement the ripe green plum and apple skin flavors. 91 *—R.V. (9/1/2007)*

Pascal Jolivet 2000 Les Caillottes Sauvignon Blanc (Sancerre) $22. 90 Editors' Choice *(8/1/2002)*

PATRIARCHE PÈRE & FILS

Patriarche Pere & Fils 2005 Cabernet Sauvignon Cabernet Sauvignon (Vin de Pays d'Oc) $10. Dry tannins dominate this wine, which certainly shows up the firm side of this varietal. The fruit is harder to find, with hints of juicy blackcurrants underneath the tannins. Decant this before serving, which will soften the toughness. 81 *—R.V. (2/1/2007)*

Patriarche Pere & Fils 2004 Brut Chardonnay (Vin Mousseux) $16. No doubt this is meant to be a slightly more serious attempt at sparkling wine, but it merely succeeds in being pleasant. Obvious citrus and earth aromas add hints of ginger on the palate. It's slightly creamy in texture, finishing clean and fresh. 83 *—J.C. (12/15/2007)*

Patriarche Père & Fils 2004 Chardonnay (Mâcon-Villages) $13. 84 *—J.C. (11/15/2005)*

Patriarche Père & Fils 2003 Chardonnay (Vin de Pays d'Oc) $8. 83 *—J.C. (11/15/2005)*

Patriarche Père & Fils 2001 Chardonnay (Pouilly-Fuissé) $25. 83 *—J.C. (11/15/2005)*

Patriarche Père & Fils 2005 Merlot (Vin de Pays d'Oc) $10. 84 *—R.V. (12/31/2006)*

Patriarche Pere & Fils 2004 Pinot Noir (Vin de Pays d'Oc) $10. Soft, easy wine, which has some red fruit and herbal flavors, a layer of light tannins and acidity. It's simple, but great as a spicy barbecue accompaniment. 83 *—R.V. (2/1/2007)*

Patriarche Père & Fils 2003 Pinot Noir (Bourgogne) $10. 84 *—J.C. (11/15/2005)*

Patriarche Père & Fils 2000 Pinot Noir (Nuits-St.-Georges) $40. 83 *—J.C. (11/15/2005)*

Patriarche Pere & Fils 2002 Pinot Noir (Charmes-Chambertin) $102. Old-fashioned Burgundy with a light color, mature fruits and light tannins. This is a wine that has red fruit Pinot Noir flavors but misses the depth or complexity of a grand cru wine. 84 *—R.V. (3/1/2007)*

Patriarche Pere & Fils 2004 Les Malconsorts Premier Cru Pinot Noir (Vosne-Romanée) $70. Densely textured and perfumed, this has flavors of red plums, soft acidity and layered dry tannins. It's a wine that could stand some aging, but is definitely ready to drink. 87 *—R.V. (3/1/2007)*

Patriarche Pere & Fils 2004 Pinot Rosé Pinot Noir (Vin de Pays d'Oc) $9. With its dull coppery hue and scents of anise and bruised fruit, this is obviously tiring. It does still have some dried cherry or cranberry flavors, but this wine is headed south. Drink up. 82 *—J.C. (7/1/2007)*

Patriarche Pere & Fils NV Eclat Carmin Rosé Sparkling Blend (Vin Mousseux) $16. Sure it's a bit simple and fruity—the flavors run toward berries and citrus—but it's also cleanly made, with a slightly creamy mouthfeel and a soft, easy-drinking finish. 84 *—J.C. (12/15/2007)*

Patriarche Père & Fils 2005 Syrah (Vin de Pays d'Oc) $10. 85 Best Buy *—R.V. (12/31/2006)*

PAUL BLANCK

Paul Blanck 2001 Pinot Blanc (Alsace) $11. 90 Best Buy *—C.S. (11/15/2002)*

Paul Blanck 2001 Grand Cru Schlossberg Riesling (Alsace) $33. 92 *—R.V. (11/1/2005)*

Paul Blanck 2002 Patergarten Riesling (Alsace) $23. 88 *—R.V. (5/1/2005)*

PATRICK COULBOIS

Patrick Coulbois 2006 Les Cocques Sauvignon Blanc (Pouilly-Fumé) $22. Young, very fruity with green plum and currant flavors, this still has a yeasty quality from the lees. Drink in 2008; it's going to be deliciously fruity and fresh, with great ripe fruit. 89 *—R.V. (9/1/2007)*

PAUL DELANE

Paul Delane NV Brut Rosé Champagne Blend (Crémant de Bourgogne) $19. 89 Editors' Choice *—R.V. (6/1/2006)*

Paul Delane NV Brut Réserve Sparkling Blend (Crémant de Bourgogne) $18. 90 *—R.V. (6/1/2006)*

PAUL GOERG

Paul Goerg NV Premier Cru Blanc de Blancs Champagne Blend (Champagne) $28. 86 *—P.G. (12/15/2002)*

PAUL JABOULET AÎNÉ

Paul Jaboulet Aîné 1998 Domaine Raymond Roure Marsanne (Crozes-Hermitage) $33. 90 *—R.V. (6/1/2002)*

Paul Jaboulet Aîné 2001 Beaumes-de-Venise Rhône Red Blend (Côtes-du-Rhône Villages) $14. 87 *—J.C. (3/1/2004)*

Paul Jaboulet Aîné 1999 Domaine de Saint-Pierre Rhône Red Blend (Cornas) $40. 93 *—R.V. (6/1/2002)*

Paul Jaboulet Aîné 1997 La Chapelle Syrah (Hermitage) $100. 96 *(11/15/1999)*

Paul Jaboulet Aîné 2003 Le Paradou Rhône Red Blend (Beaumes-de-Venise) $16. 88 *—J.C. (2/1/2005)*

Paul Jaboulet Aîné 1998 Les Traverses Rhône Red Blend (Côtes-du-Ventoux) $9. 88 Best Buy *—M.S. (11/1/2000)*

Paul Jaboulet Aîné 2005 Le Chevalier de Sterimberg Rhône White Blend (Hermitage) $80. Rather nutty—almonds—on the nose, then broadening out on the palate into apricots and oranges. This is more focused and crisp than many white Hermitages, with a long, modestly tannic finish. It may age well, or it may be trying too hard and best consumed young. 91 *—J.C. (9/1/2007)*

Paul Jaboulet Aîné 1999 Chevalier de Sterimberg Rhône White Blend (Hermitage) $75. 94 *—R.V. (6/1/2002)*

Paul Jaboulet Aîné 2000 Parallèle 45 Rhône White Blend (Côtes-du-Rhône) $9. 86 *—R.V. (6/1/2002)*

Paul Jaboulet Aîné 2005 Domaine de Saint-Pierre Syrah (Cornas) $112. Denser and more minerally than Jaboulet's Les Grandes Terrasses bottling, this is a serious Cornas, brimming with blood and iron notes wrapped in a richly tannic cloak. Chewy but ripe, this should be long-lived. Drink from 2012. 91 *—J.C. (9/1/2007)*

Paul Jaboulet Aîné 2003 Domaine de Thalabert Syrah (Crozes-Hermitage) $33. 90 *—J.C. (11/15/2006)*

Paul Jaboulet Aîné 2001 Domaine de Thalabert Syrah (Crozes-Hermitage) $30. 85 *—J.C. (2/1/2005)*

Paul Jaboulet Aîné 1999 Domaine de Thalabert Syrah (Crozes-Hermitage) $25. 89 *—R.V. (6/1/2002)*

Paul Jaboulet Aîné 1999 Domaine Raymond Roure Syrah (Crozes-Hermitage) $33. 92 *—R.V. (6/1/2002)*

Paul Jaboulet Aîné 2005 La Chapelle Syrah (Hermitage) $215. A big step up from Jaboulet's La Petite Chapelle, this is on a par with some of Jaboulet's past efforts. It's richly concentrated, yet nuanced, with notes of blood and mineral added to ripe cassis fruit and accented by hints of vanilla and spice. The tannins form an almost creamy texture in the mouth, and the finish lingers a good long time. Drink 2012–2025. 93 Cellar Selection *—J.C. (9/1/2007)*

Paul Jaboulet Aîné 2005 La Petite Chapelle Syrah (Hermitage) $96. In effect the second wine of Jaboulet's flagship La Chapelle, this is a lightweight version of Hermitage, with creamy red berry flavors that turn crisp and cranberryish on the finish. Drink now–2015. 87 *—J.C. (9/1/2007)*

Paul Jaboulet Aîné 1999 Le Grand Pompée Syrah (Saint-Joseph) $23. 90 *—R.V. (6/1/2002)*

Paul Jaboulet Aîné 2005 Les Grandes Terrasses Syrah (Cornas) $57. Starts off with oaky notes of vanilla and spice, but then folds in slightly bloody, peppery notes. It shows plenty of red currant fruit, and is fairly powerful, yet with crisp acids and firm tannins. Hold five years. 88 *—J.C. (9/1/2007)*

Paul Jaboulet Aîné 2001 Les Jalets Syrah (Crozes-Hermitage) $14. 85 *—M.S. (9/1/2003)*

Paul Jaboulet Aîné 2005 Les Jumelles Syrah (Côte Rôtie) $80. Made from purchased grapes (Jaboulet finally acquired 1.5 hectares of Côte-Rôtie in 2006), this is a nicely textured, creamy wine that avoids tannic overload or heaviness, allowing the floral, spicy side of the appellation to shine. Drink now–2015. 89 *—J.C. (9/1/2007)*

Paul Jaboulet Aîné 1999 Les Jumelles Syrah (Côte Rôtie) $68. 91 Cellar Selection *(11/1/2001)*

PAUL MAS

Paul Mas 2003 Que Serah Sirah Syrah (Vin de Pays d'Oc) $11. 85 *—J.C. (11/15/2005)*

PAUL PRIEUR ET FILS

Paul Prieur et Fils 2005 La Croix de Perthuis Sauvignon Blanc (Sancerre) $24. From the top Monts Damnés vineyard, this crisp light wine has yeasty flavors that hide the fresh grapefruit flavors. There is pleasant acidity at the back, along with some green apple skin. Will be ready by the beginning of 2008. **85** *—R.V. (9/1/2007)*

PAVILLON ROUGE DE CHÂTEAU MARGAUX

Pavillon Rouge de Château Margaux 2003 Bordeaux Blend (Margaux) $65. **90** *—R.V. (5/1/2006)*

PÈRE ANSELME

Père Anselme 2006 Domaine de la Grivelière Rhône Red Blend (Côtes-du-Rhône) $11. A high-volume wine, this is nonetheless a solid effort. Light and fresh, it combines a slightly herbal, stemmy note with simple red cherry fruit. Drink now. **84** *(8/1/2007)*

Père Anselme 2005 Fiole Réserve Rhône Red Blend (Châteauneuf-du-Pape) $43. Despite the different branding, this is a selection from the family's Domaine Barville in Châteauneuf-du-Pape. Dusty scents of dried spices and red plums turn ripe and creamy in the mouth, layering in black cherry and plum flavors. Finishes lush and long, a modern-styled wine that may be consumed young. **90** *(8/1/2007)*

Père Anselme NV La Fiole du Pape Rhône Red Blend (Châteauneuf-du-Pape) $30. This is a nonvintage Châteauneuf-du-Pape, with several bottlings released each year to retain consistency and freshness in the market. It's round and slightly alcoholic, marked by flavors of dried fruit and leather and finishing spicy and warm. Drink now. **85** *(8/1/2007)*

Père Anselme 2006 La Fiole Rhône White Blend (Châteauneuf-du-Pape) $30. Crisp and clean, with citrus notes to go with flavors of almond and acacia blossom. Finishes with a fresh touch of ripe apples. Drink now. **86** *(8/1/2007)*

PERRIER JOUËT

Perrier Jouët NV Blason Brut Rosé Champagne Blend (Champagne) $80. Full, rich, quite heavy in style, this is only just brut, with its crushed strawberry flavor and low acidity. It works, as a fine wine for a red-fruit dessert, the balance remaining right up to the very soft aftertaste. **87** *—R.V. (12/31/2007)*

Perrier Jouët NV Blason Brut Rosé Champagne Blend (Champagne) $76. **87** *—R.V. (12/1/2005)*

Perrier Jouët NV Blason Brut Rosé Champagne Blend (Champagne) $76. **93** *—P.G. (12/1/2006)*

Perrier Jouët 2000 Fleur de Champagne Blanc de Blancs Brut Chardonnay (Champagne) $400. This is full, perhaps heavy, but certainly with a fine, powerful character. The acidity and the green-apple texture are at one with the white-fruit flavors, which gives extra richness to the wine. Just a hint of mineral can be detected. **89** *—R.V. (12/31/2007)*

Perrier Jouët 1993 Fleur de Champagne Blanc de Blancs Brut Champagne Blend (Champagne) $125. **93** *(12/15/2001)*

Perrier Jouët 1999 Fleur de Champagne Brut Champagne Blend (Champagne) $140. This is a heavy, rather clumsy wine, that seems to be too soft. The weight shows through the almonds and green plum fruits, while the acidity seems somewhat forced. To finish, the softness returns. Bottle age may help this wine to liven up. **88** *—R.V. (12/31/2007)*

Perrier Jouët 1998 Fleur de Champagne Brut Champagne Blend (Champagne) $125. Ripe, full, and just hinting at maturity, this remains P-J's flagship Champagne. It's poised, elegant and fresh, with signs of nuttiness. A vibrant, joyful wine, it continues to live up to its exuberant bottle. **93** *—R.V. (12/1/2007)*

Perrier Jouët 1996 Fleur de Champagne Brut Champagne Blend (Champagne) $120. **93** *—R.V. (12/1/2004)*

Perrier Jouët 1995 Fleur de Champagne Brut Champagne Blend (Champagne) $120. **90** *—M.M. (12/1/2000)*

Perrier Jouët 2002 Fleur de Champagne Brut Rosé Champagne Blend (Champagne) $300. Are delicate and full-bodied a contradiction? Not here, with this ripe, red-fruit-flavored wine, which still creeps delicately around the palate. From its just pink color to its soft, yet still crisp aftertaste, this is a well-balanced wine, which could probably age well for 2–3 years. **90** *—R.V. (12/31/2007)*

Perrier Jouët 1997 Fleur de Champagne Brut Rosé Champagne Blend (Champagne) $140. **91** *—R.V. (12/15/2003)*

Perrier Jouët 1995 Fleur de Champagne Brut Rosé Champagne Blend (Champagne) $150. **90** *(12/15/2001)*

Perrier Jouët NV Grand Brut Champagne Blend (Champagne) $35. **88** *—S.H. (12/15/2000)*

Perrier Jouët NV Grand Brut Champagne Blend (Champagne) $40. **87** *—M.S. (12/15/2003)*

Perrier Jouët NV Grand Brut Champagne Blend (Champagne) $40. **88** *—J.C. (12/1/2004)*

PERRIN

Perrin 2004 Réserve Rhône Red Blend (Côtes-du-Rhône) $11. **87 Best Buy** *—J.C. (11/15/2006)*

PERRIN & FILS

Perrin & Fils 2004 Grenache-Syrah (Côtes-du-Rhône Villages) $15. **87** *—J.C. (11/15/2006)*

Perrin & Fils 2003 L'Andéol Rasteau Grenache-Syrah (Côtes-du-Rhône Villages) $23. **85** *—J.C. (11/15/2005)*

Perrin & Fils 2003 La Gille Grenache-Syrah (Gigondas) $22. **90 Editors' Choice** *—J.C. (11/15/2005)*

Perrin & Fils 2004 Les Christins Grenache-Syrah (Vacqueyras) $22. **90 Editors' Choice** *—J.C. (11/15/2006)*

Perrin & Fils 1999 Red Blend (Vacqueyras) $19. **90** *—M.S. (2/1/2003)*

Perrin & Fils 1996 Rhône Red Blend (Gigondas) $22. **86** *—J.C. (7/1/2000)*

Perrin & Fils 2000 Perrin L'Andéol Rasteau Rhône Red Blend (Côtes-du-Rhône Villages) $16. **91 Editors' Choice** *—M.S. (9/1/2003)*

Perrin & Fils 2006 Réserve Rosé Rhône Red Blend (Côtes-du-Rhône) $11. This is 60% Cinsault—an unusually high proportion—but perhaps that is why this wine shows so much freshness. The balance is a blend of Syrah, Grenache and Mourvèdre, and the result is a very fruit-forward wine with loads of watermelon and cherry fruit upfront, followed by hints of peach and chocolate on the finish. **88 Best Buy** *—J.C. (7/1/2007)*

Perrin & Fils 2000 Vinsobres Rhône Red Blend (Côtes-du-Rhône Villages) $16. **84** *—M.S. (9/1/2003)*

Perrin & Fils 2002 Réserve Rhône White Blend (Côtes-du-Rhône) $10. **83** *—J.C. (3/1/2004)*

Perrin & Fils 2003 Les Cornuds Vinsobres Syrah-Grenache (Côtes-du-Rhône Villages) $23. **88** *—J.C. (11/15/2005)*

PEZAT

Pezat 2004 Bordeaux Blend (Bordeaux Supérieur) $NA. From vineyards just outside the Saint-Emilion appellation, this oak-aged, Merlot-dominated wine is rich and well-padded, layered with sweet blackberry fruits, and soft, ripe tannins. It is easy to drink now, fruity although it should age over 3–4 years. **87** *—R.V. (6/1/2007)*

PHILIPPE GONET

Philippe Gonet NV Le Mesnil sur Oger Réserve Brut Champagne Blend (Champagne) $33. **90** *—R.V. (12/1/2005)*

Philippe Gonet NV Roy Soleil Grand Cru Blanc de Blancs Chardonnay (Champagne) $41. **91** *—R.V. (12/1/2005)*

PHILIPPE PORTIER

Philippe Portier 2006 Sauvignon Blanc (Quincy) $20. This ripe, creamy wine is well-rounded with herbal and apple skin flavors. It's delicious now, and shouldn't age more than a few months. **88** *—R.V. (10/1/2007)*

PHILIPPONNAT

Philipponnat 2000 Cuvée 1522 Grand Cru Champagne Blend (Champagne) $85. **94** *—R.V. (11/1/2006)*

Philipponnat 1997 Réserve Brut Champagne Blend (Champagne) $63. **93** *—R.V. (12/1/2005)*

Philipponnat NV Royale Réserve Brut Champagne Blend (Champagne) $40. **91** *—R.V. (12/1/2005)*

Philipponnat 2000 Grand Blanc Brut Chardonnay (Champagne) $75. A very floral wine, poised and creamy. Already there is an almond character as the wine develops, but it still hasn't lost sight of the initial fresh green fruits. Drink now; it will only develop slightly. **89** *—R.V. (12/1/2007)*

PIERRE AMADIEU

Pierre Amadieu 2003 Domaine Grand Romane Cuvée Prestige Rhône Red Blend (Gigondas) $25. **84** *—J.C. (11/15/2006)*

Pierre Amadieu 2005 Roulepierre Rhône Red Blend (Côtes-du-Rhône) $10. **87 Best Buy** *—J.C. (11/15/2006)*

PIERRE ANDRE

Pierre Andre 2001 Reserve Vieilles Vignes Pinot Noir (Bourgogne) $14. **81** *—J.C. (10/1/2003)*

PIERRE BESINET

Pierre Besinet 2003 Le Bosc Chardonnay-Sauvignon (Vin de Pays d'Oc) $NA. **80** *—R.V. (12/1/2004)*

Pierre Besinet 2003 Le Bosc Rosé Blend (Vin de Pays d'Oc) $NA. **86** *—R.V. (12/1/2004)*

PIERRE BONIFACE

Pierre Boniface NV Brut de Savoie Sparkling Blend (Vin de Savoie) $18. Light and frothy, this clean, palate-refreshing sparkler seems ideally suited to be an apéritif. Citrus and apple notes are gentle, underscored by some chalky minerality. **84** *—J.C. (12/15/2007)*

PIERRE COURSODON

Pierre Coursodon 2000 Le Paradis Saint-Pierre Marsanne (Saint-Joseph) $23. 91 *—R.V. (6/1/2002)*

PIERRE FRICK

Pierre Frick 2001 Grand Cru Steinert Gewürztraminer (Alsace) $43. 88 *—R.V. (4/1/2005)*

Pierre Frick 2002 Cuvée Precieuse Tokay Pinot Gris (Alsace) $NA. 86 *—R.V. (4/1/2005)*

PIERRE GAILLARD

Pierre Gaillard 2004 Clos de Cuminaille Syrah (Saint-Joseph) $30. 87 *—J.C. (11/15/2006)*

PIERRE GIMMONET ET FILS

Pierre Gimmonet et Fils NV Cuis Premier Cru Blanc de Blancs Brut Champagne Blend (Champagne) $34. 88 *—R.V. (12/1/2002)*

Pierre Gimmonet et Fils 1997 Special Club Brut Champagne Blend (Champagne) $53. 90 *—R.V. (12/1/2002)*

Pierre Gimmonet et Fils NV Cuis Premier Cru Blanc de Blancs Brut Chardonnay (Champagne) $52. Cuis is among the first villages on the Côte des Blancs after leaving Epernay. While it doesn't have the reputation of the Grand Cru villages further along the slope, it can produce delicious wines. This fine, lightly creamy, white currant-flavored Champagne, shows a good mineral texture, a crispness and a refreshing aftertaste. **92 Editors' Choice** *—R.V. (12/1/2007)*

Pierre Gimmonet et Fils 2002 Fleuron Premier Cru Blanc de Blancs Brut Chardonnay (Champagne) $64. This recently released 2002 is still showing its youth, with a firm, mineral edge to it. But it does have the right refreshingly crisp character, along with intense fruits, and acidity that just powers right through. Wait 3–4 years. **93 Cellar Selection** *—R.V. (12/1/2007)*

Pierre Gimmonet et Fils 1999 Fleuron Premier Cru Blanc de Blancs Brut Chardonnay (Champagne) $55. 93 Editors' Choice *—R.V. (11/1/2006)*

Pierre Gimmonet et Fils 1999 Oenophile Premier Cru Extra Brut Chardonnay (Champagne) $66. For those who like their Champagnes extra dry, this is a good example because it has some richness to balance that intense grapefruit shock on the palate. It is beginning to get some good age as well, as the structure and the toast begin to kick in. Another year, and it will be delicious. **93** *—R.V. (12/1/2007)*

Pierre Gimmonet et Fils 1998 Oenophile Extra Brut Chardonnay (Champagne) $55. 90 *—R.V. (11/1/2006)*

Pierre Gimmonet et Fils 1999 Premier Cru Special Club Brut Chardonnay (Champagne) $38. A blend of Grand Cru wines from Cramant and Chouilly and Premier Cru from Cuis (which is why it is only premier cru), this is all about freshness. It's more of a soft year, so this has a lightness and crispness while giving an open character over the creamy fruit. **94** *—R.V. (12/1/2007)*

PIERRE GONON

Pierre Gonon 2004 Syrah (Saint-Joseph) $32. 87 *—J.C. (11/15/2006)*

PIERRE JEAN

Pierre Jean 2000 Cabernet Sauvignon (Vin de Pays de L'Aude) $7. 83 *—D.T. (2/1/2002)*

PIERRE MONCUIT

Pierre Moncuit NV Cuvée Hugues de Coulmet Blanc de Blancs Brut Chardonnay (Champagne) $40. A good wine, this is a young, aromatic Chardonnay with lively white fruits bursting from the acidity. **88** *—R.V. (12/31/2007)*

Pierre Moncuit 1999 Cuvée Millesimé Grand Cru Brut Chardonnay (Champagne) $62. The softness of the 1999 vintage is very apparent in this approachable wine. It is full, round, only just touched by minerality, white fruits and some almonds giving weight and character. **88** *—R.V. (12/31/2007)*

Pierre Moncuit 1996 Cuvée Millesimé Grand Cru Brut Chardonnay (Champagne) $75. The 1996 vintage really brings out the minerality in a wine. This grand cru is still austere, very crisp, with some smokiness, apple-skin flavors and intense freshness. Give it another 5–6 years. **93 Cellar Selection** *—R.V. (12/31/2007)*

Pierre Moncuit NV Cuvée Moncuit-Delos Grand Cru Brut Chardonnay (Champagne) $46. From 90-year-old vines in Le Mesnil-sur-Oger, this is a superbly ripe wine, full-bodied, concentrated with a great swathe of minerality going through. This is still young, based on the 2004 vintage, but shows every sign of developing into a beautifully toasty maturity. **92** *—R.V. (12/31/2007)*

Pierre Moncuit 1996 Non-Dosé Brut Chardonnay (Champagne) $100. Very intense, very nervy wine, living on a thin wire of grapefruit and other citrus flavors but much more about pure structure. The aftertaste shows great concentration. **89** *—R.V. (12/31/2007)*

PIERRE MOREY

Pierre Morey 2004 Chardonnay (Meursault) $68. 89 *—R.V. (12/1/2006)*

Pierre Morey 2004 Les Tessons Chardonnay (Meursault) $80. 91 *—R.V. (12/1/2006)*

Pierre Morey 2005 Pinot Noir (Bourgogne) $24. A rather rustic wine, with red fruits and acidity dominating. It is mineral and austere, with a very fresh, crisp aftertaste. **84** *—R.V. (3/1/2007)*

PIERRE PRIEUR ET FILS

Pierre Prieur et Fils 2005 Domaine de Saint-Pierre Sauvignon Blanc (Sancerre) $NA. Flavored with almonds and pistachios, and touched with honey, this is already mature. There's almost a sweetness here, certainly softness, with apricot ripeness. **86** *—R.V. (9/1/2007)*

PIERRE SPARR

Pierre Sparr 2001 Gewürztraminer (Alsace) $13. 88 *—M.S. (6/1/2003)*

Pierre Sparr 2003 Reserve Gewürztraminer (Alsace) $17. 87 *—J.C. (2/1/2005)*

Pierre Sparr 2004 Réserve Gewürztraminer (Alsace) $16. 88 Editors' Choice *—J.C. (11/1/2005)*

Pierre Sparr 2001 Reserve Pinot Blanc (Alsace) $10. 89 Best Buy *—M.S. (10/1/2003)*

Pierre Sparr NV Brut Réserve Pinot Blanc-Pinot Noir (Crémant d'Alsace) $18. 86 *—R.V. (6/1/2006)*

Pierre Sparr 2003 Pinot Gris (Alsace) $15. 85 *—J.C. (2/1/2005)*

Pierre Sparr 2002 Grand Cru Mambourg Pinot Gris (Alsace) $30. 90 *—R.V. (2/1/2006)*

Pierre Sparr 2003 Réserve Pinot Gris (Alsace) $17. 87 *—J.C. (2/1/2005)*

Pierre Sparr 2004 Réserve Pinot Gris (Alsace) $17. 86 *—J.C. (11/1/2005)*

Pierre Sparr 2000 Vendanges Tardives Pinot Gris (Alsace) $NA. 88 *—R.V. (2/1/2006)*

Pierre Sparr NV Brut Rosé Pinot Noir (Crémant d'Alsace) $16. Dark pink with a slight coppery tinge to its hue, Sparr's Brut Rosé is a bit of disappointment. It boasts plum- and berry-scented aromas, but it comes across as heavy on the palate and a bit sweet, lacking freshness and verve. **81** *—J.C. (7/1/2007)*

Pierre Sparr 2005 Riesling (Alsace) $13. Though the finish falls off a bit, notes of juicy honeydew, pear and petrol open up for a sublime mouthful of pineapple and lime pulp. Medium-full-bodied, this is a well-balanced and structured offering promising pleasure and satisfaction. **88 Best Buy** *(9/1/2007)*

Pierre Sparr 2003 Riesling (Alsace) $14. 85 *—J.C. (2/1/2005)*

Pierre Sparr 2001 Altenbourg Riesling (Alsace) $25. 89 *—R.V. (5/1/2005)*

Pierre Sparr 2000 Grand Cru Schoenenbourg Riesling (Alsace) $35. 90 *—R.V. (11/1/2005)*

Pierre Sparr 2005 Réserve Riesling (Alsace) $17. Starts off with aromas of petrol, paraffin and melon. On the palate, pineapple, under-ripe stone fruit and lemon pith complement the full body. The medium length of the citrusy finish brings it all together nicely. **88** *(9/1/2007)*

Pierre Sparr 2001 Reserve Riesling (Alsace) $13. 85 *—M.S. (12/1/2003)*

Pierre Sparr 2003 Réserve Riesling (Alsace) $16. 87 *—R.V. (5/1/2005)*

Pierre Sparr 2000 Dynastie Brut Sparkling Blend (Crémant d'Alsace) $20. 90 *—R.V. (6/1/2006)*

Pierre Sparr NV Marquis de Perlade Blanc de Blancs Brut Sparkling Blend (Vin Mousseux) $13. This is on the fullish side, lacking crispness and refreshment factor. Fortunately, the ripe apple and pear flavors are charming enough to pull it through. **83** *—J.C. (12/15/2007)*

Pierre Sparr NV Réserve Brut Sparkling Blend (Crémant d'Alsace) $16. A light-bodied, somewhat austere sparkler that's short on fruit but long on mineral and earthy notes suggesting wet clay and chalk. Finishes fresh. **84** *—J.C. (12/15/2007)*

Pierre Sparr 1997 Brand Tokay Pinot Gris (Alsace) $25. 89 *(8/1/1999)*

Pierre Sparr 1997 Reserve Tokay Pinot Gris (Alsace) $13. 91 Best Buy *(8/1/1999)*

Pierre Sparr 2003 One White Blend (Alsace) $12. 84 *—J.C. (2/1/2005)*

PINK CRIQUET

Pink Criquet 2006 Bordeaux Blend (Bordeaux Rosé) $15. From the St-Emilion estate of Château Lassègue, owned by Jess Jackson, this is typical of the caramel and vanilla style that seems to be Bordeaux Rosés own. Vivid pink candy in color, full, ripe, but with some good acidity from Merlot. Screwcap. **87** *—R.V. (7/1/2007)*

PINK FLAMINGO

Pink Flamingo NV Gris de Gris Rosé Blend (Vin de Pays des Sables du Golfe du Lion) $9. 85 Best Buy *—J.C. (6/21/2006)*

PIPER-HEIDSIECK

Piper-Heidsieck NV Brut Champagne Blend (Champagne) $35. 90 Editors' Choice *—P.G. (12/15/2003)*

Piper-Heidsieck NV Brut Champagne Blend (Champagne) $35. 92 Editors' Choice *—R.V. (12/1/2005)*

Piper-Heidsieck 1998 Brut Champagne Blend (Champagne) $65. 92 Cellar Selection *—M.S. (12/31/2005)*

Piper-Heidsieck 1995 Brut Champagne Blend (Champagne) $50. 89 *(12/31/2000)*

Piper-Heidsieck 1990 Brut Champagne Blend (Champagne) $50. 89 *—M.S. (12/1/1999)*

Piper-Heidsieck NV Brut Rosé Champagne Blend (Champagne) $44. 91 *—P.G. (1/1/2004)*

Piper-Heidsieck NV Cuvée Jean-Paul Gaultier Brut Champagne Blend (Champagne) $98. 90 *—R.V. (12/15/2001)*

Piper-Heidsieck NV Cuvée Jean-Paul Gaultier Brut Champagne Blend (Champagne) $100. 90 *—R.V. (12/1/2004)*

Piper-Heidsieck NV Cuvée Rare Brut Champagne Blend (Champagne) $120. 92 *—P.G. (12/1/2006)*

Piper-Heidsieck 1990 Cuvée Rare Réservée Brut Champagne Blend (Champagne) $70. 91 *—P.G. (12/15/2003)*

Piper-Heidsieck 1988 Cuvée Rare Réservée Brut Champagne Blend (Champagne) $65. 94 *—E.M. (11/15/1999)*

Piper-Heidsieck NV Extra Dry Champagne Blend (Champagne) $35. 89 *—P.G. (12/15/2003)*

Piper-Heidsieck NV Sauvage Brut Rosé Champagne Blend (Champagne) $45. 83 *—R.V. (12/1/2004)*

Piper-Heidsieck NV Special Cuvée Brut Champagne Blend (Champagne) $100. 91 *—P.G. (12/15/2000)*

POL ROGER

Pol Roger 1995 Brut Champagne Blend (Champagne) $59. 89 *—P.G. (12/15/2002)*

Pol Roger 1995 Cuvée Sir Winston Churchill Brut Champagne Blend (Champagne) $194. 90 *—J.C. (12/15/2003)*

Pol Roger 1993 Cuvée Sir Winston Churchill Brut Champagne Blend (Champagne) $166. 89 *(12/15/2002)*

Pol Roger NV Extra Cuvée de Réserve Brut Champagne Blend (Champagne) $35. 92 Editors' Choice *—J.C. (12/1/2004)*

Pol Roger 1996 Extra Cuvée de Réserve Brut Champagne Blend (Champagne) $67. 94 *—R.V. (12/1/2004)*

Pol Roger 1996 Extra Cuvée de Réserve Brut Rosé Champagne Blend (Champagne) $70. 90 *—R.V. (12/1/2004)*

Pol Roger 1996 Réserve Brut Rosé Champagne Blend (Champagne) $71. 94 *—R.V. (1/1/2004)*

Pol Roger 1999 Blanc de Blancs Brut Chardonnay (Champagne) $106. Still very young, this wine needs time to develop its intense minerality. Now it is more about grapefruit and yeast, although it is also full-bodied, a sign of the 1999 vintage. Wait five years at least. **90** *—R.V. (12/31/2007)*

Pol Roger 1996 Blanc de Chardonnay Brut Chardonnay (Champagne) $83. 91 *—M.S. (12/15/2003)*

Pol Roger 1998 Extra Cuvée de Réserve Blanc de Chardonnay Brut Chardonnay (Champagne) $99. 94 Cellar Selection *—R.V. (11/1/2006)*

POMMERY

Pommery 1995 Champagne Blend (Champagne) $55. 90 Editors' Choice *(12/1/2000)*

Pommery 1998 Brut Champagne Blend (Champagne) $70. 92 *—R.V. (11/1/2006)*

Pommery NV Brut Apanage Champagne Blend (Champagne) $38. 87 *—J.C. (12/15/2001)*

Pommery NV Brut Rosé Champagne Blend (Champagne) $50. 86 *—P.G. (12/15/2002)*

Pommery NV Brut Rosé Champagne Blend (Champagne) $60. 90 *—J.C. (12/1/2004)*

Pommery NV Brut Rosé Champagne Blend (Champagne) $45. 88 *—J.C. (12/15/2001)*

Pommery NV Brut Royal Champagne Blend (Champagne) $42. This is in Pommery's relatively delicate style, a finely balanced, elegant Champagne. It has some lively acidity; the balance between this and the white fruits and touch of maturity works. Great non-vintage. **90** *—R.V. (12/1/2007)*

Pommery NV Brut Royal Champagne Blend (Champagne) $33. 89 *—P.G. (12/15/2002)*

Pommery NV Brut Royal Champagne Blend (Champagne) $34. 85 *—J.C. (12/1/2004)*

Pommery NV Brut Royal Champagne Blend (Champagne) $33. 87 *—J.C. (12/15/2001)*

Pommery 1998 Cuvée Louise Brut Champagne Blend (Champagne) $185. As it ages in bottle, this Champagne is showing real class. It remains as delicate as when reviewed last year, but it is now showing much more mature toastiness and bread flavors, and less of the green fruits. Elegance is still the main character; a fine, pure wine. **92** *—R.V. (12/1/2007)*

Pommery 1998 Grand Cru Brut Champagne Blend (Champagne) $80. A fine vintage, which shows some age from a relatively fast-maturing year, but is now nicely poised between the initial fresh green fruits and grapefruit flavors, and the elements of toast and yeast that are developing well. This is a great food wine, with some weight and ripeness. **93** *—R.V. (12/1/2007)*

Pommery 1998 Louise Champagne Blend (Champagne) $180. 91 *—R.V. (11/1/2006)*

Pommery 1990 Louise Champagne Blend (Champagne) $140. 93 Cellar Selection *(12/1/2000)*

Pommery 1989 Louise Champagne Blend (Champagne) $NA. 83 *—R.V. (12/1/2004)*

Pommery 1992 Louise Rosé Champagne Blend (Champagne) $240. 92 *(12/15/2001)*

Pommery NV Pop Extra Dry Champagne Blend (Champagne) $50. It's good that Pommery has given this wine some bottle age, despite the young image the label suggests. The result is dry, but with less fruit and more secondary toast and nut flavors, a finely textured wine. It also has some weight, which balances the acidity well. **89** *—R.V. (12/1/2007)*

Pommery NV Pop Champagne Blend (Champagne) $11. 89 *—R.V. (12/1/2005)*

Pommery NV Pop Rosé Extra Dry Champagne Blend (Champagne) $50. Putting aside the chic lipstick pink bottle (and the pink plastic box it comes in), this is a pleasing, soft wine, with white fruit flavors which lend crisp point to the easy palate. It is certainly dry, but it is also relatively soft, a well thought out blend. **87** *—R.V. (12/1/2007)*

Pommery NV Brut Rosé Champagne Blend (Champagne) $70. This is the palest of pinks. To taste, also, it is more a white than a rosé. There's just that touch of structure to add complexity to the deliciously fresh green-apple fruit flavors. **89** *—R.V. (12/1/2007)*

Pommery NV Summertime Blanc de Blancs Brut Chardonnay (Champagne) $50. This has certainly benefited from some bottle age, bringing out the nutty, lightly toasty character of older Chardonnay, while still preserving great white fruit flavors. **90** *—R.V. (12/1/2007)*

POTEL-AVIRON

Potel-Aviron 2001 Château Gaillard Vieilles Vignes Gamay (Morgon) $19. 85 *—J.C. (11/15/2003)*

Potel-Aviron 2001 Vieilles Vignes Gamay (Moulin-à-Vent) $19. 85 *—J.C. (11/15/2003)*

Potel-Aviron 2000 Vieilles Vignes Gamay (Fleurie) $17. 84 *—M.M. (11/15/2002)*

Potel-Aviron 2001 Gamay (Juliénas) $17. 85 *—J.C. (11/15/2003)*

PREMIÈRE

Première 2004 Chenin Blanc (Vouvray) $13. 83 *—J.C. (8/1/2006)*

PREMIUS

Premius 2005 Bordeaux Blend (Bordeaux) $10. Solid, wood-flavored tannins give this wine a good, smooth texture. Flavors of red cherries dominate what is an attractively fruity wine. **84** *—R.V. (11/1/2007)*

Premius 1998 Bordeaux Blend (Bordeaux) $10. 86 Best Buy *—J.C. (3/1/2001)*

Premius 2005 Merlot-Cabernet Franc (Bordeaux Clairet) $10. A 50-50 blend of Merlot and Cabernet Franc, this isn't as attractive as the other

Clairet bottling from Premius. This one lacks a bit of textural interest, but does feature clean strawberry and raspberry fruit. Imported by Freixenet USA. 83 *—J.C. (7/1/2007)*

Premius 2005 Merlot-Cabernet Sauvignon (Bordeaux Clairet) $10. A 50-50 blend of Merlot and Cabernet Sauvignon, this is a full-bodied rosé. Assertive chocolate and cherry aromas and flavors finish dry and slightly dusty with tannin, making it a solid choice with grilled meats, less so with fish. **86 Best Buy** *—J.C. (7/1/2007)*

Premius 2006 Sauvignon Blanc (Bordeaux Blanc) $10. A creamy textured wine, with fresh green apples, herbs, pink grapefruit and a fresh, crisp zing. It is full-bodied, intense and packed with fruit. **85 Best Buy** *—R.V. (12/31/2007)*

PRIEURÉ DE MONTÉZARGUES

Prieuré de Montézargues 2005 Grenache (Tavel) $24. Tavel is the one rosé which needs an extra year in bottle. This one, with its caramel toffee aroma and dense structure, along with the red berry flavors is now well integrated, all ripe fruits and smoothness. 89 *—R.V. (7/1/2007)*

PRIEURE SAINT-HIPPOLYTE

Prieure Saint-Hippolyte 2004 Rosé Blend (Coteaux du Languedoc) $13. 86 *—J.C. (6/19/2006)*

PRIEURÉ SAINT-SIXTE

Prieuré Saint-Sixte 2005 Cuvée des Premices Rhône Red Blend (Lirac) $NA. 87 *—J.C. (11/15/2006)*

PRODUCTEURS PLAIMONT

Producteurs Plaimont 2006 Colombelle Rosé Rosé Blend (Vin de Pays des Côtes de Gascogne) $8. A blend of Merlot, Tannat and Cabernet Sauvignon from Gascony, this is an attractive but somewhat simple rosé, featuring a plump mouthfeel and herb-tinged cherry-berry flavors. **85 Best Buy** *—J.C. (7/1/2007)*

PROSPER MAUFOUX

Prosper Maufoux 1999 Aligoté (Bourgogne) $11. 84 *(7/1/2001)*

Prosper Maufoux 2005 Chardonnay (Viré-Clessé) $16. 88 *(11/15/2006)*

Prosper Maufoux 2004 Chardonnay (Bourgogne) $12. 84 *(11/15/2006)*

Prosper Maufoux 1998 Chardonnay (Puligny-Montrachet) $55. 88 *(7/1/2001)*

Prosper Maufoux 2003 Comme Dessus Chardonnay (Santenay) $24. 85 *(11/15/2006)*

Prosper Maufoux 1999 Domaine des Combelières Chardonnay (Viré-Clessé) $14. 86 *(7/1/2001)*

Prosper Maufoux 2002 Les Folatieres Premier Cru Chardonnay (Puligny-Montrachet) $72. 87 *(11/15/2006)*

Prosper Maufoux 1999 Mont de Milieu Premier Cru Chardonnay (Chablis) $29. **89 Editors' Choice** *(7/1/2001)*

Prosper Maufoux 2004 Pinot Noir (Bourgogne) $12. 84 *(11/15/2006)*

Prosper Maufoux 1997 Pinot Noir (Gevrey-Chambertin) $40. 87 *(7/1/2001)*

Prosper Maufoux 1997 Bourgogne Pinot Noir (Burgundy) $14. 85 *(11/15/1999)*

Prosper Maufoux 2004 Clos Paradis Premier Cru Pinot Noir (Mercurey) $23. 82 *(11/15/2006)*

Prosper Maufoux 2003 Les Gravieres Premier Cru Pinot Noir (Santenay) $36. 89 *(11/15/2006)*

Prosper Maufoux 2003 Les Gravières Premier Cru Pinot Noir (Santenay) $36. 89 *(11/15/2006)*

Prosper Maufoux 1997 Premier Cru Beaumonts Pinot Noir (Vosne-Romanée) $57. 90 *(7/1/2001)*

Prosper Maufoux 1998 Sauvignon Blanc (Sancerre) $18. 84 *(5/1/2000)*

RAYMOND BECK

Raymond Beck NV Cuvée Prestige Sparkling Blend (Clairette de Die Méthode Dioise Ancestrale) $12. 87 *—P.G. (12/15/2000)*

RAYMOND HENRIOT

Raymond Henriot NV Brut Champagne Blend (France) $21. **94 Editors' Choice** *—P.G. (12/15/2002)*

RED BERET

Red Beret 2004 Rosé Blend (Côtes-du-Rhône) $11. **86 Best Buy** *—J.C. (6/19/2006)*

RED BICYCLETTE

Red Bicyclette 2004 Chardonnay (Vin de Pays d'Oc) $NA. A full, buttery style of Chardonnay, made from grapes grown in the cool Limoux region of Languedoc, soft and ripe. There's spice and toast, with quince and white pear flavors. 85 *—R.V. (12/15/2007)*

Red Bicyclette 2003 Merlot (Vin de Pays d'Oc) $12. 84 *(12/1/2004)*

Red Bicyclette 2005 Rosé Rosé Blend (Vin de Pays d'Oc) $11. Attractive, dry rosé, just brushed with sweetness. Herbs and fresh raspberries give a lift to the wine, while the layer of acidity is still there, leaving an easy, clean aftertaste. 85 *—R.V. (12/15/2007)*

Red Bicyclette 2003 Syrah (Vin de Pays d'Oc) $12. **85 Best Buy** *(12/1/2004)*

RÉGNARD

Régnard 1999 Pinot Noir (Bourgogne) $15. 80 *—J.C. (10/1/2003)*

Régnard 1998 Pinot Noir (Chambolle-Musigny) $57. 89 *—C.S. (11/1/2002)*

Reignac 2001 Blanc Bordeaux White Blend (Bordeaux) 86 *—J.C. (6/1/2005)*

REMY-PANNIER

Remy-Pannier 2005 Cabernet Franc (Chinon) $14. A good, sturdy wine, fruity with blueberries structured with soft tannins. This has some good ripe fruit and a layer of dryness. To finish, there are dry figs and dark plums. 87 *—R.V. (10/1/2007)*

Remy-Pannier 2000 Cabernet Franc (Chinon) $9. 87 *—S.H. (9/12/2002)*

Remy-Pannier 2005 Vallée des Jardins Cabernet Franc (Saumur) $11. Good, spicy Cabernet Franc, loaded with dry plums and stalky fruit flavors. It's soft, with a streak of acidity to give freshness, but mainly juicy and fruity. **86 Best Buy** *—R.V. (10/1/2007)*

Remy-Pannier 2000 Chardonnay (Vin de Pays du Jardin de la France) $6. 87 *—S.H. (9/12/2002)*

Remy-Pannier 2006 Vallée des Jardins Chardonnay (Vin de Pays du Jardin de la France) $10. A soft, smooth, apples-and-cream-flavored wine, shot with acidity and some green fruit. It's a light wine, very crisp and clean, better with food than as an apéritif. 84 *—R.V. (10/1/2007)*

Remy-Pannier 2000 Chenin Blanc (Vouvray) $8. 85 *—S.H. (9/12/2002)*

Remy-Pannier 2006 Haiku Bridge Chenin Blanc (Vin de Pays du Jardin de la France) $10. This is restrained, with very crisp apple-skin acidity, and a generally light, fresh texture. Certainly a food wine. Screwcap. **85 Best Buy** *—R.V. (10/1/2007)*

Remy-Pannier 2006 Vallée des Jardins Chenin Blanc (Vouvray) $12. A medium-sweet wine, with a delicious, sweet, apple flavor, finely balanced with good acidity, and a lifted fresh aftertaste. This makes a great apéritif. **87 Best Buy** *—R.V. (10/1/2007)*

Remy-Pannier 2000 Melon (Muscadet Sèvre Et Maine) $6. 85 *—S.H. (9/12/2002)*

Remy-Pannier 2006 Vallée des Jardins Melon (Muscadet Sèvre Et Maine) $10. Rather fat, this misses the essential freshness of good Muscadet. The flavors are of white pears, a touch of almonds and kiwis; needs more lift. 84 *—R.V. (10/1/2007)*

Remy-Pannier 2006 Vallée des Jardins Rosé Blend (Rosé d'Anjou) $10. On the sweet side, but balanced with acidity, this wine shows all the freshness of just picked strawberries, and a very pure, clean, crisp aftertaste. No pretensions, just pleasure. **85 Best Buy** *—R.V. (7/1/2007)*

Remy-Pannier 2005 Vallée des Jardins Rosé Blend (Rosé d'Anjou) $9. This is a honeyed, rather sweet rosé. Modest peach and cherry fruit turns honeyed on the finish. 81 *—J.C. (7/1/2007)*

Remy-Pannier 2005 Sauvignon Blanc (Pouilly-Fumé) $22. Full, ripe fruit, flavored with green plum skins and gooseberries. There's great fresh acidity, but there is also a good structure suggesting the wine will age another year. Attractive weight as well. 86 *—R.V. (9/1/2007)*

Remy-Pannier 2005 Sauvignon Blanc (Sancerre) $22. Crisp, clean and herbaceous, with grapefruit and citrus flavors. It's a light wine, with good acidity, grassy aromas and the scents of summer flowers. 84 *—R.V. (9/1/2007)*

Remy-Pannier 2005 Sauvignon Blanc (Sancerre) $22. 83 *—R.V. (8/1/2006)*

Remy-Pannier 2000 Sauvignon Blanc (Sancerre) $13. 86 *—S.H. (9/12/2002)*

Remy-Pannier 2006 Vallée des Jardins Sauvignon Blanc (Touraine) $11. A classically crisp, herbaceous wine, full of poised fruit, flavors of pink grapefruit and acidity. There's a good texture, touch of tannins, white pear skins. Screwcap. **87 Best Buy** *—R.V. (9/1/2007)*

RENE GEOFFROY

Rene Geoffroy NV Cuvée Prestige Premier Cru Brut Champagne Blend (Champagne) $51. 84 *—R.V. (12/1/2002)*

RENÉ MURÉ

René Muré NV Champagne Blend (Crémant d'Alsace) $20. 89 *—R.V. (6/1/2006)*

René Muré 2000 Domaine du Clos St Landelin Vendanges Tardives Grand Cru Vorbourg Gewürztraminer (Alsace) $45. 91 *—M.S. (6/1/2003)*

René Muré 2002 Clos de Rouffach Riesling (Alsace) $17. 91 Editors' Choice *—R.V. (11/1/2005)*

René Muré 2002 Grand Cru Clos Saint Landelin Riesling (Alsace) $50. 94 Cellar Selection *—R.V. (11/1/2005)*

René Muré 2004 Tradition Riesling (Alsace) $23. A beautiful example of Alsace Riesling. Notes of honey, petrol and sweet spice invite you in to a full-bodied mouthful of minerality, honeydew and baked apple. The crisp acidity complements the inherent sweeter characteristics of the wine, bringing everything into perfect harmony. With a clean, lingering finish, this Riesling only leaves you ready for more. **90 Editors' Choice** *(9/1/2007)*

RENE-NOEL LEGRAND

Rene-Noel Legrand 2004 Les Rogelins Cabernet Franc (Saumur-Champigny) $NA. Legrand's top wine needs aging, as it is a little austere when young. But to compensate there are some good red berry fruits, with fresh layers of acidity. The aromas, too, are already enticing. There is a touch of toast, finishing with red currants and cranberries. **89** *—R.V. (4/1/2007)*

Rene-Noel Legrand 2005 Les Terrages Cabernet Franc (Saumur-Champigny) $NA. A big, firm wine, matured in stainless steel and packed with fruit tannins and dry layers. But between these are great red fruits, depth of flavor and some velvet ripeness. This wine could age for a year. **87** *—R.V. (4/1/2007)*

RESERVE ST. MARTIN

Reserve St. Martin 2002 Cabernet Sauvignon (Vin de Pays d'Oc) $8. 82 *—R.V. (12/1/2004)*

Reserve St. Martin 2003 Merlot (Vin de Pays d'Oc) $8. 84 Best Buy *—R.V. (12/1/2004)*

Reserve St. Martin 2005 Rosé Syrah (Vin de Pays d'Oc) $7. 86 Best Buy *—J.C. (6/21/2006)*

RICHARD BOURGEOIS

Richard Bourgeois 2005 Sauvignon Blanc (Sancerre) $19. 84 *—R.V. (8/1/2006)*

RIEFLÉ

Rieflé 2004 Classique Pinot Blanc (Alsace) $20. With its slightly petrol-like aromas and baked-apple flavors, this could almost pass for Riesling, but for its plump, juicy texture. Finishes with hints of honey, cinnamon and clove that lend added interest. Drink now. **88** *—J.C. (7/1/2007)*

Rieflé 2004 Classique Pinot Gris (Alsace) $25. 85 *—R.V. (2/1/2006)*

Rieflé 2003 Grand Cru Steinert Pinot Gris (Alsace) $40. 91 *—R.V. (2/1/2006)*

Rieflé 1997 Côte de Rouffach Tokay Pinot Gris (Alsace) $19. 88 *—M.M. (11/1/2000)*

Rieflé 1996 Steinert Tokay Pinot Gris (Alsace) $30. 89 *—J.C. (11/1/2000)*

RIVEFORT DE FRANCE

Rivefort de France 1997 Viognier (Vin de Pays d'Oc) $10. 81 *—J.C. (10/1/1999)*

ROBERT GIRAUD

Robert Giraud 2000 Cepages Cabernet Sauvignon (Vin de Pays d'Oc) $7. 81 *—M.S. (9/1/2003)*

ROC DE CAMBES

Roc de Cambes 1996 Bordeaux Blend (Côtes de Bourg) $29. 90 *—M.S. (12/31/1999)*

ROPITEAU

Ropiteau 2000 Les Perrieres Chardonnay (Meursault) $49. 90 *(10/1/2002)*

Ropiteau 2000 Les Tillets Chardonnay (Meursault) $37. 88 *(10/1/2002)*

Ropiteau 2000 Meursault de Ropiteau Chardonnay (Meursault) $32. 85 *(10/1/2002)*

Ropiteau 2000 Premier Cru Chardonnay (Rully) $18. 86 *(10/1/2002)*

Ropiteau 2000 Pinot Noir (Chassagne-Montrachet) $18. 84 *(10/1/2002)*

ROUX PÈRE ET FILS

Roux Père et Fils 2005 Chardonnay (Chablis) $19. 85 *—R.V. (12/1/2006)*

Roux Père et Fils 2004 Chardonnay (Meursault) $39. 89 *—R.V. (12/1/2006)*

Roux Père et Fils 2004 La Pucelle Chardonnay (St.-Aubin) $28. 88 *—R.V. (12/1/2006)*

Roux Père et Fils 2004 Les Cortons Premier Cru Chardonnay (St.-Aubin) $42. 90 *—R.V. (12/1/2006)*

Roux Père et Fils 2005 Les Murelles Chardonnay (Bourgogne) $12. 85 *—R.V. (12/1/2006)*

Roux Père et Fils 2004 Pinot Noir (Gevrey-Chambertin) $39. A firm, solid wine with dry layers of tannin between the red berry and plum fruit flavors. There's plenty of the right richness, along with acidity, and some bold textures. For a village wine, this is just right. **88** *—R.V. (3/1/2007)*

Roux Père et Fils 2004 Corton Les Renardes Grand Cru Pinot Noir (Corton Les Renardes) $99. From high above the village of Ladoix, at the end of the run of grand crus on the Corton hill, this Les Renardes is in a soft style: It's open, generous, full of red fruit flavors and soft, dusty tannins. It's already delicious, a great mouthful of fruit and ripeness. **92** *—R.V. (3/1/2007)*

RUINART

Ruinart NV Brut Champagne Blend (Champagne) $48. 88 *(12/1/2003)*

Ruinart NV Brut Champagne Blend (Champagne) $48. 87 *—J.C. (12/15/2001)*

Ruinart NV Brut Rosé Champagne Blend (Champagne) $83. 87 *—J.C. (12/15/2001)*

Ruinart NV Brut Rosé Champagne Blend (Champagne) $83. 87 *(12/1/2003)*

Ruinart 1993 Dom Ruinart Champagne Blend (Champagne) $130. 92 Cellar Selection *(12/31/2003)*

Ruinart 1990 Dom Ruinart Brut Rosé Champagne Blend (Champagne) $NA. 91 *—R.V. (12/1/2004)*

Ruinart 1993 R de Ruinart Brut Champagne Blend (Champagne) $72. 82 *(12/15/1999)*

Ruinart NV Blanc de Blancs Brut Chardonnay (Champagne) $65. Toasty, floral and full-bodied, with a soft aftertaste, this has a great aromatic swathe initially, with only hints of Chardonnay minerality. The wine is delicious, with ripe white fruits and light acidity to finish. **89** *—R.V. (12/31/2007)*

Ruinart 1996 Dom Ruinart Blanc de Blancs Brut Chardonnay (Champagne) $180. Made entirely from grand cru grapes, this is a beautiful wine, layering toast and ripe fruit with a proper minerality from the year. Flavors of honey, toast and nougat soften the aftertaste. It is ready to drink now, but it has still a ways to go, as the intense concentration of fruit opens out. **93** *—R.V. (12/31/2007)*

Ruinart 1990 Dom Ruinart Blanc de Blancs Brut Chardonnay (Champagne) $130. 86 *—J.C. (12/15/2001)*

SAINT COSME

Saint Cosme 2005 Les Deux Albion Rhône Red Blend (Côtes-du-Rhône) $20. 89 *—J.C. (11/15/2006)*

Saint Cosme 2005 Syrah (Côtes-du-Rhône) $15. 88 *—J.C. (11/15/2006)*

Saint Cosme 2004 Syrah (Saint-Joseph) $35. 88 *—J.C. (11/15/2006)*

SAINT SAVIN

Saint Savin 2003 Bordeaux White Blend (Bordeaux) $11. 83 *—J.C. (6/1/2005)*

SAINT-HILAIRE

Saint-Hilaire 2002 Blanc de Blancs Brut Sparkling Blend (Blanquette de Limoux) $12. 87 Best Buy *—M.S. (12/31/2005)*

SALON LE MESNIL

Salon Le Mesnil 1996 Blanc de Blancs Chardonnay (Champagne) $350. The latest release from Salon, this just explodes in the mouth with mineral, steel and flint. The tiny mousse has flavors of yeast and just a touch of toast. It is rich, but so austere and structured. Like many Salon Champagnes, this will age for 20 years or more. **97** *—R.V. (12/31/2007)*

Salon Le Mesnil 1996 Blanc de Blancs Brut Chardonnay (Champagne) $300. 95 Editors' Choice *—R.V. (11/1/2006)*

Salon Le Mesnil 1995 Blanc de Blancs Brut Chardonnay (Champagne) $225. 97 *—M.S. (12/31/2005)*

Salon Le Mesnil 1990 Blanc de Blancs Brut Chardonnay (Champagne) $200. 91 *(12/15/2001)*

Salon Le Mesnil 1985 Blanc de Blancs Brut Chardonnay (Champagne)

$216. 96 *(12/1/2000)*

SANTA DUC

Santa Duc 2003 Les Buissons Cairanne Rhône Red Blend (Côtes-du-Rhône Villages) $17. 90 Editors' Choice *—J.C. (11/15/2006)*

SAUVION

Sauvion 2005 Rosé d'Anjou Cabernet Franc (Anjou) $11. A simple wine, with scents of peach and cantaloupe and sweet fruity flavors that seem slightly cloying on the finish. 82 *—J.C. (7/1/2007)*

Sauvion 2003 Baronne du Cléray Melon (Muscadet Sèvre Et Maine) $NA. 86 *—R.V. (1/1/2004)*

Sauvion 2001 Sauvignon Blanc (Sancerre) $15. 83 *(8/1/2002)*

SCHRÖDER ET SCHYLER

Schröder et Schyler 2003 Signatures en White Blend (Bordeaux) $NA. 84 *—R.V. (6/1/2005)*

SEIGNEURS DE BERGERAC

Seigneurs de Bergerac 2006 Rosé Rosé Blend (Bergerac) $10. This bright pink rosé is a blend of 50% Merlot, 40% Cabernet Sauvignon and 10% Cabernet Franc, and its varietal makeup shows in its slightly herbal aromas and flavors. But there's also plenty of watermelon and cherry-berry fruit. It's a fruit-forward wine that's not simply fruity, with the herbal notes lending freshness to the finish. 87 Best Buy *—J.C. (7/1/2007)*

Seigneurs de Bergerac 2002 White Blend (Bergerac Sec) $8. 80 *—J.C. (12/1/2004)*

SERGE DAGUENEAU ET FILLES

Serge Dagueneau et Filles 2006 Les Pentes Sauvignon Blanc (Pouilly-Fumé) $23. A delicious and richly creamy wine, full-bodied, with green plum and pink grapefruit flavors. There's freshness, but also power. Still young, just bottled, this wine will develop over 4–5 years. Les Pentes, slopes, refers to the slope of the vineyard. 90 *—R.V. (9/1/2007)*

SERGE MATHIEU

Serge Mathieu NV Blanc de Noirs Cuvée Tradition Brut Champagne Blend (Champagne) $30. 89 *—R.V. (12/1/2002)*

Serge Mathieu NV Cuvée Prestige Brut Champagne Blend (Champagne) $34. 91 *—R.V. (12/1/2002)*

SIEUR D'ARQUES

Sieur d'Arques 2001 Vichon Mediterranean Chardonnay (Vin de Pays d'Oc) $7. 85 Best Buy *—R.V. (11/15/2002)*

Sieur d'Arques 2000 Grande Cuvée Millénaire Sparkling Blend (Crémant de Limoux) $NA. 89 *—R.V. (6/1/2006)*

Sieur d'Arques NV Toques et Clochers Sparkling Blend (Crémant de Limoux) $16. 86 *—J.C. (12/31/2004)*

SIMONNET-FEBVRE

Simonnet-Febvre 1999 Chevaliere (Vin de Table) Bordeaux Blend (France) $8. 86 *—P.G. (11/1/2002)*

Simonnet-Febvre 1999 Red Blend (Bourgogne) $15. 85 *—P.G. (11/1/2002)*

SIRIUS

Sirius 2003 Bordeaux Blend (Bordeaux) $NA. Shows how good branded Bordeaux can be if the vinification was done carefully. A 50-50 blend of Merlot and Cab Sauvignon backed up by wood and balanced with red fruits, black cherries and some dense fruit tannins. 88 *—R.V. (11/1/2007)*

TAITTINGER

Taittinger 1999 Brut Champagne Blend (Champagne) $65. 92 *—R.V. (11/1/2006)*

Taittinger 1998 Brut Champagne Blend (Champagne) $70. 88 *—R.V. (12/1/2004)*

Taittinger 1995 Brut Champagne Blend (Champagne) $56. 92 *—P.G. (12/1/2000)*

Taittinger 1996 Comtes de Champagne Blanc de Blancs Brut Champagne Blend (Champagne) $130. 90 *—P.G. (12/15/2003)*

Taittinger 1995 Comtes de Champagne Blanc de Blancs Brut Champagne Blend (Champagne) $130. 90 *—P.G. (12/15/2002)*

Taittinger 1994 Comtes de Champagne Blanc de Blancs Brut Champagne Blend (Champagne) $170. 89 *(12/31/2000)*

Taittinger 1999 Comtes de Champagne Brut Rosé Champagne Blend (Champagne) $210. 92 *—R.V. (11/1/2006)*

Taittinger 1995 Comtes de Champagne Brut Rosé Champagne Blend (Champagne) $204. 95 *—M.S. (12/15/2000)*

Taittinger NV La Française Brut Champagne Blend (Champagne) $35. 91 *—P.G. (12/1/2006)*

Taittinger NV La Française Brut Champagne Blend (Champagne) $43. 92 *—S.H. (12/1/2000)*

Taittinger NV La Française Brut Champagne Blend (Champagne) $35. 91 *—P.G. (12/15/2002)*

Taittinger NV La Française Brut Champagne Blend (Champagne) $45. 85 *(12/15/1999)*

Taittinger NV Prélude Grands Crus Brut Champagne Blend (Champagne) $70. 94 Cellar Selection *—R.V. (12/1/2005)*

Taittinger NV Prélude Grands Crus Brut Champagne Blend (Champagne) $65. 88 *—M.S. (12/15/2003)*

Taittinger NV Prestige Brut Rosé Champagne Blend (Champagne) $70. 89 *—R.V. (12/1/2005)*

Taittinger NV Prestige Brut Rosé Champagne Blend (Champagne) $52. 88 *—J.C. (12/15/2000)*

Taittinger 1998 Comtes de Champagne Blanc de Blancs Brut Chardonnay (Champagne) $150. 94 *—R.V. (11/1/2006)*

TARDIEU-LAURENT

Tardieu-Laurent 2004 Guy-Louis Rhône Red Blend (Côtes-du-Rhône) $24. 87 *—J.C. (11/15/2006)*

Tardieu-Laurent 2004 Vieilles Vignes Rhône Red Blend (Gigondas) $34. 88 *—J.C. (11/15/2006)*

TARLANT

Tarlant 1997 Brut Prestige Champagne Blend (Champagne) $60. Look beyond the grapes and leaves which decorate the bottle. This is a solidly ripe wine, dominated by Chardonnay, full of generous fruit, but not losing sight of its elegance and creaminess. This could age for a couple more years, but is ready now. 91 *—R.V. (2/1/2007)*

TERRE DE MISTRAL

Terre de Mistral 2004 Red Blend (Côtes-du-Rhône) $11. 85 *—J.C. (11/15/2006)*

TERRES NOIRES

Terres Noires 2003 Chardonnay (Vin de Pays d'Oc) $NA. 83 *—R.V. (12/1/2004)*

THE FRENCHHOUSE

The Frenchhouse 2005 Rosé Rosé Blend (Vin de Pays d'Oc) $10. A fresh, medium-bodied rosé filled with mixed berries, this is an easy-drinking wine perfect for poolside sipping. No, it's not complex, but it's clean, refreshing and inexpensive. 84 *—J.C. (7/1/2007)*

THIERRY & GUY

Thierry & Guy 2003 Fat Bastard Chardonnay (Vin de Pays d'Oc) $11. 83 *—J.C. (11/15/2005)*

Thierry & Guy 2000 Fat Bastard Shiraz (Vin de Pays d'Oc) $10. 83 *(10/1/2001)*

THIERRY ALLEMAND

Thierry Allemand 2004 Chaillot Syrah (Cornas) $78. From the domaine's young vines, this offering features somewhat restrained aromatics, with just traces of violets and blackberries. But on the palate there's plenty of cassis fruit. No, it's not that rich or lush, but it's pure, supple and easy to drink right out of the gate. Drink now–2012. 87 *—J.C. (9/1/2007)*

Thierry Allemand 2004 Reynard Syrah (Cornas) $96. A step up from Allemand's Chaillot bottling, the 2004 Reynard boasts more intense cassis fruit and even some licorice and spice notes. It's rich, layered and tannic, needing some time to show its best. Drink 2010–2020. 90 *—J.C. (9/1/2007)*

TOQUES ET CLOCHERS

Toques et Clochers 2003 Clocher D'Ajac Reserve Jean-Pierre Bourret Vigneron Chardonnay (Limoux) $33. 83 *—J.C. (11/15/2005)*

Toques et Clochers 2003 Merlot-Syrah-Grenache Red Blend (Limoux) $15. 86 *—J.C. (11/15/2005)*

TORTOISE CREEK

Tortoise Creek 2004 Chardonnay (Vin de Pays d'Oc) $9. 84 *—J.C. (11/15/2005)*

Tortoise Creek 2004 Chardonnay-Viognier (Vin de Pays d'Oc) $8. 85 Best Buy *—J.C. (11/15/2005)*

Tortoise Creek 2005 Merlot (Vin de Pays d'Oc) $9. For consumers seeking inexpensive yet varietally true wines, Tortoise Creek has scored with the 2005 vintage. The Merlot may be the richest and longest of their red wine offerings, with impressive black cherry aromas backed by flavors of blackberry and espresso. Drink now. **85 Best Buy** *—J.C. (4/1/2007)*

Tortoise Creek 2003 Merlot (Vin de Pays d'Oc) $8. **86 Best Buy** *—J.C. (12/1/2004)*

Tortoise Creek 2005 Pinot Noir (Vin de Pays d'Oc) $9. A fresh, red-fruited wine with supple tannins, this will scratch your itch for inexpensive Pinot Noir. It's medium-bodied, with simple cherry-berry aromas and flavors. Drink now. **84** *—J.C. (4/1/2007)*

Tortoise Creek 2000 Les Ámoureux Red Blend (Vin de Pays d'Oc) $8. **80** *—M.M. (2/1/2002)*

Tortoise Creek 2006 Rosé d'Une Nuit Rosé Blend (Vin de Pays d'Oc) $10. Easy, soft, crisp fruit, just sweetened to finish. Attractive red currant fruit flavors add to a simple, drinkable wine. Screwcap. **83** *—R.V. (7/1/2007)*

Tortoise Creek 2003 Sauvignon Blanc (Vin de Pays d'Oc) $8. **84 Best Buy** *—J.C. (12/1/2004)*

Tortoise Creek 2000 Les Ámoureux Sauvignon Blanc (Vin de Pays d'Oc) $8. **83** *—M.M. (2/1/2002)*

Tortoise Creek 2005 Syrah (Vin de Pays d'Oc) $9. A fruit-forward, friendly wine that boasts admirably concentrated cassis and blackberry flavors. It's medium-bodied, with enough supple tannin to accompany burgers and the like. **85 Best Buy** *—J.C. (4/1/2007)*

Tortoise Creek 2000 Les Ámoureux White Blend (Vin de Pays d'Oc) $8. **84** *—M.M. (2/1/2002)*

TRIENNES

Triennes 1996 Syrah (Vin de Pays Var) $15. **89** *(11/15/1999)*

TRIMBACH

Trimbach 2000 Gewürztraminer (Alsace) $18. **86** *(1/1/2004)*

Trimbach 1994 Selection de Grains Nobles Gewürztraminer (Alsace) $130. **92** *(1/1/2004)*

Trimbach 2001 Pinot Blanc (Alsace) $11. **85** *—R.V. (11/15/2003)*

Trimbach 2000 Hommage à Jeanne Pinot Gris (Alsace) $60. **92** *—R.V. (2/1/2006)*

Trimbach 2002 Réserve Pinot Gris (Alsace) $20. **87** *—R.V. (2/1/2006)*

Trimbach 1997 Reserve Personnelle Pinot Gris (Alsace) $40. **90** *(1/1/2004)*

Trimbach 2000 Sélection de Grains Nobles Pinot Gris (Alsace) $150. **94** *—R.V. (2/1/2006)*

Trimbach 2002 Riesling (Alsace) $17. **88** *—R.V. (11/1/2005)*

Trimbach 1998 Clos Ste Hune Riesling (Alsace) $100. **93** *(1/1/2004)*

Trimbach 2001 Cuvée Frédéric Emile Grand Cru Riesling (Alsace) $40. Well balanced with medium weight, this conjures up notes of honey, bergamot, lime pith and red apple. A tangy, medium-length finish brings it all together. Imported by Diageo Chateau & Estate Wines. **86** *(9/1/2007)*

Trimbach 2000 Cuvée Frédéric Emile Riesling (Alsace) $42. **95** *—R.V. (11/1/2005)*

Trimbach 2002 Réserve Riesling (Alsace) $20. **90 Editors' Choice** *—R.V. (11/1/2005)*

VAL D'ORBIEU

Val d'Orbieu 2001 Reserve St. Martin Cabernet Sauvignon (Languedoc) $8. **82** *—M.S. (9/1/2003)*

Val d'Orbieu 2001 Reserve St. Martin Merlot (Languedoc) $8. **83** *—M.S. (9/1/2003)*

Val d'Orbieu 2001 Les Deux Rives Rouge Red Blend (Corbières) $8. **84** *—M.S. (9/1/2003)*

Val d'Orbieu 2001 Reserve St. Martin Syrah (Languedoc) $8. **82** *—M.S. (9/1/2003)*

Val d'Orbieu 2001 Les Deux Rives Blanc White Blend (Corbières) $8. **84** *—M.S. (9/1/2003)*

VERBAU

Verbau 2000 Cabernet Sauvignon (Bordeaux) $12. **83** *—M.S. (6/1/2003)*

Verbau 2001 Grand Cru Gewürztraminer (Alsace) $12. **87 Best Buy** *—M.S. (6/1/2003)*

VEUVE AMBAL

Veuve Ambal NV Blanc de Blancs Brut Sparkling Blend (Vin Mousseux) $13. **85** *—R.V. (6/1/2006)*

VEUVE CLICQUOT PONSARDIN

Veuve Clicquot Ponsardin NV Brut Champagne Blend (Champagne) $50. **87** *—J.C. (12/1/2004)*

Veuve Clicquot Ponsardin NV Brut Champagne Blend (Champagne) $50. **88** *—P.G. (12/1/2006)*

Veuve Clicquot Ponsardin 1998 Brut Champagne Blend (Champagne) $76. **89** *(12/1/2005)*

Veuve Clicquot Ponsardin NV Brut Rosé Champagne Blend (Champagne) $50. **88** *—P.G. (12/1/2006)*

Veuve Clicquot Ponsardin 1985 Brut Rosé Champagne Blend (Champagne) $250. **93** *(12/1/2005)*

Veuve Clicquot Ponsardin NV Demi-Sec Champagne Blend (Champagne) $50. **87** *(12/1/2005)*

Veuve Clicquot Ponsardin 1998 La Grande Dame Brut Champagne Blend (Champagne) $120. **92** *—R.V. (11/1/2006)*

Veuve Clicquot Ponsardin 1996 La Grande Dame Brut Champagne Blend (Champagne) $150. **91 Cellar Selection** *—J.C. (12/1/2004)*

Veuve Clicquot Ponsardin 1993 La Grande Dame Brut Champagne Blend (Champagne) $150. **91 Cellar Selection** *(12/15/2001)*

Veuve Clicquot Ponsardin 1989 La Grande Dame Brut Champagne Blend (Champagne) $NA. **90** *(12/1/2005)*

Veuve Clicquot Ponsardin 1995 La Grande Dame Brut Rosé Champagne Blend (Champagne) $200. **92** *(12/1/2005)*

Veuve Clicquot Ponsardin 1995 La Grande Dame Brut Rosé Champagne Blend (Champagne) $230. **92** *—P.G. (12/15/2003)*

Veuve Clicquot Ponsardin 1998 Réserve Brut Champagne Blend (Champagne) $75. **90** *—J.C. (12/1/2004)*

Veuve Clicquot Ponsardin 1995 Réserve Brut Champagne Blend (Champagne) $68. **88** *(12/15/2001)*

Veuve Clicquot Ponsardin 1999 Réserve Brut Rosé Champagne Blend (Champagne) $86. **89** *(12/1/2005)*

Veuve Clicquot Ponsardin 1996 Réserve Brut Rosé Champagne Blend (Champagne) $75. **89** *—P.G. (12/15/2003)*

Veuve Clicquot Ponsardin 1993 Réserve Brut Rosé Champagne Blend (Champagne) $75. **92** *—M.S. (12/1/1999)*

Veuve Clicquot Ponsardin NV Yellow Label Brut Champagne Blend (Champagne) $50. **88** *—P.G. (12/15/2003)*

VEUVE DU VERNAY

Veuve du Vernay NV Blanc de Blancs Brut Champagne Blend (Bordeaux) $10. **86 Best Buy** *—M.M. (12/31/2000)*

Veuve du Vernay NV Brut Blanc de Blancs Champagne Blend (France) $10. **84** *—P.G. (12/15/2002)*

VF

VF 2002 Lasira Red Wine Rhône Red Blend (Costières de Nimes) $9. **88 Best Buy** *—P.G. (11/15/2004)*

VICHON

Vichon 1997 Mediterranean Chardonnay (Vin de Pays d'Oc) $10. **82** *—S.H. (7/1/2000)*

Vichon 1998 Mediterranean Sauvignon Blanc (Vin de Pays d'Oc) $10. **82** *—S.H. (7/1/2000)*

VIEUX CHÂTEAU CERTAN

Vieux Château Certan 2006 Barrel Sample Bordeaux Blend (Pomerol) $NA. 95-97 Barrel Sample. A ripe, perfumed wine with spice and sweet, delicious fruit, sustained by dense, opulent tannins and red fruits. A greater dominance of Merlot in the wine in 2006 has resulted in a richer, fatter wine than usual. **96** *—R.V. (6/1/2007)*

VIEUX CHÂTEAU GAUBERT

Vieux Château Gaubert 2003 Benjamin Bordeaux White Blend (Graves) $14. **87** *—R.V. (6/1/2005)*

VIGNERONS DE BUZET

Vignerons de Buzet 2000 Baron d'Ardeuil Bordeaux Blend (Buzet) $15. **88** *—R.V. (3/1/2006)*

Vignerons de Buzet 2003 Château de Padère Bordeaux Blend (Buzet) $NA. **89** *—R.V. (9/1/2005)*

Vignerons de Buzet 2004 Le Lys Bordeaux Blend (Buzet) $NA. **85** *—R.V. (9/1/2005)*

VIGNERONS DE CARACTERE

Vignerons de Caractere 2001 Bois du Ménestral Rhône Red Blend (Vacqueyras) $16. 84 —*J.C. (11/15/2006)*

Vignerons de Caractere 2004 Domaine Mas du Bouquet Rhône Red Blend (Vacqueyras) $16. 83 —*J.C. (11/15/2006)*

Vignerons de Caractere 2004 Les Hautes Restangues Rhône Red Blend (Gigondas) $18. 84 —*J.C. (11/15/2006)*

Vignerons de Caractere 2004 Privilege des Vignerons Rhône Red Blend (Côtes-du-Rhône) $NA. 83 —*J.C. (11/15/2006)*

VIGNERONS DE GRIMAUD

Vignerons de Grimaud 2006 Cuvée du Golfe de Saint-Tropez Rosé Blend (Côtes de Provence) $NA. Talk about riding on the back of a famous name, but to be fair Grimaud village does overlook Saint-Tropez. Sadly, the wine lacks the pizazz of high society, a flat, simple wine that is clean but not much else. 82 —*R.V. (7/1/2007)*

VIGNOBLES ALAIN JAUME & FILS

Vignobles Alain Jaume & Fils 2005 Clos de Sixte Rhône Red Blend (Lirac) $23. 92 **Editors' Choice** —*J.C. (11/15/2006)*

Vignobles Alain Jaume & Fils 2004 Grande Garrigue Rhône Red Blend (Vacqueyras) $19. 89 —*J.C. (11/15/2006)*

Vignobles Alain Jaume & Fils 2004 Clos de Sixte Rosé Blend (Lirac) $23. 86 —*J.C. (11/15/2006)*

VIGNOBLES COSTE

Vignobles Coste 2004 Domaine de la Charité Rhône Red Blend (Côtes-du-Rhône) $13. 84 —*J.C. (11/15/2006)*

VIGNOBLES DE FRANCE

Vignobles de France 2000 Cabernet Sauvignon (Vin de Pays d'Oc) $6. 80 —*S.H. (7/1/2001)*

Vignobles de France 2000 Merlot (Vin de Pays d'Oc) $6. 82 —*S.H. (7/1/2001)*

Vignobles de France 2000 Sauvignon Blanc (Entre-Deux-Mers) $7. 83 —*S.H. (7/1/2001)*

VILLA SYMPOSIA

Villa Symposia 2003 Red Blend (Coteaux du Languedoc) $NA. 92 —*R.V. (12/1/2004)*

Villa Symposia 2003 White Blend (Coteaux du Languedoc) $10. 88 **Best Buy** —*R.V. (12/1/2004)*

VINCENT DELAPORTE

Vincent Delaporte 2003 Chavignol Sauvignon Blanc (Sancerre) $26. 89 *(7/1/2005)*

VINSOBRAISE

Vinsobraise 2005 Cuvée Ambre Rhône Red Blend (Vinsobres) $NA. 83 —*J.C. (11/15/2006)*

Vinsobraise 2005 Cuvée Grenat Rhône Red Blend (Vinsobres) $NA. 84 —*J.C. (11/15/2006)*

VITTEAUT-ALBERTI

Vitteaut-Alberti NV Blanc de Blancs Sparkling Blend (Crémant de Bourgogne) $19. 87 —*R.V. (6/1/2006)*

VRANKEN

Vranken 2000 Demoiselle Brut Champagne Blend (Champagne) $100. 85 —*R.V. (11/1/2006)*

Vranken 2000 Demoiselle La Parisienne Premier Cru Brut Champagne Blend (Champagne) $120. A rich wine, creamy, with nut and toast flavors following fresher, crisper aromas. It is softening and coming well into its own, but still keeping a fine structure, along with ripe apple tastes. This should certainly develop further. 90 —*R.V. (12/1/2007)*

Vranken NV Demoiselle Brut Rosé Champagne Blend (Champagne) $38. 86 —*P.G. (12/15/2002)*

Vranken NV Demoiselle Cuvée 2000 Blanc de Blancs Champagne Blend (Champagne) $30. 88 *(12/15/1999)*

Vranken 1995 Demoiselle Cuvée 21 Champagne Blend (Champagne) $80. 86 —*P.G. (12/15/2003)*

Vranken NV Demoiselle E.O. Tête de Cuvée Brut Champagne Blend (Champagne) $35. 87 —*J.C. (12/1/2004)*

Vranken NV Demoiselle E.O. Tête de Cuvée Brut Champagne Blend (Champagne) $33. 84 —*R.V. (12/1/2005)*

Vranken NV Demoiselle Grande Cuvée Brut Rosé Champagne Blend (Champagne) $45. 86 —*J.C. (12/1/2004)*

Vranken NV Demoiselle Grande Cuvée Brut Rosé Champagne Blend (Champagne) $43. 86 —*P.G. (12/15/2003)*

Vranken NV Demoiselle Premier Choix de Cuvées Brut Champagne Blend (Champagne) $30. 88 —*P.G. (12/15/2002)*

Vranken 1996 Demoiselle Tête de Cuvée Champagne Blend (Champagne) $90. 87 —*R.V. (12/1/2004)*

Vranken 1994 Demoiselle Tête de Cuvée Grand Reserve Brut Champagne Blend (Champagne) $30. 85 —*P.G. (12/15/2002)*

Vranken 1999 Diamant Blanc Champagne Blend (Champagne) $120. 88 —*R.V. (11/1/2006)*

Vranken NV Diamant Brut Champagne Blend (Champagne) $50. For those who like their non-vintage with some bottle age, this is a fine wine. While it has lost its early freshness, it certainly has gained in complexity, offering ripe, soft, toasty flavors to add to the green plum fruits and acidity. 89 —*R.V. (12/1/2007)*

Vranken 1998 Diamant Rosé Brut Champagne Blend (Champagne) $160. A mature, toasty wine, perhaps too toasty. There are still hints of ripe strawberries as well as the more mature flavors. The wine shows a full-bodied character and an attractive onion skin color. 86 —*R.V. (12/1/2007)*

Vranken 1998 Diamant Rosé Champagne Blend (Champagne) $135. 85 —*R.V. (11/1/2006)*

Vranken NV La Demoiselle de Champagne Rosé Brut Champagne Blend (Champagne) $50. Considerable bottle aging shows with the nutty, toasty flavors of this wine. The fruit has gone, leaving structured maturity, somewhat austere, but a definite appeal to those who like older Champagne. 85 —*R.V. (12/1/2007)*

Vranken NV La Demoiselle de Champagne Tête de Cuvée Champagne Blend (Champagne) $37. Fully rounded, and crisply dry, this has a great foamy, creamy texture, filled out with red apple skins, pink grapefruit and an open aftertaste. Is the aftertaste just a touch sweet? Perhaps, but that seems to be part of the balance, and not out of place. 89 —*R.V. (12/1/2007)*

Vranken NV Tête de Cuvée Tradition Grande Reserve Champagne Blend (Champagne) $22. 88 **Editors' Choice** —*P.G. (12/15/2003)*

Vranken 1999 Diamant Blanc Brut Chardonnay (Champagne) $140. A soft, very open, lightweight wine, that has some richness along with its white fruits. It tastes sweet, from what appears to be a relatively high dosage. 85 —*R.V. (12/1/2007)*

W. GISSELBRECHT

W. Gisselbrecht 2002 Franstein Grand Cru Gewürztraminer (Alsace) $25. 87 —*J.C. (8/1/2006)*

W. Gisselbrecht 2005 Pinot Blanc (Alsace) $11. A light, dry style of Pinot Blanc, with apple, melon and mineral hints backed by citrus and wet stones that finish crisp and dry. As prices for Riesling and Pinot Gris have edged upward, Pinot Blanc has remained the bargain variety of Alsace, and this is a solid example, best served as an apéritif or with light fish dishes. 87 **Best Buy** —*J.C. (7/1/2007)*

W. Gisselbrecht 2004 Pinot Blanc (Alsace) $11. 87 **Best Buy** —*J.C. (8/1/2006)*

W. Gisselbrecht 2005 Riesling (Alsace) $12. Inherent wet stone and lively citrus entice you with the promise of refreshment. The palate delivers as well with bright green apple and lemon rind. Plump and medium weight in the mouth, it finishes as clean and minerally as anticipated. Imported by Paramount Brands. 87 **Best Buy** *(9/1/2007)*

W. Gisselbrecht 2002 Grand Cru Muenchberg Riesling (Alsace) $21. 85 —*J.C. (8/1/2006)*

WILLM

Willm 2004 Pinot Blanc (Alsace) $12. 85 —*J.C. (8/1/2006)*

Willm 2004 Pinot Gris (Alsace) $15. 86 —*R.V. (2/1/2006)*

Willm NV Blanc de Noirs Pinot Noir (Crémant d'Alsace) $15. 87 —*M.S. (6/1/2003)*

WOLFBERGER

Wolfberger NV Sparkling Blend (Crémant d'Alsace) $19. 84 —*R.V. (6/1/2006)*

YANN CHAVE

Yann Chave 2005 Cuvée Traditionnelle Syrah (Crozes-Hermitage) $NA. 86 —*J.C. (11/15/2006)*

YANNICK AMIRAULT

Yannick Amirault 2005 Les Malgagnes Cabernet Franc (Saint-Nicolas-de-Bourgueil) $NA. This is Amirault's top wine from St-Nicolas. For an appellation normally seen as making light wines, this is stunning. There are dense, dusty tannins, layers of blackberry jelly flavors and rich wood tastes that balance with the fruit. **93 Editors' Choice** —*R.V. (4/1/2007)*

Yannick Amirault 2005 Les Quartiers Cabernet Franc (Bourgueil) $NA. From 40-year-old Cabernet Franc vines, this impressive wine rolls around the mouth. There is a touch of mint and spicy wood that coat the core of intense black fruits and rich tannins. Big and fruity, but with its tannins, this is likely to age well. **92** —*R.V. (4/1/2007)*

YVECOURT

Yvecourt 2005 Bordeaux Blend (Bordeaux) $10. Vanilla aromas and fresh red currant fruit flavors give this wine a freshness as well as a simple, easy structure. The acidity could be less dominant. **83** —*R.V. (11/1/2007)*

Yvecourt 2006 Bordeaux White Blend (Bordeaux Blanc) $11. A really green, grassy wine that owes a lot to New Zealand. It is fresh, crisp, squeaky clean and a great aperitif wine. **84** —*R.V. (12/31/2007)*

YVES CUILLERON

Yves Cuilleron 2003 Cuvée Saint-Pierre Marsanne (Saint-Joseph) $44. 89 —*R.V. (2/1/2005)*

Yves Cuilleron 2003 Le Lombard Marsanne (Saint-Joseph) $40. 90 —*R.V. (2/1/2005)*

Yves Cuilleron 2005 Saint-Pierre Roussanne (Saint-Joseph) $48. 88 —*J.C. (11/15/2006)*

Yves Cuilleron 2004 L'Amarybelle Syrah (Saint-Joseph) $40. 90 —*J.C. (11/15/2006)*

Yves Cuilleron 2002 Les Pierres Sèches Syrah (Saint-Joseph) $32. 89 —*R.V. (2/1/2005)*

Yves Cuilleron 2002 Les Serines Syrah (Saint-Joseph) $58. 90 —*R.V. (2/1/2005)*

Yves Cuilleron 1999 Terres Sombres Syrah (Côte Rôtie) $65. 91 —*R.V. (6/1/2002)*

Yves Cuilleron 2003 La Petite Côte Viognier (Condrieu) $58. 87 —*R.V. (2/1/2005)*

Yves Cuilleron 2000 Les Chaillets Viognier (Condrieu) $65. 90 —*R.V. (6/1/2002)*

YVETTE ET MICHEL BECK-HARTWEG

Yvette et Michel Beck-Hartweg 2002 Cuvée Prestige Riesling (Alsace) $12. A bit flat and lifeless with a bouquet composed only of petrol and stone. A touch of honey might present itself to some, but the fruit character is sorely missed. **84** *(9/1/2007)*

YVON MAU

Yvon Mau 2002 Yvecourt Bordeaux Blend (Médoc) $15. 84 —*J.C. (6/1/2005)*

Yvon Mau 2004 Yvecourt Bordeaux White Blend (Bordeaux) $10. 85 —*R.V. (6/1/2005)*

Yvon Mau 2004 Premius Sauvignon Blanc (Bordeaux) $10. 85 Best Buy —*R.V. (6/1/2005)*

ZOÉMIE DE SOUSA

Zoémie De Sousa NV Précieuse Grand Cru Brut Champagne Blend (Champagne) $NA. 92 —*R.V. (12/1/2005)8*

Germany

German wine labels can be intimidating: long foreign words and ornate gothic script are enough to make many consumers head for a different section of the wine shop. But for the initiated—and you'll qualify after reading this quick primer—German wine labels are among the most descriptive out there.

As on any wine label, you'll find the name of the producer, the vintage, the region, and sometimes the name of the grape.

In addition to the grape-growing region (see below), most labels will show the names of the town and the vineyard in large type, such as Graacher Himmelreich (the town of Graach, Himmelreich vineyard). In much smaller type will be the terms *Qualitätswein bestimmter Anbaugebiete* (often just Qualitätswein, or QbA), indicating a "quality wine," or *Qualitätswein mit Prädikat (QmP)*, denoting a quality wine picked at designated minimum ripeness levels that vary by grape variety and growing region. These ripeness levels will be indicated on the label as follows:

Label on a bottle of Zimmermann-Graeff.

Kabinett The least ripe of the *prädikat* levels, and typically the lightest of a grower's offerings. With their low alcohol levels and touch of sweetness, these wines make ideal picnic quaffs and mouth-watering apéritifs. Most often consumed in their youth, they can last for ten years or more.

Spätlese Literally, "late picked." These grapes are generally only late-picked with respect to those grapes that go into Kabinett or QbA wines. If vinified dry (an increasingly popular style), they can still seem less than optimally ripe. Traditionally made, with some residual sugar left in, they are extremely food friendly. Try them with anything from Asian food to baked ham and roast fowl. Most should be consumed before age twenty.

Auslese Made from "select" bunches of grapes left on the vine until they achieve high sugar readings, these wines often carry a hint or more of botrytis (see Glossary). While some are sweet enough to serve with simple fruit desserts, others are best sipped alone. With age, some of the sugar seems to melt away, yielding wines that can ably partner with roast pork or goose. Thirty-year-old auslesen can smell heavenly, but sometimes fall flat on the palate. Enjoy them on release for their luscious sweet fruit, or cellar for ten to twenty years.

Beerenauslese "Berry select" wines are harvested berry by berry, taking only botrytis-affected fruit. While auslesen are usually sweet, this level of ripeness elevates the wine to the dessert-only category. Hold up to 50 years.

Trockenbeerenauslese These "dried berry select" wines are made from individually harvested, shriveled grapes that have been heavily affected by botrytis. Profoundly sweet and honeyed, their over-the-top viscosity and sweetness can turn off some tasters, while others revel in the complex aromas and flavors.

Eiswein Made from frozen grapes that are at least equivalent in sugar levels to beerenauslese, but which produce wines with much racier levels of acidity. The intense sugars and acids enable these wines to easily endure for decades.

Aside from the ripeness levels denoted by the QmP system, you can expect to see the terms *trocken* and *halbtrocken* on some labels (their use is optional). *Trocken*, or dry, may be used on wines with fewer than 9g/L residual sugar (less than 0.9 percent); *halbtrocken* (half-dry) refers to wines with between 9 and 18g/L. Given the allowable ranges, these wines may be truly dry or verging on sweet, depending on acid-sugar balance.

In an effort to simplify German labels, a few relatively new terms have cropped up that supplement, replace, or partially replace the traditional labeling system. *Erstes Gewächs* wines, or "first growths," come only from designated sites in the Rheingau. Classic wines must be "harmoniously dry" and must omit references to specific villages or vineyards. Selection wines bear a single-vineyard designation on the label and must be dry.

GERMAN WINE REGIONS

Most of the classic German wine regions are closely identified with river valleys, the slopes of which provide the proper exposure for ripening grapes at this northern latitude. Virtually all of Germany's best wines come from the Riesling grape, but there are several exceptions, like the fine Gewürztraminers from Fitz-Ritter in the Pfalz and Valckenberg in Rheinhessen and the exquisite Rieslaners and Scheurebes from Müeller-Catoir in the Pfalz.

Mosel-Saar-Ruwer The coolest of the German growing regions, and home to Germany's crispest, raciest, and most delicate Rieslings. Green apples, floral notes, and citrus are all likely descriptors, but the best wines also display fine mineral notes that express their slate-driven terroirs.

Rheingau Steep slate slopes and slightly warmer temperatures than found in the Mosel-Saar-Ruwer yield powerful, sturdy wines, with ripe fruit flavors underscored by deep minerality.

Rheinhessen Source for much of Germany's production, quality here can vary from generic *liebfraumilch* to fine single-estate wines.

Nahe This small side valley is the only rival to the Mosel-Saar-Ruwer for elegance and finesse, with Rieslings that balance lightness of body with mineral-based tensile strength.

Pfalz One of Germany's warmest winegrowing regions, with a great diversity of soils, microclimates, and grape varieties. Dry styles, whether made from Riesling or other white grapes, are more common here, and show better balance than those from cooler regions. Spätburgunder (Pinot Noir) is also more successful here than elsewhere.

Wines from other German winegrowing regions, such as the Ahr, Baden, Franken, and Württemberg, are infrequently seen in the United States.

GERMANY

2 BROTHERS

2 Brothers 2006 Kabinett Riesling (Mosel-Saar-Ruwer) $12. Light in weight, but distressingly lacking in flavor as well, with modest melon and anise notes that finish soft and short. 82 *—J.C. (11/15/2007)*

2 Brothers 2003 Big Tattoo White QbA White Blend (Nahe) $9. 84 *—J.C. (5/1/2005)*

A. CHRISTMANN

A. Christmann 1997 Konigsbacher Idig Spätburgunder Pinot Noir (Pfalz) $50. 93 *(12/31/2001)*

A. Christmann 2005 Kalkstein Terrassen Trocken Riesling (Pfalz) $35. An intriguing wine, this offers honeyed, apricot-like aromas and a broad, mouthfilling texture. The flavors of stone fruit and corn oil are mouthcoating but not particularly fresh, lacking a bit of verve, yet still finishing dry and persistent. 86 *—J.C. (8/1/2007)*

A. Christmann 1999 Konigsbacher Idig Spätlese Trocken Riesling (Pfalz) $40. 93 Editors' Choice *—P.G. (12/31/2001)*

A. Christmann 2004 Königsbacher Idig Spätlese Trocken Riesling (Pfalz) $54. 90 *—J.C. (5/1/2006)*

A. Christmann 2002 Königsbacher Idig Spätlese Trocken Riesling (Pfalz) $48. 83 *—J.C. (11/1/2004)*

A. Christmann 2003 Konigsbacher Idig Trocken Riesling (Pfalz) $60. 90 *—J.C. (5/1/2005)*

A. Christmann 2004 QbA Riesling (Pfalz) $21. 84 *—J.C. (5/1/2006)*

A. Christmann 2001 QbA Riesling (Pfalz) $17. 88 *—J.C. (3/1/2003)*

A. Christmann 2002 Qualitätswein Riesling (Pfalz) $20. 85 *—J.C. (11/1/2004)*

A. Christmann 2005 Ruppertsberger Reiterpfad Auslese Riesling (Pfalz) $65. Intrigues on the nose, offering tantalizing hints of smoke, nuts and honey. But this wine is thick and sweet, and it clings to the sides of the glass, defying attempts to shake it out afterwards. The gooey marmalade flavors finish long and sticky. 92 *—J.C. (10/1/2007)*

A. Christmann 2003 Ruppertsberger Reiterpfad Auslese Riesling (Pfalz) $40. 91 *—J.C. (5/1/2005)*

A. Christmann 2001 Ruppertsberger Reiterpfad Auslese Riesling (Pfalz) $32. 89 *—J.C. (3/1/2003)*

A. Christmann 1999 Ruppertsberger Reiterpfad Auslese Riesling (Pfalz) $50. 94 Editors' Choice *—P.G. (12/31/2001)*

A. Christmann 2003 Trocken Riesling (Pfalz) $20. 85 *—J.C. (5/1/2005)*

ADELSECK

Adelseck NV Juwel Brut Riesling (Nahe) $15. 84 *—P.G. (12/31/2002)*

ALFRED MERKELBACH

Alfred Merkelbach 2001 Ürziger Würzgarten Auslese Fuder 15 Riesling (Mosel-Saar-Ruwer) $23. 91 Editors' Choice *—J.C. (3/1/2003)*

Alfred Merkelbach 2001 Ürziger Würzgarten Spätlese Fuder 11 Riesling (Mosel-Saar-Ruwer) $17. 90 Editors' Choice *—J.C. (3/1/2003)*

AM TURM

Am Turm NV Turm-Exquisit Brut Sekt Chardonnay (Pfalz) $25. 88 *—J.C. (6/1/2006)*

Am Turm NV Turm-Exquisit Brut Sekt Pinot Blanc de Noir Pinot Noir (Pfalz) $25. 82 *—J.C. (6/1/2006)*

Am Turm NV Trocken Sekt Riesling (Pfalz) $21. 85 *—J.C. (6/1/2006)*

Am Turm NV Turm-Exquisit Brut Sekt Weissburgunder (Pfalz) $23. 84 *—J.C. (6/1/2006)*

ANTHONY HAMMOND

Anthony Hammond 2005 Estate QbA Riesling (Rheingau) $13. 85 *—J.C. (2/1/2007)*

Anthony Hammond 2003 Estate Rüdesheimer Burgweg Riesling (Rheingau) $14. 89 Best Buy *—J.C. (2/1/2007)*

Anthony Hammond 2004 Rüdesheimer Berg Roseneck Spätlese Riesling (Rheingau) $25. 86 *—J.C. (2/1/2007)*

Anthony Hammond 2004 Rüdesheimer Drachenstein Kabinett Riesling (Rheingau) $18. 91 Editors' Choice *—J.C. (2/1/2007)*

Anthony Hammond 2004 Rüdesheimer Drachenstein Spätlese Riesling (Rheingau) $15. 89 *—J.C. (2/1/2007)*

ARTUR STEINMANN

Artur Steinmann 2004 Sommerhäuser Steinbach Riesling (Franken) $29. 88 *—J.C. (12/1/2006)*

BALDUIN VON HOVEL

Balduin von Hovel 2002 Estate QbA Riesling (Mosel-Saar-Ruwer) $14. 87 *—J.C. (8/1/2004)*

BALTHASAR RESS

Balthasar Ress 2001 Hattenheimer Engelmannsberg Eiswein Riesling (Rheingau) $160. 85 *—R.V. (1/1/2004)*

Balthasar Ress 2001 Hattenheimer Nussbrunnen Auslese Riesling (Rheingau) $25. 89 *—R.V. (1/1/2004)*

Balthasar Ress 2001 Hattenheimer Nussbrunnen Beerenauslese Riesling (Rheingau) $120. 91 *—R.V. (4/1/2003)*

Balthasar Ress 2001 Hattenheimer Nussbrunnen Spätlese Riesling (Rheingau) $18. 91 *—R.V. (1/1/2004)*

Balthasar Ress 2001 Hattenheimer Nussbrunnen Trockenbeerenauslese Riesling (Rheingau) $170. 94 *—R.V. (1/1/2004)*

Balthasar Ress 2001 Hattenheimer Schützenhaus Kabinett Riesling (Rheingau) $12. 89 *—R.V. (3/1/2003)*

Balthasar Ress 2001 Rüdesheimer Berg Roseneck Auslese Riesling (Rheingau) $23. 90 *—R.V. (1/1/2004)*

Balthasar Ress 2001 Rüdesheimer Berg Rottland Beerenauslese Riesling (Rheingau) $120. 92 *—R.V. (1/1/2004)*

Balthasar Ress 2001 Rüdesheimer Berg Rottland Spätlese Riesling (Rheingau) $19. 89 *—J.C. (8/1/2004)*

Balthasar Ress 2001 Rüdesheimer Berg Rottland Trockenbeerenauslese Riesling (Rheingau) $170. 93 *—R.V. (1/1/2004)*

Balthasar Ress 2001 Schloss Reichartshausen Kabinett Riesling (Rheingau) $14. 88 *—R.V. (3/1/2003)*

Balthasar Ress 2001 Schloss Reichartshausen Spätlese Riesling (Rheingau) $14. 91 *—R.V. (1/1/2004)*

BARON KNYPHAUSEN

Baron Knyphausen 2006 Riesling (Rheingau) $14. Almost tropically fruity, with hints of banana and pineapple adding nuance to the peach flavors. It's slightly creamy in texture but not heavy, a pleasant sipper or companion to mildly spicy dishes. 86 *—J.C. (11/15/2007)*

Baron Knyphausen 2006 Baron K Kabinett Riesling (Rheingau) $15. In contrast to Knyphausen's 2006 Riesling, the 2006 kabinett is restrained and minerally, offering crisp pineapple and green apple flavors underscored by mouthwatering acidity. It's slightly lighter in body as well, with a raciness that would work well served alongside sautéed trout. 86 *—J.C. (11/15/2007)*

Baron Knyphausen 2005 Baron K' Kabinett Riesling (Rheingau) $15. 82 *—J.C. (2/1/2007)*

Baron Knyphausen 2005 QbA Riesling (Rheingau) $14. 82 *—J.C. (2/1/2007)*

BARON ZU KNYPHAUSEN

Baron zu Knyphausen 2004 Baron K Riesling Kabinett Riesling (Rheingau) $15. 80 *—J.C. (7/1/2006)*

Baron zu Knyphausen 2005 Kiedricher Sandgrub Spätlese Riesling (Rheingau) $23. 91 Editors' Choice *—J.C. (12/1/2006)*

Baron zu Knyphausen 2004 Kiedricher Sandgrub Spätlese Riesling (Rheingau) $23. 85 *—J.C. (5/1/2006)*

Baron zu Knyphausen 2004 QbA Riesling (Rheingau) $14. 84 *—J.C. (5/1/2006)*

Baron zu Knyphausen 2001 Charta Kabinett Riesling (Rheingau) $18. 85 *—J.C. (5/1/2005)*

Baron zu Knyphausen 2003 Erbacher Steinmorgen Kabinett Riesling (Rheingau) $24. 87 *—J.C. (5/1/2005)*

Baron zu Knyphausen 2001 Erbacher Steinmorgen Kabinett Riesling (Rheingau) $14. 86 *—J.C. (3/1/2003)*

Baron zu Knyphausen 2003 Erbacher Steinmorgen Riesling Kabinett Riesling (Rheingau) $17. 82 *—J.C. (12/15/2004)*

Baron zu Knyphausen 2001 Erbacher Steinmorgen Spätlese Riesling (Rheingau) $22. 91 Editors' Choice *—J.C. (3/1/2003)*

Baron zu Knyphausen 2001 Hattenheimer Wisselbrunnen Erstes Gewächs Riesling (Rheingau) $28. 89 *—J.C. (3/1/2003)*

Baron zu Knyphausen 2003 Hattenheimer Wisselbrunnen Riesling Auslese Riesling (Rheingau) $51. 85 *—J.C. (12/15/2004)*

Baron zu Knyphausen 2003 Kiedricher Sandgrub Spätlese Riesling (Rheingau) $23. 84 *—J.C. (5/1/2005)*

Baron zu Knyphausen 2003 QbA Riesling (Rheingau) $13. 87 *—J.C. (12/15/2004)*

Baron zu Knyphausen 2001 QbA Riesling (Rheingau) $12. 86 *—J.C. (3/1/2003)*

BAUER HAUS

Bauer Haus 2006 Riesling (Nahe) $8. Plump and sweet, with confected apple, melon and cotton candy aromas and flavors. 82 *—J.C. (8/1/2007)*

BEND IN THE RIVER

Bend In The River 2001 QbA Riesling (Rheinhessen) $10. 83 *—J.C. (3/1/2003)*

BERNHARD EIFEL

Bernhard Eifel 2005 Longuicher Maximiner Herrenberg Spätlese Riesling (Mosel-Saar-Ruwer) $28. Surprisingly taut and fresh for a 2005, this spätlese starts off a bit leesy and smoky, then opens up to reveal pear, melon and spice flavors. Shows great verve and energy on the citrusy finish. 88 *—J.C. (4/1/2007)*

Bernhard Eifel 2003 Longuicher Maximiner Herrenberg Spätlese Riesling (Mosel-Saar-Ruwer) $25. 90 *—J.C. (11/1/2004)*

Bernhard Eifel 2004 Maximilian E Trocken Riesling (Mosel-Saar-Ruwer) $23. 86 *—J.C. (7/1/2006)*

Bernhard Eifel 2003 Maximillian Classic Qualitätswein Riesling (Mosel-Saar-Ruwer) $16. 88 *—J.C. (11/1/2004)*

Bernhard Eifel 2004 Trittenheimer Apotheke Kabinett Halbtrocken Riesling (Mosel-Saar-Ruwer) $22. 86 *—J.C. (7/1/2006)*

BLACK TOWER

Black Tower 2004 Pinot Grigio (Rheinhessen) $8. 86 **Best Buy** *(2/1/2006)*

Black Tower 2003 QbA Riesling (Pfalz) $8. 84 **Best Buy** *—J.C. (12/15/2004)*

Black Tower 2006 Rosé Blend (Deutscher Tafelwein Rhein) $9. Seems to be aiming at the Rosé d'Anjou or white Zinfandel market, as it's slightly sweet, only partly balanced by citrusy acids. 82 *—J.C. (7/1/2007)*

BLOOM

Bloom 2004 Petals Müller-Thurgau (Mosel-Saar-Ruwer) $7. 83 *—J.C. (7/1/2006)*

Bloom 2005 Pinot Gris (Nahe) $8. Made specifically for the U.S. market, this simple, fruity, medium-bodied wine combines apple, melon and citrus flavors. Clean, with hints of ripe pears on the finish. 84 **Best Buy** *—J.C. (11/15/2007)*

Bloom 2004 Pinot Gris (Nahe) $7. 83 *—J.C. (7/1/2006)*

Bloom 2004 Riesling (Mosel-Saar-Ruwer) $7. 83 *—J.C. (7/1/2006)*

Bloom 2005 QbA Riesling (Mosel-Saar-Ruwer) $8. 84 **Best Buy** *—J.C. (12/1/2006)*

BLUE FISH

Blue Fish 2006 Estate Bottled Riesling (Pfalz) $10. Melon and spice aromas and flavors are clean and pleasant, just lacking a bit of concentration on the palate. Finishes almost dry. 83 *—J.C. (11/15/2007)*

Blue Fish 2006 Estate Bottled Sweet Riesling (Pfalz) $10. The extra residual sugar in this wine helps round out the midpalate, giving it a minor leg up over the Blue Fish Estate Bottled Riesling. Melon and apple flavors pick up a hint of anise, finishing clean and fresh. 84 *—J.C. (11/15/2007)*

Blue Fish 2004 Estate Riesling (Pfalz) $10. 86 **Best Buy** *—J.C. (10/1/2005)*

BLUE NUN

Blue Nun 2002 Eiswein Riesling (Rheinhessen) $36. 88 *—J.C. (12/15/2004)*

Blue Nun 2001 QbA Riesling (Pfalz) $7. 84 *—J.C. (8/1/2004)*

Blue Nun 2003 Qualitätswein Riesling (Rheinhessen) $7. 85 **Best Buy** *—J.C. (11/1/2004)*

BOLLIG-LEHNERT

Bollig-Lehnert 2003 Trittenheimer Apotheke Eiswein Riesling (Mosel-Saar-Ruwer) $42. Sweet and lithe, this is a wonderfully clean and pure expression of Riesling eiswein. There's no botrytis, only sweet pineapple, apple and citrus flavors that finish on lingering notes of orange and lemon. This should last a while in the cellar, but there's really no reason to delay gratification. 90 *—J.C. (12/15/2007)*

C.H. BERRES

C.H. Berres 1990 Erdener Treppchen Beerenauslese Riesling (Mosel-Saar-Ruwer) $80. 91 **Editors' Choice** *—J.C. (9/1/2006)*

C.H. Berres 2004 Erdener Treppchen Kabinett Riesling (Mosel-Saar-Ruwer) $21. 88 *—J.C. (7/1/2006)*

C.H. Berres 2005 Impulse Estate Riesling (Mosel-Saar-Ruwer) $13. Starts off well, featuring scents of green apples and honey. But the flavors are simple and it's a bit on the weighty side, with ample (12%) alcohol and some residual sugar as well. 83 *—J.C. (8/1/2007)*

C.H. Berres 2004 Impulse (Gold) QbA Riesling (Mosel-Saar-Ruwer) $14. 86 *—J.C. (5/1/2006)*

C.H. Berres 2004 Impulse (Sapphire) QbA Riesling (Mosel-Saar-Ruwer) $14. 87 *—J.C. (12/1/2006)*

C.H. Berres 2004 Ürziger Goldwingert Auslese Riesling (Mosel-Saar-Ruwer) $48. 90 *—J.C. (5/1/2006)*

CARL EHRHARD

Carl Ehrhard 2004 Rüdesheimer Berg Roseneck QbA Trocken Pinot Noir (Rheingau) $22. This is one of the more impressive German Pinot Noirs we've reviewed at Wine Enthusiast. No, it's not the most complex Pinot, but the flavors are true and it nails Pinot's elusive mouthfeel. The silky texture delivers cherry and vanilla flavors, then turns crisp on the finish. 87 *—J.C. (6/1/2007)*

Carl Ehrhard 2005 Rüdesheimer Blanc de Noir Pinot Noir Trocken Pinot Noir (Rheingau) $15. Despite a laudable pale copper color, this wine has a rather coarse, tannic texture that dampens its melon and appleskin flavors. Turns slightly bitter on the finish. 80 *—J.C. (11/15/2007)*

Carl Ehrhard 2004 Rüdesheimer Berg Rottland Auslese Riesling (Rheingau) $24. Reasonably priced, this fruit-bowl auslese boasts hints of dried apricot, heaps of ultraripe stone fruit and just enough citrusy notes for balance. It's a more classic vintage, so not as rich or unctuous as the 2003s or 2005s, but leaner and more focused, with a balanced, fresh finish. Drink now–2020. 91 *—J.C. (10/1/2007)*

Carl Ehrhard 2004 Rüdesheimer Berg Rottland Spätlese Feinherb Riesling (Rheingau) $18. Reasonably priced for a Riesling of this quality, this off-dry wine is filled with spiced baked apple flavors. Touches of petrol and stone dust impart a sense of minerality, while the finish is long and mouthwatering. 89 *—J.C. (9/1/2007)*

Carl Ehrhard 2005 Rüdesheimer Kabinett Feinherb Riesling (Rheingau) $15. Lime, honey and slate aromas mingle easily on the nose of this medium-bodied Riesling, while the flavors show hints of melon rind and plenty of peppery spice. Finshes crisp, with zesty acids balancing a touch of sweetness. Drink now. 88 *—J.C. (9/1/2007)*

Carl Ehrhard 2004 Rüdesheimer Kabinett Feinherb Riesling (Rheingau) $14. 86 *—J.C. (7/1/2006)*

CARL GRAFF

Carl Graff 2003 Erdener Pralat Auslese Riesling (Mosel-Saar-Ruwer) $25. 89 *—J.C. (5/1/2005)*

Carl Graff 2001 Erdener Prälat Auslese Riesling (Mosel-Saar-Ruwer) $14. 88 **Best Buy** *—J.C. (3/1/2003)*

Carl Graff 2001 Erdener Treppchen Spätlese Riesling (Mosel-Saar-Ruwer) $11. 85 *—J.C. (3/1/2003)*

Carl Graff 2003 Graacher Himmelreich Spätlese Riesling (Mosel-Saar-Ruwer) $15. 86 *—J.C. (5/1/2005)*

Carl Graff 2001 Graacher Himmelreich Spätlese Riesling (Mosel-Saar-Ruwer) $12. 85 *—J.C. (3/1/2003)*

Carl Graff 2001 Kabinett Riesling (Mosel-Saar-Ruwer) $8. 83 *—J.C. (1/1/2004)*

Carl Graff 2001 Piesporter Goldtropfchen Kabinett Riesling (Mosel-Saar-Ruwer) $12. 85 *—J.C. (3/1/2003)*

Carl Graff 2001 Piesporter Goldtropfchen Spätlese Riesling (Mosel-Saar-Ruwer) $15. 86 *—J.C. (3/1/2003)*

Carl Graff 2001 Piesporter Michelsberg Auslese Riesling (Mosel-Saar-Ruwer) $14. 86 *—J.C. (3/1/2003)*

Carl Graff 2001 QbA Riesling (Mosel-Saar-Ruwer) $7. 82 *—J.C. (1/1/2004)*

Carl Graff 2003 Riesling Kabinett Riesling (Mosel-Saar-Ruwer) $11. 85 *—J.C. (12/15/2004)*

Carl Graff 2001 Urziger Wurzgarten Auslese Riesling (Mosel-Saar-Ruwer) $17. 84 *—J.C. (3/1/2003)*

Carl Graff 2003 Ürziger Würzgarten Auslese Riesling (Mosel-Saar-Ruwer) $22. 84 *—J.C. (5/1/2005)*

Carl Graff 2003 Ürziger Würzgarten Spätlese Riesling (Mosel-Saar-Ruwer) $19. 85 *—J.C. (5/1/2005)*

Carl Graff 2001 Wehlener Sonnenuhr Spätlese Riesling (Mosel-Saar-Ruwer) $12. 87 **Best Buy** *—J.C. (3/1/2003)*

CARL LOEWEN

Carl Loewen 2004 Leiwener Klostergarten Kabinett Riesling (Mosel-Saar-Ruwer) $19. 91 **Editors' Choice** *—J.C. (10/1/2005)*

Carl Loewen 2001 Thörnicher Ritsch Spätlese Riesling (Mosel-Saar-Ruwer) $20. 90 **Editors' Choice** *—J.C. (3/1/2003)*

CARL SCHMITT-WAGNER

Carl Schmitt-Wagner 2001 Longuicher Maximiner Herrenberg Auslese Riesling (Mosel-Saar-Ruwer) $26. 90 *—J.C. (3/1/2003)*

Carl Schmitt-Wagner 2001 Longuicher Maximiner Herrenberg Spätlese Riesling (Mosel-Saar-Ruwer) $19. 89 *—J.C. (3/1/2003)*

CARL SITTMANN

Carl Sittmann 2005 QbA Riesling (Mosel-Saar-Ruwer) $10. Simple and sweet; ripe apple flavors tinged with just a hint of rock dust. 83 *—J.C. (4/1/2007)*

CASTELL

Castell 2004 Frenzy Müller-Thurgau Trocken Müller-Thurgau (Franken) $12. 86 *—J.C. (7/1/2006)*

Castell 2003 Riesling QbA Trocken Riesling (Franken) $14. 89 Best Buy *—J.C. (12/15/2004)*

Castell 2006 Trocken Silvaner (Franken) $14. Like a mildly spicy Traminer (one of its parent varieties), this Silvaner is medium-bodied, with modest pear and melon fruit and hints of ginger and pepper. Finishes short. 83 *—J.C. (11/15/2007)*

CLEAN SLATE

Clean Slate 2005 Riesling (Mosel-Saar-Ruwer) $11. Fills the need for a light poolside quaffer, combining aromas of fresh greens, lime and apple with a hint of slate-driven minerality. Green apple and citrus flavors could use a little more length and intensity, but overall it's nicely balanced, crisp and focused. 86 Best Buy *—J.C. (6/1/2007)*

CLUSSERATH-WEILER

Clusserath-Weiler 2005 HC Riesling (Mosel-Saar-Ruwer) $22. Similar to the Alte Reben bottling from the Apotheke vineyard, Clüsserath-Weiler's HC Riesling combines petrol and mineral oil notes with baked apples and clover blossom, in a slightly more open and obvious manner. It's slightly oily in texture, ending on notes of crushed stone and grated cinnamon. 89 *—J.C. (6/1/2007)*

Clusserath-Weiler 2004 HC Riesling QbA Riesling (Mosel-Saar-Ruwer) $21. 86 *—J.C. (2/1/2006)*

Clusserath-Weiler 2005 Trittenheimer Apotheke Alte Reben Riesling (Mosel-Saar-Ruwer) $40. From 60–80-year-old vines, this is a mostly dry Riesling with unusual heft for the Mosel. The aromas start off a bit understated, then open with air to reveal some apple and citrus, but the flavors are more like spiced baked apples and mineral oil. Picks up hints of clover blossom and honey on the steely, lime-driven finish. 90 *—J.C. (6/1/2007)*

Clusserath-Weiler 2004 Trittenheimer Apotheke Auslese Riesling (Mosel-Saar-Ruwer) $42 375 ml. 90 *—J.C. (9/1/2006)*

Clusserath-Weiler 2003 Trittenheimer Apotheke Spätlese Riesling (Mosel-Saar-Ruwer) $25. 85 *—J.C. (11/1/2004)*

Clusserath-Weiler 2003 Trittenheimer Apotheke Spätlese Riesling (Mosel-Saar-Ruwer) $33. 86 *—J.C. (11/1/2004)*

Clusserath-Weiler 2003 Trittenheimer Apotheke Spätlese Trocken Riesling (Mosel-Saar-Ruwer) $24. 86 *—J.C. (11/1/2004)*

Clusserath-Weiler 2005 Trittenheimer Apotheke Spätlese Riesling (Mosel-Saar-Ruwer) $31. 89 *—J.C. (12/1/2006)*

DEINHARD

Deinhard 2002 Hanns Christof Liebfraumilch (Rheinhessen) $6. 83 *—J.C. (8/1/2004)*

Deinhard 2003 Classic Pinot Blanc (Pfalz) $8. 84 Best Buy *—J.C. (11/1/2004)*

Deinhard 2003 Classic Riesling (Rheinhessen) $8. 84 Best Buy *—J.C. (11/1/2004)*

Deinhard 2002 Classic Riesling (Rheinhessen) $8. 82 *—J.C. (8/1/2004)*

Deinhard 2002 Green Label QbA Riesling (Mosel-Saar-Ruwer) $6. 84 Best Buy *—J.C. (8/1/2004)*

Deinhard 2003 Green Label Qualitätswein Riesling (Mosel-Saar-Ruwer) $6. 82 *—J.C. (11/1/2004)*

Deinhard 2004 Piesporter QbA Riesling (Mosel-Saar-Ruwer) $8. 86 Best Buy *—J.C. (5/1/2006)*

Deinhard 2002 Piesporter QbA Riesling (Mosel-Saar-Ruwer) $9. 86 Best Buy *—J.C. (8/1/2004)*

Deinhard 2003 Piesporter Qualitätswein Riesling (Mosel-Saar-Ruwer) $9. 85 Best Buy *—J.C. (11/1/2004)*

Deinhard NV Cabinet Traditions-Cuvée Sekt Trocken Sparkling Blend (Germany) $8. 84 Best Buy *—J.C. (12/31/2004)*

Deinhard NV Feiner Fruchtiger Sekt Halbtrocken Sparkling Blend (Germany) $9. 83 *—J.C. (12/31/2004)*

Deinhard NV Lila Riesling Brut Sekt Sparkling Blend (Germany) $11. 86 Best Buy *—J.C. (12/31/2004)*

Deinhard NV Rose de Blanc et Noir Feiner Fruchtiger Sekt Halbtrocken Sparkling Blend (Germany) $8. 82 *—J.C. (12/31/2004)*

DES GRAFEN NEIPPERG

Des Grafen Neipperg 2001 Neipperger Schlossberg Kabinett Trocken Riesling (Württemberg) $14. 83 *—J.C. (1/1/2004)*

Des Grafen Neipperg 2001 Hemma QbA White Blend (Württemberg) $17. 82 *—J.C. (1/1/2004)*

DOMDECHANT WERNER

Domdechant Werner 2005 Hochheim Classic Riesling (Rheingau) $17. 86 *—J.C. (2/1/2007)*

Domdechant Werner 2002 Hochheim Classic Riesling (Rheingau) $17. 89 *—J.C. (8/1/2004)*

Domdechant Werner 2002 Hochheim Domdechaney QbA Erstes Gewachs Riesling (Rheingau) $44. 91 *—J.C. (8/1/2004)*

Domdechant Werner 2005 Hochheimer Domdechaney Auslese Riesling (Rheingau) $41. Rich, lush and slightly oily in texture, this may lack the exotic notes of the goldkap bottling, but it's still an exceptional wine. Dried apricot notes provide sweetness and flavor, balanced by ripe citrus and a slightly pithy note on the long finish. Drink now–2020. 92 **Editors' Choice** *—J.C. (10/1/2007)*

Domdechant Werner 2002 Hochheimer Domdechaney Auslese Riesling (Rheingau) $49. 88 *—J.C. (8/1/2004)*

Domdechant Werner 1999 Hochheimer Domdechaney Auslese Riesling (Rheingau) $35. 90 *(8/1/2001)*

Domdechant Werner 2005 Hochheimer Domdechaney Auslese Goldkap Riesling (Rheingau) $60. This is wonderfully exotic on the nose, blasting forth with waves of mango and peach, then settles down a bit on the palate, where the flavors are of honeyed peaches, dripping with nectar, framed by just enough citrus for balance. Moderately rich, with a long, squeaky-clean finish. Drink now–2025 or beyond. 94 *—J.C. (10/1/2007)*

Domdechant Werner 1999 Hochheimer Domdechaney Beerenauslese Riesling (Rheingau) $126. 92 *(8/1/2001)*

Domdechant Werner 2005 Hochheimer Domdechaney Erstes Gewachs Riesling (Rheingau) $41. It's rather expensive, but also undeniably good, with a light, almost delicate feel that belies its inner strength. Lime, crushed stones and green apple flavors end dry, with a tactile sensation of dusty minerality. Terroir naysayers should compare this to Werner's Kirchenstück bottling, then see if they're still skeptical. 89 *—J.C. (6/1/2007)*

Domdechant Werner 2004 Hochheimer Domdechaney Spätlese Riesling (Rheingau) $27. 90 *—J.C. (9/1/2006)*

Domdechant Werner 2003 Hochheimer Domdechaney Spätlese Riesling (Rheingau) $29. 86 *—J.C. (5/1/2005)*

Domdechant Werner 2001 Hochheimer Domdechaney Spätlese Riesling (Rheingau) $21. 92 *—R.V. (1/1/2004)*

Domdechant Werner 1999 Hochheimer Domdechaney Spätlese Riesling (Rheingau) $24. 87 *(8/1/2001)*

Domdechant Werner 2001 Hochheimer Domdechaney Spätlese Trocken Riesling (Rheingau) $23. 85 *—R.V. (1/1/2004)*

Domdechant Werner 1999 Hochheimer Domdechaney Trockenbeerenauslese Riesling (Rheingau) $227. 91 *(8/1/2001)*

Domdechant Werner 2005 Hochheimer Hölle Kabinett Riesling (Rheingau) $17. 88 *—J.C. (2/1/2007)*

Domdechant Werner 2004 Hochheimer Hölle Kabinett Riesling (Rheingau) $17. 88 *—J.C. (7/1/2006)*

Domdechant Werner 2003 Hochheimer Hölle Kabinett Riesling (Rheingau) $19. 86 *—J.C. (5/1/2005)*

Domdechant Werner 2002 Hochheimer Hölle Kabinett Riesling (Rheingau) $19. 85 *—J.C. (8/1/2004)*

Domdechant Werner 2001 Hochheimer Hölle Kabinett Riesling (Rheingau) $12. 88 *—R.V. (1/1/2004)*

Domdechant Werner 1999 Hochheimer Hölle Kabinett Riesling (Rheingau) $14. 88 *(8/1/2001)*

Domdechant Werner 2005 Hochheimer Hölle Kabinett Trocken Riesling (Rheingau) $17. Although this wine boasts a viscous, slightly oily texture, the aromas and flavors are somewhat stony and unyielding. Hints of apple, peach and spice finish with a hard edge. 86 *—J.C. (9/1/2007)*

Domdechant Werner 2003 Hochheimer Hölle Kabinett Trocken Riesling (Rheingau) $19. 84 *—J.C. (5/1/2005)*

Domdechant Werner 1999 Hochheimer Hölle Kabinett Trocken Riesling (Rheingau) $14. 89 Best Buy *(8/1/2001)*

Domdechant Werner 2003 Hochheimer Kirchenstück Auslese Riesling (Rheingau) $46. 89 *—J.C. (2/1/2006)*

Domdechant Werner 2002 Hochheimer Kirchenstück Auslese Riesling (Rheingau) $49. 89 *—J.C. (8/1/2004)*

Domdechant Werner 2003 Hochheimer Kirchenstück Beerenauslese 375 ml Riesling (Rheingau) $300. 96 Cellar Selection *—J.C. (5/1/2005)*

Domdechant Werner 2002 Hochheimer Kirchenstück Eiswein Riesling (Rheingau) $149. 91 *—J.C. (8/1/2004)*

Domdechant Werner 2001 Hochheimer Kirchenstück Eiswein Riesling (Rheingau) $126. 92 *—R.V. (1/1/2004)*

Domdechant Werner 1999 Hochheimer Kirchenstück Eiswein Riesling (Rheingau) $126. 89 *(8/1/2001)*

Domdechant Werner 2005 Hochheim Kirchenstuck Erstes Gewachs Riesling (Rheingau) $41. Seemingly hard, stony and unyielding in texture, with scents of petrol, slate and lime, not giving a lot of roundness or flesh in which to sink your teeth. It's like crystallized citrus or lime-flavored rock—a coldly impressive wine worthy of a salute. **88** *—J.C. (6/1/2007)*

Domdechant Werner 2002 Hochheimer Kirchenstück QbA Erstes Gewachs Riesling (Rheingau) $44. 89 *—J.C. (8/1/2004)*

Domdechant Werner 2005 Hochheimer Kirchenstück Spätlese Riesling (Rheingau) $25. 91 *—J.C. (2/1/2007)*

Domdechant Werner 2003 Hochheimer Kirchenstück Spätlese Riesling (Rheingau) $29. 88 *—J.C. (5/1/2005)*

Domdechant Werner 2002 Hochheimer Kirchenstück Spätlese Riesling (Rheingau) $30. 84 *—J.C. (8/1/2004)*

Domdechant Werner 1999 Hochheimer Kirchenstück Spätlese Riesling (Rheingau) $22. 87 *(8/1/2001)*

Domdechant Werner 2005 Hochheimer Kirchenstück Spätlese Trocken Riesling (Rheingau) $25. A medium-bodied dry Riesling, this offers rather simple, fruity flavors of apple and pineapple. Although it lacks a great deal of complexity, it's well-balanced and harmonious; easy to drink. **86** *—J.C. (9/1/2007)*

Domdechant Werner 2003 Hochheimer Kirchenstuck Spätlese Trocken Riesling (Rheingau) $29. 84 *—J.C. (5/1/2005)*

Domdechant Werner 1999 Hochheimer Kirchenstück Spätlese Trocken Riesling (Rheingau) $20. 87 *(8/1/2001)*

Domdechant Werner 2005 Hochheimer Stein Kabinett Halbtrocken Riesling (Rheingau) $17. Off-dry, as expected from a halbtrocken, marrying stony, underripe peach notes with hints of oil and honey. The combination of sugar and tartness gives it a tangy finish. **88** *—J.C. (9/1/2007)*

Domdechant Werner 2004 Hochheimer Stein Kabinett Halbtrocken Riesling (Rheingau) $17. 87 *—J.C. (7/1/2006)*

DÖNNHOFF

Dönnhoff 2001 Schlossböckelheimer Kupfergrube Spätlese Riesling (Nahe) $42. 93 *—J.C. (3/1/2003)*

DR. BÜRKLIN-WOLF

Dr. Bürklin-Wolf 2006 Estate Riesling (Pfalz) $17. Medium-bodied and round in the mouth, this is readily approachable Riesling with slightly smoky aromas of diesel fuel and corn oil. Orange zest and spice flavors flesh out the package, finishing a bit soft. **85** *—J.C. (8/1/2007)*

Dr. Bürklin-Wolf 1999 Bürklin Estate Red Blend (Pfalz) $20. 88 *—P.G. (8/1/2001)*

Dr. Bürklin-Wolf 2001 Bürklin Estate Riesling (Pfalz) $16. 90 Editors' Choice *—J.C. (3/1/2003)*

Dr. Bürklin-Wolf 1999 Bürklin Estate Riesling (Pfalz) $15. 87 *—P.G. (8/1/2001)*

Dr. Bürklin-Wolf 2002 Bürklin Estate Qualitätswein Riesling (Pfalz) $20. 83 *—J.C. (11/1/2004)*

Dr. Bürklin-Wolf 2004 Deidesheimer Hohenmorgen GC Fass 23 QbA Riesling (Pfalz) $50. 91 *—J.C. (5/1/2006)*

Dr. Bürklin-Wolf 2003 Estate QbA Riesling (Pfalz) $19. 85 *—J.C. (5/1/2005)*

Dr. Bürklin-Wolf 2004 Forster Kirchenstück GC Riesling QbA Trocken Riesling (Pfalz) $80. 88 *—J.C. (5/1/2006)*

Dr. Bürklin-Wolf 2004 Old Vines Estate Riesling (Pfalz) $19. 86 *—J.C. (7/1/2006)*

Dr. Bürklin-Wolf 2002 Qualitätswein Riesling (Pfalz) $12. 83 *—J.C. (11/1/2004)*

Dr. Bürklin-Wolf 2002 Ruppertsberger Gaisbohl Qualitätswein Trocken Riesling (Pfalz) $48. 88 *—J.C. (11/1/2004)*

Dr. Bürklin-Wolf 1998 Ruppertsberger Gaisbohl Spätlese Trocken Riesling (Pfalz) $37. 92 Cellar Selection *(8/1/2001)*

Dr. Bürklin-Wolf 2003 Ruppertsberger Gaisböhl Trocken Riesling (Pfalz) $50. 84 *—J.C. (5/1/2005)*

Dr. Bürklin-Wolf 2001 Ruppertsberger Gaisböhl Trocken Riesling (Pfalz) $37. 87 *—J.C. (3/1/2003)*

Dr. Bürklin-Wolf 1998 Ruppertsberger Hoheburg Spätlese Trocken Riesling (Pfalz) $23. 91 Editors' Choice *—P.G. (8/1/2001)*

Dr. Bürklin-Wolf 1990 Wachenheimer Rechbächel 'R' Riesling (Pfalz) $44. 91 *(8/1/2001)*

Dr. Bürklin-Wolf 2002 Wachenheimer Rechbächel Qualitätswein Trocken Riesling (Pfalz) $26. 90 *—J.C. (11/1/2004)*

Dr. Bürklin-Wolf 1998 Wachenheimer Rechbächel Spätlese Trocken Riesling (Pfalz) $28. 90 *(8/1/2001)*

DR. FISCHER

Dr. Fischer 2005 Classic Riesling (Mosel-Saar-Ruwer) $14. 89 Best Buy *—J.C. (12/1/2006)*

Dr. Fischer 2003 Classic QbA Riesling (Mosel-Saar-Ruwer) $14. 82 *—J.C. (11/1/2004)*

Dr. Fischer 2003 Ockfener Bockstein Kabinett Riesling (Mosel-Saar-Ruwer) $17. 84 *—J.C. (11/1/2004)*

Dr. Fischer 2003 Ockfener Bockstein Spätlese Riesling (Mosel-Saar-Ruwer) $20. 82 *—J.C. (11/1/2004)*

Dr. Fischer 2002 Wawerner Herrenberger Spätlese Riesling (Mosel-Saar-Ruwer) $20. 85 *—J.C. (11/1/2004)*

DR. H. THANISCH (ERBEN MÜLLER-BURGGRAEF)

Dr. H. Thanisch (Erben Müller-Burggraef) 2002 Berncasteler Doctor Auslese Riesling (Mosel-Saar-Ruwer) $42. 87 *—J.C. (11/1/2004)*

Dr. H. Thanisch (Erben Müller-Burggraef) 2005 Berncasteler Doctor Auslese Goldkapsel Riesling (Mosel-Saar-Ruwer) $50. A bit full-bodied and slightly syrupy in texture, this heavily concentrated auslese lacks the elegance and complexity of the vintage's best examples, yet it's still an excellent wine. Pretty floral and mineral scents lead the way, followed by flavors of baked apple and honey. Sweet, but balanced on the finish by hints of grapefruit pith. **91** *—J.C. (2/1/2007)*

Dr. H. Thanisch (Erben Müller-Burggraef) 2006 Berncasteler Doctor Beerenauslese Goldkap Riesling (Mosel-Saar-Ruwer) $160. The wonderful minerality imparted by the Doctor vineyard is somehow able to keep this intensely sweet, rich wine from being heavy or cloying. Dried apricot notes mark the nose, followed by scents of mango, peach and pineapple; this wine virtually gushes with sweet tropical fruit and honey, yet maintains a wonderful sense of balance throughout. **96 Cellar Selection** *—J.C. (12/15/2007)*

Dr. H. Thanisch (Erben Müller-Burggraef) 2005 Berncasteler Doctor Kabinett Riesling (Mosel-Saar-Ruwer) $38. 89 *—J.C. (2/1/2007)*

Dr. H. Thanisch (Erben Müller-Burggraef) 2002 Berncasteler Doctor Kabinett Riesling (Mosel-Saar-Ruwer) $29. 86 *—J.C. (8/1/2004)*

Dr. H. Thanisch (Erben Müller-Burggraef) 2001 Berncasteler Doctor Kabinett Riesling (Mosel-Saar-Ruwer) $27. 90 *—J.C. (3/1/2003)*

Dr. H. Thanisch (Erben Müller-Burggraef) 2005 Berncasteler Doctor Spätlese Riesling (Mosel-Saar-Ruwer) $50. A top-notch effort, this wine blends fruit and minerality almost inseparably. Stone fruit and honey notes provide the weight, while apple and pineapple are the muscle and a powerful slaty minerality is the spine. This is rich, even a little bit heavy, but luscious, and surprisingly clean and fresh on the finish. **92** *—J.C. (6/1/2007)*

Dr. H. Thanisch (Erben Müller-Burggraef) 2002 Berncasteler Doctor Spätlese Riesling (Mosel-Saar-Ruwer) $46. 88 *—J.C. (8/1/2004)*

Dr. H. Thanisch (Erben Müller-Burggraef) 2005 Bernkasteler Badstube Kabinett Riesling (Mosel-Saar-Ruwer) $19. 87 *—J.C. (2/1/2007)*

Dr. H. Thanisch (Erben Müller-Burggraef) 2004 Bernkasteler Badstube Kabinett Riesling (Mosel-Saar-Ruwer) $19. 84 *—J.C. (7/1/2006)*

Dr. H. Thanisch (Erben Müller-Burggraef) 2003 Bernkasteler Badstube Kabinett Riesling (Mosel-Saar-Ruwer) $19. 87 *—J.C. (5/1/2005)*

Dr. H. Thanisch (Erben Müller-Burggraef) 2002 Bernkasteler Badstube Kabinett Riesling (Mosel-Saar-Ruwer) $17. 86 *—J.C. (8/1/2004)*

Dr. H. Thanisch (Erben Müller-Burggraef) 2005 Bernkasteler Graben Spätlese Riesling (Mosel-Saar-Ruwer) $26. 90 *—J.C. (2/1/2007)*

Dr. H. Thanisch (Erben Müller-Burggraef) 2001 Bernkasteler Graben Spätlese Riesling (Mosel-Saar-Ruwer) $18. 89 *—J.C. (3/1/2003)*

Dr. H. Thanisch (Erben Müller-Burggraef) 2005 Bernkasteler Lay Auslese Riesling (Mosel-Saar-Ruwer) $35. The price is right on this auslese from one of the Mosel's historic estates. Aromas and flavors of spiced baked apples provide ample fruit, while citrus notes give balance and hints of corn oil give the impression of minerality. Lush and creamy on the palate, with mouth-tingling acidity on the finish. **93 Editors' Choice** *—J.C. (2/1/2007)*

Dr. H. Thanisch (Erben Müller-Burggraef) 2005 Bernkasteler Lay Spätlese Riesling (Mosel-Saar-Ruwer) $26. 88 *—J.C. (12/1/2006)*

Dr. H. Thanisch (Erben Müller-Burggraef) 2005 Brauneberger Juffer-Sonnenuhr Auslese Riesling (Mosel-Saar-Ruwer) $35. 93 Editors' Choice *—J.C. (12/1/2006)*

Dr. H. Thanisch (Erben Müller-Burggraef) 2005 Brauneberger Juffer-Sonnenuhr Spätlese Riesling (Mosel-Saar-Ruwer) $26. 92 Editors' Choice *—J.C. (12/1/2006)*

Dr. H. Thanisch (Erben Müller-Burggraef) 2003 Brauneberger Juffer-Sonnenuhr Spätlese Riesling (Mosel-Saar-Ruwer) $24. 87 *—J.C. (5/1/2005)*

Dr. H. Thanisch (Erben Müller-Burggraef) 2002 Brauneberger Juffer-Sonnenuhr Spätlese Riesling (Mosel-Saar-Ruwer) $21. 88 *—J.C. (8/1/2004)*

Dr. H. Thanisch (Erben Müller-Burggraef) 2006 Classic Riesling (Mosel-Saar-Ruwer) $17. Soft and round in the mouth, this is rather alcoholic for a Mosel (12%), but carries it well, balancing the weight with flinty, citrusy aromas and flavors that fall off rapidly on the finish. **84** *—J.C. (8/1/2007)*

Dr. H. Thanisch (Erben Müller-Burggraef) 2004 Classic Riesling (Mosel-Saar-Ruwer) $17. 85 *—J.C. (2/1/2006)*

Dr. H. Thanisch (Erben Müller-Burggraef) 2005 Classic QbA Riesling (Mosel-Saar-Ruwer) $17. 88 *—J.C. (12/1/2006)*

Dr. H. Thanisch (Erben Müller-Burggraef) 2004 Graacher Himmelreich Spätlese Riesling (Mosel-Saar-Ruwer) $26. 87 *—J.C. (9/1/2006)*

Dr. H. Thanisch (Erben Müller-Burggraef) 2005 Wehlener Sonnenuhr Auslese Riesling (Mosel-Saar-Ruwer) $35. On the big side, with fairly high alcohol and not as much residual sugar as most of this vintage's auslesen. There's apple, melon and citrus, but the fruit is relegated to the background behind layers of spice and minerality. Finishes with hints of white pepper and anise. **90** *—J.C. (2/1/2007)*

Dr. H. Thanisch (Erben Müller-Burggraef) 2006 Wehlener Sonnenuhr Beerenauslese Riesling (Mosel-Saar-Ruwer) $105. This winery has turned out a couple of terrific BAs in 2006 as the family focuses its efforts on its estate wines. Pear, peach, pineapple and spice notes lead the way, garnished by hints of dried apricots in this rich, viscous offering. Finishes long and mouthwatering, not cloying at all—a remarkable achievement in a wine this sweet. Drink now–2040 or beyond. **94 Cellar Selection** *—J.C. (12/15/2007)*

Dr. H. Thanisch (Erben Müller-Burggraef) 2004 Wehlener Sonnenuhr Kabinett Riesling (Mosel-Saar-Ruwer) $19. 87 *—J.C. (7/1/2006)*

Dr. H. Thanisch (Erben Müller-Burggraef) 2002 Wehlener Sonnenuhr Kabinett Riesling (Mosel-Saar-Ruwer) $17. 89 *—J.C. (8/1/2004)*

DR. H. THANISCH (ERBEN THANISCH)

Dr. H. Thanisch (Erben Thanisch) 2004 Berncasteler Doctor Auslese Riesling (Mosel-Saar-Ruwer) $64. 94 Editors' Choice *—J.C. (9/1/2006)*

Dr. H. Thanisch (Erben Thanisch) 2003 Berncasteler Doctor Kabinett Riesling (Mosel-Saar-Ruwer) $47. 84 *—J.C. (5/1/2005)*

Dr. H. Thanisch (Erben Thanisch) 2003 Bernkasteler Badstube Kabinett Riesling (Mosel-Saar-Ruwer) $23. 88 *—J.C. (12/15/2004)*

Dr. H. Thanisch (Erben Thanisch) 2001 Bernkasteler Badstube Kabinett Riesling (Mosel-Saar-Ruwer) $30. 87 *—R.V. (3/1/2003)*

Dr. H. Thanisch (Erben Thanisch) 2001 Bernkasteler Doctor Auslese Riesling (Mosel-Saar-Ruwer) $60. 93 *—R.V. (3/1/2003)*

Dr. H. Thanisch (Erben Thanisch) 2004 QbA Riesling (Mosel-Saar-Ruwer) $21. 88 *—J.C. (2/1/2006)*

Dr. H. Thanisch (Erben Thanisch) 2003 QbA Riesling (Mosel-Saar-Ruwer) $19. 90 *—J.C. (12/15/2004)*

Dr. H. Thanisch (Erben Thanisch) 2001 QbA Riesling (Mosel-Saar-Ruwer) $16. 86 *—J.C. (3/1/2003)*

DR. HEYDEN

Dr. Heyden 2005 Oppenheimer Kabinett Riesling (Rheinhessen) $13. A relatively dry kabinett, with slightly nutty scents of vegetable oil followed by flavors of peach pit and underripe melon. But the sum of the parts is actually better than they sound alone, offering fresh, lemony refreshment with mineral underpinnings. Drink now. **85** *—J.C. (11/15/2007)*

DR. LOOSEN

Dr. Loosen 2004 Villa Wolf Pinot Gris (Pfalz) $11. 84 *—J.C. (7/1/2006)*

Dr. Loosen 1999 Riesling (Mosel-Saar-Ruwer) $10. 86 Best Buy *(8/1/2001)*

Dr. Loosen 2006 Beerenauslese Riesling (Mosel-Saar-Ruwer) $55. Made from an early picking of botrytized grapes from the Bernkasteler Lay vineyard, this is a sweet, plump wine, filled to the brim with lush tropical fruit flavors. The aromas show remarkably pure pear and pineapple scents, with just a touch of dried apricots but also a sense of slate-driven minerality. With 300 cases imported, it should prove relatively easy to find. **93 Editors' Choice** *—J.C. (12/15/2007)*

Dr. Loosen 2005 Beerenauslese Riesling (Mosel-Saar-Ruwer) $55. An affordable BA, presumably from a variety of vineyard sites, this is relatively light in body, but it's still a sweet little wine. Fresh apple and citrus aromas and flavors fold in touches of cinnamon, finishing clean and fresh. The bright acidity suggests this may work best as a foil for foie gras or cheeses rather than as a true dessert wine. **92 Editors' Choice** *—J.C. (10/1/2007)*

Dr. Loosen 1999 Bernkasteler Lay Riesling (Mosel-Saar-Ruwer) $17. 84 *—C.S. (5/1/2002)*

Dr. Loosen 2003 Bernkasteler Lay Kabinett Riesling (Mosel-Saar-Ruwer) $20. 82 *—J.C. (5/1/2005)*

Dr. Loosen 2002 Bernkasteler Lay Kabinett Riesling (Mosel-Saar-Ruwer) $17. 88 *—J.C. (8/1/2004)*

Dr. Loosen 2001 Bernkasteler Lay Kabinett Riesling (Mosel-Saar-Ruwer) $17. 90 *—R.V. (3/1/2003)*

Dr. Loosen 1999 Bernkasteler Lay Kabinett Riesling (Mosel-Saar-Ruwer) $12. 87 *(8/1/2001)*

Dr. Loosen 2005 Dr. L Riesling (Mosel-Saar-Ruwer) $12. 86 *—J.C. (2/1/2007)*

Dr. Loosen 2002 Dr. L QbA Riesling (Mosel-Saar-Ruwer) $11. 87 Best Buy *—J.C. (8/1/2004)*

Dr. Loosen 2001 Dr. L QbA Riesling (Mosel-Saar-Ruwer) $10. 85 *—J.C. (3/1/2003)*

Dr. Loosen 2003 Dr. L Qualitätswein Riesling (Mosel-Saar-Ruwer) $10. 86 Best Buy *—J.C. (11/1/2004)*

Dr. Loosen 2005 Erdener Prälat Auslese Riesling (Mosel-Saar-Ruwer) $65. Very clean and precise, with each of the aromatic elements clearly delineated and imbued with wonderful freshness: apples, honey and citrus. Flavors follow right along with no untoward surprises, only a welcome touch of peaches to help round out the palate. Lush and lingering on the finish. This is immediately attractive, but shows the balance to last 20 years or more. **93** *—J.C. (6/1/2007)*

Dr. Loosen 2002 Erdener Prälat Auslese Riesling (Mosel-Saar-Ruwer) $48. 90 *—J.C. (8/1/2004)*

Dr. Loosen 2005 Erdener Prälat Auslese Goldkapsel Riesling (Mosel-Saar-Ruwer) $55. Unlike many botrytis-affected wines, this wine retains a strong sense of minerality, with oily aromas that remain strong amid the swirl of dried apricot and poached pear scents. Sweet and viscous, but beautifully balanced by lively acidity and a stony core. Long and mouthwatering on the finish. **95 Cellar Selection** *—J.C. (2/1/2007)*

Dr. Loosen 2001 Erdener Prälat Auslese Gold Capsule Riesling (Mosel-Saar-Ruwer) $48. 88 *—J.C. (3/1/2003)*

Dr. Loosen 2005 Erdener Treppchen Auslese Riesling (Mosel-Saar-Ruwer) $40. Dried apricot notes on the nose mingle with pineapple, vanilla and smoky-slatey notes. Flavors of apricot, pineapple, melon and citrus form a veritable fruit bowl, but they're all anchored by stony minerality. This is beautifully balanced, with honeyed sweetness kept in check by bright acidity. **92** *—J.C. (2/1/2007)*

Dr. Loosen 2003 Erdener Treppchen Auslese Riesling (Mosel-Saar-Ruwer) $40. 90 *—J.C. (5/1/2005)*

Dr. Loosen 2005 Erdener Treppchen Auslese Goldkapsul Riesling (Mosel-Saar-Ruwer) $40. Another of the stellar Loosen auslesen from '05, this one features scents of crushed stone and fresh greens, giving less weight and botrytis character than the other goldkapsel offerings. Intense minerality and apple and citrus flavors make an almost crunchy-fresh impression, yet the wine's texture is smooth and creamy. **93** *—J.C. (2/1/2007)*

Dr. Loosen 2001 Erdener Treppchen Eiswein Riesling (Mosel-Saar-Ruwer) $200. 94 *—R.V. (3/1/2003)*

Dr. Loosen 2005 Erdener Treppchen Kabinett Riesling (Mosel-Saar-Ruwer) $22. Leesy and minerally, but there's also plenty of fruit to go alongside, ranging from lime custard to ripe melons and pears. This is medium-bodied, ripe and rich, but balanced by exquisite acidity and minerality. The mouth-tingling finish is long, imbued with great energy. **92 Editors' Choice** *—J.C. (2/1/2007)*

Dr. Loosen 2002 Erdener Treppchen Kabinett Riesling (Mosel-Saar-Ruwer) $18. 87 *—J.C. (8/1/2004)*

Dr. Loosen 2001 Erdener Treppchen Kabinett Riesling (Mosel-Saar-Ruwer) $18. 89 *—J.C. (3/1/2003)*

Dr. Loosen 1999 Erdener Treppchen Kabinett Riesling (Mosel-Saar-Ruwer) $18. 90 Editors' Choice *(8/1/2001)*

Dr. Loosen 2005 Erdener Treppchen Spätlese Riesling (Mosel-Saar-Ruwer) $30. Another success from Loosen, the 2005 Erdener Treppchen Spätlese artfully combines honey, melon and citrus flavors with aromas of wet slate. It's a bit chunky, but should slim down in a few years. It finishes well, with a long, tactile, minerally feel. 92 *—J.C. (6/1/2007)*

Dr. Loosen 2001 Erdener Treppchen Spätlese Riesling (Mosel-Saar-Ruwer) $25. 89 *—R.V. (3/1/2003)*

Dr. Loosen 2005 Graacher Himmelreich Kabinett Riesling (Mosel-Saar-Ruwer) $22. Can a wine be simultaneously light in weight yet dense and concentrated? This one is—then it adds complex flavors of apples, peaches and lemon to terroir-driven notes of slate and spice for a magical result. Finishes with lush, creamy citrus flavors that seem almost like lemon custard. 92 Editors' Choice *—J.C. (6/1/2007)*

Dr. Loosen 2005 Graacher Himmelreich Spätlese Riesling (Mosel-Saar-Ruwer) $30. This has surprisingly restrained fruit for a Loosen wine, but is none the worse for it, as the honeyed apple and citrus flavors allow slaty, minerally notes to play a leading role. Despite its considerable weight, and sweetness, the wine is balanced by zippy acids and a powerful green apple component on the finish. Terrific. 93 *—J.C. (6/1/2007)*

Dr. Loosen 1999 Ürziger Würzgarten Riesling (Mosel-Saar-Ruwer) $25. 89 *(8/1/2001)*

Dr. Loosen 2005 Ürziger Würzgarten Auslese Riesling (Mosel-Saar-Ruwer) $40. The bouquet of apple, pear, citrus and honey become more minerally and complex with air, developing into a delicate interplay of tree fruit, honeyed sweetness and a hint of petrol on the palate. Long on the finish, where it hints at mild citrus, such as tangerine. 91 *—J.C. (2/1/2007)*

Dr. Loosen 2001 Urziger Wurzgarten Auslese Riesling (Mosel-Saar-Ruwer) $42. 90 *—R.V. (3/1/2003)*

Dr. Loosen 2003 Ürziger Würzgarten Auslese Riesling (Mosel-Saar-Ruwer) $40. 85 *—J.C. (5/1/2005)*

Dr. Loosen 2002 Ürziger Würzgarten Auslese Riesling (Mosel-Saar-Ruwer) $42. 90 *—J.C. (8/1/2004)*

Dr. Loosen 2005 Ürziger Würzgarten Auslese Goldkapsel Riesling (Mosel-Saar-Ruwer) $36. On first pass, this wine features wonderfully pristine scents of green apple and lime blended with mineral-laden rainwater. On second nosing, tropical fruit emerges, revealing this wine's sweet nature. Dried apricot, honey, apple and mild citrus flavors are not laser-precise, but rather softly rounded and voluptuous. Finishes long, leaving an elegant, delicate impression. 93 *—J.C. (2/1/2007)*

Dr. Loosen 2005 Ürziger Würzgarten Beerenauslese Riesling (Mosel-Saar-Ruwer) $110. Loosen excelled in 2005, and this beerenauslese is no exception. Brilliantly pure scents of pineapple and honey zoom from the glass, then turn lush and voluptuous on the palate, adding alluring hints of peaches and baked apple. Rich and viscous, it lingers on the finish like wildflower honey. 94 Cellar Selection *—J.C. (10/1/2007)*

Dr. Loosen 2005 Ürziger Würzgarten Kabinett Riesling (Mosel-Saar-Ruwer) $22. Zesty lime notes anchor the bouquet, which touches on green apple and spring flowers as well. Green apple, crushed stone and lime flavors are crisp and sharply focused without being lean or angular. 90 *—J.C. (2/1/2007)*

Dr. Loosen 2004 Ürziger Würzgarten Kabinett Riesling (Mosel-Saar-Ruwer) $20. 90 *—J.C. (5/1/2006)*

Dr. Loosen 2005 Ürziger Würzgarten Spätlese Riesling (Mosel-Saar-Ruwer) $30. Loosen hit a home run in 2005, nailing virtually every wine in his expansive portfolio. Floral, apple and citrus aromas give way to flavors of superripe apples and pears, lively tangerines, even a hint of strawberry. Acids are soft, making this luscious to drink young. 90 *—J.C. (4/1/2007)*

Dr. Loosen 2001 Urziger Wurzgarten Spätlese Riesling (Mosel-Saar-Ruwer) $25. 90 *—J.C. (3/1/2003)*

Dr. Loosen 2003 Ürziger Würzgarten Spätlese Riesling (Mosel-Saar-Ruwer) $28. 85 *—J.C. (5/1/2005)*

Dr. Loosen 2002 Ürziger Würzgarten Spätlese Riesling (Mosel-Saar-Ruwer) $25. 91 Editors' Choice *—J.C. (8/1/2004)*

Dr. Loosen 1999 Wehlener Sonnenuhr Riesling (Mosel-Saar-Ruwer) $17. 88 *(8/1/2001)*

Dr. Loosen 1999 Wehlener Sonnenuhr Riesling (Mosel-Saar-Ruwer) $30. 93 *—P.G. (8/1/2001)*

Dr. Loosen 2005 Wehlener Sonnenuhr Auslese Riesling (Mosel-Saar-Ruwer) $40. Despite being sweet, with a rounded, full mouthfeel, this isn't cloying at all; a testament to its fine balance. Smoky, leesy, fuel oil and slate scents lead off, followed by pristine flavors of apple, pineapple, lime and honey. Finishes long and clean; this should age 20 years or more. 92 *—J.C. (6/1/2007)*

Dr. Loosen 2001 Wehlener Sonnenuhr Auslese Riesling (Mosel-Saar-Ruwer) $38. 90 *—J.C. (3/1/2003)*

Dr. Loosen 2005 Wehlener Sonnenuhr Auslese Goldkapsel Riesling (Mosel-Saar-Ruwer) $36. A magnificent auslese, featuring plenty of botrytis character, but also pronounced wet-slate aromas. Sweet flavors of dried apples and honey are balanced by lively citrus notes and underlying minerality. Despite being rich and viscous, it doesn't come across as heavy; instead it ends long and exquisite balanced. 95 Editors' Choice *—J.C. (2/1/2007)*

Dr. Loosen 2001 Wehlener Sonnenuhr Goldkapsel Auslese Riesling (Mosel-Saar-Ruwer) $33. 92 *—R.V. (3/1/2003)*

Dr. Loosen 2005 Wehlener Sonnenuhr Kabinett Riesling (Mosel-Saar-Ruwer) $22. Light and fresh, this is a wonderfully appealing kabinett, true to its prädikat despite having an abundance of sugar. Lime and green apple aromas set the tone, while the flavors of peaches, apples and citrus fruit never seem heavy. Pure fruit finishes crisp and refreshing. 91 Editors' Choice *—J.C. (6/1/2007)*

Dr. Loosen 2001 Wehlener Sonnenuhr Kabinett Riesling (Mosel-Saar-Ruwer) $35. 89 *—R.V. (1/1/2004)*

Dr. Loosen 2005 Wehlener Sonnenuhr Spätlese Riesling (Mosel-Saar-Ruwer) $30. 92 *—J.C. (2/1/2007)*

Dr. Loosen 2003 Wehlener Sonnenuhr Spätlese Riesling (Mosel-Saar-Ruwer) $28. 86 *—J.C. (5/1/2005)*

Dr. Loosen 2002 Wehlener Sonnenuhr Spätlese Riesling (Mosel-Saar-Ruwer) $25. 91 Editors' Choice *—J.C. (8/1/2004)*

Dr. Loosen 2001 Wehlener Sonnenuhr Spätlese Riesling (Mosel-Saar-Ruwer) $25. 88 *—R.V. (3/1/2003)*

DR. PAULY BERGWEILER

Dr. Pauly Bergweiler 2006 Bernkasteler Badstube Beerenauslese Riesling (Mosel-Saar-Ruwer) $44. A soft, lush, sweet Riesling, but one that lacks the precision and cut of crisp acidity. The avalanche of honeyed fruit—nectarine, peach and pineapple—ends up being merely very enjoyable instead of transporting. Drink now–2015. 89 *—J.C. (12/15/2007)*

Dr. Pauly Bergweiler 2005 Bernkasteler Badstube Kabinett Riesling (Mosel-Saar-Ruwer) $17. 89 *—J.C. (2/1/2007)*

Dr. Pauly Bergweiler 2000 Berkasteler Badstube Spätlese Riesling (Mosel-Saar-Ruwer) $21. 85 *—D.T. (5/1/2002)*

Dr. Pauly Bergweiler 2003 Bernkasteler alte Badstube am Doctorberg Auslese Riesling (Mosel-Saar-Ruwer) $50. 92 *—J.C. (11/1/2004)*

Dr. Pauly Bergweiler 2002 Bernkasteler alte Badstube am Doctorberg Auslese Riesling (Mosel-Saar-Ruwer) $46. 92 *—J.C. (8/1/2004)*

Dr. Pauly Bergweiler 2001 Bernkasteler alte Badstube am Doctorberg Auslese Riesling (Mosel-Saar-Ruwer) $36. 87 *—J.C. (3/1/2003)*

Dr. Pauly Bergweiler 2003 Bernkasteler alte Badstube am Doctorberg Beerenauslese Riesling (Mosel-Saar-Ruwer) $150. 93 *—J.C. (12/15/2004)*

Dr. Pauly Bergweiler 2004 Bernkasteler alte Badstube am Doctorberg Beerenauslese Riesling (Mosel-Saar-Ruwer) $90 375 ml . 93 *—J.C. (2/1/2006)*

Dr. Pauly Bergweiler 2005 Bernkasteler alte Badstube am Doctorberg Kabinett Riesling (Mosel-Saar-Ruwer) $21. 89 *—J.C. (12/1/2006)*

Dr. Pauly Bergweiler 2004 Bernkasteler alte Badstube am Doctorberg Kabinett Riesling (Mosel-Saar-Ruwer) $23. 87 *—J.C. (10/1/2005)*

Dr. Pauly Bergweiler 2003 Bernkasteler alte Badstube am Doctorberg Kabinett Riesling (Mosel-Saar-Ruwer) $21. 89 *—J.C. (11/1/2004)*

Dr. Pauly Bergweiler 2002 Bernkasteler alte Badstube am Doctorberg Kabinett Riesling (Mosel-Saar-Ruwer) $20. 88 *—J.C. (8/1/2004)*

Dr. Pauly Bergweiler 2001 Bernkasteler alte Badstube am Doctorberg Kabinett Riesling (Mosel-Saar-Ruwer) $16. 88 *—J.C. (3/1/2003)*

Dr. Pauly Bergweiler 2005 Bernkasteler alte Badstube am Doctorberg Spätlese Riesling (Mosel-Saar-Ruwer) $27.89 *—J.C. (12/1/2006)*

Dr. Pauly Bergweiler 2004 Bernkasteler alte Badstube am Doctorberg Spätlese Riesling (Mosel-Saar-Ruwer) $30. 87 *—J.C. (10/1/2005)*

Dr. Pauly Bergweiler 2003 Bernkasteler alte Badstube am Doctorberg Spätlese Riesling (Mosel-Saar-Ruwer) $28. 90 *—J.C. (11/1/2004)*

Dr. Pauly Bergweiler 2002 Bernkasteler alte Badstube am Doctorberg Spätlese Riesling (Mosel-Saar-Ruwer) $26. 90 *—J.C. (8/1/2004)*

Dr. Pauly Bergweiler 2001 Bernkasteler alte Badstube am Doctorberg Spätlese Riesling (Mosel-Saar-Ruwer) $20. 87 *—J.C. (3/1/2003)*

Dr. Pauly Bergweiler 2005 Bernkasteler alte Badstube am Doctorberg Trockenbeerenauslese Riesling (Mosel-Saar-Ruwer) $200. Honeyed and viscous—this practically pours like syrup—this is a rich dessert wine, filled with flavors of dried apricots and ultraripe peaches. It's long and sugary on the finish, just lacks a bit of acid balance, and while the hints of caramelized nuts may add complexity, they could also be a hint of oxidation. Drink now, in small doses. 90 *—J.C. (10/1/2007)*

Dr. Pauly Bergweiler 2001 Bernkasteler alte Badstube am Doctorberg Trockenbeerenauslese Riesling (Mosel-Saar-Ruwer) $150. 92 *—J.C. (3/1/2003)*

Dr. Pauly Bergweiler 2000 Bernkasteler alte Badtube am Doctobergretail Kabinett Riesling (Mosel-Saar-Ruwer) $21. 85 *—J.C. (5/1/2002)*

Dr. Pauly Bergweiler 2000 Bernkasteler alte Badtube am Doctorberg Auslese Riesling (Mosel-Saar-Ruwer) $42. 86 *—D.T. (5/1/2002)*

Dr. Pauly Bergweiler 2003 Bernkasteler Badstube Auslese Riesling (Mosel-Saar-Ruwer) $30. 91 Editors' Choice *—J.C. (11/1/2004)*

Dr. Pauly Bergweiler 2001 Bernkasteler Badstube Beerenauslese Riesling (Mosel-Saar-Ruwer) $115. 92 *—R.V. (3/1/2003)*

Dr. Pauly Bergweiler 2003 Bernkasteler Badstube Eiswein Riesling (Mosel-Saar-Ruwer) $175. 96 *—J.C. (12/15/2004)*

Dr. Pauly Bergweiler 2002 Bernkasteler Badstube Eiswein Riesling (Mosel-Saar-Ruwer) $75. 90 *—J.C. (8/1/2004)*

Dr. Pauly Bergweiler 2001 Bernkasteler Badstube Eiswein Riesling (Mosel-Saar-Ruwer) $115. 89 *—J.C. (3/1/2003)*

Dr. Pauly Bergweiler 2004 Bernkasteler Badstube Eiswein 375 ml Riesling (Mosel-Saar-Ruwer) $90. 96 Editors' Choice *—J.C. (9/1/2006)*

Dr. Pauly Bergweiler 2004 Bernkasteler Badstube Kabinett Riesling (Mosel-Saar-Ruwer) $23. 86 *—J.C. (10/1/2005)*

Dr. Pauly Bergweiler 2003 Bernkasteler Badstube Kabinett Riesling (Mosel-Saar-Ruwer) $19. 86 *—J.C. (11/1/2004)*

Dr. Pauly Bergweiler 2002 Bernkasteler Badstube Kabinett Riesling (Mosel-Saar-Ruwer) $18. 87 *—J.C. (8/1/2004)*

Dr. Pauly Bergweiler 2001 Bernkasteler Badstube Kabinett Riesling (Mosel-Saar-Ruwer) $14. 84 *—J.C. (1/1/2004)*

Dr. Pauly Bergweiler 2005 Bernkasteler Badstube Spätlese Riesling (Mosel-Saar-Ruwer) $24. 89 *—J.C. (12/1/2006)*

Dr. Pauly Bergweiler 2004 Bernkasteler Badstube Spätlese Riesling (Mosel-Saar-Ruwer) $30. 89 *—J.C. (10/1/2005)*

Dr. Pauly Bergweiler 2003 Bernkasteler Badstube Spätlese Riesling (Mosel-Saar-Ruwer) $24. 90 *—J.C. (11/1/2004)*

Dr. Pauly Bergweiler 2002 Bernkasteler Badstube Spätlese Riesling (Mosel-Saar-Ruwer) $23. 89 *—J.C. (8/1/2004)*

Dr. Pauly Bergweiler 2001 Bernkasteler Badstube Spätlese Riesling (Mosel-Saar-Ruwer) $18. 87 *—J.C. (3/1/2003)*

Dr. Pauly Bergweiler 2002 Erdener Prälat Auslese Riesling (Mosel-Saar-Ruwer) $48. 89 *—J.C. (8/1/2004)*

Dr. Pauly Bergweiler 2002 Erdener Treppchen Spätlese Riesling (Mosel-Saar-Ruwer) $25. 87 *—J.C. (8/1/2004)*

Dr. Pauly Bergweiler 2001 Graacher Himmelreich Eiswein Riesling (Mosel-Saar-Ruwer) $100. 94 *—R.V. (3/1/2003)*

Dr. Pauly Bergweiler 2001 Graacher Himmelreich Kabinett Riesling (Mosel-Saar-Ruwer) $14. 88 *—J.C. (3/1/2003)*

Dr. Pauly Bergweiler 2005 Noble House Riesling (Mosel-Saar-Ruwer) $10. The house style at Pauly-Bergweiler is one of ripeness and sugar, so it's no surprise that even its entry-level wine shows plenty of weight and sucrosity. Corn oil and acacia blossom scents accent baked apple, cinnamon and honey flavors that linger on the finish. Drink now. 87 Best Buy *—J.C. (6/1/2007)*

Dr. Pauly Bergweiler 2006 Noble House QbA Riesling (Mosel-Saar-Ruwer) $12. Round and soft in the mouth, yet without much flavor, just hints of peach and melon. 82 *—J.C. (8/1/2007)*

Dr. Pauly Bergweiler 2002 Noble House QbA Riesling (Mosel-Saar-Ruwer) $11. 84 *—J.C. (8/1/2004)*

Dr. Pauly Bergweiler 2001 Noble House QbA Riesling (Mosel-Saar-Ruwer) $8. 88 Best Buy *—J.C. (3/1/2003)*

Dr. Pauly Bergweiler 2004 Noble House Qualitatswein Riesling (Mosel-Saar-Ruwer) $12. 87 Best Buy *—J.C. (10/1/2005)*

Dr. Pauly Bergweiler 2003 Noble House Qualitätswein Riesling (Mosel-Saar-Ruwer) $11. 84 *—J.C. (11/1/2004)*

Dr. Pauly Bergweiler 2000 Urziger Wurzgarten Spätlese Riesling (Mosel-Saar-Ruwer) $23. 83 *—D.T. (5/1/2002)*

Dr. Pauly Bergweiler 2001 Urziger Wurzgarten Trockenbeerenauslese Riesling (Mosel-Saar-Ruwer) $265. 94 Cellar Selection *—J.C. (3/1/2003)*

Dr. Pauly Bergweiler 2002 Ürziger Würzgarten Trockenbeernauslese Riesling (Mosel-Saar-Ruwer) $175. 92 *—J.C. (8/1/2004)*

Dr. Pauly Bergweiler 2005 Wehlener Sonnenuhr Spätlese Riesling (Mosel-Saar-Ruwer) $27. Ripe and full-bodied, with sweet, honeyed flavors of baked apple and petrol. This is a bit rich and heavy for its prädikat, with a low-acid finish that lingers thanks to some dried-spice notes. 88 *—J.C. (6/1/2007)*

Dr. Pauly Bergweiler 2000 Wehlener Sonnehur Spätlese Riesling (Mosel-Saar-Ruwer) $23. 85 *—D.T. (5/1/2002)*

Dr. Pauly Bergweiler 2005 Wehlener Sonnenuhr Auslese Riesling (Mosel-Saar-Ruwer) $37. 90 *—J.C. (12/1/2006)*

Dr. Pauly Bergweiler 2004 Wehlener Sonnenuhr Auslese Riesling (Mosel-Saar-Ruwer) $40. 89 *—J.C. (9/1/2006)*

Dr. Pauly Bergweiler 2003 Wehlener Sonnenuhr Auslese Riesling (Mosel-Saar-Ruwer) $37. 90 *—J.C. (11/1/2004)*

Dr. Pauly Bergweiler 2001 Wehlener Sonnenuhr Auslese Riesling (Mosel-Saar-Ruwer) $26. 87 *—J.C. (3/1/2003)*

Dr. Pauly Bergweiler 2004 Wehlener Sonnenuhr Kabinett Riesling (Mosel-Saar-Ruwer) $23. 86 *—J.C. (10/1/2005)*

Dr. Pauly Bergweiler 2003 Wehlener Sonnenuhr Kabinett Riesling (Mosel-Saar-Ruwer) $22. 84 *—J.C. (11/1/2004)*

Dr. Pauly Bergweiler 2001 Wehlener Sonnenuhr Kabinett Riesling (Mosel-Saar-Ruwer) $10. 86 Best Buy *—R.V. (1/1/2004)*

Dr. Pauly Bergweiler 2004 Wehlener Sonnenuhr Spätlese Riesling (Mosel-Saar-Ruwer) $30. 86 *—J.C. (10/1/2005)*

Dr. Pauly Bergweiler 2003 Wehlener Sonnenuhr Spätlese Riesling (Mosel-Saar-Ruwer) $28. 90 *—J.C. (11/1/2004)*

Dr. Pauly Bergweiler 2002 Wehlener Sonnenuhr Spätlese Riesling (Mosel-Saar-Ruwer) $25. 85 *—J.C. (8/1/2004)*

Dr. Pauly Bergweiler 2001 Wehlener Sonnenuhr Spätlese Riesling (Mosel-Saar-Ruwer) $20. 88 *—J.C. (3/1/2003)*

Dr. Pauly Bergweiler 2002 Wehlener Sonneuhr Kabinett Riesling (Mosel-Saar-Ruwer) $21. 88 *—J.C. (8/1/2004)*

DR. WAGNER

Dr. Wagner 2004 Ockfener Bockstein Kabinett Riesling (Mosel-Saar-Ruwer) $19. 89 *—J.C. (5/1/2006)*

Dr. Wagner 2001 Ockfener Bockstein Kabinett Riesling (Mosel-Saar-Ruwer) $17. 87 *—J.C. (3/1/2003)*

Dr. Wagner 2003 Ockfener Bockstein Riesling Kabinett Riesling (Mosel-Saar-Ruwer) $18. 87 *—J.C. (12/15/2004)*

Dr. Wagner 2004 Ockfener Bockstein Spätlese Riesling (Mosel-Saar-Ruwer) $22. 86 *—J.C. (2/1/2006)*

Dr. Wagner 2001 Ockfener Bockstein Spätlese Riesling (Mosel-Saar-Ruwer) $20. 85 *—J.C. (3/1/2003)*

DR. WEINS-PRÜM

Dr. Weins-Prüm 2005 Graacher Himmelreich Auslese Riesling (Mosel-Saar-Ruwer) $44. This may seem a bit sweet and heavy next to J.J. Prüm's bottling from the same vineyard, but it's still a darn good wine, with hints of dried apricots to accent pear, melon and spice flavors. It's thick and viscous, with a finish that lingers sweetly. Drink 2013–2020. 90 *—J.C. (10/1/2007)*

DR. ZENZEN

Dr. Zenzen 2001 Valwiger Herrenberg Auslese Riesling (Mosel-Saar-Ruwer) $29. Light to medium in body, this is a clean, fresh auslese, not a big, sugary blockbuster. Pineapple and honey aromas lead the way, adding green apple, mint and citrus flavors as the wine crosses the palate. To some, it may seem a bit green and underripe despite the ample residual sugar, while to others it will be a welcome respite from many of the over-ripe ausleses that are actually declassified BAs. 88 *—J.C. (10/1/2007)*

DUIJN

Duijn 2004 Jannin Pinot Noir (Baden) $46. Light to medium in body, this wine's modest cherry fruit is largely submerged under a layer of smoky oak. Cola and coffee flavors dominate, ending on a tart note. 84 *—J.C. (6/1/2007)*

Duijn 2003 Jannin Trocken Spätburgunder (Baden) $45. 84 *—J.C. (7/1/2006)*

EGON MULLER

Egon Muller 2002 Scharzhof QbA Riesling (Mosel-Saar-Ruwer) $17. 84 *—J.C. (11/1/2004)*

Egon Muller 2002 Scharzhofberger Kabinett Riesling (Mosel-Saar-Ruwer) $40. 87 *—J.C. (11/1/2004)*

EGON MÜLLER-SCHARZHOF

Egon Müller-Scharzhof 2001 Kabinett Riesling (Mosel-Saar-Ruwer) $34. 92 Cellar Selection *—J.C. (3/1/2003)*

Egon Müller-Scharzhof 2001 Scharzhof QbA Riesling (Mosel-Saar-Ruwer) $17. 89 *—J.C. (3/1/2003)*

EILENZ

Eilenz 2001 Ayler Kupp Kabinett Riesling (Mosel-Saar-Ruwer) $12. 88 Best Buy *—J.C. (3/1/2003)*

Eilenz 2001 Ayler Kupp QbA Riesling (Mosel-Saar-Ruwer) $12. 81 *—J.C. (1/1/2004)*

Eilenz 2001 Ayler Kupp Spätlese Riesling (Mosel-Saar-Ruwer) $16. 83 *—J.C. (1/1/2004)*

EMRICH-SCHONLEBER

Emrich-Schonleber 2004 Monzinger Frülingsplätzchen Kabinett Riesling (Nahe) $31. An interesting, characterful kabinett, with scents of smoke and scorched oil that mingle with lime and apple notes. On the palate, it delivers plenty of zippy citrus flavors, wrapped in a confounding veil of smoke and tar. Might prove better in time; give it 3–4 years of cellaring. 85 *—J.C. (10/1/2007)*

Emrich-Schonleber 2003 Monzinger Frühlingsplätzchen Kabinett Riesling (Nahe) $25 86 *—J.C. (5/1/2005)*

Emrich-Schonleber 2003 Monzinger Halenberg Auslese Riesling (Nahe) $35. 90 *—J.C. (2/1/2006)*

ERICH BENDER

Erich Bender 2004 Trockenbeerenauslese 375 ml Huxelrebe (Pfalz) $37. 88 *—J.C. (9/1/2006)*

ERNST BRETZ

Ernst Bretz 2003 Eiswein Riesling (Rheinhessen) $33. A lush, somewhat soft eiswein, with aromas and flavors of superripe oranges or orange marmalade, balanced by a touch of dry, minerally extract on the finish. 89 *—J.C. (12/15/2007)*

EUGEN WEHRHEIM

Eugen Wehrheim 2001 Niersteiner Bildstock Kabinett Riesling (Rheinhessen) $13. 84 *—J.C. (1/1/2004)*

Eugen Wehrheim 2003 Niersteiner Bildstock Riesling Kabinett Riesling (Rheinhessen) $13. 86 *—J.C. (12/15/2004)*

Eugen Wehrheim 2003 Niersteiner Oelberg Auslese Riesling (Rheinhessen) $24. 89 *—J.C. (5/1/2006)*

Eugen Wehrheim 2003 Niersteiner Orbel Riesling Spätlese Riesling (Rheinhessen) $16. 87 *—J.C. (12/15/2004)*

Eugen Wehrheim 2001 Niersteiner Orbel Spätlese Riesling (Rheinhessen) $15. 89 *—J.C. (3/1/2003)*

EYMANN

Eymann 2003 Classic Riesling (Pfalz) $12. 87 Best Buy *—R.V. (4/1/2005)*

Eymann 1999 Gönnheimer Mandelgarten Eiswein Riesling (Pfalz) $74. 91 *—R.V. (4/1/2005)*

Eymann 2001 Selektion Toreye Gönnheimer Sonnenberg Trocken Spätburgunder (Pfalz) $26. 86 *—R.V. (4/1/2005)*

FALCON HILL

Falcon Hill 2006 Dry Riesling (Rheinhessen) $10. Despite the "dry" label, this wine boasts sweet-tasting flavors that are fruity and simple, favoring apple and pineapple, then turning tart and citrusy on the finish. Cleanly made. 84 *—J.C. (9/1/2007)*

Falcon Hill 2005 Dry Riesling (Rheinhessen) $9. 83 *—J.C. (12/1/2006)*

FISCHER

Fischer 2004 Pinot Noir (Baden) $18. This lightweight Pinot could use a larger helping of fruit. There's plenty of the earthy complexity you want in Pinot Noir—smoke, earth, beet root, mushrooms—but it all fades quickly, turning dull, with drying tannins on the finish. 81 *—J.C. (6/1/2007)*

Fischer 2004 Kabinett Trocken Riesling (Baden) $18. 86 *—J.C. (12/1/2006)*

Fischer 2005 QbA Riesling (Baden) $18. A reasonably dry, full-bodied style of Riesling, Fischer's 2005 shows bold aromas of lemon and quince, then rounds them out with a bit of apple on the palate. Crisp; a good partner for seafood. 85 *—J.C. (4/1/2007)*

FITZ-RITTER

Fitz-Ritter 2003 Spätlese Gewürztraminer (Pfalz) $18. 88 *—J.C. (12/15/2004)*

Fitz-Ritter 2005 Dürkheimer Abtsfronhof Kabinett Trocken Riesling (Pfalz) $16. 86 *—J.C. (12/1/2006)*

Fitz-Ritter 2003 Dürkheimer Abtsfronhof Riesling Spätlese Halbtrocken Riesling (Pfalz) $18. 87 *—J.C. (12/15/2004)*

Fitz-Ritter 2005 QbA Riesling (Pfalz) $13. 84 *—J.C. (2/1/2007)*

Fitz-Ritter NV Extra Trocken Sekt Riesling (Pfalz) $15. 87 *—J.C. (6/1/2006)*

FORSTMEISTER GELTZ ZILLIKEN

Forstmeister Geltz Zilliken 2001 Ockfener Bockstein Kabinett Riesling (Mosel-Saar-Ruwer) $NA. 88 *—R.V. (1/1/2004)*

Forstmeister Geltz Zilliken 2001 Saarburger Rausch Kabinett Riesling (Mosel-Saar-Ruwer) $NA. 89 *—R.V. (1/1/2004)*

FRANZ KÜNSTLER

Franz Künstler 2001 Hochheimer Holle Auslese Riesling (Rheingau) $60. 92 *—R.V. (1/1/2004)*

Franz Künstler 2001 Hochheimer Hölle Eiswein Riesling (Rheingau) $140. 90 *—R.V. (1/1/2004)*

Franz Künstler 2001 Hochheimer Holle Spätlese Trocken Riesling (Rheingau) $40. 84 *—R.V. (1/1/2004)*

Franz Künstler 2001 Hochheimer Kirchenstück Eiswein Riesling (Rheingau) $150. 94 *—R.V. (1/1/2004)*

Franz Künstler 2002 Hochheimer Reichestal Kabinett Riesling (Rheingau) $20. 85 *—J.C. (8/1/2004)*

Franz Künstler 2001 Hochheimer Reichestal Kabinett Riesling (Rheingau) $20. 84 *—R.V. (1/1/2004)*

FRED PRINZ

Fred Prinz 2003 Hallgartener Jungfer Kabinett Riesling (Rheingau) $21. 87 *—J.C. (5/1/2005)*

Fred Prinz 2001 Hallgartner Jungfer Spätlese Riesling (Rheingau) $NA. 87 *—R.V. (1/1/2004)*

Fred Prinz 2001 Hallgartner Schonhell Spätlese Trocken Riesling (Rheingau) $NA. 89 *—R.V. (1/1/2004)*

Fred Prinz 2001 Hallgartner Jungfer Kabinett White Blend (Rheingau) $NA. 92 *—R.V. (1/1/2004)*

FREIHERR HEYL ZU HERRNSHEIM

Freiherr Heyl zu Herrnsheim 2005 Baron Heyl Estate QbA Riesling (Rheinhessen) $17. 87 *—J.C. (2/1/2007)*

Freiherr Heyl zu Herrnsheim 2003 Baron Heyl Estate Riesling QbA Riesling (Rheinhessen) $15. 86 *—J.C. (12/15/2004)*

Freiherr Heyl zu Herrnsheim 2005 Baron Heyl Kabinett Riesling (Rheinhessen) $19. 91 Editors' Choice *—J.C. (12/1/2006)*

Freiherr Heyl zu Herrnsheim 2004 Baron Heyl Nierstein Kabinett Riesling (Rheinhessen) $19. 90 Editors' Choice *—J.C. (7/1/2006)*

Freiherr Heyl zu Herrnsheim 2003 Baron Heyl Nierstein Kabinett Riesling (Rheinhessen) $16. 86 *—J.C. (12/15/2004)*

Freiherr Heyl zu Herrnsheim 2003 Baron Heyl Nierstein Riesling Spätlese Riesling (Rheinhessen) $24. 91 Editors' Choice *—J.C. (12/15/2004)*

Freiherr Heyl zu Herrnsheim 2001 Baron Heyl Nierstein Spätlese Riesling (Rheinhessen) $11. 87 Best Buy *—J.C. (3/1/2003)*

Freiherr Heyl zu Herrnsheim 2001 Nierstein Kabinett Riesling (Rheinhessen) $14. 86 *—J.C. (3/1/2003)*

Freiherr Heyl zu Herrnsheim 2001 Nierstein Pettental QbA Trocken Riesling (Rheinhessen) $30. 88 *—J.C. (3/1/2003)*

Freiherr Heyl zu Herrnsheim 2001 Red Slate Spätlese Trocken Riesling (Rheinhessen) $25. 84 *—J.C. (3/1/2003)*

FRIEDRICH-WILHELM-GYMNASIUM

Friedrich-Wilhelm-Gymnasium 2004 Bernkasteler Badstube Kabinett Halbtrocken Riesling (Mosel-Saar-Ruwer) $14. 87 *—J.C. (7/1/2006)*

Friedrich-Wilhelm-Gymnasium 2005 Graacher Himmelreich Auslese Riesling (Mosel-Saar-Ruwer) $25. This wine blends intense green apple and lime fruit aromas with scents of rock dust and petrol. It's medium-bodied and plump in texture, easily gliding along with flavors of apple seed oil, honey and ripe citrus, finishing soft, yet persistent. Imported by Chatham Imports, Inc. 91 *—J.C. (6/1/2007)*

Friedrich-Wilhelm-Gymnasium 2001 Graacher Himmelreich Auslese Riesling (Mosel-Saar-Ruwer) $24. 92 *—R.V. (1/1/2004)*

Friedrich-Wilhelm-Gymnasium 2005 Graacher Himmelreich Kabinett Riesling (Mosel-Saar-Ruwer) $15. Light in weight, this is a refreshing throwback to the kabinett style of the '70s and '80s rather than the declassified spätlesen that pass for kabinett so often these days. Lemon and lime aromas are followed by citrus and green apple flavors and a lightly off-dry finish. Crisp and focused. Imported by Chatham Imports, Inc. 86 *—J.C. (4/1/2007)*

Friedrich-Wilhelm-Gymnasium 2001 Graacher Himmelreich Kabinett Riesling (Mosel-Saar-Ruwer) $18. 90 *—R.V. (1/1/2004)*

Friedrich-Wilhelm-Gymnasium 2004 Graacher Himmelreich Spätlese Riesling (Mosel-Saar-Ruwer) $19. 90 Editors' Choice *—J.C. (9/1/2006)*

Friedrich-Wilhelm-Gymnasium 2001 Graacher Himmelreich Spätlese Riesling (Mosel-Saar-Ruwer) $18. 91 *—R.V. (1/1/2004)*

Friedrich-Wilhelm-Gymnasium 2000 Graacher Himmelreich Spätlese Riesling (Mosel-Saar-Ruwer) $18. 83 *—D.T. (5/1/2002)*

Friedrich-Wilhelm-Gymnasium 2001 Trittenheimer Apotheke Ausles Riesling (Mosel-Saar-Ruwer) $20. 90 *—R.V. (1/1/2004)*

Friedrich-Wilhelm-Gymnasium 2000 Trittenheimer Apotheke Kabinett Riesling (Mosel-Saar-Ruwer) $14. 84 *—J.C. (5/1/2002)*

Friedrich-Wilhelm-Gymnasium 2001 Trittenheimer Apotheke Spätlese Riesling (Mosel-Saar-Ruwer) $18. 92 *—R.V. (1/1/2004)*

Friedrich-Wilhelm-Gymnasium 2000 Trittenheimer Apothke Spätlese Riesling (Mosel-Saar-Ruwer) $18. 86 *—C.S. (5/1/2002)*

FÜRST VON METTERNICH

Fürst von Metternich NV Brut Riesling Sekt Riesling (Germany) $23. 86 *—J.C. (12/31/2004)*

Fürst von Metternich NV Cuvée Trocken Riesling Sekt Riesling (Germany) $15. 85 *—J.C. (12/31/2004)*

FURST ZU HOHENLOHE

Furst zu Hohenlohe 2002 Verrenberger Verrenberg Butzen QbA Trocken Riesling (Württemberg) $13. 87 *—J.C. (8/1/2004)*

Furst zu Hohenlohe 2002 Verrenberger Verrenberg Butzen Spätlese Riesling (Oehringen) $24. 84 *—J.C. (8/1/2004)*

G&M MACHMER

G&M Machmer 2001 Bechtheimer Rosengarten Eiswein Gewürztraminer (Rheinhessen) $32. An eiswein that's different—and affordable. Made from Gewürz, it boasts aromas and flavors of caramel or butterscotch, maple syrup and caramelized peaches. It is sweet, without the crispness of a Riesling eiswein, but enjoyable nonetheless. Drink it over the near term. 90 *—J.C. (12/15/2007)*

G. DICKENSHEID

G. Dickensheid 2003 Riesling Kabinett Riesling (Rheinhessen) $10. 84 Best Buy *—J.C. (12/15/2004)*

GEH. RAT DR. VON BASSERMANN-JORDAN

Geh. Rat Dr. von Bassermann-Jordan 2004 Deidesheimer Paradiesgarten Kabinett Riesling (Pfalz) $19. 86 *—J.C. (5/1/2006)*

Geh. Rat Dr. von Bassermann-Jordan 2001 Deidesheimer Paradiesgarten Kabinett Riesling (Pfalz) $16. 83 *—J.C. (1/1/2004)*

Geh. Rat Dr. von Bassermann-Jordan 2003 Deidesheimer Paradiesgarten Riesling Kabinett Riesling (Pfalz) $19. 84 *—J.C. (12/15/2004)*

Geh. Rat Dr. von Bassermann-Jordan NV Deutscher Sekt Brut Riesling (Pfalz) $NA. 87 *—J.C. (6/1/2006)*

Geh. Rat Dr. von Bassermann-Jordan 2003 Forster Jesuitengarten Riesling Spätlese Riesling (Pfalz) $29. 89 *—J.C. (12/15/2004)*

Geh. Rat Dr. von Bassermann-Jordan 2004 Forster Jesuitengarten Spätlese Riesling (Pfalz) $28. 90 *—J.C. (2/1/2006)*

Geh. Rat Dr. von Bassermann-Jordan 2001 Forster Jesuitengarten Spätlese Riesling (Pfalz) $26. 86 *—J.C. (3/1/2003)*

Geh. Rat Dr. von Bassermann-Jordan 2003 Forster Ungeheuer Riesling Spätlese Trocken Riesling (Pfalz) $27. 87 *—J.C. (12/15/2004)*

Geh. Rat Dr. von Bassermann-Jordan 2001 QbA Riesling (Pfalz) $14. 83 *—J.C. (1/1/2004)*

Geh. Rat Dr. von Bassermann-Jordan 2006 Trocken Riesling (Pfalz) $17. Understated on the nose, but there are some pretty hints of melon, spice and crushed stone. Light in body, with modest fruit flavors on the palate, but some finishing anise and clove. 84 *—J.C. (8/1/2007)*

Geh. Rat Dr. von Bassermann-Jordan 2004 QbA Trocken Riesling (Pfalz) $17. 88 *—J.C. (10/1/2005)*

Geh. Rat Dr. von Bassermann-Jordan 2001 QbA Trocken Riesling (Pfalz) $14. 85 *—J.C. (3/1/2003)*

Geh. Rat Dr. von Bassermann-Jordan 2005 Trocken QbA Riesling (Pfalz) $16. 85 *—J.C. (12/1/2006)*

GEORG BREUER

Georg Breuer 2004 Spätburgunder Rouge Pinot Noir (Rheingau) $20. 83 *—J.C. (7/1/2006)*

Georg Breuer 2004 Berg Schlossberg Auslese 375 ml Riesling (Rheingau) $95. 92 *—J.C. (9/1/2006)*

Georg Breuer 2003 Berg Schlossberg Auslese 375 ml Riesling (Rheingau) $80. 88 *—J.C. (5/1/2005)*

Georg Breuer 2003 Berg Schlossberg Trockenbeerenauslese Riesling (Rheingau) $250. 91 *—J.C. (5/1/2005)*

Georg Breuer 2002 Charm Riesling (Rheingau) $14. 87 *—J.C. (11/1/2004)*

Georg Breuer 2004 Estate Rüdesheim QbA Riesling (Rheingau) $20. 85 *—J.C. (5/1/2006)*

Georg Breuer 1999 GB Riesling (Rheingau) $13. 88 Best Buy *—P.G. (8/1/2001)*

Georg Breuer 1999 Montosa Riesling (Rheingau) $23. 88 *(8/1/2001)*

Georg Breuer 1998 Rauenthal Nonnenberg Riesling (Rheingau) $36. 89 *(8/1/2001)*

Georg Breuer 2004 Rauenthal Nonnenberg QbA Riesling (Rheingau) $50. 85 *—J.C. (7/1/2006)*

Georg Breuer 2002 Rauenthal Nonnenberg QbA Riesling (Rheingau) $46. 85 *—J.C. (11/1/2004)*

Georg Breuer 2003 Rauenthaler Nonnenberg Auslese 375 ml Riesling (Rheingau) $79. 93 *—J.C. (2/1/2006)*

Georg Breuer 2005 Rauenthal Nonnenberg Auslese Gold Cap Riesling (Rheingau) $65. Intensely sweet, as you might expect, with scents of honey, dried apricots and clover. But there's also a hint of vinyl or plastic that mars the nose and the palate, so although this is sticky and long on the finish, it doesn't quite make top marks. 89 *—J.C. (10/1/2007)*

Georg Breuer 2003 Rauenthaler Nonnenberg Riesling Trockenbeerenauslese 375 ml Riesling (Rheingau) $283. 94 *—J.C. (9/1/2006)*

Georg Breuer 2004 Rüdesheim Berg Schlossberg QbA Riesling (Rheingau) $55. Big and full-bodied, with just a touch of sugar in evidence, while the alcohol is up to 13%. Petrol and slate notes mark the nose, while the fruit features pineapple, nectarine and melon. Long, powerful and citrusy on the finish, with underlying minerality and spice that provides fascinating complexity. Great now, but there's no reason this shouldn't age well for five or more years. 91 *—J.C. (10/1/2007)*

Georg Breuer 2002 Rudesheim Berg Schlossberg QbA Riesling (Rheingau) $50. 85 *—J.C. (11/1/2004)*

Georg Breuer 1998 Rüdeshemier Berg Schlossberg Riesling (Rheingau) $40. 92 *(8/1/2001)*

Georg Breuer 2001 Terra Montosa Riesling (Rheingau) $20. 90 Editors' Choice *—J.C. (3/1/2003)*

Georg Breuer 2002 Terra Montosa Qualitätswein Riesling (Rheingau) $22. 89 *—J.C. (11/1/2004)*

GRAFF

Graff 2004 Wehlener Sonnenuhr Kabinett Riesling (Mosel-Saar-Ruwer) $12. 89 Best Buy *—J.C. (10/1/2005)*

GRANS-FASSIAN

Grans-Fassian 2005 QbA Riesling (Mosel-Saar-Ruwer) $17. 88 *—J.C. (2/1/2007)*

Grans-Fassian 2003 QbA Riesling (Mosel-Saar-Ruwer) $17. 86 *—J.C. (5/1/2005)*

Grans-Fassian 2001 Trittenheimer Apotheke Riesling (Mosel-Saar-Ruwer) $21. 87 *—J.C. (3/1/2003)*

Grans-Fassian 2005 Trittenheimer Apotheke Auslese Riesling (Mosel-Saar-Ruwer) $40. 94 Editors' Choice *—J.C. (12/1/2006)*

Grans-Fassian 2004 Trittenheimer Apotheke Auslese Riesling (Mosel-Saar-Ruwer) $40. 90 *—J.C. (9/1/2006)*

Grans-Fassian 2005 Trittenheimer Apotheke Spätlese Riesling (Mosel-Saar-Ruwer) $31. 91 *—J.C. (2/1/2007)*

Grans-Fassian 2004 Trittenheimer Apotheke Spätlese Riesling (Mosel-Saar-Ruwer) $31. 86 *—J.C. (5/1/2006)*

Grans-Fassian 2003 Trittenheimer Apotheke Spätlese Riesling (Mosel-Saar-Ruwer) $30. 91 *—J.C. (12/15/2004)*

Grans-Fassian 2005 Trittenheimer Kabinett Riesling (Mosel-Saar-Ruwer) $21. 91 Editors' Choice *—J.C. (12/1/2006)*

Grans-Fassian 2004 Trittenheimer Kabinett Riesling (Mosel-Saar-Ruwer) $21. 88 *—J.C. (7/1/2006)*

Grans-Fassian 2001 Trittenheimer Kabinett Riesling (Mosel-Saar-Ruwer) $14. 91 Best Buy *—J.C. (3/1/2003)*

GROEBE

Groebe 2003 Westhofener Kabinett Trocken Riesling (Rheinhessen) $17. 84 *—J.C. (11/1/2004)*

Groebe 2003 Westhofener Kirchspiel Spätlese Riesling (Rheinhessen) $26. 87 *—J.C. (11/1/2004)*

Groebe 2004 Westhofener Riesling Kabinett Riesling (Rheinhessen) $18. 84 —*J.C. (7/1/2006)*

GUNDERLOCH

Gunderloch 2004 Diva Spätlese Riesling (Rheinhessen) $21. 86 —*J.C. (10/1/2005)*

Gunderloch 2002 Diva Spätlese Riesling (Rheinhessen) $20. 85 —*J.C. (8/1/2004)*

Gunderloch 2005 Dry Riesling (Rheinhessen) $19. Strikes a lovely balance between fruit and minerality, marrying ripe apple and orangey citrus notes with hints of petrol or diesel. Reasonably full-bodied, turning crisp and zesty on the spice-inflected finish. Drink now. 90 Editors' Choice —*J.C. (9/1/2007)*

Gunderloch 2004 Dry Qualitätswein Riesling (Rheinhessen) $19. 87 —*J.C. (10/1/2005)*

Gunderloch 2002 Jean Baptiste Kabinett Riesling (Rheingau) $18. 86 —*J.C. (8/1/2004)*

Gunderloch 2004 Jean-Baptiste Kabinett Riesling (Rheinhessen) $20. 87 —*J.C. (10/1/2005)*

GUSTAV ADOLPH SCHMITT

Gustav Adolph Schmitt 2005 Niersteiner Rehlbach Spätlese Riesling (Rheinhessen) $10. Fans of sweet Riesling should scoop this bargain up. The aromas and flavors of honey, superripe apples and pears are lusciously sugary, the mouthfeel is thick and concentrated, and the finish long and mouthcoating. It could use a touch more zest, but at this price, who's arguing? 87 Best Buy —*J.C. (11/15/2007)*

GYSLER

Gysler 2004 Weinheimer Kabinett Riesling (Rheinhessen) $17. 89 —*J.C. (10/1/2005)*

H. & R. LINGENFELDER

H. & R. Lingenfelder 2001 Freinsheimer Goldberg Spätlese Scheurebe (Pfalz) $26. 85 —*J.C. (1/1/2004)*

HANS LANG

Hans Lang 2001 Hallgartner Jungfer Eiswein Riesling (Rheingau) $NA. 91 —*R.V. (1/1/2004)*

Hans Lang 2001 Hattenheimer Wisselbrunnen Auslese Riesling (Rheingau) $NA. 85 —*R.V. (1/1/2004)*

Hans Lang 2001 Hattenheimer Wisselbrunnen Beerenauslese Riesling (Rheingau) $NA. 94 —*R.V. (1/1/2004)*

Hans Lang 2001 Hattenheimer Wisselbrunnen Spätlese Riesling (Rheingau) $NA. 88 —*R.V. (1/1/2004)*

Hans Lang 2001 Kabinett Riesling (Rheingau) $NA. 88 —*R.V. (1/1/2004)*

Hans Lang 2001 Spätlese Riesling (Rheingau) $NA. 83 —*R.V. (1/1/2004)*

HANS WIRSCHING

Hans Wirsching 2005 Iphöfer Kronsberg Spätlese Trocken Riesling (Franken) $33. Make no mistake—this is full-bodied, but it carries its 14.5% alcohol without any sign of warmth, just mouthcoating layers of flavor. Petrol and oily notes mark the nose and palate, but there's enough apple-y fruit and dried-spice notes to achieve complexity and balance. Dry essence of Riesling. 92 Editors' Choice —*J.C. (9/1/2007)*

HEINRICH SEEBRICH

Heinrich Seebrich 2001 Niersteiner Hipping Spätlese Riesling (Rheinhessen) $13. 85 —*J.C. (3/1/2003)*

HEINZ SCHMITT

Heinz Schmitt 2005 Halbtrocken Riesling (Mosel-Saar-Ruwer) $15. Based on the last two vintages of this wine, Schmitt seems to have settled into a rather oily, minerally style for this wine, marrying kerosene and honeyed richness with baked apple and pear flavors. Drink now. 87 —*J.C. (4/1/2007)*

Heinz Schmitt 2004 Halbtrocken Riesling (Mosel-Saar-Ruwer) $13. 86 —*J.C. (7/1/2006)*

HELMUT HEXAMER

Helmut Hexamer 2001 Meddersheimer Rheingrafenberg Spätlese S Riesling (Nahe) $26. 90 —*J.C. (3/1/2003)*

HELMUT HEXAMER

Helmut Hexamer 2004 Quarzit Meddersheimer Rheingrafenberg Qualitätswein Riesling (Nahe) $22. 91 Editors' Choice —*J.C. (10/1/2005)*

HENKELL

Henkell 2000 Chardonnay Brut Sekt Chardonnay (Germany) $23. 80 —*J.C. (12/31/2004)*

Henkell NV Rosé Feiner Sekt Trocken Rosé Blend (Germany) $11. 83 —*J.C. (12/31/2004)*

Henkell 2002 Gamay Rose Brut Sekt Sparkling Blend (Germany) $25. 84 —*J.C. (12/31/2004)*

Henkell NV Trocken Sekt White Blend (Germany) $12. 84 —*J.C. (6/1/2006)*

HESS. STAATSWEINGÜTER

Hess. Staatsweingüter 2001 Rauenthaler Baiken Kabinett Riesling (Rheingau) $17. 88 —*J.C. (3/1/2003)*

Hess. Staatsweingüter 2001 Steinberg QbA Riesling (Rheingau) $14. 88 Best Buy —*J.C. (3/1/2003)*

Hess. Staatsweingüter 2001 Steinberger Spätlese Riesling (Rheingau) $34. 90 —*J.C. (3/1/2003)*

I.Q.

I.Q. 2002 QbA Riesling (Rheinhessen) $9. 83 —*J.C. (11/1/2004)*

IMMICH-BATTERIEBERG

Immich-Batterieberg 2004 Blauschiefer QbA Riesling (Mosel-Saar-Ruwer) $23. 88 —*J.C. (7/1/2006)*

Immich-Batterieberg 2005 Detonation Riesling (Rhein-Mosel) $11. 84 —*J.C. (12/1/2006)*

Immich-Batterieberg 2004 Enkircher Batterieberg Spätlese Riesling (Mosel-Saar-Ruwer) $38. 90 —*J.C. (9/1/2006)*

Immich-Batterieberg 2005 Kabinett Riesling (Mosel-Saar-Ruwer) $20. 83 —*J.C. (2/1/2007)*

Immich-Batterieberg 2003 Kabinett Riesling (Mosel-Saar-Ruwer) $20. 89 —*J.C. (5/1/2005)*

Immich-Batterieberg 2004 Rotschiefer Trocken Riesling (Mosel-Saar-Ruwer) $20. 90 Editors' Choice —*J.C. (7/1/2006)*

Immich-Batterieberg 2003 Rotschiefer Trocken Riesling (Mosel-Saar-Ruwer) $20. 87 —*J.C. (5/1/2005)*

IRONSTONE

Ironstone 2005 QbA Riesling (Pfalz) $10. 82 —*J.C. (7/1/2006)*

J. & H.A. STRUB

J. & H.A. Strub 2004 Niersteiner Brückchen Kabinett Riesling (Rheinhessen) $20. 89 —*J.C. (7/1/2006)*

J.L. WOLF

J.L. Wolf 2000 Forster Jesuitengarten Spätlese Trocken Riesling (Pfalz) $30. 87 —*J.C. (3/1/2003)*

J.L. Wolf 2003 Forster Pechstein Spätlese Riesling (Pfalz) $28. 84 —*J.C. (5/1/2005)*

J.L. Wolf 2005 Ungeheuer Spätlese Trocken Riesling (Pfalz) $30. 88 —*J.C. (2/1/2007)*

J.L. Wolf 2005 Wachenheimer Riesling (Pfalz) $14. 87 —*J.C. (2/1/2007)*

J.L. Wolf 2001 Wachenheimer Riesling (Pfalz) $14. 86 —*J.C. (3/1/2003)*

J.L. Wolf 2002 Wachenheimer Belz QbA Riesling (Pfalz) $18. 86 —*J.C. (8/1/2004)*

J.L. Wolf 2003 Wachenheimer Belz Spätlese Riesling (Pfalz) $20. 85 —*J.C. (5/1/2005)*

J.L. Wolf 2001 Wachenheimer Gerumpel QbA Riesling (Pfalz) $18. 84 —*J.C. (1/1/2004)*

J.L. Wolf 2003 Wachenheimer Kabinett Riesling (Pfalz) $13. 82 —*J.C. (5/1/2005)*

J.L. Wolf 2002 Wachenheimer QbA Riesling (Pfalz) $14. 86 —*J.C. (8/1/2004)*

J.u.H.A. STRUB

J.u.H.A. Strub 2001 Niersteiner Kabinett Riesling (Rheinhessen) $13. 87 Best Buy —*J.C. (3/1/2003)*

J.u.H.A. Strub 2001 Niersteiner Paterberg Spätlese Three-Star Riesling (Rheinhessen) $27. 91 —*J.C. (3/1/2003)*

JOH. HAART

Joh. Haart 2003 Piersporter Riesling (Mosel-Saar-Ruwer) $15. 87 —*J.C. (5/1/2005)*

Joh. Haart 2003 Piersporter Goldtröpfchen Riesling Auslese Riesling (Mosel-Saar-Ruwer) $31. 92 Editors' Choice —*J.C. (12/15/2004)*

JOH. JOS. CHRISTOFFEL

Joh. Jos. Christoffel 2001 Erdener Treppchen Kabinett Riesling (Mosel-Saar-Ruwer) $23. 91 Editors' Choice —*J.C. (3/1/2003)*

GERMANY

Joh. Jos. Christoffel 2001 Ürziger Würzgarten Auslese Two-Star Riesling (Mosel-Saar-Ruwer) $48. 92 —*J.C. (3/1/2003)*

Joh. Jos. Christoffel 2004 Ürziger Würzgarten Kabinett Riesling (Mosel-Saar-Ruwer) $27. 86 —*J.C. (10/1/2005)*

JOH. JOS. PRÜM

Joh. Jos. Prüm 2005 Bernkasteler Badstube Auslese Riesling (Mosel-Saar-Ruwer) $NA. In contrast to Prüm's Wehlener Sonnenuhr auslese, this wine is less flamboyant, more taciturn in character. The bouquet is rather sulfury and leesy but clearly suggests great potential. It's dense and powerful on the palate, with apple, citrus and vanilla flavors that finish long and crisp. It may seem redundant to go on gushing about each of Prüm's 2005 bottlings, but each is majestic in its own way—a tremendous success. Like the other offerings, this one should last 30 or more years. 94 —*J.C. (6/1/2007)*

Joh. Jos. Prüm 2005 Graacher Himmelreich Auslese Riesling (Mosel-Saar-Ruwer) $38. Strongly marked by rather stinky aromas at first, this wine reveals its full majesty on the palate, where it's lush and round without being soft, filled with baked apple, vanilla, honey and spice notes balanced by ripe acidity. Layered and long on the finish, where it reveals more complexity with every sip. Give it a vigorous decanting if you open a bottle now, or wait 10–20 years, maybe longer. 94 Editors' Choice —*J.C. (10/1/2007)*

Joh. Jos. Prüm 2005 Graacher Himmelreich Riesling Auslese Gold Cap Riesling (Mosel-Saar-Ruwer) $NA. Prüm has hit a grand slam in 2005, with every bottling we've tasted coming in at 90-plus points. This offering has the house's trademark yeasty, leesy scents, but also layer after layer of dense, slaty fruit balanced by crisp acidity. It's a bit sweet for most dishes, but pairing it with foie gras or mild cheeses will allow it to shine. Should evolve gracefully for decades. 97 Cellar Selection —*J.C. (6/1/2007)*

Joh. Jos. Prüm 2005 Graacher Himmelreich Spätlese Riesling (Mosel-Saar-Ruwer) $NA. Pungent at first, with diesel notes to go with smoky, leesy scents. But give this wine time, because on the palate the quality is immediately obvious. There's great intensity and depth married to elegance and persistence, complexity combined with purity. Flavors of apple, slate and citrus linger seemingly forever. A masterpiece that should easily last until at least 2030. 95 Editors' Choice —*J.C. (6/1/2007)*

Joh. Jos. Prüm 2001 Graacher Himmelreich Spätlese Riesling (Mosel-Saar-Ruwer) $35. 91 —*J.C. (3/1/2003)*

Joh. Jos. Prüm 2005 Wehlener Sonnenuhr Auslese Riesling (Mosel-Saar-Ruwer) $NA. Tasted blind in the same flight as Prüm's Bernkasteler Badstube auslese, this wine is flashier, more of an attention-grabber, with amazing purity and intensity of fruit backed by great length. The fruit flavors of green apple, pineapple and lime are underscored by slate-driven minerality, and the wine, although plump and amply endowed, is well balanced, with superb posture provided by sinewy acids. Surprisingly approachable now, but could last as long as 50 years. 95 —*J.C. (6/1/2007)*

Joh. Jos. Prüm 2005 Wehlener Sonnenuhr Spätlese Riesling (Mosel-Saar-Ruwer) $NA. Leesy and sulfury, this wine is fully possessed of the "Prüm stink", yet equally obvious is its incredible intensity and depth. Waves of tropical fruit—think guava and pineapple—cascade over the palate, yet the sweetness is beautifully balanced by acidity. Tremendously concentrated and long on the finish, this should easily live 20 years or more. 95 —*J.C. (6/1/2007)*

Joh. Jos. Prüm 2001 Wehlener Sonnenuhr Kabinett Riesling (Mosel-Saar-Ruwer) $25. 90 —*J.C. (3/1/2003)*

Joh. Jos. Prüm 2001 Wehlener Sonnenuhr Spätlese Riesling (Mosel-Saar-Ruwer) $37. 90 Cellar Selection —*J.C. (3/1/2003)*

JOHANN HAART

Johann Haart 2001 Piersporter Goldtropfchen Kabinett Riesling (Mosel-Saar-Ruwer) $17. 89 —*J.C. (3/1/2003)*

Johann Haart 2001 Piersporter Goldtropfchen QbA Riesling (Mosel-Saar-Ruwer) $13. 84 —*J.C. (1/1/2004)*

Johann Haart 2001 Piersporter Goldtropfchen Spätlese Riesling (Mosel-Saar-Ruwer) $20. 91 Editors' Choice —*J.C. (3/1/2003)*

JOHANN RUCK IPHOFEN

Johann Ruck Iphofen 2002 Iphöfer Julius-Echter-Berg Kabinett trocken Riesling (Franken) $24. 84 —*J.C. (8/1/2004)*

Johann Ruck Iphofen 2002 Iphofer Julius-Echter-Berg Spätlese Trocken Riesling (Franken) $36. 85 —*J.C. (8/1/2004)*

JOHANNISHOF

Johannishof 2002 Charta Riesling (Rheingau) $14. 90 *(11/15/2003)*

Johannishof 2001 Charta QbA Riesling (Rheingau) $14. 90 Best Buy —*J.C. (3/1/2003)*

Johannishof 2005 Johannisberg G Kabinett Riesling (Rheingau) $19. 88 —*J.C. (12/1/2006)*

Johannishof 2005 Johannisberg V Kabinett Riesling (Rheingau) $20. This has the power and weight of the Rheingau, but also the delicate floral nuances of the Mosel. Scents of flower-shop greens, crushed-stone and lime easily glide into flavors of melon and citrus, underscored by a strong mineral component. Long, intense and refreshing on the finish. 92 Editors' Choice —*J.C. (2/1/2007)*

Johannishof 2004 Johannisberg V Kabinett Riesling (Rheingau) $18. 88 —*J.C. (7/1/2006)*

Johannishof 2003 Johannisberg V Kabinett Riesling (Rheingau) $17. 88 —*J.C. (12/15/2004)*

Johannishof 2001 Johannisberger Goldatzel Kabinett Riesling (Rheingau) $11. 88 Best Buy —*J.C. (3/1/2003)*

Johannishof 2003 Johannisberger Hölle Beerenauslese 375 ml Riesling (Rheingau) $132. 95 —*J.C. (2/1/2006)*

Johannishof 2005 Johannisberger Klaus Spätlese Riesling (Rheingau) $25. 87 —*J.C. (2/1/2007)*

Johannishof 2004 Johannisberger Klaus Spätlese Riesling (Rheingau) $24. 88 —*J.C. (5/1/2006)*

Johannishof 2001 Johannisberger Vogelsang Kabinett Riesling (Rheingau) $11. 90 Best Buy —*J.C. (3/1/2003)*

Johannishof 2003 Rudesheimer Berg Rottland Spätlese Riesling (Rheingau) $26. 92 Editors' Choice —*J.C. (12/15/2004)*

Johannishof 2005 Rüdesheimer Berg Rottland Spätlese Riesling (Rheingau) $27. 90 —*J.C. (12/1/2006)*

JOSEF BIFFAR

Josef Biffar 2001 Deidesheimer Kieselberg Kabinett Riesling (Pfalz) $16. 87 —*J.C. (3/1/2003)*

Josef Biffar 2001 Wachenheimer Altenburg Spätlese Riesling (Pfalz) $32. 86 —*J.C. (3/1/2003)*

JOSEF LEITZ

Josef Leitz 2004 Dragonstone Qualitätswein Riesling (Rheingau) $18. 88 Editors' Choice —*J.C. (10/1/2005)*

Josef Leitz 2001 Rüdesheimer Berg Rottland Spätlese Trocken Riesling (Rheingau) $33. 90 —*J.C. (3/1/2003)*

Josef Leitz 2001 Rüdesheimer Drachenstein Riesling (Rheingau) $12. 89 Best Buy —*J.C. (11/15/2002)*

Josef Leitz 2002 Rudesheimer Drachenstein Riesling QbA Riesling (Rheingau) $12. 90 Best Buy —*J.C. (11/15/2003)*

JOSEPH MÜLLER

Joseph Müller 2003 Qualitätswein Riesling (Pfalz) $6. 82 —*J.C. (11/1/2004)*

JUL. FERD. KIMICH

Jul. Ferd. Kimich 2001 Deidecheimer Paradiesgarten Kabinett Halbtrocken Riesling (Pfalz) $15. 87 —*J.C. (1/1/2004)*

JULIUSSPITAL

Juliusspital 2001 Iphofer Julius-Echter-Berg Auslese Riesling (Franken) $24. 89 —*J.C. (3/1/2003)*

KARL ERBES

Karl Erbes 2005 Erbes Riesling Trocken Sekt Riesling (Mosel-Saar-Ruwer) $29. This light, fresh-tasting sparkler tastes something like a still Riesling from the Mosel, with zesty lime and lemon zest flavors enlivened by bubbles and a bit of underlying minerality. Imported by Chapin Cellars, LLC. 86 —*J.C. (12/15/2007)*

Karl Erbes 2004 Ürziger Würzgarten Auslese Gold Capsule 375 ml Riesling (Mosel-Saar-Ruwer) $40. 89 —*J.C. (9/1/2006)*

Karl Erbes 2006 Ürziger Würzgarten Beerenauslese Riesling (Mosel-Saar-Ruwer) $79. Dried apricot notes dominate this wine from start to finish, making it a bit one-dimensional. Still, it features impressive sugar-acid balance so despite the sweetness it's not cloying; finishes long, with lip-smacking notes of honeyed pineapple. Imported by Chapin Cellars, LLC. 92 —*J.C. (12/15/2007)*

Karl Erbes 2001 Ürziger Würzgarten Kabinett Riesling (Mosel-Saar-Ruwer) $12. 88 Best Buy —*J.C. (3/1/2003)*

Karl Erbes 2003 Ürziger Würzgarten Auslese Riesling (Mosel-Saar-Ruwer) $29. 88 —*J.C. (12/15/2004)*

Karl Erbes 2003 Ürziger Würzgarten Spätlese Riesling (Mosel-Saar-Ruwer) $18. 88 —*J.C. (12/15/2004)*

Karl Erbes 2004 Ürziger Würzgarten Spätlese Riesling (Mosel-Saar-Ruwer) $19. 87 —*J.C. (2/1/2006)*

Karl Erbes 2001 Ürziger Würzgarten Spätlese Riesling (Mosel-Saar-Ruwer) $14. 89 Best Buy *—J.C. (3/1/2003)*

KARTHAUSERHOF

Karthauserhof 2002 Kabinett Riesling (Mosel-Saar-Ruwer) $20. 88 *—J.C. (8/1/2004)*

KASSNER SIMON

Kassner Simon 1998 Brut Riesling (Pfalz) $17. 87 *—P.G. (12/31/2002)*

Kassner Simon 2001 Freinsheimer Oschelkopf Spätlese Scheurebe (Pfalz) $16. 87 *—J.C. (1/1/2004)*

KELLER

Keller 2003 Kabinett Riesling (Rheinhessen) $33. 87 *—J.C. (5/1/2005)*

Keller 2003 Pius Beerenauslese Riesling (Rheinhessen) $36. 90 *—J.C. (2/1/2006)*

KENDERMANNS

Kendermanns 2004 Kalkstein Dry QbA Riesling (Pfalz) $21. 85 *—J.C. (7/1/2006)*

Kendermanns 2004 Schiefer Riesling QbA Trocken Riesling (Mosel-Saar-Ruwer) $21. 88 *—J.C. (5/1/2006)*

KIRSTEN

Kirsten 1998 Brut Riesling (Mosel-Saar-Ruwer) $16. 88 *—P.G. (12/31/2002)*

KNIPSER

Knipser 2003 Auslese Gewürztraminer-Riesling (Pfalz) $30. 90 *—J.C. (5/1/2005)*

Knipser 2005 Im Großen Garten Großkarlbacher Burgweg Spätlese Trocken Riesling (Pfalz) $48. Full-bodied and rich, even a little oily in texture, this is a big mouthful of Riesling, yet it's spicy and floral, making for an elegant presentation. Drink it now to make the most of its intricate bouquet. 89 *—J.C. (9/1/2007)*

Knipser 2005 Laumersheimer Kapellenberg Kabinett Trocken Riesling (Pfalz) $20. This is a crisp, tongue-tingling Riesling. It starts with scents of oiled apples, but quickly turns lemony, racing across the palate with zesty acids. 87 *—J.C. (9/1/2007)*

Knipser 2004 Steinbuckel Grosses Gewächs Spätlese Trocken Riesling (Pfalz) $46. 90 *—J.C. (12/1/2006)*

Knipser 2005 Steinbuckel Laumersheimer Mandelberg Spätlese Trocken Riesling (Pfalz) $48. This wine lacks the richness and texture of Knipser's Im Großen Garten bottling, but more than makes up for it with complex notes of spring flowers, bergamot, spice and mineral. Long and crisp on the finish, with potential to possibly improve up to 10 years. 90 *—J.C. (9/1/2007)*

Knipser 2004 Blauer Trocken Spätburgunder (Pfalz) $24. Excessively woody, with powerful smoke and cedar notes that cover modest beet flavors. The bouquet features additional oak-derived scents of vanilla and an odd, marzipan-like quality. Oak fans will think this wine's been underrated. 82 *—J.C. (6/1/2007)*

Knipser 2003 Chardonnay & Weissburgunder Trocken White Blend (Pfalz) $27. 83 *—J.C. (5/1/2005)*

KÖSTER-WOLF

Köster-Wolf 2006 Halbtrocken Müller-Thurgau (Rheinhessen) $13. Despite the grape variety—one not known for producing great wines—this wine presents an attractive blend of citrus and crushed-rock aromas and flavors. Virtually dry, it's also light in body and clean and refreshing on the finish—a fine apéritif wine. Imported by Chapin Cellars, LLC. 85 Best Buy *—J.C. (11/15/2007)*

Köster-Wolf 2004 Müller-Thurgau Halbtrocken 1 Liter Müller-Thurgau (Rheinhessen) $12. 83 *—J.C. (7/1/2006)*

Köster-Wolf 2004 Riesling QbA Trocken 1 Liter Riesling (Rheinhessen) $12. 85 Best Buy *—J.C. (7/1/2006)*

Köster-Wolf 2006 Trocken Riesling (Rheinhessen) $15. With its pure, clean scents and flavors of green apple, lime and mineral, slightly creamy texture and long, mouthwatering finish, this nearly dry Riesling offers a lot to like. No, it's not that complex, but it is admirably concentrated and eminently satisfying. Imported by Chapin Cellars, LLC. 87 Best Buy *—J.C. (11/15/2007)*

Köster-Wolf 2003 Trocken 1 L Riesling (Rheinhessen) $11. 86 *—J.C. (5/1/2005)*

Köster-Wolf 2006 Wolfs Frischer Weissherbst Feinherb Spätburgunder (Rheinhessen) $14. Pale copper in color, this is a lean, angular rosé that's rather neutral on the nose, then offers only sour cherry flavors on the tart finish. 81 *—J.C. (11/15/2007)*

KOWERICH LUDWIG VON BEETHOVEN

Kowerich Ludwig von Beethoven 1998 Brut Riesling (Mosel-Saar-Ruwer) $17. 87 Best Buy *—P.G. (12/31/2002)*

KRUGER-RUMPF

Kruger-Rumpf 2001 Münsterer Rheinberg Kabinett Riesling (Nahe) $17. 88 *—J.C. (3/1/2003)*

KÜHL

Kühl 2006 Riesling (Mosel-Saar-Ruwer) $11. Off-dry but still lacking in midpalate depth, this is a soft Riesling that offers up scents of kerosene, followed by flavors of melon and spice. Imported by Chapin Cellars, LLC. 83 *—J.C. (11/15/2007)*

Kühl 2003 Kabinett Riesling (Mosel-Saar-Ruwer) $9. 83 *—J.C. (12/15/2004)*

Kühl 2005 Way Kühl Dry Riesling (Mosel-Saar-Ruwer) $11. This medium-bodied, off-dry Riesling boasts attractive packaging and a clever name, but the wine itself lacks depth, offering little more than modest green apple, melon and lime flavors. Imported by Chapin Cellars, LLC. 83 *—J.C. (11/15/2007)*

KÜNSTLER

Künstler 2004 Estate Qualitatswein Riesling (Rheingau) $18. 88 *—J.C. (10/1/2005)*

Künstler 2004 Hochheimer Reichestal Kabinett Riesling (Rheingau) $25. 88 *—J.C. (10/1/2005)*

KURT HAIN

Kurt Hain 2003 Piesporter Goldtröpfchen Spätlese Riesling (Mosel-Saar-Ruwer) $23. 89 *—J.C. (5/1/2005)*

LANDSHUT

Landshut 2004 QbA Riesling (Mosel-Saar-Ruwer) $5. 82 *—J.C. (7/1/2006)*

Landshut 2002 Qualitätswein Riesling (Mosel-Saar-Ruwer) $5. 83 Best Buy *—J.C. (11/1/2004)*

LOOSEN BROS.

Loosen Bros. 2006 Dr. L Riesling (Mosel-Saar-Ruwer) $12. A bit leaner in style than the 2005—as you might expect—with attractive aromas of pineapple and fresh greens giving way to flavors of honey, spice and melon. The fruit drops away on the finish, leaving tart acids to linger. 84 *—J.C. (8/1/2007)*

Loosen Bros. 2000 Dr. L Riesling (Mosel-Saar-Ruwer) $10. 83 *—C.S. (5/1/2002)*

LOSEN-BOCKSTANZ

Losen-Bockstanz 2001 Wittlicher Lay Spätlese Riesling (Mosel-Saar-Ruwer) $18. 86 *—R.V. (1/1/2004)*

Losen-Bockstanz 2001 Wittlicher Portnersberg Kabinett Riesling (Mosel-Saar-Ruwer) $10. 87 *—R.V. (1/1/2004)*

LOTHAR FRANZ

Lothar Franz 2001 Hattenheimer Pfaffenberg Spätlese Riesling (Rheingau) $NA. 86 *—R.V. (1/1/2004)*

LOUIS GUNTRUM

Louis Guntrum 2006 Dry Riesling (Rheinhessen) $12. Rather full and round in the mouth—the combined effect of 12.5% alcohol and a touch (0.6%) of residual sugar—this nevertheless does taste pretty dry. It's a minerally version, with smoky minerality and powdered—almost liquified—stone notes fleshed out by hints of tangerine and peach. Drink now. 88 Best Buy *—J.C. (9/1/2007)*

Louis Guntrum 2005 Dry Riesling (Rheinhessen) $11. Light and rather innocuous, this dry Riesling just manages to have enough going on to make it recommendable. Some waxy, kerosene-like notes intrigue on the nose, while hints of apple and citrus impart tartness to the finish. 83 *—J.C. (4/1/2007)*

Louis Guntrum 2004 Dry Riesling (Rheinhessen) $11. 82 *—J.C. (12/1/2006)*

Louis Guntrum 2005 Niersteiner Rehbach Spätlese Riesling (Rheinhessen) $23. 91 *—J.C. (12/1/2006)*

Louis Guntrum 2003 Niersteiner Rehbach Spätlese Riesling (Rheinhessen) $19. 87 *—J.C. (11/1/2004)*

Louis Guntrum 2005 Oppenheimer Herrenberg Auslese Riesling (Rheinhessen) $28. 87 *—J.C. (12/1/2006)*

Louis Guntrum 2002 Oppenheimer Herrenberg Auslese Riesling (Rheinhessen) $23. 88 *—J.C. (12/15/2004)*

Louis Guntrum 2002 Oppenheimer Sackträger Riesling Auslese Riesling (Rheinhessen) $23. 87 —*J.C. (12/15/2004)*

Louis Guntrum 2004 Oppenheimer Sackträger Spätlese Trocken Riesling (Rheinhessen) $26. Although the aromas of this wine are largely neutral, showing just hints of apple and citrus, the flavors come alive on the palate, offering up ripe apple, lime, nectarine and spice notes. It's slightly oily in texture, finishing softly tart, accented by dried spices. 88 —*J.C. (9/1/2007)*

Louis Guntrum 2002 Oppenheimer Sackträger Riesling Spätlese Trocken Riesling (Rheinhessen) $19. 87 —*J.C. (12/15/2004)*

Louis Guntrum 2005 Royal Blue Riesling (Rheinhessen) $11. Honey, spice and a suggestion of smoke on the nose are intriguing, but this wine is lacking in flavor intensity, finishing clean but short. 82 —*J.C. (4/1/2007)*

Louis Guntrum 2005 Spicy White Scheurebe Kabinett Scheurebe (Rheinhessen) $13. The aromas speak to the uniqueness of the grape variety, offering up funky pink grapefruit and ginger notes, but the flavors are overly sweet, lacking proper balance. 81 —*J.C. (11/15/2007)*

Louis Guntrum 2002 Penguin Eiswein Silvaner (Rheinhessen) $52. 81 —*J.C. (5/1/2005)*

Louis Guntrum 2004 Trocken Spätburgunder (Rheinhessen) $20. Tastes better than it smells, with strongly herbal aromas that seem almost cabbage-like giving way to flavors of cola and black cherries. Light in weight, it finishes crisply acidic, without much tannin. 83 —*J.C. (6/1/2007)*

LUCASHOF

Lucashof 2002 QbA Riesling (Pfalz) $11. 84 —*J.C. (8/1/2004)*

LUDWIG NEUHAUS

Ludwig Neuhaus 2000 Piesporter Michelsberg Riesling (Mosel-Saar-Ruwer) $5. 82 —*J.C. (5/1/2002)*

MARKUS MOLITOR

Markus Molitor 2005 Bernkasteler Badstube Kabinett Feinherb Riesling (Mosel-Saar-Ruwer) $16. Makes an interesting contrast to Molitor's spätlese feinherb from the same vineyard, being lighter in body and driertasting. Clover, honey and green apple aromas are matched by mineral and melon-rind flavors and a touch of vanilla. Dry and stony on the finish. Imported by Schmitt-Sohne Inc. 87 —*J.C. (4/1/2007)*

Markus Molitor 2005 Bernkasteler Badstube Spätlese Feinherb Riesling (Mosel-Saar-Ruwer) $25. Feinherb—a rarely seen designation—wines are similar in style to halbtrocken, rather dry. This is an excellent example, marrying the Mosel's green apple and citrus fruit with slaty, minerally notes in a medium-bodied, rich Riesling that tops out at 11.5% alcohol. Imported by Schmitt-Sohne Inc. 90 —*J.C. (4/1/2007)*

Markus Molitor 2002 Bernkasteler Badstube Spätlese Feinherb Riesling (Mosel-Saar-Ruwer) $18. 86 —*J.C. (12/15/2004)*

Markus Molitor 2002 Bernkasteler Bratenhöfchen Kabinett Riesling (Mosel-Saar-Ruwer) $13. 86 —*J.C. (12/15/2004)*

Markus Molitor 2003 Erdener Treppchen Auslese Riesling (Mosel-Saar-Ruwer) $45. 86 —*J.C. (2/1/2006)*

Markus Molitor 2001 Graacher Himmelreich Spätlese Riesling (Mosel-Saar-Ruwer) $16. 91 —*J.C. (12/15/2004)*

Markus Molitor 2002 QbA Feinherb Riesling (Mosel-Saar-Ruwer) $12. 84 —*J.C. (12/15/2004)*

Markus Molitor 2002 QbA Trocken Riesling (Mosel-Saar-Ruwer) $12. 84 —*J.C. (12/15/2004)*

Markus Molitor 2001 Wehlener Klosterberg Eiswein Riesling (Mosel-Saar-Ruwer) $46. 89 —*J.C. (12/15/2004)*

Markus Molitor 2005 Wehlener Sonnenuhr Auslese ** Riesling (Mosel-Saar-Ruwer) $40. Sweet, rich and creamy, this is an easy-to-enjoy auslese that packs in the flavor. Poached apples and pears pick up hints of clove, cinnamon and vanilla, and end on a ripe citrus note that's best described as tangerine. Imported by Schmitt-Sohne Inc. 90 —*J.C. (2/1/2007)*

Markus Molitor 2005 Wehlener Sonnenuhr Spätlese Riesling (Mosel-Saar-Ruwer) $25. Light and vivacious, this has loads of tropical fruit aromas and flavors, but also vivid slate notes. The acidity is ripe and rounded rather than crisp, but the wine still comes across as refreshingly balanced. Drink now–2025. Imported by Schmitt-Sohne Inc. 92 Editors' Choice —*J.C. (6/1/2007)*

Markus Molitor 2002 Zeltinger Sonnenuhr Auslese Feinherb Riesling (Mosel-Saar-Ruwer) $28. 90 —*J.C. (12/15/2004)*

Markus Molitor 2005 Zeltinger Sonnenuhr Kabinett Riesling (Mosel-Saar-Ruwer) $17. Light in body and very easy to drink, with pristine flavors of flower greens, green apples and lime and a clean, fresh finish. The only clue that this is from an exceptionally ripe vintage is the hint of tropical fruit—verging on banana and melon—that may be found amidst the flavors. Imported by Schmitt-Sohne Inc. 90 Editors' Choice —*J.C. (2/1/2007)*

Markus Molitor 2002 Zeltinger Sonnenuhr Kabinett Riesling (Mosel-Saar-Ruwer) $15. 87 —*J.C. (12/15/2004)*

Markus Molitor 2005 Zeltinger Sonnenuhr Spätlese Riesling (Mosel-Saar-Ruwer) $26. Broad, mouthfilling and weighty, this is an atypically rich spätlese, but one that delivers a dizzying array of aromas and flavors. Diesel and mineral oil notes provide gravitas, while lime zest adds spark. Ripe melon, baked apple and powdered cinnamon round out the chassis of this low-rider. Imported by Schmitt-Sohne Inc. 91 —*J.C. (6/1/2007)*

Markus Molitor 2002 Zeltinger Sonnenuhr Spätlese Riesling (Mosel-Saar-Ruwer) $20. 91 —*J.C. (12/15/2004)*

MAX FERD. RICHTER

Max Ferd. Richter 2001 Braueneberger Juffer Auslese Riesling (Mosel-Saar-Ruwer) $40. 91 —*R.V. (1/1/2004)*

Max Ferd. Richter 2001 Braueneberger Juffer Kabinett Riesling (Mosel-Saar-Ruwer) $20. 88 —*R.V. (4/1/2003)*

Max Ferd. Richter 2001 Braueneberger Juffer Spätlese Riesling (Mosel-Saar-Ruwer) $28. 89 —*R.V. (1/1/2004)*

Max Ferd. Richter 2001 Braueneberger Juffer-Sonnenuhr Auslese Riesling (Mosel-Saar-Ruwer) $55. 92 —*R.V. (1/1/2004)*

Max Ferd. Richter 2001 Braueneberger Juffer-Sonnenuhr Spätlese Riesling (Mosel-Saar-Ruwer) $30. 87 —*R.V. (1/1/2004)*

Max Ferd. Richter 2001 Graacher Himmelreich Kabinett Riesling (Mosel-Saar-Ruwer) $20. 87 —*R.V. (1/1/2004)*

Max Ferd. Richter 2001 Graacher Himmelreich Spätlese Riesling (Mosel-Saar-Ruwer) $28. 90 —*R.V. (1/1/2004)*

Max Ferd. Richter 2001 Veldenzer Eisenberg Auslese Riesling (Mosel-Saar-Ruwer) $40. 90 —*R.V. (1/1/2004)*

Max Ferd. Richter 2001 Veldenzer Eisenberg Spätlese Riesling (Mosel-Saar-Ruwer) $28. 91 —*R.V. (1/1/2004)*

MAXIMIN GRÜNHÄUSER

Maximin Grünhäuser 2005 Abstberg Auslese Riesling (Mosel-Saar-Ruwer) $40. 92 Editors' Choice —*J.C. (12/1/2006)*

Maximin Grünhäuser 2004 Abstberg Auslese Riesling (Mosel-Saar-Ruwer) $40. 92 —*J.C. (2/1/2006)*

Maximin Grünhäuser 2006 Abtsberg Beerenauslese Riesling (Mosel-Saar-Ruwer) $204. For a beerenauslese, usually dominated by honeyed fruit, this shows a surprising degree of stony minerality, which helps to balance the rich, sweet flavors of orange marmalade, dried apricots and honey. Viscous in texture, yet the citrus and mineral notes keep it from becoming cloying. Drink now–2035. 93 —*J.C. (12/15/2007)*

Maximin Grünhäuser 2005 Abstberg Beerenauslese Riesling (Mosel-Saar-Ruwer) $177. A stunningly rich yet balanced dessert wine, this beauty starts with hints of paraffin and almonds, then unleashes waves of sweet dried-apricot and orange-marmalade flavors. Despite the intense, honeyed sweetness, there's enough lime-like acidity to prevent it from being cloying. This tour de force should age effortlessly for 40 or more years. 95 Cellar Selection —*J.C. (10/1/2007)*

Maximin Grünhäuser 2004 Abstberg Beerenauslese Riesling (Mosel-Saar-Ruwer) $167. 93 —*J.C. (2/1/2006)*

Maximin Grünhäuser 2005 Abstberg Spätlese Riesling (Mosel-Saar-Ruwer) $28. 92 Editors' Choice —*J.C. (12/1/2006)*

Maximin Grünhäuser 2004 Abstberg Spätlese Riesling (Mosel-Saar-Ruwer) $28. 91 Editors' Choice —*J.C. (5/1/2006)*

Maximin Grünhäuser 2003 Abtsberg Auslese 122 375 ml Riesling (Mosel-Saar-Ruwer) $32. 91 —*J.C. (2/1/2006)*

Maximin Grünhäuser 2003 Abtsberg Beerenauslese Riesling (Mosel-Saar-Ruwer) $167. 95 —*J.C. (12/15/2004)*

Maximin Grünhäuser 2003 Abtsberg Auslese Riesling (Mosel-Saar-Ruwer) $40. 90 —*J.C. (12/15/2004)*

Maximin Grünhäuser 2003 Abtsberg Auslese 155 Riesling (Mosel-Saar-Ruwer) $38. 88 —*J.C. (12/15/2004)*

Maximin Grünhäuser 2003 Abtsberg Riesling Auslese 70 Riesling (Mosel-Saar-Ruwer) $36. 91 —*J.C. (12/15/2004)*

Maximin Grünhäuser 2003 Abtsberg Spätlese Riesling (Mosel-Saar-Ruwer) $28. 90 —*J.C. (5/1/2005)*

Maximin Grünhäuser 2005 Herrenberg Auslese 30 Riesling (Mosel-Saar-Ruwer) $32. Seems almost pungent in its minerally intensity, featuring hints of smoke and brown butter, then adds pure green apple and lime flavors on the palate. Lithe and wiry, this is powerful without being muscular and on the crisp, less-sweet side for the vintage. 91 —*J.C. (2/1/2007)*

Maximin Grünhäuser 2001 Herrenberg QbA Trocken Riesling (Mosel-Saar-Ruwer) $12. 85 —*J.C. (1/1/2004)*

Maximin Grünhäuser 2005 Herrenberg Kabinett Riesling (Mosel-Saar-Ruwer) $23. 88 *—J.C. (2/1/2007)*

Maximin Grünhäuser 2003 Herrenberg Kabinett Riesling (Mosel-Saar-Ruwer) $22. 89 *—J.C. (12/15/2004)*

Maximin Grünhäuser 2003 Herrenberg Spätlese Riesling (Mosel-Saar-Ruwer) $28. 92 *—J.C. (12/15/2004)*

Maximin Grünhäuser 2005 Herrenberg Superior QbA (Auslese?) Riesling (Mosel-Saar-Ruwer) $37. A stunning, close to dry Riesling from Von Schubert, this boasts a powerful, assertively mineral bouquet laced with smoke, diesel fuel and honey that will startle tasters expecting a light, blossomy Riesling. It's broad and mouthfilling, with spicy, minerally flavors that just hint at baked fruit and honey, finishing long and intense. 92 Editors' Choice *—J.C. (6/1/2007)*

Maximin Grünhäuser 2004 QbA Riesling (Mosel-Saar-Ruwer) $19. 88 *—J.C. (2/1/2006)*

Maximin Grünhäuser 2003 QbA Riesling (Mosel-Saar-Ruwer) $19. 90 *—J.C. (12/15/2004)*

MEILEN

Meilen 2006 Kabinett Riesling (Mosel-Saar-Ruwer) $11. Light in weight, as expected from the Mosel, but it also lacks richness or depth. There's a burnt matchstick note to the aromas, then simple, short-lived flavors of melon and citrus. Imported by Chapin Cellars, LLC. 81 *—J.C. (11/15/2007)*

Meilen 2003 Kabinett Riesling (Mosel-Saar-Ruwer) $9. 86 Best Buy *—J.C. (12/15/2004)*

MILZ-LAURETIUSHOF

Milz-Lauretiushof 2005 180 Degree Riesling (Mosel-Saar-Ruwer) $15. Smoky, intense and petrolly on the nose, this medium-bodied Riesling goes 180 degrees on the palate, where the flavors are the more typical apple and lemon-lime. It's a touch oily, finishing with a tangy, citrusy edge. 86 *—J.C. (8/1/2007)*

MÖNCHHOF

Mönchhof 2002 Astor Kabinett Riesling (Mosel-Saar-Ruwer) $18. 85 *—J.C. (8/1/2004)*

Mönchhof 2006 Estate Riesling (Mosel-Saar-Ruwer) $15. Boasts classic Mosel Riesling aromas and flavors—lime, pineapple, green apple, maybe a touch of honey—all at an eminently reasonable price. Though richer and creamier than you might expect, the weight is balanced by crisp acidity on the long finish. 89 Editors' Choice *—J.C. (8/1/2007)*

Mönchhof 2003 Estate QbA Riesling (Mosel-Saar-Ruwer) $14. 86 *—J.C. (8/1/2004)*

Mönchhof 2004 Estate Qualitatswein Riesling (Mosel-Saar-Ruwer) $16. 86 *—J.C. (10/1/2005)*

Mönchhof 2004 Mosel Slate Spätlese Riesling (Mosel-Saar-Ruwer) $21. 90 Editors' Choice *—J.C. (10/1/2005)*

Mönchhof 2004 Ürzig Würzgarten Kabinett Riesling (Mosel-Saar-Ruwer) $20. This delectable kabinett starts off with amazingly pure scents of crushed stone, lime and apple, then follows up with flavors of strawberries to go with more apples and limes. It's medium-bodied, slightly sweet but with the crispness to balance its sugars. Finishes pristine and fresh. Drink now-2016. 90 *—J.C. (10/1/2007)*

ORIGIN

Origin 2005 Rhein Tafelwein Riesling (Rheingau) $7. Bargain-hunting shoppers should be happy to find this in their local stores. Presumably a blend from different Rhein regions—hence the lowly Tafelwein designation—it is nevertheless a tasty, balanced wine. Lime and slate notes power the bouquet, while the flavors are rounder and more lush. Off dry; drink now. 85 Best Buy *—J.C. (6/1/2007)*

P.J. VALCKENBERG

P.J. Valckenberg 2001 QBA Gewürztraminer (Pfalz) $10. 87 Best Buy *—J.C. (1/1/2004)*

P.J. Valckenberg 2006 V Gewürztraminer (Pfalz) $11. This speaks of Gewürztraminer from the get-go, offering up hallmark scents of lychees and spice, but it also suffers from the low acidity of the variety, coming up soft and short on the honeyed finish. 84 *—J.C. (11/15/2007)*

P.J. Valckenberg 2003 QbA Pinot Grigio (Pfalz) $11. 85 *—J.C. (5/1/2005)*

P.J. Valckenberg 2003 1808 Wormser Liebfrauenstift-Kirchenstück Spätlese Trocken Riesling (Rheinhessen) $27. 85 *—J.C. (12/15/2004)*

P.J. Valckenberg 2006 Estate Dry Riesling (Rheinhessen) $14. Valckenberg has simplified the front label by moving the vineyard information to the back—this wine is from the Wormser Liebfrauenstift-Kirchenstück. Despite some hints of honey on the nose, it's pretty darn dry, with flavors of citrus and underripe peach that finish zesty and crisp. 85 *—J.C. (11/15/2007)*

P.J. Valckenberg 2004 Estate Dry Riesling (Rheinhessen) $12. 84 *—J.C. (10/1/2005)*

P.J. Valckenberg 2005 Estate Kabinett Riesling (Rheinhessen) $18. In an attempt to unclutter the label, this wine no longer features the vineyard name, which is the Wormser Liebfrauenstift-Kirchenstück. It's medium-bodied, but with a crisp backbone to support the ripe green apple, lime and flower green notes. Long and minerally on the finish. 90 Editors' Choice *—J.C. (2/1/2007)*

P.J. Valckenberg 2004 Estate Kabinett Riesling (Rheinhessen) $18. 86 *—J.C. (5/1/2006)*

P.J. Valckenberg 2004 Estate Spätlese Riesling (Rheinhessen) $22. 86 *—J.C. (9/1/2006)*

P.J. Valckenberg 2001 Liebfrauenstift-Kirchenstück Kabinett Riesling (Rheinhessen) $14. 87 *—J.C. (3/1/2003)*

P.J. Valckenberg 2001 Liebfrauenstift-Kirchenstück Spätlese Riesling (Rheinhessen) $18. 87 *—J.C. (3/1/2003)*

P.J. Valckenberg 2003 Liebfrauenstift-Kirchenstück Spätlese Riesling (Rheinhessen) $22. 87 *—J.C. (5/1/2005)*

P.J. Valckenberg 2001 Liebfrauenstift-Kirchenstück Spätlese Trocken Riesling (Rheinhessen) $18. 86 *—J.C. (3/1/2003)*

P.J. Valckenberg 2003 QbA Riesling (Rheinhessen) $11. 84 *—J.C. (12/15/2004)*

P.J. Valckenberg 2001 QbA Riesling (Rheinhessen) $7. 84 Best Buy *—J.C. (3/1/2003)*

P.J. Valckenberg 2001 QbA Trocken Riesling (Rheinhessen) $10. 89 Best Buy *—J.C. (3/1/2003)*

P.J. Valckenberg 2003 QbA Trocken Riesling (Rheinhessen) $14. 84 *—J.C. (12/15/2004)*

P.J. Valckenberg 2005 Spätlese Trocken Riesling (Rheinhessen) $22. 88 *—J.C. (12/1/2006)*

P.J. Valckenberg 2005 Trocken Riesling (Rheinhessen) $14. 84 *—J.C. (12/1/2006)*

P.J. Valckenberg 2006 V Riesling (Rheinhessen) $11. Plump, moderately rich and slightly sweet, featuring scents of ripe peaches underscored by citrus. Stone fruit, melon and lime flavors mingle easily on the palate, ending on lingering fruit and mineral notes. 86 Best Buy *—J.C. (11/15/2007)*

P.J. Valckenberg 2003 Wormser Liebfrauenstift Kirchenstück Sekt Brut Riesling (Rheinhessen) $25. 82 *—J.C. (6/1/2006)*

P.J. Valckenberg 2003 Wormser Liebfrauenstift-Kirchenstück Kabinett Riesling (Rheinhessen) $16. 84 *—J.C. (12/15/2004)*

P.J. Valckenberg 2003 Wormser Liebfrauenstift-Kirchenstück Riesling Spätlese Trocken Riesling (Rheinhessen) $22. 88 *—J.C. (12/15/2004)*

PAZEN

Pazen 2001 Zeltinger Himmelreich Kabinett Riesling (Mosel-Saar-Ruwer) $14. 91 Best Buy *—J.C. (3/1/2003)*

Pazen 2001 Zeltinger Himmelreich Spätlese Riesling (Mosel-Saar-Ruwer) $18. 88 *—J.C. (3/1/2003)*

PETER BRUM

Peter Brum 2005 Noblesse Riesling (Rheinhessen) $10. This medium-bodied, off-dry Riesling starts well with its zesty citrus aromas, but falls off a bit on the palate, where the flavors come across as understated apple, pear and citrus. Ends on a spicy, peppery note, but could use a touch more freshness as well. 83 *—J.C. (11/15/2007)*

PETER JAKOB KUHN

Peter Jakob Kuhn 1999 Oestricher Lenchen Kabinett Riesling (Rheingau) $12. 87 *—S.H. (6/1/2001)*

PETER NICOLAY

Peter Nicolay 2001 Berkasteler Badstube Kabinett Riesling (Mosel-Saar-Ruwer) $15. 88 *—R.V. (3/1/2003)*

Peter Nicolay 2001 Bernkasteler alte Badstube am Doctorberg Auslese Riesling (Mosel-Saar-Ruwer) $47. 87 *—R.V. (3/1/2003)*

Peter Nicolay 2001 Bernkasteler alte Badstube am Doctorberg Spätlese Riesling (Mosel-Saar-Ruwer) $27. 90 *—R.V. (3/1/2003)*

Peter Nicolay 2001 Bernkasteler Badstube Spätlese Riesling (Mosel-Saar-Ruwer) $21. 87 *—R.V. (3/1/2003)*

Peter Nicolay 2005 Erdener Prälat Auslese Riesling (Mosel-Saar-Ruwer) $48. Starts off with a somewhat austere and steely bouquet, and the flavors play a fancy riff off of that, ending up like spice-laden minerals coated in honey. It's incredibly complex, without being obviously fruity. The rich, viscous mouthfeel yields to a long, sweet finish tinged with cinnamon, clove and pepper and just a touch of warmth. Opt for drinking this on the young side—within 10 years or so. 93 *—J.C. (2/1/2007)*

Peter Nicolay 2004 Erdener Prälat Auslese Riesling (Mosel-Saar-Ruwer) $48. 92 *—J.C. (2/1/2006)*

Peter Nicolay 2005 Estate Riesling (Mosel-Saar-Ruwer) $14. A top-notch value, Nicolay's Estate Riesling shows bold notes of mineral oil and wet stones to complement flavors of ripe pears and melons. It's round in the mouth without being fat, gaining focus on the citrus- and spice-inflected finish. Drink now–2012. 89 **Best Buy** *—J.C. (6/1/2007)*

Peter Nicolay 2004 Estate QbA Riesling (Mosel-Saar-Ruwer) $14. 84 *—J.C. (7/1/2006)*

Peter Nicolay 2001 Ürziger Goldwingert Auslese Riesling (Mosel-Saar-Ruwer) $32. 92 *—R.V. (3/1/2003)*

Peter Nicolay 2005 Ürziger Goldwingert Spätlese Riesling (Mosel-Saar-Ruwer) $27. A broad, mouthfilling wine that comes across as a bit low acid and weighty. Honey, spice and citrus flavors are rich and sweet, balanced by a hint of bitterness on the finish. 87 *—J.C. (6/1/2007)*

Peter Nicolay 2001 Ürziger Goldwingert Spätlese Riesling (Mosel-Saar-Ruwer) $26. 92 *—R.V. (3/1/2003)*

Peter Nicolay 2004 Ürziger Würzgarten Auslese Riesling (Mosel-Saar-Ruwer) $40. 90 *—J.C. (2/1/2006)*

Peter Nicolay 2004 Ürziger Würzgarten Eiswein 375 ml Riesling (Mosel-Saar-Ruwer) $125. 95 **Cellar Selection** *—J.C. (9/1/2006)*

Peter Nicolay 2005 Ürziger Würzgarten Kabinett Riesling (Mosel-Saar-Ruwer) $16. A bit gold in color, this is an atypical Mosel kabinett, with a broad, verging on fat, mouthfeel and sweet flavors of honey and spice. 85 *—J.C. (4/1/2007)*

Peter Nicolay 2004 Ürziger Würzgarten Kabinett Riesling (Mosel-Saar-Ruwer) $16. 87 *—J.C. (7/1/2006)*

Peter Nicolay 2005 Ürziger Würzgarten Spätlese Riesling (Mosel-Saar-Ruwer) $23. 89 *—J.C. (2/1/2007)*

Peter Nicolay 2004 Ürziger Würzgarten Spätlese Riesling (Mosel-Saar-Ruwer) $23. 90 *—J.C. (2/1/2006)*

PFEFFINGEN

Pfeffingen 2005 Dry Riesling (Pfalz) $15. Full and soft for a Riesling, with appealing aromas of corn oil, ripe apples, pears and limes and flavors of minerals and spice. Attractive, but lacks a bit of vibrancy and zest on the finish. 86 *—J.C. (8/1/2007)*

Pfeffingen 2002 Pfeffo Kabinett Riesling (Pfalz) $18. 87 *—J.C. (8/1/2004)*

PRINZ

Prinz 2004 Hallgartener Jungfer Auslese Riesling (Rheingau) $43. 91 *—J.C. (2/1/2006)*

Prinz 2004 Hallgartener Jungfer Spätlese 375 ml Riesling (Rheingau) $19. 88 *—J.C. (9/1/2006)*

Prinz 2005 Hallgartener Jungfer Gold Capsule Spätlese Riesling (Rheingau) $23. 90 *—J.C. (2/1/2007)*

Prinz 2006 Trocken Riesling (Rheingau) $15. Reasonably plump in the mouth and maybe even showing a touch of sweetness, this is a clean, well-crafted Riesling with straightforward green apple and citrus flavors. A squirt of lime gives the finish a tangy quality. Drink now. 86 *—J.C. (9/1/2007)*

Prinz 2005 Trocken Riesling (Rheingau) $14. It's a bit muscular, weighing in at over 12% alcohol, but dry and fruit-filled. The bouquet offers hints of apricot, marmalade and fresh citrus, while the flavors emphasize stone fruit and lemon. A strong effort at a fair price. 87 *—J.C. (6/1/2007)*

Prinz 2004 Riesling Trocken Riesling (Rheingau) $14. 86 *—J.C. (7/1/2006)*

PRINZ ZU SALM-DALBERG

Prinz zu Salm-Dalberg 2003 Johannisberg Wallhausen Auslese Riesling (Nahe) $50. 90 *—J.C. (5/1/2005)*

Prinz zu Salm-Dalberg 2001 Roxheimer Berg Spätlese Riesling (Nahe) $26. 86 *—J.C. (3/1/2003)*

Prinz zu Salm-Dalberg 2003 Schloss Wallhausen Berg Roxheim Spätlese Riesling (Nahe) $29. 85 *—J.C. (5/1/2005)*

Prinz zu Salm-Dalberg 2001 Schloss Wallhausen Kabinett Riesling (Nahe) $16. 85 *—J.C. (3/1/2003)*

Prinz zu Salm-Dalberg 2001 Wallhäuser Johannisberg QbA Riesling (Nahe) $31. 90 *—J.C. (3/1/2003)*

RATZENBERGER

Ratzenberger 1998 Bacharacher Kloster Furstenal Riesling (Mittelrhein) $17. 87 *—P.G. (12/31/2002)*

REICHSGRAF VON KESSELSTATT

Reichsgraf von Kesselstatt 2001 Graacher QbA Trocken Riesling (Mosel-Saar-Ruwer) $NA. 86 *—J.C. (1/1/2004)*

Reichsgraf von Kesselstatt 2005 Josephshöfer Kabinett Riesling (Mosel-Saar-Ruwer) $22. 88 *—J.C. (2/1/2007)*

Reichsgraf von Kesselstatt 2004 Josephshöfer Spätlese Riesling (Mosel-Saar-Ruwer) $33. 91 *—J.C. (9/1/2006)*

Reichsgraf von Kesselstatt 2001 Josephshöfer Spätlese Monopol Riesling (Mosel-Saar-Ruwer) $20. 90 **Editors' Choice** *—J.C. (3/1/2003)*

Reichsgraf von Kesselstatt 2001 Kaseler Nies'chen Kabinett Riesling (Mosel-Saar-Ruwer) $19. 86 *—J.C. (3/1/2003)*

Reichsgraf von Kesselstatt 2001 Piesporter Goldtropfchen Kabinett Riesling (Mosel-Saar-Ruwer) $19. 89 *—J.C. (3/1/2003)*

Reichsgraf von Kesselstatt 2005 Piesporter Goldtröpfchen Kabinett Riesling (Mosel-Saar-Ruwer) $22. 89 *—J.C. (12/1/2006)*

Reichsgraf von Kesselstatt 2003 Piesporter Goldtröpfchen Riesling Kabinett Riesling (Mosel-Saar-Ruwer) $22. 86 *—J.C. (12/15/2004)*

Reichsgraf von Kesselstatt 2001 Piesporter Goldtropfchen Spätlese Riesling (Mosel-Saar-Ruwer) $24. 88 *—J.C. (3/1/2003)*

Reichsgraf von Kesselstatt 2006 RK Riesling (Mosel-Saar-Ruwer) $15. This lightweight, off-dry Riesling captures a bit of the region's slaty minerality, then balances that with ginger, spice and citrus flavors. Remains fresh and clean on the finish. 84 *—J.C. (11/15/2007)*

Reichsgraf von Kesselstatt 2005 RK QbA Riesling (Mosel-Saar-Ruwer) $13. 84 *—J.C. (2/1/2007)*

Reichsgraf von Kesselstatt 2004 RK QbA Riesling (Mosel-Saar-Ruwer) $13. 87 *—J.C. (5/1/2006)*

Reichsgraf von Kesselstatt 2003 RK QbA Riesling (Mosel-Saar-Ruwer) $13. 84 *—J.C. (5/1/2005)*

Reichsgraf von Kesselstatt 2001 RK QbA Riesling (Mosel-Saar-Ruwer) $9. 88 **Best Buy** *—J.C. (3/1/2003)*

Reichsgraf von Kesselstatt 2002 Scharzhofberger Auslese Riesling (Mosel-Saar-Ruwer) $84. 92 *—J.C. (12/15/2004)*

Reichsgraf von Kesselstatt 2004 Scharzhofberger Auslese Fuder 4 Riesling (Mosel-Saar-Ruwer) $46. 92 *—J.C. (2/1/2006)*

Reichsgraf von Kesselstatt 2004 Scharzhofberger Kabinett Riesling (Mosel-Saar-Ruwer) $22. 85 *—J.C. (7/1/2006)*

Reichsgraf von Kesselstatt 2003 Scharzhofberger Kabinett Riesling (Mosel-Saar-Ruwer) $22. 88 *—J.C. (12/15/2004)*

Reichsgraf von Kesselstatt 2001 Scharzhofberger Spätlese Riesling (Mosel-Saar-Ruwer) $25. 90 *—J.C. (3/1/2003)*

ROBERT WEIL

Robert Weil 2006 Estate Dry Riesling (Rheingau) $24. Like all of the Weil wines, even this entry-level effort places an emphasis on ripeness. Hints of smoke and diesel add complexity to the nose, while on the palate it's broad and slightly off-dry, with sun-drenched flavors of nectarine and melon that coat the mouth on the finish. 89 *—J.C. (9/1/2007)*

Robert Weil 2004 Estate Dry QbA Riesling (Rheingau) $25. 89 *—J.C. (10/1/2005)*

Robert Weil 2002 QbA Trocken Riesling (Rheingau) $20. 86 *—J.C. (8/1/2004)*

ROYAL RHEINGAU

Royal Rheingau Riesling 2004 RRR QbA Riesling (Rheingau) $13. Fairly big and full-bodied for a branded Riesling, this collaboration between several Rheingau estates successfully blends peach and melon nuances with hints of mineral oil and spice. The only quibble is a lack of persistence on the nearly dry finish. 87 *—J.C. (6/1/2007)*

RUDI WIEST

Rudi Wiest 2001 Mosel River QbA Riesling (Mosel-Saar-Ruwer) $9. 84 *—J.C. (8/1/2004)*

Rudi Wiest 2002 Rhein River QbA Riesling (Rheingau) $10. 85 *—J.C. (8/1/2004)*

RUDOLF EILENZ

Rudolf Eilenz 2004 Ayler Kupp Kabinett Riesling (Mosel-Saar-Ruwer) $15. 89 *—J.C. (7/1/2006)*

Rudolf Eilenz 2004 Ayler Kupp Spätlese Feinherb Riesling (Mosel-Saar-Ruwer) $18. 86 *—J.C. (9/1/2006)*

Rudolf Eilenz 2003 Ayler Kupp Spätlese Feinherb Riesling (Mosel-Saar-Ruwer) $17. 87 *—J.C. (5/1/2005)*

RUDOLF MÜLLER

Rudolf Müller 2006 Auslese Riesling (Mosel-Saar-Ruwer) $14. A hint of dried apricot underscores the ripe apple aromas in this fresh and appealing auslese. It's sweet but not overly so, with apple and melon flavors that are plesantly round without becoming soft. 86 *—J.C. (11/15/2007)*

Rudolf Müller 2005 Auslese Riesling (Mosel-Saar-Ruwer) $13. Citrus and green apple flavors mark this rather light-bodied auslese. It's crisp, clean and fresh, with tart lemon-lime flavors on the finish and some modestly minerally undercurrents. Drink now. 88 Best Buy *—J.C. (10/1/2007)*

Rudolf Müller 2004 Eiswein 375 ml Riesling (Pfalz) $19. 90 Editors' Choice *—J.C. (9/1/2006)*

Rudolf Müller 2006 Kabinett Riesling (Mosel-Saar-Ruwer) $11. Sweet and plump, this apple and melon-scented Riesling offers no great character or length but is cleanly made, fresh and fruity. 83 *—J.C. (11/15/2007)*

Rudolf Müller 2005 Kabinett Riesling (Mosel-Saar-Ruwer) $11. This thick, oily-textured wine lacks the freshness and vibrance expected from a Mosel Riesling, but does offer some suggestion of minerality and some vaguely apple-like fruit. 81 *—J.C. (11/15/2007)*

Rudolf Müller 2004 Mainzer Domherr Eiswein Riesling (Rheinhessen) $20. There's a slight hint of mushroominess to this wine's aromas, but otherwise it's rather clean, featuring apricot and candied orange aromas and flavors. Offers plenty of depth without being syrupy, ending with a pithy note to help balance the sweetness. Drink now. 90 Editors' Choice *—J.C. (10/1/2007)*

Rudolf Müller 2005 Piesporter Goldtröpfchen Kabinett Riesling (Mosel-Saar-Ruwer) $13. From a large négociant, this is a light-bodied kabinett that shows traces of the region's floral character layered over notes of apple, chalk and citrus. 83 *—J.C. (11/15/2007)*

Rudolf Müller 2006 Spätlese Riesling (Mosel-Saar-Ruwer) $12. This is a bit sweet and heavy, but it combines honeyed fruit with underripe green notes of herbs and limes to make a reasonably flavorful package. 84 *—J.C. (11/15/2007)*

Rudolf Müller 2005 Spätlese Riesling (Mosel-Saar-Ruwer) $12. Scents of ripe apples and a hint of dried apricot are pleasant enough, but the wine is simple and sweet, lacking richness or depth. 82 *—J.C. (11/15/2007)*

Rudolf Müller 2005 The Bishop of Riesling Riesling (Mosel-Saar-Ruwer) $9. Light and lacking substance, with simple lime and apple flavors that finish short. 81 *—J.C. (8/1/2007)*

S.A. PRÜM

S.A. Prüm 2003 Blue Slate Kabinett Riesling (Mosel-Saar-Ruwer) $16. 88 *—J.C. (5/1/2005)*

S.A. Prüm 2006 Essence Riesling (Mosel-Saar-Ruwer) $11. This plump, succulent Riesling offers up scents of honey, ripe pears and even some slate-driven minerality, then follows through on the palate with crisp pear and citrus flavors, underscored by wet stones. Fresh and clean, it's an ideal apéritif, but would also work well with various Asian dishes. 86 Best Buy *—J.C. (11/15/2007)*

S.A. Prüm 2005 Essence Riesling (Mosel-Saar-Ruwer) $10. 85 Best Buy *—J.C. (7/1/2006)*

S.A. Prüm 2004 Essence Riesling (Mosel-Saar-Ruwer) $10. 86 Best Buy *—J.C. (2/1/2006)*

S.A. Prüm 2003 Essence QbA Riesling (Mosel-Saar-Ruwer) $10. 84 *—J.C. (5/1/2005)*

S.A. Prüm 2001 Graacher Domprobst Eiswein Riesling (Mosel-Saar-Ruwer) $175. 90 *—J.C. (3/1/2003)*

S.A. Prüm 2002 Graacher Domprobst Trockenbeerenauslese Fass 61 Riesling (Mosel-Saar-Ruwer) $360. 95 Cellar Selection *—J.C. (8/1/2004)*

S.A. Prüm 2001 Graacher Hammelreich Eiswein Riesling (Mosel-Saar-Ruwer) $165. 89 *—J.C. (3/1/2003)*

S.A. Prüm 2002 Graacher Himmelreich Eiswein Fass 56 Riesling (Mosel-Saar-Ruwer) $195. 94 *—J.C. (8/1/2004)*

S.A. Prüm 1998 Graacher Himmelreich Eiswein Vat 28 Riesling (Mosel-Saar-Ruwer) $140. 84 *—J.C. (5/1/2005)*

S.A. Prüm 2001 Graacher Himmelreich Eiswein Vat 46 Riesling (Mosel-Saar-Ruwer) $143. Sweet and bracingly tart at the same time, with racy acidity framing sweet orange and lime flavors. Flourishes of bergamot and cinnamon add complexity on the nose and reprise on the long finish. 93 *—J.C. (12/15/2007)*

S.A. Prüm 2003 Graacher Himmelreich Spätlese Riesling (Mosel-Saar-Ruwer) $26. 86 *—J.C. (5/1/2005)*

S.A. Prüm 2001 Kabinett Halbtrocken Riesling (Mosel-Saar-Ruwer) $20. 89 *—J.C. (3/1/2003)*

S.A. Prüm 2001 QbA trocken Riesling (Mosel-Saar-Ruwer) $19. 88 *—J.C. (3/1/2003)*

S.A. Prüm 2001 Spätlese trocken Riesling (Mosel-Saar-Ruwer) $23. 87 *—J.C. (3/1/2003)*

S.A. Prüm 2002 Wehlener Sonnenuhr Auslese Riesling (Mosel-Saar-Ruwer) $65. 93 Editors' Choice *—J.C. (8/1/2004)*

S.A. Prüm 2001 Wehlener Sonnenuhr Auslese Riesling (Mosel-Saar-Ruwer) $53. 87 *—J.C. (3/1/2003)*

S.A. Prüm 2005 Wehlener Sonnenuhr Kabinett Riesling (Mosel-Saar-Ruwer) $20. 87 *—J.C. (7/1/2006)*

S.A. Prüm 2003 Wehlener Sonnenuhr Kabinett Riesling (Mosel-Saar-Ruwer) $20. 85 *—J.C. (5/1/2006)*

S.A. Prüm 2001 Wehlener Sonnenuhr Kabinett Riesling (Mosel-Saar-Ruwer) $23. 88 *—J.C. (3/1/2003)*

S.A. Prüm 2001 Wehlener Sonnenuhr Spätlese Riesling (Mosel-Saar-Ruwer) $24. 86 *—J.C. (3/1/2003)*

S.A. Prüm 2001 Wehlener Sonnenuhr Spätlese Halbtrocken Riesling (Mosel-Saar-Ruwer) $35. 86 *—J.C. (3/1/2003)*

S.A. Prüm 2001 Wehlener Sonnenuhr Spätlese Trocken Riesling (Mosel-Saar-Ruwer) $35. 87 *—J.C. (3/1/2003)*

S.A. Prüm 2001 Wehlener Sonnenuhr Vat 10 Riesling Beerenauslese Riesling (Mosel-Saar-Ruwer) $160. Viscous, almost oily in texture, this is several vintages older than most of the recent samples, yet seems so unevolved that it's not out of place. Honey and dried spices are the predominant themes, with citrusy fruit making up the core. Should evolve glacially through at least 2025. 91 *—J.C. (12/15/2007)*

SAINT M

Saint M 2006 Riesling (Pfalz) $12. Simple but fresh and appealing, this offering—made in conjunction with Washington State's Chateau Ste. Michelle—is a light, entry-level Riesling filled with green apple and citrus flavors. Drink now. 84 *—J.C. (8/1/2007)*

Saint M 2004 Qualitatswein Riesling (Pfalz) $12. 83 *—J.C. (10/1/2005)*

SANDER

Sander 2002 Terravita Dornfelder (Rheinhessen) $18. 85 *—R.V. (4/1/2005)*

Sander NV Brut Sekt Riesling (Rheinhessen) $28. Fresh and gingery, this lightweight sparkling wine adds modest earth notes on the palate. 83 *—J.C. (12/15/2007)*

Sander 2005 Halbtrocken Riesling (Rheinhessen) $18. Smells of waxed citrus rinds, and although there's a hint of green apple to the flavors, that same citrusy note dominates. It's a light- to medium-bodied, relatively dry Riesling that could just use a touch more weight and power. 85 *—J.C. (4/1/2007)*

Sander 2003 Kabinett Halbtrocken Terravita Riesling (Rheinhessen) $13. 84 *—R.V. (4/1/2005)*

Sander 2002 QbA Riesling (Rheinhessen) $13. 84 *—J.C. (8/1/2004)*

Sander 2004 Single Vineyard Riesling (Rheinhessen) $27. From the Mettenheimer Schlossberg, this rather light, hollow offering smells a bit dirty, adding a slight funk to its honey and earth aromas. Assertively tart on the finish. 81 *—J.C. (4/1/2007)*

Sander 2003 Terravita Riesling (Rheinhessen) $13. 87 *—R.V. (4/1/2005)*

Sander 2004 Metterheimer Sauvignon Blanc (Rheinhessen) $28. 83 *(7/1/2005)*

Sander 2003 Trocken Spätburgunder (Rheinhessen) $15. 86 *—R.V. (4/1/2005)*

Sander 2003 Trocken Weissburgunder (Rheinhessen) $13. 85 *—R.V. (4/1/2005)*

Sander 2004 Mettenheimer Sauvignon Blanc-Riesling White Blend (Rheinhessen) $25. 87 *(7/1/2005)*

Sander 2003 Trio Terravita White Blend (Rheinhessen) $11. 84 *—R.V. (4/1/2005)*

SCHÄFER-FRÖHLICH

Schäfer-Fröhlich 2005 Halbtrocken Riesling (Nahe) $18. Smoky and leesy upfront, with powerful diesel notes. Yet all that seems to disappear on the palate, where apple and citrus flavors hold sway. Has a pleasantly plump, custardy texture and a crisp clean finish. 86 *—J.C. (8/1/2007)*

SCHLOSS JOHANNISBERGER

Schloss Johannisberger 2004 Kabinett Riesling (Rheingau) $28. 88 *—J.C. (7/1/2006)*

Schloss Johannisberger 2001 Kabinett Riesling (Rheingau) $18. 84 *—J.C. (1/1/2004)*

Schloss Johannisberger 2004 QbA Riesling (Rheingau) $23. 84 *—J.C. (2/1/2006)*

Schloss Johannisberger 2003 QbA Riesling (Rheingau) $23. 86 *—J.C. (12/15/2004)*

Schloss Johannisberger 2001 QbA Riesling (Rheingau) $15. 87 —*J.C. (3/1/2003)*

Schloss Johannisberger 2003 Kabinett Riesling (Rheingau) $28. 86 —*J.C. (12/15/2004)*

Schloss Johannisberger 2006 Rosa-Goldlack Beerenauslese Riesling (Rheingau) $395. With scents of dried apricots and superconcentrated pear nectar, one sniff suggests this is going to be a sumptuously sweet treat. And it is. Pear, melon and spice flavors linger elegantly on the finish, ending long and sweet. **93** —*J.C. (12/15/2007)*

Schloss Johannisberger 2003 Spätlese Riesling (Rheingau) $34. 84 —*J.C. (12/15/2004)*

Schloss Johannisberger 2006 Trockenbeerenauslese Goldlack Riesling (Rheingau) $486. So incredibly thick and sweet it's almost chewy in texture, with aromas and flavors that feature a fascinating interplay of fresh and dried apricots, peach and citrus, kept lively by healthy acidity. The finish lasts for minutes; the wine should age well for decades. **97 Cellar Selection** —*J.C. (12/15/2007)*

SCHLOSS KOBLENZ

Schloss Koblenz NV Weisslack Trocken Sekt Sparkling Blend (Germany) $12. 85 —*J.C. (6/1/2006)*

SCHLOSS SAARSTEIN

Schloss Saarstein 2005 Auslese Riesling (Mosel-Saar-Ruwer) $49. Starts off with leesy, minerally notes, including struck flint, but also ripe melon and star anise scents. This is a nicely balanced, not overly sweet auslese, with green apple and citrus fruit smoothly combining with steely acidity and petrol notes. The long finish, filled with green apple and white grapefruit, promises a long life in the cellar. **92** —*J.C. (2/1/2007)*

Schloss Saarstein 2005 Kabinett Riesling (Mosel-Saar-Ruwer) $20. 86 —*J.C. (2/1/2007)*

Schloss Saarstein 2001 QbA Trocken Riesling (Mosel-Saar-Ruwer) $11. 88 Best Buy —*J.C. (3/1/2003)*

Schloss Saarstein 2003 QbA Trocken Riesling (Mosel-Saar-Ruwer) $17. 88 —*J.C. (12/15/2004)*

Schloss Saarstein 2006 Saarstein Riesling (Mosel-Saar-Ruwer) $13. This wine features bold, assertive aromas of honeyed pineapple, but there's also a touch of dustiness—not TCA—that seems out of place. Flavors are sweet and reprise the pineapple theme, but there's also a slightly bitter character—posssibly rot. A shame, because this thick, rich, admirably concentrated wine could have been so much better. **83** —*J.C. (11/15/2007)*

Schloss Saarstein 2005 Saarstein QbA Riesling (Mosel-Saar-Ruwer) $13. 87 —*J.C. (2/1/2007)*

Schloss Saarstein 2005 Spätlese Riesling (Mosel-Saar-Ruwer) $26. 91 —*J.C. (2/1/2007)*

Schloss Saarstein 2003 Spätlese Trocken Riesling (Mosel-Saar-Ruwer) $26. 87 —*J.C. (12/15/2004)*

Schloss Saarstein 2003 Serriger Schloss Saarsteiner Auslese Riesling (Mosel-Saar-Ruwer) $39. 89 —*J.C. (12/15/2004)*

Schloss Saarstein 2004 Serriger Schloss Saarsteiner Kabinett Riesling (Mosel-Saar-Ruwer) $20. 89 —*J.C. (5/1/2006)*

Schloss Saarstein 2003 Serriger Schloss Saarsteiner Kabinett Riesling (Mosel-Saar-Ruwer) $20. 88 —*J.C. (5/1/2005)*

Schloss Saarstein 2003 Serriger Schloss Saarsteiner Spätlese Riesling (Mosel-Saar-Ruwer) $26. 88 —*J.C. (12/15/2004)*

Schloss Saarstein 2003 Weisser Burgunder QbA Weissburgunder (Mosel-Saar-Ruwer) $17. 84 —*J.C. (12/15/2004)*

SCHLOSS SCHÖNBORN

Schloss Schönborn 2001 Domanenweingut Hattenheimer Pfaffenberg Spätlese Riesling (Rheingau) $28. 90 —*R.V. (3/1/2003)*

Schloss Schönborn 2001 Erbacher Marcobrunn Kabinett Riesling (Rheingau) $14. 90 —*R.V. (3/1/2003)*

Schloss Schönborn 2001 Erbacher Marcobrunn Spätlese Riesling (Rheingau) $23. 92 —*R.V. (3/1/2003)*

Schloss Schönborn 2001 Hattenheimer Pfaffenberg Kabinett Riesling (Rheingau) $12. 90 —*R.V. (3/1/2003)*

Schloss Schönborn 2001 Hattenheimer Pfaffenberg Spätlese Riesling (Rheingau) $17. 91 —*R.V. (3/1/2003)*

Schloss Schönborn 2001 Johannisberger Klaus Spätlese Riesling (Rheingau) $16. 87 —*R.V. (3/1/2003)*

Schloss Schönborn 2001 Kabinett Riesling (Rheingau) $10. 88 —*R.V. (3/1/2003)*

Schloss Schönborn 2000 Rudesheimer Berg Rottland Auslese Riesling (Rheingau) $43. 93 —*R.V. (3/1/2003)*

SCHLOSS THORN

Schloss Thorn 2001 Spätlese Riesling (Mosel-Saar-Ruwer) $20. 89 —*R.V. (1/1/2004)*

SCHLOSS VOLLRADS

Schloss Vollrads 2003 Auslese Riesling (Rheingau) $50. 90 *(8/1/2004)*

Schloss Vollrads 2001 Auslese Riesling (Rheingau) $46. 88 —*R.V. (3/1/2003)*

Schloss Vollrads 2004 Auslese 375 ml Riesling (Rheingau) $50. 91 —*J.C. (9/1/2006)*

Schloss Vollrads 2003 Beerenauslese Riesling (Rheingau) $180. 93 *(8/1/2004)*

Schloss Vollrads 2004 Beerenauslese (375ml) Riesling (Rheingau) $170. 87 —*J.C. (9/1/2006)*

Schloss Vollrads 2002 Eiswein Riesling (Rheingau) $160. 91 *(8/1/2004)*

Schloss Vollrads 2001 Eiswein Riesling (Rheingau) $119. 90 —*R.V. (3/1/2003)*

Schloss Vollrads 2004 Kabinett Riesling (Rheingau) $19. 84 —*J.C. (5/1/2006)*

Schloss Vollrads 2003 Kabinett Riesling (Rheingau) $17. 86 *(8/1/2004)*

Schloss Vollrads 2001 Kabinett Riesling (Rheingau) $15. 87 —*R.V. (3/1/2003)*

Schloss Vollrads 2004 Kabinett Halbtrocken Riesling (Rheingau) $19. 85 —*J.C. (7/1/2006)*

Schloss Vollrads 2002 Kabinett Halbtrocken Riesling (Rheingau) $17. 87 *(8/1/2004)*

Schloss Vollrads 2001 Kabinett Halbtrocken Riesling (Rheingau) $15. 87 —*R.V. (3/1/2003)*

Schloss Vollrads 2003 Kabinett Trocken Riesling (Rheingau) $17. 85 *(8/1/2004)*

Schloss Vollrads 2004 QbA Riesling (Rheingau) $16. 88 —*J.C. (5/1/2006)*

Schloss Vollrads 2003 QbA Riesling (Rheingau) $17. 85 *(8/1/2004)*

Schloss Vollrads 2004 QbA Trocken Riesling (Rheingau) $16. 86 —*J.C. (5/1/2006)*

Schloss Vollrads 2003 QbA Trocken Riesling (Rheingau) $15. 86 *(8/1/2004)*

Schloss Vollrads 2003 Spätlese Riesling (Rheingau) $26. 89 *(8/1/2004)*

Schloss Vollrads 2001 Spätlese Riesling (Rheingau) $25. 86 —*R.V. (3/1/2003)*

Schloss Vollrads 2003 Spätlese Halbtrocken Riesling (Rheingau) $26. 88 *(8/1/2004)*

Schloss Vollrads 2002 Trockenbeerenauslese Riesling (Rheingau) $300. 92 *(8/1/2004)*

SCHLOSS WALLHAUSEN

Schloss Wallhausen 2005 Kabinett Riesling (Nahe) $19. Plump and sweet, this is a bit soft and lacking structure, although the ripe apple and pear flavors do offer plenty of immediate attraction. Drink now. **84** —*J.C. (8/1/2007)*

Schloss Wallhausen 2004 Kabinett Riesling (Nahe) $17. 88 —*J.C. (10/1/2005)*

Schloss Wallhausen 2005 Spätlese Riesling (Nahe) $23. 89 —*J.C. (12/1/2006)*

SCHMITGES

Schmitges 2006 Riesling (Mosel-Saar-Ruwer) $15. Rather weighty, with fresh green apple and citrus aromas but thick, sweet flavors. Still, there's enough zesty acidity to clean it up a bit on the finish and give it life. **84** —*J.C. (11/15/2007)*

Schmitges 2006 Erdener Prälat Alte Reben Auslese Riesling (Mosel-Saar-Ruwer) $50. Ultraripe tropical fruits—even including hints of bananas—dominate this wine's heady aromas. Acids are soft, and alcohol fairly elevated—12.5%—for a wine of this prädikat. There's ample concentration, and the peach and melon flavors linger on the finish. Drink now–2016. **88** —*J.C. (10/1/2007)*

Schmitges 2004 Erdener Prälat Spätlese Alte Reben Riesling (Mosel-Saar-Ruwer) $41. 87 —*J.C. (9/1/2006)*

Schmitges 2004 Erdener Treppchen Kabinett No. 11 Riesling (Mosel-Saar-Ruwer) $18. 86 —*J.C. (7/1/2006)*

Schmitges 2003 Erdener Treppchen Kabinett No. 7 Riesling (Mosel-Saar-Ruwer) $17. 88 —*J.C. (11/1/2004)*

Schmitges 2004 Erdener Treppchen Spätlese No. 14 Riesling (Mosel-Saar-Ruwer) $25. 89 —*J.C. (2/1/2006)*

Schmitges 2005 Grauschiefer Dry Riesling (Mosel-Saar-Ruwer) $15. 87 —*J.C. (12/1/2006)*

Schmitges 2003 Grauschiefer Qualitätswein Trocken Riesling (Mosel-Saar-Ruwer) $15. 86 —*J.C. (11/1/2004)*

Schmitges 2004 Grauschiefer Trocken Riesling (Mosel-Saar-Ruwer) $15. **89 Editors' Choice** —*J.C. (10/1/2005)*

Schmitges 2006 Grey Slate Dry Riesling (Mosel-Saar-Ruwer) $16. Round and plush, this relatively high-alcohol (13%) Mosel Riesling offers plenty of ripe fruit flavors, yet finishes dry. A smoky, leesy character on the nose wraps easily around a core of pineapple and peach fruit. Drink now. 87 —*J.C. (8/1/2007)*

Schmitges 2003 QbA Riesling (Mosel-Saar-Ruwer) $17. 88 —*J.C. (11/1/2004)*

Schmitges 2004 Qualitatswein Riesling (Mosel-Saar-Ruwer) $15. 85 —*J.C. (10/1/2005)*

Schmitges 2006 Dry Rivaner (Mosel-Saar-Ruwer) $12. Rivaner is a rarely seen grape variety, but this is awfully good. It's a full-bodied, robust wine with intense stone fruit and melon flavors, underscored by citrus and spice notes that linger delicately on the finish. Drink it now and over the next year or two. **88 Best Buy** —*J.C. (6/1/2007)*

Schmitges 2005 Dry Rivaner (Mosel-Saar-Ruwer) $11. **88 Best Buy** —*J.C. (6/1/2007)*

SCHMITT SCHENK

Schmitt Schenk 2001 Ayler Kupp Auslese Riesling (Mosel-Saar-Ruwer) $14. 86 —*R.V. (3/1/2003)*

SCHMITT SOHNE

Schmitt Sohne 2001 Piesporter Michelsberg Auslese Riesling (Mosel-Saar-Ruwer) $12. 84 —*R.V. (3/1/2003)*

Schmitt Sohne 2004 Relax QbA Riesling (Mosel-Saar-Ruwer) $8. **84 Best Buy** —*J.C. (7/1/2006)*

Schmitt Sohne 2001 Spätlese Riesling (Mosel-Saar-Ruwer) $9. 83 —*R.V. (3/1/2003)*

Schmitt Sohne 2001 Wehlener Sonnenuhr Auslese Riesling (Mosel-Saar-Ruwer) $14. 86 —*R.V. (3/1/2003)*

Schmitt Sohne 2001 Wehlener Sonnenuhr Kabinett Riesling (Mosel-Saar-Ruwer) $18. 86 —*R.V. (3/1/2003)*

Schmitt Sohne 2001 Wehlener Sonnenuhr Spätlese Riesling (Mosel-Saar-Ruwer) $11. 85 —*R.V. (3/1/2003)*

SCHUMANN-NÄGLER

Schumann-Nägler 2006 Christopher Philipp Riesling (Rheingau) $15. Filled with ripe apples, peaches and featuring some lime-like notes on the finish, this is textbook German Riesling. Clean, fresh and balanced, with a delicacy to its texture that belies its ripe succulence. Easy to drink on its own. 88 —*J.C. (11/15/2007)*

Schumann-Nägler 2004 Christopher Philipp QbA Riesling (Rheingau) $13. 83 —*J.C. (5/1/2006)*

Schumann-Nägler 2001 Christopher Philipp QbA Riesling (Rheingau) $10. 83 —*J.C. (1/1/2004)*

Schumann-Nägler 2003 Christopher Philipp Riesling QbA Riesling (Rheingau) $12. **87 Best Buy** —*J.C. (12/15/2004)*

Schumann-Nägler 2001 Johannisberger Ertenbringer Riesling (Rheingau) $15. 86 —*J.C. (3/1/2003)*

SEEBRICH

Seebrich 2004 Niersteiner Hipping Auslese Riesling (Rheinhessen) $24. 88 —*J.C. (9/1/2006)*

Seebrich 2003 Niersteiner Hipping Spätlese Riesling (Rheinhessen) $17. 86 —*J.C. (12/15/2004)*

Seebrich 2006 Niersteiner Oelberg Beerenauslese Riesling (Rheinhessen) $48. Sweet and slightly viscous in texture, this wine lacks some aromatic flourishes, sacrificing complexity for purity of its pineapple, apple and citrus flavors. Yet because of its balanced, crisp acidity, the wine still sings, finishing long and mouthwatering. Drink now–2030. **93 Editors' Choice** —*J.C. (12/15/2007)*

SELBACH

Selbach 2001 Piesporter Michelsberg Riesling Kabinett Riesling (Mosel-Saar-Ruwer) $11. **87 Best Buy** —*D.T. (11/15/2002)*

Selbach 2004 Qba Dry Riesling (Mosel-Saar-Ruwer) $14. 83 —*J.C. (2/1/2006)*

SELBACH SÖHNE

Selbach Söhne NV Blau-Gold Mild Schaumwein Sparkling Blend (Germany) $13. 81 —*J.C. (6/1/2006)*

SELBACH-OSTER

Selbach-Oster 2004 Kabinett Riesling (Mosel-Saar-Ruwer) $23. 87 —*J.C. (10/1/2005)*

Selbach-Oster 2001 Zeltinger Sonnenuhr Auslese Riesling (Mosel-Saar-Ruwer) $33. 91 —*J.C. (3/1/2003)*

Selbach-Oster 2004 Zeltinger Sonnenuhr Kabinett Riesling (Mosel-Saar-Ruwer) $26. 88 —*J.C. (10/1/2005)*

Selbach-Oster 2001 Zeltinger Sonnenuuhr Spätlese One Star Riesling (Mosel-Saar-Ruwer) $27. 91 —*J.C. (3/1/2003)*

SOMMERAU CASTLE

Sommerau Castle 2005 QbA Riesling (Mosel-Saar-Ruwer) $8. A surprisingly attractive blend of green plum and apple flavors that manages to deftly balance sweetness and tartness to yield a balanced result. It's light body and sweetness make it a fine companion for your midweek order of Chinese takeout. **85 Best Buy** —*J.C. (4/1/2007)*

Sommerau Castle 2004 QbA Riesling (Mosel-Saar-Ruwer) $7. 83 —*J.C. (7/1/2006)*

SPREITZER

Spreitzer 2001 Oestricher Lenchen Spätlese Riesling (Rheingau) $27. 89 —*J.C. (3/1/2003)*

ST. GABRIEL

St. Gabriel 2005 Auslese Riesling (Mosel-Saar-Ruwer) $11. This lightweight auslese features admirable minerality in its crisp green apple and lime aromas and flavors. Frankly sweet flavors turn tart and malic, then thin out a little on the finish, but this is a solid commercial offering. **86 Best Buy** —*J.C. (6/1/2007)*

St. Gabriel 2002 Auslese Riesling (Mosel-Saar-Ruwer) $9. **86 Best Buy** —*J.C. (12/15/2004)*

St. Gabriel 2002 Kabinett Riesling (Mosel-Saar-Ruwer) $7. 83 —*J.C. (11/1/2004)*

St. Gabriel 2002 Qualitätswein Riesling (Pfalz) $6. **84 Best Buy** —*J.C. (11/1/2004)*

St. Gabriel 2002 Spätlese Riesling (Mosel-Saar-Ruwer) $8. **84 Best Buy** —*J.C. (11/1/2004)*

ST. URBANS-HOF

St. Urbans-Hof 2006 Riesling (Mosel-Saar-Ruwer) $13. Relatively full-bodied, even though the alcohol is only 10%, this shows a touch of the botrytis influence of the vintage, with apricot notes adding interest to the straightforward melon and herb flavors. Finishes soft; drink now. 86 —*J.C. (8/1/2007)*

St. Urbans-Hof 2005 Ockfener Bockstein Auslese Riesling (Mosel-Saar-Ruwer) $40. Shows the winery's characteristic leesy notes on the nose, but unfurls on the palate to reveal wonderfully delineated flavors of melon, white peach, honey and green apples, all held together by slaty underpinnings. It's rich and mouthcoating without being heavy, ending on a spicy, minerally note that helps counter the wine's sweetness. Imported by HB Wine Merchants. **94 Editors' Choice** —*J.C. (6/1/2007)*

St. Urbans-Hof 2001 Ockfener Bockstein Auslese Riesling (Mosel-Saar-Ruwer) $16. 87 —*R.V. (1/1/2004)*

St. Urbans-Hof 2005 Ockfener Bockstein Kabinett Riesling (Mosel-Saar-Ruwer) $18. Leesy, smoky and with a note of diesel oil, this light-bodied offering from the Saar emphasizes the mineral aspects of its site, then adds graceful notes of tart green apples and citrus to perk things up. Crisp, long and mouthwatering on the finish. Imported by HB Wine Merchants. 89 —*J.C. (4/1/2007)*

St. Urbans-Hof 2001 Ockfener Bockstein Kabinett Riesling (Mosel-Saar-Ruwer) $14. 80 —*R.V. (1/1/2004)*

St. Urbans-Hof 2000 Ockfener Bockstein Kabinett Riesling (Mosel-Saar-Ruwer) $14. 86 —*J.C. (5/1/2002)*

St. Urbans-Hof 2005 Ockfener Bockstein Spätlese Riesling (Mosel-Saar-Ruwer) $25. A solid effort, but one that lacks the brilliant focus of some of Nik Weis's other offerings this year. This is broad and mouthfilling, oozing with honey, apple and petrol aromas and flavors that seem to lack a little focus, then pick up a bitter citrus pith note on the finish. Imported by HB Wine Merchants. 87 —*J.C. (4/1/2007)*

St. Urbans-Hof 2004 Ockfener Bockstein Spätlese Riesling (Mosel-Saar-Ruwer) $20. **92 Editors' Choice** —*J.C. (9/1/2006)*

St. Urbans-Hof 2001 Ockfener Bockstein Spätlese Riesling (Mosel-Saar-Ruwer) $16. 84 —*R.V. (1/1/2004)*

St. Urbans-Hof 2000 Ockfener Bockstein Spätlese Riesling (Mosel-Saar-Ruwer) $18. 86 —*C.S. (5/1/2002)*

St. Urbans-Hof 2001 Piesporter Goldtropfchen Auslese Riesling (Mosel-Saar-Ruwer) $12. 85 —*R.V. (1/1/2004)*

GERMANY

St. Urbans-Hof 2004 Piesporter Goldtröpfchen Auslese Riesling (Mosel-Saar-Ruwer) $45. 91 Cellar Selection *—J.C. (9/1/2006)*

St. Urbans-Hof 2004 Piesporter Goldtröpfchen Kabinett Riesling (Mosel-Saar-Ruwer) $18. 89 *—J.C. (7/1/2006)*

St. Urbans-Hof 2001 Piesporter Goldtröpfchen Kabinett Riesling (Mosel-Saar-Ruwer) $16. 88 *—J.C. (3/1/2003)*

St. Urbans-Hof 2005 Piesporter Goldtröpfchen Spätlese Riesling (Mosel-Saar-Ruwer) $30. A rich and exotic spätlese, with honeyed fruit that even contains a hint of apricot to go with the apple, melon and citrus flavors. Rather full-bodied (9% alcohol) and sweet, but remarkably finesse-filled as well, finishing long. Imported by HB Wine Merchants. **92 Editors' Choice** *—J.C. (4/1/2007)*

St. Urbans-Hof 2001 Piesporter Goldtropfchen Spätlese Riesling (Mosel-Saar-Ruwer) $20. 86 *—J.C. (3/1/2003)*

St. Urbans-Hof 2000 Piesporter Goldtropfchen Spätlese Riesling (Mosel-Saar-Ruwer) $21. 86 *—C.S. (5/1/2002)*

St. Urbans-Hof 2005 QbA Riesling (Mosel-Saar-Ruwer) $12. 89 Best Buy *—J.C. (11/15/2006)*

STAATSWEINGÜTER KLOSTER EBERBACH

Staatsweingüter Kloster Eberbach 2001 Erbacher Marcobrunn Kabinett Riesling (Rheingau) $19. 91 *—R.V. (3/1/2003)*

Staatsweingüter Kloster Eberbach 1998 Rauenthaler Baiken Brut Riesling (Rheingau) $17. 86 *—P.G. (12/31/2002)*

Staatsweingüter Kloster Eberbach 2001 Steinberger Kabinett Riesling (Rheingau) $18. 92 *—R.V. (3/1/2003)*

Staatsweingüter Kloster Eberbach 2001 Steinberger Spätlese Riesling (Rheingau) $34. 89 *—R.V. (3/1/2003)*

STARLING CASTLE

Starling Castle 2004 QbA Riesling (Mosel-Saar-Ruwer) $11. 84 *—J.C. (2/1/2006)*

STEPHAN EHLEN

Stephan Ehlen 2005 Erdener Treppchen Beerenauslese Riesling (Mosel-Saar-Ruwer) $99. A bit over the top, thickly layered with dried apricots, honey and dried spices. This is one rich, sweet BA, with surprisingly apparent alcohol (9.5%). It finishes a bit low in acid, making it impressive but not classic. Imported by Chapin Cellars, LLC. **90** *—J.C. (12/15/2007)*

Stephan Ehlen 2004 Erdener Treppchen Spätlese Riesling (Mosel-Saar-Ruwer) $20. 90 Editors' Choice *—J.C. (5/1/2006)*

Stephan Ehlen 2003 Erdener Treppchen Spätlese Riesling (Mosel-Saar-Ruwer) $20. 86 *—J.C. (5/1/2005)*

Stephan Ehlen 2005 Erdener Treppchen Trockenbeerenauslese Riesling (Mosel-Saar-Ruwer) $144. Rich and thickly textured, this wine features intense botrytis aromas of dried apricots, backing them up with flavors of honey and orange marmalade. Long and intensely sugary on the finish, with enough sugar to genuinely stand up to desserts. Imported by Chapin Cellars, LLC. **93** *—J.C. (12/15/2007)*

STICH DEN BUBEN

Stich den Buben 1999 Kabinett Riesling (Baden) $13. 84 *(8/1/2001)*

Stich den Buben 1999 Qualitätswein Riesling (Baden) $12. 82 *(8/1/2001)*

STUDERT-PRÜM

Studert-Prüm 2002 Maximiner Cabinet Trocken Sekt Riesling (Mosel-Saar-Ruwer) $20. 84 *—J.C. (6/1/2006)*

SUN GARDEN

Sun Garden 2005 Riesling (Mosel-Saar-Ruwer) $9. Shows the warm vintage in its array of peach, cinnamon and melon flavors and slightly elevated (10.5%) alcohol, but manages to stay off-dry and nicely balanced; it even has some crushed-stone scents to add interest. Drink now. **85 Best Buy** *—J.C. (6/1/2007)*

Sun Garden 2004 QbA Riesling (Mosel-Saar-Ruwer) $10. 84 *—J.C. (7/1/2006)*

SYBILLE KUNTZ

Sybille Kuntz 2001 Dreistern Lieser Niederberg-Helden Spätlese Trocken Riesling (Mosel-Saar-Ruwer) $NA. 89 *—R.V. (1/1/2004)*

Sybille Kuntz 2001 Wehlen Sonnenuhr Spätlese Trocken Riesling (Mosel-Saar-Ruwer) $NA. 88 *—R.V. (1/1/2004)*

TESCH

Tesch 2001 Langenlonsheimer Lohrer Berg Auslese Riesling (Nahe) $30. 90 *—J.C. (3/1/2003)*

Tesch 2001 Langenlonsheimer Lohrer Berg Eiswein Riesling (Nahe) $68. 91 *—J.C. (3/1/2003)*

Tesch 2001 Langenlonsheimer Löhrer Berg Kabinett Halbtrocken Riesling (Nahe) $15. 89 *—J.C. (3/1/2003)*

Tesch 2001 Langenlonsheimer Lohrer Berg Spätlese Riesling (Nahe) $21. 89 *—J.C. (3/1/2003)*

Tesch 2001 Laubenheimer St. Remigiusberg Spätlese Trocken Riesling (Nahe) $23. 88 *—J.C. (3/1/2003)*

Tesch 2001 QbA Halbtrocken Riesling (Nahe) $10. 84 *—J.C. (1/1/2004)*

THOMAS SCHMITT

Thomas Schmitt 2005 Private Collection Riesling (Mosel-Saar-Ruwer) $12. Floral and fresh-smelling, this is true to its Mosel origins. It may be a little higher in alcohol (11%) and rounder than expected, but it's still charming in a buxom sort of way, offering pear and melon flavors augmented by a bit of spice. Drink now. **86** *—J.C. (6/1/2007)*

TWO PRINCES

Two Princes 2006 P2 Riesling (Nahe) $11. As expected, this vintage is not as interesting as the 2005, but it still remains a decent Riesling. It's fresh and minerally, with lime zest and pineapple flavors that finish tart and refreshing. **84** *—J.C. (8/1/2007)*

Two Princes 2005 P2 Riesling (Nahe) $12. Fragrant and slightly floral or herbal, but there's also an intriguing mineral-smoke note that adds dimension to the aromas. It's light to medium-bodied, with apple, mint and lime flavors complementing a dry, stony minerality. Drink now. **87 Best Buy** *—J.C. (8/1/2007)*

Two Princes 2004 P2 Qualitatswein Riesling (Nahe) $10. 85 Best Buy *—J.C. (10/1/2005)*

ULRICH LANGGUTH

Ulrich Langguth 2001 Piesporter Goldtropfchen Auslese Riesling (Mosel-Saar-Ruwer) $28. 84 *—R.V. (1/1/2004)*

Ulrich Langguth 2001 Piesporter Goldtropfchen Spätlese Riesling (Mosel-Saar-Ruwer) $20. 82 *—R.V. (1/1/2004)*

VAN VOLXEM

Van Volxem 2001 Scharzhofberger Spätlese Riesling (Mosel-Saar-Ruwer) $30. 86 *—J.C. (3/1/2003)*

VILLA WOLF

Villa Wolf 2006 Gewürztraminer (Pfalz) $12. Varietally correct scents of rose petals and spice burst from the glass, followed by pear and melon fruit. It's all backed by acidity that's fairly crisp for Gewürztraminer and relatively modest residual sugar. The only quibble is the relatively quick fade on the finish. **87 Best Buy** *—J.C. (11/15/2007)*

Villa Wolf 2006 Pinot Gris (Pfalz) $12. The Pfalz is warm enough to ripen many grape varieties, and one that is growing in popularity is Pinot Gris. This version is round in the mouth, but not terribly assertively flavored, offering up only hints of tangerine and apple before ending with a blast of citrus. **84** *—J.C. (11/15/2007)*

Villa Wolf 2006 Rosé de Pinot Noir (Pfalz) $12. This one tries to capitalize on the trendiness of rosé and Pinot Noir but ultimately only succeeds in putting forth some vaguely melony flavors and hinting at strawberry on the sweet finish. **82** *—J.C. (11/15/2007)*

Villa Wolf 2005 Rosé de Pinot Noir (Pfalz) $12. This pale salmon-colored rosé is thickly textured and sweet, with flavors of overripe pears and a slightly cloying finish. **80** *—J.C. (7/1/2007)*

Villa Wolf 2003 Kabinett Riesling (Pfalz) $12. 87 Best Buy *—J.C. (5/1/2005)*

Villa Wolf 2005 QbA Riesling (Pfalz) $12. 85 *—J.C. (2/1/2007)*

Villa Wolf 2004 QbA Riesling (Pfalz) $11. 86 Best Buy *—J.C. (5/1/2006)*

Villa Wolf 2003 Saint M Riesling (Pfalz) $12. 87 Best Buy *—J.C. (11/1/2004)*

Villa Wolf 2006 Silvaner (Pfalz) $12. Silvaner's chief attributes are its high levels of acidity, high crop yields and early maturation, which make this bottling better than average for the variety. It does have somewhat screechy acids, but there's also some apple-like notes and vaguely citrusy flavors to go with a clean, fresh finish. Drink now. **84** *—J.C. (11/15/2007)*

VON BEULWITZ

Von Beulwitz 1999 Kaseler Nies'chen Spätlese Riesling (Mosel-Saar-Ruwer) $12. 89 *—S.H. (6/1/2001)*

VON BUHL

Von Buhl 2005 Maria Schneider Jazz Medium-Dry Riesling (Pfalz) $15. Light and fresh, with citrusy flavors dressed up by flowershop greens and a touch of dusty chalk. Finishes with a hint of ripe apple. **84** *—J.C. (8/1/2007)*

Von Buhl 2002 Maria Schneider QbA Medium-Dry Riesling (Pfalz) $14. 84 —*J.C. (8/1/2004)*

VON OTHEGRAVEN

Von Othegraven 2005 Kanzem Altenberg Alte Reben Auslese Riesling (Mosel-Saar-Ruwer) $61. Wonderfully balanced and fine, with classic honey, bergamot and dried pineapple aromas that aren't overpowering. This is on the elegant side, blending sweet honey and candied pineapple flavors with zesty citrus fruit for balance. Exquisitely long on the finish, where the balance and elegance become even more apparent. Drink now–2030. **94 Editors' Choice** —*J.C. (10/1/2007)*

Von Othegraven 2004 Kanzem Altenberg Auslese Riesling (Mosel-Saar-Ruwer) $55. 94 Cellar Selection —*J.C. (5/1/2006)*

Von Othegraven 2003 Kanzem Altenberg Auslese Riesling (Mosel-Saar-Ruwer) $50. 88 —*J.C. (5/1/2005)*

Von Othegraven 2004 Kanzem Altenberg Eiswein First Growth 375 ml Riesling (Mosel-Saar-Ruwer) $250. 97 Cellar Selection —*J.C. (9/1/2006)*

Von Othegraven 2004 Kanzem Altenberg First Growth Riesling Kabinett Riesling (Mosel-Saar-Ruwer) $21. 88 —*J.C. (7/1/2006)*

Von Othegraven 2004 Kanzem Altenberg QbA First Growth Riesling (Mosel-Saar-Ruwer) $35. 87 —*J.C. (7/1/2006)*

Von Othegraven 1999 Kanzemer Altenberg Riesling (Mosel-Saar-Ruwer) $25. 89 —*P.G. (8/1/2001)*

Von Othegraven 2001 Kanzemer Altenberg Auslese Riesling (Mosel-Saar-Ruwer) $32. 90 —*R.V. (3/1/2003)*

Von Othegraven 1999 Kanzemer Altenberg Auslese Riesling (Mosel-Saar-Ruwer) $50. 94 Cellar Selection *(8/1/2001)*

Von Othegraven 2001 Kanzemer Altenberg QbA Riesling (Mosel-Saar-Ruwer) $27. 91 Editors' Choice —*J.C. (3/1/2003)*

Von Othegraven 2001 Kanzemer Altenberg Spätlese Riesling (Mosel-Saar-Ruwer) $27. 88 —*R.V. (3/1/2003)*

Von Othegraven 2001 Maria V. O. Riesling (Mosel-Saar-Ruwer) $15. 90 Best Buy —*J.C. (3/1/2003)*

Von Othegraven 2003 Maria V.O. Riesling (Mosel-Saar-Ruwer) $17. 89 —*J.C. (11/1/2004)*

Von Othegraven 2005 Maria V.O. Kabinett Riesling (Mosel-Saar-Ruwer) $19. A strongly minerally wine, the 2005 Maria v. O. boasts perfumes of heating oil and smoke, while the flavors are of apple, pear and citrus, all wrapped in a petrolly shroud. Yet for all that, it also features sweetness balanced by lime-like acid and a clean, refreshing finish. Drink now–2015. **89** —*J.C. (10/1/2007)*

Von Othegraven 1999 Maximus Riesling (Mosel-Saar-Ruwer) $18. 87 *(8/1/2001)*

Von Othegraven 2003 Ockfen Bockstein Riesling (Mosel-Saar-Ruwer) $33. 84 —*J.C. (5/1/2005)*

Von Othegraven 2001 Ockfen Bockstein Riesling (Mosel-Saar-Ruwer) $25. 90 —*J.C. (3/1/2003)*

Von Othegraven 2004 Ockfen Bockstein QbA Riesling (Mosel-Saar-Ruwer) $30. 88 —*J.C. (7/1/2006)*

Von Othegraven 2003 Ungrafted Vines Kanzemer Altenberg Riesling Spätlese Riesling (Mosel-Saar-Ruwer) $45. 90 —*J.C. (5/1/2005)*

Von Othegraven 2000 Kanzemer Berg Brut Sekt Sparkling Blend (Mosel-Saar-Ruwer) $35. 85 —*J.C. (12/31/2004)*

WEINGUT STIFTUNG ST. NIKOLAUS-HOSPITAL

Weingut Stiftung St. Nikolaus-Hospital 2005 Cardinal Cusanus Stiftswein Graacher Himmelreich Auslese Riesling (Mosel-Saar-Ruwer) $25. A terrific value, this may be the best-priced top-quality auslese on the market. From a site that produced several other gems this vintage, this is a lush, slightly viscous wine that boasts scents of apricots, honey and crushed stone, while the flavors feature a beautifully harmonious interplay of stone fruits and ripe citrus. Long and balanced on the finish, with at least a decade or two or evolution ahead. **93 Editors' Choice** —*J.C. (10/1/2007)*

WEINGUT-PENSION H.J.&E. LEHMEN

Weingut-Pension H.J.&E. Lehmen 2006 Kerner (Mosel-Saar-Ruwer) $18. Kerner is a variety not often seen in the U.S., although it is among the top five most planted white grapes in Germany. It's a cross between Trollinger (a red grape) and Riesling, making for—in this case—a pretty, aromatic white with hints of muskmelon, tropical fruit, maybe even some red berries, all on a light frame. Long and refreshing on the finish. **90 Editors' Choice** —*J.C. (8/1/2007)*

Weingut-Pension H.J.&E. Lehmen 2006 Hochgewächs Lieblich QbA Zeller Schwarze Katz Riesling (Mosel-Saar-Ruwer) $20. Hochgewächs suggests an extra level of quality, and this is good, especially for one from the oft-maligned Zeller Schwarze Katz. Starts off a bit leesy on the nose, but offers pleasant flavors of white peaches, melon and spice before coming to a slightly attenuated close. **86** —*J.C. (8/1/2007)*

Weingut-Pension H.J.&E. Lehmen 2006 Zeller Schwarze Katz Hochgewächs Halbtrocken Riesling (Mosel-Saar-Ruwer) $20. Fruity, packed with berry and melon aromas and flavors that end up coming across as slightly confected, with a slightly syrupy texture in the mouth. **84** —*J.C. (8/1/2007)*

WERNER & SOHN

Werner & Sohn 2005 Classic Riesling (Mosel-Saar-Ruwer) $16. Light in body despite 12% alcohol, with bland, vaguely fruity white gumdrop flavors and a short finish. **80** —*J.C. (8/1/2007)*

Werner & Sohn 2005 Schweicher Annaberg Kabinett Riesling (Mosel-Saar-Ruwer) $18. Starts off a little sluggish, offering up hints of roasted sweet corn on the nose, but those aromas soon give way to scents of pineapple and dried apples. It's soft in the mouth, verging on flabby, but has some charming flavors of apple and spiced pear that make it enjoyable as a chilled apéritif. Drink now. **87** —*J.C. (10/1/2007)*

WILHELMSHOF

Wilhelmshof 1999 Siebeldingen Brut Riesling (Pfalz) $17. 83 —*P.G. (12/31/2002)*

WILLI HAAG

Willi Haag 2005 Brauneberger Juffer Auslese Riesling (Mosel-Saar-Ruwer) $24. Crisp and clean, with a long, delicately wrought finish, this is a throwback to the auslesen of earlier times, without heaps of sweetness, but instead playing off the fine balance between sugar and acid. Floral and citrus aromas weave around a core of green apple fruit, while a bass line of slatey minerality underscores the melody. **92 Editors' Choice** —*J.C. (10/1/2007)*

Willi Haag 2004 Brauneberger Juffer Kabinett Riesling (Mosel-Saar-Ruwer) $20. 88 —*J.C. (5/1/2006)*

Willi Haag 2003 Brauneberger Juffer Riesling Kabinett Riesling (Mosel-Saar-Ruwer) $18. 87 —*J.C. (12/15/2004)*

Willi Haag 2003 Brauneberger Juffer Riesling Spätlese Riesling (Mosel-Saar-Ruwer) $21. 91 Editors' Choice —*J.C. (12/15/2004)*

Willi Haag 2004 QbA Riesling (Mosel-Saar-Ruwer) $15. 87 —*J.C. (7/1/2006)*

WINZER VON ERBACH

Winzer Von Erbach 2005 Erbacher Honigberg Riesling (Rheingau) $12. Shows some pleasant earth and slate notes, but lacks much in the way of fruit, with just a slight suggestion of peaches to be found. It's medium-bodied, with a crisp finish. **83** —*J.C. (11/15/2007)*

WITTMANN

Wittmann 2003 Trocken Riesling (Rheinhessen) $23. 85 —*R.V. (4/1/2005)*

Wittmann 2003 Westhofen Aulerde Trocken Riesling (Rheinhessen) $NA. 90 —*R.V. (4/1/2005)*

Wittmann 2003 Westhofen Morstein Trocken Riesling (Rheinhessen) $NA. 88 —*R.V. (4/1/2005)*

Wittmann 2002 Westhofener Kirchspiel Auslese S Riesling (Rheinhessen) $66. 90 —*R.V. (4/1/2005)*

Wittmann 2003 Westhofener Morstein Auslese S Riesling (Rheinhessen) $NA. 87 —*R.V. (4/1/2005)*

Wittmann 2001 Westhofener Morstein Spätlese Riesling (Rheinhessen) $31. 89 —*J.C. (3/1/2003)*

Wittmann 2003 Westhofener Morstein Trockenbeerenauslese Riesling (Rheinhessen) $NA. 91 —*R.V. (4/1/2005)*

WOODBRIDGE BY ROBERT MONDAVI

Woodbridge by Robert Mondavi 2005 Riesling (Mosel-Saar-Ruwer) $8. Fresh and fruity on the nose, this wine's pear and apple flavors turn sweet and a bit heavy on the palate. There's a refreshing bite on the finish, but not quite enough to lighten the midpalate. **82** —*J.C. (11/15/2007)*

YBURG

Yburg 1999 Riesling (Baden) $12. 86 *(8/1/2001)*

ZILLIKEN

Zilliken 2006 Butterfly Riesling (Mosel-Saar-Ruwer) $16. A bit fuller and drier than you might expect from a Mosel Riesling, but there's no questioning this wine's excellent balance. Honey and cinnamon notes accent pear and melon fruit, while hints of petrol lurk in the background. It's almost dry on the long finish. **90 Editors' Choice** —*J.C. (8/1/2007)*

Zilliken 2004 Butterfly Riesling (Mosel-Saar-Ruwer) $17. 85 —*J.C. (2/1/2006)*

Italy

ITALY

In ancient times, the Italian peninsula was commonly referred to as enotria, or "land of wine," because of its rich diversity of grape varieties and many acres dedicated to cultivated vines. In more ways than one, Italy became a gigantic nursery and a commercial hub fortuitously positioned at the heart of the Mediterranean for what would become western civilization's first "globally" traded product: wine.

Italy's prominence in the global wine industry has in no way diminished despite millennia of history. The sun-drenched north-south peninsula that extends from the thirty-sixth to the forty-sixth parallel embodies pockets of geographical, geological, and climatic perfection between the Upper Adige and the island of Pantelleria for the production of quality wine. Italian tradition is so closely grafted to the vine that the good cheer and easy attitudes associated with wine culture are mirrored in the nation's temperament.

Tenuta la Volta, near Barolo, Piemonte, Italy.

Despite Italy's long affinity with *Vitis vinifera*, the Italian wine industry has experienced an invigorating rebirth over the past three decades that truly sets it apart from other European wine nations. American baby boomers may still recall watery Valpolicella or Chianti Classico in hay-wrapped flasks at neighborhood New York eateries, or the generic "white" and "red" wines of Sicily's Corvo. Wines like those cemented Italy's reputation as a quantity (as opposed to quality, like in France) producer of wines sold at attractive prices. But as Italy gained confidence during the prosperous post-war years in the areas of design, fashion, and gastronomy, it demonstrated renewed attention to wine. Thanks to a small band of primarily Tuscan vintners, Italy launched itself with aggressive determination onto the world stage as a producer of some of the best wines ever produced anywhere: Amarone, Barolo, Brunello di Montalcino, and Passito di Pantelleria.

Like a happy epidemic, modern viticulture and enological techniques swept across the Italian peninsula throughout the 1980s and 1990s: Vertical shoot positioning and bilateral cordon trellising in vineyards; stainless steel, temperature-controlled fermentation, and barrique wood aging in wineries. As profits soared, producers reinvested in technology, personnel, and high-priced consultants, and a modern Italian wine revolution had suddenly taken place.

As it stands, Italy is the world's second-largest producer of wine after France. Each year, one in fifty Italians is involved with the grape harvest. And like France, Italy has adopted a rigorously controlled appellation system that imposes strict controls, with regulations governing vineyard quality, yields per acre, and aging practices among other things. There are over three hundred DOC (Denominazioni di Origine Controllata) and DOCG (Denominazioni di Origine Controllata e Garantita) wines today, and the classifications increase to over five hundred when IGT (Indicazioni Geografica Tipica) wines are factored in. Thanks to this system, Italy's 50,000 wineries enjoy a competitive advantage when it comes to the production and sales of quality wines.

Interestingly, there is a second wine revolution underway that promises to unlock potential uniquely associated with Italy. It is the re-evaluation and celebration of Italy's rich patrimony of "indigenous" grapes. (Because some varieties actually originated outside Italy, producers often refer to them as "traditional" varieties instead.) These are grapes—like Nero d'Avola, Fiano, Sagrantino, and Teroldego—that only modern enotria can offer to world consumers. As a result, a rapidly increasing number of vintners from Italy's twenty winemaking regions are banking on "traditional" varieties to distinguish themselves in a market dominated by "international" varieties, such as Merlot, Cabernet Sauvignon, and Chardonnay.

NORTH

The Italian Alps butt against the long expanses of the Po River plains, leaving tiny pockets and microclimates along the foot of the mountains that are each linked to their own special wine. Starting in northwestern Piedmont, Nebbiolo grapes form two tall pillars of Italy's wine legacy: Barolo and Barbaresco, named in the French tradition after the hilltop hamlets where the wines were born. Like in Burgundy, the exclusivity of these wines has a lot to do with the winemakers' battle against nature and the wine's extraordinary ability to age. Rare vintages like the stellar 1985 or 1990 Barolos are the darlings of serious wine collectors.

Further east, in the Veneto region, vintners follow an ancient formula in which wine is made from raisins dried on straw mats. With its higher concentration and alcohol, silky Amarone is Italy's most distinctive wine and can command record prices for new releases. The Veneto Trentino, Alto Adige, and Friuli-Venezia Giulia are celebrated for their white wines—such as the phenomenally successful Pinot Grigio. Italy's best sparkling wine is made in Trentino and the Franciacorta area of Lombardy (known as the "Champagne of Italy") under strict regulation with Pinot Noir and Chardonnay grapes.

CENTER

With its cypress-crested hills and beautiful stone farmhouses, Tuscany is the pin-up queen of Italian enology. The region's iconic dreamscape has helped promote the image of Italian wine abroad like no other. Within Tuscany's borders is a treasure-trove of excellent wines: Chianti Classico, Brunello di Montalcino, Vino Nobile di Montepulciano, San Gimignano whites, Bolgheri and Maremma reds. Italy's wine revolution started here when storied producers like Piero Antinori worked outside appellation regulations to make wines blended with international varieties such as Cabernet Sauvignon. These wines are known as Super Tuscans and are considered on par with the top crus of Bordeaux and California.

Central Italy delivers many more exciting wines, such as Sagrantino from the Umbrian town of Montefalco, dense and dark Montepulciano from Abruzzo, and white Verdicchio from Le Marche.

SOUTH AND ISLANDS

The regions of southern Italy, and the island of Sicily in particular, are regarded as Italy's enological frontier: Relaxed regulation and increased experimentation promise a bright future for vintners and investors alike. In many ways, Italy's south is a "new world" wine region locked within the confines of an "old world" wine reality. This unique duality has many betting on its enological promise.

Campania boasts wonderful whites, such as Fiano and Greco di Tufo that embody crisp, mineral characteristics from volcanic soils. Its red is Taurasi ("the Barolo of the south"), made from Aglianico. That same grape makes Basilicata's much-hyped Aglianico del Vulture. Puglia, the "heel" of the boot of Italy, was mostly a producer of bulk wine, but holds its own today among nascent wine regions with its powerhouse Primitivo and Negroamaro grapes.

Sicily has shown keen marketing savvy in bringing media attention to its native grapes like Nero d'Avola (red) and Grillo (a white once used in the production of fortified wine Marsala) and has done a great job of promoting the south of Italy in general. Some of Europe's most sensuous dessert wines, like the honey-rich Passito di Pantelleria, come from Sicily's satellite islands. The Mediterranean's other big island, Sardinia, is steadily working on its Cannonau and Vermentino grapes to raise the bar on quality there.

A-MANO

A-Mano 2005 Primitivo (Puglia) $11. This is a ready-to-drink informal wine with fresh red fruit and spice aromas. It really comes alive in the mouth though with loads of tasty spice and a firm tannin edge. **87 Best Buy** *—M.L. (8/1/2007)*

A-Mano 2003 Primitivo (Puglia) $11. 87 Best Buy *—M.L. (9/1/2005)*

A-Mano 2002 Primitivo (Puglia) $11. 87 Best Buy *—M.S. (2/1/2005)*

A-Mano 2001 Primitivo (Puglia) $10. 88 *—M.S. (11/15/2003)*

A-Mano 2000 Primitivo (Puglia) $10. 88 Best Buy *(5/1/2002)*

A-Mano 2003 Prima Mano Primitivo (Puglia) $28. 88 *—M.L. (9/1/2005)*

A-Mano 1999 Prima Mano Primitivo (Puglia) $22. 90 *—C.S. (5/1/2002)*

A-Mano 2005 White Blend (Puglia) $12. This 50-50 Fiano and Greco blend is deeply redolent of white flowers, talc powder, pear, peach and offers an attractive fresh piquancy, almost spicy, touch in the mouth. It's also slightly sweet with noticeable residual sugar and honey-like flavors. **86** *—M.L. (11/15/2007)*

AAA

AAA NV Montenisa Brut Satèn Chardonnay (Franciacorta) $46. 88 *—M.L. (12/15/2004)*

AAA NV Montenisa Brut Sparkling Blend (Franciacorta) $30. 91 *—M.L. (12/15/2004)*

ABARBANEL

Abarbanel NV Extra Dry Kosher Prosecco (Prosecco) $20. Thumbs up to Bellenda for producing what surely must be the world's first kosher Prosecco. Sadly, as far as Proseccos go, this wine has its limits: The wine is deeply golden in appearance and has a thicker concentration of heavy peach and mature fruit aromas. There's also a touch of peanut oil and sulfur. **81** *—M.L. (12/15/2007)*

ABBAZIA DI NOVACELLA

Abbazia di Novacella 2004 Pinot Grigio (Alto Adige) $21. 88 *—M.L. (2/1/2006)*

ABBAZIA MONTE OLIVETO

Abbazia Monte Oliveto 2000 Vernaccia (San Gimignano) $10. 87 Best Buy *(12/31/2002)*

ABBAZIA SANTA ANASTASIA

Abbazia Santa Anastasia 2003 Litra Cabernet Sauvignon (Sicilia) $70. 91 *—M.L. (7/1/2006)*

Abbazia Santa Anastasia 2002 Litra Cabernet Sauvignon (Sicilia) $70. 91 *—M.L. (7/1/2006)*

Abbazia Santa Anastasia 2000 Litra Cabernet Sauvignon (Sicilia) $40. 86 *—M.S. (10/1/2003)*

Abbazia Santa Anastasia 1998 Litra Cabernet Sauvignon (Sicilia) $40. 88 *—C.S. (5/1/2002)*

Abbazia Santa Anastasia 2001 Baccante Chardonnay (Sicilia) $37. 88 *—R.V. (10/1/2003)*

Abbazia Santa Anastasia 2005 Contempo Grillo (Sicilia) $12. 86 *—M.L. (7/1/2006)*

Abbazia Santa Anastasia 2005 Contempo Inzolia (Sicilia) $12. 85 *—M.L. (7/1/2006)*

Abbazia Santa Anastasia 2002 Nero d'Avola (Sicilia) $13. 87 *—M.S. (2/1/2005)*

Abbazia Santa Anastasia 2001 Nero d'Avola (Sicilia) $11. 89 Best Buy *—M.S. (10/1/2003)*

Abbazia Santa Anastasia 2006 Contempo Nero d'Avola (Sicilia) $16. The Mediterranean island of Sicily certainly does not lack sunshine and this well-priced Nero d'Avola (Sicily's most exported native grape variety) is redolent of a hot summer day: mature berry fruit, black cherry, bramble, cola, resin, licorice, tar and spice peel back in thick, sticky layers. It is a ripe, succulent wine with a soft, chewy consistency that offers a lot of flavor and little fuss. Serve it with lamb shank tagine with couscous and stewed prunes. **87** *—M.L. (11/15/2007)*

Abbazia Santa Anastasia 2004 Contempo Nero d'Avola (Sicilia) $12. 88 Best Buy *—M.L. (7/1/2006)*

Abbazia Santa Anastasia 1998 Montenero (Sicilia) $34. 90 Cellar Selection *(5/1/2002)*

Abbazia Santa Anastasia 2002 Montenero Red Blend (Sicilia) $40. 90 *—M.L. (7/1/2006)*

Abbazia Santa Anastasia 2002 Passomaggio Red Blend (Sicilia) $19. 89 *—M.S. (2/1/2005)*

Abbazia Santa Anastasia 2001 Passomaggio Red Blend (Sicilia) $14. 92 Best Buy *—M.S. (10/1/2003)*

Abbazia Santa Anastasia 1998 Passomaggio Red Blend (Sicilia) $14. 89 Best Buy *(5/1/2002)*

Abbazia Santa Anastasia 2003 Rosso di Passomaggio Red Blend (Sicilia) $18. 89 *—M.L. (7/1/2006)*

Abbazia Santa Anastasia 2004 Baccante White Blend (Sicilia) $39. 88 *—M.L. (7/1/2006)*

Abbazia Santa Anastasia 2005 Bianco di Passomaggio White Blend (Sicilia) $14. 85 *—M.L. (7/1/2006)*

Abbazia Santa Anastasia 2002 Bianco di Passomaggio White Blend (Sicilia) $14. 88 *—M.S. (11/15/2003)*

Abbazia Santa Anastasia 2005 Sinestesìa White Blend (Sicilia) $27. 86 *—M.L. (7/1/2006)*

ABBONA

Abbona 1998 Barbera (Barbera d'Alba) $19. 90 *—M.N. (9/1/2001)*

Abbona 1997 Papa Celso Dolcetto (Dolcetto di Dogliani) $16. 89 *(4/1/2000)*

ADAMI

Adami NV Bosco di Gica Prosecco (Prosecco di Valdobbiadene) $15. Franco Adami is a true Prosecco artisan who has expertly shaped a sparkling wine that is both clean and simple, without being one-dimensional or predictable. What makes this special is its ability to express the romantic Prosecco territory with its vibrant green hills, mineral rich soils and delicate spring blossom fragrances. The fine bubbles are persistent and small, and their spicy piquancy reinforces the wine's fresh acidity. Try it with oven roasted bream fillet wrapped in tin foil with ginger, sweet peas and sesame seeds. **87 Best Buy** *—M.L. (11/15/2007)*

Adami NV Bosco di Gica Prosecco (Prosecco di Valdobbiadene) $15. 87 *—M.L. (6/1/2006)*

Adami NV Cartizze Prosecco (Prosecco di Valdobbiadene) $30. The Cartizze cru is characterized by its elegance and Adami's expression lives up to the task thanks to its notes of delicate white peach, citrus blossom and white stone. In the mouth, it boasts pulpy, creamy complexity with a playful touch of sweetness. **90** *—M.L. (12/15/2007)*

Adami NV Dei Casel Extra Dry Prosecco (Prosecco di Valdobbiadene) $19. Adami has produced an enticing and interesting sparkler with a delicate golden hue, lively perlage and aromas of almond blossom, stone fruit, jasmine and scented candle. It offers sweet fruity flavors and a spicy finish. **87** *—M.L. (12/15/2007)*

Adami NV Dei Casel Extra Dry Prosecco (Prosecco di Valdobbiadene) $15. 86 *—M.L. (6/1/2006)*

Adami NV Vigneto Giardino Dry Prosecco (Prosecco di Valdobbiadene) $22. This is a dry Prosecco, meaning it is slightly sweeter than a brut or extra dry. Traditionally, Prosecco has this level of sugar, making it a very true rendition of what the wine is intended to taste like: Fresh peach, basil, pineapple, yellow apple and even an understated touch of banana come into play. **87** *—M.L. (12/15/2007)*

Adami 2005 Vigneto Giardino Dry Prosecco (Prosecco di Valdobbiadene) $18. 86 *—M.L. (6/1/2006)*

ADRIANO MARCO & VITTORIO

Adriano Marco & Vittorio 2000 Nebbiolo (Barbaresco) $35. 90 *(4/2/2004)*

Adriano Marco & Vittorio 1999 Nebbiolo (Barbaresco) $35. 88 *(4/2/2004)*

Adriano Marco & Vittorio 1999 Nebbiolo (Barbaresco) $40. 88 *(4/2/2004)*

Adriano Marco & Vittorio 2000 Basarin Nebbiolo (Barbaresco) $40. 92 *(4/2/2004)*

AGOSTINA PIERI

Agostina Pieri 2001 Brunello (Brunello di Montalcino) $50. 90 *(4/1/2006)*

AGOSTINO PAVIA & FIGLI

Agostino Pavia & Figli 2000 Bricco Blina Barbera (Barbera d'Asti) $12. 85 *—M.S. (12/15/2003)*

Agostino Pavia & Figli 2000 Moliss Barbera (Barbera d'Asti) $14. 84 *—M.S. (12/15/2003)*

AGRICOLA ARANO

Agricola Arano 1997 Red Blend (Amarone della Valpolicella Classico) $67. 91 *(5/1/2003)*

AGRICOLA PUNICA

Agricola Punica 2002 Barrua Red Blend (Isola dei Nuraghi) $50. This is a ripe, deeply concentrated and solid wine that boasts cherries under spirit, plum preserves, humus, tobacco and tea leaf. So thick, it's almost syrupy: this is a powerhouse wine. **92 Editors' Choice** *—M.L. (4/1/2007)*

AGRICOLA QUERCIABELLA

Agricola Querciabella 2005 Sangiovese (Chianti Classico) $29. Give it a few minutes to open and you will be rewarded with small berry aromas, bramble, forest floor, spice and fresh wood oak tones. The wine's structure is elegant but solid with dusty tannins on the finish. **87** *—M.L. (11/1/2007)*

Agricola Querciabella 2004 Sangiovese (Chianti Classico) $29. The nose is rich and opulent, but it is also very ripe—just shy of too ripe. Thick and broad aromas of black cherry essence, smoked ham, leather, tobacco and beet root are direct and generous. The wine has raw intensity overall and cool freshness on the finish. **87** *—M.L. (11/1/2007)*

Agricola Querciabella 2001 Camartina Sangiovese (Toscana) $104. 88 *—M.S. (9/1/2006)*

Agricola Querciabella 2003 Querciabella Sangiovese (Chianti Classico) $31. 87 *—M.S. (10/1/2006)*

Agricola Querciabella 2003 Batàr White Blend (Toscana) $78. 88 *—M.S. (9/1/2006)*

AGRICOLA UZZANO

Agricola Uzzano 2004 Castello di Uzzano Sangiovese (Chianti Classico) $NA. This vintage delivers power and concentration over aromas of black cherries, prunes, roasted chestnuts and spice cake. It's round, soft and generous in the mouth. **88** *—M.L. (11/1/2007)*

AGRICOLE VALLONE

Agricole Vallone 1997 Riserva Vigna Flaminio Red Blend (Salice Salentino) $10. 88 Best Buy *—M.S. (11/15/2003)*

AGRICOLTORI DEL CHIANTI GEOGRAFICO

Agricoltori del Chianti Geografico 2004 Red Blend (Chianti Classico) $16. This is not a particularly complex wine, but it will win you over nonetheless thanks to its friendly fruit and cherry aromas, plum, blackberry, leather and vanilla. Medium weight in the mouth, it finishes spicy and with a fine sour point. **85** *—M.L. (5/1/2007)*

Agricoltori del Chianti Geografico 2003 Contessa di Radda Sangiovese (Chianti Classico) $20. Sangiovese with a small percentage of Canaiolo are blended to produce a vibrant wine with good intensity and distinctive notes of berry fruit, blue flowers, rose petal, graphite and warm wood tones. It is smooth and creamy in the mouth and backed by solid structure. **87** *—M.L. (11/1/2007)*

Agricoltori del Chianti Geografico 2003 Ferraiolo Sangiovese (Toscana) $25. Sangiovese and Cabernet Sauvignon are blended and aged two years in oak to shape a wine that is characterized by cherry, blueberry, minerality and cedar wood. Overall, this is a balanced, muscular wine with thick extraction and a firm consistency. **89** *—M.L. (5/1/2007)*

Agricoltori del Chianti Geografico 2003 Riserva Montegiachi Sangiovese (Chianti Classico) $20. This Riserva Chianti Classico, aged two years in barrique, seems to have lost some of its overall intensity, but not its aromas of red currant and vanilla. It's astringent on the palate and enjoyable, but not stellar. **87** *—M.L. (5/1/2007)*

Agricoltori del Chianti Geografico 1998 Riserva Montegiachi Sangiovese (Chianti Classico) $20. 88 *—R.V. (8/1/2002)*

AL BANO CARRISI

Al Bano Carrisi 1997 Negroamaro (Salice Salentino) $9. 83 *—C.S. (5/1/2002)*

Al Bano Carrisi 1997 Nostalgìa Negroamaro (Salento) $10. 85 *—C.S. (5/1/2002)*

AL VERDI

Al Verdi 2004 Pinot Grigio (Terra degli Osci) $7. 84 Best Buy *(2/1/2006)*

ALBERTO LOI

Alberto Loi 1995 Grenache (Sardinia) $15. 84 *—C.S. (5/1/2002)*

Alberto Loi 1995 Tuvara Red Blend (Sardinia) $35. 88 *—C.S. (5/1/2002)*

ALBERTO LONGO

Alberto Longo 2004 Capoposto Negroamaro (Puglia) $22. Here is a different take on Negroamaro with green, almost unripe, notes that merge with sweeter tones of forest berry, smoke and coffee. Sour cherry flavors appear on the finish. **85** *—M.L. (8/1/2007)*

Alberto Longo 2004 Le Cruste Nero di Troia (Puglia) $32. Nero di Troia, a traditional grape from Puglia, has been deftly vinified to exalt its cherry, chocolate fudge and raspberry nuances. Delicate tea leaf, balsam and tobacco notes also appear thanks to 9 months of barrique aging. Pair with pasta, roasted red peppers, white meat and lamb. **90** *—M.L. (8/1/2007)*

Alberto Longo 2004 Cacc'e Mmitte di Lucera Red Blend (Puglia) $22. You'll pick up an attractive smoked ham-like quality on the nose backed by blueberry, blackberry, lead pencil, crushed black pepper and licorice. The intensity is not huge, nor is the length, but it would make an excellent match to grilled meats and aged goat cheeses. A 55-30-15 blend of Nero di Troia, Montepulciano and Bombino Bianco. **87** *—M.L. (8/1/2007)*

Alberto Longo 2004 Calcara Vecchia Red Blend (Puglia) $28. Here's an interesting Cabernet Franc-Merlot blend that boasts cooler, green aromas of cut grass, dill, bell pepper and small forest berries. The intensity of the flavors is good and graceful, without ever seeming heavy. **88** *—M.L. (8/1/2007)*

ALBINO ARMANI

Albino Armani 2001 Pinot Grigio (Veneto) $17. 86 *—J.C. (7/1/2003)*

Albino Armani 1998 Corvara Red Blend (Veneto) $28. 88 *(5/1/2003)*

ALBINO ROCCA

Albino Rocca 1999 Vigneto Brich Ronchi Nebbiolo (Barbaresco) $65. 91 *(4/2/2004)*

ALBOLA

Albola 2005 Pinot Grigio (Friuli Aquileia) $12. 85 *—M.L. (6/1/2006)*

Albola 2004 Pinot Grigio (Friuli Aquileia) $13. 85 *—M.L. (2/1/2006)*

ALDEGHERI

Aldegheri 2003 Corvina, Rondinella, Molinara (Amarone della Valpolicella Classico) $40. As far as Amarone goes, this version delivers general satisfaction and good quality but is also muddled by ripe flavors of strawberry comfiture, mushroom and wet soil that is probably due to overly mature fruit. Beyond those aromas are penetrating cherry flavors and a solid structure. **88** *—M.L. (10/1/2007)*

Aldegheri 2006 Pinot Grigio (Veneto) $17. Here's a very fruity wine with distinct mineral veins throughout that would pair well with grilled vegetables, white meat or seafood salad marinated with lime cilantro vinaigrette. **85** *—M.L. (12/1/2007)*

Aldegheri 2004 Pinot Grigio (Veneto) $10. 85 Best Buy *—M.L. (2/1/2006)*

Aldegheri 2006 Zaleo Rosé Blend (Veronese) $NA. Fine and delicate aromas of rose petal, a light touch of raspberry and pretty almond tones make this a generous and feminine wine with high appeal among rosé enthusiasts seeking a wine from the eastern shores of Lake Garda. The wine has crisp acidity and refined nuances in the mouth that are protected and enhanced thanks to the use of a novel glass closure that fits snug into the lip of the bottle just like a traditional cork. **88** *—M.L. (7/1/2007)*

Aldegheri 2006 le Pietre White Blend (Veronese) $12. Here's a no-fuss wine for everyday dinners with loads of fresh fruit, kiwi, pineapple and a strong emphasis on floral fragrances. The flavors focus on dried fruit, sun-dried apple chips in particular. **86** *—M.L. (12/1/2007)*

ALDO CONTERNO

Aldo Conterno 1999 Barbera (Barbera d'Alba) $40. 84 *—M.S. (11/15/2002)*

Aldo Conterno 1996 Conco Tre Pile Barbera (Barbera d'Alba) $37. 91 *(4/1/2000)*

Aldo Conterno 1998 Bussia Soprana Dolcetto (Dolcetto d'Alba) $22. 83 *(4/1/2000)*

Aldo Conterno 1998 Colonello Nebbiolo (Barolo) $116. 89 *(4/2/2004)*

ALESSANDRO DI CAMPOREALE

Alessandro di Camporeale 2003 Kaid Syrah (Sicilia) $8. 86 Best Buy *—M.L. (7/1/2006)*

ALLEGRINI

Allegrini 2003 Corvina, Rondinella, Molinara (Amarone della Valpolicella Classico) $75. This is a highly intense and thickly extracted wine from one of the area's most storied producers that boast blockbuster notes of black cherry, chewy fruit comfiture, milk chocolate and vanilla-oak. At the back are interesting bacon highlights. **91** *—M.L. (10/1/2007)*

Allegrini 1998 La Poja Corvina (Veronese) $85. 90 *(5/1/2003)*

Allegrini 2004 Garganega (Soave) $15. 85 *—J.C. (10/1/2006)*

Allegrini 2001 Red Blend (Valpolicella Classico) $12. 87 Best Buy *(5/1/2003)*

Allegrini 2000 Red Blend (Amarone della Valpolicella Classico) $75. 90 *(11/1/2005)*

Allegrini 1998 Red Blend (Amarone della Valpolicella Classico) $65. 93 Cellar Selection *(5/1/2003)*

Allegrini 1999 La Grola Red Blend (Veneto) $20. 88 *(5/1/2003)*

Allegrini 1999 Palazzo della Torre Red Blend (Veronese) $19. 88 *(5/1/2003)*

Allegrini 1993 Recioto Superiore Red Blend (Amarone della Valpolicella Classico) $40. 94 *(11/15/1999)*

ALOIS LAGEDER

Alois Lageder 2003 Lindenburg Lagrein (Alto Adige) $30. Lagrein tends towards plump red cherry fruit aromas but is also an excellent vehicle for expressing territorial and winemaking distinctions. In this wine, for example, delicate flinty-mineral notes from alluvial soils from near the Talvera River and well-integrated oak (18 months) create many layers of complexity. **89** *—M.L. (9/1/2007)*

Alois Lageder 2003 Merlot (Alto Adige) $15. What distinguishes this wine is its harmony and purity: every element is tied down and polished with no sharp edges. Aromas recall red berry, cappuccino and vanilla bean. Compact, clean and crisp in the mouth, this is masterfully made. **90 Best Buy** *—M.L. (3/1/2007)*

Alois Lageder 2005 Haberlehof Pinot Bianco (Alto Adige) $22. There's a subtle elegance to this wine that really sets it apart from the rest. The aromas are defined and fresh, bringing in mixed herbs, stone fruit and crisp minerality. It's very soft and feathery light in the mouth with layers of fruity nuances: After a period on the lees, it ages six months in Slavonian oak casks. **91** *—M.L. (9/1/2007)*

Alois Lageder 2004 Pinot Grigio (Vigneti delle Dolomiti) $15. 85 *—M.L. (6/1/2006)*

Alois Lageder 1999 Pinot Grigio (Alto Adige) $15. 90 Best Buy *—M.N. (12/31/2000)*

Alois Lageder 1998 Pinot Grigio (Alto Adige) $11. 87 *—M.S. (4/1/2000)*

Alois Lageder 2004 Riff Pinot Grigio (Delle Venezie) $10. 84 *—M.L. (6/1/2006)*

Alois Lageder 2003 Krafuss Pinot Nero (Alto Adige) $40. Enhanced with polished notes of toasted nut and vanilla (the wine sees 12 month of barrique) this is a more austere Pinot Nero with delicate nuances of spice, blue fruit and white mushroom. The fruit comes from a high-density vineyard planted in 1991 with clay and rocky soils. **89** *—M.L. (9/1/2007)*

Alois Lageder 2006 Riesling (Alto Adige) $18. One of Italy's best Rieslings, this is a classic rendition of the variety with trace sweetness and opulent notes of citrus, stone fruit, white mineral and a touch of natural rubber. It ages on its lees in stainless steel for four months, which explains its creamy consistency: very enthusiastically recommended. **90** *—M.L. (9/1/2007)*

ALTEMASI

Altemasi 1995 Graal Riserva Sparkling Blend (Trento) $30. 84 *—M.S. (12/15/2005)*

Altemasi 1996 Riserva Graal Sparkling Blend (Trento) $30. 86 *—M.L. (6/1/2006)*

ALTESINO

Altesino 2001 Brunello (Brunello di Montalcino) $70. 91 Cellar Selection *(4/1/2006)*

Altesino 2000 Brunello (Brunello di Montalcino) $55. 89 *—M.S. (7/1/2005)*

Altesino 1999 Brunello (Brunello di Montalcino) $60. 93 *—M.S. (6/1/2004)*

Altesino 2001 Montosoli Brunello (Brunello di Montalcino) $106. 89 *(4/1/2006)*

Altesino 1999 Riserva Brunello (Brunello di Montalcino) $90. 90 *—M.S. (7/1/2005)*

AMBRA DELLE TORRI

Ambra Delle Torri 2002 Vernaccia (Vernaccia di San Gimignano) $10. 85 *—M.S. (8/1/2004)*

AMINEA

Aminea 2004 Fiano (Fiano di Avellino) $19. 84 *—M.L. (9/1/2005)*

Aminea 2004 Greco (Greco di Tufo) $19. 87 *—M.L. (9/1/2005)*

ANERI

Aneri NV Brut Prosecco (Prosecco di Valdobbiadene) $20. 84 *—M.S. (12/15/2005)*

ANIME

Anime 1998 Pinot Grigio (Alto Adige) $11. 83 *(8/1/1999)*

ANNA SPINATO

Anna Spinato 2004 i Vini Pinot Grigio (Marca Trevigiana) $8. 84 *(2/1/2006)*

ANSELMA

Anselma 1996 Barbera (Barbera d'Alba) $15. 86 *(4/1/2000)*

Anselma 1997 Vigna Rionda Nebbiolo (Barolo) $48. 87 *—C.S. (11/15/2002)*

ANSELMI

Anselmi 2001 Capitel Croce White Blend (Delle Venezie) $18. 91 *—R.V. (7/1/2003)*

Anselmi 2002 San Vincenzo White Blend (Delle Venezie) $11. 89 *—R.V. (7/1/2003)*

Anselmi 2001 San Vincenzo White Blend (Veneto) $10. 84 *—J.C. (7/1/2003)*

ANTICA HIRPINIA

Antica Hirpinia 2001 Riserva Aglianico (Taurasi) $35. This is a spectacular Taurasi Riserva from a 170-member cooperative that stretches far into the realm of extreme robustness, succulence and persistency. The aromas are seamlessly integrated, to incorporate ripe red cherry, chocolate fudge, licorice and a finely chiseled mineral note. The wine is layered with beautifully aromatic nuances and rock solid tannins in the mouth. **92** *—M.L. (8/1/2007)*

ANTINORI

Antinori 2004 Fattoria Aldobrandesca Aleatico (Toscana) $35. 87 Editors' Choice *—M.L. (10/1/2006)*

Antinori 2001 Pian delle Vigne Brunello (Brunello di Montalcino) $65. 94 *(4/1/2006)*

Antinori 2000 Pian delle Vigne Brunello (Brunello di Montalcino) $65. 91 *—M.S. (7/1/2005)*

Antinori 1999 Pian delle Vigne Brunello (Brunello di Montalcino) $80. 93 *—M.S. (6/1/2004)*

Antinori 1997 Pian Delle Vigne Brunello (Brunello di Montalcino) $70. 93 *—M.S. (8/1/2002)*

Antinori 1995 Pian delle Vigne Brunello (Brunello di Montalcino) $60. 89 *—M.S. (9/1/2000)*

Antinori 1998 Castello della Sala Chardonnay (Umbria) $10. 84 *—M.S. (4/1/2000)*

Antinori 1999 Guado Al Tasso Red Blend (Bolgheri) $80. 95 *—M.S. (8/1/2002)*

Antinori 1997 Guado al Tasso Red Blend (Bolgheri) $80. 91 *(9/1/2001)*

Antinori 2004 Santa Cristina Red Blend (Toscana) $11. 86 Best Buy *(9/1/2006)*

Antinori 1997 Solaia Red Blend (Toscana) $115. 97 Editors' Choice *(9/1/2001)*

Antinori 1996 Badia A Passignano Riserva Sangiovese (Chianti Classico) $38. 90 *(4/1/2001)*

Antinori 2000 Guado al Tasso Sangiovese (Bolgheri) $80. 89 *—M.S. (10/1/2004)*

Antinori 2001 Pèppoli Sangiovese (Chianti Classico) $21. 89 *(4/1/2005)*

Antinori 1999 Pèppoli Sangiovese (Chianti Classico) $23. 87 *—M.S. (8/1/2002)*

Antinori 1998 Pèppoli Sangiovese (Chianti Classico) $22. 89 *(4/1/2001)*

Antinori 1999 Riserva Sangiovese (Chianti Classico) $36. 88 *(4/1/2005)*

Antinori 2001 Santa Cristina Sangiovese (Toscana) $11. 86 Best Buy *—M.S. (12/31/2002)*

Antinori 1999 Santa Cristina Sangiovese (Toscana) $11. 86 *—J.C. (9/1/2001)*

Antinori 1998 Tenuta Marchese Antinori Riserva Sangiovese (Chianti Classico) $23. 92 *—R.V. (8/1/2002)*

Antinori 1997 Tenute Marchese Antinori Riserva Sangiovese (Chianti Classico) $38. 87 *(4/1/2001)*

Antinori 2000 Tignanello Sangiovese (Toscana) $70. 90 *—M.S. (10/1/2004)*

Antinori 1997 Tignanello Sangiovese (Toscana) $80. 93 Cellar Selection *(9/1/2001)*

Antinori 2001 Villa Antinori Sangiovese (Toscana) $23. 91 Editors' Choice *—M.S. (10/1/2004)*

Antinori 1998 Villa Antinori Riserva Sangiovese (Chianti Classico) $65. 89 *—M.S. (12/31/2002)*

Antinori 1997 Villa Antinori Riserva Sangiovese (Chianti Classico) $21. 87 *(4/1/2001)*

Antinori 2001 Conte delle Vipera Sauvignon (Umbria) $24. 85 *(7/1/2005)*

Antinori 2001 Guado al Tasso Vermentino (Bolgheri) $18. 91 *—M.S. (8/1/2002)*

Antinori 2002 Tenuta Guado al Tasso Vermentino (Bolgheri) $18. 90 *—M.S. (8/1/2004)*

Antinori 2002 Campogrande White Blend (Orvieto Classico) $11. 86 *—M.S. (11/15/2003)*

Antinori 1999 Villa Antinori White Blend (Toscana) $11. 87 Best Buy *(9/1/2001)*

ANTOLINI

Antolini 2003 Corvina, Rondinella, Molinara (Amarone della Valpolicella) $55. This is a small estate, run by brothers Pier Paolo and Stefano, that delivers big surprises. The 2003 Amarone is a gorgeous wine with compelling territory-driven characteristics such as black cherry, violets, red apple, chopped herb, white stone and delicate harmony. It has great complexity, succulence and firm, dusty tannins. 92 *—M.L. (10/1/2007)*

ANTONELLI

Antonelli 1998 Estate Bottled Red Blend (Montefalco) $15. 86 *(4/1/2001)*

Antonelli 2000 Rosso Red Blend (Montefalco) $14. 86 *—M.S. (10/1/2004)*

Antonelli 1999 Rosso Red Blend (Montefalco) $14. 88 Best Buy *—M.S. (2/1/2003)*

Antonelli 2001 Sagrantino (Sagrantino di Montefalco) $40. 88 *—M.L. (9/1/2005)*

Antonelli 1995 Sagrantino (Sagrantino) $16. 86 *(9/1/2000)*

Antonelli 1999 Estate Bottled Sagrantino (Sagrantino di Montefalco) $34. 89 *—M.S. (10/1/2004)*

Antonelli 1998 Estate Bottled Sagrantino (Sagrantino di Montefalco) $33. 90 *—C.S. (2/1/2003)*

Antonelli 1997 Estate Bottled Sagrantino (Sagrantino di Montefalco) $30. 90 Editors' Choice *(4/1/2001)*

ANTONINO TRINGALI-CASANUOVA

Antonino Tringali-Casanuova 2005 Patrimonio Rosé Blend (Bolgheri) $NA. Five grapes are blended (Cabernet Sauvignon, Merlot and Sangiovese with small percentages of Syrah and Teroldego) to achieve a light red/ruby colored wine with big cherry, blueberry, strawberry and almond aromas. There's a distinct herbal or medicinal note buried within as well. It appears slightly closed on the palate but does deliver structure and acidity. 86 *—M.L. (7/1/2007)*

ANTONIO CAGGIANO

Antonio Caggiano 1999 Aglianico (Aglianico d'Irpinia) $32. 92 *—C.S. (5/1/2002)*

Antonio Caggiano 1997 Vigna Dei Gotti Aglianico (Taurasi) $42. 84 *(5/1/2002)*

APOLLONIO

Apollonio 1997 Red Blend (Copertino) $10. 95 Best Buy *(11/15/1999)*

ARAGOSTA

Aragosta 2003 Vermentino (Vermentino di Sardegna) $13. 84 *—M.S. (7/1/2005)*

ARALDICA

Araldica 2006 La Luciana Cortese (Gavi) $11. It takes a few minutes to get the best out of this wine. By then the initial cheesiness has worn off, and aromas of mineral, stones and fruit come to the fore. On the palate, the wine shows some good complexity although a short-to-medium finish. 86 Best Buy *—M.G. (12/31/2007)*

ARANO

Arano 2000 Estate Amarone (Amarone della Valpolicella Classico) $50. 90 *(11/1/2005)*

ARCANO

Arcano 2004 Pinot Grigio (Veneto) $9. 83 *(2/1/2006)*

ARDUINI

Arduini 2003 Corvina, Rondinella, Molinara (Amarone della Valpolicella Classico) $34. This is a small producer with a grape grower past who built a new winery and started bottling just a few years ago. The 2003 vintage is ripe with strawberry preserves, cherry, maple syrup, crème caramel and light vanilla spice. It's lively and spicy in the mouth and delivers determined intensity and length. 89 *—M.L. (10/1/2007)*

ARÈLE

Arèle 1994 Vin Santo Nosiola grape White Blend (Trentino) $42. 90 *(4/1/2004)*

ARGENTIERA

Argentiera 2003 Bordeaux Blend (Bolgheri Superiore) $78. 89 *—M.S. (9/1/2006)*

Argentiera 2003 Villa Donoratico Bordeaux Blend (Bolgheri) $30. 88 *—M.S. (9/1/2006)*

Argentiera 2004 Villa Donoratico Red Blend (Bolgheri) $35. What the 2003 vintage delivers in terms of instant gratification, this wine makes up for with subtle, almost teasing, nuances of berry, clove, spice bread and toast. It's beautifully expressive in the mouth, with firm tannins and very good length. 88 *—M.L. (4/1/2007)*

ARGIANO

Argiano 2001 Brunello (Brunello di Montalcino) $61. 92 *(4/1/2006)*

Argiano 2000 Brunello (Brunello di Montalcino) $57. 90 *—M.S. (7/1/2005)*

Argiano 1999 Brunello (Brunello di Montalcino) $66. 90 *—M.S. (6/1/2004)*

ARGIOLAS

Argiolas 1997 Turriga Grenache (Sardinia) $50. 94 Cellar Selection *—C.S. (5/1/2002)*

Argiolas 1996 Isola dei Nuraghi Red Blend (Sardinia) $9. 90 *(11/15/1999)*

Argiolas 1999 Korem Red Blend (Sardinia) $34. 91 *—C.S. (5/1/2002)*

Argiolas 2001 Perdera Red Blend (Isola dei Nuraghi) $12. 89 *—M.S. (11/15/2003)*

Argiolas 2003 Costamolino Vermentino (Vermentino di Sardegna) $14. 87 *—M.S. (8/1/2004)*

Argiolas 2000 Costamolino Vermentino (Vermentino di Sardegna) $9. 86 *—J.C. (9/1/2001)*

ARMILLA

Armilla 2001 Brunello (Brunello di Montalcino) $65. 91 *(4/1/2006)*

ARNALDO CAPRAI

Arnaldo Caprai 2000 Red Blend (Montefalco) $22. 91 Editors' Choice *—M.S. (2/1/2003)*

Arnaldo Caprai 2000 Poggio Belvedere Red Blend (Umbria) $14. 88 Best Buy *—C.S. (2/1/2003)*

Arnaldo Caprai 2003 Rosso Red Blend (Montefalco) $22. 85 *—M.L. (9/1/2005)*

Arnaldo Caprai 2001 25 Anni Sagrantino (Sagrantino di Montefalco) $110. 93 Cellar Selection *—M.L. (9/1/2005)*

Arnaldo Caprai 1999 25 Anni Sagrantino (Sagrantino di Montefalco) $100. 92 Cellar Selection *—M.S. (10/1/2004)*

Arnaldo Caprai 2001 Collepiano Sagrantino (Sagrantino di Montefalco) $55. 90 *—M.L. (9/1/2005)*

Arnaldo Caprai 1999 Collepiano Sagrantino (Sagrantino di Montefalco) $50. 90 *—M.S. (10/1/2004)*

Arnaldo Caprai 1998 Collepiano Sagrantino (Sagrantino di Montefalco) $48. 92 *—C.S. (2/1/2003)*

Arnaldo Caprai 1998 Venticinque Anni 25 Sagrantino (Sagrantino di Montefalco) $88. 93 Cellar Selection *—C.S. (2/1/2003)*

ARUNDA

Arunda 1995 Riserva Brut Sparkling Blend (Alto Adige) $27. 82 *—M.S. (12/31/2004)*

ASTORIA

Astoria 2004 Cabernet Sauvignon (Piave) $14. 86 *(11/15/2006)*

Astoria 2003 Il Puro Merlot (Piave) $11. 84 *—J.C. (12/31/2004)*

Astoria 2004 Pinot Grigio (Delle Venezie) $12. 87 Best Buy *—M.L. (2/1/2006)*

Astoria 2001 Pinot Grigio (Delle Venezie) $11. 85 *—J.C. (1/1/2004)*

Astoria NV Prosecco (Prosecco del Veneto) $9. 86 Best Buy *—M.S. (12/15/2006)*

Astoria 2001 Prosecco (Prosecco di Conegliano e Valdobbiadene) $13. 89 *—M.S. (12/31/2002)*

Astoria 2004 18 Dry Prosecco (Prosecco di Conegliano) $15. 86 *—M.S. (12/15/2005)*

Astoria NV Cartizze Prosecco (Prosecco Superiore di Cartizze) $21. Here's a Cartizze Prosecco that favors yellow fruit, pear and mature peach. But this brilliant sparkler is not at all heavy or too ripe: In fact, its elegance and fine workmanship is clear. Mineral notes, kiwi and exotic fruit appear in the mouth. 90 *—M.L. (12/15/2007)*

Astoria 2006 Casa Vittorino 20 Anni Dry Prosecco (Prosecco di Conegliano e Valdobbiadene) $20. The nose here is deeply redolent of fresh fruit with distinct tones of peach, apricot, citrus, Granny Smith apple and pear. Additional complexity is added by background tones of spring flowers, almond and baked biscuits. 88 *—M.L. (12/15/2007)*

Astoria NV Casa Vittorino Diciasette Anniversario Dry Prosecco (Prosecco di Conegliano) $15. 87 *—M.S. (12/15/2004)*

Astoria NV Cuvée Lounge Prosecco (Prosecco) $10. 87 Best Buy *—M.S. (12/15/2006)*

Astoria 2004 Cuvée Tenuta Val de Brun Prosecco (Prosecco di Valdobbiadene) $13. 88 Best Buy *—M.S. (12/15/2005)*

Astoria 2002 Cuvée Tenuta Val de Brun Prosecco (Prosecco di Valdobbiadene) $15. 86 *—J.C. (12/31/2003)*

Astoria 2005 Cuvée Tenuta Val de Brun Extra Dry Prosecco (Prosecco di Valdobbiadene) $18. 88 *—M.S. (12/15/2006)*

Astoria 2003 Cuvée Tenuta Val de Brun Extra Dry Prosecco (Prosecco di Valdobbiadene) $15. 88 *—M.S. (12/15/2004)*

Astoria NV Extra Dry Prosecco (Prosecco di Valdobbiadene) $16. 86 *—M.L. (6/1/2006)*

Astoria 2001 Extra Dry Prosecco (Prosecco di Valdobbiadene) $9. 90 Best Buy *—M.S. (12/31/2002)*

Astoria 2006 Millesimato Extra Dry Prosecco (Prosecco di Conegliano e Valdobbiadene) $20. This is an almost smoky, more sophisticated Prosecco with a nutty, almond feel, bigger structure and noticeable succulence. Aromas include Golden Delicious apple and roses. It's a stately rendition that would pair well with a pasta or white meat dish. 90 *—M.L. (12/15/2007)*

Astoria 2005 Millesimato Prosecco (Prosecco di Valdobbiadene) $19. 87 *—M.L. (6/1/2006)*

Astoria 2002 Sedici Anni Dry Prosecco (Prosecco di Conegliano) $15. 87 *—J.C. (12/31/2003)*

Astoria NV Superiore di Cartizze Prosecco (Prosecco Superiore di Cartizze) $20. 88 *—M.L. (6/1/2006)*

Astoria NV Val de Brun Extra Dry Prosecco (Prosecco del Veneto) $9. 87 Best Buy *—M.S. (12/15/2004)*

Astoria 1998 Rosso Croder Red Blend (Colli di Conegliano) $18. 89 *(5/1/2003)*

Astoria 2004 Sauvignon Blanc (Delle Venezie) $20. 90 *(7/1/2005)*

Astoria 2005 Suade Sauvignon Blanc (Delle Venezie) $14. 86 *(11/15/2006)*

Astoria 2000 White Blend (Colli di Conegliano) $17. 85 *—J.C. (7/1/2003)*

ATTEMS

Attems 2003 Pinot Grigio (Collio) $20. 84 *—J.C. (12/31/2004)*

Attems 2001 Pinot Grigio (Collio) $20. 81 *—J.C. (7/1/2003)*

Attems 2001 Sauvignon Blanc (Collio) $20. 84 *—J.C. (7/1/2003)*

Attems 2003 Sauvignon Sauvignon Blanc (Collio) $20. 88 *—J.C. (12/31/2004)*

ATTILIO GHISOLFI

Attilio Ghisolfi 1998 Barbera (Barbera d'Alba) $20. 87 *—M.S. (12/15/2003)*

Attilio Ghisolfi 1997 Barbera (Barbera d'Alba) $14. 91 Best Buy *(4/1/2000)*

Attilio Ghisolfi 1996 Vigna Lisi Barbera (Barbera d'Alba) $17. 88 *(4/1/2000)*

Attilio Ghisolfi 1997 Dolcetto (Dolcetto d'Alba) $13. 86 Best Buy *(4/1/2000)*

Attilio Ghisolfi 1998 Bricco Visette Nebbiolo (Barolo) $37. 89 *(4/2/2004)*

Attilio Ghisolfi 1995 Bricco Visette Nebbiolo (Barolo) $42. 89 *(9/1/2000)*

AURELIO SETTIMO

Aurelio Settimo 1999 Nebbiolo (Barolo) $38. 91 Editors' Choice *—J.C. (11/15/2004)*

Aurelio Settimo 1999 Rocche Nebbiolo (Barolo) $45. 93 Cellar Selection *—J.C. (11/15/2004)*

AVANTI

Avanti 2004 Pinot Grigio (Delle Venezie) $8. 87 Best Buy *—M.L. (2/1/2006)*

AVIDE

Avide 2000 Cerasuolo di Vittoria Red Blend (Sicilia) $14. 83 *—M.S. (12/15/2003)*

AVIGNONESI

Avignonesi 2002 Sangiovese (Vino Nobile di Montepulciano) $25. 86 *—M.S. (7/1/2005)*

AVIGNONESI-CAPANNELLE

Avignonesi-Capannelle 1998 50 & 50 Sangiovese (Toscana) $112. 89 *—M.S. (12/15/2003)*

AZELIA

Azelia 1998 Bricco dell'Oriolo Dolcetto (Dolcetto d'Alba) $15. 90 *(4/1/2000)*

Azelia 1999 San Rocco Nebbiolo (Barolo) $71. 91 *(4/2/2004)*

AZIENDA AGRARIA SCACCIADIAVOLI

Azienda Agraria Scacciadiavoli 2000 Red Blend (Montefalco) $12. 88 Best Buy *—M.S. (2/1/2003)*

Azienda Agraria Scacciadiavoli 1998 Red Blend (Sagrantino di Montefalco) $34. 88 *—C.S. (2/1/2002)*

Azienda Agraria Scacciadiavoli 2001 Sagrantino (Sagrantino di Montefalco) $29. 86 *—M.L. (9/1/2005)*

AZIENDA AGRICOLA ADANTI

Azienda Agricola Adanti 2000 Arquata Sagrantino (Sagrantino di Montefalco) $40. 87 *—M.L. (9/1/2005)*

AZIENDA AGRICOLA BORGNOT/VIRNA

Azienda Agricola Borgnot/Virna 1998 Nebbiolo (Barolo) $NA. 90 *(4/2/2004)*

Azienda Agricola Borgnot/Virna 1998 Cannubi Boschis Nebbiolo (Barolo) $35. 92 Editors' Choice *(4/2/2004)*

AZIENDA AGRICOLA COGNO

Azienda Agricola Cogno 2004 Bricco dei Merli Barbera (Barbera d'Alba) $26. The nose is rich and easy; packed with dark fruit, a touch of oak. Not terribly serious, but beautifully balanced and very likeable. The finish is short-medium, and the fruit stays with it. A comfort wine for comfort food. 87 *—M.G. (12/31/2007)*

Azienda Agricola Cogno 2005 Vigna del Mandorlo Dolcetto (Dolcetto d'Alba) $19. This was another solid version of the modern Dolcetto, showing dark fruit, spice and a core of plum jam. The tannins need a year or so to become civilized, but overall this is a versatile wine that will be very food-friendly. 88 *—M.G. (12/31/2007)*

Azienda Agricola Cogno 1998 Ravera Nebbiolo (Barolo) $58. 93 Editors' Choice *—M.S. (11/15/2002)*

Azienda Agricola Cogno 1997 Vigna Elena Nebbiolo (Barolo) $75. 86 *—M.S. (11/15/2002)*

Azienda Agricola Cogno 2004 Montegrilli Red Blend (Langhe) $27. A skillful blending of 50% Barbera and 50% Nebbiolo, the Cogno has lovely wild strawberry aromas, cranberry and a touch of licorice. Light bodied but with fairly intense flavors, it was pleasant and interesting, its only fault lay in the slightly high acidity. 89 *—M.G. (12/31/2007)*

AZIENDA AGRICOLA LUISA

Azienda Agricola Luisa 2004 Tenuta Luisa Pinot Grigio (Isonzo del Friuli) $23. 88 *—M.L. (2/1/2006)*

AZIENDA AGRICOLA MONTE DEL FRÁ

Azienda Agricola Monte Del Frá 2006 Chiaretto Rosé Blend (Bardolino) $10. Light and fresh, and you can imagine how easy it would go down after a day of hiking around Lake Garda. At home, try it by the pool, where its pretty berry, peach and citrus flavors will refresh the palate or pair with chicken or fish. 84 *—J.C. (7/1/2007)*

AZIENDA AGRICOLA PALOMBO

Azienda Agricola Palombo 1999 Cabernet Atina Red Blend (Lazio) $21. 84 *—M.S. (11/15/2003)*

Azienda Agricola Palombo 1998 Cabernet Duca Cantelmi Red Blend (Lazio) $34. 85 *—M.S. (11/15/2003)*

AZIENDA AGRICOLA PIRA LUIGI

Azienda Agricola Pira Luigi 1999 Vigneto Margheria Nebbiolo (Barolo) $60. 91 *(4/2/2004)*

AZIENDA AGRICOLA PUGNANE

Azienda Agricola Pugnane 1996 Vigna Villero Barolo Nebbiolo (Barolo) $39. 89 *(11/15/2002)*

AZIENDA AGRICOLA RESSIA

Azienda Agricola Ressia 2000 Canova Nebbiolo (Barbaresco) $50. 89 *(4/2/2004)*

AZIENDA AGRICOLA ROBERTO CERAUDO STRONGOLI

Azienda Agricola Roberto Ceraudo Strongoli 2003 Imyr Chardonnay (Val di Neto) $36. 89 *—M.S. (7/1/2005)*

Azienda Agricola Roberto Ceraudo Strongoli 2001 Petraro Red Blend (Val di Neto) $39. 84 *—M.S. (7/1/2005)*

Azienda Agricola Roberto Ceraudo Strongoli 2000 Petraro Red Blend (Val di Neto) $37. 91 *—M.S. (10/1/2004)*

AZIENDA AGRICOLA SUAVIA

Azienda Agricola Suavia 2002 White Blend (Soave Classico) $15. 88 —*M.S. (10/1/2004)*

Azienda Agricola Suavia 2001 Le Rive White Blend (Soave Classico) $37. 87 —*M.S. (10/1/2004)*

AZIENDA AGRICOLA TABARRINI

Azienda Agricola Tabarrini 2001 Colle Grimaldesco Sagrantino (Montefalco) $NA. 90 —*M.L. (9/1/2005)*

AZIENDA VINICOLA FRATELLI FABIANO

Azienda Vinicola Fratelli Fabiano 2004 Pinot Grigio (Terra degli Osci) $6. 85 Best Buy —*M.L. (6/1/2006)*

BADIA A COLTIBUONO

Badia a Coltibuono 1998 Sangiovese (Chianti Classico) $20. 87 *(4/1/2001)*

Badia a Coltibuono 1999 Cetamura Sangiovese (Chianti) $11. 88 Best Buy *(4/1/2001)*

Badia a Coltibuono 1997 Cetamura Sangiovese (Chianti) $11. 90 Best Buy —*M.S. (3/1/2000)*

Badia a Coltibuono 2003 Cultus Boni Sangiovese (Chianti Classico) $30. This is an organically made Chianti Classico from one of Tuscany's most famous estates that boasts fine qualities and elegant harmony overall. The nose is redolent of cherry, red rose, vanilla and toasted nut and, in the mouth, this has a pretty, fine texture with dusty tannins and tart freshness on the finish. 90 —*M.L. (11/1/2007)*

Badia a Coltibuono 2001 Estate Sangiovese (Chianti Classico) $23. 85 *(4/1/2005)*

Badia a Coltibuono 1999 Riserva Sangiovese (Chianti Classico) $31. 83 *(4/1/2005)*

Badia a Coltibuono 2001 Roberto Stucchi Sangiovese (Chianti Classico) $19. 86 *(4/1/2005)*

Badia a Coltibuono 1999 Roberto Stucchi Sangiovese (Chianti Classico) $20. 86 *(4/1/2001)*

BADIA A PASSIGNANO

Badia a Passignano 1999 Riserva Sangiovese (Chianti Classico) $45. 86 *(4/1/2005)*

BADIA DI MORRONA

Badia di Morrona 2002 I Sodi Del Paretaio Sangiovese (Chianti) $14. 80 *(4/1/2005)*

Badia di Morrona 1998 I Sodi del Paretaio Sangiovese (Chianti) $11. 83 *(4/1/2001)*

Badia di Morrona 1997 N'Antia Sangiovese (Toscana) $30. 91 —*J.F. (9/1/2001)*

BADIOLO

Badiolo 2000 Sangiovese (Chianti) $9. 84 —*M.S. (11/15/2003)*

Badiolo 1998 Reserva Sangiovese (Chianti) $13. 84 —*M.S. (11/15/2003)*

Badiolo 2000 Riserva Sangiovese (Chianti) $14. 83 —*M.S. (10/1/2004)*

BAGLIO DI PIANETTO

Baglio di Pianetto 2002 Piana dei Salici Merlot (Sicilia) $26. 90 —*M.L. (7/1/2006)*

Baglio di Pianetto 2002 Piana dei Cembali Nero d'Avola (Sicilia) $32. 88 —*M.L. (7/1/2006)*

Baglio di Pianetto 2002 Ramione Red Blend (Sicilia) $20. 85 —*M.L. (7/1/2006)*

Baglio di Pianetto 2004 Piana del Ginolfo Viognier (Sicilia) $24. 85 —*M.L. (7/1/2006)* 85 —*M.L. (7/1/2006)*

BALESTRI VALDA

Balestri Valda 2002 Garganega (Recioto di Soave) $NA. This Recioto dessert wine is beautifully redolent of baked apple and cinnamon spice with peach cobbler, apricot and honey. Flavors of Golden Delicious apple and a sweet, sticky consistency characterize the mouthfeel. Pair with dessert or aged cheeses. 88 —*M.L. (5/1/2007)*

Balestri Valda 2003 Lungalonga Garganega (Soave Classico) $NA. This is an interesting, if somewhat awkward wine. The aromas are extremely pungent and vertical: Notes of peppermint candy, peach soda and lemon zest go straight to the nose. But the menthol freshness is long lasting and very nice in the mouth. 85 —*M.L. (5/1/2007)*

Balestri Valda 2004 Vigneto Sengialta Garganega (Soave Classico) $NA. This is a wonderful Soave with aromas of maple syrup, pine nut, pressed flowers and honeysuckle that are both layered and unique. The wine, aged six months in oak barrel, has a creamy smoothness in the mouth with medium but flavorful persistency. 88 —*M.L. (5/1/2007)*

BANEAR

Banear 2001 Rosso Merlot (Colli Orientali del Friuli) $15. 83 —*M.S. (12/15/2003)*

Banear 1997 Pinot Grigio (Grave del Friuli) $10. 84 *(8/1/1999)*

Banear 2004 Pinot Grigio (Friuli Grave) $14. 86 —*M.L. (2/1/2006)*

Banear 2001 Pinot Grigio (Friuli Grave) $13. 87 —*J.C. (7/1/2003)*

BANFI

Banfi 2005 Rosa Regale Brachetto (Brachetto d'Acqui) $23. 86 —*M.L. (6/1/2006)*

Banfi 2002 Rosa Regale Brachetto (Brachetto d'Acqui) $23. 84 —*J.C. (12/31/2003)*

Banfi 2001 Rosa Regale Brachetto (Brachetto d'Acqui) $23. 87 —*K.F. (12/31/2002)*

Banfi 2000 Rosa Regale Brachetto (Brachetto d'Acqui) $23. 82 —*M.M. (12/31/2001)*

Banfi 2004 Col Di Sasso Cabernet Sauvignon-Sangiovese (Toscana) $9. 84 —*M.S. (9/1/2006)*

Banfi 2004 Le Rime Chardonnay-Pinot Grigio (Toscana) $9. 84 —*M.S. (9/1/2006)*

Banfi 2000 Pinot Grigio (Toscana) $14. 86 —*J.F. (9/1/2001)*

Banfi 2001 Centine Red Blend (Toscana) $11. 87 Best Buy —*M.S. (10/1/2004)*

Banfi 2000 Col di Sasso Red Blend (Toscana) $9. 86 Best Buy —*R.V. (11/15/2002)*

Banfi 2003 Rosa Regale Rosé Blend (Brachetto d'Acqui) $23. 84 —*M.S. (12/15/2004)*

Banfi 2003 Sangiovese (Chianti Classico) $9. 87 Best Buy *(4/1/2005)*

Banfi 1999 Sangiovese (Brachetto d'Acqui) $23. 87 *(2/1/2001)*

Banfi 2003 Centine Sangiovese (Toscana) $11. 87 Best Buy —*M.L. (11/15/2005)*

Banfi 2002 Centine Sangiovese (Toscana) $11. 85 —*M.S. (11/15/2004)*

Banfi 2002 Col di Sasso Sangiovese (Toscana) $9. 83 —*M.S. (11/15/2004)*

Banfi 2001 Riserva Sangiovese (Chianti Classico) $18. 87 *(4/1/2005)*

Banfi 1998 Riserva Sangiovese (Chianti Classico) $17. 88 —*M.S. (12/31/2002)*

Banfi 1997 Riserva Sangiovese (Chianti Classico) $16. 87 *(4/1/2001)*

Banfi NV Brut Sparkling Blend (Piedmont) $24. 89 —*M.L. (6/1/2006)*

BANOLIS

Banolis 1998 Merlot (Grave del Friuli) $11. 84 *(3/1/2000)*

Banolis 1998 Pinot Grigio (Grave del Friuli) $13. 87 *(8/1/1999)*

BARBERANI

Barberani 2005 Grechetto (Umbria) $NA. Grechetto is an excellent alternative for those looking for a crisp, easy wine with body and more structure than your standard Italian white. This rendition is particularly attractive with lemon, melon, honey, almond skin and mineral notes on the nose. 85 —*M.L. (2/1/2007)*

Barberani 2004 Grechetto (Umbria) $22. 86 —*M.L. (9/1/2005)*

Barberani 2003 Villa Monticelli Grechetto (Umbria) $28. 82 —*M.L. (9/1/2005)*

Barberani 2004 Castagnolo Grechetto, Chardonnay, Trebiano (Orvieto Classico Superiore) $15. 85 —*M.L. (9/1/2005)*

Barberani 2004 Passito Villa Monticelli Moscato (Umbria) $NA. Luminous and amber-colored, here is a dessert wine made from fragrant Moscato grapes that were intentionally left to over-ripen both on the vine and on drying mats. This process helps develop deeply etched notes of honey, dried flowers and nuts. The wine is creamy and smooth with well-balanced acidity. 90 —*M.L. (2/1/2007)*

Barberani 2003 Villa Monticelli 500ml Moscato (Umbria) $40. 91 —*M.L. (10/1/2006)*

Barberani 2003 Foresco Red Blend (Lago di Corbara) $22. Umbria is an often-overlooked wine region capable of delivering many pleasing surprises. This Sangiovese Grosso-Cabernet Sauvignon blend, aged one year in oak, boasts clove, exotic spice, crushed black pepper and wild mushroom, all rounded off by a cool splash of bell pepper. Its tight tannins and succulence make it ideal to pair with red meat. 88 —*M.L. (5/1/2007)*

Barberani 2005 Rosato Vallesanta Rosé Blend (Umbria) $NA. Aromas are focused on cranberry and raspberry fruit, but there's also a uniquely creamy quality that is offset by fresh fruit crispness. Drink with seafood, salads and light pasta dishes. **85** *—M.L. (5/1/2007)*

Barberani 2003 Calcaia Dolce White Blend (Orvieto Classico Superiore) $NA. This is a truly delicious and exciting dessert wine made from botrytisized grapes that are blanketed with fog on the banks of the Tiber River in Umbria. The wine's intensity, peach, honey and almond aromas are simply outstanding. Instead of pairing this with dessert, try it with goat cheese or foie gras. **92** *—M.L. (2/1/2007)*

Barberani 2002 Calcaia Muffa Nobile 500ml White Blend (Orvieto Classico Superiore) $40. **90** *—M.L. (10/1/2006)*

Barberani 2005 Castagnolo White Blend (Orvieto Classico Superiore) $NA. There's a delicate balance on the nose of this straw-colored wine with notes of dried sage, stone fruit and lavender honey. No one aroma outshines the others; the wine shows good fruit-acidity equilibrium in the mouth. Made from a blend of Grechetto, Trebbiano, Verdello, Malvasia, Drupeggio, Chardonnay and Riesling. **86** *—M.L. (2/1/2007)*

ITALY

BARBI

Barbi 2001 Brunello (Brunello di Montalcino) $50. **89** *(4/1/2006)*

Barbi 2000 Brunello (Brunello di Montalcino) $50. **88** *—M.S. (7/1/2005)*

Barbi 2000 Riserva Brunello (Brunello di Montalcino) $100. **86** *(4/1/2006)*

BARBOLINI

Barbolini NV Lambrusco Grasparossa di Castelvetro Lambrusco (Emilia-Romagna) $11. **86 Best Buy** *—J.C. (12/31/2003)*

BARICCI

Baricci 2001 Brunello (Brunello di Montalcino) $49. **90** *(4/1/2006)*

BARON DI PAULI

Baron di Pauli 2003 Arzio Red Blend (Alto Adige) $60. This Alto Adige Merlot, Cabernet Sauvignon and Cabernet Franc blend is a powerful but elegant wine with decisive notes of fudge, chocolate dipped cherries and just the right level of toast. It opens beautifully with time and delivers polished, chewy tannins, long persistency and menthol notes on the close. **91** *—M.L. (5/1/2007)*

BARONCINI

Baroncini 1999 Sangiovese (Chianti Colli Senesi) $9. **89 Best Buy** *(4/1/2001)*

Baroncini 1999 Sangiovese (Toscana) $10. **85** *—J.C. (9/1/2001)*

Baroncini 1999 Sangiovese (Chianti) $8. **86 Best Buy** *(4/1/2001)*

Baroncini 1998 Casina Del Giglio Sangiovese (Chianti Classico) $14. **85** *(4/1/2001)*

Baroncini 2001 Chianti Sangiovese (San Gimignano) $10. **83** *—M.S. (11/15/2003)*

Baroncini 2002 La Mandorlae Sangiovese (Morellino di Scansano) $17. **84** *—M.S. (11/15/2003)*

Baroncini 1998 Le Mandorlae Sangiovese (Morellino di Scansano) $11. **80** *—M.S. (8/1/2002)*

Baroncini 1997 Le Mandorlae Riserva Sangiovese (Morellino di Scansano) $23. **86** *—J.C. (9/1/2001)*

Baroncini 1999 White Blend (Vernaccia di San Gimignano) $10. **86** *—J.C. (9/1/2001)*

BARONE

Barone 1998 Pinot Grigio (Del Veneto) $6. **86 Best Buy** *(8/1/1999)*

BARONE FINI

Barone Fini 2002 Merlot (Trentino) $14. **86** *—J.C. (12/31/2004)*

Barone Fini 1998 Pinot Grigio (Valdadige) $10. **87 Best Buy** *(8/1/1999)*

Barone Fini 2003 Pinot Grigio (Valdadige) $12. **84** *—J.C. (12/31/2004)*

Barone Fini 2002 Pinot Grigio (Valdadige) $11. **84** *—J.C. (7/1/2003)*

Barone Fini 2001 Pinot Grigio (Valdadige) $10. **83** *—J.C. (1/1/2004)*

Barone Fini 2000 Pinot Grigio (Valdadige) $11. **83** *—M.N. (9/1/2001)*

BARONE RICASOLI

Barone Ricasoli 2001 1141 Sangiovese (Chianti Classico) $15. **84** *—M.S. (11/15/2003)*

Barone Ricasoli 2000 1141 Sangiovese (Chianti Classico) $13. **86 Best Buy** *—M.S. (12/31/2002)*

Barone Ricasoli 1998 1141 Sangiovese (Chianti Classico) $18. **86** *(4/1/2001)*

Barone Ricasoli 2002 Brolio Sangiovese (Chianti Classico) $22. **88** *(12/15/2004)*

Barone Ricasoli 2002 Brolio Sangiovese (Chianti Classico) $22. **89** *(4/1/2005)*

Barone Ricasoli 2001 Brolio Sangiovese (Chianti Classico) $17. **87** *—M.S. (11/15/2003)*

Barone Ricasoli 2002 Campo Ceni Sangiovese (Toscana) $20. **87** *(12/15/2004)*

Barone Ricasoli 2000 Casalferro Sangiovese (Toscana) $40. **88** *—M.S. (11/15/2003)*

Barone Ricasoli 2000 Casalferro Sangiovese (Toscana) $40. **89** *(12/15/2004)*

Barone Ricasoli 2000 Castello di Brolio Sangiovese (Chianti Classico) $50. **90** *(12/15/2004)*

Barone Ricasoli 2000 Castello di Brolio Sangiovese (Chianti Classico) $55. **92 Cellar Selection** *(4/1/2005)*

Barone Ricasoli 1999 Castello di Brolio Sangiovese (Chianti Classico) $45. **92** *—M.S. (11/15/2003)*

Barone Ricasoli 2000 Formulae Sangiovese (Toscana) $10. **85 Best Buy** *—M.S. (12/31/2002)*

Barone Ricasoli 2001 Formulæ Sangiovese (Toscana) $10. **87 Best Buy** *—M.S. (11/15/2003)*

Barone Ricasoli 1998 Rocca Guicciarda Riserva Sangiovese (Chianti Classico) $18. **87** *—M.S. (12/31/2002)*

Barone Ricasoli 1999 Rocca Guicciarda Riserva Sangiovese (Chianti Classico) $20. **90 Editors' Choice** *—M.S. (11/15/2003)*

Barone Ricasoli 1997 Rocca Guicciarda Riserva Sangiovese (Chianti Classico) $22. **89** *(4/1/2001)*

Barone Ricasoli 1999 San Ripolo Sangiovese (Chianti) $13. **86** *(4/1/2001)*

BARTENURA

Bartenura 1998 Barbera (Barbera d'Asti) $10. **87 Best Buy** *(4/1/2000)*

Bartenura 2003 Moscato (Moscato d'Asti) $12. **85** *—J.M. (4/3/2004)*

Bartenura 2000 Moscato (Moscato d'Asti) $10. **90 Best Buy** *(4/1/2001)*

Bartenura NV Spumante Moscato (Asti) $15. **86** *—J.M. (4/3/2004)*

Bartenura NV Spumante Kosher Moscato (Asti) $15. **86** *—M.S. (6/1/2005)*

Bartenura 1998 Pinot Grigio (Veneto) $10. **86** *—S.H. (9/1/2000)*

Bartenura 2002 Pinot Grigio (Pavia) $12. **82** *—J.M. (4/3/2004)*

Bartenura 2000 Pinot Grigio (Veneto) $10. **82** *—J.C. (7/1/2003)*

Bartenura 1999 Pinot Grigio (Veneto) $7. **85 Best Buy** *(4/1/2001)*

Bartenura NV Prosecco (Prosecco di Valdobbiadene) $12. **85** *—J.M. (4/3/2004)*

Bartenura 1998 Sangiovese (Chianti) $11. **86** *(4/1/2001)*

Bartenura NV Prosecco Brut Kosher Sparkling Blend (Italy) $12. **87 Best Buy** *—M.S. (6/1/2005)*

BASTÍA

Bastía 1998 Chardonnay (Langhe) $34. **86** *—M.M. (9/1/2001)*

BATASIOLO

Batasiolo 1997 Barbera (Barbera d'Alba) $11. **87 Best Buy** *(4/1/2000)*

Batasiolo 2003 Barbera (Barbera d'Alba) $15. **87** *—J.C. (3/1/2006)*

Batasiolo 2001 Barbera (Barbera d'Alba) $12. **86 Best Buy** *(4/1/2003)*

Batasiolo 2001 Sabri Barbera (Barbera d'Asti) $13. **86** *—M.S. (12/15/2003)*

Batasiolo 2004 Sovrana Barbera (Barbera d'Alba) $18. **86** *(12/1/2006)*

Batasiolo 2001 Sovrana Barbera (Barbera d'Alba) $18. **89 Editors' Choice** *(4/1/2003)*

Batasiolo 1996 Sovrana Barbera (Barbera d'Alba) $18. **85** *(4/1/2000)*

Batasiolo 2002 Serbato Chardonnay (Langhe) $12. **85** *—M.S. (12/15/2003)*

Batasiolo 2000 Vigneto Morino Chardonnay (Langhe) $17. **86** *(4/1/2003)*

Batasiolo 2005 Granée Cortese (Gavi) $14. **87** *(12/1/2006)*

Batasiolo 2004 Granée Cortese (Gavi di Gavi) $15. **87** *—J.C. (3/1/2006)*

Batasiolo 2002 Granée Gavi del Comune di Gavi Cortese (Gavi) $15. **87** *—M.S. (12/15/2003)*

Batasiolo 1998 Dolcetto (Dolcetto d'Alba) $11. **86 Best Buy** *(4/1/2000)*

Batasiolo 2001 Bricco di Vergne Dolcetto (Dolcetto d'Alba) $14. **86** *(4/1/2003)*

Batasiolo 2002 Vigneto Bricco di Vergne Dolcetto (Dolcetto d'Alba) $14. **87** *—M.S. (12/15/2003)*

Batasiolo 2005 Bosc Dla Rei Moscato (Moscato d'Asti) $12. **86** *(12/1/2006)*

Batasiolo 2004 Bosc Dla Rei Moscato (Moscato d'Asti) $12. 89 Best Buy —*M.L. (12/15/2005)*

Batasiolo 2001 Bosc Dla Rei Moscato (Moscato d'Asti) $12. 85 *(4/1/2003)*

Batasiolo 2000 Muscatel Tardi Moscato (Piedmont) $40. 86 *(4/1/2003)*

Batasiolo 2003 Nebbiolo (Barbaresco) $35. 87 *(12/1/2006)*

Batasiolo 2001 Nebbiolo (Barbaresco) $40. 88 *—J.C. (3/1/2006)*

Batasiolo 2001 Nebbiolo (Barolo) $38. 89 *(12/1/2006)*

Batasiolo 2001 Nebbiolo (Barolo) $37. 90 Editors' Choice *—J.C. (3/1/2006)*

Batasiolo 2000 Nebbiolo (Barbaresco) $33. 89 *(4/2/2004)*

Batasiolo 1999 Nebbiolo (Barbaresco) $27. 89 *—M.S. (11/15/2002)*

Batasiolo 1999 Nebbiolo (Barolo) $33. 85 *(4/2/2004)*

Batasiolo 1998 Nebbiolo (Barolo) $32. 88 *(4/1/2003)*

Batasiolo 2002 Arsigà Nebbiolo (Dolcetto d'Alba) $15. 88 *—M.S. (12/15/2003)*

Batasiolo 1997 Vigneto Bofani Nebbiolo (Piedmont) $52. 89 *—R.V. (11/15/2002)*

Batasiolo 1997 Vigneto Boscarecto Nebbiolo (Piedmont) $52. 87 *—R.V. (11/15/2002)*

Batasiolo 1998 Vigneto Cerequio Nebbiolo (Barolo) $63. 90 *(4/1/2003)*

Batasiolo 1997 Vigneto Cerequio Nebbiolo (Piedmont) $52. 90 *—R.V. (11/15/2002)*

Batasiolo 2001 Vigneto Corda della Briccolina Nebbiolo (Barolo) $NA. 92 *(12/1/2006)*

Batasiolo 1998 Vigneto Corda della Briccolina Nebbiolo (Barolo) $70. 91 Cellar Selection *(4/1/2003)*

Batasiolo 1997 Vingna Corda della Briccolini Nebbiolo (Piedmont) $60. 91 *—R.V. (11/15/2002)*

BAVA

Bava 1996 Piano Alto Vigneti Bava d'Agl Barbera D'Asti Superiore Barbera (Barbera d'Asti) $38. 84 *(4/1/2000)*

Bava 1995 Stradivario Barbera D'Asti Superiore Barbera (Barbera d'Asti) $38. 85 *(4/1/2000)*

Bava 2003 Thou Bianc Chardonnay (Piedmont) $15. 86 *—J.C. (3/1/2006)*

Bava 1998 Controvento Dolcetto (Dolcetto d'Asti) $13. 87 Best Buy *(4/1/2000)*

Bava 2004 Bass Tuba Moscato (Moscato d'Asti) $25. 87 *—M.L. (12/15/2005)*

Bava 1997 Barolo di Castiglione Falletto Nebbiolo (Barolo) $60. 89 *—R.V. (11/15/2002)*

BEGALI

Begali 1999 Red Blend (Amarone della Valpolicella Classico) $55. 91 *(11/1/2005)*

Begali 1999 Monte Ca'Bianca Red Blend (Amarone della Valpolicella Classico) $75. 91 *(11/1/2005)*

BELLA ROSA

Bella Rosa 2003 Pinot Grigio (Veneto) $8. 84 Best Buy *—J.C. (12/31/2004)*

Bella Rosa 2002 Sangiovese (Chianti) $13. 84 *(4/1/2005)*

BELLA SERA

Bella Sera 2006 Pinot Grigio (Delle Venezie) $NA. This is an easy, low-impact Grigio with aromas of peach, citrus and yellow flowers. It's lean, almost watery, in the mouth with bright acidity suggesting a successful pairing at informal outdoor meals. 84 *—M.L. (12/1/2007)*

Bella Sera 2003 Pinot Grigio (Delle Venezie) $7. 84 Best Buy *—J.C. (12/31/2004)*

Bella Sera 2002 Tre Venezie Pinot Grigio (Delle Venezie) $7. 84 *—J.C. (7/1/2003)*

Bella Sera 2005 Pinot Nero (Delle Venezie) $15. A successful Italian Pinot Noir that offers a lot of aromatic intensity, this wine boasts a garnet-ruby color and an emphasis on small berry fruit, blue flowers, spice and honey-roasted almonds. Polished, compact and crisp, it would make a perfect companion to pork, poultry or pasta. Thanks to its light, delicate fruity aromas and streamlined body, you could serve it with tender roasted pork with stewed figs and forest berry coulis. 86 *—M.L. (11/15/2007)*

BELLAVISTA

Bellavista NV Brut Champagne Blend (Franciacorta) $30. 85 *—M.M. (12/31/2001)*

Bellavista NV Cuvée Brut Champagne Blend (Franciacorta) $26. 86 *—M.S. (6/1/2003)*

Bellavista NV Cuvée Brut Champagne Blend (Franciacorta) $26. 87 *(12/31/2000)*

Bellavista 1991 Vittorio Moretti Reserve Cuvée Champagne Blend (Franciacorta) $100. 83 *(12/31/2000)*

Bellavista 2002 Convento SS Annunciata Chardonnay (Franciacorta) $50. Terre di Franciacorta is an area east of Milan that produces crisp, clean whites boasting many of the same nutty and yellow fruit characteristics that this primarily sparkling wine-based region is celebrated for. This version has a brilliant, luminous appearance and notes of almond, stone fruit and dried hay. 88 *—M.L. (5/1/2007)*

Bellavista NV Gran Cuvée Satèn Chardonnay (Franciacorta) $61. This satèn boasts a pretty, brilliant golden color and aromas of dried apricot, peach, white stone and banana. More grandiose and opulent in style, it has great succulence, fine acidity and playful perlage. 90 *—M.L. (12/15/2007)*

Bellavista NV Gran Cuvée Satén Chardonnay (Franciacorta) $58. 90 *—M.L. (6/1/2006)*

Bellavista NV Cuvèe Brut Sparkling Blend (Franciacorta) $38. This is a lightweight, tonic wine with yeasty aromas surrounded by ripe peach, dried hay and warm, nutty tones. Dig deep to uncover accents of green apple, white stone, flowers and exotic fruit. It ends with fresh lemon flavors and bright acidity. 90 *—M.L. (12/15/2007)*

Bellavista NV Cuvée Brut Sparkling Blend (Franciacorta) $37. 90 *—M.S. (12/15/2004)*

Bellavista NV Cuvée Brut Sparkling Blend (Franciacorta) $34. 92 *—M.L. (6/1/2006)*

Bellavista NV Cuvée Brut Sparkling Blend (Franciacorta) $36. 91 Editors' Choice *—M.S. (12/15/2005)*

Bellavista 1999 Gran Cuvée Brut Sparkling Blend (Franciacorta) $53. 87 *—M.S. (12/15/2004)*

Bellavista 1998 Gran Cuvée Brut Sparkling Blend (Franciacorta) $39. 89 *—J.C. (12/31/2003)*

Bellavista 2001 Gran Cuvée Brut Sparkling Blend (Franciacorta) $53. 90 *—M.L. (6/1/2006)*

Bellavista 2000 Gran Cuvée Brut Sparkling Blend (Franciacorta) $54. 89 *—M.S. (12/15/2005)*

Bellavista 1999 Gran Cuvée Brut Rose Sparkling Blend (Franciacorta) $59. 88 *—M.S. (12/15/2004)*

Bellavista 2000 Gran Cuvée Brut Rosé Sparkling Blend (Franciacorta) $59. 89 *—M.S. (12/15/2005)*

Bellavista 2001 Gran Cuvée Pas Operé Sparkling Blend (Franciacorta) $63. This sophisticated metodo classico sparkler has deep complexity thanks to well-rendered notes of yeast and toast that recall apple pie crust or fresh baking bread. It's a full, generous wine with round tones, lively perlage and a fine point of acidity on the close. 92 *—M.L. (12/15/2007)*

Bellavista 2002 Grand Cuvée Rosé Sparkling Blend (Franciacorta) $61. Persistent and lively perlage sets the stage for a complex wine with deeper dimension and well-balanced acidity. Aromas include peach, melon and yeast and translate seamlessly to the palate. Drink with oven-baked shellfish with parsley and garlic. 88 *—M.L. (7/1/2007)*

Bellavista 2001 Gran Cuvée Rosé Sparkling Blend (Franciacorta) $58. 89 *—M.L. (6/1/2006)*

Bellavista NV Gran Cuvée Satèn Sparkling Blend (Franciacorta) $59. 90 *—J.C. (12/15/2004)*

Bellavista NV Gran Cuvée Satèn Sparkling Blend (Franciacorta) $59. 93 Editors' Choice *—M.S. (12/15/2005)*

Bellavista 1998 Grand Cuvée Brut Rosé Sparkling Blend (Franciacorta) $45. 88 *—J.C. (12/31/2003)*

Bellavista 1999 Pas Operé Gran Cuvée Sparkling Blend (Franciacorta) $62. 87 *—M.S. (12/15/2005)*

BELLENDA

Bellenda 2006 Brut San Fermo Prosecco (Prosecco di Conegliano e Valdobbiadene) $19. You'll get the field flowers and white mineral tones that you expect from this category of Italian sparkling wine, but you also get a hint of cardboard and sulfur that doesn't seem to blow away completely. 82 *—M.L. (12/15/2007)*

Bellenda 2006 Extra Dry Miraval Prosecco (Prosecco di Conegliano e Valdobbiadene) $19. Bellenda is an innovative and hardworking winery that is not afraid to go against the grain. You can taste that this Prosecco is different that the rest: it has more warm, toasted, nutty aromas but it also suffers from a slightly pungent matchstick-like aroma that disturbs an otherwise pretty picture. 82 *—M.L. (12/15/2007)*

Bellenda NV Rosè di Valmonte Col di Luna Brut Rosé Blend (Veneto) $17. Made with Raboso and Pinot Nero, this is a perky sparkling rosé with a vibrant, brilliant appearance and aromas of pink grapefruit, peach, rose, current berry and a strong emphasis on strawberry. The flavors are simple, with strawberry emerging as most evident, and the wine tastes sweet in the mouth. **85** *—M.L. (7/1/2007)*

BELLUSSI

Bellussi NV Belcanto Cartizze Prosecco (Prosecco Superiore di Cartizze) $NA. This Prosecco is slightly more rustic or chunky in character but that quality does not necessarily take away from its overall performance, especially if you like this more robust style of sparkler. It is redolent of sweet exotic fruit, pear and melon. **88** *—M.L. (12/15/2007)*

Bellussi NV Belcanto Cartizze Prosecco (Prosecco Superiore di Cartizze) $24. 89 *—M.L. (6/1/2006)*

Bellussi NV Belcanto Extra Dry Prosecco (Prosecco di Valdobbiadene) $18. 87 *—M.L. (6/1/2006)*

Bellussi NV Dry Prosecco (Prosecco di Conegliano e Valdobbiadene) $NA. This dry Prosecco is dominated by lemon and lime sorbet aromas with less intense tones of kiwi and white peppercorn on the rear. Those lime flavors appear again in the mouth and are reinforced by the wine's delicate sweetness and creamy texture. **87** *—M.L. (12/15/2007)*

Bellussi NV Dry Prosecco (Prosecco di Valdobbiadene) $16. 87 *—M.L. (6/1/2006)*

Bellussi NV Extra Dry Belcanto Prosecco (Prosecco di Conegliano e Valdobbiadene) $NA. This is an extremely fresh and easy sparkler with an emphasis on floral aromas such as jasmine and simple peach tones. It has a creamy consistency thanks to its frothy bubbling and a sweet streak throughout. **87** *—M.L. (12/15/2007)*

Bellussi NV Extra Dry Prosecco (Prosecco di Valdobbiadene) $16. 86 *—M.L. (6/1/2006)*

BELMONDO

Belmondo 2004 Pinot Grigio (Pavia) $6. 83 *—M.L. (6/1/2006)*

Belmondo 1999 Pinot Grigio (Oltrepò Pavese) $5. 81 *—M.N. (12/31/2000)*

BELTRAME

Beltrame 1997 Pinot Grigio (Friuli Aquileia) $15. 84 *(8/1/1999)*

BENANTI

Benanti 2001 Il Monovitigno Nerello Mascalese (Sicilia) $34. 87 *—M.L. (7/1/2006)*

Benanti 2000 Il Monovitigno Nerello Mascalese (Sicilia) $30. 87 *—M.L. (7/1/2006)*

Benanti 2000 Il Monovitigno Nero d'Avola (Sicilia) $30. 88 *—M.L. (7/1/2006)*

Benanti 2000 Lamorémio Red Blend (Sicilia) $32. 89 *—M.L. (7/1/2006)*

Benanti 2001 Rosso di Verzella Red Blend (Etna) $15. 89 *—M.L. (7/1/2006)*

Benanti 2000 Rovittello Red Blend (Etna) $33. 90 *—M.L. (7/1/2006)*

Benanti 2000 Serra della Contessa Red Blend (Etna) $38. 93 Editors' Choice *—M.L. (7/1/2006)*

Benanti 2004 Bianco di Caselle White Blend (Etna) $15. 86 *—M.L. (7/1/2006)*

Benanti 2003 Edélmio White Blend (Sicilia) $22. 87 *—M.L. (7/1/2006)*

Benanti 2001 Pietramarina White Blend (Etna) $33. 89 *—M.L. (7/1/2006)*

BENINCASA

Benincasa 2000 Sagrantino (Sagrantino di Montefalco) $NA. 85 *—M.L. (9/1/2005)*

BERLUCCHI

Berlucchi 2002 Cellarius Brut Sparkling Blend (Franciacorta) $NA. 87 *—M.L. (6/1/2006)*

Berlucchi 2002 Cellarius Rose Sparkling Blend (Franciacorta) $NA. 90 Editors' Choice *—M.L. (6/1/2006)*

Berlucchi NV Cuvée Imperiale Brut Sparkling Blend (Franciacorta) $NA. 88 *—M.L. (6/1/2006)*

Berlucchi NV Cuvée Storica Brut Sparkling Blend (Franciacorta) $32. 89 *—M.L. (6/1/2006)*

BERSANO

Bersano 1997 Costalunga Barbera (Barbera d'Asti) $12. 89 Best Buy *(4/1/2000)*

Bersano 1997 Cremosina Barbera (Barbera d'Asti) $17. 86 *(4/1/2000)*

Bersano 1997 Generala Barbera (Barbera d'Asti) $34. 91 *(4/1/2000)*

Bersano 2001 Cortese (Gavi) $12. 88 Best Buy *—M.S. (12/15/2003)*

Bersano 2001 Raggio Cortese (Gavi) $23. 82 *—M.S. (12/15/2003)*

Bersano 2004 Moscato (Moscato d'Asti) $8. 88 Best Buy *—M.L. (12/15/2005)*

Bersano 2003 San Michele Moscato (Moscato d'Asti) $10. 84 *—M.L. (12/15/2005)*

Bersano 1997 Badarina Nebbiolo (Barolo) $49. 88 *—M.S. (12/15/2003)*

Bersano 1998 Nirvasco Nebbiolo (Barolo) $35. 88 *(4/2/2004)*

BERTANI

Bertani 1999 Corvina, Rondinella, Molinara (Amarone della Valpolicella Classico) $70. Here is a beautifully aged Amarone that shows profound grace and elegance on all levels. The nose is expertly weaved with cherry, licorice, white truffle, caramel and butterscotch nuances. A tight, fine grain texture characterizes the mouthfeel, and bolsters the wine's enormous intensity and persistency of flavor. It is aged six years in oak casks. **94** *—M.L. (12/1/2007)*

Bertani 1998 Corvina, Rondinella, Molinara (Amarone della Valpolicella Classico) $70. There's a particular elegance here that is impossible to beat: The wine is spectacular overall, but never too ornate, and earns high praise for its purity. Aromas of resin, tar, apple and almond are distinct and vibrant and the wine delivers firm, dusty tannins and excellent length. **95** *—M.L. (12/1/2007)*

Bertani 2004 Villa Arvedi Corvina, Rondinella, Molinara (Amarone della Valpolicella Valpantena) $25. The Valpantena Valley produces hearty, structured wines that are usually priced more competitively than those from the Classico zone. Bertani's Villa Arvedi is a case in point. It delivers all the qualities you look for in excellent Amarone: intensity and diversity of aromas such as almond paste, currant berry, Indian spice and deep oak tones. It has polished tannins and a playful note of sour cherry on the finish. **90 Editors' Choice** *—M.L. (10/1/2007)*

Bertani 2003 Villa Arvedi Corvina, Rondinella, Molinara (Amarone della Valpolicella Valpantena) $25. For this attractive price and this classy presentation, you can't go wrong. This delivers mature aromas of cherry compote, brown sugar, maple syrup and spice over firm, chewy concentration. Pair it with strewed rabbit and sage or meat ravioli. **89 Editors' Choice** *—M.L. (10/1/2007)*

Bertani 2004 Velante Pinot Grigio (Veneto) $12. 87 Best Buy *—M.L. (2/1/2006)*

Bertani 1997 Red Blend (Amarone della Valpolicella Classico) $90. 85 *(11/1/2005)*

Bertani 1995 Red Blend (Amarone della Valpolicella Classico) $75. 87 *(5/1/2003)*

Bertani 2000 Villa Arvedi Red Blend (Amarone della Valpolicella Valpantena) $54. 88 *(11/1/2005)*

Bertani 2002 White Blend (Soave Classico Superiore) $14. 86 *—R.V. (7/1/2003)*

Bertani 2002 Due Uve White Blend (Delle Venezie) $13. 85 *—R.V. (7/1/2003)*

Bertani 2001 Le Lave White Blend (Delle Venezie) $23. 89 *—R.V. (7/1/2003)*

BERTELLI

Bertelli 1995 Montetusa Barbera (Barbera d'Alba) $13. 83 *(4/1/2000)*

BIAGINI MANRICO

Biagini Manrico 2000 Signano Sangiovese (Chianti Colli Senesi) $11. 86 *—M.S. (12/31/2002)*

BIGI

Bigi 2003 Amabile White Blend (Orvieto Classico) $9. 84 *—M.L. (10/1/2006)*

BIONDI-SANTI

Biondi-Santi 1997 Il Greppo Brunello (Brunello di Montalcino) $120. 93 Cellar Selection *—R.V. (8/1/2002)*

Biondi-Santi 2000 Sassoalloro Sangiovese (Toscana) $30. 87 *—M.S. (8/1/2002)*

Biondi-Santi 1995 Sassoalloro Sangiovese (Toscana) $25. 91 *—M.G. (5/1/1999)*

BISOL

Bisol NV Cartizze Prosecco (Prosecco Superiore di Cartizze) $41. An emphasis on yellow fruit, pear and measured banana almost makes you think Bisol employs a different yeast selection on their Cartizze Cru. The wine is thick and creamy, with excellent opulence and just the right measure of sweetness. **90 Editors' Choice** *—M.L. (12/15/2007)*

Bisol NV Cartizze Prosecco (Prosecco di Valdobbiadene Superiore) $44. 88 *—M.S. (12/15/2005)*

Bisol NV Crede Prosecco (Prosecco di Valdobbiadene) $12. 90 Best Buy *—M.S. (12/31/2002)*

Bisol NV Crede Prosecco (Prosecco di Valdobbiadene) $18. 90 Editors' Choice *—M.S. (6/1/2005)*

Bisol 2005 Crede Prosecco (Prosecco di Valdobbiadene) $15. 89 Best Buy *—M.L. (6/1/2006)*

Bisol NV Brut Crede Prosecco (Prosecco di Valdobbiadene) $19. Great execution and delivery: This lively Brut layers on stone fruit, floral and mineral tones in well-measured doses. The mouthfeel is creamy and soft, gliding over the palate in an attractive and refreshing way. 89 *—M.L. (12/15/2007)*

Bisol NV Crede Brut Prosecco (Prosecco di Valdobbiadene) $18. 88 *—M.S. (12/15/2005)*

Bisol NV Jeio Prosecco (Prosecco di Valdobbiadene) $14. Clean, fresh and tonic, here is a lively Italian sparkler with very good intensity and fresh notes of peach and citrus. It has a touch of sweetness in the mouth and perfect Prosecco crispness on the close. 87 *—M.L. (12/15/2007)*

Bisol NV Desiderio Jeio Brut Prosecco (Veneto) $15. 87 *—M.S. (6/1/2005)*

Bisol NV Jeio Brut Prosecco (Prosecco) $15. 87 *—M.S. (12/15/2005)*

Bisol 2004 Superiore di Cartizze Dry Prosecco (Prosecco Superiore di Cartizze) $44. 88 *—M.L. (6/1/2006)*

Bisol NV Vigneti del Fol Extra Dry Prosecco (Prosecco di Valdobbiadene) $NA. 87 *—M.L. (6/1/2006)*

BIXIO

Bixio 2000 Ripasso Red Blend (Valpolicella Classico Superiore) $17. 86 *—J.C. (12/31/2004)*

BOCCADIGABBIA

Boccadigabbia 2001 Akronte Cabernet Sauvignon (Marche) $52. 93 Editors' Choice *—M.L. (9/1/2006)*

Boccadigabbia 2004 La Castelletta Pinot Grigio (Marche) $17. 87 *—M.L. (2/1/2006)*

Boccadigabbia 2003 La Castelletta Pinot Grigio (Marche) $17. 86 *—M.L. (2/1/2006)*

Boccadigabbia 2004 Red Blend (Rosso Piceno) $16. There's an attractive smoky or dusty mineral quality to this wine that comes on the heels of fresh red fruit, blackberry and exotic spice. Velvety and caressing in the mouth, this red boasts great structure and length on the finish. 88 *—M.L. (12/1/2007)*

BOLLA

Bolla 2001 Cabernet Sauvignon (Delle Venezie) $9. 82 *(5/1/2003)*

Bolla 1999 Creso Cabernet Sauvignon (Delle Venezie) $27. 83 *—M.S. (12/15/2003)*

Bolla 1998 Creso Cabernet Sauvignon (Delle Venezie) $27. 84 *(5/1/2003)*

Bolla 2001 Corvina (Amarone della Valpolicella Classico) $45. 88 *(11/1/2005)*

Bolla 2002 Merlot (Delle Venezie) $9. 83 *—M.S. (12/15/2003)*

Bolla 2001 Merlot (Delle Venezie) $9. 82 *(5/1/2003)*

Bolla 2000 Colforte Merlot (Delle Venezie) $15. 83 *(5/1/2003)*

Bolla 2004 Nero d'Avola (Sicilia) $9. 87 Best Buy *—M.L. (7/1/2006)*

Bolla 2004 Pinot Grigio (Delle Venezie) $9. 85 Best Buy *—M.L. (6/1/2006)*

Bolla 2001 Pinot Grigio (Delle Venezie) $8. 81 *—J.C. (7/1/2003)*

Bolla 2001 Arcale Pinot Grigio (Collio) $10. 84 *—J.C. (7/1/2003)*

Bolla 2002 Red Blend (Bardolino) $10. 81 *—M.S. (12/15/2003)*

Bolla 2001 Red Blend (Bardolino) $10. 82 *(5/1/2003)*

Bolla 2001 Red Blend (Valpolicella) $9. 81 *(5/1/2003)*

Bolla 1999 Red Blend (Bardolino) $8. 82 *(5/1/2003)*

Bolla 1999 Red Blend (Valpolicella) $9. 84 *—J.C. (12/31/2000)*

Bolla 1998 Red Blend (Valpolicella) $8. 80 *(5/1/2003)*

Bolla 1997 Red Blend (Amarone della Valpolicella Classico) $50. 88 *(5/1/2003)*

Bolla 1996 Red Blend (Amarone della Valpolicella Classico) $50. 86 *—M.N. (12/31/2000)*

Bolla 1998 Le Poiane Red Blend (Valpolicella Classico) $15. 83 *(5/1/2003)*

Bolla 2002 White Blend (Soave) $9. 83 *—M.S. (10/1/2004)*

Bolla 2001 White Blend (Soave) $9. 82 *—J.C. (7/1/2003)*

Bolla 2004 Grillo White Blend (Sicilia) $9. 86 Best Buy *—M.L. (7/1/2006)*

Bolla 2000 Tufaie White Blend (Soave Classico Superiore) $8. 84 *—J.C. (7/1/2003)*

BOLLINI

Bollini 2005 Barricato 40 Chardonnay (Trentino) $11. Natural nuttiness and generous tones of baked apple, cinnamon, mature apricot, honey and white peppercorn come together to form a wine with good depth, balance and personality. Indeed, this tastes more expensive than it is and that will please lovers of delicately oaked Chardonnay. Its caressing mouthfeel suggests a pairing with spicy jalapeño cheese gratin or chicken marinated in a mole poblano sauce. 86 Best Buy *—M.L. (11/15/2007)*

Bollini 2004 Merlot (Trentino) $11. It's light, ruby appearance promises a lean, easy Merlot for weeknight dinners, and in fact, the nose delivers blueberry, forest fruit and linear mineral tones. This is not a hugely intense wine, but crisp acidity and a lighter consistency make it a friendly companion to pasta with meat ragù or roast beef. 86 Best Buy *—M.L. (3/1/2007)*

Bollini 2005 Pinot Grigio (Trentino) $14. 88 *—M.L. (6/1/2006)*

Bollini 2004 Pinot Grigio (Trentino) $13. 89 Best Buy *—M.L. (6/1/2006)*

Bollini 1999 Pinot Grigio (Trentino) $11. 80 *—J.F. (9/1/2001)*

Bollini 1998 Pinot Grigio (Trentino) $11. 87 *(8/1/1999)*

Bollini 2004 Reserve Selection Pinot Grigio (Friuli Grave) $18. 87 *—M.L. (6/1/2006)*

Bollini 2003 Reserve Selection Pinot Grigio (Friuli Grave) $13. 86 *—M.L. (2/1/2006)*

BONFIGLIO

Bonfiglio 2001 Cabernet Sauvignon (Colli Bolognesi) $24. 91 Editors' Choice *—M.L. (9/1/2006)*

Bonfiglio 2003 Il Passito Pignoletto (Colli Bolognesi) $NA. The sweet, honey-like flavors present here are rich, opulent and reinforced by floral aromas of honeysuckle, acacia and bee's wax. This wine is thick and creamy in the mouth but leaves a crisp clean feel on the palate nonetheless. 89 *—M.L. (5/1/2007)*

BOOTLEG

Bootleg 2004 Pinot Grigio (Venezie) $15. 83 *(2/1/2006)*

Bootleg 2004 Sangiovese (Chianti) $15. 85 *—M.S. (10/1/2006)*

Bootleg 2003 Grande Tuscan Sangiovese (Tuscany) $20. 85 *—M.S. (9/1/2006)*

BORGO AL CASTELLO

Borgo al Castello 1999 Mother Zin Primitivo (Apulia) $11. 82 *—C.S. (5/1/2002)*

BORGO CONVENTI

Borgo Conventi 1997 Pinot Grigio (Collio) $22. 87 *(8/1/1999)*

Borgo Conventi 2002 I Fiori del Borgo Pinot Grigio (Collio) $NA. 86 *—R.V. (7/1/2003)*

Borgo Conventi 2005 Sauvignon Blanc (Collio) $18. Pungent, but not aggressively so, with scents of boxwood, grapefruit and currant. It's medium-bodied on the palate, where hints of tomato leaf add nuance to the citrus and berry flavors. Long and minerally on the finish. 88 *—J.C. (3/1/2007)*

Borgo Conventi 2002 Sauvignon Blanc (Collio) $15. 91 *—R.V. (7/1/2003)*

Borgo Conventi 2002 I Fiori del Borgo Sauvignon Blanc (Collio) $15. 88 *—R.V. (7/1/2003)*

BORGO DEI VASSALLI

Borgo dei Vassalli 2004 Pinot Grigio (Venezia Giulia) $10. 87 Best Buy *—M.L. (6/1/2006)*

BORGO PRETALE

Borgo Pretale 1999 Sangiovese (Chianti Classico) $17. 81 *(4/1/2005)*

Borgo Pretale 1998 Borgato Sangiovese (Colli della Toscana Centrale) $50. 89 *—M.S. (11/15/2004)*

Borgo Pretale 1999 Riserva Sangiovese (Chianti Classico) $22. 81 *(4/1/2005)*

Borgo Pretale 1998 Riserva Sangiovese (Chianti Classico) $22. 86 *(4/1/2005)*

BORGO SALCETINO

Borgo Salcetino 1998 Lucarello Riserva Red Blend (Chianti) $32. 85 *—M.S. (12/31/2002)*

Borgo Salcetino 2000 Sangiovese (Chianti Classico) $22. 84 *—M.S. (10/1/2004)*

Borgo Salcetino 1999 Sangiovese (Chianti Classico) $18. 83 *—M.S. (11/15/2003)*

Borgo Salcetino 1998 Sangiovese (Chianti Classico) $17. 84 *(4/1/2001)*

Borgo Salcetino 1999 Lucarello Riserva Sangiovese (Chianti Classico) $40. 87 *—M.S. (10/1/2004)*

Borgo Salcetino 1997 Lucarello Riserva Sangiovese (Chianti Classico) $33. 88 *(10/1/2001)*

Borgo Salcetino 1999 RosSole Sangiovese (Chianti) $28. 91 *—M.S. (11/15/2003)*

Borgo Salcetino 1998 RosSole Sangiovese (Chianti) $16. 84 *—M.S. (12/31/2002)*

BORGO SAN DANIELE

Borgo San Daniele 2004 Pinot Grigio (Isonzo del Friuli) $24. 87 *—M.L. (2/1/2006)*

BORGO SCOPETO

Borgo Scopeto 1998 Red Blend (Chianti Classico) $20. 87 *(4/1/2001)*

Borgo Scopeto 2003 Sangiovese (Chianti Classico) $18. 87 *—M.S. (10/1/2006)*

Borgo Scopeto 2000 Sangiovese (Chianti Classico) $15. 86 *(3/1/2005)*

Borgo Scopeto 2001 Borgonero Sangiovese (Toscana) $35. 89 *—M.S. (9/1/2006)*

Borgo Scopeto 1999 Borgonero Sangiovese (Toscana) $35. 89 *(3/1/2005)*

Borgo Scopeto 1998 Borgonero Sangiovese (Toscana) $35. 93 *—M.S. (8/1/2002)*

Borgo Scopeto 1998 Misciano Riserva Sangiovese (Chianti Classico) $35. 93 *—M.S. (8/1/2002)*

Borgo Scopeto 1999 Misciano Riserva Sangiovese (Chianti Classico) $35. 90 *(3/1/2005)*

Borgo Scopeto 2001 Riserva Sangiovese (Chianti Classico) $29. 88 *—M.S. (10/1/2006)*

Borgo Scopeto 1999 Riserva Sangiovese (Chianti Classico) $21. 88 *(3/1/2005)*

Borgo Scopeto 1998 Riserva Sangiovese (Chianti Classico) $28. 92 *—M.S. (8/1/2002)*

BORGOGNO

Borgogno 1993 Sangiovese (Barolo) $29. 90 *—M.G. (5/1/1999)*

BOROLI

Boroli 1998 Nebbiolo (Barolo) $38. 91 *(4/2/2004)*

BORTOLIN

Bortolin 2006 Brut Prosecco (Prosecco di Valdobbiadene) $16. The first thing you notice about this lively sparkler is its nice consistency of bubbles and pretty perlage. White peach, stone fruit, and herbal tones ride over mouthfeel that is more opulent and fat than others. 86 *—M.L. (12/15/2007)*

Bortolin NV Cartizze Prosecco (Prosecco Superiore di Cartizze) $21. This expression of the Prosecco grape is not as fragrant as others but what it lacks in intensity, it makes up for in elegance. It's a linear, direct wine with herbal, musky notes, anise seed and creamy fruit. 87 *—M.L. (12/15/2007)*

Bortolin NV Dry Prosecco (Prosecco di Valdobbiadene) $15. This is a pretty wine to behold in the glass; Its bubbly effervescence is persistent and even. The nose is subdued, but elegant, with stone fruit and white peach in center stage. Lean and compact in the mouth, this sweet sparkler would work well with buttery puff pastry appetizers. 85 *—M.L. (12/15/2007)*

Bortolin NV Extra Dry Prosecco (Prosecco di Valdobbiadene) $16. Dried apple skin, apricot and almond nut emerge with measured intensity. Delicate and light, this is a no-fuss sparkler with interesting sweet and sour contrasts that would pair well with most appetizers or spicy dishes. 86 *—M.L. (12/15/2007)*

Bortolin NV Rù Extra Dry Prosecco (Prosecco di Valdobbiadene) $15. There's nice golden brilliance here and sweet notes of citrus blossom and yellow peach. The wine doesn't have huge dimension but it does have a fine point of acidity on the close that really livens up the finish. 85 *—M.L. (12/15/2007)*

BORTOLOMIOL

Bortolomiol NV Alta Badia Riserva Speciale Extra Dry Prosecco (Veneto) $12. 89 *—M.L. (6/1/2006)*

Bortolomiol 2006 Banda Rossa Millesimato Extra Dry Prosecco (Prosecco di Valdobbiadene) $25. This is creamier than the norm, thanks to its tight, persistent bubbles that feel frothy and soft in the mouth. Lemongrass, fresh field flowers, citrus and white stone characterize its typical Prosecco aromas. 88 *—M.L. (12/15/2007)*

Bortolomiol 2005 Brut Millesimato Motus Vitae Prosecco (Prosecco di Valdobbiadene) $37. The idea here is to present a more structured and sophisticated Brut with emphasis on the nutty tones and mature peach. The wine succeeds in this regard but the whole point of Prosecco is to be light and fun; this ultimately lacks those sharp, well-defined fruit tones you might expect. 87 *—M.L. (12/15/2007)*

Bortolomiol 2006 Cartizze Prosecco (Prosecco Superiore di Cartizze) $35. This is a beautiful sparkler with outstanding purity of aromas: Peach blossom, kiwi, exotic fruit, floral tones and caramel candy form a delicate embroidery. It boasts perky sweetness in the mouth with refreshing crispness on the close. 90 **Editors' Choice** *—M.L. (12/15/2007)*

Bortolomiol 2005 Cartizze Prosecco (Prosecco Superiore di Cartizze) $33. 91 *—M.L. (6/1/2006)*

Bortolomiol 2005 Millesimato Selezione Banda Rossa Prosecco (Prosecco di Valdobbiadene) $19. 89 *—M.L. (6/1/2006)*

Bortolomiol 2006 Prior Brut Prosecco (Prosecco di Valdobbiadene) $13. It's hard to imagine a wine more ingeniously engineered for good times and easy drinking than Italy's bubbly Prosecco. Of the many expressions on the market today, Bortolomiol's Prior Brut (lowest in terms of sweetness) is a fantastic bargain thanks to delicate floral, lime, citrus and cut-grass aromas. But there's sophistication here too, thanks to the pale wine's pretty perlage and it's creamy mouthfeel (a small percentage of Pinot Bianco is used in the blend for added structure). Pair it with appetizers and finger foods, or better yet, with a full course of pan seared ahi tuna and wild fennel reduction sauce. 87 **Best Buy** *—M.L. (11/15/2007)*

Bortolomiol NV Prior Brut Prosecco (Prosecco di Valdobbiadene) $17. 86 *—M.L. (6/1/2006)*

Bortolomiol NV Senior Extra Dry Prosecco (Prosecco di Valdobbiadene) $17. 87 *—M.L. (6/1/2006)*

BORTOLOTTI

Bortolotti NV Brut Prosecco (Prosecco di Valdobbiadene) $16. Here is a lighter, paler shade of Prosecco with opulent and cheerful soapy and herbal qualities (thanks to 10% Pinot Bianco) backed by lemon candy and polished mineral. Yellow apple and chalk are immediately recognizable. The mouthfeel is creamy and foamy with fresh crispness that is noticeable but not exaggerated. 87 *—M.L. (12/15/2007)*

Bortolotti NV Cartizze Prosecco (Prosecco Superiore di Cartizze) $28. Here is an extremely floral and tonic tasting Prosecco with layered aromas of sweet fruit and drying minerals. Its sweetish mouthfeel is rendered more buoyant by the wine's sparkling effervescence. 88 *—M.L. (12/15/2007)*

Bortolotti NV Cartizze Dry Prosecco (Prosecco Superiore di Cartizze) $28. 89 *—M.L. (6/1/2006)*

Bortolotti NV Dry Prosecco (Prosecco di Conegliano e Valdobbiadene) $16. Something is slightly off in this wine: tea leaf, or even tobacco leaf, seems to mask background tones of creamy peach and apricot. In the mouth, however, it offers loads of zesty crispness. 82 *—M.L. (12/15/2007)*

Bortolotti NV Prosecco 47 Extra Dry Prosecco (Prosecco di Valdobbiadene) $19. A distinctly different Prosecco with a colorful aromatic lineup that sets it apart: Yellow fruit, green tea, white stone and nutty almond (10% Chardonnay is added). It delivers a clean, crunchy texture and sweet peach flavors. 87 *—M.L. (12/15/2007)*

Bortolotti NV Brut Sparkling Blend (Prosecco di Valdobbiadene) $16. 87 *—M.L. (6/1/2006)*

Bortolotti NV Extra Dry Selezione Sparkling Blend (Prosecco di Valdobbiadene) $19. 87 *—M.L. (6/1/2006)*

BORTOLUSSO

Bortolusso 2004 Pinot Grigio (Friuli) $15. 89 *—M.L. (2/1/2006)*

BORTOLUZZI

Bortoluzzi 2002 Chardonnay (Isonzo del Friuli) $17. 85 *—J.C. (12/31/2004)*

Bortoluzzi 2001 Chardonnay (Isonzo del Friuli) $15. 82 *—J.C. (7/1/2003)*

Bortoluzzi 2005 Pinot Grigio (Venezia Giulia) $17. 87 *—M.L. (6/1/2006)*

Bortoluzzi 2004 Pinot Grigio (Venezia Giulia) $17. 87 *—M.L. (6/1/2006)*

Bortoluzzi 2001 Pinot Grigio (Isonzo del Friuli) $15. 87 *—J.C. (7/1/2003)*

Bortoluzzi 1997 Pinot Grigio (Isonzo del Friuli) $13. 82 *(8/1/1999)*

BOSCAINI

Boscaini 1996 Amarone Marano Corvina (Valpolicella) $35. 87 *—J.C. (9/1/2000)*

Boscaini 1999 La Cros Pinot Grigio (Valdadige) $12. 86 *—J.C. (9/1/2000)*

Boscaini 1993 Ca' de Loi Red Blend (Amarone della Valpolicella Classico) $52. 90 *—J.F. (9/1/2001)*

BOSCARELLI

Boscarelli 2002 Sangiovese (Vino Nobile di Montepulciano) $33. 86 —*M.S. (7/1/2005)*

Boscarelli 1999 Sangiovese (Vino Nobile di Montepulciano) $68. 90 —*M.S. (11/15/2003)*

Boscarelli 1994 Sangiovese (Vino Nobile di Montepulciano) $18. 87 —*M.M. (5/1/1999)*

Boscarelli 1999 35 Anni Sangiovese (Toscana) $51. 94 Editors' Choice —*M.S. (11/15/2003)*

Boscarelli 2001 Nocio dei Boscarelli Sangiovese (Vino Nobile di Montepulciano) $69. 92 Cellar Selection —*M.S. (7/1/2005)*

Boscarelli 1999 Rosso Sangiovese (Toscana) $67. 89 —*M.S. (12/31/2002)*

Boscarelli 1996 Vino Nobile Di Montepulciano Sangiovese (Toscana) $27. 85 —*M.S. (7/1/2000)*

BOSCO DEL MERLO

Bosco del Merlo 2004 Pinot Grigio (Lison-Pramaggiore) $16. 86 —*M.L. (2/1/2006)*

BOTROMAGNO

Botromagno 2005 Primitivo (Puglia) $11. A bit thorny on the initial impact; notes of apple cider, prunes, dried currant, chocolate, almond and black pepper chime in harmoniously. There's a sour note on the finish but otherwise it's a perfect everyday dinner wine. 86 Best Buy —*M.L. (8/1/2007)*

Botromagno 1999 Apulian Zinfandel Primitivo (Puglia) $10. 84 —*C.S. (5/1/2002)*

Botromagno 2001 Pier delle Vigne Red Blend (Murgia) $13. Murky sulfur notes are a distraction, especially at the beginning, but soften later to reveal cherry and chocolate aromas. This 60-40 Aglianico and Montepulciano blend is characterized by a firm, creamy mouthfeel with smoke (24 months in oak) and some sourness on the close. 84 —*M.L. (8/1/2007)*

Botromagno 2005 Gravina White Blend (Puglia) $11. This 60-40 Greco and Malvasia blend is among the most representative quality white wines from the Puglia region. Aromas of pear, stone fruit and white mineral are backed by creamy warm-climate nuances and a thick consistency. The wine is not oak fermented or aged although it tastes as if it had been. Botromagno was founded in 1991 by the D'Agostino family, following a long history as a cooperative winery. 87 Best Buy —*M.L. (11/15/2007)*

Botromagno 2004 Gravina White Blend (Puglia) $10. 87 Best Buy —*M.L. (9/1/2005)*

Botromagno 2000 Gravina White Blend (Apulia) $9. 88 Best Buy —*M.N. (9/1/2001)*

Botromagno 2000 Passito di Malvasia Gravisano White Blend (Puglia) $30. 88 —*M.L. (10/1/2006)*

BOTTEGA VINAIA

Bottega Vinaia 2001 Chardonnay (Trentino) $20. 87 *(4/1/2004)*

Bottega Vinaia 2003 Lagrein (Trentino) $19. 86 —*M.L. (9/1/2005)*

Bottega Vinaia 2002 Lagrein (Trentino) $21. 85 —*J.C. (12/31/2004)*

Bottega Vinaia 2000 Lagrein (Trentino) $21. 90 Editors' Choice *(4/1/2004)*

Bottega Vinaia 2000 Merlot (Trentino) $21. 87 *(4/1/2004)*

Bottega Vinaia 2006 Pinot Grigio (Trentino) $17. Cavit's Bottega Vinaia line offers an extremely likeable and creamy wine that will more than satisfy adoring fans of Italian Pinot Grigio. The layered aromas are both opulent and pristine and recall acacia flower, yellow fruit, butterscotch and honey—loads of honey. In the mouth, it is lean and fresh with perky spice on the finish. 88 Editors' Choice —*M.L. (12/1/2007)*

Bottega Vinaia 2005 Pinot Grigio (Trentino) $18. 88 —*M.L. (6/1/2006)*

Bottega Vinaia 2004 Pinot Grigio (Trentino) $18. 87 —*M.L. (6/1/2006)*

Bottega Vinaia 2003 Pinot Grigio (Trentino) $20. 86 —*J.C. (12/31/2004)*

Bottega Vinaia 2002 Pinot Grigio (Trentino) $20. 87 *(4/1/2004)*

Bottega Vinaia 2001 Pinot Noir (Trentino) $21. 84 *(4/1/2004)*

Bottega Vinaia 2004 Teroldego (Teroldego Rotaliano) $19. The concentrated, big, blackberry fruit is almost over the top but deftly brought into balance thanks to more austere nuances of licorice, black tar and worn leather. The wine leaves a big impact in the mouth thanks to its good structure and length. 88 —*M.L. (12/1/2007)*

Bottega Vinaia 2002 Teroldego (Rotaliano) $21. 86 —*J.C. (12/31/2004)*

Bottega Vinaia 2003 Teroldego Rotaliano (Trentino) $19. 88 —*M.L. (9/1/2005)*

BOTTER

Botter 2006 Al Verdi Pink Rosé Blend (Veneto) $8. Here is an unusual rosé blend of Merlot and Pinot Grigio that tastes much sweeter than most. High sugar helps shape pretty aromas of delicate forest fruits, peach and strawberry: Pale pink in color. Made only for U.S. consumption. 85 —*M.L. (7/1/2007)*

BRAIDA DI GIACOMO BOLOGNA

Braida di Giacomo Bologna 2004 Vigna Senza Nome Moscato (Moscato d'Asti) $16. 88 —*M.L. (12/15/2005)*

BRANCAIA

Brancaia 2002 Sangiovese (Chianti Classico) $32. 91 Editors' Choice *(4/1/2005)*

Brancaia 2001 Sangiovese (Chianti Classico) $32. 90 —*M.S. (10/1/2004)*

Brancaia 2000 Sangiovese (Chianti Classico) $30. 90 —*M.S. (11/15/2003)*

Brancaia 2001 Il Blu Sangiovese (Toscana) $72. 88 —*M.S. (10/1/2004)*

BRESSAN

Bressan 2001 Merlot (Venezia Giulia) $34. Medium consistency with deep notes of sour cherry, pine forest and black licorice. Crisp acidity makes it a bit thorny or sharp in the mouth but the wine would pair well with cream- or butter- based dishes. 87 —*M.L. (4/1/2007)*

Bressan 2004 Pinot Grigio (Venezia Giulia) $35. Bressan proves that Pinot Grigio can obtain sky high levels of sophistication. This saturated, almost amber-colored wine is rich with opulent honey, apricot, maple syrup, baked pear and pungent pinesap. It's extremely rich, long-lasting and sports a complex, almost prickly personality. 92 —*M.L. (12/1/2007)*

Bressan 2003 Pinot Grigio (Venezia Giulia) $40. 93 Editors' Choice —*M.L. (2/1/2006)*

Bressan 2002 Pinot Nero (Venezia Giulia) $45. The depth and dimension of this wine are extraordinary and so are its aromas of plum, fresh berry, exotic spice, resin, pine forest, vanilla, bramble and chopped herb. These many nuances blend together to form a complex, balanced whole backed by solid structure and good intensity of flavors. The wine undergoes long maceration on the grape skins and ages two years in oak barrel. 90 —*M.L. (12/1/2007)*

Bressan 2001 Pinot Nero (Venezia Giulia) $34. The wine opens with dark concentration and segues into aromas of red fruit, peppermill, resin, pine, rhubarb and smoked ham. The exotic, almost spicy, flavors are very attractive as are its dusty tannins. 89 —*M.L. (12/1/2007)*

Bressan 2004 Carat Tocai Friulano (Venezia Giulia) $35. Here's a white wine that is so rich and creamy it could stand up to the most demanding pairing situations, from pasta with béchamel sauce to honey-roasted pork. It is deep gold in color and viscous in consistency with fragrant aromas of summer flowers, mature yellow fruit, mineral tones and loads of golden honey. It's alluring and complex with more honey flavors in the mouth. 91 —*M.L. (12/1/2007)*

Bressan 2004 Verduzzo (Venezia Giulia) $38. This is a strange but enticing wine with an army of solid aromas that include apricot, dried peach, white stone, honey-nut and a fragrant pine forest-like element. You won't find many wines with this aromatic profile but you can't help but applaud its complex ensemble. 88 —*M.L. (12/1/2007)*

Bressan 2003 Verduzzo (Venezia Giulia) $30. There's a unique quality to Bressan whites that almost always gives them away. You could describe it as sappy pine nut or chestnut honey and this Verduzzo is a prime example of what I mean. Make no mistake, this is a sophisticated and evolved wine with excellent length and deep golden saturation. But it's also an acquired taste. 87 —*M.L. (12/1/2007)*

Bressan 2003 Carat White Blend (Venezia Giulia) $28. Loaded with strong personality and distinctive characteristics, Carat is a savory white blend with penetrating aromas of honey, almonds, oat and fragrant yellow flower. It boasts a solid build and creamy opulence that suggests a pairing with lobster or clam chowder. 89 —*M.L. (12/1/2007)*

BRIGALDARA

Brigaldara 2003 Corvina, Rondinella, Molinara (Amarone della Valpolicella Classico) $60. This is an extremely opulent wine with rich notes of chocolate fudge, cherry liquor and accents of black peppercorn, ginger and oak. It's bright and lively in the mouth with excellent intensity and durable persistency. 92 —*M.L. (10/1/2007)*

Brigaldara 2003 Case Vece Corvina, Rondinella, Molinara (Amarone della Valpolicella) $60. You can tell this is a blockbuster Valpolicella blend just by looking at it. Dense concentration and generous complexity set a somber mood, followed by smoked bacon, beet root, honey, maple syrup, prune and dried fig. In general this is a broad, horizontal wine (no thorny spikes here) with a silky-smooth finish. 90 —*M.L. (12/1/2007)*

Brigaldara 2000 Red Blend (Amarone della Valpolicella Classico) $65. 85 *(11/1/2005)*

BROGAL VINI

Brogal Vini 2001 Antigniano Sagrantino (Montefalco) $16. 87 *—M.L. (9/1/2005)*

BROGLIA

Broglia 2006 La Meirana Cortese (Gavi di Gavi) $21. Usually a strong performer, this wine proved slightly disappointing; showing plenty of alcohol and lacking the fruit to balance it. The second bottle had more fruit, but the alcohol was still too dominant. 81 *—M.G. (12/31/2007)*

BRUNELLI

Brunelli 2004 Corvina, Rondinella, Molinara (Amarone della Valpolicella Classico) $NA. This modern Amarone seems to have sunshine within: Mature ripe berry fruit is highlighted by exotic spice, cedar and roasted nut. The wine delivers good intensity and clarity of flavors that last long on the palate thanks to its excellent persistency. 89 *—M.L. (10/1/2007)*

Brunelli 2001 Campo del Titari Corvina, Rondinella, Molinara (Amarone della Valpolicella Classico) $NA. Thick concentration and extraction set the tone for what proves to be a meaty, raw, chunky wine with chewy succulence and a creamy texture. Not much is subtle especially the blockbuster nose, which is redolent of smoked ham, beef jerky, black fruit and spicy barbecue sauce. 89 *—M.L. (12/1/2007)*

Brunelli 2001 Cengia Campo Inferi Corvina, Rondinella, Molinara (Amarone della Valpolicella Classico) $NA. Cherry, blueberry and vanilla are weaved together to create a solid nose with delicate balances between fruit and oak. In general, the nose is not as lively as other wines from this vintage but many of those wines lack this ease and approachability. Dusty, firm tannins suggest a pairing with lamb shanks and garlic roasted potatoes. 88 *—M.L. (12/1/2007)*

BRUNO FRANCO

Bruno Franco 2000 Barbera (Barbera d'Alba) $NA. 80 *—M.S. (12/15/2003)*

Bruno Franco 2000 Nebbiolo (Nebbiolo d'Alba) $NA. 83 *—M.S. (12/15/2003)*

BRUNO GIACOSA

Bruno Giacosa 2004 Arneis (Roero Arneis) $30. In 2004, Giacosa fashioned a stylish Arneis with a pretty nose of honeysuckle, spice and dried apricot. The palate does not quite live up to the nose, showing a slight hollowness, but the wine blossoms at the end, and it finishes with real aplomb in a rush of sweet fruit. 88 *—M.G. (4/1/2007)*

Bruno Giacosa 1997 Barbera (Barbera d'Alba) $20. 87 *(4/1/2000)*

Bruno Giacosa 1996 Dino Nero Spumante Champagne Blend (Piedmont) $36. 90 *—P.G. (12/15/2000)*

Bruno Giacosa 1994 Extra Champagne Blend (Piedmont) $38. 91 *—E.M. (11/15/1999)*

Bruno Giacosa 1997 Falletto di Serralunga Dolcetto (Dolcetto d'Alba) $19. 80 *(4/1/2000)*

Bruno Giacosa 1999 Nebbiolo (Barbaresco) $95. 90 *(4/2/2004)*

Bruno Giacosa 1999 Falletto Nebbiolo (Barolo) $155. 88 *(4/2/2004)*

Bruno Giacosa 1999 Le Rocche del Falletto Nebbiolo (Barolo) $175. 93 Cellar Selection *(4/2/2004)*

Bruno Giacosa 1999 Santo Stefano Nebbiolo (Barbaresco) $160. 91 *(4/2/2004)*

Bruno Giacosa 2000 Extra Brut Pinot Nero (Piedmont) $38. 90 *—M.L. (12/15/2004)*

BRUNO NICODEMI

Bruno Nicodemi 1998 Colline Teramane Riserva Montepulciano (Abruzzo) $23. 85 *—M.S. (11/15/2003)*

Bruno Nicodemi 1997 Dei Colli Venia Red Blend (Montepulciano d'Abruzzo) $11. 87 Best Buy *—J.F. (9/1/2001)*

BRUNO PORRO

Bruno Porro 2005 Vigna Ribote Dolcetto (Dolcetto di Dogliani) $23. The Porro is a big, lusty wine with plenty of appeal. Pure, simple dark fruit is combined with a solid if unobtrusive structure. Just before the end, all that fruit seemed spent, the wine became slightly hollow, but it recovered in time, and it had a solid medium finish. 87 *—M.G. (12/31/2007)*

BRUNO ROCCA

Bruno Rocca 1997 Barbera (Barbera d'Alba) $32. 85 *(4/1/2000)*

Bruno Rocca 2000 Barbera (Barbera d'Alba) $45. 91 *—M.S. (12/15/2003)*

Bruno Rocca 1999 Estate Bottled Barbera (Barbera d'Alba) $40. 90 *—M.S. (11/15/2002)*

Bruno Rocca 1999 Coparossa Nebbiolo (Barbaresco) $85. 90 *(4/2/2003)*

Bruno Rocca 1996 Coparossa Nebbiolo (Barbaresco) $60. 89 *—J.C. (9/1/2000)*

Bruno Rocca 1998 Coparossa Nebbiolo (Barbaresco) $42. 90 *—M.S. (11/15/2002)*

Bruno Rocca 1999 Rabajà Nebbiolo (Barbaresco) $85. 95 Editors' Choice *(4/2/2004)*

Bruno Rocca 1996 Rabaja Nebbiolo (Barbaresco) $62. 88 *—M.S. (7/1/2000)*

BUCCI

Bucci 2003 Pongelli Red Blend (Rosso Piceno) $21. 86 *—M.S. (10/1/2006)*

Bucci 2002 Pongelli Red Blend (Rosso Piceno) $19. 84 *—M.S. (6/1/2005)*

Bucci 2005 Tenuta Pongelli Red Blend (Rosso Piceno) $21. Here's a 50-50 Montepulciano and Sangiovese blend that genuinely reflects the territory it comes from: Aromas of wet earth, blackberry, leather, spice and red beets are woven tightly together. Well-built and firm, the wine shows good persistency on the finish and can stand up to stewed meats or aged cheeses. 86 *—M.L. (12/1/2007)*

Bucci 2004 Verdicchio (Verdicchio dei Castelli di Jesi Classico Superiore) $21. 87 *—M.S. (10/1/2006)*

Bucci 2002 Verdicchio (Verdicchio dei Castelli di Jesi Classico Superiore) $19. 86 *—M.S. (8/1/2004)*

Bucci 1997 Verdicchio (Verdicchio dei Castelli di Jesi Classico) $16. 85 *(11/1/1999)*

Bucci 2000 Villa Bucci Riserva Verdicchio (Verdicchio dei Castelli di Jesi) $35. 87 *—M.S. (8/1/2004)*

Bucci 1994 Villa Bucci Riserva Verdicchio (Verdicchio dei Castelli di Jesi Classico) $22. 88 *(11/1/1999)*

BUGLIONI

Buglioni 2003 L'Amarone Corvina, Rondinella, Molinara (Amarone della Valpolicella Classico) $NA. Alfredo Buglioni, formally in textiles, bought this beautiful property in 1993 and is now completely dedicated to wine. L'Amarone is hard to read at this young stage, but does delivery thickly extracted fruit and good primary aromas of cherry and chocolate powder. 88 *—M.L. (10/1/2007)*

BURCHINO

Burchino 2002 Sangiovese (Chianti Superiore) $13. 86 *—M.S. (10/1/2006)*

Burchino 2001 Sangiovese (Chianti Superiore) $13. 84 *(4/1/2005)*

Burchino 1999 Sangiovese (Chianti Superiore) $13. 84 *—M.S. (12/31/2002)*

Burchino 1997 Sangiovese (Chianti Superiore) $15. 87 *(4/1/2001)*

Burchino 2003 Genius Loci Sangiovese (Toscana) $26. 90 *—M.S. (9/1/2006)*

Burchino 1999 Genius Loci Sangiovese (Toscana) $17. 85 *—M.S. (12/31/2002)*

BUSSIA SOPRANA

Bussia Soprana 2000 Dolcetto (Dolcetto d'Alba) $18. 83 *—M.S. (12/15/2003)*

Bussia Soprana 1998 Nebbiolo (Barolo) $55. 88 *(4/2/2004)*

Bussia Soprana 1997 Bussia Nebbiolo (Barolo) $70. 87 *—R.V. (11/15/2002)*

Bussia Soprana 1997 Moscani Nebbiolo (Barolo) $76. 88 *—R.V. (11/15/2002)*

Bussia Soprana 1998 Mosconi Nebbiolo (Barolo) $68. 89 *(4/2/2004)*

Bussia Soprana 1998 Vigna Colonnello Nebbiolo (Barolo) $68. 87 *(4/2/2004)*

Bussia Soprana 2001 Vigne del Rio White Blend (Piedmont) $23. 87 *—M.S. (12/15/2003)*

CÀ DEL SARTO

Cà del Sarto 2004 Pinot Grigio (Friuli Grave) $13. 84 *—M.L. (6/1/2006)*

CA' BERTOLDI

Ca' Bertoldi 1998 Red Blend (Amarone della Valpolicella) $30. 89 *(11/1/2005)*

CA' BIANCA

Ca' Bianca 2002 Barbera (Barbera d'Asti) $14. 88 *—J.C. (11/15/2004)*

Ca' Bianca 2001 Barbera (Barbera d'Asti) $15. 80 *—M.S. (12/15/2003)*

Ca' Bianca 2000 Cortese (Gavi) $13. 84 *—M.S. (12/15/2003)*

Ca' Bianca 1995 Nebbiolo (Barolo) $35. 92 *(7/1/2000)*

Ca' Bianca 1999 Nebbiolo (Barolo) $36. 86 *(4/2/2004)*

Ca' Bianca 1998 Nebbiolo (Barolo) $42. 90 *(4/2/2004)*

Ca' Bianca 1997 Nebbiolo (Barbaresco) $33. 86 *—M.S. (11/15/2002)*

CA' BOLANI

Ca' Bolani 2005 Pinot Grigio (Friuli Aquileia) $10. 86 Best Buy *—M.L. (6/1/2006)*

Ca' Bolani 2004 Pinot Grigio (Friuli Aquileia) $11. 86 Best Buy *—M.L. (2/1/2006)*

Ca' Bolani 2002 Pinot Grigio (Friuli Aquileia) $10. 85 *—R.V. (7/1/2003)*

Ca' Bolani 2000 Aquileia Pinot Grigio (Friuli Aquileia) $15. 86 *(12/31/2002)*

Ca' Bolani 2002 Traminer (Friuli Aquileia) $NA. 87 *—R.V. (1/1/2004)*

CA' BRUZZO

Ca' Bruzzo 2000 La Sperugola Merlot (Veneto) $15. 89 Editors' Choice *(5/1/2003)*

CA' DEL BOSCO

Ca' del Bosco NV Champagne Blend (Franciacorta) $44. 85 *—J.C. (12/31/2001)*

Ca' del Bosco NV Champagne Blend (Franciacorta) $44. 88 *—C.S. (12/31/2002)*

Ca' del Bosco 1993 Cuvée Annamaria Clementi Champagne Blend (Franciacorta) $120. 90 Editors' Choice *—C.S. (12/31/2002)*

Ca' del Bosco NV Carmenero Red Blend (Italy) $126. 85 *—M.S. (11/15/2004)*

Ca' del Bosco 1998 Maurizio Zanella Red Blend (Sebino) $87. 86 *—M.S. (10/1/2006)*

Ca' del Bosco NV Brut Sparkling Blend (Franciacorta) $39. 86 *—M.S. (12/15/2005)*

Ca' del Bosco NV Brut Sparkling Blend (Franciacorta) $44. 91 *—M.L. (6/1/2006)*

Ca' del Bosco NV Brut Sparkling Blend (Franciacorta) $32. 86 *—J.C. (12/31/2003)*

Ca' del Bosco 1999 Brut Sparkling Blend (Franciacorta) $65. 89 *—M.S. (12/15/2004)*

Ca' del Bosco 1997 Brut Sparkling Blend (Franciacorta) $65. 87 *—J.C. (12/31/2003)*

Ca' del Bosco 2001 Brut Millesimato Sparkling Blend (Franciacorta) $88. 91 *—M.L. (6/1/2006)*

Ca' del Bosco 1994 Cuvée Annamaria Clementi Sparkling Blend (Franciacorta) $99. 88 *—M.S. (12/15/2004)*

Ca' del Bosco 1999 Cuvée Annamaria Clementi Sparkling Blend (Franciacorta) $157. 93 *—M.L. (6/1/2006)*

Ca' del Bosco 1994 Cuvée Annamaria Clementi Sparkling Blend (Franciacorta) $120. 91 *—J.C. (12/31/2003)*

Ca' del Bosco 1998 Dosage Zero Sparkling Blend (Franciacorta) $65. 87 *—M.S. (12/15/2004)*

Ca' del Bosco 1998 Dosage Zero Sparkling Blend (Franciacorta) $65. 91 Editors' Choice *—J.C. (12/31/2003)*

Ca' del Bosco 2001 Dosage Zéro Sparkling Blend (Franciacorta) $90. 90 *—M.L. (6/1/2006)*

Ca' del Bosco 1998 Rosé Sparkling Blend (Franciacorta) $67. 88 *—M.S. (12/15/2004)*

Ca' del Bosco 1998 Rosé Sparkling Blend (Franciacorta) $67. 88 *—J.C. (12/31/2003)*

Ca' del Bosco 1997 Rosé Sparkling Blend (Franciacorta) $67. 88 *—J.C. (12/31/2003)*

Ca' del Bosco 1993 Satèn Sparkling Blend (Franciacorta) $68. 90 *—J.C. (12/31/2003)*

Ca' del Bosco 1993 Satèn Sparkling Blend (Franciacorta) $68. 89 *—M.S. (12/15/2004)*

Ca' del Bosco 2001 Satén Sparkling Blend (Franciacorta) $68. 91 *—M.L. (6/1/2006)*

CA' DEL MONTE

Ca' del Monte 1994 Corvina (Amarone della Valpolicella Classico) $35. 84 *—J.C. (9/1/2000)*

Ca' del Monte 1993 Vigneto Scaiso Corvina (Valpolicella Classico Superiore) $18. 87 *—J.C. (9/1/2000)*

Ca' del Monte 1995 Vigneto Scaiso Red Blend (Valpolicella Classico Superiore) $19. 86 *(5/1/2003)*

CA' DEL VISPO

Ca' del Vispo 2003 Sangiovese (Chianti Colli Senesi) $16. 90 Editors' Choice *(4/1/2005)*

Ca' del Vispo 2002 Sangiovese (Chianti Colli Senesi) $12. 83 *(4/1/2005)*

Ca' del Vispo 2001 Sangiovese (Chianti Colli Senesi) $15. 82 *—M.S. (10/1/2004)*

CÀ LA BIONDA

Cà La Bionda 2003 Vigneti di Ravazzol Corvina, Rondinella, Molinara (Amarone della Valpolicella Classico) $70. Run by the Castellani family, this is a promising estate and one consumers should keep an eye on. This vineyard-designate cru strikes all the right chords: It's traditional and clearly territory-driven, yet it remains lush, generous and pleasing thanks to 32 months in oak casks and native yeasts. Chocolate, spice, black pepper, almond, earth, ginger, apple and wild herbs characterize a complex wine with velvety texture. 92 *—M.L. (10/1/2007)*

CA' MARCANDA

Ca' Marcanda 2001 Magari Sangiovese (Toscana) $70. 88 *(7/1/2005)*

CA' MONTINI

Ca' Montini 2004 L'Aristocratico Pinot Grigio (Trentino) $16. 86 *—M.L. (2/1/2006)*

Ca' Montini 2001 L'Aristocratico Sauvignon Blanc (Trentino) $15. 85 *—J.C. (7/1/2003)*

CA' RUGATE

Ca' Rugate 2003 Corvina, Rondinella, Molinara (Amarone della Valpolicella) $55. Started in the Soave region, this producer bought vineyards in Valpolicella to include hearty reds in its portfolio. In some distant way, those white winemaking techniques seem to be behind this Amarone. Its aromas are floral and soapy—wild rose and lavender—and very fragrant with undertones of scented candle or incense. The tannins are firm and the finish is long. 88 *—M.L. (10/1/2007)*

Ca' Rugate 1999 Monte Fiorntine Soave Classico White Blend (Soave) $13. 89 Best Buy *—M.M. (9/1/2001)*

Ca' Rugate 2000 Soave Classico White Blend (Soave) $12. 86 *(9/1/2001)*

CA' VIOLA

Ca' Viola 2005 Brichet Barbera (Barbera d'Alba) $27. The Ca' Viola has a simple nose of coffee and fruit. Easy and soft on the palate, the coffee flavors are a little too much for the fruit. Finishes a little hot. 83 *—M.G. (12/31/2007)*

Ca' Viola 2003 Brichet Barbera (Barbera d'Alba) $38. 84 *—J.C. (3/1/2006)*

Ca' Viola 2005 Vilot Dolcetto (Dolcetto d'Alba) $20. A well-made wine that offers plenty of dark fruit, violets and spices. Rich, big, fat and tasty, this is a wine that, while not overly serious, will still make for delicious drinking over the next five years. 89 *—M.G. (12/31/2007)*

CA'NTELE

Ca'ntele 1999 Riserva Negroamaro (Salice Salentino) $11. 87 Best Buy *—M.S. (2/1/2005)*

Ca'ntele 2002 Primitivo (Salento) $11. 90 Best Buy *—M.S. (2/1/2005)*

Ca'ntele 2001 Amativo Red Blend (Salento) $32. 88 *—M.S. (10/1/2006)*

CA'ROME

Ca'Rome 2003 La Gamberaja Barbera (Barbera d'Alba) $33. 84 *—J.C. (3/1/2006)*

Ca'Rome 1998 Nebbiolo (Barbaresco) $50. 88 *—M.M. (11/15/2002)*

Ca'Rome 1999 Sori Rio Sordo Nebbiolo (Barbaresco) $60. 90 *—M.M. (11/15/2002)*

Ca'Rome 2003 Calimpia Nebbiolo (Langhe) $44. This rich, jammy wine will appeal to many, with its sweet core of raspberry fruit candy. The texture is soft, fat and very rich, although there is sufficient acid and tannin to keep the wine in balance. No great complexity here, but it's easygoing and opulent. 86 *—M.G. (12/31/2007)*

Ca'Rome 2001 Maria di Brun Nebbiolo (Barbaresco) $83. 90 *—J.C. (11/15/2004)*

Ca'Rome 2001 Rapet Nebbiolo (Barolo) $42. 90 Editors' Choice *—J.C. (3/1/2006)*

Ca'Rome 1998 Rapet Romano Morengo Nebbiolo (Barolo) $59. 88 *—C.S. (11/15/2002)*

Ca'Rome 2001 Söri Rio Sordo Nebbiolo (Barbaresco) $76. 86 *—J.C. (11/15/2004)*

Ca'Rome 2000 Söri Rio Sordo Nebbiolo (Barbaresco) $76. 91 *(4/2/2004)*

Ca'Rome 2001 Vigna Cerretta Nebbiolo (Barolo) $78. 91 *(3/1/2006)*

Ca'Rome 2000 Vigna Cerretta Nebbiolo (Barolo) $81. 92 Cellar Selection *—J.C. (11/15/2004)*

Ca'Rome 1998 Vigna Cerretta Nebbiolo (Barolo) $62. 92 *—C.S. (11/15/2002)*

CABREO

Cabreo 2003 La Pietra Chardonnay (Toscana) $26. 85 *—M.S. (9/1/2006)*

Cabreo 2001 Il Borgo Sangiovese (Toscana) $47. 90 *—M.S. (9/1/2006)*

CADIS-CANTINA DI SOAVE

Cadis-Cantina di Soave 1997 Pinot Grigio (Veneto) $6. 83 *(8/1/1999)*

CAIREL

Cairel 1996 Vigneto Caveia Barbera (Barbera d'Alba) $15. 87 *(4/1/2000)*

Cairel 1998 Vigneto del Mandorlo Dolcetto (Dolcetto d'Alba) $15. 83 *(4/1/2000)*

CALA SILENTE

Cala Silente 2000 White Blend (Vermentino di Sardegna) $13. 89 *—D.T. (9/1/2001)*

CALATRASI

Calatrasi 2003 Accademia del Sole Cabernet Sauvignon (Sicilia) $15. 87 *—M.L. (7/1/2006)*

Calatrasi 2003 D'Istinto Magnifico Cabernet Sauvignon-Merlot (Sicilia) $31. 90 *—M.L. (7/1/2006)*

Calatrasi 2003 Terre di Ginestra Catarratto (Sicilia) $19. 86 *—M.L. (7/1/2006)*

Calatrasi 2003 D'Istinto Chardonnay (Sicilia) $13. 87 *—M.L. (7/1/2006)*

Calatrasi 2004 TDG 651 Chardonnay (Sicilia) $29. 87 *—M.L. (7/1/2006)*

Calatrasi 2003 Accademia del Sole Merlot (Sicilia) $15. 87 *—M.L. (7/1/2006)*

Calatrasi 2003 Terre di Ginestra Nero d'Avola (Sicilia) $19. 88 *—M.L. (7/1/2006)*

Calatrasi 2002 Terrale Primitivo (Puglia) $8. Loads of toasted notes, vanilla, cherry, leather, almond and melted butter. There's also an earthy tone to the nose, followed by a creamy consistency in the mouth. The wine would make an excellent match to almost any pasta dish. 85 *—M.L. (4/1/2007)*

Calatrasi 2004 Solese Red Blend (Sicilia) $17. 89 *—M.L. (7/1/2006)*

Calatrasi 2003 TDG 651 Red Blend (Sicilia) $29. 90 *—M.L. (7/1/2006)*

Calatrasi 2003 D'Istinto Shiraz (Sicilia) $13. 89 Best Buy *—M.L. (7/1/2006)*

Calatrasi 2004 Accademia del Sole Viognier (Sicilia) $15. 87 Editors' Choice *—M.L. (7/1/2006)*

Calatrasi 2004 Baglio Badami Vioca White Blend (Sicilia) $17. 85 *—M.L. (7/1/2006)*

CALDARO

Caldaro 2004 Pinot Grigio (Alto Adige) $15. 87 *—M.L. (2/1/2006)*

Caldaro 2004 Söll Pinot Grigio (Alto Adige) $28. 86 *—M.L. (2/1/2006)*

CAMIGLIANO

Camigliano 2001 Brunello (Brunello di Montalcino) $57. 91 *(4/1/2006)*

Camigliano 2000 Brunello (Brunello di Montalcino) $53. 90 *—M.S. (7/1/2005)*

Camigliano 1997 Estate Bottled Brunello (Brunello di Montalcino) $48. 84 *—M.S. (11/15/2003)*

Camigliano 2000 Red Blend (Rosso di Montalcino) $19. 88 *—M.S. (11/15/2003)*

CAMPANILE

Campanile 1998 Pinot Grigio (Grave del Friuli) $11. 87 *(8/1/1999)*

Campanile 2004 Pinot Grigio (Delle Venezie) $10. 86 Best Buy *—M.L. (10/1/2006)*

Campanile 2003 Pinot Grigio (Delle Venezie) $10. 85 Best Buy *—J.C. (12/31/2004)*

Campanile 2002 Pinot Grigio (Delle Venezie) $12. 85 *—J.C. (7/1/2003)*

Campanile 2001 Pinot Grigio (Friuli Grave) $10. 87 *—S.H. (1/1/2002)*

Campanile 2000 Pinot Grigio (Friuli) $10. 85 *—J.F. (9/1/2001)*

CAMPO AL MARE

Campo al Mare 2003 Bordeaux Blend (Bolgheri) $30. 84 *—M.S. (9/1/2006)*

Campo al Mare 2004 Vermentino (Vermentino di Toscana) $17. 86 *—M.S. (10/1/2006)*

CAMPO ALLA SUGHERA

Campo alla Sughera 2004 Adèo Red Blend (Bolgheri) $25. Here is a Cabernet Sauvignon-Merlot blend that borrows on Bordeaux inspiration but delivers an all-Italian personality. Earthy smells are woven seamlessly with notes of forest berry, blackberry and cedar wood; there's also an appealing hint of smoked bacon. The wine appears firm and solid in the mouth. 90 *—M.L. (4/1/2007)*

Campo alla Sughera 2003 Arnione Red Blend (Bolgheri Superiore) $47. Blackberry, cherry, moist earth and vanilla notes emerge from the nose of this Cab Sauvignon-Merlot-Petit Verdot blend. Modern and solid, pair it with grilled meat or hearty stew. 91 *—M.L. (4/1/2007)*

CAMPO DI SASSO

Campo di Sasso 2005 Insoglio del Cinghiale Red Blend (Toscana) $27. Surprisingly rich and complex for such a young wine, this blend of Syrah and other red varieties flaunts its sun-drenched Bibbona (central Italy) origins with penetrating and polished aromas of forest berry fruit, peppercorn and Mediterranean sage. From brothers Piero and Ludovico Antinori. 89 Editors' Choice *—M.L. (5/1/2007)*

CAMPO MASERI

Campo Maseri 2006 Sclave Pinot Bianco (Trentino) $NA. Tonic and vibrant, this delivers measured tones of yellow fruit, almond blossom and background mineral etchings over a lean, crisp mouthfeel. 85 *—M.L. (12/1/2007)*

CAMPO VERDE

Campo Verde 1996 Barrel Aged Barbera (Barbera d'Asti) $14. 84 *(4/1/2000)*

Campo Verde 1997 Dolcetto (Dolcetto d'Alba) $12. 83 *(4/1/2000)*

Campo Verde 1999 Nebbiolo (Barbaresco) $44. 88 *(4/2/2004)*

CAMPOBELLO

Campobello 2004 Villa di Campobello Sangiovese (Chianti) $10. 83 *—M.S. (10/1/2006)*

Campobello 2003 Villa di Campobello Sangiovese (Chianti) $10. 90 Best Buy *(4/1/2005)*

CAMPOGIOVANNI

Campogiovanni 2000 Brunello (Brunello di Montalcino) $65. 88 *—M.S. (7/1/2005)*

Campogiovanni 1999 Brunello (Brunello di Montalcino) $NA. 91 *—M.S. (6/1/2004)*

CAMPOMAGGIO

Campomaggio 2003 Red Blend (Toscana) $20. 84 *—M.S. (9/1/2006)*

Campomaggio 2000 Sangiovese (Chianti Classico) $14. 87 *(4/1/2005)*

Campomaggio 1999 Sangiovese (Toscana) $18. 86 *—M.S. (10/1/2004)*

Campomaggio 1998 Sangiovese (Chianti Classico) $16. 82 *(4/1/2001)*

Campomaggio 1999 Riserva Sangiovese (Chianti Classico) $22. 88 *—M.S. (10/1/2004)*

Campomaggio 1999 Riserva Sangiovese (Chianti Classico) $18. 83 *(4/1/2005)*

Campomaggio 1997 Riserva Sangiovese (Chianti Classico) $24. 91 *(4/1/2001)*

Campomaggio 1995 Riserva Sangiovese (Chianti Classico) $19. 87 *(9/1/2000)*

CAMPRIANO

Campriano 2003 Sangiovese (Chianti Colli Senesi) $16. 89 *(4/1/2005)*

CANALETTO

Canaletto 2000 Winemaker's Collection Chardonnay (Puglia) $9. 84 *(5/1/2001)*

Canaletto 1999 Winemaker's Collection Montepulciano (Abruzzo) $9. 85 *(5/1/2001)*

Canaletto 1998 Pinot Grigio (Venezie) $7. 87 Best Buy *(8/1/1999)*

Canaletto 2005 Winemaker's Collection Pinot Grigio (Delle Venezie) $10. Here is a clean and easy-to-drink Grigio with notes of citrus candy, Granny Smith apple and stone fruit. It's everything you should expect from a wine at this price point. The mouthfeel is lean but refreshing acidity comes through at the end. 85 Best Buy *—M.L. (5/1/2007)*

Canaletto 2004 Winemaker's Selection Pinot Grigio (Delle Venezie) $10. 86 Best Buy *—M.L. (2/1/2006)*

Canaletto 2003 Winemaker's Collection Primitivo (Puglia) $10. 85 Best Buy *—M.L. (11/15/2006)*

Canaletto 1999 Winemaker's Collection Primitivo (Puglia) $9. 85 *(5/1/2001)*

Canaletto 2000 Winemaker's Collection Red Blend (Sicilia) $9. 85 *(5/1/2002)*

CANALICCHIO

Canalicchio 2001 Brunello (Brunello di Montalcino) $51. 90 *(4/1/2006)*

Canalicchio 2000 Brunello (Brunello di Montalcino) $60. 92 *—M.S. (7/1/2005)*

Canalicchio 1999 Brunello (Brunello di Montalcino) $75. 94 *—M.S. (6/1/2004)*

Canalicchio di Sopra 2001 Brunello (Brunello di Montalcino) $74. 88 *(4/1/2006)*

CANDIDO

Candido 1997 Capello Di Prette Negroamaro (Salento) $8. 83 *—C.S. (5/1/2002)*

Candido 1995 Duca D'Aragona Negroamaro (Salento) $25. 84 *—C.S. (5/1/2002)*

Candido 1998 Immensum Negroamaro (Salento) $18. 86 *—C.S. (5/1/2002)*

Candido 2000 Red Blend (Salice Salentino) $10. 87 Best Buy *—M.L. (11/15/2005)*

Candido 1997 Riserva Red Blend (Salice Salentino) $8. 84 *—M.N. (12/31/2000)*

CANDONI

Candoni 2001 Pinot Grigio (Friuli Venezia Giulia) $13. 81 *—J.C. (7/1/2003)*

Candoni NV Prosecco (Veneto) $13. 86 *—M.S. (6/1/2003)*

CANELLA

Canella NV Champagne Blend (Prosecco di Conegliano e Valdobbiadene) $11. 87 Best Buy *—P.G. (12/15/2000)*

Canella NV Extra Dry Champagne Blend (Prosecco di Conegliano e Valdobbiadene) $11. 83 *—D.T. (12/31/2001)*

Canella NV Extra Dry Champagne Blend (Prosecco di Conegliano) $11. 90 Best Buy *—M.S. (6/1/2003)*

Canella NV Vino Spumante Brut Chardonnay (Italy) $18. As a brut sparkler, you'll notice this wine's dryer mouthfeel and the finely etched qualities to its nose: herbs, white peach, almond skin and minerals set the stage. Pair this wine with appetizers or fish dishes. **86** *—M.L. (12/15/2007)*

Canella NV Spumante Rosé Pinot Nero (Veneto) $18. This producer tends to make deeply aromatic wines and this Pinot Noir-based rosé is no exception. Floral tones of pink rose, honeysuckle, peach blossom and white stone are generous and inviting. It's lean but creamy in the mouth. **86** *—M.L. (7/1/2007)*

Canella NV Prosecco (Prosecco di Conegliano) $15. This is a popular and trustworthy Prosecco brand that delivers stone fruit, lemon zest, crushed sage leaf and a vitamin-mineral note at the back. There is enough complexity and crispness here to guarantee this as an anytime, anywhere wine. **87** *—M.L. (12/15/2007)*

Canella NV Prosecco (Prosecco di Conegliano) $11. 89 Best Buy *—M.L. (6/1/2006)*

Canella NV Prosecco (Prosecco di Conegliano) $15. 89 Editors' Choice *—M.S. (12/15/2004)*

Canella NV Extra Dry Prosecco (Prosecco di Conegliano) $NA. You'll love this sparkler's peachy-mineral tones and its sweet, fruity essences (both in the mouth and on the nose). A tonic mouthfeel and persistent bubbles are capped by clean freshness on the close. **87** *—M.L. (12/15/2007)*

CANEVELE

Canevele NV Brut Prosecco (Prosecco di Valdobbiadene) $13. 89 Best Buy *—M.S. (12/15/2004)*

CANNETA

Canneta 2000 Brunello (Brunello di Montalcino) $NA. 86 *—M.S. (7/1/2005)*

CANNETO

Canneto 2002 Sangiovese (Vino Nobile di Montepulciano) $22. 88 *—M.S. (7/1/2005)*

Canneto 2001 Riserva Sangiovese (Vino Nobile di Montepulciano) $22. 89 *—M.S. (7/1/2005)*

CANONICA A CERRETO

Canonica a Cerreto 2004 Riserva Sangiovese (Chianti Classico) $32. Ten percent Cabernet Sauvignon is blended into Sangiovese to give this additional power and structure. Yet those delicate Sangiovese characteristics of pressed blue flower, cherry, blueberry and prune do shine through. Two years of barrique aging have added rich notes of chocolate and leather. **89** *—M.L. (11/1/2007)*

CANTALICI L'ANTICA FORNACE DI RIDOLFO

Cantalici L'Antica Fornace di Ridolfo 2004 Messer Ridolfo Sangiovese (Chianti Classico) $32. This has a sweet nose with fresh red fruit, blueberries and loads of exotic spice. In all, it is a compact, well-integrated wine with a lean mouthfeel, solid grip and texture and a sour cherry note on the finish. **89** *—M.L. (11/1/2007)*

CÁNTELE

Cántele 2003 Chardonnay (Salento) $11. 83 *—J.C. (12/31/2004)*

Cántele 1998 Primitivo (Salento) $6. 82 *—C.S. (5/1/2002)*

Cántele 1996 Primitivo (Salice Salentino) $12. 89 *(11/15/1999)*

Cántele 1998 Riserva Red Blend (Salice Salentino) $10. 88 *—M.S. (11/15/2003)*

CANTINA BEATO BARTOLOMEO

Cantina Beato Bartolomeo 2004 Savardo Pinot Grigio (Breganze) $10. 85 Best Buy *—M.L. (2/1/2006)*

Cantina Beato Bartolomeo 2004 Superiore Pinot Grigio (Breganze) $11. 85 *—M.L. (6/1/2006)*

Cantina Beato Bartolomeo 2004 Savardo Vespaiolo (Breganze) $10. 84 *—M.L. (10/1/2006)*

CANTINA BERA

Cantina Bera 2001 Moscato (Moscato d'Asti) $10. 90 Best Buy *—S.H. (11/15/2002)*

CANTINA DEL VERMENTINO

Cantina del Vermentino 2004 Aghilóia Vermentino (Vermentino di Gallura) $NA. 87 *—M.L. (10/1/2006)*

Cantina del Vermentino 2003 Arakena Vermentino (Vermentino di Gallura) $NA. 87 *—M.L. (10/1/2006)*

Cantina del Vermentino 2004 Funtanaliras Vermentino (Vermentino di Gallura) $19. 84 *—M.L. (10/1/2006)*

Cantina del Vermentino 2004 S'Éleme Vermentino (Vermentino di Gallura) $NA. 87 *—M.L. (10/1/2006)*

CANTINA DELLA PORTA ROSSA

Cantina della Porta Rossa 1997 Vigna Bruni Dolcetto (Dolcetto d'Alba) $20. 87 *(4/1/2000)*

CANTINA DI CUSTOZA

Cantina di Custoza 2003 Trebbiano (Lugana) $12. 86 Best Buy *—M.L. (11/15/2005)*

CANTINA DI MONTALCINO

Cantina di Montalcino 2000 Brunello (Brunello di Montalcino) $48. 85 *—M.S. (7/1/2005)*

Cantina di Montalcino 2000 Riserva Brunello (Brunello di Montalcino) $50. 91 *(4/1/2006)*

Cantina di Montalcino 2000 Villa di Corsano Red Blend (Toscana) $39. 81 *—M.S. (9/1/2006)*

Cantina di Montalcino 2003 Sangiovese (Chianti) $10. 90 Best Buy *(4/1/2005)*

Cantina di Montalcino 2001 Sangiovese (Chianti Classico) $17. 84 *(4/1/2005)*

Cantina di Montalcino 2001 Riserva Sangiovese (Chianti) $15. 85 *(4/1/2005)*

CANTINA DI MONTEFIASCONE

Cantina di Montefiascone 2004 Secco White Blend (Est! Est!! Est!!!) $10. 85 Best Buy *—M.S. (10/1/2006)*

CANTINA DI NEGRAR

Cantina di Negrar 2004 Corvina, Rondinella, Molinara (Amarone della Valpolicella Classico) $NA. Cantina di Negrar is an ambitious, quality-minded cooperative with 200 members totaling 1,200 acres of vineyard. Here is a base Amarone with plum, fresh prune, almond, mineral notes and distant Porcini mushroom. It has dried fruit flavors, chewy tannins and very good intensity over a long finish. **90** *—M.L. (10/1/2007)*

Cantina di Negrar 2004 Vigneti di Negrar Corvina, Rondinella, Molinara (Amarone della Valpolicella Classico) $NA. The Cantina Negrar line (this cooperative is also responsible for the well-known Domìni Veneti line) offers good value and this delivers dark concentration and ripe aromas of mature fruit, raisin, coffee grounds and leather. Despite being young, it tastes older with tobacco and earth flavors and chewy tannins. **88** *—M.L. (10/1/2007)*

CANTINA DI SOAVE

Cantina di Soave 2004 Rocca Alata Corvina, Rondinella, Molinara (Amarone della Valpolicella) $48. This is a dark, plush and richly concentrated wine with cherry, blueberry, spice, resin and distinct mineral elements. Seventy percent sees oak casks for 18 months and 30% sees 12 months of barrique. **91** *—M.L. (10/1/2007)*

CANTINA DI VENOSA

Cantina di Venosa 1997 Carato Venusio Aglianico (Aglianico del Vulture) $18. 90 Editors' Choice *—M.S. (12/15/2003)*

Cantina di Venosa 2003 Terre di Orazio Aglianico (Aglianico del Vulture) $12. This is a very fragrant wine named after Latin poet Horace that delivers vibrant tones of blackberry, prunes, plums, freshly milled peppercorn and black volcanic soil. It has rock solid tannins and is a bit gritty in texture suggesting a pairing with succulent foods, such as grilled steak. **86** *—M.L. (11/15/2007)*

Cantina di Venosa 2005 Terre di Orazio Dry Muscat (Basilicata) $10. Basilicata, the "arch" of the boot of Italy, is one of the country's most fascinating and little-known regions. Insular, superstitious and rustic, it is also a territory deeply linked to its wine growing traditions. Here's an openly aromatic white with soapy floral notes and flavors of dried apricot and honey. You'd think it was a dessert wine, but it's not. **86 Best Buy** *—M.L. (11/15/2007)*

CANTINA GALLURA

Cantina Gallura 2004 Dolmen Red Blend (Sardinia) $12. The wine is dominated by apple aromas, which suggest volatility. A small space is allocated for interesting almond and mineral notes, but not nearly enough. More successful in the mouth, you'll encounter dusty tannins and pleasingly adequate length. The wine is made with Nebbiolo grapes and 10% Sangiovese. **83** *—M.L. (11/15/2007)*

Cantina Gallura 2005 Karana Red Blend (Sardinia) $5. Vibrant cherry aromas and berry fruit are backed by flinty-mineral tones and toasted nuances. This Nebbiolo-based wine (with 10% Sangiovese and Caricagiola) delivers cola and tealeaf tones but is lean in the mouth with medium persistency. **85 Best Buy** *—M.L. (11/15/2007)*

Cantina Gallura 2005 Canayli Vermentino (Vermentino di Gallura) $17. This is a nice, crisp summer wine with rather unusual notes of dandelions or field flowers, chopped herbs, basil, minerals and some white fruit as well. It's lean, slightly watery in the mouth, but will wash down pasta salad, fish or finger foods without a fuss. **84 Best Buy** *—M.L. (8/1/2007)*

Cantina Gallura 2005 Piras Vermentino (Vermentino di Gallura) $17. Distinctive, with fresh notes of cut grass or pine forest backed by evident minerality and white fruit aromas. This pale wine offers decent acidity. **84** *—M.L. (8/1/2007)*

CANTINA NALS MARGREID

Cantina Nals Margreid 2003 Baron Salvadori Merlot (Alto Adige) $58. A tad overripe and funky at the start, this needs a few minutes to come into its own. When it does, it is redolent of cherry preserves, sweet spice cake, Porcino mushroom and cookie dough. The aromas are wide and dispersed but the mouthfeel is more compact. **87** *—M.L. (4/1/2007)*

CANTINA PRODUTTORI BOLZANO S. MADDALENA

Cantina Produttori Bolzano S. Maddalena/Gries 2004 Riserva Taber Lagrein (Alto Adige) $40. Massive cherry and blueberry aromas are released with licorice, toasted almond, earthy mushroom and a pretty note of chalk or flint. Inky-black in color, this is almost chunky in feeling and enhanced by sweet floral tones in the mouth. **89** *—M.L. (9/1/2007)*

Cantina Produttori Bolzano S. Maddalena/Gries 2003 Riserva Prestige Line Merlot (Alto Adige) $50. You'll find pretty, feminine aromas here that fall within the realm of cherry blossom, vanilla bean and almond nut with a touch of chocolate fudge. The nose is very floral and fragrant, yet fresh red fruit makes a strong appearance in its flavor profile. A very well made wine, this Merlot has chewy tannins and a velvety texture. **90** *—M.L. (4/1/2007)*

Cantina Produttori Bolzano S. Maddalena/Gries 2005 Dellago Pinot Bianco (Alto Adige) $20. A beautiful and generous wine, you'll get notes of exotic fruit, peach, yellow flowers and banana (a small percentage sees oak). The mouthfeel is refreshing and crisp thanks to well-balanced acidity, yet it also has a sweet, creamy consistency that washes evenly over the palate. **89** *—M.L. (9/1/2007)*

Cantina Produttori Bolzano S. Maddalena/Gries 2004 Riserva Pinot Nero (Alto Adige) $25. Pretty blue flowers and small forest berries set the stage for what is a cushiony, feminine wine with well-balanced acidity and very good length on the finish: A textbook expression of this Noir grape from the mountainous Alto Adige region. **90** *—M.L. (9/1/2007)*

CANTINA PRODUTTORI DI VALDOBBIADENE

Cantina Produttori di Valdobbiadene NV Brut Val d'Oca Prosecco (Prosecco di Valdobbiadene) $NA. Lemon-lime candy, white peach, chalky mineral tones and sweet herbs, especially sage and basil, are vibrant and penetrating aromas. Pair this bubbly with exotic foods, such as roasted eggplant with Indian spice. **87** *—M.L. (12/15/2007)*

Cantina Produttori di Valdobbiadene 2006 Millesimato Val d'Oca Extra Dry Prosecco (Prosecco di Valdobbiadene) $NA. Pretty citrus tones are backed by white peach and soapy floral notes to produce a clean, fresh sparkler that is easy and approachable. The wine is beautifully crisp with smooth citrus flavors that leave a lasting impression. **86** *—M.L. (12/15/2007)*

Cantina Produttori di Valdobbiadene NV Uvaggio Storico Val d'Oca Extra Dry Prosecco (Prosecco) $NA. This has everything going for it: good intensity, variety of aromas and fresh acidity. It would have scored higher, only it seems to lack that tonic, bubbly edge of other Prosecco—maybe because 15% of other grapes are used. Aromas include lemon zest, sweet basil, peach and white stone. **85** *—M.L. (12/15/2007)*

CANTINA PRODUTTORI S. PAOLO

Cantina Produttori S. Paolo 2004 Eggleiten Pinot Grigio (Alto Adige) $NA. 85 *—M.L. (6/1/2006)*

CANTINA PRODUTTORI SAN MICHELE APPIANO

Cantina Produttori San Michele Appiano 2003 St. Valentin Lagrein (Alto Adige) $50. Big in depth and hidden nooks and crannies, this is a fabulously chewy red wine with carefully etched aromas of blueberry, currants, cookie dough, toasted oak and chalky minerals. It would make an easy match to stewed rabbit (use half a cup of the wine in the sauce). **89** *—M.L. (9/1/2007)*

Cantina Produttori San Michele Appiano 2004 St. Valentin Pinot Bianco (Alto Adige) $36. Beautifully integrated wood tones enhance aromas of vanilla, banana, spice and stone fruit. There's even a subtle note of melted butter or bacon fat in there. Like Chardonnay, Pinot Bianco has the natural consistency to match longer periods of oak aging. **90** *—M.L. (9/1/2007)*

Cantina Produttori San Michele Appiano 2003 St. Valentin Pinot Nero (Alto Adige) $50. Enticing and very feminine, here is a wine with deeply fragrant floral tones of violet, lilac and jasmine. Firm but yielding with crisp acidity and impressive length. Pair with lamb with mint sauce. **90** *—M.L. (9/1/2007)*

Cantina Produttori San Michele Appiano 2006 Montiggl Riesling (Alto Adige) $18. This is textbook Riesling with clean citrus aromas and good intensity through and through. Background flavors of almond skin and stone fruit add depth and character. In the mouth, this is smooth and silky with a touch of sweetness. **87** *—M.L. (9/1/2007)*

Cantina Produttori San Michele Appiano 2005 St. Valentin Sauvignon Blanc (Alto Adige) $36. Characterized by its crystalline luminosity, this delivers aromas of tomato leaf, white stone and white fruit. There's a cooling blast of refreshing crispness on the close. One of the best Sauvignon Blancs you'll find in Italy. **91** *—M.L. (9/1/2007)*

CANTINA SANTADI

Cantina Santadi 2004 Grotta Rossa Carignano (Carignano del Sulcis) $12. Here is a very ripe wine with dense concentration and generous fruit shadings that only sees stainless steel: The nose is sweet smelling and redolent of strawberry jam. In the mouth, it showcases a firm structure and chewy persistency. **86** *—M.L. (11/15/2007)*

Cantina Santadi 2003 Grotta Rossa Carignano (Carignano del Sulcis) $14. 86 Best Buy *—M.L. (11/15/2005)*

Cantina Santadi 2002 Grotta Rossa Carignano (Carignano del Sulcis) $11. 87 Best Buy *—M.S. (2/1/2005)*

Cantina Santadi 2002 Rocca Rubia Riserva Carignano (Carignano del Sulcis) $24. 86 *—M.S. (10/1/2006)*

Cantina Santadi 2001 Rocca Rubia Riserva Carignano (Carignano del Sulcis) $28. 92 Editors' Choice *—M.S. (2/1/2005)*

Cantina Santadi 2000 Rocca Rubia Riserva Carignano (Carignano del Sulcis) $25. 87 *—M.S. (11/15/2004)*

Cantina Santadi 2000 Shardana Carignano (Valli di Porto Pino) $32. 90 *—M.S. (10/1/2006)*

Cantina Santadi 1999 Shardana Carignano (Valli di Porto Pino) $31. 90 *—M.S. (2/1/2005)*

Cantina Santadi 2001 Terre Brune Superiore Carignano (Carignano del Sulcis) $66. 92 Editors' Choice *—M.S. (10/1/2006)*

Cantina Santadi 1999 Terre Brune Superiore Carignano (Carignano del Sulcis) $63. 88 *—M.S. (11/15/2004)*

Cantina Santadi 2006 Tre Torri Carignano (Carignano del Sulcis) $12. This rosé has a nice way about it thanks to small berry fruit flavors and rich almond aromas. It's compact but with enough structure to make it an interesting companion to pork, white meat or shellfish. **87 Best Buy** *—M.L. (7/1/2007)*

Cantina Santadi 2005 Tre Torri Carignano (Carignano del Sulcis) $12. This rose-colored Sardinian wine has very good depth and complexity and appears luminous in the glass thanks to gorgeous pink highlights. The nose offers small berries, crushed pomegranate, ripe fruit and a dash of medicinal herbs: From the island's Carignano grape variety. **87 Best Buy** *—M.L. (7/1/2007)*

Cantina Santadi 2005 Antigua Red Blend (Monica di Sardegna) $14. This is not a very intense wine and initial sulfuric notes (that eventually blow) are distracting. The 85-15 Monica and Carignano blend does however gain clarity and purity with a few swirls of the glass to reveal pomegranate, earth and exotic spice. No wood is used. **84** *—M.L. (11/15/2007)*

Cantina Santadi 2005 Cala Silente Vermentino (Vermentino di Sardegna) $16. Crisp, fruity and full of mineral nuances, this faithfully represents Sardinia's winemaking potential, especially when it comes to easy-drinking white wines. Vanilla, stone fruit, apple-nut, citrus peel and honey flavors boost a creamy, almost viscous consistency. **88** *—M.L. (8/1/2007)*

Cantina Santadi 2004 Cala Silente Vermentino (Vermentino di Sardegna) $18. 88 *—M.S. (7/1/2006)*

Cantina Santadi 2003 Cala Silente Vermentino (Vermentino di Sardegna) $18. 85 *—M.S. (2/1/2005)*

Cantina Santadi 2002 Cala Silente Vermentino (Vermentino di Sardegna) $16. 91 Editors' Choice *—M.S. (8/1/2004)*

Cantina Santadi 2005 Villa Solais Vermentino (Vermentino di Sardegna) $11. Brilliant golden highlights and penetrating aromas of honey, acacia and stone fruit; the fragrant honey notes are particularly opulent and refined. In the mouth, the wine boasts good intensity, medium length and bright acidity. **87 Best Buy** *—M.L. (8/1/2007)*

Cantina Santadi 2004 Villa di Chiesa White Blend (Valli di Porto Pino) $35. There's a saturated, almost amber-like tinge to this oak-driven Sardinia Vermentino and Chardonnay blend. It boasts good structure and lovely notes of vanilla, butter, butterscotch, banana and pineapple (wood-fermented and aged). Creamy in the mouth with nutty-apple flavors folded within. **88** *—M.L. (8/1/2007)*

CANTINA SOCIALE COOPERATIVA

Cantina Sociale Cooperativa 2002 PIRAS Vermentino (Vermentino di Gallura) $16. 82 *—M.S. (8/1/2004)*

CANTINA SOCIALE DELLA VALPANTENA

Cantina Sociale della Valpantena 2003 Torre del Falasco Corvina, Rondinella, Molinara (Amarone della Valpolicella) $40. The Cantina's top wines are from its Falasco line and this Amarone delivers complex renderings of black cherry, cola and an elegant use of wood that produces unique cedar highlights. It is a bright, intense wine with a welcoming, drinkable approach. **90** *—M.L. (10/1/2007)*

CANTINA TAVAGNACCO

Cantina Tavagnacco 2004 Pinot Grigio (Colli Orientali del Friuli) $10. 82 *—M.L. (2/1/2006)*

CANTINA TERLANO

Cantina Terlano 2006 Terlaner Chardonnay (Alto Adige) $18. For crisp, easy-to-drink Italian whites from a cooler northern climate, you can count on the Terlano cooperative of wine growers to deliver good value. Notes of exotic fruit, yellow flower and toasted almond distinguish this creamy, chewy Chardonnay. **87** *—M.L. (12/1/2007)*

Cantina Terlano 2006 Gewürztraminer (Alto Adige) $25. You'll love the beautiful clarity of aromas that this pristine, fragrant wine offers: citrus fruit, peach, honey and sweet exotic fruit. It's definitely a compact wine with a streamlined mouthfeel, but those pretty aromas will get you in the mood for Thai lemongrass curry. **88 Editors' Choice** *—M.L. (12/1/2007)*

Cantina Terlano 2005 Lunare Gewürztraminer (Alto Adige) $49. An evolved aromatic white with deeply saturated color and generous notes of butterscotch, vanilla and distilled flower perfume. It showcases big fruit in the mouth and is a tad heavy or waxy on the palate. **88** *—M.L. (12/1/2007)*

Cantina Terlano 2001 Lunare Gewürztraminer (Alto Adige) $43. 87 *—J.C. (7/1/2003)*

Cantina Terlano 2004 Porphyr Riserva Lagrein (Alto Adige) $47. Deeply ruby, almost purple, in appearance, this is a thickly concentrated wine with a massive load of blueberry in center stage. Just enough room is left to allow delicate nuances of chalk, almond skin and garden herbs at the periphery. Excellent solid structure and good length on the finish make this a showcase Lagrein. **90** *—M.L. (9/1/2007)*

Cantina Terlano 2006 Rosé Lagrein (Alto Adige) $16. The brilliant garnet-pink color of this wine makes a great first impression but the wine loses a few points on the nose where Camembert cheese or Parmigiano-like aromas are a distraction. Red-berry fruit fragrances do work their way to the top and the wine has an attractive crisp, spicy close. **86** *—M.L. (12/1/2007)*

Cantina Terlano 2005 Rosé Lagrein (Alto Adige) $15. One of Italy's reliable rosés year after year, the 2005 is getting a bit long in the tooth, but still boasts scents of dried rose petals tinged with leather and earth. There's plenty of richness, weight and complexity, but drink up, or look for the 2006, which should arrive in the U.S. this summer. **88** *—J.C. (7/1/2007)*

Cantina Terlano 2006 Müller-Thurgau (Alto Adige) $18. This pale-colored get by with standard aromas of stone fruit, kiwi and passion fruit. Easy-to-drink and decidedly uncomplicated, it offers simple, fruit-driven flavors. **84** *—M.L. (12/1/2007)*

Cantina Terlano 2006 Pinot Bianco (Alto Adige) $18. Definitely more neutral than other Pinot Biancos from the same vintage, this wine delivers measured aromas of apple, pear, peach and natural rubber that is consistent with the variety's traditional characteristics. It's an approachable, everyday wine. **86** *—M.L. (12/1/2007)*

Cantina Terlano 2002 Pinot Bianco (Alto Adige) $16. 91 Editors' Choice *—J.C. (7/1/2003)*

Cantina Terlano 2000 Vorberg Pinot Bianco (Alto Adige) $21. 88 *—J.C. (7/1/2003)*

Cantina Terlano 2004 Vorberg Riserva Pinot Bianco (Alto Adige) $27. Fleshier and sexier than some of the other Pinot Biancos from Alto Adige, this is ripe with aromatic fruit and floral tones. It has great persistency and would make an excellent match to quiche, asparagus, lobster or pasta. **90** *—M.L. (9/1/2007)*

Cantina Terlano 2006 Pinot Grigio (Alto Adige) $19. Cantina Terlano delivers textbook Pinot Grigio that is fruity, fragrant and creamy smooth in the mouth without ever appearing heavy or flat. You'll get aromas of yellow fruit, mature lemon and natural rubber with sweet peach flavors in the mouth. **87** *—M.L. (12/1/2007)*

Cantina Terlano 2004 Pinot Grigio (Alto Adige) $19. 85 Best Buy *—M.L. (6/1/2006)*

Cantina Terlano 2002 Pinot Grigio (Alto Adige) $17. 90 *—J.C. (1/1/2004)*

Cantina Terlano 2005 Pinot Nero (Alto Adige) $20. A smoky, dusty mineral quality sets the tone for this elegantly polished Pinot Nero that, ultimately, delivers high intensity thanks to its assorted aromas of blue flowers, cola and rose tea. It's silky-textured in the mouth, with a sour note on the finish. **87** *—M.L. (12/1/2007)*

Cantina Terlano 2004 Montigl Riserva Pinot Nero (Alto Adige) $27. Like many Alto Adige Pinot Noirs, the beautiful floral aromas hit you first to be followed by a delicately choreographed ensemble of white almond, berry fruit, licorice root and white mushroom. Very good length and intensity in the mouth: This calls out for baked saltwater fish. **89** *—M.L. (9/1/2007)*

Cantina Terlano 2005 Quarz Sauvignon Blanc (Alto Adige) $47. This interpretation of Northern Italian Sauvignon Blanc puts more emphasis on a creamy mouthfeel and smooth consistency than it does on bursting aromatics and fragrance. You'll get big, broad brushstrokes of stone fruit and chopped nuts, but the real action here is in the mouth. **89** *—M.L. (9/1/2007)*

Cantina Terlano 2001 Quarz Sauvignon Blanc (Alto Adige) $43. 90 *—J.C. (7/1/2003)*

Cantina Terlano 1992 Riserva Sauvignon Blanc (Alto Adige) $95. 90 *—J.C. (7/1/2003)*

Cantina Terlano 2006 Winkl Sauvignon Blanc (Alto Adige) $25. Pristine and luminous in appearance, this typical northern Italian Sauvignon Blanc is clear and clean with enticing aromas of exotic fruit, peach and kiwi. Peach flavors flood the mouth and are cut clean by zesty acidity on the finish. **89** *—M.L. (12/1/2007)*

Cantina Terlano 2001 Winkl Sauvignon Blanc (Alto Adige) $22. 89 *—J.C. (7/1/2003)*

Cantina Terlano 2000 Winkle Sauvignon Blanc (Alto Adige) $18. 89 *(8/1/2002)*

Cantina Terlano 2000 Classico White Blend (Alto Adige) $15. 83 *—J.C. (7/1/2003)*

Cantina Terlano 1997 Classico White Blend (Alto Adige) $12. 87 *—M.S. (4/1/2000)*

Cantina Terlano 2003 Nova Domus Riserva White Blend (Alto Adige) $49. A blend of Pinot Bianco, Chardonnay and Sauvignon Blanc that was given more time in wood and bottle, this is a satisfying and sophisticated wine. Its thick concentration and creamy fruit nuances provide loads of pleasure. **91** *—M.L. (12/1/2007)*

Cantina Terlano 2006 Terlaner Classico Cuvée White Blend (Alto Adige) $18. Pinot Bianco, Chardonnay and Sauv Blanc are blended in a light, fresh style that puts an emphasis on the purity of fruit and green, grassy accents. Pair with swordfish carpaccio or shrimp cocktail. **87** *—M.L. (12/1/2007)*

Cantina Terlano 2002 Terlano Classico White Blend (Alto Adige) $15. 88 Editors' Choice *—J.C. (7/1/2003)*

CANTINA TOLLO

Cantina Tollo 1999 Villa Diana Red Blend (Montepulciano d'Abruzzo) $7. 86 Best Buy *—M.N. (9/1/2001)*

CANTINA TRAMIN

Cantina Tramin 2004 Lagrein (Alto Adige) $33. 85 *—M.L. (9/1/2005)*

Cantina Tramin 2002 Pinot Bianco (Alto Adige) $13. 87 *—R.V. (7/1/2003)*

Cantina Tramin 2002 Pinot Grigio (Alto Adige) $13. 86 *—R.V. (7/1/2003)*

CANTINA TUDERNUM

Cantina Tudernum 2006 Grechetto (Colli Martani) $NA. Golden in color with faint amber highlights, this is a somewhat neutral-smelling Grechetto with measured aromas of pear, almond and dried mint. The mouthfeel is definitely out of the ordinary with sharp astringency making this an almost tannic-tasting white wine. **82** *—M.L. (12/1/2007)*

CANTINA VALLE ISARCO

Cantina Valle Isarco 2004 Aristos Pinot Grigio (Alto Adige) $25. 86 *—M.L. (6/1/2006)*

CANTINE BARBERA

Cantine Barbera 2004 Nero d'Avola (Sicilia) $13. 87 *—M.L. (7/1/2006)*

CANTINE DEL NOTAIO

Cantine del Notaio 2003 Il Rogito Rosato Aglianico (Basilicata) $21. 84 *—M.L. (9/1/2005)*

Cantine del Notaio 2003 L'Autentica 500mL White Blend (Basilicata) $25. 88 *—M.L. (10/1/2006)*

CANTINE FLORIO

Cantine Florio 2003 Malvasia Bianca (Malvasia delle Lipari) $NA. 91 *—M.L. (2/1/2006)*

Cantine Florio 1992 Baglio Florio White Blend (Marsala) $NA. 89 *—M.L. (2/1/2006)*

Cantine Florio NV Vino Marsala Fine Ambra Dry White Blend (Marsala) $12. 88 *—M.L. (7/1/2006)*

Cantine Florio NV Vino Marsala Fine Ambra Sweet White Blend (Marsala) $12. 88 *—M.L. (7/1/2006)*

Cantine Florio 2002 Zibibbo (Passito di Pantelleria) $NA. 93 Editors' Choice *—M.L. (2/1/2006)*

Cantine Florio 2002 Morsi di Luce Zibibbo (Sicilia) $NA. 92 *—M.L. (2/1/2006)*

CANTINE GEMMA

Cantine Gemma 1997 Bricco Angelini Barbera (Barbera d'Alba) $14. 85 *(4/1/2000)*

Cantine Gemma 1998 Madonna Della Neve Dolcetto (Dolcetto d'Alba) $11. 90 *(4/1/2000)*

CANTINE LENOTTI DI LENOTTI

Cantine Lenotti di Lenotti 2003 Corvina, Rondinella, Molinara (Amarone della Valpolicella Classico) $25. This wine is a bruiser and a pleaser with loads of spice and excellent intensity that is feathered out by herbaceous highlights, almond, coffee, cedar, root beer and cherry cola. It has good acidity, freshness and persistency. **91** *—M.L. (10/1/2007)*

Cantine Lenotti di Lenotti 2000 Di Carlo Corvina, Rondinella, Molinara (Amarone della Valpolicella Classico) $35. This Amarone delivers a high spice quota with layered notes of cumin, clove and black pepper backed by berry, bramble, chestnut and almond nut. The complexity and intensity are remarkable as are its thick structure and dusty, firm tannins. **92** *—M.L. (12/1/2007)*

CANTINE LUCIANI

Cantine Luciani 1997 Brunello (Brunello di Montalcino) $32. 84 *—M.S. (11/15/2003)*

CANTINE PICHIERI

Cantine Pichieri 1999 Traditione del Nonno Primitivo (Primitivo Di Manduria) $24. 85 *—C.S. (5/1/2002)*

CANTINE RIUNITE

Cantine Riunite NV Lambrusco (Emilia-Romagna) $5. 82 *—M.L. (12/15/2006)*

Cantine Riunite NV Vivante Lambrusco (Emilia-Romagna) $10. 83 *—M.L. (12/15/2006)*

CANTINE TALAMONTI

Cantine Talamonti 2005 Rosé Cerasuolo Montepulciano (Abruzzo) $9. Red berry fruit, raspberry and almonds characterize the nose but there's also a hint of sherry that may denote overripe fruit. The wine is lean but vibrant in the mouth and would pair well with informal foods. **86 Best Buy** *—M.L. (7/1/2007)*

Cantine Talamonti 2004 Tre Saggi Montepulciano (Montepulciano d'Abruzzo) $16. Nice concentration and pretty aromas characterize this brawny red: red fruit, forest berries, licorice, mineral tones, toasted nut and black slate are identifying elements. There's good ripeness and succulence to the wine followed by solid tannins. **89** *—M.L. (12/1/2007)*

CANTININO

Cantinino 2000 Cantinino de Renzis Sonnino Sangiovese (Tuscany) $30. 86 *—M.S. (11/15/2003)*

CAPANNA

Capanna 2001 Brunello (Brunello di Montalcino) $50. 90 *(4/1/2006)*

Capanna 2000 Riserva Brunello (Brunello di Montalcino) $70. 91 *(4/1/2006)*

CAPANNELLE

Capannelle 1998 Solare Vino di Tavola Red Blend (Toscana) $95. 91 *—M.S. (9/1/2006)*

Capannelle 2000 Riserva Sangiovese (Chianti Classico) $42. 87 *(4/1/2005)*

Capannelle 1999 Solare Sangiovese (Toscana) $85. 92 *—M.S. (9/1/2006)*

Capannelle 1997 Solare Sangiovese (Toscana) $83. 89 *—M.S. (9/1/2006)*

Capannelle 1997 Solare Sangiovese (Toscana) $74. 85 *—M.S. (11/15/2003)*

Capannelle 1998 Vino di Tavola Rosso Sangiovese (Toscana) $78. 89 *—M.S. (9/1/2006)*

CAPARZO

Caparzo 2000 Brunello (Brunello di Montalcino) $48. 89 *—M.S. (7/1/2005)*

Caparzo 2000 La Casa Brunello (Brunello di Montalcino) $75. 90 *(4/1/2006)*

Caparzo 1994 La Casa Brunello di Montalcino Brunello (Brunello di Montalcino) $76. 93 *—M.S. (11/15/1999)*

Caparzo 1999 La Vigna Brunello (Brunello di Montalcino) $66. 91 *—M.S. (6/1/2004)*

Caparzo 2003 Red Blend (Toscana) $15. 88 *—M.S. (9/1/2006)*

Caparzo 2006 Rosato Rosé Blend (Toscana) $14. A blend of 60% Sangiovese and 40% Syrah, this darkly hued rosé offers plenty of weight; it's muscular, filled with mineral and citrus flavors with just touches of berry and watermelon. **85** *—J.C. (7/1/2007)*

Caparzo 1997 Cà del Pazzo Sangiovese (Toscana) $33. 88 *(9/1/2001)*

CAPESTRANO

Capestrano 2001 Red Blend (Montepulciano d'Abruzzo) $10. 89 Best Buy *—M.S. (10/1/2004)*

CAPEZZANA

Capezzana 2004 Barco Reale di Carmignano Red Blend (Toscana) $15. Sangiovese's delicate nuances meet Cabernet Sauvignon's muscle to shape a ruby wine with notes of red fruit, blueberry and wood spice. The wine showcases its fruity youthfulness and approachability and has drying tannins at the close. **86** *—M.L. (5/1/2007)*

Capezzana 2001 Barco Reale Red Blend (Carmignano) $15. 87 *—M.S. (11/15/2003)*

Capezzana 2000 Ghiaie dell Furba Red Blend (Rosso di Toscana) $50. 91 *—M.S. (9/1/2006)*

Capezzana 1999 Ghiaie Della Furba Red Blend (Tuscany) $49. 90 *—M.S. (8/1/2002)*

Capezzana 1998 Ghiaie della Furba Red Blend (Toscana) $52. 88 *—J.C. (9/1/2001)*

Capezzana 2000 Trefiano Red Blend (Carmignano) $40. There's definitely a sweet, ripe, almost jammy quality to the nose that is pleasantly offset by austere aromas of espresso, resin, plum and blueberry. With good balance and harmony between fruit and toast, the wine has a touch of tannic bitterness on the close. **88** *—M.L. (5/1/2007)*

Capezzana 2003 Villa di Capezzana Red Blend (Carmignano) $30. Overall this wine is fruity and pleasant but there are a few elements left hanging. The nose delivers pretty blueberry and cherry but also present is chopped dill or soy sauce that may not appeal to all. Textured with firm tannins, it would pair well with barbeque sauce and ribs. **86** *—M.L. (5/1/2007)*

Capezzana 2002 Sangiovese (Barco Reale di Carmignano) $14. 86 *—M.S. (11/15/2003)*

Capezzana 1999 Sangiovese (Carmignano) $21. 91 *—M.S. (8/1/2002)*

Capezzana 1998 Sangiovese (Carmignano) $23. 83 *—J.C. (9/1/2001)*

Capezzana 1997 Sangiovese (Carmignano) $23. 91 *—M.S. (9/1/2000)*

Capezzana 2000 Barco Reale Sangiovese (Carmignano) $14. 86 *—M.S. (8/1/2002)*

Capezzana 2004 Conti Contini Sangiovese (Toscana) $10. 85 Best Buy *—M.L. (11/15/2006)*

Capezzana 2000 Conti Contini Sangiovese (Carmignano) $10. 85 *—M.S. (8/1/2002)*

Capezzana 1995 Ghiaie della Furba Sangiovese (Toscana) $53. 95 *—M.S. (11/15/1999)*

Capezzana 1995 Riserva Sangiovese (Carmignano) $41. 91 *—M.S. (11/15/1999)*

CAPICHERA

Capichera 2002 Assajé Carignano (Isola dei Nuraghi) $42. 91 Editors' Choice *—M.S. (2/1/2005)*

Capichera 2001 Mantenghja Carignano (Isola dei Nuraghi) $91. 94 Editors' Choice *—M.S. (10/1/2006)*

Capichera 2003 Vermentino (Isola dei Nuraghi) $50. 88 *—M.S. (2/1/2005)*

Capichera 2005 Classico Vermentino (Sardinia) $33. A pretty crystalline appearance and aromas of stone fruit, kiwi, minerals, apple-nut and mint, this is fragrant and intense without being cloying. In fact, there's a lively piquancy in the mouth that drives a long, spicy finish. **89** *—M.L. (8/1/2007)*

Capichera 2004 Vendemmia Tardiva Vermentino (Isola dei Nuraghi) $48. Late harvest, with beautiful luminosity and aromas of stone peach, apricot, vanilla and light toast. Bright acidity leaves the palate clean and refreshed. With 5.3 grams of residual sugar, you'll also taste its perky sweetness. **88** *—M.L. (8/1/2007)*

CAPOCROCE

Capocroce 2005 Pulvino Grillo (Sicilia) $13. Grillo, a native Sicilian white grape, is usually employed to make fresh, easy, food-friendly wines and this, minimally oaked expression from Capocroce is a perfect example. For salads or light fish dishes, you can't go wrong thanks to its crisp acidity and refreshing fruit flavors. **86** *—M.L. (11/15/2007)*

Capocroce 2005 Sapiri White Blend (Sicilia) $11. Two native Sicilian grapes—Catarratto and Inzolia—are blended here to produce an easy, well-priced drinking wine with fresh aromas of citrus, peach and stone fruit. The wine is light in color and consistency and would make an excellent informal luncheon companion. **85** *—M.L. (11/15/2007)*

CAPOVERSO

Capoverso 2005 Sangiovese (Rosso di Montepulciano) $NA. Fresh cherries, blackberries and blueberries come through loud and clear and are backed by almond nuttiness and mild toast. This is an attractive, fruity and fresh wine of medium consistency that would make a perfect match to grilled meats or lasagna. **86** *—M.L. (5/1/2007)*

Capoverso 2003 Sangiovese (Vino Nobile di Montepulciano) $NA. It's easy to appreciate the almond marzipan and black berry fruit aromas that characterize this ripe, ruby red. Other aromas of Indian spice, roasted chestnut and rubber put in brief appearances and add layers of complexity. This is an approachable, food-friendly Tuscan red. **89** *—M.L. (5/1/2007)*

CAPPELLANO

Cappellano 1996 Barbera (Barbera d'Alba) $17. 89 *(4/1/2000)*

Cappellano 1994 Nebbiolo (Barolo) $40. 85 *—M.S. (7/1/2000)*

CAPRILI

Caprili 1997 Brunello (Brunello di Montalcino) $54. 90 *—R.V. (8/1/2002)*

CAPUTO

Caputo 1999 Sannio Aglianico (Campania) $13. 85 *—C.S. (5/1/2002)*

Caputo 1999 Zicorra Aglianico (Campania) $20. 84 *—C.S. (5/1/2002)*

Caputo 2000 Piedirosso (Lacryma Christi del Vesuvio) $13. 83 *—C.S. (5/1/2002)*

Caputo 2002 Rosso Red Blend (Lacryma Christi del Vesuvio) $11. 82 *—M.S. (11/15/2004)*

Caputo 2002 White Blend (Lacryma Christi del Vesuvio) $11. 85 *—M.S. (10/1/2004)*

CARLO BOSCAINI

Carlo Boscaini 2003 S. Giorgio Corvina, Rondinella, Molinara (Amarone della Valpolicella Classico) $40. Located at the foot of the town of San Giorgio in western Valpolicella, Boscaini's top cru seems to have been affected by the hot vintage. Aromas include ripe cherry with strawberry comfiture, dried prune, raisin and finely etched mineral tones. It's slightly lighter in color and concentration but slides like silk over the palate and is not cloying or too chewy. **88** *—M.L. (10/1/2007)*

CARLO DI PRADIS

Carlo di Pradis 2004 Pinot Grigio (Isonzo del Friuli) $15. 87 *—M.L. (6/1/2006)*

CARLO GANCIA

Carlo Gancia NV Rosé Integral Metodo Classico Brut Pinot Nero (Piedmont) $NA. The persistence and intensity of the perlage is very good and the wine's light pink hue is very pretty yet the nose is dominated by distinct apple cider aromas that overpower any delicate nuances: Bright and lively in the mouth. Tasted both bottles with consistent notes. **83** *—M.L. (7/1/2007)*

CARMINA

Carmina NV Brut Prosecco (Prosecco di Conegliano e Valdobbiadene) $13. The wine opens with a foamy, fun personality but does not ultimately provide that extreme vibrancy you usually get with Prosecco. This is a chewy, broad and opulent wine with mature fruit and a dusty quality. **86** *—M.L. (12/15/2007)*

Carmina NV Brut Prosecco (Prosecco di Conegliano) $NA. 88 *—M.L. (6/1/2006)*

Carmina NV Cartizze Prosecco (Prosecco Superiore di Cartizze) $NA. 87 *—M.L. (6/1/2006)*

Carmina NV Cuvée C Extra Dry Prosecco (Prosecco di Conegliano e Valdobbiadene) $15. Toasted nuts and mature peach are, unfortunately, matched by hints of sulfur and cardboard box. The mouthfeel is good with creamy texture and medium acidity. **81** *—M.L. (12/15/2007)*

Carmina NV Extra Dry Prosecco (Prosecco di Conegliano e Valdobbiadene) $13. Floral aromas, white peach and mineral tones make for a harmonious and elegant sparkler with a pretty, vibrant appearance in the glass. Fruity, nutty flavors add sophistication and elegance in the mouth. **86** *—M.L. (12/15/2007)*

Carmina NV Extra Dry Prosecco (Prosecco di Conegliano) $13. 87 *—M.L. (6/1/2006)*

CARPARZO

Carparzo 1993 Brunello di Montalcino Brunello (Brunello di Montalcino) $52. 90 *—M.S. (11/15/1999)*

Carparzo 1997 Le Grance Sant'Antimo White Blend (Tuscany) $25. 91 *—M.M. (9/1/2001)*

CARPENÈ MALVOLTI

Carpenè Malvolti NV Prosecco (Prosecco di Conegliano) $12. 88 Best Buy *—M.S. (6/1/2003)*

Carpenè Malvolti NV Cuvée Brut Prosecco (Prosecco) $15. 87 *—M.L. (6/1/2006)*

Carpenè Malvolti NV Dry Cuvée Oro Prosecco (Prosecco di Conegliano e Valdobbiadene) $NA. This sparkler opens with a pretty, foamy crest and medium intensity of aromas: stone fruit, talc powder, dried sage and crushed white pepper tones are subdued but intricate. It ends on a creamy, sweet note. **86** *—M.L. (12/15/2007)*

Carpenè Malvolti NV Extra Dry Prosecco (Prosecco) $15. 86 *—M.L. (6/1/2006)*

CARPINETO

Carpineto 2000 Farnito Cabernet Sauvignon (Toscana) $30. 86 *(8/1/2006)*

Carpineto 1999 Farnito Cabernet Sauvignon (Toscana) $35. 89 *(11/1/2003)*

Carpineto NV Farnito Brut Chardonnay (Tuscany) $35. 84 *—M.S. (6/1/2003)*

Carpineto NV Dolce Moscato (Tuscany) $17. 83 *—M.S. (6/1/2003)*

Carpineto 2006 Rosato Rosé Blend (Toscana) $10. A 80-20 Sangiovese and Canaiolo rosè blend, this light ruby-colored wine is richly redolent of white cherry, forest berries, white flowers, chalky minerals and herbal tones too. It's floral and fresh in the mouth, clean, informal and easy to drink. **85 Best Buy** *—M.L. (7/1/2007)*

Carpineto 2002 Sangiovese (Chianti Classico) $20. 87 *(4/1/2005)*

Carpineto 2001 Sangiovese (Chianti Classico) $20. 86 *—M.S. (10/1/2004)*

Carpineto 2000 Sangiovese (Chianti Classico) $20. 91 Editors' Choice *—M.S. (11/15/2003)*

Carpineto 1999 Sangiovese (Chianti Classico) $19. 85 *(4/1/2001)*

Carpineto 2004 Dogajolo Sangiovese (Tuscany) $10. 85 Best Buy *(8/1/2006)*

Carpineto 2001 Dogajolo Sangiovese (Toscana) $10. 86 *—M.S. (11/15/2003)*

Carpineto 2000 Dogajolo Sangiovese (Tuscany) $11. 82 *—M.S. (11/15/2003)*

Carpineto 1986 Farnito Vin Santo Sangiovese (Toscana) $55. 90 *(11/1/2003)*

Carpineto 1999 Molin Vecchio Sangiovese (Toscana) $75. 92 *(11/1/2003)*

Carpineto 1999 Poggio Sant'Enrico Sangiovese (Toscana) $70. 91 *(11/1/2003)*

Carpineto 2001 Riserva Sangiovese (Vino Nobile di Montepulciano) $30. 90 *—M.S. (7/1/2005)*

Carpineto 2000 Riserva Sangiovese (Vino Nobile di Montepulciano) $30. 90 *(8/1/2006)*

Carpineto 2000 Riserva Sangiovese (Chianti Classico) $25. 90 *(4/1/2005)*

Carpineto 1999 Riserva Sangiovese (Chianti Classico) $26. 88 *—M.S. (10/1/2004)*

Carpineto 1998 Riserva Sangiovese (Vino Nobile di Montepulciano) $33. 88 *(11/1/2003)*

Carpineto 1998 Riserva Sangiovese (Chianti Classico) $22. 90 *—R.V. (8/1/2002)*

Carpineto 1998 Riserva Sangiovese (Chianti Classico) $28. Dessert Wine. 87 *(11/1/2003)*

Carpineto 1997 Riserva Sangiovese (Vino Nobile di Montepulciano) $69. 91 *(8/1/2006)*

Carpineto 1996 Riserva Sangiovese (Chianti Classico) $24. 90 *(4/1/2001)*

Carpineto 1995 Riserva Sangiovese (Vino Nobile di Montepulciano) $55. 90 *(8/1/2006)*

Carpineto 1990 Riserva Sangiovese (Vino Nobile di Montepulciano) $95. 89 *(8/1/2006)*

Carpineto 1988 Riserva Sangiovese (Vino Nobile di Montepulciano) $99. 90 *(8/1/2006)*

Carpineto 1999 Sillano Sangiovese (Toscana) $75. 91 *(11/1/2003)*

Carpineto 2002 Vernaccia (Vernaccia di San Gimignano) $17. 86 *—M.S. (8/1/2004)*

CASA ALLE VACCHE

Casa alle Vacche 2001 Sangiovese (Chianti Colli Senesi) $11. 84 *—M.S. (11/15/2003)*

Casa alle Vacche 1999 Cinabro Sangiovese (Chianti Colli Senesi) $20. 88 *—M.S. (11/15/2003)*

CASA BALOCCA

Casa Balocca 1998 Dolcetto (Dolcetto d'Alba) $13. 89 **Best Buy** *(4/1/2000)*

Casa Balocca 1997 Nebbiolo (Barbaresco) $64. 88 *—J.C. (11/15/2004)*

CASA CATELLI

Casa Catelli 2006 Pinot Grigio (Veneto) $10. Very pale hay in color with greenish reflections, this is a fresh, citrus-driven Pinot Grigio with background nuances of crisp green apple, kiwi and white stone. It constitutes a perfect appetizer, salad, white meat or light seafood wine thanks to its crisp, clean acidity. 85 **Best Buy** *—M.L. (11/15/2007)*

CASA CONTINI

Casa Contini 2001 Red Blend (Salice Salentino) $7. 86 **Best Buy** *—M.S. (1/1/2004)*

CASA DI ROCCO

Casa di Rocco 2005 Pinot Grigio (Delle Venezie) $10. 86 **Best Buy** *—M.L. (6/1/2006)*

Casa di Rocco 2004 Pinot Grigio (Venezie) $10. 86 **Best Buy** *(2/1/2006)*

Casa di Rocco 2004 Sangiovese (Chianti) $10. 84 *—M.S. (10/1/2006)*

CASA GIRELLI

Casa Girelli 1998 Fontella Chianti Red Blend (Tuscany) $8. 85 **Best Buy** *(4/1/2001)*

Casa Girelli 2001 Virtuoso Syrah (Sicilia) $20. 87 *—R.V. (10/1/2003)*

CASA VINO

Casa Vino 2003 Nero d'Avola (Sicilia) $9. 85 **Best Buy** *—M.S. (7/1/2005)*

Casa Vino 2002 Sangiovese (Chianti) $10. 83 *(4/1/2005)*

Casa Vino 2000 Riserva Sangiovese (Chianti) $13. 86 *(4/1/2005)*

CASA ZULIANI

Casa Zuliani 2004 Pinot Grigio (Collio) $18. 87 *—M.L. (2/1/2006)*

Casa Zuliani 2004 Pinot Grigio (Isonzo del Friuli) $15. 86 *—M.L. (2/1/2006)*

CASABIANCA

Casabianca NV Brut Prosecco (Montello e Colli Asolani) $14. 85 *—M.S. (12/15/2004)*

CASALE DEL DUCCIO

Casale del Duccio 2004 Sangiovese (Chianti) $NA. This wine has a slightly aged appearance thanks to its garnet color and its aromas of ripe cherry, prunes, toast, tobacco and black stone. It boasts nice dimension and a smooth structure. 86 *—M.L. (11/1/2007)*

CASALE DELLO SPARVIERO

Casale dello Sparviero 1997 Sangiovese (Chianti Classico) $16. 85 *(4/1/2001)*

Casale dello Sparviero 1997 Riserva Sangiovese (Chianti Classico) $27. 88 *(4/1/2001)*

CASALE TRIOCCO

Casale Triocco 2001 Sagrantino (Sagrantino di Montefalco) $NA. 85 *—M.L. (9/1/2005)*

CASALFARNETO

Casalfarneto 2002 Fontevecchia Verdicchio (Verdicchio dei Castelli di Jesi Classico Superiore) $14. 83 *—M.S. (8/1/2004)*

Casalfarneto 2001 Grancasale Verdicchio (Verdicchio dei Castelli di Jesi Classico Superiore) $22. 86 *—M.S. (8/1/2004)*

CASALI DI BIBBIANO

Casali di Bibbiano 2000 Argante Sangiovese (Toscana) $32. 82 *—M.S. (10/1/2004)*

Casali di Bibbiano 2001 Capannino Riserva Sangiovese (Chianti Classico) $30. 91 **Editors' Choice** *(4/1/2005)*

Casali di Bibbiano 2002 Montornello Sangiovese (Chianti Classico) $18. 86 *(4/1/2005)*

CASALNOVA

Casalnova NV Extra Dry Prosecco (Prosecco del Veneto) $15. 86 *—M.S. (12/15/2006)*

CASALOSTE

Casaloste 2000 Sangiovese (Chianti Classico) $30. 82 *—M.S. (10/1/2004)*

Casaloste 1999 Sangiovese (Chianti Classico) $28. 87 *—M.S. (12/31/2002)*

Casaloste 1998 Sangiovese (Chianti Classico) $26. 85 *(4/1/2001)*

Casaloste 1999 Don Vincenzo Riserva Sangiovese (Chianti Classico) $80. 91 *(4/1/2005)*

Casaloste 1999 Riserva Sangiovese (Chianti Classico) $38. 87 *(4/1/2005)*

Casaloste 1998 Riserva Sangiovese (Chianti Classico) $45. 87 *—M.S. (12/31/2002)*

Casaloste 1997 Riserva Sangiovese (Chianti Classico) $44. 88 *(4/1/2001)*

CASANOVA DI NERI

Casanova di Neri 2000 Brunello (Brunello di Montalcino) $56. 91 *—M.S. (7/1/2005)*

Casanova di Neri 1999 Brunello (Brunello di Montalcino) $70. 93 *—M.S. (6/1/2004)*

Casanova di Neri 2000 Cerretalto Brunello (Brunello di Montalcino) $130. 96 *(4/1/2006)*

Casanova di Neri 2001 Tenuta Nuova Brunello (Brunello di Montalcino) $65. 91 *(4/1/2006)*

Casanova di Neri 1994 Tenuta Nuova Brunello (Brunello di Montalcino) $50. 87 *—M.S. (3/1/2000)*

CASANUOVA DELLE CERBAIE

Casanuova delle Cerbaie 2001 Brunello (Brunello di Montalcino) $65. 88 *(4/1/2006)*

Casanuova delle Cerbaie 1999 Brunello (Brunello di Montalcino) $NA. 92 *—M.S. (6/1/2004)*

CASANUOVA DI NITTARDI

Casanuova di Nittardi 2001 Sangiovese (Chianti Classico) $26. 81 *(4/1/2005)*

Casanuova di Nittardi 1999 Riserva Sangiovese (Chianti Classico) $48. 88 *(4/1/2005)*

CASCINA ADELAIDE

Cascina Adelaide 2004 Le Mie Donne Barbera (Barbera d'Alba) $24. Le Mie Donne has a complex nose of smoked meat, musky fruit and earthiness. Although they carry through to the palate, they come in a less intense form, and the finish is short to medium. Could have used a little more concentration, but a pleasant complex wine. **87** *—M.G. (12/31/2007)*

Cascina Adelaide 2004 Vigna Preda Barbera (Barbera d'Alba Superiore) $32. A big, rich, modernist effort; a nose of harness leather, candied rose and dark fruit. Nothing shy and retiring about this wine, it is big, hefty and full flavored. **88** *—M.G. (12/31/2007)*

Cascina Adelaide 2004 Nebbiolo (Langhe) $29. The smell of chemicals, reminiscent of the plastic in a new car, never really evaporated, and the wine displayed a disturbing amount of volatility. On the plus side, there is fruit. **81** *—M.G. (12/31/2007)*

CASCINA BALLARIN

Cascina Ballarin 1996 Giuli Barbera (Barbera d'Alba) $16. 83 *(4/1/2000)*

Cascina Ballarin 1995 Nebbiolo (Barolo) $45. 85 *(9/1/2000)*

CASCINA BONGIOVANNI

Cascina Bongiovanni 2006 Arneis (Langhe) $16. There's a palate of apricot and pear and a pleasant smokiness. Lively and pleasant on the front of the palate and it becomes a little too sharp and thin at the finish. **84** *—M.G. (12/31/2007)*

Cascina Bongiovanni 2005 Arneis (Langhe) $17. This light Arneis initially showed a fair amount of sulfur, which blew off with time. Underneath, it revealed some summer fruit flavors and vanilla, but also an odd nuance of wintergreen mint. **83** *—M.G. (12/31/2007)*

Cascina Bongiovanni 2004 Barbera (Barbera d'Alba) $33. The Bongiovanni is a modernist take on Barbera; it is a big, ripe wine, spiced with oak. With some time in the glass, it showed complexity, with flavors of violets and smokiness but the fruit still dominated. There was a slight hollowness two thirds in, but the wine came back and finished with some aplomb. **86** *—M.G. (12/31/2007)*

Cascina Bongiovanni 2005 Dolcetto (Dolcetto d'Alba) $17. The Bongiovanni is a pretty wine showing lots of dark jammy fruit. A few stray violet flavors give it some added complexity but overall a pleasant food wine. **86** *—M.G. (12/31/2007)*

Cascina Bongiovanni 1998 Dolcetto (Dolcetto d'Alba) $18. 89 *(4/1/2000)*

Cascina Bongiovanni 2002 Dolcetto (Dolcetto d'Alba) $31. 86 *—J.C. (11/15/2004)*

Cascina Bongiovanni 2003 Nebbiolo (Barolo) $59. A big, fat, jolly wine with many of the warm, friendly qualities of the '03 vintage. On the nose it shows dark jammy fruit, coffee and spices. On the palate, it is solid and slightly rustic, with a medium finish although there is a touch of alcohol at the end. **90** *—M.G. (12/31/2007)*

Cascina Bongiovanni 2000 Nebbiolo (Barolo) $60. 89 *—J.C. (11/15/2004)*

Cascina Bongiovanni 1998 Nebbiolo (Barolo) $45. 88 *(4/2/2004)*

Cascina Bongiovanni 1997 Nebbiolo (Barolo) $59. 88 *—M.S. (12/15/2003)*

Cascina Bongiovanni 1998 Pernanno Nebbiolo (Barolo) $57. 88 *—C.S. (11/15/2002)*

Cascina Bongiovanni 2001 Faletto Red Blend (Langhe) $46. 86 *—J.C. (11/15/2004)*

CASCINA CHICCO

Cascina Chicco 1999 Bric Loira Barbera (Barbera d'Alba) $28. 89 *—M.S. (12/15/2003)*

Cascina Chicco 1997 Bric Loira Barbera (Barbera d'Alba) $26. 93 *(4/1/2000)*

Cascina Chicco 1997 Valmaggiore Nebbiolo (Roero) $25. 89 *—M.M. (9/1/2000)*

CASCINA CUCCO

Cascina Cucco 1998 Cerrati Nebbiolo (Barolo) $64. 87 *—C.S. (11/15/2002)*

Cascina Cucco 1998 Vigna Cucco Nebbiolo (Barolo) $64. 90 *—M.S. (11/15/2002)*

CASCINA LA GHERSA

Cascina La Ghersa 1999 Camparo-Superiore Barbera (Barbera d'Asti) $14. 88 Best Buy *—M.S. (11/15/2002)*

Cascina La Ghersa 1999 Vignassa Barbera D'Asti Superiore Barbera (Barbera d'Asti) $40. 89 *—M.S. (11/15/2002)*

Cascina La Ghersa 2004 Giorgia Moscato (Moscato d'Asti) $15. 88 *—M.L. (12/15/2005)*

CASCINA LUISIN

Cascina Luisin 1999 Rabaja Nebbiolo (Barbaresco) $65. 88 *(4/2/2004)*

Cascina Luisin 1998 Rabaja Nebbiolo (Barbaresco) $50. 91 *—M.M. (11/15/2002)*

Cascina Luisin 1999 Sori Paolin Nebbiolo (Barbaresco) $65. 90 *(4/2/2004)*

Cascina Luisin 1998 Sori Paolin Nebbiolo (Barbaresco) $56. 88 *—M.S. (11/15/2002)*

CASCINA PIAN D'OR

Cascina Pian d'Or 2004 Bricco Riella Moscato (Moscato d'Asti) $12. 87 *—M.L. (12/15/2005)*

CASCINACASTLE'T

Cascinacastle't 2004 Moscato (Moscato d'Asti) $13. 87 *—M.L. (12/15/2005)*

CASCINETTA VIETTI

Cascinetta Vietti 2006 Moscato (Moscato d'Asti) $15. Vietti's 2006 Moscato has a lovely if slightly muted nose of white peaches and green plum. On the palate, the lack of concentration shows; it is pleasant and quite complex, but the flavors are a little wispy. **85** *—M.G. (12/15/2007)*

Cascinetta Vietti 2004 Moscato (Moscato d'Asti) $14. 86 *—M.L. (12/15/2005)*

CASISANO COLOMBAIO

Casisano Colombaio 2001 Brunello (Brunello di Montalcino) $40. 91 Editors' Choice *(4/1/2006)*

Casisano Colombaio 1999 Brunello (Brunello di Montalcino) $NA. 87 *—M.S. (6/1/2004)*

CASTEL SALLEGG

Castel Sallegg 2003 Riserva Merlot (Alto Adige) $27. An extremely floral Merlot, this wine is redolent of violet, lavender and is almost soapy in fragrance. Berry and sweet vanilla flavors also put in an appearance and the wine boasts good structure, chewy tannins and a long finish. **87** *—M.L. (4/1/2007)*

Castel Sallegg 2002 Riserva Merlot (Alto Adige) $26. Firm and fragrant overall, with a few elements slightly out of place. For example, the nose delivers Indian spice, incense candle, almond, cherry cola and clove but it also has a hint of apple cider that disrupts the overall harmony. It's tannic and solid in the mouth with a bitter finish. **85** *—M.L. (4/1/2007)*

CASTELCOSA

Castelcosa 1997 Pinot Grigio (Venezia Giulia) $NA. 83 *(8/1/1999)*

CASTELGIOCONDO

Castelgiocondo 2001 Brunello (Brunello di Montalcino) $56. 89 *(4/1/2006)*

Castelgiocondo 1999 Brunello (Brunello di Montalcino) $NA. 90 *—M.S. (6/1/2004)*

Castelgiocondo 2000 Riserva Ripe al Convento Brunello (Brunello di Montalcino) $95. 94 *(4/1/2006)*

CASTELL'IN VILLA

Castell'In Villa 1998 Sangiovese (Chianti Classico) $30. 86 *(4/1/2005)*

Castell'In Villa 1998 Poggio Delle Rose Riserva Sangiovese (Chianti Classico) $75. 89 *(4/1/2005)*

Castell'In Villa 1996 Poggio delle Rose Riserva Sangiovese (Chianti Classico) $63. 87 *(4/1/2001)*

Castell'In Villa 1997 Riserva Sangiovese (Chianti Classico) $48. 88 *(4/1/2005)*

CASTELLANI

Castellani 2005 Pinot Grigio (Delle Venezie) $9. 84 *—M.L. (6/1/2006)*

Castellani 2005 Biagio Pinot Grigio (Venezie) $8. 84 *—M.L. (6/1/2006)*

Castellani 2000 Arbos Primitivo (Puglia) $10. 84 *—C.S. (5/1/2002)*

Castellani 2000 Essenza Primitivo (Puglia) $9. 85 Best Buy *—C.S. (5/1/2002)*

Castellani 2000 Red Blend (Monteregio di Massa Maritima) $17. 88 *—M.S. (10/1/2004)*

Castellani 2003 Sangiovese (Chianti) $7. 84 Best Buy *(4/1/2005)*

Castellani 1999 Sangiovese (Chianti) $7. 85 Best Buy *(4/1/2001)*

Castellani 1998 Sangiovese (Chianti Classico) $12. 87 Best Buy *(4/1/2001)*

Castellani 1997 Beni Duilio Castellani Riserva Sangiovese (Chianti Classico) $18. 90 *(4/1/2001)*

Castellani 2004 Biagio Sangiovese (Chianti) $8. 82 *—M.S. (10/1/2006)*

Castellani 2000 Biagio Sangiovese (Toscana) $11. 84 *—M.S. (10/1/2004)*

Castellani 1999 Biagio Sangiovese (Toscana) $11. 85 *—M.S. (12/31/2002)*

Castellani 2001 Biagio Riserva Sangiovese (Chianti) $12. 84 *—M.S. (10/1/2006)*

Castellani 2002 Biagio Sangiovese-Cabernet Sauvignon Sangiovese (Toscana) $12. 82 *—M.S. (9/1/2006)*

Castellani 1998 Riserva Sangiovese (Chianti Classico) $18. 84 *—M.S. (12/31/2002)*

Castellani 1997 Riserva Sangiovese (Chianti) $12. 83 *(4/1/2001)*

Castellani 1997 Villa Teseo Sangiovese (Toscana) $13. 87 Best Buy *(8/1/2002)*

CASTELLANI MICHELE & FIGLI

Castellani Michele & Figli 2003 I Castei Campo Casalin Corvina, Rondinella, Molinara (Amarone della Valpolicella Classico) $80. Celebrated for its excellent Recioto dessert wine, this quality-minded producer presents a big, brawny red with deep concentration, oversized wood notes, toasted nut, sizzling bacon fat and barbecue aromas. It's so modern, but also so lively, it definitely represents a departure from traditional Amarone. **90** *—M.L. (10/1/2007)*

CASTELLARE

Castellare 1999 Poggio ai Merli Merlot (Colli della Toscana Centrale) $89. 91 *—M.S. (8/1/2002)*

Castellare 2002 Sangiovese (Chianti Classico) $22. 84 *(4/1/2005)*

Castellare 1998 Sangiovese (Chianti Classico) $19. 85 *(4/1/2001)*

Castellare 2000 Il Poggiale Riserva Sangiovese (Chianti Classico) $36. 85 *(4/1/2005)*

Castellare 1996 Riserva Sangiovese (Chianti Classico) $26. 83 *(4/1/2001)*

CASTELLARE DI CASTELLINA

Castellare di Castellina 2002 Coniale Cabernet Sauvignon (Toscana) $50. 88 *—M.L. (9/1/2006)*

Castellare di Castellina 2004 Poggio ai Merli Merlot (Toscana) $65. You can tell you're in for a bruiser just by looking at it: Thick and extracted, the wine packs lush notes of cherry, cassis, spice, clove, white mushroom and lead pencil. It's expressive and intense in the mouth but those rock-hard tannins suggest that it should be consumed after 2009. **90** *—M.L. (3/1/2007)*

Castellare di Castellina 2004 Sangiovese (Chianti Classico) $18. Here's a Chianti that ups the ante in terms of aromatic intensity: The red berry, blue flower, humus and porcino mushroom are framed by cedar, clove and spice thanks to six months of wood aging: Nice spice flavors on the palate. **87** *—M.L. (2/1/2007)*

Castellare di Castellina 2003 Sangiovese (Chianti Classico) $23. Has mature notes of red fruit, exotic spice, blueberry comfiture and thick balsam notes and offers refreshing red fruit tones in the mouth and a very fine, dusty quality of tannin. **87** *—M.L. (11/1/2007)*

Castellare di Castellina 2002 I Sodi di San Niccolas Sangiovese (Toscana) $73. This is a blend of Sangioveto (85%) and Malvasia Nera that results in layered notes of cherry fruit, roasted coffee and black plum thanks to two years of oak aging. It's an attractive, silky wine with toasted overtones and very firm tannins. Drink now. **89** *—M.L. (5/1/2007)*

Castellare di Castellina 2003 Riserva Sangiovese (Chianti Classico) $25. This is a fruit-forward wine (95 percent Sangiovese with a small component of Canaiolo) with nice nuances of cherry and forest berry backed by white mushroom, an herbaceous or dill-like note at the back and a smoky note on the finish. In line with traditional Chianti Classico, it's an easy match to most foods. **86** *—M.L. (2/1/2007)*

Castellare di Castellina 2003 Vigna Il Poggiale Riserva Sangiovese (Chianti Classico) $35. Here's a vineyard-designate Chianti Classico with a pretty ruby red color and a wide offering of aromatic intensity: you'll get plums, dark berry, licorice and tar. The tannins are supple and smooth and create just enough structure to match grilled meats or sausages. **88** *—M.L. (2/1/2007)*

Castellare di Castellina 2000 San Niccolas Vin Santo White Blend (Vin Santo del Chianti Classico) $35. Malvasia and Trebbiano grapes are blended in this traditional Vin Santo from Tuscany that imparts rich and vibrant notes of almond, honey, apricot and vanilla. Oak tones emerge steadily and are rounded off by a slightly musky note: Great nutty flavors and long persistency in the mouth. **90** *—M.L. (5/1/2007)*

CASTELLARIN

Castellarin 2001 Cabernet Sauvignon (Delle Venezie) $10. 82 *(5/1/2003)*

Castellarin 2004 Pinot Grigio (Delle Venezie) $7. 86 Best Buy *—M.L. (6/1/2006)*

Castellarin 2001 Pinot Grigio (Delle Venezie) $8. 86 Best Buy *—J.C. (7/1/2003)*

Castellarin 1998 Pinot Grigio (Venezia Giulia) $8. 86 Best Buy *(8/1/1999)*

CASTELLO BANFI

Castello Banfi 1998 Excelsus Bordeaux Blend (Sant'Antimo) $73. 90 *—M.S. (8/1/2002)*

Castello Banfi 1994 Brunello (Brunello di Montalcino) $43. 88 *—M.S. (3/1/2000)*

Castello Banfi 2001 Brunello (Brunello di Montalcino) $68. 91 *(4/1/2006)*

Castello Banfi 2000 Brunello (Brunello di Montalcino) $68. 90 *—M.S. (7/1/2005)*

Castello Banfi 1999 Brunello (Brunello di Montalcino) $66. 91 *—M.S. (6/1/2004)*

Castello Banfi 1998 Brunello (Brunello di Montalcino) $59. 89 *(11/15/2003)*

Castello Banfi 1997 Brunello (Brunello di Montalcino) $59. 92 *—R.V. (8/1/2002)*

Castello Banfi 1995 Brunello (Brunello di Montalcino) $54. 92 Cellar Selection *(2/1/2001)*

Castello Banfi 1997 Poggio all'Oro Riserva Brunello (Brunello di Montalcino) $125. 93 Cellar Selection *—M.S. (11/15/2003)*

Castello Banfi 1993 Poggio all'Oro Riserva Brunello (Brunello di Montalcino) $125. 92 *—J.C. (3/1/2000)*

Castello Banfi 1999 Poggio All'Oro Riserva Brunello (Brunello di Montalcino) $150. 94 Cellar Selection *—M.S. (7/1/2005)*

Castello Banfi 1999 Poggio alla Mura Brunello (Brunello di Montalcino) $75. 93 *—M.S. (6/1/2004)*

Castello Banfi 2001 Poggio Alle Mura Brunello (Brunello di Montalcino) $75. 91 *(4/1/2006)*

Castello Banfi 2000 Poggio Alle Mura Brunello (Brunello di Montalcino) $75. 92 *—M.S. (7/1/2005)*

Castello Banfi 1998 Poggio Alle Mura Brunello (Brunello di Montalcino) $70. 89 *—M.S. (11/15/2003)*

Castello Banfi 2000 Tavernelle Cabernet Sauvignon (Sant'Antimo) $41. 88 *—M.S. (11/15/2003)*

Castello Banfi 1998 Tavernelle Cabernet Sauvignon (Sant'Antimo) $41. 89 *—M.S. (8/1/2002)*

Castello Banfi 1996 Tavernelle Cabernet Sauvignon (Montalcino) $38. 87 *—M.S. (7/1/2000)*

Castello Banfi 2001 Excelsus Cabernet Blend (Sant'Antimo) $78. Cabernet Sauvignon's green pepper aromas do arise but are delicately reigned in by the soft, yielding and plush Merlot component, which adds cherry, blackberry, spice cake and nutmeg. But what really makes this a standout wine is the texture: creamy and concentrated with solid tannins and loads of cherry flavors. **92** *—M.L. (2/1/2007)*

Castello Banfi 2000 Excelsus Cabernet Sauvignon-Merlot (Sant'Antimo) $78. 87 *—M.S. (9/1/2006)*

Castello Banfi 1999 Excelsus Cabernet Sauvignon-Merlot (Sant'Antimo) $73. 92 *—M.S. (11/15/2003)*

Castello Banfi 1997 Excelsus Cabernet Sauvignon-Merlot (Montalcino) $73. 89 *(2/1/2001)*

Castello Banfi 1995 Excelsus Cabernet Sauvignon-Merlot (Toscana) $50. 93 *—M.S. (3/1/2000)*

Castello Banfi 2002 Fontanelle Chardonnay (Montalcino) $19. 85 *—M.S. (10/1/2004)*

Castello Banfi 2003 Mandrielle Merlot (Sant'Antimo) $35. Twelve months of aging in French oak help shape inviting aromas of red berry, sweet spice bread, slate roof and forest floor. The toasted tones are pronounced and add to this Merlot's overall richness and flavor. An easy match to most meat dishes. **89** *—M.L. (4/1/2007)*

Castello Banfi 2002 Mandrielle Merlot (Sant'Antimo) $35. 85 *—M.S. (9/1/2006)*

Castello Banfi 1999 Mandrielle Merlot (Sant'Antimo) $35. 86 *—M.S. (11/15/2003)*

Castello Banfi 2005 San Angelo Pinot Grigio (Toscana) $18. 87 *—M.L. (6/1/2006)*

Castello Banfi 2004 San Angelo Pinot Grigio (Toscana) $18. 87 *—M.L. (6/1/2006)*

Castello Banfi 2004 San Angelo Pinot Grigio (Toscana) $18. 84 *(2/1/2006)*

Castello Banfi 1999 San Angelo Pinot Grigio (Toscana) $13. 88 Best Buy *(2/1/2001)*

Castello Banfi 2004 Centine Red Blend (Toscana) $11. Fresh, clean and approachable, this wine offers simple linearity in terms of structure and concentration but holds its own in terms of aromas. Buried within are notes of ripe cherry, forest floor and white mushroom. **87 Best Buy** *—M.L. (2/1/2007)*

Castello Banfi 2003 Centine Red Blend (Tuscany) $NA. 87 Best Buy *—M.L. (11/15/2005)*

Castello Banfi 2001 Summus Red Blend (Sant'Antimo) $66. 90 *—M.S. (9/1/2006)*

Castello Banfi 2006 Centine Rosé Rosé Blend (Toscana) $12. Here's a rosato from Tuscany that is vibrant and clean and richly redolent of forest fruit, red berry, dried sage and minerals. In fact, the herbal quality is unique and impressive. It's clean and fresh in the mouth with medium persistency. **87 Best Buy** *—M.L. (7/1/2007)*

Castello Banfi 1998 Sangiovese (Rosso di Montalcino) $22. 89 *(2/1/2001)*

Castello Banfi 2000 Cum Laude Sangiovese (Sant'Antimo) $36. 86 *—M.S. (11/15/2003)*

Castello Banfi 1999 Cum Laude Sangiovese (Sant'Antimo) $35. 87 *—M.S. (8/1/2002)*

Castello Banfi 2002 Riserva Sangiovese (Chianti Classico) $18. A nice, soft Riserva from a difficult vintage that exhibits resin notes, pine nut, some mineral intensity, cherry flavors and dusty tannins. You'll get a chalky, velvety feel in the mouth. **87** *—M.L. (2/1/2007)*

Castello Banfi 2000 Summus Red Blend (Montalcino) $63. 87 *—M.S. (10/1/2004)*

Castello Banfi 1999 Summus Red Blend (Sant'Antimo) $63. 94 Editors' Choice *—M.S. (11/15/2003)*

Castello Banfi 1997 Summus Red Blend (Sant'Antimo) $63. 91 *(2/1/2001)*

Castello Banfi 1998 Colvecchio Syrah (Sant'Antimo) $36. 86 *—M.S. (8/1/2002)*

Castello Banfi 1997 Colvecchio Single Vyd Syrah (Sant'Antimo) $35. 88 *(11/1/2001)*

CASTELLO D'ALBOLA

Castello d'Albola 2002 Sangiovese (Chianti Classico) $15. 84 *(4/1/2005)*

Castello d'Albola 2000 Sangiovese (Chianti Classico) $14. 86 *(3/1/2004)*

Castello d'Albola 1998 Sangiovese (Chianti Classico) $15. 87 *(4/1/2001)*

Castello d'Albola 2000 Acciaiolo Sangiovese (Toscana) $50. 90 *(3/1/2004)*

Castello d'Albola 1997 Acciaiolo Sangiovese (Chianti Classico) $40. 87 *(9/1/2001)*

Castello d'Albola 1995 Acciaiolo Sangiovese (Toscana) $44. 92 *—M.S. (3/1/2000)*

Castello d'Albola 1993 Acciaiolo Sangiovese (Toscana) $33. 92 *—M.G. (5/1/1999)*

Castello d'Albola 1999 Le Ellere Sangiovese (Chianti Classico) $20. 88 *(12/31/2002)*

Castello d'Albola 2000 Riserva Sangiovese (Chianti Classico) $25. 86 *(4/1/2005)*

Castello d'Albola 1999 Riserva Sangiovese (Chianti Classico) $23. 91 Editors' Choice *(3/1/2004)*

Castello d'Albola 1996 Trebbiano-Malvasia (Vin Santo del Chianti Classico) $62. 90 *—M.L. (10/1/2006)*

Castello d'Albola 1992 Trebbiano-Malvasia (Vin Santo del Chianti Classico) $50. 91 *(3/1/2004)*

CASTELLO DE CAMIGLIANO

Castello de Camigliano 1999 Brunello (Brunello di Montalcino) $58. 94 *—M.S. (6/1/2004)*

CASTELLO DEI RAMPOLLA

Castello dei Rampolla 2000 Sangiovese (Chianti Classico) $29. 86 *(4/1/2005)*

Castello dei Rampolla 1998 Sangiovese (Chianti Classico) $26. 86 *(4/1/2001)*

Castello dei Rampolla 1997 Riserva Sangiovese (Chianti Classico) $43. 88 *(4/1/2001)*

Castello dei Rampolla 2000 Sammarco Sangiovese (Toscana) $116. 89 *—M.S. (9/1/2006)*

CASTELLO DEL POGGIO

Castello del Poggio 2003 Barbera (Barbera d'Asti) $13. The Poggio is a friendly wine with plenty of superripe blackberry fruit, a big, thick almost chunky structure that finishes with a burst of fruit. No great subtlety, but immensely likeable. **88** *—M.G. (4/1/2007)*

Castello del Poggio 2000 Barbera (Barbera d'Asti) $13. 87 *(12/31/2002)*

Castello del Poggio NV Brachetto (Piedmont) $18. 85 *—M.L. (11/15/2006)*

Castello del Poggio 2003 Dolcetto (Dolcetto di Monferrato) $12. 89 Best Buy *—J.C. (3/1/2006)*

Castello del Poggio NV Moscato (Asti) $12. 84 *—J.C. (12/15/2004)*

Castello del Poggio 2004 Moscato (Moscato d'Asti) $12. 87 Best Buy *—M.L. (12/15/2005)*

Castello del Poggio NV Dolce Moscato (Asti) $15. 84 *—M.L. (11/15/2006)*

Castello del Poggio NV Brachetto Sparkling Blend (Piedmont) $12. 83 *—J.C. (12/15/2004)*

CASTELLO DEL TERRICCIO

Castello del Terriccio 2003 Lupicaia Cabernet Sauvignon (Toscana) $134. 92 *—M.L. (9/1/2006)*

Castello del Terriccio 2001 Lupicaia Cabernet Sauvignon (Toscana) $140. 93 *—M.L. (9/1/2006)*

Castello del Terriccio 1998 Lupicaia Cabernet Sauvignon (Toscana) $90. 93 *—M.S. (8/1/2002)*

Castello del Terriccio 2005 Rondinaia Chardonnay (Toscana) $30. Here's a fresh straw-colored Chardonnay (that only sees stainless steel) with vibrant tones of stone fruit, yellow flower, melon, peach and drying minerals. Lean and crisp on the palate, it closes with nice spice and a touch of lemon zest. **88** *—M.L. (5/1/2007)*

Castello del Terriccio 2003 Castello del Terriccio Red Blend (Toscana) $118. A nice performance from Tuscany, this extracted and rich wine (made from a blend of mostly Syrah and Petit Verdot) boasts penetrating aromas of herbs, roasted nut, spice and clove. Red fruit is in there, too, but in smaller doses. It's a big, brawny wine with drying tannins and a robust constitution. **90** *—M.L. (5/1/2007)*

Castello del Terriccio 2001 Castello del Terriccio Red Blend (Toscana) $118. You may pick up slightly musty notes but they happily add to the wine's complexity. Espresso bean, blackberry, resin, toast and balsamic vinegar come to mind and the wine delivers power in the mouth boosted by nicely etched tannins. **91** *—M.L. (4/1/2007)*

Castello del Terriccio 2002 Tassinaia Red Blend (Toscana) $43. 91 *—M.L. (11/15/2006)*

Castello del Terriccio 2001 Tassinaia Red Blend (Toscana) $45. 92 Editors' Choice *—M.S. (9/1/2006)*

Castello del Terriccio 1999 Tassinaia Red Blend (Toscana) $35. 90 *—M.S. (10/1/2004)*

Castello del Terriccio 2000 Rondinaia Sangiovese (Toscana) $18. 91 *—M.S. (8/1/2002)*

Castello del Terriccio 1998 Tassinaia Red Blend (Toscana) $55. 92 *—M.S. (8/1/2002)*

Castello del Terriccio 2005 Con Vento Sauvignon Blanc (Toscana) $32. Stainless steel fermentation and refining helps shape clean and fresh aromas of exotic fruit, lime, kiwi, chopped sage and white stone. It is lean but incredibly clean and crisp on the palate and is exactly the kind of wine you want in ample supply during summer months. **85** *—M.L. (5/1/2007)*

Castello del Terriccio 2003 Con Vento Sauvignon Blanc (Toscana) $36. 83 *(7/1/2005)*

CASTELLO DELLA PANERETTA

Castello della Paneretta 2005 Sangiovese (Chianti Classico) $26. Clean and elegant, with deeply etched mineral notes that add a dry, linear quality to abundant cherry and forest berry aromas. This is vibrant wine with red fruit flavors, chewy tannins and good length. **89** *—M.L. (11/1/2007)*

CASTELLO DI AMA

Castello di Ama 1997 Al Poggio Chardonnay (Toscana) $27. 88 *—J.C. (11/15/1999)*

Castello di Ama 2001 L'Apparita Merlot (Toscana) $150. Gorgeous, elegant, deeply layered and full of nuances, this delivers cherry candy, espresso and toasted notes with a refined herbal edge. Tones of rosemary, sage and thyme are weaved in with a careful touch and appear only in the background as a delicious afterthought. Dusty tannins and a firm consistency mean this wine will age well for years to come. **93 Cellar Selection** *—M.L. (4/1/2007)*

Castello di Ama 1995 L' Apparita Merlot (Toscana) $150. 93 *—J.C. (11/15/1999)*

Castello di Ama 2000 Sangiovese (Chianti Classico) $38. 90 Editors' Choice *(4/1/2005)*

Castello di Ama 1998 Sangiovese (Chianti Classico) $42. 87 *(4/1/2001)*

Castello di Ama 1997 Sangiovese (Chianti Classico) $39. 90 *—J.C. (11/15/1999)*

Castello di Ama 1995 Cru Bellavista Sangiovese (Chianti Classico) $150. 93 *—J.C. (11/15/1999)*

Castello di Ama 1995 Cru La Casuccia Sangiovese (Chianti Classico) $150. 91 *—J.C. (11/15/1999)*

Castello di Ama 1995 Il Chiuso Pinot Nero Sangiovese (Toscana) $47. 87 *—J.C. (11/15/1999)*

Castello di Ama 1998 Rosato Sangiovese (Toscana) $16. 87 *—J.C. (11/15/1999)*

CASTELLO DI BOLGHERI

Castello di Bolgheri 2001 Superiore Sangiovese (Bolgheri) $79. 86 *—M.S. (10/1/2004)*

CASTELLO DI BOSSI

Castello di Bossi 2000 Girolamo Merlot (Toscana) $50. 89 *—M.S. (9/1/2006)*

Castello di Bossi 2001 Sangiovese (Chianti Classico) $25. 88 *(4/1/2005)*

Castello di Bossi 2000 Berardo Riserva Sangiovese (Chianti Classico) $38. 91 Editors' Choice *(4/1/2005)*

Castello di Bossi 2000 Corbaia Sangiovese (Toscana) $50. 91 *—M.S. (9/1/2006)*

CASTELLO DI BROLIO

Castello di Brolio 1999 Sangiovese (Chianti Classico) $16. 88 *—M.S. (12/31/2002)*

Castello di Brolio 1998 Sangiovese (Chianti Classico) $50. 90 *—M.S. (12/31/2002)*

Castello di Brolio 1997 Sangiovese (Chianti Classico) $17. 85 *(4/1/2001)*

Castello di Brolio 1997 Sangiovese (Chianti Classico) $40. 89 *(4/1/2001)*

CASTELLO DI CACCHIANO

Castello di Cacchiano 1998 Sangiovese (Chianti Classico) $21. 88 *(4/1/2001)*

CASTELLO DI FARNETELLA

Castello di Farnetella 2002 Sangiovese (Chianti Colli Senesi) $14. 88 *(4/1/2005)*

CASTELLO DI FONTERUTOLI

Castello di Fonterutoli 2001 Sangiovese (Chianti Classico) $26. 91 *—M.S. (10/1/2004)*

Castello di Fonterutoli 2004 Fonterutoli Sangiovese (Chianti Classico) $25. Thanks to careful Sangiovese clone selection and expert winemaking, this is a generous, full wine with layered aromas of berry, bramble, red cherry and blue flower. Smooth and silky, the fresh berry flavors on the finish leave a lasting impression. 89*—M.L. (11/1/2007)*

Castello di Fonterutoli 1998 Riserva Sangiovese (Chianti Classico) 91 Cellar Selection *—R.V. (8/1/2002)*

Castello di Fonterutoli 1997 Riserva Sangiovese (Chianti Classico) $49. 90 *(4/1/2001)*

CASTELLO DI GABBIANO

Castello di Gabbiano 2004 Pinot Grigio (Delle Venezie) $10. 84 *(2/1/2006)*

Castello di Gabbiano 1997 Sangiovese (Chianti Classico) $13. 84 *—M.S. (3/1/2000)*

Castello di Gabbiano 2003 Sangiovese (Chianti) $10. 84 *(4/1/2005)*

Castello di Gabbiano 2001 Sangiovese (Chianti) $14. 86 *—M.S. (11/15/2003)*

Castello di Gabbiano 2000 Sangiovese (Chianti) $10. 85 *—M.S. (11/15/2003)*

Castello di Gabbiano 2000 Sangiovese (Chianti Classico) $12. 85 *—S.H. (1/1/2002)*

Castello di Gabbiano 1999 Sangiovese (Chianti Classico) $12. 86 *—S.H. (9/1/2002)*

Castello di Gabbiano 1999 Alleanza Sangiovese (Toscana) $35. 85 *—M.S. (10/1/2004)*

Castello di Gabbiano 1997 Alleanza Sangiovese (Toscana) $40. 88 *—M.S. (11/15/2003)*

Castello di Gabbiano 1999 Bellezza Sangiovese (Toscana) $30. 86 *—M.S. (10/1/2004)*

Castello di Gabbiano 1997 Bellezza Sangiovese (Toscana) $35. 85 *—M.S. (11/15/2003)*

Castello di Gabbiano 1999 Riserva Sangiovese (Chianti Classico) $17. 90 *—S.H. (12/31/2002)*

Castello di Gabbiano 1997 Riserva Sangiovese (Chianti Classico) $16. 87 *(4/1/2001)*

Castello di Gabbiano 1995 Riserva Sangiovese (Chianti Classico) $16. 86 *—M.S. (3/1/2000)*

Castello di Gabbiano 2000 Bellezza Sangiovese Grosso (Toscana) $30. 86 *—M.S. (9/1/2006)*

CASTELLO DI LISPIDA

Castello di Lispida 1999 Terraforte Red Blend (Veneto) $40. 89 *(5/1/2003)*

CASTELLO DI MELETO

Castello di Meleto 2001 Sangiovese (Chianti Classico) $21. 87 *(4/1/2005)*

Castello di Meleto 2000 Sangiovese (Chianti Classico) $20. 88 *—M.S. (11/15/2003)*

Castello di Meleto 1999 Sangiovese (Chianti Classico) $17. 83 *—M.S. (12/31/2002)*

Castello di Meleto 1998 Sangiovese (Chianti Classico) $23. 89 *(4/1/2001)*

Castello di Meleto 1998 Fiore Sangiovese (Toscana) $36. 88 *—M.S. (12/31/2002)*

Castello di Meleto 2001 Rainero Sangiovese (Toscana) $39. 87 *—M.S. (9/1/2006)*

Castello di Meleto 1997 Riserva Sangiovese (Chianti Classico) $36. 90 *(4/1/2001)*

Castello di Meleto 1999 Vigna Casi Riserva Sangiovese (Chianti Classico) $34. 85 *—M.S. (10/1/2004)*

CASTELLO DI MONASTERO

Castello di Monastero 2001 Sangiovese (Chianti Classico) $17. 89 *(4/1/2005)*

Castello di Monastero 1998 Sangiovese (Chianti Classico) $16. 89 *(4/1/2001)*

Castello di Monastero 2001 Montetondo Sangiovese (Chianti Superiore) $15. 88 *(4/1/2005)*

Castello di Monastero 1998 Montetondo Sangiovese (Chianti Superiore) $13. 88 *(4/1/2001)*

Castello di Monastero 1999 Riserva Sangiovese (Chianti Classico) $30. 90 *(4/1/2005)*

Castello di Monastero 1996 Riserva Sangiovese (Chianti Classico) $24. 88 *(4/1/2001)*

CASTELLO DI MONSANTO

Castello di Monsanto 2003 Nemo Cabernet Sauvignon (Toscana) $35. A big, bold Cabernet executed in a modern, New World style, this wine layers on generous amounts of cherry fruit, toasted wood, vanilla and black berry. The oak element is anything but understated, yet it does not distract from the fruit. Let it rest two or three years in your cellar. 88 *—M.L. (2/1/2007)*

Castello di Monsanto 2001 Nemo Cabernet Sauvignon (Toscana) $50. 90 *—M.L. (9/1/2006)*

Castello di Monsanto 1999 Nemo Cabernet Sauvignon (Tuscany) $44. 87 *—M.S. (12/31/2002)*

Castello di Monsanto 1998 Nemo Cabernet Sauvignon (Toscana) $38. 87 *—M.S. (8/1/2002)*

Castello di Monsanto 2004 Fabrizio Bianchi Chardonnay (Toscana) $20. This light, straw-colored Chard offers rich notes of stone fruit, honey, vanilla and toasted oak. It is half oak and half steel fermented for structure and freshness. Thanks to its easy-going, approachable style, creamy texture and crisp acidity, this wine would pair wonderfully with pasta, fish and vegetables. 87 *—M.L. (5/1/2007)*

Castello di Monsanto 2003 Fabrizio Bianchi Collection Chardonnay (Toscana) $22. 87 *—M.L. (10/1/2006)*

Castello di Monsanto 2002 Chianti Classico Riserva Red Blend (Chianti Classico) $20. From a difficult vintage, this Riserva successfully brings forward red cherry, porcino mushroom, and mineral notes. The ensemble lacks overall intensity but that's absolutely fine for an approachable wine like that that could back pork or roast turkey. 86 *—M.L. (2/1/2007)*

Castello di Monsanto 2005 Monrosso Red Blend (Chianti) $10. 85 Best Buy *—M.L. (11/15/2006)*

Castello di Monsanto 2003 Riserva Red Blend (Chianti Classico) $20. What works nicely here are the cherry, forest berry, charcoal, black licorice and plum aromas. You'll get candied cherry flavors in the mouth and dusty tannins although the wine lacks that extra dimension to boost it up to the excellent category. 87 *—M.L. (5/1/2007)*

Castello di Monsanto 2005 Sangiovese (Chianti Classico) $24. The style here is light and lean with subtle but distinct aromas of berry fruit, blue flowers, exotic spice and cedar wood. In the mouth, this is a medium-bodied wine with fine, tight texture and noticeable freshness on the finish. 86 —*M.L. (11/1/2007)*

Castello di Monsanto 2002 Alaura Sangiovese (Chianti) $11. 89 Best Buy *(4/1/2005)*

Castello di Monsanto 1995 Chianti Classico Riserva Sangiovese (Chianti Classico) $22. 86 —*M.S. (11/15/1999)*

Castello di Monsanto 2001 Fabrizio Bianchi Sangiovese (Toscana) $35. 90 —*M.L. (11/15/2006)*

Castello di Monsanto 1999 Fabrizio Bianchi Sangiovese (Tuscany) $39. 92 Editors' Choice —*M.S. (12/31/2002)*

Castello di Monsanto 2003 Il Poggio Riserva Sangiovese (Chianti Classico) $35. Here's a wine that showcases a nice evolution: Initial fruit aromas give way to toasted wood, vanilla and bramble. Overall, it shows a clean, linear quality, although it does end strong with oak notes; astringent but very persistent on the finish. 90 —*M.L. (5/1/2007)*

Castello di Monsanto 2001 Il Poggio Riserva Sangiovese (Chianti Classico) $40. Deep and layered with some barnyard or Band-Aid that doesn't distract from a solid core of ripe cherry, red fruit, coffee, toast and vanilla bean. I liked the toasted notes that add dimension and softness. This is a wine that would pair well with braised lamb. 90 —*M.L. (2/1/2007)*

Castello di Monsanto 1995 Il Poggio Chianti Classico Sangiovese (Chianti Classico) $45. 88 —*M.S. (11/15/1999)*

Castello di Monsanto 1999 Il Poggio Riserva Sangiovese (Chianti Classico) $55. 92 —*M.S. (12/31/2002)*

Castello di Monsanto 1997 Il Poggio Riserva Sangiovese (Chianti Classico) $44. 87 *(4/1/2001)*

Castello di Monsanto 2004 Riserva Sangiovese (Chianti Classico) $24. A generous and modern wine with plush aromas of sweet vanilla, black cherry, ripe blueberry, spice and a healthy wallop of chocolate fudge that proves to be a true crowd pleaser. Beautiful in the glass, with brilliant ruby reflections, the wine is silky-smooth in the mouth with bright berries flavors that ride over a long, soft finish. 90 —*M.L. (11/1/2007)*

Castello di Monsanto 2000 Riserva Sangiovese (Chianti Classico) $22. 86 —*M.S. (10/1/2004)*

Castello di Monsanto 1999 Riserva Sangiovese (Chianti Classico) $23. 90 —*M.S. (12/31/2002)*

Castello di Monsanto 1998 Riserva Sangiovese (Chianti Classico) $23. 87 —*M.S. (8/1/2002)*

Castello di Monsanto 1997 Riserva Sangiovese (Chianti Classico) $22. 86 *(4/1/2001)*

Castello di Monsanto 1999 Tinscvil Sangiovese (Toscana) $35. 91 —*M.S. (8/1/2002)*

Castello di Monsanto 1997 Tinscvil Sangiovese (Toscana) $34. 87 *(9/1/2001)*

Castello di Monsanto 1998 Il Poggio Riserva Sangiovese Grosso (Chianti Classico) $50. 88 —*M.S. (8/1/2002)*

CASTELLO DI MONTEPÒ

Castello di Montepò 1997 Montepaone Cabernet Sauvignon (Toscana) $45. 89 —*M.S. (8/1/2002)*

Castello di Montepò 1998 Schidione Sangiovese (Toscana) $125. 93 *(11/15/2003)*

CASTELLO DI NEIVE

Castello di Neive 2000 Mattarello Barbera (Barbera d'Alba) $18. 90 Editors' Choice —*J.C. (3/1/2006)*

Castello di Neive 1998 Basarin Dolcetto (Dolcetto d'Alba) $12. 91 Best Buy *(4/1/2000)*

Castello di Neive 1998 Messoirano Dolcetto (Dolcetto d'Alba) $12. 89 Best Buy *(4/1/2000)*

Castello di Neive 2005 Moscato (Moscato d'Asti) $16. 85 —*M.L. (12/15/2006)*

Castello di Neive 2001 Santo Stefano Nebbiolo (Barbaresco) $40. 88 —*J.C. (3/1/2006)*

Castello di Neive 2000 Santo Stefano Nebbiolo (Barbaresco) $38. 90 Editors' Choice —*J.C. (3/1/2006)*

Castello di Neive 2002 Metodo Classico Pinot Nero (Piedmont) $37. 88 —*M.L. (12/15/2006)*

Castello di Neive 2001 Metodo Classico Pinot Nero (Piedmont) $37. 88 —*M.L. (12/15/2006)*

CASTELLO DI POPPIANO

Castello di Poppiano 1998 Riserva Red Blend (Chianti Colli Fiorentini) $18. 87 —*M.S. (12/31/2002)*

Castello di Poppiano 2004 Il Cortile Sangiovese (Chianti Colli Fiorentini) $15. This is an attractively priced wine with defined notes of sweet chocolate, cinnamon biscuit, cherry fruit and spice. Measured oak tones are balanced well against bright fruit to create a soft, plush mouthfeel. 87 —*M.L. (11/1/2007)*

Castello di Poppiano 2003 Il Cortile Sangiovese (Chianti Colli Fiorentini) $14. 86 *(4/1/2005)*

Castello di Poppiano 2001 Il Cortile Sangiovese (Chianti Colli Fiorentini) $12. 87 Best Buy —*M.S. (10/1/2004)*

Castello di Poppiano 2000 Riserva Sangiovese (Chianti Colli Fiorentini) $22. 90 Editors' Choice *(4/1/2005)*

Castello di Poppiano 2003 Riserva Conte Ferdinando Guicciardini Sangiovese (Chianti Colli Fiorentini) $23. Colli Fiorentini is considered the lesser of the Chianti subzones, but the overall quality of this wine shows the enormous potential of the area. This is chewy and succulent with mature red fruit and spice over firm, dusty tannins. 89 —*M.L. (11/1/2007)*

Castello di Poppiano 2000 Tosco Forte Sangiovese (Colli della Toscana Centrale) $18. 84 —*M.S. (12/31/2002)*

Castello di Poppiano 2000 Tricorno Sangiovese (Colli della Toscana Centrale) $50. 92 —*M.S. (11/15/2004)*

Castello di Poppiano 1999 Tricorno Sangiovese (Colli della Toscana Centrale) $35. 92 Editors' Choice —*M.S. (11/15/2003)*

Castello di Poppiano 1998 Tricorno Sangiovese (Colli della Toscana Centrale) $35. 86 —*M.S. (12/31/2002)*

Castello di Poppiano 2000 Conte Ferdinando Guicciardini Syrah (Colli della Toscana Centrale) $19. 81 —*M.S. (12/31/2002)*

Castello di Poppiano 2005 Camposegreto Viognier (Toscana) $15. Floral and stone fruit aromas offer a pretty prelude to this luminous, fresh white wine. Yet the mouthfeel is lean and thin and offers good but not great persistency. It would be nice to see more Viognier from Italy. 83 —*M.L. (5/1/2007)*

CASTELLO DI QUERCETO

Castello di Querceto 2003 Cignale Cabernet Sauvignon (Colli della Toscana Centrale) $68. 91 —*M.L. (9/1/2006)*

Castello di Querceto 2001 Cignale Cabernet Sauvignon-Merlot (Colli della Toscana Centrale) $69. 93 —*M.L. (9/1/2006)*

Castello di Querceto 2005 Sangiovese (Chianti Classico) $NA. A wine with nicely measured aromas of blueberry, cherry, almonds and dusty chalk. It's easy-going, with a great pairing potential with most foods. 86 —*M.L. (11/1/2007)*

Castello di Querceto 1999 Il Picchio Riserva Sangiovese (Chianti Classico) $33. 88 *(4/1/2005)*

CASTELLO DI SPESSA

Castello di Spessa 1997 Pinot Grigio (Collio) $20. 86 *(11/1/1999)*

Castello di Spessa 1997 Tocai (Collio) $22. 87 *(11/1/1999)*

CASTELLO DI TASSAROLO

Castello di Tassarolo 2001 S Cortese (Gavi) $18. 82 —*M.S. (12/15/2003)*

Castello di Tassarolo 2005 Tassarolo S. Cortese (Cortese di Gavi) $13. 86 Best Buy —*M.L. (11/15/2006)*

Castello di Tassarolo 2002 Villa Rosa Cortese (Gavi) $17. 84 —*M.S. (12/15/2003)*

CASTELLO DI VALIANO

Castello di Valiano 1999 Sangiovese (Chianti Classico) $15. 88 Best Buy —*M.M. (11/15/2001)*

Castello di Valiano 1998 Poggio Teo Riserva Sangiovese (Chianti Classico) $24. 91 Editors' Choice *(11/15/2001)*

Castello di Valiano 1998 Riserva Sangiovese (Chianti Classico) $24. 90 *(11/15/2001)*

CASTELLO DI VERRAZZANO

Castello di Verrazzano 1998 Sangiovese (Chianti Classico) $21. 85 *(4/1/2001)*

Castello di Verrazzano 1999 Riserva Sangiovese (Chianti Classico) $40. 84 *(4/1/2005)*

Castello di Verrazzano 1997 Riserva Sangiovese (Chianti Classico) $38. 87 *(4/1/2001)*

Castello di Verrazzano 2000 Sassello Sangiovese (Toscana) $60. 89 —*M.S. (9/1/2006)*

CASTELLO DI VOLPAIA

Castello di Volpaia 1995 Sangiovese (Chianti Classico) $15. 88 —*M.M. (5/1/1999)*

Castello di Volpaia 2002 Sangiovese (Chianti Classico) $17. 87 *(4/1/2005)*

Castello di Volpaia 2000 Sangiovese (Chianti Classico) $19. 90 Editors' Choice —*M.S. (11/15/2003)*

Castello di Volpaia 1999 Balifico Sangiovese (Toscana) $46. 91 —*M.S. (11/15/2003)*

Castello di Volpaia 1995 Balifico Sangiovese (Toscana) $40. 90 *(2/1/2000)*

Castello di Volpaia 2002 Borgianni Sangiovese (Chianti) $10. 82 *(4/1/2005)*

Castello di Volpaia 2001 Borgianni Sangiovese (Chianti) $10. 88 Best Buy —*M.S. (11/15/2003)*

Castello di Volpaia 1997 Classico Sangiovese (Toscana) $17. 87 *(2/1/2000)*

Castello di Volpaia 1996 Classico Sangiovese (Toscana) $17. 84 *(2/1/2000)*

Castello di Volpaia 1995 Classico Riserva Sangiovese (Toscana) $24. 88 *(2/1/2000)*

Castello di Volpaia 1995 Coltassala Sangiovese (Toscana) $40. 91 *(2/1/2000)*

Castello di Volpaia 2000 Coltassala Riserva Sangiovese (Chianti Classico) $36. 87 *(4/1/2005)*

Castello di Volpaia 1999 Coltassala Riserva Sangiovese (Chianti Classico) $46. 91 —*M.S. (11/15/2003)*

Castello di Volpaia 2000 Riserva Sangiovese (Chianti Classico) $26. 90 *(4/1/2005)*

Castello di Volpaia 1999 Riserva Sangiovese (Chianti Classico) $29. 89 —*M.S. (11/15/2003)*

Castello di Volpaia 1996 Riserva Sangiovese (Chianti Classico) $26. 89 *(4/1/2001)*

CASTELLO MONTAÚTO

Castello Montaúto 2004 Vernaccia (Vernaccia di San Gimignano) $13. 85 —*M.S. (10/1/2006)*

Castello Montaúto 2003 Vernaccia (Vernaccia di San Gimignano) $13. 87 —*M.S. (8/1/2004)*

CASTELLO MONTE VIBIANO VECCHIO

Castello Monte Vibiano Vecchio 2003 L'Andrea Red Blend (Colli Perugini Rosso) $45. A blend of Sangiovese, Sagrantino, Merlot, Cabernet Sauvignon and Syrah, this is a wine that imparts great intensity and a wide range of aromas including red fruit, dried mint leaf, root beer and white truffle. It boasts a beautiful color, firm tannins and smoky flavors in the mouth. **91** —*M.L. (12/1/2007)*

Castello Monte Vibiano Vecchio 2003 MonVí Red Blend (Colli Perugini Rosso) $19. Here's a less austere but fruity Sangiovese-Merlot-Cab Sauvignon blend that is redolent of forest berries, wild cherry and strawberry preserves. It's not a wine of huge complexity, but it is a fantastically easy-to-drink wine especially with pasta, meats and cheeses. **87** —*M.L. (12/1/2007)*

CASTELLO ROMITORIO

Castello Romitorio 2001 Brunello (Brunello di Montalcino) $55. 92 *(4/1/2006)*

Castello Romitorio 2000 Brunello (Brunello di Montalcino) $50. 91 —*M.S. (7/1/2005)*

Castello Romitorio 1999 Brunello (Brunello di Montalcino) $59. 94 —*M.S. (6/1/2004)*

Castello Romitorio 1997 Brunello (Brunello di Montalcino) $55. 92 —*R.V. (8/1/2002)*

Castello Romitorio 1999 Riserva Brunello (Brunello di Montalcino) $65. 93 —*M.S. (7/1/2005)*

Castello Romitorio 2002 Sangiovese (Rosso di Montalcino) $23. 89 —*M.S. (6/1/2004)*

Castello Romitorio 1998 Sangiovese (Chianti Colli Senesi) $10. 88 Best Buy *(4/1/2001)*

CASTELLO VICCHIOMAGGIO

Castello Vicchiomaggio 2001 La Prima Riserva Sangiovese (Chianti Classico) $39. 87 *(4/1/2005)*

Castello Vicchiomaggio 2001 Ripa Delle More Sangiovese (Toscana) $44. 91 —*M.S. (9/1/2006)*

Castello Vicchiomaggio 1998 Riserva La Prima Sangiovese (Chianti Classico) $25. 92 Editors' Choice —*R.V. (12/31/2002)*

Castello Vicchiomaggio 2001 Riserva Petri Sangiovese (Chianti Classico) $30. 91 Editors' Choice *(4/1/2005)*

Castello Vicchiomaggio 1998 Riserva Petri Sangiovese (Chianti Classico) $24. 90 —*R.V. (12/31/2002)*

CASTELVERO

Castelvero 1996 Barbera (Barbera d'Asti) $12. 87 Best Buy *(4/1/2000)*

Castelvero 2003 Barbera (Piedmont) $9. 87 Best Buy —*J.C. (11/15/2004)*

Castelvero 2001 Barbera (Piedmont) $10. 80 —*M.S. (12/15/2003)*

Castelvero 1998 Barbera (Barbera di Piemonte) $8. 88 Best Buy *(4/1/2000)*

Castelvero 2006 Cortese (Piedmont) $10. This light-colored Cortese is an easy-going white that manages to be both very light and quite complex. The aromas of roasted peaches and apricots is lovely but low in intensity. The same can be said for the palate; complex and a touch dilute. The finish on this surprising, it has a real persistence to it. **84** —*M.G. (12/31/2007)*

Castelvero 2001 Cortese (Piedmont) $9. 84 —*M.S. (12/15/2003)*

CASTIGLION DEL BOSCO

Castiglion del Bosco 2001 Brunello (Brunello di Montalcino) $45. 93 *(4/1/2006)*

Castiglion del Bosco 1997 Brunello (Brunello di Montalcino) 89 —*R.V. (8/1/2002)*

Castiglion del Bosco 2000 Campo del Drago Brunello (Brunello di Montalcino) $75. 93 *(4/1/2006)*

CAVALIER BARTOLOMEO

Cavalier Bartolomeo 1998 Vigneti Solanotto Altinasso Nebbiolo (Barolo) $65. 90 *(4/2/2004)*

CAVALLERI

Cavalleri NV Brut Blanc de Blancs Champagne Blend (Franciacorta) $15. 86 —*J.C. (12/31/2001)*

Cavalleri 1995 Collezione Blanc de Blancs Champagne Blend (Franciacorta) $22. 84 —*J.C. (12/31/2001)*

Cavalleri NV Satèn Blanc de Blancs Champagne Blend (Franciacorta) $18. 84 *(12/31/2001)*

CAVIT

Cavit 1999 Merlot (Trentino) $9. 81 —*S.H. (9/1/2001)*

Cavit 2000 Pinot Grigio (Trentino) $8. 84 —*S.H. (9/1/2001)*

Cavit 1998 Pinot Grigio (Trentino) $8. 86 Best Buy *(8/1/1999)*

Cavit 2005 Cavit Collection Pinot Grigio (Delle Venezie) $9. 86 Best Buy —*M.L. (6/1/2006)*

Cavit 2004 Collection Pinot Grigio (Delle Venezie) $9. 86 Best Buy —*M.L. (6/1/2006)*

Cavit 1999 Pinot Noir (Delle Venezie) $9. 82 —*S.H. (9/1/2001)*

Cavit NV Lunetta Prosecco (Italy) $11. Cavit is relatively new to the Prosecco genre and this sparkler provides all the fresh fruit flavors you'd expect from this popular category of Italian wine. It's a low-intensity wine, with notes of peach, honeydew kiwi and white peppercorn. There's also a slightly soapy-musky tone at the back. **86 Best Buy** —*M.L. (12/15/2007)*

Cavit 2001 Quattro Vicariati Red Blend (Trentino) $24. Blueberry and vanilla sum up this wine nicely; despite its beautiful packaging and brilliant ruby color, it doesn't offer much more. That said, it is an enjoyable and easy wine with enough palate-cleaning acidity to boost its appeal as a companion to most hearty foods. **86** —*M.L. (5/1/2007)*

Cavit 2006 Riesling (Provincia di Pavia) $10. An easy wine that will go down nicely with spicy appetizers. Its color is a paler shade of straw and the aromas focus on citrus, lime and stone fruit. The residual sugar is high, making for sweet peach flavors in the mouth. **85 Best Buy** —*M.L. (9/1/2007)*

Cavit 2004 Teroldego (Vigneti delle Dolomiti) $10. 84 —*M.L. (9/1/2005)*

Cavit 1995 Arèle Vin Santo White Blend (Trentino) $42. 90 —*M.L. (10/1/2006)*

CCHIA

Cchia 2001 Corvina, Rondinella, Molinara (Amarone della Valpolicella) $30. 87 —*J.C. (10/1/2006)*

Cchia 2004 Garganega (Soave Colli Scaligeri) $10. 82 —*J.C. (10/1/2006)*

CECCHETTO

Cecchetto 2003 Sante Rosso Merlot (Piave) $39. A saturated, pretty color sets the stage for lush and ripe notes of red fruit, moist earth, tobacco and tealeaf. There's also a touch of cherry preserve or jamminess that works

ITALY

fine with the wine's chewy, expressive flavors. Notes of tar, resin and plum appear on the close (grapes are harvested slightly overripe). **88** —*M.L. (3/1/2007)*

Cecchetto 2004 Pinot Grigio (Piave) $9. 87 Best Buy —*M.L. (2/1/2006)*

CECCHI

Cecchi 2002 Sangiovese (Chianti Classico) $12. 85 *(4/1/2005)*

Cecchi 1999 Sangiovese (Chianti) $9. 85 Best Buy *(4/1/2001)*

Cecchi 1998 Sangiovese (Toscana) $9. 83 —*J.C. (9/1/2001)*

Cecchi 1998 Sangiovese (Vino Nobile di Montepulciano) $27. 87 —*M.S. (5/1/2002)*

Cecchi 1998 Sangiovese (Chianti Classico) $12. 84 *(4/1/2001)*

Cecchi 2002 Arcano Sangiovese (Chianti Classico) $14. 84 —*M.S. (10/1/2004)*

Cecchi 1999 Arcano Sangiovese (Chianti Colli Senesi) $12. 87 Best Buy *(4/1/2001)*

Cecchi 1997 Messr Pietro di Teuzzo Riserva Sangiovese (Chianti Classico) $28. 88 *(4/1/2001)*

Cecchi 2001 Spargolo Sangiovese (Toscana) $38. 89 —*M.S. (9/1/2006)*

Cecchi 2000 Spargolo Sangiovese (Toscana) $38. 89 —*M.S. (10/1/2004)*

Cecchi 2000 Teuzzo Riserva Sangiovese (Chianti Classico) $32. 87 —*M.S. (10/1/2004)*

Cecchi 1999 Teuzzo Riserva Sangiovese (Chianti Classico) $31. 86 —*M.S. (8/1/2002)*

Cecchi 2002 Toscana Sangiovese (Sangiovese di Toscana) $9. 81 —*M.S. (11/15/2004)*

Cecchi 2004 Trebbiano (Orvieto Classico) $11. 85 —*M.L. (10/1/2006)*

Cecchi 2004 Litorale Vermentino (Maremma) $17. 87 —*M.S. (10/1/2006)*

Cecchi 2003 Litorale Vermentino (Maremma) $17. 88 —*M.S. (8/1/2004)*

Cecchi 1999 Vernaccia (Vernaccia di San Gimignano) $11. 84 —*J.C. (9/1/2001)*

Cecchi 2003 White Blend (Orvieto Classico) $10. 85 Best Buy —*M.S. (11/15/2004)*

CECILIA BERETTA

Cecilia Beretta 2003 Terre di Cariano Corvina, Rondinella, Molinara (Amarone della Valpolicella Classico) $59. Cecilia Beretta is the top line of the Pasqua estate and this wine delivers the heat and power you'd normally expect from Amarone. It also imparts expansive notes of maple syrup, earth, cassis berry and distinct peanut or cashew aromas. It's chunky and chewy in the mouth with good length. Pair with game meat or aged cheese. **91** —*M.L. (10/1/2007)*

Cecilia Beretta 2001 Terre di Cariano Corvina, Rondinella, Molinara (Amarone della Valpolicella Classico) $NA. An exciting achievement, this select cru throbs with powerful intensity and complexity awarding a long list of adjectives to describe its aromatic qualities: black cherry and cherry liquor, leather, cola, milk chocolate and almond. Berry and bramble flavors make the mouthfeel lively and sophisticated and are a delicate segue into chewy-tart tannins and a spice driven finale. **93 Cellar Selection** —*M.L. (12/1/2007)*

Cecilia Beretta 1998 Terre di Cariano Red Blend (Amarone della Valpolicella Classico) $30. 93 Editors' Choice *(5/1/2003)*

CELLI

Celli 2003 Solara Albana (Albana di Romagna) $18. Its color is deep amber and its nose is redolent of dried lemon peel and orange zest. It lacks big, dried fruit aromas like other Albana di Romagna passitos, but makes up for it with a creamy, almost viscous mouthfeel and just the right amount of acidity to cleans the palate. **86** —*M.L. (2/1/2007)*

Celli 2004 Bron & Rusèval Red Blend (Romagna) $13. Etched toasted notes linger over candied cherry, espresso, almond and an unexpected note of crushed laurel leaf. Mixed spice notes –like clove and white pepper – add more nuances. The tannins are firm and the finish is spice-driven. **86** —*M.L. (2/1/2007)*

CENNATOIO

Cennatoio 1997 Sangiovese (Chianti Classico) $22. 87 *(4/1/2001)*

Cennatoio 1995 O'Leandro Riserva Sangiovese (Chianti Classico) $43. 84 *(4/1/2001)*

Cennatoio 1996 Riserva Sangiovese (Chianti Classico) $37. 85 *(4/1/2001)*

Cennatoio 1998 Riserva O'leandro Sangiovese (Chianti Classico) $NA. 88 —*R.V. (8/1/2002)*

CERBAIA

Cerbaia 2001 Brunello (Brunello di Montalcino) $55. 90 *(4/1/2006)*

Cerbaia 2000 Brunello (Brunello di Montalcino) $55. 85 —*M.S. (7/1/2005)*

CERBAIONA

Cerbaiona 2001 Brunello (Brunello di Montalcino) $135. 91 *(4/1/2006)*

CERETTO

Ceretto 2006 Blange Arneis (Langhe) $17. The Ceretto was surprisingly evolved for a 2006. A big, ripe, rich wine with flavors of pear, lychee and a hint of lime peel. Structurally, this is a wine that probably won't hold up well, but at the moment it is a pleasant wine. Just make sure you drink it over the next few months. **86** —*M.G. (12/31/2007)*

Ceretto 2002 Blangé Arneis (Piedmont) $20. 86 —*M.S. (12/15/2003)*

Ceretto 2000 Blangé Arneis (Piedmont) $30. 87 —*D.T. (9/1/2001)*

Ceretto 1999 Piana Barbera (Barbera d'Alba) $27. 89 —*M.M. (11/15/2002)*

Ceretto 1998 Monsordo Rosso Cabernet Blend (Langhe) $38. 89 —*J.C. (9/1/2001)*

Ceretto 2005 Rossana Dolcetto (Dolcetto d'Alba) $21. Not your everyday Docetto, the nose is far more aromatic than the typical version, while the fruit takes a supporting role to the tarry earthiness of the more traditional main flavors, which follows through to a medium finish. Lovely, complex and delicious. **90** —*M.G. (12/31/2007)*

Ceretto 2003 Rossana Dolcetto (Dolcetto d'Alba) $21. 84 —*J.C. (3/1/2006)*

Ceretto 2002 Rossana Dolcetto (Dolcetto d'Alba) $19. 84 —*J.C. (11/15/2004)*

Ceretto 2001 Rossana Dolcetto (Dolcetto d'Alba) $18. 84 —*M.S. (12/15/2003)*

Ceretto 1999 Rossana Dolcetto (Dolcetto d'Alba) $19. 82 —*M.N. (9/1/2001)*

Ceretto 1998 Rossana Dolcetto (Dolcetto d'Alba) $17. 90 *(4/1/2000)*

Ceretto 2005 I Vignaioli di Santo Stefano Moscato (Moscato d'Asti) $20. 87 —*M.L. (12/15/2006)*

Ceretto 2003 I Vignaioli di Santo Stefano Moscato (Moscato d'Asti) $19. 85 —*J.C. (11/15/2004)*

Ceretto 2002 I Vignaioli di Santo Stefano Moscato D'Asti Muscat Canelli (Piedmont) $20. 89 —*M.S. (12/15/2003)*

Ceretto 1998 Nebbiolo (Barbaresco) $111. 91 Cellar Selection *(9/1/2001)*

Ceretto 2004 Asij Nebbiolo (Barbaresco) $40. In 2004, Ceretto has made a pleasant, fragrant Barbaresco; on the nose it had dark fruit aromas mingled with dried roses and a hint of mint. On the palate, the fruit is soft and the floral quality more pronounced. Nice, medium finish. Needs a couple more years. **89** —*M.G. (12/31/2007)*

Ceretto 1999 Asij Nebbiolo (Barbaresco) $37. 88 *(4/2/2004)*

Ceretto 1998 Asij Nebbiolo (Barbaresco) $44. 88 —*M.S. (11/15/2002)*

Ceretto 1997 Asij Nebbiolo (Barbaresco) $44. 92 —*M.S. (9/1/2000)*

Ceretto 2001 Bernardot Nebbiolo (Barbaresco) $62. 92 —*J.C. (3/1/2006)*

Ceretto 2000 Bernardot Nebbiolo (Barbaresco) $67. 93 Editors' Choice *(4/2/2004)*

Ceretto 1999 Bernardot Nebbiolo (Barbaresco) $87. 91 —*M.S. (11/15/2002)*

Ceretto 1998 Bernardot Nebbiolo (Barbaresco) $74. 87 *(9/1/2001)*

Ceretto 1997 Bernardot Nebbiolo (Barbaresco) $74. 89 *(9/1/2000)*

Ceretto 2001 Bricco Asili Nebbiolo (Barbaresco) $116. 90 —*J.C. (3/1/2006)*

Ceretto 2000 Bricco Asili Nebbiolo (Barbaresco) $122. 91 *(4/2/2004)*

Ceretto 1997 Bricco Asili Nebbiolo (Barbaresco) $111. 92 —*J.C. (9/1/2000)*

Ceretto 1995 Bricco Asili Nebbiolo (Barbaresco) $105. 90 —*M.S. (11/15/1999)*

Ceretto 2001 Bricco Rocche Nebbiolo (Barolo) $200. 94 —*J.C. (3/1/2006)*

Ceretto 1999 Bricco Rocche Nebbiolo (Barolo) $200. 90 *(4/2/2004)*

Ceretto 1998 Bricco Rocche Nebbiolo (Barolo) $221. 94 Editors' Choice —*R.V. (11/15/2002)*

Ceretto 1997 Bricco Rocche Nebbiolo (Barolo) $147. 92 *(9/1/2001)*

Ceretto 1995 Bricco Rocche Nebbiolo (Barolo) $140. 96 Cellar Selection *(3/1/2000)*

Ceretto 1998 Brunate Nebbiolo (Barolo) $90. 91 —*R.V. (11/15/2002)*

Ceretto 1998 Prapó Nebbiolo (Barolo) $90. 88 —*R.V. (11/15/2002)*

Ceretto 2001 Brunate Nebbiolo (Barolo) $75. 92 —*J.C. (3/1/2006)*

Ceretto 1999 Brunate Nebbiolo (Barolo) $80. 91 *(4/2/2004)*

Ceretto 1997 Brunate Nebbiolo (Barolo) $74. 90 *(9/1/2001)*

Ceretto 2000 Fasêt Nebbiolo (Barbaresco) $67. 88 *(4/2/2004)*

Ceretto 1998 Fasêt Nebbiolo (Barbaresco) $74. 90 *(9/1/2001)*

Ceretto 1996 Fasêt Nebbiolo (Barbaresco) $70. 93 *—M.S. (11/15/1999)*

Ceretto 1995 Prapo Nebbiolo (Barolo) $70. 92 *—M.S. (7/1/2000)*

Ceretto 2001 Prapó Nebbiolo (Barolo) $75. 92 *—J.C. (3/1/2006)*

Ceretto 1999 Prapó Nebbiolo (Barolo) $80. 90 *(4/2/2004)*

Ceretto 1997 Prapó Nebbiolo (Barolo) $74. 92 *(9/1/2001)*

Ceretto 1999 Zonchera Nebbiolo (Barolo) $40. 89 *(4/2/2004)*

Ceretto 1998 Zonchera Nebbiolo (Barolo) $40. 93 Editors' Choice *—R.V. (11/15/2002)*

Ceretto 2001 Monsordo Red Blend (Langhe) $35. Took its time to emerge from the glass, then settled into a lovely, rich and complex wine, with plenty of dark fruit, an earthy, floral core, nice balance and a medium finish. 88 *—M.G. (12/31/2007)*

CERRAIA

Cerraia 1996 Sangiovese (Vino Nobile di Montepulciano) $27. 83 *—M.S. (9/1/2000)*

CERRI DEL PALAGIO

Cerri del Palagio 2002 Sangiovese (Chianti Classico) $12. 85 *(4/1/2005)*

Cerri del Palagio 2000 Riserva Sangiovese (Chianti Classico) $20. 84 *(4/1/2005)*

CESANI

Cesani 2006 Sangiovese (Chianti Colli Senesi) $NA. This Chianti sees six months of wood aging to render distinct oak-related aromas that come on the heels of, and almost overwhelm, the red fruit and cherry. The tannins are hard, just shy of astringent. 84 *—M.L. (11/1/2007)*

CESARI

Cesari 1999 Mara Corvina (Valpolicella Classico) $13. 90 Best Buy *(5/1/2003)*

Cesari 2004 Corvina, Rondinella, Molinara (Amarone della Valpolicella Classico) $45. Big intensity and power is delivered from this brawny Amarone that imparts distinctive, yet not overwhelmingly intense, aromas of black cherry, plum, resin, tar, pine and black pepper. The wine boasts good freshness, consistency and length on the finish. 89 *—M.L. (10/1/2007)*

Cesari 2001 Il Bosco Corvina, Rondinella, Molinara (Amarone della Valpolicella) $65. Cesari hits all the right marks with this single-vineyard wine and presents a gorgeous, proudly modern wine with soft plush notes of chocolate, vanilla coffee, smoked ham and natural rubber. It is chewy and firm in the mouth but ends on a fresh note, leaving the palate glossed and clean. 93 *—M.L. (12/1/2007)*

Cesari 2004 Due Torri Pinot Grigio (Delle Venezie) $10. 88 Best Buy *—M.L. (2/1/2006)*

Cesari 2005 Fiorile Pinot Grigio (Delle Venezie) $16. 87 *—M.L. (6/1/2006)*

Cesari 1998 Fiorile Pinot Grigio (Trentino) $11. 84 *(8/1/1999)*

Cesari 2000 Red Blend (Amarone della Valpolicella Classico) $40. 90 *(11/1/2005)*

Cesari 1998 Red Blend (Amarone della Valpolicella Classico) $40. 92 Editors' Choice *(5/1/2003)*

Cesari 1997 Bosan Red Blend (Amarone della Valpolicella) $80. 90 *(11/1/2005)*

Cesari 2000 Il Bosco Red Blend (Amarone della Valpolicella) $60. 93 *(11/1/2005)*

Cesari 1997 Il Bosco Red Blend (Amarone della Valpolicella) $52. 89 *(5/1/2003)*

Cesari 2000 Recioto della Valpolicella Red Blend (Valpolicella) $30. 89 *(5/1/2003)*

CEUSO

Ceuso 1998 Custera Bordeaux Blend (Sicilia) $37. 86 *—C.S. (5/1/2002)*

Ceuso 2004 Scurati Nero d'Avola (Sicilia) $18. 87 *—M.L. (7/1/2006)*

Ceuso 2003 Scurati Nero d'Avola (Sicilia) $19. 91 *—M.S. (2/1/2005)*

Ceuso 2001 Ceuso Red Blend (Sicilia) $41. 90 *—M.L. (7/1/2006)*

Ceuso 2000 Custera Red Blend (Sicilia) $39. 89 *—M.S. (7/1/2005)*

Ceuso 2000 Fastaia Red Blend (Sicilia) $31. 88 *—M.S. (10/1/2003)*

CEUSO DI MELIA VIGNA CUSTERA

Ceuso di Melia Vigna Custera 1996 Vino da Tavola Red Blend (Sicilia) $23. 90 *—M.S. (11/15/1999)*

CHIANTI TRAMBUSTI

Chianti Trambusti 1998 Celsus Sangiovese (Sangiovese di Toscana) $22. 84 *—M.S. (11/15/2003)*

Chianti Trambusti 1999 Il Perticato Sangiovese (Chianti Classico) $17. 86 *—M.S. (11/15/2003)*

Chianti Trambusti 2001 Val Serena Sangiovese (Chianti Rufina) $12. 82 *(4/1/2005)*

CHIGI SARACINI

Chigi Saracini 2001 Poggiassai Sangiovese (Toscana) $40. 93 Editors' Choice *—M.S. (9/1/2006)*

Chigi Saracini 2003 Villachigi Sangiovese (Chianti) $13. 92 Best Buy *(4/1/2005)*

CHIORRI

Chiorri 2006 Grechetto (Umbria) $NA. This is a fine example of Grechetto's potential as a structured, food-friendly, white wine. It offers vibrant intensity and deep aromas of mature fruit, peach, pear and pecan butter with a creamy, soft texture and playful citrus on the finish. Try it with an avocado and crabmeat salad. 87 *—M.L. (12/1/2007)*

CIACCI PICCOLOMINI D'ARAGONA

Ciacci Piccolomini d'Aragona 2000 Brunello (Brunello di Montalcino) $65. 87 *—M.S. (7/1/2005)*

Ciacci Piccolomini d'Aragona 1999 Brunello (Brunello di Montalcino) $65. 89 *—M.S. (6/1/2004)*

Ciacci Piccolomini d'Aragona 2001 Vigna di Pianrosso Brunello (Brunello di Montalcino) $65. 91 *(4/1/2006)*

CIAO BELLA

Ciao Bella 2004 Pinot Grigio (Delle Venezie) $10. 84 *(2/1/2006)*

CIELO

Cielo 2001 Pinot Grigio (Veneto) $8. 83 *—J.C. (7/1/2003)*

Cielo 1997 Red Blend (Veneto) $7. 85 *(11/15/1999)*

CIELO BLEU

Cielo Bleu 2001 Vermentino (Vermentino di Sardegna) $14. 85 *—M.S. (8/1/2004)*

CISPIANO

Cispiano 1998 Sangiovese (Chianti Classico) $16. 86 *(4/1/2001)*

CITILLE DI SOPRA

Citille di Sopra 2001 Brunello (Brunello di Montalcino) $NA. 91 *(4/1/2006)*

CITRA

Citra 2002 Montepulciano (Montepulciano d'Abruzzo) $5. 81 *—M.S. (11/15/2003)*

CLERICO

Clerico 1997 Trevigne Barbera (Barbera d'Alba) $20. 89 *(4/1/2000)*

Clerico 1999 Ciabot Mentin Ginestra Nebbiolo (Barolo) $75. 90 *(4/2/2004)*

CLETO CHIARLI

Cleto Chiarli 2005 Pruno Nero Lambrusco (Lambrusco Grasparossa di Castelvetro) $10. 84 *—M.L. (12/15/2006)*

Cleto Chiarli 2005 Vigneto Enrico Cialoini Lambrusco (Lambrusco Grasparossa di Castelvetro) $18. 84 *—M.L. (12/15/2006)*

COCCINELLA

Coccinella 1999 Pinot Grigio (Veneto) $11. 82 *—M.M. (9/1/2001)*

COL D'ORCIA

Col d'Orcia 2001 Brunello (Brunello di Montalcino) $46. 89 *(4/1/2006)*

Col d'Orcia 2000 Brunello (Brunello di Montalcino) $49. 88 *—M.S. (7/1/2005)*

Col d'Orcia 1999 Brunello (Brunello di Montalcino) $50. 87 *—M.S. (6/1/2004)*

Col d'Orcia 1999 Banditella Red Blend (Rosso di Montalcino) $18. 87 *—M.S. (12/31/2002)*

Col d'Orcia 2004 Spezieri Red Blend (Toscana) $13. 83 *—M.S. (9/1/2006)*

Col d'Orcia 1997 Sangiovese (Rosso di Montalcino) $14. 89 *(11/15/1999)*

COL DE' SALICI

Col de' Salici NV Extra Dry Champagne Blend (Prosecco di Valdobbiadene) $15. 87 *—S.H. (12/31/2000)*

Col de' Salici NV Extra Dry Prosecco (Prosecco di Valdobbiadene) $15. 81 *—M.S. (12/31/2002)*

COL DI LUNA

Col di Luna NV Cuvée Brut White Blend (Italy) $12. 85 *—M.S. (6/1/2005)*

COL VETORAZ SPUMANTI

Col Vetoraz Spumanti NV Brut Prosecco (Prosecco di Conegliano e Valdobbiadene) $16. Attractive creamy foam and bubbles set the stage, followed by pungent herbal intensity that definitely sets this Prosecco apart from the rest. Background notes include stone fruit, white flowers and dusty mineral. This is a laid-back sparkler with a creamy, less-acidic mouthfeel. 86 *—M.L. (12/15/2007)*

Col Vetoraz Spumanti NV Brut Prosecco (Prosecco di Valdobbiadene) $23. 86 *—M.L. (6/1/2006)*

Col Vetoraz Spumanti NV Cartizze Prosecco (Prosecco Superiore di Cartizze) $36. There's a nutty, smoky quality to this Cartizze Prosecco that adds depth and dimension beyond the wine's more characteristic floral and fresh fruit notes. This is a well-balanced wine, thanks to a playful harmony between delicate sweetness and spicy crispness on the finish. 88 *—M.L. (12/15/2007)*

Col Vetoraz Spumanti 2006 Dry Millesimato Prosecco (Prosecco di Conegliano e Valdobbiadene) $23. This is an extremely fragrant and floral dry Prosecco (meaning it tastes sweeter), with distinct notes of honey, apricot, honeysuckle and exotic fruit. Thanks to its lively perlage, it feels creamy, soft and foamy in the mouth. 87 *—M.L. (12/15/2007)*

Col Vetoraz Spumanti NV Extra Dry Prosecco (Prosecco di Conegliano e Valdobbiadene) $16. Soapy lavender and floral tones are followed by loads of citrus fruit. This is a perky, lively sparkler with a sharp point of acidity on the close and a determined, linear personality. Pair it with spicy finger foods. 87 *—M.L. (12/15/2007)*

Col Vetoraz Spumanti NV Extra Dry Prosecco (Prosecco di Valdobbiadene) $23. 87 *—M.L. (6/1/2006)*

COLDISOLE

Coldisole 2001 Brunello (Brunello di Montalcino) $NA. 91 *(4/1/2006)*

COLI

Coli 1995 Brunello (Brunello di Montalcino) $34. 85 *(11/1/2002)*

Coli 2000 Montepulciano (Montepulciano d'Abruzzo) $7. 84 Best Buy *(11/1/2002)*

Coli 1999 Primo di Montignana Red Blend (Toscana) $48. 87 *—M.S. (11/15/2003)*

Coli 2001 Sangiovese (Orvieto) $7. 85 Best Buy *(11/1/2002)*

Coli 2000 Sangiovese (Chianti) $10. 83 *(11/1/2002)*

Coli 2000 Sangiovese (Chianti Classico) $13. 85 *(11/1/2002)*

Coli 1999 Sangiovese (Chianti) $7. 85 Best Buy *(4/1/2001)*

Coli 1998 Sangiovese (Chianti Classico) $10. 83 *(4/1/2001)*

Coli 1998 Montignana Riserva Sangiovese (Tuscany) $23. 84 *—M.S. (11/15/2003)*

Coli 1998 Pratale Sangiovese (Chianti Classico) $22. 86 *(11/1/2002)*

Coli 1997 Pratale Sangiovese (Chianti Classico) $19. 84 *(4/1/2001)*

Coli 1999 Riserva Sangiovese (Chianti Classico) $18. 87 *—M.S. (11/15/2003)*

Coli 1998 Riserva Sangiovese (Chianti) $12. 84 *(11/1/2002)*

Coli 1997 Riserva Sangiovese (Chianti) $11. 86 *(4/1/2001)*

Coli 1995 Villa Montignana Riserva Sangiovese (Chianti Classico) $23. 88 *(4/1/2001)*

Coli 2003 Vernaccia (Vernaccia di San Gimignano) $10. 85 *—M.S. (8/1/2004)*

Coli 1999 Vernaccia (Vernaccia di San Gimignano) $8. 83 *—J.C. (9/1/2001)*

COLLAVINI

Collavini 2004 Villa Canlungo Pinot Grigio (Collio) $17. 87 *—M.L. (6/1/2006)*

COLLE NERO

Colle Nero 2003 Sangiovese (Chianti) $8. 85 Best Buy *—M.L. (10/1/2006)*

COLLE S. MUSTIOLA DI FABIO CENNI

Colle S. Mustiola di Fabio Cenni 1999 Poggio Ai Chiari Sangiovese (Toscana) $48. 88 *—M.S. (12/31/2002)*

COLLELCETO

Collelceto 2001 Brunello (Brunello di Montalcino) $50. 90 *(4/1/2006)*

COLLI AMERINI

Colli Amerini 1998 Carbio Red Blend (Umbria) $18. 88 *—C.S. (2/1/2003)*

COLLI DEL SOLIGO

Colli del Soligo NV Brut Prosecco (Italy) $14. This Prosecco-based sparkler (with fruit from outside the traditional Prosecco zone) offers creamy froth and sweet notes of peach, mint leaf and almond nut. It has medium intensity, nice crispness and a slightly sour note on the finish. 84 *—M.L. (12/15/2007)*

Colli del Soligo 2006 Millesimato Extra Dry Prosecco (Italy) $23. This is a low-intensity sparkler made with the Prosecco grape that offers measured aromas of stone fruit and citrus. Despite a lean, watery structure, it does have vibrant crispness and a sweet, fruity finish. 85 *—M.L. (12/15/2007)*

COLLI DELLA MURGIA

Colli della Murgia 1998 Selvato Red Blend (Apulia) $11. 84 *(9/1/2000)*

COLLOSORBO

Collosorbo 2001 Brunello (Brunello di Montalcino) $59. 92 *(4/1/2006)*

Collosorbo 1999 Brunello (Brunello di Montalcino) $56. 92 *—M.S. (6/1/2004)*

Collosorbo 1999 Riserva Brunello (Brunello di Montalcino) $65. 91 *—M.S. (7/1/2005)*

COLMELLO DI GROTTA

Colmello di Grotta 2004 Pinot Grigio (Collio) $9. 84 *—M.L. (2/1/2006)*

Colmello di Grotta 2004 Pinot Grigio (Isonzo del Friuli) $10. 83 *—M.L. (6/1/2006)*

COLOGNOLE

Colognole 2001 Sangiovese (Chianti Rufina) $12. 88 Best Buy *(4/1/2005)*

Colognole 1997 Chianti Rufina Sangiovese (Chianti Rufina) $12. 81 *(4/1/2001)*

COLONNARA

Colonnara 2003 Cuprese Verdicchio (Verdicchio dei Castelli di Jesi Classico) $15. 91 Best Buy *—M.S. (8/1/2004)*

Colonnara 2003 Lyricus Verdicchio (Verdicchio dei Castelli di Jesi Classico) $11. 88 Best Buy *—M.S. (8/1/2004)*

COLOSI

Colosi 1999 Nero d'Avola (Sicilia) $12. 87 *—J.C. (5/1/2002)*

Colosi 2002 Red Blend (Sicilia) $11. 83 *—M.S. (2/1/2005)*

Colosi 2001 Red Blend (Sicilia) $10. 85 *—M.S. (10/1/2003)*

CÒLPETRONE

Còlpetrone 1999 Red Blend (Montefalco) $14. 91 Best Buy *—M.S. (2/1/2003)*

Còlpetrone 2001 Sagrantino (Sagrantino di Montefalco) $65. 89 *—M.L. (9/1/2005)*

COLSANTO

Colsanto 2002 Sagrantino (Sagrantino di Montefalco) $NA. 87 *—M.L. (9/1/2005)*

COLTERENZIO

Colterenzio 2001 Lafoa Cabernet Sauvignon (Alto Adige) $65. 93 *—M.L. (9/1/2006)*

Colterenzio 2003 Mantsch Riserva Lagrein (Alto Adige) $20. There's plenty of berry fruit upfront, cherry, vanilla and chopped herbs in particular. The wine has a forward, very full and round mouthfeel; it's plush and ripe but not jammy or simple. Supported by solid structure and tannins. 89 *—M.L. (9/1/2007)*

Colterenzio 2000 Cornell Merlot (Alto Adige) $35. You can taste the savory nuances of time and oak aging thanks to this wine's gorgeous notes of forest floor, cassis, slate roof and licorice. The wine remains thick and austere on the palate with bitter tannins and a velvety finish. It promises to age beautifully for many more years. 90 *—M.L. (3/1/2007)*

Colterenzio 2003 Riserva Siebeneich Merlot (Alto Adige) $22. Round and supple, plush and bright; here is a wine with deep and penetrating aromas of red berry, tobacco and spice. It's intense and voluptuous—down to the thick streaks of glycerin on the glass—with firm structure, great taste and a long, spice-driven finish. 91 *—M.L. (3/1/2007)*

Colterenzio 2004 Pinot Grigio (Alto Adige) $12. 87 Best Buy *—M.L. (2/1/2006)*

Colterenzio 1997 Praedium Pinot Grigio (Alto Adige) $17. 82 *(8/1/1999)*

Colterenzio 2004 Puiten Pinot Grigio (Alto Adige) $18. 87 *—M.L. (6/1/2006)*

Colterenzio 2004 St. Daniel Riserva Pinot Nero (Alto Adige) $20. The appearance is marked by brilliant, ruby luminosity and its consistency warms over the palate with delicate flavors of violets, lavender and forest berry. The bouquet is refined, delicate and intense and the finish is long and persistent. Pair with roasted lamb. **88** *—M.L. (9/1/2007)*

Colterenzio 2005 Prail Sauvignon Blanc (Alto Adige) $17. Snappy and crisp with wonderful persistency, this Sauv Blanc delivers all of the high aromatic notes that you should expect from this fragrant variety. Try it with sesame-seasoned salad, fish or finger foods. **88** *—M.L. (9/1/2007)*

COLUTTA

Colutta 2006 Pinot Grigio (Colli Orientali del Friuli) $12. Initial sulfur smells—that do blow off after a few minutes to reveal stone fruit and white mineral tones—denote possible bottle shock. But Colutta's track record for delicious Pinot Grigio is good, so we should look forward to the next vintage. **84** *—M.L. (11/15/2007)*

Colutta 2004 Pinot Grigio (Colli Orientali del Friuli) $12. 87 Best Buy *—M.L. (6/1/2006)*

Colutta 2006 Sauvignon (Colli Orientali del Friuli) $12. Thanks to a special clone of Sauvignon, Giorgio Colutta has successfully paired this international variety to his unique territory, creating a distinctively Italian wine. Fresh aromas include citrus zest, wild sage, chopped herbs and kiwi yet the sharp edges you might find in French or New Zealand versions are absent. The wine boasts good acidity and a bright, zesty finish that cleans the palate and would pair perfectly with vegetable based exotic appetizers. Fire roasted eggplant with cumin, potato samosa or red lentil patties would stand up to the wine's gentle aromatic intensity. **87 Best Buy** *—M.L. (11/15/2007)*

Colutta 2006 Tocai Friulano (Colli Orientali del Friuli) $12. Fresh green fruit, lime and kiwi emerge on the heels of broader aromas of ripe peach and banana. This is a lush and thick wine with a lively mouthfeel and loads of delicate spice on the finish. **87 Best Buy** *—M.L. (11/15/2007)*

Colutta 2002 Tocai Friulano Tocai (Friuli) $17. 86 *—S.H. (10/1/2004)*

CONCILIO

Concilio 2001 Chardonnay (Trentino) $10. 85 *—J.C. (7/1/2003)*

Concilio 2001 Riserva Merlot (Trentino) $10. 88 Best Buy *—M.L. (11/15/2005)*

Concilio 2004 Pinot Grigio (Delle Venezie) $11. 85 *—M.L. (6/1/2006)*

Concilio 1998 Pinot Grigio (Trentino) $9. *(8/1/1999)*

Concilio 2003 Contessa Manci Pinot Grigio (Trentino) $15. 83 *(2/1/2006)*

Concilio 1997 Single Vineyard-Manci DOC Pinot Grigio (Trentino) $13. 85 *(8/1/1999)*

CONSORZIO VINI TIPICI DI SAN MARINO

Consorzio Vini Tipici di San Marino 2001 Tessano Riserva Red Blend (Emilia-Romagna) $25. Here is an unusual Sangiovese blend with red berry aromas but also thicker, compelling notes of Graham cracker, caramel, cookie dough and cinnamon snaps. The tannins are chewy and you'll get milk chocolate flavors on the finish. **87** *—M.L. (2/1/2007)*

Consorzio Vini Tipici di San Marino 2003 Brugneto Sangiovese (Emilia-Romagna) $14. Here's a Sangiovese that is light and lean in the mouth with a vibrant ruby color and pretty aromas of forest berry, tar, licorice and chopped herbs. There is also slight astringency that promises to soften up with a bit of aeration. **86** *—M.L. (2/1/2007)*

Consorzio Vini Tipici di San Marino 2004 Caldese White Blend (Emilia-Romagna) $20. From the tiny republic of San Marino, this is a 70-30 blend of Chardonnay and Ribolla with well-integrated fruit and toasted tones. Vanilla and butter aromas come on the heels of apricot, peach, beeswax and acacia flower. Nice acidity and persistence, too. **86** *—M.L. (2/1/2007)*

Consorzio Vini Tipici di San Marino 2004 Roncale White Blend (Emilia-Romagna) $14. Made with Chardonnay and the local Ribolla grape, this is a dry, fragrant and easy-to-drink white. The aromas span fruit and honeysuckle to dried hay and mineral notes. Would pair with salads or grilled vegetables. **85** *—M.L. (2/1/2007)*

CONTADI CASTALDI

Contadi Castaldi NV Brut Champagne Blend (Terre di Franciacorta) $13. 86 Best Buy *—M.S. (12/31/2002)*

Contadi Castaldi 1998 Rose Sparkling Blend (Terre di Franciacorta) $27. 83 *—M.S. (12/31/2002)*

Contadi Castaldi 1997 Saten Sparkling Blend (Terre di Franciacorta) $27. 82 *—M.S. (12/31/2002)*

Contadi Castaldi NV Chardonnay (Terre di Franciacorta) $11. 84 *—J.C. (9/1/2000)*

Contadi Castaldi NV Brut Sparkling Blend (Franciacorta) $24. 91 *—M.L. (6/1/2006)*

Contadi Castaldi NV Brut Sparkling Blend (Franciacorta) $28. 90 *—J.C. (12/31/2003)*

Contadi Castaldi 2001 Rosé Sparkling Blend (Franciacorta) $46. 88 *—M.L. (6/1/2006)*

Contadi Castaldi 1999 Rosé Sparkling Blend (Franciacorta) $35. 84 *—J.C. (12/31/2003)*

Contadi Castaldi 1999 Satèn Sparkling Blend (Franciacorta) $35. 89 *—J.C. (12/31/2003)*

Contadi Castaldi 2001 Satén Sparkling Blend (Franciacorta) $26. 91 *—M.L. (6/1/2006)*

CONTE COLLALTO

Conte Collalto NV Brut Prosecco (Prosecco di Conegliano e Valdobbiadene) $19. Sweet peach, passionfruit and fragrant green apple make for a pretty nose with a soapy, perfumed quality. This sparkler boasts a smooth texture and a playful touch of sweetness in the mouth. **86** *—M.L. (12/15/2007)*

Conte Collalto NV Prosecco (Prosecco di Conegliano e Valdobbiadene) $10. 86 *—M.L. (12/15/2006)*

Conte Collalto NV Brut Prosecco (Prosecco di Conegliano e Valdobbiadene) $15. 86 *—M.L. (6/1/2006)*

Conte Collalto NV Brut Prosecco (Prosecco di Conegliano e Valdobbiadene) $14. 86 *—M.L. (12/15/2006)*

Conte Collalto NV Extra Dry Prosecco (Prosecco di Conegliano e Valdobbiadene) $19. Thanks to its buoyant aromas of field flower, green apple, pear and dried sage leaf, you could definitely describe this as a multidimensional wine with noticeable elegance. There are musky, sweet fruit flavors on the finish. **87** *—M.L. (12/15/2007)*

Conte Collalto NV Extra Dry Prosecco (Prosecco di Conegliano e Valdobbiadene) $13. 87 *—M.L. (12/15/2006)*

Conte Collalto NV Extra Dry Prosecco (Prosecco di Conegliano e Valdobbiadene) $15. 87 *—M.L. (6/1/2006)*

Conte Collalto NV Frizzante Prosecco (Prosecco di Conegliano e Valdobbiadene) $19. Frizzante Proseccos are made with less atmospheric pressure and therefore taste extremely smooth and silky in the mouth. The aromas here are not particularly intense but do reveal good fruit and mineral notes. **85** *—M.L. (12/15/2007)*

CONTE DELLA VIPERA

Conte della Vipera 2001 Sauvignon Blanc (Umbria) $22. 81 *—M.S. (10/1/2004)*

CONTE FERDINANDO GUICCIARDINI

Conte Ferdinando Guicciardini 2002 Massi Di Mandorlaia Red Blend (Morellino di Scansano) $NA. 84 *—M.S. (10/1/2004)*

Conte Ferdinando Guicciardini 2001 Massi di Mandorlaia Riserva Sangiovese (Morellino di Scansano) $40. 91 *—M.S. (11/15/2004)*

CONTE LEOPARDI

Conte Leopardi 2001 Pigmento Dittajuti Red Blend (Rosso Conero) $NA. This hearty, late harvest Montepulciano-based wine is only made in the best years. This barrique-aged vintage delivers red cherry, toasted nut, tobacco, leather and black chocolate. The tannins are firm, but not astringent, leaving this a natural choice for grilled red meat. **90** *—M.L. (12/1/2007)*

Conte Leopardi 2004 Vigneti del Coppo Red Blend (Rosso Conero) $NA. Dark, dense concentration sets this Conero apart from the crowd as do the penetrating notes of red fruit, plum, beets, leather and tobacco. The wine delivers structure, power and would be best paired with grilled meat. **89** *—M.L. (12/1/2007)*

CONTERNO FANTINO

Conterno Fantino 2005 Vignota Barbera (Barbera d'Alba) $29. A grapy, easy-going wine that is pleasant to drink but comes across as quite simple. Short, medium-intensity finish. **83** *—M.G. (12/31/2007)*

Conterno Fantino 2003 Vignota Barbera (Barbera d'Alba) $27. 91 Editors' Choice *—J.C. (3/1/2006)*

Conterno Fantino 2002 Vignota Barbera (Barbera d'Alba) $28. 85 *—J.C. (11/15/2004)*

Conterno Fantino 1999 Vignota Barbera (Barbera d'Alba) $22. 87 *—M.N. (9/1/2001)*

Conterno Fantino 2005 Bricco Bastia Dolcetto (Dolcetto d'Alba) $23. The Conterno Fantino is one of the lighter, grapier Dolcettos tasted. Plenty of dark fruit, an easygoing personality and nicely balanced with a solid finish. Amiable rather than profound. **84** *—M.G. (12/31/2007)*

Conterno Fantino 1998 Bricco Bastia Dolcetto (Dolcetto d'Alba) $19. 88 *(4/1/2000)*

Conterno Fantino 2002 Monprà Red Blend (Langhe) $46. 90 *—J.C. (3/1/2006)*

Conterno Fantino 2001 Parussi Nebbiolo (Barolo) $81. 89 *—J.C. (3/1/2006)*

Conterno Fantino 2000 Parussi Nebbiolo (Barolo) $81. 92 *—J.C. (11/15/2004)*

Conterno Fantino 1998 Parussi Nebbiolo (Barolo) $65. 87 *—C.S. (11/15/2002)*

Conterno Fantino 2000 Sorì Ginestra Nebbiolo (Barolo) $99. 89 *—J.C. (11/15/2004)*

Conterno Fantino 1998 Sorì Ginestra Nebbiolo (Barolo) $99. 88 *(4/2/2004)*

Conterno Fantino 2001 Sorí Ginestra Nebbiolo (Barolo) $99. 93 *—J.C. (3/1/2006)*

Conterno Fantino 2001 Monprà Red Blend (Langhe) $59. 87 *—J.C. (11/15/2004)*

CONTI COSTANTI

Conti Costanti 2001 Brunello (Brunello di Montalcino) $74. 92 *(4/1/2006)*

Conti Costanti 2000 Brunello (Brunello di Montalcino) $70. 89 *(4/1/2006)*

Conti Costanti 1998 Brunello (Brunello di Montalcino) $62. 88 *(11/15/2003)*

Conti Costanti 1997 Riserva Brunello (Brunello di Montalcino) $97. 92 *—M.S. (11/15/2003)*

Conti Costanti 1998 Vermiglio Red Blend (Toscana) $46. 89 *—M.S. (12/31/2002)*

CONTI FORMENTINI

Conti Formentini 2000 Torre di Tramontana Chardonnay (Collio) $25. 89 *—R.V. (7/1/2003)*

Conti Formentini 1999 Torre di Tramontana Chardonnay (Collio) $25. 83 *—J.C. (7/1/2003)*

Conti Formentini 2004 Pinot Grigio (Collio) $15. 87 *—M.L. (2/1/2006)*

Conti Formentini 2001 Pinot Grigio (Collio) $15. 84 *—J.C. (7/1/2003)*

Conti Formentini 1999 Pinot Grigio (Collio) $14. 85 *—J.F. (9/1/2001)*

Conti Formentini 1996 Pinot Grigio (Collio) $13. 84 *(8/1/1999)*

Conti Formentini 2001 Rylint White Blend (Collio) $NA. 87 *—R.V. (7/1/2003)*

CONTI ZECCA

Conti Zecca 2004 Cantalupi Negroamaro (Salento) $10. You'd expect this southern Italian wine to be on the extraripe side, but instead it offers a nice balance of green notes including herbs, eucalyptus, licorice, carob, vanilla and delicate forest berry. It's an easy drink with noticeable but not overpowering tannins and medium consistency. **87 Best Buy** *—M.L. (8/1/2007)*

Conti Zecca 2003 Cantalupi Negroamaro (Salento) $10. 86 Best Buy *—M.S. (10/1/2006)*

Conti Zecca 2004 Primitivo (Salento) $20. Very ripe and succulent red fruit here with background notes of licorice, prunes and balsamic sauce. This unfiltered wine beautifully recalls the charms of Puglia, including its rustic edge, strong colors and decisive flavors. **88** *—M.L. (8/1/2007)*

Conti Zecca 2003 Primitivo (Primitivo del Salento) $18. 88 *—M.S. (10/1/2006)*

Conti Zecca 2004 Cantalupi Primitivo (Salento) $11. Here's a wine that faithfully reflects the personality of its origin: Prune, black fruit, plump cherry, leather, coffee, Mediterranean herb and exotic spice are all components of an intense and intriguing nose. In the mouth, this wine offers sweet berry flavors, spice and dusty tannins. **87 Best Buy** *—M.L. (8/1/2007)*

Conti Zecca 2003 Cantalupi Primitivo (Salento) $10. 86 Best Buy *—M.S. (10/1/2006)*

Conti Zecca 2004 Nero Red Blend (Salento) $45. A 70-30 blend of Negroamaro grape and hearty Cabernet Sauvignon, this is a highly successful rendition with succulent concentration, a pretty purplish hue and a nice balance between ripe fruit and tar-like aromas. You'll detect blackberry, leather, spice, licorice and asphalt. A characteristic Cabernet Sauvignon note of bell pepper appears as well. **91** *—M.L. (8/1/2007)*

Conti Zecca 2002 Nero Red Blend (Rosso del Salento) $45. 90 *—M.S. (10/1/2006)*

Conti Zecca 2003 Terra Riserva Red Blend (Leverano) $30. This Negroamaro-Aglianico blend opens slowly, then suddenly releases a rush of red cherry, toast, prune, leather and red earth. The tannins are velvety (the wine sees 14 months of oak) and you'll get lavender, blueberry and dill-like flavors on the finish. **90** *—M.L. (8/1/2007)*

Conti Zecca 2001 Terra Riserva Red Blend (Leverano) $30. 88 *—M.S. (10/1/2006)*

CONTINI

Contini 2002 Vermentino (Vermentino di Sardegna) $15. 88 *—M.S. (8/1/2004)*

Contini 2002 Karmis Vernaccia (Vernaccia delle Valle del Tirso) $15. 86 *—M.S. (8/1/2004)*

CONTRATTO

Contratto 1997 Panta Rei Barbera (Barbera d'Asti) $15. 86 *(4/1/2000)*

CONVIVIALE

Conviviale 2006 Pinot Grigio (Pavia) $8. A light, easy quaffing wine that typifies the Pinot Grigio available in the U.S. market, offering modest apple, peach and citrus flavors. It's cleanly made and priced right for the quality. **84 Best Buy** *(10/1/2007)*

COPPO

Coppo 1997 Camp du Rouss Barbera (Barbera d'Asti) $18. 88 *(4/1/2000)*

Coppo 1997 L'Avvocata Barbera (Barbera d'Asti) $14. 85 *(4/1/2000)*

Coppo 1996 Pomorosso Barbera (Barbera d'Asti) $35. 92 *(4/1/2000)*

Coppo 1997 Monteriolo Chardonnay (Piedmont) $43. 84 *(9/1/2000)*

CORDERO DI MONTEZEMOLO

Cordero di Montezemolo 1998 Annata Barbera (Barbera d'Alba) $25. 90 *(4/1/2000)*

Cordero di Montezemolo 1998 Dolcetto (Dolcetto d'Alba) $17. 88 *(4/1/2000)*

CORINO

Corino 1999 Vecchie Vigne Nebbiolo (Barolo) $105. 90 *(4/2/2004)*

Corino 1999 Vigneto Rocche Nebbiolo (Barolo) $70. 88 *(4/2/2004)*

CORMÒNS

Cormòns 2004 Pinot Grigio (Collio) $16. 85 *—M.L. (6/1/2006)*

Cormòns 2004 Pinot Grigio (Friuli Isonzo) $14. 86 *—M.L. (6/1/2006)*

Cormòns 2004 Rosänder Pinot Grigio (Friuli Isonzo) $14. 87 *—M.L. (6/1/2006)*

CORNAREA

Cornarea 2005 Arneis (Roero Arneis) $22. This Arneis displays some muted lime and leather aromas, but on the palate the leathery quality becomes a touch sweaty. It is well balanced, and shows a solid finish. **82** *—M.G. (12/31/2007)*

CORTE CAMPAGNOLA

Corte Campagnola 2004 Gli Archi Corvina, Rondinella, Molinara (Amarone della Valpolicella Classico) $40. From a small, quality-minded producer who buys grapes and also grows them, here is a gorgeous wine with amazing intensity and refined nuances of small berry fruit, cassis, wild apple, nut, white peppercorn and pine. It is a traditional Amarone with great length, durability and bright acidity on the close that ages in wood for 24 months. **92** *—M.L. (10/1/2007)*

Corte Campagnola 2003 Gli Archi Corvina, Rondinella, Molinara (Amarone della Valpolicella Classico) $40. Gli Archi is a beautiful, modern Amarone with thick and syrupy notes of chocolate fudge, bright red fruit, roasted chestnut and freshly brewed coffee. But it's not sticky or cloying; in fact, it's firm and compact with dusty tannins, good length and a wonderful ability to slide smoothly over the palate. **92** *—M.L. (10/1/2007)*

CORTE LENGUIN

Corte Lenguin 2003 Corvina, Rondinella, Molinara (Amarone della Valpolicella Classico) $35. You'll notice the wine's thick concentration first and its layered aromatic intensity second. There's a bit of everything here: big, meaty tones, dried herbs, white mushroom, vanilla-cherry and savory black currant. It's complex in the mouth too, with chewy tannins and very good length. **87** *—M.L. (10/1/2007)*

Corte Lenguin 2003 La Coeta Corvina, Rondinella, Molinara (Amarone della Valpolicella Classico) $60. Here's a winery founded at the start of the 1900s that has morphed over the decades to enthusiastically embrace modern use of oak. In fact, the wood here is almost too much of a good thing with carpentry and cedar notes that mask much of the cherry fruit. In the mouth, it has a chewy texture, smoke favors and a spice-driven finish. **88** *—M.L. (10/1/2007)*

CORTE PAVONE

Corte Pavone 2001 Brunello (Brunello di Montalcino) $45. 92 Editors' Choice *(4/1/2006)*

CORTE RUGOLIN

Corte Rugolin 2003 Crosàra de le Strìe Coati Bruno Corvina, Rondinella, Molinara (Amarone della Valpolicella Classico) $41. You'll find genuine Amarone typicity here with poached black cherries, maple syrup, chocolate dust, rose petal and almond nut. The mouthfeel is characterized by dusty tannins, fresh menthol and good length. **88** —*M.L. (10/1/2007)*

Corte Rugolin 2000 Vigna Monte Danieli Corvina, Rondinella, Molinara (Amarone della Valpolicella Classico) $62. Definitely on the ripe side, this wine showcases mature aromas of berry jam, raspberry fruit roll-up, tar, licorice and lingering strawberry. Ripe flavors in the mouth are backed by spice, smoke, mineral and velvety consistency. Pair this wine with Cajun blackened meat. **90** —*M.L. (12/1/2007)*

CORTE SANT' ALDA

Corte Sant' Alda 2003 Corvina, Rondinella, Molinara (Amarone della Valpolicella) $100. Marinella Camerani's dedication to tradition (with organic and biodynamic farming principles) is legendary. Hers are delicate, sometimes difficult wines, yet they are always prized for authenticity. Distinctive aromas include crushed raspberry, raisins, almond cookie, molasses and cooked pears in reduction sauce. The wine ends with lively, refreshing acidity. **90 Cellar Selection** —*M.L. (10/1/2007)*

Corte Sant' Alda 1999 Corvina (Amarone della Valpolicella) $94. 87 *(11/1/2005)*

CORTE VECCHIA

Corte Vecchia 1997 Red Blend (Amarone della Valpolicella Classico) $45. 90 *(5/1/2003)*

CORTEFORTE

Corteforte 2001 Terre di San Zeno Corvina, Rondinella, Molinara (Amarone della Valpolicella Classico) $40. Here is a subtle, delicate style that emphasizes cherry cola, apple, root beer, nutty-green aromas such as dried chopped herbs or tea leaf, with currant berry and dried prunes. The fruit tastes very ripe in the mouth and this sensation is underlined by the wine's natural succulence and chewy consistency. **90** —*M.L. (12/1/2007)*

Corteforte 2000 Vigneti di Osan Corvina, Rondinella, Molinara (Amarone della Valpolicella Classico) $40. Carlo Maria Cerutti's powerful wine boasts strong vertical intensity (you feel it at the back of the nose) with blackberry, mulberry and bramble-like notes. It has a unique, polished personality and is determined but not overpowering in the mouth. **92** —*M.L. (10/1/2007)*

Corteforte 1995 Amarone Riserva Red Blend (Amarone della Valpolicella) $33. 88 *(5/1/2003)*

Corteforte 1998 Ripasso Red Blend (Valpolicella Classico Superiore) $17. 87 *(5/1/2003)*

CORVO

Corvo 2003 Bianco Inzolia (Sicilia) $10. 86 —*M.S. (10/1/2004)*

Corvo 2004 Rosso Red Blend (Sicilia) $9. 86 Best Buy —*M.L. (7/1/2006)*

Corvo 2002 Rosso Red Blend (Sicilia) $10. 86 Best Buy —*M.S. (11/15/2004)*

Corvo 2001 Rosso Red Blend (Sicilia) $10. 86 —*R.V. (11/15/2004)*

Corvo 2000 Rosso Red Blend (Sicilia) $10. 86 Best Buy —*M.S. (10/1/2003)*

Corvo 2005 Bianco White Blend (Sicilia) $9. 85 Best Buy —*M.L. (7/1/2006)*

Corvo 2004 Bianco White Blend (Sicilia) $10. 86 Best Buy —*M.L. (7/1/2006)*

Corvo 2002 Bianco White Blend (Sicilia) $10. 83 —*R.V. (10/1/2003)*

COSTANZA MALFATTI

Costanza Malfatti 2001 Sangiovese (Morellino di Scansano) $47. 89 —*M.S. (11/15/2004)*

Costanza Malfatti 2000 Sangiovese (Morellino di Scansano) $39. 86 —*M.S. (10/1/2004)*

COSTARIPA

Costaripa 2003 Mazane Marzemino (Benaco Bresciano) $17. A hot vintage translates into jammy fruit and berry preserves backed by rich toasted notes. Ripeness definitely overtakes elegance in this case, yet this juicy red would do well with aged cheese or red meat. **84** —*M.L. (4/1/2007)*

COTTANERA

Cottanera 2002 Barbazzale Inzolia (Sicilia) $18. 85 —*J.C. (10/1/2003)*

Cottanera 2000 Grammonte Merlot (Sicilia) $50. 81 —*M.S. (10/1/2003)*

Cottanera 1999 L'Ardenza Mondeuse (Sicilia) $38. 89 —*C.S. (5/1/2002)*

Cottanera 2002 Barbazzale Nerello Mascalese (Sicilia) $17. 84 —*M.S. (7/1/2005)*

Cottanera 2001 Fatagione Nerello Mascalese (Sicilia) $28. 87 —*M.S. (7/1/2005)*

Cottanera 1999 Fatagione Nerello Mascalese (Sicilia) $25. 90 —*C.S. (5/1/2002)*

Cottanera 2001 Barbazzale Red Blend (Sicilia) $19. 87 —*M.S. (10/1/2003)*

Cottanera 1999 Grammonte Red Blend (Sicilia) $38. 91 Editors' Choice —*C.S. (5/1/2002)*

Cottanera 2001 L'Ardenza Red Blend (Sicilia) $45. 85 —*M.S. (7/1/2005)*

Cottanera 2000 Sole di Sesta Syrah (Sicilia) $50. 83 —*M.S. (10/1/2003)*

Cottanera 1999 Sole Di Sesta Syrah (Sicilia) $38. 87 —*C.S. (5/1/2002)*

CROCE DI MEZZO

Croce di Mezzo 2001 Brunello (Brunello di Montalcino) $NA. 90 *(4/1/2006)*

CUSLANUS

Cuslanus 2003 Corvina, Rondinella, Molinara (Amarone della Valpolicella Classico) $NA. Introducing the newest player in Valpolicella: Cuslanus is a fresh start-up with a fresh approach. The vineyard is located 400 meters in altitude, which is high by Valpolicella standards. That altitude has helped safeguard aromas of wild apple, white cherry, vanilla-spice, nutmeg and peppercorn. Keep your eye on this producer. **90** —*M.L. (10/1/2007)*

CUSUMANO

Cusumano 2002 Nadarìa Alcamo (Alcamo) $10. 88 —*J.C. (10/1/2003)*

Cusumano 2004 Jal Chardonnay (Sicilia) $18. 87 —*M.L. (7/1/2006)*

Cusumano 2001 Jalé Chardonnay (Sicilia) $28. 84 —*J.C. (10/1/2003)*

Cusumano 2005 Insolia (Sicilia) $10. 86 Best Buy —*M.L. (7/1/2006)*

Cusumano 2004 Insolia (Sicilia) $11. 86 Best Buy —*M.L. (7/1/2006)*

Cusumano 2004 Cubià Insolia (Sicilia) $13. 87 —*M.L. (7/1/2006)*

Cusumano 2004 Cubià Insolia (Sicilia) $11. 88 —*M.L. (9/1/2005)*

Cusumano 2001 Cubìa Inzolia (Sicilia) $20. 84 —*J.C. (10/1/2003)*

Cusumano 2002 Nadarìa Inzolia (Sicilia) $10. 87 —*J.C. (10/1/2003)*

Cusumano 2005 Merlot (Sicilia) $10. 87 Best Buy —*M.L. (7/1/2006)*

Cusumano 2005 Rosato Nerello Mascalese (Sicilia) $10. 86 Best Buy —*M.L. (6/21/2006)*

Cusumano 2004 Nero d'Avola (Sicilia) $10. 87 Best Buy —*M.L. (7/1/2006)*

Cusumano 2002 Nadarìa Nero d'Avola (Sicilia) $10. 87 —*J.C. (10/1/2003)*

Cusumano 2005 Nero d'Avola (Sicilia) $10. 87 Best Buy —*M.L. (7/1/2006)*

Cusumano 2003 Sagana Nero d'Avola (Sicilia) $NA. 88 —*M.L. (7/1/2006)*

Cusumano 2004 Sàgana Nero d'Avola (Sicilia) $30. 87 —*M.L. (7/1/2006)*

Cusumano 2001 Sàgana Nero d'Avola (Sicilia) $21. 85 —*J.C. (10/1/2003)*

Cusumano 2005 Benuara Red Blend (Sicilia) $15. 88 —*M.L. (7/1/2006)*

Cusumano 2001 Benuara Red Blend (Sicilia) $15. 88 —*J.C. (10/1/2003)*

Cusumano 2004 Noa Red Blend (Sicilia) $28. 88 —*M.L. (7/1/2006)*

Cusumano 2001 Noa Red Blend (Sicilia) $30. 84 —*J.C. (10/1/2003)*

Cusumano 2005 Syrah (Sicilia) $10. 86 Best Buy —*M.L. (7/1/2006)*

Cusumano 2005 Alcamo White Blend (Sicilia) $10. 85 Best Buy —*M.L. (7/1/2006)*

Cusumano 2005 Angimbé White Blend (Sicilia) $13. 87 —*M.L. (7/1/2006)*

Cusumano 2002 Angimbé / Insolia-Chardonnay White Blend (Sicilia) $15. 86 —*J.C. (10/1/2003)*

D'ANGELO

D'Angelo 1997 Canneto Aglianico (Aglianico del Vulture) $23. 84 —*C.S. (5/1/2002)*

D'Angelo 2001 Sacravite Aglianico (Aglianico del Vulture) $12. 88 Best Buy —*M.S. (2/1/2005)*

DA VINCI

Da Vinci 2001 Brunello (Brunello di Montalcino) $70. 89 *(4/1/2006)*

Da Vinci 2001 S. to Ippolito Merlot-Syrah (Toscana) $42. 86 *(12/31/2004)*

Da Vinci 2005 Sangiovese (Chianti) $16. This really is the quintessential pizza or pasta wine: It offers medium intensity and build, just as Chianti should, and big notes of cherry fruit, tobacco, smoke and leather. **87** —*M.L. (11/1/2007)*

Da Vinci 2004 Sangiovese (Chianti) $16. Da Vinci delivers attractive ruby brilliance with sweet notes of red berry, leather, spice, espresso and toasted oak. This is approachable on every level and promises to make an excellent match to pasta and meat dishes. **87** —*M.L. (11/1/2007)*

Da Vinci 2003 Sangiovese (Chianti) $14. 85 *(12/31/2004)*

Da Vinci 2002 Sangiovese (Chianti Classico) $17. 82 *(4/1/2005)*

Da Vinci 2001 Sangiovese (Chianti Classico) $17. 88 *(12/31/2004)*

Da Vinci 2003 Riserva Sangiovese (Chianti) $24. A distinct herbal or spice note is the first thing you'll notice in this Sangiovese-based Riserva. Medicinal herbs, Indian spice, cinnamon, cumin and dried sage or oregano are very abundant and set it apart from the rest. In the mouth, this is a firm wine with a solid tannic grip suggesting a successful pairing with grilled meats marinated in rosemary oil. 89 *—M.L. (11/1/2007)*

Da Vinci 2001 Riserva Sangiovese (Chianti) $20. 87 *(12/31/2004)*

Da Vinci 2000 Riserva Sangiovese (Chianti) $20. 88 *—M.S. (10/1/2004)*

DAL FORNO ROMANO

Dal Forno Romano 1999 Corvina, Rondinella, Molinara (Amarone della Valpolicella) $459. 95 Cellar Selection *(11/1/2005)*

Dal Forno Romano 2002 Vigneto di Monte Lodoletta Corvina, Rondinella, Molinara (Amarone della Valpolicella) $535. Winemaker Romano Dal Forno fearlessly confronted the soggy 2002 vintage with high extraction techniques and barrique aging (36 months). This is an inky, dense wine (more syrupy than it is vinous) with black currant, peppermill, chocolate fudge and big, firm wood tannins. It is so monolithic, a viable food match is virtually impossible. As always, Dal Forno straddles a fine line between brilliance and exaggeration. 90 Cellar Selection *—M.L. (10/1/2007)*

Dal Forno Romano 1997 Red Blend (Valpolicella Superiore) $70. 90 *(5/1/2003)*

Dal Forno Romano 1996 Red Blend (Amarone della Valpolicella) $300. 91 *(5/1/2003)*

DALFIUME

Dalfiume 1999 Rubicone Sangiovese (Emilia-Romagna) $6. 87 Best Buy *—M.N. (12/31/2000)*

DAMILANO

Damilano 2006 Arneis (Langhe) $16. At first, the Damilano seemed fairly nondescript; a little fruit and earth, a tight short palate and little finish. But once it had been swirled and aired, it became more interesting; the fruit became more pronounced showing an attractive apricot and floral quality, while the earthiness became smoky and nutty. The wine still finished a little short, but overall an attractive package. 85 *—M.G. (12/31/2007)*

Damilano 2005 Barbera (Barbera d'Alba) $18. The Damilano is a modern take on Barbera; a big, very ripe, chunky wine that is easy to like. The fruit is thick with dark jammy flavors, and although there are hints of something more exotic lurking, at the moment all you have is a hint of spice. Easy to drink now, but worth cellaring for a couple of years, as it will prove to be more interesting with some bottle age. 88 *—M.G. (12/31/2007)*

Damilano 1999 Barbera (Barbera d'Alba) $25. 90 *—M.S. (12/15/2003)*

Damilano 1999 Cannubi Nebbiolo (Barolo) $72. 88 *(4/2/2004)*

Damilano 1998 Cannubi Nebbiolo (Barolo) $70. 91 *—C.S. (11/15/2002)*

Damilano 2003 Liste Nebbiolo (Barolo) $63. A muted nose but a pleasant combination of sweet dark fruit, violets and earth. The wine shows more concentration on the palate, but the finish is quite short. Pleasant and commercial. 86 *—M.G. (12/31/2007)*

Damilano 1999 Liste Nebbiolo (Barolo) $65. 85 *(4/2/2004)*

Damilano 1998 Liste Nebbiolo (Barolo) $98. 93 Editors' Choice *—C.S. (11/15/2002)*

DANZANTE

Danzante 2001 Merlot (Sicilia) $11. 81 *—M.S. (10/1/2004)*

Danzante 2000 Merlot (Sicilia) $11. 84 *(9/1/2002)*

Danzante 1999 Merlot (Sicilia) $11. 86 Best Buy *—C.S. (5/1/2002)*

Danzante 2005 Pinot Grigio (Delle Venezie) $10. You can usually count on this popular Grigio to deliver good value thanks to its no-fuss approach, fresh citrus and white fruit aromas. This release is less convincing because of a slightly muddled nose and watery mouthfeel. 84 *—M.L. (11/15/2007)*

Danzante 2004 Pinot Grigio (Delle Venezie) $10. 87 Best Buy *—M.L. (6/1/2006)*

Danzante 2003 Pinot Grigio (Delle Venezie) $10. 83 *—J.C. (12/31/2004)*

Danzante 2001 Pinot Grigio (Delle Venezie) $10. 86 *(9/1/2002)*

Danzante 2002 Sangiovese (Marche) $10. 84 *—M.S. (6/1/2005)*

Danzante 2000 Sangiovese (Marche) $11. 84 *(9/1/2002)*

DARDANO

Dardano 1999 Nebbiolo (Barolo) $25. 89 *—J.C. (11/15/2004)*

Dardano 1997 Nebbiolo (Barolo) $23. 87 *—C.S. (11/15/2002)*

Dardano 2000 Primitivo (Salento) $9. 86 Best Buy *—C.S. (5/1/2002)*

DAVID STERZA

David Sterza 2003 Corvina, Rondinella, Molinara (Amarone della Valpolicella Classico) $42. Every once in a while, wine writers are awarded a producer like David Sterza: young, relatively unknown and full of promise for the future. His Amarone is a genuine "discovery" with beautiful, bright fruit, good cheer, cherry cough drop, red apple, coffee and dried herbs. This is a bright, lively wine and a wonderful expression of the territory. 92 Editors' Choice *—M.L. (10/1/2007)*

DEGANI

Degani 2003 Corvina, Rondinella, Molinara (Amarone della Valpolicella Classico) $48. This is a richly concentrated, velvety wine with chewy characteristics and excellent length. The nose, on the other hand, is slightly disjointed and murky with contrasting aromas of coffee grind and medicinal herbs. 88 *—M.L. (10/1/2007)*

Degani 2003 La Rosta Corvina, Rondinella, Molinara (Amarone della Valpolicella Classico) $56. This is a big, brawny, plush, "international" Amarone that sees four years of oak and delivers thick layers of espresso coffee, chocolate fudge, wood toast and honey nut. It has a chewy, viscous mouthfeel, rounded off by caressing spice flavors and very good length on the finish. 91 *—M.L. (10/1/2007)*

DEI

Dei 1999 Red Blend (Rosso di Montepulciano) $15. 87 *—M.N. (9/1/2001)*

Dei 2002 Sangiovese (Vino Nobile di Montepulciano) $30. 87 *—M.S. (7/1/2005)*

Dei 2001 Bossona Sangiovese (Vino Nobile di Montepulciano) $45. 91 Editors' Choice *—M.S. (7/1/2005)*

DELLA STAFFA

Della Staffa 1997 Chardonnay (Alto Adige) $15. 86 *(9/1/2000)*

DELLATORRI

Dellatorri 2003 Pinot Grigio (Delle Venezie) $12. 82 *—M.L. (2/1/2006)*

DESSILANI

Dessilani 1997 Reserve Selection Barbera (Barbera di Piemonte) $16. 86 *(4/1/2000)*

DEZZANI

Dezzani 2000 Gli Scaglioni Barbera (Barbera d'Asti) $17. 90 Editors' Choice *—J.C. (11/15/2004)*

Dezzani 2004 Il Gavi Cortese (Gavi) $15. 88 *—J.C. (3/1/2006)*

Dezzani 2004 I Morelli Moscato (Moscato d'Asti) $12. 88 Best Buy *—M.L. (12/15/2005)*

DI LENARDO

Di Lenardo 2004 Pinot Grigio (Friuli Grave) $10. 87 Best Buy *—M.L. (2/1/2006)*

DI MAJO NORANTE

Di Majo Norante 2001 Contado Aglianico (Molise) $12. 89 Best Buy *—M.S. (2/1/2005)*

Di Majo Norante 2002 Ramitello Red Blend (Terra degli Osci) $14. 89 Best Buy *—M.L. (11/15/2005)*

Di Majo Norante 2001 Ramitello Red Blend (Terra degli Osci) $14. 87 *—M.S. (2/1/2005)*

Di Majo Norante 2003 Sangiovese (Terra degli Osci) $10. 86 Best Buy *—M.S. (2/1/2005)*

Di Majo Norante 2002 Apianae 500ml White Blend (Molise) $19. 93 *—M.L. (10/1/2006)*

Di Majo Norante 1999 Biblos White Blend (Molise) $11. 81 *—M.N. (9/1/2001)*

DI MEO

Di Meo 2004 A Aglianico (Irpinia) $16. Deep, ripe and rich red fruit flavors characterize a wine that offers generous aromas of sweet cherry, pipe tobacco, mint, licorice and lingering smoke tones over firm, mouth-drying tannins. Aglianico, aged in oak for 12 months. 87 *—M.L. (8/1/2007)*

Di Meo 2003 A Aglianico (Irpinia) $16. This is a raw and nervous Aglianico with firm tannins and finely etched mineral tones spread over red fruit nuances and toast. The nose offers blackberry, pomegranate and ash. It begs for a pairing with stewed game meat or crunchy roasted lamb. 87 *—M.L. (8/1/2007)*

Di Meo 2000 T Aglianico (Taurasi) $32. Despite its seven years of age (two of which were spent in oak), this is a seemingly youthful wine with bright and lively fruity tones of berries, cherry soda or candy, red apple backed by a supporting cast of vanilla, cedar and roasted nuts. It offers chewy, firm tannins and good length on the finish. 90 —*M.L. (8/1/2007)*

Di Meo 2005 C Coda di Volpe (Coda di Volpe d'Irpinia) $14. This little-known grape from the Campania region of southern Italy boasts many nutty, almost pine-like aromas over melon, peach and pear. Medium intensity and freshness characterize the mouth and suggest a pairing with simple grilled fish or vegetables. 85 —*M.L. (11/15/2007)*

Di Meo 2005 S Falanghina (Sannio) $15. Pear, Golden Delicious apple and mineral notes reminiscent of talc powder are the most compelling aromas of this fresh and zesty Falanghina-based wine. Pair it with pasta, or fish dishes. 86 —*M.L. (11/15/2007)*

Di Meo 2004 G Greco (Greco di Tufo) $NA. 88 Best Buy —*M.L. (11/15/2005)*

Di Meo 2000 Don Generoso Red Blend (Irpinia) $65. This is deeply rich and concentrated, with notes of ripe fruit, tobacco, leather, spice, smoke and sweet black cherry. It's soft and full on the palate with spice, clove flavors and firm tannins. 91 —*M.L. (8/1/2007)*

Di Meo 2004 Isso Red Blend (Irpinia) $13. This is a fine and compact southern red that lacks big intensity but that delivers aromas of prunes, blackberries, red fruit and a background touch of dill weed. It has a firm build but seems somewhat lean on the palate. 85 —*M.L. (8/1/2007)*

ITALY

DIEVOLE

Dievole 2001 Dieulele Riserva Red Blend (Chianti Classico) $55. A blockbuster red from a beautiful Chianti Classico estate that drinks like a slab of succulent charred steak. Billboard-sized aromas of cherry and espresso bean still manage to be overwhelmed by notes of burnt wood. If you can get past the woodshop tones, the mouthful is divinely velvety and supple with soft tannins and firm structure. Drink now. 89 —*M.L. (2/1/2007)*

Dievole 2001 Novecento Riserva Red Blend (Chianti Classico) $32. With an international team and winemaker, Dievole presents modern, succulent and irresistible Chianti Classicos with concentration, coffee, nutmeg, leather, cherry under spirits, chocolate and toasted almond. You will love this big, bold style: Chewy in the mouth and soft as silky on the taste buds. 91 —*M.L. (2/1/2007)*

Dievole 2003 Vendemmia Chianti Classico Red Blend (Chianti Classico) $14. You can't go wrong with a wine like this: It goes down smooth, is food-friendly and offers a complete package of alluring aromas. There's cherry, graphite, tobacco, chopped mint and licorice. It has a medium consistency and a polished finish. 87 —*M.L. (2/1/2007)*

Dievole 2001 Sangiovese (Chianti Classico) $20. 86 *(4/1/2005)*

Dievole 1999 Broccato Sangiovese (Toscana) $29. 88 —*M.S. (9/1/2006)*

Dievole 2000 Novecento Riserva Sangiovese (Chianti Classico) $37. 93 Editors' Choice *(4/1/2005)*

Dievole 1998 Riserva Sangiovese (Chianti Classico) $35. 92 —*R.V. (8/1/2002)*

DILEO

DiLeo 1996 Cabernet Sauvignon (Sicilia) $22. 85 —*J.C. (10/1/2003)*

DiLeo 1998 Achilles Nero d'Avola (Sicilia) $14. 80 *(10/1/2003)*

DiLeo 1999 Sangiovese (Sicilia) $20. 84 —*J.C. (10/1/2003)*

DOLMEN

Dolmen 2000 Nebbiolo (Colli del Limbara) $24. 88 —*M.S. (12/15/2003)*

DOMENICO DE BERTIOL

Domenico de Bertiol NV Prosecco (Prosecco di Conegliano) $13. 86 —*J.C. (12/31/2003)*

DOMÌNI VENETI

Domìni Veneti 2000 Corvina (Amarone della Valpolicella Classico) $39. 89 *(11/1/2005)*

Domìni Veneti 2003 Corvina, Rondinella, Molinara (Amarone della Valpolicella Classico) $NA. Like the vineyard select Vigneti di Jago by the same producer, this wine showcases heavily toasted notes of oak, nut and spice, although here they seem more balanced. The wine has solid tannins and a chewy consistency that is pleasantly accented by cherry-berry flavors. 90 —*M.L. (10/1/2007)*

Domìni Veneti 2000 Corvina, Rondinella, Molinara (Amarone della Valpolicella Classico) $NA. Beautiful density and color characterize this wine as do its layered notes of exotic spice, cardamom, curry and roasted nut. Plush, full red fruit and cherry build in intensity, especially on the palate, creating a rich wine with a firm backbone, smooth texture and dusty notes on the finish. 92 —*M.L. (12/1/2007)*

Domìni Veneti 2003 Vigneti di Jago Corvina, Rondinella, Molinara (Amarone della Valpolicella Classico) $NA. Despite its deep concentration and evident power, here is a food-friendly wine (think pheasant stuffed with mushrooms or polenta with wild boar) that balances brawn with soft tones of vanilla, nut and bright fruit. The only distraction on the nose is heavily toasted oak. 89 —*M.L. (10/1/2007)*

Domìni Veneti 1997 Vigneti di Jago Corvina (Amarone della Valpolicella Classico) $52. 88 *(11/1/2005)*

Domìni Veneti 2002 Ca' de napa Garganega (Soave Classico) $17. 86 —*M.S. (10/1/2004)*

Domìni Veneti 2002 Red Blend (Amarone della Valpolicella Classico) $39. 91 Editors' Choice *(11/1/2005)*

Domìni Veneti 1999 Red Blend (Amarone della Valpolicella Classico) $39. 93 Editors' Choice *(5/1/2003)*

Domìni Veneti 1999 La Casetta Ripasso Red Blend (Valpolicella Classico Superiore) $20. 91 Editors' Choice *(5/1/2003)*

Domìni Veneti 2000 Vigneti di Jago Red Blend (Amarone della Valpolicella Classico) $60. 88 *(11/1/2005)*

Domìni Veneti 1997 Vigneti di Lago Red Blend (Valpolicella Classico) $48. 89 *(5/1/2003)*

Domìni Veneti NV Vigneti di Moron Red Blend (Recioto della Valpolicella) $23. 90 Editors' Choice *(5/1/2003)*

DON GATTI

Don Gatti NV Amabile Frizzante Malvasia Bianca (Colli Piacentini) $9. 82 —*M.S. (12/31/2002)*

DONATELLA CINELLI COLOMBINI

Donatella Cinelli Colombini 2001 Brunello (Brunello di Montalcino) $55. 95 Editors' Choice *(4/1/2006)*

Donatella Cinelli Colombini 2000 Brunello (Brunello di Montalcino) $49. 92 —*M.S. (7/1/2005)*

Donatella Cinelli Colombini 1999 Brunello (Brunello di Montalcino) $45. 88 —*M.S. (6/1/2004)*

Donatella Cinelli Colombini 1997 Brunello (Brunello di Montalcino) $38. 91 —*R.V. (8/1/2002)*

Donatella Cinelli Colombini 2000 Prime Donne Brunello (Brunello di Montalcino) $65. 90 —*M.S. (7/1/2005)*

Donatella Cinelli Colombini 2000 Riserva Brunello (Brunello di Montalcino) $65. 94 Editors' Choice *(4/1/2006)*

Donatella Cinelli Colombini 1999 Riserva Brunello (Brunello di Montalcino) $65. 95 Cellar Selection —*M.S. (7/1/2005)*

Donatella Cinelli Colombini 2001 Prime Donne Sangiovese (Brunello di Montalcino) $65. This is a wine that starts off restrained yet hints at the enormity of what's to come. It offers a quick blast of creamy espresso, cherry, licorice and ripe blackberry at first and the intensity of the aromas grow to gigantic proportions without ever losing their clarity and harmony. This is a big, bruising Brunello with firm, dusty tannins and good length. 92 —*M.L. (2/1/2007)*

DONNA CRISTINA

Donna Cristina 2004 Pinot Grigio (Lazio) $8. 85 —*M.L. (2/1/2006)*

DONNA OLGA

Donna Olga 2001 Brunello (Brunello di Montalcino) $75. 87 *(4/1/2006)*

DONNAFUGATA

Donnafugata 2004 Vigna di Gabri Ansonica (Sicilia) $NA. 87 —*M.L. (7/1/2006)*

Donnafugata 2004 Sedàra Nero d'Avola (Sicilia) $15. 87 —*M.L. (7/1/2006)*

Donnafugata 2003 Sedàra Nero d'Avola (Sicilia) $15. 87 —*M.L. (7/1/2006)*

Donnafugata 2003 Mille e Una Notte Red Blend (Contessa Entellina) $60. 92 Cellar Selection —*M.L. (7/1/2006)*

Donnafugata 2002 Mille e Una Notte Red Blend (Sicilia) $69. 91 —*M.L. (7/1/2006)*

Donnafugata 1999 Mille e Uno Notte Red Blend (Contessa Entellina) $65. 90 —*R.V. (10/1/2003)*

Donnafugata 2002 Sedàra Red Blend (Sicilia) $12. 86 —*R.V. (10/1/2003)*

Donnafugata 2003 Tancredi Red Blend (Contessa Entellina) $30. 90 —*M.L. (7/1/2006)*

Donnafugata 2002 Tancredi Red Blend (Contessa Entellina) $30. 91 Editors' Choice —*M.L. (7/1/2006)*

Donnafugata 2001 Tancredi Red Blend (Contessa Entellina) $25. 88 —*R.V. (10/1/2003)*

Donnafugata 2003 Anthilia White Blend (Sicilia) $15. 86 —*M.S. (10/1/2004)*

Donnafugata 2005 Anthìlia White Blend (Sicilia) $15. 86 *—M.L. (7/1/2006)*

Donnafugata 2004 Anthìlia White Blend (Sicilia) $15. 86 *—M.L. (7/1/2006)*

Donnafugata 2002 Anthìlia White Blend (Sicilia) $12. 84 *—R.V. (10/1/2003)*

Donnafugata 2001 Chiarandà del Merlon Contessa Entellina White Blend (Sicilia) $35. 89 *—R.V. (10/1/2003)*

Donnafugata 2004 Chiarandé White Blend (Contessa Entellina) $36. 88 *—M.L. (7/1/2006)*

Donnafugata 2004 Ben Ryé Zibibbo (Passito di Pantelleria) $38. 95 Editors' Choice *—M.L. (7/1/2006)*

Donnafugata 2004 Kabir Zibibbo (Moscato di Pantelleria) $NA. 90 *—M.L. (7/1/2006)*

DRAGANI

Dragani 1996 Selva de' Canonici Montepulciano (Montepulciano d'Abruzzo) $14. 87 *—J.F. (9/1/2001)*

DREI DONA TENUTA LA PALAZZA

Drei Dona Tenuta La Palazza 2003 Vigneti delle Rosenere Albana (Albana di Romagna) $20. A deep, amber-colored dessert wine that boasts a gorgeous aromatic embroidery of honey, citrus rind, apricot and vanilla. Those same flavors are skillfully integrated in the mouth and leave a lasting impression thanks to the wine's lengthy persistency. Albana grapes are dried on straw mats and refined in oak for 18 months. 91 Editors' Choice *—M.L. (2/1/2007)*

Drei Dona Tenuta La Palazza 2001 Magnificat Cabernet Sauvignon (Emilia-Romagna) $35. A score of interesting notes strive to push though to the nose such as leather, coffee, tar, almond paste, licorice and berry fruit but come off slightly muddled instead. There's an interesting chalky or dusty feel in the mouth with solid tannins and medium length. The wine is aged 20 months in French oak. 87 *—M.L. (2/1/2007)*

Drei Dona Tenuta La Palazza 1997 Graf Noir Red Blend (Emilia-Romagna) $60. A charming treat from enologist Franco Bernabei, this Sangiovese-Cabernet Franc and Negretto Longanesi blend is a layered and intense red with green or vegetal notes, leather, licorice and black plum. The tannins are firm, yielding a solid sensation in the mouth making this a perfect pairing partner to roasted leg of lamb. Drink now. 87 *—M.L. (2/1/2007)*

Drei Dona Tenuta La Palazza 2004 Notturno Sangiovese (Emilia-Romagna) $15. Notes of blackberry and blueberry emerge first and are quickly followed by marzipan, licorice and cedar wood. This wine boasts a nice, firm structure that comes off clean, not heavy. 86 *—M.L. (2/1/2007)*

Drei Dona Tenuta La Palazza 2001 Pruno Superiore Riserva Sangiovese (Sangiovese di Romagna) $30. The high quality of this wine is obvious as soon as you raise your glass to your nose: Cherry and forest berry are nicely balanced by toasted wood notes and the mouth is characterized by intense spice, chewy tannins and coffee liquor or spice cake flavors on the finish. 91 *—M.L. (2/1/2007)*

Drei Dona Tenuta La Palazza 2004 Vigneti delle Rosenere Sangiovese (Sangiovese di Romagna) $12. Sangiovese grown in the central Romagna region of Italy is often a deeper and darker expression of the variety with distinct aromas of blackberry and cherry fruit. This wine is no exception. It's tame in the mouth with firm tannins and medium persistency. 85 *—M.L. (2/1/2007)*

DRIUS

Drius 2004 Pinot Grigio (Isonzo del Friuli) $NA. 86 *—M.L. (2/1/2006)*

DRUSIAN

Drusian NV Brut Prosecco (Prosecco di Conegliano e Valdobbiadene) $15. Here is a more opulent style of Prosecco with floral and mineral tones backed by an attractive herbal accent. The mouthfeel is creamy and thick so this expression will appeal less to those looking for zippy freshness. 87 *—M.L. (12/15/2007)*

Drusian NV Brut Prosecco (Prosecco di Valdobbiadene) $15. 88 *—M.L. (6/1/2006)*

Drusian NV Extra Dry Prosecco (Prosecco di Conegliano e Valdobbiadene) $15. Soapy, floral tones come forward, followed by tempered white peach, kiwi and pear. In the mouth, this sparkler registers medium intensity and has a lean, crisp feel. 86 *—M.L. (12/15/2007)*

Drusian NV Extra Dry Prosecco (Prosecco di Valdobbiadene) $15. 86 *—M.L. (6/1/2006)*

DUCA DI CASTELMONTE

Duca di Castelmonte 2002 Notorious Syrah (Sicilia) $16. 86 *—M.S. (11/15/2004)*

DUCA DI SALAPARUTA

Duca di Salaparuta 2002 Bianca di Valguarnera Insolia (Sicilia) $40. 88 *—M.L. (7/1/2006)*

Duca di Salaparuta 2004 Colomba Platino Insolia (Sicilia) $18. 87 *—M.L. (7/1/2006)*

Duca di Salaparuta 2003 Colomba Platino Insolia (Sicilia) $18. 87 *—M.S. (2/1/2005)*

Duca di Salaparuta 2000 Bianca di Valguarnera Inzolia (Sicilia) $35. 88 *—R.V. (10/1/2003)*

Duca di Salaparuta 2001 Duca Enrico Nero d'Avola (Sicilia) $50. 91 Cellar Selection *—M.L. (7/1/2006)*

Duca di Salaparuta 1999 Duca Enrico Nero d'Avola (Sicilia) $55. 89 *—R.V. (10/1/2003)*

Duca di Salaparuta 2000 Terra D'Agala Red Blend (Sicilia) $18. 84 *—M.S. (7/1/2005)*

Duca di Salaparuta 2002 Terre d'Agala Red Blend (Sicilia) $14. 89 Best Buy *—M.L. (7/1/2006)*

Duca di Salaparuta 1999 Terre D'Agala Red Blend (Sicilia) $16. 87 *—M.S. (10/1/2003)*

Duca di Salaparuta 2000 Trislelè Red Blend (Sicilia) $NA. 88 *—R.V. (10/1/2003)*

Duca di Salaparuta 2003 Vajasindi Làvico Red Blend (Etna) $15. This historic Sicilian estate presents its first vintage of its newest wine from the volcanic slopes of the Etna volcano. Indigenous grape Nerello Mascalese is blended with a touch of Merlot to achieve a medium-structured wine with delicate and refined aromas of blue flower, black stone, campfire, cherry and small forest berry. The wine is big in intensity and delicacy. 90 Best Buy *—M.L. (4/1/2007)*

Duca di Salaparuta 2002 Colomba Platino White Blend (Sicilia) $15. 85 *—R.V. (10/1/2003)*

Duca di Salaparuta 2001 Colomba Platino White Blend (Sicilia) $16. 86 *—J.C. (10/1/2003)*

DUCA LEONARDO

Duca Leonardo 2000 La Gioiosa Montepulciano (Montepulciano d'Abruzzo) $6. 83 *—M.S. (11/15/2003)*

DUCAROSSO

Ducarosso 2001 Riserva Sangiovese (Chianti) $11. 86 Best Buy *—M.L. (10/1/2006)*

ECCO DOMANI

Ecco Domani 2000 Merlot (Delle Venezie) $10. 83 *(5/1/2003)*

Ecco Domani 2005 Pinot Grigio (Delle Venezie) $11. 86 *—M.L. (6/1/2006)*

Ecco Domani 2006 Pinot Grigio (Delle Venezie) $11. This is the perfect wine for washing down pasta salad and easy dishes. Peach, citrus and pink grapefruit are delivered in measured doses and the wine is light and lean in the mouth with a brilliant sparkle of acidity on the close. 85 *—M.L. (11/15/2007)*

Ecco Domani 2003 Pinot Grigio (Delle Venezie) $10. 82 *—J.C. (12/31/2004)*

Ecco Domani 2002 Pinot Grigio (Delle Venezie) $10. 85 *—J.C. (7/1/2003)*

Ecco Domani 2001 Maso Canali Pinot Grigio (Trentino) $17. 84 *—J.C. (7/1/2003)*

Ecco Domani 2005 Sangiovese (Chianti) $12. After a slow start, this reveals vibrant notes of red fruit, mineral and toasted nut. There's a nice overall roundness that makes it soft in the mouth and an easy, pleasant drinking experience. 85 *—M.L. (11/1/2007)*

Ecco Domani 2004 Sangiovese (Chianti) $11. 84 *—M.S. (10/1/2006)*

Ecco Domani 2000 Sangiovese (Chianti) $10. 84 *(8/1)*

ELENA WALCH

Elena Walch 2002 Castel Ringberg Chardonnay (Alto Adige) $18. 86 *—R.V. (7/1/2003)*

Elena Walch 2004 Castel Ringberg Riserva Chardonnay (Alto Adige) $34. If you love Italy and love elegantly oaked Chardonnay, this is your wine. Deep gold in color, Elena Walch delivers generous notes of apple, nut, spring flowers over lavish honey aromas. Opulent, modern and seductively smooth in the mouth, pair it with butter squash, turkey or roasted pork. 92 Editors' Choice *—M.L. (12/1/2007)*

Elena Walch 2001 Cashmere Gewürztraminer (Alto Adige) $25. 91 *—R.V. (7/1/2003)*

Elena Walch 2005 Kastelaz Gewürztraminer (Alto Adige) $28. Extremely floral and fragrant, Elena Walch's Gewürztraminer boasts generous layers of jasmine, passion fruit, fresh apricot and honey. This is a very feminine expression of a naturally aromatic variety that ends on a very crisp, fresh note. 88 *—M.L. (12/1/2007)*

Elena Walch 2002 Kastelatz Gewürztraminer (Alto Adige) $25. 89 *—R.V. (7/1/2003)*

Elena Walch 2003 Castel Ringberg Riserva Lagrein (Alto Adige) $38. This is a gorgeous juicy-red-fruit driven wine with complex and interwoven nuances of blueberry, cherry, cookie dough, chocolate chip and soft vanilla oak playing a supporting role (the wine sees 18 months of oak). Deep and dark in color, this about as creamy-smooth on the palate as they come. 91 *—M.L. (9/1/2007)*

Elena Walch 2003 Riserva Kastelaz Merlot (Alto Adige) $35. An outstanding Merlot with notes of blueberry, red fruit and light vanilla bean. It also has a touch of leather and tobacco, which add personality. The wine is solid in the mouth with a medium build, finesse and long persistency on the finish. 91 *—M.L. (4/1/2007)*

Elena Walch 2002 Riserva Kastelaz Merlot (Alto Adige) $35. Here's a wine that scores sky high in drinkability: It is a modern Merlot but avoids being big or brawny. In fact, its structure is just right—solid without being heavy—and the many delicate aromatic nuances are the finishing touches on a pretty picture. Look for forest berry fruit, light toast and loads of almond (refined in oak for 18 months). 91 *—M.L. (4/1/2007)*

Elena Walch 2002 Pinot Bianco (Alto Adige) $13. 86 *—R.V. (7/1/2003)*

Elena Walch 2005 Kastelaz Pinot Bianco (Alto Adige) $21. Here is a gorgeous and very fragrant Pinot Bianco with loads of stone fruit, floral and mineral nuances. Spicy acidity livens up the mouth and is fueled by the wine's creamy and smooth consistency (one third is aged in oak). This is a very drinkable wine: Try it with shellfish, pasta, white meat or with appetizers. 90 *—M.L. (9/1/2007)*

Elena Walch 2002 Kastelatz Pinot Bianco (Alto Adige) $23. 87 *—R.V. (7/1/2003)*

Elena Walch 2006 Pinot Grigio (Alto Adige) $17. There's a mellow, soft quality to this cool-climate Grigio that helps it stand out in a crowd. This is a round wine—no sharp edges here—that offers generous peachy cream, apricot, amaretto and just enough acidity to be zesty and mouth-cleansing. 88 *—M.L. (12/1/2007)*

Elena Walch 2004 Pinot Grigio (Alto Adige) $14. 87 *—M.L. (2/1/2006)*

Elena Walch 2002 Pinot Grigio (Alto Adige) $12. 85 *—R.V. (7/1/2003)*

Elena Walch 1997 Pinot Grigio (Alto Adige) $13. 87 *(8/1/1999)*

Elena Walch 2005 Castel Ringberg Pinot Grigio (Alto Adige) $23. Honey, sweet peach, vanilla-almond, hay, banana and yellow flower best describe this smooth, creamy Pinot Grigio from northern Italy. The wine closes with refreshing crispness making for an extremely enjoyable experience. 90 *—M.L. (12/1/2007)*

Elena Walch 2004 Castel Ringberg Pinot Grigio (Alto Adige) $18. 87 *—M.L. (2/1/2006)*

Elena Walch 2004 Ludwig Pinot Nero (Alto Adige) $25. You'll notice a brownish tinge in the glass that gives way to aromas of plum, prune, blue flower and mineral. The wine delivers full and round flavors of forest berries and toasted nuts. Fermented in steel and aged in oak for one year. 87 *—M.L. (9/1/2007)*

Elena Walch 2005 Castel Ringberg Sauvignon Blanc (Alto Adige) $21. There's a playful touch of smoky toast and dusty minerality that adds a deeper dimension to this modern and beautifully constructed wine (one third is aged in barrique). Pair it with leafy greens, seafood and white meat. 88 *—M.L. (9/1/2007)*

Elena Walch 2004 Beyond the Clouds White Blend (Alto Adige) $36. Put your nose to the glass and you will be rewarded with extreme floral fragrances that suggest naturally aromatic grapes are used over a Chard base. Ultimately, this is a very feminine, lady-like wine busting with white flowers and naturally sweet aromas. 90 **Editors' Choice** *—M.L. (12/1/2007)*

Elena Walch 2002 Castel Ringberg Pinot Grigio (Alto Adige) $16. 86 *—R.V. (7/1/2003)*

Elena Walch 1998 Castel Ringberg Pinot Grigio (Alto Adige) $20. 87 *(8/1/1999)*

Elena Walch 2002 Castel Ringberg Sauvignon Blanc (Alto Adige) $23. 88 *—R.V. (7/1/2003)*

Elena Walch 2001 Beyond the Clouds White Blend (Alto Adige) $40. 90 *—R.V. (7/1/2003)*

ELIO ALTARE

Elio Altare 1996 Larigi Barbera (Langhe) $70. 90 *(4/1/2000)*

Elio Altare 1998 Dolcetto (Dolcetto d'Alba) $19. 89 *(4/1/2000)*

Elio Altare 1998 Nebbiolo (Barolo) $60. 90 *(4/2/2004)*

ELIO GRASSO

Elio Grasso 1996 Vigna Martini Barbera (Barbera d'Alba) $21. 87 *(4/1/2000)*

Elio Grasso 1998 Vigna Dei Grassi Dolcetto (Dolcetto d'Alba) $14. 88 *(4/1/2000)*

Elio Grasso 1999 Ginestra Vigna Casa Maté Nebbiolo (Barolo) $53. 93 **Editors' Choice** *(4/2/2004)*

ELIO PERRONE

Elio Perrone 2004 Clartè Moscato (Moscato d'Asti) $18. 85 *—M.L. (12/15/2005)*

Elio Perrone 2004 Sourgal Moscato (Moscato d'Asti) $16. 87 *—M.L. (12/15/2005)*

ELISABETTA

Elisabetta 1998 Le Marze Bordeaux Blend (Toscana) $40. 89 *—M.S. (8/1/2002)*

Elisabetta 1999 Aulo Sangiovese (Toscana) $12. 86 *—M.S. (8/1/2002)*

ELORINA

Elorina 1999 Eloro Nero d'Avola (Sicilia) $11. 83 *—M.S. (10/1/2003)*

Elorina 1998 Pachino Nero d'Avola (Sicilia) $17. 84 *—M.S. (10/1/2003)*

ELVIO COGNO

Elvio Cogno 1999 Bricco dei Merli Barbera (Barbera d'Alba) $34. 90 *—M.S. (11/15/2002)*

Elvio Cogno 1997 Bricco del Merli Barbera (Barbera d'Alba) $30. 87 *(4/1/2000)*

Elvio Cogno 2003 Vigna Del Mandorlo Dolcetto (Dolcetto d'Alba) $20. 90 **Editors' Choice** *—J.C. (3/1/2005)*

Elvio Cogno 1998 Vigna del Mandorlo Dolcetto (Dolcetto d'Alba) $16. 88 *(4/1/2000)*

Elvio Cogno 1999 Ravera Nebbiolo (Barolo) $63. 91 *(4/2/2004)*

ENRICO

Enrico NV Brut Prosecco (Prosecco di Valdobbiadene) $11. 84 *—M.S. (12/15/2005)*

ENRICO SANTINI

Enrico Santini 2004 Poggio al Moro Red Blend (Bolgheri) $25. 82 *—M.S. (9/1/2006)*

Enrico Santini 2001 Montepergoli Sangiovese (Bolgheri) $65. 87 *—M.S. (9/1/2006)*

Enrico Santini 2004 Campo alla Casa White Blend (Bolgheri) $20. 86 *—M.S. (9/1/2006)*

ENZO BOGLIETTI

Enzo Boglietti 1999 Barbera (Barbera d'Alba) $17. 84 *—M.N. (9/1/2001)*

Enzo Boglietti 1998 Brunate Nebbiolo (Piedmont) $60. 89 *—R.V. (11/15/2002)*

Enzo Boglietti 1998 Casa Nere Nebbiolo (Piedmont) $60. 88 *—R.V. (11/15/2002)*

Enzo Boglietti 1998 Fossati Nebbiolo (Piedmont) $60. 90 *—R.V. (11/15/2002)*

Enzo Boglietti 1998 Buio Red Blend (Langhe) $35. 91 *—J.C. (9/1/2001)*

ERBALUNA

Erbaluna 1999 Organic Nebbiolo (Barolo) $70. The excellent 1999 vintage in Piedmont has been somewhat overlooked because it fell between some even better vintages. Erbaluna has crafted an interesting aromatic wine that shows sweet jammy fruit, licorice and violets. It still seems young, and has the structure to benefit from a few more years of bottle age, but it drinks well now. 88 *—M.G. (12/31/2007)*

ERIK BANTI

Erik Banti 2005 Sangiovese (Morellino di Scansano) $12. Sangiovese and 15% Merlot-Cab Sauvignon are combined to produce an attractive and approachable wine that goes down without a fuss, just like Morellino di Scansano should. The many identifiable aromas include fresh red fruit, almond, Mediterranean herbs and cherry candy. 88 **Best Buy** *—M.L. (11/1/2007)*

Erik Banti 2004 Ciabatta Riserva Sangiovese (Morellino di Scansano) $25. This 100% Sangiovese Morellino delivers great intensity, ripe red fruit, raspberry, licorice and dried herbs. It is a real charmer thanks to vibrant fruity flavors and a solid, firm built. Aged 13 months in barrique, it would pair well with roasted meats or lamb stew. 90 *—M.L. (11/1/2007)*

ESPERTO

Esperto 2004 Pinot Grigio (Delle Venezie) $12. 85 *—M.L. (6/1/2006)*

Esperto 2001 Pinot Grigio (Delle Venezie) $13. 86 *—J.C. (7/1/2003)*

EUGENIO COLLAVINI

Eugenio Collavini 2005 Dei Sassi Cavi Chardonnay (Collio) $NA. Vanilla cream, banana, Golden Delicious apple and a rubbery note characterize the intense aromas of this northern Italian wine that moves over the palate in a pleasing way, thanks to its creamy smoothness. 89 *—M.L. (12/1/2007)*

Eugenio Collavini 2002 Merlot Dal Pic Merlot (Collio) $NA. Very nice use of oak here: bottle aging enhances sweet vanilla aromas to the right point without overwhelming fresh berry fruit. An intriguing and complex nose is rounded off by notes of blueberry, menthol and licorice. Characterized by elegance and finesse; good structure and very dry tannins appear on the close. 90 *—M.L. (3/1/2007)*

Eugenio Collavini 2005 Villa Canlungo Pinot Grigio (Collio) $NA. The wine opens with an attractive, saturated golden color and segues into ripe aromas of apricot, mature peach, honey and melon. There are loads of honey-like flavors in the mouth and the wine is pleasantly round and creamy overall. 87 *—M.L. (12/1/2007)*

Eugenio Collavini 2005 Broy White Blend (Collio) $40. A blend of Chardonnay, Tocai Friulano and Sauvignon, the wine is supple, soft and creamy in the mouth and accented by bright fruit tones such as pineapple, banana, lemon soda and an unexpected—albeit totally appealing—touch of cracked white peppercorn. 90 *—M.L. (5/1/2007)*

F PRINCIPIANO

F Principiano 1996 La Romualda Barbera (Barbera d'Alba) $36. 87 *(4/1/2000)*

F Principiano 2000 Sant'Anna Dolcetto (Dolcetto d'Alba) $19. 85 *—M.S. (12/15/2003)*

F Principiano 1997 Sant'Anna Dolcetto (Dolcetto d'Alba) $17. 90 *(4/1/2000)*

FABIANO

Fabiano 1999 Corvina, Rondinella, Molinara (Amarone della Valpolicella) $39. 89 *(11/1/2005)*

Fabiano 1998 Corvina, Rondinella, Molinara (Amarone della Valpolicella Classico) $39. 87 *(11/1/2005)*

Fabiano 1999 I Fondatori Corvina, Rondinella, Molinara (Amarone della Valpolicella Classico) $55. 89 *(11/1/2005)*

Fabiano 1997 I Fondatori Corvina, Rondinella, Molinara (Amarone della Valpolicella Classico) $55. 86 *(11/1/2005)*

Fabiano 1998 IGT Del Veneto Pinot Grigio (Del Veneto) $7. 85 *(8/1/1999)*

Fabiano 2000 Red Blend (Amarone della Valpolicella Classico) $37. 87 *(11/1/2005)*

Fabiano 1998 I Fondatori Red Blend (Amarone della Valpolicella Classico) $50. 91 *(11/1/2005)*

FALCHINI

Falchini 2002 Vigna a Solatio Vernaccia (Vernaccia di San Gimignano) $14. 86 *—M.S. (8/1/2004)*

Falchini 2001 Vinea Doni Vernaccia (Vernaccia di San Gimignano) $25. 83 *—M.S. (8/1/2004)*

FALESCO

Falesco 2003 Marciliano Cabernet Blend (Umbria) $50. 93 **Editors' Choice** *—M.L. (9/1/2006)*

Falesco 2004 Montiano Merlot (Lazio) $40. One of the best Montianos ever, this is as dark as a moonless night. Its appearance alone bears the mark of Merlot master Riccardo Cotarella. It is a bold overstatement—backed by mindbending complexity—with aromas of black cherry, milk chocolate, red brick, campfire and bacon. Velvety in look and taste, it delivers chewy tannins, a solid consistency and a long, spice-driven finish. 93 *—M.L. (3/1/2007)*

Falesco 2005 Pesano Merlot (Umbria) $16. The overall intensity and concentration is nothing less than stratospheric and its aromatic profile reaches deep into the darkest and plushest of enological possibilities: Fudge, cinnamon, ginger, blackberry, espresso and vanilla come at you one thick layer after another. 90 **Editors' Choice** *—M.L. (4/1/2007)*

Falesco 2003 Vitiano Rosso Red Blend (Umbria) $10. 88 **Best Buy** *—M.S. (7/1/2005)*

Falesco 2001 Vitiano Rosso Red Blend (Umbria) $10. 88 **Best Buy** *—C.S. (2/1/2003)*

Falesco 2003 Ferentano Roscetto (Lazio) $25. 90 **Editors' Choice** *—M.L. (9/1/2005)*

Falesco 2006 Vitiano Rosé Blend (Umbria) $10. The wine's color is vibrant ruby pink and its aromas recall candied berry fruit, blueberries and dusty minerals. In all, it offers many layers of nuances and boasts a nice, velvety mouthfeel. 87 **Best Buy** *—M.L. (7/1/2007)*

FANTI

Fanti 2001 Brunello (Brunello di Montalcino) $90. 93 *(4/1/2006)*

Fanti 2000 Brunello (Brunello di Montalcino) $75. 91 *—M.S. (7/1/2005)*

Fanti 1999 Brunello (Brunello di Montalcino) $80. 92 *—M.S. (6/1/2004)*

Fanti 1997 Brunello (Brunello di Montalcino) $58. 90 *—R.V. (8/1/2002)*

Fanti 2000 Sangiovese (Sant'Antimo) $17. 88 *—M.S. (8/1/2002)*

Fassati 2000 Selciaia Sangiovese (Rosso di Montepulciano) $11. 81 *—M.S. (11/15/2004)*

FARINA

Farina 2003 Corvina, Rondinella, Molinara (Amarone della Valpolicella Classico) $40. This wine is a bit strange, especially on the nose where it yields too generous notes of cocoa butter, sun tanning lotion, butterscotch, cherry and sweet vanilla. The nose is definitely sweet, bordering on cloying, and tight tannins will need time to soften. 86 *—M.L. (10/1/2007)*

Farina 2001 Monte Fante Corvina, Rondinella, Molinara (Amarone della Valpolicella Classico) $60. The Farina family was among the first to market this unique wine abroad. The Monte Fante cru smells like an opulent dessert: crème brûlée, brown sugar, sweet chocolate, toasted coconut, butterscotch, poached cherries and caramel candy. 91 *—M.L. (10/1/2007)*

FARNESE

Farnese 2006 Farneto Valley Chardonnay (Terre di Chieti) $9. Citrus blossom, apricot, peach, minerals and white peppercorn emerge from the nose of this attractively priced Chard. It boasts medium build and persistency with nice acidity and a spice-filled finish. 86 **Best Buy** *—M.L. (11/15/2007)*

Farnese 2005 Farneto Valley Chardonnay (Terre di Chieti) $7. Here's a pale, straw-colored white with melon, honey, citrus, white minerals and fresh, clean aromas overall. It also has attractive creaminess in the mouth that denotes good structure and persistency. 85 **Best Buy** *—M.L. (2/1/2007)*

Farnese 2006 Opis Chardonnay (Terre di Chieti) $NA. This is a fine example of a sun-drenched Chardonnay from central Italy that boasts a saturated, golden color and savory exotic fruit, vanilla, butter and natural rubber. It's viscous with streaks of glycerin that slowly make their way down the side of the glass and offers a creamy, sweet, sensation in the mouth. 88 *—M.L. (11/15/2007)*

Farnese 2003 Montepulciano (Montepulciano d'Abruzzo Colline Teramane) $21. Montepulciano is a late-ripening grape packed solid with color, flavor and tannins. It never lends itself to flimsy, fragile wines, but brings brawn and power instead. This wine is a showcase example of the variety with deep tones of coffee, black cherry, charcoal and wet asphalt. The tannins are firm and there's a slightly sour note on the finish. 87 *—M.L. (2/1/2007)*

Farnese 2005 Casale Vecchio Montepulciano (Montepulciano d'Abruzzo) $15. This is a solid, easy wine with familiar Montepulciano grape characteristics including ripe berry, cherry and dark fruit aromas and a chunky, masculine build in the mouth. Thanks to six months in oak, it shows very rich fruit with smoke and espresso-like flavors and bitter tannins on the close. 86 *—M.L. (2/1/2007)*

Farnese 2005 Farneto Valley Montepulciano (Montepulciano d'Abruzzo) $7. This light and informal interpretation of Montepulciano is thinner and less intense than other wines in the Farnese lineup. In fact, it ages only in stainless steel in order to preserve its fresh fruit. There's a pleasant candied note on the nose with rich espresso in the mouth. 84 **Best Buy** *—M.L. (2/1/2007)*

Farnese 2001 Opis Montepulciano (Montepulciano d'Abruzzo Colline Teramane) $33. Here's a nicely aged Riserva Montepulciano (it sees ten months in oak) that oozes darkness: dark burgundy in color with blackberry, plum, black cherry, tar, mocha-fudge and exotic spice aromas. Built like a rock: it's plush and concentrated in the mouth with tight tannins. 90 *—M.L. (2/1/2007)*

Farnese 2005 Casale Vecchio Pecorino (Terre di Chieti) $15. Fresh and fragrant, this straw-colored white wine is redolent of honeysuckle, apricot, dried herbs and has some lemon soda on the end. This is a simple, nicely layered wine with a good deal of pizazz and personality that sees seven months in barrique to give it a soft edge. 86 *—M.L. (2/1/2007)*

Farnese 2006 Casale Vecchio Pecorino Pecorino (Terre di Chieti) $16. A sweet-smelling, rich wine with thick glycerin streaks and fragrant aromas of vanilla, honey, nut and chopped basil. It's a forthcoming and generous wine with a heavy texture that avoids being fat or flat, thanks to natural crispness. **87** *—M.L. (11/15/2007)*

Farnese 2005 Don Camillo Red Blend (Terre di Chieti) $15. Sangiovese and Cabernet Sauvignon (15 percent) from the central Abruzzo region are blended to yield an easy and approachable wine with notes of toasted oak, blueberry, black pepper, dried herbs and sour cherry. **85** *—M.L. (2/1/2007)*

Farnese 2003 Edizione Cinque Autoctoni Red Blend (Abruzzo) $39. You could call this a "concept" wine: five indigenous grapes (Montepulciano, Primitivo, Negroamaro, Sangiovese and Malvasia Nera) offer huge ripe red fruit, blueberry muffin and mocha fudge aromas. Unfiltered, it drinks like a young wine, but probably doesn't have long-lived aging potential. **87** *—M.L. (2/1/2007)*

Farnese 2005 Farneto Valley Sangiovese (Terre di Chieti) $7. Terre di Chieti is a relatively unknown winemaking region from central Italy where wine consumers can often find great value. Here's a good example with ripe notes of cherry, chocolate and chestnut. **84 Best Buy** *—M.L. (2/1/2007)*

Farnese 2006 Farneto Valley Trebbiano (Trebbiano d'Abruzzo) $9. Lemon candy and tonic soda-like aromas are fresh without being particularly complex or compelling, make this a no-fuss wine that should be consumed on easy, informal occasions. It has vibrant flavors of stone fruit, white stone and sweet basil and is watery in the mouth. **84** *—M.L. (11/15/2007)*

Farnese 2005 Farneto Valley Trebbiano (Trebbiano d'Abruzzo) $7. Apricot, peach, nuts, honey and cut grass emerge first on the nose of this pale straw-colored wine. It's equally fragrant and clean in the mouth with medium to lean structure and dimension. **85 Best Buy** *—M.L. (2/1/2007)*

FASSATI

Fassati 2001 Gersemi Sangiovese (Vino Nobile di Montepulciano) $35. Good concentration and red fruit aromas set the tone and are embellished by background notes of vanilla and cedar. Drying tannins characterize the mouthfeel but the wine also has a pointed vein of tartness that hits the mid-palate. Tiny percentages of Merlot and Cabernet Sauvignon are added. **88** *—M.L. (5/1/2007)*

Fassati 2002 Pasiteo Sangiovese (Vino Nobile di Montepulciano) $25. Good aromatic intensity helps shape aromas of blackberry, forest floor and white mushroom. Overall there is nice harmony to this wine with well-integrated oak notes, thanks to 24 months of wood aging and vibrant fruit. It's slightly tart in the mouth with firm tannins. **87** *—M.L. (5/1/2007)*

Fassati 1999 Salarco Riserva Sangiovese (Vino Nobile di Montepulciano) $50. Nice concentration and color reinforces aromas of dried currant berry, fruit preserves, tar, resin and exotic spice. The wine is extremely ripe and succulent and delivers notes of toasted oak throughout. Good acidity fuels a long, rich finish. Pair with game meats or stews and don't wait any longer to drink. **90** *—M.L. (5/1/2007)*

FATTOI

Fattoi 2001 Brunello (Brunello di Montalcino) $NA. 89 *(4/1/2006)*

FATTORIA CARPINETA FONTALPINO

Fattoria Carpineta Fontalpino 1997 Gioia Sangiovese (Chianti Colli Senesi) $13. 86 *(4/1/2001)*

FATTORIA CORONCINO

Fattoria Coroncino 1999 Gaiospino Verdicchio (Verdicchio dei Castelli di Jesi Classico) $27. 90 *—M.S. (8/1/2004)*

Fattoria Coroncino 2001 Il Coroncino Verdicchio (Verdicchio dei Castelli di Jesi Classico Superiore) $18. 89 *—M.S. (8/1/2004)*

Fattoria Coroncino 1999 Gaiospino White Blend (Marche) $25. 84 *—D.T. (9/1/2001)*

FATTORIA DEI BARBI

Fattoria dei Barbi 2004 Sangiovese (Morellino di Scansano) $15. This wine offers pretty red fruit, almond flavors, firm structure and ages six months in medium oak casks. **88** *—M.L. (11/1/2007)*

Fattoria dei Barbi 2004 Sole Sangiovese (Morellino di Scansano) $20. There's a very attractive vitality to this ruby-colored wine, and complexity too, thanks to well-integrated aromas of ripe cherry, blueberry, licorice and tar. This 85-15 Sangiovese and Merlot blend ages 12 months in barrique. In the mouth, it delivers firm tannins and good length on the finish. **89 Editors' Choice** *—M.L. (11/1/2007)*

FATTORIA DEL CERRO

Fattoria del Cerro 1999 Prugnolo Gentile (Rosso di Montepulciano) $14. 90 Best Buy *—M.S. (11/15/2003)*

Fattoria del Cerro 2002 Sangiovese (Vino Nobile di Montepulciano) $28. 85 *—M.S. (7/1/2005)*

Fattoria del Cerro 1999 Sangiovese (Vino Nobile di Montepulciano) $30. 87 *—M.S. (10/1/2004)*

Fattoria del Cerro 1996 Sangiovese (Vino Nobile di Montepulciano) $17. 82 *—J.C. (9/1/2000)*

Fattoria del Cerro 1995 Antica Chiusina Sangiovese (Vino Nobile di Montepulciano) $35. 86 *—J.C. (7/1/2000)*

Fattoria del Cerro 2001 Riserva Sangiovese (Vino Nobile di Montepulciano) $NA. 87 *—M.S. (7/1/2005)*

FATTORIA DI BASCIANO

Fattoria di Basciano 2001 Riserva Sangiovese (Chianti Rufina) $22. 89 *(4/1/2005)*

FATTORIA DI CINCIANO

Fattoria di Cinciano 1999 Sangiovese (Chianti Classico) $12. 85 *—M.S. (12/31/2002)*

FATTORIA DI FELSINA

Fattoria di Felsina 1995 Fontalloro Sangiovese (Tuscany) $60. 93 *(11/15/1999)*

FATTORIA DI GRACCIANO SVETONI

Fattoria di Gracciano Svetoni 1999 Calvano Sangiovese (Vino Nobile di Montepulciano) $20. 88 *—M.S. (10/1/2004)*

FATTORIA DI LUCIGNANO

Fattoria di Lucignano 2002 Sangiovese (Chianti Colli Fiorentini) $12. 80 *(4/1/2005)*

FATTORIA FIBBIANO

Fattoria Fibbiano 2006 Sangiovese (Chianti Classico) $13. Small percentages of Canaiolo and Malvasia Nera help render a classic-tasting wine with berry fruit intensity, cherries, amaretto and a vibrant ruby color. The wine is clean and genuine in the mouth with succulent fruit flavors, dusty tannins and good intensity. **87** *—M.L. (11/1/2007)*

FATTORIA IL COLLE

Fattoria il Colle 2001 Leone Rosso Sangiovese (Toscana) $17. 87 *—M.S. (10/1/2004)*

FATTORIA IL PALAGIO

Fattoria il Palagio 2002 Chardonnay (Toscana) $15. 83 *—M.S. (6/1/2005)*

Fattoria il Palagio 2003 Sangiovese (Chianti) $12. 87 Best Buy *(4/1/2005)*

Fattoria il Palagio 2001 Sauvignon Blanc (Toscana) $12. 88 Best Buy *(12/31/2002)*

FATTORIA LA LECCIAIA

Fattoria la Lecciaia 2001 Brunello (Brunello di Montalcino) $38. 89 *(4/1/2006)*

Fattoria la Lecciaia 2001 Manapetra Brunello (Brunello di Montalcino) $45. 93 Editors' Choice *(4/1/2006)*

FATTORIA LA LECCIAIA DI PACINI MAURO

Fattoria la Lecciaia di Pacini Mauro 1999 Brunello (Brunello di Montalcino) $43. 85 *—M.S. (10/1/2004)*

FATTORIA LE SORGENTI

Fattoria le Sorgenti 1998 Sangiovese (Chianti Colli Fiorentini) $12. 91 Best Buy *(4/1/2001)*

FATTORIA LICIA

Fattoria Licia 2000 Il Colle Ruzzo Red Blend (Montepulciano d'Abruzzo) $10. 86 Best Buy *—M.S. (1/1/2004)*

FATTORIA NITTARDI

Fattoria Nittardi 2004 Ad Astra Red Blend (Maremma) $21. Full of pleasant surprises, this red blend offers high intensity in the form of blackberry, green bell pepper and crushed peppercorn backed by chocolate, cigar and toast. A fine, modern wine with firm structure but also with a plush, velvety mouthfeel despite only five months in oak. **89** *—M.L. (4/1/2007)*

Fattoria Nittardi 2004 Nectar Dei Red Blend (Maremma) $52. If you like richly oaked reds, this is your wine. The toasted notes are pungent but they don't completely mask the fresh plum, cherry and currant. Vanilla and clove flavors are reinforced by rock-solid tannins and excellent persistency on the finish. Drink after 2008. **90** *—M.L. (4/1/2007)*

Fattoria Nittardi 2005 Casanuova di Nittardi Sangiovese (Chianti Classico) $NA. Yoko Ono designed the "Imagine You" label, which has been printed in six different collectors' colors. The nose is as distinctive as its packaging with deep notes of Indian spice, cumin, cardamom, tobacco, leather and bright cherry at the core. Palate-wise, it is lush and opulent with a solid build and firm tannins. **88** *—M.L. (11/1/2007)*

Fattoria Nittardi 2004 Casanuova di Nittardi Sangiovese (Chianti Classico) $27. You can't help but admire the beautifully vibrant ruby color of this Chianti Classico that ages six months in oak. Red fruit aromas also show very well, especially dried currant berry. Flavors include coffee and toast and are followed by tight tannins. 87 —*M.L. (2/1/2007)*

Fattoria Nittardi 2003 Nectar Dei Sangiovese (Maremma) $90. 90 —*M.S. (9/1/2006)*

Fattoria Nittardi 2003 Riserva Sangiovese (Chianti Classico) $46. Deep and incisive, two years of slow barrique aging create rich toasted notes such as charcoal, cigar box, licorice and vanilla although, thankfully, enough room is left for fresh cherry and berry fruit flavors. The wine is 95 percent Sangiovese with a small component of Merlot for softness: A brawny, oak-powered wine best enjoyed now. 88 —*M.L. (2/1/2007)*

Fattoria Nittardi 2004 Riserva Nittardi Sangiovese (Chianti Classico) $NA. Modern in delivery and approach, this boasts deep and penetrating notes of coffee, vanilla-nut, sweet fudge, espresso and a dark core of mature black cherry. It is extremely velvety and caressing in the mouth with soft tannins and mature fruit flavors on the finish. 91 —*M.L. (11/1/2007)*

FATTORIA POGGIO CAPPONI

Fattoria Poggio Capponi 2005 Red Blend (Chianti) $10. Following in Chianti tradition, this is a Sangiovese, Canaiolo Nero, Trebbiano and Malvasia blend that offers nice ruby concentration, and youthful but pungent aromas of cherry and apple backed by cookie dough. It seems tight and a bit nervous on the palate. 84 —*M.L. (11/15/2007)*

Fattoria Poggio Capponi 2004 Montespertoli Petriccio Sangiovese (Chianti) $20. Although the general ensemble works, this wine is a bit lean and thorny in places. Aromas include forest floor, white mushroom, wild flower and sour cherry. The mouthfeel is lean but does offer simple fruit flavors. 85 —*M.L. (11/1/2007)*

Fattoria Poggio Capponi 2002 Vin Santo White Blend (Colli Etruria Centrale) $20. There's a lot going on in this little bottle: Resin and toasted pinenut appear over rich notes of maple syrup and dried fruit. Flavors of toasted wood add dimension and the wine closes with a soft and feminine touch of melted lavender honey. 91 —*M.L. (5/1/2007)*

FATTORIA POGGIOPIANO

Fattoria Poggiopiano 1998 Sangiovese (Chianti Classico) $21. 86 *(4/1/2001)*

FATTORIA RODANO

Fattoria Rodano 2001 Sangiovese (Chianti Classico) $18. 86 *(4/1/2005)*

Fattoria Rodano 1999 Riserva Viacoste Sangiovese (Chianti Classico) $28. 92 Editors' Choice *(4/1/2005)*

FATTORIA SAN FRANCESCO

Fattoria San Francesco 1998 Ronco Dei QuatroVenti Red Blend (Cirò Classico) $28. 85 —*C.S. (5/1/2002)*

FATTORIA SAN LORENZO

Fattoria San Lorenzo 2002 di Gino Verdicchio (Verdicchio dei Castelli di Jesi Classico) $10. 85 —*M.S. (8/1/2004)*

Fattoria San Lorenzo 2001 Vigna delle Oche Verdicchio (Verdicchio dei Castelli di Jesi Classico Superiore) $15. 89 —*M.S. (8/1/2004)*

FATTORIA SCOPONE

Fattoria Scopone 2001 Brunello (Brunello di Montalcino) $39. 91 Editors' Choice *(4/1/2006)*

FATTORIA SELVANOVA

Fattoria Selvanova 2003 Selvanova Aglianico (Terre del Volturno) $45. This is a new, promising estate from Campania (southern Italy) that makes "one bottle equals one vine" its operating philosophy. With that kind of intense concentration, you can expect deeply etched tones of blackberry, figs and cherry preserves. But that's not all: toasted cedar, vanilla, tobacco and campfire aromas are also prominent, thanks to 18 months of barrique aging. 89 —*M.L. (4/1/2007)*

Fattoria Selvanova 2004 Silicata Aglianico (Terre del Volturno) $39. With 15% Cab Sauvignon, this is a meaty, red fruit-driven red that delivers lingering notes of exotic spice, clove, cherry cola and roasted espresso bean. Nutmeg-like flavors appear in the mouth, followed by tight tannins and a rock-solid structure. 90 —*M.L. (4/1/2007)*

Fattoria Selvanova 2005 Vignantica Aglianico (Terre del Volturno) $15. Notes of chocolate fudge, cherry, plum and espresso are embellished by the wine's smooth roundness and compact mouthfeel. Chewy, sweet tannins call out for red meat and hearty winter cooking. 86 —*M.L. (4/1/2007)*

Fattoria Selvanova 2003 Sopralago Cabernet Sauvignon (Terre del Volturno) $20. A concentrated, unfiltered Cabernet with rich notes of wet tobacco, earth, blackberry, Graham cracker and succulent black fruit; this is a chewy and structured wine with firm tannins. 87 —*M.L. (4/1/2007)*

Fattoria Selvanova 2004 Acquavigna White Blend (Campania) $20. I had been looking forward to tasting the rare Pallagrello variety but needed more convincing once I did. Yes, the kiwi, green apple, acacia and mineral characteristics are crisp and refreshing but the appearance is slightly cloudy (to be fair, it reads "light filter" on the label) and the flavors are simplistic. Saved from near extinction, only 5,000 cases of Pallagrello are made per year by 10 producers. This estate produces 200 cases. 83 —*M.L. (4/1/2007)*

FATTORIA SONNINO

Fattoria Sonnino 2001 Chianti Montespertoli Sangiovese (Chianti Montespertoli) $12. 87 —*M.S. (11/15/2003)*

FATTORIA SOVESTRO

Fattoria Sovestro 1998 San Domenico Vineyard Sangiovese (Chianti Colli Senesi) $13. 85 *(4/1/2001)*

FATTORIA ZERBINA

Fattoria Zerbina 2003 Scaccomatto Albana (Albana di Romagna) $60. This is one of the best passito dessert wines from central Italy: It's plush and silky in the mouth and deliciously sweet without being sticky or heavy. The aromas span a large spectrum, from dried apricot and honey to toasted nuts and caramel, thanks to 14 months of aging in new oak. Absolutely beautiful. 92 —*M.L. (2/1/2007)*

Fattoria Zerbina 2001 Marzieno Rosso Red Blend (Romagna) $45. Sangiovese is blended with Cabernet Sauvignon, Merlot and Syrah to produce a finely layered red wine redolent of espresso bean, licorice, mint and toast. The mouthfeel is long-lasting with cherry flavors and firm tannins. A surprise hit from Romagna. 91 —*M.L. (2/1/2007)*

Fattoria Zerbina 2004 Ceregio Sangiovese (Sangiovese di Romagna) $15. This Sangiovese has an earthy, porcino mushroom note that doesn't distract from the variety's characteristic notes of pressed violet and cherry. Mineral notes also shine through and the wine shows nice crispness on the close. 85 —*M.L. (2/1/2007)*

Fattoria Zerbina 2003 Pietramora Superiore Riserva Sangiovese (Sangiovese di Romagna) $40. Definitely on the lush, ripe side, this wine has thick aromas of black chocolate fudge, cherry liquor and espresso bean. In fact, the wine's flavors recall a dark chocolate cake with cherry filling. The wine has firm tannins, succulence and good persistency. 90 —*M.L. (2/1/2007)*

Fattoria Zerbina 2003 Torre di Ceparano Superiore Sangiovese (Sangiovese di Romagna) $22. This Sangiovese from Italy's central, eastern flank boasts clean and distinct aromas of blackberry, forest floor, marzipan and some black pepper. It's a medium-structured wine with a firm backbone and persistent, fruity flavors. 87 —*M.L. (2/1/2007)*

FATTORIE AZZOLINO

Fattorie Azzolino 2002 Chardonnay (Sicilia) $27. 87 —*M.S. (2/1/2005)*

Fattorie Azzolino 2002 Nero d'Avola (Sicilia) $15. 87 —*M.S. (2/1/2005)*

Fattorie Azzolino 2001 Di'More Red Blend (Sicilia) $27. 86 —*M.S. (2/1/2005)*

Fattorie Azzolino 2003 Tranùi White Blend (Sicilia) $15. 87 —*M.S. (2/1/2005)*

FAUNUS

Faunus 1998 Riserva Red Blend (Salice Salentino) $11. 84 —*M.S. (1/1/2004)*

FAUSTO GEMME

Fausto Gemme 1998 La Merlina Cortese (Gavi di Gavi) $16. 83 *(4/1/2000)*

FAZI BATTAGLIA

Fazi Battaglia 2002 Passo del Lupo Riserva Montepulciano (Rosso Conero) $35. This Marche red shows the aging potential of Conero wines. Notes of raw plum and red currants are enhanced by carefully executed oak-use (12 months in barrique) to render soft layers of exotic spice and leather. Drink this wine with stewed rabbit or red meat. 88 —*M.L. (12/1/2007)*

Fazi Battaglia 1998 Passo Del Lupo Riserva Red Blend (Rosso Conero) $34. 82 —*M.S. (10/1/2004)*

Fazi Battaglia 2004 Verdicchio (Verdicchio dei Castelli di Jesi Classico) $10. 87 Best Buy —*M.L. (11/15/2005)*

Fazi Battaglia 2002 Verdicchio (Verdicchio dei Castelli di Jesi Classico) $10. 86 Best Buy —*M.S. (8/1/2004)*

Fazi Battaglia 2002 Arkezia Muffo di San Sisto Verdicchio (Marche) $70. Sweet wines like this complex and intense nectar from central Italy add the final, necessary touch to a complete dining experience. Fifty percent of the grapes are altered by Noble Rot to render primary aromas of fresh stone fruit and white flowers backed by peach cobbler and dried herbs.

Cinnamon and lively fruit flavors characterize the mouthfeel. With more than 10 passes in the vineyard during harvest, this is an extremely labor-intensive and precious wine. **92 Cellar Selection** *—M.L. (5/1/2007)*

Fazi Battaglia 2001 Arkezia Muffa di San Sisto Verdicchio (Marche) $65. 92 Editors' Choice *—M.L. (7/1/2006)*

Fazi Battaglia 2005 Le Moie Verdicchio (Verdicchio dei Castelli di Jesi Classico Superiore) $20. Italy's first cru Verdicchio, Le Moie offers loads of citrus-and lime-like nuances on the heels of stone fruit, field flowers and fruit candy. Sweet fruit notes create a lively, tangy impression. A tiny percentage is aged in wood. **87** *—M.L. (12/1/2007)*

Fazi Battaglia 2004 Massaccio Verdicchio (Verdicchio dei Castelli di Jesi Classico Superiore) $30. This is one of the producer's top wines and its quality is immediately confirmed thanks to well-integrated notes of melon, honey, peach, citrus and exotic fruit. It has vibrant crispness on the close. **89** *—M.L. (12/1/2007)*

Fazi Battaglia 2001 San Sisto Riserva Verdicchio (Verdicchio dei Castelli di Jesi Classico) $30. From a historic producer who has done much work to promote Verdicchio and the Marche region around the world, San Sisto is among the most sophisticated expressions of the variety. Matured in barrel, the deeply golden colored and saturated wine is redolent of vanilla, nut, mature melon and chewy caramel. **90** *—M.L. (12/1/2007)*

Fazi Battaglia 2006 Titulus Verdicchio (Verdicchio dei Castelli di Jesi Classico) $13. Fazi Battaglia's amphora-shaped bottle is a museum worthy legend of Italian design. The contents, on the other hand, express simplicity and ease. This is a no-fuss wine that, over the years, has proudly adorned the checkered tablecloths of neighborhood trattorias all over Italy. Linear and compact, aromas include jasmine, peach blossom and dusty mineral. **85** *—M.L. (11/15/2007)*

FAZIO

Fazio 2005 Insolia (Sicilia) $16. 86 *—M.L. (7/1/2006)*

Fazio 2004 Insolia (Sicilia) $17. 85 *—M.L. (7/1/2006)*

Fazio 2004 Torre dei Venti Nero d'Avola (Sicilia) $19. 87 *—M.L. (7/1/2006)*

Fazio 2002 Torre dei Venti Nero d'Avola (Sicilia) $21. 86 *—M.L. (7/1/2006)*

Fazio 2004 Capo Soprano White Blend (Sicilia) $11. 86 Best Buy *—M.L. (11/15/2005)*

FELLINE

Felline 2000 Alberello Negroamaro (Salento) $15. 84 *(5/1/2002)*

Felline 2000 Primitivo (Primitivo Di Manduria) $19. 87 *— (1/1/2004)*

Felline 2000 Vigna Del Feudo Red Blend (Puglia) $28. 88 *—C.S. (5/1/2002)*

FELSINA

Felsina 2002 Berardenga Sangiovese (Chianti Classico) $23. 87 *(4/1/2005)*

Felsina 1996 Berardenga Sangiovese (Chianti Classico) $18. 90 *—M.M. (5/1/1999)*

Felsina 2000 Berardenga Rancia Reserva Sangiovese (Chianti Classico) $46. 87 *(4/1/2005)*

Felsina 2000 Berardenga Riserva Sangiovese (Chianti Classico) $32. 89 *(4/1/2005)*

Felsina 1995 Riserva Sangiovese (Chianti Classico) $25. 92 *—M.M. (5/1/1999)*

FENECH

Fenech 2004 Red Blend (Sicilia) $NA. 87 *—M.L. (7/1/2006)*

Fenech 2004 Passito White Blend (Malvasia delle Lipari) $NA. 89 *—M.L. (7/1/2006)*

FERDINANDO GUCCIARDINI

Ferdinando Gucciardini 1999 Castello di Poppiano Riserva Sangiovese (Chianti Colli Fiorentini) $18. 90 *—M.S. (10/1/2004)*

FERESIN DAVIDE

Feresin Davide 2004 Pinot Grigio (Isonzo del Friuli) $NA. 87 *—M.L. (2/1/2006)*

FERRARI

Ferrari NV Brut Chardonnay (Trento) $25. 88 *—M.L. (12/15/2004)*

Ferrari NV Brut Chardonnay (Trento) $28. 92 *—M.L. (6/1/2006)*

Ferrari 1996 Giulio Ferrari Riserva del Fondatore Chardonnay (Trento) $90. 93 *—M.L. (6/1/2006)*

Ferrari 1997 Giulio Riserva del Fondatore Chardonnay (Trento) $90. 93 *—M.L. (12/15/2006)*

Ferrari 2001 Perlé Chardonnay (Trento) $30. 92 *—M.L. (6/1/2006)*

Ferrari 1998 Perlé Chardonnay (Trento) $30. 89 *—M.L. (12/15/2004)*

Ferrari NV Rosé Metodo Classico Pinot Noir (Trento) $28. 87 *—M.L. (12/15/2004)*

Ferrari NV Maximum Rosé Sparkling Blend (Trento) $34. 89 *—M.L. (12/15/2006)*

Ferrari 1994 Riserva del Fondatore Brut Sparkling Blend (Trento) $75. 92 *(12/15/2004)*

Ferrari NV Rosé Sparkling Blend (Trento) $30. 88 *—M.L. (6/1/2006)*

FERRERO

Ferrero 2001 Brunello (Brunello di Montalcino) $45. 89 *(4/1/2006)*

FEUDI DI SAN GIULIANO

Feudi di San Giuliano 2004 Cjatomé Chardonnay (Sicilia) $NA. 87 *—M.L. (7/1/2006)*

Feudi di San Giuliano 2004 Nicasio Nero d'Avola (Sicilia) $NA. 85 *—M.L. (7/1/2006)*

Feudi di San Giuliano 2003 Kundisa Red Blend (Sicilia) $NA. 87 *—M.L. (7/1/2006)*

Feudi di San Giuliano 2005 Vento di Majo White Blend (Sicilia) $NA. 86 *—M.L. (7/1/2006)*

FEUDI DI SAN GREGORIO

Feudi di San Gregorio 1994 Aglianico (Taurasi) $25. 92 *—M.S. (11/15/1999)*

Feudi di San Gregorio 2000 Patrimo Aglianico (Irpinia) $115. 91 *(12/1/2002)*

Feudi di San Gregorio 2000 Piano di Monte Vergine Riserva Aglianico (Taurasi) $62. A blockbuster wine: big, bold and opulent on every front, you'll be seduced and subdued by its concentrated and immediate aromas of black berry fruit, pencil lead, licorice, chocolate fudge and the pretty ashen nuances. It's a masculine and multi-layered wine with expertly extracted flavors, hearty enough to cellar for many more years. **93** *—M.L. (8/1/2007)*

Feudi di San Gregorio 2000 Rabrato Aglianico (Irpinia) $17. 87 *(12/1/2002)*

Feudi di San Gregorio 2002 Selve di Luoti Aglianico (Taurasi) $44. Year after year, Feudi's Taurasi delivers amazing intensity and volcanic soil aromas that are so distinctive they immediately give its Campania roots away. This boasts bold cherry, with deep tones of sweet-smelling blue flower, licorice, pinecone, tobacco, campfire and charcoal. The wine is plush and velvety on the palate and those fantastic mineral notes emerge on the finale. **90** *—M.L. (8/1/2007)*

Feudi di San Gregorio 1998 Selve di Luoti Aglianico (Taurasi) $36. 88 Cellar Selection *(12/1/2002)*

Feudi di San Gregorio 1997 Selve di Lvoti Aglianico (Taurasi) $38. 88 *—C.S. (5/1/2002)*

Feudi di San Gregorio 2000 Serpico Aglianico (Irpinia) $62. 89 *(12/1/2002)*

Feudi di San Gregorio 1999 Serpico Aglianico (Irpinia) $57. 94 Editors' Choice *—C.S. (5/1/2002)*

Feudi di San Gregorio 1997 Serpico Aglianico (Campania) $60. 92 Cellar Selection *—M.N. (9/1/2001)*

Feudi di San Gregorio 2004 Falanghina (Campania) $18. 87 *—M.L. (9/1/2005)*

Feudi di San Gregorio 2001 Falanghina (Falanghina) $16. 87 *(12/1/2002)*

Feudi di San Gregorio 2004 Fiano (Fiano di Avellino) $23. 89 *—M.L. (9/1/2005)*

Feudi di San Gregorio 2004 Fiano (Fiano di Avellino) $18. 84 *—M.S. (10/1/2006)*

Feudi di San Gregorio 2001 Fiano (Fiano di Avellino) $21. 89 *(12/1/2002)*

Feudi di San Gregorio 2000 Fiano (Fiano di Avellino) $20. 86 *—M.N. (9/1/2001)*

Feudi di San Gregorio 1999 Privilegio Fiano (Irpinia) $55. 90 *(12/1/2002)*

Feudi di San Gregorio 2004 Greco (Greco di Tufo) $23. 87 *—M.L. (9/1/2005)*

Feudi di San Gregorio 2001 Greco (Greco di Tufo) $21. 88 *(12/1/2002)*

Feudi di San Gregorio 2000 Greco (Greco di Tufo) $20. 83 *—M.N. (9/1/2001)*

Feudi di San Gregorio 2003 Patrimo Merlot (Irpinia) $115. A first-rate Merlot that is dense, concentrated, chewy and packed tight with red cherry, Indian spice, chopped mint and roasted espresso bean. But there is also a subtle and delicate floral tone that adds to its wonderful complexity. This

ITALY

wine is full of nuances and finesse and is silky smooth on the palate. **91** —*M.L. (3/1/2007)*

Feudi di San Gregorio 2001 White Blend (Falanghina) $12. 87 Best Buy —*D.T. (11/15/2002)*

Feudi di San Gregorio 1999 White Blend (Fiano di Avellino) $20. 91 —*M.N. (12/31/2000)*

Feudi di San Gregorio 2004 Campanaro White Blend (Fiano di Avellino) $40. 90 —*M.L. (9/1/2005)*

Feudi di San Gregorio 2002 Campanaro White Blend (Fiano di Avellino) $40. 89 —*M.S. (11/17/2005)*

Feudi di San Gregorio 2001 Campanaro White Blend (Irpinia) $36. 87 *(12/1/2002)*

Feudi di San Gregorio 1998 Falanghina White Blend (Campania) $10. 88 —*M.S. (11/15/1999)*

Feudi di San Gregorio 2000 Falanghina Sannio White Blend (Campania) $15. 89 Editors' Choice —*M.N. (9/1/2001)*

Feudi di San Gregorio 2002 Privilegio White Blend (Campania) $56. 87 —*M.L. (10/1/2006)*

FEUDO ARANCIO

Feudo Arancio 2004 Cabernet Sauvignon (Sicilia) $9. 87 Best Buy —*M.L. (7/1/2006)*

Feudo Arancio 2006 Chardonnay (Sicilia) $9. Sweet stone fruit, peach, banana and yellow flowers characterize this well-conceived and executed Sicilian white wine. Thanks to balanced acidity, it would make a perfect partner to shellfish, pasta and white meat. **87 Best Buy** —*M.L. (8/1/2007)*

Feudo Arancio 2005 Chardonnay (Sicilia) $8. 87 Best Buy —*M.L. (7/1/2006)*

Feudo Arancio 2004 Chardonnay (Sicilia) $8. 87 Best Buy —*M.S. (7/1/2005)*

Feudo Arancio 2003 Chardonnay (Sicilia) $9. 85 Best Buy *(2/1/2005)*

Feudo Arancio 2002 Chardonnay (Sicilia) $10. 87 Best Buy —*J.C. (10/1/2003)*

Feudo Arancio 2006 Grillo (Sicilia) $8. Light in color and lean in consistency, this is a refreshing white made from a traditional Sicilian variety called Grillo. Aromas of citrus, peach and stone fruit are clean and intense and the wine has a slightly sour touch on the finish. **86 Best Buy** —*M.L. (8/1/2007)*

Feudo Arancio 2005 Grillo (Sicilia) $8. 86 Best Buy —*M.L. (7/1/2006)*

Feudo Arancio 2004 Grillo (Sicilia) $7. 86 Best Buy —*M.S. (7/1/2005)*

Feudo Arancio 2003 Grillo (Sicilia) $7. 84 Best Buy *(2/1/2005)*

Feudo Arancio 2002 Grillo (Sicilia) $10. 84 —*J.C. (10/1/2003)*

Feudo Arancio 2005 Merlot (Sicilia) $9. Red berry fruit, tobacco, wet leaf and nuts work well together to create a fine and compact aromatic portfolio. A food-friendly red with a lean structure and clean execution. There's also a touch of bitterness on the finish. **87 Best Buy** —*M.L. (4/1/2007)*

Feudo Arancio 2004 Merlot (Sicilia) $8. 87 Best Buy —*M.L. (7/1/2006)*

Feudo Arancio 2001 Merlot (Sicilia) $10. 88 Best Buy —*M.S. (10/1/2003)*

Feudo Arancio 2001 Merlot (Sicilia) $9. 83 *(2/1/2005)*

Feudo Arancio 2001 Merlot (Sicilia) $9. 83 *(2/1/2005)*

Feudo Arancio 2004 Nero d'Avola (Sicilia) $8. 88 Best Buy —*M.L. (7/1/2006)*

Feudo Arancio 2003 Nero d'Avola (Sicilia) $7. 87 Best Buy —*M.S. (7/1/2005)*

Feudo Arancio 2002 Nero d'Avola (Sicilia) $7. 84 Best Buy *(2/1/2005)*

Feudo Arancio 2001 Nero d'Avola (Sicilia) $10. 87 Best Buy —*M.S. (10/1/2003)*

Feudo Arancio 2004 Syrah (Sicilia) $8. 87 Best Buy —*M.L. (7/1/2006)*

Feudo Arancio 2002 Syrah (Sicilia) $7. 86 Best Buy *(2/1/2005)*

Feudo Arancio 2001 Syrah (Sicilia) $10. 88 Best Buy —*M.S. (10/1/2003)*

Feudo Arancio 2004 Hekate Passito White Blend (Sicilia) $29. 89 —*M.L. (7/1/2006)*

FEUDO DI SANTA TERESA

Feudo di Santa Teresa 2001 Nivuro Red Blend (Sicilia) $15. 88 —*R.V. (10/1/2003)*

FEUDO MACCARI

Feudo Maccari 2003 Saia Nero d'Avola (Sicilia) $33. 91 —*M.L. (9/1/2005)*

Feudo Maccari 2002 Saia Nero d'Avola (Sicilia) $35. 90 —*M.S. (2/1/2005)*

Feudo Maccari 2006 Re Noto Rosé Blend (Sicilia) $NA. The wine's color is a darker shade of raspberry and its nose is expansive and intense with raspberry soda like aromas, almond paste, mint cream and white stone. The red berry fruit is less vibrant but the wine remains full and tasty, thanks to hot climate Sicilian roots. Pair this wine with more structured foods like oven roasted chicken, potatoes au gratin or pasta with red sauce. 86 —M.L. (7/1/2007)

Feudo Maccari 2004 Re Noto Red Blend (Sicilia) $13. 88 Best Buy —*M.L. (7/1/2006)*

FEUDO MONACI

Feudo Monaci 2000 Negroamaro (Salice Salentino) $9. 83 —*C.S. (5/1/2002)*

Feudo Monaci 2003 Primitivo (Puglia) $9. 85 Best Buy *(8/1/2005)*

Feudo Monaci 2002 Primitivo (Puglia) $9. 89 Best Buy —*M.S. (2/1/2005)*

Feudo Monaci 2000 Primitivo (Puglia) $9. 87 Best Buy —*C.S. (5/1/2002)*

Feudo Monaci 2003 Red Blend (Salice Salentino) $9. 87 Best Buy *(8/1/2005)*

FEUDO MONTONI

Feudo Montoni 2003 Classico Nero d'Avola (Sicilia) $16. 90 Editors' Choice —*M.L. (7/1/2006)*

Feudo Montoni 2003 Vrucara Nero d'Avola (Sicilia) $32. 92 Editors' Choice —*M.L. (7/1/2006)*

FEUDO PRINCIPI DI BUTERA

Feudo Principi di Butera 2004 Cabernet Sauvignon (Sicilia) $13. 87 —*M.L. (7/1/2006)*

Feudo Principi di Butera 2001 Cabernet Sauvignon (Sicilia) $20. 85 —*M.S. (10/1/2003)*

Feudo Principi di Butera 2001 San Rocco Cabernet Sauvignon (Sicilia) $50. 90 —*M.L. (9/1/2006)*

Feudo Principi di Butera 2000 San Rocco Cabernet Sauvignon (Sicilia) $60. 90 *(12/31/2002)*

Feudo Principi di Butera 2005 Chardonnay (Sicilia) $13. 86 —*M.L. (7/1/2006)*

Feudo Principi di Butera 2001 Chardonnay (Sicilia) $26. 85 —*R.V. (10/1/2003)*

Feudo Principi di Butera 2005 Insolia (Sicilia) $13. 87 —*M.L. (7/1/2006)*

Feudo Principi di Butera 2004 Insolia (Sicilia) $13. 86 —*M.L. (7/1/2006)*

Feudo Principi di Butera 2002 Inzolia (Sicilia) $20. 88 —*M.S. (2/1/2005)*

Feudo Principi di Butera 2001 Inzolia (Sicilia) $20. 84 —*R.V. (10/1/2003)*

Feudo Principi di Butera 2004 Merlot (Sicilia) $13. 87 —*M.L. (7/1/2006)*

Feudo Principi di Butera 2001 Merlot (Sicilia) $26. 84 —*R.V. (1/1/2004)*

Feudo Principi di Butera 2000 Merlot (Sicilia) $20. 90 —*M.S. (10/1/2003)*

Feudo Principi di Butera 2001 Calat Merlot (Sicilia) $25. If you like extra toasty notes in your Merlot, here is an excellent alternative from southern Italy: the aromas are intense and pronounced and focus mainly on blackberry, plum, roasted nuts, campfire, pencil lead, peanut and oak. Mineral notes come through on the palate and the wine has very good length. **90** —*M.L. (4/1/2007)*

Feudo Principi di Butera 2000 Calat Merlot (Sicilia) $25. Thick, dark concentration sets the tone for this expressive wine redolent of cherry or strawberry preserves, dried figs, tobacco, leather, licorice and tar. Yes, bottle aging has done this wine well. Fig flavors appear once again in the mouth, where the wine proves to be textured, heavy and persistent. **90** —*M.L. (3/1/2007)*

Feudo Principi di Butera 2000 Calat Merlot (Sicilia) $60. 89 —*M.S. (10/1/2003)*

Feudo Principi di Butera 2004 Nero d'Avola (Sicilia) $13. 87 —*M.L. (7/1/2006)*

Feudo Principi di Butera 2003 Nero d'Avola (Sicilia) $NA. 86 —*M.L. (7/1/2006)*

Feudo Principi di Butera 2000 Nero d'Avola (Sicilia) $20. 86 —*M.S. (10/1/2003)*

Feudo Principi di Butera 2002 Deliella Nero d'Avola (Sicilia) $NA. 87 —*M.L. (7/1/2006)*

Feudo Principi di Butera 2001 Deliella Nero d'Avola (Sicilia) $30. 88 —*M.L. (7/1/2006)*

Feudo Principi di Butera 2000 Deliella Nero d'Avola (Sicilia) $60. 85 —*M.S. (10/1/2003)*

Feudo Principi di Butera 2004 Iperion Red Blend (Sicilia) $18. 88 —*M.L. (7/1/2006)*

Feudo Principi di Butera 2004 Syrah (Sicilia) $13. 87 *—M.L. (7/1/2006)*

FIBBIANO

Fibbiano 2003 Sangiovese (Chianti) $13. 85 *—M.S. (10/1/2006)*

Fibbiano 2000 Ceppatella Sangiovese (Tuscany) $18. 83 *—M.S. (12/31/2002)*

Fibbiano 2002 L'Aspetto Sangiovese (Toscana) $18. 87 *—M.S. (9/1/2006)*

Fibbiano 2000 L'Aspetto Sangiovese (Tuscany) $14. 80 *—M.S. (12/31/2002)*

Fibbiano 2004 Le Pianette Sangiovese (Rosso di Toscana) $10. 83 *—M.S. (9/1/2006)*

FILIPPO GALLINO

Filippo Gallino 2001 Barbera (Barbera d'Alba) $13. 83 *—M.S. (12/15/2003)*

Filippo Gallino 1998 Barbera (Barbera d'Alba Superiore) $25. 84 *—M.S. (12/15/2003)*

Filippo Gallino 2000 Superiore Nebbiolo (Roero) $27. 84 *—M.S. (12/15/2003)*

FLOURISH

Flourish 2003 Pinot Grigio (Veneto) $11. 85 *—M.L. (2/1/2006)*

FOFFANI

Foffani 2004 Pinot Grigio (Friuli Aquileia) $14. 84 *—M.L. (6/1/2006)*

Foffani 2000 Pinot Grigio (Friuli Aquileia) $14. 86 *—J.C. (7/1/2003)*

Foffani 2000 Sauvignon Blanc (Friuli Aquileia) $19. 88 *(8/1/2002)*

Foffani 1999 Superiore Sauvignon Blanc (Friuli Aquileia) $13. 83 *(9/1/2001)*

FOLONARI

Folonari 2003 Garganega (Soave) $8. 84 Best Buy *—J.C. (12/31/2004)*

Folonari 2004 Pinot Grigio (Delle Venezie) $8. 85 Best Buy *—M.L. (2/1/2006)*

Folonari 2003 Pinot Grigio (Delle Venezie) $8. 83 *—J.C. (12/31/2004)*

Folonari NV Brio Prosecco (Prosecco del Veneto) $10. 87 Best Buy *—M.S. (12/15/2006)*

Folonari 2004 Sangiovese (Chianti) $9. 83 *—M.S. (10/1/2006)*

FONGOLI

Fongoli 2002 Sagrantino (Montefalco) $21. 86 *—M.L. (9/1/2005)*

FONTALEONI

Fontaleoni 2003 Sangiovese (Chianti Colli Senesi) $12. 86 *(4/1/2005)*

Fontaleoni 1999 Sangiovese (Chianti Colli Senesi) $11. 86 *(4/1/2001)*

FONTANA

Fontana 1996 Dolcetto (Dolcetto d'Alba) $19. 84 *(4/1/2000)*

FONTANA CANDIDA

Fontana Candida 2004 Pinot Grigio (Delle Venezie) $9. 84 *—M.L. (2/1/2006)*

Fontana Candida 2001 Pinot Grigio (Veneto) $8. 83 *—J.C. (7/1/2003)*

FONTANAFREDDA

Fontanafredda 2004 Millesimato Moscato (Asti) $23. 87 *—M.L. (11/15/2006)*

Fontanafredda 2004 Moncucco Moscato (Moscato d'Asti) $23. 90 *—M.L. (12/15/2005)*

Fontanafredda 2000 Coste Rubín Nebbiolo (Barbaresco) $48. 86 *(4/2/2004)*

Fontanafredda 1998 La Rosa Nebbiolo (Piedmont) $68. 90 *—R.V. (11/15/2002)*

Fontanafredda 1998 Lazzarito Nebbiolo (Piedmont) $68. 90 *—R.V. (11/15/2002)*

Fontanafredda 1998 Serralunga d'Alba Nebbiolo (Piedmont) $44. 89 *—R.V. (11/15/2002)*

FONTERUTOLI

Fonterutoli 2002 Sangiovese (Chianti Classico) $26. 89 *(4/1/2005)*

Fonterutoli 2000 Sangiovese (Chianti Classico) $26. 93 Editors' Choice *—M.S. (11/15/2003)*

Fonterutoli 1999 Sangiovese (Chianti Classico) $25. 91 Cellar Selection *—M.S. (1/1/2004)*

Fonterutoli 1998 Sangiovese (Chianti Classico) $27. 86 *(4/1/2001)*

Fonterutoli 2001 Poggio Alle Badiola Sangiovese (Toscana) $13. 87 *—M.S. (11/15/2003)*

FONTEVECCHIA

Fontevecchia 2001 Brunello (Brunello di Montalcino) $50. 90 *(4/1/2006)*

Fontevecchia 1998 Brunello (Brunello di Montalcino) $40. 89 *—M.S. (10/1/2004)*

Fontevecchia 2001 Sangiovese (Rosso di Montalcino) $16. 81 *—M.S. (12/15/2003)*

Fontevecchia 2000 Sangiovese Grosso (Brunello di Montalcino) $50. 90 *—M.L. (11/15/2006)*

Fontevecchia 1997 Riserva Sangiovese Grosso (Brunello di Montalcino) $65. 92 *—M.L. (11/15/2006)*

FONTODI

Fontodi 2001 Sangiovese (Chianti Classico) $32. 90 *(4/1/2005)*

Fontodi 2000 Vigna del Sorbo Riserva Sangiovese (Chianti Classico) $63. 92 Editors' Choice *(4/1/2005)*

FORACI

Foraci 2004 Galhasi Nero d'Avola (Sicilia) $12. 85 *—M.L. (10/1/2006)*

Foraci 2002 Tenute Dorrasita Nero d'Avola (Sicilia) $29. 88 *—M.L. (10/1/2006)*

Foraci 2004 Galhasi Nero d'Avola-Syrah Red Blend (Sicilia) $15. 86 *—M.L. (10/1/2006)*

Foraci 2005 Conte Ruggero White Blend (Alcamo) $11. 87 Best Buy *—M.L. (10/1/2006)*

Foraci 2005 Galhasi Inzolia-Catarratto White Blend (Sicilia) $12. 86 *—M.L. (10/1/2006)*

FORADORI

Foradori 2002 Teroldego (Rotaliano) $23. 84 *—J.C. (12/31/2004)*

Foradori 2001 Granato Teroldego (Vigneti delle Dolomiti) $60. 90 *—J.C. (12/31/2004)*

FORCHIR

Forchir 2004 Rosadis Pinot Grigio (Friuli Grave) $10. 87 Best Buy *—M.L. (6/1/2006)*

Forchir 2004 Villa del Borgo Pinot Grigio (Friuli Grave) $10. 86 Best Buy *—M.L. (6/1/2006)*

FORNACINA

Fornacina 2001 Brunello (Brunello di Montalcino) $60. 92 *(4/1/2006)*

FORTETO DELLA LUJA

Forteto della Luja 2004 Piasa Sanmaurizio Moscato (Moscato d'Asti) $18. 85 *—M.L. (12/15/2005)*

FOSS MARAI

Foss Marai NV Prosecco (Prosecco di Valdobbiadene) $12. 88 Best Buy *—P.G. (12/15/2000)*

Foss Marai NV Dry Prosecco (Prosecco Superiore di Cartizze) $30. 90 *—M.S. (12/15/2005)*

Foss Marai NV Extra Dry Prosecco (Prosecco di Valdobbiadene) $12. 88 Best Buy *—M.S. (12/15/2005)*

Foss Marai NV Cuvée Vino Spumante Brut Sparkling Blend (Italy) $18. 85 *—M.S. (6/1/2005)*

Foss Marai NV Cuvée Brut Sparkling Blend (Italy) $18. 88 *—M.S. (12/15/2005)*

FOSSACOLLE

Fossacolle 2001 Brunello (Brunello di Montalcino) $64. 89 *(4/1/2006)*

FOURPLAY

Fourplay 2001 No 1 Red Blend (Sicilia) $12. 86 *—M.S. (7/1/2005)*

FRANCESCO BOSCHIS

Francesco Boschis 1998 Vigna del Prey Dolcetto (Dolcetto di Dogliani) $19. 90 *(4/1/2000)*

FRANZ GOJER-GLÖGGLHOF

Franz Gojer-Glögglhof 2004 Spitz Merlot (Alto Adige) $NA. Loads of sweet spice, cumin and curry round off a red fruit-driven nose, but are never overstated. The cooler climate helps shape delicate aromas and keeps the wine's structure firm yet refreshing. This will prove a perfect match to Indian and exotic foods. 88 *—M.L. (4/1/2007)*

FRANZ HAAS

Franz Haas 2003 Lagrein (Alto Adige) $33. 87 *—M.L. (9/1/2005)*

Franz Haas 2004 Kris Pinot Grigio (Delle Venezie) $10. 87 Best Buy *—M.L. (2/1/2006)*

Franz Haas 2002 Kris Pinot Grigio (Delle Venezie) $9. 85 *—R.V. (7/1/2003)*

Franz Haas 2001 Manna Bianco di Mitterberg White Blend (Alto Adige) $24. 92 *—R.V. (7/1/2003)*

FRASCOLE

Frascole 2004 Sangiovese (Chianti Rufina) $13. Although this is fresh and genuine in the mouth, it loses points for a nose that seems tired and redolent of mature fruit. As tradition dictates, the Chianti blend sees smaller percentages of Canaiolo and Colorino to back a Sangiovese base. **84** *—M.L. (11/1/2007)*

Frascole 2003 Riserva Sangiovese (Chianti Rufina) $32. Unexpected notes of soy sauce and ginger are awkward at first, but fall comfortably within a greater aromatic context of black fruit, plum, cherry, prune and licorice. There's deep berry succulence in the mouth, with oak tones at the back that glide over polished texture and feel. **87** *—M.L. (11/1/2007)*

FRATELLI BERLUCCHI

Fratelli Berlucchi 1999 Brut Champagne Blend (Franciacorta) $27. 85 *—M.S. (12/15/2004)*

Fratelli Berlucchi 2000 Satèn Champagne Blend (Franciacorta) $NA. 88 *—M.L. (12/15/2004)*

Fratelli Berlucchi 2000 Pas Dosé Chardonnay (Franciacorta) $NA. 89 *—M.L. (12/15/2004)*

Fratelli Berlucchi 2000 Brut Sparkling Blend (Franciacorta) $30. 90 *—M.L. (12/15/2004)*

Fratelli Berlucchi 2000 Brut Rosé Sparkling Blend (Franciacorta) $30. 87 *—M.L. (12/15/2004)*

Fratelli Berlucchi NV Cuvée Imperiale Brut Sparkling Blend (Franciacorta) $NA. 89 *—M.L. (12/15/2004)*

Fratelli Berlucchi NV Cuvée Imperiale Max Rosé Sparkling Blend (Franciacorta) $NA. 91 *—M.L. (12/15/2004)*

FRATELLI FICI

Fratelli FICI 2000 Baglio Fici Syrah (Sicilia) $NA. 87 *(10/1/2003)*

FRATELLI GANCIA

Fratelli Gancia 2000 Carlo Gancia Cuvée del Fondatore Brut Champagne Blend (Asti) $20. 83 *—M.S. (12/15/2004)*

Fratelli Gancia NV Castello Gancia Brut Champagne Blend (Piedmont) $12. 85 *(11/15/1999)*

Fratelli Gancia NV Gancia Moscato (Asti) $13. 85 *—M.S. (12/15/2004)*

Fratelli Gancia NV Gancia Spumante Moscato (Piedmont) $9. 83 *—M.S. (12/15/2004)*

Fratelli Gancia 1999 Marchesi Spinola Nebbiolo (Nebbiolo d'Alba) $15. 84 *—J.C. (11/15/2004)*

Fratelli Gancia 1998 Marchesi Spinola Nebbiolo (Barolo) $35. 87 *(4/2/2004)*

Fratelli Gancia 2000 Torrebianco Negroamaro (Salento) $8. 85 *—M.S. (11/15/2004)*

Fratelli Gancia 2002 Della Serenissima Pinot Grigio (Friuli) $22. 83 *—J.C. (12/31/2004)*

Fratelli Gancia 2000 Torrebianco Primitivo (Salento) $9. 86 Best Buy *—M.S. (11/15/2004)*

Fratelli Gancia NV Gancia Extra Dry Prosecco (Veneto) $10. 86 Best Buy *—M.S. (12/15/2004)*

Fratelli Gancia 1999 Della Serenissima Red Blend (Amarone della Valpolicella) $34. 83 *(11/1/2005)*

Fratelli Gancia 2002 Torrebianco Red Blend (Sicilia) $6. 84 Best Buy *—M.S. (10/1/2004)*

Fratelli Gancia NV Prosè Brut Rosato Rosé Blend (Oltrepò Pavese) $NA. A sparkling rosé Pinot Noir from Piedmont, this is a cheerful, easy-to-drink wine that can be served before dinner or on informal occasions. It is a pale rose color, with aromas of small berry and white almond and tastes zesty fresh in the mouth. **84** *—M.L. (12/15/2007)*

Fratelli Gancia 2001 Torrebianco Locorotondo White Blend (Italy) $7. 82 *—M.S. (10/1/2004)*

FRATELLI GIULIARI

Fratelli Giuliari 1998 Red Blend (Valpolicella Classico Superiore) $9. 84 *(5/1/2003)*

Fratelli Giuliari 2000 La Piccola Botte Red Blend (Amarone della Valpolicella Classico) $45. 89 *(11/1/2005)*

Fratelli Giuliari 1998 La Piccola Botte Red Blend (Recioto della Valpolicella Classico) $31. 85 *(5/1/2003)*

Fratelli Giuliari 1995 La Piccola Botte Red Blend (Amarone della Valpolicella Classico) $37. 84 *(5/1/2003)*

FRATELLI MARTINI

Fratelli Martini 2004 Superiore Barbera (Barbera d'Asti) $13. A modern take on Barbera, the Martini has aromas of ripe fruit with an overlay of vanilla on the palate. While not particularly complex, the big fruit character makes for an undemanding but pleasant wine. **88** *—M.G. (4/1/2007)*

FRATELLI ZENI

Fratelli Zeni 1998 Red Blend (Bardolino Classico) $12. 84 *(5/1/2003)*

Fratelli Zeni 1995 Red Blend (Amarone della Valpolicella Classico) $38. 88 *(5/1/2003)*

Fratelli Zeni 1998 Vigne Alte Red Blend (Valpolicella Classico) $11. 83 *(5/1/2003)*

Fratelli Zeni 2000 Vigne Alte White Blend (Bianco di Custoza) $11. 88 Best Buy *—J.C. (7/1/2003)*

FRATTA PASINI

Fratta Pasini 2002 Corvina, Rondinella, Molinara (Amarone della Valpolicella) $53. 89 *(11/1/2005)*

FRESCOBALDI

Frescobaldi 1998 Nipozanno Riserva Red Blend (Chianti Rufina) $15. 88 Best Buy *—M.S. (12/31/2002)*

Frescobaldi 1999 Castiglioni Sangiovese (Chianti) $13. 89 Best Buy *(4/1/2001)*

Frescobaldi 1995 Montesodi Sangiovese (Chianti Rufina) $49. 87 *—M.M. (5/1/1999)*

Frescobaldi 1999 Montesodi Castello Di Nipozzano Sangiovese (Chianti Rufina) $40. 90 *—M.S. (12/31/2002)*

Frescobaldi 1997 Montesodi Castello di Nipozzano Sangiovese (Chianti Rufina) $54. 92 Cellar Selection *(4/1/2001)*

Frescobaldi 1995 Mormoreto Sangiovese (Toscana) $45. 87 *—M.M. (5/1/1999)*

Frescobaldi 1997 Nipozzano Riserva Sangiovese (Chianti Rufina) $22. 91 *(4/1/2001)*

Frescobaldi 1996 Nipozzano Riserva Sangiovese (Chianti Rufina) $20. 86 *—M.S. (7/1/2000)*

Frescobaldi 1999 Pomino Rosso Sangiovese (Pomino) $25. 89 *—M.S. (12/31/2002)*

Frescobaldi 1996 Pomino Rosso Sangiovese (Pomino) $25. 86 *—L.W. (3/1/2000)*

Frescobaldi 2001 Remole Sangiovese (Toscana) $9. 87 *—M.S. (10/1/2004)*

Frescobaldi 1998 Remole Sangiovese (Toscana) $9. 87 *(11/15/1999)*

Frescobaldi 1997 Remole Sangiovese (Toscana) $9. 83 *—L.W. (3/1/2000)*

Frescobaldi 2001 Benefizio White Blend (Pomino) $NA. 86 *—M.S. (10/1/2004)*

FULIGNI

Fuligni 2001 Brunello (Brunello di Montalcino) $74. 92 *(4/1/2006)*

Fuligni 2000 Brunello (Brunello di Montalcino) $74. 93 Editors' Choice *—M.S. (7/1/2005)*

Fuligni 1999 Brunello (Brunello di Montalcino) $82. 95 *—M.S. (6/1/2004)*

Fuligni 1998 Brunello (Brunello di Montalcino) $65. 92 *(11/15/2003)*

Fuligni 1997 Riserva Brunello (Brunello di Montalcino) $100. 94 Editors' Choice *—M.S. (11/15/2003)*

Fuligni 1999 S.J. Red Blend (Tuscany) $37. 89 *—M.S. (12/31/2002)*

FURLAN

Furlan 2000 Castelcosa Pinot Grigio (Friuli) $12. 83 *—J.C. (7/1/2003)*

Furlan 2000 Castelcosa Sauvignon Blanc (Friuli Venezia Giulia) $12. 84 *—J.C. (7/1/2003)*

Furlan 2000 Cuvée Tai White Blend (Friuli) $14. 82 *—J.C. (7/1/2003)*

G CONTRATTO

G Contratto 1995 Solus Ad Superiore (Barbera d'Asti) $24. 89 *(4/1/2000)*

G D VAJRA

G D Vajra 1997 Barbera (Barbera d'Alba) $17. 88 *(4/1/2000)*

G D Vajra 1997 Dolcetto (Dolcetto d'Alba) $13. 86 Best Buy *(4/1/2000)*

G D Vajra 1997 Coste & Fossati Dolcetto (Dolcetto d'Alba) $18. 87 *(4/1/2000)*

G.A. ROSSI DI MEDELENA

G.A. Rossi di Medelena 2000 Lupicaia Cabernet Sauvignon-Merlot (Toscana) $120. 89 *—M.S. (10/1/2004)*

GABBIANO

Gabbiano 2003 Pinot Grigio (Delle Venezie) $10. 85 Best Buy *—J.C. (12/31/2004)*

Gabbiano 2003 Bonello Red Blend (Sicilia) $9. 87 Best Buy *—M.L. (11/15/2005)*

Gabbiano 2001 Sangiovese (Chianti Classico) $14. 82 *(4/1/2005)*

Gabbiano 2001 Riserva Sangiovese (Chianti Classico) $17. 88 *(4/1/2005)*

GAGLIOLE

Gagliole 2001 Red Blend (Colli della Toscana Centrale) $56. 92 Editors' Choice *—M.S. (11/15/2003)*

Gagliole 2003 Pecchia Red Blend (Colli della Toscana Centrale) $155. 93 *—M.S. (9/1/2006)*

Gagliole 2003 Rosso Red Blend (Colli della Toscana Centrale) $75. 91 *—M.S. (9/1/2006)*

Gagliole 1999 Pecchia Sangiovese (Colli della Toscana Centrale) $93. 85 *—M.S. (11/15/2003)*

GAIERHOF

Gaierhof 2004 Pinot Grigio (Trentino) $17. 86 *—M.L. (6/1/2006)*

Gaierhof 2001 Pinot Grigio (Trentino) $11. 83 *—J.C. (7/1/2003)*

GAJA

Gaja 1999 Darmagi Cabernet Sauvignon (Langhe) $224. 94 Cellar Selection *—M.L. (9/1/2006)*

Gaja 2001 Nebbiolo (Barbaresco) $185. 92 *(7/1/2005)*

Gaja 2001 Conteisa Red Blend (Langhe) $205. 94 *(7/1/2005)*

Gaja 2001 Costa Russi Red Blend (Langhe) $350. 95 *(7/1/2005)*

Gaja 2003 Rossj-Bass Red Blend (Langhe) $57. 89 *(7/1/2005)*

Gaja 2001 Sorì San Lorenzo Red Blend (Langhe) $350. 95 *(7/1/2005)*

Gaja 2001 Sorì Tildìn Red Blend (Langhe) $350. 95 *(7/1/2005)*

Gaja 2001 Sperss Refosco (Langhe) $200. 94 *(7/1/2005)*

GALLI & BROCCATELLI

Galli & Broccatelli 1998 Sagrantino di Montefalco Sagrantino (Sagrantino di Montefalco) $25. 85 *—C.S. (2/1/2003)*

GALTAROSSA

Galtarossa 2000 Red Blend (Amarone della Valpolicella) $54. 84 *(11/1/2005)*

GAROFOLI

Garofoli 2000 Grosso Agontano Riserva Montepulciano (Rosso Conero) $25. 88 *—M.S. (6/1/2005)*

Garofoli 2001 Piancarda Montepulciano (Rosso Conero) $13. 85 *—M.S. (6/1/2005)*

Garofoli 2001 Podium Classico Superiore Verdicchio (Verdicchio dei Castelli di Jesi Classico) $15. 88 Best Buy *—M.S. (8/1/2004)*

Garofoli 2002 Serra del Conte Verdicchio (Verdicchio dei Castelli di Jesi Classico) $8. 85 Best Buy *—M.S. (8/1/2004)*

GASTALDI

Gastaldi 1997 Moriolo Dolcetto (Dolcetto d'Alba) $18. 85 *(4/1/2000)*

GATTAVECCHI

Gattavecchi 1998 Sangiovese (Chianti Colli Senesi) $11. 84 *(4/1/2001)*

GATTINARA

Gattinara 1997 Estate Bottled Nebbiolo (Gattinara) $30. 82 *—M.S. (12/15/2003)*

GERETTO

Geretto 2001 Merlot (Delle Venezie) $10. 83 *(5/1/2003)*

Geretto 2005 Pinot Grigio (Delle Venezie) $10. 86 Best Buy *—M.L. (6/1/2006)*

Geretto 2004 Pinot Grigio (Delle Venezie) $10. 86 Best Buy *—M.L. (2/1/2006)*

Geretto 2001 Pinot Grigio (Delle Venezie) $9. 87 Best Buy *—J.C. (7/1/2003)*

GERMANO ETTORE

Germano Ettore 2001 Pra Di Po Dolcetto (Dolcetto d'Alba) $17. 86 *—M.S. (12/15/2003)*

Germano Ettore 1998 Cerretta Nebbiolo (Barolo) $45. 91 *(4/2/2004)*

GHIONE

Ghione 2005 Piccole Gioie Moscato (Moscato d'Asti) $17. 87 *—M.L. (11/15/2006)*

GIACOMO ASCHERI

Giacomo Ascheri 2006 Cristina Ascheri Arneis (Langhe) $22. The Ascheri is a light-colored wine with a lovely nose of honeysuckle, pear and lychees. On the palate, the fruit flavors were less intense but it showed good balance and a medium finish. An attractive wine which probably should be drunk fairly soon. **86** *—M.G. (12/31/2007)*

Giacomo Ascheri 1998 Podere di Sorano Barolo Bordeaux Blend (Barolo) $40. 89 *—R.V. (11/15/2002)*

Giacomo Ascheri 2006 Cristina Ascheri Cortese (Gavi di Gavi) $20. A pleasant wine that shows a sweet, spicy apricot nose; on the palate it has an interesting smokiness that works well with the fruit, and although there is a fair amount of alcohol, the fruit just manages to cover it, and the wine moves to a pleasant, if not particularly long, finish. **85** *—M.G. (12/31/2007)*

Giacomo Ascheri 2004 Bricco S. Giacomo Nebbiolo (Nebbiolo d'Alba) $25. Showing very young, it has an unusual nose of puréed violets, pencil lead and dark fruit. The palate is still very primary, very full-bodied, and although it drinks well now, will develop well over the next 3–5 years. **89** *—M.G. (12/31/2007)*

Giacomo Ascheri 2003 Bricco S. Giacomo Nebbiolo (Nebbiolo d'Alba) $29. The wine has evolved quickly, and the color is showing some browning on the edge. Almost fully mature now, it shows aromas of marzipan, strawberries and roses. Complex and pretty, the wine has a solid midpalate, and the finish is shorter than I would have expected. Still a nice, well-made wine for lovers of older Nebbiolos. **88** *—M.G. (12/31/2007)*

Giacomo Ascheri 1997 Poderi di Sorano Nebbiolo (Barolo) $40. 87 *—R.V. (11/15/2002)*

Giacomo Ascheri 1996 Poderi di Sorano Nebbiolo (Barolo) $40. 87 *—R.V. (11/15/2002)*

Giacomo Ascheri 1999 Sorano Coste & Bricco Nebbiolo (Barolo) $55. 89 *(4/2/2004)*

Giacomo Ascheri 1999 Vigna dei Pola Nebbiolo (Barolo) $55. 90 *(4/2/2004)*

GIACOMO BREZZA

Giacomo Brezza 1996 Cannubi Muscatel Barbera (Barbera d'Alba) $20. 90 *(4/1/2000)*

Giacomo Brezza 1998 San Lorenzo Dolcetto (Dolcetto d'Alba) $16. 87 *(4/1/2000)*

GIACOMO BREZZA & FIGLI

Giacomo Brezza & Figli 1997 Nebbiolo (Piedmont) $45. 91 *—R.V. (11/15/2002)*

Giacomo Brezza & Figli 1998 Cannubi Nebbiolo (Piedmont) $55. 85 *—R.V. (11/15/2002)*

Giacomo Brezza & Figli 1998 Sarmassa Nebbiolo (Piedmont) $55. 87 *—R.V. (11/15/2002)*

GIACOMO CONTERNO

Giacomo Conterno 1998 Cascina Francia Barbera (Barbera d'Alba) $24. 90 *(4/1/2000)*

Giacomo Conterno 1998 Cascina Francia Dolcetto (Dolcetto d'Alba) $22. 88 *(4/1/2000)*

GIACOMO FENOCCHIO

Giacomo Fenocchio 1999 Bussia Nebbiolo (Barolo) $45. 82 *(4/2/2004)*

GIACOMO MARENGO

Giacomo Marengo 2001 Castello Di Rapale Sangiovese (Chianti) $23. 83 *(4/1/2005)*

Giacomo Marengo 2002 Le Tornanie Sangiovese (Chianti) $19. 82 *(4/1/2005)*

Giacomo Marengo 1998 Tenuta del Fondatore La Commenda Riserva Sangiovese (Chianti) $33. 87 *(4/1/2005)*

GIACOMO MORI

Giacomo Mori 2002 Sangiovese (Chianti) $18. 87 *(4/1/2005)*

Giacomo Mori 1999 Sangiovese (Chianti) $15. 87 *(4/1/2001)*

Giacomo Mori 2001 Castelrotto Sangiovese (Chianti) $30. 88 *(4/1/2005)*

Giacomo Mori 1998 Castelrotto Sangiovese (Chianti) $26. 83 *(4/1/2001)*

GIACOSA FRATELLI

Giacosa Fratelli 1997 Vigna Mandorlo Borolo Nebbiolo (Barolo) $NA. 93 —*R.V. (11/15/2002)*

GIANNI BRUNELLI

Gianni Brunelli 2001 Brunello (Brunello di Montalcino) $NA. 89 *(4/1/2006)*

Gianni Brunelli 2000 Brunello (Brunello di Montalcino) $75. 90 —*M.S. (7/1/2005)*

Gianni Brunelli 1999 Brunello (Brunello di Montalcino) $NA. 91 —*M.S. (6/1/2004)*

Gianni Brunelli 2003 Amor Costante Merlot (Toscana) $65. The standout wine of the Dancing Bear portfolio, this is 90% Merlot, 10% Sangiovese. As might be expected from a 2003, it's superripe, with black cherry fuit flavors that verge on prune without actually tipping over the edge. Vanilla, smoke and toast from aging in small oak frames and supports the fruit without overwhelming it, while helping to shape the lush, velvety texture. Drink now–2015. 92 *(10/1/2007)*

GIANNI DOGLIA

Gianni Doglia 2004 Moscato (Moscato d'Asti) $15. 90 Editors' Choice —*M.L. (12/15/2005)*

GIANNI VESCOVO

Gianni Vescovo 1997 Pinot Grigio (Isonzo del Friuli) $12. 86 *(8/1/1999)*

GIANNI VOERZIO

Gianni Voerzio 1996 Ciabot della Luna Barbera (Barbera d'Alba) $27. 88 *(4/1/2000)*

Gianni Voerzio 1998 La Serra Nebbiolo (Piedmont) $93. 91 —*R.V. (11/15/2002)*

GIANNINA

Giannina 2002 Vernaccia (Vernaccia di San Gimignano) $11. 89 Best Buy —*M.S. (8/1/2004)*

Giannina 2002 Villa Laura Vernaccia (Vernaccia di San Gimignano) $15. 83 —*M.S. (8/1/2004)*

GIGI ROSSO

Gigi Rosso 1997 Cascina Rocca Giovino Barbera (Barbera d'Alba) $12. 87 Best Buy *(4/1/2000)*

Gigi Rosso 1998 Moncolombetto Dolcetto (Dolcetto d'Alba) $14. 87 *(4/1/2000)*

Gigi Rosso 1999 Arione Nebbiolo (Barolo) $48. 89 *(4/2/2004)*

GILIA

Gilia 2004 Pinot Grigio (Delle Venezie) $8. 82 *(2/1/2006)*

GINI

Gini 2000 Sorai Chardonnay (Delle Venezie) $24. 89 —*R.V. (7/1/2003)*

Gini 1999 La Frosca Soave Classico Superiore Garganega (Soave) $18. 90 Editors' Choice —*M.N. (12/31/2000)*

Gini 1998 La Frosca Soave Classico Superiore Garganega (Soave) $18. 89 *(4/1/2000)*

Gini 2003 Villa Fortuna Sangiovese (Chianti) $9. 83 —*M.S. (10/1/2006)*

Gini 1999 Villa Fortunato Sangiovese (Chianti) $7. 86 Best Buy *(4/1/2001)*

Gini 2002 Classico White Blend (Soave) $10. 88 —*R.V. (7/1/2003)*

Gini 2001 Contrada Salavrenza Vecchie Vigne White Blend (Soave Classico Superiore) $24. 91 —*R.V. (7/1/2003)*

Gini 2001 La Frosca Classico White Blend (Soave) $18. 89 —*R.V. (7/1/2003)*

Gini 2000 Soave Classico Superiore White Blend (Soave) $12. 88 Best Buy —*M.N. (9/1/2001)*

GIOVELLO

Giovello 2004 Pinot Grigio (Veneto) $10. 86 Best Buy —*M.L. (6/1/2006)*

GIRIBALDI

Giribaldi 2004 Barbera (Barbera d'Alba) $14. The Giribaldi's distinctive bottle houses an easygoing, pleasant wine. The fruit is just ripe, showing clear strawberry and red cherries. There is plenty of acid, and a short medium finish. 84 —*M.G. (4/1/2007)*

Giribaldi 1997 Barbera (Barbera d'Asti) $10. 84 *(4/1/2000)*

Giribaldi 1999 Barbera (Barbera d'Alba Superiore) $11. 87 Best Buy —*M.S. (11/15/2002)*

Giribaldi 2004 Rié Barbera (Barbera d'Alba Superiore) $17. The wine begins well with aromas of dark fruit and spice, but the palate is less exciting; the burst of fruit gives way to a hollow midpalate, although it does come back to a solid if dull finish. 86 —*M.G. (12/31/2007)*

Giribaldi NV Selezioni Rodellisa Dolce Brachetto (Piedmont) $15. 88 Best Buy —*K.F. (12/31/2002)*

Giribaldi 2000 Cortese (Gavi) $16. 87 —*M.S. (12/15/2003)*

Giribaldi 1997 Dolcetto (Dolcetto d'Alba) $14. 85 *(4/1/2000)*

Giribaldi 2004 Vigna Campo del Pero Dolcetto (Dolcetto d'Alba) $14. The winemakers at Giribaldi went for a more ambitious wine, with intense jammy fruit, licorice and earth. On the palate the wine was quite extracted, showing plenty of black fruit and the earthy character taking a more central role. Imported by Global E. Selections, LLC. 89 —*M.G. (12/31/2007)*

Giribaldi 2000 Vigna Cason Dolcetto (Dolcetto d'Alba) $14. 85 —*M.S. (12/15/2003)*

Giribaldi 2003 Nebbiolo (Barbaresco) $36. In a year where so many Barbarescos are heavy and slightly plummy, this is lighter and the fruit aromas are more primary. On the palate, the flavors show elements of wild strawberries, lavender and smoke, and the wine is balanced and finishes well. A really pleasant Barbaresco that will evolve for a few more years. 88 —*M.G. (12/31/2007)*

Giribaldi 2002 Nebbiolo (Barolo) $49. A fine example of a Barolo, and a marvel considering the problems of the 2002 harvest. The fruit is dark and juicy with plenty of concentration, with the added complexity of roses and pencil shavings. Nicely textured, with a medium to long finish. Imported by Global E. Selections, LLC. 92 —*M.G. (12/31/2007)*

Giribaldi 1999 Nebbiolo (Barolo) $39. 86 —*J.C. (11/15/2004)*

Giribaldi 1998 Nebbiolo (Barbaresco) $28. 91 —*M.M. (11/15/2002)*

Giribaldi 1997 Nebbiolo (Barolo) $30. 90 —*C.S. (11/15/2002)*

Giribaldi 2004 Conca D'Oro Nebbiolo (Langhe) $20. This has textbook aromas of smoke, earth and cherry. On the palate, the flavors come through, and if in the final analysis, it lacked a little concentration, the complexity was here, and the finish is decent. Imported by Global E. Selections, LLC. 87 —*M.G. (12/31/2007)*

Giribaldi 1998 Riserva Nebbiolo (Barolo) $37. 92 Editors' Choice *(4/2/2004)*

GIRLAN

Girlan 2006 Aimé Gewürztraminer (Alto Adige) $22. Pretty golden hues set the tone and segue into floral aromas of acacia and honey. There are some soapy, Moscato-like qualities to this aromatic white and its floral fragrances transfer to the mouth, where there's a smooth, creamy texture. 87 —*M.L. (12/1/2007)*

Girlan 2006 San Martino Pinot Bianco (Alto Adige) $15. Cool-climate origins help shape aromas of Granny Smith apple, citrus, exotic fruit and peach. This is a very likeable, crisp and enjoyable wine to pair with chicken southwestern salad. 87 —*M.L. (12/1/2007)*

Girlan 2004 Pinot Grigio (Alto Adige) $15. 84 —*M.L. (6/1/2006)*

Girlan 2006 AltoPiano Pinot Grigio (Alto Adige) $17. In a return to tradition, some enterprising Pinot Grigio producers allow more skin contact during winemaking, which results in a slightly copper-colored wine (as the name implies, Pinot Grigio's natural skin color is copper-gray). This is one of those wines, and besides the unique color, you'll appreciate its aromas of peach, citrus, almond and natural rubber. 86 —*M.L. (12/1/2007)*

Girlan 2005 Altopiano Pinot Grigio (Alto Adige) $16. Sweet yellow melon, honeysuckle, pear and peach are delivered first, followed by lemon zest and lingering honey-like flavors. This is an attractive ensemble with clean acidity; pair with pasta salads or light fish dishes. 87 —*M.L. (4/1/2007)*

Girlan 2006 Filadonna Pinot Grigio (Valdadige) $15. Here's a bottle of standard, easy-to-drink Pinot Grigio with abundant aromas of delicate white flower, stone fruit, sage leaf and some soapy-lavender like notes. The wine is not huge in intensity, but it does offer nice balance between creamy fruit and bright acidity over a lean, somewhat thin mouthfeel. 86 —*M.L. (12/1/2007)*

Girlan 2004 Filadonna Pinot Grigio (Valdadige) $14. 86 —*M.L. (2/1/2006)*

Girlan 2004 Filadonna Pinot Grigio (Alto Adige) $15. 87 —*M.L. (2/1/2006)*

Girlan 2006 Indra Sauvignon (Alto Adige) $20. This wine offers a nice mix of typical Sauvignon aromas such as fresh fruit, sage and tomato leaf, and also appears less sharp than other versions of the grape with low-key acidity that is never pointed or thorny. 87 —*M.L. (12/1/2007)*

Girlan 2006 Toretta Classico White Blend (Alto Adige) $14. You'll love the delicate floral fragrances of this feminine, cool-climate northern Italian white. Acacia, jasmine and honeysuckle play a leading role with a supporting cast of stone fruit and pear. In the mouth, it's not particularly intense or thick. **86** *—M.L. (12/1/2007)*

GIROLAMO DORIGO

Girolamo Dorigo 2000 Chardonnay (Colli Orientali del Friuli) $35. 87 *—R.V. (7/1/2003)*

Girolamo Dorigo 2001 Ronc di Juri Sauvignon Blanc (Colli Piacentini) $35. 85 *—R.V. (7/1/2003)*

Girolamo Dorigo 1999 Ronc di Juri Sauvignon Blanc (Friuli) $37. 82 *(1/1/2004)*

GIULIO FERRARI

Giulio Ferrari 1994 Riserva del Fondatore Chardonnay (Trento) $75. 92 *—M.L. (12/15/2004)*

GIUNTI

Giunti 2001 Il Monte Riserva Sangiovese (Chianti) $25. 88 *(4/1/2005)*

GIUSEPPE CAMPAGNOLA

Giuseppe Campagnola 2003 Caterina Zardini Corvina, Rondinella, Molinara (Amarone della Valpolicella Classico) $60. This is a high intensity wine with a lot going on aroma-wise: Red cherry, vanilla, roasted peanut, chestnut, Indian spice, cola and some cooked green notes are distinguishable elements in a complex package. Although the nose has complexity, it's a hair shy of absolute harmony. **92** *—M.L. (10/1/2007)*

Giuseppe Campagnola 2003 Centenario Corvina, Rondinella, Molinara (Amarone della Valpolicella Classico) $45. Celebrating 100 years of activity, Giuseppe Campagnola is one of Valpolicella's oldest and biggest producers. The company has a refurbished winery and three enormous hangers dedicated to grape appassimento. This anniversary wine delivers black berry fruit, chocolate, cherry cough drop and a smidgeon of cooked fruit and is aged in both barrique and oak cask. **90** *—M.L. (10/1/2007)*

GIUSEPPE CORTESE

Giuseppe Cortese 1998 Trifolera Dolcetto (Dolcetto d'Alba) $15. 88 *(4/1/2000)*

Giuseppe Cortese 2000 Rabajá Nebbiolo (Barbaresco) $45. 89 *(4/2/2004)*

GIUSEPPE LONARDI

Giuseppe Lonardi 2003 Corvina, Rondinella, Molinara (Amarone della Valpolicella Classico) $60. With a background in the hospitality industry, Giuseppe Lonardi started making wine in 1984 and favors tonneaux-aged Amarone with deep complexity and elegance. Chocolate, red apple skin, cherry, prunes, dried figs, cardamom spice, eucalyptus, mint and cough drop add brilliance and depth. **90** *—M.L. (10/1/2007)*

GORETTI

Goretti 2000 Le Mura Saracene Sagrantino (Sagrantino di Montefalco) $NA. 90 Editors' Choice *—M.L. (9/1/2005)*

GOTTARDI

Gottardi 2004 Mazzon Pinot Nero (Alto Adige) $48. There's a lot going on in the glass thanks to penetrating aromas of red fruit, smoky toast and white chocolate. Although the nose in intense, it's a bit awkward with a few thorny spots along the way. But the wine does boast a beautiful ruby color and a silky, caressing mouthfeel. **87** *—M.L. (9/1/2007)*

GRADIS'CIUTTA

Gradis'ciutta 2000 Chardonnay (Collio) $13. 80 *—J.C. (7/1/2003)*

Gradis'ciutta 2000 del Bratinus Bianco White Blend (Collio) $13. 81 *—J.C. (7/1/2003)*

GRASSO FRATELLI

Grasso Fratelli 1999 Nebbiolo (Barbaresco) $30. 89 *(4/2/2004)*

Grasso Fratelli 1999 Bricco Spessa Nebbiolo (Barbaresco) $36. 89 *(4/2/2004)*

GRU

Gru 2003 Montepulciano (Montepulciano d'Abruzzo) $7. 81 *—M.S. (10/1/2006)*

GUALDO DEL RE

Gualdo del Re 2003 Federico Primo Cabernet Sauvignon (Val di Cornia Suvereto) $36. Inky, modern and deeply concentrated, this is a bruiser; delivers lavish notes of blueberry preserves, plum, prunes, pipe tobacco, smoked bacon and cigar box. Game meat or duck will enhance the dusty tannins and creamy mouthfeel. **91** *—M.L. (4/1/2007)*

Gualdo del Re 2003 L'Rennero Merlot (Val di Cornia Suvereto) $50. The toasted tones are deep and penetrating thanks to 15 months of oak aging and are backed by blueberry, coffee and vanilla. There is attractive dimension to this wine shaped by lavish exotic spice, firm tannins, chewy sweetness and vibrant fruit flavors: An excellent red meat Merlot. **90** *—M.L. (3/1/2007)*

Gualdo del Re 2005 Eliseo Rosato Red Blend (Val di Cornia Suvereto) $14. Definitely a cheerful rosé with a brilliant ruby color and subtle amber reflections, this easy-to-drink wine delivers cranberries, rose petal, white chocolate and sweet raspberry. It's simplistic but refreshing and tart in the mouth. **85** *—M.L. (4/1/2007)*

Gualdo del Re 2004 Eliseo Rosso Red Blend (Val di Cornia Suvereto) $14. Here's another powerful red (80% Sangiovese and 20% Canaiolo) with aromas of moist tobacco, leather, blackberry, dusty minerality and a thick, extracted mouthfeel. It scores well in texture and persistency and would pair wonderfully with grilled meat. **87** *—M.L. (4/1/2007)*

Gualdo del Re 2002 Sangiovese Grosso (Val di Cornia Suvereto) $29. How do you get Sangiovese to taste like this? Dense, unfiltered and concentrated, this is smoky, ripe and intense, with blackberry, pipe tobacco, charcoal, moist earth and a chewy, almost sticky, feel in the mouth. It sees 18 months in barrique and one year of bottle aging; made with the same Sangiovese clone that produces Brunello. **90 Editors' Choice** *—M.L. (4/1/2007)*

Gualdo del Re 1994 Val Di Cornia Suvereto Riserva Sangiovese (Barolo) $27. 88 *—J.S. (5/1/1999)*

Gualdo del Re 2005 Valentina Vermentino (Val di Cornia Suvereto) $16. Exotic fruit, banana and yellow rose are embellished by toasted almond, vanilla, maple syrup and herbal tones. But the wine is too watery and light-weight in the mouth to score higher. **84** *—M.L. (4/1/2007)*

GUARNIERI

Guarnieri 1999 Le Masse di Greve Sangiovese (Chianti Classico) $19. 84 *—M.S. (12/31/2002)*

Guarnieri 1998 Le Masse di Greve Sangiovese (Chianti Classico) $19. 85 *(4/1/2001)*

GUASTI CLEMENTE

Guasti Clemente 2004 Moscato (Moscato d'Asti) $12. 87 *—M.L. (12/15/2005)*

Guasti Clemente 2001 Nebbiolo (Nebbiolo d'Alba) $21. Showing its age, this has lost most of its fruit, and the earthy flavors now dominate. Saved from total extinction, by one or two stray shards of fruit, it is a wine that needs to be drunk and drunk quickly. **82** *—M.G. (4/1/2007)*

GUERRIERI RIZZARDI

Guerrieri Rizzardi 2001 Villa Rizzardi Corvina, Rondinella, Molinara (Amarone della Valpolicella Classico) $40. This is a very ripe wine with dirty notes of strawberry jam and moist earth. The mouthfeel, on the other hand, is definitely more balanced and polished with chiseled tannins and a good spice-driven finish. **85** *—M.L. (12/1/2007)*

Guerrieri Rizzardi 1998 Red Blend (Amarone della Valpolicella Classico) $70. 84 *(11/1/2005)*

Guerrieri Rizzardi 1997 Red Blend (Amarone della Valpolicella Classico) $59. 87 *(5/1/2003)*

Guerrieri Rizzardi 1998 Calcarole Red Blend (Amarone della Valpolicella Classico) $95. 86 *(11/1/2005)*

Guerrieri Rizzardi 1995 Calcarole Red Blend (Amarone della Valpolicella Classico) $82. 87 *(5/1/2003)*

Guerrieri Rizzardi 2000 Estate Bottled Classico Superiore Red Blend (Bardolino) $12. 81 *(5/1/2003)*

Guerrieri Rizzardi 2000 Pojega Red Blend (Valpolicella Classico Superiore) $15. 82 *(5/1/2003)*

Guerrieri Rizzardi 2001 Tacchetto Estate Bottled Classico Red Blend (Bardolino) $15. 82 *(5/1/2003)*

GUICCIARDINI STROZZI

Guicciardini Strozzi 2000 Millanni 994 Red Blend (Toscana) $55. 84 *—M.S. (9/1/2006)*

Guicciardini Strozzi 2001 Selvascura Red Blend (Toscana) $29. 90 *—M.S. (9/1/2006)*

Guicciardini Strozzi 2003 Titolato Sangiovese (Chianti Colli Senesi) $10. 88 Best Buy *(4/1/2005)*

GULFI

Gulfi 2000 Nero Bufaleffi Nero d'Avola (Sicilia) $33. 91 *—J.C. (10/1/2003)*

Gulfi 2000 Nero Ibleo Nero d'Avola (Sicilia) $16. 90 Editors' Choice —*J.C. (10/1/2003)*

Gulfi 2000 Nero Maccari Nero d'Avola (Sicilia) $33. 92 —*J.C. (10/1/2003)*

Gulfi 2002 Nerobaronj Nero d'Avola (Sicilia) $40. 87 —*M.L. (7/1/2006)*

Gulfi 2002 Nerobufaleffj Nero d'Avola (Sicilia) $40. 87 —*M.L. (7/1/2006)*

Gulfi 1999 Neroibleo Nero d'Avola (Sicilia) $12. 90 Best Buy —*C.S. (5/1/2002)*

Gulfi 2003 Nerojbleo Nero d'Avola (Sicilia) $18. 89 —*M.L. (7/1/2006)*

Gulfi 2002 Nerosanlorenzj Nero d'Avola (Sicilia) $40. 88 —*M.L. (7/1/2006)*

Gulfi 2001 Rosso Ibleo Nero d'Avola (Sicilia) $11. 88 Best Buy —*J.C. (10/1/2003)*

Gulfi 2005 Rossojbleo Nero d'Avola (Sicilia) $15. 86 —*M.L. (7/1/2006)*

Gulfi 2000 Caricanti White Blend (Sicilia) $22. 85 —*J.C. (10/1/2003)*85 —*M.L. (7/1/2006)*

Gulfi 2001 Valcanziria White Blend (Sicilia) $11. 88 Best Buy —*J.C. (10/1/2003)*

Gulfi 2005 Valcanzjria White Blend (Sicilia) $15. 86 —*M.L. (7/1/2006)*

H. LUN WINERY

H. Lun Winery 2004 Pinot Grigio (Alto Adige) $16. 84 —*M.L. (6/1/2006)*

HAUNER

Hauner 1999 Agave Red Blend (Sicilia) $15. 86 *(5/1/2002)*

I CASALI SELECTION

I Casali Selection 2004 Pinot Grigio (Friuli Grave) $14. 87 —*M.L. (2/1/2006)*

I FEUDI DI ROMANS

I Feudi di Romans 2004 Pinot Grigio (Isonzo del Friuli) $14. 87 —*M.L. (6/1/2006)*

I GIUSTI E ZANZA

I Giusti e Zanza 2003 Dulcamara Cabernet Blend (Toscana) $55. 92 —*M.L. (9/1/2006)*

I Giusti e Zanza 1999 Belcore Sangiovese (Toscana) $24. 89 —*M.S. (8/1/2002)*

I Giusti e Zanza 1999 Dulcamara Sangiovese (Toscana) $55. 88 —*M.S. (8/1/2002)*

I VIGNAIOLI DI SANTO STEFANO

I Vignaioli di Santo Stefano 2004 Moscato (Moscato d'Asti) $20. 88 —*M.L. (12/15/2005)*

IL BORRO

Il Borro 2004 Il Borro Red Blend (Toscana) $36. This is the flagship wine of the Ferragamo family's beautiful Il Borro property in Tuscany and it does the estate proud. A blend of Merlot, Cabernet Sauvignon, and smaller percentages of Syrah and Petit Verdot, it's a concentrated wine with tones of earth, chocolate, exotic spice, prunes and red fruit. Consulting enologist Nicolò D'Afflitto has shaped the wine with 12 months of oak aging, adding deeper notes of spice, vanilla and clove. 93 —*M.L. (2/1/2007)*

Il Borro 2004 Pian di Nova Red Blend (Toscana) $19. This is a 75-25 percent Syrah and Sangiovese blend that goes down smoothly and comfortably. The nose offers notes of cherry, currant berry and spice that are attractive albeit simple. Syrah with its richness, and Sangiovese with its berry freshness make an interesting blend. 86 —*M.L. (2/1/2007)*

Il Borro 2004 Polissena Sangiovese (Toscana) $24. This is a beautiful and unique rendition of Sangiovese with a vibrant ruby color, berry notes, menthol freshness and tight, dusty tannins on the finish. This part of Tuscany is hotter, less hilly and has different soils than Chianti Classico; these distinctions create a more robust and intense Sangiovese. 89 —*M.L. (2/1/2007)*

IL CARPINO

Il Carpino 2003 Red Blend (Friuli) $37. Aromas of cherry, spice cake and vanilla are nicely integrated, forward and dense. Very delicate menthol notes also come into play at the fringe. A succulent wine boasting soft tannins. 87 —*M.L. (5/1/2007)*

Il Carpino 2003 Ribolla Gialla (Collio) $27. The saturated, golden color is perplexing because you might think the wine is oxidized. Yet, once you bring your nose to the glass, you will be happily surprised by pine nut, melon, Golden Delicious apple and a touch of maple syrup. It's creamy in the mouth with toasted notes that ride over a long finish. Pair with roasted pork. 86 —*M.L. (5/1/2007)*

IL CASCINONE

Il Cascinone 2006 Sorilaria Arneis (Roero Arneis) $26. The color is darker than the other 2006 Arneis' tasted, and the wine is very evolved. It is pleasant but top heavy; the lack of acidity makes it soft, rich but blowsy, so little carries on to the finish. 81 —*M.G. (12/31/2007)*

IL CIRCO

Il Circo 2001 La Violetta Uva di Troia (Castel del Monte) $15. 88 —*M.S. (10/1/2004)*

Il Circo 2000 La Violetta Uva di Troia (Castel del Monte) $15. 86 —*S.H. (1/1/2002)*

Il Conte 2006 Villa Prandone Pecorino (Marche) $NA. An interesting aromatic ensemble of exotic fruit, white mineral, natural rubber, almond skin and perfumed flowers set the tone. In the mouth, this unique wine made from the little-known Pecorino grape offers ripe yellow fruit flavors, and a waxy, creamy texture. 86 —*M.L. (12/1/2007)*

Il Conte 2002 Marinus Red Blend (Rosso Piceno) $14. 83 —*M.S. (7/1/2005)*

Il Conte 2005 Villa Prandone Red Blend (Rosso Piceno) $NA. Here is a fresh and immediate Rosso Piceno that offers notes of forest berry, blueberry, savory spice and salad greens. This wine makes a very nice impact in the mouth: Firm structure and good intensity are backed by flavors of almond nut and chopped herbs. 87 —*M.L. (12/1/2007)*

Il Conte 2000 Zipolo Red Blend (Marche) $24. 85 —*M.S. (7/1/2005)*

Il Conte 2003 Donello Sangiovese (Marche) $13. 85 —*M.S. (7/1/2005)*

Il Conte 2003 Aurato White Blend (Falerio del Colli Ascolani) $10. 86 Best Buy —*M.S. (7/1/2005)*

Il Conte 2005 Villa Prandone Aurato White Blend (Falerio dei Colli Ascolani) $NA. A blend of three native grapes (Trebbiano, Pecorino and Passerina), this refreshing wine is redolent of mature fruit, almond, honey and finely chopped garden herbs. It boasts a smooth, silky quality in the mouth and ends on a tart, crisp note. 86 —*M.L. (12/1/2007)*

Il Conte d'Alba NV Moscato (Moscato d'Asti) $10. 87 Editors' Choice —*M.L. (12/15/2005)*

IL FALCHETTO

Il Falchetto 2006 Arneis (Langhe) $21. The Il Falchetto offers lovely aromas of fresh peach, honeysuckle and lime peel. The palate is more delicate but the wine is beautifully balanced, and initially, there is more than enough intensity of flavor. But as it moves towards the finish, it begins to run out of steam. 88 —*M.G. (12/31/2007)*

Il Falchetto 2006 Chardonnay (Langhe) $17. This alluring Chardonnay displayed a gorgeous nose of vanilla and candied apricot. While it is relatively simple on the palate, the flavors are concentrated and it finishes well. Overall an easy-going bottle of wine that will match most foods. 87 —*M.G. (12/31/2007)*

Il Falchetto 2004 Ciombi (Not Imported) Moscato (Moscato d'Asti) $NA. 87 —*M.L. (12/15/2005)*

Il Falchetto 2006 Tenuta Del Fant Moscato (Moscato d'Asti) $19. Very laid back, the nose shows some mango and pear, but you really have to go looking for them. In contrast, the palate is almost pushy–this is a big, fat intense wine. Essentially quite simple, but very tasty. Short to medium finish. 85 —*M.G. (12/31/2007)*

Il Falchetto 2004 Tenuta del Fant Moscato (Moscato d'Asti) $17. 86 —*M.L. (12/15/2005)*

IL FEUDUCCIO DI S. MARIA D'ORNI

Il Feuduccio Di S. Maria D'Orni 2001 Montepulciano (Montepulciano d'Abruzzo) $29. 90 Editors' Choice —*M.S. (10/1/2006)*

Il Feuduccio Di S. Maria D'Orni 1999 Margae Montepulciano (Montepulciano d'Abruzzo) $75. 90 —*M.S. (10/1/2006)*

Il Feuduccio Di S. Maria D'Orni 1999 Ursonia Montepulciano (Montepulciano d'Abruzzo) $39. 91 —*M.S. (11/15/2003)*

Il Feuduccio Di S. Maria D'Orni 1998 Ursonia Montepulciano (Montepulciano d'Abruzzo) $31. 90 —*M.S. (11/15/2003)*

Il Feuduccio Di S. Maria D'Orni 2005 Ocumare Sauvignon (Colline Teatine) $15. Here's an interesting Sauvignon from central Italy with distinctive notes of chopped herbs and honey on the fringe of crisp, zesty fruit. There's good dimension and balance here and a thin mouthfeel is capped by vibrant spice on the close. 87 —*M.L. (12/1/2007)*

Il Feuduccio Di S. Maria D'Orni 2003 White Blend (Colline Teatine) $18. 80 —*M.S. (7/1/2005)*

Il Feuduccio Di S. Maria D'Orni 2004 Yare White Blend (Colline Teatine) $33. It's always a pleasure to encounter a white wine with this level of softness and intensity. Banana, pineapple, exotic fruit, pear and Golden

Delicious apple sum up the nose and evolve into honey-nut flavors in the mouth. Drink it with saffron risotto. 89 *—M.L. (12/1/2007)*

IL GRILLESINO

Il Grillesino 1999 Sangiovese (Morellino di Scansano) $14. 86 *—M.S. (8/1/2002)*

Il Grillesino 1999 Ceccante Sangiovese (Toscana) $43. 90 *—M.S. (8/1/2002)*

IL MARRONETO

Il Marroneto 2001 Brunello (Brunello di Montalcino) $NA. 87 *(4/1/2006)*

IL NURAGHE

Il Nuraghe 1999 Chio Red Blend (Cannonau di Sardegna) $22. 88 *—M.S. (12/15/2003)*

Il Nuraghe 2000 Colle Moresco Red Blend (Monica di Sardegna) $12. 87 *—M.S. (12/15/2003)*

Il Nuraghe 1998 Nabui Red Blend (Monica di Sardegna) $21. 89 *—M.S. (12/15/2003)*

Il Nuraghe 2000 San Bernardino Red Blend (Monica di Sardegna) $15. 83 *—M.S. (1/1/2004)*

Il Nuraghe 2001 Vignaruja Red Blend (Cannonau di Sardegna) $15. 87 *—M.S. (12/15/2003)*

IL PALAGIONE

Il Palagione 2002 Hydra Vernaccia (Vernaccia di San Gimignano) $14. 85 *—M.S. (8/1/2004)*

IL PALAZZINO

Il Palazzino 1998 Sangiovese (Chianti Classico) $18. 90 Editors' Choice *(4/1/2001)*

Il Palazzino 1997 Grosso Sanese Riserva Sangiovese (Chianti Classico) $35. 90 *(4/1/2001)*

IL PALAZZONE

Il Palazzone 2001 Brunello (Brunello di Montalcino) $85. 92 *(4/1/2006)*

Il Palazzone 2000 Brunello (Brunello di Montalcino) $85. 92 *—M.S. (7/1/2005)*

Il Palazzone 1999 Riserva Brunello (Brunello di Montalcino) $95. 96 Editors' Choice *—M.S. (7/1/2005)*

IL PICCOLO BORGO

IL Piccolo Borgo 2002 Sangiovese (Chianti Classico) $16. 87 *—M.S. (10/1/2006)*

IL POGGIOLINO

Il Poggiolino 1998 Riserva Sangiovese (Chianti Classico) $25. 87 *—R.V. (8/1/2002)*

IL POGGIONE

Il Poggione 2001 Brunello (Brunello di Montalcino) $62. 89 *(4/1/2006)*

Il Poggione 2000 Brunello (Brunello di Montalcino) $60. 91 *—M.S. (7/1/2005)*

Il Poggione 1999 Brunello (Brunello di Montalcino) $62. 93 *—M.S. (6/1/2004)*

Il Poggione 1998 Brunello (Brunello di Montalcino) $63. 90 *—M.S. (11/15/2003)*

Il Poggione 1997 Brunello (Brunello di Montalcino) $60. 91 *—R.V. (8/1/2002)*

Il Poggione 1999 Riserva Brunello (Brunello di Montalcino) $80. 94 *—M.S. (7/1/2005)*

Il Poggione 1997 Riserva Brunello (Brunello di Montalcino) $71. 92 Cellar Selection *—M.S. (11/15/2003)*

Il Poggione 2002 Sangiovese (Rosso di Montalcino) $28. 90 *—M.S. (6/1/2004)*

Il Poggione 1999 Sangiovese (Rosso di Montalcino) $19. 90 *—M.S. (8/1/2002)*

Il Poggione 1999 San Leopoldo Sangiovese (Toscana) $41. 92 Editors' Choice *—M.S. (12/31/2002)*

IL ROVERONE

Il Roverone 2000 Corvina, Rondinella, Molinara (Amarone della Valpolicella Classico) $47. 92 *—J.C. (10/1/2006)*

Il Roverone 1999 Corvina, Rondinella, Molinara (Amarone della Valpolicella Classico) $47. 89 *—J.C. (10/1/2006)*

IL SOGNO DI ANNIBALE

Il Sogno di Annibale NV Extra Dry Prosecco (Prosecco di Conegliano e Valdobbiadene) $13. 87 *—M.L. (6/1/2006)*

IL TASSO

Il Tasso 1999 Sangiovese (Chianti) $11. 86 *(4/1/2001)*

IL VESCOVADO

Il Vescovado 2001 Sangiovese (Chianti) $10. 81 *(4/1/2005)*

IL VIGNALE

Il Vignale 1997 Pinot Grigio (Veneto) $10. 86 *(8/1/1999)*

IMPERO

Impero 2001 Red Blend (Amarone della Valpolicella Classico) $48. 90 *(11/1/2005)*

INAMA

Inama 2001 Vulcaia Sauvignon Blanc (Delle Venezie) $21. 88 *—R.V. (7/1/2003)*

Inama 2001 White Blend (Soave Classico Superiore) $13. 89 *—R.V. (7/1/2003)*

Inama 2001 Vigneti di Foscarino White Blend (Soave Classico Superiore) $19. 90 *—R.V. (7/1/2003)*

INNOCENTI

Innocenti 2001 Brunello (Brunello di Montalcino) $49. 90 *(4/1/2006)*

INSTITUO ENOLOGICO ITALIANO

Instituo Enologico Italiano 2001 Duca di Camastra Nero d'Avola (Sicilia) $9. 85 Best Buy *—M.S. (10/1/2004)*

ISIDORO POLENCIC

Isidoro Polencic 2004 Pinot Grigio (Collio) $20. 83 *—M.L. (6/1/2006)*

ISOLE E OLENA

Isole e Olena 2001 Collezione de Marchi Cabernet Sauvignon (Toscana) $60. 92 *—M.L. (9/1/2006)*

J. HOFSTATTER

J. Hofstatter 2002 Chardonnay (Alto Adige) $NA. 86 *—R.V. (7/1/2003)*

J. Hofstatter 2002 Kolbenhof Gewürztraminer (Alto Adige) $26. 89 *—R.V. (7/1/2003)*

J. Hofstatter 1997 Pinot Grigio (Alto Adige) $18. 80 *(8/1/1999)*

J. Hofstatter 2002 Barthenau Vigna San Michele White Blend (Alto Adige) $16. 88 *—R.V. (7/1/2003)*

JASCI

Jasci 2006 Cerasuolo Montepulciano (Abruzzo) $14. Here is a raspberry colored rosé (fermented on the skins for 12 hours) with berry aromas and notes of white chocolate, almond and wild cherry. Overall, it offers nice intensity despite a tiny point of sulfur that never blows off. Crisp and clean on the finish. 86 *—M.L. (7/1/2007)*

JERMANN

Jermann 2002 Mjzzu Blau & Blau Blaufränkisch (Delle Venezie) $36. 88 *—M.L. (9/1/2005)*

Jermann 2003 Chardonnay (Venezia Giulia) $32. 86 *—J.C. (12/31/2004)*

Jermann 2001 Chardonnay (Venezia Giulia) $27. 85 *—J.C. (7/1/2003)*

Jermann 2000 Were Dreams, Now it is Just Wine Chardonnay (Venezia Giulia) $55. 85 *—J.C. (7/1/2003)*

Jermann 2001 Pignacolusse Pignolo (Venezia Giulia) $52. 94 Editors' Choice *—M.L. (9/1/2005)*

Jermann 2001 Pinot Bianco (Venezia Giulia) $25. 89 *—J.C. (7/1/2003)*

Jermann 2004 Pinot Grigio (Venezia Giulia) $34. 88 *—M.L. (2/1/2006)*

Jermann 2003 Pinot Grigio (Venezia Giulia) $32. 87 *—J.C. (12/31/2004)*

Jermann 2001 Pinot Grigio (Venezia Giulia) $27. 90 *—J.C. (7/1/2003)*

Jermann 2006 Afix Riesling (Delle Venezie) $39. This wine boasts beautiful purity of aromas, starting with crisp citrus, lime, kiwi and cut grass before evolving to reveal layers of almond blossom and white mineral. A trace of sweetness on the palate is backed by zesty freshness, citrus flavors and overall vigor. This would make an excellent companion to Thai dishes with lemongrass or peanut sauce. 88 *—M.L. (9/1/2007)*

Jermann 2005 Afix Riesling (Delle Venezie) $39. An extra year in the bottle has helped define this wine's mineral qualities, which are reinforced by aromas of citrus, lime lollipop and jasmine. Detectable sweetness suggests an excellent pairing with exotic or spicy foods. 87 *—M.L. (9/1/2007)*

Jermann 2003 Sauvignon (Venezia Giulia) $33. 87 *(7/1/2005)*

Jermann 2000 Capo Martino in Ruttaris White Blend (Venezia Giulia) $48. 86 *—J.C. (7/1/2003)*

Jermann 2001 Vintage Tunina White Blend (Venezia Giulia) $49. 90 *—J.C. (7/1/2003)*

Jermann 1997 Vintage Tunina White Blend (Collio) $43. 87 *(11/1/1999)*

JERZU ANTICHI PODERI

Jerzu Antichi Poderi 1998 Josto Miglior Riserva Grenache (Cannonau di Sardegna) $32. 89 *—C.S. (5/1/2002)*

Jerzu Antichi Poderi 1998 Marghia Red Blend (Cannonau di Sardegna) $17. 82 *—C.S. (5/1/2002)*

JOSÉ MARIA DA FONSECA

José Maria da Fonseca 1999 Alambre Moscatel (Abruzzo) $19. 88 *—R.V. (12/31/2002)*

JOSEF BRIGL

Josef Brigl 1997 Pinot Grigio (Alto Adige) $10. 84 *(8/1/1999)*

Josef Brigl 2004 Altanuta Pinot Grigio (Alto Adige) $17. 86 *(2/1/2006)*

JOSEF NIEDERMAYR

Josef Niedermayr 2004 Pinot Grigio (Alto Adige) $NA. 86 *—M.L. (2/1/2006)*

JOSEF WEGER

Josef Weger 2004 Pinot Grigio (Alto Adige) $9. 85 Best Buy *—M.L. (6/1/2006)*

Josef Weger 2004 Maso delle Rosé Rulânder Pinot Grigio (Alto Adige) $11. 86 Best Buy *—M.L. (6/1/2006)*

KELLEREI KALTERN CALDARO

Kellerei Kaltern Caldaro 2005 Lasón Merlot (Alto Adige) $NA. Offers pretty aromatic intensity, finesse and cheerful notes of red berry fruit, almond and fine spice. The ensemble is nicely layered and elegant and a solid core of red fruit is embellished by a touch of cracked black pepper and nutmeg. 89 *—M.L. (3/1/2007)*

KHÁRISMA

Khárisma 2005 Vermentino (Sardinia) $17. This is a particularly likeable and approachable (with 5% Chardonnay), delivering crisp stone-fruit flavors backed by honey, yellow flower, smoke, clove and a playful dash of herb. The aromas linger over the palate and close with a smoky aftertaste. 87 *—M.L. (8/1/2007)*

KISMET CELLARS

Kismet Cellars 2002 Montepulciano (Montepulciano d'Abruzzo) $10. 84 *—M.S. (11/15/2003)*

Kismet Cellars 2004 Pinot Grigio (Veneto) $9. 83 *(2/1/2006)*

Kismet Cellars 2002 Sangiovese (Veneto) $10. 84 *—M.S. (12/15/2003)*

KRIS

Kris 2003 Pinot Grigio (Delle Venezie) $11. 90 Best Buy *—P.G. (11/15/2004)*

KRIZIA

Krizia 1996 Pinot Grigio (Colli Orientali del Friuli) $23. 82 *(8/1/1999)*

KUPELWIESER

Kupelwieser 2004 Pinot Grigio (Alto Adige) $13. 87 *—M.L. (6/1/2006)*

LA BRACCESCA

La Braccesca 1996 Sangiovese (Vino Nobile di Montepulciano) $26. 86 *—J.C. (7/1/2000)*

LA CARRAIA

La Carraia 2001 Fobiano Cabernet Sauvignon-Merlot (Umbria) $40. 84 *—M.S. (7/1/2005)*

La Carraia 1999 Fobiano Red Blend (Umbria) $35. 89 *—C.S. (2/1/2003)*

La Carraia 2003 White Blend (Orvieto Classico) $9. 83 *—M.S. (7/1/2005)*

LA CASA DELL'ORCO

La Casa Dell'Orco 1996 Red Blend (Taurasi) $25. 83 *—C.S. (5/1/2002)*

LA COLOMBAIA

La Colombaia 1997 Monopolio Montresor Pinot Grigio (Valdadige) $11. 88 Best Buy *(8/1/1999)*

La Colombaia 2000 Red Blend (Amarone della Valpolicella) $50. 89 *(11/1/2005)*

La Colombaia 2006 Albarosa Rosé Blend (Veneto) $14. Here's a wine with pretty rosy vibrancy, elegance and spectacular freshness across the palate. The wine imparts attractive notes of blueberry, small forest berries, stone fruit and minerals. It is zesty in the mouth with good persistency and would pair with seafood, pasta and salads. 87 Editors' Choice *—M.L. (7/1/2007)*

LA COLOMBINA

La Colombina 2001 Brunello (Brunello di Montalcino) $45. 91 *(4/1/2006)*

La Colombina 2000 Brunello (Brunello di Montalcino) $45. 92 Editors' Choice *—M.S. (7/1/2005)*

La Colombina 1999 Brunello (Brunello di Montalcino) $NA. 89 *—M.S. (6/1/2004)*

LA CONTEA

La Contea 1999 Ripa Sorita Nebbiolo (Barbaresco) $40. 89 *(4/2/2004)*

LA CORTE

La Corte 2004 Anfora Primitivo (Puglia) $14. 86 *—M.L. (9/1/2005)*

La Corte 2002 Zinfandel Primitivo (Puglia) $25. 87 *—M.L. (9/1/2005)*

La Corte 2003 Red Blend (Salento) $49. 87 *—M.L. (9/1/2005)*

LA DIACCETA

La Diacceta 2000 Vernaccia (San Gimignano) $11. 87 *—M.S. (8/1/2002)*

LA FIAMMENGA

La Fiammenga 2005 Dolcetto (Dolcetto d'Alba) $12. The La Fiammenga is a beautifully made wine; its aromas of dark fruit, almonds and violets give it a lushness that stops just short of jamminess. On the palate, it is rich, and quite meaty but let down by a slightly short finish. Imported by Sapori Italiani, Inc. 88 *—M.G. (4/1/2007)*

La Fiammenga 2004 Nebbiolo (Nebbiolo d'Alba) $14. Made to a traditional formula, the Clemente shows some fruit, but also funky stale earth aromas. On the palate, the wine takes on the stale character of the nose, and the fruit disappears quickly. Imported by Sapori Italiani, Inc. 82 *—M.G. (4/1/2007)*

La Fiammenga 2003 Nebbiolo (Barbaresco) $28. Typical of this hot vintage, La Fiammenga is already quite mature. The fruit is on the plummy side, it has the added complexity of licorice and road tar. On the palate, it is soft and rich, but it does need a touch of acid to liven it up. Imported by Sapori Italiani, Inc. 87 *—M.G. (12/31/2007)*

La Fiammenga 2002 Nebbiolo (Barolo) $40. Browning slightly at the edge, and already fully mature, this shows some pretty aromatics of strawberry, flowers and wintergreen mint. Quite light on the palate, but the aromatic thrust gives it plenty of interest. While it will not improve, it is a nice example of a good Barolo that should be drunk over the next five years. Imported by Sapori Italiani, Inc. 89 *—M.G. (12/31/2007)*

La Fiammenga 2003 Pas de Deux Red Blend (Monferrato) $28. The Passepied is a pretty, chunky wine displaying bright raspberry flavors and a rich easygoing personality. Pleasant to drink, but with the potential to age gracefully for another five years. Imported by Sapori Italiani, Inc. 88 *—M.G. (12/31/2007)*

La Fiammenga 2003 Passepied Red Blend (Monferrato) $30. A well-made wine from the relatively obscure subregion of Piedmont, Monferrato. A modernist wine, where the wine shows very ripe fruit flavors, coffee and a touch of earth, a soft but solid structure, and a medium finish. Imported by Sapori Italiani, Inc. 87 *—M.G. (12/31/2007)*

LA FORTUNA

La Fortuna 2000 Brunello (Brunello di Montalcino) $48. 90 *—M.S. (7/1/2005)*

La Fortuna 1999 Riserva Brunello (Brunello di Montalcino) $70. 93 *—M.S. (7/1/2005)*

LA FRANCESCA

La Francesca 2001 Cabernet Sauvignon (Veneto) $6. 80 *(5/1/2003)*

La Francesca 2001 Chardonnay (Veneto) $6. 82 *—J.C. (7/1/2003)*

La Francesca 2002 Merlot (Veneto) $6. 84 Best Buy *—M.S. (12/15/2003)*

La Francesca 2001 Merlot (Veneto) $6. 84 *(5/1/2003)*

La Francesca 1998 Pinot Grigio (Veneto) $5. 86 Best Buy *(8/1/1999)*

La Francesca 2003 Pinot Grigio (Veneto) $7. 84 Best Buy *—J.C. (12/31/2004)*

La Francesca 2001 Pinot Grigio (Veneto) $6. 84 Best Buy *—J.C. (7/1/2003)*

La Francesca 2000 Pinot Grigio (Veneto) $5. 83 *(9/1/2001)*

La Francesca 2001 Red Blend (Valpolicella) $6. 84 *(5/1/2003)*

LA GERLA

La Gerla 1993 Brunello (Brunello di Montalcino) $45. 88 *—M.M. (5/1/1999)*

La Gerla 2001 Brunello (Brunello di Montalcino) $45. 92 Editors' Choice *(4/1/2006)*

La Gerla 2000 Brunello (Brunello di Montalcino) $60. 88 *—M.S. (7/1/2005)*

La Gerla 1999 Brunello (Brunello di Montalcino) $NA. 88 *—M.S. (6/1/2004)*

La Gerla 1997 Brunello (Brunello di Montalcino) $55. 93 Editors' Choice *—R.V. (8/1/2002)*

La Gerla 1999 Riserva Brunello (Brunello di Montalcino) $100. 91 *—M.S. (7/1/2005)*

La Gerla 2001 Vigne gli Angeli Brunello (Brunello di Montalcino) $65. 90 *(4/1/2006)*

LA GIARETTA

La Giaretta 2003 Corvina, Rondinella, Molinara (Amarone della Valpolicella Classico) $23. La Giaretta is an up-and-coming winery in full evolution with a modern approach and excellent pricing. There are deep oak aromas here that thankfully do not overwhelm delicate notes of cherry cola, cough drop, Indian spice, herbal infusion and almond. This is a spice-driven wine with a velvety texture and lively fruit on the finish. 91 Editors' Choice *—M.L. (10/1/2007)*

La Giaretta 2000 I Quadretti Corvina, Rondinella, Molinara (Amarone della Valpolicella Classico) $35. Pretty color and density are backed by mismatched aromas of soy sauce, ginger, steak sauce and beef jerky. It's a big, chewy wine in the mouth with attractive succulence and a fresh, long-lasting finish. 88 *—M.L. (12/1/2007)*

La Gioiosa NV Cartizze Prosecco (Prosecco Superiore di Cartizze) $NA. A delicately balanced Prosecco with a touch of white pepper and dried herbs that make a pretty frame to peach cream aromas. The wine has a fine point of sweetness in the mouth and would pair well with Thai curry dishes. 88 *—M.L. (12/15/2007)*

La Gioiosa NV Extra Dry Prosecco (Prosecco di Conegliano e Valdobbiadene) $NA. This is a classic Prosecco in terms of the wine's soapy, citrusy aromas: Jasmine, peach, pear, melon and cut grass make for a fragrant ensemble. It delivers round, soft tones in the mouth followed by a fine point of cooling acidity. 86 *—M.L. (12/15/2007)*

LA GUARDIENSE

La Guardiense 2003 Greco (Sannio) $10. 84 *—M.L. (10/1/2006)*

LA LASTRA

La Lastra 2005 Sangiovese (Chianti Colli Senesi) $18. The nose is very fruity and ripe with intense notes of forest berry, cherry and blueberry that play a leading role next to spice and church incense. From an estate founded in 1994 by Nadia Betti and Renato Spanu near San Gimignano, Tuscany's "City of Towers," this is a simple, genuine red that would pair well with informal meals. 87 *—M.L. (11/1/2007)*

La Lastra 1999 Sangiovese (Chianti Colli Senesi) $12. 87 Best Buy *(4/1/2001)*

LA MANNELLA

La Mannella 2001 Brunello (Brunello di Montalcino) $45. 91 *(4/1/2006)*

La Mannella 2001 I Poggiarelli Brunello (Brunello di Montalcino) $50. 90 *(4/1/2006)*

LA MARCA

La Marca 1998 Pinot Grigio (Veneto) $8. 84 *(8/1/1999)*

La Marca 2003 Winemaker's Collection Pinot Grigio (Piave) $11. 83 *—J.C. (12/31/2004)*

La Marca NV Extra Dry Prosecco (Prosecco di Conegliano e Valdobbiadene) $10. 87 Best Buy *—M.L. (6/1/2006)*

La Marca NV Cuvée Extra Dry Prosecco (Prosecco di Conegliano e Valdobbiadene) $13. There's less aromatic intensity here although you can catch whiffs of sweet fruit and peach. It does have body and length and a firmly tonic feel in the mouth. Pair with informal picking foods. 85 *—M.L. (12/15/2007)*

La Marca NV Extra Dry San Nicola Prosecco (Prosecco di Conegliano e Valdobbiadene) $12. On appearance, this sparkler is light in color with delicate golden reflections and the nose is similarly understated with aromas of pulpy white fruit and dusty mineral. The wine comes alive in the mouth thanks to its lively freshness. 87 Best Buy *—M.L. (12/15/2007)*

La Marca 2004 Prestige Cuvée Prosecco (Prosecco di Conegliano e Valdobbiadene) $13. 88 Best Buy *—M.L. (6/1/2006)*

LA MASSA

La Massa 2003 Sangiovese (Toscana) $29. 91 *—M.S. (9/1/2006)*

La Massa 2001 Sangiovese (Toscana) $37. 93 Editors' Choice *—M.S. (9/1/2006)*

La Massa 2001 Giorgio Primo Sangiovese (Chianti Classico) $75. 92 *(4/1/2005)*

LA MODA

La Moda 2006 Pinot Grigio Blush Pinot Grigio (Delle Venezie) $7. The movie Pretty in Pink comes to mind thanks to this semi-sparkler's pale rose hue and its smart girlie-fashionista packaging. It recalls Prosecco with a sweet twist thanks to aromas of jasmine, peach and honeysuckle. 84 Best Buy *—M.L. (7/1/2007)*

LA MONACESCA

La Monacesca 2002 Verdicchio (Verdicchio di Matelica) $19. 85 *—M.S. (8/1/2004)*

LA MONTECCHIA

La Montecchia 1997 Red Blend (Colli Euganei) $13. 85 *—M.S. (9/1/2000)*

LA NUNSIO

La Nunsio 1997 Barbera (Barbera d'Asti) $22. 89 *(4/1/2000)*

LA PALAZZOLA

La Palazzola 1999 Rubino Grilli Red Blend (Umbria) $40. 86 *—C.S. (2/1/2002)*

LA PESCAIA

La Pescaia 2001 Brunello (Brunello di Montalcino) $NA. 90 *(4/1/2006)*

La Pisara 2004 Primitivo (Salento) $9. 83 *—M.S. (10/1/2006)*

La Pisara 2003 Red Blend (Salice Salentino) $8. 83 *—M.S. (10/1/2006)*

LA PISARA

La Pisara 2004 Negroamaro (Salento) $8. If you like wines marked by fragrant, incense-like perfumes, this is a bottle for you. Indian spice, clove, red rose, ginger and sandalwood surround a core of brandied cherries. It's a corpulent wine that slides easily across the palate. 85 Best Buy *—M.L. (8/1/2007)*

La Pisara 2004 Primitivo (Salento) $9. Inky black, dense and concentrated, that's a lot of extraction at just $9 per bottle. Ripe fruit, prunes, dried figs, blackberry confiture and chocolate notes characterize the nose; in the mouth the wine is chewy, with sweet cherry flavors. At 3.7 grams per liter of residual sugar, it definitely has a sweet note. 86 Best Buy *—M.L. (8/1/2007)*

La Pisara 2004 Salice Salentino Red Blend (Salento) $9. There's chewy ripeness in this 80-20 Negroamaro-Malvasia Nera blend with aromas of freshly brewed coffee grinds, blackberries, plum and cherry. Not hugely intense, but it is genuine with good structure and many food-friendly elements. Try it with barbecued meats. 85 Best Buy *—M.L. (8/1/2007)*

LA PODERINA

La Poderina 2001 Brunello (Brunello di Montalcino) $75. 91 *(4/1/2006)*

La Poderina 2000 Brunello (Brunello di Montalcino) $65. 90 *—M.S. (7/1/2005)*

La Poderina 1999 Brunello (Brunello di Montalcino) $69. 88 *—M.S. (6/1/2004)*

La Poderina 2000 Poggio Banale Brunello (Brunello di Montalcino) $118. 91 *(4/1/2006)*

La Poderina 1999 Poggio Banale Brunello (Brunello di Montalcino) $125. 91 *—M.S. (6/1/2004)*

LA RASINA

La Rasina 2001 Brunello (Brunello di Montalcino) $56. 91 *(4/1/2006)*

LA RIVA

La Riva dei Frati NV Hi! Prosecco (Prosecco di Valdobbiadene) $13. Despite its name, Hi! is actually an understated Prosecco with elegant qualities that translate into delicate tones of lemongrass, white stone and peach. It boasts bright acidity and medium intensity and is very refreshing overall. 86 *—M.L. (12/15/2007)*

LA ROCCA

La Rocca 1998 Pinot Grigio (Collio) $10. 81 *(8/1/1999)*

LA RONCAIA

La Roncaia 1999 Il Fusco Red Blend (Friuli Venezia Giulia) $50. 89 *(5/1/2003)*

La Roncaia 2002 Eclisse Sauvignon-Picolit Sauvignon (Colli Orientali del Friuli) $34. 90 *(7/1/2005)*

LA SCOLCA

La Scolca 1999 Cortese (Gavi di Gavi) $19. 84 *(9/1/2001)*

La Scolca 2001 Bianco Secco Cortese (Gavi di Gavi) $19. 83 *—M.S. (12/15/2003)*

La Scolca 2002 Black Label Cortese (Gavi di Gavi) $42. 84 *—J.C. (11/15/2004)*

La Scolca 2002 Il Valentino Cortese (Gavi di Gavi) $14. 84 *—J.C. (11/15/2004)*

La Scolca 2001 il Valentino White Blend (Gavi) $13. 80 *—M.S. (12/15/2003)*

La Scolca NV Soldati LaScolca Brut White Blend (Gavi) $26. 87 *—M.S. (12/31/2002)*

LA SELVACCIA

La Selvaccia 2001 Brunello (Brunello di Montalcino) $55. 91 *(4/1/2006)*

La Selvaccia 2000 Brunello (Brunello di Montalcino) $50. 90 *—M.L. (11/15/2006)*

LA SERA

La Sera 1997 Barbera (Barbera del Monferrato) $12. 87 Best Buy *(4/1/2000)*

La Sera 2004 Il Cielo Barbera (Barbera d'Alba) $20. The Il Cielo offers a complex nose of marzipan, licorice and dark fruit. On the palate, the fruit shows more of a plumminess and the licorice and marzipan notes are less pronounced. A solid medium finish. Overall, this is a well made, balanced pleasant wine with plenty of character. 88 *—M.G. (12/31/2007)*

La Sera 1997 Il Cielo Barbera (Barbera d'Alba) $17. 89 *(4/1/2000)*

LA SERENA

La Serena 2001 Brunello (Brunello di Montalcino) $NA. 90 *(4/1/2006)*

La Serena 2000 Brunello (Brunello di Montalcino) $NA. 94 Editors' Choice *—M.S. (7/1/2005)*

La Serena 1999 Brunello (Brunello di Montalcino) $NA. 92 *—M.S. (6/1/2004)*

LA SPINETTA

La Spinetta 2004 Bricco Quaglia Moscato (Moscato d'Asti) $18. 88 *—M.L. (12/15/2005)*

La Spinetta 2000 Oro Moscato Passito Moscato (Piedmont) $NA. 93 Editors' Choice *—M.L. (11/15/2006)*

LA SPINONA

La Spinona 1999 Vigna Qualin Dolcetto (Dolcetto d'Alba) $15. 86 *—M.N. (9/1/2001)*

La Spinona 1998 Vigneto Qualin Dolcetto (Dolcetto d'Alba) $15. 83 *(4/1/2000)*

LA TORDERA

La Tordera NV Brut Prosecco (Prosecco di Valdobbiadene) $19. This Brut is noticeably sweet with deep floral tones, backed by fragrant bee's wax, honey and peach. It has a fatter, thicker feel in the mouth with very good intensity of flavors and a lively, refreshing finish. 89 *—M.L. (12/15/2007)*

La Tordera 2006 Cartizze Prosecco (Prosecco di Valdobbiadene Superiore) $33. A creamy, voluptuous sparkler, this delivers sweet, peach fragrances with background notes of chopped basil, mango and kiwi. Pair it with smoked salmon canapés. 88 *—M.L. (12/15/2007)*

La Tordera NV Dry Cru Prosecco (Prosecco di Valdobbiadene Superiore) $22. Definitely on the sweet side, this lively Prosecco offers white peach, citrus, melon and distant notes of dried hay. Creamy peach flavors follow. 85 *—M.L. (12/15/2007)*

La Tordera NV Extra Dry Prosecco (Prosecco di Valdobbiadene) $19. There's a lot going on in the glass starting with lively perlage in the form of small, persistent bubbling. Also very enjoyable are the aromas, which recall white fruit, chopped sweet basil, almond blossom and soapy floral tones. The wine ends on a sweet note with mature pear flavors. 88 *—M.L. (12/15/2007)*

LA TORRE

La Torre 1999 Brunello (Brunello di Montalcino) $NA. 88 *—M.S. (6/1/2004)*

LA TOSA

La Tosa 2003 Luna Selvatica Cabernet Blend (Colli Piacentini) $27. An interesting wine: Bright and concentrated, this Cabernet Sauvignon with 10 percent Merlot delivers green notes like minced herbs followed by cough drop and menthol freshness. Seven months of barrique add depth and complexity. Menthol notes follow to the mouth making this a first-class palate-cleanser. 87 *—M.L. (2/1/2007)*

La Tosa 2005 Sorriso di Cielo Malvasia Bianca (Colli Piacentini) $17. "Sorriso di Cielo" means "sky's smile" and this light, other-worldly image is nicely illustrated by this Malvasia-based wine. The aromas are clean, fresh and floral with white flowers and exotic fruit. It's slightly sweet in the mouth without too much fuss or complexity. 86 *—M.L. (2/1/2007)*

La Tosa 2005 Gutturnio Red Blend (Colli Piacentini) $11. Here's an intensely cherry-flavored wine with vinous and menthol like notes. It's also and easy wine with medium intensity and a spicy touch on the finish. Nicely integrated acidity too. 85 *—M.L. (2/1/2007)*

La Tosa 2004 Luna Selvatica Red Blend (Colli Piacentini) $27. Dark, concentrated and intense, this is a modern and inviting Cabernet Sauvignon (with 10% Merlot) with notes of milk chocolate, blackberry and plum. Impressive in the mouth too: It's succulent, creamy and has presence and personality. 88 *—M.L. (2/1/2007)*

La Tosa 2004 Vignamorello Red Blend (Colli Piacentini) $21. La Tosa is an interesting winery to watch out for from one of Italy's lesser-known wine-making regions. A blend of native Barbera and Bonarda grapes that see two months of oak, this is a young, concentrated wine with chocolate fudge and cherry preserves. It's dark, thick, structured and creamy in the mouth. 87 *—M.L. (2/1/2007)*

La Tosa 2004 Sauvignon Blanc (Colli Piacentini) $15. Here's a Sauvignon from northern Italy with herbal notes, sweet basil leaf and white stone aromas that accent a clean, lean and fresh mouthfeel. This is a quaffable, easy-to-enjoy wine. 85 *—M.L. (2/1/2007)*

LA VELONA

La Velona 2001 Brunello (Brunello di Montalcino) $NA. 91 *(4/1/2006)*

LA VIARTE

La Viarte 2003 Sauvignon Blanc (Colli Orientali del Friuli) $20. 83 *(7/1/2005)*

LA VILLA

La Villa 2005 Pinot Grigio (Veneto) $8. 84 Best Buy *—M.L. (6/1/2006)*

LA VILLA VENETA

La Villa Veneta 2000 Merlot (Veneto) $8. 83 *(5/1/2003)*

La Villa Veneta 2001 Pinot Grigio (Veneto) $8. 83 *—J.C. (7/1/2003)*

LA VIS

La Vis 2001 Chardonnay (Trentino) $11. 86 *—J.C. (1/1/2004)*

La Vis 2006 Dipinti Chardonnay (Trentino) $11. You'll find all the pleasing aromas that you normally associate with a no-fuss Chardonnay such as apricot, honey and white stone in this wine. This is an easy, quaffable wine that lacks great depth but would pair well with light, casual meals. 86 Best Buy *—M.L. (12/1/2007)*

La Vis 2000 Ritratti Chardonnay (Trentino) $13. 84 *—J.C. (7/1/2003)*

La Vis 2006 Dipinti Müller-Thurgau (Trentino) $11. Awkwardly focused on pineapple-like aromas, this makes little room for other fragrances. Despite being lean and thin in the mouth, it delivers a lot of fruity freshness on the finish. 84 *—M.L. (12/1/2007)*

La Vis 2000 Maso Roncador Müller-Thurgau (Trentino) $14. 86 *—J.C. (7/1/2003)*

La Vis 2005 Pinot Grigio (Vigneti delle Dolomiti) $11. 87 Best Buy *—M.L. (6/1/2006)*

La Vis 2006 Dipinti Pinot Grigio (Vigneti delle Dolomiti) $11. This is a textbook Italian white with an upbeat personality shaped by cheerful notes of peach, citrus, lemon grass, white stone and that distinctive rubber-like aroma often associated with Pinot Grigio. America has fallen in love with these characteristics precisely because wines like this are clean, easy, food-friendly and utterly unpretentious. It closes on a crisp, clean note with bright acidity and would pair well with pasta, pizza or Chinese food. 86 Best Buy *—M.L. (11/15/2007)*

La Vis 2004 Ritratti Pinot Grigio (Trentino) $15. 87 *—M.L. (2/1/2006)*

La Vis 2006 Dipinti Pinot Nero (Trentino) $11. This is a leaner, lighter expression of Pinot Nero that is slightly weighed down by bulky tones of charred wood that come on the heels of the variety's natural small berry fruit, herbs, white mushroom and peppermint nuances. 86 Best Buy *—M.L. (12/1/2007)*

La Vis 2001 Rosso dei Sorni Red Blend (Trentino) $15. 85 *—M.S. (12/15/2003)*

La Vis 2005 Dipinti Riesling (Trentino) $11. This wine hits all the right buttons: Its pricing is unbeatable, the packaging is fun with a Paola de Manincor painting on the label and its overall quality is very good. Delicious honey, acacia, polished stone, pink grapefruit and peach are obvious components of an opulent aromatic ensemble. It is lean and racy in the mouth with prominent crispness and good length. Pair it with Indian dishes. **87 Best Buy** *—M.L. (9/1/2007)*

La Vis 2005 Dipinti Sauvignon (Trentino) $11. La Vis's Dipinti series has preformed well thanks to attractive pricing. This expression of Sauvignon offers evident herbal characteristics, as well as mineral ones. Think chopped sage and basil and drying white stone. **86 Best Buy** *—M.L. (12/1/2007)*

La Vis 2000 Masso Tratta Sauvignon Blanc (Trentino) $13. 88 Best Buy *—J.C. (7/1/2003)*

La Vis 2001 Bianco dei Sorni White Blend (Trentino) $15. 88 *—J.C. (7/1/2003)*

LAGARIA

Lagaria 2003 Chardonnay (Delle Venezie) $10. 87 Best Buy *—J.C. (12/31/2004)*

Lagaria 2001 Chardonnay (Delle Venezie) $8. 87 Best Buy *—J.C. (7/1/2003)*

Lagaria 2000 Merlot (Delle Venezie) $8. 83 *(5/1/2003)*

Lagaria 2005 Pinot Grigio (Delle Venezie) $10. 86 Best Buy *—M.L. (6/1/2006)*

Lagaria 2004 Pinot Grigio (Delle Venezie) $10. 84 *—M.L. (2/1/2006)*

Lagaria 2001 Pinot Grigio (Delle Venezie) $8. 83 *—J.C. (7/1/2003)*

Lagaria 1999 Pinot Grigio (Trentino) $7. 83 *—M.N. (9/1/2001)*

Lagaria 1997 Pinot Grigio (Trentino) $8. 82 *(8/1/1999)*

LAIMBURG

Laimburg 2005 Riesling (Alto Adige) $22. Aromas of lemon rind, white stone fruit and natural rubber are backed by a nutty note that adds dimension and depth. In the mouth, this is tangy but not tart and delivers citrus flavors over a lean consistency. **87** *—M.L. (9/1/2007)*

LAMBARDI

Lambardi 2001 Brunello (Brunello di Montalcino) $NA. 90 *(4/1/2006)*

LAMBERTI

Lamberti 2001 Santepietre Merlot (Delle Venezie) $9. 81 *(5/1/2003)*

Lamberti 1998 Corte Rubini Red Blend (Amarone della Valpolicella) $30. 84 *(5/1/2003)*

Lamberti 2001 Tenuta Pule Red Blend (Amarone della Valpolicella) $31. 86 *(11/1/2005)*

LAMBORGHINI

Lamborghini 2004 Campoleone Red Blend (Umbria) $50. Like the previous vintage, this Sangiovese-Merlot blend boasts great intensity and purity of aromas, including chocolate fudge, espresso, red berry, cracked peppercorn and a touch of fresh dill. It has plush tannins and fantastic persistency and will win you over with its vigor and vitality. **93** *—M.L. (12/1/2007)*

Lamborghini 2003 Campoleone Red Blend (Umbria) $50. The best word to describe this impressive Sangiovese-Merlot blend from Umbria is "healthy." It has a vibrant, ruby red color and delivers absolutely immaculate aromas of succulent cherry, violet, balsamic notes, earth and root beer. It imparts soft, silky tannins, bright acidity and ends only after having carefully caressed each taste bud. **93 Editors' Choice** *—M.L. (12/1/2007)*

Lamborghini 2000 Campoleone Red Blend (Umbria) $75. 91 *—C.S. (2/1/2003)*

Lamborghini 2004 Trescone Red Blend (Umbria) $20. This is great value for your dollar. You'll find bright red fruit, candied cherry, sweet blueberry muffin as well as thick succulence, firm tannins and good length. A very convivial wine, it's perfect for informal dinners and large groups of friends. **88** *—M.L. (12/1/2007)*

Lamborghini 2000 Trescone Red Blend (Umbria) $12. 87 Best Buy *—C.S. (2/1/2003)*

LAMOLE DI LAMOLE

Lamole Di Lamole 2001 Sangiovese (Chianti Classico) $18. 86 *(4/1/2005)*

Lamole Di Lamole 2000 Blue Label Sangiovese (Chianti Classico) $20. 85 *(4/1/2005)*

Lamole Di Lamole 2000 Riserva Sangiovese (Chianti Classico) $24. 89 *(4/1/2005)*

Lamole Di Lamole 1999 Vigneto di Campolungo Riserva Sangiovese (Chianti Classico) $36. 89 *(4/1/2005)*

LANARI

Lanari 2002 Red Blend (Rosso Conero) $20. 83 *—M.S. (6/1/2005)*

Lanari 2001 Fibbio Red Blend (Rosso Conero) $47. 91 *—M.S. (6/1/2005)*

LANCIOLA

Lanciola 2001 Sangiovese (Chianti Colli Fiorentini) $16. 86 *(4/1/2005)*

Lanciola 1999 Sangiovese (Chianti Colli Fiorentini) $9. 87 *—M.S. (12/31/2002)*

Lanciola 1998 Sangiovese (Chianti Colli Fiorentini) $12. 87 Best Buy *(4/1/2001)*

Lanciola 1999 Antiche Terre De' Ricci Terricci Sangiovese (Toscana) $37. 89 *—M.S. (9/1/2006)*

Lanciola 1998 Antiche Terre de' Ricci Terricci Sangiovese (Toscana) $40. 87 *—M.S. (9/1/2006)*

Lanciola 2002 Le Masse Di Greve Sangiovese (Chianti Classico) $29. 83 *(4/1/2005)*

LAZZERETTI

Lazzeretti 2001 Brunello (Brunello di Montalcino) $NA. 88 *(4/1/2006)*

LE BELLERIVE

Le Bellerive NV Di Cartizze Prosecco (Prosecco di Valdobbiadene Superiore) $47. 85 *—M.S. (12/15/2005)*

Le Bellerive NV Frizzante Prosecco (Prosecco di Valdobbiadene) $19. 85 *—M.S. (12/15/2005)*

LE BERTAROLE

Le Bertarole 2000 Podere Le Marognole Corvina, Rondinella, Molinara (Amarone della Valpolicella Classico) $45. Giordano Venturini delivers a fantastic wine, and although it is beginning to show its age, it successfully embodies all the unique qualities of the traditional Amarone school of winemaking. The nose is penetrating and intensely aromatic of apple-cherry, dusty licorice, almond amaretto and a splattering of black asphalt. This is an ethereal expression with fine, textured tannins and pristine elegance on the close. **94 Editors' Choice** *—M.L. (12/1/2007)*

LE BERTOLE

Le Bertole NV Brut Prosecco (Prosecco di Conegliano e Valdobbiadene) $NA. White stone, almond tones, dried oats and white peach describe a wine with good volume and one that makes a great impression in the mouth. The finish is short and simple, but definitely in line with traditional Prosecco. **87** *—M.L. (12/15/2007)*

LE BOCCE

Le Bocce 1998 Sangiovese (Chianti Classico) $14. 87 *(4/1/2001)*

Le Bocce 1997 Riserva Sangiovese (Chianti Classico) $24. 89 *(4/1/2001)*

LE CALVANE

Le Calvane 1999 Trecione Riserva Sangiovese (Chianti Colli Fiorentini) $25. 87 *(4/1/2005)*

LE CHIUSE

Le Chiuse 2001 Brunello (Brunello di Montalcino) $50. 90 *(4/1/2006)*

Le Chiuse 2000 Brunello (Brunello di Montalcino) $55. 86 *—M.S. (7/1/2005)*

Le Chiuse 1999 Brunello (Brunello di Montalcino) $NA. 89 *—M.S. (6/1/2004)*

Le Chiuse 2000 Riserva Brunello (Brunello di Montalcino) $70. 84 *(4/1/2006)*

LE CINCIOLE

Le Cinciole 1998 Sangiovese (Chianti Classico) $18. 89 *(4/1/2001)*

Le Cinciole 2000 Petresco Riserva Sangiovese (Chianti Classico) $33. 80 *(4/1/2005)*

Le Cinciole 1997 Petresco Riserva Sangiovese (Chianti Classico) $30. 88 *(4/1/2001)*

LE COLTURE

Le Colture NV Cartizze Prosecco (Prosecco Superiore di Cartizze) $38. This is a very feminine sparkler with a beautiful bouquet of fresh white rose and jasmine. It has a delicate, pulpy consistency and would pair well with zucchini flowers stuffed with mozzarella cheese. **89** *—M.L. (12/15/2007)*

Le Colture NV Cartizze Prosecco (Prosecco Superiore di Cartizze) $35. 87 *—M.L. (6/1/2006)*

Le Colture NV Cruner Dry Prosecco (Prosecco di Conegliano e Valdobbiadene) $17. Lively perlage and measured aromatic intensity set the stage for this friendly, no-fuss sparkler. It offers caressing effervescence and fresh tones of white peach, melon and lime. **86** *—M.L. (12/15/2007)*

Le Colture NV Cruner Dry Prosecco (Prosecco di Conegliano e Valdobbiadene) $19. 87 *—M.L. (6/1/2006)*

ITALY

Le Colture 2006 Fagher Prosecco (Prosecco di Conegliano e Valdobbiadene) $17. This is a very beautiful and intense sparkler with delicate floral tones that come on the heels of white peach and Golden Delicious apple (10% Chardonnay is blended in). Traces of distinct minerality add elegance and dimension. **88** *—M.L. (12/15/2007)*

Le Colture NV Fagher Brut Prosecco (Prosecco di Conegliano e Valdobbiadene) $19. 87 *—M.L. (6/1/2006)*

Le Colture NV Mas Spago Frizzante Prosecco (Prosecco di Conegliano e Valdobbiadene) $14. As tradition dictates, white string forms the bottle's closure to lock in aromas of exotic fruit, blooming flowers and peachy cream. A slight touch of acidity helps give this wine more structure and staying power. **85** *—M.L. (12/15/2007)*

Le Colture 2006 Pianer Extra Dry Prosecco (Prosecco di Conegliano e Valdobbiadene) $17. Here is a very likeable Prosecco with lime flavors and aromas of mint leaf and lemon ice sorbet. It has a remarkably creamy and smooth texture in the mouth—like citrus cream—and a nervous touch of crisp acidity on the close. **88** *—M.L. (12/15/2007)*

Le Colture NV Pianer Extra Dry Prosecco (Prosecco di Conegliano e Valdobbiadene) $19. 87 *—M.L. (6/1/2006)*

LE CORTE

Le Corte 2001 Anfora Zinfandel (Puglia) $11. 87 Best Buy *—R.V. (11/15/2002)*

LE CORTI

Le Corti 2000 Sangiovese (Chianti Classico) $15. 84 *—M.S. (12/31/2002)*

Le Corti 1999 Cortevecchia Riserva Sangiovese (Chianti Classico) $23. 86 *—M.S. (12/31/2002)*

Le Corti 2000 Don Tommaso Sangiovese (Chianti Classico) $29. 86 *—M.S. (12/31/2002)*

Le Corti 2000 Marsiliana Sangiovese (Toscana) $15. 86 *—M.S. (12/31/2002)*

LE DUE TERRE

Le Due Terre 2000 Sacrisassi Bianco White Blend (Colli Orientali del Friuli) $42. 88 *—J.C. (7/1/2003)*

LE FILIGARE

Le Filigare 1997 Sangiovese (Chianti Classico) $19. 85 *(4/1/2001)*

LE FIORAIE

Le Fioraie 2000 Sangiovese (Chianti Classico) $20. 81 *—M.S. (10/1/2004)*

Le Fioraie 1998 Riserva Sangiovese (Toscana) $28. 85 *—M.S. (10/1/2004)*

LE FONTI

Le Fonti 1999 Fontissimo Sangiovese (Toscana) $46. 85 *—M.S. (10/1/2004)*

LE GINESTRE

Le Ginestre 1997 Pian Romaldo Barbera (Barbera d'Alba) $19. 85 *(4/1/2000)*

Le Ginestre 1998 Chardonnay (Langhe) $13. 85 *(9/1/2000)*

Le Ginestre 1999 Madonna di Como Dolcetto (Dolcetto d'Alba) $16. 88 *—M.N. (9/1/2001)*

Le Ginestre 1997 Madonna Di Como Dolcetto (Dolcetto d'Alba) $16. 84 *(4/1/2000)*

Le Ginestre 1998 Nebbiolo (Barolo) $45. 87 *(4/2/2004)*

LE GODE

Le Gode 2001 Brunello (Brunello di Montalcino) $67. 87 *(4/1/2006)*

LE MACCHIOCHE

Le Macchioche 2000 Brunello (Brunello di Montalcino) $60. 89 *—M.S. (7/1/2005)*

LE MACCHIOLE

Le Macchiole 1998 Paleo Cabernet Blend (Bolgheri) $84. 87 *—M.S. (8/1/2002)*

LE MACIOCHE

Le Macioche 2001 Brunello (Brunello di Montalcino) $65. 89 *(4/1/2006)*

Le Macioche 1999 Brunello (Brunello di Montalcino) $NA. 92 *—M.S. (6/1/2004)*

LE MANZANE

Le Manzane NV Brut Prosecco (Prosecco di Conegliano e Valdobbiadene) $13. Despite its pretty golden brilliance, this wine doesn't deliver the bubbly piquancy of traditional Prosecco. Instead, it offers flatter, broader tones of yellow apple and mature fruit. There's a sour almondlike note on the finish. **85** *—M.L. (12/15/2007)*

LE MICCINE

Le Miccine 2003 Sangiovese (Chianti Classico) $20. This is a streamlined Chianti Classico with less heft and concentration on the palate and more light elegance. The nose imparts a sensation of cool harmony thanks to its measured tones of fruit, vanilla and toast. This is a clean, crisp wine with polished tannins and a smooth texture. **88** *—M.L. (11/1/2007)*

Le Miccine 2002 Sangiovese (Chianti Classico) $20. 85 *(4/1/2005)*

Le Miccine 2001 Sangiovese (Chianti Classico) $20. 86 *—M.S. (10/1/2004)*

Le Miccine 2000 Sangiovese (Chianti Classico) $22. 87 *—M.S. (11/15/2003)*

Le Miccine 1999 Sangiovese (Chianti Classico) $24. 86 *—M.S. (8/1/2002)*

Le Miccine 2003 Riserva Don Alberto Sangiovese (Chianti Classico) $40. This lavishes on decadent aromas of lively blueberry, sweet chocolate and vanilla cream, creating an ensemble that is rich and intense but not overwhelming in concentration or density. Le Miccine is an American- owned winery in Gaiole-in-Chianti, run by Clifford and Donna Meneghetti Weaver, with help from legendary enologist Vittorio Fiore. **91** *—M.L. (11/1/2007)*

Le Miccine 2001 Riserva Don Alberto Sangiovese (Chianti Classico) $40. 88 *(4/1/2005)*

Le Miccine 2000 Don Alberto Riserva Sangiovese (Chianti Classico) $40. 83 *—M.S. (10/1/2004)*

Le Miccine 1999 Riserva Don Alberto Sangiovese (Chianti Classico) $40. 90 *—M.S. (11/15/2003)*

Le Miccine 1998 Riserva Don Alberto Sangiovese (Chianti Classico) $40. 88 *—M.S. (8/1/2002)*

Le Miccine 1997 Riserva Don Alberto Sangiovese (Chianti Classico) $40. 89 *(9/1/2000)*

LE MUSE

Le Muse 1997 Pinot Grigio (Piave) $7. 81 *(8/1/1999)*

LE POTAZZINE

Le Potazzine 2001 Gorelli Brunello (Brunello di Montalcino) $55. 86 *(4/1/2006)*

LE RAGOSE

Le Ragose 2001 Corvina, Rondinella, Molinara (Amarone della Valpolicella) $62. Le Ragose makes Classico and non-Classico Amarone. This is the non-Classico version with notes of toast, vanilla and raspberry fruit roll-up. It also shows nice aged qualities such as dark mineral, tar, resin and dried prune, making it ready to drink immediately. It has great length on the finish, firm tannins and bright acidity. **91** *—M.L. (12/1/2007)*

Le Ragose 2001 Corvina, Rondinella, Molinara (Amarone della Valpolicella Classico) $NA. The vineyards of Le Ragose are located on beautiful hillside terrain at good altitudes and are rigorously planted in the traditional pergola system. Compared to the non-Classico version, this wine seems more youthful with sweet cherry flavors, wild apple and vanilla backed by good acidity and a spice-driven finish which means it has a bright future ahead even if you age it 5–10 more years. **90** *—M.L. (12/1/2007)*

Le Ragose 1999 Estate Bottled Red Blend (Valpolicella Classico Superiore) $14. 89 Best Buy *(5/1/2003)*

Le Ragose 1999 Estate Bottled Red Blend (Amarone della Valpolicella) $60. 91 *(11/1/2005)*

Le Ragose 1997 Estate Bottled Red Blend (Amarone della Valpolicella) $53. 89 *(5/1/2003)*

LE SALETTE

Le Salette 2003 La Marega Corvina, Rondinella, Molinara (Amarone della Valpolicella Classico) $67. Le Salette, run by a cheerful husband-and-wife team, hits all the right marks. What makes this wine special is its vibrant, tonic personality backed by brilliant ruby coloring, bright cherry-apple aromas and a polished, streamlined finish, achieved by 10% Sangiovese. It's a benchmark Amarone and one that grooves seamlessly with meat, risotto and cheese based pasta. **93** *—M.L. (10/1/2007)*

Le Salette 2000 La Marega Amarone (Amarone della Valpolicella Classico) $63. 91 *(11/1/2005)*

Le Salette 2003 Pergole Vece Corvina, Rondinella, Molinara (Amarone della Valpolicella Classico) $118. This first-rate Amarone by Franco Scamperle earns an "A" for typicity and intensity. The aromas are enticing and pristine, with nuances of forest berry, red apple, chocolate, espresso, resin, chopped herbs and cherry pie. It boasts a lively ruby color, spice-driven flavors (the wine ages three years in barrique) and excellent persistence in the mouth. **95 Cellar Selection** —*M.L. (10/1/2007)*

Le Salette 1999 Pergole Vece Amarone (Amarone della Valpolicella Classico) $120. 89 *(11/1/2005)*

Le Salette 2000 Ca' Camocchio Red Blend (Valpolicella Classico Superiore) $35. 88 *(5/1/2003)*

Le Salette 2000 I Progni Red Blend (Valpolicella Classico Superiore) $25. 90 *(5/1/2003)*

Le Salette 1999 La Marega Red Blend (Amarone della Valpolicella Classico) $60. 90 *(5/1/2003)*

Le Salette 1998 Pergole Vece Red Blend (Amarone della Valpolicella Classico) $115. 93 Cellar Selection *(5/1/2003)*

LE TORRI

Le Torri 1998 Sangiovese (Chianti Colli Fiorentini) $10. 84 *(4/1/2001)*

LE VIGNE

Le Vigne 2003 Sangiovese (Chianti) $12. 85 *(4/1/2005)*

Le Vigne 2002 Sangiovese (Chianti) $12. 82 *(4/1/2005)*

LEONE DE CASTRIS

Leone de Castris 1996 Donna Lisa Riserva Negroamaro (Salice Salentino) $30. 86 —*C.S. (5/1/2002)*

Leone de Castris 2005 Five Roses Negroamaro (Salento) $12. Here's a style of rosé that takes you straight to the sunny deep south of Italy thanks to its bouquet of ripe red fruit and its velvety mouthfeel. The cherry and fruit aromas are penetrating and long lasting. First made in 1943, many consider this Italy's first-ever quality rosato. **86** —*M.L. (7/1/2007)*

Leone de Castris 1999 Riserva Negroamaro (Salice Salentino) $12. 85 —*P.G. (5/1/2002)*

Leone de Castris 1998 Riserva Negroamaro (Salice Salentino) $12. 85 —*C.S. (5/1/2002)*

Leone de Castris 1999 Santera Primitivo (Primitivo Di Manduria) $15. 81 —*C.S. (5/1/2002)*

LEPORE

Lepore 1996 Montepulciano (Colonella) $13. 85 *(9/1/2000)*

LETRARI

Letrari 1995 Brut Riserva Champagne Blend (Trento) $19. 91 Best Buy *(12/31/2000)*

LIBRANDI

Librandi 2006 Gaglioppo (Cirò) $NA. This Calabria-based producer is a tireless advocate of indigenous grapes such as Gaglioppo and has skillfully produced a southern Italian red with the sweeter, ripe red fruit aromas you'd expect and with delicate cola and mineral tones as well. There's a touch of astringency in the mouth. **87** —*M.L. (7/1/2007)*

Librandi 1999 Gaglioppo (Cirò Classico) $10. 84 —*M.N. (9/1/2001)*

Librandi 1997 Duca Sanfelice Riserva Gaglioppo (Calabria) $13. 86 —*M.N. (9/1/2001)*

Librandi 1996 Gravello Gaglioppo (Calabria) $29. 88 —*M.N. (9/1/2001)*

Librandi 2000 Rosso Classico Gaglioppo (Cirò) $10. 81 —*C.S. (5/1/2002)*

Librandi 1999 Magno Megonio Magliocco (Calabria) $35. 85 —*C.S. (5/1/2002)*

Librandi 1998 Gravello Red Blend (Calabria) $29. 89 —*C.S. (5/1/2002)*

LIS NERIS

Lis Neris 2005 Pinot Grigio (Venezia Giulia) $21. Here is a white wine with brilliant clarity to its appearance and aromas of stone fruit, citrus and almond skin. This is a straightforward and well-made P.G. that would pair well with Chinese or spicy Indian food. **88** —*M.L. (5/1/2007)*

Lis Neris 2004 Pinot Grigio (Venezia Giulia) $15. 88 —*M.L. (2/1/2006)*

Lis Neris 2003 Pinot Grigio (Venezia Giulia) $16. 88 Editors' Choice —*M.L. (2/1/2006)*

Lis Neris 2004 Gris Pinot Grigio (Venezia Giulia) $24. This is a truly beautiful Grigio with notes of baked apple, pear, nuts and added layers redolent of minerals and dried herbs. It delivers rich intensity in the mouth with a creamy texture, sweetness and refreshing spice on the close. The wine ferments and matures in French oak. **90** —*M.L. (5/1/2007)*

Lis Neris 2005 Sauvignon (Venezia Giulia) $21. This important name in Italian white wine delivers a delightfully expressive Sauvignon Blanc that puts emphasis on the sweet, toasted notes, not the variety's characteristic green ones: Almond nut, peach and dried hay are framed by smoke and campfire notes. It's creamy in the mouth with good consistency. **87** —*M.L. (5/1/2007)*

Lis Neris 2003 Confini White Blend (Venezia Giulia) $35. Off-dry, aromatic and floral, this is better classified as a dessert wine; would pair with foie gras or aged blue cheese. Floral notes abound, so do peach, apricot and cream custard: A late-harvest blend of Pinot Grigio, Traminer and Riesling. **88** —*M.L. (5/1/2007)*

Lis Neris 2003 Lis White Blend (Venezia Giulia) $32. I served this wine with endive salad and smoked salmon and it was absolutely divine. The blend of white grapes delivers delicious aromas of yellow flower, peach, creamy vanilla and crushed almond. It leaves a silky but rich impression in the mouth thanks to tonneau aging and traces of residual sugar; has enough body to match the smoky flavors of salmon. **91 Editors' Choice** —*M.L. (5/1/2007)*

LISINI

Lisini 2001 Brunello (Brunello di Montalcino) $60. 90 *(4/1/2006)*

Lisini 2000 Brunello (Brunello di Montalcino) $69. 90 —*M.S. (7/1/2005)*

Lisini 1999 Ugolaia Brunello (Brunello di Montalcino) $122. 92 —*M.S. (7/1/2005)*

LIVIO FELLUGA

Livio Felluga 1997 Esperto Chardonnay (Friuli) $16. 86 *(9/1/2000)*

Livio Felluga 1995 Sosso Riserva Merlot (Colli Orientali del Friuli) $35. 89 —*M.S. (9/1/2000)*

Livio Felluga 2000 Vertigo Merlot-Cabernet Sauvignon (Friuli Venezia Giulia) $21. 89 *(5/1/2003)*

Livio Felluga 2000 Illivio Pinot Bianco (Colli Orientali del Friuli) 89 —*R.V. (1/1/2004)*

Livio Felluga 1999 Pinot Grigio (Friuli Venezia Giulia) $21. 90 —*M.S. (9/1/2000)*

Livio Felluga 1997 Pinot Grigio (Friuli Venezia Giulia) $20 85 — *(8/1/1999)*

Livio Felluga 2004 Pinot Grigio (Collio) $25. 87 —*M.L. (2/1/2006)*

Livio Felluga 2002 Pinot Grigio (Friuli Venezia Giulia) $23. 90 —*J.C. (7/1/2003)*

Livio Felluga 2001 Pinot Grigio (Friuli Venezia Giulia) $24. 90 Editors' Choice —*J.C. (7/1/2003)*

Livio Felluga 2000 Pinot Grigio (Friuli Venezia Giulia) $21. 88 —*M.M. (9/1/2001)*

Livio Felluga 2002 Sauvignon Blanc (Colli Orientali del Friuli) $NA. 88 —*R.V. (1/1/2004)*

Livio Felluga 1998 Tocai (Colli Orientali del Friuli) $20. 86 *(9/1/2000)*

Livio Felluga 2002 Tocai (Friuli Venezia Giulia) $22. 88 —*J.C. (7/1/2003)*

Livio Felluga 2001 Tocai (Friuli Venezia Giulia) $24. 90 Editors' Choice —*J.C. (7/1/2003)*

Livio Felluga 2000 Terre Alte Rosazzo Bianco White Blend (Colli Orientali del Friuli) $41. 86 —*J.C. (7/1/2003)*

LIVIO SASSETTI

Livio Sassetti 2001 Pertimali Brunello (Brunello di Montalcino) $NA. 88 *(4/1/2006)*

LIVON

Livon 1997 Pinot Grigio (Collio) $15. 85 *(8/1/1999)*

Livon Erte 1997 Braide Grande Vineyard Pinot Grigio (Collio) $20. 83 *(8/1/1999)*

LOAKER

Loacker 2004 Norital Pinot Nero (Alto Adige) $NA. This is impressive on many fronts, not least of which is the fact that it is one of the first wines in Italy to boast a glass cork. The glass works wonders helping to preserve a wine with intense and pristine floral, nutty—especially almonds—and mineral aromas. **91** —*M.L. (9/1/2007)*

LOBSTER COVE

Lobster Cove 2004 Pinot Grigio (Veneto) $11. 84 *(2/1/2006)*

LODOLA NUOVA

Lodola Nuova 2002 Sangiovese (Vino Nobile di Montepulciano) $22. 84 —*M.S. (7/1/2005)*

Lodola Nuova 2001 Riserva Sangiovese (Vino Nobile di Montepulciano) $35. 86 —*M.S. (7/1/2005)*

LODOVICO ANTINORI

Lodovico Antinori 1995 Ornellaia Bordeaux Blend (Bolgheri) $63. 96 —*M.S. (5/1/1999)*

LOHSA

Lohsa 2000 Sangiovese (Morellino di Scansano) $18. 88 —*M.S. (8/1/2002)*

LOREDAN GASPARINI

Loredan Gasparini 2005 Pinot Grigio (Delle Venezie) $16. 87 —*M.L. (6/1/2006)*

Loredan Gasparini 2004 Pinot Grigio (Delle Venezie) $16. 88 —*M.L. (2/1/2006)*

LORENZO BEGALI

Lorenzo Begali 2003 Corvina, Rondinella, Molinara (Amarone della Valpolicella Classico) $45. The Begali family started off selling grapes to Bolla before embarking on their own brand and they remain firm believers in the traditional pergola (an overhead trellis system). This successful Amarone imparts flavors of chocolate, sweet vanilla, Indian spice, cola and Mediterranean herb. It is soft and caressing, thanks to three years in tonneaux, with bright acidity and lengthy persistency. 91 —*M.L. (10/1/2007)*

Lorenzo Begali 2001 Monte Cà Bianca Corvina, Rondinella, Molinara (Amarone della Valpolicella Classico) $58. This vintage of Begali's top cru is very ripe and comes close to being too ripe: Think black tones of espresso, mature berry fruit and plum comfiture. But it is also a well-made and expertly extracted wine with big chewy tannins, soft sweetness and a long, fruit-driven finish that is ultimately very satisfying. 90 —*M.L. (12/1/2007)*

LORENZON

Lorenzon 2004 Grigio Mascalzone Pinot Grigio (Friuli Isonzo) $16. 87 —*M.L. (6/1/2006)*

LOSI

Losi 1997 Millennium Riserva Sangiovese (Chianti Classico) $30. 85 *(4/1/2005)*

LOSI QUERCIAVALLE

Losi Querciavalle 2004 Sangiovese (Chianti Classico) $24. This is slightly disjointed on the nose with unripe, thorny berry notes next to bitter black chocolate and raw spice. But it seems to pick up speed and charm in the mouth, thanks to its spicy chocolate cookie dough flavors and smooth, creamy finish. 84 —*M.L. (11/1/2007)*

Losi Querciavalle 2003 Riserva Sangiovese (Chianti Classico) $30. Aged in large oak casks, this is a lively wine with obvious but not overwhelming wood flavors on the heels of mature fruit, black cherry, chopped herbs and a subtle medicinal note that adds dimension. The wine is fresh and tonic in the mouth with juicy fruit flavors, nice freshness and good length. 88 —*M.L. (11/1/2007)*

Losi Querciavalle 2001 Riserva Millennium Sangiovese (Chianti Classico) $33. Beautifully aged up to four years in oak casks and redolent of dried red currant berry, prune and exotic spice, this Riserva has a compelling menthol and licorice element that makes it all the more interesting and complex. It boasts good structure, silky tannins and loads of dried fruit flavors. 90 —*M.L. (11/1/2007)*

LUCCIO

Luccio 2002 Merlot (Veneto) $7. 82 —*J.C. (12/31/2004)*

Luccio NV Moscato (Moscato d'Asti) $9. 87 Best Buy —*J.C. (11/15/2004)*

Luccio NV Spumante Moscato (Asti) $8. 86 Best Buy —*M.S. (12/15/2004)*

Luccío 2002 Sangiovese (Chianti) $7. 84 Best Buy *(4/1/2005)*

Luccío 1998 Reserva Sangiovese (Chianti Rufina) $14. 84 *(4/1/2005)*

LUCE

Luce 1998 Red Blend (Toscana) $75. 84 —*S.H. (9/12/2002)*

Luce 2001 della Vite Sangiovese (Toscana) $75. 92 Editors' Choice —*M.S. (9/1/2006)*

Luce 2000 Della Vite Sangiovese (Toscana) $75. 92 —*M.S. (10/1/2004)*

Luce 1999 della Vite Sangiovese (Toscana) $75. 90 *(9/1/2002)*

Luce 2001 Lucente Sangiovese (Toscana) $25. 89 —*M.S. (10/1/2004)*

LUCE DELLA VITE

Luce della Vite 2003 Luce Red Blend (Toscana) $75. This vintage of Frescobaldi's superstar Luce della Vite makes a bold statement thanks to its ruby concentration and intensely inviting aromas of cherry, cola, leather, vanilla and blackberry. It is a big, modern wine (50-50 Sangiovese and Merlot) that flaunts many deep layers of intensity and flavor with firm tannins and excellent persistency on the finish. 92 Cellar Selection —*M.L. (5/1/2007)*

LUCENTE

Lucente 1999 Sangiovese (Toscana) $28. 85 *(9/1/2002)*

Lucente 1998 Sangiovese (Toscana) $28. 89 —*S.H. (8/1/2002)*

Lucente 2001 La Vite Sangiovese (Toscana) $26. 90 —*M.S. (9/1/2006)*

LUCIANO SANDRONE

Luciano Sandrone 2003 Dolcetto (Dolcetto d'Alba) $20. 90 —*J.C. (8/1/2005)*

Luciano Sandrone 1998 Cannubi Boschis Nebbiolo (Barolo) $125. 93 Cellar Selection *(4/2/2004)*

LUIANICO

Luianico 2003 Rosso Sangiovese (Toscana) $8. 85 Best Buy —*M.S. (9/1/2006)*

LUIANO

Luiano 2002 Sangiovese (Chianti Classico) $16. 83 *(4/1/2005)*

Luiano 2000 Sangiovese (Chianti Classico) $16. 89 —*M.S. (11/15/2003)*

Luiano 1998 Estate Bottled Sangiovese (Chianti Classico) $16. 89 *(4/1/2001)*

Luiano 1998 Gold Label Sangiovese (Chianti Classico) $25. 86 —*M.S. (11/15/2003)*

Luiano 1999 Gold Label Riserva Sangiovese (Chianti Classico) $24. 84 *(4/1/2005)*

Luiano 1996 Riserva Sangiovese (Chianti Classico) $23. 91 *(4/1/2001)*

LUIGI EINAUDI

Luigi Einaudi 1997 Vigna Tecc Dolcetto (Dolcetto di Dogliani) $20. 89 *(4/1/2000)*

Luigi Einaudi 2001 Costa Grimaldi Nebbiolo (Barolo) $86. 91 *(3/1/2006)*

Luigi Einaudi 2001 Nei Cannubi Nebbiolo (Barolo) $100. 90 *(3/1/2006)*

LUIGI RIGHETTI

Luigi Righetti 2000 Capital de Roari Amarone (Amarone della Valpolicella) $24. 90 Editors' Choice *(11/1/2005)*

Luigi Righetti 1995 Capitel de' Roari Corvina (Amarone della Valpolicella) $25. 87 —*M.N. (12/31/2000)*

Luigi Righetti 1995 Ca' del Monte Red Blend (Amarone della Valpolicella) $36. 86 —*J.F. (9/1/2001)*

Luigi Righetti 1999 Campolieti Red Blend (Valpolicella Classico) $12. 87 Best Buy *(5/1/2003)*

Luigi Righetti 2001 Capitel de Roari Red Blend (Amarone della Valpolicella Classico) $26. 84 *(11/1/2005)*

LUNA DI LUNA

Luna Di Luna 2002 White Blend (Veneto) $10. 83 —*J.C. (7/1/2003)*

Luna Di Luna NV Extra Dry White Blend (Veneto) $12. 82 —*M.M. (12/31/2000)*

LUNGAROTTI

Lungarotti 2001 Cabernet Sauvignon (Torgiano) $22. 84 —*M.S. (11/15/2004)*

Lungarotti 2002 Chardonnay (Umbria) $16. 87 —*M.S. (6/1/2005)*

Lungarotti 2002 Aurente Chardonnay (Umbria) $40. 89 —*M.S. (6/1/2005)*

Lungarotti 2005 Pinot Grigio (Umbria) $14. Here's a Pinot Grigio from Umbria that boasts a ripe, sunny disposition and aromas of peach, honey and almond nut. It has a distinct purity of fruit aromas, good intensity and a chewy consistency. Because it has less acidity than Grigios from northern Italy, it would pair with creamy, slightly sweet dishes like cool cream of tomato soup. 86 —*M.L. (11/15/2007)*

Lungarotti 1998 Pinot Grigio (Umbria) $12. 83 *(8/1/1999)*

Lungarotti 2004 Pinot Grigio (Umbria) $17. 86 —*M.L. (2/1/2006)*

Lungarotti 2000 Giubilante Red Blend (Umbria) $18. 85 —*M.S. (12/15/2003)*

Lungarotti 1998 Giubilante Red Blend (Umbria) $18. 85 —*M.S. (2/1/2003)*

Lungarotti 2003 Rubesco Red Blend (Torgiano) $19. A Sangiovese and Canajolo blend from one of Umbria's most esteemed estates, Rubesco—as its name would imply—boasts a glowing ruby color and fresh berry notes of cherry, bramble and blueberry. A layer of complexity is added by tones of blue flower and toasted nut. It's a genuine yet simple ensemble with spicy notes on the close. 87 —*M.L. (12/1/2007)*

Lungarotti 1998 Rubesco Red Blend (Torgiano) $15. 87 —*M.S. (2/1/2003)*

Lungarotti 1992 Rubesco Vigna Monticchio Red Blend (Torgiano Rosso Riserva) $43. 89 —*M.S. (2/1/2003)*

Lungarotti 1997 San Giorgio Red Blend (Umbria) $67. 88 *—M.S. (11/15/2004)*

Lungarotti 1993 San Giorgio Red Blend (Umbria) $58. 90 *—M.S. (2/1/2003)*

Lungarotti 1990 San Giorgio Red Blend (Rosso dell'Umbria) $49. 90 *—M.S. (3/1/2000)*

Lungarotti 1990 Rubesco Monticchio Sangiovese (Torgiano Rosso Riserva) $35. 95 *(3/1/2000)*

Lungarotti 2005 Torre di Giano White Blend (Torgiano) $18. Trebbiano and Grechetto are combined to produce a hearty white blend redolent of soapy flower, scented candle and sweet fruit. Umbria's warm sunshine has shaped a creamy wine with good length and body. **87** *—M.L. (12/1/2007)*

Lungarotti 2002 Torre di Giano White Blend (Torgiano) $18. 81 *—M.S. (10/1/2004)*

ITALY

LUWA

Luwa 1997 Selezione Luwa Collio DOC Pinot Grigio (Collio) $14. 80 *(8/1/1999)*

MACCARI SPUMANTI

Maccari Spumanti NV Cartizze Prosecco (Prosecco Superiore di Cartizze) $NA. Delicate mineral nuances frame a refined, sweet sparkler redolent of white peach, spring flowers and sweet herbs. The pretty aromatic layering that this Prosecco offers is its distinguishing characteristic. **88** *—M.L. (12/15/2007)*

Maccari Spumanti 2006 Dry Millesimato Prosecco (Prosecco di Conegliano e Valdobbiadene) $NA. This is a creamy, sweet Prosecco with fragrant aromas of peach, apricot and citrus that you can expect from this kind of informal sparkler. It has a tonic, soda-like like feel in the mouth and clean freshness on the close. **86** *—M.L. (12/15/2007)*

Maccari Spumanti NV Extra Dry Prosecco (Prosecco di Conegliano e Valdobbiadene) $NA. An easy-going, simple Prosecco with drying notes of talc powder, kiwi fruit and fresh lime. It's light and buoyant in the mouth with good freshness on the close. **86** *—M.L. (12/15/2007)*

MACHIAVELLI

Machiavelli 1998 Riserva Fontalle Sangiovese (Chianti Classico) $NA. 85 *—R.V. (8/1/2002)*

MACULAN

Maculan 2003 Fratta Cabernet Sauvignon (Veneto) $80. 94 Editors' Choice *—M.L. (9/1/2006)*

Maculan 2001 Brentino Cabernet Sauvignon-Merlot (Veneto) $14. 87 *(5/1/2003)*

Maculan 1999 Fratta Cabernet Sauvignon-Merlot (Veneto) $80. 91 Cellar Selection *(5/1/2003)*

Maculan 1999 Breganze di Breganze White Blend (Veneto) $15. 84 *—M.N. (9/1/2001)*

Maculan 2002 Pino & Toi White Blend (Veneto) $10. 87 Best Buy *—J.C. (7/1/2003)*

Maculan 2000 Pino & Toi White Blend (Veneto) $11. 85 *—M.N. (9/1/2001)*

Maculan 2001 Pino & Toi White Blend (Veneto) $11. 88 Best Buy *—C.S. (11/15/2002)*

MADONNA ALTA

Madonna Alta 2002 Sagrantino (Montefalco) $NA. 85 *—M.L. (9/1/2005)*

MADONNA DELLE GRAZIE

Madonna delle Grazie 2001 Selezione Brunello (Brunello di Montalcino) $NA. 91 *(4/1/2006)*

MALGRA

Malgra 2001 Cortese (Gavi di Gavi) $16. 85 *—M.S. (12/15/2003)*

Malgra 2005 Cugnexio Moscato (Moscato d'Asti) $17. The moment you smell the wine you are assailed by a very pure, very intense aroma of apricot liqueur. On the palate, it is rich, fat, soft and thick. Very simple, extremely tasty, a perfect foil to spicy Szechuan food. **86** *—M.G. (12/15/2007)*

MALIBRAN

Malibran NV Gorio Extra Dry Prosecco (Prosecco di Valdobbiadene) $NA. 86 *—M.L. (6/1/2006)*

Malibran 2005 Ruio Brut Prosecco (Prosecco di Valdobbiadene) $NA. 85 *—M.L. (6/1/2006)*

MANARA

Manara 2003 Corvina, Rondinella, Molinara (Amarone della Valpolicella Classico) $34. Manara's base Amarone is a slow, cautious wine that evolves to reveal apple-nut, chewy cherry and lavish dustings of chocolate powder. Less successful, however, is the mouthfeel: tight and firm but also slightly astringent. Any hard edges will surely diminish with time. **88** *—M.L. (10/1/2007)*

Manara 2003 Postera Corvina, Rondinella, Molinara (Amarone della Valpolicella Classico) $40. Following a generational change, Manara is another small producer who sparks buzz and renewal in Valpolicella. Made with carefully selected fruit, Postera is a confident, sassy wine with baked apple, root beer, rose petal, mineral notes and characteristic Amarone intensity. **90** *—M.L. (10/1/2007)*

MANDRAROSSA

MandraRossa 2004 Cabernet Sauvignon-Shiraz (Sicilia) $9. 86 Best Buy *—M.L. (7/1/2006)*

MandraRossa 2005 Chardonnay (Sicilia) $9. 86 Best Buy *—M.L. (7/1/2006)*

MandraRossa 2003 Chardonnay (Sicilia) $9. 86 Best Buy *—M.S. (2/1/2005)*

MandraRossa 2005 Fiano (Sicilia) $9. 86 Best Buy *—M.L. (7/1/2006)*

MandraRossa 2004 Fiano (Sicilia) $9. 86 Best Buy *—M.L. (9/1/2005)*

MandraRossa 2003 Fiano (Sicilia) $9. 85 Best Buy *—M.S. (2/1/2005)*

MandraRossa 2004 Nero d'Avola (Sicilia) $9. 86 Best Buy *—M.L. (9/1/2005)*

MandraRossa 2004 Shiraz (Sicilia) $9. 87 Best Buy *—M.L. (7/1/2006)*

MandraRossa 2005 Pinot Grigio Grecanico White Blend (Sicilia) $9. 85 Best Buy *—M.L. (7/1/2006)*

MARCARINI

Marcarini 2004 Ciabot Camerano Barbera (Barbera d'Alba) $18. This is a traditional old-fashioned Barbera; with aromas of bright red cherry fruit, wood smoke and roses. The cherries dominated the palate and although the mid-palate was slightly acidic, it came back with a pleasant medium finish. **84** *—M.G. (12/31/2007)*

Marcarini 2003 Ciabot Camerano Barbera (Barbera d'Alba) $17. 86 *—J.C. (3/1/2006)*

Marcarini 2002 Ciabot Camerano Barbera (Barbera d'Alba) $18. 83 *—J.C. (11/15/2004)*

Marcarini 1998 Ciabot Camerano Barbera (Barbera d'Asti) $15. 86 *(4/1/2000)*

Marcarini 2005 Fontanazza Dolcetto (Dolcetto d'Alba) $17. The Marcarini is a luscious, grapy Dolcetto. A bright fruit-driven nose, with a touch of spice, richly textured and an easy if not particularly long finish. Solid Dolcetto with a winning personality. **86** *—M.G. (12/31/2007)*

Marcarini 2003 Fontanazza Dolcetto (Dolcetto d'Alba) $15. 83 *—J.C. (3/1/2006)*

Marcarini 1998 Fontanazza Dolcetto (Dolcetto d'Alba) $14. 85 *(4/1/2000)*

Marcarini 2003 Moscato (Moscato d'Asti) $16. 87 *—J.C. (11/15/2004)*

Marcarini 2001 Brunate Nebbiolo (Barolo) $54. 93 *—J.C. (3/1/2006)*

Marcarini 2000 Brunate Nebbiolo (Barolo) $64. 93 Cellar Selection *—J.C. (11/15/2004)*

Marcarini 1998 Brunate Nebbiolo (Barolo) $50. 89 *—C.S. (11/15/2002)*

Marcarini 2001 La Serra Nebbiolo (Barolo) $54. 92 Editors' Choice *—J.C. (3/1/2006)*

Marcarini 2000 La Serra Nebbiolo (Barolo) $65. 90 *—J.C. (11/15/2004)*

Marcarini 1998 La Serra Nebbiolo (Barolo) $50. 92 *—C.S. (11/15/2002)*

Marcarini 2001 Donald Red Blend (Langhe) $28. 84 *—J.C. (11/15/2004)*

MARCHESATO DEGLI ALERAMICI

Marchesato degli Aleramici 2000 Brunello (Brunello di Montalcino) $45. 91 *—M.S. (7/1/2005)*

Marchesato degli Aleramici 1999 Brunello (Brunello di Montalcino) $45. 90 *—M.S. (6/1/2004)*

Marchesato degli Aleramici 1999 Riserva Brunello (Brunello di Montalcino) $60. 93 *—M.S. (7/1/2005)*

MARCHESE ALFIERI

Marchese Alfieri 1996 Alfiera Barbera D'Asti Superiore Barbera (Barbera d'Asti) $28. 85 *(4/1/2000)*

MARCHESE ANTINORI

Marchese Antinori NV Nature Sparkling Blend (Oltrepò Pavese) $25. 87 *—M.L. (12/15/2004)*

MARCHESE CARLO GUERRIERI GONZAGA

Marchese Carlo Guerrieri Gonzaga 1999 San Leonardo Bordeaux Blend (Vallagarina) $75. 83 *—M.S. (12/15/2003)*

Marchese Carlo Guerrieri Gonzaga 1998 Merlot di San Leonardo Estate Bottled Merlot (Trento) $18. 83 *—M.S. (12/15/2003)*

MARCHESE DE PETRI

Marchese de Petri 1997 Il Valore Riserva Sangiovese (Chianti) $15. 87 *(4/1/2001)*

MARCHESI ANTINORI

Antinori 2003 Guado al Tasso Red Blend (Bolgheri Superiore) $80. The first thing you'll notice here is the outstanding quality of this wine (forget talk of 2003 being a difficult vintage). Thick and lush, notes of blackberry, blueberry, cherry and chocolate abound, but so does Mediterranean sage and herb that adds dimension and complexity. Fabulously taut and firm: drink after 2010. 92 Cellar Selection *—M.L. (4/1/2007)*

Antinori 2003 Solaia Cabernet Blend (Toscana) $155. 92 *—M.L. (9/1/2006)*

Antinori 2000 Guado al Tasso Red Blend (Bolgheri Superiore) $80. 95 Cellar Selection *—M.L. (11/15/2006)*

Antinori 2000 Tenute Marchesi Antinori Riserva Sangiovese (Chianti Classico) $30. 91 *—M.L. (10/1/2006)*

Antinori 2001 Tignanello Red Blend (Toscana) $70. 93 *—M.L. (11/15/2006)*

Antinori 2002 Villa Antinori Red Blend (Toscana) $22. 88 *(9/1/2006)*

Antinori 2004 Tenuta Guado al Tasso Vermentino (Bolgheri) $20. 90 *—M.L. (10/1/2006)*

Antinori 2003 Cervaro della Sala White Blend (Umbria) $42. 92 Editors' Choice *—M.L. (10/1/2006)*

MARCHESI BISCARDO

Marchesi Biscardo 2000 Red Blend (Amarone della Valpolicella) $65. 86 *(11/1/2005)*

MARCHESI CATTANEO DI BELFORTE

Marchesi Cattaneo di Belforte 2001 Etichetta Bianca Brunello (Brunello di Montalcino) $40. 90 Editors' Choice *(4/1/2006)*

Marchesi Cattaneo di Belforte 2000 Etichetta Bianca Brunello (Brunello di Montalcino) $40. 89 *(4/1/2006)*

Marchesi Cattaneo di Belforte 2001 Riserva Sangiovese (Chianti Classico) $23. 87 *—M.S. (10/1/2006)*

MARCHESI DE' FRESCOBALDI

Marchesi de' Frescobaldi 2000 Castelgiocondo Brunello (Brunello di Montalcino) $55. 92 *—M.S. (7/1/2005)*

Marchesi de' Frescobaldi 1999 Castelgiocondo Riserva Brunello (Brunello di Montalcino) $100. 97 Cellar Selection *—M.S. (7/1/2005)*

Marchesi de' Frescobaldi 2003 Remole Cabernet Sauvignon-Sangiovese (Toscana) $10. This is a nicely priced Sangiovese and Cabernet Sauvignon blend that appears extra toasty and ripe thanks to a hot vintage. The nose yields exotic spice, raspberry preserves, prune and plum. The wine has medium structure in the mouth and is an easy drink overall. 86 Best Buy *—M.L. (5/1/2007)*

Marchesi de' Frescobaldi 2000 Metodo Classical Brut Champagne Blend (Trento) $25. 87 *—M.S. (12/15/2004)*

Marchesi de' Frescobaldi 2002 Benefizio Bianco Chardonnay (Pomino) $27. 83 *—M.S. (6/1/2005)*

Marchesi de' Frescobaldi 2003 Lamaione Merlot (Toscana) $75. From Frescobaldi's Castelgiocondo vineyard in Montalcino, here is an intriguing and seductive Merlot with forest fruit, menthol notes and beautifully integrated exotic spice. Its standout qualities are elegance, succulence and careful fruit extraction. Yet this is a powerful wine with firm tannins and structure: Drink after 2008. 92 Cellar Selection *—M.L. (4/1/2007)*

Marchesi de' Frescobaldi 1999 Lamaione Merlot (Toscana) $85. 92 Cellar Selection. *(9/1/2002)*

Marchesi de' Frescobaldi 1998 Lamaione Merlot (Toscana) $64. 92 Cellar Selection *—M.S. (12/31/2002)*

Marchesi de' Frescobaldi 2000 Campo ai Sasso Red Blend (Rosso di Montalcino) $NA. 87 *(9/1/2002)*

Marchesi de' Frescobaldi 2005 Castiglioni Red Blend (Chianti) $13. Fresh plum, ripe cherry, almond, lavender and cinnamon all figure into the layered nose of this vibrant Sangiovese with 15% Merlot. The wine only sees stainless steel, leaving it fruity, fresh and clean on the finish. 86 *—M.L. (11/15/2007)*

Marchesi de' Frescobaldi 2000 Castiglioni Red Blend (Chianti) $13. 85 *—M.S. (12/31/2002)*

Marchesi de' Frescobaldi 2004 Castello di Nipozzano Vigneto Montesodi Sangiovese (Chianti Rufina) $45. This is a bold, modern wine that confidently presents savory notes of plump cherry, toasted nut and mineral shadings that are well balanced and flawlessly integrated. Nor is the wine shy in the mouth, where it boasts black fruit flavors and a firm, tight composition. Aged in new oak for 18 months. 92 *—M.L. (11/1/2007)*

Marchesi de' Frescobaldi 2002 Castiglioni Sangiovese (Chianti) $13. 85 *(4/1/2005)*

Marchesi de' Frescobaldi 2003 Nipozzano Riserva Sangiovese (Chianti Rufina) $22. The nose is heavy and bold and delivers hearty notes of smoked ham, prunes, plums, spice and deep earthy shades. The mouthfeel is dominated by thick concentration, polished tannins and very good persistency of flavor on the finish. Small amounts of Cabernet Sauvignon, Malvasia Nera, Merlot and Colorino are added to this Sangiovese-based (90%) wine. 88 *—M.L. (11/1/2007)*

Marchesi de' Frescobaldi 2001 Nipozzano Riserva Sangiovese (Chianti Rufina) $22. 90 *—M.S. (10/1/2006)*

Marchesi de' Frescobaldi 2000 Nipozzano Riserva Sangiovese (Chianti Rufina) $22. 86 *(4/1/2005)*

Marchesi de' Frescobaldi 2000 Remole Sangiovese (Toscana) $9. 83 *(9/1/2002)*

Marchesi de' Frescobaldi 2001 Vigneto Montesodi Castello di Nipozzano Sangiovese (Chianti Rufina) $45. 93 Editors' Choice *(4/1/2005)*

MARCHESI DI BAROLO

Marchesi Di Barolo 1998 Barbera (Monferrato) $10. 84 *(3/1/2001)*

Marchesi Di Barolo 1999 Le Lune Cortese (Gavi) $14. 86 *(3/1/2001)*

Marchesi Di Barolo 2005 Madonna di Como Dolcetto (Dolcetto d'Alba) $17. Marchese di Barolo has come out with a dark, powerful and slightly syrupy wine. The fruit brings back memories of old-fashioned canned black fruits. It is a simple, soft, rich, low-acid wine with plenty of appeal. 85 *—M.G. (12/31/2007)*

Marchesi Di Barolo 2004 Nebbiolo (Barbaresco) $43. An odd black currant candy flavor totally dominated this wine both on the nose and palate. It seemed in balance, but the sweet cassis quality overwhelmed the wine. 84 *—M.G. (12/31/2007)*

Marchesi Di Barolo 1999 Nebbiolo (Barbaresco) $39. 89 *(4/2/2004)*

Marchesi Di Barolo 1996 Nebbiolo (Barolo) $40. 89 *(3/1/2001)*

Marchesi Di Barolo 1995 Nebbiolo (Barolo) $50. 92 Cellar Selection *(3/1/2001)*

Marchesi Di Barolo 1998 Cannubi Nebbiolo (Piedmont) $65. 90 *—R.V. (11/15/2002)*

Marchesi Di Barolo 1998 Sarmassa Nebbiolo (Piedmont) $55. 89 *—R.V. (11/15/2002)*

Marchesi Di Barolo 1998 Vigne di Proprieta Nebbiolo (Barolo) $45. 90 *(4/2/2004)*

MARCHESI DI GRESY

Marchesi di Gresy 1998 Monte Arribaldo Dolcetto (Dolcetto d'Alba) $15. 88 *(4/1/2000)*

Marchesi di Gresy 2004 La Serra Moscato (Moscato d'Asti) $13. 89 Editors' Choice *—M.L. (12/15/2005)*

Marchesi di Gresy 2000 Martinenga Nebbiolo (Barbaresco) $45. 87 *(4/2/2004)*

MERCHETTI

Marchetti 2004 Villa Bonomi Red Blend (Rosso Conero) $NA. There's nothing not to like about this wine with its generous aromas of cherry fruit, plum, forest berry, spice and roasted chestnut. Smooth and caressing, the wine is easy to drink but could also be considered for a pairing with more elaborate meat dishes. 88 *—M.L. (12/1/2007)*

MARCO BONFANTE

Marco Bonfante 2001 Dolcetto (Dolcetto d'Alba) $17. 86 *—J.C. (11/15/2004)*

Marco Bonfante 2000 Nebbiolo (Nebbiolo d'Alba) $18. 83 *—J.C. (11/15/2004)*

MARCO CECCHINI

Marco Cecchini 2004 Pinot Grigio (Venezia Giulia) $16. 90 Editors' Choice *—M.L. (6/1/2006)*

Marco Cecchini 1999 Careme Red Blend (Colli Orientali del Friuli) $23. 86 *—M.S. (12/15/2003)*

MARCO DE BARTOLI

Marco de Bartoli 2003 Grappoli Del Grillo (Sicilia) $34. 87 *—M.S. (7/1/2005)*

MARCO FELLUGA

Marco Felluga 2004 Pinot Grigio (Collio) $15. 85 *—M.L. (6/1/2006)*

Marco Felluga 2004 Russiz Superiore Pinot Grigio (Collio) $20. 87 *—M.L. (6/1/2006)*

MARCO NEGRI

Marco Negri 2002 Marsillo Moscato (Moscato d'Asti) $13. 90 **Best Buy** *—M.S. (12/15/2003)*

MAREA

Marea 2005 Pinot Grigio (Delle Venezie) $10. 87 **Best Buy** *—M.L. (6/1/2006)*

MAREGA

Marega 1998 Chardonnay (Collio) $15. 88 **Best Buy** *(4/1/2001)*

Marega 1998 Malvasia Istriana (Collio) $15. 84 *—J.C. (7/1/2003)*

Marega 1997 Merlot (Collio) $14. 87 *—M.S. (5/1/1999)*

Marega 2004 Pinot Grigio (Collio) $15. 85 *—M.L. (2/1/2006)*

Marega 1998 Holbar Red Blend (Friuli Venezia Giulia) $25. 87 *—M.S. (12/15/2003)*

Marega 1994 Holbar Red Blend (Friuli Venezia Giulia) $20. 91 **Editors' Choice** *(4/1/2001)*

Marega 1993 Holbar Rosso Red Blend (Friuli) $25. 90 *—M.S. (5/1/1999)*

Marega 1995 Holbar White Blend (Friuli Venezia Giulia) $20. 89 *(4/1/2001)*

MARENCO

Marenco 2004 Scrapona Moscato (Moscato d'Asti) $17. 90 *—M.S. (8/1/2005)*

Marenco 2003 Scrapona Moscato (Moscato d'Asti) $17. 84 *—J.C. (11/15/2004)*

Marenco 2002 Scrapona Moscato (Moscato d'Asti) $16. 89 *—M.S. (12/15/2003)*

MARETIMA

Maretima 1999 Fabula Sangiovese (Tuscany) $16. 91 **Editors' Choice** *—M.S. (11/15/2003)*

MARIO SCHIOPETTO

Mario Schiopetto 2005 Pinot Bianco (Collio) $34. Stone fruit, melon, white stone and a touch of lemon zest on the nose shape a wine with good dimension and persistency that ages on the lees for eight months. The mouthfeel is particularly attractive and skillfully achieved with an extremely soft and smooth quality. Pair it with pasta, fish, and chicken. 89 *—M.L. (12/1/2007)*

Mario Schiopetto 2001 Pinot Bianco (Collio) $35. 90 *—R.V. (7/1/2003)*

Mario Schiopetto 2005 Pinot Grigio (Collio) $37. A distinctive PG that puts a high priority on elegance and refinement. The aromas are characterized by white flower, minerals, almond skin and peaches; and the wine rests on its lees for eight months to render a broader, creamier mouthfeel. 88 *—M.L. (4/1/2007)*

Mario Schiopetto 2004 Pinot Grigio (Collio) $37. 88 **Editors' Choice** *—M.L. (2/1/2006)*

Mario Schiopetto 2001 Pinot Grigio (Collio) $32. 91 *—R.V. (7/1/2003)*

Mario Schiopetto 2005 Sauvignon (Collio) $37. This historic family-run winery (now run by Maria Angela, Carlo and Giorgio) presents a clean and completely refreshing Sauvignon with grapefruit, citrus, sage, green notes and a remote background aroma that recalls almond marzipan. It has nice consistency and some interesting succulence in the mouth. 88 *—M.L. (5/1/2007)*

Mario Schiopetto 2001 Tocai (Collio) $35. 93 *—R.V. (7/1/2003)*

Mario Schiopetto 2004 Tocai Friulano (Collio) $37. Although you might encounter some initial sulfur, this wine later portrays yellow rose, peach, almond, cut grass and honey. It doesn't have huge flavor intensity but just enough to keep your attention. 86 *—M.L. (12/1/2007)*

Mario Schiopetto 2004 Bianco White Blend (Venezia Giulia) $49. Here is a beautifully executed northern white (mostly barrel-fermented Chardonnay and Tocai Friulano) with pristine notes of stone fruit, banana, pineapple, vanilla and yellow flowers. It has good intensity in the mouth with a silky, creamy feel and very good persistency on the finish. 91 *—M.L. (5/1/2007)*

Mario Schiopetto 2005 Blanc des Rosis White Blend (Venezia Giulia) $34. Excellent acidity and drying minerality are framed by feminine notes of citrus, pineapple and dried grass. Zest and crispness suggest this complex white blend would pair with quiche or puff pastry appetizers. 89 *—M.L. (5/1/2007)*

Mario Schiopetto 2001 Blanc des Rosis White Blend (Friuli Venezia Giulia) $31. 89 *—R.V. (7/1/2003)*

MARION

Marion 2001 Corvina, Rondinella, Molinara (Amarone della Valpolicella) $70. Deep complexity is the first quality you'll notice in this wine. Dig deep to encounter penetrating notes of black cherry, nutty apple flavors, rose petals, crème brûlèe, carob powder, leather, exotic spice and dark chocolate. This is a wine painted in big brush strokes, with a vibrant personality, succulent tannins and great length. Pair it with roasted duck or grilled red meat. 92 *—M.L. (12/1/2007)*

Marion 1999 Corvina, Rondinella, Molinara (Amarone della Valpolicella) $80. 93 *(11/1/2005)*

MARISA CUOMO

Marisa Cuomo 1997 Furore Riserva Piedirosso (Campania) $32. 91 *—C.S. (5/1/2002)*

Marisa Cuomo 1996 Ravello Riserva Piedirosso (Campania) $30. 89 *—C.S. (5/1/2002)*

MAROTTI CAMPI

Marotti Campi 2002 Luzano Classico Verdicchio (Verdicchio dei Castelli di Jesi Classico) $11. 86 *—M.S. (8/1/2004)*

MARTINI & ROSSI

Martini & Rossi NV Moscato (Asti) $12. 86 **Best Buy** *—M.L. (12/15/2006)*

Martini & Rossi NV Asti Moscato (Piedmont) $13. 88 *(11/15/1999)*

Martini & Rossi NV Asti Spumante Moscato (Moscato d'Asti) $10. 87 *—S.H. (12/31/2000)*

Martini & Rossi NV Vino Frizzante Prosecco (Marca Trevigiana) $14. 83 *—M.S. (12/15/2004)*

MASCHIO DEI CAVALIERI

Maschio dei Cavalieri NV Brut Prosecco (Prosecco di Valdobbiadene) $20. 85 *—M.L. (6/1/2006)*

MASCIARELLI

Masciarelli 2004 Marina Cvetic Chardonnay (Colline Teatine) $50. Gianni Masciarelli has mastered the tricky art of growing Chardonnay in the Abruzzo and this sophisticated, barrique-aged wine shows his enormous talent. Dedicated to his wife, layered aromas here include vanilla extract, pineapple, honey and almond backed by elegant mineral nuances. Wood-driven flavors are underplayed in the mouth, allowing the quality of the fruit to show. 92 *—M.L. (12/1/2007)*

Masciarelli 2003 Marina Cvetic Chardonnay (Colline Teatine) $50. This is a showcase wine for the region of Abruzzo that delivers mature notes of peach, rounded toasted notes of honey and pear. As a whole, it is harmonious and flowing and is surprisingly fresh and tonic despite the hot vintage. 91 *—M.L. (12/1/2007)*

Masciarelli 2003 Marina Cvetic Montepulciano (Montepulciano d'Abruzzo) $30. Here is a wonderful, masterfully made wine that Gianni Masciarelli has dedicated to his wife Marina. This expression of the hearty Montepulciano grape showcases soft cherry nuances backed by spicy, wood, deep succulence and a long finish. 90 *—M.L. (12/1/2007)*

Masciarelli 2003 Masciarelli Montepulciano (Montepulciano d'Abruzzo) $10. Spicy, fruity and nicely rounded, this wine boasts great flavor intensity without the sharp points sometimes associated with Montepulciano. It's an easy, approachable wine perfect for everyday dining with solid tannins and good length. 86 **Best Buy** *—M.L. (11/15/2007)*

Masciarelli 2005 Valori Montepulciano (Montepulciano d'Abruzzo) $11. If you are not familiar with the hearty Montepulciano grape variety from central Italy but adore modern, structured, New World reds, you should considered adding this wine to your weekly shopping list. Thick in power, extracts and color, Montepulciano has rock-solid tannins and blockbuster aromas of blackberry, prune, chocolate, spice and toast that appear naturally, even without wood aging. This is a big value wine that should pair with a big value meal of barbecued baby back ribs in smoked sauce and spicy potato salad. 86 **Best Buy** *—M.L. (11/15/2007)*

Masciarelli 2001 Villa Gemma Montepulciano (Montepulciano d'Abruzzo) $90. This is one of those "wow" wines you encounter on fortunate but rare occasions that radically changes the way you think about a relatively unknown, workhorse grape like Montepulciano d'Abbruzzo. Gianni Masciarelli is a solid and passionate winemaker who has expertly extracted both elegance and complexity: Black cherry, espresso, chocolate and licorice are reinforced by impenetrable concentration, raw intensity, solid tannins and extreme persistency on the finish. **95 Cellar Selection** *—M.L. (12/1/2007)*

Masciarelli 2000 Villa Gemma Montepulciano (Montepulciano d'Abruzzo) $80. 90 Cellar Selection *—M.L. (9/1/2005)*

Masciarelli 2004 Trebbiano (Trebbiano d'Abruzzo) $8. 86 Best Buy *—M.L. (9/1/2005)*

Masciarelli 2004 Castello di Semivicoli Trebbiano (Trebbiano d'Abruzzo) $40. This is special, with uniquely distinctive undertones of smoky warm honey, lavender essence, acacia flower, baked apple and barbecue spice. In the mouth, you get pure lavender honey and pungent rosemary oil. **89** *—M.L. (12/1/2007)*

Masciarelli 2004 Marina Cvetic Trebbiano (Trebbiano d'Abruzzo) $50. This wine brings the Trebbiano grape to a whole new level of sophistication. You'll get stone fruit, melon and apricot, but you'll also be rewarded with radically unique aromas of melted butter, brown sugar and crunchy crème caramel. The texture is smooth and firm and the wine's persistency can be counted in minutes. **93** *—M.L. (12/1/2007)*

Masciarelli 2002 Marina Cvetic' Trebbiano (Trebbiano d'Abruzzo) $55. 89 *—M.L. (9/1/2005)*

Masciarelli 2005 Valori Trebbiano (Trebbiano d'Abruzzo) $10. The nose is more neutral than other Trebbianos from the same vintage but it does offer a pretty embroidery of fresh fruit, nut and dusty mineral. Lean and somewhat watery in the mouth, the wine closes on a tart citrus note. **85 Best Buy** *—M.L. (11/15/2007)*

MASI

Masi 2003 Costasera Corvina, Rondinella, Molinara (Amarone della Valpolicella Classico) $55. This is a solid, steady wine that deftly delivers perfectly measured doses of cherry, plum, black currant, brown sugar, chocolate dust and almond nut. Fruit flavors are integrated seamlessly and come on the heels of the wine's solid structure. Drink it with crispy pork roast or pasta with a meat reduction sauce. **90** *—M.L. (10/1/2007)*

Masi 2000 Campolongo di Torbe Amarone (Amarone della Valpolicella Classico) $126. 92 *—J.C. (12/31/2006)*

Masi 1990 Campolongo di Torbe Amarone (Amarone della Valpolicella Classico) $NA. 93 *—J.C. (12/31/2006)*

Masi 2001 Costasera Amarone (Amarone della Valpolicella Classico) $55. 90 *—J.C. (12/31/2006)*

Masi 1990 Costasera Amarone (Amarone della Valpolicella Classico) $NA. 90 *—J.C. (12/31/2006)*

Masi 2000 Mazzano Amarone (Amarone della Valpolicella Classico) $140. 95 *—J.C. (12/31/2006)*

Masi 1990 Mazzano Amarone (Amarone della Valpolicella Classico) $NA. 97 *—J.C. (12/31/2006)*

Masi 2000 Serego Alighieri Vaio Armaron Amarone (Amarone della Valpolicella Classico) $75. 92 *—J.C. (12/31/2006)*

Masi 1990 Serego Alighieri Vaio Armaron Amarone (Amarone della Valpolicella Classico) $NA. 91 *—J.C. (12/31/2006)*

Masi 1998 Brolo di Campofiorin Corvina (Rosso del Veronese) $24. 89 *(12/1/2004)*

Masi 1997 Brolo di Campofiorin Corvina (Rosso del Veronese) $NA. 89 *(12/1/2004)*

Masi 1995 Brolo di Campofiorin Corvina (Rosso del Veronese) $NA. 90 *(12/1/2004)*

Masi 2001 Campofiorin Corvina (Rosso del Veronese) $16. 90 Editors' Choice *(12/1/2004)*

Masi 1999 Campofiorin Corvina (Rosso del Veronese) $15. 89 *(12/1/2004)*

Masi 1997 Campofiorin Corvina (Rosso del Veronese) $NA. 88 *(12/1/2004)*

Masi 1995 Campofiorin Corvina (Rosso del Veronese) $NA. 89 *(12/1/2004)*

Masi 1993 Campofiorin Corvina (Rosso del Veronese) $NA. 86 *(12/1/2004)*

Masi 1985 Campofiorin Corvina (Rosso del Veronese) $NA. 91 *(12/1/2004)*

Masi 1983 Campofiorin Corvina (Rosso del Veronese) $NA. 87 *(12/1/2004)*

Masi 1977 Campofiorin Corvina (Rosso del Veronese) $NA. 85 *(12/1/2004)*

Masi 1983 Campofiorion Corvina (Rosso del Veronese) $NA. 87 *(12/1/2004)*

Masi 1977 Campofiorion Corvina (Rosso del Veronese) $NA. 85 *(12/1/2004)*

Masi 2003 Bonacosta Corvina, Rondinella, Molinara (Valpolicella Classico) $14. 86 *—M.L. (9/1/2005)*

Masi 2002 Colbaraca Classico Garganega (Soave) $11. 87 *—R.V. (7/1/2003)*

Masi 2000 Colbaraca Soave Classico Superiore Garganega (Soave) $12. 89 Best Buy *(9/1/2001)*

Masi 2001 Brolo di Campofiorin Red Blend (Rosso del Veronese) $25. 89 *—J.C. (12/31/2006)*

Masi 1998 Brolo di Campofiorin Red Blend (Rosso del Veronese) $24. 91 Editors' Choice *(5/1/2003)*

Masi 2003 Campofiorin Red Blend (Rosso del Veronese) $15. 88 *—J.C. (12/31/2006)*

Masi 1997 Campofiorin Red Blend (Rosso del Veronese) $16. 88 *(9/1/2001)*

Masi 1999 Campofiorin Ripasso Red Blend (Rosso del Veronese) $15. 90 Best Buy *(5/1/2003)*

Masi 1999 Campolongo di Torbe Red Blend (Amarone della Valpolicella Classico) $110. 91 *(11/1/2005)*

Masi 1997 Campolongo di Torbe Red Blend (Amarone della Valpolicella) $70. 92 Editors' Choice *(5/1/2003)*

Masi 1993 Campolongo di Torbe Red Blend (Amarone della Valpolicella Classico) $62. 88 *(5/1/2003)*

Masi 2001 Costasera Red Blend (Amarone della Valpolicella) $53. 86 *(11/1/2005)*

Masi 1999 Costasera Red Blend (Amarone della Valpolicella Classico) $40. 91 *(5/1/2003)*

Masi 1997 Costasera Red Blend (Amarone della Valpolicella) $41. 91 Cellar Selection *(9/1/2001)*

Masi 1999 Mazzano Red Blend (Amarone della Valpolicella Classico) $140. 93 *(11/1/2005)*

Masi 2000 Modello Red Blend (Delle Venezie) $10. 87 Best Buy *(5/1/2003)*

Masi 2003 Modello delle Venezie Red Blend (Delle Venezie) $11. A deep, ruby colored wine with aromas of cherry, plum, leather, tar and some dried fruit; this Rabosa-Corvina blend is easy to drink and full of personality. It would pair beautifully with red meat, stews, aged cheeses or roasted vegetables. **86** *—M.L. (5/1/2007)*

Masi 1998 Serego Alighieri Red Blend (Valpolicella Classico Superiore) $15. 85 *(5/1/2003)*

Masi 1995 Serègo Alighieri Red Blend (Amarone della Valpolicella) $54. 87 *—J.F. (9/1/2001)*

Masi 1999 Serego Alighieri Possessioni Red Blend (Valpolicella Classico Superiore) $17. 88 *(5/1/2003)*

Masi 1997 Serego Alighieri Vaio Red Blend (Amarone della Valpolicella) $60. 93 *(5/1/2003)*

Masi 1996 Serego Alighieri Vaio Red Blend (Amarone della Valpolicella) $55. 89 *(5/1/2003)*

Masi 1999 Serego Alighieri Vaio Amaron Red Blend (Amarone della Valpolicella) $75. 91 *(11/1/2005)*

Masi 2002 Classico White Blend (Soave) $15. 86 *—R.V. (7/1/2003)*

Masi 2006 Levarie White Blend (Soave) $10. Creamy peach and stone fruit are backed by a subtle touch of crushed white pepper and some herbal tones. In the mouth, this is a simple, lean wine with fresh vibrant flavors that would pair well with salads and appetizers. **85 Best Buy** *—M.L. (11/15/2007)*

Masi 2005 Levarie White Blend (Soave Classico) $13. A lovely floral, fresh and fruity wine, this Soave is simple and clean with a pretty embroidery of peach blossom and citrus aromas. It goes down easy with a delicate but crisp touch along the way. **86** *—M.L. (5/1/2007)*

Masi 2006 Masianco White Blend (Delle Venezie) $13. Year after year, Masi rolls out one of the most interesting Pinot Grigio blends to come out of northern Italy. The Masianco difference is the slightly overripe Verduzzo component (25%) that adds mature fruit intensity and structure. Masianco is a clean and genuine wine, with floral fragrances and a crisp close. **88 Best Buy** *—M.L. (11/15/2007)*

Masi 2005 Masianco White Blend (Delle Venezie) $12. 89 Best Buy *—M.L. (11/15/2006)*

Masi 2004 Masianco White Blend (Delle Venezie) $14. 89 Best Buy *—M.L. (9/1/2005)*

Masi 2002 Masianco White Blend (Delle Venezie) $12. 90 *—R.V. (7/1/2003)*

Masi 2006 Serego Alighieri Possessioni White Blend (Veneto) $15. Native Italian grape Garganega and Sauvignon Blanc are blended to produce a layered white wine with fresh tones of stone fruit, kiwi, melon and lemon zest. This interesting combination offers good, fresh acidity and vibrant fruit flavors. **87** *—M.L. (11/15/2007)*

Masi 2005 Serego Alighieri Possessioni White Blend (Veneto) $15. Presenting a beautiful Garganega-Sauvignon blend that boldly brings on aromas of citrus, grapefruit, melon, apples, white stone and a touch of chopped green herb. These clean, linear notes promise a food-friendly wine that would pair nicely with seafood, vegetables and appetizers. 88 —*M.L. (5/1/2007)*

Masi 2001 Serego Alighieri Possessioni White Blend (Veneto) $15. 87 *(5/1/2003)*

MASO CANALI

Maso Canali 2005 Pinot Grigio (Trentino) $23. 88 —*M.L. (6/1/2006)*

MASO POLI

Maso Poli 1997 Pinot Grigio (Trentino) $13. 85 *(8/1/1999)*

Maso Poli 2004 Pinot Grigio (Trentino) $21. 87 —*M.L. (6/1/2006)*

Maso Poli 2003 Estate Bottled Pinot Grigio (Trentino) $21. 87 —*J.C. (12/31/2004)*

MASOTTINA

Masottina 1997 Montesco Bordeaux Blend (Colli di Conegliano) $35. 87 *(5/1/2003)*

Masottina 2005 Vigneto ai Palazzi Chardonnay (Piave) $NA. This is a simple, friendly wine with a pretty dusty, mineral quality that frames fresher aromas of pear, peach and golden apple. It's a bit toned down in terms of flavors intensity but does end on a playful spicy note. 86 —*M.L. (12/1/2007)*

Masottina 2002 Riserva Vigneto ai Palazzi Merlot (Piave) $32. Distinct notes of blueberry, black fruit and sweet spice; yet despite the intensity of the aromas, this is anything but heavy or austere. Thanks to only stainless steel aging it has many delicate touches such as pressed red rose petal and fresh currant flavors. 88 —*M.L. (4/1/2007)*

Masottina 2005 Pinot Grigio (Piave) $NA. The nose is deeply penetrating with gorgeous notes of honey, luscious stone fruit, apricot and almonds. Thick streaks of glycerin slide down the glass denoting a deliciously creamy structure. 88 —*M.L. (12/1/2007)*

Masottina 2003 Pinot Grigio (Piave) $14. 87 —*M.L. (6/1/2006)*

Masottina 2005 Ai Palazzi Pinot Grigio (Piave) $NA. Pineapple, banana, peach and apricot are followed by a dusty mineral quality that adds extra dimension. This is a tasty, fruit-forward wine that closes with tingling, spicy crispness. 87 —*M.L. (12/1/2007)*

Masottina 2003 Ai Palazzi Pinot Grigio (Piave) $21. 81 *(2/1/2006)*

Masottina 2001 Vigneto Ai Palazzi Pinot Grigio (Piave) $15. 87 —*J.C. (7/1/2003)*

Masottina NV Prosecco (Prosecco di Conegliano e Valdobbiadene) $14. 89 —*M.S. (6/1/2003)*

Masottina NV Cartizze Dry Prosecco (Prosecco Superiore di Cartizze) $30. Sweet, musky aromas are immediate and generous and come on the heels of mature peach, apricot and exotic fruit. This is an easy, simple wine that goes down beautifully at cocktail hour. 88 —*M.L. (12/15/2007)*

Masottina 2004 Cartizze Dry Prosecco (Prosecco Superiore di Cartizze) $35. 90 —*M.L. (6/1/2006)*

Masottina NV Dry Prosecco (Prosecco di Conegliano) $20. Here's an easy-going Italian sparkler with a strong emphasis on floral aromas such as jasmine and honeysuckle as well as fruity tones of peach, apricot and melon. It smells very sweet and tastes so as well. 85 —*M.L. (12/15/2007)*

Masottina 2004 Extra Dry Prosecco (Prosecco di Conegliano e Valdobbiadene) $15. 88 —*M.L. (6/1/2006)*

Masottina NV Extra Dry Prosecco (Prosecco di Conegliano e Valdobbiadene) $21. This sparkler has a touch of playful sweetness without being sticky or cloying. As far as its aromas are concerned, you'll detect citrus, floral notes, minerals and a slightly smoky or musky quality on the periphery. 87 —*M.L. (12/15/2007)*

Masottina NV Frizzante Prosecco (Prosecco di Conegliano e Valdobbiadene) $16. The nice thing about this Frizzante sparkler is its etched mineral tone that gives it backbone and purpose. Also present are well-rendered notes of citrus and lime. 85 —*M.L. (12/15/2007)*

Masottina NV Spumante Extra Dry Prosecco (Prosecco di Conegliano e Valdobbiadene) $NA. 86 —*M.S. (6/1/2005)*

Masottina 2002 Vigneto Rizzardo White Blend (Colli di Conegliano) $NA. Notes of fresh melon and peach come as a big surprise if you consider the wine's age. Apparently, its built to last thanks to tones of vanilla, banana and toasted nut. It has a raw, nutty characteristic and a spice-driven finish. Drink now. 87 —*M.L. (12/1/2007)*

Masottina 1999 Vigneto Rizzardo White Blend (Colli di Conegliano) $25. 89 —*J.C. (7/1/2003)*

MASSERIA ALTEMURA

Masseria Altemura 2005 Aglianico (Puglia) $15. Perfumed on the nose, with hints of truffle and mineral mingling easily with black cherry fruit. Tannins are soft, but the impression is one of taut minerality on the palate, as the flavors finish crisp and dusty, marked by hints of crushed stone. Drink now–2012, possibly longer. 89 *(11/15/2007)*

Masseria Altemura 2006 Fiano (Salento) $15. Made entirely in stainless steel, this is only the second vintage for this wine, and it's a good start. Flavors are bold and assertive, with notes of green apple and citrus that finish lemony and mouthwatering. Drink now. 87 *(11/15/2007)*

Masseria Altemura 2005 Negroamaro (Salento) $15. The warmth of Italy's heel is evident in this wine's slightly roasted notes of chocolate and coffee, but those flavors marry easily with flavors of black cherry and caramel. Soft and creamy on the palate, yet the wine finishes with decent acidity. Drink now. 88 *(11/15/2007)*

Masseria Altemura 2005 Rosato Negroamaro (Salento) $14. Here is a well-recommended southern Italian rosè with genuine aromas of peach candy, stone fruit, white chocolate and pink flower. It is a deservedly popular wine, thanks to its affordability and easy approach. 86 —*M.L. (7/1/2007)*

Masseria Altemura 2004 Rosato Negroamaro (Salento) $14. This southern Italian rosé boasts a pretty pink rose color and inviting aromas of stone fruit, cranberry, flower petal and almond. It has a creamy texture, sweetness and a broader structure that promises to match to appetizers and summer barbequed foods. 86 —*M.L. (7/1/2007)*

Masseria Altemura 2005 Sasseo Primitivo (Salento) $15. Smoky cola and plum flavors feature some intriguingly briary notes, but also veer toward prune and cooked fruit. Tannins are soft, but the wine is surprisingly tart on the finish. With its crisp acidity, expect it to pair well with tomato-based sauces. 86 *(11/15/2007)*

Masseria Altemura 2006 Rosato Rosé Blend (Salento) $15. Made from Negroamaro, this coppery, peach-hued rosé is rather weighty, with flavors that run toward cherries and chocolate. You could serve it with rich seafood dishes, but it can also stand up to grilled beef. 87 *(11/15/2007)*

MASSERIA DEL FEUDO GROTTAROSSA

Masseria del Feudo Grottarossa 2003 Haermosa Chardonnay (Sicilia) $30. 84 —*M.L. (7/1/2006)*

Masseria del Feudo Grottarossa 2004 Nero d'Avola (Sicilia) $14. 87 —*M.L. (7/1/2006)*

Masseria del Feudo Grottarossa 2003 Rosso delle Rose Red Blend (Sicilia) $20. 88 Editors' Choice —*M.L. (7/1/2006)*

MASSOLINO

Massolino 1995 Vigna Margheria Nebbiolo (Barolo) $60. 82 —*M.S. (9/1/2000)*

MASTROBERARDINO

Mastroberardino 2003 Aglianico (Irpinia) $22. 87 *(12/1/2005)*

Mastroberardino 2005 Lacrimarosa Aglianico (Campania) $18. This pleasing Aglianico-based rosé from Campania offers tingling acidity and a refreshing palate-cleansing quality throughout. The nose is redolent of rose petal, cranberry-raspberry and white stone. It's a simple wine, but also a well executed one. 86 —*M.L. (4/1/2007)*

Mastroberardino 2000 Radici Aglianico (Taurasi) $41. 91 Cellar Selection —*M.L. (9/1/2005)*

Mastroberardino 1995 Radici Aglianico (Taurasi) $42. 89 *(3/1/2000)*

Mastroberardino 2005 Coda di Volpe (Lacryma Christi del Vesuvio) $19. The mineral component here is downright fantastic, as are the fresh aromas of pink grapefruit, lemon zest and green apple. Delightful notes of white stone appear again in the mouth to render a chalky, dry finish. 88 —*M.L. (4/1/2007)*

Mastroberardino 2002 Coda di Volpe (Lacryma Christi del Vesuvio) $18. 88 —*M.S. (10/1/2004)*

Mastroberardino 2005 Falanghina (Sannio) $19. There is a beautifully polished pear and Golden Delicious apple component to the nose, but there is also an attractive mineral side that adds dimension and contrast. Additional aromas include kiwi, honeydew, dried herbs and even a tiny hint of bubble gum or rock candy. Tasty pear flavors characterize the mouth. 89 —*M.L. (4/1/2007)*

Mastroberardino 2004 Falanghina (Sannio) $19. 86 —*M.L. (9/1/2005)*

Mastroberardino 2005 Radici Fiano (Fiano di Avellino) $25. The strong suit here is elegance and grace: Light stone fruit and green apple aromas mingle seamlessly with drying mineral, almost chalk-like tones. The wine is somewhat neutral in the mouth but has clean, sharp angles and an absolutely pristine mouthfeel. 89 —*M.L. (4/1/2007)*

Mastroberardino 2004 Radici Fiano (Fiano di Avellino) $25. 90 Editors' Choice —*M.L. (9/1/2005)*

Mastroberardino 1998 Radici Fiano (Fiano di Avellino) $26. 89 —*M.M. (9/1/2001)*

Mastroberardino 1997 Radici Fiano (Fiano di Avellino) $26. 84 —*M.S. (4/1/2000)*

Mastroberardino 1997 Greco (Greco di Tufo) $25. 92 *(4/1/2000)*

Mastroberardino 2005 NovaSerra Greco (Greco di Tufo) $24. Immaculate pear, apple, melon, almond and citrus emerge on the nose of this brilliantly luminous barrel-fermented Greco di Tufo. The aromas are very pretty and distinct and the same holds true for the wine's flavors. This is a showcase wine for Campania. 90 —*M.L. (4/1/2007)*

Mastroberardino 2004 NovaSerra Greco (Greco di Tufo) $25. 88 —*M.L. (9/1/2005)*

Mastroberardino 2005 Piedirosso (Lacryma Christi del Vesuvio) $22. True to form for the Piedirosso grape, this is redolent of raspberries, sandalwood, lavender, volcanic soils and soapy-scented tones. Flinty flavors in the mouth are backed by bright acidity and a sour note. 85 —*M.L. (8/1/2007)*

Mastroberardino 1998 Piedirosso (Lacryma Christi del Vesuvio) $23. 86 —*L.W. (3/1/2000)*

Mastroberardino 1997 Piedirosso (Lacryma Christi del Vesuvio) $23. 91 —*M.S. (3/1/2000)*

Mastroberardino 1997 Red Blend (Aglianico d'Irpinia) $22. 91 *(11/15/1999)*

Mastroberardino 2004 Red Blend (Lacryma Christi del Vesuvio) $22. 87 *(12/1/2005)*

Mastroberardino 2000 Red Blend (Lacryma Christi del Vesuvio) $20. 86 —*C.S. (5/1/2002)*

Mastroberardino 1998 Mastro Red Blend (Campania) $17. 82 —*C.S. (5/1/2002)*

Mastroberardino 2000 Naturalis Historia Red Blend (Irpinia) $65. 90 *(12/1/2005)*

Mastroberardino 1998 Naturalis Historia Red Blend (Irpinia) $70. 88 —*M.S. (12/15/2003)*

Mastroberardino 1997 Naturalis Historia Red Blend (Irpinia) $70. 90 —*C.S. (5/1/2002)*

Mastroberardino 2002 Villa dei Misteri Red Blend (Pompeiano) $217. 89 *(12/1/2005)*

Mastroberardino 1998 White Blend (Coda di Volpe d'Irpinia) $13.88 —*L.W. (4/1/2000)*

Mastroberardino 2004 Bianco White Blend (Lacryma Christi del Vesuvio) $19. 88 *(12/1/2005)*

Mastroberardino 1998 Sireum White Blend (Campania) $NA. 87 —*L.W. (4/1/2000)*

MASTROJANNI

Mastrojanni 2001 Brunello (Brunello di Montalcino) $55. 90 Cellar Selection *(4/1/2006)*

Mastrojanni 2000 Brunello (Brunello di Montalcino) $50. 88 —*M.S. (7/1/2005)*

Mastrojanni 1999 Brunello (Brunello di Montalcino) $55. 89 —*M.S. (6/1/2004)*

Mastrojanni 1997 Brunello (Brunello di Montalcino) $60. 93 Cellar Selection —*R.V. (8/1/2002)*

MASÙT DA RIVE

Masùt da Rive 2004 Pinot Grigio (Isonzo del Friuli) $19. 89 —*M.L. (2/1/2006)*

Masùt Da Rive 2001 Sauvignon (Isonzo del Friuli) $22. 82 *(7/1/2005)*

MAURO BUSSI

Mauro Bussi 2000 Nebbiolo (Barbaresco) $55. 90 *(4/2/2004)*

MAURO MOLINO

Mauro Molino 1997 Vigna Gettere Barbera (Barbera d'Alba) $33. 89 *(4/1/2000)*

MAURO SEBASTE

Mauro Sebaste 1999 Brunate Nebbiolo (Barolo) $75. 91 *(4/2/2004)*

Mauro Sebaste 1999 La Serra Nebbiolo (Barolo) $54. 87 *(4/2/2004)*

Mauro Sebaste 1995 Monvigliero Nebbiolo (Barolo) $66. 86 *(7/1/2000)*

Mauro Sebaste 2001 Parigi Nebbiolo (Nebbiolo d'Alba) $32. 84 —*M.S. (12/15/2003)*

Mauro Sebaste 1999 Prapo Nebbiolo (Barolo) $75. 90 *(4/2/2004)*

MAURO VEGLIO

Mauro Veglio 1998 Castelletto Nebbiolo (Barolo) $60. 87 *(4/2/2004)*

MAZZEI

Mazzei 2000 Badiola Sangiovese (Toscana) $13. 85 —*M.S. (12/31/2002)*

Mazzei 2003 Castello di Fonterutoli Sangiovese (Chianti Classico) $50. You can taste the touch of consulting enologist Carlo Ferrini here: This is an opulent, modern and plush rendition of Chianti Classico with deep tones of cherry, vanilla and chocolate fudge. It's rich and plush in the mouth with velvety tannins and dark concentration. 92 —*M.L. (11/1/2007)*

Mazzei 1999 Fonterutoli Sangiovese (Chianti Classico) $27. 91 —*M.S. (8/1/2002)*

MAZZI

Mazzi 2003 Punta di Villa Corvina, Rondinella, Molinara (Amarone della Valpolicella Classico) $30. This is difficult to score because its aromas dart off in opposite directions making it hard to discern the quality of the fruit. I picked up citrus notes, like pink grapefruit and lemon zest, on one side of the spectrum and heavy notes of tar, resin and asphalt on the other. The 24 months in barrique add soft layers of chocolate and spice in the mouth. 87 —*M.L. (10/1/2007)*

Mazzi 2001 Punta di Villa Red Blend (Amarone della Valpolicella Classico) $60. 87 *(11/1/2005)*

MAZZINO

Mazzino 1998 Barbera (Barbera d'Alba) $12. 82 —*M.S. (12/15/2003)*

Mazzino 1997 Nebbiolo (Barolo) $35. 86 —*M.S. (12/15/2003)*

MEDICI ERMETE

Medici Ermete 2005 Concerto Lambrusco Reggiano Secco Lambrusco (Emilia-Romagna) $21. 86 —*M.L. (12/15/2006)*

Medici Ermete 2005 Solo Lambrusco Reggiano Secco Lambrusco (Emilia-Romagna) $15. 85 —*M.L. (12/15/2006)*

Medici Ermete 2005 Daphne Malvasia Frizzante Malvasia Bianca (Emilia-Romagna) $21. 85 —*M.L. (12/15/2006)*

MELINI

Melini 1997 Coltri 2 Cabernet Blend (Tuscany) $33. 90 —*M.S. (11/15/2003)*

Melini 1999 Bonorli Merlot (Tuscany) $35. 88 —*M.S. (11/15/2003)*

Melini 2002 Borghi D'Elsa Sangiovese (Chianti) $10. 84 *(4/1/2005)*

Melini 1998 Borghi D'Elsa Sangiovese (Chianti) $9. 87 Best Buy *(4/1/2001)*

Melini 2000 Isassi Sangiovese (Chianti Classico) $16. 87 —*M.S. (11/15/2004)*

Melini 1999 Isassi Sangiovese (Chianti Classico) $15. 87 —*M.S. (11/15/2003)*

Melini 1997 Isassi Sangiovese (Chianti Classico) $13. 85 *(4/1/2001)*

Melini 1999 Laborel Riserva Sangiovese (Chianti Classico) $19. 86 —*M.S. (11/15/2004)*

Melini 1998 Laborel Riserva Sangiovese (Chianti Classico) $19. 85 —*M.S. (11/15/2003)*

Melini 1995 Massovecchio dai Vigneti Terrarossa Riserva Sangiovese (Chianti Classico) $35. 91 *(11/15/1999)*

Melini 1998 Riserva La Selvanella Sangiovese (Chianti Classico) $23. 87 —*R.V. (8/1/2002)*

Melini 1999 Riserva Massovecchio Sangiovese (Chianti Classico) $30. 90 —*M.S. (10/1/2004)*

Melini 1999 Vigneti La Selvanella Riserva Sangiovese (Chianti Classico) $24. 86 —*M.S. (10/1/2004)*

Melini 2002 Vernaccia (Vernaccia di San Gimignano) $12. 85 —*M.S. (8/1/2004)*

Melini 2002 Le Grillaie Vernaccia (Vernaccia di San Gimignano) $20. 87 —*M.S. (8/1/2004)*

MELONI

Meloni 2001 Le Ghiaie Cannonau (Cannonau di Sardegna) $21. 88 —*M.S. (2/1/2005)*

Meloni 2005 Omarus Vermentino (Vermentino di Sardegna) $15. This is an awkward wine with aromas of peach, melon and honey, but it also has slightly oxidized aromas of Marsala or pinecone. The wine definitely has valid points but might prove difficult to pair with the seafood dishes Vermentino is usually designed for. Tasted both bottles with consistent notes. 83 —*M.L. (11/15/2007)*

MERK

Merk 2001 Pinot Bianco (Friuli Aquileia) $16. 86 —*J.C. (7/1/2003)*

Merk 2004 Pinot Grigio (Friuli Aquileia) $16. 89 —*M.L. (6/1/2006)*

Merk 2001 Pinot Grigio (Friuli Aquileia) $16. 85 —*J.C. (7/1/2003)*

Merk 2001 Tocai (Friuli Aquileia) $16. 87 *—J.C. (7/1/2003)*

MERONI

Meroni 1997 Il Velluto Red Blend (Valpolicella Classico Superiore) $24. 83 *(5/1/2003)*

Meroni 1997 Il Velluto Riserva Red Blend (Amarone della Valpolicella Classico) $80. 83 *(11/1/2005)*

MESA

Mesa 2005 Opale Vermentino (Sardinia) $37. Vermentino is one of Italy's most versatile and food-friendly white grapes; this rendition boasts notes of exotic fruit, acacia, honey and mineral tones. It is delightfully refreshing—with some nutty flavors—and buoyant. Only 10% is aged in oak and the rest in stainless steel. 87 *—M.L. (4/1/2007)*

MEZZACORONA

Mezzacorona 2004 Cabernet Sauvignon (Vigneti delle Dolomiti) $9. 87 **Best Buy** *—M.L. (10/1/2006)*

Mezzacorona 2003 Cabernet Sauvignon (Vigneti delle Dolomiti) $8. 85 **Best Buy** *(6/1/2005)*

Mezzacorona 2006 Chardonnay (Vigneti delle Dolomiti) $8. There's a real clean and genuine quality that comes through thanks to aromas of peach, yellow fruit and Golden Delicious apple. It drinks well too—easy and forthcoming—and would make an excellent match to grilled chicken, spicy asian food or stay-at-home pasta. 86 **Best Buy** *—M.L. (11/15/2007)*

Mezzacorona 2005 Chardonnay (Vigneti delle Dolomiti) $9. 86 **Best Buy** *—M.L. (10/1/2006)*

Mezzacorona 2004 Chardonnay (Vigneti delle Dolomiti) $7. 85 **Best Buy** *(6/1/2005)*

Mezzacorona 2003 Chardonnay (Vigneti delle Dolomiti) $8. 84 **Best Buy** *—J.C. (12/31/2004)*

Mezzacorona 2002 Vigneti delle Dolomiti Chardonnay (Trentino) $8. 85 **Best Buy** *—J.C. (7/1/2003)*

Mezzacorona 2005 Merlot (Vigneti delle Dolomiti) $9. Here's a Merlot with a medium build that offers more fruity freshness on the nose: Notes of red berry, blueberry and cherry call out loud and clear. A firm structure and nice cherry-berry flavors leave a lasting impression in the mouth. 87 **Best Buy** *—M.L. (3/1/2007)*

Mezzacorona 2004 Merlot (Vigneti delle Dolomiti) $9. The nose offers cherry, chocolate mocha and smoke backed by moist earth and white mushroom. You get a lot of great flavor for your dollar plus chewy, sweet tannins and medium length on the finish. Informal and friendly this is the kind of red wine you want handy for when friends pop over. 87 **Best Buy** *—M.L. (3/1/2007)*

Mezzacorona 2003 Merlot (Vigneti delle Dolomiti) $10. 85 **Best Buy** *—J.C. (12/31/2004)*

Mezzacorona 2001 Merlot (Trentino) $8. 86 **Best Buy** *—M.S. (12/15/2003)*

Mezzacorona 1998 Merlot (Trentino) $8. 86 *(1/1/2004)*

Mezzacorona 2004 Castel Firmian Merlot (Trentino) $13. An easy red with medium concentration and measured aromatic intensity. Blueberry, almond and mineral aromas with an impressive mouthfeel, thanks to the wine's noticeable structure and persistence. 85 *—M.L. (3/1/2007)*

Mezzacorona 2006 Pinot Grigio (Vigneti delle Dolomiti) $9. This is a pristine albeit easy wine with clean and compact aromas of stone fruit, yellow flower and zesty citrus. Genuine and aromatic, this is textbook Pinot Grigio with pleasing creaminess on the palate. Pair with pasta salad, grilled white meats and finger foods. 87 **Best Buy** *—M.L. (11/15/2007)*

Mezzacorona 2005 Pinot Grigio (Vigneti delle Dolomiti) $9. 86 **Best Buy** *—M.L. (6/1/2006)*

Mezzacorona 2004 Pinot Grigio (Vigneti delle Dolomiti) $8. 84 **Best Buy** *(6/1/2005)*

Mezzacorona 1999 Pinot Grigio (Trentino) $7. 83 *—M.N. (12/31/2000)*

Mezzacorona 1998 Pinot Grigio (Trentino) $8. 86 **Best Buy** *(8/1/1999)*

Mezzacorona 2005 Castel Firmian Pinot Grigio (Trentino) $11. With its pretty medley of honey and peach aromas and a crystalline appearance, this is a quintessential Italian Pinot Grigio. It's easy, crisp, refreshing, slightly sour in the mouth and without pretense: A great match to summer eating. 86 **Best Buy** *—M.L. (12/1/2007)*

Mezzacorona 2001 Millesimato Pinot Grigio (Trentino) 85 *—R.V. (7/1/2003)*

Mezzacorona 2004 Riserva Pinot Grigio (Trentino) $13. 89 **Best Buy** *—M.L. (2/1/2006)*

Mezzacorona 2003 Riserva Pinot Grigio (Trentino) $13. 88 **Best Buy** *—M.L. (2/1/2006)*

Mezzacorona 2002 Riserva Pinot Grigio (Trentino) $14. 85 *—J.C. (12/31/2004)*

Mezzacorona 2006 Rosato Rosé Blend (Vigneti delle Dolomiti) $8. Forest berry and strawberry nuances take center stage leaving delicate mineral aromas in the background. But there a nice simplicity and understated quality to this raspberry-copper colored rosé that evokes summer picnics and outdoor lunches. There's also a touch of sweetness in the mouth: This is Mezzacorona's first rosé. 85 **Best Buy** *—M.L. (7/1/2007)*

Mezzacorona 2000 Riserva Teroldego (Italy) $14. 85 *—J.C. (12/31/2004)*

Mezzacorona 2000 Riserva Superiore Teroldego (Teroldego Rotaliano) $NA. 89 *(6/1/2005)*

Mezzacorona 2005 Castel Firmian Traminer (Trentino) $11. This is a crisp wine with pretty brilliance and aromatic floral notes, peach, white mineral and a very enticing hint of crushed basil leaf. This is a very approachable fresh and drinkable wine with medium length and plenty of fruity flavors on the finish. 86 **Best Buy** *—M.L. (12/1/2007)*

MICHELE CHIARLO

Michele Chiarlo 1998 Barbera (Barbera d'Asti) $13. 87 **Best Buy** *(4/1/2000)*

Michele Chiarlo 1997 Barbera (Barbera d'Asti) $12. 83 *(4/1/2000)*

Michele Chiarlo 2003 La Court Barbera (Barbera d'Asti) $40. An immense hefty Barbera showing a good deal of dark fruit, smoked meat and licorice. On the palate, it is still a little fragmented, but with another year of bottle age, it will make a very nice bottle of wine. 90 *—M.G. (4/1/2007)*

Michele Chiarlo 2000 La Court Barbera (Barbera d'Asti) $35. 88 *—J.C. (11/15/2004)*

Michele Chiarlo 1996 La Court Barbera (Barbera d'Asti) $46. 87 *(4/1/2000)*

Michele Chiarlo 1999 La Court Superiore Barbera (Barbera d'Asti) $NA. 91 **Editors' Choice** *—M.S. (11/15/2002)*

Michele Chiarlo 2004 Le Orme Barbera (Barbera d'Asti) $13. The light-bodied Chiarlo showes plenty of fruit, and the earthiness of a traditional Barbera. The finish was a little less exciting, marred by a sweet bubble gum character. 86 *—M.G. (4/1/2007)*

Michele Chiarlo 2001 Le Orme Barbera (Barbera d'Asti) $11. 86 **Best Buy** *—J.C. (11/15/2004)*

Michele Chiarlo 2000 Superiore Barbera (Barbera d'Asti) $10. 86 **Best Buy** *—M.S. (11/15/2002)*

Michele Chiarlo 1995 Valle del Sole Barbera (Barbera d'Asti) $29. 88 *(4/1/2000)*

Michele Chiarlo 1998 Cortese (Gavi) $15. 86 *(4/1/2000)*

Michele Chiarlo 2002 Cortese (Gavi) $14. 87 *—M.S. (11/15/2003)*

Michele Chiarlo 1998 Rovereto Cortese (Gavi di Gavi) $24. 86 *(4/1/2000)*

Michele Chiarlo 2005 Nivole Moscato (Moscato d'Asti) $12. There is something a little funky about this wine. At first, it has a creamy quality that mixes well with the peach and apricot flavors and gives the wine a certain complexity, but over time, that edge becomes a little dank and begins to overwhelm the fruit. 82 *—M.G. (12/31/2007)*

Michele Chiarlo 2004 Nivole Moscato (Moscato d'Asti) $12. 89 **Best Buy** *—M.L. (12/15/2005)*

Michele Chiarlo 1998 Nebbiolo (Piedmont) $30. 90 *—R.V. (11/15/2002)*

Michele Chiarlo 1995 Nebbiolo (Barbaresco) $35. 88 *—M.M. (5/1/1999)*

Michele Chiarlo 2001 Brunate Nebbiolo (Barolo) $90. A really old-fashioned Barolo; the nose is all plums, road tar and roses, with the road tar becoming dominant after a few minutes in the glass. On the palate, it is light-bodied, perfumed and very pretty, with the fruit making a good comeback. Although it could use a touch more concentration, it is a fine example of a traditional Barolo. 90 *—M.G. (4/1/2007)*

Michele Chiarlo 2000 Brunate Nebbiolo (Barolo) $85. 88 *—J.C. (11/15/2004)*

Michele Chiarlo 1998 Brunate Nebbiolo (Piedmont) $81. 93 **Cellar Selection** *—R.V. (11/15/2002)*

Michele Chiarlo 1999 Cannubi Nebbiolo (Barolo) $81. 87 *(4/2/2004)*

Michele Chiarlo 1998 Cannubi Nebbiolo (Piedmont) $81. 92 *—R.V. (11/15/2002)*

Michele Chiarlo 2000 Cerequio Nebbiolo (Barolo) $85. 87 *—J.C. (11/15/2004)*

Michele Chiarlo 1999 Cerequio Nebbiolo (Barolo) $84. 88 *(4/2/2004)*

Michele Chiarlo 1998 Cerequio Nebbiolo (Barolo) $45. 90 *—C.S. (11/15/2002)*

Michele Chiarlo 1995 Cerequio Nebbiolo (Barolo) $89. 88 *(7/1/2000)*

Michele Chiarlo 2004 Reyna Nebbiolo (Barbaresco) $35. Browning slightly at the edge, the Chiarlo has already evolved beautifully. The smoky red fruit is combined with clove, anise and rose petals. Well balanced and with a medium finish, over the next five years, this will drink beautifully. **91** —*M.G. (12/31/2007)*

Michele Chiarlo 2001 Tortoniano Nebbiolo (Barolo) $50. The Veglio is a big, slightly raw wine with flavors of fruit cake, smoke, almonds and roses. The palate begins solidly, but quickly thins out, leaving little in the finish. Needs a few years. **89** —*M.G. (4/1/2007)*

Michele Chiarlo 1998 Tortoniano Nebbiolo (Barolo) $44. 90 *(4/2/2004)*

Michele Chiarlo 1995 Countacc Red Blend (Monferrato) $40. 91 —*M.M. (5/1/1999)*

Michele Chiarlo 2005 Le Monache Red Blend (Monferrato) $13. Chiarlo tends to be one of the more reliable producers in Piedmont, and this comes across as a pleasant everyday wine. The fruit is very ripe, bordering on the superripe; but on the palate, the wine has some interesting flavors, dark cherry fruit and hints of licorice and green olive. **85** —*M.G. (12/31/2007)*

MIONETTO

Mionetto NV Champagne Blend (Prosecco di Valdobbiadene) $24. 89 *(11/15/2002)*

Mionetto NV Cartizze Champagne Blend (Prosecco di Valdobbiadene) $47. 88 *(11/15/2002)*

Mionetto NV Casada Extra Dry Spumante Champagne Blend (Prosecco di Valdobbiadene) $14. 85 —*M.M. (12/31/2001)*

Mionetto NV Frizzante (Soft White Wine) Champagne Blend (Prosecco di Valdobbiadene) $12. 88 Best Buy —*M.M. (12/31/2001)*

Mionetto NV Sergio Extra Dry Champagne Blend (Prosecco di Valdobbiadene) $18. 88 Best Buy —*D.T. (12/31/2001)*

Mionetto NV Sergio Extra Dry Spumante Champagne Blend (Prosecco di Valdobbiadene) $16. 92 *(11/15/2002)*

Mionetto NV Spumante Champagne Blend (Prosecco di Valdobbiadene) $12. 87 *(11/15/2002)*

Mionetto NV Spumante Brut Champagne Blend (Prosecco di Valdobbiadene) $11. 89 Best Buy *(11/15/2002)*

Mionetto NV Superiore di Cartizze Champagne Blend (Prosecco di Valdobbiadene) $47. 84 —*M.M. (12/31/2001)*

Mionetto NV Il Moscato (Moscato delle Venezie) $10. 84 —*J.C. (12/31/2003)*

Mionetto NV Prosecco (Prosecco di Valdobbiadene) $13. 85 —*M.L. (12/15/2004)*

Mionetto NV Prosecco (Prosecco di Valdobbiadene) $15. 85 —*M.S. (6/1/2005)*

Mionetto NV Prosecco (Prosecco di Conegliano e Valdobbiadene) $13. 85 —*M.L. (12/15/2006)*

Mionetto NV Brut Prosecco (Prosecco di Valdobbiadene) $11. 87 —*M.L. (12/15/2006)*

Mionetto NV Brut Prosecco (Prosecco di Valdobbiadene) $12. 88 Best Buy —*M.L. (12/15/2004)*

Mionetto NV Brut Spumante Prosecco (Prosecco di Valdobbiadene) $12. 87 Best Buy —*M.S. (6/1/2005)*

Mionetto NV Cartizze Prosecco (Prosecco Superiore di Cartizze) $24. Delicately sweet and redolent of honey, acacia and exotic fruit, this would go down easily in casual settings or during the holidays. It has a creamy mouthfeel with peach and pear flavors. **89** —*M.L. (12/15/2007)*

Mionetto NV Cartizze Prosecco (Prosecco Superiore di Cartizze) $24. 90 Editors' Choice —*M.L. (6/1/2006)*

Mionetto NV Cartizze Dry Prosecco (Prosecco di Valdobbiadene) $25. 89 —*M.S. (6/1/2005)*

Mionetto NV Extra Dry Prosecco (Prosecco di Valdobbiadene) $13. 87 —*M.L. (6/1/2006)*

Mionetto 2005 Extra Dry Prosecco (Prosecco di Conegliano e Valdobbiadene) $17. 87 —*M.L. (12/15/2006)*

Mionetto NV Extra Dry Linea Mó Prosecco (Prosecco di Conegliano e Valdobbiadene) $19. Makers of textbook Prosecco, Mionetto's Extra Dry sparkler is lush and pulpy with aromas of lemon blossom, melon, bee's wax, pear and oats. Count on good freshness in the mouth reinforced by lemon candy flavors. **88** —*M.L. (12/15/2007)*

Mionetto NV Extra Dry Linea Mó Prosecco (Prosecco di Valdobbiadene) $15. 88 —*M.L. (6/1/2006)*

Mionetto NV Frizzante Prosecco (Prosecco di Valdobbiadene) $12. 88 Best Buy —*M.S. (6/1/2005)*

Mionetto NV Il Prosecco (Prosecco di Valdobbiadene) $11. 86 Best Buy —*M.L. (12/15/2006)*

Mionetto NV Il Prosecco (Prosecco del Veneto) $10. 86 Best Buy —*M.S. (6/1/2005)*

Mionetto NV Il Prosecco (Prosecco del Veneto) $11. 86 Best Buy —*M.S. (12/15/2004)*

Mionetto NV Il Prosecco (Prosecco del Veneto) $10. 85 —*J.C. (12/31/2003)*

Mionetto NV Prestige Extra Dry Prosecco (Prosecco di Conegliano e Valdobbiadene) $14. This is a tonic, almost crunchy sparkler with citrus tones, pristine mineral renderings and even a touch of dried bread crust. It is a polished wine with many angles, good dimension and just the right dose of sweetness. **87** —*M.L. (12/15/2007)*

Mionetto NV Sergio Extra Dry Prosecco (Prosecco di Valdobbiadene) $18. 87 —*M.L. (12/15/2004)*

Mionetto NV Sergio Extra Dry Prosecco (Prosecco del Veneto) 89 —*J.C. (12/31/2003)*

Mionetto NV Sergio Extra Dry Spumante Prosecco (Prosecco di Valdobbiadene) $18. 88 —*M.S. (6/1/2005)*

Mionetto 2002 Marca Trevigiana Novello '02 Red Blend (Marca Trevigiana) $10. 83 *(5/1/2003)*

Mionetto 2006 Il Rosé Rosé Blend (Veneto) $10. Low in alcohol and high in drinkability, this is the kind of fun, informal sparkling rosè you want to pack for a summer picnic (the closure is a bottlecap). The pink hues are more saturated and deeper than most and the nose has some chopped herbs backed by fresh fruit, raspberry, strawberry and cotton candy. **85 Best Buy** —*M.L. (7/1/2007)*

Mionetto NV Extra Dry Sergio (Prosecco del Veneto) $17. 88 —*M.L. (12/15/2006)*

Mionetto NV Sergio Rosé Extra Dry Sparkling Blend (Veneto) $22. Made from Raboso and Lagrein grapes native to northern Italy, this is a brilliant, raspberry-colored sparkler with pretty and well-defined aromas of cranberry juice, white almond and roses. Among the trendy new pink Prosecco-styled wines to hit the U.S. market, Mionetto is one of the best. Interesting mineral nuances that recall chalk or white stone add a patina of elegance and femininity to a fun and informal wine otherwise characterized by red berry fruit, white cherry and flower petal. Creamy, fresh, fruity and tangy in the mouth, this approachable sparkler delivers everything you should expect. **87** —*M.L. (7/1/2007)*

MOCALI

Mocali 2001 Brunello (Brunello di Montalcino) $45. 91 *(4/1/2006)*

Mocali 2001 Vigna delle Raunate Brunello (Brunello di Montalcino) $23. 91 *(4/1/2006)*

MOCCAGATTA

Moccagatta 2000 Cole Nebbiolo (Barbaresco) $60. 83 *(4/2/2004)*

MOLETTO

Moletto 2000 Selecti Cabernet Sauvignon (Veneto Orientale) $62. 92 —*M.L. (9/1/2006)*

Moletto 1999 Merlot (Veneto) $10. 86 Best Buy *(5/1/2002)*

Moletto 1998 Merlot (Piave) $20. 87 *(9/1/2001)*

Moletto 2004 Brut Millesimato Pinot Bianco (Italy) $NA. Thanks to its vertical aromatic delivery, you can enjoy this sparkler's upfront fresh notes of green apple, peach, crushed white pepper and mineral. Beyond those is an extra layer of honey and toast thanks to some oak aging; bubbly effervescence adds a piquant touch on the palate backed by sweet fruit flavors. **89** —*M.L. (12/15/2007)*

Moletto 2004 Pinot Bianco (Veneto Orientale) $13. 85 —*M.L. (12/15/2006)*

Moletto 2005 Pinot Grigio (Piave) $13. 85 —*M.L. (6/1/2006)*

Moletto 2004 Pinot Grigio (Piave) $13. 87 —*M.L. (2/1/2006)*

Moletto 2003 Pinot Grigio (Veneto) $11. 86 Best Buy —*J.C. (12/31/2004)*

Moletto 2000 Pinot Grigio (Veneto) $10. 87 Best Buy *(9/1/2001)*

Moletto 1998 Pinot Grigio (Piave) $10. 86 *(8/1/1999)*

Moletto NV Prosecco (Marca Trevigiana) $8. 88 Best Buy —*M.L. (11/15/2005)*

Moletto 2000 Prosecco (Veneto) $10. 85 *(5/1/2002)*

Moletto NV Extra Dry Prosecco (Prosecco di Valdobbiadene) $14. 84 —*J.C. (12/31/2003)*

Moletto NV Extra Dry Spumante Prosecco (Veneto) $13. 87 —*M.L. (12/15/2004)*

Moletto NV Frizzante Prosecco (Marca Trevigiana) $13. 87 —*M.S. (12/15/2004)*

Moletto NV Frizzante Prosecco (Marca Trevigiana) $13. 87 —*M.L. (6/1/2006)*

Moletto NV Extra Dry Spumante Prosecco (Veneto) $15. 87 —*M.L. (6/1/2006)*

Moletto 2005 Raboso Frizzante Raboso (Veneto Orientale) $14. More of a red frizzante than a rosé, this deeply ruby semi-sparkler delivers bold and potent medicinal and balsam aromas: Cherry cough drop is in center stage. The herbal flavors come in awkward contrast to the wine's sweet, plush mouthfeel. **83** *—M.L. (7/1/2007)*

Moletto 1998 Colmello Rosso Red Blend (Veneto) $20. 89 *(5/1/2002)*

Moletto NV Rosa Tocai Rosso (Veneto Orientale) $13. Bright and vibrant in appearance with ruby highlights, this pretty rosé sparkler has drying aromas of white chalk and stone fruit to make for an elegant ensemble. The wine is simple, genuine, sweet and would make a great appetite opener. **85** *—M.L. (7/1/2007)*

Moletto 2005 Rosa Tocai Rosso (Veneto Orientale) $13. 85 Best Buy *—M.L. (11/15/2006)*

MONASTERO DI CORIANO

Monastero di Coriano 1996 White Blend (Vin Santo del Chianti) $21. 84 *—S.H. (1/1/2002)*

Monastero di Coriano 1994 Regina White Blend (Tuscany) $24. 84 *—S.H. (1/1/2002)*

MONCARO

Moncaro 2002 Terrazzo Verdicchio (Verdicchio dei Castelli di Jesi Classico Superiore) $13. 84 *—M.S. (8/1/2004)*

MONCHIERO

Monchiero 2003 Barbera (Barbera d'Alba Superiore) $20. The color is light, but the Monchiero has pungent earthy aromas over a backdrop of fruit. On the palate, it is soft and quite chunky, and dominated by its earthiness. The wine has evolved completely, and should be drunk reasonably quickly. **85** *—M.G. (12/31/2007)*

MONCHIERO CARBONE

Monchiero Carbone 1996 Mon Birone Barbera (Barbera d'Alba) $20. 86 *(4/1/2000)*

MONDORO

Mondoro NV Moscato (Asti) $14. 82 *—J.C. (12/31/2001)*

MONROSSO

Monrosso 2005 Red Blend (Chianti) $10. 85 Best Buy *—M.L. (11/15/2006)*

Monrosso 2004 Red Blend (Chianti) $10. The nose is muddled by Band-Aid and wine cellar smells opposite cherry and herbaceous notes that bring up the rear. Not terribly exciting in the mouth but clean and lean nonetheless. **84** *—M.L. (2/1/2007)*

MONTE ANTICO

Monte Antico 2000 Red Blend (Toscana) $8. 84 *—M.S. (12/31/2002)*

Monte Antico 1998 Sangiovese (Toscana) $10. 85 *(10/1/2001)*

Monte Antico 2003 Rosso Sangiovese (Toscana) $12. 86 *—M.S. (9/1/2006)*

MONTE CAMPO

Monte Campo 2005 Pinot Grigio (Delle Venezie) $10. 86 Best Buy *—M.L. (6/1/2006)*

Monte Campo 2004 Pinot Grigio (Delle Venezie) $8. 85 Best Buy *—M.L. (2/1/2006)*

MONTE DALL'ORA

Monte dall'Ora 2003 Corvina, Rondinella, Molinara (Amarone della Valpolicella Classico) $NA. Although the wine lacks overall intensity, its measured, composed approach is very refreshing in this land of powerhouse wines. Dig deep and give it time to allow for sweet chocolate, black fruit, spice and cherry liquor. The wine is smooth, with chewy chocolate flavors and excellent length. **90** *—M.L. (10/1/2007)*

Monte dall'Ora 2001 Stropa Corvina, Rondinella, Molinara (Amarone della Valpolicella Classico) $NA. Sharp mineral and vitamin notes are not inviting when considered individually but they do form a good frame to chewy blueberry muffin, cherry-pie and earthy aromas. It's probably better to drink this wine sooner rather than later before the mineral tones become too prominent. **87** *—M.L. (12/1/2007)*

MONTE DEL FRÁ

Monte del Frá 2003 Corvina, Rondinella, Molinara (Amarone della Valpolicella Classico) $50. The wine opens with a pretty ruby color and offers typical Amarone aromas of candied cherry, blueberry, almond and spice. It exhibits a clean, simple style with juicy candied fruit flavors and freshness on the finish. **87** *—M.L. (12/1/2007)*

Monte del Frá 2006 Garganega (Soave) $15. Pale gold highlights illuminate this fresh that is redolent of citrus, pear, green grass, mineral tones and very light butter. It has a creamy, sweet opulence in the mouth backed by zesty crispness on the finish. **87** *—M.L. (11/15/2007)*

Monte del Frá 2006 White Blend (Custoza) $13. This blend of Garganega, Trebbiano, Tocai, Cortese, Chardonnay and Riesling delivers clean simplicity and crisp aromas of stone fruit, lemon drop and mint leaf. It's lean and easy on the palate and would pair nicely with vegetable wraps, bite-sized quiche or any other finger food. **85** *—M.L. (11/15/2007)*

Monte del Frá 2005 Cà del Magro White Blend (Custoza Superiore) $16. One of the most attractive aspects of this fresh white blend is its structure: The wine is silky and smooth and seemingly weightless at the same time. That kind of structure is a good platform for flavors of pear, exotic fruit, honey and almond. Try it with grilled shrimp in a cilantro pesto sauce. **87** *—M.L. (12/1/2007)*

MONTE FAUSTINO

Monte Faustino 2001 Corvina, Rondinella, Molinara (Amarone della Valpolicella Classico) $130. Although this wine opens with a lively ruby color, it segues into tired, somewhat lifeless aromas of resin, tar, cherry liquor, earth and deep toasted notes. The wine seems to be very influenced by the wood in which it aged. **87** *—M.L. (12/1/2007)*

Monte Faustino 1998 Red Blend (Amarone della Valpolicella Classico) $75. 90 *(11/1/2005)*

MONTE ROSSA

Monte Rossa NV Brut Saten Champagne Blend (Franciacorta) $30. 81 *—S.H. (6/1/2001)*

Monte Rossa NV Satén Chardonnay (Franciacorta) $38. 90 *—M.L. (6/1/2006)*

Monte Rossa 2001 Cabochon Brut Sparkling Blend (Franciacorta) $53. 92 *—M.L. (6/1/2006)*

Monte Rossa NV Prima Cuvée Brut Sparkling Blend (Franciacorta) $28. 90 *—M.L. (6/1/2006)*

MONTE ZOVO

Monte Zovo 1999 Corvina, Rondinella, Molinara (Amarone della Valpolicella Classico) $55. Smoke, coffee, leather, tobacco, spice, dried prune and currant berry characterize a modern, nicely aged wine with deep complexity and depth. It's also a distinctive wine with noticeable sweetness, firm tannins and excellent length. It's ready to drink now and would make a fine companion to any red meat dish. **92** *—M.L. (12/1/2007)*

Monte Zovo 2003 Riserva Corvina, Rondinella, Molinara (Amarone della Valpolicella) $60. This 2003 Riserva emphasizes oak-related aromas of black pepper, spice and cedar thanks to 36 months of French barrique. It has an inherently nervous quality, which will no doubt unwind with a few more years of cellar aging. **88** *—M.L. (10/1/2007)*

MONTECARBELLO

Montecarbello 2001 Brunello (Brunello di Montalcino) $NA. 89 *(4/1/2006)*

MONTECARIANO

Montecariano 2003 Corvina, Rondinella, Molinara (Amarone della Valpolicella Classico) $34. Here's a ripe, sun-drenched Amarone with big power and heat and mature aromas of raisin, resin, dried figs, prunes, coffee and dried apple. It tastes great, thanks to sweet fruit flavors and a chewy texture. **90** *—M.L. (10/1/2007)*

MONTEFORCHE

Monteforche 2005 Cabernet Franc (Veneto) $15. Spice, leather, smoked ham and slate roof are backed by lush red berry aromas. This deep, dark Cabernet Franc also imparts seductive notes of vanilla and mocha fudge that recall New World winemaking; very tight tannins and firm structure. Good value. **87** *—M.L. (5/1/2007)*

Monteforche 2004 Vigna del Vento Red Blend (Veneto) $38. Here's a Cab Franc-Merlot blend with rich notes of moist earth, espresso bean, Porcino mushroom and almost iron-like minerality. Fruit is here too but appears as plum, prune and blackberry: Tasty and thick with good length. **89** *—M.L. (5/1/2007)*

MONTELVINI

Montelvini 2004 Pinot Grigio (Delle Venezie) $12. 85 *—M.L. (6/1/2006)*

Montelvini NV Spumante Extra Dry Prosecco (Montello e Colli Asolani) $12. 85 *—M.S. (6/1/2005)*

MONTEMARO

Montemaro 2004 Pinot Grigio (Veneto) $8. 86 Best Buy *—M.L. (2/1/2006)*

MONTENISA

Montenisa NV Satén Chardonnay (Franciacorta) $44. 90 *—M.L. (6/1/2006)*

Montenisa NV Brut Sparkling Blend (Franciacorta) $30. 92 Editors' Choice *—M.S. (12/15/2005)*

Montenisa NV Brut Sparkling Blend (Franciacorta) $30. 90 *—M.L. (6/1/2006)*

Montenisa 2000 Riserva Contessa Maggi Sparkling Blend (Franciacorta) $NA. 92 *—M.L. (6/1/2006)*

MONTESEL RENZO

Montesel Renzo 2004 Brut Prosecco (Prosecco di Conegliano e Valdobbiadene) $20. 86 *—M.L. (6/1/2006)*

Montesel Renzo 2006 Dry Millesimato Prosecco (Prosecco di Conegliano e Valdobbiadene) $21. This sparkler opens with a very pale golden color and lively bubbling. But looks can be deceiving because its intense aromas are anything but plain: Sweet floral tones mingle with peach, herbal notes and beeswax. 86 *—M.L. (12/15/2007)*

Montesel Renzo 2004 Dry Millesimato Prosecco (Prosecco di Conegliano e Valdobbiadene) $20. 88 *—M.L. (6/1/2006)*

Montesel Renzo NV Riva dei Fiori Brut Prosecco (Prosecco di Conegliano e Valdobbiadene) $21. There's the slightest trace of oxidation on this wine that adds a cardboardlike characteristic to what would otherwise have been a pristine Prosecco. And despite its peach and citrus flavors, the mouthfeel lacks a tonic, crisp edge. 82 *—M.L. (12/15/2007)*

Montesel Renzo NV Vigna del Paradiso Extra Dry Prosecco (Prosecco di Conegliano e Valdobbiadene) $21. There's a lemon sodalike quality to this wine that is reinforced by its citrus flavors and mouth-cleansing acidity. It delivers a tonic, crisp mouthfeel with good creamy density and silky sweetness on the finish. 86 *—M.L. (12/15/2007)*

Montesel Renzo 2005 Vigna del Paradiso Extra Dry Prosecco (Prosecco di Conegliano e Valdobbiadene) $20. 85 *—M.L. (6/1/2006)*

MONTESOLE

Montesole 2003 Fiano (Fiano di Avellino) $18. 88 *—M.S. (2/1/2005)*

MONTEVETRANO

Montevetrano 2003 Montevetrano Red Blend (Campania) $90. This 60-30-10 Cabernet Sauvignon, Merlot and Aglianico blend is a real treat from southern Italy with interesting complexity and flushed out tones of small berry fruit, exotic spice, vanilla, espresso and leather. The Cabernet aromas shine brightest. It's modern, vibrant and a fine example of successful winemaking. 91 *—M.L. (8/1/2007)*

Montevetrano 1999 Montevetrano Red Blend (Campania) $70. 94 Cellar Selection *—C.S. (5/1/2002)*

MONTI

Monti 2001 Barbera (Barbera d'Alba) $NA. 86 *—J.C. (11/15/2004)*

Monti 1999 Barbera (Barbera d'Alba) $37. 92 *—M.N. (9/1/2001)*

Monti 1997 Barbera (Barbera d'Alba) $35. 85 *(4/1/2000)*

Monti 2000 Bussia Nebbiolo (Barolo) $NA. 87 *—J.C. (11/15/2004)*

Monti 2000 L'Aura White Blend (Langhe) $28. 88 *—M.M. (9/1/2001)*

MONTICELLO VINEYARDS

Monticello Vineyards 2001 Riserva Sangiovese (Chianti Classico) $25. 89 *(4/1/2005)*

Monticello Vineyards 1997 Riserva Sangiovese (Chianti Classico) $16. 90 Best Buy *(4/1/2001)*

MONTIPAGANO

Montipagano 2003 Costamorro Montepulciano (Montepulciano d'Abruzzo Colline Teramane) $30. Bold and brawny, vibrant and intense, this is a hearty wine with hickory tones, smoked bacon, loads of fresh cherry and shadings of black peppercorn and spice. It imparts a velvety texture in the mouth, thanks to solid tannins, and closes with a sour note that recalls sour cherry. 89 *—M.L. (12/1/2007)*

Montipagano 2005 Trebbiano (Trebbiano d'Abruzzo) $10. There's an attractive buoyancy to this white wine that evokes floral fragrances, stone fruit, mature apple and lemon peel. The wine's color is golden and saturated and its mouthfeel is abundantly smooth and silky. 85 Best Buy *—M.L. (11/15/2007)*

MONTRESOR

Montresor 1999 CS del Veneto Campo Madonna Cabernet Sauvignon (Veneto) $17. 87 *(5/1/2003)*

Montresor 2001 Garganega (Bianco di Custoza) $11. 88 Best Buy *—J.C. (7/1/2003)*

Montresor 2004 La Colombaia Pinot Grigio (Valdadige) $13. 87 *(2/1/2006)*

Montresor 2004 La Colombaia Pinot Grigio (Valdadige) $12. 87 *—M.L. (2/1/2006)*

Montresor 2002 La Colombaia Pinot Grigio (Valdadige) $13. 87 *—M.S. (11/15/2003)*

Montresor 1997 Capitel della Crosara Red Blend (Amarone della Valpolicella Classico) $55. 90 *(5/1/2003)*

Montresor 1998 Recioto re Tiodorico Red Blend (Amarone della Valpolicella) $33. 89 *(5/1/2003)*

Montresor 1999 Valpolicalla Capitel della Crosara Red Blend (Veneto) $13. 83 *(5/1/2003)*

MORELLONE

Morellone 1999 Le Caniette Red Blend (Rosso Piceno) $23. 83 *—M.S. (12/15/2003)*

MORGANTE

Morgante 2004 Nero d'Avola (Sicilia) $18. 87 Best Buy *—M.L. (9/1/2005)*

Morgante 2002 Nero d'Avola (Sicilia) $15. 84 *—R.V. (10/1/2003)*

Morgante 1999 Nero d'Avola (Sicilia) $12. 88 Best Buy *—C.S. (5/1/2002)*

Morgante 2003 Don Antonio Nero d'Avola (Sicilia) $30. 87 *—M.L. (9/1/2005)*

Morgante 2003 Don Antonio Nero d'Avola (Sicilia) $28. 91 Editors' Choice *—M.L. (7/1/2006)*

Morgante 2001 Don Antonio Nero d'Avola (Sicilia) $30. 88 *—R.V. (10/1/2003)*

Morgante 1999 Don Antonio Nero d'Avola (Sicilia) $30. 90 *—C.S. (5/1/2002)*

MOSSIO

Mossio 2000 Dolcetto (Dolcetto d'Alba) $19. 90 *—M.S. (12/15/2003)*

MOTTA

Motta 1999 Sangiovese (Morellino di Scansano) $15. 89 Best Buy *—M.M. (1/1/2004)*

Motta 1998 Morellino Di Scansano Sangiovese (Morellino di Scansano) $14. 86 *(9/1/2000)*

MURI-GRIES

Muri-Gries 2004 Pinot Grigio (Alto Adige) $19. 87 *—M.L. (6/1/2006)*

MUSELLA

Musella 2003 Corvina, Rondinella, Molinara (Amarone della Valpolicella) $37. Members of the Pasqua family bought this historic property (with an adorable bed & breakfast) and founded a new wine estate in 1995. Since then, Musella has emerged as one of the best Amarone producers outside the Classico zone. This wine delivers incredible intensity and purity of aromas: Distinct notes of coffee, cherry and roasted nut comprise a compact and clean presentation. It's chewy and sweet with a velvety, soft texture in the mouth. 93 Editors' Choice *—M.L. (10/1/2007)*

Musella 1999 Corvina, Rondinella, Molinara (Amarone della Valpolicella) $32. 93 Editors' Choice *(11/1/2005)*

Musella 1997 Red Blend (Amarone della Valpolicella) $45. 87 *(11/1/2005)*

MUSSO

Musso 1999 Bricco Rio Sordo Nebbiolo (Barbaresco) $38. 92 *(4/2/2004)*

Musso 1999 Pora Nebbiolo (Barbaresco) $38. 90 *(4/2/2004)*

MUSTILLI

Mustilli 2003 Briccone Aglianico (Sannio) $40. A small portion of Merlot (15%) is blended into this Aglianico-based wine to achieve plush concentration and inviting aromas of forest berry, cookie dough, peppermint, Porcini mushroom, spice and loads of licorice. It's a very solid and tannic wine that would pair well with hearty meat or game dishes: Oak-aged for 12 months. 91 *—M.L. (8/1/2007)*

Mustilli 2003 Cesco di Nece Aglianico (Sant' Agata dei Goti) $23. This Aglianico imparts bright berry fruit, candied cherry, blueberry, licorice, white mushroom and a hearty dose of licorice. Dark, mysterious and dense, it has a solid structure and good length and would pair well with stewed rabbit or roasted lamb. 88 *—M.L. (8/1/2007)*

Mustilli 2005 Falanghina (Campania) $16. A very enticing ensemble, here is a fruity-floral white with fresh tones of yellow rose, acacia, melon, pear and Golden Delicious apple. It is lean and crisp in the mouth with lingering mineral tones over a lengthy finish. 88 *—M.L. (4/1/2007)*

MUZIC

Muzic 2001 Moresco Pinot Grigio (Collio) $NA. 81 *—J.C. (1/1/2004)*

NANDO

Nando 2000 Corvina (Amarone della Valpolicella Classico) $42. 92 Editors' Choice *(11/1/2005)*

Nando NV Moscato (Asti) $9. 80 *—M.S. (1/1/2004)*

Nando NV Moscato (Asti) $9. 84 *—M.S. (12/15/2004)*

Nando 1998 Nebbiolo (Barolo) $41. 85 *(4/2/2004)*

Nando 2004 Pinot Grigio (Isonzo del Friuli) $11. 85 *(2/1/2006)*

Nando 2001 Pinot Grigio (Isonzo del Friuli) $10. 83 *—J.C. (7/1/2003)*

Nando 1997 Red Blend (Amarone della Valpolicella Classico) $36. 86 *(5/1/2003)*

Nando 2002 Sangiovese (Chianti Classico) $12. 86 *(4/1/2005)*

Nando 2001 Sangiovese (Chianti Classico) $11. 84 *(4/1/2005)*

Nando 2000 Sangiovese (Chianti Classico) $11. 89 Best Buy *—M.S. (11/15/2003)*

Nando 1998 Sangiovese (Chianti Classico) $11. 83 *(4/1/2001)*

NATURA IBLEA

Natura Iblea 2004 Archimede Nero d'Avola (Sicilia) $35. 87 *—M.L. (7/1/2006)*

Natura Iblea 2004 Don Pasquale Nero d'Avola (Sicilia) $23. 84 *—M.L. (7/1/2006)*

Natura Iblea 2004 Don Paolo Red Blend (Sicilia) $25. 87 *—M.L. (7/1/2006)*

Natura Iblea 2005 Impronta White Blend (Sicilia) $20. 86 *—M.L. (7/1/2006)*

NEIRANO

Neirano 2003 Barbera (Barbera d'Asti) $9. Even a low-acid vintage such as 2003 should not be this mature. Despite its premature aging, the Neirano is a pretty, seamless wine that should be consumed fairly quickly. Strawberry compote, earth and spice give the wine an interesting complexity. Drink now. 87 *—M.G. (4/1/2007)*

Neirano 2000 Barbera (Barbera d'Asti) $10. 85 *—M.S. (12/15/2003)*

Neirano 1998 Le Croci Superiore Barbera (Barbera d'Asti) $24. 91 *—M.M. (11/15/2002)*

Neirano NV Spumante Dolce Brachetto (Brachetto d'Acqui) $12. 82 *—J.C. (1/1/2004)*

Neirano 2003 Dolcetto (Dolcetto d'Alba) $10. Despite the deep crimson color, the nose is surprisingly delicate; showing strawberries and red cherry. Pleasant, easy drinking and well balanced, but not particularly concentrated, this is a wine that will work easily with a wide variety of food without drawing much attention to itself. 85 *—M.G. (12/31/2007)*

Neirano 2002 Dolcetto (Dolcetto d'Alba) $10. 85 *—M.S. (12/15/2003)*

Neirano 2004 Pitulè Moscato (Moscato d'Asti) $11. 83 *—M.L. (11/15/2006)*

Neirano 2001 Nebbiolo (Barolo) $28. The delicious Neirano is near maturity and ready to drink. It is showing plenty of plummy, dried fruit, spices, herb and smoked meat. It is a pleasant wine, but with a little more concentration could be an outstanding one. 87 *—M.G. (4/1/2007)*

Neirano 1997 Nebbiolo (Barolo) $32. 89 *—C.S. (11/15/2002)*

Neirano 1995 Nebbiolo (Barolo) $18. 86 *(9/1/2000)*

NICOLIS

Nicolis 2003 Corvina, Rondinella, Molinara (Amarone della Valpolicella Classico) $60. This base Amarone comes from a company in rapid expansion thanks to smart investments in the vineyard (100 acres) and winery. The nose is characterized by poached cherries, brown sugar and deep minerals that recall crushed vitamins. The length is good and so is the quality of its finish. 89 *—M.L. (10/1/2007)*

Nicolis 2000 Red Blend (Amarone della Valpolicella Classico) $52. 91 *(11/1/2005)*

Nicolis 1998 Red Blend (Amarone della Valpolicella Classico) $50. 87 *(5/1/2003)*

Nicolis 2000 Ambrosan Red Blend (Amarone della Valpolicella Classico) $75. 93 *(11/1/2005)*

Nicolis 1998 Ambrosian Red Blend (Amarone della Valpolicella) $75. 90 *(5/1/2003)*

Nicolis 2001 Classico Red Blend (Valpolicella Classico) $11. 80 *(5/1/2003)*

Nicolis 2000 Seccal Red Blend (Valpolicella Classico Superiore) $20. 84 *(5/1/2003)*

Nicolis 2000 Testal Red Blend (Veronese) $28. 86 *(5/1/2003)*

NINO FRANCO

Nino Franco NV Brut Champagne Blend (Prosecco di Valdobbiadene) $14. 83 *—D.T. (12/31/2001)*

Nino Franco 2000 Primo Franco Champagne Blend (Prosecco di Valdobbiadene) $16. 84 *—M.M. (12/31/2001)*

Nino Franco 2000 Rive di San Floriano Champagne Blend (Prosecco di Valdobbiadene) $15. 83 *—D.T. (12/31/2001)*

Nino Franco NV Rustico Champagne Blend (Prosecco di Valdobbiadene) $12. 84 *—M.M. (12/31/2001)*

Nino Franco NV Rustico Champagne Blend (Prosecco di Valdobbiadene) $12. 87 *—M.S. (12/31/2002)*

Nino Franco 2002 Primo Franco Prosecco (Prosecco di Valdobbiadene) $17. 86 *—J.C. (12/31/2003)*

Nino Franco 2001 Rive di San Floriano Brut Prosecco (Prosecco di Valdobbiadene) $17. 84 *—J.C. (12/31/2003)*

Nino Franco NV Rustico Prosecco (Prosecco di Valdobbiadene) $10. 83 *—M.S. (11/15/2003)*

NINO NEGRI

Nino Negri 1995 Inferno Nebbiolo (Valtellina Superiore) $16. 88 *—R.V. (5/1/1999)*

Nino Negri 1996 Mazer Inferno Nebbiolo (Valtellina Superiore) $16. 88 *(7/1/2000)*

NOCIANO

Nociano 1998 Red Blend (Umbria) $9. 90 *—M.S. (2/1/2003)*

NOTTOLA

Nottola 1996 Vigna del Fattore Sangiovese (Vino Nobile di Montepulciano) $24. 84 *(7/1/2000)*

NOVAIA

Novaia 2003 Corte Vaona Corvina, Rondinella, Molinara (Amarone della Valpolicella Classico) $42. Brothers Cesare and Giampaolo Vaona bring us a modern Amarone with a tonic, tight consistency and loads of exotic spice—from cardamom to cinnamon—backed by cherry cola, cassis and dried prune. Those intense spice flavors are what set this wine, aged 24 months in barrique, apart. 90 *—M.L. (10/1/2007)*

Novaia 2001 Le Balze Corvina, Rondinella, Molinara (Amarone della Valpolicella Classico) $60. This winery is taking quick steps forward and carving out its own identity for quality wines. This nicely aged vineyard designate boasts sweet cherry, marzipan, vanilla and loads of raspberry candy aromas. Instead of berry candy, the mouth is dominated by exotic spice, root beer and crushed pepper. Despite these distinctive characteristics, it remains a harmonious whole. 90 *—M.L. (12/1/2007)*

OCONE

Ocone 2000 Aglianico (Aglianico del Taburno) $12. 86 *—M.S. (11/15/2004)*

Ocone 2003 Greco (Taburno) $11. 85 *—M.S. (11/15/2004)*

Ocone 2003 Piedirosso (Taburno) $12. 87 Best Buy *—M.S. (2/1/2005)*

ODOARDI

Odoardi 1998 Garrone Red Blend (Calabria) $30. 82 *—C.S. (5/1/2002)*

OGNISSOLE

Ognissole 2005 Primitivo (Primitivo Di Manduria) $18. This is a simpatico wine with perky notes of candied cherry, sweet spice, spring flowers, cocoa and vanilla. In fact, it smells a lot like chocolate cake. In the mouth it is smooth and velvety with a medium-long finish. 87 *—M.L. (8/1/2007)*

Ognissole 2003 Primitivo (Primitivo Di Manduria) $22. 83 *—M.L. (9/1/2005)*

ORIEL

Oriel 2003 Palio Montepulciano (Montepulciano d'Abruzzo) $15. 83 *—M.S. (10/1/2006)*

ORIGIN

Origin 2002 Collection Series Montepulciano (Montepulciano d'Abruzzo) $22. 86 *—M.S. (10/1/2006)*

Origin 2003 Pinot Grigio (Delle Venezie) $9. 82 *—M.L. (2/1/2006)*

Origin 2002 Pinot Grigio (Delle Venezie) $NA. 81 *—M.L. (2/1/2006)*

Origin 2002 Riserva Sangiovese (Chianti) $20. 86 *—M.S. (10/1/2006)*

PALA

Pala 2004 Essentija Bovale (Isola dei Nuraghi) $45. Some occasions call for a simple, genuine wine and this Sardinian red made with the Bovale grape fits the bill just fine. Aromas include red fruit, berries, vanilla, cedar and toast. In the mouth, it imparts a succulent, creamy feel and good length. 85 *—M.L. (8/1/2007)*

Pala 2005 Triente Cannonau (Cannonau di Sardegna) $18. Thick in concentration and color, this ripe-and-ready wine delivers notes of sweet cherry cola, smoked ham, toast and red rose. It's big, jammy and chewy in the mouth with nice succulence and medium structure. 87 *—M.L. (8/1/2007)*

Pala 2005 Elima Monica (Monica di Sardegna) $NA. A nice, vibrant ruby color makes a good first impression as do the raspberry, blueberry and crushed peppercorn notes. This is not a wine of huge complexity, but it is the kind of simple and genuine wine you want with pasta, white meat and easy cuisine. **84** *—M.L. (5/1/2007)*

Pala 2003 S'arai Red Blend (Isola dei Nuraghi) $40. This is a beautifully crafted 40-30-30 blend of Cannonau, Carignano and Bovale with dark concentration and vibrant cherry fruit, bold espresso and background notes of toast, vanilla bean and cedar thanks to 12 months in barrique. All these aromas are contained within an elegant whole and the wine's quality is evident. Firm in structure: drink after 2008. **90** *—M.L. (8/1/2007)*

Pala 2006 Crabilis Vermentino (Vermentino di Sardegna) $14. A pristine Sardinian white, Crabilis is loaded with abundant notes of dried herb, stone fruit, chopped mint and honeysuckle. Its herbal-Mediterranean characteristics make it really unique. Lean and clean in the mouth, it ends on a sharp, crisp note. **86** *—M.L. (11/15/2007)*

Pala 2005 Crabilis Vermentino (Vermentino di Sardegna) $14. The nose is almost neutral save for subtle notes of white stone, honey and pear. But on the palate, the wine proves itself, thanks to its smooth and silky consistency. **85** *—M.L. (4/1/2007)*

Pala 2005 Stellato Vermentino (Vermentino di Sardegna) $25. Hats off to this wine's beautiful clear-bottle packaging that reinforces its crystalline brilliance and polished angles. Accents of white flower, honeycomb and melon make this late-harvest wine (that ages on its lees for three months) immediately attractive. It's creamy and fruit-driven in the mouth with a great finish. **88** *—M.L. (4/1/2007)*

Pala 2005 Assoluto White Blend (Isola dei Nuraghi) $43. This is a lovely dessert wine that should be served very chilled. Its aromas are intense and inviting and recall almond, plush peach, apricot and honey. Smooth and creamy in the mouth, the wine delivers extra richness and a luscious mouthfeel (grapes are left to dry on the vine). **89** *—M.L. (4/1/2007)*

Pala 2005 Entemari White Blend (Isola dei Nuraghi) $NA. Added structure, thanks to a blend of Vermentino, Malvasia and Chardonnay and power due to higher alcohol, create a robust Sardinian white that would pair beautifully with elaborate seafood (think lobster). The fruit is there but is not overstated and comes on the heels of pristine mineral tones. **88** *—M.L. (4/1/2007)*

Pala 2005 Sàlnico White Blend (Nuragus di Cagliari) $NA. The sun-drenched island of Sardinia is gaining an excellent reputation for extremely food-friendly white wines. With stone fruit, honey and floral tones, this is a perfect example; pairs well with seafood. **85** *—M.L. (4/1/2007)*

Pala 2005 Silenzi White Blend (Isola dei Nuraghi) $NA. There's nothing not to like about this 50-50 Vermentino-Nuragus blend: Honey, pear, exotic fruit, yellow flower and pine nut appear with confidence on the nose and the wine's consistency in the mouth is creamy, cool and refreshing. Drink with shellfish or light pasta dishes. **87** *—M.L. (4/1/2007)*

PALADIN

Paladin 2004 Pinot Grigio (Delle Venezie) $14. 86 *—M.L. (2/1/2006)*

PALARI

Palari 1998 Faro Red Blend (Sicilia) $45. 93 Cellar Selection *—C.S. (5/1/2002)*

Palari 1998 Rosso Del Soprano Red Blend (Sicilia) $31. 91 *—C.S. (5/1/2002)*

PALAZZETTI

Palazzetti 1995 Brunello (Brunello di Montalcino) $56. 82 *—M.S. (11/15/2003)*

Palazzetti 1998 Sangiovese (Rosso di Montalcino) $23. 88 *—M.S. (11/15/2003)*

PALAZZI

Palazzi 2004 Pinot Grigio (Veneto) $9. 86 Best Buy *—M.L. (2/1/2006)*

PALAZZINA

Palazzina 1993 Le Macioche Brunello (Brunello di Montalcino) $41. 88 *—J.C. (3/1/2000)*

PALAZZO

Palazzo 2001 Brunello (Brunello di Montalcino) $74. 92 *(4/1/2006)*

Palazzo 2000 Brunello (Brunello di Montalcino) $69. 84 *—M.S. (7/1/2005)*

PALAZZO ROSSO

Palazzo Rosso 1999 Brunello (Brunello di Montalcino) $36. 95 *—M.S. (6/1/2004)*

PALLADINO

Palladino 2006 Cortese (Gavi di Gavi) $18. At first the Palladino showed some sour apple notes, but with air became a little more friendly, with low intensity summer fruit. The wine seemed to peter out and finish short. **80** *—M.G. (12/31/2007)*

Palladino 2003 Serralunga Nebbiolo (Barolo) $44. A beautiful, complex wine, it begins with dense aromas of dark jammy fruit, anise, wax polish and leather. The palate is well balanced and the flavors are intense and have evolved well. The finish is medium long. **92** *—M.G. (12/31/2007)*

PALLADIO

Palladio 2003 Sangiovese (Chianti) $10. 84 *(4/1/2005)*

PALMADINA

Palmadina 2004 Pinot Grigio (Friuli Isonzo) $12. 85 *—M.L. (6/1/2006)*

PANZANELLO

Panzanello 2001 Sangiovese (Chianti Classico) $27. 89 *(4/1/2005)*

Panzanello 2000 Riserva Sangiovese (Chianti Classico) $35. 90 *(4/1/2005)*

PAOLO BEA

Paolo Bea 2000 Sagrantino (Sagrantino di Montefalco) $NA. 86 *—M.L. (9/1/2005)*

PAOLO RODARO

Paolo Rodaro 2004 Pinot Grigio (Colli Orientali del Friuli) $26. 84 *—M.L. (6/1/2006)*

PAOLO SCAVINO

Paolo Scavino 1998 Dolcetto (Dolcetto di Diano d'Alba) $20. 91 *(4/1/2000)*

Paolo Scavino 1999 Nebbiolo (Barolo) $60. 90 *(4/2/2004)*

Paolo Scavino 1999 Bric dël Fiasc Nebbiolo (Barolo) $85. 91 *(4/2/2004)*

PAOLO TOSCANO

Paolo Toscano 2000 Red Blend (Chianti) $8. 80 *—M.S. (12/31/2002)*

PARUSSO

Parusso 1998 Piani Noce Dolcetto (Dolcetto d'Alba) $15. 90 *(4/1/2000)*

Parusso 1999 Bussia Vigna Fiurin Nebbiolo (Barolo) $70. 94 Editors' Choice *(4/2/2004)*

Parusso 2001 Bricco Rovella Sauvignon Blanc (Langhe) $36. 85 *(7/1/2005)*

PASQUA

Pasqua 2003 Villa Borghetti Corvina, Rondinella, Molinara (Amarone della Valpolicella Classico) $29. Chewy and chunky, with more emphasis on power and concentration than elegance. Nonetheless, it imparts seductive aromas of coffee, cedar, cherry, smoked bacon, plum, herbs and sweet oak. **88** *—M.L. (10/1/2007)*

Pasqua 1998 Vigneti del Sole Pinot Grigio (Pavia) $8. 82 *(8/1/1999)*

Pasqua 1999 Sagramoso Red Blend (Valpolicella Classico Superiore) 86 *(5/1/2003)*

Pasqua 1998 Sagramoso Red Blend (Amarone della Valpolicella) $30. 91 *(5/1/2003)*

Pasqua 2002 Vigneti Del Sole Red Blend (Montepulciano d'Abruzzo) $7. 85 *—M.S. (11/15/2003)*

PATERNOSTER

Paternoster 1997 Aglianico (Aglianico del Vulture) $20. 86 *—C.S. (5/1/2002)*

Paternoster 2000 Don Anselmo Aglianico (Aglianico del Vulture) $47. 92 Cellar Selection *—M.L. (9/1/2005)*

PATRIARCA DI PICCINI

Patriarca di Piccini 1998 Rosso Sangiovese (Toscana) $16. 88 *(11/15/2001)*

PATRIGLIONE

Patriglione 1994 Red Blend (Salento) $NA. 83 *—D.T. (5/1/2002)*

PECCHENINO

Pecchenino 1996 Bricco Botti Dolcetto di Dogliani Superiore Dolcetto (Dolcetto di Dogliani) $27. 89 *(4/1/2000)*

Pecchenino 2005 San Luigi Dolcetto (Dolcetto di Dogliani) $18. The Pecchenino begins with promising dark berry fruit aromas, mixed with black pepper. Rich and fruit forward, with soft tannins, and good structure. There is, however, a slight volatility to the wine which is more pronounced on the palate. The fruit still dominates, but the wine fades to a short finish. **83** *—M.G. (12/31/2007)*

Pecchenino 2002 San Luigi Dolcetto (Dolcetto di Dogliani) $18. 90 Editors' Choice *—J.C. (11/15/2004)*

Pecchenino 2005 Sirì d'Jermu Dolcetto (Dolcetto di Dogliani) $29. Some wines have a personality that makes you want to smile. This is one of them. A big, rich, friendly wine full of fruit that's approachable and easy to drink. It is not particularly serious, nor should it be put down for long aging. But drink it now with a burger or roast chicken and it will give pleasure. 85 *—M.G. (12/31/2007)*

Pecchenino 2003 Siri D'Jermu Dolcetto (Dolcetto d'Alba) $29. 90 *—J.C. (3/1/2006)*

PERE ALESSANDRO

Pere Alessandro 1999 Barbera (Barbera d'Alba) $16. 82 *—M.S. (12/15/2003)*

Pere Alessandro 2001 Barbera (Barbera d'Alba) $15. 82 *—J.C. (11/15/2004)*

Pere Alessandro 2001 Moscato (Moscato d'Asti) $16. 87 *—M.S. (12/15/2003)*

Pere Alessandro 1998 Nebbiolo (Barolo) $49. 86 *(4/2/2004)*

Pere Alessandro 1997 Nebbiolo (Barolo) $44. 90 *—M.S. (12/15/2003)*

Pere Alessandro 2000 Vigna Giaia Nebbiolo (Barbaresco) $55. 89 *(4/2/2004)*

PERLAGE

Perlage NV Canah Brut Prosecco (Prosecco di Valdobbiadene) $14. Here's an organic Prosecco with a wide variety of adjectives that can be attributed to its aromas: peach, lemon blossom, white peppercorn and talc powder. It boasts good personality and freshness on the close. 88 *—M.L. (12/15/2007)*

Perlage NV Canah Brut Prosecco (Prosecco di Valdobbiadene) $14. 88 *—M.L. (6/1/2006)*

Perlage NV Col di Manza Prosecco (Prosecco di Valdobbiadene) $16. Here's an intriguing wine with many interesting contrasts: It offers mineral dryness on the nose and sweet fruit in the mouth; and a lean tonic feel against opulent texture. This organic sparkler has a fine, chiseled quality and a pretty ensemble of flavors. 88 *—M.L. (12/15/2007)*

Perlage 2005 Col di Manza Extra Dry Prosecco (Prosecco di Valdobbiadene) $12. 87 *—M.L. (6/1/2006)*

Perlage NV Quorum Extra Dry Prosecco (Prosecco di Conegliano e Valdobbiadene) $18. This organic Prosecco is very focused on soapy, floral aromas that recall lavender honey, honeysuckle and ripe melon. But it also has pretty opulence, or roundness, despite its spicy acidity. 87 *—M.L. (12/15/2007)*

Perlage 2006 Riva Moretta Frizzante Prosecco (Prosecco di Valdobbiadene) $12. Here's an organic Frizzante with good dimension and clear notes of citrus, orange blossom and almond skin. Lively bubbling achieves a creamy, silky feel in the mouth. 85 *—M.L. (12/15/2007)*

PERTICAIA

Perticaia 2001 Sagrantino (Sagrantino di Montefalco) $46. 87 *—M.L. (9/1/2005)*

PERTINACE

Pertinace 2006 Arneis (Roero Arneis) $16. The Pertinace evolves nicely in the glass; at first there are simple lime peel aromas, but over time, they become richer and slightly more complex. On the palate there is pear, as well as the lime and an interesting smoky quality. Crisp and with good balance, the finish is a little short. Imported by MW Imports. 85 *—M.G. (12/31/2007)*

Pertinace 2005 Barbera (Barbera d'Alba) $15. This is lighter Barbera showing a pleasant very ripe, plummy character. The wine has evolved early, and gives a seamless backdrop to the pretty flavors of spice and Christmas pudding. Easygoing and complex. Imported by MW Imports. 87 *—M.G. (12/31/2007)*

Pertinace 2006 Dolcetto (Dolcetto d'Alba) $15. The Pertinace offers a a soft, spicy nose of blackberry jam, vanilla and cinnamon. A pleasant, everyday, food-friendly wine that can be drunk now but has the structure to improve for a year or so. Imported by MW Imports. 85 *—M.G. (12/31/2007)*

Pertinace 2004 Dolcetto (Dolcetto d'Alba) $14. 84 *—J.C. (3/1/2006)*

Pertinace 2001 Nebbiolo (Barbaresco) $32. 87 *—J.C. (3/1/2006)*

Pertinace 2001 Nebbiolo (Barolo) $32. 89 *—J.C. (3/1/2006)*

Pertinace 2001 Vigneto Marcarini Nebbiolo (Barbaresco) $45. 91 *—J.C. (3/1/2006)*

PETER ZEMMER

Peter Zemmer 2005 Merlot (Alto Adige) $12. Unmistakably fruity on the nose, this mellow and fresh Merlot is full of red berry fruit, blueberry, cassis and red rock candy. It's a clean and compact package with beautiful brilliance to its ruby color and a sour note on the mid-palate. From a territory that the producer describes as "both Alpine and Mediterranean." 87 Best Buy *—M.L. (3/1/2007)*

Peter Zemmer 2004 Pinot Grigio (Alto Adige) $14. 86 *—M.L. (2/1/2006)*

Peter Zemmer 1998 Pinot Grigio (Alto Adige) $11. 88 *(8/1/1999)*

Peter Zemmer 2004 La Lot Pinot Grigio (Vigneti delle Dolomiti) $11. 87 Best Buy *—M.L. (2/1/2006)*

Peter Zemmer 2006 Riesling (Alto Adige) $18. Lemon soda, dry minerals, sage and stone fruit characterize the nose and although all the elements are correct and in place, the wine never seems to reach its full potential. This is a good, dry Riesling, but you do get the impression that there could be more to it. 86 *—M.L. (9/1/2007)*

PETRA

Petra 1999 Riserva Cabernet Sauvignon-Merlot (Toscana) $50. 92 *—M.S. (11/15/2003)*

Petra 1998 Riserva Cabernet Sauvignon-Merlot (Toscana) $50. 95 *—M.S. (8/1/2002)*

Petra 2000 Val di Cornia Suvereto Sangiovese (Toscana) $29. 84 *—M.S. (11/15/2003)*

PETROLO

Petrolo 2003 Galatrona Red Blend (Toscana) $84. 90 *—M.S. (9/1/2006)*

Petrolo 1999 Terre di Galatrona Sangiovese (Toscana) $16. 87 *—M.S. (12/31/2002)*

Petrolo 2003 Torrione Sangiovese (Toscana) $36. 88 *—M.S. (9/1/2006)*

Petrolo 2001 Torrione Sangiovese (Toscana) $47. 90 *—M.S. (9/1/2006)*

Petrolo 2000 Torrione Sangiovese (Toscana) $47. 80 *—M.S. (10/1/2004)*

PETRUSSA

Petrussa 2003 Sauvignon (Colli Orientali del Friuli) $27. 88 *(7/1/2005)*

Petrussa 2005 Tocai Friulano (Colli Orientali del Friuli) $19. This starts off a little funky and sweaty-smelling, but that blows off with some time to reveal a tropical, fruit-laden wine that's round in the mouth yet finishes with a refreshing burst of nectarine, mango and white pepper. Drink now–2010. 87 *(10/1/2007)*

PIANCORNELLO

PianCornello 2001 Brunello (Brunello di Montalcino) $50. 92 Editors' Choice *(4/1/2006)*

PIANTATE

Piantate Lunghe 2005 Red Blend (Rosso Conero) $NA. The nose is greeted with vibrant cherry fruit, blueberry, fresh plum, ash and tobacco setting the tone for what proves to be a refreshing and tasty red from central Italy. A food-friendly nature is reinforced by soft tannins and firm structure. 87 *—M.L. (12/1/2007)*

PIAZZANO

Piazzano 1997 Rio Camerata Riserva Sangiovese (Chianti) $12. 89 Best Buy *(4/1/2001)*

PIAZZO ARMANDO

Piazzo Armando 2005 Moscato (Moscato d'Asti) $17. 85 *—M.L. (12/15/2006)*

Piazzo Armando 2004 Moscato (Moscato d'Asti) $15. 89 *—M.L. (12/15/2005)*

PICCIAU

Picciau 1998 Vermentino (Vermentino di Sardegna) $13. 84 *—D.T. (9/1/2001)*

PICCINI

Piccini 2004 Sangiovese (Chianti) $8. 87 Best Buy *—M.L. (11/15/2005)*

Piccini 2003 Sangiovese (Chianti) $8. 86 Best Buy *(4/1/2005)*

Piccini 2002 Sangiovese (Vernaccia di San Gimignano) $10. 85 *(7/1/2003)*

Piccini 2001 Sangiovese (Chianti Superiore) $10. 84 *(7/1/2003)*

Piccini 2001 Sangiovese (Chianti) $10. 83 *(7/1/2003)*

Piccini 2000 Sangiovese (Chianti Superiore) $10. 86 *(11/15/2001)*

Piccini 2000 Sangiovese (Chianti) $8. 85 Best Buy *(11/15/2001)*

Piccini 1999 Sangiovese (Chianti) $6. 82 *(4/1/2001)*

Piccini 1998 Sangiovese (Chianti Classico) $11. 84 *(4/1/2001)*

Piccini 1999 Patriale Sangiovese (Toscana) $10. 86 Best Buy *(7/1/2003)*

Piccini 2000 Riserva Sangiovese (Chianti) $10. 85 *(7/1/2003)*

Piccini 1998 Riserva Sangiovese (Chianti Classico) $16. 84 *—R.V. (8/1/2002)*

Piccini 1997 Riserva Sangiovese (Chianti Classico) $13. 83 *(4/1/2001)*

Piccini 2003 Selezione Oro Riserva Sangiovese (Chianti) $17. Forest floor, bramble, red earth, plum, black fruit, mineral, leather, tobacco and cherry preserves: This Chianti Riserva delivers the whole gamut of aromatic possibilities. The intensity and purity of these aromas is good and the wine has tight, plush feel in the mouth. 88 *—M.L. (11/1/2007)*

Piccini 2005 Solco Sangiovese (Chianti Classico) $10. There's a lot of action in the glass in the form of contrasting aromas and flavors: Chocolate, caramel, carob pod, balsamic sauce and Porcini mushroom offset cherry and berry candy. Some notes are slightly off key but the wine delivers good consistency and persistency on the palate. 85 Best Buy *—M.L. (11/1/2007)*

PIERO BUSSO

Piero Busso 2003 Majano Barbera (Barbera d'Alba) $30. 85 *—J.C. (3/1/2006)*

Piero Busso 1996 Vigna Majano Barbera (Barbera d'Alba) $20. 90 *(4/1/2000)*

Piero Busso 1997 Vigna Majano Dolcetto (Dolcetto d'Alba) $19. 84 *(4/1/2000)*

Piero Busso 1999 Gallina Nebbiolo (Barbaresco) $174. 92 *(4/2/2004)*

Piero Busso 1999 Vigna Borgese Nebbiolo (Barbaresco) $57. 87 *(4/2/2004)*

PIEROPAN

Pieropan 2004 Garganega (Soave Classico) $18. 86 *—M.L. (9/1/2005)*

Pieropan 2003 La Rocca Garganega (Soave) $43. 88 *—M.L. (9/1/2005)*

Pieropan 1997 Soave Classico Superiore Garganega (Soave) $13. 84 *(11/1/1999)*

Pieropan 1997 Soave Classico Superiore Garganega (Soave) $17. 88 *(11/1/1999)*

Pieropan 2001 White Blend (Soave Classico Superiore) $14. 90 Best Buy *—J.C. (7/1/2003)*

Pieropan 2003 Calvarino White Blend (Soave) $30. 87 *—M.L. (9/1/2005)*

Pieropan 2001 Calvarino White Blend (Soave Classico Superiore) $20. 91 Editors' Choice *—J.C. (7/1/2003)*

Pieropan 2000 La Rocca White Blend (Soave Classico Superiore) $30. 89 *—J.C. (7/1/2003)*

Pieropan 1998 La Rocca Soave Classico Superiore White Blend (Soave) $25. 91 *—M.N. (9/1/2001)*

Pieropan 1999 Soave Classico Superiore White Blend (Soave) $15. 88 *—M.N. (12/31/2000)*

PIERPAOLO PECORARI

Pierpaolo Pecorari 1997 Pinot Grigio (Venezia Giulia) $17. 83 *(8/1/1999)*

Pierpaolo Pecorari 2004 Pinot Grigio (Venezia Giulia) $10.85 Best Buy *—M.L. (2/1/2006)*

Pierpaolo Pecorari 2004 Olivers Pinot Grigio (Venezia Giulia) $20. 87 *—M.L. (6/1/2006)*

Pierpaolo Pecorari 2000 Isonzio Sauvignon Blanc (Friuli Venezia Giulia) $15. 82 *(8/1/2002)*

PIETRACOLATA

Pietracolata 2003 White Blend (Orvieto Classico) $8. 84 Best Buy *—M.S. (11/15/2004)*

Pietracolata 2002 White Blend (Orvieto) $8. 84 *—M.S. (10/1/2004)*

Pietracolata 2004 Secco White Blend (Orvieto Classico) $10. 82 *—M.S. (10/1/2006)*

PIETRAFITTA

Pietrafitta 2000 La Sughera Rosso Red Blend (San Gimignano) $25. 83 *—M.S. (9/1/2006)*

Pietrafitta 2003 Sangiovese (Chianti Colli Senesi) $12. 85 *(4/1/2005)*

Pietrafitta 2001 Sangiovese (Chianti Colli Senesi) $11. 85 *—M.S. (10/1/2004)*

Pietrafitta 2000 Sangiovese (Chianti Colli Senesi) $11. 85 Best Buy *—M.S. (12/31/2002)*

Pietrafitta 1998 Sangiovese (Chianti Colli Senesi) $10. 88 Best Buy *(4/1/2001)*

Pietrafitta 1999 La Sughera Sangiovese (San Gimignano) $18. 86 *—M.S. (12/31/2002)*

Pietrafitta 1998 La Sughera Rosso Sangiovese (San Gimignano) $18. 89 *(4/1/2001)*

Pietrafitta 2004 Vernaccia (Vernaccia di San Gimignano) $13. 85 *—M.S. (10/1/2006)*

Pietrafitta 2002 Vernaccia (Vernaccia di San Gimignano) $12. 86 *—M.S. (8/1/2004)*

Pietrafitta 2002 Borghetto Vernaccia (Vernaccia di San Gimignano) $16. 87 *—M.S. (8/1/2004)*

Pietrafitta 1999 Borghetto White Blend (Vernaccia di San Gimignano) $15. 88 *(4/1/2001)*

Pietrafitta 1992 Vin Santo White Blend (Colli della Toscana Centrale) $16. 90 Editors' Choice *(4/1/2001)*

PIETRASERENA

Pietraserena 2003 Sangiovese (Chianti Colli Senesi) $11. 85 *(4/1/2005)*

PIETRATORCIA

Pietratorcia 1998 Riserva Red Blend (Ischia) $36. 87 *—C.S. (5/1/2002)*

PIETRO BARBERO

Pietro Barbero 1996 Bricco Verlenga Barbera D'Asti Superiore Barbera (Barbera d'Asti) $20. 86 *(4/1/2000)*

Pietro Barbero 1996 La Vignassa Barbera D'Asti Superiore Barbera (Barbera d'Asti) $35. 90 *(4/1/2000)*

PIETRO ZARDINI

Pietro Zardini 2001 Corvina, Rondinella, Molinara (Amarone della Valpolicella Classico) $57. An impressive ensemble from the newest generation of a winemaking family, this rich wine boasts great Amarone typicity and does so in a confident, determined manner. Almond, black cherry and ripe blueberry are backed by just enough acidity to appear taut and fresh. The wine conveys warmth and harmony over a long, dusty finish. 93 *—M.L. (12/1/2007)*

PIETROSO

Pietroso 2001 Brunello (Brunello di Montalcino) $NA. 89 *(4/1/2006)*

PIEVE DI SPALTENNA

Pieve di Spaltenna 2000 Sangiovese (Chianti Classico) $15. 83 *(4/1/2005)*

PIEVE SANTA RESTITUTA

Pieve Santa Restituta 1999 Rennina Brunello (Brunello di Montalcino) $95. 92 *(7/1/2005)*

Pieve Santa Restituta 2001 Rennina Sangiovese (Brunello di Montalcino) $125. Elegance, finesse and deeply layered nuances are this Brunello's strongest suits. The aromas are tightly etched: The mineral tones are exact and fine, the fruit is fleshly and cushioned by tones of moist tobacco and earth. The menthol notes are divine and penetrating: A beautiful, vineyard-designate wine from Angelo Gaja. 93 Cellar Selection *—M.L. (2/1/2007)*

Pieve Santa Restituta 2001 Sugarille Sangiovese (Brunello di Montalcino) $155. A gorgeous single-vineyard Brunello from Angelo Gaja's Tuscan estate, this wine is slightly more round and fleshy than Rennina but equally as complex and elegant. This is truly a great wine with velvet-like smoothness on the palate and intense black fruit and balsam aromas. It's pensive yet yielding, refined and powerful all at once. 93 Cellar Selection *—M.L. (2/1/2007)*

PIGHIN

Pighin 2006 Pinot Grigio (Friuli Grave) $16. Rich texture and concentration are layered with aromas of stone fruit, toasted nut and a distinctive herbal accent. This is a vibrant, golden wine with a round, silky essence and attractive crispness. 87 *—M.L. (12/1/2007)*

Pighin 2006 Pinot Grigio (Collio) $23. The color here is a deeper shade of gold and the fragrant aromas are characteristic of a well-made, concentrated Pinot Grigio: honey, peach and Golden Delicious apple ride over a creamy, supple mouthfeel. Fresh flavors include caramel and peach. 87 *—M.L. (12/1/2007)*

Pighin 2004 Pinot Grigio (Collio) $23. 85 *(2/1/2006)*

Pighin 2004 Pinot Grigio (Friuli Grave) $15. 84 *(2/1/2006)*

Pighin 1998 Pinot Grigio (Grave del Friuli) $13. 85 *(8/1/1999)*

Pighin 1997 Pinot Grigio (Collio) $13. 82 *(8/1/1999)*

Pighin 2006 Terre di Risano White Blend (Friuli Grave) $16. A mix of white grapes including Pinot Bianco, Tocai Friulano and Sauvignon, Terre di Risano is a crisp, clean wine that calls out for grilled salmon fillet. There are a ton of flavors here from peach to pear to dusty talc powder. 87 *—M.L. (12/1/2007)*

PININO

Pinino 2001 Brunello (Brunello di Montalcino) $NA. 89 *(4/1/2006)*

PINOCCHIO

Pinocchio 2003 Nero d'Avola (Sicilia) $9. 88 Best Buy *—M.S. (7/1/2005)*

PINTAR

Pintar 1997 Single Vineyard Pinot Grigio (Collio) $20. 85 *(8/1/1999)*

PIO CESARE

Pio Cesare 2006 Arneis (Langhe) $19. The Pio Cesare has a pleasant nose of apple and pear with smoky nuances. On the palate, though, it proves less interesting. Extremely soft, lacking acidity and grip; pleasant, but drink soon. **82** *—M.G. (12/31/2007)*

Pio Cesare 1998 Arneis (Langhe) $23. 88 *—L.W. (11/15/1999)*

Pio Cesare 2004 Barbera (Barbera d'Alba) $21. The Pio Cesare basic Barbera is a lean wine, with aromas of tart cherries and road tar. On the palate, the fruit and aromatics have melded together quite nicely, but despite a decent finish, the acidity is a little high. **84** *—M.G. (12/31/2007)*

Pio Cesare 2001 Barbera (Barbera d'Alba) $26. 86 *—M.S. (12/15/2003)*

Pio Cesare 2004 Fides Barbera (Barbera d'Alba) $39. The Pio Cesare starts well; a fat opulent nose of rich fruit mixed with a strong mocha character. It is also big on the palate; plummy and powerful, with good acidity. Towards the end, however, the wine runs out of steam, and it finishes somewhat abruptly and with a slight sourness. **85** *—M.G. (12/31/2007)*

Pio Cesare 2003 Fides Barbera (Barbera d'Alba) $41. Pio Cesare's Fides is several steps up from its basic Barbera. It shows a pretty, complex nose of black cherry, fennel and bacon, while on the palate, there is plenty of rich fruit, layered by the aromatics. Good levels of concentration and a long, solid finish. **90** *—M.G. (12/31/2007)*

Pio Cesare 2000 Fides Barbera (Barbera d'Alba) $40. 90 *—M.S. (12/15/2003)*

Pio Cesare 1996 Fides Barbera (Barbera d'Alba) $38. 89 *(4/1/2000)*

Pio Cesare 1998 Chardonnay (Piedmont) $18. 88 *—M.S. (4/1/2000)*

Pio Cesare 1998 Chardonnay (Piedmont) $18. 84 *—L.W. (11/15/1999)*

Pio Cesare 2003 L'Altro Chardonnay (Piedmont) $24. 88 *—J.C. (3/1/2006)*

Pio Cesare 2002 L'Altro Chardonnay (Piedmont) $20. 82 *—M.S. (12/15/2003)*

Pio Cesare 1999 Piemonte Chardonnay (Piedmont) $19. 83 *—M.M. (9/1/2001)*

Pio Cesare 2003 Piodilei Chardonnay (Langhe) $49. 90 *—J.C. (3/1/2006)*

Pio Cesare 2001 Piodilei Chardonnay (Langhe) $40. 83 *—M.S. (12/15/2003)*

Pio Cesare 1997 Piodilei Chardonnay (Langhe) $39. 90 *—M.M. (9/1/2001)*

Pio Cesare 1998 Cortese (Cortese di Gavi) $20. 86 *(4/1/2000)*

Pio Cesare 2003 Cortese (Cortese di Gavi) $23. 87 *—J.C. (11/15/2004)*

Pio Cesare 2002 Cortese (Cortese di Gavi) $20. 83 *—M.S. (12/15/2003)*

Pio Cesare 2005 Dolcetto (Dolcetto d'Alba) $21. For a Dolcetto, the Pio Cesare is a strong, fairly extracted wine. The fruit is here, but the wine is marked more by its power than its friendliness. **84** *—M.G. (12/31/2007)*

Pio Cesare 2003 Dolcetto (Dolcetto d'Alba) $24. 88 *—J.C. (11/15/2004)*

Pio Cesare 2002 Dolcetto (Dolcetto d'Alba) $26. 86 *—M.S. (12/15/2003)*

Pio Cesare 1998 Dolcetto (Dolcetto d'Alba) $19. 85 *—L.W. (11/15/1999)*

Pio Cesare 2003 Moscato (Moscato d'Asti) $26. 85 *—J.C. (11/15/2004)*

Pio Cesare 2004 Nebbiolo (Nebbiolo d'Alba) $30. Pio Cesare's Langhe 2004 is more open and easier to taste than the 2003. The nose is big and plummy with a strong floral component, while on the palate, the fruit possesses an inner core of bright strawberry giving the wine a nice lift in the finish. **88** *—M.G. (12/31/2007)*

Pio Cesare 2003 Nebbiolo (Nebbiolo d'Alba) $30. A big, chunky wine that begins with pleasant aromas of dark, lush fruit and rose petals, it cannot sustain its promise on the palate. It starts well enough, but by midpalate, most of the fruit has gone, and the finish is short and a little dour. **84** *—M.G. (12/31/2007)*

Pio Cesare 2003 Nebbiolo (Barbaresco) $61. The 2003 Barbaresco is evolving well, if quickly. It shows mature flavors of smoky fruit, sweet plums, graphite and a touch of rubber. Soft on the palate, and delicious now, it should drink well for another five years. **87** *—M.G. (12/31/2007)*

Pio Cesare 2002 Nebbiolo (Barolo) $61. The Pio Cesare is dominated by the smell of diesel. Beyond that are a few shards of fruit, but overall this is a throwback for those who like the tarriness that characterized old-fashioned Barolos. **86** *—M.G. (12/31/2007)*

Pio Cesare 2001 Nebbiolo (Barbaresco) $35. 90 *—J.C. (3/1/2006)*

Pio Cesare 2000 Nebbiolo (Nebbiolo d'Alba) $23. 84 *—M.S. (12/15/2003)*

Pio Cesare 1999 Nebbiolo (Barolo) $79. 89 *(4/2/2004)*

Pio Cesare 1999 Nebbiolo (Barbaresco) $71. 89 *(4/2/2004)*

Pio Cesare 1998 Nebbiolo (Barbaresco) $60. 89 *—M.S. (11/15/2002)*

Pio Cesare 1998 Nebbiolo (Barolo) $58. 87 *—R.V. (11/15/2002)*

Pio Cesare 1997 Nebbiolo (Nebbiolo d'Alba) $23. 88 *—L.W. (11/15/1999)*

Pio Cesare 1997 Nebbiolo (Barbaresco) $60. 89 *(9/1/2001)*

Pio Cesare 1999 Il Bricco Nebbiolo (Barbaresco) $137. 91 *—J.C. (11/15/2004)*

Pio Cesare 1996 Il Bricco Nebbiolo (Barbaresco) $105. 91 Cellar Selection *(9/1/2001)*

Pio Cesare 2001 Ornato Nebbiolo (Barolo) $146. 90 *—J.C. (3/1/2006)*

Pio Cesare 1999 Ornato Nebbiolo (Barolo) $110. 91 *(4/2/2004)*

Pio Cesare 1998 Ornato Nebbiolo (Barolo) $135. 89 *(4/2/2004)*

Pio Cesare 1997 Ornato Nebbiolo (Barolo) $110. 90 *—R.V. (11/15/2002)*

Pio Cesare 1996 Ornato Nebbiolo (Barolo) $110. 90 *(9/1/2001)*

Pio Cesare 1995 Ornato Nebbiolo (Barolo) $100. 87 *(7/1/2000)*

PIOIERO

Pioiero 2006 Cascina Pioiero Arneis (Roero Arneis) $17. Begins beautifully with a hint of honey, white flowers and fruit. The palate shows good acidity and the finish is longer than the other Arneis tasted. The problem is that within five minutes, a slightly sour note could be detected, which although not particularly strong never really disappeared. Overall a very nice wine that could have been very special. **84** *—M.G. (12/31/2007)*

PLACIDO

Placido 2004 Pinot Grigio (Delle Venezie) $9. 86 Best Buy *M.L. (6/1/2006)*

Placido 1998 Pinot Grigio (Veneto) $8. 85 Best Buy *(8/1/1999)*

Placido 2003 Sangiovese (Chianti) $9. 87 Best Buy *(4/1/2005)*

Placido 1998 Sangiovese (Chianti) $8. 89 Best Buy *(4/1/2001)*

PLANETA

Planeta 2000 Burdese Cabernet Sauvignon (Sicilia) $38. 89 *—R.V. (10/1/2003)*

Planeta 2004 Chardonnay (Sicilia) $43. 90 *—M.L. (7/1/2006)*

Planeta 2001 Chardonnay (Sicilia) $16. 88 *—R.V. (10/1/2003)*

Planeta 2004 Cometa Fiano (Sicilia) $43. 90 *—M.L. (7/1/2006)*

Planeta 2003 Merlot (Sicilia) $43. 90 *—M.L. (7/1/2006)*

Planeta 2001 Merlot (Sicilia) $38. 90 *—R.V. (10/1/2003)*

Planeta 1999 Merlot (Sicilia) $39. 87 *—C.S. (5/1/2002)*

Planeta 2003 Santa Cecilia Nero d'Avola (Sicilia) $43. 92 Cellar Selection *—M.L. (7/1/2006)*

Planeta 2002 Santa Cecilia Nero d'Avola (Sicilia) $41. 86 *—M.S. (7/1/2005)*

Planeta 2004 Red Blend (Cerasuolo di Vittoria) $26. 87 *—M.L. (7/1/2006)*

Planeta 2003 Red Blend (Cerasuolo di Vittoria) $26. 89 *—M.S. (7/1/2005)*

Planeta 2002 Red Blend (Cerasuolo di Vittoria) $12. 87 *—R.V. (10/1/2003)*

Planeta 2003 Burdese Red Blend (Sicilia) $43. 91 *—M.L. (7/1/2006)*

Planeta 2005 La Segreta Red Blend (Sicilia) $16. 88 *—M.L. (7/1/2006)*

Planeta 2002 La Segreta Red Blend (Sicilia) $16. 88 Editors' Choice *—M.S. (10/1/2003)*

Planeta 2000 La Segreta Red Blend (Sicilia) $16. 88 Best Buy *—C.S. (5/1/2002)*

Planeta 2003 La Segreta Rosso Red Blend (Sicilia) $17. 87 *—M.S. (7/1/2005)*

Planeta 1999 Santa Cecilia Red Blend (Sicilia) $39. 90 *—C.S. (5/1/2002)*

Planeta 2003 Syrah (Sicilia) $43. 90 *—M.L. (7/1/2006)*

Planeta 2001 Syrah (Sicilia) $38. 88 *—R.V. (10/1/2003)*

Planeta 2005 La Segreta White Blend (Sicilia) $16. 87 *—M.L. (7/1/2006)*

Planeta 2002 La Segreta White Blend (Sicilia) $15. 86 *—R.V. (10/1/2003)*

Planeta 2003 La Segreta Bianco White Blend (Sicilia) $17. 84 *—M.S. (7/1/2005)*

Planeta 2004 Moscato di Noto White Blend (Sicilia) $46. 91 *—M.L. (7/1/2006)*

PLOZNER

Plozner 2003 Chardonnay (Friuli Grave) $14. 82 *—J.C. (12/31/2004)*

Plozner 1997 Pinot Grigio (Friuli Grave) $12. 84 *(8/1/1999)*

Plozner 2001 Pinot Grigio (Friuli Grave) $13. 85 *—J.C. (7/1/2003)*

Plozner 1999 Pinot Grigio (Friuli Grave) $10. 84 *—J.F. (9/1/2001)*

Plozner 2001 Tocai (Friuli Grave) $10. 86 Best Buy *—J.C. (7/1/2003)*

PODERE IL CAIO

Podere il Caio 2004 Grechetto (Umbria) $13. 83 *—M.S. (10/1/2006)*

PODERE IL PALAZZINO

Podere IL Palazzino 2002 Argenina Sangiovese (Chianti Classico) $20. 88 *(4/1/2005)*

PODERE LA CAPPELLA

Podere La Cappella 1997 Querciolo Riserva Sangiovese (Chianti Classico) $22. 84 *(4/1/2001)*

PODERE LA VIGNA

Podere La Vigna 2001 Brunello (Brunello di Montalcino) $NA. 90 Cellar Selection *(4/1/2006)*

PODERP POGGIO SCALETTE

Podere Poggio Scalette 2003 Il Carbonaione Sangiovese (Toscana) $60. Enologist Vittorio Fiore has crafted a very distinctive wine with a vibrant ruby color, nice concentration and full-force aromas of blueberry, chocolate and smoked bacon. But what won me over was an elegant and precise point of white mineral or chalk that appears on the nose. It ages for 44 months and is succulent and chewy with firm tannins. Drink after 2008. 92 Cellar Selection *—M.L. (5/1/2007)*

PODERE PROVINCIALE CANTINA LAIMBURG

Podere Provinciale Cantina Laimburg 2004 Pinot Grigio (Alto Adige) $18. 84 *—M.L. (6/1/2006)*

PODERE RUGGERI CORSINI

Podere Ruggeri Corsini 1999 Nebbiolo (Barolo) $45. 87 *(4/2/2004)*

Podere Ruggeri Corsini 1996 Corsini-Barolo Nebbiolo (Barolo) $45. 91 *(11/15/2002)*

PODERI ALASIA

Poderi Alasia 2003 Rive Barbera (Barbera d'Asti) $26. 87 *—J.C. (3/1/2006)*

Poderi Alasia 2000 Rive Barbera (Barbera d'Asti) $22. 91 Editors' Choice *—M.S. (12/15/2003)*

Poderi Alasia 2000 Luca Monaca Red Blend (Monferrato) $27. 90 *—M.S. (12/15/2003)*

Poderi Alasia 2003 Camillona Sauvignon Blanc (Monferrato) $28. 85 *(7/1/2005)*

PODERI ALDO CONTERNO

Poderi Aldo Conterno 2003 Printanie Chardonnay (Langhe) $35. 84 *—J.C. (3/1/2006)*

Poderi Aldo Conterno 1998 Nebbiolo (Barolo) $100. 89 *(4/2/2004)*

Poderi Aldo Conterno 1999 Cicala Nebbiolo (Barolo) $126. 93 *(4/2/2004)*

Poderi Aldo Conterno 1998 Cicala Nebbiolo (Barolo) $112. 95 Editors' Choice *—R.V. (11/15/2002)*

Poderi Aldo Conterno 1999 Colonello Nebbiolo (Barolo) $126. 91 *(4/2/2004)*

Poderi Aldo Conterno 1998 Colonnello Nebbiolo (Barolo) $116. 89 *(4/2/2004)*

Poderi Aldo Conterno 1999 Monforte Bussia Nebbiolo (Barolo) $100. 87 *(4/2/2004)*

Poderi Aldo Conterno 1998 Monforte Bussia Nebbiolo (Barolo) $86. 89 *—R.V. (11/15/2002)*

PODERI BRIZIO

Poderi Brizio 1998 Brunello (Brunello di Montalcino) $70. 91 *—M.S. (11/15/2003)*

Poderi Brizio 2000 Sangiovese (Colli della Toscana Centrale) $50. 87 *—M.S. (11/15/2003)*

PODERI COLLA

Poderi Colla 1997 Barbera (Barbera d'Alba) $18. 88 *(4/1/2000)*

Poderi Colla 2004 Costa Bruna Barbera (Barbera d'Alba) $23. A big wine that has plenty of oak, some blueberry fruit and spices. It is promising on the palate, if a little clumsy, but shows good structure and length. 86 *—M.G. (4/1/2007)*

Poderi Colla 2001 Costa Bruna Barbera (Barbera d'Alba) $20. 86 *—J.C. (11/15/2004)*

Poderi Colla 1996 Dolcetto (Dolcetto d'Alba) $17. 83 *(4/1/2000)*

Poderi Colla 2001 Bricco del Drago Dolcetto (Langhe) $35. 92 Editors' Choice *—J.C. (3/1/2006)*

Poderi Colla 2005 Pian Balbo Dolcetto (Dolcetto d'Alba) $16. The Colla offers a pleasant nose of bright fruit, but on the palate the wine is light and lacks complexity. Easy drinking, but with not enough structure to hold the wine together. Drink soon. 83 *—M.G. (12/31/2007)*

Poderi Colla 2003 Pian Balbo Dolcetto (Dolcetto d'Alba) $17. 86 *—J.C. (3/1/2006)*

Poderi Colla 2002 Pian Balbo Dolcetto (Dolcetto d'Alba) $17. 87 *—J.C. (11/15/2004)*

Poderi Colla 2004 Nebbiolo (Nebbiolo d'Alba) $26. The nose was interesting; earthy with plenty of plummy fruit and a touch of musk. On the palate, with the fruit more muted, the earthiness became more apparent, and what fruit remained thinned out even more as it reached the finish. 84 *—M.G. (12/31/2007)*

Poderi Colla 2002 Nebbiolo (Nebbiolo d'Alba) $24. 88 *—J.C. (3/1/2006)*

Poderi Colla 1999 Bussia Dardi le Rose Nebbiolo (Barolo) $60. 86 *(4/2/2004)*

Poderi Colla 1998 Bussia Dardi le Rose Nebbiolo (Barolo) $48. 90 *—C.S. (11/15/2002)*

Poderi Colla 2001 Dardi Le Rose Bussia Nebbiolo (Barolo) $60. 91 *—J.C. (3/1/2006)*

Poderi Colla 2000 Dardi le Rose Bussia Nebbiolo (Barolo) $64. 89 *—J.C. (11/15/2004)*

Poderi Colla 2001 Roncaglie Nebbiolo (Barbaresco) $56. 90 *—J.C. (11/15/2004)*

Poderi Colla 2000 Roncaglie Nebbiolo (Barbaresco) $56. 87 *(4/2/2004)*

Poderi Colla 1999 Tenuta Roncaglia Nebbiolo (Barbaresco) $46. 91 *—M.S. (11/15/2002)*

Poderi Colla 2000 Bricco del Drago Red Blend (Langhe) $35. 85 *—J.C. (11/15/2004)*

Poderi Colla 1996 Dardi Le Rose Bussia Red Blend (Barolo) $46. 87 *—J.C. (9/1/2001)*

PODERI LUIGI EINAUDI

Poderi Luigi Einaudi 2005 Dolcetto (Dolcetto di Dogliani) $19. This was somewhat disappointing, lots of structure but little or no fruit. On the palate the flavors were muted; the wine seemed dull, and it finished softly and with little impact. 82 *—M.G. (12/31/2007)*

Poderi Luigi Einaudi 2004 Dolcetto (Dolcetto di Dogliani) $21. The Einaudi is a fairly hefty version of a Dolcetto, having lost some fruit but gaining an interesting earthy character to the palate. Structurally a little on the chunkier side, but with good concentration. The finish is solid but dominated by the earthiness. Should be drunk soon. 85 *—M.G. (12/31/2007)*

Poderi Luigi Einaudi 2005 Vigna Tecc Superiore Dolcetto (Dolcetto di Dogliani) $29. Unlike most Dolcettos, this is laid back; it doesn't announce itself with a great blast of fruit. Instead it offers a package of spices and blackberry jam throughout the palate. No great intensity here but there is an easy elegance to the wine, culminating in a solid, medium finish. 86 *—M.G. (12/31/2007)*

Poderi Luigi Einaudi 2003 Vigna Tecc Dolcetto (Dolcetto di Dogliani) $27. 91 Editors' Choice *—J.C. (3/1/2006)*

Poderi Luigi Einaudi 2002 Vigna Tecc Dolcetto (Dolcetto di Dogliani) $26. 89 *—J.C. (11/15/2004)*

Poderi Luigi Einaudi 2000 Nebbiolo (Barolo) $73. 90 *—J.C. (11/15/2004)*

Poderi Luigi Einaudi 1999 Nebbiolo (Barolo) $68. 88 *(4/2/2004)*

Poderi Luigi Einaudi 1998 Nebbiolo (Barolo) $52. 91 *—C.S. (11/15/2002)*

Poderi Luigi Einaudi 2003 Costa Grimaldi Nebbiolo (Barolo) $89. This wine needed time in the glass to really show its stuff. At first, a touch volatile and funky, this soon blew off, and the wine showed plenty of sweet fruit, rose petal and licorice. Fairly evolved, this is a wine that should be enjoyed over the next five years. 87 *—M.G. (12/31/2007)*

Poderi Luigi Einaudi 2000 Costa Grimaldi Nebbiolo (Barolo) $90. 88 *—J.C. (11/15/2004)*

Poderi Luigi Einaudi 1999 Costa Grimaldi Nebbiolo (Barolo) $81. 91 *(4/2/2004)*

Poderi Luigi Einaudi 2000 Nei Cannubi Nebbiolo (Barolo) $100. 91 Cellar Selection *—J.C. (11/15/2004)*

Poderi Luigi Einaudi 1999 Nei Cannubi Nebbiolo (Barolo) $93. 90 *(4/2/2004)*

Poderi Luigi Einaudi 1998 Nei Cannubi Nebbiolo (Barolo) $50. 93 Cellar Selection *—C.S. (11/15/2002)*

Poderi Luigi Einaudi 2001 Luigi Einaudi Red Blend (Langhe) $73. 88 *—J.C. (11/15/2004)*

PODERI SALVAROLO

Poderi Salvarolo 1997 Ser Milion Cabernet Sauvignon-Merlot (Veneto Orientale) $27. 84 *(5/1/2003)*

POGGIO AI CHIARI

Poggio Ai Chiari 2001 Sangiovese (Toscana) $43. 89 *—M.S. (9/1/2006)*

POGGIO AL CASONE

Poggio al Casone 2004 La Cattura Red Blend (Toscana) $22. 85 *—M.S. (9/1/2006)*

Poggio al Casone 2001 Sangiovese (Chianti Superiore) $13. 86 *(4/1/2005)*

Poggio al Casone 1997 Sangiovese (Chianti Superiore) $15. 87 *(4/1/2001)*

Poggio al Casone 1999 Pog Sangiovese (Chianti Superiore) $12. 86 Best Buy *—M.S. (12/31/2002)*

Poggio al Casone 2002 Poggio al Casone Sangiovese (Chianti Superiore) $13. 85 *—M.S. (10/1/2006)*

POGGIO AL MULINO

Poggio Al Mulino 1997 Pancarta Sangiovese (Toscana) $32. 91 *—M.S. (8/1/2002)*

POGGIO ALLE SUGHERE

Poggio alle Sughere 2001 Splendido Sangiovese (Toscana) $45. 88 *—M.S. (9/1/2006)*

POGGIO ANTICO

Poggio Antico 2001 Brunello (Brunello di Montalcino) $74. 91 *(4/1/2006)*

Poggio Antico 2000 Brunello (Brunello di Montalcino) $72. 93 *—M.S. (7/1/2005)*

Poggio Antico 1999 Brunello (Brunello di Montalcino) $76. 94 *—M.S. (6/1/2004)*

Poggio Antico 1998 Brunello (Brunello di Montalcino) $58. 89 *(11/15/2003)*

Poggio Antico 1997 Brunello (Brunello di Montalcino) $60. 84 *—R.V. (8/1/2002)*

Poggio Antico 2001 Altero Brunello (Brunello di Montalcino) $82. 91 *(4/1/2006)*

Poggio Antico 2000 Altero Brunello (Brunello di Montalcino) $74. 90 *(4/1/2006)*

Poggio Antico 1998 Altero Brunello (Brunello di Montalcino) $57. 92 *(11/15/2003)*

Poggio Antico 2000 Riserva Brunello (Brunello di Montalcino) $129. 94 Cellar Selection *(4/1/2006)*

Poggio Antico 1999 Riserva Brunello (Brunello di Montalcino) $125. 95 Cellar Selection *—M.S. (7/1/2005)*

Poggio Antico 1995 Riserva Brunello (Brunello di Montalcino) $56. 84 *—M.S. (8/1/2002)*

Poggio Antico 2001 Madre Cabernet Sauvignon-Sangiovese (Toscana) $64. 94 Editors' Choice *—M.S. (10/1/2004)*

POGGIO ARGENTIERA

Poggio Argentiera 2002 Finisterre Red Blend (Toscana) $62. 85 *—M.S. (9/1/2006)*

Poggio Argentiera 2002 Bellamarsilia Sangiovese (Morellino di Scansano) $18. 86 *—M.S. (11/15/2004)*

POGGIO BERTAIO

Poggio Bertaio 2000 Cimbolo Sangiovese (Umbria) $20. 90 *—M.S. (2/1/2003)*

POGGIO BONELLI

Poggio Bonelli 2001 Sangiovese (Chianti Classico) $30. 90 Cellar Selection *(4/1/2005)*

POGGIO DEI POGGI

Poggio Dei Poggi 1997 Sangiovese Grosso (Chianti Classico) $13. 85 *(4/1/2001)*

Poggio Dei Poggi 1995 Riserva Sangiovese Grosso (Chianti Classico) $20. 85 *(4/1/2001)*

POGGIO DI SOTTO

Poggio di Sotto 2001 Brunello (Brunello di Montalcino) $NA. 88 *(4/1/2006)*

Poggio di Sotto 1999 Riserva Brunello (Brunello di Montalcino) $NA. 91 *(4/1/2006)*

POGGIO IL CASTELLARE

Poggio il Castellare 2001 Brunello (Brunello di Montalcino) $NA. 89 *(4/1/2006)*

POGGIO NARDONE

Poggio Nardone 2001 Brunello (Brunello di Montalcino) $65. 92 *(4/1/2006)*

Poggio Nardone 2005 Sangiovese (Morellino di Scansano) $18. The wood tones are very evident although vibrant fruit notes are not totally masked: You'll encounter cherry, forest berries and a very pleasing blast of menthol freshness. The wine drinks a bit young, with loads of oak nuances, thanks to 10 months in tonneaux, and ends on a slightly sour note. 87 *—M.L. (11/1/2007)*

POGGIO SALVI

Poggio Salvi 1998 Sangiovese (Chianti Colli Senesi) $15. 84 *(4/1/2001)*

POGGIO SAN POLO

Poggio San Polo 2001 Brunello (Brunello di Montalcino) $NA. 89 *(4/1/2006)*

POGGIO VALPAZZA

Poggio Valpazza 1997 Monteregio Sangiovese Grosso (Monteregio Rosso) $47. 88 *(7/1/2000)*

POGGIO VERRANO

Poggio Verrano 2004 Dròmos Red Blend (Maremma) $60. 92 *—M.L. (11/15/2006)*

Poggio Verrano 2003 Dròmos Red Blend (Maremma) $60. 90 *(9/1/2006)*

POJER & SANDRI

Pojer & Sandri NV Cuvée Vino Spumante Extra Brut Champagne Blend (Trento) $30. 82 *—M.S. (12/31/2002)*

Pojer & Sandri 2001 Müller-Thurgau (Trentino) $16. 88 *—R.V. (7/1/2003)*

Pojer & Sandri 2001 Traminer (Trentino) $18. 90 *—R.V. (7/1/2003)*

POLIZIANO

Poliziano 2002 Sangiovese (Vino Nobile di Montepulciano) $25. 87 *—M.S. (7/1/2005)*

Poliziano 2001 Sangiovese (Rosso di Montepulciano) $16. 86 *—M.S. (11/15/2003)*

Poliziano 2000 Sangiovese (Rosso di Montepulciano) $20. 87 *—M.S. (8/1/2002)*

Poliziano 1999 Sangiovese (Vino Nobile di Montepulciano) $23. 87 *—M.S. (11/15/2003)*

Poliziano 1998 Sangiovese (Vino Nobile di Montepulciano) $29. 87 *(8/1/2002)*

Poliziano 2001 Asinone Sangiovese (Vino Nobile di Montepulciano) $40. 91 Cellar Selection *—M.S. (7/1/2005)*

Poliziano 1999 Asinone Sangiovese (Vino Nobile di Montepulciano) $43. 87 *—M.S. (12/15/2003)*

Poliziano 1998 Asinone Sangiovese (Vino Nobile di Montepulciano) $45. 89 *(8/1/2002)*

POWERS

Powers 1998 Merlot (Colonella) $12. 89 Best Buy *—P.G. (12/31/2001)*

POZZI

Pozzi 2001 Merlot (Delle Venezie) $9. 82 *(5/1/2003)*

Pozzi 2002 Rosso Nero d'Avola (Sicilia) $10. 83 *—M.S. (10/1/2004)*

Pozzi 2001 Rosso Nero d'Avola (Sicilia) $10. 83 *(10/1/2003)*

Pozzi 1999 Rosso Nero d'Avola (Sicilia) $9. 82 *—C.S. (5/1/2002)*

Pozzi 2001 Pinot Grigio (Delle Venezie) $10. 84 *—J.C. (7/1/2003)*

PRADIO

Pradio 1999 Teraje Chardonnay (Friuli Grave) $10. 87 Best Buy *—J.C. (7/1/2003)*

PRIMA & NUOVA CANTINA

Prima & Nuova Cantina 2004 Pinot Grigio (Alto Adige) $12. 83 *—M.L. (6/1/2006)*

PRIMA TERRA

Prima Terra 2004 Pinot Grigio (Lazio) $6. 85 Best Buy *—M.L. (2/1/2006)*

PRIMOSIC

Primosic 1997 Gmajne Pinot Grigio (Collio) $18. 85 *(8/1/1999)*

Primosic 2004 I Classici Pinot Grigio (Collio) $16. 87 *—M.L. (6/1/2006)*

Primosic 2004 Murno Pinot Grigio (Collio) $20. 89 *—M.L. (6/1/2006)*

PRINCIPE DI CORLEONE

Principe di Corleone 2004 Inzolia (Sicilia) $18. 86 *—M.L. (7/1/2006)*

Principe di Corleone 2002 Nero d'Avola (Sicilia) $18. 87 *—M.L. (7/1/2006)*

Principe di Corleone 2003 Red Blend (Sicilia) $18. 86 *—M.L. (7/1/2006)*

Principe di Corleone 2005 White Blend (Alcamo) $18. 86 *—M.L. (7/1/2006)*

PRINCIPESSA GAVIA

Principessa Gavia 2004 Cortese (Gavi) $14. 85 *—J.C. (3/1/2006)*

Principessa Gavia 2003 Cortese (Gavi) $12. 87 Best Buy *—J.C. (11/15/2004)*

Principessa Gavia 2002 Cortese (Gavi) $12. 88 Best Buy *—M.S. (12/15/2003)*

Principessa Gavia 1999 Cortese (Gavi) $18. 87 *(2/1/2001)*

Principessa Gavia 1998 Cortese (Gavi) $11. 85 *—M.S. (4/1/2000)*

PRINCIPI DI SPADAFORA

Principi di Spadafora 2004 Don Pietro Red Blend (Sicilia) $24. 90 *—M.L. (7/1/2006)*

Principi di Spadafora 2004 Monreale Syrah Red Blend (Sicilia) $18. 88 *—M.L. (7/1/2006)*

Principi di Spadafora 2002 Sole dei Padri Syrah (Sicilia) $80. 93 Editors' Choice *—M.L. (7/1/2006)*

Principi di Spadafora 2002 Syrah Schietto Syrah (Sicilia) $42. 92 *—M.L. (7/1/2006)*

Principi di Spadafora 2005 Don Pietro Bianco White Blend (Sicilia) $17. 86 *—M.L. (7/1/2006)*

PRINCIPIANO FERDINANDO

Principiano Ferdinando 2003 La Romualda Barbera (Barbera d'Alba) $30. The Romualda is a lovely wine that has evolved nicely. It has some of the plumminess of the year, but there is also some freshness and a pretty floral quality. Big, rich and pleasant. **87** *—M.G. (12/31/2007)*

Principiano Ferdinando 1999 Boscareto Nebbiolo (Barolo) $60. 91 *(4/2/2004)*

PRINSI

Prinsi 2004 Gaia Principe Nebbiolo (Barbaresco) $45. There is plenty to like in this wine with its rich dark fruit, Indian spices and leather but it also showed a slightly dank, wet fur character. On the palate, the animal quality had retreated to the side, and the fruit was dominant. Medium finish, a nice wine with a question mark. **85** *—M.G. (12/31/2007)*

PRODUTTORI COLTERENZIO

Produttori Colterenzio 2001 Cornell Chardonnay (Alto Adige) $33. 89 *—R.V. (7/1/2003)*

Produttori Colterenzio 1997 Pinot Grigio (Alto Adige) $12. 85 *(8/1/1999)*

Produttori Colterenzio 2001 Cornell Pinot Grigio (Alto Adige) $24. 89 *—R.V. (7/1/2003)*

Produttori Colterenzio 2001 Lafoa Sauvignon Blanc (Alto Adige) $35. 90 *—R.V. (7/1/2003)*

Produttori Colterenzio 2002 Praedium Sauvignon Blanc (Alto Adige) $19. 89 *—R.V. (7/1/2003)*

PRODUTTORI DEL BARBARESCO

Produttori del Barbaresco 2003 Nebbiolo (Langhe) $18. 87 *—J.C. (3/1/2006)*

Produttori del Barbaresco 2001 Nebbiolo (Barbaresco) $33. 87 *—J.C. (3/1/2006)*

Produttori del Barbaresco 1999 Nebbiolo (Barbaresco) $20. 86 *(4/2/2004)*

PRODUTTORI MOSCATO D'ASTI ASSOCIATI

Produttori Moscato d'Asti Associati 2004 Moscato (Moscato d'Asti) $NA. 87 *—M.L. (12/15/2005)*

PROMESSA

Promessa 2003 Negroamaro (Puglia) $9. 86 Best Buy *—M.S. (2/1/2005)*

Promessa 2003 Rosso Salento Red Blend (Apulia) $9. 90 Best Buy *—P.G. (11/15/2004)*

Promessa 2001 Rosso Salento Red Blend (Salento) $8. 88 Best Buy *—M.S. (12/15/2003)*

Promessa 2000 Rosso Salento Red Blend (Puglia) $8. 87 Best Buy *(5/1/2002)*

PROVOLO

Provolo 2001 Corvina, Rondinella, Molinara (Amarone della Valpolicella) $55. From a little-known producer outside the Classico zone, here is a pretty wine with notes of cherry, chocolate, spice and subtle shadings of vanilla. In the mouth, it delivers soft tannins and good persistency of spice and fruit flavors. **89** *—M.L. (12/1/2007)*

Provolo 1994 Riserva Corvina, Rondinella, Molinara (Amarone della Valpolicella) $130. Great pleasure is derived from this wine's elegant, aged tones. This is a graceful wine with ethereal notes of blue flower, dried berry, cedar, leather, mushroom and soy sauce. You'll taste its delicate sweetness and its smooth, long-lasting finish. This is the kind of precious wine you'll want to drink with good friends. **94** *—M.L. (12/1/2007)*

Provolo 2001 Red Blend (Valpolicella) $12. 84 *(5/1/2003)*

Provolo 1999 Red Blend (Amarone della Valpolicella) $54. 88 *(11/1/2005)*

Provolo 1997 Red Blend (Amarone della Valpolicella) $49. 89 *(5/1/2003)*

Provolo 1998 Campotorbian Red Blend (Valpolicella Classico Superiore) $19. 85 *(5/1/2003)*

PRUNETO

Pruneto 1996 Riserva Sangiovese (Chianti Classico) $28. 82 *(4/1/2001)*

PRUNOTTO

Prunotto 2003 Fiulot Barbera (Barbera d'Asti) $13. 88 Best Buy *—R.V. (11/15/2004)*

Prunotto 1997 Pian Romualdo Barbera (Barbera d'Alba) $28. 90 *(4/1/2000)*

Prunotto 1997 Dolcetto (Dolcetto d'Alba) $15. 84 *(4/1/2000)*

Prunotto 2004 Moscato (Moscato d'Asti) $21. 88 *—M.L. (12/15/2005)*

Prunotto 1996 Nebbiolo (Barbaresco) $43. 84 *(9/1/2000)*

Prunotto 1999 Nebbiolo (Barolo) $45. 86 *(4/2/2004)*

Prunotto 1998 Nebbiolo (Piedmont) $42. 91 *—R.V. (11/15/2002)*

Prunotto 1998 Bussia Nebbiolo (Piedmont) $70. 93 *—R.V. (11/15/2002)*

PUIATTI

Puiatti 2004 Ruttars Pinot Grigio (Collio) $18. 85 *—M.L. (6/1/2006)*

PUNSET

Punset 1996 Nebbiolo (Barbaresco) $38. 86 *—J.C. (9/1/2000)*

QUADRA

Quadra 2003 Brut Sparkling Blend (Franciacorta) $35. 87 *—M.L. (6/1/2006)*

QUADRI

Quadri 2005 Mátraalja Pinot Grigio (Trento) $8. 87 Best Buy *—M.L. (6/1/2006)*

QUERCETO

Querceto 1997 Sangiovese (Chianti Classico) $11. 90 Best Buy *(7/1/2000)*

Querceto 2004 Sangiovese (Chianti) $8. 87 Best Buy *—M.S. (10/1/2006)*

Querceto 2003 Sangiovese (Chianti) $9. 88 Best Buy *(4/1/2005)*

Querceto 2003 Sangiovese (Chianti Classico) $13. 83 *(4/1/2005)*

Querceto 2002 Sangiovese (Chianti Classico) $12. 84 *—M.S. (10/1/2004)*

Querceto 2001 Sangiovese (Chianti) $8. 86 Best Buy *—M.S. (11/15/2003)*

Querceto 2000 Sangiovese (Chianti Classico) $11. 83 *—M.S. (8/1/2002)*

Querceto 2000 Riserva Sangiovese (Chianti Classico) $20. 87 *(4/1/2005)*

Querceto 1996 Riserva Sangiovese (Chianti Classico) $18. 84 *(4/1/2001)*

Querceto 1995 Riserva Sangiovese (Chianti Classico) $18. 88 *(7/1/2000)*

QUERCIAVALLE

Querciavalle 1997 Sangiovese (Chianti Classico) $18. 89 *(4/1/2001)*

Querciavalle 1999 Riserva Sangiovese (Chianti Classico) $28. 84 *(4/1/2005)*

Querciavalle 1995 Riserva Sangiovese (Chianti Classico) $25. 86 *(4/1/2001)*

QUINTARELLI

Quintarelli 1998 Corvina, Rondinella, Molinara (Amarone della Valpolicella Classico) $NA. There's something magical about this wine: the purity, the elegance, the harmony, the immediate rush of intensity. This is one of Italy's iconic wines thanks to the profound purity it delivers with notes of chocolate, leather, cherry, apple, cola and spice. It imparts loads of succulent flavor and is simply beautiful. **96 Editors' Choice** *—M.L. (12/1/2007)*

Quintarelli 1997 Corvina, Rondinella, Molinara (Amarone della Valpolicella Classico) $300. 89 *(11/1/2005)*

Quintarelli 1999 Primofiore Red Blend (Veronese) $32. 86 *(5/1/2003)*

RAIMONDI

Raimondi 1998 Villa Monteleone Corvina, Rondinella, Molinara (Amarone della Valpolicella Classico) $49. 88 *(11/1/2005)*

Raimondi 1997 Red Blend (Amarone della Valpolicella Classico) $53. 91 *(5/1/2003)*

RAMPOLDI

Rampoldi 2000 Riserva Negroamaro (Copertino) $9. 84 *—M.S. (10/1/2006)*

RASHI

Rashi 2003 Moscato (Moscato d'Asti) $11. 83 *—J.C. (4/1/2005)*

Rashi 2002 Moscato (Moscato d'Asti) $11. 84 *—J.M. (4/3/2004)*

Rashi NV Kosher Moscato (Asti) $12. 82 *—M.S. (6/1/2005)*

Rashi 1999 Select Nebbiolo (Barolo) $38. 83 *—J.M. (4/3/2004)*

Rashi NV Pinot Brut Kosher Pinot Blanc (Italy) $12. 82 *—M.S. (6/1/2005)*

RE MANFREDI

Re Manfredi 2000 Aglianico (Aglianico del Vulture) $30. 90 *(8/1/2005)*

RECCHIA

Recchia 2003 Corvina, Rondinella, Molinara (Amarone della Valpolicella Classico) $NA. This is a beautiful style of Amarone: Powdered chocolate and cherry aromas are made more buoyant and vibrant by a colorful supporting cast of root beer, cola, menthol, wild apple and almond amaretto. A wine like this offers enormous intensity to both the nose and the palate and leaves a long-lasting trail of harmony and freshness. 90 *—M.L. (10/1/2007)*

Recchia 2001 Cà Bertoldi Corvina, Rondinella, Molinara (Amarone della Valpolicella Classico) $NA. The Recchia brothers, Riccardo and Roberto, are among the area's largest private owners. They sell fruit and juice but keep the best selections for their own production. The 2001 Amarone boasts a pretty ruby color and is redolent of cherry, cedar wood, almond paste, cola, resin and coffee. It has a chewy, sticky consistency and excellent purity of flavors. 91 *—M.L. (10/1/2007)*

REMO FARINA

Remo Farina 2000 Red Blend (Amarone della Valpolicella Classico) $40. 86 *(11/1/2005)*

Remo Farina 1998 Red Blend (Amarone della Valpolicella Classico) $34. 89 *(5/1/2003)*

Remo Farina 1998 Corte Conti Cavalli Red Blend (Rosso del Veronese) $45. 88 *(5/1/2003)*

Remo Farina 2000 Montecorna Red Blend (Valpolicella) $19. 90 Editors' Choice *(5/1/2003)*

Remo Farina 2000 Ripasso Red Blend (Valpolicella Classico Superiore) $13. 87 Best Buy *(5/1/2003)*

Remo Farina 1997 Ripasso Red Blend (Valpolicella Classico Superiore) $12. 82 *—M.N. (12/31/2000)*

Remo Farina 1999 Soave Classico Superiore White Blend (Soave) 86 *—M.S. (1/1/2004)*

RENATO RATTI

Renato Ratti 1997 Barbera (Barbera di Piemonte) $14. 86 *(4/1/2000)*

Renato Ratti 2005 Torriglione Barbera (Barbera d'Alba) $17. This is one of the more exotic Barberas. The dark fruit is mixed with scents of licorice, curry and violets. On the palate, there is plenty of dark fruit, but it still retains its likeable spicy character. Although the finish is short to medium, this is a pleasant wine, and a natural match with a good juicy steak. 87 *—M.G. (12/31/2007)*

Renato Ratti 1997 Torriglione Barbera (Barbera d'Alba) $14. 88 Best Buy *(4/1/2000)*

Renato Ratti 1998 Dolcetto (Dolcetto d'Alba) $14. 87 *(4/1/2000)*

Renato Ratti 2004 Colombè Dolcetto (Dolcetto d'Alba) $15. A pleasant Dolcetto with plenty of fruit, and an interesting inner core of licorice and spice. Easy to drink, but with enough structure to allow it to mature gracefully over the next couple of years. 86 *—M.G. (12/31/2007)*

Renato Ratti 2003 Conco Marcenasco Nebbiolo (Barolo) $62. While more structured than the other Ratti Barolos, it does not have quite enough fruit to keep it balanced. The nose has muted plum, wood-smoke, cloves and licorice. The flavors are not intense enough to balance the hard tannins and the alcohol. The relatively short finish suggests that even with time, it will never really come into balance. 85 *—M.G. (4/1/2007)*

Renato Ratti 1998 Conca Marcenasco Nebbiolo (Piedmont) $62. 95 Editors' Choice *—R.V. (11/15/2002)*

Renato Ratti 2003 Marcenasco Nebbiolo (Barolo) $47. The least expensive of the Ratti Barolos tasted, it shows very well, with pretty aromas of plums, thyme and mushroom. Light bodied, it has enough structure and concentration to carry it, and the flavors of plum and thyme come through the palate to a soft, layered finish. 90 *—M.G. (4/1/2007)*

Renato Ratti 2001 Marcenasco Nebbiolo (Barolo) $47. While the Ratti is currently a little disjointed, the elements are all there; will make a lovely bottle of wine in five years or so. Built on a large scale, great concentration, plenty of fruit, roses and smoked meat. A long, easy finish. 91 *—M.G. (4/1/2007)*

Renato Ratti 1998 Marcenasco Nebbiolo (Piedmont) $40. 93 *—R.V. (11/15/2002)*

Renato Ratti 2004 Ochetti Nebbiolo (Nebbiolo d'Alba) $18. Ratti has made a lovely Nebbiolo, thick and rich and very friendly. It shows plenty of ripe fruit, spices and anise. On the palate, the fruit takes center stage, so the complexity noted on the nose seems muted; finishes well. A pleasant enough wine now, it will become more interesting with another year of cellaring. 88 *—M.G. (4/1/2007)*

Renato Ratti 2003 Rocche Marcenasco Nebbiolo (Barolo) $73. The most structured of the Ratti wines, this begins with the heady perfume of jasmine, roses and plums. On the palate, the heavy structure is balanced by the fruit, as well as more traditional flavors of tar and roses; medium-long finish. A really lovely wine in what has proved to be a patchy vintage; needs a good five years of cellaring. 92 *—M.G. (4/1/2007)*

Renato Ratti 1998 Rocche Marcenasco Nebbiolo (Piedmont) $60. 96 Cellar Selection *—R.V. (11/15/2002)*

Renato Ratti 2004 Villa Pattono Red Blend (Monferrato) $26. The Ratti proved to be a rich, pleasant, gentle wine, showing lots of plummy fruit, not much acidity and a medium finish. The wine will marry well with a variety of foods, thanks to its hefty texture and easygoing personality. 85 *—M.G. (12/31/2007)*

Renato Ratti 2005 I Cedri Sauvignon Blanc (Monferrato) $15. Little doubt from the nose what the grape was: archetypal Sauvignon Blanc. Lots of hay, wet grass a touch of green plums. Promising a lot, but really fell down on the palate, which was light and totally lacked the oomph and intensity promised by the nose. 85 *—M.G. (12/31/2007)*

RENZO MARINAI

Renzo Marinai 2003 Sangiovese (Chianti Classico) $NA. Here's a distinctive nose for a Chianti Classico: coffee, leather, Indian spice, beef broth, wet earth and an unexpected hint of bay leaf. In the mouth, this is a chewy wine with tart blueberry flavors and a nice quality of tannins. 89 *—M.L. (11/1/2007)*

RENZO MASI

Renzo Masi 2003 Sangiovese (Chianti) $8. 84 Best Buy *(4/1/2005)*

Renzo Masi 1999 Sangiovese (Chianti Rufina) $8. 85 Best Buy *(4/1/2001)*

Renzo Masi 1997 Riserva Sangiovese (Chianti) $10. 87 Best Buy *(4/1/2001)*

RICCARDO ARRIGONI

Riccardo Arrigoni 2003 Ampelos Vermentino (Colli di Luni) $17. 86 *—M.S. (8/1/2004)*

RICCI

Ricci 2001 Brunello (Brunello di Montalcino) $52. 92 *(4/1/2006)*

RIECINE

Riecine 1998 Sangiovese (Chianti Classico) $23. 87 *(4/1/2001)*

Riecine 1997 Riserva Sangiovese (Chianti Classico) $35. 90 *(4/1/2001)*

RISECCOLI

Riseccoli 1998 Sangiovese (Chianti Classico) $18. 88 *(4/1/2001)*

Riseccoli 1997 Riserva Sangiovese (Chianti Classico) $26. 90 *(4/1/2001)*

RIVALTA

Rivalta NV Brut Convivio Rivalta Prosecco (Prosecco di Valdobbiadene) $18. 86 *—M.L. (6/1/2006)*

Rivalta NV Incontri Extra Dry Prosecco (Prosecco di Valdobbiadene) $18. 87 *—M.L. (6/1/2006)*

RIVE DELLA CHIESA

Rive Della Chiesa NV Frizzante Prosecco (Colli Trevigiani) $12. 85 *—J.C. (12/15/2004)*

Rive Della Chiesa NV Frizzante Prosecco (Colli Trevigiani) $10. 85 *—M.S. (6/1/2003)*

Rive Della Chiesa NV Spumante Extra Dry Prosecco (Montello e Colli Asolani) $12. 87 *—M.S. (6/1/2003)*

Rive Della Chiesa NV Spumante Extra Dry Prosecco (Montello e Colli Asolani) $14. 87 *—J.C. (12/15/2004)*

RIVETTO

Rivetto 2001 Zio Nando Barbera (Barbera d'Alba) $20. 89 *—M.S. (12/15/2003)*

Rivetto 2002 Ercolino Dolcetto (Dolcetto d'Alba) $15. 86 *—M.S. (12/15/2003)*

Rivetto 1999 Nebbiolo (Barbaresco) $30. 91 Editors' Choice *(4/2/2004)*

Rivetto 1999 Giulin Nebbiolo (Barolo) $38. 88 *(4/2/2004)*

Rivetto 1999 Leon Nebbiolo (Barolo) $45. 87 *(4/2/2004)*

Rivetto 2001 Lirano Nebbiolo (Nebbiolo d'Alba) $11. 85 *—M.S. (12/15/2003)*

RIZZI

Rizzi 2000 Nebbiolo (Barbaresco) $42. 89 *(4/2/2004)*

Rizzi 2000 Boito Nebbiolo (Barbaresco) $45. 92 *(4/2/2004)*

Rizzi 2000 Fondetta Nebbiolo (Barbaresco) $45. 86 *(4/2/2004)*

ROBERTO COSIMI

Roberto Cosimi 2001 Beato Brunello (Brunello di Montalcino) $30. 91 Editors' Choice *(4/1/2006)*

Roberto Cosimi 2001 Podere il Poggiolo Brunello (Brunello di Montalcino) $50. 93 Editors' Choice *(4/1/2006)*

ROCCA

Rocca 2000 Mitico Red Blend (Salento) $22. 83 *—M.S. (10/1/2004)*

ROCCA DELLE MACÌE

Rocca delle Macìe 1997 Ser Gioveto Cabernet Sauvignon (Toscana) $30. 92 Cellar Selection *(8/1/2001)*

Rocca delle Macìe 2000 Roccato Cabernet Sauvignon-Sangiovese (Toscana) $46. 85 *—M.S. (9/1/2006)*

Rocca delle Macìe 2005 Campomaccione Red Blend (Morellino di Scansano) $15. This is a youthful, perky wine with generous notes of cherry, blueberry and chiseled mineral notes that overlap, layer over layer, to form a harmonious whole. The mouthfeel is lean and powerful but also extremely fruity and it speaks of its sunny, southern Tuscan origins. Morellino di Scansano is Italy's quintessential pasta wine. 87 *—M.L. (11/15/2007)*

Rocca delle Macìe 2003 Sangiovese (Chianti Classico) $16. 87 *—M.S. (10/1/2006)*

Rocca delle Macìe 2002 Sangiovese (Chianti Classico) $16. 86 *(4/1/2005)*

Rocca delle Macìe 1998 Sangiovese (Chianti Classico) $13. 87 *(8/1/2001)*

Rocca delle Macìe 1999 Campomaccione Sangiovese (Morellino di Scansano) $14. 87 Best Buy *(8/1/2001)*

Rocca delle Macìe 2000 Riserva Sangiovese (Chianti Classico) $22. 86 *(4/1/2005)*

Rocca delle Macìe 1998 Riserva Sangiovese (Chianti Classico) $18. 90 *—R.V. (8/1/2002)*

Rocca delle Macìe 1997 Riserva Sangiovese (Chianti Classico) $21. 89 *(8/1/2001)*

Rocca delle Macìe 2000 Riserva Di Fizzano Sangiovese (Chianti Classico) $29. 90 *(4/1/2005)*

Rocca delle Macìe 1997 Riserva di Fizzano Sangiovese (Chianti Classico) $25. 90 *(8/1/2001)*

Rocca delle Macìe 1997 Roccato Sangiovese (Toscana) $25. 92 Editors' Choice *(8/1/2001)*

Rocca delle Macìe 2001 Rubizzo Sangiovese (Sangiovese di Toscana) $12. 86 *—M.S. (11/15/2003)*

Rocca delle Macìe 1999 Rubizzo Sangiovese (Toscana) $12. 87 Best Buy *(8/1/2001)*

Rocca delle Macìe 2000 Ser Gioveto Sangiovese (Toscana) $42. 91 *—M.S. (9/1/2006)*

Rocca delle Macìe 2000 Tenuta Sant'Alfonso Sangiovese (Chianti Classico) $23. 86 *(4/1/2005)*

Rocca delle Macìe 1999 Ser Gioveto Sangiovese Grosso (Toscana) $42. 90 *—M.S. (9/1/2006)*

Rocca delle Macìe 2003 Vernaccia (Vernaccia di San Gimignano) $11. 84 *—M.S. (8/1/2004)*

Rocca delle Macìe 1999 Vernaccia (Vernaccia di San Gimignano) $12. 85 *(8/1/2001)*

Rocca delle Macìe 1999 White Blend (Orvieto Classico) $10. 84 *(8/1/2001)*

ROCCA DI CASTAGNOLI

Rocca di Castagnoli 1998 Sangiovese (Chianti Classico) $13. 87 *(4/1/2001)*

ROCCA DI FABBRI

Rocca di Fabbri 1999 Red Blend (Sagrantino di Montefalco) $35. 88 *—C.S. (2/1/2002)*

Rocca di Fabbri 2000 Rosso di Montefalco Red Blend (Montefalco) $20. 90 *—M.S. (2/1/2003)*

Rocca di Fabbri 2001 Sagrantino (Sagrantino di Montefalco) $NA. 88 *—M.L. (9/1/2005)*

Rocca di Fabbri 2000 Satiro Sangiovese (Colli Martani) $12. 88 Best Buy *—M.S. (2/1/2003)*

ROCCA DI MONTEGROSSI

Rocca di Montegrossi 2003 Sangiovese (Chianti Classico) $NA. Toasted wood notes are wide and penetrating and leave a heavy mark of espresso, spice and leather. There are also fruity notes, albeit very ripe ones, of red cherry and strawberry preserves. Made in Gaiole in Chianti, the wine has good intensity and dusty tannins. 86 *—M.L. (11/1/2007)*

Rocca di Montegrossi 2001 Sangiovese (Chianti Classico) $23. 86 *(4/1/2005)*

Rocca di Montegrossi 1998 Sangiovese (Chianti Classico) $18. 88 *(4/1/2001)*

Rocca di Montegrossi 1999 Geremia Sangiovese (Toscana) $35. 91 *—M.S. (9/1/2006)*

Rocca di Montegrossi 1998 Riserva Sangiovese (Chianti Classico) $NA. 85 *—R.V. (8/1/2002)*

Rocca di Montegrossi 1997 San Marcellino Sangiovese (Chianti Classico) $30. 88 *(4/1/2001)*

Rocca di Montegrossi 1999 Vigneto San Marcellino Sangiovese (Chianti Classico) $40. 84 *(4/1/2005)*

ROCCA DI MONTEMASSI

Rocca di Montemassi 2005 Le Focaie Sangiovese (Maremma) $13. Why reach for a lean, tart Chianti when you could have this varietally correct but friendlier Sangiovese? Aged half in stainless steel and half in large Slavonian oak casks, this wine's black cherry and plum fruit flavors are carried by soft tannins, but still show hints of tobacco leaf on the finish. 88 Best Buy *(11/15/2007)*

Rocca di Montemassi 2005 Sassabruna Sangiovese (Monteregio di Massa Maritima) $30. A blend of 80% Sangiovese, 10% Merlot and 10% Syrah, this was our favorite of the Montemassi wines. Spice and meat accents plum and chocolate flavors, while the mouthfeel is full and velvety smooth. Drink now–2015. 90 *(11/15/2007)*

Rocca di Montemassi 2006 Vermentino (Maremma) $15. "A gentle wine for gentle foods," according to Francesco Zonin, this is a plump, easygoing white with hints of peach, brine and almond, finishing clean and fresh. Try it with simple white fish dishes. 87 *(11/15/2007)*

ROCCHE CASTAMAGNA

Rocche Castamagna 1999 Annunziata Barbera (Barbera d'Alba) $17. 88 *—M.M. (9/1/2001)*

Rocche Castamagna 1997 Annunziata Barbera (Barbera d'Alba) $20. 86 *(4/1/2000)*

Rocche Castamagna 2000 Annunziata 2000 Barbera (Barbera d'Alba) $20. 84 *—M.S. (12/15/2003)*

Rocche Castamagna 1996 Rocche delle Rocche Barbera (Barbera d'Alba) $27. 89 *(4/1/2000)*

Rocche Castamagna 1998 Dolcetto (Dolcetto d'Alba) $14. 82 *(4/1/2000)*

Rocche Castamagna 2001 Dolcetto (Dolcetto d'Alba) $13. 90 Best Buy *—M.S. (12/15/2003)*

Rocche Castamagna 1999 Dolcetto (Dolcetto d'Alba) $13. 87 *—M.M. (9/1/2001)*

Rocche Castamagna 1998 Bricco Francesco Nebbiolo (Barolo) $50. 87 *(4/2/2004)*

Rocche Castamagna 1998 Rocche Dell'Annunziata Nebbiolo (Barolo) $39. 90 *(4/2/2004)*

ROCCOLO GRASSI

Roccolo Grassi 2003 Corvina, Rondinella, Molinara (Amarone della Valpolicella) $90. The winds of change are blowing over Valpolicella and this boutique winery is one of the protagonists behind a new wave of excellence. The family winery has been around for 50 years and young Marco Sartori took over in 1996, proposing wines like this one: Brawny intensity is delivered over notes of espresso, almond, black fruit and tea leaf. Despite its concentrated appearance, this is a delicate wine with subtle nuances around a solid core of excellent fruit. **93 Cellar Selection** *—M.L. (10/1/2007)*

ROMOLO BUCCELLATO

Romolo Buccellato 1999 Tre Vigne Frappato (Sicilia) $11. **82** *—M.S. (12/15/2003)*

Romolo Buccellato 1999 Il Cigno Nero White Blend (Cerasuolo di Vittoria) $10. **87 Best Buy** *—M.S. (10/1/2003)*

RONCHI DI GIANCARLO ROCCA

Ronchi di Giancarlo Rocca 1999 Nebbiolo (Barbaresco) $40. **92** *(4/2/2004)*

RONCHI DI MANZANO

Ronchi di Manzano 2004 Pinot Grigio (Colli Orientali del Friuli) $16. **82** *—M.L. (2/1/2006)*

Ronchi di Manzano 1999 Colli Orientale del Friuli Superiore Tocai (Colli Orientali del Friuli) **91** *—M.N. (12/31/2000)*

RONCO BLANCHIS

Ronco Blanchis 2004 Pinot Grigio (Collio) $17. **85** *—M.L. (2/1/2006)*

RONCO DE TASSI

Ronco de Tassi 1997 Pinot Grigio (Collio) $15. **84** *(8/1/1999)*

RONCO DEI PINI

Ronco Dei Pini 2004 Pinot Grigio (Collio) $16. **84** *—M.L. (2/1/2006)*

RONCO DEL GELSO

Ronco del Gelso 1999 Chardonnay (Friuli) $21. **88** *—J.C. (7/1/2003)*

Ronco del Gelso 2004 Pinot Grigio (Isonzo del Friuli) $25. **87** *—M.L. (2/1/2006)*

Ronco del Gelso 2004 Sot Lis Rivis Pinot Grigio (Isonzo del Friuli) $22. **86** *—M.L. (2/1/2006)*

Ronco del Gelso 2006 Riesling (Friuli Isonzo) $22. What sets this wine apart is the intensity of its aromas: Citrus blossom, creamy lime and honeysuckle are immediate and generous, almost pungent. This showcases many of the prized characteristics associated with the Friuli region of northeastern Italy, which is home to some of the country's most elegant whites. The mouthfeel is rich, refined and silky but there is enough fresh acidity to keep it lively and cool. Pair it with delicate dishes like sea bass or lake fish. **88** *—M.L. (9/1/2007)*

Ronco del Gelso 2006 Rive Alte Tocai Friulano (Isonzo del Friuli) $22. Deep, golden saturation is backed by big power and structure and bountiful shadings of creamy vanilla, peach, apricot and honeysuckle. This is a naturally creamy wine, visibly thick and viscous, with tangy fruit flavors through and through. **89** *—M.L. (12/1/2007)*

RONCO DEL GNEMIZ

Ronco del Gnemiz 2003 Sauvignon (Colli Orientali del Friuli) $23. **87** *(7/1/2005)*

RONCO DELLE BETULLE

Ronco delle Betulle 2005 Pinot Grigio (Colli Orientali del Friuli) $NA. Here is a luminous, golden-hued Grigio with opulent notes of honey, savory apricot and apple-nut. It's a sophisticated, high-quality wine that boasts a caressing, creamy quality and long, silky persistency. Drink with smoked salmon. **87** *—M.L. (12/1/2007)*

Ronco delle Betulle 1997 Pinot Grigio (Colli Orientali del Friuli) $21. **85** *(8/1/1999)*

Ronco delle Betulle 2005 Ribolla Gialla (Colli Orientali del Friuli) $NA. In line with the best of Friuli winemaking tradition, this Ribolla Gialla boasts a luminous golden color and broad, wide-reaching notes of stone fruit, melon and honey. There's nice heft to its texture that helps drive a chewy, spicy finish. **86** *—M.L. (12/1/2007)*

Ronco delle Betulle 2005 Sauvignon (Colli Orientali del Friuli) $NA. Penetrating and deeply refreshing, this wine reaches mouth-cleansing acidity levels without being sharp or thorny. The nose is fragrant and clean and redolent of green fruit, kiwi, lime, lemon zest and green-apple candy. **87** *—M.L. (12/1/2007)*

Ronco delle Betulle 2005 Tocai Friulano (Colli Orientali del Friuli) $NA. Mature peach and stone fruit, honeysuckle and pine nut come to mind as do dried Mediterranean herbs. These aromas are forthcoming and generous, but also a bit muddy on first impact, which is why this wine hasn't scored higher. **85** *—M.L. (12/1/2007)*

ROSA DEL GOLFO

Rosa Del Golfo 1997 Portulano Red Blend (Salento) $15. **88** *—J.F. (5/1/2002)*

Rosa Del Golfo 1999 Scaliere Red Blend (Salento) $10. **83** *—J.F. (5/1/2002)*

ROTARI

Rotari NV Arte Italiana Champagne Blend (Trento) $11. **83** *(7/1/2000)*

Rotari NV Arte Italiana Brut Champagne Blend (Trento) $11. **85** *(6/1/2005)*

Rotari NV Arte Italiana Brut Champagne Blend (Trento) $11. **86 Best Buy** *—M.S. (12/31/2002)*

Rotari NV Blanc de Noir Brut Champagne Blend (Trentino) $11. **87 Best Buy** *—M.M. (12/31/2001)*

Rotari NV Blanc de Noir Brut Champagne Blend (Trentino) $11. **87 Best Buy** *—M.S. (12/15/2000)*

Rotari NV Blanc de Noir Brut Rose Champagne Blend (Trento) $11. **80** *—M.S. (12/31/2002)*

Rotari NV Brut Champagne Blend (Trento) $11. **86** *—S.H. (12/15/2000)*

Rotari 1997 Brut Riserva Sparkling Blend (Trento) $15. **87** *—M.S. (12/31/2002)*

Rotari 1995 Brut Riserva Champagne Blend (Trento) $15. **87 Best Buy** *(7/1/2000)*

Rotari 1995 Brut Riserva Sparkling Blend (Trentino) $15. **86** *—M.M. (12/31/2001)*

Rotari 2000 Riserva Brut Champagne Blend (Trento) $14. **84** *—M.S. (6/1/2005)*

Rotari 1999 Flavio Riserva Brut Blanc de Blanc Chardonnay (Trento) $38. This is one of the most beautiful wines yet to come from Rotari, in Italy's northern Trento region. Barrique-fermented Chardonnay offers balanced and enticing notes of apricot, nuts, honey, crushed stone and toast over a broad, creamy mouthfeel. This is a sophisticated wine that makes for a lively, elegant presence. **93** *—M.L. (12/15/2007)*

Rotari NV Arte Italiana Brut Chardonnay (Trento) $11. **85** *—M.S. (12/15/2004)*

Rotari NV Arte Italiana Brut Chardonnay (Trentino) $11. **84** *—M.M. (12/31/2001)*

Rotari 1999 Riserva Brut Chardonnay (Trento) $15. **85** *—M.S. (12/15/2004)*

Rotari NV Blanc de Noir Pinot Noir (Trento) $11. **86 Best Buy** *—M.S. (12/15/2004)*

Rotari NV Arte Italiana Sparkling Blend (Trento) $12. This Chardonnay-based sparkler (with 10% Pinot Nero) offers generous and penetrating aromas of Golden Delicious apple, toasted almond and mature peach and is extra smooth and silky in the mouth. Nice crispness over a long finish. Pair it with seafood risotto. **88 Best Buy** *—M.L. (12/15/2007)*

Rotari NV Arte Italiana Sparkling Blend (Trento) $11. **86 Best Buy** *—J.C. (12/31/2003)*

Rotari NV Arte Italiana Sparkling Blend (Trento) $11. **88 Best Buy** *—M.L. (6/1/2006)*

Rotari NV Arte Italiana Brut Sparkling Blend (Trento) $11. **87 Best Buy** *—M.S. (12/15/2005)*

Rotari NV Blanc de Noir Sparkling Blend (Trento) $11. **85** *—J.C. (12/31/2003)*

Rotari 1998 Brut Riserva Sparkling Blend (Trento) $13. **86** *—J.C. (12/31/2003)*

Rotari NV Demi-Sec Sparkling Blend (Trento) $11. **84** *(6/1/2005)*

Rotari NV Demi-Sec Sparkling Blend (Trento) $12. **84** *—M.S. (12/15/2005)*

Rotari 2001 Riserva Sparkling Blend (Trento) $13. **89 Best Buy** *—M.L. (6/1/2006)*

Rotari 2001 Riserva Brut Sparkling Blend (Trento) $16. The blend sees 90% Chardonnay and 10% Pinot Nero and the wine rests for 36 long months on the lees to produce an extremely creamy and inviting sparkler that is elegant and sophisticated yet genuine at the same time. Yeasty notes of bread crust and apple pie are the most obvious aromas but are soon followed by stone fruit, honey and well-balanced mineral tones. **90 Editors' Choice** *—M.L. (12/15/2007)*

Rotari 2000 Riserva Brut Sparkling Blend (Trento) $15. **87** *—M.S. (12/15/2005)*

Rotari NV Rosé Sparkling Blend (Trento) $11. **87 Best Buy** *—M.L. (6/1/2006)*

Rotari NV Rosé Brut Sparkling Blend (Trento) $12. Wonderful on all fronts: The wine opens with a delicate pale pink color and segues into aromas of peach juice, pink grapefruit, fresh flowers, small red berries and fuller, rounder tones of yeast and freshly baked bread. The acidity is excellently integrated and this bottle-fermented pink sparkler is elegant through and through. Pair with smoked salmon canapé appetizers. **89 Best Buy** *—M.L. (7/1/2007)*

RUFFINO

Ruffino 2000 Greppone Mazzi Brunello (Brunello di Montalcino) $65. 87 *—M.S. (7/1/2005)*

Ruffino 1999 Greppone Mazzi Brunello (Brunello di Montalcino) $65. 92 *—M.S. (6/1/2004)*

Ruffino 1997 Greppone Mazzi Brunello (Brunello di Montalcino) $70. 89 *—R.V. (8/1/2002)*

Ruffino 1997 Greppone Mazzi Brunello (Brunello di Montalcino) $60. 90 *—M.S. (8/1/2002)*

Ruffino 1996 Greppone Mazzi Brunello (Brunello di Montalcino) $60. 87 *(3/1/2002)*

Ruffino 1999 Greppone Mazzi Riserva Brunello (Brunello di Montalcino) $95. 91 *—M.S. (7/1/2005)*

Ruffino 1998 La Solatìa Chardonnay (Toscana) $20. 86 *(3/1/2002)*

Ruffino 2000 Libaio Chardonnay (Toscana) $9. 84 *(3/1/2002)*

Ruffino 2004 Tenuta La Solatìa Chardonnay (Toscana) $23. Weighty and slightly oily in texture, this is not a cookie-cutter Chardonnay. The 10% Viognier adds spice and floral lift to the aromas, while the melon flavors easily handle the restrained oak. Drink now. **90 Editors' Choice** *—J.C. (3/1/2007)*

Ruffino 2005 Lumina Pinot Grigio (Venezia Giulia) $13. Basic Pinot Grigio—light in body, with simple fruity flavors of apple, pear, melon and citrus. Very clean and fresh. **84** *—J.C. (3/1/2007)*

Ruffino 2004 Lumina Pinot Grigio (Venezia Giulia) $13. 86 *—M.L. (6/1/2006)*

Ruffino 2002 Lumina Pinot Grigio (Venezia Giulia) $13. 85 *—J.C. (1/1/2004)*

Ruffino 2000 Lumina Pinot Grigio (Toscana) $12. 84 *(3/1/2002)*

Ruffino 1997 Modus Red Blend (Toscana) $40. 88 *(3/1/2002)*

Ruffino 2003 Romitorio di Santedame Red Blend (Toscana) $70. A unique blend of 60% Colorino and 40% Merlot, this wine features a drying finish loaded with firm tannins. It's dense and packed with plummy fruit as well, plus lashings of smoke and tobacco, making it complex and chewy—a good option with a simple grilled steak. **88** *—J.C. (3/1/2007)*

Ruffino 2001 Romitorio di Santedame Red Blend (Toscana) $70. 89 *—M.S. (9/1/2006)*

Ruffino 1999 Romitorio di Santedame Red Blend (Toscana) $NA. 91 Cellar Selection *(3/1/2002)*

Ruffino 1997 Tenuta Lodola Nuova Red Blend (Vino Nobile di Montepulciano) $17. 88 Editors' Choice *(3/1/2002)*

Ruffino 2006 Concento Rosé Blend (Toscana) $NA. The wine opens with a pretty pink color and delivers a rush of sweet, fruity aromas that recall raspberry, blueberry and strawberry. This is a simple wine with a vibrant liveliness backed by sweet flavors. **84** *—M.L. (7/1/2007)*

Ruffino 1999 Aziano Sangiovese (Chianti Classico) $15. 84 *(4/1/2001)*

Ruffino 2000 Fonte al Sole Sangiovese (Toscana) $8. 84 Best Buy *(3/1/2002)*

Ruffino 2001 Greppone Mazzi Sangiovese (Brunello di Montalcino) $63. Ruffino's Montalcino estate, Greppone Mazzi is—in our opinion—the source for the company's best wine. Cedary cigar box aromas are backed by layers of black cherry and plum fruit and a velvety mouthfeel. The finish is long and lush, yet structured. Drink 2008–2020. **91** *—J.C. (3/1/2007)*

Ruffino 2003 Il Ducale Sangiovese (Toscana) $20. Dusty and a bit leathery on the nose, but there's fruit enough on the palate, fleshing out with black cherry and plum flavors and picking up touches of tobacco on the finish. At 80% Sangiovese and the rest Cabernet Sauvignon and Merlot, it's a harmonious blend designed to introduce new drinkers to Tuscan wines. **86** *—J.C. (3/1/2007)*

Ruffino 2004 Il Leo Sangiovese (Chianti Superiore) $12. This plump, medium-bodied red makes a nice introduction to the company's style. Black cherry, chocolate and cinnamon flavors add leathery notes on the finish, yet remain clean and crisp. **86** *—J.C. (3/1/2007)*

Ruffino 2000 Il Leo Sangiovese (Chianti Superiore) $10. 86 Best Buy *(3/1/2002)*

Ruffino 1999 Modus Sangiovese (Toscana) $40. 88 *—M.S. (8/1/2002)*

Ruffino 2001 Riserva Ducale Sangiovese (Chianti Classico) $27. 85 *(4/1/2005)*

Ruffino 2001 Riserva Ducale Oro Sangiovese (Chianti Classico) $40. Ruffino's most famous label is the gold-label Chianti Classico Riserva Ducale, first produced in 1947. The 2001 rendition capably maintains the tradition, combining coffee, prune and tobacco scents with flavors of ripe plums and dark earth. Tannins give a richly textured feel in the mouth, the drying finish balanced by ample fruit. Drink 2008–2015. **90 Cellar Selection** *—J.C. (3/1/2007)*

Ruffino 2000 Riserva Ducale Oro Sangiovese (Chianti Classico) $39. 86 *(4/1/2005)*

Ruffino 1997 Riserva Ducale Tan Label Sangiovese (Chianti Classico) $20. 89 *(4/1/2001)*

Ruffino 1995 Tenuta Lodola Nuova Sangiovese (Vino Nobile di Montepulciano) $20. 86 *—M.S. (7/1/2000)*

Ruffino 1998 Tenuta Santedame Sangiovese (Chianti Classico) $16. 85 *(3/1/2002)*

Ruffino 1997 Tenuta Santedame Sangiovese (Chianti Classico) $18. 87 *(4/1/2001)*

Ruffino 2005 White Blend (Orvieto Classico) $7. Light and fresh, this wine hints at pear and apple; anise and almond on the nose, then turns citrusy on the palate. It's modest in intensity, but clean and refreshing on the finish. **84 Best Buy** *—J.C. (3/1/2007)*

RUGGERI & C.

Ruggeri & C. NV Extra Dry Giall Oro Gold Label Prosecco (Prosecco di Conegliano e Valdobbiadene) $18. This sparker's name, Gialloro, (yellow-gold) accurately sums up its brilliant appearance in the glass. More enticing, perhaps, are its aromas: sweet peach, fresh apricot, sage and crushed white pepper. It's a simple, fresh wine that cleans your palate and gets the job done. **86** *—M.L. (12/15/2007)*

Ruggeri & C. NV Extra Dry Gold Label Prosecco (Prosecco di Valdobbiadene) $18. 86 *—M.L. (6/1/2006)*

Ruggeri & C. NV Frizzante Gentile Prosecco (Prosecco di Conegliano e Valdobbiadene) $16. This is a very sweet-smelling frizzante with intense aromas of peach, exotic fruit and kiwi. The mouthfeel is lean and somewhat watery but the wine cleans the palate thanks to its natural crispness. **84** *—M.L. (12/15/2007)*

Ruggeri & C. NV Quartese Prosecco (Prosecco di Valdobbiadene) $NA. 86 *—M.L. (6/1/2006)*

Ruggeri & C. NV Santo Stefano Dry Prosecco (Prosecco di Valdobbiadene) $21. 87 *—M.L. (6/1/2006)*

RUGGERI GIULIANO

Ruggeri Giuliano NV Santo Stefano Champagne Blend (Prosecco di Valdobbiadene) $16. 85 *—M.S. (6/1/2003)*

Ruggeri Giuliano 2001 Giustino B. Extra Dry Prosecco (Prosecco di Valdobbiadene) $20. 87 *—M.S. (6/1/2003)*

Ruggeri Giuliano NV Gold Label Prosecco (Prosecco di Valdobbiadene) $15. 86 *—M.S. (6/1/2003)*

Ruggeri Giuliano 1999 Rosso Sagrantino (Montefalco) $15. 84 *—M.S. (2/1/2003)*

Ruggeri Giuliano 1998 Sagrantino di Montefalco Sagrantino (Sagrantino di Montefalco) $35. 89 *—C.S. (2/1/2002)*

SALADINI PILASTRI

Saladini Pilastri 2003 White Blend (Falerio) $10. 88 Best Buy *—R.V. (11/15/2004)*

SALICUTTI

Salicutti 2000 Brunello (Brunello di Montalcino) $95. 92 Editors' Choice *—M.S. (7/1/2005)*

Salicutti 2001 Piaggione Brunello (Brunello di Montalcino) $110. 90 *(4/1/2006)*

Salicutti 1999 Sangiovese (Rosso di Montalcino) $33. 90 *—M.S. (8/1/2002)*

SALUSTRI

Salustri 2002 Grotte Rosse Sangiovese (Montecucco) $40. 89 *—M.S. (9/1/2006)*

Salustri 2004 Marleo Rosso Sangiovese (Montecucco) $19. 87 *—M.S. (9/1/2006)*

Salustri 2003 Santa Marta Sangiovese (Montecucco) $28. 92 *—M.S. (9/1/2006)*

SALVANO

Salvano 1998 Dolcetto (Dolcetto di Diano d'Alba) $9. 87 *(4/1/2000)*

SALVATERRA

SalvaTerra 2001 Corvina, Rondinella, Molinara (Amarone della Valpolicella Classico) $65. SalvaTerra is a relatively new estate with high altitude vineyards at the back of the Classico zone, just before the hills of Valpolicella soar up to the Dolomites. It will be interesting to see how the winery and its wines evolve over time. This vintage tastes a bit tired, with milky chocolate, almost lactic aromas, thick inky concentration and rock-solid tannins. 87 *—M.L. (12/1/2007)*

SALVATORE MOLETTIERI

Salvatore Molettieri 1996 Vigna Cinque Querce Aglianico (Taurasi) $32. 85 *—C.S. (5/1/2002)*

SALVIANO

Salviano 1999 Turlo Red Blend (Umbria) $10. 86 *—M.S. (2/1/2003)*

Salviano 2003 White Blend (Orvieto Classico Superiore) $13. 85 *—M.S. (7/1/2005)*

Salviano 2003 Superiore White Blend (Orvieto Classico) $13. 87 *—M.S. (11/15/2004)*

SAN ANGELO

San Angelo 1998 Single Vineyard Pinot Grigio (Toscana) $13. 87 *(8/1/1999)*

SAN BONIFACIO

San Bonifacio 1998 Pinot Grigio (Veneto) $10. 86 *(8/1/1999)*

SAN CARLO

San Carlo 1999 Brunello (Brunello di Montalcino) $NA. 86 *—M.S. (6/1/2004)*

SAN FABIANO

San Fabiano 2002 Sangiovese (Chianti) $12. 82 *(4/1/2005)*

San Fabiano 1998 Sangiovese (Chianti) $8. 85 *(4/1/2001)*

San Fabiano 2000 Borghini Baldovinetti (Armaiolo) Sangiovese (Colli della Toscana Centrale) $43. 84 *—M.S. (9/1/2006)*

SAN FABIANO CALCINAIA

San Fabiano Calcinaia 2005 Sangiovese (Chianti Classico) $21. This is a pretty, feminine wine with foreground tones of blue flower, white cherry and delicate forest berry that also has a few unripe notes of bramble and fresh grass at the back. It has good crispness in the mouth and a few more of those green tones on the finish. 87 *—M.L. (11/1/2007)*

San Fabiano Calcinaia 2002 Sangiovese (Chianti Classico) $23. 89 *(4/1/2005)*

San Fabiano Calcinaia 2001 Sangiovese (Chianti Classico) $23. 86 *—M.S. (11/15/2003)*

San Fabiano Calcinaia 2000 Sangiovese (Chianti Classico) $19. 86 *—M.S. (12/31/2002)*

San Fabiano Calcinaia 1998 Sangiovese (Chianti Classico) $18. 87 *(4/1/2001)*

San Fabiano Calcinaia 2004 Cellole Riserva Sangiovese (Chianti Classico) $33. Blueberry, sweet cherry and forest fruit set the tone, followed by a distinctly perfumed aroma. Musky, spicy favors appear in the mouth and seem to reinforce the firm tannins and a slightly sour finish. 89 *—M.L. (11/1/2007)*

San Fabiano Calcinaia 2001 Cellole Riserva Sangiovese (Chianti Classico) $38. 93 Editors' Choice *(4/1/2005)*

San Fabiano Calcinaia 2000 Cerviolo Sangiovese (Toscana) $63. 93 *—M.S. (10/1/2004)*

San Fabiano Calcinaia 1999 Cerviolo Sangiovese (Toscana) $45. 90 *—M.S. (12/31/2002)*

San Fabiano Calcinaia 1997 Cerviolo Sangiovese (Toscana) $45. 90 *—J.F. (9/1/2001)*

San Fabiano Calcinaia 1996 Cerviolo Sangiovese (Toscana) $37. 90 *—M.S. (9/1/2000)*

San Fabiano Calcinaia 2000 Cerviolo Rosso Sangiovese (Tuscany) $65. 88 *—M.S. (11/15/2003)*

San Fabiano Calcinaia 1998 Riserva Cellole Sangiovese (Chianti Classico) $31. 89 *—M.S. (12/31/2002)*

San Fabiano Calcinaia 1997 Riserva Cellole Sangiovese (Chianti Classico) $28. 87 *(4/1/2001)*

SAN FELICE

San Felice 2001 Campogiovanni Brunello (Brunello di Montalcino) $70. 90 Cellar Selection *(4/1/2006)*

San Felice 2002 Sangiovese (Chianti Classico) $18. 86 *(4/1/2005)*

San Felice 2000 Sangiovese (Chianti Classico) $18. 86 *(1/1/2004)*

San Felice 2000 Il Grigio Riserva Sangiovese (Chianti Classico) $26. 83 *(4/1/2005)*

San Felice 1999 Il Grigio Riserva Sangiovese (Chianti Classico) $26. 89 *(1/1/2004)*

San Felice 1999 Poggio Rosso Riserva Sangiovese (Chianti Classico) $55. 91 *(1/1/2004)*

San Felice 1999 Poggio Rosso Riserva Sangiovese (Chianti Classico) $50. 86 *(4/1/2005)*

San Felice 1999 Vigorello Sangiovese (Toscana) $43. 90 *(1/1/2004)*

SAN FILIPPO DI GIANNELLI

San Filippo di Giannelli 2001 Brunello (Brunello di Montalcino) $56. 85 *(4/1/2006)*

SAN FRANCESCO

San Francesco 1999 Rosso Gaglioppo (Cirò Classico) $12. 80 *—C.S. (5/1/2002)*

SAN GIORGIO A LAPI

San Giorgio a Lapi 2003 Sangiovese (Chianti Colli Senesi) $10. Shows the heat of the vintage in its slightly cooked-fruit aromas and flavors. Think dried cherries, prune and molasses, but without being too heavy; balanced by supple tannins and a dusty sensation on the finish. 85 Best Buy *(10/1/2007)*

SAN GIULIO

San Giulio 2004 Pinot Grigio (Delle Venezie) $10. 82 *—M.L. (2/1/2006)*

SAN GIUSEPPE

San Giuseppe 2003 Corvina, Rondinella, Molinara (Amarone della Valpolicella Classico) $36. There's a nice aromatic ensemble here of spice, clove, oak, prune and cherry. But the oak nuances are a bit over-powering. More wood flavors appear in the mouth as well as dried berry flavors. 88 *—M.L. (12/1/2007)*

San Giuseppe 2001 Merlot (Veneto) $9. 81 *(5/1/2003)*

San Giuseppe 2004 Pinot Grigio (Veneto) $11. 87 Best Buy *(2/1/2006)*

San Giuseppe 2003 Pinot Grigio (Piave) $18. 83 *—J.C. (12/31/2004)*

San Giuseppe 2002 Pinot Grigio (Veneto) $9. 83 *—J.C. (7/1/2003)*

San Giuseppe 2001 Pinot Grigio (Veneto) $9. 82 *—J.C. (7/1/2003)*

San Giuseppe 2004 Pink Pinot Grigio (Veneto) $11. 86 Best Buy *(2/1/2006)*

San Giuseppe 2005 Brut Prosecco (Prosecco di Conegliano) $NA. 85 *—M.L. (6/1/2006)*

San Giuseppe 2005 Extra Dry Prosecco (Prosecco di Conegliano) $NA. 85 *—M.L. (6/1/2006)*

San Giuseppe 2002 Sangiovese (Chianti) $10. 83 *(4/1/2005)*

SAN GIUSTO A RENTENNANO

San Giusto a Rentennano 1998 Sangiovese (Chianti Classico) $19. 92 Editors' Choice *(4/1/2001)*

SAN JACOPO DA VICCHIOMAGGIO

San Jacopo da Vicchiomaggio 2003 Sangiovese (Chianti Classico) $18. 89 *—M.S. (10/1/2006)*

SAN LUCIANO

San Luciano 2005 Resico White Blend (Toscana) $11. This is a highly like-able wine with unique aromas of orange peel, dried fruit, apricot and fragrant pear. Those flavors carry through to the mouth, creating a sensa-tion of opulence and chewy sweetness. 86 Best Buy *—M.L. (11/15/2007)*

SAN MICHELE EPPAN

San Michele Eppan 2002 Sanct Valentin Gewürztraminer (Alto Adige) $30. 88 *—R.V. (7/1/2003)*

San Michele Eppan 2002 Sanct Valentin Pinot Bianco (Alto Adige) $30. 88 *—R.V. (7/1/2003)*

San Michele Eppan 2002 Sanct Valentin Sauvignon Blanc (Alto Adige) $29. 87 *—R.V. (7/1/2003)*

SAN PATRIGNANO

San Patrignano 2001 Montepirolo Cabernet Sauvignon (Colli di Rimini) $45. 87 *—M.S. (7/1/2005)*

San Patrignano 2003 Montepirolo Red Blend (Colli di Rimini) $38. San Patrignano is among Romagna's best and most respected producers and offers Bordeaux-inspired wines like this succulent Cabernet (with smaller percentages of Merlot and Cabernet Franc). The nose is rich with leather, vanilla, moist earth, coffee and licorice but there's enough ripe black red fruit to keep it fresh and lively. A beautiful Cabernet from a hot vintage and enologist Riccardo Cotarella. 90 *—M.L. (2/1/2007)*

San Patrignano 2004 Noi Red Blend (Colli di Rimini) $28. Noi means "us" in Italian and refers to the community of recovering drug addicts that produces this wine. With the help of consulting enologist Riccardo Cotarella, this is a delicious deep and concentrated wine that boasts a gorgeous nose of blackberry, plum, pressed violets and toasted notes: Sophisticated and succulent in the mouth. 87 —*M.L. (2/1/2007)*

San Patrignano 2002 Noi Red Blend (Colli di Rimini) $36. 86 —*M.S. (7/1/2005)*

San Patrignano 2001 Avi Sangiovese (Sangiovese di Romagna) $45. 87 —*M.S. (7/1/2005)*

San Patrignano 2003 Avi Superiore Riserva Sangiovese (Sangiovese di Romagna) $38. Full throttle Sangiovese with beautifully integrated toasted notes (thanks to 12 months in French oak) that frame aromas of prune, black cherry, plum, leather and vanilla: This is a modern, deep and smooth wine with rock-solid structure. 92 Editors' Choice —*M.L. (2/1/2007)*

SAN QUIRICO

San Quirico 2003 Sangiovese (Chianti Colli Senesi) $12. 83 *(4/1/2005)*

San Quirico 1999 Sangiovese (Chianti Colli Senesi) $12. 86 *(4/1/2001)*

San Quirico 2004 Riserva Proprietà Vecchione Vernaccia (Vernaccia di San Gimignano) $16. 86 —*M.L. (9/1/2005)*

SAN RUSTICO

San Rustico 2003 Corvina, Rondinella, Molinara (Amarone della Valpolicella Classico) $45. Founded in 1870, San Rustico has recently done a lot of work in the winery and vineyard to maintain a quality edge. This Amarone boasts great intensity and delicacy of aromas. You'll get layers of apple, cherry cola, mint, blue flowers, licorice, raisin and almond. In the mouth, those flavors are lively and fresh and the mouthfeel is caressing and long lasting. 91 —*M.L. (10/1/2007)*

San Rustico 2001 Gaso Corvina, Rondinella, Molinara (Amarone della Valpolicella Classico) $50. There's a fun, chunky, slightly hefty quality to this wine, accented by blocky aromas of coffee, vanilla, poached cherries, cola, roasted chestnut and brown sugar. If you're an Amarone purist, you might find these qualities muddled and lacking in grace. But if you love big, meaty wines that you can sink your teeth into, it's for you. The mouthfeel is chewy, sticky and long lasting. 90 —*M.L. (12/1/2007)*

SAN SIMONE

San Simone 2004 Pinot Grigio (Friuli) $15. 84 *(2/1/2006)*

SAN VALENTINO

San Valentino 2003 Luna Nuova Red Blend (Romagna) $NA. Another surprise hit from central Italy with bright, vibrant color, modern-style concentration and lush notes of roasted coffee, mocha, plum, black cherry and cedar wood (thanks to 14 months of oak aging). It's equally big and bold in the mouth with chewy tannins and a robust, meaty quality. This is a wine worth looking out for. 89 —*M.L. (2/1/2007)*

San Valentino 2005 Scabi Red Blend (Sangiovese di Romagna) $NA. Milk chocolate, clove and cinnamon meet aromas of moist earth and distant notes of rhubarb too. The wine has a leaner consistency in the mouth but shows plenty of power and purity. 85 —*M.L. (2/1/2007)*

San Valentino 2003 Terre di Covignano Superiore Riserva Sangiovese (Sangiovese di Romagna) $NA. A surprise hit from Romagna: This is a fine and elegant red with toasted notes, soft vanilla and Asian spice. It boasts a solid structure that washes over the palate with firm tannins, persistence and loads of intensity. It scores high in overall intensity; pair it with something of equal or greater strength like paprika beef stew. 91 —*M.L. (2/1/2007)*

SANDRA LOTTI

Sandra Lotti 2000 Saporita Sangiovese (Toscana) $23. 86 —*M.S. (10/1/2004)*

SANDRONE

Sandrone 2004 Barbera (Barbera d'Alba) $30. The Sandrone is a great example of a modern Barbera: hefty black fruit, violets and smoked meats under a thin mantle of oak. Despite the exuberance of the fruit, the wine shows plenty of finesse, as it moves seamlessly through the palate to a medium finish. 90 —*M.G. (4/1/2007)*

Sandrone 2003 Barbera (Barbera d'Alba) $29. 90 Editors' Choice —*J.C. (3/1/2006)*

Sandrone 2005 Dolcetto (Dolcetto d'Alba) $22. As with many of the wines of Sandrone, it is easy to be beguiled by the fruit and miss the underlying structure holding it together. This is true of the Dolcetto, where the wine initially shows plenty of dark fruit and a touch of mint, but gains a spicy complexity as it takes in air. The wine will benefit from a couple of years in the bottle, but is delicious now. 90 —*M.G. (12/31/2007)*

Sandrone 2004 Dolcetto (Dolcetto d'Alba) $19. 86 —*J.C. (3/1/2006)*

Sandrone 1998 Dolcetto (Dolcetto d'Alba) $25. 93 *(4/1/2000)*

Sandrone 2001 Cannubi Boschis Nebbiolo (Barolo) $135. 97 Editors' Choice —*J.C. (3/1/2006)*

Sandrone 2002 Le Vigne Nebbiolo (Barolo) $118. Sandrone has crafted a pleasant if slightly less ambitious wine than usual. It is a rich wine, with plenty of fruit, but overall is a little straightforward and lacks complexity. 86 —*M.G. (12/31/2007)*

Sandrone 2001 Le Vigne Nebbiolo (Barolo) $120. 96 —*J.C. (3/1/2006)*

Sandrone 2004 Valmaggiore Nebbiolo (Nebbiolo d'Alba) $45. Sandrone's Nebbiolos are usually minor versions of his great Barolos, but the 2004 did not show particularly well. The tannins are hard, the wine overly structured for the amount of fruit, and the finish is short to medium. 84 —*M.G. (4/1/2007)*

Sandrone 2003 Valmaggiore Nebbiolo (Nebbiolo d'Alba) $45. 87 —*J.C. (3/1/2006)*

SANGERVASIO

Sangervasio 1998 Le Stoppie Sangiovese (Chianti Colli Pisani) $9. 85 Best Buy *(4/1/2001)*

SANSONINA

Sansonina 1998 Merlot (Veneto) $60. 90 *(5/1/2003)*

SANT' ELENA

Sant' Elena 1998 Pinot Grigio (Venezia Giulia) $15. 86 *(8/1/1999)*

SANT'EVASIO

Sant'Evasio 1999 Cortese (Gavi di Gavi) $13. 84 *(9/1/2001)*

Sant'Evasio 1995 Nebbiolo (Barolo) $34. 91 —*J.C. (9/1/2001)*

SANTA ANASTASIA

Santa Anastasia 1999 Passomaggio Red Blend (Sicilia) $14. 90 Best Buy —*C.S. (11/15/2002)*

SANTA MARGHERITA

Santa Margherita 2006 Chardonnay (Trentino) $22. Poolside lunches, seafood salads and quick finger foods call out for a simple, un-oaked Chardonnay and this crisp white from northern Italy fits the bill perfectly. The wine is light as a feather with cool crispness on the close that reinforces distinct citrus flavors. 86 —*M.L. (12/1/2007)*

Santa Margherita 2003 Chardonnay (Veneto Orientale) $16. 83 —*J.C. (12/31/2004)*

Santa Margherita 2003 Chardonnay (Alto Adige) $21. 86 —*J.C. (12/31/2004)*

Santa Margherita 2001 Versato Merlot (Veneto) $21. 85 —*J.C. (12/31/2004)*

Santa Margherita 2006 Vino Frizzante Müller-Thurgau (Vigneti delle Dolomiti) $NA. Light fizz and a touch of sweetness tickle your palate and open the way for fragrant floral tones and exotic fruit. The mouthfeel is lean and watery but fruity flavors are raised one notch up in intensity thanks to the wine's easy effervescence. 84 —*M.L. (12/1/2007)*

Santa Margherita 2002 Pinot Bianco (Alto Adige) 84 —*R.V. (7/1/2003)*

Santa Margherita 2006 Pinot Grigio (Valdadige) $25. If any one single estate turned America on to Pinot Grigio, Santa Margherita did. The reason for the outstanding success of this wine is its clean simplicity. This is a no-fuss wine that invites casual drinking situations and a global range of pairing possibilities, from pizza to Thai spicy beef. Fresh aromas include citrus, passion fruit and white stone. 86 —*M.L. (12/1/2007)*

Santa Margherita 2005 Pinot Grigio (Alto Adige) $25. This cooler climate Pinot Grigio is elegant and pristine with fine notes of citrus, stone fruit, peach and white stone. The mouthfeel is lean, watery and refreshing. 86 —*M.L. (9/1/2007)*

Santa Margherita 2004 Pinot Grigio (Alto Adige) $22. 85 —*M.L. (2/1/2006)*

Santa Margherita 2003 Pinot Grigio (Alto Adige) $25. 86 —*J.C. (12/31/2004)*

Santa Margherita 2002 Pinot Grigio (Valdadige) $22. 87 —*R.V. (7/1/2003)*

Santa Margherita 1998 Pinot Grigio (Valdadige) $19. 84 *(8/1/1999)*

Santa Margherita NV Brut Prosecco (Prosecco di Valdobbiadene) $NA. Frothy bubbles and a luminous color set the stage for this lively Prosecco redolent of peachy cream and white mineral. The carbonization is pungent and direct and underlines the wine's fruity flavors and bright acidity. Santa Margherita is one of only two producers permitted to bottle DOC Prosecco, despite the fact they are located outside the DOC zone. 87 —*M.L. (12/15/2007)*

Santa Margherita NV Brut Prosecco (Prosecco di Valdobbiadene) $21. 88 —*M.L. (6/1/2006)*

Santa Margherita NV Brut Prosecco (Prosecco di Valdobbiadene) $21. 87 —*M.S. (12/15/2004)*

Santa Margherita NV Brut Prosecco (Prosecco di Valdobbiadene) $21. 88 —*M.S. (12/15/2005)*

Santa Margherita NV Cartizze Prosecco (Prosecco Superiore di Cartizze) $NA. True to the spirit of the Cartizze cru, this sparkler is elegant and refined, while being slightly sweet on the nose and mouth. Peach blossom, acacia, basil and exotic fruit set the tone. 88 —*M.L. (12/15/2007)*

Santa Margherita NV Extra Dry Prosecco (Prosecco di Conegliano e Valdobbiadene) $NA. Known for its popular Pinot Grigio, Santa Margherita sounds off in the Prosecco market with this sweet, fresh sparkler redolent of kiwi, pineapple and fragrant flowers. A distant herbal or anise seed note adds dimension and character. 85 —*M.L. (12/15/2007)*

SANTA SOFIA

Santa Sofia 2004 Garganega (Soave Classico) $11. 83 —*J.C. (10/1/2006)*

Santa Sofia 2000 Red Blend (Valpolicella Classico) $10. 83 *(5/1/2003)*

Santa Sofia 2000 Red Blend (Amarone della Valpolicella Classico) $55. 92 *(11/1/2005)*

Santa Sofia 1997 Classico Red Blend (Amarone della Valpolicella Classico) $40. 92 *(5/1/2003)*

Santa Sofia 1998 Gioé Red Blend (Amarone della Valpolicella Classico) $72. 92 *(11/1/2005)*

Santa Sofia 1995 Gioé Red Blend (Amarone della Valpolicella Classico) $45. 89 *(5/1/2003)*

Santa Sofia 1998 Monte Gradella Red Blend (Valpolicella Classico Superiore) $20. 86 *(5/1/2003)*

SANTA TRINITA

Santa Trinita 2004 Sangiovese (Chianti Classico) $NA. This is executed in a traditional style that can be recognized by its light ruby color and vibrant cherry aromas. The pretty nose is well balanced and clean, and the wine is lively in the mouth with fresh acidity on the close. 86 —*M.L. (11/1/2007)*

SANTADI

Santadi 1997 Terre Brune Carignane (Sardinia) $37. 89 —*C.S. (5/1/2002)*

Santadi 1998 Grotta Rossa Grenache (Cannonau di Sardegna) $10. 85 Best Buy —*C.S. (5/1/2002)*

Santadi 1998 Rocca Rubia Riserva Red Blend (Sardinia) $19. 86 —*C.S. (5/1/2002)*

Santadi 1997 Shardana Red Blend (Valli di Porto Pino) $24. 90 Editors' Choice —*C.S. (5/1/2002)*

Santadi 1996 Shardana Red Blend (Valli di Porto Pino) $21. 86 —*C.S. (5/1/2002)*

SANTI

Santi 2003 Corvina, Rondinella, Molinara (Amarone della Valpolicella) $45. Managed by Italy's leading wine company, GIV, this is a traditional Amarone with sweet spice aromas, white stone, brown sugar and pulsing forest berry. The aromatic intensity is not huge, but it is balanced and the wine delivers fine, dusty tannins on the close. 88 —*M.L. (10/1/2007)*

Santi 2003 Proemio Corvina, Rondinella, Molinara (Amarone della Valpolicella) $65. Here is a refreshing approach to Amarone only because this wine is not overextracted or concentrated. It charges forward with a leaner, more elegant approach that allows distinct berry, spice and crushed black pepper notes to appear without too much power or weight. The mouthfeel is smooth, caressing and leaves lasting sweet berry flavors. 90 —*M.L. (10/1/2007)*

Santi 1999 Merlot (Delle Venezie) $10. 83 *(5/1/2003)*

Santi 2005 Sortesele Pinot Grigio (Delle Venezie) $14. 87 —*M.L. (6/1/2006)*

Santi 2004 Sortesele Pinot Grigio (Delle Venezie) $12. 87 Best Buy —*M.L. (2/1/2006)*

Santi 2002 Sortesele Pinot Grigio (Trentino) $13. 85 —*R.V. (7/1/2003)*

Santi 2001 Sortesele Pinot Grigio (Trentino) $12. 83 —*J.C. (7/1/2003)*

Santi 2001 Red Blend (Amarone della Valpolicella) $40. 86 *(11/1/2005)*

Santi 2006 L'Infinito Chiaretto Red Blend (Bardolino) $NA. Here's a pale pink rosé made with traditional Veronese grapes (Corvina, Rondinella and Molinara) that imparts nice floral tones and aromas of small forest fruit. Delicate overall, there are some sharper, spicier highlights in the mouth where the wine shows good length. 86 —*M.L. (7/1/2007)*

Santi 1996 Proemio Red Blend (Amarone della Valpolicella) $51. 91 —*J.F. (9/1/2001)*

Santi 1999 Solane Red Blend (Valpolicella Classico) $10. 83 *(5/1/2003)*

SANTINI

Santini NV Spumante Moscato (Moscato d'Asti) $7. 84 —*P.G. (12/31/2000)*

SAPÍENS

Sapíens 2003 Chardonnay (Sicilia) $10. 83 —*M.S. (7/1/2005)*

SARACCO

Saracco 2004 Moscato (Moscato d'Asti) $15. 90 Best Buy —*M.L. (12/15/2005)*

SARDUS PATER

Sardus Pater 2002 Vermentino (Vermentino di Sardegna) $15. 84 —*M.S. (8/1/2004)*

Sardus Pater 2003 Albus Vermentino (Vermentino di Sardegna) $14. 80 —*M.S. (7/1/2006)*

SARTARELLI

Sartarelli 2003 Verdicchio (Verdicchio dei Castelli di Jesi Classico) $13. 87 —*M.S. (8/1/2004)*

Sartarelli 1999 White Blend (Verdicchio dei Castelli di Jesi Classico) $11. 83 —*M.N. (12/31/2000)*

SARTORI

Sartori 1991 Corte Brá Corvina (Amarone della Valpolicella) $40. 94 —*M.G. (5/1/1999)*

Sartori 2000 Corvina, Rondinella, Molinara (Amarone della Valpolicella Classico) $33. 91 Editors' Choice —*J.C. (12/31/2004)*

Sartori 1995 Corvina, Rondinella, Molinara (Amarone della Valpolicella Classico) $31. 87 —*M.S. (9/1/2000)*

Sartori 2001 Corte Brà Corvina, Rondinella, Molinara (Amarone della Valpolicella Classico) $40. This wine has a leg up on the competition thanks to its elegance. Vibrant ruby red in color, its aromas include ripe cherry, milk chocolate, leather, tobacco and Indian spice. Yes, the aromas are intense, but they are weaved together in a seamless, harmonious fashion, creating a polished and pristine whole. Try it with roast leg of lamb and broad bean purée. 91 —*M.L. (12/1/2007)*

Sartori 2003 Estate Collection Corvina, Rondinella, Molinara (Amarone della Valpolicella) $34. This is a compact and clean wine that boasts pretty mineral tones on the fringe of a solid fruit core of cherry and plum. It is nicely made, with crisp freshness, good structure and length. 88 —*M.L. (10/1/2007)*

Sartori 1997 Merlot (Friuli Venezia Giulia) $9. 83 —*M.S. (9/1/2000)*

Sartori 1997 Pinot Grigio (Grave del Friuli) $9. 80 *(8/1/1999)*

Sartori 2004 Pinot Grigio (Delle Venezie) $9. 86 Best Buy —*M.L. (6/1/2006)*

Sartori 2003 Pinot Grigio (Delle Venezie) $9. 85 Best Buy —*J.C. (12/31/2004)*

Sartori 2002 Pinot Grigio (Delle Venezie) $9. 81 —*J.C. (7/1/2003)*

Sartori 2005 Giulietta Blush Pinot Grigio (Delle Venezie) $9. A concept wine made with the American market in mind, Giuliette recalls the pink marble of Verona and, of course, Shakespeare's lovelorn protagonist. The wine drinks well: It's correct and clean albeit lean and watery in the mouth. Aromas recall red berries, peach and white stone. 85 Best Buy —*M.L. (7/1/2007)*

Sartori 2001 Red Blend (Amarone della Valpolicella) $34. 88 *(11/1/2005)*

Sartori 1995 Cent'Anni Red Blend (Valpolicella) $33. 84 —*M.S. (9/1/2000)*

Sartori 1998 Corte Brà Red Blend (Amarone della Valpolicella Classico) $40. 89 *(11/1/2005)*

SASSO

Sasso 1997 Covo dei Briganti Aglianico (Aglianico del Vulture) $15. 85 —*C.S. (5/1/2002)*

SCAGLIOLA

Scagliola 2004 Volo di Farfalle Moscato (Moscato d'Asti) $17. 88 —*M.L. (12/15/2005)*

SCARLATTA

Scarlatta 1997 Merlot (Veneto) $5. 81 —*M.S. (9/1/2000)*

Scarlatta 1997 Pinot Grigio (Veneto) $5. 84 *(8/1/1999)*

SCARPA

Scarpa 1990 Tettimorra Barolo Nebbiolo (Barolo) $NA. 81 —*R.V. (11/15/2002)*

SCARZELLO

Scarzello 1998 Vigna Merenda Nebbiolo (Barolo) $75. 85 *(4/2/2004)*

SCIARRA

Sciarra 1998 Roccarosso Red Blend (Marche) $18. 83 —*M.S. (10/1/2006)*

SCOPETANI

Scopetani 2000 Nemus Red Blend (Toscana) $14. Sweet black fruit, roasted almonds, pine and slate roof characterize the nose of this Sangiovese-Cabernet Sauvignon Tuscan blend. The wine has measured intensity and a solid build with smooth tannins. Drink now. 85 —*M.L. (5/1/2007)*

Scopetani 2004 Sangiovese (Chianti Rufina) $6. 86 Best Buy —*M.L. (11/15/2006)*

Scopetani 2004 Angelicus Sangiovese (Chianti) $9. 85 Best Buy —*M.S. (10/1/2006)*

Scopetani 2003 Angelicus Sangiovese (Chianti) $8. 89 Best Buy *(4/1/2005)*

Scopetani 2004 Risasso Sangiovese (Chianti Rufina) $12. Cherries, candied fruit and blue flowers denote a traditional Chainti and add a touch of sweetness to the nose. This wine has good persistency and presents more cherry-berry flavors on the finish. IMPORTED BY USA WINE IMPORTS? 87 Best Buy —*M.L. (2/1/2007)*

Scopetani 2001 813 Riserva Sangiovese (Chianti Rufina) $14. 85 *(11/15/2006)*

Scopetani 2001 Riserva Vigna Macereto Sangiovese (Chianti Rufina) $14. This is a wine with bursting red fruit and a solid dose of minerality that hits the nose in a solid and decisive fashion. Dig a bit deeper, and subtle notes of prune, coffee, dark chocolate, dried violet and rose petal appear. Tannins and acidity fall nicely into place. 87 —*M.L. (2/1/2007)*

SECCO-BERTANI

Secco-Bertani 2000 Red Blend (Valpolicella Valpantena) $13. 88 *(5/1/2003)*

SEGHESIO

Seghesio 1997 Vigneto della Chiesa Barbera (Barbera d'Alba) $30. 91 *(4/1/2000)*

SELLA & MOSCA

Sella & Mosca 1995 Marchese Di Villamarina Cabernet Sauvignon (Sardinia) $35. 84 —*M.N. (12/31/2000)*

Sella & Mosca 2004 Riserva Cannonau (Cannonau di Sardegna) $14. Light in color and thin in extraction, this Cannonau opens with aromas of forest berry, red candy, blue flowers, white stone, fennel seed and walnut nuttiness. There's enough dimension and structure here to pair with roasted pork, fried chicken or cheese-topped pasta. 86 —*M.L. (5/1/2007)*

Sella & Mosca 1996 Raím Red Blend (Isola dei Nuraghi) $12. 85 —*M.N. (12/31/2000)*

Sella & Mosca 2002 Riserva Red Blend (Cannonau di Sardegna) $16. 82 —*M.S. (10/1/2006)*

Sella & Mosca 1997 Riserva Red Blend (Cannonau di Sardegna) $11. 86 —*M.N. (12/31/2000)*

Sella & Mosca 1995 Tanca Farra Red Blend (Sardinia) $16. 88 —*M.N. (12/31/2000)*

Sella & Mosca 1999 Le Arenarie Sauvignon Blanc (Sardinia) $12. 88 —*M.N. (12/31/2000)*

Sella & Mosca 2005 Terre Bianche Torbato (Alghero) $22. This offers an excellent opportunity to taste Sardinia's Torbato grape. The flavors are inviting and intense, including yellow fruit, nuts, roasted chestnuts and honey. Bottom line: It's a wine with loads of personality. 87 —*M.L. (8/1/2007)*

Sella & Mosca 2006 La Cala Vermentino (Vermentino di Sardegna) $14. An informal, easy-to-drink wine with medium aromatic intensity rallied mostly around fragrant fresh fruit, white stone and Mediterranean herbs. The structure is lean and the acidity is bright: You can't ask for more. 86 —*M.L. (8/1/2007)*

Sella & Mosca 2003 La Cala Vermentino (Vermentino di Sardegna) $13. 87 —*M.S. (8/1/2004)*

Sella & Mosca 1999 La Cala White Blend (Sardinia) $11. 88 Best Buy —*M.N. (12/31/2000)*

SELVO DEL MORO

Selvo del Moro 2001 Sangiovese (Chianti Classico) $22. 85 *(4/1/2005)*

SEMIFONTE

Semifonte 1997 Riserva Sangiovese (Chianti Classico) $31. 86 *(4/1/2001)*

SERGIO MOTTURA

Sergio Mottura 2004 La Tour a Civitella Grechetto (Civitella d'Agliano) $20. The region of Lazio, in central Italy, is not known for its wines. However, it does have a few aces up its sleeve and this Grechetto-based wine (with fruit sourced from five different vineyards) is one of them. Thanks to its brilliant golden color and rich aromas of stone fruit, honey and caramel, this is a wine that pairs majestically with lobster, crab and smoked salmon. 90 Editors' Choice —*M.L. (12/1/2007)*

Sergio Mottura 2005 Poggio della Costa Grechetto (Civitella d'Agliano) $20. This Grechetto-based wine has a pretty straw appearance and definitely puts an emphasis on nuts, melon and stone fruit. Thanks to a smooth mouthfeel and spicy finish, it does liven up in the mouth. 86 —*M.L. (11/15/2007)*

Sergio Mottura 2005 Vigna Tragugnano White Blend (Orvieto) $16. Aromas of stone fruit, melon and almond skin lend this Procanico-Verdello-Grechetto blend a sophisticated touch, and the wine delivers nutty nuances in the mouth. 86 —*M.L. (11/15/2007)*

SESTA DI SOPRA

Sesta di Sopra 2001 Brunello (Brunello di Montalcino) $55. 91 *(4/1/2006)*

SESTI

Sesti 2001 Brunello (Brunello di Montalcino) $60. 88 *(4/1/2006)*

Sesti 2000 Phenomena Riserva Brunello (Brunello di Montalcino) $45. 90 *(4/1/2006)*

SIGNANO

Signano 2001 Sangiovese (Chianti Colli Senesi) $14. 82 *(4/1/2005)*

Signano 2002 Vernaccia (Vernaccia di San Gimignano) $17. 84 —*M.S. (8/1/2004)*

SIMONE SANTINI

Simone Santini 2003 Tenute Le Calcinaie Sangiovese (Chianti Colli Senesi) $20. 88 *(4/1/2005)*

SINFAROSA

Sinfarosa 1998 Zinfandel (Puglia) $24. 82 —*C.S. (5/1/2002)*

SIRO PACENTI

Siro Pacenti 2001 Brunello (Brunello di Montalcino) $70. 89 *(4/1/2006)*

Siro Pacenti 2000 Brunello (Brunello di Montalcino) $75. 93 Editors' Choice —*M.S. (7/1/2005)*

Siro Pacenti 1999 Brunello (Brunello di Montalcino) 95 —*M.S. (6/1/2004)*

Siro Pacenti 2002 Sangiovese (Rosso di Montalcino) $NA. 91 —*M.S. (6/1/2004)*

SOLARIA

Solaria 2001 Brunello (Brunello di Montalcino) $45. 89 *(4/1/2006)*

Solaria 2000 Brunello (Brunello di Montalcino) $70. 92 —*M.S. (7/1/2005)*

Solaria 1998 Brunello (Brunello di Montalcino) $70. 92 Cellar Selection —*M.S. (11/15/2003)*

Solaria 2002 Sangiovese (Rosso di Montalcino) $29. 89 —*M.S. (6/1/2004)*

Solaria 2001 Sangiovese (Rosso di Montalcino) $30. 87 —*M.S. (11/15/2003)*

SOLDIMELA

Soldimela 1999 Sangiovese Grosso (Monteregio di Massa Maritima) $8. 87 Best Buy —*M.M. (11/15/2001)*

Soldimela 2000 Vermentino (Maremma) $8. 87 Best Buy —*M.M. (11/15/2001)*

SOLDO

Soldo 2001 Cabernet Sauvignon (Veneto) $6. 83 *(5/1/2003)*

Soldo 2001 Merlot (Veneto) $6. 80 *(5/1/2003)*

Soldo 2001 Pinot Grigio (Veneto) $6. 83 —*J.C. (7/1/2003)*

Soldo 2000 Red Blend (Valpolicella) $6. 85 Best Buy *(5/1/2003)*

Soldo 2000 Red Blend (Montepulciano d'Abruzzo) $6. 81 —*M.S. (11/15/2003)*

Soldo 2000 White Blend (Soave) $6. 82 —*J.C. (7/1/2003)*

SORELLE BRONCA

Sorelle Bronca NV Extra Dry Prosecco (Prosecco di Valdobbiadene) $14. 86 —*J.C. (12/31/2003)*

SPADINA

Spadina 2002 Nero d'Avola (Sicilia) $10. 86 Best Buy —*M.S. (2/1/2005)*

Spadina 2002 Una Rosa Signature Nero d'Avola (Sicilia) $15. 88 —*M.S. (2/1/2005)*

SPALLETTI

Spalletti 2004 Sangiovese (Chianti) $11. 84 *—M.S. (10/1/2006)*

Spalletti 1997 Riserva Sangiovese (Chianti Rufina) $20. 90 *(4/1/2001)*

SPANO

Spano 1996 Annata Red Blend (Salento) $40. 84 *—C.S. (5/1/2002)*

SPERI

Speri 2000 Corvina (Amarone della Valpolicella Classico) $60. 91 *(11/1/2005)*

Speri 2001 Corvina, Rondinella, Molinara (Amarone della Valpolicella Classico) $60. 91 *(11/1/2005)*

Speri 2003 Vigneto Monte Sant'Urbano Corvina, Rondinella, Molinara (Amarone della Valpolicella Classico) $75. This vineyard designate wine straddles a fine line between Old and New World. On the traditional side is a coulis of blackberry fruit (a pergola trellis is used for better grape aeration) and sweet spice. On the modern front are deep oak shadings. The final result is an excellent package and an example of very good winemaking. 90 *—M.L. (10/1/2007)*

Speri 1997 Red Blend (Amarone della Valpolicella Classico) $48. 91 *(5/1/2003)*

Speri 2003 La Roverina Red Blend (Valpolicella Classico Superiore) $16. 86 *—M.L. (9/1/2005)*

Speri 1999 Sant'urbano Red Blend (Valpolicella Classico Superiore) $21. 86 *(5/1/2003)*

Speri 1998 Sant'urbano Red Blend (Valpolicella Classico Superiore) $22. 85 *(5/1/2003)*

Speri 2000 Vigneto La Roverina Red Blend (Valpolicella Classico Superiore) $12. 85 *(5/1/2003)*

SPORTOLETTI

Sportoletti 2004 Grechetto (Assisi) $12. 87 *—M.L. (9/1/2005)*

Sportoletti 2001 Assisi Rosso Red Blend (Umbria) $15. 86 *—C.S. (2/1/2003)*

Sportoletti 2000 Villa Fidelia Rosso Red Blend (Umbria) $55. 92 Editors' Choice *—C.S. (2/1/2003)*

ST. MICHAEL EPPAN

St. Michael Eppan 1998 Pinot Grigio (Alto Adige) $10. 86 *(8/1/1999)*

St. Michael Eppan 2000 Sanct Valentin Sauvignon Blanc (Alto Adige) $28. 87 *(8/1/2002)*

St. Michael-Eppan 2004 Pinot Grigio (Alto Adige) $11. 85 *—M.L. (2/1/2006)*

St. Michael-Eppan 2004 Anger Pinot Grigio (Alto Adige) $14. 86 *—M.L. (2/1/2006)*

St. Michael-Eppan 2003 Sanct Valentin Pinot Grigio (Alto Adige) $22. 86 *—M.L. (2/1/2006)*

STEFANO ACCORDINI

Stefano Accordini 2004 Acinatico Corvina, Rondinella, Molinara (Amarone della Valpolicella Classico) $NA. The Accordini family is ripe with excellent winemakers and this young Amarone showcases their expertise. What it lacks in overt intensity it makes up for with elegance and tonic aromas of small fruit berries, polished stone, bramble and smoke. Tight and clean in structure, there's a nice wholeness to this wine. 92 *—M.L. (10/1/2007)*

Stefano Accordini 2001 Vigneto il Fornetto Corvina, Rondinella, Molinara (Amarone della Valpolicella Classico) $NA. This is a genuine, powerful wine that fully embodies the fundamental aromatic tenets of Amarone: cherry, chocolate and spice. You might pick up slight variations on this basic theme such as cherry liquor, dark fudge and powdered licorice. Ultimately, it is a very intense and extracted wine with a modern, supple approach and lively acidity on the finish. 93 *—M.L. (12/1/2007)*

STEFANO FERRUCCI

Stefano Ferrucci 2004 Domus Aurea Albana (Albana di Romagna) $39. Lavish aromas of honey infused with herbs or dried flowers emerge boldly from the nose at first, but subtle tones of melon, almond, apricot and white stone soon follow. This golden-hued dessert wine, made from dried grapes and aged eight months in oak, has a beautifully creamy mouthfeel and a perky, crisp close. 88 *—M.L. (2/1/2007)*

Stefano Ferrucci 2003 Domvs Caia Superiore Riserva Sangiovese (Sangiovese di Romagna) $35. Here is a very attractive, fleshy wine with deep layers of fudge, chocolate and succulent black cherry. You'll also be pleasantly surprised by the firm mouthfeel, chewy tannins and rich red fruit flavor. Grapes are slightly appassiti, or dried before being pressed; the wine sees 14 months of oak. 90 *—M.L. (2/1/2007)*

Stefano Ferrucci 2005 Chiaro della Serra White Blend (Colli di Faenza) $12. An easy, refreshing white (60% Bianchino Faentino and 40% Chardonnay) with yellow fruit, fresh apricot, peach and citrus tones. Pretty aromas are successfully embellished by a touch of green grass or minced herb. It's lightweight in the mouth, but crisp on the close. 86 *—M.L. (2/1/2007)*

STELLA

Stella 1998 Pinot Grigio (Umbria) $8. 83 *(8/1/1999)*

Stella 2000 Pinot Grigio (Umbria) $6. 87 *—P.G. (11/15/2001)*

Stella 2003 Sangiovese (Puglia) $7. 80 *—M.S. (2/1/2005)*

STIVAL

Stival 2000 Cabernet Sauvignon (Veneto) $6. 85 Best Buy *(5/1/2002)*

Stival 2000 Chardonnay (Veneto) $6. 85 Best Buy *(5/1/2002)*

Stival 2000 Merlot (Veneto) $6. 86 Best Buy *(5/1/2002)*

Stival 1998 Pinot Grigio (Veneto) $6. 85 Best Buy *(8/1/1999)*

Stival 2005 Pinot Grigio (Veneto) $7. 85 Best Buy *—M.L. (6/1/2006)*

Stival 2004 Pinot Grigio (Veneto) $7. 85 Best Buy *—M.L. (2/1/2006)*

Stival 2003 Pinot Grigio (Veneto) $6. 84 Best Buy *—J.C. (12/31/2004)*

Stival 2000 2000 Pinot Grigio (Veneto) $6. 84 *(5/1/2002)*

STRACCALI

Straccali 2003 Sangiovese (Chianti) $9. 84 *(4/1/2005)*

Straccali 2001 Sangiovese (Chianti Classico) $13. 82 *(4/1/2005)*

Straccali 1999 Sangiovese (Chianti) $10. 85 *(4/1/2001)*

Straccali 1998 Sangiovese (Sangiovese di Toscana) $8. 84 *(8/1/2001)*

SUBERLI

Suberli 2005 Sangiovese (Morellino di Scansano) $16. Well-rendered oak tones gained during 10 months of tonneaux aging deliver layers of toast, vanilla and leather over the wine's natural aromas of cherry fruit and dried herbs. Red fruit flavors shine through in the mouth, and the wine boasts very good structure and length. 88 *—M.L. (11/1/2007)*

Suberli 2003 Riserva Sangiovese (Morellino di Scansano) $30. A lively Morellino Riserva with very ripe cherry fruit, blueberry and delicate nuances of toasted nut, spice, cherry cough drop, mint and asphalt. It's a wine that grabs your attention and is a bit high strung but ultimately goes down smoothly, thanks to 24 months in tonneaux. 90 *—M.L. (11/1/2007)*

TALAMONTI

Talamonti 2004 Trebì Trebbiano (Trebbiano d'Abruzzo) $NA. 86 *—M.L. (9/1/2005)*

TALENTI

Talenti 2000 Brunello (Brunello di Montalcino) $60. 88 *—M.S. (7/1/2005)*

Talenti 1997 Brunello (Brunello di Montalcino) $NA. 95 Editors' Choice *—R.V. (8/1/2002)*

Talenti 2001 Pian di Conte Brunello (Brunello di Montalcino) $53. 92 *(4/1/2006)*

Talenti 1998 Reserva Brunello (Brunello di Montalcino) $NA. 88 *—M.S. (6/1/2004)*

Talenti 1999 Riserva Brunello (Brunello di Montalcino) $85. 90 *—M.S. (7/1/2005)*

TALIANO

Taliano NV Birbet Red Blend (Piedmont) $14. Similar to Bracchetto, this is a pinkish-red slightly sparkling wine that's sweet, but in this case, the sugar is capably balanced by a sense of minerality. Slightly floral and earthy, with flavors of dust-covered black cherries. Drink now. 88 *(10/1/2007)*

TASCA D'ALMERITA

Tasca d'Almerita 2003 Cabernet Sauvignon (Contea di Sclafani) $60. 91 Editors' Choice *—M.L. (9/1/2006)*

Tasca d'Almerita 1998 Cabernet Sauvignon (Sicilia) $48. 85 *—D.T. (5/1/2002)*

Tasca d'Almerita 1998 Cabernet Sauvignon (Sicilia) $48. 85 *—C.S. (5/1/2002)*

Tasca d'Almerita 2000 Chardonnay (Sicilia) $50. 87 *—R.V. (10/1/2003)*

Tasca d'Almerita 2004 Chardonnay Chardonnay (Contea di Sclafani) $29. 87 *—M.L. (7/1/2006)*

Tasca d'Almerita 2001 Regaleali Bianco Inzolia (Sicilia) $11. 86 *(6/1/2003)*

Tasca d'Almerita 2006 Regaleali Le Rosé Nerello Mascalese (Sicilia) $10. Sicily's Count Tasca delivers a Nerello Mascalese-based rosé that reflects the ripe red fruit of his sun-drenched island. Mature aromas of red berries and raspberry set it apart from northern rosés. **85 Best Buy** *—M.L. (7/1/2007)*

Tasca d'Almerita 2005 Le Rosé Nerello Mascalese (Sicilia) $12. 86 *—M.L. (6/21/2006)*

Tasca d'Almerita 2004 Lamuri Nero d'Avola (Sicilia) $19. 89 *—M.L. (7/1/2006)*

Tasca d'Almerita 2004 Regaleali Nero d'Avola (Sicilia) $15. 87 *—M.L. (7/1/2006)*

Tasca d'Almerita 2003 Regaleali Nero d'Avola (Sicilia) $15. 87 *—M.L. (9/1/2005)*

Tasca d'Almerita 2002 Regaleali Nero d'Avola (Sicilia) $14. 88 *—M.S. (2/1/2005)*

Tasca d'Almerita 2003 Rosso del Conte Nero d'Avola (Contea di Sclafani) $49. 92 Cellar Selection *—M.L. (7/1/2006)*

Tasca d'Almerita 2001 Rosso del Conte Nero d'Avola (Contea di Sclafani) $45. 90 *—M.S. (2/1/2005)*

Tasca d'Almerita 1998 Rosso Del Conte Nero d'Avola (Sicilia) $42. 91 *—C.S. (5/1/2002)*

Tasca d'Almerita 2003 Camastra Red Blend (Sicilia) $NA. 90 *—M.L. (7/1/2006)*

Tasca d'Almerita 2000 Camastra Red Blend (Sicilia) $24. 87 *—R.V. (10/1/2003)*

Tasca d'Almerita 2003 Cygnus Red Blend (Sicilia) $30. 91 Editors' Choice *—M.L. (7/1/2006)*

Tasca d'Almerita 1999 Cygnus Red Blend (Sicilia) $21. 90 Editors' Choice *(6/1/2003)*

Tasca d'Almerita 1997 Regaleali Red Blend (Sicilia) $12. 90 Best Buy *—M.N. (12/31/2000)*

Tasca d'Almerita 2001 Regaleali Rosso Red Blend (Sicilia) $16. 84 *—R.V. (10/1/2003)*

Tasca d'Almerita 2000 Regaleali Rosso Red Blend (Sicilia) $9. 86 Best Buy *—R.V. (11/15/2002)*

Tasca d'Almerita 2000 Rosso del Conte Red Blend (Sicilia) $37. 91 *—R.V. (10/1/2003)*

Tasca d'Almerita 1998 Rosso del Conte Red Blend (Sicilia) $40. 91 *(6/1/2003)*

Tasca d'Almerita 2001 Rose di Regaleali Rosé Blend (Sicilia) $11. 90 Best Buy *(6/1/2003)*

Tasca d'Almerita 2005 Leone d'Almerita White Blend (Sicilia) $16. 87 *—M.L. (7/1/2006)*

Tasca d'Almerita 2002 Leone d'Almerita White Blend (Sicilia) $18. 86 *—R.V. (10/1/2003)*

Tasca d'Almerita 2001 Leone d'Almerita White Blend (Sicilia) $15. 87 *(6/1/2003)*

Tasca d'Almerita 2000 Nozze d'Oro White Blend (Sicilia) $23. 90 *(6/1/2003)*

Tasca d'Almerita 2005 Regaleali White Blend (Sicilia) $12. 86 *—M.L. (7/1/2006)*

Tasca d'Almerita 2004 Regaleali White Blend (Sicilia) $13. 90 Best Buy *—M.L. (9/1/2005)*

Tasca d'Almerita 2002 Regaleali Bianco White Blend (Sicilia) $12. 84 *—R.V. (10/1/2003)*

Tasca d'Almerita 1998 Regaleali Bianco White Blend (Sicilia) $10. 90 *(11/15/1999)*

TASSAROLO

Tassarolo 1997 S Cortese (Gavi) $17. 86 *(11/1/1999)*

Tassarolo 1996 Vigneto Alborina Cortese (Gavi) $30. 89 *(11/1/1999)*

TAURINO

Taurino 2000 Notarpanaro Negroamaro (Puglia) $17. This is not the inky-viscous powerhouse you'd expect from this sun-drenched territory. Rather, it is an understated expression of the hearty Negroamaro grape (some Malvasia Nera too) with blackberry, ash, and cherry that are fleshed out over a firm structure with bright acidity. 88 *—M.L. (8/1/2007)*

Taurino 1999 Patriglione Negroamaro (Puglia) $61. Who says southern Italian wines won't age gracefully? Here is an eight-year-old specimen that delivers generous expressions of dried currants, tar, leather, licorice and refined toasted notes without seeming tired or old. It has firm tannins and a long finish but probably won't last too much longer. Drink now. 91 *—M.L. (8/1/2007)*

Taurino 1994 Patriglione Negroamaro (Salento) $41. 85 *(5/1/2002)*

Taurino 1998 Riserva Negroamaro (Salice Salentino) $10. 85 Best Buy *—C.S. (5/1/2002)*

Taurino 2001 Riserva Red Blend (Salice Salentino) $12. Inviting and finely complex, this Negroamaro-Malvasia Nera-based wine boasts thick, aromatic layers of black fruit, prune, tar, sweet balsamic, charcoal, licorice and well-integrated toast. It's a high-intensity wine and a real charmer, with a brawny build and bright acidity. 90 Best Buy *—M.L. (8/1/2007)*

Taurino 1997 Riserva Red Blend (Salice Salentino) $9. 85 *—S.H. (7/1/2001)*

Taurino 1996 Salice Salentino Riserva Red Blend (Apulia) $9. 90 *(11/15/1999)*

TEDESCHI

Tedeschi 2003 Corvina, Rondinella, Molinara (Amarone della Valpolicella Classico) $50. Tedeschi's base Amarone made with grapes from various vineyards is distinctive, unique and extremely succulent. The wine boasts chewy cherries, milky chocolate, natural rubber, raisin, pine, tar, maple syrup and black stone. In fact, there is no Amarone quite like it, especially considering the immediate, incredibly intense rush of aromas that it offers. 90 *—M.L. (10/1/2007)*

Tedeschi 2001 Corvina, Rondinella, Molinara (Amarone della Valpolicella) $49. 91 Cellar Selection *—J.C. (10/1/2006)*

Tedeschi 2003 Capitel Monte Olmi Corvina, Rondinella, Molinara (Amarone della Valpolicella Classico) $83. Although this is a deeply extracted wine with dense concentration and intense aromas, it is fundamentally too sweet and too astringent to score higher. Aromas of dried fruits, earth, black cherry and black truffles are sharp and linear and the wine imparts cherry candy sweetness in the mouth. 86 *—M.L. (10/1/2007)*

Tedeschi 1999 Capitel Monte Olmi Red Blend (Amarone della Valpolicella Classico) $82. 89 *(11/1/2005)*

Tedeschi 2003 La Fabriseria Corvina, Rondinella, Molinara (Amarone della Valpolicella Classico) $200. You either like it or you don't, and I am not a fan: The wine is so sweet it drinks more like a Recioto dessert wine than an Amarone; it closes with biting astringency, making it nearly impossible to pair with food. It does boast incredible concentration and impenetrable blackness with aromas of hot pepper, beets, carrot root, earth and espresso. 85 *—M.L. (10/1/2007)*

Tedeschi 2005 Vigneto Monte Tenda Garganega (Soave Classico) $15. At face value, this Soave Classico might seem like a simple wine. Aromas of peach, yellow fruit and mineral are straightforward and easy to read. On second consideration, however, it reveals a deeper, more complex side made evident by piquant layers of white peppercorn and frothy lime frosting. 88 *—M.L. (11/15/2007)*

TENIMENTI ANGELINI

Tenimenti Angelini 2000 Brunello (Brunello di Montalcino) $64. 87 *—M.S. (7/1/2005)*

Tenimenti Angelini 2001 Val di Suga Brunello (Brunello di Montalcino) $53. 92 *(4/1/2006)*

Tenimenti Angelini 1997 Val di Suga Brunello (Brunello di Montalcino) $80. 92 *—R.V. (8/1/2002)*

Tenimenti Angelini 1999 Vigna del Lago Riserva Brunello (Brunello di Montalcino) $134. 92 Cellar Selection *—M.S. (7/1/2005)*

Tenimenti Angelini 2000 Vigna Spuntali Brunello (Brunello di Montalcino) $86. 93 *(4/1/2006)*

Tenimenti Angelini 2004 TuttoBene Red Blend (Toscana) $11. 83 *—M.S. (9/1/2006)*

Tenimenti Angelini 2002 Sangiovese (Vino Nobile di Montepulciano) $22. 87 *—M.S. (7/1/2005)*

Tenimenti Angelini 2001 La Villa Sangiovese (Vino Nobile di Montepulciano) $41. 90 *—M.S. (7/1/2005)*

Tenimenti Angelini 2003 San Leonino Riserva Sangiovese (Chianti Classico) $37. Intense and penetrating, this wine delivers lavish layers of berry fruit, cherry cough drop, coffee and plum. It is an evolved wine that still has plenty to offer in terms of vibrant fruit flavors. In the mouth, it is plush and soft with cherry oak tones on the finish. 90 *—M.L. (11/1/2007)*

Tenimenti Angelini 2001 San Leonino Sangiovese (Chianti Classico) $17. 86 *(4/1/2005)*

Tenimenti Angelini 1999 San Leonino Riserva Sangiovese (Chianti Classico) $34. 87 *(4/1/2005)*

Tenimenti Angelini 2004 Sanleonino Sangiovese (Chianti Classico) $18. This no-fuss Chianti Classico delivers all kinds of small berry fruit, from blueberries to cranberries, and finishes with fresh crispness and delicate fruit flavors. This has a natural ability to pair with most foods. 86 *—M.L. (11/1/2007)*

Tenimenti Angelini 2002 Sanleonino Sangiovese (Chianti Classico) $18. 88 —*M.S. (10/1/2006)*

TENIMENTI CA'BIANCA

Tenimenti Ca'Bianca 2003 Anté Barbera (Barbera d'Asti) $14. 84 —*J.C. (3/1/2006)*

Tenimenti Ca'Bianca 2004 Cortese (Gavi) $14. 86 —*J.C. (3/1/2006)*

Tenimenti Ca'Bianca 2004 Moscato (Moscato d'Asti) $15. 90 Best Buy —*M.L. (12/15/2005)*

TENIMENTI LUIGI D'ALESSANDRO

Tenimenti Luigi D'Alessandro 2003 Il Bosco Syrah (Cortona) $49. 87 —*M.S. (9/1/2006)*

TENUTA ALZATURA

Tenuta Alzatura 2001 Uno di Quattro Sagrantino (Sagrantino di Montefalco) $45. 87 —*M.L. (9/1/2005)*

TENUTA BELGUARDO

Tenuta Belguardo 1999 Sangiovese (Morellino di Scansano) $20. 89 —*M.S. (8/1/2002)*

Tenuta Belguardo 2001 Poggio Bronzone Sangiovese (Morellino di Scansano) $29. 90 —*M.S. (10/1/2004)*

Tenuta Belguardo 2001 Serrata di Belguardo Sangiovese (Maremma) $44. 90 —*M.S. (10/1/2004)*

TENUTA BELTRAME

Tenuta Beltrame 2004 Pinot Grigio (Friuli Aquileia) $19. 86 —*M.L. (2/1/2006)*

TENUTA CA' VESCOVO

Tenuta Ca' Vescovo 2005 Pinot Grigio (Friuli Aquileia) $12. 86 —*M.L. (6/1/2006)*

Tenuta Ca' Vescovo 2004 Pinot Grigio (Friuli Aquileia) $12. 84 —*M.L. (2/1/2006)*

Tenuta Ca' Vescovo 2002 Sauvignon Blanc (Friuli Aquileia) $12. 83 —*J.C. (12/31/2004)*

TENUTA CAPARZO

Tenuta Caparzo 2001 Brunello (Rosso di Montalcino) $18. 88 *(3/1/2005)*

Tenuta Caparzo 2001 Brunello (Brunello di Montalcino) $64. 88 *(4/1/2006)*

Tenuta Caparzo 1999 Brunello (Brunello di Montalcino) $60. 90 *(3/1/2005)*

Tenuta Caparzo 1997 Brunello (Brunello di Montalcino) $65. 92 —*R.V. (8/1/2002)*

Tenuta Caparzo 1999 La Casa Brunello (Brunello di Montalcino) $120. 93 Cellar Selection *(3/1/2005)*

Tenuta Caparzo 2001 Vigna La Casa Brunello (Brunello di Montalcino) $120. 89 *(4/1/2006)*

Tenuta Caparzo 2002 Sangiovese (Toscana) $10. 83 *(3/1/2005)*

Tenuta Caparzo 2000 Sangiovese (Rosso di Montalcino) $21. 90 —*M.S. (11/15/2003)*

Tenuta Caparzo 2000 Sangiovese (Toscana) $14. 86 —*M.S. (11/15/2003)*

Tenuta Caparzo 1999 Borgo Scopeto Sangiovese (Chianti Classico) $20. 86 —*M.S. (11/15/2003)*

Tenuta Caparzo 1999 Borgo Scopeto Borgonero Sangiovese (Toscana) $35. 83 —*M.S. (11/15/2003)*

Tenuta Caparzo 1999 Borgo Scopeto Riserva Misciano Sangiovese (Chianti Classico) $35. 87 —*M.S. (11/15/2003)*

Tenuta Caparzo 1994 Ca del Pazzo Sangiovese (Toscana) $33. 87 —*J.C. (3/1/2000)*

Tenuta Caparzo 1999 Ca' del Pazzo Sangiovese (Sant'Antimo) $40. 92 Editors' Choice *(3/1/2005)*

Tenuta Caparzo 2000 La Grance White Blend (Sant'Antimo) $21. 85 *(3/1/2005)*

Tenuta Caparzo 1998 Le Crete White Blend (Toscana) $15. 81 —*J.C. (9/1/2001)*

TENUTA CARRETTA

Tenuta Carretta 2002 Dolcetto (Dolcetto d'Alba) $16. 83 —*M.S. (12/15/2003)*

Tenuta Carretta 2001 Nebbiolo (Barbaresco) $35. The basic Barbaresco is a pleasant, light, complex wine, with flavors of bright strawberry fruit, road tar and minerals. The acidity is high, but just about held in check, and the wines finishes well. Fully mature now, and probably not getting any better. 86 —*M.G. (12/31/2007)*

Tenuta Carretta 2000 Cannubi Nebbiolo (Barolo) $65. A big-boned, structured wine, the Caretta has aromas of ripe cherry, soy sauce and violets. The nose is a little more open than the palate; at the moment the wine is a little dour, with structure and flavors centring around the mid-palate. It certainly needs time, but the finish is short. Potentially a good, rather than great, wine. 88 —*M.G. (4/1/2007)*

Tenuta Carretta 1997 Cannubi Nebbiolo (Barolo) $54. 85 —*M.S. (12/15/2003)*

Tenuta Carretta 1998 Cannubi Barolo Nebbiolo (Barolo) $NA. 89 —*R.V. (11/15/2002)*

TENUTA COCCI GRIFONI

Tenuta Cocci Grifoni NV Passerina Champagne Blend (Marche) $10. 88 Best Buy —*S.H. (12/15/2000)*

Tenuta Cocci Grifoni 2006 Colle Vecchio Pecorino (Offida Pecorino) $24. Only a few producers import wines made with the Pecorino variety, and if you like fresh, light Italian whites they are definitely worth trying. This expression is redolent of fresh pear, honey and Golden Delicious apple and even has a slightly greenish hue within its pretty golden highlights. 86 —*M.L. (12/1/2007)*

Tenuta Cocci Grifoni 2001 Il Grifone Red Blend (Offida Rosso) $49. 91 —*M.S. (10/1/2006)*

Tenuta Cocci Grifoni 2000 Il Grifone Red Blend (Rosso Piceno Superiore) $48. 88 —*M.S. (7/1/2005)*

Tenuta Cocci Grifoni 2004 Le Torri Red Blend (Rosso Piceno Superiore) $13. Ripe red fruit, cherry and forest berry mingle with darker, opulent tones of resin and leather to produce a wine of dimension and character. It is aged 18 months in oak. There's good complexity here and an evenly textured mouthfeel that is accented by bright fruit flavors and dusty tannins. 88 Best Buy —*M.L. (11/15/2007)*

Tenuta Cocci Grifoni 2000 Vigna Messieri Red Blend (Rosso Piceno Superiore) $12. 86 —*M.S. (7/1/2005)*

Tenuta Cocci Grifoni 1997 Sangiovese (Rosso Piceno Superiore) $10. 83 *(9/1/2000)*

Tenuta Cocci Grifoni 1997 Il Grifone Sangiovese (Rosso Piceno Superiore) $36. 87 *(10/1/2001)*

Tenuta Cocci Grifoni 2003 Le Torri Sangiovese (Rosso Piceno Superiore) $13. 88 Best Buy —*M.S. (10/1/2006)*

Tenuta Cocci Grifoni 2001 Vigna Messieri Sangiovese (Rosso Piceno Superiore) $24. 90 —*M.S. (10/1/2006)*

Tenuta Conti Attems 2004 Cicinis White Blend (Collio) $38. A sparkling appearance with brilliant golden highlights sets the stage for this rich and vibrant wine that delivers notes of fresh pineapple, melon, citrus flower, pear and apricot. The mouthfeel is lush and intense and boosted by peach and almond flavors. Sauvignon, Tocai and Pinot Bianco are aged in new French and American oak. 91 —*M.L. (5/1/2007)*

Tenuta Cocci Grifoni 2004 Podere Colle Vecchio White Blend (Offida Pecorino) $23. 86 —*M.L. (10/1/2006)*

Tenuta Conti Attems 2004 Pinot Grigio (Collio) $19. 87 —*M.L. (2/1/2006)*

TENUTA DEL NANFRO

Tenuta del Nanfro 2001 San Mauro Nero d'Avola (Sicilia) $18. 81 —*M.S. (10/1/2003)*

Tenuta del Nanfro 2000 Cerasuolo di Vittoria Red Blend (Sicilia) $18. 82 —*M.S. (12/15/2003)*

TENUTA DELL'ORNELLAIA

Tenuta dell'Ornellaia 2000 Ornellaia Bordeaux Blend (Bolgheri) $145. 94 Cellar Selection —*M.S. (11/15/2003)*

Tenuta dell'Ornellaia 2000 Le Serre Nuove Cabernet Sauvignon-Merlot (Bolgheri) $50. 90 —*M.S. (11/15/2003)*

Tenuta dell'Ornellaia 2003 Masseto Merlot (Toscana) $250. Produced in limited numbers, this showcases fine winemaking on all levels despite a hot vintage. The raspberry fruit and chocolate nuances are fragrant and intense; the oak is so well integrated you only feel its presence in the mouth, where the wine is opulent but also extremely silky. But the most exciting elements to this wine are its distinctive Mediterranean accents of menthol, wild sage and seaside shrubbery that beautifully recall its coastal Tuscan roots. 92 —*M.L. (4/1/2007)*

Tenuta dell'Ornellaia 2002 Le Serre Nuove Red Blend (Bolgheri) $50. 86 —*M.S. (9/1/2006)*

Tenuta dell'Ornellaia 1996 Masseto Red Blend (Bolgheri) $138. 93 —*R.V. (12/31/2001)*

Tenuta dell'Ornellaia 1999 Ornellaia Red Blend (Bolgheri) $125. 96 —*M.S. (8/1/2002)*

Tenuta dell'Ornellaia 1995 Sangiovese (Toscana) $63. 96 —*M.S. (5/1/1999)*

Tenuta dell'Ornellaia NV Le Volte Sangiovese (Toscana) $20. 87 —*M.S. (3/1/2000)*

Tenuta dell'Ornellaia 1996 Ornellaia Sangiovese (Bolgheri) $73. 92 —*M.S. (7/1/2000)*

TENUTA DI ARCENO

Tenuta di Arceno 2002 Arcanum I Cabernet Blend (Toscana) $96. 83 —*M.S. (9/1/2006)*

Tenuta di Arceno 2002 Arcanum II Merlot (Toscana) $96. 85 —*M.S. (9/1/2006)*

Tenuta di Arceno 2003 Arcanum III Red Blend (Toscana) $100. 88 —*M.S. (9/1/2006)*

Tenuta di Arceno 2003 Ataison Sangiovese (Toscana) $40. 84 —*M.S. (9/1/2006)*

Tenuta di Arceno 2002 Ataison Sangiovese (Toscana) $48. 83 —*M.S. (11/15/2004)*

Tenuta di Arceno 2003 PrimaVoce Sangiovese (Toscana) $20. 86 —*M.S. (9/1/2006)*

Tenuta di Arceno 2003 Riserva Sangiovese (Chianti Classico) $25. Winemaker Seillan prefers not to use much new oak with Sangiovese, and this wine is more than 80% Sangiovese, so the fruit shines through. Sour cherries and tobacco are classic Chianti flavors and they're here, picking up darker notes of loamy earth and a hint of charcoal on the finish. **88** —*J.C. (6/1/2007)*

TENUTA DI ARGIANO

Tenuta di Argiano 1997 Brunello (Brunello di Montalcino) $56. 92 **Cellar Selection** —*R.V. (8/1/2002)*

TENUTA DI BLASIG

Tenuta di Blasig 2004 Pinot Grigio (Isonzo del Friuli) $NA. 86 —*M.L. (2/1/2006)*

TENUTA DI NOZZOLE

Tenuta di Nozzole 2001 Il Pareto Cabernet Sauvignon (Toscana) $60. 90 —*M.L. (9/1/2006)*

Tenuta di Nozzole 2004 Le Bruniche Chardonnay (Chardonnay di Toscana) $14. 6 —*M.S. (10/1/2006)*

Tenuta di Nozzole 2002 Le Bruniche Chardonnay (Toscana) $12. 86 —*M.S. (11/15/2003)*

Tenuta di Nozzole 2003 Sangiovese (Chianti Classico) $26. Strawberry jam comes to mind and this is no surprise considering the sweltering-hot vintage. The wine tastes overripe in the mouth but also imparts a sour note. **82** —*M.L. (2/1/2007)*

Tenuta di Nozzole 2001 Riserva Sangiovese (Chianti Classico) $22. 89 *(4/1/2005)*

Tenuta di Nozzole 2000 Riserva Sangiovese (Tuscany) $22. 88 —*M.S. (10/1/2004)*

Tenuta di Nozzole 1997 Riserva Sangiovese (Chianti Classico) $38. 86 *(4/1/2001)*

TENUTA DI PIETRA PORZIA

Tenuta di Pietra Porzia 2006 Regillo White Blend (Frascati Superiore) $NA. Here's a fresh, quaffable white wine from Lazio with muddled stone fruit aromas, citrus and melon. It doesn't offer huge intensity and is slightly watery in the mouth, but it does taste fresh and zesty. **84** —*M.L. (12/1/2007)*

TENUTA DI RISECCOLI

Tenuta di Riseccoli 2001 Sangiovese (Chianti Classico) $26. 89 *(4/1/2005)*

Tenuta di Riseccoli 1999 Sangiovese (Chianti Classico) $12. 89 **Best Buy** —*M.S. (12/31/2002)*

Tenuta di Riseccoli 2000 Riserva Sangiovese (Chianti Classico) $43. 89 *(4/1/2005)*

Tenuta di Riseccoli 2000 Saeculum Sangiovese (Tuscany) $75. 91 **Cellar Selection** —*M.S. (9/1/2006)*

TENUTA DI SESTA

Tenuta di Sesta 2001 Brunello (Brunello di Montalcino) $75. 87 *(4/1/2006)*

Tenuta di Sesta 1997 Brunello (Brunello di Montalcino) $45. 94 **Cellar Selection** —*R.V. (8/1/2002)*

TENUTA FARNETA

Tenuta Farneta 2001 Bentivoglio Sangiovese (Toscana) $18. 81 —*M.S. (9/1/2006)*

Tenuta Farneta 2000 Bongoverno Sangiovese (Toscana) $38. 83 —*M.S. (9/1/2006)*

TENUTA FARNETA DI COLLATO

Tenuta Farneta di Collato 2002 Sangiovese (Chianti Colli Senesi) $8. 85 **Best Buy** —*M.S. (10/1/2004)*

Tenuta Farneta di Collato 2003 Tenuta Farneta Sangiovese (Chianti Colli Senesi) $8. 86 **Best Buy** *(4/1/2005)*

Tenuta Farneta di Collato 2003 Vendemmia Sangiovese (Chianti Colli Senesi) $9. 86 **Best Buy** *(4/1/2005)*

TENUTA FRIGGIALI

Tenuta Friggiali 2001 Brunello (Brunello di Montalcino) $66. 89 *(4/1/2006)*

TENUTA I SALTARI

Tenuta i Saltari 2001 Le Vigne di Turano Corvina, Rondinella, Molinara (Amarone della Valpolicella) $62. The Sartori family is behind this wonderful vineyard select wine with deep concentration and intense aromatic of savory plum, cherry, natural rubber, almond nut and mineral shadings. The wine is well-rounded in the mouth with fresh acidity at the back and dusty mineral flavors on the finish. **92** —*M.L. (12/1/2007)*

TENUTA IL BOSCO

Tenuta Il Bosco NV Philèo Pinot Nero (Oltrepò Pavese) $15. 86 —*M.L. (6/1/2006)*

Tenuta Il Bosco 1997 Millesimato Brut Sparkling Blend (Oltrepò Pavese) $25. 88 —*M.L. (6/1/2006)*

Tenuta Il Bosco NV Philèo Brut Sparkling Blend (Oltrepò Pavese) $NA. 84 —*M.L. (12/15/2004)*

TENUTA IL POGGIONE

Tenuta Il Poggione 1993 Riserva Brunello (Brunello di Montalcino) $67. 84 —*J.C. (3/1/2000)*

TENUTA IL TESORO

Tenuta Il Tesoro 2000 La Fonte Red Blend (Toscana) $15. 86 —*M.S. (12/31/2002)*

TENUTA LA FUGA

Tenuta La Fuga 2001 Brunello (Brunello di Montalcino) $65. 90 **Cellar Selection** *(4/1/2006)*

Tenuta La Fuga 1997 Brunello (Brunello di Montalcino) $NA. 90 —*R.V. (8/1/2002)*

Tenuta La Fuga 1999 Sangiovese (Rosso di Montalcino) $NA. 83 —*M.S. (8/1/2002)*

TENUTA LE QUERCE

Tenuta Le Querce 2001 Il Viola Aglianico (Aglianico del Vulture) $18. 85 —*M.S. (2/1/2005)*

Tenuta Le Querce 2000 Rosso di Costanza Aglianico (Aglianico del Vulture) $40. 90 —*M.S. (10/1/2006)*

Tenuta Le Querce 1999 Il Viola Red Blend (Aglianico del Vulture) $11. 86 **Best Buy** —*C.S. (5/1/2002)*

Tenuta Le Querce 1999 Rosso Di Costanza Red Blend (Aglianico del Vulture) $26. 88 *(5/1/2002)*

TENUTA MONACI

Tenuta Monaci 1997 Simposia Negroamaro (Puglia) $12. 85 —*C.S. (5/1/2002)*

TENUTA OLIVETO

Tenuta Oliveto 2001 Brunello (Brunello di Montalcino) $48. 92 **Editors' Choice** *(4/1/2006)*

Tenuta Oliveto 2005 Il Leccio Sangiovese (Toscana) $12. Here's a delightfully voluptuous and chewy Sangiovese from Montalcino in southern Tuscany that offers lavish layers of succulent cherry, plum, spice and natural rubber. Thick, ripe fruit aromas are elaborated by 15 months of oak aging that adds background dimension and renderings of vanilla, cinnamon and toasted almond. It's a soft, velvety wine with plush consistency and drying tannins that would pair beautifully with tender venison medallions, wild mushroom risotto or meat ragout. **88 Best Buy** —*M.L. (11/15/2007)*

TENUTA PETER SÖLVA & SÖHNE

Tenuta Peter Sölva & Söhne 2003 De Silva Riserva Merlot (Alto Adige) $25. Big and brooding, here is a masculine Merlot with thick color concentration, big berry flavors, chocolate fudge and pipe tobacco. Layered under the intensity and heat is also a fragrant forest floor-like note that reminds you of its cooler climate, Alto Adige origins. **90** —*M.L. (3/1/2007)*

ITALY

TENUTA RAPITALA

Tenuta Rapitala 2001 Bianco Chardonnay (Sicilia) $10. 88 *—R.V. (10/1/2003)*

Tenuta Rapitala 2003 Hugonis Red Blend (Sicilia) $37. 89 *—M.L. (7/1/2006)*

Tenuta Rapitala 2002 Hugonis Red Blend (Sicilia) $37. 88 *(8/1/2005)*

Tenuta Rapitala 2002 Nu har Red Blend (Sicilia) $11. 87 Best Buy *—M.S. (11/15/2004)*

Tenuta Rapitala 2002 Nu-har Red Blend (Sicilia) $13. 87 *(8/1/2005)*

Tenuta Rapitala 2001 Nuhar Red Blend (Sicilia) $11. 86 *—M.S. (10/1/2003)*

Tenuta Rapitala 2004 Nadir Syrah (Sicilia) $15. 89 *—M.L. (7/1/2006)*

Tenuta Rapitala 2003 Solinero Syrah (Sicilia) $41. 91 *—M.L. (7/1/2006)*

Tenuta Rapitala 2002 Solinero Syrah (Sicilia) $42. 89 *(8/1/2005)*

Tenuta Rapitala 2000 Solinero Syrah (Sicilia) 90 *—R.V. (10/1/2003)*

Tenuta Rapitala 2004 Casalj White Blend (Sicilia) $11. 87 *—M.L. (7/1/2006)*

Tenuta Rapitala 2003 Casalj White Blend (Sicilia) $11. 87 Best Buy *—M.S. (11/15/2004)*

Tenuta Rapitala 2003 Casalj White Blend (Sicilia) $13. 88 Best Buy *(8/1/2005)*

Tenuta Rapitala 2001 Casalj White Blend (Sicilia) $11. 83 *—R.V. (10/1/2003)*

TENUTA ROCCA

Tenuta Rocca 2004 Barbera (Barbera d'Alba) $19. An old fashioned Barbera; the wine is not totally ripe, but on the plus side it has bright strawberry flavors if a little too much acidicity. The finish, although quite long, is also a little sour. 83 *—M.G. (4/1/2007)*

Tenuta Rocca 2003 Vigna Ròca Neira Barbera (Barbera d'Alba) $28. The Vigna Ròca Neira is no shrinking violet. It weighs in at 14.5% alcohol, and is a massive wine with blackberry liqueur aromas, big plummy super-ripe flavors and a dense finish. A wine of little subtlety, but a good deal of character, it should be served with grilled meat, the more raw the better. 87 *—M.G. (12/31/2007)*

Tenuta Rocca 2000 Nebbiolo (Barolo) $59. The Tenuta boasts a mature gorgeous nose of plums, smoked meat, chocolate and road tar. The complexity comes through on the palate, but it is confined to the midpalate, leaving little for the finish. While the flavors seem fully mature, the structure is not; hence the slight disconnect on the palate. 90 *—M.G. (4/1/2007)*

Tenuta Rocca 2003 Vigna Sorì Ornati Nebbiolo (Nebbiolo d'Alba) $26. A wine where the nose is stunning and the palate non-descript. The nose is really beautiful: ripe fruit, thyme, licorice, mocha and a hint of lavender. Unfortunately it doesn't quite carry through to the palate, where the flavors are so muted that it is a struggle to find them. Little structure and practically no grip, and yet that nose is so haunting. 87 *—M.G. (4/1/2007)*

Tenuta Rocca 2003 Ornati Red Blend (Langhe) $28. Began with unpleasant swampy aromas, but they blew off, revealing dark fruit, spices and an earthiness that had nothing to do with the initial smells. As the wine opened up, it grew more interesting and ended up as quite an impressive wine, with pleasant flavors and good length. 90 *—M.G. (12/31/2007)*

TENUTA ROVEGLIA

Tenuta Roveglia 2000 Vigne di Catullo White Blend (Lugana) $17. 82 *—J.C. (7/1/2003)*

TENUTA SAN GIORGIO

Tenuta San Giorgio 2001 Ugolforte Brunello (Brunello di Montalcino) $50. 88 *(4/1/2006)*

TENUTA SAN GUIDO

Tenuta San Guido 2003 Sassicaia Cabernet Sauvignon (Bolgheri) $180. 91 Cellar Selection *—M.L. (9/1/2006)*

Tenuta San Guido 2002 Sassicaia Cabernet Sauvignon (Bolgheri) $180. 90 *—M.L. (9/1/2006)*

Tenuta San Guido 2004 Guidalberto Sangiovese (Toscana) $50. 90 *—M.L. (11/15/2006)*

Tenuta San Guido 2003 Guidalberto Sangiovese (Toscana) $50. 89 *—M.S. (9/1/2006)*

Tenuta San Guido 2000 Guidalberto Sangiovese (Bolgheri) $52. 89 *—M.S. (10/1/2004)*

TENUTA SAN VITO

Tenuta San Vito 2005 Sangiovese (Chianti) $NA. This is a disjointed wine with a few elements out of place, especially on the nose: Aromas include cherry, cooked vegetable, mushroom and a drop of iodine. It's a lean wine with medium consistency and persistency. 82 *—M.L. (11/1/2007)*

Tenuta San Vito 2005 Darno Sangiovese (Chianti Colli Fiorentini) $NA. Starts off a bit funky with sulfur-like smells and never seems to recuperate. Its ruby appearance is attractive, but the wine proves too lean and thin to give it much staying power. 81 *—M.L. (11/1/2007)*

TENUTA SANT'ANTONIO

Tenuta Sant'Antonio 2002 Capitel del Monte Cabernet Blend (Veneto) $NA. Although this is probably not the most successful vintage of this otherwise pristine, powerhouse wine, you will get thickly layered notes of blackberry, black cherry, cracked black pepper and humus. Slightly less intense than the 2001 vintage, this Veneto Cabernet Sauvignon does boast a very long, supple finish. 88 *—M.L. (5/1/2007)*

Tenuta Sant'Antonio 2001 Capitel Del Monte Cabernet Sauvignon (Veneto) $35. Here is a powerful and succulent Cabernet Sauvignon from the same area that makes Amarone. This wine is characterized by penetrating notes of blackberry, granite, forest berry, humus and moist soil. It's an excellent red with powerful concentration and a spice-driven close. 90 *—M.L. (5/1/2007)*

Tenuta Sant'Antonio 1999 Capitello Cabernet Sauvignon (Veneto) $45. 86 *(5/1/2003)*

Tenuta Sant'Antonio 1998 Capitello Chardonnay (Friuli) $27. 89 *—J.C. (7/1/2003)*

Tenuta Sant'Antonio 2003 Campo dei Gigli Corvina, Rondinella, Molinara (Amarone della Valpolicella) $90. Deep dark concentration sets the tone for a shapely wine accented by black cherry, almond-amaretto, resin and dark chocolate. It's not the intensity of these aromas that sets this wine apart, but the quality. Together, they form a seamless, elegant whole with mouth-watering succulence and a polished feel. 93 *—M.L. (10/1/2007)*

Tenuta Sant'Antonio 1999 Campo dei Gigli Corvina, Rondinella, Molinara (Amarone della Valpolicella) $98. 86 *(11/1/2005)*

Tenuta Sant'Antonio 1998 Campo dei Gigli Corvina, Rondinella, Molinara (Amarone della Valpolicella) $64. 88 *(5/1/2003)*

Tenuta Sant'Antonio 2003 Selezione Antonio Castagnedi Corvina, Rondinella, Molinara (Amarone della Valpolicella) $50. Run by four jolly brothers, Tenuta Sant'Antonio was originally purchased as grazing land before the family decided to try its luck with grapevines. Thankfully they did: This is one of the most exciting estates outside the Classico zone. This special selection wine delivers clean cherry nuances, soft toast and enduring coffee-vanilla flavors. 90 *—M.L. (10/1/2007)*

Tenuta Sant'Antonio 2002 Selezione Antonio Castagnedi Corvina, Rondinella, Molinara (Amarone della Valpolicella) $50. 92 *—J.C. (10/1/2006)*

Tenuta Sant'Antonio 2000 Selezione Antonio Castagnedi Corvina, Rondinella, Molinara (Amarone della Valpolicella) $50. 93 *(11/1/2005)*

Tenuta Sant'Antonio 1998 La Bandina Red Blend (Valtellina Superiore) $34. 88 *(5/1/2003)*

Tenuta Sant'Antonio 2004 White Blend (Soave) $11. 88 Best Buy *—J.C. (10/1/2006)*

Tenuta Sant'Antonio 2003 Monte Ceriani White Blend (Soave) $18. 85 *—J.C. (10/1/2006)*

TENUTA SANTOMÉ

Tenuta Santomé NV Extra Dry Prosecco (Veneto) $13. 84 *—M.L. (12/15/2006)*

TENUTA SETTE PONTI

Tenuta Sette Ponti 2003 Poggio al Lupo Red Blend (Toscana) $55. 89 *—M.S. (9/1/2006)*

Tenuta Sette Ponti 2001 Poggio Al Lupo Red Blend (Toscana) $50. 91 *—M.S. (9/1/2006)*

Tenuta Sette Ponti 2003 Crognolo Sangiovese (Toscana) $35. 88 *—M.S. (9/1/2006)*

Tenuta Sette Ponti 2001 Crognolo Sangiovese (Toscana) $32. 91 Editors' Choice *—M.S. (10/1/2004)*

Tenuta Sette Ponti 2000 Crognolo Sangiovese (Toscana) $32. 92 *—M.S. (8/1/2002)*

Tenuta Sette Ponti 2003 Oreno Sangiovese (Toscana) $100. 90 *—M.S. (9/1/2006)*

Tenuta Sette Ponti 1999 Oreno Sangiovese (Toscana) $90. 91 *—M.S. (8/1/2002)*

TENUTA SETTEN

Tenuta Setten 2001 Vigneto S. Antonio Pinot Grigio (Piave) $14. 84 *(5/1/2003)*

TENUTA TERACREA

Tenuta Teracrea 1999 Tocai Italiano Tocai (Lison-Pramaggiore) $13. 88 —*M.M. (9/1/2001)*

TENUTA VALDIPIATTA

Tenuta Valdipiatta 2002 Sangiovese (Vino Nobile di Montepulciano) $29. 84 —*M.S. (7/1/2005)*

Tenuta Valdipiatta 2001 Vigna d'Alfiero Sangiovese (Vino Nobile di Montepulciano) $50. 85 —*M.S. (7/1/2005)*

TENUTA VIGLIONE

Tenuta Viglione 2003 Primitivo (Gioia del Colle) $15. Here's a deeply fruity, purple wine with loads of dark berry and blueberry jam on the nose. Almost too much of a good thing, you'll get spice, nutmeg, red beets and a touch of minerality. A nice but not totally harmonious wine. 84 —*M.L. (4/1/2007)*

TENUTA VITANZA

Tenuta Vitanza 2005 Sangiovese (Chianti Colli Senesi) $10. Vitanza is better known for its excellent Brunello di Montalcino, yet this traditionally styled Chianti also holds its own. The wine is a light shade of ruby with ripe berries and nutty aromas over a delicately structured whole. 85 Best Buy —*M.L. (11/1/2007)*

Tenuta Vitanza 2003 Casale del Duccio Riserva Sangiovese (Chianti Classico) $14. Lovely and extremely well-priced, with excellent power and spice behind mature notes of cherry, red fruit, blueberry, almond amaretto, chopped mint and violets. It's feminine, compact, racy and showcases enormous purity of aromas and flavors. 90 Best Buy —*M.L. (11/1/2007)*

Tenuta Vitanza 1999 Riserva Sangiovese (Brunello di Montalcino) $NA. Brunello di Montalcino is celebrated for its amazing capacity to age gracefully. This Riserva has done just that and pours beautifully: Blackberry, espresso, licorice, tar and cola are integrated seamlessly with vanilla, toast and campfire tones. It is velvety, yet firm in the mouth, with a long, long licorice-driven finish. 93 —*M.L. (5/1/2007)*

TENUTA WEINGUT KORNELL

Tenuta Weingut Kornell 2004 Riserva Staves Merlot (Alto Adige) $NA. This wine boasts big fruit,especially blueberry, framed by delicate notes of menthol and almond. It's a dense, ruby wine that reflects brilliant red highlights and tastes fresh in the mouth thanks to vibrant fruit, good acidity and structure. 90 —*M.L. (4/1/2007)*

TENUTE DEI VALLARINO

Tenute dei Vallarino 2001 Bricco Asinari Superiore Barbera (Barbera d'Asti) $36. 88 —*J.C. (11/15/2004)*

Tenute dei Vallarino 2001 La Ladra Barbera (Barbera d'Asti) $18. 86 —*J.C. (11/15/2004)*

Tenute dei Vallarino 2004 Castello di Canelli Moscato (Moscato d'Asti) $15. 88 —*M.L. (12/15/2005)*

Tenute dei Vallarino 2001 Dialogo Red Blend (Monferrato) $41. 84 —*J.C. (11/15/2004)*

TENUTE DETTORI

Tenute Dettori 2004 Badde Nigolosu Cannonau (Romangia) $80. This is a distinctly uncommon wine with delicate nuances of pressed flowers, violets, leather, spice, nutmeg and licorice that sees no wood. High heat (and a whopping 17% alcohol) does not disturb as much as you'd think, although there is a disjointed spicy, peppery hot sensation on the palate. 85 —*M.L. (8/1/2007)*

Tenute Dettori 2001 Badde Nigolosu Tenores Cannonau (Romangia) $91. 87 —*M.S. (7/1/2005)*

Tenute Dettori 2001 Badde Nigolosu Tuderi Cannonau (Romangia) $57. 90 —*M.S. (7/1/2005)*

Tenute Dettori 2005 Badde Nigolosu Moscadeddu Uve Stramature Moscato (Sardinia) $20. Here is a deeply aromatic wine with wonderful notes of honeysuckle, beeswax, peach, apricot and lavender honey. The nose of this dessert wine is simply beautiful; there's enough acidity for a successful pairing with lightly frosted carrot cake or spice bread. 89 —*M.L. (8/1/2007)*

Tenute Dettori 2005 Badde Nigolosu Vermentino (Romangia) $34. Slightly cloudy in appearance with disjointed aromas of vitamin, mineral and soapy floral tones, this is an awkward wine. Nice crispness comes though in the mouth but it lacks the big, round flavors you need in order to balance the high alcohol. 83 —*M.L. (8/1/2007)*

Tenute Dettori 2003 Badde Nigolosu Bianco Vermentino (Romangia) $40. 86 —*M.S. (7/1/2005)*

TENUTE GLATAROSSA

Tenute Galtarossa 2003 Corvina, Rondinella, Molinara (Amarone della Valpolicella) $60. A beautiful Venetian villa is surrounded by 200 acres of vineyard and is the setting in which this fine Amarone is crafted. Rhubarb, plum, black cherry exotic spice, espresso and caramel are backed by toast and cedar notes. It has chewy length, refreshing crispness and good power on the finish. 88 —*M.L. (10/1/2007)*

TENUTE NICCOLAI

Tenute Niccolai 2001 Podere Bellarina Brunello (Brunello di Montalcino) $NA. 91 *(4/1/2006)*

Tenute Niccolai 2005 Palagetto Santa Chiara Vernaccia (Vernaccia di San Gimignano) $15. An initial touch of sulfur blows off quickly to reveal stone fruit, fresh cantaloupe and pear. The mouthfeel is lean and not particularly intense. 85 —*M.L. (11/15/2007)*

TENUTE RUBINO

Tenute Rubino 2004 Punta Aquila Primitivo (Puglia) $NA. Here is a dense and intense Primitivo with exotic spice, clove, ground cinnamon and nutmeg backed by plump red fruit and toasted notes. A very nice ensemble with roundness and harmony and a rock-solid build. Cellar the wine for at least two more years. 90 —*M.L. (8/1/2007)*

Tenute Rubino 2004 Marmorelle Red Blend (Salento) $10. An initial blast of musky earth wears off to reveal blueberry, blackberry and ripe red fruit. The wine performs well in the mouth thanks to firm tannins and good acidity. 85 —*M.L. (8/1/2007)*

Tenute Rubino 2002 Marmorelle Red Blend (Salento) $10. 88 Best Buy —*M.S. (11/15/2004)*

Tenute Rubino 2003 TorreTesta Susumaniello (Salento) $60. This is an excellent wine from a grape few people have ever heard of—Susumaniello—with inky, concentrated extracts and intense aromas of dried currants, fruit preserves, root beer, plums, blackberry and sweet cookie dough. It's sticky and creamy in the mouth with molasses and herbal notes over the long, luscious finish. 92 —*M.L. (8/1/2007)*

Tenute Rubino 2005 Marmorelle White Blend (Salento) $10. A luminous, fruity 80-20 Chardonnay-Malvasia blend from the southern Puglia region that showcases aromas of white fruit pulp, peach and citrus. You'll get pretty, pear-like flavors in the mouth, good intensity and refreshing crispness on the close. 88 Best Buy —*M.L. (4/1/2007)*

TENUTE SILVIO NARDI

Tenute Silvio Nardi 2001 Brunello (Brunello di Montalcino) $50. 89 *(4/1/2006)*

Tenute Silvio Nardi 2000 Brunello (Brunello di Montalcino) $55. 91 —*M.S. (7/1/2005)*

Tenute Silvio Nardi 1999 Brunello (Brunello di Montalcino) $55. 93 —*M.S. (6/1/2004)*

Tenute Silvio Nardi 1997 Brunello (Brunello di Montalcino) $60. 92 —*R.V. (8/1/2002)*

Tenute Silvio Nardi 1998 Manachiara Brunello (Brunello di Montalcino) $65. 92 —*M.S. (10/1/2004)*

Tenute Silvio Nardi 2002 Sangiovese (Rosso di Montalcino) $22. 90 —*M.S. (6/1/2004)*

TENUTE SOLETTA

Tenute Soletta 1997 Soletta/Reserva Grenache (Cannonau di Sardegna) $24. 85 —*C.S. (5/1/2002)*

Tenute Soletta 2002 Prestizu Vermentino (Vermentino di Sardegna) $17. 86 —*M.S. (8/1/2004)*

TERCIC

Tercic 2004 Pinot Grigio (Collio) $22. 86 *(2/1/2006)*

TERESA RAIZ

Teresa Raiz 2005 Le Marsure Merlot (Venezia Giulia) $14. One of my favorite Merlots at this price point, this vineyard-designate red boasts a plethora of tender, delicate aromas that recall cassis, forest berry, blue flowers and exotic spice. No wood is used so the vibrant fruit really shows. A smooth and feminine wine with medium length and intensity but plenty of elegance. 87 —*M.L. (3/1/2007)*

Teresa Raiz 2005 Pinot Grigio (Colli Orientali del Friuli) $15. The aromatic intensity certainly helps it stand out within a vast sea of Italian PGs. Feminine and fun, with fresh-cut flowers, sweet, cool exotic fruit, pear and citrus. The close is crisp; mouthfeel is playfully sweet. 87 —*M.L. (4/1/2007)*

Teresa Raiz 2004 Pinot Grigio (Colli Orientali del Friuli) $15. 89 Editors' Choice *—M.L. (2/1/2006)*

Teresa Raiz 2005 Le Marsure Pinot Grigio (Venezia Giulia) $14. A straightforward PG with an attractive, easy personality: almonds, green apple and dried herbs come forth; the wine closes with citrus-like zest. Great with light meals or appetizers. 87 *—M.L. (4/1/2007)*

Teresa Raiz 2004 Le Marsure Pinot Grigio (Venezia Giulia) $13. 87 *—M.L. (2/1/2006)*

Teresa Raiz 2005 Ribolla Gialla (Delle Venezie) $18. Ribolla Gialla is a naturally creamy, soft variety, but this expression favors tonic soda aromas and tart lemon candy that help shape a racy and zesty impression overall. 85 *—M.L. (12/1/2007)*

Teresa Raiz 2005 Le Marsure Sauvignon Blanc (Venezia Giulia) $15. Round and rewarding, this Sauvignon Blanc is a traditional expression of the variety thanks to herbaceous notes, green apple and clean mineral tones. Crisp and dry in the mouth, it promises excellent food pairing potential. 88 *—M.L. (5/1/2007)*

TERLAN

Terlan 2005 Pinot Grigio (Alto Adige) $19. 90 Editors' Choice *—M.L. (6/1/2006)*

Terlan 2003 Sauvignon (Alto Adige) $30. 86 *(7/1/2005)*

TERRA DEI REI

Terra dei Rei 2001 Divinus Aglianico (Aglianico del Vulture) $35. 89 *M.S. (10/1/2006)*

Terra dei Rei 2001 Vultur Aglianico (Aglianico del Vulture) $20. 83 *—M.S. (10/1/2006)*

TERRA ROSSA

Terra Rossa 2001 Brunello (Brunello di Montalcino) $50. 92 Cellar Selection *(4/1/2006)*

TERRA SERENA

Terra Serena NV Extra Dry Prosecco (Prosecco di Conegliano e Valdobbiadene) $15. 84 *—M.L. (6/1/2006)*

TERRABIANCA

Terrabianca 2003 Ceppate Cabernet Blend (Toscana) $37. 92 *—M.L. (9/1/2006)*

Terrabianca 1999 Campaccio Red Blend (Toscana) $24. 89 *—M.S. (12/31/2002)*

Terrabianca 2001 Campaccio Sangiovese (Toscana) $38. 87 *M.S. (11/15/2004)*

Terrabianca 2000 Campaccio Sangiovese (Toscana) $24. 85 *—M.S. (10/1/2004)*

Terrabianca 2001 Campaccio Selezione Riserva Sangiovese (Toscana) $72. 88 *—M.S. (9/1/2006)*

Terrabianca 1998 Ceppate Sangiovese (Tuscany) $22. 86 *—M.S. (12/31/2002)*

Terrabianca 2004 Croce Riserva Sangiovese (Chianti Classico) $29. This is Sangiovese-based with a just 3% Canaiolo, exhibiting modern, ripe flavors of sweet mocha chocolate, vanilla, cherry and mature blueberry. The nose is sweet smelling and some of that sweetness transfers to the mouth. The wine has a velvety, soft texture and tasty finish. 89 *—M.L. (11/1/2007)*

Terrabianca 2001 Croce Riserva Sangiovese (Chianti Classico) $31. 87 *(4/1/2005)*

Terrabianca 2000 Croce Riserva Sangiovese (Chianti Classico) $25. 90 *—M.S. (10/1/2004)*

Terrabianca 1997 Croce Riserva Sangiovese (Chianti Classico) $25. 87 *(4/1/2001)*

Terrabianca 2001 La Fonte Sangiovese (Toscana) $20. 85 *—M.S. (10/1/2004)*

Terrabianca 2000 Piano del Cipresso Sangiovese (Toscana) $22. 88 *—M.S. (10/1/2004)*

Terrabianca 1999 Piano Del Cipresso Sangiovese (Tuscany) $22. 90 *—M.S. (12/31/2002)*

Terrabianca 2005 Scassino Sangiovese (Chianti Classico) $26. Sangiovese is enhanced with a tiny quota of Canaiolo to produce a traditional-style Chianti Classic with high appeal and drinkability. In measured doses, you'll recognize black currant, mulberries and slate-like mineral flavors over a cool, fresh finish. 87 *—M.L. (11/1/2007)*

Terrabianca 2003 Scassino Sangiovese (Chianti Classico) $24. 82 *—M.S. (10/1/2006)*

Terrabianca 2002 Scassino Sangiovese (Chianti Classico) $22. 86 *(4/1/2005)*

Terrabianca 2001 Scassino Sangiovese (Chianti Classico) $20. 85 *—M.S. (10/1/2004)*

Terrabianca 2000 Scassino Sangiovese (Chianti Classico) $20. 87 *(8/1/2002)*

Terrabianca 1999 Scassino Sangiovese (Chianti Classico) $14. 87 *—M.S. (12/31/2002)*

Terrabianca 1998 Scassino Sangiovese (Chianti Classico) $18. 87 *(4/1/2001)*

TERRALE

Terrale 2002 Catarratto (Sicilia) $8. 83 *—R.V. (10/1/2003)*

Terrale 2000 Primitivo (Puglia) $8. 85 Best Buy *(5/1/2002)*

Terrale 1998 Primitivo (Puglia) $5. 83 *—M.N. (12/31/2000)*

Terrale 2000 Nero D'Avola/Syrah Red Blend (Sicilia) $8. 86 Best Buy *(5/1/2002)*

Terrale 2000 Sangiovese (Puglia) $8. 84 *(5/1/2002)*

Terrale 1998 Bianco White Blend (Sicilia) $5. 82 *—M.N. (12/31/2000)*

TERRALSOLE

Terralsole 2001 Brunello (Brunello di Montalcino) $NA. 89 *(4/1/2006)*

TERRAZZE DELLA LUNA

Terrazze Della Luna 2004 Pinot Grigio (Trentino) $12. 86 *—M.L. (6/1/2006)*

TERRAZZO

Terrazzo 2000 Sangiovese-Montepulciano Sangiovese (Marche) $7. 83 *—M.S. (11/15/2003)*

TERRE DA VINO

Terre da Vino 1998 Barbera (Barbera d'Asti) $11. 88 Best Buy *(4/1/2000)*

Terre da Vino 2003 La Bella Estate Moscato Passito Moscato (Piedmont) $NA. 87 *—M.L. (11/15/2006)*

Terre da Vino 2004 La Gatta Moscato (Moscato d'Asti) $12. 87 Editors' Choice *—M.L. (12/15/2005)*

Terre da Vino 2004 Monti Furchi Moscato (Asti) $NA. 89 *—M.L. (11/15/2006)*

TERRE DE TRINCI

Terre de Trinci 2000 Ugolino Sagrantino (Sagrantino di Montefalco) $35. 87 *—M.L. (9/1/2005)*

TERRE DEGLI SVEVI

Terre Degli Svevi 1999 Re Manfredi Aglianico (Aglianico del Vulture) $30. 90 *—M.S. (11/15/2004)*

TERRE DEL PRINCIPE

Terre del Principe 1998 Sangiovese (Chianti) $11. 84 *(4/1/2001)*

Terre del Principe 2002 Vernaccia (Vernaccia di San Gimignano) $13. 84 *—M.S. (8/1/2004)*

TERRE DI GENESTRA

Terre di Genestra 1999 Catarratto (Sicilia) $13. 87 *(4/1/2002)*

Terre di Genestra 2002 Nero d'Avola (Sicilia) $13. 87 *—R.V. (10/1/2003)*

Terre di Genestra 1999 Nero d'Avola (Sicilia) $13. 88 Best Buy *(5/1/2002)*

TERRE DI GER

Terre di Ger 2004 Pinot Grigio (Friuli) $15. 84 *(2/1/2006)*

TERRE DI GINESTRA

Terre di Ginestra 2002 Catarratto Chardonnay (Sicilia) $9. 87 *—R.V. (10/1/2003)*

TERRE DI GIURFO

Terre di Giurfo 2004 Kuntéri Nero d'Avola (Sicilia) $11. 87 *—M.L. (7/1/2006)*

Terre di Giurfo 2004 Maskarìa Red Blend (Cerasuolo di Vittoria) $10. 85 *—M.L. (7/1/2006)*

Terre di Giurfo 2004 Ronna Syrah (Sicilia) $10. 87 *—M.L. (7/1/2006)*

TERRE DI TALAMO

Terre di Talamo 2006 Piano Rosé Blend (Maremma) $NA. Chianti's Castello Bossi owns this coastal Tuscany estate and has released a very attractive rosé with pretty floral tones, fresh fruit and a touch of menthol-cherry for extra dimension. Try it with pasta, fish or white meat. 87 *—M.L. (7/1/2007)*

TERREDORA

Terredora 2004 Aglianico (Irpinia) $15. 87 —*M.L. (10/1/2006)*

Terredora 2000 Fatica Contadina Aglianico (Taurasi) $48. 91 Cellar Selection —*M.L. (10/1/2006)*

Terredora 2002 Il Principio Aglianico (Irpinia) $NA. 89 —*M.L. (10/1/2006)*

Terredora 1998 Il Principio Aglianico (Aglianico d'Irpinia) $9. 85 Best Buy —*C.S. (5/1/2002)*

Terredora 2003 Red Blend (Lacryma Christi del Vesuvio) $27. 86 —*M.L. (10/1/2006)*

Terredora 1999 Red Blend (Aglianico d'Irpinia) $12. 87 Best Buy —*M.N. (12/31/2000)*

Terredora 1996 Fatica Contadina Aglianico (Taurasi) $38. 89 —*M.N. (12/31/2000)*

Terredora 2004 White Blend (Lacryma Christi del Vesuvio) $NA. Here is an interesting wine from Campania with a bigger, broader build and alluring notes of melon, white stone, peach, vanilla and almond. It's full-flavored and creamy, almost thick, in the mouth. 86 —*M.L. (4/1/2007)*

Terredora 1999 Terre di Dora White Blend (Fiano di Avellino) $20. 91 —*M.N. (12/31/2000)*

TERREDORA DI PAOLO

Terredora Di Paolo 2003 Aglianico (Irpinia) $14. 87 —*M.S. (2/1/2005)*

Terredora Di Paolo 2003 Loggia Della Serra Greco (Greco di Tufo) $21. 83 —*M.S. (2/1/2005)*

Terredora Di Paolo 1999 Fatica Contadina Aglianico (Taurasi) $49. 89 —*M.S. (2/1/2005)*

TERUZZI & PUTHOD

Teruzzi & Puthod 2001 Peperino Sangiovese (Toscana) $15. 83 —*M.S. (10/1/2004)*

Teruzzi & Puthod 2004 Vernaccia (Vernaccia di San Gimignano) $13. 85 —*M.L. (9/1/2005)*

Teruzzi & Puthod 2003 Vernaccia (Vernaccia di San Gimignano) 84 —*M.L. (9/1/2005)*

Teruzzi & Puthod 2002 Vernaccia (Vernaccia di San Gimignano) $12. 85 —*M.S. (8/1/2004)*

Teruzzi & Puthod 1997 Vernaccia (Vernaccia di San Gimignano) $11. 84 *(11/1/1999)*

Teruzzi & Puthod 1997 Terre di Tufi Vernaccia (Vernaccia di San Gimignano) $21. 86 *(11/1/1999)*

Teruzzi & Puthod 2004 Terre di Tufi White Blend (Toscana) $25. 88 —*M.S. (9/1/2006)*

TESEO

Teseo 2002 Chardonnay (Terre di Chieti) $15. 83 —*M.S. (10/1/2004)*

TEZZA

Tezza 2002 Brolo delle Giare Corvina, Rondinella, Molinara (Amarone della Valpolicella Valpantena) $50. This producer fought against Mother Nature and the wet 2002 vintage with 36 months of barrique aging. The wood tones almost overwhelm the fruit and leave only glimmering remnants of vibrant cherry and raspberry liquor. The wine also tastes very sweet and end with good freshness. 88 —*M.L. (10/1/2007)*

TIAMO

Tiamo 2005 Pinot Grigio (Delle Venezie) $11. With much more personality than past vintages, the wine's aromas include banana, yellow flower, peach and spice. There's good dimension and personality to this crisp, friendly white that would pair well with vegetables, fish and white meat. 85 —*M.L. (11/15/2007)*

Tiamo 2004 Pinot Grigio (Delle Venezie) $10. 84 *(2/1/2006)*

Tiamo 2004 Pinot Grigio (Delle Venezie) $10. 84 —*M.L. (2/1/2006)*

TIBERINI

Tiberini 1998 Podere le Caggiole Prugnolo Gentile (Vino Nobile di Montepulciano) $20. 86 —*M.S. (11/15/2003)*

Tiberini 2000 Virgulto Prugnolo Gentile (Rosso di Montepulciano) $30. 84 —*M.S. (11/15/2003)*

TIEFENBRUNNER

Tiefenbrunner 1999 Linticlarus Chardonnay (Alto Adige) $20. 89 —*R.V. (7/1/2003)*

Tiefenbrunner 2003 Castel Turmhof Lagrein (Alto Adige) $18. 88 —*M.L. (9/1/2005)*

Tiefenbrunner 2003 Linticlarus Riserva Lagrein (Alto Adige) $18. Blueberry and cherry fruit are the protagonist with delicately toasted oak in a supporting role. There's a sweet note in the mouth with flavors of balsamic sauce, pine nut, licorice and red cedarwood. Pair with grilled lamb or game. 89 —*M.L. (9/1/2007)*

Tiefenbrunner 2002 Feldmarschall von Fenner Vino da Tavola Müller-Thurgau (Alto Adige) $27. 87 —*R.V. (7/1/2003)*

Tiefenbrunner 2005 Pinot Bianco (Alto Adige) $14. Generous and fragrant aromas of sweet fruit, peach, melon and a dusty mineral note are derived from the Cortaccia and Magrè chalk gravel vineyards in Alto Adige. Lean and crisp in the mouth, this is one of those drink-anytime wines that pairs with a long list of foods. 87 —*M.L. (9/1/2007)*

Tiefenbrunner 2004 Pinot Grigio (Delle Venezie) $15. 87 —*M.L. (6/1/2006)*

Tiefenbrunner 2003 Linticlarus Riserva Pinot Nero (Alto Adige) $35. Delicately layered and fragrant throughout, this softly delivers small, steady doses of berry fruit, blue flower and vanilla fragrances. It has greater intensity in the mouth with crisp, polished acidity. 89 —*M.L. (9/1/2007)*

Tiefenbrunner 2005 Kirchleiten Sauvignon Blanc (Alto Adige) $25. What a wonderful treat from Herbert and son Christof Tiefenbrunner. Beautifully fragrant floral aromas mingle gently with kiwi, tomato leaf, exotic fruit and mineral tones from the vineyard's loamy, chalky soils. This is a truly beautiful portrait of Sauvignon from northern Italy. 89 —*M.L. (9/1/2007)*

Tiefenbrunner 2002 Kirchleiten Sauvignon Blanc (Alto Adige) $21. 86 —*R.V. (7/1/2003)*

Tieffenbrunner 2000 Pinot Bianco (Alto Adige) $12. 83 —*M.N. (9/1/2001)*

Tieffenbrunner 2000 delle Venezie Pinot Grigio (Alto Adige) $13. 86 —*M.N. (9/1/2001)*

TIEZZI

Tiezzi 2001 Brunello (Brunello di Montalcino) $50. 88 *(4/1/2006)*

Tiezzi 2000 Brunello (Brunello di Montalcino) $50. 87 —*M.S. (7/1/2005)*

Tiezzi 1999 Brunello (Brunello di Montalcino) $NA. 85 —*M.S. (6/1/2004)*

TINAZZI

Tinazzi 2004 La Bastia Ca' de' Rocchi Corvina, Rondinella, Molinara (Amarone della Valpolicella Classico) $40. This producer buys wine to age and bottle under the estate label. La Bastia Cà de' Rocchi is a top cru and boasts broader, meatier, sun-drenched characteristics that translate into black cherry, blueberries and cola. The wine has good power and concentration, yet is soft, sweet and velvety in the mouth with quality tannins. 89 —*M.L. (10/1/2007)*

Tinazzi 2003 Tenuta Valleselle Aurum Corvina, Rondinella, Molinara (Amarone della Valpolicella Classico) $45. This presents an aromatic wall of chocolate, cherry, toasted almonds, crème caramel and spice. In the mouth, it offers a long extension of flavors, chewy consistency and a solid backbone of sweet primary fruit. 88 —*M.L. (10/1/2007)*

TIZIANO

Tiziano 2003 Sangiovese (Chianti) $10. 87 Best Buy *(4/1/2005)*

Tiziano 2001 Sangiovese (Chianti) $8. 85 Best Buy —*M.S. (11/15/2003)*

Tiziano 1999 Sangiovese (Chianti) $7. 83 *(4/1/2001)*

Tiziano 2001 Gold Sangiovese (Chianti Classico) $16. 86 *(4/1/2005)*

Tiziano 2001 Riserva Sangiovese (Chianti) $12. 85 *(4/1/2005)*

Tiziano 1999 Riserva Sangiovese (Chianti) $10. 86 Best Buy —*M.S. (11/15/2003)*

TOFFOLI

Toffoli NV Brut Prosecco (Prosecco di Conegliano e Valdobbiadene) $15. By its saturated, golden shine, you can tell that is a bolder, bigger Prosecco style and aromas of orange blossom, lemon candy and white stone reinforce that impression. Also a notch up in terms of concentration, the wine's mouthfeel is creamy and quite sweet for a Brut. 86 —*M.L. (12/15/2007)*

Toffoli 2005 Brut Prosecco (Prosecco di Conegliano e Valdobbiadene) $12. 85 —*M.L. (6/1/2006)*

Toffoli NV Extra Dry Prosecco (Prosecco di Conegliano e Valdobbiadene) $15. This opens with a golden hue and pretty perlage followed by fragrant aromas of lime, lemon zest, pear and green apple. There's a simple, genuine feel to it that is reinforced by the wine's lean, crisp finish. 86 —*M.L. (12/15/2007)*

Toffoli 2005 Extra Dry Prosecco (Prosecco di Conegliano e Valdobbiadene) $12. 86 —*M.L. (6/1/2006)*

TOLAINI

Tolaini 2002 Tenuta S. Giovanni Duesanti Bordeaux Blend (Toscana) $40. 88 —*M.S. (9/1/2006)*

TOLLOY

Tolloy 1998 Pinot Bianco (Alto Adige) $11. 86 *(7/1/2000)*

Tolloy 2005 Pinot Grigio (Alto Adige) $10. 88 Best Buy *—M.L. (6/1/2006)*

Tolloy 2004 Pinot Grigio (Alto Adige) $12. 87 *—M.L. (2/1/2006)*

Tolloy 1999 Pinot Grigio (Alto Adige) $10. 88 Best Buy *—M.N. (12/31/2000)*

Tolloy 2003 Cantina Salorno Pinot Grigio (Alto Adige) $12. 86 *—J.C. (12/31/2004)*

Tolloy 1997 Pinot Nero (Alto Adige) $11. 86 *(7/1/2000)*

TOMMASI

Tommasi 2001 Vigneto Santa Cecilia Chardonnay (Valdadige) $9. 88 *—J.C. (7/1/2003)*

Tommasi 2001 Rafael Corvina (Valpolicella Classico Superiore) $11. 86 Best Buy *—J.C. (12/31/2004)*

Tommasi 2001 Ripasso Corvina (Valpolicella Classico Superiore) $18. 88 *—J.C. (12/31/2004)*

Tommasi 2003 Corvina, Rondinella, Molinara (Amarone della Valpolicella Classico) $60. You'll feel the heat in this sun-drenched Amarone that offers a chewy consistency and a pleasingly firm but smooth texture. Aroma-wise, there's a lot going on: First are notes of mature cherry fruit, but there are also green, almost eucalyptus-like renderings. On top of those are coffee, bacon and cocoa. 90 *—M.L. (10/1/2007)*

Tommasi 2001 Corvina, Rondinella, Molinara (Amarone della Valpolicella Classico) $60. 92 *—J.C. (10/1/2006)*

Tommasi 2000 Corvina, Rondinella, Molinara (Amarone della Valpolicella Classico) $60. 90 *—J.C. (12/31/2004)*

Tommasi 1997 Corvina, Rondinella, Molinara (Amarone della Valpolicella Classico) $49. 88 *(5/1/2003)*

Tommasi 2003 Cà Florian Corvina, Rondinella, Molinara (Amarone della Valpolicella Classico) $70. This Amarone offers a very distinctive and evolved nose that recalls espresso grinds, cola and tealeaf with menthol-balsam renderings. Dark concentration, power and great intensity are reinforced by thick berry flavors, coffee and excellent durability on the palate. 92 *—M.L. (10/1/2007)*

Tommasi 2001 Ca' Florian Corvina, Rondinella, Molinara (Amarone della Valpolicella Classico) $68. 92 *—J.C. (10/1/2006)*

Tommasi 2000 Ca' Florian Corvina, Rondinella, Molinara (Amarone della Valpolicella Classico) $60. 90 *(11/1/2005)*

Tommasi 1997 Ca'Florian Corvina, Rondinella, Molinara (Amarone della Valpolicella) $55. 93 Editors' Choice *(5/1/2003)*

Tommasi 2003 Il Sestante Vigneto Monte Masua Corvina, Rondinella, Molinara (Amarone della Valpolicella Classico) $65. Now in its fourth generation, Tommasi is one of the most ardent ambassadors of Valpolicella wine tradition. And although the wines are always top notch, this particular vintage of Monte Masua seems to have suffered from the heat. Stewy notes are a distraction and appear on the coat tails of attractive spice, ginger, cherry and smoked ham. 87 *—M.L. (10/1/2007)*

Tommasi 2000 Il Sestante Vigneto Monte Masua Corvina, Rondinella, Molinara (Amarone della Valpolicella Classico) $58. 89 *(11/1/2005)*

Tommasi 1997 Vigneto Il Sestante Corvina, Rondinella, Molinara (Amarone della Valpolicella) $50. 87 *(5/1/2003)*

Tommasi 2006 Le Volpare Garganega (Soave Classico) $13. This is a well-priced Soave with a luminous golden color and creamy aromas of peach, melon and honey. The wine offers sweet fruit flavors, nice consistency and a crisp finish making it a good choice for informal, light meals. 87 *—M.L. (12/1/2007)*

Tommasi 2003 Le Volpare Garganega (Soave Classico) $10. 87 Best Buy *—J.C. (12/31/2004)*

Tommasi 2006 Le Rosse Pinot Grigio (Delle Venezie) $15. This is textbook Pinot Grigio Delle Venezie—meaning that fruit is sourced from anywhere within the region—with characteristic aromas of Golden Delicious apple, pear, natural rubber, yellow fruit, honey and a playful touch of citrus zest. Broad dimension and a spicy finish call for a dish like sweet and sour pork. 86 *—M.L. (12/1/2007)*

Tommasi 2004 Le Rosse Pinot Grigio (Delle Venezie) $10. 85 *—M.L. (2/1/2006)*

Tommasi 2003 Le Rosse Pinot Grigio (Delle Venezie) $10. 86 Best Buy *—J.C. (12/31/2004)*

Tommasi 1997 Le Rosse Pinot Grigio (Colli Orientali del Friuli) $10. 85 *(8/1/1999)*

Tommasi 1997 Campo Fiorato Red Blend (Recioto di Soave) $20. 87 *(5/1/2003)*

Tommasi 2000 Crearo della Concaa d'Oro Red Blend (Veronese) $25. 89 *(5/1/2003)*

Tommasi 1998 Ripasso Red Blend (Valpolicella Classico Superiore) $30. 87 *(5/1/2003)*

Tommasi 2004 Poggio al Tufo Vigneto Rompicollo Sangiovese (Maremma) $12. 85 *—M.S. (9/1/2006)*

Tommasi 2001 Vigneto Le Volpare White Blend (Soave Classico Superiore) $9. 82 *—J.C. (7/1/2003)*

Tommasi 2001 Vigneto San Martino White Blend (Lugana) $NA. 84 *—J.C. (7/1/2003)*

TOMMASO BUSSOLA

Tommaso Bussola 2002 Corvina, Rondinella, Molinara (Amarone della Valpolicella Classico) $NA. Tommaso Bussola successfully delivers Amarone typicity in the form of white cherry, fragrant almond blossom and vanilla-apple. This is a wine with personality and a vertical, direct approach that ends with firm structure and good length. 90 *—M.L. (10/1/2007)*

Tommaso Bussola 2001 Corvina, Rondinella, Molinara (Amarone della Valpolicella Classico) $NA. Lovers of traditional Amarone can appreciate a pinch of volatility (it sometimes appears as apple or cider) because it can add vibrancy, buoyancy and life to a wine when applied in measured doses. This is a good example of a wine enhanced by pungent apple that will appeal to those who like this style. Tommaso Bussola is a winemaking legend in these parts and is a leader in Valpolicella tradition. 90 *—M.L. (12/1/2007)*

Tommaso Bussola 2000 Vigneto Alto Corvina, Rondinella, Molinara (Amarone della Valpolicella Classico) $NA. Opulent, harmonious and confident in its typicity, this Amarone's pretty nose is bolstered by dried red currant berries, tea leaf, coffee and chocolate nuances. It imparts ripe fruit flavors and noticeable sweetness in the mouth and also delivers clean freshness and firm structure. 93 *—M.L. (12/1/2007)*

TORMARESCA

Tormaresca 2002 Bocca di Lupo Aglianico (Castel del Monte) $27. 91 Editors' Choice *—M.L. (10/1/2006)*

Tormaresca 2000 Bocca di Lupo Aglianico (Castel del Monte) $28. 93 Editors' Choice *—M.S. (12/15/2003)*

Tormaresca 2004 Chardonnay (Puglia) $8. 87 Best Buy *—M.L. (10/1/2006)*

Tormaresca 2002 Chardonnay (Puglia) $10. 82 *—M.S. (10/1/2004)*

Tormaresca 2003 Masseria Maìme Negroamaro (Salento) $27. I'm a fan of Antinori's Puglia estate and the work that enologist Renzo Cotarella does with the region's native varieties. These wines deliver power and aromatic intensity without losing their delicate balance between fruit and tobacco. The wine also shows a nice evolution in the glass with rose petal and vanilla not far behind. Drink now. 90 *—M.L. (4/1/2007)*

Tormaresca 2002 Masseria Maime Negroamaro (Salento) $28. 90 *—M.S. (10/1/2006)*

Tormaresca 2000 Masseria Maime Negroamaro (Salento) $28. 92 *—M.S. (12/15/2003)*

Tormaresca 2004 Torcicoda Primitivo (Salento) $20. A sophisticated and seductive expression of the Primitivo grape, this Antinori-made Puglian wine boasts thick concentration, fruity extracts, ripe cherry flavors, strawberry and a thick inky appearance. The tannins are rock solid, suggesting a pairing with roasted meats, steak or aged cheeses. 88 *—M.L. (8/1/2007)*

Tormaresca 2003 Torcicoda Primitivo (Salento) $20. 88 *—M.L. (9/1/2005)*

Tormaresca 2001 Torcicoda Primitivo (Salento) $20. 89 *—M.S. (11/15/2004)*

Tormaresca 2003 Red Blend (Puglia) $8. Usually a consistent value wine from southern Italy, this Negroamaro-Cabernet blend offers a fully charged nose with Indian spice, iron, cherry and leather. You will also pick up an earthy or barnyard-like note that doesn't distract too much. 85 Best Buy *—M.L. (4/1/2007)*

Tormaresca 2000 Red Blend (Puglia) $11. 86 Best Buy *—C.S. (5/1/2002)*

TORNESI

Tornesi 2001 Brunello (Brunello di Montalcino) $44. 90 *(4/1/2006)*

TORRE DI LUNA

Torre di Luna 1997 Pinot Grigio (Trentino) $8. 83 *(8/1/1999)*

Torre di Luna 2004 Pinot Grigio (Delle Venezie) $12. 85 *—M.L. (6/1/2006)*

Torre di Luna 2003 Pinot Grigio (Delle Venezie) $13. 84 *—J.C. (12/31/2004)*

Torre di Luna 2001 Pinot Grigio (Delle Venezie) $12. 84 *—J.C. (7/1/2003)*

TORRE DI MONTE

Torre di Monte 2001 Pinot Grigio (Umbria) $10. 82 *—M.S. (10/1/2004)*

TORRE MASCOLI

Torre Mascoli 2001 Niró Red Blend (Murgia) $10. 83 *—M.S. (10/1/2006)*

TORRE ROSAZZA

Torre Rosazza 1997 Pinot Grigio (Colli Orientali del Friuli) $12. 86 *(8/1/1999)*

TORRE SVEVA

Torre Sveva 1998 Castel del Monte Red Blend (Apulia) $8. 85 Best Buy *—L.W. (3/1/2000)*

TORRE VIGNE

Torre Vigne 1997 Aglianico (Taurasi) $20. 86 *—M.S. (2/1/2005)*

TORRESELLA

Torresella 2000 Cabernet Sauvignon (Veneto) $10. 82 *(5/1/2003)*

Torresella 2002 Chardonnay (Veneto) $14. 83 *—J.C. (12/31/2004)*

Torresella 2000 Merlot (Veneto) $10. 83 *(5/1/2003)*

Torresella 2003 Pinot Grigio (Veneto) $10. 82 *—J.C. (12/31/2004)*

Torresella 2001 Pinot Grigio (Veneto) $10. 83 *—J.C. (7/1/2003)*

Torresella 2002 Sauvignon Blanc (Veneto) $14. 84 *—J.C. (12/31/2004)*

TOSCA

Tosca 2004 Pinot Grigio (Friuli Grave) $9. 86 Best Buy *—M.L. (6/1/2006)*

TOSCOLO

Toscolo 2004 Sangiovese (Chianti) $11. 88 Best Buy *—M.S. (10/1/2006)*

Toscolo 2003 Sangiovese (Chianti) $11. 84 *(4/1/2005)*

Toscolo 2003 Sangiovese (Chianti Classico) $20. 84 *—M.S. (10/1/2006)*

Toscolo 2001 Sangiovese (Chianti Classico) $20. 87 *(4/1/2005)*

Toscolo 2001 Sangiovese (Chianti) $9. 86 *—M.S. (11/15/2003)*

Toscolo 2000 Sangiovese (Chianti) $8. 84 *(10/1/2001)*

Toscolo 2000 Sangiovese (Chianti Classico) $19. 85 *—M.S. (10/1/2004)*

Toscolo 1999 Sangiovese (Chianti Classico) $14. 86 *(10/1/2001)*

Toscolo 2001 Riserva Sangiovese (Chianti Classico) $24. 87 *—M.S. (10/1/2006)*

Toscolo 1999 Riserva Sangiovese (Chianti Classico) $24. 84 *—M.S. (10/1/2004)*

Toscolo 1997 Riserva Sangiovese (Chianti Classico) $17. 87 *(10/1/2001)*

TRABUCCHI

Trabucchi 2000 Corvina, Rondinella, Molinara (Amarone della Valpolicella) $50. 89 *(11/1/2005)*

Trabucchi 2003 L'Amarone di Marchetto Corvina, Rondinella, Molinara (Amarone della Valpolicella) $100. This is beautiful but so atypical, it's difficult to place within the wider range of Amarone styles. Very extracted and almost impenetrable in appearance, the wine offers Cab-like smells of green pepper, herb and licorice. It also delivers sweet chocolate, vanilla-nut and spice. **87** *—M.L. (10/1/2007)*

TRAMIN

Tramin 2003 Sauvignon (Alto Adige) $20. 91 Editors' Choice *(7/1/2005)*

TRANCHERO OSVALDO

Tranchero Osvaldo 2004 Casot Moscato (Moscato d'Asti) $15. 84 *—M.L. (12/15/2005)*

TRAVAGLINI

Travaglini 1997 Nebbiolo (Gattinara) $30. 87 *—S.H. (11/15/2002)*

Travaglini 1995 Nebbiolo (Gattinara) $29. 92 *(11/15/1999)*

Travaglini 1996 Riserva Nebbiolo (Gattinara) $35. 89 *—S.H. (11/15/2002)*

Travaglini 1997 Tre Vigne Nebbiolo (Gattinara) $40. 88 *—S.H. (11/15/2002)*

TREFIANO

Trefiano 1997 Sangiovese (Carmignano) $37. 84 *—J.C. (9/1/2001)*

Trefiano 1995 Sangiovese (Carmignano) $37. 88 *—M.S. (11/15/1999)*

TREVISIOL

Trevisiol NV Vino Spumante Brut Champagne Blend (Prosecco di Valdobbiadene) $14. 86 *—M.M. (12/31/2001)*

TRE MONTI

Tre Monti 2004 Albana (Albana di Romagna) $23. This dessert wine scores in the â€œacceptableâ€? range because of a slight cloudiness in its appearance and a thin, simplistic mouthfeel. On the upside are distinct lemon rind and herbal aromas. **82** *—M.L. (2/1/2007)*

Tre Monti 2005 Superiore Sangiovese (Sangiovese di Romagna) $12. This wine is broad on the palate despite only seeing stainless steel and offers a pretty medley of coffee, chocolate and red cherry. The nose is bold, but the mouthfeel is less so with a lighter imprint and medium tannins. **84** *—M.L. (2/1/2007)*

Tre Monti 2003 Superiore Riserva Sangiovese (Sangiovese di Romagna) $16. A solid, clean and straightforward red with lighter ruby hue and consistency: This is the kind of wine you need for informal occasions. Cherry, chocolate and herbal aromas are backed by medium tannins. **85** *—M.L. (2/1/2007)*

Tre Monti 2004 Thea Superiore Sangiovese (Sangiovese di Romagna) $23. Cherry, toasted almond and herbal notes characterize a wine that comes close to hitting optimal equilibrium if it weren't for the alcohol heat. Some wine enthusiasts may appreciate that quality especially if paired with a winter dish like hearty beef stew. **87** *—M.L. (2/1/2007)*

Tre Monti 2005 Vigna del Rio Trebbiano (Emilia-Romagna) $12. This is a light and luminous Trebbiano with herbal notes, lavender honey and stone fruit. It's an easily drinkable wine with a somewhat broad, creamy and viscous mouthfeel. **84** *—M.L. (2/1/2007)*

Tre Monti 2004 Thea White Blend (Colli d' Imola) $23. A structured, golden-hued blend of grapes that only sees stainless steel; there are notes of honey, beeswax, melon and dried straw. The wine could pair with white meat or more elaborately prepared vegetables. It has nutty flavors in the mouth and a creamy consistency without being syrupy. **87** *—M.L. (2/1/2007)*

TRIACCA

Triacca 1998 La Palaia Red Blend (Chianti Classico) $NA. 84 *—M.S. (8/1/2002)*

TUA RITA

Tua Rita 2004 Redigaffi Merlot (Toscana) $275. This 100% Merlot's top-notch performance starts off with a beautiful, saturated ruby red color and continues with soft, well-defined aromas of sweet milk chocolate, clove, ground cinnamon and forest berries. Secondary aromas are of vanilla, licorice and toast; the wine is amazingly lively in the mouth with voluptuous, liquid chocolate-like flavors and an extra-long finish. **95 Cellar Selection** *—M.L. (4/1/2007)*

TURNING LEAF

Turning Leaf 1997 Pinot Grigio (Delle Venezie) $12. 82 *(8/1/1999)*

UCCELLIERA

Uccelliera 2001 Brunello (Brunello di Montalcino) $65. 93 Cellar Selection *(4/1/2006)*

Uccelliera 2000 Brunello (Brunello di Montalcino) $62. 92 Editors' Choice *—M.S. (7/1/2005)*

Uccelliera 1999 Brunello (Brunello di Montalcino) $NA. 92 *—M.S. (6/1/2004)*

Uccelliera 1999 Riserva Brunello (Brunello di Montalcino) $90. 94 Editors' Choice *—M.S. (7/1/2005)*

UGO LEQUIO

Ugo Lequio 2000 Gallina Nebbiolo (Barbaresco) $50. 90 *(4/2/2004)*

Ugo Lequio 1999 Gallina Nebbiolo (Barbaresco) $49. 88 *(4/2/2004)*

UMANI RONCHI

Umani Ronchi 2003 Cumaro Montepulciano (Rosso Conero) $30. Here's a wine to look out for (in pretty packaging too) if you want to impress your friends with a selection from a little-known region of Italy that is ripe with enological potential. The aromatic layers here are generous and intense: You'll get loads of red fruit, leather, tar and menthol flavors. **90** *—M.L. (12/1/2007)*

Umani Ronchi 2002 Jorio Montepulciano (Montepulciano d'Abruzzo) $13. 86 Best Buy *—M.L. (11/15/2006)*

Umani Ronchi 2003 San Lorenzo Montepulciano (Rosso Conero) $14. One of the most attractive characteristics of this vineyard-designated wine is the particular clarity in which its mineral nuances are delivered. They give the wine a linear, vertical quality that is enhanced by broader tones of red fruit and wet tobacco. **89 Best Buy** *—M.L. (11/15/2007)*

Umani Ronchi 2003 Maximo Botrytis Cinerea Sauvignon Blanc (Marche) $30. There are only a few pockets of vineyard land in Italy with the correct levels of fog or moisture for noble rot (botrytis) and the Marche is one of them. But 2003 was a sweltering hot year and as a result this Sauvignon-based dessert wine lacks its characteristic intensity. You do get apricot, peach and honey over the wine's lean consistency and there's a slightly sour taste on the finish. **86** *—M.L. (12/1/2007)*

Umani Ronchi 2005 Casal di Serra Verdicchio (Verdicchio dei Castelli di Jesi Classico Superiore) $14. Pear, Golden Delicious apple, natural smoke and mineral form a fine, elegant whole. Verdicchio has natural creaminess and the plush consistency of this wine demonstrates this fact. Pair it with pork, poultry or pasta. **87** *—M.L. (11/15/2007)*

Umani Ronchi 2002 Casal di Serra Verdicchio (Verdicchio dei Castelli di Jesi Classico Superiore) $14. **87** *—M.S. (8/1/2004)*

Umani Ronchi 2004 Casal di Serra Vecchie Vigne Verdicchio (Verdicchio dei Castelli di Jesi Classico Superiore) $22. This is a fabulous take on Verdicchio from 30-year-old vines that boasts a golden color and generous tones of sweet honey, passion fruit, perfumed white flower and mature peach. Feminine and silky in texture, it also has a viscous, creamy side that aids in establishing a broader, richer mouthfeel. **89 Editors' Choice** *—M.L. (12/1/2007)*

Umani Ronchi 2003 Casal di Serra Vecchie Vigne Verdicchio (Verdicchio dei Castelli di Jesi Classico Superiore) $22. **87** *—M.L. (10/1/2006)*

Umani Ronchi 2003 Plenio Riserva Verdicchio (Verdicchio dei Castelli di Jesi Classico Superiore) $22. One third of Umani Ronchi's celebrated Plenio Riserva is fermented in wood barrel which leads to rich aromas of vanilla, almond and apricot. Overall, those oak nuances are delicately balanced by rich fruit and fragrant floral tones. **89** *—M.L. (12/1/2007)*

Umani Ronchi 2002 Plenio Riserva Verdicchio (Verdicchio dei Castelli di Jesi Classico) $22. **87** *—M.L. (10/1/2006)*

Umani Ronchi 2005 Villa Bianchi Verdicchio (Verdicchio dei Castelli di Jesi Classico Superiore) $10. Villa Bianchi is a pristine white wine from the Marche region with a pretty aromatic ensemble that reveals stone fruit, fragrant melon, pear and dusty white stone. It would make a great companion to grilled vegetables or chicken salad. **85 Best Buy** *—M.L. (11/15/2007)*

Umani Ronchi 2004 Villa Bianchi Verdicchio (Verdicchio dei Castelli di Jesi Classico Superiore) $10. **85 Best Buy** *—M.L. (10/1/2006)*

Umani Ronchi 2002 Villa Bianchi Verdicchio (Verdicchio dei Castelli di Jesi Classico Superiore) $12. **86** *—M.S. (8/1/2004)*

Umani Ronchi 2004 Le Busche White Blend (Marche) $22. A barrique-fermented blend of Verdicchio and Chardonnay, Le Busche is the kind of wine you'll want to serve with roast turkey or lasagna with crusty melted cheese. Its color is solid gold and notes of banana, vanilla, yellow apple and exotic spice create an ensemble that is steady enough to pair with hearty dishes. **90** *—M.L. (12/1/2007)*

Umani Ronchi 2003 Le Busche White Blend (Marche) $25. **90** *—M.L. (10/1/2006)*

UMBERTO CESARI

Umberto Cesari 2005 Colle del Re Albana (Albana di Romagna) $10. This is a nice, refreshing wine, but it does have certain elements that need to be tucked back into place. One example is the sour note on the finish that distracts from the wine's pleasant flavors of stone fruit, melon and cut grass. **84** *—M.L. (2/1/2007)*

Umberto Cesari 2003 Colle del Re Albana (Albana di Romagna) $28. Dried peach and apricot with luscious honey-like tones describe both the aromas and flavors of this Romagna dessert wine made from dried grapes. It is aged in oak for one year to add nuances of toast and almond nut. **89** *—M.L. (2/1/2007)*

Umberto Cesari 2003 Colle Del Re Albana (Albana di Romagna) $8. **85 Best Buy** *—M.S. (7/1/2005)*

Umberto Cesari 2003 Liano Red Blend (Emilia-Romagna) $30. One-third Cabernet Sauvignon gives this Sangiovese-based wine enough power and structure to pair with game meat or barbecue. Red fruit, exotic spice, leather and roasted coffee characterize the aromas. The mouthfeel is thicker and meatier with soft tannins, nice intensity and mint on the finish. **88** *—M.L. (2/1/2007)*

Umberto Cesari 2003 Riserva Red Blend (Sangiovese di Romagna) $15. This wine has loads of balsam and menthol-like notes, which I find particularly attractive. Candied cherry almond and a brambly quality add more interesting layers. The wine's impression on the palate is balanced yet lean with spicy crispness and a sour note on the finish. **86** *—M.L. (2/1/2007)*

Umberto Cesari 2001 Tauleto Red Blend (Rubicone) $50. Give this wine a few moments to open and you'll be greeted by red fruit, roasted chestnut, coffee and vanilla. Made with Sangiovese and the Bursona Longanesi grape and aged in wood for two years, the wine is soft and round in the mouth with sour cherry on the finish. **88** *—M.L. (2/1/2007)*

VAGNONI

Vagnoni 2000 Riserva Sangiovese (Chianti Colli Senesi) $24. **85** *(4/1/2005)*

Vagnoni 1997 Riserva Sangiovese (Chianti Colli Senesi) $14. **87** *(4/1/2001)*

Vagnoni 2002 Vernaccia (Vernaccia di San Gimignano) $15. **84** *—M.S. (8/1/2004)*

VAL D'OCA

Val d'Oca 2004 Pigià Pinot Grigio (Marca Trevigiana) $9. **85 Best Buy** *—M.L. (10/1/2006)*

Val d'Oca NV Brut Prosecco (Prosecco di Valdobbiadene) $14. **85** *—M.S. (12/15/2004)*

Val d'Oca 2004 Brut Prosecco (Prosecco di Valdobbiadene) $16. **86** *—M.S. (12/31/2005)*

Val d'Oca 2004 Extra Dry Prosecco (Prosecco di Valdobbiadene) $16. **87** *—M.S. (12/31/2005)*

Val d'Oca 2003 Millesimato Extra Dry Prosecco (Prosecco di Valdobbiadene) $14. **85** *—M.S. (12/15/2004)*

Val d'Oca NV VSAQ Extra Dry Prosecco (Italy) $11. **89 Best Buy** *—M.S. (12/15/2004)*

VAL DELLE ROSE

Val delle Rose 2003 Sangiovese (Morellino di Scansano) $15. **84** *—M.S. (11/15/2004)*

Val delle Rose 2002 Sangiovese (Morellino di Scansano) $15. **82** *—M.S. (10/1/2004)*

Val delle Rose 1999 Sangiovese (Morellino di Scansano) $14. **88** *—M.S. (8/1/2002)*

Val delle Rose 2000 Riserva Sangiovese (Morellino di Scansano) $19. **87** *—M.S. (11/15/2004)*

Val delle Rose 1998 Riserva Sangiovese (Morellino di Scansano) $19. **88** *—M.S. (8/1/2002)*

VAL DI SUGA

Val di Suga 1999 Brunello (Brunello di Montalcino) $54. **91** *—M.S. (6/1/2004)*

Val di Suga 1993 Vigna del Lago Brunello (Brunello di Montalcino) $92. **93** *—M.S. (3/1/2000)*

Val di Suga 1998 Vigna del Lago Riserva Brunello (Brunello di Montalcino) $120. **91** *—M.S. (6/1/2004)*

Val di Suga 1999 Vigna Spuntali Brunello (Brunello di Montalcino) $50. **91** *—M.S. (6/1/2004)*

VALCHIARÒ

Valchiarò 2000 Sauvignon Blanc (Colli Orientali del Friuli) $15. **83** *(8/1/2002)*

VALDICAVA

Valdicava 2001 Brunello (Brunello di Montalcino) $110. **91** *(4/1/2006)*

Valdicava 2000 Brunello (Brunello di Montalcino) $89. **93** *—M.S. (7/1/2005)*

Valdicava 1999 Brunello (Brunello di Montalcino) $NA. **89** *—M.S. (6/1/2004)*

Valdicava 1997 Brunello (Brunello di Montalcino) $90. **88** *—R.V. (8/1/2002)*

Valdicava 1999 Madonna del Piano Riserva Brunello (Brunello di Montalcino) $130. **97 Editors' Choice** *—M.S. (7/1/2005)*

VALDINERRA

Valdinera 2006 Arneis (Roero Arneis) $21. The Valdinaria has evolved quickly. The nose is muted, there are low intensity aromas of pear and green plums with a touch of earthiness. It is crisp with plenty of acidity, but there is not enough fruit to give it balance, resulting in a slightly angular wine. **83** *—M.G. (12/31/2007)*

Valdinera 2005 Barbera (Barbera d'Alba Superiore) $23. The Valdinara is a soft, seductive wine showing plenty of jammy fruit, and a pleasant smoky spice. On the finish it is a touch stemmy, but it is so slight that it adds an exotic edge to the wine. Pleasant, not very intense and easy to like. **85** *—M.G. (12/31/2007)*

Valdinera 2006 Favorita (Langhe) $21. The Favorita (known as Vermentino in other regions of Italy) is not a particularly common grape in Piedmont. This Valdinera is a light, friendly, somewhat simple wine with flavors of grapefruit and flowers. A natural match with seafood. **83** *—M.G. (12/31/2007)*

Valdinera 2006 Chiaro di Luna Nebbiolo (Piedmont) $19. This Nebbiolo-based rosé from northern Italy offers a brilliant color and refreshing zest in the mouth but lacks overall intensity. There are however delicate notes of small red fruit and white stone and a cookie or peach-cobbler-like tone. Pair with light appetizers and salads. **85** *—M.L. (7/1/2007)*

VALDIPIATTA

Valdipiatta 1998 Sangiovese (Rosso di Montepulciano) $15. 88 *—M.M. (9/1/2000)*

VALDO

Valdo NV Brut Cuvée del Fondatore Prosecco (Prosecco di Conegliano e Valdobbiadene) $NA. This has huge floral tendencies with fragrant notes of jasmine and honeysuckle. Sweet peach, tea leaf and chopped herbs also make an appearance, and the wine boasts a lean, spicy finish. 88 *—M.L. (12/15/2007)*

Valdo NV Brut Cuvée di Boj Prosecco (Prosecco di Conegliano e Valdobbiadene) $NA. This is a tonic, almost crunchy, Prosecco with spicy effervescence and lingering notes of candied lemon drops, lavender and honey. Its overall intensity is high without being pungent and there are loads of peach-like flavors over the crisp finish. 88 *—M.L. (12/15/2007)*

Valdo NV Cartizze Cuvée Viviana Prosecco (Prosecco Superiore di Cartizze) $NA. An attractive element here is the distinct mineral tone that adds a vein of dryness to what is otherwise a sweet sparkler ripe with peach and apricot-like aromas. It has frothy texture and cleansing crispness on the close. 88 *—M.L. (12/15/2007)*

Valdo NV Cartizze Cuvée Viviana Prosecco (Prosecco Superiore di Cartizze) $25. 87 *—M.L. (6/1/2006)*

Valdo NV Cuvée di Boj Prosecco (Prosecco di Valdobbiadene) $19. 87 *—M.L. (6/1/2006)*

Valdo NV Marca Oro Prosecco (Prosecco di Valdobbiadene) $15. 87 *—M.L. (6/1/2006)*

Valdo NV Marca Oro Extra Dry Prosecco (Prosecco di Valdobbiadene) $12. 87 *—J.C. (12/31/2003)*

Valdo NV Selezzione Oro Brut Prosecco (Prosecco di Valdobbiadene) $14. 86 *—J.C. (12/31/2003)*

VALENTINA CUBI

Valentina Cubi 2001 Morar Corvina, Rondinella, Molinara (Amarone della Valpolicella Classico) $40. Valentina Cubi is a quality Amarone producer to look out for especially if you like big and brawny wines with skyscraping intensity. A beautiful Bordeaux-inspired cellar and barrique regimen has recently been installed and the producer is entering the market with four vintages at once. The 2001 is the youngest and boasts nutty spice, poached apple and pure integrity of fruit with firm tannins and long cherry flavors on the finish. 93 Editors' Choice *—M.L. (12/1/2007)*

Valentina Cubi 2000 Morar Corvina, Rondinella, Molinara (Amarone della Valpolicella Classico) $40. Red apple and cherry-nut notes are prominent here, but in this vintage seem less vibrant compared to the others. Spice, sour cherry, leather and vanilla-nut describe a pretty aromatic portfolio. This is a modern wine rooted in tradition. 90 *—M.L. (12/1/2007)*

Valentina Cubi 1998 Morar Corvina, Rondinella, Molinara (Amarone della Valpolicella Classico) $44. Oak aging imparts distinct notes of vanilla, spice and roasted coffee bean but the wine offers plenty more. There are nicely integrated herbal notes and you'll pick up a hints of balsamic vinegar and caramel candy too. The wine delivers great intensity and good length over a firm, spice-driven finish. 92 *—M.L. (12/1/2007)*

Valentina Cubi 1997 Morar Corvina, Rondinella, Molinara (Amarone della Valpolicella Classico) $50. Although this aged Amarone offers rich notes of dried prune, spice, resin and leather, you should not wait to drink it. Behind the fruit notes are somewhat tired notes of old spice and dried flowers. It has firm tannins and good length. 91 *—M.L. (12/1/2007)*

VALFIERI

Valfieri 2001 Arneis (Roero Arneis) $17. 84 *—M.S. (12/15/2003)*

Valfieri 2001 Cortese (Gavi di Gavi) $17. 85 *—M.S. (12/15/2003)*

Valfieri 1997 Nebbiolo (Barbaresco) $42. 82 *—M.S. (11/15/2002)*

VALIANO

Valiano 2001 Sangiovese (Chianti Classico) $15. 87 *(7/1/2003)*

Valiano 1997 Sangiovese (Chianti Classico) $15. 81 *(4/1/2001)*

Valiano 2000 Poggio Teo Sangiovese (Chianti Classico) $20. 88 *(4/1/2005)*

Valiano 1999 Poggio Teo Sangiovese (Chianti Classico) $20. 87 *—J.C. (7/1/2003)*

Valiano 2000 Riserva Sangiovese (Chianti Classico) $25. 88 *(4/1/2005)*

Valiano 1999 Riserva Sangiovese (Chianti Classico) $25. 86 *(7/1/2003)*

Valiano 1995 Riserva Sangiovese (Chianti Classico) $22. 83 *(4/1/2001)*

Valiano 1999 Vino in Musica Sangiovese (Toscana) $40. 90 *(7/1/2003)*

Valiano 1997 Vino in Musica Sangiovese (Toscana) $40. 88 *(7/1/2003)*

VALLE DELL'ACATE

Valle dell'Acate 2004 Frappato (Sicilia) $20. 86 *—M.L. (7/1/2006)*

Valle dell'Acate 2002 Il Frappato Frappato (Sicilia) $19. 86 *—J.C. (10/1/2003)*

Valle dell'Acate 2004 Il Moro Nero d'Avola (Sicilia) $24. 88 Editors' Choice *—M.L. (7/1/2006)*

Valle dell'Acate 2000 Il Moro Nero d'Avola (Sicilia) $23. 88 *—J.C. (10/1/2003)*

Valle dell'Acate 2004 Poggio Bidini Nero d'Avola (Sicilia) $12. 87 Best Buy *—M.L. (7/1/2006)*

Valle dell'Acate 2002 Poggio Bidini Nero d'Avola (Sicilia) $12. 86 *—J.C. (10/1/2003)*

Valle dell'Acate 2001 Poggio Bidini Nero d'Avola (Sicilia) $9. 88 Best Buy *—C.S. (11/15/2002)*

Valle dell'Acate 2000 Poggio Bidini Nero d'Avola (Sicilia) $11. 89 Best Buy *—C.S. (5/1/2002)*

Valle dell'Acate 2004 Red Blend (Cerasuolo di Vittoria) $24. 86 *—M.L. (7/1/2006)*

Valle dell'Acate 1999 Cerasuolo Di Vittoria Red Blend (Sicilia) $24. 88 *—C.S. (5/1/2002)*

Valle dell'Acate 2000 Cerasuolo della Vittoria Red Blend (Sicilia) $20. 90 *—J.C. (10/1/2003)*

Valle dell'Acate 2000 Frappato (Sicilia) $22. 84 *—C.S. (5/1/2002)*

Valle dell'Acate 2003 Tané Red Blend (Sicilia) $60. 90 *—M.L. (7/1/2006)*

Valle dell'Acate 2002 Tané Red Blend (Sicilia) $60. 91 *—M.L. (7/1/2006)*

Valle dell'Acate 2004 Bidis White Blend (Sicilia) $25. 88 *—M.L. (7/1/2006)*

Valle dell'Acate 2006 Zagra Grillo (Sicilia) $15. This island wine offers hot climate notes of butterscotch, stone fruit and melon backed by lemon blossom and white flower. It has deep, golden saturation and sweet floral flavors on the finish. 86 *—M.L. (11/15/2007)*

VALLE REALE

Valle Reale 2003 Montepulciano (Montepulciano d'Abruzzo) $15. 87 *—M.L. (9/1/2005)*

VALLEBELBO

Vallebelbo 2004 Moscato (Moscato d'Asti) $11. 86 Best Buy *—M.L. (12/15/2005)*

VALLEROSA

Vallerosa 2001 Carpaneto Vineyard Verdicchio (Verdicchio dei Castelli di Jesi Classico) $12. 86 *—M.S. (8/1/2004)*

VALORI

Valori 2005 Montepulciano (Montepulciano d'Abruzzo) $20. If you are not familiar with the hearty Montepulciano grape variety from central Italy but adore modern, structured New World reds, you should considered adding this wine to your weekly shopping list. Thick in power, extracts and color, Montepulciano has rock solid tannins and blockbuster aromas of blackberry, prune, chocolate, spice and toast that appear naturally, even without wood aging. This is a big-value wine that should pair with a big-value meal of barbecued baby back ribs in smoked sauce and spicy potato salad. 86 *—M.L. (11/15/2007)*

VAONA

Vaona 2004 Corvina, Rondinella, Molinara (Amarone della Valpolicella Classico) $35. Dark tones of black cherry and raisin are immediate and upfront but are soon followed by fresh notes of blackberry, mulberry and almond amaretto. Those pretty almond notes (the wine ages 18 months in oak casks) help flesh out a soft wine with excellent dimension and long, caressing flavors. 90 *—M.L. (10/1/2007)*

Vaona 2003 Pegrandi Corvina, Rondinella, Molinara (Amarone della Valpolicella Classico) $44. Here's a vineyard-designate wine that boasts all the special characteristics you look for in quality Amarone. It's densely concentrated and extracted, yet refined and elegant with cherry-apple, almond paste and vibrant red fruit. In the mouth, it delivers great intensity, a firm build and long-lasting persistency. It is aged 24 months in oak casks. 92 *—M.L. (10/1/2007)*

Vaona 2000 Pegrandi Corvina, Rondinella, Molinara (Amarone della Valpolicella Classico) $95. Gorgeous color and concentration with brilliant ruby highlights make this a beautiful wine to contemplate in the glass. The aromas are broad and far-reaching with a high mineral component, small berry fruit, spice and a distinct soapy-lavender element. Chewy, firm and succulent, it's a mouth-watering bruiser that leaves a lasting imprint on the palate. Only 60 cases made. 93 *—M.L. (12/1/2007)*

VARALDO

Varaldo 1999 Bricco Libero Nebbiolo (Barbaresco) $62. 90 *(4/2/2004)*

Varaldo 1999 Sorì Loreto Nebbiolo (Barbaresco) $62. 89 *(4/2/2004)*

Varaldo 1995 Vigua di Aldo-Barolo Nebbiolo (Barolo) $45. 87 *(11/15/2002)*

VARRAMISTA

Varramista 1997 Syrah (Toscana) $51. 89 *(11/1/2001)*

VASARI

Vasari 1998 Sangiovese (Chianti Colli Aretini) $11. 84 *(4/1/2001)*

VASCO SASSETTI

Vasco Sassetti 2001 Brunello (Brunello di Montalcino) $30. 88 *(4/1/2006)*

Vasco Sassetti 2000 Brunello (Brunello di Montalcino) $NA. 86 *—M.S. (7/1/2005)*

VECCHIE TERRE DI MONTEFILI

Vecchie Terre di Montefili 1998 Sangiovese (Chianti Classico) $21. 87 *(4/1/2001)*

VEGLIO

Veglio 2004 Barbera (Barbera d'Alba) $12. The nose is complex, showing smoky dark cherry fruit, roses and cinnamon. A pleasant wine on the palate, it shows the same complexity, but lacks concentration. A medium finish. A good wine that will work well with food, but it needs a little extra on the palate to make it special. **86** *—M.G. (4/1/2007)*

Veglio 2004 Sori dei Bertinetti Dolcetto (Diano d'Alba) $14. From the small hilltop town of Diano d'Aba, the wine has two very distinct personalities; the nose is fully mature with beautiful deep blackberry aromas mingled with smoke and violets, but the palate, which had little fruit, was soft and lacked definition, not to mention much finish. **83** *—M.G. (4/1/2007)*

Veglio 2001 Nebbiolo (Barolo) $32. Shows very ripe, roasted fruit and brown sugar. It verges on overripeness, but has the acidity to keep it in balance. For a Barolo from a top vintage, it lacks complexity, but it is an easy-drinking wine. **85** *—M.G. (4/1/2007)*

Veglio NV Baric Red Blend (Diano d'Alba) $13. A pleasant wine showing some jammy fruit, with interesting nuances of burnt sugar. Already at its apogee, and probably should be drunk quickly. **84** *—M.G. (12/31/2007)*

VELENOSI

Velenosi 2005 Vigna Solaria White Blend (Falerio) $NA. The nice thing is how this wine delivers so much fruit, especially peach, apricot and mature pear. The mouthfeel is creamy and sophisticated but the overall emphasis is on the purity and intensity of the fruit fragrances. Grapes are harvested late, at the end of October, for extra flavor. **89** *—M.L. (12/1/2007)*

VENEGAZZU

Venegazzu NV Venegazzu Brut Champagne Blend (Prosecco del Montello e Colli Asolani) $11. 86 *—M.M. (12/31/2001)*

VENICA

Venica 2000 Bottaz Collio Refosco (Venezia Giulia) $30. 86 *—M.L. (9/1/2005)*

VENICA & VENICA

Venica & Venica 2004 Jesera Pinot Grigio (Collio) $17. 90 **Editors' Choice** *—M.L. (2/1/2006)*

VENTURINI MASSIMINO

Venturini Massimino 2003 Corvina, Rondinella, Molinara (Amarone della Valpolicella Classico) $50. This is a hardworking producer with a recently refurbished winery and a new tonneaux regimen that seems to have suffered from the hot vintage. Those typical Amarone apple-volatility notes are more apparent and the nose is not completely clean. Nonetheless, the wine performs well in the mouth thanks to its cherry flavors and fine texture. **87** *—M.L. (10/1/2007)*

Venturini Massimino 2001 Campomasua Corvina, Rondinella, Molinara (Amarone della Valpolicella Classico) $60. Here is a lively, buoyant wine that affords room for a wide array of aromatic nuances. Apple, almond, cherry cobbler and penetrating black tar are foreground notes with red fruit and sweet vanilla as soft background shadings. The intensity is as remarkable as its persistency. **92** *—M.L. (12/1/2007)*

Venturini Massimino 2001 Red Blend (Valpolicella Classico) $12. 85 *(5/1/2003)*

Venturini Massimino 1998 Red Blend (Amarone della Valpolicella Classico) $42. 91 *(5/1/2003)*

VERBENA

Verbena 2001 Brunello (Brunello di Montalcino) $NA. 89 *(4/1/2006)*

VERETO

Vereto 1995 Red Blend (Salice Salentino) $8. 85 **Best Buy** *—L.W. (3/1/2000)*

VETTORI

Vettori NV Extra Dry Prosecco (Prosecco di Conegliano e Valdobbiadene) $NA. Very pretty in a flute thanks to its persistent perlage and luminous color, this is a delicate, light wine that aims to please without making any grand statements. Fresh and clean, its aromas include white fruit, citrus and field flowers. **87** *—M.L. (12/15/2007)*

VEZZANI

Vezzani 2000 Rosso Red Blend (Salice Salentino) $6. 82 *—C.S. (5/1/2002)*

Vezzani 2002 Sangiovese (Rubicone) $7. 83 *—M.S. (10/1/2004)*

Vezzani 2002 Bianco White Blend (Sicilia) $7. 81 *—M.S. (10/1/2004)*

VIA FIRENZE

Via Firenze 2004 Pinot Grigio (Venezie) $9. 84 *(2/1/2006)*

VIBERTI

Viberti 1999 Bricco Airoli Barbera (Barbera d'Alba) $27. 81 *—M.S. (12/15/2003)*

Viberti 2001 Toni 'D Giuspin Dolcetto (Dolcetto d'Alba) $21. 87 *—M.S. (12/15/2003)*

Viberti 1999 Buon Padre Nebbiolo (Barolo) $42. 90 **Cellar Selection** *—J.C. (11/15/2004)*

Viberti 1998 Buon Padre Nebbiolo (Barolo) $42. 88 *(4/2/2004)*

VICARA

Vicara 1996 Barbera (Barbera del Monferrato) $15. 87 *(4/1/2000)*

Vicara 1999 Cantico della Crosia Barbera (Monferrato) $23. 88 *—M.S. (11/15/2002)*

Vicara 1997 Cantico della Crosia Barbera (Barbera del Monferrato) $21. 85 *(4/1/2000)*

VICCHIOMAGGIO

Vicchiomaggio 2002 La Lellera Sangiovese (Chianti Classico) $15. 84 *(4/1/2005)*

Vicchiomaggio 2003 La Lellera di Vicchiomaggio Sangiovese (Chianti Classico) $15. 88 *—M.S. (10/1/2006)*

Vicchiomaggio 2000 La Prima Riserva Sangiovese (Chianti Classico) $35. 90 *(11/15/2004)*

Vicchiomaggio 2000 Petri Riserva Sangiovese (Chianti Classico) $27. 89 *(11/15/2004)*

Vicchiomaggio 2000 Ripa delle Mandorle Sangiovese (Toscana) $20. 86 *(11/15/2004)*

Vicchiomaggio 2000 Ripa delle More Sangiovese (Toscana) $NA. 89 *(11/15/2004)*

Vicchiomaggio 2001 San Jacopo da Vicchiomaggio Sangiovese (Toscana) $18. 87 *(11/15/2004)*

VIDUSSI

Vidussi 2006 Ribolla Gialla (Collio) $NA. Ribolla Gialla offers excellent pairing potential with cream-based dishes, and all kinds of roasted white meat. That's because it has the natural structure to stand up to those dishes without being overwhelmed. This expression offers pretty tones of peach, white flower and vanilla seed as well. **87** *—M.L. (12/1/2007)*

Vidussi 2006 Sauvignon (Collio) $NA. There's a lot a personality here thanks to perky aromas of lemon zest, chopped herbs, fresh sage, yellow pepper and cheerful crisp flavors. This is textbook Sauvignon—easy Italian style—with an emphasis on smoothness. **86** *—M.L. (12/1/2007)*

VIE DE ROMANS

Vie de Romans 2001 Ciampaign Vieris Chardonnay (Friuli Isonzo) $24. 90 *—R.V. (7/1/2003)*

Vie de Romans 2004 Dessimis Pinot Grigio (Friuli Isonzo) $24. 90 **Editors' Choice** *—M.L. (6/1/2006)*

Vie de Romans 2003 Dessimis Pinot Grigio (Friuli Isonzo) $24. 89 *—M.L. (6/1/2006)*

Vie de Romans 2001 Dessimis Pinot Grigio (Friuli Isonzo) $28. 87 *—R.V. (7/1/2003)*

Vie de Romans 2001 Piere Sauvignon Blanc (Friuli Isonzo) $29. 86 *—R.V. (7/1/2003)*

Vie de Romans 2001 Flors di Uis White Blend (Friuli Isonzo) $27. 88 *—R.V. (7/1/2003)*

VIETTI

Vietti 1996 La Crena Barbera (Barbera d'Asti) $30. 90 *(4/1/2000)*

Vietti 2003 Scarrone Vigna Vecchia Barbera (Barbera d'Alba) $78. 89 *—M.L. (11/15/2006)*

Vietti 1998 Tre Vigne Barbera (Barbera d'Alba) $18. 90 *(4/1/2000)*

Vietti 1998 Lazzarito Dolcetto (Dolcetto d'Alba) $19. 90 *(4/1/2000)*

Vietti 2003 Sant'Anna Dolcetto (Dolcetto d'Alba) $20. 90 *—M.L. (11/15/2006)*

Vietti 1998 Sant'anna Dolcetto (Dolcetto d'Alba) $19. 89 *(4/1/2000)*

Vietti 1998 Tre Vigne Dolcetto (Dolcetto d'Alba) $18. 86 *(4/1/2000)*

Vietti 2002 Cascinetta Moscato (Moscato d'Asti) $12. 89 *—M.S. (11/15/2003)*

Vietti 1998 Brunate Nebbiolo (Piedmont) $84. 85 *—R.V. (11/15/2002)*

Vietti 2000 Lazzarito Nebbiolo (Barolo) $100. 93 Editors' Choice *—M.L. (11/15/2006)*

Vietti 1998 Lazzarito Nebbiolo (Piedmont) $84. 88 *—R.V. (11/15/2002)*

Vietti 2001 Masseria Nebbiolo (Barbaresco) $92. 91 *—M.L. (11/15/2006)*

Vietti 2000 Rocche Nebbiolo (Barolo) $100. 91 *—M.L. (11/15/2006)*

Vietti 1998 Rocche Nebbiolo (Piedmont) $84. 84 *—R.V. (11/15/2002)*

Vietti 1996 Villero Riserva Nebbiolo (Piedmont) $145. 93 *—R.V. (11/15/2002)*

VIGNA PICCOLA

Vigna Piccola 1996 Sangiovese (Chianti Classico) $18. 83 *(4/1/2001)*

Vigna Piccola 1997 Riserva Sangiovese (Chianti Classico) $26. 89 *(4/1/2001)*

VIGNE &VINI

Vigne & Vini 2004 Schiaccianoci Negroamaro (Salento) $11. Hearty Negroamaro with 15% Malvasia Nera produce a wine that delivers surprisingly delicate tones of blue flowers, blueberry and vanilla. With time, the fragrances become perfume-like in intensity with notes of violet spray and lavender soap. The wine has medium length, sweet flavors and a crisp close. 86 Best Buy *—M.L. (8/1/2007)*

Vigne & Vini 2003 Schiaccianoci Negroamaro (Salento) $13. A very nice rendition of the robust Negroamaro variety from a hot vintage. Ripe, velvety and brawny, you'll get strawberry preserve, minerality, Porcino mushroom and Puglia's trademark iron note. Toasted, soft and velvety in the mouth and ready to drink immediately. 87 *—M.L. (4/1/2007)*

Vigne & Vini 2001 Schiaccianoci Riserva Negroamaro (Salento) $18. Vibrant fruit, red apple and blue flowers appear with intensity on the nose to create a racy, clean red wine. The acidity is good, as is the structure, but the 15% alcohol does hit the palate hard. Pair it with cream-based pasta (to counter the alcohol), white meat and roasted winter vegetables. 88 *—M.L. (8/1/2007)*

Vigne & Vini 2002 Chicca Vino Dolce Naturale Primitivo (Primitivo Di Manduria) $20. From 50-year-old vines, here is a unique, sweet red wine bursting with aromas of blackberry, cherry, pine forest, licorice and a playful touch of espresso. The wine is creamy and compact in the mouth and deliciously sweet: Pair with spice cake or ginger snaps. 89 *—M.L. (8/1/2007)*

Vigne & Vini 2003 Papale Primitivo (Primitivo Di Manduria) $15. Solid red fruit makes an excellent first impression and aromas of rose petal, red earth, cedar and mint are both pleasing and long lasting. The wine sees 10 months of oak and embodies all the vibrancy of this dynamic, young-in-spirit Puglia wine estate. 88 *—M.L. (8/1/2007)*

Vigne & Vini 2002 Papale Primitivo (Puglia) $17. Iron, earth and ripe pomegranate fruit are backed by a brackish, almost marine-like tone. It's a simple but clean wine with soft tannins and menthol notes on the finish. 88 *—M.L. (4/1/2007)*

Vigne & Vini 2004 Tatu Primitivo (Primitivo del Tarantino) $12. An attractively priced Primitivo-Aglianico blend that delivers a surprisingly delicate aromatic ensemble of forest berry, marzipan aromas. Firm tannins do need to unwind though. Pair with lamb, roasted pork or aged cheeses. 87 Best Buy *—M.L. (8/1/2007)*

Vigne & Vini 2003 Tatu Primitivo (Primitivo del Tarantino) $13. Loads of berry fruit are backed by white mushroom, red earth, bitter chocolate, exotic spice and granite. This Primitivo, with a small amount of Aglianico blended in, is a genuine, simple wine with nice, ripe flavors and a spicy finish. 86 *—M.L. (4/1/2007)*

VIGNE DI MEZZO

Vigne di Mezzo 2004 Aglianico (Aglianico del Vulture) $16. A very characteristic wine of southern Italy, the nose delivers cherry, berry, tobacco, root beer, balsamic, red earth and linseed oil aromas. In fact, there's a lingering perfume reminiscent of paints in an artist's studio. The wine is elegant in the mouth with crisp acidity and a long finish. 88 *—M.L. (8/1/2007)*

Vigne di Mezzo 2003 Efesto Aglianico (Aglianico del Vulture) $40. This is a very attractive wine with loads of personality and a long list of aromatic characteristics: Porcino mushroom, cedar, spice, licorice and scented candle. It's a bit shy on the fruit though: Very modern and intense in the mouth with waxy flavors on the close. 89 *—M.L. (8/1/2007)*

VIGNE REGALI

Vigne Regali 2003 L'Ardi Dolcetto (Dolcetto d'Acqui) $9. 88 Best Buy *—J.C. (3/1/2006)*

VIGNETI DI UMBERTO FRANCASSI RATTI MENTONE

Vigneti di Umberto Francassi Ratti Mentone 1998 Nebbiolo (Barolo) $47. 90 *(4/2/2004)*

VIGNETI VILLABELLA

Vigneti Villabella 2001 Corvina, Rondinella, Molinara (Amarone della Valpolicella Classico) $38. This is one of the most fruit-forward Amarones I have tasted from this vintage. The concentration and extraction is very good and the nose is richly redolent of plump black cherry, plum, blackberry and blueberry supported by shadings of chocolate, tar and caramel. Creamy succulence and a long, drying finish characterize the mouthfeel. Imported by Wine Wave. 90 Editors' Choice *—M.L. (12/1/2007)*

Vigneti Villabella 2000 Fracastoro Corvina, Rondinella, Molinara (Amarone della Valpolicella Classico) $47. This is a densely concentrated wine with lush and traditional notes of apple-cherry, cherry liquor, black chocolate and spice cake. What you notice most in the mouth is the wine's almost excessive sweetness that is well framed within a context of firm tannins and good length. Imported by Wine Wave. 90 *—M.L. (12/1/2007)*

VIGNOLE

Vignole 1998 Sangiovese (Chianti Classico) $13. 88 *(4/1/2001)*

VILLA ABA

Villa Aba 1998 Pinot Grigio (Grave del Friuli) $13. 84 *(8/1/1999)*

VILLA ARCENO

Villa Arceno 1999 Pozzo di San Donato Cabernet Sauvignon (Toscana) $35. 88 *—S.H. (1/1/2002)*

Villa Arceno 1999 Merlot (Toscana) $35. 86 *—S.H. (1/1/2002)*

Villa Arceno 1998 Merlot (Toscana) $20. 86 *—S.H. (1/1/2002)*

Villa Arceno 1999 Arguzzio Red Blend (Toscana) $60. 91 *—S.H. (1/1/2002)*

Villa Arceno 1999 Riserva Red Blend (Chianti Classico) $25. 87 *—S.H. (1/1/2002)*

Villa Arceno 1998 Arguzzio Sangiovese (Toscana) $50. 86 *—M.S. (12/31/2002)*

Villa Arceno 1997 Riserva Sangiovese (Chianti Classico) $20. 91 *—S.H. (1/1/2002)*

Villa Arceno 1999 Syrah (Toscana) $20. 88 *—S.H. (1/1/2002)*

Villa Arceno 2000 Il Boschetto Syrah (Toscana) $35. 87 *—S.H. (1/1/2002)*

VILLA BANFIO

Villa Banfio 2000 Il Torrione Sangiovese (Tuscany) $20. 87 *—M.S. (11/15/2003)*

VILLA BETTA

Villa Betta 2002 Pinot Grigio (Sicilia) $9. 80 *—M.S. (10/1/2004)*

VILLA BORGHETTI

Villa Borghetti 1998 Grigio Luna Pinot Grigio (Valdadige) $9. 81 *(8/1/1999)*

VILLA BRANCA

Villa Branca 2001 Alef Kosher Sangiovese (Chianti Classico) $29. 85 *—J.C. (4/1/2006)*

VILLA CAFAGGIO

Villa Cafaggio 1997 Cortaccio Cabernet Sauvignon (Tuscany) $50. 90 *(5/1/2001)*

Villa Cafaggio 1998 Sangiovese (Chianti Classico) $17. 88 *(4/1/2001)*

Villa Cafaggio 1997 Chianti Classico Riserva Sangiovese (Tuscany) $30. 89 *(5/1/2001)*

Villa Cafaggio 2001 Riserva Sangiovese (Chianti Classico) $30. Made near Panzano, in the famed "golden amphitheatre"—regarded as Chianti Classico's best vineyard site—this is a gorgeous wine with bold, opulent characteristics and deeply penetrating aromas. It exhibits beautiful saturation of color and notes of plum, prune, resin, pine and natural rubber. The structure is solid and firm and so are the polished tannins. 92 *—M.L. (11/1/2007)*

Villa Cafaggio 1997 San Martino Sangiovese (Tuscany) $50. 91 Cellar Selection *(5/1/2001)*

Villa Cafaggio 2004 Villa Cafaggio Sangiovese (Chianti Classico) $20. Despite its youthful appearance, this delivers aged notes of leather, tobacco, granite, black fruit and plum. Mature fruit flavors, backed by zesty spice, are noticeable in the mouth and reinforce chewy, succulent consistency. 87 *—M.L. (11/1/2007)*

VILLA CALCINAIA

Villa Calcinaia 2000 Casarsa Rosso Merlot (Colli della Toscana Centrale) $38. 88 *—M.S. (9/1/2006)*

Villa Calcinaia 2003 Sangiovese (Chianti Classico) $18. 88 *—M.S. (10/1/2006)*

Villa Calcinaia 2001 Sangiovese (Chianti Classico) $15. 88 *(4/1/2005)*

Villa Calcinaia 2001 Riserva Sangiovese (Chianti Classico) $24. 89 *(4/1/2005)*

Villa Calcinaia 2000 Riserva Sangiovese (Chianti Classico) $24. 85 *—M.S. (10/1/2004)*

VILLA CARRA

Villa Carra 2001 Selection Castellarin Merlot (Delle Venezie) $7. 80 *(5/1/2003)*

Villa Carra 2001 Pinot Grigio (Friuli Grave) $11. 87 *—J.C. (7/1/2003)*

VILLA CERNA

Villa Cerna 2001 Riserva Sangiovese (Chianti Classico) $22. 90 Editors' Choice *(4/1/2005)*

Villa Cerna 2000 Riserva Sangiovese (Chianti Classico) $22. 87 *—M.S. (10/1/2004)*

Villa Cerna 1997 Riserva Sangiovese (Chianti Classico) $21. 89 *(4/1/2001)*

VILLA DANTE

Villa Dante 1997 Vocato Red Blend (Toscana) $10. 86 *(9/1/2000)*

Villa Dante 1995 Sangiovese (Vino Nobile di Montepulciano) $18. 84 *(7/1/2000)*

Villa Dante 2000 Oak Aged Sangiovese (Toscana) $12. 85 *—M.S. (9/1/2006)*

VILLA DEI LECCI

Villa dei Lecci 1999 Sangiovese (Chianti Colli Senesi) $9. 85 Best Buy *(4/1/2001)*

VILLA DI BAGNOLO

Villa di Bagnolo 1997 Marchesi Pancrazi Pinot Noir (Toscana) $43. 86 *—M.S. (8/1/2002)*

VILLA ERBICE

Villa Erbice 2001 Vigneto Tremenel Corvina, Rondinella, Molinara (Amarone della Valpolicella) $65. On appearance the wine boasts a healthy, vibrant ruby color and the nose is characterized by chewy chocolate and cookie-dough aromas. On the periphery of that fibrous core are subtle spottings of espresso bean, herb, cedar, and black stone. It ends with chalky tannins and licorice flavors. 90 *—M.L. (12/1/2007)*

VILLA FIORE

Villa Fiore 2004 Pinot Grigio (Delle Venezie) $7. 82 *(2/1/2006)*

VILLA FRATTINA

Villa Frattina 1997 Pinot Grigio (Lison-Pramaggiore) $12. 81 *(8/1/1999)*

VILLA GIADA

Villa Giada 2004 Andrea Moscato (Moscato d'Asti) $15. 86 *—M.L. (12/15/2005)*

VILLA GIRARDI

Villa Girardi 1997 San Giuseppe Pinot Grigio (Valdadige) $11. 81 *(8/1/1999)*

VILLA GIULIA

Villa Giulia 2001 Alaura Sangiovese (Chianti) $10. 85 *—M.S. (11/15/2003)*

Villa Giulia 2000 Alaura Sangiovese (Chianti) $9. 85 *—M.S. (8/1/2002)*

Villa Giulia 1998 Alaura Sangiovese (Chianti) $10. 86 Best Buy *—M.S. (3/1/2000)*

VILLA IL MEXXINO

Villa il Mexxino 1998 Nebbiolo (Barolo) $NA. 90 *(4/2/2004)*

VILLA ILARIA

Villa Ilaria 2000 Nebbiolo (Barbaresco) $18. 85 *—J.C. (11/15/2004)*

Villa Ilaria 1999 Nebbiolo (Barolo) $24. 87 *—J.C. (11/15/2004)*

VILLA LA SELVA

Villa La Selva 1997 Selvamaggio Cabernet Sauvignon (Toscana) $27. 88 *—M.S. (8/1/2002)*

Villa La Selva 2001 Merlo Rosso Cabernet Sauvignon-Sangiovese (Toscana) $54. 90 *—M.S. (9/1/2006)*

Villa La Selva 2001 Felciaia Sangiovese (Toscana) $28. 90 *—M.S. (9/1/2006)*

Villa La Selva 1998 Felciaia Sangiovese (Toscana) $20. 88 *—M.S. (12/31/2002)*

Villa La Selva 1999 Feliciaia Sangiovese (Toscana) $23. 88 *—M.S. (10/1/2004)*

Villa La Selva 1999 Selvamaggio Sangiovese (Toscana) $28. 89 *—M.S. (11/15/2003)*

Villa La Selva 1998 Selvamaggio Sangiovese (Toscana) $27. 86 *—M.S. (12/31/2002)*

VILLA LANATA

Villa Lanata 1998 Sucule Barbera (Barbera d'Alba) $18. 87 *—M.S. (11/15/2002)*

Villa Lanata 2004 Cardinale Lanata Moscato (Moscato d'Asti) $13. 87 *—M.L. (12/15/2005)*

VILLA MAISANO

Villa Maisano 1997 Sangiovese (Chianti Classico) $15. 85 *(4/1/2001)*

Villa Maisano 1997 Questo Sangiovese (Chianti Classico) $30. 90 *(4/1/2001)*

Villa Maisano 1997 Riserva Sangiovese (Chianti Classico) $27. 90 *(4/1/2001)*

VILLA MALIZIA

Villa Malizia 2004 Pinot Grigio (Venezie) $6. 83 *—M.L. (2/1/2006)*

VILLA MASSETO

Villa Masseto 2004 La Quarta Luna Chardonnay (Toscana) $NA. 86 *—M.L. (10/1/2006)*

VILLA MATILDE

Villa Matilde 1999 Aglianico (Falerno del Massico) $15. 84 *—C.S. (5/1/2002)*

Villa Matilde 1998 Camarato Aglianico (Falerno del Massico) $45. 92 Cellar Selection *—C.S. (5/1/2002)*

Villa Matilde 2005 Tenuta Rocca dei Leoni Aglianico (Aglianico del Beneventano) $20. Thanks to a thick, purple-hued appearance you know you're in for a ripe and concentrated wine with thick layers of sweet red fruit aromas. The fruit is in fact very forthcoming but is also rendered more complex by background notes of graphite and chestnut. It's a youthful wine with a bright future. 87 *—M.L. (8/1/2007)*

Villa Matilde 2005 Falanghina (Falerno del Massico) $19. Pear, green apple and a prominent mineral theme produce a very nice and polished wine that boasts a brilliant straw color and golden highlights. It's a fantastic palate cleanser that would work wonders next to white meat, fish or salads. 87 *—M.L. (4/1/2007)*

Villa Matilde 2004 Falanghina (Falerno del Massico) $15. 86 *—M.L. (9/1/2005)*

Villa Matilde 2000 Falanghina (Falerno del Massico) $14. 82 *—M.N. (9/1/2001)*

Villa Matilde 2003 Caracci Falanghina (Falerno del Massico) $29. Falanghina grapes are nourished by potassium and phosphorus-rich volcanic soils to produce this wonderfully clean wine and its strong mineral component. Tropical fruit, kiwi, banana, passion fruit, pine nut and even a touch of maple syrup follow, thanks to five months in barrique. It's structured enough to pair with elaborate pasta dishes, white meat and pork. 88 *—M.L. (4/1/2007)*

Villa Matilde 2005 Tenuta Rocca dei Leoni Falanghina (Falanghina del Beneventano) $15. Mineral-rich volcanic soils help render a clean, polished and linear white with loads of candied fruit and LifeSaver-like tones. What it lacks in persistency, it makes up for in purity and freshness. 86 *—M.L. (4/1/2007)*

Villa Matilde 2003 Tenuta Rocca dei Leoni Falanghina (Falanghina del Beneventano) $14. 82 *—M.S. (7/1/2005)*

Villa Matilde 2005 Tenute di Altavilla Greco (Greco di Tufo) $26. For those who still need convincing, this wine affirms Greco di Tufo's prominence as one of Southern Italy's most versatile white wines. With good intensity and complexity, the nose yields Granny Smith apple, white stone, basil leaf and more herbal flavors in the mouth: from the relatively new Tenute di Altavilla property in the province of Avellino. **89 Editors' Choice** —*M.L. (4/1/2007)*

Villa Matilde 2004 Red Blend (Falerno del Massico) $20. Here is a firm, extracted and well-built Aglianico (80%) and Piedirosso blend that benefits from decanting a few hours before being served. Aromas of ruby pomegranate, black cherry and blueberry are backed by territory-driven notes of ash and granite slate. A balanced wine; it should be enjoyed with beef, lamb or cheese-based dishes. **89** —*M.L. (8/1/2007)*

Villa Matilde 2002 Red Blend (Falerno del Massico) $20. 87 —*M.S. (2/1/2005)*

Villa Matilde 2001 Camarato Red Blend (Falerno del Massico) $64. Dark in color and deep in concentration, this is a ripe Aglianico-Piedirosso (80-20) blend with tones of mature red cherry, beets, roasted peanut, espresso and roasted red pepper. It's a big wine in every sense with a sticky, almost syrupy consistency, power and firm tannins. **91** —*M.L. (8/1/2007)*

Villa Matilde 2004 Cecubo Red Blend (Roccamonfina) $34. There's a nice use of wood here with creamy concentration and toasted notes that are made obvious but do not overwhelm the fruit. The nose spins black fruit, prune, sweet chewy cherry, vanilla, cider, almond and coffee. The blend is all native grapes: 45-35-20 Abbuoto, Primitivo and Piedirosso. **90 Editors' Choice** —*M.L. (8/1/2007)*

Villa Matilde 1999 Cecubo Red Blend (Campania) $28. 87 —*C.S. (5/1/2002)*

Villa Matilde 1998 Rosso Red Blend (Falerno del Massico) $16. 88 —*M.N. (9/1/2001)*

VILLA MONTELEONE

Villa Monteleone 2001 Campo San Paolo Corvina, Rondinella, Molinara (Amarone della Valpolicella Classico) $100. The protagonist here is oak, which is identified by overwhelming aromas of toast, vanilla, roasted almond, crème caramel, mesquite shavings and barbecue spice flavors. That's not to say that the fruit is totally gone: Wade through the wood and you'll find a healthy dose of fresh cherries at the back. **90** —*M.L. (12/1/2007)*

Villa Monteleone 2003 Villa Monteleone Corvina, Rondinella, Molinara (Amarone della Valpolicella Classico) $60. Rather than vertical and direct aromas, this Amarone offers plush, broad ones that glide over the senses with vanilla-honey, powdered chocolate, black cherry and spice. American Tony Raimondi and his wife Lucia present a modern wine with good presence and endurance. **90** —*M.L. (10/1/2007)*

VILLA PATRIZIA

Villa Patrizia 2000 Orto di Boccio Sangiovese (Montecucco) $36. 88 —*M.S. (11/15/2003)*

VILLA PETRIOLO

Villa Petriolo 2002 Sangiovese (Chianti) $13. 86 *(4/1/2005)*

VILLA PILLO

Villa Pillo 1998 Vivaldaia Cabernet Franc (Toscana) $16. 84 —*M.S. (12/31/2002)*

Villa Pillo 2003 Borgoforte Cabernet Sauvignon-Sangiovese (Toscana) $12. 89 Best Buy —*M.S. (9/1/2006)*

Villa Pillo 1998 Estate Bottled Merlot (Tuscany) $16. 84 —*M.S. (12/31/2002)*

Villa Pillo 2000 Sant' Adele Merlot (Toscana) $23. 83 —*M.S. (12/31/2002)*

Villa Pillo 2004 Sant'Adele Merlot (Toscana) $13. 86 Best Buy —*M.L. (11/15/2006)*

Villa Pillo 2003 Sant'Adele Merlot (Toscana) $16. 87 —*M.S. (9/1/2006)*

Villa Pillo 2004 Borgoforte Red Blend (Toscana) $11. From an estate located between Florence and Pisa, this is a chocolate-charged wine with good intensity and coffee, leather, blackberry and plum aromas. There's also a lactic-like note buried within and the balance between acidity and dusty tannins hits the mark. **87 Best Buy** —*M.L. (5/1/2007)*

Villa Pillo 2001 Borgoforte Sangiovese (Tuscany) $12. 88 Best Buy —*M.S. (11/15/2003)*

Villa Pillo 2000 Borgoforte Sangiovese (Tuscany) $12. 89 —*M.S. (11/15/2003)*

Villa Pillo 2003 Syrah (Toscana) $16. 85 —*M.S. (9/1/2006)*

Villa Pillo 2000 Syrah (Tuscany) $15. 86 —*M.S. (11/15/2003)*

Villa Pillo 1998 Syrah (Tuscany) $15. 87 Editors' Choice *(10/1/2001)*

Villa Pillo 1998 Vin Santo del Chianti White Blend (Vin Santo del Chianti) $22. This brilliant, amber-colored Vin Santo boasts intense notes of dried apricot, almond paste, pine nuts, honey and baked peach pie. The aromas are rich and layered and the wine's thicker consistency is a real pleasure on the palate. **90** —*M.L. (5/1/2007)*

VILLA POGGIO SALVI

Villa Poggio Salvi 2000 Brunello (Brunello di Montalcino) $65. 90 —*M.S. (7/1/2005)*

Villa Poggio Salvi 1999 Brunello (Brunello di Montalcino) $NA. 87 —*M.S. (6/1/2004)*

VILLA PUCCINI

Villa Puccini 2005 Pinot Grigio (Friuli Grave) $10. 85 —*M.L. (6/1/2006)*

Villa Puccini 2004 Pinot Grigio (Friuli Grave) $10. 85 Best Buy —*M.L. (2/1/2006)*

VILLA RUSSIZ

Villa Russiz 2001 Gräfin de la Tour Chardonnay (Collio) $31. 92 —*R.V. (7/1/2003)*

Villa Russiz 2002 Graf de la Tour Merlot (Collio) $71. Tertiary aromas from bottle aging such as licorice, balsam notes and dried black fruit best describe this Merlot's bouquet; but there's are also notes of moist earth, melted chocolate or spice that add character and complexity. This is a food-friendly wine with power, a medium consistency and firm structure. **88** —*M.L. (3/1/2007)*

Villa Russiz 2002 Pinot Bianco (Collio) $22. 88 —*R.V. (7/1/2003)*

Villa Russiz 1999 Pinot Bianco (Collio) $19. 87 *(9/1/2001)*

Villa Russiz 2004 Pinot Grigio (Collio) $28. 84 *(2/1/2006)*

Villa Russiz 2003 Pinot Grigio (Collio) $28. 85 —*M.L. (2/1/2006)*

Villa Russiz 2001 Pinot Grigio (Collio) $22. 86 —*J.C. (7/1/2003)*

Villa Russiz 2003 Sauvignon (Collio) $28. 87 *(7/1/2005)*

Villa Russiz 2002 Sauvignon (Collio) $28. 86 —*J.C. (12/31/2004)*

Villa Russiz 1997 Sauvignon Blanc (Collio) $21. 88 *(11/1/1999)*

Villa Russiz 2002 Sauvignon Blanc (Collio) $22. 87 —*R.V. (7/1/2003)*

Villa Russiz 2002 Sauvignon de la Tour Sauvignon Blanc (Collio) $47. 89 —*J.C. (12/31/2004)*

Villa Russiz 2001 Sauvignon de la Tour Sauvignon Blanc (Collio) $38. 87 —*J.C. (7/1/2003)*

Villa Russiz 1998 Tocai (Collio) $21. 87 *(11/1/1999)*

Villa Russiz 2002 Tocai (Collio) $22. 90 —*R.V. (7/1/2003)*

Villa Russiz 2001 Tocai (Collio) $22. 87 —*J.C. (7/1/2003)*

VILLA SANDI

Villa Sandi 2002 Marinali Cabernet Blend (Marca Trevigiana) $20. 89 —*M.L. (11/15/2006)*

Villa Sandi 1998 Marinali Rosso Cabernet Blend (Veneto) $20. 86 *(5/1/2003)*

Villa Sandi 1999 CS Glaxa Cabernet Sauvignon (Piave) $10. 81 *(5/1/2003)*

Villa Sandi NV Champagne Blend (Prosecco di Valdobbiadene) $10. 82 —*J.C. (12/31/2001)*

Villa Sandi 2000 Estate Bottled Merlot (Piave) $10. 85 *(5/1/2003)*

Villa Sandi 2005 Pinot Grigio (Piave) $14. 87 —*M.L. (6/1/2006)*

Villa Sandi 2003 Pinot Grigio (Piave) $12. 86 —*J.C. (12/31/2004)*

Villa Sandi 2001 Estate Bottled Pinot Grigio (Veneto) $10. 84 —*J.C. (7/1/2003)*

Villa Sandi NV Prosecco (Prosecco di Valdobbiadene) $10. 86 —*M.S. (12/31/2002)*

Villa Sandi NV Prosecco (Prosecco di Valdobbiadene) $20. 86 —*M.S. (12/15/2004)*

Villa Sandi NV Brut Prosecco (Prosecco di Conegliano e Valdobbiadene) $15. Villa Sandi consistently delivers well-priced Proseccos, designed to be easy and fun to drink. This expression has notes of hay, flowers and peach and is succulent without appearing cloying or sticky. **87** —*M.L. (12/15/2007)*

Villa Sandi NV Brut Prosecco (Prosecco di Valdobbiadene) $12. 87 Best Buy —*M.L. (6/1/2006)*

Villa Sandi NV Cartizze Prosecco (Prosecco Superiore di Cartizze) $25. This elegant sparkler achieves a nice balance between sweet, fruit flavors and lively crispness. Peach, pear, jasmine and white stone characterize the nose and make for a very approachable, friendly wine. **89** —*M.L. (12/15/2007)*

Villa Sandi NV Dry Cuvée Prosecco (Prosecco di Conegliano e Valdobbiadene) $19. Villa Sandi's dry Prosecco registers high in sweetness, an impression reinforced by the wine's fragrant floral aromas—you'll detect loads of jasmine. It's chewy-sweet in the mouth with medium zest on the close. **86** —*M.L. (12/15/2007)*

Villa Sandi NV Dry Cuvée Prosecco (Prosecco di Conegliano e Valdobbiadene) $19. 88 —*M.L. (12/15/2006)*

Villa Sandi NV Extra Dry Prosecco (Prosecco di Conegliano e Valdobbiadene) $15. Here's a cheerful, textbook Prosecco with musky-fruity flavors and undertones of peach, pear, jasmine and apricot. It has a simple, fresh mouthfeel and piquant crispness on the close: Pair it with fried shrimp appetizers. **87** —*M.L. (12/15/2007)*

Villa Sandi NV Extra Dry Prosecco (Prosecco di Conegliano e Valdobbiadene) $15. 87 —*M.L. (12/15/2006)*

Villa Sandi NV Extra Dry Prosecco (Prosecco di Valdobbiadene) $12. 88 Best Buy —*M.L. (6/1/2006)*

Villa Sandi NV Il Fresco Prosecco (Veneto) $12. 86 —*M.L. (12/15/2006)*

Villa Sandi NV Brut Sparkling Blend (Prosecco di Valdobbiadene) $12. 87 Best Buy —*M.S. (12/15/2005)*

Villa Sandi NV Cuvée Sparkling Blend (Prosecco di Valdobbiadene) $20. 89 —*M.S. (12/15/2005)*

Villa Sandi NV Extra Dry Sparkling Blend (Prosecco di Valdobbiadene) $12. 89 Best Buy —*M.L. (11/15/2005)*

Villa Sandi NV Opere Trevigiane Brut Sparkling Blend (Veneto) $23. 90 —*M.L. (12/15/2006)*

Villa Sandi NV Opere Trevigiane Rosé Blend (Veneto) $28. I had this wine in the early evening with a group of my closest girlfriends and it proved to be a real charmer. It's informal, refreshing and recalls aromas of peach, citrus, raspberry and cranberry. It's not huge in intensity but has lively effervescence and good acidity. **87** —*M.L. (7/1/2007)*

Villa Sandi NV Cuvée Prosecco White Blend (Prosecco di Valdobbiadene) $15. 88 —*M.S. (12/31/2002)*

Villa Sandi 2000 Marinali Bianco White Blend (Marca Trevigiana) $20. 84 —*J.C. (7/1/2003)*

VILLA SELVAPIANA

Villa Selvapiana 2000 Vigneto Bucerchiale Riserva Sangiovese (Chianti Rufina) $31. 90

Villa Selvapiana 2000 Vigneto Bucerchiale Riserva (Chianti Rufina); $31. 90 *(4/1/2005)*

VILLA SPARINA

Villa Sparina 1996 Rivalta Barbera (Barbera del Monferrato) $40. 85 *(4/1/2000)*

Villa Sparina 1997 Bric Maioli Dolcetto (Dolcetto d'Acqui) $7. 85 *(4/1/2000)*

Villa Sparina 1997 D Giusep Dolcetto (Dolcetto d'Acqui) $11. 88 Best Buy *(4/1/2000)*

VILLA SPINOSA

Villa Spinosa 2000 Corvina, Rondinella, Molinara (Amarone della Valpolicella Classico) $55. Villa Spinosa owns some of the most beautiful vineyards in Valpolicella and selects the best fruit for this intense, succulent Amarone. The nose offers notes of milk chocolate, vanilla-cherry and spice as well as warmer tones of white mushroom, earth and baked apple. The mouthfeel is subdued, but balanced. **92** —*M.L. (12/1/2007)*

Villa Spinosa 1999 Corvina, Rondinella, Molinara (Amarone della Valpolicella Classico) $55. The emphasis here is on elegance, not power or intensity. The wine offers carefully measured notes of apple-nut, cherry, vanilla, mineral, dried lavender and no clear aromatic protagonist. The wine's age is discernable in the mouth and this suggests that you should not wait to drink it. **91** —*M.L. (12/1/2007)*

Villa Spinosa 1998 Corvina, Rondinella, Molinara (Amarone della Valpolicella Classico) $60. This wine exhibits fine spice and nicely measured notes of cinnamon, cumin, leather, espresso and dried prune. Its aromas are those you'd expect from a Turkish bazaar. There's a slightly brown hue to its color but overall it is thick and concentrated with sweet, sticky flavors and noticeable succulence. **93** —*M.L. (12/1/2007)*

VILLA VISTARENNI

Villa Vistarenni 2000 Codirosso Cabernet Sauvignon-Sangiovese (Toscana) $33. 88 —*M.S. (9/1/2006)*

Villa Vistarenni 1999 Riserva Sangiovese (Chianti Classico) $25. 89 *(4/1/2005)*

VILLABELLA

Villabella 2000 Red Blend (Amarone della Valpolicella Classico) $20. 86 *(11/1/2005)*

Villabella 1999 Fracastoro Red Blend (Amarone della Valpolicella Classico) $60. 87 *(11/1/2005)*

VILLADORIA

Villadoria 2000 Arneis (Roero Arneis) $9. 80 —*M.S. (12/15/2003)*

Villadoria 1999 Barbera (Barbera d'Alba Superiore) $9. 86 Best Buy —*M.S. (11/15/2002)*

Villadoria 1997 Barbera (Barbera d'Alba Superiore) $10. 87 *(1/1/2000)*

Villadoria 1999 Nebbiolo (Barbaresco) $21. 87 *(4/2/2004)*

Villadoria 1997 Nebbiolo (Barolo) $23. 88 —*C.S. (11/15/2002)*

Villadoria 1995 Nebbiolo (Serralunga D'Alba) $NA. 90 Best Buy *(1/1/2000)*

VILLADORO

Villadoro 2002 Montepulciano (Montepulciano d'Abruzzo) $12. 83 —*M.S. (10/1/2004)*

VILLANOVA

Villanova 2004 Pinot Grigio (Friuli Isonzo) $NA. 88 *M.L. (2/1/2006)*

Villanova 1997 Pinot Grigio (Isonzo del Friuli) $12. 82 *(8/1/1999)*

Villanova 2004 Ronco Cucco Pinot Grigio (Collio) $20. 86 *(2/1/2006)*

VINAGRI PUGLIA

Vinagri Puglia SRL 2000 Limitone Dei Greci Primitivo (Salento) $30. 84 —*M.S. (12/15/2003)*

VINARTE

VinArte 1998 Sangiovese (Chianti) $7. 84 *(4/1/2001)*

VITANZA

Vitanza 2001 Brunello (Brunello di Montalcino) $40. 92 *(4/1/2006)*

VITICCIO

Viticcio 1998 Sangiovese (Chianti Classico) $12. 88 Best Buy *(4/1/2001)*

Viticcio 1997 Lucius Riserva Sangiovese (Chianti Classico) $25. 90 *(4/1/2001)*

Viticcio 1998 Riserva Sangiovese (Chianti Classico) $18. 85 —*M.S. (8/1/2002)*

Viticcio 1997 Riserva Sangiovese (Chianti Classico) $20. 87 *(4/1/2001)*

Viticcio 2000 Rosarossa Sangiovese (Toscana) $9. 85 —*M.S. (8/1/2002)*

VOGA

Voga 2004 Pinot Grigio (Delle Venezie) $13. 85 —*M.L. (6/1/2006)*

VOLPAIA

Volpaia 1998 Sangiovese (Chianti Classico) $19. 85 *(4/1/2001)*

VOLPE PASINI

Volpe Pasini 2004 Focus Zuc di Volpe Merlot (Venezia Giulia) $38. Truly wonderful, with a creamy, smooth texture and lavish notes of ripe blackberry, chocolate fudge, cedar and smoke that grow in intensity and succulence as it warms. Exciting and vibrant in the mouth, with an excellent, firm structure, elegance and a polished quality throughout. **91 Editors' Choice** —*M.L. (4/1/2007)*

Volpe Pasini 2005 Zuc di Volpe Pinot Bianco (Colli Orientali del Friuli) $28. Solid, luscious and silky smooth, this white wine from the northern Friuli region is one of the most beautiful expressions of the Pinot Bianco grape you'll find. Stone fruit and nutty tones are rich and penetrating and backed by more fruit and white flowers. Half the wine sees four months of oak to shape its creamy consistency and heightened complexity. **92** —*M.L. (12/1/2007)*

Volpe Pasini 2004 Pinot Grigio (Colli Orientali del Friuli) $12. 86 —*M.L. (6/1/2006)*

Volpe Pasini 2005 Grivò Pinot Grigio (Colli Orientali del Friuli) $17. There's a very attractive mineral component to this wine that helps create a sensation of dryness and purity to both the nose and mouth. Dig deeper and other aromas of exotic fruit, citrus and ground clover add roundness and fullness. **86** —*M.L. (5/1/2007)*

Volpe Pasini 2001 Ipso Pinot Grigio (Friuli Venezia Giulia) $18. 91 —*R.V. (7/1/2003)*

Volpe Pasini 2005 Zuc di Volpe Pinot Grigio (Colli Orientali del Friuli) $25. Pretty almond nut, peach, pear and honeydew tones reflect the best of this northeastern Italian region already associated with excellent whites. This wine sparkles thanks to lush honey and dried herb aromas: It's clean and crisp with spice on the close. **87** —*M.L. (5/1/2007)*

Volpe Pasini 2002 Zuc de Volpe Pinot Grigio (Colli Orientali del Friuli) $18. 88 —*R.V. (7/1/2003)*

Volpe Pasini 2003 Zuc di Volpe Pinot Grigio (Venezia Giulia) $23. 88 —*M.L. (6/1/2006)*

Volpe Pasini 2005 Zuc di Volpe Ribolla Gialla (Colli Orientali del Friuli) $26. Sometimes, white wines pick up natural gas or chemical rubber aromas and this is definitely the case here. It's fair to say that some wines from the Friuli region of northern Italy naturally emit those characteristics as well as mature yellow fruit, ripe peach and melon like you will find here. **83** *—M.L. (12/1/2007)*

Volpe Pasini 2002 Zuc de Volpe Ribolla Gialla (Colli Orientali del Friuli) $18. 86 *—R.V. (7/1/2003)*

Volpe Pasini 2005 Zuc di Volpe Tocai Friulano (Colli Orientali del Friuli) $26. An absolute pleasure to drink, especially with fresh pasta topped with grated Parmigiano cheese, this is a soft, yielding wine with mature pear, Golden Delicious apple, apricot and white stone. An attractive bouquet is followed by creamy consistency and good persistency. **87** *—M.L. (12/1/2007)*

Volpe Pasini 2002 Luc de Volpe Tocai Friulano Tocai (Colli Orientali del Friuli) $18. 89 *—R.V. (7/1/2003)*

VUOLO

Vuolo 2005 Fiano di Mila Vuolo Fiano (Campania) $24. Here is a fragrant, floral rendition of Fiano that bursts with pretty notes of acacia, honeysuckle and beeswax. The fragrances are sweet, almost sticky, but the wine is lighter in the mouth overall and imparts crisp acidity over a satisfying finish. **87** *—M.L. (4/1/2007)*

WALTER FILIPUTTI

Walter Filiputti 1997 Pinot Grigio (Venezia Giulia) $24. 83 *(8/1/1999)*

ZAMUNER

Zamuner 1999 Brut Rosè Sparkling Blend (Veneto) $34. Very difficult to decipher, this is an awkward wine mostly because of its age. Some of the fresh fruitiness you'd expect from a sparkling rosé is left intact thanks to nicely integrated acidity. Yet, the nose also imparts duller, graham cracker notes. Yeasty flavors help shape complexity in the mouth. **85** *—M.L. (7/1/2007)*

ZANETTI

Zanetti NV Brut Vigna del Cuc Prosecco (Prosecco di Conegliano e Valdobbiadene) $NA. This is a fantastic Prosecco, enthusiastically recommended, with a crisp, clean style and an elegant aromatic weave that combines garden flowers, violets, chalky mineral and stone fruit. Thanks to its silky mouthfeel and lively bubbles, it's a real pleasure to drink. **88** *—M.L. (12/15/2007)*

Zanetti NV Case Bianche Extra Dry Prosecco (Prosecco di Conegliano e Valdobbiadene) $NA. This Prosecco stands out in a crowd thanks to its strong concentration of pear-like aromas. That pear note is embellished by similar tones of Golden Delicious apple, almond and melon. Great personality and persistency in the mouth. **88** *—M.L. (12/15/2007)*

ZARDETTO

Zardetto NV Brut Prosecco (Italy) $11. Here's another terrific no-fuss Italian sparkler with a tight, tonic mouthfeel. There's nice linearity and coherency to the aromas that recall stone fruits and lemon drops. **88 Best Buy** *—M.L. (12/15/2007)*

Zardetto NV Prosecco Brut DOC Prosecco (Veneto) $11. 89 *—M.S. (6/1/2003)*

Zardetto 2004 Zeta Prosecco (Prosecco di Conegliano) $19. 87 *—M.S. (12/15/2005)*

Zardetto NV Zeta Dry Prosecco (Prosecco di Conegliano) $17. This is a pleasant, no-fuss sparkler with textbook aromas of peach, flowers and citrus fruit. Overall, it lacks intensity but its crisp, lean mouthfeel helps it end on a high, zesty note. **86** *—M.L. (12/15/2007)*

Zardetto 2004 Zeta Dry Prosecco (Prosecco di Conegliano) $20. 87 *—M.L. (6/1/2006)*

ZENATO

Zenato 2003 Corvina, Rondinella, Molinara (Amarone della Valpolicella Classico) $65. This vintage shows the heat, with big, ripe cherry intensity, power and beefy aromas of barbecue, red beets, resin, tar and toasted chestnut. The wine boasts deep concentration, almost viscous consistency and a sweet finish. **90** *—M.L. (10/1/2007)*

Zenato 2001 Corvina, Rondinella, Molinara (Amarone della Valpolicella Classico) $60. Amarone enthusiasts will be delighted by the resin, cola, menthol and pressed raisin notes that this gorgeous wine delivers. It's a big, bold wine that doesn't hold back in terms of heat, power and general intensity: A challenge to pair with food, but an enological treat nonetheless. **92** *—M.L. (5/1/2007)*

Zenato 2000 Sergio Zenato Corvina, Rondinella, Molinara (Amarone della Valpolicella Classico) $90. 92 *(11/1/2005)*

Zenato 2004 Pinot Grigio (Delle Venezie) $12. 87 Best Buy *—M.L. (6/1/2006)*

Zenato 1998 Pinot Grigio (Delle Venezie) $10. 85 *(8/1/1999)*

Zenato 2002 Red Blend (Valpolicella Superiore) $13. The traditional Valpolicella blend of Corvina and Rondinella from the hills north of Verona usually delivers red currant, apple cider, mineral tones and Indian spice. This wine is no exception. There's a nice intensity in the mouth and the wine promises to make a good match to meat ragù. **85** *—M.L. (5/1/2007)*

Zenato 2000 Red Blend (Amarone della Valpolicella Classico) $65. 88 *(11/1/2005)*

Zenato 1998 Red Blend (Amarone della Valpolicella Classico) $50. 91 *(5/1/2003)*

Zenato 2003 Ripassa Red Blend (Valpolicella Superiore) $25. Amarone pomace is added to a Valpolicella base wine to trigger a second fermentation that yields more color, extracts and aromatic intensity. Cherry, vanilla, Mediterranean dried herbs and exotic spice come together to create harmony; it also has very dry tannins, thanks to 24 months in wood. **89** *—M.L. (5/1/2007)*

Zenato 1999 Ripassa Superiore Red Blend (Valpolicella) $19. 91 Editors' Choice *(5/1/2003)*

Zenato 2001 San Benedetto Trebbiano (Lugana) $10. 87 Best Buy *—R.V. (11/15/2002)*

Zenato 2004 Vigneto San Benedetto Trebbiano (Lugana) $13. A golden hued wine with deep aromas of peanut skin, graham cracker, cookie dough and dried tobacco leaf; this white from near Lake Garda would make a good companion to white meat or shellfish-based dishes. It's very nut-driven and heavy in the mouth although its fresh crispness comes through on the close. **85** *—M.L. (5/1/2007)*

Zenato 2002 San Benedetto White Blend (Lugana) $NA. 86 *—R.V. (7/1/2003)*

ZENI

Zeni 2003 Barriques Corvina, Rondinella, Molinara (Amarone della Valpolicella) $NA. This historic estate on the shores of Lake Garda is one of Amarone's biggest ambassadors when it comes to foreign markets. Good fruit sourcing has shaped a pretty 2003 vintage wine with a nice full nose and no sharp points. You'll encounter plum, black cherry, roasted nut, vanilla-coffee and exotic spice. **91** *—M.L. (10/1/2007)*

ZENNER

Zenner 1999 Nero d'Avola (Sicilia) $20. 86 *—C.S. (5/1/2002)*

ZISOLA

Zisola 2004 Nero d'Avola (Sicilia) $NA. 90 *—M.L. (7/1/2006)*

ZONIN

Zonin 1999 Amarone (Amarone della Valpolicella) $35. 90 *(11/1/2005)*

Zonin NV Chardonnay (Italy) $10. 84 *—M.S. (12/15/2005)*

Zonin NV Brut Chardonnay (Italy) $10. 85 Best Buy *—J.C. (12/15/2004)*

Zonin NV Brut Blanc de Blanc Chardonnay (Piedmont) $15. 87 *—M.L. (6/1/2006)*

Zonin 2003 Corvina, Rondinella, Molinara (Amarone della Valpolicella) $25. As Italy's largest family-run wine estate, Zonin knows the Valpolicella territory well enough to guarantee successful sourcing of fruit and juice. This Amarone delivers polished tones of cherry, chocolate and apple-nut. Pair it with truffle gnocchi or stewed game meat. **90** *—M.L. (10/1/2007)*

Zonin 2000 Corvina, Rondinella, Molinara (Amarone della Valpolicella) $35. 90 *—J.C. (10/1/2006)*

Zonin 2004 Il Giangio Garganega (Gambellara Classico) $12. 87 *—M.L. (9/1/2005)*

Zonin 2002 Podere il Giangio Garganega (Gambellara Classico) 86 *—R.V. (7/1/2003)*

Zonin 2002 Podere il Giangio Recioto Garganega (Gambellara Classico) $NA. 88 *—M.L. (10/1/2006)*

Zonin 2002 Terre Mediterranee Insolia (Sicilia) $9. 82 *—M.S. (2/1/2005)*

Zonin 2000 Terre Mediterranee Insolia (Sicilia) 84 *—J.C. (10/1/2003)*

Zonin NV Lambrusco dell'Emilia Lambrusco (Emilia-Romagna) $6. 81 *—M.L. (12/15/2006)*

Zonin 2001 Merlot (Veneto) $7. 84 *(5/1/2003)*

Zonin 2005 Terre Palladiane Merlot (Veneto) $7. Lean and youthful, a great value thanks to layers of exotic spice, sweet berry, red apple and cinnamon. Bright fruit appears in the mouth, and the close is marked by a note of sour cherry. **85 Best Buy** *—M.L. (3/1/2007)*

Zonin 2000 Montepulciano (Montepulciano d'Abruzzo) $7. 85 Best Buy *—M.S. (11/15/2003)*

Zonin NV Moscato (Asti) $7. 80 *—J.C. (1/1/2004)*

Zonin NV Dolce Moscato (Asti) $11. 84 *—M.L. (11/15/2006)*

Zonin NV Dolce Moscato (Italy) $10. 84 *—M.S. (12/15/2005)*

Zonin NV Moscato Dolce Moscato (Asti) $11. 85 *—M.L. (11/15/2006)*

Zonin NV Spumante Moscato (Asti) $10. 83 *—J.C. (12/15/2004)*

Zonin 2000 Terre Mediterranee Nero d'Avola (Sicilia) $9. 85 Best Buy *(12/31/2002)*

Zonin 2004 Pinot Grigio (Friuli Aquileia) $10. 86 Best Buy *—M.L. (2/1/2006)*

Zonin 2003 Pinot Grigio (Delle Venezie) $9. 83 *—J.C. (12/31/2004)*

Zonin 2001 Pinot Grigio (Delle Venezie) $7. 84 *(12/31/2002)*

Zonin 2005 Terre Palladiane Pinot Grigio (Delle Venezie) $8. 85 Best Buy *—M.L. (6/1/2006)*

Zonin 2004 Terre Palladiane Pinot Grigio (Delle Venezie) $8. 85 Best Buy *—M.L. (2/1/2006)*

Zonin NV Brut Prosecco (Veneto) $10. 87 Best Buy *—M.L. (6/1/2006)*

Zonin NV Brut Prosecco (Italy) $10. 84 *—M.S. (12/15/2005)*

Zonin NV Special Cuvée Brut Prosecco (Italy) $10. 86 Best Buy *—J.C. (12/15/2004)*

Zonin NV Special Cuvée Brut Prosecco (Italy) $10. 87 Best Buy *—M.S. (12/15/2005)*

Zonin NV Special Cuvée Extra Dry Prosecco (Prosecco di Conegliano) $13. 86 Best Buy *—J.C. (12/31/2003)*

Zonin 1997 Red Blend (Amarone della Valpolicella) $35. 89 *(5/1/2003)*

Zonin NV Baccorosa Sparkling Blend (Asti) $10. 84 *—M.L. (11/15/2006)*

Zonin NV Baccorosa Dolce Sparkling Blend (Italy) $10. 82 *—J.C. (12/15/2004)*

Zonin 2002 Classico White Blend (Soave) 84 *—R.V. (7/1/2003)*

ITALY

New Zealand

In recent years, the New Zealand wine industry has mushroomed in size like no other. New Zealand now boasts more than five hundred wineries in a country with a total human population of only four million. The reason behind this growth has been exports. From 1995 to 2005, United States imports of New Zealand wine went from just over NZ$1 million to more than NZ$113 million. The result is that consumers in the United States are seeing more and more New Zealand wines on store shelves and restaurant wine lists. Thankfully, quality has remained generally excellent, thanks to a rigorous export certification process, a solid technological base, and a rapidly expanding understanding of viticulture.

Fairhall Downs Estate produces wine in the Brancott Valley, Marlborough, New Zealand.

NEW ZEALAND WINE REGIONS

Marlborough The engine driving New Zealand's growth, Marlborough wine production is dominated by Sauvignon Blanc. With its crisp, grassy, herbal-yet-tropical style, it has become the hallmark of New Zealand. Yet Marlborough is also capable of making other fine aromatic white wines, as well as Pinot Noir and Chardonnay.

Hawkes Bay Known for its Bordeaux-style reds from Merlot and Cabernet Sauvignon, which can be very fine in warm vintages, but excessively herbal in others. Alternative reds, such as Malbec and Syrah, are gaining in popularity, with Syrah in particular likely to emerge as a star.

Martinborough Together with the surrounding Wairarapa, Martinborough is Pinot Noir country. The wines marry cherry fruit with an often intense, wiry-herbal character that adds character and staying power.

Central Otago The world's southernmost wine-growing region has gained a repu-ta-tion for its bold, dramatically fruity Pinot Noirs, but also makes some surprisingly good Rieslings.

Other important parts of New Zealand include Waipara for Riesling and Burgundy varieties, Gisborne for Chardonnay, and Nelson for a spectrum of grape varieties similar to Marlborough's.

AKARUA

Akarua 2003 Pinot Noir (Central Otago) $40. 88 —*J.C. (12/1/2005)*

Akarua 2003 The Gullies Pinot Noir (Central Otago) $33. 85 —*J.C. (12/1/2005)*

ALANA ESTATE

Alana Estate 2003 Pinot Noir (Martinborough) $40. 84 —*J.C. (12/1/2005)*

ALEXANDRA WINE COMPANY

Alexandra Wine Company 2002 Davishon Pinot Noir (Central Otago) $35. 84 —*J.C. (12/1/2005)*

Alexandra Wine Company 2001 Davishon Alexandra Pinot Noir (Central Otago) $35. 90 —*J.C. (9/1/2003)*

Alexandra Wine Company 2001 Crag an Oir Riesling (Central Otago) $20. 88 —*J.C. (8/1/2003)*

ALEXIA

Alexia 2001 Chardonnay (Nelson) $20. 86 —*J.C. (9/1/2003)*

Alexia 2002 Sauvignon Blanc (Nelson) $18. 87 —*J.C. (9/1/2003)*

ALLAN SCOTT

Allan Scott 2000 Chardonnay (Marlborough) $20. 87 —*D.T. (12/15/2001)*

Allan Scott 1999 Chardonnay (Marlborough) $18. 88 —*J.C. (5/1/2001)*

Allan Scott 2002 Vineyard Select Chardonnay (Marlborough) $15. 88 —*J.C. (7/1/2005)*

Allan Scott 2002 Pinot Noir (Marlborough) $24. 83 —*J.C. (7/1/2005)*

Allan Scott 2001 Pinot Noir (Marlborough) $23. 87 —*J.C. (9/1/2003)*

Allan Scott 2006 Riesling (Marlborough) $14. This has all the Riesling basics: crushed-stone and lime aromas, citrus zest and melon rind flavors and a zippy, fresh finish. There's an almost crystalline quality to this wine's fruit, a slightly hard, teutonic edge that snaps the taster to attention rather than seducing with charm. 87 —*J.C. (9/1/2007)*

Allan Scott 2001 Riesling (Marlborough) $14. 87 —*J.C. (8/1/2003)*

Allan Scott 2000 Riesling (Marlborough) $14. 86 —*J.C. (5/1/2001)*

Allan Scott 2007 Sauvignon Blanc (Marlborough) $14. Wines like this are why Americans can't get enough Marlborough Sauvignon Blanc. passion-fruit and nectarine are joined by spicy hints of jalapeño, creating a fine balance of round, tropical fruit with peppery piquancy that leaves the mouth watering. 89 Best Buy —*J.C. (12/1/2007)*

Allan Scott 2006 Sauvignon Blanc (Marlborough) $14. A crisp, lean style, with herb and citrus aromas with the emphasis on white grapefruit. Shows more intensity and freshness than many Marlbortough Savvies in the price range, with an almost saline quality on the finish. Drink now. 89 Best Buy —*J.C. (3/1/2007)*

Allan Scott 2000 Sauvignon Blanc (Marlborough) $15. 87 —*J.C. (5/1/2001)*

Allan Scott 2004 Vineyard Select Sauvignon Blanc (Marlborough) $15. 90 Best Buy —*J.C. (7/1/2005)*

ALPHA DOMUS

Alpha Domus 2002 The Aviator Bordeaux Blend (Hawke's Bay) $50. 87 —*J.C. (7/1/2006)*

Alpha Domus 2000 The Aviator Bordeaux Blend (Hawke's Bay) $37. 88 —*J.C. (4/1/2004)*

Alpha Domus 2002 The Navigator Bordeaux Blend (Hawke's Bay) $20. 87 —*J.C. (7/1/2006)*

Alpha Domus 2001 The Navigator Bordeaux Blend (Hawke's Bay) $23. 87 —*J.C. (4/1/2004)*

Alpha Domus 2004 Chardonnay (Hawke's Bay) $13. 86 —*J.C. (7/1/2005)*

Alpha Domus 2002 Chardonnay (Hawke's Bay) $14. 86 —*J.C. (9/1/2003)*

Alpha Domus 2001 Chardonnay (North Island) $14. 85 —*J.C. (7/1/2002)*

Alpha Domus 2005 Unoaked Chardonnay (Hawke's Bay) $14. 84 —*J.C. (7/1/2006)*

Alpha Domus 2004 Merlot (Hawke's Bay) $14. 85 —*J.C. (11/1/2006)*

Alpha Domus 2002 Merlot (Hawke's Bay) $16. 84 —*J.C. (12/15/2003)*

Alpha Domus 2004 Sauvignon Blanc (Hawke's Bay) $13. 84 —*J.C. (7/1/2005)*

AMISFIELD

Amisfield 2005 Pinot Gris (Central Otago) $24. 88 —*J.C. (11/1/2006)*

Amisfield 2004 Pinot Gris (Central Otago) $20. 83 —*J.C. (7/1/2005)*

Amisfield 2006 Pinot Noir (Central Otago) $39. A strong followup to the excellent 2005, Amisfield's 2006 Pinot Noir seems riper and weightier, marrying dark black cherry and plum fruit with hints of chocolate and spice cake. Finishes with soft tannins and a slightly dusty feel. Drink now–2015. 91 —*J.C. (12/1/2007)*

Amisfield 2005 Pinot Noir (Central Otago) $35. Winemaker Jeff Sinnott showed an elegant touch with Pinot Noir when he worked at Isabel Estate in Marlborough, and he continues that at Amisfield, crafting a wonderfully elegant, silky-textured wine from the concentrated 2005 vintage. Dusty floral notes beguile on the nose, while cola and coffee notes add depth and richness to the black cherry and plum flavors. Drink now–2012. 90 —*J.C. (5/1/2007)*

Amisfield 2004 Pinot Noir (Central Otago) $32. 88 —*J.C. (12/1/2005)*

Amisfield 2003 Pinot Noir (Central Otago) $30. 88 —*J.C. (12/1/2005)*

Amisfield 2005 Sauvignon Blanc (Central Otago) $24. 85 —*J.C. (9/1/2006)*

Amisfield 2004 Sauvignon Blanc (Central Otago) $20. 91 Editors' Choice *(7/1/2005)*

AMOR-BENDALL

Amor-Bendall 2005 Chardonnay (Gisborne) $20. Despite hints of dried spices and a touch of butter, this Chardonnay was made without the use of oak, according to the winery. Apple and citrus flavors finish on an almost peppery clove note. 86 —*J.C. (11/1/2007)*

ASHWELL

Ashwell 2003 Pinot Noir (Martinborough) $NA. 83 —*J.C. (12/1/2005)*

ATA RANGI

Ata Rangi 2003 Pinot Noir (Martinborough) $39. 90 Cellar Selection —*J.C. (12/1/2005)*

Ata Rangi 2001 Pinot Noir (Martinborough) $55. 88 —*J.C. (9/1/2003)*

Ata Rangi 1999 Célèbre Red Blend (Martinborough) $36. 87 —*J.C. (12/15/2003)*

Ata Rangi 2006 Sauvignon Blanc (Martinborough) $23. With flavors that range from nectarine through grapefruit and brush up against bell pepper, this is a broad-spectrum Sauvignon Blanc that should prove versatile with food. It's medium-bodied, with a dry, slightly minerally finish. 86 —*J.C. (12/1/2007)*

AUNTSFIELD

Auntsfield 2005 Long Cow Sauvignon Blanc (Marlborough) $17. 88 —*J.C. (5/1/2006)*

AURUM

Aurum 2006 Riesling (Central Otago) $17. This new winery—founded in only 2002—has turned out a wonderfully delicate off-dry Riesling. Floral hints accent lemon and green apple aromas, while the finish lingers elegantly, hitting some lime top notes. 89 —*J.C. (9/1/2007)*

BABICH

Babich 1998 Chardonnay (Gisborne) $10. 87 Best Buy —*S.H. (8/1/1999)*

Babich 1996 Irongate Chardonnay (Hawke's Bay) $22. 91 —*S.H. (8/1/1999)*

Babich 2000 Unwooded Chardonnay (Hawke's Bay) $11. 87 —*J.C. (11/15/2003)*

Babich 1998 Sauvignon Blanc (Marlborough) $10. 87 Best Buy —*S.H. (8/1/1999)*

Babich 2005 Sauvignon Blanc (Marlborough) $13. 84 —*J.C. (5/1/2006)*

BALD HILLS

Bald Hills 2004 Pinot Noir (Bannockburn) $40. 87 —*J.C. (9/1/2006)*

Bald Hills 2006 Last Light Riesling (Central Otago) $28. From a small Bannockburn winery, this is an idiosyncratic Riesling that's fun to taste. To begin, there's a slightly vegetal note to its aromas and flavors that's not dissimilar from corn or vegetable oil. This is given focus by powerful citrus notes and complexity through a pinch of dried spices. Off-dry, but it finishes crisp, suggesting it would be a fine partner to sweet-fleshed crustaceans like shrimp or prawns. 87 —*J.C. (9/1/2007)*

BANNOCK BRAE

Bannock Brae 2005 Barrel Selection Pinot Noir (Central Otago) $40. With its soft, wonderfully silky texture, this is a real seductress of a Pinot. And its charms aren't limited to its mouthfeel—the aromas of dusty earth, dried mushrooms, black cherries and truffle are complex, and the flavors linger elegantly on the finish. Balanced to drink now and over the next few years. 91 —*J.C. (11/1/2007)*

Bannock Brae 2003 Barrel Selection Pinot Noir (Central Otago) $36. 86 —*J.C. (12/1/2005)*

Bannock Brae 2002 Barrel Selection Pinot Noir (Central Otago) $38. 87 —*J.C. (7/1/2005)*

BELMONTE

Belmonte 2006 Sauvignon Blanc (Marlborough) $18. Modestly herbal, this is instead laden with layers of tropical and stone fruits. There's passion-fruit, pineapple, some nectarine and melon, all well put together and pleasantly balanced. Drink now. **89** *—J.C. (11/1/2007)*

Belmonte 2004 Sauvignon Blanc (Marlborough) $20. 89 *(7/1/2005)*

BILANCIA

Bilancia 2003 Syrah-Viognier Shiraz-Viognier (Hawke's Bay) $30. 89 *—J.C. (5/1/2006)*

Bilancia 2002 La Collina Syrah (Hawke's Bay) $80. 91 *—J.C. (5/1/2006)*

BIRD

Bird 2006 Old Schoolhouse Vineyard Riesling (Marlborough) $17. Relatively full-bodied and muscular as well as dry, this new effort from winemaker Steve Bird features plenty of brawny citrus and spice flavors that finish long. There's no real track record, so it's probably best to drink now. **90 Editors' Choice** *—J.C. (9/1/2007)*

BLADEN

Bladen 2000 Riesling (Marlborough) $11. 86 *—J.C. (8/1/2002)*

Bladen 2001 Sauvignon Blanc (Marlborough) $11. 85 *—S.H. (11/15/2002)*

BLIND RIVER

Blind River 2003 Sauvignon Blanc (Marlborough) $13. 89 Best Buy *—J.C. (8/1/2004)*

BLIND TRAIL

Blind Trail 2003 Pinot Noir (Central Otago) $25. 87 *—J.C. (12/15/2006)*

BORTHWICK VINEYARD

Borthwick Vineyard 2004 Pinot Noir (Wairarapa) $25. Boasts plenty of savory, mushroomy character, but lacks fruit and turns crisp on the finish. **80** *—J.C. (3/1/2007)*

Borthwick Vineyard 2005 Sauvignon Blanc (Wairarapa) $17. 90 Editors' Choice *—J.C. (12/15/2006)*

Borthwick Vineyard 2004 Sauvignon Blanc (Wairarapa) $18. 90 *—J.C. (7/1/2005)*

BOULDERVINES

Bouldervines 2005 Single Vineyard Sauvignon Blanc (Marlborough) $NA. 86 *—J.C. (5/1/2006)*

BRANCOTT

Brancott 1997 Fairhall Estate Cabernet Sauvignon (Marlborough) $22. 87 *—J.C. (5/1/2001)*

Brancott 2002 Chardonnay (Gisborne) $11. 85 *—J.C. (8/1/2004)*

Brancott 2000 Chardonnay (Gisborne) $10. 85 Best Buy *—J.C. (5/1/2001)*

Brancott 2004 Ormond Chardonnay (Gisborne) $24. 90 *—J.C. (5/1/2006)*

Brancott 1999 Ormond Estate Chardonnay (Gisborne) $30. 87 *—J.C. (8/1/2002)*

Brancott 1998 Ormond Estate Chardonnay (Gisborne) $25. 88 *—J.C. (5/1/2001)*

Brancott 1998 Renwick Estate Chardonnay (Marlborough) $25. 89 *—J.C. (5/1/2001)*

Brancott 1999 Reserve Chardonnay (Gisborne) $17. 88 *—D.T. (12/15/2001)*

Brancott 1999 Reserve Chardonnay (Gisborne) $NA. 90 *—S.H. (1/1/2002)*

Brancott 1998 Reserve Chardonnay (Gisborne) $15. 84 *—J.C. (5/1/2001)*

Brancott 2004 Unoaked Chardonnay (Gisborne) $12. 85 *—J.C. (5/1/2006)*

Brancott 2004 Patutahi Estate Gewürztraminer (Hawke's Bay) $25. 89 *—J.C. (5/1/2006)*

Brancott 1998 Patutahi Estate Gewürztraminer (Gisborne) $25. 86 *—J.C. (5/1/2001)*

Brancott 1999 Reserve Merlot (Marlborough) $17. 86 *—J.C. (5/1/2001)*

Brancott 2006 Pinot Noir (South Island) $13. A lightweight, delicate Pinot Noir, with a light ruby hue and pretty cherry and herb flavors framed by oaky notes of brown sugar and vanilla. Good value. Imported by Pernod Ricard USA. **86** *—J.C. (12/1/2007)*

Brancott 2004 Pinot Noir (Marlborough) $11. 84 *—J.C. (7/1/2006)*

Brancott 2003 Pinot Noir (Marlborough) $11. 85 *(12/31/2004)*

Brancott 2002 Pinot Noir (Marlborough) $11. 86 Best Buy *—J.C. (8/1/2004)*

Brancott 2005 Reserve Pinot Noir (Marlborough) $19. This is a bit earthy and muted at first, showing some molasses and sous-bois character, but comes around in time to deliver modest cherry flavors as well. Solid, if somewhat unexceptional. Imported by Pernod Ricard USA. **84** *—J.C. (5/1/2007)*

Brancott 2000 Reserve Pinot Noir (Marlborough) $20. 86 *—J.C. (8/1/2002)*

Brancott 1999 Reserve Pinot Noir (Marlborough) $17. 88 Best Buy *—J.C. (5/1/2001)*

Brancott 2003 Terraces Estate Pinot Noir (Marlborough) $25. 88 *—J.C. (12/1/2005)*

Brancott 2002 Terraces Estate Pinot Noir (Marlborough) $22. 88 *(12/31/2004)*

Brancott 2007 Sauvignon Blanc (Marlborough) $13. Light and fresh, with modest grapefruit flavors matched by herbal notes and some flowery aromatics. Probably best as an apéritif. Imported by Pernod Ricard, USA. **86** *—J.C. (12/31/2007)*

Brancott 2006 Sauvignon Blanc (Marlborough) $13. Why the price had to jump $2 in a year that produced ample yields is a mystery, but the quality is still in the bottle from this perennial Best Buy. It's plump in feel, with ripe citrus—orange and tangerine—accented by zippy lime and grassy notes. Could be longer on the finish, but this is still a very good value. Imported by Pernod Ricard USA. **88 Best Buy** *—J.C. (5/1/2007)*

Brancott 2005 Sauvignon Blanc (Marlborough) $11. 88 Best Buy *—J.C. (7/1/2006)*

Brancott 2004 Sauvignon Blanc (Marlborough) $11. 86 Best Buy *(12/31/2004)*

Brancott 2003 Sauvignon Blanc (Marlborough) $11. 86 *—J.C. (8/1/2004)*

Brancott 2001 Sauvignon Blanc (Marlborough) $13. 85 *(8/1/2002)*

Brancott 2000 Sauvignon Blanc (Marlborough) $22. 86 Best Buy *—J.C. (5/1/2001)*

Brancott 1999 Sauvignon Blanc (Marlborough) $24. 84 *—D.T. (12/15/2001)*

Brancott 1998 Brancott Estate Sauvignon Blanc (Marlborough) $25. 87 *—J.C. (5/1/2001)*

Brancott 2007 B Sauvignon Blanc (Marlborough) $23. Slightly grassy, gooseberry notes bring a hint of herbaceousness to this medium-bodied Sauvignon Blanc, but the core is based around lively melon and grapefruit flavors. Plump in the mouth, yet it finishes crisp and clean; more vibrant than Brancott's Reserve bottling, making it go down that much easier. Imported by Pernod Ricard, USA. **90** *—J.C. (12/31/2007)*

Brancott 2000 Brancott Estate ("B") Sauvignon Blanc (Marlborough) $30. 83 *(8/1/2002)*

Brancott 2007 Reserve Sauvignon Blanc (Marlborough) $17. Nicely concentrated, with dense fruit flavors packed into a refined package. Melon, fig and grapefruit aromas and flavors finish long, picking up hints of smoke and herbs. Imported by Pernod Ricard, USA. **88** *—J.C. (12/31/2007)*

Brancott 2006 Reserve Sauvignon Blanc (Marlborough) $17. Fresh, grassy and citrusy on the nose, this is a wonderfully clean and elegant Marlborough Sauvignon Blanc that should be widely available. Grapefruit and fresh herb flavors are pretty much what we've come to expect, perhaps a little less overtly tropical than some and less pungent than some others. Drink now. Imported by Pernod Ricard USA. **90 Editors' Choice** *—J.C. (11/1/2007)*

Brancott 2005 Reserve Sauvignon Blanc (Marlborough) $19. Has all the typical ingredients of Marlborough Sauvignon Blanc: tropical fruit, citrus flavors and herbal notes. What distinguishes this wine is that they're all in relative balance, with no single element dominating. It's simultaneously plump in the mouth, yet clean and refreshing on the finish. Imported by Pernod Ricard. USA. **90 Editors' Choice** *—J.C. (5/1/2007)*

Brancott 2004 Reserve Sauvignon Blanc (Marlborough) $18. 89 *(12/31/2004)*

Brancott 2002 Reserve Sauvignon Blanc (Marlborough) $18. 88 *—S.H. (1/1/2002)*

Brancott 2001 Reserve Sauvignon Blanc (Marlborough) $18. 88 *(8/1/2002)*

Brancott 2000 Reserve Sauvignon Blanc (Marlborough) $15. 88 *—J.C. (5/1/2001)*

BURINGS

Burings 2004 Pinot Noir (Martinborough) $NA. 84 *—J.C. (12/1/2005)*

C.J. PASK

C.J. Pask 2002 Reserve Syrah (Hawke's Bay) $NA. 84 *—J.C. (5/1/2006)*

CADWALLADERS RIVERSIDE

Cadwalladers Riverside 2004 Chardonnay (Hawke's Bay) $15. 85 *—J.C. (7/1/2005)*

Cadwalladers Riverside 2004 Sauvignon Blanc (Hawke's Bay) $15. 86 —*J.C. (7/1/2005)*

CAIRNBRAE

Cairnbrae 2000 Chardonnay (Marlborough) $14. 86 —*J.C. (7/1/2002)*

Cairnbrae 1999 Chardonnay (Marlborough) $15. 85 —*J.C. (5/1/2001)*

Cairnbrae 2001 Pinot Noir (Marlborough) $NA. 84 —*J.C. (4/1/2004)*

Cairnbrae 2000 Old River Riesling (Marlborough) $12. 87 Best Buy —*J.C. (5/1/2001)*

Cairnbrae 1998 Sauvignon Blanc (Marlborough) $12. 87 —*S.H. (8/1/1999)*

Cairnbrae 2003 The Stones Sauvignon Blanc (Marlborough) $13. 87 —*J.C. (4/1/2004)*

Cairnbrae 2001 The Stones Sauvignon Blanc (Marlborough) $15. 90 Editors' Choice *(8/1/2002)*

Cairnbrae 1999 The Stones Sauvignon Blanc (Marlborough) $13. 86 —*J.C. (5/1/2001)*

CAMERON HUGHES

Cameron Hughes 2006 Lot 26 Sauvignon Blanc (Marlborough) $11. Boasting typical passionfruit and herb aromas in a light- to medium-bodied format, this is a decent value in low-end Marlborough Sauvignon Blanc. Crisp and herbal on the finish. **85** —*J.C. (11/1/2007)*

CANTERBURY HOUSE

Canterbury House 2000 Chardonnay (Waipara) $17. 84 —*M.M. (12/15/2001)*

Canterbury House 2000 Pinot Gris (Waipara) $14. 82 —*J.C. (8/1/2002)*

Canterbury House 1999 Pinot Noir (Waipara) $19. 82 —*M.S. (12/15/2001)*

Canterbury House 1999 Riesling (Waipara) $13. 84 —*J.C. (8/1/2002)*

Canterbury House 2000 Sauvignon Blanc (Waipara) $14. 82 *(1/1/2004)*

CAROLINE BAY

Caroline Bay 2000 Cabernet Sauvignon (Hawke's Bay) $20. 85 —*J.C. (8/1/2002)*

Caroline Bay 2000 Chardonnay (Hawke's Bay) $16. 86 —*J.C. (7/1/2002)*

Caroline Bay 2003 Sauvignon Blanc (Marlborough) $18. 86 —*J.C. (8/1/2004)*

Caroline Bay 2002 Sauvignon Blanc (Marlborough) $16. 88 —*J.C. (9/1/2003)*

Caroline Bay 2001 Sauvignon Blanc (Marlborough) $16. 90 Editors' Choice *(8/1/2002)*

CARRICK

Carrick 2003 Pinot Noir (Central Otago) $40. 87 —*J.C. (12/1/2005)*

Carrick 2002 Pinot Noir (Central Otago) $40. 89 —*J.C. (12/1/2005)*

Carrick 2001 Bannock Burn Pinot Noir (Central Otago) $40. 87 —*J.C. (9/1/2003)*

Carrick 2001 Bannockburn Riesling (Central Otago) $20. 90 Editors' Choice —*J.C. (8/1/2003)*

CATALINA SOUNDS

Catalina Sounds 2006 Sauvignon Blanc (Marlborough) $20. Fans of tropical fruit will love this wine, as it's filled with variations on that theme: guava, banana, passionfruit and lime all play roles here in this zesty mouthful. The lime gives it a sense of focus and freshness on the finish. **86** —*J.C. (5/1/2007)*

CHANCELLOR ESTATES

Chancellor Estates 2000 Mt. Cass Road Chardonnay (Waipara) $17. 84 —*J.C. (7/1/2002)*

Chancellor Estates 2000 Mt. Cass Road Pinot Noir (Waipara) $24. 83 —*J.C. (8/1/2002)*

Chancellor Estates 2000 Mt. Cass Road Riesling (Waipara) $13. 84 —*J.C. (8/1/2002)*

Chancellor Estates 2000 Mt. Cass Road Sauvignon Blanc (Waipara) $15. 88 *(8/1/2002)*

CHARLES WIFFEN

Charles Wiffen 2000 Chardonnay (Marlborough) $15. 88 Best Buy —*M.S. (12/15/2001)*

Charles Wiffen 2000 Riesling (Marlborough) $12. 85 —*M.S. (12/15/2001)*

Charles Wiffen 2001 Sauvignon Blanc (Marlborough) $30. 89 —*S.H. (11/15/2002)*

Charles Wiffen 2000 Sauvignon Blanc (Marlborough) $14. 89 —*D.T. (12/15/2001)*

CHURTON

Churton 2004 Pinot Noir (Marlborough) $25. Shows the weakness of the vintage in its prematurely browning rim and tired, slightly stewed fruit aromas. It's light in body, with dried cherry, cinnamon and clove flavors that finish crisp and lemony. **82** —*J.C. (5/1/2007)*

Churton 2005 Sauvignon Blanc (Marlborough) $17. An odd duck, but not an unenjoyable one, this is a slightly viscous Sauvignon with a deep straw color and some unusual flavors of canned corn and honey. It's more about texture and weight than forward fruit, with some herbal, capsicum notes on the finish. **84** —*J.C. (5/1/2007)*

CJ PASK

CJ Pask 2004 Declaration Bordeaux Blend (Hawke's Bay) $40. C.J. Pask is a top Hawkes Bay winery that has struggled with various importers here in the States. From a top vintage, this lushly textured blend of 55% Cabernet Sauvignon, 30% Merlot and 15% Malbec should start to give U.S. consumers something to notice. It is a little wood-dominated right now, but should come into better balance in the next couple of years, as the dried spices and cedar merge with the black cherry and cassis underneath. Drink 2008–2015. **89** —*J.C. (11/1/2007)*

CLAYRIDGE

Clayridge 2005 Pinot Noir (Marlborough) $28. Starts off distinctly herbal, but also gushing with cherry fruit—a complex, intriguing blend. The flavors seem somewhat simpler, combining black cherries with chocolate, but also a lemony streak of acidity. Finishes crisp, without much tannin. Drink now. **86** —*J.C. (7/1/2007)*

Clayridge 2005 Excalibur Pinot Noir (Marlborough) $36. Features scents of coffee, meat, button mushrooms and brown sugar. It's a savory style that's earthy and complex, with undercurrents of cherries and cola. Nicely rounded and supple in the mouth, this seems ready to go, with no need for further aging. **89** —*J.C. (7/1/2007)*

Clayridge 2006 Pinot Rosé Pinot Noir (Marlborough) $16. Slightly rubbery or tarry on the nose, this wine does show some simple, ripe cherry flavors on the palate. It's rather full-bodied, not enlivened quite enough by a prickle of carbon dioxide. **84** —*J.C. (7/1/2007)*

Clayridge 2006 Sauvignon Blanc (Marlborough) $20. Winemaker Mike Just, formerly of Lawson's Dry Hills, has gone out on his own and this new release is a terrific effort in a riper style. Melon and fig flavors are honeyed and round in the mouth, finishing long with touches of spice. **91 Editors' Choice** —*J.C. (7/1/2007)*

CLEARVIEW

Clearview 2004 Old Olive Block Bordeaux Blend (Hawke's Bay) $37. 87 —*J.C. (11/1/2006)*

Clearview 2004 Reserve Chardonnay (Hawke's Bay) $46. 91 —*J.C. (11/1/2006)*

Clearview 2002 Reserve Chardonnay (Hawke's Bay) $42. 89 —*J.C. (8/1/2004)*

Clearview 2001 Reserve Chardonnay (Hawke's Bay) $45. 83 —*J.C. (4/1/2004)*

Clearview 2005 Unwooded Chardonnay (Hawke's Bay) $28. 90 Editors' Choice —*J.C. (11/1/2006)*

Clearview 2004 Unwooded Chardonnay (Hawke's Bay) $27. 87 —*J.C. (7/1/2006)*

CLIFFORD BAY ESTATE

Clifford Bay Estate 2004 Single Vineyard Pinot Noir (Marlborough) $NA. 85 —*J.C. (12/1/2005)*

CLOS MARGUERITE

Clos Marguerite 2006 Sauvignon Blanc (Marlborough) $20. More pungent than expected, with nettle and tomato-leaf notes on the nose. Yet in the mouth, the wine is full-bodied, weighty without being particularly tropical or fruity and combines a lush mouthfeel with intriguing herbal complexity. Drink now. **90 Editors' Choice** —*J.C. (11/1/2007)*

Clos Marguerite 2005 Sauvignon Blanc (Marlborough) $19. 86 —*J.C. (9/1/2006)*

Clos Marguerite 2003 Sauvignon Blanc (Marlborough) $17. 86 —*J.C. (7/1/2005)*

CLOUDY BAY

Cloudy Bay 2005 Chardonnay (Marlborough) $30. Cloudy Bay has been remarkably consistent over the years, and is no exception, offering up aromas of toasted grain and a hint of butter to marry with citrus and custard notes. It's toasty throughout, but layered with varied fruit and a rich, velvety texture. Drink now. **90** —*J.C. (12/1/2007)*

Cloudy Bay 2004 Chardonnay (Marlborough) $29. 87 —*J.C. (9/1/2006)*

Cloudy Bay 2003 Chardonnay (Marlborough) $28. 89 *(12/15/2005)*

Cloudy Bay 2002 Chardonnay (Marlborough) $29. 88 *—J.C. (8/1/2004)*

Cloudy Bay 1999 Chardonnay (Marlborough) $28. 89 *—J.C. (5/1/2001)*

Cloudy Bay 2004 Pinot Noir (Marlborough) $30. 86 *—J.C. (9/1/2006)*

Cloudy Bay 2003 Pinot Noir (Marlborough) $29. 88 *(12/15/2005)*

Cloudy Bay 2002 Pinot Noir (Marlborough) $29. 88 *—J.C. (8/1/2004)*

Cloudy Bay 2006 Sauvignon Blanc (Marlborough) $27. Marlborough's standard-bearer continues to turn out vintage after vintage of worthy wines. CB's 2006 Sauvignon is marginally less rich than the 2005, but still offers plenty of crisp, tangy tropical flavors. Pineapple and grapefruit notes finish with a grassy edge. **90** *—J.C. (3/1/2007)*

Cloudy Bay 2005 Sauvignon Blanc (Marlborough) $25. 91 *(12/15/2005)*

Cloudy Bay 2004 Sauvignon Blanc (Marlborough) $26. 89 *(7/1/2005)*

Cloudy Bay 2003 Sauvignon Blanc (Marlborough) $29. 88 *—J.C. (8/1/2004)*

Cloudy Bay 2001 Sauvignon Blanc (Marlborough) $22. 89 *(8/1/2002)*

Cloudy Bay 2000 Sauvignon Blanc (Marlborough) $24. 90 Editors' Choice *—J.C. (5/1/2001)*

Cloudy Bay 2002 Te Koko Sauvignon Blanc (Marlborough) $35. 90 *(12/15/2005)*

COOPERS CREEK

Coopers Creek 1998 Reserve Cabernet Sauvignon-Merlot (Hawke's Bay) $24. 88 *—J.C. (5/1/2001)*

Coopers Creek 1998 Swamp Reserve Chardonnay (Hawke's Bay) $26. 91 *—J.C. (5/1/2001)*

Coopers Creek 1998 Merlot (Hawke's Bay) $14. 86 *—J.C. (5/1/2001)*

Coopers Creek 2006 Riesling (Marlborough) $15. Plump and soft in the mouth, with ripe apple and pear flavors underscored by tangy notes of passionfruit. **85** *—J.C. (9/1/2007)*

Coopers Creek 1998 Riesling (Hawke's Bay) $9. 88 Best Buy *—S.H. (8/1/1999)*

Coopers Creek 2000 Riesling (Hawke's Bay) $12. 87 Best Buy *—J.C. (5/1/2001)*

Coopers Creek 1997 Sauvignon Blanc (Marlborough) $11. 87 *—S.H. (8/1/1999)*

Coopers Creek 2005 Sauvignon Blanc (Marlborough) $15. 87 *—J.C. (5/1/2006)*

Coopers Creek 2000 Sauvignon Blanc (Marlborough) $10. 86 *—J.C. (5/1/2001)*

Coopers Creek 2001 Reserve Sauvignon Blanc (Marlborough) $15. 88 *—S.H. (11/15/2002)*

Coopers Creek 1999 Reserve Sauvignon Blanc (Marlborough) $18. 90 *—J.C. (5/1/2001)*

CORBANS

Corbans 1998 Winemaker's Cottage Block Bordeaux Blend (Hawke's Bay) $22. 90 Editor's Choice *—J.C. (5/1/2001)*

Corbans 1998 Winemaker's Private Bin Bordeaux Blend (Hawke's Bay) $20. 88 *—J.C. (5/1/2001)*

Corbans 1999 Winemaker's Private Bin Chardonnay (Gisborne) $18. 86 *—J.C. (5/1/2001)*

Corbans 1999 Winemaker's Selection Chardonnay (East Coast) $13. 85 *—J.C. (5/1/2001)*

Corbans 1999 Winemaker's Selection Merlot (East Coast) $13. 87 *—J.C. (5/1/2001)*

Corbans 1999 Winemaker's Private Bin Sauvignon Blanc (Marlborough) $18. 83 *—J.C. (5/1/2001)*

Corbans 1999 Winemaker's Selection Sauvignon Blanc (Marlborough) $13. 85 *—J.C. (5/1/2001)*

COTTIER

Cottier 2005 Trillo Sauvignon Blanc (Wairarapa) $20. 81 *—J.C. (11/1/2006)*

COURTNEY'S POST

Courtney's Post 2002 Sauvignon Blanc (Marlborough) $16. 84 *—J.C. (4/1/2004)*

CRAGGY RANGE

Craggy Range 2004 Sophia Gimblett Gravels Bordeaux Blend (Hawke's Bay) $60. 90 *—J.C. (12/15/2006)*

Craggy Range 2002 Sophia Gimblett Gravels Bordeaux Blend (Hawke's Bay) $55. 92 *—J.C. (7/1/2005)*

Craggy Range 2004 Te Kahu Gimblett Gravels Vineyard Bordeaux Blend (Hawke's Bay) $25. Not quite up to the quality of the winery's excellent 2004 Sophia (a recent bottle of which suggested that its 90-point score may be stingy), but at one-third the price, who's complaining? This is a richly textured Merlot-based blend, loaded with scents and flavors of mocha, earth, plum and brown sugar that's built to please. Drink now–2012. Imported by Kobrand Corporation. **88** *—J.C. (5/1/2007)*

Craggy Range 2002 Les Beaux Cailloux Chardonnay (Hawke's Bay) $50. 89 *—J.C. (7/1/2005)*

Craggy Range 2004 Les Beaux Cailloux Gimblett Gravels Chardonnay (Hawke's Bay) $60. 89 *—J.C. (12/15/2006)*

Craggy Range 2000 Seven Poplars Vineyard Chardonnay (Hawke's Bay) 85 *—J.C. (11/15/2002)*

Craggy Range 2003 Gimblett Gravels Vineyard Merlot (Hawke's Bay) $35. 86 *—J.C. (7/1/2006)*

Craggy Range 2002 Gimblett Gravels Vineyard Merlot (Hawke's Bay) $35. 86 *—J.C. (8/1/2004)*

Craggy Range 1999 Seven Poplars Vineyard Merlot (Hawke's Bay) 90 *—J.C. (8/1/2002)*

Craggy Range 2003 Te Muna Block 1 Doug Wisor Memorial Pinot Noir (Martinborough Terrace) $60. 93 *—J.C. (12/1/2005)*

Craggy Range 2005 Te Muna Road Vineyard Pinot Noir (Martinborough) $35. A slight disappointment from this highly-touted winery, the 2005 Te Muna Road Pinot is certainly complex enough on the nose, where it shows pleasant meaty, peppery, cedary and smoky notes, but features rather tart cherry flavors and a crisply acidic finish. Imported by Kobrand. **86** *—J.C. (7/1/2007)*

Craggy Range 2004 Te Muna Road Vineyard Pinot Noir (Martinborough) $40. 89 *—J.C. (9/1/2006)*

Craggy Range 2003 Te Muna Road Vineyard Pinot Noir (Martinborough) $40. 88 *—J.C. (12/1/2005)*

Craggy Range 2006 Fletcher Family Vineyard Riesling (Marlborough) $23. This distinctive Riesling starts with a blast of crushed stone and lime zest, then settles down to offer strident lime-sherbet flavors—slightly sweet—that end on a dry, tactile note. Imported by Kobrand Corporation. **89** *—J.C. (9/1/2007)*

Craggy Range 2005 Fletcher Family Vineyard Riesling (Marlborough) $24. A top example of the kind of balance Marlborough Riesling can achieve, this is simultaneously full-bodied and round, off-dry yet crisp. Citrusy aromas reminiscent of lemon curd lead the way, while the fruit flavors that unfold on the palate offer melon, apple and citrus. **90** *—J.C. (9/1/2007)*

Craggy Range 2005 Te Muna Road Vineyard Riesling (Martinborough) $24. Drier-tasting and slightly more austere than the Fletcher Family Vineyard bottling, this Riesling from Craggy's own vineyard in Martinborough features zesty lemon and lime aromas and flavors backed by various spices, including ginger and clove. It's medium-bodied, with a long spice-and-citrus finish. **90** *—J.C. (9/1/2007)*

Craggy Range 2001 Old Renwick Vineyard Sauvignon Blanc (Marlborough) $17. 90 Editors' Choice *(8/1/2002)*

Craggy Range 2006 Te Muna Road Vineyard Sauvignon Blanc (Martinborough) $23. After a slightly rubbery or tarry note when first poured, this wine cleans up nicely to present grassy herbal notes balanced by stone fruit. It's tightly focused and a bit more minerally than many NZ Sauvignon Blancs, without being overly tart or lemony. Should drink well through the end of 2008. Imported by Kobrand Corporation. **89** *—J.C. (11/1/2007)*

Craggy Range 2005 Te Muna Road Vineyard Sauvignon Blanc (Martinborough) $22. \90 Editors' Choice *—J.C. (9/1/2006)*

Craggy Range 2004 Te Muna Road Vineyard Sauvignon Blanc (Martinborough) $20. 90 Editors' Choice *(7/1/2005)*

Craggy Range 2003 Te Muna Road Vineyard Sauvignon Blanc (Martinborough) $18. 90 Editors' Choice *—J.C. (4/1/2004)*

Craggy Range 2004 Le Sol Gimblett Gravels Syrah (Hawke's Bay) $65. This is an inky purple-hued Syrah, with the power to match its intense color. Scents of toast, vanilla and black cherries set the stage, while the flavors build on that, adding hints of cured meat and cinnamon. This is full-bodied, with ripe tannins, yet isn't soft. Give it a couple years in the cellar to allow the wood to integrate, and this will be even tastier. **92** *—J.C. (7/1/2007)*

Craggy Range 2002 Le Sol Syrah (Hawke's Bay) $60. 92 *—J.C. (7/1/2005)*

CRONEY ESTATES

Croney Estates 2006 Three Ton Sauvignon Blanc (Marlborough) $15. Pretty standard Marlborough Sauvignon Blanc, marrying herbal qualities with hints of honeyed stone fruit. It's medium-bodied, with the tart flavors of underripe nectarines on the finish. Imported by Davies & Co., Inc. 86 —*J.C. (9/1/2007)*

CROSSROADS

Crossroads 2002 RGF Bordeaux Blend (Hawke's Bay) $30. 87 —*J.C. (5/1/2006)*

Crossroads 2004 Chardonnay (Hawke's Bay) $17. 86 —*J.C. (5/1/2006)*

Crossroads 2005 Gewürztraminer (Hawke's Bay) $NA. 85 —*J.C. (5/1/2006)*

Crossroads 2003 Merlot-Cabernet Sauvignon (Hawke's Bay) $NA. 85 —*J.C. (5/1/2006)*

Crossroads 2005 Destination Series Sauvignon Blanc (Marlborough) $14. 85 —*J.C. (5/1/2006)*

Crossroads 2004 Destination Series Sauvignon Blanc (Marlborough) $14. 85 —*J.C. (7/1/2005)*

DANIEL SCHUSTER

Daniel Schuster 2002 Selection Chardonnay (Waipara) $29. 87 —*J.C. (5/1/2006)*

Daniel Schuster 2003 Pinot Noir (Waipara) $27. 89 —*J.C. (12/1/2005)*

Daniel Schuster 2002 Omihi Hills Vineyard Selection Pinot Noir (Waipara) $30. 90 —*J.C. (12/1/2005)*

Daniel Schuster 2004 Twin Vineyards Pinot Noir (Waipara) $18. 87 —*J.C. (12/1/2005)*

Daniel Schuster 2004 Riesling (Waipara) $NA. 85 —*J.C. (5/1/2006)*

Daniel Schuster 2004 Hull Family Vineyard Late Harvest Riesling (Waipara) $30. 87 —*J.C. (5/1/2006)*

DASHWOOD

Dashwood 2006 Pinot Noir (Marlborough) $18. A lightweight, lean Pinot with an herbal streak. Scents of cherries, strawberries and dried mushrooms set the stage for tart berry flavors that finish tangy and crisp. 84 —*J.C. (11/1/2007)*

Dashwood 2005 Pinot Noir (Marlborough) $17. A good value in Pinot Noir, this effort features notes of beet greens and underbrush but also plenty of bright raspberry fruit on the nose. Flavors are complex and well-integrated, and there's a reasonably full and soft mouthfeel. Hints of sassafras and vanilla underline the finish. Drink now. 87 —*J.C. (3/1/2007)*

Dashwood 2004 Pinot Noir (Marlborough) $17. Already showing signs of aging, this modest Pinot features herb-infelected strawberry flavors to go with slightly earthy, meaty aromas. It's a bit lean and thins out on the finish. Drink yesterday. 84 —*J.C. (3/1/2007)*

Dashwood 2007 Sauvignon Blanc (Marlborough) $18. Pineapple and grapefruit flavors are accented by hints of tomato leaf, meaning this conforms to the basic Marlborough profile that blends fruit with grassy, herbal notes. Pretty good, it just fades a bit quickly on the finish. 86 —*J.C. (12/31/2007)*

Dashwood 2006 Sauvignon Blanc (Marlborough) $18. Round, easily approachable Sauvignon Blanc, with pink grapefruit aromas and flavors that verge on red berries. A hint of grassiness keeps it true to type, with citrus flavors that define the finish. Drink now. 88 —*J.C. (5/14/2007)*

Dashwood 2005 Sauvignon Blanc (Marlborough) $15. 85 —*J.C. (9/1/2006)*

Dashwood 2001 Sauvignon Blanc (Marlborough) 88 —*S.H. (11/15/2002)*

DAVIS FAMILY

Davis Family 2002 Gusto Sauvignon Blanc (Marlborough) $18. 83 —*J.C. (7/1/2005)*

DELTA VINEYARD

Delta Vineyard 2006 Pinot Noir (Marlborough) $19. A bit of a letdown after the 2005, this lean, slightly astringent Pinot Noir offers tart cherry flavors touched with black tea leaves. Finishes on a pomegranate note. 84 —*J.C. (11/1/2007)*

Delta Vineyard 2005 Pinot Noir (Marlborough) $19. 89 —*J.C. (9/1/2006)*

Delta Vineyard 2005 Hatter's Hill Pinot Noir (Marlborough) $29. 90 Editors' Choice —*J.C. (11/1/2006)*

DISCOVERY

Discovery 2005 Sauvignon Blanc (Marlborough) $15. 88 —*J.C. (9/1/2006)*

DOMAINE GEORGES MICHEL

Domaine Georges Michel 2004 Golden Mile Chardonnay (Marlborough) $23. 85 —*J.C. (9/1/2006)*

Domaine Georges Michel 2000 Golden Mile Chardonnay (Marlborough) $16. 88 —*J.C. (9/1/2003)*

Domaine Georges Michel 2001 Golden Mile Pinot Noir (Marlborough) $25. 82 —*J.C. (9/1/2003)*

Domaine Georges Michel 2005 Golden Mile Sauvignon Blanc (Marlborough) $18. 89 —*J.C. (5/1/2006)*

Domaine Georges Michel 2002 Golden Mile Sauvignon Blanc (Marlborough) $15. 83 —*J.C. (9/1/2003)*

DRY GULLY

Dry Gully 2001 Alexandra Pinot Noir (Central Otago) $35. 86 —*J.C. (9/1/2003)*

DRY RIVER

Dry River 2004 Chardonnay (Martinborough) $45. 92 —*J.C. (11/1/2006)*

Dry River 1999 Pinot Gris (New Zealand) $NA. 90 —*J.C. (5/1/2001)*

Dry River 2004 Pinot Noir (Martinborough) $NA. 92 —*J.C. (11/1/2006)*

Dry River 1999 Amaranth Pinot Noir (Martinborough) $NA. 87 —*J.C. (11/1/2006)*

Dry River 2000 Arapoff Syrah (Martinborough) $NA. 88 —*J.C. (11/1/2006)*

DRYLANDS

Drylands 2005 Pinot Noir (Marlborough) $18. The price of this wine has moved up, but it's still under $20, and still represents a good value in Pinot Noir. It's medium-bodied, and like most Marlborough Pinots these days, very supple. Blends slightly mushroomy, savory components with hints of cedar and strawberry. Drink now. 87 —*J.C. (3/1/2007)*

Drylands 2004 Pinot Noir (Marlborough) $14. 86 —*J.C. (12/1/2005)*

Drylands 2006 Dry Riesling (Marlborough) $15. This dry Riesling manages to tie together several disparate elements into a nicely cohesive whole. Strands of honey, baked apples and dusty minerality are all bound together by citrusy acids on the long, clean finish. Drink now. 89 —*J.C. (9/1/2007)*

Drylands 2006 Sauvignon Blanc (Marlborough) $15. A nicely balanced, complex Sauvignon, this wine is mouthfilling and round, but not soft, with a blend of tropical fruit—mango and papaya—and grasssy, herbal nuances. Finishes long, crisp and herbal; should be versatile at the table. Drink now. 90 Best Buy —*J.C. (3/1/2007)*

Drylands 2005 Sauvignon Blanc (Marlborough) $16. 87 *(3/1/2006)*

Drylands 2001 Winemakers Reserve Sauvignon Blanc (Marlborough) $19. 90 —*S.H. (11/15/2002)*

DRYSTONE

Drystone 2003 Pinot Noir (Central Otago) $30. 90 —*J.C. (12/1/2005)*

DYED-IN-THE-WOOL

Dyed-In-The-Wool 2005 Ram's Reserve Pinot Noir (Marlborough) $16. 84 —*J.C. (12/15/2006)*

Dyed-In-The-Wool 2003 Ram's Reserve Pinot Noir (Marlborough) $20. 85 —*J.C. (12/1/2005)*

Dyed-In-The-Wool 2002 Ram's Reserve Pinot Noir (Marlborough) $20. 86 —*J.C. (4/1/2004)*

Dyed-In-The-Wool 2003 Unchangeable Pinot Noir (Canterbury) $14. 83 —*J.C. (12/1/2005)*

Dyed-In-The-Wool 2002 Unchangeable Pinot Noir (Canterbury) $14. 87 Best Buy —*J.C. (8/1/2004)*

Dyed-In-The-Wool 2005 Sauvignon Blanc (Marlborough) $10. 86 Best Buy —*J.C. (11/1/2006)*

Dyed-In-The-Wool 2001 Estate Grown Unchangable Sauvignon Blanc (Marlborough) $12. 87 Best Buy —*J.C. (9/1/2003)*

Dyed-In-The-Wool 2003 Unchangeable Sauvignon Blanc (Marlborough) $12. 87 Best Buy —*J.C. (8/1/2004)*

Dyed-In-The-Wool 2002 Unchangeable Sauvignon Blanc (Marlborough) $13. 85 —*J.C. (4/1/2004)*

ELSTREE

Elstree 1998 Reserve Riesling (Marlborough) $20. 90 —*S.H. (8/1/1999)*

Elstree 1998 Reserve Sauvignon Blanc (Marlborough) $19. 87 —*S.H. (8/1/1999)*

ERADUS

Eradus 2006 Sauvignon Blanc (Marlborough) $18. From the Awatere Valley, this is an exciting new discovery. It's pungent, even sweaty at times, but also boasts plenty of passionfruit, and hints of melon and nectarine. The texture is rich and slightly oily, yet with a chalky, minerally component as well. Sure it's herbal, but it's also of undeniable quality for those who appreciate the style. 91 Editors' Choice —*J.C. (7/1/2007)*

ESCARPMENT

Escarpment 2006 Pinot Gris (Martinborough) $30. Barrel-fermented Pinot Gris is a bit of a rarity, but this one is good if you like the style. Buttered apples and nuts lead the way, backed by tangerine fruit and outlined by oaky spice. Tough to know whether aging it will result in slightly better integration, or if you're better off drinking this one young. 86 —*J.C. (12/31/2007)*

Escarpment 2004 Pinot Gris (Martinborough) $30. 88 —*J.C. (2/1/2006)*

Escarpment 2002 Station Bush Vineyard Pinot Gris (Martinborough) $31. 84 —*J.C. (8/1/2004)*

Escarpment 2001 Station Bush Vineyard Pinot Gris (Martinborough) $23. 85 —*J.C. (9/1/2003)*

Escarpment 2005 Pinot Noir (Martinborough) $37. This is like a scaled-down version of the Kupe bottling—or is that one a scaled-up version of this wine? Smoky and peppery notes mark the nose, framing black cherry and plum flavors in a wire cage of cured meats, yet the texture is supple and silky. Drink now–2012. 90 Editors' Choice —*J.C. (11/1/2007)*

Escarpment 2004 Pinot Noir (Martinborough) $35. 86 —*J.C. (9/1/2006)*

Escarpment 2003 Pinot Noir (Martinborough) $45. 88 —*J.C. (12/1/2005)*

Escarpment 2002 Pinot Noir (Martinborough) $42. 86 —*J.C. (8/1/2004)*

Escarpment 2005 Kupe Pinot Noir (Martinborough) $60. Since its debut in 2003, this has been one of New Zealand's top Pinot Noirs, combining power, structure and complexity. Smoky and richly peppery at first, it turns more floral with aeration, and while it's big in the mouth, it's also silky in texture. The black cherry, plum, vanilla and spice flavors fan out on the long, layered finish. Drink now–2015. 93 —*J.C. (11/1/2007)*

Escarpment 2003 Kupe Pinot Noir (Martinborough) $60. 93 —*J.C. (12/1/2005)*

ESK VALLEY

Esk Valley 2002 Chardonnay (Hawke's Bay) $15. 88 —*J.C. (9/1/2003)*

Esk Valley 2000 Red Blend (Hawke's Bay) $15. 84 —*J.C. (12/15/2003)*

Esk Valley 2000 Reserve Red Blend (Hawke's Bay) $40. 89 —*J.C. (12/15/2003)*

Esk Valley 2002 Riesling (Hawke's Bay) $19. 90 —*J.C. (8/1/2003)*

Esk Valley 2002 Sauvignon Blanc (Hawke's Bay) $19. 90 Editors' Choice —*J.C. (9/1/2003)*

Esk Valley 2001 Sauvignon Blanc (Hawke's Bay) $19. 89 *(8/1/2002)*

FAIRHALL DOWNS

Fairhall Downs 2000 Pinot Gris (Marlborough) $20. 87 —*J.C. (5/1/2001)*

Fairhall Downs 2004 NA in US Pinot Noir (Marlborough) $NA. 90 —*J.C. (12/1/2005)*

Fairhall Downs 2005 Single Vineyard Pinot Noir (Marlborough) $27. This shows concentrated fruit together with plenty of savory complexity—black cherry and plum flavors blend with meaty-mushroomy notes and just a touch of herb. Creamy-smooth tannins give it a lush mouthfeel, yet it retains a sense of delicacy on the long, silky finish. 90 Editors' Choice —*J.C. (7/1/2007)*

Fairhall Downs 2005 Sauvignon Blanc (Marlborough) $16. 90 Editors' Choice —*J.C. (7/1/2006)*

Fairhall Downs 2001 Sauvignon Blanc (Marlborough) $18. 91 —*S.H. (11/15/2002)*

Fairhall Downs 2000 Sauvignon Blanc (Marlborough) $18. 88 —*J.C. (5/1/2001)*

Fairhall Downs 2006 Single Vineyard Sauvignon Blanc (Marlborough) $15. Made in a slightly leaner style than what has become the norm for Marlborough, this starts with scents of passionfruit and a hint of bell pepper, then adds riper melon notes. Flavors of underripe pineapple and passionfruit are crisp, and would provide a good foil for various shellfish dishes. Long and refreshing on the finish. 87 —*J.C. (7/1/2007)*

FAUNA

Fauna 2005 Sauvignon Blanc (Marlborough) $12. 88 Best Buy —*J.C. (7/1/2006)*

FELTON ROAD

Felton Road 2004 Barrel Fermented Chardonnay (Central Otago) $NA. 90 —*J.C. (5/1/2006)*

Felton Road 2002 Barrel Fermented Chardonnay (Central Otago) $30. 90 —*J.C. (4/1/2004)*

Felton Road 2000 Barrel Fermented Chardonnay (Central Otago) $30. 88 —*J.C. (7/1/2002)*

Felton Road 1999 Barrel Fermented Chardonnay (Central Otago) $34. 90 —*J.C. (5/1/2001)*

Felton Road 2004 Block 6 Chardonnay (Central Otago) $44. 88 —*J.C. (9/1/2006)*

Felton Road 2006 Pinot Noir (Central Otago) $43. A bit disjointed at this early stage of its evolution, this shows plenty of brown sugar and plum sweetness, but also crisp acids and some dry, dusty tannins. Give it a couple of years to round into form and drink it over the next 5–6 years. 88n—*J.C. (12/1/2007)*

Felton Road 2005 Pinot Noir (Central Otago) $43. Another top effort from winemaker Blair Walter, Felton Road's 2005 Pinot Noir features masses of plum and blackberry fruit, hints of tea and smoke, and a long, mouthwatering finish. It's a big, muscular wine that keeps a sense of elegance to its robust personality and flavors. Drink now–2015. The most plentiful of the Felton Road Pinot Noirs, with 150 cases imported. 90 —*J.C. (5/1/2007)*

Felton Road 2004 Pinot Noir (Central Otago) $44. 90 —*J.C. (12/1/2005)*

Felton Road 2002 Pinot Noir (Central Otago) $43. 91 —*J.C. (4/1/2004)*

Felton Road 2000 Pinot Noir (Central Otago) $40. 90 —*J.C. (8/1/2002)*

Felton Road 1999 Pinot Noir (Central Otago) $45. 89 —*J.C. (5/1/2001)*

Felton Road 2006 Block 3 Pinot Noir (Central Otago) $63. Full-bodied and well-structured, this is the rare New Zealand Pinot that warrants cellaring for a few years prior to enjoyment. Dusty earth, cedar, cola and plum notes mingle easily, but seem a bit reined in. Shows good length, auguring well for improvement over the next five years. Drink 2010–2018. 91 Cellar Selection —*J.C. (11/1/2007)*

Felton Road 2005 Block 3 Pinot Noir (Central Otago) $63. This is showing some lovely complexity on the nose, with hints of spice, maple syrup and hickory smoke all showing through the weighty plum and chocolate fruit. It's lush and soft on the palate, just firming up a bit on the finish, where it picks up elegant oak-spice notes. 90 —*J.C. (11/1/2007)*

Felton Road 2004 Block 3 Pinot Noir (Central Otago) $60. 91 —*J.C. (12/1/2005)*

Felton Road 2002 Block 3 Pinot Noir (Central Otago) $53. 90 —*J.C. (4/1/2004)*

Felton Road 2000 Block 3 Pinot Noir (Central Otago) $50. 89 —*J.C. (8/1/2002)*

Felton Road 1999 Block 3 Pinot Noir (Central Otago) $70. 91 —*J.C. (5/1/2001)*

Felton Road 2005 Block 5 Pinot Noir (Central Otago) $63. Despite a slight hint of reduction on the nose, this often burly bottling is fairly open and accessible. The complex bouquet includes hints of green tobacco, dried spices and dark chocolate to go along with ripe plum fruit, while the mouthfeel is supple and richly textured. Drink now–2012, if you can manage to track down one of the less than 300 bottles imported to the U.S. 91 —*J.C. (5/1/2007)*

Felton Road 2004 Block 5 Pinot Noir (Central Otago) $62. 90 —*J.C. (9/1/2006)*

Felton Road 2003 Block 5 Pinot Noir (Central Otago) $62. 91 Cellar Selection —*J.C. (12/1/2005)*

Felton Road 1999 Block 5 Pinot Noir (Central Otago) $80. 91 —*J.C. (5/1/2001)*

Felton Road 2006 Calvert Pinot Noir (Central Otago) $54. A new offering from Felton Road, with a creamy, almost syrupy texture and aromas and flavors that lean toward red fruit, versus the dark fruits so often found in their other Pinot Noirs. Turns tart and snappy on the finish, almost cranberryish. 88 —*J.C. (11/1/2007)*

Felton Road 2006 Riesling (Central Otago) $27. Broad and sweet, but the sugars are amply balanced by this wine's dusty minerality and dried-spice character. Honey, spice and apple shadings on the nose glide easily into flavors of baked apple on the palate, while the finish possesses a tactile minerality that precisely brings all of the components into harmony. Drink now–2016. 91 —*J.C. (9/1/2007)*

Felton Road 2005 Riesling (Central Otago) $26. 90 —*J.C. (7/1/2006)*

Felton Road 2002 Riesling (Central Otago) $23. 91 Editors' Choice —*J.C. (8/1/2003)*

Felton Road 2000 Riesling (Central Otago) $26. 88 —*J.C. (5/1/2001)*

Felton Road 2002 Block 1 Riesling (Central Otago) $25. 90 —*J.C. (8/1/2003)*

Felton Road 2002 Dry Riesling (Central Otago) $23. 92 Editors' Choice —*J.C. (8/1/2003)*

Felton Road 2000 Dry Riesling (Central Otago) $21. 91 Editors' Choice —*J.C. (5/1/2001)*

FERNLEAF

Fernleaf 2005 Sauvignon Blanc (East Coast) $10. Seems to be tiring a bit, with slightly dull, earthy flavors enlivened by crisp citrusy notes and hints of apple. Imported by North Lake Wines. 83 —*J.C. (4/12/2007)*

FIRSTLAND

Firstland 2000 Pinot Noir (Marlborough) $25. 83 —*J.C. (9/1/2003)*

Firstland 2002 Sauvignon Blanc (Marlborough) $19. 86 —*J.C. (9/1/2003)*

Firstland 2001 Sauvignon Blanc (Marlborough) $NA. 91 *—S.H. (11/15/2002)*

FOREFATHERS

Forefathers 2005 Sauvignon Blanc (Marlborough) $16. 89 *—J.C. (9/1/2006)*

Forefathers 2002 Sauvignon Blanc (Marlborough) $13. 90 *—J.M. (1/1/2003)*

Forefathers 2000 Sauvignon Blanc (Marlborough) $13. 91 *—J.M. (11/15/2001)*

Forefathers 1999 Sauvignon Blanc (Marlborough) $14. 84 *—J.C. (5/1/2001)*

FORREST ESTATE

Forrest Estate 2004 John Forrest Collection Cabernet Sauvignon (Hawke's Bay) $50. With its hefty price tag and limited production (150 cases), consumers aren't likely to stumble across this wine, but it's worth a try, if only to see what the NZ possibilities are for Cabernet Sauvignon. Herb-tinged cassis aromas and flavors are framed by vanilla oak, soft tannins and balanced acidity. Finishes long, picking up hints of tea and tobacco leaves. Drink now–2015. **90** *—J.C. (11/1/2007)*

Forrest Estate 2000 Cornerstone Cabernet Sauvignon-Merlot (Hawke's Bay) $25. 84 *—J.C. (12/15/2003)*

Forrest Estate 1997 Chardonnay (Marlborough) $15. 90 *—S.H. (8/1/1999)*

Forrest Estate 2006 Gewürztraminer (Marlborough) $18. Relatively restrained aromatically, with rose petal scents that set the stage for pear, peach and modest spice flavors. It's slightly off dry, a modest Gewürztraminer that's unlikely to offend but also unlikely to be loved. **85** *—J.C. (11/1/2007)*

Forrest Estate 2006 Pinot Gris (Marlborough) $15. A medium-bodied, rather sweet Pinot Gris that manages to retain a sense of balance to its luscious honey, peach and apple flavors. The finish lingers elegantly, picking up intriguing notes of dried spices along the way. Ready to drink now, although it could surprise in another year or two. **90 Best Buy** *—J.C. (11/1/2007)*

Forrest Estate 2005 Pinot Noir (Marlborough) $20. A lithe, light-bodied Pinot with tart berry flavors and some slightly tomato-like flavors. Finishes with cranberry fruit and a bit of tea. Drink now. **84** *—J.C. (7/1/2007)*

Forrest Estate 2004 Pinot Noir (Marlborough) $20. 86 *—J.C. (11/1/2006)*

Forrest Estate 2003 Pinot Noir (Marlborough) $20. 87 *—J.C. (12/1/2005)*

Forrest Estate 2001 Pinot Noir (Marlborough) $20. 88 *—J.C. (4/1/2004)*

Forrest Estate 2005 Riesling (Marlborough) $16. No, this isn't that complex, but it does offer a mouthful of assertive Riesling flavor. Intense notes of green apple, lime and honey coat the palate, leaving a long, slightly sweet finish in their wake. Drink now. **89** *—J.C. (9/1/2007)*

Forrest Estate 2001 Riesling (Marlborough) $15. 85 *—J.C. (8/1/2004)*

Forrest Estate 2005 John Forrest Collection Riesling (Marlborough) $40. Lean and crisp, yet still holding on to a hint of residual sugar, this zesty Riesling boasts aromas and flavors of green apple, lime and honey, then turns chalky and tart on the finish. **87** *—J.C. (9/1/2007)*

Forrest Estate 2006 Sauvignon Blanc (Marlborough) $16. Starts off a bit slow, with scents of underripe peach or melon that are a bit unyielding, and a hint of matchstick-like, Fumé character. Green pepper and citrus flavors take firm hold of the slightly oily palate, then turn crisp and tart on the finish. **87** *—J.C. (7/1/2007)*

Forrest Estate 1997 Sauvignon Blanc (Marlborough) $15. 88 *—S.H. (8/1/1999)*

Forrest Estate 2005 Sauvignon Blanc (Marlborough) $16. 91 Editors' Choice *—J.C. (7/1/2006)*

Forrest Estate 2002 Sauvignon Blanc (Marlborough) $15. 90 Best Buy *—J.C. (4/1/2004)*

Forrest Estate 2001 Sauvignon Blanc (Marlborough) $19. 88 *—S.H. (11/15/2002)*

Forrest Estate 2004 John Forrest Collection Syrah (Hawke's Bay) $50. Big and full-bodied, boasting heaps of rather unformed fruit, framed by vanilla but not showing much complexity or silkiness. Instead, it's crisp and firm, and needs a few years to show its true colors. **87** *—J.C. (7/1/2007)*

FOXES ISLAND

Foxes Island 2004 Chardonnay (Marlborough) $37. 91 Editors' Choice *J.C. (12/1/2005)*

Foxes Island 2002 Chardonnay (Marlborough) $30. 87 *—J.C. (7/1/2005)*

Foxes Island 2001 Chardonnay (Marlborough) $32. 86 *—J.C. (8/1/2004)*

Foxes Island 2000 Chardonnay (Marlborough) $26. 85 *—J.C. (9/1/2003)*

Foxes Island 1999 Chardonnay (Marlborough) $21. 86 *—J.C. (7/1/2002)*

Foxes Island 1998 Chardonnay (Marlborough) $28. 83 *—J.C. (5/1/2001)*

Foxes Island 2004 Pinot Noir (Marlborough) $42. 84 *—J.C. (11/1/2006)*

Foxes Island 2002 Pinot Noir (Marlborough) $40. 88 *—J.C. (7/1/2005)*

Foxes Island 2001 Pinot Noir (Marlborough) $38. 89 *—J.C. (8/1/2004)*

Foxes Island 2000 Pinot Noir (Marlborough) $28. 87 *—J.C. (9/1/2003)*

Foxes Island 1999 Pinot Noir (Marlborough) $24. 88 *—J.C. (8/1/2002)*

Foxes Island 1998 Pinot Noir (Marlborough) $30. 81 *—J.C. (5/1/2001)*

Foxes Island 2005 Sauvignon Blanc (Marlborough) $25. 85 *—J.C. (11/1/2006)*

Foxes Island 2004 Sauvignon Blanc (Marlborough) $NA. 91 Editors' Choice *—J.C. (11/1/2006)*

FRAMINGHAM

Framingham 2000 Chardonnay (Marlborough) $16. 87 *—D.T. (12/15/2001)*

Framingham 2004 Pinot Noir (Marlborough) $26. 86 *—J.C. (12/1/2005)*

Framingham 2001 Classic Riesling (Marlborough) $15. 88 *—J.C. (8/1/2002)*

Framingham 2005 Sauvignon Blanc (Marlborough) $17. 86 *—J.C. (5/1/2006)*

Framingham 2001 Sauvignon Blanc (Marlborough) $14. 88 *—S.H. (11/15/2002)*

FREEFALL

Freefall 2006 Sauvignon Blanc (Marlborough) $15. An interesting mix of frankly vegetal notes—green bean and asparagus—with ripe melon and stone fruit. Doesn't sound that good, but it's plump and round in the mouth and somehow pulls together on the finish, which is crisp, refreshing and carries a peppery, arugula bite. **87** *—J.C. (11/1/2007)*

Freefall 2005 Sauvignon Blanc (Marlborough) $15. Solid Marlborough Savvy, with tropical aromas intertwined with grassy, herbal notes. It's medium-bodied, with melon and citrus flavors that reveal just a hint of bell pepper on the mouthwatering finish. Drink now. **88** *—J.C. (12/1/2007)*

FROMM WINERY

Fromm Winery 2002 Clayvin Vineyard Pinot Noir (Marlborough) $49. 88 *—J.C. (7/1/2005)*

Fromm Winery 2002 Fromm Vineyard Pinot Noir (Marlborough) $55. 87 *—J.C. (7/1/2005)*

Fromm Winery 2002 La Strada Pinot Noir (Marlborough) $36. 85 *—J.C. (7/1/2005)*

Fromm Winery 2004 La Strada Riesling (Marlborough) $31. 84 *—J.C. (7/1/2006)*

GIBBSTON VALLEY

Gibbston Valley 2001 Pinot Gris (Central Otago) $22. 88 *—S.H. (1/1/2002)*

Gibbston Valley 2000 Pinot Noir (Central Otago) $30. 88 *—S.H. (1/1/2002)*

GIESEN

Giesen NV Voyage Special Cuvée Brut Champagne Blend (Canterbury) $10. 86 Best Buy *—J.C. (5/1/2001)*

Giesen 1999 Reserve Barrel Selection Chardonnay (Marlborough) $20. 88 *—J.C. (5/1/2001)*

Giesen 1998 Reserve Barrel Selection Chardonnay (Canterbury) $20. 88 *—J.C. (5/1/2001)*

Giesen 1999 Pinot Noir (Canterbury) $16. *—J.C. (5/1/2001)*

Giesen 2005 Riesling (East Coast) $13. A blend of fruit sourced from Canterbury and Marlborough, Giesen's 2005 Riesling is an excellent value in off-dry Riesling. Ripe notes of melon and peach round out the wine's citrusy core, adding a bit of flesh to the zesty lemon and pineapple components. Drink now. **88 Best Buy** *—J.C. (9/1/2007)*

Giesen 2004 Riesling (East Coast) $13. 85 *—J.C. (7/1/2006)*

Giesen 2000 Riesling (Canterbury) $12. 86 *—J.C. (5/1/2001)*

Giesen 1999 Noble School Road Late Harvest Riesling (Canterbury) $18. 88 *—J.C. (5/1/2001)*

Giesen 2006 Sauvignon Blanc (Marlborough) $13. 85 *—J.C. (12/15/2006)*

Giesen 2005 Sauvignon Blanc (Marlborough) $12. 87 Best Buy *—J.C. (5/1/2006)*

Giesen 2000 Sauvignon Blanc (Marlborough) $10. 85 Best Buy *—J.C. (5/1/2001)*

Giesen 2003 Single Vineyard Selection Sauvignon Blanc (Marlborough) $20. 82 *(7/1/2005)*

GLADSTONE

Gladstone 2003 Auld Alliance Bordeaux Blend (Wairarapa) $20. 84 —*J.C. (7/1/2006)*

Gladstone 2004 Pinot Gris (Wairarapa) $20. 89 —*J.C. (2/1/2006)*

GLAZEBROOK

Glazebrook 2002 Chardonnay (Gisborne) $16. 85 —*J.C. (8/1/2004)*

Glazebrook 2000 Chardonnay (Gisborne) $11. 87 —*J.C. (7/1/2002)*

Glazebrook 2000 Merlot-Cabernet Sauvignon (Hawke's Bay) $18. 84 —*J.C. (12/15/2003)*

Glazebrook 1999 Merlot-Cabernet Sauvignon (Hawke's Bay) $19. 87 —*J.C. (5/1/2001)*

Glazebrook 2003 Sauvignon Blanc (Marlborough) $14. 86 —*J.C. (8/1/2004)*

Glazebrook 2002 Sauvignon Blanc (Marlborough) $13. 88 Best Buy —*J.C. (9/1/2003)*

Glazebrook 2000 Sauvignon Blanc (Hawke's Bay) $12. 88 Best Buy —*J.C. (5/1/2001)*

GOLDWATER

Goldwater 1998 Bordeaux Blend (Waiheke Island) $60. 89 —*J.C. (5/1/2001)*

Goldwater 1997 Cabernet Sauvignon-Merlot (Waiheke Island) $60. 84 —*J.C. (12/15/2003)*

Goldwater 2002 Roseland Chardonnay (Marlborough) $24. 89 —*J.C. (4/1/2004)*

Goldwater 2001 Roseland Chardonnay (Marlborough) $22. 90 —*J.C. (9/1/2003)*

Goldwater 1999 Roseland Chardonnay (Central Otago) $27. 90 —*J.C. (5/1/2001)*

Goldwater 1998 Roseland Chardonnay (Marlborough) $20. 87 —*J.C. (10/1/2000)*

Goldwater 2002 Zell Chardonnay (Waiheke Island) $40. 90 —*J.C. (8/1/2004)*

Goldwater 2000 Zell Chardonnay (Waiheke Island) $40. 89 —*D.T. (12/15/2001)*

Goldwater 2002 Esslin Merlot (Waiheke Island) $100. 86 —*J.C. (7/1/2005)*

Goldwater 1999 Esslin Merlot (Waiheke Island) $98. 87 —*J.C. (12/15/2003)*

Goldwater 1998 Esslin Merlot (Waiheke Island) $99. 87 —*J.C. (5/1/2001)*

Goldwater 2007 Sauvignon Blanc (Marlborough) $20. Less flamboyant and herbal than many of its brethren, Goldwater's 2007 Sauvignon Blanc features grapefruit and gooseberry aromas and flavors, a soft, lush mouthfeel and a minerally, textured finish. **88** —*J.C. (12/31/2007)*

Goldwater 2006 Sauvignon Blanc (Marlborough) $18. Light and a bit lacking in concentration, but this wine makes up for that with fun, fruit-forward flavors. Tropical fruit—including hints of mango and banana—lead the way, backed by fresh gooseberries. Certainly, this is easy to drink. **86** —*J.C. (5/1/2007)*

Goldwater 2005 Sauvignon Blanc (Marlborough) $20. 84 —*J.C. (5/1/2006)*

Goldwater 2000 Sauvignon Blanc (Marlborough) $20. 89 —*J.C. (5/1/2001)*

Goldwater 2002 Dog Point Sauvignon Blanc (Marlborough) $20. 89 —*J.C. (9/1/2003)*

Goldwater 2001 Dog Point Sauvignon Blanc (Marlborough) $20. 85 *(8/1/2002)*

Goldwater 2004 New Dog Sauvignon Blanc (Marlborough) $20. 84 *(7/1/2005)*

Goldwater 2003 New Dog Sauvignon Blanc (Marlborough) $20. 89 —*J.M. (4/1/2004)*

GOOSE BAY

Goose Bay 2006 Kosher Sauvignon Blanc (Marlborough) $18. Marginally better than last year's bottling, this kosher Kiwi is a touch too vegetal, with scents of cooked green beans intruding on the nectarine and honey aromas. Tart and lemony on the finish. **82** —*J.C. (4/1/2007)*

GRAVITAS

Gravitas 2004 Saint Arnaud's Vineyard Reserve Chardonnay (Marlborough) $20. 85 —*J.C. (11/1/2006)*

Gravitas 2005 Pinot Noir (Marlborough) $20. 82 —*J.C. (12/15/2006)*

Gravitas 2005 Saint Arnaud's Vineyard Sauvignon Blanc (Marlborough) $NA. 89 —*J.C. (5/1/2006)*

GREENHOUGH

Greenhough 2004 Chardonnay (Nelson) $20. 87 —*J.C. (12/15/2006)*

Greenhough 2004 Pinot Noir (Nelson) $25. 85 —*J.C. (12/15/2006)*

Greenhough 2000 Riesling (Nelson) $12. 86 —*M.S. (12/15/2001)*

Greenhough 2000 Sauvignon Blanc (Nelson) $12. 82 —*M.M. (12/15/2001)*

GROVE MILL

Grove Mill 2001 Chardonnay (Marlborough) $18. 87 —*J.C. (9/1/2003)*

Grove Mill 1999 Chardonnay (Marlborough) $18. 86 —*J.C. (5/1/2001)*

Grove Mill 2006 Pinot Gris (Marlborough) $20. Soft and honeyed, with ultraripe apples and mild citrus fruits sharing the spotlight. There's some residual sugar, suggesting a match with Asian dishes, or perhaps using it as an apéritif. **86** —*J.C. (12/31/2007)*

Grove Mill 2005 Pinot Gris (Marlborough) $20. 88 —*J.C. (2/1/2006)*

Grove Mill 2002 Pinot Gris (Marlborough) $18. 86 —*J.C. (9/1/2003)*

Grove Mill 2000 Pinot Gris (Marlborough) $19. 86 —*J.C. (5/1/2001)*

Grove Mill 2005 Pinot Noir (Marlborough) $23. Abnormally structured for a Pinot Noir from this producer, with firm tannins and crisp acids that highlight the wine's cola and sour plum flavors. **86** —*J.C. (11/1/2007)*

Grove Mill 2004 Pinot Noir (Marlborough) $25. 82 —*J.C. (12/1/2005)*

Grove Mill 2002 Pinot Noir (Marlborough) $23. 89 Editors' Choice —*J.C. (8/1/2004)*

Grove Mill 2001 Pinot Noir (Marlborough) $23. 90 —*J.C. (9/1/2003)*

Grove Mill 1999 Pinot Noir (Marlborough) $27. 86 —*J.C. (5/1/2001)*

Grove Mill 2004 Wairau Valley Reserve Pinot Noir (Marlborough) $30. 86 —*J.C. (11/1/2006)*

Grove Mill 2005 Riesling (Marlborough) $17. 86 —*J.C. (7/1/2006)*

Grove Mill 2002 Riesling (Marlborough) $15. 89 —*J.C. (8/1/2004)*

Grove Mill 2001 Riesling (Marlborough) $15. 84 —*J.C. (8/1/2003)*

Grove Mill 2000 Riesling (Marlborough) $16. 88 —*J.C. (5/1/2001)*

Grove Mill 2006 Sauvignon Blanc (Marlborough) $17. This widely available brand continues to turn out reliable bottlings vintage after vintage. The 2006 Sauvignon Blanc features restrained gooseberry and peach aromatics, then turns up the stone-fruit volume on the palate and adds some slightly pithy citrus notes. **86** —*J.C. (11/1/2007)*

Grove Mill 2005 Sauvignon Blanc (Marlborough) $16. 86 —*J.C. (5/1/2006)*

Grove Mill 2002 Sauvignon Blanc (Marlborough) $17. 85 —*J.C. (9/1/2003)*

Grove Mill 2000 Sauvignon Blanc (Marlborough) $17. 87 —*J.C. (5/1/2001)*

Grove Mill 2005 17 Valley Reserve Sauvignon Blanc (Marlborough) $22. 87 —*J.C. (11/1/2006)*

GUNN ESTATE

Gunn Estate 1998 Skeetfield Chardonnay (Ohiti Valley) $17. 84 —*J.C. (5/1/2001)*

Gunn Estate 1998 Woolshed Merlot-Cabernet Sauvignon (Ohiti Valley) $17. 86 —*J.C. (5/1/2001)*

Gunn Estate 2006 Sauvignon Blanc (New Zealand) $15. The winery is located in Hawke's Bay, but the label doesn't make clear the fruit sourcing for this wine, which is a bit of an odd bird. Some sour lime and green vegetable notes vie with honey on the palate, ending on a heavy note. Probably past its "best by" date. **83** —*J.C. (12/31/2007)*

Gunn Estate 2006 Skippers Pool Sauvignon Blanc (Marlborough) $18. Leafy and herbal on the nose, with complementary flavors of crushed tomato leaf, melon and fig. Despite the green notes, it shows reasonably high alcohol and ample weight on the palate, finishing long. Drink now. **89** —*J.C. (9/1/2007)*

Gunn Estate 2005 Silistria Syrah (Hawke's Bay) $28. Another promising Syrah from Hawke's Bay, this is a rich, velvety wine, if somewhat wood-dominated at this stage of its development. The 2005 Silistria Syrah boasts scents of toast and cedar, then adds flavors of cola and baking spices, ending with a hint of licorice. Ready to drink now. **88** —*J.C. (7/1/2007)*

GYPSY DANCER

Gypsy Dancer 2004 Pinot Noir (Central Otago) $40. 87 —*J.C. (12/1/2005)*

Gypsy Dancer 2003 Gibbston Home Estate Vineyard Pinot Noir (Central Otago) $50. 88 —*J.C. (7/1/2005)*

HATTON ESTATE

Hatton Estate 2003 Carsons Cabernets Cabernet Blend (Hawke's Bay) $25. 82 —*J.C. (12/15/2006)*

Hatton Estate 2005 EC2 Gimblett Gravels Chardonnay (Hawke's Bay) $20. 86 —*J.C. (12/15/2006)*

HAWKDON RISE

Hawkdon Rise 2001 Red Barnais Alexandra Pinot Noir (Central Otago) $40. 86 —*J.C. (9/1/2003)*

HERZOG

Herzog 1999 Bordeaux Blend (Marlborough) $45. 85 —*J.C. (4/1/2004)*

Herzog 2001 Chardonnay (Marlborough) $30. 88 —*J.C. (4/1/2004)*

Herzog 2001 Montepulciano-Cabernet Fanc Montepulciano (Marlborough) $34. 86 —*J.C. (4/1/2004)*

Herzog 2002 Pinot Noir (Marlborough) $35. 83 —*J.C. (7/1/2005)*

HIGHFIELD ESTATE

Highfield Estate 2001 Pinot Noir (Marlborough) $23. 86 —*J.C. (8/1/2004)*

Highfield Estate 1998 Riesling (Marlborough) $12. 87 —*S.H. (8/1/1999)*

Highfield Estate 2004 Sauvignon Blanc (Marlborough) $20. 89 *(7/1/2005)*

Highfield Estate 2002 Sauvignon Blanc (Marlborough) $18. 89 —*J.C. (9/1/2003)*

Highfield Estate 2001 Sauvignon Blanc (Marlborough) 90 —*S.H. (11/15/2002)*

Highfield Estate 1998 Elstree Cuvée Brut Sparkling Blend (Marlborough) $30. 87 —*M.S. (6/1/2003)*

HOLMES

Holmes 2003 Pinot Noir (Nelson) $25. 84 —*J.C. (12/1/2005)*

HOUSE OF NOBILO

House of Nobilo 1998 Fall Harvest Chardonnay (Gisborne) $12. 90 Best Buy —*S.H. (8/1/1999)*

House of Nobilo 2004 Regional Collection Chardonnay (East Coast) $12. 87 Best Buy —*J.C. (7/1/2005)*

House of Nobilo 2005 Icon Pinot Gris (Marlborough) $22. 88 —*J.C. (2/1/2006)*

House of Nobilo 2004 Icon Pinot Gris (Marlborough) $20. 87 —*J.C. (7/1/2005)*

House of Nobilo 2002 Icon Pinot Noir (Marlborough) $20. 88 —*J.C. (4/1/2004)*

House of Nobilo 2005 Icon Riesling (Marlborough) $20. 84 —*J.C. (11/1/2006)*

House of Nobilo 2001 Fall Harvest Sauvignon Blanc (Marlborough) $10. 85 Best Buy —*D.T. (12/15/2001)*

House of Nobilo 2000 Fall Harvest Sauvignon Blanc (Marlborough) $10. 86 Best Buy —*J.C. (5/1/2001)*

House of Nobilo 1998 Fall Harvest Sauvignon Blanc (Marlborough) $11. 88 Best Buy —*S.H. (8/1/1999)*

House of Nobilo 2006 Icon Sauvignon Blanc (Marlborough) $22. A solid effort, but given the resources of the parent company, there's no reason why this couldn't be better. passionfruit and grapefruit aromas lead off, followed by modest peach and melon flavors that finish sternly citric and somewhat green. Imported by Pacific Wine Partners. 86 —*J.C. (7/1/2007)*

House of Nobilo 2005 Icon Sauvignon Blanc (Marlborough) $20. 89 *(3/1/2006)*

House of Nobilo 2004 Icon Sauvignon Blanc (Marlborough) $20. 85 *(7/1/2005)*

House of Nobilo 2006 Regional Collection Sauvignon Blanc (Marlborough) $12. This is crisp, stylish Marlborough SB. Markedly pungent on the nose, but then it settles down a bit to offer a blend of pink grapefruit and gooseberry fruit with some leafy, herbal nuances. Clean and fresh on the finish. Drink now. 89 Best Buy —*J.C. (3/1/2007)*

HUIA

Huia 2001 Chardonnay (Marlborough) $19. 87 —*J.C. (4/1/2004)*

Huia 2003 Gewürztraminer (Marlborough) $19. 85 —*J.C. (7/1/2005)*

Huia 2002 Gewürztraminer (Marlborough) $17. 87 —*J.C. (9/1/2003)*

Huia 2004 Pinot Gris (Marlborough) $19. 86 —*J.C. (7/1/2005)*

Huia 2003 Pinot Noir (Marlborough) $26. 90 —*J.C. (12/1/2005)*

Huia 2002 Pinot Noir (Marlborough) $27. 86 —*J.C. (8/1/2004)*

Huia 2001 Pinot Noir (Marlborough) $24. 83 —*J.C. (9/1/2003)*

Huia 2000 Pinot Noir (Marlborough) $24. 90 —*J.C. (8/1/2002)*

Huia 2004 Riesling (Marlborough) $18. 84 —*J.C. (7/1/2005)*

Huia 2002 Riesling (Marlborough) $15. 89 —*J.C. (8/1/2003)*

Huia 2004 Sauvignon Blanc (Marlborough) $18. 87 —*J.C. (7/1/2005)*

Huia 2003 Sauvignon Blanc (Marlborough) $18. 91 Editors' Choice —*J.C. (4/1/2004)*

Huia 2001 Sauvignon Blanc (Marlborough) $16. 86 *(8/1/2002)*

Huia 2000 Brut Sparkling Blend (Marlborough) $33. 83 —*J.C. (6/1/2005)*

HUNTAWAY

Huntaway 1998 Reserve Limited Edition Bordeaux Blend (North Island) $15. 87 —*J.C. (5/1/2001)*

Huntaway 1998 Reserve Chardonnay (North Island) $15. 82 —*J.C. (5/1/2001)*

HUNTER'S

Hunter's 1996 Chardonnay (Marlborough) $21. 90 —*S.H. (8/1/1999)*

Hunter's 2003 Pinot Noir (Marlborough) $18. 87 —*J.C. (12/1/2005)*

Hunter's 2005 Sauvignon Blanc (Marlborough) $15. 86 —*J.C. (5/1/2006)*

Hunter's 2002 Sauvignon Blanc (Marlborough) $19. 88 —*J.C. (9/1/2003)*

Hunter's 1999 Sauvignon Blanc (Marlborough) $12. 90 —*S.H. (6/1/2001)*

ISABEL ESTATE

Isabel Estate 1999 Chardonnay (Marlborough) $22. 89 —*J.C. (5/1/2001)*

Isabel Estate 1997 Chardonnay (Marlborough) $20. 91 —*S.H. (8/1/1999)*

Isabel Estate 2006 Pinot Gris (Marlborough) $22. Not terrible aromatic, and the flavors are somewhat austere as well, offering little more than underripe melon and peach notes. Clean and stony, with hints of apple creeping in on the finish. 84 —*J.C. (11/1/2007)*

Isabel Estate 2005 Pinot Gris (Marlborough) $22. 88 —*J.C. (2/1/2006)*

Isabel Estate 2000 Pinot Gris (Marlborough) $16. 87 —*J.C. (5/1/2001)*

Isabel Estate 2004 Pinot Noir (Marlborough) $29. 82 —*J.C. (11/1/2006)*

Isabel Estate 2001 Pinot Noir (Marlborough) $30. 86 —*J.C. (9/1/2003)*

Isabel Estate 1999 Pinot Noir (Marlborough) $26. 90 Editors' Choice —*J.C. (5/1/2001)*

Isabel Estate 2000 Riesling (Marlborough) $18. 90 —*J.C. (5/1/2001)*

Isabel Estate 2006 Sauvignon Blanc (Marlborough) $22. This label has been a reliable source of Marlborough Sauvignon for years, and the 2006 is on form, offering bold grapefruit and passionfruit aromas. Melon and fig join on the palate, underscored by a touch of grassiness. Soft, round and easy to drink, this is a summertime staple. 88 —*J.C. (7/1/2007)*

Isabel Estate 2005 Sauvignon Blanc (Marlborough) $22. 89 —*J.C. (9/1/2006)*

Isabel Estate 2004 Sauvignon Blanc (Marlborough) $21. 91 Editors' Choice *(7/1/2005)*

Isabel Estate 2002 Sauvignon Blanc (Marlborough) $20. 88 —*J.C. (9/1/2003)*

Isabel Estate 2001 Sauvignon Blanc (Marlborough) $18. 92 —*S.H. (11/15/2002)*

Isabel Estate 2000 Sauvignon Blanc (Marlborough) $18. 89 —*J.C. (5/1/2001)*

Isabel Estate 1998 Sauvignon Blanc (Marlborough) $18. 89 —*S.H. (8/1/1999)*

Isabel Estate 1999 Noble Sauvage Sauvignon Blanc (Marlborough) $35. 92 —*J.C. (5/1/2001)*

JACKSON ESTATE

Jackson Estate 1999 Chardonnay (Marlborough) $15. 84 —*J.C. (9/1/2003)*

Jackson Estate 1998 Reserve Chardonnay (Marlborough) $25. 84 —*J.C. (5/1/2001)*

Jackson Estate 2005 Shelter Belt Chardonnay (Marlborough) $18. 87 —*J.C. (12/15/2006)*

Jackson Estate 2003 Unoaked Chardonnay (Marlborough) $16. 86 —*J.C. (7/1/2006)*

Jackson Estate 2002 Unoaked Chardonnay (Marlborough) $15. 85 —*J.C. (9/1/2003)*

Jackson Estate 2001 Unoaked Chardonnay (Marlborough) $15. 82 —*J.C. (11/15/2002)*

Jackson Estate 2000 Pinot Noir (Marlborough) $30. 87 —*M.S. (12/15/2001)*

Jackson Estate 2005 Vintage Widow Pinot Noir (Marlborough) $23. 89 —*J.C. (12/15/2006)*

Jackson Estate 2000 Dry Riesling (Marlborough) $15. 87 —*J.C. (8/1/2003)*

Jackson Estate 1999 Dry Riesling (Marlborough) $15. 86 —*J.C. (5/1/2001)*

Jackson Estate 2005 Sauvignon Blanc (Marlborough) $20. 90 Editors' Choice *—J.C. (5/1/2006)*

Jackson Estate 2004 Sauvignon Blanc (Marlborough) $13. 85 *—J.C. (7/1/2005)*

Jackson Estate 2003 Sauvignon Blanc (Marlborough) $17. 90 *—J.C. (8/1/2004)*

Jackson Estate 2002 Sauvignon Blanc (Marlborough) $17. 90 Editors' Choice *—J.C. (9/1/2003)*

Jackson Estate 2000 Sauvignon Blanc (Marlborough) $15. 85 *—J.C. (5/1/2001)*

KAHURANGI

Kahurangi 2004 Mt. Arthur Chardonnay (Moutere) $22. 89 *—J.C. (5/1/2006)*

Kahurangi 2004 Unwooded Chardonnay (Nelson) $17. 87 *—J.C. (5/1/2006)*

Kahurangi 2004 Moutere Gewürztraminer (Nelson) $24. 87 *—J.C. (5/1/2006)*

Kahurangi 2004 Pinot Noir (Nelson) $24. 84 *—J.C. (12/1/2005)*

Kahurangi 2003 Late Harvest Riesling (Moutere) $20. 92 *—J.C. (5/1/2006)*

Kahurangi 2004 Old Vines Riesling (Moutere) $20. 84 *—J.C. (5/1/2006)*

Kahurangi 2004 Sauvignon Blanc (Nelson) $18. 85 *—J.C. (5/1/2006)*

KAIKOURA

Kaikoura 2002 Sauvignon Blanc (Marlborough) $14. 87 *—J.C. (9/1/2003)*

KATHY LYNSKEY

Kathy Lynskey 2005 Godfrey Reserve Chardonnay (Marlborough) $29. Shows good concentration of tropical and citrus fruit, but also a heavy veneer of vanillin oak, ending on notes of tangerine and slightly bitter roasted coffee. It's still a good wine, and if your preferences run toward dark, oaky flavors on the finish, you may like it more than this. 86 *—J.C. (12/1/2007)*

Kathy Lynskey 2004 Godfrey Reserve Chardonnay (Marlborough) $29. 90 *—J.C. (7/1/2006)*

Kathy Lynskey 2003 Godfrey Reserve Chardonnay (Marlborough) $29. 87 *—J.C. (7/1/2005)*

Kathy Lynskey 2006 Single Vineyard Gewürztraminer (Marlborough) $24. An oily, weighty rendition of Gewürztraminer, with proper varietal aromas of pear and spice. Yet this isn't terribly aromatic or fruity, being more about texture and a unique peppery, nasturtium-like spice. Seems almost dry, with a touch of alcoholic warmth on the finish. Drink now. 89 *—J.C. (11/1/2007)*

Kathy Lynskey 2004 Single Vineyard Gewürztraminer (Marlborough) $25. 85 *—J.C. (7/1/2005)*

Kathy Lynskey 2005 15 Rows Reserve Merlot (Marlborough) $45. In contrast to the highly successful 2004, this wine shows some of the slightly sour, rhubarby notes that can mar Marlborough Merlot. The tart cherry flavors are not without appeal, but lack richness and ripeness. 84 *—J.C. (5/1/2007)*

Kathy Lynskey 2004 15 Rows Reserve Merlot (Marlborough) $45. 90 *—J.C. (11/1/2006)*

Kathy Lynskey 2006 Single Vineyard Pinot Gris (Marlborough) $25. Given the richness and weight of Lynskey's 2006 Gewürztraminer, the freshness of this Pinot Gris is a bit of a surprise. It's off-dry and effusively fruity in style, with pineapple, peach and melon all playing roles. Good as a cocktail sipper. 88 *—J.C. (11/1/2007)*

Kathy Lynskey 2005 Single Vineyard Pinot Gris (Marlborough) $25. 85 *—J.C. (11/1/2006)*

Kathy Lynskey 2004 Single Vineyard Pinot Gris (Marlborough) $25. 87 *—J.C. (7/1/2005)*

Kathy Lynskey 2005 Block 36 Reserve Pinot Noir (Marlborough) $39. This is a full-bodied, rather muscular Pinot Noir, with some resinous or medicinal hints on the nose and chunky cherry and chocolate flavors. Picks up a citrusy tang on the finish. 86 *—J.C. (3/1/2007)*

Kathy Lynskey 2004 Block 36 Reserve Pinot Noir (Marlborough) $39. 85 *—J.C. (7/1/2006)*

Kathy Lynskey 2003 Block 36 Reserve Pinot Noir (Marlborough) $39. 86 *—J.C. (12/1/2005)*

Kathy Lynskey 2006 Vineyard Select Sauvignon Blanc (Marlborough) $19. This wine is herbal and dangerously close to vegetal, without the accompanying rich fruit needed to completely balance it. A slightly oily, heavy texture gives the impression of weight and richness, but the fruit seems quiescent. 84 *—J.C. (3/1/2007)*

Kathy Lynskey 2005 Vineyard Select Sauvignon Blanc (Marlborough) $19. 88 *—J.C. (5/1/2006)*

Kathy Lynskey 2004 Vineyard Select Sauvignon Blanc (Marlborough) $19. 90 Editors' Choice *—J.C. (7/1/2005)*

KEMBLEFIELD

Kemblefield 2002 Winemakers Signature Cabernet Sauvignon-Merlot (Hawke's Bay) $12. 81 *—J.C. (5/1/2006)*

Kemblefield 2002 Distinction Chardonnay (Hawke's Bay) $16. 87 *—J.C. (5/1/2006)*

Kemblefield 2004 Winemakers Signature Chardonnay (Hawke's Bay) $13. 87 *—J.C. (5/1/2006)*

Kemblefield 2004 Distinction Gewürztraminer (Hawke's Bay) $14. 86 *—J.C. (5/1/2006)*

Kemblefield 2002 Reserve Malbec-Merlot (Hawke's Bay) $16. 87 *—J.C. (5/1/2006)*

Kemblefield 2002 Distinction Merlot (Hawke's Bay) $14. 86 *—J.C. (5/1/2006)*

Kemblefield 2005 Distinction Pinot Gris (Hawke's Bay) $15. 87 *—J.C. (2/1/2006)*

Kemblefield 2005 Winemakers Signature Sauvignon Blanc (Hawke's Bay) $14. 88 Best Buy *—J.C. (5/1/2006)*

Kemblefield 2004 Distinction Sémillon (Hawke's Bay) $16. 86 *—J.C. (5/1/2006)*

Kemblefield 2002 Reserve Zinfandel (Hawke's Bay) $25. 90 *—J.C. (5/1/2006)*

KENNEDY POINT

Kennedy Point 2006 Sauvignon Blanc (Marlborough) $22. This is a round, mouthfilling Marlborough Sauvignon, with clean scents of grasses, passionfruit and hints of melon and peach, but it lacks flavor intensity despite its size, coming off as slightly lacking concentration. It's nice, but needs more intensity to shine. 85 *—J.C. (3/1/2007)*

KIM CRAWFORD

Kim Crawford 2000 Tané Bordeaux Blend (Hawke's Bay) $25. 90 *—J.C. (5/1/2006)*

Kim Crawford 1999 Tané Cabernet Franc (Hawke's Bay) $30. 89 *—J.C. (5/1/2001)*

Kim Crawford 1996 Rory Brut Champagne Blend (Marlborough) $NA. 87 *—J.C. (5/1/2001)*

Kim Crawford 1999 Pia Chardonnay (Hawke's Bay) $30. 90 *—J.C. (5/1/2001)*

Kim Crawford 2000 Tietjen Chardonnay (Gisborne) $20. 91 Editors' Choice *—J.C. (5/1/2001)*

Kim Crawford 2004 Tietjen-Briant Chardonnay (Gisborne) $25. 89 *—J.C. (5/1/2006)*

Kim Crawford 2005 Unoaked Chardonnay (Marlborough) $17. 84 *—J.C. (11/1/2006)*

Kim Crawford 2002 Unoaked Chardonnay (Marlborough) $18. 85 *—J.C. (4/1/2004)*

Kim Crawford 2000 Unoaked Chardonnay (Marlborough) $17. 88 *—J.C. (5/1/2001)*

Kim Crawford 1999 Unoaked Chardonnay (Marlborough) $15. 89 *—M.S. (10/1/2000)*

Kim Crawford 1998 Unoaked Chardonnay (Marlborough) $15. 90 *(11/15/1999)*

Kim Crawford 2002 Merlot (East Coast) $18. 84 *—S.H. (1/1/2002)*

Kim Crawford 1999 Te Awanga Merlot (Hawke's Bay) $21. 88 *—J.C. (5/1/2001)*

Kim Crawford 2005 Pinot Gris (Marlborough) $17. 87 *—J.C. (11/1/2006)*

Kim Crawford 2004 Pinot Gris (Marlborough) $17. 88 *—J.C. (7/1/2005)*

Kim Crawford 2000 Boyzown Vineyard Pinot Gris (Marlborough) $18. 88 *—J.C. (5/1/2001)*

Kim Crawford 2006 Pinot Noir (Marlborough) $17. It's a simple, fruit-driven Pinot, but it's well done in its idiom, with black cherry fruit carried by a plump mouthfeel and supple tannins. Finishes crisp, making it versatile at the table and worth trying with salmon or tuna. Drink now. 86 *—J.C. (5/1/2007)*

Kim Crawford 2005 Pinot Noir (Marlborough) $17. 89 *—J.C. (11/1/2006)*

Kim Crawford 2004 Pinot Noir (Marlborough) $17. 86 *—J.C. (12/1/2005)*

Kim Crawford 2002 Pinot Noir (Marlborough) $14. 86 *—J.C. (4/1/2004)*

Kim Crawford 2000 Pinot Noir (Hawke's Bay) $NA. 87 *—J.C. (5/1/2001)*

Kim Crawford 2000 Anderson Vineyard Pinot Noir (Marlborough) $35. 90 —*M.S. (12/15/2001)*

Kim Crawford 2006 Dry Riesling (Marlborough) $17. A stalwart of the New Zealand Riesling firmament, Kim Crawford's 2006 version is a solid effort that boasts some beautiful pink-grapefruit aromas and flavors. Ultimately, this lacks a bit of complexity, but it nicely balances sugar and acid in a plump, easy-to-drink wine with no hard edges. **87** —*J.C. (9/1/2007)*

Kim Crawford 2004 Dry Riesling (Marlborough) $17. 87 —*J.C. (12/1/2005)*

Kim Crawford 2000 Dry Riesling Riesling (Marlborough) $16. 90 Editors' Choice —*J.C. (5/1/2001)*

Kim Crawford 2000 Reka Riesling (Marlborough) $NA. 90 —*J.C. (5/1/2001)*

Kim Crawford 2007 Sauvignon Blanc (Marlborough) $17. This iconic New Zealand winery's Sauvignon Blanc hits all the right notes in 2007, featuring lush stone-fruit flavors accented by less ripe notes of fresh herbs and capsicum. A fine apéritif, or try served with herb-seasoned shellfish. Drink now and over the next six months. Imported by Icon Estates. **89** —*J.C. (12/31/2007)*

Kim Crawford 2006 Sauvignon Blanc (Marlborough) $17. The Kim Crawford Sauvignon is a reliable wine, year in and year out. This vintage shows pungent, almost sweaty aromatics, backed by hints of stone fruit and melon. Medium-bodied in the mouth, where the flavors turn toward citrus while picking up chalky notes and a hint of pepper on the finish. Imported by Vincor USA. **87** —*J.C. (3/1/2007)*

Kim Crawford 2005 Sauvignon Blanc (Marlborough) $17. 87 —*J.C. (5/1/2006)*

Kim Crawford 2004 Sauvignon Blanc (Marlborough) $17. 88 —*J.C. (7/1/2005)*

Kim Crawford 2002 Sauvignon Blanc (Marlborough) $18. 89 —*S.H. (1/1/2002)*

Kim Crawford 2000 Sauvignon Blanc (Marlborough) $17. 87 —*J.C. (5/1/2001)*

Kim Crawford 1999 Sauvignon Blanc (Marlborough) $15. 92 —*L.W. (4/1/2000)*

Kim Crawford 1998 Sauvignon Blanc (Wairau) $15. 88 —*S.H. (8/1/1999)*

Kim Crawford 1998 Awatere Sauvignon Blanc (Awatere Valley) $20. 89 —*S.H. (8/1/1999)*

KINGSLEY ESTATE

Kingsley Estate 2000 Cabernet Sauvignon-Merlot (Hawke's Bay) $55. 88 —*J.C. (7/1/2005)*

KIWI

Kiwi 2004 White Table Wine Chardonnay (New Zealand) $14. 86 —*J.C. (5/1/2006)*

Kiwi 2004 Red Table Wine Pinot Noir (New Zealand) $15. 83 —*J.C. (7/1/2006)*

KONO

Kono 2005 Unoaked Chardonnay (Marlborough) $17. 86 —*J.C. (11/1/2006)*

Kono 2004 Unoaked Chardonnay (Marlborough) $15. 86 —*J.C. (7/1/2006)*

Kono 2005 Pinot Noir (Marlborough) $17. 84 —*J.C. (9/1/2006)*

Kono 2005 Sauvignon Blanc (Marlborough) $15. 84 —*J.C. (9/1/2006)*

Kono 2004 Sauvignon Blanc (Marlborough) $15. 88 —*J.C. (7/1/2006)*

KONRAD

Konrad 2005 Sauvignon Blanc (Marlborough) $18. 84 —*J.C. (12/15/2006)*

KONRAD & CONRAD

Konrad & Conrad 2001 Sauvignon Blanc (Marlborough) $15. 90 Editors' Choice *(8/1/2002)*

KOURA BAY

Koura Bay 2001 Whalesback Awatere Valley Sauvignon Blanc (Marlborough) $18. 85 —*S.H. (11/15/2002)*

KUMEU RIVER

Kumeu River 2005 Chardonnay (Kumeu) $33. Always more precocious than Kumeu River's Maté's Vineyard Chardonnay, this bottling nevertheless seems to be moving in a tighter, more restrained direction. The citrus and pineapple flavors are reined in by structure, finishing lean and citrusy, with just enough peach to provide flesh. Drink now–2012. **90** —*J.C. (12/1/2007)*

Kumeu River 2004 Chardonnay (Kumeu) $33. 91 Editors' Choice —*J.C. (7/1/2006)*

Kumeu River 2003 Chardonnay (Kumeu) $32. 89 —*J.C. (7/1/2005)*

Kumeu River 2002 Chardonnay (Kumeu) $26. 90 —*J.C. (4/1/2004)*

Kumeu River 1999 Chardonnay (Kumeu) $23. 90 Editors' Choice —*J.C. (5/1/2001)*

Kumeu River 1998 Chardonnay (Kumeu) $33. 91 —*J.C. (10/1/2000)*

Kumeu River 1997 Chardonnay (Kumeu) $25. 90 —*S.H. (8/1/1999)*

Kumeu River 2004 Matés Vineyard Chardonnay (Kumeu) $43. 90 —*J.C. (7/1/2006)*

Kumeu River 1997 Matés Vineyard Chardonnay (Kumeu) $40. 90 —*J.C. (10/1/2000)*

Kumeu River 2003 Mate's Vineyard Chardonnay (Kumeu) $37. 91 Editors' Choice —*J.C. (7/1/2005)*

Kumeu River 1999 Mate's Vineyard Chardonnay (Kumeu) $33. 92 —*J.C. (5/1/2001)*

Kumeu River 2006 Village Chardonnay (Kumeu) $19. Kumeu River's entry-level Chardonnay boasts plenty of tropical fruit and citrus flavors, all rolled into a fresh, crisp wine. It's a simple fruit cocktail, but with well-judged balance and zesty, food-friendly acids. **87** —*J.C. (12/1/2007)*

Kumeu River 2005 Village Chardonnay (Kumeu) $19. 85 —*J.C. (11/1/2006)*

Kumeu River 2004 Village Chardonnay (Kumeu) $19. 84 —*J.C. (9/1/2006)*

Kumeu River 2005 Pinot Gris (Kumeu) $19. 87 —*J.C. (11/1/2006)*

Kumeu River 2004 Pinot Gris (Kumeu) $19. 88 —*J.C. (2/1/2006)*

Kumeu River 2000 Pinot Gris (Kumeu) $15. 85 —*J.C. (5/1/2001)*

Kumeu River 2003 Pinot Noir (Kumeu) $30. 85 —*J.C. (11/1/2006)*

Kumeu River 2002 Pinot Noir (Kumeu) $30. 86 —*J.C. (6/6/2005)*

Kumeu River 1999 Pinot Noir (Kumeu) $30. 90 —*J.C. (5/1/2001)*

Kumeu River 1998 Pinot Noir (Kumeu) $18. 87 —*M.S. (10/1/2000)*

Kumeu River 1998 Melba Red Blend (Kumeu) $23. 90 —*J.C. (5/1/2001)*

Kumeu River 2006 Sauvignon Blanc (Marlborough) $19. A fresh, fruit-forward style, this wine offers bold passionfruit and gooseberry flavors with just a hint of nectarine. It's not terribly complex, but the refreshing flavors linger nicely on the finish. **87** —*J.C. (12/1/2007)*

Kumeu River 2004 Sauvignon Blanc (Marlborough) $19. 87 —*J.C. (7/1/2005)*

Kumeu River 1997 Sauvignon Blanc (Kumeu) $17. 88 —*S.H. (8/1/1999)*

KUSUDA

Kusuda 2003 C Pinot Noir (Martinborough) $NA. 89 —*J.C. (12/1/2005)*

Kusuda 2003 G Pinot Noir (Martinborough) $NA. 88 —*J.C. (12/1/2005)*

Kusuda 2002 Syrah (Martinborough) $NA. 84 —*J.C. (5/1/2006)*

LAKE CHALICE

Lake Chalice 2003 Pinot Noir (Marlborough) $20. 86 —*J.C. (7/1/2005)*

Lake Chalice 2002 Pinot Noir (Marlborough) $22. 87 —*J.C. (4/1/2004)*

Lake Chalice 2004 Riesling (Marlborough) $16. 87 —*J.C. (7/1/2005)*

Lake Chalice 2002 Falcon Vineyard Botrytised Riesling (Marlborough) $20. 84 —*J.C. (8/1/2003)*

Lake Chalice 2001 Falcon Vineyard Late Harvest Riesling (Marlborough) $17. 83 —*J.C. (8/1/2003)*

Lake Chalice 2006 New Zealand Falcon Riesling (Marlborough) $16. A plump, off-dry Riesling, this wine kicks off with scents of passionfruit as well as hints of honey and grapefruit. Honeyed citrus and green apple flavors take over on the palate, finishing long and clean. **87** —*J.C. (9/1/2007)*

Lake Chalice 2005 Sauvignon Blanc (Marlborough) $17. 88 —*J.C. (5/1/2006)*

Lake Chalice 2004 Sauvignon Blanc (Marlborough) $16. 86 —*J.C. (7/1/2005)*

Lake Chalice 2001 Sauvignon Blanc (Marlborough) $15. 84 *(8/1/2002)*

LAWSON'S DRY HILLS

Lawson's Dry Hills 2001 Chardonnay (Marlborough) $22. 87 —*J.C. (4/1/2004)*

Lawson's Dry Hills 2004 Gewürztraminer (Marlborough) $16. 90 Editors' Choice —*J.C. (7/1/2005)*

Lawson's Dry Hills 2002 Gewürztraminer (Marlborough) $15. 90 Best Buy —*J.C. (8/1/2004)*

Lawson's Dry Hills 2004 Pinot Noir (Marlborough) $22. 87 —*J.C. (12/1/2005)*

Lawson's Dry Hills 2002 Pinot Noir (Marlborough) $18. 88 —*J.C. (4/1/2004)*

Lawson's Dry Hills 2005 Sauvignon Blanc (Marlborough) $16. 90 Editors' Choice —*J.C. (5/1/2006)*

Lawson's Dry Hills 2004 Sauvignon Blanc (Marlborough) $16. 84 —*J.C. (7/1/2005)*

Lawson's Dry Hills 2003 Sauvignon Blanc (Marlborough) $16. 86 —*J.C. (8/1/2004)*

Lawson's Dry Hills 2002 Sauvignon Blanc (Marlborough) $16. 88 —*J.C. (4/1/2004)*

Lawson's Dry Hills 2001 Sauvignon Blanc (Marlborough) $16. 87 *(8/1/2002)*

LEGRYS

LeGrys 2000 Adam's Estate Pinot Noir (Marlborough) $26. 83 —*J.C. (9/1/2003)*

LeGrys 2001 Sauvignon Blanc (Marlborough) $17. 85 —*J.C. (9/1/2003)*

LINACRE LANE

Linacre Lane 2003 Pinot Noir (Martinborough) $NA. 83 —*J.C. (12/1/2005)*

LINDAUER

Lindauer NV Brut (New Zealand) $13. 85 —*J.C. (12/31/2004)*

LINDEN ESTATE

Linden Estate 2000 Merlot (Hawke's Bay) $13. 83 —*J.C. (12/15/2003)*

Linden Estate 2002 Sauvignon Blanc (Hawke's Bay) $11. 90 Best Buy —*J.C. (9/1/2003)*

LOBSTER KEY

Lobster Key 2004 Pinot Noir (East Coast) $14. 82 —*J.C. (7/1/2006)*

LONGRIDGE

Longridge 1999 Chardonnay (Hawke's Bay) $10. 81 —*J.C. (5/1/2001)*

Longridge 1998 Sauvignon Blanc (Hawke's Bay) $10. 89 Best Buy —*S.H. (8/1/1999)*

LYNSKEYS WAIRAU PEAKS

Lynskeys Wairau Peaks 2002 Chardonnay (Marlborough) $25. 90 —*J.C. (9/1/2003)*

Lynskeys Wairau Peaks 1999 Chardonnay (Marlborough) $20. 84 —*J.C. (5/1/2001)*

Lynskeys Wairau Peaks 2001 Reserve Chardonnay (Marlborough) $25. 87 —*J.C. (9/1/2003)*

Lynskeys Wairau Peaks 2002 Gewürztraminer (Marlborough) $18. 87 —*J.C. (9/1/2003)*

Lynskeys Wairau Peaks 2000 Gewürztraminer (Marlborough) $17. 87 —*J.C. (5/1/2001)*

Lynskeys Wairau Peaks 2003 Single Vineyard Gewürztraminer (Marlborough) $25. 85 —*J.C. (8/1/2004)*

Lynskeys Wairau Peaks 2002 15 Rows Reserve Merlot (Marlborough) $49. 87 —*J.C. (4/1/2004)*

Lynskeys Wairau Peaks 2001 Merlot (Marlborough) $45. 88 —*J.C. (12/15/2003)*

Lynskeys Wairau Peaks 2002 Pinot Noir (Marlborough) $33. 87 —*J.C. (4/1/2004)*

Lynskeys Wairau Peaks 2000 Pinot Noir (Marlborough) $33. 87 —*J.C. (8/1/2002)*

Lynskeys Wairau Peaks 1999 Pinot Noir (Marlborough) $33. 82 —*J.C. (5/1/2001)*

Lynskeys Wairau Peaks 2002 Sauvignon Blanc (Marlborough) $18. 86 —*J.C. (9/1/2003)*

Lynskeys Wairau Peaks 2001 Sauvignon Blanc (Marlborough) $17. 87 *(8/1/2002)*

Lynskeys Wairau Peaks 2000 Sauvignon Blanc (Marlborough) $17. 84 —*J.C. (5/1/2001)*

Lynskeys Wairau Peaks 2003 Vineyard Select Sauvignon Blanc (Marlborough) $19. 84 —*J.C. (8/1/2004)*

MAIN DIVIDE

Main Divide 2005 Chardonnay (Waipara Valley) $18. Starts with a blast of toasted nut aromas, but also hints of butter and citrus, then adds some lactic notes, Muscat-like spice and vanilla flavors jump into the mix before finishing with flavors of tangerines and roasted coffee. It's a bit oaky, but attractive nonetheless. Imported by Meadowbank Estates. **87** —*J.C. (12/1/2007)*

Main Divide 2002 Chardonnay (Waipara) $20. 84 —*J.C. (8/1/2004)*

Main Divide 2005 Pinot Noir (Waipara Valley) $23. From the makers of Pegasus Bay, this is a dark, plummy Pinot Noir that's plump and easygoing in the mouth. Hints of leather, chocolate and wintergreen spice it up a little, adding a mouthwatering freshness to the finish. Imported by Meadowbank Estates. **89** —*J.C. (12/1/2007)*

Main Divide 2004 Pinot Noir (Canterbury) $25. 86 —*J.C. (12/1/2005)*

Main Divide 2005 Riesling (New Zealand) $18. Sort of a second label from Pegasus Bay, Main Divide's 2005 Riesling is made in a slightly sweet style that recalls some weighty Rheingau spätlesen. Baked apple and clover-blossom honey are perked up by the addition of lime and petrol. Drink now. **88** —*J.C. (9/1/2007)*

Main Divide 2002 Sauvignon Blanc (Canterbury & Marlborough) $15. 86 —*J.C. (4/1/2004)*

MANA

Mana 2005 Pinot Noir (Marlborough) $15. A considerable step up from the mediocre 2004, this vintage of Mana Pinot Noir features a pleasant mix of savory and fruity flavors that includes hints of strawberries, cola, cinnamon and toast. It's fairly full in the mouth, but soft, with a hint of raisiny overripeness on the finish. **85** —*J.C. (3/1/2007)*

Mana 2004 Pinot Noir (Marlborough) $15. 81 —*J.C. (7/1/2006)*

MARGRAIN

Margrain 2003 Pinot Noir (Martinborough) $25. 86 —*J.C. (12/1/2005)*

MARLBOROUGH WINES

Marlborough Wines 2003 Pinot Noir (Marlborough) $23. 85 —*J.C. (12/1/2005)*

Marlborough Wines 2005 Sauvignon Blanc (Marlborough) $16. 84 —*J.C. (7/1/2006)*

Marlborough Wines 2003 Sauvignon Blanc (Marlborough) $16. 88 —*J.C. (7/1/2005)*

MARTINBOROUGH VINEYARD

Martinborough Vineyard 1997 Chardonnay (Martinborough) $26. 93 —*S.H. (8/1/1999)*

Martinborough Vineyard 2003 Pinot Noir (Martinborough) $40. 85 —*J.C. (12/1/2005)*

Martinborough Vineyard 2002 Pinot Noir (Martinborough) $NA. 88 —*J.C. (11/1/2006)*

Martinborough Vineyard 2001 Riesling (Martinborough) $15. 86 —*J.C. (8/1/2003)*

Martinborough Vineyard 1999 Late Harvest Riesling (Martinborough) $29. 93 —*J.C. (5/1/2001)*

MATAHIWI

Matahiwi 2004 Pinot Noir (Wairarapa) $NA. 86 —*J.C. (12/1/2005)*

Matahiwi 2004 Holly Pinot Noir (Wairarapa) $NA. 86 —*J.C. (12/1/2005)*

MATARIKI

Matariki 1999 Chardonnay (Hawke's Bay) $22. 89 —*J.C. (5/1/2001)*

Matariki 1997 Chardonnay (Hawke's Bay & Waipara) $23. 93 —*S.H. (8/1/1999)*

Matariki 1999 Merlot (Hawke's Bay) $25. 83 —*J.C. (5/1/2001)*

Matariki 2004 Pinot Noir (Hawke's Bay) $31. 86 —*J.C. (12/15/2006)*

Matariki 2001 Quintology Red Blend (Hawke's Bay) $33. 89 —*J.C. (8/1/2004)*

Matariki 2000 Quintology Red Blend (Hawke's Bay) $26. 86 —*J.C. (12/15/2003)*

Matariki 2000 Late Harvest Riesling (Hawke's Bay) $30. 87 —*J.C. (8/1/2003)*

Matariki 1997 Sauvignon Blanc (Hawke's Bay) $19. 88 —*S.H. (8/1/1999)*

Matariki 2005 Sauvignon Blanc (Hawke's Bay) $18. 84 —*J.C. (11/1/2006)*

Matariki 2004 Sauvignon Blanc (Hawke's Bay) $18. 90 —*J.C. (7/1/2005)*

Matariki 2003 Sauvignon Blanc (Hawke's Bay) $19. 87 —*J.C. (8/1/2004)*

Matariki 2002 Sauvignon Blanc (Hawke's Bay) $14. 84 —*J.C. (9/1/2003)*

Matariki 2001 Sauvignon Blanc (Hawke's Bay) $15. 91 —*S.H. (11/15/2002)*

Matariki 2000 Sauvignon Blanc (Hawke's Bay) $16. 87 —*J.C. (5/1/2001)*

Matariki 1999 Reserve Sauvignon Blanc (Hawke's Bay) $25. 90 —*J.C. (5/1/2001)*

Matariki 2001 Syrah (Hawke's Bay) $30. 89 —*J.C. (4/1/2004)*

Matariki 1999 Gimblett Road Syrah (Hawke's Bay) $30. 90 —*J.C. (5/1/2001)*

MATUA VALLEY

Matua Valley 1998 Bordeaux Blend (Hawke's Bay) $16. 87 *—J.C. (10/1/2000)*

Matua Valley 1996 Ararimu Bordeaux Blend (Hawke's Bay) $45. 86 *—J.C. (10/1/2000)*

Matua Valley 1998 Matheson Vineyard Bordeaux Blend (Hawke's Bay) $20. 87 *—J.C. (10/1/2000)*

Matua Valley 1999 Cabernet Sauvignon-Merlot (Hawke's Bay) $17. 84 *—J.C. (5/1/2001)*

Matua Valley 2001 Ararimu Cabernet Sauvignon-Merlot (Hawke's Bay) $23. 86 *—J.C. (12/15/2003)*

Matua Valley 1999 Matheson Vineyard Cabernet Sauvignon-Merlot (Hawke's Bay) $17. 89 *—J.C. (5/1/2001)*

Matua Valley 2004 Chardonnay (Gisborne) $12. 84 *—J.C. (12/1/2005)*

Matua Valley 2003 Chardonnay (Gisborne) $11. 86 *—J.C. (4/1/2004)*

Matua Valley 1999 Chardonnay (Eastern Bays) $15. 86 *—J.C. (5/1/2001)*

Matua Valley 1998 Ararimu Chardonnay (Gisborne) $45. 90 *—J.C. (5/1/2001)*

Matua Valley 2004 Judd Estate Chardonnay (Gisborne) $17. 86 *—J.C. (11/1/2006)*

Matua Valley 2003 Judd Estate Chardonnay (Gisborne) $17. 87 *—J.C. (5/1/2006)*

Matua Valley 2002 Judd Estate Chardonnay (Gisborne) $17. 89 *—J.C. (4/1/2004)*

Matua Valley 1999 Judd Estate Chardonnay (Gisborne) $20. 89 *—J.C. (5/1/2001)*

Matua Valley 1998 Judd Estate Chardonnay (Gisborne) $18. 89 *—J.C. (10/1/2000)*

Matua Valley 1997 Judd Estate Hand Picked Chardonnay (Gisborne) $40. 90 *—J.C. (10/1/2000)*

Matua Valley 1998 Judd Estate Innovator Handpicked Chardonnay (Gisborne) $45. 90 *—J.C. (5/1/2001)*

Matua Valley 1999 Matheson Vineyard Chardonnay (Hawke's Bay) $20. 88 *—J.C. (5/1/2001)*

Matua Valley 2002 Bullrush Merlot (Hawke's Bay) $20. 85 *—J.C. (4/1/2004)*

Matua Valley 2003 Bullrush Vineyard Merlot (Hawke's Bay) $20. 88 *—J.C. (5/1/2006)*

Matua Valley 1998 Smith Dartmoor Estate Merlot (Hawke's Bay) $18. 87 *—J.C. (5/1/2001)*

Matua Valley 1996 Smith-Dartmoor Estate Merlot (Hawke's Bay) $18. 82 *—J.C. (10/1/2000)*

Matua Valley 1998 Ararimu Merlot-Cabernet Sauvignon (Hawke's Bay) $44. 90 *—J.C. (5/1/2001)*

Matua Valley 2003 Matheson Merlot-Cabernet Sauvignon (Hawke's Bay) $NA. 86 *—J.C. (5/1/2006)*

Matua Valley 2000 Late Harvest Muscat (Eastern Bays) $13. 86 *—J.C. (5/1/2001)*

Matua Valley 1996 Late Harvest Muscat (Gisborne) $12. 86 *—J.C. (10/1/2000)*

Matua Valley 2004 Pinot Gris (Marlborough) $12. 87 Best Buy *—J.C. (7/1/2005)*

Matua Valley 2004 Pinot Noir (Marlborough) $15. 85 *—J.C. (12/1/2005)*

Matua Valley 2002 Pinot Noir (Marlborough) $11. 83 *—J.C. (8/1/2004)*

Matua Valley 2005 Estate Series Pinot Noir (Marlborough) $20. This New Zealand outpost of Foster's Wine Estates has turned in an impressive performance at an enviable price point. Cola, sassafras, vanilla and plum shadings all merge gracefully together in this full-bodied, seriously endowed Pinot that should drink well now and over the next few years. **89** *—J.C. (5/1/2007)*

Matua Valley 2004 Estate Series Pinot Noir (Marlborough) $20. 87 *—J.C. (11/1/2006)*

Matua Valley 2002 Ararimu Merlot-Syrah-Cabernet Red Blend (Hawke's Bay) $25. 88 *—J.C. (8/1/2004)*

Matua Valley 2006 Sauvignon Blanc (Marlborough) $12. More open and giving than the upscale Paretai bottling, with fruit that's forward and enjoyable, ranging from passionfruit to mango and from nectarine to melon. Sauvignon's trademark herbaceousness is here, but in the background, as an accent rather than as the centerpiece. **89 Best Buy** *—J.C. (5/1/2007)*

Matua Valley 2005 Sauvignon Blanc (Marlborough) $12. 88 Best Buy *—J.C. (12/1/2005)*

Matua Valley 2003 Sauvignon Blanc (Marlborough) $13. 88 Best Buy *—J.C. (4/1/2004)*

Matua Valley 2002 Sauvignon Blanc (Hawke's Bay) $11. 88 Best Buy *—S.H. (11/15/2002)*

Matua Valley 2000 Sauvignon Blanc (Hawke's Bay) $12. 85 *—J.C. (5/1/2001)*

Matua Valley 1999 Matheson Vineyard Sauvignon Blanc (Hawke's Bay) $15. 88 *—J.C. (5/1/2001)*

Matua Valley 2006 Paretai Sauvignon Blanc (Marlborough) $17. Paretai remains a bit of an extreme style, giving even more herbaceous and grassy flavors than many N.Z. Sauvignons. It's leaner, drier and more focused as well, with passionfruit upfront and strident lime notes on the finish. **88** *—J.C. (5/1/2007)*

Matua Valley 2005 Paretai Sauvignon Blanc (Marlborough) $17. 87 *—J.C. (7/1/2006)*

Matua Valley 2004 Paretai Sauvignon Blanc (Marlborough) $17. 84 *—J.C. (7/1/2005)*

Matua Valley 2003 Innovator Bullrush Syrah (Hawke's Bay) $NA. 85 *—J.C. (5/1/2006)*

Matua Valley 2004 Matheson Syrah (Hawke's Bay) $NA. 84 *—J.C. (5/1/2006)*

MAVEN

Maven 2006 Chardonnay (Marlborough) $18. Textbook New World Chard, blending tropical fruit with hints of toasty oak. It's medium-bodied, with flavors of pineapple and citrus touched with caramel and smoke, ending on a lingering note of grilled pineapple. **88** *—J.C. (12/1/2007)*

Maven 2005 Pinot Noir (Marlborough) $20. This dusty mélange of cherries, beets, herbs and mushrooms shows some complexity but also a slightly lean, tart profile. It finishes clean and fresh, with a hint of wintergreen. **83** *—J.C. (5/1/2007)*

Maven 2006 Sauvignon Blanc (Marlborough) $18. A bit sweaty and herbal on the nose, but the flavors are riper than that, leaning toward the melon and nectarine side of the Sauvignon spectrum. This wine is lean and a bit minerally in feel, with a clean, fresh finish. **85** *—J.C. (5/1/2007)*

Maven 2005 Sauvignon Blanc (Marlborough) $17. 85 *—J.C. (11/1/2006)*

MEBUS

Mebus 2000 Dakins Road Bordeaux Blend (Wairarapa) $25. 87 *—J.C. (12/15/2003)*

Mebus 2001 Dakins Road Cabernet-Merlot-Malbec Bordeaux Blend (Wairarapa) $21. 82 *—J.C. (5/1/2006)*

MILLS REEF

Mills Reef 1998 Elspeth Cabernet Sauvignon-Merlot (Hawke's Bay) $30. 90 *—J.C. (10/1/2000)*

Mills Reef 1999 Reserve Chardonnay (Hawke's Bay) $17. 84 *—J.C. (5/1/2001)*

Mills Reef 2000 Mere Road Elspeth Merlot (Hawke's Bay) $30. 93 Editors' Choice *—S.H. (11/15/2002)*

Mills Reef 2004 Reserve Merlot-Malbec (Hawke's Bay) $20. 85 *—J.C. (12/15/2006)*

Mills Reef 2002 Elspeth One Red Blend (Hawke's Bay) $35. 87 *—J.C. (8/1/2004)*

Mills Reef 2000 Elspeth One Red Blend (Hawke's Bay) $35. 94 Cellar Selection *—S.H. (11/15/2002)*

Mills Reef 1998 Sauvignon Blanc (Hawke's Bay) $13. 87 *—S.H. (8/1/1999)*

Mills Reef 2005 Reserve Sauvignon Blanc (Hawke's Bay) $15. 89 *—J.C. (12/15/2006)*

Mills Reef 2003 Reserve Sauvignon Blanc (Hawke's Bay) $14. 88 *—J.C. (8/1/2004)*

Mills Reef 2002 Reserve Sauvignon Blanc (Hawke's Bay) $14. . 87 *—J.C. (9/1/2003)*

Mills Reef 2001 Reserve Sauvignon Blanc (Hawke's Bay) $15. 88 *(8/1/2002)*

Mills Reef 2000 Reserve Sauvignon Blanc (Hawke's Bay) $14. 83 *—J.C. (5/1/2001)*

Mills Reef 1999 Reserve Sauvignon Blanc (Hawke's Bay) $13. 87 *—J.C. (10/1/2000)*

Mills Reef 1998 Reserve Sauvignon Blanc (Hawke's Bay) $13. 90 Best Buy *—L.W. (8/1/1999)*

Mills Reef 2002 Elspeth Syrah (Hawke's Bay) $NA. 87 *—J.C. (5/1/2006)*

Mills Reef 2001 Elspeth Syrah (Hawke's Bay) $29. 88 *—J.C. (4/1/2004)*

Mills Reef 2000 Mere Road Elspeth Syrah (Hawke's Bay) $30. 92 Editors' Choice *—S.H. (11/15/2002)*

Mills Reef 1999 Mere Road Vineyard Syrah (Hawke's Bay) $28. 89 *(11/1/2001)*

MONKEY BAY

Monkey Bay 2004 Chardonnay (Gisborne) $10. 84 *(3/1/2006)*

Monkey Bay 2006 Rosé Blend (East Coast) $11. This is mainly Merlot, although it does include bits of Malbec, Pinotage and Syrah in the blend. Smells of cinnamon-dusted citrus, then adds some berry flavors on the slightly creamy palate. There's a touch of sweetness on the finish. **84** *—J.C. (7/1/2007)*

Monkey Bay 2006 Sauvignon Blanc (Marlborough) $11. Produced in huge quantities, this mainstream Marlborough Sauvignon remains a good value, offering an easy introduction to thousands of American consumers. A slightly smoky, fumé character gives way to round, ripe flavors of stone fruit, melon and fig, finishing soft. Drink now. **86 Best Buy** *—J.C. (3/1/2007)*

Monkey Bay 2005 Sauvignon Blanc (Marlborough) $10. 84 *(3/1/2006)*

Monkey Bay 2004 Sauvignon Blanc (Marlborough) $10. 87 Best Buy *—J.C. (7/1/2005)*

MORWORTH ESTATE

Morworth Estate 2000 Chardonnay (Marlborough) $25. 83 *—J.C. (11/15/2002)*

Morworth Estate 1999 Pinot Noir (Canterbury) $NA. 82 *—J.C. (8/1/2002)*

Morworth Estate 1999 Riesling (Canterbury) $NA. 85 *—J.C. (8/1/2002)*

Morworth Estate 2001 Sauvignon Blanc (Marlborough) $11. 85 *—J.C. (9/1/2003)*

MOUNT CASS

Mount Cass 2004 Chardonnay (Waipara) $20. 91 Editors' Choice *—J.C. (5/1/2006)*

Mount Cass 2004 Late Harvest Chardonnay (Waipara) $20. 86 *—J.C. (5/1/2006)*

Mount Cass 2004 Unoaked Chardonnay (Waipara) $NA. 88 *—J.C. (5/1/2006)*

Mount Cass 2003 Pinot Noir (Waipara) $27. 87 *—J.C. (12/1/2005)*

Mount Cass 2002 Pinot Noir (Waipara) $NA. 85 *—J.C. (11/1/2006)*

Mount Cass 2004 Riesling (Waipara) $16. 87 *—J.C. (5/1/2006)*

Mount Cass 2004 Waipara Gravels Reserve Riesling (Waipara) $18. 89 *—J.C. (5/1/2006)*

Mount Cass 2004 Sauvignon Blanc (Waipara) $17. 88 *—J.C. (5/1/2006)*

Mount Cass 2004 Sauvignon Blanc (Marlborough) $15. 87 *—J.C. (5/1/2006)*

MOUNT EDWARD

Mount Edward 2003 Pinot Noir (Central Otago) $39. 89 *—J.C. (12/1/2005)*

MOUNT NELSON

Mount Nelson 2006 Sauvignon Blanc (Marlborough) $17. Pungent on the nose, this is even a touch garlicky, making it hard to warm up to. And that's too bad, because there appears to be some nicely rounded melon and fig flavors that struggle to emerge. **83** *—J.C. (11/1/2007)*

Mount Nelson 2005 Sauvignon Blanc (Marlborough) $16. 90 Editors' Choice *—J.C. (9/1/2006)*

Mount Nelson 2004 Sauvignon Blanc (Marlborough) $16. 88 *—J.C. (7/1/2005)*

MOUNT RILEY

Mount Riley 2001 Chardonnay (Marlborough) $13. 91 Best Buy *—S.H. (11/15/2002)*

Mount Riley 2005 Pinot Noir (Marlborough) $17. 87 *—J.C. (12/15/2006)*

Mount Riley 2004 Pinot Noir (South Island) $17. 87 *—J.C. (12/1/2005)*

Mount Riley 2001 Pinot Noir (Marlborough) $20. 87 *—J.C. (9/1/2003)*

Mount Riley 2005 Sauvignon Blanc (Marlborough) $13. 88 Best Buy *—J.C. (7/1/2006)*

Mount Riley 2004 Sauvignon Blanc (Marlborough) $16. 88 *—J.C. (7/1/2005)*

Mount Riley 2001 Sauvignon Blanc (Marlborough) $15. 90 Editors' Choice *(8/1/2002)*

MOUNTFORD

Mountford 1999 Chardonnay (Waipara) $25. 89 *—J.C. (7/1/2002)*

MT. DIFFICULTY

Mt. Difficulty 1999 Chardonnay (Central Otago) $17. 88 *—J.C. (5/1/2001)*

Mt. Difficulty 2003 Not imported Chardonnay (Central Otago) $NA. 88 *—J.C. (5/1/2006)*

Mt. Difficulty 2004 Pinot Gris (Central Otago) $24. 87 *—J.C. (5/1/2006)*

Mt. Difficulty 2000 Pinot Gris (Central Otago) $15. 88 Best Buy *—M.S. (12/15/2001)*

Mt. Difficulty 2003 Pinot Noir (Central Otago) $30. 88 *—J.C. (12/1/2005)*

Mt. Difficulty 1999 Pinot Noir (Central Otago) $24. 88 *—J.C. (5/1/2001)*

Mt. Difficulty 2004 Roaring Meg Pinot Noir (Central Otago) $20. 86 *—J.C. (12/1/2005)*

Mt. Difficulty 2003 Target Gully Pinot Noir (Central Otago) $80. 90 *—J.C. (12/1/2005)*

Mt. Difficulty 2000 Riesling (Central Otago) $15. 84 *—D.T. (12/15/2001)*

Mt. Difficulty 2004 Dry Riesling (Central Otago) $NA. 90 *—J.C. (5/1/2006)*

Mt. Difficulty 2004 Long Gully Riesling (Central Otago) $NA. 90 *—J.C. (5/1/2006)*

Mt. Difficulty 2004 Target Gully Riesling (Central Otago) $NA. 90 *—J.C. (5/1/2006)*

Mt. Difficulty 2004 Sauvignon Blanc (Central Otago) $19. 88 *—J.C. (5/1/2006)*

Mt. Difficulty 2001 Sauvignon Blanc (Central Otago) $16. 93 *—S.H. (11/15/2002)*

Mt. Difficulty 2000 Sauvignon Blanc (Central Otago) $13. 88 *—J.C. (5/1/2001)*

MUD HOUSE WINE COMPANY

Mud House Wine Company 2000 Chardonnay (Marlborough) $17. 86 *—J.C. (9/1/2003)*

Mud House Wine Company 1999 Black Swan Reserve Merlot (Marlborough) $25. 82 *—J.C. (12/15/2003)*

Mud House Wine Company 2001 Pinot Noir (Marlborough) $33. 85 *—J.C. (9/1/2003)*

Mud House Wine Company 2002 Sauvignon Blanc (Marlborough) $16. 83 *—J.C. (9/1/2003)*

MUDDY WATER

Muddy Water 2000 Chardonnay (Waipara) $20. 90 *—J.C. (7/1/2002)*

Muddy Water 2003 Pinot Noir (Waipara) $31. 84 *—J.C. (12/1/2005)*

Muddy Water 1999 Pinot Noir (Waipara) $25. 87 *—J.C. (5/1/2001)*

Muddy Water 2006 James Hardwick Riesling (Waipara) $21. A plump, round Riesling with honeyed pineapple aromas, Muddy Water's James Hardwick is made from nonbotrytized fruit so it retains a wonderfully clear citrus character. Melon and pineapple flavors give it some fat, but the long finish is dominated by peals of lime-ridden fruit. **89** *—J.C. (9/1/2007)*

MURDOCH JAMES

Murdoch James 2004 Pinot Noir (Martinborough) $20. 87 *—J.C. (12/1/2005)*

Murdoch James 2003 Salesyards Syrah (Martinborough) $33. 85 *—J.C. (5/1/2006)*

MURDOCH JAMES ESTATE

Murdoch James Estate 2002 Blue Rock Pinot Noir (Martinborough) $36. 85 *—J.C. (7/1/2005)*

Murdoch James Estate 2001 Waiata Pinot Noir (Martinborough) $27. 86 *—J.C. (9/1/2003)*

Murdoch James Estate 2002 Sauvignon Blanc (Martinborough) $17. 83 *—J.C. (9/1/2003)*

Murdoch James Estate 2001 Syrah (Martinborough) $27. 82 *—J.C. (12/15/2003)*

NAUTILUS

Nautilus 1999 Chardonnay (Marlborough) $18. 86 *—J.C. (5/1/2001)*

Nautilus 1998 Chardonnay (Marlborough) $17. 86 *—J.C. (10/1/2000)*

Nautilus 2002 Pinot Gris (Marlborough) $18. 89 *—S.H. (1/1/2002)*

Nautilus 2001 Pinot Gris (Marlborough) $18. 88 *—S.H. (11/15/2002)*

Nautilus 2006 Pinot Noir (Marlborough) $20. Soft, with a lush, friendly texture, this wine's black cherry and cola flavors are pleasant enough, if slightly simple. Given the relatively modest price point, it could be a find on restaurant lists filled with overpriced domestic Pinot Noirs. **86** —*J.C. (11/1/2007)*

Nautilus 2005 Pinot Noir (Marlborough) $20. 84 —*J.C. (12/15/2006)*

Nautilus 2003 Pinot Noir (Marlborough) $23. 87 —*J.C. (12/1/2005)*

Nautilus 2001 Pinot Noir (Marlborough) $20. 89 —*J.C. (9/1/2003)*

Nautilus 1999 Pinot Noir (Marlborough) $25. 84 —*J.C. (5/1/2001)*

Nautilus 2005 Awatere River Vineyard Pinot Noir (Marlborough) $40. Slightly confected strawberry and cherry fruit on the nose segue easily into flavors that trend darker—toward black cherries and earth. Tannins are rounded and smooth, finishing soft and easy. **86** —*J.C. (11/1/2007)*

Nautilus 2004 Awatere River Vineyard Pinot Noir (Marlborough) $40. 84 —*J.C. (12/1/2007)*

Nautilus 1999 Sauvignon Blanc (Marlborough) $16. 86 —*M.M. (10/1/2000)*

Nautilus 2005 Sauvignon Blanc (Marlborough) $17. 88 —*J.C. (12/15/2006)*

Nautilus 2002 Sauvignon Blanc (Marlborough) $17. 87 —*S.H. (1/1/2002)*

Nautilus 2001 Sauvignon Blanc (Marlborough) $18. 88 *(8/1/2002)*

Nautilus 2000 Sauvignon Blanc (Marlborough) $16. 82 —*J.C. (5/1/2001)*

NEUDORF

Neudorf 2006 Chardonnay (Nelson) $32. Lovely scents of toasted hazelnuts, apple and lime set the stage for a top-flight Chardonnay. It's medium- to full-bodied, round and broad in the mouth, then gains focus on the lime-driven finish. Delicious now, and should hold up well in the cellar for up to six years. **90** —*J.C. (12/1/2007)*

Neudorf 2004 Chardonnay (Nelson) $30. 90 —*J.C. (5/1/2006)*

Neudorf 2003 Moutere Chardonnay (Nelson) $NA. 92 —*J.C. (5/1/2006)*

Neudorf 2003 Moutere Chardonnay (New Zealand) $53. 90 Editors' Choice —*J.C. (7/1/2005)*

Neudorf 2001 Moutere Chardonnay (New Zealand) $49. 91 —*J.C. (9/1/2003)*

Neudorf 2004 Pinot Gris (Moutere) $NA. 90 —*J.C. (2/1/2006)*

Neudorf 2004 Pinot Noir (Nelson) $30. 86 —*J.C. (11/1/2006)*

Neudorf 2003 Pinot Noir (Nelson) $46. 89 —*J.C. (12/1/2005)*

Neudorf 2003 Pinot Noir (Moutere) $55. 91 —*J.C. (12/1/2005)*

Neudorf 2003 Home Vineyard Pinot Noir (Moutere) $NA. 94 —*J.C. (12/1/2005)*

Neudorf 2003 Riesling (Moutere) $NA. 88 —*J.C. (5/1/2006)*

Neudorf 2004 Brightwater Riesling (Nelson) $22. 85 —*J.C. (5/1/2006)*

Neudorf 2004 Sauvignon Blanc (Nelson) $24. 83 *(7/1/2005)*

Neudorf 2003 Sauvignon Blanc (Nelson) $23. 89 —*J.C. (8/1/2004)*

Neudorf 2002 Sauvignon Blanc (Marlborough) $22. 88 —*J.C. (9/1/2003)*

NEVIS BLUFF

Nevis Bluff 2003 Pinot Noir (Central Otago) $24. 87 —*J.C. (12/1/2005)*

Nevis Bluff 2002 Pinot Noir (Central Otago) $24. 90 Editors' Choice —*J.C. (12/1/2005)*

NEW Z LAND

New Z Land 2002 Merlot (Wairarapa) $17. 81 —*J.C. (11/1/2006)*

New Z Land 2005 Sauvignon Blanc (Marlborough) $11. 86 Best Buy —*J.C. (7/1/2006)*

NEWHAVEN

Newhaven 2006 Sauvignon Blanc (Marlborough) $12. Plump and round, with some residual sugar a distinct possibility, this wine boasts honey and melon flavors, accented with just enough tomato-leaf herbaceousness to maintain its varietal character. Drink now. **87 Best Buy** —*J.C. (9/1/2007)*

NEWTON FORREST ESTATE

Newton Forrest Estate 2004 Cornerstone of Gimblett Road Cabernet-Merlot-Malbec Bordeaux Blend (Hawke's Bay) $30. A solid, well-made blend, this packs in plenty of tobacco, vanilla and earth into a compact package. Some cherry fruit stands out on the palate, but but this is in a rather sturdy, earthy style. Try with herbed meats to help accentuate the fruit in the wine. **85** —*J.C. (11/1/2007)*

Newton Forrest Estate 2002 Gimblett Gravels Cabernet-Merlot-Malbec Bordeaux Blend (Hawke's Bay) $31. 89 —*J.C. (7/1/2006)*

NGA WAKA

Nga Waka 2000 Chardonnay (Martinborough) $30. 86 —*J.C. (7/1/2002)*

Nga Waka 1999 Chardonnay (Martinborough) $25. 87 —*J.C. (5/1/2001)*

Nga Waka 2003 Pinot Noir (Martinborough) $NA. 81 —*J.C. (12/1/2005)*

Nga Waka 2001 Pinot Noir (Martinborough) $35. 88 —*J.C. (9/1/2003)*

Nga Waka 2001 Riesling (Martinborough) $20. 87 —*J.C. (8/1/2003)*

Nga Waka 2002 Sauvignon Blanc (Martinborough) $17. 84 —*J.C. (8/1/2004)*

Nga Waka 2001 Sauvignon Blanc (Martinborough) $20. 87 *(8/1/2002)*

Nga Waka 2000 Sauvignon Blanc (Martinborough) $20. 88 —*J.C. (5/1/2001)*

NGATARAWA

Ngatarawa 2006 Glazebrook Sauvignon Blanc (Marlborough) $15. Grassy and herbal on the nose, but those elements are balanced by stone fruit and citrus notes. On the palate, there's the merest hint of asparagus, but ultimately, this is a soft, fruit-driven style, round and easy to drink. **87** —*J.C. (11/1/2007)*

Ngatarawa 2005 Glazebrook Sauvignon Blanc (Marlborough) $14. 86 —*J.C. (9/1/2006)*

Ngatarawa 2004 Glazebrook Sauvignon Blanc (Marlborough) $14. 87 —*J.C. (7/1/2005)*

NO 1 FAMILY ESTATE

No 1 Family Estate NV Cuvée No 1 Blanc de Blancs Chardonnay (Marlborough) $25. 88 —*J.C. (12/15/2003)*

No 1 Family Estate NV Cuvée Number Eight Brut Sparkling Blend (Marlborough) $20. 90 Editors' Choice —*J.C. (12/15/2003)*

NOBILO

Nobilo 2002 Chardonnay (East Coast) $10. 86 —*J.C. (4/1/2004)*

Nobilo 2000 Fall Harvest Chardonnay (Gisborne) $10. 83 —*J.C. (5/1/2001)*

Nobilo 1999 Poverty Bay Chardonnay (Gisborne) $NA. 87 —*J.C. (5/1/2001)*

Nobilo 2004 Regional Collection Merlot (East Coast) $12. 85 *(3/1/2006)*

Nobilo 2003 Icon Pinot Gris (Marlborough) $20. 87 —*J.C. (8/1/2004)*

Nobilo 2005 Icon Pinot Noir (Marlborough) $22. 88 —*J.C. (12/15/2006)*

Nobilo 2003 Icon Pinot Noir (Marlborough) $20. 88 —*J.C. (7/1/2005)*

Nobilo 2003 Sauvignon Blanc (Marlborough) $12. 88 Best Buy —*J.C. (4/1/2004)*

Nobilo 2000 Sauvignon Blanc (Marlborough) $NA. 88 —*J.C. (5/1/2001)*

Nobilo 2000 Fall Harvest Sauvignon Blanc (Marlborough) $10. 86 Best Buy —*J.C. (5/1/2001)*

Nobilo 2000 Icon Series Sauvignon Blanc (Marlborough) $19. 88 —*S.H. (11/15/2002)*

Nobilo 1999 Icon Series Sauvignon Blanc (Marlborough) $NA. 89 —*J.C. (5/1/2001)*

Nobilo 2005 Regional Collection Sauvignon Blanc (Marlborough) $12. 87 Best Buy —*J.C. (12/1/2005)*

Nobilo 2004 Regional Collection Sauvignon Blanc (Marlborough) $12. 87 Best Buy —*J.C. (7/1/2005)*

OLSSENS

Olssens 2001 Barrel Fermented Chardonnay (Central Otago) $NA. 85 —*J.C. (5/1/2006)*

Olssens 2004 Gewürztraminer (Central Otago) $17. 87 —*J.C. (7/1/2005)*

Olssens 2004 Gewürztraminer (Central Otago) $17. 86 —*J.C. (5/1/2006)*

Olssens 2004 Jackson Barry Pinot Noir (Central Otago) $33. 88 —*J.C. (12/1/2005)*

Olssens 2002 Jackson Barry Pinot Noir (Central Otago) $29. 89 —*J.C. (7/1/2005)*

Olssens 2003 Slap Jack Creek Pinot Noir (Central Otago) $48. 89 —*J.C. (12/1/2005)*

Olssens 2004 Riesling (Central Otago) $17. 88 —*J.C. (7/1/2005)*

Olssens 2004 Riesling (Central Otago) $17. 88 —*J.C. (5/1/2006)*

Olssens 2003 Desert Gold Late Harvest Riesling (Central Otago) $NA. 86 —*J.C. (5/1/2006)*

OMAKA SPRINGS

Omaka Springs 2002 Chardonnay (Marlborough) $18. 85 —*J.C. (9/1/2003)*

Omaka Springs 1998 Reserve Chardonnay (Marlborough) $NA. 80 —*J.C. (5/1/2001)*

Omaka Springs 2002 Winemaker's Selection Chardonnay (Marlborough) $24. 90 Editors' Choice —*J.C. (7/1/2005)*

Omaka Springs 2001 Merlot (Marlborough) $18. 84 —*J.C. (12/15/2003)*

Omaka Springs 1999 Merlot (Marlborough) $15. 85 *—J.C. (5/1/2001)*

Omaka Springs 2007 Pinot Gris (Marlborough) $18. A sweet, medium-bodied style of Pinot Gris, with honeyed flavors of apple, pear and pineapple. Despite the sweetness, the finish is nicely balanced, with a lush texture. Even prettier is the wine's pale copper hue. **87** *—J.C. (12/31/2007)*

Omaka Springs 2006 Pinot Gris (Marlborough) $17. Round and weighty, this is a well-made Pinot Gris in a soft, slightly sweet style. Baked apple flavors pick up hints of cinnamon and caramel, accented by a squeeze of citrus. **87** *—J.C. (11/1/2007)*

Omaka Springs 2005 Pinot Gris (Marlborough) $17. 88 *—J.C. (2/1/2006)*

Omaka Springs 2002 Pinot Gris (Marlborough) $15. 88 *—J.C. (11/15/2003)*

Omaka Springs 2006 Falveys Pinot Noir (Marlborough) $28. A savory style, one that focuses on woodsy, mushroomy, meaty complexity. If most New World Pinot Noirs are too fruity for your tastes, try this, as the the tannins are soft, the flavors complex. Drink now. **85** *—J.C. (12/31/2007)*

Omaka Springs 1998 Reserve Pinot Noir (Marlborough) $NA. 85 *—J.C. (5/1/2001)*

Omaka Springs 2001 Winemaker's Selection Pinot Noir (Marlborough) $19. 83 *—J.C. (4/1/2004)*

Omaka Springs 2005 Riesling (Marlborough) $15. A light, dry style of Riesling—clean and refreshing—with simple green apple and citrus flavors. It's leaner and more linear than most Marlborough Rieslings, making it a solid bet with raw shellfish. **86** *—J.C. (9/1/2007)*

Omaka Springs 2004 Riesling (Marlborough) $17. 88 *—J.C. (7/1/2005)*

Omaka Springs 2003 Riesling (Marlborough) $17. 89 *—J.C. (8/1/2004)*

Omaka Springs 2002 Riesling (Marlborough) $15. 85 *—J.C. (8/1/2003)*

Omaka Springs 2001 Riesling (Marlborough) $14. 88 *—J.C. (8/1/2002)*

Omaka Springs 1998 Riesling (Marlborough) $NA. 85 *—J.C. (5/1/2001)*

Omaka Springs 2007 Sauvignon Blanc (Marlborough) $18. Typical Marlborough Sauvignon Blanc, pairing ripe, honeyed stone-fruit flavors with slightly grassy, herbal notes. It's softer and lusher than many of its competitors, with less biting acidity and a soft, mouthwatering finish. **86** *—J.C. (12/31/2007)*

Omaka Springs 2006 Sauvignon Blanc (Marlborough) $14. This wine's bouquet is strongly marked by bell pepper, but the flavors veer toward stone fruit and melon, with a broad, fat mouthfeel and a surprisingly soft finish. **85** *—J.C. (3/1/2007)*

Omaka Springs 2005 Sauvignon Blanc (Marlborough) $17. 87 *—J.C. (7/1/2006)*

Omaka Springs 2004 Sauvignon Blanc (Marlborough) $17. 86 *—J.C. (7/1/2005)*

Omaka Springs 2003 Sauvignon Blanc (Marlborough) $17. 83 *—J.C. (4/1/2004)*

Omaka Springs 2002 Sauvignon Blanc (Marlborough) $18. 86 *—J.C. (9/1/2003)*

Omaka Springs 2001 Sauvignon Blanc (Marlborough) $17. 89 *(8/1/2002)*

Omaka Springs 1999 Sauvignon Blanc (Marlborough) $15. 86 *—J.C. (5/1/2001)*

Omaka Springs 2007 Falveys Sauvignon Blanc (Marlborough) $21. Blends ripe tropical fruit—even including hints of mango and banana—with more pungent notes in a full-bodied, almost sweet-seeming Sauvignon Blanc. Flashy upfront, then fades a bit on the finish. **88** *—J.C. (12/31/2007)*

Omaka Springs 2006 Falveys Sauvignon Blanc (Marlborough) $24. This is very nice, with just enough herbaceousness to mark it as New Zealand, yet not so much as to be overwhelming. Green pea scents are interspersed with hints of honey and fig, while the finish is a bit short but crisp and filled with citrus and chalk. **89** *—J.C. (3/1/2007)*

ORIGIN

Origin 2004 Sauvignon Blanc (Marlborough) $14. 88 *—J.C. (7/1/2005)*

OVERSTONE

Overstone 2007 Sauvignon Blanc (Marlborough) $13. Winemaker Grant Edmonds is based in Hawke's Bay, but sources the fruit for the Overstone Sauvignon Blanc from Marlborough. The 2007 features ripe, tropical fruit—guava and passionfruit—allied to a slightly herbaceous character, and a slightly creamy mouthfeel that nonetheless finishes brisk and fresh. **88 Best Buy** *—J.C. (12/1/2007)*

OYSTER BAY

Oyster Bay 2005 Chardonnay (Marlborough) $13. 82 *—J.C. (12/15/2006)*

Oyster Bay 2004 Chardonnay (Marlborough) $13. 86 *—J.C. (5/1/2006)*

Oyster Bay 2002 Chardonnay (Marlborough & Hawke's Bay) $15. 86 *—J.C. (9/1/2003)*

Oyster Bay 2004 Merlot (Hawke's Bay) $13. 84 *—J.C. (5/1/2006)*

Oyster Bay 2005 Pinot Noir (Marlborough) $13. 87 *—J.C. (9/1/2006)*

Oyster Bay 2004 Pinot Noir (Marlborough) $17. 85 *—J.C. (12/1/2005)*

Oyster Bay 2005 Sauvignon Blanc (Marlborough) $13. 87 *—J.C. (5/1/2006)*

PALLISER ESTATE

Palliser Estate 2004 Chardonnay (Martinborough) $NA. 88 *—J.C. (5/1/2006)*

Palliser Estate 1999 Chardonnay (Marlborough) $23. 87 *—J.C. (5/1/2001)*

Palliser Estate 2004 Pencarrow Chardonnay (Martinborough) $NA. 87 *—J.C. (5/1/2006)*

Palliser Estate 2004 Pinot Gris (Martinborough) $19. 86 *—J.C. (7/1/2005)*

Palliser Estate 2002 Pinot Gris (Martinborough) $19. 84 *—J.C. (9/1/2003)*

Palliser Estate 2000 Pinot Gris (Martinborough) $20. 85 *—J.C. (5/1/2001)*

Palliser Estate 2005 Pinot Noir (Martinborough) $27. Far and away the best Palliser Pinot Noir we've ever reviewed, the 2005 boasts complex, savory aromas and flavors that match ripe black cherry and plum fruit with peppery-herbal notes and hints of smoke, meat and brown sugar. The creamy, supple tannins are balanced by crisp acids and concentrated fruit on the long finish. Drink now–2015. **91 Editors' Choice** *—J.C. (7/1/2007)*

Palliser Estate 1998 Pinot Noir (Martinborough) $24. 87 *—M.S. (10/1/2000)*

Palliser Estate 2003 Pinot Noir (Martinborough) $27. 86 *—J.C. (12/1/2005)*

Palliser Estate 2000 Pinot Noir (Marlborough) $26. 88 *—S.H. (11/15/2002)*

Palliser Estate 1999 Pinot Noir (Martinborough) $26. 88 *—J.C. (5/1/2001)*

Palliser Estate 2005 Pencarrow Pinot Noir (Martinborough) $18. Even Palliser's second label, Pencarrow, is very good in 2005, although it doesn't show quite the intensity or complexity of its big brother. Black cherry fruit takes on a subtly herbal tang, with plenty of earthy, mushroomy notes as well. Finishes with silky, lingering hints of black tea and vibrant acidity. Drink now. **87** *—J.C. (7/1/2007)*

Palliser Estate 2003 Pencarrow Pinot Noir (Martinborough) $18. 84 *—J.C. (12/1/2005)*

Palliser Estate 2002 Pencarrow Pinot Noir (Martinborough) $18. 81 *—J.C. (12/1/2005)*

Palliser Estate 2001 Pencarrow Pinot Noir (Martinborough) $20. 84 *—J.C. (9/1/2003)*

Palliser Estate 2005 The Great George Pinot Noir (Martinborough) $50. Palliser's attempt at a luxury bottling of Pinot Noir features plenty of oak and some noticeably sturdy tannins. Put those things together and they suggest cellaring 2–3 years prior to consumption. For now, there's cedar, brown sugar and soy notes, plus flavors of earth and mushroom to go along with black cherry fruit. **90** *—J.C. (11/1/2007)*

Palliser Estate 2000 Riesling (Martinborough) $NA. 87 *—J.C. (5/1/2001)*

Palliser Estate 1999 Sauvignon Blanc (Martinborough) $17. 89 *—J.C. (10/1/2000)*

Palliser Estate 2006 Sauvignon Blanc (Martinborough) $19. Palliser's wines seem to be improving across the range over recent vintages, with this being their best Sauvignon Blanc yet. A smoky, slightly fumé character marks the nose, then ripe peaches and nectarines wash across the palate, with just enough grassiness to impart varietal character. Plump and round, it's soft and approachable without being sloppy, ending on a note of ripe tangerines. Drink now. **91 Editors' Choice** *—J.C. (11/1/2007)*

Palliser Estate 2005 Sauvignon Blanc (Martinborough) $19. 87 *—J.C. (12/15/2006)*

Palliser Estate 2004 Sauvignon Blanc (Martinborough) $19. 87 *—J.C. (12/1/2005)*

Palliser Estate 2002 Sauvignon Blanc (Martinborough) $17. 83 *—J.C. (9/1/2003)*

Palliser Estate 2001 Sauvignon Blanc (Marlborough) $18. 91 *—S.H. (11/15/2002)*

Palliser Estate 2000 Sauvignon Blanc (Martinborough) $19. 89 *—J.C. (5/1/2001)*

Palliser Estate 2006 Pencarrow Sauvignon Blanc (Martinborough) $14. Slightly sweaty on the nose, but this wine shows much better on the palate, delivering assertive flavors of melon, fig and green tomatoes. Overall, it's a bit strident and tart, but clean and refreshing; a suitable wine with herbed seafood preparations. **87** *—J.C. (11/1/2007)*

Palliser Estate 2004 Pencarrow Sauvignon Blanc (Martinborough) $14. 85 *—J.C. (5/1/2006)*

Palliser Estate 2002 Pencarrow Sauvignon Blanc (Martinborough) $13. 86 —*J.C. (9/1/2003)*

PEGASUS BAY

Pegasus Bay 2005 Sauvignon-Sémillon Bordeaux White Blend (Waipara Valley) $25. 92 Editors' Choice —*J.C. (11/1/2006)*

Pegasus Bay 1998 Maestro Cabernet Sauvignon-Merlot (Waipara) $52. 92 Cellar Selection —*J.C. (8/1/2002)*

Pegasus Bay 2005 Chardonnay (Waipara Valley) $35. 90 —*J.C. (11/1/2006)*

Pegasus Bay 2004 Chardonnay (Waipara) $35. 88 —*J.C. (12/1/2005)*

Pegasus Bay 2001 Chardonnay (Waipara) $34. 89 —*J.C. (8/1/2004)*

Pegasus Bay 2000 Chardonnay (Waipara) $30. 91 —*J.C. (7/1/2002)*

Pegasus Bay 1998 Whole Bunch Pressed Chardonnay (Waipara) $33. 90 —*J.C. (5/1/2001)*

Pegasus Bay 2001 Maestro Merlot-Malbec (Waipara) $NA. 90 —*J.C. (5/1/2006)*

Pegasus Bay 2005 Pinot Noir (Waipara Valley) $41. This vintage of Peg Bay's Pinot shows the firm structure of the year, suggesting 2–3 years of cellaring. But while the black cherry fruit may not be immediately accessible, there's plenty of it, touched with herbal, minty complexity and a touch of oaky toast on the finish. **90** —*J.C. (12/1/2007)*

Pegasus Bay 2003 Pinot Noir (Waipara) $40. 87 —*J.C. (12/1/2005)*

Pegasus Bay 2001 Pinot Noir (Waipara) $48. 91 —*J.C. (9/1/2003)*

Pegasus Bay 1999 Pinot Noir (Waipara) $39. 91 —*J.C. (5/1/2001)*

Pegasus Bay 2004 Prima Donna Pinot Noir (Waipara Valley) $78. Full-bodied and surprisingly muscular for a Prima Donna, the 2004 features big plum and black cherry fruit, wrapped in hints of hickory smoke, mint and cola. Finishes with enough dusty tannins to suggest cellaring another year or two. Imported by Meadowbank Estates. **90** —*J.C. (12/1/2007)*

Pegasus Bay 2003 Prima Donna Pinot Noir (Waipara) $74. 88 —*J.C. (12/1/2005)*

Pegasus Bay 2001 Prima Donna Pinot Noir (Waipara) $88. 88 —*J.C. (8/1/2004)*

Pegasus Bay 1999 Prima Donna Pinot Noir (Waipara) $63. 87 —*J.C. (9/1/2003)*

Pegasus Bay 2006 Riesling (Waipara Valley) $23. Peg Bay continues to push the ripeness envelope on its Rieslings. The 2006 is honeyed and rather sweet, with baked apple flavors at the core, surrounded by hints of spice and apricot. Lime-like acids seem a bit strident on the finish right now; give it a couple of years in the cellar. Imported by Meadowbank Estates. **90** —*J.C. (9/1/2007)*

Pegasus Bay 2005 Riesling (Waipara Valley) $25. 88 —*J.C. (11/1/2006)*

Pegasus Bay 2004 Riesling (Waipara) $24. 90 —*J.C. (12/1/2005)*

Pegasus Bay 2003 Riesling (Waipara) $25. 90 Editors' Choice —*J.C. (7/1/2005)*

Pegasus Bay 2002 Riesling (Waipara) $24. 90 Editors' Choice —*J.C. (8/1/2003)*

Pegasus Bay 2000 Riesling (Waipara) $20. 89 —*J.C. (5/1/2001)*

Pegasus Bay 2004 Sauvignon Blanc (Waipara) $24. 87 —*J.C. (12/1/2005)*

Pegasus Bay 2002 Sauvignon Blanc (Waipara) $26. 88 —*J.C. (8/1/2004)*

Pegasus Bay 2001 Sauvignon Blanc (Waipara) $19. 88 —*J.C. (9/1/2003)*

Pegasus Bay 2000 Sauvignon Blanc (Waipara) $19. 89 *(8/1/2002)*

Pegasus Bay 1999 Sauvignon Blanc (Waipara) $20. 85 —*J.C. (5/1/2001)*

PENINSULA ESTATE WINES

Peninsula Estate Wines 1998 Hauraki Bordeaux Blend (Waiheke Island) $45. 84 —*J.C. (8/1/2004)*

Peninsula Estate Wines 2000 Zeno Syrah (Waiheke Island) $40. 85 —*J.C. (8/1/2004)*

PEREGRINE

Peregrine 1999 Gewürztraminer (Central Otago) $NA. 90 —*J.C. (5/1/2001)*

Peregrine 2005 Pinot Gris (Central Otago) $29. 84 —*J.C. (11/1/2006)*

Peregrine 2003 Pinot Gris (Central Otago) $26. 85 —*J.C. (8/1/2004)*

Peregrine 2002 Pinot Gris (Central Otago) $19. 88 —*J.C. (9/1/2003)*

Peregrine 2006 Pinot Noir (Central Otago) $42. A pleasant stylistic change from Peregrine, whose wines have been somewhat chunky in the past, this vintage nicely captures Pinot's elusive silky texture and complex aromas. It's highly perfumed, with hints of herbs and roses wrapped around a soft core of lush black-cherry fruit. Finishes long, framed by soft tannins. Drink now–2015. **92 Editors' Choice** —*J.C. (12/1/2007)*

Peregrine 2005 Pinot Noir (Central Otago) $38. A bit linear in style, but although it lacks a bit of the silky texture that makes Pinot so attractive, it does deliver plenty of Pinot flavor and punch. Black cherries, cola, dried spices and a bit of beet greens mark the nose, and the flavors develop some slightly sappy, resinous notes before ending with black tea leaves. Hold two years, then drink it over the next 5–8. **89** —*J.C. (11/1/2007)*

Peregrine 2003 Pinot Noir (Central Otago) $38. 88 —*J.C. (12/1/2005)*

Peregrine 2002 Pinot Noir (Central Otago) $34. 89 —*J.C. (8/1/2004)*

Peregrine 2001 Pinot Noir (Central Otago) $34. 85 —*J.C. (9/1/2003)*

Peregrine 2005 Rastasburn Riesling (Central Otago) $25. 90 Editors' Choice —*J.C. (11/1/2006)*

PHEASANT GROVE

Pheasant Grove 2004 Sauvignon Blanc (Marlborough) $15. 88 —*J.C. (7/1/2005)*

PISA RANGE

Pisa Range 2003 Black Poplar Block Pinot Noir (Central Otago) $35. 87 —*J.C. (12/1/2005)*

POND PADDOCK

Pond Paddock 2003 Hawk's Flight Pinot Noir (Martinborough) $NA. 85 —*J.C. (12/1/2005)*

QUARTZ REEF

Quartz Reef 2004 Pinot Gris (Central Otago) $26. 87 —*J.C. (5/1/2006)*

Quartz Reef 2002 Pinot Gris (Central Otago) $20. 87 —*J.C. (9/1/2003)*

Quartz Reef 2004 Pinot Noir (Central Otago) $NA. 89 —*J.C. (11/1/2006)*

Quartz Reef 2003 Pinot Noir (Central Otago) $30. 87 —*J.C. (12/1/2005)*

Quartz Reef 2002 Pinot Noir (Central Otago) $NA. 91 Editors' Choice —*J.C. (11/1/2006)*

Quartz Reef 2001 Pinot Noir (Central Otago) $30. 86 —*J.C. (9/1/2003)*

Quartz Reef 2004 Bendigo Estate Vineyard Pinot Noir (Central Otago) $NA. 90 —*J.C. (11/1/2006)*

Quartz Reef 2003 Bendigo Estate Vineyard Pinot Noir (Central Otago) $NA. 88 —*J.C. (12/1/2005)*

Quartz Reef 2002 Bendigo Estate Vineyard Pinot Noir (Central Otago) $NA. 91 —*J.C. (11/1/2006)*

Quartz Reef 2001 Chauvet Sparkling Blend (Central Otago) $28. 90 —*J.C. (5/1/2006)*

RAIN

Rain 2008 Sauvignon Blanc (Marlborough) $14. 87 —*J.C. (12/15/2006)*

REBECCA SALMOND

Rebecca Salmond 2000 Cabernet Sauvignon-Merlot (Kumeu) $18. 88 —*J.C. (12/15/2003)*

Rebecca Salmond 2001 Reserve Chardonnay (Gisborne) $25. 84 —*J.C. (9/1/2003)*

Rebecca Salmond 2002 Merlot (Kumeu) $18. 86 —*J.C. (12/15/2003)*

Rebecca Salmond 2001 Sauvignon Blanc (Marlborough) $15. 83 —*J.C. (9/1/2003)*

RED HILL

Red Hill (NZ) 2001 Riesling (Marlborough) $NA. 84 —*J.C. (8/1/2002)*

Red Hill (NZ) 2001 Sauvignon Blanc (Marlborough) $11. 83 —*M.M. (12/15/2001)*

REDCLIFFE

Redcliffe 2006 Sauvignon Blanc (Marlborough) $12. Lightweight and fresh, this is a crisp, peppery Sauvignon Blanc with a core of grapefruit and a touch of sweatiness to its aromas. Probably best with potent shellfish preparations, like mussels steamed in white wine and herbs. **85** —*J.C. (12/1/2007)*

Redcliffe 2005 Sauvignon Blanc (Marlborough) $11. 87 Best Buy —*J.C. (9/1/2006)*

Redcliffe 2004 Sauvignon Blanc (Marlborough) $10. 86 Best Buy —*J.C. (7/1/2005)*

RIMU GROVE

Rimu Grove 2005 Pinot Gris (Nelson) $27. 87 —*J.C. (2/1/2006)*

Rimu Grove 2004 Pinot Gris (Nelson) $19. 82 —*J.C. (7/1/2005)*

Rimu Grove 2003 Pinot Noir (Nelson) $30. 87 —*J.C. (12/1/2005)*

Rimu Grove 2001 Pinot Noir (Nelson) $35. 84 —*J.C. (4/1/2004)*

RIPPON

Rippon 2003 Pinot Noir (Central Otago) $25. 87 *—J.C. (12/1/2005)*

RIVER FORD

River Ford 1999 Saint Clair Estate Sauvignon Blanc (Marlborough) $16. 87 *—M.M. (10/1/2000)*

RIVERSIDE

Riverside 1998 Chardonnay (Gisborne) $13. 81 *—J.C. (10/1/2000)*

Riverside 1997 Reserve Chardonnay (Stirling) $20. 83 *—J.C. (10/1/2000)*

Riverside 1999 Sauvignon Blanc (Hawke's Bay) $12. 85 *—J.C. (10/1/2000)*

ROARING MEG

Roaring Meg 2002 Pinot Noir (Central Otago) $25. 84 *—J.C. (8/1/2004)*

ROCKBURN

Rockburn 2003 Chardonnay (Central Otago) $23. 86 *—J.C. (5/1/2006)*

Rockburn 2003 Pinot Noir (Central Otago) $30. 87 *—J.C. (12/1/2005)*

Rockburn 2002 Pinot Noir (Central Otago) $38. 89 *—J.C. (8/1/2004)*

Rockburn 2005 Riesling (Central Otago) $20. Weighty and slightly oily in the mouth, this is a big, broad-shouldered Riesling that's completely dry. Apple and spice flavors lack the sweetness you might expect, underlined by lemony notes that impart focus to the wine's finish. **89** *—J.C. (9/1/2007)*

Rockburn 2003 Riesling (Central Otago) $21. 85 *—J.C. (5/1/2006)*

ROWLAND

Rowland 2001 Jill's Vineyard Pinot Noir (Central Otago) $26. 87 *—J.C. (9/1/2003)*

Rowland 2000 Jill's Vineyard Pinot Noir (Central Otago) $28. 87 *—J.C. (8/1/2002)*

Rowland 1999 Jill's Vineyard Pinot Noir (Central Otago) $22. 84 *—J.C. (5/1/2001)*

Rowland 1998 Jill's Vineyard Pinot Noir (Central Otago) $22. 86 *—J.C. (10/1/2000)*

SACRED HILL

Sacred Hill 1997 Basket Press Cabernet Sauvignon (Hawke's Bay) $20. 87 *(9/1/2000)*

Sacred Hill 1998 Helmsman Cabernet Sauvignon (Hawke's Bay) $40. 87 *—J.C. (5/1/2001)*

Sacred Hill 1999 Barrel Fermented Chardonnay (Hawke's Bay) $20. 88 *—J.C. (5/1/2001)*

Sacred Hill 1998 Barrel Fermented Chardonnay (Hawke's Bay) $20. 88 *(9/1/2000)*

Sacred Hill 1997 Barrel Fermented Chardonnay (Hawke's Bay) $21. 89 *—S.H. (8/1/1999)*

Sacred Hill 1999 Rifleman's Chardonnay (Hawke's Bay) $36. 90 *—J.C. (5/1/2001)*

Sacred Hill 1997 Rifleman's Chardonnay (Hawke's Bay) $33. 92 *(9/1/2000)*

Sacred Hill 1998 Whitecliff Chardonnay (Marlborough & Hawkes Bay) $16. 89 *(9/1/2000)*

Sacred Hill 1998 Broken Stone Merlot (Hawke's Bay) $40. 92 *—J.C. (5/1/2001)*

Sacred Hill 1999 Whitecliff Merlot (Hawke's Bay) $16. 87 *(9/1/2000)*

Sacred Hill 1999 Basket Press Merlot-Cabernet Sauvignon (Hawke's Bay) $20. 86 *—J.C. (5/1/2001)*

Sacred Hill 2005 Sauvignon Blanc (Marlborough) $22. 87 *—J.C. (11/1/2006)*

Sacred Hill 1997 Barrel Fermented Sauvignon Blanc (Hawke's Bay) $20. 88 *(9/1/2000)*

Sacred Hill 1998 Sauvage Sauvignon Blanc (Hawke's Bay) $32. 91 *—J.C. (5/1/2001)*

Sacred Hill 1999 Whitecliff Sauvignon Blanc (Hawke's Bay) $13. 88 *(9/1/2000)*

Sacred Hill 2000 Whitecliff Vineyards Sauvignon Blanc (Hawke's Bay) $20. 85 *—J.C. (5/1/2001)*

SAINT CLAIR

Saint Clair 2004 Omaka Reserve Chardonnay (Marlborough) $25. 90 Editors' Choice *—J.C. (9/1/2006)*

Saint Clair 2005 Unoaked Chardonnay (Marlborough) $16. 85 *—J.C. (11/1/2006)*

Saint Clair 2005 Vicar's Choice Chardonnay (Marlborough) $14. 84 *—J.C. (11/1/2006)*

Saint Clair 2006 Pinot Noir (Marlborough) $18. This is a big-boned Pinot, with a crisp, almost citrusy framework to the bold cherry flavors. Hints of cola and dried flowers add complexity, while the finish is tangy and mouthcoating. Give it another few months to settle down, then drink now–2012. **87** *—J.C. (5/1/2007)*

Saint Clair 2005 Pinot Noir (Marlborough) $16. 85 *—J.C. (9/1/2006)*

Saint Clair 2004 Pinot Noir (Marlborough) $16. 87 *—J.C. (7/1/2006)*

Saint Clair 2006 Doctor's Creek Reserve Pinot Noir (Marlborough) $29. Aromatically, this wine excels, offering perfumy notes of ripe cherries and flowers. But it doesn't quite deliver on the palate, where the cherry and herbal flavors are rather lightweight and tart, finishing with overtones of pomegranate and cranberry. **86** *—J.C. (12/31/2007)*

Saint Clair 2005 Doctor's Creek Reserve Pinot Noir (Marlborough) $26. Reasonably full-bodied and rich, Saint Clair's 2005 Doctor's Creek blends the mushroomy, savory elements found in some clones with the fruitier black cherry and plum flavors found in others. Picks up hints of cola on the long, silky finish. **90 Editors' Choice** *—J.C. (5/1/2007)*

Saint Clair 2004 Doctor's Creek Reserve Pinot Noir (Marlborough) $26. 88 *—J.C. (9/1/2006)*

Saint Clair 2005 Omaka Reserve Pinot Noir (Marlborough) $30. Saint Clair's top Pinot is gorgeous in the successful 2005 vintage, marrying oaky complexity—cedar, sandalwood and dried spices—with lush black cherry fruit. The wood and fruit are beatifully integrated, making it hard to tell where one leaves off and the other begins, and the flavors come to a long, elegant close. Drink now–2012. **90 Editors' Choice** *—J.C. (5/1/2007)*

Saint Clair 2004 Omaka Reserve Pinot Noir (Marlborough) $29. 88 *—J.C. (9/1/2006)*

Saint Clair 2006 Pioneer Block 4 Sawcut Pinot Noir (Marlborough) $29. A blend of Dijon clones 667 and 777, this wine offers intense aromas of cherries, root beer, cola and chocolate. The texture is silky-smooth, while the flavors take on an intriguing herbal edge that adds welcome dimension to the ripe fruit and ample oak. Finishes complex, herbal and lingering; drink now–2012. **90 Editors' Choice** *—J.C. (12/31/2007)*

Saint Clair 2006 Vicar's Choice Pinot Noir (Marlborough) $16. Saint Clair's entry-level Pinot Noir is light in body but features subtle floral aromas and understated cherry flavors. An herbal streak enhances rather than detracts from the overall impression, adding the suggestion of sinewy power to an otherwise delicate wine. **85** *—J.C. (5/1/2007)*

Saint Clair 2004 Vicar's Choice Pinot Noir (Marlborough) $13. 85 *—J.C. (7/1/2006)*

Saint Clair 2002 Vicar's Choice Pinot Noir (Marlborough) $15. 83 *—J.C. (4/1/2004)*

Saint Clair 2002 Riesling (New Zealand) $14. 87 *—J.C. (8/1/2003)*

Saint Clair 2007 Sauvignon Blanc (Marlborough) $19. The only problem with this bottling from Saint Clair is that the price just keeps inching up. It's a plump SB with a mouthwatering finish and varietal flavors of stone fruit, gooseberries and grapefruit and a touch of peppery spice. **87** *—J.C. (12/1/2007)*

Saint Clair 2006 Sauvignon Blanc (Marlborough) $16. 88 *—J.C. (12/15/2006)*

Saint Clair 2005 Sauvignon Blanc (Marlborough) $16. 84 *—J.C. (5/1/2006)*

Saint Clair 2002 Sauvignon Blanc (Marlborough) $13. 87 *—J.C. (9/1/2003)*

Saint Clair 2006 Block 7 Sauvignon Blanc (Marlborough) $25. Assertively pungent and grassy, this is a statement-making rendition of Sauvignon Blanc. Although there are some white grapefruit flavors, this wine is aggressively herbal and may prove too much for some. That said, it is admirably concentrated and long on the finish, so fans of this style will likely love it. **89** *—J.C. (3/1/2007)*

Saint Clair 2007 Pioneer Block 2 Swamp Block Sauvignon Blanc (Marlborough) $26. The Saint Clair style usually features prominent herbaceous notes, but this special block bottling tones down that influence, instead relying more on melon, fig and mineral notes for impact. It's full-bodied, broad and mouthfilling in the context of Sauvignon Blanc, with a long, white grapefruit finish. Drink through the end of 2008. **91 Editors' Choice** *—J.C. (12/31/2007)*

Saint Clair 2007 Vicar's Choice Sauvignon Blanc (Marlborough) $16. A lightweight Sauvignon Blanc that fits the standard Marlborough profile, with slightly grassy notes layered over grapefruit and pineapple flavors. Drink now. **85** *—J.C. (12/31/2007)*

Saint Clair 2006 Vicar's Choice Sauvignon Blanc (Marlborough) $14. 87 *—J.C. (12/15/2006)*

Saint Clair 2005 Wairau Reserve Sauvignon Blanc (Marlborough) $25. 90 Editors' Choice *—J.C. (7/1/2006)*

Saint Clair 2006 Wairau Reserve Sauvignon Blanc (Marlborough) $26. Steers an herbal path dangerously close to asparagus. This is on the green side, but adequately balanced by tropical fruit flavors, while the mouthfeel is slightly oily and concentrated, ending in a long, decidedly herbal finish. **90** *—J.C. (3/1/2007)*

SANCTUARY

Sanctuary 1997 Sauvignon Blanc (Marlborough) $12. 87 *—S.H. (8/1/1999)*

SANDIHURST

Sandihurst 2004 Pinot Noir (Canterbury) $18. 87 *—J.C. (12/1/2005)*

Sandihurst 1998 Premier Pinot Noir (Canterbury) $18. 86 *—J.C. (5/1/2001)*

SAUVIGNON REPUBLIC

Sauvignon Republic 2007 Sauvignon Blanc (Marlborough) $18. This ambitious international effort has yet to really take off—at least in its New Zealand incarnation. Chunky tropical-fruit flavors are pleasant, and they're accented by some grassy notes, but that's all there is to it. **85** *—J.C. (12/31/2007)*

Sauvignon Republic 2006 Sauvignon Blanc (Marlborough) $18. Grassy and herbal—verging on vegetal—but with just enough ripe nectarine flavors to help provide a sense of balance. It's nicely round in the mouth, with a soft, easy-going finish. **86** *—J.C. (11/1/2007)*

Sauvignon Republic 2005 Sauvignon Blanc (Marlborough) $18. 85 *—J.C. (9/1/2006)*

SCHUBERT

Schubert 1999 Cabernet Sauvignon (Hawke's Bay) $40. 85 *—J.C. (12/15/2003)*

Schubert 2003 Pinot Noir (Wairarapa) $50. 84 *—J.C. (12/1/2005)*

Schubert 2004 Block B Pinot Noir (Wairarapa) $50. The aromas feature a subtle interplay between roses, red fruit and earthier elements, with the flavors following along in a similar vein. But where this wine excels is in its texture—supremely silky—and finish, which shows excellent persistence. A complex and elegant expression of North Island Pinot Noir. **91** *—J.C. (12/1/2007)*

Schubert 2002 Syrah (Wairarapa) $54. 89 *—J.C. (5/1/2006)*

Schubert 1999 Syrah (New Zealand) $24. 90 Editors' Choice *—J.C. (12/15/2003)*

Schubert 2000 Tribianco White Blend (New Zealand) $10. 83 *—J.C. (9/1/2003)*

SEIFRIED

Seifried 2002 Bordeaux Blend (Nelson) $16. 87 *—J.C. (8/1/2004)*

Seifried 2004 Malbec-Merlot-Cabernet Bordeaux Blend (Nelson) $15. 84 *—J.C. (12/15/2006)*

Seifried 2002 Malbec-Merlot-Cabernet Bordeaux Blend (Nelson) $16. 87 *—J.C. (8/1/2004)*

Seifried 2004 Chardonnay (Nelson) $NA. 86 *—J.C. (5/1/2006)*

Seifried 2003 Unoaked Chardonnay (Nelson) $16. 85 *—J.C. (8/1/2004)*

Seifried 2004 Winemakers Collection Barrique Fermented Chardonnay (Nelson) $NA. 89 *—J.C. (5/1/2006)*

Seifried 2006 Gewürztraminer (Nelson) $17. A bit on the sweet side, Seifried's 2006 Gewürztraminer features scents of lychee fruit and rose petals, then adds flavors of honey, peach and pear on the palate. Lingers elegantly on the finish. Drink now. **89** *—J.C. (11/1/2007)*

Seifried 2005 Gewürztraminer (Nelson) $NA. 86 *—J.C. (5/1/2006)*

Seifried 2005 Winemakers Collection Gewürztraminer (Nelson) $NA. 88 *—J.C. (5/1/2006)*

Seifried 2005 Pinot Gris (Nelson) $17. 86 *—J.C. (2/1/2006)*

Seifried 2005 Pinot Noir (Nelson) $25. Possibly a bit too sternly tannic for its own good, this starts off with attractive meaty, mushroomy scents, then adds cherry and tea leaf flavors that seem a bit herbal and green. Medium in body, the wine finishes crisp, with drying tannins. **84** *—J.C. (5/1/2007)*

Seifried 2004 Pinot Noir (Nelson) $25. 86 *—J.C. (12/1/2005)*

Seifried 2002 Pinot Noir (Nelson) $25. 86 *—J.C. (8/1/2004)*

Seifried 2004 Winemakers Collection Pinot Noir (Nelson) $35. 89 *—J.C. (12/1/2005)*

Seifried 2005 Riesling (Nelson) $25. 86 *—J.C. (5/1/2006)*

Seifried 2004 Riesling (Nelson) $15. 90 Best Buy *—J.C. (7/1/2005)*

Seifried 2003 Riesling (Nelson) $16. 87 *—J.C. (8/1/2004)*

Seifried 2005 Winemakers Collection Riesling (Nelson) $NA. 89 *—J.C. (5/1/2006)*

Seifried 2008 Sauvignon Blanc (Nelson) $17. 86 *—J.C. (11/1/2006)*

Seifried 2005 Sauvignon Blanc (Nelson) $17. 86 *—J.C. (5/1/2006)*

Seifried 2004 Sauvignon Blanc (Nelson) $17. 89 *—J.C. (7/1/2005)*

Seifried 2003 Sauvignon Blanc (Nelson) $18. 88 *—J.C. (8/1/2004)*

Seifried 2005 Winemakers Collection Sauvignon Blanc (Nelson) $NA. 86 *—J.C. (5/1/2006)*

Seifried 2004 Sylvia Zweigelt (Nelson) $NA. 86 *—J.C. (5/1/2006)*

SELAKS

Selaks 2000 Chardonnay (Marlborough) $15. 88 Best Buy *—J.C. (5/1/2001)*

Selaks 2000 Drylands Chardonnay (Marlborough) $NA. 89 *—J.C. (5/1/2001)*

Selaks 1999 Drylands Merlot (Marlborough) $NA. 86 *—J.C. (5/1/2001)*

Selaks 1998 Founders Estate Merlot (Hawke's Bay) $NA. 88 *—J.C. (5/1/2001)*

Selaks 2000 Drylands Pinot Gris (Marlborough) $NA. 88 *—J.C. (5/1/2001)*

Selaks 2002 Founders Reserve Pinot Noir (Marlborough) $NA. 89 *—J.C. (12/1/2005)*

Selaks 1999 Riesling (Marlborough) $NA. 85 *—J.C. (5/1/2001)*

Selaks 2001 Sauvignon Blanc (Marlborough) $14. 88 *—S.H. (11/15/2002)*

Selaks 2000 Sauvignon Blanc (Marlborough) $11. 88 Best Buy *—J.C. (5/1/2001)*

Selaks 2000 Drylands Sauvignon Blanc (Marlborough) $18. 90 *—J.C. (5/1/2001)*

Selaks 1998 Founders Reserve Sauvignon Blanc (Marlborough) $NA. 90 *—J.C. (5/1/2001)*

SENTINEL

Sentinel 2005 Sauvignon Blanc (Marlborough) $NA. 86 *—J.C. (5/1/2006)*

SERESIN

Seresin 2005 Chardonnay (Marlborough) $22. 92 Editors' Choice *—J.C. (11/1/2006)*

Seresin 2005 Sauvignon Blanc (Marlborough) $21. 92 Editors' Choice *—J.C. (11/1/2006)*

Seresin 2004 Sauvignon Blanc (Marlborough) $20. 85 *—J.C. (11/1/2006)*

Seresin 2003 Sauvignon Blanc (Marlborough) $23. 91 Editors' Choice *(7/1/2005)*

Seresin 2001 Sauvignon Blanc (Marlborough) $20. 91 *(8/1/2002)*

Seresin 2004 Márama Sauvignon Blanc (Marlborough) $32. 88 *—J.C. (11/1/2006)*

SEVEN TERRACES

Seven Terraces 2005 Pinot Noir (Marlborough) $20. 86 *—J.C. (12/15/2006)*

Seven Terraces 2004 Pinot Noir (Marlborough) $20. 87 *—J.C. (12/1/2005)*

Seven Terraces 2005 Sauvignon Blanc (Marlborough) $15. 86 *—J.C. (11/1/2006)*

Seven Terraces 2004 Sauvignon Blanc (Marlborough) $15. 88 *—J.C. (12/1/2005)*

Seven Terraces 2003 Sauvignon Blanc (Marlborough) $14. 89 Best Buy *—J.C. (7/1/2005)*

SHAKY BRIDGE

Shaky Bridge 2003 Pinot Noir (Central Otago) $36. 90 *—J.C. (12/1/2005)*

Shaky Bridge 2006 Rosé Pinot Noir (Central Otago) $16. A rosé of Pinot Noir, Shaky Bridge's 2006 offers floral aromas along with scents of candied cherries. It's plump and juicy in the mouth, lacking complexity but making up for that with vibrant fruit. Drink now. **84** *—J.C. (7/1/2007)*

SHEPHERDS RIDGE

Shepherds Ridge 2006 Sauvignon Blanc (Marlborough) $10. Boasts textbook gooseberry notes—sort of a cross between pink grapefruit and tangerine—to go along with slightly grassy aromas and flavors. Shows surprising punch on the finish for such an inexpensive Sauvignon. **89 Best Buy** *—J.C. (3/1/2007)*

Shepherds Ridge 2004 Sauvignon Blanc (Marlborough) $15. 84 *—J.C. (7/1/2005)*

Shepherds Ridge 2002 Sauvignon Blanc (Marlborough) $15. 86 *—J.C. (9/1/2003)*

Shepherds Ridge 2001 Sauvignon Blanc (Marlborough) $15. 90 Editors' Choice *(8/1/2002)*

SHERWOOD ESTATE

Sherwood Estate 2000 Reserve Chardonnay (Canterbury) $20. 89 —*J.C. (7/1/2002)*

Sherwood Estate 2005 Pinot Noir (Marlborough) $18. 88 —*J.C. (12/15/2006)*

Sherwood Estate 2005 Sauvignon Blanc (Marlborough) $15. 88 —*J.C. (12/15/2006)*

SHINGLE PEAK

Shingle Peak 2000 Pinot Noir (Marlborough) $15. 92 —*S.H. (6/1/2001)*

Shingle Peak 2001 Sauvignon Blanc (Marlborough) $12. 90 —*S.H. (11/15/2002)*

SILENI

Sileni 1998 EV Merlot-Cabernet Franc (Hawke's Bay) $80. 92 —*J.C. (5/1/2001)*

Sileni 2006 Cellar Selection Pinot Noir (Hawke's Bay) $18. This is a nicely made, varietally correct Pinot Noir from a region known more for its Bordeaux varieties (and increasingly Syrah). Delicate scents of tea, rose petals and cranberries set the stage for a light-bodied wine that features juicy raspberry and cranberry flavors with some herbal notes. 86 —*J.C. (5/1/2007)*

Sileni 2004 Cellar Selection Pinot Noir (Hawke's Bay) $16. 86 —*J.C. (7/1/2006)*

Sileni 2006 Cellar Selection Sauvignon Blanc (Marlborough) $15. Bright and fruity, with candied red berry, pineapple and gooseberry aromas upfront, followed by flavors of currant, melon and nectarine. It's on the full side for Marlborough Sauvignon, with a tangerine-tinged finish. Drink now. 88 —*J.C. (5/1/2007)*

Sileni 2005 Cellar Selection Sauvignon Blanc (Marlborough) $14. 87 —*J.C. (5/1/2006)*

SILVER BEACH

Silver Beach 2006 Sauvignon Blanc (Marlborough) $14. Loud on the nose, where bold lime and herbal notes strike a brassy impression, and that intensity continues throughout. Focused citrus and pineapple flavors are assertive on the palate, finishing clean and crisp. Pair with boldly flavored seafood dishes, or savor it on its own. 88 —*J.C. (5/1/2007)*

SILVER BIRCH

Silver Birch 2005 Sauvignon Blanc (Marlborough) $14. 86 —*J.C. (7/1/2006)*

SOUTHBANK ESTATE

Southbank Estate 2005 Pinot Gris (Hawke's Bay) $NA. 86 —*J.C. (2/1/2006)*

Southbank Estate 2004 Pinot Noir (Marlborough) $10. 84 —*J.C. (12/1/2005)*

Southbank Estate 2004 Sauvignon Blanc (Marlborough) $12. 84 —*J.C. (5/1/2006)*

Southbank Estate 2004 Syrah (Hawke's Bay) $NA. 84 —*J.C. (5/1/2006)*

SPY VALLEY

Spy Valley 2004 Chardonnay (Marlborough) $25. 85 —*J.C. (7/1/2006)*

Spy Valley 2003 Chardonnay (Marlborough) $25. 86 —*J.C. (7/1/2005)*

Spy Valley 2005 Gewürztraminer (Marlborough) $20. 88 —*J.C. (5/1/2006)*

Spy Valley 2004 Gewürztraminer (Marlborough) $17. 82 —*J.C. (7/1/2005)*

Spy Valley 2001 Gewürztraminer (Marlborough) $12. 88 —*J.C. (8/1/2002)*

Spy Valley 2001 Gewürztraminer (Marlborough) $12. 88 Best Buy —*J.C. (11/15/2002)*

Spy Valley 2006 Pinot Gris (Marlborough) $25. Thickly textured and rather sweet, with superripe apples and pears that at times seem almost drenched in honey. Probably best on its own, well-chilled as a hot-weather apéritif. 85 —*J.C. (12/31/2007)*

Spy Valley 2005 Pinot Gris (Marlborough) $23. 87 —*J.C. (2/1/2006)*

Spy Valley 2004 Pinot Gris (Marlborough) $20. 87 —*J.C. (7/1/2005)*

Spy Valley 2005 Pinot Noir (Marlborough) $29. 88 —*J.C. (12/15/2006)*

Spy Valley 2003 Pinot Noir (Marlborough) $30. 89 —*J.C. (12/1/2005)*

Spy Valley 2005 Riesling (Marlborough) $20. 90 Editors' Choice —*J.C. (7/1/2006)*

Spy Valley 2004 Riesling (Marlborough) $14. 90 Best Buy —*J.C. (7/1/2005)*

Spy Valley 2006 Sauvignon Blanc (Marlborough) $18. Spy Valley's Riesling and Gewürz have consistently scored well, so it is nice to see the Sauvignon finally reach this level of quality. It's crisp and well-structured, with grassy, herbal notes to the fig and grapefruit flavors, and has an authoritative, rich finish. 90 Editors' Choice —*J.C. (3/1/2007)*

Spy Valley 2005 Sauvignon Blanc (Marlborough) $18. 87 —*J.C. (5/1/2006)*

Spy Valley 2004 Sauvignon Blanc (Marlborough) $18. 87 —*J.C. (7/1/2005)*

Spy Valley 2001 Sauvignon Blanc (Marlborough) $13. 88 Best Buy —*S.H. (11/15/2002)*

Spy Valley 2000 Sauvignon Blanc (Marlborough) $12. 90 —*S.H. (6/1/2001)*

STAETE LANDT

Staete Landt 2005 Pinot Gris (Marlborough) $23. An interesting take on Pinot Gris, barrel-fermented in older French oak. The result accentuates the variety's smoky, nutty characters and adds heft and texture. Apple and honey flavors give it enough fruit to carry the weight, and the wine picks up pleasant spice notes on the finish. Drink now. 89 —*J.C. (11/1/2007)*

Staete Landt 2004 Pinot Noir (Marlborough) $25. A plump, round Pinot lavished with oak, this seemed slightly off, in that the fruit had a bit of cooked character to it. Otherwise, this is a very nice Pinot, easily marrying cola, mint and maple syrup notes and ending quite long. 85 —*J.C. (3/1/2007)*

Staete Landt 2005 Sauvignon Blanc (Marlborough) $17. Not a strong effort, this shows overt bell pepper and honey on the nose, then follows that up with flavors of peach, green pepper and sour citrus. It's an odd mix of vegetal and honeyed that doesn't quite come together. 81 —*J.C. (5/1/2007)*

STONE PADDOCK

Stone Paddock 2005 Sauvignon Blanc (Hawke's Bay) $16. Shows decent weight and concentration, but plays a bit of a one-note tune, primarily lemony citrus flavors. There's a hint of flintiness to the nose and an orangy, pith-like tinge to the finish. 85 —*J.C. (4/12/2007)*

STONECROFT

Stonecroft 2000 Chardonnay (Hawke's Bay) $22. 89 —*J.C. (7/1/2002)*

Stonecroft 2003 Syrah (Hawke's Bay) $30. 87 —*J.C. (5/1/2006)*

STONECROP

Stonecrop 2006 Sauvignon Blanc (Martinborough) $18. A plump, ripe style of New Zealand Sauvignon Blanc, Stonecrop's 2006 boasts peach, melon and citrus scents followed by gooseberry and stone fruit flavors. Rounder and fleshier than you might expect, but without being heavy or unbalanced. Drink now. 89 —*J.C. (5/1/2007)*

STONECUTTER

StoneCutter 2003 Pinot Noir (Martinborough) $35. 87 —*J.C. (11/1/2006)*

STONELEIGH

Stoneleigh 1998 Chardonnay (Marlborough) $10. 87 Best Buy —*S.H. (8/1/1999)*

Stoneleigh 2003 Chardonnay (Marlborough) $15. 88 —*J.C. (7/1/2005)*

Stoneleigh 1999 Chardonnay (Marlborough) $12. 84 —*J.C. (5/1/2001)*

Stoneleigh 2006 Pinot Noir (Marlborough) $16. A medium-bodied, softly structured Pinot Noir, with earth and black cherry notes that come across as cola or chocolate. Drink now–2010. Imported by Pernod Ricard USA. 85 —*J.C. (11/1/2007)*

Stoneleigh 2004 Pinot Noir (Marlborough) $16. 85 —*J.C. (12/1/2005)*

Stoneleigh 2003 Pinot Noir (Marlborough) $15. 87 —*J.C. (12/1/2005)*

Stoneleigh 1999 Pinot Noir (Marlborough) $15. 83 —*J.C. (5/1/2001)*

Stoneleigh 2003 Rapaura Series Pinot Noir (Marlborough) $19. 87 —*J.C. (12/1/2005)*

Stoneleigh 2004 Riesling (Marlborough) $16. 89 —*J.C. (7/1/2006)*

Stoneleigh 2003 Riesling (Marlborough) $15. 87 —*J.C. (7/1/2005)*

Stoneleigh 2007 Sauvignon Blanc (Marlborough) $16. Light and fresh, with slightly pungent notes accenting crisp grapefruit flavors. A bit too light to stand up to most foods, so try it on its own as an apéritif. Imported by Pernod Ricard, USA. 85 —*J.C. (12/31/2007)*

Stoneleigh 2006 Sauvignon Blanc (Marlborough) $16. Starts off with plenty of sweaty, passionfruit aromas, but delivers ripe citrus and pink grapefruit flavors. It's plump and round on the palate, finishing crisp and citrusy. Imported by Pernod Ricard USA. 87 —*J.C. (5/1/2007)*

Stoneleigh 2004 Sauvignon Blanc (Marlborough) $15. 85 —*J.C. (7/1/2005)*

STRATFORD

Stratford 2003 Pinot Noir (Martinborough) $40. 86 —*J.C. (12/1/2005)*

SUNSHINE BAY

Sunshine Bay 2004 Pinot Noir (Marlborough) $15. 87 —*J.C. (12/1/2005)*

SYREN

Syren 2001 Pinot Noir (Central Otago) $27. 89 —*J.C. (9/1/2003)*

TE AWA

Te Awa 2002 Boundary Bordeaux Blend (Hawke's Bay) $32. 89 —*J.C. (11/1/2006)*

Te Awa 2001 Boundary Bordeaux Blend (Hawke's Bay) $25. 89 —*J.C. (5/1/2006)*

Te Awa 2004 Chardonnay (Hawke's Bay) $21. 91 Editors' Choice —*J.C. (5/1/2006)*

Te Awa 2005 Longlands Chardonnay (Hawke's Bay) $16. Despite this wine's ample weight, it lacks a bit of generosity, instead leaving behind dry, minerally impressions of pencil shavings and citrus fruits. 85 —*J.C. (11/1/2007)*

Te Awa 2002 Merlot (Hawke's Bay) $16. 89 —*J.C. (5/1/2006)*

Te Awa 2003 Zone 6 Merlot-Cabernet Sauvignon (Hawke's Bay) $30. A blend of 61% Merlot and 37% Cabernet Sauvignon, this medium-bodied red comes across as a bit firm and earthy. It sure smells fine, combining tobacco, earth, red currants and vanilla, but doesn't seem to have the richness of fruit to stand up to the structure in the long run. Drink now, with rare beef or lamb. 86 —*J.C. (11/1/2007)*

Te Awa 2006 Sauvignon Blanc (Hawke's Bay) $20. A lovely departure from most New Zealand Sauvignons, Te Awa's version offers ripe fruit—peaches and nectarines—brushed with a touch of oak. Relatively full-bodied, with grilled-fruit flavors that bring summer immediately to mind. 89 —*J.C. (7/1/2007)*

Te Awa 2005 Sauvignon Blanc (Hawke's Bay) $20. 91 Editors' Choice —*J.C. (11/1/2006)*

Te Awa 2004 Sauvignon Blanc (Hawke's Bay) $16. 90 Editors' Choice —*J.C. (5/1/2006)*

Te Awa 2004 Syrah (Hawke's Bay) $27. 88 —*J.C. (11/1/2006)*

Te Awa 2002 Syrah (Hawke's Bay) $20. 90 Editors' Choice —*J.C. (5/1/2006)*

TE AWA FARM

Te Awa Farm 1998 Boundary Bordeaux Blend (Hawke's Bay) $23. 91 Editors' Choice —*J.C. (5/1/2001)*

Te Awa Farm 1999 Longlands Bordeaux Blend (Hawke's Bay) $16. 87 —*J.C. (5/1/2001)*

Te Awa Farm 1998 Frontier Chardonnay (Hawke's Bay) $20. 89 —*J.C. (5/1/2001)*

Te Awa Farm 2000 Longlands Chardonnay (Hawke's Bay) $14. 87 Best Buy —*M.M. (12/15/2001)*

Te Awa Farm 1999 Longlands Chardonnay (Hawke's Bay) $16. 88 —*J.C. (5/1/2001)*

Te Awa Farm 1999 Longlands Merlot (Hawke's Bay) $16. 88 —*J.C. (5/1/2001)*

Te Awa Farm 1999 Pinotage (Hawke's Bay) $16. 88 —*J.C. (5/1/2001)*

Te Awa Farm 2000 Frontier Sauvignon Blanc (Hawke's Bay) $20. 89 —*J.C. (5/1/2001)*

Te Awa Farm 2000 Longlands Sauvignon Blanc (Hawke's Bay) $12. 85 —*J.C. (5/1/2001)*

Te Awa Farm 2000 Longlands Syrah (Hawke's Bay) $21. 89 *(11/1/2001)*

TE HERA

Te Hera 2004 Pinot Noir (Martinborough) $NA. 89 —*J.C. (12/1/2005)*

TE KAIRANGA

Te Kairanga 1999 Cabernet Sauvignon (Martinborough) $15. 80 —*J.C. (5/1/2001)*

Te Kairanga 2004 Chardonnay (Martinborough) $20. 87 *(12/15/2006)*

Te Kairanga 2002 Chardonnay (Martinborough) $18. 89 —*J.C. (9/1/2003)*

Te Kairanga 2005 Casarina Reserve Chardonnay (Martinborough) $30. 91 *(12/15/2006)*

Te Kairanga 1999 Reserve Chardonnay (Martinborough) $20. 88 —*J.C. (5/1/2001)*

Te Kairanga 2006 Pinot Noir (Martinborough) $20. One of the less exensive bottlings from the tiny region of Martinborough, Te Kairanga's regular bottling represents a solid value. The sappy plum and black cherry flavors carry mushroomy, savory undertones characteristic of the region, finishing snappy and fresh, with good persistence. Tasty now, but should last a few years, too. 88 —*J.C. (5/1/2007)*

Te Kairanga 2004 Pinot Noir (Martinborough) $20. 88 *(12/15/2006)*

Te Kairanga 2003 Pinot Noir (Wairarapa) $20. 84 —*J.C. (12/1/2005)*

Te Kairanga 2002 Pinot Noir (Martinborough) $26. 87 —*J.C. (4/1/2004)*

Te Kairanga 2000 Pinot Noir (Martinborough) $23. 84 —*M.S. (12/15/2001)*

Te Kairanga 2005 John Martin Reserve Pinot Noir (Martinborough) $42. 90 *(12/15/2006)*

Te Kairanga 2003 Reserve Pinot Noir (Martinborough) $42. 88 —*J.C. (12/1/2005)*

Te Kairanga 1999 Reserve Pinot Noir (Martinborough) $35. 85 —*J.C. (5/1/2001)*

Te Kairanga 2005 Runholder Pinot Noir (Martinborough) $30. 89 *(12/15/2006)*

Te Kairanga 2004 Runholder Pinot Noir (Martinborough) $30. 90 Editors' Choice —*J.C. (9/1/2006)*

Te Kairanga 2008 Sauvignon Blanc (Martinborough) $18. 89 *(12/15/2006)*

Te Kairanga 2001 Sauvignon Blanc (Martinborough) $14. 93 Best Buy —*S.H. (11/15/2002)*

Te Kairanga 2000 Sauvignon Blanc (Martinborough) $15. 86 —*J.C. (5/1/2001)*

TE MATA

Te Mata 2004 Woodthorpe Pinot Noir (Hawke's Bay) $25. 87 —*J.C. (11/1/2006)*

Te Mata 2006 Woodthorpe Vineyard Sauvignon Blanc (Hawke's Bay) $18. Fresh and fruity, featuring pear and melon accented by floral notes. Finishes with hints of pineapple and grapefruit. Lightweight and refreshing. 87 —*J.C. (7/1/2007)*

Te Mata 2005 Woodthorpe Sauvignon Blanc (Hawke's Bay) $18. 86 —*J.C. (11/1/2006)*

Te Mata 2002 Woodthorpe Sauvignon Blanc (Hawke's Bay) $18. 86 —*J.C. (9/1/2003)*

TERRACE HEIGHTS ESTATE

Terrace Heights Estate 2005 Pinot Noir (Marlborough) $29. A suave, fruit-driven wine that's deceptively easy to drink. It isn't very complex, but it's still a pleasure, offering plenty of plum, black cherry and cola flavors, medium body and a creamy-smooth texture. Finishes clean and fresh without being excessively tart. Drink now. 87 —*J.C. (7/1/2007)*

Terrace Heights Estate 2003 Pinot Noir (Marlborough) $NA. 85 —*J.C. (12/1/2005)*

Terrace Heights Estate 2006 Sauvignon Blanc (Marlborough) $19. Combines ripe flavors of honey-dipped grapefruit with less-ripe flavors of green pepper in a zesty mouthful. Despite a slightly oily mouthfeel, it finishes green and fresh, making it an ideal counterpoint to the local green-lipped mussels. 87 —*J.C. (7/1/2007)*

Terrace Heights Estate 2005 Sauvignon Blanc (Marlborough) $20. 85 —*J.C. (7/1/2006)*

TERRACE ROAD

Terrace Road 2001 Sauvignon Blanc (Marlborough) $17. 91 —*S.H. (11/15/2002)*

TERRAVIN

Terravin 2003 Pinot Noir (Omaka Valley) $36. 87 —*J.C. (12/1/2005)*

Terravin 2003 Hillside Selection Pinot Noir (Omaka Valley) $59. 88 —*J.C. (12/1/2005)*

Terravin 2004 Sauvignon Blanc (Omaka Valley) $21. 87 —*J.C. (5/1/2006)*

THE CROSSINGS

The Crossings 2006 Unoaked Chardonnay (Marlborough) $16. Like most unoaked Chardonnays, this is a bit simply fruity, but it's also clean and fresh. Apple, melon and citrus flavors are easily carried by its medium body and mouthwatering finish. 86 —*J.C. (12/1/2007)*

The Crossings 2006 Pinot Noir (Marlborough) $20. A fruit-driven style, showing plenty of black cherries, accented by cola, herb and spice notes. The palate is pleasantly smooth and satiny in texture before turning tart on the finish. Drink now-2010. 87 —*J.C. (11/1/2007)*

The Crossings 2005 Pinot Noir (Marlborough) $20. 88 —*J.C. (12/15/2006)*

The Crossings 2004 Pinot Noir (Marlborough) $20. 89 —*J.C. (12/1/2005)*

The Crossings 2003 Pinot Noir (Marlborough) $20. 88 —*J.C. (8/1/2004)*

The Crossings 2006 Sauvignon Blanc (Marlborough) $16. Very crisp and fresh, this is filled with citrusy pleasures—lime and grapefruit—but also features passionfruit and a pungent, herbal streak. Zingy and refreshing. 87 —*J.C. (7/1/2007)*

The Crossings 2005 Sauvignon Blanc (Marlborough) $16. 91 Editors' Choice —*J.C. (7/1/2006)*

The Crossings 2004 Sauvignon Blanc (Marlborough) $17. 89 —*J.C. (12/1/2005)*

The Crossings 2003 Sauvignon Blanc (Marlborough) $16. 90 Editors' Choice —*J.C. (8/1/2004)*

The Crossings 2002 Sauvignon Blanc (Awatere Valley) $16. 90 Editors' Choice —*J.C. (9/1/2003)*

The Crossings 2001 Awatere Valley Sauvignon Blanc (Marlborough) $16. 90 Editors' Choice *(8/1/2002)*

The Crossings 2004 Catherine's Run Sauvignon Blanc (Awatere Valley) $20. 91 Editors' Choice —*J.C. (5/1/2006)*

The Crossings 2002 Catherine's Run Reserve Sauvignon Blanc (Awatere Valley) $25. 87 —*J.C. (9/1/2003)*

THE JIBE

The Jibe 2004 Pinot Noir (Marlborough) $15. 85 —*J.C. (12/1/2005)*

The Jibe 2005 Sauvignon Blanc (Marlborough) $15. 86 *(3/1/2006)*

THE RED SQUARE

The Red Square 2004 For The People Pinot Noir (Hawke's Bay) $20. 84 —*J.C. (12/15/2006)*

The Red Square 2006 For The People Sauvignon Blanc (Marlborough) $16. This charitable endeavor that helps fund student scholarships in Hawkes Bay has yet to really strike gold with any of its wines. This Sauvignon features pleasant herbal and passionfruit shadings but finishes with a touch of sweetness and just lacks zip. 84 —*J.C. (3/1/2007)*

THORNBURY

Thornbury 2005 Chardonnay (Gisborne) $19. Textbook Gisborne Chardonnay, marrying ripe peach and pineapple aromas with oaky notes of toasted grain. It's full and lush, the mouthcoating fruit set off by judicious oak. Finishes toasty and tropical, with plenty of length. Drink now. 90 —*J.C. (11/1/2007)*

Thornbury 2006 Pinot Gris (Marlborough) $0. Thick and slightly sweet—the residual sugar here clocks in at 9.7g/L—this is a ripe, well-rounded Pinot Gris filled with flavors of apple, pear and melon. Cantaloupe is especially noticeable on the finish. Try well-chilled as an apéritif, or perhaps with slightly spicy foods. 86 *(7/1/2007)*

Thornbury 2004 Pinot Gris (Marlborough) $21. 86 —*J.C. (7/1/2005)*

Thornbury 2005 Pinot Noir (Central Otago) $0. Made in a full-bodied, slightly beefy style, with broad shoulders, this does show typical Central Otago flavors of black cherries, beets, cola and coffee. A solid effort from Bannockburn fruit. 87 *(7/1/2007)*

Thornbury 2004 Pinot Noir (Marlborough) $24. 86 —*J.C. (11/1/2006)*

Thornbury 2003 Pinot Noir (Marlborough) $NA. 83 —*J.C. (12/1/2005)*

Thornbury 2002 Pinot Noir (Marlborough) $25. 87 —*J.C. (4/1/2004)*

Thornbury 2006 Sauvignon Blanc (Marlborough) $17. Thornbury is a brand developed by winemaker Steve Bird, then later acquired by Villa Maria's George Fistonich. This is an intensely aromatic wine, with scents of passionfruit, lime and bell pepper that burst from the glass. On the palate, it's crisp and medium-bodied, with hints of peach to balance the bit of capsicum. Lively and tangy on the finish. 88 *(7/1/2007)*

Thornbury 2005 Sauvignon Blanc (Marlborough) $17. 86 —*J.C. (11/1/2006)*

Thornbury 2004 Sauvignon Blanc (Marlborough) $19. 85 —*J.C. (7/1/2005)*

Thornbury 2002 Sauvignon Blanc (Marlborough) $17. 89 —*J.C. (9/1/2003)*

Thornbury 2001 Sauvignon Blanc (Marlborough) $17. 87 *(8/1/2002)*

THREE MINERS

Three Miners 2003 Pinot Noir (Central Otago) $38. 85 —*J.C. (12/1/2005)*

TOHU

Tohu 2001 Chardonnay (Gisborne) $15. 88 *(9/1/2003)*

Tohu 2000 Chardonnay (Gisborne) $16. 88 —*D.T. (12/15/2001)*

Tohu 2005 Unoaked Chardonnay (Gisborne) $16. Fresh and lively, combining peach, apple and citrus flavors in a fruit cocktail of a wine that's just complex enough to stand up sip after sip. It's medium-bodied, with a juicy, mouthwatering finish. Pair it with grilled chicken or fish and a fruit-based salsa. 88 —*J.C. (11/1/2007)*

Tohu 2002 Reserve Chardonnay (Gisborne) $22. 88 *(9/1/2003)*

Tohu 2000 Reserve Chardonnay (Gisborne) $22. 85 —*J.C. (7/1/2002)*

Tohu 2003 Unoaked Chardonnay (Gisborne) $10. 88 Best Buy —*J.C. (8/1/2004)*

Tohu 2005 Pinot Noir (Marlborough) $23. Like many 2005s, this is a considerable step up over the previous vintage, boasting better concentration and ripeness than the somewhat lackluster 2004. While there's a lot of savory notes of cola, meat and spice to this wine, it gets a lift on the finish from hints of raspberry and vanilla. Drink now. 89 —*J.C. (3/1/2007)*

Tohu 2004 Pinot Noir (Marlborough) $20. 85 —*J.C. (7/1/2006)*

Tohu 2002 Pinot Noir (Marlborough) $20. 90 *(9/1/2003)*

Tohu 2001 Pinot Noir (Marlborough) $25. 91 *(9/1/2003)*

Tohu 2006 Sauvignon Blanc (Marlborough) $16. This Sauvignon from a Maori-owned venture is a bit extreme in style, but well-made. It leans toward the vegetal side of Sauv Blanc, hinting at string beans and green tomatoes, then closes with a powerful blast of white-grapefruity tartness. Drink now. 87 —*J.C. (9/1/2007)*

Tohu 2005 Sauvignon Blanc (Marlborough) $16. 85 —*J.C. (11/1/2006)*

Tohu 2003 Sauvignon Blanc (Marlborough) $14. 88 Best Buy —*J.C. (8/1/2004)*

Tohu 2002 Sauvignon Blanc (Marlborough) $14. 89 Best Buy *(9/1/2003)*

Tohu 2001 Sauvignon Blanc (Marlborough) $15. 87 —*M.S. (12/15/2001)*

Tohu 1999 Sauvignon Blanc (Marlborough) $15. 88 —*M.S. (10/1/2000)*

TOM EDDY

Tom Eddy 2004 Tenz Sauvignon Blanc (Marlborough) $17. 87 —*J.C. (7/1/2005)*

TORLEESE

Torlesse 2002 Sauvignon Blanc (Waipara) $16. 87 —*J.C. (9/1/2003)*

Torlesse 2004 Pinot Noir (Canterbury) $23. 85 —*J.C. (12/1/2005)*

Torlesse 2002 Pinot Noir (Canterbury) $18. 84 —*J.C. (7/1/2005)*

Torlesse 2004 Riesling (Waipara) $18. 87 —*J.C. (11/1/2006)*

Torlesse 2004 Riesling (Canterbury) $13. 87 —*J.C. (7/1/2006)*

Torlesse 2003 Riesling (Marlborough) $16. 89 —*J.C. (7/1/2005)*

Torlesse 2005 Sauvignon Blanc (Waipara) $19. 89 —*J.C. (9/1/2006)*

Torlesse 2004 Sauvignon Blanc (Waipara) $15. 84 —*J.C. (7/1/2005)*

TRINITY HILL

Trinity Hill 1998 Gimblett Road Cabernet Sauvignon (Hawke's Bay) $30. 90 —*J.C. (5/1/2001)*

Trinity Hill 1998 Gimblett Road Chardonnay (Hawke's Bay) $30. 90 —*J.C. (5/1/2001)*

Trinity Hill 1999 Gimblett Merlot (Hawke's Bay) $35. 86 —*J.C. (5/1/2001)*

Trinity Hill 2003 High Country Pinot Noir (Hawke's Bay) $30. 87 —*J.C. (12/1/2005)*

Trinity Hill 2004 Riesling (Marlborough) $15. 88 —*J.C. (7/1/2006)*

Trinity Hill 1999 Gimblett Road Syrah (Hawke's Bay) $35. 87 —*J.C. (5/1/2001)*

Trinity Hill 2002 Homage Syrah (Hawke's Bay) $100. 90 —*J.C. (5/1/2006)*

TROUT VALLEY

Trout Valley 2001 Chardonnay (Nelson) $12. 82 —*J.C. (9/1/2003)*

Trout Valley 2001 Chardonnay (Marlborough) $14. 84 —*J.C. (8/1/2004)*

TUATARA

Tuatara 2001 Chardonnay (Nelson) $16. 85 —*J.C. (9/1/2003)*

Tuatara 2001 Pinot Noir (Nelson) $NA. 84 —*J.C. (4/1/2004)*

Tuatara 2002 Sauvignon Blanc (Nelson) $12. 86 —*J.C. (9/1/2003)*

TWIN ISLANDS

Twin Islands 2001 Pinot Noir (Marlborough) $13. 84 —*S.H. (1/1/2002)*

Twin Islands 2002 Sauvignon Blanc (Marlborough) $12. 85 —*S.H. (1/1/2002)*

TWO PADDOCKS

Two Paddocks 2004 Last Chance Pinot Noir (Central Otago) $35. This wine seems prematurely tired, with dried fruit scents and flavors, some mushroomy notes and tart, lemony acids. 81 —*J.C. (3/1/2007)*

Two Paddocks 2004 Picnic Pinot Noir (Central Otago) $28. Medium-bodied and supple, but the fruit seems to fading, offering up modest black cherry flavors and notes of sous-bois and rhubarb. 83 —*J.C. (3/1/2007)*

TWO TAILS

Two Tails 2004 Sauvignon Blanc (Marlborough) $9. 88 —*J.C. (7/1/2005)*

UNISON VINEYARD

Unison Vineyard 1999 Unison Red Blend (Hawke's Bay) $25. 83 —*J.C. (12/15/2003)*

Unison Vineyard 1999 Unison Selection Red Blend (Hawke's Bay) $25. 85 —*J.C. (12/15/2003)*

VAVASOUR

Vavasour 1999 Awatere Valley Chardonnay (Marlborough) $23. 90 —*J.C. (5/1/2001)*

Vavasour 2006 Pinot Noir (Awatere Valley) $24. A bold, assertive Pinot Noir, with a lattice of briary, herbal complexity layered over a base of ripe black cherries. Together, they make a fascinating intertwined contrast that lingers on the crisp finish. 89 —*J.C. (12/31/2007)*

Vavasour 2004 Pinot Noir (Marlborough) $24. This medium-bodied Pinot shows a touch of clove and saddle leather to go with coffee and earthy black cherry flavors. Picks up a bit of Band-Aid® on the finish, which is nicely textured, with a dusting of silky tannins. 84 —*J.C. (5/1/2007)*

Vavasour 1999 Pinot Noir (Marlborough) $19. 86 —*J.C. (5/1/2001)*

Vavasour 2005 Awatere Valley Pinot Noir (Marlborough) $23. Right now this wine presents itself as being rather light and lacking intensity, but it does have some pretty black cherry fruit and intriguing spice notes, and it should fill out a bit and put on weight over the next year or two. Finishes clean and long, with mild peppery notes and slightly dusty tannins. 89 —*J.C. (3/1/2007)*

Vavasour 2007 Sauvignon Blanc (Awatere Valley) $20. The Awatere is a subregion of Marlborough receiving more and more notice for its distinctive Sauvignons and Pinots. Vavasour was an early pioneer, and the 2007 is especially successful, offering up some slightly sweaty, nettle-y aromas to go along with hints of ripe melons and nectarines. It's nicely concentrated, with a slightly oily mouthfeel and good persistence. **90 Editors' Choice** —*J.C. (12/31/2007)*

Vavasour 2006 Awatere Valley Sauvignon Blanc (Marlborough) $15. Standard Marlborough Sauvignon done well, although in this case the wine comes from the slightly more extreme Awatere Valley. The bouquet features passionfruit, lime and grassy notes, while the flavors are also greenish, but with hints of stone fruit and melon to round them out. The long, herb-inflected finish confirms this wine's quality. 89 —*J.C. (3/1/2007)*

Vavasour 1999 Awatere Valley Sauvignon Blanc (Marlborough) $19. 89 —*J.C. (5/1/2001)*

Vavasour 1999 Single Vineyard Sauvignon Blanc (Awatere Valley) $23. 90 —*J.C. (5/1/2001)*

VIDAL

Vidal 2005 Pinot Noir (Marlborough) $28. Seems a bit more structured than most Marlborough Pinot Noirs, with black cherry fruit and root beer and cola notes buttressed by crisp acids and firm tannins. Give this one a couple of years to mellow before opening. Drink 2008–2012. 89 —*J.C. (3/1/2007)*

Vidal 2006 Sauvignon Blanc (Marlborough) $20. This sister label to Villa Maria better known for its Hawkes Bay red wines has turned out a plump, medium-weight Sauvignon Blanc. It starts with scents of crushed tomato leaf, then folds in grapefruit and a hint of honey on the palate. Turns more powerfully grassy and herbal on the finish, ending on a slightly bitter note. 87 —*J.C. (5/1/2007)*

Vidal 2003 Syrah (Hawke's Bay) $NA. 85 —*J.C. (5/1/2006)*

Vidal 2004 Estate Syrah (Hawke's Bay) $26. After a lack of international success with Merlot and Cabernet, Syrah is being touted as the next hot red from Hawkes Bay. From a top-notch vintage, this wine offers scents of tar, prune and white pepper, then flavors of blackberry, prune and pepper. Finishes with crisp acids and soft tannins. 87 *(7/1/2007)*

Vidal 2004 Soler Syrah (Hawke's Bay) $40. A selection of the best lots, Vidal's Solar Syrah is a big step up from the regular bottling, not showing any overripeness and revealing more complexity. Subtle peppery notes kick-start the bouquet of cedar, vanilla and blackberries, while an intriguing herbal-peppery note winds through the flavors, adding nuance to the bold blueberry and raspberry mix. Creamy-textured, yet with a long, fresh, spice-tinged finish, this is a fine example of Hawkes Bay Syrah. Unfortunately, there are only 50 cases for the U.S. 90 *(7/1/2007)*

VILLA MARIA

Villa Maria 2001 Cellar Selection Cabernet Sauvignon-Merlot Cabernet Blend (Hawke's Bay) $20. 88 —*J.C. (8/1/2004)*

Villa Maria 2002 Private Bin Cabernet Sauvignon-Merlot Cabernet Blend (Hawke's Bay) $13. 86 —*J.C. (8/1/2004)*

Villa Maria 2000 Cellar Selection Cabernet Sauvignon-Merlot (Hawke's Bay) $23. 86 —*J.C. (12/15/2003)*

Villa Maria 2001 Private Bin Cabernet Sauvignon-Merlot (East Coast) $13. 83 —*J.C. (12/15/2003)*

Villa Maria 2000 Private Bin Cabernet Sauvignon-Merlot (Hawke's Bay) $19. 88 —*J.C. (8/1/2002)*

Villa Maria 1999 Private Bin Cabernet Sauvignon-Merlot (Hawke's Bay) $13. 85 —*M.S. (12/15/2001)*

Villa Maria 2005 Keltern Single Vineyard Chardonnay (Hawke's Bay) $30. From a relatively young vineyard in Hawkes Bay, this is a round, fruit-filled Chardonnay framed by toasty, mealy flavors from barrel fermentation and lees stirring. Orange, melon and apricot fruit are just slightly buttery, with a touch of warmth on the finish. 90 *(7/1/2007)*

Villa Maria 2005 Private Bin Chardonnay (Hawke's Bay) $15. 85 —*J.C. (7/1/2006)*

Villa Maria 2003 Private Bin Chardonnay (Marlborough) $13. 85 —*J.C. (7/1/2005)*

Villa Maria 2002 Private Bin Chardonnay (Marlborough) $15. 85 —*J.C. (9/1/2003)*

Villa Maria 2001 Private Bin Chardonnay (Marlborough) $15. 87 —*J.C. (7/1/2002)*

Villa Maria 2000 Private Bin Chardonnay (Marlborough) $13. 86 —*M.M. (12/15/2001)*

Villa Maria 1999 Private Bin Chardonnay (East Coast) $15. 86 —*J.C. (5/1/2001)*

Villa Maria 2005 Single Vineyard Waikahu Vineyard Chardonnay (Hawke's Bay) $35. Villa Maria's single-vineyard wines are usually incredibly expressive, and this flashy Chardonnay from Hawke's Bay is no exception. Bold nectarine and citrus notes are skillfully framed by toasty oak. There's a woody wallop here, but also plenty of fruit, and rather than being heavy, it finishes long and fresh. Delicious now, so there's no need to defer gratification. 92 —*J.C. (11/1/2007)*

Villa Maria 2006 Private Bin Gewürztraminer (East Coast) $15. The equal of Villa Maria's Keltern Vineyard Gewürztraminer for its grace and balance. The nose is floral and perfumed, carrying the essence of the variety home in a medium-bodied, off-dry package. Pear and peach flavors fill out the midpalate, making this very easy to drink. Try with lightly spiced curries or Thai food. 87 —*J.C. (11/1/2007)*

Villa Maria 2004 Single Vineyard Keltern Vineyard Gewürztraminer (Hawke's Bay) $35. Rich, verging on heavy, this barrel-fermented Gewürztraminer may be just too much of a good thing. Honeyed peach and modest spice flavors are palate-coating, then fade abruptly on the finish. 87 —*J.C. (11/1/2007)*

Villa Maria 2004 Twyford Gravels Single Vineyard Merlot (Hawke's Bay) $49. This vineyard was planted in only 2000, yet the wine already shows ample depth. Ripe black cherry flavors are framed by toast, smoke and vanilla shadings from oak aging. Tannins are soft, and the wine relies more on its crisp acidity for structure. Ready to drink. 89 *(7/1/2007)*

Villa Maria 2005 Private Bin Merlot-Cabernet Sauvignon (Hawke's Bay) $15. Merlot dominates the blend by about a 2:1 ratio, yielding a smooth, supple wine that firms up just enough on the dusty finish to give it the proper structure. The cherry fruit flavors are clean and fresh, anchored by darker berry notes and hints of bittersweet chocolate. Drink now–2010. 87 —*J.C. (5/1/2007)*

Villa Maria 2004 Private Bin Merlot-Cabernet Sauvignon (Hawke's Bay) $15. 87 —*J.C. (12/15/2006)*

Villa Maria 2006 Seddon Single Vineyard Pinot Gris (Marlborough) $0. At their cellar door, Villa actually has several single-vineyard Pinot Gris for sale, all of impeccable quality. This example is rich and weighty, slightly sweet, but balanced by great acidity. Aromas of lime sherbet and melon blend easily into fruit flavors that carry more than a hint of berries. Complex, balanced and long. 91 *(7/1/2007)*

Villa Maria 2005 Cellar Selection Pinot Noir (Marlborough) $28. On the full side for Marlborough Pinot Noir, with a round mouthfeel and creamy texture. Flavors are rich and meaty, with notes of cola, smoke and plum and cherry fruit that lingers elegantly on the finish, picking up hints of dried flowers and tea leaves. 90—*J.C. (3/1/2007)*

Villa Maria 2003 Cellar Selection Pinot Noir (Marlborough) $28. 88 —*J.C. (12/1/2005)*

Villa Maria 2002 Cellar Selection Pinot Noir (Marlborough) $28. 87 *(8/1/2004)*

Villa Maria 2006 Private Bin Pinot Noir (Marlborough) $20. Sturdy and chunky, with pleasant notes of black cherries and plums set off by cola and coffee. It's mouthfilling and ripe—a pleasant red that doesn't show the silky, seductive side of Pinot Noir, but a rather more muscular physique. 86 —*J.C. (12/31/2007)*

Villa Maria 2005 Private Bin Pinot Noir (Marlborough) $20. Light- to medium-bodied with a pleasantly creamy texture, Villa's entry-level Pinot remains a consistent performer. Mushroom and cinnamon notes accent tart cherry-berry fruit, finishing with dark chocolate shadings. Drink now. 87 —*J.C. (3/1/2007)*

Villa Maria 2004 Private Bin Pinot Noir (Marlborough) $19. 86 *—J.C. (9/1/2006)*

Villa Maria 2005 Reserve Pinot Noir (Marlborough) $37. Despite some spicy, herbal nuances on the nose, this is surprisingly one-dimensional on the palate, offering little more than bold black cherry fruit and maybe a hint of sassafras. Some dusty tannins on the finish suggest cellaring one or two years in the hopes that more complexity will emerge. **88** *—J.C. (5/1/2007)*

Villa Maria 2003 Reserve Pinot Noir (Marlborough) $37. 90 *—J.C. (12/1/2005)*

Villa Maria 2002 Reserve Pinot Noir (Marlborough) $35. 88 *—J.C. (8/1/2004)*

Villa Maria 2001 Reserve Pinot Noir (Marlborough) $37. 87 *—J.C. (9/1/2003)*

Villa Maria 2005 Taylors Pass Single Vineyard Pinot Noir (Marlborough) $49. Shows that Marlborough shouldn't be discounted when discussing New Zealand's best Pinot Noir regions. It's wonderfully floral and complex on the nose, dealing scents of rose petals, cola and black cherry, wrapped in a silky filigree of herbal notes. It's full-bodied, yet elegant and finely textured, with excellent persistence. Drink now, but it should last a few more years. **91** *(7/1/2007)*

Villa Maria 2002 Botrytis Selection Reserve Noble Riesling (Marlborough) $45. 90 *(8/1/2004)*

Villa Maria 2006 Cellar Selection Riesling (Marlborough) $19. Wonderfully forward and fruity, this is simply a delight to taste. Apple and lime aromas are rounded out by just a hint of peach, while the flavors of ripe peaches and apples are kept focused by stabs of citrus. Medium-bodied, with a touch of sweetness to balance the crisp acids, this would make a great apéritif. **90** *—J.C. (9/1/2007)*

Villa Maria 2005 Cellar Selection Riesling (Marlborough) $19. With more than 20g/L residual sugar, you might expect this wine to be rather sweet, but because of its high acidity it only registers as off dry. Lime and grapefruit flavors are flecked with green apple and petrol, finishing soft but with a citrusy edge. Drink now. **87** *—J.C. (9/1/2007)*

Villa Maria 2001 Cellar Selection Riesling (Marlborough) $22. 91 *—J.C. (8/1/2002)*

Villa Maria 2006 Private Bin Riesling (Marlborough) $15. All of Villa Maria's 2006 Rieslings hit the target, balancing modest residual sugar with crisp acids. Even this entry-level offering boasts bold fruit—apple and citrus—plus hints of crushed stone and a lingering finish. Drink now. **89** *—J.C. (9/1/2007)*

Villa Maria 2005 Private Bin Riesling (Marlborough) $15. 88 *—J.C. (7/1/2006)*

Villa Maria 2004 Private Bin Riesling (Marlborough) $13. 89 Best Buy *—J.C. (7/1/2005)*

Villa Maria 2003 Private Bin Riesling (Marlborough) $13. 88 Best Buy *—J.C. (8/1/2004)*

Villa Maria 2001 Private Bin Riesling (Marlborough) $15. 86 *—J.C. (8/1/2002)*

Villa Maria 2000 Private Bin Riesling (Marlborough) $14. 85 *—J.C. (5/1/2001)*

Villa Maria 1999 Private Bin Riesling (Marlborough) $12. 87 *—M.S. (10/1/2000)*

Villa Maria 2006 Waldron Vineyard Riesling (Marlborough) $35. With its relatively modest alcohol (10.5%) and lovely sugar-acid balance, this Riesling could pass for an excellent spätlese. Aromas are floral and fruit-filled, yielding hints of apple, pineapple and even a suggestion of red berries, while the flavors echo with apples, stone fruit and strawberries. Clean and fresh on the finish. This is delicious now, but should hold at least 5–6 years, maybe longer. **91** *—J.C. (9/1/2007)*

Villa Maria 2004 Cellar Selection Sauvignon Blanc (Marlborough) $20. 89 *(7/1/2005)*

Villa Maria 2003 Cellar Selection Sauvignon Blanc (Marlborough) $19. 88 *—J.C. (8/1/2004)*

Villa Maria 2002 Cellar Selection Sauvignon Blanc (Marlborough) $22. 85 *—J.C. (9/1/2003)*

Villa Maria 2001 Cellar Selection Sauvignon Blanc (Marlborough) $22. 86 *(8/1/2002)*

Villa Maria 2000 Cellar Selection Sauvignon Blanc (Marlborough) $22. 87 *—J.C. (5/1/2001)*

Villa Maria 2006 Clifford Bay Reserve Sauvignon Blanc (Marlborough) $27. This is supremely perfumed, almost pungent in its intensity, with plenty of presence on the palate and bold flavors of peach, pineapple and complex layers of herbaceousness. Despite its power and weight, it remains surprisingly elegant on the long finish. **92 Editors' Choice** *(7/1/2007)*

Villa Maria 2005 Clifford Bay Reserve Sauvignon Blanc (Marlborough) $31. A good warning against holding Marlborough Sauvignon Blanc too long. This wine is already losing some fruit, showing a touch of asparagus or green bean. It's still impressively complex and weighty, with a rich, slightly oily mouthfeel, but deserved to be tasted earlier in its life. **87** *—J.C. (12/1/2007)*

Villa Maria 2004 Clifford Bay Reserve Sauvignon Blanc (Marlborough) $32. 88 *(7/1/2005)*

Villa Maria 2003 Clifford Bay Reserve Sauvignon Blanc (Marlborough) $30. 90 *—J.C. (8/1/2004)*

Villa Maria 2002 Clifford Bay Reserve Sauvignon Blanc (Marlborough) $30. 88 *—J.C. (9/1/2003)*

Villa Maria 2000 Clifford Bay Reserve Sauvignon Blanc (Marlborough) $30. 89 *—J.C. (5/1/2001)*

Villa Maria 2006 Gateway Vineyard Sauvignon Blanc (Marlborough) $30. This is the first year that this wine is available in the U.S. Scents of passionfruit and orange zest burst from the glass, while the flavors are ripe—more toward the melon and fig side of the SB spectrum. It's round in the mouth, just lightly green, with an underlying sense of minerality that closes long and crisp. **91** *—J.C. (7/1/2007)*

Villa Maria 2007 Private Bin Sauvignon Blanc (Marlborough) $16. This medium-bodied Sauvignon Blanc doesn't have the lush tropical fruit of some versions, or the sharp pungency of others. What it does have is a balanced, minerally mouthfeel and crisp, citrusy flavors ideal for matching with simple seafood dishes. **88** *—J.C. (12/1/2007)*

Villa Maria 2006 Private Bin Sauvignon Blanc (Marlborough) $19. 90 *—J.C. (9/1/2006)*

Villa Maria 2005 Private Bin Sauvignon Blanc (Marlborough) $15. 88 *—J.C. (5/1/2006)*

Villa Maria 2004 Private Bin Sauvignon Blanc (Marlborough) $13. 86 *—J.C. (7/1/2005)*

Villa Maria 2003 Private Bin Sauvignon Blanc (Marlborough) $13. 86 *—J.C. (8/1/2004)*

Villa Maria 2002 Private Bin Sauvignon Blanc (Marlborough) $13. 86 *—J.C. (9/1/2003)*

Villa Maria 2001 Private Bin Sauvignon Blanc (Marlborough) $15. 90 Editors' Choice *(8/1/2002)*

Villa Maria 2000 Private Bin Sauvignon Blanc (Marlborough & Hawke's Bay) $12. 86 *—J.C. (5/1/2001)*

Villa Maria 2001 Reserve Sauvignon Blanc (Clifford Bay) $29. 93 *—S.H. (11/15/2002)*

Villa Maria 1998 Reserve Sauvignon Blanc (Clifford Bay) $25. 89 *—S.H. (8/1/1999)*

Villa Maria 2006 Taylors Pass Vineyard Sauvignon Blanc (Marlborough) $35. This is a wonderfully expressive NZ SAuvignon Blanc, oozing with tropical fruit, but with greenish overtones of fresh herbs and tomato leaves. Bold passionfruit rules the nose, with the herbal notes providing balance. Medium- to full-bodied, with a long finish, this should drink well over the next year or so. **92 Editors' Choice** *—J.C. (11/1/2007)*

Villa Maria 2004 Cellar Selection Syrah (Hawke's Bay) $21. A complex, relatively soft Syrah that's a new offering for Villa Maria here in the U.S. The aromas feature smoke, vanilla, meat and mushroom, while the flavors add cola to the mix. It's a creamy-textured wine that seems destined for early consumption. **89** *—J.C. (7/1/2007)*

VINOPTIMA

Vinoptima 2003 Reserve Ormond Gewürztraminer (Gisborne) $53. 89 *—J.C. (5/1/2006)*

VOSS

Voss 2005 Pinot Noir (Martinborough) $39. An atypically lush, full-bodied Pinot, this harkens back to the winery's excellent 2001 in style, ripe and plummy, yet with complex notes of coffee, meat, dried herbs and cracked pepper. Long on the finish, where hints of black tea emerge. Imported by Meadowbank Estates. **92** *—J.C. (7/1/2007)*

Voss 2003 Pinot Noir (Martinborough) $40. 87 *—J.C. (12/1/2005)*

Voss 2002 Pinot Noir (Martinborough) $41. 87 *—J.C. (8/1/2004)*

Voss 2001 Pinot Noir (Martinborough) $40. 92 *—J.C. (9/1/2003)*

Voss 2005 Riesling (Martinborough) $21. 86 *—J.C. (11/1/2006)*

Voss 2004 Riesling (Martinborough) $20. 87 *—J.C. (7/1/2006)*

VYNFIELDS

Vynfields 2003 Reserve Pinot Noir (Martinborough) $NA. 89 *—J.C. (12/1/2005)*

WAIHEKE VINEYARD

Waiheke Vineyard 1998 Te Motu (The Island) Cabernet Sauvignon-Merlot (Waiheke Island) $48. 82 —*J.C. (12/15/2003)*

WAIRAU RIVER

Wairau River 1998 Chardonnay (Marlborough) $25. 84 —*J.C. (7/1/2002)*

Wairau River 1997 Chardonnay (Marlborough) $20. 87 —*J.C. (5/1/2001)*

Wairau River 1997 Reserve Chardonnay (Marlborough) $22. 89 —*J.C. (5/1/2001)*

Wairau River 2004 Home Block Pinot Noir (Marlborough) $25. 85 —*J.C. (9/1/2006)*

Wairau River 1999 Reserve Botrytised Riesling (Marlborough) $24. 93 Editors' Choice —*J.M. (12/1/2002)*

Wairau River 1998 Reserve Botrytised Riesling (Marlborough) $58. 90 —*J.C. (5/1/2001)*

Wairau River 2006 Sauvignon Blanc (Marlborough) $19. Starts off with aromas of passionfruit and lime, then adds a hint of green pea to the tropical fruit and citrus flavors. Medium-bodied, with a zesty, fresh finish. Drink now. 87 —*J.C. (11/1/2007)*

Wairau River 2005 Sauvignon Blanc (Marlborough) $19. 86 —*J.C. (5/1/2006)*

Wairau River 2002 Sauvignon Blanc (Marlborough) $17. 87 —*J.C. (9/1/2003)*

Wairau River 2001 Sauvignon Blanc (Marlborough) $17. 87 *(8/1/2002)*

Wairau River 2000 Sauvignon Blanc (Marlborough) $20. 86 —*J.C. (5/1/2001)*

Wairau River 2004 Home Block Sauvignon Blanc (Marlborough) $25. 82 —*J.C. (12/15/2006)*

Wairau River 2002 Reserve Sauvignon Blanc (Marlborough) $25. 83 *(7/1/2005)*

Wairau River 2001 Reserve Sauvignon Blanc (Marlborough) $24.84 —*J.C. (9/1/2003)*

Wairau River 2000 Reserve Sauvignon Blanc (Marlborough) $24. 89 *(8/1/2002)*

Wairau River 1999 Reserve Sauvignon Blanc (Marlborough) $28. 86 —*(11/15/2002)*

Wairau River 1998 Reserve Sauvignon Blanc (Marlborough) $24. 86 —*J.C. (5/1/2001)*

WHITEHAVEN

Whitehaven 2005 Pinot Noir (Marlborough) $30. This may not have the complexity of some of the country's best Pinots, but this is still a fine example of what New Zealand can do with the variety. Clean black cherry fruit is accented by touches of vanilla and dried spices, while the mouthfeel is soft, with well-concealed tannin. The finish is finely textured, adding lingering notes of cinnamon and clove. 88 —*J.C. (7/1/2007)*

Whitehaven 2004 Pinot Noir (Marlborough) $30. 88 —*J.C. (7/1/2006)*

Whitehaven 2003 Pinot Noir (Marlborough) $28. 86 —*J.C. (12/1/2005)*

Whitehaven 2002 Pinot Noir (Marlborough) $29. 89 —*J.C. (8/1/2004)*

Whitehaven 2000 Pinot Noir (Marlborough) $22. 92 Editors' Choice —*M.S. (12/15/2001)*

Whitehaven 2001 Estate Grown Pinot Noir (Marlborough) $24. 87 —*J.C. (9/1/2003)*

Whitehaven 2006 Sauvignon Blanc (Marlborough) $22. Intense passionfruit and citrus aromas blast from the glass, leaving no doubt about the intensity. Thankfully, it's harmonious as well, blending ripe notes of melon and fig with strident citrus flavors and a hint of jalapeño on the finish. 90 —*J.C. (7/1/2007)*

Whitehaven 2005 Sauvignon Blanc (Marlborough) $20. 84 —*J.C. (9/1/2006)*

Whitehaven 2004 Sauvignon Blanc (Marlborough) $16. 87 —*J.C. (7/1/2005)*

Whitehaven 2003 Sauvignon Blanc (Marlborough) $17. 87 —*J.C. (8/1/2004)*

Whitehaven 2001 Sauvignon Blanc (Marlborough) $16. 90 Editors' Choice *(8/1/2002)*

Whitehaven 2000 Sauvignon Blanc (Marlborough) $15. 80 —*M.M. (1/1/2004)*

Whitehaven 2002 Estate Grown Sauvignon Blanc (Marlborough) $15. 86 —*J.C. (9/1/2003)*

WILD EARTH

Wild Earth 2004 Pinot Noir (Central Otago) $30. 89 —*J.C. (12/15/2006)*

WILD ROCK

Wild Rock 2006 Cupids Arrow Pinot Noir (Central Otago) $18. Plummy yet herbal at the same time, this Pinot from the folks at Craggy Range hints at rhubarb and beet greens, but relies on a sturdy core of sour plum to carry it. It's a bit chunky, with a dusting of tannins on the finish. Imported by Kobrand Corporation. 87 —*J.C. (12/1/2007)*

Wild Rock 2006 The Infamous Goose Sauvignon Blanc (Marlborough) $15. This is a round, approachable white, with just enough leafy notes to let you know it's Sauvignon Blanc. A hint of honey adds softness to the melon and citrus flavors, which gain tartness on the finish. Drink now. Imported by Kobrand Corporation. 88 —*J.C. (11/1/2007)*

WILLOW CREEK

Willow Creek 2000 Pinot Noir (Canterbury) $16. 80 —*J.C. (9/1/2003)*

WITHER HILLS

Wither Hills 2002 Chardonnay (Marlborough) $20. 87 —*J.C. (8/1/2004)*

Wither Hills 2005 Pinot Noir (Marlborough) $30. Sweetly oaky, this Pinot doesn't seem to have quite the stuffing it needs to stand up to the heavy coat of brown sugar, cedar and vanilla. Some cherry and cola flavors peek through, ending on crisp, lemony note. A bit disappointing compared to the last few vintages, but at least the suggested retail price has come down. 84 —*J.C. (5/1/2007)*

Wither Hills 2004 Pinot Noir (Marlborough) $36. 88 —*J.C. (12/1/2005)*

Wither Hills 2003 Pinot Noir (Marlborough) $NA. 87 —*J.C. (11/1/2006)*

Wither Hills 2002 Pinot Noir (Marlborough) $32. 87 —*J.C. (8/1/2004)*

Wither Hills 2006 Sauvignon Blanc (Marlborough) $15. Plagued by controversy back home because of different bottlings, the one imported to the U.S. is a plump, fruit-filled wine. Lime and passionfruit aromas and tropical flavors show no signs of Sauvignon's sometime vegetal side, finishing short and arguably a little sweet. 87 —*J.C. (5/1/2007)*

Wither Hills 2005 Sauvignon Blanc (Marlborough) $20. 89 —*J.C. (5/1/2006)*

Wither Hills 2004 Sauvignon Blanc (Marlborough) $23. 89 *(7/1/2005)*

Wither Hills 2003 Sauvignon Blanc (Marlborough) $20. 88 —*J.C. (8/1/2004)*

WOOING TREE

Wooing Tree 2005 Pinot Noir (Central Otago) $35. This wine was a big award winner back in New Zealand, and it's easy to see why. It's full-bodied and rich but never heavy, with complex aromas and flavors that include cola and coffee, black cherries and plums, cinnamon and clove. Finishes long, with mouthwatering acids and a fine coating of silky tannins. Delicious now, but should last through at least 2012, maybe longer. 92 Editors' Choice —*J.C. (5/1/2007)*

WOOLLASTON

Woollaston 2004 Pinot Noir (Nelson) $30. 86 —*J.C. (12/1/2005)*

Woollaston 2005 Pinot Rosé Pinot Noir (Nelson) $16. 87 —*J.C. (12/1/2005)*

Woollaston 2005 Sauvignon Blanc (Nelson) $NA. 89 —*J.C. (5/1/2006)*

Woollaston 2005 Morgan Leigh Sauvignon Blanc (Nelson) $NA. 86 —*J.C. (5/1/2006)*

Woollaston 2001 Sémillon-Sauvignon Blanc (Nelson) $14. 82 —*J.C. (9/1/2003)*

WYCROFT

Wycroft 2003 Old River Terrace Pinot Noir (Wairarapa) $NA. 88 —*J.C. (12/1/2005)*

ZEAL

Zeal 2007 Sauvignon Blanc (Marlborough) $12. Citrus and herb aromas set the mouth watering, anticipating a crisp, bracing wine. But this one's surprisingly soft in the mouth, filling out with tropical fruit flavors that could use a bit more zest. 84 —*J.C. (12/31/2007)*

Zeal 2005 Sauvignon Blanc (Marlborough) $13. 82 —*J.C. (5/1/2006)*

ZENITH

Zenith 2001 Sauvignon Blanc (Marlborough) $11. 81 —*J.C. (9/1/2003)*

Portugal

Portugal has always had Port. Vintage Port and Late Bottled Vintage Port are the best sellers in the United States, but aged tawnies should command increasing interest. With the great strides in winemaking techniques and the results of great research into grape varieties and vineyard sites being put into practice, Portugal's Port is entering a golden age.

What makes Portugal so exciting at the moment is that the same can now be said of Portuguese table wines. The days of Portugal being known for only lightly sparkling Rosé are long gone, although the wines themselves are still widely available. Increasingly, wines with the quality to be poured at the top international tables are arriving in America from Portugal, and the number of these wines is increasing with each new harvest.

Terraced vineyards at Taylor's Quinta da Vargellas, high in the Dours Valley east of Prinhão, Portugal

Encouragingly, Portugal has not copied the rest of the world. As with the Italians, Portuguese winemakers have not capitulated to international grape varieties and tastes. But, unlike the Italians, who enjoy playing with Cabernet, Chardonnay, and have acres of Merlot, Portuguese vineyards are still almost entirely planted with the great native varietals.

The boiler house of new developments in Portugal is the Douro Valley. Many of the same people who also make Port are making the greatest table wines. They use Portugal's greatest red grape varieties, Touriga Nacional, Tinta Roriz, Tinta Franca, Souzão, Tinta Cão, and Tinta Barroca, generally blended, invariably wood aged (although often in large wood barrels). The tastes are powerful, intense, tannic; the wines are long-lived.

South of the Douro, the Dão region also makes reds, which can be ageworthy (see Glossary). The Dão, lacking the same wealth of winemaking talent, has lagged behind, but there are now enough producers of quality to show that the style of the reds is going to be less intense than the Douro, more mineral, more herbal.

But Portugal is not only a red wine country. One of the country's most famous wines, Vinho Verde, produced in the far north of the country, is normally seen overseas in its white version (the tart, acid red stays at home and is drunk with sardines). At its best, Vinho Verde can equal some of the whites of the Rías Baixas region of Spain.

More southerly regions of Portugal bring us back to red wine. The Alentejo, the Ribatejo, and Estremadura are three vineyards that straddle the center of the country. These are the good value areas, which can often reach fascinating heights of quality. Warmer and softer wines than the tannic giants of the Douro are produced in greater quantities, making these regions the best way of starting into the adventure of today's Portuguese wines.

ADEGA COOPERATIVA DE VILA NOVA DE TAZEM

Adega Cooperativa de Vila Nova de Tazem 2000 Alfrocheiro Red Blend (Dão) $18. 86 *—J.C. (11/15/2003)*

Adega Cooperativa de Vila Nova de Tazem 2000 Touriga Nacional (Dão) $18. 90 Editors' Choice *—J.C. (11/15/2003)*

ADEGA COOPERATIVA PONTE DE LIMA

Adega Cooperativa Ponte de Lima 2005 Portuguese White (Vinho Verde) $9. 83 *—R.V. (7/1/2006)*

Adega Cooperativa Ponte de Lima 2005 Adamado Portuguese White (Vinho Verde) $9. 84 *—R.V. (7/1/2006)*

ADEGA DE MONSÃO

Adega de Monsão 2005 Alvarinho Deu la Deu Alvarinho (Vinho Verde) $16. 90 Editors' Choice *—R.V. (7/1/2006)*

Adega de Monsão 2005 Danaide Branco Portuguese White (Vinho Verde) $NA. 87 *—R.V. (7/1/2006)*

Adega de Monsão 2005 Muralhas de Monsão Portuguese White (Vinho Verde) $11. 89 *—R.V. (7/1/2006)*

ALENTEX

Alentex 2004 Portuguese Red (Alentejo) $NA. Lightweight wine, tasting of fresh raspberries and Morello cherries, with a high layer of acidity. It's pleasant, but dilute. 82 *—R.V. (12/15/2007)*

Alentex 2004 Trincadeira-Aragonez Portuguese Red (Alentejo) $NA. Firm and tannic with balanced, juicy red fruits—sweet strawberry and red-plum skins. This could age 2–3 years. Its structure is supported by the fruit and wood flavors. 85 *—R.V. (12/15/2007)*

Alentex 2006 Antão Vaz-Arinto Portuguese White (Alentejo) $NA. One of the principle grapes of the Alentejo, Antão Vaz blends easily with the Arinto of neighboring Ribatejo. There is an attractive citrus element to this wood-aged wine, soft, open, but remaining fresh, the tropical fruit flavors well under control. 87 *—R.V. (12/15/2007)*

Alentex 2005 Rosé Blend (Alentejo) $NA. Pink grey in color, this cranberry and cherry cordial flavored wine is full-bodied, rich but still dry. There is some sweetness there, a touch of caramel. 83 *—R.V. (7/1/2007)*

ALTANO

Altano 2000 Portuguese Blend (Douro) $8. 87 Best Buy *—R.V. (12/31/2002)*

Altano 2003 Tinta Roriz-Touriga Franca Portuguese Red (Douro) $7. 84 Best Buy *—J.C. (11/1/2006)*

Altano 2001 Tinta Roriz-Touriga Franca Portuguese Red (Douro) $7. 85 Best Buy *—R.V. (11/1/2004)*

Altano 1999 Portuguese Red (Douro) $8. 82 *—D.T. (12/31/2001)*

Altano 2003 Reserva Portuguese Red (Douro) $18. 90 Editors' Choice *—J.C. (11/1/2006)*

Altano 2000 Reserva Portuguese Red (Douro) $NA. 87 *—R.V. (11/1/2004)*

ANDREZA

Andreza 2003 Reserva Red Blend (Douro) $15. 88 *—J.C. (11/1/2006)*

Andreza 2003 Vinho Tinto Red Blend (Douro) $13. 85 *—J.C. (11/1/2006)*

ANSELMO MENDES

Anselmo Mendes 2005 Muros Antigos Alvarinho (Vinho Verde) $16. 91 Editors' Choice *—R.V. (7/1/2006)*

Anselmo Mendes 2004 Muros de Melgaço Alvarinho (Vinho Verde) $20. 89 *—R.V. (7/1/2006)*

ANTONIO ESTEVES FERREIRA

Antonio Esteves Ferreira 2001 Soalheiro Alvarinho (Vinho Verde) $15. 83 *—J.C. (11/15/2003)*

AVELEDA

Aveleda 2005 Alvarinho (Vinho Verde) $11. 90 Best Buy *—R.V. (7/1/2006)*

Aveleda 2000 Alvarinho (Vinho Verde) $11. 85 *—J.C. (12/31/2001)*

Aveleda 2000 Loureiro (Vinho Verde) $8. 84 *—M.S. (12/31/2001)*

Aveleda 2005 Grinalda Portuguese White (Vinho Verde) $9. 88 Best Buy *—R.V. (7/1/2006)*

Aveleda NV White Blend (Vinho Verde) $6. 86 Best Buy *—D.T. (12/31/2001)*

Aveleda NV Casal Garcia White Blend (Vinho Verde) $6. 85 Best Buy *—M.S. (12/31/2001)*

BACALHÔA WINES OF PORTUGAL

Bacalhôa Wines of Portugal 2003 Quinta da Bacalhôa Cabernet Sauvignon (Terras do Sado) $29. 89 *—R.V. (3/1/2006)*

Bacalhôa Wines of Portugal 2003 Tinto da Anfora Red Portuguese Red (Alentejano) $10. 87 Best Buy *—R.V. (3/1/2006)*

Bacalhôa Wines of Portugal 2003 Tinto da Anfora Grande Escolha Red Blend (Alentejano) $29. 90 *—R.V. (3/1/2006)*

Bacalhôa Wines of Portugal 2003 Só Syrah (Terras do Sado) $25. 91 *—R.V. (3/1/2006)*

Bacalhôa Wines of Portugal 2003 Só Touriga Nacional (Terras do Sado) $25. 87 *—R.V. (3/1/2006)*

BARÃO DE VILAR

Barão de Vilar NV 10-Year Old Tawny Port $26. 90 Editors' Choice *—R.V. (8/1/2006)*

Barão de Vilar NV 20-Year Old Tawny Port $42. 92 *—R.V. (8/1/2006)*

Barão de Vilar 2003 Vintage Port $38. 90 *—R.V. (11/15/2005)*

BARROS

Barros NV 10 Years Old Port $25. 90 *—J.C. (11/15/2003)*

Barros NV 10-Year Old Tawny Port $22. 88 *—R.V. (8/1/2006)*

Barros NV 20-year old Tawny Port (Port) $48. A surprisingly fresh wine for a 20-year-old, but there is still some good burnt toffee character, enlivened by fresh citrus and a firm, slightly austere base of wood and acidity. 86 *—R.V. (11/1/2007)*

Barros NV 20 Years Old Port $35. 90 *—J.C. (11/15/2003)*

Barros 1996 Colheita Port (Port) $23. Although with its vintage date, this is only 10 years' old, don't think of this as another 10-year-old aged tawny. Like most colheitas, aged in wood and not topped up with new wine as are aged tawnies, this is much more concentrated, like syrup. It has some sweetness, but the dominant character is dark Belgian chocolate. Very dense, with a very dry aftertaste. 90 *—R.V. (11/1/2007)*

Barros 1977 Colheita Bottled 2002 Port $75. 91 *—J.C. (11/15/2003)*

Barros NV Hutcheson Porto Rocha Vintage Character Port $17. 83 *—R.V. (3/1/2005)*

Barros 1994 LBV Bottled 2000 Traditional Unfiltered Port $24. 88 *—J.C. (11/15/2003)*

Barros 1996 LBV Bottled 2001 Port $20. 85 *—J.C. (11/15/2003)*

Barros 1997 LBV Bottled 2002 Port $19. 86 *—R.V. (3/1/2003)*

Barros NV Special Reserve Port $NA. 84 *—R.V. (3/1/2005)*

Barros 2003 Vintage Port (Port) $49. A light, soft, sweet modern style of Port, flavored with raisins and some fresh acidity. There are stalky currant flavors, wood tannins, but the main emphasis is on an easy, soon-to-drink character. 88 *—R.V. (11/1/2007)*

BARROS ALMEIDA

Barros Almeida NV 20-Year Old Tawny Port $42. 85 *—R.V. (8/1/2006)*

Barros Almeida NV 30-Year Old Tawny Port $85. 86 *—R.V. (8/1/2006)*

Barros Almeida NV 40-Year Old Tawny Port $130. 82 *—R.V. (8/1/2006)*

Barros Almeida 2003 Vintage Port $40. 88 *—R.V. (11/15/2005)*

BERCO DO INFANTE

Berco Do Infante 2003 Reserva Portuguese Red (Estremadura) $6. 85 Best Buy *—J.C. (6/1/2006)*

BLANDY'S

Blandy's NV Alvada 5 Year Old Rich Madeira Blend (Madeira) $15. 86 *—J.C. (3/1/2005)*

Blandy's NV 10 Years Old Rich Malmsey (Madeira) $37. 91 *—J.C. (11/1/2006)*

Blandy's NV 5 Year Sercial (Madeira) $21. 91 Editors' Choice *—J.C. (11/1/2006)*

Blandy's NV 5 Year Verdelho (Madeira) $21. 87 *—J.C. (11/1/2006)*

BOA NOVA

Boa Nova 2002 Tinto Portuguese Red (Alentejano) $16. 82 *—J.C. (11/1/2006)*

BORGES

Borges 2003 Vintage Port $30. 81 *—R.V. (11/15/2005)*

Borges 2000 Meia Encosta Red Blend (Dão) $5. 85 Best Buy *—J.C. (11/15/2003)*

Borges NV Gatão White Blend (Vinho Verde) $6. 83 *—R.V. (8/1/2004)*

BROADBENT

Broadbent 2003 Vintage Port $85. 90 —*R.V. (11/15/2005)*

BURMEISTER

Burmeister NV Sotto Voce Port $NA. 90 —*R.V. (3/1/2005)*

Burmester 2003 Vintage Port $NA. 85 —*R.V. (11/15/2005)*

Burmester 2002 Tavedo Red Blend (Douro) $8. 82 —*J.C. (11/1/2006)*

BURMESTER

Burmester NV 10-Year Old Tawny Port (Port) $35. Soft and very smooth, perfumed with rosehips and black figs. There's some burnt character, but more of the soft, sweet, treacly style of tawny. 87 —*R.V. (11/1/2007)*

Burmester 1998 Colheita Port (Port) $35. This is too young to have the true taste of a vintage-dated Colheita. It is almost a young tawny, both in color and taste. As such, it is a pleasant wine, with good ripe, sweet fruits, sultanas. At the finish, the spirit is too dominant. 84 —*R.V. (11/1/2007)*

Burmester 2001 Late Bottled Vintage Port (Port) $27. Sweet with flavors of molasses and sweet chocolate, this is for lovers of a gentler side of Port. It is full, certainly, but it glides over the palate, easily and softly. 87 —*R.V. (11/1/2007)*

Burmester 2004 Reserva Portuguese Red (Douro) $23. A firm, very straightforward wine that shows dark tannins, juicy black fruits and an impressive structure. It opens well, with powered intensity and refreshing acidity that balances the richness. 87 —*R.V. (3/1/2007)*

C DA SILVA

C da Silva NV Presidential 20-Year Old Tawny Port $50. 84 —*R.V. (8/1/2006)*

C da Silva NV Presidential 30-Year Old Tawny Port $80. 87 —*R.V. (8/1/2006)*

C da Silva NV Presidential 40-Year Old Tawny Port $100. 89 —*R.V. (8/1/2006)*

CALÇOS DO TANHA

Calços do Tanha 1997 Reserva Portuguese Red (Douro) $19. 86 —*M.S. (12/31/2001)*

Calços do Tanha 1996 Tinto Portuguese Red (Douro) $14. 86 —*J.C. (12/15/2000)*

Calços do Tanha 1999 Touriga Francesa Portuguese Red (Douro) $26. 86 —*J.C. (12/31/2001)*

Calços do Tanha 1998 Vinho Tinto Portuguese Red (Douro) $15. 84 —*J.C. (12/31/2001)*

CÁLEM

Cálem NV 40-Year Old Tawny Port (Port) $130. A golden, glowing wine, very concentrated. The burnt vanilla and dark chocolate flavors are intense. Like many 40-year olds, this has just a hint of a medicinal character, suggesting, and rightly so, that it should be sipped rather than drunk. 92 —*R.V. (11/1/2007)*

Cálem 1994 LBV Bottled 1998 Port (Douro) $19. 89 —*R.V. (3/1/2003)*

Cálem 1997 LBV Bottled 2002 Port $23. 90 —*R.V. (3/1/2003)*

Cálem 1990 Colheita Port (Port) $45. With its dark gold color, this fits the part of an aged, vintage-dated tawny even before tasting. It has great concentration, black raisin flavors, and hugely dense texture, leavened by an equally important layer of acidity. An impressive wine that leaves a very dry aftertaste. 92 Editors' Choice —*R.V. (11/1/2007)*

Cálem 2004 Curva Reserva Portuguese Red (Douro) $0. The main Cálem property is at a curve of the Douro, by the town of Pinhão, hence the name of the wine. It's an earthy, traditional style, not bad for that, but definitely for those who enjoy wines with a touch of volatility. It does go well with rich meat dishes. 84 —*R.V. (3/1/2007)*

Cálem NV Old Friends Fine Ruby Port $14. 85 —*J.C. (11/1/2006)*

Cálem NV Reserva Ruby Port (Port) $17. A full and rich style, with sweetness and jammy red fruits lifted by a citrus touch. This is full-bodied, red currant cordial, very fruity. 85 —*R.V. (11/1/2007)*

Cálem NV Reserva Ruby Port $NA. 86 —*R.V. (3/1/2005)*

Cálem 2003 Vintage Port $85. 89 —*R.V. (11/15/2005)*

Cálem 2000 Vintage Port (Port) $48. Impressively structured, packed with dark, heavy tannins, this is an aromatic Port. The initial black plum fruit and spice flavors are dominated by the structure, promising a good aging potential. 90 —*R.V. (11/1/2007)*

Cálem 2000 Vintage Port $80. 89 —*J.C. (11/1/2006)*

CALHEIROS CRUZ

Calheiros Cruz 1999 Touriga Nacional Tinta Roriz (Douro) $26. 87 —*D.T. (12/31/2001)*

Calheiros Cruz 1999 Touriga Nacional (Douro) $25. 86 —*M.M. (12/31/2001)*

CAMPO ARDOSA

Campo Ardosa 2000 Quinta da Carvalhosa Red Blend (Douro) $28. 94 —*R.V. (12/31/2002)*

CANTANHEDE

Cantanhede 2000 Marquês de Marialva Reserva Baga (Bairrada) $10. 85 —*R.V. (12/31/2002)*

Cantanhede 2001 Marquês de Marialva Reserva Seleccionada Baga (Bairrada) $17. 86 —*R.V. (12/31/2002)*

Cantanhede 1999 Marquês de Marialva Reserva Red Blend (Bairrada) $10. 83 —*R.V. (12/31/2002)*

Cantanhede 2001 Marquês de Marialva White Blend (Bairrada) $NA. 85 —*R.V. (8/1/2004)*

CARDOSO DE MENEZES

Cardoso de Menezes 1999 Quinta da Murqueira Red Blend (Dão) 85 —*R.V. (12/31/2002)*

Cardoso de Menezes 1998 Quinta da Murqueira Reserva Red Blend (Dão) 83 —*R.V. (12/31/2002)*

Cardoso de Menezes 2000 Quinta da Murqueira Touriga Nacional (Dão) 91 —*R.V. (12/31/2002)*

Cardoso de Menezes 2001 Quinta da Murqueira Reserva White Blend (Dão) $5. 87 —*R.V. (8/1/2004)*

CARTUXA

Cartuxa 2006 EA Colheita Seleccionada Portuguese Red (Alentejano) $NA. With its proportion of barrel-aged Trincadeira, this special selection has some pretensions, which are generally fulfilled. There is a great juicy character, from stalky red fruits, acidity and dense tannins. The edge of bitterness is only just apparent, a flaw in an otherwise pleasant wine. 85 —*R.V. (12/15/2007)*

Cartuxa 2006 EA Rosado Portuguese Red (Alentejano) $NA. Pleasantly fresh, touched by caramel. Fresh pink color with very soft, lightly sweet strawberry flavors. 84 —*R.V. (12/15/2007)*

Cartuxa 2006 EA Tinto Portuguese Red (Alentejano) $NA. The least interesting wine in the normally excellent Cartuxa range, this has black currant aromas, but disappoints with its leather character, and tannic, bitter cranberry flavors. 80 —*R.V. (12/15/2007)*

Cartuxa 2005 Foral de Evora Portuguese Red (Alentejano) $NA. A ripe, dense, very serious wine, with a powerful element from the wood aging, dark red fruits and dense tannins. There are black figs, dry blueberry juice flavors and a shot of acidity. It's going to develop, certainly over the next five years. 90 —*R.V. (12/15/2007)*

Cartuxa 2003 Pêra-Manca Portuguese Red (Alentejo) $NA. Made from old vines, this top wine from Cartuxa (the name means a rough, stony place) is revered in Portugal. Only nine vintages have been made since 1986, a selection of a selection. Figs, superripe black plums, dense tannins, and bitter chocolate are all here. An impressive wine; likely to age over 5–10 years. 92 Cellar Selection —*R.V. (12/15/2007)*

Cartuxa 2003 Tinto Portuguese Red (Alentejano) $NA. A gentle wine, surprisingly soft within the context of other reds from Cartuxa. There are dried fruit, sweet acidity, topped by superripe, velvet-textured flavors. Drink now. 87 —*R.V. (12/15/2007)*

Cartuxa 2005 Branco Colheita Portuguese White (Alentejano) $NA. It's the Antão Vaz, the Chardonnay of Portugal, that gives this such class. It is full, tasty and complex, with acidity and superripeness, but still elegant white fruits. Additional richness comes from lees-stirring after fermentation, giving a fine depth of flavor. 88 —*R.V. (12/15/2007)*

Cartuxa 2006 EA Branco Portuguese White (Alentejano) $NA. A blend of Roupeiro, Perrum and Antão Vaz, this is a wine that shows how crisp and fresh (and light) whites from the hot Alentejo can be. There's simple, fresh, crisp fruit, with green plum and tropical fruit flavors, just great for chilling and drinking. 86 —*R.V. (12/15/2007)*

Cartuxa 2005 Pêra-Manca Portuguese White (Alentejo) $NA. The white and red Pêra-Manca are cult wines in Portugal, only released in the best years. The white has partial barrel fermentation, giving great richness and depth of flavor, as well as smooth toastiness. With its high proportion of Antão Vaz, it is very white Burgundy in its richness and sense of mineral terroir. Delicious acidity rounds the wine out. 93 Editors' Choice —*R.V. (12/15/2007)*

CASA CADAVAL

Casa Cadaval 1999 Muge Merlot (Ribatejano) $13. 83 —*J.C. (11/15/2003)*

CASA DA ALORNA

Casa da Alorna 2003 Colheita Seleccionada Portuguese Red (Ribatejo) $14. 90 Best Buy —*J.C. (11/1/2006)*

CASA DE CASAL DE LOIVOS

Casa de Casal de Loivos 2004 Portuguese Red (Douro) $NA. One of the wines produced by Cristiano van Zeller, this comes from a village high above the Pinhao valley. It is deliciously ripe, spicy, with a dense structure and packed flavors of thyme and black berries. Still young, give this another two years at least. 90 Cellar Selection —*R.V. (3/1/2007)*

CASA DE SANTAR

Casa de Santar 2001 Outono de Santar Vindima Tardia Encruzado (Dão) $14. 87 —*J.C. (3/1/2005)*

Casa de Santar 1999 Castas de Santar Portuguese Red (Dão) $8. 83 —*M.M. (12/31/2001)*

Casa de Santar 2000 Reserva Portuguese Red (Dão) $20. 92 —*R.V. (11/1/2004)*

Casa de Santar 1998 Reserva Portuguese Red (Dão) $16. 85 —*M.S. (12/31/2001)*

Casa de Santar 2001 Castas de Santar Red Blend (Dão) $8. 86 Best Buy —*J.C. (11/15/2003)*

Casa de Santar 2000 Castas de Santar Red Blend (Dão) $8. 87 Best Buy —*R.V. (12/31/2002)*

Casa de Santar 1999 Reserva Red Blend (Dão) $15. 90 —*R.V. (12/31/2002)*

Casa de Santar 2001 Tinto Superior Red Blend (Dão) $14. 85 —*J.C. (11/1/2004)*

Casa de Santar 2000 Touriga Nacional (Dão) $43. 88 —*R.V. (11/1/2004)*

Casa de Santar 2000 Touriga Nacional (Dão) $43. 91 —*J.C. (11/15/2003)*

Casa de Santar 2001 Castas de Santar Touriga Nacional (Dão) $10. 88 Best Buy —*R.V. (11/1/2004)*

Casa de Santar 2001 Reserva Touriga Nacional Blend (Dão) $19. 86 —*J.C. (11/1/2004)*

CASA DE SEZIM

Casa de Sezim 2003 Portuguese White (Vinho Verde) $NA. 87 —*R.V. (8/1/2005)*

Casa de Sezim 2005 Grande Escolha Portuguese White (Vinho Verde) $8. 89 Best Buy —*R.V. (7/1/2006)*

Casa de Sezim NV Sezim Portuguese White (Vinho Verde) $7. 84 Best Buy —*R.V. (7/1/2006)*

Casa de Sezim 2001 Sociedade Agricola Pecuaria White Blend (Vinho Verde) $NA. 89 —*R.V. (8/1/2004)*

CASA DE VILA VERDE

Casa de Vila Verde 2005 Alvarinho (Vinho Verde) $12. 85 —*R.V. (7/1/2006)*

Casa de Vila Verde 2004 Alvarinho (Minho) $14. 90 Best Buy —*R.V. (8/1/2005)*

Casa de Vila Verde 2005 Portuguese White (Vinho Verde) $8. 82 —*R.V. (7/1/2006)*

Casa de Vila Verde 2003 White Blend (Vinho Verde) $9. 86 Best Buy —*J.C. (3/1/2005)*

Casa de Vila Verde 2004 Estate White Blend (Vinho Verde) $10. 84 —*J.C. (12/31/2005)*

CASA DI TONDA

Casa di Tonda 2004 Quinta dos Grilos Portuguese Red (Dão) $11. 89 Best Buy —*R.V. (11/15/2006)*

CASA FERREIRINHA

Casa Ferreirinha 2001 Esteva Portuguese Red (Douro) $10. 85 Best Buy —*J.C. (12/1/2004)*

Casa Ferreirinha 1991 Barca Velha Red Blend (Douro) $80. 90 *(10/1/2000)*

Casa Ferreirinha 1997 Esteva Red Blend (Douro) $10. 87 Best Buy *(10/1/2000)*

Casa Ferreirinha 2004 Quinta da Leda Portuguese Red (Douro) $60. The Quinta da Leda is high up the Douro, in the remote regions of Douro Superior. This 2004 shows the concentration of the fruit in the dark tannins, the toasty new wood and the ripe dark plum fruits. It is smooth enough to drink now, but the tannins promise 5–6 years aging. 90 Cellar Selection —*R.V. (9/1/2007)*

Casa Ferreirinha 1989 Reserva Red Blend (Douro) $46. 87 *(10/1/2000)*

Casa Ferreirinha 2002 Vinha Grande Portuguese Red (Douro) $20. From Ferreira's own vineyards in the Douro, this smooth, ripe, wood laden wine is spicy, with blackberry fruits, a shot of dark tannins, and fresh, juicy acidity. Age for another 2–3 years before drinking. 88 —*R.V. (9/1/2007)*

Casa Ferreirinha 1994 Vinha Grande Red Blend (Douro) $19. 88 *(11/15/1999)*

CASA SANTA EUFEMIA

Casa Santa Eufemia NV 10-Year Old Tawny Port $39. 88 —*R.V. (8/1/2006)*

Casa Santa Eufemia NV 20-Year Old Tawny Port $NA. 82 —*R.V. (8/1/2006)*

Casa Santa Eufemia NV 30-Year Old Tawny Port $NA. 84 —*R.V. (8/1/2006)*

Casa Santa Eufemia NV 40-Year Old Tawny Port $NA. 85 —*R.V. (8/1/2006)*

CASA SANTOS LIMA

Casa Santos Lima 2006 Fernão Pires Fernão Pires (Estremadura) $0. Freshly aromatic, this is a Portuguese equivalent of a Gewürztraminer. It has all the lychees and spice as well as a thick, almost viscous texture. Good acidity helps the balance. Delicious, as an apéritif or with Asian food. 89 —*R.V. (12/15/2007)*

Casa Santos Lima 2005 Palha-Canas Portuguese Red (Estremadura) $11. An elegant, understated wine that shows balanced red fruits, vanilla and touches of chocolate. Its attractiveness lies in the balance, with structure and acidity keeping the exuberant fruit flavors in check. Worth aging for 1–2 years. 89 —*R.V. (12/15/2007)*

Casa Santos Lima 2006 Palha-Canas Portuguese White (Estremadura) $7. A delicious, ripe and creamy wine, tasting of white fruits. An esoteric blend of Arinto, Fernão Pires, Vital and Chardonnay. It has a good, mineral edge along with lifted, fresh acidity. 87 Best Buy —*R.V. (12/15/2007)*

Casa Santos Lima 2000 Palha-Cana Vinho Tinto Red Blend (Estremadura) $9. 85 Best Buy —*D.T. (11/15/2002)*

Casa Santos Lima 2005 Quinta de Bons-Ventos Portuguese Red (Estremadura) $7. Touched by the ocean breezes, this vineyard has long ripening, cool-climate characteristics. And this blend of Castelão, Camarate, Tinta Miúda and Touriga Nacional is elegant, with soft, velvet tannins balancing well with the plum skin and the refreshing acidity. It all holds together very well. 88 —*R.V. (12/15/2007)*

Casa Santos Lima 2004 Touriz Portuguese Red (Estremadura) $14. No prizes from Portuguese varietal experts for guessing that this is a blend with Touriga (Nacional and Franca) and Tinta Roriz. The wine itself is rounded, soft and sweet, with sweet black plums just touched by acidity, but more about open tannins and rich, dried fruits. 87 —*R.V. (12/15/2007)*

Casa Santos Lima 2004 Sousão (Estremadura) $14. Bitter chocolate and dried apricots vie with each other in this curious wine. It is certainly too big and rich for its own good, a blockbuster of a wine, but without the complexity that could compensate. What is here are very ripe plums and a layer of dry, bitter tannins. 84 —*R.V. (12/15/2007)*

CASAL DE VALLE PRADINHOS

Casal de Valle Pradinhos 2001 Porta Velha Red Blend (Trás-os-Montes) $10. 86 Best Buy —*J.C. (3/1/2004)*

Casal de Valle Pradinhos 2000 Valle Pradinhos Red Blend (Trás-os-Montes) $15. 85 —*J.C. (3/1/2004)*

CASAL DOS JORDÕES

Casal dos Jordões NV Finest Reserve Port $NA. 82 —*R.V. (3/1/2005)*

Casal dos Jordões 2000 Vintage Port) $NA. 80 —*J.C. (11/1/2006)*

Casal dos Jordões 2003 Reserva Touriga Franca (Douro) $NA. 89 —*R.V. (3/1/2006)*

CASTELLO D'ALBA

Castello d'Alba 2003 Colheita Seleccionada Red Blend (Douro) $12. 86 —*J.C. (11/1/2006)*

Castello d'Alba 2003 Tinto Reserva Red Blend (Douro) $12. 86 —*J.C. (11/1/2006)*

Castello d'Alba 2005 Branco Reserva White Blend (Douro) $12. 90 Best Buy —*J.C. (11/1/2006)*

Castello d'Alba 2004 Vinhas Velhas Branco White Blend (Douro) $17. 87 —*J.C. (11/1/2006)*

CAVES ALIANÇA

Caves Aliança 2004 Galeria Bical (Bairrada) $8. 85 Best Buy —*R.V. (8/1/2005)*

Caves Aliança 2001 Alabastro Portuguese Red (Alentejano) $8.5. 84 —*R.V. (12/1/2004)*

Caves Aliança 2004 Alabastro Reserva Portuguese Red (Alentejano) $14. A hugely rich wine, packed with dried fruit flavors and spice from aging in American oak. This is a dense blend of Aragonez, Trincadeira and

Cabernet Sauvignon, merging well together, the Cabernet giving structure, the other grapes the rich, smooth texture and black fruits. **88** *—R.V. (9/1/2007)*

Caves Aliança 2003 Alabastro Reserva Portuguese Red (Alentejano) $14. **86** *—R.V. (3/1/2006)*

Caves Aliança 2001 Alabastro Reserva Portuguese Red (Alentejano) $13. **89** *—R.V. (12/1/2004)*

Caves Aliança 2005 Aliança Foral Portuguese Red (Douro) $8. A fruity, juicy wine, all ripe raspberries and red plum skins. It is fresh, with a layer of dry tannins, but more fruit than structure. **85 Best Buy** *—R.V. (9/1/2007)*

Caves Aliança 2004 Aliança Particular Portuguese Red (Dão) $11. Beefy, burly wine, shot through with dry Dão tannins, dry and firm. The fruit is juicy, lightly rustic, with high acidity coming through its rich meat gravy flavors. **86 Best Buy** *—R.V. (9/1/2007)*

Caves Aliança 2000 Aliança Particular Portuguese Red (Dão) $10. **89 Best Buy** *—R.V. (11/1/2004)*

Caves Aliança 1996 Particular Portuguese Red (Dão) $11. **87 Best Buy** *—M.S. (10/1/1999)*

Caves Aliança 2005 Aliança Reserva Portuguese Red (Dão) $8. A firm, dry lean wine, with some tough tannins, but also with great red fruits and good freshness. This young Dão, with its blend of Tinta Roriz, Jaen and Touriga Nacional, is likely to develop, with its tannins and acidity softening. At the moment, freshness is the key. **87 Best Buy** *—R.V. (9/1/2007)*

Caves Aliança 2004 Quinta da Terrugem Portuguese Red (Alentejo) $23. From Aliança's Alentejo Terrugem vineyard, this dense, tannin-packed wine has powerful flavors of dark fruits, a very dry backbone and layer upon layer of tarry, smoky tastes. Initially it overwhelms with its richness, but that softens and the acidity gives the wine a lifted vibrancy. **90** *—R.V. (9/1/2007)*

Caves Aliança 2001 Quinta da Terrugem Portuguese Red (Alentejo) $20. **88** *—R.V. (3/1/2006)*

Caves Aliança 2000 Quinta da Terrugem Portuguese Red (Alentejo) $24. **87** *—R.V. (12/1/2004)*

Caves Aliança 2004 Quinta das Baceladas Portuguese Red (Bairrada) $25. A rare Portuguese Merlot and Cabernet Sauvignon blend, made with the involvement of Bordeaux winemaker Pascal Chatonnet, working with Caves Aliança's winemaker Francisco Antunes. Does it work? Yes, as a delicious curiosity. There is no connection with Portugal, but there is smooth new wood, and some pepper from alcohol. Then tannins are dry, the fruit is very ripe and very rich. **90** *—R.V. (9/1/2007)*

Caves Aliança 2001 Quinta das Baceladas Portuguese Red (Beiras) $25. **91** *—R.V. (11/1/2004)*

Caves Aliança 2001 Quinta dos Quatro Ventos Reserva Portuguese Red (Douro) $45. **90** *—R.V. (11/1/2004)*

Caves Aliança 2001 T da Terrugem Portuguese Red (Alentejo) $60. **90** *—R.V. (12/1/2004)*

Caves Aliança 2002 T Quinta da Terrugem Portuguese Red (Alentejo) $57. **92** *—R.V. (3/1/2006)*

Caves Aliança 2004 Portuguese White (Dão) $7. **83** *—R.V. (8/1/2005)*

Caves Aliança 1998 Alianca Classico Reserva Red Blend (Beiras) $9. **87** *—R.V. (12/31/2002)*

Caves Aliança 1999 Alianca Floral Reserva Red Blend (Douro) $7. **84** *—R.V. (12/31/2002)*

Caves Aliança 1999 Alianca Particular Red Blend (Palmela) $15. **88** *—R.V. (12/31/2002)*

Caves Aliança 1998 Alianca Particular Red Blend (Dão) $13. **83** *—R.V. (12/31/2002)*

Caves Aliança 1998 Alianca Reserva Red Blend (Dão) $7. **82** *—R.V. (12/31/2002)*

Caves Aliança 1998 Floral Grande Escolha Red Blend (Douro) $13. **88** *—R.V. (12/31/2002)*

Caves Aliança 1995 Floral Grande Escolha Red Blend (Douro) $13. **87** *(11/15/1999)*

Caves Aliança 1996 Foral Reserva Red Blend (Douro) $9. **85** *(11/15/1999)*

Caves Aliança 1997 Quinta da Terrugem Red Blend (Alentejo) $20. **90** *—R.V. (12/31/2002)*

Caves Aliança 1999 Quinta das Baceladas Single Estate Red Blend (Beiras) $26. **89** *—R.V. (12/31/2002)*

Caves Aliança 1999 Quinta dos Quatro Ventos Red Blend (Douro) $30. **88** *—R.V. (12/31/2002)*

Caves Aliança 1999 Galeria Tinta Roriz (Douro) $9. **90 BestBuy** *—R.V. (12/31/2002)*

CAVES DO CERCA

Caves do Cerca 2005 Famega Portuguese White (Vinho Verde) $7. **85** *—R.V. (7/1/2006)*

CAVES DO SOLAR DE SÃO DOMINGOS

Caves do Solar de São Domingos 2000 Prestígio Red Blend (Beiras) $14. **81** *—J.C. (11/15/2003)*

CAVES DOM TEODOSIO

Caves Dom Teodosio 2005 Lagosta Portuguese White (Vinho Verde) $7. **85** *—R.V. (7/1/2006)*

Caves Dom Teodosio 1995 Quinta de S. Joao Batista Reserva Red Blend (Douro) $13. **82** *—M.S. (11/15/2002)*

CAVES MESSIAS

Caves Messias 2003 Vintage Port $NA. **86** *—R.V. (11/15/2005)*

CAVES SÃO JOÃO

Caves São João 1990 Quinta do Poço do Lobo Cabernet Sauvignon (Bairrada) $20. **89** *(10/1/1999)*

CHARAMBA

Charamba 1999 Portuguese Red (Douro) $6. **84 Best Buy** *—M.M. (12/31/2001)*

CHURCHILL'S

Churchill's NV 10-Year Old Tawny Port $30. **87** *—R.V. (8/1/2006)*

Churchill's NV 20-Year Old Tawny Port $51. **89** *—R.V. (8/1/2006)*

Churchill's NV Finest Vintage Character Port $17. **83** *—J.C. (12/1/2004)*

Churchill's NV Finest Vintage Character Port $17. **86** *—R.V. (3/1/2005)*

Churchill's 1998 LBV Port $24. **87** *—J.C. (12/1/2004)*

Churchill's 1996 LBV Port $24. **89** *—M.S. (11/15/2002)*

Churchill's 1997 LBV Bottled 2001 Port $21. **87** *—R.V. (3/1/2003)*

Churchill's 1998 Quinta Da Agua Alta Port $60. **89** *—M.S. (11/15/2002)*

Churchill's 1999 Quinta da Gricha Port $64. **89** *—M.S. (11/15/2002)*

Churchill's 2003 Quinta da Gricha Vintage Port $85. **83** *—R.V. (11/15/2005)*

Churchill's 2001 Quinta da Gricha Vintage Port $80. **88** *—J.C. (12/1/2004)*

Churchill's 2000 Quinta da Gricha Vintage Port $83. **87** *—J.C. (11/15/2003)*

Churchill's NV Tawny Ten Years Old Port $30. **88** *—J.C. (11/15/2003)*

Churchill's NV Tawny Ten Years Old Port $30. **87** *—M.S. (7/1/2002)*

Churchill's NV Ten Years Old Tawny Port $30. **85** *—J.C. (12/1/2004)*

Churchill's 2003 Vintage Port $95. **92** *—R.V. (11/15/2005)*

Churchill's NV Vintage Character Port $17. **86** *—M.S. (11/15/2002)*

Churchill's 2000 Vintage Port $82. **93 Cellar Selection** *—J.C. (11/15/2003)*

Churchill's 1997 Vintage Port $82. **87** *—M.S. (11/15/2002)*

Churchill's NV White Port $17. **83** *—M.S. (11/15/2002)*

CISTUS

Cistus 2002 Reserva Red Blend (Douro) $14. **88** *—J.C. (6/1/2006)*

COCKBURN'S

Cockburn's NV 10-Year Old Tawny Port $30. **83** *—R.V. (8/1/2006)*

Cockburn's NV 20-Year Old Tawny Port $50. **82** *—R.V. (8/1/2006)*

Cockburn's 1996 LBV Port $20. **85** *—J.C. (3/1/2004)*

Cockburn's 1998 Quinta dos Canais Port $50. **88** *—M.S. (11/15/2002)*

Cockburn's 2003 Quinta dos Canais Vintage Port $56. **87** *—R.V. (11/15/2005)*

Cockburn's 2001 Quinta dos Canais Vintage Port $NA. **93** *—J.C. (3/1/2004)*

Cockburn's 2000 Quinta dos Canais Vintage Port $60. **91** *—J.C. (3/1/2004)*

Cockburn's 1999 Quinta dos Canais Vintage Port $NA. **92** *—J.C. (3/1/2004)*

Cockburn's 1995 Quinta dos Canais Vintage Port $NA. **89** *—J.C. (3/1/2004)*

Cockburn's NV Special Reserve Port $16. **83** *—J.C. (11/1/2006)*

Cockburn's 2003 Vintage Port $65. **86** *—R.V. (11/15/2005)*

Cockburn's 2000 Vintage Port $90. **92** *—J.C. (3/1/2004)*

Cockburn's 1994 Vintage Port $NA. **88** *—J.C. (3/1/2004)*

Cockburn's 1977 Vintage Port $NA. **93** *—J.C. (3/1/2004)*

Cockburn's 1970 Vintage Port $NA. **91** *—J.C. (3/1/2004)*

Cockburn's 1963 Vintage Port $NA. **90** *—J.C. (3/1/2004)*

Cockburn's 1955 Vintage Port $NA. **96** *—J.C. (3/1/2004)*

Cockburn's 1947 Vintage Port $NA. 93 —*J.C. (3/1/2004)*

Cockburn's 1935 Vintage Port $NA. 88 —*J.C. (3/1/2004)*

Cockburn's 1927 Vintage Port $NA. 97 —*J.C. (3/1/2004)*

Cockburn's 1912 Vintage Port $NA. 89 —*J.C. (3/1/2004)*

Cockburn's NV Fine Tawny Red Blend (Port) $12. 82 —*J.C. (11/15/2003)*

COMPANHIA DAS QUINTAS

Companhia das Quintas 2001 Quinta da Romeira Arinto (Bucelas) $NA. 87 —*R.V. (8/1/2004)*

Companhia das Quintas 2002 Tradição Tinto Castelão (Palmela) $10. 84 —*J.C. (6/1/2006)*

Companhia das Quintas 2000 Cado Portuguese Red (Douro) $14. 87 —*J.C. (3/1/2005)*

Companhia das Quintas 2004 Quinta da Romeira Prova Régia Portuguese White (Bucelas) $7. 88 Best Buy —*R.V. (8/1/2005)*

Companhia das Quintas 2004 Quinta do Cardo Portuguese White (Beira Interior) $6. 88 Best Buy —*R.V. (8/1/2005)*

Companhia das Quintas 2004 Quinta do Cardo Síria Portuguese White (Beira Interior) $7. 89 Best Buy —*R.V. (8/1/2005)*

Companhia das Quintas 2000 Aristocrata Red Blend (Estremadura) $6. 82 —*R.V. (12/31/2002)*

Companhia das Quintas 1999 Fronteira Red Blend (Douro) $NA. 87 —*R.V. (12/31/2002)*

Companhia das Quintas 1999 Fronteira Reserva Red Blend (Douro) $NA. 89 —*R.V. (12/31/2002)*

Companhia das Quintas 2000 Quinta do Cardo Red Blend (Beira Interior) $10. 85 —*R.V. (12/31/2002)*

Companhia das Quintas 2000 Tradicao Red Blend (Palmela) $6. 85 —*R.V. (12/31/2002)*

Companhia das Quintas 2000 Tradicao Red Blend (Beira Interior) $6. 82 —*R.V. (12/31/2002)*

Companhia das Quintas 1999 Quinta do Cardo Touriga Nacional (Beira Interior) $14. 88 —*R.V. (12/31/2002)*

Companhia das Quintas 1999 Quinta do Cardo Reserva Touriga Nacional Blend (Beira Interior) $11. 86 —*R.V. (12/31/2002)*

Companhia das Quintas 2001 Calhandriz White Blend (Estremadura) $NA. 82 —*R.V. (8/1/2004)*

Companhia das Quintas 2001 Quinta do Cardo White Blend (Beira Interior) $NA. 81 —*R.V. (8/1/2004)*

COOPERATIVA AGRICOLA DE SANTO ISIDRO DE PEGOES

Cooperativa Agricola de Santo Isidro de Pegoes 2000 Fontanario de Pegoes Portuguese Red (Palmela) 88 —*R.V. (12/31/2002)*

Cooperativa Agricola de Santo Isidro de Pegoes 2000 Adega de Pegoes Colheita Seleccionada Touriga Nacional-Cabernet Sauvignon (Terras do Sado) $13. 90 —*R.V. (12/31/2002)*

Cooperativa Agricola de Santo Isidro de Pegoes 2001 Adega de Pegoes Colheita Seleccionada White Blend (Terras do Sado) $NA. 90 —*R.V. (8/1/2004)*

Cooperativa Agricola de Santo Isidro de Pegoes 2001 Vale de Judia White Blend (Terras do Sado) $NA. 89 —*R.V. (8/1/2004)*

CORTES DE CIMA

Cortes de Cima 2004 Aragonês (Alentejano) $NA. A soft, but spicy wine made from the Portuguese version of Tempranillo, giving rounded, silky tannins, balanced with fresh red berry fruits. With its acid highlights, it needs time to calm down, but it should be attractively ripe in one year. 89 —*R.V. (12/15/2007)*

Cortes de Cima 2003 Aragonês (Alentejano) $NA. Big and dense, the tannins showing a dusty character from the heat of 2003 and the long, dry harvest. The wine shows plenty of structure, the fruits are big and jammy, very hot and ripe. Acidity seems to be missing, though, with all this ripe fruit around. 88 —*R.V. (12/15/2007)*

Cortes de Cima 2004 Portuguese Red (Alentejano) $NA. A finely balanced wine that shows structure as well as rich fruits. It has ripe red fruits, spice and toast that hang well together, the fruit held in check by the structure of the wine. This would be worth aging for two years or more. 90 Editors' Choice —*R.V. (12/15/2007)*

Cortes de Cima 2002 Portuguese Red (Alentejano) $18. 91 —*R.V. (3/1/2006)*

Cortes de Cima 2001 Portuguese Red (Alentejano) $18. 88 —*R.V. (12/1/2004)*

Cortes de Cima 2006 Chaminé Portuguese Red (Alentejano) $NA. Dominated by Aragonez and Syrah, this is a fresh, fruity wine, tasting of delicious red fruits, light acidity, soft tannins. An earthy edge adds vigor. 85 —*R.V. (12/15/2007)*

Cortes de Cima 2004 Chaminé Portuguese Red (Alentejano) $11. 86 Best Buy —*R.V. (3/1/2006)*

Cortes de Cima 2002 Chamine Portuguese Red (Alentejano) $12. 86 Best Buy —*R.V. (12/1/2004)*

Cortes de Cima 2002 Incognito Portuguese Red (Alentejano) $NA. 88 —*R.V. (12/1/2004)*

Cortes de Cima 2003 Incógnito Portuguese Red (Alentejano) $45. 87 —*R.V. (3/1/2006)*

Cortes de Cima 2003 Reserva Portuguese Red (Alentejano) $58. Made from a selection of the best parcels in the Cortes de Cima vineyard, this is a heady blend of raisins, dark plums and firm, dark tannins. It layers superripe, almost sweet, concentrated flavors along with a core of dryness that stops the wine being too jammy, and gives it a splendid structure. A blend of Syrah, Aragonez and Touriga Nacional. 91 —*R.V. (3/1/2007)*

Cortes de Cima 2001 Reserva Portuguese Red (Alentejano) $NA. 92 Editors' Choice —*R.V. (12/1/2004)*

Cortes de Cima 2001 Red Blend (Alentejo) $21. 89 —*J.C. (3/1/2004)*

Cortes de Cima 2000 Red Blend (Alentejano) $20. 87 —*R.V. (12/31/2002)*

Cortes de Cima 2000 Chamine Red Blend (Alentejo) $12. 87 Best Buy —*J.C. (1/1/2004)*

Cortes de Cima 2000 Chamine Red Blend (Alentejano) $11. 86 Best Buy —*R.V. (12/31/2002)*

Cortes de Cima 2000 Incognito Red Blend (Alentejano) $33. 88 —*R.V. (12/31/2002)*

Cortes de Cima 1998 Reserva Red Blend (Alentejano) $45. 91 —*R.V. (12/31/2002)*

Cortes de Cima 2003 Syrah (Alentejano) $NA. A wine that is quite over the top, with perfumed fruit, dark, dusty tannins, layers of toast, dark, juicy plums and an aftertaste of black figs and bitter chocolate. Hold for a year or two. 87 —*R.V. (12/15/2007)*

Cortes de Cima 2004 Icognito Syrah (Alentejano) $46. This is called Icognito because Syrah was not allowed in the Alentejo at the time it was launched. It has since become a signature wine for Hans Jorgensen at Cortes de Cima. It's a great mouthful of soft, ripe fruit, full-bodied with flavors of cranberries and dark raisins. 88 —*R.V. (3/1/2007)*

Cortes de Cima 2001 Incógnito Syrah (Alentejo) $37. 88 —*J.C. (1/1/2004)*

Cortes de Cima 2004 Syrah Syrah (Alentejano) $NA. A gentle giant of a wine, this powers through the tannins and the acidity to give great ripe black damson and plum fruits, a juicy richness, just lifted by a touch of toast. The aftertaste is impressive, lifted with acidity and freshness after all that power. 90 —*R.V. (12/15/2007)*

Cortes de Cima 2003 Touriga Nacional (Alentejano) $43. 90 —*R.V. (3/1/2006)*

Cortes de Cima 2002 Touriga Nacional (Alentejano) $NA. 85 —*R.V. (12/1/2004)*

Cortes de Cima 2004 Trincadeira Trincadeira (Alentejano) $NA. A high-perfumed, highly individualistic wine, with beetroot and sweet red cherry flavors, leaving freshness and lively acidity. The 100% Trincadeira gives character to a wine that would go well with rich stews in the winter. 87 —*R.V. (12/15/2007)*

Cortes de Cima 2003 Trincadeira Trincadeira (Alentejano) $43. With its fresh, fruity, herbal aromas and flavors of thyme, basil and red fruits, this is an easily accessible, pleasurable wine. There is a touch of oak from nine months' French oak aging, but the overall effect is of great, fresh, dense fruit. 88 —*R.V. (3/1/2007)*

COSSART GORDON

Cossart Gordon NV 15 year Medium Rich Bual (Madeira) $34/500ml. 88 —*J.C. (11/1/2006)*

Cossart Gordon 1990 Colheita Medium Rich500ml. Bual (Madeira) $32/500ml. 90 —*J.C. (11/1/2006)*

Cossart Gordon NV 5 year Malmsey (Madeira) $21. 90 Editors' Choice —*J.C. (11/1/2006)*

Cossart Gordon NV Rainwater Medium Dry Tinta Negra Mole (Madeira) $15. 85 —*J.C. (11/1/2006)*

CROFT

Croft NV 10-Year Old Tawny Port $30. 89 —*R.V. (8/1/2006)*

Croft NV 20-Year Old Tawny Port $53. 82 —*R.V. (8/1/2006)*

Croft NV Distinction Special Reserve Port $17. 88 —*R.V. (3/1/2005)*

Croft 2001 Late Bottled Vintage Port (Port) $19. Dry, firm and structured, with balancing acidity. Enjoy its solid tannins, spice and dried fruits. Croft, now in the same group as Taylor Fladgate, is becoming a brand to buy again. 89 —*R.V. (11/1/2007)*

Croft 1997 LBV Bottled 2002 Port $19. 87 —*R.V. (3/1/2003)*

Croft 1983 Quinta da Roeda Port $56. 82 —*M.S. (11/15/2002)*

Croft 2003 Vintage Port $72. 85 —*R.V. (11/15/2005)*

DÃO SUL

Dao Sul 2005 Berço do Infante Portuguese Red (Estremadura) $7. An impressive, dense wine, this is a wood-aged, smooth blend of Aragonez and Castelão grapes. This has ripe tannins and fruit, and a rich blend of blackberries and dark plums. **88 Best Buy** —*R.V. (12/15/2007)*

Dão Sul 2004 Berco do Infante Portuguese Red (Estremadura) $6. 88 Best Buy —*R.V. (3/1/2006)*

Dao Sul 2004 Cabriz Colheita Seleccionada Portuguese Red (Dão) $8. A big, hearty, robust and juicy red wine that layers typical dry Portuguese tannins with dark red fruits, herbs and acidity. This blend of Alfrocheiro, Touriga Nacional and Tinta Roriz is from one of the increasing number of enterprising producers to emerge in the Dão region of central Portugal. Touches of wood add complexity to a big-hearted wine. **89 Best Buy** —*R.V. (3/1/2007)*

Dão Sul 2003 Monte de Cal Reserva Portuguese Red (Alentejano) $15. 89 —*R.V. (3/1/2006)*

Dão Sul 2002 Quinta das Tecedeiras Reserva Portuguese Red (Douro) $20. 89 —*R.V. (11/1/2004)*

Dão Sul 2002 Quinta de Cabriz Colheita Seleccionada Portuguese Red (Dão) $7. 87 Best Buy —*R.V. (11/1/2004)*

Dão Sul 2000 Quinta de Cabriz Reserva Portuguese Red (Dão) $14. 91 Best Buy —*R.V. (11/1/2004)*

Dão Sul 2001 Quinta do Encontro Portuguese Red (Bairrada) $7. 89 Best Buy —*R.V. (11/1/2004)*

Dao Sul 2003 Quinta do Gradil Portuguese Red (Estremadura) $6. 90 Best Buy —*R.V. (3/1/2006)*

Dao Sul 2000 Quinta da Cabriz Colheita Seleccionada Red Blend (Dão) $6. 89 Best Buy —*R.V. (12/31/2002)*

Dao Sul 1999 Quinta de Cabriz/Alfrocheiro Preto Red Blend (Dão) $16. 91 —*R.V. (12/31/2002)*

Dao Sul 2003 Quinta de Cabriz Touriga Nacional Touriga Nacional (Dão) $24. If any proof were needed that Touriga Nacional is one of Portugal's greatest vinous treasures, this wine offers it. It is both elegant and densely powerful, a many-layered wine that has firmly dry tannins (give it another 2–3 years of aging), herbs and black fruits and a big, chunky aftertaste that trails a lift of acidity. **90 Editors' Choice** —*R.V. (3/1/2007)*

Dão Sul 2000 Quinta de Cabriz Touriga Nacional (Dão) $19. 91 —*R.V. (12/31/2002)*

Dao Sul 2005 Sul South Portuguese Red (Estremadura) $5. An earthy, rustic blend of Aragonez and Castelão grapes, soft and ripe, touched with black figs and plum skins. For a hearty stew, this is certainly a fine wine, but there's nothing sophisticated about it. 84—*R.V. (12/15/2007)*

DELAFORCE

Delaforce NV 20-Year Old Tawny Port $35. 89 —*R.V. (8/1/2006)*

Delaforce 1997 Curious & Ancient 20-Year Old Port $46. 91 —*M.S. (7/1/2002)*

Delaforce NV His Eminence's Choice 10-Year Old Tawny Port $23. 88 —*R.V. (8/1/2006)*

Delaforce 1992 LBV Port $19. 87 —*M.S. (11/15/2002)*

Delaforce 1996 LBV Bottled 2002 Port $17. 86 Editors' Choice —*R.V. (3/1/2003)*

Delaforce 2003 Vintage Port $58. 89 —*R.V. (11/15/2005)*

DFJ VINHOS

DFJ Vinhos 2005 Grand'Arte Alicante Bouschet (Estremadura) $16. The juiciness of Alicante Bouschet shows well in this full-bodied wine, packed with black berries and soft tannins. The dry finish suggests some aging—maybe onr year. 89 —*R.V. (12/15/2007)*

DFJ Vinhos 2004 Grand'Arte Alicante Bouschet (Estremadura) $15. 89 —*R.V. (3/1/2006)*

DFJ Vinhos DFJ Vinhos 2000 Grand Arte Alicante Bouschet (Estremadura) $20. 91 —*R.V. (12/31/2002)*

DFJ Vinhos 2000 DJF Cabernet Blend (Estremadura) $9. 90 Best Buy —*R.V. (12/31/2002)*

DFJ Vinhos 2000 Grand Arte Cabernet Sauvignon (Estremadura) $20. 88 —*R.V. (12/31/2002)*

DFJ Vinhos 1999 Grand Arte Caladoc (Estremadura) $20. 86 —*R.V. (12/31/2002)*

DFJ Vinhos 2004 Grand'Arte Caladoc (Estremadura) $15. 86 —*R.V. (3/1/2006)*

DFJ Vinhos 2006 Grand'Arte Chardonnay (Estremadura) $NA. Big, fat and very soft, this wood-aged wine shows just hints of minerality underneath rich creaminess. The acidity, though, is missing, the white fruits overripe. 85 —*R.V. (12/15/2007)*

DFJ Vinhos 2004 Grand'Arte Merlot (Estremadura) $15. 85 —*R.V. (3/1/2006)*

DFJ Vinhos 2005 Caladoc-Alicante Boushet Portuguese Red (Estremadura) $NA. A big, burly, juicy wine, focusing on powerful red fruits and layers of acidity. The tannins are dense, but the fruit is more dominant. There are smoky flavors, spiked with licorice and blueberries. Caladoc is a cross between Malbec and Grenache, developed in France, rarely planted. 87 —*R.V. (12/15/2007)*

DFJ Vinhos 2003 Consensus Portuguese Red (Ribatejo) $35. 90 —*R.V. (3/1/2006)*

DFJ Vinhos 2003 Francos Portuguese Red (Alenquer) $35. 88 —*R.V. (3/1/2006)*

DFJ Vinhos 2002 Merlot-Touriga Franca Portuguese Red (Estremadura) $NA. A firm, tannic wine with elegant structure. The red fruits from the Merlot are a great foil for the tannins of the Touriga Franca. Even at five years, this is still fruit dominated, although the wood and spice element is well integrated. 88 —*R.V. (12/15/2007)*

DFJ Vinhos 2006 Monte Alentejano Portuguese Red (Alentejano) $8. Fresh wine, crisp with plenty of sunny red fruits and light acidity. There's a good red currant element, giving a lively lift, with a touch of caramel to finish. 85 —*R.V. (12/15/2007)*

DFJ Vinhos 2006 Monte Alentejano Trincadeira and Aragonez Portuguese Red (Alentejano) $9. A simple fruity red wine, with spice, red-berry fruit flavors, lively acidity and some stalky tannins. This is great quaffing wine, all red fruits and freshness. 85 —*R.V. (12/15/2007)*

DFJ Vinhos 2004 Tinta Roriz-Cabernet Sauvignon Portuguese Red (Estremadura) $NA. It is curious how the Cabernet, presumably ripe, tastes austere. It is young, and the tannins will certainly soften, but this is a hard wine at the moment, all edges. Blueberries and cranberries are the dominant fruits, while the wood shows as toastiness. 85 —*R.V. (12/15/2007)*

DFJ Vinhos 2005 Tinta Roriz-Merlot Portuguese Red (Estremadura) $NA. Black currants and plums dominate this ripe, soft, open wine. There are delicious flavors of dark chocolate, spice and bacon, which add to the fruit. The tannins are subservient, lending support but not dominant. 89 —*R.V. (12/15/2007)*

DFJ Vinhos 2005 Touriga Nacional e Touriga Franca Portuguese Red (Estremadura) $NA. Perfumed, soft, easy wine, showing the juicy, fresh side of the two grapes. The fruits are more red than black, open and ripe, but still with youthful exuberance and great freshness. 88 —*R.V. (12/15/2007)*

DFJ Vinhos 2006 Alvarinho-Chardonnay Portuguese White (Estremadura) $NA. In his continual quest for unusual blends, DFJ winemaker José Neiva has come up with this mix of the Vinho Verde grape Alvarinho and Chardonnay. When it is young, as here, the fresh, crisp Alvarinho dominates, giving lively, vibrant green-fruit flavors. Some weight underneath hints at the Chardonnay. 88 —*R.V. (12/15/2007)*

DFJ Vinhos 2006 Monte Alentejano Portuguese White (Alentejano) $NA. Fresh green-apple aromas and some ripe, mango flavors, this is well rounded, showing some acidity, but more of open, fresh fruits. This is a wine that will be perfect to drink over the next few months. 87 —*R.V. (12/15/2007)*

DFJ Vinhos 2000 Red Blend (Estremadura) $10. 91 Best Buy —*R.V. (12/31/2002)*

DFJ Vinhos 2004 Tinta Roriz and Merlot Red Blend (Estremadura) $11. An unexpected combination perhaps, but it works to give a fresh, flavorful wine, with soft tannins, juicy fruit and flavors of red cherries and vanilla. Not complex, and ready to drink now. 87 —*R.V. (12/15/2007)*

DFJ Vinhos 2005 Grand'Arte Shiraz Shiraz (Estremadura) $16. Dark plums and bitter chocolate on this wine along with powerful structure and tannins. It is ripe, spicy and finely perfumed with full black fruits. The tannins are boosted by wood aging, rounding it out and giving it extra richness. 90 —*R.V. (12/15/2007)*

DFJ Vinhos 2000 Grand Arte Touriga Franca (Estremadura) $20. 88 —*R.V. (12/31/2002)*

DFJ Vinhos 2004 Grand'Arte Touriga Franca (Estremadura) $15. 88 —*R.V. (3/1/2006)*

DFJ Vinhos 2005 Grand'Arte Touriga Nacional (Estremadura) $17. Firm and ripe, with dense, juicy fruit, this shows the exuberant side of Touriga

Nacional. It has solid tannins, but the fruit is full of bright berries, herbs and a touch of pepper. The wood aging has rounded the fruit out. 90 —*R.V. (12/15/2007)*

DFJ Vinhos 2003 Grand'Arte Touriga Nacional (Estremadura) $15. 90 Best Buy —*R.V. (3/1/2006)*

DFJ Vinhos 2000 Grand Arte Touriga Nacional (Estremadura) $30. 92 —*R.V. (12/31/2002)*

DFJ Vinhos 2000 DFJ Touriga Nacional Blend (Estremadura) $23. 90 —*R.V. (12/31/2002)*

DFJ Vinhos 2000 Grand Arte Trincadeira (Ribatejano) $20. 85 —*R.V. (12/31/2002)*

DFJ Vinhos 2003 Grand' Arte Trincadeira (Ribatejano) $15. 87 —*R.V. (3/1/2006)*

DOMINGOS ALVES DE SOUSA

Domingos Alves de Sousa 2003 Quinta da Gaivosa Vintage Port $42. 89 —*R.V. (11/15/2005)*

DONA MARIA

Dona Maria 2003 Reserva Red Blend (Alentejano) $39. 86 —*J.C. (11/1/2006)*

DONA MARIA ANTONIA FERREIRA

Dona Maria Antonia Ferreira 2000 Vallado Red Blend (Douro) $22. 86 —*R.V. (12/31/2002)*

DOW'S

Dow's NV 10-Year Old Tawny Port $29. 90 —*R.V. (8/1/2006)*

Dow's NV 20-Year Old Tawny Port $50. 89 —*R.V. (8/1/2006)*

Dow's NV 30-Year Old Tawny Port $98. 94 Editors' Choice —*R.V. (8/1/2006)*

Dow's NV 40-Year Old Tawny Port $148. 93 —*R.V. (8/1/2006)*

Dow's 1992 Colheita Port $30. 84 —*J.C. (12/1/2004)*

Dow's NV Crusted Porto, Bottled 1998 Port $23. 84 —*J.C. (11/15/2003)*

Dow's 2001 Late Bottled Vintage Port (Port) $20. A great LBV, intense and concentrated, with dark plum skin flavors, dried raisins and cocoa. This is very much a wine that is in the dry style of Dow's Ports. 91 —*R.V. (11/1/2007)*

Dow's 2000 LBV Port $20. 89 —*J.C. (6/1/2006)*

Dow's 1998 LBV Port $19. 85 —*J.C. (12/1/2004)*

Dow's 1996 LBV Bottled 2002 Port $20. 90 —*R.V. (3/1/2003)*

Dow's 1997 LBV Port $18. 89 Editors' Choice —*J.C. (11/15/2003)*

Dow's 1986 Quinta Do Bomfim Vintage Port $36. 88 —*J.C. (12/1/2004)*

Dow's 2001 Senhora da Ribeira Vintage Port $50. 92 —*J.C. (11/15/2003)*

Dow's NV Trademark Finest Reserve Port $17. 83 —*R.V. (3/1/2005)*

Dow's 2003 Vintage Port $80. 93 —*R.V. (11/15/2005)*

Dow's 2004 Vale do Bomfim Reserva Portuguese Red (Douro) $12. 88 Best Buy —*J.C. (6/1/2006)*

DUAS QUINTAS

Duas Quintas 1996 Vinho Tinto Portuguese Red (Douro) $11. 85 *(11/15/1999)*

ENCOSTAS DO DOURO

Encostas do Douro 2001 Vinha Palestra Portuguese Red (Douro) $NA. 84 —*R.V. (11/1/2004)*

ERMELINDA FREITAS

Ermelinda Freitas 2003 Dona Ermelinda Red Blend (Palmela) $7. 84 Best Buy —*J.C. (6/1/2006)*

Ermelinda Freitas 2000 Dona Ermelinda Red Blend (Palmela) $7. 84 —*J.C. (11/15/2003)*

EVEL

Evel 2002 Red Portuguese Red (Douro) $9. 83 —*J.C. (6/1/2006)*

Evel 2004 White Portuguese White (Douro) $9. 86 Best Buy —*J.C. (12/31/2005)*

Evel 2001 Vinho Tinto Red Blend (Douro) $10. 86 Best Buy —*J.C. (3/1/2004)*

Evel 2002 Vinho Branco White Blend (Douro) $NA. 85 —*J.C. (1/1/2004)*

FALDAS DA SERRA

Faldas da Serra 2000 Quinta das Maias Red Blend (Dão) $13. 85 —*R.V. (12/31/2002)*

Faldas da Serra 2000 Quinta das Maias Jaen Red Blend (Dão) $22. 91 —*R.V. (12/31/2002)*

Faldas da Serra 2001 Quinta das Maias Verdelho (Dão) $14. 88 —*R.V. (8/1/2004)*

Faldas da Serra 2001 Quinta das Maias Malvasia Fina (Dão) $14. 88 —*R.V. (8/1/2004)*

FALUA

Falua 2005 Conde de Vimioso Tinto Portuguese Red (Ribatejano) $0. Under the watchful eye of leading Portuguese oenologist João Portugal Ramos, this blended wine adds Cabernet Sauvignon to a blend of Touriga Nacional and Tinta Roriz. The Cabernet changes the nature of the dry Portuguese tannins, giving a very firm, dark wine that has brooding intensity under a polished surface. 87 —*R.V. (3/1/2007)*

Falua 2005 Conde de Vimioso Branco Portuguese White (Ribatejano) $0. For a hot country white wine, this is deliciously fresh. Based on the Arinto grape, the wine's floral aromas, flavors of ripe apricots and fresh aftertaste just burst out of the glass. Oenologist João Portugal Ramos also makes his own wines in the Alentejo. 86 —*R.V. (3/1/2007)*

Falua 1999 Duas Castas Portuguese Red (Ribatejo) $9. 85 *(12/31/2001)*

FAZENDA DO MOSTEIRO

Fazenda do Mosteiro 2003 Reserva Portuguese Red (Douro) $0. A finely balanced wine, which brings together good intensity of fruit and dark, dusty tannins in a harmonious whole. There's great acidity, fig and black fruit flavors and depth of structure. A great success. 89 —*R.V. (3/1/2007)*

Fazenda do Mosteiro 2004 Selecção Portuguese Red (Douro) $0. The vineyard of the monastery of Fazenda, run by Quinta do Ventozello, has produced a simple, fruity, jammy blackberry-flavored wine with some acidity. It is easy, juicy, with a fine, dry, food-friendly aftertaste. 86 —*R.V. (3/1/2007)*

FEIST

Feist NV 10-Year-Old Port $19. 89 Best Buy *(3/1/2000)*

Feist NV 10-Year Old Tawny Port $23. 82 —*R.V. (8/1/2006)*

Feist NV 20-Year Old Tawny Port $49. 81 —*R.V. (8/1/2006)*

Feist NV 30-Year Old Tawny Port $98. 90 —*R.V. (8/1/2006)*

Feist NV 40-Year Old Tawny Port $150. 89 —*R.V. (8/1/2006)*

Feist 1997 LBV Bottled 2002 Port $18. 85 —*R.V. (3/1/2003)*

Feist 2003 Vintage Port $NA. 90 —*R.V. (11/15/2005)*

Feist NV Vintage Character Port $NA. 84 —*R.V. (3/1/2005)*

FERREIRA

Ferreira NV 10-Year Old Tawny Port $NA. 84 —*R.V. (8/1/2006)*

Ferreira NV Doña Antonia Reserva Port (Port) $22. This Reserva shows the beginnings of a tawny character while still keeping some of the freshness of young ruby. The color is beginning to go pale, the spirit is showing through, but the red fruits are still there. 86 —*R.V. (11/1/2007)*

Ferreira NV Dona Antonia Personal Reserve Port $22. 83 —*M.S. (7/1/2002)*

Ferreira NV Duque de Bragança 20-Year Old Tawny Port (Port) $70. Always great, this is softer, less intense than in the past. But there is still great richness, and power as well as smoothness, burnt caramel blending well with the spirit, and finishing with its inimitable fresh acidity. 93 —*R.V. (11/1/2007)*

Ferreira NV Duque de Bragança 20-Year Old Tawny Port $70. 94 Editors' Choice —*R.V. (8/1/2006)*

Ferreira 2000 Late Bottled Vintage Port (Port) $70. There is great balance between the ripeness, dark plum flavors and fine acidity. An intense wine, with easy tannins that are dusty, rather than dry. 90 —*R.V. (11/1/2007)*

Ferreira 1999 Late Bottled Vintage Port (Port) $22. Big and ripe, but also well structured, this is the style of LBV that could age in bottle. It has powerful black fruits, acidity and a dry core surrounded by the rich sweetness. 89 —*R.V. (11/1/2007)*

Ferreira 1997 LBV Bottled 2001 Port (Douro) $34. 86 —*R.V. (3/1/2003)*

Ferreira NV Quinta do Porto 10-Year Old Tawny Port (Port) $35. Mature beyond its claimed 10 years, this is a wine that balances fine burnt and caramel flavors with some good fresh acidity. It's dry, showing some citrus as well as wood flavors, a perfumed wine and very elegant. 89 —*R.V. (11/1/2007)*

Ferreira NV Ruby Port (Port) $14. The simplest of the Ferreira range of Ports, but still a bright fresh red fruit-flavored wine with a smooth texture. Good raisins and very soft tannins. 84 —*R.V. (11/1/2007)*

Ferreira NV Tawny Port (Port) $14. With its red gold color and fresh aromas, this is the youngest style of tawny Port. But in its class, it is smoothly made, a soft, ripe and sweet wine, just hinting at spirits. **84** —*R.V. (11/1/2007)*

Ferreira NV Tawny Port $14. 86 —*M.S. (7/1/2002)*

Ferreira 1994 Traditional LBV Port $20. 89 —*M.S. (11/15/2002)*

Ferreira 2003 Vintage Port $78. 82 —*R.V. (11/15/2005)*

FONSECA

Fonseca NV 10-Year Old Tawny Port $30. 90 —*R.V. (8/1/2006)*

Fonseca NV 20-Year Old Tawny Port $50. 91 —*R.V. (8/1/2006)*

Fonseca NV 40-Year Old Tawny Port $157. 88 —*R.V. (8/1/2006)*

Fonseca NV Bin 27 Port $20. 88 —*R.V. (3/1/2005)*

Fonseca 1984 Guimaraens Port $44. 90 —*M.S. (11/15/2002)*

Fonseca 2000 LBV Port $25. 90 Editors' Choice —*J.C. (6/1/2006)*

Fonseca 1996 Port $21. 91 Editors' Choice —*R.V. (3/1/2003)*

Fonseca 2001 Quinta Do Panascal Vintage Port $50. 91 Cellar Selection —*J.C. (12/1/2004)*

Fonseca 2001 Unfiltered Late Bottled Vintage Port (Port) $22. This is all about power and rich fruit. A great depth of flavor, dark and brooding, but also with great sweetness and richness. This is an outstanding powerful wine, which will age. **92** —*R.V. (11/1/2007)*

Fonseca 2003 Vintage Port $92. 97 —*R.V. (11/15/2005)*

FRANCISCO NUNES GARCIA

Francisco Nunes Garcia 1999 Colheita Seleccionada Aragonês (Alentejo) $45. 87 —*J.C. (3/1/2004)*

FUNDAÇÃO EUGENIO ALMEIDA

Fundação Eugenio Almeida 1994 Pera-Manca Portuguese Red (Alentejo) $60. 91 *(10/1/1999)*

GLORIA

Gloria 2002 Tinto Portuguese Red (Douro) $16. 88 —*J.C. (6/1/2006)*

GOULD CAMPBELL

Gould Campbell NV 10-Year Old Tawny Port $24. 90 Editors' Choice —*R.V. (8/1/2006)*

Gould Campbell 2001 Late Bottled Vintage Port (Port) $17. A pleasant, fresh wine with light raisin, spice and a warm rounded texture. Drink this easily, with pleasure. **87** —*R.V. (11/1/2007)*

Gould Campbell 1996 LBV Bottled 2002 Port $20. 91 —*R.V. (3/1/2003)*

Gould Campbell 2003 Vintage Port $50. 91 —*R.V. (11/15/2005)*

GRANTOM

Grantom 2001 Reserva Portuguese Red (Trás-os-Montes) $40. 89 —*R.V. (11/1/2004)*

HERDADE DA CALADA

Herdade da Calada 2000 Baron de B Reserva Red Blend (Alentejo) $25. 85 —*J.C. (11/15/2003)*

Herdade da Calada 2000 Vale da Calada Red Blend (Alentejano) $11. 83 —*R.V. (12/31/2002)*

HERDADE DA MADEIRA

Herdade da Madeira 1999 Roquevale Red Blend (Alentejo) $16. 82 —*R.V. (12/31/2002)*

Herdade da Madeira 2000 Roquevale Chao de Xisto Red Blend (Alentejano) $6. 81 —*R.V. (12/31/2002)*

HERDADE DA MALHADINA NOVA

Herdade da Malhadina Nova 2004 Aragonês de Peceguina Aragonês (Alentejo) $NA. 90 —*R.V. (3/1/2006)*

Herdade da Malhadina Nova 2005 Portuguese Red (Alentejano) $90. Malhadinha Nova continues on its impressive way. This 2005 is big and powerful, yes, but it also has complexity, even some elegance in a muscular way. There are bitter chocolate flavors, black fruits, layered with wood, needing aging. A great wine. **93 Cellar Selection** —*R.V. (12/15/2007)*

Herdade da Malhadina Nova 2004 Portuguese Red (Alentejano) $90. It may be the 15% Cabernet in this blend, it may just be the natural structure of the wine, but this is a powerful, structured, firmly tannic wine that is enveloped by a rich robe of super-ripe black fruits. As always with a fine Portuguese wine, this fruit is balanced with dusty tannins and a dry, lingering aftertaste. **92** —*R.V. (3/1/2007)*

Herdade da Malhadina Nova 2004 Malhadina Portuguese Red (Alentejo) $NA. 92 —*R.V. (3/1/2006)*

Herdade da Malhadina Nova 2006 Monte de Peceguina Portuguese Red (Alentejano) $30. The second wine from Malhadinha Nova is lively and fruity, packed with red fruits, sweet strawberry flavors and easy, ripe texture. Drink now. **87** —*R.V. (12/15/2007)*

Herdade da Malhadina Nova 2005 Monte de Peceguina Portuguese Red (Alentejano) $30. A blend that includes Aragonès, Alicante Bouschet, Touriga Nacional and Syrah, this deliciously fruity and juicy wine bursts with freshness and ripeness. It may be young, but the vibrant red fruits and spice flavors are all ready for drinking. **87** —*R.V. (3/1/2007)*

Herdade da Malhadina Nova 2004 Monte da Peceguina Portuguese Red (Alentejano) $NA. 89 —*R.V. (3/1/2006)*

HERDADE DE ESPORÃO

Herdade de Esporão 2003 Alicante Bouschet (Alentejano) $19. 86 —*R.V. (3/1/2006)*

Herdade de Esporão 2003 Aragonês (Alentejano) $18. 89 —*R.V. (3/1/2006)*

Herdade de Esporão 2002 Aragonês (Alentejano) $20. 89 Best Buy —*R.V. (12/1/2004)*

Herdade de Esporão 2000 Aragonês (Alentejano) $14. 88 —*R.V. (12/31/2002)*

Herdade de Esporão 2002 Esporão Reserva Portuguese Red (Alentejo) $16. 91 —*R.V. (3/1/2006)*

Herdade de Esporão 2001 Esporão Reserva Portuguese Red (Alentejo) $17. 88 —*R.V. (12/1/2004)*

Herdade de Esporão 2000 Garrafeira Portuguese Red (Alentejo) $38. 91 Cellar Selection —*R.V. (12/1/2004)*

Herdade de Esporão 2001 Garrafeira Private Selection Portuguese Red (Alentejo) $38. 93 —*R.V. (3/1/2006)*

Herdade de Esporão 2003 Monte Velho Portuguese Red (Alentejano) $8. 85 —*R.V. (12/1/2004)*

Herdade de Esporão 2002 Quatro Castas Reserva Portuguese Red (Alentejano) $20. 88 —*R.V. (3/1/2006)*

Herdade de Esporão 2003 Vinha da Defesa Portuguese Red (Alentejano) $11. 85 —*R.V. (12/1/2004)*

Herdade de Esporão 2004 Monte Velho Portuguese White (Alentejano) $8. 90 Best Buy —*R.V. (11/15/2005)*

Herdade de Esporão 2003 Reserva Portuguese White (Alentejo) $12. 91 Best Buy —*R.V. (11/15/2005)*

Herdade de Esporão 2004 Vinha da Defesa Portuguese White (Alentejo) $11. 87 Best Buy —*R.V. (8/1/2005)*

Herdade de Esporão 2000 Esporao Reserva Red Blend (Alentejo) $15. 91 —*R.V. (12/31/2002)*

Herdade de Esporão 2001 Monte Velho Tinto Red Blend (Alentejano) $6. 84 —*R.V. (12/31/2002)*

Herdade de Esporão 2000 Quatro Castas Reserva Red Blend (Alentejano) $21. 86 —*J.C. (11/15/2003)*

Herdade de Esporão 2000 Vinha da Defesa Red Blend (Alentejano) $14. 85 —*R.V. (12/31/2002)*

Herdade de Esporão 2003 Syrah (Alentejano) $19. 89 —*R.V. (3/1/2006)*

Herdade de Esporão 2000 Syrah (Alentejano) $11. 89 —*R.V. (12/31/2002)*

Herdade de Esporão 2003 Touriga Nacional (Alentejano) $19. 90 —*R.V. (3/1/2006)*

Herdade de Esporão 2002 Touriga Nacional (Alentejano) $22. 88 —*R.V. (12/1/2004)*

Herdade de Esporão 2000 Touriga Nacional (Alentejano) $15. 90 —*R.V. (12/31/2002)*

Herdade de Esporão 2003 Trincadeira (Alentejano) $19. 88 —*R.V. (3/1/2006)*

Herdade de Esporão 2000 Trincadeira (Alentejano) $14. 86 —*R.V. (12/31/2002)*

Herdade de Esporão 2004 Verdelho (Alentejano) $11. 86 Best Buy —*R.V. (8/1/2005)*

Herdade de Esporão 2001 Reserva White Blend (Alentejo) $14. 86 —*J.C. (11/15/2003)*

HERDADE DE SANTA MARTA

Herdade de Santa Marta 1999 Red Blend (Alentejano) $10. 84 —*J.C. (3/1/2004)*

HERDADE DE SÃO MIGUEL

Herdade de São Miguel 2005 Reserva Portuguese Red (Alentejano) $0. From a winery that only started operations in 2001, one of the new wave in the Alentejo. This Reserva is in a modern, smooth style, big and powerful. But there's one welcome wrinkle in all this smooth fruit, and that is a dash of Cabernet Sauvignon which gives just the right amount of tannins and interestingly fresh acidity. 89 —*R.V. (12/15/2007)*

HERDADE DO ESPORÃO

Herdade do Esporão 2004 Alicante Bouschet Alicante Bouschet (Alentejano) $18. A juicy wine with cranberry fruit flavors, spice, and exotic berries, spoiled by a rustic, earthy, meaty edge. Not for aging. 83 —*R.V. (12/15/2007)*

Herdade do Esporão 2004 Aragonês (Alentejano) $18. The local version of the Spanish Tempranillo, this is a firm, but wood- tinged wine, a core of acidity and black skin flavors giving a dense concentration to the wine, and contrasting with the great finishing acidity. 89 —*R.V. (12/15/2007)*

Herdade do Esporão 2004 Herdade Reserva Portuguese Red (Alentejo) $18. Smooth and elegant, this is an impressive wine with its powered black fruits, concentrated dark, brooding tannins and spice. The wood element is held in check with acidity, plum skin textures and a dry core. 90 —*R.V. (12/15/2007)*

Herdade do Esporão 2006 Monte Velho Portuguese Red (Alentejano) $9. With its 5 million bottle production, this is one of Portugal's leading brands. It is a ripe wine, but with a stalky element, giving freshness, although the aftertaste is soft, perhaps sweet, very easy, ripe. 86 Best Buy —*R.V. (12/15/2007)*

Herdade do Esporão 2004 Reserva Private Selection Portuguese Red (Alentejo) $39. The top-of-the-line red from Esporão, this partners the white Private Selection. The comparative restraint of this wine is admirable, with ripe, bright fruits, smoothed by wood. The dark, dry tannins and the dense, almost impenetrable texture hint at the power; finishing with wood spice and acidity. 92 Cellar Selection —*R.V. (12/15/2007)*

Herdade do Esporão 2006 Vinha de Defesa Portuguese Red (Alentejano) $12. Very soft, smooth and polished, this favors ripe plums and figs, and ripe, lightweight tannins. It is designed as an easy-going, soft wine, and does the job very well. 84 —*R.V. (12/15/2007)*

Herdade do Esporão 2006 Monte Velho Portuguese White (Alentejano) $8. A simple, fruity with great freshness and flavors of lemons, mangos and spice. Attractive, and easy drinking. 84 Best Buy —*R.V. (12/15/2007)*

Herdade do Esporão 2006 Private Selection Reserva Portuguese White (Alentejo) $22. Very New World in its ripe, tropical fruit flavors, rounded toasty element, and impressive concentration. Yet the elegance also remains, finishing with spice and light acidity, adding shape to this rich wine. 90 Editors' Choice —*R.V. (12/15/2007)*

Herdade do Esporão 2006 Reserva Portuguese White (Alentejano) $16. The white Reserva from Esporão is full-bodied, with a judicious mix of softness and toasty creaminess. There's a great touch of lime to freshen it all up, as well as spice to go with the wood. Aging potential for the next 2–3 years. 89 —*R.V. (12/15/2007)*

Herdade do Esporão 2006 Vinha da Defesa Portuguese White (Alentejano) $10. Creamy and full-bodied wine layered with lime and other citrus flavors that highlight acidity although the aftertaste is sweet. 84 —*R.V. (12/15/2007)*

Herdade do Esporão 2004 Syrah (Alentejano) $18. That the Syrah performs well in the Alentejo is proved by producer after producer. Here it has produced a big, beefy wine, full of black, silky fruits, concentrated ripe fruits and floating perfumes. 90 —*R.V. (12/15/2007)*

Herdade do Esporão 2004 Touriga Nacional (Alentejano) $19. The aromas are the thing here, as so often with Touriga Nacional, keeping the soft tannins and ripe, sweet fruit buoyant and lively. There is acidity, but there's more, maybe too much, of blackberry jam flavor. 86 —*R.V. (12/15/2007)*

Herdade do Esporão 2006 Verdelho (Alentejano) $14. Spicy, aromatic, touched by minerality and chalk, with an intense texture, the wine remains fresh, though, a fine apéritif wine, ending softly. 85 —*R.V. (12/15/2007)*

HERDADE DOS COELHEIROS

Herdade dos Coelheiros 2001 Tapada de Coelheiros Chardonnay (Alentejano) $NA. 81 —*R.V. (8/1/2004)*

Herdade dos Coelheiros 1999 Tapada de Coelheiros Red Blend (Alentejano) $32. 87 —*R.V. (12/31/2002)*

Herdade dos Coelheiros 1999 Tapada de Coelheiros Garrafeira Red Blend (Alentejano) $42. 90 —*R.V. (12/31/2002)*

Herdade dos Coelheiros 2000 Vinha da Tapada Red Blend (Alentejano) $15. 81 —*R.V. (12/31/2002)*

Herdade dos Coelheiros 2001 Tapada de Coelheiros White Blend (Alentejano) $NA. 83 —*R.V. (8/1/2004)*

HERDADE GRANDE

Herdade Grande 2003 Portuguese Red (Alentejano) $11. 86 Best Buy —*J.C. (11/1/2006)*

Herdade Grande 2003 Condado das Vinhas Portuguese Red (Alentejano) $8. 86 Best Buy —*J.C. (11/1/2006)*

Herdade Grande 2005 Colheita Seleccionada White Blend (Alentejano) $11. 86 Best Buy —*J.C. (11/1/2006)*

Herdade Grande 2004 Condado das Vinhas White Blend (Alentejano) $8. 82 —*J.C. (11/1/2006)*

HOOPERS

Hoopers 2003 Vintage Port $NA. 90 —*R.V. (11/15/2005)*

HUTCHESON FEUERHEERD

Hutcheson Feuerheerd 2003 Vintage Port $NA. 83 —*R.V. (11/15/2005)*

J. & F. LURTON

J. & F. Lurton 2004 Pilheiros Portuguese Red (Douro) $19. The Lurton brothers, who make wines from France to South America, have now started to produce two Douro wines, with the help, they say, of the Lavradores de Feitoria group of producers. This is the simpler of the two wines, dominated by spicy flavors, very soft and round, ready to drink now. 87 —*R.V. (3/1/2007)*

J. & F. Lurton 2004 Pilheiros Grande Escolha Portuguese Red (Douro) $38. The top wine of the pair produced by the Lurton brothers, this is a bomb of a wine, exploding fruit and superripe tannins in the mouth. It has the proper dry layer over this fruit, but it's more about velvet and smoothness. It shows great structure, and could certainly age for five years. 90 —*R.V. (3/1/2007)*

J. H. ANDERSEN

J. H. Andersen NV Special Reserve Port $15. 86 —*R.V. (3/1/2005)*

J. H. Andresen 2003 Vintage Port $32. 90 —*R.V. (11/15/2005)*

J. PORTUGAL RAMOS

J. Portugal Ramos 2005 Aragonês (Alentejano) $20. Smooth, wood-polished wine, packed with a ripe, comfortable texture, very ripe red fruits, highlights of tannins. There are black figs, balanced with sweet acidity and fattened with some bacon flavors. 88 —*R.V. (12/15/2007)*

J. Portugal Ramos 2004 Aragonês (Alentejano) $15. 86 —*R.V. (3/1/2006)*

J. Portugal Ramos 2002 Conde de Vimioso Portuguese Red (Ribatejano) $8. 87 Best Buy —*R.V. (11/1/2004)*

J. Portugal Ramos 2001 Conde de Vimioso Reserva Portuguese Red (Ribatejano) $20. 90 —*R.V. (3/1/2006)*

J. Portugal Ramos 2001 Conde de Vimioso Reserva Portuguese Red (Ribatejano) $20. 91 Editors' Choice —*R.V. (11/1/2004)*

J. Portugal Ramos 2006 Marquès de Borba Portuguese Red (Alentejo) $NA. Red fruits andsoft tannins with wood hints give this wine a fresh, immediate appeal. The fruit structure is slightly hot and leathery, but this is balanced with ripeness and very soft acidity. 87 —*R.V. (12/15/2007)*

J. Portugal Ramos 2005 Marquès de Borba Portuguese Red (Alentejo) $NA. Rounded, open soft raisin and dense black fruit flavors, make this an intense, solidly structured wine. It is big and powered by generous fruits, finishing with black plums. 88 —*R.V. (12/15/2007)*

J. Portugal Ramos 2004 Marquês de Borba Portuguese Red (Alentejo) $10. 86 Best Buy —*R.V. (3/1/2006)*

J. Portugal Ramos 2003 Marquès de Borba Reserva Portuguese Red (Alentejo) $NA. The huge concentration of this wine reflects the hot 2003 vintage. There are aromas of ripe fruit skins, and flavors of big, juicy, hugely rich black fruits, with dark tannins and a hot texture. 87 —*R.V. (12/15/2007)*

J. Portugal Ramos 2003 Marquês de Borba Portuguese Red (Alentejo) $12. 83 —*J.C. (12/1/2004)*

J. Portugal Ramos 2001 Marquês de Borba Portuguese Red (Alentejo) $10. 85 —*J.C. (11/15/2003)*

J. Portugal Ramos 1999 Marquês de Borba Portuguese Red (Alentejo) $11. 86 —*J.C. (12/31/2001)*

J. Portugal Ramos 2000 Marquês de Borba Reserva Portuguese Red (Alentejo) $50. 90 —*R.V. (12/1/2004)*

J. Portugal Ramos 2000 Marquês de Borba Reserva Portuguese Red (Alentejo) $48. 90 —*R.V. (3/1/2006)*

J. Portugal Ramos 2000 Marquês de Borba Reserva Portuguese Red (Alentejo) $45. 89 —*R.V. (12/31/2002)*

J. Portugal Ramos 1999 Marquês de Borba Reserva Portuguese Red (Alentejo) $45. 88 —*M.S. (12/31/2001)*

J. Portugal Ramos 1999 Sinfonia Portuguese Red (Alentejo) $9. 86 Best Buy —*J.C. (12/31/2001)*

J. Portugal Ramos 2005 Vila Santa Portuguese Red (Alentejano) $20. Mint aromas, followed by young, fresh fruit topped with firm tannins, make an impressively dense wine from one of Portugal's top winemakers. Flavors of mint and eucalyptus go with dark black fruits and concentration. **91 Editors' Choice** —*R.V. (12/15/2007)*

J. Portugal Ramos 2004 Vila Santa Portuguese Red (Alentejano) $16. 87 —*R.V. (3/1/2006)*

J. Portugal Ramos 2003 Vila Santa Portuguese Red (Alentejano) $18. 90 Editors' Choice —*R.V. (12/1/2004)*

J. Portugal Ramos 2004 Antão Vaz Portuguese White (Alentejano) $10. 87 Best Buy —*R.V. (8/1/2005)*

J. Portugal Ramos 2006 Marquès de Borba Portuguese White (Alentejo) $0. A soft, full, creamy wine, with light acidity and a touch of green structure. The white version of one of Portugal's most famous brands, this has fresh flavors of peas, green fruits. **85** —*R.V. (12/15/2007)*

J. Portugal Ramos 2005 Marquês de Borba Portuguese White (Alentejo) $13. 89 Best Buy —*J.C. (11/1/2006)*

J. Portugal Ramos 2004 Marquês de Borba Portuguese White (Alentejo) $14. 88 —*R.V. (8/1/2005)*

J. Portugal Ramos 2003 Marquês de Borba Portuguese White (Alentejo) $11. 85 —*J.C. (11/1/2004)*

J. Portugal Ramos 2001 Aragones Red Blend (Alentejano) $18. 88 —*R.V. (12/31/2002)*

J. Portugal Ramos 2000 Falua Duas Castas Red Blend (Ribatejo) $9. 86 Best Buy —*J.C. (11/15/2003)*

J. Portugal Ramos 2001 Tinta Caiada Red Blend (Alentejano) $18. 89 —*R.V. (12/31/2002)*

J. Portugal Ramos 2002 Vila Santa Red Blend (Alentejano) $15. 85 —*J.C. (12/31/2005)*

J. Portugal Ramos 2001 Vila Santa Red Blend (Alentejano) $20. 90 —*R.V. (12/31/2002)*

J. Portugal Ramos 2004 Syrah (Alentejano) $16. 90 —*R.V. (3/1/2006)*

J. Portugal Ramos 2003 Syrah (Alentejano) $19. 89 —*R.V. (12/1/2004)*

J. Portugal Ramos 2001 Syrah (Alentejano) $18. 90 —*R.V. (12/31/2002)*

J. Portugal Ramos 2006 Vila Santa Syrah (Alentejano) $20. The perfumes are the central theme of this wine, aromas of roses and flavors of spice, cinnamon, going through the ripe fruit and suggestions of wood. It is a superripe wine, but one which manages to keep in balance. **89** —*R.V. (12/15/2007)*

J. Portugal Ramos 2004 Tinta Caiada (Alentejano) $16. 87 —*R.V. (3/1/2006)*

J. Portugal Ramos 2003 Quinta da Viçosa Touriga Merlot Touriga Nacional Blend (Alentejano) $26. 88 —*R.V. (3/1/2006)*

J. Portugal Ramos 2003 Quinta da Viçosa Touriga Nacional Blend (Alentejano) $NA. From the hot 2003 vintage, this has big, superripe fruit, but manages to keep everything in check with vibrant fruit and elegance. The black fruits, powered and concentrated, also have acidity and great perfumes from the Touriga Nacional. **91** —*R.V. (12/15/2007)*

J. Portugal Ramos 2004 Trincadeira (Alentejano) $15. 89 —*R.V. (3/1/2006)*

J. Portugal Ramos 2003 Trincadeira (Alentejano) $17. 87 —*R.V. (12/1/2004)*

J. Portugal Ramos 2006 Vila Santa Trincadeira Trincadeira (Alentejano) $20. A big, juicy wine with balancing acidity and bright red fruit flavors. This is full of freshness and fruit flavors, with only soft tannins to hold the flavors together. **87** —*R.V. (12/15/2007)*

JOSÉ MARIA DA FONSECA

José Maria da Fonseca 2003 Domingos Soares Franco & Cristiano Van Zeller Domini Portuguese Red (Douro) $18. This joint venture between the inspired winemaker Domingos Soares Franco and Cristiano van Zeller produces fascinatingly idiosyncratic wines. Big and bold, but then lean and tannic, with sunshine-filled fruit over dark tannins. Consumers wanting an action-packed wine, needing time to come together (when it will be superb), should go for this. **90** —*R.V. (9/1/2007)*

José Maria da Fonseca 2004 Periquita Portuguese Red (Terras do Sado) $10. This is one of Portugal's big brands. Soft, easy and juicy, this has just a touch of dryness and great, fresh aftertaste. **86 Best Buy** —*R.V. (9/1/2007)*

J.M. DA FONSECA AND VAN ZELLER

J.M. da Fonseca and Van Zeller 2003 Vintage Port $NA. 83 —*R.V. (11/15/2005)*

J.P. VINHOS

J.P. Vinhos 2000 Quinta da Bacalhôa Cabernet Blend (Terras do Sado) $27. 89 —*R.V. (11/1/2004)*

J.P. Vinhos NV J.P. Branco Moscatel (Terras do Sado) $NA. 83 —*R.V. (8/1/2004)*

J.P. Vinhos 1999 Herdade de Santa Marta Portuguese Red (Alentejano) $10. 84 —*R.V. (12/1/2004)*

J.P. Vinhos NV J.P. Tinto Portuguese Red (Terras do Sado) $7. 83 —*R.V. (11/1/2004)*

J.P. Vinhos 2003 Santa Fé de Arraiolos Portuguese Red (Alentejano) $9. 85 Best Buy —*J.C. (12/31/2005)*

J.P. Vinhos 2003 Serras de Azeitão Portuguese Red (Terras do Sado) $8. 86 Best Buy —*R.V. (11/1/2004)*

J.P. Vinhos 1994 Tinto da Anfora Portuguese Red (Alenteo) $11. 87 Best Buy *(10/1/1999)*

J.P. Vinhos 2001 Tinto da Anfora Grande Escolha Portuguese Red (Alentejano) $29. 90 —*R.V. (12/1/2004)*

J.P. Vinhos 2004 Catarina Portuguese White (Terras do Sado) $9. 86 Best Buy —*J.C. (12/31/2005)*

J.P. Vinhos 2003 Catarina Portuguese White (Terras do Sado) $10. 88 Best Buy —*R.V. (8/1/2005)*

J.P. Vinhos 2003 J.P. Branco Portuguese White (Terras do Sado) $7. 83 —*R.V. (8/1/2005)*

J.P. Vinhos 2004 Serras de Azeitão Portuguese White (Terras do Sado) $9. 89 Best Buy —*R.V. (8/1/2005)*

J.P. Vinhos 2003 Serras de Azeitão Portuguese White (Terras do Sado) $8. 85 Best Buy —*R.V. (11/1/2004)*

J.P. Vinhos 1999 Herdade de Santa Marta Red Blend (Alentejano) $8. 84 —*R.V. (12/31/2002)*

J.P. Vinhos 1995 J.P. Garrafeira Red Blend (Palmela) $10. 91 Best Buy —*R.V. (12/31/2002)*

J.P. Vinhos 2000 Monte das Anforas Red Blend (Alentejano) $9. 85 —*R.V. (12/31/2002)*

J.P. Vinhos 2001 Monte das Anforas Vinho Tinto Red Blend (Alentejano) $8. 84 —*J.C. (3/1/2004)*

J.P. Vinhos 2000 Quinta da Bacalhoa Red Blend (Terras do Sado) $20. 86 —*R.V. (12/31/2002)*

J.P. Vinhos 2001 Tinto da Anfora Red Blend (Alentejano) $12. 90 Best Buy —*J.C. (3/1/2004)*

J.P. Vinhos 1999 Tinto da Anfora Red Blend (Alentejano) $13. 87 —*R.V. (12/31/2002)*

J.P. Vinhos 1999 Tinto da Anfora Grande Escohla Red Blend (Alentejano) $30. 90 —*R.V. (12/31/2002)*

J.P. Vinhos 2000 Só Syrah (Terras do Sado) $18. 85 —*J.C. (3/1/2004)*

J.P. Vinhos 2002 Catarina White Blend (Terras do Sado) $8. 85 —*J.C. (3/1/2004)*

J.P. Vinhos 2001 Monte das Ânforas White Blend (Alentejano) $NA. 87 —*R.V. (8/1/2004)*

JOÃO PIRES

João Pires 1997 Muscat (Terras do Sado) $11. 85 *(10/1/1999)*

João Pires 2004 Muscat (Terras do Sado) $14. 86 —*J.C. (11/1/2006)*

João Pires 2003 Muscat (Terras do Sado) $13. 85 —*J.C. (3/1/2005)*

João Pires 1999 Muscat (Terras do Sado) $9. 84 —*M.S. (12/31/2001)*

João Pires 1998 Muscat (Terras do Sado) $7. 87 Best Buy —*J.C. (12/15/2000)*

João Pires 2002 Dry Muscat (Terras do Sado) $11. 88 Best Buy —*J.C. (11/15/2003)*

João Pires 2001 Muscat of Alexandria Muscat (Terras do Sado) $10. 87 —*J.C. (7/1/2003)*

JOSÉ MARIA DA FONSECA

José Maria da Fonseca 2001 Periquita Castelão (Palmela) $7. 85 Best Buy —*R.V. (11/1/2004)*

José Maria da Fonseca NV Alambre 20 Anos Moscatel (Setubal) $45. 93 —*R.V. (12/31/2002)*

José Maria da Fonseca NV Alambre 20 Anos Moscatel (Moscatel de Setúbal) $62. 92 —*R.V. (11/15/2005)*

José Maria da Fonseca 2001 Domingos Soares Franco Colecção Privado Moscatel (Moscatel de Setúbal) $NA. 92 —*R.V. (11/15/2005)*

José Maria da Fonseca NV Moscatel Roxo 20 Anos Moscatel (Moscatel de Setúbal) $NA. 94 —*R.V. (11/15/2005)*

José Maria da Fonseca 2003 Domingos Soares Franco Colecção Privado Portuguese Red (Terras do Sado) $NA. 93 Editors' Choice *—R.V. (11/15/2005)*

José Maria da Fonseca 2001 Domini Portuguese Red (Douro) $14. 89 *—R.V. (11/1/2004)*

José Maria da Fonseca 2001 Domini Plus Portuguese Red (Douro) $26. 92 *—R.V. (11/1/2004)*

José Maria da Fonseca 2001 DPT Garrafeira Portuguese Red (Palmela) $NA. 92 *—R.V. (11/1/2004)*

José Maria da Fonseca 2001 FSF Fernando Soares Franco Portuguese Red (Terras do Sado) $NA. 94 Editors' Choice *—R.V. (11/15/2005)*

José Maria da Fonseca 1999 Garrafeira CO Portuguese Red (Palmela) $20. 89 *—R.V. (11/1/2004)*

José Maria da Fonseca 2000 Hexagon Portuguese Red (Terras do Sado) $50. 92 *—R.V. (11/1/2004)*

José Maria da Fonseca 2003 Jose de Sousa Portuguese Red (Alentejano) $NA. 88 *—R.V. (11/15/2005)*

José Maria da Fonseca 2001 José de Sousa Mayor Portuguese Red (Alentejano) $NA. 91 *—R.V. (11/15/2005)*

José Maria da Fonseca 2001 Periquita Portuguese Red (Terras do Sado) $10. 87 Best Buy *—R.V. (11/15/2005)*

José Maria da Fonseca 2001 Periquita Classico Portuguese Red (Terras do Sado) $19. 90 *—R.V. (11/15/2005)*

José Maria da Fonseca 1996 Primum Portuguese Red (Terras do Sado) $11. 89 *(11/15/1999)*

José Maria da Fonseca 2003 Septimus Portuguese Red (Terras do Sado) $12. 87 *—R.V. (11/1/2004)*

José Maria da Fonseca 2000 Domini Red Blend (Douro) $15. 89 *—R.V. (12/31/2002)*

José Maria da Fonseca 2000 Domini Plus Red Blend (Douro) $25. 93 *—R.V. (12/31/2002)*

José Maria da Fonseca 1999 Periquita Red Blend (Azeitao) $8. 85 Best Buy *—D.T. (11/15/2002)*

José Maria da Fonseca 1995 Periquita Classico Red Blend (Terras do Sado) $19.87 *—R.V. (12/31/2002)*

José Maria da Fonseca 2000 Primum Touriga Nacional Blend (Terras do Sado) $13. 88 *—R.V. (12/31/2002)*

José Maria da Fonseca 2001 Primum White Blend (Terras do Sado) $15. 90 *—R.V. (8/1/2004)*

José Maria da Fonseca 2002 Primum Sauvignon-Arinto White Blend (Terras do Sado) $15. 87 *—J.C. (11/15/2003)*

KOPKE

Kopke 2004 Arinto (Douro) $18. The Arinto grape makes full-bodied white wines, sometimes just a touch creamy. This wine is typical, with rich flavors balanced with some apple skin acidity and tannins, but showing a wide open, creamy texture. There's just a touch of wood. 85 *—R.V. (3/1/2007)*

Kopke NV 10-Year Old Tawny Port $28. 88 *—R.V. (8/1/2006)*

Kopke NV 20-Year Old Tawny Port $56. 92 *—R.V. (8/1/2006)*

Kopke NV 30-Year Old Tawny Port (Port) $NA. The wood leaps out over the delicate, sweet fruit. The burnt character touched with caramel is fine, but less wood would definitely help. 84 *—R.V. (11/1/2007)*

Kopke NV 30-Year Old Tawny Port $122. 87 *—R.V. (8/1/2006)*

Kopke NV 40-Year Old Tawny Port $180. 83 *—R.V. (8/1/2006)*

Kopke NV Barão de Massarelos Ruby Reserve Port $NA. 83 *—R.V. (3/1/2005)*

Kopke 2004 Quinta São Luiz Vintage Port (Port) $58. A great mouthful of sweet fruit, flavors of ripe figs and tannins are almost lost in this delicious wine. This is hardly a classic, long-term vintage, but it's almost ready to be a hugely enjoyable wine. For lovers of rich, almost sweet Zinfandel, go back to the original model with this wine. 90 *—R.V. (11/1/2007)*

Kopke 2003 Vintage Port $NA. 86 *—R.V. (11/15/2005)*

Kopke NV Vintage Character Port $NA. 87 *—R.V. (3/1/2005)*

Kopke 2003 Tinta Roriz (Douro) $25. Owned by Barros Almeida, Kopke is one of the oldest Port houses. Now it has branched into table wines, with grapes from its own quintas. This is enticingly aromatic, with a big weight of black fruit, and dusty tannins. It's very ripe, toasty and ready to drink. 88 *—R.V. (3/1/2007)*

LAVRADORES DE FEITORIA

Lavradores de Feitoria 2001 Portuguese Red (Douro) $9. 90 Best Buy *—R.V. (11/15/2005)*

LEACOCK'S

Leacock's NV 10 Year Medium Rich Bual (Madeira) $36. 88 *—J.C. (11/1/2006)*

Leacock's NV Rainwater Tinta Negra Mole (Madeira) $13. 86 *—J.C. (11/1/2006)*

LEMOS & VAN ZELLER

Lemos & Van Zeller 2004 Curriculum Vitae Portuguese Red (Douro) $NA. From a special lot of wine that showed, as the producers put it, "new flavors and characters," this wine has been named Curriculum Vitae in recognition of its importance "in our winemaking lives." Luckily, this hype is justified. It's initially austere, with dry black fruits and firm tannins. But it shows great long-term qualities. A powerful wine that, with its wood and rich, almost Porty fruit, promises to keep for many years. 93 Cellar Selection *—R.V. (3/1/2007)*

LUIS MARGARIDE

Luis Margaride 1996 Dom Hermano Reserva Portuguese Red (Ribatejo) $9. 83 *—D.T. (12/31/2001)*

LUIS PATO

Luis Pato 2003 Casta Baga (Beiras) $9. 87 Best Buy *—R.V. (11/15/2006)*

Luis Pato 2001 Casta Baga (Beiras) $14. 85 *—J.C. (11/15/2003)*

Luis Pato 2001 Casta Baga (Beiras) $8. 86 *—R.V. (11/1/2004)*

Luis Pato 2001 Quinta do Moinho Baga (Beiras) $60. 91 *—J.C. (11/15/2003)*

Luis Pato 2003 Vinha Formal Bical (Beiras) $19. 90 *—R.V. (8/1/2005)*

Luis Pato 2004 Maria Gomes (Beiras) $8. 86 Best Buy *—R.V. (8/1/2005)*

Luis Pato 2002 Maria Gomes (Bairrada) $13. 85 *—J.C. (11/15/2003)*

Luis Pato 2001 Quinta do Ribeirinho Primeira Escolha Portuguese Red (Beiras) $20. 89 *—R.V. (11/1/2004)*

Luis Pato 2001 Vinha Barrosa Portuguese Red (Beiras) $NA. 88 *—R.V. (11/1/2004)*

Luis Pato 2001 Vinha Pan Portuguese Red (Beiras) $50. 91 *—R.V. (11/1/2004)*

Luis Pato 2001 Vinhas Velhas Portuguese Red (Beiras) $19. 91 Editors' Choice *—R.V. (11/1/2004)*

Luis Pato 2001 Vinha Formal Portuguese White (Beiras) $NA. 88 *—R.V. (11/1/2004)*

Luis Pato 2000 Red Blend (Beiras) $13. 86 *—R.V. (12/31/2002)*

Luis Pato 1999 Quinta do Moinho Red Blend (Beiras) $45. 88 *—R.V. (12/31/2002)*

Luis Pato 2000 Quinta do Ribeirinho Red Blend (Beiras) $30. 85 *—R.V. (12/31/2002)*

Luis Pato 2000 Quinta do Ribeirinho Primeira Escolha Red Blend (Beiras) $29. 90 *—R.V. (12/31/2002)*

Luis Pato 2000 Vinha Barrio Red Blend (Beiras) $29. 87 *—R.V. (12/31/2002)*

Luis Pato 2000 Vinha Barrosa Vina Velha Red Blend (Beiras) $29. 92 *—R.V. (12/31/2002)*

Luis Pato 2000 Vinha Pan Red Blend (Beiras) $13. 90 *—R.V. (12/31/2002)*

Luis Pato 2000 Vinhas Velhas Red Blend (Beiras) $13. 88 *—R.V. (12/31/2002)*

Luis Pato 1997 Vinhas Velhas Red Blend (Bairrada) $20. 90 *(11/15/1999)*

Luis Pato 2000 Vinha Formal White Blend (Beiras) $NA. 87 *—R.V. (11/1/2004)*

Luis Pato 2001 Vinhas Velhas White Blend (Beiras) $15. 90 *—R.V. (11/1/2004)*

MARCOLINO SEBO

Marcolino Sebo 2006 Visconde de Borba Portuguese Red (Alentejo) $10. The juicy fruit is dominated by Aragones and Trincadeira. This is a soft wine, simple, open and fresh, touched with acidity. 83 *—R.V. (12/15/2007)*

Marcolino Sebo 2004 Visconde de Borba Reserva Portuguese Red (Alentejo) $14. With 4–6 months' wood aging, here is a wine that is smooth, ripe, layered with black, juicy fruits, spoiled by an aftertaste of cured ham from volatility. 84 *—R.V. (12/15/2007)*

Marcolino Sebo 2006 Visconde de Borba Portuguese White (Alentejo) $9. Initially fresh, with a creamy, white-fruit texture, this has acidity, but it finishes fat and rather hot, with pepper. 83 *—R.V. (12/15/2007)*

MARGARIDA CABACO

Margarida Cabaco 2001 Monte dos Cabacos Portuguese Red (Alentejano) $19. 84 *—J.C. (12/31/2005)*

MARQUÉS DE BORBA

Marqués de Borba 2000 Portuguese White (Alentejo) $11. 85 *—D.T. (12/31/2001)*

MARTINEZ GASSIOT

Martinez Gassiot 2001 Late Bottled Vintage Port (Port) $NA. This combines the structured definition of Martinez with a youthful freshness. It is relatively light, but finely balanced, and immediately attractive. 89 *—R.V. (11/1/2007)*

Martinez Gassiot 2000 Late Bottled Vintage Port (Port) $NA. Very structured, dense and powerful, this wine is finely shaped, with acidity balancing the solid fruit. 90 *—R.V. (11/1/2007)*

Martinez Gassiot 1995 Quinta da Chousa Port $40. 86 *—J.C. (3/1/2000)*

Martinez Gassiot 1995 Quinta da Eira Velha Port $43. 89 *—J.C. (3/1/2000)*

MESSIAS

Messias NV 10-Year Old Tawny Port) $20. 82 *—R.V. (8/1/2006)*

Messias NV 20-Year Old Tawny Port) $40. 81 *—R.V. (8/1/2006)*

Messias NV 30-Year Old Tawny Port $60. 84 *—R.V. (8/1/2006)*

MONTEZ CHAMPALIMAUD

Montez Champalimaud 1999 Quinta do Cotto Red Blend (Douro) $20. 80 *—R.V. (12/31/2002)*

Montez Champalimaud10-Year Old Tawny Port $44. 93 Editors' Choice *—R.V. (8/1/2006)*

NIEPOORT

Niepoort NV 20-Year Old Tawny Port $40. 92 *—R.V. (8/1/2006)*

Niepoort NV 30-Year Old Tawny Port $174. 92 *—R.V. (8/1/2006)*

Niepoort 1995 Colheita Port (Port) $NA. Don't let the medicinal aromas put you off because on the palate it is a hugely dense wine, concentrated, like dark, old toffee, with bitter coffee flavors. It's best taken in small quantities, savoring the richness and complexity. 93 *—R.V. (11/1/2007)*

Niepoort NV Junior Tinto Port (Port) $20. A ripe, intense, dry fruit-flavored ruby Port that has depth of fruit and well-integrated spirit. A great, everyday drinking Port. 85 *—R.V. (11/1/2007)*

Niepoort 2001 Late Bottled Vintage Port (Port) $24. This is like a junior vintage. Because Niepoort bottles its LBVs unfiltered, they have ripeness and balance, while the fruit has great concentration of flavor. This is very rich with many black fruit and dark plum flavors, but at the same time it has a core of structure and tannin, which suggests that it could age. Bottled in 2006. 90 *—R.V. (11/1/2007)*

Niepoort 1997 LBV Bottled 2001 Port $22. 90 *—R.V. (3/1/2003)*

Niepoort 1998 LBV Bottled 2002 Port $22. 90 *—R.V. (3/1/2003)*

Niepoort 2003 Secundum Vintage Port $58. 93 *—R.V. (11/15/2005)*

Niepoort NV Senior Tawny Port (Port) $20. Fresh and fruity, this is a prime example of good tawny. It has flavors of currants and figs, along with some wood acidity which gives it a great tawny character. 87 *—R.V. (11/1/2007)*

Niepoort 2003 Vintage Port $84. 95 *—R.V. (11/15/2005)*

Niepoort NV Vintage Character Port $18. 88 *—R.V. (3/1/2005)*

Niepoort 2000 Vintage Port $80. 97 Cellar Selection *(11/15/2003)*

Niepoort 2004 Batuta Portuguese Red (Douro) $90. It is appropriate that the name "Batuta" means conductor's baton. This is certainly the leader (and the finest) of the three reds made by Niepoort. That's because, while it remains as powerful a statement as the other two (Redoma and Vertente), it also has better balance of rich fruits, sweet tannins and the dark chocolate flavors. Age for six years at least. 93 *—R.V. (3/1/2007)*

Niepoort 2001 Batuta Portuguese Red (Douro) $71. 94 *—R.V. (11/1/2004)*

Niepoort 2001 Redoma Portuguese Red (Douro) $NA. North-facing vineyards are the source for this impressively structured, layered wine. Its tannins are huge, but dusty rather than dry, sustaining big, rich fruits. Coffee flavors vie with the dry toast and acidity. This is a wine that just narrowly avoids being over the top, and in doing so turns into something great. 91 *—R.V. (3/1/2007)*

Niepoort 2001 Redoma Portuguese Red (Douro) $43. 90 *—R.V. (11/1/2004)*

Niepoort 2004 Vertente Portuguese Red (Douro) $NA. This is a new label from Niepoort. It's action-packed, velvety with both deliciously sweet fruit and bone-dry tannins. It is round and smooth on top of black, dense fruits. Licorice and acidity dominate the aftertaste. 90 *—R.V. (3/1/2007)*

Niepoort 2001 Vertente Portuguese Red (Douro) $26. 89 *—R.V. (11/1/2004)*

Niepoort 1999 Batuta Red Blend (Douro) $60. 92 *—R.V. (12/31/2002)*

Niepoort 1999 Redoma Red Blend (Douro) $41. 92 *—R.V. (12/31/2002)*

Niepoort 2000 Redoma Reserva White Blend (Douro) $41. 91 Editors' Choice *—R.V. (11/1/2004)*

NOVAL

Noval NV LB Finest Reserve Port $18. 85 *—R.V. (3/1/2005)*

OFFLEY

Offley NV 10-Year Old Tawny Port $26. 86 *—R.V. (8/1/2006)*

Offley NV 20-Year Old Tawny Port $48. 89 *—R.V. (8/1/2006)*

Offley NV 30-Year Old Tawny Port $45. 90 *—R.V. (8/1/2006)*

Offley NV Baron de Forrester Reserva Port $NA. 87 *—R.V. (3/1/2005)*

Offley 1997 Boa Vista Port $19. 84 *—M.S. (7/1/2002)*

Offley 2003 Boa Vista Vintage Port $50. 90 *—R.V. (11/15/2005)*

Offley 1997 LBV Bottled 2001 Port) $23. 89 *—R.V. (3/1/2003)*

Offley 2000 Late Bottled Vintage Port (Port) $20. A dry, powerful wine, almost austere initially, dominated by bitter chocolate and dried raisins. This is a great, firm, structured style. 89 *—R.V. (11/1/2007)*

OSBORNE

Osborne NV 10-Year Old Tawny Port $25. 88 *—J.C. (3/1/2005)*

Osborne 1997 LBC Port $16. 86 *—J.C. (3/1/2004)*

Osborne 1999 LBV Port $14. 84 *—J.C. (3/1/2005)*

Osborne NV Special Reserve Master of Port $16. 87 *—M.S. (7/1/2002)*

Osborne 2003 Vintage Port $50. 84 *—R.V. (11/15/2005)*

Osborne 2000 Vintage Port $45. 87 *—J.C. (3/1/2004)*

Osborne 1995 Vintage Port $40. 88 *—M.S. (11/15/2002)*

PALACIO DE BREJOEIRA

Palacio de Brejoeira 2004 Alvarinho (Vinho Verde) $24. 90 *—R.V. (7/1/2006)*

PENINSULA

Peninsula 2003 Red Blend (Estremadura) $9. 84 *—J.C. (11/1/2006)*

PINHAL DA TORRE

Pinhal da Torre 2003 Two Worlds Portuguese Red (Ribatejano) $16. 89 *—R.V. (7/1/2006)*

Pinhal da Torre 2003 Quinta do Alqueve Touriga Nacional (Ribatejano) $29. 92 Editors' Choice *—R.V. (7/1/2006)*

Pinhal da Torre 2003 Quinta do Alqueve Touriga Nacional-Syrah (Ribatejano) $32. 92 Cellar Selection *—R.V. (7/1/2006)*

PINTAS

Pintas 2002 Portuguese Red (Douro) $NA. 88 *—R.V. (11/1/2004)*

Pintas 2001 Portuguese Red (Douro) $60. 91 *—R.V. (11/1/2004)*

PONTUAL

Pontual 2004 Reserva Portuguese Red (Alentejano) $38. 90 *—J.C. (11/1/2006)*

Pontual 2004 Touriga Nacional-Trincadeira Portuguese Red (Alentejano) $23. 84 *—J.C. (11/1/2006)*

Pontual 2004 Syrah (Alentejano) $23. 89 *—J.C. (11/1/2006)*

PORCA DE MURCA

Porca de Murca 2000 Reserve Red Blend (Douro) $16. 83 *—J.C. (3/1/2004)*

Porca de Murca 2001 Tinto Red Blend (Douro) $10. 85 *—J.C. (3/1/2004)*

Porca de Murca 2002 Branco Reserva White Blend (Douro) $10. 84 *—J.C. (3/1/2004)*

PORTAL

Portal NV Cellar Reserve Port $NA. 86 *—R.V. (3/1/2005)*

PORTAL DO FIDALGO

Portal do Fidalgo 2004 Alvarinho (Vinho Verde) $15. 84 *—J.C. (12/31/2005)*

Portal do Fidalgo 2002 Alvarinho (Vinho Verde) $15. 87 Editors' Choice *—J.C. (3/1/2004)*

PORTO POÇAS

Porto Poças NV 10-Year Old Tawny Port $20. 86 *—R.V. (8/1/2006)*

Porto Poças NV 20-Year Old Tawny Port $50. 87 *—R.V. (8/1/2006)*

Porto Poças NV 30-Year Old Tawny Port $60. 89 *—R.V. (8/1/2006)*

Poças NV 40-Year Old Tawny Port $130. 84 *—R.V. (8/1/2006)*

Poças 2003 Director's Choice Vintage Port $19. 91 *—R.V. (11/15/2005)*

Poças 2003 Vintage Port $46. 91 *—R.V. (11/15/2005)*

Porto Poças NV Director's Choice Tawny Port $20. 89 *—J.C. (3/1/2005)*

Porto Poças 1998 LBV Port $23. 88 *—J.C. (3/1/2005)*

Porto Poças NV Quinta Vale de Cavalos Special Reserve Ruby Port $19. 88 *—R.V. (3/1/2005)*

Porto Poças NV Ruby Port $14. 85 *—J.C. (3/1/2005)*

Porto Poças NV Tawny Port $14. 84 *—J.C. (3/1/2005)*

Porto Poças 2001 Vintage Port $70. 89 *—J.C. (6/1/2006)*

PORTO SOLENE

Porto Solene NV Ruby Special Reserve Port $40/500 ml. 88 *—J.C. (11/1/2006)*

PRATS & SYMINGTON LDA

Prats & Symington LDA 2003 Chryseia Portuguese Red (Douro) $66. 92 *—J.C. (11/1/2006)*

Prats & Symington LDA 2000 Chryseia (Douro) $45. 92 *—R.V. (12/31/2002)*

Prats & Symington LDA 2004 Post Scriptum de Chryseia Portuguese Red (Douro) $24. 89 *—J.C. (11/1/2006)*

Prats & Symington LDA 2001 Chryseia Portuguese Red (Douro) $25. 91 Editors' Choice *—R.V. (11/1/2004)*

Prats & Symington LDA 2002 Post Scriptum de Chryseia Portuguese Red (Douro) $NA. 88 *—R.V. (11/1/2004)*

PRESIDENTIAL

Presidential 2000 LBV Port $20. 87 *—J.C. (6/1/2006)*

Presidential 2003 Vintage Port $55. 88 *—R.V. (11/15/2005)*

PROVAM

Provam 2005 Alvarinho Portal do Fidalgo Alvarinho (Vinho Verde) $15. 90 Best Buy *—R.V. (7/1/2006)*

Provam 2005 Varanda do Conde Portuguese White (Vinho Verde) $10. 89 *—R.V. (7/1/2006)*

QUARLES HARRIS

Quarles Harris NV 10-Year Old Tawny Port $NA. 85 *—R.V. (8/1/2006)*

Quarles Harris 2003 Vintage Port $NA. 88 *—R.V. (11/15/2005)*

QUINTA D'AGUIEIRA

Quinta d'Aguieira 2000 Alvarinho Chardonnay (Beiras) $10. 84 *—M.M. (12/31/2001)*

Quinta d'Aguieira 2001 Touriga Nacional-Cabernet Sauvignon (Beiras) $13. 84 *(1/1/2004)*

Quinta d'Aguieira 1999 Touriga Nacional-Cabernet Sauvignon (Bairrada) $13. 80 *—M.S. (12/31/2001)*

Quinta d'Aguieira 2002 White Blend (Beiras) $8. 86 Best Buy *(12/15/2003)*

Quinta d'Aguieira 2000 White Blend (Beiras) $8. 85 Best Buy *—J.C. (12/31/2001)*

QUINTA DA ALORNA

Quinta da Alorna 2004 Red Blend (Ribatejano) $10. Features a bright, bouncy bouquet of red fruit married to a light to medium-weight palate. Dark, chocolaty flavors add a warming bass note. Shows some dry tannins on the finish, but doesn't seem particularly ageworthy; drink now and over the next two years. 85 Best Buy *—J.C. (3/1/2007)*

QUINTA DA AVELEDA

Quinta da Aveleda 2000 Alvarinho Alvarinho (Vinho Verde) $12. 88 *—R.V. (8/1/2004)*

Quinta da Aveleda 2001 Loureiro (Vinho Verde) $7. 84 *—J.C. (7/1/2003)*

Quinta da Aveleda 2005 Portuguese White (Vinho Verde) $8. 89 Best Buy *—R.V. (7/1/2006)*

Quinta da Aveleda 2000 Aveleda Red Blend (Estremadura) $6. 86 Best Buy *—R.V. (12/31/2002)*

Quinta da Aveleda 2000 Charamba Red Blend (Douro) $7. 85 Best Buy *(1/1/2004)*

Quinta da Aveleda 1999 Charamba Red Blend (Douro) $7. 83 *—R.V. (12/31/2002)*

Quinta da Aveleda 2000 Quinta da Aguieira Touriga Nacional (Beiras) $26. 85 *—R.V. (12/31/2002)*

Quinta da Aveleda 2000 Quinta d'Aguiera Touriga Nacional-Cabernet Sauvignon (Beiras) $16. 84 *—R.V. (12/31/2002)*

Quinta da Aveleda 2001 Trajadura (Vinho Verde) $7. 86 *—J.C. (7/1/2003)*

Quinta da Aveleda 2002 Aveleda Trajadura (Vinho Verde) $8. 84 *(12/15/2003)*

Quinta da Aveleda 2000 White Blend (Vinho Verde) $9. 85 *—M.M. (12/31/2001)*

Quinta da Aveleda 2002 Alvarinho White Blend (Vinho Verde) $12. 86 *(12/15/2003)*

Quinta da Aveleda NV Aveleda White Blend (Vinho Verde) $6. 83 *(12/15/2003)*

Quinta da Aveleda NV Aveleda White Blend (Vinho Verde) $6. 84 *—R.V. (8/1/2004)*

Quinta da Aveleda NV Casal Garcia White Blend (Vinho Verde) $6. 82 *—J.C. (7/1/2003)*

Quinta da Aveleda NV Casal Garcia White Blend (Vinho Verde) $6. 84 *(12/15/2003)*

Quinta da Aveleda 2001 Grinalda White Blend (Vinho Verde) $8. 87 *—R.V. (8/1/2004)*

Quinta da Aveleda 2000 Grinalda White Blend (Vinho Verde) $9. 84 *—J.C. (12/31/2001)*

Quinta da Aveleda 2002 Quinta da Aveleda White Blend (Vinho Verde) $7. 84 *(12/15/2003)*

Quinta da Aveleda 2001 Quinta de Aveleda White Blend (Vinho Verde) $7. 88 *—R.V. (8/1/2004)*

QUINTA DA CARVALHOSA

Quinta da Carvalhosa 2002 Ardosino Portuguese Red (Douro) $18. 88 *—R.V. (11/1/2004)*

Quinta da Carvalhosa 2001 Campo Ardosa Portuguese Red (Douro) $30. 94 Editors' Choice *—R.V. (11/1/2004)*

Quinta da Carvalhosa 2001 Ardosino Red Blend (Douro) $22. 87 *—J.C. (3/1/2004)*

QUINTA DA CORTEZIA

Quinta da Cortezia 2005 Vinho Branco Arinto (Estremadura) $12. 86 *—J.C. (11/1/2006)*

Quinta da Cortezia 2004 Reserve Red Blend (Estremadura) $16. 86 *—J.C. (11/1/2006)*

Quinta da Cortezia 2004 Vinha Conchas Red Blend (Estremadura) $8. 87 Best Buy *—J.C. (11/1/2006)*

Quinta da Cortezia 2004 Vinha Conchas Special Selection Red Blend (Estremadura) $11. 88 Best Buy *—J.C. (11/1/2006)*

Quinta da Cortezia 2004 Touriga Nacional (Estremadura) $16. This wine seems to have slipped somewhat since we last reviewed it (back in 1999 the 1997 vintage scored 91 points), but at least the price has fallen considerably since then. Medium-bodied, dark berry fruit is couched in a charred barrel and roasted coffee frame. Drink 2007–2010. 85 *—J.C. (3/1/2007)*

Quinta da Cortezia 1997 Touriga Nacional (Estremadura) $33. 91 *(10/1/1999)*

Quinta da Cortezia 1999 Reserva Touriga Nacional Blend (Estremadura) $32. 90 *—R.V. (12/31/2002)*

QUINTA DA ESTEVEIRA

Quinta da Esteveira 2003 Colheita Seleccionada Portuguese Red (Douro) $NA. 92 *—R.V. (3/1/2006)*

QUINTA DA FOZ

Quinta da Foz 1996 Vintage Port $50. 90 *—R.V. (3/1/2004)*

Quinta da Foz 1992 Vintage Port $NA. 89 *—R.V. (3/1/2004)*

QUINTA DA MANUELA

Quinta da Manuela 2000 Portuguese Red (Douro) $61. 90 *—J.C. (3/1/2005)*

QUINTA DA MIMOSA

Quinta da Mimosa 2001 Periquita (Palmela) $16. 88 *—J.C. (11/15/2003)*

Quinta da Mimosa 2000 Tinto Red Blend (Palmela) $15. 88 *—J.C. (7/1/2003)*

QUINTA DA MURTA

Quinta da Murta 2005 Vinho Branco Seco Arinto (Bucelas) $10. 86 Best Buy *—J.C. (11/1/2006)*

QUINTA DA PACHECA

Quinta da Pacheca 2003 Vintage Port $NA. 91 *—R.V. (11/15/2005)*

QUINTA DA PEDRA

Quinta da Pedra 2005 Alvarinho (Vinho Verde) $13. 89 Best Buy —*R.V. (7/1/2006)*

QUINTA DA ROMEIRA

Quinta da Romeira 2003 Arinto (Bucelas) $9. 85 Best Buy —*J.C. (3/1/2005)*

Quinta da Romeira 2002 Arinto (Bucelas) $8. 85 —*J.C. (11/15/2003)*

Quinta da Romeira 2001 Estate Bottled Arinto (Bucelas) $7. 83 —*J.C. (7/1/2003)*

Quinta da Romeira 2001 Morgado de Santa Catherina Arinto (Bucelas) $14. 90 —*R.V. (8/1/2004)*

Quinta da Romeira 1999 Morgado de Sta. Catherina Arinto (Bucelas) $13. 83 —*J.C. (12/31/2001)*

Quinta da Romeira 2004 Arinto Portuguese White (Bucelas) $NA. 86 —*R.V. (8/1/2005)*

Quinta da Romeira 2003 Morgado de Santa Catherina Portuguese White (Bucelas) $NA. 88 —*R.V. (8/1/2005)*

Quinta da Romeira 2000 Calhandriz Red Blend (Estremadura) $7. 82 —*R.V. (12/31/2002)*

Quinta da Romeira 1999 Tradicão Red Blend (Palmela) $7. 87 Best Buy —*J.C. (12/15/2000)*

Quinta da Romeira 1999 Prova Regia Touriga Nacional (Estremadura) $13. 88 —*J.C. (7/1/2003)*

QUINTA DAS BALDIAS

Quinta das Baldias 2003 Vintage Port $NA. 93 —*R.V. (11/15/2005)*

QUINTA DAS HEREDIAS

Quinta das Heredias NV 10-Year Old Tawny Port $28. 86 —*R.V. (8/1/2006)*

Quinta das Heredias NV 20-Year Old Tawny Port $50. 80 —*R.V. (8/1/2006)*

Quinta das Heredias NV 40-Year Old Tawny Port $130. 83 —*R.V. (8/1/2006)*

QUINTA DAS MAIAS

Quinta das Maias 2003 Malvasia Fina (Dão) $15. 87 —*R.V. (8/1/2005)*

Quinta das Maias 2001 Portuguese Red (Dão) $18. 89 —*R.V. (11/1/2004)*

Quinta das Maias 2000 Jaen Portuguese Red (Dão) $29. 89 —*R.V. (11/1/2004)*

Quinta das Maias 2000 Reserva Portuguese Red (Dão) $29. 90 —*R.V. (11/1/2004)*

Quinta das Maias 2003 Portuguese White (Dão) $10. 86 Best Buy —*R.V. (8/1/2005)*

QUINTA DAS TECEDEIRAS

Quinta das Tecedeiras 2003 Vintage Port $35. 88 —*R.V. (11/15/2005)*

Quinta das Tecedeiras 2001 Reserva Red Blend (Douro) $NA. 86 —*J.C. (11/15/2003)*

QUINTA DE CABRIZ

Quinta de Cabriz 2003 Colheita Seleccionada Portuguese Red (Dão) $7. 89 Best Buy —*J.C. (6/1/2006)*

Quinta de Cabriz 2000 Colheita Seleccionada Red Blend (Dão) $20. 85 —*J.C. (11/15/2003)*

QUINTA DE CHOCAPALHA

Quinta de Chocapalha 2005 Cabernet Sauvignon Cabernet Sauvignon-Syrah (Estremadura) $22. With its addition of 10% Syrah, this is a deliciously rounded wine, the Cabernet firmness mellowed into mature, ripe fruit. The acidity gives it shape, the tannins act as a focus for the rich fruit. 90 —*R.V. (12/15/2007)*

Quinta de Chocapalha 2005 Portuguese Red (Estremadura) $18. A powerful expression of Portuguese varieties, with dense tannins, dark fruit flavors and ripeness. If the alcohol is too high—and it shows in the pepper edge to the wine—it still has a sense of shape and structure. 88 —*R.V. (12/15/2007)*

Quinta de Chocapalha 2001 Portuguese Red (Estremadura) $NA. 91 Editors' Choice —*R.V. (11/1/2004)*

Quinta de Chocapalha 2005 Chocopalha Reserva Portuguese Red (Estremadura) $38. A blend of Touriga Nacional and Tinta Roriz, fermented in open lagers with new barrique aging. All that goes to make a mature, superripe wine, with intense violet and vanilla perfumes, packed with blackberry flavors and dark, brooding, dry tannins. Age for five years. 91 Cellar Selection —*R.V. (12/15/2007)*

Quinta de Chocapalha 2006 Branco Portuguese White (Estremadura) $17. Deliciously fresh, full of floral aromas, citrus and white fruit flavors, and long, ripe acidity. Blending Arinto, Viosinho and Vital, this is has minerality and a complexity from lees aging. 89 —*R.V. (12/15/2007)*

QUINTA DE COVELA

Quinta de Covela 2001 Colheita Seleccionada Portuguese Red (Portugal) $NA. 87 —*R.V. (11/1/2004)*

Quinta de Covela 2002 Tinto Escolha Portuguese Red (Portugal) $NA. 84 —*R.V. (11/1/2004)*

Quinta de Covela 2003 Branco Escolha Portuguese White (Portugal) $NA. 88 —*R.V. (11/1/2004)*

Quinta de Covela 2002 Colheita Seleccionada Portuguese White (Portugal) $NA. 90 —*R.V. (11/1/2004)*

Quinta de Covela 2004 Covela Portuguese White (Minho) $21. 86 —*R.V. (8/1/2005)*

Quinta de Covela 2003 Covela Colheita Seleccionada Portuguese White (Minho) $NA. 89 Best Buy —*R.V. (8/1/2005)*

Quinta de Covela 2003 Covela Fantástico Portuguese White (Minho) $NA. 90 —*R.V. (8/1/2005)*

Quinta de Covela 1999 Vinho Branco White Blend (Portugal) $13. 83 —*M.S. (12/31/2001)*

QUINTA DE LA ROSA

Quinta de la Rosa NV 10-Year Old Tawny Port $37. 88 —*R.V. (3/1/2004)*

Quinta de la Rosa NV Finest Reserve Port $28. 88 —*R.V. (3/1/2005)*

Quinta de la Rosa 1997 LBV Bottled 2002 Port $26. 87 —*R.V. (3/1/2003)*

Quinta de la Rosa 1999 Vale do Inferno Vintage Port $52. 92 Cellar Selection —*R.V. (3/1/2004)*

Quinta de la Rosa 2003 Vintage Port $NA. 94 —*R.V. (11/15/2005)*

Quinta de la Rosa 2000 Vintage Port $NA. 89 —*R.V. (3/1/2004)*

Quinta de la Rosa 2001 Portuguese Red (Douro) $NA. 89 —*R.V. (11/1/2004)*

Quinta de la Rosa 2001 Vale de Clara Portuguese Red (Douro) $NA. 86 —*R.V. (11/1/2004)*

Quinta de la Rosa 2001 Quinta la Rosa Red Blend (Douro) $18. 90 —*R.V. (12/31/2002)*

QUINTA DE PANCAS

Quinta de Pancas 1996 Cabernet Sauvignon (Estremadura) $13. 83 —*(10/1/1999)*

Quinta de Pancas 2003 Cabernet Sauvignon (Estremadura) $15. 84 —*J.C. (11/1/2006)*

Quinta de Pancas 2003 Special Selection Cabernet Sauvignon (Estremadura) $35. 89 —*R.V. (3/1/2006)*

Quinta de Pancas 2003 Assemblage Touriga Nacional-Cabernet Sauvignon (Estremadura) $12. It's called Assemblage because the wine is a blend of Touriga Nacional and Cabernet Sauvignon. This big wine, with its dense structure, texture and superripe fruit, is certainly rich. The tannins and the acidity do hold everything in check. But it's not a wine for aging. 89 —*R.V. (12/15/2007)*

Quinta de Pancas 2003 Premium Red Portuguese Red (Estremadura) $80. 94 —*R.V. (3/1/2006)*

Quinta de Pancas 2003 Reserva Especial Red Portuguese Red (Estremadura) $38. 93 —*R.V. (3/1/2006)*

QUINTA DE PARROTES

Quinta de Parrotes 2002 Red Wine Portuguese Red (Alenquer) $9. 82 —*J.C. (6/1/2006)*

Quinta de Parrotes 2001 Red Blend (Alenquer) $9. 86 Best Buy —*J.C. (11/1/2004)*

QUINTA DE RORIZ

Quinta de Roriz 1999 Vintage Port $50. 91 —*M.S. (11/15/2002)*

Quinta de Roriz 2003 Vintage Port $57. 87 —*R.V. (11/15/2005)*

Quinta de Roriz 2002 Vintage Port $52. 90 —*J.C. (12/1/2004)*

Quinta de Roriz 2001 Vintage Port $48. 92 Editors' Choice —*J.C. (11/15/2003)*

Quinta de Roriz 2005 Prazo de Roriz Portuguese Red (Douro) $15. The second wine from the Quinta de Roriz, an estate managed and marketed by the Symington family. This blend of the classic Port varieties is a good, fresh, attractively balanced wine, slightly lean but with some fine tannins, and fresh acidity. The finish is full of fresh red berries. 87 —*R.V. (3/1/2007)*

Quinta de Roriz 2004 Prazo de Roriz Portuguese Red (Douro) $14. 89 Best Buy —*J.C. (6/1/2006)*

Quinta de Roriz 2003 Prazo de Roriz Portuguese Red (Douro) $13. 87 —*J.C. (12/31/2005)*

Quinta de Roriz 2002 Prazo de Roriz Portuguese Red (Douro) $13. 85 —*R.V. (11/1/2004)*

Quinta de Roriz 2003 Reserva Portuguese Red (Douro) $29. This estate, managed by the Symington family, is a great Douro property by any standard. This hot 2003 vintage is properly big and dense, but the elegance and style of the estate shows through, with delicious ripe plum flavors over the new wood. Age this for at least 6 years. **92 Cellar Selection** —*R.V. (9/1/2007)*

Quinta de Roriz 2002 Reserva Portuguese Red (Douro) $26. 87 —*J.C. (11/1/2006)*

Quinta de Roriz 2001 Reserva Portuguese Red (Douro) $23. 90 Editors' Choice —*R.V. (11/1/2004)*

Quinta de Roriz 2001 Reserva Portuguese Red (Douro) $24. 86 —*J.C. (12/31/2005)*

Quinta de Roriz 2000 Reserva Portuguese Red (Douro) $23. 91 Editors' Choice —*R.V. (11/1/2004)*

Quinta de Roriz 2001 Prazo de Roriz Red Blend (Douro) $13. 88 —*R.V. (12/31/2002)*

Quinta de Roriz 2000 Quinta de Roriz Reserva Red Blend (Douro) $29. 91 —*R.V. (12/31/2002)*

QUINTA DE SAES

Quinta de Saes 1996 Vinho Tinto Red Blend (Dão) $25. 87 *(10/1/1999)*

QUINTA DE VENTOZELO

Quinta de Ventozelo 2000 LBV Port $19. 89 —*J.C. (6/1/2006)*

Quinta de Ventozelo NV Reserva Port $15. 83 —*R.V. (3/1/2005)*

Quinta de Ventozelo NV Tawny Reserva Port (Port) $18. A raisin- and fresh fig-flavored wine, light and open. There's a hint of cocoa, acidity and some citrus. **84** —*R.V. (11/1/2007)*

Quinta de Ventozelo 2004 Vintage Port (Port) $65. Generally, 2004 is not a classic vintage Port year, but there are some very good ones around. This is soft, ripe and with good tannins. It will not age over many years, but its fresh red fruits and layer of dryness suggest it will be at its best in 3–4 years. **88** —*R.V. (11/1/2007)*

Quinta de Ventozelo 2003 Vintage Port $60. 92 —*J.C. (6/1/2006)*

Quinta de Ventozelo 2002 Vintage Port $50. 92 —*J.C. (6/1/2006)*

Quinta de Ventozelo 2001 Vintage Port $50. 88 —*J.C. (6/1/2006)*

Quinta de Ventozelo 2000 Vintage Port $50. 89 —*J.C. (11/1/2006)*

Quinta de Ventozelo 2000 Portuguese Red (Douro) $12. 86 —*J.C. (12/1/2004)*

Quinta de Ventozelo 2003 Amostra de Casco Portuguese Red (Douro) $15. 84 —*J.C. (12/31/2005)*

Quinta de Ventozelo 2001 Cister da Ribeira Portuguese Red (Douro) $9. 87 Best Buy —*J.C. (12/31/2005)*

Quinta de Ventozelo 2000 Cistera da Ribeira Tinto Portuguese Red (Douro) $9. 84 —*J.C. (12/1/2004)*

Quinta de Ventozelo 2003 Reserva Portuguese Red (Douro) $25. A wine that shows firm, slightly vegetal characters initially, but then does open up to give ripe, but very dry, tannins and some intense power. The acidity is prominent at this stage in its evolution, so it should age well over 5–10 years. **89** —*R.V. (3/1/2007)*

Quinta de Ventozelo 2001 Reserva Portuguese Red (Douro) $22. 89 —*J.C. (12/31/2005)*

Quinta de Ventozelo 2002 Tinto Portuguese Red (Douro) $15. 87 —*J.C. (6/1/2006)*

Quinta de Ventozelo 2000 Tinto Reserva Portuguese Red (Douro) $45. 85 —*J.C. (12/1/2004)*

Quinta de Ventozelo 2003 Tinta Roriz (Douro) $16. 85 —*J.C. (6/1/2006)*

Quinta de Ventozelo 2003 Touriga Franca (Douro) $16. 86 —*J.C. (12/31/2005)*

Quinta de Ventozelo 2003 Tinto Touriga Nacional (Douro) $16. 90 Editors' Choice —*J.C. (12/31/2005)*

QUINTA DO AMEAL

Quinta do Ameal 2004 Loureiro (Vinho Verde) $13. 91 Best Buy —*R.V. (7/1/2006)*

Quinta do Ameal 2003 Escolha Loureiro (Vinho Verde) $25. 92 Editors' Choice —*R.V. (7/1/2006)*

QUINTA DO CARMO

Quinta do Carmo 2004 Portuguese Red (Alentejano) $26. Ripe fruit, good, even high acidity, a touch of wood: everything is here, except for the nagging edge of rusticity that often pervades the Carmo estate wine. It needs more polish. **86** —*R.V. (12/15/2007)*

Quinta do Carmo 2003 Portuguese Red (Alentejano) $26. Superripe, with sweet black fruit, and ripe, soft tannins. The structure is here, but the acidity seems to have missed out with such richly ripe black fig flavors. **86** —*R.V. (12/15/2007)*

Quinta do Carmo 2002 Portuguese Red (Alentejano) $26. A finely perfumed, but also rough-edged wine, with acidity and very dry tannins. It is beginning to show maturity, the tannins edging out the fruit and chocolate flavors and old leather aromas coming through. Drink now. **85** —*R.V. (12/15/2007)*

Quinta do Carmo 2002 Portuguese Red (Alentejano) $23. 82 —*J.C. (11/1/2006)*

Quinta do Carmo 2001 Portuguese Red (Alentejano) $30. 86 —*J.C. (12/31/2005)*

Quinta do Carmo 2000 Portuguese Red (Alentejano) $25. 87 —*R.V. (12/1/2004)*

Quinta do Carmo 2004 Dom Martinho Portuguese Red (Alentejano) $13. This open, juicy wine is a blend dominated by Aragonez and Alicante Bouschet that gives it sweetness and flavors of red berries with a firm underlay of tannin. A wine to drink with spicy foods on a cold day. **84** —*R.V. (12/15/2007)*

Quinta do Carmo 2003 Dom Martinho Portuguese Red (Alentejano) $13. 84 —*J.C. (11/1/2006)*

Quinta do Carmo 2001 Dom Martinho Portuguese Red (Alentejano) $11. 84 —*R.V. (12/1/2004)*

Quinta do Carmo 2004 Reserva Portuguese Red (Alentejano) $55. The most satisfying of recent offerings from this Lafite-managed estate. It is certainly tough and young, but with its great black berry fruits and ripe plum flavors, it also shows elegant tannins and balanced acidity. Excellent aging potential. **90** —*R.V. (12/15/2007)*

Quinta do Carmo 2003 Reserva Portuguese Red (Alentejano) $55. A wine that seems weighed down by its own structure. It is all solid tannins, darkness, the fruit not really able to express itself. Powerful and concentrated, this needs more time to develop, although the direction of the wine is still problematic. **87** —*R.V. (12/15/2007)*

Quinta do Carmo 2003 Reserva Portuguese Red (Alentejano) $55. 87 —*J.C. (11/1/2006)*

Quinta do Carmo 2001 Reserva Portuguese Red (Alentejano) $40. 89 —*R.V. (12/1/2004)*

Quinta do Carmo 2000 Red Blend (Alentejano) $25. 86 —*J.C. (12/10/2003)*

Quinta do Carmo 1999 Red Blend (Alentejano) $24. 85 —*R.V. (12/31/2002)*

Quinta do Carmo 1998 Red Blend (Alentejo) $30. 85 —*M.S. (11/15/2002)*

Quinta do Carmo 2002 Dom Martinho Red Blend (Alentejano) $12. 85 —*J.C. (6/1/2006)*

Quinta do Carmo 2000 Dom Martinho Red Blend (Alentejano) $10. 84 —*J.C. (3/1/2004)*

Quinta do Carmo 1999 Dom Martinho Red Blend (Alentejano) $10. 82 —*R.V. (12/31/2002)*

Quinta do Carmo 1998 Dom Martinho Red Blend (Alentejo) $15. 84 —*M.S. (11/15/2002)*

Quinta do Carmo 2002 Reserva Red Blend (Alentejano) $40. 87 —*J.C. (12/31/2005)*

Quinta do Carmo 2001 Reserva Red Blend (Alentejano) $40. Try in 2007. **88** —*J.C. (3/1/2004)*

Quinta do Carmo 2000 Reserva Red Blend (Alentejano) $NA. 87 —*J.C. (7/1/2003)*

QUINTA DO CASAL BRANCO

Quinta do Casal Branco 1999 Capucho Cabernet Sauvignon (Ribatejo) $20. 88 —*R.V. (12/31/2002)*

Quinta do Casal Branco 2002 Falcoaria Fernão Pires (Ribatejo) $9. 87 Best Buy —*R.V. (8/1/2005)*

Quinta do Casal Branco 2002 Capucho Merlot Merlot (Ribatejo) $NA. 83 —*R.V. (11/1/2004)*

Quinta do Casal Branco 1999 Falcoaria Portuguese Red (Ribatejo) $15. 85 —*R.V. (11/1/2004)*

Quinta do Casal Branco 2001 Falcoaria Reserva Portuguese Red (Ribatejo) $NA. 89 —*R.V. (11/1/2004)*

Quinta do Casal Branco 2000 Globus Portuguese Red (Ribatejano) $NA. 86 —*R.V. (11/1/2004)*

Quinta do Casal Branco 2002 Terra de Lobos Portuguese Red (Ribatejano) $7. 84 **Best Buy** —*R.V. (11/1/2004)*

Quinta do Casal Branco 2003 Portuguese White (Ribatejano) $6. 91 **Best Buy** —*R.V. (11/15/2005)*

Quinta do Casal Branco 2002 Falcoaria Branco Portuguese White (Ribatejo) $10. 88 **Best Buy** —*R.V. (11/1/2004)*

Quinta do Casal Branco 1999 Falcoaria Red Blend (Ribatejo) $15. 90 —*R.V. (12/31/2002)*

Quinta do Casal Branco 2001 Falcoaria White Blend (Ribatejo) $NA. 91 —*R.V. (8/1/2004)*

QUINTA DO CÔA

Quinta do Côa 2004 Red Blend (Douro) $16. 83 —*J.C. (11/1/2006)*

QUINTA DO CÔTTO

Quinta do Côtto 2002 Paço de Texeiró Avesso (Minho) $26. 87 —*R.V. (11/1/2004)*

Quinta do Côtto 2001 Paço de Texeiró Avesso (Minho) $18. 88 —*R.V. (11/1/2004)*

Quinta do Côtto 2002 Portuguese Red (Douro) $19. 87 —*R.V. (11/1/2004)*

QUINTA DO CRASTO

Quinta do Crasto 1998 Late Bottled Vintage Port $14. 88 **Best Buy** —*R.V. (3/1/2004)*

Quinta do Crasto 1997 LBV Bottled 2001 Port $20. 89 —*R.V. (3/1/2003)*

Quinta do Crasto 1996 LBV Bottled 2000 Port $20. 90 —*R.V. (3/1/2003)*

Quinta do Crasto 2003 Vintage Port $94. 88 —*R.V. (11/15/2005)*

Quinta do Crasto 1995 Vintage Port $33. 90 —*R.V. (3/1/2004)*

Quinta do Crasto 2001 Vintage Port) $63. 90 —*R.V. (3/1/2004)*

Quinta do Crasto 1999 Vintage Port $NA. 89 —*R.V. (3/1/2004)*

Quinta do Crasto 2005 Portuguese Red (Douro) $20. A wine that relies on delicious primary fruit flavors, fresh and lively, with acidity, soft but typically dry Douro tannins and red fruit flavors. A delicious, fresh wine. 87 —*R.V. (9/1/2007)*

Quinta do Crasto 2002 Portuguese Red (Douro) $15. 86 —*R.V. (11/1/2004)*

Quinta do Crasto 1996 Reserva Portuguese Red (Douro) $18. 90 *(11/15/1999)*

Quinta do Crasto 2004 Reserva Old Vines Portuguese Red (Douro) $40. Old vines in this case means 70-year-old vines. Featuring blackberry fruit flavors, along with plums, sweet and rich, this shows a dense, herbal character, dry tannins, lifted by acidity to finish. 90 —*R.V. (9/1/2007)*

Quinta do Crasto 2001 Reserva Old Vines Portuguese Red (Douro) $33. 90 —*R.V. (11/1/2004)*

Quinta do Crasto 2004 Vinha da Ponte Portuguese Red (Douro) $125. From a single vineyard at Quinta do Crasto, this wine was fermented in open lagars. It is big, perfumed, packed with superripe fruit. It could almost be too much, but the spice, pepper and dense tannins are restrained by an edge of acidity. It promises long-term aging. 92 —*R.V. (9/1/2007)*

Quinta do Crasto 2003 Vinha Maria Teresa Portuguese Red (Douro) $150. Dark, dense and concentrated, with power and elegance. But somehow this complex wine also shows restraint and style. It has much to do with the pure richness of the fruit (from 90-year-old vines) as the acidity which lifts and restrains the power. 94 **Editors' Choice** —*R.V. (9/1/2007)*

Quinta do Crasto 2001 Vinha Maria Teresa Portuguese Red (Douro) $125. 91 **Cellar Selection** —*J.C. (3/1/2005)*

Quinta do Crasto 1997 Reserva Red Blend (Douro) $22. 89 —*J.C. (10/1/2000)*

Quinta do Crasto 1999 Vinho Tinto Red Blend (Douro) $14. 87 —*J.C. (12/31/2001)*

Quinta do Crasto 1998 Vinho Tinto Red Blend (Douro) $14. 86 —*J.C. (10/1/2000)*

Quinta do Crasto 2004 Touriga Nacional (Douro) $100. The fine, ripe, structured character of Touriga Nacional is well evident here. It may be big in alcohol, but the wine wears that easily, going more for fresh tannins and acidity, for black currant and dark plum flavors and smooth, vanilla flavors from the French wood aging. 91 —*R.V. (9/1/2007)*

Quinta do Crasto 2001 Touriga Nacional (Douro) $100. 92 —*R.V. (11/1/2004)*

QUINTA DO ESTANHO

Quinta do Estanho 1996 Vintage Port $28. 88 —*R.V. (3/1/2004)*

QUINTA DO FOJO

Quinta do Fojo 2000 Fojo Portuguese Red (Douro) $84. 87 —*J.C. (3/1/2005)*

Quinta do Fojo 1999 Vinha do Fojo Portuguese Red (Douro) $51. 84 —*J.C. (3/1/2005)*

QUINTA DO GRADIL

Quinta do Gradil 2005 Cortello Aragonês (Estremadura) $8. Dense tannins dominate this wine. The black currant and blackberries are layered under this intense structure, with wood and acidity giving the wine backbone and a vibrant, juicy aftertaste. 87 **Best Buy** —*R.V. (12/15/2007)*

Quinta do Gradil 2006 Portuguese Red (Estremadura) $10. Vinified by the winemaking team of Dão Sul, this is a blend of Touriga Nacional, Alicante Bouschet and Syrah, a rich, wild blend, with smooth blackberry jelly fruits, an edge of astringency, and a layer of toast from the eight months wood aging. 88 —*R.V. (12/15/2007)*

Quinta do Gradil 2005 Cortello Syrah (Estremadura) $8. A lean, edgy wine, which shows bramble fruits, red berries and tense tannins. There's fine structure and, given a few months, the acidity will turn this into a good food wine. 86 **Best Buy** —*R.V. (12/15/2007)*

Quinta do Gradil 2005 Cortello Touriga Nacional (Estremadura) $12. A fresh, red, fruity wine, with flavors of herbs. The tannins are light, leaving an aftertaste of red berries and acidity. Easy and attractive. 84 —*R.V. (12/15/2007)*

QUINTA DO GRIFO

Quinta do Grifo 2004 Reserva Portuguese Red (Douro Superior) $16. 85 —*J.C. (11/1/2006)*

QUINTA DO INFANTADO

Quinta do Infantado NV 10-year old Tawny Port $35. 86 —*R.V. (3/1/2004)*

Quinta do Infantado LBV Port 1998 $23. 87 —*R.V. (3/1/2004)*

Quinta do Infantado 2003 Vintage Port $52. 86 —*R.V. (11/15/2005)*

Quinta do Infantado 2000 Vintage Port $50. 91 —*R.V. (3/1/2004)*

Quinta do Infantado 1997 Vintage Port $NA. 86 —*R.V. (3/1/2004)*

Quinta do Infantado 1995 Vintage Port $NA. 89 —*R.V. (3/1/2004)*

QUINTA DO JUDEU

Quinta do Judeu 2003 Portuguese Red (Douro) $15. 85 —*J.C. (12/31/2005)*

QUINTA DO NOVAL

Quinta do Noval NV 10-Year Old Tawny Port $28. 91 **Editors' Choice** —*R.V. (8/1/2006)*

Quinta do Noval NV 20-Year Old Tawny Port $60. 89 —*R.V. (8/1/2006)*

Quinta do Noval NV 40-Year Old Tawny Port $125. 94 —*R.V. (8/1/2006)*

Quinta do Noval 1971 Colheita Port $40. 85 —*M.S. (3/1/2000)*

Quinta do Noval 1997 LBV Bottled 2001 Port $23. 85 —*R.V. (3/1/2003)*

Quinta do Noval 2003 Silval Vintage Port $45. 88 —*R.V. (11/15/2005)*

Quinta do Noval 2000 Silval Vintage Port $37. 90 —*J.C. (11/15/2003)*

Quinta do Noval 2004 Vintage Port (Port) $115. With its inky dark color, this is darkly dense, a huge mouthful of black fruits and dark, initially medicinal flavors and firm, concentrated tannins. It will age 20 years at least, but its sweet, ripe fruit suggest it could be drunk much earlier than that. 93 —*R.V. (11/1/2007)*

Quinta do Noval 2003 Vintage Port $95. 90 —*R.V. (11/15/2005)*

Quinta do Noval 2000 Vintage Port $65. 95 **Cellar Selection** —*J.C. (11/15/2003)*

QUINTA DO PASSADOURO

Quinta do Passadouro 2000 Vintage Port $70. 91 *(11/15/2003)*

QUINTA DO PORTAL

Quinta do Portal NV 10-Year Old Tawny Port $22. 85 —*R.V. (8/1/2006)*

Quinta do Portal NV 20-Year Old Tawny Port $52. 92 —*R.V. (8/1/2006)*

Quinta do Portal NV Cellar Reserve Port $16. 83 —*J.C. (3/1/2004)*

Quinta do Portal 1995 Colheita Port (Port) $NA. As distinct from the normal 10- or 20-year aged tawny, this is made from wine from a single year. It is like a 10-year-old, but fresher, a lively but balanced sweet wine, touched with raisins and citrus honey. 88 —*R.V. (11/1/2007)*

Quinta do Portal 1994 Colheita Port $28. 90 —*R.V. (3/1/2004)*

Quinta do Portal 2001 Late Bottled Vintage Port (Port) $NA. A very sweet, fruity style, soft, rich and velvety. There are tannins, but they seem lost in the rounded fruit and sweet blackberries. Just at the end does the wine become more serious with a dry, tannic aftertaste. 88 —*R.V. (11/1/2007)*

Quinta do Portal 1996 LBV Port $15. 87 *—J.C. (11/15/2003)*

Quinta do Portal 2000 Portal Vintage Port $33. 89 *—R.V. (3/1/2004)*

Quinta do Portal NV Tawny Reserve Port $14. 87 *—J.C. (11/15/2003)*

Quinta do Portal NV Ten Year Old Aged Tawny Port $24. 89 *—J.C. (11/15/2003)*

Quinta do Portal NV Twenty Year Old Aged Tawny Port $49. 87 *—J.C. (11/15/2003)*

Quinta do Portal 2004 Vintage Port (Port) $NA. Portal's 2004 vintage is a powerful effort from an average year. The dark structures are all here: the rich, sweet fruit is dense and concentrated, flavored with currants and black figs. This should age well, with its present dominant dry structure. **90** *—R.V. (11/1/2007)*

Quinta do Portal 2003 Vintage Port $60. 95 *—R.V. (11/15/2005)*

Quinta do Portal 2003 Vintage Port $57. 94 *—R.V. (11/15/2005)*

Quinta do Portal 1999 Vintage Port $33. 87 *—J.C. (11/15/2003)*

Quinta do Portal 1997 Vintage Port $54. 90 *—J.C. (11/15/2003)*

Quinta do Portal 1995 Vintage Port $33. 89 *—J.C. (11/15/2003)*

Quinta do Portal 2003 Auru Portuguese Red (Douro) $70. The top wine in the Quinta do Portal range is in its second vintage. With 12 months aging in French oak, the power is all there in very dark, heavy tannins that dominate the fruit. This is a powerful expression of the richness and the structure of great Douro wines, all granite and mineral in character, dark and tough, sure to age well. **93 Cellar Selection** *—R.V. (9/1/2007)*

Quinta do Portal 2001 Auru Portuguese Red (Douro) $75. 91 *—R.V. (11/1/2004)*

Quinta do Portal 2003 Colheita Portuguese Red (Douro) $12. Very dense tannins dominate big ripe blackberry jam flavors. The wine is hugely rich, but sustains itself by the structure which is dry, dusty tannin-dominated, with just a hint of fruit. To finish, there are juicy, fresh flavors. **89** *—R.V. (9/1/2007)*

Quinta do Portal 2003 Grande Reserva Portuguese Red (Douro) $29. A hugely juicy wine, dominated by Touriga Nacional, leavened by dry tannins. It's big, ripe, with vivid red fruits giving spice and power. Immediately attractive now, it is likely to age well over the next 5–8 years. **92** *—R.V. (9/1/2007)*

Quinta do Portal 2000 Grande Reserva Portuguese Red (Douro) $35. 90 *—R.V. (11/1/2004)*

Quinta do Portal 2000 Portal Portuguese Red (Douro) $13. 87 *—R.V. (11/1/2004)*

Quinta do Portal 2006 Portal Rosé Portuguese Red (Douro) $NA. For a rosé, the alcohol is too much at 14%. And this shows through in a pepper, hot character. But if power in rosés is what you like, the rest of the wine is enjoyable with ripe strawberry flavors. And the richness of the wine leaves a very soft aftertaste. **83** *—R.V. (7/1/2007)*

Quinta do Portal 2003 Reserva Portuguese Red (Douro) $17. Structured, rich, but also with good fresh acidity, this is one of the best wines in the Quinta do Portal range. It has lively, vibrant red fruit, along with dry tannins, some vanilla from wood aging. Great acidity in the aftertaste. **91** *—R.V. (9/1/2007)*

Quinta do Portal 2000 Reserva Portuguese Red (Douro) $17. 88 *—R.V. (11/1/2004)*

Quinta do Portal 1999 Red Blend (Douro) 86 *—R.V. (12/31/2002)*

Quinta do Portal 2000 Grande Reserva Red Blend (Douro) 91 *—R.V. (12/31/2002)*

Quinta do Portal 1996 Grande Reserva Red Blend (Douro) $29. 88 *—J.C. (11/15/2003)*

Quinta do Portal 1996 Mural Red Blend (Douro) $7. 84 *—J.C. (11/15/2003)*

Quinta do Portal 1999 Muros de Vinha Red Blend (Douro) $8. 85 *—J.C. (11/15/2003)*

Quinta do Portal 1999 Quinta do Portal Reserva Red Blend (Douro) 90 *—R.V. (12/31/2002)*

Quinta do Portal 2001 Tinta Roriz (Douro) $35. 88 *—R.V. (11/1/2004)*

Quinta do Portal 2001 Touriga Franca (Douro) $35. 89 *—R.V. (11/1/2004)*

Quinta do Portal 2003 Touriga Nacional (Douro) $20. A huge wine, full of soft fruit. The layers of tannins sit gently on the plum and cassis fruits, lifted by acidity. If it wasn't 15.5%, this would be impressive, but the high alcohol makes the wine very Port-like, giving an extra layer of pepper from the alcohol. **88** *—R.V. (9/1/2007)*

Quinta do Portal 2001 Touriga Nacional (Douro) $35. 88 *—R.V. (11/1/2004)*

QUINTA DO REGUENGO DE MELGACO

Quinta do Reguengo de Melgaco 2005 Alvarinho (Vinho Verde) $15. 88 *—R.V. (7/1/2006)*

QUINTA DO TEDO

Quinta do Tedo NV Finest Reserve Port $NA. 85 *—R.V. (3/1/2005)*

Quinta do Tedo 1997 Late Bottled Vintage Port $22. 86 *—R.V. (3/1/2004)*

Quinta do Tedo 2000 Savedra Vintage Port $55. 88 *—R.V. (3/1/2004)*

Quinta do Tedo 1999 Traditional Single Quinta Port $NA. 89 *—R.V. (3/1/2004)*

Quinta do Tedo 2000 Vintage Port $45. 85 *—R.V. (3/1/2004)*

QUINTA DO VALE MEÃO

Quinta do Vale Meão 2004 Vintage Port (Port) $NA. Still with all its primary fruit flavors, ripe blackberries and figs, this wine currently only hints at its density of structure. While 2004 is certainly not the greatest Port vintage year, the concentration of this wine is good. The tannins are here, but at the moment it is the fruit that powers this wine. **90** *—R.V. (11/1/2007)*

Quinta do Vale Meão 2003 Vintage Port $30. 87 *—J.C. (6/1/2006)*

Quinta do Vale Meão 2001 Vintage Port $35. 88 *—R.V. (3/1/2004)*

Quinta do Vale Meão 2000 Vintage Port $45. 92 Editors' Choice *—J.C. (11/15/2003)*

Quinta do Vale Meão 2004 Portuguese Red (Douro) $19. This is the greatest of the quintas planted by Dona Antonia Ferreira in the 19th century. It is in the Douro Superior, the driest, most remote part of the Douro. The Olazabal family, descendants of Dona Antonia, produce this hugely impressive, dark-hued wine, packed with dense, brooding tannins and solid, initially tough fruits, which open out to opulence and richness. **94 Editors' Choice** *—R.V. (9/1/2007)*

Quinta do Vale Meão 2003 Portuguese Red (Douro) $55. 94 Editors' Choice *—J.C. (12/31/2005)*

Quinta do Vale Meão 2002 Portuguese Red (Douro) $50. 88 *—J.C. (12/31/2005)*

Quinta do Vale Meão 2001 Portuguese Red (Douro) $49. 93 Cellar Selection *—R.V. (11/1/2004)*

Quinta do Vale Meão 2000 Portuguese Red (Douro) $65. 93 Editors' Choice *—J.C. (11/15/2003)*

Quinta do Vale Meão 2003 Meandro Portuguese Red (Douro) $20. 91 Editors' Choice *—J.C. (12/31/2005)*

Quinta do Vale Meão 2002 Meandro Portuguese Red (Douro) $20. 87 *—J.C. (12/31/2005)*

Quinta do Vale Meão 2001 Meandro Portuguese Red (Douro) $19. 87 *—R.V. (11/1/2004)*

Quinta do Vale Meão 2000 Meandro Portuguese Red (Douro) $19. 90 Editors' Choice *—J.C. (11/15/2003)*

Quinta do Vale Meão 2004 Meandro do Vale Meão Portuguese Red (Douro) $49. The name refers to the big meander the Douro river takes around the quinta's vineyards, forming a long peninsula. Like its big brother, the quinta wine, this reflects the heat and the concentrated fruit that comes from this famed vineyard. Its tannins are almost impenetrable at this stage, deep and dry, needing several years of aging to reveal the solid, ripe dark, spicy flavors. **91 Cellar Selection** *—R.V. (9/1/2007)*

QUINTA DO VALLADO

Quinta do Vallado NV 10-Year Old Tawny Port $NA. 87 *—R.V. (8/1/2006)*

Quinta do Vallado NV 20-Year Old Tawny Port $NA. 88 *—R.V. (8/1/2006)*

Quinta do Vallado 2005 Portuguese Red (Douro) $0. Young, fresh and fruity, with vivid acidity, flavors of red currants and layered tannins. This is a good, simple, fresh wine, likely to develop fast. **85** *—R.V. (9/1/2007)*

Quinta do Vallado 2004 Portuguese Red (Douro) $20. Vallado's simplest wine is all big, black, crisp fruit leaping out of the glass. While it is not light, it certainly has a lilt and freshness to it, despite the dry tannins which underlie the flavors. Herbs and spices add to the pleasure. **87** *—R.V. (9/1/2007)*

Quinta do Vallado 2004 Reserva Portuguese Red (Douro) $50. An impressively powerful wine, with concentrated fruit from old vines. It packs dense tannins, layers flavors of ripe figs, plums and raisins, along with wood flavors. The quinta is close to Regua in the western part of the Douro vineyards, a region particularly well suited to powerful but still elegant table wines. **92** *—R.V. (9/1/2007)*

Quinta do Vallado 2004 Sousão Portuguese Red (Douro) $38. The Olazabal/Ferreira family owns two Douro quintas, this and Vale Meão, high up-river. Vallado is in a cooler, wetter climate, and produces elegant wines, in a modern, smooth style. Based on one of the lesser Port grapes, the Sousão, this is full of black currant fruits and new wood flavors. **89** *—R.V. (9/1/2007)*

Quinta do Vallado 2002 Vallado Portuguese Red (Douro) $NA. 85 *—R.V. (11/1/2004)*

Quinta do Vallado 2003 Portuguese White (Douro) $18. 89 —*R.V. (8/1/2005)*

Quinta do Vallado 2002 Vallado Branco Portuguese White (Douro) $NA. 87 —*R.V. (11/1/2004)*

QUINTA DO VENTOZELO

Quinta do Ventozelo NV 10-Year Old Tawny Port $30. 87 —*R.V. (8/1/2006)*

Quinta do Ventozelo NV 20-Year Old Tawny Port $40. 88 —*R.V. (8/1/2006)*

QUINTA DO VESUVIO

Quinta do Vesuvio 2003 Vintage Port $78. 93 —*R.V. (11/15/2005)*

Quinta do Vesuvio 2000 Vintage Port $NA. 93 —*R.V. (3/1/2004)*

Quinta do Vesuvio 2001 Vintage Port $56. 91 —*J.C. (11/15/2003)*

Quinta do Vesuvio 1998 Vintage Port $50. 90 —*R.V. (2/1/2001)*

QUINTA DOS ACIPRESTES

Quinta dos Acipreste 2003 Portuguese Red (Douro) $12. 87 Best Buy —*J.C. (6/1/2006)*

Quinta dos Acipreste 2001 Portuguese Red (Douro) $12. 87 Best Buy —*R.V. (11/1/2004)*

QUINTA DOS ROQUES

Quinta dos Roques 2003 Alfrocheiro Alfrocheiro (Dão) $25. The Alfrocheiro grape is a native to Portugal, found in the Dão and in the Beiras in the center of the country. This is a good example of its anise aromas and juicy ripe strawberry with mint character, not showing huge tannins, but with a touch of pepper. 88 —*R.V. (3/1/2007)*

Quinta dos Roques 2000 Alfrocheiro (Dão) $29. 88 —*R.V. (11/1/2004)*

Quinta dos Roques 2004 Portuguese Red (Dão) $15. The estate wine from Quinta dos Roques is a vanilla-soft wine, with ripe tannins and an intense flavor of blackberry jelly. It is a good reflection of 2004, likely to be ready to drink soon, the tannins just an easy layer rather than being dry, the fruit being fresh and juicy. 89 —*R.V. (3/1/2007)*

Quinta dos Roques 2003 Portuguese Red (Dão) $15. A hugely dark wine, with solid bitter chocolate flavors and layers of dry tannins. It comes from the granite soils of the home estate of Quinta dos Roques, a blend of Touriga Nacional, Jaen and Alfrocheiro. There are dry wood flavors and black plum fruits. Age for five years at least. 91 Best Buy —*R.V. (3/1/2007)*

Quinta dos Roques 2000 Garrafeira Portuguese Red (Dão) $39. 91 —*R.V. (11/1/2004)*

Quinta dos Roques 2003 Quinta do Correio Portuguese Red (Dão) $9. One of the properties owned by dynamic Dão producer Quinta dos Roques, this blend dominated by Touriga Nacional and Jaen, is soft, fruity and fresh. In Portuguese terms, this is a light wine, with its easy tannins and raspberry fruit flavors. 86 Best Buy —*R.V. (3/1/2007)*

Quinta dos Roques 2003 Reserva Portuguese Red (Dão) $25. A fine barrique-aged wine, dominated by Touriga Nacional. It is solidly structured without being too powerful, with ripe, black currant fruits and aromas of freshly fallen leaves. With its new wood element, this is a wine that is potentially long-lasting. It certainly deserves attention. 90 —*R.V. (3/1/2007)*

Quinta dos Roques 2000 Reserva Portuguese Red (Dão) $29. 90 —*R.V. (11/1/2004)*

Quinta dos Roques 2003 Encruzado Portuguese White (Dão) $18. 90 —*R.V. (8/1/2005)*

Quinta dos Roques 2000 Red Blend (Dão) $13. 84 —*R.V. (12/31/2002)*

Quinta dos Roques 2000 Alfrocheiro Preto Red Blend (Dão) $22. 88 —*R.V. (12/31/2002)*

Quinta dos Roques 2000 Tinta Roriz (Dão) $29. 86 —*R.V. (11/1/2004)*

Quinta dos Roques 2000 Tinta Roriz (Dão) $22. 90 —*R.V. (12/31/2002)*

Quinta dos Roques 2003 Touriga Nacional Touriga Nacional (Dão) $25. One of a range of varietal wines from top Dão producer Quinta dos Roques, this takes Portugal's most famous grape and turns it into a firmly tannic, almost mineral wine. It has big, black juicy fruit and finely balanced acidity. 89 —*R.V. (3/1/2007)*

Quinta dos Roques 2000 Touriga Nacional (Dão) $22. 89 —*R.V. (12/31/2002)*

Quinta dos Roques 2000 Touriga Nacional (Dão) $29. 89 —*R.V. (11/1/2004)*

Quinta dos Roques 2001 White Blend (Dão) $9. 90 —*R.V. (12/31/2002)*

QUINTA SANTA EUFEMIA

Quinta Santa Eufemia NV 10-Year Old Tawny Port $23. 88 —*R.V. (8/1/2006)*

Quinta Santa Eufemia NV 20-Year Old Tawny Port $40. 88 —*R.V. (8/1/2006)*

Quinta Santa Eufemia NV 30-Year Old Tawny Port $43. 87 —*R.V. (8/1/2006)*

QUINTA SEARA D'ORDENS

Quinta Seara d'Ordens 2003 Vintage Port $NA. 83 —*R.V. (11/15/2005)*

QUINTA VALE D. MARIA

Quinta Vale D. Maria 2002 Late Bottled Vintage Port (Port) $NA. Initially dry, with dense and dark tannins, this opens in the mouth to give a richly concentrated array of ripe fruits and sweetness. It is likely that this could age. 90 —*R.V. (11/1/2007)*

Quinta Vale D. Maria NV Reserve Port $NA. 89 —*R.V. (3/1/2005)*

Quinta Vale D. Maria 2002 Vintage Port (Port) $NA. Ripe, soft and beautifully perfumed. There's density, but aims more for the sweet, blackberry jam style. Only towards the aftertaste is there a layer of dry tannin. Drink now or hold 10 years. 89 —*R.V. (11/1/2007)*

Quinta Vale D. Maria 2003 Vintage Port $NA. 85 —*R.V. (11/15/2005)*

Quinta Vale D. Maria 2001 Vintage Port $55. 92 —*R.V. (3/1/2004)*

Quinta Vale D. Maria 2005 Portuguese Red (Douro) $NA. Big, warm and richly tannic, this wine has both power and intensity of fruit. The flavors are dark and solid, with some dryness, but also intense, sweet acidity. Sweet raisins go with the dusty tannins to evoke a warm, rich feel. 90 —*R.V. (3/1/2007)*

Quinta Vale D. Maria 2001 Portuguese Red (Douro) $NA. 90 —*R.V. (11/1/2004)*

QUINTAS DE MELGACO

Quintas de Melgaco 1998 Couto de Frades Alvarinho (Vinho Verde) $10. 85 —*J.C. (12/15/2000)*

Quintas de Melgaco 1998 QM Alvarinho (Vinho Verde) $11. 82 —*J.C. (12/15/2000)*

Quintas de Melgaco 1998 Torre de Menagem White Blend (Vinho Verde) $8. 83 —*J.C. (12/15/2000)*

RAMOS-PINTO

Ramos-Pinto NV 30 Year Tawny Port (Douro) $90. 92 *(10/1/2004)*

Ramos-Pinto NV Collector Reserva Port $19. 86 —*J.C. (3/1/2004)*

Ramos-Pinto NV Collector Reserva Port $19. 85 *(11/1/2004)*

Ramos-Pinto 1997 LBV Port $21. 88 *(10/1/2004)*

Ramos-Pinto 1996 LBV Port $19. 89 —*M.S. (11/15/2002)*

Ramos-Pinto 1995 LBV Bottled 1999 Port $15. 88 —*R.V. (3/1/2003)*

Ramos-Pinto 1998 LBV Bottled 2002 Port (Douro) $18. 86 —*R.V. (3/1/2003)*

Ramos-Pinto NV Quinta Bom Retiro 20-Year Old Tawny Port $75. 91 —*R.V. (8/1/2006)*

Ramos-Pinto NV Quinta da Ervamoira Port $34. 90 *(3/1/2000)*

Ramos-Pinto 1994 Quinta da Ervamoira Port $45. 88 —*M.S. (11/15/2002)*

Ramos-Pinto NV Quinta Ervamoira 10-Year Old Tawny Port $41. 89 —*R.V. (8/1/2006)*

Ramos-Pinto NV Reserva Collector Port $19. 84 —*R.V. (3/1/2005)*

Ramos-Pinto NV Urtiga Vintage Character Port $16. 88 —*M.S. (11/15/2002)*

Ramos-Pinto 2003 Vintage Port $65. 94 —*R.V. (11/15/2005)*

Ramos-Pinto 2000 Vintage Port $63. 91 *(10/1/2004)*

Ramos-Pinto 1997 Vintage Port $50. 86 —*J.C. (11/15/2003)*

Ramos-Pinto 1994 Vintage Port $NA. 91 *(10/1/2004)*

Ramos-Pinto 1983 Vintage Port $NA. 91 *(10/1/2004)*

Ramos-Pinto 2005 Adriano Portuguese Red (Douro) $13. A structured, ripe wine, leavened with a base of dry tannins. It is full of ripe blueberry fruit flavors and juicy freshness. A little stalky, but easy, soft and ready to drink. 86 —*R.V. (9/1/2007)*

Ramos-Pinto 2004 Adriano Portuguese Red (Douro) $13. At three years, Ramos-Pinto's branded Adriano (named after the founder of the company) is at its best. This 2004 vintage is big-hearted, with bitter chocolate and blackberry fruits, as well as generous tannins. Good, dry structure and fresh acidity complete a rounded picture. 87 —*R.V. (9/1/2007)*

Ramos-Pinto 2003 Adriano Estate Bottled Red Wine Portuguese Red (Douro) $15. 86 —*J.C. (12/31/2005)*

Ramos-Pinto 2003 Duas Quintas Portuguese Red (Douro) $13. Ramos-Pinto's benchmark wine, a classic in the Douro, made from the two quintas of Ervamoira and Bons Ares, is as good as ever. It is firm but but not powerful, with black fruits, freshened by acidity, leaving a wine that is a touch mineral. **88 Best Buy** *—R.V. (9/1/2007)*

Ramos-Pinto 2003 Duas Quintas Reserva Portuguese Red (Douro) $32. The two Ramos-Pinto quintas of Ervamoira and Bons Ares provide contrasting fruit—the hot, dry conditions of Ervamoira and the more temperate climate of Bons Ares. Together, with this coffee and oak flavored wine, built upon ripe fruits, they make an impressive combination of dark, spicy flavors. **89** *—R.V. (9/1/2007)*

Ramos-Pinto 2003 Duas Quintas Reserva Especial Portuguese Red (Douro) $54. The darkest, most impressive version of the Duas Quintas brand, this Reserva is made in the open lagars, from foot-trodden grapes in the tradition still used by major Port houses. It gives a ripe, sweet, almost Port-like character, but still firmed by structure and dusty tannins to go with the superripe plums. **91 Cellar Selection** *—R.V. (9/1/2007)*

Ramos-Pinto 2006 Adriano Portuguese White (Douro) $13. A fresh, lively, citrus-flavored wine with touches of white peaches and a soft structure. Give this six months in bottle for the freshness to peak. **86** *—R.V. (9/1/2007)*

Ramos-Pinto 2005 Adriano Portuguese White (Douro) $13. Zingy, touched with honey and ripe, soft fruits. Flavors of green plum, thyme and lime gives this lift and a light, white aftertaste. **87** *—R.V. (9/1/2007)*

Ramos-Pinto 2000 Duas Quintas Red Blend (Douro) $12. 86 Best Buy *—R.V. (11/15/2002)*

Ramos-Pinto 1999 Duas Quintas Red Blend (Douro) $12. 85 *—M.S. (11/15/2002)*

Ramos-Pinto 2000 Duas Quintas Reserva Red Blend (Douro) $34. 92 *—R.V. (12/31/2002)*

Ramos-Pinto 1999 Duas Quintas Reserva Red Blend (Douro) $34. 91 *—R.V. (12/31/2002)*

Ramos-Pinto 1999 Duas Quintas Reserva Especial Red Blend (Douro) $11. 85 *—J.C. (11/15/2003)*

Ramos-Pinto 1997 Duas Quintas Reserva Touriga Nacional (Douro) $34. 85 *—J.C. (7/1/2003)*

Ramos-Pinto 2001 Duas Quintas Touriga Nacional Blend (Douro) $NA. 86 *(10/1/2004)*

Ramos-Pinto 2000 Duas Quintas Reserva Touriga Nacional Blend (Douro) $37. 90 *(10/1/2004)*

Ramos-Pinto NV Fine White Port (Douro) $14. 88 Editors' Choice *—J.C. (3/1/2004)*

REAL COMPANHIA VELHA

Real Companhia Velha 2003 Quinta de Cidrô Reserva Chardonnay (Trás-os-Montes) $12. 87 *—R.V. (8/1/2005)*

Real Companhia Velha 2002 Quinta do Cidrô Chardonnay (Trás-os-Montes) $12. 87 Best Buy *—R.V. (12/1/2004)*

Real Companhia Velha 2001 Evel Grande Escholha Portuguese Red (Douro) $22. 86 *—R.V. (11/1/2004)*

Real Companhia Velha 2001 Porca de Murça Portuguese Red (Douro) $8. 88 Best Buy *—R.V. (11/1/2004)*

Real Companhia Velha 2004 Quinta de Cidrô Sauvignon Blanc (Trás-os-Montes) $10. 85 Best Buy *—R.V. (8/1/2005)*

Real Companhia Velha 2003 Porca de Murça White Blend (Douro) $12. 88 Best Buy *—R.V. (8/1/2005)*

REAL VINICOLA

Real Vinicola 1998 Porca de Murça Reserva Red Blend (Douro) $17. 89 *(10/1/1999)*

Real Vinicola 1997 Porca de Murça Reserva Red Blend (Douro) $17. 87 *(10/1/1999)*

RED FOX

Red Fox 2004 Portuguese Red (Alentejo) $7. A blend of Aragonez and Trincadeira, produced by a group of cooperatives in the Alentejo region. It is a simple wine, but has good red fruits, soft, velvet structure and a finishing edge of acidity. Good barbecue wine. **83** *—R.V. (12/15/2007)*

ROBEREDO MADEIRA

Roberedo Madeira 2000 Carm Classico Red Blend (Douro) $18. 87 *—J.C. (11/15/2003)*

Roberedo Madeira 1999 Carm Praemium Touriga Nacional (Douro) $27. 89 *—J.C. (11/15/2003)*

Roberedo Madeira 2000 Carm Reserva Touriga Nacional (Douro) $23. 90 Editors' Choice *—J.C. (11/15/2003)*

ROMARIZ

Romariz 2003 Vintage Port $NA. 84 *—R.V. (11/15/2005)*

ROQUETTE E CAZES

Roquette e Cazes 2003 Xisto Portuguese Red (Douro) $56. The joint venture between the Cazes family of Bordeaux and the Roquette family of Quinta do Crasto in the Douro is in its second released vintage. This is made using Bordeaux techniques, resulting in a style that is more structured than many Douro wines, exploiting ripe fruit with solid tannins, leavened by sweetness and sweet red fruits. The wood shows through on the finish. **93 Cellar Selection** *—R.V. (9/1/2007)*

ROQUEVALE

Roquevale 1999 Redondo Portuguese Red (Alentejo) $6. 83 *—M.M. (12/31/2001)*

ROYAL OPORTO

Royal Oporto NV 10-Year Old Tawny Port $29. 90 *—R.V. (8/1/2006)*

Royal Oporto NV 20-Year Old Tawny Port $48. 87 *—R.V. (8/1/2006)*

Royal Oporto NV 40-Year Old Tawny Port $128. 88 *—R.V. (8/1/2006)*

Royal Oporto 2003 Vintage Port $44. 88 *—R.V. (11/15/2005)*

ROZES

Rozes NV 10-Year Old Tawny Port $27. 86 *—R.V. (8/1/2006)*

Rozes NV 20-Year Old Tawny Port $50. 87 *—R.V. (8/1/2006)*

Rozes NV 40-Year Old Tawny Port $120. 83 *—R.V. (8/1/2006)*

Rozes 1994 Reserve Edition LBV Port $19. 86 *—M.S. (3/1/2000)*

Rozes NV Reserve Port $NA. 88 *—R.V. (3/1/2005)*

Rozes 2000 Vintage Port $90. 88 *—J.C. (11/1/2006)*

Rozes 1997 Vintage Port $60. 92 Cellar Selection *—M.S. (11/15/2002)*

SANDEMAN

Sandeman NV 20-Year Old Tawny Port $50. 85 *—R.V. (8/1/2006)*

Sandeman NV 40-Year Old Tawny Port $135. 93 Editors' Choice *—R.V. (8/1/2006)*

Sandeman NV Founder's Reserve Port $17. 86 *—R.V. (3/1/2005)*

Sandeman 2000 Late Bottled Vintage Port (Port) $23. Ripe, soft and sweet, with easy acidity along with balanced tannins, fig flavors and a great lift of freshness to finish. **87** *—R.V. (11/1/2007)*

Sandeman 1997 LBV Bottled 2001 Port (Douro) $19. 84 *—R.V. (3/1/2003)*

Sandeman 1997 Quinta do Vau Port $38. 93 *(12/15/1999)*

Sandeman NV Ruby Port $12. 86 *—J.C. (11/1/2006)*

Sandeman NV Tawny Port $12. 83 *—J.C. (12/1/2004)*

Sandeman 2000 Vau Vintage Port $45. 90 *—J.C. (11/15/2003)*

Sandeman 1999 Vau Vintage Port $30. 88 Editors' Choice *—J.C. (12/1/2004)*

Sandeman 2003 Vintage Port $60. 87 *—R.V. (11/15/2005)*

Sandeman 2000 Vintage Port $60. 86 *—J.C. (11/15/2003)*

SANTA VITORIA

Santa Vitoria 2004 Red Blend (Alentejano) $13. 88 Best Buy *—J.C. (11/1/2006)*

Santa Vitoria 2004 Reserva Red Blend (Alentejano) $25. 90 *—J.C. (11/1/2006)*

Santa Vitoria 2004 Versátil Red Blend (Alentejano) $13. 82 *—J.C. (11/1/2006)*

SAO PEDRO

Sao Pedro 1995 das Águias LBV Port $NA. 84 *—J.C. (11/15/2003)*

SENHORA DO CONVENTO

Senhora do Convento NV Quinta das Heredias Ruby Special Reserve Port $NA. 85 *—R.V. (3/1/2005)*

Senhora do Convento 2003 Vintage Port $NA. 89 *—R.V. (11/15/2005)*

SENTUS

Sentus 1997 Portuguese Red (Douro) $18. 84 *—J.C. (12/31/2001)*

SMITH WOODHOUSE

Smith Woodhouse NV 10-Year Old Tawny Port $28. 90 *—R.V. (8/1/2006)*

Smith Woodhouse 1986 Colheita Port $41. 90 Editors' Choice *—J.C. (12/1/2004)*

Smith Woodhouse 1976 Colheita Single Year Tawny Port $43. 87 *—J.C. (11/15/2003)*

Smith Woodhouse 1999 Late Bottled Vintage Port (Port) $0. Dried raisins, intense and concentrated, drive this impressive wine. It is dry, structured and packs big tannins. It has the density to suggest aging. **89** —*R.V. (11/1/2007)*

Smith Woodhouse 1995 Late Bottled Vintage Port (Port) $30. Somewhat rustic on the nose, but the palate opens up with structured, ripe, dense tannins. It has a good backbone of freshness, finishing light and fruity. **86** —*R.V. (11/1/2007)*

Smith Woodhouse 1994 LBV Port $25. 87 —*R.V. (3/1/2004)*

Smith Woodhouse 1992 LBV Port $25. 85 —*J.C. (12/1/2004)*

Smith Woodhouse 1990 LBV Bottled 1994 Port $27. 88 —*R.V. (3/1/2003)*

Smith Woodhouse NV Lodge Reserve Port $16. 85 —*R.V. (3/1/2005)*

Smith Woodhouse 1999 Quinta de Madelena Vintage Port $32. 87 —*M.S. (11/15/2002)*

Smith Woodhouse 2003 Vintage Port $60. 90 —*R.V. (11/15/2005)*

SOGRAPE

Sogrape 2004 Morgadio da Torre Alvarinho (Vinho Verde) $12. 89 Best Buy —*R.V. (7/1/2006)*

Sogrape 1998 Morgadio da Torre Alvarinho (Vinho Verde) $13. 87 Best Buy —*M.S. (10/1/1999)*

Sogrape 2004 Callabriga Portuguese Red (Alentejo) $17. A rich, robust blend of Aragonês and Alicante Bouschet, this wine offers red fruits, spice and vanilla from wood aging. It is certainly rich, but there is elegance here as well; the exuberant fruit is tempered by acidity and some intensely firm tannins. Age for 4–5 years. **90** —*R.V. (12/15/2007)*

Sogrape 2003 Callabriga Portuguese Red (Douro) $NA. 90 —*R.V. (11/15/2005)*

Sogrape 2003 Callabriga Portuguese Red (Alentejo) $NA. 89 —*R.V. (11/15/2005)*

Sogrape 1997 Duque de Viseu White Table Win Portuguese Red (Dão) $10. 84 —*M.S. (10/1/1999)*

Sogrape NV Duque du Viseu Portuguese Red (Dão) $11. 87 Best Buy —*M.S. (10/1/1999)*

Sogrape 1997 Grão Vasco Portuguese Red (Dão) $6. 86 Best Buy —*M.S. (10/1/1999)*

Sogrape 2003 Herdade do Peso Vinha do Monte Portuguese Red (Alentejano) $9. 89 Best Buy —*R.V. (3/1/2006)*

Sogrape 2002 Reserva Portuguese Red (Alentejo) $15. 92 Best Buy —*R.V. (3/1/2006)*

Sogrape 1996 Reserva Portuguese Red (Douro) $13. 87 —*M.S. (10/1/1999)*

Sogrape 1999 Vinha do Monte Portuguese Red (Alentejo) $9. 84 *(12/31/2001)*

Sogrape 1997 Vinha do Monte Portuguese Red (Alentejo) $10. 85 —*M.S. (10/1/1999)*

Sogrape NV Gazela Portuguese White (Vinho Verde) $6. 84 Best Buy —*R.V. (7/1/2006)*

Sogrape 1999 Casa do Douro Reserva Red Blend (Douro) $13. 87 —*R.V. (12/31/2002)*

Sogrape 1999 Duque de Viseu Red Blend (Dão) $11. 85 —*R.V. (12/31/2002)*

Sogrape 1999 Reserva Red Blend (Alentejo) $9. 90 —*R.V. (12/31/2002)*

Sogrape 2000 Vinha do Monte Red Blend (Alentejano) $11. 87 Best Buy —*R.V. (12/31/2002)*

Sogrape 1996 Quinta dos Carvalhais Touriga Nacional (Dão) $39. 89 —*M.S. (10/1/1999)*

Sogrape 2001 Duque de Viseu White Blend (Vinho Verde) $11. 85 —*R.V. (8/1/2004)*

TAMARA

Tamara NV Tinto Portuguese Red (Portugal) $10. If this is a simple table wine, then Portugal is doing plenty right. It is ripe, fruity, accessible, packed with red fruits. But it is also firm, with dry tannins to give structure, a great food wine that demands big winter dishes. **83** —*R.V. (3/1/2007)*

TAYLOR FLADGATE

Taylor Fladgate NV 10-Year Old Tawny Port $30. 91 —*R.V. (8/1/2006)*

Taylor Fladgate NV 20-Year Old Tawny Port $53. 90 —*R.V. (8/1/2006)*

Taylor Fladgate NV 30-Year Old Tawny Port $115. 88 —*R.V. (8/1/2006)*

Taylor Fladgate NV 40-Year Old Tawny Port) $154. 95 Editors' Choice —*R.V. (8/1/2006)*

Taylor Fladgate NV Fine Ruby Porto Cordovero Kosher Port (Douro) $27. Deep raisin, raspberry and anise waft from this kosher Port from Taylor Fladgate. Prune and black cherry on the palate are appealing but there's an excess of anise and the mouthfeel is overly syrupy. A good Port, but a little overloaded. **83** —*S.K. (4/1/2007)*

Taylor Fladgate NV First Estate Reserve Port $18. 87 —*R.V. (3/1/2005)*

Taylor Fladgate 2002 Late Bottled Vintage Port (Port) $23. For freshness, it is worth buying this young LBV. It has all the structure needed, a dark chocolate undertone, but it is the fresh black fruits and the lift of acidity that make it so attractive. **91** —*R.V. (11/1/2007)*

Taylor Fladgate 2000 Late Bottled Vintage Port (Port) $23. This is a mature, deliciously perfumed and structured wine. There is a great milk chocolate flavor that balances the flavors of candied fruits. **90** —*R.V. (11/1/2007)*

Taylor Fladgate 2000 LBV Port $25. 88 —*J.C. (6/1/2006)*

Taylor Fladgate 1997 LBV Bottled 2002 Port $21. 89 —*R.V. (3/1/2003)*

Taylor Fladgate 2001 Quinta De Vargellas Port $50. 89 —*J.C. (12/1/2004)*

Taylor Fladgate 1998 Quinta de Vargellas Port $42. 90 —*R.V. (2/1/2001)*

Taylor Fladgate 1995 Quinta de Vargellas Vinha Velha Port $NA. 97 Cellar Selection —*J.C. (12/1/2004)*

Taylor Fladgate 2004 Vargellas Vinhas Velhas Vintage Port (Port) $240. Bottled in July 2006, this wine remains deliciously open, showcasing floral, violet scents intertwined with rich layers of plum and chocolate. Although the firm structure is evident, there's more than adequate fruit for balance. A lovely combination of power and elegance. Hold. **97 Cellar Selection** —*J.C. (2/1/2007)*

Taylor Fladgate 2000 Vargellas Vinhas Velhas Vintage Port (Port) $270. The hue of this wine takes dark and inky to a new level—and this wine's intensity isn't confined to its color. This is simply huge in every way, yet because every component is in proportion, the balance is impeccable. Incredibly rich, dense fruit picks up hints of tar and chocolate, while the finish lasts for what must be minutes. Hold. **100** —*J.C. (2/1/2007)*

Taylor Fladgate 1997 Vargellas Vinha Velha Port $NA. 94 Cellar Selection —*J.C. (12/1/2004)*

Taylor Fladgate 2000 Vargellas Vinha Velha Vintage Port $NA. 95 Cellar Selection —*J.C. (12/1/2004)*

Taylor Fladgate 2003 Vintage Port (Port) $100. Inky purple in color, this youngest Taylor vintage Port boasts a floral, wonderfully open and appealing bouquet, backed by layers of rich fruit. What makes this wine extra special is the seductive texture—somewhere between creamy and syrupy—and ample length. Hold. **97** —*J.C. (2/1/2007)*

Taylor Fladgate 2003 Vintage Port $92. 95 —*R.V. (11/15/2005)*

Taylor Fladgate 2000 Vintage Port (Port) $0. This was perhaps the most prototypically "Taylor" wine of the vertical, with complex floral and spice aromas backed by firm, black cherry and berry fruit. The fruit is fresh and almost crunchy in character, underscored by solid tannins and a long, dusty finish. Immense power combines with intricate nuance and a supremely ageworthy structure. Hold. **96** —*J.C. (2/1/2007)*

Taylor Fladgate 1997 Vintage Port (Port) $180. This is rather flashy for Taylor, with plenty of upfront appeal to its floral, spicy aromas and gobs of fruit. It's very lush and soft on the palate, almost overloaded with blackberries and plums, then firms up and begins to show that Taylor reserve on the dusty finish. Hold. **96** —*J.C. (2/1/2007)*

Taylor Fladgate 1994 Vintage Port (Port) $290. This is very much in the mold of the 1992—maybe slightly less rich but just by a whisker. It's dense without being heavy, with a beautifully spice-filled and long finish. Flavors of chocolate, mint and plum pudding linger elegantly for a few seconds longer than the '92. Hold. **99** —*J.C. (2/1/2007)*

Taylor Fladgate 1985 Vintage Port (Port) $165. Dark garnet in color with some bricking apparent, this was "not a particularly good example," according to Fladgate Partnership CEO Adrian Bridge. It was still enjoyable, but seemed to lack midpalate lushness, ending green and firm. **87** —*J.C. (2/1/2007)*

Taylor Fladgate 1977 Vintage Port (Port) $260. The most prominently floral wine in the vertical, but that delicacy is amply backed by plush chocolate and dried fruit flavors. The finish is deceptively soft and welcoming, but still shows great backbone and the ability to go many more years. **95** —*J.C. (2/1/2007)*

Taylor Fladgate 1970 Vintage Port (Port) $255. This wine's dark garnet color with minimal bricking suggests a relatively youthful wine and this certainly could age longer, although it's also delicious now. Wonderfully complex floral and herbal scents easily move into deep, rich flavors of chocolate and cherries, sprinkled with a healthy dose of Douro minerality and spice. Drink or hold. **99** —*J.C. (2/1/2007)*

Taylor Fladgate 1963 Vintage Port (Port) $430. A tough wine to confidently evaluate. This showed masses of dried fruit and maple syrup flavors, all of which seemed to dry up a bit on the finish to reveal spice, alcohol and a certain degree of austerity. It may just be in an awkward stage, as the components are fine, just a little disjointed. Hold? **92** *—J.C. (2/1/2007)*

Taylor Fladgate 1955 Vintage Port (Port) $NA. This bottle was at a lovely point in its life, balancing savory, mushroom and spice notes against sweet caramel and dried fruit flavors on the long finish. Tannins resolved, potent alcohol totally concealed by the richness of the wine—there's simply nothing out of place. Drink. **95** *—J.C. (2/1/2007)*

Taylor Fladgate 1948 Vintage Port (Port) $NA. Most houses declared 1947 instead, but this '48 is beautiful to taste now. Starts off almost meaty or coffee-like, then shows more plum and prune notes, while delicate herb and floral notes emerge only after prolonged aeration. It's richly textured in the mouth, with a seamless mouthfeel and no alcohol evident amid the dense, chocolaty flavors. Drink or hold. **98** *—J.C. (2/1/2007)*

Taylor Fladgate 1945 Vintage Port (Port) $NA. Remarkably dark and well-preserved in color, this wine's dark brick-garnet hue suggests a powerful, youthful wine. Complex aromas of flowers, mint, cherry and plum also carry hints of spice cake. On the palate, there's ample spice, with plenty of power and tannin still evident on the long, long finish. Drink or hold. **96** *—J.C. (2/1/2007)*

Taylor Fladgate 1935 Vintage Port (Port) $NA. The lightest of the first few wines, lighter even than the 1900, with no hints of russet remaining. It's a mellow Port, almost tawny in character, with nutty aromas and flavors tinged with figs and caramel. Drink up. **88** *—J.C. (2/1/2007)*

Taylor Fladgate 1927 Vintage Port (Port) $NA. By far the darkest of the first few vintages in this vertical, with intense dried fruit and maple syrup aromas marked by slightly nutty, toffee notes. It seems still youthful if that's possible in a wine nearly 80 years old, with great power and freshness and minerally notes. Doesn't have quite the spicy complexity of the '08, but it's still superb. **95** *—J.C. (2/1/2007)*

Taylor Fladgate 1908 Vintage Port (Port) $NA. Darker than the 1900, with a notable reddish tint toward the center, but still rather amber. This shows appreciably more richness and weight, as well as hints of dried cherries and mushrooms to go along with the sweet caramel and maple syrup flavors. Where it really shines is on the finish, with a burst of licorice and freshness. Drinking well now. **96** *—J.C. (2/1/2007)*

Taylor Fladgate 1900 Vintage Port (Port) $NA. Medium amber in color, this wine shows aged notes of honey, caramel and dried fig, picking up hints of heat and spice on the finish. Relative to the 1908 and 1927 it lacks body and richness; at this stage of its evolution, it's a wine of historic significance rather than any great hedonistic value. **86** *—J.C. (2/1/2007)*

TERRACOTA

Terracota 2003 Fernão Pires (Ribatejo) $9. 86 Best Buy *—R.V. (8/1/2005)*

Terracota 2001 Portuguese Red (Ribatejo) $NA. 86 *—R.V. (11/1/2004)*

Terracota 2003 Branco Portuguese White (Ribatejo) $9. 87 *—R.V. (12/1/2004)*

TERRAS DE PAUL

Terras de Paul 2004 Portuguese Red (Ribatejano) $17. 84 *—J.C. (6/1/2006)*

TERRAS DO GRIFO

Terras do Grifo 2005 Selected Harvest Malvasia Fina (Douro) $16. 82 *—J.C. (11/1/2006)*

THE RARE WINE CO.

The Rare Wine Co. NV Historic Series Boston Bual Special Reserve (Madeira) $40. 93 Editors' Choice *—J.C. (11/1/2006)*

The Rare Wine Co. NV Historic Series Charleston Sercial Special Reserve (Madeira) $40. 93 Editors' Choice *—J.C. (11/1/2006)*

The Rare Wine Co. NV Historic Series New York Malmsey Special Reserve (Madeira) $40. 93 Editors' Choice *—J.C. (11/1/2006)*

VALLEGRE

Vallegre 2003 Valle Longo Vintage Port $NA. 82 *—R.V. (11/15/2005)*

VARANDA DO CONDE

Varanda do Conde 2004 Alvarinho (Vinho Verde) $10. 85 Best Buy *—J.C. (12/31/2005)*

VEIGA TEIXEIRA

Veiga Teixeira 2001 Horta da Nazaré Castelão Red Blend (Ribatejo) $13. 88 Best Buy *—J.C. (11/1/2004)*

Veiga Teixeira 2002 Quinta de Santo André Red Blend (Ribatejo) $9. 87 Best Buy *—J.C. (11/1/2004)*

Veiga Teixeira 2003 Quinta de Santo André White Blend (Ribatejo) $8. 84 Best Buy *—J.C. (11/1/2004)*

VIDIGAL

Vidigal 2005 Reserva dos Amigos Cabernet Sauvignon (Estremadura) $NA. A green wine, the Cabernet that dominates is obviously not ripe. There is structure though, which just gives pleasure when drinking with food. **80** *—R.V. (12/15/2007)*

Vidigal 1999 Casa do Cónego Reserva Portuguese Red (Estremadura) $NA. A mature wine with dry tannins and flavors of leather, spice and fresh herbs. It is certainly ready to drink and is on the edge of drying out, with the tannins dominating. **82** *—R.V. (12/15/2007)*

Vidigal 2006 Reserva dos Amigos Sauvignon Blanc (Estremadura) $NA. This Sauvignon Blanc has some herbal character, touches of green acidity and grapefruit flavors. It finishes hard, though somewhat metallic. **80** *—R.V. (12/15/2007)*

VINHOS BORGES

Vinhos Borges 2005 Alvarinho (Vinho Verde) $15. 89 *—R.V. (7/1/2006)*

Vinhos Borges NV Gatão Portuguese White (Vinho Verde) $6. 82 *—R.V. (7/1/2006)*

Vinhos Borges 2000 Meia Encosta Red Blend (Dão) $8. 83 *—R.V. (12/31/2002)*

VINHOS JUSTINO HENRIQUES, FILHOS

Vinhos Justino Henriques, Filhos 1996 Colheita Sweet Madeira Blend (Madeira) $25. 88 *—J.C. (3/1/2005)*

VINHOS MESSIAS

Vinhos Messias 2000 Quinta do Cachao Tinta Roriz (Douro) $20. 83 *—R.V. (12/31/2002)*

Vinhos Messias 1999 Quinta do Cachão Touriga Nacional (Douro) $5. 85 Best Buy *—J.C. (12/31/2001)*

Vinhos Messias 2000 Quinta do Cachão/Colheita Touriga Nacional (Douro) $20. 87 *—R.V. (12/31/2002)*

Vinhos Messias 2001 Quinta do Valdoeiro Touriga Nacional (Beiras) $20. 87 *—R.V. (12/31/2002)*

Vinhos Messias NV Santola White Blend (Vinho Verde) $11. 85 *—M.S. (12/31/2001)*

VISTA ALEGRE

Vista Alegre 1995 LBV Bottled 2000 Port $NA. 86 *—R.V. (11/1/2004)*

Vista Alegre 1996 LBV Bottled 2002 Port $NA. 86 *—R.V. (11/1/2004)*

Vista Alegre 2003 Single Estate Vintage Port $NA. 88 *—R.V. (11/15/2005)*

Vista Alegre NV Vintage Character Port $NA. 85 *—R.V. (3/1/2005)*

W. & J. GRAHAM'S

W. & J. Graham's NV 10-Year Old Tawny Port $31. 92 Editors' Choice *—R.V. (8/1/2006)*

W. & J. Graham's NV 20-Year Old Tawny Port $52. 90 *—R.V. (8/1/2006)*

W. & J. Graham's NV 30-Year Old Tawny Port (Port) $102. Remarkably, this is able to show age and long cask aging, but the flavor is still here: figs and honey, balanced out with burnt caramel aged acidity and a rich (but not sweet) finish. Excellent, top-quality aged tawny. **95 Editors' Choice** *—R.V. (11/1/2007)*

W. & J. Graham's NV 40-Year Old Tawny Port $152. 94 *—R.V. (8/1/2006)*

W. & J. Graham's NV Aged 20 Years Finest Cask Matured Tawny Port $45. 90 *—J.C. (11/15/2003)*

W. & J. Graham's NV Crusted Port Bottled 1999 Port $NA. 89 *—R.V. (11/1/2004)*

W. & J. Graham's 2001 Late Bottled Vintage Port (Port) $21. Sweet, fragrant, very luscious and soft. It is fruity and easy with some youthful freshness, and stalky, dried currant flavors. Certainly not intense, but immediately appealing. **88** *—R.V. (11/1/2007)*

W. & J. Graham's 2000 Late Bottled Vintage Port (Port) $21. A firm, dry wine, very upright and elegant. It has power, but it's the initially austere perfumes that dominate. Dried currants go with black plum skins and definite tannins. **89** *—R.V. (11/1/2007)*

W. & J. Graham's 1995 LBV Bottled 2000 Port $20. 88 *—R.V. (3/1/2003)*

W. & J. Graham's 1996 Malvedos Vintage Port $42. 86 *—J.C. (11/15/2003)*

W. & J. Graham's NV Six Grapes Reserve Port $21. 89 *—R.V. (3/1/2005)*

W. & J. Graham's 2003 Vintage Port $100. 96 *—R.V. (11/15/2005)*

WARRE'S

Warre's NV King's Tawny Port $13. 85 *(3/1/2000)*

Warre's 1992 LBV Bottled 1996 Port $23. 92 *—R.V. (3/1/2003)*

Warre's NV Otima 10-Year Old Tawny Port $25. 91 *—R.V. (8/1/2006)*

Warre's NV Otima 20-Year Old Tawny Port $42. 90 *—R.V. (8/1/2006)*

Warre's NV Plus 20-Year Old Tawny Port $46. 85 *—R.V. (8/1/2006)*

Warre's 1986 Quinta Da Cavadinha Port $42. 87 *—J.C. (3/1/2000)*

Warre's 1987 Reserve Tawny Port $28. 93 *(1/1/2004)*

Warre's 1961 Reserve Tawny Port $111. 89 *(3/1/2000)*

Warre's NV Sir William 10-Year Old Tawny Port $26. 83 *—R.V. (8/1/2006)*

Warre's 1995 Traditional Late Bottled Vintage Port (Port) $26. Traditional here means that this is bottled unfiltered, giving it a good aging ability. Bottled in 1999, this is smooth and velvety in texture, showing signs of maturity. It has many of the complex flavors of a vintage Port. **93 Editors' Choice** *—R.V. (11/1/2007)*

Warre's 2003 Vintage Port $82. 90 *—R.V. (11/15/2005)*

Warre's NV Warrior Special Reserve Port $16. 82 *—J.C. (11/1/2006)*

WIESE & KROHN

Wiese & Krohn NV 10-Year Old Tawny Port $25. 88 *—R.V. (8/1/2006)*

Wiese & Krohn NV 20-Year Old Tawny Port $50. 90 *—R.V. (8/1/2006)*

Wiese & Krohn 2003 Vintage Port $NA. 89 *—R.V. (11/15/2005)*

WINE & SOUL

Wine & Soul 2003 Pintas Vintage Port $55. 90 *—R.V. (11/15/2005)*

ZIMBRO

Zimbro 2004 Tinto Red Blend (Douro) $16. 84 *—J.C. (11/1/2006)*

South Africa

After a slow start, South Africa's wines have reached international heights. The wines are sold at an impressively good value, and the country offers styles and tastes that are special and—importantly—enjoyable.

South Africa has been producing wine since the first vineyards were planted by the French in the seventeenth century, brought to the country by the Dutch governors of Cape Colony. At one time, the sweet wine of Constantia was the most prized in the world. For decades, South Africa, as part of the British Empire, sent shiploads of fortified wines to London.

This luxurious past can still be seen in the stunningly beautiful Cape vineyards, and the elegant, gabled Dutch Cape houses that form the centerpieces of many wine estates. But the future has also made its mark in South Africa's vineyards, where local winemakers (joined by an increasing number of European and American winemakers and investors) are creating a new generation of wines.

Boschendal Estate, Groot Drakenstein Valley, Franschhoek, Cape Province, South Africa.

The style, the character of the wines, is somewhere between California or Australia and Europe. Food friendly and equally elegant and powerful, there are many wines here for drinkers tired of alcoholic blockbusters.

All South Africa's vineyards are within an hour or three of Cape Town, in the southwest corner of the country. South Africa has its own appellation system, Wine of Origin, which is indicated on the label and on a government-issued neck sticker.

The most important quality wine areas are around the two cities of Stellenbosch and Paarl. All wine styles are made here: the country's greatest reds are from Stellenbosch, but Paarl's sub-district of Franschhoek runs a close second. Increasingly, other areas are being developed: the west coast, which makes great cooler-climate Sauvignon Blanc and red wines under the Darling and Swartland Wine of Origin, and the south coast at Walker Bay and Elgin, from which the country's best Pinot Noir comes.

The other famed quality area (although tiny in volume) is Constantia, almost in the suburbs of Cape Town. The original Cape vineyards now make impressive reds and whites in the country's most historic wine estates.

Larger-volume areas are further north and east than these classic heartland areas: Robertson, known for its Chardonnay, Worcester, for inexpensive volume wines, and Oliphants River, better known for reds and fortified wines.

South Africa's wine styles are evolving. Chenin Blanc, the local white workhorse grape, is also capable of making some impressive dry and sweet wines. Sauvignon Blanc has the potential to be more exciting than Chardonnay.

For reds, Pinotage, South Africa's own red grape (a cross between Pinot Noir and Cinsaut) still leaves wine critics divided, but can make great things, especially if found in Cape Blend wines (Pinotage blended with other red grapes). Shiraz is seen as the new hope for red wine, but Cabernet Sauvignon, Merlot, and Bordeaux blend wines are still the country's top reds.

ABRAHAM PEROLD

Abraham Perold 1998 Shiraz (Paarl) $155. Powerful and assertive but poised, this exemplary Shiraz from Abraham Perold is a study in balance. Beautiful and subtle berry, pepper and spice mingle, set aloft by a restrained wave of minerality. The wine is structured but delicate, unfolding quietly on the palate. A lovely meeting of Old and New World styles. **94** *—S.K. (11/15/2007)*

Abraham Perold 1996 Op Die Berg Shiraz (Paarl) $145. 90 *(1/1/2004)*

ALEXANDERFONTEIN

Alexanderfontein 2003 Chenin Blanc (Coastal Region) $10. 88 Editors' Choice *—M.M. (7/1/2005)*

ALLESVERLOREN

Allesverloren 1999 Estate Cabernet Sauvignon (Swartland) $22. 86 *—K.F. (8/1/2003)*

Allesverloren 2005 Shiraz (Swartland) $13. Elegant, earthy and unique—this wine is rich with dark berry, clove and spice flavors, but the intermingled stonefruit adds unexpected finesse. Firm tannins indicate the wine could age another few years and still be delicious. **88 Best Buy** *—S.K. (3/1/2007)*

ALTO

Alto 2003 Cabernet Sauvignon (Stellenbosch) $20. Mocha, coffee, mint and spice in the nose and on the palate make this unique offering from South Africa a true expression of the country's diverse terroir. It has a friendly character, with its minerality and soft tannins, making it great for a meal of lighter dishes. **85** *—S.K. (11/15/2007)*

AMANI

Amani 2002 Merlot (Stellenbosch) $18. 81 *—S.K. (9/1/2007)*

AMBELOUI

Ambeloui 2000 Valley Road Hout Bay Christo Champagne Blend (Constantia) $20. 84 *—S.H. (12/1/2002)*

ANURA

Anura 2004 Private Cellar Chenin Blanc (Paarl) $18. 88 *—M.D. (7/1/2006)*

Anura 2004 Private Cellar Syrah-Mourvèdre Red Blend (Paarl) $30. 87 *—M.D. (7/1/2006)*

ARNISTON BAY

Arniston Bay 2003 Chenin Blanc-Chardonnay (Western Cape) $10. 85 Best Buy *—M.M. (7/1/2005)*

Arniston Bay 2003 Merlot-Shiraz (Western Cape) $11. 82 *—M.M. (7/1/2005)*

Arniston Bay 2004 Rosé Pinotage (Western Cape) $10. 84 *—M.M. (7/1/2005)*

ASARA

Asara 1999 Bell Tower Bordeaux Blend (Stellenbosch) $35. Smoke, spice and rustic herbs lead on the nose of this assertive blend. On the palate a touch of South African smoke and alkaline flavors adds to the earthy feel of the wine, but pairing it with roasted meat or game will create a compelling meal. **86** *—S.K. (12/15/2007)*

Asara 2004 Reserve Chardonnay (Stellenbosch) $22. Subtle aromas of creamy vanilla and citrus on the nose of this appealing Chardonnay, and on the palate, waves of French oak, toast and fruit are integrated and elegant. Minerality adds a restraint that further recommends the wine. **86** *—S.K. (11/15/2007)*

Asara 2001 Cape Fusion Red Blend (Stellenbosch) $26. Rich plum and cherry roused by a touch of spicy Pinotage and red fruit exuberance make this Merlot, Cabernet and Pinotage blend both elegant and adventurous. It has good structure and is hearty enough to hold its own against smoked meat and game dishes. **87** *—S.K. (9/1/2007)*

ASHANTI

Ashanti 2001 Chiwara Red Blend (Paarl) $24. 87 *—K.F. (9/1/2003)*

Ashanti 2001 Joseph's Hat Red Blend (Paarl) $10. 86 *—K.F. (9/1/2003)*

Ashanti 2001 Nicole's Hat White Blend (Paarl) $10. 85 *—K.F. (9/1/2003)*

AVONDALE

Avondale 2004 Chenin Blanc (Coastal Region) $NA. 89 *—R.V. (11/15/2005)*

BACKSBERG

Backsberg 2002 Cabernet Sauvignon (Paarl) $12. 86 *—M.M. (11/15/2004)*

Backsberg 1997 Cabernet Sauvignon (Paarl) $14. 85 *—M.M. (3/1/2001)*

Backsberg 2002 Klein Babylons Toren Cabernet Sauvignon-Merlot (Paarl) $15. 87 *—M.M. (11/15/2004)*

Backsberg 2003 Chardonnay (Paarl) $10. 86 Best Buy *—M.D. (3/1/2006)*

Backsberg 2002 Chardonnay (Paarl) $10. 84 *—M.M. (7/4/2004)*

Backsberg 2001 Chardonnay (Paarl) $13. 84 *—M.M. (4/1/2002)*

Backsberg 2000 Chardonnay (Paarl) $13. 85 *—M.M. (4/1/2002)*

Backsberg 1999 Chardonnay (Paarl) $14. 82 *—M.N. (3/1/2001)*

Backsberg 2002 Babylons Toren Chardonnay (Paarl) $25. 91 Editors' Choice *—M.M. (11/15/2004)*

Backsberg 2004 Kosher Chardonnay (Paarl) $12. There's some toasted oak on the nose but overall, this wine tends towards watery and lean, with very little flavor or finish to make an impact, especially for a Chardonnay. **81** *—S.K. (4/1/2007)*

Backsberg 2005 Chenin Blanc (Western Cape) $12. 85 *—M.D. (7/1/2006)*

Backsberg 2003 Chenin Blanc (Paarl) $10. 86 *—M.M. (7/4/2004)*

Backsberg 1998 Merlot (Paarl) $14. 82 *—M.N. (3/1/2001)*

Backsberg 1998 Klein Babylonstoren Merlot-Cabernet Sauvignon (Paarl) $18. 87 *—M.S. (4/1/2002)*

Backsberg 2005 Pinotage (Coastal Region) $13. The wines of Backsberg have a distinctive, artistic quality to them that makes them ideal for collectors and drinkers who seek wines with style. This Pinotage has those qualities, with its layers of cinnamon and deep berry on the nose and smooth, integrated berry and smoke flavors. This is a real Pinotage so expect the rubbery smoke that goes along with it—but it's also elegant, offering structure and complexity with a gentle touch. **87** *—S.K. (12/15/2007)*

Backsberg 2004 Kosher Pinotage (Paarl) $14. 84 *—M.D. (4/1/2006)*

Backsberg 2002 Babylons Toren Red Blend (Paarl) $30. 87 *—M.M. (7/1/2005)*

Backsberg 2005 Elba Red Blend (Paarl) $NA. This blend of seven grape cultivars has an arresting aroma of violet and unfolds on the palate layer by layer, revealing alternately floral and fruity facets. The combined qualities of the grapes is intriguing and seamless—it is both easy to love and mysterious. **89** *—S.K. (7/1/2007)*

Backsberg 2005 Sauvignon Blanc (Western Cape) $12. 86 *—M.D. (3/1/2006)*

Backsberg 2003 Sauvignon Blanc (Western Cape) $10. 85 Best Buy *—M.M. (11/15/2004)*

Backsberg 2005 John Martin Reserve Sauvignon Blanc (Paarl) $NA. This compelling wooded Sauvignon Blanc is spicy and complex but still very fresh, striking a delicious balance between curvy and classic. Tropical fruit and vanilla meld together with a crisp minerality that lends itself to creative food pairing and refreshing summer sips. **90 Editors' Choice** *—S.K. (7/1/2007)*

Backsberg 2003 John Martin Sauvignon Blanc (Paarl) $15. 90 Best Buy *—M.M. (11/15/2004)*

Backsberg 1998 Shiraz (Paarl) $14. 82 *(10/1/2001)*

Backsberg 2003 Pumphouse Shiraz (Paarl) $20. 88 *—M.D. (5/1/2006)*

Backsberg 2002 Pumphouse Shiraz (Paarl) $18. 87 *—M.M. (11/15/2004)*

Backsberg 2004 Babylons Toren Viognier (Paarl) $30. 89 *—M.D. (9/1/2006)*

Backsberg 2003 Babylons Toren Viognier (South Africa) $25. 88 *—M.S. (11/15/2004)*

BAOBAB

Baobab 2002 Chardonnay (Western Cape) $8. 84 *—S.H. (1/1/2002)*

Baobab 2001 Chenin Blanc (Western Cape) $7. 85 *—S.H. (4/1/2002)*

Baobab 2004 Merlot (Western Cape) $10. 85 Best Buy *—J.C. (11/15/2005)*

Baobab 2002 Merlot (Western Cape) $8. 87 Best Buy *—M.M. (11/15/2004)*

Baobab 1998 Merlot (Western Cape) $10. 87 *—S.H. (1/1/2002)*

Baobab 2004 Pinotage (Western Cape) $10. 84 *—M.D. (3/1/2006)*

Baobab 2001 Pinotage (Western Cape) $10. 88 Best Buy *—K.F. (4/1/2003)*

Baobab 2001 Sauvignon Blanc (Western Cape) $8. 84 *—S.H. (4/1/2002)*

BEAU JOUBERT

Beau Joubert 2004 Cabernet Sauvignon (Stellenbosch) $17. Integrated, elegant flavors characterize this full-bodied Cab from premium producer Beau Joubert. Mocha and blackberry on the nose and palate, paired with soft, smooth tannins, create layers of flavor that linger. A wine with dimension and class. **90 Editors' Choice** *—S.K. (11/15/2007)*

Beau Joubert 2002 Cabernet Sauvignon (Stellenbosch) $17. 89 *—M.D. (7/1/2006)*

Beau Joubert 2006 Chardonnay (Stellenbosch) $14. A classy Chardonnay with a balance of fresh citrus flavors and spice. It's lively and clean in a manner that keeps it light, but there's a brain behind the fun. The overall character is simple and pleasing to the palate; this would be delicious with crab cakes or Caribbean cooking. **85** *—S.K. (6/1/2007)*

Beau Joubert 2005 Chardonnay (Stellenbosch) $14. 86 *—M.D. (7/1/2006)*

Beau Joubert 2004 Merlot (Stellenbosch) $16. Wine has been made on the Beau Joubert property since the early 19th century, and today, the Joubert family makes consistently good wines that flourish in the mineral-rich soils of the Stellenbosch farm. This Merlot is no exception: rich, integrated flavors of berry and chocolate are both smooth and balanced and the wine is lovely when paired with roasted meat or game. **88** *—S.K. (9/1/2007)*

Beau Joubert 2005 Oak Lane Chenin Blanc-Sauvignon Blanc (Stellenbosch) $8. 85 Best Buy *—M.D. (7/1/2006)*

Beau Joubert 2005 Oak Lane Merlot-Cabernet Sauvignon (Stellenbosch) $8. Balanced and subtle but with good character, this blend offers flavors of tobacco, leather and clove. Fruit-driven and accessible, it's both elegant and ageable. **87 Best Buy** *—S.K. (11/15/2007)*

Beau Joubert 2004 Oak Lane Merlot-Cabernet Sauvignon (Stellenbosch) $8. 86 Best Buy *—M.D. (5/1/2006)*

Beau Joubert 2006 Oak Lane Rosé Pinot Noir (Stellenbosch) $8. A lovely nose of berry and spice, followed by integrated, medium-bodied flavors, characterize this rosé from 17th-century Stellenbosch producer Beau Joubert. A good everyday wine at an attractive price—perfect for pairing with seafood or grilled poultry. **84 Best Buy** *—S.K. (7/1/2007)*

Beau Joubert 2006 Sauvignon Blanc (Stellenbosch) $13. Fresh, grassy and clean, this Sauvignon Blanc offers light citrus and tropical fruit flavors and is a fitting companion to fresh seafood dishes and chicken summer salads. The finish is zippy with a touch of spice and the price is right for everyday drinking. **86** *—S.K. (7/1/2007)*

Beau Joubert 2005 Sauvignon Blanc (Stellenbosch) $13. 87 *—M.D. (7/1/2006)*

Beau Joubert 2005 Oak Lane Shiraz (Stellenbosch) $8. 83 *—M.D. (7/1/2006)*

BEAUMONT

Beaumont 2001 Ariane Bordeaux Blend (Walker Bay) $20. 87 *—K.F. (8/1/2003)*

Beaumont 2004 Chenin Blanc (Walker Bay) $15. 88 *—R.V. (11/15/2005)*

Beaumont 2004 Hope Marguerite Chenin Blanc (Walker Bay) $21. 91 *—R.V. (11/15/2005)*

Beaumont 2002 Cape Vintage Red Blend (Walker Bay) $37. 88 *—S.K. (7/1/2007)*

Beaumont 2000 Shiraz (South Africa) $18. 88 *—K.F. (8/1/2003)*

BELLINGHAM

Bellingham 2003 Our Founder's Cabernet Sauvignon (Coastal Region) $12. 84 *—M.D. (3/1/2006)*

Bellingham 2004 Our Founder's Chardonnay (Coastal Region) $11. 84 *—M.D. (3/1/2006)*

Bellingham 2003 Our Founder's Pinotage (Coastal Region) $12. 84 *—M.D. (5/1/2006)*

Bellingham 2004 Our Founder's Sauvignon Blanc (Coastal Region) $11. 85 *—M.D. (3/1/2006)*

Bellingham 2004 Our Founder's Shiraz (Coastal Region) $15. This wine starts with an extremely pretty nose—heady, dense and spicy aromas mingle with fruit in a poised dance. On the palate, the touch is soft, with smoke and berry unfolding in the mouth nicely. There's a touch of angularity to the wine—it's not terribly complex—but it's very approachable. **85** *—S.K. (11/15/2007)*

Bellingham 2003 Shiraz (Coastal Region) $12. 83 *—M.D. (5/1/2006)*

BERGSIG

Bergsig 2003 Pinotage (Breede River Valley) $13. 84 *—M.D. (12/31/2006)*

Bergsig 2001 Pinotage (South Africa) $12. 87 *—K.F. (4/1/2003)*

Bergsig 2004 Sauvignon Blanc (Breede River Valley) $9. 84 *—M.D. (12/31/2006)*

Bergsig 2002 Sauvignon Blanc (Breede River Valley) $10. 84 *—M.M. (3/1/2004)*

BEYERSKLOOF

Beyerskloof 2001 Cabernet Sauvignon-Merlot (Stellenbosch) $35. 93 Editors' Choice *—R.V. (11/1/2006)*

Beyerskloof 2005 Pinotage (Stellenbosch) $12. 86 *—M.D. (12/31/2006)*

Beyerskloof 2000 Pinotage (Stellenbosch) $10. 89 Best Buy *(9/1/2001)*

Beyerskloof 2003 Cape Blend Red Blend (Stellenbosch) $20. 88 *—M.D. (9/1/2006)*

BILTON

Bilton 2004 Cabernet Sauvignon (Stellenbosch) $27. A spicy tobacco and dark fruit nose leads on this elegant Cabernet, followed by luscious flavors of plum, clove, tobacco and a touch of oak. Layered and smooth, the wine has a stylish complexity that will develop nicely in the cellar. Overall, a compelling wine that will call for more than one glass. **89** *—S.K. (11/15/2007)*

Bilton 1999 Merlot (Stellenbosch) $18. 89 *—M.M. (4/1/2002)*

Bilton 2004 Shiraz (Stellenbosch) $27. This traditional Shiraz displays aromas of prune and toasted spice, followed by flavors of cheerful cherry and vanilla. Though young, the wine has a balanced, silky texture and good finish. **85** *—S.K. (11/15/2007)*

Bilton 2002 Shiraz (Stellenbosch) $25. 85 *—J.C. (11/15/2005)*

BLAAUWKLIPPEN

Blaauwklippen 2003 Shiraz (Coastal Region) $27. Dark berry and trademark South African smoke comprise the nose and the flavors of this wine from this historic Stellensbosch producer, and while the tannins are soft, the wine has enough complexity to hold its own against heartier dishes. There's some exotic spice on the palate, too, offering an interesting extra facet to the wine. **84** *—S.K. (6/1/2007)*

Blaauwklippen 2000 Barrel Selection Zinfandel (Stellenbosch) $19. 85 *—K.F. (9/1/2003)*

BLACK PEARL

Black Pearl 2003 Shiraz (Paarl) $33. 92 Editors' Choice *—M.D. (12/31/2006)*

Black Pearl 2003 Oro Shiraz-Cabernet Sauvignon (Paarl) $20. Intense and exotic, this wine has an earthy, beguiling nose and flavors of bright, juicy fruit. Subtle hints of anise and herbs add character. Smooth and elegant, this wine has backbone, but the gentle finish borders on weak. Overall the wine is very good and would pair well with chicken and vegetarian dishes. **87** *—S.K. (3/1/2007)*

BLACK ROCK

Black Rock 2004 Red Blend (Swartland) $25. 92 Cellar Selection *—S.K. (6/19/2007)*

Black Rock 2005 White Blend (Swartland) $25. This refreshing, citric blend of Chenin, Viognier and Chardonnay is lush but light, with an underlying minerality that offers restraint and clarity. The nose and palate are full of tropical fruit, lemon and lime and flowers. A classic, infectious wine. **90** *—S.K. (7/1/2007)*

Black Rock 2004 White Blend (Swartland) $24. 91 *—R.V. (11/15/2005)*

BLUE COVE

Blue Cove 2006 Cabernet Sauvignon (Western Cape) $10. This is a good everyday wine at an attractive price. Packed full of mint, mocha and some juicy berry, the wine offers simple, mouthwatering flavors on the palate and a touch of toasted spice. It's not terribly complex but it's fun and easy to like. **84** *—S.K. (12/15/2007)*

BLUE GROVE HILL

Blue Grove Hill 2005 Merlot-Cabernet Sauvignon (Philadelphia) $16. Opulent fruit, roasted meat and spice typify this cuvée from Capaia winery, located in the Philadelphia wine-growing region near Durbanville. Aged in French oak, there is a pleasant balance of young fruit and backbone, and fans of more tannic wines could drink now. Even better if it ages another three years. **85** *—S.K. (3/1/2007)*

BOEKENHOUTSKLOOF

Boekenhoutskloof 2004 Cabernet Sauvignon (Franschhoek) $47. 92 *—R.V. (11/1/2006)*

Boekenhoutskloof 2003 Cabernet Sauvignon (Franschhoek) $46. 94 *—R.V. (11/1/2006)*

Boekenhoutskloof 2004 Chocolate Block Red Blend (Franschhoek) $39. The name is enticing enough—and in the glass, this red blend from innovator Marc Kent delivers with style and grace. Spice and, appropriately, chocolate waft on the nose, and on the palate, the wine is rich, structured and full of red berry, cocoa and pepper flavors. Syrah, Grenache Noir, Cabernet Sauvignon, Viognier and Cinsault offer ripeness and a juicy character. **88** *—S.K. (7/1/2007)*

Boekenhoutskloof 2004 Sémillon (Franschhoek) $29. Semillon is an excellent food wine and this vibrant selection from South Africa will pair beautifully with everything from lobster salad to a Moroccan chicken tagine. Playful citrus flavors mingled with honey give the wine weight as well as life, while the dryness and acidity on the palate leave a clean finish. A versatile wine with character. **89** *—S.K. (7/1/2007)*

Boekenhoutskloof 2002 Sémillon (Franschhoek) $29. You would be hard-pressed to go wrong with any of winemaker Marc Kent's wines, and this pretty Semillon is no exception. A lovely, aromatic nose leads into a wine with good weight, balanced acidity and layers of citrus, fruit and herbs that are smooth and complex. Solid and accessible, this wine will pair well with shellfish or a variety of cheeses. **87** —*S.K. (7/1/2007)*

BON CAP

Bon Cap 2005 Organic Cabernet Sauvignon (Robertson) $15. Spicy berry aromas followed by smoke, tobacco spice and blackberry make this a good wine for pairing with hearty dishes or drinking on its own. A touch of acidity adds restraint and balance. Ample tannins mean it will age well, but it's good to drink now. **84** —*S.K. (12/15/2007)*

Bon Cap 2005 Organic Pinotage (Robertson) $15. This organic Pinotage from Bon Cap offers red berry and pepper flavors that, though a touch angular, are soft and food-friendly. The minerality gives this an attractive restraint. **83** —*S.K. (11/15/2007)*

BOSCHENDAL

Boschendal 2001 Cabernet Sauvignon (Coastal Region) $16. 85 —*M.M. (7/1/2005)*

Boschendal 2000 Reserve Cabernet Sauvignon (Coastal Region) $20. 88 —*M.M. (7/1/2005)*

Boschendal NV Le Grand Pavillon Blanc de Blancs Champagne Blend (Coastal Region) $15. 87 *(12/1/2001)*

Boschendal NV Le Grand Pavillon Brut Champagne Blend (Coastal Region) $13. 87 —*M.M. (3/1/2004)*

Boschendal 2004 Chardonnay (Western Cape) $16. 85 —*M.D. (9/1/2006)*

Boschendal 2003 Chardonnay (Coastal Region) $14. 86 —*M.M. (4/1/2005)*

Boschendal 2000 Chardonnay (Coastal Region) $NA. 85 —*R.V. (7/1/2002)*

Boschendal 2003 Reserve Chardonnay (Coastal Region) $18. 86 —*M.D. (11/1/2006)*

Boschendal 2001 Reserve Chardonnay (Coastal Region) $16. 87 —*K.F. (4/1/2003)*

Boschendal 2005 Le Pavillon Chardonnay-Semillon (Western Cape) $9. 87 Best Buy —*M.D. (11/1/2006)*

Boschendal 2001 Reserve Merlot (Coastal Region) $20. 84 —*M.M. (7/1/2005)*

Boschendal 2001 Lanoy Red Blend (Coastal Region) $15. 88 —*M.M. (7/1/2005)*

Boschendal 2006 The Pavillion Rosé Red Blend (Coastal Region) $9. Rose petals and strawberries on the nose and palate, balanced with a clean acidity, make this Rosé from consistently solid producer Boschendal a great choice for sipping on the patio or pairing with a multitude of warm-weather dishes. Think chicken salad, grilled salmon—it will all harmonize well with this fun wine. **85 Best Buy** —*S.K. (7/1/2007)*

Boschendal 2004 Sauvignon Blanc (Coastal Region) $12. 86 —*M.M. (4/1/2005)*

Boschendal 2002 Sauvignon Blanc (Coastal Region) $12. 88 Best Buy —*K.F. (4/1/2003)*

Boschendal 2006 1685 Grande Cuvée Sauvignon Blanc (Coastal Region) $17. Lush, tropical fruit flavors meet a clean, steely edge in this delicious wine from historic producer Boschendal. Intense aromas in the nose and an overall rounded, full character give it presence, but it's still clean and balanced. **90** —*S.K. (7/1/2007)*

Boschendal 2003 Grand Cuvée Sauvignon Blanc (Franschhoek) $14. 90 Editors' Choice —*M.M. (4/1/2005)*

Boschendal 2004 Grande Cuvée Sauvignon Blanc (Franschhoek) $14. 90 Best Buy —*M.M. (4/1/2005)*

Boschendal 2005 Grande Cuvée Sauvignon Blanc (Coastal Region) $17. 89 Editors' Choice —*M.D. (12/31/2006)*

Boschendal 2002 Grande Cuvée Sauvignon Blanc (Coastal Region) $14. 89 —*K.F. (1/1/2004)*

Boschendal 1999 Grande Cuvée Sauvignon Blanc (Coastal Region) $12. 88 Best Buy *(9/1/2001)*

Boschendal 2005 Reserve Sauvignon Blanc (Coastal Region) $12. 87 Best Buy —*M.D. (3/1/2006)*

Boschendal 2004 Le Pavillon Semillon-Chardonnay (Western Cape) $9. 83 —*M.M. (4/1/2005)*

Boschendal 2004 1685 Shiraz (Coastal Region) $19. This New World-style Shiraz has a subtle touch but is true to the varietal, with its pepper, spice and red berry flavors. The nose is elegant and integrated, and overall, the wine is pleasant and accessible and a good cohort to grilled meats or game. **84** —*S.K. (7/1/2007)*

Boschendal 2003 Shiraz (Coastal Region) $19. 88 —*M.D. (9/1/2006)*

Boschendal 2002 Shiraz (Coastal Region) $16. 87 —*M.M. (7/1/2005)*

Boschendal 2001 Grand Pavillon Sparkling Blend (Franschhoek) $15. 86 —*K.F. (12/1/2003)*

BOSCHKLOOF

Boschkloof 1999 Cabernet Sauvignon-Merlot (Vlootenburg) $15. 84 —*K.F. (4/1/2003)*

Boschkloof 1998 Reserve Cabernet Sauvignon-Merlot (Vlootenburg) $20. 85 —*K.F. (4/1/2003)*

Boschkloof 2000 Syrah (Vlootenburg) $18. 85 —*K.F. (8/1/2003)*

BOUCHARD FINLAYSON

Bouchard Finlayson 2004 Crocodile's Lair/Kaaimansgat Chardonnay (Walker Bay) $25. A spritely, alluring citric and floral nose is the first impression, but in the mouth, the wine opens up into a combination of clean minerality and juicy, rounded flavors. The marriage is successful—great acidity and ample body create an intriguing result. **88** —*S.K. (7/1/2007)*

Bouchard Finlayson 2000 Crocodile's Lair/Kaaimansgat Chardonnay (Overberg) $20. 88 —*K.F. (4/1/2003)*

Bouchard Finlayson 2001 Sans Barrique Chardonnay (Overberg) $18. 86 —*K.F. (4/1/2003)*

Bouchard Finlayson 2001 Blanc de Mer Meritage (Hemel en Aarde) $12. 87 —*K.F. (4/1/2003)*

Bouchard Finlayson 2005 Mission Vale Chardonnay (Walker Bay) $29. Soft, balanced, with flowery aromatics and layers of vanilla and apricot that are luscious but subtle. The wine is gentle but makes its mark because the quality of the fruit is excellent. Drink now or let it age—there's complexity here and the wine still has room for development. **89** —*S.K. (7/1/2007)*

Bouchard Finlayson 2005 Galpin Peak Pinot Noir (Walker Bay) $45. Soft, subtle tannins, a touch of pepper, and elegant flavors of sweet raspberry and spice comprise this Pinot Noir. A pretty, perfumed nose and lingering finish add to the appeal of the wine. There's enough structure here to allow for aging, but it's very good now. **87** —*S.K. (7/1/2007)*

Bouchard Finlayson 2001 Galpin Peak Pinot Noir (Walker Bay) $40. 86 —*K.F. (9/1/2003)*

Bouchard Finlayson 2004 Hannibal Red Blend (Walker Bay) $39. Brooding dark cherry, deep spices and waves of chocolate coating make this intense and intriguing blend of Italian and French grapes a rare treat. The nose is dark and layered with aromas of wood and dark fruit. The lush tannins and slow finish adds to the overall appeal of the wine. Lots of character here. **89 Editors' Choice** —*S.K. (7/1/2007)*

Bouchard Finlayson 2001 Hannibal Cuvée Red Blend (Walker Bay) $30. 87 —*K.F. (9/1/2003)*

BOUWLAND

Bouwland 2003 Chenin Blanc (Stellenbosch) $NA. 88 —*R.V. (11/15/2005)*

BOWE JOUBERT VINEYARD & WINERY

Bowe Joubert Vineyard & Winery 2001 Cabernet Sauvignon (Stellenbosch) $18. 88 —*K.F. (4/1/2003)*

Bowe Joubert Vineyard & Winery 2002 Cuvée Emmerentia Chardonnay (Stellenbosch) $13. 87 —*M.M. (3/1/2004)*

Bowe Joubert Vineyard & Winery 2001 Cuvée Emmerentia Chardonnay (Stellenbosch) $15. 85 —*K.F. (4/1/2003)*

Bowe Joubert Vineyard & Winery 2001 Oaked Chenin Blanc (Stellenbosch) $10. 86 —*K.F. (4/1/2003)*

Bowe Joubert Vineyard & Winery 2001 Merlot (Stellenbosch) $18. 87 —*K.F. (4/1/2003)*

Bowe Joubert Vineyard & Winery 2001 Sauvignon Blanc (Stellenbosch) $11. 87 —*K.F. (4/1/2003)*

Bowe Joubert Vineyard & Winery 2003 JB Sauvignon Blanc (Stellenbosch) $12. 88 Best Buy —*M.M. (3/1/2004)*

Bowe Joubert Vineyard & Winery 2001 Mosaïc White Blend (Stellenbosch) $8. 84 —*K.F. (4/1/2003)*

BRADGATE

Bradgate 2002 White Blend (Stellenbosch) $9. 85 —*K.F. (4/1/2003)*

Bradgate 2005 Chenin Blanc/Sauvignon Blanc White Blend (Stellenbosch) $9. 89 Best Buy —*R.V. (11/15/2005)*

BRAHMS

Brahms 2004 Chenin Blanc (Paarl) $17. 87 —*R.V. (11/15/2005)*

Brahms 2004 Pinotage (Paarl) $24. Rich, rounded and full of flavor, this successful Pinotage has an assertive, spicy nose and equally energetic flavors of red berry and smoke. It's structured and serious, needing some time in the cellar, and should be paired with foods that can hold their own, like grilled lamb or a beef stew. **86** *—S.K. (11/15/2007)*

BRAMPTON

Brampton 2004 Cabernet Sauvignon (Stellenbosch) $14. **87** *—R.V. (11/1/2006)*

Brampton 1996 Cabernet Sauvignon-Merlot (Stellenbosch) $14. **86** *(9/1/1999)*

Brampton 2006 Unoaked Chardonnay (Coastal Region) $10. This is alluring from the start with its slightly sweet, floral aromas of peach and ginger and lush fruit flavors of melon and pear. The elements are fresh and full at the same time, creating an intricate and diverse impression on the palate. This is a wine to be enjoyed at leisure—it needs time to unfold. **87** *—S.K. (6/1/2007)*

Brampton 2005 Unoaked Chardonnay (Coastal Region) $10. **87 Best Buy** *—M.D. (12/31/2006)*

Brampton 2001 Red Blend (Stellenbosch) $15. **84** *—K.F. (4/1/2003)*

Brampton 2006 Rosé Rosé Blend (Coastal Region) $11. Heady aromas of rose petal and strawberry lead on this memorable wine from South Africa's Brampton, the sister label to top-tier producer Rustenberg. The color is a gorgeous dark pink, and the flavors assertive. It's a likeable wine that will appeal to rose drinkers with a taste for something a little more substantial. **84** *—S.K. (7/1/2007)*

Brampton 1997 Sauvignon Blanc (Stellenbosch) $14. **86** *—M.S. (9/1/1999)*

Brampton 2004 Shiraz (Coastal Region) $12. **89 Best Buy** *—M.D. (9/1/2006)*

Brampton 2005 Viognier (Coastal Region) $14. **88** *—M.D. (9/1/2006)*

BUITENVERWACHTING

Buitenverwachting 2001 Chardonnay (Constantia) $15. **85** *—K.F. (9/1/2003)*

Buitenverwachting 2005 Rhine Riesling (Constantia) $12. **85** *—M.D. (12/31/2006)*

Buitenverwachting 2005 Sauvignon Blanc (Constantia) $12. **88 Best Buy** *—M.D. (9/1/2006)*

Buitenverwachting 2002 Sauvignon Blanc (Constantia) $13. **83** *—K.F. (9/1/2003)*

Buitenverwachting 2005 Beyond Sauvignon Blanc (Coastal Region) $12. The nose is luxuriant and fragrant and the flavors crisp, clean and full of zing—a unique combination. Strains of lemon and lime give the wine tang but it has a weightier complexity and full body, too. The finish is lingering and refreshing. Pair with seafood. **89 Best Buy** *—S.K. (3/1/2007)*

CAMBERLEY

Camberley 2000 Cabernet Sauvignon-Merlot (Stellenbosch) $18. **85** *—K.F. (8/1/2003)*

CAPAIA

Capaia 2005 Capaia Bordeaux Blend (Philadelphia) $42. Dark, rich fruit, luscious spice and a velvety overall texture make this flagship wine from Capaia a benchmark Bordeaux blend for South Africa. Assertive but refined, layered but delicate, the wine unfolds gently on the palate and is the perfect cohort to myriad meat and poultry dishes. Minerality gives it lift and clarity. **92 Editors' Choice** *—S.K. (11/15/2007)*

CAPE CHAMONIX

Cape Chamonix 2004 Troika Bordeaux Blend (Franschhoek) $NA. A blend of Cabernet, Cabernet Franc and Merlot, this Bordeaux-style red has beautiful, layered aromatics leading into poised flavors of pepper and spice, and the structure is both assertive and balanced. A great food wine, it will pair well with everything from salmon to grilled steak. **89** *—S.K. (7/1/2007)*

Cape Chamonix 2005 Reserve Chardonnay (Franschhoek) $NA. This structured, creamy wine displays all of the hallmakers of a great Chardonnay: appetizing toasted wood, elegant, integrated flavors and a natural acid that gives the wine excellent balance. A great food wine. **89** *—S.K. (7/1/2007)*

Cape Chamonix 2005 Reserve Pinot Noir (Franschhoek) $NA. Stylish and reserved like most of Chamonix's wines, this is a unique selection since Pinot Noir is not a prevalent grape in South Africa. A lovely floral nose, subtle but distinctive, is followed by fruit-forward berries and a lively, Burgundian-style acid lift. The finish is long but gentle. **88** *—S.K. (7/1/2007)*

Cape Chamonix 2005 Reserve Sauvignon Blanc (Franschhoek) $NA. An opulent nose of peach and pineapple leads on this full, round, wooded Sauvignon Blanc from lauded winemaker Gottfried Mocke. Ripe melon mingles with wooded spice in a delicious marriage that is both elegant and distinctive among the more prevalent lean and green New World style of SB. This is clearly a food-driven wine, meant to hold its own against stronger dishes. The finish is long and touched with spice. Delightful and distinctive. **90 Editors' Choice** *—S.K. (7/1/2007)*

CAPE COLLECTION

Cape Collection 2004 Ingwe Merlot (Swartland) $8. Gamey spice and smooth tannins recommend this affordable Merlot to drinkers who enjoy softer flavors and an elegant, integrated style. It's approachable and a great food pairing wine as well—think veal shank, cioppino or a salad with duck breast. **84 Best Buy** *—S.K. (7/1/2007)*

Cape Collection 2005 Idube Sauvignon Blanc (Swartland) $8. This has some delicious heft in the nose, with all of the tropical, citric notes desired in a Sauv Blanc, but on the palate it's clunky. The mouthfeel is overly viscous, weighing down the lively flavors beneath. Needs more complexity, but at the same time, a lighter touch. **82** *—S.K. (6/1/2007)*

CAPE HAVEN

Cape Haven 2004 Chenin Blanc (Swartland) $12. **88 Best Buy** *—R.V. (11/15/2005)*

CAPE INDABA

Cape Indaba 1998 Chardonnay (Western Cape) $10. **82** *(9/1/1999)*

Cape Indaba 1998 Pinotage (Coastal Region) $10. **86** *—J.C. (11/15/1999)*

Cape Indaba 1998 Sauvignon Blanc (Robertson) $8. **82** *(9/1/1999)*

CAPE POINT VINEYARDS

Cape Point Vineyards 2004 Chardonnay (Cape Point) $0. Delightful aromas of citrus and apricot and a balance of toasty creaminess and minerally zip are found in this wonderful coastal Chardonnay. Great balance and body are topped off with a kiss of lime on the finish, which has length and personality. **93** *—S.K. (7/1/2007)*

Cape Point Vineyards 2006 Stonehaven Sauvignon Blanc (Cape Point) $20. Fresh, zesty, and edged with the superb minerally and lime character that typifies Cape Point's wines, this classy Sauvignon Blanc delivers on every level. Flirty and fresh, but full of elegance. **90** *—S.K. (7/1/2007)*

Cape Point Vineyards 2005 Sémillon (Cape Point) $35. The discovery of some wines could be caled epiphanic. Your first sip of this Sémillon may qualify as such. An exquisite balance between rich, round fruit flavors and a zesty, clean minerality gives this Cape Point offering the kind of intriguing character that sets it apart from the pack. A full, complex midpalate and beautiful tropical fruit flavors are lifted by the spin of lime on the finish. Poised and blue-blooded, the wine makes an outstanding accompaniment to both rich and delicate dishes. This is a unique offering and a beautiful reflection of Cape terroir. **93 Editors' Choice** *—S.K. (7/1/2007)*

CAPE VIEW

Cape View 1999 Merlot (Stellenbosch) $23. **86** *—K.F. (4/1/2003)*

Cape View 1999 Pinotage (Stellenbosch) $28. **84** *—K.F. (4/1/2003)*

CATHERINE MARSHALL

Catherine Marshall 2003 Cabernet Sauvignon (Paarl) $NA. South African winemaker Catherine Marshall specializes in subtle, refined wines, and this displays her deft touch. Elegant, integrated spice and berry flavors, a clean, dry minerality and a very soft overall character make this a wine to savor slowly. Its restraint means it will pair well with more delicate flavors and can be enjoyed alone without blasting the palate in two sips. Imported by The Wild Grape. **90** *—S.K. (7/1/2007)*

CEDERBERG

Cederberg 2003 Cabernet Sauvignon (Cederberg) $28. **89** *—R.V. (11/1/2006)*

Cederberg 2002 Cabernet Sauvignon (South Africa) $25. **88** *—M.M. (12/15/2004)*

Cederberg 2003 Five Generations Cabernet Sauvignon (Cederberg) $49. **93 Cellar Selection** *—R.V. (11/1/2006)*

Cederberg 2005 Chenin Blanc (Cederberg) $17. **89** *—R.V. (11/15/2005)*

Cederberg 2004 Chenin Blanc (South Africa) $15. **86** *—M.M. (7/1/2005)*

Cederberg 2003 Dry Chenin Blanc (South Africa) $15. **90 Editors' Choice** *—M.M. (12/15/2004)*

Cederberg 2003 Five Generations Chenin Blanc (Cederberg) $35. **93** *—R.V. (11/15/2005)*

Cederberg 2003 Cederberger Red Blend (Cederberg) $20. **87** *—M.D. (7/1/2006)*

Cederberg 2005 Sauvignon Blanc (Cederberg) $19. **87** *—M.D. (12/31/2006)*

Cederberg 2004 Shiraz (Cederberg) $29. **90** *—M.D. (12/31/2006)*

Cederberg 2003 Shiraz (South Africa) $30. **86** *—J.C. (11/15/2005)*

Cederberg 2002 Shiraz (South Africa) $25. 88 *—M.M. (12/15/2004)*

CHAMONIX

Chamonix 2000 Troika Bordeaux Blend (Franschhoek) $25. 86 *—K.F. (8/1/2003)*

Chamonix 2005 Cabernet Sauvignon (Franschhoek) $17. Chamonix is known for its stylish touch and this offers all of the hallmarks of a good Cabernet—deep berry, menthol, layered smoke and spice—in an approachable style. The fruit is bright and appealing and the wine relatively soft and easy to drink. 84 *—S.K. (12/15/2007)*

Chamonix 1998 Chardonnay (Franschhoek) $16. 85 *—K.F. (9/1/2003)*

Chamonix 1998 Reserve Chardonnay (Franschhoek) $25. 87 *—K.F. (9/1/2003)*

Chamonix 2000 Pinot Noir (Franschhoek) $25. 85 *—K.F. (9/1/2003)*

Chamonix 2001 Pinotage (Franschhoek) $17. 88 *—K.F. (9/1/2003)*

CIRRUS

Cirrus 2005 Syrah (Coastal Region) $NA. A collboration between Ernie Els, Jean Englebrecht, and Californian Silver Oak Cellars owner Ray Duncan, this South African Shiraz contains a touch of Viognier, which lends a lovely floral component to the nose. On the palate, there's blackberry and plum with a gentle spiciness. Unique and velvety, the wine displays the clean minerality that typifies South African wines. 89 *—S.K. (7/1/2007)*

Cirrus 2004 Syrah (Coastal Region) $58. The touch of Viognier (6 %)adds extra character to this rich Syrah, which is lead by white pepper on the nose and assertive, floral aromatics. Flavors of violet, plum and dark berry on the palate are big, but the overall character is balanced. 87 *—S.K. (7/1/2007)*

CLOS MALVERNE

Clos Malverne 1998 Cabernet-Pinotage Cabernet Blend (Stellenbosch) $17. 85 *—K.F. (4/1/2003)*

Clos Malverne 2000 Basket Pressed Cabernet Sauvignon (Stellenbosch) $16. 83 *—K.F. (9/1/2003)*

Clos Malverne 2004 Cabernet Sauvignon-Merlot (Stellenbosch) $NA. 92 *—R.V. (11/1/2006)*

Clos Malverne 2001 Limited Release Cabernet Sauvignon-Merlot (Stellenbosch) $67. 90 *—R.V. (11/1/2006)*

Clos Malverne 2002 Cabernet Sauvignon-Shiraz (Stellenbosch) $16. 88 *—M.M. (4/1/2005)*

Clos Malverne 1999 Basket Pressed Cabernet Sauvignon-Shiraz (Stellenbosch) $16. 83 *—K.F. (9/1/2003)*

Clos Malverne 2001 Pinotage (Stellenbosch) $16. 82 *—M.M. (4/1/2005)*

Clos Malverne 2002 Reserve Pinotage (Stellenbosch) $17. 86 *—M.D. (5/1/2006)*

Clos Malverne 2001 Reserve Pinotage (Stellenbosch) $17. 86 *—K.F. (9/1/2003)*

Clos Malverne 2000 Reserve Pinotage (Stellenbosch) $17. 84 *—K.F. (9/1/2003)*

Clos Malverne 2001 Auret Red Blend (Stellenbosch) $17. 85 *—M.M. (4/1/2005)*

Clos Malverne 1999 Auret Red Blend (Stellenbosch) $17. 84 *—K.F. (1/1/2004)*

Clos Malverne 2001 Sauvignon Blanc (Stellenbosch) $15. 88 *—K.F. (4/1/2003)*

Clos Malverne 1999 Shiraz (Stellenbosch) $13. 83 *(10/1/2001)*

CONSTANTIA GLEN

Constantia Glen 2006 Sauvignon Blanc (Constantia) $0. Intense minerality melds with lush, tropical fruit—an apt reflection of the cool-climate Constantia terroir. The wine is elegant and expressive with a clean, fresh character that's wonderfully food-friendly. Imported by Frederick Wildman & Sons, Ltd. 89 *—S.K. (7/1/2007)*

CULRAITHIN

Culraithin 2003 Merlot (Paarl) $34. This Merlot is a hit from start to finish, with its herbal, earthy and spiced meat notes, elegant, savory fruit and spice flavors and good finish. It's restrained but deliciously classy. 91 Editors' Choice *—S.K. (7/1/2007)*

Culraithin 2002 Syrah (Paarl) $34. 91 Cellar Selection *—M.D. (12/31/2006)*

DANIE DE WET

Danie de Wet 2003 Bateleur Chardonnay (Robertson) $45. This wine has a restrained, elegant character that offers minerality and deep Chardonnay fruit on the palate. Aromas of lemon and spice on the nose are followed by full-bodied flavors and a toasted nut finish. Poised and pretty, it will pair well with most dishes. 87 *—S.K. (11/15/2007)*

Danie de Wet 2000 Bateleur Chardonnay (Robertson) $31. 88 *—K.F. (4/1/2003)*

Danie de Wet 2005 Limestone Hill Chardonnay (Robertson) $15. Aromas of green apples and grass take the lead on this unwooded Chardonnay from pioneer South African Chardonnay vintner Danie de Wet. A Chablis-style character follows, with flavors of peaches and nuts, and the citrus adds a pleasurable zing to the finish. 85 *—S.K. (3/1/2007)*

DARLING CELLARS

Darling Cellars 1999 DC Cabernet Sauvignon (Coastal Region) $13. 87 *—K.F. (4/1/2003)*

Darling Cellars 1999 Onyx Cabernet Sauvignon (Groenekloof) $20. 82 *—K.F. (4/1/2003)*

Darling Cellars 2000 DC Chardonnay (Swartland-GroeneKloof) $13. 84 *—K.F. (4/1/2003)*

Darling Cellars 1999 Onyx Chardonnay (Groenekloof) $15. 85 *—K.F. (9/1/2003)*

Darling Cellars 1999 DC Merlot (Swartland-GroeneKloof) $13. 84 *—K.F. (4/1/2003)*

Darling Cellars 1999 DC Pinotage (Coastal Region) $22. 85 *—K.F. (4/1/2003)*

Darling Cellars 1999 Onyx Pinotage (Swartland-GroeneKloof) $22. 83 *—K.F. (4/1/2003)*

Darling Cellars 2001 Onyx Kroon Red Blend (Groenekloof) $25. 85 *—K.F. (9/1/2003)*

Darling Cellars 2001 DC Sauvignon Blanc (Swartland-GroeneKloof) $13. 84 *—K.F. (4/1/2003)*

DASHBOSCH

Dashbosch 2005 Chenin Blanc (Worcester) $NA. 85 *—R.V. (11/15/2005)*

Dashbosch 2005 Cape Concert Seaside White Chenin Blanc (Worcester) $NA. 84 *—R.V. (11/15/2005)*

DAVID FROST

David Frost 2000 Chardonnay (Western Cape) $NA. 87 *—S.H. (1/1/2002)*

David Frost 2001 Sauvignon Blanc (Western Cape) $NA. 87 *—S.H. (1/1/2002)*

DC

DC 1999 Shiraz (Coastal Region) $23. 88 *—K.F. (4/1/2003)*

DE GRENDEL

De Grendel 2006 Merlot (Durbanville) $NA. Licorice, currant and an enticing combination of spices characterize this cool-climate Merlot. Round and seamless, but with plenty of character. The finish lingers. 88 *—S.K. (7/1/2007)*

De Grendel 2005 Tijgerberg Merlot (Durbanville) $20. Winemaker Charles Hopkins has a fondness for the more austere Saint-Émilion style, and it shows in this taut but expressive Merlot. Though restrained and elegant, the wine exhibits energetic aromas of red fruit and spice, and on the palate is rounded out by hints of chocolate and coffee. Pair with lamb or duck. 86 *—S.K. (7/1/2007)*

De Grendel 2006 Tijgerberg Sauvignon Blanc (Durbanville) $17. Rich, tropical fruit and flowers intermingle on the nose of this elegant white from Durbanville. On the palate, it's a combination of full and flavorful—white fruits and fragrant flowers—as well as crisp and clean. the overall character is delicate and balanced. 89 *—S.K. (7/1/2007)*

DE MEYE

De Meye 1999 Cabernet Sauvignon (Stellenbosch) $16. 85 *—K.F. (4/1/2003)*

De Meye 2006 Rosé Shiraz (Stellenbosch) $10. The lovely pale salmon color of this Stellenbosch Rosé speaks of its delicate nature, and on the nose and palate, the wine is light and playful. Good acidity, fresh fruit flavors and a crisp, clean finish make this a fun and friendly summer wine that will pair well with a variety of dishes. 85 Best Buy *—S.K. (7/1/2007)*

De Meye 2000 Shiraz (South Africa) $16. 86 *—K.F. (4/1/2003)*

DE TOREN

De Toren 2004 Fusion V Bordeaux Blend (Stellenbosch) $45. Complex, rich and full of smoky clove and dark fruit, this impressive blend is food friendly and will age beautifully. Warming spices like cinnamon on the nose and palate mingle with toasted oak and anise, and the overall mouthfeel is supple and smooth. Attractive to varied palates but also has a South African character that sets it apart. 88 *—S.K. (11/15/2007)*

De Toren 2004 Z Bordeaux Blend (Coastal Region) $30. Plum and rose on the nose introduces this beautiful blend from De Toren, and on the palate, it shows ample structure and firm tannins with a shock of acidity that brings freshness to the overall flavor profile. Subtle, reserved strains of spice and soft fruit flavors end up with a clean and fresh twist. A unique and attractive wine at a good price. **91** *—S.K. (11/15/2007)*

DE TRAFFORD

de Trafford 1999 Reserve Bordeaux Blend (Helderberg) $35. 87 *—K.F. (8/1/2003)*

de Trafford 2004 Chenin Blanc (Stellenbosch) $25. 91 *—R.V. (11/15/2005)*

de Trafford 2002 Chenin Blanc (Helderberg) $17. 86 *—K.F. (4/1/2003)*

de Trafford 2001 Straw Wine Chenin Blanc (Helderberg) $25. 88 *—K.F. (12/1/2003)*

de Trafford 2001 Pinot Noir (Helderberg) $40. 86 *—K.F. (9/1/2003)*

de Trafford 2000 Shiraz (Helderberg) $40. 88 *—K.F. (8/1/2003)*

DE WETSHOF

De Wetshof 2000 Bateleur Chardonnay (Robertson) $20. 90 *—R.V. (7/1/2002)*

De Wetshof 2005 Bon Vallon Chardonnay (Robertson) $16. Strong citrus aromas and flavors—predominately lemon—permeate this offering from De Wetshof. There's some cream on the nose, too, joined by mild spice tones on the palate. It finishes clean with little bother. Simple but appetizing. **86** *—S.K. (3/1/2007)*

De Wetshof 2002 Bon Vallon Chardonnay (Robertson) $14. 87 *—K.F. (4/1/2003)*

De Wetshof 2001 Bon Vallon Chardonnay (Robertson) $12. 90 Best Buy *—R.V. (7/1/2002)*

De Wetshof 2000 Bon Vallon Chardonnay (Robertson) $10. 89 Best Buy *(9/1/2001)*

De Wetshof 2002 D'Honneur Chardonnay (Robertson) $24. 91 Editors' Choice *—M.M. (4/1/2005)*

De Wetshof 2002 Lesca Chardonnay (Robertson) $16. 86 *—K.F. (4/1/2003)*

De Wetshof 2001 Lesca Chardonnay (Robertson) $14. 87 *—R.V. (7/1/2002)*

De Wetshof 2000 Edeloes Noble Late Harvest Riesling (Robertson) $65. 88 *—K.F. (12/1/2003)*

De Wetshof 2002 Rhine Riesling (Robertson) $12. 85 *—K.F. (8/1/2003)*

DELAIRE

Delaire 2005 Sauvignon Blanc (Stellenbosch) $19. Tropical fruit and herbal notes comprise this well-balanced, lively wine. Citrus and spice linger on the palate and the wine has more complexity than many of its SB cohorts. Ideal with shellfish. **87** *—S.K. (3/1/2007)*

DEWAAL/VITERWYK ESTATE

DeWaal/Viterwyk Estate 2001 Pinotage (Stellenbosch) $17. 88 *—K.F. (4/1/2003)*

DeWaal/Viterwyk Estate 2001 Top of the Hill Pinotage (Stellenbosch) $45. 88 *—K.F. (4/1/2003)*

DIEMERSDAL

Diemersdal 2003 Cabernet Sauvignon (Durbanville) $25. From Tygerberg, this attractive Cabernet offers smoked sausage and spice on the nose and a wonderful balance of pepper, smoke and juicy fruit on the palate. It's assertive and ageable but good now. A hint of restrained minerality means it will pair well with myriad foods. **86** *—S.K. (11/15/2007)*

Diemersdal 2003 Pinotage (Durbanville) $24. Plum, ripe blackberry and gamey spice give this Pinotage a nice balance of elegant and exotic flavors, with notes of herb and an overall pretty berry character adding dimension. The wine is accessible and its minerality gives it good food-pairing potential. **84** *—S.K. (12/15/2007)*

Diemersdal 2004 Matys Red Blend (Durbanville) $18. Herbs, spice and an earthy undertone of leather give this affordable sipper character and weight. The flavors of raspberry and blueberry are integrated but vibrant, and the texture smooth. An elegant choice that will pair well with almost any meat-driven dish. **89** *—S.K. (11/15/2007)*

Diemersdal 2003 Shiraz (Durbanville) $25. Subtle, smooth and elegant on the finish, this is both approachable and distinctive. The wine is balanced with bright fruit and an underpinning of smoke and spice. A very versatile food pairing choice. **88** *—S.K. (11/15/2007)*

DIEU DONNE

Dieu Donne 2000 Merlot (Franschhoek) $18. 86 *—K.F. (8/1/2003)*

Dieu Donne 1999 Merlot (Franschhoek) $17. 88 *—K.F. (4/1/2003)*

Dieu Donne 1999 Pinotage (Franschhoek) $17. 88 *—K.F. (4/1/2003)*

Dieu Donne 2001 Sauvignon Blanc (Franschhoek) $15. 87 *(8/1/2002)*

DOUGLAS GREEN

Douglas Green 2004 Sauvignon Blanc (Western Cape) $10. 87 Best Buy *—M.D. (3/1/2006)*

Douglas Green 2003 Shiraz (Western Cape) $10. 81 *—M.D. (5/1/2006)*

DU PREEZ ESTATE

Du Preez Estate 2000 Merlot (Goudini) $11. 88 Best Buy *—K.F. (4/1/2003)*

Du Preez Estate 2001 Sauvignon Blanc (Goudini) $9. 88 Best Buy *—K.F. (4/1/2003)*

Du Preez Estate 2000 Shiraz (Goudini) $11. 86 *—K.F. (4/1/2003)*

Du Preez Estate 1999 Hanepoot Estate Wine White Blend (South Africa) $10. 86 *—K.F. (11/15/2003)*

DURBANVILLE HILLS

Durbanville Hills 2005 Sauvignon Blanc (Durbanville) $12. 83 *—M.D. (3/1/2006)*

Durbanville Hills 2003 Sauvignon Blanc (Durbanville) $12. 87 Best Buy *—M.M. (11/15/2004)*

Durbanville Hills 2002 Durbanville Hills Sauvignon Blanc (Durbanville) $12. 86 *—K.F. (4/1/2003)*

Durbanville Hills 2001 Rhinofields Sauvignon Blanc (Durbanville) $17. 88 *—K.F. (4/1/2003)*

Durbanville Hills 2003 Shiraz (Durbanville) $14. 84 *—M.D. (5/1/2006)*

Durbanville Hills 2001 Durbanville Hills Shiraz (South Africa) $15. 87 *—K.F. (4/1/2003)*

EIKENDAL

Eikendal 2000 Classique Bordeaux Blend (Stellenbosch) $30. 87 *—M.M. (11/15/2004)*

Eikendal 2003 Chardonnay (Stellenbosch) $22. 87 *—M.M. (12/15/2004)*

ENGELBRECHT ELS VINEYARDS

Engelbrecht Els Vineyards 2003 Red Blend (Western Cape) $45. 89 *—M.D. (7/1/2006)*

Engelbrecht Els Vineyards 2004 Proprietor's Blend Red Blend (Western Cape) $44. A collaboration between Rust en Vrede's Jean Engelbrecht and golf star Ernie Els, this blend is a balance of fruity, spicy Shiraz and earthy Bordeaux—a testament to the two styles the winemaking partners enjoy. On the nose are hints of mint and spice, and on the palate, heavy oak adds a woody element. Ample structure but still smooth. **89** *—S.K. (3/1/2007)*

ERNIE ELS

Ernie Els 2003 Limited Release Bordeaux Blend (Stellenbosch) $93. 95 Editors' Choice *—R.V. (11/1/2006)*

EVENTIDE CELLAR

Eventide Cellar 2004 Cabernet Sauvignon (Wellington) $17. An aroma bursting with jammy fruit—think black currant and blueberry—is followed by a full-bodied palate with hints of cinnamon spice. It's wildly fruity but at the same time dry on the finish, and hearty tannins insure that the fruit does not completely steamroll the whole production. Lots to like here but perhaps just a little too fruity and one-dimensional for any truly serious contemplation. **84** *—S.K. (3/1/2007)*

Eventide Cellar 2006 Sauvignon Blanc (Wellington) $NA. Bright citrus notes of lemon and pineapple start the show with this cheerful, versatile white from the lesser-known winemaking region of Wellington, and in the glass, you'll find delicious flavors of tropical passionfruit and lemon. Clean and light but with some dimension in the midpalate. **89** *—S.K. (7/1/2007)*

Eventide Cellar 2004 Shiraz (Wellington) $17. Deep, rich aromas of cinnamon, mocha and pepper are followed by a burst of berry fruit and firm tannins. It's not a very complex wine, but its fruity, ripe flavors are enjoyable and dense. **85** *—S.K. (3/1/2007)*

Eventide Cellar 2002 Wellington Shiraz (South Africa) $15. 87 *—J.C. (11/15/2005)*

Eventide Cellar 2006 Viognier (Wellington) $16. Spicy, fresh and floral, the nose on this Viognier immediately marks it as a wine to be savored. On the palate, it's lighter and fresher than the typical Viognier, with its white peach and lemon, but still full of dimension. Balanced acids keep it dancing on the tongue. Pair with chicken or fish. **90** *—S.K. (7/1/2007)*

EXCELSIOR

Excelsior 2006 Chardonnay (Robertson) $10. Mouthwatering apple and a lively acidity make this a Chardonnay that will appeal to vinophiles who like a crisper white wine. But for the tartness and clean edge there's a weight and creaminess on the palate that rounds this wine out. A good, accessible Chardonnay at a very good price, it could become a favorite weekday wine. **86** —*S.K. (6/1/2007)*

Excelsior 2005 Chardonnay (Robertson) $10. Apple pie and fig, along with some lemon, lime and peach, are found in this friendly wine from the De Wet family estate dating back to the 17th century. The finish is broad with toasted oak and vanilla. Pair with seafood. **84** —*S.K. (3/1/2007)*

Excelsior 2002 Estate Chardonnay (Robertson) $8. 85 —*K.F. (9/1/2003)*

Excelsior 2004 Paddock Shiraz (Robertson) $10. 85 Best Buy —*M.D. (9/1/2006)*

FAIRVALLEY

Fairvalley 2004 Cabernet Sauvignon (Western Cape) $9. 85 Best Buy —*M.D. (12/31/2006)*

Fairvalley 2005 Chenin Blanc (Coastal Region) $8. This crisp style of Chenin features tropical fruit, pineapple and pear flavors and an overall balanced, rounded character. At this price and with its food-friendly balance of acid and weight, the wine is a great everyday choice and will pair well with chicken salad or hard cheeses like an English Derby. **86** —*S.K. (7/1/2007)*

Fairvalley 2004 Pinotage (Coastal Region) $9. 88 Best Buy —*M.D. (11/15/2006)*

FAIRVIEW

Fairview 2002 Pegleg Carignane (Paarl) $23. 88 —*M.M. (12/15/2004)*

Fairview 2001 Pegleg Carignane (Paarl) $25. 89 —*K.F. (4/1/2003)*

Fairview 2004 Mourvèdre (Coastal Region) $17. 86 —*M.D. (7/1/2006)*

Fairview 2006 Pinotage (Coastal Region) $15. Subtle scents and flavors of dark berry, cedar and spice make this Pinotage both embraceable and friendly, though it's still full of the distinctive Pinotage smoke and rubber that tend to divide drinkers when it comes to this grape. The wine has ample body and structure and will age nicely. **84** —*S.K. (12/15/2007)*

Fairview 2003 Pinotage (Coastal Region) $14. 85 —*M.D. (3/1/2006)*

Fairview 2002 Pinotage (Coastal Region) $12. 86 —*M.M. (12/15/2004)*

Fairview 2001 Pinotage (Coastal Region) $13. 87 —*K.F. (4/1/2003)*

Fairview 2005 Pinotage (Paarl) $14. This is for real Pinotage lovers, so bashful drinkers, beware. The nose bursts with ripe red fruit and spice—Pinotage hallmarks—and on the palate, lively, spicy and smoky flavors of berry and savory spice abound. It's a wine full of personality and is best enjoyed with a dish of grilled spicy ribs or ethnic food that can tame its wildness. **86** —*S.K. (11/15/2007)*

Fairview 2001 Primo Pinotage (Paarl) $8. 86 —*K.F. (4/1/2003)*

Fairview 2001 SMV Red Blend (Coastal Region) $17. 88 —*M.M. (12/15/2004)*

Fairview 2005 Sauvignon Blanc (Coastal Region) $12. 84 —*M.D. (3/1/2006)*

Fairview 2002 Sauvignon Blanc (Coastal Region) $10. 85 —*K.F. (4/1/2003)*

Fairview 2001 Oom Pagel Sémillon (Paarl) $25. 89 —*K.F. (4/1/2003)*

Fairview 2004 Shiraz (Coastal Region) $15. Black fruit and white pepper on the nose, followed by pronounced oak and spice. There's an interesting earthiness here—cedar, nuts—but the fruit gets a little lost. Lingering finish. **85** —*S.K. (3/1/2007)*

Fairview 2001 Shiraz (Paarl) $13. 86 —*M.M. (11/15/2004)*

Fairview 1999 Shiraz (Paarl) $15. 84 *(10/1/2001)*

Fairview 2003 The Beacon Shiraz (Paarl) $36. The minerality of this wine is clear from the start, mingling with round layers of cherry, violet and spice. Good structure in the mouth. The wine is both bold and juicy while at the same time showing an elegant restraint. A very interesting choice for the glass or the table. **87** —*S.K. (11/15/2007)*

Fairview 2002 Beacon Shiraz (Paarl) $28. 90 Cellar Selection —*M.M. (11/15/2004)*

Fairview 2001 Beacon Shiraz (Paarl) $30. 87 —*K.F. (4/1/2003)*

Fairview 2001 Cyril Back Shiraz (Paarl) $26. 85 —*M.M. (11/15/2004)*

Fairview 1999 Cyril Back Shiraz (South Africa) $24. 88 *(11/1/2001)*

Fairview 2000 Cyril Back Shiraz Shiraz (Paarl) $20. 85 —*K.F. (4/1/2003)*

Fairview 2003 Jakkalsfontein Shiraz (Swartland) $35. 91 —*M.D. (7/1/2006)*

Fairview 2002 Jakkalsfontein Shiraz (Swartland) $28. 88 —*M.M. (11/15/2004)*

Fairview 2002 Solitude Shiraz (Paarl) $34. 89 —*M.D. (5/1/2006)*

Fairview 2001 Solitude Shiraz (Paarl) $20. 87 —*K.F. (4/1/2003)*

Fairview 2004 Viognier (Coastal Region) $19. 88 —*M.D. (9/1/2006)*

Fairview 2003 Viognier (South Africa) $18. 85 —*M.M. (12/15/2004)*

Fairview 2002 Viognier (Paarl) $18. 83 —*K.F. (9/1/2003)*

FALSE BAY

False Bay 2002 Chardonnay (South Africa) $NA. 85 —*M.M. (7/4/2004)*

False Bay 2000 Chenin Blanc (Coastal Region) $9. 84 —*M.S. (4/1/2002)*

False Bay 2002 Merlot (South Africa) $NA. 84 —*M.M. (7/4/2004)*

False Bay 2002 Pinotage (South Africa) $NA. 85 —*M.M. (7/4/2004)*

False Bay 2000 Pinotage (Coastal Region) $9. 85 —*M.S. (4/1/2002)*

False Bay 2000 Rhône Red Blend (Coastal Region) $9. 85 —*M.M. (4/1/2002)*

False Bay 2002 Sauvignon Blanc (South Africa) $NA. 84 —*M.M. (7/4/2004)*

FISH HOEK

Fish Hoek 2005 Sauvignon Blanc (Western Cape) $11. 85 —*M.D. (7/1/2006)*

FISH HOOK

Fish Hook 2005 Merlot (Western Cape) $11. 83 —*M.D. (11/1/2006)*

FLAGSTONE

Flagstone 2003 The Music Room Cabernet Sauvignon (South Africa) $40. 87 —*M.D. (9/1/2006)*

Flagstone 2004 Dark Horse Shiraz (Western Cape) $40. 89 —*M.D. (7/1/2006)*

FLAMINGO BAY

Flamingo Bay 2001 Red Blend (Coastal Region) $7. 84 —*K.F. (4/1/2003)*

Flamingo Bay 2001 White Blend (Coastal Region) $7. 84 —*K.F. (4/1/2003)*

FLAT ROOF MANOR

Flat Roof Manor 2004 Pinot Grigio (Stellenbosch) $NA. 87 *(2/1/2006)*

FLEUR DU CAP

Fleur Du Cap 2001 Cabernet Sauvignon (Stellenbosch) $14. Tobacco spice and cherry dominate this unfiltered Cabernet. It's full-bodied with moderately sturdy tannins and the finish is persistent and pleasurable. A good, accessible Cabernet that is just right and does not require a great amount of philosophizing. Pair it with a rack of lamb and leave the rest to nature. **86** —*S.K. (6/1/2007)*

Fleur du Cap 2001 Cabernet Sauvignon (Coastal Region) $14. 86 —*M.D. (12/31/2006)*

Fleur du Cap 2000 Cabernet Sauvignon (Coastal Region) $13. 85 —*K.F. (4/1/2003)*

Fleur du Cap 1998 Cabernet Sauvignon (Stellenbosch) $10. 84 *(11/15/2002)*

Fleur du Cap 1992 Cabernet Sauvignon (Coastal Region) $12. 84 *(9/1/1999)*

Fleur du Cap 2000 Unfiltered Cabernet Sauvignon (Stellenbosch) $15. 87 *(11/15/2002)*

Fleur du Cap 1998 Unfiltered Cabernet Sauvignon (Coastal Region) $23. 84 —*K.F. (8/1/2003)*

Fleur Du Cap 2005 Chardonnay (Stellenbosch) $13. This barrel-fermented Chardonnay has a lively nose of apricot and melon. It's zesty, but has a balanced weight and complexity of nut and toasted oak that gives it substance. Delicious and intriguing, it will pair well with oysters and smoked seafood. **88 Best Buy** —*S.K. (3/1/2007)*

Fleur du Cap 2001 Chardonnay (Stellenbosch) $9. 85 *(11/15/2002)*

Fleur du Cap 2000 Chardonnay (South Africa) $9. 85 —*M.M. (4/1/2002)*

Fleur du Cap 1998 Chardonnay (Coastal Region) $9. 85 —*M.S. (9/1/1999)*

Fleur du Cap 2000 Unfiltered Chardonnay (Coastal Region) $15. 86 —*K.F. (9/1/2003)*

Fleur du Cap 2001 Unfilterted Chardonnay (Stellenbosch) $15. 86 *(11/15/2002)*

Fleur du Cap 2003 Chenin Blanc (Stellenbosch) $10. 83 —*R.V. (11/15/2005)*

Fleur du Cap 2004 Merlot (Stellenbosch) $12. 87 Best Buy —*M.D. (12/31/2006)*

Fleur du Cap 2001 Merlot (Coastal Region) $15. 86 —*K.F. (8/1/2003)*

Fleur du Cap 2000 Merlot (Stellenbosch) $10. 84 *(11/15/2002)*

Fleur du Cap 1996 Merlot (South Africa) $12. 82 *(9/1/1999)*

Fleur du Cap 2001 Unfiltered Merlot (Coastal Region) $23. 88 —*M.D. (12/31/2006)*

Fleur du Cap 2000 Unfiltered Merlot (Stellenbosch) $15. 86 *(11/15/2002)*

Fleur du Cap 1998 Unfiltered Merlot (Coastal Region) $15. 85 *—K.F. (8/1/2003)*

Fleur Du Cap 2004 Pinotage (Coastal Region) $12. A very enjoyable Pinotage at a good price. Plum and a rounded, juicy nose lead into balanced, elegant flavors of red berry, smoke and spice. The wine is balanced with good acid, flavor and structure but not aggressive, making it not only a good food wine, but also a great intro to Pinotage. Imported by Maisons Marques & Domaines USA. **86** *—S.K. (11/15/2007)*

Fleur du Cap 2000 Pinotage (Coastal Region) $13. 86 *—K.F. (4/1/2003)*

Fleur du Cap 1993 Pinotage (Coastal Region) $12. 83 *(9/1/1999)*

Fleur du Cap 2004 Pinotage (Stellenbosch) $14. 85 *—M.D. (12/31/2006)*

Fleur Du Cap 2005 Sauvignon Blanc (Stellenbosch) $10. Tropical fruit flavors of melon and passionfruit shine on the nose of this approachable SB. The wine is medium-bodied and multi-layered, but the acidity creates a clean, cutting edge that plays off of the fruit. Both lively and robust. **87 Best Buy** *—S.K. (7/1/2007)*

Fleur du Cap 2004 Sauvignon Blanc (Coastal Region) $11. 87 Best Buy *—M.M. (4/1/2005)*

Fleur du Cap 2003 Sauvignon Blanc (Coastal Region) $10. 86 Best Buy *—M.M. (11/15/2004)*

Fleur du Cap 2002 Sauvignon Blanc (Stellenbosch) $9. 86 Best Buy *— (11/15/2002)*

Fleur du Cap 2000 Sauvignon Blanc (Coastal Region) $13. 85 *—M.S. (4/1/2002)*

Fleur Du Cap 2006 Unfiltered Sauvignon Blanc (Stellenbosch) $18. This full-bodied Sauvignon Blanc offers a heady nose of gooseberry and mango, while on the palate, tropical fruit mingles with herbs, giving it weight and dimension. The mouthfeel is full but not heavy. Imported by Maisons Marques & Domaines USA. **85** *—S.K. (7/1/2007)*

Fleur Du Cap 2005 Unfiltered Sauvignon Blanc (Stellenbosch) $16. Arresting aromas of orange peel and peach start this clean, fresh and minerally wine. A decidedly firm acidity keeps the wine crisp and refreshing, and its tropical flavors are appetizing, but it may be too austere and even on the lean side for palates that prefer a little more curve to their SB. Still, a delicious food wine and great for a hot day. **84** *—S.K. (6/1/2007)*

Fleur du Cap 2002 Unfiltered Sauvignon Blanc (Stellenbosch) $15. 87 *(11/15/2002)*

Fleur du Cap 2001 Unfiltered Sémillon (Stellenbosch) $15. 87 *(11/15/2002)*

Fleur Du Cap 2003 Shiraz (Stellenbosch) $14. Just looking at this wine whets the appetite, with its dark, dense ruby color hinting at the rich fruit that awaits. The nose is ripe and lush, with a touch of oaky spice and the flavors sturdy and round. A substantial backbone means the wine can age, but it's very good now, especially if paired with duck or grilled steak. **87** *—S.K. (6/1/2007)*

Fleur du Cap 2000 Shiraz (Coastal Region) $15. 85 *—K.F. (4/1/2003)*

Fleur du Cap 1996 Noble Late Harvest White Blend (Coastal Region) $8. 87 Best Buy *(9/1/1999)*

FORRESTER'S

Forrester's 2002 Petit Chenin Chenin Blanc (Stellenbosch) $9. 87 Best Buy *—K.F. (4/1/2003)*

FORT SIMON

Fort Simon 2004 Chenin Blanc (Stellenbosch) $NA. 85 *—R.V. (11/15/2005)*

GENERAL BILIMORIA

General Bilimoria 2002 Pinotage (Stellenbosch) $11. 84 *—M.M. (7/4/2004)*

General Bilimoria 2003 Olifants River Red Blend (Olifants River) $8. 80 *—M.M. (7/4/2004)*

General Bilimoria 2003 Olifants River White Blend (Olifants River) $8. 82 *—M.M. (7/4/2004)*

GENESIS

Genesis 1999 Shiraz (Stellenbosch) $25. 89 *—M.M. (4/1/2002)*

GILGA

Gilga 2000 Shiraz (Stellenbosch) $45. 87 *—K.F. (8/1/2003)*

GLEN CARLOU

Glen Carlou 2005 Chardonnay (Paarl) $16. Citrus and grassy notes lead into a somewhat one-dimensional tropical fruit and spice flavors. The finish is round and lingering, but overall, the wine needs more character and substance. **82** *—S.K. (3/1/2007)*

Glen Carlou 2004 Chardonnay (Paarl) $16. 81 *—M.D. (3/1/2006)*

Glen Carlou 2001 Chardonnay (Paarl) $14. 83 *—K.F. (4/1/2003)*

Glen Carlou 2000 Chardonnay (Paarl) $14. 86 *—R.V. (7/1/2002)*

Glen Carlou 1999 Chardonnay (Coastal Region) $14. 87 *—R.V. (7/1/2002)*

Glen Carlou 2003 Grand Classique Meritage (Paarl) $20. Glen Carlou's wines are far from shy and this delicious Meritage from Paarl has all of the bold notes you'd expect from this producer. The nose is elegant, with waves of cinnamon, tobacco and spice, and on the palate, flavors of red berry, spice and smoke are distinctive but harmonious. This is a wine that will continue to unfold as it ages. **91 Editors' Choice** *—S.K. (12/15/2007)*

Glen Carlou 2002 Grand Classique Meritage (Paarl) $18. 87 *—M.D. (5/1/2006)*

Glen Carlou 2005 Syrah (Paarl) $22. This assertive wine has spicy notes of chocolate, mulberry and oak on the nose, and ripe berry and clove flavors on the palate. The mouthfeel is full and round. The wine is rich and balanced but needs some time. **87** *—S.K. (3/1/2007)*

GOATS DO ROAM WINE CO.

Goats do Roam Wine Co. 2005 Bored Doe Bordeaux Blend (Coastal Region) $13. Enticing aromas of raspberry, spice and smoke immediately attract with this Bordeaux blend. Bright, deep fruit flavors are cheerful and approachable without being too simple. A light touch of oak adds further character. **86** *—S.K. (11/15/2007)*

Goats do Roam Wine Co. 2004 Bored Doe Bordeaux Blend (Coastal Region) $14. 84 *—M.D. (9/1/2006)*

Goats do Roam Wine Co. 2005 Goat Door Chardonnay (Coastal Region) $14. 85 *—M.D. (9/1/2006)*

Goats do Roam Wine Co. 2001 Goat-Roti Red Blend (Western Cape) $17. 86 *—K.F. (9/1/2003)*

Goats do Roam Wine Co. 2003 Goats do Roam Red Blend (Western Cape) $10. 85 Best Buy *—M.M. (4/1/2005)*

Goats do Roam Wine Co. 2002 Goats do Roam Red Blend (Paarl) $10. 84 *—K.F. (1/1/2004)*

Goats do Roam Wine Co. 2005 The Goatfather Red Blend (Coastal Region) $15. This coastal region red from the cleverly named Goats do Roam winery is named from the Barbera and Primitivo grapes that comprise it. It's a somewhat lean offering but for the oak and spice on the nose and some bright berry flavors, needing more balance and flavior to really assert itself. **83** *—S.K. (3/1/2007)*

Goats do Roam Wine Co. 2003 Goat-Roti Rhône Red Blend (Western Cape) $18. 88 *—M.D. (7/1/2006)*

Goats do Roam Wine Co. 2004 Goats do Roam in Villages Rhône Red Blend (Coastal Region) $13. 87 *—M.D. (7/1/2006)*

Goats do Roam Wine Co. 2006 Goats do Roam Rosé Rosé Blend (Coastal Region) $10. A shocking pink color and sweet, playful nose prepare you for the vibrant cherry and strawberry flavors to follow. It's full-flavored and balanced with some citrus, but not the most complex wine in the world. Good for pairing with summer salads and light dishes. **84** *—S.K. (3/1/2007)*

Goats do Roam Wine Co. 2003 Goats do Roam Rosé Blend (South Africa) $10. 87 Best Buy *—M.M. (12/15/2004)*

Goats do Roam Wine Co. 2002 Goats do Roam White Blend (Western Cape) $10. 86 *—K.F. (1/1/2004)*

Goats do Roam Wine Co. 2003 Goats do Roam in Villages White Blend (Western Cape) $14. 87 *—M.M. (4/1/2005)*

GÔIYA

Gôiya 2004 Cabernet Sauvignon (Western Cape) $8. 86 Best Buy *—M.D. (3/1/2006)*

Gôiya 2004 Chardonnay (Western Cape) $7. 82 *—J.C. (11/15/2005)*

Gôiya 2004 Chardonnay-Sauvignon (Olifants River) $7. 84 Best Buy *—J.C. (11/15/2005)*

Gôiya 2004 Merlot (Western Cape) $8. 85 Best Buy *—M.D. (3/1/2006)*

Gôiya 2003 Merlot (Western Cape) $7. 84 Best Buy *—M.M. (7/1/2005)*

Gôiya 2004 Shiraz (Western Cape) $7. 85 Best Buy *—J.C. (11/15/2005)*

GOLDEN KAAN

Golden Kaan 2004 Cabernet Sauvignon (Western Cape) $10. 85 Best Buy *—M.D. (3/1/2006)*

Golden Kaan 2003 Cabernet Sauvignon (Western Cape) $10. 84 *—J.C. (11/15/2005)*

Golden Kaan 2003 Reserve Selection Cabernet Sauvignon (Western Cape) $14. 88 *—M.D. (7/1/2006)*

Golden Kaan 2005 Chardonnay (Western Cape) $10. 84 *—M.D. (12/31/2006)*

Golden Kaan 2004 Chardonnay (Western Cape) $10. 84 *—J.C. (11/15/2005)*

Golden Kaan 2005 Chenin Blanc (Western Cape) $10. 85 Best Buy *—R.V. (11/15/2005)*

Golden Kaan 2004 Merlot (Western Cape) $10. 84 *—M.D. (3/1/2006)*

Golden Kaan 2003 Merlot (Western Cape) $10. 82 *—J.C. (11/15/2005)*

Golden Kaan 2004 Pinotage (Western Cape) $10. 85 Best Buy *—M.D. (3/1/2006)*

Golden Kaan 2003 Pinotage (Western Cape) $10. 84 *—M.M. (12/15/2004)*

Golden Kaan 2006 Rosé Pinotage (Western Cape) $10. There's a pleasant combination of sweetness and citrus in this easy-drinking Pinotage rose, though its candied edge pushes the wine into the "garden party" sphere despite valiant efforts to keep it grounded. Strawberry, banana and lemon on the nose lead into a fresh burst of fruit and flowers on the palate. It lends itself to summertime drinking with salads and seafood. 83 *—S.K. (3/1/2007)*

Golden Kaan 2005 Sauvignon Blanc (Western Cape) $9. 85 Best Buy *—M.D. (11/15/2006)*

Golden Kaan 2004 Sauvignon Blanc (Western Cape) $10. 84 *—J.C. (11/15/2005)*

Golden Kaan 2003 Sauvignon Blanc (Western Cape) $10. 84 *—M.M. (12/15/2004)*

Golden Kaan 2005 Reserve Selection Sauvignon Blanc (Western Cape) $14. 84 *—M.D. (5/1/2006)*

Golden Kaan 2004 Shiraz (Western Cape) $10. 83 *—M.D. (3/1/2006)*

Golden Kaan 2003 Shiraz (Western Cape) $10. 85 Best Buy *—M.M. (12/15/2004)*

Golden Kaan 2003 Reserve Selection Shiraz (Western Cape) $14. 85 *—M.D. (5/1/2006)*

GRAHAM BECK

Graham Beck 2005 Gamekeeper's Reserve Cabernet Sauvignon (Robertson) $17. Soft spice and blackberry on the nose are followed by rich, balanced layers of mint, toast and berry. The wine has a minerality that adds a fresh note to the mix. A big wine but not overly complex, this is a Cabernet for spicy dishes and beef stew. Imported by GBW, LLC. 87 *—S.K. (12/15/2007)*

Graham Beck NV Brut Champagne Blend (Western Cape) $15. This offers very pretty flavors at a reasonable price, making it a good choice for everyday drinking or a celebration where quantity is needed. Buttery, warm aromas mingle with a crisp, flinty sparkle in the nose and on the palate. It's on the sweet side but that lively zip keeps the wine aloft. Half Pinot Noir, half Chardonnay. Imported by GBW, LLC. 85 *—S.K. (12/15/2007)*

Graham Beck 2005 Brut Rosé Champagne Blend (Western Cape) $18. An appealing ripe strawberry nose leads on this flirty, easy-drinking sparkling wine from South Africa. Freshness and a touch of delicate minerality in the aromas, followed by light, elegant flavors of strawberry and yeast, make it a lovely wine for a summer day or to pair with myriad dishes. Creamy but fresh on the tongue, the wine has good body for a rosé. Imported by GBW, LLC. 87 *—S.K. (12/15/2007)*

Graham Beck 2000 Chardonnay (Robertson) $10. 85 *—R.V. (9/10/2002)*

Graham Beck 2002 Premier Cuvée Blanc de Blancs Brut Chardonnay (Robertson) $22. An enticing nose of buttery oak and flavors of toast, minerality and yeast makes this ample-bodied sparkler an impressive solo sip or great when paired with richer foods like oysters or cream-based dishes. Creamy on the tongue and full of flavor, the wine is classic in style and well priced. Imported by GBW, LLC. 86 *—S.K. (12/15/2007)*

Graham Beck 2003 The William Barrel Selection Red Blend (Coastal Region) $17. Dusty, red berry aromas introduce this blend packed with soft, red berry fruit and a hint of rubber typical of Pinotage. Approachable and fun. Imported by GBW, LLC. 85 *—S.K. (12/15/2007)*

Graham Beck 2003 The Joshua Barrel Selection Shiraz (Coastal Region) $45. A smoky, spicy nose leads to a lovely integration of tannin and balance in this elegant wine. The touch of Viognier adds a pretty floral quality to the anise and smoke of the Shiraz. Long and lively finish. Imported by GBW, LLC. 90 *—S.K. (11/15/2007)*

GRANGEHURST

Grangehurst 1997 Cabernet Sauvignon-Merlot (Stellenbosch) $30. 84 *—M.S. (4/1/2002)*

Grangehurst 2000 Pinotage (Stellenbosch) $20. 87 *—M.D. (9/1/2006)*

Grangehurst 2000 Nikela Red Blend (Stellenbosch) $30. 84 *—M.D. (7/1/2006)*

GREAT WHITE WINES

Great White Wines 2004 Chardonnay (Western Cape) $9. 83 *—M.M. (12/15/2004)*

Great White Wines 2004 Chenin Blanc (Western Cape) $9. 86 Best Buy *—M.M. (12/15/2004)*

Great White Wines 2004 Sauvignon Blanc (Western Cape) $9. 84 *—M.M. (12/15/2004)*

GROENLAND

Groenland 2000 Cabernet Sauvignon (Stellenbosch) $13. 84 *—K.F. (9/1/2003)*

Groenland 2001 Shiraz (Stellenbosch) $13. 82 *—M.M. (3/1/2004)*

GROOT CONSTANTIA

Groot Constantia 2003 Gouverneurs Reserve Bordeaux Blend (Constantia) $32. 89 *—M.D. (9/1/2006)*

Groot Constantia 2003 Cabernet Sauvignon (Constantia) $20. From a producer of famed whites comes a beautiful Cabernet with an elegant, poised character. Mint, clove and deep berry on the nose are followed on the palate, where balanced tannins and spice offer serious flavor. The overall character is rich but softer, making it a lovely food wine. 88 *—S.K. (11/15/2007)*

Groot Constantia 2001 Cabernet Sauvignon (Constantia) $14. 81 *—M.M. (3/1/2004)*

Groot Constantia 2001 Gouverneur's Reserve Cabernet Sauvignon-Merlot (Constantia) $19. 85 *—M.M. (3/1/2004)*

Groot Constantia 2005 Merlot (Constantia) $21. This displays structured but elegant layers of cinnamon spice and soft berry and the finish is long and gentle. The nose is gamey and spicy but classically subdued. A delicious food wine with aging potential. 88 *—S.K. (7/1/2007)*

Groot Constantia 2002 Merlot (Constantia) $21. Cinnamon and spice on the nose and soft, integrated flavors on the palate characterize this wine from Groot Constantia, a producer of elegant, food-friendly wines. The wine is structured but balanced and mellow in style. Pair with pasta dishes and game. 86 *—S.K. (7/1/2007)*

Groot Constantia 2001 Merlot (Constantia) $17. 82 *—M.M. (7/1/2005)*

Groot Constantia 2002 Pinotage (Constantia) $21. 89 *—M.D. (9/1/2006)*

Groot Constantia 2001 Pinotage (Constantia) $16. 86 *—M.M. (3/1/2004)*

Groot Constantia 2004 Sauvignon Blanc (Constantia) $16. 86 *—M.D. (3/1/2006)*

Groot Constantia 2003 Sauvignon Blanc (Constantia) $16. 86 *—M.M. (3/1/2004)*

Groot Constantia 2000 Sauvignon Blanc (Constantia) $11. 83 *(1/1/2004)*

Groot Constantia 1997 Shiraz (Constantia) $12. 82 *—M.S. (5/1/2000)*

Groot Constantia 2001 Shiraz (Constantia) $17. 86 *—M.M. (4/1/2005)*

Groot Constantia 1999 Shiraz (Constantia) $13. 82 *(10/1/2001)*

Groot Constantia 2001 Gouverneurs Shiraz (Constantia) $36. 89 *—M.D. (7/1/2006)*

GROOTE POST

Groote Post 2005 Unwooded Chardonnay (Darling) $15. Grown on an historic 18th-century farm in the southwestern Cape, this unusual unoaked Chardonnay offers lime, pineapple and banana on the nose and a combination of resin, lime and apple on the palate. Medium-bodied and intensely flavored, it would pair well with seafood and light meats. 83 *—S.K. (3/1/2007)*

Groote Post 2006 Chenin Blanc (Darling) $14. From the emerging wine growing region of Darling, this Chenin Blanc is cheerful and bright, but substantive. Crisp apple and bright tropical fruit on the nose lead into a creamy palate of melon and guava. There's a nice spiciness on the finish, which is long. The wine has a light character but has plenty of dimension. 88 *—S.K. (7/1/2007)*

Groote Post 2005 Chenin Blanc (Coastal Region) $12. 86 *—M.D. (11/1/2006)*

Groote Post 2004 Chenin Blanc (Coastal Region) $11. 88 Best Buy *—R.V. (11/15/2005)*

Groote Post 2002 Darling Hills Road Chenin Blanc (Coastal Region) $13. 86 *—K.F. (4/1/2003)*

Groote Post 2004 Darling Hills Road Sauvignon Blanc (Coastal Region) $13. 86 *—M.M. (7/1/2005)*

Groote Post 2004 The Old Man's Blend Red Blend (Coastal Region) $16. Aromas of mint and white pepper are followed by a blend of red berry, savory spice and smoke. The successful play between juicy fruit and oak makes for a layered and affordable everyday drinking choice. **88** —*S.K. (11/15/2007)*

Groote Post 2006 Sauvignon Blanc (Darling) $15. The cool climate of Darling adds a crisp, fresh quality to this wonderful SB. Rich fruit paired with zesty acidity and snappy hints of citrus balance the wine, giving it complexity without weighing it down. **89 Editors' Choice** —*S.K. (7/1/2007)*

Groote Post 2005 The Old Man's Blend White Blend (Coastal Region) $15. 90 Best Buy —*M.D. (11/1/2006)*

GUARDIAN

Guardian 2002 Chardonnay (Western Cape) $7. 85 —*K.F. (9/1/2003)*

GUARDIAN PEAK

Guardian Peak 2005 Lapa Cabernet Sauvignon (Western Cape) $NA. Big, bold and in the style of a Napa Cabernet, this offering has a no-nonsense nose of raspberry and spice that jumps out of the glass. On the palate, the wine is powerful but smooth, with flavors of toasted oak, cinnamon and bright berry, and the finish is impressive. Hold for 2–5 years. Imported by Terlato Wines International. **88 Cellar Selection** —*S.K. (7/1/2007)*

Guardian Peak 2004 Lapa Cabernet Sauvignon (Stellenbosch) $33. 89 —*R.V. (11/1/2006)*

Guardian Peak 2004 Lapa Cabernet Sauvignon (Western Cape) $36. Powerful spice, cigar, cinnamon and lead pencil join bright raspberry aromas in this assertive Cab from Ernie Els and Jean Engelbrecht. Nutty spice typifies the palate; buttery toast on the finish. A hearty, enjoyable wine that could age comfortably for five more years. **87** —*S.K. (3/1/2007)*

Guardian Peak 2001 Cabernet Sauvignon-Syrah (Stellenbosch) $10. 89 Best Buy —*K.F. (4/1/2003)*

Guardian Peak 2005 Red Blend (Stellenbosch) $NA. 85 —*S.K. (7/1/2007)*

Guardian Peak 2005 Frontier Red Blend (Stellenbosch) $NA. This Cabernet-Shiraz-Merlot blend is another example of how South African winemakers have mastered the art of the blend. A lighter-style red with great structure, bright fruit flavors and a juicy overall character, it is both accessible and adaptable to varied tastes. There's complexity but the wine has a soft touch. Drink now. **86** —*S.K. (7/1/2007)*

Guardian Peak 2004 Frontier Red Blend (Western Cape) $13. Cedar, juicy red berry and spice are on the wine's nose, while chocolate and plum are touched with toasty oak on the palate. It's accessible and pleasurable, though it could use a little more complexity. Overall good flavor and structure. Produced by Engelbrecht Els Vineyards. **85** —*S.K. (3/1/2007)*

Guardian Peak 2002 Frontier Red Blend (Western Cape) $13. 82 —*M.M. (4/1/2005)*

Guardian Peak 2005 SMG Red Blend (Western Cape) $NA. This is unique not only because it's the first such blend to be produced in South Africa (Syrah-Mourvèdre-Grenache) but also because of its exotic palate of dark chocolate, plum and spice flavors. The wine is fun and vibrant but also elegant and complex enough to stand on its own in the glass, and it still exhibits the measured restraint for which the French, and many South African wines, are known. Imported by Terlato Wines International. **87** —*S.K. (7/1/2007)*

Guardian Peak 2004 SMG Rhône Red Blend (Western Cape) $28. 86 —*S.K. (7/1/2007)*

Guardian Peak 2004 Shiraz (Western Cape) $12. 83 —*M.D. (3/1/2006)*

Guardian Peak 2001 Shiraz (Western Cape) $9. 88 Best Buy —*K.F. (4/1/2003)*

HAMILTON RUSSELL

Hamilton Russell 2006 Chardonnay (Walker Bay) $28. This French-style Chardonnay from a premium producer in Walker Bay shows how well New World and Old World styles can work together with the help of excellent winemaking. Delicious toasty aromas lead into a minerally, restrained flavor profile, but the wine has a creamy texture which balances well with lively acidity. A lovely wine at a good price. **89** —*S.K. (7/1/2007)*

Hamilton Russell 2005 Chardonnay (Walker Bay) $27. 90 —*M.D. (7/1/2006)*

Hamilton Russell 2003 Chardonnay (Walker Bay) $25. 88 —*M.M. (4/1/2005)*

Hamilton Russell 2000 Chardonnay (Walker Bay) $22. 92 —*R.V. (7/1/2002)*

Hamilton Russell 2005 Pinot Noir (Walker Bay) $36. Dark fruit, licorice and spice give this wine depth but the overall character is very soft and integrated. There's intensity—the wine can age—but right now, it's a sophisticated sip that will pair beautifully with food. **89** —*S.K. (7/1/2007)*

HAVANA HILLS

Havana Hills 2000 Merlot (Western Cape) $33. 85 —*K.F. (1/1/2004)*

Havana Hills 2000 Du Plessis Reserve Merlot (Western Cape) $33. 83 —*M.M. (3/1/2004)*

Havana Hills 2000 Sauvignon Blanc (Western Cape) $15. 84 —*K.F. (9/1/2003)*

Havana Hills 2000 Shiraz (Western Cape) $33. 85 —*K.F. (8/1/2003)*

Havana Hills 1999 Shiraz (Western Cape) $33. 86 —*K.F. (8/1/2003)*

Havana Hills 2000 Du Plessis Reserve Shiraz (Western Cape) $33. 87 —*K.F. (8/1/2003)*

HELDERBERG

Helderberg 2003 Chardonnay (Western Cape) $9. 87 Best Buy —*M.D. (3/1/2006)*

Helderberg 2000 Chardonnay (Stellenbosch) $8. 81 —*R.V. (1/1/2003)*

Helderberg 2001 Chenin Blanc (Stellenbosch) $6. 87 Best Buy —*M.S. (1/1/2003)*

Helderberg 1999 Shiraz (Stellenbosch) $9. 86 Best Buy *(1/1/2003)*

HELGERSON

Helgerson 2002 Reserve Cabernet Sauvignon (Franschhoek) $9. 86 Best Buy —*J.C. (11/15/2005)*

HERCULES PARAGON

Hercules Paragon 2003 Cabernet Sauvignon (Western Cape) $20. A mingling of toasty oak and mocha on the nose lead into earthy flavors of mint and spice on this affordable Cabernet from South Africa. The warming spices and inviting touch of smoke make this a delicious choice for steak or grilled lamb. **84** —*S.K. (11/15/2007)*

Hercules Paragon 2002 Shiraz (Western Cape) $20. Truly a unique Shiraz, with its smoky, leathery and black olive aromas, followed by flavors of black cherry and spice. While appealing overall, it has a slightly syrupy, raisiny quality and some roughness on the palate that distracts slightly from the flavors. This is not really a problem for fans of wines that push the envelope a bit. **84** —*S.K. (6/1/2007)*

HERDING CATS

Herding Cats 2005 Chenin Blanc-Chardonnay (Western Cape) $9. 83 —*M.D. (7/1/2006)*

Herding Cats 2004 Merlot/Pinotage Red Blend (Western Cape) $9. 83 —*M.D. (7/1/2006)*

HIDDEN VALLEY

Hidden Valley 2000 Limited Release Cabernet Sauvignon (Stellenbosch) $25. 89 —*M.D. (7/1/2006)*

Hidden Valley 2001 Limited Release Pinotage (Stellenbosch) $20. 83 —*M.D. (5/1/2006)*

Hidden Valley 2003 Hidden Agenda Red Blend (Stellenbosch) $15. 84 —*M.D. (7/1/2006)*

HOOPENBURG

Hoopenburg 1998 Winemaker's Selection Cabernet Sauvignon (Stellenbosch) $18. 86 —*K.F. (4/1/2003)*

Hoopenburg 1999 Merlot (Stellenbosch) $18. 83 —*K.F. (4/1/2003)*

INDABA

Indaba 2005 Chardonnay (Western Cape) $9. 86 Best Buy —*M.D. (11/15/2006)*

Indaba 2002 Chardonnay (Western Cape) $9. 84 —*K.F. (9/1/2003)*

Indaba 2002 Chenin Blanc (Western Cape) $7. 83 —*K.F. (9/1/2003)*

Indaba 2005 Merlot (Western Cape) $9. 81 —*M.D. (11/1/2006)*

Indaba 2006 Pinotage (Western Cape) $10. Dark berry and a light, tropical fruit quality on the nose add to the appeal of this Pinotage. On the palate, the flavors of juicy berry and banana are rounded and smooth, offering assertive spice but in a gentle package. **84** —*S.K. (12/15/2007)*

Indaba 2005 Sauvignon Blanc (Western Cape) $9. 86 Best Buy —*M.D. (12/31/2006)*

Indaba 2002 Sauvignon Blanc (Western Cape) $8. 83 —*K.F. (9/1/2003)*

Indaba 2004 Shiraz (Western Cape) $10. 83 —*M.D. (9/1/2006)*

IONA VINEYARDS

Iona Vineyards 2004 Cabernet Sauvignon-Merlot (Elgin) $NA. Red berry fruit and restrained wood mingle in a soft, elegant wine that is more about poise than power. There's structure and complexity to be sure, which means pairing it with meat or game dishes will be delicious, but the style is gentle enough that this wine is very nice to drink on its own. **89** —*S.K. (7/1/2007)*

Iona Vineyards 2006 Sauvignon Blanc (Elgin) $NA. A stellar example of what cool-climate South African vineyards can produce, this crisp, minerally Sauvignon Blanc is steely and clean in the true Sauvignon style. Tropical fruit flavors are subtle but delicious, and the finish is lingering and impressive. At this price, you can't get much better, whether you're looking for a solo sip or a food-friendly cohort. Imported by Martin Scott. **91 Best Buy** *—S.K. (7/1/2007)*

JABULANI

Jabulani 2006 Chardonnay (Western Cape) $9. Tropical fruit and vanilla flavors are led by a toasty nose on this creamy, accessible wine from Jabulani. It's not terribly complex but at this price, with its fresh but rounded flavors and long finish, you can't go wrong. Pair this with shellfish or salmon. Imported by American Wine Distributors, Inc. **86 Best Buy** *—S.K. (7/1/2007)*

Jabulani 2004 Chardonnay (Western Cape) $10. 84 *—M.D. (5/1/2006)*

Jabulani 2004 Merlot (Western Cape) $10. 85 Best Buy *—M.D. (3/1/2006)*

Jabulani 2005 Merlot-Cabernet Sauvignon (Western Cape) $9. With its full raspberry flavors and enticing floral nose, this is an easy-drinking wine, flavorful yet soft. It's not terribly complex but will pair well with an array of food, most likely meat dishes. Imported by American Wine Distributors, Inc. **86 Best Buy** *—S.K. (3/1/2007)*

Jabulani 2003 Merlot-Cabernet Sauvignon (Western Cape) $10. 87 Best Buy *—M.D. (5/1/2006)*

Jacobsdal 2003 Pinotage (Stellenbosch) $15. Jacobsdal has been making wine for nearly four decades and with this Pinotage, the producer's years of experience show. The aromas are typical of South African Pinotage: smoke, banana, red berry and plum. Flavors of raspberry and cherry are framed by structured but subtle tannins. The wine is assertive but avoids the edge of many Pinotages. **87** *—S.K. (9/1/2007)*

Jabulani 2004 Shiraz (Western Cape) $10. 82 *—M.D. (3/1/2006)*

JACOBSDAL

Jacobsdal 1998 Pinotage (Stellenbosch) $17. 87 *—K.F. (9/1/2003)*

Jacobsdal 1996 Pinotage (Stellenbosch) $15. 83 *(3/1/2001)*

JARDIN

Jardin 2003 Cobblers Hill Bordeaux Blend (Stellenbosch) $38. 91 *—R.V. (11/1/2006)*

Jardin 2004 Cabernet Sauvignon (Stellenbosch) $20. 93 Best Buy *—R.V. (11/1/2006)*

Jardin 2004 Chardonnay (Stellenbosch) $16. Deep flavors of hazelnut, French oak and citrus characterize this bold offering that will please fans of buttery, round Chardonnays. Its deep golden color, heady nose and assertive flavors add appeal, though backing off on the butter would have added balance. **84** *—S.K. (3/1/2007)*

Jardin 1998 Chardonnay (Stellenbosch) $17. 92 Editors' Choice *(3/1/2001)*

Jardin 2004 Nine Yards Chardonnay (Stellenbosch) $38. Vanilla toast and a compelling yeasty character on the nose entice. It's a little brighter on the palate, offering a balanced combination of minerality, acid and cream that lingers. **87** *—S.K. (11/15/2007)*

Jardin 1999 Fumé Blanc (Stellenbosch) $13. 88 *—M.M. (3/1/2001)*

Jardin 1998 Merlot (Stellenbosch) $17. 90 Editors' Choice *(3/1/2001)*

Jardin 2005 Sauvignon Blanc (Stellenbosch) $15. 85 *—M.D. (12/31/2006)*

Jardin 2002 Sauvignon Blanc (Stellenbosch) $12. 85 *—K.F. (9/1/2003)*

Jardin 1999 Chameleon White Blend (Stellenbosch) $16. 83 *—M.M. (3/1/2001)*

JEAN TAILLEFERT

Jean Taillefert 2002 Shiraz (Paarl) $68. 91 *—M.D. (5/1/2006)*

Jean Taillefert 2001 Shiraz (Paarl) $66. 90 *—M.M. (11/15/2004)*

JOHN B.

John B. 2003 Bouquet Rouge Cabernet Blend (Robertson) $9. 86 Best Buy *—M.M. (12/15/2004)*

KAAPZICHT

Kaapzicht 2001 Estate Cabernet Sauvignon (Stellenbosch) $NA. 90 *—R.V. (11/1/2006)*

KANONKOP

Kanonkop 2003 Paul Sauer Bordeaux Blend (Stellenbosch) $39. Cigar, coffee and mocha on the nose, followed by smoke and tobacco on the palate, give this ageable wine a masculine, restrained edge. The fruit is soft and integrated but the structure good. Imagine sipping this one by a roaring fire—it has that kind of character. **87** *—S.K. (12/15/2007)*

Kanonkop 2002 Paul Sauer Bordeaux Blend (Simonsberg-Stellenbosch) $39. 86 *—M.D. (9/1/2006)*

Kanonkop 2002 Cabernet Sauvignon (Stellenbosch) $33. 85 *—M.D. (9/1/2006)*

Kanonkop 2000 Cabernet Sauvignon (Stellenbosch) $30. 89 *—M.M. (3/1/2004)*

Kanonkop 2003 Pinotage (Simonsberg-Stellenbosch) $33. 87 *—M.D. (9/1/2006)*

Kanonkop 2001 Pinotage (Stellenbosch) $28. 88 *—M.M. (3/1/2004)*

Kanonkop 2000 Pinotage (Stellenbosch) $27. 86 *—K.F. (1/1/2004)*

Kanonkop 2001 Kadette Red Blend (Stellenbosch) $12. 86 *—M.M. (3/1/2004)*

Kanonkop 2000 Paul Sauer Red Blend (Stellenbosch) $35. 90 Cellar Selection *—M.M. (3/1/2004)*

KANU

Kanu 2004 Chardonnay (Stellenbosch) $17. 87 *—M.D. (9/1/2006)*

Kanu 2004 Chenin Blanc (Stellenbosch) $10. 90 Best Buy *—R.V. (11/15/2005)*

Kanu 2004 Limited Release Wooded Chenin Blanc (Stellenbosch) $18. 91 *—R.V. (11/15/2005)*

Kanu 2005 Sauvignon Blanc (Stellenbosch) $12. 84 *—M.D. (12/31/2006)*

KEN FORRESTER

Ken Forrester 2005 Chenin Blanc (Stellenbosch) $15. 90 Best Buy *—R.V. (11/15/2005)*

Ken Forrester 2003 Forrester Meinert Chenin Chenin Blanc (Stellenbosch) $65. 88 *—R.V. (11/15/2005)*

Ken Forrester 2002 Helderberg Chenin Blanc (Stellenbosch) $14. 87 *—K.F. (4/1/2003)*

Ken Forrester 2004 Petit Chenin Chenin Blanc (Stellenbosch) $9. 90 Best Buy *—R.V. (11/15/2005)*

Ken Forrester 2001 Helderberg Grenache-Syrah (Stellenbosch) $20. 84 *—K.F. (4/1/2003)*

Ken Forrester 2000 Helderberg Grenache-Syrah (Stellenbosch) $20. 86 *—K.F. (4/1/2003)*

Ken Forrester 2001 Merlot (Stellenbosch) $20. 85 *—K.F. (8/1/2003)*

Ken Forrester 2002 Sauvignon Blanc (Stellenbosch) $14. 86 *—K.F. (4/1/2003)*

KLEIN CONSTANTIA

Klein Constantia 1999 Estate Cabernet Sauvignon (Constantia) $22. 85 *—K.F. (8/1/2003)*

Klein Constantia 2005 Marlbrook Cabernet Sauvignon (Constantia) $NA. 90 *—R.V. (11/1/2006)*

Klein Constantia 2001 Vin de Constance Muscat (Constantia) $50. Beloved by everyone from Dickens to Napolean, this exquisite dessert wine, which was produced in the 18th and 19th centuries in Constantia and is now being revived at Klein Constantia, is a wonderful treat. It's made from ripe Muscat de Frontignan, a naturally sweet grape with charm and complexity. Layers of honey, orange and spice coat the tongue in a sumptuous wave, but the wine still has a delicate quality that begs for another glass. Pair it with rich dishes like foie gras or crème brûlée and you'll see why Jane Austen lauded it in Sense & Sensibility as the sure-fire cure for a broken heart. **91** *—S.K. (7/1/2007)*

Klein Constantia 2005 Riesling (Constantia) $15. 83 *—M.D. (12/31/2006)*

Klein Constantia 2005 Sauvignon Blanc (Constantia) $0. A beautiful nose of flowers and tropical fruit is paired with an interplay of bright acidity and gooseberry/grapefruit flavors. Restrained and subtle with a steely minerality that keeps it clean, the wine is delicate but full of character. **92** *—S.K. (7/1/2007)*

Klein Constantia 2005 Sauvignon Blanc (South Africa) $17. From centuries-old producers Klein Constantia, this wine is fresh and elegant with a lovely floral nose, long, minerally flavors and a crisp finish. Semillon adds an extra level of richness and complexity. **88** *—S.K. (3/1/2007)*

Klein Constantia 2004 Marlbrook White Blend (Constantia) $20. 89 *—M.D. (11/1/2006)*

KLEINE ZALZE

Kleine Zalze 2004 Bush Vines Chenin Blanc (Stellenbosch) $NA. 89 *—R.V. (11/15/2005)*

KUMALA

Kumala 2004 Cabernet Sauvignon (Western Cape) $9. 83 *—J.C. (11/15/2005)*

Kumala 2004 Chardonnay (Western Cape) $9. 85 Best Buy —*J.C. (11/15/2005)*

Kumala 2004 Merlot (Western Cape) $9. 81 —*J.C. (11/15/2005)*

Kumala 2005 Sauvignon Blanc (Western Cape) $9. 83 —*M.D. (7/1/2006)*

Kumala 2004 Shiraz (Western Cape) $9. 83 —*J.C. (11/15/2005)*

KUMKANI

Kumkani 2000 Cabernet Sauvignon-Shiraz (Stellenbosch) $13. 90 Best Buy —*M.M. (4/1/2002)*

Kumkani 2005 Chenin Blanc (Coastal Region) $10. Kumkani offers a very fresh style of Chenin here, with melon, pear and balanced minerality on the palate. There's also a nuance of honey and spice in the wine, which adds complexity. This is a great value and the perfect wine to pair with ethnic Moroccan, Indian or Asian dishes. **85 Best Buy** —*S.K. (7/1/2007)*

Kumkani 2004 Pinotage (Stellenbosch) $14. 86 —*M.D. (12/31/2006)*

Kumkani 2005 Sauvignon Blanc (Coastal Region) $14. Grassy and herbaceous, this wine is full of gooseberry and green pepper and is an interesting alternative to the tropical fuit flavors of many SBs. The fruit grows in the Helderberg Hills, a coastal area that yields wines with an intense flavor and fuller body. Great for seafood. **85** —*S.K. (3/1/2007)*

Kumkani 2004 Sauvignon Blanc (Stellenbosch) $12. 86 —*M.M. (7/1/2005)*

Kumkani 2001 Sauvignon Blanc (Stellenbosch) $11. 80 —*M.S. (1/1/2003)*

Kumkani 2005 Single Vineyard Lanner Hill Sauvignon Blanc (Groenekloof) $22. 88 —*M.D. (12/31/2006)*

Kumkani 2003 Shiraz (Stellenbosch) $16. Spice and vanilla, a reflection of its oak, plays a lead with this friendly wine. The nose is soft and elegant and the flavors rounded and for the most part, successfully integrated. The finish is substantial. A good everyday Shiraz. **85** —*S.K. (6/1/2007)*

Kumkani 2002 Shiraz (Stellenbosch) $15. 85 —*J.C. (11/15/2005)*

Kumkani 2000 Shiraz (Stellenbosch) $15. 88 —*M.M. (4/1/2002)*

Kumkani 2004 Shiraz-Cabernet Sauvignon (Stellenbosch) $11. There's not a lot of fanfare here, just a smooth blend of clove, plum and smoke flavors, but the oak adds texture and it's more subtle than one would expect from these varieties. There's a faint feel of juicy fruit but it fades and leaves just toasted oak. **84** —*S.K. (3/1/2007)*

Kumkani 2002 Shiraz-Cabernet Sauvignon (Stellenbosch) $13. 87 Best Buy —*M.M. (7/1/2005)*

KWV

KWV 2003 Cathedral Cellar Triptych Bordeaux Blend (Coastal Region) $NA. 89 —*R.V. (11/1/2006)*

KWV 2003 Cabernet Sauvignon (Western Cape) $9. 81 —*J.C. (11/15/2005)*

KWV 2002 Cabernet Sauvignon (Western Cape) $10. 85 —*M.M. (3/1/2004)*

KWV 2001 Cabernet Sauvignon (Western Cape) $10. 89 Best Buy —*K.F. (11/15/2003)*

KWV 2000 Cabernet Sauvignon (Western Cape) $10. 90 Best Buy —*K.F. (4/1/2003)*

KWV 2002 Cathedral Cellar Cabernet Sauvignon (Coastal Region) $18. 90 Editors' Choice —*R.V. (11/1/2006)*

KWV 2001 Cathedral Cellar Cabernet Sauvignon (Paarl) $17. 87 —*M.D. (11/1/2006)*

KWV 2000 Cathedral Cellar Cabernet Sauvignon (Coastal Region) $15. 83 —*M.M. (7/1/2005)*

KWV 1999 Cathedral Cellar Cabernet Sauvignon (Coastal Region) $15. 88 —*K.F. (4/1/2003)*

KWV 1997 Cathedral Cellar Cabernet Sauvignon (Stellenbosch) $15. 90 Editors' Choice *(9/1/2001)*

KWV 2003 Reserve Cabernet Sauvignon (Stellenbosch) $NA. 88 —*R.V. (11/1/2006)*

KWV 2005 Chardonnay (Western Cape) $9. 86 Best Buy —*M.D. (11/15/2006)*

KWV 2004 Chardonnay (Western Cape) $10. 83 —*J.C. (11/15/2005)*

KWV 2003 Chardonnay (Western Cape) $10. 83 —*M.M. (3/1/2004)*

KWV 2004 Cathedral Cellar Chardonnay (Coastal Region) $14. 82 —*M.D. (3/1/2006)*

KWV 2003 Cathedral Cellar Chardonnay (Coastal Region) $17. 87 —*M.M. (4/1/2005)*

KWV 2002 Cathedral Cellar Chardonnay (Coastal Region) $16. 87 —*M.M. (3/1/2004)*

KWV 2001 Cathedral Cellar Chardonnay (Western Cape) $12. 90 Best Buy —*R.V. (7/1/2002)*

KWV 2000 Cathedral Cellar Chardonnay (Western Cape) $12. 89 Editors' Choice *(9/1/2001)*

KWV 2002 KWV Chardonnay (Western Cape) $10. 86 —*K.F. (4/1/2003)*

KWV 2004 Steen Chenin Blanc (Western Cape) $8. 85 Best Buy —*M.M. (4/1/2005)*

KWV 2003 Steen Chenin Blanc (Western Cape) $8. 84 —*M.M. (3/1/2004)*

KWV 2002 Steen Chenin Blanc (Western Cape) $8. 85 —*K.F. (4/1/2003)*

KWV 2003 Merlot (Western Cape) $9. 84 —*M.D. (9/1/2006)*

KWV 2002 Merlot (Western Cape) $10. 85 Best Buy —*M.M. (4/1/2005)*

KWV 2001 Merlot (Western Cape) $10. 88 Best Buy —*K.F. (4/1/2003)*

KWV 2002 Cathedral Cellar Merlot (Coastal Region) $17. 86 —*M.D. (9/1/2006)*

KWV 1996 Cathedral Cellar Merlot (Coastal Region) $15. 86 *(9/1/2001)*

KWV 2004 Pinotage (Western Cape) $11. This starts with a soft, unintimidating nose of red berry and spice, and on the palate, the wine offers true Pinotage flavors. This means one will either embrace it and love it or find it a touch angular and heavy on dry, white pepper flavors and a touch of tropical fruit. Fans of Pinotage will commend the effort. **84** —*S.K. (11/15/2007)*

KWV 2003 Pinotage (Western Cape) $9. 85 Best Buy —*M.D. (3/1/2006)*

KWV 2002 Pinotage (Western Cape) $10. 85 —*M.M. (3/1/2004)*

KWV 2001 Pinotage (Western Cape) $10. 85 —*K.F. (9/1/2003)*

KWV 2000 Pinotage (Western Cape) $11. 86 —*K.F. (4/1/2003)*

KWV 1999 Pinotage (Western Cape) $9. 86 *(9/1/2001)*

KWV 1999 Cathedral Cellar Pinotage (Western Cape) $17. 84 —*K.F. (9/1/2003)*

KWV NV Full Ruby Port (Western Cape) $9. 87 —*K.F. (12/1/2003)*

KWV NV Full Tawny Port (Western Cape) $9. 87 —*K.F. (12/1/2003)*

KWV 1993 Late Bottled Vintage Port (Western Cape) $15. 88 —*K.F. (12/1/2003)*

KWV 2005 Sauvignon Blanc (Western Cape) $9. 84 —*M.D. (12/31/2006)*

KWV 2001 Cathedral Cellar Sauvignon Blanc (Western Cape) $15. 87 —*K.F. (4/1/2003)*

KWV 2002 Shiraz (Western Cape) $10. 84 —*M.M. (4/1/2005)*

KWV 2000 Shiraz (Western Cape) $10. 84 —*K.F. (9/1/2003)*

KWV 1999 Shiraz (Western Cape) $9. 84 *(10/1/2001)*

KWV 1999 Cathedral Cellar Shiraz (Western Cape) $15. 81 —*D.T. (1/1/2002)*

KWV 1999 Cathedral Cellar Shiraz (Coastal Region) $17. 83 —*M.M. (3/1/2004)*

KWV 1998 Cathedral Cellar Shiraz (Coastal Region) $15. 83 *(10/1/2001)*

KWV 2005 Steen (Western Cape) $7. 86 Best Buy —*R.V. (11/15/2005)*

L'AVENIR

L'Avenir 2005 Chenin Blanc (Stellenbosch) $NA. 91 —*R.V. (11/15/2005)*

L'Avenir 2004 Pinotage (Stellenbosch) $20. 87 —*R.V. (11/1/2006)*

L'Avenir 2004 Grand Vin Pinotage (Stellenbosch) $NA. 89 —*R.V. (11/1/2006)*

L'Avenir 2005 Sauvignon Blanc (Stellenbosch) $NA. 87 —*R.V. (11/1/2006)*

LA MOTTE

La Motte 2002 Cabernet Sauvignon (Stellenbosch) $23. The clove and leather on the nose of this Cab from Stellenbosch introduce it appropriately: On the palate flavors of plum and dark berry impress. There's good fruit here and the finish is long, but overall, the wine lacks some punch and one wants more of the juicy, lush character. This depends on your taste, though—fans of more subtle styles may enjoy it. **84** —*S.K. (6/1/2007)*

La Motte 1999 Estate Cabernet Sauvignon (Franschhoek) $20. 84 —*K.F. (8/1/2003)*

La Motte 2004 Shiraz (Western Cape) $22. La Motte's quality-oriented winemaking shows with this classic Shiraz, redolent of spicy, dark berry aromas. Textured flavors of red fruit and pepper a robust body give this wine some heft. Great with a rack of roasted lamb or grilled steak. **86** —*S.K. (7/1/2007)*

LABORIE

Laborie 2001 Estate Cabernet Sauvignon (Paarl) $12. 89 Best Buy —*K.F. (1/1/2004)*

Laborie 1998 Blanc de Noir Champagne Blend (Paarl) $18. 83 —*J.M. (12/1/2002)*

Laborie 1995 Cap Classique Brut Champagne Blend (Paarl) $18. 85 *—J.M. (12/1/2002)*

Laborie 2003 Chardonnay (Paarl) $11. 83 *—M.M. (3/1/2004)*

Laborie 2001 Chardonnay (Paarl) $11. 84 *—R.V. (7/1/2002)*

Laborie 1998 Cap Classique Chardonnay (Paarl) $18. 86 *—K.F. (12/1/2003)*

Laborie 2001 Estate Wine Merlot-Cabernet Sauvignon (Paarl) $12. 85 *—K.F. (9/1/2003)*

Laborie 1998 Pineau de Laborie Pinotage (Paarl) $16. 87 *—K.F. (12/1/2003)*

Laborie 2003 Sauvignon Blanc (Paarl) $11. 84 *—M.M. (3/1/2004)*

Laborie 2002 Sauvignon Blanc (Paarl) $11. 87 *—K.F. (11/15/2003)*

Laborie 1999 Blanc de Noir Sparkling Blend (Paarl) $13. 87 Best Buy *—K.F. (12/1/2003)*

LAMMERSHOEK

Lammershoek 2001 Barrique Chenin Blanc (Coastal Region) $10. 87 *—K.F. (1/1/2004)*

Lammershoek 2001 Red Blend (Coastal Region) $13. 84 *—M.M. (3/1/2004)*

Lammershoek 2002 Roulette Red Blend (Coastal Region) $28. 86 *—M.M. (7/1/2005)*

Lammershoek 2005 Aprilskloof Sauvignon Blanc (Coastal Region) $10. 84 *—M.D. (3/1/2006)*

LANDSKROON

Landskroon 2002 Cabernet Sauvignon (Paarl) $16. 85 *—M.D. (9/1/2006)*

Landskroon 2001 Cabernet Sauvignon (Paarl) $15. 85 *—M.M. (11/15/2004)*

Landskroon 2000 Cabernet Sauvignon (Paarl) $16. 87 *—K.F. (4/1/2003)*

Landskroon 2000 Merlot (Paarl) $16. 86 *—K.F. (4/1/2003)*

Landskroon 2003 Jerepico Morio Muskat (Paarl) $15. 87 *—M.M. (11/15/2004)*

Landskroon 1999 Pinotage (Paarl) $15. 83 *—K.F. (4/1/2003)*

Landskroon 1999 Cape Vintage Port (Paarl) $20. 88 *—M.M. (11/15/2004)*

Landskroon 2002 Shiraz (Paarl) $16. 86 *—M.M. (11/15/2004)*

Landskroon 2000 Shiraz (Paarl) $18. 84 *—K.F. (4/1/2003)*

LANZERAC

Lanzerac 1998 Cabernet Sauvignon (Stellenbosch) $27. 86 *—M.M. (11/15/2004)*

Lanzerac 2003 Chardonnay (Stellenbosch) $20. 89 *—M.M. (11/15/2004)*

Lanzerac 1999 Chardonnay (Stellenbosch) $22. 85 *—K.F. (4/1/2003)*

Lanzerac 2000 Pinotage (Stellenbosch) $26. 80 *—M.M. (12/15/2004)*

Lanzerac 2004 Sauvignon Blanc (Stellenbosch) $21. 87 *(7/1/2005)*

LE BONHEUR

Le Bonheur 2000 Cabernet Sauvignon (Simonsberg-Stellenbosch) $25. 85 *—M.M. (4/1/2005)*

Le Bonheur 1997 Cabernet Sauvignon (Stellenbosch) $18. 82 *—M.S. (1/1/2004)*

Le Bonheur 1996 Cabernet Sauvignon (Stellenbosch) $9. 89 Best Buy *—M.N. (1/1/2004)*

Le Bonheur 2004 Chardonnay (Stellenbosch) $13. Fresh, while maintaining a spicy, oaky character, this is an everyday sip that will pair well with creamy, opulent dishes and fresh seafood. On the palate, it's round and subtle with good spice but has a nice lively feel. **84** *—S.K. (11/15/2007)*

Le Bonheur 2003 Chardonnay (Simonsberg-Stellenbosch) $13. 84 *—M.M. (4/1/2005)*

Le Bonheur 1999 Chardonnay (Stellenbosch) $11. 81 *—M.N. (1/1/2004)*

Le Bonheur 2001 Landgoed Chardonnay (Stellenbosch) $12. 83 *—K.F. (9/1/2004)*

Le Bonheur 2001 Prima Merlot-Cabernet Sauvignon (Stellenbosch) $16. 86 *—M.D. (12/31/2006)*

Le Bonheur 2000 Prima Merlot-Cabernet Sauvignon (Simonsberg-Stellenbosch) $15. 88 *—M.M. (4/1/2005)*

Le Bonheur 1999 Prima Merlot-Cabernet Sauvignon (Stellenbosch) $15. 87 *—M.M. (3/1/2004)*

Le Bonheur 1998 Prima Red Blend (Stellenbosch) $15. 86 *—K.F. (1/1/2004)*

Le Bonheur 2006 Sauvignon Blanc (Stellenbosch) $14. Lively citrus character with a balanced, elegant overall feel make this SB from Stellenbosch producer Le Bonheur a winner for those who want more complexity along with zesty lift. There's a flinty, grassy quality here, alongside richer tropical flavors that make it ideal with poultry and fresh summer dishes. **85** *—S.K. (6/1/2007)*

Le Bonheur 2005 Sauvignon Blanc (Stellenbosch) $12. 83 *—M.D. (12/31/2006)*

Le Bonheur 2003 Sauvignon Blanc (Stellenbosch) $11. 84 *—M.M. (11/15/2004)*

Le Bonheur 2000 Sauvignon Blanc (Stellenbosch) $13. 85 *—M.S. (1/1/2004)*

Le Bonheur 2004 Landgoed Sauvignon Blanc (Simonsberg-Stellenbosch) $13. 87 *—M.M. (4/1/2005)*

Le Bonheur 2002 Landgoed Sauvignon Blanc (Stellenbosch) $11. 87 *—K.F. (1/1/2004)*

LE RICHE

Le Riche 2002 Reserve Cabernet Sauvignon (Stellenbosch) $45. This reserve Cabernet from Stellensbosch displays aromas of oak spice and currant and its berry flavors are subtle and elegant. Could use a touch more tannic backbone and complexity of flavor, but it has a gentle touch that will please people who favor Old World wines over younger, more aggressive styles. **86** *—S.K. (6/1/2007)*

Le Riche 1999 Reserve Cabernet Sauvignon (Stellenbosch) $30. 86 *—M.M. (3/1/2001)*

LEIDERSBURG

Leidersburg 2005 Vintner's Reserve Sauvignon Blanc (Coastal Region) $18. 84 *—M.D. (3/1/2006)*

Leidersburg 2004 Vintner's Reserve Sauvignon Blanc (Coastal Region) $23. 87 *(7/1/2005)*

Leidersburg 2005 Vintner's Reserve Sur Lie Sauvignon Blanc (Walker Bay) $15. Round and upfront with flavors of grapefruit, mango and lemon, this will please fans of a denser style of SB. Because of its structure, it can stand up to heartier dishes and hold its own well against spicy cuisine. **84** *—S.K. (6/1/2007)*

Leidersburg 2003 Vintner's Reserve Sur Lie Sauvignon Blanc (Coastal Region) $19. 85 *—M.M. (7/1/2005)*

LEOPARD'S LEAP

Leopard's Leap 2004 Cabernet Sauvignon (Western Cape) $15. Cherry, blueberry and cassis backed by earthy coffee give this wine flavor and heft, but it's not a terribly complex pour. It would pair well with exotic dishes like spiced lamb or assertive cheeses. Grown in vineyards visited by the indigenous leopard population of the Franschhoek Valley/Western Cape Winelands area. Imported by Confluence Wine Importers. **84** *—S.K. (3/1/2007)*

Leopard's Leap 2006 Chardonnay (Western Cape) $13. Vanilla oak leads on this luscious Chard from Leopard's Leap, and will please anyone with a taste for a more voluptuous white wine. There are also touches of melon here, but it's mostly about the soft oak flavors. Good acidity keeps it from going too far in the wooded direction, and there's an elegant balance overall. **85** *—S.K. (6/1/2007)*

Leopard's Leap 2006 Lookout Rosé Pinotage (Western Cape) $10. This is a good example of how to work with Pinotage's assertive character in a way that is both inventive and accessible. Here, it adds body and a clean, dry character that balances the appetizing strawberry and honey flavors of the wine. Good acidity adds a lively punch. Overall, this is a great wine with a unique character. **85 Best Buy** *—S.K. (7/1/2007)*

Leopard's Leap 2004 Shiraz (Western Cape) $13. Black pepper, spice, and the unique touch of violet are the hallmarks of this Shiraz from South Africa. The wine has plenty of muscular kick in the flavors but its overall nature is smooth and integrated, and will only get better with aging. Pair with typical Shiraz compliments like lamb or grilled meats. **85** *—S.K. (7/1/2007)*

Leopard's Leap 2004 Shiraz-Pinotage (Western Cape) $15. 88 *—S.K. (7/1/2007)*

LINDHORST

Lindhorst 2003 Cabernet Sauvignon (Coastal Region) $34. Lovely aromas of cinnamon and clove mean this Cabernet is of a serious mind, and the flavors of smoke, mocha and tobacco confirm it. The wine shows very good structure and layers of delicious flavors. Cellar it and enjoy the unfolding character in years to come. **87 Cellar Selection** *—S.K. (11/15/2007)*

Lindhorst 2003 Pinotage (Coastal Region) $29. Pinotage, with its often rustic, eccentric character, is typically a hard sell outside of South Africa. But producers like Lindhorst are proving that the variety can be just as appealing as any other red. This shows appetizing aromas of spiced meat and soft red berry, and on the palate, it has a round, velvety mouthfeel that is atypical of the sometimes prickly Pinotage. Pretty and full of dimension, the wine is a great introduction to the grape. **89** —*S.K. (12/15/2007)*

Lindhorst 2003 Max's Shiraz (Coastal Region) $29. Minty eucalyptus on the nose is followed by a fusion of lively plum and spice on the palate. A warming backbone of oak gives the wine weight. The finish is smooth and supple. Drink now or hold up to 4–5 years. **87** —*S.K. (11/15/2007)*

LONG NECK

Long Neck 2003 Cabernet Sauvignon (Western Cape) $8. 85 Best Buy —*M.M. (12/15/2004)*

Long Neck 2003 Chardonnay (Western Cape) $8. 84 Best Buy —*M.M. (12/15/2004)*

Long Neck 2003 Merlot (Western Cape) $8. 80 —*M.M. (12/15/2004)*

Long Neck 2003 Shiraz (Western Cape) $8. 82 —*M.M. (12/15/2004)*

LONGRIDGE

Longridge 1998 Merlot (Stellenbosch) $20. 84 —*M.M. (3/1/2001)*

Longridge 1999 Bay View Merlot (Stellenbosch) $10. 87 Best Buy *(3/1/2001)*

Longridge 1998 Pinotage (Stellenbosch) $20. 87 *(3/1/2001)*

Longridge 1999 Bayview Pinotage (South Africa) $10. 86 *(3/1/2001)*

Longridge 1999 Bayview Syrah (Stellenbosch) $10. 80 *(10/1/2001)*

Longridge (S.Af) 1999 Chardonnay (Stellenbosch) $19. 87 —*M.M. (3/1/2001)*

LONGRIDGE BAY VIEW

Longridge Bay View 1999 Merlot (Stellenbosch) $10. 87 Best Buy *(3/1/2001)*

LOST HORIZONS

Lost Horizons 2001 Cabernet Sauvignon-Merlot (Western Cape) $8. 85 *K.F. (4/1/2003)*

LOUISVALE

Louisvale 2000 Chardonnay (Stellenbosch) $NA. 87 —*R.V. (9/10/2002)*

MAKULU

Makulu 2006 Rosé Pinotage (Wellington) $6. Crisp, fruity and likeable, this full-bodied Pinotage rosé is a great value and will pair well with almost any food. The Pinotage adds spice and body to the berry flavors and the mouthfeel is rounded without being heavy. A good, lasting finish adds to the mix. Another example of the good quality, affordable wines coming out of this category. **84 Best Buy** —*S.K. (7/1/2007)*

MALAN

Malan 2000 Family Vinter's Chardonnay (Stellenbosch) $8. 86 Best Buy —*R.V. (7/1/2002)*

Malan 1999 Pinotage (Stellenbosch) $9. 88 Best Buy —*M.M. (4/1/2002)*

Malan 2001 Family Vinters Sauvignon Blanc (Stellenbosch) $8. 89 Best Buy —*M.M. (4/1/2002)*

MAN VINTNERS

MAN Vintners 2005 Cabernet Sauvignon (Coastal Region) $10. 85 Best Buy —*R.V. (11/1/2006)*

MAN Vintners 2004 Cabernet Sauvignon (Western Cape) $10. 85 Best Buy —*M.D. (3/1/2006)*

MAN Vintners 2005 Chardonnay (Coastal Region) $10. 83 —*M.D. (5/1/2006)*

MAN Vintners 2006 Chenin Blanc (Coastal Region) $10. This is an example of a Chenin that balances all of its components extremely well. Tropical fruit and melon on the nose lead into flavors of citrus and more of the tropical lushness on the palate. The wine is lively and given a touch of restraint because of its minerality. A very appealing food wine at a very attractive price, once again proving that South Africa is a great source for high-quality value wines. **87 Best Buy** —*S.K. (7/1/2007)*

MAN Vintners 2005 Chenin Blanc (Coastal Region) $9. 86 Best Buy —*R.V. (11/15/2005)*

MAN Vintners 2005 Pinotage (Coastal Region) $10. Pinotage can be a notoriously edgy grape to handle and South Africa's biggest challenge has been in learning how to properly cultivate it, and how to create a wine that is true to the varietal but pleasing to international palates. This Pinotage, with its assertive cherry and spice flavors and smooth tannins, is a step in the right direction. It's approachable, enjoyable and appetizing. There's still a touch of the dry, spicy Pinotage character, but the wine is generally friendly. **84** —*S.K. (7/1/2007)*

MAN Vintners 2004 Pinotage (Western Cape) $10. 81 —*M.D. (5/1/2006)*

MAN Vintners 2005 Sauvignon Blanc (Western Cape) $10. 83 —*M.D. (5/1/2006)*

MAN Vintners 2005 Shiraz (Coastal Region) $10. Aromas of ripe berry, cola, anise and herbs invite on the nose, while the wine is bold and juicy on the palate. There's some leather and spice for grip, but in general, it's soft and smooth. The wine loses a little steam at the end, but has a nice balance. **85** —*S.K. (3/1/2007)*

MAN Vintners 2004 Shiraz (Western Cape) $10. 83 —*M.D. (3/1/2006)*

MAS NICOLAS

Mas Nicolas 2000 Cape Shiraz-Cabernet Sauvignon (Stellenbosch) $34. 86 —*K.F. (8/1/2003)*

MATUBA

Matuba 2003 Premium Select Cabernet Sauvignon (Coastal Region) $12. 85 —*M.D. (9/1/2006)*

Matuba 2004 Premium Select Chardonnay (Coastal Region) $12. 84 —*M.D. (11/1/2006)*

Matuba 2004 Vineyards Specific Chardonnay (Coastal Region) $15. 84 —*M.D. (9/1/2006)*

Matuba 2004 Premium Select Chenin Blanc (Western Cape) $12. 85 —*M.D. (11/1/2006)*

Matuba 2006 Premium Select Sauvignon Blanc (Western Cape) $15. Soft and subtle tropical fruit aromas are anchored by some spice on the nose of this pleasing but straightforward wine from Matuba. There's pineapple, lemon and grapefruit on the palate, and the finish is clean and refreshing. Imported by American Wine Distributors, Inc. **84** —*S.K. (6/1/2007)*

Matuba 2005 Premium Select Sauvignon Blanc (Coastal Region) $12. With fruit picked high on the slopes of Groenberg at Wellington, this wine is driven by lively, crisp, tropical fruit flavors like grapefruit and has a pleasant floral and zingy fruit nose. It's a little lean and nondescript in general character, but would pair well with a mildly flavored fish entree. Imported by American Wine Distributors. **83** —*S.K. (3/1/2007)*

Matuba 2004 Premium Select Shiraz (Western Cape) $12. A hint of unoaked Viognier was added (6%) to this approachable Shiraz for depth and body, but despite some appealing flavors of plum, spice and chocolate, the wine lacks soul. There's some heft in the midpalate but it fades without the kind of vibrancy sought for in this variety. Imported by American Wine Distributors. **83** —*S.K. (3/1/2007)*

Matuba 2005 Vineyards Specific Shiraz-Viognier (Western Cape) $20. 85 —*S.K. (7/1/2007)*

MEERLUST

Meerlust 2001 Rubicon Bordeaux Blend (Stellenbosch) $30. 94 Editors' Choice —*R.V. (11/1/2006)*

Meerlust 2003 Chardonnay (Stellenbosch) $19. 88 —*M.D. (3/1/2006)*

Meerlust 1998 Chardonnay (Stellenbosch) $20. 83 —*K.F. (9/1/2003)*

Meerlust 2000 Merlot (Stellenbosch) $25. 90 —*M.D. (12/31/2006)*

Meerlust 2000 Rubicon Red Blend (Stellenbosch) $30. 90 —*M.D. (7/1/2006)*

Meerlust 1997 Rubicon Red Blend (Stellenbosch) $28. 87 —*K.F. (9/1/2003)*

MEINERT

Meinert 2000 Cabernet Sauvignon (Devon Valley) $25. 84 —*K.F. (8/1/2003)*

Meinert 2000 Merlot (Devon Valley) $20. 84 —*K.F. (8/1/2003)*

Meinert 2000 Synchronicity Red Blend (Devon Valley) $35. 90 —*K.F. (9/1/2003)*

MIDDELVLEI

Middelvlei 1995 Cabernet Sauvignon (Stellenbosch) $17. 87 —*M.N. (3/1/2001)*

Middelvlei 1996 Pinotage (Stellenbosch) $17. 84 *(3/1/2001)*

Middelvlei 1998 Red Blend (Stellenbosch) $16. 86 *(3/1/2001)*

Middelvlei 1996 Syrah (Stellenbosch) $17. 81 *(10/1/2001)*

MILES MOSSOP

Miles Mossop 2004 Max Bordeaux Blend (Coastal Region) $35. Elegant, integrated and balanced, this Bordeaux blend from lauded winemaker Miles Mossop offers an Old World-style experience that is both subtle and stylish. A touch of spice and oak on the nose lead into taut but tasty flavors of smoky spice and fruit. **85** —*S.K. (11/15/2007)*

Miles Mossop 2004 Saskia White Blend (Coastal Region) $35. 87 —*M.D. (11/1/2006)*

MISCHA

Mischa 2003 Cabernet Sauvignon (Wellington) $NA. Already established as a leading vine nursery, the Mischa Estate is now making wines of top quality. This intriguing and original Cab is packed with delicious black currant and clove aromas, and the flavors of chocolate and rich berry mingle with elegance. The oak treatment adds sweetness too, but it's subtle. This wine could use some time in the cellar but it's excellent now. **91 Editors' Choice** *—S.K. (7/1/2007)*

Mischa 2006 Eventide Sauvignon Blanc (Wellington) $NA. Beautiful, clean and bright citrus notes set this wine apart from first sniff, and the impression continues with flavors of passionfruit and tropical fruit on the palate. It's light and elegant but there's complexity and some weight on the midpalate which works suprisingly well. This is a lovely wine that's perfect for simple patio sipping or as the pairing to an elegant meal. **90** *—S.K. (7/1/2007)*

Mischa 2004 Shiraz (Wellington) $27. 87 *—M.D. (12/31/2006)*

MISSIONVALE

Missionvale 2000 Walker Bay Chardonnay (South Africa) $NA. 91 *—R.V. (9/10/2002)*

MONTEROSSO

Monterosso 2005 Bush Vine Chenin Blanc (Stellenbosch) $NA. 84 *—R.V. (11/15/2005)*

MONTESTELL

Montestell 2002 Reserve Cabernet Sauvignon (Paarl) $18. 82 *—M.D. (3/1/2006)*

Montestell 2000 Reserve Cabernet Sauvignon (Paarl) $20. 88 *—K.F. (4/1/2003)*

Montestell 2001 Reserve Pinotage (Paarl) $14. 82 *—M.M. (11/15/2004)*

Montestell 2000 Reserve Pinotage (Paarl) $16. 84 *—K.F. (4/1/2003)*

Montestell 2002 Reserve Shiraz (Paarl) $18. 86 *—M.M. (11/15/2004)*

MOOIUITZICHT

Mooiuitzicht NV Old Tawny Port (Western Cape) $16. 85 *—M.M. (11/15/2004)*

MÔRESON

Môreson 2003 Magia Bordeaux Blend (Coastal Region) $27. 87 *—R.V. (11/1/2006)*

Môreson 2004 Cabernet Sauvignon (Coastal Region) $27. 89 *—R.V. (11/1/2006)*

Môreson 1998 Cabernet Sauvignon (Coastal Region) $20. 87 *—K.F. (8/1/2003)*

Môreson 1997 Cabernet Sauvignon (Franschhoek) $25. 88 *—K.F. (4/1/2003)*

Môreson 2004 Premium Chardonnay (Franschhoek) $19. 87 *—M.D. (11/1/2006)*

Môreson 2004 Chenin Blanc (Franschhoek) $14. 85 *—R.V. (11/15/2005)*

Môreson 2001 Chenin Blanc (Franschhoek) $13. 86 *—K.F. (4/1/2003)*

Môreson 1999 Merlot (Franschhoek) $23. 88 *—K.F. (4/1/2003)*

Môreson 2004 Pinotage (Coastal Region) $20. 86 *—M.D. (11/1/2006)*

Môreson 1999 Magia Red Blend (Coastal Region) $25. 87 *—K.F. (9/1/2003)*

Môreson 2001 Sauvignon Blanc (Franschhoek) $16. 85 *(8/1/2002)*

Môreson NV Blanc de Blanc Brut Sparkling Blend (Franschhoek) $19. 83 *—M.D. (12/31/2006)*

MORGENHOF

Morgenhof 2001 Premiere Selection Bordeaux Blend (Stellenbosch) $35. 91 *—R.V. (11/1/2006)*

Morgenhof 1997 Premiere Selection Cabernet Blend (Stellenbosch) $20. 90 Editors' Choice *—M.M. (4/1/2002)*

Morgenhof 2001 Reserve Cabernet Sauvignon (Stellenbosch) $45. 89 *—R.V. (11/1/2006)*

Morgenhof 1999 Estate Chardonnay (Stellenbosch) $12. 90 Best Buy *—R.V. (7/1/2002)*

Morgenhof 1998 Merlot (Stellenbosch) $16. 88 *—M.M. (4/1/2002)*

Morgenhof 2001 Sauvignon Blanc (Stellenbosch) $9. 85 *—M.S. (4/1/2002)*

MOUNTAIN GATE

Mountain Gate 2000 Cabernet Sauvignon (Stellenbosch) $15. 86 *—M.M. (3/1/2004)*

Mountain Gate 2001 Sauvignon Blanc (Stellenbosch) $9. 87 *—K.F. (9/1/2003)*

MULDERBOSCH

Mulderbosch 2006 Rosé Cabernet Sauvignon (Stellenbosch) $12. With its elegant pale pink color, light but layered nose of strawberries, grapefruit and guava and its reasonable price, this rose from consistently solid Stellenbosch producer Mulderbosch is an accessible and affordable food wine that will please multiple palates. Flavors of cherry, herbs and strawberry on the palate coat the tongue with the slightly viscous mouthfeel, but it's not overwhelming. Drink now. **87 Best Buy** *—S.K. (7/1/2007)*

Mulderbosch 2005 Rosé Cabernet Sauvignon (Stellenbosch) $12. The strawberry jam, honey and grapefruit notes on the nose make for an alluring invitation, and on the palate, the wine is fun and fruity, with balanced flavors that match its aroma. It's on the drier side, too—a break for those who prefer a cleaner rosé. **85** *—S.K. (3/1/2007)*

Mulderbosch 2003 Chardonnay (Stellenbosch) $24. 88 *—M.D. (9/1/2006)*

Mulderbosch 2002 Barrel Fermented Chardonnay (Stellenbosch) $38. 89 *—M.D. (9/1/2006)*

Mulderbosch 1999 Barrel Fermented Chardonnay (Stellenbosch) $23. 91 *—R.V. (7/1/2002)*

Mulderbosch 2004 Chenin Blanc (Stellenbosch) $14. 87 *—R.V. (11/15/2005)*

Mulderbosch 2003 Faithful Hound Red Blend (Stellenbosch) $22. This supple Bordeaux blend of 50% Cabernet, 35% Merlot with Petit Verdot, Malbec and Cabernet Franc from Stellenbosch's Mulderbosch Vineyards is packed with flavorful berry, coffee and allspice character but is also rather soft and elegant. The vanilla from oak aging balances well with the vibrant blackberry and cassis. **85** *—S.K. (3/1/2007)*

Mulderbosch 2006 Sauvignon Blanc (Stellenbosch) $20. This wine is immediately likeable and pleases from the nose right through to the elegant finish. Its tropical fruit nose is flecked with fig, lemon and snappy green pepper, while the flavors are ripe and round, with enough acidity to keep it light on the tongue. An overall freshness here makes this wine fun, but it's interesting enough to be memorable after the last drop is gone. Imported by Cape Classics. **86** *—S.K. (6/1/2007)*

Mulderbosch 2003 Shiraz (Western Cape) $35. Delicious aromas of pepper and smoked meat introduce this elegant, but assertive Shiraz. Flavors of clove and nutmeg intertwined with lush fruit balance the wine well, offering a long and complex finish. A great example of a South African Shiraz—unique to its terroir, but also possessing all of the appealing aspects of the variety. **88** *—S.K. (6/1/2007)*

Mulderbosch 2002 Shiraz (Western Cape) $69. 87 *—M.D. (9/1/2006)*

NATURAL STATE

Natural State 1999 Cape Soleil Shiraz (Coastal Region) $12. 82 *(10/1/2001)*

NEDERBURG

Nederburg 2002 Cabernet Sauvignon (Western Cape) $10. 85 Best Buy *—M.M. (4/1/2005)*

Nederburg 2001 Cabernet Sauvignon (Western Cape) $11. 82 *—M.M. (3/1/2004)*

Nederburg 2001 Private Bin Cabernet Sauvignon (South Africa) $18. 84 *—M.M. (3/1/2004)*

Nederburg 2002 Edelrood Cabernet Sauvignon-Merlot (Western Cape) $11. 83 *—M.M. (4/1/2005)*

Nederburg 2001 Chardonnay (Western Cape) $10. 86 *—K.F. (4/1/2003)*

Nederburg 2004 Pinotage (Western Cape) $9. This Pinotage goes the classic route and embraces the upfront, somewhat eccentric character of the grape well. Pepper, spice and a dry finish mingle with a smoky overall aroma and flavor, and though the wine has a touch of angularity and kick, with grilled meat or spicy dishes, it will pair well. Imported by Dreyfus Ashby & Co. **84** *—S.K. (11/15/2007)*

Nederburg 2003 Pinotage (Western Cape) $11. 88 Best Buy *—M.D. (3/1/2006)*

Nederburg 2003 Paarl Riesling (Western Cape) $10. 85 Best Buy *—M.M. (7/1/2005)*

Nederburg 2005 Sauvignon Blanc (Western Cape) $11. 87 Best Buy *—M.D. (3/1/2006)*

Nederburg 2003 Sauvignon Blanc (Western Cape) $9. 87 Best Buy *—M.M. (3/1/2004)*

Nederburg 2003 Private Bin Sauvignon Blanc (South Africa) $15. 87 *—M.M. (3/1/2004)*

Nederburg 2002 Shiraz (Western Cape) $11. 88 Best Buy *—M.D. (5/1/2006)*

Nederburg 2001 Shiraz (Paarl) $11. 80 —*M.M. (3/1/2004)*

Nederburg 2001 Private Bin Shiraz (South Africa) $18. 85 —*M.M. (3/1/2004)*

Nederburg 2005 Lyric White Blend (Western Cape) $11. 87 Best Buy —*M.D. (11/1/2006)*

Nederburg 2004 Lyric White Blend (Western Cape) $10. 83 —*M.M. (4/1/2005)*

Nederburg 2003 Special Late Harvest White Blend (Western Cape) $10. 85 Best Buy —*M.M. (4/1/2005)*

Nederburg 2005 Stein White Blend (Western Cape) $11. 87 Best Buy —*M.D. (7/1/2006)*

NEIL ELLIS

Neil Ellis 2003 Cabernet Sauvignon (Stellenbosch) $23. 90 —*M.D. (7/1/2006)*

Neil Ellis 1999 Cabernet Sauvignon (Stellenbosch) $17. 87 —*M.S. (4/1/2002)*

Neil Ellis 2003 Vineyard Selection Cabernet Sauvignon (Jonkershoek Valley) $43. 88 —*M.D. (9/1/2006)*

Neil Ellis 2003 Cabernet Sauvignon-Merlot (Stellenbosch) $20. 87 —*M.D. (7/1/2006)*

Neil Ellis 2002 Cabernet Sauvignon-Merlot (Stellenbosch) $15. 86 —*M.M. (11/15/2004)*

Neil Ellis 2004 Chardonnay (Stellenbosch) $20. 87 —*M.D. (7/1/2006)*

Neil Ellis 2004 Chardonnay (Elgin) $23. 90 Editors' Choice —*M.D. (7/1/2006)*

Neil Ellis 2003 Chardonnay (Stellenbosch) $17. 89 Editors' Choice —*M.M. (11/15/2004)*

Neil Ellis 2000 Chardonnay (Elgin) $20. 91 —*R.V. (7/1/2002)*

Neil Ellis 2005 Sauvignon Blanc (Stellenbosch) $18. 85 —*M.D. (7/1/2006)*

Neil Ellis 2004 Sauvignon Blanc (Groenekloof) $14. 89 Best Buy —*M.M. (4/1/2005)*

Neil Ellis 2003 Sauvignon Blanc (Groenekloof) $14. 88 —*M.M. (11/15/2004)*

Neil Ellis 2001 Sauvignon Blanc (Groenekloof) $15. 85 —*M.S. (4/1/2002)*

Neil Ellis 2000 Sauvignon Blanc (Groenekloof) $15. 90 —*M.M. (3/1/2001)*

Neil Ellis 2005 Sincerely Sauvignon Blanc (Western Cape) $15. 84 —*M.D. (7/1/2006)*

Neil Ellis 2004 Shiraz (Groenekloof) $23. Warming spices and smoke on the nose lead into an elegant balance of juicy berry, firm tannins and pepper. There's an earthy backbone to the wine but overall, it's bright and approachable. Pair with grilled meats. **88** —*S.K. (11/15/2007)*

Neil Ellis 2003 Shiraz (Stellenbosch) $23. 88 —*M.D. (7/1/2006)*

Neil Ellis 1999 Shiraz (Stellenbosch) $19. 86 *(10/1/2001)*

Neil Ellis 2005 Sincerely Shiraz (Western Cape) $15. Flavors of cherry, blackberry, mocha, roasted meat and spice star in this soft, elegant wine. The mouthfeel is rounded and gentle, the finish light. A wine for those with a taste for lighter, less fruit-forward Shiraz. Drink now. **86** —*S.K. (3/1/2007)*

Neil Ellis 2004 Sincerely Shiraz (Western Cape) $15. 86 —*M.D. (7/1/2006)*

Neil Ellis 2003 Vineyard Selection Syrah (Jonkershoek Valley) $43. 89 —*M.D. (7/1/2006)*

NEW WORLD

New World 2002 Sémillon-Chardonnay (Western Cape) $9. 85 —*K.F. (4/1/2003)*

New World 2002 Syrah (Western Cape) $10. 86 —*K.F. (8/1/2003)*

NIEL JOUBERT

Niel Joubert 2001 African Tradition Collection Leopard Cabernet Sauvignon (Paarl) $12. 86 —*K.F. (8/1/2003)*

Niel Joubert 2002 African Tradition Collection Buffalo Chardonnay (Paarl) $12. 86 —*K.F. (9/1/2003)*

Niel Joubert 2000 African Tradition Collection Lion Merlot (Paarl) $12. 87 —*K.F. (8/1/2003)*

Niel Joubert 2001 African Tradition Collection Rhinoceros Red Blend (Paarl) $12. 87 —*K.F. (9/1/2003)*

Niel Joubert 2000 African Tradition Collection Elephant Shiraz (Paarl) $12. 86 —*K.F. (8/1/2003)*

NIELS VERBURG

Niels Verburg 2004 Shiraz (Western Cape) $44. From the former Beaumont winemaker Niels Verburg, this cool and collected Shiraz has lovely layers of mint, chocolate and spice, with raspberry fruit that is expressive but elegant. There's length and body but the wine has a tempered touch. **88** —*S.K. (7/1/2007)*

NITÍDA

Nitída 2003 Calligraphy Bordeaux Blend (Durbanville) $25. 87 —*M.D. (5/1/2006)*

Nitída 2006 Pinotage (Durbanville) $0. Voluptuous and elegant but still true to the rustic nature of Pinotage, this is a true expression of South African terroir. Sweet black currant, licorice and cool-climate-derived mint mingled with smoke and spice create dimension and depth. The finish is firm and a touch edgy—again, a Pinotage characteristic. **88** —*S.K. (7/1/2007)*

Nitída 2002 Pinotage (Durbanville) $15. 81 —*M.M. (12/15/2004)*

Nitída 2005 Sauvignon Blanc (Durbanville) $15. 85 —*M.D. (5/1/2006)*

Nitída 2003 Sauvignon Blanc (Durbanville) $15. 88 —*M.M. (12/15/2004)*

Nitída 2003 Sémillon (Durbanville) $13. 82 —*M.M. (12/15/2004)*

OMNIA

Omnia 2005 Arniston Bay Bush Vines Chenin Blanc (Coastal Region) $NA. 84 —*R.V. (11/15/2005)*

ONE STROKE ONE

One Stroke One 2003 Cabernet Sauvignon (Stellenbosch) $28. 87 —*M.D. (11/1/2006)*

ONYX

Onyx 2000 Shiraz (Groenekloof) $20. 85 —*K.F. (4/1/2003)*

ORACLE

Oracle 2002 Cabernet Sauvignon (Western Cape) $8. 81 —*M.M. (11/15/2004)*

Oracle 2002 Pinotage (Western Cape) $8. 87 Best Buy —*M.M. (7/4/2004)*

Oracle 2003 Sauvignon Blanc (Western Cape) $8. 88 —*M.M. (7/4/2004)*

Oracle 2002 Shiraz (Western Cape) $8. 87 —*M.M. (7/4/2004)*

Oracle 2006 Of The Sun Shiraz (Western Cape) $10. The earthy cigar box, tobacco and spice aromas on the nose of this Shiraz are both distinctive and attractive, though on the palate, the wine could use a touch more complexity. It's a good wine with enticing flavors of berry, smoke and spice—I just want more of what's working here. A great selection for everything from grilled meat to Mexican dishes. **85 Best Buy** —*S.K. (11/15/2007)*

ORIGIN

Origin 2005 Sauvignon Blanc (Western Cape) $10. 82 —*M.D. (7/1/2006)*

Origin 2004 Syrah (Western Cape) $10. 83 —*M.D. (9/1/2006)*

OUT OF AFRICA

Out of Africa 2002 Cabernet Sauvignon (Western Cape) $9. 82 —*M.M. (11/15/2004)*

Out of Africa 2003 Chardonnay (Western Cape) $9. 84 —*M.M. (7/4/2004)*

Out of Africa 2002 Pinotage (Western Cape) $9. 85 —*M.M. (7/4/2004)*

Out of Africa 2003 Sauvignon Blanc (Western Cape) $9. 85 —*M.M. (7/4/2004)*

Out of Africa 2003 Shiraz (Western Cape) $9. 86 —*M.M. (7/4/2004)*

PAUL CLUVER

Paul Cluver 2005 Gewürztraminer (Elgin) $13. 88 Best Buy —*M.D. (12/31/2006)*

Paul Cluver 2005 Riesling (Elgin) $13. 87 —*M.D. (12/31/2006)*

Paul Cluver 2006 Noble Late Harvest Riesling (Elgin) $24. Lush honey, apricots and pineapple come together in this luxuriant dessert wine It displays a mouthwatering apple character that adds a clean spin to the decadent richness. Balanced and very elegant. **90 Editors' Choice** —*S.K. (7/1/2007)*

Paul Cluver 2005 Sauvignon Blanc (Elgin) $15. Green pepper, paired with berries and flowers, comprise the nose of this typical cool-climate Sauvignon Blanc. The full flavors are carried on a slightly more viscous mouthfeel and end with a long, minerally finish. **85** —*S.K. (3/1/2007)*

PEACOCK RIDGE

Peacock Ridge 2005 Chardonnay (Stellenbosch) $19. 84 —*M.D. (11/1/2006)*

Peacock Ridge 2005 Merlot (Stellenbosch) $19. 83 —*M.D. (11/1/2006)*

Peacock Ridge 2005 Sauvignon Blanc (Stellenbosch) $19. 87 —*M.D. (9/1/2006)*

PEARLY BAY

Pearly Bay NV Celebration Champagne Blend (South Africa) $7. 82 *—M.M. (12/1/2001)*

Pearly Bay NV Celebration Champagne Blend (South Africa) $7. 84 *—J.M. (12/1/2002)*

PECAN STREAM

Pecan Stream 2004 Cabernet Sauvignon-Shiraz (Stellenbosch) $14. This wine, made by respected winemaker Kevin Arnold (who has released Pecan Stream as a second label to Waterford Estate) is a balanced blend of 50% Cabernet and 42% Shiraz with some Cabernet Franc, Mourvèdre, Cinsaut and Merlot. On the nose, there's clove, chocolate and herbal notes, and on the palate, some smokiness with oak and berry. Likeable and easy to drink. **86** *—S.K. (3/1/2007)*

Pecan Stream 2005 Chenin Blanc (Stellenbosch) $14. 90 Best Buy *—R.V. (11/15/2005)*

PETER ANDREW

Peter Andrew 2003 Ingenium Reserve Bordeaux Blend (Stellenbosch) $52. This is a beautiful Bordeaux blend, offering the kind of classic poise and exotic flair that South Africans are so good at delivering. On the nose, soft mint, chocolate, cedar and black currant beckon, and on the palate, spice and minerality mingle with the earthier elements. The structure is good, and there's ample complexity, but the wine is still approachable. **90 Editors' Choice** *—S.K. (12/15/2007)*

PINE CREST

Pine Crest 2004 Cabernet Sauvignon (Coastal Region) $15. 87 *—R.V. (11/1/2006)*

Pine Crest 2003 Cabernet Sauvignon (Coastal Region) $15. 84 *—M.D. (11/1/2006)*

Pine Crest 2001 Chardonnay (Coastal Region) $13. 84 *—K.F. (9/1/2003)*

Pine Crest 2000 Chardonnay (Franschhoek) $13. 88 *—K.F. (4/1/2003)*

Pine Crest 2001 Chenin Blanc (Franschhoek) $10. 85 *—K.F. (4/1/2003)*

Pine Crest 2004 Pinotage (Coastal Region) $14. 85 *—M.D. (11/1/2006)*

PLAISIR DE MERLE

Plaisir De Merle 1998 Merlot (Paarl) $22. 86 *—K.F. (8/1/2003)*

Plaisir De Merle 2005 Sauvignon Blanc (Coastal Region) $22. 90 *—M.D. (12/31/2006)*

PORCUPINE RIDGE

Porcupine Ridge 2006 Cabernet Sauvignon (Coastal Region) $13. The smoked meat and spice on the nose of this consistently good Cabernet give it an exotic South African appeal, but the wine goes beyond merely unique. Balanced tannins and good acidity give this poise and dimension, its smoke and berry layers soft and approachable. A very nice wine at a good price. **87** *—S.K. (12/15/2007)*

Porcupine Ridge 2005 Cabernet Sauvignon (Coastal Region) $12. 83 *—M.D. (12/31/2006)*

Porcupine Ridge 2004 Cabernet Sauvignon (Coastal Region) $12. 86 *—M.D. (3/1/2006)*

Porcupine Ridge 2001 Cabernet Sauvignon (Coastal Region) $13. 84 *—K.F. (4/1/2003)*

Porcupine Ridge 2005 Merlot (Coastal Region) $13. Vibrant red fruits, raspberry and dark chocolate meet in this Merlot from South Africa. The structure and acids are good and the wine overall has a firm but balanced character. The finish is long and lush. **85** *—S.K. (7/1/2007)*

Porcupine Ridge 2004 Merlot (Coastal Region) $12. 86 *—M.D. (3/1/2006)*

Porcupine Ridge 2003 Merlot (Coastal Region) $11. 83 *—M.M. (11/15/2004)*

Porcupine Ridge 2001 Merlot (Coastal Region) $13. 88 *—K.F. (4/1/2003)*

Porcupine Ridge 2005 Sauvignon Blanc (Western Cape) $10. 85 Best Buy *—M.D. (3/1/2006)*

Porcupine Ridge 2003 Sauvignon Blanc (Western Cape) $9. 86 Best Buy *—M.M. (11/15/2004)*

Porcupine Ridge 2002 Sauvignon Blanc (Western Cape) $10. 87 Best Buy *—K.F. (4/1/2003)*

Porcupine Ridge 2006 Syrah (Coastal Region) $13. A full, rich nose of blackberry, cinnamon and black pepper introduces this impressive Shiraz from mover and shaker Marc Kent. Balanced and elegant with a restrained minerality, this is a food-friendly and structured without being rugged. **84** *—S.K. (11/15/2007)*

Porcupine Ridge 2005 Syrah (Coastal Region) $12. Vibrant berry fruit and smoke hit the nose, followed by chocolate, cherry and spice on the palate. Plenty of chewy texture, sure to even out with a little aging, gives the wine backbone. Needs time but is well-balanced and flavorful. **86** *—S.K. (3/1/2007)*

Porcupine Ridge 2004 Syrah (Coastal Region) $12. Marc Kent gets it right again with this intense, elegant Syrah. Waves of dark berry and vanilla hit the palate, with an edge of coffee and pepper. The aromas are great too: plum, herbs and cassis. This wine can be enjoyed today but it has enough structure to age very nicely. Imported by Vineyard Brands. **89 Best Buy** *—S.K. (7/1/2007)*

Porcupine Ridge 2004 Syrah (Coastal Region) $12. 88 Best Buy *—M.D. (7/1/2006)*

Porcupine Ridge 2003 Syrah (Coastal Region) $11. 82 *—M.M. (11/15/2004)*

Porcupine Ridge 2000 Syrah (Coastal Region) $13. 84 *(10/1/2001)*

POSITIVELY ZINFUL

Positively Zinful 2001 Zinfandel (Coastal Region) $10. 87 *—K.F. (11/15/2003)*

POST HOUSE CELLAR

Post House Cellar 2002 Chenin Blanc (Stellenbosch) $NA. 87 *—R.V. (11/15/2005)*

PROSPECT

Prospect 1870 1998 Cabernet Sauvignon (Robertson) $30. 85 *—K.F. (8/1/2003)*

RAATS FAMILY

Raats Family 2004 Chenin Blanc (Stellenbosch) $23. 93 *—R.V. (11/15/2005)*

Raats Family 2005 Original Chenin Blanc (South Africa) $13. 89 Best Buy *—M.D. (11/1/2006)*

Raats Family 2004 Original Chenin Blanc (Stellenbosch) $13. 89 Best Buy *—R.V. (11/15/2005)*

RADFORD DALE

Radford Dale 2004 Shiraz (Stellenbosch) $20. 88 *—M.D. (12/31/2006)*

RAKA

Raka 2002 Biography Shiraz (Western Cape) $23. 91 Editors' Choice *—M.D. (5/1/2006)*

RAWSON'S

Rawson's 2002 Chardonnay (Worcester) $9. 87 Best Buy *—K.F. (4/1/2003)*

Rawson's 2001 Pinotage (Breede River Valley) $10. 85 *—K.F. (9/1/2003)*

Rawson's 2002 Shiraz (Breede River Valley) $10. 86 *—K.F. (8/1/2003)*

Rawson's 2001 Revelry White Blend (Worcester) $8. 86 *—K.F. (4/1/2003)*

REMHOOGTE

Remhoogte 2003 Bonne Nouvelle Cabernet Blend (Stellenbosch) $45. 92 *—R.V. (11/1/2006)*

Remhoogte 2002 Bonne Nouvelle Cabernet Blend (Stellenbosch) $40. 89 *—R.V. (11/1/2006)*

Remhoogte 2003 Estate Wine Cabernet Blend (Simonsberg-Stellenbosch) $28. 92 Editors' Choice *—R.V. (11/1/2006)*

Remhoogte 2000 Cabernet Sauvignon (Stellenbosch) $22. 81 *—M.M. (3/1/2004)*

RIETVALLEI ESTATE WINE

Rietvallei Estate Wine 2004 Cabernet Sauvignon (Robertson) $15. Grown in the Robertson region, this full-bodied wine has a bright berry nose with hints of woodsy spice, and on the palate offers chocolate, coffee, some leather and toasted oak. It's an elegant wine with ample structure—very good on its own or when paired with heartier dishes like steak or venison. **88** *—S.K. (3/1/2007)*

Rietvallei Estate Wine 2002 Cabernet Sauvignon (Robertson) $13. 86 *—M.M. (11/15/2004)*

Rietvallei Estate Wine 2006 Rosé Cabernet Sauvignon (Robertson) $15. This is a full-bodied, refreshing rosé from Rietvallei, one of South Africa's oldest Muscadel producers. Made from 100% Cab, this is rife with fresh berry aromas and on the palate, a mixture of weight and racy citrus adds appeal. A great warm weather wine but not to be dismissed as simple. **87** *—S.K. (3/1/2007)*

Rietvallei Estate Wine 2006 Chardonnay (Robertson) $13. This is a sophisticated Chardonnay that balances vibrant fruit flavors with light, spicy oak. Lime and citrus on the nose are backed by flavors of rounded fruit and a toasty wooded character. Understated and elegant, but with a lingering finish, this wine makes an impact because it gets everything right in a memorable way. **88** *—S.K. (6/1/2007)*

Rietvallei Estate Wine 2003 Chardonnay (Robertson) $11. 84 *—M.M. (11/15/2004)*

Rietvallei Estate Wine 2003 Gewürztraminer (Robertson) $10. 82 *—M.M. (12/15/2004)*

Rietvallei Estate Wine 2002 Muscadel (Robertson) $11. 88 Editors' Choice *—M.M. (11/15/2004)*

Rietvallei Estate Wine 2004 Shiraz (Robertson) $17. With aromas of cinnamon, chocolate, cigar and plum, this wine promises to be interesting. For the most part, it delivers, with flavors of pert, peppery fruit, spice, and toasted oak. The finish is smooth and elegant, but faint. Overall, a full-bodied, flavorful wine that would pair well with meats and pastas. 86 *—S.K. (3/1/2007)*

Rietvallei Estate Wine 2002 Shiraz (Robertson) $15. 87 *—M.M. (11/15/2004)*

Rietvallei Estate Wine 2003 John B. Bouquet Blanc White Blend (Robertson) $9. 84 *—M.M. (12/15/2004)*

RIJK'S PRIVATE CELLAR

Rijk's Private Cellar 2004 Chenin Blanc (Tulbagh) $NA. 85 *—R.V. (11/15/2005)*

Rijk's Private Cellar 2003 Chenin Blanc (Tulbagh) $35. 93 *—R.V. (11/15/2005)*

ROBERT'S ROCK

Robert's Rock 2004 Cabernet Sauvignon-Merlot (Western Cape) $8. 84 Best Buy *—J.C. (11/15/2005)*

Robert's Rock 2003 Cabernet Sauvignon-Merlot (Western Cape) $9. 84 *—M.M. (4/1/2005)*

Robert's Rock 2002 Cabernet Sauvignon-Merlot (Western Cape) $8. 84 *—K.F. (8/1/2003)*

Robert's Rock 2005 Chenin Blanc-Chardonnay (Western Cape) $8. 86 Best Buy *—M.D. (11/1/2006)*

Robert's Rock 2004 Chenin Blanc-Chardonnay (Western Cape) $8. 84 Best Buy *—M.M. (4/1/2005)*

Robert's Rock 2003 Chenin Blanc-Chardonnay (Western Cape) $8. 85 Best Buy *—M.M. (3/1/2004)*

Robert's Rock 2000 Chenin Blanc-Chardonnay (Western Cape) $6. 84 *(9/1/2001)*

Robert's Rock 2003 Shiraz-Cabernet Sauvignon (Western Cape) $9. 83 *—M.M. (4/1/2005)*

Robert's Rock 2003 Shiraz-Malbec (Western Cape) $9. 85 Best Buy *—M.M. (4/1/2005)*

Robert's Rock 2001 Shiraz-Malbec (Western Cape) $9. 85 Best Buy *—J.C. (7/1/2004)*

ROBERTSON WINERY

Robertson Winery 2006 Cabernet Sauvignon (Robertson) $18. Bright berry aromas and a palate of spicy, dry flavors give this Cab an attractive, varietally correct character. Tobacco, mint and berry mingle nicely with a touch of sweet oak. Easy and good to pair with grilled meat. 86 *—S.K. (12/15/2007)*

Robertson Winery 2004 Cabernet Sauvignon (Robertson) $10. 88 Best Buy *—M.D. (3/1/2006)*

Robertson Winery 2003 Cabernet Sauvignon (Robertson) $10. 80 *—M.M. (11/15/2004)*

Robertson Winery 2002 Cabernet Sauvignon (Robertson) $10. 87 *—K.F. (8/1/2003)*

Robertson Winery 2004 Prospect Hill Cabernet Sauvignon (Robertson) $18. This wine's beautiful nose, with waves of flowers, brambly fruit and earthy, woodsy spice, makes it an enticing choice from the get-go. On the palate, ripe berries and a soft, round character with chew but no edge continue to please. An elegant, approachable wine that would pair well with roasted meat. 86 *—S.K. (3/1/2007)*

Robertson Winery 2003 Prospect Hill Cabernet Sauvignon (Robertson) $20. 86 *—M.M. (7/1/2005)*

Robertson Winery 2005 Chardonnay (Robertson) $10. 82 *—M.D. (5/1/2006)*

Robertson Winery 2003 Chardonnay (Robertson) $10. 82 *—M.M. (7/4/2004)*

Robertson Winery 2002 Chardonnay (Robertson) $9. 84 *—K.F. (9/1/2003)*

Robertson Winery 2003 Kings River Chardonnay (Robertson) $19. 87 *—M.M. (7/4/2004)*

Robertson Winery 2005 Chenin Blanc (Robertson) $10. 87 Best Buy *—R.V. (11/15/2005)*

Robertson Winery 2004 Chenin Blanc (Robertson) $10. 84 *—M.M. (12/15/2004)*

Robertson Winery 2003 Chenin Blanc (Robertson) $9. 80 *—M.M. (7/4/2004)*

Robertson Winery 2004 Special Late Harvest Gewürztraminer (Robertson) $10. 85 Best Buy *—M.M. (12/15/2004)*

Robertson Winery 2003 Special Late Harvest Gewürztraminer (Robertson) $10. 86 Best Buy *—M.M. (12/15/2004)*

Robertson Winery 2003 Merlot (Robertson) $10. 80 *—J.C. (11/15/2005)*

Robertson Winery 2002 Merlot (Robertson) $10. 85 Best Buy *—M.M. (11/15/2004)*

Robertson Winery 2001 Merlot (Robertson) $10. 84 *—K.F. (8/1/2003)*

Robertson Winery 2005 Pinotage (Robertson) $10. Typical Pinotage flavors of banana, plums and cherry characterize this wine from Robertson Winery, a producer in South Africa since 1941. Oak treatment mellows the edges and offers a smooth overall style. The finish is easy and soft. 84 *—S.K. (7/1/2007)*

Robertson Winery 2003 Pinotage (Robertson) $10. 85 *—M.M. (7/4/2004)*

Robertson Winery 2002 Pinotage (Robertson) $10. 84 *—K.F. (9/1/2003)*

Robertson Winery 2005 Phanto Ridge Pinotage (Robertson) $18. This is an extremely appealing, accessible Pinotage—instantly likeable and elegant. On the nose, heady aromas of chocolate and plum; on the palate, lush, velvety, soft tannins and substantial structure. Not sure you'll like Pinotage? Give this one a shot. With food, it will be even better. 87 *—S.K. (7/1/2007)*

Robertson Winery 2004 Phanto Ridge Pinotage (Robertson) $20. 85 *—M.D. (3/1/2006)*

Robertson Winery 2003 Almond Grove Noble Late Harvest Riesling (Robertson) $18. 88 Editors' Choice *—M.M. (12/15/2004)*

Robertson Winery 2005 Sauvignon Blanc (Robertson) $10. 87 Best Buy *—M.D. (3/1/2006)*

Robertson Winery 2004 Sauvignon Blanc (Robertson) $10. 83 *—M.M. (12/15/2004)*

Robertson Winery 2003 Sauvignon Blanc (Robertson) $10. 84 *—M.M. (7/4/2004)*

Robertson Winery 2002 Sauvignon Blanc (Robertson) $9. 84 *—K.F. (9/1/2003)*

Robertson Winery 2004 Retreat Sauvignon Blanc (Robertson) $20. 90 Editors' Choice *—M.M. (12/15/2004)*

Robertson Winery 2004 Shiraz (Robertson) $10. 84 *—M.D. (3/1/2006)*

Robertson Winery 2003 Shiraz (Robertson) $10. 82 *—J.C. (11/15/2005)*

Robertson Winery 2002 Shiraz (Robertson) $10. 87 *—K.F. (8/1/2003)*

Robertson Winery 2004 Wolfkloof Shiraz (Robertson) $18. An intriguing nose of mint, dark fruit and smoke lead to flavors of mulberry, leather and spice. Good tannins and structure, with a soft finish. Elegant but full of backbone. 88 *—S.K. (3/1/2007)*

Robertson Winery 2003 Wolfkloof Shiraz (Robertson) $20. 86 *—M.M. (12/15/2004)*

ROCKFIELDS

Rockfields 2005 Chenin Blanc (Worcester) $NA. 81 *—R.V. (11/15/2005)*

ROODEBERG

Roodeberg 2003 Red Blend (Western Cape) $12. This blend of Cabernet Sauvignon, Merlot and Shiraz is an all-around winner. Cinnamon spice, dark berry and pepper on the nose creates a complex aromatic character, while the combination of earthy, woody flavors are complemented by touches of lush mocha. This will pair beautifully with red meat dishes and robust cheeses. 89 Best Buy *—S.K. (7/1/2007)*

Roodeberg 2002 Red Blend (Western Cape) $13. 87 *—M.M. (3/1/2004)*

Roodeberg 2001 Red Blend (Western Cape) $13. 88 *—K.F. (1/1/2004)*

Roodeberg 1998 Red Blend (Western Cape) $11. 88 *(9/1/2001)*

Roodeberg 1997 Red Blend (Western Cape) $12. 91 Best Buy *—M.S. (1/1/2004)*

RUDERA

Rudera 2004 Cabernet Sauvignon (Stellenbosch) $44. 89 *—R.V. (11/1/2006)*

Rudera 2003 Cabernet Sauvignon (Stellenbosch) $46. 85 *—M.D. (9/1/2006)*

Rudera 2004 Chenin Blanc (Stellenbosch) $20. 89 *—R.V. (11/15/2005)*

Rudera 2002 Robusto Chenin Blanc (Stellenbosch) $NA. 92 *—R.V. (11/15/2005)*

Rudera 2004 Syrah (Stellenbosch) $27. Earthy tobacco, smoke and spice on the nose and a fruit-forward palate make this expressive Shiraz an attractive cohort to smoked meat dishes and cheese assortments. The wine has a backbone of toasted oak and a smooth character. **85** *—S.K. (11/15/2007)*

Rudera 2003 Syrah (Stellenbosch) $27. 87 *—M.D. (9/1/2006)*

RUDI SCHULTZ

Rudi Schultz 2004 Syrah (Stellenbosch) $37. This wine has an exuberant, juicy quality to it that is extremely attractive for solo sipping. Bright berry and spice on the nose are followed by mouthwatering, round fruit in the mouth. Pepper and spice mingle with good structure and a long finish, making this an impressive showing from Schultz. **87 Editors' Choice** *—S.K. (11/15/2007)*

RUPERT & ROTHSCHILD

Rupert & Rothschild 1999 Baron Edmund Bordeaux Blend (Coastal Region) $45. 88 *—M.M. (12/15/2004)*

Rupert & Rothschild 2001 Classique Bordeaux Blend (Coastal Region) $19. 87 *—M.M. (12/15/2004)*

Rupert & Rothschild 2000 Classique Bordeaux Blend (Coastal Region) $20. 88 *—M.M. (3/1/2004)*

Rupert & Rothschild 1998 Classique Bordeaux Blend (Coastal Region) $20. 87 *(2/1/2002)*

Rupert & Rothschild 2001 Baron Edmond Cabernet Sauvignon-Merlot (Coastal Region) $45. 88 *—J.C. (7/1/2005)*

Rupert & Rothschild 2003 Baroness Nadine Chardonnay (Western Cape) $25. 87 *—M.D. (3/1/2006)*

Rupert & Rothschild 2000 Baroness Nadine Chardonnay (Coastal Region) $26. 85 *—S.H. (1/1/2002)*

Rupert & Rothschild 1999 Baroness Nadine Chardonnay (Coastal Region) $26. 89 *(2/1/2002)*

Rupert & Rothschild 2003 Classique Merlot-Cabernet Sauvignon (Western Cape) $20. Produced on an historic French Huguenot farm by the Rupert family and Baron Benjamin de Rothschild, son of the late Baron Edmond de Rothschild of France, this wine beckons with a blackberry and pepper nose but falls flat on the palate with one-dimensional angularity. The parts feel disparate, though the oak and some earthy tones add some complexity. **83** *—S.K. (3/1/2007)*

Rupert & Rothschild 1999 Classique Red Blend (Coastal Region) $20. 86 *—K.F. (4/1/2003)*

RUST EN VREDE

Rust en Vrede 1998 Estate Wine Bordeaux Blend (Stellenbosch) $33. 87 *—M.S. (1/1/2004)*

Rust en Vrede 2002 Cabernet Sauvignon (Stellenbosch) $29. 93 Editors' Choice *—R.V. (11/1/2006)*

Rust en Vrede 1999 Cabernet Sauvignon (Stellenbosch) $20. 83 *—K.F. (4/1/2003)*

Rust en Vrede 1998 Cabernet Sauvignon (Stellenbosch) $23. 88 *—M.M. (4/1/2002)*

Rust en Vrede 2005 Merlot (Stellenbosch) $0. This is a traditional, terroir-driven Merlot, heavy on the dark berry and mocha and with smooth, balanced tannins. Soft, warming spices are intertwined throughout, and the finish dry. There's structure and tannin here, but the wine is approachable. Imported by Terlato Wines International. **88** *—S.K. (7/1/2007)*

Rust en Vrede 2004 Merlot (Stellenbosch) $21. 91 Editors' Choice *—M.D. (12/31/2006)*

Rust en Vrede 2003 Merlot (Stellenbosch) $23. 88 *—M.D. (9/1/2006)*

Rust en Vrede 2001 Merlot (Stellenbosch) $14. 85 *—K.F. (8/1/2003)*

Rust en Vrede 2003 Estate Wine Red Blend (Stellenbosch) $44. Dark and inky in color, this blend of Cab, Shiraz and Merlot comes from respected Stellenbosch producer Rust en Vrede. There's an earthy nose of leather and spice that gives way to berries and crisp herbs. On the palate, the wine is balanced and structured, with a toasty nut finish. **87** *—S.K. (3/1/2007)*

Rust en Vrede 2002 Estate Wine Red Blend (Stellenbosch) $46. 92 Editors' Choice *—M.D. (7/1/2006)*

Rust en Vrede 1999 Shiraz (Stellenbosch) $35. 87 *—K.F. (4/1/2003)*

Rust en Vrede 1998 Shiraz (Stellenbosch) $22. 87 *(11/1/2001)*

RUSTENBERG

Rustenberg 2004 John X Merriman Bordeaux Blend (Stellenbosch) $30. 93 *—R.V. (11/1/2006)*

Rustenberg 2003 John X Merriman Bordeaux Blend (Stellenbosch) $30. A serious wine with real aging potential, this Bordeaux blend from on-the-radar vintner Adi Badenhorst marries muscular strength with a softer, savvy style. Smoke, mocha, berry and spice create a seamless mosaic of flavor, while firmly structured tannins offer an assertive edge. The wine has all the hallmarks of a classic Bordeaux with a few added exotic touches, making it a great gift for wine lovers who already have everything. **91** *—S.K. (12/15/2007)*

Rustenberg 2002 John X Merriman Bordeaux Blend (Stellenbosch) $30. 87 *—M.D. (9/1/2006)*

Rustenberg 2004 Peter Barlow Cabernet Sauvignon (Stellenbosch) $48. Rustenberg makes delicious, serious wines that will age beautifully, and this Cabernet is included, though it needs some time to mellow and unfurl. 100% Cabernet Sauvignon, it has an assertive nose of cherry and herbs, and on the palate, it's taut and intense with spicy fruit flavors and firm tannins. This wine should be cellared for a good 5-10 years for maximum enjoyment. **91 Cellar Selection** *—S.K. (7/1/2007)*

Rustenberg 2003 Peter Barlow Cabernet Sauvignon (Stellenbosch) $48. 87 *—M.D. (9/1/2006)*

Rustenberg 2003 Five Soldiers Chardonnay (Stellenbosch) $38. 90 *—M.D. (9/1/2006)*

Rustenberg 1999 Five Soldiers Chardonnay (Stellenbosch) $33. 91 *—R.V. (7/1/2002)*

Rustenberg 2005 John X Merriman Red Blend (Stellenbosch) $0. This wine is renegade winemaker Adi Badenhorst's favorite in his portfolio, and for good reason. In line with the best Bordeaux blends, it leads with an earthy, mineral-driven nose, and on the palate, it's both juicy and restrained. Expressive flavors of pepper, mocha and spice and elegant tannins give the wine a stately and sophisticated style. It will keep getting better in the bottle. **92 Cellar Selection** *—S.K. (7/1/2007)*

SADIE

Sadie 2004 Sequillo Red Blend (Swartland) $30. Eben Sadie continues to put Swartland on the map with this excellent SMG blend, displaying savory spices, delicious red fruit and a great tannin structure. There's also that siganture South African touch of minerality, which adds to the elegance. It's ready to drink now but will age with grace. Imported by Vinnovative Imports. **90 Cellar Selection** *—S.K. (7/1/2007)*

Sadie 2005 Palladius White Blend (Swartland) $0. Loosely based on the white wines of southern France, this wine—fresh and creamy blend of Viognier, Chenin Blanc, Chardonnay and Grenache Blanc, offers toast and spice with an interplay of fresh fruit giving an intense, lush character to the wine. Good natural acidity is an added bonus. The flavors are big but very pretty. Imported by European Cellars. **89** *—S.K. (7/1/2007)*

SANCTUM

Sanctum 2003 Shiraz (Western Cape) $48. 90 *—M.D. (9/1/2006)*

SAUVIGNON REPUBLIC

Sauvignon Republic 2006 Sauvignon Blanc (Stellenbosch) $0. From Stellenbosch producer Sauvignon Republic Cellars, this wine has an undeniably South Africa character, with its tropical fruit aromas and flavors mingled with a crisp minerality. It's clean and crisp but full of upfront flavor. Imported by Sauvignon Republic, Inc. **88** *—S.K. (7/1/2007)*

Sauvignon Republic 2005 Sauvignon Blanc (Stellenbosch) $18. 88 *—M.D. (7/1/2006)*

SAXENBURG ESTATE

Saxenburg Estate 2003 Private Collection Cabernet Sauvignon (Stellenbosch) $NA. 89 *—R.V. (11/1/2006)*

Saxenburg Estate 2000 Private Collection Chardonnay (Stellenbosch) $15. 84 *—J.M. (7/1/2002)*

Saxenburg Estate 1998 Merlot (Coastal Region) $15. 82 *—M.M. (3/1/2001)*

Saxenburg Estate 1998 Private Selection Merlot (Stellenbosch) $20. 86 *—M.M. (4/1/2002)*

Saxenburg Estate 1999 Private Collection Sauvignon Blanc (Stellenbosch) $14. 85 *—M.N. (3/1/2001)*

Saxenburg Estate 1998 Private Collection Shiraz (Stellenbosch) $30. 86 *(11/1/2001)*

SCALI

Scali 1999 Pinotage (Paarl) $25. 86 *—K.F. (4/1/2003)*

Scali 2005 Blanc White Blend (Swartland) $30. This blend of Chenin Blanc, Chardonnay and Viognier is delicious, delicate and floral with notes of honey and a minerally, crisp acidity. It's soft but rich with a sweet, luscious character. The Scali family is dedicated to traditional farming and winemaking with little interference; that purity comes through in the glass. **91** *—S.K. (7/1/2007)*

SEBEKA

Sebeka 2006 Shiraz (Western Cape) $8. Blueberry and raspberry on the nose of this impressive, well-priced Shiraz entice, and on the palate, a balance of lively fruit, bright flavors and spice make this an attractive everyday sip. A touch of smoke and blackberry add to its appeal. **86 Best Buy** —*S.K. (11/15/2007)*

Sebeka 2006 Cape Blend Shiraz-Pinotage (Western Cape) $9. This Cape Blend (so-called because it has Pinotage in it) is juicy, structured and easy-drinking. An enjoyable food wine to boot, it has an expressive, approachable character—jammy fruit of the Shiraz gives it life—but has Pinotage reserve and backbone, too. Pair this with grilled ribs or lamb or drink it alone. **88 Best Buy** —*S.K. (7/1/2007)*

SEIDELBERG

Seidelberg 2000 Roland's Reserve Estate Wine Cabernet Sauvignon (Paarl) $32. 87 —*K.F. (4/1/2003)*

Seidelberg 2001 Chardonnay (Paarl) $15. 87 —*K.F. (4/1/2003)*

Seidelberg 2005 Estate Chenin Blanc (Paarl) $12. 86 —*M.D. (7/1/2006)*

Seidelberg 2000 Roland's Reserve Estate Wine Merlot (Paarl) $32. 87 —*K.F. (4/1/2003)*

Seidelberg 2003 Pinotage (Paarl) $13. 87 —*M.D. (7/1/2006)*

Seidelberg 2003 Roland's Reserve Pinotage (Paarl) $22. 88 —*M.D. (7/1/2006)*

Seidelberg 2001 Roland's Reserve Estate Wine Pinotage (Paarl) $32. 89 —*K.F. (4/1/2003)*

Seidelberg 2002 Un Deux Trois Red Blend (Paarl) $22. 88 —*M.D. (5/1/2006)*

Seidelberg 2005 Sauvignon Blanc (Paarl) $14. 85 —*M.D. (9/1/2006)*

Seidelberg 2004 Sauvignon Blanc (Paarl) $12. 88 Best Buy —*M.D. (3/1/2006)*

Seidelberg 2002 Estate Wine Sauvignon Blanc (Paarl) $13. 86 —*K.F. (4/1/2003)*

Seidelberg 2003 Roland's Reserve Syrah (Paarl) $24. 86 —*M.D. (5/1/2006)*

Seidelberg 2001 Roland's Reserve Estate Wine Syrah (Paarl) $32. 88 —*K.F. (4/1/2003)*

SERENGETI

Serengeti 2004 Cabernet Sauvignon-Merlot (Coastal Region) $10. This is a great example of how an affordable wine can still offer quality and character. A compelling nose of tobacco, berry and spice is followed by a play of plum and clean minerality. Balanced and slightly restrained, the wine will pair well with heartier foods like steak or stew. **87 Best Buy** —*S.K. (11/15/2007)*

Serengeti 2004 Pinotage (Coastal Region) $10. Serengeti continues to produce good quality wines at a friendly price and this Pinotage continues the tradition. The nose is peppery, spicy and a little spikey in the true Pinotage fashion, but on the palate, the wine is prettier. It's soft and rounded with nice red berry and spice components that finish in a soft but lingering manner. **86 Best Buy** —*S.K. (11/15/2007)*

Serengeti 2003 Pinotage (Coastal Region) $13. 83 —*M.D. (3/1/2006)*

Serengeti 2005 Rosé Pinotage (Coastal Region) $10. Fragrant, tropical fruit on the nose and a combination of sweet and exotic flavors makes this appealing rosé an easy, everyday wine that will pair well with spicy dishes and grilled poultry. **83** —*S.K. (7/1/2007)*

Serengeti 2005 Sauvignon Blanc (Coastal Region) $10. A heavy dose of orange and lemon leads the nose of this affordable Sauvignon Blanc from coastal South Africa, but it's slightly heavy-handed and lacks some of the acidity that gives this variety its lift. The mouthfeel is viscous and needs a lighter, fresher touch, but in general, the wine is good and displays a unique character. Imported by Hemingway & Hale. **83** —*S.K. (6/1/2007)*

Serengeti 2004 Sauvignon Blanc (Coastal Region) $13. 82 —*J.C. (11/15/2005)*

Serengeti 2003 Shiraz (Coastal Region) $13. 87 —*J.C. (11/15/2005)*

SHARK TRUST

Shark Trust 2005 Great White Unwooded Chardonnay (Western Cape) $10. 85 Best Buy —*M.D. (12/31/2006)*

Shark Trust 2005 Whale Shark Chenin Blanc (Western Cape) $10. 87 Best Buy —*M.D. (11/1/2006)*

SIGNAL HILL

Signal Hill 2003 Tete Blanche Chenin Blanc (Stellenbosch) $15. 88 —*R.V. (11/15/2005)*

Signal Hill 2000 Gamay Noir (Stellenbosch) $10. 87 —*K.F. (9/1/2003)*

Signal Hill 2000 Petite Verdot (Western Cape) $25. 87 —*K.F. (9/1/2003)*

SIMONSIG

Simonsig 2000 Tiara Bordeaux Blend (Stellenbosch) $30. 90 —*R.V. (11/1/2006)*

Simonsig 1996 Tiara Bordeaux Blend (Stellenbosch) $25. 86 —*M.S. (5/1/2000)*

Simonsig 1996 Cabernet Sauvignon (Stellenbosch) $14. 82 —*M.S. (5/1/2000)*

Simonsig 1998 Cabernet Sauvignon (Stellenbosch) $15. 93 Editors' Choice —*M.N. (3/1/2001)*

Simonsig 2002 Cabernet Sauvignon Cabernet Sauvignon (Stellenbosch) $18. 88 —*R.V. (11/1/2006)*

Simonsig 2000 Chardonnay (Stellenbosch) $14. 88 —*R.V. (7/1/2002)*

Simonsig 1998 Chenin Blanc (Stellenbosch) $8. 87 —*M.S. (11/15/1999)*

Simonsig 2005 Chenin Blanc (Stellenbosch) $10. 87 Best Buy —*R.V. (11/15/2005)*

Simonsig 2004 Chenin Blanc (Stellenbosch) $10. 86 Best Buy —*M.M. (7/1/2005)*

Simonsig 2003 Chenin Blanc (Stellenbosch) $8. 88 Best Buy —*M.S. (11/15/2004)*

Simonsig 2001 Estate Wine Chenin Blanc (Stellenbosch) $7. 85 —*M.S. (4/1/2002)*

Simonsig 2003 Pinotage (Stellenbosch) $14. Raspberry and cherry pervade in this well-rounded Pinotage, which exhibits touches of plum and that spciy dryness that typifies the variety. The fruit keeps the edges soft though, and the wine is structured but balanced. Pair with smoked meat or enjoy on its own—it's an embraceable Pinotage from a dependable producer. Imported by Quintessential Family of Wines, LLC. **87** —*S.K. (9/1/2007)*

Simonsig 2002 Pinotage (Stellenbosch) $14. 88 —*M.D. (9/1/2006)*

Simonsig 2005 Redhill Pinotage (Stellenbosch) $30. Soft mint, spice, cocoa and smoke on the nose lead into like flavors on the palate, creating a smooth, integrated combination of elegant and structured components that are assertive but friendly. The finish is lingering and the wine has aging potential. **89** —*S.K. (12/15/2007)*

Simonsig 2004 Redhill Pinotage (Stellenbosch) $30. This rich, ruby-colored red goes in the softer, smoother direction for a Pinotage, making it more appealing to American palates. The dry, spicy Pinotage character is still present, but it's rounded by a softer, fuller blanket of pretty fruit. Simonsig gets it right and this wine will pair well with grilled meats or can be enjoyed on its own. Hold for aging. Imported by Quintessential Family of Wines, LLC. **88** —*S.K. (9/1/2007)*

Simonsig 2003 Redhill Pinotage (Stellenbosch) $30. 89 —*M.D. (7/1/2006)*

Simonsig 2006 Sauvignon Blanc (Stellenbosch) $13. Tropical fruit and apple on the nose and palate place this wine firmly on South African soil, and that's a good thing—Sauvignon Blancs from South Africa are the perfect balance of lush fruit and crisp, clean minerality. The wine is fresh and friendly, but has character. Imported by Quintessential Family of Wines, LLC. **86** —*S.K. (7/1/2007)*

Simonsig 2005 Sauvignon Blanc (Stellenbosch) $13. 85 —*M.D. (3/1/2006)*

Simonsig 2000 Sauvignon Blanc (Stellenbosch) $13. 90 Best Buy —*M.N. (3/1/2001)*

Simonsig 2001 Estate Wine Sauvignon Blanc (Stellenbosch) $11. 84 —*M.S. (4/1/2002)*

Simonsig 1998 Shiraz (Stellenbosch) $15. 80 *(10/1/2001)*

Simonsig 1998 Merindol Shiraz (Stellenbosch) $45. 86 *(11/1/2001)*

SIMONSVLEI

Simonsvlei 2005 Lifestyle Chenin Blanc (Western Cape) $NA. 85 —*R.V. (11/15/2005)*

Simonsvlei 2005 Premier Chenin Blanc (Western Cape) $NA. 86 —*R.V. (11/15/2005)*

SINNYA

Sinnya 1998 Bordeaux Blend (Robertson) $11. 85 *(9/1/1999)*

Sinnya 1998 Chardonnay (Robertson) $11. 82 *(9/1/1999)*

Sinnya 2002 Chardonnay (Robertson) $10. 83 —*K.F. (9/1/2003)*

Sinnya 2001 Merlot-Cabernet Sauvignon (Robertson) $10. 84 —*K.F. (8/1/2003)*

Sinnya 2002 Pinotage (Robertson) $10. 85 —*K.F. (9/1/2003)*

SIYABONGA

Siyabonga 2001 Cabernet Sauvignon-Merlot (Western Cape) $28. 84 —*K.F. (1/1/2004)*

Siyabonga 2001 Severney White Blend (Western Cape) $16. 84 —*K.F. (1/1/2004)*

SLALEY

Slaley 2003 Hunting Family Chardonnay (Stellenbosch) $17. Peach and lemon mingled with toasted oak make this wine a compelling choice for fans of Chardonnays with character. This has weight and presence but is still approachable, with the fresh touch that makes South African whites so food friendly. **86** —*S.K. (11/15/2007)*

Slaley 2003 Hunting Family Pinotage (Stellenbosch) $24. The gripping, earthy flavors of this impressive Pinotage are true to the variety without frightening off fans of softer wine. Pinotage has a tendency toward angularity, but this wine, with its deep leather and coffee flavors and elegant minerality is accessible and, paired with meats like pork or grilled steak, will please palates overall. It needs to age though—at least four years. **89** —*S.K. (9/1/2007)*

Slaley 2003 Lindsay's Whimsy Cape Blend Red Blend (Stellenbosch) $15. This blend of 40% Cabernet and 60% Pinotage is not for the faint-hearted, with its bold aromas and flavors of spice and spiky fruit. The Cabernet takes the edge off the Pinotage without changing its nature, making this a great wine for pairing with a big plate of ribs or a spicy ethnic dish. **84** —*S.K. (12/15/2007)*

Slaley 2002 Hunting Family Shiraz (Stellenbosch) $25. Chocolate and spice on the nose are subtle but seductive, and there's a generous amount of white pepper in the aroma and on the palate, along with blackberry and cherry. Layered and elegant but a touch too restrained, this wine will pair well with duck and lamb. **86** —*S.K. (6/1/2007)*

Slaley 1999 Hunting Family Shiraz (Stellenbosch) $28. 89 *(11/1/2001)*

SLALEY ESTATE

Slaley Estate 2002 Broken Stone Pinotage (Stellenbosch) $15. Subtle oak, strawberry, raspberry and mocha flavors come together in a rich swirl in this unique Pinotage. Juicy and smooth, with elegant tannins and a lingering finish, this is a very nice example of what South African Pinotage can achieve, and how it can please multiple palates. **87** —*S.K. (9/1/2007)*

Slaley Estate 2003 Broken Stone Shiraz (Stellenbosch) $15. Deep cherry, smoke and spice on the nose lead this exuberant but balanced wine. More cherry and smoke on the palate is elegantly integrated; the wine has great structure and will age well. Mouthwatering and quite delicious from beginning to end. **88** —*S.K. (6/1/2007)*

SLANGHOEK

Slanghoek 2001 Private Reserve Pinotage (South Africa) $13. 84 —*M.M. (3/1/2004)*

Slanghoek 2002 Private Reserve Sauvignon Blanc (South Africa) $11. 86 —*K.F. (11/15/2003)*

Slanghoek 2000 Private Reserve Shiraz (South Africa) $14. 84 —*M.M. (3/1/2004)*

Slanghoek NV Vin Doux Sparkling Blend (South Africa) $14. 86 —*K.F. (12/1/2003)*

SONOP

Sonop 2006 Organic Chardonnay (Western Cape) $10. Crisp, clean and lively, this is a fresh-style Chardonnay with flavors of grapefruit and lemon. Good acidity and weight and lots of flavor make it an exciting everyday choice and good food-pairing wine. **86 Best Buy** —*S.K. (7/1/2007)*

SOUTHERN RIGHT

Southern Right 2004 Pinotage (Walker Bay) $20. 84 —*M.D. (11/1/2006)*

Southern Right 2002 Pinotage (Western Cape) $15. 86 —*M.M. (11/15/2004)*

Southern Right 2003 Sauvignon Blanc (Western Cape) $10. 87 Best Buy —*M.M. (11/15/2004)*

SPICE ROUTE

Spice Route 2005 Chenin Blanc (Swartland) $18. Tropical fruit, pear and honey typify this distinctive Chenin from South Africa's Swartland region. It's round and smooth but not heavy, making it an excellent wine for diverse food pairing. Think hard, salty cheeses or seafood. **87** —*S.K. (7/1/2007)*

Spice Route 2004 Chenin Blanc (Coastal Region) $17. 82 —*R.V. (11/15/2005)*

Spice Route 2000 Flagship Merlot (Swartland) $35. 88 —*K.F. (4/1/2003)*

Spice Route 2005 Mourvèdre (Swartland) $20. This Mourvèdre has a lovely nose of chocolate and mint and is both soft and layered. Flavors of blackberry are jammy and integrated, and there's a facet of spice, all of which creates an easy-drinking and accessible wine. A softer wine with character. **88 Editors' Choice** —*S.K. (7/1/2007)*

Spice Route 2004 Mourvèdre (Swartland) $18. 89 —*M.D. (7/1/2006)*

Spice Route 2006 Pinotage (Swartland) $23. Blackberry, red berry and tobacco, along with exotic spiced meat and coriander flavors, offer complexity and intrigue in this concentrated treat. Good structure and a light touch of minerality—complete with a wave of the varietal alkaline—give the wine a distinctive character. Pair with grilled meat. **86** —*S.K. (12/15/2007)*

Spice Route 2005 Pinotage (Swartland) $23. Brambly plum and red berry aromas and a lush, full palate make this both approachable and great to drink on its own. Plum, berry and pepper on the palate are smooth and elegant, and the finish is soft and poised. **87** —*S.K. (11/15/2007)*

Spice Route 2004 Pinotage (Swartland) $23. 88 —*M.D. (3/1/2006)*

Spice Route 2000 Flagship Pinotage (Swartland) $23. 86 —*K.F. (9/1/2003)*

Spice Route 2005 Sauvignon Blanc (Coastal Region) $15. 85 —*M.D. (7/1/2006)*

Spice Route 1999 Shiraz (Swartland) $20. 80 *(10/1/2001)*

Spice Route 2001 Flagship Syrah (Swartland) $34. 87 —*M.D. (5/1/2006)*

Spice Route 2000 Flagship Syrah (Swartland) $34. 83 —*M.M. (11/15/2004)*

Spice Route 1999 Flagship Syrah (Swartland) $35. 88 *(11/1/2001)*

Spice Route 2005 Viognier (Swartland) $23. 85 —*M.D. (9/1/2006)*

SPIER

Spier 2005 Classic Chenin Blanc (Western Cape) $9. 87 Best Buy —*R.V. (11/15/2005)*

Spier 2005 Discover Steen (Western Cape) $7. 83 —*R.V. (11/15/2005)*

SPRINGFIELD ESTATE

Springfield Estate 2001 The Work of Time Bordeaux Blend (Robertson) $30. 90 —*R.V. (11/1/2006)*

Springfield Estate 1999 Cabernet Sauvignon Methode Ancienne Cabernet Sauvignon (Robertson) $52. 92 —*R.V. (11/1/2006)*

Springfield Estate 2004 Whole Berry Cabernet Sauvignon Cabernet Sauvignon (Robertson) $22. 89 —*R.V. (11/1/2006)*

STARK-CONDÉ

Stark-Condé 2004 Condé Cabernet Sauvignon (Stellenbosch) $42. 89 —*R.V. (11/1/2006)*

Stark-Condé 2003 Condé Cabernet Sauvignon (Stellenbosch) $42. 87 —*M.D. (7/1/2006)*

Stark-Condé 2004 Stark Cabernet Sauvignon (Stellenbosch) $27. 90 —*R.V. (11/1/2006)*

Stark-Condé 2003 Stark Cabernet Sauvignon (Stellenbosch) $27. 89 —*M.D. (7/1/2006)*

Stark-Condé 2005 Unfined and Unfiltered Cabernet Sauvignon (Stellenbosch) $27. From small-batch, handcraft producer Stark-Condé, this unfiltered Cab offers personality and elegance. Berry, herbs, fennel and spice on the nose lead into a red that's extremely pretty in the mouth. Good integration of tannins and fruit, and a light minerality throughout give the wine a soft, balanced appeal. Though it will pair well with spiced meat and bolder dishes, the wine is great on its own. **89 Editors' Choice** —*S.K. (12/15/2007)*

Stark-Condé 2003 Condé Syrah (Stellenbosch) $35. 90 —*M.D. (7/1/2006)*

Stark-Condé 2003 Stark Syrah (Stellenbosch) $26. 89 —*M.D. (7/1/2006)*

STEENBERG

Steenberg 2004 Cabernet Sauvignon (Coastal Region) $11. Red berry, cinnamon and vanilla mingle playfully in this personality-laden Cab. The combo of pretty and slightly wild flavors works well—and firm tannins and structure mean the wine will age nicely. Imported by Monsieur Touton. **87 Best Buy** —*S.K. (11/15/2007)*

STELLAR ORGANICS

Stellar Organics 2003 Cabernet Sauvignon (Western Cape) $9. 80 —*J.C. (11/15/2005)*

STELLEKAYA

Stellekaya 2002 Cabernet Sauvignon (Stellenbosch) $29. 88 —*M.D. (11/1/2006)*

STELLENRYCK

Stellenryck 1996 Cabernet Sauvignon (Coastal Region) $16. 87 —*M.M. (3/1/2001)*

STELLENZICHT

Stellenzicht 2002 Golden Triangle Chardonnay (Stellenbosch) $15. 88 Editors' Choice —*M.M. (7/4/2004)*

Stellenzicht 2001 Golden Triangle Pinotage (Stellenbosch) $18. 88 —*M.M. (7/4/2004)*

Stellenzicht 2003 Golden Triangle Sauvignon Blanc (Stellenbosch) $13. 87 —*M.M. (7/4/2004)*

Stellenzicht 2002 Reserve Sémillon (Stellenbosch) $25. 90 Editors' Choice —*M.M. (11/15/2004)*

Stellenzicht 2001 Golden Triangle Shiraz (Stellenbosch) $18. 89 —*M.M. (7/4/2004)*

Stellenzicht 2000 Syrah (Stellenbosch) $60. 83 —*M.M. (11/15/2004)*

STORMHOEK

Stormhoek 2006 Pinot Grigio (Coastal Region) $10. Light, clean and uncomplicated, the way most people like their Pinot Grigio's, this wine still has depth. It offers great acidity and lift as well as easy-to-savor tropical fruit and citrus flavors. Despite its popularity in the U.S., Pinot Grigio is a rare find in South Africa, and winemaker Graham Knox is getting it right. 87 Best Buy —*S.K. (7/1/2007)*

Stormhoek 2005 Pinotage (Western Cape) $10. The great Pinotage debate in South Africa continues: How do you appeal to the American palate with a variety that has an eccentric, spicy and rustic edge? Stormhoek may have found the answer with this soft and friendly version, which has managed to extract the best of the variety without stripping it of its unique character. Bright and juicy with a soft, integrated spice mélange, the wine offers plum and smoke too, making it an excellent choice for grilled ribs or steak. 88 Best Buy —*S.K. (7/1/2007)*

Stormhoek 2006 Sauvignon Blanc (Western Cape) $10. Bright, tropical fruit flavors mingled with a fresh, lively, cut grass character typify this playful wine from the hills of South Africa's Wellington region. Good acidity and lift ensure this is a refreshing wine for warm weather repasts. 87 Best Buy —*S.K. (7/1/2007)*

Stormhoek 2004 Sémillon (Wellington) $10. Not currently imported into the U.S. 89 Best Buy —*S.K. (7/1/2007)*

STORYTELLER

Storyteller 2005 Chapter IV The Sea Serpent Chardonnay (Western Cape) $9. Apricot, melon and peach on the nose lead to a viscous but slightly thin-tasting Chardonnay with some sweetness. Not terribly complex but an enjoyable, everyday drinking wine. 84 —*S.K. (3/1/2007)*

Storyteller 2005 Chapter III Eliza 1868 Merlot (Western Cape) $9. From the producer whose labels read like assorted chapters from Melville, this affordable Merlot is good enough, and inexpensive enough, to drink with everything from Tuesday night pizza to Sunday night duck breast medallions. Smooth and mellow with gamey spice and cherry aromas and flavors. Soft finish. Can drink now. 85 —*S.K. (7/1/2007)*

SUMARIDGE

Sumaridge 2005 Chardonnay (Walker Bay) $18. A balanced Chardonnay with finesse, offering expressive flavors of grapefruit and pineapple paired with a toasty roundness. The wine has a racy cleanness but is still full-bodied. Will pair well with a variety of foods. 86 —*S.K. (3/1/2007)*

Sumaridge 2004 Merlot (Walker Bay) $18. A traditional, structured Merlot with smooth, soft tannins and flavors of spice, chocolate and dark fruit. The wine has a good finish and an elegant character. 84 —*S.K. (7/1/2007)*

Sumaridge 2006 Dry Rosé Rosé Blend (Hemel en Aarde) $14. Simple and easygoing, this dry rosé exhibits strawberry and red fruit. It's not complex and lacks some of the delicate nuances that make a rosé shine, but paired with a summer salad or seafood, it will make a nice addition to the table. 82 —*S.K. (7/1/2007)*

Sumaridge 2005 Sauvignon Blanc (Hemel en Aarde) $15. Lively, bright aromas and clean flavors of citrus and tropical fruit make this a fun wine to sip on its own or pair with dishes like seafood or Chinese chicken salad. There's pineapple on the palate too, giving the wine a playful edge. It's not to be mulled upon—it's too lighthearted for such contemplation—but meant to be enjoyed on a hot summer day with some rays beating on your back. Good, clean finish. 85 —*S.K. (6/1/2007)*

Sumaridge 2004 Syrah (Walker Bay) $25. A wine with character, this Syrah from the oceanside Walker Bay region is full of classic flavors like pepper, spice and chocolate, and while assertive, has a soft, clean finish. Paired with grilled lamb or beef, it's even better. 84 —*S.K. (7/1/2007)*

SWARTLAND

Swartland 1997 Cabernet Sauvignon (Swartland) $12. 85 *(9/1/1999)*

Swartland 2004 Indalo Cabernet Sauvignon (Swartland) $14. 87 —*M.D. (12/31/2006)*

Swartland 1997 Chardonnay (Swartland) $10. 81 *(9/1/1999)*

Swartland 2005 Chenin Blanc (Swartland) $NA. 83 —*R.V. (11/15/2005)*

Swartland 2005 Indalo Chenin Blanc (Swartland) $14. 86 —*R.V. (11/15/2005)*

Swartland 1997 Merlot (Swartland) $12. 82 *(9/1/1999)*

Swartland 2003 Indalo Pinotage (Swartland) $14. 86 —*M.D. (7/1/2006)*

Swartland 1997 Shiraz (Swartland) $10. 86 *(9/1/1999)*

Swartland 2003 Indalo Shiraz (Swartland) $15. Earthy, leathery and peppery scents on this Swartland offering will appeal to fans of a more grounded Shiraz, and the flavors follow suit. Berry and tobacco layers are folded into smooth tannins, but the wine has structure. It's a little on the rustic side, though with a good barbecue the edge might be evened out. 84 —*S.K. (6/1/2007)*

TALL HORSE

Tall Horse 2005 Cabernet Sauvignon (Western Cape) $8. Raspberry, cherry and spice on the nose and a good balance of rounded-fruit flavors recommend this value-driven Cab from South Africa. Friendly, approachable and touched with oak for complexity, the wine will hold its own well against spicy meat dishes. Imported by Cape Wine Ventures, LLC. 84 Best Buy —*S.K. (11/15/2007)*

Tall Horse 2004 Cabernet Sauvignon (Western Cape) $8. A lush nose of mocha, tobacco and tea, followed by flavors of juicy blackberry and spice, make this wine an easy choice for everyday drinking. The finish falls slightly short but the layered flavors offer quality and character at a very reasonable price. 84 Best Buy —*S.K. (11/15/2007)*

Tall Horse 2003 Cabernet Sauvignon (South Africa) $8. 82 —*M.D. (3/1/2006)*

Tall Horse 2004 Chardonnay (Western Cape) $8. 84 Best Buy —*M.D. (3/1/2006)*

Tall Horse 2005 Merlot (Western Cape) $8. Aromas of cherry, plum and flint introduce this fun Merlot from South Africa. Elegant, soft and supple on the palate, this offers good fruit flavors and a pleasant finish. Not terribly complex but certainly enjoyable. Imported by Cape Wine Ventures, LLC. 85 Best Buy —*S.K. (11/15/2007)*

Tall Horse 2004 Merlot (Western Cape) $8. Smoke and clove on the nose and a toasty, soft berry flavor profile make this Merlot a good choice for everyday sipping. Try with tomato-based pasta dishes or duck. 83 —*S.K. (11/15/2007)*

Tall Horse 2003 Merlot (Western Cape) $8. 84 Best Buy —*M.D. (3/1/2006)*

Tall Horse 2005 Shiraz (Western Cape) $8. A floral nose of violets offers an intriguing start to a wine that's both a value and a fun find. On the palate, red wild berry, spice and smoke are balanced, and though this has a rusticity that tells of its terroir, overall it's simply pretty. Imported by Cape Wine Ventures, LLC. 85 Best Buy —*S.K. (11/15/2007)*

Tall Horse 2003 Shiraz (South Africa) $8. 84 Best Buy —*M.D. (5/1/2006)*

TEDDY HALL

Teddy Hall 2005 Chenin Blanc (Stellenbosch) $12. 88 Best Buy —*R.V. (11/15/2005)*

THANDI

Thandi 2001 Cabernet Sauvignon (Coastal Region) $14. 83 —*M.M. (12/15/2004)*

Thandi 2002 Chardonnay (Western Cape) $13. 85 —*M.M. (12/15/2004)*

Thandi 2002 Pinot Noir (Elgin) $15. 84 —*M.M. (12/15/2004)*

THE BERRIO

The Berrio 2003 Cabernet Sauvignon (South Africa) $20. 87 —*M.D. (9/1/2006)*

The Berrio 2005 Sauvignon Blanc (Elim) $20. 85 —*M.D. (7/1/2006)*

THE BIG FIVE COLLECTION

The Big Five Collection 2006 Lion Cabernet Sauvignon (Western Cape) $10. A soft, delicate nose of spice and mocha lead on this approachable Cab from South Africa. Simple flavors of berry and tobacco and an overall integrated character make it an easy choice for everyday sipping. Could use some structure and complexity but for the price, it's a good buy. 83 —*S.K. (12/15/2007)*

The Big Five Collection 2003 Lion Cabernet Sauvignon (Western Cape) $10. 84 —*M.M. (4/1/2005)*

The Big Five Collection 2004 Leopard Chardonnay (Western Cape) $10. 87 Best Buy —*M.M. (4/1/2005)*

The Big Five Collection 2006 Elephant Pinotage (Western Cape) $10. This is a friendly, mainstream approach to Pinotage that makes a lot of sense; with its balanced flavors of pepper, red berry and spice it has exotic appeal but is still easy to drink. The price is reasonable, making it a fun pick for ethnic dishes or grilled meats. **85 Best Buy** —*S.K. (12/15/2007)*

The Big Five Collection 2003 Elephant Pinotage (Western Cape) $10. 83 —*M.M. (4/1/2005)*

The Big Five Collection 2004 Rhino Sauvignon Blanc (Western Cape) $10. 85 Best Buy —*M.M. (4/1/2005)*

The Big Five Collection 2006 Buffalo Shiraz (Western Cape) $10. Another attractively priced Shiraz from South Africa, which is becoming a bigger player in terms of both value and prestige Shiraz. Luscious spice and dark berry on the nose are touched with smoke and black pepper and lead into a spicy, rounded fruit character. There's complexity here and with age, this will become an elegant, integrated choice. **86 Best Buy** —*S.K. (11/15/2007)*

The Big Five Collection 2003 Buffalo Shiraz (Western Cape) $10. 85 Best Buy —*M.M. (4/1/2005)*

THE FOUNDRY

The Foundry 2003 Cape of Good Hope Syrah (Coastal Region) $41. 89 —*M.D. (9/1/2006)*

The Foundry 2005 Cape of Good Hope Viognier (Coastal Region) $20. 87 —*M.D. (9/1/2006)*

THE WOLFTRAP

The Wolftrap 2003 Red Blend (Western Cape) $10. 85 Best Buy —*M.M. (12/15/2004)*

THELEMA

Thelema 2005 Cabernet Sauvignon (Stellenbosch) $41. Gamey spice, cigar and tobacco notes make this a classic choice. It also has a touch of alkaline smoke—an indigenous spin that will attract or dissuade, depending on a person's palate. Overall, the wine has a facet of eccentric appeal, making it a poised choice for the cellar. **85** —*S.K. (12/15/2007)*

Thelema 2004 Cabernet Sauvignon (Stellenbosch) $41. Focused flavors of mint and black currant come together in this distinctive Cabernet. There's a touch of oak, too, that adds spice, and the overall character is elegant. The wine will benefit from some aging to further integrate its parts. **87** —*S.K. (11/15/2007)*

Thelema 2003 Cabernet Sauvignon (Stellenbosch) $41. 88 —*M.D. (9/1/2006)*

Thelema 1995 Cabernet Sauvignon (Stellenbosch) $30. 85 *(9/1/1999)*

Thelema 2005 The Mint Cabernet Sauvignon (Stellenbosch) $45. As the name would suggest, this is redolent of mint on the nose and on the palate. Pair that up with cocoa, herbs and some spiced wood and you'll see why the wine is a keeper for fans of new flavor combinations. Memorable and immediately appealing, it's also ageworthy. South African character with a classic spin. **88** —*S.K. (12/15/2007)*

Thelema 2004 The Mint Cabernet Sauvignon (Stellenbosch) $45. Smoked meat, herbs and mint on the nose lead into a melange of soft, elegant and complex flavors of black currant and mocha. The wine has structure but is subtle. Drink now or hold for 4–5 years. **89** —*S.K. (11/15/2007)*

Thelema 2004 Chardonnay (Stellenbosch) $25. 88 —*M.D. (9/1/2006)*

Thelema 2002 Chardonnay (Stellenbosch) $25. 83 —*M.D. (9/1/2006)*

Thelema 2000 Chardonnay (Stellenbosch) $25. 90 —*R.V. (7/1/2002)*

Thelema 2004 Merlot (Stellenbosch) $29. This is a Merlot that asserts itself rather than hanging back in the wings like many other examples of the variety. Bright fruit flavors and sturdy tannins are rounded out by coffee and spice and an overall integrated character. Not terribly intellectual but definitely fun and full of flavor. **86** —*S.K. (9/1/2007)*

Thelema 2003 Merlot (Stellenbosch) $29. 89 —*M.D. (9/1/2006)*

Thelema 1999 Merlot (Stellenbosch) $22. 86 —*K.F. (8/1/2003)*

Thelema 2004 Rhine Riesling (Stellenbosch) $17. 84 —*M.D. (12/31/2006)*

Thelema 2005 Sauvignon Blanc (Stellenbosch) $19. 89 —*M.D. (12/31/2006)*

Thelema 2006 Sutherland Sauvignon Blanc (Elgin) $20. With the lush nose of pineapple, melon and tropical fruit in this intriguing wine from Elgin's Thelema, you'd expect a wine that's sweet and slightly viscous in the mouth. This wine is actually bone-dry with a firm acidity; perhaps even a touch too tight for this reviewer, but its citric, clean flavors are pleasurable regardless. Try this with oysters or seafood salad and drink it young. **85** —*S.K. (6/1/2007)*

THEUNISKRAAL

Theuniskraal 2005 Ixia Shiraz (Tulbagh) $9. Smoke, smoke and more smoke—but paired with spice, clove and licorice, that's not such a bad thing. The regular plum and blackberry Shiraz flavors are here, but they take a back seat to an earthy ashiness that is very distinctive, though perhaps not for the fainthearted. **84** —*S.K. (3/1/2007)*

THORNTREE

Thorntree 2004 Chardonnay (Western Cape) $9. 85 Best Buy —*M.D. (5/1/2006)*

Thorntree 2003 Merlot (Western Cape) $9. 85 Best Buy —*M.D. (9/1/2006)*

Thorntree 2004 Sauvignon Blanc (Western Cape) $9. 84 —*M.D. (5/1/2006)*

Thorntree 2003 Shiraz (Western Cape) $9. 83 —*M.D. (5/1/2006)*

TOKARA

Tokara 2004 Chardonnay (Stellenbosch) $36. 86 —*M.D. (11/1/2006)*

Tokara 2003 Zondernaam Chardonnay (Stellenbosch) $20. 86 —*M.D. (9/1/2006)*

Tokara 2005 Zondernaam Sauvignon Blanc (Western Cape) $17. 86 —*M.D. (12/31/2006)*

Tokara 2003 Zondernaam Shiraz (Stellenbosch) $20. 88 —*M.D. (9/1/2006)*

TRIBAL

Tribal 2003 Chardonnay (Western Cape) $7. 83 —*M.M. (7/4/2004)*

Tribal 2003 Merlot (Western Cape) $7. 80 —*M.M. (7/4/2004)*

Tribal 2003 Pinot Noir (Western Cape) $7. 83 —*M.M. (7/4/2004)*

Tribal 2002 Pinotage (Western Cape) $7. 85 —*M.M. (7/4/2004)*

TUKULU

Tukulu 2003 Chenin Blanc (Groenekloof) $12. 87 Best Buy —*M.M. (11/15/2004)*

Tukulu 2005 Papkuilsfontein Chenin Blanc (Darling) $13. 90 Best Buy —*R.V. (11/15/2005)*

TUMARA

Tumara 2002 Titan Bordeaux Blend (Stellenbosch) $16. 88 —*M.D. (5/1/2006)*

Tumara 2002 Malbec (Stellenbosch) $13. 85 —*M.M. (4/1/2005)*

Tumara 2005 Bellevue Estate Wine Pinotage (Stellenbosch) $17. An instantly recommendable Pinotage, with soft, pretty aromas of berry and spice and a balanced, integrated overall flavor. It's approachable and full of juicy red berry that plays along with spice. Many Pinotages verge on tongue-stripping; this one is both playful and serious. Will pair well with grilled meat. **87** —*S.K. (11/15/2007)*

Tumara 2004 Bellevue Estate Pinotage (Stellenbosch) $16. 86 —*M.D. (11/1/2006)*

Tumara 2003 Bellevue Estate Pinotage (Stellenbosch) $12. 87 Best Buy —*M.D. (3/1/2006)*

Tumara 2002 Bellevue Estate Pinotage (Stellenbosch) $13. 85 —*M.M. (4/1/2005)*

Tumara 2001 Bellevue Estate Pinotage (Stellenbosch) $13. 85 —*M.M. (3/1/2004)*

TWEE JONGE GEZELLEN

Twee Jonge Gezellen NV The Rosé Brut Sparkling Blend (Tulbagh) $17. 85 —*M.D. (12/31/2006)*

TWO OCEANS

Two Oceans 2004 Cabernet Sauvignon-Merlot (Western Cape) $8. 87 Best Buy —*M.D. (5/1/2006)*

Two Oceans 2006 Chardonnay (Western Cape) $8. Toasty vanilla meets bright fruit aromas and flavors in this solid, affordable Chardonnay. It has roundness and complexity, but a good amount of acid keeps it in balance. A well-executed, dependable white that will pair well with almost anything and should be a no-brainer everyday favorite. **85 Best Buy** —*S.K. (7/1/2007)*

Two Oceans 2004 Chardonnay (Western Cape) $8. 87 Best Buy —*M.D. (5/1/2006)*

Two Oceans 2003 Chardonnay (Western Cape) $8. 83 —*M.M. (7/4/2004)*

Two Oceans 2002 Chardonnay (Western Cape) $7. 87 Best Buy —*K.F. (4/1/2003)*

Two Oceans 2005 Sauvignon Blanc (Western Cape) $8. 82 —*M.D. (5/1/2006)*

Two Oceans 2006 Shiraz (Western Cape) $8. Pretty berry fruit and mineral on the nose give this affordable Shiraz character, and on the palate it's dominated by a smoky, simple offering of Shiraz flavors. Not terribly complex, but unique and good for everyday enjoyment. **84 Best Buy** —*S.K. (11/15/2007)*

Two Oceans 2004 Shiraz (Western Cape) $8. 87 Best Buy —*M.D. (7/1/2006)*

Two Oceans 2002 Shiraz (Western Cape) $8. 85 —*M.M. (7/4/2004)*

Two Oceans 2001 Shiraz (Western Cape) $7. 88 Best Buy —*K.F. (4/1/2003)*

UITKYK

Uitkyk 1998 Cabernet Sauvignon (Stellenbosch) $17. 84 —*K.F. (4/1/2003)*

Uitkyk 1999 Estate Cabernet Sauvignon (Stellenbosch) $18. 83 —*M.M. (4/1/2005)*

Uitkyk 2003 Chardonnay (Stellenbosch) $18. 89 —*M.M. (4/1/2005)*

Uitkyk 2001 Chardonnay (Stellenbosch) $17. 85 —*K.F. (4/1/2003)*

Uitkyk 2004 Sauvignon Blanc (Stellenbosch) $18. 84 —*M.M. (4/1/2005)*

Uitkyk 2002 Sauvignon Blanc (Stellenbosch) $11. 84 —*K.F. (9/1/2003)*

Uitkyk 2001 Sauvignon Blanc (Stellenbosch) $11. 84 —*K.F. (4/1/2003)*

UITSIG CONSTANTIA

Uitsig Constantia 2003 Christine Bordeaux Blend (Constantia) $0. You'll want to decant this dense, dark gem of a wine before drinking it, because it needs to time to unfurl its many layers of chocolate, pepper and spice. It's a Bordeaux-style red—traditional, Old World, restrained—but still has strength and personality enough to hold its own against bolder dishes. Very unique and elegant at the same time. **90** —*S.K. (7/1/2007)*

UMKHULU

Umkhulu 2001 Tian Bordeaux Blend (Stellenbosch) $20. Smoke, toast and red fruit flavors come together gracefully in this approachable Bordeaux blend. There are plenty of aromas and flavors to contemplate—think roasted lamb and black fruit—but overall the wine is one you can feel comfortable savoring with a big bowl of stew or a plate of cheese. The price is right, too. **89** —*S.K. (9/1/2007)*

Umkhulu 2001 Akira Red Blend (Stellenbosch) $16. Cabernet and Pinotage give this a hearty edge, but balanced oak and vanilla flavors soften the punch. Add to the toast a mélange of blackberry, plum and currant flavors and the result is a classic wine with character. **86** —*S.K. (9/1/2007)*

Umkhulu 2003 Shiraz (Stellenbosch) $25. The nose on this Shiraz is deep and opulent in character, wafting of mulberry, vanilla and oak, and the flavors are rich and integrated. The tannins are firm but the wine is elegant and enjoyable. An approachable Shiraz that will pair well with everything from grilled ribs to pizza. **84** —*S.K. (6/1/2007)*

Umkhulu 2004 Dry White White Blend (Stellenbosch) $NA. 89 —*R.V. (11/15/2005)*

URBANE

Urbane 2005 Chenin Blanc (Walker Bay) $NA. 84 —*R.V. (11/15/2005)*

Urbane 2002 Sauvignon Blanc (Stellenbosch) $10. 83 —*M.M. (3/1/2004)*

Urbane 2002 Shiraz (Stellenbosch) $10. 84 —*M.M. (3/1/2004)*

VAN LOVEREN

Van Loveren 2003 Reserve Chardonnay (Robertson) $15. 80 —*M.M. (11/15/2004)*

Van Loveren 2002 Reserve Chardonnay (Robertson) $16. 80 —*M.M. (7/4/2004)*

Van Loveren 2001 Reserve Chardonnay (Robertson) $16. 84 —*K.F. (4/1/2003)*

Van Loveren 2002 Riesling (Robertson) $13. 87 —*K.F. (4/1/2003)*

Van Loveren 2003 Sauvignon Blanc (Robertson) $10. 83 —*M.M. (12/15/2004)*

VEENWOUDEN

Veenwouden 1998 Classic Bordeaux Blend (Paarl) $37. 91 —*M.S. (4/1/2002)*

Veenwouden 1998 Merlot (Paarl) $37. 90 —*M.S. (4/1/2002)*

VERGELEGEN

Vergelegen 2004 Mill Race Bordeaux Blend (Stellenbosch) $23. Bold but balanced, rustic but poised, this assertive Bordeaux blend has an appealing nose of plum, mocha and pepper. The flavors of mint, berry and spice are full and lingering, and the tannins are firm but elegant. A beautful wine with real aging potential, and further proof that Vergelegen is a leader in South African wines. **90** —*S.K. (11/15/2007)*

Vergelegen 2001 Red Cabernet Blend (Stellenbosch) $59. 88 —*M.D. (5/1/2006)*

Vergelegen 2001 Red Cabernet Blend (Stellenbosch) $59. 82 —*J.C. (11/15/2005)*

Vergelegen 2001 V Cabernet Blend (Stellenbosch) $145. 92 —*M.D. (9/1/2006)*

Vergelegen 2003 Cabernet Sauvignon (Stellenbosch) $34. 88 —*M.D. (3/1/2006)*

Vergelegen 2003 Reserve Chardonnay (Stellenbosch) $31. 88 —*M.D. (3/1/2006)*

Vergelegen 2003 Mill Race Merlot-Cabernet Sauvignon (Stellenbosch) $22. 89 —*M.D. (5/1/2006)*

Vergelegen 2005 Sauvignon Blanc (Western Cape) $22. 86 —*M.D. (9/1/2006)*

Vergelegen 2004 Sauvignon Blanc (Western Cape) $22. 87 *(7/1/2005)*

Vergelegen 2004 Flagship White Blend (Stellenbosch) $49. Beautiful aromas lead on this white blend from venerable producer Vergelegen. The nose is spicy with a minerally edge. Though time will unfurl the complex flavors of the wine, it's currently exhibiting lovely layers of spicy sweet orange and peach, and the mouthfeel is substantial—coating the tongue but not heavy. Wait until this wine has time to unwind . . . it will be worth it. **90** —*S.K. (7/1/2007)*

VERGENOEGD

Vergenoegd 2001 Estate Wine Bordeaux Blend (Stellenbosch) $35. 92 —*R.V. (11/1/2006)*

Vergenoegd 2001 Cabernet Sauvignon (Stellenbosch) $28. 91 —*R.V. (11/1/2006)*

Vergenoegd 2000 Estate Cabernet Sauvignon (Stellenbosch) $32. 82 —*J.C. (11/15/2005)*

Vergenoegd 2000 Estate Merlot (Stellenbosch) $31. 84 —*M.M. (11/15/2004)*

Vergenoegd 1998 Old Cape Colony Port (Stellenbosch) $30. 86 —*M.M. (11/15/2004)*

Vergenoegd 2000 Estate Shiraz (Stellenbosch) $40. 82 —*M.M. (12/15/2004)*

VILAFONTÉ

Vilafonté 2004 Series C Bordeaux Blend (Paarl) $70. 94 —*R.V. (11/1/2006)*

Vilafonté 2003 Series C Bordeaux Blend (Paarl) $70. 92 *(11/15/2005)*

Vilafonté 2004 Series M Bordeaux Blend (Paarl) $50. 93 —*R.V. (11/1/2006)*

Vilafonté 2003 Series M Bordeaux Blend (Paarl) $50. 91 *(11/15/2005)*

VILLIERA

Villiera NV Tradition Brut Champagne Blend (Paarl) $16. 86 —*M.S. (6/1/2003)*

Villiera 2005 Chenin Blanc (Stellenbosch) $12. 89 —*R.V. (11/15/2005)*

Villiera 2004 Cellar Door Chenin Blanc (Stellenbosch) $24. 85 —*R.V. (11/15/2005)*

VINAY

Vinay NV Rosé Blend (South Africa) $12. 84 —*M.M. (3/1/2004)*

VINUM AFRICA

Vinum Africa 2004 Cabernet Sauvignon (Stellenbosch) $14. 89 Best Buy —*M.D. (11/15/2006)*

Vinum Africa 2005 Chenin Blanc (Stellenbosch) $12. Is Chenin experiencing a renaissance in South Africa? This wine would suggest so, with its taut, layered elegance and sophisticated overall style. The nose is complex, with varying degrees of crisp citrus, flowers and spice. On the palate, it unfolds subtly, with lime, spice and honeyed fruit all sparkling and in sync. It goes without saying that this wine is food-friendly, but it's good enough to be savored on its own. **89 Best Buy** —*S.K. (7/1/2007)*

Vinum Africa 2004 Chenin Blanc (Stellenbosch) $12. 89 Best Buy —*R.V. (11/15/2005)*

Vinum Africa 2002 Chenin Blanc (Stellenbosch) $12. 84 —*K.F. (9/1/2003)*

VREDE EN LUST

Vrede en Lust 2003 Classic Bordeaux Blend (Simonsberg-Paarl) $20. 87 —*M.D. (12/31/2006)*

Vrede en Lust 2003 Simond Red Blend (Simonsberg-Paarl) $15. A blend of Merlot, Cabernet Sauvignon and Shiraz from the Paarl region, this wine is lightly wooded and medium-bodied with ash, smoke, and raspberry on the nose, and on the palate, more ashy, earthy, smoky heft and a bit of chocolate and tea. It's unusual and tough to tackle—the fruit is overpowered. **82** —*S.K. (3/1/2007)*

WARWICK

Warwick 2002 Reserve Bordeaux Blend (Stellenbosch) $32. 90 *—M.M. (7/1/2005)*

Warwick 2003 Tilogy (Estate Reserve) Bordeaux Blend (Stellenbosch) $30. 90 *—M.D. (5/1/2006)*

Warwick 2001 Tilogy (Estate Reserve) Bordeaux Blend (Simonsberg-Stellenbosch) $30. 88 *—M.M. (11/15/2004)*

Warwick 1998 Tilogy (Estate Reserve) Bordeaux Blend (Stellenbosch) $22. 86 *—M.M. (4/1/2002)*

Warwick 2004 Trilogy (Estate Reserve) Bordeaux Blend (Stellenbosch) $32. 95 Editors' Choice *—R.V. (11/1/2006)*

Warwick 2004 Chardonnay (Stellenbosch) $25. 85 *—M.D. (3/1/2006)*

Warwick 1999 Chardonnay (Stellenbosch) $18. 89 *—R.V. (9/10/2002)*

Warwick 1998 Merlot (Stellenbosch) $19. 87 *—M.M. (4/1/2002)*

Warwick 1997 Merlot (Stellenbosch) $18. 87 *—M.N. (3/1/2001)*

Warwick 2005 Old Bush Vines Pinotage (Stellenbosch) $23. An exemplary Pinotage, with its cigarbox, clove and plum aromas and rounded flavors of plum and flowers. Unique and pretty, this is balanced, layered and friendly. Pinotage is a tough customer, but Warwick has, in its usual way, gotten it right. 89 Editors' Choice *—S.K. (11/15/2007)*

Warwick 2004 Old Bush Vines Pinotage (Stellenbosch) $17. 86 *—M.D. (3/1/2006)*

Warwick 2003 Old Bush Vines Pinotage (Stellenbosch) $21. 88 *—M.M. (11/15/2004)*

Warwick 1999 Old Bush Vines Pinotage (Stellenbosch) $17. 89 *—M.M. (4/1/2002)*

Warwick 1998 Old Bush Vines Pinotage (Stellenbosch) $18. 84 *—M.M. (3/1/2001)*

Warwick 2001 Three Cape Ladies Red Blend (Simonsberg-Stellenbosch) $21. 86 *—M.M. (11/15/2004)*

Warwick 2003 Three Cape Ladies Cape Blend Red Blend (Stellenbosch) $25. 85 *—M.D. (7/1/2006)*

Warwick 2002 Three Cape Ladies Cape Blend Red Blend (Stellenbosch) $29. 88 *—M.M. (7/1/2005)*

Warwick 2004 Winemaker Guild Blend Red Blend (Stellenbosch) $60. 92 *—R.V. (11/1/2006)*

Warwick 2006 Professor Black Sauvignon Blanc (Stellenbosch) $20. Enticing aromas of herb, peach and pear lead this delicious SB from centuries-old winery Warwick, whose vineyards are situated on the slopes of Stellenbosh-Simonsberg. The flavors are zesty, with more peach, pear and citrus on the palate, but the overall feel is one of poise and integration. This is a very good example of a wine in which flirty and focused elements marry successfully. 87 *—S.K. (6/1/2007)*

Warwick 2005 Professor Black Sauvignon Blanc (Stellenbosch) $17. 88 *—M.D. (12/31/2006)*

Warwick 2004 Professor Black Sauvignon Blanc (Simonsberg-Stellenbosch) $18. 90 Editors' Choice *—M.M. (11/15/2004)*

Warwick 2001 Estate Shiraz (Simonsberg-Stellenbosch) $20. 84 *—M.M. (11/15/2004)*

WATERFORD

Waterford 2004 Cabernet Sauvignon (Stellenbosch) $29. 92 *—R.V. (11/1/2006)*

Waterford 2003 Cabernet Sauvignon (Stellenbosch) $27. 93 Cellar Selection *—R.V. (11/1/2006)*

Waterford 2001 Cabernet Sauvignon (Stellenbosch) $27. 89 *—R.V. (11/1/2006)*

Waterford 2000 Cabernet Sauvignon (Stellenbosch) $22. 87 *—K.F. (4/1/2003)*

Waterford 1999 Chardonnay (Stellenbosch) $15. 90 Best Buy *—M.M. (3/1/2001)*

Waterford 2005 Estate Chardonnay (Stellenbosch) $22. A zippy tropical fruit character firmly places this wine in the South African Cape, but it also features an elegant degree of French oak, which adds a touch of creaminess. The finish is slightly racy and the overall feel dry, but there's enough weight here to make it more than just merely fun. 87 *—S.K. (3/1/2007)*

Waterford 2000 Sauvignon Blanc (Stellenbosch) $13. 90 Best Buy *—M.M. (3/1/2001)*

Waterford 2003 Kevin Arnold Shiraz (Stellenbosch) $38. Deep aromas of coffee and spice mean this is a Shiraz to be taken seriously, but on the palate, it's simply delicious and not terribly intellectual. The Mourvèdre adds a mocha silkiness to the mix, balancing the dry pepper character of the Shiraz. Great to drink now, but will age gracefully. 87 *—S.K. (6/1/2007)*

Waterford 1999 Kevin Arnold Shiraz (Stellenbosch) $30. 88 *—M.M. (3/1/2001)*

Waterford 2001 Nadine Shiraz (Stellenbosch) $34. 89 *—K.F. (4/1/2003)*

WATERKLOOF

Waterkloof 2005 Sauvignon Blanc (Stellenbosch) $45. 87 *—M.D. (9/1/2006)*

WEBERSBURG

Webersburg 1999 Cabernet Sauvignon (Stellenbosch) $35. 84 *—J.C. (11/15/2005)*

WILD RUSH

Wild Rush 2003 Cape Red Cabernet Blend (Robertson) $9. 85 *—M.M. (11/15/2004)*

Wild Rush 2003 Cape White White Blend (Robertson) $8. 83 *—M.M. (11/15/2004)*

WILDEKRANS

Wildekrans 2005 Chenin Blanc (Walker Bay) $15. 86 *—R.V. (11/15/2005)*

Wildekrans 2001 Reserve Estate Wine Chenin Blanc (Walker Bay) $9. 85 *—K.F. (4/1/2003)*

Wildekrans 2001 Barrel Selection Estate Wine Pinotage (Walker Bay) $25. 87 *—K.F. (9/1/2003)*

Wildekrans 2001 Estate Wine Pinotage (Walker Bay) $15. 87 *—K.F. (9/1/2003)*

Wildekrans 2001 Estate Wine - Cabernet Franc/Merlot Red Blend (Walker Bay) $13. 83 *—K.F. (9/1/2003)*

Wildekrans 2000 Warrant Estate Wine Red Blend (Walker Bay) $25. 84 *—K.F. (9/1/2003)*

Wildekrans 2002 Estate Wine Sauvignon Blanc (Walker Bay) $8. 85 *—K.F. (4/1/2003)*

Wildekrans 2001 Estate Wine Sémillon (Walker Bay) $15. 84 *—K.F. (4/1/2003)*

WINERY OF GOOD HOPE

Winery of Good Hope 2006 Chenin Blanc (Helderberg) $9. Restrained and stately, this impressive Chenin Blanc is also complex and full of flavor. Though there's weight and round layers of flavor on the palate, the minerality gives the wine a delicate, ephemeral touch that is truly elegant. 90 Best Buy *—S.K. (7/1/2007)*

Winery of Good Hope 2005 Chenin Blanc (Stellenbosch) $9. 91 Best Buy *—R.V. (11/15/2005)*

ZELPHI WINES

Zelphi Wines 2001 Simunye Sauvignon Blanc (Coastal Region) $17. 85 *—K.F. (4/1/2003)*

ZEVENWACHT

Zevenwacht 2005 Chenin Blanc (Stellenbosch) $NA. 88 *—R.V. (11/15/2005)*

ZONNEBLOEM

Zonnebloem 2003 Chardonnay (Western Cape) $10. 87 Best Buy *—M.M. (4/1/2005)*

Zonnebloem 2000 Chardonnay (Stellenbosch) $10. 86 *—K.F. (4/1/2003)*

Zonnebloem 2004 Merlot (Stellenbosch) $11. 80 *—M.D. (11/1/2006)*

Zonnebloem 2004 Pinotage (Stellenbosch) $10. 87 Best Buy *—M.D. (11/1/2006)*

Zonnebloem 2005 Sauvignon Blanc (Western Cape) $11. 87 Best Buy *—M.D. (11/15/2006)*

Zonnebloem 2004 Shiraz (Stellenbosch) $10. Ash, berry, smoked meat and spice on the nose lead into flavors of gamey leather and dark fruit. Good with smoked meat entrees. Hold for 3–4 years. 86 Best Buy *—S.K. (3/1/2007)*

Zonnebloem 2002 Shiraz (Stellenbosch) $10. 85 Best Buy *—M.M. (4/1/2005)*

Spain

Among European countries with long winemaking histories, no country has come further in recent years than Spain. As the nation with more acreage under vine than any of its continental mates, Spain is no longer simply a producer of overcropped, basic wines destined for domestic consumption. Just the opposite: in less than two decades, Spain has evolved into one of Europe's most exciting and progressive wine producers.

Today, Spanish winemakers are making sought-after wines at almost every price point and quality level, and in most of the country's sixty-plus denominated regions. From everyday reds made from grapes including Tempranillo, Monastrell, and Garnacha, to crisp whites like Albariño and Verdejo, to frothy Cava and some of the world's finest and richest red and dessert wines, Spain is offering the consumer variety and value at almost every turn.

Harvesting Xarel-lo grapes in a vineyard at Cavas Chandon, the Spanish branch of Moët et Chandon.

Talk about a 180-degree turnabout; twenty years ago, nobody thought much of Spain's wines. In those early post-Franco years, the country featured one collectable red—the idiosyncratic and esoteric Vega Sicilia (still one of the world's great red wines). Meanwhile, Rioja boasted a few highly traditional wines (read: not that fruity, with a lot of American oak flavor) in López de Heredia's Viña Tondonia, Marqués de Riscal, and CUNE, among others. Beyond that, there wasn't much to talk about besides Torres' Sangre de Toro and the dry and sweet fortified wines coming from Jerez in the south.

By the middle of the 1990s and into the twenty-first century, however, the world's thirst for better, more distinctive wines gave Spain the necessary spur in the side that it needed to push the envelope. Younger winemakers, many trained outside the country, started to replace their more traditional predecessors. Older regions that had fallen out of style were invigorated with new plantings and the construction of modern wineries. And almost before you could say Olé, quality wines were emerging from all four corners of the country and quite a few places in between.

SPAIN'S WINES AND REGIONS

There are currently more than sixty regulated wine regions in Spain. The most prominent denominaciones de origen, as the regions are called, have been around for decades if not longer; places like Rioja, Ribera Del Duero, Jerez, Rías Baixas, Priorat, Penedès, Navarra, La Mancha, and Valdepeñas. Others have risen to prominence during the aforementioned growth boom: Rueda, Bierzo, Toro, Cigales, Somontano, Yecla, Jumilla, and Montsant, while not all young, fit the mold of up and coming. And there are still a few DOs that seem stuck in time; outposts like Extremadura, located along the border with Portugal, and Utiel-Requena (inland from Valencia) that may have their day down the line.

Among red-wine regions, the spotlight is shining brightest on Rioja, Ribera Del Duero, Priorat, and, to a lesser degree, Toro and Bierzo. Rioja is one of Spain's larger DOs, and the focus here is on Tempranillo. Rioja came to prominence in the 1800s when French winemakers fled their country's phylloxera (see Glossary) epidemic, and over time three main styles of red wine have evolved: crianzas, which are wood-aged wines generally of lighter stature; reservas, which spend extended time in barrel; and gran reserva, theoretically the ripest and most ageworthy of wines. Look for modern, extracted, flavorful wines from the likes of Allende, LAN, Muga, Remelluri, Remírez de Ganuza, Roda, and a host of other newcomers. Marqués de Murrieta, Marqués de Cáceres, Montecillo, and the previously mentioned CUNE and Riscal comprise the respected old guard.

Ribera Del Duero, Toro, Cigales, and other sections of Castilla y León province are also prime Tempranillo areas. Modern wineries like Alion, Pingus, Viña Sastre, and others in Ribera, as well as Numanthia-Termes in Toro are the new-wave leaders, while Vega Sicilia, Pesquera, Protos, and Pérez Pascuas have been plying their trade in Ribera for longer, with commendable results.

Just to the southwest of Barcelona lies Penedès, the heart of Spain's sparkling wine industry. Here wineries harvest the white grapes Macabeo, Parellada, and Xarello before blending them into what's known as Cava. This sparkling wine is made similarly to Champagne but is lighter and far less complex than France's prized bubbly. Penedès is also home to Miguel Torres S.A., one of Spain's preeminent wineries, a survivor of the Spanish Civil War, and for many years when Spain was overlooked, a major exporter to the United States.

A little further southwest of Penedès are Priorat and Montsant, regions that can trace their winemaking roots back to the Romans and later Carthusian monks. Here Garnacha and old Cariñena vines yield powerful wines, and the current crop of winemakers is, almost to a person, young, ambitious, and iconoclastic. Today Priorat is producing some of the world's finest red wines, ones that compare with the best of France, Italy, and California.

Lastly, Sherry is the fortified sipper of Andalusia. From crisp fino and manzanilla up to richer, nuttier amontillado and oloroso, Sherry is a unique wine for either before a meal or after. Sherry predates Spain's vinous renaissance by centuries, but never has it gone out of style.

1+1=3

1+1=3 2005 Rosé Cabernet Sauvignon (Penedès) $16. Almost red in color, with sweet, juicy aromas of red fruits that bring to mind Beaujolais Nouveau. The palate is fairly unctuous for a rosado, with thick flavors of red apples, berry pie and sweet butter. For a fuller-bodied dry pink wine, it's pretty hefty stuff. **85** —*M.S. (4/1/2007)*

1+1=3 NV Brut Sparkling Blend (Cava) $13. We've tried this nonvintage brut cava for three years running, and it has registered similarly each time. It's a touch flat in terms of feel but the lemon-lime aromas and flavors are solid, if unspectacular. Overall, the wine is fine, with no major faults. **85** —*M.S. (12/15/2007)*

1+1=3 NV Brut Sparkling Blend (Cava) $13. **86** —*M.S. (12/15/2006)*

7 LUNAS

7 Lunas 2003 Campo Góticos Tempranillo (Ribera del Duero) $55. **90** —*M.S. (11/1/2006)*

AALTO

Aalto 2001 PS Tinto del Pais (Ribera del Duero) $105. **95 Editors' Choice** —*M.S. (6/1/2005)*

Aalto 2003 PS Tempranillo (Ribera del Duero) $100. Aalto is one of Ribera's high flyers, and this vintage exhibits coconut, toast and marinated beef aromas in front of bold, round berry flavors. With a lot of oak and the warmth of 2003 behind it, this is a softer, less exact rendition than the amazing 2001 Aalto PS. But it still shows that excellent rugged fruit character and power that define Ribera del Duero. **92** —*M.S. (6/1/2007)*

ABAD DOM BUENO

Abad Dom Bueno 2006 Godello (Bierzo) $13. A little too much canned fruit cocktail and grapefruit juice on the nose, but overall it's generous with its sweetness. The palate offers ripe nectarine, although the feel runs perilously close to being cloying. Better if you don't mind some stickiness to your white wines. **83** —*M.S. (11/1/2007)*

Abad Dom Bueno 2001 Crianza Mencía (Bierzo) $25. Spicy and inviting on the nose, with no shortage of oak. The palate holds that spiciness as bramble and some tartness enter the fray. More of a ready-to-go food wine; it doesn't really have the depth or complexity to go further. **86** —*M.S. (11/1/2007)*

Abad Dom Bueno 2003 Roble Mencía (Bierzo) $14. Hard smoke and raspberry aromas are balanced and pure, and the mouth is ripe, juicy and bright. This makes its point with subtlety and smoothness. It's not a bumpy, aggressive wine as it holds its balance all the way to the end. **88** —*M.S. (11/1/2007)*

ABADIA RETUERTA

Abadia Retuerta 1996 Pago Valdebellon Cabernet Sauvignon (Vino de Mesa de Castilla y León) $100. **92** —*J.C. (11/1/2001)*

Abadia Retuerta 1998 Red Blend (Sardon de Duero) $10. **86** —*M.M. (8/1/2000)*

Abadia Retuerta 1997 Red Blend (Sardon de Duero) $26. **89** —*M.M. (8/1/2000)*

Abadia Retuerta 2000 Primicia Red Blend (Vino de la Tierra de Castilla y León) $10. **87 Best Buy** —*J.C. (11/1/2001)*

Abadia Retuerta 1998 Rívola Red Blend (Sardon de Duero) $12. **90** *(11/15/1999)*

Abadia Retuerta 1998 Selección Especial Red Blend (Vino de Mesa de Castilla y León) $24. **87** —*J.C. (11/1/2001)*

Abadia Retuerta 1999 Selección Especial Unfiltered Red Blend (Sardon de Duero) $27. **89** —*M.S. (3/1/2004)*

Abadia Retuerta 1997 Cuvée El Campanario Tempranillo (Sardon de Duero) $50. **95** —*M.M. (8/1/2000)*

Abadia Retuerta 1998 Cuvée El Campanario Tempranillo (Vino de Mesa de Castilla y León) $50. **91 Cellar Selection** —*J.C. (11/1/2001)*

Abadia Retuerta 1997 Cuvée El Palomar Tempranillo (Sardon de Duero) $48. **89** —*M.M. (8/1/2000)*

Abadia Retuerta 1997 Lapsus Tempranillo (Sardon de Duero) $130. **90** —*M.M. (8/1/2000)*

Abadia Retuerta 1996 Pago Negralada Tempranillo (Sardon de Duero) $140. **90** *(8/1/2000)*

Abadia Retuerta 1999 Rívola Tempranillo (Sardon de Duero) $12. **88** —*M.M. (8/1/2000)*

Abadia Retuerta 2001 Selección Especial Tempranillo (Vino de la Tierra de Castilla y León) $21. Quite ripe and savory, but also perilously close to stewy. The palate offers blackberry, plum and cured beef in a ripe package propelled by pronounced acidity. Finishes buttery and fairly short. This blend of Tempranillo, Cabernet and Merlot is ready to drink now. **87** —*M.S. (4/1/2007)*

Abadia Retuerta 1998 Cuvée El Palomar Tempranillo-Cabernet Sauvignon (Vino de Mesa de Castilla y León) $45. **89** —*J.C. (11/1/2001)*

Abadia Retuerta 2000 Cuvée Palomar Tempranillo-Cabernet Sauvignon (Vino de la Tierra de Castilla y León) $48. **88** —*M.S. (12/15/2006)*

Abadia Retuerta 2003 Rívola Tempranillo-Cabernet Sauvignon (Vino de la Tierra de Castilla y León) $13. Spicy but a bit green, this value label from Abadia Retuerta seems to have fallen off in recent years. The 2003, despite being from a hot year, has light vegetal aromas and flavors to go with cherry, plum and a mild saltiness. Not bad, but nothing special. **84** —*M.S. (4/1/2007)*

Abadia Retuerta 2001 Rívola Tempranillo-Cabernet Sauvignon (Vino de la Tierra de Castilla y León) $14. **88** —*M.S. (3/1/2004)*

Abadia Retuerta 1999 Rívola Tempranillo-Cabernet Sauvignon (Vino de Mesa de Castilla y León) $11. **89 Editors' Choice** —*J.C. (11/1/2001)*

ABANDO

Abando 2001 Crianza Tempranillo (Rioja) $NA. **86** —*M.S. (8/1/2005)*

ABRAZO

Abrazo 2003 Garnacha (Cariñena) $7. **81** —*M.S. (12/31/2004)*

Abrazo 2001 Garnacha (Cariñena) $5. **84 Best Buy** —*M.S. (8/1/2003)*

Abrazo 1999 Crianza Garnacha-Tempranillo Red Blend (Cariñena) $8. **81** —*M.S. (6/1/2005)*

Abrazo 1996 Gran Reserva Red Blend (Cariñena) $13. **82** —*M.S. (6/1/2005)*

Abrazo 1996 Gran Reserva Red Blend (Cariñena) $11. **86** —*S.H. (1/1/2002)*

Abrazo 1997 Reserva Garnacha-Tempranillo Red Blend (Cariñena) $10. **80** —*M.S. (6/1/2005)*

ADEGA MARTÍNEZ SERANTES

Adega Martínez Serantes 2005 Alba Rosa Albariño (Rías Baixas) $15. **87** —*M.S. (9/1/2006)*

Adega Martínez Serantes 2005 Dona Rosa Albariño (Rías Baixas) $17. **91 Editors' Choice** —*M.S. (9/1/2006)*

ADEGAS D'ALTAMIRA

Adegas D'Altamira 2005 Albariño (Rías Baixas) $25. There's not much difference between this wine and the label's less expensive Brandal. This is a bit richer, with chunky melon aromas and peach melba flavors. But it may suffer a bit from additional ripeness and lower acidity. For best results, get at it fast. **87** —*M.S. (8/1/2007)*

Adegas D'Altamira 2005 Brandal Albariño (Rías Baixas) $15. A little weighty, with ripe apple and peach aromas. Fairly succulent in the mouth, with apple and citrus flavors that are both sweet and a touch chewy. Some pith on the finish adds complexity and overall you can't knock the wine's character. Drink now. **87** —*M.S. (8/1/2007)*

ADEGAS GALEGAS

Adegas Galegas 2003 O Deus Dionisos Albariño (Rías Baixas) $22. **86** —*M.S. (9/1/2004)*

ADEGAS GRAN VINUM

Adegas Gran Vinum 2006 Esencia Diviña Albariño (Rías Baixas) $19. A heavier, sweeter style with cider-like aromas followed by apple and lime flavors. In the mouth, this is a more citric wine that may go well with shellfish. It's sturdy and zesty, but not that evolved. Tasted twice, with this note reflecting the better of the two bottles. **85** —*M.S. (11/1/2007)*

Adegas Gran Vinum 2005 Gran Vinum Albariño (Rías Baixas) $24. Beeswax, roast squash and vanilla are the dominant aromas, and all indicate a fading wine that was borderline overripe to begin with. The flavors are of apple and melon, and the finish is pithy and turns bitter toward the final stages. Not really what we're looking for from Rías Baixas. **82** —*M.S. (12/15/2007)*

Adegas Gran Vinum 2005 Mar De Viñas Albariño (Rías Baixas) $22. **82** —*M.S. (9/1/2006)*

Adegas Gran Vinum 2006 Nessa Albariño (Rías Baixas) $12. Nice Albariño, no ifs, ands or buts. The nose is floral and clean, and that's backed by a no-fuss palate of citrus, namely orange and grapefruit. As it holds form from front to back, you know this is a good wine. Will go great with light salads and shellfish. Drink immediately. **88** —*M.S. (11/1/2007)*

ADEGAS VALMIÑOR

Adegas Valmiñor 2005 Davila White Blend (Rías Baixas) $15. **88** —*M.S. (9/1/2006)*

AGNUSDEI

Agnusdei 2005 Albariño (Rías Baixas) $17. Clean, pure and a touch slight, but fine in terms of minerality and zest. This is nice with lots of melon, lemon verbena and almond notes. It finishes very long and nutty, showing good acidity. Drink as soon as possible for best results. 88 *—M.S. (11/1/2007)*

AGRAMONT

Agramont 2000 Chardonnay (Navarra) $9. 81 *—M.S. (11/1/2002)*

AGREST DE GUITARD

Agrest de Guitard 2003 Cabernet Sauvignon-Merlot (Penedès) $10. 82 *—M.S. (3/1/2005)*

AGRIBERGIDVM

Agribergidvm 2005 Fructus Odorus Godello (Bierzo) $10. Bierzo in northwest Spain is best known for the red Mencía grape, but here we find organic Godello with hay, corn and other slightly overripe aromas. To continue on the theme, the palate is a touch baked and soft, with spongy melon and papaya flavors. A pliable wine that may already be past its prime. Imported by Newton Land Development, Inc. 84 *—M.S. (11/1/2007)*

Agribergidvm 2003 Castro Bergidum Roble Mencía (Bierzo) $9. Rubbery and not all that convincing on the nose. The palate is sizable but also acidic, which leads to a tart, almost sour flavor profile that is dominated by tangy cherry skins and citrus zest. Imported by Newton Land Development, Inc. 82 *—M.S. (11/1/2007)*

Agribergidvm 2001 Encomienda Templaria Reserva Mencía (Bierzo) $17. Blackberry and raisin with a sharp smokiness carries the nose. The palate is not overly generous, but it does house berry, spice and vanilla flavors along with some clipped tannins. Has the components but not the harmony. Imported by Newton Land Development, Inc. 84 *—M.S. (11/1/2007)*

AGRICOLA CASTELLANA

Agricola Castellana 2005 Veliterra Joven White Blend (Rueda) $9. 81 *—M.S. (12/15/2006)*

AGRICOLA FALSET-MARCA

Agricola Falset-Marca 2001 Etim Garnacha (Montsant) $14. 88 *—M.S. (3/1/2004)*

AGRO DE BAZÁN

Agro de Bazán 2005 Contrapunto Albariño (Rías Baixas) $13. 82 *—M.S. (12/15/2006)*

Agro de Bazán 1999 Granbazán Albariño (Rías Baixas) $19. 83 *—M.S. (1/1/2004)*

Agro de Bazán 1999 Granbazán Albariño (Rías Baixas) $13. 83 *—M.S. (3/1/2004)*

Agro de Bazán 2003 Granbazán Ambar Limousin Albariño (Rías Baixas) $35. Stylistically and individually, this is not what this critic is looking for in Albariño. The wine is moderately but noticeably oaked, and seeing that it dates from 2003, it has aged to the point that there's butterscotch and canned-corn aromas reminiscent of warm-climate Chardonnay. Lots of vanilla and butterscotch work the finish, and the acidity seems forced. Not poorly made but not really what Albariño should be. 83 *—M.S. (12/15/2007)*

Agro de Bazán 2005 Mas de Bazan Rosé Blend (Utiel-Requena) $8. Full in color and size, with round aromas. The base grape is Bobal, a rubbery, lively variety that when made into a rosado yields melon, nectarine and berry flavors. It's also kind of hard, rubbery and pithy. Requires some getting used to. 84 *—M.S. (2/1/2007)*

AGUSTÍ TORELLÓ

Agustí Torelló 1999 Barrica Reserva Extra Brut Macabeo (Penedès) $25. 89 *—M.S. (12/31/2002)*

Agustí Torelló 1999 Kripta Gran Reserva Brut Nature Sparkling Blend (Cava) $52. 90 *—M.S. (6/1/2005)*

Agustí Torelló 1999 Brut Riserva White Blend (Penedès) $12. 88 Best Buy *—M.S. (12/31/2002)*

Agustí Torelló 1998 Gran Reserva Extra Brut White Blend (Penedès) $16. 89 *—M.S. (12/31/2002)*

Agustí Torelló 1997 Kripta Extra Brut White Blend (Penedès) $45. 91 Editors' Choice *—M.S. (12/31/2002)*

AL MUVEDRE

AL Muvedre 2005 Tinto Joven Monastrell (Alicante) $9. This Alicante red from Telmo Rodriguez is a giant with grapy, medicinal aromas followed by huge plum and blackberry flavors. This broad, mildly tannic red with tons of finishing coffee and leather notes fits the bill. 87 *—M.S. (4/1/2007)*

ALABANZA

Alabanza 2001 Crianza Tempranillo (Rioja) $15. 87 *—M.S. (8/1/2005)*

Alabanza 1999 Reserva Tempranillo (Rioja) $24. 86 *—M.S. (8/1/2005)*

Alabanza 2001 Selección Tempranillo (Rioja) $42. 85 *—M.S. (8/1/2005)*

Alabanza 2002 Selección Tempranillo Blend (Rioja) $40. 89 *—M.S. (11/1/2006)*

ALBA

Alba 2004 de Los Infantes Roble Tempranillo (Valdepeñas) $10. Raspberry and strawberry aromas offer a reasonably good opening, backed by sweet strawberry and vanilla flavors. A bit sticky and candied, but overall it's friendly and round enough to make the grade. 84 *—M.S. (8/1/2007)*

ALBADA

Albada 2001 Garnacha (Calatayud) $12. 85 *—M.S. (12/31/2004)*

Albada 2000 Garnacha (Calatayud) $8. 81 *—M.S. (10/1/2003)*

ALBET I NOYA

Albet I Noya 2000 Lignum Negre Red Blend (Penedès) $11. 87 Best Buy *—M.S. (3/1/2004)*

Albet I Noya 1999 Cava Brut Reserva Sparkling Blend (Cava) $14. 84 *—J.C. (12/31/2003)*

ALCEÑO

Alceño 2003 Selección Crianza Red Blend (Jumilla) $18. 90 Editors' Choice *—M.S. (12/15/2006)*

Alceño 2003 Selección Roble Red Blend (Jumilla) $13. 89 Best Buy *—M.S. (12/15/2006)*

Alceño 2005 Tinto Red Blend (Jumilla) $10. 87 Best Buy *—M.S. (12/15/2006)*

Alceño 2005 Rosado Rosé Blend (Jumilla) $10. 84 *—M.S. (12/15/2006)*

Alceño 2004 Syrah (Jumilla) $15. 90 Best Buy *—M.S. (12/15/2006)*

ALCONDE

Alconde 2001 Reserva Tempranillo Blend (Navarra) $34. 84 *—M.S. (11/15/2005)*

ALDOR

Aldor 2005 Verdejo (Rueda) $11. Quite heavy; in fact, a touch too much. The nose is defined by corn and apple cider, while the palate is heavy and melony, with a lot of unbounded sweetness and softness. Needs more overt acidity and citrus to achieve proper balance. 83 *—M.S. (8/1/2007)*

Aldor 2003 Verdejo (Rueda) $11. 83 *—M.S. (8/1/2005)*

ALENZA

Alenza 1999 Gran Reserva Tinto del Pais (Ribera del Duero) $87. 87 *—M.S. (10/1/2005)*

ALIDIS

Alidis 2000 Crianza Tempranillo (Ribera del Duero) $22. 86 *—M.S. (3/1/2004)*

Alidis 1999 Crianza Tempranillo (Ribera del Duero) $20. 88 *—M.S. (3/1/2004)*

Alidis 2001 Tinto Roble Tempranillo (Ribera del Duero) $15. 85 *—M.S. (3/1/2004)*

ALION

Allende 2003 Tempranillo (Rioja) $27. This wine is not typical of Allende. It suffered from the heat of 2003 and thus it's overtly aromatic in a prune-like way and out of balance on the palate. If it weren't for the unusual but intriguing molasses aromas and the occasional blast of quality berry fruit, we'd dismiss it outright. Better to wait for the 2004. 83 *—M.S. (9/1/2007)*

Alion 2002 Tempranillo (Ribera del Duero) $65. Robust and pretty dense for an '02, with sweet aromas of baked plums, blueberry, sandalwood and exotic spices. The palate is ripe and fairly pure, showing black cherry and dark plum flavors. Really good for an off year, with a touch of spice, chocolate and vanilla. Not a complicated RdD; best from 2008–2010. 90 *—M.S. (6/1/2007)*

Alion 1999 Tempranillo (Ribera del Duero) $50. 88 *—M.S. (3/1/2004)*

Alion 1996 Crianza Tempranillo (Ribera del Duero) $45. 95 *(8/1/2000)*

Alion 2000 Tinto del Pais (Ribera del Duero) $65. 91 *—M.S. (6/1/2005)*

ALLENDE

Allende 1997 Aurus Red Blend (Rioja) $155. 91 *—M.M. (11/1/2002)*

Allende 1999 Calvario Red Blend (Rioja) $45. 93 Editors' Choice *—M.M. (11/1/2002)*

SPAIN

Allende 1999 Tempranillo (Rioja) $20. 91 Editors' Choice —*M.S. (3/1/2004)*

Allende 1997 Tempranillo (Rioja) $18. 91 —*M.M. (8/1/2000)*

Allende 2000 Calvario Tempranillo (Rioja) $50. 91 —*M.S. (3/1/2004)*

Allende 2002 Estate White Blend (Rioja) $25. 87 —*M.S. (8/1/2005)*

Allende 2000 Special Reserve Dealu Mare-Ploiesti White Blend (Rioja) $18. 86 —*M.S. (3/1/2004)*

ALMA DE TOBIA

Alma de Tobia 2002 Estate Bottled Tempranillo (Rioja) $54. Dense and fairly earthy, with a big coating of chocolate and char courtesy of full-force oak. The palate is dark and heavy with blackberry fruit, compact tannins and some burnt notes, while the finish is a little salty but long. Not stellar but showing a lot of qualities. **88** —*M.S. (11/1/2007)*

ALONSO DEL YERRO

Alonso del Yerro 2004 Tempranillo (Ribera del Duero) $31. Not an easy wine to appreciate. It begins with a ton of funk, leather and sulfuric aromas. Time tames the beast, and with patience you get rich, meaty flavors of bouillon, plum, herbs and earth. Never quite achieves a level of brightness but has qualities along the way. **87** —*M.S. (2/1/2007)*

ALQUÉZAR

Alquézar 2004 Moristel (Somontano) $12. 84 —*M.S. (9/1/2006)*

ALTA ALELLA

Alta Alella 2005 Lanius White Blend (Alella) $34. Chardonnay, Muscadet and something known as Pansa Blanca comprise this Catalonian oddball, which is so severely oaked that you have no idea what the grapes might actually taste like. No, it's not badly made, meaning there's mouthfeel, acidity and stages to the wine. But the aromas, flavors and overall package are weird and confusing. **82** —*M.S. (12/15/2007)*

ALTA MARCA

Alta Marca 2004 Tempranillo - Cabernet Sauvignon - Shiraz Red Blend (Madrid) $12. A bit charred and hot on the nose, but with some tempering richness finds its way. The mouth is dominated by blackberry flavors with raisin accents, while the finish is a touch oaky and pulpy. Bold and meaty but not endowed with much finesse or variety. **86** —*M.S. (12/15/2007)*

ALTANZA

Altanza 1998 Lealtanza Gran Reserva Tempranillo (Rioja) $33. 84 —*M.S. (12/31/2004)*

Altanza 1999 Lealtanza Reserva Tempranillo (Rioja) $25. 85 —*M.S. (3/1/2005)*

Altanza 1999 Reserva Tempranillo (Rioja) $68. 82 —*M.S. (11/1/2006)*

Altanza 1998 Reserva Tempranillo (Rioja) $47. 86 —*M.S. (6/1/2005)*

ALTICO

Altico 2003 Red Blend (Jumilla) $19. 82 —*M.S. (10/1/2005)*

ALTO MONCAYO

Alto Moncayo 2003 Garnacha (Campo de Borja) $43. Campo de Borja can produce some strange wines, and at the head of the class would be this rooty, tomato-laden wine that's at one point sweet but then bland and cooked at the next. A varietal Garnacha from a hot vintage that just isn't worth the price. **82** —*M.S. (8/1/2007)*

Alto Moncayo 2003 Veraton Garnacha (Campo de Borja) $22. Burnt and seemingly weedy at first, this heavily oaked 100% Garnacha is initially downright weird and baked. In the final analysis it's all wood and medicinal fruit. Not a personal favorite. **82** —*M.S. (8/1/2007)*

ALTOS DE TAMARON

Altos de Tamaron 2003 Tinto del Pais (Ribera del Duero) $10. 85 Best Buy —*M.S. (11/15/2005)*

Altos de Tamaron 2002 Crianza Tinto del Pais (Ribera del Duero) $14. 87 —*M.S. (11/15/2005)*

ALVAREZ Y DIEZ

Alvarez y Diez 2002 Nava Real Verdejo (Rueda) $11. 83 —*M.S. (9/1/2004)*

ALVARO PALACIOS

Alvaro Palacios 2003 Finca Dofí Red Blend (Priorat) $70. 94 Editors' Choice —*M.S. (10/1/2005)*

Alvaro Palacios 2003 L'Ermita Red Blend (Priorat) $440. 98 —*M.S. (10/1/2005)*

Alvaro Palacios 2003 Les Terrasses Red Blend (Priorat) $32. 91 —*M.S. (10/1/2005)*

ALVEAR

Alvear NV Solera 1830 Pedro Ximenez (Montilla-Moriles) $NA. 90 —*M.S. (6/1/2005)*

Alvear 2004 Añada Pedro Ximénez (Montilla-Moriles) $18. Molasses, spice, chocolate and pure raisins define this as classic P.X. It's syrupy but not too much so, with maple, cinnamon and brown sugar flavors. For a sweet and candied dessert wine, it has excellent balance and persistence. A star among many in this category; these wines are hard not to like. **92** —*M.S. (12/15/2007)*

Alvear 2003 Fino En Rama Pedro Ximénez (Montilla-Moriles) $11. Fino Sherry rarely has this kind of weight and complexity. It's full of spunk, grab and length, and that's probably due to the fact that it's made from Pedro Ximenez grapes and not the more common Palomino. Likely marvelous with garlic shrimp or langostinos. **90 Editors' Choice** —*M.S. (12/15/2007)*

ALVIDES

Alvides 2002 Crianza Tempranillo (Ribera del Duero) $27. Maybe more savory and sautéed than overtly fresh and fruity, but still there's enough ripeness, purity and acidity to keep this wine in line. That said, the wine runs more heavy and less vibrant than some. Which only means that it's incredibly easy to drink now and doesn't require further aging. **87** —*M.S. (6/1/2007)*

Alvides 2004 Vendima Seleccionada Tempranillo (Ribera del Duero) $15. Ripe, saturated and raring to go, this tyke takes no prisoners as it pumps forward with berry aromas and then robust flavors of black cherry and bitter chocolate. There's little to no finesse on this fruit ball, but it will go with any grilled meat. **86** —*M.S. (6/1/2007)*

ALZANIA

Alzania 2002 Crianza Red Blend (Navarra) $30. 89 —*M.S. (10/1/2005)*

Alzania 2002 Selección Privada Red Blend (Navarra) $70. 88 —*M.S. (10/1/2005)*

ANECOOP

Anecoop NV Flare Método Charmat Moscatel (Valencia) $12. This seems to be an attempt to mock the Moscato d'Asti style from Italy, but it doesn't quite pull it off. The nose is powdery and full of gardenias, but the feel is thick and it doesn't have that clean, ethereal personality that the best Moscatos exhibit. Not a bad wine by any means, and probably best with desserts. **84** —*M.S. (12/15/2007)*

ANIMA NEGRA

Anima Negra 1999 Red Blend (Vi de Taula de Balears) $30. 86 —*M.N. (4/1/2002)*

ANNOSUS

Annosus 2004 Tempranillo (Ribera del Duero) $10. Given the prices of Ribera Del Duero's wines these days, this one is a steal. The bouquet pumps black cherry mixed with licorice and vanilla, while the palate has some minerally shale notes to accent fundamental cherry flavors. Finishes with notes of toast, coffee and earth. **87 Best Buy** —*M.S. (2/1/2007)*

ANTAÑO

Antaño 1997 Crianza Red Blend (Rioja) $10. 80 —*M.M. (9/1/2002)*

Antaño 2000 Tempranillo (Rioja) $7. 83 —*M.M. (9/1/2002)*

ARADON

Aradon 2004 Rosado Tempranillo Blend (Rioja) $10. 86 Best Buy —*M.S. (8/1/2005)*

Aradon 2003 Joven Blanco Viura (Rioja) $10. 84 —*M.S. (8/1/2005)*

ARBANTA

Arbanta 2002 Tempranillo (Rioja) $10. 85 —*M.S. (9/1/2004)*

ARCO DE GUÍA

Arco de Guía 2003 Jóven Tinta de Toro (Toro) $10. 84 —*M.S. (10/1/2005)*

ARCS

Arcs 2004 Carinyena (Terra Alta) $11. 81 —*M.S. (9/1/2006)*

ARES

Ares 2001 Crianza Tempranillo (Rioja) $16. 87 —*M.S. (4/1/2006)*

ARRIBEÑO

Arribeño 2003 Roble Tempranillo (Ribera del Duero) $9. 81 —*M.S. (11/15/2005)*

Arribeño 2004 Tinto del Pais (Ribera del Duero) $7. 81 —*M.S. (4/1/2006)*

ARROCAL

Arrocal 2005 Tempranillo (Ribera del Duero) $15. On the verge of heavy, but good in a stocky, straightforward way. Blackberry and chocolate lead, and the body leans toward weighty but doesn't go entirely heavy. A good, fuller-bodied selection with toast and tannin on the back end. **87** —*M.S. (6/1/2007)*

Arrocal 2004 Tempranillo (Ribera del Duero) $36. Seductive like a trap, meaning the nose is lush and full of bacon, cola and blackberry, yet the palate is tannic and shows some serious teeth. The fruit is bold and ripe, and the structure dictates that it be drunk with hearty foods like steak, lamb or burgers. **87** —*M.S. (6/1/2007)*

ARROYO

Arroyo 1998 Crianza Red Blend (Ribera del Duero) $32. 84 —*J.C. (11/1/2001)*

Arroyo 1995 Reserva Red Blend (Ribera del Duero) $18. 85 —*J.C. (11/1/2001)*

Arroyo 2000 Jóven Tempranillo (Ribera del Duero) $11. 88 Best Buy —*J.C. (11/1/2001)*

ARTADI

Artadi 2004 Pagos Viejos Tempranillo (Rioja) $95. Classic in color, and backed by aromatics of lavender, graphite and pure blackberry. This is not overly weighty, as the acidity keeps it pointed and pure. There's a lot of elegance and balance to this wine; a perfect example of how to blend multiple vineyards into one excellent whole. **95 Cellar Selection** —*M.S. (9/1/2007)*

Artadi 2002 Pagos Viejos Tempranillo (Rioja) $70. 91 —*M.S. (6/1/2005)*

Artadi 2002 Viña El Pisón Tempranillo (Rioja) $145. 90 —*M.S. (6/1/2005)*

ARTEAGA

Arteaga 2000 Crianza Red Blend (Navarra) $19. 85 —*M.S. (9/1/2006)*

ARX

Arx 2003 Tempranillo-Cabernet Sauvignon (Navarra) $12. 82 —*M.S. (10/1/2005)*

ARZUAGA

Arzuaga 1996 Crianza Tempranillo (Ribera del Duero) $27. 88 *(8/1/2000)*

Arzuaga 1995 Crianza Tempranillo (Ribera del Duero) $23. 92 —*S.H. (11/15/1999)*

Arzuaga 2002 La Planta Tempranillo (Ribera del Duero) $15. 87 —*M.S. (9/1/2004)*

Arzuaga 1995 Reserva Tempranillo (Ribera del Duero) $60. 89 —*S.H. (11/15/1999)*

Arzuaga 2000 Tinto Crianza Tempranillo (Ribera del Duero) $28. 86 —*M.S. (9/1/2004)*

AS LAXAS

As Laxas 2006 Albariño (Rías Baixas) $15. Hints of peanut and caramel vie with mineral and acacia blossom for center stage on the nose, while the palate deals nut skins, lime, kiwi and gooseberry. In the end, this is a tangy, streamlined wine that's refreshing. It has some style but it's mostly just racy and lean. **87** —*M.S. (11/1/2007)*

As Laxas 2005 Bágoa do Miño Albariño (Rías Baixas) $NA. 88 —*M.S. (9/1/2006)*

As Laxas 2005 Laxas Albariño (Rías Baixas) $NA. 89 —*M.S. (9/1/2006)*

As Laxas 2005 Val do Sosego Albariño (Rías Baixas) $NA. 89 —*M.S. (9/1/2006)*

ÁSTER

áster 2001 Crianza Tempranillo (Ribera del Duero) $25. Starts off with unusual aromas of sandalwood, bath oils and nail polish, and never does the bouquet find a true groove. But the palate is sturdy and the flavors of red plum, cherry and spice win you over once you get used to them. More unconventional than many Ribera fans might like. **86** —*M.S. (6/1/2007)*

áster 2000 Reserva Tempranillo (Ribera del Duero) $32. The fruit component is starting to fade as this wine hits maturity, but it's still there and what you get from it is raspberry, cherry and strawberry. Supporting that triumvirate is drying oak that leaves vanilla and dill on the finish. More loose and less tannic than many, so it goes down easily. **88** —*M.S. (6/1/2007)*

ASTRALES

Astrales 2003 Tempranillo (Ribera del Duero) $55. This is a full-bodied, modern-style RDD that teeters on the edge of heavy and sun-baked but manages to keep itself upright. Very ripe and jammy on the palate, with concentrated dark-fruit flavors. Meaty and a bit soft. A wine that shows the typicity of the vintage. **88** —*M.S. (2/1/2007)*

AURA

Aura 2004 Verdejo (Rueda) $18. 85 —*M.S. (9/1/2006)*

AURUS

Aurus 1996 Aurus Tempranillo (Rioja) $130. 96 —*M.M. (8/1/2000)*

AVINYÓ

Avinyó 2001 Cabernet Sauvignon (Penedès) $NA. 86 —*M.S. (3/1/2003)*

Avinyó NV Brut Reserva Sparkling Blend (Cava) $16. 85 —*M.S. (6/1/2006)*

Avinyó NV Rosado Brut Reserva Sparkling Blend (Cava) $20. 87 —*M.S. (6/1/2006)*

AZAGADOR

Azagador 2002 Viñedos Propios Crianza Tempranillo Blend (La Mancha) $13. The nose deals perfume, sawdust and even some fruit, while tobacco, cassis and blackberry flavors are adequate if not overly impressive. More interesting than some in its class, with a few flaws along with virtues. **84** —*M.S. (8/1/2007)*

BACASIS

Bacasis 2002 Crianza Cabernet Sauvignon-Merlot (Pla de Bages) $14. 84 —*M.S. (9/1/2006)*

BALBAS

Balbas 2004 Crianza Tempranillo (Ribera del Duero) $29. Quite dry and woody, with old-school dill and sawdust aromas. The palate also runs dry and mature, but only at first. Later red fruit, vanilla, mocha and leathery accents come up and make themselves noticed. More traditional in style as it steers clear of any overt richness and weight. **86** —*M.S. (6/1/2007)*

Balbas 1996 Gran Reserva Tempranillo (Ribera del Duero) $85. As this wine hits prime age, it's showing cumin and other Middle Eastern spice notes. The flavor profile deals raspberry, plum and some mushroom, while the feel is tight as a drum, which is impressive given that the wine is 10 years old and counting. Drink now through 2010. **88** —*M.S. (6/1/2007)*

Balbas 2001 Reserva Tempranillo (Ribera del Duero) $45. Heavy and earthy, with more pepper and moss than brightness. In the mouth, there's black cherry, dark plum and tobacco flavors, while the feel is dictated by stern tannins. Overall it's a fairly serious wine but it doesn't offer the love that we'd like to see. With 10% Cabernet Sauvignon. 12,500 cases made. **86** —*M.S. (6/1/2007)*

Balbas 2003 Tradición Tempranillo (Ribera del Duero) $17. 86 —*M.S. (11/15/2005)*

Balbas 2004 Roble Tinto del Pais (Ribera del Duero) $19. 88 —*M.S. (11/1/2006)*

BARBADILLO

Barbadillo NV Solear Manzanilla Sherry (Jerez) $9. 89 —*M.S. (6/1/2005)*

BARON DE LEY

Baron De Ley 2000 Finca Monasterio Red Blend (Rioja) $42. 86 —*M.S. (10/1/2003)*

Baron De Ley 1996 Gran Reserva Tempranillo (Rioja) $34. 86 —*M.S. (4/1/2006)*

Baron De Ley 1995 Gran Reserva Tempranillo (Rioja) $32. 81 —*M.S. (10/1/2003)*

Baron De Ley 2001 Reserva Tempranillo (Rioja) $20. Stewed fruit aromas with some baked beans on the side just isn't alluring, and the lean, raw, acidic palate that some might describe as traditional isn't clicking in my book. Saving graces include milk chocolate on the finish. **82** —*M.S. (9/1/2007)*

Baron De Ley 2000 Reserva Tempranillo (Rioja) $20. 86 —*M.S. (12/15/2006)*

Baron De Ley 1998 Reserva Tempranillo (Rioja) $19. 82 —*M.S. (10/1/2003)*

Baron De Ley 2004 Finca Monasterio Tempranillo Blend (Rioja) $42. It has taken this bodega a few years to get it right, but in 2004 this blend of 80% Tempranillo and 20% Cabernet is dark and rocking. The nose offers that modern but increasingly familiar blast of bacon, baked fruit pastry and leather, and the palate works its magic with black plum and smoked game flavors. If it were just a touch longer and richer toward the finish it might rank as a nuevo classico. **91** —*M.S. (9/1/2007)*

Baron De Ley 2003 Finca Monasterio Tempranillo Blend (Rioja) $43. As per usual, this wine carries a leafiness and peppery quality that runs ahead of its fruit quotient. That doesn't mean it's a poor wine; but it emphasizes dry oak and saucy flavors as opposed to richness and ripeness. Best for

Rioja traditionalists and those who might drink it with robust foods. **85** —*M.S. (9/1/2007)*

Baron De Ley 2002 Finca Monasterio Tempranillo-Cabernet Sauvignon (Rioja) $44. 83 —*M.S. (4/1/2006)*

Baron De Ley 2001 Finca Monasterio Tempranillo-Cabernet Sauvignon (Rioja) $45. 83 —*M.S. (8/1/2005)*

BARÓN DE OÑA

Barón de Oña 1997 Reserva Tempranillo (Rioja) $24. 87 —*M.S. (3/1/2004)*

BARZAGOSO

Barzagoso 2001 Crianza Tempranillo Blend (Rioja) $14. 87 —*M.S. (10/1/2005)*

Barzagoso 2000 Reserva Tempranillo Blend (Rioja) $25. 87 —*M.S. (11/15/2005)*

BASA

Basa 2005 White Blend (Rueda) $11. For several years running, one of our favorite bargain whites has been Basa. This '05 is still kicking with citrus and tropical-fruit aromas as well as defined flavors of pink grapefruit, melon and green herbs. With minerality and white pepper on the finish, it has closing complexity. 89 —*M.S. (4/1/2007)*

BENJAMIN ROMEO

Benjamin Romeo 2003 La Cueva del Contador Tempranillo (Rioja) $99. After a rough, almost chemical nose, the palate holds onto a personality that's overly sour. Rarely do you find such a tangy, tart wine in this price range. In its defense, airing and time serve it better. But we wouldn't expect you to drop a hundred and wait that long for something special that's not going to come. 82 —*M.S. (2/1/2007)*

Benjamin Romeo 2003 La Viña de Andrés Romeo Tempranillo (Rioja) $157. Given the prices of Benjamin Romeo's wines, one should expect more. His Cueva del Contador isn't that impressive, and while this wine is better it's still a bit flat and raisiny, with molasses and a stewed black-cherry character. Romeo's wines just don't seem on the ball. 86 —*M.S. (2/1/2007)*

Benjamin Romeo 2001 La Viña de Andrés Romeo Tempranillo (Rioja) $140. 90 —*M.S. (9/1/2004)*

Benjamin Romeo 2004 Qué Bonito Cacareaba White Blend (Rioja) $74. Benjamin Romeo makes nothing but big, idiosyncratic wines. And some are big hits while others may not be your thing. This modern, round, polished blend is creamy and smooth but also loaded with almond, pear, citrus and toast flavors. Certainly there's a strong wood element, but it handles it with aplomb and oozes class. Drink as soon as possible. It won't age much past 2007. Only 25 cases made. **92 Editors' Choice** —*M.S. (9/1/2007)*

BERBERANA

Berberana 1997 Viña Alarde Reserva Red Blend (Rioja) $18. 89 —*D.T. (4/1/2003)*

Berberana 2005 Number One Shiraz-Tempranillo (Tierra de Castilla) $8. This offers chewy plum and berry flavors along with a finishing wave of vanilla, chocolate and coconut. It's fruity and forward, if a bit rubbery on the finish. **85 Best Buy** —*M.S. (8/1/2007)*

Berberana 2002 Dragon Tempranillo (Rioja) $10. 85 —*M.S. (5/1/2004)*

Berberana 2001 Dragón Tempranillo (Vino de la Tierra de Castilla y León) $8. 84 —*M.S. (3/1/2004)*

Berberana 2000 Dragón Tempranillo (Rioja) $8. 85 —*D.T. (4/1/2003)*

Berberana 2005 Number One Tempranillo (Tierra de Castilla) $8. Initial sweet-plum aromas are as good as it gets. Raisin enters the picture, and eventually you've got a heavy, clumsy, overly ripe wine that tastes and smells mostly of sappy oak and coconut. 82 —*M.S. (8/1/2007)*

Berberana 2002 Viña Alarde Tempranillo (Rioja) $13. 80 —*M.S. (6/1/2005)*

Berberana 2001 Vina Alarde Reserva Tempranillo (Rioja) $18. 85 —*M.S. (3/1/2004)*

Berberana 1999 Vina Alarde Reserva Tempranillo Blend (Rioja) $20. 86 —*M.S. (5/1/2004)*

BERNARD MAGREZ

Bernard Magrez 2004 Herència del Padrí Red Blend (Priorat) $75. Rustic fruit aromas led by the native Samso grape cause a stir, and the wine, which also has Garnacha, Cabernet and Merlot, carries forth in the mouth, where lush blackberry and plum flavors are supported by healthy, spicy, minty oak. With tight tannins and comfortable acidity, it will drink better in a few years. Imported by Bernard Magrez. **90 Cellar Selection** —*M.S. (8/1/2007)*

Bernard Magrez 2004 Paciencia Tempranillo (Toro) $75. It seems that all of Monsieur Magrez's new wines from around the world have a similar DNA: size, ripeness, plenty of new oak and ultimately quality. This big-boned Toro shows tons of ripe black cherry flavors darkened by bitter chocolate and espresso. It's immensely oaky now and should benefit from a couple to 10 years on its side. Imported by Bernard Magrez. **91 Cellar Selection** —*M.S. (11/1/2007)*

BLANCO NIEVA

Blanco Nieva 2006 Verdejo (Rueda) $13. Serious and true-to-form Verdejo, with dry lime and green fruits on the nose and lots of green apple, apricot and citrus in the mouth. This wine packs a lot of flavor and power into a fairly regular, unadulterated package. And that's basically why we like it. Drink now. 87 —*M.S. (11/1/2007)*

Blanco Nieva 2006 Pie Franco Verdejo (Rueda) $20. Old-vines Verdejo from Rueda can amount to something special, and this vineyard-select beauty has it going on. The bouquet is clean, with touches of saline, mineral and lime. The palate is mostly about freshness, but soon power and depth of fruit take over. And the finish is a whopper in terms of length and purity. 90 —*M.S. (11/1/2007)*

BLASÓN DE SAN JUAN

Blasón de San Juan 2000 Crianza Tinto del Pais (Ribera del Duero) $19. 87 —*M.S. (6/1/2005)*

Blasón de San Juan 2000 Jóven Tinto del Pais (Ribera del Duero) $10. 83 —*M.S. (10/1/2005)*

Blasón de San Juan 1999 Reserva Tinto del Pais (Ribera del Duero) $27. 84 —*M.S. (6/1/2005)*

Blasón de San Juan 2000 Roble Tinto del Pais (Ribera del Duero) $13. 86 —*M.S. (6/1/2005)*

BLECUA

Blecua 2001 Vino Tinto Red Blend (Somontano) $NA. 91 —*M.S. (6/1/2005)*

BODEGA DEL ABAD

Bodega del Abad 2005 Carracedo Mencía (Bierzo) $75. From 80-year-old vines planted on steep slopes, this shows an early blast of buttery oak, but underneath there's mineral, coffee, lemon peel and potent fruit. Power and tightness define the palate, which is also intensely mineral as it teeters on the border of overoaked and leathery. 91 —*M.S. (11/1/2007)*

Bodega del Abad 2003 Carracedo Mencía (Bierzo) $67. Deep and clear in color, and very solid smelling; the prune and mineral aromas form the base, with woodsy notes offering complexity. The palate is chiseled and juicy, with plum, berry, tobacco and espresso flavors. Best to drink now. Only 600 cases made; 125 imported. 90 —*M.S. (11/1/2007)*

BODEGA JARIO

Bodega Jario 1998 Reserva Red Blend (Rioja) $14. 87 —*M.S. (6/1/2005)*

BODEGAS ABEL DE MENDOZA

Bodegas Abel de Mendoza 2003 Jarrarte Tempranillo (Rioja) $29. Bouquet is nice and smooth, with an earthy warmth surrounding scents of purple flowers and crushed berries. The palate is lively and acidic, with semi-sweet red-fruit flavors that are more generic. No reticence here; the wine is racy to the end as it finishes with oak and vanilla. 88 —*M.S. (9/1/2007)*

Bodegas Abel de Mendoza 1999 Jarrarte Tempranillo (Rioja) $26. 91 —*M.S. (3/1/2004)*

Bodegas Abel de Mendoza 2004 Seleccion Personal Tempranillo (Rioja) $49. Blackberry and cola are the prime aromas that comprise the alluring bouquet. And as you'd expect, there's also leather and spicy wood thrown in. In the mouth, it's an intense ride of rich black cherry and plum. For now it's a little closed on the finish; will likely be better in three years. 89 —*M.S. (9/1/2007)*

BODEGAS AGAPITO RICO

Bodegas Agapito Rico 2004 Monastrell (Jumilla) $9. **87 Best Buy** —*M.S. (10/1/2005)*

Bodegas Agapito Rico 2000 Monastrell (Jumilla) $9. 85 —*M.M. (9/1/2002)*

Bodegas Agapito Rico 2005 Carchelo Monastrell (Jumilla) $11. Carchelo is at its best in this vintage. This is loaded with wild blackberry and leathery sass, too. Typical of Jumilla, it's big, saturated and packed with ripe berry flavors, jabbing tannins and warmth. A true hot-climate country wine but one with polish and pizazz. **88 Best Buy** —*M.S. (8/1/2007)*

Bodegas Agapito Rico 2002 Carchelo Red Blend (Jumilla) $9. 84 —*M.S. (3/1/2004)*

Bodegas Agapito Rico 2000 Carchelo Red Blend (Jumilla) $8. **85 Best Buy** —*M.M. (9/1/2002)*

Bodegas Agapito Rico 1999 Carchelo Red Blend (Jumilla) $9. 86 —*M.S. (8/1/2000)*

Bodegas Agapito Rico 1999 Carchelo Syrah (Jumilla) $13. 84 —*M.S. (8/1/2000)*

BODEGAS AGUSTÍN CUBERO

Bodegas Agustín Cubero 2005 Unus Joven Cabernet Sauvignon (Calatayud) $8. For a basic, broad-framed Cabernet from Central Spain, this wine does the trick. The nose sports leather, Balsamic vinegar and some barnyard, while the dark-fruited palate is edged by licorice, tobacco and a smack of green. Good size and tannins keep it balanced. 84 Best Buy —*M.S. (2/1/2007)*

BODEGAS ALEJANDRO FERNANDEZ

Bodegas Alejandro Fernandez 2004 Pesquera Tempranillo (Ribera del Duero) $33. Early aromas of jelly donut, hot asphalt and leather are scattershot, but with time and airing the wine pulls itself together to show deep berry flavors, prune and a touch of burnt toast. It's a firm, serious Tempranillo, but at $33 it makes you long for the time when it was half the price and just as good, if not better. 88 —*M.S. (6/1/2007)*

BODEGAS ARESAN

Bodegas Aresan 2003 6 meses en barrica Red Blend (Tierra de Castilla) $35. A blend of 55% Tempranillo, 20% Cabernet, 20% Merlot and Syrah. But in the end it comes up a bit barnyardy and bretty, with animal aromas giving way to a racy, almost lemony palate that also offers some wild raspberry. For $35 it's scattered and faulty. 82 —*M.S. (11/1/2007)*

Bodegas Aresan 2002 9 meses en barrica Red Blend (Tierra de Castilla) $40. Smells whole, so you're hopeful going in. But the palate is stark and rather raw, while the flavors of raspberry and cherry are limited. A palate slammer with harsh tannins. Tempranillo 65%/Cabernet Sauvignon 35%. 82 —*M.S. (8/1/2007)*

BODEGAS ANGEL LORENZO CACHAZO

Bodegas Angel Lorenzo Cachazo 2002 Martivilli Superior Verdejo (Rueda) $10. 90 Best Buy —*M.S. (3/1/2004)*

Bodegas Angel Lorenzo Cachazo 2002 Las Brisas White Blend (Rueda) $9. 89 Best Buy —*M.S. (3/1/2004)*

BODEGAS ANTANO

Bodegas Antano 2005 Viña Mocen White Blend (Rueda) $10. 85 Best Buy —*M.S. (9/1/2006)*

BODEGAS ARAGONESAS

Bodegas Aragonesas 2001 Don Ramon Tinto Barrica Garnacha (Campo de Borja) $8. 84 —*M.S. (9/1/2004)*

Bodegas Aragonesas 2002 La Riada Old Vines Garnacha (Campo de Borja) $11. 82 —*M.S. (9/1/2004)*

Bodegas Aragonesas 2000 Don Ramon Red Blend (Campo de Borja) $6. 83 —*M.S. (5/1/2004)*

BODEGAS ARTAZU

Bodegas Artazu 2006 Artazuri Rosado Garnacha (Navarra) $10. Typcial of Navarran rosado, this is fuller in color and weight but still holds true to the region's textbook crispness and freshness. It has fairly big flavors or raspberry and citrus, with a rousing finish. A little more elegance and refinement and we'd be even happier. 86 Best Buy —*M.S. (7/1/2007)*

BODEGAS ARTESANAS

Bodegas Artesanas 2000 Campo Viejo Crianza Red Blend (Rioja) $9. 84 —*M.S. (3/1/2004)*

Bodegas Artesanas 1998 Campo Viejo Crianza Red Blend (Rioja) $9. 85 —*D.T. (4/1/2003)*

Bodegas Artesanas 1997 Campo Viejo Reserva Red Blend (Rioja) $15. 83 —*D.T. (4/1/2003)*

BODEGAS B.G.

Bodegas B.G. 2001 Gueta-Lupia Red Blend (Priorat) $66. 83 —*M.S. (3/1/2005)*

BODEGAS BALCONA

Bodegas Balcona 1999 Partal Crianza Red Blend (Bullas) $23. 88 —*M.S. (3/1/2004)*

BODEGAS BARRIOSA

Bodegas Barriosa 2006 Sombrero Rojo Tempranillo (Rioja) $11. Purple in tint, with volatile aromas of pickled fruit and rhubarb. The palate feel is wet and dilute, with no real substance. Finishes mildly green, with generic sweetness as an offset. 80 —*M.S. (12/15/2007)*

Bodegas Barriosa 2003 Sombrero Rojo Crianza Tempranillo (Rioja) $13. Nothing to swoon over but much better than the label's unpalatable 2005 and '06 wines. This has warm, earthy, mulchy aromas of baked fruit and cola, while the palate is a touch burnt to the taste, leaving caramel to mingle with raspberry. Not a bad midlevel wine if you catch it on a good day. 84 —*M.S. (12/15/2007)*

BODEGAS BERCEO

Bodegas Berceo 2000 Los Dominios de Berceo Reserva 36 Tempranillo (Rioja) $67. 88 —*M.S. (8/1/2005)*

Bodegas Berceo 2003 Viña Berceo Crianza Tempranillo (Rioja) $13. From a hot year, this wine adheres to tradition. It's 85% Tempranillo with Mazuelo and Graciano, so it's straight from central casting. The wine offers clean red-fruit flavors that pop across the palate, and the finish is racy and spicy. Not a show-stopper but worth stopping for. 85 —*M.S. (12/15/2007)*

BODEGAS BERNABE NAVARRO

Bodegas Bernabe Navarro 2003 Beryna Red Blend (Alicante) $17. 90 —*M.S. (11/1/2006)*

BODEGAS BILBAINAS

Bodegas Bilbainas 1994 Viña Pomal Reserva Red Blend (Rioja) $15. 86 *(8/1/2000)*

Bodegas Bilbainas 1994 La Vicalanda Gran Reserva Tempranillo (Rioja) $46. 89 —*D.T. (4/1/2003)*

Bodegas Bilbainas 2001 La Vicalanda Reserva Tempranillo (Rioja) $20. Gets out of the starting blocks with raw, peppery aromas that soon fold in cinnamon and other powdered spice notes. The palate offers red cherry and wild strawberry flavors along with touches of dill and chocolate. 87 —*M.S. (2/1/2007)*

Bodegas Bilbainas 1999 La Vicalanda Reserva Tempranillo (Rioja) $20. 86 —*M.S. (8/1/2005)*

Bodegas Bilbainas 1996 La Vicalanda Reserva Tempranillo (Rioja) $20. 88 —*D.T. (4/1/2003)*

Bodegas Bilbainas 1995 La Vicalanda Reserva Tempranillo (Rioja) $20. 88 —*J.C. (8/1/2000)*

Bodegas Bilbainas 2000 Viña Pomal Crianza Tempranillo (Rioja) $10. 84 —*M.S. (3/1/2005)*

Bodegas Bilbainas 1998 Viña Pomal Reserva Tempranillo (Rioja) $16. 86 —*M.S. (8/1/2005)*

Bodegas Bilbainas 1996 La Vicalanda Gran Reserva Tempranillo Blend (Rioja) $30. 87 —*M.S. (9/1/2004)*

Bodegas Bilbainas 1999 La Vicalanda Reserva Tempranillo Blend (Rioja) $22. 87 —*M.S. (9/1/2004)*

Bodegas Bilbainas 2003 Vicuana Tempranillo Blend (Rioja) $24. 87 —*M.S. (10/1/2005)*

Bodegas Bilbainas 2003 Viña Pomal Crianza Tempranillo (Rioja) $11. Mildly warm and roasted upfront, with aromatics similar to tomato, spice, leather and reserved red fruits. The palate is a bit streamlined and tart, with cherry and raspberry flavors. Tight and borderline hard on the finish; this wine needs food to smooth out its harsher elements. 84 —*M.S. (4/1/2007)*

Bodegas Bilbainas 1999 Viña Pomal Reserva Tempranillo (Rioja) $16. Early nosing reveals some stewy, raisiny qualities along with hints of cinnamon and red bell pepper. The palate is heavy, with no ifs, ands or buts about it. And sticking to that theme, the finish is flat and soft. Has its good points but seems tired and slightly overripe. 85 —*M.S. (2/1/2007)*

Bodegas Bilbainas 1997 Viña Pomal Reserva Tempranillo Blend (Rioja) $10. 88 Best Buy —*M.S. (9/1/2004)*

BODEGAS BLEDA

Bodegas Bleda 2002 Divus Monastrell (Jumilla) $28. 82 —*M.S. (10/1/2005)*

BODEGAS BRETON

Bodegas Breton 1998 Loriñon Reserva Red Blend (Rioja) $14. 85 —*M.S. (10/1/2003)*

Bodegas Breton 2001 Alba de Breton Reserva Tempranillo (Rioja) $54. 83 —*M.S. (11/15/2005)*

Bodegas Breton 1998 Alba de Breton Tempranillo (Rioja) $50. 90 —*M.S. (9/1/2004)*

Bodegas Breton 1996 Alba de Breton Tempranillo (Rioja) $55. 90 —*(9/1/2002)*

BODEGAS CAMPANTE

Bodegas Campante 2003 Gran Reboreda White Blend (Ribeiro) $16. 83 —*M.S. (9/1/2004)*

Bodegas Campante 2005 Viña Reboreda White Blend (Ribeiro) $9. Burning hay field, roasted corn and other over-the-hill aromas put this one on life support. The palate isn't much livelier; there's dry, bland citrus and more canned corn. Not a total mess but not very fresh or attractive. 81 *—M.S. (11/1/2007)*

Bodegas Campante 2003 Viña Reboreda White Blend (Ribeiro) $9. 85 *—M.S. (9/1/2004)*

BODEGAS CARLOS MAGAÑA S.L.

Bodegas Carlos Magaña S.L. 2004 Melius Merlot-Cabernet Sauvignon (Navarra) $11. Heavy and quite herbal, with strong tomato and molasses flavors. The feel of this wine is chunky and broad, yet the edges are sheer and sharp. It requires too much patience and shows too many flaws to rate better. 81 *—M.S. (8/1/2007)*

BODEGAS CARMELO RODERO

Bodegas Carmelo Rodero 2000 Tempranillo (Ribera del Duero) $13. 86 *—D.T. (4/1/2003)*

Bodegas Carmelo Rodero 1998 Crianza Tempranillo (Ribera del Duero) $20. 85 *—D.T. (4/1/2003)*

BODEGAS CASTEJÓN

Bodegas Castejón 2002 NOBUL red Tempranillo (Madrid) $7. 83 *—M.S. (9/1/2004)*

Bodegas Castejón 2001 Viña Rey Tempranillo (Madrid) $6. 83 *—D.T. (4/1/2003)*

Bodegas Castejón 2002 Viña Rey 70 Barricas Tempranillo (Madrid) $9. 84 *—M.S. (9/1/2004)*

BODEGAS CERROSOL

Bodegas Cerrosol 2002 Verdejo (Rueda) $11. 86 *—M.S. (3/1/2004)*

Bodegas Cerrosol 2001 Verdejo (Rueda) $9. 80 *—M.S. (3/1/2004)*

Bodegas Cerrosal 2000 Verdejo (Rueda) $9. 84 *—M.M. (9/1/2002)*

BODEGAS CONCAVINS

Bodegas Concavins 2000 Proyecto 4 Red Blend (Conca de Barberà) $10. 85 *—M.S. (8/1/2003)*

BODEGAS CONDE

Bodegas Conde 2001 Neo Punta Esencia Tinto del Pais (Ribera del Duero) $96. 91 *—M.S. (6/1/2005)*

BODEGAS DE LOS RIOS PRIETO

Bodegas de los Rios Prieto 2003 Prios Maximus Crianza Tempranillo (Ribera del Duero) $26. Plenty of intense new oak sets the nose in a direction toward mint, licorice and black pepper. And that's all good, because the palate backs it up with prime blackberry and cassis flavors. This is a solid wine with slightly pronounced acids and tannins. Not for those averse to a little grab and kick. 88 *—M.S. (8/1/2007)*

BODEGAS DIOS BACO S.L.

Bodegas Dios Baco S.L. NV Pedro Ximénez (Jerez) $15. It's easy to throw high scores at almost any well-made P.X. because the wines are so viscous and overwhelmingly sweet. And while this one fits that bill, it has a couple of holes in it, namely a nose that stumbles out of the gate and a mouthfeel that's almost too thick and rich. Very nice but not at that ultra-high level. 89 *—M.S. (12/15/2007)*

Bodegas Dios Baco S.L. NV Pedro Ximenez (Jerez) $18. 88 *—M.S. (10/1/2005)*

Bodegas Dios Baco S.L. NV 1970 Oxford Pedro Ximenez (Jerez) $40. 85 *—M.S. (12/31/2004)*

Bodegas Dios Baco S.L. NV 20 Yr. Imperial Amontillado Sherry (Jerez) $75. 90 *—M.S. (10/1/2005)*

Bodegas Dios Baco S.L. NV 20 yr. Baco Imperial Amontillado Sherry (Jerez) $90. Smooth and nutty, with deep secondary aromatics of apricot and orange peel. For a dry, aged Sherry, you can't object to the wine's intense citrus core and outlying toffee and hazelnut flavors. And then on the finish come those classic mushroom and bitter chocolate notes. A real dandy made for connoisseurs more than novices. 92 *—M.S. (12/15/2007)*

Bodegas Dios Baco S.L. NV 30-Year Imperial Oloroso Sherry (Jerez) $90. 89 *—M.S. (10/1/2005)*

Bodegas Dios Baco S.L. NV Amontillado Sherry (Jerez) $20. This is sweet Amontillado in fine form. The nose is centered around a core of molasses and brown sugar, while the palate bubbles with maple and toffee. Yes, it's a sweeter-styled Amontillado, but the sugar fades on the palate, leaving only the complex residue of caramel, espresso and burnt cinnamon. A lovely wine for any fan of serious Sherry. 93 Editors' Choice *—M.S. (12/15/2007)*

Bodegas Dios Baco S.L. NV Amontillado Sherry (Jerez) $20. 91 *—M.S. (10/1/2005)*

Bodegas Dios Baco S.L. NV Cream Sherry (Jerez) $18. The first whiff yields mostly raisins, but subsequent sniffs force up lush caramel and malt notes along with a blast of molasses. Cream Sherries by nature are sweet, and this one fits the bill with the full allotment of fig, date and carob flavors. Mocha and espresso on the finish cement this wine's pedigree. Great if you have a sweet tooth and fine even if you don't. 90 *—M.S. (12/15/2007)*

Bodegas Dios Baco S.L. NV Cream Sherry (Jerez) $20. 90 *—M.S. (10/1/2005)*

Bodegas Dios Baco S.L. NV Fino Sherry Sherry (Jerez) $18. 87 *—M.S. (4/1/2006)*

Bodegas Dios Baco S.L. NV Manzanilla Sherry (Jerez) $9. 91 Editors' Choice *—M.S. (4/1/2006)*

Bodegas Dios Baco S.L. NV Oloroso Sherry (Jerez) $18. If at first the wine seems sweet and scattered, just give it time. Soon the nose will knit together to show mocha and that lightly oxidized elegance that is Oloroso. After that there's a palate of coffee, caramel and brown sugar, and a tight, grabby palate that's like your tongue is attached to a magnet. Give this one plenty of air for best results. 91 *—M.S. (12/15/2007)*

Bodegas Dios Baco S.L. NV Oloroso Sherry (Jerez) $20. 89 *—M.S. (10/1/2005)*

BODEGAS EL MOLAR

Bodegas El Molar 2001 Araviñas Semi-Crianza Tempranillo (Ribera del Duero) $14. 86 *—M.S. (3/1/2004)*

BODEGAS ENTREMONTES

Bodegas Entremontes 2006 Clavelito Rosado Tempranillo (La Mancha) $10. Any winning notes soon evaporate as this wine shows little to zero staying power. The nose is simple but innocuous, while the palate has some raspberry flavors but no definition or character. Adequate but vacuous. 82 *—M.S. (7/1/2007)*

BODEGAS FONTANA

Bodegas Fontana 2002 Fontal Crianza Tempranillo (La Mancha) $6. Ripe and rich, with some prune on the nose; it shows a good mix of berry and earth characteristics in front of a mildly oaky finish that holds its form. Sort of heavy and overripe but still pretty good. Drink now. 85 Best Buy *—M.S. (4/1/2007)*

Bodegas Fontana 1999 Fontal Crianza Tempranillo (La Mancha) $11. 84 *—M.S. (5/1/2004)*

Bodegas Fontana 2001 Fontal Roble Tempranillo (La Mancha) $9. 86 *—M.S. (5/1/2004)*

Bodegas Fontana 2002 Mesta Tempranillo (Vino de la Tierra de Castilla) $6. 87 Best Buy *—M.S. (5/1/2004)*

BODEGAS FUENTESPINA

Bodegas Fuentespina 1998 Crianza Red Blend (Ribera del Duero) $17. 85 *—J.C. (11/1/2001)*

Bodegas Fuentespina 1998 Reserva Red Blend (Ribera del Duero) $25. 88 *—D.T. (4/1/2003)*

Bodegas Fuentespina 1996 Reserva Especial Red Blend (Ribera del Duero) $65. 87 *J.C. (11/1/2001)*

Bodegas Fuentespina 2002 Tempranillo (Ribera del Duero) $12. 87 Best Buy *—M.S. (3/1/2004)*

Bodegas Fuentespina 2001 Tempranillo (Ribera del Duero) $12. 87 *—M.S. (3/1/2004)*

Bodegas Fuentespina 2000 Tempranillo (Ribera del Duero) $12. 86 *—D.T. (4/1/2003)*

Bodegas Fuentespina 2003 Crianza Tempranillo (Ribera del Duero) $16. Quite smoky and tough at first, but airing unleashes earthy fruit aromas along with some road tar and char. In the mouth, the wine delivers enough fruit and acidity to keep it fresh, while the finish is your typical blend of young oak and chocolate. Drink now through 2009. 89 *—M.S. (6/1/2007)*

Bodegas Fuentespina 1999 Crianza Tempranillo (Ribera del Duero) $22. 90 *—M.S. (3/1/2004)*

Bodegas Fuentespina 2004 Granate Tempranillo (Ribera del Duero) $10. Drier and lighter than this winery's Crianzas and reservas, Granate shows rubber and red-fruit aromas and then lean cherry flavors. It's rather chalky and grabby late, and by then some of the thrill is gone. 84 *—M.S. (6/1/2007)*

Bodegas Fuentespina 2001 Reserva Tempranillo (Ribera del Duero) $21. Full and bold on the bouquet, where grilled meat and leather blend with ripe fruit to create an alluring, inviting whole. Black cherry and raspberry flavors are smooth and serious, while at the core there's a jammy, syrupy richness that conveys total ripeness. Best from 2008–2011. 92 *—M.S. (6/1/2007)*

Bodegas Fuentespina 1997 Reserva Tempranillo (Ribera del Duero) 88 —*J.C. (11/1/2001)*

Bodegas Fuentespina 2001 Reserva Especial Tempranillo (Ribera del Duero) $50. Anyone fond of great red wine should swoon over this lovely thoroughbred that's just beginning to enter its prime. The nose offers hard hickory, pure red fruit, a touch of leather and herbs, and much more. Vital and serious in the mouth, with pulsing raspberry and plum flavors. Strapped on the finish, with tannic bite but also sweet flavors of mocha and vanilla. Drink now through 2013. 93 —*M.S. (6/1/2007)*

Bodegas Fuentespina 1998 Reserva Especial Tempranillo (Ribera del Duero) $72. 92 —*M.S. (3/1/2004)*

Bodegas Fuentespina 2003 Roble Tempranillo (Ribera del Duero) $13. Warm, fruity and full of blackberry aromas as well as touches of citrus peel. The palate is lean and firm in the middle and tannic on the sides, and it's carrying flavors of raspberry and black cherry. This wine has good stuff but it also runs choppy, jagged and rough. Flavorful but lacks finesse. 50,000 cases made. 85 —*M.S. (6/1/2007)*

Bodegas Fuentespina 1999 Cosecha Tempranillo Blend (Ribera del Duero) $12. 85 —*J.C. (11/1/2001)*

BODEGAS GODEVAL

Bodegas Godeval 2001 Viña Godeval Godello (Valdeorras) $14. 90 Best Buy —*M.S. (3/1/2004)*

BODEGAS GUELBENZU

Bodegas Guelbenzu 2002 EVO Cabernet Blend (Ribera del Queiles) $22. 87 —*M.S. (9/1/2004)*

Bodegas Guelbenzu 1999 Guelbenzu EVO Cabernet Blend (Navarra) $22. 89 —*C.S. (4/1/2002)*

Bodegas Guelbenzu 2002 Azul Tempranillo Blend (Ribera del Queiles) $14. 86 —*M.S. (9/1/2004)*

Bodegas Guelbenzu 1999 Guelbenzu Azul Tempranillo Blend (Navarra) $13. 88 Best Buy *(1/1/2004)*

BODEGAS GUTIÉRREZ DE LA VEGA

Bodegas Gutiérrez de la Vega 2000 Casta Diva Reserva Real Moscatel (Alicante) $NA. 90 —*M.S. (6/1/2005)*

Bodegas Gutiérrez de la Vega 2003 Casta Diva Cosecha Miel Muscat (Alicante) $25. 85 —*M.S. (8/1/2005)*

BODEGAS HEREDEROS RIBAS

Bodegas Herederos Ribas 1998 Ribas de Cabrera Red Blend (Vi de Taula de Balears) $53. 92 —*M.S. (3/1/2004)*

BODEGAS HIDALGO

Bodegas Hidalgo NV La Gitana Manzanilla Sherry (Jerez) $10. 89 Best Buy —*M.S. (11/15/2004)*

BODEGAS HNOS. PÉREZ PASCUAS

Bodegas Hnos. Pérez Pascuas 2004 Viña Pedrosa Tempranillo (Ribera del Duero) $22. More complex than many, and lighter in bouquet and body, this semitraditional RdD starts with smoky, leathery aromas but also some dill and coconut from the barrel regimen. It keeps that "American oak" character through the sweet-berry palate and onto the vanilla-tinged finish. Gets better with airing but could use another year or two of bottle age. 89 —*M.S. (6/1/2007)*

BODEGAS INVIOSA

Bodegas Inviosa 1999 Lar de Barros Crianza Tempranillo (Ribera del Guadiana) $10. 83 —*D.T. (4/1/2003)*

Bodegas Inviosa 1998 Lar de Barros Crianza White Blend (Ribera del Guadiana) $10. 87 Best Buy —*C.S. (4/1/2002)*

BODEGAS IRANZO

Bodegas Iranzo 2004 Mi Niña Tempranillo (Utiel-Requena) $11. 84 —*M.S. (12/15/2006)*

Bodegas Iranzo 2002 Vertus Reserva Tempranillo-Cabernet Sauvignon (Utiel-Requena) $35. 80 —*M.S. (12/15/2006)*

BODEGAS JULIÁN CHIVITE

Bodegas Julián Chivite 2003 Colección 125 Chardonnay (Navarra) $NA. 89 —*M.S. (10/1/2004)*

Bodegas Julián Chivite 2000 Colección 125 Chardonnay (Navarra) $50. 90 *(4/1/2003)*

Bodegas Julián Chivite 1999 Colección 125 Chardonnay (Navarra) $49. 89 *(4/1/2003)*

Bodegas Julián Chivite 2005 Gran Feudo Rosé Garnacha (Navarra) $12. 85 —*M.S. (12/15/2006)*

Bodegas Julián Chivite 2002 Colección 125 Vendimia Tardía Moscatel (Navarra) $40. 92 —*M.S. (6/1/2005)*

Bodegas Julián Chivite 2000 Colección 125 Vendimia Tardía Muscat (Navarra) $35. 91 *(4/1/2003)*

Bodegas Julián Chivite 2001 Colección 125 Reserva Tempranillo Blend (Navarra) $NA. 92 —*M.S. (10/1/2004)*

Bodegas Julián Chivite 2000 Colección 125 Reserva Tempranillo Blend (Navarra) $NA. 90 *(4/1/2003)*

Bodegas Julián Chivite 1999 Colección 125 Reserva Tempranillo Blend (Navarra) $46. 90 *(4/1/2003)*

Bodegas Julián Chivite 1998 Colección 125 Reserva Tempranillo Blend (Navarra) $42. 88 *(4/1/2003)*

Bodegas Julián Chivite 2002 Gran Feudo Crianza Tempranillo Blend (Navarra) $11. 85 —*M.S. (12/15/2006)*

Bodegas Julián Chivite 2001 Gran Feudo Reserva Tempranillo Blend (Navarra) $15. 87 —*M.S. (12/15/2006)*

Bodegas Julián Chivite 2000 Señorio de Arinzano Tempranillo Blend (Navarra) $NA. 93 Cellar Selection *(4/1/2003)*

BODEGAS LA CERCA

Bodegas La Cerca 2001 Don Cecilio Red Blend (Mentrida) $10. 85 —*D.T. (4/1/2003)*

Bodegas La Cerca 2000 Milino Viejo Crianza Red Blend (Mentrida) $18. 87 —*M.S. (3/1/2004)*

Bodegas La Cerca 1999 Molino Viejo Crianza Red Blend (Mentrida) $20. 88 —*D.T. (4/1/2003)*

BODEGAS LA PURÍSIMA

Bodegas La Purísima 2003 Trapío Monastrell (Yecla) $0. Smooth on the nose, with baked-fruit aromas along with touches of forest and mineral. For a previously untried Monastrell from southern Yecla, we like the wine's light fruit character and apple-skin tannins. Finishes with spice and cinnamon. Drinking very well now. 88 —*M.S. (12/15/2007)*

PRICE?

BODEGAS LAN

Bodegas LAN 2003 Crianza Red Blend (Rioja) $11. 84 —*M.S. (12/15/2006)*

Bodegas LAN 1998 Gran Reserva Red Blend (Rioja) $25. 83 —*M.S. (11/1/2006)*

Bodegas LAN 1999 Reserva Red Blend (Rioja) $17. 86 —*M.S. (11/1/2006)*

Bodegas LAN 1999 Crianza Tempranillo (Rioja) $11. 83 —*M.S. (6/1/2005)*

Bodegas LAN 2004 Edicion Limitada Tempranillo (Rioja) $45. The color and mouthfeel on this modern-styled, expensive Rioja are both very nice. On the palate, it's cushioned and healthy, with smooth tannins and proper acidity. But aromatically and flavorwise, the wine is green almost to the point of vegetal. And there's only so much tobacco leaf, bell pepper and rosemary that one should have to take. Imported by Monsieur Touton Selection, Ltd. 86 —*M.S. (11/1/2007)*

Bodegas LAN 1996 Gran Reserva Tempranillo (Rioja) $25. 84 —*M.S. (6/1/2005)*

Bodegas LAN 1999 Viña Lanciano Reserva Red Blend (Rioja) $25. 87 —*M.S. (12/15/2006)*

Bodegas LAN 2000 Crianza Tempranillo (Rioja) $10. 84 —*M.S. (6/1/2005)*

Bodegas LAN 1994 Culmen de LAN Tempranillo (Rioja) $162. 89 —*M.M. (9/1/2002)*

Bodegas LAN 2003 Edición Limitada Tempranillo (Rioja) $45. 89 —*M.S. (11/1/2006)*

Bodegas LAN 2002 Edición Limitada Tempranillo (Rioja) $38. 91 —*M.S. (3/1/2005)*

Bodegas LAN 2001 Edición Limitada Tempranillo (Rioja) $38. 95 Editors' Choice —*M.S. (3/1/2005)*

Bodegas LAN 1996 Viña Lanciano Reserva Tempranillo (Rioja) $30. 89 —*M.S. (3/1/2005)*

Bodegas LAN 2001 Viña Lanciano Single Vineyard Reserva Tempranillo Blend (Rioja) $25. From what will go down as a legendary vintage, the '01 Lanciano is a full-boned but elegant wine with deftly balanced aromas of chocolate, mint, graphite and berry compote. The feel is satisfying and chewy, while the flavors of cherry cola, black plum and cocoa are pure and lasting. Good now through 2012. Imported by Monsieur Touton Selection, Ltd. 91 —*M.S. (11/1/2007)*

Bodegas LAN 2001 Culmen Tempranillo Blend (Rioja) $75. 90 —*M.S. (3/1/2005)*

Bodegas LAN 1996 Edición Limitada Reserva Tempranillo Blend (Rioja) $39. 86 —*M.S. (9/1/2004)*

Bodegas LAN 1998 Reserva Tempranillo Blend (Rioja) $17. 89 *—M.S. (6/1/2005)*

Bodegas LAN 1999 Viña Lanciano Tempranillo Blend (Rioja) $30. 90 *—M.S. (6/1/2005)*

Bodegas LAN 1998 Viña Lanciano Reserva Tempranillo Blend (Rioja) $30. 92 Editors' Choice *—M.S. (3/1/2005)*

BODEGAS LEDA

Bodegas Leda 2002 Viñas Viejas Tempranillo (Viño de la Tierra de Castilla y León) $60. 89 *—M.S. (6/1/2005)*

Bodegas Leda 2000 Viñas Viejas Tempranillo (Viño de la Tierra de Castilla y León) $50. 92 Editors' Choice *—M.S. (3/1/2004)*

BODEGAS LÓPEZ PANACH

PRICE?

Bodegas López Panach 2002 Man Quixot Tempranillo (Vino de la Tierra de Castilla) $13. Prune and other overweight aromas carry the nose, and the palate is raisiny. Not rough by any means, but a lot of dead weight drags it down. **81** *—M.S. (8/1/2007)*

BODEGAS LOS LLANOS

Bodegas Los Llanos 2000 Pata Negra Gran Reserva Tempranillo (Valdepeñas) $15. The hefty nose forces out spice and mildly-baked aromas of blackberries, while the palate delivers legitimate berry flavors touched up by accents of dill and butter. The finish is expansive and drying, with solid tannins. This is the best of what's on offer from Bodegas Los Llanos. **85** *—M.S. (12/15/2007)*

Bodegas Los Llanos 2005 Pata Negra Roble Tempranillo (Valdepeñas) $10. Stewy and sweet on the nose, with clumsy black-fruit flavors. This shows all the rough and tumble characteristics of young Tempranillo: It's hard as nails, with big, forceful tannins and awkward, gummy flavors. **82** *—M.S. (12/15/2007)*

Bodegas Los Llanos 1999 Señorío de los Llanos Gran Reserva Tempranillo (Valdepeñas) $13. Opens with spice notes of cinnamon and anise before transitioning to fuller cherry and plum flavors. The mouthfeel is warm and fatty, while the finish still holds some buttery notes and tannic grip. Nothing spectacular but not bad for a 1999 wine from Valdepeñas. **84** *—M.S. (12/15/2007)*

Bodegas Los Llanos 2001 Señorío de los Llanos Reserva Tempranillo (Valdepeñas) $11. Transparent in color, with rustic aromas of leather, dried leaves and tea-like berries. The palate is rather thin but refreshing, with red-fruit flavors and a smack of citrus. Might take well to a light chilling. **83** *—M.S. (12/15/2007)*

BODEGAS LUIS GURPEGUI MUGA

Bodegas Luis Gurpegui Muga 2004 Saludo Garnacha (Navarra) $9. A big surprise! This shows that it rates many levels higher than what $9 usually buys. The nose is smooth, clean and fresh, with a hint of lemon peel to accent raspberry. The palate is exuberant and balanced, with three-star feel. For unoaked Garnacha that's sure to please, this is where you should turn. **90 Best Buy** *—M.S. (11/1/2007)*

Bodegas Luis Gurpegui Muga 2004 Primi Red Blend (Rioja) $10. Roasted and woodsy on the nose, with a base scent of raisins. The palate pushes tight cherry flavors and a little citrus, while the feel is uncomplicated and light. **83** *—M.S. (9/1/2007)*

Bodegas Luis Gurpegui Muga 2006 Pintoresco Tempranillo (Extremadura) $10. Opens with scents of pine needle, citrus peel and punch-bowl generic fruit aromas, and it keeps those characteristics on the palate while adding olive and pickle notes. Has good size and texture supporting a mundane flavor profile. **84** *—M.S. (12/15/2007)*

BODEGAS LUZON

Bodegas Luzon 2005 Verde Monastrell (Jumilla) $8. A young Monastrell with no measurable oak, which means there's only grapy, juvenile aromas of berries preceding juicy black plum and berry flavors. Very ripe and better balanced than previous vintages; look for notes of chocolate and leather in between the dominant fruit character. **86 Best Buy** *—M.S. (4/1/2007)*

Bodegas Luzon 2004 Verde Monastrell (Jumilla) $8. 82 *—M.S. (11/15/2005)*

BODEGAS MARCELINO DIAZ

Bodegas Marcelino Diaz 2006 Puerta Palma Pardina (Ribera del Guadiana) $11. This is made from an obscure grape called Pardina, and what results is a moderately pleasant but soft product. Hailing from hot, dry land in east-central Spain, it's largely dilute and innocuous but at the same time wet, melony and mildly refreshing. **83** *—M.S. (12/15/2007)*

Bodegas Marcelino Diaz 2004 Puerta Palma Red Blend (Ribera del Guadiana) $15. Austere aromas of wintergreen, lemon peel and cola don't allow for much fruit to escape, and the palate is literally as hard as nails. The mix is Tempranillo, Graciano and Cabernet Sauvignon and it's anything but a mellow ride. Extremely tannic and tough to swallow. **80** *—M.S. (12/15/2007)*

BODEGAS MARTINEZ LACUESTA

Bodegas Martinez Lacuesta 1996 Campeador Reserva Tempranillo (Rioja) $18. 84 *(8/1/2000)*

BODEGAS MARTINEZ PAYVA

Bodegas Martinez Payva 2003 Payva Tempranillo (Ribera del Guadiana) $8. 84 *—M.S. (9/1/2004)*

BODEGAS MAURO

Bodegas Mauro 1999 Red Blend (Viño de la Tierra de Castilla y León) $37. 90 Editors' Choice *—J.C. (11/1/2001)*

Bodegas Mauro 1998 Vendimmia Seleccionada Red Blend (Viño de la Tierra de Castilla y León) $90. 91 Cellar Selection *—J.C. (11/1/2001)*

BODEGAS MAURODOS

Bodegas Maurodos 2000 San Roman, Unfiltered Tinta de Toro (Toro) $38. 92 Editors' Choice *—M.S. (3/1/2004)*

BODEGAS MURIEL

Bodegas Muriel 1995 Reserva Tempranillo (Rioja) $13. 86 *(8/1/2000)*

BODEGAS MURVIEDRO

Bodegas Murviedro 2003 Tinto Bobal (Valencia) $6. 84 Best Buy *—M.S. (8/1/2005)*

Bodegas Murviedro 2000 Los Monteros Crianza Monastrell (Valencia) $11. 85 *—D.T. (4/1/2003)*

Bodegas Murviedro 1996 Reserva Red Blend (Valencia) $15. 84 *—D.T. (4/1/2003)*

Bodegas Murviedro 1999 Tinto Crianza Red Blend (Valencia) $10. 83 *—D.T. (4/1/2003)*

Bodegas Murviedro 2003 Agarena Tempranillo-Cabernet Sauvignon (Utiel-Requena) $7. 87 Best Buy *—M.S. (8/1/2005)*

Bodegas Murviedro 2001 Agarena Tempranillo-Cabernet Sauvignon (Utiel-Requena) $8. 87 Best Buy *—D.T. (4/1/2003)*

Bodegas Murviedro 2003 Blanco White Blend (Valencia) $6. 88 Best Buy *—M.S. (8/1/2005)*

BODEGAS NAIA

Bodegas Naia 2004 Las Brisas White Blend (Rueda) $10. 89 Best Buy *—M.S. (8/1/2005)*

BODEGAS NAVAJAS

Bodegas Navajas 2002 Vega del Rio Crianza Red Blend (Rioja) $14. 82 *—M.S. (11/1/2006)*

Bodegas Navajas 2003 Vega del Rio Crianza Tempranillo Blend (Rioja) $14. From Bodegas Navajas, this basic Rioja shows savory barbecued aromas along with brambly fruit notes, while the flavor profile veers toward red fruits and tomato leaf. Light in terms of mouthfeel, with some finishing oak flavor. A fresh sort of wine. **85** *—M.S. (4/1/2007)*

Bodegas Navajas 2003 Vega del Rio-Jóven Tempranillo Blend (Rioja) $10. 82 *—M.S. (2/1/2006)*

Bodegas Navajas 2003 Vega del Rio Crianza Viura (Rioja) $14. 80 *—M.S. (11/1/2006)*

BODEGAS NAVARRO LÓPEZ

Bodegas Navarro López 2005 Rojo Granrojo Garnacha (Tierra de Castilla) $9. The sweet, oddly spicy nose stirs some intrigue, and that's likely derived from the Grenache. Yet despite reasonably good flavors, it bounces along like a truck on a gravel road. It just doesn't have much balance, mouthfeel or charm. **83** *—M.S. (8/1/2007)*

Bodegas Navarro López 2001 Old Vines Crianza Tempranillo (Valdepeñas) $13. Foxy and rough, with a nose that is reminiscent of a wet dog. The palate is blanched out and rather green, while any sweetness the wine has comes across as burnt brown sugar. **80** *—M.S. (8/1/2007)*

Bodegas Navarro López 1999 Old Vines Gran Reserva Tempranillo (Valdepeñas) $22. Not often do you come across an aged Valdepeñas red, especially one with style, structure and character. The nose of dried fruits and spices also features cigar box and tomato, while the palate of red plum, cherry and tomato is mature. With some length and intensity to the finish, this is perfect to drink now. **89** *—M.S. (8/1/2007)*

Bodegas Navarro López 2000 Old Vines Reserva Tempranillo (Valdepeñas) $17. Classic in every sense, from the early aromas of dill butter to the dry, acid-driven palate to the light, crisp finish. In a world where so many wines are going ripe and heavy, this one holds steady to the traditional. So if you're looking for an old-school Spanish red to go with tortilla espanola or lamb chops, this will do the trick. **87** *—M.S. (8/1/2007)*

Bodegas Navarro López 2005 Rojo Granrojo Tempranillo (Tierra de Castilla) $9. There's more than enough to like about this red-fruit driven middleweight. It's surehanded and fruity, with enough grip, balance and character that it doesn't sway from that base-level quality line. **85 Best Buy** —*M.S. (8/1/2007)*

Bodegas Navarro López 2005 Rojo Granrojo Tempranillo-Cabernet Sauvignon (Tierra de Castilla) $9. This Cabernet-Tempranillo blend is even-keeled and solid from start to finish. The palate shows good raspberry and cherry fruit, and the mouthfeel holds its form until the very end, when a touch of tomato and oak enter the picture. A nice wine for the money. **86 Best Buy** —*M.S. (8/1/2007)*

Bodegas Navarro López 2005 Rojo Granrojo Tempranillo-Garnacha (Tierra de Castilla) $9. Peppery and tough smelling, with tomato-leaf aromas. This is a bland, innocuous wine with a touch of berry sweetness on the midpalate but no complexity or follow through. **81** —*M.S. (11/1/2007)*

BODEGAS NEKEAS

Bodegas Nekeas 2003 Vega Sindoa Cabernet Sauvignon-Tempranillo (Navarra) $10. 85 Best Buy —*M.S. (11/15/2005)*

Bodegas Nekeas 2001 Vega Sindoa Cabernet Sauvignon-Tempranillo (Navarra) $11. 82 —*M.S. (3/1/2004)*

Bodegas Nekeas 2001 Vega Sindoa Chardonnay (Navarra) $10. 85 —*M.S. (3/1/2004)*

Bodegas Nekeas 2005 Vega Sindoa El Chaparral Old Vines Grenache (Navarra) $11. Nice slate and mineral aromas meld with exotic spice and black-fruit scents; next up is a palate of lively cherry, raspberry and citrus zest. You get plenty of depth and spunk for a good price—wines with this much kick and verve usually don't sell for this little. **88 Best Buy** —*M.S. (4/1/2007)*

Bodegas Nekeas 2001 Vega Sindoa El Chaparral Old Vines Garnacha (Navarra) $11. 89 Best Buy —*M.S. (3/1/2004)*

Bodegas Nekeas 2000 Vega Sindoa Merlot (Navarra) $12. 81 —*M.S. (3/1/2004)*

Bodegas Nekeas 2002 Vega Sindoa Rosé Blend (Navarra) $7. 88 Best Buy —*M.S. (3/1/2004)*

Bodegas Nekeas 2002 Vega Sindoa White Blend (Navarra) $7. 82 —*M.S. (3/1/2004)*

BODEGAS OLIVARES

Bodegas Olivares 2005 Altos de la Hoya Monastrell (Jumilla) $11. Big and sun-baked, with large berry aromas and flavors that come up nice but a touch hollow. Ample acidity ensures that the wine doesn't register as dull, but in the long run there isn't much substance to it; there's color, flavor and tannins but no individuality. **85** —*M.S. (4/1/2007)*

BODEGAS ONTANON

Bodegas Ontanon 1998 Crianza Tempranillo (Rioja) $NA. 86 —*M.M. (9/1/2002)*

Bodegas Ontanon 1994 Gran Reserva Tempranillo (Rioja) $NA. 91 —*M.M. (9/1/2002)*

BODEGAS ORVALAIZ

Bodegas Orvalaiz 1998 Cabernet Sauvignon (Navarra) $8. 82 *(1/1/2004)*

Bodegas Orvalaiz 1999 Merlot (Navarra) $8. 82 *(1/1/2004)*

Bodegas Orvalaiz 1999 Tempranillo (Navarra) $8. 85 —*C.S. (4/1/2002)*

Bodegas Orvalaiz 1999 Viña Orvalaiz Tempranillo Blend (Navarra) $9. 84 —*C.S. (4/1/2002)*

BODEGAS OTTO BESTUE

Bodegas Otto Bestue 2002 Finca Rableros Tempranillo-Cabernet Sauvignon (Somontano) $13. 87 —*M.S. (5/1/2004)*

BODEGAS PALACIO

Bodegas Palacio 2004 Tempranillo (Rioja) $9. 84 —*M.S. (11/1/2006)*

Bodegas Palacio 2002 Crianza Tempranillo (Rioja) $10. 85 Best Buy —*M.S. (11/1/2006)*

Bodegas Palacio 1998 Gran Reserva Tempranillo (Rioja) $28. 86 —*M.S. (11/1/2006)*

Bodegas Palacio Especial 2000 Reserva Tempranillo (Rioja) $33. 84 —*M.S. (11/15/2005)*

BODEGAS PIRINEOS

Bodegas Pirineos 2005 Pirineos Rosado Merlot-Cabernet Sauvignon (Somontano) $11. This wine has its qualities, namely cantaloupe and peach flavors, minerality and a spongy but semi fresh mouthfeel. But it's also fading in terms of acidity and our bet is that you'd be better off waiting for the 2006. The blend is 50-50 Cabernet and Merlot, and it seems to be on the right path even if it's slightly over the hill. **84** —*M.S. (7/1/2007)*

Bodegas Pirineos 2002 Montesierra Macabeo (Somontano) $7. 82 —*M.S. (3/1/2004)*

Bodegas Pirineos 2001 Moristel (Somontano) $13. 84 —*M.S. (3/1/2004)*

Bodegas Pirineos 1999 Moristel (Somontano) $10. 87 Best Buy —*J.C. (4/1/2002)*

Bodegas Pirineos 1999 Marbore Red Blend (Somontano) $28. 86 —*D.T. (4/1/2003)*

Bodegas Pirineos 2001 Marboré Red Blend (Somontano) $34. 87 —*M.S. (6/1/2005)*

Bodegas Pirineos 2000 Marboré Red Blend (Somontano) $28. 82 —*M.S. (3/1/2004)*

Bodegas Pirineos 1999 Montesierra Tinto Red Blend (Somontano) $7. 81 —*M.M. (9/1/2002)*

Bodegas Pirineos 2002 Montesierra Rosado Rosé Blend (Somontano) $10. 83 —*M.S. (3/1/2004)*

Bodegas Pirineos 2005 Mesache Blanco White Blend (Somontano) $11. Macabeo, Gewürz and Chardonnay all in one . . . and what's the point? The wine tastes of apricots and other chunky fruits. Basically it's unfamiliar stuff that doesn't strike a chord despite the fact that it seems reasonably well made. **81** —*M.S. (11/1/2007)*

Bodegas Pirineos 2006 Montesierra Chardonnay-Macabeo White Blend (Somontano) $9. Strange that a 2006 wine will already seem old, but thus is the bane of Somontano, a region striving for better wines but not always hitting the target. This Macabeo-Chardonnay blend goes heavy on the melon and apple character, and in the end it teeters on cider-like. **82** —*M.S. (11/1/2007)*

BODEGAS REAL

Bodegas Real 2000 Vega Ibor Crianza Tempranillo (Valdepeñas) $10. 85 —*M.S. (5/1/2004)*

BODEGAS REMIREZ DE GANUZA

Bodegas Remirez de Ganuza 1998 Reserva Tempranillo Blend (Rioja) $65. 92 Cellar Selection —*M.S. (3/1/2004)*

BODEGAS REYES

Bodegas Reyes 2004 Tamiz Joven Tempranillo (Ribera del Duero) $15. Heavy fruit in the form of raisin controls the nose, while cranberry and rhubarb flavors anchor a surprisingly tart, red-fruit driven palate. Not sour per se, because there is core sweetness, but it just seems rough, snappy and sharp throughout. **83** —*M.S. (6/1/2007)*

Bodegas Reyes 2002 Teófilo Reyes Tinto Crianza Tempranillo (Ribera del Duero) $30. More earthy and chunky than you might expect for an '02 Crianza. The nose belts forth with cola, leather and brambly red fruit, and the palate is mostly fresh raspberry and oak-based vanilla. Fairly tight on the finish, with a nuttiness akin to popcorn or peanuts. The mouthfeel is sort of scouring so we recommend drinking this wine with grilled meat or something along those lines. **87** —*M.S. (6/1/2007)*

BODEGAS RIOJANAS

Bodegas Riojanas 2001 Gran Albina Tempranillo Blend (Rioja) $35. 89 —*M.S. (10/1/2005)*

Bodegas Riojanas 2000 Puerta Vieja Crianza Tempranillo Blend (Rioja) $13. 85 —*M.S. (2/1/2006)*

Bodegas Riojanas 1999 Reserva Viña Albina Tempranillo Blend (Rioja) $20. 87 —*M.S. (2/1/2006)*

BODEGAS RODA

Bodegas Roda 2004 Cirsion Tempranillo (Rioja) $273. Char and chocolate, then a dollop of rum raisin and black cherry, and there is your nose. This version of Cirsion, one of our very favorite modern Riojas, is relatively soft, raisiny and simple, and for that it doesn't quite rate with some of the past vintages, which were spectacular. But that doesn't mean you won't love the wine's smooth texture, cocoa and baked berry flavors, and its overall generous character. Drink now through 2010. **92** —*M.S. (9/1/2007)*

Bodegas Roda 2001 Cirsion Tempranillo (Rioja) $200. 97 Editors' Choice —*M.S. (9/1/2004)*

Bodegas Roda 1998 Cirsion Tempranillo (Rioja) $215. 94 *(8/1/2000)*

Bodegas Roda 2003 Roda I Tempranillo (Rioja) $73. A sweet, ripe, jammy style for Roda I, with smooth tannins, corpulence and more than adequate minerality and power. This is not a flabby wine despite the heat of the vintage, and the lush cassis, blackberry and mocha notes come together on the back palate and finish. **91** —*M.S. (9/1/2007)*

Bodegas Roda 2002 Roda I Reserva Tempranillo (Rioja) $67. Clearly Bodegas Roda threw all its best fruit at its '02 Roda I: it's as smooth, succulent and ripe as we've come to expect from this front-line alta expression Tempranillo. There's oak, vanilla, tannin, resin and lots of studly red and black fruit to give you something to ponder. Good now and better in a couple of years. **91** —*M.S. (11/1/2007)*

Bodegas Roda 2003 Roda Reserva Tempranillo (Rioja) $48. Alert and snappy on the nose, with no "hot" or stewy characteristics from the steamy year. Raspberry and cassis flavors are supported by tight, crisp oak, while the finish offers mineral, coffee and cherry essence. A solid wine from a hellishly warm vintage. **88** —*M.S. (9/1/2007)*

Bodegas Roda 2002 Roda Reserva Tempranillo (Rioja) $44. Typical of many 2002 Riojas, this packs a punch but doesn't hit many high marks. The nose is heavy and dark, while the plum and cherry flavors that carry the palate also have touches of green and bramble. Ample oak covers the wine and its weaknesses, and in Roda's skilled hands the wine isn't bad. **85** —*M.S. (11/1/2007)*

Bodegas Roda 2000 Roda I Tempranillo Blend (Rioja) $60. 95 Cellar Selection —*M.S. (9/1/2004)*

BODEGAS SILVANO GARCIA

Bodegas Silvano Garcia 2003 Dulce Monastrell (Jumilla) $24. 86 —*M.S. (6/1/2006)*

Bodegas Silvano Garcia 2004 Viña Honda Red Blend (Jumilla) $12. 81 —*M.S. (9/1/2006)*

BODEGAS TINTORALBA

Bodegas Tintoralba 2000 Crianza Red Blend (Almansa) $19. 87 —*M.S. (9/1/2006)*

Bodegas Tintoralba 2003 Higueruela Red Blend (Almansa) $10. 83 —*M.S. (9/1/2006)*

BODEGAS TOBIA

Bodegas Tobia 2001 Oscar Tobia Tempranillo (Rioja) $35. Raisin, baking spices and other soft, cooked aromas set the stage for a dense palate that's easy but flabby. In between the folds there's molasses and raisin flavors backed by a soft, fading palate. It's a sweet and inoffensive wine, but one with little future. **84** —*M.S. (11/1/2007)*

Bodegas Tobia 2005 Viña Tobia Tempranillo (Rioja) $11. Sweaty and pickled at first, although airing reveals some hidden dark fruit aromas. The palate is grapy and accented by black plum, yet it finishes salty and cheeky, with grabby tannins. Has it good points but lacks direction and elegance. **84** —*M.S. (12/15/2007)*

BODEGAS TORO ALBALA

Bodegas Toro Albala, SL 2004 Don PX Pedro Ximénez (Montilla-Moriles) $29. Ultra concentrated and sticky, with unctuous but wholesome raisin aromas taken to a level that's almost heavenly. In the mouth, the maple, cinnamon and brown sugar flavors are lusty and satisfying, and the finish never ends. This is P.X. in awesome form. **93 Editors' Choice** —*M.S. (12/15/2007)*

Bodegas Toro Albala, SL 2003 La Noría Pedro Ximénez (Montilla-Moriles) $23. Pure and unblocked by anything other than raisin, maple and brown sugar aromas and flavors. It's thick as motor oil, with a mile-long finish and lasting notes of pecan pie and cinnamon coffee cake. Maybe it's a little candied and easygoing, but who's complaining? **90** —*M.S. (12/15/2007)*

BODEGAS TORREDUERO

Bodegas Torreduero 2002 Peñamonte Tinta de Toro (Toro) $10. 86 —*M.S. (2/1/2006)*

BODEGAS VALDEÁGUILA

Bodegas Valdeáguila 2003 Viña Salamanca Rufete (Sierra de Salamanca) $8. 83 —*M.S. (9/1/2004)*

Bodegas Valdeáguila 2003 Viña Salamanca Verdejo (Sierra de Salamanca) $8. 82 —*M.S. (9/1/2004)*

BODEGAS VALDEMAR

Bodegas Valdemar 2006 Esencia Valdemar Garnacha (Rioja) $8. Sweet and creamy goes this ruby=tinted Garnacha-based rosado. All the way through, it pounds the palate with a grabby fistful of red-fruit flavor and sugar. Colorful and generous, but with no finesse. **82** —*M.S. (7/1/2007)*

Bodegas Valdemar 2004 Esencia Valdemar Rosé Garnacha (Rioja) $7. 83 —*M.S. (2/1/2006)*

Bodegas Valdemar 2001 Inspiración Valdemar Graciano (Rioja) $95. 86 —*M.S. (4/1/2006)*

Bodegas Valdemar 2003 Conde de Valdemar Crianza Tempranillo (Rioja) $12. Smooth upfront, with a light veil of oak sitting on top of black fruit. In the mouth, flavors of raspberry and plum satisfy in a juicy, medium-depth sort of way, while the finish is cushioned by chocolate and vanilla notes. A crianza that gets it right. **87 Best Buy** —*M.S. (9/1/2007)*

Bodegas Valdemar 2001 Inspiración Valdemar V.O.4 Tempranillo Blend (Rioja) $45. 85 —*M.S. (10/1/2005)*

BODEGAS VALDERROA

Bodegas Valderroa 2005 Montenovo Godello (Valdeorras) $10. 87 Best Buy —*M.S. (9/1/2006)*

Bodegas Valderroa 2004 Pedrouzos 1.5L Godello (Valdeorras) $80. 92 —*M.S. (9/1/2006)*

Bodegas Valderroa 2004 Val de Sil Godello (Valdeorras) $18. 90 Editors' Choice —*M.S. (9/1/2006)*

Bodegas Valderroa 2004 Pezas da Portela White Blend (Valdeorras) $35. 92 —*M.S. (9/1/2006)*

BODEGAS VENTURA DE VEGA

Bodegas Ventura De Vega 2006 Cadencias de Vega Esteban Shiraz-Tempranillo (Ribera del Guadiana) $13. Saucy dark fruit leads toward a palate that's hard, tight and full of rambunctious cherry, raspberry and plum flavors. The tannins get fiercer as the game runs on, and in the end it's probably too tight and tannic to really enjoy. **83**—*M.S. (12/15/2007)*

Bodegas Ventura De Vega 2004 Leyendas de Vega Esteban Crianza Tempranillo (Ribera del Guadiana) $20. Peppery raisin is the dominant aroma on this condensed, sun-baked wine that surprisingly shows spiky acidity and a rugged mouthfeel. Seems like the winery was shooting for a riper, bigger style than its regular Vega Esteban crianza, and that heft and kick don't really help. **82** —*M.S. (11/1/2007)*

Bodegas Ventura De Vega 2002 Leyendas de Vega Esteban Crianza Tempranillo (Ribera del Guadiana) $12. A wine in discord. The nose shows raisiny P.X. Sherry hints, while the palate is underdeveloped and tart. Shallow and almost too sour. **80** —*M.S. (11/1/2007)*

Bodegas Ventura De Vega 2004 Vega Esteban Crianza Tempranillo (Ribera del Guadiana) $17. The west-central plains of Spain get hot and that heat is evident in almost every Ribera del Guadiana wine I've tried. In this case, the prune, leather and dry earthy aromas are controlled and solid, as is the blackberry flavor that works the palate, which is full, tannic and offers pretty good feel. **87** —*M.S. (11/1/2007)*

Bodegas Ventura De Vega 2002 Vega Esteban Crianza Tempranillo (Ribera del Guadiana) $10. Spice and warm leather on the nose are worthy aromas, but there isn't much fruit and the palate runs gritty and acidic. It's got freshness and fairly good purity; but it's also kind of narrow. **83** —*M.S. (11/1/2007)*

Bodegas Ventura De Vega 2005 Vega Esteban Blanco Viura (Ribera del Guadiana) $8. Rather dilute and basic, with a touch of buttercup to the sweet, mellow nose. In the mouth there's almond skin, melon and mild citrus flavors, while the finish is fresh enough despite being fleshy. Simple but fine; drink immediately. **83** —*M.S. (8/1/2007)*

BODEGAS VIDAL SOBLECHERO

Bodegas Vidal Soblechero 2001 Viña Clavidor Tempranillo (Rueda) $11. 88 Best Buy —*M.S. (5/1/2004)*

Bodegas Vidal Soblechero 2002 Viña Clavidor Verdejo (Rueda) $11. 82 —*M.S. (5/1/2004)*

BODEGAS VIRGEN DEL ÁGUILA

Bodegas Virgen del Águila 2006 ía Garnacha (Cariñena) $10. Here's a fruity wine that wants to jump out of the glass at you. It's loaded with sweet, candied aromas that are typical of young Garnacha, and the palate is chewy, creamy and bullish with the red-berry flavors. It shows bubble gum sweetness on the finish, but it's exactly what you'd expect as a whole. **85 Best Buy** —*M.S. (12/15/2007)*

Bodegas Virgen del Águila 2003 ía Crianza Garnacha (Cariñena) $11. A simple, crisp and slightly stripped-back wine. The nose has red fruit, leather and light wood, while the palate races with cranberry and red cherry flavors. Overall it is fairly sheer and drying, but it will accent food without much effort. **85** —*M.S. (12/15/2007)*

BODEGAS Y VIÑEDOS DE JALÓN

Bodegas y Vinedos de Jalón 2002 Viña Alarba Old Vines Grenache Grenache (Catalonia) $6. 87 —*M.S. (3/1/2004)*

Bodegas y Viñedos Garcia Revalo 2005 Casamaro Verdejo (Rueda) $10. Light and floral on the nose, and medium in intensity and acidity. Flavors of apple, green melon and citrus are clean and crisp, and overall the wine is a model of freshness. Drink it sooner rather than later; it's a touch on the soft side. **87 Best Buy** —*M.S. (8/1/2007)*

BODEGAS Y VINEDOS DE RIBERA DEL DURATON

Bodegas y Vinedos de Ribera del Duraton 2000 Duraton Red Blend (Vino de la Tierra de Castilla y León) $18. 89 —*M.S. (3/1/2004)*

BODEGAS Y VIÑEDOS DEL JARO

Bodegas y Viñedos del Jaro 2001 Sed de Caná Tinto del Pais (Ribera del Duero) $NA. 92 —*M.S. (6/1/2005)*

BOHIGAS

Bohigas 1999 Brut Champagne Blend (Cava) $11. 84 —*M.S. (12/31/2002)*

Bohigas 2000 Chardonnay (Catalonia) $12. 80 —*M.M. (9/1/2002)*

Bohigas 1999 Brut Nature-Reserva Limitada Chardonnay (Cava) $12. 84 —*M.S. (12/31/2002)*

Bohigas NV Gran Reserva Brut Nature Sparkling Blend (Cava) $18. 84 —*M.S. (12/15/2006)*

Bohigas NV Rosado Sparkling Blend (Cava) $14. 85 —*M.S. (12/15/2006)*

Bohigas 1999 Tempranillo Blend (Catalonia) $10. 88 Best Buy —*C.S. (4/1/2002)*

BONAL

Bonal 2005 Tempranillo (Valdepeñas) $10. Fruity and punchy, with bright, no-nonsense aromas in front of fresh, clean flavors of cherry and raspberry. More juicy and simple than intense and complicated. The wine is all about fruit and flow. 85 Best Buy —*M.S. (2/1/2007)*

BORSAO

Borsao 2004 Tres Picos Garnacha (Campo de Borja) $12. For several years running this Garnacha from the Borsao winery has been popular among those seeking size, balance and affordability. The 2004 is a bit oaky and modern, but with its bacon, leather and dark-berry aromas and flavors it'll win you over. Lush enough but with good spine. 89 Best Buy —*M.S. (4/1/2007)*

Borsao 2000 Tres Picos Garnacha (Campo de Borja) $13. 91 Editors' Choice —*M.M. (4/1/2002)*

Borsao 2005 Rosé Garnacha (Campo de Borja) $7. Already past its prime, this Garnacha-based rosado has sweet nectarine aromas along with a sugary, creamy palate. If it had more zest upon release, that's mostly gone at this stage. Wait for the 2006. 82 —*M.S. (8/1/2007)*

Borsao 2002 Red Blend (Campo de Borja) $6. 87 Best Buy —*M.S. (3/1/2004)*

BOUZA DO REI

Bouza do Rei 2005 Albariño (Rías Baixas) $15. 91 Best Buy —*M.S. (9/1/2006)*

BOUZA GRANDE

Bouza Grande 2003 Condado de Tea Albariño (Rías Baixas) $22. 89 —*M.S. (3/1/2005)*

BUIL & GINÉ

Buil & Giné 2002 17-XI Red Blend (Montsant) $23. 84 —*M.S. (10/1/2005)*

Buil & Giné 2000 Pleret Red Blend (Priorat) $45. 86 —*M.S. (3/1/2004)*

Buil & Giné 2004 Nosis Verdejo (Rueda) $19. 86 —*M.S. (10/1/2005)*

BURGÁNS

Burgáns 2005 Albariño (Rías Baixas) $12. 90 Best Buy —*M.S. (9/1/2006)*

Burgáns 2000 Albariño (Rías Baixas) $16. 86 —*M.M. (4/1/2002)*

CALDERONA

Calderona 1999 Crianza Red Blend (Cigales) $12. 86 —*D.T. (4/1/2003)*

Calderona 1996 Reserva Red Blend (Cigales) $17. 87 —*M.S. (8/1/2003)*

CALIU

Caliu 2001 1+1=3 U més U fan tres Tempranillo-Cabernet Sauvignon (Penedès) $13. 84 —*M.S. (9/1/2006)*

CALLEJO

Callejo 2004 Crianza Tempranillo (Ribera del Duero) $30. Black fruit and olive aromas vie for center stage on the nose, while in the mouth there's black cherry but not much nuance or background. Overall, the wine comes across linear and a bit green. And it's brutally tannic as it transitions from midpalate to finish. 85 —*M.S. (6/1/2007)*

Callejo 2003 Crianza Tempranillo (Ribera del Duero) $30. Pure dark plum and blackberry aromas define the bouquet, while accents of coconut and mushroom get into the game. An intense palate of cherry, plum and buttery oak finishes in a cascade of dark fruit and medium-weight tannins. Give it a year to come together. 89 —*M.S. (4/1/2007)*

Callejo 2002 Crianza Tempranillo (Ribera del Duero) $26. 88 —*M.S. (2/1/2006)*

Callejo 2005 Cuatro Meses en Barrica Tempranillo (Ribera del Duero) $19. Wide and ranging, the bouquet on this young, lightly oaked RdD starts with campfire aromas before moving on to black cherry and earth. Convincing in the mouth, with chunky berry flavors that lead into peppery, vanilla-based finishing notes. Plump and easy. 87 —*M.S. (4/1/2007)*

Callejo 2004 Cuatro Meses en Barrica Tempranillo (Ribera del Duero) $18. The muscularity and meatiness of the nose indicate ripeness, while the aromas veer toward drying oak and a bit of raisin. The palate is chunky and dark, with subdued berry flavors front and center. And the weight is up there, especially for a youngster that spent only four months in oak. 85 —*M.S. (6/1/2007)*

Callejo 2001 Reserva Tempranillo (Ribera del Duero) $42. 89 —*M.S. (2/1/2006)*

Callejo 2002 Reserve Tempranillo (Ribera del Duero) $44. 88 —*M.S. (12/15/2006)*

CAMPILLO

Campillo 1994 Gran Reserva Tempranillo (Rioja) $32. 88 *(5/1/2004)*

Campillo 1998 Pago Cuesta Clara Raro Reserva Tempranillo (Rioja) $NA. 92 *(5/1/2004)*

Campillo 1996 Reserva Tempranillo (Rioja) $24. 88 *(5/1/2004)*

Campillo 1991 Rioja Gran Reserva Tempranillo (Rioja) $75. 92 Cellar Selection *(5/1/2001)*

Campillo 1995 Rioja Reserva Tempranillo (Rioja) $24. 90 *(5/1/2001)*

Campillo 1996 Reserva Especial Tempranillo Blend (Rioja) $56. Healthy in look, with tobacco, dried spices and pure wood notes on the nose. The palate is drizzled with plum and berry flavors, but there's also ample tobacco and tomato-leaf accents. Overall this aging Rioja is healthy and has enough of the nuances and subtleties to make the grade. 87 —*M.S. (9/1/2007)*

Campillo 1995 Reserva Especial Tempranillo Blend (Rioja) $50. 90 *(5/1/2004)*

CAMPO ELISEO

Campo Eliseo 2002 Tinta de Toro (Toro) $50. 91 —*M.S. (10/1/2005)*

CAMPO VIEJO

Campo Viejo 1995 Gran Reserva Red Blend (Rioja) $25. 90 —*C.S. (11/1/2002)*

Campo Viejo 1994 Gran Reserva Red Blend (Rioja) $25. 88 —*M.M. (9/1/2002)*

Campo Viejo 1996 Reserva Red Blend (Rioja) $13. 83 —*C.S. (11/1/2002)*

Campo Viejo 2004 Crianza Tempranillo (Rioja) $10. For unafflicted plum and berry character, this young, fresh Rioja has the goods. The sweet berry and cherry palate is at peak drinking condition, and the finish runs longer than expected courtesy of a beam of bright acidity. A wine with Zinfandel-like charm. Imported by Pernod Ricard USA. 85 Best Buy —*M.S. (9/1/2007)*

Campo Viejo 2003 Crianza Tempranillo (Rioja) $10. A nominally sweet red-candy note helps define the upbeat nose, and it all makes sense once you know that there's 20% Garnacha in the wine along with 75% Tempranillo and Mazuelo. With airing you get nice pie cherry and raspberry flavors, while the mouthfeel is juicy and correct. A good wine for pizza or hamburgers. Imported by Pernod Ricard, USA. 86 Best Buy —*M.S. (9/1/2007)*

Campo Viejo 2002 Crianza Tempranillo (Rioja) $10. 85 Best Buy —*M.S. (11/1/2006)*

Campo Viejo 2000 Gran Reserva Tempranillo (Rioja) $20. Racy on the nose, with tea, pepper and pine scents along with basic red-fruit aromas. The palate is zingy and fairly trim, with strawberry and raspberry flavors. Finishes fresh and snappy, with a shot of tartness. Drink now. Imported by Pernod Ricard, USA. 86 —*M.S. (9/1/2007)*

Campo Viejo 2000 Reserva Tempranillo (Rioja) $13. 85 —*M.S. (11/1/2006)*

Campo Viejo 1998 Gran Reserva Tempranillo Blend (Rioja) $20. 90 —*M.S. (4/1/2006)*

CAMPOS REALES

Campos Reales 2005 Tempranillo (La Mancha) $7. A strong peppery quality infiltrates the nose, which otherwise has some simple berry aromas to offer. And the palate is scouring and sour. La Mancha can do better than this. 81 —*M.S. (8/1/2007)*

Campos Reales 2004 Tempranillo (La Mancha) $6. 84 Best Buy —*M.S. (11/15/2005)*

CAÑO

Caño 2002 Selección Tempranillo (Toro) $15. Noticeably sharp and a touch green on the nose, with earthy, richer accents such as leather and chocolate making an appearance. The mouth is tangy and lean, with strawberry and raspberry flavors. Very un-Toro in its skinny, tight approach. **83** —*M.S. (11/1/2007)*

Caño 2005 Cosecha Tempranillo-Garnacha (Toro) $9. Dry and piercing on the nose, and then crisp and snappy on the palate. For those opposed to overextracted, heavy reds, this could be up your alley. More modern-influenced palates will probably find it a bit lean, stripped down and tart, especially for Toro, which is known for bigger, riper wines. **84** —*M.S. (11/1/2007)*

CANTOFINO

Cantofino 2003 Joven Garnacha (Vino de la Tierra de Castilla) $9. 82 —*M.S. (10/1/2005)*

CAPAFONS-OSSÓ

Capafons-Ossó 2003 Mas de Masos Red Blend (Priorat) $70. Big, brawny and not entirely welcoming: this Priorat heavyweight is full of licorice and cool black-fruit and cola aromas. The palate is hard as nails, and only time will tell if it softens and finds a sweeter spot. We think it will; in five years it should trade in the current burnt steak notes and fierce tannins for softer touches and more complex flavors. **91 Cellar Selection** —*M.S. (12/15/2007)*

Capafons-Ossó 2003 Masos d'en Cubells Red Blend (Priorat) $55. Time will only help this tough, rough Priorato that isn't offering a whole lot now besides tannin, dark-fruit flavors and searing oak. The flavors are middle-of-the-road in terms of friendliness and complexity, so expect a forward, hard-hitting wine. Should be more revealing in a few years. **86** —*M.S. (12/15/2007)*

CAPÇANES

Capçanes 2001 Cabrida Garnacha (Priorat) $60. 91 —*M.S. (10/1/2005)*

Capçanes 2001 Costers del Gravet Red Blend (Montsant) $20. 88 —*M.S. (10/1/2005)*

Capçanes 2003 Mas Donís Barrica Red Blend (Montsant) $12. 86 —*M.S. (10/1/2005)*

Capçanes 2003 Peraj Ha'Abib Flor de Primavera Kosher Red Blend (Montsant) $42. This old-vine Grenache is unique and surprising, with its touch of lilac and currant on the nose, followed by full-bodied, lush berry and currant flavors. It's tannic and needs to age, but should develop into a velvety, integrated treat with a few years on it. One of the better kosher wines on the market. **86** —*S.K. (4/1/2007)*

CAPITOSO

Capitoso 2003 Tempranillo (Rioja) $14. Rather stocky, with beef bouillon, blackberry and rubber on the nose. The feel is solid while the plum, berry and leathery flavors display some of the heat of the year. Not a refined wine but good in an easy, drink-me-now way. Could use cheese or some roasted meat. **85** —*M.S. (2/1/2007)*

Capitoso 2002 Tempranillo (Rioja) $12. 84 —*M.S. (8/1/2005)*

CARE

Care 2001 Tinto Red Blend (Cariñena) $20. 84 —*M.S. (6/1/2005)*

CARMELO RODERO

Carmelo Rodero 2001 Crianza Tempranillo (Ribera del Duero) $25. 87 —*M.S. (10/1/2005)*

Carmelo Rodero 2000 Crianza Tempranillo (Ribera del Duero) $24. 84 —*M.S. (9/1/2004)*

Carmelo Rodero 2000 Reserva Tempranillo (Ribera del Duero) $43. 87 —*M.S. (10/1/2005)*

Carmelo Rodero 1999 Reserva Tempranillo (Ribera del Duero) $45. 90 —*M.S. (9/1/2004)*

Carmelo Rodero 2003 Roble Tempranillo (Ribera del Duero) $15. 87 —*M.S. (10/1/2005)*

Carmelo Rodero 2002 Roble Tempranillo (Ribera del Duero) $17. 85 —*M.S. (9/1/2004)*

CARREDUEÑAS

Carredueñas 2003 Tinto Roble Tempranillo (Cigales) $14. 86 —*M.S. (8/1/2005)*

CASA CASTILLO

Casa Castillo 2005 Monastrell (Jumilla) $11. Young, dark and handsome, this is an example of what Jumilla can do when good grapes and winemaking come together. The palate is chewy and full of earthy blackberry flavors, while the finish is smooth, ripe and long. Drink now–2008. One of the best Jumillas you're likely to find. **90 Best Buy** —*M.S. (4/1/2007)*

CASA DE LA REINA

Casa de la Reina 2003 Tempranillo Blend (Rioja) $8. 83 —*M.S. (11/1/2006)*

Casa de la Reina 2001 Crianza Tempranillo Blend (Rioja) $12. 85 —*M.S. (4/1/2006)*

Casa de la Reina 1996 Gran Reserva Tempranillo Blend (Rioja) $21. 89 —*M.S. (4/1/2006)*

Casa de la Reina 1998 Reserva Tempranillo Blend (Rioja) $18. 88 —*M.S. (4/1/2006)*

Casa de la Reina 2004 Viura (Rioja) $8. 82 —*M.S. (11/1/2006)*

CASA SOLAR

Casa Solar 2000 Plata Red Blend (Rioja) $6. 83 —*M.S. (10/1/2003)*

Casa Solar 1999 Plata - Vino de la Tierra del bajo Aragon Red Blend (Bajo Aragon) $6. 86 —*M.S. (11/1/2002)*

Casa Solar 1997 Tempranillo (Bajo Aragon) $4. 84 *(3/1/2000)*

Casa Solar 2003 3 Months in Oak Tempranillo (Vino de la Tierra de Castilla) $6. 81 Best Buy —*M.S. (12/15/2006)*

Casa Solar 1994 Oro Tempranillo (Sacedon-Mondejar) $6. 87 Best Buy *(3/1/2000)*

Casa Solar 2006 Rosado Tempranillo (Vino de la Tierra de Castilla) $5. Alert and rosy, with touches of red berry snazzing up the bouquet. For $5 this is as much as one could reasonably expect out of a rosado from the high plains of Spain. And with modest melon and peach notes on the finish, it concludes with a hint of style. **84 Best Buy** —*M.S. (7/1/2007)*

Casa Solar 1994 Plata Tempranillo (Sacedon-Mondejar) $5. 86 *(3/1/2000)*

Casa Solar 2005 Viura (Vino de la Tierra de Castilla) $6. The yellowish color is an indicator that it may be over the top, and it is. Honey and mealy apple aromas and flavors are out of whack with what Viura/Macabeo should be. Enough said. **80** —*M.S. (2/1/2007)*

Casa Solar 2004 Viura (Vino de la Tierra de Castilla) $5. 84 Best Buy —*M.S. (10/1/2005)*

CASAJÚS

Casajús 2004 Tempranillo (Ribera del Duero) $17. A little oily and nutty on the nose, but there's also deep, dark fruit aromas and some leather to keep it on an even keel. The palate features moderate black cherry and coffee flavors with medium tannins, and the finish is dry, peppery and warm. **86** —*M.S. (6/1/2007)*

Casajús 2003 Antiguos Viñedos Tempranillo (Ribera del Duero) $33. A nice hue entices you, and the nose is meaty, tight and well oaked. With solid blackberry, dark cherry and chocolate flavors, this old-vines wine delivers the goods and manages to stay on course from start to finish. Almost everything about the wine is solid and commendable, even if it doesn't have the chops of something from the top echelon. **88** —*M.S. (6/1/2007)*

Casajús 2005 Vendimia Seleccionada Tempranillo (Ribera del Duero) $21. Alongside open, hefty berry aromas are bramble and toasted oak notes. The palate pushes pure cherry and plum flavors, while the toasty back end finishes with chocolate and espresso. A perfectly good wine with medium tannins and depth. **87** —*M.S. (6/1/2007)*

Casajús 2004 Vendimia Seleccionada Tempranillo (Ribera del Duero) $21. Heavy and a touch nutty at first, with coconut and earth. Then it opens to a palate of black cherry, plum, mocha and coffee. Has breadth and medium tannic grab, with a solid feel and density. A little big at 14.5% but quite good overall. **88** —*M.S. (6/1/2007)*

CASAL CAEIRO

Casal Caeiro 2003 Albariño (Rías Baixas) $16. 85 —*M.S. (8/1/2005)*

CASAR DE BURBIA

Casar de Burbia 2003 Hombros Mencia (Bierzo) $26. 86 *(11/15/2006)*

Casar de Burbia 2002 Hombros Mencia (Bierzo) $22. 85 —*M.S. (6/1/2005)*

CASTAÑO

Castaño 2000 Monastrell (Yecla) $9. 87 Best Buy —*J.C. (11/15/2002)*

Castaño 2001 Hécula Monastrell (Yecla) $12. 90 —*M.S. (11/15/2003)*

Castaño 2006 Rosado Monastrell (Yecla) $9. Dry, full and with integrity, this mild-mannered rosado sings in a steady, firm voice. It doesn't go beyond the basics of semicrisp berry flavors and a touch of pepper. It's good wine made from the local Monastrell (Mourvedre), but dialed back; expect no bells or whistles. **85 Best Buy** —*M.S. (7/1/2007)*

CASTEL DE BOUZA

Castel de Bouza 2005 Albariño (Rías Baixas) $17. 87 —*M.S. (9/1/2006)*

CASTELL DE FALSET

Castell de Falset 1998 Tempranillo Blend (Tarragona) $19. **86** —*M.M. (4/1/2002)*

CASTELL ROIG

Castell Roig NV Brut Nature Sparkling Blend (Cava) $20. **87** —*M.S. (6/1/2006)*

Castell Roig NV Brut Rosat Sparkling Blend (Cava) $18. Smooth and simple stuff. It's quite fresh and clean, with more citrus and cherry than what you'd get from a Catalonian Pinot Noir. And that's because this is made entirely from the Trepat grape, which results in a racy, zippy personality. A refreshing cava for fans of leaner, crisper styles. **86** —*M.S. (12/15/2007)*

CASTELLBLANCH

Castellblanch NV Brut Zero Reserva Sparkling Blend (Cava) $10. **89 Best Buy** —*M.S. (12/15/2006)*

Castellblanch NV Extra Brut Sparkling Blend (Cava) $8. **87 Best Buy** —*M.S. (12/15/2006)*

Castellblanch NV Rosado Seco Sparkling Blend (Cava) $10. **86 Best Buy** —*M.S. (12/15/2006)*

Castellblanch NV Semi-Seco Sparkling Blend (Cava) $10. **87 Best Buy** —*M.S. (12/15/2006)*

Castellblanch NV Brut Zero Brut Reserva White Blend (Cava) $9. **85** —*K.F. (12/31/2002)*

CASTELLFLORIT

Castellflorit 1999 Tinto Garnacha (Priorat) $17. **84** —*M.S. (11/1/2002)*

CASTILLO CATADAU

Castillo Catadau 1996 Reserva Tempranillo Blend (Valencia) $9. **85 Best Buy** —*M.M. (9/1/2002)*

CASTILLO DE ALMANSA

Castillo de Almansa 1994 Reserva Cencibel (Almansa) $10. **87** —*J.C. (8/1/2000)*

Castillo de Almansa 2005 Tintorera Garnacha (Almansa) $9. **86 Best Buy** —*M.S. (12/15/2006)*

Castillo de Almansa 2002 Reserva Red Blend (Almansa) $11. **88 Best Buy** —*M.S. (9/1/2006)*

Castillo de Almansa 1995 Reserva Red Blend (Almansa) $10. **84** —*M.M. (9/1/2002)*

Castillo de Almansa 1993 Reserva Tempranillo (Almansa) $10. **87 Best Buy** —*J.C. (11/15/1999)*

CASTILLO DE CUZCURRITA

Castillo de Cuzcurrita 2001 Cerrado del Castillo Tempranillo (Rioja) $75. All in all this is a perfectly good wine. But in this pricey class and category we get picky, and we're finding some reduced, raisiny aromas and a slightly flat, edgeless mouthfeel. However, we do like the wine's berry and plum core and its intensity; too bad it's not more evenly balanced. **88** —*M.S. (11/1/2007)*

Castillo de Cuzcurrita 2002 Señorío de Cuzcurrita Tempranillo (Rioja) $40. Black cherry and toasty oak aromas greet you, followed by racy raspberry flavors. There's a lot of acid, but there's also ample berry flesh and texture to handle it. Shows good quality overall but also some of 2002's lean character. Drink now with food and it won't be any trouble. **88** —*M.S. (9/1/2007)*

CASTILLO DE FUENDEJALON

Castillo de Fuendejalon 2000 Crianza Garnacha (Campo de Borja) $8. **86** —*M.S. (9/1/2004)*

Castillo de Fuendejalon 2000 Crianza Red Blend (Campo de Borja) $7. **84** —*M.S. (5/1/2004)*

CASTILLO DE FUENMAYOR

Castillo de Fuenmayor 2004 Gran Familia Tempranillo (Rioja) $10. Oak, cherry and raisin make for a warm bouquet, and there's initial weight to the palate. But then grabby tannins and cutting acidity take over, pushing the fruit toward zesty, even thin. A light and ready style, for certain. **84** —*M.S. (9/1/2007)*

CASTILLO DE JUMILLA

Castillo de Jumilla 2001 Reserva Red Blend (Jumilla) $16. From a region where sweet, ripe wines rule, you're not going to get much from this tangy, tart wine dominated by minty aromas and sharp cranberry and raspberry flavors. It's choppy and needling. **82** —*M.S. (12/15/2007)*

Castillo de Jumilla 1999 Reserva Red Blend (Jumilla) $17. **84** —*M.S. (10/1/2005)*

CASTILLO DE MONJARDIN

Castillo de Monjardin 2005 El Cerezo Chardonnay (Navarra) $10. Gold in color, with papaya, almond and orange on the nose. The palate features a heavy mix of citrus and apples, and in the end it's a style that leaves you questioning its intention. It's dense and wet, but also reduced and clumsy. **83** —*M.S. (11/1/2007)*

Castillo de Monjardin 1999 Reserva Barrel Fermented Chardonnay (Navarra) $20. **87** —*M.S. (5/1/2004)*

Castillo de Monjardin 2002 Unoaked Chardonnay (Navarra) $11. **86** —*M.S. (5/1/2004)*

Castillo de Monjardin 2002 Deyo Merlot (Navarra) $18. **82** —*M.S. (12/15/2006)*

Castillo de Monjardin 2001 Deyo Merlot (Navarra) $18. **90** —*M.S. (12/31/2004)*

Castillo de Monjardin 2000 Deyo Merlot (Navarra) $15. **91 Best Buy** —*M.S. (5/1/2004)*

Castillo de Monjardin 2000 Crianza Red Blend (Navarra) $11. **88 Best Buy** —*M.S. (5/1/2004)*

Castillo de Monjardin 2005 Tintico Tempranillo (Navarra) $8. A mixed bag of red-fruit aromas are brought down by a hint of sour pickle, yet the palate is uplifting as it delivers nothing but snappy red-cherry flavors. Grippy and scouring courtesy of live-wire tannins and acidity, but there's enough weight and sweetness to ensure balance. A good tapas wine. **85 Best Buy** —*M.S. (2/1/2007)*

CASTILLO DE MONSÉRAN

Castillo de Monséran 2005 Garnacha (Cariñena) $6. **84 Best Buy** —*M.S. (12/15/2006)*

Castillo de Monséran 2002 Garnacha (Cariñena) $7. **85 Best Buy** —*M.S. (9/1/2004)*

CASTILLO DE OLITE

Castillo de Olite 1998 Crianza Red Blend (Navarra) $8. **85** —*M.S. (11/1/2002)*

CASTILLO DE PERELADA

Castillo de Perelada NV Cresta Rosa Rosé Blend (Emporadà-Costa Brava) $18. **81** —*M.S. (9/1/2004)*

CASTILLO DE URA

Castillo de Ura 1998 Tinto Tempranillo (Ribera del Arlanza) $16. **85** —*D.T. (4/1/2002)*

CASTILLO DE URTAU

Castillo de Urtau 2001 Crianza Tempranillo (Ribera del Duero) $34. **84** —*M.S. (8/1/2005)*

Castillo de Urtau 2003 Joven Tempranillo (Ribera del Duero) $19. Not sure why an '03 Joven would still be on the market, but since it is we'll review it. The bouquet deals cinnamon and rubber along with basic berry aromas, while the palate is tangy and racy as it pumps cherry and raspberry fruit. Full on the finish but modest in flavor and style. Still seems fresh and ready to go. **85** —*M.S. (6/1/2007)*

Castillo de Urtau 1998 Reserva Tempranillo (Ribera del Duero) $80. Plenty of spice, citrus peel and leather on the nose. In fact, there's a lot more of those types of scents than anything you would describe as fruity. And in the mouth there's an herbal, mildly green character. Still, as a whole the wine has a nice feel and some liveliness. **86** —*M.S. (6/1/2007)*

CASTILLO LABASTIDA

Castillo Labastida 2003 Crianza Tempranillo (Rioja) $14. Fine aromas that announce balance and completeness draw you in, and right away you will like the cherry, red currant and cassis flavors. But as that fruit sits and the acidity builds, the wine goes racy initially and then almost haywire. By the end it almost falls off toward sour. Best right out of the bottle, and with food. **85** —*M.S. (9/1/2007)*

Castillo Labastida 2002 Crianza Tempranillo (Rioja) $13. More spicy and savory on the bouquet than flat-out fruity, with marinade and BBQ sauce outweighing the berry aromas. The palate is medium in power and depth, with raspberry and red cherry flavors. Overall it's smooth, light and refreshing. **86**—*M.S. (4/1/2007)*

Castillo Labastida 2001 Manuel Quintano Reserva Tempranillo (Rioja) $56. A swaggering, slightly traditional holdover from the amazing 2001 vintage. This wine delivers cumin, pepper, turned earth and vanilla-infused berry aromas in front of a juicy, forward, complex palate featuring prime red-berry flavors along with hints of red pepper flake and tobacco. It still shows ample oak and vanilla but the fruit quality, tannins and structure can handle it. Drink now–2015. **92 Editors' Choice** —*M.S. (11/1/2007)*

Castillo Labastida 1999 Reserva Tempranillo (Rioja) $18. 87 *—M.S. (12/15/2006)*

CASTRO BREY

Castro Brey 2004 Albariño (Rías Baixas) $14. 83 *—M.S. (11/15/2005)*

CATALINO

Catalino 2003 Tempranillo-Cabernet Sauvignon (Catalunya) $10. 84 *—M.S. (8/1/2005)*

CAVA BLANCHER

Cava Blancher NV Capdevila Pujol Reserva Especial Brut Natural Sparkling Blend (Cava) $15. Light citrus and a hint of baby powder is about all you get from the neutral nose. And seeing that it's a brut natural wine (meaning no dosage), you sort of expect it to have a clean, dry, tart character. Added notes of peach and green melon point it in the right direction, especially if you're not expecting any surprises along the way. 85 *—M.S. (12/15/2007)*

CAVAS HILL

Cavas Hill 2000 Chardonnay (Penedès) $NA. 83 *—D.T. (4/1/2003)*

Cavas Hill 2001 Gran Civet Hill Crianza Red Blend (Penedès) $10. 85 **Best Buy** *—M.S. (8/1/2005)*

Cavas Hill 2000 Gran Civet Hill Crianza Red Blend (Penedès) $11. 86 *—M.S. (3/1/2004)*

Cavas Hill 1999 Gran Civet Hill Crianza Red Blend (Penedès) $8. 83 *—M.S. (11/1/2002)*

Cavas Hill 1998 Gran Reserva Hill Red Blend (Penedès) $25. 87 *—M.S. (3/1/2004)*

Cavas Hill 1997 Gran Toc Hill Reserva Red Blend (Penedès) $13. 83 *—M.S. (11/1/2002)*

Cavas Hill 2001 Sauvignon Blanc Hill Sauvignon Blanc (Penedès) $13. 83 *—M.S. (3/1/2004)*

CELLAR MARTI FABRA CARRERAS

Cellar Marti Fabra Carreras 1999 Masia Carreras Red Blend (Emporadà-Costa Brava) $29. 87 *—M.S. (3/1/2004)*

CELLER CECILIO

Celler Cecilio 2001 L'Espill Red Blend (Priorat) $40. 90 *—M.S. (4/1/2006)*

Celler Cecilio 2003 Negre Red Blend (Priorat) $17. 88 *—M.S. (4/1/2006)*

CELLERS BARONIA DEL MONTSANT

Cellers Baronia del Montsant 2001 Clos D'Englora Red Blend (Montsant) $40. 83 *—M.S. (12/15/2006)*

CELLERS UNIO

Cellers Unio 2001 Roureda llicorella Red Blend (Priorat) $27. 85 *—M.S. (3/1/2004)*

Cellers Unio 1999 Tendral Red Blend (Priorat) $22. 84 *—M.S. (3/1/2004)*

CERMEÑO

Cermeño 2004 Tinto Jóven Tinta de Toro (Toro) $11. 84 *—M.S. (12/15/2006)*

CIMS DE PORRERA

Cims de Porrera 2001 Classic Red Blend (Priorat) $98. 94 **Editors' Choice** *—M.S. (10/1/2005)*

Cims de Porrera 2003 Solanes Red Blend (Priorat) $29. On the cusp of unbridled excellence, but since it's Cims' second wine it has its limitations. It's a bit woody and needs to broaden out with time in bottle, but even now the licorice, mineral and ripe plum/prune flavors are delightful. And the oak-driven finish of mocha and coffee seals the package. 90 *—M.S. (12/15/2007)*

CLIO

Clio 2003 Monastrell-Cabernet Sauvignon Red Blend (Jumilla) $42. If all you're after is size, then sign on the dotted line. This blend is a monster that weighs in at 15.5%, so be ready for intensely sweet flavors of grape essence and licorice. To this judge, the wine has a lot of gumption but isn't what I'd want to drink glass after glass, day after day. It's lumbering, heavy but oh, so sweet and dessert-like. 87 *—M.S. (12/15/2007)*

CLOS CYPRES

Clos Cypres 2002 Tinto Red Blend (Priorat) $48. 86 *—M.S. (10/1/2005)*

CLOS DE L'OBAC

Clos de L'Obac 2000 Costers del Siurana Red Blend (Priorat) $55. 93 *—M.S. (3/1/2004)*

Clos de L'Obac 2000 Dolç de L'Obac Red Blend (Priorat) $100. 91 *—M.N. (3/1/2003)*

CLOS DELS CODULS

Clos Dels Coduls 2001 Red Blend (Montsant) $19. 86 *—M.S. (6/1/2005)*

CLOS ERASMUS

Clos Erasmus 2002 Tinto Grenache (Priorat) $125. 93 *—M.S. (10/1/2005)*

Clos Erasmus 1996 Grenache (Priorat) $50. 94 *(11/15/1999)*

CLOS FIGUERAS

Clos Figueras 2002 Font de la Figuera Red Blend (Priorat) $30. 86 *—M.S. (10/1/2005)*

CLOS MOGADOR

Clos Mogador 2002 Manyetes Red Blend (Priorat) $NA. 89 *—M.S. (10/1/2005)*

Clos Mogador 2001 Manyetes Red Blend (Priorat) $70. 91 *—M.S. (10/1/2005)*

Clos Mogador 2001 Tinto Red Blend (Priorat) $75. 95 **Editors' Choice** *—M.S. (10/1/2005)*

Clos Mogador 2002 Vino Tinto Red Blend (Priorat) $75. 93 *—M.S. (6/1/2005)*

CLOS VILÓ

Clos Viló 2002 Costers del Priorat Red Blend (Priorat) $40. 81 *—M.S. (10/1/2005)*

CODICE

Codice 1999 Red Blend (Vino de la Tierra de Manchuela) $9. 87 *—M.M. (4/1/2002)*

Codice 2004 Tempranillo (Vino de la Tierra de Castilla) $9. The Eguren brothers of Sierra Cantabria and other projects always do a nice job with this Tempranillo from central Spain. It's a no-frills, bulky red with rich fruit and bacon aromas backed by bold boysenberry and blackberry flavors. There's no shortage of voltage in this tight, jabby, slightly clumsy red. 86 **Best Buy** *—M.S. (8/1/2007)*

Codice 2003 Tempranillo (Vino de la Tierra de Castilla) $9. 84 *—M.S. (8/1/2005)*

CODORNÍU

Codorníu NV Brut Pinot Noir (Cava) $14. 87 *—M.S. (12/15/2006)*

Codorníu NV Brut Rosé Pinot Noir (Cava) $15. This one takes on an orange tint, and the aromas are akin to chocolate, spice cake and even some baked beans. The palate is quite crisp and healthy, with berry fruit, citrus and length. A good wine with a racy, cleansing feel. It's not spectacular but it ranks highly among similar competitors. 87 *—M.S. (12/15/2007)*

Codorníu NV Jaume de Codorníu Brut Sparkling Blend (Cava) $NA. 89 *—M.S. (6/1/2005)*

Codorníu NV Original Brut Sparkling Blend (Cava) $10. The nose begins with wheat grass and chopped chive before folding in peach, clover and honey. The palate runs toward melon, pear and green herbs, while the finish is dry, crisp and perfectly solid. As a whole, it's an easy, straightforward, mass-market cava that gets it more right than wrong. 85 **Best Buy** *—M.S. (12/15/2007)*

Codorníu NV Original Brut Sparkling Blend (Cava) $9. 87 **Best Buy** *—M.S. (12/15/2006)*

Codorníu NV Reserva Raventós Brut Sparkling Blend (Cava) $15. Ginger ale and Sprite are the first things that come to mind when you give it a sniff. The palate shows ripe and sweet orange, tangerine and pink grapefruit, while the back end is lean and citrusy but far short of complex. Good in a standard way. 87 *—M.S. (12/15/2007)*

Codorníu NV Reserva Raventós Brut Sparkling Blend (Cava) $14. 88 *—M.S. (6/1/2006)*

COMENGE

Comenge 2004 Tempranillo (Ribera del Duero) $30. This is not a blow-you-away RDD, but it is a smooth, well-composed red wine with clean, alluring aromas and ripe-styled fruit flavors that touch on raisin but then pull back to black cherry and dark plum. With its integrated tannins and mild finish, this is ready to go now and should hold form for about five years, maybe eight. 90 *—M.S. (11/1/2007)*

CONDADO DE HAZA

Condado de Haza 2003 Tempranillo (Ribera del Duero) $25. 87 *—M.S. (11/1/2006)*

Condado de Haza 2002 Tempranillo (Ribera del Duero) $23. 87 *—M.S. (10/1/2005)*

Condado de Haza 1999 Estate Bottled Tempranillo (Ribera del Duero) $20. 88 *—C.S. (11/1/2002)*

Condado de Haza 1999 Alenza Gran Reserva Tempranillo (Ribera del Duero) $89. A couple of years ago the wine seemed heavy and stewy, but as it ages it seems to be showing the ripeness and richness from before, as well as intriguing notes of tobacco, chocolate and baked plum. More than the flavors, the wine impressed this time around courtesy of smooth tannins, flushness and mouthfeel. In a word, it has found a groove. **91** *—M.S. (6/1/2007)*

CONDE ANSUREZ

Conde Ansurez 1996 Tinto Crianza Red Blend (Cigales) $13. 89 *—M.S. (8/1/2003)*

CONDE DE LA SALCEDA

Conde de la Salceda 2001 Reserva Tempranillo (Rioja) $50. Smoky, alluring and sexy; this is a fine holdover from the excellent 2001 vintage. The bouquet is subtle and dusty, while the palate builds in power as the blackberry and plum flavors jump back and forth between lush and dynamic. An excellent Rioja reserva from the Rioja property of Julian Chivite. **91 Editors' Choice** *—M.S. (11/1/2007)*

Conde de la Salceda 2000 Reserva Tempranillo (Rioja) $40. 90 *—M.S. (12/15/2006)*

Conde de la Salceda 1998 Reserva Tempranillo Blend (Navarra) $49. 86 *(4/1/2003)*

CONDE DE OLZINELLAS

Conde de Olzinellas 2001 Crianza Cabernet Sauvignon-Merlot (Penedès) $18. 82 *—M.S. (9/1/2006)*

CONDE DE SIRUELA

Conde de Siruela 1996 Crianza Red Blend (Ribera del Duero) $23. 84 *—K.F. (11/1/2002)*

CONDE DE VALDEMAR

Conde de Valdemar 2002 Crianza Tempranillo (Rioja) $12. 81 *—M.S. (12/15/2006)*

Conde de Valdemar 2001 Crianza Tempranillo Blend (Rioja) $12. 86 *—M.S. (9/1/2004)*

Conde de Valdemar 1998 Gran Reserva Tempranillo (Rioja) $25. A little tight and reticent, but airing reveals aromas of raisin, marzipan and earth. The palate is measurably peppier, with lean but healthy red-fruit flavors stepping up and demanding to be noticed. As for feel, expect grabby tannins and shortness. Probably at its best now but will hold steady for at least five more years. **87** *—M.S. (9/1/2007)*

Conde de Valdemar 2001 Reserva Tempranillo (Rioja) $20. Functional Rioja Reserva is what this is. The nose starts out smoky and powerful, but the fruit is lean and on the snappy and tart side, with orange peel and cherry skins getting into the game. For a stellar year like 2001, it's surprisingly lean and basic. **84** *—M.S. (11/1/2007)*

Conde de Valdemar 1996 Gran Reserva Tempranillo Blend (Rioja) $21. 89 *—M.S. (12/31/2004)*

Conde de Valdemar 2002 Reserva Tempranillo Blend (Rioja) $20. The bouquet of cassis, liqueur and molasses would seem to portend a lush, deep, very ripe wine. But emblematic of the cool, wet 2002 harvest, this wine is crisp to the point of sharp, with oak coming up late and on the finish. Falls off with more time in the glass. **86** *—M.S. (11/1/2007)*

Conde de Valdemar 1999 Reserva Tempranillo Blend (Rioja) $18. 88 *—M.S. (2/1/2006)*

Conde de Valdemar 1998 Reserva Tempranillo Blend (Rioja) $15. 87 *—M.S. (9/1/2004)*

Conde de Valdemar 2002 Viura (Rioja) $15. 83 *—M.S. (11/15/2005)*

Conde de Valdemar 2005 Blanco Viura (Rioja) $15. 85 *—M.S. (12/15/2006)*

CONDES DE ALBAREI

Condes de Albarei 2006 Albariño (Rías Baixas) $15. Now this is Albariño! The nose sings a pretty tune, backed by aromas of white fruits, candle wax and flower blossoms. The mouth is perfectly racy but balanced, with forward apple, mineral and honeyed flavors. Get at this as soon as possible to enjoy Albariño's classic crisp, oceanic qualities. You won't be disappointed. **90 Best Buy** *—M.S. (11/1/2007)*

Condes de Albarei 2005 Albariño (Rías Baixas) $16. 88 *—M.S. (9/1/2006)*

Condes de Albarei 2004 Albariño (Rías Baixas) $15. 87 *—M.S. (10/1/2005)*

Condes de Albarei 2003 Albariño (Rías Baixas) $12. 86 *—M.S. (12/31/2004)*

Condes de Albarei 2000 Albariño (Rías Baixas) $13. 87 *—M.M. (9/1/2002)*

Condes de Albarei 1999 Albariño (Rías Baixas) $13. 86 *(8/1/2000)*

Condes de Albarei 2005 Carballo Galego Albariño (Rías Baixas) $20. Peachy and waxy on the nose, with dry lemon and green-melon flavors. This is a small-production wine (1,000 cases total) that leans on core acidity to keep it propped and steady. It's not the most complex game in town, and maybe it's on its way to having seen better days even if 2005 was a benchmark vintage. Limited in its scope of flavors but lively, courtesy of an extra boost of acidity. **86** *—M.S. (12/15/2007)*

Condes de Albarei 2006 Salneval Albariño (Rías Baixas) $10. Salneval is the so-called baby Albariño from Condes de Albarei, and it's lively and complete. Aromas of honeydew and peach nectar are appropriate and welcoming, while the apple, orange and pineapple flavors are fresh and agile. A wine for salads and seafood. **87 Best Buy** *—M.S. (11/1/2007)*

Condes de Albarei 2005 Salneval Albariño (Rías Baixas) $10. 86 **Best Buy** *—M.S. (9/1/2006)*

CONDESA DE LEGANZA

Condesa de Leganza 2002 Crianza Tempranillo (La Mancha) $10. Light and rubbery on the nose, but thin, tight and not very exciting on the palate. Cranberry, apple skins and some herbal weediness control the flavor profile and it never offers much pleasure. **81** *—M.S. (8/1/2007)*

Condesa de Leganza 2001 Crianza Tempranillo (La Mancha) $10. 86 *—M.S. (8/1/2005)*

Condesa de Leganza 1998 Crianza Tempranillo (La Mancha) $9. 88 **Best Buy** *—S.H. (11/1/2002)*

Condesa de Leganza 1999 Crianza Estate Bottled Finca los Trenzones Tempranillo (La Mancha) $9. 88 **Best Buy** *—M.S. (8/1/2003)*

Condesa de Leganza 1998 Los Trezones Tempranillo (La Mancha) $9. 84 *—M.M. (9/1/2002)*

Condesa de Leganza 1998 Reserva Tempranillo (La Mancha) $13. Leafy and minty upfront, with jumpy fruit that runs toward tomato and pepper. It's a rugged little wine with hot and spicy oak notes along with some dill and burnt coffee. Not offensive but not exactly regal. **84** *—M.S. (8/1/2007)*

CONRERIA D'SCALA DEI

Conreria d'Scala Dei 2004 Les Brugueres Garnacha (Priorat) $25. 90 *—M.S. (10/1/2005)*

CONSEJO DE LA ALTA

Consejo de la Alta 2001 Cata de Consejero Tempranillo (Rioja) $58. With its spice and fig aromas, this registers as a rich, mature Rioja reserva. The palate runs toward sweet plums and blackberry, while the finish is mildly toasty and full, with coffee as the lasting flavor. This has many good qualities, not the least of which is balance and a touch of citrus peel. Best now–2010. 525 cases produced. **91** *—M.S. (9/1/2007)*

Consejo de la Alta 2003 Crianza Tempranillo (Rioja) $20. This wine is not up there with the bodega's top bottlings. It's rather sweet and soft, with mildly green and minty aromas. In the mouth, there's size and power but also a strong medicinal overtone that dampens the fiesta. In the end it's big and fruity but there's no sense of path or purpose. **84** *—M.S. (9/1/2007)*

Consejo de la Alta 2001 Reserva Tempranillo (Rioja) $29. Earthy and fully ripe, with classic Rioja aromas of sweet leather, herbs and a touch of raisin. But once you get it onto the palate you'll be impressed with the roundness of the body and the depth of the cola, cherry and plum flavors. Finishes with cocoa, buttered toast and width. Drink now through 2008. **90** *—M.S. (9/1/2007)*

CONTADOR

Contador 2003 Tempranillo (Rioja) $354. Never let the price tag dictate perceived quality; you may be disappointed. This tart, choppy, clumsily extracted Tempranillo is a case in point. Where's the balance and mouthfeel? This is why we blind-taste; save your $350. **81** *—M.S. (9/1/2007)*

CONTINO

Contino 2001 Single Vineyard Graciano (Rioja) $95. 84 *—M.S. (11/1/2006)*

Contino 2000 Single Vineyard Graciano (Rioja) $95. 89 *—M.S. (8/1/2005)*

Contino 2001 Reserva Red Blend (Rioja) $42. Closed early on, the nose eventually opens to reveal earthy fruit aromas backed by cinnamon, clay and red pepper flake. Bright cherry fruit flavors on the palate are envigorating, while background raspberry notes are intensified by chocolate and a touch of oak-based dill. Modern but still sort of classical; nice in an approachable way. **91** *—M.S. (2/1/2007)*

Contino 1996 Gran Reserva Tempranillo (Rioja) $50. 90 *—M.S. (3/1/2004)*

Contino 1996 Gran Reserva Tempranillo (Rioja) $65. 88 *—M.S. (8/1/2005)*

Contino 1999 Reserva Tempranillo (Rioja) $42. 89 *—M.S. (8/1/2005)*

SPAIN

Contino 2000 Reserva Tempranillo Blend (Rioja) $42. 89 —*M.S. (2/1/2006)*

Contino 1997 Single Vineyard Crianza Tempranillo Blend (Rioja) $20. 84 —*D.T. (4/1/2003)*

Contino 2001 Viña del Olivo Tempranillo Blend (Rioja) $120. 90 —*M.S. (6/1/2005)*

CONVENTO SAN FRANCISCO

Convento San Francisco 2003 Crianza Tempranillo (Ribera del Duero) $39. If a roasted, fully oaked nose is not your thing, then this is not your wine. But if some barrel-busting char, toast and mocha is fine by you, then this youthful, rambunctious wine will do the trick. It's got power and pedigree but the heat of the vintage resulted in a softness that encourages near-term drinking. Best prior to 2009. **88** —*M.S. (6/1/2007)*

Convento San Francisco 2002 Crianza Tempranillo (Ribera del Duero) $38. 90 —*M.S. (12/15/2006)*

COOPERATIVO SAN ISIDRO

Cooperativo San Isidro 2002 Campo de Camarena Garnacha (Mentrida) $9. 82 —*M.S. (3/1/2004)*

Cooperativo San Isidro 2001 Campo de Camarena Garnacha (Mentrida) $9. 85 —*D.T. (4/1/2003)*

Cooperativo San Isidro 2001 Bastión de Camarena Red Blend (Mentrida) $11. 84 —*D.T. (4/1/2003)*

CORONA DE ARAGÓN

Corona de Aragón 2005 Cariñena (Cariñena) $12. A bit bulky and forward, but there's enough ripe, solid red-fruit aromas to keep you interested. The palate is full of cherry and crisp raspberry, while the finish shows a hint of citrus peel. The blend is Carignan with portions of Tempranillo and Syrah. **84** —*M.S. (2/1/2007)*

Corona de Aragón 2004 Syrah (Cariñena) $12. 82 —*M.S. (12/15/2006)*

CORONA DE CASTILLA

Corona de Castilla 2003 Prestigio Tempranillo (Ribera del Duero) $22. A very smoky, meaty, heavily oaked style of Ribera Del Duero, and one that never reaches a level where the fruit can escape the oak boundaries. Yes, the palate has berry flavors and snap, but there's also a ton of pepper, vanilla and burnt spices that keep it under wraps. And the bet here is that time will not make it better. **84** —*M.S. (6/1/2007)*

CORONILLA

Coronilla 2002 Crianza Bobal (Utiel-Requena) $12. 85 —*M.S. (8/1/2005)*

Coronilla 2000 Reserva Bobal (Utiel-Requena) $23. 88 —*M.S. (8/1/2005)*

Coronilla 2000 Crianza Red Blend (Utiel-Requena) $15. 85 —*D.T. (4/1/2003)*

CORTE REAL

Corte Real 2000 Platinum Cabernet Sauvignon-Merlot (Extremadura) $34. 84 —*M.S. (2/1/2006)*

Corte Real 2000 Tempranillo-Cabernet Sauvignon (Extremadura) $16. 80 —*M.S. (10/1/2005)*

COSME PALACIO Y HERMANOS

Cosme Palacio y Hermanos 2004 Tempranillo (Rioja) $13. 83 —*M.S. (12/15/2006)*

Cosme Palacio y Hermanos 2001 Tempranillo (Rioja) $12. 85 —*M.S. (9/1/2004)*

Cosme Palacio y Hermanos 2001 Reserva Privada Tempranillo (Rioja) $25. 83 —*M.S. (11/15/2005)*

Cosme Palacio y Hermanos 2003 Viura (Rioja) $12. 81 —*M.S. (11/15/2005)*

Cosme Palacio y Hermanos 2002 Viura (Rioja) $12. 83 —*M.S. (9/1/2004)*

COSTERS DEL PRIORAT

Costers del Priorat 2004 Abadia Mediterrània Red Blend (Priorat) $30. 83 —*M.S. (12/15/2006)*

Costers del Priorat 2003 Gran Abadia Mediterrània Red Blend (Priorat) $65. Spicy and savory smelling, with interesting aromas that encompass maple, chili powder, smoked meat and mildly baked berries. The palate is round and a little rough in the tannic category. But overall this wine is exceedingly pleasant, well made and pretty much ready to drink now. **89** —*M.S. (8/1/2007)*

COSTERS DEL SIURANA

Costers del Siurana 2003 Clos de L'Obac Red Blend (Priorat) $75. Mildly sweet and candied, with accents of rose petal, red licorice and high-quality raisin. As always, it's an intense wine with red raspberry, cherry and plum flavors in front of finishing vanilla and butter. It's a bit grabby and tannic, but it seems to have harnessed correct ripeness in what was a difficult, hot year. **90** —*M.S. (8/1/2007)*

Costers del Siurana 2001 Clos de L'Obac Red Blend (Priorat) $67. 90 —*M.S. (10/1/2005)*

Costers del Siurana 2001 Dolç de L'Obac Red Blend (Priorat) $98. 92 —*M.S. (10/1/2005)*

Costers del Siurana 2003 Miserere Red Blend (Priorat) $68. Generally speaking, this is a respectable Priorat from a tough year. The nose is berry packed, while the flavors run toward toast-covered raspberry. It's typically grabby and expansive, as any good young wine from the area will be, yet you can drink it now with meat. **88** —*M.S. (8/1/2007)*

Costers del Siurana 2001 Miserere Red Blend (Priorat) $60. 88 —*M.S. (10/1/2005)*

COTA

Cota 585 2005 Tempranillo (Rioja) $10. Nice upfront, with cherry, chocolate and rose petals to the nose. The palate peels off flavors of cherry and red plums coasting on a wave of tough acidity and tight tannins. Tastes and smells pretty good but struggles with mouthfeel. **84** —*M.S. (2/1/2007)*

COTO DE HAYAS

Coto de Hayas 2006 Chardonnay (Campo de Borja) $8. The nose is floral and tropical, while the palate is clean, zesty and full of melon and papaya. For a basic, straight-ahead wine with no acidic curves or oaky bumps, this is commendable. Best if served well chilled, and in less serious settings. **85 Best Buy** —*M.S. (11/1/2007)*

Coto de Hayas 2002 Centenaria Garnacha (Campo de Borja) $14. 86 —*M.S. (5/1/2004)*

Coto de Hayas 2001 Centenaria Garnacha (Tarragona) $10. 86 —*M.M. (9/1/2002)*

Coto de Hayas 2003 Fagus Garnacha (Campo de Borja) $37. 82 —*M.S. (11/1/2006)*

Coto de Hayas 2001 Fagus Garnacha (Campo de Borja) $30. 83 —*M.S. (9/1/2004)*

Coto de Hayas 2001 Reserva Garnacha (Campo de Borja) $18. 84 —*M.S. (2/1/2006)*

Coto de Hayas 1998 Reserva Garnacha (Campo de Borja) $13. 84 —*M.S. (9/1/2004)*

Coto de Hayas 2006 Rosado Garnacha (Campo de Borja) $8. Clean and fresh, and isn't that the first prerequisite for any decent rosé? The palate offers citrus and peppery apple skin flavors, while the finish is long and loud. Pretty good Garnacha that's ready for the summer and early fall. Drink now. **85 Best Buy** —*M.S. (11/1/2007)*

Coto de Hayas 2005 Rosado Grenache (Campo de Borja) $7. Earthy raspberry aromas get it going, and they're backed by red-apple, nectarine and cherry-skin flavors. Medium in body and fairly smooth in mouthfeel; it's a solid, simple, fuller-styled pink wine. **84 Best Buy** —*M.S. (2/1/2007)*

Coto de Hayas 2004 Rosado Grenache (Campo de Borja) $7. 81 —*M.S. (11/1/2006)*

Coto de Hayas 2003 Rosado Garnacha (Campo de Borja) $6. 83 Best Buy —*M.S. (8/1/2005)*

Coto de Hayas 2005 Tinto Garnacha (Campo de Borja) $8. In 2005 this winery got a great harvest and it's evident in this ripe, clean Garnacha that hits with jammy aromas and a ton of fresh-fruit flavors. Juicy, smooth and earnest is how to describe this tasty bargain from a region that doesn't always shine this bright. **87 Best Buy** —*M.S. (8/1/2007)*

Coto de Hayas 2000 Crianza Red Blend (Campo de Borja) $8. 85 —*M.S. (5/1/2004)*

Coto de Hayas 1998 Crianza Red Blend (Campo de Borja) $7. 85 Best Buy —*M.S. (11/1/2002)*

Coto de Hayas 2004 Tinto Red Blend (Campo de Borja) $7. 85 Best Buy *M.S. (2/1/2006)*

Coto de Hayas 2002 Tinto Jóven Red Blend (Campo de Borja) $6. 87 Best Buy —*M.S. (5/1/2004)*

Coto de Hayas 2002 Tempranillo-Cabernet Sauvignon (Campo de Borja) $9. 87 Best Buy —*M.S. (5/1/2004)*

Coto de Hayas 2003 Tempranillo-Cabernet Sauvignon (Campo de Borja) $10. 84 —*M.S. (2/1/2006)*

Coto de Hayas 2002 Blanco White Blend (Campo de Borja) $6. 84 Best Buy —*M.S. (5/1/2004)*

COTO DE IMAZ

Coto de Imaz 1996 Selección Pedro Guasch Reserva Red Blend (Rioja) $45. 90 Cellar Selection —*M.M. (9/1/2002)*

Coto de Imaz 1994 Gran Reserva Tempranillo (Rioja) $29. 87 —*M.M. (9/1/2002)*

CRATER

Crater 1998 Barrica Red Blend (Tacoronte-Acentejo) $38. 90 —*M.M. (4/1/2002)*

CRISTALINO

Cristalino NV Brut Sparkling Blend (Cava) $9. 85 Best Buy —*M.S. (12/15/2005)*

Cristalino 2001 Brut Nature Sparkling Blend (Cava) $15. 87 —*M.S. (6/1/2006)*

Cristalino 1998 Brut Nature Sparkling Blend (Cava) $12. 85 —*J.C. (12/31/2003)*

Cristalino NV Extra Dry Sparkling Blend (Cava) $9. 86 Best Buy —*M.S. (12/15/2005)*

Cristalino NV Rosé Brut Sparkling Blend (Cava) $9. 81 —*M.S. (12/15/2005)*

CRUCILLON

Crucillon 2003 Garnacha (Campo de Borja) $6. 85 Best Buy —*M.S. (6/1/2005)*

Crucillon 2004 Tinto Garnacha (Campo de Borja) $6. 85 Best Buy —*M.S. (2/1/2006)*

Crucillon 2002 Tinto Garnacha (Campo de Borja) $5. 85 Best Buy —*M.S. (5/1/2004)*

Crucillon 2005 Macabeo (Campo de Borja) $6. There are good 83s and bad ones, and honestly, this is a perfectly good one. It's not too deep on fruit and it's a touch low-acid and pudgy, but the apple, papaya and peach flavors are okay and the finish is clean and crisp. **83 Best Buy** —*M.S. (2/1/2007)*

CRUZ DE PIEDRA

Cruz de Piedra 2002 Garnacha (Calatayud) $7. 84 —*M.S. (12/31/2004)*

Cruz de Piedra 2003 Macabeo (Calatayud) $7. 86 Best Buy —*M.S. (8/1/2005)*

CUATRO PASOS

Cuatro Pasos 2004 Mencia (Bierzo) $12. 88 Best Buy —*M.S. (11/15/2006)*

CUATRO RAYAS

Cuatro Rayas 2005 Verdejo (Rueda) $13. Prickly and generic, with flat, cushy citrus flavors that don't hold court for long. Finishes mealy and pithy, with the essence of lemon juice. **82** —*M.S. (2/1/2007)*

CUETO

Cueto 2004 Tempranillo (Rioja) $10. 80 —*M.S. (12/15/2006)*

CVNE

CVNE 2001 Rosado Grenache (Rioja) $11. 82 —*D.T. (4/1/2003)*

CVNE 2006 Cune Rosado Rosé Blend (Rioja) $12. Frankly this is nothing to swoon over. The color is salmon and the nose is like matchstick sulfur. The wine is surprisingly sweet for being 80% Tempranillo and 20% Garnacha, and it's borderline cloying on the finish. Has its moments but I'm not really sure what the point is. **83** —*M.S. (11/1/2007)*

CVNE 2005 Rosado Rosé Blend (Rioja) $9. 84 —*M.S. (11/1/2006)*

CVNE 2003 Crianza Tempranillo (Rioja) $16. 85 —*M.S. (11/1/2006)*

CVNE 1996 Imperial Gran Reserva Tempranillo (Rioja) $60. CVNE is a throwback bodega whose wines won't appeal to followers of the new wave. And since I consider myself a backer of the modern style, I found this wine too obtuse, funky and borderline dirty to rate higher. It's full of mossy, stewy flavors and the feel is heavy. Traditionalist, however, may find it worthy of greater praise. **84** —*M.S. (9/1/2007)*

CVNE 1995 Imperial Gran Reserva Tempranillo (Rioja) $43. 88 —*M.S. (3/1/2004)*

CVNE 1996 Imperial Reserva Tempranillo (Rioja) $31. 87 —*D.T. (4/1/2003)*

CVNE 1998 Imperial Reserva 125 Anniversary Tempranillo (Rioja) $45. 87 —*M.S. (8/1/2005)*

CVNE 2004 Pagos de Viña Real Tempranillo (Rioja) $125. Leather, baked berry fruit and coffee make up the nose, while the palate is tight with cherry, raspberry and zesty acidity. This wine could use a few more years of bottle time, and then maybe that pronounced acidity will soften. If not, it is going to seem a little thinner than it should be for $125. **89** —*M.S. (11/1/2007)*

CVNE 2001 Pagos de Viña Real Tempranillo (Rioja) $119. 91 Cellar Selection —*M.S. (8/1/2005)*

CVNE 2003 Viña Real Crianza Tempranillo (Rioja) $18. 86 —*M.S. (11/1/2006)*

CVNE 1996 Viña Real Gran Reserva Tempranillo (Rioja) $48. 83 —*M.S. (8/1/2005)*

CVNE 2000 Viña Real Oro Reserva Tempranillo (Rioja) $33. 87 —*M.S. (8/1/2005)*

CVNE 2002 Viña Real Plata Crianza Tempranillo (Rioja) $19. 82 —*M.S. (8/1/2005)*

CVNE 2001 Viña Real Reserva Tempranillo (Rioja) $30. This wine reflects the great vintage and CVNE's long-standing status as a quality Rioja winery; the final product zips along with lively blackberry and plum flavors before slowing into a smooth, mellow and lengthy finish. A blue chip wine with style and finesse. **91 Editors' Choice** —*M.S. (11/1/2007)*

CVNE 1996 Vina Real Reserva Tempranillo (Rioja) $29. 86 —*D.T. (4/1/2003)*

CVNE 2004 Cune Crianza Tempranillo Blend (Rioja) $15. Savory mint and herbal aromas accent leafy, classic red fruit on the bouquet, while plum, berry, mineral, black olive and herbs work the palate. The wine transitions from one stage to the next without much trouble, and within the folds there are some complexities. A measurable step up from the bargain barrel milieu. **88** —*M.S. (12/15/2007)*

CVNE 2002 Cune Reserva Tempranillo Blend (Rioja) $27. CVNE must have done a strict selection in chilly, wet 2002 to get a reserva that's this sound. The nose is a lovely, traditional blend of earth, leather, coffee, spicy wood and red fruits. The palate follows suit, showing raspberry, strawberry, plum and vanilla flavors. A great, understated wine from what was a forgettable year for most Rioja producers. **91 Editors' Choice** —*M.S. (11/1/2007)*

CVNE 2001 Imperial Reserva Tempranillo Blend (Rioja) $48. The traditional side of Rioja is exhibited in the wine's vanilla, dill and peppery aromas, but the palate shows lots of red fruit, butter and a core of perfect acidity and tannins. This is a consistent wine that doesn't overwhelm. If you're looking for Nuevo Classico heft, color and power, look elsewhere. Best from 2008–2014. **91** —*M.S. (11/1/2007)*

CVNE 2000 Imperial Reserva Tempranillo Blend (Rioja) $45. 91 —*M.S. (11/1/2006)*

CVNE 1998 Imperial Reserva Tempranillo Blend (Rioja) $38. 89 —*M.S. (9/1/2004)*

CVNE 2000 Real de Asúa Reserva Tempranillo Blend (Rioja) $120. 92 —*M.S. (6/1/2005)*

CVNE 2006 Cune Monopole Viura (Rioja) $16. This wine shows Viura at its most elegant and expressive. It has weight, balance and body along with tangy lemon drop flavors. If you like pure but weighty citrus with a touch of mineral and brine, this has it. Better than most Viura by leaps and bounds. **89** —*M.S. (11/1/2007)*

CVNE 2005 Monopole White Blend (Rioja) $15. 85 —*M.S. (11/1/2006)*

D. PEDRO DE SOUTOMAIOR

D. Pedro de SoutoMaior 2003 Albariño (Rías Baixas) $19. 87 —*M.S. (3/1/2005)*

DAMALISCO

Damalisco 1999 Reserva Tempranillo Blend (Toro) $26. 86 —*M.S. (9/1/2004)*

DARIEN

Darien 2005 Tempranillo (Rioja) $10. A standard but solid Tempranillo is what you're looking at. The nose pushes red fruit and some American oak aromas like pickle and dill. The feel is fresh and young, but also a little fleshy and substantive. Finishes friendly and smooth. **85 Best Buy** —*M.S. (9/1/2007)*

Darien 2004 Tempranillo (Rioja) $10.82 —*M.S. (12/15/2006)*

Darien 2002 Tempranillo (Rioja) $9. 83 —*M.S. (9/1/2004)*

Darien 2000 Crianza Tempranillo Blend (Rioja) $14. 84 —*M.S. (5/1/2004)*

Darien 2000 Reserva Tempranillo Blend (Rioja) $28. 88 —*M.S. (6/1/2005)*

Darien 2001 Reserve Tempranillo Blend (Rioja) $28. 87 —*M.S. (11/1/2006)*

Darien 2000 Selección Tempranillo Blend (Rioja) $32. 86 —*M.S. (5/1/2004)*

Darien 2001 Selección Tempranillo Blend (Rioja) $36. 89 —*M.S. (9/1/2004)*

DE LOZAR

De Lozar 2005 Tempranillo (Ribera del Duero) $13. Fairly heavy on the nose, with aromas of tire rubber and blackberry. The palate is full, with black fruit, mineral and ample depth. Finishes with chocolate, heat and spice. Pretty serious and pretty good, with ripeness and balance. **86** —*M.S. (4/1/2007)*

De Lozar 2004 Tinto del Pais (Ribera del Duero) $13. 88 Best Buy —*M.S. (4/1/2006)*

DE MULLER

De Muller 1998 Legitim Red Blend (Priorat) $15. 80 —*D.T. (4/1/2003)*

DEHESA LA GRANJA

Dehesa la Granja 2000 Selección Tempranillo (Zamora) $35. 86 —*M.S. (10/1/2005)*

DELIUS

Delius 2001 Reserva Tempranillo Blend (Rioja) $60. 87 —*M.S. (11/1/2006)*

DESCENDIENTES DE J. PALACIOS

Descendientes de J. Palacios 2001 Corullón Villa Mencia (Bierzo) $40. 92 —*M.S. (6/1/2005)*

Descendientes de J. Palacios 2006 Petalos Mencía (Bierzo) $22. This is Descendientes' so-called starter Bierzo, but it rises above the tried and true value zone to exhibit mineral, crushed violet petals, graham cracker and pure dark-fruit aromas. The palate is smooth and plush, with lush black-fruit flavors, easygoing tannins and some creamy length. It's not as vivid as the 2005, but it's still mighty impressive. **91** —*M.S. (11/1/2007)*

Descendientes de J. Palacios 2004 Villa de Corullon Mencía (Bierzo) $50. This is about as aromatically complex as Bierzo gets. It shows radical minerality, bright berry fruit, purity and passion. The palate is a fast and exciting ride highlighted by excellent acidity, kick and ripe but restrained flavors. Corullon gets better and better with each passing vintage. **94 Editors' Choice** —*M.S. (11/1/2007)*

DÍA NACIENTE

Día Naciente 2004 Shiraz (Castilla La Mancha) $10. 84 —*M.S. (12/15/2006)*

Día Naciente 2004 Shiraz-Tempranillo (Castilla La Mancha) $10. 85 Best Buy —*M.S. (12/15/2006)*

Día Naciente 2004 Tempranillo (Castilla La Mancha) $10. 83 —*M.S. (12/15/2006)*

Día Naciente 2000 Tempranillo (La Mancha) $10. 80 —*M.S. (6/1/2005)*

DIEGO DE ALMAGRO

Diego de Almagro 1991 Gran Reserva Tempranillo (Valdepeñas) $19. 87 —*J.C. (8/1/2000)*

DIEZ LLORENTE

Diez Llorente 2005 Tempranillo (Ribera del Duero) $11. Bring on da funk; this offering has barrel-based, oily aromas that don't inspire much confidence in what's to come. The berry flavors are savory but not very precise, while the finish is baked and rhubarb-driven. Not a lot of fun. **81** —*M.S. (2/1/2007)*

Diez Llorente 2005 Barrel Aged Tempranillo (Ribera del Duero) $13. Weak in color, with chunky, oily aromas. The palate performs better than the bouquet, with brambly fruit and some burning field aromas. Decent mouthfeel is a plus. Not a very good wine but not a disaster. **83** —*M.S. (4/1/2007)*

Diez Llorente 2001 Crianza Tinto del Pais (Ribera del Duero) $25. 88 —*M.S. (10/1/2005)*

Diez Llorente 2001 Reserva Tinto del Pais (Ribera del Duero) $29. 84 —*M.S. (11/1/2006)*

DINASTÍA VIVANCO

Dinastía Vivanco 1998 Reserva Tempranillo Blend (Rioja) $20. 84 —*M.S. (9/1/2004)*

DO FERREIRO

Do Ferreiro 2005 Albariño (Rías Baixas) $24. Waxy melon and apple aromas are intricate and welcoming, while the melon and citrus flavors are just as they should be. Do Ferreiro is a consistent high-end producer in Rias Baixas and its '05 Albariño is great. It picks up steam as it goes along and will go great with salads and seafood. Drink now. **90** —*M.S. (8/1/2007)*

Do Ferreiro 2001 Albariño (Rías Baixas) $20. 85 —*M.S. (11/1/2002)*

Do Ferreiro 2003 Cepas Vellas Albariño (Rías Baixas) $33. 92 Editors' Choice —*M.S. (6/1/2005)*

DOMAINE PEDRO DE SOUTOMAIOR

Domaine Pedro De Soutomaior 2000 Albariño (Rías Baixas) $15. 89 —*M.M. (9/1/2002)*

DOMECQ

Domecq NV La Ina Fino Sherry (Jerez) $14. 88 —*M.S. (4/1/2006)*

Domecq NV Light, Very Dry Manzanilla Sherry (Jerez) $14. 87 —*M.S. (4/1/2006)*

DOMINIO DE ATAUTA

Dominio de Atauta 2002 Tinto del Pais (Ribera del Duero) $40. 89 —*M.S. (6/1/2005)*

Dominio de Atuata 2000 Tempranillo (Ribera del Duero) $30. 89 —*M.S. (3/1/2004)*

DOMINIO DE CONTE

Dominio de Conte 2001 Reserva Tempranillo Blend (Rioja) $30. A throwback Rioja that sports tobacco, mulch and some true Old World aromas that make you question the wine's health. But airing breathes life and tilts it toward dried cherries. Finally you discover core power hammered home by hard tannins, sharp acidity and an odd nuttiness. Not a wine for all tastes. **86** —*M.S. (9/1/2007)*

DOMINIO DE EGUREN

Dominio de Eguren 1999 Protocolo Rosado Rosé Blend (Tierra Manchuela) $6. 87 Best Buy —*M.M. (8/1/2000)*

Dominio de Eguren 2001 Codice Tempranillo (Tierra Manchuela) $9. 85 —*M.S. (3/1/2004)*

Dominio de Eguren 1998 Codice Tinto Tempranillo (Tierra Manchuela) $8. 87 —*M.M. (8/1/2000)*

Dominio de Eguren 2001 Protocolo Tempranillo (Tierra Manchuela) $6. 86 Best Buy —*M.S. (3/1/2004)*

Dominio de Eguren 2004 Protocolo Tinto Tempranillo (Vino de la Tierra de Castilla) $6. With its black plum, blackberry and other bold, juvenile aromas, this bargain-priced Spaniard shows flavors of chocolate, natural bitterness and good overall balance. A little big and brawny, but better than washed out and weak. A classic chorizo or hamburger wine. **86 Best Buy** —*M.S. (8/1/2007)*

Dominio de Eguren 1998 Protocolo Tinto Tempranillo (Tierra Manchuela) $6. 85 Best Buy —*M.M. (8/1/2000)*

Dominio de Eguren 2005 Protocolo Rosado Tempranillo Blend (Vino de la Tierra de Castilla) $6. Some cinnamon spice aids the nose, which otherwise seems a bit dull and faded. The palate is chunky and monotone in its creaminess and depth of flavor. Sweet and standard, but lacking in pop. **83** —*M.S. (4/1/2007)*

Dominio de Eguren 2005 Protocolo Blanco White Blend (Vino de la Tierra de Castilla) $6. With this Airen and Macabeo blend you'll get almondy aromas in front of apricot and peach flavors. It's a solid, fairly well-balanced wine that won't hurt your budget or your appetizers. **85 Best Buy** —*M.S. (11/1/2007)*

Dominio de Eguren 1999 Protocolo Blanca White Blend (Tierra Manchuela) $6. 86 —*M.M. (8/1/2000)*

Dominio de Eguren 2002 Protocolo Blanco White Blend (Vino de la Tierra de Castilla) $6. 87 Best Buy —*M.S. (3/1/2004)*

DOMINIO DE PINGUS

Dominio de Pingus 2001 Flor de Pingus Tinto del Pais (Ribera del Duero) $50. 93 Editors' Choice —*M.S. (6/1/2005)*

Dominio de Pingus 2001 Pingus Tinto del Pais (Ribera del Duero) $320. 94 —*M.S. (6/1/2005)*

DOMINIO DE TARES

Dominio de Tares 2003 Mencia (Bierzo) $16. 90 Editors' Choice —*M.S. (6/1/2005)*

Dominio de Tares 2003 Albares Mencia (Bierzo) $11. 88 Best Buy —*M.S. (6/1/2005)*

Dominio de Tares 2005 Baltos Mencía (Bierzo) $16. Mineral, crushed flowers, black olive, dark fruit and herbs carry the hefty bouquet toward a round, earthy and fully packed palate that offers accents of cured meat, leather, creamy oak and some heat. It's definitely a big wine that's warm on the finish, but not tannic. A good deal at $16. **89** —*M.S. (11/1/2007)*

Dominio de Tares 2004 Baltos Mencia (Bierzo) $16. 90 —*M.S. (9/1/2006)*

Dominio de Tares 2004 Bembibre Mencía (Bierzo) $50. This blend of six vineyards is great. It's dense and full of minerality, finely polished leather and pure berry aromas. The palate sings a melodious tune that begins with creamy oaky notes and expands to more defined plum, vanilla and fine herb flavors. The '04 Bembibre is a rounder, more complete version than the impressive but more austere 2002 (the last Bembibre we reviewed). It is immediately pleasing and keeps you on the hook to the end. **93 Editors' Choice** —*M.S. (11/1/2007)*

Dominio de Tares 2002 Bembibre Mencia (Bierzo) $45. 91 *—M.S. (6/1/2005)*

Dominio de Tares 2001 Cepas Viejas Mencia (Bierzo) $26. 91 *—M.S. (12/31/2004)*

Dominio de Tares 2003 Exaltos Mencia (Bierzo) $28. 90 *—M.S. (9/1/2006)*

Dominio de Tares 2004 Tares P.3 Mencía (Bierzo) $90. Very dark for Mencía, which indicates that it is an old-vines wine of pedigree. The nose is composed of cigar box, licorice gumdrop, balsam wood and berry fruit. In a word it's hedonistic, and the richness and full-bodied berry and plum flavors may just bowl you over. It's definitely more oaky than many, but it still qualifies as Bierzo at its most bountiful. **92 Editors' Choice** *—M.S. (11/1/2007)*

DON OLEGARIO

Don Olegario 2005 Albariño (Rías Baixas) $22. Sharp and sweaty on the nose, with bulky passionfruit, scallion and citrus flavors. This wine is on its last legs; it's soft, fleshy and starting to lose its final vestiges of freshness. You'll be better off waiting for the 2006, assuming it gets to market soon. 83 *—M.S. (11/1/2007)*

Don Olegario 2004 Albariño (Rías Baixas) $21. 84 *—M.S. (12/15/2006)*

DON PEDRO DE SOUTOMAIOR

Don Pedro de Soutomaior 2002 Albariño (Rías Baixas) $19. 87 *—M.S. (9/1/2004)*

DON RAMÓN

Don Ramón 2002 Tinto Red Blend (Campo de Borja) $7. 83 *—M.S. (6/1/2005)*

Don Ramón 2003 Tinto Barrica Red Blend (Campo de Borja) $7. 83 *—M.S. (11/1/2006)*

Don Ramón 2002 Tempranillo (Rioja) $15. 83 *—M.S. (6/1/2005)*

DON ROMÁN

Don Román 2004 Tempranillo Blend (Rioja) $15. A bit leafy upfront, with aromas of carob, forest floor and standard berry. The palate deals expected cherry and raspberry flavors, while the tight finish leaves a snappy sensation. A standard food wine. 85 *—M.S. (4/1/2007)*

DOS VICTORÍAS

Dos Victorias 2006 José Pariente Verdejo (Rueda) $17. An excellent Verdejo from Rueda is as good as fresh, crisp white wine from Spain gets. And the two Victorias that make José Pariente know their stuff. After an overly ripe 2005, this vintage shows more of Pariente's patented lemon, citrus and mango flavors. The feel of the wine is super solid and the finish is long and properly acidic. It's a treat for fans of Spanish whites. 91 *—M.S. (11/1/2007)*

Dos Victorias 2005 José Pariente Verdejo (Rueda) $17. Significantly more bulky, aggressive and unrefined than previous vintages, and overall fairly disappointing given that this was one of our favorite Verdejos the past couple of years. The 2005 version offers mostly chunky melon and pithy citrus. It lacks the verve, clarity and pure fruit that we fell in love with. Tasted twice with consistent notes. 84 *—M.S. (2/1/2007)*

Dos Victorías 2004 José Pariente Verdejo (Rueda) $17. **91 Editors' Choice** *—M.S. (9/1/2006)*

Dos Victorías 2003 José Pariente Verdejo (Rueda) $16. **91 Editors' Choice** *—M.S. (6/1/2005)*

Dos Victorias 2005 José Pariente - Fermentado en Barrica Verdejo (Rueda) $31. This is truly a unique wine in the sense that hardly any Verdejos are fermented in oak. Not only that, the end result is stellar. There's soft buttercup aromas leading into a layered, vanilla-edged palate of spiced apple, melon and greens. The wine is round, substantive and it stirs interest. And for that we're grateful. Drink now through 2008. 91 *—M.S. (11/1/2007)*

DUQUE DE SEVILLA

Duque de Sevilla 1998 Reserva Garnacha (Campo de Borja) $11. 83 *—M.S. (9/1/2004)*

EL ARTE DE VIVIR

El Arte de Vivir 2004 Tempranillo (Ribera del Duero) $14. Once you get by some early baked-bean and bacon-fat aromas, the wine settles and unleashes lean-figured, dark-fruit flavors backed by a mildly herbal, charred finish. Covers a lot of ground but never really makes that grand statement you're hoping to find from Ribera Del Duero. 85 *—M.S. (2/1/2007)*

EL BURRO

El Burro 2005 Kickass Garnacha (Navarra) $12. Once you get by the early sulfur this is mostly a nicely made, chewy Garnacha that has brawn and balance before going a bit hot and stewy on the finish. 85 *—M.S. (11/1/2007)*

EL COPERO

El Copero 2004 Tinto Bobal (Valencia) $6. 83 *—M.S. (8/1/2005)*

El Copero 2001 Vino Rosado Rosé Blend (Valencia) $7. 82 *—D.T. (4/1/2003)*

El Copero 2001 White Blend (Valencia) $7. 82 *—D.T. (4/1/2003)*

El Copero 2004 Blanco White Blend (Valencia) $6. **88 Best Buy** *—M.S. (8/1/2005)*

EL COTO

El Coto 2004 Rosé Blend (Rioja) $12. **87 Best Buy** *—M.S. (11/1/2006)*

El Coto 2001 Rosado Rosé Blend (Rioja) $9. 82 *—M.S. (10/1/2003)*

El Coto 1996 Coto de Imaz Gran Reserva Tempranillo (Rioja) $39. Broad-shouldered and muscled-up, this hearty wine seems more youthful than it is. The nose is spicy and full of lively berry aromas, while the palate is laced with red cherry, raspberry and vanilla. It's a classic gran reserva with dried qualities and spice. It's right on the money. **91 Editors' Choice** *—M.S. (9/1/2007)*

El Coto 1995 Coto de Imaz Gran Reserva Tempranillo (Rioja) $38. 91 *—M.S. (4/1/2006)*

El Coto 1994 Coto de Imaz Gran Reserva Tempranillo (Rioja) $30. 85 *—D.T. (4/1/2003)*

El Coto 2001 Coto De Imaz Reserva Tempranillo (Rioja) $23. Tilts a bit toward the ripe side, with sweet, mature aromas of blueberry, raisin and vanilla. It's fleshy and soft in terms of feel, with earthy, warm flavors of fig, berry and molasses. Drink now for its traditional integrity and tobacco-like qualities; it's not improving. 87 *—M.S. (9/1/2007)*

El Coto 2000 Coto de Imaz Reserva Tempranillo (Rioja) $21. 84 *—M.S. (11/1/2006)*

El Coto 1999 Coto de Imaz Reserva Tempranillo (Rioja) $21. 88 *—M.S. (11/1/2006)*

El Coto 1997 Coto de Imaz Reserva Tempranillo (Rioja) $18. 88 *—D.T. (4/1/2003)*

El Coto 1997 Coto Real Reserva Tempranillo (Rioja) $45. 90 *—D.T. (4/1/2003)*

El Coto 2004 Crianza Tempranillo (Rioja) $13. The kick and acidic foundation of this crianza work in its favor. They balance some of the heavier elements and emphasize the berry core and also the finish. Is it narrow and limited? Yes. But it fits the traditional mold and doesn't disappoint. 85 *—M.S. (9/1/2007)*

El Coto 2003 Crianza Tempranillo (Rioja) $12. Light and rosy in color, with spicy, peppery aromas blending with hints of raspberry and rhubarb. Very much in the leaner, spicier mold; the palate is slight and the finish dry and peppery. 84 *—M.S. (4/1/2007)*

El Coto 2000 Crianza Tempranillo (Rioja) $12. **87 Best Buy** *—M.S. (10/1/2003)*

El Coto 1999 Crianza Tempranillo (Rioja) $12. 85 *—D.T. (4/1/2003)*

El Coto 1998 Crianza Tempranillo (Rioja) $12. 85 *—M.M. (9/1/2002)*

El Coto 2001 Coto Real Reserva Tempranillo Blend (Rioja) $46. You're going to like this masculine, well-oaked blend of 80% Tempranillo with 10% each Graciano and Garnacha. It's got modern touches but a lot of tradition as well. The wine is rich and round, with tobacco, coffee, chocolate and earth creating depth and character. With fine mouthfeel and a solid finish, you can drink now or hold a few more years. 91 *—M.S. (9/1/2007)*

El Coto 2000 Coto Real Reserva Tempranillo Blend (Rioja) $48. 89 *—M.S. (11/1/2006)*

El Coto 1998 Coto Real Reserva Tempranillo Blend (Rioja) $42. 88 *—M.S. (6/1/2005)*

El Coto 2005 Rosado Tempranillo Blend (Rioja) $12. 84 *—M.S. (11/1/2006)*

El Coto 2006 Viura (Rioja) $10. Lemon-lime and ginger ale are the opening aromas, while the palate carries green melon and passionfruit flavors. Not terribly intense or complex, with a cider-like spritz to the mouthfeel and finish. 84 *—M.S. (9/1/2007)*

El Coto 2005 Blanco Viura (Rioja) $11. 83 *—M.S. (11/1/2006)*

El Coto 2004 Blanco Viura (Rioja) $12. 80 *—M.S. (11/1/2006)*

El Coto 2001 Blanco Viura (Rioja) $9. 84 *—M.S. (10/1/2003)*

EL CURATO

El Curato 2005 Old Vines Tinta de Toro (Toro) $13. Juicy and aromatic, but not particularly complex or refined. The palate deals a blast of snappy berry and plum flavors, while the finish seems racy, courtesy of slick tannins and forward acidity. Shows much more power than finesse. 86 *—M.S. (4/1/2007)*

EL PUNTIDO

El Puntido 2001 Tempranillo (Rioja) $51. 94 Editors' Choice —*M.S. (8/1/2005)*

EL VINCULO

El Vinculo 1999 Red Blend (La Mancha) $21. 85 —*D.T. (4/1/2003)*

El Vinculo 2002 Tempranillo (La Mancha) $25. 87 —*M.S. (8/1/2005)*

El Vinculo 2000 Crianza Tempranillo (La Mancha) $27. 87 —*M.S. (3/1/2004)*

El Vinculo 2001 Reserva Tempranillo (La Mancha) $40. 88 —*M.S. (8/1/2005)*

El Vinculo 1999 Reserva Tempranillo (La Mancha) $19. 88 —*M.S. (3/1/2004)*

ELIAS MORA

Elias Mora 2003 Tinta de Toro (Toro) $22. 84 —*M.S. (2/1/2006)*

Elias Mora 2001 Crianza Tinta de Toro (Toro) $30. 90 —*M.S. (2/1/2006)*

EMILIO MORO

Emilio Moro 1998 Crianza Tempranillo (Ribera del Duero) $24. 91 Editors' Choice —*J.C. (11/1/2001)*

Emilio Moro 1997 Crianza Tempranillo (Ribera del Duero) $25. 89 —*M.M. (8/1/2000)*

Emilio Moro 1998 Malleolus Tempranillo (Ribera del Duero) $40. 91 —*J.C. (11/1/2001)*

Emilio Moro 2004 Tinta Fina (Ribera del Duero) $34. The nose is hefty and full of molten berry and bacon aromas, while the palate is rough, with young tannins and plush with plum and cassis flavors. Finishes with the taste of mocha and tannic clamp. Give it until 2008 for best results. 88 —*M.S. (4/1/2007)*

Emilio Moro 2000 Crianza Tinto del Pais (Ribera del Duero) $28. 89 —*M.S. (3/1/2004)*

Emilio Moro 1999 Malleolus Tinto del Pais (Ribera del Duero) $40. 91 —*M.S. (3/1/2004)*

Emilio Moro 2002 Malleolus de Valderramiro Tinto del Pais (Ribera del Duero) $166. 92 —*M.S. (6/1/2005)*

EMILIO ROJO

Emilio Rojo 2001 White Blend (Ribeiro) $35. 82 —*M.S. (11/1/2002)*

Emilio Rojo 2005 Blanco White Blend (Ribeiro) $40. 92 —*M.S. (9/1/2006)*

Emilio Rojo 2003 Blanco White Blend (Ribeiro) $35. 89 —*M.S. (6/1/2005)*

EMINA

Emina 2003 12 Meses en Barrica Tinto del Pais (Ribera del Duero) $17. 84 —*M.S. (11/1/2006)*

Emina 2003 Atio Tinto del Pais (Ribera del Duero) $44. 87 —*M.S. (11/1/2006)*

Emina 2003 Prestigio Tinto del Pais (Ribera del Duero) $26. 88 —*M.S. (11/1/2006)*

ENATE

Enate 2000 Reserva Cabernet Sauvignon-Merlot (Somontano) $NA. 88 —*M.S. (6/1/2005)*

Enate 2002 Fermentado en Barrica de Roble Chardonnay (Somontano) $NA. 85 —*M.S. (6/1/2005)*

ENRIQUE MENDOZA

Enrique Mendoza 2003 Moscatel de la Marina Moscatel (Alicante) $NA. 89 —*M.S. (6/1/2005)*

Enrique Mendoza 2000 Reserva Santa Rosa Red Blend (Alicante) $35. 90 —*M.S. (6/1/2005)*

EOLO

Eolo 2000 Crianza Tempranillo Blend (Navarra) $13. 89 Best Buy —*M.S. (9/1/2006)*

ERMITA VERACRUZ

Ermita Veracruz 2004 Verdejo (Rueda) $16. 85 —*M.S. (9/1/2006)*

ESPELT

Espelt 2006 Corali Garnacha (Emporda) $10. This is the type of rosé that once you get started on it you can't put it down. Ethereal smelling, pretty to look at and gracefully balanced: when Spain gets it right with its Garnacha, a case in point being the '06 Coralí, the pleasure quotient is high. The bouquet here is wet and inviting, the palate lusty and elegant. Beyond that there's a full mouthfeel, juicy acidity and length. It's all here. 91 Best Buy —*M.S. (7/1/2007)*

ESPERANZA

Esperanza 2003 Sauvignon Blanc (Rueda) $10. 80 —*M.S. (3/1/2005)*

Esperanza 2003 Verdejo (Rueda) $10. 87 —*M.S. (12/31/2004)*

Esperanza 2003 Verdejo-Viura White Blend (Rueda) $9. 87 —*M.S. (12/31/2004)*

ESSENCIA VENDIMA

Essencia Vendima 2005 Albariño (Rías Baixas) $16. 88 —*M.S. (12/15/2006)*

ESTANCIA PIEDRA

Estancia Piedra 2000 Paredinas Tinta de Toro (Toro) $80. This starts with a strong blast of black olives, leather and blackberry, followed by condensed fruit flavors and a tinge of black cherry. A nice wine with character, but for $80 it comes up short of thrilling. 88 —*M.S. (11/1/2007)*

Estancia Piedra 2001 Roble Tinta de Toro (Toro) $28. Molasses, saddle leather and black olive aromas add complexity and masculinity to the bouquet, while flavors of black cherry, roasted plum and vanilla fit correctly into the wine's meaty, firm style. With obvious oak and raw tannins, this wine is still kicking and should drink well for another 3–5 years. 88 —*M.S. (11/1/2007)*

Estancia Piedra 2000 Selección Tinta de Toro (Toro) $39. A touch grassy and raisiny at first, but soon it gets into step and shows cleaner, fresher spice and cherry notes. For an average vintage, this is a nice wine with pepper, mildly jabby tannins and lots of oak. With air it settles nicely, and with food it should make for a good partner. 88 —*M.S. (11/1/2007)*

ESTOLA

Estola 1991 Gran Reserva Red Blend (La Mancha) $16. 86 —*M.S. (11/1/2002)*

Estola 1997 Reserva 1997 Tempranillo (La Mancha) $8. 83 —*M.S. (11/1/2002)*

FAUSTINO

Faustino 1994 Faustino de Autor Reserva Tempranillo (Rioja) $50. 91 *(5/1/2004)*

Faustino 2000 Faustino de Crianza Tempranillo (Rioja) $13. 87 —*M.S. (10/1/2005)*

Faustino 1999 Faustino de Crianza Tempranillo (Rioja) $12. 86 —*M.S. (3/1/2004)*

Faustino 1998 Faustino de Crianza Tempranillo (Rioja) $10. 85 *(5/1/2004)*

Faustino 1999 Faustino V Reserva Tempranillo (Rioja) $19. 87 —*M.S. (10/1/2005)*

Faustino 1995 Gran Reserva Tempranillo (Rioja) $36. 89 *(5/1/2004)*

Faustino 2003 Faustino VII Tempranillo Blend (Rioja) $11. 84 —*M.S. (10/1/2005)*

Faustino 1997 Crianza Tempranillo Blend (Rioja) $15. 88 *(5/1/2001)*

Faustino 1995 Faustino de Autor Reserva Especial Tempranillo (Rioja) $50. 88 —*M.S. (4/1/2006)*

Faustino 1996 Faustino I Rioja Gran Reserva Tempranillo (Rioja) $30. A little bit leafy and light, but that's traditional Rioja for you. The color is a mix of orange and red, while the palate of snappy red fruits is beginning to slip toward peach and nectarine. If you like a leaner, racier style of wine, then drink this now. It's probably at its peak. 88 —*M.S. (9/1/2007)*

Faustino 1994 Faustino I Rioja Gran Reserva Tempranillo (Rioja) $26. 92 Editors' Choice *(5/1/2001)*

Faustino 1982 Faustino I Rioja Gran Reserva Tempranillo (Rioja) $72. 89 *(5/1/2001)*

Faustino 1970 Faustino I Rioja Gran Reserva Tempranillo (Rioja) $125. 92 *(5/1/2001)*

Faustino 1964 Faustino I Rioja Gran Reserva Tempranillo (Rioja) $185. 94 *(5/1/2001)*

Faustino 1999 Faustino V Rosado Rosé Blend (Rioja) $12. 84 *(5/1/2001)*

Faustino 1998 Faustino V Reserva Tempranillo (Rioja) $18. 86 *(5/1/2004)*

Faustino 1995 Faustino V Rioja Riserva Tempranillo (Rioja) $17. 89 *(5/1/2001)*

Faustino 2002 Faustino V Rosé Tempranillo (Rioja) $9. 83 —*M.S. (3/1/2004)*

Faustino 2003 Faustino V Blanco Seco Viura (Rioja) $10. 85 Best Buy —*M.S. (11/15/2005)*

Faustino 2002 Faustino V Blanco Seco White Blend (Rioja) $8. 85 —*M.S. (3/1/2004)*

Faustino 2000 Faustino VII Tempranillo (Rioja) $10. 86 —*M.S. (3/1/2004)*

Faustino 1998 Faustino VII Tempranillo (Rioja) $12. 86 *(5/1/2001)*

FELIX CALLEJO

Felix Callejo 2003 Selección de Viñedos de la Familia Tempranillo (Ribera del Duero) $112. A very dense version of Tempranillo, with brooding aromas of pencil lead, mossy earth and full-stock black fruit. The palate is exceedingly rich, such that it's perilously close to raisiny. But in the end the wine holds its line and delivers all the chocolate and baked fruit a New World junkie might want. 89 *—M.S. (2/1/2007)*

Felix Callejo 2002 Selección de Vinedos de la Familia Tempranillo (Ribera del Duero) $108. 84 *—M.S. (11/15/2005)*

FELIX SOLIS

Felix Solis 2001 Los Molinos Airen (Valdepeñas) $6. 81 *—D.T. (4/1/2003)*

Felix Solis 2001 Los Molinos Tempranillo (Valdepeñas) $7. 85 Best Buy *—M.S. (11/1/2002)*

Felix Solis 1995 Vina Albali Gran Reserva Tempranillo (Valdepeñas) $14. 84 *—M.S. (11/1/2002)*

Felix Solis 1998 Vina Albali Los Molinos Crianza Tempranillo (Valdepeñas) $9. 82 *—M.S. (11/1/2002)*

FIGUERO

Figuero 2001 Vendimia Seleccionada Tempranillo (Ribera del Duero) $60. 89 *—M.S. (8/1/2005)*

FILLABOA

Fillaboa 2006 Albariño (Rías Baixas) $17. This is what Albariño is all about! The nose issues a salinic combo of salt water and sea shells along with green banana and melon, while the palate is jumpy, fresh, balanced and intriguing. The flavors of just-ripe bananas and Meyer lemon are true, while the mouthfeel is both smooth and refreshing. Get after this one as soon as you can. 91 Editors' Choice *—M.S. (11/1/2007)*

Fillaboa 2002 Finca Monte Alto Albariño (Rías Baixas) $27. 91 Editors' Choice *—M.S. (6/1/2005)*

FINCA ALLENDE

Finca Allende 2001 Tempranillo (Rioja) $24. 91 *—M.S. (9/1/2004)*

Finca Allende 2004 Allende Tempranillo (Rioja) $30. Stylish and alluring nose; quite sexy. The malolactic fermentation took place in barrel, so the wine has mouthfeel and richness. Yet it's a juicy, friendly, fruit-forward style of Tempranillo, one that finishes with mocha and wood-driven spice notes. 20,000 cases made. Imported by Tempranillo, Inc. 90 *—M.S. (9/1/2007)*

Finca Allende 2004 Aurus Tempranillo (Rioja) $212. One half of the wine is lush and opulent, the other juicy, fresh and pulsing with the essence of old-vines Rioja fruit. So for every note of molasses, burnt toast, chocolate or baked berry pie, there's a twinge of acidity, a spike of tannin and a dollop of earthy terroir. Tempranillo with 15% Graciano. 500 cases made. Imported by Tempranillo, Inc. 94 *—M.S. (9/1/2007)*

Finca Allende 2001 Aurus Tempranillo (Rioja) $184. 96 Editors' Choice *—M.S. (6/1/2005)*

Finca Allende 2004 Calvario Tempranillo (Rioja) $105. The bouquet explodes with tobacco, leather, dry oak and waves of berry fruit. In the mouth, the wine sits comfortably on the tongue, with firm tannins offering structure to the bedazzling boysenberry, black cherry and cassis flavors. Long and intoxicating on the finish. It's 90% Tempranillo and 10% Garnacha and Graciano. 650 cases made. Imported by Tempranillo, Inc. 95 *—M.S. (9/1/2007)*

Finca Allende 2000 Aurus Tempranillo Blend (Rioja) $25. 92 *—M.S. (9/1/2004)*

Finca Allende 2001 Calvario Tempranillo Blend (Rioja) $88. 94 Editors' Choice *—M.S. (6/1/2005)*

FINCA ANTIGUA

Finca Antigua 2004 Merlot (La Mancha) $10. 85 Best Buy *—M.S. (12/15/2006)*

Finca Antigua 2003 Crianza Red Blend (La Mancha) $12. 85 *—M.S. (12/15/2006)*

Finca Antigua 2001 Crianza Red Blend (La Mancha) $10. 84 *—M.S. (6/1/2005)*

Finca Antigua 2002 Reserva Red Blend (La Mancha) $15. 85 *—M.S. (12/15/2006)*

Finca Antigua 2001 Reserva Red Blend (La Mancha) $15. 88 *—M.S. (4/1/2006)*

Finca Antigua 2003 Syrah (La Mancha) $10. 83 *—M.S. (11/15/2005)*

Finca Antigua 2003 Tempranillo (La Mancha) $10. 83 *—M.S. (11/15/2005)*

Finca Antigua 2002 Tempranillo (La Mancha) $10. 85 Best Buy *—M.S. (6/1/2005)*

Finca Antigua 2002 Clavis Tempranillo Blend (La Mancha) $95. 82 *—M.S. (4/1/2006)*

Finca Antigua 2005 Viura (La Mancha) $10. 86 Best Buy *—M.S. (12/15/2006)*

FINCA EL ENCINAL

Finca El Encinal 1999 Reserva Tempranillo (Ribera del Duero) $32. 84 *—M.S. (11/1/2006)*

Finca El Encinal 2003 Roble Tempranillo (Ribera del Duero) $10. 83 *—M.S. (11/1/2006)*

FINCA LA ESTACADA

Finca La Estacada 2002 Oak Aged 12 Months Tempranillo (Vino de la Tierra de Castilla) $16. 82 *—M.S. (11/1/2006)*

Finca La Estacada 2004 Oak Aged 6 Months Tempranillo (Vino de la Tierra de Castilla) $13. 83 *—M.S. (11/1/2006)*

Finca La Estacada 2003 Oak Aged 6 Months Tempranillo (Vino de la Tierra de Castilla) $13. 83 *—M.S. (12/15/2006)*

FINCA LUZÓN

Finca Luzón 2002 Merlot (Jumilla) $8. 88 Best Buy *—M.S. (3/1/2004)*

Finca Luzón 2001 Merlot (Jumilla) $8. 87 Best Buy *—J.C. (11/15/2002)*

Finca Luzón 2000 Merlot (Jumilla) $10. 86 *—M.M. (4/1/2002)*

Finca Luzón 2005 Red Blend (Jumilla) $8. Rarely do you find muscle-bound, intense reds priced at $8 that are this good. But Luzon manages to give you a 65/35 blend of Monastrell and Syrah that is lively, loaded and eminently likable. It's all about hefty black fruit, bold tannins and flash. Only 5,000 cases made. 88 Best Buy *—M.S. (8/1/2007)*

Finca Luzón 2001 Red Blend (Jumilla) $14. 90 Best Buy *—M.S. (3/1/2004)*

Finca Luzón 2004 Altos de Luzón Red Blend (Jumilla) $16. One of the best efforts we've tried from Jumilla, Luzon's luxury blend starts with coconut, mint, char and fudge, and below that is a treasure trove of deep black fruit. Huge blackberry and black cherry flavors are potent as they ride on a wave of jolting tannins. An affordable shining star for a rising region. 91 Editors' Choice *—M.S. (8/1/2007)*

Finca Luzón 2002 Altos de Luzon Red Blend (Jumilla) $10. 89 Best Buy *—M.S. (3/1/2004)*

FINCA MINATEDA

Finca Minateda 2000 Selección Pedro Sarrion Garnacha (Vino de la Tierra de Castilla) $18. 85 *—M.S. (10/1/2005)*

Finca Minateda 2001 Tinto Roble Garnacha (Vino de la Tierra de Castilla) $13. 85 *—M.S. (10/1/2005)*

FINCA SANDOVAL

Finca Sandoval 2002 Syrah (Tierra Manchuela) $39. 90 *—M.S. (6/1/2005)*

Finca Sandoval 2001 Syrah (Tierra Manchuela) $29. 90 *—M.S. (3/1/2004)*

FINCA VILLACRECES

Finca Villacreces 2004 Tempranillo (Ribera del Duero) $35. With 14% Cabernet and Merlot added to prime Tempranillo, this wine jabs early with toasty oak, forest floor and roasted berry aromas, and then follows it up with full-bodied blackberry fruit accented by tobacco, leather and warm earth. It has body but also a firm, acidic core; and the tannins are totally manageable. Already drinking well but will improve over the next 2–5 years. 92 Editors' Choice *—M.S. (5/22/2007)*

Finca Villacreces 2003 Tempranillo (Ribera del Duero) $35. Leathery and earthy, with some heavier, muddled characteristics that reflect the vintage. Overall, this wine is not on the same level as the superior 2004, but as it opens it shows a willing mouthfeel and finishing flavors of red currant and cranberry. If you own this along with the 2004, drink this one before the other. 87 *—M.S. (6/1/2007)*

Finca Villacreces 2004 Nebro Tempranillo (Ribera del Duero) $185. An intense, dark-styled Tempranillo with a ton of oak. In fact, this might have more wood and toast than many people are looking for. That said, this is a generous wine with huge blackberry and plum flavors. And as it finishes with unctuous cream and vanilla, you are again reminded of how much the barrel influenced the final product. Excellent but so heavily oaked that we prefer the basic wine from this producer. 91 *—M.S. (6/1/2007)*

FINCA ZUBASTÍA

Finca Zubastía 2003 ADA Cabernet Sauvignon-Merlot (Navarra) $10. 84 *—M.S. (12/31/2004)*

Finca Zubastía 2003 ADA Tempranillo Blend (Navarra) $10. 86 Best Buy *—M.S. (6/1/2005)*

FLEUR DE NUIT

Fleur de Nuit NV Brut Sparkling Blend (Cava) $7. 85 Best Buy —*M.S. (12/15/2005)*

FLOURISH

Flourish 2002 Tempranillo (Rioja) $11. 81 —*M.S. (8/1/2005)*

FORTIUS

Fortius 1999 Tierra de Estella Merlot (Navarra) $12. 85 —*M.S. (8/1/2003)*

Fortius 1998 Tierra de Estella Tempranillo (Navarra) $12. 86 —*M.S. (8/1/2003)*

FRA GUERAU

Fra Guerau 2002 Red Blend (Montsant) $12. 87 Best Buy —*M.S. (6/1/2005)*

Fra Guerau 2006 Rosé Rosé Blend (Montsant) $14. Spicy strawberries on the nose lead straight to a full-bodied, totally balanced and healthy palate that is eager to deliver zesty raspberry and tea-like flavors. Not hard to enjoy, with peppery rosé tannins and good length. Freshness is key to this wine, and as of June 2007 it was drinking perfectly. Imported by Freixenet USA. 88 —*M.S. (12/15/2007)*

Fra Guerau 2005 Rosé Rosé Blend (Montsant) $12. This Freixenet-owned label from Montsant opts to use Syrah, Tempranillo and Merlot in the blend, and hence the wine is very red in color and rather weighty. The nose has some green character and earthiness, while the palate deals stewed plum and apple skin. Putting it nicely: It's not the freshest piece of fruit in the bowl. 83 —*M.S. (7/1/2007)*

FRANCESC SANCHEZ BAS

Francesc Sanchez Bas 2002 Montgarnatx Garnacha (Priorat) $45. 88 —*M.S. (10/1/2005)*

Francesc Sanchez Bas 2001 Montgarnatx Garnacha (Priorat) $38. 91 *M.S. (5/1/2004)*

Francesc Sanchez Bas 2001 Montsalvat Red Blend (Priorat) $72. 91 —*M.S. (10/1/2005)*

Francesc Sanchez Bas 2000 Montsalvat Red Blend (Priorat) $60. 92 —*M.S. (5/1/2004)*

Francesc Sanchez Bas 2005 Blanc de Montsalvat White Blend (Priorat) $45. This vintage seems lighter on its feet than previous versions, but it's still a strange, atypical wine made from Garnacha Blanca and other Priorato white varieties. The bouquet is heavy and dusty, while the palate is thick and woody, with white pepper, peach and melon notes. Pithy bitterness weighs down the finish. Unusual but stirs interest. 85 —*M.S. (12/15/2007)*

Francesc Sanchez Bas 2002 Blanc de Montsalvat White Blend (Priorat) $32. 84 —*M.S. (5/1/2004)*

FREIXENET

Freixenet NV Cordon Negro Brut Sparkling Blend (Cava) $10. 88 Best Buy —*M.S. (12/15/2006)*

Freixenet NV Brut de Noirs Sparkling Blend (Cava) $10. Salmon colored, with forward aromas of dust, earth, spice and red fruits. The palate is nicely decorated with cherry notes and brown sugar, while the finish moves quickly from fruit to vanilla and cream soda. Nice but a touch confected. 86 Best Buy —*M.S. (12/15/2007)*

Freixenet NV Brut de Noirs Sparkling Blend (Cava) $10. 83 —*M.S. (12/15/2006)*

Freixenet 2000 Brut Nature Sparkling Blend (Cava) $14. 88 —*M.S. (6/1/2006)*

Freixenet 1999 Brut Nature Sparkling Blend (Cava) $NA. 81 —*J.C. (1/1/2004)*

Freixenet NV Carta Nevada Brut Sparkling Blend (Cava) $9. 87 Best Buy —*M.S. (12/15/2006)*

Freixenet NV Carta Nevada Semi Dry Sparkling Blend (Cava) $9. 85 Best Buy —*M.S. (12/15/2006)*

Freixenet NV Cordon Negro Extra Dry Sparkling Blend (Cava) $10. Some things never change. Put this sturdy, mildly nutty and fairly bright cava on that list. Year after year, the palate remains comfortably sweet and bubbly, but not too much so. And the round apple, pear and lime flavors even bring a shade of spice along for the ride. Imported by Freixenet USA. 87 Best Buy —*M.S. (12/15/2007)*

Freixenet NV Cordon Negro Extra Dry Sparkling Blend (Cava) $10. 88 Best Buy —*M.S. (12/15/2006)*

Freixenet 1999 Cuvée D.S. Brut Nature Sparkling Blend (Cava) $NA. 90 —*M.S. (6/1/2005)*

Freixenet NV Spumante Sparkling Blend (Cava) $10. 86 —*M.S. (12/15/2006)*

Freixenet NV XXI Brut Sparkling Blend (Cava) $25. 85 —*M.S. (12/15/2006)*

FUENTE DEL CONDE

Fuente del Conde 2002 Rosado Rosé Blend (Cigales) $9. 86 Best Buy —*M.S. (3/1/2004)*

Fuente del Conde 2004 Rosado Tempranillo (Cigales) $10. 80 —*M.S. (8/1/2005)*

FUENTES

Fuentes 2000 Gran Clos de J.M. Fuentes Red Blend (Priorat) $50. 93 Editors' Choice —*M.S. (3/1/2004)*

G

G 2005 Dehesa Gago Tinta de Toro (Toro) $13. From Telmo Rodriguez, this Toro is full of eraser, violet and other candied, floral aromas. The palate, meanwhile, is hard and rubbery, with tannins that are bullish and flavors that run dark to almost bitter. A big wine in need of some manners. 84 —*M.S. (4/1/2007)*

GABA DO XIL

Gaba do Xil 2005 Godello (Valdeorras) $13. This wine is at its peak and you may wish to wait for the 2006, but if you encounter this toasty, mineral-influenced Godello, go for it. The palate is loaded with peach, papaya and green melon, while the finish is creamy and smooth. With Gaba do Xil, the stateliness and simple pleasures of Valdeorras on are on full display. From Vinos de Telmo Rodriguez. 90 Best Buy —*M.S. (11/1/2007)*

GAGO

Gago 1999 Red Blend (Toro) $20. 90 —*M.M. (4/1/2002)*

Gago 2000 Dehesa Gago Tinta de Toro (Toro) $12. 88 —*M.M. (4/1/2002)*

GANDIA

Gandia 2003 Fusta Nova Moscatel (Valencia) $12. 86 —*M.S. (8/1/2005)*

Gandia 2002 Hoya De Cadenas Reserva Tempranillo (Utiel-Requena) $9. 85 Best Buy —*M.S. (9/1/2006)*

GAZUR

Gazur 2005 Tinta Fina (Ribera del Duero) $13. Quite pleasant in its style, which is extracted, colorful and grapy. To call it fruit-forward is almost an understatement. In the mouth, there's huge boysenberry fruit accented by coffee and mocha. Finishes toasty and warm. Yet another wine from the camp of Telmo Rodriguez. 86 —*M.S. (4/1/2007)*

GENIUM CELLAR

Genium Celler 2004 Red Blend (Priorat) $32. This muscular youth proves that Priorat can deliver fleshy, modern wines. Or maybe it's the 20% Merlot that's softening the Garnacha and Carignan. Either way, look for lush plum and black cherry flavors floating on a rich, heady palate. This is more Escalade or Range Rover than sports car. 89 —*M.S. (8/1/2007)*

Genium Celler 2004 Ecològic Red Blend (Priorat) $39. You want color and heft? You get that here, and more. Dark, grapy aromas are lush more than rough and tight, while the palate is full of sassy black cherry fruit and a fair share of richness. No doubt this jam-packed blend of Garnacha, Merlot and Carignan is solid and rewarding. 250 cases produced. 91 —*M.S. (8/1/2007)*

GIRÓ RIBOT

Giró Ribot NV Masia Parera Brut Sparkling Blend (Penedès) $11. Nothing wrong with this pleasant, friendly Cava. The nose boasts frosted breakfast cereal and lemon curd, while the palate is defined by spiced apple and baked citrus. It gets more honeyed and fat as it opens, although a good chilling will keep that in check. 87 Best Buy —*M.S. (8/1/2007)*

GLORIOSO

Glorioso 2003 Crianza Tempranillo (Rioja) $11. 86 Best Buy —*M.S. (12/15/2006)*

Glorioso 2001 Crianza Tempranillo (Rioja) $11. 85 —*M.S. (12/31/2004)*

Glorioso 2001 Reserva Tempranillo (Rioja) $15. 90 Best Buy —*M.S. (11/1/2006)*

Glorioso 2000 Reserva Tempranillo (Rioja) $15. 88 Best Buy —*M.S. (12/31/2004)*

Glorioso 2003 Roble Tempranillo (Rioja) $9. 82 —*M.S. (2/1/2006)*

GONDOMAR DEL REINO

Gondomar Del Reino 1996 Gran Reserva Tempranillo (Ribera del Duero) $43. 83 —*M.S. (10/1/2005)*

Gondomar Del Reino 2002 Roble Tempranillo (Ribera del Duero) $19. 83 —*M.S. (8/1/2005)*

GONZALEZ BYASS

Gonzalez Byass NV Noe Muy Viejo Pedro Ximenez (Jerez) $NA. 88 *—M.S. (6/1/2005)*

Gonzalez Byass NV Tio Pepe Fino Sherry (Jerez) $NA. 88 *—M.S. (6/1/2005)*

GORDONZELLO

Gordonzello 2005 Peregrino Verdejo (Vino de Calidad de Tierras de León) $11. A bit flowery but dense; it lacks a certain expected zest. The palate is plump but straightforward in its apple flavor. And the finish keeps the theme of weight without freshness. Low-acid and clunky. 83 *—M.S. (2/1/2007)*

GOTIN

Gotin 2005 Mencía (Bierzo) $12. Nice and fruity, with a touch of spice to the nose. The palate is plump and dark, with nothing besides all-natural fruit. A hearty and healthy wine that boasts freshness and purity but no oak. 87 Best Buy *—M.S. (8/1/2007)*

Gotin 2001 Crianza Mencía (Bierzo) $26. An older wine with more oak than jazzy fruit, so the aromas are heavy with the scent of cinnamon and the palate is more drying and spicy than it is rich and rewarding. Still, with the right food you may be able to appreciate the wine's smoke and vanilla qualities. 84 *—M.S. (8/1/2007)*

GOSALBEZ ORTI

Gosalbez Orti 2001 Qubel Barrica Tempranillo Blend (Vinos de Madrid) $47. 92 Editors' Choice *—M.S. (9/1/2004)*

GRAMONA

Gramona NV Brut Rosado Pinot Noir (Cava) $NA. 83 *—M.S. (6/1/2005)*

Gramona 2003 Gran Cuvée Sparkling Blend (Cava) $18. 86 *—M.S. (6/1/2006)*

Gramona 2003 Grand Cuvée Rosé Sparkling Blend (Cava) $35. 87 *—M.S. (6/1/2006)*

Gramona 1998 III Lustros Gran Reserva Sparkling Blend (Cava) $NA. 91 *—M.S. (6/1/2005)*

Gramona 2001 Imperial Gran Reserva Sparkling Blend (Cava) $48. 90 *—M.S. (6/1/2006)*

GRAN CERMEÑO

Gran Cermeño 1997 Crianza Tinta de Toro (Toro) $14. 84 *—D.T. (4/1/2002)*

Gran Cermeño 1996 Reserva Tinta de Toro (Toro) $19. 91 Editors' Choice *—M.M. (9/1/2002)*

GRAN GESTA

Gran Gesta NV Brut Sparkling Blend (Cava) $14. 90 Best Buy *—M.S. (6/1/2005)*

Gran Gesta NV Brut Rosé Sparkling Blend (Cava) $17. Darker red in color, with a dusty, full bouquet. Flavors of plum, raspberry and apple skins are appealing and on the money, as is the mouthfeel and the fresh, drying finish. There seems to be a little bit of everything running through this cava, and the end result is rock solid. 88 *—M.S. (12/15/2007)*

GRAN METS

Gran Mets 2001 Red Blend (Montsant) $15. 88 *—M.S. (5/1/2004)*

GRAN ORISTAN

Gran Oristan 1992 Gran Reserva Cencibel (La Mancha) $13. 84 *—J.C. (8/1/2000)*

Gran Oristan 1995 Gran Reserva Red Blend (La Mancha) $14. 85 *—D.T. (4/1/2002)*

GRAN VEIGADARES

Gran Veigadares 2001 Blanco Albariño (Rías Baixas) $110. 88 *—M.S. (3/1/2005)*

GRAN VEREMA

Gran Verema 2000 Old Vines Reserva Tempranillo (Utiel-Requena) $9. 84 *—M.S. (10/1/2005)*

GRANBAZÁN

Granbazán 2005 Ambar Albariño (Rías Baixas) $19. 90 *—M.S. (9/1/2006)*

Granbazán 2005 Don Alvaro de Bazán Albariño (Rías Baixas) $24. 87 *—M.S. (9/1/2006)*

Granbazán 2005 Verde Albariño (Rías Baixas) $15. 88 *—M.S. (9/1/2006)*

GRANJA NTRA, SRA. DE REMELLURI

Granja Ntra, Sra. de Remelluri 2002 Colección Jaime Rodríguez Tempranillo (Rioja) $104. Smooth berries and plenty of dark licorice carry the seductive bouquet. And seeing that this is Remelluri's signature high-priced red, you should expect the fine berry, plum and chocolate flavors that rest comfortably on the palate. But like many '02s, the wine has a hard mouthfeel and pronounced acidity, so it doesn't quite trigger all the pleasure points that it might in a better vintage. 89 *—M.S. (9/1/2007)*

Granja Ntra, Sra. de Remelluri 2002 Remelluri Tempranillo (Rioja) $31. Bramble bush, graphite, leather and medium-depth fruit are the opening notes on this qualm-free, fairly muscular Rioja. Dark cherry and raspberry flavors run the palate, and they are followed by a warm, milk chocolate-tinged finish. Very nice for a 2002. 89 *—M.S. (9/1/2007)*

Granja Ntra, Sra. de Remelluri 2000 Tempranillo Blend (Rioja) $28. 90 *—M.S. (3/1/2004)*

Granja Ntra, Sra. de Remelluri 2004 Remelluri White Blend (Rioja) $52. This multi-grape white blend is aged in a fair amount of new and once-used oak, and it has the aromas and mouthfeel of a good Burgundy or California Chardonnay. With 14.5% alcohol, it's quite New World in its delivery of apricot and peach flavors, riding on powerful vanilla and toast notes. Excellent but oaky; somewhere a beaver is smiling. 90 *—M.S. (4/1/2007)*

Granja Ntra, Sra. de Remelluri 2001 Remelluri Blanco White Blend (Rioja) $40. 88 *—M.S. (3/1/2004)*

GREGO

Grego 2004 Centenaria Garnacha (Madrid) $13. Not too bright in color, with oily, earthy, raisiny aromas. Typical of the warm region it comes from, the wine is pruney and candied, with chocolate in the rear. Lacks an edge or pronounced tannins, but has enough good fruit quality to warrant a taste or two. 84 *—M.S. (2/1/2007)*

Grego 2004 Old Vines Tempranillo (Madrid) $13. A touch woody and fiery to start, and then graphite and earthy-leathery aromas come up. The palate is mostly attractive, with solid plum and berry flavors along with tannins that are full but don't fight you. The finish seems a touch hollow and bitter, but overall the wine has good Tempranillo quality. 86 *—M.S. (12/15/2007)*

GUELBENZU

Guelbenzu 2003 EVO Cabernet Blend (Ribera del Queiles) $25. 86 *—M.S. (8/1/2005)*

Guelbenzu 2001 Azul Red Blend (Navarra) $13. 87 *—M.S. (3/1/2004)*

Guelbenzu 2000 Azul Red Blend (Ribera del Arlanza) $13. 88 Best Buy *—M.S. (11/1/2002)*

Guelbenzu 2001 EVO Red Blend (Navarra) $20. 88 *—M.S. (3/1/2004)*

Guelbenzu 1999 Lautus Red Blend (Navarra) $45. 90 *—M.S. (3/1/2004)*

Guelbenzu 1998 Tempranillo Blend (Navarra) $13. 84 *(1/1/2004)*

Guelbenzu 2003 Azul Tempranillo Blend (Ribera del Queiles) $15. 85 *—M.S. (8/1/2005)*

Guelbenzu 1998 EVO Tempranillo Blend (Navarra) $22. 89 *—C.S. (4/1/2002)*

Guelbenzu 1996 Lautus Tempranillo Blend (Navarra) $58. 90 *—C.S. (4/1/2002)*

GUITIÁN

Guitián 2006 Joven Godello (Valdeorras) $23. With red wines joven usually means a few months in oak. It seems as though this wine was made the same way; there's a kiss of popcorn and buttered toast to the lemon and melon nose, while the palate has life, texture and complexity. Flavorwise, you should enjoy the wine's papaya, green banana and other tempered tropical flavors. Balanced and pleasing, and proof that certain Spanish whites can take some oaking. 90 *—M.S. (11/1/2007)*

Guitián 2002 Sobre Lias Godello (Valdeorras) $NA. 90 *—M.S. (6/1/2005)*

GUNDIAN

Gundian 2006 Albariño (Rías Baixas) $17. Young and vibrant; it's straightforward Albariño from a good vintage. In the mouth, expect green melon and stone-fruit flavors backed by solid acidity and a bit of fleshy weight. It's comfortable around the edges, and overall it's sure to satisfy fans of this type of crisp, clean white wine. 89 *—M.S. (11/1/2007)*

Gundian 2004 Albariño (Rías Baixas) $15. 87 *—M.S. (11/15/2005)*

GUZMÁN ALDAZABAL

Guzmán Aldazabal 2000 Tempranillo Blend (Rioja) $27. 90 *—M.S. (2/1/2006)*

HACIENDA LA CONCORDIA

Hacienda la Concordia 1999 Reserva Tempranillo (Rioja) $25. 83 *—M.S. (5/1/2004)*

HACIENDA MONASTERIO

Hacienda Monasterio 1997 Crianza Red Blend (Ribera del Duero) $30. 83 —*J.C. (11/1/2001)*

Hacienda Monasterio 1995 Crianza Tempranillo (Ribera del Duero) $30. 92 *(11/15/1999)*

HACIENDAS DURIUS

Haciendas Durius 2002 Durius Tempranillo (Ribera del Duero) $10. 89 Best Buy —*M.S. (5/1/2004)*

Haciendas Durius 2003 Alto Duero Viura-Sauvignon Blanc (Vino de la Tierra de Castilla y León) $13. 84 —*M.S. (3/1/2005)*

Haciendas Durius 2002 White Blend (Ribera del Duero) $10. 88 Best Buy —*M.S. (5/1/2004)*

HARVEYS

Harveys NV Reserve Rare Cream Sherry (Jerez) $15. Any fan of sweet Sherry should not turn a cheek against this jammy, figgy, rich wine that could use a cut of ice and citrus peel but isn't at all bad on its own. Aromas of burnt caramel are just right, while the finish dries out long before turning cloying. 88 —*M.S. (12/15/2007)*

HERAS CORDON

Heras Cordon 2001 Reserva Tempranillo (Rioja) $42. Having never tasted Heras Cordon's wines, the verdict is in: the current releases are all winners. This basic Reserva is lighter in frame, buttery and full of dill and red fruit; with air it settles to show ripe strawberry and raspberry notes as well as good structure. Perfect for drinking now. 89 —*M.S. (11/1/2007)*

Heras Cordon 2001 Reserva Vendimia Seleccionada Tempranillo (Rioja) $55. For an old-school highlight, look for this lesser known selection-based Reserva, because good grapes from a good year should add up to good wine. And in this case, the wine is better than good; it's ripe, spicy, chocolaty and pushes all the right buttons. A sure thing with the right foods: meats, stews, etc. 91 Editors' Choice —*M.S. (11/1/2007)*

Heras Cordon 2002 Vendimia Seleccionada Tempranillo (Rioja) $28. This is a nice, traditionally styled Rioja. Delivers smooth, earthy, leathery aromas and then spicy dry fruit that's right out of Rioja 101. With good acidity, it's a very respectable table wine from a weak vintage. 87 —*M.S. (11/1/2007)*

HEREDEROS DE MARTÍNEZ FUENTE

Herederos de Martínez Fuente 2005 Pucho Mencía (Bierzo) $15. Moderately dark and dense, but hardly brooding and deep. This is a nice, zesty version of Mencia that highlights the grape's cherry and raspberry character. It's flush and features good fruit-to-acid balance. 86 —*M.S. (8/1/2007)*

Herederos de Martínez Fuente 2002 Pucho Mencia (Bierzo) $13. 86 —*M.S. (3/1/2004)*

HERENCIA ANTICA

Herencia Antica 2000 Reserva Tempranillo (Utiel-Requena) $8. 81 —*M.S. (10/1/2005)*

Herencia Antica 1998 Reserva Tempranillo (Utiel-Requena) $8. 85 Best Buy —*M.S. (3/1/2004)*

HERMANOS LURTON

Hermanos Lurton 2006 Red Blend (Vino de la Tierra de Castilla y León) $13. Round and smooth upfront, with fairly pure berry aromas along with hints of leather, chocolate and warm earth. You are getting your money's worth with this medium-rich, balanced, semicomplex wine. The feel is right, the tannins smooth but present, and the finish touched up by coffee and mocha. 87 —*M.S. (11/1/2007)*

Hermanos Lurton 2004 Rosado Tempranillo Blend (Vino de la Tierra de Castilla y León) $11. 88 Best Buy —*M.S. (11/15/2005)*

Hermanos Lurton 2006 White Blend (Rueda) $13. While not that distinct, there's nothing wrong with this plump blend of 70% Verdejo and 30% Viura. The wine offers standard green melon and apple flavors, with sweet grapefruit notes on the finish. Better in the near-term; drink well chilled. 85 —*M.S. (11/1/2007)*

Hermanos Lurton 2005 White Blend (Rueda) $13. Scattered and fading, this soft white features candied aromas in front of mango and cantaloupe flavors. Lacks snap and pop, as it finishes with a soft feel and a strong taste of banana pudding. 84 —*M.S. (4/1/2007)*

Hermanos Lurton 2004 White Blend (Rueda) $13. 83 —*M.S. (9/1/2006)*

HERMANOS SASTRE

Hermanos Sastre 1999 Crianza Tempranillo (Ribera del Duero) $25. 89 —*C.S. (11/1/2002)*

Hermanos Sastre 2000 Roble Tempranillo (Ribera del Duero) $14. 88 Best Buy —*C.S. (11/1/2002)*

HIDALGO

Hidalgo NV Oloroso Viejo Sherry (Jerez) $116. 93 Editors' Choice —*M.S. (6/1/2005)*

HI WINES

Hi Wines 2005 Hi. Garnacha (Navarra) $11. A touch saucy and soupy to start with, but airing sends it to a better place. This wine falls into the chunky and ripe category, with good but heavy black cherry and black plum flavors. All the way through it's a wide load, but generally speaking an appealing wine to drink now. 85 —*M.S. (11/1/2007)*

HIGUERUELA

Higueruela 2005 Garnacha (Almansa) $10. Mostly Garnacha (with 12% Syrah), this Mediterranean-styled wine is locked and loaded on the nose: There's a ton of mineral, sunshine and earthy blackberry aromas. The palate is full with cherry and raspberry, and the acidity is strong enough to keep the wine stable. In the end it's almost lean and perky. 87 Best Buy —*M.S. (12/15/2007)*

HUGUET DE CAN FEIXES

Huguet de Can Feixes 2000 Brut Nature Reserva Champagne Blend (Cava) $23. 89 Editors' Choice —*M.S. (12/15/2004)*

Huguet de Can Feixes 2003 Negre Selecció Red Blend (Penedès) $19. Baked, stewy and very much in the warm Penedès style. The nose is herbal and green, while tobacco, tomato and other reedy flavors just don't cut it. Mouthfeel and intent are the saving graces; we know this isn't meant to be a green wine but it tastes that way. 82 —*M.S. (12/15/2007)*

Huguet de Can Feixes 2000 Negre Selecció Red Blend (Penedès) $22. 86 —*M.S. (3/1/2004)*

Huguet de Can Feixes 2001 Gran Reserva Brut Nature Sparkling Blend (Cava) $25. 87 —*M.S. (6/1/2006)*

Huguet de Can Feixes 1999 Brut Nature Sparkling Blend (Cava) $18. 85 —*M.S. (12/31/2002)*

Huguet de Can Feixes 2000 Can Feixes Blanc Selecció White Blend (Catalonia) $10. 87 Best Buy —*M.M. (9/1/2002)*

IBERNOBLE

Ibernoble 1995 Reserva Tempranillo (Ribera del Duero) $42. 87 —*J.C. (11/1/2001)*

Ibernoble 1999 Cosecha Tempranillo Blend (Ribera del Duero) $17. 83 —*J.C. (11/1/2001)*

IGLESIA VIEJA

Iglesia Vieja 1997 La Purisima Red Blend (Yecla) $13. 87 —*D.T. (4/1/2002)*

INFINITUS

Infinitus 2004 Cabernet Sauvignon (Vino de la Tierra de Castilla) $7.

Infinitus 2005 Merlot (Vino de la Tierra de Castilla) $7. 83 —*M.S. (12/15/2006)*

Infinitus 2005 Syrah (Vino de la Tierra de Castilla) $7. Round and basic, with sweet black plum and raisins on the nose. Dark fruit, chocolate and some earth work the palate, followed by a medium-length finish with moderate tannins. Basic but solid. 84 Best Buy —*M.S. (2/1/2007)*

Infinitus 2004 Syrah (Vino de la Tierra de Castilla) $7. 81 —*M.S. (11/15/2005)*

Infinitus 2006 Tempranillo (Tierra de Castilla) $7. Deep purple in color; this is a classic young grapeball across the bouquet, with sweet candied fruit aromas. The palate is plump and full of youthful blackberry flavors, while the finish is moderately chewy and substantive. Not a finesse-driven wine by any means, but good if you like simple, forward fruit character. 84 Best Buy —*M.S. (11/1/2007)*

Infinitus 2005 Tempranillo (Vino de la Tierra de Castilla) $7. 86 Best Buy —*M.S. (12/15/2006)*

Infinitus 2004 Tempranillo-Cabernet Sauvignon (Vino de la Tierra de Castilla) $7. 84 Best Buy —*M.S. (12/15/2006)*

Infinitus 2006 Viura (Tierra de Castilla) $7. This is a nice little Viura (with 15% Chardonnay) that smells nutty and smooth and tastes of tangy citrus and other white stone fruits. It has more acidity than body and it locks onto that citrusy profile and doesn't let go. But overall it's a good quaff for the price. 85 Best Buy —*M.S. (11/1/2007)*

Infinitus 2005 Chardonnay-Viura White Blend (Vino de la Tierra de Castilla) $7. 84 Best Buy —*M.S. (12/15/2006)*

Infinitus 2004 Viura and Chardonnay White Blend (Vino de la Tierra de Castilla) $7. 82 —*M.S. (10/1/2005)*

INSPIRACIÓN PAMPANO

Inspiración Pampano 2004 White Blend (Rueda) $10. 83 —*M.S. (12/15/2006)*

INURRIETA

Inurrieta 2002 Norte Cabernet Sauvignon-Merlot (Navarra) $13. 88 —*M.S. (10/1/2004)*

ITSAS MENDI

Itsas Mendi 2006 Hondarrabi Zuri (Bizkaiko Txakolina) $20. Bright apple, pear and pineapple aromas are indicative of the sharp white fruits this wine has to offer. The flavors of apple, pear and lime are refreshing, and like any Txakoli it hits with quick jabs and a lot of zest. Drink now. 88 —*M.S. (11/1/2007)*

J. & F. LURTON

J. & F. Lurton 2001 El Albar Barricas Tempranillo (Toro) $20. 88 —*M.S. (12/31/2004)*

J. & F. Lurton 2001 El Albar Excelencia Tempranillo (Toro) $43. 89 —*M.S. (8/1/2005)*

J. & F. Lurton 2000 El Albar Excelencia Tempranillo (Toro) $43. 86 —*M.S. (3/1/2005)*

J. & F. Lurton 2006 Rosado Tempranillo (Vino de la Tierra de Castilla y León) $11. Nectarine aromas lead into a tart palate that offers white peach and citrus flavors. This is an aggressively styled wine with pulsing acidity and touches of pie cherry and tangerine on the finish. Too sharp in the long run. 83 —*M.S. (7/1/2007)*

J. & F. Lurton 2004 Campo Eliseo Tinta de Toro (Toro) $73. With each vintage this bruising Toro gets more comfortable and familiar. Yes, it's still a tannic behemoth with a ton of new oak, but under all that bluster there's wonderful Tinta de Toro blackberry, licorice and tobacco flavors. And the finish of mocha and more is better than any visit to Starbucks. Hold until 2009. 92 Cellar Selection —*M.S. (11/1/2007)*

J. & F. Lurton 2003 Campo Eliseo Tinta de Toro (Toro) $60. Let's face it, the raw power of this wine is impressive. At 15.5% it cannot claim to pull punches; in fact, it's jam-packed with balsam and cedar aromas bolstered by dark, seductive fruit and marzipan flavors. A true knife-and-fork wine that finishes with licorice so potent it's reminiscent of Samnbuca. Drink through 2010. 93 —*M.S. (2/1/2007)*

J. & F. Lurton 2001 Campo Eliseo Tinta de Toro (Toro) $50. 88 —*M.S. (9/1/2004)*

J. & F. Lurton 2003 El Albar Tinta de Toro (Toro) $20. 88 —*M.S. (12/15/2006)*

J. & F. Lurton 2002 El Albar Barricas Tinta de Toro (Toro) $20. 87 —*M.S. (2/1/2006)*

J. & F. Lurton 2003 El Albar Excelencia Tinta de Toro (Toro) $40. 84 —*M.S. (12/15/2006)*

J. & F. Lurton 2002 El Albar Excellencia Tinta de Toro (Toro) $40. 90 Cellar Selection —*M.S. (2/1/2006)*

J. & F. Lurton 2003 Hermanos Lurton White Blend (Rueda) $12. 85 —*M.S. (12/31/2004)*

J.C. CONDE

J.C. Conde 2005 Sentido Tempranillo (Ribera del Duero) $24. The broad, rich nose draws you in; unfortunately, the palate doesn't deliver, as it seems jagged, tannic and spiky in its blackberry, plum, raisin and chocolate flavors. A good but unspectacular wine that's devoid of touch and elegance. 85 —*M.S. (6/1/2007)*

JANÉ VENTURA

Jané Ventura 2000 Finca Els Camps Macabeo (Penedès) $21. 82 —*M.S. (11/1/2002)*

Jané Ventura 1998 Gran Reserva Brut Nature Sparkling Blend (Cava) $21. 91 —*M.S. (6/1/2005)*

Jané Ventura 2006 White Blend (Penedès) $11. Jané Ventura is known for its sparkling cavas, but this table wine from Xarello, Muscat and the obscure Subirat Parent grape is appealing because it doesn't bite off more than it can chew. There's no oak so what you get is lean, transparent lemon and lime flavors and a ready mouthfeel. Interesting but not for everyone. 85 —*M.S. (12/15/2007)*

JARRARTE

Jarrarte 1998 Red Blend (Rioja) $24. 89 —*M.M. (11/1/2002)*

Jarrarte 2001 Tempranillo (Rioja) $29. 87 —*M.S. (8/1/2005)*

JARRERO

Jarrero 2001 Red Blend (Rioja) $16. 84 —*M.S. (11/1/2006)*

JAUME LLOPART ALEMANY

Jaume Llopart Alemany NV Artesanal Brut Nature Sparkling Blend (Cava) $14. 83 *(12/31/2001)*

Jaume Llopart Alemany NV Artesanal Brut Reserva Sparkling Blend (Penedès) $12. 82 *(12/31/2001)*

JAUME SERRA

Jaume Serra NV Seco Reserva Sparkling Blend (Penedès) $9. 82 *(12/15/2000)*

Jaume Serra NV Semi Seco Reserva Sparkling Blend (Penedès) $9. 86 —*S.H. (6/1/2001)*

Jaume Serra 2000 Estate Bottled Chardonnay (Penedès) $9. 82 —*M.S. (11/1/2002)*

JEAN LEÓN

Jean León 2003 Zemis Bordeaux Blend (Penedès) $140. Not a great Zemis. It's woody, lemony and doesn't have the flesh, depth or complexity that we've seen before. The oak is heavy and the resulting coffee, burnt toast and charred aromas and flavors are a little too much. 250 cases made. 85 —*M.S. (12/15/2007)*

Jean León 2000 Zemis Bordeaux Blend (Penedès) $126. 91 —*M.S. (6/1/2005)*

Jean León 1998 Cabernet Sauvignon (Penedès) $26. 87 —*M.S. (12/31/2004)*

Jean León 1994 Gran Reserva Cabernet Sauvignon (Penedès) $33. 92 *(2/1/2003)*

Jean León 1996 Reserva Cabernet Sauvignon (Penedès) $23. 88 *(2/1/2003)*

Jean León 1995 Reserva Cabernet Sauvignon (Penedès) $23. 90 *(2/1/2003)*

Jean León 2002 Chardonnay (Penedès) $26. 81 —*M.S. (12/31/2004)*

Jean León 2000 Chardonnay (Penedès) $21. 88 *(2/1/2003)*

Jean León 2002 Terrasola Chardonnay (Catalonia) $14. 80 —*M.S. (12/31/2004)*

Jean León 2002 Vinya Gigi Chardonnay (Penedès) $29. 86 —*M.S. (6/1/2005)*

Jean León 2001 Merlot (Penedès) $26. 86 —*M.S. (12/31/2004)*

Jean León 1999 Merlot (Penedès) $20. 87 *(2/1/2003)*

Jean León 2002 Terrasola Syrah (Catalunya) $16. 83 —*M.S. (9/1/2006)*

JM ORTEA

JM Ortea 2000 Crianza Tempranillo (Ribera del Guadiana) $23. 83 —*M.S. (10/1/2005)*

JOAN D'ANGUERA

Joan D'Anguera 2002 El Bugader Red Blend (Montsant) $60. 89 —*M.S. (10/1/2005)*

Joan D'Anguera 2002 Finca L'Argata Red Blend (Montsant) $25. 88 —*M.S. (10/1/2005)*

Joan D'Anguera 1999 Finca L'Argata Red Blend (Tarragona) $21. 90 —*C.S. (4/1/2002)*

Joan D'Anguera 2000 Finca L'Argatà Red Blend (Montsant) $21. 90 Editors' Choice —*M.S. (3/1/2004)*

Joan D'Anguera 2003 La Planella Red Blend (Montsant) $18. 84 —*M.S. (10/1/2005)*

Joan D'Anguera 2002 La Planella Red Blend (Montsant) $19. 87 —*M.S. (3/1/2004)*

Joan D'Anguera 2000 La Planella Red Blend (Tarragona) $19. 88 —*C.S. (4/1/2002)*

Joan D'Anguera 1998 Vi Dolç Red Blend (Tarragona) $70. 88 —*C.S. (4/1/2002)*

Joan D'Anguera 1999 El Bugader Shiraz (Tarragona) $50. 93 Cellar Selection —*C.S. (4/1/2002)*

Joan D'Anguera 2000 El Bugader Syrah (Montsant) $50. 92 —*M.S. (3/1/2004)*

JOAN SARDÀ

Joan Sardà 2001 Criança Cabernet Sauvignon (Penedès) $13. 82 —*M.S. (2/1/2006)*

JOAN SIMÓ

Joan Simó 2003 Les Eres Vinyes Velles Red Blend (Priorat) $68. Carignan and Grenache lead the way on this old-vines classic that is typically excellent but not quite as generous, round and whole as in previous vintages.

Still, you will be impressed by the compact nose of thyme, sage and tobacco along with dry red fruit. In addition, the palate of cassis and blackberry is pure and tannic as a rock. Needs time; best in 2009–10. **91** —*M.S. (8/1/2007)*

Joan Simó 2002 Les Eres Vinyas Velles Red Blend (Priorat) $66. 91 —*M.S. (10/1/2005)*

Joan Simó 2000 Les Eres Vinyes Velles Red Blend (Priorat) $59. 89 —*M.S. (3/1/2004)*

Joan Simó 2003 Les Sentius Red Blend (Priorat) $35. This younger-vines mix of Garnacha, Carignan, Cab Sauvignon and Syrah is very attractive and loaded with graphite, schisty mineral and black cherry aromas. The palate comes in waves, with the first delivering plum and berry and the second offering chocolate, herbs and lavender. Quite pretty and very tannic. Hold until 2008, if possible. **91** —*M.S. (8/1/2007)*

Joan Simó 2002 Les Sentius Red Blend (Priorat) $34. 85 —*M.S. (10/1/2005)*

JORGE ORDOÑEZ & CO.

Jorge Ordoñez & Co. 2004 Old Vines Moscatel (Málaga) $66. An ultrarich, TBA-styled Moscatel, syrupy and dripping with concentrated peach, pineapple and mango flavors. Almost overdone but still in balance, courtesy of good acidity. **89** —*M.S. (4/1/2007)*

Jorge Ordoñez & Co. 2004 Seleccion Especial Moscatel (Málaga) $20. Smooth, oily and nice upfront, with sweet orange marmalade and some pith on the back palate. Plenty of zest to this, it comes across much like a German Auslese. Not too unctuous or difficult. **88** —*M.S. (4/1/2007)*

Jorge Ordoñez & Co. 2004 Victoria Moscatel (Málaga) $44. Hand's down, the best of Jorge Ordoñez's dessert-styled Moscatels is the Victoria. It's floral and piercing on the nose, while the palate is ripe and smooth, with honeyed mango and pineapple flavors. Balanced like a gymnast on the beam, this sweetie is textured, rich and also a little bit racy. **93 Editors' Choice** —*M.S. (4/1/2007)*

JUAN GIL

Juan Gil 2004 Monastrell (Jumilla) $16. Sweet and welcoming; a good deal among pedigreed red wines. The nose on this 100% Monastrell from older vines is mammoth, toasty and dark, while the palate is chunky and virtually melts with blackberry, plum and cherry flavors. A real-deal red with breadth and class. 1,000 cases made. **90** —*M.S. (8/1/2007)*

JULIA ROCH E HIJOS

Julia Roch e Hijos 2000 Las Gravas Red Blend (Jumilla) $19. 89 —*M.S. (3/1/2004)*

JULIO IGLESIAS

Julio Iglesias NV Julio Brut Sparkling Blend (Cava) $15. 83 *(12/31/2001)*

JUVÉ Y CAMPS

Juvé y Camps NV Brut Rosé Pinot Noir (Cava) $11. Dry and spicy on the nose, but also a little cooked smelling. The flavors of this 100% Pinot Noir, but the flavors seem confected as they conjure memories of cherry Coke. The finish is short and leaks flavor, and always does the wine seem a bit strained. **84** —*M.S. (12/15/2007)*

Juvé y Camps NV Brut Rosé Pinot Noir (Cava) $16. 86 —*M.S. (12/15/2006)*

Juvé y Camps 2001 Reserva de la Familia Brut Nature Sparkling Blend (Cava) $20. 87 —*M.S. (6/1/2005)*

Juvé y Camps 2003 Brut Nature Reserva De La Familia Sparkling Blend (Cava) $15. For a consistently pleasing brut nature (no added sweetness), Juvé y Camps is one place to turn. This wine is dominated by matchstick, apple, pear and light vanilla aromas, which are backed by meet-in-the-middle flavors of citrus, apple and celery. It's a bit sheer and tangy, but it's also genuinely refreshing and not the least bit sweet. **87** —*M.S. (12/15/2007)*

Juvé y Camps 2003 Reserva Brut Sparkling Blend (Cava) $13. Give this stylish wine a few minutes to rev its engine and you'll be rewarded with warm pear and apple aromas. The palate is equally nice as it focuses on apple, pear and peach flavors. The finish is relatively long, clean and pretty, and overall it's a very nice wine with a hint of intricacy and complexity. **89 Best Buy** —*M.S. (12/15/2007)*

Juvé y Camps 2002 Brut Nature Reserva de la Familia White Blend (Cava) $22. 86 —*M.S. (6/1/2006)*

Juvé y Camps 2005 Ermita d'Espiells White Blend (Penedès) $12. Peach pit, almond skin and other dry, waxy aromas carry the nose on this Macabeo-Xarello-Parellada blend. Flavors of lime and nettle are playful and acid-based, while the finish seems wet and fresh. Overall it is much like a cava without the bubbles. **86** —*M.S. (12/15/2007)*

Juvé y Camps 2000 Gran Brut White Blend (Cava) $42. 89 —*M.S. (6/1/2006)*

LA LEGUA

La Legua 1999 Crianza Tempranillo (Cigales) $10. 84 —*M.S. (8/1/2003)*

La Legua 1998 Reserva Tempranillo (Cigales) $19. 89 —*M.S. (8/1/2003)*

LA RIADA

La Riada 2004 Old Vines Garnacha (Campo de Borja) $10. 81 —*M.S. (12/15/2006)*

LA RIOJA ALTA

La Rioja Alta 1987 Gran Reserva 890 Tempranillo (Rioja) $120. 90 —*M.S. (10/1/2003)*

La Rioja Alta 1994 Gran Reserva 904 Tempranillo (Rioja) $53. 88 —*M.S. (9/1/2004)*

La Rioja Alta 1989 Gran Reserva 904 Tempranillo (Rioja) $48. 92 *(11/15/1999)*

La Rioja Alta 1998 Vina Alberdi Reserva Tempranillo (Rioja) $23. 88 —*M.S. (3/1/2004)*

La Rioja Alta 1996 Vina Ardanza Reserva Tempranillo (Rioja) $28. 88 —*M.S. (10/1/2003)*

La Rioja Alta 1990 Vina Ardanza Reserva Tempranillo (Rioja) $27. 86 —*J.C. (11/15/1999)*

LA VAL

La Val 2005 Albariño (Rías Baixas) $NA. 85 —*M.S. (9/1/2006)*

La Val 2005 Finca de Arantei Albariño (Rías Baixas) $NA. 89 —*M.S. (9/1/2006)*

La Val 2005 Orballo Albariño (Rías Baixas) $19. 87 —*M.S. (9/1/2006)*

LACATUS

Lacatus 2003 Tempranillo (Penedès) $8. 85 Best Buy —*M.S. (8/1/2005)*

Lacatus 2001 Tempranillo (Penedès) $7. 81 —*M.S. (3/1/2004)*

Lacatus NV Gold Brut Nature White Blend (Cava) $13. 86 —*M.S. (12/15/2005)*

Lacatus NV Semi Seco White Blend (Cava) $12. 85 —*M.S. (12/15/2005)*

LAGAR DE CERVERA

Lagar de Cervera 2002 Albariño (Rías Baixas) $21. 87 —*M.S. (3/1/2004)*

LAGAR DE COSTA

Lagar de Costa 2005 Albariño (Rías Baixas) $13. 85 —*M.S. (12/15/2006)*

LAGUNA DE LA NAVA

Laguna de la Nava 1999 Gran Reserva Tempranillo Blend (Valdepeñas) $14. Opens with aromas of tobacco and dried leaves as well as plum and cherry, and that's backed by raspberry, plum and cherry tomato flavors. For an older wine, it's showing life, acidity and some old-school style. What it doesn't have are any of those New World characteristics, i.e. black fruit, chocolate and weight. **86** —*M.S. (8/1/2007)*

Laguna de la Nava 2000 Reserva Tempranillo (Valdepeñas) $11. 84 —*M.S. (12/15/2006)*

LAS BRISAS

Las Brisas 2005 White Blend (Rueda) $10. This wine was better last year, but in its defense we tasted the '04 several months earlier in the year, so it came across fresher. And with Rueda whites, which are vintage-to-vintage wines, that makes a difference. Here, look for tropical-fruit aromas with a pure citrus palate. It's good, straight-forward stuff that shouldn't surprise or disappoint. Drink immediately. **87** —*M.S. (4/1/2007)*

LAS GRAVAS

Las Gravas 1999 Red Blend (Jumilla) $18. 85 —*M.M. (4/1/2002)*

LAURONA

Laurona 2000 Red Blend (Montsant) $20. 91 Editors' Choice —*M.S. (3/1/2004)*

Laurona 2000 6 Vinyes de Laurona Red Blend (Montsant) $45. 90 —*M.S. (10/1/2005)*

Laurona 2001 Tinto Red Blend (Montsant) $28. 90 —*M.S. (10/1/2005)*

LEALTANZA

Lealtanza 2001 Crianza Tempranillo (Rioja) $20. 84 —*M.S. (11/15/2005)*

Lealtanza 2000 Crianza Tempranillo (Rioja) $16. 87 —*M.S. (6/1/2005)*

Lealtanza 2000 Gran Reserva Tempranillo (Rioja) $44. 87 —*M.S. (11/1/2006)*

Lealtanza 1999 Gran Reserva Tempranillo (Rioja) $45. 85 —*M.S. (4/1/2006)*

Lealtanza 2000 Reserva Tempranillo (Rioja) $29. 85 *—M.S. (11/1/2006)*

Lealtanza 2001 Reserva Selección Tempranillo (Rioja) $135. 84 *—M.S. (11/1/2006)*

Lealtanza 2005 Rosé Tempranillo (Rioja) $14. 86 *—M.S. (11/1/2006)*

LEGADO MUNOZ

Legado Munoz 2004 Chardonnay (Vino de la Tierra de Castilla) $13. Soft and smooth, with a bouquet of apples and caramel that's entirely appealing. This is not a complex Chardonnay, but for this varietal out of central Spain we shouldn't complain. The palate is balanced and offers good cantaloupe and peach flavors, while the finish is wide and features butterscotch and cinnamon. 87 *—M.S. (2/1/2007)*

Legado Munoz 2003 Chardonnay (Vino de la Tierra de Castilla) $13. Gold as a nugget, with all the full-on toast, butter and nut oil that stems from oak aging. Aromas of baked peach and apricot lead into a heavy but solid palate of Golden Delicious apple, white raisin and vanilla flavors. From a hot vintage; meaning it's ready to go right now or already past its prime. 86 *—M.S. (2/1/2007)*

Legado Munoz 2004 Garnacha (Vino de la Tierra de Castilla) $10. 81 *—M.S. (11/1/2006)*

Legado Munoz 2005 Macabeo (Vino de la Tierra de Castilla) $10. Adequate aromas of citrus and tropical fruits fall onto a flat palate holding orange, melon and banana flavors. The finish is heavy, with an apple-cider taste and feel. Doesn't stir much interest. 81 *—M.S. (2/1/2007)*

Legado Munoz 2004 Merlot (Vino de la Tierra de Castilla) $10. 85 Best Buy *—M.S. (12/15/2006)*

Legado Munoz 2005 Tempranillo (Vino de la Tierra de Castilla) $10. 84 *—M.S. (12/15/2006)*

LEGARIS

Legaris 2004 Crianza Tempranillo (Ribera del Duero) $16. Coconut, mint and plenty of raw oak aromas precede vanilla, toast and bullish fruit flavors. It runs kind of sticky and grabby on the palate, but all in all it's of good quality even if the total package isn't that complex or intriguing. It's a drink-now kind of Ribera. 87 *—M.S. (6/1/2007)*

Legaris 2000 Crianza Tempranillo (Ribera del Duero) $15. 87 *—M.S. (3/1/2004)*

Legaris 2003 Reserva Tempranillo (Ribera del Duero) $21. Dark, smoky and loaded with baked berry aromas indicative of a warm vintage. The flavors are sturdy yet superficial, with toast, vanilla and coconut shadings. Shows good chocolate and some depth, but not much length on the finish. Drink now. 87 *—M.S. (6/1/2007)*

Legaris 1999 Reserva Tempranillo (Ribera del Duero) $28. 93 Editors' Choice *—M.S. (3/1/2004)*

Legaris 2003 Crianza Tinta Fina (Ribera del Duero) $16. The first sniff is all about buttered popcorn on top of dill, while airing reveals deeper berry aromas. The palate is nice but standard, with plum and zesty berry aromas riding on a bed of firm tannins. Finishes long and rather oaky, with modest depth and not much complexity. Drink now. 86 *—M.S. (4/1/2007)*

Legaris 2001 Reserva Tinta Fina (Ribera del Duero) $20. Starts out rough and almost rubbery, but patience will be rewarded with tight cherry, cassis and cola flavors jumping on a bed of cheek-starching tannins. Airing and food are key to enjoying this serious Tempranillo. Drink now–2011. 90 *—M.S. (4/1/2007)*

Legaris 2002 Crianza Tinto del Pais (Ribera del Duero) $17. 83 *—M.S. (10/1/2005)*

Legaris 2000 Reserva Tinto del Pais (Ribera del Duero) $25. 85 *—M.S. (10/1/2005)*

LEGÓN

Legón 2004 Roble Tempranillo (Ribera del Duero) $0. More oak than anything, with aromas of cinnamon, clove and char. The palate runs fairly sour, which confirms that wood cannot cure all ills. And the finish shows little love although there is ample spearmint and leftover resin. 83 *—M.S. (2/1/2007)*

LELIA

Lelia 2005 Garnacha (Cariñena) $8. A raisiny wine with hot-weather characteristics throughout. The nose is baked and the palate offers mostly prune and burnt oak. There is a limited scope to the mouthfeel, which remains heavy and deep throughout. 82 *—M.S. (12/15/2007)*

LÍCIA

Lícia 2005 Albariño (Rías Baixas) $13. Round and sweet, with heavy buttercup and honeyed aromas. This is what we call a candied Albariño; it's loaded up with canned pineapple, melon and mango. The feel is plump and the acid level fairly low. Ripe and ready as it's ever going to be. 85 *—M.S. (11/1/2007)*

LLOPART

Llopart 1994 Brut Leopardi Sparkling Blend (Cava) $26. 85 *(12/31/2001)*

Llopart 2000 Leopardi Brut Nature Sparkling Blend (Cava) $18. 87 *—M.S. (6/1/2006)*

Llopart 2003 Rosé Brut Reserva Sparkling Blend (Cava) $18. Heat from the 2003 vintage aside, this is one sweet, forward, dark-colored Cava. The nose is all about cheeky, sweet fruit, while the palate offers more berry sweetness along with vanilla. Normally this bottling is more restrained and striated, but 2003 was a warm year. May be better with desserts than appetizers, given the ripeness. 87 *—M.S. (8/1/2007)*

Llopart 2002 Rosé Brut Reserva Sparkling Blend (Cava) $25. 91 Editors' Choice *—M.S. (6/1/2006)*

LÓPEZ HERMANOS

López Hermanos NV Don Juan Trasañejo Pedro Ximenez (Málaga) $NA. 94 Editors' Choice *—M.S. (6/1/2005)*

LORCA

Lorca 2006 Rosé Monastrell (Bullas) $10. Wet and wild, with raspberry aromas that sweeten into red licorice. The palate is kind of sweet, but it's also sturdy and full of ultraripe, almost sugary Monastrell flavors. You wouldn't call this precise or particular but it works. Drink now. 87 Best Buy *—M.S. (12/15/2007)*

LORIÑON

PRICE?

Loriñon 1997 Gran Reserva Tempranillo (Rioja) $34. 86 *—M.S. (10/1/2005)*

Loriñon 2000 Reserva Tempranillo (Rioja) $20. 86 *—M.S. (8/1/2005)*

Loriñon 2003 Crianza Tempranillo Blend (Rioja) $13. Early leather and animal aromas soon yield to brighter fruit scents, and that's followed up by a palate detailed by cherry and plum flavors. This nice, comfortable wine offers freshness and texture; it's a very good Crianza that nails the relationship between fruit and oak. 88 Best Buy *—M.S. (9/1/2007)*

Loriñon 2002 Crianza Tempranillo Blend (Rioja) $13. 84 *—M.S. (11/1/2006)*

Loriñon 2001 Crianza Tempranillo Blend (Rioja) $13. 85 *—M.S. (6/1/2005)*

Loriñon 2004 Viura (Rioja) $12. 82 *—M.S. (11/1/2006)*

LOS CUCOS DE LA ALBERQUILLA

Los Cucos de la Alberquilla 2005 Cabernet Sauvignon (Jumilla) $12. Bursting, powerful Cabernet from Jumilla is not an everyday event, so keep an eye out for this dark, sweet blackberry- and chocolate-driven youngster that only saw a few months in oak. The finish is like mud pie and it darts comfortably between exuberance and balance. 88 Best Buy *—M.S. (12/15/2007)*

LOS MONTEROS

Los Monteros 2004 Tinto Red Blend (Valencia) $10. 83 *—M.S. (8/1/2005)*

Los Monteros 2004 Blanco White Blend (Valencia) $10. 86 Best Buy *M.S. (8/1/2005)*

LOZANO

Lozano 2002 Anoranza Crianza Tempranillo (La Mancha) $8. Sweet, simple cherry aromas greet you, and they are backed by hints of almond candy. The palate is snappy as it deals strawberry and raspberry flavors. The mouthfeel is fresh, the weight light, and overall it's a clean, lighter-bodied wine that's ready to go now. 86 Best Buy *—M.S. (4/1/2007)*

Lozano 2005 Añoranza Rosé Tempranillo (La Mancha) $6. Basement-level pricing is matched by fleeting qualities. The nose is one part baked beans and one part rhubarb compote, while the palate is sharp. It's a high-acid wine that goes on forever but never shows much style or charm. 82 *—M.S. (2/1/2007)*

Lozano 2002 Oristan Crianza Tempranillo Blend (La Mancha) $10. Ripe, warm and spicy on the nose, with standard red berry aromas and flavors. The mix is Tempranillo, Cab and Syrah, which is unusual. Yet the wine tastes perfectly open and familiar, as if you've had it and enjoyed it before. Nothing special but it's good and fruity. 84 *—M.S. (8/1/2007)*

LUBERRI

Luberri 2001 Finca los Meriños Tempranillo (Rioja) $60. An attempt at high-end Tempranillo that comes across rough and tough and not too friendly. The nose is rubbery and dark, while the palate is big and generic, with chocolate on the back end. But where this wine gets you is in feel: it's a tannic monster. 83 *—M.S. (9/1/2007)*

Luberri 2005 Seis de Luberri Tempranillo (Rioja) $14. A heavier, more elevated style, but still well-priced relative to the competition. Expect lusty toast and berry aromas along with a round but juicy palate that delivers chewy berry and plum flavors and some "grasa," which means fat in Spanish. A cut above most wines in this price range. 88 *—M.S. (9/1/2007)*

LUNA BEBERIDE

Luna Beberide 2006 Mencía (Bierzo) $13. Young and a bit fiery at first, but give it time in the glass and it unfolds in a way that you would never expect for a wine of this price. Medium-bodied without any harshness, it has Mencía's typical soft tannins and berry compote flavors backed by a touch of char and vanilla. A super good wine that proudly represents Bierzo at the value level. **90 Best Buy** *—M.S. (11/1/2007)*

Luna Beberide 2005 Mencía (Bierzo) $13. Here's a really good, young Mencia that is sure to win you over. The nose is fully ripe and loaded with pure berry aromas. The juicy mouth is warm and meaty, with pure fruit and chewy tannins. Luna Beberide's Mencia pinpoints the essence of modern Bierzo. **90 Best Buy** *—M.S. (8/1/2007)*

Luna Beberide 2004 Mencía (Bierzo) $13. 88 Best Buy *—M.S. (9/1/2006)*

Luna Beberide 2003 Daniel Mencía (Bierzo) $50. Earth, leather and mildly stewed aromas greet you, and right away one can tell this wine came from a warm vintage. It has integrity and depth but maybe it still couldn't escape what 2003 threw at it. Why do we say that? The acidity seems higher than normal, maybe because of early picking, and it lacks the pure-pleasure quotient that we look for in higher-priced Bierzo wines. **87** *—M.S. (11/1/2007)*

Luna Beberide 2000 Tinto Red Blend (Vino de la Tierra de Castilla y León) $46. 90 *—M.S. (4/1/2006)*

LUSCO

Lusco 2005 Albariño (Rías Baixas) $24. Very nice apple blossom and lightly stony aromas greet you, and the apple and apricot flavors are juicy and ripe. This is an all-fruit wine with just enough acidity and minerality to keep it in shape. Finishes with citrus and melon. Drink now. **89** *—M.S. (8/1/2007)*

Lusco 2004 Albariño (Rías Baixas) $23. 85 *—M.S. (11/15/2005)*

Lusco 2003 Pazo Piñeiro Albariño (Rías Baixas) $35. 88 *—M.S. (6/1/2005)*

Lusco 2002 Albariño (Rías Baixas) $20. 85 *—M.S. (3/1/2004)*

Lusco 2000 Albariño (Rías Baixas) $20. 89 *—M.M. (9/1/2002)*

LZ

LZ 2005 Tempranillo (Rioja) $12. Dark, modern and a tiny bit funky. The round palate boasts medium-strength plum and berry, while the finish is defined by vanilla and warmth. Nothing special but good in this price range. **87 Best Buy** *—M.S. (4/1/2007)*

MAD DOGS & ENGLISHMEN

Mad Dogs & Englishmen 2004 Red Blend (Jumilla) $10. 83 *—M.S. (9/1/2006)*

Mad Dogs & Englishmen 2005 Shiraz - Cabernet - Monastrell Red Blend (Jumilla) $10. This catchy named, three-grape blend is a nice wine that's sinewy and leathery; overall it ranks as a natural and controlled reflection of Jumilla. The nose is forward and fiery, while the palate has berry-driven ripeness and plenty of oak. Better with food; the tannins are kind of scratchy with nothing to absorb them. **86 Best Buy** *—M.S. (12/15/2007)*

Mad Dogs & Englishmen 2003 Shiraz Cabernet Monastrell Red Blend (Jumilla) $10. 88 Best Buy *—P.G. (11/15/2004)*

MAJAZUL

Majazul 1999 Crianza Tempranillo (Mentrida) $13. 82 *—D.T. (4/1/2003)*

MANO A MANO

Mano A Mano 2005 Tempranillo (La Mancha) $10. Dense in color, this pours on the sugar beet and wild field aromas to the point that the nose isn't very appealing. Equally challenged is the sour, monotone palate. Peppy, but not much to offer. **82** *—M.S. (4/1/2007)*

Mano A Mano 2004 Tempranillo (La Mancha) $10. 86 Best Buy *—M.S. (11/15/2005)*

MANYANA

Manyana 2003 Tempranillo (Cariñena) $7. 80 *—M.S. (8/1/2005)*

MAR DE CASTILLA

Mar de Castilla 2005 Tempranillo Blend (Vino de la Tierra de Castilla y León) $9. 80 *—M.S. (12/15/2006)*

Mar de Castilla 2005 Verdejo (Vino de la Tierra de Castilla y León) $9. 84 *—M.S. (11/1/2006)*

MAR DE FRADES

Mar de Frades 2006 Albariño (Rías Baixas) $28. Full to the tipping point, with sweet aromas of pears and peaches. Is it over done? Maybe a little, but in between the folds of very ripe fruit there's some mineral and citrus pith. Bottom line: the funky blue bottle catches your eye and the wine is fine. But the 2005 cost $15 and this one is going for $28. Can somebody please explain the drastic price hike? **87** *—M.S. (11/1/2007)*

Mar de Frades 2005 Albariño (Rías Baixas) $15. 87 *—M.S. (12/15/2006)*

Mar de Frades 2004 Albariño (Rías Baixas) $15. 82 *—M.S. (9/1/2006)*

Mar de Frades 2002 Albariño (Rías Baixas) $16. 87 *—M.S. (3/1/2004)*

MAR DE LEÓN

Mar de León 2004 Joven Tempranillo (Vino de la Tierra de Castilla y León) $7. 81 *—M.S. (11/1/2006)*

MARIA CASANOVAS

Maria Casanovas 2004 Brut Nature Gran Reserva Sparkling Blend (Cava) $40. Disappointing considering the price. There's no good reason to pay $40 for a Cava that's cidery and offers hints of vinegar along the way. That said, this is not a cheaply made disaster unworthy of a rating; still, it's austere and hints at sauerkraut. **80** *—M.S. (12/15/2007)*

MARQUÉS DE ALELLA

Marqués de Alella 1999 White Blend (Alella) $10. 87 Best Buy *(8/1/2000)*

Marqués de Alella 2000 Classico White Blend (Alella) $10. 87 Best Buy *—M.M. (9/1/2002)*

MARQUÉS DE ARIENZO

Marqués de Arienzo 2001 Crianza Tempranillo (Rioja) $23. 87 *—M.S. (11/1/2006)*

Marqués de Arienzo 1999 Crianza Tempranillo (Rioja) $10. 85 *—M.S. (3/1/2004)*

Marqués de Arienzo 1998 Crianza Tempranillo (Rioja) $10. 88 Best Buy *—C.S. (11/1/2002)*

Marqués de Arienzo 1996 Gran Reserva Tempranillo (Rioja) $15. 84 *—M.S. (11/1/2006)*

Marqués de Arienzo 1994 Gran Reserva Tempranillo (Rioja) $25. 90 Editors' Choice *—M.M. (9/1/2002)*

Marqués de Arienzo 1999 Reserva Tempranillo (Rioja) $13. 83 *—M.S. (11/1/2006)*

Marqués de Arienzo 1998 Reserva Tempranillo (Rioja) $15. 84 *—M.S. (3/1/2004)*

Marqués de Arienzo 1996 Reserva Tempranillo (Rioja) $16. 84 *—M.M. (9/1/2002)*

Marqués de Arienzo 1997 Reserva Tempranillo Blend (Rioja) $15. 86 *—S.H. (1/1/2002)*

MARQUÉS DE CÁCERES

Marqués de Cáceres 2000 Crianza Red Blend (Rioja) $13. 87 *—M.S. (3/1/2004)*

Marqués de Cáceres 2000 Gaudium Gran Vino Red Blend (Rioja) $50. 90 *—M.S. (11/1/2006)*

Marqués de Cáceres 1994 Gran Reserva Red Blend (Rioja) $26. 89 *—D.T. (4/1/2003)*

Marqués de Cáceres 1998 Reserva Red Blend (Rioja) $22. 88 *—M.S. (11/1/2006)*

Marqués de Cáceres 1994 Reserva Red Blend (Rioja) $21. 89 *(8/1/2000)*

Marqués de Cáceres 2005 Dry Rosé Blend (Rioja) $8. 87 Best Buy *—M.S. (6/21/2006)*

Marqués de Cáceres 2004 Dry Rosé Rosé Blend (Rioja) $8. 88 Best Buy *—M.S. (8/1/2005)*

Marqués de Cáceres 2003 Dry Rosé Rosé Blend (Rioja) $7. 84 *(10/1/2004)*

Marqués de Cáceres 2006 Rosé Blend (Rioja) $8. Baked pastry and warm berry aromas are the opening salvo, with dry, almost toasty fruit sitting on the palate. It's not oak-aged yet it has that type of weighty personality. Finishes fairly flat and weighty, with lower-than-expected acidity. **84 Best Buy** *—M.S. (7/1/2007)*

Marqués de Cáceres 2002 Rosé Blend (Rioja) $7. 85 *—M.S. (3/1/2004)*

Marqués de Cáceres 1999 Rosé Blend (Rioja) $7. 84 *—M.M. (8/1/2000)*

Marqués de Cáceres 2004 MC Tempranillo (Rioja) $38. 83 *—M.S. (12/15/2006)*

Marqués de Cáceres 2003 Crianza Tempranillo (Rioja) $15. Round, clean and a touch leathery, but not penetrating or dense. For a nice, smooth red wine with some plum and cinnamon spice, look no further. This Crianza is easy-going, lightly oaked and good throughout. **87** *—M.S. (9/1/2007)*

Marqués de Cáceres 2002 MC Tempranillo (Rioja) $37. 89 *(10/1/2004)*

Marqués de Cáceres 1995 Rioja Crianza Tempranillo (Rioja) $12. 82 *—J.C. (11/15/1999)*

Marqués de Cáceres 1992 Rioja Reserva Tempranillo (Rioja) $18. 88 *—J.C. (11/15/1999)*

Marqués de Cáceres 2002 Crianza Tempranillo Blend (Rioja) $14. 86 —*M.S. (11/1/2006)*

Marqués de Cáceres 2001 Crianza Tempranillo Blend (Rioja) $13. 86 *(10/1/2004)*

Marqués de Cáceres 1998 Gaudium Gran Vino Tempranillo Blend (Rioja) $50. 88 —*M.S. (8/1/2005)*

Marqués de Cáceres 1996 Gaudium Gran Vino Tempranillo Blend (Rioja) $60. 90 *(10/1/2004)*

Marqués de Cáceres 2000 Gran Reserva Tempranillo Blend (Rioja) $30. Rich and a bit syrupy on the nose, with pepper and black cherry notes that keep things moving along. The palate is deep and round, with broad tannins housing beefy dark-fruit flavors and reasonable depth. A stocky wine that's ready to drink now or over the next few years. 88 —*M.S. (11/1/2007)*

Marqués de Cáceres 1995 Gran Reserva Tempranillo Blend (Rioja) $28. 84 —*M.S. (10/1/2005)*

Marqués de Cáceres 1994 Gran Reserva Tempranillo Blend (Rioja) $25. 90 Editors' Choice *(10/1/2004)*

Marqués de Cáceres 2001 Reserva Tempranillo Blend (Rioja) $23. Plump and ripe in style, with a lot of charm to its personality. This is very nice and simple Tempranillo (with 15% Garnacha and Graciano), and it's ready to drink now. The feel is on the flush side, and there's jamminess to the palate along with light pickle notes and vanilla on the finish. Coming along nicely; this review reflects an improvement over a tasting done in May 2007. 90 —*M.S. (11/1/2007)*

Marqués de Cáceres 1996 Reserve Tempranillo Blend (Rioja) $22. 88 —*M.S. (10/1/2005)*

Marqués de Cáceres 1995 Reserva Tempranillo Blend (Rioja) $21. 89 *(10/1/2004)*

Marqués de Cáceres 2006 Viura (Rioja) $7. As always, this gracious white wine made from the Viura grape delivers the goods. In this case, it's pineapple and pear aromas in front of pleasant apple and fresh celery flavors. There's even some honeyed apple to the finish. Light, liquidy and never bad when served properly chilled. 86 Best Buy —*M.S. (9/1/2007)*

Marqués de Cáceres 2005 Viura (Rioja) $7. 85 Best Buy —*M.S. (11/1/2006)*

Marqués de Cáceres 2004 Viura (Rioja) $7. 86 Best Buy —*M.S. (8/1/2005)*

Marqués de Cáceres 2003 Viura (Rioja) $7. 84 *(10/1/2004)*

Marqués de Cáceres 2002 Viura (Rioja) $7. 85 —*M.S. (11/15/2003)*

Marqués de Cáceres 2000 Viura (Rioja) $7. 85 Best Buy —*M.M. (9/1/2002)*

Marqués de Cáceres 1999 Viura (Rioja) $7. 84 —*M.S. (8/1/2000)*

Marqués de Cáceres 2003 Antea White Blend (Rioja) $10. 81 —*M.S. (8/1/2005)*

Marqués de Cáceres 2002 Antea White Blend (Rioja) $9. 84 *(10/1/2004)*

Marqués de Cáceres 2001 Antea White Blend (Rioja) $9. 87 —*M.S. (11/1/2002)*

Marqués de Cáceres 1998 Antea White Blend (Rioja) $10. 84 *(8/1/2000)*

Marqués de Cáceres 2005 Barrel Fermented White Blend (Rioja) $10. Heavy feline aromas matched to full oak scents don't amount to anything alluring, and the amorphous, woody palate doesn't save the day. This wine helps confirm the sketchy track record of barrel-fermented Viura from Rioja. 80 —*M.S. (2/1/2007)*

Marqués de Cáceres 2003 Satinela White Blend (Rioja) $7. 83 *(10/1/2004)*

Marqués de Cáceres 2001 Satinela White Blend (Rioja) $9. 84 —*D.T. (4/1/2003)*

Marqués de Cáceres 2005 Satinela Medium-Sweet White Blend (Rioja) $8. This semisweet white can come across likable or awful, depending on your mood and the shape of the bottle you're drinking. The sample we tried for this review was in perfect shape, and it showed tropical fruit and pineapple aromas in front of sugary mango and melon flavors. 84 —*M.S. (9/1/2007)*

Marqués de Cáceres 2000 Satinela Medium Sweet White Blend (Rioja) $7. 81 —*M.M. (9/1/2002)*

Marqués de Cáceres 2004 Satinela Medium Sweet White Blend (Rioja) $8. 80 —*M.S. (8/1/2005)*

MARQUÉS DE GELIDA

Marqués de Gelida 1997 Brut Sparkling Blend (Cava) $10. 86 Best Buy —*M.M. (12/31/2001)*

Marques de Gelida 2002 Brut Exclusive Reserva Sparkling Blend (Cava) $13. Toasty, yeasty and quite composed given the price point. If you like green apples, ripe pears or lychee fruit, chances are you're going to like this well-blended and fairly smooth Cava. It's persistent and structured enough to go with appetizers or main courses. 88 Best Buy —*M.S. (8/1/2007)*

Marqués de Gelida 2001 Brut Exclusive Reserva Sparkling Blend (Cava) $12. 89 Best Buy —*M.S. (6/1/2006)*

Marques de Gelida NV Rosé Brut Reserva Sparkling Blend (Cava) $15. Dry, smoky and lightly fruity, this Pinot Noir-based Cava is about as good as it gets in the price range. The nose delivers distant brown sugar and burnt leaves, while the palate lays on the orange rind, peach and cherry skin flavors. Try this classy sparkler; you won't be disappointed. 89 —*M.S. (8/1/2007)*

MARQUÉS DE GRIÑON

Marqués de Griñon 2002 Cabernet Sauvignon (Dominio de Valdepusa) $40. 88 —*M.S. (2/1/2006)*

Marqués de Griñon 2001 Dominio de Valdepusa Cabernet Sauvignon (Toledo) $35. 83 —*M.S. (12/31/2004)*

Marqués de Griñon 2000 Dominio de Valdepusa Cabernet Sauvignon (Toledo) $35. 89 —*M.S. (5/1/2004)*

Marqués de Griñon 1999 Dominio de Valdepusa Cabernet Sauvignon (Vino da Mesa de Toledo) $28. 84 —*M.M. (9/1/2002)*

Marqués de Griñon 2002 Petite Verdot (Dominio de Valdepusa) $40. 92 —*M.S. (2/1/2006)*

Marqués de Griñon 1999 Dominio de Valdepusa Petite Verdot (Vino da Mesa de Toledo) $30. 88 —*M.M. (9/1/2002)*

Marqués de Griñon 2000 Emeritus Red Blend (Vino da Mesa de Toledo) $60. 90 —*M.S. (3/1/2005)*

Marqués de Griñon 1998 Emeritus Red Blend (Toledo) $50. 87 —*D.T. (4/1/2003)*

Marqués de Griñon 1999 Enartis Red Blend (Rioja) $30. 85 —*D.T. (4/1/2003)*

Marqués de Griñon 2002 Syrah (Dominio de Valdepusa) $40. 92 —*M.S. (2/1/2006)*

Marqués de Griñon 2000 Dominio de Valdepusa Syrah (Vino da Mesa de Toledo) $34. 86 —*M.S. (3/1/2004)*

Marqués de Griñon 1999 Dominio de Valdepusa Syrah (Vino da Mesa de Toledo) $34. 83 *(11/1/2001)*

Marqués de Griñon 2000 Durius Tempranillo (Douro) $9. 84 —*D.T. (4/1/2003)*

Marqués de Griñon 2001 Durius White Blend (Douro) $9. 83 —*D.T. (4/1/2003)*

Marqués de Griñon 2000 Tempranillo (Rioja) $12. 86 —*D.T. (4/1/2003)*

Marqués de Griñon 1997 Colección Personal Reserva Tempranillo (Rioja) $26. 88 —*D.T. (4/1/2003)*

MARQUÉS DE LA CONCORDIA

Marques de la Concordia 2004 Tempranillo (Rioja) $11. Right from the start you know this wine is challenged. The nose is lean and green, with hints of tea and citrus peel. In the mouth, it's snappy and traditional, meaning there's American oak dill notes brushing up against rhubarb and red cherry. Proponents will cite its "classic" character while others will call it thin and not very rewarding. 83 —*M.S. (9/1/2007)*

Marques de la Concordia 2004 Crianza Tempranillo (Rioja) $13. Lemon peel and citrus aromas are the proper foreshadowing of what's to come: a tart, lean, old-style wine that is ultimately lean and grabby. These days you have to give the consumer more richness and flavor than this. 81 —*M.S. (11/1/2007)*

Marques de la Concordia 2003 Crianza Tempranillo (Rioja) $14. A little leafy, a little spicy and a little bit of a throwback to the days when Rioja wasn't taken so seriously. This has light cinnamon oak shadings followed by cola, tobacco and sweet berry flavors. Somewhat acidic and sheer, so better with food; drink now. 87 —*M.S. (9/1/2007)*

Marqués de la Concordia 2000 Crianza Tempranillo (Rioja) $15. 80 —*M.S. (5/1/2004)*

Marqués de la Concordia 2001 Hacienda de Susar Tempranillo (Rioja) $15. 87 —*M.S. (6/1/2005)*

Marques de la Concordia 2002 Reserva Tempranillo (Rioja) $19. Spicy and reedy in an old-fashioned way. This wine represents traditional Riojano winemaking: it's tight, acidic and endowed with racy rhubarb, raspberry and dill flavors. Pretty full and big on the palate, with touches of green herb and spice on the finish. 85 —*M.S. (9/1/2007)*

MARQUÉS DE MONISTROL

Marqués de Monistrol 1999 Masia Monistrol Single Vineyard Reserva Especial Cabernet Sauvignon-Merlot (Penedès) $20. 90 Editors' Choice —*D.T. (4/1/2003)*

Marqués de Monistrol 2000 Cabernet Sauvignon-Tempranillo (Penedès) $7. 88 Best Buy —*D.T. (4/1/2003)*

Marqués de Monistrol NV Brut Reserva Sparkling Blend (Cava) $9. 88 Best Buy —*M.S. (12/31/2002)*

Marqués de Monistrol NV Masia Monistrol Sparkling Blend (Cava) $7. 86 Best Buy —*M.S. (12/31/2002)*

Marqués de Monistrol 1998 Reserva Privada Red Blend (Penedès) $10. 88 Best Buy —*D.T. (4/1/2003)*

Marqués de Monistrol 1999 Brut Reserva Privada Sparkling Blend (Cava) $15. 90 Best Buy —*M.S. (6/1/2006)*

MARQUÉS DE MURRIETA

Marqués de Murrieta 1994 Castillo Ygay Reserva Especial Red Blend (Rioja) $24. 87 *(2/1/2000)*

Marqués de Murrieta 1989 Castillo Ygay Gran Reserva Esp Red Blend (Rioja) $35. 89 *(2/1/2000)*

Marqués de Murrieta 1998 Colección 2100 Tinto Red Blend (Rioja) $11. 86 *(2/1/2000)*

Marqués de Murrieta 1997 Colección 2100 Tinto Red Blend (Rioja) $10. 83 *(2/1/2000)*

Marqués de Murrieta 1995 Dalmau Reserva Red Blend (Rioja) $75. 89 *(2/1/2000)*

Marqués de Murrieta 1995 Prado Lagar Reserva Especial Red Blend (Rioja) $27. 89 *(2/1/2000)*

Marqués de Murrieta 1995 Reserva Red Blend (Rioja) $20. 89 *(2/1/2000)*

Marqués de Murrieta 1995 Castillo Ygay Gran Reserva Tempranillo (Rioja) $45. 91 —*M.S. (9/1/2004)*

Marqués de Murrieta 2003 Dalmau Tempranillo (Rioja) $100. Dark mineral, toasted French oak and black fruit carry the nose. This is a sturdy, nicely made high-end Rioja, but due to the heat of the year its range of flavors is narrow as it settles on baked plum and molasses. Medium long on the finish, with a lasting taste of chocolate. **90** —*M.S. (9/1/2007)*

Marqués de Murrieta 1999 Dalmau Tempranillo Blend (Rioja) $80. 91 —*M.S. (9/1/2004)*

Marqués de Murrieta 2000 Dalmau Reserva Tempranillo Blend (Rioja) $NA. 92 —*M.S. (6/1/2005)*

MARQUÉS DE REALA

Marqués de Reala 2004 Grenache (Campo de Borja) $9. 84 —*M.S. (2/1/2006)*

Marqués de Reala 2003 Rosado Grenache (Campo de Borja) $7. 84 Best Buy —*M.S. (3/1/2005)*

Marqués de Reala 2005 Rosé Joven Grenache (Campo de Borja) $9. 81 —*M.S. (11/1/2006)*

Marqués de Reala 2003 Tinto Grenache (Campo de Borja) $7. 84 Best Buy —*M.S. (6/1/2005)*

Marqués de Reala 2005 Joven White Blend (Campo de Borja) $9. Sort of waxy and odd, with heavy floral notes but no discernible fruit on the nose. The taste profile runs all over the map, first offering lumbering spiced apple and then things that are totally foreign to white wine, i.e. wax. Not impressive. **81** —*M.S. (2/1/2007)*

MARQUÉS DE RISCAL

Marqués de Riscal 2004 Sauvignon (Rueda) $8. 87 —*M.S. (10/1/2005)*

Marqués de Riscal 2004 Riscal 1860 Tempranillo (Vino de la Tierra de Castilla y León) $8. 88 Best Buy —*M.S. (11/15/2006)*

Marqués de Riscal 2001 Riscal 1860 Tempranillo (Vino de la Tierra de Castilla y León) $9. 86 Best Buy *(12/31/2004)*

Marqués de Riscal 2000 Riscal 1860 Tempranillo (Vino de la Tierra de Castilla y León) $8. 84 —*M.S. (8/1/2003)*

Marqués de Riscal 2005 Rosé Tempranillo (Rioja) $10. This Tempranillo-based wine has seen its day, or maybe it never had one. The color is dark and murky, while freshness appears to have gone on permanent vacation. Best to wait for the 2006. **81** —*M.S. (4/1/2007)*

Marqués de Riscal 2001 Baron de Chirel Reserva Tempranillo Blend (Rioja) $50. 91 —*M.S. (10/1/2005)*

Marqués de Riscal 1999 Baron de Chirel Reserva Tempranillo Blend (Rioja) $60. 90 *(12/31/2004)*

Marqués de Riscal 1996 Baron de Chirel Reserva Tempranillo Blend (Rioja) $60. 90 —*M.M. (9/1/2002)*

Marqués de Riscal 1998 Gran Reserva Tempranillo Blend (Rioja) $36. 90 —*M.S. (10/1/2005)*

Marqués de Riscal 1996 Gran Reserva Tempranillo Blend (Rioja) $35. 90 *(11/1/2004)*

Marqués de Riscal 1996 Gran Reserva Tempranillo Blend (Rioja) $36. 92 —*M.S. (10/1/2003)*

Marqués de Riscal 1995 Gran Reserva Tempranillo Blend (Rioja) $36. 88 —*C.S. (11/1/2002)*

Marqués de Riscal 2001 Reserva Tempranillo Blend (Rioja) $15. Given the production (65,000 cases) and price, you can't come down on this wine. It's spicy and traditional as can be, with cured meat, cinnamon and snappy red fruit on the nose. The palate is just as zesty as the bouquet, but there's some depth and richness as well. Great for chorizo, grilled meats, cheeses and the like. **89** —*M.S. (2/1/2007)*

Marqués de Riscal 2000 Reserva Tempranillo Blend (Rioja) $17. 87 *(12/31/2004)*

Marqués de Riscal 1998 Reserva Tempranillo Blend (Rioja) $15. 86 —*C.S. (11/1/2002)*

Marqués de Riscal 2003 Verdejo (Rueda) $8. 87 Best Buy *(12/31/2004)*

Marqués de Riscal 2005 White Blend (Rueda) $8. Fleshy, ripe and going soft, but in the fold is tasty pineapple, honey, apple and citrus aromas and flavors. Nothing complicated from nose to tail; it shows standard passion-fruit and grapefruit characteristics and not much more. **85 Best Buy** —*M.S. (2/1/2007)*

Marqués de Riscal 2000 White Blend (Rueda) $9. 85 —*M.M. (9/1/2002)*

MARQUÉS DE TOMARES

Marqués de Tomares 2005 Don Roman Tempranillo (Rioja) $15. An earthy style with pickle barrel and leather on the nose. Dark berry flavors are muddled, and there's an odd twinge of citrus to the flavor profile. Never really gets it going and seems murky. Two samples tasted. **82** —*M.S. (9/1/2007)*

Marqués de Tomares 2002 Crianza Tempranillo Blend (Rioja) $19. Raisin, licorice and sawdust are the primary aromas, while the palate runs dry and slightly overdone with oak. It's a decent wine that's neither funky nor faulty; but it is dried out and lean, with apple skin and hard-spice flavors. **84** —*M.S. (9/1/2007)*

Marqués de Tomares 2001 Crianza Tempranillo Blend (Rioja) $19. 88 —*M.S. (6/1/2005)*

Marqués de Tomares 1999 Crianza Tempranillo Blend (Rioja) $19. 84 —*M.S. (12/31/2004)*

Marqués de Tomares 1996 Gran Reserva Tempranillo Blend (Rioja) $50. 88 —*M.S. (12/31/2004)*

Marqués de Tomares 1995 Gran Reserva Tempranillo Blend (Rioja) $50. 89 —*M.S. (12/31/2004)*

MARQUÉS DE ULIA

Marqués de Ulia 1998 Reserva Tempranillo (Rioja) $15. 87 —*M.S. (6/1/2005)*

MARQUÉS DE VARGAS

Marqués de Vargas 1998 Reserva Tempranillo Blend (Rioja) $70. 86 —*M.S. (3/1/2005)*

MARQUÉS DE VILLALBA

Marqués de Villalba 2000 Crianza Tempranillo (Ribera del Guadiana) $15. 85 —*M.S. (12/31/2004)*

MARQUÉS DE VILLAMAGNA

Marqués de Villamagna 1997 Gran Reserva Tempranillo (Rioja) $NA. 87 —*M.S. (9/1/2004)*

MARQUÉS DE VIZHOJA

Marqués de Vizhoja 2005 Torre La Moreira Albariño (Rías Baixas) $19. 90 —*M.S. (9/1/2006)*

Marqués de Vizhoja 2005 Señor da Folla Verde White Blend (Rías Baixas) $21. 88 —*M.S. (9/1/2006)*

MARQUÉS DEL PUERTO

Marqués del Puerto 1997 Crianza Red Blend (Rioja) $12. 81 —*M.S. (8/1/2000)*

Marqués del Puerto 1991 Gran Reserva Red Blend (Rioja) $21. 84 *(8/1/2000)*

Marqués del Puerto 1996 Reserva Red Blend (Rioja) $13. 85 —*C.S. (11/1/2002)*

Marqués del Puerto 1995 Reserva Red Blend (Rioja) $17. 85 *(8/1/2000)*

Marqués del Puerto 1985 Roman Paladino Gran Reserva Red Blend (Rioja) $130. 87 *(8/1/2000)*

Marqués del Puerto 1996 Selección Especial MM-Reserva Red Blend (Rioja) $40. 90 *(11/1/2002)*

Marqués del Puerto 1994 Selección Especial MM Reserva Red Blend (Rioja) $NA. 87 *(8/1/2000)*

Marqués del Puerto 2002 Rosado Rosé Blend (Rioja) $9. 83 *—M.S. (10/1/2003)*

Marqués del Puerto 2000 Crianza Tempranillo (Rioja) $14. 84 *—M.S. (10/1/2003)*

Marqués del Puerto 1999 Crianza Tempranillo (Rioja) $12. 89 *—C.S. (11/1/2002)*

Marqués del Puerto 1995 Gran Reserva Tempranillo (Rioja) $25. 83 *—M.S. (10/1/2003)*

Marqués del Puerto 1999 Rosado Tempranillo (Rioja) $10. 85 *(8/1/2000)*

Marqués del Puerto 2003 Rosado Tempranillo Blend (Rioja) $10. 86 Best Buy *—M.S. (9/1/2004)*

Marqués del Puerto 2003 Blanco Viura (Rioja) $9. 83 *—M.S. (12/31/2004)*

Marqués del Puerto 2002 Blanco Viura (Rioja) $9. 86 Best Buy *—M.S. (10/1/2003)*

Marqués del Puerto 2000 Cosecha 2000 White Blend (Rioja) $17. 81 *—M.S. (11/1/2002)*

MARQUÉS DEL REAL TESORO

Marqués del Real Tesoro NV Del Principe Amontillado Muy Viejo Sherry (Jerez) $22. 84 *—M.S. (12/31/2004)*

Marqués del Real Tesoro NV Pedro Ximenez Viejo Sherry (Jerez) $16. 88 *—M.S. (12/31/2004)*

Marqués del Real Tesoro NV Tio Mateo Fino Seco y Suave Sherry (Jerez) $15. 82 *—M.S. (12/31/2004)*

MARTÍN CÓDAX

Martín Códax 2006 Albariño (Rías Baixas) $15. Light and limpid, with mild almond, palm butter and citrus aromas. This is a basic, clean wine that offers citrus, pineapple and mango flavors. It's a bit sweet and monotone in its delivery, but it doesn't offend and it goes down easy if properly chilled. Imported by Martín Códax USA. 87 *—M.S. (11/1/2007)*

Martín Códax 2005 Albariño (Rías Baixas) $16. 88 *—M.S. (9/1/2006)*

Martín Códax 1999 Albariño (Rías Baixas) $13. 88 Best Buy *—M.M. (8/1/2000)*

Martín Códax 1999 Burgans Albariño (Rías Baixas) $12. 85 *—M.M. (8/1/2000)*

Martín Códax 1998 Organistrum Albariño (Rías Baixas) $17. 87 *—M.M. (8/1/2000)*

Martín Códax 2005 Ergo Tempranillo (Rioja) $15. Dill and butter aromas announce aging in American oak, while the berry aromas are solid but common. This is a tightly wound wine with black cherry and olive flavors followed by length on the palate. It's not edgy, complex or beguiling, but it is full of fruit and has good balance. Imported by Martín Códax USA. 86 *—M.S. (12/15/2007)*

MARTINEZ BUJANDA

Martinez Bujanda 2001 Finca Antigua Cabernet Sauvignon (La Mancha) $8. 85 *(11/1/2003)*

Martinez Bujanda 1997 Conde de Valdemar Garnacha Reserva Garnacha (Rioja) $26. 82 *—M.S. (10/1/2003)*

Martinez Bujanda 1999 Conde de Valdemar Reserva Garnacha (Rioja) $25. 90 Editors' Choice *(11/1/2003)*

Martinez Bujanda 2002 Valdemar Vino Rosado Garnacha (Rioja) $8. 85 Best Buy *(11/1/2003)*

Martinez Bujanda 2000 Conde de Valdemar Crianza Red Blend (Rioja) $10. 85 *—M.S. (3/1/2004)*

Martinez Bujanda 1998 Finca Valpiedra Reserva Red Blend (Rioja) $32. 87 *—M.S. (3/1/2004)*

Martinez Bujanda 1998 Conde de Valdemar Crianza Tempranillo (Rioja) $9. 86 *—M.M. (9/1/2002)*

Martinez Bujanda 1994 Conde de Valdemar Gran Reserva Tempranillo (Rioja) $21. 89 *—M.M. (9/1/2002)*

Martinez Bujanda 1998 Conde de Valdemar Reserva Tempranillo (Rioja) $15. 87 *(11/1/2003)*

Martinez Bujanda 2001 Finca Antigua Tempranillo (La Mancha) $9. 87 Best Buy *(11/1/2003)*

Martinez Bujanda 2000 Finca Antigua Crianza Tempranillo (La Mancha) $10. 86 *(11/1/2003)*

Martinez Bujanda 2004 Finca Valpiedra Reserva Tempranillo (Rioja) $30. Red fruit is the dominant player on both the raspberry-driven bouquet and the currant- and cherry-laced palate. In the mouth there's integrity, natural acidity and restrained oak as opposed to heft and unnecessary burnt coffee and chocolate notes. Very clean and well-made wine with aging potential. Good upon release and will hold through 2015. 90 *—M.S. (11/1/2007)*

Martinez Bujanda 1997 Finca Valpiedra Reserva Tempranillo (Rioja) $30. 87 *(11/1/2003)*

Martinez Bujanda 1997 Conde de Valdemar Gran Reserva Tempranillo Blend (Rioja) $25. 83 *—M.S. (10/1/2005)*

Martinez Bujanda 1999 Finca Valpiedra Reserva Tempranillo Blend (Rioja) $32. 90 *—M.S. (9/1/2004)*

Martinez Bujanda 1996 Gran Reserva Tempranillo Blend (Rioja) $22. 89 *(11/1/2003)*

MARTINEZ LAORDEN

Martinez Laorden 2004 El Talud Tempranillo (Rioja) $13. 81 *—M.S. (2/1/2006)*

MARTINSANCHO

Martinsancho 2005 Verdejo (Rueda) $15. Plump, melony and ripe on the nose, with creamy pear, melon and banana flavors. Normally this wine is more racy and acidic than this, but the '05 seems tropical relative to previous years. Still, it's a good wine that will go down nicely if properly chilled. Drink now. 86 *—M.S. (8/1/2007)*

Martinsancho 2004 Verdejo (Rueda) $15. 86 *—M.S. (8/1/2005)*

Martinsancho 2003 Verdejo (Rueda) $14. 89 *—M.S. (9/1/2004)*

Martinsancho 2002 Verdejo (Rueda) $12. 85 *—M.S. (3/1/2004)*

Martinsancho 2000 Rueda Superior Verdejo (Rueda) $13. 84 *—M.M. (9/1/2002)*

MARTIVILLI

Martivilli 2000 Verdejo (Rueda) $10. 87 Best Buy *—M.M. (4/1/2002)*

MAS DELS FRARES

Mas Dels Frares 2004 Red Blend (Priorat) $17. 88 *—M.S. (12/15/2006)*

Mas Dels Frares 2002 Crianza Red Blend (Priorat) $70. 84 *—M.S. (10/1/2005)*

MAS DOIX

Mas Doix 2002 Doix Costers de Vinyes Velles Red Blend (Priorat) $85. 91 *—M.S. (10/1/2005)*

MAS FRANCH

Mas Franch 2003 Red Blend (Montsant) $35. 89 *—M.S. (12/15/2006)*

MAS IGNEUS

Mas Igneus 2001 Mas Igneus-Garnacha Blanca Old Vines Garnacha (Priorat) $18. 83 *—M.S. (3/1/2004)*

Mas Igneus 2001 Barranc Dels Closos Red Blend (Priorat) $15. 91 Editors' Choice *—M.S. (3/1/2004)*

Mas Igneus 2000 FA 112 Red Blend (Priorat) $32. 92 *—M.S. (3/1/2004)*

Mas Igneus 1999 FA 104 Blanco White Blend (Priorat) $19. 88 *—M.M. (4/1/2002)*

MAS MARÇAL

Mas Marçal 2003 Tinto Red Blend (Catalonia) $9. 86 Best Buy *—M.S. (6/1/2005)*

MAS MARTINET

Mas Martinet 2002 Clos Martinet Red Blend (Priorat) $58. 92 *—M.S. (10/1/2005)*

MAS VILÓ

Mas Viló 2003 Red Blend (Priorat) $26. 87 *—M.S. (10/1/2005)*

MAS DE L'ABUNDÀNCIA

Mas de l'Abundància 2003 Red Blend (Montsant) $42. From a brutally hot vintage, this shows plenty of mineral, schist and cola aromas along with impeccably smooth fruit. It's a little racy and sheer in the mouth, but food will balance that without a problem. And along the way you should enjoy the licorice, cherry, kirsch and other crafty nuances that this fine blend of Cabernet, Garnacha and Carignan has to offer. Drink now through 2009. 91 *—M.S. (8/1/2007)*

Mas de l'Abundància 2004 Flvminis Red Blend (Montsant) $28. After a couple of rough years, all Fluminus needed was the good 2004 vintage. And the result is splendid. This blend of Cab, Garnacha and Carignan is pure as can be, with polished leather and fine tobacco aromas entering the fray. The whole is complete and big-boned, but in the end it's more tight and compact than plush. Give it two years to show its best side. 90 *—M.S. (8/1/2007)*

SPAIN

MAS DE MONISTROL

Mas de Monistrol NV MPX Brut Sparkling Blend (Cava) $11. Pretty pear, apple and other dusty white-fruit aromas start this cleansing Cava on its way to pure citrus, Granny Smith apple and lime flavors. It has a mildly linear, angular feel but it doesn't come across sheer or sour; to the contrary, it's balanced and generous with its fruit. **88 Best Buy** *—M.S. (12/15/2007)*

Mas de Monistrol NV MPX Brut Rosé Sparkling Blend (Cava) $11. Mas de Monistrol always seems to please. This rosado is dusty and smoky on the nose, with lightly roasted fruit aromas peeking through. The flavors are more in the cherry and cranberry field, so in terms of mouthfeel it leans toward tangy, racy and pulsing. And who would want it any other way? **89 Best Buy** *—M.S. (12/15/2007)*

MASET DEL LLEÓ

Maset del Lleó NV Semi-Dulce Rosé Blend (Penedès) $11. 83 *—M.S. (8/1/2005)*

Maset del Lleó NV Brut Sparkling Blend (Cava) $13. 83 *—M.S. (12/15/2004)*

Maset del Lleó NV Brut Nature Sparkling Blend (Cava) $14. 84 *—M.S. (12/15/2004)*

Maset del Lleó NV Brut Nature Reserva Sparkling Blend (Cava) $16. 86 *—M.S. (12/15/2004)*

Maset del Lleó NV Brut Reserva Sparkling Blend (Cava) $15. 87 *—M.S. (12/15/2004)*

Maset del Lleó NV Semi Seco Sparkling Blend (Cava) $12. 88 Best Buy *—M.S. (12/15/2004)*

Maset del Lleó NV Semi Seco Reserva Sparkling Blend (Cava) $14. 87 *—M.S. (12/15/2004)*

Maset del Lleó NV Semi-Sweet White Blend (Penedès) $11. 84 *—M.S. (8/1/2005)*

MASIA BACH

Masia Bach 1997 Bach Cabernet Sauvignon (Catalonia) $12. 86 *—R.V. (11/1/1999)*

Masia Bach 1997 Merlot (Catalonia) 88 *—R.V. (11/1/1999)*

Masia Bach 1996 Bach Tempranillo (Catalonia) $8. 89 Best Buy *—R.V. (11/1/1999)*

MASIES D'AVINYO

Masies d'Avinyo 2005 Abadal Rosado Cabernet Sauvignon (Pla de Bages) $17. This Catalonian winery is proving itself year after year, wine after wine. Abadal's dry Cabernet-based rosado starts with sweet strawberry and raspberry aromas, while next up you get pure, enticing watermelon, nectarine and raspberry flavors. Too bad you missed it over the summer but it's still healthy enough to drink before the 2006 arrives. **88** *—M.S. (2/1/2007)*

Masies d'Avinyo 2003 Abadal Crianza Cabernet Sauvignon-Merlot (Pla de Bages) $15. For the most part this is smooth, ripe red wine. At 50% Cabernet and 50% Merlot the flavors and style should be familiar, but still this wine has its own Catalonian personality. It's concentrated and ripe but not all that heavy. Overall it's very Mediterranean/mountainous and not very New World at all. A fine match for good food. **88** *—M.S. (12/15/2007)*

Masies d'Avinyo 2002 Abadal Crianza Cabernet Sauvignon-Merlot (Pla de Bages) $14. 85 *—M.S. (2/1/2006)*

Masies d'Avinyo 2000 Abadal 3.9 Reserva Cabernet Sauvignon-Syrah (Pla de Bages) $33. Ripeness in inland Catalonia is always going to be challenging, so it is no surprise that the wine features snappy red-fruit aromas and flavors, with herbal touches and lots of length. Neither outrageous nor extraordinary; just good wine. 85% Cabernet and 15% Syrah. **87** *—M.S. (12/15/2007)*

Masies d'Avinyo 2001 Abadal Merlot (Pla de Bages) $16. 89 *—M.S. (9/1/2006)*

Masies D'Avinyo 2003 Red Blend (Pla de Bages) $12. 91 Best Buy *—M.S. (4/1/2006)*

Masies d'Avinyo 2004 Abadal Red Blend (Pla de Bages) $13. Tempranillo and Cabernet Franc aren't often thrown together, but here the marriage works. The nose offers herbal, leafy aromas from the CF, while berry fruit and oak carry the rest of the show. The palate is slightly crisp and racy, but its lightweight character is welcome. This is yet another well-made, interesting wine from one of our favorite obscure Spanish labels. **88 Best Buy** *—M.S. (12/15/2007)*

Masies d'Avinyo 2000 Abadal Reserva Red Blend (Pla de Bages) $24. Merlot, Cabernet and a splash of Syrah are brought together in solid, inspiring fashion by this Catalonian winery. Cherry and raspberry aromas are hoisted by full oak, while the finish deals a basket of berry flavors and ripeness. For the most part this is an in-your-face wine that's clearly been made from good grapes. **89** *—M.S. (12/15/2007)*

Masies d'Avinyo 2002 Abadal Selecció Red Blend (Pla de Bages) $49. Serious wines from a tiny inland appellation in Catalonia—that's Abadal, a maker of true terroir wines that succeed way more often than they disappoint. This blend of Cab Sauvignon, Cab Franc and Syrah is minerally and full of red fruit and vanilla aromas. The palate is husky but correct, with full tannins, a kick of acidity and pure, ripe berry flavors. Even from a tough vintage it justifies its selected status. **91** *—M.S. (12/15/2007)*

Masies d'Avinyo 2005 Abadal Blanc White Blend (Pla de Bages) $16. Fresh, light and peachy is this three-way blend of Chardonnay, Sauvignon Blanc and the native Picapoll. The nose is clean and alluring, with no oak, while the flavors run toward pineapple, green apple and wet stones. More crisp than heavy, with a good feel and full, bracing acidity. **86** *—M.S. (2/1/2007)*

MATARROMERA

Matarromera 2003 Crianza Tinto del Pais (Ribera del Duero) $28. 83 *—M.S. (11/1/2006)*

Matarromera 1999 Crianza Tinto del Pais (Ribera del Duero) $30. 91 Editors' Choice *—M.S. (3/1/2004)*

Matarromera 1999 Grand Reserva Tinto del Pais (Ribera del Duero) $105. 87 *—M.S. (11/1/2006)*

Matarromera 1999 Prestigio Tinto del Pais (Ribera del Duero) $60. 85 *—M.S. (11/1/2006)*

Matarromera 2001 Prestigio Pago de las Solanas Tinto del Pais (Ribera del Duero) $300. 89 *—M.S. (11/1/2006)*

Matarromera 2002 Reserva Tinto del Pais (Ribera del Duero) $40. 88 *—M.S. (12/15/2006)*

Matarromera 1998 Reserva Tinto del Pais (Ribera del Duero) $49. 90 *—M.S. (3/1/2004)*

MAURO

Mauro 2004 Tempranillo (Vino de la Tierra de Castilla y León) $47. Sweet, succulent aromas draw you in and while the wine doesn't deliver much nuance on either the nose or palate, we can't quibble with the power, purity and intensity of the blackberry fruit. It's young, tannic and tough now, so give it two years and it should be an excellent wine. **90** *—M.S. (8/1/2007)*

Mauro 2000 Tempranillo (Vino de la Tierra de Castilla y León) $32. 92 Editors' Choice *—M.S. (3/1/2004)*

MAYORAL

Mayoral 2000 Cosecha Tempranillo Blend (Jumilla) $7. 87 Best Buy *M.M. (9/1/2002)*

MEDERAÑO

Mederaño 2003 Linea d'Oro Cabernet Sauvignon-Tempranillo (Catalunya) $10. 85 Best Buy *—M.S. (4/1/2006)*

Mederaño 2000 Tinto Red Blend (Tierra de Castilla) $7. 83 *—D.T. (4/1/2003)*

Mederaño 2001 White Blend (Tierra de Castilla) $7. 80 *—D.T. (4/1/2003)*

Mederaño 2004 Linea d'Oro Chardonnay & Xarel-Lo White Blend (Catalunya) $10. 82 *—M.S. (9/1/2006)*

MELIS

Melis 2004 Red Blend (Priorat) $90. Powerful is almost an understatement in describing this big boy. The nose starts out fiery and rough before settling to intense. It's all guns blazing on the palate, where tight, racy raspberry fruit holds court. With intense oak and a molten core generating 15.5% alcohol you may want to tread carefully. The ride is not for the weak. Garnacha with Carignan, Syrah and Cab Sauvignon. **92** *—M.S. (8/1/2007)*

MERUM

Merum 2005 Old Vines Grenache-Syrah (Spain) $16. 85 *—M.S. (12/15/2006)*

Merum 2003 Monastrell (Jumilla) $9. 83 *—M.S. (6/1/2005)*

Merum 2002 Unico Monastrell (Jumilla) $27. 84 *—M.S. (6/1/2005)*

Merum 2005 Tempranillo (Madrid) $10. 85 Best Buy *—M.S. (12/15/2006)*

Merum 2002 Tempranillo (Madrid) $7. 87 Best Buy *—M.S. (9/1/2004)*

Merum 1999 Crianza Tempranillo (Madrid) $10. 86 Best Buy *—M.S. (9/1/2004)*

MIRONE

Mirone 2005 Seleccion Old Vines Garnacha (Campo de Borja) $9. Raspberry and a touch of citrus peel make for a light, appealing nose, while the red cherry and red apple skin flavors are cheerful, bouncy and attractive. For a basic Garnacha from Campo de Borja, this has it all: color, fresh fruit, balance and character. **88 Best Buy** *—M.S. (8/1/2007)*

MM MASIA L'HEREU

MM Masia L'Hereu 2000 Reserva Privada Cabernet Blend (Penedès) $10. 90 Best Buy *—M.S. (5/1/2004)*

MM Masia L'Hereu 1999 1882 Reserva Privada Red Blend (Penedès) $10. 88 Best Buy *—M.S. (5/1/2004)*

MONASTERIO DE LAS VIÑAS

Monasterio de las Viñas 2001 Reserva Red Blend (Cariñena) $16. A four-grape blend that's a touch rooty and charred upfront, while the palate is brighter and juicier as it gives fresh tomato, savory red berry and spice flavors. The more it opens the more grabby and tannic it gets, so expect some good ol' country grip as it goes down. **84** *—M.S. (12/15/2007)*

MONOPOLE

Monopole 2001 Blanco Seco Viura (Rioja) $20. 86 *—D.T. (4/1/2003)*

MONT MARÇAL

Mont Marçal NV Brut Sparkling Blend (Cava) $11. 89 *(11/15/1999)*

Mont Marçal 2003 Reserva Brut Sparkling Blend (Cava) $12. 88 Best Buy *—M.S. (6/1/2006)*

Mont Marçal 2001 Brut Reserva Sparkling Blend (Cava) $12. 89 Best Buy *—M.S. (11/15/2005)*

Mont Marçal 1999 Brut Reserva Sparkling Blend (Cava) $9. 86 *—K.F. (12/31/2002)*

Mont Marçal 1998 Brut Reserva Sparkling Blend (Cava) $9. 86 Best Buy *(12/31/2001)*

Mont Marçal NV Brut Reserva Rosé Sparkling Blend (Cava) $15. 86 *—M.S. (12/15/2005)*

Mont Marçal NV Extremarium Brut Sparkling Blend (Cava) $18. 88 *—M.S. (6/1/2006)*

MONTALVO WILMONT

Montalvo Wilmont 2003 Tempranillo-Cabernet Sauvignon (La Mancha) $11 84 *—M.S. (8/1/2005)*

Montalvo Wilmot 2003 Gran Baco de Oro Cabernet Sauvignon (La Mancha) $12. 82 *—M.S. (10/1/2005)*

MONTE DON LUCIO

Monte Don Lucio 2000 Reserva Tempranillo-Cabernet Sauvignon (La Mancha) $8. 84 Best Buy *—M.S. (4/1/2006)*

MONTE NEGRO

Monte Negro 2005 Tempranillo (Ribera del Duero) $16. Blackberry and bramble work the nose, with a medium-bodied, generously oaked palate to follow. In the mouth, buttery oak leads the way with dark fruit, wood resin and chewiness coming next. Not overly tannic, but short on the finish. Pretty easygoing as a whole. **85** *—M.S. (6/1/2007)*

Monte Negro 2004 Tempranillo (Ribera del Duero) $16. Generic and maturing, but still juicy and showing proper tannins and mouthfeel. A middleweight with securing balance and decent fruit intensity, it's mouth-filling and uncomplicated, with finishing notes of coconut and mocha. **86** *—M.S. (6/1/2007)*

Monte Negro 2001 Crianza Tempranillo (Ribera del Duero) $28. Freshness is in demand as the nose shows dampness, tobacco and wood more than bright fruit. In the mouth, there's oak-driven flavors of vanilla and tobacco accenting basic red fruit. Has a lot of snap and zest but comes off kind of thin and on the mature side. Drink now for best results; its lifespan appears limited. **85** *—M.S. (6/1/2007)*

MONTE PINADILLO

Monte Pinadillo 1997 Crianza Tempranillo (Ribera del Duero) $20. 82 *—J.C. (11/1/2001)*

MONTEBACO

Montebaco 2001 Crianza Red Blend (Ribera del Duero) $20. 88 *—M.S. (11/1/2006)*

Montebaco 2001 Selección Especial Red Blend (Ribera del Duero) $40. 89 *—M.S. (11/1/2006)*

Montebaco 2003 Selección Especial Tempranillo Blend (Ribera del Duero) $40. 89 *(11/15/2006)*

Montebaco 2003 Semele Tempranillo Blend (Ribera del Duero) $16. 86 *(11/15/2006)*

MONTECASTRO

Montecastro 2004 Tempranillo (Ribera del Duero) $45. Moist soil, cola and molasses aromas all indicate depth, oak and ripeness, while the palate is full, fairly juicy and saturated with serious black fruit flavors. Additional prune and chocolate notes come on toward the finish, cementing this wine's meaty, somewhat modern personality. It gets better with airing and will not suffer from a few years in the cellar. **91** *—M.S. (6/1/2007)*

Montecastro 2003 y Llanahermosa Tempranillo (Ribera del Duero) $36. Flat, murky and mildly vegetal on the nose, and no matter how many times you swirl and sniff that's what comes out of it. Bottom line: it's a stewy, pruny Tempranillo with baked flavors and hard tannins. **81** *—M.S. (6/1/2007)*

Montecastro 2003 Tinto del Pais (Ribera del Duero) $36. 83 *—M.S. (12/15/2006)*

MONTECILLO

Montecillo 1994 130 Edicion Limitada Gran Reserva Tempranillo (Rioja) $50. 83 *—M.S. (8/1/2005)*

Montecillo 2003 Crianza Tempranillo (Rioja) $11. Smooth, savory and spicy, but with enough red-fruit character to ensure that it doesn't taste dull. The palate offers orderly berry and pepper flavors, while it ends with vanilla and a hint of campfire. Juicy and fairly fresh, but a little thin and watery across the palate. Imported by W.J. Deutsch & Sons. **85** *—M.S. (12/15/2007)*

Montecillo 2002 Crianza Tempranillo (Rioja) $11. Red cherry, cough drop and a touch of mushroom work the nose, while in the mouth it's crisp and pointed, with light red fruit and citrus-influenced flavors. A lean, lithe wine very much in the pie cherry realm. **84** *—M.S. (9/1/2007)*

Montecillo 2001 Crianza Tempranillo (Rioja) $10. 85 Best Buy *—M.S. (6/1/2005)*

Montecillo 1998 Crianza Tempranillo (Rioja) $10. 85 *—M.M. (9/1/2002)*

Montecillo 1998 Gran Reserva Tempranillo (Rioja) $26. 89 *—M.S. (11/1/2006)*

Montecillo 1996 Gran Reserva Tempranillo (Rioja) $23. 87 *—M.S. (6/1/2005)*

Montecillo 1994 Gran Reserva Tempranillo (Rioja) $23. 89 *—M.M. (9/1/2002)*

Montecillo 2001 Reserva Tempranillo (Rioja) $20. Plenty of dusty, spicy aromas run the nose, almost to the exclusion of ripe fruit. But once it opens the wine displays savory flavors as well as some pure dark berry. On the finish, it's a touch lean and crisp, but overall this is a balanced Rioja reserva with spunk. **87** *—M.S. (9/1/2007)*

Montecillo 2000 Reserva Tempranillo (Rioja) $16. 86 *—M.S. (11/1/2006)*

Montecillo 1997 Reserva Tempranillo (Rioja) $17. 86 *—M.M. (11/1/2002)*

Montecillo 1996 Reserva Tempranillo (Rioja) $17. 86 *—M.M. (9/1/2002)*

Montecillo 1991 Selección Especial Gran Reserva Tempranillo (Rioja) $65. 92 Cellar Selection *—M.S. (12/31/2004)*

Montecillo 1985 Selección Especial Gran Reserva Tempranillo (Rioja) $65. 89 *—M.S. (12/31/2004)*

Montecillo 1982 Selección Especial Gran Reserva Tempranillo (Rioja) $75. 90 *—M.S. (12/31/2004)*

Montecillo 1981 Selección Especial Gran Reserva Tempranillo (Rioja) $75. 91 *—M.S. (12/31/2004)*

Montecillo 2006 Viura (Rioja) $9. Bland as they come, with tangy white fruit and green veggies doctoring up the palate. Try as you may, there's just nothing much to latch on to. Imported by W.J. Deutsch & Sons. **80** *—M.S. (11/1/2007)*

Montecillo 2005 Viura (Rioja) $8. Creamy vanilla and apple aromas are not upheld on the poorly defined, watery palate. All you get in terms of flavor is citrus peel and some mineral. Not offensive or aggressive; but it leaves you bored. Imported by W.J. Deutsch & Sons. **82** *—M.S. (2/1/2007)*

Montecillo 2004 Viura (Rioja) $8. 80 *—M.S. (7/1/2005)*

Montecillo 2003 Viura (Rioja) $8. 80 *—M.S. (12/31/2004)*

Montecillo 2002 Viura (Rioja) $10. 84 *—M.S. (9/1/2004)*

MONTECRUZ

Montecruz 2005 Tempranillo (Valdepeñas) $10. Cloudy red in color, with musky berry aromas. The palate shows some cherry and raspberry, while the feel is sort of rough. A classic country wine that isn't about to rock anyone's world. **82** *—M.S. (8/1/2007)*

MONTEGAREDO

Montegaredo 2000 Piramide Red Blend (Ribera del Duero) $20. 83 *—C.S. (11/1/2002)*

Montegaredo 1999 Crianza Tempranillo (Ribera del Duero) $19. 88 *—K.F. (11/1/2002)*

Montegaredo 1999 Tinto Tempranillo (Ribera del Duero) $13. 88 Best Buy *—K.F. (11/1/2002)*

MONTESIERRA

Montesierra 1999 Tinta de Toro (Somontano) $7. 81 —*M.M. (9/1/2002)*

MONTSARRA

Montsarra NV Brut Sparkling Blend (Cava) $16. More in the Champagne style, meaning the nose is yeasty and toasty, and the color is more gold than pale yellow. The palate offers wholesome apple, lemon and green herb flavors, and the finish is dry and peppery, with some bitterness. Strives for more complexity than most Cavas, and it gets there for the most part. 87 —*M.S. (12/15/2007)*

Montsarra NV Brut Sparkling Blend (Cava) $15. 84 —*M.S. (6/1/2005)*

MORGADIO

Morgadio 2004 Albariño (Rías Baixas) $20. 88 —*M.S. (11/15/2005)*

Morgadio 2003 Albariño (Rías Baixas) $19. 86 —*M.S. (9/1/2004)*

Morgadio 2002 Albariño (Rías Baixas) $18. 87 —*M.S. (3/1/2004)*

Morgadio 2000 Albariño (Rías Baixas) $19. 85 —*M.M. (9/1/2002)*

Morgadio 1999 Albariño (Rías Baixas) $20. 89 —*M.M. (8/1/2000)*

MORLANDA

Morlanda 2001 Criança Red Blend (Priorat) $48. 84 —*M.S. (3/1/2005)*

Morlanda 1998 Crianza Red Blend (Priorat) $46. 84 —*M.M. (9/1/2002)*

Morlanda 2002 Vi de Guarda Red Blend (Priorat) $48. 85 —*M.S. (10/1/2005)*

Morlanda 2000 Vi de Guarda Red Blend (Priorat) $48. 88 —*M.S. (3/1/2004)*

MUGA

Muga 1996 Reserva Tempranillo Blend (Rioja) $17. 89 —*M.M. (8/1/2000)*

Muga 2006 Rosé Blend (Rioja) $11. Despite some tempered oak aging, this one will whet your whistle and then some. Talk about cutting acidity and being fit and trim; it's like a hard-bodied personal trainer. It doesn't have an ounce of fat on it, so the aromas are tight and minerally and the flavors lean and crisp. Will plow through grilled vegetables and chicken or tuna salad with ease. Made primarily from Garnacha, with some Viura and Tempranillo. 88 **Best Buy** —*M.S. (7/1/2007)*

Muga 2005 Rosé Blend (Rioja) $11. Muga always makes one of Spain's most ethereal, balanced pink wines; and the 2005, while starting to show its age, is quite nice and still offering plenty. The color and aromas are light and attractive, while the zesty peach, tangerine and strawberry flavors will bring you back to summer. 88 —*M.S. (4/1/2007)*

Muga 2002 Rosé Blend (Rioja) $9. 89 **Best Buy** —*M.S. (11/15/2003)*

Muga 1999 Rosada Rosé Blend (Rioja) $10. 87 —*M.M. (8/1/2000)*

Muga 2004 Aro Tempranillo (Rioja) $194. Plant-by-plant fruit selection leads to intensity, concentration and structure. Aro shows gripping tannins and juicy acidity, and overall it reeks of power and precision. At this young stage it seems like it could last forever. In reality, it should be just right in about seven years. Imported by Tempranillo, Inc. 94 —*M.S. (9/1/2007)*

Muga 1991 Prado Enea Gran Reserva Tempranillo (Rioja) $41. 92 —*M.M. (8/1/2000)*

Muga 1994 Reserva Seleccion Especial Tempranillo (Rioja) $29. 91 —*M.M. (8/1/2000)*

Muga 2004 Torre Muga Tempranillo (Rioja) $90. This seems eminently ageworthy; it has the strong foundation and pulsing acidity required of a true cellar dweller. The raspberry and plum fruit have a beam of acidity and the tannins are not shy. Shows all the hallmarks of a fine modern Rioja: power, purity and balance. Imported by Tempranillo, Inc. 91 **Cellar Selection** —*M.S. (9/1/2007)*

Muga 1996 Torre Muga Tempranillo (Rioja) $60. 92 —*M.M. (8/1/2000)*

Muga 2001 Aro Tempranillo Blend (Rioja) $179. 90 —*M.S. (6/1/2005)*

Muga 1995 Prado Enea Gran Reserva Tempranillo Blend (Rioja) $41. 90 —*M.S. (3/1/2004)*

Muga 2002 Reserve Tempranillo Blend (Rioja) $23. A good effort in a tough year, and frankly we're happy that Muga decided to make a reserva in 2002. The wine shows lean aromas of dried red fruit, tomato leaf and dill. In fact, dill is a recurring theme from front to back. And along the way there's acids, red cherries, plums and currants. Good but leaner than a normal Muga effort. 87 —*M.S. (9/1/2007)*

Muga 1999 Reserva Tempranillo Blend (Rioja) $19. 89 —*M.S. (3/1/2004)*

Muga 1996 Reserva Selección Especial Tempranillo Blend (Rioja) $31. 90 —*M.S. (3/1/2004)*

Muga 2001 Selección Especial Reserva Tempranillo Blend (Rioja) $37. Robust and sexy, with smoke, leather and pure berry and plum aromas that make for a sensational bouquet. The palate is up to the precedent set by the nose, as the cherry and cola flavors are outright lovely. For what you get, this is almost a value. It shows us what that Muga can do in a great vintage. 92 **Editors' Choice** —*M.S. (9/1/2007)*

Muga 1998 Torre Muga Tempranillo Blend (Rioja) $45. 93 **Editors' Choice** —*M.S. (3/1/2004)*

Muga 2005 Viura (Rioja) $13. For a good price you get a lot of white wine here. Muga barrel ferments this Viura, so there's popcorn and richness to the nose, but it's not overwhelming. And in the mouth, the lemon, orange and tangerine flavors are flat-out lovely. Pour a glass of this with your next platter of sizzling garlic shrimp and you'll be in heaven. 89 **Best Buy** —*M.S. (9/1/2007)*

Muga 1999 Barrel Fermented White Blend (Rioja) $11. 88 **Best Buy** —*M.M. (8/1/2000)*

Muga 2002 Blanco White Blend (Rioja) $11. 87 —*M.S. (3/1/2004)*

MURUVE

Muruve 1998 Crianza Tinta de Toro (Toro) $12. 82 —*D.T. (4/1/2003)*

Muruve 1996 Crianza Tinta de Toro (Toro) $13. 91 **Best Buy** —*M.S. (8/1/2000)*

MUSEUM

Museum 2000 Crianza Tempranillo (Cigales) $14. 84 —*M.S. (9/1/2004)*

Museum 2002 Real Reserva Tempranillo (Cigales) $25. 86 —*M.S. (12/15/2006)*

Museum 2001 Real Reserva Tempranillo (Cigales) $24. 88 —*M.S. (4/1/2006)*

Museum 2000 Real Reserva Tempranillo (Cigales) $23. 86 —*M.S. (8/1/2005)*

Museum 2001 Crianza Tinto del Pais (Cigales) $14. 86 —*M.S. (11/1/2006)*

MUTUO

Mutuo 2001 Crianza Organic Tempranillo Blend (Rioja) $17. 85 —*M.S. (11/1/2006)*

NAIA

Naia 2005 Verdejo (Rueda) $13. Slightly heavy and seemingly ripe based on the apple cider and citrus blossom aromas. The palate confirms its health by showing baked apple and sweet citrus flavors. A proper wine that's big and peachy but not overdone. 86 —*M.S. (2/1/2007)*

Naia 2004 Verdejo (Rueda) $13. 88 **Best Buy** —*M.S. (11/15/2005)*

Naia 2003 Verdejo (Rueda) $13. 86 —*M.S. (8/1/2005)*

Naia 2004 Naiades Verdejo (Rueda) $28. Big and yellow, which is evidence of the oak aging on this plump, modern Verdejo that's made in small quantity and will appeal to those who like things such as Sémillon and Chenin Blanc. The body is full, there's fruit, weight and grip, and the ripeness versus minerality is just right. Drink now with cheese or fish. 300 cases produced. 89 —*M.S. (8/1/2007)*

NEO

Neo 2004 Tempranillo (Ribera del Duero) $58. Smooth as silk and deep as night, this is a wonderful new-age wine with voluminous tree bark, maple and cassis aromas as well as a sweet undertext of perfume. The palate presents the truest mix of weight and finesse, and the finish is coffee, fine-knit tannins and length. Drinkable now with food, or hold for up to five years. 93 **Editors' Choice** —*M.S. (6/1/2007)*

Neo 2003 Tempranillo (Ribera del Duero) $58. If the name doesn't say it clearly enough, then the excellent color, ripeness and well-toasted nose indicate that Neo is a modern-style wine. It's from old vines, and the cherry, cassis and cola flavors are the real deal as far as Tempranillo goes. A really well-made wine that's not too complicated or tannic to drink now. Best by mid-2008. 91 —*M.S. (6/1/2007)*

NESSA

Nessa 2005 Albariño (Rías Baixas) $12. At this price, you can't go wrong. At least not with this wine, which veers toward the lush and sweet as it pumps out aromas of melon, pear and almonds. The palate is crisp enough, but not jagged. Flavors of apple and citrus are zesty and correct. Act fast to get it while it's fresh. 88 —*M.S. (4/1/2007)*

NOBUL RED

Nobul Red 2003 Tempranillo (Vinos de Madrid) $7. 82 —*M.S. (6/1/2005)*

NORA

Nora 2005 Albariño (Rías Baixas) $16. Buttercup and apple pie aromas are inviting, while the round palate offers apple, pear, melon and even banana flavors. Slightly more soft than others in the class, but it's tasty and long on the finish. Drink up now and enjoy. 87 —*M.S. (4/1/2007)*

Nora 2004 Albariño (Rías Baixas) $16. 85 —*M.S. (11/15/2005)*

Nora 2003 Albariño (Rías Baixas) $16. 88 *—M.S. (8/1/2005)*

Nora 2002 Albariño (Rías Baixas) $13. 86 *—M.S. (3/1/2004)*

NORA DE NEVE

Nora da Neve 2004 Albariño (Rías Baixas) $28. At first whiff you may not be impressed; the nose offers abnormal butterscotch and honey. But once you get into the wine you'll encounter feminine orange, lemon, melon and custard flavors sitting on the plumpest, most comfortable palate in Galicia. Purity of fruit is by far the wine's leading attribute. 90 *—M.S. (4/1/2007)*

NOS RIQUEZA

Nos Riqueza 2003 9 Meses Tinto del Pais (Ribera del Duero) $33. A little peppery and lean, but time unleashes more heft, char and fruit than what's initially evident. In the mouth, it's full of plump berry and cherry notes, and maybe a touch of raisin (2003 was a hot year). Not the most agile, finesse-based red but still very good. 88 *—M.S. (6/1/2007)*

NUMANTHIA-TERMES, S.L.

Numanthia-Termes, S.L. 2003 Numanthia Tinta de Toro (Toro) $57. Mammoth from the beginning. The nose practically bleeds black fruit, fine leather and charcoal. Calling the bouquet alluring would be conservative. In the mouth, the wine pumps black cherry, cassis and enough acidity to coax out plenty of complexity and vitality. Huge but not a clod, with finishing flavors of mocha and bitter chocolate. 94 Editors' Choice *—M.S. (2/1/2007)*

Numanthia-Termes, S.L. 2003 Termanthia Tinta de Toro (Toro) $201. Sly in the early innings and then menthol, forest, spice, charcoal and earthy black-fruit aromas emerge to rally this bruiser into its prime, which entails monster fruit flavors, rugged tannins, and a stout, peppery finish. The core power on this wine is beyond reproach. Will cellar nicely for at least five years, possibly more. 96 Cellar Selection *—M.S. (2/1/2007)*

Numanthia-Termes, S.L. 2003 Termes Tinta de Toro (Toro) $26. The warmth of 2003 infused this wine with weight, power and lusciousness. On the other hand, there's a slight bit of raisin, marzipan and bitter chocolate that come from the vintage. In between you'll find Termes' patented dark berry flavors, earthiness and tannins. An excellent effort that should be best in 2008. 92 *—M.S. (2/1/2007)*

Numanthia-Termes, S.L. 2000 Numanthia Tinta de Toro (Toro) $45. 89 *—M.S. (3/1/2004)*

Numanthia-Termes, S.L. 2001 Termanthia Tinta de Toro (Toro) $175. 95 Cellar Selection *—M.S. (6/1/2005)*

Numanthia-Termes, S.L. 2000 Termes Tinta de Toro (Toro) $21. 93 Editors' Choice *—M.S. (3/1/2004)*

Numanthia-Termes, S.L. 1999 Termes Tinta de Toro (Toro) $21. 90 *—M.S. (3/1/2004)*

O. FOURNIER

O. Fournier 2004 AlfaSpiga Tinto del Pais (Ribera del Duero) $54. Twenty months in oak has created coconut aromas to go with the ripe, sappy boysenberry scents that are draped on this studly, full-force RDD. The palate is a powder keg of massive blackberry, boysenberry and chocolate flavors, and the finish is like a retaining wall that keeps everything focused on the impressive midpalate. Great if you like 'em big. Imported by Fine Wines from Spain. 93 Editors' Choice *—M.S. (11/1/2007)*

O. Fournier 2003 AlfaSpiga Tinto del Pais (Ribera del Duero) $49. Intense and deep, with plenty of licorice, leather and pepper encasing serious dark-berry aromas. The wine runs round and full in the mouth, with chewy berry flavors, meaty tannins and a generous finish that's long and just a touch lemony from the wine's 20 months in barrel. A wine that speaks to you. 91 *—M.S. (8/1/2007)*

O. Fournier 2004 Ribera del Duero Tinto del Pais (Ribera del Duero) $85. Rock-solid Tempranillo that wows with its richness and depth, but also shows a touch of ripeness-based sweetness that critics could see as candied and simple. But that's splitting hairs, and we prefer to compliment the wine's dynamite intensity and its rangy finish. Maybe a touch bigger and less complex than Fournier's AlfaSpiga, but still excellent. Imported by Fine Wines from Spain. 92 *—M.S. (11/1/2007)*

O. Fournier 2004 Spiga Tinto del Pais (Ribera del Duero) $33. Some early gas and sulfuric aromas blow off from the nose, leaving meaty berry scents. This wine sports a natural personality; it mixes leather and herb notes with polished but not overdone berry and plum flavors. And the finish is rich with molasses and leather. Probably best from 2008 through 2012. Imported by Fine Wines from Spain. 91 *—M.S. (11/1/2007)*

O. Fournier 2003 Spiga Tinto del Pais (Ribera del Duero) $30. Bring on the funk, at least at first. This new-to-America wine gets out of the gate with wild leather, stable and bramble aromas, and there's always an aggressive, untamed quality to it. But with air it settles, and eventually true Tempranillo flavors emerge. More challenging than it should be. 85 *—M.S. (8/1/2007)*

OCHOA

Ochoa 2003 Rosado Rosé Blend (Navarra) $10. 88 Best Buy *—M.S. (10/1/2004)*

Ochoa 2003 Viura-Chardonnay White Blend (Navarra) $10. 87 Best Buy *—M.S. (10/1/2004)*

OLIVER CONTI

Oliver Conti 1999 Bordeaux Blend (Emporadà-Costa Brava) $43. 89 *—M.S. (3/1/2004)*

Oliver Conti 1998 Bordeaux Blend (Emporadà-Costa Brava) $39. 89 *—M.M. (4/1/2002)*

ONIX

Onix 1999 Red Blend (Priorat) $12. 88 Best Buy *—M.M. (4/1/2002)*

Onix 2005 Clàssic Tempranillo (Priorat) $13. Dark cherry, raspberry, mineral and black pepper aromas start this value-driven Priorat on its way. The palate features high-toned, borderline tart black cherry and plum flavors, while the finish shows a bit of resiny oak that translates into spice and vanilla. A reasonable wine; juicy but not very rich. 85 *—M.S. (4/1/2007)*

ORBALLO

Orballo 2003 Albariño (Rías Baixas) $17. 87 *—M.S. (8/1/2005)*

OREADES

Oreades 2005 Tempranillo (Navarra) $9. No matter how you slice it, this wine shows a lot of muddled compost on both the nose and palate. It has decent texture and an adequate mouthfeel, but as you chew on the wine you can't escape the cooked, saucy flavors that point to overripeness. 82 *—M.S. (12/15/2007)*

Oreades 2003 Tempranillo (Navarra) $9. Simple red fruit gives way to raisiny aromas on the burly, fairly sedate nose. Raisin and plum flavors emerge on the palate, and they are followed by lasting notes of licorice and sherry. Not exactly jazzy but has its merits. 84 *—M.S. (2/1/2007)*

ORIEL

Oriel 2004 Barona Albariño (Rías Baixas) $20. 84 *—M.S. (9/1/2006)*

Oriel 2001 Alma de Llicorella Red Blend (Priorat) $35. 87 *—M.S. (10/1/2005)*

Oriel 2003 Setena Red Blend (Terra Alta) $18. 81 *—M.S. (10/1/2005)*

ORIGIN

Origin 2003 Tempranillo (Tierra de Castilla) $11. 80 *—M.S. (8/1/2005)*

Origin 1998 Reserva Tempranillo Blend (Rioja) $24. 85 *—M.S. (6/1/2005)*

ORISTAN

Oristan 1993 Reserva Cabernet Sauvignon-Tempranillo (La Mancha) $10. 86 *—J.C. (11/15/1999)*

Oristan 1995 Reserva Cencibel (La Mancha) $10. 83 *(8/1/2000)*

OSBORNE

Osborne 2001 Dominio de Malpica Cabernet Sauvignon (Tierra de Castilla) $13. 84 *—M.S. (12/31/2004)*

Osborne 2000 Solaz Cabernet Sauvignon-Tempranillo (Tierra de Castilla) $7. 85 Best Buy *—M.M. (11/1/2002)*

Osborne 2005 Solaz Merlot-Tempranillo Red Blend (Vino de la Tierra de Castilla) $9. A blend of 65% Merlot with 35% Tempranillo; the nose offers olive, black plum and a touch of resiny young oak. Black fruit, coffee and juicy acidity work the palate, and then some medium tannins and grab come up late. Not that complex but entirely satisfying, and consistent with past vintages that offered very good value for money. 87 Best Buy *—M.S. (11/1/2007)*

Osborne NV Fino Quinta Palomino (Jerez) $14. 90 Best Buy *—M.S. (6/1/2005)*

Osborne NV Rare Sherry Pedro Ximénez Viejo (Jerez) $120. 91 *—M.S. (6/1/2005)*

Osborne NV 10RF Oloroso Medium Sherry (Jerez) $14. 90 Best Buy *—M.S. (8/1/2003)*

Osborne NV Bailen Dry Oloroso Sherry (Jerez) $14. 90 Best Buy *—M.S. (10/1/2005)*

Osborne NV Cream Sherry (Jerez) $10. 86 Best Buy *—M.S. (10/1/2005)*

Osborne NV Manzanilla Sherry (Jerez) $14. 87 *—M.S. (8/1/2005)*

Osborne NV Medium Amontillado Sherry (Jerez) $10. 88 Best Buy *—M.S. (8/1/2005)*

Osborne NV Pale Dry Fino Sherry (Jerez) $10. 87 Best Buy *—M.S. (8/1/2005)*

Osborne NV Pedro Ximénez 1827 Sweet Sherry (Jerez) $14. 94 Best Buy —*M.S. (8/1/2003)*

Osborne NV Solera AOS Rare Amontillado Sherry (Jerez) $60. 87 —*M.S. (8/1/2005)*

Osborne NV Solera Primera Rare Amontillado Sherry (Jerez) $90. 90 —*M.S. (8/1/2005)*

Osborne 2004 Solaz Shiraz-Tempranillo (Vino de la Tierra de Castilla) $8. 84 Best Buy —*M.S. (11/1/2006)*

Osborne 2001 Señorio del Cid Crianza Tempranillo (Ribera del Duero) $21. Classic in many ways, this wine shows maturity and much of what Ribera del Duero is known for. It offers a nice balance between Old World leather and tomato notes and more modern plum, meat and oak characteristics. It has good tannins and the right amount of vanilla. Drink now or over the next year or two. 89 —*M.S. (6/1/2007)*

Osborne 1999 Solaz Tempranillo Blend (Tierra de Castilla) $7. 82 —*M.M. (9/1/2002)*

Osborne 2001 Tempranillo-Cabernet Sauvignon (Tierra de Castilla) $8. 88 —*P.G. (11/15/2004)*

Osborne 2004 Solaz Tempranillo-Cabernet Sauvignon (Viño de la Tierra de Castilla) $8. 83 —*M.S. (11/1/2006)*

Osborne 2003 Solaz Tempranillo-Cabernet Sauvignon (Tierra de Castilla) $8. 86 Best Buy —*M.S. (10/1/2005)*

Osborne 2001 Solaz Tempranillo-Cabernet Sauvignon (Viño de la Tierra de Castilla) $8. 87 Best Buy —*M.S. (9/1/2004)*

Osborne 2005 Solaz Blanco Viura (Viño de la Tierra de Castilla) $8. 87 Best Buy —*M.S. (11/15/2006)*

Osborne 2004 Solaz Blanco Viura (Viño de la Tierra de Castilla) $8. 83 —*M.S. (11/1/2006)*

Osborne Selección 2002 Dominio de Malpica Cabernet Sauvignon (Viño de la Tierra de Castilla) $15. 84 —*M.S. (11/15/2005)*

Osborne Selección 2000 Señorio del Cid Crianza Tempranillo (Ribera del Duero) $20. 85 —*M.S. (12/31/2004)*

OSTATU

Ostatu 2004 Crianza Tempranillo (Rioja) $19. Fans of big, blocky reds that offer punch, extract and tannins should jump on this now, and then watch it age nicely for the next four or five years. That's the type of meaty, tannic, fruit-infused Tempranillo this is. It's always going to be short and stocky, but still it will round into shape as it matures. 88 —*M.S. (9/1/2007)*

Ostatu 2000 Crianza Tempranillo (Rioja) $16. 87 —*M.S. (3/1/2004)*

Ostatu 2003 Gloria de Ostatu Tempranillo (Rioja) $75. Full and ready, this fabulous wine from Rioja Alavesa sets the bar very high for any of its Vanguardia co-runners. Gloria hits hard with bacon, tire rubber, tobacco and pastry crust aromas, but also pure dark fruit. Then it's wave after wave of boysenberry and crisped brown sugar flavors prior to a finale of heady European chocolate. Need we say more? 750 cases produced; best now through 2011. 95 Editors' Choice —*M.S. (9/1/2007)*

Ostatu 2002 Reserva Tempranillo (Rioja) $28. A dense wine from the start, and each subsequent whiff of the oaky but vital nose is convincing. The palate here is exemplary, especially for an '02; there's dark berry and plum flavors backed by notes of black licorice and pepper. An exceedingly nice wine with a textbook mix of tannins, flesh and acidity. 91 —*M.S. (9/1/2007)*

Ostatu 2005 Cosecha White Blend (Rioja) $11. This is an easy, sweeter style of Viura that emits aromas of peaches and pears. The palate is lively enough but not exactly zesty, and the flavors run toward pink grapefruit and other citrus fruits; but think sweet, nice fruits—not sour ones. Has all the hallmarks of a good apéritif wine. 86 Best Buy —*M.S. (9/1/2007)*

OTANON

Otanon 1998 Crianza 1998 Red Blend (Rioja) $14. 86 —*M.M. (9/1/2002)*

OTAZU

Otazu 2000 Chardonnay (Navarra) $11. 86 —*C.S. (4/1/2002)*

Otazu 1999 Barriqua Chardonnay (Navarra) $14. 89 Best Buy —*C.S. (4/1/2002)*

Otazu 2002 Palacio de Otazu Chardonnay (Navarra) $14. 86 —*M.S. (10/1/2004)*

Otazu 1997 Palacio de Erite-Crianza Red Blend (Navarra) $12. 86 —*C.S. (4/1/2002)*

Otazu 1997 Palacio de Otazu-Crianza Red Blend (Navarra) $16. 86 —*C.S. (11/1/2002)*

Otazu 1997 Reserva Red Blend (Navarra) $19. 90 Cellar Selection —*C.S. (4/1/2002)*

PAGO DE CARRAOVEJAS

Pago de Carraovejas 2004 Crianza Tempranillo-Cabernet Sauvignon (Ribera del Duero) $44. Almost jolting in how the nose differs from the competition. Here, you get an early blast of rhubarb and wet dog along with herbal strawberry. Never does the wine shed that herbal character, so at all points there's a touch of tobacco, bell pepper and bramble. 85 —*M.S. (6/1/2007)*

PAGO DE LA JARABA

Pago de la Jaraba 2003 Crianza Tempranillo Blend (La Mancha) $10. 82 —*M.S. (12/15/2006)*

PAGO DE LOS CAPELLANES

Pago de los Capellanes 1996 Crianza Red Blend (Ribera del Duero) $25. 88 —*J.C. (11/1/2001)*

Pago de los Capellanes 2001 Jóven Roble Tempranillo (Ribera del Duero) $28. 90 Best Buy —*R.V. (11/15/2002)*

Pago de los Capellanes 2003 Parcela El Picón Tempranillo (Ribera del Duero) $225. This high-priced 2003 parcel-based Tempranillo hits with funky citrus peel and wet clay aromas, which are followed by cherry and savory, almost stewy berry flavors. The heat of 2003 is evidenced on the soft, hollow finish. It's a very good wine with character and typicity—but for $225? 89 —*M.S. (11/1/2007)*

Pago de los Capellanes 1998 Reserva Tempranillo (Ribera del Duero) $22. 90 Editors' Choice —*M.S. (11/1/2002)*

Pago de los Capellanes 2004 Tinto Crianza Tempranillo (Ribera del Duero) $34. A mile deep on the nose. The palate starts out grapy and jammy and then develops to show herb-infused plum and berry flavors. The finish of chocolate and black truffle ensures that this is a top-level wine. Drink now through 2014. 90 —*M.S. (11/1/2007)*

Pago de los Capellanes 1996 Reserva Tinto del Pais (Ribera del Duero) $37. 89 —*J.C. (11/1/2001)*

Pago de los Capellanes 1999 Tinto Jóven Tinto del Pais (Ribera del Duero) $13. 84 —*J.C. (11/1/2001)*

PAGO DEL VOSTAL

Pago del Vostal 2002 Crianza Tinto del Pais (Ribera del Duero) $14. 83 —*M.S. (2/1/2006)*

Pago del Vostal 2001 Reserva Tinto del Pais (Ribera del Duero) $20. This wine delivers a touch too much barnyard, and even when it settles, what's left is slightly leafy and murky. Beyond that, it's a holdover from a good vintage, so along with stark tannins and old-style Ribera ruggedness there's cranberry, pine and leather notes. Drink now. 85 —*M.S. (4/1/2007)*

Pago del Vostal 2004 Tinto Jóven Tinto del Pais (Ribera del Duero) $10. 84 —*M.S. (4/1/2006)*

PAGOS DE VALDE ORCA

Pagos de Valde Orca 2000 Tempranillo (Rioja) $45. 84 —*M.S. (4/1/2006)*

PAGOS DEL REY

Pagos Del Rey 2002 Condado de Oriza Reserva Tempranillo (Ribera del Duero) $15. Vanilla and dill aromas are front and center. The palate imparts plum skin and red-apple flavors, with lots of rough tannins holding the feel hostage. There just isn't a lot of meat on the bones, so it comes across like a mouth full of hardware. Imported by Luneau USA, Inc. 84 —*M.S. (8/1/2007)*

PAIXAR

Paixar 2004 Mencía (Bierzo) $80. This small-production, ultraexpressive Bierzo features dynamite structure and intensity, a clear reflection of old vines grown at altitude. The nose exudes minerality and dense black fruit along with a good whack of fine French oak. The palate runs for miles while distributing warmth, richness, chocolate, minerality and length. Already drinking well but will age nicely for another 3–5 years. 92 Cellar Selection —*M.S. (11/1/2007)*

PALACIO DE BORNOS

Palacio de Bornos 2004 Verdejo (Rueda) $14. 88 —*M.S. (9/1/2006)*

Palacio de Bornos 2003 Verdejo (Rueda) $10. 86 Best Buy —*M.S. (9/1/2004)*

PALACIO DE FEFIÑANES

Palacio de Fefiñanes 2005 Albariño (Rías Baixas) $20. 87 —*M.S. (9/1/2006)*

PALACIO DE LA VEGA

Palacio de La Vega 2000 Conde de La Vega Selección Privada Cabernet Blend (Navarra) $20. 86 —*M.S. (12/31/2004)*

Palacio de La Vega 2000 Reserva Cabernet Sauvignon (Navarra) $13. 85 —*M.S. (12/31/2004)*

Palacio de La Vega 2000 Crianza Cabernet Sauvignon-Tempranillo (Navarra) $9. 82 —*M.S. (12/31/2004)*

Palacio de La Vega 1999 Reserva Tempranillo (Navarra) $13. 81 —*M.S. (3/1/2005)*

PALACIO DE VILLACHICA

Palacio de Villachica 2003 3T Tinta de Toro (Toro) $12. 82 —*M.S. (10/1/2005)*

Palacio de Villachica 2001 4T Tinta de Toro (Toro) $14. 81 —*M.S. (10/1/2005)*

Palacio de Villachica 2001 5T Tinta de Toro (Toro) $19. 87 —*M.S. (10/1/2005)*

PALACIOS REMONDO

Palacios Remondo 2001 Propiedad Herencia Remondo Red Blend (Rioja) $28. 92 —*M.S. (6/1/2005)*

Palacios Remondo 2003 La Montesa Crianza Tempranillo (Rioja) $15. More earthy, ripe and bulky than normal, with a lot of smoky/savory aromas. The cherry and apple-skin palate is propelled initially by acidity, and then core depth comes up. For a hot vintage, this wine is expectedly melting and warm. But it still has enough gusto and acid to keep it moving. Drink now through 2008 (with food) and you'll be happy. 88 —*M.S. (2/1/2007)*

Palacios Remondo 2005 La Vendimia Tempranillo (Rioja) $30. Early aromas of leather, rubber and char sort of shadow the fruit component. But in the mouth there's ample blackberry, cherry and pepper, all of which bring the wine into form. In terms of mouthfeel, it's good. And on the finish it's got some of that espresso bitterness that sings of toasted barrels. 87 —*M.S. (9/1/2007)*

Palacios Remondo 2003 Propiedad Tempranillo (Rioja) $19. Good Rioja from a challenging vintage; the nose deals cherry and a dusting of spices, before turning sharper and leaner with air. Like in previous years, the wine veers toward elegance as it shows red fruit and tea flavors before a grabby, firm finish. Not the best Propiedad but once again, the year was problematic. 87 —*M.S. (4/1/2007)*

Palacios Remondo 2001 Propiedad Herencia Remondo Tempranillo Blend (Rioja) $25. 92 —*M.S. (9/1/2004)*

PANARROZ

Panarroz 2005 Red Red Blend (Jumilla) $10. No matter how you slice this up, it comes out smelling and tasting sharp and burnt. The nose is brambly and fiery, while the mouth is peppery and rough. Hard and jagged at every turn, thus you need the pan y arroz (bread and rice), to absorb the wine's kick. 82 —*M.S. (8/1/2007)*

PAÑUELO

Pañuelo 2002 Merlot-Cabernet Sauvignon (Navarra) $11. 84 —*M.S. (10/1/2005)*

Pañuelo 2002 Garnacha-Tempranillo Tempranillo Blend (Navarra) $11. 84 —*M.S. (10/1/2005)*

PÁRAMO DE GUZMÁN

Páramo de Guzmán 2000 Crianza Tempranillo (Ribera del Duero) $31. 87 —*M.S. (6/1/2005)*

Páramo de Guzmán 2003 Roble Tempranillo (Ribera del Duero) $19. 85 —*M.S. (8/1/2005)*

PARDEVALLES

Pardevalles 2005 Gamonal Prieto Picudo (Vino de Calidad de Tierras de León) $20. Prieto Picudo is a variety unknown to most wine drinkers. And that's probably a good thing, because the grape yields acidic, tight, astringent wines like this. Yes, there's color and size here, but there's not much balance or charm. 80 —*M.S. (11/1/2007)*

PARTAL

Partal 1998 Crianza Monastrell (Bullas) $25. 88 —*M.M. (4/1/2002)*

PARXET

Parxet 2004 Marqués de Alella Clasico Pansa Blanca (Alella) $10. 82 —*M.S. (2/1/2006)*

Parxet NV Brut Pinot Noir (Cava) $12. 88 Best Buy —*M.S. (6/1/2006)*

Parxet NV Cuvée Dessert Dulce Pinot Noir (Cava) $20. 86 —*M.S. (6/1/2006)*

Parxet NV Aniversario PA 84 Brut Nature Sparkling Blend (Cava) $70. 86 —*M.S. (6/1/2005)*

Parxet NV Cuvée 21 Brut Sparkling Blend (Cava) $10. 85 —*M.S. (12/31/2003)*

Parxet 1999 Tionio Crianza Tinto del Pais (Ribera del Duero) $20. 87 —*D.T. (4/1/2003)*

Parxet 2002 Marqués de Alella Clasico White Blend (Alella) $10. 88 —*M.S. (8/1/2003)*

PASANAU GERMANS

Pasanau Germans 2002 Finca la Planeta Cabernet Sauvignon (Priorat) $46. 88 —*M.S. (10/1/2005)*

Pasanau Germans 2001 Finca la Planeta Cabernet Sauvignon (Priorat) $46. 88 —*M.S. (3/1/2005)*

Pasanau Germans 1998 Pasanau La Planeta Cabernet Blend (Priorat) $40. 88 —*C.S. (4/1/2002)*

Pasanau Germans 2003 Ceps Nous Red Blend (Priorat) $20. 85 —*M.S. (10/1/2005)*

Pasanau Germans 2000 Finca la Planeta Red Blend (Priorat) $34. 92 Editors' Choice —*M.S. (3/1/2004)*

Pasanau Germans 1999 Finca La Planeta Red Blend (Priorat) $34. 87 —*C.S. (11/1/2002)*

Pasanau Germans 2001 La Morera de Montsant Red Blend (Priorat) $34. 90 —*M.S. (10/1/2005)*

Pasanau Germans 2000 La Morera de Montsant Red Blend (Priorat) $29. 90 —*M.S. (3/1/2004)*

PAUL CHENEAU

Paul Cheneau NV Brut Sparkling Blend (Cava) $11. 85 —*M.S. (6/1/2006)*

PAZO DE BARRANTES

Pazo de Barrantes 2005 Albariño (Rías Baixas) $14. 87 —*M.S. (9/1/2006)*

Pazo de Barrantes 2003 Albariño (Rías Baixas) $NA. 89 —*M.S. (6/1/2005)*

PAZO DE EIRAS

Pazo de Eiras 2004 Albariño (Rías Baixas) $27. 87 —*M.S. (9/1/2006)*

Pazo de Eiras 2003 Albariño (Rías Baixas) $25. 89 —*M.S. (8/1/2005)*

PAZO DE SEÑORANS

Pazo de Señorans 2005 Albariño (Rías Baixas) $22. 91 Editors' Choice —*M.S. (9/1/2006)*

PAZO DE VILLAREI

Pazo De Villarei 2000 Albariño (Rías Baixas) $15. 82 —*M.S. (11/1/2002)*

PAZO PONDAL

Pazo Pondal 2004 Albariño (Rías Baixas) $22. 89 —*M.S. (9/1/2006)*

PAZO SAN MAURO

Pazo San Mauro 2005 Albariño (Rías Baixas) $19. 89 —*M.S. (9/1/2006)*

Pazo San Mauro 2003 Albariño (Rías Baixas) $17. 87 —*M.S. (3/1/2005)*

Pazo San Mauro 2002 Albariño (Rías Baixas) $18. 88 —*M.S. (9/1/2004)*

Pazo San Mauro 2001 Albariño (Rías Baixas) $17. 86 —*D.T. (4/1/2003)*

PAZO SERANTELLOS

Pazo Serantellos 2006 Albariño (Rías Baixas) $10. Melon, honey and white stone-fruit aromas carry the nose, with a touch of sulfuric match stick sneaking in late. The palate deals good lime, citrus and spiced apple, and while the finish is lean and short, it's also clean and scouring. A nice wine for near-term consumption. 86 Best Buy —*M.S. (11/1/2007)*

PAZO VILADOMAR

Pazo Viladomar 2004 Albariño (Rías Baixas) $15. 82 —*P.P. (11/15/2005)*

Pazo Viladomar 2005 White Blend (Rías Baixas) $17. Don't expect a lot from this fruity but fading blend of Treixadura and Albariño. It offers heavy green plum and melon flavors, yet it's losing steam as it turns heavy and briny. 83 —*M.S. (11/1/2007)*

PECIÑA

Peciña 1997 Reserve Tempranillo (Rioja) $60. 85 —*M.S. (4/1/2006)*

PEDRO ESCUDERO

Pedro Escudero 2006 Fuente Elvira Verdejo (Rueda) $14. Basic and fresh, yet not very individual in its aromas or flavors. The nose is your standard mineral and snappy citrus, while the palate offers nice apple, lemon and grapefruit flavors. It's more of tangy, cleansing wine than anything deep or cerebral. Drink now with salads or grilled shrimp. 87 —*M.S. (11/1/2007)*

Pedro Escudero 2005 Fuente Elvira Verdejo (Rueda) $14. Solid and spunky, with tight mineral-driven apple and nectarine aromas. The palate yields citrus and dried fruits, while the mouthfeel and finish are smooth and satisfying but nothing extraordinary. Simply a good white wine made right. **87** —*M.S. (2/1/2007)*

Pedro Escudero 2003 Fuente Elvira Verdejo (Rueda) $22. 86 —*M.S. (9/1/2006)*

Pedro Escudero 2006 Valdelainos Verdejo (Rueda) $11. Consistency is a virtue in this business, and this wine tastes almost exactly like the highly recommended 2005. The nose blends green grass and golden fruits, while the palate is clean, intense and snappy. This is a wine that sings, and the interspersed notes of bell pepper, grapefruit and mineral are just right for Verdejo. Drink right away for maximum freshness. **90 Best Buy** —*M.S. (11/1/2007)*

PEDROSA

Pedrosa 1995 Gran Reserva Red Blend (Ribera del Duero) $79. 90 Cellar Selection —*J.C. (11/1/2001)*

Pedrosa 1997 Reserva Red Blend (Ribera del Duero) $45. 87 —*J.C. (11/1/2001)*

Pedrosa 1998 Crianza Tempranillo (Ribera del Duero) $28. 88 —*J.C. (11/1/2001)*

PEGASO

Pegaso 2002 Barrancos de Pizarra Garnacha (Vino de la Tierra de Castilla y León) $36. With can't-miss aromas of coconut and prune, this wine stirs memories of tanning oil and fruitcake. It's big, bold and earthy, but also mildly herbal. The palate tastes of black fruit as well as dill and pepper, and the mouthfeel is convincing. Too bad the oak is still so pronounced. **87** —*M.S. (4/1/2007)*

PENASCAL

Penascal 2005 Sauvignon Blanc (Viño de la Tierra de Castilla y León) $7. 84 Best Buy —*M.S. (11/1/2006)*

Penascal 2004 Sauvignon Blanc (Viño de la Tierra de Castilla y León) $6. 84 Best Buy —*M.S. (10/1/2005)*

Penascal 2002 Sauvignon Blanc (Viño de la Tierra de Castilla y León) $7. 88 Best Buy —*M.S. (3/1/2004)*

Penascal 2004 Shiraz (Viño de la Tierra de Castilla y León) $7. 85 Best Buy —*M.S. (11/1/2006)*

Penascal 2003 Shiraz (Viño de la Tierra de Castilla y León) $6. 86 Best Buy —*M.S. (11/15/2005)*

Penascal 2004 Tempranillo (Viño de la Tierra de Castilla y León) $7. 86 Best Buy —*M.S. (11/1/2006)*

Penascal 2000 Tempranillo (Viño de la Tierra de Castilla y León) $7. 85 Best Buy —*M.S. (3/1/2004)*

Penascal 2006 Rosé Tempranillo (Vino de la Tierra de Castilla y León) $8. If a little left-over sugar doesn't bother you than this wine will register in a positive way. For beginners, the bouquet dances with rose hip, red licorice and cherry notes, and next the palate has real flavor and layering. Yes, it's kind of sweet and manufactured. But it's also got zest and pleasant pomegranate and pink-grapefruit flavors. **85 Best Buy** —*M.S. (7/1/2007)*

Penascal 2005 Rosé Tempranillo (Viño de la Tierra de Castilla y León) $7. 85 Best Buy —*M.S. (11/1/2006)*

PERELADA

Perelada 1996 Gran Claustro Extra Brut Champagne Blend (Cava) $14. 83 *(12/31/2001)*

PESQUERA

Pesquera 1999 Crianza Tempranillo (Ribera del Duero) $23. 85 —*K.F. (11/1/2002)*

Pesquera 2000 Crianza Tempranillo (Ribera del Duero) $25. 85 —*M.S. (3/1/2004)*

Pesquera 1999 Tinto Reserva Tempranillo (Ribera del Duero) $40. 90 —*M.S. (3/1/2004)*

Pesquera 1998 Crianza Tempranillo (Ribera del Duero) $25. 89 —*J.C. (11/1/2001)*

Pesquera 1995 Gran Reserva Tempranillo (Ribera del Duero) $99. 91 Cellar Selection —*J.C. (11/1/2001)*

Pesquera 1996 Millennium Reserva Tempranillo (Ribera del Duero) $799. 92 *(8/1/2000)*

Pesquera 1997 Reserva Tempranillo (Ribera del Duero) $40. 89 —*J.C. (11/1/2001)*

Pesquera 1996 Reserva Tempranillo (Ribera del Duero) $49. 91 *(8/1/2000)*

Pesquera 2001 Reserva Tempranillo Blend (Ribera del Duero) $44. 91 —*M.S. (10/1/2005)*

Pesquera 2002 Crianza Tempranillo (Ribera del Duero) $27. 86 —*M.S. (10/1/2005)*

Pesquera 2001 Crianza Tempranillo (Ribera del Duero) $25. 88 —*M.S. (9/1/2004)*

PICO MADAMA

Pico Madama 2003 Monastrell / Petit Verdot Red Blend (Jumilla) $36. It's not easy assessing this blend of Monastrell and Petit Verdot from a warm vintage. It's fiery and almost citric on the nose, while the palate is ripe as can be, with spicecake and blackberry syrup flavors. It's not missing any potency or ripeness, but the longer you work with it the larger and more medicinal it gets. Think big Zinfandel from California when you take this on. **89** —*M.S. (12/15/2007)*

PINTIA

Pintia 2002 Vino Tinto Tinta de Toro (Toro) $50. 90 —*M.S. (6/1/2005)*

PIRAMIDE

Piramide 1999 Piramide Crianza Red Blend (Ribera del Duero) $20. 86 —*K.F. (11/1/2002)*

PISSARRES

Pissarres 2003 Red Blend (Priorat) $25. 83 —*M.S. (10/1/2005)*

POMAR VIÑEDOS

Pomar Viñedos 2001 Pomar de Burgos Crianza Tempranillo (Ribera del Duero) $24. Musky and leathery at first, with a hint of cough drop. And it never really gains its legs. The palate shows a pruny character along with some wayward acidity, while the finish is indifferent. Adequate but lacks elegance and appeal. **84** —*M.S. (6/1/2007)*

Pomar Viñedos 2005 Pomar de Burgos Joven Tempranillo (Ribera del Duero) $14. A lot of wood sits upfront, and in back of that things seem a touch murky and lactic. Freshness and precision are not this wine's best attributes, but there is decent weight and body carrying berry, tobacco and vanilla flavors. Would be better with more purity. **84** —*M.S. (6/1/2007)*

Pomar Viñedos 2000 Pomar de Burgos Reserva Tempranillo (Ribera del Duero) $40. Hickory, maple and light berry aromas are act one. Next there's mild fruit flavors, tobacco and tomato notes on the palate. Finishes chunky, round and with mocha flavors. It's a touch warm and sweet, but overall it hangs in there. **87** —*M.S. (6/1/2007)*

PONTALIE

Pontalie 1998 Crianza Red Blend (Mentrida) $17. 82 —*D.T. (4/1/2003)*

Pontalie 1998 Crianza Syrah-Cabernet (Mentrida) $18. 81 —*D.T. (4/1/2003)*

PRADO REY

Prado Rey 1998 Reserva (Ribera del Duero) 90 Cellar Selection —*J.C. (11/1/2001)*

Prado Rey 1999 Roble (Ribera del Duero) $11. 86 —*J.C. (11/1/2001)*

Prado Rey 2003 Crianza Tempranillo (Ribera del Duero) $18. Coffee, wood grain and berry fruit combine to create a standard trio of aromas, while the palate is medium in weight, with strawberry, raspberry and vanilla flavors. This wine offers a reasonably good mouthfeel and finishing notes of coconut, dill and vanilla. Good but ordinary. Imported by Dana Importers, Inc. **85** —*M.S. (6/1/2007)*

Prado Rey 2001 Crianza Tempranillo (Ribera del Duero) $19. 86 —*M.S. (6/1/2005)*

Prado Rey 1997 Crianza Tempranillo (Ribera del Duero) $17. 88 —*M.M. (8/1/2000)*

Prado Rey 2003 Elite Tempranillo (Ribera del Duero) $50. Elite more in name than product. This wine shows a lot of espresso and blackened leather aromas. In the mouth, it's a touch green and listing, with short fruit flavors sitting in front of a toasty, woody finish. Firm but short, with only a modicum of flesh and flourish. Overall it's good but hard to justify at $50. 1,000 cases produced. Imported by Dana Importers, Inc. **86** —*M.S. (6/1/2007)*

Prado Rey 1999 Elite Tempranillo (Ribera del Duero) $55. 86 —*M.S. (6/1/2005)*

Prado Rey 1999 Gran Reserva Tempranillo (Ribera del Duero) $60. The nose shows some tire rubber and burnt toast, but the biggest component of the bouquet is black coffee. The fruit on the palate has a high-toned, acidic edge to it, but the flavors are solid. If there's any one thing that raises questions, it's the strong, persistent nuttiness to the finish. The wine tastes a lot like roasted almonds or cashews as it fades away. Imported by Dana Importers, Inc. **87** —*M.S. (6/1/2007)*

Prado Rey 1999 Real Sitio Tempranillo (Ribera del Duero) 91 —*J.C. (11/1/2001)*

Prado Rey 2001 Reserva Tempranillo (Ribera del Duero) $35. There's really no good reason why a reserva from such a fine year like 2001 should be so thin and tart. But in this case, that's what we're dealing with. The nose offers earth, tobacco and red fruit aromas, but the palate is all acid and in the end everything seems stripped down and sour. Imported by Dana Importers, Inc. 81 *—M.S. (6/1/2007)*

Prado Rey 1999 Reserva Tempranillo (Ribera del Duero) $35. 83 *—M.S. (6/1/2005)*

Prado Rey 2005 Roble Tempranillo (Ribera del Duero) $14. Plum and dark berry aromas are offset by typical American oak aromas of pickle and dill. But the wine is generally ripe and whole, with blackberry flavors balanced by chocolate and black pepper on the finish. Medium to full in weight, with no noticeable holes in the fabric. At 83,000 cases, this is a really good wine given the quantity. Imported by Dana Importers, Inc. 87 *—M.S. (6/1/2007)*

Prado Rey 2002 Roble Tempranillo (Ribera del Duero) $14. 83 *—M.S. (6/1/2005)*

Prado Rey 1998 Roble Tempranillo (Ribera del Duero) $11. 85 *—M.M. (8/1/2000)*

Prado Rey 1998 Crianza Tempranillo (Ribera del Duero) $18. 87 *—J.C. (11/1/2001)*

Prado Rey 1999 Crianza Tempranillo (Ribera del Duero) $18. 83 *—M.S. (8/1/2003)*

Prado Rey 2005 Rosé Tempranillo-Merlot (Ribera del Duero) $15. As pink wine goes, this Tempranillo-Merlot is extremely forward, heavy and aggressive. The nose is loaded with raspberry and cherry aromas, but there's also alcoholic heat reflective of its 14.8% alcohol. In many ways this drinks like a medium-bodied red wine, meaning it's fuller and beefier than your usual lighter-framed rosado. Imported by Dana Importers, Inc. 84 *—M.S. (6/1/2007)*

Prado Rey 2000 Roble Tinto del Pais (Ribera del Duero) $13. 84 *—M.S. (8/1/2003)*

PRIMA

Prima 2004 Tinta de Toro (Toro) $18. From the guys that do Mauro, one of Spain's better ultrapremium reds, comes this heavy, forward, youthful red with chunky, lush aromas of fruitcake and licorice along with bruising flavors of black cherry and berry skins. A ton of new oak rests on top of chocolate, vanilla and cedar subtleties. Very tannic and rough after spending 11 months in barrel. 87 *—M.S. (4/1/2007)*

PRINCIPE DE VIANA

Principe de Viana 1996 Tempranillo (Navarra) $11. 85 *—J.C. (11/15/1999)*

PROTOS

Protos 1994 Gran Reserva Red Blend (Ribera del Duero) $75. 87 *—J.C. (11/1/2001)*

Protos 2000 Jóven Roble Tempranillo (Ribera del Duero) $11. 87 Best Buy *—J.C. (11/1/2001)*

PUERTA COLORADA

Puerta Colorada 2004 Tempranillo (Rioja) $10. Earthy and mossy initially, with notes of coffee and mocha. The flavors of spiced red fruit are solid and fresh, but the wine comes up short on flesh and feel. In fact, it's quite lean and acidic, which means a food partner is almost mandatory. 84 *—M.S. (12/15/2007)*

PUERTA DE GRANADA

Puerta de Granada 1997 Monastrell Crianza 1997 Monastrell (Jumilla) $15. 86 *—M.S. (11/1/2002)*

Puerta de Granada 1996 Puerta de Granada-Reserva Monastrell (Jumilla) $20. 82 *—D.T. (4/1/2003)*

Puerta de Granada 2000 Vino Tinto Tempranillo (Jumilla) $9. 83 *—M.S. (11/1/2002)*

PUERTA DEL SOL

Puerta Del Sol 2002 Blanco Fermentado en Roble Malvar (Madrid) $16. 81 *—M.S. (12/31/2004)*

PUERTA PALMA

Puerta Palma 2001 Estate Bottled Red Blend (Ribera del Guadiana) $15. 83 *—M.S. (3/1/2004)*

Puerta Palma 2000 Vino Tinto Tempranillo (Ribera del Guadiana) 87 *—M.S. (11/1/2002)*

Puerta Palma 2003 Estate Tempranillo Blend (Ribera del Guadiana) $13. 80 *—M.S. (8/1/2005)*

Puerta Palma 2000 Finca El Campillo Reserva de la Familia Tempranillo Blend (Ribera del Guadiana) $12. 82 *—M.S. (12/31/2004)*

PUJANZA

Pujanza 2003 Tempranillo (Rioja) $30. Ripe and heavy, with a chunky overtone to the nose that's perfectly right for the earth and spice that's present. This wine is almost two-faced in character: It has zest, acidity and red fruit that make you think along traditional lines; but the weight and a raisiny underbelly remind you of the vintage. Best now through 2008. 89 *—M.S. (2/1/2007)*

Pujanza 2001 Tempranillo (Rioja) $30. 88 *—M.S. (4/1/2006)*

QUINTA COUSELO

Quinta Couselo 2005 Turonia Albariño (Rías Baixas) $20. May be getting old but still welcoming and mostly fresh. Citrus, melon and mango flavors are flush and clean, and the finish is racy and fluid. Normally Albariño is a one-year wine, meaning you should drink it in the year immediately after harvest. Here's an '05 that's hanging in there and still showing kick. Drink now for best results. 88 *—M.S. (12/15/2007)*

QUINTA SARDONIA

Quinta Sardonia 2004 Red Blend (Vino de la Tierra de Castilla y León) $50. Earthy and heavily toasted, especially upon first take. This is a serious multigrape wine from the outskirts of RDD that needs a few years in the cellar and then a decanting. With that TLC you will get saucy berry flavors, aggressive spice and tannins, and a dynamic, multifaceted finish. Drink it too soon or without airing and it may seem overoaked, hot and bitter. 90 *—M.S. (11/1/2007)*

R. DE AYALA LETE E HIJOS

R. de Ayala Lete E Hijos 2003 Viña Santurnia Crianza Tempranillo (Rioja) $15. Fits the mold of traditional Rioja Crianza. The nose has oaky warmth and a slight mulchy quality that probably comes from the hot vintage. But it's holding in there with ripe black cherry and berry flavors that are accented by chocolate, vanilla and cola. Has grabby tannins and is ready to go now. 86 *—M.S. (12/15/2007)*

R. de Ayala Lete E Hijos 2001 Viña Santurnia Reserva Tempranillo (Rioja) $20. This shows classic dill, vanilla and brambly fruit aromas. Meanwhile, the palate deals wave after wave of vanilla-infused red fruit. For classicists this will constitute a trip down memory lane; a testament to the greatness of 2001. 91 *—M.S. (11/1/2007)*

R. LOPEZ DE HEREDIA

R. Lopez de Heredia 1996 Viña Tondonia Reserva Red Blend (Rioja) $36. 89 *—M.S. (9/1/2004)*

R. Lopez de Heredia 1995 Viña Tondonia Rosé Blend (Rioja) $27. Part of you will be complexed by this unique-for-the-sake-of-unique oak-aged "rosé" while the rest of you, the less generous part, will want to pour it down the drain. It's oxidized, loaded with resiny wood, and tastes as much like sherried orange juice as fine wine. Yet on the other hand, it has apricot and almondy flavors and pulsing acidity that make you give it some thought. Definitely not for everyone but someone out there probably loves it. 84 *—M.S. (7/1/2007)*

R. Lopez de Heredia 1996 Viña Bosconia Reserva Tempranillo (Rioja) $21. 86 *—M.S. (3/1/2004)*

R. Lopez de Heredia 1996 Viña Bosconia Reserva Tempranillo Blend (Rioja) $32. 84 *—M.S. (9/1/2004)*

R. Lopez de Heredia 2000 Viña Cubillo Crianza Tempranillo Blend (Rioja) $25. 88 *—M.S. (11/1/2006)*

R. Lopez de Heredia 1997 Viña Tondonia Reserva Tempranillo Blend (Rioja) $39. 86 *—M.S. (6/1/2005)*

RAFAEL PALACIOS

Rafael Palacios 2005 As Sortes Godello (Valdeorras) $35. 92 *—M.S. (9/1/2006)*

RAIMAT

Raimat 1998 Cabernet Sauvignon (Costers del Segre) $13. 82 *—D.T. (4/1/2003)*

Raimat 1994 El Moli Cabernet Sauvignon (Costers del Segre) $29. 93 *—R.V. (11/1/1999)*

Raimat 1994 Mas Castell Cabernet Sauvignon (Costers del Segre) $29. 90 *—R.V. (11/1/1999)*

Raimat 1995 Mas Castell Reserva Cabernet Sauvignon (Costers del Segre) $20. 81 *—D.T. (4/1/2003)*

Raimat 1994 Vallorba Cabernet Sauvignon (Costers del Segre) $12. 94 Best Buy *—R.V. (11/1/1999)*

Raimat 2003 Chardonnay (Costers del Segre) $9. 82 *—M.S. (12/31/2004)*

Raimat 2002 Chardonnay (Costers del Segre) $8. 84 *—M.S. (3/1/2004)*

Raimat 2005 Unoaked Chardonnay (Costers del Segre) $10. Mild citrus and basic stone-fruit aromas get going, with sweet, slightly candied white-fruit flavors taking up the cause. Talk about a simple, easygoing wine; this is it. **84** *—M.S. (2/1/2007)*

Raimat 1996 Merlot (Costers del Segre) $12. 88 *—R.V. (11/1/1999)*

Raimat 1996 Tempranillo (Costers del Segre) $14. 89 *—R.V. (11/1/1999)*

Raimat 2000 Tempranillo (Costers del Segre) $14. 85 *—M.S. (3/1/2004)*

Raimat 1999 Tempranillo (Costers del Segre) $13. 83 *—D.T. (4/1/2003)*

Raimat 1999 Abadia Tempranillo-Cabernet Sauvignon (Costers del Segre) $10. 85 *—D.T. (4/1/2003)*

RAIZ DE GUZMAN

Raiz de Guzman 2000 Tempranillo (Ribera del Duero) $61. 86 *—M.S. (10/1/2005)*

RAMIREZ DE LA PISCINA

Ramirez de la Piscina 1999 Crianza Tempranillo (Rioja) $12. 83 *—M.S. (3/1/2004)*

Ramirez de la Piscina 1997 Crianza Tempranillo (Rioja) $15. 87 *—M.M. (8/1/2000)*

Ramirez de la Piscina 1995 Reserva Tempranillo (Rioja) $21. 90 *—M.M. (8/1/2000)*

RAMÓN BILBAO

Ramón Bilbao 2000 Tempranillo (Rioja) $11. 85 *—M.S. (3/1/2004)*

Ramón Bilbao 1999 Tempranillo (Rioja) $10. 88 Best Buy *—D.T. (4/1/2003)*

Ramón Bilbao 2004 Crianza Tempranillo (Rioja) $13. Plenty of red berry and jam greet you on the nose, and beyond that there's sweet barrel notes and a little wood smoke. It's smart and snappy on the palate, but not all that long or complex. Finishing notes of tobacco add interest. Tasty and ready to go now. **87** *—M.S. (9/1/2007)*

Ramón Bilbao 2003 Crianza Tempranillo (Rioja) $10. Luxe raspberry and blackberry aromas blend with some leather to create a solid, soothing bouquet. The palate is fairly deep and pure, with sophisticated berry, cherry and mild herb flavors. Long and spicy late. No frills but a complete wine for a good price. **87 Best Buy** *—M.S. (2/1/2007)*

Ramón Bilbao 1996 Gran Reserva Tempranillo (Rioja) $20. 86 *—M.S. (3/1/2004)*

Ramón Bilbao 1995 Gran Reserva Tempranillo (Rioja) $20. 84 *—D.T. (4/1/2003)*

Ramón Bilbao 2004 Limited Edition Tempranillo (Rioja) $20. Good color and intriguing aromas of baked fruit, tobacco and mint indicate that you're getting some modern-styled ripeness along with traditional Rioja earth, spice and old man's library. The palate is juicy and mildy fruity, while the finish pushes chocolate, vanilla, baking spice and tannins. Drinkable now but will age for another five years without a problem. **89** *—M.S. (9/1/2007)*

Ramón Bilbao 2003 Limited Edition Crianza Tempranillo (Rioja) $14. Bold berry fruit is the opening salvo, while next in line are aromas of mint and dried spices. The palate pours on the raspberry and cherry flavors, while strong but youthful tannins create a gritty but masculine mouthfeel and finish. Rough and ready, but satisfying. **87** *—M.S. (2/1/2007)*

Ramón Bilbao 1999 Limited Edition Crianza Tempranillo (Rioja) $13. 88 *—D.T. (4/1/2003)*

Ramón Bilbao 2004 Mirto Tempranillo (Rioja) $65. Color and size are readily apparent but gaps appear between the layers. For starters, the nose doesn't have the purity and density that it could; and the palate also shows some weakness where structure and quality of fruit meet. Otherwise, it's a ripe and modern red wine with some lushness and depth. **87** *—M.S. (9/1/2007)*

Ramón Bilbao 1998 Reserva Tempranillo (Rioja) $15. 86 *—M.S. (3/1/2004)*

Ramón Bilbao 1996 Reserva Tempranillo (Rioja) $15. 84 *—D.T. (4/1/2003)*

Ramón Bilbao 1998 Gran Reserva Tempranillo Blend (Rioja) $38. Vanilla, raisin and carob aromas announce a level of heft and overripeneness that is never lost or compensated for. It's a jammy, soft, well-aged specimen that doesn't have much life or kick. It does offer ripe, sweet berry flavors, however, and some molasses. **84** *—M.S. (9/1/2007)*

Ramón Bilbao 2001 Limited Edition Crianza Tempranillo Blend (Rioja) $13. 88 *—M.S. (9/1/2004)*

Ramón Bilbao 2002 Mirto Tempranillo Blend (Rioja) $38. Stout and generally quite pure, with aromas of leather and berries that thicken and gather density with airing. The palate is your standard new-age blend of dark cherry and raspberry, while the finish is oaky, warm and spicy. Very nice, if a touch jammy and simple. **88** *—M.S. (9/1/2007)*

Ramón Bilbao 2001 Mirto Tempranillo Blend (Rioja) $37. 89 *—M.S. (9/1/2004)*

Ramón Bilbao 1999 Mirto Tempranillo Blend (Rioja) $37. 88 *—M.S. (3/1/2004)*

Ramón Bilbao 2001 Reserva Tempranillo Blend (Rioja) $25. Aromas of cherry sucking candy, sangria and citrus peel are easy and clean but not what you'd call sophisticated. The palate is forward and basic, with tangy cherry and plum skin flavors. It thickens a bit on the finish but always has a racy personality. Better with food due to grabby tannins and acids. **85** *—M.S. (9/1/2007)*

RAMÓN CARDOVA

Ramón Cardova 2002 Tempranillo (Rioja) $12. 83 *—J.C. (4/1/2005)*

Ramón Cardova 2001 Tempranillo (Rioja) $10. 82 *—M.S. (10/1/2003)*

Ramón Cardova 2001 Crianza Tempranillo (Rioja) $18. 83 *—J.C. (4/1/2005)*

RAVENTÓS I BLANC

Raventós I Blanc 1998 Gran Reserva Personal Brut Nature Sparkling Blend (Cava) $NA. 90 *—M.S. (6/1/2005)*

REINO DE LOS MALLOS

Reino de los Mallos 2003 Red Blend (Vino de la Tierra Ribera del Gállego-Cinco Villas) $20. 81 *—M.S. (12/15/2006)*

REJADORADA

Rejadorada 2001 Crianza Tinta de Toro (Toro) $27. 89 *—M.S. (4/1/2006)*

Rejadorada 2001 Sango Tinta de Toro (Toro) $55. 85 *—M.S. (9/1/2006)*

Rejadorada 2003 Tinto Roble Tinta de Toro (Toro) $20. 90 *—M.S. (12/15/2006)*

REMÍREZ DE GANUZA

Remírez de Ganuza 2003 Reserva Tempranillo (Rioja) $77. Thick, brooding and aromatically mature, this delivers heft, grab and balance. It has developed black-fruit flavors followed by a cushioned, soft finish. Drink now and over the next several years as the 2001 gets better and the promising but not yet released 2004 begins to settle. Imported by Tempranillo, Inc. **91** *—M.S. (9/1/2007)*

Remírez de Ganuza 2002 Reserva Tempranillo (Rioja) $77. A juicy, prickly wine with pungent red-fruit aromas backed by tangy cherry, raspberry and currant flavors. It's firm and tight, entirely reflective of the cool vintage, and the bet here is that it's unlikely to ever lose that inherent toughness. Needs food to absorb the crispness. Imported by Tempranillo, Inc. **87** *—M.S. (9/1/2007)*

Remírez de Ganuza 2001 Reserva Tempranillo Blend (Rioja) $74. 94 Editors' Choice *—M.S. (6/1/2005)*

RENÉ BARBIER

René Barbier 2002 Cabernet Sauvignon (Penedès) $7. 82 *—M.S. (3/1/2004)*

René Barbier 1996 Selección Crianza Cabernet Sauvignon (Penedès) $14. 83 *—C.S. (4/1/2002)*

René Barbier 2002 Chardonnay (Penedès) $7. 84 *—M.S. (3/1/2004)*

René Barbier 2001 Chardonnay (Penedès) $10. 83 *—M.S. (3/1/2004)*

René Barbier 1999 Selección Chardonnay (Penedès) $14. 83 *—M.M. (9/1/2002)*

René Barbier NV Mediterranean Red Blend (Penedès) $6. 81 *—D.T. (4/1/2002)*

René Barbier NV Mediterranean Rosé Blend (Catalunya) $6. If you catch this salmon-colored sweety when it's fresh and chilled, it will fit the bill with ease. It offers spicy gumdrop aromas offset by strawberry, while the flavor profile centers around peach, cherry and melon. Has residual sugar but also enough natural fruit and acids to handle it. **85 Best Buy** *—M.S. (7/1/2007)*

René Barbier 2003 Tempranillo (Penedès) $7. 83 *—M.S. (9/1/2006)*

René Barbier 2002 Tempranillo (Penedès) $7. 84 *—M.S. (3/1/2004)*

René Barbier NV Mediterranean Rosé Tempranillo Blend (Catalunya) $6. 82 *—M.S. (2/1/2006)*

René Barbier NV Mediterranean White Blend (Catalunya) $6. By the sheer fact that this wine costs $6 and never really goes up in price, it holds onto its tenuous value status via clean tropical aromas and mild flavors of lime, pineapple and citrus. It's a touch hot and burning on the finish, but finish isn't what you're banking on with a wine like this. Imported by Freixenet USA. **83 Best Buy** *—M.S. (12/15/2007)*

René Barbier NV Mediterranean White Blend (Catalunya) $6. 85 Best Buy *—M.S. (10/1/2005)*

RENTO

Rento 2003 Tinto del Pais (Ribera del Duero) $60. 82 *—M.S. (11/1/2006)*

REQUIEM

Requiem 2003 Crianza Tempranillo (Ribera del Duero) $57. The aromas veer toward grilled hamburger, pepper and roasted black fruit, and the bouquet never gets more fruity or expressive than that. The fact is that this is a full, weighty product of a warm year. There's not much acidity and the flavors run perilously close to raisin. Still, if you get at it now there's likable prune, tobacco and dark chocolate characteristics. 86 *—M.S. (6/1/2007)*

RESALTE

Resalte 2001 Crianza Tempranillo (Ribera del Duero) $35. First impressions say this wine is overdone and charred. But patience is rewarded with secondary aromas of baked fruit, earth and leather, and that package is backed up by black cherry, plum and rhubarb flavors. Yes, it's a bit racy and scattered, but there's enough quality here to make it good. Whether it's worth $35 is another story. 87 *—M.S. (6/1/2007)*

RIBERAL

Riberal 2003 4 Meses Barrica Tinto del Pais (Ribera del Duero) $13. 81 *—M.S. (11/1/2006)*

RIMARTS

Rimarts 2001 Cabernet Sauvignon-Merlot (Penedès) $14. 86 *—M.S. (5/1/2004)*

Rimarts 2002 Merlot Rosé Blend (Penedès) $11. 82 *—M.S. (5/1/2004)*

Rimarts 1998 Brut Nature Sparkling Blend (Cava) $15. 85 *—J.C. (12/31/2003)*

Rimarts 1996 Brut Nature Gran Reserva Sparkling Blend (Cava) $21. 83 *—J.C. (1/1/2004)*

Rimarts 1994 Reserva Especial Brut Nature Sparkling Blend (Cava) $30. 80 *—J.C. (1/1/2004)*

RIOJA VEGA

Rioja Vega 2000 Red Blend (Rioja) $8. 87 Best Buy *—D.T. (4/1/2003)*

Rioja Vega 2004 Tempranillo (Rioja) $8. 81 *—M.S. (12/15/2006)*

Rioja Vega 2003 Crianza Tempranillo Blend (Rioja) $12. Spearmint and untamed wild berry aromas start it down a slope that ends with a palate that's hot and heavy with fruit but devoid of balance and touch. There's a lot of this and that, namely vanilla and oak. But overall the wine just gets it together. 83 *—M.S. (9/1/2007)*

Rioja Vega 2001 Reserva Tempranillo Blend (Rioja) $19. Standard but nicely done. This is a solid representative of 2001, and it's showing nice, mature cherry flavors along with integrated tannins, vanilla and an easygoing plumpness. Drink now. 88 *—M.S. (11/1/2007)*

Rioja Vega 2005 Tempranillo-Garnacha (Rioja) $8. Cheerful but basic raspberry aromas and flavors is what this young Rioja is about. It feels a little bulky at first, and then acids swell up to cut it short. Almost snappy in the late innings. 83 *—M.S. (9/1/2007)*

RONDEL

Rondel NV Extreme Brut Sparkling Blend (Cava) $6. 81 *—M.S. (12/15/2004)*

ROQUERO

Roquero 1995 Reserva Monastrell (Jumilla) $12. 83 *—M.M. (9/1/2002)*

Roquero 1994 Reserva Monastrell (Jumilla) $12. 86 *—J.C. (8/1/2000)*

Roquero 1998 Tinto Monastrell (Jumilla) $9. 87 *—J.C. (8/1/2000)*

ROTLLAN TORRA

Rotllan Torra 2003 Amadis Red Blend (Priorat) $60. A barrel buster, with huge barrique qualities including char, chocolate and vanilla along with ripe black-fruit aromas. Spirited is the best way to describe this masculine, tannic bruiser, which is a blend of old-vines Garnacha and Carignan. Hold a couple of years to let it settle, then enjoy. 92 *—M.S. (8/1/2007)*

Rotllan Torra 2002 Amadis Red Blend (Priorat) $55. 86 *—M.S. (10/1/2005)*

Rotllan Torra 1998 Amadis Red Blend (Priorat) $45. 93 Editors' Choice *—K.F. (11/1/2002)*

Rotllan Torra 1998 Balandra Red Blend (Priorat) $32. 91 *—K.F. (11/1/2002)*

Rotllan Torra 1997 Reserva Red Blend (Priorat) $15. 89 Best Buy *—C.S. (11/15/2002)*

Rotllan Torra 2000 Sellecció Red Blend (Priorat) $15. 83 *—M.S. (3/1/2004)*

Rotllan Torra 2003 Tirant Red Blend (Priorat) $87. In no way is this up to the high standards of other Tirants. The 2003 is overly woody and shy on the rich, saturated fruit that it's supposed to deliver. It's okay, but very leafy, dry and tight. 83 *—M.S. (8/1/2007)*

Rotllan Torra 2002 Tirant Red Blend (Priorat) $75. 91 *—M.S. (10/1/2005)*

Rotllan Torra 1998 Tirant Red Blend (Priorat) $70. 94 Cellar Selection *(11/1/2002)*

RUBIEJO

Rubiejo 2005 Tempranillo (Ribera del Duero) $17. Baseball card bubble gum and leafy spearmint aromas shade dark, dusty fruit notes, while the tannic palate houses mildly tart cherry flavors followed by hints of sucking candy and finally coffee. Decent but a bit overoaked and out of sorts. 84 *—M.S. (6/1/2007)*

Rubiejo 2002 Crianza Tempranillo (Ribera del Duero) $22. 88 *—M.S. (9/9/1999)*

Rubiejo 2004 Oak Aged Tempranillo (Ribera del Duero) $17. 89 *—M.S. (11/1/2006)*

Rubiejo 2003 Oak Aged Tempranillo (Ribera del Duero) $17. 89 *—M.S. (11/15/2005)*

Rubiejo 2002 Reserva Tempranillo (Ribera del Duero) $45. Dark cherry is the lead aroma, and behind that there's a supporting wave of vanilla and dill. The palate is snappy for a reserve, with clean raspberry and cherry flavors. While we wouldn't call it "lean," the wine isn't super rich or extracted. So enjoy it now for its medium weight, admirable purity and true Ribera character. 89 *—M.S. (6/1/2007)*

Rubiejo 2005 Young Tempranillo (Ribera del Duero) $12. Rubiejo seems to have a way with young, spunky, simple wines. Their Jovenes of the past few years have been fruity and broad, but also balanced and down to earth. This grapy youngster shows floral, fleshy aromas backed by black fruit flavors that are likable but impossible to distinguish. It's big but weightless, meaning it's like a pastry with lots of calories that isn't that filling. 88 Best Buy *—M.S. (6/1/2007)*

Rubiejo 2004 Young Tempranillo (Ribera del Duero) $12. 85 *—M.S. (11/1/2006)*

Rubiejo 2002 Crianza Tinto del Pais (Ribera del Duero) $29. 84 *—M.S. (10/1/2005)*

Rubiejo 2003 Jóven Tinto del Pais (Ribera del Duero) $13. 88 Best Buy *—M.S. (10/1/2005)*

RUBINES

Rubines 2003 Albariño (Rías Baixas) $21. 86 *—M.S. (3/1/2005)*

RUIZ VILLANUEVA

Ruiz Villanueva 2003 maceracion carbonica Cencibel (Vino de la Tierra de Castilla) $12. Violet in color, with full red-berry aromas. The grape is called Cencibel, and the wine is sweet, structured, a bit medicinal and quite pleasant overall. Not too tannic but structured enough to be balanced. A good mainstream red from a variety that's not common. 86 *—M.S. (2/1/2007)*

S'FORNO

S'forno 2003 Estate Godello (Valdeorras) $15. 80 *—J.C. (4/1/2005)*

S'forno 2002 Estate Mourvedre Monastrell (Yecla) $10. 82 *—J.C. (4/1/2005)*

S. ARROYO

S. Arroyo 2001 Tinto Jóven Tempranillo (Ribera del Duero) $9. 86 Best Buy *—M.S. (3/1/2004)*

SALNEVAL

Salneval 2004 Albariño (Rías Baixas) $10. 86 Best Buy *—M.S. (10/1/2005)*

SAN GABRIEL

San Gabriel 2001 Crianza Tempranillo (Ribera del Duero) $20. A snappy, jumpy type of wine that delivers aromas of red fruit and spice, but there's something piercing about it, too. The palate is clean and tight, with lots of cranberry/raspberry flavors framed by citrusy notes. Best if you prefer a leaner, shorter, crisper type of red. 85 *—M.S. (6/1/2007)*

San Gabriel 2001 Reserva Tempranillo (Ribera del Duero) $26. This a nice wine that's at peak maturity. The nose offers an old-time blend of cinnamon and dried fruit, while the palate has a good feel and lively raspberry and vanilla flavors. A more traditionally styled wine that's ready to drink now. 87 *—M.S. (6/1/2007)*

SAN PEDRO

San Pedro 1999 Vallobera Crianza Tempranillo (Rioja) $15. 87 *—M.S. (8/1/2003)*

SAN ROMAN

San Roman 1998 Tempranillo (Toro) $40. 92 *(8/1/2000)*

San Roman 2003 Tinta de Toro (Toro) $50. Despite the hot vintage, we're fairly blown away by this Toro red. It's dense, dark and the nose is coated with mineral, crude oil and perfectly ripe black-fruit. Consistent with the region's track record, San Roman delivers uncomplicated but powerful fruit character strengthened by serious tannins. Drink from 2007–2012. **94 Editors' Choice** *—M.S. (2/1/2007)*

SAN VICENTE

San Vicente 2002 Tempranillo (Rioja) $49. 89 *—M.S. (4/1/2006)*

San Vicente 2001 Tempranillo (Rioja) $51. **94 Editors' Choice** *—M.S. (8/1/2005)*

San Vicente 2000 Tempranillo Blend (Rioja) $49. 91 *—M.S. (9/1/2004)*

SANCHEZ ROMATE

Sanchez Romate NV Cardenal Cisneros Reservas Pedro Ximénez (Jerez) $15. **94 Best Buy** *—M.S. (10/1/2005)*

Sanchez Romate NV Don José Oloroso Sherry (Jerez) $17. 93 *—M.S. (10/1/2005)*

Sanchez Romate NV Fino Marismeno Reservas Sherry (Jerez) $15. **90 Editors' Choice** *—M.S. (4/1/2006)*

Sanchez Romate NV Iberia Cream Sherry (Jerez) $15. **93 Editors' Choice** *—M.S. (10/1/2005)*

Sanchez Romate NV Imported Cream Sherry (Jerez) $7. **88 Best Buy** *—M.S. (10/1/2005)*

Sanchez Romate NV NPU Amontillado Sherry (Jerez) $17. 92 *—M.S. (10/1/2005)*

Sanchez Romate NV Romate Medium Dry Amontillado Sherry (Jerez) $7. **84 Best Buy** *—M.S. (10/1/2005)*

SANDEMAN

Sandeman NV Royal Ambrosante Aged 20 Years Old Solera Pedro Ximénez (Jerez) $24. **93 Editors' Choice** *—M.S. (6/1/2005)*

Sandeman NV Royal Corregidor Rich Old Oloroso Sherry (Jerez) $25. 94 *—M.S. (8/1/2003)*

Sandeman NV Royal Esmeralda Fine Dry Amontillado Sherry (Jerez) $25. 91 *—M.S. (8/1/2003)*

SANGENÍS I VAQUÉ

Sangenís I Vaqué 2000 Clos Monlleó Red Blend (Priorat) $60. 90 *—M.S. (4/1/2006)*

Sangenís I Vaqué 2000 Coranya Red Blend (Priorat) $45. 89 *—M.S. (4/1/2006)*

Sangenís I Vaqué 2002 Crianza Dara Red Blend (Priorat) $14. 85 *—M.S. (11/1/2006)*

Sangenís I Vaqué 2001 Vall Por Red Blend (Priorat) $13. **88 Best Buy** *—M.S. (4/1/2006)*

Sangenís I Vaqué 2000 Vall Por Red Blend (Priorat) $34. 90 *—M.S. (3/1/2004)*

SANTA QUITERIA

Santa Quiteria 2005 Loma Gorda Garnacha (Almansa) $12. Dark in color and seemingly packed on the nose, this wine pulls a no-show on the palate. There's really nothing here but acidity and tart currant and wild raspberry flavors. It only gets more astringent with each sip. 81 *—M.S. (12/15/2007)*

SANTANA

Santana 2004 Tempranillo (Castilla La Mancha) $6. Tastes and smells like the large-production, central plains wine that it is. The nose is basic but reasonably fresh; the palate is scratchy and hard, with dull cherry and cranberry flavors. 81 *—M.S. (8/1/2007)*

Santana 1998 Tempranillo (Rioja) $7. 84 *(5/1/2001)*

Santana 1999 Viura (Tierra Manchuela) $7. **86 Best Buy** *(5/1/2001)*

SANTIAGO RUIZ

Santiago Ruiz 2005 O Rosal White Blend (Rías Baixas) $18. 89 *—M.S. (9/1/2006)*

SANTONEGRO

Santonegro 2005 Monastrell (Jumilla) $9. **87 Best Buy** *—M.S. (12/15/2006)*

Santonegro 2002 Crianza Red Blend (Jumilla) $12. **87 Best Buy** *—M.S. (12/15/2006)*

SCALA DEI

Scala Dei 2002 Negre Garnacha (Priorat) $13. 85 *—M.S. (12/31/2004)*

Scala Dei 2000 Prior Criança Garnacha (Priorat) $20. 86 *—M.S. (12/31/2004)*

Scala Dei 2003 Negre Grenache (Priorat) $15. 83 *—M.S. (10/1/2005)*

Scala Dei 2001 Prior Criança Grenache (Priorat) $22. 89 *—M.S. (10/1/2005)*

Scala Dei 2003 Cartoixa Red Blend (Priorat) $36. Scala Dei seems to have managed 2003's tough conditions, and this is endowed with sweet Garnacha-driven aromas that touch up against raisiny but don't cross the line. The palate is plump and loaded with strawberry and vanilla flavors, then chocolate shows up on the finish. The blend is 41% Garnacha, 41% Syrah and 18% Cab Sauvignon. 89 *—M.S. (8/1/2007)*

Scala Dei 2001 Cartoixa Red Blend (Priorat) $30. 91 *—M.S. (10/1/2005)*

Scala Dei 2000 Cartoixa Reserva Red Blend (Priorat) $26. 90 *—M.S. (12/31/2004)*

Scala Dei 1998 Cartoixa Reserva Red Blend (Priorat) $22. 86 *—D.T. (4/1/2003)*

Scala Dei 2003 Prior Red Blend (Priorat) $25. No doubt this wine possesses peppery, herbal qualities. But before it's dismissed as green we'd like to note that there's also a nice savory side to it. More herbal than vegetal, and with decent balance. With food this wine will do just fine; on its own it may seem a touch reedy and rough. 86 *—M.S. (8/1/2007)*

SEGURA VIUDAS

Segura Viudas NV Aria Brut Rosé Pinot Noir (Cava) $12. 87 *—M.S. (12/15/2006)*

Segura Viudas NV Aria Estate Brut Sparkling Blend (Cava) $12. Crushed vitamins and frothy notes work the nose, while the palate is fairly fresh and clean, with apple as the lead flavor. The body is solid if standard, as is the depth of fruit and overall quality. By now Aria brut is a known entity; always a safe bet. Imported by Freixenet USA. 86 *—M.S. (12/15/2007)*

Segura Viudas NV Aria Estate Brut Sparkling Blend (Cava) $12. **89 Best Buy** *—M.S. (12/15/2006)*

Segura Viudas NV Aria Extra Dry Sparkling Blend (Cava) $12. **88 Best Buy** *—M.S. (12/15/2006)*

Segura Viudas NV Aria Estate Extra Dry Sparkling Blend (Cava) $12. The bouquet seems nutty and salinic, and overall this extra dry (meaning fairly sweet) focuses on soft and sugary mango and melon flavors. It's not as lively as it needs to be to balance the sweetness, so ultimately the wine comes up a touch flat. Imported by Freixenet USA. 84 *—M.S. (12/15/2007)*

Segura Viudas NV Brut Reserva Sparkling Blend (Cava) $10. Baked apple and spice aromas form a recognizable bouquet, while the palate oozes with grapefruit and tart apple flavors. This is zesty, clean, a little bit lean and fresh. It doesn't offer much in the way of range or complexity, but it's more than serviceable at the price point. Imported by Freixenet USA. **86 Best Buy** *—M.S. (12/15/2007)*

Segura Viudas NV Brut Reserva Sparkling Blend (Cava) $14. 88 *—M.S. (12/15/2006)*

Segura Viudas NV Brut Heredad Reserva Sparkling Blend (Cava) $20. 89 *—M.S. (6/1/2006)*

Segura Viudas NV Brut Rosé Sparkling Blend (Cava) $10. A very solid and consistent rosé cava. Opening aromas of spiced fruit, pepper and juicy citrus raise this to a higher level, and the raspberry and nectarine flavors are snappy and sure. A pleasant bubbly with a dash of complexity. Imported by Freixenet USA. **87 Best Buy** *—M.S. (12/15/2007)*

Segura Viudas NV Brut Rosé Sparkling Blend (Cava) $10. **87 Best Buy** *—M.S. (12/15/2006)*

Segura Viudas NV Extra Dry Sparkling Blend (Cava) $10. A perennial Best Buy among cavas. The Segura Viudas Extra Dry is a light, easy taste of lemon-lime and sweet apples. It finishes just crisp enough and with some juiciness. Not overly sugary, although it is pretty sweet. Imported by Freixenet USA. **86 Best Buy** *—M.S. (12/15/2007)*

Segura Viudas NV Extra Dry Sparkling Blend (Cava) $10. **89 Best Buy** *—M.S. (12/15/2006)*

Segura Viudas NV Reserva Heredad Brut Sparkling Blend (Cava) $20. Always one of Catalonia's more elevated cavas, this version opens with spiced dried apple aromas and a bit of yeast and dough. The palate is both sweet and tangy, with tangerine as the lead fruit. And the finish is consistent and moderately deep. A handsome wine with character. Imported by Freixenet USA. 88 *—M.S. (12/15/2007)*

Segura Viudas 2000 Torre Galimany Brut Nature Sparkling Blend (Cava) $NA. 88 *—M.S. (6/1/2005)*

Segura Viudas 2001 Mas D'Aranyó Reserva Tempranillo (Penedès) $15. 82 *—M.S. (10/1/2005)*

Segura Viudas 1998 Mas D'Aranyo Reserva Tempranillo (Penedès) $12. **87 Best Buy** *—M.S. (11/1/2002)*

Segura Viudas 1997 Mas D'Aranyó Riserva Tempranillo (Penedès) $15. 83 —*M.M. (9/1/2002)*

Segura Viudas 2005 Creu de Lavit Xarel-lo (Penedès) $15. This Freixenet brand consists of 100% Xarello grapes, and it's nice on the nose and clean as a whistle. Flavors of apple cider, peach and melon are subdued and a bit sweet, while the feel is juicy and tightly wrapped. Nice for a Catalonian white table wine. Imported by Freixenet USA. **87** —*M.S. (12/15/2007)*

Segura Viudas 2004 Creu de Lavit Xarel-lo (Penedès) $15. 86 —*M.S. (10/1/2005)*

Segura Viudas 2003 Creu de Lavit Xarel-lo (Penedès) $15. 84 —*M.S. (12/31/2004)*

Segura Viudas 2002 Creu de Lavit Xarel-lo (Penedès) $15. 84 —*M.S. (9/1/2004)*

Segura Viudas 2000 Creu de Lavit Xarel-lo (Penedès) $15. 84 —*M.M. (9/1/2002)*

Segura Viudas 2001 Creu de Lavit Xarel-lo (Penedès) $15. 87 —*D.T. (4/1/2003)*

SEIS DE AZUL Y GARANZA

Seis de Azul y Garanza 2004 Cabernet Sauvignon-Merlot (Navarra) $21. This Cab-Merlot blend delivers nice tobacco, char and dark fruit aromas, which are backed by plum, blackberry and chocolate flavors. Like most Navarran reds, there's some lettuce and other green characteristics. But for the most part the wine's balance, charm and mouthfeel win you over. **86** —*M.S. (8/1/2007)*

SEÑORIO DE AYLÉS

Señorio de Aylés 2004 Garnacha (Cariñena) $10. 80 —*M.S. (9/1/2006)*

Señorio de Aylés 2004 Tinto Jóven Red Blend (Cariñena) $11. 80 —*M.S. (9/1/2006)*

Señorio de Aylés 2003 Tempranillo-Merlot (Cariñena) $15. 87 —*M.S. (4/1/2006)*

SEÑORÍO DE CRUCES

Señorio de Cruces 2002 Albariño (Rías Baixas) $17. 87 —*M.S. (12/31/2004)*

SEÑORÍO DE CUZCURRITA

Señorío de Cuzcurrita 2001 Tempranillo (Rioja) $39. 90 —*M.S. (9/1/2004)*

Señorío de Cuzcurrita 2000 Tempranillo (Rioja) $35. 87 —*M.S. (5/1/2004)*

SEÑORÍO DE P. PECIÑA

Señorío de P. Peciña 2003 Tempranillo (Rioja) $15. 81 —*M.S. (2/1/2006)*

SEÑORÍO DE SAN VINCENTE

Senorio de San Vincente 2004 San Vicente Tempranillo (Rioja) $57. Slightly tighter and more complex than previous years, this single- vineyard wine delivers a ton of spice and herbs on a masculine bouquet and palate. Well-blended acids and tannins allow for it to be drunk now or over the next 5–8 years. About 4,000 cases made. Imported by Tempranillo, Inc. **93** —*M.S. (9/1/2007)*

Señorío de San Vincente 1997 San Vincente Tempranillo (Rioja) $36. 89 —*M.M. (8/1/2000)*

SEÑORIO DE SARRIA

Señorío de Sarria 1996 Cabernet Sauvignon (Navarra) $12. 86 —*D.T. (4/1/2003)*

Señorío de Sarria 2001 Chardonnay (Navarra) $12. 86 —*D.T. (4/1/2003)*

Señorío de Sarria 2001 Vinedo No 7 Graciano (Navarra) $15. 81 —*D.T. (4/1/2003)*

Señorío de Sarria 2001 Vinedo No 4 Merlot (Navarra) $15. 83 —*D.T. (4/1/2003)*

Señorío de Sarria 1998 Reserva Merlot-Cabernet Sauvignon (Navarra) $18. 81 —*M.S. (9/1/2006)*

Señorío de Sarria 1997 Reserva Red Blend (Navarra) $18. 88 Best Buy —*D.T. (4/1/2003)*

Señorío de Sarria 2001 Vinedo No 5 Rosé Blend (Navarra) $15. 85 —*D.T. (4/1/2003)*

Señorío de Sarria 2001 Reserva Especial Tempranillo Blend (Navarra) $65. 87 —*M.S. (4/1/2006)*

SEÑORIO DEL AGUILA

Señorio del Aguila 1994 Reserva Tempranillo Blend (Cariñena) $12. 84 —*M.M. (9/1/2002)*

SEÑORIO DEL VAL

Señorio del Val 2000 Tempranillo (Valdepeñas) $7. 85 —*M.S. (11/1/2002)*

SERRA DA ESTRELA

Serra da Estrela 2004 Albariño (Rías Baixas) $15. 86 —*M.S. (9/1/2006)*

Serra da Estrela 2003 Albariño (Rías Baixas) $15. 88 —*M.S. (12/31/2004)*

Serra da Estrela 2002 Albariño (Rías Baixas) $17. 85 —*M.S. (9/1/2004)*

SESTERO

Sestero 2003 Tempranillo-Cabernet Sauvignon (Navarra) $7. 83 —*M.S. (10/1/2005)*

SIDESHOW

Sideshow 2003 The Barker Garnacha (Calatayud) $9. 87 Best Buy —*M.S. (9/1/2006)*

Sideshow 2004 La Rosa Rosé Blend (Campo de Borja) $9. 84 —*M.S. (11/1/2006)*

SIERRA CANTABRIA

Sierra Cantabria 2003 Tempranillo (Rioja) $10. 84 —*M.S. (11/15/2005)*

Sierra Cantabria 2002 Tempranillo (Rioja) $9. 87 Best Buy —*M.S. (9/1/2004)*

Sierra Cantabria 2001 Tempranillo (Rioja) $9. 88 Best Buy —*M.S. (3/1/2004)*

Sierra Cantabria 2001 Amancio Tempranillo (Rioja) $138. 93 —*M.S. (8/1/2005)*

Sierra Cantabria 2000 Colección Privada, Unfiltered Tempranillo (Rioja) $38. 88 —*M.S. (3/1/2004)*

Sierra Cantabria 1998 Crianza Tempranillo (Rioja) $13. 86 —*M.S. (3/1/2004)*

Sierra Cantabria 1999 Cuvée Especial, Unfiltered Tempranillo (Rioja) $19. 90 Editors' Choice —*M.S. (3/1/2004)*

Sierra Cantabria 2002 El Bosque Tempranillo (Rioja) $138. 91 —*M.S. (6/1/2005)*

Sierra Cantabria 2001 Finca El Bosque Tempranillo (Rioja) $140. 92 —*M.S. (9/1/2004)*

Sierra Cantabria 1996 Reserva Tempranillo (Rioja) $19. 88 —*M.S. (3/1/2004)*

Sierra Cantabria 2003 Organza White Blend (Rioja) $23. 87 —*M.S. (8/1/2005)*

Sierra Cantabria 2001 Organza White Blend (Rioja) $17. 85 —*M.S. (3/1/2004)*

SIGLO

Siglo 1998 Crianza Red Blend (Rioja) $9. 82 —*C.S. (11/1/2002)*

SIGLO SACO

Siglo Saco 2001 Crianza Tempranillo (Rioja) $NA. 84 —*M.S. (9/1/2004)*

SOLABAL

Solabal 2003 Crianza Tempranillo (Rioja) $16. Condensed leather and spice aromas are upfront, while oak and fruit sit in the bouquet's second row. With raspberry and plum flavors balanced by dry spice and vanilla notes, there's complexity to the palate. Overall it's a nicely balanced wine with the full allotment of oak character. Not a boutique wine at 25,000 cases. **88** —*M.S. (4/1/2007)*

Solabal 1999 Crianza Tempranillo (Rioja) $13. 86 —*M.S. (3/1/2004)*

Solabal 2001 Reserva Tempranillo (Rioja) $23. Seems like Solabal let its reserva-level grapes get a little too soft before picking. The wine has color and potential, but the nose is a little flat and syrupy. The palate delivers ripe dark fruit flavors but also a touch of medicinality. Balance can be fleeting and this wine doesn't have it all the way. **85** —*M.S. (9/1/2007)*

Solabal 1997 Reserva Tempranillo (Rioja) $20. 89 —*M.M. (8/1/2000)*

SOLANES

Solanes 2000 Red Blend (Priorat) $24. 92 Editors' Choice —*M.S. (3/1/2004)*

SOLAR DE LA VEGA

Solar de la Vega 2004 Verdejo (Rueda) $8. 83 —*M.S. (10/1/2005)*

Solar de la Vega 2004 Verdejo (Rueda) $10. 82 —*M.S. (12/15/2006)*

SOLAR DE MUNOSANCHO

Solar de Munosancho 2005 Prius de Moraña Verdejo (Rueda) $14. Clean and minerally on the nose, with hints of pear and apple. The palate is a touch sharp and jumpy, with notes of nettle tangling with more common grapefruit flavors. Seems to start confidently but loses steam along the path. Tiny production of 210 cases. **85** —*M.S. (2/1/2007)*

SOLAR DE RANDEZ

Solar de Randez 2001 Crianza Tempranillo (Rioja) $18. 83 *—M.S. (11/1/2006)*

SOLEIRA

Soleira 2004 Albariño (Rías Baixas) $20. 81 *—M.S. (9/1/2006)*

SOLO

Solo 2003 Tempranillo Blend (Utiel-Requena) $20. 85 *—M.S. (9/1/2006)*

SOMBRERO

Sombrero 2005 Tempranillo Syrah Red Blend (Madrid) $17. Lots of charred oak and leathery fruit start it out, and then you get runaway berry flavors and screechy, almost grabby tannins. It finally settles and smooths out with airing, but requires too much compromise on the part of the drinker. Has its good points but not enough of them. **83** *—M.S. (12/15/2007)*

SONSIERRA

Sonsierra 2006 Tempranillo (Rioja) $10. Lucent to the eye and graced with fresh aromas of watermelon, flowers and fresh green herbs. A bit more candied that desired in the mouth, but still it delivers plum and raspberry flavors. Shows good kick all the way to the finish. **85 Best Buy** *—M.S. (7/1/2007)*

SUMARROCA

Sumarroca 2006 Estate Bottled Chardonnay (Penedès) $13. Citrus, barrel spice and vanilla are the primary aromas on this fresh, slightly watery Chard from Catalonia. The palate is dominated by pineapple and green apple flavors, while the tail end is clean and quiet. **86** *—M.S. (12/15/2007)*

Sumarroca 2005 Brut Nature Gran Reserva Cava Sparkling Blend (Penedès) $15. Dry, pure and attractive on the nose, with crisp apple and lemon-lime flavors. This wine performs on an even keel from start to finish, and it's dry, tangy and correct as far as brut nature cavas go. Verges on elegant. **88** *—M.S. (12/15/2007)*

Sumarroca 2004 Brut Reserva Cava Sparkling Blend (Penedès) $12. Nothing really sticks out on this perfectly good brut. It offers the basic aromas of green apple and lime, followed by flavors of apple juice, citrus and pineapple. It takes on weight as it opens and then finishes a bit sweet. **86** *—M.S. (12/15/2007)*

TANDEM

Tandem 2004 Ars Nova Red Blend (Navarra) $25. 86 *—M.S. (12/15/2006)*

TAPEÑA

Tapeña 2005 Garnacha (Tierra de Castilla) $10. Nothing earth-shattering here, but this Garnacha is sweet and syrupy, with jammy berry and black plum flavors. It's totally round and soft, with no hard tannins or confounding complexities. It's a sound, uneventful red wine. **84** *—M.S. (11/1/2007)*

Tapeña 2005 Tempranillo (Tierra de Castilla) $10. Dark and resiny, with aromas of leather, black olive and jammy berries. The palate runs quite sweet and without the backbone needed to prop things up. Hence the mouthfeel is lacking and the finish peters out quickly. Tasty enough, but short on feel and structure. **83** *—M.S. (11/1/2007)*

TARSUS

Tarsus 1999 Red Blend (Ribera del Duero) $25. 85 *—M.S. (11/1/2006)*

TELMO RODRÍGUEZ

Telmo Rodríguez 1999 Alma Garnacha (Navarra) $10. 86 *—M.M. (8/1/2000)*

Telmo Rodríguez 2005 MR Moscatel (Málaga) $21. MR is a heavy Moscatel with smoky, slightly burnt aromas that almost get into popcorn territory. In the mouth, it's round and honeyed, but again, there's a mild acrid quality to it. Very concentrated but not totally harmonious. **86** *—M.S. (4/1/2007)*

Telmo Rodríguez 2002 Molino Real Mountain Wine Moscatel (Málaga) $50. 90 *—M.S. (8/1/2005)*

Telmo Rodríguez 2001 Molino Real Mountain Wine Moscatel (Málaga) $48. 88 *—M.S. (6/1/2005)*

Telmo Rodríguez 2003 MR Mountain Wine Moscatel (Málaga) $19. 90 *—M.S. (8/1/2005)*

Telmo Rodríguez 2001 Matallana Red Blend (Ribera del Duero) $93. 93 Editors' Choice *—M.S. (6/1/2005)*

Telmo Rodríguez 2004 Altos de Lanzaga Tempranillo (Rioja) $105. Masculine and heady stuff, as leather, espresso, smoked meat, mocha and intense blackberry aromas set the stage for an intense, driven, structured palate that's full of coconut, vanilla bean, cocoa and pure plum and berry. A serious nuevo classico Rioja if there ever was one. **95 Cellar Selection** *—M.S. (9/1/2007)*

Telmo Rodríguez 2003 Altos de Lanzaga Tempranillo (Rioja) $82. Right away this shows the requisite signs of excellence. The meaty, earthy, leathery, full-fruit nose is just right, and the palate is elevated in how it is infused with pure blackberry and plum as well as chocolate and fine herbs. Finishes with class and kick. Best from 2008–2011. **92** *—M.S. (9/1/2007)*

Telmo Rodríguez 1998 Altos Lanzaga Tempranillo (Rioja) $20. 91 *—M.M. (8/1/2000)*

Telmo Rodríguez 1999 Dehesa Gago Tempranillo (Toro) $12. 87 *—M.M. (8/1/2000)*

Telmo Rodríguez 2000 Lanzaga Tempranillo (Rioja) $20. 90 *—M.S. (3/1/2004)*

Telmo Rodríguez 1998 Valderiz Tempranillo Blend (Ribera del Duero) $25. 92 *—M.M. (8/1/2000)*

Telmo Rodríguez 2002 G Dehesa Gago Tinta de Toro (Toro) $13. 86 *—M.S. (3/1/2004)*

Telmo Rodríguez 2003 Gago Tinta de Toro (Toro) $25. Coffee grounds, some minty wood and lots of ripe fruit greet you, and the lower levels contain all the sweet, dark fruit and oak-based chocolate and vanilla one could ever ask for. This is new-age wine to the max, and some might call it overdone. But if you like ripeness and a rowdy mix of body, tannins and acidity, this is it. **91** *—M.S. (11/1/2007)*

Telmo Rodríguez 2003 Pago la Jara Tinta de Toro (Toro) $57. This small-batch, single-vineyard heavyweight has a lot of stuffing, power and tannin, but it's also a rough ride, meaning the fruit and tannins hit like a jackhammer. But with good fatty foods and some decanting, the beast can be tamed. As for flavors, it delivers mostly plum and chocolate. **89** *—M.S. (11/1/2007)*

Telmo Rodríguez 2002 Basa White Blend (Rueda) $9. 88 Best Buy *—M.S. (11/15/2003)*

Telmo Rodríguez 1999 Basa White Blend (Rueda) $8. 88 Best Buy *—M.M. (8/1/2000)*

TEOFILO REYES

Teofilo Reyes 1999 Crianza Red Blend (Ribera del Duero) $26. 92 Editors' Choice *—J.C. (11/1/2001)*

Teofilo Reyes 1998 Tempranillo (Ribera del Duero) $36. 89 *—M.M. (8/1/2000)*

Teofilo Reyes 1996 Reserva Tempranillo (Ribera del Duero) $150. 94 *—M.M. (8/1/2000)*

TERRAS GAUDA

Terras Gauda 2005 Abadía de San Campio Albariño (Rías Baixas) $16. 89 *—M.S. (9/1/2006)*

Terras Gauda 2004 Abadía de San Campio Albariño (Rías Baixas) $18. 84 *—M.S. (2/1/2006)*

Terras Gauda 2004 O Rosal Albariño (Rías Baixas) $20. 83 *—M.S. (12/31/2005)*

Terras Gauda 2005 O Rosal White Blend (Rías Baixas) $19. 88 *—M.S. (9/1/2006)*

TIBERIO

Tiberio 2003 Tinto Tinto del Pais (Ribera del Duero) $10. 82 *—M.S. (11/15/2005)*

TIENEN DUENDE

Tienen Duende 2005 Garnacha (Campo de Borja) $9. Big and bulky with giant, untamed red-fruit aromas. The palate is equally loud and pretty much anonymous in terms of its flavors. A bumpy ride with size and power but zero finesse. **81** *—M.S. (8/1/2007)*

Tienen Duende 2005 Verdejo (Vino de la Tierra de Castilla y León) $9. Very fresh and citrusy, which is a style that Rueda can do well. The nose is pure citrus blossom and mineral, and the crisp palate never loses focus while delivering quick bursts of lemon, orange and green apple. A wine that's good and easy to comprehend. **87 Best Buy** *—M.S. (2/1/2007)*

TIERRA ADENTRO

Tierra Adentro 2002 Valdunes Tempranillo (Ribera del Duero) $20. If you don't mind some heavy barrel char, then you'll probably like this rough rider. It has espresso and asphalt on the nose, and then you get leathery plum and berry fruit on the palate. A good wine, with a long finish, lots of oak and overall balance. In a nutshell, there's plenty going on. **89** *—M.S. (8/1/2007)*

TINAR

Tinar 2000 Crianza Tempranillo (Ribera del Duero) $32. 85 *—M.S. (8/1/2005)*

TIONIO

Tionio 2000 Crianza Red Blend (Ribera del Duero) $20. 86 —*M.S. (8/1/2003)*

Tionio 1998 Crianza Tempranillo (Ribera del Duero) $17. 86 —*J.C. (11/1/2001)*

TORNASOL

Tornasol 2002 Tempranillo (Rioja) $25. 81 —*M.S. (8/1/2005)*

TORRE ORIA

Torre Oria NV Brut Rosado Grenache (Cava) $13. Light cherry and berry aromas are a bit candied, and the palate is more so. It's almost sugary sweet, but fortunately the wine has good acidity and bounce, so it's not cloying or sticky. Definitely for fans of white Zin and other sweet rosés. 84 —*M.S. (12/15/2007)*

Torre Oria NV Brut Sparkling Blend (Cava) $13. First, second and third nosings all result in the same finding: that this Cava smells a lot like lettuce. In the mouth, scattered citrus and apple flavors are acceptable, and while the mouthfeel is fine, it just doesn't hit the spot or trigger much excitement. 83 —*M.S. (8/1/2007)*

Torre Oria NV Brut Nature Sparkling Blend (Cava) $20. 85 —*M.M. (12/31/2001)*

Torre Oria NV Brut Sparkling Blend (Cava) $11. 85 —*M.S. (6/1/2005)*

Torre Oria NV Brut Reserve Tannat (Cava) $15. 81 —*M.S. (6/1/2005)*

Torre Oria 1997 Gran Reserva Tempranillo (Utiel-Requena) $19. No way around the fact that this is funky, starchy and full of dry oak and tannins. The nose is rubbery and earthy, while the palate shows some green tobacco and herbal flavors. Gets better with airing, but the pleasure factor remains low. 81 —*M.S. (12/15/2007)*

Torre Oria 1999 Reserva Tempranillo (Utiel-Requena) $15. Cola, root beer and herbal fruit carry the nose into a fairly balanced, old-school palate that features crisp cherry, raspberry and citrus flavors. This is made from Tempranillo and it's a bit like an '80s model cru bourgeois Bordeaux. 84 —*M.S. (12/15/2007)*

Torre Oria 1996 Reserva Tempranillo (Utiel-Requena) $15. 80 —*M.S. (9/1/2004)*

Torre Oria 1998 Reserve Tempranillo (Utiel-Requena) $15. 81 —*M.S. (10/1/2005)*

Torre Oria 2005 Superior Tempranillo (Utiel-Requena) $9. Dusty and peppery aromas alert you to the fact that this will be a lean, tight ride. The palate delivers on the promise, showing tart cherry and raspberry flavors in front of a wave of vanilla on the choppy, acidic finish. Decent fruit and clean, but lean and clipped. 83 —*M.S. (12/15/2007)*

Torre Oria 2003 Superior Tempranillo (Utiel-Requena) $9. 80 —*M.S. (9/1/2006)*

TORREDEROS

Torrederos 2004 Selección Tempranillo (Ribera del Duero) $46. The greeting is nothing but pure green coconut, and that essence of powerful, almost overpowering oak persists all the way through. Along the way, and amidst the resin and sawdust, the wine offers dark fruit, potency and flash. But the depth isn't here, thus the wood stands out. 86 —*M.S. (11/1/2007)*

TORRES

Torres 2000 Reserva Real Bordeaux Blend (Penedès) $150. 88 —*M.S. (3/1/2005)*

Torres 1998 Gran Coronas Cabernet Sauvignon (Penedès) $19. 86 —*M.S. (11/1/2002)*

Torres 1999 Gran Coronas Reserva Cabernet Sauvignon (Penedès) $20. 88 —*M.S. (3/1/2004)*

Torres 1997 Gran Coronas Reserva Cabernet Sauvignon (Penedès) $19. 87 —*M.M. (9/1/2002)*

Torres 2003 Mas La Plana Cabernet Sauvignon (Penedès) $50. Brutal heat didn't do a lot for Mas La Plana in 2003. While still a worthy wine, this one shows some green on the nose and palate, while the balance is weightier than normal. In its favor, there's bold blackberry and a touch of cola on the palate. Good but not up to the wine's usual high standards. 88 —*M.S. (8/1/2007)*

Torres 2001 Mas La Plana Cabernet Sauvignon (Penedès) $50. 91 Cellar Selection *(11/15/2005)*

Torres 2000 Mas La Plana Cabernet Sauvignon (Penedès) $49. 88 —*M.S. (3/1/2004)*

Torres 1998 Mas La Plana Cabernet Sauvignon (Penedès) $49. 87 —*M.S. (3/1/2004)*

Torres 1997 Mas La Plana Cabernet Sauvignon (Penedès) $25. 92 Cellar Selection —*M.M. (4/1/2002)*

Torres 1995 Gran Coronas Cabernet Sauvignon-Tempranillo (Penedès) $18. 87 —*J.C. (8/1/2000)*

Torres 2006 Gran Viña Sol Chardonnay (Penedès) $15. The bouquet deals some peach, custard and a slight hint of oak, while the palate runs racy, fresh and citrusy. If you like a fresher style with strong orange and tropical fruit flavors, this is your ticket. It's a controlled wine that meets expectations. With 15% Parellada. 87 —*M.S. (12/15/2007)*

Torres 2003 Gran Viña Sol Chardonnay (Penedès) $15. 86 —*M.S. (12/31/2004)*

Torres 2002 Gran Viña Sol Chardonnay (Penedès) $14. 86 —*M.S. (3/1/2004)*

Torres 2001 Gran Viña Sol Chardonnay (Penedès) $14. 83 —*D.T. (4/1/2003)*

Torres 2005 Milmanda Chardonnay (Conca de Barberà) $53. As long as the price keeps creeping up on this wine, we're happy to say that the quality seems better and the oak level lower than in past years. This version of Milmanda offers roasted corn, walnut and other smoky, barrel-based aromas. Throughout the fruit is shy but the mouthfeel and oak are smooth. Finishes with a blast of white pepper and toast. 88 —*M.S. (12/15/2007)*

Torres 2002 Milmanda Chardonnay (Conca de Barberà) $47. 86 —*M.S. (12/31/2004)*

Torres 2001 Milmanda Chardonnay (Conca de Barberà) $50. 84 —*M.S. (3/1/2004)*

Torres 2000 Milmanda Chardonnay (Conca de Barberà) $50. 86 —*M.S. (11/1/2002)*

Torres 1999 Milmanda Chardonnay (Conca de Barberà) $48. 85 —*M.M. (9/1/2002)*

Torres 2005 Malena Garnacha (Catalunya) $10. 89 Best Buy —*M.S. (12/15/2006)*

Torres 2003 Atrium Merlot (Penedès) $16. 82 —*M.S. (12/31/2004)*

Torres 2001 Atrium Merlot (Penedès) $15. 86 —*D.T. (4/1/2003)*

Torres 1999 Atrium Merlot (Penedès) $14. 86 —*M.S. (11/1/2002)*

Torres 2005 Viña Esmeralda Moscatel (Catalunya) $14. For ages this Moscatel-Gewürztraminer blend has been Torres's prescription for light Mediterranean seafood and Pan Asian cuisine. A total lightweight, it's defined by simplistic lime, pineapple and mango flavors. Clean and crisp on the finish, with little to no aftertaste. 84 —*M.S. (4/1/2007)*

Torres 2004 Viña Sol Paralleda (Penedès) $8. 84 Best Buy —*M.S. (10/1/2005)*

Torres 2003 Viña Sol Paralleda (Catalonia) $9. 85 Best Buy —*M.S. (12/31/2004)*

Torres 2000 Viña Sol Paralleda (Penedès) $11. 83 —*M.M. (9/1/2002)*

Torres 2002 Mas Borràs Pinot Noir (Penedès) $30. 82 —*M.S. (6/1/2005)*

Torres 2001 Mas Borràs Pinot Noir (Penedès) $32. 85 —*M.S. (3/1/2004)*

Torres 1994 Mas Borràs Pinot Noir (Penedès) $30. 90 —*R.V. (11/1/1999)*

Torres 2003 Celeste Red Blend (Ribera del Duero) $22. 86 *(11/15/2005)*

Torres 2001 Gran Sangre de Toro Red Blend (Catalunya) $15. 86 —*M.S. (11/15/2005)*

Torres 2000 Gran Sangre de Toro Red Blend (Catalonia) $14. 86 —*M.S. (3/1/2004)*

Torres 1998 Gran Sangre de Toro Red Blend (Catalonia) $13. 87 Best Buy —*D.T. (4/1/2002)*

Torres 1996 Gran Sangre de Toro Reserva Red Blend (Penedès) $11. 89 —*M.S. (8/1/2000)*

Torres 1995 Gran Sangre de Toro Reserva Red Blend (Penedès) $11. 90 —*R.V. (11/1/1999)*

Torres 2000 Grans Muralles Red Blend (Conca de Barberà) $100. 91 —*M.S. (4/1/2006)*

Torres 1999 Grans Muralles Red Blend (Conca de Barberà) $98. 88 —*M.S. (3/1/2005)*

Torres 1998 Grans Muralles Red Blend (Conca de Barberà) $106. 87 —*D.T. (4/1/2003)*

Torres 1997 Grans Muralles Red Blend (Rioja) $103. 90 —*M.M. (9/1/2002)*

Torres 2003 Nerola Xarello-Garnacha Red Blend (Catalunya) $18. 85 *(11/15/2005)*

Torres 2002 Nerola Red Blend (Catalonia) $20. 88 —*M.S. (12/31/2004)*

Torres 2001 Nerola Red Blend (Catalonia) $20. 84 —*M.S. (6/1/2005)*

Torres 1998 Reserva Real Red Blend (Penedès) $150. 92 —*M.S. (3/1/2004)*

SPAIN

Torres 2003 50th Aniversario Sangre de Toro Red Blend (Catalonia) $10. 85 Best Buy —*M.S. (6/1/2005)*

Torres 2002 Sangre de Toro Red Blend (Catalonia) $10. 84 —*M.S. (3/1/2004)*

Torres 2001 Sangre de Toro Red Blend (Catalonia) $10. 84 —*D.T. (4/1/2003)*

Torres 2000 Sangre do Toro Red Blend (Catalonia) $11. 84 —*M.S. (11/1/2002)*

Torres 1999 Sangre de Toro Red Blend (Catalonia) $11. 83 —*D.T. (4/1/2002)*

Torres 1998 Waltroud Riesling (Penedès) $13. 88 —*L.W. (11/15/1999)*

Torres 2006 DeCasta Rosado Rosé Blend (Catalunya) $10. Clean, dry and ripe she goes, and that's just the way we like it. The nose on this Garnacha-Carignan blend is precise and easygoing, and the raspberry flavors are pure. It finishes dry and peppery, but always there's some fruit to assure its friendliness. **87 Best Buy** —*M.S. (7/1/2007)*

Torres 2004 De Casta Rosé Blend (Catalunya) $8. 86 Best Buy —*M.S. (2/1/2006)*

Torres 2005 Fransola Sauvignon Blanc (Penedès) $27. This is over the hill and showing mostly vegetal papaya and green melon aromas and flavors. There's not much spunk or style left, so wait for the 2006 and drink that wine upon release; Fransola has never aged well. **81** —*M.S. (8/1/2007)*

Torres 2003 Fransola Sauvignon Blanc (Penedès) $26. 83 —*M.S. (3/1/2005)*

Torres 2002 Fransola Sauvignon Blanc (Penedès) $25. 86 —*M.S. (3/1/2004)*

Torres 2001 Fransola Sauvignon Blanc (Penedès) $25. 87 —*D.T. (4/1/2003)*

Torres 2000 Fransola Sauvignon Blanc (Penedès) $22. 88 *(8/1/2002)*

Torres 1998 Fransola Sauvignon Blanc (Penedès) $22. 84 *(8/1/2000)*

Torres 2004 Celeste Tempranillo (Ribera del Duero) $22. Torres claims to be serious about Ribera del Duero, but early on the Celeste wines, made from purchased grapes, are so-so at best. The 2004 is a touch damp and leathery on the nose, with toasty dark cherries as the driving flavor. It's got some weight but it's also drying and oaky on the finish. Needs some fine tuning. **84** —*M.S. (6/1/2007)*

Torres 2003 Coronas Tempranillo (Catalunya) $10. 85 Best Buy —*M.S. (10/1/2005)*

Torres 2002 Coronas Tempranillo (Catalonia) $10. 83 —*M.S. (6/1/2005)*

Torres 2001 Coronas Tempranillo (Catalonia) $10. 88 Best Buy —*M.S. (3/1/2004)*

Torres 2000 Coronas-Tempranillo (Penedès) $10. 87 Best Buy —*M.S. (11/1/2002)*

Torres 1999 Coronas Tempranillo (Catalonia) $11. 85 —*D.T. (4/1/2002)*

Torres 1997 Coronas Tempranillo (Penedès) $9. 84 —*R.V. (11/1/1999)*

Torres 2002 Nerola White Blend (Catalonia) $15. 85 —*M.S. (12/31/2004)*

Torres 2002 Viña Esmeralda White Blend (Penedès) $13. 87 —*M.S. (3/1/2004)*

Torres 2001 Viña Esmeralda White Blend (Penedès) $13. 87 Best Buy —*M.S. (11/1/2002)*

Torres 2002 Viña Sol White Blend (Penedès) $10. 86 —*M.S. (8/1/2003)*

Torres 2001 Vina Sol White Blend (Penedès) $10. 85 —*M.S. (11/1/2002)*

TORRES DE ANGUIX

Torres de Anguix 2004 A Tinto del Pais (Ribera del Duero) $10. 85 Best Buy —*M.S. (4/1/2006)*

Torres de Anguix 2000 A Tinto del Pais (Ribera del Duero) $20. 83 —*M.S. (6/1/2005)*

Torres de Anguix 2002 Crianza Tinto del Pais (Ribera del Duero) $14. 85 —*M.S. (6/1/2005)*

Torres de Anguix 2003 Tinto Tinto del Pais (Ribera del Duero) $10. 84 —*M.S. (6/1/2005)*

TORROXAL

Torroxal 2004 Albariño (Rías Baixas) $25. 85 —*M.S. (9/1/2006)*

TR3

TR3 2002 Tinta de Toro (Toro) $30. 83 —*M.S. (2/1/2006)*

TRASLANZAS

Traslanzas 2000 Tinto del Pais Tempranillo (Cigales) $35. 90 —*M.S. (5/1/2004)*

Traslanzas 2001 Tinto del Pais (Cigales) $46. There is much to like about this wine, particularly the cola and roasted fruit flavors that control the palate. But in front and back of that likable intermezzo is a sharp, prickly bouquet and a mouthfeel that's slightly grabby, tannic and elastic. Good but you want it to be better. Drink now. **86** —*M.S. (8/1/2007)*

TRAVITANA

Travitana 2003 Old Vines Monastrell (Alicante) $10. 85 Best Buy —*M.S. (8/1/2005)*

TRES BARCOS

Tres Barcos 2004 Tinta de Toro (Toro) $15. This granular, mildly earthy Toro falls into the everyday category, but within that market segment it'll do just fine with steaks, burgers and lamb chops. It offers viscosity, blackberry fruit and a long, chocolaty finish. It's not ultra-refined but it has plenty of stuffing and kick. **86** —*M.S. (11/1/2007)*

TRES LUNAS

Tres Lunas 2003 Tempranillo (Toro) $17. 87 —*M.S. (12/15/2006)*

TRESANTOS

Tresantos 2000 Roble Red Blend (Tierra del Viños de Zamora) $13. 85 —*M.M. (4/1/2002)*

TXOMÍN ETXANÍZ

Txomín Etxaníz 1999 Txakoli (Getariako Txakolina) $17. 87 —*M.M. (8/1/2000)*

Txomín Etxaníz 2005 White Blend (Getariako Txakolina) $19. A native Basque white that's way past its prime. Txakoli wines barely last a year and need to be attacked very young, and this '05 is pretty much DOA. It still has some character and perfume, but it's getting heavier and duller by the minute. Look for the 2006 or wait until the spring/summer for the 2007. **81** —*M.S. (11/1/2007)*

Txomín Etxaníz 2002 White Blend (Getariako Txakolina) $14. 81 —*M.S. (3/1/2004)*

Txomín Etxaníz 2000 White Blend (Getariako Txakolina) $16. 85 —*M.M. (4/1/2002)*

URBINA

Urbina 2001 Selección Especial Tempranillo (Rioja) $35. 84 —*M.S. (8/1/2005)*

VAL DE LOS FRAILES

Val de Los Frailes 2003 Jóven Tempranillo (Cigales) $8. 83 —*M.S. (8/1/2005)*

Val de Los Frailes 2001 Pago de las Costanas Tempranillo (Cigales) $35. 87 —*M.S. (11/1/2006)*

Val de Los Frailes 2001 Prestigio Tempranillo (Cigales) $25. 90 —*M.S. (8/1/2005)*

Val de Los Frailes 2001 Vendimia Seleccionada Tempranillo (Cigales) $15. 86 —*M.S. (8/1/2005)*

Val de Los Frailes 2002 Prestigio Tinta Fina (Cigales) $23. 84 —*M.S. (11/1/2006)*

Val de Los Frailes 2003 Vendimia Seleccionada Tinta Fina (Cigales) $15. Complex, with all sorts of aromas, flavors and textures coming from every direction. The color is lighter and the feel more delicate than many; and the flavors are pure cherry and chocolate, while the finish is long, minty and echoing some of the barrels it once saw. Drink now–2008. **90 Best Buy** —*M.S. (4/1/2007)*

VAL MONTIUM

Val Montium 2005 Mencía (Bierzo) $18. Fairly bold and ripe upfront, with dark berry aromas and an almond candy undercurrent. The palate is a bit more red-fruit based than the bouquet, and the flavors of raspberry and red plums are satisfying a touch tangy. Interesting, with drying tannins on the finish. **87** —*M.S. (8/1/2007)*

VAL SOTILLO

Val Sotillo 1998 Crianza Temparillo (Ribera del Duero) $28. 88 Cellar Selection —*J.C. (11/1/2001)*

Val Sotillo 1997 Tempranillo (Ribera del Duero) $29. 88 —*M.M. (8/1/2000)*

Val Sotillo 1996 Reserva Tempranillo (Ribera del Duero) $55. 93 —*M.M. (8/1/2000)*

Val Sotillo 1995 Gran Reserva Red Blend (Ribera del Duero) $75. 89 —*J.C. (11/1/2001)*

Val Sotillo 1994 Gran Reserva Red Blend (Ribera del Duero) $80. 96 —*M.M. (8/1/2000)*

SPAIN

VALCANTARA

Valcantara 2004 Old Vine Garnacha (Cariñena) $8. 84 Best Buy *—M.S. (9/1/2006)*

VALCORTES

Valcortes 2006 Cosecha Tempranillo (Rioja) $10. Cheerful at first, with bubble gum and berry drink mix aromas. The fun pretty much stops there; what follows is astringent berry flavors and a lean, choppy finish. Juicy but lacks sytle and finesse. **82** *—M.S. (12/15/2007)*

Valcortes 2001 Crianza Tempranillo (Rioja) $15. 84 *—M.S. (6/1/2005)*

VALDAMOR

Valdamor 2005 Albariño (Rías Baixas) $20. 86 *—M.S. (9/1/2006)*

VALDEAURUM

Valdeaurum 2000 Crianza Tempranillo (Ribera del Guadiana) $15. 85 *—M.S. (3/1/2005)*

VALDEGRACIA

Valdegracia 1998 Tinto Crianza Tempranillo (Ribera del Guadiana) $14. 87 *—M.M. (9/1/2002)*

VALDELAINOS

Valdelainos 2005 Verdejo (Rueda) $11. Delicous Verdejo with no pretenses. The nose is big and oily, but still fresh and full of green herbs and citrus fruits. Solid, stand-up flavors of melon and peach are nice, and there's even some nuttiness to the stone-fruit dominated finish. A bargain white that touches the right notes. **89 Best Buy** *—M.S. (2/1/2007)*

VALDELANA

Valdelana 2001 Red Blend (Rioja) $8. 83 *—M.S. (11/1/2002)*

Valdelana 1999 Crianza Red Blend (Rioja) $11. 84 *(11/1/2002)*

Valdelana 2003 Agnus Crianza Tempranillo (Rioja) $25. 87 *—M.S. (12/15/2006)*

VALDELAPINTA

Valdelapinta 2006 Verdejo (Rueda) $12. Crisp, green and friendly, with aromas of celery and fairway grass. The palate also has some green to it, namely celery and edamame, but there's adequate melon and grapefruit to balance things off. The finish is dry and pithy, with a lasting flavor of pink grapefruit. Imported by USA Wine Imports, Inc. **88 Best Buy** *—M.S. (11/1/2007)*

Valdelapinta 2004 Verdejo (Rueda) $12. 85 *—M.S. (9/1/2006)*

VALDEMAR

Valdemar 2003 Rosado Garnacha (Rioja) $9. 83 *—M.S. (3/1/2005)*

VALDEMORAL

Valdemoral 1998 Tinto del Pais (Ribera del Duero) $17. 85 *(8/1/2000)*

VALDERIZ

Valderiz 2003 Tempranillo (Ribera del Duero) $29. Round, meaty, colorful and full of oak, chocolate and ripe fruit aromas. The palate is big and broad, with plum and boysenberry leading the troops. The mouthfeel deals some choppy tannins but all in all the wine has the right stuff, meaning it tastes fairly regal and offers a well-rounded feel. **90** *—M.S. (5/22/2007)*

Valderiz 2005 Señorío de Valdehermoso Tempranillo (Ribera del Duero) $12. More deep and muscular than average, with a smooth and fruity nose that settles nicely. The palate is somewhat crisp and juicy as acidity and ripe tannins drive red apple and raspberry flavors. Call it a classic, young, food-friendly Tempranillo. **87 Best Buy** *—M.S. (6/1/2007)*

Valderiz 2003 Señorío de Valdehermoso Crianza Tempranillo (Ribera del Duero) $20. One whiff reveals deep, ripe, lush black-fruit aromas, and the palate is as chunky, rich and full of berries and dark plums as the nose indicates. Like most '03s, this is broad and a touch soft. It has just enough acid and tannin to keep it lively now and for the next year or so. **89** *—M.S. (6/1/2007)*

Valderiz 2005 Señorío de Valdehermoso Roble Tempranillo (Ribera del Duero) $16. A look and a sniff confirm that this is a potent brew with full ripeness. The color is opaque and the aromas of baked fruits and bacon are staunch. One could say this makes its impression upfront and then holds onto that goodwill while not improving. A jammy young wine made to drink now and into 2008. **88** *—M.S. (6/1/2007)*

Valderiz 2001 Tomás Esteban Tempranillo (Ribera del Duero) $105. Deep and ripe, with smooth black-fruit aromas in front of a generous palate that deals cherry, tobacco and vanilla flavors. In terms of feel, this wine isn't overly dense or tannic; in fact, it's modest at the core and getting very close to peak drinkability. Best now through 2009. **91** *—M.S. (6/1/2007)*

VALDETAN

Valdetan 2000 Roble Tinto Red Blend (Cigales) $10. 83 *—M.S. (3/1/2004)*

Valdetan 2001 Tinto Red Blend (Cigales) $NA. 87 *—M.S. (8/1/2003)*

VALDRINAL

Valdrinal 2002 Roble Tempranillo (Ribera del Duero) $20. Smells a lot like a pot of baked beans, meaning it's not that fresh and probably too earthy for most tastes. The palate offers mostly cherry tomato and green herbs on top of dried cherry, while the finish, which has a good feel to it, tastes too much like tomato. **82** *—M.S. (6/1/2007)*

Valdrinal 2004 6 Tinto del Pais (Ribera del Duero) $14. Light in terms of fruit potency, but heavy on the spicy oak. This is your typical dry, lean, somewhat shallow Tempranillo with spice and vanilla as the dominant forces. Some red cherry is evident in the mix. **83** *—M.S. (6/1/2007)*

Valdrinal 2002 Crianza Tinto del Pais (Ribera del Duero) $17. 88 *—M.S. (12/15/2006)*

Valdrinal 2005 Valdrinal de Santamaria Verdejo (Rueda) $11. Quite chunky, with an aromatic personality defined by canned peaches and very ripe melon. The palate, however, offers nothing but dried, stripped-down citrus, while the finish is clean but short as a whistle blast. Acceptable but dull. **83** *—M.S. (2/1/2007)*

VALDUBÓN

Valdubón 2003 Tempranillo (Ribera del Duero) $14. 86 *—M.S. (6/1/2005)*

Valdubón 1999 Tempranillo (Ribera del Duero) $14. 85 *—J.C. (11/1/2001)*

Valdubón 2004 Cosecha Tempranillo (Ribera del Duero) $14. Fairly dark and chocolaty on the nose, with some vanilla oak notes that help it along. The mouthfeel, however, is a bit choppy and tangy as red fruit and acidity come up and take over the game. Short on the finish, with oak filling any gaps left by the fading fruit. Good and ready to go now. Imported by Freixenet USA. **85** *—M.S. (6/1/2007)*

Valdubón 2004 Cosecha Tempranillo (Ribera del Duero) $17. 83 *—M.S. (4/1/2006)*

Valdubón 2002 Cosecha Tempranillo (Ribera del Duero) $14. 87 *—M.S. (3/1/2004)*

Valdubón 2002 Crianza Tempranillo (Ribera del Duero) $18. We tried this wine a couple of years ago and it came in at exactly the same level. Now, it's showing mature aromas of vanilla, tobacco, leather and dried berry fruits, while the palate is offering tight cherry and raspberry flavors backed by tobacco and perky acidity. It's probably at its classic best now as it's registering more traditional than modern. Imported by Freixenet USA. **87** *—M.S. (6/1/2007)*

Valdubón 2002 Crianza Tempranillo (Ribera del Duero) $18. 87 *—M.S. (11/15/2005)*

Valdubón 2001 Crianza Tempranillo (Ribera del Duero) $18. 89 *—M.S. (12/31/2004)*

Valdubón 1999 Crianza Tempranillo (Ribera del Duero) $18. 86 *—D.T. (4/1/2003)*

Valdubón 1998 Crianza Tempranillo (Ribera del Duero) $18. 88 *—J.C. (11/1/2001)*

Valdubón 2002 Reserva Tempranillo (Ribera del Duero) $24. Fairly earthy but also smooth and inviting. This wine shows a reserva's higher oak level but also a higher level of fruit quality than the winery's 2002 Crianza. The palate is all about red berries, while the feel and finish are crisp and integrated. Nearly mature and pretty much ready to drink now. 250 cases made. Imported by Freixenet USA. **88** *—M.S. (6/1/2007)*

Valdubón 2001 Reserva Tempranillo (Ribera del Duero) $24. Starts out a touch earthy and funky, but that's the way mature Ribera is supposed to be. And as this one opens up it shows a good mix of traditional sous bois and earth matched by core ripeness and balance. If you like Spanish reds with subtle fruit flavors offset by touches of dill, vanilla and herbal essence, this is for you. Imported by Freixenet USA. **88** *—M.S. (6/1/2007)*

Valdubón 2000 Reserva Tempranillo (Ribera del Duero) $24. 87 *—M.S. (6/1/2005)*

Valdubón 1999 Reserva Tempranillo (Ribera del Duero) $24. 90 *—M.S. (3/1/2004)*

VALENCISO

Valenciso 2001 Reserva Tempranillo (Rioja) $35. 89 *—M.S. (11/1/2006)*

Valenciso 2000 Reserva Tempranillo (Rioja) $34. 87 *—M.S. (6/1/2005)*

VALL LLACH

Vall Llach 2004 Red Blend (Priorat) $85. Stand up and take note: this is great wine from Priorat. And that's regardless of whether it is typically Priorato in style. It trades textbook minerality for lushness, and the fruit is star quality. In the mouth, there's an explosion of grape matter that leaves coffee, chocolate, peanut brittle and vanilla. Almost drinkable right now but best from 2009. **96 Editors' Choice** —*M.S. (8/1/2007)*

Vall Llach 2000 Celler Red Blend (Priorat) $88. 95 Cellar Selection —*M.S. (3/1/2004)*

Vall Llach 2004 Embruix Red Blend (Priorat) $34. Lovers of full-bodied, extracted Priorat wines know Vall Llach, and that cult sees Embruix as a good value. The 2004 is on the right track: the nose is almost impenetrable as it oozes blackberry, tar and fine leather. Meanwhile, the palate is like warm berry compote followed by espresso and dark chocolate. Very rich although not overly complex. Best now with steak or cheese, or hold until 2008. **92** —*M.S. (8/1/2007)*

Vall Llach 2002 Embruix Red Blend (Priorat) $33. 88 —*M.S. (10/1/2005)*

Vall Llach 2000 Embruix Red Blend (Priorat) $28. 94 Editors' Choice —*M.S. (3/1/2004)*

Vall Llach 1998 Embruix Red Blend (Priorat) $80. 87 —*M.M. (4/1/2002)*

Vall Llach 2004 Idus Red Blend (Priorat) $55. Deep and dark, this is an excellent kitchen-sink blend (it includes Carignan, Merlot, Cabernet, Garnacha and Syrah). For those who like expressive, fruity, no-holds-barred wines, you're gonna swoon for this. The palate is super lush and full of dark cherry, tobacco, herbs and spice, while the finish is mile-long. Outwardly impressive in a modern style. **93 Editors' Choice** —*M.S. (8/1/2007)*

Vall Llach 2002 Idus Red Blend (Priorat) $62. 90 —*M.S. (10/1/2005)*

Vall Llach 2002 Vino Tinto Red Blend (Priorat) $94. 91 —*M.S. (6/1/2005)*

VALLE ROJO

Valle Rojo 2002 Crianza Grenache-Tempranillo Red Blend (Cariñena) $13. At 70% Garnacha and 30% Tempranillo, this hold-over from the sketchy 2002 harvest starts with an odd blend of clove and shaved wood notes, while the palate pushes basic cherry and tangy raspberry flavors. **83** —*M.S. (12/15/2007)*

VALLFORMOSA

Vallformosa 2000 Clos Maset Selección Especial Cabernet Sauvignon (Penedès) $30. 85 —*M.S. (9/1/2006)*

Vallformosa 1999 Masia Freyes Collección Especial Merlot (Penedès) $30. 81 —*M.S. (9/1/2006)*

Vallformosa 1992 Gran Reserva Red Blend (Penedès) $18. 86 —*M.M. (9/1/2002)*

Vallformosa NV Chantal Brut Rosé Sparkling Blend (Cava) $19. There's a bit of bramble, hard spice and forest fire smoke on the nose, but the palate is largely fresh, with red-fruit flavors such as plum and wild raspberry. The wine is ripe, a bit sweet and solid on the finish. Imported by Altuve Foods and Beverage. **86** —*M.S. (12/15/2007)*

Vallformosa 2000 Mas La Roca Selección Especial Syrah (Penedès) $30. 83 —*M.S. (9/1/2006)*

Vallformosa 2003 Primum Vitae Crianza Tempranillo (Rioja) $17. Ready as it will ever be, this mildly baked red starts with minty aromas and chocolate. The palate is saturated and full of fruit, but the feel is a touch thin given the color and the lightly cooked aromas. Drink now with food and it will satisfy. **86** —*M.S. (9/1/2007)*

Vallformosa 2001 Primum Vitae Crianza Tempranillo (Rioja) $19. 83 —*M.S. (11/1/2006)*

Vallformosa 2001 Primum Vitae Reserva Tempranillo (Rioja) $20. 86 —*M.S. (11/1/2006)*

Vallformosa NV Chantal Brut Rosé White Blend (Cava) $20. 85 —*M.S. (6/1/2006)*

Vallformosa 2006 Claudia White Blend (Penedès) $13. Honeysuckle, talcum powder, melon and tangerine all work the nose, while the palate comes at you sweet and almost sticky. Flavors of white fruits and canned peaches are good if that's your thing, while the finish teeters on cloying but manages to hold the line. For a sweet Parellada-Muscat wine it isn't bad. Imported by Altuve Foods and Beverage. **83** —*M.S. (12/15/2007)*

Vallformosa NV Eric Brut Nature White Blend (Cava) $22. 87 —*M.S. (6/1/2006)*

VALLOBERA

Vallobera 1998 Reserva Tempranillo (Rioja) $20. 88 —*M.S. (6/1/2005)*

Vallobera 2001 Crianza Tempranillo Blend (Rioja) $15. 88 —*M.S. (6/1/2005)*

Vallobera 2002 Pago Malarina Tempranillo Blend (Rioja) $10. 85 Best Buy —*M.S. (10/1/2005)*

Vallobera 1999 Tinto Crianza Tempranillo Blend (Rioja) $15. 84 —*S.H. (1/1/2002)*

VALMIÑOR

Valmiñor 2005 Albariño (Rías Baixas) $15. 87 —*M.S. (9/1/2006)*

VALPICULATA

Valpiculata 2003 Tinta de Toro (Toro) $45. 85 —*M.S. (12/15/2006)*

VALSACRO

Valsacro 2001 Dioro Tempranillo Blend (Rioja) $36. 93 —*M.S. (9/1/2004)*

VALSANZO

Valsanzo 2006 T-Sanzo Rosado Tempranillo (Vino de la Tierra de Castilla y León) $10. Acceptable, but barely. There's a strange citric, grassy tinge to the nose that makes it smell like Verdejo or Sauvignon Blanc. And it tastes pickled and briny. Decent mouthfeel and sensory balance save it from even lower depths. **80** —*M.S. (11/1/2007)*

VALTOSCA

Valtosca 2004 Syrah (Jumilla) $23. Really good and interesting Syrah, with chocolate, campfire, menthol and prune on the nose. With airing the wine quickly settles into a deep, smooth berry and chocolate groove, while the finish deals pure tannins and comfort. Ripe but not raisiny; a really nice example of Jumilla Syrah, with 4% Viognier blended in for lightness (and it still weighs in at 14.9%). **90** —*M.S. (12/15/2007)*

VALTRAVIESO

Valtravieso 2003 Crianza Tempranillo (Ribera del Duero) $20. Ultra sweet and loaded with aromas of marzipan, shoe polish and warm earth, this is a soft, chewy wine with low acidity but rewarding flavors of dark plum, fruit cake and chocolate. It's plump and ready to drink now. **87** —*M.S. (6/1/2007)*

Valtravieso 2005 Dominio De Nogara Tempranillo (Ribera del Duero) $10. Pretty good except for some hardness and a touch of chemical that runs onto the finish. Along the way there are heavy aromas and rugged blackberry and dark plum flavors. Finishes full but drying toward the end. **84** —*M.S. (6/1/2007)*

VEGA BARCELONA

Vega Barcelona NV Brut Reserva Sparkling Blend (Cava) $13. The palate touches both the sweet and sour, as it offers green apple and then candied white fruit flavors. The feel is a touch flat and pithy, but all in all it shows what it should. **86** —*M.S. (12/15/2007)*

VEGA CARCHE

Vega Carche 2001 Crianza Tempranillo Blend (Jumilla) $14. Fires out of the blocks with rubbery, fiery aromas that later settle into leather, campfire and baked black fruit. The palate, typical for Jumilla, is beefy and stout, with dark fruit and hard-spice flavors. Chocolate emerges on the full, healthy, mildly tannic finish. **87** —*M.S. (4/1/2007)*

VEGA DE CASTILLA

Vega de Castilla 2000 Tempranillo (Ribera del Duero) $11. 86 —*D.T. (4/1/2003)*

VEGA GITANIA

Vega Gitania 2003 Premium Rosé Tempranillo Blend (Mentrida) $15. 81 —*M.S. (2/1/2006)*

VEGA PRIVANZA

Vega Privanza 1999 Tinto Jóven Tempranillo (Ribera del Duero) $11. 83 —*J.C. (11/1/2001)*

VEGA RIAZA

Vega Riaza 2002 Tempranillo (Ribera del Duero) $12. 87 —*M.S. (5/1/2004)*

Vega Riaza 2002 Roble Tempranillo (Ribera del Duero) $15. 85 —*M.S. (5/1/2004)*

VEGA SAUCO

Vega Sauco 2002 Roble Tinta de Toro (Toro) $10. 86 Best Buy —*M.S. (10/1/2005)*

Vega Sauco 1998 Adoremus Reserva Tinta de Toro (Toro) $22. 87 —*M.S. (9/1/2004)*

Vega Sauco 2000 Crianza Tinta de Toro (Toro) $15. 85 —*M.S. (9/1/2004)*

Vega Sauco 2001 Roble Tinta de Toro (Toro) $10. 86 Best Buy —*M.S. (9/1/2004)*

Vega Sauco 1999 Wences Reserva Tinta de Toro (Toro) $60. 84 —*M.S. (3/1/2005)*

VEGA SICILI

Vega Sicilia 1987 Unico Red Blend (Ribera del Duero) $200. 90 —*J.C. (11/1/2001)*

Vega Sicilia 1997 Valbuena Tempranillo (Ribera del Duero) $90. 92 Cellar Selection *—J.C. (11/1/2001)*

Vega Sicilia 1994 Unico Gran Reserva Tempranillo Blend (Ribera del Duero) $325. 95 Editors' Choice *—M.S. (6/1/2005)*

VEGA SINDOA

Vega Sindoa 2003 Rosé Cabernet Blend (Navarra) $8. 87 Best Buy *—M.S. (10/1/2004)*

Vega Sindoa 2004 Cabernet Sauvignon-Tempranillo (Navarra) $11. Nicely balanced and a better example of the upside of Navarra than the wines that are based on or include Merlot. The nose shows some herbal character but more deep fruit notes. And in the mouth there's ripe cherry, cassis and plum. Texturally, it's very nice, and when you get down to the nuts and bolts it's a very good value. 88 Best Buy *—M.S. (8/1/2007)*

Vega Sindoa 1998 Cabernet Sauvignon-Tempranillo (Navarra) $7. 84 *—M.M. (8/1/2000)*

Vega Sindoa 2000 Barrel Fermented Chardonnay (Navarra) $11. 87 *—M.M. (4/1/2002)*

Vega Sindoa 1999 Barrel Fermented Chardonnay (Navarra) $10. 86 *—M.M. (8/1/2000)*

Vega Sindoa 1998 Cuvée Allier Chardonnay (Navarra) $12. 89 Best Buy *—M.M. (8/1/2000)*

Vega Sindoa 2004 Merlot (Navarra) $12. Navarran Merlot often leans toward the vegetal. There's bell pepper and tomato on the nose, but also balancing red plum, cherry and raspberry on the palate. It's a touch sheer, scratchy and green, but the effort is there and by no means is it a bad, herbaceous wine. 84 *—M.S. (8/1/2007)*

Vega Sindoa 2002 Merlot (Navarra) $8. 87 Best Buy *—M.S. (10/1/2004)*

Vega Sindoa 1998 Merlot (Navarra) $12. 90 Best Buy *—M.M. (8/1/2000)*

Vega Sindoa 1996 Reserva Red Blend (Navarra) $16. 86 *—M.M. (8/1/2000)*

Vega Sindoa 2005 Rosé Blend (Navarra) $7. Heavy and mildly pickled on the nose. This 50/50 blend of Garnacha and Cabernet has already lost its freshness, and while it's acceptable you're best off waiting for the 2006 to arrive in the spring or summer. This version is now mealy and over the hill. 80 *—M.S. (4/1/2007)*

Vega Sindoa 2001 Rosé Blend (Navarra) $7. 86 Best Buy *—D.T. (11/15/2002)*

Vega Sindoa 2000 Rosé Blend (Navarra) $7. 87 Best Buy *—M.M. (4/1/2002)*

Vega Sindoa 1999 Rosé Blend (Navarra) $7. 86 *—M.M. (8/1/2000)*

Vega Sindoa 2005 Tempranillo-Merlot (Navarra) $7. Young and bouncy, with jammy aromas of raspberries and strawberries. Immediately you know this has Tempranillo at the core, and fans should appreciate the pleasant combination of meaty flavors, a round body, solid ripeness and a good price. 86 Best Buy *—M.S. (8/1/2007)*

Vega Sindoa 2002 Tempranillo-Merlot (Navarra) $7. 86 Best Buy *—M.S. (11/15/2003)*

Vega Sindoa 1999 Tempranillo-Merlot (Navarra) $7. 88 Best Buy *—M.M. (8/1/2000)*

Vega Sindoa 2000 White Blend (Navarra) $7. 86 Best Buy *—M.M. (4/1/2002)*

Vega Sindoa 2005 Viura-Chardonnay White Blend (Navarra) $7. Unusual from the beginning, with custard and citrus aromas that don't totally mesh. The palate is dry and devoid of potency; all you really get is blanched almond, green banana and papaya. And it's not getting better as it ages. 83 *—M.S. (4/1/2007)*

Vega Sindoa 1999 Viura Chardonnay White Blend (Navarra) $7. 87 Best Buy *—M.M. (8/1/2000)*

VEGAVAL PLATA

Vegaval Plata 1996 Crianza Cencibel (Valdepeñas) $10. 86 *—J.C. (8/1/2000)*

Vegaval Plata 1993 Gran Reserva Cencibel (Valdepeñas) $17. 85 *—D.T. (4/1/2002)*

Vegaval Plata 1993 Reserva Tempranillo (Valdepeñas) $12. 82 *—J.C. (11/15/1999)*

Vegaval Plata 1989 Reserva Tempranillo (Valdepeñas) $12. 83 *—J.C. (11/15/1999)*

VEIGADARES

Veigadares 2002 Albariño (Rías Baixas) $18. 84 *—M.S. (12/31/2004)*

VENTA LA OSSA

Venta la Ossa 2004 Tempranillo (La Mancha) $26. Strange how sour and unappealing this tastes when it smells pretty decent. It's not a well-balanced specimen; the acidity is up there and the mouthfeel is stark. 80 *—M.S. (8/1/2007)*

VENTA MAZZARON

Venta Mazzaron 2004 Tinta de Toro (Vino de Calidad de Tierras de León) $15. Fans of hammering new oak will take to this charred, barrel-driven Tempranillo that hits forcefully with coffee, bacon and toast. It's loud, aggressive and amplified as it pumps black fruit, chocolate and drying tannins. Good for its power and potency but not deserving of style points. 87 *—M.S. (4/1/2007)*

Venta Mazzaron 2000 Tinta de Toro (Toro) $10. 90 *—M.M. (4/1/2002)*

VÍ DE NULLES

Ví de Nulles 2006 Rosat Rosé Blend (Tarragona) $10. Dry, dusty and fairly full in fruit, this is a solid entry from Tarragona. The fruit is ripe and veers toward raspberry, while the finish is bolstered by proper acidity. If there's any fault, it's that the palate is a touch pulpy and weighty. 85 Best Buy *—M.S. (7/1/2007)*

VICENTE GANDIA

Vicente Gandia 2004 Fusta Nova Moscatel (Valencia) $11. 84 *—M.S. (9/1/2006)*

Vicente Gandia 2001 Generacion 1 Red Blend (Utiel-Requena) $19. 83 *—M.S. (6/1/2005)*

Vicente Gandia 2002 Tempranillo (Utiel-Requena) $7. 84 Best Buy *—M.S. (6/1/2005)*

Vicente Gandia 2002 Ceremonia Reserva De Autor Tempranillo (Utiel-Requena) $15. 85 *—M.S. (9/1/2006)*

Vicente Gandia 2004 El Miracle 120 Tempranillo Blend (Valencia) $10. 86 Best Buy *—M.S. (12/15/2006)*

Vicente Gandia 2000 Hoya De Cadenas Reserva Prevada Tempranillo-Cabernet Sauvignon (Utiel-Requena) $11. 85 *—M.S. (6/1/2005)*

VILLACAMPA DEL MARQUÉS

Villacampa del Marqués 2002 Roble Tempranillo Blend (Ribera del Duero) $14. 82 *—M.S. (6/1/2005)*

VILLACEZAN

Villacezan 2003 Doce Meses Prieto Picudo (Viño Tierra de León) $15. 87 *—M.S. (9/1/2006)*

Villacezan 2003 Molendores Prieto Picudo (Viño Tierra de León) $12. 80 *—M.S. (3/1/2005)*

Villacezan 2005 Molendores Rosado Prieto Picudo (Viño Tierra de León) $11. 83 *—M.S. (9/1/2006)*

Villacezan 2004 VCZ Molendores Prieto Picudo (Viño Tierra de León) $15. 83 *—M.S. (9/1/2006)*

Villacezan 2003 Dehesa de Villacezan Red Blend (Viño Tierra de León) $11. 84 *—M.S. (6/1/2005)*

Villacezan 2001 Doce Meses Red Blend (Viño Tierra de León) $17. 84 *—M.S. (6/1/2005)*

Villacezan 2002 Seis Meses Red Blend (Viño Tierra de León) $14. 83 *—M.S. (6/1/2005)*

Villacezan 2005 Elverite Verdejo (Viño Tierra de León) $11. 84 *—M.S. (9/1/2006)*

Villacezan 2003 Elverite Verdejo (Viño de la Tierra de Castilla y León) $11. 82 *—M.S. (12/31/2004)*

VILLAREI

Villarei 2003 Albariño (Rías Baixas) $20. 83 *—M.S. (9/1/2006)*

VILLARROYA DE LA SIERRA

Villarroya de la Sierra 2004 la Garnacha (Calatayud) $9. 83 *—M.S. (9/1/2006)*

VIÑA ALARBA

Viña Alarba 2001 Old Vines Grenache (Catalonia) $6. 88 Best Buy *—J.C. (11/15/2002)*

VIÑA ALBALI

Viña Albali 1998 Gran Reserva Tempranillo (Valdepeñas) $11. 83 *—M.S. (10/1/2005)*

Viña Albali 2000 Reserva Tempranillo (Valdepeñas) $8. 82 *—M.S. (10/1/2005)*

SPAIN

VIÑA ARNÁIZ

Viña Arnáiz 2001 Crianza Tinto del Pais (Ribera del Duero) $28. 85 *—M.S. (2/1/2006)*

Viña Arnáiz 2000 Reserva Tinto del Pais (Ribera del Duero) $30. 84 *—M.S. (11/1/2006)*

Viña Arnáiz 1999 Crianza Tinto del Pais (Ribera del Duero) $19. 87 *—C.S. (11/1/2002)*

Viña Arnáiz 1998 Reserva Tinto del Pais (Ribera del Duero) $30. 89 *—M.S. (3/1/2004)*

VIÑA BORGIA

Viña Borgia 2005 Garnacha (Campo de Borja) $5. A distinguished little red wine. It's all Garnacha, and it's round and a touch citrusy on the nose, while the palate delivers pure, ripe cherry and raspberry flavors. Generous, balanced and shapely. What more could you ask for five bucks? **87 Best Buy** *—M.S. (4/1/2007)*

Viña Borgia 2000 Garnacha (Campo de Borja) $6. 86 Best Buy *—M.M. (4/1/2002)*

VIÑA BOSQUERA

Viña Bosquera 2005 Red Blend (Madrid) $17. Solid black cherry aromas distinguish this wine from the competition. It has poise for a Madrid wine, and the mix of Tempranillo, Syrah and Cabernet Sauvignon delivers a saturated palate with natural, full-bodied flavors that aren't too infused with oak. Concentrated and well made, with good size. **88** *—M.S. (12/15/2007)*

VIÑA CANCHAL

Viña Canchal 2003 Tempranillo (Ribera del Guadiana) $6. 83 *—M.S. (8/1/2005)*

Viña Canchal 2003 Crianza Tempranillo (Ribera del Guadiana) $11. A strong whiff of wintergreen cements the wine's herbal status; it seems as though the grapes were likely picked to beat the heat but maybe weren't fully ripe. Hence the wine shows lean strawberry and raspberry characteristics, and always there's that shot of green. **82** *—M.S. (11/1/2007)*

Viña Canchal 2002 Crianza Tempranillo (Ribera del Guadiana) $12. 85 *—M.S. (2/1/2006)*

Viña Canchal 2001 Crianza Tempranillo (Ribera del Guadiana) $9. 86 Best Buy *—M.S. (3/1/2005)*

VIÑA CAROSSA

Viña Carossa NV Tinto Red Blend (Spain) $6. 83 *—M.S. (5/1/2004)*

Viña Carossa NV Brut Sparkling Blend (Spain) $8. 82 *—M.S. (5/1/2004)*

VIÑA COLLADO

Viña Collado 1999 Tinto Tempranillo Blend (Campo de Borja) $8. 85 *—M.M. (9/1/2002)*

VIÑA CONCEJO

Viña Concejo 2001 Crianza Tempranillo (Cigales) $19. 83 *—M.S. (11/1/2006)*

Viña Concejo 1999 Crianza Tempranillo (Cigales) $20. 87 *—M.S. (12/31/2004)*

VIÑA DEL FRADE

Viña del Frade 2005 Roble Tempranillo (Ribera del Duero) $13. Seems a little raw and fiery but there's also attractive red licorice and raspberry aromas to balance things out. In the mouth, the strawberry and raspberry flavors are real and likable, albeit kind of thin. So while it's not in the heavily extracted style, it's still got good fruit and integrity. **86** *—M.S. (6/1/2007)*

VIÑA FUENTENARRO

Viña Fuentenarro 2003 Cuatro Meses Barrica Tempranillo (Ribera del Duero) $14. 82 *—M.S. (11/1/2006)*

VIÑA GODEVAL

Viña Godeval 2005 Godello (Valdeorras) $15. 89 *—M.S. (9/1/2006)*

Viña Godeval 2003 Godello (Valdeorras) $15. 87 *—M.S. (10/1/2005)*

Viña Godeval 2000 Godello (Valdeorras) $16. 89 *—M.M. (4/1/2002)*

VIÑA GORMAZ

Viña Gormaz 2005 Tempranillo (Ribera del Duero) $9. Sweet, fruity and much like you've seen many times before, this is a satisfying, nicely made fruitball with lots of oomph and admirable richness and balance. It's young and grabby, but gets better with some airing. Good with ham and/or chorizo. **86 Best Buy** *—M.S. (6/1/2007)*

Viña Gormaz 2004 Tempranillo (Ribera del Duero) $0. A sweet, clumsy wine with gumball aromas in front of a funky palate that deals hints of vinegar and olives along with candied fruit flavors. Not a very good wine but drinkable. **80** *—M.S. (6/1/2007)*

VIÑA HERMOSA

Viña Hermosa 2001 Crianza Tempranillo (Rioja) $14. 85 *—M.S. (4/1/2006)*

Viña Hermosa 1997 Gran Reserva Tempranillo (Rioja) $30. 88 *—M.S. (4/1/2006)*

Viña Hermosa 1998 Reserva Tempranillo (Rioja) $20. 88 *—M.S. (4/1/2006)*

VIÑA IJALBA

Viña Ijalba 2000 Múrice Crianza Tempranillo (Rioja) $13. 83 *—M.S. (8/1/2005)*

Viña Ijalba 1998 Reserva Tempranillo Blend (Rioja) $20. 82 *—M.S. (10/1/2005)*

VIÑA IZADI

Viña Izadi 2000 Crianza Tempranillo (Rioja) $14. 86 *—M.S. (10/1/2003)*

Viña Izadi 1998 Expresión Tempranillo (Rioja) $60. 91 *—K.F. (11/1/2002)*

Viña Izadi 1998 Reserva Tempranillo (Rioja) $20. 85 *—M.S. (10/1/2003)*

Viña Izadi 1997 Selección Tempranillo (Rioja) $45. 89 *—M.M. (9/1/2002)*

Viña Izadi 2000 Blanco Viura (Rioja) $13. 86 *—M.M. (9/1/2002)*

Viña Izadi 2001 White Blend (Rioja) $14. 83 *—M.S. (10/1/2003)*

VIÑA JARABA

Viña Jaraba 2002 Crianza Tempranillo Blend (La Mancha) $13. 83 *—M.S. (12/15/2006)*

VIÑA LUCIA

Viña Lucia 1998 Cabernet Sauvignon-Tempranillo (Cadiz) $10. 88 *—C.S. (4/1/2002)*

VIÑA MAGAÑA

Viña Magaña 2001 Baron de Magana Merlot (Navarra) $22. 83 *—M.S. (12/31/2004)*

Viña Magaña 2000 Calchetas Crianza Red Blend (Navarra) $40. 84 *—M.S. (3/1/2005)*

Viña Magaña 1998 Dignus Red Blend (Navarra) $12. 82 *—M.S. (9/1/2004)*

VIÑA MAYOR

Viña Mayor 1994 Gran Reserva Red Blend (Ribera del Duero) $32. 86 *—J.C. (11/1/2001)*

Viña Mayor 1996 Reserva Red Blend (Ribera del Duero) $16. 84 *—J.C. (11/1/2001)*

Viña Mayor 1999 Secreto Reserva Red Blend (Ribera del Duero) $18. 87 *—M.S. (9/1/2004)*

Viña Mayor 2003 Crianza Tempranillo (Ribera del Duero) $15. A bit light and lucent at the edges, with raspberry/strawberry aromas that are hardly demanding nor overbearing. The palate on this middleweight shows lighter cherry and apple skins, while pepper and scratchy acids reign on the finish. Drink now or wait for the better 2004s and 2005s. **86** *—M.S. (6/1/2007)*

Viña Mayor 2002 Crianza Tempranillo (Ribera del Duero) $15. 87 *—M.S. (9/9/1999)*

Viña Mayor 2002 Crianza Tempranillo (Ribera del Duero) $14. 86 *—M.S. (12/15/2006)*

Viña Mayor 2000 Crianza Tempranillo (Ribera del Duero) $13. 83 *—M.S. (12/31/2004)*

Viña Mayor 1998 Crianza Tempranillo (Ribera del Duero) $13. 87 Best Buy *—J.C. (11/1/2001)*

Viña Mayor 1999 Gran Reserva Tempranillo (Ribera del Duero) $40. A little candied and sweet upfront, which is surprising for a wine of eight years. But this one does not seem to be fading, as cherry, tobacco and chocolate flavors float on a bed of zesty acidity. As a result, the wine offers both richness and deftness. Best to drink it soon before it really does start to head south. **89** *—M.S. (6/1/2007)*

Viña Mayor 1996 Gran Reserva Tempranillo (Ribera del Duero) $30. 86 *—M.S. (6/1/2005)*

Viña Mayor 2001 Reserva Tempranillo (Ribera del Duero) $20. If it weren't for the drying oak and old-fashioned tart acidity, this would be even more approachable and hence even more likable. But as is, it's spicy and true to its roots, with pepper and rooty aromas preceding raspberry and cherry flavors. Best with food because it has tightness and snap more than, say, flesh, extract and richness. **89** *—M.S. (6/1/2007)*

Viña Mayor 2000 Reserva Tempranillo (Ribera del Duero) $20. Shows nice size and pop given that it's now almost seven years old. There are warm berry, leather and maple aromas, and after that ample red-fruit flavors rise up and make a statement. On the finish there's some wayward buttery oak and mint, but overall this is a good wine that can be drunk now or held for another few years at most. **88** *—M.S. (6/1/2007)*

Viña Mayor 1999 Reserva Tempranillo (Ribera del Duero) $19. 86 *—M.S. (3/1/2005)*

Viña Mayor 2005 Roble Tempranillo (Ribera del Duero) $10. Viña Mayor has been around for ages; in 2005 its young wines show huge fruit, nuance and quality. This basic youngster rides high with boysenberry flavors followed by toast, earth and mushroom on the finish. Smells and tastes better than its price. **88 Best Buy** *—M.S. (5/22/2007)*

Viña Mayor 2005 Secreto Tempranillo (Ribera del Duero) $17. Having tasted Mayor's wines over the past decade, this might be one of the winery's best efforts. First off, it doesn't cost an arm and a leg, like some RdDs can. But it does give woodsy oak on top of deep berry aromas and flavors. And all the way through the balance, feel and complexities are here. Drink now through 2009. **89** *—M.S. (6/1/2007)*

Viña Mayor 2004 Tinto Roble Tempranillo (Ribera del Duero) $10. Lighter bodied and more traditional than the new-age heavyweights, this peppery wine shows earth and leather on the nose along with rustic red-fruit aromas. The palate is pure cherry and berry, while the tannic finish is smoky and right. Nothing extraordinary; just good RDD the way it used to be made. **86** *—M.S. (2/1/2007)*

VIÑA MAYTE

Viña Mayte 2005 Vino de Mesa Red Blend (Valdepeñas) $6. Interesting in that this fresh, snappy table wine includes 60% Airen (a white grape) in addition to Tempranillo. This odd combo results in a light-bodied, almost translucent wine that's easy to drink but offers little in the way of heft or complexity. **83** *—M.S. (8/1/2007)*

VIÑA MEIN

Viña Mein 2001 White Blend (Ribeiro) $16. 86 *—M.S. (3/1/2004)*

Viña Mein 2004 Barrica White Blend (Ribeiro) $21. 91 *—M.S. (9/1/2006)*

Viña Mein 2005 Blanco White Blend (Ribeiro) $18. 91 Editors' Choice *—M.S. (9/1/2006)*

Viña Mein 2003 Blanco White Blend (Ribeiro) $19. 90 Editors' Choice *—M.S. (8/1/2005)*

Viña Mein 2000 Blanco White Blend (Ribeiro) $16. 86 *—M.M. (4/1/2002)*

VIÑA MOCEN

Viña Mocen 2005 Verdejo (Rueda) $12. 85 *—M.S. (12/15/2006)*

VIÑA PRÓDIGUS

Viña Pródigus 1998 Reserva Tinta de Toro (Toro) $38. 88 *—M.S. (10/1/2005)*

Viña Pródigus 2001 Roble Tinta de Toro (Toro) $18. 85 *—M.S. (10/1/2005)*

VIÑA RUFINA

Viña Rufina 2000 Alta Gama Reserva Tempranillo (Cigales) $28. 83 *—M.S. (11/1/2006)*

VIÑA SALAMANCA

Viña Salamanca 2004 Viura/Verdejo White Blend (Viño de la Tierra de Castilla y León) $10. 84 *—M.S. (10/1/2005)*

VIÑA SALCEDA

Viña Salceda 2002 Crianza Tempranillo Blend (Rioja) $16. 87 *—M.S. (12/15/2006)*

VIÑA SANTA MARINA

Viña Santa Marina 2005 Alicena White Blend (Extremadura) $9. The average American wine drinker is probably not interested in a three-grape white blend from hot and dry Extremadura, Spain, but in case you are, this wine is neutral on the nose and lean on the palate. Flavors of green apple, pineapple and lemon are scouring and seem designed for fried seafood. **82** *—M.S. (12/15/2007)*

VIÑA SARDASOL

Viña Sardasol 2005 Rosado de Lagrima Garnacha (Navarra) $9. 85 Best Buy *—M.S. (12/15/2006)*

Viña Sardasol 2004 Rosado de Lagrima Garnacha (Navarra) $9. 87 Best Buy *—M.S. (2/1/2006)*

Viña Sardasol 2005 Tempranillo (Navarra) $7. Sweet and ripe, with bubble gum and berry jam on the nose. Flavors of raspberry and blackberry are nice but narrow in scope, while the finish holds on to the fruit shown on the palate. Fruity but not very challenging. **84 Best Buy** *—M.S. (2/1/2007)*

Viña Sardasol 2004 Tempranillo (Navarra) $7. 84 Best Buy *—M.S. (11/15/2005)*

Viña Sardasol 2002 Crianza Tempranillo Blend (Navarra) $10. 81 *—M.S. (12/15/2006)*

Viña Sardasol 2001 Crianza Tempranillo Blend (Navarra) $10. 87 Best Buy *—M.S. (11/15/2005)*

Viña Sardasol 2001 Reserva Tempranillo Blend (Navarra) $11. 89 Best Buy *—M.S. (11/15/2006)*

Viña Sardasol 2000 Reserva Tempranillo Blend (Navarra) $11. 85 *—M.S. (11/15/2005)*

Viña Sardasol 2004 Tempranillo-Merlot (Navarra) $9. 86 Best Buy *—M.S. (11/15/2005)*

VIÑA SASTRE

Viña Sastre 2003 Crianza Tempranillo (Ribera del Duero) $30. Lots of size and smoothness are on display, and the bouquet is ample and fruity. In the mouth, there's forward berry fruit and snappy cherry riding more on the surface than down below. In fact, this wine runs more racy than hefty, with a touch of herbal essence blending with chocolate on the finish. **89** *—M.S. (6/1/2007)*

Viña Sastre 2001 Pago de Santa Cruz Tempranillo (Ribera del Duero) $70. Smoky and subtle on the nose, except for some robust coconut that had to come from the barrel aging. In the mouth, vanilla and coconut remain present, sitting alongside stately berry fruit and tobacco flavors. This is a rock-steady wine with all the characteristics of a high-flying Ribera del Duero. While it's an excellent example, does it sing to the tune of $70? You be the judge. 208 cases produced. **90** *—M.S. (6/1/2007)*

Viña Sastre 1999 Regina Vides Tempranillo (Ribera del Duero) $175. 95 Cellar Selection *(4/1/2003)*

Viña Sastre 1999 Regina Vides 1998 Tempranillo (Ribera del Duero) $175. 93 *(4/1/2003)*

Viña Sastre 1999 Pago de Santa Cruz Tempranillo (Ribera del Duero) $85. 92 *(4/1/2003)*

Viña Sastre 1998 Pago de Santa Cruz Tempranillo (Ribera del Duero) $85. 91 *(4/1/2003)*

Viña Sastre 1996 Pago de Santa Cruz Gran Reserva Tempranillo (Ribera del Duero) $175. 90 *(4/1/2003)*

Viña Sastre 1995 Pago de Santa Cruz Gran Reserva Tempranillo (Ribera del Duero) $150. 87 *(4/1/2003)*

Viña Sastre 2000 Reserva Tempranillo (Ribera del Duero) $45. A really nice, mature offering considering that 2000 was an average year at best. This wine delivers earthy, savory aromas along with background dark fruit, while in the mouth there's toast, forest and leather to accompany a good core of red-fruit flavors. Well made and balanced, with a creamy finish housing graceful tannins. Drink now or hold for another couple of years. **90** *—M.S. (6/1/2007)*

Viña Sastre 2005 Roble Tempranillo (Ribera del Duero) $19. Sastre does not make mass-market, inexpensive wines; this is the base-level offering. And it's a delicious, moderately complex Ribera that is fat and fruity but also exotic and a touch beguiling. It will make an excellent accompaniment to basic grilled meats; drink now or through 2008. 1,600 cases produced. **90** *—M.S. (6/1/2007)*

Viña Sastre 1999 Pesus Tempranillo Blend (Ribera del Duero) $375. 94 Cellar Selection *(4/1/2003)*

Viña Sastre 2001 Pesus Tinto del Pais (Ribera del Duero) $395. 95 *—M.S. (6/1/2005)*

VIÑA SILA

Viña Sila 2003 Naia Des Verdejo (Rueda) $28. 88 *—M.S. (6/1/2005)*

VIÑA SOLEDAD

Viña Soledad 2001 Crianza Tempranillo Blend (Rioja) $18. 84 *—M.S. (4/1/2006)*

VIÑA SOLORCA

Viña Solorca 1998 Crianza Tempranillo (Ribera del Duero) $19. 87 *—C.S. (11/1/2002)*

Viña Solorca 1999 Roble Tempranillo (Ribera del Duero) $12. 85 *—C.S. (11/1/2002)*

VIÑA SOMOZA

Viña Somoza 2004 Godello (Valdeorras) $18. 85 *—M.S. (9/1/2006)*

VIÑA VERMETA

Viña Vermeta 1996 Reserva Roble Nuevo Monastrell (Alicante) $10. 82 *—C.S. (4/1/2002)*

VIÑA VILANO

Viña Vilano 2006 Rosado Tempranillo (Ribera del Duero) $9. Nothing about this empty, heavy wine will instill confidence in Ribera del Duero's ability to produce good rosado. The wine is pulpy and offers watery, saline notes as opposed to bright, viviacious fruit. What's the point, really? **80** —*M.S. (7/1/2007)*

Viña Vilano 2005 Rosado Tempranillo (Ribera del Duero) $10. 81 —*M.S. (12/15/2006)*

VIÑALCASTA

Viñalcasta 2000 Crianza Tempranillo (Toro) $14. 86 —*M.S. (12/31/2004)*

Viñalcasta 1999 Reserva Tempranillo (Toro) $18. 84 —*M.S. (12/31/2004)*

Viñalcasta 2001 Reserva Tinta de Toro (Toro) $20. 81 —*M.S. (9/1/2006)*

VIÑAS DEL CENIT

Viñas del Cenit 2003 Venta Mazzaron Tempranillo (Viño de la Tierra de Manchuela) $15. 90 Best Buy —*M.S. (11/15/2005)*

VIÑAS DEL MONTSAN

Viñas del Montsant 2001 Fra Gueralu Red Blend (Montsant) $NA. 85 —*M.S. (3/1/2004)*

VIÑAS DEL VERO

Viñas del Vero 2003 Clarion White Blend (Somontano) $NA. 88 —*M.S. (6/1/2005)*

VIÑEDOS DE PAGANOS

Viñedos de Paganos 2004 El Puntido Tempranillo (Rioja) $57. As expected, the wine exhibits a dense black color, with mineral, burnt toast and dark fruit on the bouquet. The flavor profile offers cured meat, leather, graphite and plenty of blackberry, mocha, caramel and coffee. Beautiful modern Rioja. 4,000 cases made. Imported by Tempranillo, Inc. **96** —*M.S. (9/1/2007)*

Viñedos de Paganos 2002 El Puntido Tempranillo (Rioja) $54. Stylish and serious, with polished, fancy oak sitting like royalty atop dark fruit that is almost pruney. The palate hits with a solid smack of blackberry, while a secondary layer delivers chocolate, mocha and spice. Not quite at the level of the classic 2001 but still excellent. **92 Editors' Choice** —*M.S. (9/1/2007)*

Viñedos de Paganos 2005 La Nieta Tempranillo (Rioja) $150. The best new release in the Eguren family's collection of modern Rioja wines is this small-production, 100% Tempranillo. It's a true nuevo classico with proper touches of smoked meat, herbs and sweet black fruits as well as a lush, round mouthfeel that culminates in a mile-long finish. Destined to rock your socks off. Just over 300 cases produced. Imported by Tempranillo, Inc. **97** —*M.S. (9/1/2007)*

Viñedos de Paganos 2004 La Nieta Tempranillo (Rioja) $145. This is yet another magnetic example from the Eguren stable that includes El Puntido, San Vicente, Finca El Bosque and the many Sierra Cantabria wines. It's a racy, red-fruit dominated Tempranillo with raspberry, plum and cassis flavors accented by firm, almost blazing acidity. It's definitely tighter and more compact than the more generous, richer 2005 La Nieta. Imported by Tempranillo, Inc. **93** —*M.S. (9/1/2007)*

VIÑEDOS Y BODEGAS GARCIA FIGUERO

Viñedos y Bodegas Garcia Figuero 2003 Tinto Figuero 12 Tempranillo (Ribera del Duero) $30. Young and jumpy at first, with early lactic notes. Airing allows this wine to show ripe berry aromas and flavors with ample shadings of oak-based vanilla and chocolate. Saturated and full; this wine gets it right. Drink through 2008. **89** —*M.S. (6/1/2007)*

Viñedos y Bodegas Garcia Figuero 2003 Tinto Figuero 15 Tempranillo (Ribera del Duero) $55. Plenty ripe, in fact it's on the edge of raisiny but not quite over the line. The palate runs surprisingly racy with a lot of acidity, yet the flavor profile is short and drying. Shows a flash or two but it's not a complete wine and not worth the high price tag. **84** —*M.S. (6/1/2007)*

Viñedos y Bodegas Garcia Figuero 2005 Tinto Figuero 4 Tempranillo (Ribera del Duero) $20. Sort of sweet and jammy, but nice overall. The nose is your average young, candied easiness, while the plump berry and plum flavors are pretty much where they should be. Shows juiciness and a spunky mouthfeel, as it was aged only four months in oak. **85** —*M.S. (6/1/2007)*

VINÍCOLA HIDALGO

Vinícola Hidalgo NV Pastrana Manzanilla Pasada Sherry (Jerez) $18. 92 Editors' Choice —*M.S. (8/1/2003)*

VIÑOS JEROMIN

Viños Jeromin 1999 Cosecha de Familia Félix Martinez Reserva Red Blend (Vinos de Madrid) $45. 84 —*M.S. (6/1/2005)*

Viños Jeromin 2000 Manu Crianza Red Blend (Madrid) $60. 85 —*M.S. (3/1/2005)*

Viños Jeromin 2005 Vega Madroño Tempranillo-Garnacha (Vinos de Madrid) $8. A Tempranillo-Garnacha blend that shows fiery aromas and raspberry followed by sweet and granular plum and red berry flavors. If you like juicy, lively, higher-acid wines, then give this a try. It's not bad for the money and ranks as the type of wine you'd get by the glass in Spain. **84** —*M.S. (12/15/2007)*

VIÑOS SANZ

Viños Sanz 2004 Finca La Colina Sauvignon Blanc (Rueda) $NA. 90 —*M.S. (6/1/2005)*

VIÑOS VALTUILLE

Viños Valtuille 2005 Pago de Valdoneje Mencía (Bierzo) $14. Here's an affordable Bierzo red that earns big points for its straightforward, no-nonsense accessibility and balance. The bouquet offers ample minerality, a sprinkle of burnt toast and friendly red fruit. The palate is moderately deep and pure, with spice, pepper and vanilla on the finish. A fine reflection of the region and the 2005 harvest. **90 Best Buy** —*M.S. (11/1/2007)*

VINYA L'HEREU

Vinya L'Hereu 2002 Flor de Grealo Red Blend (Costers del Segre) $33. 89 —*M.S. (11/1/2006)*

Vinya L'Hereu 2002 Petit Grealo Red Blend (Costers del Segre) $16. 83 —*M.S. (11/1/2006)*

VIONTA

Vionta 2005 Albariño (Rías Baixas) $18. 90 —*M.S. (9/1/2006)*

Vionta 2004 Albariño (Rías Baixas) $18. 84 —*M.S. (10/1/2005)*

Vionta 2000 Albariño (Rías Baixas) $12. 81 —*M.M. (9/1/2002)*

Vionta 2003 Single Vineyard Albariño (Rías Baixas) $18. 84 —*M.S. (12/31/2004)*

Vionta 2006 Estate Bottled Single Vineyard Limited Release Albariño (Rías Baixas) $18. Vionta aims for the racy, lively style of Albariño, and for the most part it nails it. Aromas of peach and nectarine are youthful and pure, while the flavors of apple, peach and lime are pleasant. Not over the top but instead it achieves balance and ease. Imported by Freixenet USA. **88** —*M.S. (12/15/2007)*

Vionta 2002 Estate Botted Single Vineyard Limited Release Albariño (Rías Baixas) $15. 86 —*M.S. (3/1/2004)*

Vionta 2001 Estate Bottled-Single Vineyard-Limited Edition White Blend (Rías Baixas) $16. 87 —*D.T. (4/1/2003)*

VITICULTORES BERCIANOS

Viticultores Bercianos 2001 Gran Riocua Mencia (Bierzo) $65. 80 —*M.S. (6/1/2005)*

VITICULTORES DEL PRIORAT

Viticultores del Priorat 1998 Prior Terrae Red Blend (Priorat) $200. 84 —*M.S. (3/1/2005)*

VIVIR, VIVIR

Vivir, Vivir 2004 Tempranillo (Ribera del Duero) $10. Hard-driving aromas of smoke and graphite drown out shy fruit, while in the mouth the flavors are more distant than ideal. The feel is typically deep and and tannic, while a lasting flavor of chocolate is a welcome finishing touch. **84** —*M.S. (6/1/2007)*

Vivir, Vivir 2004 Tempranillo (Ribera del Duero) $10. 86 —*M.S. (9/9/1999)*

VIZCONDE DE AYALA

Vizconde de Ayala 1999 Crianza Tempranillo (Rioja) $12. 81 —*M.S. (8/1/2005)*

Vizconde de Ayala 1994 Gran Reserva Tempranillo (Rioja) $50. 84 —*M.S. (8/1/2005)*

WRONGO DONGO

Wrongo Dongo 2005 Monastrell (Jumilla) $8. A country-style red made from Monastrell. The nose is chubby and deeply fruity, while the plump palate offers a wave or two of blackberry and currant flavors. Flush and full, and totally uncomplicated. **86** —*M.S. (4/1/2007)*

YLLERA

Yllera 1986 Black Label Red Blend (Viño da Mesa de Toledo) $28. 86 —*J.C. (11/1/2001)*

Yllera 1995 Red Label Red Blend (Viño de Mesa de Castilla y León) $23. 86 —*J.C. (11/1/2001)*

Yllera 1999 Oak Selection Tempranillo (Viño de Mesa de Castilla y León) $9. 87 Best Buy —*J.C. (11/1/2001)*

YSIOS

Ysios 1999 Reserva Red Blend (Rioja) $30. 85 *—M.S. (11/1/2006)*

Ysios 2001 Reserva Tempranillo (Rioja) $30. Ysios is one of the most visually pleasing wineries you'll see. It was designed by Santiago Calatrava and it's the town of Laguardia's modern stamp. But until now the wines were just average. This one, however, is far better than that, with pure dried cherry and raspberry flavors bolstered by spicy oak, vanilla and perfect acidity. Drink now–2009. Imported by Pernod Ricard USA. 89 *—M.S. (9/1/2007)*

ZARATE

Zarate 2004 Albariño (Rías Baixas) $18. It's already too late for an '04 Albariño, but this one still has some life and kick in it. The nose has some peanut and lacquer, but overall apple aromas ride high. In the mouth, it shows the oily quality of an aging white along with peach, citrus and nut flavors. 86 *—M.S. (8/1/2007)*

ZAZA

Zaza 2006 Rosé Garnacha (Campo de Borja) $8. Very red in color, an ominous indicator of what's to come. The aromas are close to raisiny and baked, while the palate sort of lugs along. There's nothing terribly off-putting about this wine, yet it doesn't offer any thrill or chill. 80 *—M.S. (11/1/2007)*

ZITUA

Zitua 2000 Crianza Tempranillo (Rioja) $16. 85 *—M.S. (6/1/2005)*

ZUMAYA

Zumaya 1999 Crianza Tempranillo (Ribera del Duero) $17. 83 *—M.S. (12/31/2004)*

Zumaya 1999 Reserva Tempranillo (Ribera del Duero) $25. 84 *—M.S. (12/31/2004)*

Zumaya 1998 Reserva Tempranillo (Ribera del Duero) $25. 80 *—M.S. (1/1/2005)*

Other International

BULGARIA AND ROMANIA

These two countries have been upgrading their vineyards and wineries for several years. Bulgaria has some 200,000 acres of vinifera vines in production, Romania has about the same. Look for good-value Chardonnays, Merlots, and Cabernets from Bulgaria in particular. Merlot and Cabernet show promise in Romania, along with indigenous reds such as Feteasca Neagra.

CANADA

The Canadian wine industry divides neatly in half. In eastern Canada, the Niagara Peninsula north of Lake Ontario produces the vast majority of the region's wines. The government-funded switch to vinifera vines in the early 1990s revolutionized the region, which produces roughly four-fifths of Canada's wine grapes. Though a wide range of varietal white and red wines are made, it is the region's ice wines, marketed in super-tall, slim, 375 ml bottles, that have brought it global acclaim. Meanwhile, British Columbia has been quietly building a substantial wine industry of its own, especially on the bluffs surrounding Lake Okanagan, where a compelling blend of wine and recreational tourism draws visitors year-round. Everything from Germanic Rieslings to Burgundian Pinots to Bordeaux-style red wines and even Syrah can be ripened here. More than one hundred wineries call British Columbia home, with more opening every month.

CROATIA

Original homeland to Zinfandel—known on the Dalmatian coast as Crljenik Kasteljanski. Plavac Mali is a similar grape, making sometimes tough, tannic wines.

GREECE

Greece's best, most distinctive wines are indigenous grape varieties that are unknown elsewhere. Moschofilero is Greece's answer to Pinot Grigio—a light, attractively fruity white that can be charming when cleanly made. Reds tend to be more rustic, whether made from Agiorgitiko or Xinomavro.

HUNGARY

Although home to the storied wines of Tokaji and Egri Bikaver (Bull's Blood), quality was stunted by the chaos that supplanted Communism. Western investment and heroic individual efforts are just beginning to bear fruit.

ISRAEL

High-tech farming is a hallmark of Israeli agriculture, and grape growing is no different, with carefully metered irrigation of international grape varieties the rule rather than the exception. A new generation of carefully sculpted reds is raising the bar.

LEBANON

For years, Lebanese wine was synonymous with Château Musar, but now other names have joined the Hochar family in making wine amidst the ruins. Reds show the most promise.

SLOVENIA

Bordering Italy's Collio region, Slovenia produces many of the same grape varieties, including pungent Sauvignon and classy Tocai, as well as blended whites.

URUGUAY

Uruguay is South America's fourth-largest wine producer (behind Chile, Argentina, and Brazil), and, in global wine terms, is best described as an emerging market.

With a couple hundred years of grape-growing history to its name, and 135 years of commercial winemaking history, Uruguay has never quite caught on the way Argentina and Chile have. Nonetheless, many vinifera grapes, most imported from France, are grown in Uruguay, including Cabernet Sauvignon, Merlot, Pinot Noir, Riesling, and Gewürztraminer. That said, the calling-card grape for the country is Tannat, a rustic variety hailing from Madiran, in southwest France. Somewhat of a chameleon, Uruguayan Tannat can be made in a racier, fruity style or in a more international, barrel-aged style.

Brazil

CORDELIER

Cordelier NV White Sparkling Wine Muscat (Brazil) $11. 82 —*M.S. (12/31/2005)*

Cordelier NV Brut Sparkling Blend (Brazil) $13. 84 —*M.S. (6/1/2006)*

SALTON

Salton NV Demi-Sec Sparkling Blend (Brazil) $7. 84 Best Buy —*M.S. (12/31/2005)*

Bulgaria

BALKAN HILLS

Balkan Hills 2003 Muscat (Targovishte) $8. 85 Best Buy —*J.C. (6/1/2005)*

DAMIANITZA

Damianitza 2002 Reserva Melnik (Melnik) $10. 81 —*J.C. (6/1/2005)*

DOMAINE BOYAR

Domaine Boyar 2000 Reserve Cabernet Sauvignon (Sliven) $8. 85 Best Buy —*J.C. (6/1/2005)*

KANOV VINEYARD

Kanov Vineyard 2003 Reserve Unfiltered Cabernet Sauvignon (Danube Hills Valley) $15. 86 —*J.C. (6/1/2005)*

SUN VALLEY

Sun Valley 2003 Cabernet Sauvignon (Bulgaria) $10. 83 —*J.C. (6/1/2005)*

Sun Valley 2003 Merlot (Bulgaria) $10. 83 —*J.C. (6/1/2005)*

Sun Valley 2003 Sauvignon Blanc (Bulgaria) $10. 82 —*J.C. (6/1/2005)*

TCHERGA

Tcherga 2004 Red Blend (Thracian Valley) $10. A blend of Cabernet Sauvignon, Merlot and Rubin, this wine offers full, ripe blackberry and chocolate flavors and soft tannins. Simple but easy going. **81** —*S.K. (8/1/2007)*

TODOROFF

Todoroff 2005 Gallery Cabernet Sauvignon (Thracian Valley) $19. Bright berry and spices take the lead in this Cabernet from Bulgaria, which is slightly rustic on the palate but likeable. Pair with grilled lamb or ribs. **83** —*S.K. (8/1/2007)*

Todoroff 2005 Teres Special Selection Cabernet Sauvignon (Thracian Valley) $19. Spicy cigarbox aromas and expressive, jammy and earthy flavors on the palate make this Cabernet an intriguing alternative for fans seeking new finds. On the palate, it's balanced and full of flavor. **83** —*S.K. (8/1/2007)*

Todoroff 2005 Gallery Mavrud (Thracian Valley) $15. 81 —*S.K. (8/1/2007)*

Todoroff 2005 Gallery Merlot (Thracian Valley) $15. Balanced and soft, this Merlot from Bulgaria's Thracian Valley has subtle spicy and meaty notes and a lingering finish. Pleasant and approachable, and good with duck or roast chicken with thyme. **82** —*S.K. (8/1/2007)*

VINI

Vini 2004 Cabernet Sauvignon (Thracian Valley) $8. 84 Best Buy —*M.D. (6/1/2006)*

Vini 2002 Cabernet Sauvignon (Sliven) $7. 82 —*J.C. (6/1/2005)*

Vini 2002 Meritage (Sliven) $7. 86 Best Buy —*M.D. (6/1/2006)*

Vini 2004 Merlot (Thracian Valley) $8. 80 —*M.D. (6/1/2006)*

Canada

CAVE SPRING

Cave Spring 1997 Estate Chardonnay (Niagara Peninsula) $12. 84 —*J.C. (8/1/1999)*

Cave Spring 1997 Gamay (Niagara Peninsula) $9. 84 —*J.C. (8/1/1999)*

Cave Spring 2005 Riesling (Niagara Peninsula) $12. Pear, peach and lemon aromas lead on this elegant Riesling. On the palate, it's a combination of sultry sweetness and zip, and the finish is pretty and lingering. It's affordable, too, making it a great everyday wine. Imported by Eber Bros. Wine & Liquor Corp. **86** —*S.K. (7/1/2007)*

Cave Spring 1997 Dry Reserve Riesling (Niagara Peninsula) $12. 87 —*J.C. (8/1/1999)*

Cave Spring 1999 Ice Wine Riesling (Niagara Peninsula) $50. 88 —*J.C. (3/1/2001)*

Cave Spring 1997 Ice Wine Riesling (Niagara Peninsula) $48. 86 —*J.C. (8/1/1999)*

Cave Spring 1997 Indian Summer Riesling (Niagara Peninsula) $18. 92 —*J.C. (8/1/1999)*

Cave Spring 2003 Reserve Riesling (Niagara Peninsula) $13. 87 —*J.C. (8/1/2005)*

Cave Spring 2005 Reserve Estate Bottled Riesling (Niagara Peninsula) $15. Ripe pear and citrus notes and a good minerality make this an attractive choice. It could use a little more lift and there's a bit of heaviness on the palate, but the flavors are fresh and the finish long. A good Riesling with unique qualities. Imported by Eber Bros. Wine & Liquor Corp. **84** —*S.K. (7/1/2007)*

COLIO

Colio 1998 Icewine Riesling (Lake Erie) $NA. 90 —*J.C. (3/1/2001)*

Colio 1998 Select Late Harvest Riesling (Lake Erie) $18. 86 —*J.C. (3/1/2001)*

HENRY OF PELHAM

Henry of Pelham 1998 Botrytis Affected Riesling (Niagara Peninsula) $30. 88 —*J.C. (3/1/2001)*

Henry of Pelham 2004 Icewine Riesling (Niagara Peninsula) $50. Spicy, floral and with a touch of minerality, this is poised and layered. It's dense and honeyed on the palate but overall, has a balanced, attractive character. Imported by Bayfield Importing, Ltd. **85** —*S.K. (12/1/2007)*

Henry of Pelham 1999 Icewine Riesling (Niagara Peninsula) $50. 91 —*J.C. (3/1/2001)*

Henry of Pelham 2006 Reserve Riesling (Short Hills Bench) $13. A soft and elegant nose of apple and citrus, followed by a dry and spicy palate, recommend this reserve wine from Pelham. The wine wants a touch more complexity but aging may allow for more layers to develop. **84** —*S.K. (9/1/2007)*

Henry of Pelham 1998 Select Late Harvest Riesling (Niagara Peninsula) $23. 87 —*J.C. (3/1/2001)*

Henry of Pelham 1999 Special Select Late Harvest Vidal Blanc (Niagara Peninsula) $25. 87 —*J.C. (3/1/2001)*

INNISKILLIN

Inniskillin 2004 Icewine Cabernet Franc (Niagara Peninsula) $100. 86 —*M.D. (8/1/2006)*

Inniskillin 2005 Icewine Riesling (Niagara Peninsula) $80. Delicate flowers, honey and a touch of apricot typify this lovely dessert wine. On the palate, the flavors are set aloft by a touch of spice and acid. The character is serious but feminine, and the finish lingering, but clean. **90** —*S.K. (12/1/2007)*

Inniskillin 2003 Icewine Riesling (Niagara Peninsula) $80. 92 —*J.C. (9/1/2005)*

Inniskillin 2005 Icewine Vidal Blanc (Niagara Peninsula) $60. This Vidal icewine is packed with aromas of lemon, grapefruit and flowers, and offers a racy but luscious intermingling of lemon and apricot. The flavors are heady but never heavy—the wine has a delicate touch and an elegant, integrated character that would please almost any wine drinker. **91** —*S.K. (7/1/2007)*

Inniskillin 2003 Icewine Vidal Blanc (Niagara Peninsula) $59. 94 —*J.C. (9/1/2005)*

Inniskillin 2005 Icewine Gold Vidal Blanc (Niagara Peninsula) $80. There's a classic, elegant nose of apricot, apple and spice on this rich, golden dessert wine, and the flavors of mango, fig and honey have a touch of raciness and spice that balances the components beautifully. A lingering finish and overall exquisite play of flavors ensures that Inniskillin is still one os the best producers of ice wine in the world. **93** —*S.K. (7/1/2007)*

Inniskillin 1997 Oak Aged Ice Wine Vidal Blanc (Niagara Peninsula) $80. 89 —*J.C. (3/1/2001)*

Inniskillin 2003 Oak Aged Icewine Vidal Blanc (Niagara Peninsula) $80. 91 —*J.C. (9/1/2005)*

Inniskillin 2004 Sparkling Icewine Vidal Blanc (Niagara Peninsula) $90. Honey, mango and butter on the nose hint at the opulence that's ahead, but on the palate, the wine takes a delightful, lively turn. Apple, honey and apricot create complexity, but a balanced acidity lifts the flavors and adds a refreshing edge. Flavors unfold in the mouth, so keep coming back. Imported by Icon Estates. **89** *—S.K. (7/1/2007)*

Inniskillin 2002 Sparkling Icewine Vidal Blanc (Niagara Peninsula) $90. 91 *—J.C. (9/1/2005)*

Inniskillin 1998 Sparkling Icewine Vidal Blanc (Niagara Peninsula) $83. 84 *—J.C. (3/1/2001)*

JACKSON-TRIGGS

Jackson-Triggs 2002 Proprietor's Reserve Cabernet Sauvignon (Okanagan Valley) $15. 85 *—J.C. (9/1/2005)*

Jackson-Triggs 2004 Proprietors' Grand Reserve Okanagan Estate Meritage (Okanagan Valley) $25. The 5 classic Bordeaux grape varietals of Cabernet Sauvignon (40%), Merlot (40%), Cabernet Franc (7%), Malbec (10%) and Petit Verdot (3%) comprise this reserve Meritage from Okanagan Valley producer Jackson-Triggs. A bright, young nose of raspberry and coffee is followed by pleasant flavors of spicy pepper and berries, but the mouthfeel is dry and tannic, giving the wine a rough character. Aging will help but there's still a lack of elegance here that might turn off lovers of balanced, softer wines. Imported by The Meritage Association. **84** *—S.K. (5/1/2007)*

Jackson-Triggs 2002 Proprietor's Grand Reserve Okanagan Estate Meritage (Okanagan Valley) $25. 88 *—J.C. (9/1/2005)*

Jackson-Triggs 1998 Proprietor's Grand Reserve Ice Wine Riesling (Okanagan Valley) $60. 92 *—J.M. (12/1/2002)*

Jackson-Triggs 2003 Proprietor's Grande Reserve Sauvignon Blanc (Okanagan Valley) $20. 87 *(7/1/2005)*

Jackson-Triggs 2005 Proprietors' Reserve Icewine Vidal Blanc (Niagara Peninsula) $20. It's no surprise that excellent icewine is being made in the Niagara region of Canada, but this Vidal offering from Jackson-Triggs is a pleasure nonetheless. With its layered aromas and flavors of orange, apricot and honey lifted by crisp acidity, this is both approachable and collectible. A serious wine with a fun and flirty side. Imported by Icon Estates. **91 Editors' Choice** *—S.K. (12/1/2007)*

Jackson-Triggs 2003 Proprietors' Reserve Icewine (187mL) Vidal Blanc (Niagara Peninsula) $20. 87 *—J.C. (9/1/2005)*

KONZELMANN

Konzelmann 2003 Grand Reserve Classic Riesling (Niagara Peninsula) $28. Peach, orange and tropical fruit on the nose and a balance of acid and sweetness are appealing, but this wine is a touch watery and needs more substance. Imported by Specialty Cellars. **82** *—S.K. (9/1/2007)*

MAGNOTTA

Magnotta 2001 Iced Apple Apple (Niagara Peninsula) $20. A heady baked apple and spice nose on this unusual dessert wine, but the flavors of cinnamon, apple and honey are a bit heavy. It's tasty, but slightly clumsy in its intense sweetness. A lighter touch with these appetizing flavors would have improved the wine's accessibility. **84** *—S.K. (7/1/2007)*

Magnotta 2004 Limited Edition Icewine Cabernet Franc (Niagara Peninsula) $50. The nose is luscious, packed with heady floral and ripe fruit notes. The wine is viscous; fruit flavors of cranberry and melon give it an interesting character that's not too sweet or cloying. Pair it with sharp cheese or fruit desserts. **85** *—S.K. (7/1/2007)*

Magnotta 2004 Limited Edition Icewine Vidal Blanc (Niagara Peninsula) $40. Has a pleasurable nose of toasted oak, pear and pineapple, but on the palate, there's a burst of apricot and a syrupy, honeyed weight that overrides its more delicate features. Needs more balance and acidity, but overall, it will be enjoyed by fans of a heavier style of dessert wine. **84** *—S.K. (7/1/2007)*

MALIVOIRE

Malivoire 2004 Estate Bottled Pinot Gris (Niagara Peninsula) $16. 82 *—J.C. (2/1/2006)*

MISSION HILL

Mission Hill 1999 Merlot (Okanagan Valley) $9. 82 *—P.G. (12/31/2001)*

Mission Hill 2003 S.L.C. Merlot (Okanagan Valley) $40. There's serious cedar on the nose here, which leads into flavors of plum, berries and more cedar. It's slightly tart and tannic and lacking softness or subtlety, but the finish is lingering and satisfying. Imported by Mark Anthony Wine Merchants. **83** *—S.K. (5/1/2007)*

Mission Hill 1999 Bin 99 Pinot Noir (Okanagan Valley) $8. 85 *—P.G. (12/31/2001)*

Mission Hill 2004 Five Vineyards Icewine 187ML Riesling (Okanagan Valley) $20. 91 *—M.D. (8/1/2006)*

Mission Hill 2004 Reserve Icewine Riesling (Okanagan Valley) $60. 90 *—M.D. (8/1/2006)*

Mission Hill 2004 S.L.C. Icewine Riesling (Okanagan Valley) $85. 92 Cellar Selection *—M.D. (8/1/2006)*

Mission Hill 1999 Estate Syrah (Okanagan Valley) $16. 85 *(10/1/2001)*

Mission Hill 2003 S.L.C. Syrah (Okanagan Valley) $40. This wine from Mission Hill in the Okanagan Valley has a spicy, gamey character on the nose—think plums and leather and the flavors are enjoyable, albeit a bit watery. Blackberry and chocolate mingled with spices would make more of an impact with more structure and a bolder array of fruit. Overall, the wine has pleasant flavors but needs more personality. Imported by Mark Anthony Wine Merchants. **83** *—S.K. (5/1/2007)*

OSOYOOS LAROSE

Osoyoos Larose 2003 Le Grand Vin Bordeaux Blend (Okanagan Valley) $35. Marrying Okanagan grapes and French winemaking styles, this Bordeaux blend is a joint venture between industry giant Vincor and the Bordeaux wine company Groupe Tailan. Rich strawberry and spice on the nose and a firm combination of white pepper, smoke and vanilla make for an unusual offering that could probably age a bit to soften its edges. **85** *—S.K. (5/1/2007)*

Osoyoos Larose 2002 Le Grand Vin Bordeaux Blend (Okanagan Valley) $35. 87 *—J.C. (9/1/2005)*

PENINSULA RIDGE

Peninsula Ridge 2003 Sauvignon Blanc (Niagara Peninsula) $25. 90 *(7/1/2005)*

PILLITTERI

Pillitteri 2004 Icewine Cabernet Franc (Niagara Peninsula) $60. Elegant and integrated, this pale pink icewine has a complex nose of flowers, maple syrup and strawberry, followed by round, lush flavors of strawberry, raspberry and tropical fruit. It's a touch sweet and heavy on the mouth, but the flavors are lively and the finish lingering with a light finesse. A lovely picnic wine that will pair well with most foods. **86** *—S.K. (7/1/2007)*

Pillitteri 2002 Icewine Cabernet Franc (Niagara Peninsula) $60. A heady fragrance of strawberry, orange peel and red berries immediately entices, and the flavors that follow do not disappoint. The wine is elegant and flavorful, with a balanced amount of acidity and sweetness, and the mouthfeel is creamy as well as lively—a tough balance to strike but one that is successfully achieved here. Delicious and accessible. **87** *—S.K. (7/1/2007)*

Pillitteri 2002 Family Reserve Merlot (Niagara Peninsula) $50. Ripe berry, cinnamon and clove spices and a touch of tobacco on the nose lead to subtle, integrated flavors of dark chocolate, raspberries and spice on the palate. The wine is assertive but elegant. Imported by Wine Emporium. **84** *—S.K. (5/1/2007)*

Pillitteri 2004 Icewine Riesling (Niagara Peninsula) $50. Apricot and honey lead this delicate Riesling, and on the palate, a poised balance of sweet and spicy keeps the wine aloft. Citrus and a floral note are woven throughout, creating complexity and elegance. Imported by Wine Emporium. **85** *—S.K. (12/1/2007)*

Pillitteri 2004 Select Late Harvest Riesling (Niagara Peninsula) $24. Intense flavors of mango, melon and apricot lead on this lively but rich dessert. The palate is bursting with flavor but layered spice softens and adds depth. The sweetness is enhanced by a pretty floral character that lingers through the finish. Imported by Wine Emporium. **87** *—S.K. (12/1/2007)*

Pillitteri 2004 Icewine Vidal Blanc (Niagara Peninsula) $40. The pineapple, honey and lemon aromas of this elegant, golden wine are delicate, but on the palate, the wine is assertive and complex. Buttery and rich, but lightened by tropical fruit flavors, it has a balanced acidity and a lengthy, pleasureable finish. **87** *—S.K. (7/1/2007)*

Pillitteri 2003 Sparkling Icewine Vidal Blanc (Niagara Peninsula) $60. Clean, elegant and with a poised balance of creaminess and spice, this is a delicate but luscious summer sip. Apricots and cloves on the nose and palate are complex but not overwhelming, and the honeyed finish lingers without unwanted weight, thanks in part to a measured acidity. Will pair well with desserts, but is good on its own. **88** *—S.K. (7/1/2007)*

CHINA

CHINA SILK

Chateau Changyu-Castel 1995 Cabernet Gernischt (China) $30. Appetizing smoked meat, pepper and berries on the nose of this Chinese Cabernet relative are varietally-correct, but on the palate, the wine turns a little bitter and there's a thinness that suggests that aging may be a problem. Pair it with red meat or stew to round it out. **80** —*S.K. (8/1/2007)*

Chateau Changyu-Castel 2001 Cabernet Sauvignon (China) $27. Earthy herbs and smoked sausage on the nose of this Cab are followed by elegant flavors of cinnamon spice and plum. The wine has decent structure and a lovely deep color, but there's a hint of bitterness that is tough to throw your arms around. Though not a complex wine, it has character. **81** —*S.K. (8/1/2007)*

Chateau Changyu-Castel 2003 Chardonnay (China) $27. Toasted oak and candy on the nose lead into flavors of butterscotch and vanilla in this appraochable but rather simple Chardonnay. There's a leanness to the wine but the finish is good. Try with salmon or cream-based dishes. **82** —*S.K. (8/1/2007)*

China Silk NV Marco Polo White Wine White Blend (China) $7. 82 —*M.D. (8/1/2006)*

CROATIA

CARA

Cara 2001 Posip (Croatia) $16. 87 —*S.H. (10/1/2004)*

FERA VINO

Fera Vino NV Grasevina (Slavonija) Welschriesling (Croatia) $9. 86 —*S.H. (10/1/2004)*

KATUNAR

Katunar 2002 Zlahtina (Croatia) $15. 87 —*S.H. (10/1/2004)*

CYPRUS

DOMAINE NICOLAIDES

Domaine Nicolaides NV Xinisteri (Lemesos) $10. 80 —*M.D. (12/15/2006)*

K&K VASILIKON

K&K Vasilikon 2003 Agios Onoufrios Red Blend (Kathikas) $10. 81 —*M.D. (12/15/2006)*

TSIAKKAS

Tsiakkas 2003 Oak Aged Cabernet Sauvignon (Pitsilia Mountains) $22. 88 —*M.D. (12/15/2006)*

GEORGIA

ALAVERDI

Alaverdi 2005 Akhasheni Saperavi (Kakheti) $12. Fruity with flavors of red cherry and berry, this semisweet Georgian red is balanced with woodsy flavors such as cedar, spice and herbs. **83** —*S.K. (11/15/2007)*

Alaverdi 2005 Kindzmarauli Saperavi (Kakheti) $15. This semisweet wine from Georgia exhibits bright red berry and cherry aromas and flavors, and a layer of woodsy, earthy spice and herbs. The combination of sweet and savory makes for an interesting sip, but it might be a touch exotic for traditionalists to fully embrace. **82** —*S.K. (11/15/2007)*

Alaverdi 2001 Mukuzani Saperavi (Kakheti) $11. Saperavi has its wild side—high acidity, exotic, incense-like spice—and this Georgian red is true to that variety. Its aroma is lovely but on the palate the wine is a tad too angular. The premise is good and the fruit nice, so pair it with food and the wrinkles will iron out a bit. **81** —*S.K. (11/15/2007)*

Alaverdi 2005 Pirosmani Saperavi (Kakheti) $11. Made from the indigenous red grape Saperavi of Georgia, this attractive wine starts with hot spice and red berry fruit on the nose, then unfolds into a soft combination of sweet fruit and earthy spice. There's still an underpinning of rustic terroir character here, but overall, the wine is pretty and appealing. **85** —*S.K. (11/15/2007)*

Alaverdi 2005 Shirakis Veli Saperavi (Kakheti) $11. Semisweet with grapy, red-cherry flavors, this has a strain of acidity that keeps it from becoming too sappy. Earthy spices unfold nicely, but the wine could use a touch more tannin and dimension. A fun and character-driven dip. **82** —*S.K. (11/15/2007)*

TELAVI

Telavi 2002 Saperavi (Napareuli) $13. 85 —*M.D. (6/1/2006)*

Telavi 2000 Saperavi (Georgia) $13. 84 —*M.D. (6/1/2006)*

Telavi 2002 Tsinandali White Blend (Georgia) $9. 81 —*M.D. (6/1/2006)*

GREECE

A. BABATZIM

A. Babatzim 2002 Domaine Anestis Babatzimopoulos Malvasia Bianca (Vin de Pays de Macedoine) $22. 84 —*J.C. (9/2/2004)*

A. PARPAROUSSIS

A. Parparoussis 1999 Muscat de Rio Patras Muscat (Muscat of Patras) $26. 87 —*J.C. (9/2/2004)*

ACHAIA CLAUSS

Achaia Clauss 2003 Agiorgitiko (Nemea) $11. The nose on this Greek red is inviting, with its hearth spice, plum and smoke, but on the palate, there's a sharp edge that overrides the fruit. There's a nice subtlety about the wine—the tannins are soft, and the finish delicate, but overall, the wine wants more flavor. **81** —*S.K. (11/15/2007)*

Achaia Clauss 2000 Agiorgitiko (Corinth) $10. 83 —*J.C. (9/2/2004)*

Achaia Clauss NV Danielis Agiorgitiko (Patras) $10. A spicy, minerally nose offers an interesting introduction to this Cabernet-style red from Greece, but on the palate, rounded fruit gives way to bitterness and lack of structure. It's soft with some appealing spice, so the wine has good potential, just needs a little more dimension. **82** —*S.K. (11/15/2007)*

Achaia Clauss NV Danielis Agiorgitiko (Greece) $10. 85 Best Buy —*M.D. (10/1/2006)*

Achaia Clauss NV Demestica Red Agiorgitiko (Greece) $9. 81 —*M.D. (10/1/2006)*

Achaia Clauss NV Demestica Rosé Agiorgitiko (Greece) $9. 82 —*M.D. (12/15/2006)*

Achaia Clauss 1998 Château Clauss Cabernet Blend (Peloponnese) $12. 82 —*J.C. (9/2/2004)*

Achaia Clauss 2005 Imperial Mavrodaphne (Mavrodaphne of Patras) $10. This unusual dessert wine from Greece has soft red berry and herbal aromas and pretty flavors of caramel, toasted nut and spice. The overall character is sweet and subtle with a hint of barnyardy hay and earth tones. **84** —*S.K. (11/15/2007)*

Achaia Clauss 1996 Mavrodaphne of Patras Reserve Mavrodaphne (Peloponnese) $20. 86 —*J.C. (9/2/2004)*

Achaia Clauss NV Muscat (Muscat of Patras) $9. 84 —*J.C. (9/2/2004)*

Achaia Clauss NV Muscat de Patras Muscat (Patras) $9. 84 —*J.C. (9/1/2004)*

Achaia Clauss 2003 Château Clauss Red Blend (Patras) $13. Exotic and assertive, this red blend from Greece shows red berry and brambly fruit as well as a wave of spice. It's slightly sharp and smoky though, making it a tough one to sip on its own. Pair with food to soften the edges. **82** —*S.K. (11/15/2007)*

AGROS

Agros 2003 Agiorgitiko (Peloponnese) $10. 84 —*J.C. (9/2/2004)*

Agros 2003 Assyrtico (Santorini) $14. 85 —*J.C. (9/2/2004)*

Agros 2002 Muscat de Rio Patras Muscat (Patras) $7. 84 —*J.C. (9/2/2004)*

ALEXANDROS MEGAPANOS

Alexandros Megapanos 2002 Savatiano (Spata) $8. 85 Best Buy —*J.C. (9/2/2004)*

Alexandros Megapanos 2003 Xinomavro (Amindeo) $10. 81 —*J.C. (9/2/2004)*

ALPHA ESTATE

Alpha Estate 2004 Estate Red Blend (Macedonia) $35. 87 —*M.D. (10/1/2006)*

Alpha Estate 2003 One Red Blend (Greece) $65. 86 *—M.D. (10/1/2006)*

Alpha Estate 2005 Sauvignon Blanc (Florina) $28. 89 *—M.D. (10/1/2006)*

ANTONOPOULOS

Antonopoulos 2001 Cabernet-Nea Dris Cabernet Blend (Greece) $23. 87 *—M.D. (10/5/2006)*

Antonopoulos 2002 Cabernet-Nea Dris Cabernet Sauvignon-Cabernet Franc (Greece) $26. 88 *—M.D. (12/15/2006)*

Antonopoulos 2002 Chardonnay in New Oak Chardonnay (Greece) $25. 83 *—J.C. (9/2/2004)*

Antonopoulos 2002 Moschofilero (Mantinia) $10. 84 *—J.C. (9/2/2004)*

Antonopoulos 2003 Collection White Dry Table Wine White Blend (Greece) $15. 86 *—J.C. (9/2/2004)*

ARGYROS

Argyros 2003 Canava Assyrtico (Santorini) $19. 86 *—J.C. (9/2/2004)*

Argyros 2004 Estate Assyrtico (Santorini) $26. 87 *—M.D. (10/1/2006)*

Argyros 2004 Estate Barrel Assyrtico (Santorini) $33. 88 *—M.D. (10/1/2006)*

Argyros NV Atlantis Mandilaria (Santorini) $17. 88 *—J.C. (9/2/2004)*

Argyros NV Atlantis White Blend (Santorini) $15. 85 *—J.C. (9/2/2004)*

Argyros 2004 Atlantis White Blend (Santorini) $16. 85 *—M.D. (10/1/2006)*

AVANTIS

Avantis 2005 Roditis (Beotia) $17. 81 *—M.D. (10/1/2006)*

Avantis 2005 Fumé Sauvignon Blanc (Beotia) $18. 87 *—M.D. (10/1/2006)*

Avantis 2002 Syrah (Beotia) $25. 85 *—M.D. (10/1/2006)*

BOUTARI

Boutari 2000 Agiorgitiko (Corinth) $20. 87 *—J.C. (9/2/2004)*

Boutari 2004 Agiorgitiko Agiorgitiko (Nemea) $20. 84 *—M.D. (12/15/2006)*

Boutari 2004 Nemea Agiorgitiko (Nemea) $14. 83 *—M.D. (12/15/2006)*

Boutari 2003 Assyrtico (Santorini) $15. 85 *—J.C. (9/2/2004)*

Boutari 2001 Assyrtico (Cyclades) $15. 88 *— (11/15/2002)*

Boutari 2004 Kallisti Assyrtico (Santorini) $24. 85 *—M.D. (10/1/2006)*

Boutari 2002 Kallisti Assyrtico (Santorini) $19. 87 *—J.C. (9/2/2004)*

Boutari 2000 Ode Cabernet Sauvignon-Agiorgitiko Cabernet Blend (Corinth) $25. 88 *—J.C. (9/2/2004)*

Boutari 2005 Moschofilero (Mantinia) $17. 87 *—M.D. (12/15/2006)*

Boutari 2003 Moschofilero (Mantinia) $15. 86 *—J.C. (9/2/2004)*

Boutari 2001 Moschofilero (Mantinia) $12. 88 *(11/15/2002)*

Boutari NV Muscat (Samos) $14. 87 *—J.C. (9/2/2004)*

Boutari 2003 Evinos Red Blend (Macedonia) $25. Good structure and body with elegant flavors typify this 50-50 blend of Merlot and Xinomavro. The Merlot offers deep color and a velvety mouthfeel, while Xinomavro's elegant tannic structure ensures softness without weakness. 85 *—S.K. (4/1/2007)*

Boutari 2002 Skalani Red Blend (Crete) $25. 89 *—J.C. (9/2/2004)*

Boutari 1999 Xinomavro Merlot Red Blend (Imathia) $18. 86 *— (11/15/2002)*

Boutari 2003 Domaine Matsa Savatiano (Attica) $20. 86 *—J.C. (9/2/2004)*

Boutari 2005 Kretikos Vilana (Crete) $10. 81 *—M.D. (12/15/2006)*

Boutari 2003 Fantaxometocho White Blend (Paros) $20. 88 *—J.C. (9/2/2004)*

Boutari 2004 Xinomavro (Naoussa) $15. 88 *—M.D. (12/15/2006)*

Boutari 1999 Grande Reserve Xinomavro (Naoussa) $17. 88 *—J.C. (9/2/2004)*

CALLIGA

Calliga NV Rubis Agiorgitiko (Greece) $10. 83 *—M.D. (10/1/2006)*

CHÂTEAU JULIA

Château Julia 2000 Merlot (Adriani) $23. 87 *—C.S. (11/15/2002)*

CHÂTEAU NICO LAZARIDI

Château Nico Lazaridi 2003 White Dry Wine White Blend (Drama) $22. 80 *(7/1/2005)*

DOMAINE CONSTANTIN LAZARIDI

Domaine Constantin Lazaridi 1998 Amethystos Cabernet Sauvignon (Drama) $30. 89 *—C.S. (11/15/2002)*

Domaine Costa Lazaridi 2002 Amethystos Cabernet Blend (Vin de Pays de Macedoine) $19. 85 *—J.C. (9/2/2004)*

Domaine Costa Lazaridi 2003 Amethystos Red Cabernet Blend (Macedonia) $18. 85 *—M.D. (12/15/2006)*

Domaine Costa Lazaridi 2002 Oenodea Cabernet Blend (Vin de Pays de Macedoine) $10. 84 *—J.C. (9/2/2004)*

Domaine Costa Lazaridi 2005 Amethystos Rosé Cabernet Sauvignon (Drama) $14. 83 *—M.D. (12/15/2006)*

Domaine Costa Lazaridi 2001 Cava Amethystos Cabernet Sauvignon (Drama) $30. 85 *—M.D. (10/1/2006)*

Domaine Costa Lazaridi 2002 Château Julia Chardonnay (Drama) $14. 83 *—J.C. (9/2/2004)*

Domaine Costa Lazaridi 2005 Château Julia Chardonnay (Drama) $15. 83 *—M.D. (10/1/2006)*

Domaine Costa Lazaridi 2004 Amethystos Fumé Sauvignon Blanc (Drama) $16. 88 *—M.D. (10/1/2006)*

Domaine Costa Lazaridi 2003 Amethystos White White Blend (Vin de Pays de Macedoine) $14. 86 *—J.C. (9/2/2004)*

Domaine Costa Lazaridi 2005 Amethystos White White Blend (Drama) $14. 87 *—M.D. (10/1/2006)*

Domaine Costa Lazaridi 2002 Oenodea White Blend (Vin de Pays de Macedoine) $10. 85 *—J.C. (9/2/2004)*

DOMAINE EVHARIS

Domaine Evharis 2004 Assyrtiko (Gerania) $22. 84 *—M.D. (10/1/2006)*

Domaine Evharis 2003 Red Blend (Gerania) $28. 88 *—M.D. (10/1/2006)*

Domaine Evharis 2005 White Blend (Gerania) $22. 85 *—M.D. (10/1/2006)*

DOMAINE GEROVASSILIOU

Domaine Gerovassiliou 2004 Chardonnay (Epanomi) $32. 89 *—M.D. (10/1/2006)*

Domaine Gerovassiliou 2003 Malagauzia (Greece) $22. 88 *—J.C. (9/2/2004)*

Domaine Gerovassiliou 2002 Syrah (Epanomi) $24. 90 Editors' Choice *—M.D. (10/1/2006)*

Domaine Gerovassiliou 2001 Syrah (Greece) $24. 88 *—J.C. (9/2/2004)*

DOMAINE KARYDAS

Domaine Karydas 2003 Xinomavro (Naoussa) $25. 85 *—M.D. (12/15/2006)*

Domaine Karydas 2001 Xinomavro (Naoussa) $20. 88 *—J.C. (9/2/2004)*

DOMAINE MERCOURI

Domaine Mercouri 1999 Refosco Red Blend (Ilias) $15. 89 *— (11/15/2002)*

DOMAINE SKOURAS

Domaine Skouras 2006 Zoë! Rosé Blend (Peloponnese) $11. This pretty, medium-cranberry-colored rose from Domaine Skouras in Greece's Pelopponese is lively but not flimsy—it features earthy, mouthwatering flavors of raspberry and spice, set aloft by playful acid and citrus undertones. Like many of Greece's affordable white and rose wines, this quaff is food-friendly and refreshing—perfect for a warm-weather lounge and paired with nearly every dish imaginable. Think a pasta with spicy red sauce or a more delicate seafood entree. Imported by Diamond Importers Inc. 86 Best Buy *—S.K. (7/1/2007)*

DOUGOS

Dougos 2003 Methistanes Red Blend (Greece) $29. 82 *—M.D. (10/1/2006)*

ESTATE BIBLIA CHORA

Estate Biblia Chora 2002 Areti Red Agiorgitiko (Greece) $18. 85 *—M.D. (10/1/2006)*

Estate Biblia Chora 2004 Areti White Assyrtico (Pangeon) $18. 82 *—M.D. (10/1/2006)*

Estate Biblia Chora 2005 Ovilos White Blend (Pangeon) $40. 87 *—M.D. (10/1/2006)*

Estate Biblia Chora 2005 Sauvignon Blanc-Assyrtico White Blend (Pangeon) $16. 87 *—M.D. (10/1/2006)*

GAIA ESTATE

Gaia Estate 2002 Agiorgitiko (Corinth) $30. 87 —*J.C. (9/2/2004)*

Gaia Estate 2003 14-18h Agiorgitiko (Peloponnese) $10. 83 —*J.C. (9/2/2004)*

Gaia Estate 2001 14-18h Koutsi Nemea Agiorgitiko (Corinth) $9. 87 Best Buy *(11/15/2002)*

Gaia Estate 2002 Notios Agiorgitiko (Peloponnese) $11. 86 —*M.S. (11/15/2003)*

Gaia Estate 2000 Superior Agiorgitiko (Corinth) $20. 90 *(11/15/2002)*

GENTILINI

Gentilini 2003 Robola (Cephalonia) $15. 87 —*J.C. (9/2/2004)*

Gentilini 2003 Classico White Blend (Cephalonia) $15. 85 —*J.C. (9/2/2004)*

GLINAVOS

Glinavos 1999 Red Velvet Red Blend (Greece) $17. 82 —*J.C. (9/2/2004)*

Glinavos 2006 Primus White Blend (Zitsa) $15. Made in Zitsa, the only area within Epirus, Greece entitled to an appellation, this sparkler is made with a traditional white wine variety called Debina. True to the grape, the wine has a lively acidity, good minerality and an overall attractive quality. It's a touch clunky and hard to embrace for a sparkling wine, though—and needs to be paired with food. **82** —*S.K. (12/15/2007)*

Glinavos 2001 Primus White Blend (Zitsa) $17. 87 —*J.C. (9/2/2004)*

HAGGIPAVLU

Haggipavlu 2004 Agiorgitiko (Nemea) $12. A minty, spicy nose and smooth, integrated flavors of berry, oak and pepper make this red from Greece a no-brainer choice for fans of unusual wines. Mild, mellow and friendly, the wine is a good example of the variety that, along with Xinomavro, has put Greek wine on the map. **84** —*S.K. (11/15/2007)*

Haggipavlu 2000 Agiorgitiko (Corinth) $14. 84 —*J.C. (9/2/2004)*

Haggipavlu 2004 Cabernet Sauvignon (Peloponnese) $12. Black pepper and a juicy red berry nose recommend this red from Greece, but on the palate, there's a one-dimensional simplicity and slight bitterness that's hard to embrace. That said, paired with food, this wine might soften up and prove to be a decent quaffer. **82** —*S.K. (11/15/2007)*

Haggipavlu 2002 Moschofilero (Mantinia) $12. 87 Best Buy —*J.C. (9/2/2004)*

HARLAFTIS

Harlaftis 2001 Argilos Agiorgitiko (Corinth) $12. 81 —*J.C. (9/2/2004)*

HATZI MICHALIS

Hatzi Michalis 2001 Kapnias Cabernet Blend (Opuntia Locris) $30. 87 —*J.C. (9/2/2004)*

Hatzi Michalis 2002 Chardonnay (Atalanti Valley) $15. 83 —*J.C. (9/2/2004)*

Hatzi Michalis 2003 Laas White Blend (Opuntia Locris) $25. 85 —*J.C. (9/2/2004)*

HELIOPOULOS

Heliopoulos 2003 White Blend (Santorini) $16. 87 —*J.C. (9/2/2004)*

KARIPIDIS

Karipidis 2003 Cabernet Sauvignon (Thessalikos) $22. 89 —*M.D. (12/15/2006)*

KATOGI & STROFILIA

Katogi & Strofilia 2000 Averoff Estate Bordeaux Blend (Metsovo) $23. 91 Cellar Selection —*J.C. (9/2/2004)*

Katogi & Strofilia 2001 Purple Earth Red Blend (Nemea) $22. 80 —*M.D. (12/15/2006)*

KEO

Keo NV Domaine D'Ahera Mavro Red Blend (Cyprus) $11. 84 — *(11/15/2002)*

KIR-YIANNI

Kir-Yianni 2004 Paranga Red Blend (Vin de Pays de Macedoine) $13. 84 —*M.D. (10/1/2006)*

Kir-Yianni 2001 Paranga Red Blend (Vin de Pays de Macedoine) $15. 82 —*J.C. (9/2/2004)*

Kir-Yianni 2003 Yianakohori Red Blend (Vin de Pays d'Imithia) $25. 82 —*M.D. (10/1/2006)*

Kir-Yianni 2003 Syrah (Vin de Pays d'Imithia) $40. 89 —*M.D. (10/1/2006)*

Kir-Yianni 2005 Samaropetra White Blend (Florina) $14. 87 —*M.D. (12/15/2006)*

Kir-Yianni 2003 Samaropetra White Blend (Florina) $13. 87 —*J.C. (9/2/2004)*

Kir-Yianni 2006 Akakies Xinomavro (Amyndeon) $12. This delightful, medium-bodied rose made from the typically tannic Xinomavro grape of northern Greece is a pleasant surprise, though Kir-Yianni has a solid reputation for making good wine. This is an exotic alternative for both casual wine lovers and serios vinophiles looking for something out of the ordinary, The wine is fresh, fruity and lively, with a tart strawberry nose and a combination of juicy fruit and clean, minerally acidity on the palate. Its body and acidity ensures that it will match bolder foods like roast lamb and beef, but will also be delicious with lighter fare like seafood and poultry. Its beautiful dark pink color is a selling point as well. **88 Best Buy** —*S.K. (7/1/2007)*

Kir-Yianni 2005 Akakies Xinomavro (Amyndeon) $11. 85 —*M.D. (12/15/2006)*

Kir-Yianni 2003 Akakies Xinomavro (Amyntaion) $11. 87 —*J.C. (9/2/2004)*

Kir-Yianni 2001 Ramnista Xinomavro (Naoussa) $22. 89 —*M.D. (12/15/2006)*

KOUROS

Kouros 2000 Agiorgitiko (Corinth) $9. 80 —*J.C. (9/2/2004)*

Kouros 2003 Red Agiorgitiko (Nemea) $9. 85 Best Buy —*M.D. (10/1/2006)*

Kouros 1999 Red Blend (Corinth) $9. 85 Best Buy —*C.S. (11/15/2002)*

Kouros 2002 Roditis (Patras) $9. 84 —*J.C. (9/2/2004)*

Kouros 2004 White Roditis (Patras) $9. 80 —*M.D. (10/1/2006)*

KOURTAKI

Kourtaki NV Muscat (Samos) $9. 86 Best Buy —*J.C. (9/2/2004)*

Kourtaki 2003 Vin de Crete Red Red Blend (Crete) $8. 80 —*M.D. (10/1/2006)*

KTIMA VOYATZI

Ktima Voyatzi 2001 Red Blend (Greece) $24. 85 —*J.C. (9/2/2004)*

Ktima Voyatzi 2003 Red Red Blend (Vin de Pays de Velvendo) $28. 85 —*M.D. (10/1/2006)*

KYR-YIANNI

Kyr-Yianni 1997 Ramnista Xinomavro (Naoussa) $15. 87 — *(11/15/2002)*

LAFAZANIS

Lafazanis 2005 Roditis (Peloponnese) $10. 86 Best Buy —*M.D. (11/15/2006)*

LAFAZANIS

Lafazanis 2005 St. George (Peloponnese) $10. 83 —*M.D. (10/1/2006)*

Lathazanni 2003 Roditis (Corinth) $10. 85 —*J.C. (9/2/2004)*

MANOLESAKI ESTATE

Manolesaki Estate 2001 Cabernet Blend (Drama) $22. 86 —*J.C. (9/2/2004)*

Manolesaki Estate 2001 Cabernet Sauvignon (Drama) $23. 87 —*J.C. (9/2/2004)*

Manolesaki Estate 2001 Merlot (Drama) $23. 88 —*J.C. (9/2/2004)*

Manolesaki Estate 2002 Sauvignon Blanc-Chardonnay White Blend (Drama) $22. 85 —*J.C. (9/2/2004)*

Manolesaki Estate 2002 Sauvignon Blanc-Roditis White Blend (Drama) $18. 87 —*J.C. (9/2/2004)*

MANOUSAKIS

Manousakis 2002 Nostos Rhône Red Blend (Crete) $19. 89 —*M.D. (10/1/2006)*

MARRAS

Marras 2003 Cabernet Sauvignon (Peloponnese) $13. A pleasant nose of red cherry and pepper is followed by soft, mingled waves of strawberry, cherry and herbs in this expressive Greek Cabernet. It's not complex but it is approachable, making it a fun option for red wine fans. **83** —*S.K. (11/15/2007)*

Marras 2003 Merlot (Peloponnese) $13. The typical Merlot qualities of soft spice and gamey notes apply here in this wine from Greece, with the addition of the slightly smoky and bitter quality found in some Greek red wines. Good balance and oak integration make this an interesting red on it own or paired with roasted lamb or chicken souvlaki. **82** —*S.K. (11/15/2007)*

Marras 2003 St. George (Peloponnese) $10. A soft, subtle nose of hearth spices and oak is followed by flavors of red cherry, pepper and nut. The wine is approachable and affordable, and will pair well with lamb and beef dishes. **83** *—S.K. (11/15/2007)*

MERCOURI ESTATE

Mercouri Estate 2005 Folói Roditis (Pisatis) $15. 88 *—M.D. (12/15/2006)*

MINOS

Minos 2002 Vilana Vilana (Crete) $16. 85 *—J.C. (9/2/2004)*

NASIAKOS

Nasiakos 2006 Agiorgitiko (Peloponnese) $15. Sweet, jammy aromas and flavors of red berry, spice and pepper are attractive, but overall, this red wine from the Peloponnese fails to impress. There's a bitter, somewhat indigenous edge to the wine that requires softening, probably with a spicy meat dish like lamb kebobs. **82** *—S.K. (11/15/2007)*

Nasiakos 2004 Agiorgitiko (Nemea) $20. Clove and cinnamon on the nose and a slightly smoky flavor profile recommend this Greek red for everyday sipping and pairing with like-flavored dishes such as spice-rubbed ribs. The finish is rustic but the overall character likeable. **83** *—S.K. (11/15/2007)*

Nasiakos 2005 Mantinia Moschofilero (Mantinia) $17. 87 *—M.D. (12/15/2006)*

Nasiakos 2003 Mantinia Moschofilero (Mantinia) $16. 84 *—J.C. (9/2/2004)*

Nasiakos 2005 Moschofilero White Label Moschofilero (Mantinia) $14. 85 *—M.D. (12/15/2006)*

Nasiakos 2003 Moschofilero White Label Moschofilero (Mantinia) $13. 87 *—J.C. (9/2/2004)*

NICO LAZARIDI

Nico Lazaridi 2001 Château Nico Lazaridi Bordeaux Blend (Peloponnese) $17. 83 *—J.C. (9/2/2004)*

Nico Lazaridi 1999 Magic Mountain Red Bordeaux Blend (Drama) $50. 86 *—J.C. (9/2/2004)*

Nico Lazaridi 2004 Lion d'Or Cabernet Sauvignon (Greece) $15. 86 *—M.D. (12/15/2006)*

Nico Lazaridi 2003 Merlot (Drama) $16. An earthy but slightly sweet nose leads into flavors of meat, clove and dark fruit in this beautifully colored, well-balanced Merlot. The structure is good and the finish lingers with lush fruit. **84** *—S.K. (4/1/2007)*

Nico Lazaridi 2001 Merlot (Drama) $17. 81 *—J.C. (9/2/2004)*

Nico Lazaridi 2001 Moushk Muscat d'Alexandrie (Drama) $23. 85 *—J.C. (9/2/2004)*

Nico Lazaridi 2003 Magic Mountain Sauvignon Blanc (Drama) $30. 88 *(7/1/2005)*

Nico Lazaridi 2002 Magic Mountain White Sauvignon Blanc (Drama) $33. 84 *—J.C. (9/2/2004)*

OENOFOROS

Oenoforos 2003 Cabernet Sauvignon (Aigialias Slopes) $12. 86 *—M.D. (10/1/2006)*

Oenoforos 2001 Chardonnay (Egilias Slopes) $12. 82 *—M.D. (10/1/2006)*

Oenoforos 2005 Asprolithi Roditis (Patras) $10. 82 *—M.D. (10/1/2006)*

Orphanos 2005 Assyrtico Assyrtico (Santorini) $17. 84 *—M.D. (10/1/2006)*

PALIVOU

Palivou 2006 Agiorgitiko (Peloponnese) $15. A floral character adds interesting dimension to the red berry and pepper aromas, and on the palate, it shows a zip and spice that mingles well with the earthier aspects of the grape. There's still a touch of that indigenous rusticity but the floral and minerally elements, added to the spice, are fun and exotic. **84** *—S.K. (11/15/2007)*

Papagiannakos 2005 Agiorgitiko (Attica) $20. One of the two most commercially important red grapes grown in Greece, Agiorgitiko is a light, lively variety that does especially well in the Pelopponese, where Papagiannakos is located. This wine exhibits a nose of playful spice and appetizing flavors of red berry and black currant. Mellow and balanced, it will pair well with heartier meat dishes as well as tomato-based pastas and poultry. **85** *—S.K. (11/15/2007)*

Palivou 2003 Agiorgitiko (Nemea) $25. 87 *—M.D. (10/1/2006)*

Palivou 2005 Agiorgitiko (St. George) Agiorgitiko (Peloponnese) $14. 85 *—M.D. (10/1/2006)*

Palivou 2005 Agiorgitiko (St. George) Rosé Agiorgitiko (Corinth) $14. 81 *—M.D. (12/15/2006)*

Palivou 2003 Ammos Agiorgitiko (Nemea) $35. 88 *—M.D. (12/15/2006)*

Palivou 2001 Nemea Agiorgitiko (Nemea) $20. 88 *—J.C. (9/2/2004)*

Palivou 2001 St. George Agiorgitiko (Corinth) $13. 85 *—J.C. (9/2/2004)*

Palivou 2002 St. George (Rose) Agiorgitiko (Corinth) $13. 81 *—J.C. (9/2/2004)*

Palivou 2001 Chardonnay (Corinth) $16. 85 *—J.C. (9/2/2004)*

Palivou 2005 White Fox Roditis (Corinth) $14. 82 *—M.D. (10/1/2006)*

Palivou 2003 White Fox White Blend (Corinth) $13. 85 *—J.C. (9/2/2004)*

PAPAGIANNAKOS

Papagiannakos 2000 St. George Agiorgitiko (Attica) $18. 84 *—J.C. (9/2/2004)*

Papagiannakos 2005 Savatiano (Attica) $14. 86 *—M.D. (12/15/2006)*

Papagiannakos 2003 Savatiano (Attica) $13. 88 Best Buy *—J.C. (9/2/2004)*

PAVLIDIS

Pavlidis 2001 Cabernet Blend (Drama) $18. 85 *—J.C. (9/2/2004)*

Pavlidis 2002 White Blend (Drama) $15. 82 *—J.C. (9/2/2004)*

PORTO CARRAS

Porto Carras 2003 Melisanthi Assyrtico (Côtes de Meliton) $15. 83 *—J.C. (9/2/2004)*

Porto Carras 2001 Château Porto Carras Cabernet Blend (Côtes de Meliton) $30. 90 *—J.C. (9/2/2004)*

Porto Carras 2001 Lidia (Côtes de Meliton) $15. 84 *—J.C. (9/2/2004)*

Porto Carras 2003 Regional Wine of Sithonia Malagousia (Halkidiki) $20. 84 *—J.C. (9/2/2004)*

Porto Carras 1999 Syrah (Halkidiki) $80. 86 *—J.C. (9/2/2004)*

Porto Carras 2003 Blanc de Blancs White Blend (Côtes de Meliton) $10. 85 *—J.C. (9/2/2004)*

PROVENZA

Provenza 2001 White Blend (Naoussa) $12. 84 *—J.C. (7/1/2003)*

ROBOLA

Robola 2003 Robola (Cephalonia) $10. 83 *—J.C. (9/2/2004)*

SAMOS

Samos 2000 Grand Cru Vin Doux Naturel White Blend (Samos) $10. 88 *— (11/15/2002)*

SKOURAS

Skouras 2004 Grande Cuvée Agiorgitiko (Nemea) $25. 87 *—M.D. (10/1/2006)*

Skouras 2003 Saint George Agiorgitiko (Nemea) $13. 84 *—M.D. (10/1/2006)*

Skouras 2004 Saint George-Cabernet Sauvignon Agiorgitiko (Peloponnese) $8. 85 Best Buy *—M.D. (10/1/2006)*

Skouras 2004 Cuvée Prestige Cabernet Sauvignon (Peloponnese) $16. 85 *—M.D. (10/1/2006)*

Skouras 2004 Chardonnay (Peloponnese) $14. 85 *—M.D. (10/1/2006)*

Skouras 2005 Moschofilero (Peloponnese) $14. 84 *—M.D. (12/15/2006)*

Skouras 2005 Zoë! Rosé Blend (Peloponnese) $10. 87 Best Buy *—M.D. (12/15/2006)*

Skouras 2005 White Blend (Peloponnese) $8. 84 Best Buy *—M.D. (10/1/2006)*

SPIROPOULOS

Spiropoulos 2000 Red Stag Agiorgitiko (Peloponnese) $15. 80 *—J.C. (9/2/2004)*

SPYROS HATZIYIANNIS

Spyros Hatziyiannis 2002 White Blend (Cyclades) $10. 88 Best Buy *—J.C. (9/2/2004)*

TECHNI ALIPIAS 2

Techni Alipias 2002 Regional Wine Sauvignon Blanc (Drama) $19. 83 *—J.C. (9/2/2004)*

TSANTALI

Tsantali 2002 Athiri (Vin de Pays de Macedoine) $10. 84 *—J.C. (9/2/2004)*

Tsantali 1998 Cava Tsantalis Cabernet Blend (Halkidiki) $15. 89 Best Buy *—J.C. (9/2/2004)*

Tsantali 2001 Metoxi Cabernet Blend (Mount Athos) $20. 89 *—M.D. (12/15/2006)*

Tsantali 1999 Metoxi Cabernet Blend (Mount Athos) $NA. 89 *—J.C. (9/1/2004)*

Tsantali 1996 Metoxi Reserve Cabernet Blend (Mount Athos) $44. 85 *—J.C. (9/2/2004)*

Tsantali 2001 Organics Cabernet Sauvignon (Halkidiki) $22. 91 Editors' Choice *—M.D. (12/15/2006)*

Tsantali 2000 Organics Cabernet Sauvignon (Halkidiki) $24. 88 *—J.C. (9/2/2004)*

Tsantali NV Cellar Reserve Mavrodaphne (Patras) $13. 84 *—J.C. (9/2/2004)*

Tsantali 2003 Maronia Vineyard Mavroudi (Thraki) $12. This 100% Mavroudi, a regional red wine of Thrace, has an expressive, red-fruit nose with warm hints of vanilla and smoky spice. Grown in northeastern Greece on an ancient site overlooking the Aegean Sea, this is smooth and velvety with rich, spicy flavors and a lingering finish. Its texture and complexity lends it to pairings with more opulent dishes like rack of lamb and beef stew, but alternately, consider its Mediterranean roots and sip alongside a plate of spicy black olives or a Greek salad. 87 Best Buy *—S.K. (11/15/2007)*

Tsantali 2000 Halkidiki Vineyards Merlot (Halkidiki) $12. 86 *—J.C. (9/2/2004)*

Tsantali 2003 Organic Merlot (Halkidiki) $18. There's little beyond the light fruit and spice on the nose here—it's followed by angular fruit flavors and a lack of the spice and warmth that gives Merlot its mellow, blended smoothness. This wine is acceptable, just on the thin side. 82 *—S.K. (4/1/2007)*

Tsantali 2003 Muscat (Lemnos) $7. 81 *—J.C. (9/2/2004)*

Tsantali 1998 Epilegmenos Reserve Red Blend (Rapsani) $18. 88 *—J.C. (9/2/2004)*

Tsantali 1997 Epilegmenos Reserve Red Blend (Naoussa) $14. 89 Best Buy *—J.C. (9/2/2004)*

Tsantali 1997 Epilegmenos Reserve Red Blend (Rapsani) $13. 88 *— (11/15/2002)*

Tsantali 1995 Epilegmenos Reserve Red Blend (Rapsani) $35. 87 *—J.C. (9/2/2004)*

Tsantali 1992 Rapsani Grand Reserve Red Blend (Rapsani) $43. 83 *—J.C. (9/2/2004)*

Tsantali 2002 Agiroritikos Rosé Blend (Greece) $15. 81 *—J.C. (9/2/2004)*

Tsantali 1999 Syrah (Greece) $17. 85 *—J.C. (9/2/2004)*

Tsantali 2002 Agioritikos White Blend (Greece) $15. 84 *—J.C. (9/2/2004)*

Tsantali 2003 Ambelonas White Blend (Halkidiki) $23. 86 *(7/1/2005)*

Tsantali 2002 Ambelonas White Blend (Halkidiki) $15. 85 *—J.C. (9/2/2004)*

Tsantali 2002 Chromitsa White Blend (Mount Athos) $16. 84 *—J.C. (9/2/2004)*

Tsantali 2003 Xinomavro (Naoussa) $13. 87 *—M.D. (12/15/2006)*

Tsantali 1992 Nauosa Reserve Xinomavro (Naoussa) $33. 84 *—J.C. (9/2/2004)*

Tsantali 2002 Xinomavro (Macedonia) $14. 86 *—M.D. (12/15/2006)*

TSELEPOS

Tselepos 2000 Agiorgitiko (Corinth) $15. 90 *— (11/15/2002)*

Tselepos 2001 Moschofilero (Mantinia) $12. 87 *— (11/15/2002)*

UNION DE COOPERATIVES VINICOLES DE SAMOS

Union de Cooperatives Vinicoles de Samos 1999 Nectar Vin de Paille Muscat (Samos) $20. 90 Editors' Choice *—J.C. (9/2/2004)*

Union de Cooperatives Vinicoles de Samos NV Samena Golden White Blend (Samos) $9. 86 *—J.C. (9/2/2004)*

VATISTAS

Vatistas 2002 Assyrtico (Peloponnese) $20. 84 *—J.C. (9/2/2004)*

Vatistas 2002 Athiri (Peloponnese) $20. 85 *—J.C. (9/2/2004)*

Vatistas 2001 Cabernet-Aghiorgitiko Cabernet Blend (Peloponnese) $15. 83 *—J.C. (9/2/2004)*

Vatistas 2002 Petroulianos (Peloponnese) $20. 86 *—J.C. (9/2/2004)*

Vatistas 2000 Regional Wine Red Blend (Peloponnese) $14. 82 *—J.C. (9/2/2004)*

Vatistas 2002 White Blend (Peloponnese) $14. 87 *—J.C. (9/2/2004)*

ZENATO

Zenato 2001 Vigneto Massoni White Blend (Naoussa) $NA. 88 *—R.V. (7/1/2003)*

HUNGARY

BOCK

Bock 1999 Bock Cuvée Barrique Bordeaux Blend (Villány) $52. The price is a bit steep for this attractive Bordeaux blend from Hungary, but it does deliver on many levels. Appealing pepper and mocha on the nose, and a balanced blend of pepper, spice and fruit on the palate, will satisfy versatile palates. It feels slightly tired, but the overall structure is good and the finish lingers. 83 *—S.K. (8/1/2007)*

Bock 2000 Royal Cuvée Bordeaux Blend (Villány) $28. A great example of what can be done with Bordeaux-style wines in Hungary. Heady and deep spice and plum aromas are followed by a restrained, elegant mesh of soft fruit and pepper in the mouth. Integrated and poised. 87 *—S.K. (8/1/2007)*

Bock 2000 Capella Cuvée Cabernet Sauvignon-Cabernet Franc (Villány) $90. What a lovely wine this is from Hungary, with its heady cedar/cigarbox and plum aromas and elegant, plush flavors. Soft tannins, good structure, and ageability add to the wine's appeal. Complexity without a headache—a wine with class. 88 *—S.K. (8/1/2007)*

Bock 2004 Hárslevelü (Villány) $13. Earthier mint and toasted oak on the nose lead this unique white wine from Hungary. On the palate, toasty butter and cream are pleasant and balanced. Slightly one-dimensional but overall a pretty nice everyday sipper. 82 *—S.K. (8/1/2007)*

CRAFTSMAN

Craftsman 2003 Cabernet Franc (Szekszárd) $9. 85 Best Buy *—M.D. (6/1/2006)*

Craftsman 2006 Cserszegi Fuszeres (Neszmély) $9. Another good and affordable white from Hungary. Pretty floral and flirty aromas and a bright, tropical fruit flavor profile make this wine accessible and good for stand-alone sipping or pairing with spicy cuisine. Imported by MHW Ltd. 84 *—S.K. (8/1/2007)*

Craftsman 2004 Cserszegi Fuszeres (Neszmély) $9. 83 *—M.D. (6/1/2006)*

Craftsman 2004 Gewürztraminer (Neszmély) $9. 84 *—M.D. (6/1/2006)*

Craftsman 2006 Grüner Veltliner (Neszmély) $9. White pepper, bright and zippy tropical fruit flavors and a clean, food-friendly finish make this enjoyable Gruner from Hungary a great new everyday wine. It's affordable too, adding to its appeal. Imported by MHW Ltd. 85 Best Buy *—S.K. (8/1/2007)*

Craftsman 2006 Hárslevelü (Neszmély) $9. Affordable and fun, this wine has assertive flavors of grapefruit and luscious tropical fruit. It's a touch sweet but the citrus cuts any sap. Overall, a yummy wine with mass appeal. Imported by MHW Ltd. 84 *—S.K. (8/1/2007)*

Craftsman 2006 Királyleányka (Neszmély) $9. A delicate floral nose leads with this native Hungarian variety, followed by flavors which are clean, crisp and citric—perhaps a touch limey for some tastes. Overall, the wine is balanced and the finish dry. Affordable and food-friendly. Imported by MHW Ltd. 84 *—S.K. (8/1/2007)*

Craftsman 2004 Királyleányka (Neszmély) $9. 84 *—M.D. (6/1/2006)*

Craftsman 2004 Pinot Grigio (Neszmély) $9. 86 Best Buy *(2/1/2006)*

Craftsman 2003 Falconers Cuvée Red Blend (Neszmély) $9. 83 *—M.D. (6/1/2006)*

Craftsman 2004 Sauvignon Blanc (Neszmély) $9. 86 Best Buy *—M.D. (6/1/2006)*

DISZNÓKÖ

Disznókö 1999 Aszú 5 Puttonyos Tokaji (Tokaji) $33. 91 *(6/1/2006)*

Disznókö 1999 Aszú 6 Puttonyos Tokaji (Tokaji) $43. 90 *(6/1/2006)*

° DOBOGÓ

Dobogó 2004 Furmint (Tokaj) $32. 88 *—M.D. (6/1/2006)*

Dobogó 2003 Mylitta Furmint (Tokaji) $36. 87 *(6/1/2006)*

Dobogó 2000 Aszú 6 Puttonyos Tokaji (Tokaji) $87. 90 *(6/1/2006)*

Dobogó 1999 Aszú 6 Puttonyos Tokaji (Tokaji) $87. 89 *(6/1/2006)*

DUNAVAR

Dunavar 2004 Connoisseur Collection Pinot Gris (Felso-Magyarország) $7. 84 Best Buy *—M.D. (6/1/2006)*

Dunavar 2003 Egri Bikaver Red Blend (Eger) $8. 84 Best Buy *—M.D. (6/1/2006)*

GERE ATTILA

Gere Attila 2003 Kopár Cuvée Bordeaux Blend (Villány) $52. Hungarian red wines continue to impress, and this selection from Villany is no exception. Soft and elegant fruit aromas are followed by restrained pepper and spice on the palate. The wine is a touch angular in its tautness but with food, will be a hit. 86 *—S.K. (8/1/2007)*

Gere Attila 2003 Barrique Cabernet Sauvignon (Villány) $29. Soft and integrated aromas and taut flavors of blackberry, blackcurrant and smoke give this French-style wine class and poise. Its dry, clean quality, good structure and flavorful fruit means it will age well, but drink now and you will not be disappointed. Another thumbs up for Hungarian winemaking. 87 *—S.K. (8/1/2007)*

HILLTOP NESZMÉLY

Hilltop Neszmély 1993 Aszú 5 Puttonyos Tokaji (Tokaji) $45. 87 *(6/1/2006)*

OREMUS

Oremus 2000 Furmint (Tokaji) $10. 89 Best Buy *—R.V. (11/15/2002)*

Oremus 2003 Mandolás Furmint (Tokaji) $17. 82 *—M.D. (6/1/2006)*

Oremus 1999 Aszú 5 Puttonyos Tokaji (Tokaji) $60. 88 *(6/1/2006)*

Oremus 2002 Late Harvest Tokaji (Tokaji) $24. 89 *(6/1/2006)*

ROYAL TOKAJI

Royal Tokaji 2003 Aszú 5 Puttonyos Tokaji (Tokaji) $39. Honeyed apricot and orange peel on the nose and palate typify this elegant but playful botrytis wine. The wine's lively acidity gives it a bounce on the tongue, adding dimension to the citrus components and lending it more to food pairing with desserts or a cheese plate. 89 *—S.K. (12/1/2007)*

Royal Tokaji 2000 Aszú 5 Puttonyos 500 ml Tokaji (Tokaji) $32. 94 Editors' Choice *(6/1/2006)*

Royal Tokaji 1995 Aszú Essencia Tokaji (Tokaji) $167. 92 *(6/1/2006)*

Royal Tokaji 1999 Betsek Aszú 6 Puttonyos Tokaji (Tokaji) $67. 93 *(6/1/2006)*

Royal Tokaji 2000 Birsalmás Aszú 5 Puttonyos Tokaji (Tokaji) $54. From a small single vineyard called Birsalmas (Hungarian for quince), this fresh, delicate dessert wine offers elegant flavors of quince (naturally), honey and melon. Its lively acids keep it light on the palate—refreshing but indulgent. 89 *—S.K. (12/1/2007)*

Royal Tokaji 1999 Birsalmás Aszú 5 Puttonyos Tokaji (Tokaji) $52. 88 *(6/1/2006)*

Royal Tokaji 1995 Mézes Mály Aszú 6 Puttonyos Tokaji (Tokaji) $115. 88 *(6/1/2006)*

Royal Tokaji 1996 Nyulászó Aszú 6 Puttonyos Tokaji (Tokaji) $54. Elegant flavors of apricot and honey are light and delicate, with a lively acidity keeping the wine dancing on the palate. Though the wine shows intense depth of flavors, it's never heavy and has a clean, poised finish. From start to finish, the wine is balanced and refined, with a character that speaks of its unique terroir. 90 *—S.K. (12/1/2007)*

Royal Tokaji 1995 Nyulászó Aszú 6 Puttonyos Tokaji (Tokaji) $85. 91 *(6/1/2006)*

Royal Tokaji 1999 Szt. Tamás Aszú 6 Puttonyos Tokaji (Tokaji) $77. This unique and delicious dessert wine from Hungary offers apricot and honey on the nose and palate, as well as an earthier element of tobacco and mocha. It's dense but delicate, too, with a weight and complexity that unfolds in the mouth. 90 *—S.K. (12/1/2007)*

Royal Tokaji 1996 Szt. Tamás Aszú 6 Puttonyos Tokaji (Tokaji) $77. This opulent wine, with its honeyed apricot and resiny flavors, is layered with wood and spice, giving it extra life. It also has a hint of mocha—an earthiness that adds weight but not heaviness to the overall character. Poised and pretty, but also substantial. 91 Editors' Choice *—S.K. (12/1/2007)*

Royal Tokaji 1995 Szt. Tamás Aszú 6 Puttonyos Tokaji (Tokaji) $77. 91 *(6/1/2006)*

SZEPSY

Szepsy 2002 Aszú 6 Puttonyos Tokaji (Tokaj) $0. Though this dessert wine is already excellent, it's quite exciting to imagine how good it will be as its delicate flavors mingle over time. Made by the Szepsy family, whose roots go centuries (perhaps 1,000 years) deep in Hungary, the wine starts with a dense, slightly musky but floral nose. On the tongue, apricot, honey and spice mingle in a rich, opulent union, buoyed by a sparkling acidity that keeps the wine light and pretty. 93 *—S.K. (12/1/2007)*

TIBOR GAL

Tibor Gal 2002 Chardonnay (Eger) $12. 80 *—M.D. (6/1/2006)*

Tibor Gal 2001 Chardonnay (Eger) $12. 86 *—J.C. (6/1/2005)*

Tibor Gal 2002 Egri Bikaver Red Blend (Eger) $11. 83 *—M.D. (6/1/2006)*

TÖRLEY

Törley NV Charmant Rosé Sparkling Blend (Hungary) $10. A heady strawberry nose leads into waves of honey and strawberry, touched with a hint of spice. This is rather sweet on the palate and could use a more delicate touch, but overall it's enjoyable and accessible. Imported by MHW Ltd. 83 *—S.K. (12/31/2007)*

Törley NV Fortuna Sparkling Blend (Hungary) $10. This is a stylish, sparkling dessert wine at a good price. Lush and lovely on the nose, with layers of perfumed flowers and spice, the wine offers sweet but delicate flavors on the palate. It's not overly complicated or complex, but simply good and a fitting apéritif for everyday. Imported by MHW Ltd. 85 Best Buy *—S.K. (12/31/2007)*

Törley NV Gála Sparkling Blend (Hungary) $10. A very pretty, opulent floral nose with hints of spice lead on this Hungarian sparkler. On the palate, it has a clean, minerally flavor that lacks some of the dimension and finesse that the nose would lead one to expect. A good food wine, though—and fun. Imported by MHW Ltd. 83 *—S.K. (12/31/2007)*

Törley NV Grande Cuvée Brut Sparkling Blend (Hungary) $12. Clean, citric and minerally on the nose, this Hungarian sparkler follows with good, medium-bodied flavors of toast and mineral on the palate. It has a restrained style but the fruit still flirts with the tongue and leaves a finish that is both pert and sweet. Imported by MHW Ltd. 84 *—S.K. (12/31/2007)*

ISRAEL

BARKAN

Barkan 2000 Reserve Cabernet Sauvignon (Galil) $20. 88 *—J.C. (4/1/2005)*

Barkan 1996 Reserve Cabernet Sauvignon (Galil) $19. 80 *(4/1/2001)*

Barkan 2000 Superieur Cabernet Sauvignon (Galilee) $75. Kosher. 89 *—J.M. (4/3/2004)*

Barkan 2000 Reserve Chardonnay (Barkan) $15. 84 *—J.C. (4/1/2005)*

Barkan 1998 Reserve Chardonnay (Galil) $8. 84 *(4/1/2001)*

Barkan 2000 Superieur Merlot (Galil) $75. 86 *—J.C. (4/1/2005)*

Barkan 2002 Reserve Kosher Pinotage (Judea) $20. 84 *—J.C. (4/1/2006)*

BINYAMINA

Binyamina 2002 Special Reserve Chardonnay (Galilee) $15. 81 *—J.C. (4/1/2005)*

Binyamina 1999 Special Reserve Merlot (Galilee) $25. 85 *—J.M. (4/3/2004)*

CARMEL

Carmel 2003 Limited Edition Kosher Bordeaux Blend (Judean Hills) $60. Smoke, black currant and chocolate are evident in this kosher Bordeaux blend from Israel's Carmel Winery, but the flavors are slightly-one-dimensional and the price point high. Despite that, it's a delicate, enjoyable wine with unique flavors. 83 *—S.K. (4/1/2007)*

Carmel 2002 Ben Zimra Single Vineyard Cabernet Sauvignon (Upper Galilee) $25. 87 *—J.C. (4/1/2005)*

Carmel 1999 Private Collection Cabernet Sauvignon (Judean Hills) $26. Kosher. 83 *—J.M. (4/3/2004)*

Carmel 1998 Private Collection Cabernet Sauvignon (Galil) $12. 81 *—M.S. (4/1/2002)*

Carmel 2003 Private Collection Kosher Cabernet Sauvignon (Galilee) $19. 83 *—J.C. (4/1/2006)*

Carmel 2002 Ramat Arad Single Vineyard Cabernet Sauvignon (Negev Hills) $28. 86 *—J.C. (4/1/2005)*

Carmel 2002 Zarit Single Vineyard Cabernet Sauvignon (Upper Galilee) $25. 85 *—J.C. (4/1/2005)*

Carmel 2003 Private Collection Cabernet Sauvignon-Merlot (Galilee) $15. 84 *—J.C. (4/1/2005)*

Carmel 2002 Private Collection Cabernet Sauvignon-Shiraz (Galilee) $16. 85 *—J.C. (4/1/2006)*

Carmel 2002 Kerem Single Vineyard Merlot (Shomron) $25. 87 *—J.C. (4/1/2005)*

Carmel 1998 Private Collection Merlot (Judean Hills) $12. 84 *(4/1/2001)*

Carmel 1999 Valley Wines Petite Sirah (Shomron) $9. 83 *(4/1/2001)*

Carmel 2003 Ramat Arad Vineyard Sauvignon Blanc (Negev Hills) $15. 82 *—J.C. (4/1/2005)*

Carmel 1998 Vineyards Selected Shiraz (Shomron) $12. 82 *(4/1/2001)*

CASTEL

Castel 1999 Petite Castel Cabernet Sauvignon (Haut-Judeé) $21. 87 *— (11/15/2002)*

Castel 1996 Grand Vin Cabernet Sauvignon-Merlot (Haut-Judeé) $41. 91 *— (11/15/2002)*

CHILLAG

Chillag 2003 Orna Riserva Kosher Cabernet Sauvignon (Galilee) $20. 87 *—J.C. (4/1/2006)*

DALTON

Dalton 1999 Reserve Cabernet Sauvignon (Galilee) $37. 83 *—J.M. (4/3/2004)*

Dalton 2002 Reserve Chardonnay (Galilee) $21. Kosher. 87 *—J.M. (4/3/2004)*

Dalton 2000 Merlot (Galilee) $24. Kosher. 82 *—J.M. (4/3/2004)*

Dalton 2000 Reserve Merlot (Galilee) $37. Kosher. 86 *—J.M. (4/3/2004)*

Dalton NV Admon Portah Port (Galilee) $16. Kosher. 87 *—J.M. (4/3/2004)*

Dalton 2002 Reserve Sauvignon Blanc (Galilee) $18. Kosher. 81 *—J.M. (4/3/2004)*

DOMAINE DU CASTEL

Domaine du Castel 2003 Blanc du Castel Kosher Chardonnay (Judean Hills) $40. 82 *—J.C. (4/1/2006)*

GALIL MOUNTAIN

Galil Mountain 2003 Cabernet Sauvignon (Galilee) $17. 86 *—J.C. (4/1/2005)*

Galil Mountain 2001 Yiron Cabernet Sauvignon-Merlot (Galilee) $26. 84 *—J.C. (4/1/2005)*

Galil Mountain 2003 Merlot (Galilee) $16. 85 *—J.C. (4/1/2006)*

GAMLA

Gamla 1996 Cabernet Sauvignon (Galilee) $12. 87 Best Buy *(4/1/2000)*

Gamla 2000 Cabernet Sauvignon (Galilee) $16. 83 *—J.C. (4/1/2005)*

Gamla 1997 Cabernet Sauvignon (Galilee) $14. 88 *(4/1/2001)*

Gamla 1998 Chardonnay (Galilee) $12. 84 *(4/1/2001)*

GOLAN HEIGHTS

Golan Heights 2002 Golan Cabernet Sauvignon (Galilee) $16. 86 *—J.C. (4/1/2005)*

Golan Heights 2003 Golan Chardonnay (Galilee) $15. 84 *—J.C. (4/1/2005)*

Golan Heights 2003 Golan Sion Creek Red Red Blend (Galilee) $10. 84 *—J.C. (4/1/2005)*

Golan Heights 2003 Golan Emerald Riesling (Galilee) $11. 81 *—J.C. (4/1/2005)*

Golan Heights 2003 Sion Creek White White Blend (Galilee) $10. 85 Best Buy *—J.C. (4/1/2005)*

GUSH ETZION

Gush Etzion 2000 Cabernet Sauvignon-Merlot (Judean Hills) $27. 86 *—J.C. (4/1/2005)*

HEVRON HEIGHTS WINERY

Hevron Heights Winery 2002 Isaac's Ram Kosher Cabernet Sauvignon (Judean Hills) $31. Ripe berries and spice aromas entice, and the palate continues to please with more raspberry and black pepper. The wine could use more dimension but the lively flavors and substantial finish add weight. 84 *—S.K. (4/1/2007)*

Hevron Heights Winery 2001 Isaac's Ram Kosher Cabernet Sauvignon (Judean Hills) $25. 85 *—J.C. (4/1/2006)*

Hevron Heights Winery 2002 Jerusalem Heights Barrel Selection Kosher Cabernet Sauvignon-Merlot (Judean Hills) $14. 80 *—J.C. (4/1/2006)*

Hevron Heights Winery 2001 Makhpelah Judean Vineyards Kosher Cabernet Sauvignon-Merlot (Judean Hills) $54. 83 *—J.C. (4/1/2006)*

Hevron Heights Winery 2002 Paradess Kosher Merlot (Judean Hills) $31. Black pepper, spice and smoke on the nose are followed by fruit-forward flavors of plum and cherry. Full-bodied but not overpowering, the wine has a lingering finish and overall elegant character. 84 *—S.K. (4/1/2007)*

Hevron Heights Winery 2001 Pardess Kosher Merlot (Judean Hills) $25. 86 *—J.C. (4/1/2006)*

Hevron Heights Winery 2002 Megiddo Kosher Red Blend (Judean Hills) $84. 89 *—J.C. (4/1/2006)*

Hevron Heights Winery 2002 Special Reserve Lasportas Brother's Selection Kosher Red Blend (Judean Hills) $70. This deep garnet, kosher red blend from Israel has an exuberant, slightly hot nose of cherry and chocolate and follows with a medium-bodied mixture of blackberry, cherry and cocoa. The finish is lingering with a touch of sweetness. Overall a classy wine, though for this price, perhaps a little basic. 84 *—S.K. (4/1/2007)*

Hevron Heights Winery 2001 Special Reserve Lasportas Brother's Selection Kosher Red Blend (Judean Hills) $69. 84 *—J.C. (4/1/2006)*

Hevron Heights Winery 2003 Kosher Syrah (Judean Hills) $31. Produced from grapes grown in the Northern Negev/Southern Hebron Hills at Kibbutz Kramim, this rounded kosher Syrah is well-integrated with bright berry and pepper flavors and a lingering finish. Good structure and tannins mean it will age well and can hold its own against bolder dishes. 84 *—S.K. (4/1/2007)*

NOAH

Noah 2002 Kosher Cabernet Sauvignon (Judean Hills) $15. 83 *—J.C. (4/1/2006)*

Noah 2004 Gedeon Beth Shemesh Vineyards Kosher Cabernet Sauvignon (Judean Hills) $12. Toast and powerful fruit on the nose are misleading—this tends toward the soft side and has well-balanced flavors of berry and tobacco. It's not a complex wine, though. 83 *—S.K. (4/1/2007)*

Noah 2002 Kosher Merlot (Judean Hills) $15. 81 *—J.C. (4/1/2006)*

Noah 2004 Tevel Kosher Merlot (Judean Hills) $14. Has a slightly musty and stewed fruit nose, with medium-bodied structure and primarily one-dimensional rhubarb flavors. 82 *—S.K. (4/1/2007)*

Noah 2005 Kosher Muscat (Judean Hills) $14. White peach and honey on the nose are followed by apricots, nuts and sugar on the palate. The wine is not terribly elegant but is flavorful and quite delicious. It's powerful enough to age for several years. 85 *—S.K. (4/1/2007)*

Noah 2004 Gedeon Judean Hills Vineyards Kosher Petite Sirah (Judean Hills) $12. Grown in the hills outside Jerusalem, this has a light touch, with a fruity nose that opens into straightforward strawberry and cherry flavors. Pleasant but not too memorable; finish needs length. 82 *—S.K. (4/1/2007)*

RECANATI

Recanati 2004 Barbera (Galilee) $15. Black cherry, spice and tobacco lead on the nose, but the fall slightly flat on the palate. Bright plum and cherry flavors touched with chocolate are pleasant, but the wine generally tends toward the angular side. Good but needs more structure in the mouth. 83 *—S.K. (4/1/2007)*

Recanati 2004 Kosher Cabernet Sauvignon (Galilee) $15. 84 *—J.C. (4/1/2006)*

Recanati 2002 Reserve Kosher Cabernet Sauvignon (Galilee) $25. 85 *—J.C. (4/1/2006)*

Recanati 2001 Special Reserve Kosher Cabernet Sauvignon (Galilee) $35. 89 *—J.C. (4/1/2006)*

Recanati 2004 Kosher Chardonnay (Galilee) $14. 84 *—J.C. (4/1/2006)*

Recanati 2004 Kosher Merlot (Galilee) $15. 84 *—J.C. (4/1/2006)*

Recanati 2002 Reserve Kosher Merlot (Galilee) $25. 83 *—J.C. (4/1/2006)*

Recanati 2004 Reserve Red Blend (Galilee) $22. Blueberry, plum and pepper create a subtle but supple combination in this kosher red blend from Recanati. Oak adds warmth and the finish is long, giving the wine power without compromising its sophisticated style. 84 *—S.K. (4/1/2007)*

Recanati 2005 Sauvignon Blanc (Shomron) $13. A subtle floral nose is followed by tropical fruit flavors of pear, banana and citrus in this kosher offering from Israeli winery Recanati. The feel of the wine is slightly watery and the finish is short, but the overall quality of the wine is good. 83 *—S.K. (4/1/2007)*

Recanati 2003 Kosher Shiraz (Galilee) $15. 85 *—J.C. (4/1/2006)*

SEGAL'S

Segal's 2002 Dishon Single Vineyard Kosher Cabernet Sauvignon (Galil) $35. Cigar, grilled meat and cedar on the nose lead into a full-bodied, flavorful Cab packed with berries, pepper and spice. Complex and integrated, with great structure and a mineral edge on the finish. 86 *—S.K. (4/1/2007)*

Segal's 2000 Special Reserve Cabernet Sauvignon (Galilee) $15. 90 Best Buy *—J.C. (4/1/2005)*

Segal's 2002 Unfiltered Cabernet Sauvignon (Galil) $60. 84 —*J.C. (4/1/2005)*

Segal's 2002 Special Reserve Chardonnay (Galilee) $13. Kosher. **87** —*J.M. (4/3/2004)*

Segal's 2002 Dovev Single Vineyard Kosher Merlot (Galil) $33. Sweet aromas of cherry and spice start this medium-bodied wine, rife with overriding fruit flavors. Not very complex beyond these initial flavors, but the blackberry character is appealing and the spices add dimension. **82** —*S.K. (4/1/2007)*

Segal's 2000 Special Reserve Merlot (Galilee) $15. 89 Editors' Choice —*J.C. (4/1/2005)*

TISHBI ESTATE

Tishbi Estate 2000 Chardonnay (Golan Heights) $16. 87 — *(11/15/2002)*

Tishbi Estate 2000 Baron Chenin Blanc (Galilee) $9. 82 — *(11/15/2002)*

YARDEN

Yarden 1996 Cabernet Sauvignon (Galilee) $20. 90 *(4/1/2000)*

Yarden 1998 Cabernet Sauvignon (Galilee) $26. 87 — *(11/15/2002)*

Yarden NV Champagne Blend (Galilee) $22. 88 *(4/1/2000)*

Yarden NV Brut Champagne Blend (Galilee) $20. 86 *(4/1/2000)*

Yarden NV Brut NV Champagne Blend (Galilee) $24. 88 *(4/1/2001)*

Yarden 2000 Chardonnay (Galilee) $17. 85 — *(11/15/2002)*

Yarden 1998 Chardonnay (Galilee) $15. 85 *(4/1/2001)*

Yarden 1998 Blanc de Blancs Chardonnay (Galilee) $20. Kosher. **86** —*J.C. (12/31/2004)*

Yarden 2002 Katzrin Chardonnay (Galilee) $30. 86 —*J.C. (4/1/2005)*

Yarden 2002 Odem Organic Vineyard Chardonnay (Galilee) $19. 88 —*J.C. (4/1/2005)*

Yarden 1996 Merlot (Galilee) $20. 88 *(4/1/2000)*

Yarden 1999 Yarden Merlot (Galilee) $23. 86 —*M.S. (11/15/2002)*

Yarden 2003 Mount Hermon Red Blend (Galilee) $11. 84 —*J.C. (4/1/2005)*

Yarden 1998 Mt. Hermon Red Blend (Galilee) $11. 87 Best Buy *(4/1/2000)*

Yarden 2001 Syrah (Galilee) $23. 83 —*J.C. (4/1/2005)*

YATIR

Yatir 2003 Yatir Forest Kosher Cabernet Sauvignon-Merlot (Judean Hills) $65. Blackberries and black currants aromas are followed by smoked oak and a slightly dry character on the palate. There's also a tartness here, but that will likely be tempered by a few years in the cellar. Overall, a good wine, especially when paired with food, which should take the edge off of it. **83** —*S.K. (4/1/2007)*

Yatir 2002 Yatir Forest Kosher Cabernet Sauvignon (Judean Hills) $50. 86 —*J.C. (4/1/2006)*

Yatir 2001 Cabernet Sauvignon-Merlot (Judean Hills) $30. 81 —*J.C. (4/1/2005)*

Yatir 2001 Forest Cabernet Sauvignon-Merlot (Judean Hills) $49. 87 —*J.C. (4/1/2005)*

JAPAN

CROIX TORIINO

Croix Toriino 2005 Nigori Yamanashi Limited Edition Unfiltered Koshu (Kyoto) $24. What a fun and intriguing discovery is to be found in the unfiltered version of this Japanese variety. Mouthwatering aromas of grapefruit and apple are followed by sweet but balanced grapefruit and citrus flavors. Interestingly, the flavors are fresh but the mouthfeel creamy. The finish is light. Drink as an aperitif or pair with spicy food. **85** —*S.K. (8/1/2007)*

Croix Toriino 2005 Yamanashi Limited Edition Koshu (Kyoto) $24. On the nose of this unique variety native to Japan, fresh herbal notes pervade. The favors are clean and light—think grapefruit and citrus, but a tad astringent and prickly for American tastes. An interesting wine with a natural ability to pair with—you guessed it—sushi and seafood. **80** —*S.K. (8/1/2007)*

LEBANON

CHÂTEAU KEFRAYA

Château Kefraya 1997 Cabernet Blend (Bekaa Valley) $23. 91 — *(11/15/2002)*

CHÂTEAU KEFRAYA

Château Kefraya 2000 La Dame Blanche Chardonnay (Bekaa Valley) $13. 82 — *(11/15/2002)*

CHÂTEAU MUSAR

Château Musar 2004 Cuvée Rosé Cinsault (Bekaa Valley) $20. Founded north of Beirut, Lebanon in the Bekaa Valley in 1930, Chateau Musar is a historic, respected producer of red wines in the Bordeaux style. Given the winery's track record, this rose underwhelms. The fresh strawberry and fruit flavors have potential but fade quickly on a watery foundation. **81** —*S.K. (7/1/2007)*

Château Musar 1997 Red Blend (Bekaa Valley) $49. 88 —*J.C. (4/1/2005)*

Château Musar 2000 Hochar Red Blend (Bekaa Valley) $25. 89 —*J.C. (4/1/2005)*

Château Musar 1998 White Blend (Bekaa Valley) $28. 82 —*J.C. (4/1/2005)*

TISHBI ESTATE

Tishbi Estate 2000 Baron Cabernet Sauvignon (Bekaa Valley) $12. 88 Best Buy — *(11/15/2002)*

Tishbi Estate 2000 Tishbi Vineyards Cabernet Sauvignon (Bekaa Valley) $16. 90 — *(11/15/2002)*

Tishbi Estate 1999 Jonathan Tishbi Merlot (Bekaa Valley) $46. 92 Cellar Selection — *(11/15/2002)*

LITHUANIA

ALITA

Alita NV Exclusive Semi-Dry Sparkling Blend (Lithuania) $10. Waves of citrus, apple and pear, balanced by a crisp minerality that keeps the wine aloft on the palate, recommend this semi-dry sparkler from Lithuania. The wine offers elegance and a delicate touch at a reasonable price, and will pair well with spicy cuisine or summer salads. **85 Best Buy** —*S.K. (8/1/2007)*

Alita NV Gold Sparkling Blend (Lithuania) $10. Snappy aromas of citrus mingle with orange and honey on the nose of this sweet sparkling wine from Lithuania. On the palate, the wine is rich and appealing, though perhaps a touch opulent for fans of drier wines. A great companion to Asian cuisine or paired up with an assortment of salty cheeses. **84** —*S.K. (8/1/2007)*

Alita NV Semi-Dry Sparkling Blend (Lithuania) $10. Apple, lemon, apricot and honey come together in a fresh but lush combination with this sparkling wine from Alita. It's sweet but balanced with minerality and bubbles, making it a fun option for everyday drinking. **84** —*S.K. (8/1/2007)*

Alita NV Sweet Sparkling Blend (Lithuania) $10. Heady floral and honey scents mingled with a freshness give this sparkler a distinctive edge, and on the palate, the lush sweetness is lifted by good acidity. The wine is undeniably sweet, but minerality keeps it from being cloying. **84** —*S.K. (8/1/2007)*

MACEDONIA

BOVIN

Bovin 2000 Alexandar Red Blend (Tikves) $12. 84 —*M.D. (6/1/2006)*

Bovin 2000 Venus Red Blend (Tikves) $12. 81 —*M.D. (6/1/2006)*

Bovin 2000 Vranec (Tikves) $12. 83 —*M.D. (6/1/2006)*

Bovin 2000 Dissan Vranec (Tikves) $25. 85 —*M.D. (6/1/2006)*

MEXICO

L.A. CETTO

L.A. Cetto 1996 Private Reserve Cabernet Sauvignon (Valle de Guadalupe) $18. 87 *(7/1/2003)*

L.A. Cetto 2001 Chardonnay (Valle de Guadalupe) $10. 84 *(7/1/2003)*

L.A. Cetto 2000 Private Reserve Chardonnay (Valle de Guadalupe) $14. 84 *(7/1/2003)*

L.A. Cetto 1996 Private Reserve Nebbiolo (Valle de Guadalupe) $18. 88 *(7/1/2003)*

L.A. Cetto 1999 Petite Sirah (Valle de Guadalupe) $8. 83 *(7/1/2003)*

L.A. Cetto 2001 Zinfandel (Valle de Guadalupe) $8. 83 *(7/1/2003)*

MOLDOVA

ACOREX

Acorex 2003 Reserve Cabernet Sauvignon (Moldova) $16. Game, red berry, spice and a hint of mint characterize this attractive Cabernet. Tannins are sturdy and though not terribly complex, this has personality and a good finish. Great with smoked meats or a winter stew. 84 *—S.K. (11/15/2007)*

Acorex 2004 Reserve Cabernet Sauvignon-Merlot (Moldova) $16. This blend from Moldova shows promising aromas of red berry, black pepper and cinnamon spice on the nose but on the palate, the fruit expression is lacking. Still, there are appealing hints of oak and spice and the wine has an exotic overall character that will pair well with ethnic and meat dishes. 82 *—S.K. (11/15/2007)*

Acorex 2003 Amaro Red Blend (Moldova) $59. An appealing nose of leather and tobacco on this wine is followed by elegant flavors of red berry, cigar and game. Good structure, complexity and spice means the wine can age, but it's ready to drink now. An applaudable effort from an historic wine-producing region. 86 *—S.K. (11/15/2007)*

Acorex 2004 Cuvée Aleksandr Blanc de Blancs Brut Sparkling Blend (Moldova) $23. A sweet, heady nose of citrus and minerals leads on this pretty but simple sparkler. Robust flavors of toast and minerals offer roundness, character and a food-friendly slant, but the wine needs some complexity. 82 *—S.K. (12/31/2007)*

CHÂTEAU VARTELY

Château Vartely 2005 Rezerva Cabernet Sauvignon (Moldova) $17. Black pepper, cinnamon and clove spice meet balanced fruit expression in this elegant Cab from Moldova. The wine is balanced and friendly, but exhibits a reserved edge that makes it especially good with varied foods. 85 *—S.K. (11/15/2007)*

Château Vartely 2005 Rezerva Merlot (Moldova) $17. Soft aromas of tobacco, game and spice are followed on the palate with smooth, balanced Merlot flavors and a touch of smoke. An easy-drinking wine from an interesting region. 84 *—S.K. (11/15/2007)*

CRICOVA

Cricova 2002 Cabernet Sauvignon (Moldova) $8. 83 *—M.D. (12/15/2006)*

Cricova 1993 Collection Cabernet Cabernet Sauvignon (Moldova) $23. 86 *—M.D. (12/15/2006)*

Cricova 2003 Cuvée Prestige Spumant Clasic Rosu Dulce Cabernet Sauvignon (Moldova) $17. A bit of berry, raisin and spice on the nose lead into a red sparkling wine that offers body, structure, sweetness and acidity on the palate. Do the earthy flavors of Cabernet marry well with acidity and zip? It's somewhat tricky. The wine overall has trouble with harmony, though the berry, spice and wood flavors are good. 81 *—S.K. (12/31/2007)*

Cricova 2001 Prestige Cabernet Sauvignon (Moldova) $16. 84 *—M.D. (12/15/2006)*

Cricova 2000 Codru Cabernet Sauvignon-Merlot (Moldova) $8. 84 **Best Buy** *—M.D. (12/15/2006)*

Cricova 1990 Collection Codru Cabernet Sauvignon-Merlot (Moldova) $22. 85 *—M.D. (12/15/2006)*

Cricova 2001 Prestige Codru Cabernet Sauvignon-Merlot (Moldova) $16. 82 *—M.D. (12/15/2006)*

Cricova 2001 Collection Semidry Champagne Blend (Moldova) $12. Minerally and a touch earthy on the nose, this follows with toast and sweet fruit on the palate, which is both simple and friendly. Overall, the wine has an array of good, clean flavors and a zippy finish. 83 *—S.K. (12/31/2007)*

Cricova 1992 Collection Dionis Red Blend (Moldova) $22. 84 *—M.D. (12/15/2006)*

Cricova 2000 Dionis Red Blend (Moldova) $10. 81 *—M.D. (12/15/2006)*

CRICOVA ACOREX

Cricova Acorex 1999 Riesling (Moldova) $6. 82 *(9/1/2004)*

Cricova Acorex 1999 Sauvignon Blanc (Moldova) $6. 83 *(9/1/2004)*

GRAYSTONE

Graystone 2004 Select Cabernet Sauvignon (Cahul) $13. 83 *—M.D. (12/15/2006)*

Graystone 2005 Select Chardonnay (Cahul) $13. 83 *—M.D. (12/15/2006)*

Graystone 2004 Select Merlot (Cahul) $13. 83 *—M.D. (12/15/2006)*

Graystone 2005 Select Pinot Gris (Cahul) $13. 83 *—M.D. (12/15/2006)*

Graystone 2004 Select Pinot Noir (Cahul) $13. 81 *—M.D. (12/15/2006)*

VINA LAVINA

Vina LaVina 2000 Chardonnay (Chisinau County) $9. 81 *—M.D. (6/1/2006)*

VINO VISTA COLLECTION

Vino Vista Collection 2005 Mirodia Semidry Red Blend (Codru Region) $9. 82 *—M.D. (12/15/2006)*

MOROCCO

BOULAOUANE

Boulaouane 2006 Vin Gris Rosé Blend (Morocco) $8. Blending Cinsault, Grenache and Cabernet Sauvignon grown in the foothills of the Atlas Mountains in Morocco, this is ripe, soft, with some attractive flavors of caramel and strawberries. 84 *—R.V. (7/1/2007)*

HICKORY RIDGE

Hickory Ridge 1999 Special Cuvée Shiraz (Beni M'Tir) $6. 82 *(10/1/2001)*

ROMANIA

BELOARÉ

Beloaré 2005 Selection Semi-Sweet Riesling (Romania) $11. A dancing, fragrant nose and appealing flavors of apple and flowers makes this semi-sweet selection from Romania a fun wine to try with spicy and seafood dishes. It's a little heavy on the palate but it's adaptable and an interesting alternative from a lesser-known wine-producing country. 82 *—S.K. (9/1/2007)*

BLACK C

Black C 2001 Feteasca Neagra (Romania) $9. 80 *—M.D. (6/1/2006)*

Black C 2000 Pinot Gris (Romania) $9. 83 *—J.C. (2/1/2006)*

BONVINO

Bonvino 2005 Riesling Italico Demi-Dulce Riesling (Vânju Mare) $12. Light, lively and with appealing flavors and aromas of flowers, citrus and apple, this semisweet wine from Romania is great as an after-dinner treat or paired with cheese. It's fun and versatile, and a friendly entry into wine from a region unknown to many American wine drinkers. Imported by Vidalco International, LLC. 84 *—S.K. (9/1/2007)*

BYZANTIUM

Byzantium 2000 Cabernet Sauvignon (Dealu Mare) $15. 83 *—M.D. (6/1/2006)*

Byzantium 2004 Chardonnay (Murfatlar Cernavoda) $15. 80 *—M.D. (6/1/2006)*

Byzantium 2002 Rosso di Valachia Red Blend (Dealu Mare) $15. 84 *—M.D. (6/1/2006)*

Byzantium 2004 Blanc de Transylvanie White Blend (Transylvanian Plateau) $15. 84 *—M.D. (6/1/2006)*

CHERRY TREE HILL

Cherry Tree Hill 2003 Merlot (Dealu Mare) $20. 84 —*M.D. (6/1/2006)*

CRAMELE HALEWOOD

Cramele Halewood 2000 Prahova Valley Special Reserve Cabernet Sauvignon (Dealu Mare) $14. 83 —*M.D. (6/1/2006)*

Cramele Halewood 2001 Prahova Valley Special Reserve Feteasca Neagra (Dealu Mare) $14. 83 —*M.D. (6/1/2006)*

DREAMER

Dreamer 2004 Premier Harvest Riesling (Dealu Mare) $10. Sappy sweet flavors of orange and flowers meet somewhat clumsily in this wine from Vanju Mare. Heavy and musky on the palate, the wine nonetheless has a nice, lingering finish and an appealing aroma. **82** —*S.K. (9/1/2007)*

HEAVENLY RETREAT

Heavenly Retreat 2005 Semi-Sweet Riesling (Romania) $8. A pretty nose and delicate, balanced flavors of apple and honeysuckle make this reasonably priced wine from Romania a nice surprise. It's sweet and not terribly complex, but the mouthfeel is luscious and the overall character enjoyable. A commendable effort that will appeal to American palates. **84 Best Buy** —*S.K. (9/1/2007)*

LA BELLE AMIE

La Belle Amie 2002 Special Reserve Cabernet Sauvignon (Dealu Mare) $15. 86 —*M.D. (12/15/2006)*

La Belle Amie 2001 Special Reserve Pinot Noir (Dealu Mare) $18. 83 —*M.D. (12/15/2006)*

SEVRUGA

Sevruga 2005 Demi-Dulce Riesling (Vânju Mare) $14. Citrus and peach aromas lead with this semisweet wine from Vanju Mare, the wine region situated in southern Romania. In the mouth, the wine is lively and light with flavors of peach and citrus that are expressive, but still need a slight boost. Imported by Vidalco International, LLC. **82** —*S.K. (9/1/2007)*

Sevruga 2005 Sec Riesling (Vânju Mare) $14. There's an appealing minerality and subtle touch of apple in this wine from Romania, but the overall character lacks cohesion and elegance. Riesling should certainly have a light touch at its best, but this wine just feels tired. Imported by Vidalco International, LLC. **81** —*S.K. (9/1/2007)*

SIRENA

Sirena Dunarii 2000 Dulce Riesling (Vânju Mare) $320. This collectible botrytis Riesling grown on the banks of the Danube in Romania is very concentrated, with heady flavors of honey, caramel and apricot and a nutty overall character. The finish is crisp and there's some acidity to keep the wine light on the palate. An unusual dessert wine and perhaps not for every wine lover, but definitely worthy of tasting and discussion. Imported by Vidalco International, LLC. **85** —*S.K. (12/1/2007)*

TERRA ROMANA

Terra Romana 2003 Muscat Ottonel Muskat Ottonel (Tarnave) $10. 84 —*J.C. (6/1/2005)*

Terra Romana 2002 Cuvée Charlotte Red Blend (Dealu Mare) $20. 83 —*J.C. (6/1/2005)*

Terra Romana 2000 Reserve Red Blend (Dealu Mare) $9. 80 —*J.C. (6/1/2005)*

Terra Romana 2002 Sauvignon Blanc-Feteasca White Blend (Romania) $10. 80 —*J.C. (6/1/2005)*

VAL DUNÁ

Val Duná 2004 Sauvignon Blanc/Feteasca Regala White Blend (Plaiurile Drancei) $7. 84 Best Buy —*M.D. (6/1/2006)*

VINARTE

VinArte 2005 Terase Danubiane Cuvée d'Excellence Sauvignon Blanc (Vânju Mare) $30. With its exuberant, fruity nose and flavors of grapefruit and flowers, this makes an interesting and fun sip. The primary qualities are appealing but there's not much dimension. Pair it with a nice plate of seafood and drink now. **82** —*S.K. (12/15/2007)*

VOX POPULI

Vox Populi 2004 Chardonnay (Dealu Mare) $10. 81 —*M.D. (12/15/2006)*

Vox Populi 2003 Pinot Noir (Dealu Mare) $10. 84 —*M.D. (12/15/2006)*

SLOVAKIA

CHÂTEAU BELA

Château Bela 2003 Riesling (Muzla) $15. Slovakian winemaker Miroslav Petrech and German Riesling notable Egon Müller grow the grapes for this pretty, floral Riesling on the banks of the Danube River. It's fine for a warm-weather quaff but missing the delicate layers of an exemplary Riesling. Great nose. **82** —*S.K. (9/1/2007)*

SLOVENIA

MOVIA

Movia 2002 Sauvignon (Brda) $24. 89 *(7/1/2005)*

SOUTH KOREA

KEUM HWA WINERY

Keum Hwa Winery 2003 Ajakae Wild Grape Sweet Meoru (Jiri Valley) $6. This sweet version of the wild-at-heart Meoru grape of South Korea's Mt. Jiri might be a little touch to love for American palates, though its jammy and spicy aromas and flavors are not unappealing. A little rustic and sappy but with dessert or after a meal, a fun find. **80** —*S.K. (8/1/2007)*

Keum Hwa Winery 2004 Castle Wild Grape Dry Meoru (Jiri Valley) $11. Meoru is an indigenous red grape grown on Mt. Jiri in South Korea. The aromas are spicy and smoky, and on the palate, the wine is spicy and bright, if a little dry and wild. Meoru is reputed to have extraordinary antioxidant strength, so beyond possibly doing something good for your body, you'll also find this wine an exotic discovery. **81** —*S.K. (8/1/2007)*

Keum Hwa Winery 2003 Wild Grape Dry Meoru (Jiri Valley) $16. This is an approachable version of the slightly wild and dry red Meoru grape of South Korea. Spicy and bright on the nose, the wine follows with vibrant fruit flavors that are a touch pointed when not paired with food. A great way to explore a lesser-known wine-producing region. **82** —*S.K. (8/1/2007)*

TUNISIA

DOMAINE NEFERIS

Domaine Neferis 2005 Selian Rosé Mystère Rosé Blend (Tunisia) $NA. 87 —*M.L. (7/1/2006)*

Domaine Neferis 2005 Selian White Blend (Tunisia) $NA. 85 —*M.L. (7/1/2006)*

TERRALE

Terrale 2000 Syrah/Carignan Red Blend (Tunisia) $8. 85 *(5/1/2002)*

URUGUAY

ARIANO

Ariano 2002 Cabernet Sauvignon (Canelones) $7. 80 —*M.S. (11/15/2004)*

Ariano 2003 Merlot (Canelones) $7. 82 —*M.S. (11/15/2004)*

Ariano 2003 Selección Red Blend (Canelones) $10. 83 —*M.S. (11/15/2004)*

Ariano 2002 Tannat (Canelones) $9. 82 —*M.S. (10/1/2004)*

BODEGA CARLOS PIZZORNO

Bodega Carlos Pizzorno 2004 Don Próspero Tannat (Uruguay) $12. 82 —*M.S. (11/1/2006)*

BODEGAS CARRAU

Bodegas Carrau 2002 De Reserva Tannat (Uruguay) $13. 82 —*M.S. (11/1/2006)*

BODEGONES DEL SUR

Bodegones Del Sur 1999 Selección de Barricas Red Blend (Juanico) $22. 81 —*M.S. (11/1/2006)*

Bodegones Del Sur 2003 Sauvignon Blanc (Juanico) $9. 82 —*M.S. (9/1/2004)*

Bodegones Del Sur 2000 Oak Aged Tannat (Juanico) $15. 83 —*M.S. (9/1/2004)*

Bodegones Del Sur 2000 Reserve Tannat (Juanico) $12. 86 —*M.S. (9/1/2004)*

BOUZA

Bouza 2004 Tannat-Merlot Red Blend (Canelones) $24. 86 —*M.S. (11/1/2006)*

Bouza 2004 Special Barrel Tannat (Uruguay) $50. 89 Editors' Choice —*M.S. (11/1/2006)*

CASTILLO VIEJO

Castillo Viejo 2002 Catamayor Red Blend (San Jose) $13. 83 —*M.S. (11/1/2006)*

Castillo Viejo 2004 Catamayor Sauvignon Blanc (San Jose) $10. 83 —*M.S. (4/1/2006)*

DANTE IRURTIA

Dante Irurtia 2000 Reserva del Virrey Tannat (Uruguay) $18. 80 —*M.S. (11/1/2006)*

Dante Irurtia 2004 Posada del Virrey Reserva Viognier (Uruguay) $14. 83 —*M.S. (11/1/2006)*

DELUCCA

DeLucca 2001 Red Blend (El Colorado) $10. 85 —*M.S. (1/1/2004)*

DeLucca 2000 Tannat (El Colorado) $10. 85 —*M.S. (1/1/2004)*

DON ADELIO ARIANO

Don Adelio Ariano 2002 Reserve Oak Barrel Tannat (Uruguay) $12. 83 —*M.S. (11/1/2006)*

LOS CERROS DE SAN JUAN

Los Cerros de San Juan 2002 S Torrens Oak Reserve Tannat (Uruguay) $18. 81 —*M.S. (11/1/2006)*

MOIZO HERMANOS

Moizo Hermanos 2000 Roble Reserva Tannat (Juanico) $15. 81 —*M.S. (1/1/2004)*

STAGNARI

Stagnari 2000 Salto Premier Tannat (Uruguay) $12. 84 —*M.S. (1/1/2004)*

TOSCANINI

Toscanini 2002 Cabernet Sauvignon (Canelones) $9. 80 —*M.S. (11/15/2004)*

Toscanini 2003 Sauvignon Blanc (Canelones) $8. 80 —*M.S. (10/1/2004)*

Toscanini 2002 Tannat (Canelones) $9. 84 —*M.S. (10/1/2004)*

Toscanini 2002 Reserva Tannat (Uruguay) $30. 81 —*M.S. (11/1/2006)*

Toscanini 1999 Reserve Tannat (Canelones) $13. 80 —*M.S. (10/1/2004)*

Toscanini 2003 Trebbiano 70% Sémillon 30% White Blend (Canelones) $8. 83 —*M.S. (10/1/2004)*

VIÑA PROGRESO

Viña Progreso 2003 Reserve Chardonnay (Uruguay) $19. 85 —*M.S. (10/1/2004)*

Viña Progreso 2003 Reserve Tannat (Uruguay) $19. 86 —*M.S. (10/1/2004)*

VIÑEDO DE LOS VIENTOS

Viñedo de los Vientos 2000 Eolo Gran Reserva Red Blend (Atlantida) $15. 84 —*M.S. (1/1/2004)*

Viñedo de los Vientos 2002 Tannat (Atlantida) $18. 81 —*M.S. (11/1/2006)*

VINSON RICHARDS

Vinson Richards 2000 Estate Bottled Cabernet Sauvignon (Juanico) $9. 84 —*M.S. (9/1/2004)*

Vinson Richards 2000 Merlot (Juanico) $9. 85 —*M.S. (9/1/2004)*

Vinson Richards 2000 Shiraz (Juanico) $9. 82 —*M.S. (9/1/2004)*

Vinson Richards 2000 Reserve Tannat (Juanico) $17. 86 —*M.S. (9/1/2004)*

The United States

CALIFORNIA

Vineyard on the western slopes of the Napa Valley, Oakville, Napa County, California.

California wines account for a sixty-four percent share of the United States wine market, according to the Wine Institute, the venerable trade and lobbying group whose membership includes 840 wineries. However, *Wine Business Monthly*, a trade magazine, estimates that there are 2,445 wineries doing business in California.

Whatever the number, in 2004, California wineries produced wine grown on 440,296 acres of vineyards, with about sixty percent of them planted with red or black grapes. The most widely planted major varietals, not surprisingly, are Chardonnay and Cabernet Sauvignon, although the latter has seen a slight percentage drop in recent years, as more Syrah and Pinot Noir have been planted.

The Central Valley of California contains the majority of plantings, but grapes from this hot inland region are seldom if ever included in premium bottlings. California's reputation for world-class wine rests almost entirely on coastal bottlings, "coastal" being defined as anywhere a true maritime influence penetrates the land, through gaps in the Coast Ranges that run from Oregon down to below Los Angeles. The Pacific Ocean is a chilly body of water, even in high summer. Without the gaps, California's coastal valleys would be almost as hot as the Central Valley, and incapable of producing fine, dry table wine. With the gaps, however, come the cooling winds and fogs that make for premium grape growing.

PREDOMINANT VARIETIES

Cabernet Sauvignon The great grape of the Médoc, in France's Bordeaux region, which has been the model—and point of departure—for California claret-style wines for more than a century. Napa County dominates statewide acreage of Cabernet, as well as quality. The great estates of Napa Valley have been joined by scores of small, ambitious boutique wineries on the cutting edge of viticultural and enological—and pricing—practices. California Cabernet is rich, full-bodied, opulent, fruity, and hedonistic, matching supreme power with a velvety elegance. The best will easily age for a decade or two.

Pinot Noir Undoubtedly the great varietal success story of the late twentieth century in California wine, red or white, Pinot Noir continues to make the most astounding advances. It favors the coolest climates available, although if growing conditions are too chilly, the grapes fail to ripen. Pinot Noir is far more demanding to grow than almost any other wine grape, but when conditions are right, the wines can be majestic: lush, silky, complex, and (to use an overworked but useful word) seductive.

Chardonnay For at least fifty years, Chardonnay has

USA

been California's greatest dry white wine. Although in the 1990s the media touted an "A.B.C." phenomenon—anything but Chardonnay—the wine remains a triumph. Like Pinot Noir, Chardonnay is best grown in cool coastal conditions, although it is more forgiving, and the odd bottling from anywhere can gain praise. Full-throttle Burgundian winemaking is the norm, but lately, Australian-style unoaked Chardonnay has been enjoying favor.

Zinfandel Historians still quibble about when exactly this varietal came to California. It has been here for at least one hundred and fifty years, and always has had its admirers. Zinfandel comes into and goes out of fashion, and has been made in styles ranging from sweet and Porty to dry and tannic to "white." The current thinking leans toward balance, in the model of a good Cabernet. The best Zinfandels come from cool coastal regions, especially old vines, most usually in Sonoma and Napa, but the Sierra Foothills have many old vineyards that produce great bottlings. Paso Robles occasionally comes up with a masterpiece.

Sauvignon Blanc This great grape of Sancerre and Pouilly-Fumé, in the Loire Valley, similarly produces a dry, crisp, pleasantly clean wine in California. It can be tank fermented and entirely unoaked, or just slightly oaked, in order to preserve the variety's fresh, citrusy flavors. Some producers look to Bordeaux to craft richer, barrel-fermented wines, often mixed with Sémillon, or even Viognier. "Fumé" Blanc is a synonym. If overcropped or unripe, the wines can have unpleasant aromas.

Merlot This other great grape of Bordeaux was greeted with fanfare by critics in the 1980s and 1990s, but Merlot never really reached Cabernet's superstardom. Merlot was said to be the "soft" Cabernet, but with modern tannin management, it's no softer than Cabernet, and, in fact can be quite hard. The wines, though, can be exceptional, especially in Napa Valley, Carneros, and parts of Sonoma County and Santa Barbara.

Syrah and Rhône Varieties Plantings of Syrah have increased, as consumers and critics alike welcome these deeply fruity, richly balanced wines. Syrah grapes are remarkably adaptable, and grow well almost everywhere. The wines tend to be organized into cool-climate and warm-climate bottlings, the former drier and more tannic, the latter often soft and jammy. The other red Rhône varieties, especially Mourvèdre and Grenache, are still exotic specimens, tinkered with lovingly by a coterie of Rhône Rangers.

Other Dry Whites Viognier, the darling of the Northern Rhône, grew in popularity in the 1990s. The wine achieved fame for its exotic, full-throttle fruit, floral, and spice flavors, but proved surprisingly elusive when it came to balance. An emerging handful display true Alsatian richness and complexity. The best are from cool coastal valleys, but if the climate is too cold, the wines turn acidic and green.

MAJOR CALIFORNIA WINE REGIONS

American grape-growing regions are authorized by the federal government, upon petitioning from individuals, and are called "American Viticultural Areas" (AVAs), or "appellations." Currently, there are ninety-five AVAs in California, with more petitions filed everyday.

Napa Valley The state's oldest AVA is its most famous. Napa Valley (established in 1981), at 225,000 acres, is so large that over the years, it has developed fourteen appellations within the larger one. Napa always has been home to California's, and America's, greatest Cabernet Sauvignons and blends, an achievement not likely to be upset anytime soon. In all other varieties, it strives, usually successfully, to compete.

Sonoma County Sonoma is California's most heterogeneous wine county. So diverse is its climate, from hot and sunny inland to cool, foggy coastal, that every grape varietal in the state is grown somewhere within its borders, often as not to good effect. In warm Alexander Valley and Dry Creek Valley, Zinfandel finds few peers. Out on the coast, and the adjacent Russian River Valley, Pinot Noir first proved that California could compete with Burgundy, and Pinot's huge improvements continue to startle. Chardonnay excels everywhere; Syrah is dependable. Old-vine field blends, comprised often of obscure French varieties, have their admirers. Meanwhile, Alexander Valley Cabernet, especially from the steep, rugged west-facing slopes of the Mayacamas Mountains, is showing continuing improvement.

Monterey County This large, cool growing area originally was planted with huge vineyards, making inexpensive wine in industrial-sized quantities. Serious, boutique-oriented adventurers sought out nooks and crannies where they could produce world-class wine, and the Santa Lucia Highlands AVA (1992) has been the most noteworthy result. Its slopes and benches are home to ripe, full-bodied, high-acid Pinot Noir, Chardonnay, and, increasingly, Syrah.

San Luis Obispo County Sandwiched between Monterey to the north and Santa Barbara to the south, this coastal county often is overlooked. But its twin AVAs, Edna Valley and Arroyo Grande Valley, arguably produce some of California's most distinguished Pinots and Chardonnays. A few vintners have made enormous strides with cool-climate Syrah and other Rhône varieties.

Santa Barbara County If any county deserves the honor for greatest achievements in winemaking over the last twenty years, it is this South-Central Coast region. The action began in the inland Santa Ynez Valley, a warmish-to-hot AVA. Years of experiments have shown the valley's aptitude for lush, complex red Rhône wines and Sauvignon Blanc. Merlot has been an unexpected star; Cabernet Sauvignon has not yet shown greatness. Closer to the ocean, the newest AVA, Santa Rita Hills (2001), was on critics' radar for Pinot Noir for showing lush fruit with an acidity found in few other regions. Chardonnay follows the same pattern. As in most cool-climate growing areas, determined winemakers tinker with Syrah, often excitingly.

Mendocino County Inland Mendocino is hot and mountainous. Beyond an individual winery here and there, it has yet to make a name for itself. The county's cool AVA is Anderson Valley, which has shown great promise in Pinot Noir.

The Sierra Foothills This enormous, multi-county region sprawls along the foothills of the Sierra Nevada Mountains. At their best, Foothills wines can be varietally pure, with Zinfandel taking the lead, although Cabernet Franc has been an unexpected star. Too many Foothills vintners, unfortunately, produce wines whose rusticity and high alcohol outweigh their charm.

WASHINGTON

Mount Rainier viewed over vineyards near Zillah, Washington.

In barely three decades, the Washington wine industry has risen from a half-dozen wineries trying their hand at a bit of Riesling, Gewürztraminer, and experimental plots of Pinot Noir and Cabernet, to become a global player. The state now boasts more than 375 wineries, 30,000 vineyard acres, and a track record for producing crisply etched, vibrantly fruity Rieslings; sleek and polished Chardonnays; ripe and flavorful Sémillons; bold, luscious Merlots; well-defined, muscular Cabernets; and vivid, smoky, saturated Syrahs.

Though a distant second to California in terms of total production, Washington wines get more medals and higher scores and sell for lower average prices on a percentage basis. There are seven appellations, all but one (the Puget Sound AVA) lying east of the Cascade Mountains. The largest AVA by far is the Columbia Valley, a vast area of scrubby desert, punctuated by irrigated stretches of farmland with row crops, hops, orchards, and vineyards. The Cascade Mountains protect this inland desert from the cool, wet maritime climate of western Washington. Eastern Washington summers are hot and dry, and during the growing season, the vines average two extra hours of sunlight per day.

Inside the Columbia Valley AVA are the smaller appellations of Yakima Valley, Walla Walla Valley, Red Mountain, and Horse Heaven Hills. A sixth, the Columbia Gorge AVA, lies just to the west along the Columbia River.

Several factors account for Washington's unique winegrowing profile. Its vines are planted on their own roots,

USA

as phylloxera (see Glossary) has not been a problem in the state. Most vineyards are irrigated, and the scientifically timed application of precise amounts of water has become an important aspect of grape-growing and ripening. The lengthy fall harvest season, which can run from late August into early November, is marked by warm days and very cool nights. The 40 to 50 degree Fahrenheit daily temperature swings keep acids up as sugars rise, which means that in many vintages, no acidification is necessary. Alcohol levels for finished wines have risen, but are still below the numbers for California.

The exploration of Washington terroir is well underway, and the state actually has plantings of Cabernet as old or older than any in California, where vines have been ravaged by disease. Red Mountain in particular has proven itself as a spectacular region for Merlot and Cabernet, and the Red Mountain vineyards of Klipsun and Ciel du Cheval provide grapes to dozens of Washington's best boutique wineries.

Walla Walla has become an important tourist destination, with more than eighty wineries, 1,200 acres of vineyard, year-round recreational activities, and an active and fun-loving wine community. Pioneered in the early 1980s by Leonetti Cellar, L'Ecole No 41, and Woodward Canyon, the valley is now home to dozens of wineries producing small lots of rich, oaky red wines and ripe, succulent whites. Syrah does particularly well.

Eastern Washington has periodically suffered from arctic blasts that can devastate vineyards. The most recent, early in 2004, all but eliminated that year's harvest in Walla Walla. But much is being learned about Washington viticulture, and new plantings are better sited to survive the occasional frigid winters. Additionally, established vineyards are maturing, and older vines with deeper roots are far less likely to be killed by even severe cold.

Most of Washington's wineries produce fewer than two thousand cases of wine annually, and awareness of the state's best wines has been hampered by this lack of production. Additionally, there have been very few wineries large enough to produce soundly-made, inexpensive "supermarket" wines, the kind that help establish a national presence. The wines of Columbia Crest, Covey Run, and Precept brands are beginning to change that, challenging the huge California conglomerates with budget bottles that don't skimp on either character or quality.

Oregon

Vineyards of Domaine Serene, Dayton, Oregon.

Unlike Washington, where vineyards are scattered throughout the east, most Oregon vineyards lie in the state's western half. They are somewhat protected from ocean fogs and cloud cover by the coastal mountain range. The farther south you go, the hotter it gets. In the Rogue Valley appellation, centered around the town of Ashland, Syrah and Cabernet can be ripened, though with rather tough, chewy tannins. But it is the Pinot Noirs of the northern Willamette valley that have brought Oregon to the attention of the world.

Oregon became known as the Pinot Noir state at a time when decent Pinot was hard to come by outside of Burgundy. Pioneered by David Lett, David Adelsheim, Dick Ponzi, and Dick Erath, Oregon Pinot in the early years was indeed Burgundian, elegant and light, with modest color and relatively low alcohol levels.

Over the years, as viticulture improved and winemakers learned new techniques, Oregon Pinot became thicker, darker, more jammy, and hot in the ripe years; and more tannic and earthy in the cool ones. Recently, as Pinot Noirs from California, New Zealand, and elsewhere have risen in quality, Oregon vintners have begun turning their attention to other varietals. The Willamette Valley's two hundred-plus wineries still predominantly produce Pinot, but some of the state's most interesting wines are coming from other grapes grown outside the region.

The big challenges for Oregon Pinot are two-fold. First, vintage variation is a fact of life, and wines can range from thin, harsh, and weedy to hot, ripe, and impenetrable. Unlike California and Washington, where vintages are far more consistent, Oregon vintners can expect something different every year. Hail, rain, extreme heat, humidity, drought, and vast temperature swings during harvest are the norm, not the exception.

To some degree, this is a good thing, because it suggests that Oregon, like a handful of other winemaking regions scattered across the globe, has the ability to put its own distinct stamp on its wines. The plus side of vintage variation is that each harvest is unique, and imparts specific, unique qualities to the wines of that vintage. The minus side is that not every vintage is all that good, especially where Pinot Noir is concerned.

The second challenge is that there is no longer a generally identifiable Oregon Pinot "style." Some vintners make elegant, light, tannic Pinots that require years to open up, while others make wines so dark and jammy, they are dead ringers for Syrah. And finally, while there are plenty of pricey, single-vineyard Pinots being produced, it is still difficult for consumers to find drinkable, good value, every day bottles.

Oregon's Rieslings and Gewürztraminers remain well-kept secrets. These are lively, juicy, floral, and fragrant wines that are always good value. The state's signature white is Pinot Gris, and it's made in a lush, fruity style that tastes of fresh-cut pears and goes easy on the new oak. The Chardonnays, once clumsy and fat, have dramatically improved with the introduction of Dijon clones.

Some producers have demonstrated remarkable success with grapes not generally associated with Oregon. Syrah is grown in the south, and makes a big, tannic, rough-hewn red wine. At Abacela in central Oregon, Tempranillo has proved surprisingly good, and the old-vine Zinfandels of Sineann, from an eastern Oregon vineyard, are superb. Oregon has added several new AVAs in the past couple of years, but what is most exciting are these new wines from different grapes that promise to open up Oregon to its full potential in the decades ahead.

USA

10 KNOTS

10 Knots 2005 Atlantis Rhône Red Blend (Paso Robles) $31. A Rhône blend of Syrah, Mourvèdre, Zinfandel and Grenache, this is a soft, dry wine, with dusty tannins framing cherry, coffee and herb flavors. Shows some real class. Drink now. **86** *—S.H. (12/15/2007)*

10 Knots 2005 Moonraker Rhône Red Blend (Paso Robles) $23. A Rhône-style blend of Mourvèdre, Syrah, Grenache and Zinfandel, this red shows classic Paso personality. It's soft and dry, with cherry-berry flavors that taste a little stewed. The dash of Zin really adds a punch of spice. **85** *—S.H. (12/15/2007)*

2820 WINE CO.

2820 Wine Co. 2002 The Ghost Bordeaux Blend (Napa Valley) $42. 86 *—S.H. (12/15/2005)*

2820 Wine Co. 1998 Cabernet Sauvignon (Napa Valley) $32. 91 *—J.M. (12/1/2001)*

2820 Wine Co. 2002 Merlot (Napa Valley) $22. 85 *—S.H. (12/15/2005)*

2820 Wine Co. 1999 Tain't Hermitage Syrah (Napa Valley) $36. 88 *(11/1/2001)*

2820 Wine Co. 2003 Zinfandel (Napa Valley) $18. 82 *—S.H. (6/1/2006)*

2820 Wine Co. 2002 Zinfandel (Napa Valley) $18. 87 *—S.H. (8/1/2005)*

29 SONGS

29 Songs 2004 Soscol Ridge Vineyard Back Porch Block Syrah (Napa Valley) $55. 85 *—S.H. (11/15/2006)*

39°

39° 2005 Petite Sirah (Lake County) $14. Bone dry and ruggedly tannic, this is fine if you're not fussy about what you drink with your barbecue. **83** *—S.H. (11/1/2007)*

39° 2006 Sauvignon Blanc (Lake County) $9. This is a really great price for a Sauv Blanc of this varietal purity. It's bone dry and crisp, with stimulating flavors of lemongrass, lemons and limes, figs, peaches and melons. Makes you admire how the winery produced 12,000 cases at this quality and price. **88 Best Buy** *—S.H. (11/1/2007)*

4 BEARS

4 Bears 2002 Cabernet Sauvignon (Napa Valley) $15. 84 *—S.H. (12/1/2006)*

428 WINES

428 Wines 2004 Boulevard Red Blend (Columbia Valley (WA)) $34. Competent winemaking has delivered a pleasant, simple red, which has a little bit of a spicy kick from the Syrah. It could be simply labeled Merlot, and as such it is a straightforward effort, with moderately ripe fruit and a little bit of heat in the finish. **85** *—P.G. (12/31/2007)*

6TH SENSE

6th Sense 2003 Syrah (Lodi) $17. 83 *(9/1/2005)*

7 HEAVENLY CHARDS

7 Heavenly Chards 2006 Chardonnay (Lodi) $17. Pricey for what you get, namely an everyday Chard with ripe fruit flavors and a simple structure. The oak is unnaturally heavy and plastered on, like an eccentric overlay of makeup. **82** *—S.H. (12/15/2007)*

7 Heavenly Chards 2005 Chardonnay (Lodi) $17. 86 *—S.H. (12/15/2006)*

A DONKEY AND GOAT

A Donkey and Goat 2004 Brosseau Vineyard Chardonnay (Chalone) $40. 86 *—S.H. (5/1/2006)*

A Donkey and Goat 2006 Isabel's Cuvée Grenache Rosé Grenache (McDowell Valley) $18. Fun, with fresh, grapy flavors of cherries and raspberries. With its crisp acidity and dry finish, it's a balanced, young, easy-going blush. **85** *—S.H. (7/1/2007)*

A Donkey and Goat 2004 Carson Ridge Vineyard Syrah (El Dorado) $32. 84 *—S.H. (5/1/2006)*

A Donkey and Goat 2004 Vidmar Vineyard Syrah (Yorkville Highlands) $32. 86 *—S.H. (5/1/2006)*

A Donkey and Goat 2004 Vieilles Vignes Syrah (McDowell Valley) $34. 87 *—S.H. (5/1/2006)*

À MAURICE CELLARS

à Maurice Cellars 2005 Chardonnay (Columbia Valley (WA)) $28. This is a creamy, textural Chard. Meyer lemon, lime and grapefruit dominate the mid-palate, and there is racy acid underpinning it. Medium body, medium length, no excessive oak; a good effort all around. **88** *—P.G. (3/1/2007)*

à Maurice Cellars 2004 Premier Blend Red Blend (Columbia Valley (WA)) $32. The blend is 50% Cab Sauvignon, 25% each Merlot and Cab Franc, with a splash of Malbec. Aromas seem to shoot up from the glass, rich and chocolaty, followed by rather firm, tightly constructed fruit. The flavor components of berry, currant and cherry are expertly interwoven, well-balanced and smooth. **89** *—P.G. (3/1/2007)*

à Maurice Cellars 2005 Viognier (Columbia Valley (WA)) $25. Though barrel fermented and given eight months sur lie, this does not show excessive oak flavoring. Rather it has intense, forward fruit, emphasis on lime-driven citrus, accented with honeysuckle. It's still young and sharp, and finishes with a bit of heat but with food it settles down and works very well. **87** *—P.G. (3/1/2007)*

A. RAFANELLI

A. Rafanelli 2001 Zinfandel (Sonoma County) $26. 91 Editors' Choice *(11/1/2003)*

A.S. KIKEN

A.S. Kiken 2001 Estate Cabernet Blend (Diamond Mountain) $30. 84 *—S.H. (10/1/2005)*

A.S. Kiken 2000 Red Blend (Diamond Mountain) $75. 84 *—S.H. (11/1/2005)*

A.S. Kiken 2003 Red Table Wine Red Blend (Diamond Mountain) $35. Here's a dry, fairly tannic, but polished young red wine, rich in ripely extracted red cherry, smoky leather and oak flavors. It has the elegant mouthfeel of a fine wine, and is very nice now, especially with grilled meats, but should hold and improve for five years or so. **88** *—S.H. (5/1/2007)*

ABACELA

Abacela 2005 Albariño (Southern Oregon) $23. 89 *—P.G. (12/1/2006)*

Abacela 2004 Claret Bordeaux Blend (Southern Oregon) $35. Abacela's Claret is a well-defined Bordeaux blend of 60% Cab Sauvignon, 35% Merlot, 4% Cab Franc and a splash of Petite Verdot. Packed with plenty of firm, forward fruit, it delivers full-throttle flavors of berries and plums, highlighted with some sweeter notes. Candied raisins and brown sugar decorate the tart fruit, then lead into a smoky, earthy, tannic finish. **89** *—P.G. (4/1/2007)*

Abacela 2005 Cabernet Franc (Southern Oregon) $24. Juicy and spicy and tannic, this might be an old-vine Zinfandel—it's got that sort of briary, slightly gamy scent to it. It's going to fare well with Zin-friendly foods such as pastas and pizzas; there's an undertone of ripe tomato to the fruit. **86** *—P.G. (11/15/2007)*

Abacela 2002 Cabernet Franc (Oregon) $24. 86 *—P.G. (2/1/2005)*

Abacela 2001 Cabernet Franc (Umpqua Valley) $24. 86 *—P.G. (5/1/2004)*

Abacela 2000 Cabernet Franc (Oregon) $20. 86 *—P.G. (8/1/2003)*

Abacela 1999 Cabernet Franc (Umpqua Valley) $22. 86 *—P.G. (8/1/2002)*

Abacela 2005 Dolcetto (Southern Oregon) $20. Dark and spicy, this lovely, complex Dolcetto emphasizes black fruits, plums and black raspberries. There is a hint of graphite and the suggestion of layered fruit. It's quite acidic, and appropriately so, which makes it best when matched to some richness in the sauce. **88** *—P.G. (4/1/2007)*

Abacela 2004 Dolcetto (Southern Oregon) $18. 88 *—P.G. (9/1/2006)*

Abacela 2003 Dolcetto (Oregon) $18. 88 *—P.G. (2/1/2005)*

Abacela 2002 Dolcetto (Oregon) $18. 89 *—P.G. (5/1/2004)*

Abacela 2000 Dolcetto (Umpqua Valley) $18. 88 *—P.G. (8/1/2002)*

Abacela 2005 Grenache (Southern Oregon) $24. A cool vintage in southern Oregon has created a very tart Grenache, with the fruit showing sour plum and raspberry flavors. Spicy and almost sour, it's got good verve and snap for those who enjoy high-acid wines. The flash of black pepper in the finish adds welcome texture. **88** *—P.G. (4/1/2007)*

Abacela 2004 Grenache (Southern Oregon) $22. 88 *—P.G. (9/1/2006)*

Abacela 2003 Grenache (Umpqua Valley) $22. 87 *—P.G. (2/1/2005)*

Abacela 2004 Malbec (Southern Oregon) $23. Though Malbec makes up three-fourths, there is also a substantial amount of Cab Sauvignon and Franc, making this a sort of inverted Meritage. It is the most black and inky of the new releases, yet not as jammy as the warmer 2003 vintage. This version shows red fruits such as pomegranate and red currant, expanding into a full, spicy mid-palate. It then surprisingly turns a corner and adds licorice and gingerbread to the mix, with a hint of mint. A complex, intriguing wine. **90** *—P.G. (4/1/2007)*

Abacela 2003 Malbec (Southern Oregon) $23. 89 *—P.G. (11/15/2005)*

Abacela 2002 Malbec (Oregon) $20. 90 *—P.G. (2/1/2005)*

Abacela 2001 Malbec (Umpqua Valley) $20. 90 *—P.G. (5/1/2004)*

Abacela 2000 Malbec (Umpqua Valley) $18. 91 *—P.G. (12/31/2002)*

Abacela 1999 Malbec (Umpqua Valley) $15. 85 *—P.G. (8/1/2002)*

Abacela 2003 Meritage (Southern Oregon) $35. 91 *—P.G. (11/15/2005)*

Abacela 2005 Merlot (Southern Oregon) $18. Oregon Merlots have darker fruits and streaks of tar and smoke. Tannins are more aggressive, and must be carefully managed. This wine does a pretty good job of softening up the back end while keeping the richness up front. There is plenty of acid, and the nose carries interesting scents of sandalwood and milk chocolate. It's just a bit chalky on the finish. **88** —*P.G. (11/15/2007)*

Abacela 2004 Merlot (Southern Oregon) $19. Abacela consistently produces one of Oregon's best Merlots, avoiding the tough, green tannins that often characterize the wines. This young, tart wine includes Cabernet Sauvignon, Cabernet Franc and Petit Verdot in the blend, giving it extra weight and richness in the mid-palate. Lightly smoky, with plenty of compact but powerful black fruits. **89** —*P.G. (4/1/2007)*

Abacela 2002 Merlot (Oregon) $18. 89 —*P.G. (8/1/2005)*

Abacela 2001 Merlot (Oregon) $18. 89 —*P.G. (5/1/2004)*

Abacela 2000 Merlot (Umpqua Valley) $18. 88 —*P.G. (8/1/2003)*

Abacela 1999 Merlot (Umpqua Valley) $18. 86 —*P.G. (8/1/2002)*

Abacela 2005 Petite Verdot (Southern Oregon) $40. This is the winery's first bottling of this Bordeaux blending grape. It is a curiosity that will be of interest to those in search of the unique and rare, but this does not convince me that the grape should be the centerpiece of a varietal wine. There's tangy, plummy fruit, searing acids and very astringent tannins. But the wine is incomplete—there's no middle. **85** —*P.G. (11/15/2007)*

Abacela NV Vintner's Blend #7 Red Blend (Southern Oregon) $15. 87 —*P.G. (12/1/2006)*

Abacela NV Vintner's Blend #6 Red Blend (Oregon) $15. 88 Best Buy —*P.G. (8/1/2005)*

Abacela 1999 Vintners Blend Red Table Wine Red Blend (Umpqua Valley) $11. 86 —*P.G. (8/1/2002)*

Abacela 2006 Rosado Rosé Blend (Southern Oregon) $14. Tempranillo forms the basis for this cherry-flavored rosado, with a small percentage of Grenache. Stainless steel fermentation brings out citrus peel highlights; the fruit flavors run through strawberry, cranberry and raspberry but land squarely on bright, candy-sweet cherry. There's a nice acid-driven lift to the midpalate, and a finish that remains clean and refreshing. **88** —*P.G. (7/1/2007)*

Abacela 2003 Syrah (Southern Oregon) $25. 89 —*P.G. (12/1/2006)*

Abacela 2002 Syrah (Oregon) $29. 90 —*P.G. (8/1/2005)*

Abacela 2001 Syrah (Oregon) $29. 92 —*P.G. (5/1/2004)*

Abacela 2000 Syrah (Umpqua Valley) $25. 90 —*P.G. (9/1/2003)*

Abacela 1999 Syrah (Umpqua Valley) $27. 90 —*P.G. (8/1/2002)*

Abacela 2003 Tempranillo (Umpqua Valley) $20. 88 —*P.G. (9/1/2006)*

Abacela 2002 Tempranillo (Umpqua Valley) $20. 87 —*P.G. (8/1/2005)*

Abacela 2001 Tempranillo (Umpqua Valley) $29. 89 —*P.G. (5/1/2004)*

Abacela 1999 Tempranillo (Umpqua Valley) $29. 89 —*P.G. (8/1/2002)*

Abacela 2004 Estate Tempranillo (Southern Oregon) $32. Complex aromas mix a fragrant blend of soy, black fruits, chalk and graphite. The tannins—big, chalky and a bit rough—overshadow the fruit, which remains compact and tucked away. There is plenty of tart acid along with those tannins to warrant cellaring this wine for at least five years. If you pop it now, give it several hours of breathing time. **88** —*P.G. (4/1/2007)*

Abacela 2003 Estate Tempranillo (Southern Oregon) $30. 89 —*P.G. (11/15/2005)*

Abacela 2002 Estate Grown Tempranillo (Umpqua Valley) $30. 91 —*P.G. (8/1/2005)*

Abacela 2005 Rosado Tempranillo (Southern Oregon) $12. 87 —*P.G. (12/1/2006)*

Abacela 2005 Viognier (Southern Oregon) $19. 89 —*P.G. (12/1/2006)*

Abacela 2004 Viognier (Oregon) $19. 87 —*P.G. (11/15/2005)*

Abacela 2003 Viognier (Oregon) $25. 88 —*P.G. (2/1/2005)*

ABANDON

Abandon 2004 Chardonnay (Carneros) $18. 83 —*S.H. (12/1/2006)*

ABBEY PAGE

Abbey Page 2004 Pinot Gris (Oregon) $11. 87 Best Buy —*P.G. (2/1/2006)*

ABEJA

Abeja 2004 Cabernet Sauvignon (Columbia Valley (WA)) $38. Supple and firm, the only word for this exceptionally smooth, sexy Cabernet is suave. It's delicious and silky, pure varietal, blended from a mix of top vineyards. The wine is a portrait of grace and power, folding its berry and cassis fruit into layers of smoke, toast, ash and char. A suggestion of cigar runs through the finish, and this is a wine that is sure to reward further cellaring. **92** —*P.G. (8/1/2007)*

Abeja 2003 Cabernet Sauvignon (Columbia Valley (WA)) $35. 94 —*P.G. (6/1/2006)*

Abeja 2005 Chardonnay (Washington) $32. A supple, supremely elegant wine, displaying its diverse flavors across a fine mesh. Very pretty aromatics carry a pleasing dustiness, accented with floral, sweetly spicy high notes. The tart fruit mixes citrus, tangerine, pineapple, green apple and pear, and finishes with nicely balanced toast and butterscotch. **91** —*P.G. (8/1/2007)*

Abeja 2004 Chardonnay (Columbia Valley (WA)) $28. 93 —*P.G. (6/1/2006)*

Abeja 2004 Merlot (Columbia Valley (WA)) $35. 91 —*P.G. (12/31/2006)*

Abeja 2003 Syrah (Walla Walla (WA)) $30. 90 —*P.G. (12/31/2006)*

Abeja 2005 Viognier (Walla Walla (WA)) $26. 92 —*P.G. (12/31/2006)*

ABIOUNESS

Abiouness 2001 Stanly Ranch Pinot Noir (Carneros) $35. 92 —*J.M. (6/1/2004)*

Abiouness 2000 Stanly Ranch Pinot Noir (Carneros) $40. 87 —*S.H. (2/1/2004)*

ABUNDANCE VINEYARDS

Abundance Vineyards 2000 Clos D'Abundance Chardonnay (Clarksburg) $13. 88 Best Buy —*J.M. (12/15/2002)*

Abundance Vineyards 2000 Talmage Block Viognier (Mendocino County) $18. —*J.M. (12/15/2002)*

Abundance Vineyards 1999 Mencarini Vineyards Old Vine Zinfandel (Lodi) $15. 90 —*J.M. (9/1/2003)*

ACACIA

Acacia 1993 Brut Champagne Blend (Carneros) $35. 91 —*S.H. (6/1/2001)*

Acacia 2005 Chardonnay (Carneros) $20. Some green, herbal flavors thin down the apricots and peaches in this simple wine, while the oaky overlay is too strong for the meager fruit. **82** —*S.H. (9/1/2007)*

Acacia 2004 Chardonnay (Carneros) $23. 87 —*S.H. (3/1/2006)*

Acacia 2003 Chardonnay (Carneros) $20. 90 —*S.H. (8/1/2005)*

Acacia 2002 Chardonnay (Carneros) $20. 90 —*S.H. (6/1/2004)*

Acacia 2000 Chardonnay (Carneros) $22. 87 —*J.M. (5/1/2002)*

Acacia 1998 Chardonnay (Carneros) $21. 87 *(6/1/2000)*

Acacia 1997 Chardonnay (Carneros) $20. 86 —*M.S. (10/1/1999)*

Acacia 2002 Sangiacomo Vineyard Chardonnay (Carneros) $30. 90 —*S.H. (10/1/2004)*

Acacia 2001 Sangiacomo Vineyard Chardonnay (Carneros) $30. 91 —*S.H. (12/15/2003)*

Acacia 2005 Pinot Noir (Carneros) $28. There are some interesting things here, and also some problems. On the plus side is a dry, silky mouthfeel and a persistence of cherries into the finish. But this Pinot is overly soft, and those cherries are kind of one-dimensional. **84** —*S.H. (9/1/2007)*

Acacia 2003 Pinot Noir (Carneros) $20. 87 —*S.H. (10/1/2005)*

Acacia 2002 Pinot Noir (Carneros) $20. 84 *(11/1/2004)*

Acacia 2000 Pinot Noir (Carneros) $27. 89 Editor's Choice. *(10/1/2002)*

Acacia 1999 Pinot Noir (Napa Valley) $25. 91 —*S.H. (2/1/2001)*

Acacia 1998 Pinot Noir (Napa Valley) $25. 90 —*S.H. (5/1/2000)*

Acacia 2000 Beckstoffer-Las Amigas Vineyard Pinot Noir (Napa Valley) $62. 89 *(10/1/2002)*

Acacia 1999 Beckstoffer-Las Amigas Vineyard Pinot Noir (Carneros) $60. 86 *(10/1/2002)*

Acacia 2004 Beckstoffer Las Amigas Vineyard Pinot Noir (Carneros) $60. 90 Cellar Selection —*S.H. (12/15/2006)*

Acacia 2001 Beckstoffer Las Amigas Vineyard Pinot Noir (Carneros) $60. 89 —*S.H. (2/1/2004)*

Acacia 1996 Beckstoffer Vineyard Reserve Pinot Noir (Carneros) $42. 90 —*M.S. (6/1/1999)*

Acacia 2002 Beckstoffer-Las Amigas Vineyard Pinot Noir (Carneros) $60. 83 *(11/1/2004)*

Acacia 2000 DeSoto Vineyard Pinot Noir (Napa Valley) $52. 91 Cellar Selection *(10/1/2002)*

Acacia 1999 Desoto Vineyard Pinot Noir (Carneros) $50. 86 *(10/1/2002)*

Acacia 2002 Field Blend Estate Vineyard Pinot Noir (Carneros) $50. 86 *(11/1/2004)*

Acacia 2001 Lee Vineyard Pinot Noir (Carneros) $50. 90 —*S.H. (3/1/2004)*

Acacia 1999 Lee Vineyard Pinot Noir (Carneros) $50. 87 *(10/1/2002)*

Acacia 1997 Lee Vineyard Pinot Noir (Napa Valley) $50. 94 *—S.H. (12/15/2000)*

Acacia 2004 Lone Tree Vineyard Pinot Noir (Carneros) $50. 91 *—S.H. (12/15/2006)*

Acacia 1996 Reserve Pinot Noir (Carneros) $32. 89 *(11/15/1999)*

Acacia 2002 St. Clair Vineyard Pinot Noir (Carneros) $50. 86 *(11/1/2004)*

Acacia 2001 St. Clair Vineyard Pinot Noir (Carneros) $50. 86 *—S.H. (3/1/2004)*

Acacia 2000 St. Clair Vineyard Pinot Noir (Carneros) $50. 90 *(8/1/2003)*

Acacia 1999 St. Clair Vineyard Pinot Noir (Carneros) $50. 86 *(10/1/2002)*

Acacia 1997 St. Clair Vineyard Pinot Noir (Napa Valley) $50. 93 *—S.H. (12/15/2000)*

ACKERLY POND

Ackerly Pond 2003 Cabernet Franc (North Fork of Long Island) $20. 81 *—M.D. (8/1/2006)*

Ackerly Pond 2004 Merlot (North Fork of Long Island) $25. 86 *—M.D. (12/1/2006)*

Ackerly Pond 2003 Merlot (North Fork of Long Island) $18. 83 *—M.D. (8/1/2006)*

ACORN

Acorn 2004 Alegria Vineyards Cabernet Franc (Russian River Valley) $28. So why would you buy Cab Franc instead of Cab Sauvignon? Here's why. This has the depth and seriousness of the latter, the light body of Pinot Noir, a dry, cherried richness, and none of the tannins that lots of wine lovers can't tolerate. Plus, this wine has layers of complexity that make it a delight. 88 *—S.H. (5/1/2007)*

Acorn 2003 Alegria Vineyards Cabernet Franc (Russian River Valley) $28. 88 *—S.H. (5/1/2006)*

Acorn 2003 Alegria Vineyards Dolcetto (Russian River Valley) $26. 84 *—S.H. (6/1/2006)*

Acorn 2002 Alegria Vineyards Dolcetto (Russian River Valley) $22. 84 *—S.H. (8/1/2005)*

Acorn 2001 Alegria Vineyards Dolcetto (Russian River Valley) $22. 84 *—S.H. (10/1/2004)*

Acorn 1999 Alegria Vineyards Dolcetto (Russian River Valley) $20. 82 *—S.H. (11/15/2001)*

Acorn 2003 Alegria Vineyards Medley Red Blend (Russian River Valley) $24. 87 *—S.H. (4/1/2006)*

Acorn 2002 Alegria Vineyards Medley Red Blend (Russian River Valley) $22. 85 *—S.H. (8/1/2005)*

Acorn 2001 Alegria Vineyards Medley Rhône Red Blend (Russian River Valley) $22. 87 *—S.H. (10/1/2004)*

Acorn 1999 Alegria Vineyards-Axiom Rhône Cuvée Rhône Red Blend (Russian River Valley) $16. 82 *—S.H. (11/15/2001)*

Acorn 2003 Alegria Vineyards Sangiovese (Russian River Valley) $22. 87 *—S.H. (3/1/2006)*

Acorn 2002 Alegria Vineyards Sangiovese (Russian River Valley) $22. 84 *—S.H. (8/1/2005)*

Acorn 2000 Alegria Vineyards Sangiovese (Russian River Valley) $16. 87 *—S.H. (7/1/2003)*

Acorn 2001 Alegria Vineyards Sangiovese (Russian River Valley) $20. 87 *—S.H. (10/1/2004)*

Acorn 1999 Alegria Vineyards Sangiovese (Russian River Valley) $16. 85 *—S.H. (11/15/2001)*

Acorn 2004 Alegria Vineyards Axiom Syrah (Russian River Valley) $30. I have enjoyed this bottling from Acorn in the past, and I like this one, although it's a bit simple and soft in jammy fruit. But there's no denying the wealth of cherries, blackberries, currants, chocolate and leathery spice. Probably best now, and for a few years. 87 *—S.H. (5/1/2007)*

Acorn 2003 Alegria Vineyards Axiom Syrah (Russian River Valley) $30. 85 *—S.H. (4/1/2006)*

Acorn 2002 Alegria Vineyards Axiom Syrah (Russian River Valley) $28. 86 *—S.H. (8/1/2005)*

Acorn 2001 Alegria Vineyards Axiom Syrah (Russian River Valley) $24. 91 *—S.H. (10/1/2004)*

Acorn 2000 Alegria Vineyards Axiom Syrah Cuvée Syrah (Russian River Valley) $20. 90 **Editors' Choice** *—S.H. (12/15/2003)*

Acorn 1999 Alegria Vineyards-Axiom Syrah (Russian River Valley) $16. 86 *(10/1/2001)*

Acorn 1998 Alegria Vineyards Heritage Vin Zinfandel (Russian River Valley) $25. 86 *—S.H. (12/1/2000)*

Acorn 2001 Alegria Vineyards, Heritage Vines Zinfandel (Russian River Valley) $28. 88 *(11/1/2003)*

Acorn 2000 Heritage Vines Alegria Vineyards Zinfandel (Russian River Valley) $28. 91 *—S.H. (7/1/2003)*

Acorn 1999 Heritage Vines Alegria Vineyards Zinfandel (Russian River Valley) $28. 83 *—S.H. (12/15/2001)*

ADASTRA

Adastra 2003 Chardonnay (Carneros) $30. 83 *—S.H. (12/31/2005)*

Adastra 2002 Chardonnay (Carneros) $30. 86 *—S.H. (4/1/2005)*

Adastra 2000 Chardonnay (Carneros) $28. 86 *—S.H. (5/1/2002)*

Adastra 2001 Merlot (Carneros) $30. 86 *—S.H. (4/1/2005)*

ADDAMO

Addamo 2005 Chardonnay (Santa Barbara County) $24. Ultraclean and pure in fruit, with brisk, refreshing acidity, this is an upscale Chardonnay whose lemon-and-lime, pineapple and nectarine flavors are coated with smoky oak. The cool climate and long hangtime of the '05 vintage have conspired to make this balanced and elegant. 89 *—S.H. (6/1/2007)*

Addamo 2005 Reserve Chardonnay (Santa Barbara County) $29. This is a new winery for me, but one to watch. The grapes are from Santa Maria Valley, and the wine shows the ripe balance of this fine vintage, with a tremendous depth of tropical fruit, apricot jam and oak-inspired butterscotch flavors. Brisk acidity provides needed balance to the wealth of fruit. 92 *—S.H. (6/1/2007)*

ADEA

Adea 2000 Chardonnay (Willamette Valley) $20. 85 *—P.G. (9/1/2003)*

Adea 1999 Chardonnay (Willamette Valley) $24. 90 *—P.G. (2/1/2002)*

Adea 1999 Pinot Gris (Willamette Valley) $15. 85 *—P.G. (2/1/2002)*

Adea 2002 Pinot Noir (Willamette Valley) $25. 85 *(11/1/2004)*

Adea 2000 Pinot Noir (Willamette Valley) $35. 85 *—P.G. (4/1/2003)*

Adea 1999 Pinot Noir (Willamette Valley) $35. 85 *—P.G. (12/31/2001)*

Adea 2002 Coleman Vineyard Pinot Noir (Willamette Valley) $35. 87 *(11/1/2004)*

Adea 2002 Dean-O's Pinot Noir (Willamette Valley) $30. 85 *(11/1/2004)*

Adea 2000 Reserve Pinot Noir (Willamette Valley) $42. 85 *—P.G. (4/1/2003)*

Adea 2002 Yamhill Valley Vineyards Pinot Noir (Willamette Valley) $35. 84 *(11/1/2004)*

ADELAIDA

Adelaida 2002 Estate Reserve Cabernet Sauvignon (Paso Robles) $45. 82 *—S.H. (11/1/2006)*

Adelaida 2001 Viking Port Cabernet Sauvignon (Paso Robles) $30. 84 *—S.H. (8/1/2005)*

Adelaida 2002 Chamisal Vineyard Chardonnay (Edna Valley) $24. 87 *—S.H. (7/1/2005)*

Adelaida 2004 HMR Estate Chardonnay (Santa Lucia Highlands) $30. 87 *—S.H. (11/1/2006)*

Adelaida 2002 HMR Estate Chardonnay (Paso Robles) $30. 83 *—S.H. (7/1/2005)*

Adelaida 2002 Pavanne Chenin Blanc (Paso Robles) $20. 85 *—S.H. (7/1/2005)*

Adelaida 2003 HMR Estate Pinot Noir (Paso Robles) $55. 88 *—S.H. (11/1/2006)*

Adelaida 2002 HMR Estate Pinot Noir (Paso Robles) $25. 88 *—S.H. (4/1/2005)*

Adelaida 2002 SLO Pinot Noir (San Luis Obispo County) $15. 85 *—S.H. (4/1/2005)*

Adelaida 2003 Vin Gris de Pinot Noir Pinot Noir (Paso Robles) $15. 85 *—S.H. (7/1/2005)*

Adelaida 2003 Glenrose Vineyard Rhône Style Red Wine Rhône Red Blend (Paso Robles) $26. 82 *—S.H. (11/15/2006)*

Adelaida 2004 Glenrose Vineyard Roussanne-Grenache Blanc Rhône White Blend (Paso Robles) $25. 85 *—S.H. (11/1/2006)*

Adelaida 2002 The Glenrose Vineyard Rhône White Blend (Paso Robles) $25. 90 **Editors' Choice** *—S.H. (10/1/2005)*

Adelaida 1996 Syrah (Paso Robles) $24. 88 *—S.H. (10/1/1999)*

Adelaida 2003 Syrah (Paso Robles) $26. 86 *—S.H. (11/15/2006)*

Adelaida 2003 Glenrose Vineyard Reserve Syrah (Paso Robles) $55. 84 —S.H. (11/15/2006)

Adelaida 2003 Viking Estate Reserve Syrah (Paso Robles) $55. 83 —S.H. (11/15/2006)

Adelaida 1998 Viking Estate Vineyard Syrah (Paso Robles) $40. 87 (11/1/2001)

Adelaida 2004 Glenrose Vineyard Viognier (Paso Robles) $30. 88 —S.H. (11/15/2006)

Adelaida 1997 Zinfandel (Paso Robles) $20. 83 —S.H. (5/1/2000)

Adelaida 2001 Zinfandel (Paso Robles) $21. 86 (11/1/2003)

Adelaida 2001 Reserve Zinfandel (Paso Robles) $35. 86 (11/1/2003)

Adelaida 2001 Schoolhouse Zinfandel (Paso Robles) $19. 86 (11/1/2003)

ADELSHEIM

Adelsheim 2000 Chardonnay (Oregon) $14. 85 —P.G. (4/1/2002)

Adelsheim 2005 CH Chardonnay (Willamette Valley) $22. 89 (12/1/2006)

Adelsheim 2000 Stoller Vineyard Chardonnay (Yamhill County) $30. 92 —P.G. (8/1/2002)

Adelsheim 1996 Stoller Vineyard Chardonnay (Yamhill County) $30. 90 —P.G. (4/1/2002)

Adelsheim 1999 Stoller Vineyard Clone 76 Chardonnay (Yamhill County) $30. 88 —P.G. (4/1/2002)

Adelsheim 2005 Pinot Blanc (Willamette Valley) $19. 86 —P.G. (12/1/2006)

Adelsheim 2000 Pinot Blanc (Oregon) $12. 91 Best Buy —P.G. (4/1/2002)

Adelsheim 1998 Pinot Blanc (Oregon) $13. 88 —L.W. (12/31/1999)

Adelsheim 2005 Pinot Gris (Willamette Valley) $18. 89 —P.G. (12/1/2006)

Adelsheim 2004 Pinot Gris (Oregon) $17. 87 —P.G. (2/1/2006)

Adelsheim 2000 Pinot Gris (Oregon) $13. 85 —P.G. (4/1/2002)

Adelsheim 2004 Pinot Noir (Willamette Valley) $29. 88 —P.G. (5/1/2006)

Adelsheim 2000 Pinot Noir (Oregon) $22. 87 —P.G. (4/1/2002)

Adelsheim 1997 Pinot Noir (Oregon) $20. 85 (11/15/1999)

Adelsheim 1998 AVS Pinot Noir (Willamette Valley) $40. 91 —M.M. (12/1/2000)

Adelsheim 1999 Bryan Creek Vineyard Pinot Noir (Willamette Valley) $36. 88 —P.G. (4/1/2002)

Adelsheim 1998 Bryan Creek Vineyard Pinot Noir (Willamette Valley) $40. 88 —M.S. (12/1/2000)

Adelsheim 2005 Elizabeth's Reserve Pinot Noir (Willamette Valley) $42. An authoritative, meaty nose sets off this dense, rather tannic Pinot Noir. A firmly built wine that suggests layered fruit, still young, but tightly packed. Hints of rock and herb lie within, all waiting for some additional hours of breathing time and/or years of bottle age to pass. **90** —P.G. (7/1/2007)

Adelsheim 2002 Elizabeth's Reserve Pinot Noir (Yamhill County) $40. 84 (11/1/2004)

Adelsheim 1999 Elizabeth's Reserve Pinot Noir (Oregon) $36. 91 Editors' Choice —P.G. (4/1/2002)

Adelsheim 1998 Elizabeth's Reserve Pinot Noir (Yamhill County) $45. 90 —M.S. (12/1/2000)

Adelsheim 1999 Goldschmidt Vineyard Pinot Noir (Yamhill County) $36. 90 —P.G. (4/1/2002)

Adelsheim 1998 Penta Reserve Pinot Noir (Yamhill County) $32. 87 —P.G. (4/1/2002)

Adelsheim 2002 Ribbon Springs Vineyard Pinot Noir (Yamhill County) $45. 84 (11/1/2004)

Adelsheim 1998 Seven Springs Vineyard Pinot Noir (Polk County) $30. 90 —M.M. (12/1/2000)

Adelsheim 2004 TF Tocai Friulano (Willamette Valley) $20. 88 —P.G. (5/1/2006)

Adelsheim 2005 Auxerrois White Blend (Willamette Valley) $20. 88 —P.G. (12/1/2006)

ADLER FELS

Adler Fels 1997 Chardonnay (Sonoma County) $15. 89 —S.H. (11/1/1999)

Adler Fels 2006 Gewürztraminer (Russian River Valley) $15. I wish this Gewürz had more intensity to the fruit, because even at this everyday price, it's a little watery on the finish. The dry flavors, framed by crisp acids, suggest gingersnap cookies, figs, cinnamon-spiced apple sauce and vanilla. One wonders if limiting yields would result in a better wine, which could be sold at a higher price. **85** —S.H. (11/15/2007)

Adler Fels 2001 Gewürztraminer (Russian River Valley) $10. 87 Best Buy —S.H. (11/15/2002)

Adler Fels 2006 Sauvignon Blanc (Russian River Valley) $15. Fermented in stainless steel, this young white retains the freshness and fruity vitality of the high-quality grapes from its home vineyard. Acidity really is the key, highlighting the citrus, fig, melon and vanilla flavors that shine so brightly. This is really a wonderfully drinkable, Sancerre-like Sauvignon Blanc. **88 Editors' Choice** —S.H. (11/15/2007)

Adler Fels 1997 Sauvignon Blanc (Sonoma County) $12. 86 —S.H. (11/1/1999)

Adler Fels 1998 Sauvignon Blanc (Russian River Valley) $11. 86 —S.H. (11/15/2000)

ADOBE CREEK

Adobe Creek 2000 Merlot (Sonoma County) $14. 85 —S.H. (12/31/2003)

Adobe Creek 2001 Pinot Gris (Sonoma County) $14. 83 —S.H. (12/1/2003)

Adobe Creek 2002 Sauvignon Blanc (Contra Costa County) $12. 82 —S.H. (10/1/2003)

ADOBE ROAD

Adobe Road 2000 Cabernet Sauvignon (Alexander Valley) $39. 81 —S.H. (8/1/2005)

Adobe Road 2002 Herrerias Vineyard Pinot Noir (Sonoma Coast) $30. 84 —S.H. (8/1/2005)

Adobe Road 2001 Zinfandel (Alexander Valley) $32. 83 —S.H. (8/1/2005)

AGRARIA

Agraria 1999 Big Barn Red Bordeaux Blend (Dry Creek Valley) $52. 88 —S.H. (12/1/2004)

Agraria 1999 Big Barn Red Cabernet Sauvignon (Dry Creek Valley) $52. 82 —S.H. (10/1/2004)

AHLGREN

Ahlgren 1997 Bates' Ranch Cabernet Sauvignon (Santa Cruz Mountains) $35. 90 (11/1/2000)

Ahlgren 1997 Harvest Moon Vineyards Cabernet Sauvignon (Santa Cruz Mountains) $33. 82 (11/1/2000)

Ahlgren 1999 Ventana Vineyards Syrah (Monterey) $24. 87 (11/1/2001)

AHNFELDT

Ahnfeldt 2004 Cabernet Sauvignon (Napa Valley) $50. All the grapes come from southerly, cooler portions of Napa, and it tastes like they were picked earlier than some of their long hangtime brethren. Acidity and crunchy tannins star, lending structure to the cherry, black currant and cedar flavors, while the finish is thoroughly dry. This is an elegant, food-friendly wine that should develop over the next 8–10 years. **90** —S.H. (11/1/2007)

Ahnfeldt 2004 Merlot (Napa Valley) $45. An interesting Merlot characterized not only by complexity, but by structure. The cherry, cassis, mocha and cedary spice flavors are entirely dry, and balanced with a brisk architecture of acidity and tannins. This is an elegant table wine that will let the food star rather than drawing attention to itself. **90** —S.H. (11/1/2007)

AIRFIELD ESTATES

Airfield Estates 2005 Merlot (Yakima Valley) $22. A pretty cherry red, this tart young wine tastes like fresh raspberries and cherries. It is compactly built, varietal and clean, with a crisply defined finish. **87** —P.G. (12/31/2007)

Airfield Estates 2006 Pinot Gris (Yakima Valley) $16. This new winery located just outside of Prosser hits the ground running with a luscious, viscous, creamy Pinot Gris that tastes like a pear-flavored creamsicle. The fruit is almost tropical, right at the edge of mango/banana, but not fat or flabby. This is a perfect sipping wine. Screwcap. **89 Editors' Choice** —P.G. (12/1/2007)

Airfield Estates 2006 Icewine Riesling (Yakima Valley) $28. Very rich and unctuous, this superripe bottling has buttery honey and hints of English breakfast tea notes that add flavor interest to the sweet, almost sugary Riesling. **86** —P.G. (12/31/2007)

Airfield Estates 2006 Sauvignon Blanc (Yakima Valley) $14. Airfield's owners have been grape growers for almost 40 years—a remarkable track record in Washington state. These vines date back to the late 1970s. Crisp and light with the alcohol just over 12%, it's the sort of low-impact white wine that we rarely see made in the U.S. A perfect little café wine, that should be drunk chilled, from tumblers. **86** —P.G. (12/1/2007)

AIRLIE

Airlie 2005 Chardonnay (Willamette Valley) $12. Estate-bottled and barrel fermented, this is an aggressively oaky wine, whose rather thin fruit flavors of green apple are buried in butter. Too many chips in the broth? It's fine for an informal party, but don't try to match it to food. **83** —*P.G. (11/15/2007)*

Airlie 2002 Chardonnay (Willamette Valley) $10. 83 —*P.G. (5/1/2006)*

Airlie 2004 Gewürztraminer (Willamette Valley) $10. It's a little late to be releasing an '04, but this may actually be all the better for the extra bottle age. Richly scented with rose petal soap, chewing gum and lychee, it delivers concentrated, oily flavors with a sharply floral streak. It's bone dry and highly extracted, and tips the scale at 14.4% alcohol. **88 Best Buy** —*P.G. (11/15/2007)*

Airlie 2004 Gewürztraminer (Willamette Valley) $9. 84 —*P.G. (5/1/2006)*

Airlie 2002 Gewürztraminer (Willamette Valley) $10. 87 Best Buy —*P.G. (2/1/2005)*

Airlie 2003 Maréchal Foch (Willamette Valley) $14. 89 Best Buy —*P.G. (5/1/2006)*

Airlie 2004 Müller-Thurgau (Willamette Valley) $10. 85 Best Buy —*P.G. (5/1/2006)*

Airlie 2003 Pinot Gris (Willamette Valley) $12. 84 —*P.G. (2/1/2006)*

Airlie 2002 Pinot Gris (Willamette Valley) $12. 87 —*P.G. (2/1/2005)*

Airlie 2005 Pinot Noir (Willamette Valley) $20. This is a moderately-pleasing effort for its price, modest by Oregon standards. The wine definitely shows its herbal side—don't look for sweet Pinot fruit here—but it's balanced and taut, and has much the same shape and style as a village cru Burgundy. **84** —*P.G. (11/15/2007)*

Airlie 2003 Pinot Noir (Willamette Valley) $14. 83 —*P.G. (5/1/2006)*

Airlie 2002 Two Vineyard-Old Vines Pinot Noir (Willamette Valley) $20. 88 —*P.G. (2/1/2005)*

Airlie 2004 Riesling (Willamette Valley) $10. 86 Best Buy —*P.G. (5/1/2006)*

Airlie 2006 7 White Blend (Willamette Valley) $12. Off dry with fresh flavors of pear, grapefruit and pineapple, this blend of seven grapes surely includes some Riesling, Gewürztraminer and Pinot Gris. The wine's lightly sweet finish keeps the alcohol at just 12%, and is offset nicely with crisp acids. **86** —*P.G. (11/15/2007)*

USA

AIX MONTEREY

Aix Monterey 1999 Chardonnay (Monterey) $15. 86 —*J.M. (12/15/2002)*

AJB VINEYARDS

AJB Vineyards 1997 Syrah (Paso Robles) $21. 90 —*S.H. (7/1/2002)*

ALAPAY

Alapay 2000 Chardonnay (Central Coast) $17. 90 —*S.H. (9/1/2002)*

Alapay 2004 Edna Ranch Chardonnay (Edna Valley) $22. 89 —*S.H. (11/1/2006)*

Alapay 2004 Edna Ranch Pinot Noir (Edna Valley) $25. 88 —*S.H. (10/1/2006)*

Alapay 2000 Viognier (Santa Barbara County) $19. 88 —*S.H. (9/1/2002)*

Alapay 1999 Zinfandel (Paso Robles) $18. 90 —*S.H. (9/1/2003)*

ALBA

Alba NV Forbidden Icewine Apple (New Jersey) $15. Fans of Jolly Rancher apple flavors will enjoy this apple ice wine, but it lacks depth and true apple flavors. The nose is candied and sweet, and on the palate, it has a lack of dimension beyond syrupy sweetness. **82** —*S.K. (7/1/2007)*

Alba 2005 Chambourcin (New Jersey) $16. Chambourcin shows its true colors here with a deep, dense red color and intense, aromatic flavors. Spice and berry on the nose, followed by cherry, vanilla and toast on the palate are both integrated and opulent. There's a touch of angular smoke on the wine but overall, it's a good example of the grape. Pair with lamb or red meat dishes. **85** —*S.K. (12/1/2007)*

Alba 1998 East Coast Chardonnay (New Jersey) $10. 83 —*J.C. (1/1/2004)*

Alba 2003 Heritage Red Blend (New Jersey) $25. 86 —*M.D. (8/1/2006)*

Alba 2005 Riesling (New Jersey) $11. Intense aromas of grapefruit and pineapple and flavors of tropical fruit and honey make this a pleasurable Riesling, but the sweetness on the palate tends to overpower. There's some raciness in the mouth which saves the wine from being a complete sugar bomb, and the flavors are enjoyable, but the wine lacks some degree of sophistication and finesse. **85** —*S.K. (5/1/2007)*

Alba 2004 Riesling (New Jersey) $11. 81 —*M.D. (8/1/2006)*

Alba NV Delaware Dolce White Blend (America) $20. 85 —*M.D. (8/1/2006)*

ALBAN

Alban 1996 Estate Grenache (Edna Valley) $NA. 90 —*S.H. (6/1/2005)*

Alban 1993 Estate Grenache (Edna Valley) $NA. 94 —*S.H. (6/1/2005)*

Alban 1997 Roussanne (Edna Valley) $32. 89 —*S.H. (10/1/1999)*

Alban 2000 Roussanne (Central Coast) $25. 90 —*S.H. (6/1/2003)*

Alban 2000 Estate Vineyard Roussanne (Edna Valley) $32. 91 —*S.H. (6/1/2003)*

Alban 1998 Lorraine Syrah (Edna Valley) $45. 89 *(11/1/2001)*

Alban 1996 Reva Syrah (Edna Valley) $NA. 91 —*S.H. (6/1/2005)*

Alban 1992 Reva Syrah (Edna Valley) $NA. 90 —*S.H. (6/1/2005)*

Alban 2003 Seymour's Syrah (Edna Valley) $NA. 95 —*S.H. (7/1/2006)*

Alban 1998 Viognier (Edna Valley) $28. 91 —*S.H. (10/1/1999)*

Alban 2000 Costello T.B.A. Viognier (Edna Valley) $65. 95 —*S.H. (6/1/2003)*

Alban 2001 Estate Viognier (Edna Valley) $29. 91 Editors' Choice —*J.M. (12/15/2002)*

ALBEMARLE

Albemarle 2002 Simply Red Bordeaux Blend (America) $22. 83 —*J.C. (9/1/2005)*

ALDER RIDGE

Alder Ridge 2002 Cabernet Sauvignon (Columbia Valley (WA)) $30. 92 —*P.G. (6/1/2006)*

ALDERBROOK

Alderbrook 2004 Carignane (Dry Creek Valley) $19. 87 —*S.H. (12/31/2006)*

Alderbrook 2005 Chardonnay (Russian River Valley) $18. Alderbrook is one of those insider wineries that does a good job at a fair price. This crisp, dry Chard is an elegant example of the long hangtime '05 vintage, with spicy tropical fruit, butterscotch and vanilla cream flavors. **87** —*S.H. (8/1/2007)*

Alderbrook 2004 Chardonnay (Russian River Valley) $18. 87 —*S.H. (11/1/2006)*

Alderbrook 2003 Chardonnay (Russian River Valley) $18. 83 —*S.H. (11/1/2005)*

Alderbrook 2002 Chardonnay (Dry Creek Valley) $18. 87 —*S.H. (3/1/2005)*

Alderbrook 2000 Chardonnay (Dry Creek Valley) $NA. 85 *(6/1/2003)*

Alderbrook 1999 Chardonnay (Dry Creek Valley) $18. 88 —*S.H. (11/15/2001)*

Alderbrook 1998 Chardonnay (Dry Creek Valley) $15. 89 *(6/1/2000)*

Alderbrook 1997 Dorothy's Vineyard Chardonnay (Dry Creek Valley) $22. 88 *(6/1/2000)*

Alderbrook 2005 Pinot Noir (Russian River Valley) $26. Pale, light-bodied, fruity and dry, this is the un-Cabernet, the red for white wine lovers. So easy to enjoy, you might overlook its complexities. Red cherries, cola, pomegranate, rosehip tea, cinnamon and ginger candy, it's really delicious. Drink now for its freshness. **90** —*S.H. (8/1/2007)*

Alderbrook 2004 Pinot Noir (Russian River Valley) $25. 90 Editors' Choice —*S.H. (11/1/2006)*

Alderbrook 2003 Pinot Noir (Russian River Valley) $24. 86 —*S.H. (12/15/2005)*

Alderbrook 2002 Pinot Noir (Russian River Valley) $24. 84 —*S.H. (3/1/2005)*

Alderbrook 2000 Pinot Noir (Russian River Valley) $29. 89 —*S.H. (2/1/2003)*

Alderbrook 1999 Pinot Noir (Russian River Valley) $22. 85 *(10/1/2002)*

Alderbrook 2003 Sauvignon Blanc (Dry Creek Valley) $14. 84 —*S.H. (2/1/2005)*

Alderbrook 2000 Sauvignon Blanc (Dry Creek Valley) $NA. 87 —*S.H. (9/1/2003)*

Alderbrook 1999 Sauvignon Blanc (Dry Creek Valley) $14. 86 —*S.H. (11/15/2001)*

Alderbrook 2002 Syrah (Dry Creek Valley) $24. 84 —*S.H. (3/1/2005)*

Alderbrook 2004 Old Vine Zinfandel (Dry Creek Valley) $20. 86 —*S.H. (12/31/2006)*

Alderbrook 2003 Old Vine Zinfandel (Dry Creek Valley) $21. 89 —*S.H. (12/15/2005)*

Alderbrook 2002 Old Vine Zinfandel (Dry Creek Valley) $19. 91 —*S.H. (3/1/2005)*

Alderbrook 2001 OVOC Zinfandel (Dry Creek Valley) $18. 88 *(11/1/2003)*

Alderbrook 2000 OVOC Zinfandel (Dry Creek Valley) $25. 85 *—J.M. (3/1/2002)*

Alderbrook 1998 OVOC Zinfandel (Sonoma County) $18. 90 *—P.G. (3/1/2001)*

Alderbrook 1997 OVOC Zinfandel (Sonoma County) $16. 90 *—L.W. (9/1/1999)*

Alderbrook 2003 Reserve Zinfandel (Dry Creek Valley) $34. 91 *—S.H. (6/1/2006)*

Alderbrook 2002 Reserve Zinfandel (Dry Creek Valley) $34. 92 *—S.H. (3/1/2005)*

Alderbrook 2001 Reserve Zinfandel (Russian River Valley) $39. 90 *(11/1/2003)*

Alderbrook 2001 Reserve Zinfandel (Dry Creek Valley) $39. 87 *(11/1/2003)*

Alderbrook 2000 Reserve Zinfandel (Dry Creek Valley) $39. 89 *—P.G. (3/1/2002)*

Alderbrook 2000 Reserve Zinfandel (Russian River Valley) $39. 91 *—P.G. (3/1/2002)*

Alderbrook 2004 Wind Machine Zinfandel (Dry Creek Valley) $34. 85 *—S.H. (12/31/2006)*

ALEX SOTELO CELLARS

Alex Sotelo Cellars 2002 Dalraddy Vineyard Zinfandel (Napa Valley) $28. 81 *—S.H. (6/1/2005)*

ALEXANDER

Alexander 2000 Chestnut Hill Vineyard Chardonnay (Santa Cruz Mountains) $20. 84 *—S.H. (6/1/2003)*

Alexander 1998 Petite Sirah (Monterey) $23. 84 *—S.H. (12/31/2003)*

ALEXANDER VALLEY VINEYARDS

Alexander Valley Vineyards 2003 Cyrus Bordeaux Blend (Alexander Valley) $55. A bit direct and not in the league of the '02, the '03 Cyrus nonetheless appeals for its gentle, silky texture, grippy tannins and pleasant flavors of cherries, cassis, dried herbs and oaky spices. It's an early-drinking wine of elegance and delicacy. 87 *—S.H. (10/1/2007)*

Alexander Valley Vineyards 2002 Cyrus Cabernet Blend (Alexander Valley) $50. 89 *—S.H. (9/1/2006)*

Alexander Valley Vineyards 2001 Cyrus Cabernet Blend (Alexander Valley) $50. 92 *—S.H. (10/1/2005)*

Alexander Valley Vineyards 2000 Cyrus Cabernet Blend (Alexander Valley) $50. 89 *—S.H. (6/1/2004)*

Alexander Valley Vineyards 2001 Wetzel Family Estate Cabernet Franc (Alexander Valley) $20. 86 *—S.H. (11/15/2003)*

Alexander Valley Vineyards 2005 Cabernet Sauvignon (Alexander Valley) $20. Not the most immediately enjoyable Cab from this venerable winery, but it could improve. Right now, it's tannic and a little sweet in cherry-blackberry fruit, and finishes with a burn, despite moderate 14% alcohol. Might just need a year or so to knit together. 85 *—S.H. (10/1/2007)*

Alexander Valley Vineyards 2004 Cabernet Sauvignon (Alexander Valley) $20. Good everyday Cab, on the earthy, herbal side, and thoroughly dry. The addition of some Merlot, Cab Franc and Petit Verdot adds complexity to the berry flavors. 84 *—S.H. (2/1/2007)*

Alexander Valley Vineyards 2003 Cabernet Sauvignon (Alexander Valley) $20. 90 *—S.H. (3/1/2006)*

Alexander Valley Vineyards 2000 Estate Bottled Cabernet Sauvignon (Alexander Valley) $20. 86 *(11/15/2002)*

Alexander Valley Vineyards 2002 Wetzel Family Estate Cabernet Sauvignon (Alexander Valley) $20. 87 *—S.H. (4/1/2005)*

Alexander Valley Vineyards 2005 Chardonnay (Alexander Valley) $15. Feels overly soft and flaccid, with pear and peach flavors that have been generously oaked so that buttered toast becomes an important component. There's some acidity, but it seems added, and feels funny. 83 *—S.H. (2/1/2007)*

Alexander Valley Vineyards 2004 Chardonnay (Alexander Valley) $15. 84 *—S.H. (2/1/2006)*

Alexander Valley Vineyards 1998 Estate Bottled Chardonnay (Sonoma County) $15. 85 *(6/1/2000)*

Alexander Valley Vineyards 2003 Wetzel Family Estate Chardonnay (Alexander Valley) $15. 86 *—S.H. (3/1/2005)*

Alexander Valley Vineyards 2001 Wetzel Family Estate-Estate Bottled Chardonnay (Alexander Valley) $15. 85 *—S.H. (12/15/2002)*

Alexander Valley Vineyards 2000 Wetzel Family Estate Reserve Chardonnay (Alexander Valley) $25. 87 *—S.H. (12/15/2002)*

Alexander Valley Vineyards 1997 Wetzel Family Reserve Chardonnay (Sonoma County) $24. 87 *(6/1/2000)*

Alexander Valley Vineyards 2000 Dry Chenin Blanc (Alexander Valley) $9. 85 *—J.M. (12/15/2001)*

Alexander Valley Vineyards 2000 Gewürztraminer (Alexander Valley) $9. 87 Best Buy *—J.M. (12/15/2001)*

Alexander Valley Vineyards 2003 New Gewurz Gewürztraminer (North Coast) $9. 82 *—S.H. (5/1/2004)*

Alexander Valley Vineyards 2002 New Gewurz Gewürztraminer (North Coast) $9. 84 *—S.H. (12/31/2003)*

Alexander Valley Vineyards 2001 New Gewurz Gewürztraminer (North Coast) $9. 88 *—J.M. (6/1/2002)*

Alexander Valley Vineyards 2004 Merlot (Alexander Valley) $20. Pretty good, but not the opulently soft wine Merlot seekers want. It's dry and oaky, with a rich core of red and black cherries and plums, but very tannic. We're talking lockdown mode, and the wine isn't going anywhere. 84 *—S.H. (2/1/2007)*

Alexander Valley Vineyards 2003 Merlot (Alexander Valley) $20. 85 *—S.H. (3/1/2006)*

Alexander Valley Vineyards 1997 Estate Bottled Merlot (Sonoma County) $18. 86 *—L.W. (12/31/1999)*

Alexander Valley Vineyards 2002 Wetzel Family Estate Merlot (Alexander Valley) $20. 87 *—S.H. (4/1/2005)*

Alexander Valley Vineyards 2000 Wetzel Family Estate-Estate Bottled Merlot (Alexander Valley) $20. 85 *—S.H. (11/15/2002)*

Alexander Valley Vineyards 2002 Two Barrel Merlot-Syrah (Alexander Valley) $19. 83 *—S.H. (4/1/2005)*

Alexander Valley Vineyards 2002 Wetzel Family Estate Pinot Noir (Alexander Valley) $20. 88 *—S.H. (3/1/2005)*

Alexander Valley Vineyards 2001 Wetzel Family Estate Sangiovese (Alexander Valley) $20. 85 *—S.H. (9/1/2003)*

Alexander Valley Vineyards 1999 Syrah (Sonoma County) $18. 87 *(10/1/2001)*

Alexander Valley Vineyards 2004 Estate Syrah (Alexander Valley) $20. Nice, easy-drinking Syrah, soft in acids and tannins and dry, with pleasant marmalade flavors of cherries, rhubarbs and blackberries, with a rich edge of peppery, nutmeg spices and vanilla-accented oak. Drink now. 86 *—S.H. (10/1/2007)*

Alexander Valley Vineyards 2002 Wetzel Family Estate Syrah (Alexander Valley) $20. 86 *—S.H. (4/1/2005)*

Alexander Valley Vineyards 2000 Wetzel Family Estate Syrah (Alexander Valley) $18. 85 *—S.H. (12/1/2002)*

Alexander Valley Vineyards 2005 Redemption Zin Zinfandel (Dry Creek Valley) $25. Young and tight, this Zin shows the rustic, brawny nature of Zin's personality, with rugged tannins, peppery spices and a sweet-and-sour taste to the wild cherry, raspberry, pomegranate and rhubarb fruit. Will ride out the years, gradually softening and sweetening. 87 *—S.H. (10/1/2007)*

Alexander Valley Vineyards 2002 Redemption Zinfandel (Dry Creek Valley) $25. 89 *—S.H. (12/15/2004)*

Alexander Valley Vineyards 2001 Redemption Zin Zinfandel (Dry Creek Valley) $30. 88 *(11/1/2003)*

Alexander Valley Vineyards 2005 Sin Zin Zinfandel (Alexander Valley) $20. Rugged and kind of sweet, with candied cherry, raspberry and mint julep flavors, this Zin has dusty, briary tannins and a mouth-watering spiciness that calls for steaks and chops. 84 *—S.H. (10/1/2007)*

Alexander Valley Vineyards 2002 Sin Zin Zinfandel (Alexander Valley) $20. 88 *—S.H. (6/1/2004)*

Alexander Valley Vineyards 2001 Sin Zin Zinfandel (Alexander Valley) $20. 86 *(11/1/2003)*

Alexander Valley Vineyards 1999 Sin Zin Zinfandel (Sonoma County) $18. 82 *—P.G. (3/1/2001)*

ALEXANDRIA NICOLE

Alexandria Nicole 2004 Destiny Ridge Vineyard Cabernet Sauvignon (Horse Heaven Hills) $30. This has a buttery, creamy softness that belies the usual hardness of Washington Cab. Excellent winemaking shows off not just the plum and cherry fruit, set against a thick wash of chocolaty oak, but also the firm acid and hints of citrus and earth that elevate the wine beyond the ordinary. 91 *—P.G. (12/31/2007)*

Alexandria Nicole 2001 Lemberger (Columbia Valley (WA)) $21. 88 *—P.G. (12/15/2005)*

Alexandria Nicole 2004 Destiny Ridge Vineyard Merlot (Horse Heaven Hills) $24. This is thick and spicy, a raging bull of a wine that skates along the border of Napa Cabernet country. As this Horse Heaven Hills vineyard matures, it is becoming clear that it can deliver the big, broad and deep flavors that put Washington Merlot at the front of the class. What's especially nice about this blend is its intense bouquet of blackberry, spicy anise and cedar. For all of its power this retains its balance, its acidic spine and even a touch of grace. **90** *—P.G. (12/31/2007)*

Alexandria Nicole 2002 Destiny Ridge Vineyards Merlot (Columbia Valley (WA)) $24. 90 *—P.G. (12/15/2004)*

Alexandria Nicole 2004 Destiny Ridge Vineyard Red Blend (Horse Heaven Hills) $45. Mixed tart and racy fruit flavors of blueberry and plum, pie cherry and more are softly coddled with spicy, chocolaty oak. This is the best wine Alexandria Nicole has yet produced, and should pave the way for more Washington-made Bordeaux blends to emulate this fruit-driven, well-balanced style. **92** *—P.G. (5/1/2007)*

Alexandria Nicole 2004 Sauvignon Blanc (Columbia Valley (WA)) $20. 87 *—P.G. (12/15/2005)*

Alexandria Nicole 2004 Block 17 Syrah (Horse Heaven Hills) $35. Fascinating; this was co-fermented with 7% whole cluster Roussanne, then blended with another 4% Viognier. Inky, vivid, saturated and loaded with appealing scents of meat, smoke, cedar, pencil shavings, blackberry, black cherry and much more, this is Washington's answer to Barossa Shiraz. Yet the alcohol remains a sensible 14.3%, and the wine has impeccable balance. **92** *—P.G. (5/1/2007)*

Alexandria Nicole 2002 Destiny Ridge Vineyards Syrah (Columbia Valley (WA)) $27. 86 *(9/1/2005)*

Alexandria Nicole 2006 Viognier (Columbia Valley (WA)) $16. This is sharply perfumed, with an edgy, tight consistency that seems to emphasize both the floral and the bitter rind aspects of the grape. Viognier can fall off a cliff rapidly, and this latest vintage, though complex and complicated, has a hot intensity that pulls in the bitterness and loses the citrus. If that's the style you like, this is a fine, concentrated and intense rendition. **88** *—P.G. (12/31/2007)*

Alexandria Nicole 2005 Viognier (Columbia Valley (WA)) $18. 90 *—P.G. (8/1/2006)*

Alexandria Nicole 2004 Viognier (Columbia Valley (WA)) $16. 89 *—P.G. (12/15/2005)*

Alexandria Nicole 2003 Destiny Ridge Vineyards Viognier (Columbia Valley (WA)) $16. 90 *—P.G. (12/15/2004)*

Alexandria Nicole 2004 Reserve Viognier (Columbia Valley (WA)) $21. 86 *—P.G. (12/15/2005)*

Alexandria Nicole 2006 Destiny Ridge Vineyard 'Shepherd's Mark' White Blend (Columbia Valley (WA)) $18. This is delicious, creamy and yeasty and loaded with citrus. The midpalate expands into tropical fruit, vanilla bean and spice, and it's just flat-out delightful. Chill this one and try it out on any kind of food you can imagine; it just might work. **89 Editors' Choice** *—P.G. (12/31/2007)*

Alexandria Nicole 2005 Destiny Ridge Vineyard Shepard's Mark White Blend (Columbia Valley (WA)) $18. 88 *—P.G. (8/1/2006)*

Alexandria Nicole 2004 Destiny Ridge Vineyard Shepard's Mark White Rhône White Blend (Columbia Valley (WA)) $18. 88 *—P.G. (12/15/2005)*

ALFARO FAMILY

Alfaro Family 2005 Chardonnay (Santa Cruz Mountains) $25. Nasty and sharp, with candied LifeSaver flavors that have a weirdly medicinal, over-oaked taste. **80** *—S.H. (10/1/2007)*

Alfaro Family 2005 Pinot Noir (Santa Cruz Mountains) $35. Ripe in cherry, raspberry, root beer, spice and vanilla oak flavors, this dry wine has a good balance of acidity. On the downside is a touch of the funky, sweaty smell that affects some of the winery's other wines. **84** *—S.H. (10/1/2007)*

ALHONA

Alhona 2002 Merlot (Carmel Valley) $32. The grapes come from a warmer portion of Monterey County noted for Bordeaux varieties. This is a sophisticated, softly dry red wine, brimming with cherry, cassis and oaky-spice flavors, and is notable for its finely ground, ripe tannins. Enjoyable now, it should hold for a few years. **87** *—S.H. (3/1/2007)*

ALIENTO DEL SOL

Aliento Del Sol 2003 Bien Nacido Vineyard Chardonnay (Santa Maria Valley) $24. 89 *—S.H. (11/1/2006)*

Aliento Del Sol 1998 Bien Nacido Vineyard Chardonnay (Santa Maria Valley) $25. 85 *(6/1/2000)*

Aliento Del Sol 1998 La Colline Vineyard Pinot Noir (Arroyo Grande Valley) $30. 84 *—M.S. (5/1/2000)*

Aliento Del Sol 1999 Loma Vista Pinot Noir (California) $25. 88 *(10/1/2002)*

Aliento Del Sol 2005 Sarmento Vineyard Pinot Noir (Santa Lucia Highlands) $30. The vineyard has yielded generally good, rewarding Pinots for this Riboli-owned brand. The '05 is in that vein, a light-bodied, silky wine showing good varietal character, with cola, spicy cherry and rhubarb flavors. Drink now. **87** *—S.H. (11/1/2007)*

Aliento Del Sol 2003 Sarmento Vineyard Pinot Noir (Santa Lucia Highlands) $28. 87 *—S.H. (12/31/2005)*

Aliento Del Sol 2002 Sarmento Vineyard Pinot Noir (Santa Lucia Highlands) $28. 86 *(11/1/2004)*

ALLISON

Allison 2006 Allison Rosé of Syrah Syrah (Sonoma Coast) $18. A little heavy, with a sappy, resiny quality, this blush Syrah shows a rustic nature. Yet it's dry, and the bitter cherry and cranberry flavors work well. Try it if you like your rosés more akin to a full-bodied red wine. From Steltzner. **85** *—S.H. (7/1/2007)*

ALLORA

Allora 1999 Tresca Cabernet Sauvignon (Napa Valley) $60. 86 *—S.H. (8/1/2003)*

Allora 1999 Cielo Red Blend (Napa Valley) $45. 86 *—S.H. (8/19/2003)*

ALMA ROSA

Alma Rosa 2005 El Jabali Vineyard Chardonnay (Santa Rita Hills) $32. Here's a good, rich white Burgundy-inspired Chard, creamy in barrel-fermented vanilla custard and opulant lemon drop mousse, peach pie and smoky pie crust flavors. Balanced and dry, it's enriched with crisp, savory acidity. **90** *—S.H. (4/1/2007)*

Alma Rosa 2005 El Jagali Vineyard Chardonnay (Santa Rita Hills) $33. Shows classic Santa Rita Hills cool-climate Chard notes of very high acidity and Meyer lemon drop flavors, but both may be too much of a good thing. So sharp, so citrusy, the palate craves something softer, creamier, and richer in fruit. Maybe it was a victim of the chilly vintage in a cool area. **85** *—S.H. (4/1/2007)*

Alma Rosa 2005 Pinot Blanc (Santa Rita Hills) $32. One sniff brought back a childhood memory of orange creamsicles that were so deliciously gooey and sweet, only this wine is basically dry. The alcohol adds a pleasant, peppery burn. Fun and enjoyable. **86** *—S.H. (4/1/2007)*

Alma Rosa 2005 Pinot Blanc (Santa Rita Hills) $20. I would like to follow the progress of this wine in future years, because it shows promise. It's very crisp in acidity, with a mouth-cleansing tingly feeling and good citrus, oaky peach and honeysuckle flavors. Yet it's kind of raw and simple. **85** *—S.H. (4/1/2007)*

Alma Rosa 2005 La Encantada Vineyard Pinot Blanc (Santa Rita Hills) $28. The winery's estate vineyard has produced a fine, crisp and thoroughly delicious PB. With its bells-and-whistles barrel fermentation, sure lies aging and intensely pure Meyer lemon drop, honeysuckle and mineral flavors and steely clean texture, it's a big wine, but food-friendly. **89** *—S.H. (4/1/2007)*

Alma Rosa 2005 La Encantada Vineyard Pinot Gris (Santa Rita Hills) $28. There's not much PG planted in SRH but the region shows the promise of a unique style to this often pedestrian variety. Made dry and intense in the Alsatian way, this wine has unusual but appealing floral, apricot and citrus flavors, and what tastes like a touch of botrytis. Yet its high acidity gets the tastebuds whistling. **87** *—S.H. (4/1/2007)*

Alma Rosa 2005 Pinot Noir (Santa Rita Hills) $32. Polished and supple, this is a killer Pinot to have with food. It's not an overbearing wine or a light one, but shows restraint in the pomegranate, cherry and spice flavors that are so well integrated with tannins, acids and modest oak. The result is a balanced, elegant wine. **87** *—S.H. (4/1/2007)*

Alma Rosa 2004 Pinot Noir (Santa Rita Hills) $32. 87 *—S.H. (11/1/2006)*

Alma Rosa 2005 La Encantada Pinot Noir (Santa Rita Hills) $49. The '05 is less ripe and sharper in acidity than the '04. Still, it's a praiseworthy Pinot, rich in cherry, cola, coffee and pomegranate flavors accented by a crisp minerality. Do not be put off by the screwcap. The winery deserves great credit for taking this step. **90** *—S.H. (4/1/2007)*

Alma Rosa 2005 La Encantada Vineyard Pinot Noir (Santa Rita Hills) $48. From Richard Sanford's new brand and vineyard comes this earthy, slightly rustic Pinot Noir. The flavors are of cranberries, cola, Portobello mushroom, green tea, pomegranates and chicory. Best 2008–2012. **90** *—S.H. (4/1/2007)*

Alma Rosa 2004 La Encantada Vineyard Pinot Noir (Santa Rita Hills) $48. 92 Cellar Selection *—S.H. (11/1/2006)*

Alma Rosa 2005 Pinot Noir - Vin Gris Pinot Noir (Santa Rita Hills) $28. Dull and simple, with a stubborn sulfur smell that's slow to blow off. Tastes tired and sweet. **82** *—S.H. (4/1/2007)*

ALTAMURA

Altamura 1995 Cabernet Sauvignon (Napa Valley) $40. 91 *—L.W. (6/1/1999)*

Altamura 2001 Cabernet Sauvignon (Napa Valley) $60. 88 *—S.H. (10/1/2005)*

Altamura 2000 Cabernet Sauvignon (Napa Valley) $60. 93 *—S.H. (8/1/2004)*

Altamura 1999 Cabernet Sauvignon (Napa Valley) $60. 89 *—M.S. (5/1/2003)*

Altamura 1996 Sangiovese (California) $26. 86 *—S.H. (12/15/1999)*

Altamura 2001 Sangiovese (Napa Valley) $30. 88 *—S.H. (6/1/2005)*

Altamura 1999 Sangiovese (Napa Valley) $30. 91 *—S.H. (9/1/2003)*

ALTERRA

Alterra 1998 Syrah (Russian River Valley) $18. 84 *(10/1/2001)*

AMADOR FOOTHILL WINERY

Amador Foothill Winery 2002 Fumé Blanc (Shenandoah Valley (CA)) $11. 85 *—S.H. (2/1/2004)*

Amador Foothill Winery 2001 Fumé Blanc (Shenandoah Valley (CA)) $10. 86 *—S.H. (9/1/2003)*

Amador Foothill Winery 2000 Fumé Blanc (Shenandoah Valley (CA)) $9. 87 Best Buy *—S.H. (11/15/2001)*

Amador Foothill Winery 1999 Fumé Blanc (Shenandoah Valley (CA)) $10. 85 *—S.H. (8/1/2001)*

Amador Foothill Winery 2004 Katie's Cote Rhône Red Blend (Shenandoah Valley (CA)) $18. 84 *—S.H. (10/1/2006)*

Amador Foothill Winery 2003 Katie's Cote Rhône Red Blend (Shenandoah Valley (CA)) $18. 90 *—S.H. (12/31/2005)*

Amador Foothill Winery 2000 Sangiovese (Shenandoah Valley (CA)) $20. 86 *—S.H. (12/1/2002)*

Amador Foothill Winery 2001 Barrel Select Sangiovese (Shenandoah Valley (CA)) $18. 86 *—S.H. (11/15/2004)*

Amador Foothill Winery 2004 Estate Bottled Sangiovese (Shenandoah Valley (CA)) $19. Tough going with this wine. It's very dry, and shows the high acidity of the variety, and even some rasping tannins. Unfortunately, the fruit isn't there, despite a modest attempt by the cherry squad to come to the rescue. **83** *—S.H. (9/1/2007)*

Amador Foothill Winery 2002 Estate Sangiovese (Shenandoah Valley (CA)) $18. 83 *—S.H. (6/1/2006)*

Amador Foothill Winery 2001 Grand Reserve Sangiovese (Shenandoah Valley (CA)) $28. 88 *—S.H. (12/31/2005)*

Amador Foothill Winery 2000 Grand Reserve Sangiovese (Shenandoah Valley (CA)) $30. 89 *—S.H. (9/1/2003)*

Amador Foothill Winery 2006 Rosato of Sangiovese (Amador County) $11. Full-bodied and direct, with a potent hit of cherryskin bitterness carrying cherry, tea, tobacco and spice flavors, this is a very, very dry, crisp wine that really needs food. **85** *—S.H. (7/1/2007)*

Amador Foothill Winery 2005 Rosato of Sangiovese (Amador County) $11. 86 Best Buy *—S.H. (10/1/2006)*

Amador Foothill Winery 2004 Rosato of Sangiovese (Amador County) $10. 83 *—S.H. (10/1/2005)*

Amador Foothill Winery 2003 Rosato of Sangiovese (Amador County) $10. 83 *—S.H. (11/15/2004)*

Amador Foothill Winery 2002 Rosato of Sangiovese (Amador County) $10. 88 Best Buy *—S.H. (9/1/2003)*

Amador Foothill Winery 2001 Rosato of Sangiovese (Amador County) $9. 84 *—S.H. (9/1/2003)*

Amador Foothill Winery 2005 Sauvignon Blanc (Shenandoah Valley (CA)) $12. A wondeful Fumé-type wine, especially at this price, that reminds me of Sancerre. Bone dry and crisp, it has a minerally taste of the earth underlying the grapefruit, lime and gardenia flavors, and an exceptionally long, spicy finish. **89 Best Buy** *—S.H. (9/1/2007)*

Amador Foothill Winery 2004 Sauvignon Blanc (Shenandoah Valley (CA)) $11. 88 Best Buy *—S.H. (12/31/2005)*

Amador Foothill Winery 2000 Sémillon (Shenandoah Valley (CA)) $10. 87 *—S.H. (9/1/2003)*

Amador Foothill Winery 2002 Barrel Select Syrah (Sierra Foothills) $15. 80 *—S.H. (10/1/2006)*

Amador Foothill Winery 2000 Hollander Vineyard Syrah (Sierra Foothills) $20. 84 *—S.H. (9/1/2002)*

Amador Foothill Winery 2004 Clockspring Vineyard Zinfandel (Shenandoah Valley (CA)) $16. 82 *—S.H. (10/1/2006)*

Amador Foothill Winery 2003 Clockspring Vineyard Zinfandel (Shenandoah Valley (CA)) $14. 87 *—S.H. (10/1/2005)*

Amador Foothill Winery 2001 Clockspring Vineyard Zinfandel (Shenandoah Valley (CA)) $13. 88 *(11/1/2003)*

Amador Foothill Winery 2000 Clockspring Vineyard Zinfandel (Shenandoah Valley (CA)) $13. 86 *—S.H. (5/1/2003)*

Amador Foothill Winery 1999 Clockspring Vineyard Zinfandel (Amador County) $13. 84 *—S.H. (11/15/2001)*

Amador Foothill Winery 1997 Clockspring Vineyard Zinfandel (Amador County) $12. 84 *—P.G. (11/15/1999)*

Amador Foothill Winery 2002 Esola Vineyard Zinfandel (Shenandoah Valley (CA)) $15. 88 *—S.H. (8/1/2005)*

Amador Foothill Winery 2001 Esola Vineyard Zinfandel (Shenandoah Valley (CA)) $18. 87 *(11/1/2003)*

Amador Foothill Winery 1999 Ferraro Vineyard Zinfandel (Shenandoah Valley (CA)) $15. 87 Best Buy *—S.H. (11/1/2002)*

Amador Foothill Winery 2001 Ferrero Vineyard Zinfandel (Shenandoah Valley (CA)) $15. 87 *—S.H. (3/1/2005)*

Amador Foothill Winery 1997 Ferrero Vineyard Zinfandel (Shenandoah Valley (CA)) $12. 88 Best Buy *—S.H. (5/1/2000)*

AMAVI CELLARS

Amavi Cellars 2004 Cabernet Sauvignon (Columbia Valley (WA)) $24. A substantial wine, well-balanced and showing a good mix of dark, acid-driven fruits, smoke and graphite. There are some light hints of mushroom and leaf, a good display of clear varietal character. Beautiful balance and structure. It's not a big wine but quite approachable. **89** *—P.G. (5/1/2007)*

Amavi Cellars 2003 Cabernet Sauvignon (Walla Walla (WA)) $22. 90 *—P.G. (4/1/2006)*

Amavi Cellars 2005 Sémillon (Columbia Valley (WA)) $20. This exceptionally rich Sémillon is aged in neutral barrels. The fruit is firm and tart, showing a mix of pineapple and green citrus and berry. An underlying minerality adds texture and more firmness; the wine does not show excessive flesh, but is loaded with lovely acid and fruit, and a hint of toastiness in the finish. About one third comes from 25-year-old vines, some of the state's oldest Sémillon. **91** *—P.G. (5/1/2007)*

Amavi Cellars 2004 Sémillon (Columbia Valley (WA)) $20. 92 *—P.G. (4/1/2006)*

Amavi Cellars 2004 Syrah (Columbia Valley (WA)) $28. This is drinking quite young, with tannins that are showing strong flavors of green tea, stem and some rough spots. But apart from that little bit of jaggedness in the finish, this is really good stuff, spicy and streaked with white pepper and green herb. The slightly bitter citrusy finish is characteristic of Columbia Valley Syrah. **89** *—P.G. (5/1/2007)*

Amavi Cellars 2003 Syrah (Walla Walla (WA)) $25. 92 *—P.G. (4/1/2006)*

Amavi Cellars 2003 Syrah (Walla Walla (WA)) $25. 84 *(9/1/2005)*

Amavi Cellars 2002 Syrah (Walla Walla (WA)) $25. 91 Editors' Choice *—P.G. (11/15/2004)*

Amavi Cellars 2004 Les Collines Vineyard Syrah (Walla Walla (WA)) $32. Les Collines is in a cooler, wetter site than most Walla Walla vineyards, but managed to harvest an excellent crop in 2004. This pure Syrah is intensely aromatic, dark, herbal and meaty. It shows some earthy, funky character, but a marvelous texture, and flavors and scents of mixed mineral, compost, soy and funk. Though the style is not for everyone, it's got real depth and complexity. **91** *—P.G. (5/1/2007)*

Amavi Cellars 2004 Seven Hills Vineyard Syrah (Walla Walla (WA)) $32. Dark and ripe, with a strong smoky component. It shows plenty of muscle in this difficult vintage, along with firm acids and blackberry fruit that is broader and more open than the Les Collines. Though it falls just short of that wine's exceptional complexity, here the smoke and licorice notes add interesting streaks of darkness to the wine as it extends into a finish of dark, smoky tannins. **90** *—P.G. (5/1/2007)*

AMBERHILL

Amberhill 2000 Cabernet Sauvignon (California) $9. 86 Best Buy *—S.H. (10/1/2003)*

Amberhill 1997 Chardonnay (California) $8. 84 Best Buy *—S.H. (10/1/1999)*

Amberhill 2001 Chardonnay (California) $7. 81 *—S.H. (10/1/2003)*

Amberhill 2000 Chardonnay (California) $8. 83 *—S.H. (5/1/2002)*

AMBULLNEO

Ambullneo 2005 Big Paw Chardonnay (Santa Maria Valley) $50. This is the winery's stainless steel-fermented Chardonnay. It's a big, ripe, full-throttled wine, and without undergoing malolactic fermentation, it's also a bit raw in acidity. The flavors are enormous, suggesting baked apples, pineapple marmalade, sweet date tapenade, candied ginger and Asian spices. Could be a sleeper. Try aging it for 5–10 years. **90** *—S.H. (5/1/2007)*

Ambullneo 2005 Fang Blanc Chardonnay (Santa Maria Valley) $50. Partially barrel-fermented, this Chard is a blend of Bien Nacido and Solomon Hills. It's a heavyweight, so full-bodied, in fact, that it's one of the rare California Chardonnays that will benefit from bottle age. It has a candied, English dessert trifle flavor of apricots, peaches, citrons and green apples, baked into a custardy pudding, and the caramelized taste of charred oak. You'll even find a dusting of tannins. Best after 2007, and for another 5–7 years. **91** *—S.H. (5/1/2007)*

Ambullneo 2005 Bulldog Pinot Noir (Santa Maria Valley) $80. Fans of delicate Pinot Noir need not apply. This is a big, tough, drily tannic wine, with almost the heft of Syrah. That makes it an oddball, but there's no denying its deliciousness and complexity. You can criticize it for non-varietalness, but the wealth of cherry and blackberry jam, dark chocolate and rum punch flavors is addictive. It's a blend of some of the best Pinot vineyards in California, including Bien Nacido, Laetitia and Solomon Hills, which is owned by the family that owns Bien Nacido. Could be an ager, but we know nothing of its history. **90** *—S.H. (5/1/2007)*

Ambullneo 2005 Canis Major Pinot Noir (California) $95. Ambullneo's most expensive Pinot has a statewide appellation, but they pride themselves as masters of blending. This wine, from their portions of vineyards in Solomon Hills, Bien Nacido, Hyde and Hudson, is eloquent. It's big, rich and flamboyant, almost Rhône-like, with cherry and raspberry pie-filling flavors, and the caramelized new oak that so spicily supports it. Has the volume and upscale complexity to accompany the best dishes, and should improve for five years. **93** *—S.H. (5/1/2007)*

Ambullneo 2005 Mastiff Pinot Noir (Carneros) $80. This is one of the larger, more imponderable Pinots I've tasted this year, meaning that it has the heft of something from the Rhône, perhaps a Grenache, although it never loses Pinot's silkiness. It's tremendous and forward in jammy cherries, raspberries and cola, and while it's dry, it has the sweet finish of an extremely ripe wine. Enormously complicated, it's an eccentric Pinot, but one you'll probably reach for again and again. From the esteemed Hyde and Hudson vineyards. **93** *—S.H. (5/1/2007)*

Ambullneo 2004 Howling Syrah (Santa Maria Valley) $70. Mostly from Bien Nacido Vineyard, this is solidly in the winery's style, which is huge, fruit-forward, full-bodied wines of vast concentration and deliciousness. There is nothing at all subtle about this Syrah. It overwhelms with blackberry pie, cassis and chocolate-coated cherry candy flavors, with licorice and white pepper overtones, and is also big in tannins, although they're ripe and sweet. Racy acidity saves the day, and keeps it from being a fruit bomb. **91** *—S.H. (5/1/2007)*

USA

AMETHYST

Amethyst 2001 Cabernet Sauvignon (Napa Valley) $36. 90 *—S.H. (2/1/2004)*

Amethyst 2001 Floralia Malvasia Bianca (Monterey County) $20. 90 Editors' Choice *—S.H. (2/1/2004)*

Amethyst 2004 Pinot Grigio (Los Carneros) $18. 84 *(2/1/2006)*

Amethyst 1998 Vinalia Sangiovese (Napa Valley) $17. 88 *—S.H. (3/1/2004)*

AMICI

Amici 2002 Cabernet Sauvignon (Napa Valley) $42. 84 *—S.H. (12/1/2005)*

Amici 2001 Cabernet Sauvignon (Napa Valley) $38. 90 *—S.H. (10/3/2004)*

Amici 2004 Chardonnay (Napa Valley) $30. 90 *—S.H. (12/1/2006)*

Amici 2002 Chardonnay (Napa Valley) $25. 86 *—S.H. (4/1/2005)*

Amici 2000 Meritage (Napa Valley) $45. 92 *—S.H. (11/15/2004)*

Amici 2003 Pinot Noir (Mendocino) $42. 85 *—S.H. (12/1/2005)*

Amici 2002 Pinot Noir (Mendocino) $35. 84 *—S.H. (4/1/2005)*

AMICUS

Amicus 2004 Special Blend Bordeaux Blend (Spring Mountain) $40. This is a Cabernet-based Bordeaux blend, and quite a good one. It has a classic mountain profile of intense cassis, cherry and cedar flavors, with firm, astringent tannins. Decanting will help it soften, but you're better off cellaring this polished wine for a few years. **91** *—S.H. (12/31/2007)*

Amicus 2002 Special Blend Bordeaux Blend (Napa Valley) $38. 88 *—S.H. (12/31/2005)*

Amicus 2004 Cabernet Sauvignon (Spring Mountain) $55. Amicus has been doing a good job over the years producing richly intense mountain-style Cabs. This one, from a warm vintage, is very ripe, showing lusty red and black currant flavors. The tannins are thick, but sweet and fine, making the wine instantly drinkable, although decanting won't hurt. Best now–2010. **90** *—S.H. (12/31/2007)*

Amicus 2002 Cabernet Sauvignon (Napa Valley) $49. 89 *—S.H. (12/31/2005)*

Amicus 2001 Special Blend Cabernet Sauvignon (Napa Valley) $49. 90 *—S.H. (10/1/2005)*

AMITY

Amity 1999 Gewürztraminer (Oregon) $12. 88 *—P.G. (11/15/2001)*

Amity 2002 Dry Gewürztraminer (Oregon) $12. 86 *—P.G. (2/1/2005)*

Amity 2000 Dry Gewürztraminer (Oregon) $12. 91 Best Buy *—P.G. (12/1/2003)*

Amity 1998 Pinot Blanc (Willamette Valley) $12. 88 *—L.W. (12/31/1999)*

Amity 2003 Pinot Blanc (Willamette Valley) $14. 88 *—P.G. (2/1/2005)*

Amity 2001 Pinot Blanc (Oregon) $12. 88 *—P.G. (12/31/2002)*

Amity 1999 Pinot Blanc (Willamette Valley) $12. 85 *—D.T. (11/1/2001)*

Amity 2002 Pinot Noir (Oregon) $14. 83 *(11/1/2004)*

Amity 1999 Pinot Noir (Willamette Valley) $20. 87 *(10/1/2002)*

Amity 1998 Pinot Noir (Willamette Valley) $20. 85 *—M.S. (12/1/2000)*

Amity 1997 Pinot Noir (Willamette Valley) $16. 83 *(11/15/1999)*

Amity 1999 Eco Wine Cattrall Brothers Pinot Noir (Oregon) $14. 80 *—M.S. (12/1/2000)*

Amity 2001 Eco-Wine Pinot Noir (Oregon) $14. 85 *—P.G. (12/31/2002)*

Amity 2000 Eco-Wine Pinot Noir (Oregon) $15. 85 *—P.G. (4/1/2003)*

Amity 2002 Estate Pinot Noir (Willamette Valley) $30. 83 *(11/1/2004)*

Amity 1999 Estate Pinot Noir (Willamette Valley) $30. 90 *—P.G. (12/1/2003)*

Amity 2003 Schouten Vineyard Pinot Noir (Willamette Valley) $35. 88 *—P.G. (12/1/2006)*

Amity 2002 Schouten Vineyard Pinot Noir (Willamette Valley) $30. 84 *(11/1/2004)*

Amity 2000 Schouten Vineyard Pinot Noir (Willamette Valley) $15. 89 *—P.G. (4/1/2003)*

Amity 2000 Schouter Pinot Noir (Willamette Valley) $30. 85 *(10/1/2002)*

Amity 2002 Sunnyside Pinot Noir (Willamette Valley) $30. 85 *(11/1/2004)*

Amity 1999 Sunnyside Pinot Noir (Willamette Valley) $30. 84 *(10/1/2002)*

Amity 2003 Sunnyside Vineyard Pinot Noir (Willamette Valley) $35. 89 *—P.G. (12/1/2006)*

Amity 1998 Winemaker's Reserve Pinot Noir (Willamette Valley) $40. 85 *—M.S. (9/1/2003)*

Amity 2001 Dry Riesling (Oregon) $12. 89 Best Buy *—P.G. (12/1/2003)*

Amity 2002 Select Cluster Riesling (Oregon) $40. 90 *—P.G. (12/1/2003)*

Amity 2002 Wedding Dance Riesling (Willamette Valley) $14. 88 *—P.G. (12/1/2003)*

Amity 2002 Crown Jewel Reserve White Blend (Willamette Valley) $16. 88 *—P.G. (12/1/2003)*

AMIZETTA

Amizetta 2003 Complexity Red Wine Bordeaux Blend (Napa Valley) $39. A dry, tannic wine with some asperity, this is a blend of Cab Sauvignon, Merlot and Cab Franc. Unlikely to develop in the bottle, it's best opened now to enjoy the primary flavors of cherries and blackberries. **86** *—S.H. (6/1/2007)*

Amizetta 2003 Cabernet Sauvignon (Napa Valley) $47. This little family winery, which grows its grapes high in the Vaca Mountains outside St. Helena, is getting better with each passing vintage. Their Cabs are showing that ripeness isn't enough, but balance and structure count, especially at this price. The '03 is still a young wine, but a dramatically fruity, well-oaked one. It has all the drama of a fine Napa Cab, with the stuffing to last through 2009 before the fruit starts to fade. **91** *—S.H. (6/1/2007)*

Amizetta 2002 Estate Cabernet Sauvignon (Napa Valley) $45. 91 *—S.H. (10/1/2005)*

Amizetta 1999 Estate Bottled Vigneto del Tacchino Selvatico Cabernet Sauvignon (Napa Valley) $75. 91 *(8/1/2003)*

Amizetta 2002 Vigneto del Tacchino Selvatico Estate Reserve Cabernet Sauvignon (Napa Valley) $85. 88 *—S.H. (10/1/2005)*

Amizetta 2002 Complexity Meritage (Napa Valley) $38. 86 *—S.H. (10/1/2005)*

AMPELOS

Ampelos 2004 Pinot Noir (Santa Rita Hills) $32. Very ripe and forward, with cherry-pie filling, root beer or sassafras and cola flavors that finish a bit sweet. This is a nice, supple wine for early drinking. **86** *—S.H. (6/1/2007)*

Ampelos 2004 Gamma Syrah (Santa Rita Hills) $34. A bit too rich and ripe for me, with an almost sweet cherry-raspberry flavor that veers into rum-soaked raisins. Turns bitter on the finish. **83** *—S.H. (6/1/2007)*

AMPHORA

Amphora 2002 Jacob's Ridge Mounts Vineyard Cabernet Sauvignon (Dry Creek Valley) $45. 85 *—S.H. (10/1/2005)*

Amphora 2003 Mounts Vineyard Merlot (Dry Creek Valley) $35. 83 *—S.H. (10/1/2005)*

Amphora 2003 Mounts Vineyard Petite Sirah (Dry Creek Valley) $30. 86 *—S.H. (10/1/2005)*

Amphora 2001 Mounts Vineyard Petite Sirah (Dry Creek Valley) $30. 82 *(4/1/2003)*

Amphora 2003 Mounts Vineyard Syrah (Dry Creek Valley) $30. 84 *(9/1/2005)*

Amphora 2002 Mounts Vineyard Syrah (Dry Creek Valley) $30. 86 *—S.H. (12/1/2004)*

Amphora 2003 Mounts Vineyard Zinfandel (Dry Creek Valley) $24. 85 *—S.H. (10/1/2005)*

AMUSANT

Amusant 2002 Cabernet Sauvignon (Napa Valley) $30. 91 *—S.H. (8/1/2005)*

Amusant 2001 Cabernet Sauvignon (Napa Valley) $30. 84 *—S.H. (11/15/2003)*

Amusant 2002 Chardonnay (Napa Valley) $16. 84 *—S.H. (8/1/2005)*

Amusant 2003 Sauvignon Blanc (Napa Valley) $15. 86 *—S.H. (8/1/2005)*

AMUSE BOUCHE

Amuse Bouche 2004 Red Wine Bordeaux Blend (Napa Valley) $175. This is one of those superripe, superopulent, superfancy reds that makes tasters stop and pause. A voluptuous wine, so ripe in cassis, cherry and chocolate truffle, so smooth in tannins, yet balanced. This is truly New World wine-making at its most profound, but a bit obvious. Drink now–2010, at least. **93** *—S.H. (5/1/2007)*

Amuse Bouche 2002 Merlot-Cabernet Franc (Napa Valley) $200. 90 *—S.H. (10/1/2004)*

Amuse Bouche 2003 Red Wine Red Blend (Napa Valley) $200. 94 Editors' Choice *—S.H. (8/1/2006)*

ANAKOTA

Anakota 2002 Helena Dakota Vineyard Cabernet Sauvignon (Knights Valley) $80. 92 *—S.H. (9/1/2006)*

Anakota 2002 Helena Montana Vineyard Cabernet Sauvignon (Knights Valley) $80. 92 Cellar Selection *—S.H. (9/1/2006)*

ANAM CARA CELLARS

Anam Cara Cellars 2004 Nicholas Estate Pinot Noir (Willamette Valley) $29. Second harvest vines yield a rather light Pinot. The color shows some unexpected tawniness; the wine seems heading for an early maturity. Scents are strongly in the tomato leaf quarter, and that overpowering note continues through the finish. This is not unusual for Oregon Pinot, but seems to indicate vines that need more time to mature. Alcohol just 13.3 percent. **85** *—P.G. (2/1/2007)*

Anam Cara Cellars 2004 Nicholas Estate Reserve Pinot Noir (Willamette Valley) $39. The reserve wine is a barrel selection, limited to just 65 cases. I confess that I did not find a great difference between the reserve and the regular bottling. The same quite leafy flavors were much in evidence; this wine may have had a bit more tannin and it also finished with an unusual minty note. **85** *—P.G. (2/1/2007)*

Anam Cara Cellars 2006 Nicholas Estate Riesling (Willamette Valley) $21. This is just the second harvest from this tiny, one-acre plot in the Chehalem mountains. It is a beautifully crafted wine, which wraps its fresh, crisp citrus/apple fruit in whiffs of honey and jasmine. Though just 12.7% alcohol, there is nothing light or simple about this wine; it has a firm constitution and subtle layers of mixed fruits and mineral. **91** *—P.G. (11/15/2007)*

ANAPAMU

Anapamu 2004 Chardonnay (Monterey County) $16. 85 *—S.H. (3/1/2006)*

Anapamu 2003 Chardonnay (Monterey County) $16. 82 *—S.H. (10/1/2005)*

Anapamu 2001 Chardonnay (Monterey County) $16. 87 *—S.H. (8/1/2003)*

Anapamu 2000 Chardonnay (Monterey) $16. 86 *—S.H. (5/1/2002)*

Anapamu 2003 Pinot Noir (Monterey County) $16. 83 *—S.H. (12/15/2005)*

Anapamu 2002 Pinot Noir (Monterey County) $16. 83 *—S.H. (10/1/2005)*

Anapamu 2001 Pinot Noir (Monterey County) $16. 86 *—S.H. (7/1/2003)*

Anapamu 2000 Pinot Noir (Monterey County) $16. 84 *(10/1/2002)*

Anapamu 2001 Riesling (Monterey County) $16. 87 *—J.M. (8/1/2003)*

Anapamu 2001 Syrah (Paso Robles) $20. 85 *—S.H. (12/1/2004)*

Anapamu 2001 Syrah (Paso Robles) $22. 84 *—S.H. (12/15/2003)*

Anapamu 2000 Syrah (Paso Robles) $20. 86 *—S.H. (12/1/2002)*

Anapamu 1999 Syrah (Central Coast) $16. 88 Editors' Choice *(10/1/2001)*

ANCIEN

Ancien 2006 Sangiacomo Vineyard Pinot Gris (Carneros) $22. With spearmint, lemon-lime, Fig Newton and vanilla cream flavors, this sure is a fruity wine, showing the ripeness of the California summer sun. It's a little sweet, but those bright, crisp Carneros acids balance it. **85** *—S.H. (12/15/2007)*

Ancien 2005 Pinot Noir (Russian River Valley) $42. This Pinot is simple and on the soft, heavy side, with jammy blackberry, cherry, cola and spice flavors. It's basically dry, and would benefit from higher acidity. **84** *—S.H. (12/15/2007)*

Ancien 2000 Pinot Noir (Russian River Valley) $36. 84 *(10/1/2002)*

Ancien 2000 Pinot Noir (Carneros) $32. 87 *(10/1/2002)*

Ancien 2005 Mink Vineyard Pinot Noir (Napa Valley) $42. The vineyard is in the southerly Coombsville area, which gives the wine a crisp delicacy reminiscent of Carneros. The cherry and raspberry flavors are boosted by oak, but the wine would be better if it were drier, as it has a sugary jelly taste. **84** *—S.H. (12/15/2007)*

Ancien 1999 Steiner Vineyard Pinot Noir (Sonoma Mountain) $42. 93 *—S.H. (2/1/2003)*

Ancien 2005 Toyon Pinot Noir (Carneros) $34. Heavy and sweet, with flavors of blackberry, raspberry and cherry jam, this simple Pinot benefits from decent acids. Smoky, spicy oak rounds out the taste. **83** *—S.H. (12/15/2007)*

ANDRE

Andre NV Extra Dry Champagne Blend (California) $4. 80 *—S.H. (12/15/1999)*

Andre NV Spumante Champagne Blend (California) $4. 83 *—S.H. (12/15/1999)*

ANDRETTI

Andretti 2005 Cabernet Sauvignon (Napa Valley) $38. Rich and dry, this Cab is long on blackberry and cherry flavors, with a rich vein of sweet tobacco, carob, herbs and oaky vanilla. It's a balanced wine that is drinking well now. **87** *—S.H. (12/15/2007)*

Andretti 2005 Cabernet Sauvignon (California) $20. An awkward wine that's hard to warm up to. There's a sharpness in the mouthfeel, with minty cherry flavors and a tannic, slightly sweet, cough drop finish. **82** *—S.H. (11/1/2007)*

Andretti 2004 Cabernet Sauvignon (Napa Valley) $38. 85 *—S.H. (12/31/2006)*

Andretti 2002 Cabernet Sauvignon (Napa Valley) $30. 90 *—S.H. (12/1/2005)*

Andretti 2002 Cabernet Sauvignon (Napa Valley) $28. 92 *—S.H. (4/1/2004)*

Andretti 2000 Cabernet Sauvignon (Napa Valley) $28. 89 *—S.H. (11/15/2003)*

Andretti 1999 Cabernet Sauvignon (Napa Valley) $30. 91 *—S.H. (11/15/2002)*

Andretti 2001 Selection Series Cabernet Sauvignon (North Coast) $12. 85 *—S.H. (11/15/2003)*

Andretti 2001 Selections Cabernet Sauvignon (North Coast) $15. 83 *—S.H. (12/1/2005)*

Andretti 2006 Chardonnay (Napa Valley) $24. A little obvious in the oak, which tends to overshadow the peach and apricot flavors. The finish is a mélange of fruit and spicy butterscotch. **84** *—S.H. (12/15/2007)*

Andretti 2005 Chardonnay (Napa Valley) $24. 85 *—S.H. (12/31/2006)*

Andretti 2004 Chardonnay (Napa Valley) $19. 87 *—S.H. (12/1/2005)*

Andretti 2002 Chardonnay (Napa Valley) $16. 87 *—S.H. (12/31/2003)*

Andretti 2001 Chardonnay (Napa Valley) $16. 90 Editors' Choice *—S.H. (12/15/2002)*

Andretti 2002 Selection Series Chardonnay (Sonoma County) $10. 83 *—S.H. (4/1/2004)*

Andretti 2004 Selections Chardonnay (Central Coast) $12. 83 *—S.H. (12/1/2005)*

Andretti 2006 Selections Fumé Blanc (North Coast) $19. This refreshing wine is clean and dry, with grapefruit, peach and honeysuckle flavors boosted by high, tingly acidity. Made Sancerre-style, it leaves behind a spicy, fruity aftertaste. **87** *—S.H. (12/1/2007)*

Andretti 2005 Merlot (Napa Valley) $33. Thin and weedy, with dill and oregano flavors and just a drop of cherry or blackberry fruit. Finishes dry and tannic. **83** *—S.H. (12/1/2007)*

Andretti 2004 Merlot (Napa Valley) $26. 85 *—S.H. (7/1/2006)*

Andretti 2001 Merlot (Napa Valley) $24. 90 *—S.H. (4/1/2004)*

Andretti 2000 Merlot (Napa Valley) $23. 87 *—S.H. (12/15/2003)*

Andretti 1999 Merlot (Napa Valley) $20. 91 *—S.H. (6/1/2002)*

Andretti 1997 Merlot (Napa Valley) $23. 89 *(7/1/2000)*

Andretti 2001 Selection Series Merlot (North Coast) $11. 85 *—S.H. (2/1/2004)*

Andretti 2006 Pinot Grigio (Napa Valley) $22. There's not much going on in this wine, flavor-wise. The dryness and acidic crispness are fine. But it's watery, with just a squeeze of grapefruit and lime. **83** *—S.H. (12/1/2007)*

Andretti 2005 Pinot Grigio (Napa Valley) $18. 82 *—S.H. (7/1/2006)*

Andretti 2005 Pinot Noir (Napa Valley) $30. 86 *—S.H. (12/31/2006)*

Andretti 2004 Pinot Noir (Napa Valley) $20. 88 *—S.H. (12/1/2005)*

Andretti 2004 Zinfandel-Primitivo Red Blend (Napa Valley) $33. 80 *—S.H. (12/31/2006)*

Andretti 2005 Sangiovese (Napa Valley) $33. Acidic and simple, with medicinal cherry flavors. **80** *—S.H. (12/15/2007)*

Andretti 2003 Sangiovese (Napa Valley) $20. 85 *—S.H. (12/1/2005)*

Andretti 2001 Sangiovese (Napa Valley) $18. 88 *—S.H. (4/1/2004)*

Andretti 2000 Sangiovese (Napa Valley) $19. 85 *—S.H. (9/1/2002)*

Andretti 2006 Sauvignon Blanc (Napa Valley) $22. The 2006 vintage strikes again, causing particularly strong feline aromas and taste. **80** *—S.H. (11/1/2007)*

Andretti 2005 Sauvignon Blanc (Napa Valley) $18. 83 *—S.H. (7/1/2006)*

Andretti 2004 Sauvignon Blanc (Napa Valley) $16. 86 *—S.H. (12/1/2005)*

Andretti 2002 Sauvignon Blanc (Napa Valley) $14. 88 *—S.H. (12/15/2003)*

Andretti 2001 Sauvignon Blanc (Napa Valley) $14. 89 *—S.H. (7/1/2003)*

Andretti 2000 Sauvignon Blanc (Napa Valley) $14. 87 *—S.H. (9/1/2002)*

Andretti 2005 Syrah (Napa Valley) $33. Richness stars in this soft, voluptuous Syrah. It seduces with ripe blackberry, plum, blueberry and cherry jam flavors, veined with licorice and mocha, and dusted with peppery, cinnamon spices. It's not structured enough to be an ager, but is elegant now. **90** *—S.H. (11/1/2007)*

Andretti 2005 Selections Zinfandel (North Coast) $22. Here's a classic expression of California Zinfandel. Shows the variety's rich wild berry, cherry, spice and tobacco flavors with that slightly rustic, briary edge of wildness. Finishes dry and cleanly tannic. **87** *—S.H. (12/1/2007)*

Andretti 2004 Selections Zinfandel (California) $15. 84 *—S.H. (12/1/2005)*

ANDREW GEOFFREY

Andrew Geoffrey 2002 Cabernet Sauvignon (Diamond Mountain) $75. 91 Cellar Selection *—S.H. (2/1/2006)*

Andrew Geoffrey 2001 Cabernet Sauvignon (Diamond Mountain) $75. 92 Cellar Selection *—S.H. (6/1/2005)*

Andrew Geoffrey 2000 Cabernet Sauvignon (Diamond Mountain) $85. 88 *—S.H. (11/15/2003)*

ANDREW MURRAY

Andrew Murray 1997 Espérance Red Blend (Santa Barbara County) $18. 93 *—S.H. (6/1/1999)*

Andrew Murray 2001 Espérance Rhône Red Blend (Santa Ynez Valley) $22. 88 *—S.H. (3/1/2004)*

Andrew Murray 2004 Espérance Rhône Red Blend (Central Coast) $22. 88 *—S.H. (11/15/2006)*

Andrew Murray 2004 Enchanté Rhône White Blend (Santa Ynez Valley) $22. 87 *—S.H. (11/15/2006)*

Andrew Murray 1998 Roussanne (Santa Barbara County) $25. 90 *—S.H. (6/1/1999)*

Andrew Murray 1997 "Roasted Slope" Syrah (Santa Barbara County) $18. 88 *—S.H. (6/1/1999)*

Andrew Murray 2003 Estate Grown Syrah (Santa Ynez Valley) $25. 85 *(9/1/2005)*

Andrew Murray 2001 Estate Grown Syrah (Santa Ynez Valley) $20. 84 *—S.H. (3/1/2004)*

Andrew Murray 2000 Hillside Reserve Syrah (Santa Ynez Valley) $45. 92 *—S.H. (12/1/2003)*

Andrew Murray 1996 Hillside Reserve Syrah (Santa Barbara County) $25. 92 *—S.H. (6/1/1999)*

Andrew Murray 2000 Les Coteaux Syrah (Santa Ynez Valley) $25. 84 *—S.H. (2/1/2003)*

Andrew Murray 1999 Les Coteaux Syrah (Santa Ynez Valley) $25. 90 *—S.H. (7/1/2002)*

Andrew Murray 1997 Les Coteaux Syrah (Santa Barbara County) $20. 93 *—S.H. (10/1/1999)*

Andrew Murray 2003 Roasted Slope Syrah (Santa Ynez Valley) $25. 84 *—S.H. (11/15/2006)*

Andrew Murray 2001 Roasted Slope Syrah (Santa Ynez Valley) $32. 93 Editors' Choice *—S.H. (12/1/2004)*

Andrew Murray 2000 Roasted Slope Vineyard Syrah (Santa Ynez Valley) $30. 91 *—S.H. (2/1/2003)*

Andrew Murray 1999 Roasted Slope Vineyard Syrah (Santa Ynez Valley) $30. 85 *(11/1/2001)*

Andrew Murray 1999 Tous Les Jours Syrah (California) $16. 85 *(10/1/2001)*

Andrew Murray 2003 Westerly Vineyard Syrah (Santa Ynez Valley) $36. 86 *(9/1/2005)*

Andrew Murray 1998 Viognier (Santa Barbara County) $25. 91 *—S.H. (10/1/1999)*

Andrew Murray 1997 Viognier (Santa Barbara County) $25. 90 *—S.H. (6/1/1999)*

Andrew Murray 2005 Viognier (Central Coast) $25. 85 *—S.H. (11/15/2006)*

Andrew Murray 2001 Viognier (Santa Ynez Valley) $25. 92 *—S.H. (3/1/2003)*

Andrew Murray 2000 Viognier (Santa Ynez Valley) $25. 87 *—S.H. (12/1/2001)*

Andrew Murray 2002 Estate Viognier (Santa Ynez Valley) $25. 90 *—S.H. (10/1/2003)*

Andrew Murray 2001 Enchanté White Blend (Santa Ynez Valley) $22. 90 *—S.H. (12/1/2003)*

Andrew Murray 2000 Enchanté White Blend (Santa Ynez Valley) $22. 89 *—S.H. (12/1/2001)*

ANDREW RICH

Andrew Rich 2004 Cabernet Franc (Columbia Valley (WA)) $20. 90 *—P.G. (12/31/2006)*

Andrew Rich 1998 Les Vigneaux Corral Creek Vineyard Pinot Noir (Willamette Valley) $25. 88 *—M.S. (12/1/2000)*

Andrew Rich 2004 Red Blend (Columbia Valley (WA)) $16. 87 *—P.G. (12/31/2006)*

Andrew Rich 2004 Roussanne (Columbia Valley (WA)) $20. 90 *—P.G. (12/31/2006)*

Andrew Rich 2003 Syrah (Columbia Valley (WA)) $23. 90 *—P.G. (12/31/2006)*

ANDREW WILL

Andrew Will 2003 Champoux Vineyard Bordeaux Blend (Columbia Valley (WA)) $45. 94 *—P.G. (4/1/2006)*

Andrew Will 2001 Champoux Vineyard Bordeaux Blend (Columbia Valley (WA)) $48. 91 *—P.G. (7/1/2004)*

Andrew Will 2002 Champoux Vineyard Red Wine Bordeaux Blend (Columbia Valley (WA)) $55. 91 *—P.G. (12/15/2004)*

Andrew Will 2004 Ciel du Cheval Vineyard Bordeaux Blend (Red Mountain) $56. 89 *—P.G. (12/31/2006)*

Andrew Will 2001 Ciel du Cheval Vineyard Bordeaux Blend (Red Mountain) $48. 93 *—P.G. (7/1/2004)*

Andrew Will 2002 Ciel du Cheval Vineyard Red Wine Bordeaux Blend (Red Mountain) $55. 95 Cellar Selection *—P.G. (12/15/2004)*

Andrew Will 2004 Sheridan Vineyard Bordeaux Blend (Yakima Valley) $46. 87 *—P.G. (12/31/2006)*

Andrew Will 2003 Sheridan Vineyard Bordeaux Blend (Yakima Valley) $40. 90 *—P.G. (4/1/2006)*

Andrew Will 2003 Sorella Bordeaux Blend (Columbia Valley (WA)) $65. 93 *—P.G. (6/1/2006)*

Andrew Will 2001 Sorella Red Wine Bordeaux Blend (Columbia Valley (WA)) $56. 92 *—P.G. (7/1/2004)*

Andrew Will 2002 Klipsun Vineyard Cabernet Sauvignon (Red Mountain) $45. 92 *—P.G. (12/15/2004)*

Andrew Will 2005 Cuvée Lucia Celilo Vineyard Chardonnay (Columbia Gorge) $22. This is good juice, sappy and clean, with flavors of crisp red apple leading into light tropical fruit – citrus and pineapple. It's lush and acid-driven, with an underpinning of mineral and stone. **92** *—P.G. (2/1/2007)*

Andrew Will 1999 Ciel du Cheval Merlot (Washington) $40. 92 Cellar Selection *—P.G. (6/1/2001)*

Andrew Will 2000 Ciel du Cheval Vineyard Merlot (Washington) $40. 93 *—P.G. (9/1/2002)*

Andrew Will 1998 Ciel du Cheval Vineyard Merlot (Washington) $45. 93 *—P.G. (9/1/2000)*

Andrew Will 2002 Cuvée Lucia Merlot (Washington) $30. 89 *—P.G. (7/1/2004)*

Andrew Will 2003 Cuvée Lucia Merlot (Washington) $28. 90 *—P.G. (4/1/2006)*

Andrew Will 1999 Klipsun Merlot (Washington) $40. 90 *—P.G. (6/1/2001)*

Andrew Will 2002 Klipsun Vineyard Merlot (Red Mountain) $45. 94 *—P.G. (12/15/2004)*

Andrew Will 2000 Klipsun Vineyard Merlot (Washington) $40. 93 *—P.G. (9/1/2002)*

Andrew Will 1998 Klipsun Vineyard Merlot (Washington) $45. 92 *—P.G. (9/1/2000)*

Andrew Will 1999 Pepper Bridge Merlot (Washington) $36. 88 *—P.G. (6/1/2001)*

Andrew Will 2000 Pepper Bridge Vineyard Merlot (Washington) $36. 91 *—P.G. (9/1/2002)*

Andrew Will 1998 Pepper Bridge Vineyard Merlot (Washington) $45. 86 *—P.G. (9/1/2000)*

Andrew Will 1999 Seven Hills Merlot (Washington) $36. 87 *—P.G. (6/1/2001)*

Andrew Will 2000 Seven Hills Vineyard Merlot (Walla Walla (WA)) $36. 92 *—P.G. (9/1/2002)*

Andrew Will 1998 Seven Hills Vineyard Merlot (Walla Walla (WA)) $45. 89 *—P.G. (9/1/2000)*

Andrew Will 2000 Sheridan Vineyard Merlot (Washington) $36. 90 *—P.G. (9/1/2002)*

Andrew Will 2002 Seven Hills Vineyard Red Wine Merlot-Cabernet Sauvignon (Walla Walla (WA)) $55. 90 *—P.G. (12/15/2004)*

Andrew Will 2004 Champoux Vineyard Red Wine Red Blend (Columbia Valley (WA)) $56. 90 *—P.G. (12/31/2006)*

Andrew Will 2003 Ciel du Cheval Vineyard Red Blend (Red Mountain) $45. 95 Editors' Choice *—P.G. (4/1/2006)*

Andrew Will 2003 Klipsun Vineyard Red Blend (Red Mountain) $45. 91 *—P.G. (4/1/2006)*

Andrew Will 2002 Sheridan Vineyard Red Wine Red Blend (Yakima Valley) $55. 91 *—P.G. (12/15/2004)*

Andrew Will 2003 Two Blondes Red Blend (Yakima Valley) $40. 91 *—P.G. (4/1/2006)*

Andrew Will 2005 Ciel du Cheval Vineyard Sangiovese (Red Mountain) $25. This is a perfectly drinkable wine, with good fruit from a great vineyard. It's a bit minty and chalky; let's say rustic. The mixed flavors border on the lightly vegetal side of cool-climate fruit; not sweet but firm. **86** *—P.G. (12/1/2007)*

Andrew Will 1999 Ciel du Cheval Sangiovese (Yakima Valley) $23. 90 *—P.G. (11/15/2000)*

Andrew Will 2004 Cuvée Lucia Ciel du Cheval Vineyard Sangiovese (Red Mountain) $28. 86 *—P.G. (12/31/2006)*

Andrew Will 2002 Cuvée Lucia du Cheval Sangiovese (Red Mountain) $28. 90 *—P.G. (7/1/2004)*

Andrew Will 1999 Pepper Bridge Sangiovese (Walla Walla (WA)) $23. 91 *—P.G. (11/15/2000)*

Andrew Will 2002 Annie Camarda Syrah (Red Mountain) $58. 95 *—P.G. (11/15/2006)*

Andrew Will 2002 Cuvée Lucia Seven Hills Vineyard Syrah (Walla Walla (WA)) $28. 87 *—P.G. (7/1/2004)*

ANDRUS

Andrus 1997 Reserve Bordeaux Blend (Napa Valley) $125. 94 *(11/1/2000)*

ANGELINE

Angeline 2005 Chardonnay (Russian River Valley) $14. The winery has raised the price over the previous vintage, but this is a much better wine than the '04, showing all the hallmarks of a wonderful, long hangtime vintage. Pineapples, kiwis, limes and green apples are enriched with a touch of smoky, buttery oak and creamy lees. **86** *—S.H. (6/1/2007)*

Angeline 2006 Gewürztraminer (Mendocino County) $14. Well-acidified, the fruit shows a long hangtime character of marvelously intense tropical fruits, spices and flowers. The wine spreads a honeyed richness all around the mouth, but it's dry. **89 Best Buy** *—S.H. (11/15/2007)*

Angeline 2005 Pinot Noir (Sonoma Coast) $14. As good as many Pinots costing much more. While it's on the light side, it has a silky texture, with crisp acidity and gentle tannins that let the cola, raspberry and spice flavors glide over the palate. Finishes nice and dry. Try with meats or poultry in mushroom sauce. **85** *—S.H. (2/1/2007)*

Angeline 2005 Pinot Noir (Russian River Valley) $14. Angeline Pinots have been good over the years, offering solid varietal character at an everyday price. The '05 is better than the '04, cleaner and crisper, with cherry, cola and rosehip tea flavors folded into a delicately silky texture. **86** *—S.H. (11/1/2007)*

Angeline 2002 Zinfandel (Russian River Valley) $10. 85 Best Buy *—S.H. (11/1/2005)*

ANGELO'S

Angelo's 2001 Cabernet Sauvignon (Columbia Valley (WA)) $21. 84 *—P.G. (1/1/2004)*

Angelo's 2002 Chardonnay (Columbia Valley (WA)) $18. 86 *—P.G. (1/1/2004)*

Angelo's 2001 Merlot (Columbia Valley (WA)) $21. 83 *—P.G. (1/1/2004)*

ANGLIM

Anglim 2006 Rosé Blend (Paso Robles) $15. A little hot-country rustic in the simple structure, softness and candied sweetness, yet those raspberry, cherry, vanilla and butterscotch flavors are really tasty. It's a Rhône red blend, with some Viognier. **84** *—S.H. (7/1/2007)*

ANNE AMIE

Anne Amie 2002 Pinot Noir (Willamette Valley) $22.85 *(11/1/2004)*

Anne Amie 2002 Deux Vert Vineyard Pinot Noir (Willamette Valley) $35. 85 *(11/1/2004)*

Anne Amie 2002 Doe Ridge Vineyard Pinot Noir (Willamette Valley) $35. 86 *(11/1/2004)*

Anne Amie 2001 Doe Ridge Vineyard Pinot Noir (Willamette Valley) $40. 89 *—P.G. (12/1/2003)*

Anne Amie 2002 Hawks View Vineyard Pinot Noir (Willamette Valley) $35. 87 *(11/1/2004)*

Anne Amie 2001 Hawks View Vineyard Pinot Noir (Willamette Valley) $40. 88 *—P.G. (12/1/2003)*

Anne Amie 2002 La Colina Vineyard Pinot Noir (Willamette Valley) $35. 86 *(11/1/2004)*

Anne Amie 2001 Laurel Vineyard Pinot Noir (Willamette Valley) $40. 88 *—P.G. (12/1/2003)*

Anne Amie 2002 Yamhill Springs Vineyard Pinot Noir (Willamette Valley) $35. 84 *(11/1/2004)*

Anne Amie 2001 Yamhill Springs Vineyard Pinot Noir (Willamette Valley) $40. 86 *—P.G. (12/1/2003)*

ANOMALY

Anomaly 2003 Cabernet Sauvignon (Napa Valley) $75. Classic Cabernet character from this St. Helena wine, which contains small amounts of Cab Franc and Petite Verdot. Opens with a splashy burst of black currants, spicy cherry liqueur, charry cedar and new oak and turns elegant and complex in the mouth. Polished, delicate structure, with a round, supple feel. Finishes dry and long. Drink now–2015. **91** *—S.H. (4/1/2007)*

ANTHILL

Anthill 2005 Abbey-Harris Vineyard Pinot Noir (Anderson Valley) $46. I love this Pinot for its tense balance of acidity and fruit, which make for great complexity. The vineyard is south-facing, 1,000 feet above Boonville, and the sunshine helped enormously in this cool vintage, ripening the grapes just enough to give an edge of bitter cherry and red raspberry to the earthy cola, leather and spice flavors. Utterly dry, this is a real connoisseur's wine, one that takes some understanding to appreciate. **93** *—S.H. (12/15/2007)*

Anthill 2005 Comptche Ridge Vineyard Pinot Noir (Mendocino County) $38. You can taste in the very high acidity, and the way the grapes just barely ripened. There's a rhubarb-heirloom tomato edge, but the cherries, raspberries and spicy cola win out, lending rich complexity to this totally dry, interesting young Pinot. Probably best now and for a year or two. **91** —*S.H. (12/15/2007)*

Anthill 2005 Demuth Vineyard Pinot Noir (Anderson Valley) $38. There are suggestions of wintergreen mint and tart rhubarb, but the cherries save the day, giving enough richness to make the wine interesting. Despite the high acidity and dryness, I don't think it's an ager, but it's a beautifully complex, food-friendly Pinot. **90** —*S.H. (12/15/2007)*

Anthill 2005 Peters Vineyard Pinot Noir (Sonoma Coast) $38. The vineyard is near Sebastopol, in a cool part of this vast appellation, and the vintage was cool. The result is a lean wine with high acidity. The flavors straddle the ripeness line, with cherries and strawberries along with green tomatoes and rhubarb. **88** —*S.H. (12/15/2007)*

Anthill 2005 Tina Marie Vineyard Pinot Noir (Russian River Valley) $43. The vineyard is in Green Valley, the coolest part of the appellation. You'll find very high acidity and an austere, elegant wine in this extremely low-yield Pinot Noir. The flavors are right on the edge, balancing less ripe peppermint and tannic Chinese-tea notes with richer cherries and raspberries. This is really a thrilling young wine, and while it may hold for years, it's best now for its tense youth. **93** —*S.H. (12/15/2007)*

Anthill 2005 Windsor Oaks Vineyard Syrah (Russian River Valley) $22. Tough going now with this very dry, young Syrah. Acidity and tannins star, making the wine astringent and burying the fruit. Yes, there's a deep core of black currants and blueberries, but it's a question whether aging will allow them to emerge. **87** —*S.H. (12/15/2007)*

ANTHONY ROAD

Anthony Road 2001 Cabernet Franc (Finger Lakes) $14. 82 —*M.S. (3/1/2003)*

Anthony Road 2005 Martini Reinhardt Selection Pinot Gris (Finger Lakes) $22. Fresh, fruity and semidry, this is good for summer sipping and afternoons in the hammock. There's weight here and a nice overall balance of flavor, meaning it can be enjoyed on its own or with a light pasta dish or cheese plate. **83** —*S.K. (7/1/2007)*

Anthony Road 2006 Dry Riesling (Finger Lakes) $14. The nose on this dry Riesling is a touch sweet, with its ripe pear and pineapple aromas, but the palate is earthier and more citric. It lacks some balance on the palate but the tasty fruit flavors and a finish with zip add to the appeal. **83** —*S.K. (9/1/2007)*

Anthony Road 2005 Martini Reinhardt Selection Riesling (Finger Lakes) $24. Delicate aromas of lime and peach and a bright, clean combination of sweet and dry flavors make this Riesling an accessible, versatile choice to pair with food or sip alone. It's flavorful and full of body, but maintains an elegant touch. **87** —*S.K. (5/1/2007)*

Anthony Road 2006 Semi-Dry Riesling (Finger Lakes) $14. Delicate floral aromas and a combination of ripe pineapple and melon flavors are just part of the package with this exemplary wine from Anthony Road, which has a talent for making approachable Rieslings. Though the wine has a slightly sweet nature, there's ample acidity to keep it from falling flat on the palate. **87** —*S.K. (9/1/2007)*

Anthony Road 2002 Semi-Dry Spring Riesling (Finger Lakes) $12. 82 —*J.C. (8/1/2003)*

Anthony Road 2006 Semi-Sweet Riesling (Finger Lakes) $14. Zesty flavors and aromas of pineapple and orange are balanced with a honeyed sweetness that makes this a fun and unique apéritif or a tasty accompaniment to ethnic, spicy cuisine. It's not a wine that you need mull over but it does have character. **85** —*S.K. (9/1/2007)*

Anthony Road 2002 Semi-Sweet Riesling (Finger Lakes) $11. 81 —*J.C. (8/1/2003)*

ANTICA TERRA

Antica Terra 2002 Pinot Noir (Willamette Valley) $35. 83 *(11/1/2004)*

APEX

Apex 2000 Cabernet Sauvignon (Yakima Valley) $30. 88 —*P.G. (9/1/2004)*

Apex 1998 Cabernet Sauvignon (Columbia Valley (WA)) $30. 87 —*P.G. (6/1/2002)*

Apex 2005 Chardonnay (Yakima Valley) $17. A juicy, ripe, full-flavored Chardonnay, built upon a thick core of tropical fruit—guava, mango and papaya. It's done in what might be thought of as a mid-1980s California style—barrel fermented, full malolactic fermentation, lots of buttery oak. But there is the added vibrancy from Washington-grown grapes, which keep their acidity. This is the winery's most successful wine at retail, and it's easy to see why. It is a sure-fire pleaser. **88** —*P.G. (5/1/2007)*

Apex 2004 Chardonnay (Yakima Valley) $17. 88 —*P.G. (10/1/2006)*

Apex 2000 Chardonnay (Columbia Valley (WA)) $20. 87 —*P.G. (7/1/2002)*

Apex 2001 Outlook Vineyard Chardonnay (Yakima Valley) $25. 88 —*P.G. (9/1/2004)*

Apex 2002 Merlot (Yakima Valley) $30. Apex has just released this 2002, which makes it, as far as we know, the last of that vintage to see daylight. Dark and smoky, it is already heading into more mature, secondary fruit flavors, and has a pleasing softness throughout. Time has sanded away the rough edges of the tannins, and rounded out the herbal components as well. This is drinking very nicely, and gives you a cellared wine at a new wine price. **88** —*P.G. (12/31/2007)*

Apex 1998 Merlot (Columbia Valley (WA)) $30. 86 —*P.G. (6/1/2002)*

Apex 1998 Kestrel Vineyard Merlot (Yakima Valley) $60. 88 —*P.G. (9/1/2002)*

Apex 2006 Dry Riesling (Yakima Valley) $20. This is 100% Riesling, and the intense, floral aromas suggest a smattering of Gewürztraminer, at least in essence if not in fact. Beeswax, lemon candy, orange blossom and other juicy citrus components swirl around the palate, making this an exceptionally complex and beguiling wine. Though labeled dry, it carries an impression of fruit sweetness, rather than the bracing minerality of some other dry Rieslings. A wine that is almost Germanic in its attack, and a truly lovely bottle. **91 Editors' Choice** —*P.G. (12/1/2007)*

Apex 2000 Dry Riesling (Yakima Valley) $15. 85 —*P.G. (6/1/2002)*

Apex 2003 Syrah (Yakima Valley) $30. This is just now being released, unblended Yakima Valley Syrah, with tight, almost impenetrably hard red fruits. It's a little too volatile, with lifted scents that include touches of nail polish, and the tannins are tough and chewy. It's a wine that should be decanted for several hours if you want it to show its best. **85** —*P.G. (12/31/2007)*

Apex 2002 Syrah (Yakima Valley) $25. This is a northern Rhône style, tight, bright, and quite meaty. Along with the pure flavors of 100% Syrah fruit, it brings the tart, citrusy acids that can elevate the mouthfeel, giving it what the Australians call "lift." There's backbone here in the form of acids and a tight spine, and you get the feeling that although it's a 2002, this wine is still wrapped up in its youthful shell. **89** —*P.G. (5/1/2007)*

Apex 2001 Outlook Vineyard Syrah (Yakima Valley) $45. This single vineyard, 100% Syrah provides a clear look at why Washington state is poised to become the nation's leader in producing Rhône-style reds with genuine Rhône character. It's a barrel selection from the vineyard's oldest block (not that old, planted in 1997) but along with the usual dark fruit and pepper you find genuine scents of roasted meat and the garrigue herbs and spices that the Rhône can produce. Excellent length and concentration, but the real achievement here is the way winemaker Brian Carter has captured the essential aromas. **90** —*P.G. (5/1/2007)*

APEX II

Apex II 2004 Cabernet Sauvignon (Columbia Valley (WA)) $16. This is a straightforward style of cool-climate Washington Cabernet. The herbal character of the grape comes through cleanly, with tart red fruits, hints of mushroom and just a bit of dill. Earthy and astringent, it's a wine that would sit solidly alongside a basic bottle of Bordeaux. **86** —*P.G. (5/1/2007)*

Apex II 2001 Cabernet Sauvignon (Yakima Valley) $16. 87 —*P.G. (4/1/2005)*

Apex II 2003 Chardonnay (Yakima Valley) $11. 90 Best Buy —*P.G. (4/1/2005)*

Apex II 2002 Merlot (Yakima Valley) $16. 88 —*P.G. (4/1/2005)*

Apex II 2005 Sauvignon Blanc (Yakima Valley) $12. 88 Editors' Choice —*P.G. (10/1/2006)*

Apex II 2003 Sauvignon Blanc (Yakima Valley) $11. 90 Best Buy —*P.G. (4/1/2005)*

Apex II 2002 Syrah (Yakima Valley) $16. 86 —*P.G. (4/1/2005)*

AQUINAS

Aquinas 2004 Cabernet Sauvignon (Napa Valley) $12. 84 —*S.H. (12/1/2006)*

Aquinas 2003 Cabernet Sauvignon (Napa Valley) $13. 86 —*S.H. (12/1/2005)*

Aquinas 2002 Cabernet Sauvignon (Napa Valley) $10. 85 Best Buy *(12/1/2004)*

Aquinas 2001 Cabernet Sauvignon (Napa Valley) $10. 87 Best Buy —*S.H. (10/1/2004)*

Aquinas 2003 Chardonnay (Napa Valley) $13. 90 Best Buy —*S.H. (6/1/2005)*

Aquinas 2002 Chardonnay (Napa Valley) $10. 84 *(12/1/2004)*

Aquinas 2002 Merlot (Napa Valley) $10. 84 *(12/1/2004)*

Aquinas 2005 Pinot Noir (Napa Valley) $13. This easy going Pinot is light and silky in body, with pleasant cherry, cola and cinnamon spice flavors. It's good enough for curious consumers to find out about Pinot Noir without spending a bundle. **84** —*S.H. (2/1/2007)*

USA

Aquinas 2005 Late Harvest Sauvignon Blanc (Napa Valley) $15. 90 Best Buy —*S.H. (12/15/2006)*

ARAUJO

Araujo 2002 Eisele Vineyard Cabernet Sauvignon (Napa Valley) $185. 96 Cellar Selection —*S.H. (9/1/2006)*

ARBIOS

Arbios 2003 Cabernet Sauvignon (Alexander Valley) $27. On a par with recent vintages, this four-year old Cab is soft and pleasant, with ripe cherry, blackberry, raspberry and herb flavors that are well oaked. The tannins are crunchy, but the wine isn't an ager. Best now through 2009. **87** —*S.H. (12/15/2007)*

Arbios 2002 Cabernet Sauvignon (Alexander Valley) $27. 85 —*S.H. (12/15/2006)*

Arbios 2001 Cabernet Sauvignon (Alexander Valley) $30. 86 —*S.H. (6/1/2005)*

Arbios 2000 Cabernet Sauvignon (Alexander Valley) $30. 90 —*S.H. (11/15/2004)*

Arbios 1999 Cabernet Sauvignon (Alexander Valley) $30. 91 Editors' Choice —*C.S. (11/15/2002)*

Arbios 1997 Cabernet Sauvignon (Sonoma County) $35. 88 *(11/1/2000)*

ARBOR BROOK

Arbor Brook 2005 777 Block Pinot Noir (Chehalem Mountain) $35. This new producer, harvesting fourth-leaf fruit, delivers an interesting young wine. The nose carries scents of leather and barnyard, while in the mouth the lightly spritzy wine tastes like a black cherry soda. Some smoke and leather surface again in the finish, but in terms of weight and extract, it's pretty simple. The finish turns tannic; this will improve with decanting. **88** —*P.G. (11/15/2007)*

ARBOR CREST

Arbor Crest 2002 Dionysus Bordeaux Blend (Columbia Valley (WA)) $45. This blend is 60% Cab Sauvignon, 30% Merlot and 10% Cab Franc, much of it from some of the oldest vines in the state. The winery has given it extended aging in French oak, and despite its 2002 vintage this is a new release. It's a very dark, deep and full-bodied wine. The barrel time has softened and smoothed it, adding flavors such as maple sugar and cedar to the blackberry fruit. Offers an abundance of interesting flavors and it is rare (and laudable) that a winery will sit on such high-priced inventory until it is truly ready for consumption. **90** —*P.G. (5/1/2007)*

Arbor Crest 2002 Cabernet Franc (Columbia Valley (WA)) $16. 89 —*P.G. (4/1/2006)*

Arbor Crest 1999 Conner Lee Vineyard Cabernet Franc (Columbia Valley (WA)) $25. 85 —*P.G. (12/31/2001)*

Arbor Crest 2001 Cabernet Sauvignon (Columbia Valley (WA)) $28. 86 —*P.G. (12/1/2004)*

Arbor Crest 2000 Cabernet Sauvignon (Columbia Valley (WA)) $24. 89 —*P.G. (9/1/2003)*

Arbor Crest 1999 Cabernet Sauvignon (Columbia Valley (WA)) $25. 84 —*P.G. (12/31/2001)*

Arbor Crest 2000 Chardonnay (Columbia Valley (WA)) $14. 87 —*P.G. (9/1/2002)*

Arbor Crest 1999 Chardonnay (Columbia Valley (WA)) $10. 88 Best Buy —*P.G. (6/1/2001)*

Arbor Crest 2002 Conner Lee Chardonnay (Columbia Valley (WA)) $18. 84 —*P.G. (4/1/2005)*

Arbor Crest 1999 Conner Lee Vineyard Chardonnay (Columbia Valley (WA)) $18. 85 —*P.G. (7/1/2002)*

Arbor Crest 2000 Connor Lee Vineyard Chardonnay (Columbia Valley (WA)) $18. 84 —*P.G. (12/31/2002)*

Arbor Crest 2000 Dionysus Meritage (Columbia Valley (WA)) $48. 87 —*P.G. (12/1/2004)*

Arbor Crest 1999 Dionysus Meritage (Columbia Valley (WA)) $45. 87 —*P.G. (12/31/2003)*

Arbor Crest 2001 Dionysus Red Meritage (Columbia Valley (WA)) $40. 87 —*P.G. (4/1/2006)*

Arbor Crest 2003 Merlot (Columbia Valley (WA)) $15. 90 Best Buy —*P.G. (12/31/2006)*

Arbor Crest 2002 Merlot (Columbia Valley (WA)) $15. 87 —*P.G. (4/1/2006)*

Arbor Crest 2001 Merlot (Columbia Valley (WA)) $20. 86 —*P.G. (4/1/2005)*

Arbor Crest 2003 Sangiovese (Columbia Valley (WA)) $13. 88 Best Buy —*P.G. (4/1/2006)*

Arbor Crest 2000 Sangiovese (Columbia Valley (WA)) $18. 85 —*P.G. (12/31/2002)*

Arbor Crest 2005 Sauvignon Blanc (Columbia Valley (WA)) $8. 87 —*P.G. (12/31/2006)*

Arbor Crest 2003 Sauvignon Blanc (Columbia Valley (WA)) $8. 88 Best Buy —*P.G. (4/1/2006)*

Arbor Crest 2002 Sauvignon Blanc (Columbia Valley (WA)) $12. 85 —*P.G. (12/1/2004)*

Arbor Crest 2001 Sauvignon Blanc (Columbia Valley (WA)) $10. 88 Best Buy —*P.G. (12/31/2003)*

Arbor Crest 2000 Sauvignon Blanc (Columbia Valley (WA)) $10. 86 —*P.G. (9/1/2002)*

Arbor Crest 1999 Sauvignon Blanc (Columbia Valley (WA)) $8. 88 Best Buy —*P.G. (6/1/2001)*

Arbor Crest 2003 Syrah (Columbia Valley (WA)) $17. 88 —*P.G. (12/31/2006)*

Arbor Crest 2001 Syrah (Columbia Valley (WA)) $28. 87 —*P.G. (12/1/2004)*

Arbor Crest 1999 Syrah (Columbia Valley (WA)) $26. 83 *(11/1/2001)*

ARCADIAN

Arcadian 2000 Bien Nacido Vineyard Chardonnay (Santa Maria Valley) $25. 84 —*S.H. (5/1/2005)*

Arcadian 1998 Bien Nacido Vineyard Chardonnay (Santa Maria Valley) $30. 87 *(7/1/2001)*

Arcadian 2001 Sleepy Hollow Vineyard Chardonnay (Monterey) $30. 90 —*S.H. (6/1/2005)*

Arcadian 2002 Fiddlestix Vineyard Pinot Noir (Santa Rita Hills) $50. I didn't care much for Arcadian's '01 Fiddlestix, but with the '02, they've hit the mark, producing a Pinot that appeals for its broad, pretty fruit and supple tannins. It's enjoyable now for the ripe cherries, raspberries, tangerines and vanilla cream flavors, but the acids and tannins are such that, even though it's more than four years old, it still has another 6–8 years ahead. **91** —*S.H. (6/1/2007)*

Arcadian 2001 Fiddlestix Vineyard Pinot Noir (Santa Rita Hills) $50. 83 —*S.H. (5/1/2005)*

Arcadian 2001 Francesca Pinot Noir (Central Coast) $75. 84 —*S.H. (5/1/2005)*

Arcadian 2001 Gary's Vineyard Pinot Noir (Monterey) $50. 87 —*S.H. (5/1/2005)*

Arcadian 1999 Pisoni Pinot Noir (Monterey County) $80. 91 Cellar Selection *(10/1/2002)*

Arcadian 2001 Pisoni Vineyard Pinot Noir (Monterey) $75. 87 —*S.H. (6/1/2005)*

Arcadian 2003 Rio Vista Vineyard Pinot Noir (Santa Rita Hills) $65. There's a rich, earthy grounding to the intensely ripe cherry, cola, vanilla, cinnamon, clove and brine flavors that makes this savory wine balanced and interesting. At nearly four years of age, it tastes fresh and young, and has a good eight years ahead of complexity. **91** —*S.H. (6/1/2007)*

Arcadian 2002 Sleepy Hollow Vineyard Pinot Noir (Santa Lucia Highlands) $45. 90 —*S.H. (6/1/2005)*

Arcadian 2001 Sleepy Hollow Vineyard Pinot Noir (Santa Lucia Highlands) $45. 86 —*S.H. (5/1/2005)*

Arcadian 1999 Gary's Vineyard Syrah (Monterey) $50. 90 *(11/1/2001)*

Arcadian 2001 Gary's Vineyard Syrah (Santa Lucia Highlands) $45. 82 —*S.H. (5/1/2005)*

ARCHERY SUMMIT

Archery Summit 2000 Vireton Pinot Gris (Oregon) $26. 89 —*P.G. (2/1/2002)*

Archery Summit 1999 Archery Summit Estate Pinot Noir (Oregon) $115. 90 Cellar Selection *(10/1/2002)*

Archery Summit 2003 Arcus Estate Pinot Noir (Willamette Valley) $75. 86 —*P.G. (12/1/2006)*

Archery Summit 2000 Arcus Estate Pinot Noir (Oregon) $53. 87 —*P.G. (4/1/2003)*

Archery Summit 1999 Arcus Estate Pinot Noir (Oregon) $75. 90 —*P.G. (11/1/2001)*

Archery Summit 2004 Estate Pinot Noir (Dundee Hills) $150. This is from the vineyard that surrounds the winery, and the bottling receives both Estate and Dundee Hills designations—best of the best. It's a pungent, pleasant wine upon entry, with rather pale strawberry fruit. It quickly moves through the midpalate and turns lean, with tomato leaf and green tea astringency. There is a slight impression of alcoholic heat. Though accessible and interesting, it somehow falls short of what it could/should be, given its provenance and price. **88** *—P.G. (11/15/2007)*

Archery Summit 2003 Estate Pinot Noir (Willamette Valley) $150. 89 *—P.G. (12/1/2006)*

Archery Summit 2000 Premier Cuvée Pinot Noir (Oregon) $45. 85 *—P.G. (4/1/2003)*

Archery Summit 1999 Premier Cuvée Pinot Noir (Willamette Valley) $45. 89 *(10/1/2002)*

Archery Summit 2003 Premier Cuvée Pinot Noir (Willamette Valley) $37. 87 *—P.G. (12/1/2006)*

Archery Summit 2004 Red Hills Estate Pinot Noir (Dundee Hills) $75. Spicy and a bit rough, this is a tannic wine, hard and tart. There's a subtle undertone of metal, and a slight greenness to the fruit; overall a lack of what you might call elegance. In this price range, you hope to find more detail and precision than is offered here. This wine seems to fade away quickly, leaving a stemmy, bitter impression. **87** *—P.G. (2/1/2007)*

Archery Summit 2003 Red Hills Estate Pinot Noir (Willamette Valley) $75. 86 *—P.G. (12/1/2006)*

Archery Summit 2000 Red Hills Estate Pinot Noir (Oregon) $70. 88 *—M.S. (9/1/2003)*

Archery Summit 1999 Red Hills Estate Pinot Noir (Willamette Valley) $75. 86 *(10/1/2002)*

Archery Summit 2003 Renegade Ridge Estate Pinot Noir (Willamette Valley) $60. 88 *—P.G. (12/1/2006)*

Archery Summit 2002 Renegade Ridge Estate Pinot Noir (Oregon) $60. 84 *(11/1/2004)*

Archery Summit 2000 Renegade Ridge Estate Pinot Noir (Oregon) $60. 90 *—M.S. (9/1/2003)*

ARCHIPEL

Archipel 2002 Bordeaux Blend (Sonoma-Napa) $40. 87 *—S.H. (12/31/2006)*

ARCIERO

Arciero 1999 Chardonnay (California) $10. 83 *—S.H. (5/1/2001)*

Arciero 1998 Merlot (Central Coast) $12. 82 *—S.H. (5/1/2001)*

Arciero 1998 Petite Sirah (Paso Robles) $14. 84 *—S.H. (5/1/2001)*

Arciero 1998 Estate Bottled Pinot Grigio (Paso Robles) $12. 86 Best Buy *(8/1/1999)*

Arciero 1998 Arpeggio Red Blend (Paso Robles) $15. 81 *—S.H. (5/1/2001)*

ARDENTE

Ardente 2000 Estate Cabernet Sauvignon (Atlas Peak) $45. 85 *—S.H. (11/15/2004)*

ARGER-MARTUCCI

Arger-Martucci 2002 Cabernet Sauvignon (Napa Valley) $60. 88 Cellar Selection *—S.H. (9/1/2006)*

Arger-Martucci 2001 Cabernet Sauvignon (Napa Valley) $50. 87 *—S.H. (10/1/2004)*

Arger-Martucci 2000 Cabernet Sauvignon (Napa Valley) $50. 85 *—S.H. (11/15/2004)*

Arger-Martucci 1999 Cabernet Sauvignon (Napa Valley) $50. 85 *—S.H. (11/15/2002)*

Arger-Martucci 2002 Chardonnay (Carneros) $22. 91 *—S.H. (12/15/2004)*

Arger-Martucci 2000 Chardonnay (Carneros) $30. 89 *—S.H. (12/15/2002)*

Arger-Martucci 2002 Pinot Noir (Carneros) $30. 83 *—S.H. (10/1/2006)*

Arger-Martucci 2000 Pinot Noir (Carneros) $40. 85 *—S.H. (4/1/2003)*

Arger-Martucci 2004 Syrah (Napa Valley) $30. 89 *—S.H. (10/1/2006)*

Arger-Martucci 2003 Syrah (Napa Valley) $25. 88 *(9/1/2005)*

Arger-Martucci 2004 Viognier (Russian River Valley) $25. 84 *—S.H. (10/1/2006)*

ARGYLE

Argyle 1999 Brut Champagne Blend (Willamette Valley) $21. 88 *—P.G. (12/31/2004)*

Argyle 1997 Brut Champagne Blend (Willamette Valley) $21. 87 *—P.G. (12/1/2001)*

Argyle 1996 Brut Champagne Blend (Willamette Valley) $22. 87 *—S.H. (12/1/2000)*

Argyle 1999 Brut Rosé Champagne Blend (Willamette Valley) $21. 87 *—P.G. (12/31/2004)*

Argyle 1991 Extended Tirage-Disgorged on Demand Champagne Blend (Willamette Valley) $22. 88 *—K.F. (12/1/2002)*

Argyle 1989 Extended Tirage Brut Champagne Blend (Willamette Valley) $30. 86 *—M.M. (12/1/2000)*

Argyle 1989 Extended Tirage Brut Champagne Blend (Willamette Valley) $30. 87 *—P.G. (12/1/2001)*

Argyle 1997 Knudsen Vineyard Blanc de Blancs "Julia Lee's Block" Champagne Blend (Willamette Valley) $30. 90 *—P.G. (12/31/2004)*

Argyle 1997 Knudsen Vineyard Brut Champagne Blend (Willamette Valley) $30. 90 *—P.G. (12/31/2004)*

Argyle 1996 Knudsen Vineyard Brut Champagne Blend (Willamette Valley) $35. 89 *—P.G. (12/31/2000)*

Argyle 1996 Knudsen Vineyard Julia Lee's Block Blanc de Blancs Champagne Blend (Willamette Valley) $30. 87 *—P.G. (12/1/2000)*

Argyle 1995 Knudsen's Vineyard Julis Lee's Champagne Blend (Willamette Valley) $30. 88 *(12/15/1999)*

Argyle 1996 Knutsen Vineyard Blanc de Blancs Champagne Blend (Willamette Valley) $30. 88 *—P.G. (12/1/2001)*

Argyle 1996 Knutsen Vineyard Brut Champagne Blend (Willamette Valley) $35. 89 *—P.G. (12/1/2001)*

Argyle 1999 Nuthouse Chardonnay (Willamette Valley) $28. 89 *—P.G. (8/1/2002)*

Argyle 1997 Nuthouse Chardonnay (Willamette Valley) $28. 90 *—M.S. (4/1/2000)*

Argyle 1999 Reserve Chardonnay (Willamette Valley) $20. 90 *—P.G. (7/1/2002)*

Argyle 1997 Reserve Chardonnay (Willamette Valley) $21. 84 *—M.S. (4/1/2000)*

Argyle 2004 Pinot Noir (Willamette Valley) $20. 88 *—P.G. (11/15/2005)*

Argyle 2002 Pinot Noir (Willamette Valley) $18. 87 *(11/1/2004)*

Argyle 1998 Pinot Noir (Willamette Valley) $16. 87 Best Buy *—P.G. (9/1/2000)*

Argyle 2002 Nuthouse Pinot Noir (Willamette Valley) $40. 92 Editors' Choice *—P.G. (8/1/2005)*

Argyle 2000 Nuthouse Pinot Noir (Willamette Valley) $40. 88 *(10/1/2002)*

Argyle 1998 Nuthouse Pinot Noir (Willamette Valley) $40. 92 *(12/1/2000)*

Argyle 1997 Nuthouse Pinot Noir (Willamette Valley) $35. 91 *(10/1/1999)*

Argyle 2003 Reserve Pinot Noir (Willamette Valley) $30. 89 *—P.G. (11/15/2005)*

Argyle 2002 Reserve Pinot Noir (Willamette Valley) $30. 87 *(11/1/2004)*

Argyle 1998 Reserve Pinot Noir (Willamette Valley) $30. 91 *—M.M. (12/1/2000)*

Argyle 2000 Spirit House Pinot Noir (Willamette Valley) $50. 89 *(10/1/2002)*

Argyle 1998 Spirit House Pinot Noir (Willamette Valley) $50. 88 *—J.C. (12/1/2000)*

Argyle 2004 Riesling (Willamette Valley) $25. 86 *—P.G. (11/15/2005)*

Argyle 2000 Brut Sparkling Blend (Willamette Valley) $21. 90 *—P.G. (11/15/2005)*

Argyle 2003 Brut Rosé Sparkling Blend (Willamette Valley) $25. 88 *—P.G. (12/31/2005)*

Argyle 1994 Extended Tirage Sparkling Blend (Willamette Valley) $34. 91 Editors' Choice *—P.G. (12/31/2004)*

Argyle 1995 Extended Tirage Brut Sparkling Blend (Willamette Valley) $35. 91 *P.G. (12/31/2005)*

Argyle 1998 Knudsen Vineyard Brut Sparkling Blend (Willamette Valley) $30. 86 *—P.G. (12/31/2005)*

ARISTA

Arista 2004 Pinot Noir (Russian River Valley) $28. 87 *—S.H. (10/1/2006)*

Arista 2004 Ferrington Vineyard Pinot Noir (Anderson Valley) $54. Here's a wine that will appeal to some Pinot lovers but will leave others cold. It's not opulent, but elegant, a subtle, very dry, high acid wine that's either thin or complex, depending on your point of view. For me, the cola, sour cherry and minty flavors are too light. **84** *—S.H. (2/1/2007)*

Arista 2003 Ferrington Vineyard Pinot Noir (Anderson Valley) $50. 94 *—S.H. (2/1/2006)*

Arista 2004 Harper's Rest Pinot Noir (Russian River Valley) $38. 91 *—S.H. (10/1/2006)*

Arista 2003 Harper's Rest Pinot Noir (Russian River Valley) $35. 90 *—S.H. (2/1/2006)*

Arista 2004 Longbow Pinot Noir (Russian River Valley) $38. 93 Editors' Choice *—S.H. (10/1/2006)*

Arista 2004 Mononi Vineyard Pinot Noir (Russian River Valley) $54. Dry, crisp and elegant, with a silky texture made for food, this vineyard-designated Pinot could use more fruity substance and intensity. There are cherry, cola, rosehip tea and rhubarb flavors, but the wine is light, with a one-dimensionality. **86** *—S.H. (2/1/2007)*

Arista 2003 Mononi Vineyard Pinot Noir (Russian River Valley) $50. 93 *—S.H. (2/1/2006)*

Arista 2004 Toboni Vineyard Pinot Noir (Russian River Valley) $54. I admire the evident intentions here, to avoid overripeness and produce a more elegant Pinot Noir. While it's a good Pinot, with a nice silkiness, the wine is just too dry and acidic, with a green, minty streak that barely suggests cola and cherries. **84** *—S.H. (2/1/2007)*

Arista 2003 Toboni Vineyard Pinot Noir (Russian River Valley) $50. 94 *—S.H. (2/1/2006)*

ARMAGH

Armagh 2003 Syrah (Sonoma Coast) $25. 90 *—S.H. (12/31/2005)*

ARMIDA

Armida 1997 Chardonnay (Russian River Valley) $12. 87 *—J.C. (10/1/1999)*

Armida 2004 Keefer Ranch Chardonnay (Russian River Valley) $28. 92 *—S.H. (12/15/2006)*

Armida 1997 Merlot (Russian River Valley) $22. 83 *—J.C. (7/1/2000)*

Armida 2004 Castelli-Knight Ranch Vineyard Pinot Noir (Russian River Valley) $36. 91 *—S.H. (12/15/2006)*

Armida 2004 Sauvignon Blanc (Russian River Valley) $20. 84 *(7/1/2005)*

Armida 1996 Zinfandel (Russian River Valley) $20. 84 *—J.C. (9/1/1999)*

Armida 2001 Maple Vineyard Zinfandel (Dry Creek Valley) $30. 87 *(11/1/2003)*

Armida 1998 Maple Vineyard Zinfandel (Dry Creek Valley) $22.87 *—M.S. (5/1/2000)*

Armida 2004 PoiZin Zinfandel (Sonoma County) $25. 86 *—S.H. (12/15/2006)*

Armida 2004 Tre Torrente Vineyard Zinfandel (Dry Creek Valley) $34. 90 *—S.H. (12/15/2006)*

ARNOLD PALMER

Arnold Palmer 2004 Chardonnay (California) $15. 84 *—S.H. (5/1/2006)*

ARNS

Arns 2000 Cabernet Sauvignon (Napa Valley) $60. 92 *—J.M. (11/15/2003)*

Arns 1998 Cabernet Sauvignon (Napa Valley) $50. 85 *—S.H. (11/15/2003)*

ARROW CREEK

Arrow Creek 2004 Pinot Grigio (California) $10. 85 Best Buy *—S.H. (4/1/2006)*

ARROWOOD

Arrowood 2003 Cabernet Sauvignon (Sonoma County) $50. They kept this Cab back all this time, presumably at some cost to the company, but consumers are the beneficiaries. Everything has mellowed. The wine, with 1% Petit Verdot, is like hands of cassis, dark chocolate and oak massaging the palate. The grapes were sourced from top vineyards in the Dry Creek, Sonoma and Alexander Valleys. Drink now–2010. **93** *—S.H. (12/1/2007)*

Arrowood 2001 Cabernet Sauvignon (Sonoma County) $45. 93 Editors' Choice *—S.H. (12/1/2005)*

Arrowood 2000 Cabernet Sauvignon (Sonoma County) $45. 90 *—S.H. (12/31/2004)*

Arrowood 2001 Grand Archer Cabernet Sauvignon (Sonoma County) $22. 86 *—S.H. (10/1/2004)*

Arrowood 2000 Grand Archer Cabernet Sauvignon (Sonoma County) $20. 85 *—S.H. (2/1/2003)*

Arrowood 1999 Grand Archer Cabernet Sauvignon (Sonoma County) $22. 87 *—S.H. (7/1/2002)*

Arrowood 1999 Reserve Speciale Cabernet Sauvignon (Sonoma County) $85. 92 *—S.H. (11/15/2003)*

Arrowood 2005 Chardonnay (Sonoma County) $30. Here's a polished Chard with an elegant balance to a variety that often lacks both. Everything is here, from the ripe tropical fruit and rich oak to the crisp acidity and mineral trimmings, all poised in perfect equilibrium. **90** *—S.H. (12/1/2007)*

Arrowood 2004 Chardonnay (Sonoma County) $29. A rich, complex wine of the kind we need more of. Packed with ripe pear, peach, mango and pineapple flavors that are well-oaked, and delicately balanced with acidity. **92** *—S.H. (7/1/2007)*

Arrowood 2002 Chardonnay (Sonoma County) $29. 90 *—S.H. (9/1/2004)*

Arrowood 2001 Chardonnay (Sonoma County) $29. 87 *—S.H. (6/1/2003)*

Arrowood 1998 Chardonnay (South Coast) $25. 91 *—S.H. (12/1/2001)*

Arrowood 2002 Grand Archer Chardonnay (Sonoma County) $16. 88 *—S.H. (12/1/2005)*

Arrowood 2001 Grand Archer Chardonnay (Sonoma County) $18. 87 *—S.H. (8/1/2003)*

Arrowood 2000 Grand Archer Chardonnay (Sonoma County) $18. 85 *—S.H. (5/1/2002)*

Arrowood 1998 Reserve Speciale Cuvée Michel Berthoud Chardonnay (Sonoma County) $38. 91 *(7/1/2001)*

Arrowood 2002 Reserve Speciale, Cuvée Michel Berthoud Chardonnay (Russian River Valley) $35. 92 *—S.H. (12/1/2005)*

Arrowood 2002 Saralee's Vineyard Gewürztraminer (Russian River Valley) $20. 86 *—S.H. (7/1/2003)*

Arrowood 2002 Merlot (Sonoma County) $42. As much as I like this Merlot, it feels like they let it get too ripe and gave it too much oak. It was a great vintage, and the grapes ripened effortlessly. Yet there's a baked fruit, toothpicky oakiness that robs the wine of elegance. **86** *—S.H. (10/1/2007)*

Arrowood 2001 Merlot (Sonoma County) $42. 88 *—M.S. (12/31/2006)*

Arrowood 1998 Merlot (Sonoma County) $42. 89 *—P.G. (12/1/2001)*

Arrowood 2001 Grand Archer Merlot (Sonoma County) $16. 87 *—S.H. (12/1/2005)*

Arrowood 2000 Grand Archer Merlot (Sonoma County) $18. 86 *—S.H. (2/1/2003)*

Arrowood 1999 Grand Archer Merlot (Sonoma County) $20. 90 *—S.H. (9/1/2002)*

Arrowood 2000 Unfined & Unfiltered Merlot (Sonoma County) $42. 89 *—S.H. (12/31/2003)*

Arrowood 2001 Select Late Harvest White Riesling Riesling (Alexander Valley) $25. 84 *—S.H. (12/1/2003)*

Arrowood 2005 Special Select Late Harvest White Riesling (Alexander Valley) $45. This wine is so loaded with glycerine, it actually pours slow from the bottle, like honey. With 17.4 grams of residual sugar, it's decadently, deliriously sweet, but sugar is not its only charm. There's a fabulous flood of apricots, pineapples, peaches and limes, concentrated to their essence and geléed, enriched with pure vanilla and clover honey and dusted with cinnamon. Doesn't that sound good? **95 Editors' Choice** *—S.H. (12/1/2007)*

Arrowood 2001 Special Select Late Harvest White Riesling Hoot Owl Creek Vineyards Riesling (Alexander Valley) $40. 93 *—S.H. (12/1/2003)*

Arrowood 1999 Syrah (Sonoma Valley) $55. 85 *—J.M. (12/1/2002)*

Arrowood 2001 Grand Archer Syrah (Sonoma County) $16. 85 *—S.H. (12/1/2005)*

Arrowood 2001 Le Beau Melange Syrah (Sonoma Valley) $35. 88 *(9/1/2005)*

Arrowood 2003 Saralee's Vineyard Syrah (Russian River Valley) $40. Arrowood's Saralee's always is balanced and dry, but quality varies by vintage. The '03 is a very good wine, rich in licorice-accented cassis and pepper flavors, with a generous coating of smoky oak. It's not a big wine, or ageable, but it does have grace and elegance now and for a year or two. **87** *—S.H. (12/1/2007)*

Arrowood 2001 Saralee's Vineyard Syrah (Russian River Valley) $39. 91 Cellar Selection *(9/1/2005)*

Arrowood 1999 Saralee's Vineyard Syrah (Russian River Valley) $62. 88 *—J.M. (12/1/2002)*

Arrowood 1998 Saralee's Vineyard Syrah (Russian River Valley) $60. 89 *(11/1/2001)*

Arrowood 2000 Saralee's Vineyard-Unfined & Unfiltered Syrah (Russian River Valley) $35. 86 *—S.H. (12/1/2003)*

Arrowood 2000 Unfined & Unfiltered Syrah (Sonoma Valley) $40. 86 *—S.H. (12/1/2003)*

Arrowood 1997 Viognier (Russian River Valley) $30. 91 *—S.H. (6/1/1999)*

Arrowood 2003 Saralee's Vineyard Viognier (Russian River Valley) $30. 91 *—S.H. (2/1/2005)*

Arrowood 2001 Saralee's Vineyard Viognier (Russian River Valley) $30. 88 *—S.H. (6/1/2003)*

Arrowood 2002 Saralee's Vineyard Viognier (Russian River Valley) $30. 91 *—S.H. (6/1/2004)*

ARTESA

Artesa 2005 Albariño (Carneros) $18. Albariño is turning into my favorite dry white wine. It's what Pinot Gris/Grigio claimed to be, and so often isn't. This one's really dry and acidic, with really minerally citrus flavors. Bring on the salty tapas. **90 Editors' Choice** *—S.H. (10/1/2007)*

Artesa 2001 Elements Bordeaux Blend (Sonoma-Napa) $20. 85 *—S.H. (5/1/2005)*

Artesa 2004 Limited Release Cabernet Franc (Alexander Valley) $40. Although there's promise, this is rustic now, with very dry herb, rhubarb, cola and cherry flavors that finish with a tannic, peppery astringency. **85** *—S.H. (10/1/2007)*

Artesa 2003 Cabernet Sauvignon (Alexander Valley) $40. Not in the same league as the opulent '02, the '03 is drier and less ripe, although it has an elegant tannic structure. The cherry and cassis flavors have a strongly herbal edge of dried thyme and dill. Drink now. **87** *—S.H. (10/1/2007)*

Artesa 2003 Cabernet Sauvignon (Napa-Sonoma) $25. 86 *—S.H. (12/31/2006)*

Artesa 2002 Cabernet Sauvignon (Napa-Sonoma) $25. 83 *—S.H. (12/15/2005)*

Artesa 2002 Cabernet Sauvignon (Alexander Valley) $40. 91 *—S.H. (7/1/2006)*

Artesa 1998 Cabernet Sauvignon (Napa Valley) $30. 92 *—S.H. (11/15/2002)*

Artesa 1997 Cabernet Sauvignon (Napa Valley) $33. 89 *—S.H. (12/1/2001)*

Artesa 2003 Reserve Cabernet Sauvignon (Napa Valley) $40. 85 *—S.H. (12/31/2006)*

Artesa 1997 Reserve Cabernet Sauvignon (Napa Valley) $70. 90 *—S.H. (6/1/2002)*

Artesa 2002 Chardonnay (Napa Valley) $16. 86 *—S.H. (8/1/2005)*

Artesa 2000 Chardonnay (Carneros) $23. 86 *—S.H. (2/1/2003)*

Artesa 1999 Chardonnay (Napa Valley) $23. 87 *—S.H. (12/1/2001)*

Artesa 1999 Chardonnay (Carneros) $23. 89 *—S.H. (12/1/2001)*

Artesa 2004 Estate Chardonnay (Carneros) $30. 86 *—S.H. (6/1/2006)*

Artesa 2005 Limited Release Chardonnay (Carneros) $35. There's just too much oak on this otherwise fine Chard. It's like drinking toothpicks, all sweet vanilla char, toasted meringue and caramel. Too bad, because the underlying wine is filled with polished mineral and fruit flavors. **84** *—S.H. (10/1/2007)*

Artesa 2002 Reserve Chardonnay (Carneros) $40. 90 *—S.H. (8/1/2005)*

Artesa 1999 Reserve Chardonnay (Carneros) $30. 90 *—S.H. (12/1/2001)*

Artesa 1997 Reserve Chardonnay (Carneros) $30. 88 *(6/1/2000)*

Artesa 1999 Select Late Harvest Gewürztraminer (Russian River Valley) $28. 87 *—J.M. (12/1/2002)*

Artesa 1998 Merlot (Napa Valley) $22. 91 *—S.H. (11/15/2002)*

Artesa 1997 Merlot (Napa Valley) $24. 91 Editors' Choice *—S.H. (12/1/2001)*

Artesa 1997 Merlot (Sonoma Valley) $24. 88 *—S.H. (12/1/2001)*

Artesa 1999 Reserve Merlot (Sonoma Valley) $60. 86 *(5/1/2004)*

Artesa 1997 Reserve Merlot (Sonoma Valley) $60. 91 *—S.H. (7/1/2002)*

Artesa 2002 Pinot Noir (Carneros) $22. 88 *(11/1/2004)*

Artesa 2000 Pinot Noir (Santa Barbara County) $24. 82 *(10/1/2002)*

Artesa 2000 Pinot Noir (Russian River Valley) $24. 89 Editor's Choice. *(10/1/2002)*

Artesa 2000 Pinot Noir (Carneros) $24. 91 Editors' Choice *(10/1/2002)*

Artesa 1999 Pinot Noir (Santa Barbara County) $24. 89 *—S.H. (12/15/2001)*

Artesa 1999 Pinot Noir (Russian River Valley) $24. 88 *—S.H. (12/15/2001)*

Artesa 1999 Pinot Noir (Carneros) $24. 87 *—S.H. (12/15/2001)*

Artesa 2004 Estate Pinot Noir (Carneros) $40. 85 *—S.H. (6/1/2006)*

Artesa 2004 Reserve Pinot Noir (Carneros) $50. 91 *—S.H. (12/31/2006)*

Artesa 2002 Reserve Pinot Noir (Carneros) $40. 86 *(11/1/2004)*

Artesa 2000 Reserve Pinot Noir (Carneros) $38. 88 *(10/1/2002)*

Artesa 1999 Reserve Pinot Noir (Carneros) $40. 92 *—S.H. (12/15/2001)*

Artesa 2002 Reserve Sauvignon Blanc (Napa Valley) $20. 86 *(7/1/2005)*

Artesa 1999 Reserve Sauvignon Blanc (Napa Valley) $19. 90 *—S.H. (11/15/2001)*

Artesa 2001 Syrah (Sonoma Valley) $16. 84 *(9/1/2005)*

Artesa 1999 Syrah (Sonoma Valley) $28. 90 *(11/1/2001)*

USA

Artesa 2003 Tempranillo (Alexander Valley) $24. 87 *—S.H. (4/1/2006)*

ARTEVINO

Artevino 2005 Reserve Chardonnay (Mendocino) $32. There's a succulent richness to this Burgundian-inspired Chard that makes it delicious. It's bright in acids, the main ingredient needed to balance the opulent pineapple, peach, yellow apricot vanilla custard and smoky oak flavors. Creamy and dry, it provides pleasure all the way through. **92** *—S.H. (11/1/2007)*

Artevino 2005 Lost Creek Pinot Noir (Yorkville Highlands) $32. Dry and rather tough in tannins, this may be one to cellar. It shows bitter cherryskin, cola and tobacco flavors, enhanced with oak, in a smooth, complex texture. Could do interesting things over the next five years, but who knows? The appellation, on a high plateau of coastal Mendocino County, has yet to define itself. **87** *—S.H. (11/1/2007)*

Artevino 2001 Zinfandel (North Coast) $22. 84 *(11/1/2003)*

Artevino 2005 Largo Ridge Zinfandel (Mendocino County) $26. Technically, the wine is too soft and hot for balance, but it's so luscious, so enjoyable, you can't help but like it. The flavors just swarm all over the palate, offering cherries, blueberries, cola, violets, leather, bacon, carob and Asian spices, and the finish is satisfyingly complex and dry. **88** *—S.H. (11/1/2007)*

ARTEZIN

Artezin 2004 Zinfandel (Mendocino-Sonoma-Amador) $15. 84 *—S.H. (12/15/2006)*

Artezin 2003 Zinfandel (Mendocino-Amador-Napa) $15. 90 Best Buy *—S.H. (12/15/2005)*

ASH HOLLOW

Ash Hollow 2002 Estate Blend Bordeaux Blend (Walla Walla (WA)) $30. 88 *—P.G. (4/1/2005)*

Ash Hollow 2004 Cabernet Sauvignon (Walla Walla (WA)) $28. Sharp-edged aromatics start off the nose, but the wine takes over with good grip and texture once it hits the mouth. It fills the palate with muscular blueberry flavors, subtle, acid-driven, aromatic and textural. Woven into the fruit are some chewy leaf and earth flavors, but it's nicely integrated. Flavors extend into and through an interesting, nicely textured finish. **89** *—P.G. (11/1/2007)*

Ash Hollow 2003 Cabernet Sauvignon (Walla Walla (WA)) $28. 86 *—P.G. (4/1/2006)*

Ash Hollow 2006 Gewürztraminer (Columbia Valley (WA)) $19. This was fermented completely in stainless, and finished totally dry. Made from 12-year-old vines, it punches up the aromatics, and focuses on grapefruit and other citrus flavors. Good length and plenty of acid make it a crisp, food-friendly wine, and though it is not labeled dry, it tastes like it. **90** *—P.G. (11/1/2007)*

Ash Hollow 2004 Merlot (Columbia Valley (WA)) $24. It's scented with a pretty mix of sandalwood, toasted cracker and blackberry jam, and the flavors follow into tart berry and black cherry. There's noticeable acid and some interesting grace notes, suggestive of flint and gun metal. The flavors linger pleasantly in the back of the throat. This is not a fleshy Merlot by any means, but it is polished and evocative, and I like the suggestions of rock and iron ore that it has captured with the black cherry fruit. **89** *—P.G. (8/1/2007)*

Ash Hollow 2003 Merlot (Walla Walla (WA)) $24. 86 *—P.G. (4/1/2006)*

Ash Hollow 2006 Special Release Pinot Gris (Columbia Valley (WA)) $19. From Minick Vineyard fruit, this is quite similar to the winery's Sauvignon Blanc, but with a tilt toward pear rather than apple flavors. A high-flying, high-acid wine, it's lightly annotated with spice and citrus skin. Clean and straightforward. **87** *—P.G. (11/1/2007)*

Ash Hollow 2004 Red Blend (Columbia Valley (WA)) $38. This Bordeaux-based wine (40% Cab Sauvignon, 40% Merlot, 20% Cab Franc) is a supple, muscular red, one that retains its elegance and aromatic perfume, but works in some darker notes and moderate amounts of toast and tar. There's good balance, length and mouthfeel, with fruits trending from red on into black. The finish tails off into some lightly grainy/grassy flavors, losing its concentration. **88** *—P.G. (11/1/2007)*

Ash Hollow 2003 Terassa Red Blend (Walla Walla (WA)) $36. 87 *—P.G. (4/1/2006)*

Ash Hollow 2006 Special Release Sauvignon Blanc (Columbia Valley (WA)) $19. This is 100% varietal, and quite dry, clean and fresh, with tangy green apple/lemon fruit. It shows a bit of a Friuli influence (cold fermentation in stainless steel), but without the lush textures. Winemaker Steve Clifton has a very nice touch, cajoling out light cut grass and herb scents, while maintaining firm acids. **88** *—P.G. (11/1/2007)*

Ash Hollow 2005 Syrah (Walla Walla (WA)) $24. A lean, spicy, cool-climate Syrah, with piercing notes of herb, citrus rind and resin. The fruit is brambly and sharp, just hinting at smoked meats. Though it may become more complex and interesting with more time in the bottle, it is still very young and edgy. Give it plenty of breathing time. 89 —*P.G. (11/1/2007)*

Ash Hollow 2006 White Blend (Columbia Valley (WA)) $20. This is a full and flavorful blend of Sauvignon Blanc and Pinot Gris. The Gris carries a bit of oiliness and balances out the grassier Sauvignon. I like the wine's weight and detail, and its flavors of mixed grain, light herb, citrus and acid. Somehow it strikes me as a good sushi wine, one that could even handle a bit of vinegar. 89 —*P.G. (11/1/2007)*

Ash Hollow 2003 Somanna White Blend (Columbia Valley (WA)) $20. 87 —*P.G. (4/1/2005)*

ASHLAND VINEYARDS

Ashland Vineyards 1999 Chardonnay (Rogue Valley) $8. 83 —*P.G. (8/1/2002)*

Ashland Vineyards 1999 Pinot Gris (Rogue Valley) $10. 83 —*P.G. (2/1/2002)*

ASTRALE E TERRA

Astrale e Terra 2001 Arcturus Cabernet Blend (Napa Valley) $39. 91 —*S.H. (10/1/2005)*

Astrale e Terra 2002 Arcturus Cabernet Sauvignon (Napa Valley) $39. Great Cab, but even at four-plus years, it's young and dry, with gritty Atlas Peak tannins, so cellar it for four or five years and let it soften. Shows ripe blackberry, cassis and blueberry flavors, with a rich, spicy coating of new oak, and finishes thoroughly dry. Should develop for a decade and hold for another 10 years. 93 Cellar Selection —*S.H. (4/1/2007)*

Astrale e Terra 2002 Syrah (Napa Valley) $28. From the black color and glycerine stains, you can tell this is a high-extract wine. It's very dry, with huge blackberry pie filling and caramelly new oak flavors that flood the mouth, leading to a long finish. It's thick and immature now, and needs time. Better after mid-2007. 88 —*S.H. (4/1/2007)*

ATALON

Atalon 2002 Beckstoffer Tokalon Vineyard Cabernet Blend (Oakville) $NA. 91 —*S.H. (6/1/2005)*

Atalon 1998 Beckstoffer Vineyard Cabernet Blend (Oakville) $NA. 87 —*S.H. (6/1/2005)*

Atalon 1997 Beckstoffer Vineyard Cabernet Blend (Oakville) $NA. 92 —*S.H. (6/1/2005)*

Atalon 2000 Cabernet Sauvignon (Napa Valley) $35. 90 —*S.H. (12/31/2003)*

Atalon 1999 Beckstoffer Cabernet Sauvignon (Oakville) $90. 91 *(8/1/2003)*

Atalon 1999 Beckstoffer Tokalon Vineyard Cabernet Sauvignon (Napa Valley) $NA. 94 Cellar Selection —*S.H. (6/1/2005)*

Atalon 1997 Mountain Estates Merlot (Napa Valley) $60. 92 —*J.M. (11/15/2001)*

ATELIER

Atelier 2003 Syrah (Alexander Valley) $28. 83 —*S.H. (12/1/2005)*

ATLAS PEAK

Atlas Peak 2003 Claret Cabernet Blend (Atlas Peak) $86. 87 —*S.H. (12/15/2006)*

Atlas Peak 2003 Cabernet Sauvignon (Howell Mountain) $86. 92 Cellar Selection —*S.H. (12/15/2006)*

Atlas Peak 2003 Cabernet Sauvignon (Mount Veeder) $86. 90 Cellar Selection —*S.H. (12/15/2006)*

Atlas Peak 2003 Cabernet Sauvignon (Napa Valley) $42. 86 —*S.H. (11/15/2006)*

Atlas Peak 2003 Cabernet Sauvignon (Spring Mountain) $86. 87 —*S.H. (12/15/2006)*

Atlas Peak 2002 Cabernet Sauvignon (Napa Valley) $38. 91 —*S.H. (5/1/2006)*

Atlas Peak 1997 Consenso Cabernet Sauvignon (Atlas Peak) $30. 84 —*S.H. (6/1/2003)*

Atlas Peak 1996 Consenso Vineyard Cabernet Sauvignon (Napa Valley) $30. 84 —*S.H. (2/1/2000)*

Atlas Peak 1998 Chardonnay (Atlas Peak) $16. 88 *(6/1/2000)*

Atlas Peak 2001 Chardonnay (Atlas Peak) $16. 87 —*S.H. (6/1/2003)*

Atlas Peak 1999 Chardonnay (Atlas Peak) $16. 87 —*S.H. (5/1/2001)*

Atlas Peak 2000 Atlas Peak Chardonnay (Atlas Peak) $16. 86 —*S.H. (12/31/2001)*

Atlas Peak 2001 Sangiovese (Atlas Peak) $16. 84 —*S.H. (10/1/2005)*

Atlas Peak 2000 Sangiovese (Atlas Peak) $16. 86 —*S.H. (2/1/2003)*

Atlas Peak 1999 Sangiovese (Atlas Peak) $16. 90 —*S.H. (12/15/2001)*

Atlas Peak 1999 Sangiovese (Napa Valley) $16. 87 —*S.H. (11/15/2001)*

Atlas Peak 1997 Sangiovese (Atlas Peak) $16. 87 —*S.H. (5/1/2001)*

Atlas Peak 2000 Reserve Sangiovese (Atlas Peak) $30. 87 —*S.H. (9/1/2003)*

Atlas Peak 1997 Reserve Sangiovese (Napa Valley) $24. 92 *(11/15/1999)*

ATWATER

Atwater 2005 Riesling (America) $15. Apples and vanilla toast on the nose lead to pear, lime and honey on the palate with this easy-drinking wine from Seneca Lake producer Atwater. Harsh frosts that year forced the winery to source grapes from Columbia Valley in Washington—a fairly successful effort though there's a leanness to the overall character of the wine. A lingering finish adds some heft. Pair with crab cakes or curries. 84 —*S.K. (2/1/2007)*

Atwater 2005 Reserve Riesling (Finger Lakes) $18. Creamy, opulent aromas of honey, apricot and melon are followed by a balanced, harmonious blend of fruit and toast in this reserve Riesling from the Finger Lakes' Atwater Estate Vineyards. There's ample weight but a fun, bright raciness in the midpalate, making this a great wine for food pairing. 87 —*S.K. (5/1/2007)*

Atwater 2006 Vidal Blanc (Finger Lakes) $14. Bright apple and pear flavors mingle in this full-bodied Vidal Blanc. There's a sweetness to the wine, but it's tempered by a spicy strain that helps keep it aloft. Pretty, with unique character. 85 —*S.K. (10/1/2007)*

AU BON CLIMAT

Au Bon Climat 1997 Alban Vineyard Chardonnay (Edna Valley) $35. 92 —*S.H. (10/1/1999)*

Au Bon Climat 1997 Bien Nacido Les Nuits Blanches Chardonnay (Santa Maria Valley) $40. 92 —*S.H. (10/1/1999)*

Au Bon Climat 1997 Le Bouge D'a Côte Chardonnay (Santa Maria Valley) $25. 90 —*S.H. (10/1/1999)*

Au Bon Climat 1999 Mt. Carmel Vineyard Chardonnay (Santa Ynez Valley) $40. 86 *(7/1/2001)*

Au Bon Climat 1999 Sanford & Benedict Chardonnay (Santa Ynez Valley) $35. 86 *(7/1/2001)*

Au Bon Climat 1997 Sanford & Benedict Reserve Chardonnay (Santa Ynez Valley) $35. 91 —*S.H. (10/1/1999)*

Au Bon Climat 1995 Sanford & Benedict Vineyard Reserve Chardonnay (Santa Ynez Valley) $NA. 91 —*S.H. (6/1/2005)*

Au Bon Climat 1997 Talley Reserve Chardonnay (Arroyo Grande Valley) $25. 90 —*S.H. (10/1/1999)*

Au Bon Climat 1998 Talley Vineyard "Rincon" Chardonnay (Arroyo Grande Valley) $25. 89 *(6/1/2000)*

Au Bon Climat 1988 (Benedict Vineyard) Pinot Noir (Santa Ynez Valley) $NA. 86 —*S.H. (6/1/2005)*

Au Bon Climat 1999 Knox Alexander Pinot Noir (Santa Maria Valley) $45. 93 —*J.M. (7/1/2002)*

Au Bon Climat 1998 Knox Alexander Pinot Noir (Santa Maria Valley) $45. 94 *(12/31/2001)*

Au Bon Climat 1997 Rosemary's-Talley Vineyard Pinot Noir (Arroyo Grande Valley) $50. 93 *(10/1/1999)*

Au Bon Climat 2002 Sanford & Benedict Vineyard Pinot Noir (Santa Ynez Valley) $35. 89 —*S.H. (6/1/2005)*

Au Bon Climat 2001 Sanford & Benedict Vineyard Pinot Noir (Santa Ynez Valley) $NA. 95 Editors' Choice —*S.H. (6/1/2005)*

Au Bon Climat 2000 Sanford & Benedict Vineyard Pinot Noir (Santa Ynez Valley) $NA. 89 —*S.H. (6/1/2005)*

Au Bon Climat 1997 Sanford & Benedict Vineyard Pinot Noir (Santa Ynez Valley) $35. 90 *(10/1/1999)*

Au Bon Climat 1996 Sanford & Benedict Vineyard Pinot Noir (Santa Ynez Valley) $NA. 89 —*S.H. (6/1/2005)*

Au Bon Climat 1994 Sanford & Benedict Vineyard Pinot Noir (Santa Ynez Valley) $NA. 93 —*S.H. (6/1/2005)*

AUDELSSA

Audelssa 2001 Mountain Terraces Cabernet Sauvignon (Sonoma Valley) $33. 92 —*S.H. (3/1/2005)*

AUDELSSA SONOMA

Audelssa Sonoma 2000 Mountain Terraces Cabernet Sauvignon (Sonoma Valley) $27. 89 —*S.H. (11/15/2004)*

Audelssa Sonoma 2002 Mountain Terraces Syrah (Sonoma Valley) $32. 80 *(9/1/2005)*

Audelssa Sonoma 2001 Mountain Terraces Syrah (Sonoma Valley) $32. 91 *—S.H. (12/1/2004)*

AUDUBON CELLARS

Audubon Cellars 1997 Graeser Vineyards Cabernet Sauvignon (Napa Valley) $18. 88 *—S.H. (9/1/2000)*

Audubon Cellars 1998 Sangiacomo Vineyard Chardonnay (Carneros) $13. 84 *—S.H. (11/15/2001)*

Audubon Cellars 1997 Sangiacomo Vineyard Chardonnay (Sonoma) $15. 84 *(6/1/2000)*

Audubon Cellars 1999 Juliana Vineyard Sauvignon Blanc (Napa Valley) $12. 86 *—S.H. (11/15/2000)*

Audubon Cellars 2000 Juliana Vineyards Sauvignon Blanc (Napa Valley) $12. 83 *—S.H. (11/15/2001)*

Audubon Cellars 1997 Juliana Vineyards Sauvignon Blanc (Napa Valley) $9. 83 *—S.H. (9/1/1999)*

Audubon Cellars 1997 Picnic Hill Vineyard Late Harvest Zinfandel (Amador County) $14. 82 *—S.H. (12/31/2000)*

AUGUSTA WINERY

Augusta Winery 2003 Estate Bottled Norton (Missouri) $15. Spiced oak and red cherry fruit lead on the nose of this assertive, dry Norton. On the palate, it has a big fruit flavor with a slightly burnt, smoky edge. A touch tough to wrangle, but good when paired with assertive foods that will soften its edge. 82 *—S.K. (12/1/2007)*

Augusta Winery 2002 Estate Bottled Norton (Missouri) $15. A soft nose of mocha and berry leads into subtle tobacco, mint and spice on the palate of this native American red. The wine is not complex but is appealing; a gentler version of this sometimes aggressive variety. 83 *—S.K. (12/1/2007)*

Augusta Winery 2005 Vignoles (Missouri) $9. This clean but flowery Vignoles offers white wine lovers a unique alternative. Crisp and sweet pineapple with balanced acidity on the palate is led by a fragrant nose. 84 *—S.K. (10/1/2007)*

AUGUST BRIGGS

August Briggs 1997 Cabernet Sauvignon (Sonoma Mountain) $50. 89 *(11/1/2000)*

August Briggs 1997 Cabernet Sauvignon (Napa Valley) $50. 91 *(11/1/2000)*

August Briggs 2001 Petite Sirah (Lake County) $32. 87 *—J.M. (9/1/2004)*

August Briggs 2002 Pinot Noir (Russian River Valley) $32. 85 *—S.H. (8/1/2005)*

August Briggs 2000 Pinot Noir (Russian River Valley) $32. 90 *(10/1/2002)*

August Briggs 1997 Pinot Noir (Russian River Valley) $28. 90 *(10/1/1999)*

August Briggs 2002 Dijon Clones Pinot Noir (Napa Valley) $35. 91 *—S.H. (8/1/2005)*

August Briggs 2000 Dijon Clones Pinot Noir (Napa Valley) $35. 87 *(10/1/2002)*

August Briggs 2002 Zinfandel (Napa Valley) $32. 90 *—S.H. (8/1/2005)*

August Briggs 2001 Zinfandel (Napa Valley) $32. 89 *(11/1/2003)*

AUGUST WEST

August West 2003 Rosella's Vineyard Pinot Noir (Santa Lucia Highlands) $42. 93 Cellar Selection *—S.H. (8/1/2005)*

AURIGA

Auriga 2003 Max Vineyard Syrah (El Dorado County) $18. 85 *—S.H. (4/1/2006)*

Auriga 2004 Zinfandel (El Dorado) $17. 84 *—S.H. (4/1/2006)*

AUSTIN HOPE

Austin Hope 2005 Hope Family Vineyard Grenache (Paso Robles) $42. You'll find plenty of the red cherry flavors that mark this variety, along with lots of smoky vanilla and caramel, from 70% new oak. That said, the structure is too soft and simple. The wine would benefit from greater acidity and tannins, the lack of which make it taste sweeter than it really is. 84 *—S.H. (12/15/2007)*

Austin Hope 2003 Mer Soleil Vineyard Roussanne (Santa Lucia Highlands) $37. 92 *—S.H. (11/15/2006)*

Austin Hope 2004 Hope Family Vineyard Syrah (Paso Robles) $42. The very hot vintage took its toll on this 100% varietal Syrah. While it's nicely dry, with a finely tannic structure, it tastes a bit soft and hot. The cherry and blackberry flavors have a dessicated, raisiny edge. Drink now. 86 *—S.H. (12/15/2007)*

Austin Hope 2003 Hope Family Vineyard Syrah (Paso Robles) $42. 86 *—S.H. (11/15/2006)*

AUSTIN ROBAIRE

Austin Robaire 2000 Cabernet Sauvignon (Columbia Valley (WA)) $55. 88 *—P.G. (9/1/2003)*

Austin Robaire 2001 Elerding Vineyard Reserve Cabernet Sauvignon (Columbia Valley (WA)) $115. 90 *—J.C. (6/6/2005)*

Austin Robaire 2002 Klipsun Vineyard Cabernet Sauvignon (Red Mountain) $55. 85 *—P.G. (6/1/2005)*

Austin Robaire 2002 Le Petit Garçon Cabernet Sauvignon (Columbia Valley (WA)) $18. 86 *—P.G. (6/1/2005)*

Austin Robaire 2001 Ward Family Vineyard Pinot Noir (Washington) $26. 84 *—P.G. (9/1/2003)*

Austin Robaire 2001 Elerding Vineyard Reserve Syrah (Columbia Valley (WA)) $85. 86 *(9/1/2005)*

Austin Robaire 2002 La Petite Fille Syrah (Columbia Valley (WA)) $18. 85 *—P.G. (6/1/2005)*

Austin Robaire 2001 Charmaine Angela White Blend (Columbia Valley (WA)) $26. 85 *—P.G. (9/1/2003)*

AUTUMN HILL

Autumn Hill 1997 Cabernet Sauvignon (Monticello) $16. 85 *—J.C. (8/1/1999)*

AVALON

Avalon 2003 Cabernet Sauvignon (Napa Valley) $13. 85 *—S.H. (12/31/2005)*

AVENUE

Avenue 2003 Cabernet Sauvignon (California) $11. 83 *—S.H. (5/1/2005)*

Avenue 2003 Chardonnay (California) $11. 82 *—S.H. (5/1/2005)*

Avenue 2003 Merlot (California) $11. 84 *—S.H. (5/1/2005)*

Avenue 2002 Zinfandel (California) $11. 83 *—S.H. (5/1/2005)*

AVERY LANE

Avery Lane 2001 Cabernet Sauvignon (Columbia Valley (WA)) $8. 87 Best Buy *—P.G. (12/31/2003)*

Avery Lane 2002 Chardonnay (Washington) $8. 82 *—P.G. (7/1/2004)*

Avery Lane 2001 Chardonnay (Columbia Valley (WA)) $8. 85 Best Buy *—P.G. (12/31/2003)*

Avery Lane 2003 Gewürztraminer (Washington) $7. 85 *—P.G. (7/1/2004)*

Avery Lane 2002 Gewürztraminer (Columbia Valley (WA)) $7. 87 Best Buy *—P.G. (12/31/2003)*

Avery Lane 2002 Johannisberg Riesling (Columbia Valley (WA)) $7. 88 Best Buy *—P.G. (12/31/2003)*

Avery Lane 2001 Merlot (Columbia Valley (WA)) $8. 85 Best Buy *—P.G. (12/31/2003)*

Avery Lane NV Red Blend (Columbia Valley (WA)) $8. 87 Best Buy *—P.G. (12/31/2003)*

Avery Lane 2002 Sauvignon Blanc (Washington) $7. 85 *—P.G. (7/1/2004)*

Avery Lane 2001 Sauvignon Blanc (Columbia Valley (WA)) $7. 85 Best Buy *—P.G. (12/31/2003)*

Avery Lane 2001 Syrah (Washington) $8. 82 *—P.G. (7/1/2004)*

AVILA

Avila 2004 Cabernet Sauvignon (Santa Barbara County) $13. On the sharp, rustic side, a dry wine with a wintergreen edge to the cherries and blackberries. Gets better in the glass. 83 *—S.H. (2/1/2007)*

Avila 2004 Cabernet Sauvignon (Santa Barbara County) $13. 82 *—S.H. (3/1/2006)*

Avila 2003 Cabernet Sauvignon (Santa Barbara County) $14. 83 *—S.H. (10/1/2005)*

Avila 2002 Cabernet Sauvignon (Santa Barbara County) $11. 83 *—S.H. (2/1/2005)*

Avila 2001 Cabernet Sauvignon (Santa Barbara County) $13. 85 *—S.H. (2/1/2004)*

Avila 2000 Cabernet Sauvignon (Santa Barbara County) $12. 88 Best Buy *—S.H. (11/15/2002)*

Avila 2005 Chardonnay (Santa Barbara County) $13. There's a streak of tart green apple running through this Chard that gives it a sweet and sour tang. Minerals, too, with a suggestion of lemony gunmetal or flint; you can almost taste chalk. This is a very good price for a dry, Chablis-style wine of real style and elegance. 88 Best Buy *—S.H. (2/1/2007)*

Avila 2004 Chardonnay (Santa Barbara County) $13. 83 *—S.H. (3/1/2006)*

Avila 2003 Chardonnay (San Luis Obispo County) $11. 84 *—S.H. (2/1/2005)*

Avila 2000 Chardonnay (San Luis Obispo County) $12. 85 *—S.H. (12/15/2002)*

Avila 2004 Merlot (Santa Barbara County) $13. An odd wine, at once raw and green, then turning semisweet. Too bad, because the tannins are really lush and smooth. 82 *—S.H. (2/1/2007)*

Avila 2002 Merlot (Santa Barbara County) $11. 82 *—S.H. (2/1/2005)*

Avila 2001 Merlot (Santa Barbara County) $13. 83 *—S.H. (4/1/2004)*

Avila 2000 Merlot (Santa Barbara County) $12. 89 *—S.H. (11/15/2002)*

Avila 2003 Pinot Noir (San Luis Obispo County) $11. 85 *—S.H. (12/15/2004)*

Avila 2002 Pinot Noir (San Luis Obispo County) $13. 86 *—S.H. (4/1/2004)*

Avila 2001 Pinot Noir (San Luis Obispo County) $10. 86 *—J.M. (11/15/2003)*

Avila 2000 Pinot Noir (San Luis Obispo County) $12. 85 Best Buy *(10/1/2002)*

Avila 2001 Cote d'Avila Rhône Red Blend (Santa Barbara County) $13. 82 *—S.H. (5/1/2003)*

Avila 2002 Cote d'Avila Rhône Red Blend (Santa Barbara County) $11. 84 *—S.H. (2/1/2005)*

Avila 2004 Syrah (Santa Barbara County) $13. Kind of raw and rustic despite forward blackberry and cherry jam flavors. If you don't mind the sharp acids, try it with softening foods, like chevre, lamb, or prosciutto. 83 *—S.H. (2/1/2007)*

Avila 2003 Syrah (Santa Barbara County) $13. 84 *(9/1/2005)*

AZALEA SPRINGS

Azalea Springs 1997 Estate Grown Merlot (Napa Valley) $35.89 *—J.C. (6/1/2001)*

B CELLARS

B Cellars 2004 Blend 24 Cabernet Blend (Napa Valley) $36. Mainly Cabernet Sauvignon, with some Merlot and Syrah, this is a dry, fairly tannic wine that's a bit astringent now, and may develop in the bottle, to judge by the deep core of blackberry, cassis and cherry-chocolate. It's very elegant. 90 *—S.H. (10/1/2007)*

B Cellars 2004 Blend 25 Cabernet Sauvignon-Syrah Cabernet Blend (Napa Valley) $48. Only the second vintage for this wine, but it joins the top ranks of Cabernet-Syrah blends. Dry, rich, smooth and frankly delicious, it has incredibly complex flavors, of blackberries, violets, coffee, pomegranates, cola, cloves and oak, and a long finish. A terrific wine to drink now and over the next four years. 94 Editors' Choice *—S.H. (10/1/2007)*

B Cellars 2004 Blend 26 Cabernet Sauvignon (Napa Valley) $85. The grapes come from three vineyards: Georges III in Rutherford, Tokalon in Oakville and Stagecoach, up on Atlas Peak. That helps explain the wine's beauty. It's pure California, cult-style Cab, soft and generous, with voluptuously ripe black currant and black cherry flavors elaborately enriched with spicy, smoky, 100% new French oak. My only quibble is that it could use a little more subtlety. 94 *—S.H. (12/31/2007)*

B Cellars 2006 Blend 23 Sauvignon Blanc - Viognier - Chardonnay White Blend (Napa Valley) $28. This wonderfully rich wine combines the best of all three varieties to produce a complex white. It shows rich green apple, pineapple jam, superripe apricot, honeysuckle and smoky oak flavors, and while it's tremendously honeyed on the finish, it is basically dry. Crisp acidity, probably from the Carneros Chardonnay, provides needed balance. 91 *—S.H. (12/31/2007)*

B.R. COHN

B.R. Cohn 2004 Olive Hill Cabernet Sauvignon (Sonoma Valley) $50. This bottling has got to be one of the most seriously underpriced Cabs in California. What you get is a firmly structured, tannic, complex 100% Cabernet, rich in currants and oak, that can proudly stand on the best table. Will take some age, too. Best now through 2012. 93 *—S.H. (12/31/2007)*

B.R. Cohn 1996 Olive Hill Cabernet Sauvignon (Sonoma Valley) $35. 92 *(12/31/1999)*

B.R. Cohn 2001 Olive Hill Estate Cabernet Sauvignon (Sonoma County) $50. 91 *—S.H. (10/1/2004)*

B.R. Cohn 1999 Olive Hill Estate Vineyards-Special Selection Cabernet Sauvignon (Sonoma Valley) $100. 86 *(8/1/2003)*

B.R. Cohn 1996 Olive Hill Estate Vineyards Sp Cabernet Sauvignon (Sonoma Valley) $80. 92 *—J.C. (12/31/1999)*

B.R. Cohn 1997 Olive Hill Estate Vineyards Cabernet Sauvignon (Sonoma Valley) $38. 91 *(12/31/1999)*

B.R. Cohn 1997 Olive Hill Estate Vineyards Special Cabernet Sauvignon (Sonoma Valley) $100. 88 *(11/1/2000)*

B.R. Cohn 2002 Oliver Hill Estate Vineyards Cabernet Sauvignon (Sonoma Valley) $65. 90 Cellar Selection *—S.H. (5/1/2006)*

B.R. Cohn 2005 Silver Label Cabernet Sauvignon (Sonoma Valley) $20. Pretty run of the mill, a tannic Cab with flavors of herbs and berries. Fulfills the basic requirements of dryness and full-bodied balance. Drink now. 84 *—S.H. (12/31/2007)*

B.R. Cohn 2003 Silver Label Cabernet Sauvignon (North Coast) $20. 85 *—S.H. (5/1/2006)*

B.R. Cohn 2001 Silver Label Cabernet Sauvignon (Central Coast) $20. 83 *—S.H. (10/1/2004)*

B.R. Cohn 1998 Chardonnay (Carneros) $16. 88 *(6/1/2000)*

B.R. Cohn 2001 Chardonnay (Carneros) $35. 87 *—J.M. (2/1/2004)*

B.R. Cohn 1998 Reserve Joseph Herman Vineyard Chardonnay (Carneros) $28. 87 *(6/1/2000)*

B.R. Cohn 1997 Reserve Joseph Herman Vineyard. Chardonnay (Carneros) $24. 93 *—M.S. (2/1/2000)*

B.R. Cohn 2001 Merlot (Sonoma Valley) $28. 88 *—S.H. (12/15/2004)*

B.R. Cohn 2000 Merlot (Sonoma Valley) $28. 87 *—J.M. (2/1/2004)*

B.R. Cohn 2004 Petite Sirah (North Coast) $38. Fairly distinguished for a variety that can often be rustic, this 100% Petite Sirah is smooth and bone dry. It's heavy in tannins, with a deep core of black and blue stone fruits, berries, peppery spices and coffee. A blend of Sonoma Valley and Lake County, it will slowly age for 15 years. 90 *—S.H. (7/1/2007)*

B.R. Cohn 2005 Pinot Noir (Russian River Valley) $45. Sonoma Valley Cabernet specialist Cohn reaches to the Russian River to expand his portfolio with this Pinot Noir. It's not a stretch to call it Bordeaux-style. Although it has the variety's telltale silkiness and medium body, the blackberry, cola, coffee, leather and oak flavors, not to mention the tannins, possess density and gravity, which may make this wine ageable. Best now through 2011. 88 *—S.H. (12/31/2007)*

B.R. Cohn 2005 SyrCab Syrah-Cabernet (Sonoma Valley) $32. The name doesn't exactly roll off the tongue, but this is a pretty good wine. Smooth and velvety, with earth-tinged berry, coffee and spice flavors, this gets better as it warms and breathes in the glass. 89 *—S.H. (12/31/2007)*

B.R. Cohn 2003 Syrcab Red Blend (Sonoma Valley) $32. 87 *—S.H. (5/1/2006)*

BABCOCK

Babcock 2005 Classic Rock Cuvée Bordeaux Blend (Santa Ynez Valley) $21. Herbal, tannic and soft, with some candied cherry flavors, this Cabernet-based blend feels rustic and common in the mouth. The wine is basically dry, while 25% new oak adds vanilla sweetness. 83 *—S.H. (11/1/2007)*

Babcock 2000 Fathom Bordeaux Blend (Santa Barbara County) $40. 90 *—S.H. (11/15/2002)*

Babcock 1999 Fathom Bordeaux Blend (Santa Barbara County) $35. 93 Editors' Choice *—S.H. (12/1/2001)*

Babcock 1998 Fathom Bordeaux Blend (Santa Barbara County) $30. 89 *—S.H. (2/1/2001)*

Babcock 2002 Cabernet Sauvignon (Central Coast) $19. 85 *—S.H. (10/1/2004)*

Babcock 2004 Back Roads Cuvée Cabernet Sauvignon (Central Coast) $20. 86 *—S.H. (12/1/2006)*

Babcock 2004 New Epoch Reserve Cabernet Sauvignon (Santa Ynez Valley) $35. Sharp and rustic compared to Napa and Sonoma Cabs, with green, minty tannins. There's a lot of oak, and some ripe cherry-blackberry fruit, but work remains to be done on the tannins. 85 *—S.H. (11/1/2007)*

Babcock 2001 La Moda Toscana Cabernet Sauvignon-Sangiovese (Santa Ynez Valley) $28. 89 *—S.H. (3/1/2004)*

Babcock 1997 Chardonnay (Santa Ynez Valley) $25. 92 *—S.H. (10/1/1999)*

Babcock 2002 Chardonnay (Santa Barbara County) $19. 87 *—S.H. (2/1/2004)*

Babcock 2001 Chardonnay (Santa Barbara County) $17. 93 Editors' Choice *—S.H. (12/15/2002)*

Babcock 2000 Chardonnay (Santa Barbara County) $17. 87 *—S.H. (11/15/2001)*

Babcock 2000 Chardonnay (Santa Ynez Valley) $25. 90 *—S.H. (9/1/2002)*

Babcock 1999 Chardonnay (Santa Barbara County) $18. 88 *—S.H. (2/1/2001)*

Babcock 1998 Chardonnay (Santa Barbara County) $18. 85 *(6/1/2000)*

Babcock 2005 Grand Cuvée Chardonnay (Santa Barbara County) $30. 84 —*S.H. (11/15/2006)*

Babcock 2003 Grand Cuvée Chardonnay (Santa Rita Hills) $30. 90 —*S.H. (12/31/2005)*

Babcock 2002 Grand Cuvée Chardonnay (Santa Ynez Valley) $30. 84 —*S.H. (12/31/2004)*

Babcock 2000 Grand Cuvée Chardonnay (Santa Ynez Valley) $25. 89 —*S.H. (12/15/2002)*

Babcock 1999 Grand Cuvée Chardonnay (Santa Barbara County) $25. 89 —*S.H. (12/1/2001)*

Babcock 1998 Grand Cuvée Chardonnay (Santa Barbara County) $30. 89 *(7/1/2001)*

Babcock 1996 Grand Cuvée Chardonnay (Santa Ynez Valley) $30. 91 —*S.H. (7/1/1999)*

Babcock 1997 Grand Cuvée Estate Chardonnay (Santa Ynez Valley) $30. 92 *(8/1/2003)*

Babcock 1998 Mt. Carmel Vineyard Chardonnay (Santa Ynez Valley) $35. 86 *(7/1/2001)*

Babcock 1997 Mt. Carmel Vineyard Chardonnay (Santa Ynez Valley) $30. 92 *(11/15/1999)*

Babcock 2005 Rita's Earth Cuvée Chardonnay (Sta. Rita Hills) $20. 88 —*S.H. (11/15/2006)*

Babcock 2004 Rita's Earth Cuvée Chardonnay (Santa Rita Hills) $20. 91 Editors' Choice —*S.H. (12/31/2005)*

Babcock 2001 Cuvée Sublime Gewürztraminer (Santa Barbara County) $20. 93 Editors' Choice —*S.H. (12/1/2002)*

Babcock 2005 Pinot Grigio (Santa Rita Hills) $15. 91 Best Buy —*S.H. (11/15/2006)*

Babcock 2001 Pinot Grigio (Santa Barbara County) $14. 88 Best Buy —*S.H. (9/1/2002)*

Babcock 1998 Pinot Gris (Santa Barbara County) $14. 88 *(10/1/1999)*

Babcock 2005 Naughty Little Hillsides Pinot Gris (Sta. Rita Hills) $25. 89 —*S.H. (11/15/2006)*

Babcock 2001 Pinot Noir (Santa Barbara County) $23. 91 Editors' Choice —*S.H. (2/1/2003)*

Babcock 2000 Pinot Noir (Santa Barbara County) $22. 89 —*S.H. (12/15/2001)*

Babcock 2002 Cargasacchi Pinot Noir (Santa Ynez Valley) $40. 86 *(11/1/2004)*

Babcock 2004 Grand Cuvée Pinot Noir (Santa Rita Hills) $32. 84 —*S.H. (2/1/2006)*

Babcock 2002 Grand Cuvée Pinot Noir (Santa Rita Hills) $35. 85 —*S.H. (2/1/2005)*

Babcock 2001 Grand Cuvée Pinot Noir (Santa Ynez Valley) $35. 84 —*S.H. (2/1/2004)*

Babcock 2000 Grand Cuvée Pinot Noir (Santa Ynez Valley) $35. 87 *(10/1/2002)*

Babcock 2001 Grand Cuvée Pinot Noir Pinot Noir (Santa Ynez Valley) $30. 92 —*S.H. (4/1/2004)*

Babcock 1997 Grande Cuvée-Estate Pinot Noir (Santa Ynez Valley) $40. 93 Best Buy *(10/1/1999)*

Babcock 1997 Mt. Carmel Vineyard Pinot Noir (Santa Ynez Valley) $35. 91 *(10/1/1999)*

Babcock 2002 Fathom Red Blend (Santa Ynez Valley) $32. 91 —*S.H. (2/1/2006)*

Babcock 2001 Fathom Red Blend (Santa Ynez Valley) $32. 90 —*S.H. (2/1/2005)*

Babcock 1997 Fathom Red Table Wine Red Blend (Santa Barbara County) $30. 90 —*J.C. (11/15/1999)*

Babcock 1999 Eleven Oaks Sangiovese (Santa Barbara County) $40. 91 —*S.H. (12/1/2001)*

Babcock 1997 Eleven Oaks Sangiovese (Santa Ynez Valley) $30. 90 *(10/1/1999)*

Babcock 2002 Eleven Oaks Sauvignon Blanc (Santa Barbara County) $20. 88 —*S.H. (2/1/2004)*

Babcock 2001 Eleven Oaks Sauvignon Blanc (Santa Barbara County) $23. 86 *(8/1/2002)*

Babcock 2000 Eleven Oaks Sauvignon Blanc (Santa Barbara County) $23. 90 Editors' Choice *(8/1/2001)*

Babcock 2003 Eleven Oaks Cuvée Sauvignon Blanc (Santa Ynez Valley) $25. 90 —*S.H. (12/31/2004)*

Babcock 2005 Estate Grown Sauvignon Blanc (Sta. Rita Hills) $21. 92 Editors' Choice —*S.H. (11/15/2006)*

Babcock 2004 Estate Grown Sauvignon Blanc (Santa Rita Hills) $23. 84 —*S.H. (12/31/2005)*

Babcock 2005 Big Fat Pink Shiraz Shiraz (Santa Barbara County) $15. 88 —*S.H. (12/1/2006)*

Babcock 2000 Syrah (Santa Barbara County) $23. 90 —*S.H. (7/1/2002)*

Babcock 2002 Black Label Cuvée Syrah (Central Coast) $30. 84 —*S.H. (3/1/2006)*

Babcock 2001 Black Label Cuvée Syrah (Santa Barbara County) $30. 87 —*S.H. (2/1/2005)*

Babcock 2000 Black Label Cuvée Syrah (Santa Barbara County) $40. 93 Editors' Choice —*S.H. (12/1/2002)*

Babcock 1999 Black Label Cuvée Syrah (Santa Barbara County) $50. 88 *(11/1/2001)*

Babcock 1997 Black Label Cuvée Syrah (Santa Barbara County) $40. 91 *(10/1/1999)*

Babcock 2003 Frying Pan Syrah (Santa Barbara County) $50. 87 *(9/1/2005)*

Babcock 2003 Nook & Cranny Syrah (Santa Rita Hills) $50. 90 *(9/1/2005)*

Babcock 2003 Radical Syrah (Paso Robles) $50. 85 *(9/1/2005)*

BACCHARIS

Baccharis 2003 Cabernet Sauvignon (Alexander Valley) $28. 90 Cellar Selection —*S.H. (2/1/2006)*

Baccharis 2002 Petite Sirah (Dry Creek Valley) $23. 87 —*S.H. (2/1/2006)*

Baccharis 2002 Floodgate Vineyard Pinot Noir (Anderson Valley) $28. 87 —*S.H. (2/1/2006)*

Baccharis 2004 Sauvignon Blanc (Russian River Valley) $15. 86 —*S.H. (2/1/2006)*

Baccharis 2002 Zinfandel (Sonoma County) $16. 89 Editors' Choice —*S.H. (2/1/2006)*

BACIO DIVINO

Bacio Divino 1999 Red Blend (Napa Valley) $75. 91 —*M.S. (11/15/2003)*

Bacio Divino 2000 Pazzo Red Blend (Napa Valley) $24. 85 —*S.H. (12/31/2003)*

Bacio Divino 2000 Red Wine Red Blend (Napa Valley) $80. 85 —*S.H. (12/31/2003)*

Bacio Divino 1997 Sangiovese (Napa Valley) $75. 90 *(11/1/2000)*

BADGER MOUNTAIN

Badger Mountain 1998 Cabernet Franc (Columbia Valley (WA)) $12. 82 —*P.G. (6/1/2002)*

Badger Mountain 1998 Cabernet Sauvignon (Columbia Valley (WA)) $14. 83 —*P.G. (12/31/2001)*

Badger Mountain 1999 N.S.A. Cabernet Sauvignon (Columbia Valley (WA)) $14. 84 —*P.G. (6/1/2002)*

Badger Mountain 1999 Vintner's Estate Cabernet Sauvignon (Columbia Valley (WA)) $12. 86 —*P.G. (12/31/2003)*

Badger Mountain 2000 N.S.A. Chardonnay (Columbia Valley (WA)) $10. 86 —*P.G. (7/1/2002)*

Badger Mountain 1999 Vintner's Estate Meritage (Columbia Valley (WA)) $12. 85 —*P.G. (12/31/2003)*

Badger Mountain 1999 Merlot (Columbia Valley (WA)) $14. 82 —*P.G. (12/31/2001)*

Badger Mountain 1998 Merlot (Columbia Valley (WA)) $12. 83 —*P.G. (6/1/2002)*

Badger Mountain 2000 N.S.A Merlot (Columbia Valley (WA)) $14.86 —*P.G. (6/1/2002)*

Badger Mountain 1998 Red Blend (Columbia Valley (WA)) $12. 83 —*P.G. (6/1/2002)*

Badger Mountain 2001 N.S.A. Riesling (Columbia Valley (WA)) $8. 86 Best Buy —*P.G. (6/1/2002)*

Badger Mountain 2001 Vintner's Estate Syrah (Columbia Valley (WA)) $18. 86 —*P.G. (12/31/2003)*

Badger Mountain 2000 Seve White Blend (Columbia Valley (WA)) $8. 84 —*P.G. (6/1/2002)*

BAER

Baer 2003 Ursa Red Bordeaux Blend (Columbia Valley (WA)) $29. 92 —*P.G. (10/1/2006)*

BAILEYANA

Baileyana 1998 Chardonnay (Monterey County) $17. 85 *(6/1/2000)*

Baileyana 1997 Chardonnay (Edna Valley) $22. 86 *(6/1/2000)*

Baileyana 2001 Chardonnay (San Luis Obispo) $18. 87 *—S.H. (12/31/2003)*

Baileyana 2002 55% San Luis Obispo County/45% Monterey County Chardonnay (California) $18. 83 *—S.H. (8/1/2005)*

Baileyana 2003 Estate Chardonnay (Edna Valley) $18. 86 *—S.H. (4/1/2006)*

Baileyana 2001 Firepeak Vineyard Chardonnay (Edna Valley) $30. 90 *—S.H. (12/15/2003)*

Baileyana 1999 Firepeak Vineyard Chardonnay (Edna Valley) $30. 88 *(7/1/2001)*

Baileyana 2004 Firepeak Vineyard El Gordo Chardonnay (Edna Valley) $30. 93 *—S.H. (7/1/2006)*

Baileyana 2005 Grand Firepeak Cuvée Chardonnay (Edna Valley) $30. Notable for very high acidity, this Chard would be aggressive were it not for the ripe, honeyed flavors and creamy texture, which soften it up. The flavors are very pure and clean: of kiwi, lime, mango and papaya. 90 *—S.H. (12/1/2007)*

Baileyana 2002 Grand Firepeak Cuvée Chardonnay (Edna Valley) $30. 86 *—S.H. (10/1/2005)*

Baileyana 2003 Grand Firepeak Cuvée Chardonnay (Edna Valley) $30. 86 *—S.H. (12/15/2005)*

Baileyana 2004 Grand Firepeak Vineyard Chardonnay (Edna Valley) $30. 92 Editors' Choice *—S.H. (7/1/2006)*

Baileyana 2001 Pinot Noir (Edna Valley) $23. 86 *—S.H. (4/1/2004)*

Baileyana 2000 Pinot Noir (Edna Valley) $23. 88 *(10/1/2002)*

Baileyana 1999 Pinot Noir (Edna Valley) $23. 87 *(10/1/2002)*

Baileyana 2002 El Pico Firepeak Vineyard Clone 115 90 Editors' Choice *—S.H. (11/1/2004)*

Baileyana 2003 Firepeak Vineyard Pinot Noir (Edna Valley) $23. 84 *—S.H. (8/1/2006)*

Baileyana 2002 Firepeak Vineyard Pinot Noir (Edna Valley) $23. T92 *—S.H. (10/1/2005)*

Baileyana 2001 Firepeak Vineyard Pinot Noir (Edna Valley) $38. 87 *—S.H. (4/1/2004)*

Baileyana 1999 Firepeak Vineyard Pinot Noir (Edna Valley) $38. 92 Editors' Choice *—J.M. (12/15/2001)*

Baileyana 2000 Firepeak Vineyard-Estate Bottled Pinot Noir (Edna Valley) $38. 87 *(10/1/2002)*

Baileyana 2005 Grand Firepeak Cuvée Pinot Noir (Edna Valley) $38. Shows a classic Edna Valley or San Luis Obispo profile, namely a clean, brisk mouthfeel, a silky, light texture, and dry, rewarding flavors of cherries, cola, rhubarbs, herb tea and cinnamon spice. Not a blockbuster, but very good now, reminiscent of a fine southern Burgundy. 89 *—S.H. (12/1/2007)*

Baileyana 2004 Grand Firepeak Cuvée Pinot Noir (Edna Valley) $38. 91 *—S.H. (11/1/2006)*

Baileyana 2002 Grand Firepeak Cuvée Pinot Noir (Edna Valley) $38. 85 *—S.H. (10/1/2005)*

Baileyana 2003 Grand Firepeak Cuvée Firepeak Vineyard Pinot Noir (Edna Valley) $38. 90 *—S.H. (3/1/2006)*

Baileyana 2002 Halcon Rojo Firepeak Vineyard Pommard Clone Pinot Noir (Edna Valley) $30. 87 *—S.H. (11/1/2004)*

Baileyana 1997 La Colline Vineyard Pinot Noir (Arroyo Grande Valley) $30. 89 *(12/15/1999)*

Baileyana 2002 La Entrada Firepeak Vineyard Clone 777 Pinot Noir (Edna Valley) $30. 89 *—S.H. (11/1/2004)*

Baileyana 2004 Paragon Vineyard Sauvignon Blanc (Edna Valley) $13. 89 Best Buy *—S.H. (8/1/2006)*

Baileyana 2003 Paragon Vineyard Sauvignon Blanc (Edna Valley) $13. 88 Best Buy *—S.H. (8/1/2005)*

Baileyana 2002 Paragon Vineyard Sauvignon Blanc (Edna Valley) $13. F84 *—S.H. (4/1/2004)*

Baileyana 2001 Syrah (Edna Valley) $18. 88 *(9/1/2005)*

Baileyana 1999 Syrah (Paso Robles) $18. 87 *(10/1/2001)*

Baileyana 2003 Firepeak Vineyard Syrah (Edna Valley) $30. 86 *(9/1/2005)*

Baileyana 1999 Firepeak Vineyard Syrah (Edna Valley) $38. 89 *(11/1/2001)*

Baileyana 2003 Grand Firepeak Cuvée Syrah (Edna Valley) $38. 87 *—S.H. (12/31/2005)*

Baileyana 1998 Zinfandel (Paso Robles) $18. 86 *—D.T. (3/1/2002)*

BAILY

Baily 1999 Merlot (Temecula) $16. 88 *—S.H. (4/1/2002)*

BAITING HOLLOW FARM VINEYARD

Baiting Hollow Farm Vineyard 2004 Merlot (North Fork of Long Island) $NA. 83 *—M.D. (12/1/2006)*

BALBOA

Balboa 2004 Mith Bordeaux Blend (Columbia Valley (WA)) $40. This is the second vintage for this Bordeaux blend, the winery's reserve. The simple white label, with Mith in black letters and a black rose in silhouette, belies the quality within. Rather than go for the smooth ride, this wine seeks out the flavor hills on its way to a lightly buttery finish. Elegant and interesting, with clean, Cab-dominated red fruit flavors. 90 *—P.G. (3/1/2007)*

Balboa 2005 Cabernet Sauvignon (Walla Walla (WA)) $16. An aromatic, pretty nose softens up the entry and leads into a tasty, cranberry-flavored red wine. The addition of a small amount of Malbec stiffens up the tannins a bit and thickens up the back end. It gives the wine a bit more substantial weight than its siblings. 89 *—P.G. (3/1/2007)*

Balboa 2003 Cabernet Sauvignon (Walla Walla (WA)) $16. 88 *—P.G. (6/1/2006)*

Balboa 2005 Merlot (Columbia Valley (WA)) $16. Balboa's Thomas Glase, who also makes the wines for Beresan, offers up a very fine Merlot for the price. It's firm and tangy with strawberry and raspberry flavors; balanced with refreshing acids. There's nothing big or heavy here; just an easy-drinking young wine, fresh and flavorful, with a nice spicy kick at the end. 88 *—P.G. (3/1/2007)*

Balboa 2004 Sauvignon Blanc (Columbia Valley (WA)) $16. 88 *—P.G. (6/1/2006)*

Balboa 2005 Syrah (Columbia Valley (WA)) $16. Balboa's affordably-priced Syrah brings out flavors of cranberry and raspberry fruit. Clean and tart, these crisp red fruits hit the palate with a sharp snap and finish with a spicy tang. Tasty stuff. 88 *—P.G. (3/1/2007)*

BALCOM & MOE

Balcom & Moe 1997 Cabernet Sauvignon (Washington) $20. 83 *—P.G. (10/1/2001)*

Balcom & Moe 1998 Merlot (Washington) $20. 84 *—P.G. (10/1/2001)*

BALDACCI

Baldacci 2004 Cabernet Sauvignon (Stags Leap District) $55. This is Baldacci's regular Cab, although most wineries would be content for it to be their reserve. It's a powerful, rich young wine, massive in blackberry, currant and oak flavors, with a succulent edge of milk chocolate. The tannins are pure Stags Leap, giving a complex contrapuntal balance of grip and structure to the opulent fruit. Just fabulous in every aspect, a wine to dazzle. Drink now through 2010, at least. 95 Editors' Choice *—S.H. (12/31/2007)*

Baldacci 2003 Cabernet Sauvignon (Stags Leap District) $49. 93 Editors' Choice *(9/1/2006)*

Baldacci 2002 Cabernet Sauvignon (Stags Leap District) $44. 90 *—S.H. (12/15/2005)*

Baldacci 2001 Cabernet Sauvignon (Stags Leap District) $44. 91 *—S.H. (7/1/2005)*

Baldacci 2004 Brenda's Vineyard Cabernet Sauvignon (Stags Leap District) $85. Tastes jellied with LifeSaver candy flavors of blackberries and cherries. This one is good, but far less interesting, than Baldacci's '04 Cab. 86 *—S.H. (12/31/2007)*

Baldacci 2003 Brenda's Vineyard Cabernet Sauvignon (Stags Leap District) $70. 95 Editors' Choice *(9/1/2006)*

Baldacci 2002 Brenda's Vineyard Cabernet Sauvignon (Stags Leap District) $70. 92 Cellar Selection *—S.H. (12/15/2005)*

Baldacci 2001 Brenda's Vineyard Cabernet Sauvignon (Stags Leap District) $70. 88 *—S.H. (7/1/2005)*

BALISTRERI

Balistreri 2003 Cabernet Franc (Grand Valley) $26. 80 *—M.D. (8/1/2006)*

Balistreri 2004 Cabernet Sauvignon (Grand Valley) $28. 83 *—M.D. (8/1/2006)*

BALLATORE

Ballatore NV Gran Spumante Sparkling Blend (California) $8. Rough and gritty in texture and overtly sweet in pineapple, orange, peach and bubble gum flavors, this everyday bubbly finishes clean and honeyed. 83 —*S.H. (12/31/2007)*

Ballatore NV Gran Spumante Champagne Blend (California) $7. 82 —*S.H. (12/15/1999)*

Ballatore NV Gran Spumante Champagne Blend (California) $7. 86 Best Buy —*S.H. (12/1/2002)*

Ballatore NV Rosso Champagne Blend (California) $8. 85 —*S.H. (12/1/2002)*

Ballatore NV Gran Spumante Sparkling Blend (California) $6. 84 Best Buy —*S.H. (12/31/2005)*

Ballatore NV Gran Spumante Sparkling Blend (California) $9. 85 Best Buy —*S.H. (6/1/2006)*

Ballatore NV Rosso Red Spumante Sparkling Blend (California) $8. True to its name, the wine is crimson in color, and sweet, with honeyed raspberry, cherry and vanilla flavors. Easy to drink due to the balanced sweetness. 84 Best Buy —*S.H. (12/31/2007)*

Ballatore NV Rosso Red Spumante Sparkling Blend (California) $9. 84 Best Buy —*S.H. (6/1/2006)*

Ballatore NV Rosso Red Spumante Sparkling Blend (California) $6. 82 —*S.H. (12/31/2005)*

BALLENTINE

Ballentine 2003 Pocai Vineyard Cabernet Franc (Napa Valley) $24. 86 —*S.H. (12/31/2005)*

Ballentine 2002 Pocai Vineyard Cabernet Franc (Napa Valley) $24. 84 —*S.H. (12/31/2004)*

Ballentine 2004 Maple Lane Cabernet Sauvignon (Napa Valley) $60. Impressive by any standards, this Cab is doubly so for having such great balance from a hot-hot vintage. The acids and tannins are firm, but best of all are the flavors, rich in ripe blackberry, cassis, spicy plum pudding and sweet new oak. Just a beautiful wine right now, and should evolve interestingly for 10 years. 92 —*S.H. (8/1/2007)*

Ballentine 2006 Pocai Vineyard Old Vines Chenin Blanc (Napa Valley) $15. Ballentine's Chenins nearly always impress, and this is one of their best. Bone dry and very crisp, almost tart, in acids, the wine shows intriguing lime, wildflower and sweet French green bean flavors. 91 Best Buy —*S.H. (8/1/2007)*

Ballentine 2004 Pocai Vineyard Old Vine Chenin Blanc (Napa Valley) $14. 87 —*S.H. (7/1/2005)*

Ballentine 2005 Pocai Vineyard Old Vines Chenin Blanc (Napa Valley) $14. 92 Best Buy —*S.H. (7/1/2006)*

Ballentine 2001 Merlot (Napa Valley) $22. 88 —*S.H. (6/1/2005)*

Ballentine 1999 Merlot (Napa Valley) $25. 87 —*S.H. (11/15/2002)*

Ballentine 1997 Estate Grown Merlot (Napa Valley) $20. 87 —*J.C. (7/1/2000)*

Ballentine 2003 Pocai Vineyard Merlot (Napa Valley) $22. Ballentine continues to struggle with this bottling. It's more balanced than the '02, but still has a harsh, baked quality to the cherry-berry fruit. That accentuates the tannins, which feel hard and astringent. 83 —*S.H. (10/1/2007)*

Ballentine 2002 Pocai Vineyard Merlot (Napa Valley) $22. 82 —*S.H. (11/15/2006)*

Ballentine 2000 Integrity Merlot-Cabernet Franc (Napa Valley) $28. 86 —*S.H. (11/15/2004)*

Ballentine 2004 Petite Verdot (Napa Valley) $38. 88 —*S.H. (12/1/2006)*

Ballentine 2003 Zinfandel Port (Napa Valley) $40. 85 —*S.H. (12/15/2005)*

Ballentine 1999 Bg Reserve Red Blend (Napa Valley) $40. 91 —*S.H. (11/15/2002)*

Ballentine 1999 Syrah (Napa Valley) $28. 91 —*S.H. (12/1/2002)*

Ballentine 1998 Syrah (Napa Valley) $25. 86 *(11/1/2001)*

Ballentine 2003 Betty's Vineyard Syrah (Napa Valley) $22. 88 *(9/1/2005)*

Ballentine 1999 Zinfandel (Napa Valley) $20. 90 Editors' Choice —*S.H. (12/1/2002)*

Ballentine 1999 Bg Reserve Zinfandel (Napa Valley) $28. 90 —*S.H. (12/1/2002)*

Ballentine 2001 Bg Zinfandel Block 9 Reserve Zinfandel (Napa Valley) $27. 88 *(11/1/2003)*

Ballentine 2004 Block 11 Old Vines Zinfandel (Napa Valley) $25. 90 —*S.H. (7/1/2006)*

Ballentine 2000 Block 9 Zinfandel (Napa Valley) $27. 92 —*S.H. (9/1/2004)*

Ballentine 2002 Block 9 Reserve Zinfandel (Napa Valley) $27. 91 —*S.H. (12/1/2006)*

Ballentine 1997 Estate Grown Zinfandel (Napa Valley) $16. 82 —*P.G. (11/15/1999)*

Ballentine 2003 Old Vines Estate Grown Zinfandel (Napa Valley) $18. From century-old vines growing in a warm part of the valley comes this soft, layered Zin. It shows wild blue- and black-skinned berry fruits that approach raisins, rum punch, cherry liqueur and rosemary-thyme flavors. A tasty Zin, a little simple in structure, but nice and dry. 86 —*S.H. (10/1/2007)*

Ballentine 2002 Old Vines Zinfandel (Napa Valley) $18. 89 —*S.H. (11/15/2006)*

Ballentine 2001 Old Vines Zinfandel (Napa Valley) $18. 88 *(11/1/2003)*

Ballentine 2003 Old Vines Block 11 Zinfandel (Napa Valley) $25. 92 —*S.H. (5/1/2005)*

BALLETTO

Balletto 2004 Pinot Grigio (Sonoma Coast) $12. 87 Best Buy —*S.H. (2/1/2006)*

Balletto 2004 Estate Bottled Pinot Noir (Russian River Valley) $24. 86 —*S.H. (12/1/2006)*

Balletto 2006 Rosé of Pinot Noir Pinot Noir (Russian River Valley) $16. Uncork this pale young wine to give it a hit of air for an hour or so in the fridge before serving, to let its nerves settle. Then it turns pretty and polished, with dry, Pinot-esque flavors of cherries, cola and vanilla spice, and a rich cut of acidity. 88 —*S.H. (7/1/2007)*

BANDIERA

Bandiera 2000 Vineyard Reserve Cabernet Sauvignon (California) $10. 84 —*S.H. (11/15/2002)*

Bandiera 1999 Vineyard Reserve Cabernet Sauvignon (California) $10. 87 Best Buy —*S.H. (5/1/2001)*

Bandiera 1999 Vineyard Reserve Chardonnay (California) $10. 83 —*S.H. (5/1/2001)*

Bandiera 1999 Vineyard Reserve Merlot (California) $10. 85 Best Buy —*S.H. (5/1/2001)*

Bandiera 1998 Vineyard Reserve Merlot (California) $10. 82 —*S.H. (8/1/2001)*

BANDON

Bandon 2004 Pinot Gris (Oregon) $14. 86 —*P.G. (2/1/2006)*

BANNISTER

Bannister 2002 Chardonnay (Russian River Valley) $20. 84 —*S.H. (10/1/2005)*

Bannister 1999 Porter-Bass Chardonnay (Russian River Valley) $38. 87 —*S.H. (12/15/2002)*

Bannister 2002 Porter-Bass Vineyard Chardonnay (Russian River Valley) $28. 90 Editors' Choice —*S.H. (10/1/2005)*

Bannister 2002 Rochioli & Allen Vineyards Chardonnay (Russian River Valley) $28. 88 —*S.H. (10/1/2005)*

Bannister 1999 Rochioli and Allen Vineyards Chardonnay (Russian River Valley) $28. 90 —*S.H. (12/15/2002)*

Bannister 1999 Floodgate Vineyard Pinot Noir (Anderson Valley) $30. 87 —*S.H. (2/1/2003)*

Bannister 2002 Salzgeber Vineyard Pinot Noir (Russian River Valley) $34. 85 —*S.H. (10/1/2005)*

BANYAN

Banyan 2006 Gewürztraminer (Monterey County) $12. Shows lots to like with its dry crispness and fruity flavors, and with only 12.7% alcohol, the light, delicate mouthfeel is a pleasure. Long in apricot, pineapple, guava and floral flavors, the wine finishes in a flood of cinnamon spice. 87 Best Buy —*S.H. (8/1/2007)*

Banyan 2006 Riesling (Santa Lucia Highlands) $17. Its exceptional dryness and searing acidity make this wine a natural to drink as an apéritif or with a wide range of food. It doesn't particularly taste like Riesling, though, more like a citrusy, minerally Albariño or Pinot Grigio. 85 —*S.H. (9/1/2007)*

BARBOURSVILLE

Barboursville 1998 Chardonnay (Virginia) $12. 83 —*J.C. (8/1/1999)*

Barboursville 1998 Merlot (Monticello) $16. 85 —*J.C. (8/1/1999)*

Barboursville 1998 Pinot Grigio (Monticello) $13. 86 *(8/1/1999)*

Barboursville 1998 Riesling (Monticello) $10. 82 —*J.C. (8/1/1999)*

BAREFOOT BUBBLY

Barefoot Bubbly NV Brut Cuvée Chardonnay Champagne Sparkling Blend (California) $10. Rough and scoury in the mouth, with citrus, vanilla, honey and bread dough flavors. Not bad for this price. 83 —*S.H. (12/31/2007)*

Barefoot Bubbly NV Brut Cuvée Chardonnay Champagne Sparkling Blend (California) $9. 85 Best Buy —*S.H. (6/1/2006)*

Barefoot Bubbly NV Premium Extra Dry Chardonnay Champagne Sparkling Blend (California) $10. Simple and rough in texture, with medicinal citrus fruit and dough flavors. 82 —*S.H. (12/31/2007)*

Barefoot Bubbly NV Premium Extra Dry Chardonnay Champagne Sparkling Blend (California) $7. 84 Best Buy —*S.H. (12/31/2005)*

BAREFOOT CELLARS

Barefoot Cellars 1999 Cabernet Sauvignon (Sonoma County) $17. 83 —*S.H. (3/1/2003)*

Barefoot Cellars 2003 Reserve Cabernet Sauvignon (Dry Creek Valley) $15. 83 —*S.H. (11/15/2006)*

Barefoot Cellars 2001 Reserve Cabernet Sauvignon (Dry Creek Valley) $17. 86 —*S.H. (5/1/2004)*

Barefoot Cellars 2000 Reserve Cabernet Sauvignon (Sonoma County) $17. 85 —*S.H. (10/1/2003)*

Barefoot Cellars NV Barefoot Bubbly Champagne Blend (California) $7. 81 —*S.H. (12/1/2000)*

Barefoot Cellars NV Bubbly Champagne Blend (California) $10. 80 *(12/15/1999)*

Barefoot Cellars NV Bubbly Brut Cuvée Champagne Blend (California) $7. 81 —*S.H. (12/1/2002)*

Barefoot Cellars NV Bubbly Prenium Champagne Blend (California) $7. 80 —*S.H. (12/1/2002)*

Barefoot Cellars NV Cuvée Brut Champagne Blend (California) $8. 82 *(12/1/2001)*

Barefoot Cellars NV Chardonnay (California) $6. 83 Best Buy —*S.H. (10/1/2005)*

Barefoot Cellars NV Chardonnay (California) $6. 83 Best Buy —*S.H. (4/1/2006)*

Barefoot Cellars NV Brut Cuvée Chardonnay (California) $7. 84 —*S.H. (12/1/2003)*

Barefoot Cellars NV Brut Cuvée Chardonnay (California) $7. 86 Best Buy —*S.H. (11/15/2003)*

Barefoot Cellars 2004 Reserve Chardonnay (Russian River Valley) $15. 83 —*S.H. (3/1/2006)*

Barefoot Cellars 2003 Reserve Chardonnay (Russian River Valley) $15. 84 —*S.H. (10/1/2005)*

Barefoot Cellars 1997 Reserve Chardonnay (Sonoma) $NA. 87 —*M.M. (6/1/2003)*

Barefoot Cellars 2000 Reserve Impression Meritage (Alexander Valley) $18. 86 —*S.H. (11/15/2003)*

Barefoot Cellars NV Merlot (California) $6. A little sharp and raw, but there's so much nice blackberry, cherry and spicy cola fruit, and the wine is so dry and balanced, that at this price, it's a bargain. 84 Best Buy —*S.H. (3/1/2007)*

Barefoot Cellars 2004 Reserve Merlot (Russian River Valley) $18. Lots of blackberry and coffee fruit in this dry wine. It's not terribly complex, and in fact is a little raw, but decanting will help, and the acids will balance well against the richness of steak. 85 —*S.H. (3/1/2007)*

Barefoot Cellars 2003 Reserve Merlot (Alexander Valley) $15. T85 —*S.H. (11/15/2005)*

Barefoot Cellars 2000 Reserve Merlot (Russian River Valley) $17. 86 —*S.H. (2/1/2003)*

Barefoot Cellars 1999 Reserve Merlot (Sonoma County) $17. 86 —*S.H. (9/1/2002)*

Barefoot Cellars 2001 Pinot Noir (Russian River Valley) $15. 85 —*S.H. (2/1/2003)*

Barefoot Cellars 1999 Pinot Noir (Sonoma County) $15. 84 —*S.H. (7/1/2002)*

Barefoot Cellars 2003 Reserve Pinot Noir (Russian River Valley) $15. 87 —*S.H. (11/15/2005)*

Barefoot Cellars 2002 Reserve Pinot Noir (Russian River Valley) $16. 83 *(11/1/2004)*

Barefoot Cellars 2000 Reserve Pinot Noir (Sonoma County) $NA. 87 *(5/1/2002)*

Barefoot Cellars 1998 Reserve Pinot Noir (Sonoma County) $15. 86 —*J.C. (12/15/2000)*

Barefoot Cellars NV Barefoot on the Beach Red Blend (California) $5. 83 Best Buy —*S.H. (7/1/2006)*

Barefoot Cellars 2001 Sauvignon Blanc (California) $6. 87 Best Buy —*S.H. (1/1/2004)*

Barefoot Cellars 2004 Reserve Sauvignon Blanc (Alexander Valley) $13. 87 —*S.H. (11/15/2005)*

Barefoot Cellars 2002 Reserve Sauvignon Blanc (Alexander Valley) $15. 83 —*S.H. (12/31/2003)*

Barefoot Cellars 2001 Reserve Sauvignon Blanc (Dry Creek Valley) $13. 85 —*S.H. (3/1/2003)*

Barefoot Cellars NV Extra Dry Sparkling Blend (California) $7. 86 Best Buy —*S.H. (12/1/2003)*

Barefoot Cellars NV Syrah (California) $6. 84 Best Buy —*S.H. (11/15/2005)*

Barefoot Cellars NV Syrah (California) $6. 80 —*S.H. (3/1/2004)*

Barefoot Cellars NV Barefoot on the Beach White Blend (California) $4. 82 —*S.H. (11/15/2005)*

Barefoot Cellars NV Barefoot on the Beach White Wine White Blend (California) $5. 83 Best Buy —*S.H. (7/1/2006)*

Barefoot Cellars NV Zinfandel (California) $6. 83 —*P.G. (3/1/2001)*

Barefoot Cellars NV Zinfandel (California) $6. 84 Best Buy —*S.H. (10/1/2006)*

Barefoot Cellars NV Barefoot on the Beach White Zinfandel (California) $5. 83 Best Buy —*S.H. (7/1/2006)*

Barefoot Cellars 2001 Reserve Zinfandel (Dry Creek Valley) $10. 84 *(11/1/2003)*

Barefoot Cellars 1998 Reserve Zinfandel (Sonoma County) $17. 85 —*S.H. (12/15/2001)*

BARGETTO

Bargetto 2005 Chardonnay (Santa Cruz Mountains) $20. This Chard is a little soft and simple, but likeable. It's got forward apricot, pineapple custard, vanilla and cinnamon spice flavors, and a creamy texture. 84 —*S.H. (6/1/2007)*

Bargetto 2002 Chardonnay (Central Coast) $12. 84 —*S.H. (12/1/2004)*

Bargetto 2000 Chardonnay (Central Coast) $NA. 84 —*S.H. (9/12/2002)*

Bargetto 2000 Regan Vineyard Chardonnay (Santa Cruz Mountains) $20. 89 —*S.H. (2/1/2003)*

Bargetto 2001 Regan Vineyards Chardonnay (Santa Cruz Mountains) $18. 86 —*S.H. (6/1/2003)*

Bargetto 2004 Regan Vineyards Dolcetto (Santa Cruz Mountains) $20. Smells like cheap Port, tastes harsh and aggressive, with cherry cough medicine flavors. 81 —*S.H. (6/1/2007)*

Bargetto 2005 Gewürztraminer (Monterey County) $14. A little on the thin side, but saved by beautifully crisp acidity that makes the wine so clean, and just enough fruit, spice and wildflower notes to satisfy. Finishes dry to just off-dry, in the Alsatian style. 83 —*S.H. (3/1/2007)*

Bargetto 2000 Gewürztraminer (Monterey) $10. 85 —*S.H. (9/1/2003)*

Bargetto 2000 Dry Gewürztraminer (Santa Cruz Mountains) $12. 90 —*S.H. (9/12/2002)*

Bargetto 2006 Viento Vineyard Gewürztraminer (Monterey County) $14. You'll find Asian spice, wildflower and candied peach fruit flavors in this Gewürz, and the acidity is nice and crisp. But it's just too sweet in white sugar for a table wine. 82 —*S.H. (11/15/2007)*

Bargetto 2004 Merlot (Santa Cruz Mountains) $24. Starts off a little musty, so decant for a while, and this coastal mountain Merlot will open up to reveal mint-accented blackberry, blueberry, cocoa and clove flavors. It's rich and polished, but a little on the soft side. Drink now. 86 —*S.H. (12/31/2007)*

Bargetto 2001 Merlot (Santa Cruz Mountains) $20. 90 —*S.H. (12/15/2004)*

Bargetto 2000 Merlot (California) $12. 84 —*S.H. (4/1/2003)*

Bargetto 1999 Merlot (Santa Cruz Mountains) $20. 83 —*S.H. (4/1/2003)*

Bargetto 2003 Regan Vineyard Merlot (Santa Cruz Mountains) $35. You can taste the sun-warmed grapes that got so ripe and fruity in this fine vintage. Blackberries, cherries, chocolate, dark plums and violets flood the palate, with rich toasty oak overtones. There are bigtime tannins, too, dusty and fairly astringent, making for a puckery feeling. A dry, balanced Merlot to cellar for a couple years. 87 —*S.H. (3/1/2007)*

Bargetto 1998 Reserve Merlot (Santa Cruz Mountains) $30. 81 —*S.H. (9/12/2002)*

Bargetto 2006 Pinot Grigio (California) $14. Simple and semisweet, this PG has flavors of apple juice, ripe yellow apricots and sugar. **82** *—S.H. (11/15/2007)*

Bargetto 2005 Pinot Grigio (California) $14. There must be cool-climate grapes in this statewide-appellated wine, because there's great, crunchy acidity, which is just what you want in a nice PG. The wine is dry and minerally, with fruity, apricot and spice flavors. **84** *—S.H. (3/1/2007)*

Bargetto 2003 Pinot Grigio (California) $15. 84 *—S.H. (11/15/2004)*

Bargetto 2001 Pinot Grigio (California) $16. 84 *—S.H. (9/1/2003)*

Bargetto 2000 Pinot Grigio (California) $16. 84 *—S.H. (9/1/2002)*

Bargetto 2004 Pinot Gris (California) $14. 83 *—S.H. (2/1/2006)*

Bargetto 2004 Regan Vineyard Pinot Noir (Santa Cruz Mountains) $35. Bargetto's been working with Pinot from this vineyard for some time now, and this is their best effort to date. It shows classic coastal varietal character, with a delicately dry, silky structure, flavors of cherries, cola, pomegranates, rhubarb tea and dusty spices, and crisp acidity. Best now for its polished elegance. **92** *—S.H. (3/1/2007)*

Bargetto 2001 Regan Vineyards Pinot Noir (Santa Cruz Mountains) $20. 87 *—S.H. (12/15/2004)*

Bargetto 2000 Regan Vineyards Pinot Noir (Santa Cruz County) $30. 83 *—S.H. (5/1/2002)*

Bargetto 1999 Regan Vineyards Pinot Noir (Santa Cruz Mountains) $30. 84 *(10/1/2002)*

Bargetto 2000 Regan Vineyards Reserve Pinot Noir (Santa Cruz Mountains) $40. 87 *—S.H. (7/1/2003)*

Bargetto 2001 La Vita Red Blend (Santa Cruz Mountains) $50. Pours inky black, and even though it has some bottle age, it's still astringently tannic. The suggestion is complexity and ageworthiness. A blend of Dolcetto, Refosco and Nebbiolo, there are cherry flavors, with a rich, earthy, fresh herb and coffee edge. Really locked down now; the wine's future is uncertain. **84** *—S.H. (3/1/2007)*

Bargetto 1999 La Vita Regan Vineyards Red Blend (Santa Cruz Mountains) $50. 84 *—S.H. (12/15/2004)*

Bargetto 2002 Syrah (Monterey County) $16. 83 *(9/1/2005)*

Bargetto 2005 Zinfandel (Lodi) $14. Rustic and sweet, with Porty flavors of cherries and chocolate, this Zin has a medicinal finish. **81** *—S.H. (11/15/2007)*

Bargetto 2002 Zinfandel (Lodi) $14. 86 *—S.H. (11/15/2004)*

Bargetto 2001 Rauser Vineyard Zinfandel (Lodi) $12. 83 *—J.M. (11/1/2003)*

USA

BARLOW

Barlow 2003 Barrouge Unfiltered Red Wine Cabernet Blend (Napa Valley) $40. I liked the '02, but something went wrong with the '03, which is hot and bizarre, with artificial fruit or cough medicine flavors. It's also very sharp in acidity. **81** *—S.H. (3/1/2007)*

Barlow 2001 Red Table Wine Cabernet Blend (Napa Valley) $30. 90 *—S.H. (6/1/2004)*

Barlow 2002 Cabernet Sauvignon (Napa Valley) $40. 86 *—S.H. (12/15/2005)*

Barlow 2001 Cabernet Sauvignon (Napa Valley) $39. 92 Editors' Choice *—S.H. (10/1/2004)*

Barlow 2000 Cabernet Sauvignon (Napa Valley) $36. 90 *—S.H. (11/15/2003)*

Barlow 2003 Unfiltered Cabernet Sauvignon (Napa Valley) $45. Deep in aroma, in flavor, in depth and finish, this Cabernet fulfills your Napa Cab expectations. The mouthfeel is all velvet and silk, the tannins are perfectly sculpted, and the blackberry and coffee flavors are ripe and satisfying without being overwrought. Best now and for a decade. **91** *—S.H. (3/1/2007)*

Barlow 2002 Merlot (Napa Valley) $32. 91 *—S.H. (4/1/2005)*

Barlow 2001 Merlot (Napa Valley) $NA. 91 *—S.H. (6/1/2004)*

Barlow 2000 Merlot (Napa Valley) $28. 91 *—S.H. (8/1/2003)*

Barlow 2003 Unfiltered Merlot (Napa Valley) $32. Nice structure in this wine, wonderful tannins, so sweetly ripe and soft, and such a good overlay of oak, but the problem is fruit. It's just not there, which leaves the alcohol standing naked and hot. Why this is, is a mystery from a good winery. **83** *—S.H. (3/1/2007)*

Barlow 2002 Barrouge Red Blend (Napa Valley) $38. 91 *—S.H. (4/1/2005)*

Barlow 2001 Zinfandel (Napa Valley) $19. 87 *(11/1/2003)*

BARNARD GRIFFIN

Barnard Griffin 2000 Cabernet Franc (Columbia Valley (WA)) $30. 90 *—P.G. (6/1/2002)*

Barnard Griffin 2005 Cabernet Sauvignon (Columbia Valley (WA)) $18. These grapes come from a variety of vineyards scattered widely across the state, but they add up to a 98% pure Cabernet Sauvignon, intense, dark, plummy, rich and full-bodied. It's got all the grape's key component flavors on display: olive, light herb, and juicy purple fruits. The oak is still coming into focus, with strong notes of vanilla and clove. Give it a few hours breathing time. **90** *—P.G. (8/1/2007)*

Barnard Griffin 2003 Cabernet Sauvignon (Columbia Valley (WA)) $14. 87 *—P.G. (12/15/2005)*

Barnard Griffin 2001 Cabernet Sauvignon (Columbia Valley (WA)) $15. 87 *—P.G. (9/1/2004)*

Barnard Griffin 1999 Cabernet Sauvignon (Columbia Valley (WA)) $18. 85 *—P.G. (12/31/2001)*

Barnard Griffin 2004 Reserve Cabernet Sauvignon (Columbia Valley (WA)) $30. This can stand alongside far pricier wines, and offers the same suppleness, density, nuance and detail. Winemaker Rob Griffin's masterful blending retains the often-lost subtleties—black olive, herb, balsamic—and ties these herbal notes in seamlessly with plummy, black cherry fruit. **93** *—P.G. (8/1/2007)*

Barnard Griffin 2005 Chardonnay (Columbia Valley (WA)) $10. The Chardonnay is the largest production wine made at Barnard Griffin. It is a stellar wine, about half barrel fermented, the other half stainless; a beautiful blend of crisp, fresh, creamy, leesy, textural white peach and light citrus fruit. Consistent in style with the winery's Fumé, the Chardonnay has plenty of clean acid, great fruit, and a nice butterscotch finish in the back of the throat. **90 Best Buy** *—P.G. (8/1/2007)*

Barnard Griffin 2000 Chardonnay (Columbia Valley (WA)) $14. 86 *—P.G. (2/1/2002)*

Barnard Griffin 2000 Reserve Chardonnay (Columbia Valley (WA)) $19. 88 *—P.G. (7/1/2002)*

Barnard Griffin 2000 Wahluke Slope Vineyard Chardonnay (Columbia Valley (WA)) $19. 90 *—P.G. (9/1/2002)*

Barnard Griffin 2005 Fumé Blanc (Columbia Valley (WA)) $9. Dry, sauvage and nicely detailed, this bright, tart, citrusy wine has a truly great mouthfeel. Done entirely in stainless steel, it is packed with flavors of fresh fruit skins, lingering with crisp and textural spice. Just 12.6% alcohol puts it squarely into the Sancerre range. **90 Best Buy** *—P.G. (8/1/2007)*

Barnard Griffin 2004 Fumé Blanc (Columbia Valley (WA)) $9. 88 Best Buy *—P.G. (11/15/2005)*

Barnard Griffin 2003 Fumé Blanc (Columbia Valley (WA)) $8. 88 Best Buy *—P.G. (12/1/2004)*

Barnard Griffin 2002 Fumé Blanc (Columbia Valley (WA)) $8. 89 Best Buy *—P.G. (5/1/2004)*

Barnard Griffin 2000 Fumé Blanc (Columbia Valley (WA)) $11. 88 Best Buy *—P.G. (12/31/2001)*

Barnard Griffin 2004 Merlot (Columbia Valley (WA)) $18. This is a solid example of straight-ahead Washington Merlot. The fruit is pretty and polished, bright with raspberry and cherry flavors, forward but with the palate presence to age for some years. There's a foundation of herb and a hint of silage, adding character but finishing just a bit on the funky side. **87** *—P.G. (8/1/2007)*

Barnard Griffin 2001 Merlot (Columbia Valley (WA)) $15. 87 *—P.G. (9/1/2004)*

Barnard Griffin 2000 Merlot (Columbia Valley (WA)) $15. 89 Best Buy *—P.G. (6/1/2002)*

Barnard Griffin 1998 Merlot (Columbia Valley (WA)) $17. 90 *—P.G. (6/1/2000)*

Barnard Griffin 2003 Ciel du Cheval Merlot (Red Mountain) $30. 89 *—P.G. (12/15/2005)*

Barnard Griffin 2004 Reserve Merlot (Columbia Valley (WA)) $25. This firm, tannic Merlot is a step up in concentration from the winery's regular bottling. It's ripe, focused and still a bit tight, with stacked layers of berry, plum and cassis. Winemaker Rob Griffin retains some of the natural herbaceousness of the grape, as a background nuance, adding flavor interest. Decant it well before drinking. **89** *—P.G. (8/1/2007)*

Barnard Griffin 2002 Caroway Vineyard Sémillon (Columbia Valley (WA)) $NA. 90 *—P.G. (9/1/2004)*

Barnard Griffin 2001 Caroway Vineyard Sémillon (Columbia Valley (WA)) $13. 88 Best Buy *—P.G. (6/1/2002)*

Barnard Griffin 2006 Rosé Sangiovese (Columbia Valley (WA)) $10. From the Maury Balcom vineyard, this is a dry, fruit-forward rosé, finished at a pleasing 12.4% alcohol. It's a forward, fruity, lightly spicy springtime quaffer, packed with strawberry flavor. Slightly bigger and bolder, but perhaps less detailed, than the 2005 version. **87 Best Buy** *—P.G. (8/1/2007)*

Barnard Griffin 2006 Rosé of Sangiovese (Columbia Valley (WA)) $15. A slightly confected, extremely fruity rosé, marked by scents of rose petals, cherries and strawberries. Offers decent fruit concentration, then turns slightly chalky on the finish. **84** *(10/1/2007)*

Barnard Griffin 2005 Syrah (Columbia Valley (WA)) $18. This is tight, leafy, tannic and young, but it nicely captures the Wahluke Slope AVA style, with tight edges, crisp acids, citrus rind nuances, and a polished mouthfeel. It seems to gather strength as it sits on the palate; and it will profit from more time in bottle. But the balance is already there, the fruit is tangy but ripe, and the acids are just perfect. **89** *—P.G. (8/1/2007)*

Barnard Griffin 2002 Syrah (Columbia Valley (WA)) $14. 91 Best Buy *—P.G. (5/1/2004)*

Barnard Griffin 2000 Syrah (Columbia Valley (WA)) $30. 86 *—P.G. (6/1/2002)*

Barnard Griffin 1999 Syrah (Columbia Valley (WA)) $30. 85 *(11/1/2001)*

Barnard Griffin 2006 White Riesling (Columbia Valley (WA)) $8. Tight, bright and spicy, with light peach flavors under fresh herb. There's a slight and interesting taste of fennel that lingers in the back of the palate. Though under 12% alcohol, this does not come across as sweet, but rather as a racy, food-friendly and distinctive effort. **88 Best Buy** *—P.G. (8/1/2007)*

Barnard Griffin 2006 White Riesling (Columbia Valley (WA)) $12. Light and citrusy, this off-dry Riesling features pleasant floral and spice notes that just lack a little zip on the finish. **83** *(10/1/2007)*

Barnard Griffin 2003 Zinfandel (Columbia Valley (WA)) $22. 88 *—P.G. (12/15/2005)*

BARNETT

Barnett 2003 Cabernet Sauvignon (Spring Mountain) $65. 92 Cellar Selection *—S.H. (8/1/2006)*

Barnett 2002 Cabernet Sauvignon (Spring Mountain) $60. 91 *—S.H. (10/1/2005)*

Barnett 2003 Rattlesnake Hill Cabernet Sauvignon (Spring Mountain) $110. 94 Cellar Selection *—S.H. (8/1/2006)*

Barnett 1998 Chardonnay (Napa Valley) $25. 88 *(6/1/2000)*

Barnett 2000 Chardonnay (Napa Valley) $25. 88 *—J.M. (5/1/2002)*

Barnett 2004 Sangiacomo Vineyard Chardonnay (Carneros) $29. 87 *—S.H. (8/1/2006)*

Barnett 2004 Savoy Vineyard Chardonnay (Anderson Valley) $35. 85 *—S.H. (8/1/2006)*

Barnett 2003 Merlot (Spring Mountain) $45. 87 *—S.H. (8/1/2006)*

Barnett 1997 Pinot Noir (Santa Lucia Highlands) $25. 87 *(12/15/1999)*

Barnett 2004 Pinot Noir (Santa Barbara County) $37. 88 *—S.H. (9/1/2006)*

Barnett 2004 Pinot Noir (Russian River Valley) $37. 89 *—S.H. (9/1/2006)*

Barnett 2004 Savoy Vineyard Pinot Noir (Anderson Valley) $45. 93 *—S.H. (9/1/2006)*

Barnett 2000 Sleepy Hollow Vineyard Pinot Noir (Santa Lucia Highlands) $40. 90 *(10/1/2002)*

BARNWOOD

Barnwood 1997 Trio Bordeaux Blend (Santa Barbara County) $29. 88 *—L.W. (12/31/1999)*

Barnwood 2002 Cabernet Sauvignon (Santa Barbara County) $22. 85 *—S.H. (2/1/2005)*

Barnwood 2001 Cabernet Sauvignon (Santa Barbara County) $22. 83 *—S.H. (11/15/2003)*

Barnwood 2000 Cabernet Sauvignon (Santa Barbara County) $22. 86 *—S.H. (6/1/2003)*

Barnwood 2004 3200 Cabernet Sauvignon (Santa Barbara County) $20. 82 *—S.H. (11/15/2006)*

Barnwood 1997 Reserve Merlot (Santa Barbara County) $27. 88 *—L.W. (12/31/1999)*

Barnwood 2004 Long Shadow Petite Sirah (Santa Barbara County) $20. 82 *—S.H. (11/15/2006)*

Barnwood 2003 Long Shadow Petite Sirah (Santa Barbara County) $20. 87 *—S.H. (3/1/2006)*

Barnwood 2002 Trio Red Blend (Santa Barbara County) $35. 85 *—S.H. (2/1/2005)*

Barnwood 2000 Trio Red Blend (Santa Barbara County) $35. 86 *—S.H. (6/1/2004)*

Barnwood 2004 Sauvignon Blanc (Santa Barbara County) $14. 84 *—S.H. (3/1/2006)*

Barnwood 2003 Sauvignon Blanc (Santa Barbara County) $14. 86 *—S.H. (2/1/2005)*

Barnwood 2002 Sauvignon Blanc (Santa Barbara County) $14. 85 *—S.H. (12/31/2003)*

Barnwood 2000 Sauvignon Blanc (Santa Barbara County) $14. 87 *—S.H. (11/15/2001)*

Barnwood 2005 The Border Sauvignon Blanc (Santa Barbara County) $14. 86 *—S.H. (11/15/2006)*

Barnwood 1999 Syrah (Central Coast) $20. 87 *(10/1/2001)*

Barnwood 2004 Untamed Tempranillo (San Luis Obispo County) $20. 83 *—S.H. (11/15/2006)*

Barnwood 2003 Untamed Tempranillo (San Luis Obispo County) $22. 89 *—S.H. (6/1/2006)*

BARON HERZOG

Baron Herzog 1997 Cabernet Sauvignon (California) $13. 85 *—S.H. (7/1/1999)*

Baron Herzog 2002 Cabernet Sauvignon (California) $13. 84 *—S.H. (8/1/2005)*

Baron Herzog 1999 Cabernet Sauvignon (California) $13. 82 *—M.S. (4/1/2002)*

Baron Herzog 1996 Special Reserve Cabernet Sauvignon (Napa Valley) $30. 86 *—S.H. (9/1/1999)*

Baron Herzog 1998 Chardonnay (California) $13. 85 *—S.H. (10/1/2000)*

Baron Herzog 1997 Chardonnay (California) $13. 80 *—S.H. (7/1/1999)*

Baron Herzog 1999 Chardonnay (California) $13. 80 *—M.S. (4/1/2002)*

Baron Herzog 1999 Chenin Blanc (Clarksburg) $6. 81 *(9/1/2000)*

Baron Herzog 2003 Chenin Blanc (Clarksburg) $7. 84 Best Buy *—S.H. (7/1/2005)*

BARON HERZOG

Baron Herzog 2005 Chardonnay (Central Coast) $13. Acceptable for its apricot fruit flavors and creamy texture, but the wine has a weird taste of artificial vanilla and a medicinal sweetness in the finish. **82** *—S.H. (7/1/2007)*

Baron Herzog 2002 Chenin Blanc (Clarksburg) $7. 87 Best Buy *—S.H. (11/15/2003)*

Baron Herzog 2000 Chenin Blanc (Clarksburg) $7. 83 *—S.H. (11/15/2001)*

Baron Herzog 2005 Special Reserve Late Harvest Chenin Blanc (Clarksburg) $16. With 15.2% residual sugar, this will satisfy your sweet tooth. The flavors are of apricot jam and vanilla, and are brightened with crisp acidity. Nice with apple pie à la mode. **87** *—S.H. (7/1/2007)*

Baron Herzog 1999 Merlot (Paso Robles) $13. 85 *—J.M. (11/15/2001)*

Baron Herzog 2005 Sauvignon Blanc (Central Coast) $10. This is one of the better SBs out there at this price. It's dry and crisp in layers of citrus fruits, apricots, tart green apples, white pepper and a flowery, honeysuckle taste, flavors that change all the time. **86 Best Buy** *—S.H. (3/1/2007)*

Baron Herzog 1999 Sauvignon Blanc (California) $13. 80 *—M.S. (4/1/2002)*

Baron Herzog 2003 Syrah (California) $13. 86 *(9/1/2005)*

Baron Herzog 2004 Kosher Special Reserve Syrah (Edna Valley) $30. This wine shows real varietal character, in the Northern Rhône sense of a fairly tannic, dry offering, but also is true Edna Valley in the brisk acids and purity of fruit. Has that hard-to-describe quality of elegant complexity that is the first duty of wine. Drink now through 2010. **90** *—S.H. (3/1/2007)*

Baron Herzog 1997 Zinfandel (California) $13. 83 *—S.H. (9/1/1999)*

Baron Herzog 2001 Zinfandel (Lodi) $7. 86 *(11/1/2003)*

Baron Herzog 2004 Old Vine Zinfandel (Lodi) $13. Hard to recommend this because it's so thin and harsh. There's some cherry fruit, but it's the medicinal, cough-medicine kind, and there's annoying sweetness in the finish. **82** *—S.H. (3/1/2007)*

Baron Herzog 2001 Old Vine Zinfandel (Lodi) $13. 86 *—S.H. (8/1/2005)*

Baron Herzog 1998 Old Vine Zinfandel (California) $13. 83 *—S.H. (12/1/2000)*

BARRA

Barra 2001 Cabernet Sauvignon (Mendocino) $22. 87 *—S.H. (4/1/2004)*

Barra 1999 Muscat Canelli (Mendocino County) $12. 87 *—S.H. (5/1/2002)*

Barra 1999 Petite Sirah (Mendocino) $27. 84 *(4/1/2003)*

Barra 1998 Petite Sirah (Mendocino County) $21. 90 *—S.H. (5/1/2002)*

Barra 1999 Pinot Blanc (Mendocino) $14. 87 *—S.H. (5/1/2002)*

Barra 1999 Pinot Noir (Mendocino) $15. 84 *—S.H. (5/1/2002)*

BARRA OF MENDOCINO

Barra of Mendocino 2002 Pinot Noir (Mendocino) $16. 83 *(11/1/2004)*

BARREL 27

Barrel 27 2004 Syrah (Paso Robles) $18. 87 *—S.H. (11/15/2006)*

Barrel 27 2002 Syrah (Paso Robles) $13. 87 *—S.H. (12/1/2004)*

BARRELSTONE

Barrelstone 2003 Syrah (Columbia Valley (WA)) $10. 85 Best Buy *(9/1/2005)*

Barrelstone 2001 Syrah (Columbia Valley (WA)) $14. 86 *—P.G. (12/31/2003)*

BARRETO

Barreto 2004 Vintage Port (Lodi) $35. Sweet and simple, with milk chocolate, cherry and caramel flavors. Needs greater depth and complexity. 84 *—S.H. (12/31/2007)*

Barreto 2004 Vinho Tinto Red Blend (California) $18. A blend of Tempranillo, Tannat, Touriga and Souzao, this gentle wine appeals for its raspberry and spice flavors. It's also quite crisp, making it a good partner for roasted meats. 85 *—S.H. (12/31/2007)*

Barreto 2004 Tempranillo (Lodi) $17. Soft, simple and semisweet, this Tempranillo has cherry, raspberry and spice flavors. It can be described as rustic. 82 *—S.H. (12/31/2007)*

Barreto 2004 Tempranillo (Paso Robles) $24. There's a good streak of acidity behind this dry wine, which is fortunate because the tannins are very soft. It has just enough crispness to balance the ripe cherry and sweet green herb flavors. Similar to Sangiovese, this is a pleasant sipper now. 86 *—S.H. (12/31/2007)*

Barreto 2004 Touriga Nacional (Lodi) $24. Made from one of the classic Port varieties, this dry wine shows the possibilities of growing these grapes in a hot California climate. The wine is soft, rich and complex, with cherry, tangerine, cocoa, herb and spice flavors. 86 *—S.H. (12/31/2007)*

Barreto 2005 Verdelho (Lodi) $16. The major defect of this wine is excessive sweetness. Without the sugary flavor, it would be great, for it has wonderfully crisp acidity and flavors of citrus fruits, peaches and minerals. 83 *—S.H. (12/15/2007)*

BARRISTER

Barrister 2003 Cabernet Franc (Columbia Valley (WA)) $24. 89 *—P.G. (4/1/2006)*

Barrister 2002 Cabernet Franc (Columbia Valley (WA)) $24. 89 *—P.G. (12/1/2004)*

Barrister 2001 Cabernet Franc (Columbia Valley (WA)) $24. 87 *—P.G. (12/31/2003)*

Barrister 2002 Cabernet Sauvignon (Columbia Valley (WA)) $29. 92 *—P.G. (4/1/2006)*

Barrister 2003 Bacchus Vineyard Cabernet Sauvignon (Columbia Valley (WA)) $29. 90 *—P.G. (4/1/2006)*

Barrister 2003 Merlot (Red Mountain) $28. 91 *—P.G. (4/1/2006)*

Barrister 2003 Syrah (Walla Walla (WA)) $26. 93 Editors' Choice *—P.G. (4/1/2006)*

BARTHOLOMEW PARK

Bartholomew Park 1997 Alta Vista Vineyards Cabernet Sauvignon (Sonoma Valley) $36. 89 *(11/1/2000)*

Bartholomew Park 1997 Batto Vineyard Cabernet Sauvignon (Sonoma Valley) $36. 93 *(11/1/2000)*

Bartholomew Park 1997 Kasper Vineyard Cabernet Sauvignon (Sonoma Valley) $41. 88 *(11/1/2000)*

Bartholomew Park 1997 Parks Vineyard Cabernet Sauvignon (Napa Valley) $37. 90 *(11/1/2000)*

Bartholomew Park 1996 Weiler Vineyard Chardonnay (Sonoma Valley) $21. 86 *—S.H. (11/1/1999)*

BASALT CELLARS

Basalt Cellars 2004 Merlot (Columbia Valley (WA)) $24. Unblended, 100% Merlot, this light, tart, citrusy wine leads with a spicy, tangy toastiness. The fruit lacks substance; it's just generic light red fruit, and there is a rough, chalky edge to the acids. 85 *—P.G. (3/1/2007)*

Basalt Cellars 2004 Rim Rock Red Blend (Columbia Valley (WA)) $18. This is essentially a Cabernet, with small percentages of Merlot, Cab Franc and Syrah in the blend. Bottom line is a light, earthy, herbal Cabernet with some toasty, coffee-flavored oak. 85 *—P.G. (3/1/2007)*

BASEL CELLARS

Basel Cellars 2003 Claret Bordeaux Blend (Walla Walla (WA)) $24. 87 *—P.G. (4/1/2006)*

Basel Cellars 2001 Merriment Bordeaux Blend (Walla Walla (WA)) $48. 91 *(5/1/2004)*

Basel Cellars 2002 Merriment Red Wine Bordeaux Blend (Walla Walla (WA)) $48. 88 *—P.G. (4/1/2005)*

Basel Cellars 2004 Cabernet Sauvignon (Columbia Valley (WA)) $32. This is pure Cabernet, sourced from Ste. Michelle's Cold Creek vineyard. It's firm and solid, nicely styled and clean, pure and focused. It shows the definition and supple muscularity of the vineyard, with tight black cherry and blackberry fruit, enhanced with streaks of smoke, earth and licorice. 89 *—P.G. (5/1/2007)*

Basel Cellars 2003 Cabernet Sauvignon (Columbia Valley (WA)) $32. 89 *—P.G. (4/1/2006)*

Basel Cellars 2002 Cabernet Sauvignon (Columbia Valley (WA)) $32. 90 *—P.G. (4/1/2005)*

Basel Cellars 2003 Red Blend (Walla Walla (WA)) $36. 87 *—P.G. (4/1/2006)*

Basel Cellars 2004 Claret Red Blend (Columbia Valley (WA)) $20. Right out of the bottle come slightly hot, spicy, sharp flavors of bright raspberry and strawberry. This is all press juice from the vintage, and it carries some bite, along with lively, assertive, acidic fruit and lovely floral aromatics. It's a screwcap red—approachable and fruity, but not simple or soft. Au contraire, it's substantial and spicy, with plenty of acid and definition. 88 *—P.G. (5/1/2007)*

Basel Cellars 2004 Ode To Merriment Red Blend (Columbia Valley (WA)) $48. This Bordeaux blend has a strong herbal streak and some chewy tannins. The heavy toast in past vintages has here been a bit subdued, but there is still plenty of smoke and coffee. I like the structure—the fruit is not too sweet, and the balance suggests that this wine may evolve some interesting nuances. Right now it's lightly herbal, tight, with hints of cinnamon and toast. 88 *—P.G. (11/1/2007)*

Basel Cellars 2006 Sauvignon Blanc (Columbia Valley (WA)) $18. There is a slightly sour, slightly sweaty aspect to the nose, and it affects the palate as well. Behind it there are flavors of bubble gum, some lees contact, plenty of acid but nothing has yet completely knit together. 75% Sauvignon Blanc and 25% Sémillon. 85 *—P.G. (11/1/2007)*

Basel Cellars 2004 Syrah (Columbia Valley (WA)) $42. 93 *—P.G. (11/15/2006)*

Basel Cellars 2003 Syrah (Walla Walla (WA)) $42. 87 *—P.G. (4/1/2006)*

Basel Cellars 2002 Syrah (Columbia Valley (WA)) $48. 88 *—P.G. (4/1/2005)*

Basel Cellars 2004 Lewis Vineyard Reserve Syrah (Columbia Valley (WA)) $60. 89 *—P.G. (11/15/2006)*

BASIGNANI

Basignani 1999 Chardonnay (Maryland) $13. 80 *—J.M. (7/1/2002)*

BASK

Bask 2005 Chardonnay (North Coast) $20. 85 *—S.H. (12/31/2006)*

Bask 2006 Babcock Ranch Chardonnay (Suisun Valley) $14. There's lots of ripe, appealing green apple, vanilla and honey flavors in this Chard. What it could use is greater structure and complexity. But it does show promise for this Delta appellation that's lately been fighting for recognition. 85 *—S.H. (11/15/2007)*

Bask 2005 Viognier (North Coast) $24. 84 *—S.H. (12/31/2006)*

Bask 2006 Babcock Ranch Viognier (Suisun Valley) $16. With honeyed flavors of peaches, pineapples, wildflowers and spices, this single-vineyard Viognier has fine acidic crispness that balances its slight sweetness. 84 *—S.H. (12/31/2007)*

BATES CREEK

Bates Creek 1999 Cabernet Sauvignon (Napa Valley) $25. 92 Editors' Choice *—S.H. (11/15/2002)*

BATTLE CREEK

Battle Creek 2002 Pinot Noir (Willamette Valley) $50. 86 *—P.G. (2/1/2005)*

BAXTER

Baxter 2004 Oppenlander Vineyard Pinot Noir (Mendocino) $45. Northwest of the Anderson Valley, from an area that may someday be known as Mendocino Coast, comes this slightly rustic Pinot. The berry-cherry fruit has edges of tobacco, dill, tea, hay and spice, and the finish is fairly tannic. 87 *—S.H. (11/1/2007)*

Baxter 2004 Toulouse Vineyard Pinot Noir (Anderson Valley) $45. The grapes are clones 777 and 115, and the wine shows those ultrapure,

USA

intense Dijon flavors of cherries, raspberries, cola, cinnamon and vanilla. With no new oak, the fruit really stars in this silky, delicious wine. 91 —S.H. (11/1/2007)

BAYSTONE

Baystone 2000 Saralee's Vineyard Chardonnay (Russian River Valley) $20. 87 —S.H. (6/1/2003)

Baystone 1998 Saralee's Vineyard Chardonnay (Russian River Valley) $20. 90 (6/1/2000)

Baystone 1999 Shiraz (Dry Creek Valley) $24. 86 (11/1/2001)

BAYWOOD

Baywood 1997 Merlot (Monterey) $18. 90 Editors' Choice —S.H. (5/1/2001)

Baywood 1999 Grand Reserve Syrah (Monterey) $35. 88 (11/1/2001)

Baywood 1999 Late Harvest Symphony White Blend (California) $35. 89 (8/1/2001)

Baywood 1999 Symphony White Blend (California) $12. 83 —S.H. (5/1/2001)

BEAR CREEK

Bear Creek 2000 Petite Sirah (Lodi) $18. 84 (4/1/2003)

Bear Creek 1998 Pinot Noir (Rogue Valley) $30. 89 —M.S. (12/1/2000)

Bear Creek 2000 Zinfandel (Lodi) $18. 84 —S.H. (2/1/2003)

Bear Creek 2001 Old Vine Zinfandel (Lodi) $16. 89 (11/1/2003)

BEARBOAT

Bearboat 2004 Chardonnay (Russian River Valley) $20. A nice wine, good and dry. It has forward peach, pineapple, apricot and oaky vanilla and caramel flavors, and a finely acidic finish. 85 —S.H. (12/31/2007)

Bearboat 2002 Chardonnay (Russian River Valley) $15. 84 —S.H. (8/1/2005)

Bearboat 2000 Chardonnay (Russian River Valley) $15. 84 —S.H. (6/1/2003)

Bearboat 2002 Pinot Noir (Russian River Valley) $19. 86 —S.H. (8/1/2005)

Bearboat 2000 Pinot Noir (Russian River Valley) $19. 84 (10/1/2002)

BEAUCANON

Beaucanon 2001 Trifecta Bordeaux Blend (Napa Valley) $28. The proprietary name refers to the three major Bordeaux varieties in the blend. Cab Sauvignon gives rich color and a pronounced cassis scent. Merlot adds softness, while a dash of Cab Franc brings red cherries and silk. A rich, dramatically layered wine that's still young and fresh, and has the legs for another decade, at least. 92 —S.H. (4/1/2007)

Beaucanon 2000 Trifecta Cabernet Blend (Napa Valley) $27. 82 —S.H. (10/1/2005)

Beaucanon 1998 La Crosse Cabernet Franc (Napa Valley) $12. 86 —S.H. (7/1/2002)

Beaucanon 2002 L Cuvee Cabernet Franc (Napa Valley) $22. Dry, harsh and acidic, this is not a pleasant wine, despite some stewed cherry fruit, and aging won't solve the problem. The sticky tannins don't help. 82 —S.H. (4/1/2007)

Beaucanon 1998 Jacques de Connick Cabernet Sauvignon (Napa Valley) $65. 92 —S.H. (6/1/2002)

Beaucanon 2000 Jacques de Coninck Reserve Cabernet Sauvignon (Napa Valley) $42. Even at six-plus years, this wine tastes acidic and tannic, with a minty edge to the fruit. I reported on vegetal flavors in 2000 reds as soon as they came out, and this wine confirms that. 82 —S.H. (4/1/2007)

Beaucanon 2002 Longwood Cabernet Sauvignon (Napa Valley) $28. Tastes overripe and raisiny, with stewed blackberry and cherry fruit, but it's an awkward Cab, and lots of toasty French oak just adds that spicy oak thing to this everyday wine. 84 —S.H. (4/1/2007)

Beaucanon 2001 Longwood Cabernet Sauvignon (Napa Valley) $26. 82 —S.H. (10/1/2005)

Beaucanon 1999 Reserve Cabernet Sauvignon (Napa Valley) $20. 84 —S.H. (6/1/2002)

Beaucanon 1998 Reserve Cabernet Sauvignon (Napa Valley) $18. 84 —S.H. (5/1/2001)

Beaucanon 2002 Chardonnay (Napa Valley) $15. 84 —S.H. (10/1/2005)

Beaucanon 1999 Chardonnay (Napa Valley) $25. 90 —J.M. (6/1/2003)

Beaucanon 1997 Jacques de Coninck Chardonnay (Napa Valley) $30. 85 (6/1/2000)

Beaucanon 1998 Reserve Chardonnay (Napa Valley) $15. 87 (6/1/2000)

Beaucanon 2001 Selection Reserve Jacques de Coninck Chardonnay (Napa Valley) $27. 87 —S.H. (10/1/2005)

Beaucanon 2002 Merlot (Napa Valley) $24. Raw and minty despite some cherry fruit, this Merlot is right on the borderline, and doesn't offer much to like right now. The tannins sting, and the finish is sharp. 83 —S.H. (3/1/2007)

Beaucanon 2001 Merlot (Napa Valley) $25. 80 —S.H. (10/1/2005)

Beaucanon 1998 Jacques de Connick Merlot (Napa Valley) $75. 91 —S.H. (6/1/2002)

Beaucanon 1999 Reserve Merlot (Napa Valley) $18. 87 —S.H. (6/1/2002)

Beaucanon 1999 Selection Reserve Jacques de Conink Merlot (Napa Valley) $47. 88 —J.M. (8/1/2003)

BEAULIEU VINEYARD

Beaulieu Vineyard 2004 Tapestry Reserve Bordeaux Blend (Napa Valley) $50. This blend of all five Bordeaux varieties is consistently one of Beaulieu's most interesting but overlooked wines. The '04 is certainly a lovely, polished wine right now, with lush black currant, cherry and smoky oak flavors and a lingering finish. 92 —S.H. (12/31/2007)

Beaulieu Vineyard 2001 Tapestry Reserve Bordeaux Blend (Napa Valley) $40. 92 —S.H. (10/1/2004)

Beaulieu Vineyard 1997 Tapestry Reserve Red Table Win Bordeaux Blend (Napa Valley) $50. 92 (11/1/2000)

Beaulieu Vineyard 2003 Tapestry Reserve Cabernet Blend (Napa Valley) $50. Mainly Cabernet, this is a tough, young tannic wine. It's also fairly acidic. Combined with a dry earthiness, the wine is not particularly opulent or even drinkable now. It feels bitter and hard through the finish. But the signs of ageability are favorable. Best 2009-2015. 87 —S.H. (2/1/2007)

Beaulieu Vineyard 2002 Tapestry Reserve Cabernet Blend (Napa Valley) $50. 90 —S.H. (12/1/2005)

Beaulieu Vineyard 2003 Cabernet Sauvignon (Napa Valley) $18. 89 Editors' Choice —S.H. (9/1/2006)

Beaulieu Vineyard 2003 Cabernet Sauvignon (Rutherford) $25. 87 —S.H. (9/1/2006)

Beaulieu Vineyard 2002 Cabernet Sauvignon (Napa Valley) $17. 85 —S.H. (12/1/2005)

Beaulieu Vineyard 2002 Cabernet Sauvignon (Rutherford) $25. 90 —S.H. (12/1/2005)

Beaulieu Vineyard 2001 Cabernet Sauvignon (Rutherford) $25. 87 —S.H. (5/1/2005)

Beaulieu Vineyard 2001 Cabernet Sauvignon (Napa Valley) $17. 86 —S.H. (5/1/2005)

Beaulieu Vineyard 2000 Cabernet Sauvignon (Napa Valley) $17. 88 —S.H. (6/1/2004)

Beaulieu Vineyard 2000 Cabernet Sauvignon (Rutherford) $25. 87 —S.H. (12/31/2003)

Beaulieu Vineyard 1999 Cabernet Sauvignon (Rutherford) $25. 90 —S.H. (11/15/2002)

Beaulieu Vineyard 1998 Cabernet Sauvignon (Rutherford) $22. 87 —S.H. (8/1/2001)

Beaulieu Vineyard 1998 Cabernet Sauvignon (Napa Valley) $17. 84 —S.H. (8/1/2001)

Beaulieu Vineyard 1996 Cabernet Sauvignon (Rutherford) $12. 90 (11/15/1999)

Beaulieu Vineyard 2001 Clone 4 Cabernet Sauvignon (Rutherford) $130. 89 (12/1/2005)

Beaulieu Vineyard 1997 Clone 4 Cabernet Sauvignon (Napa Valley) $130. 93 (11/1/2000)

Beaulieu Vineyard 1995 Clone 4 Cabernet Sauvignon (Rutherford) $100. 97 Cellar Selection (6/1/1999)

Beaulieu Vineyard 2001 Clone 6 Cabernet Sauvignon (Rutherford) $130. 87 (12/1/2005)

Beaulieu Vineyard 1997 Clone 6 Cabernet Sauvignon (Napa Valley) $130. 92 (11/1/2000)

Beaulieu Vineyard 2003 Coastal Estates Cabernet Sauvignon (California) $11. 82 —S.H. (12/1/2005)

Beaulieu Vineyard 2004 Georges de Latour Private Reserve Cabernet Sauvignon (Napa Valley) $95. BV Private Reserve has been on a real roll. This Georges is enormous and impressive, gigantic in fruit, explosive in blackberry tart, cherry pie, blueberry, plum, cigar box and vanilla aromas and flavors. Structurally, it's an impeccable wine, showing the fine acidity and firm, dusty tannins that always constitute Georges. Beautiful now, and should age well for 10–20 years, in a cool cellar. **95** *—S.H. (12/15/2007)*

Beaulieu Vineyard 2003 Georges de Latour Private Reserve Cabernet Sauvignon (Napa Valley) $95. 95 Cellar Selection *—S.H. (12/31/2006)*

Beaulieu Vineyard 2002 Georges de Latour Private Reserve Cabernet Sauvignon (Napa Valley) $95. 92 Cellar Selection *—S.H. (12/1/2005)*

Beaulieu Vineyard 2001 Georges de Latour Private Reserve Cabernet Sauvignon (Rutherford) $85. 93 Cellar Selection *—S.H. (10/1/2004)*

Beaulieu Vineyard 2000 Georges de Latour Private Reserve Cabernet Sauvignon (Napa Valley) $85. 92 *(2/1/2004)*

Beaulieu Vineyard 1999 Georges de Latour Private Reserve Cabernet Sauvignon (Napa Valley) $100. 90 *—M.S. (3/1/2003)*

Beaulieu Vineyard 1998 Georges de Latour Private Reserve Cabernet Sauvignon (Napa Valley) $100. 91 Cellar Selection *—S.H. (12/31/2001)*

Beaulieu Vineyard 1997 Georges de Latour Private Reserve Cabernet Sauvignon (Napa Valley) $100. 94 *(11/1/2000)*

Beaulieu Vineyard 1998 Reserve Tapestry Cabernet Sauvignon (Napa Valley) $40. 87 *—S.H. (12/31/2001)*

Beaulieu Vineyard 2004 Dulcet Reserve Cabernet Sauvignon-Syrah (Napa Valley) $40. As the name implies, it's a soft, gentle wine. Quality has varied over the years. The '04 is one of the better vintages, a complex but accessible wine with polished black currant, dark-chocolate truffle and anise liqueur flavors. Drink now and through 2010. **89** *—S.H. (12/31/2007)*

Beaulieu Vineyard 2001 Dulcet Reserve Cabernet Sauvignon-Syrah (Napa Valley) $35. 92 Editors' Choice *—S.H. (10/1/2004)*

Beaulieu Vineyard 2000 Dulcet Reserve Cabernet Sauvignon-Syrah (Napa Valley) $35. 89 *—S.H. (2/1/2004)*

Beaulieu Vineyard 2005 Chardonnay (Napa Valley) $15. Everything is clean and properly varietal in this well-made wine, which is dry, creamy and a little bit oaky. Could use greater fruity concentration, though. **84** *—S.H. (9/1/2007)*

Beaulieu Vineyard 2005 Chardonnay (Carneros) $17. Shows the limpid quality of Carneros Chard, with its crisp acidity and tang of minerality. The fruit veers toward green apples and pineapples, and as good as it is, the palate needs to be a little stronger and more concentrated. **86** *—S.H. (9/1/2007)*

Beaulieu Vineyard 2004 Chardonnay (Napa Valley) $18. 84 *—S.H. (6/1/2006)*

Beaulieu Vineyard 2004 Chardonnay (Carneros) $20. 91 *—S.H. (6/1/2006)*

Beaulieu Vineyard 2003 Chardonnay (Carneros) $18. 86 *—S.H. (6/1/2005)*

Beaulieu Vineyard 2001 Chardonnay (Carneros) $18. 90 *—S.H. (12/15/2003)*

Beaulieu Vineyard 2000 Chardonnay (Carneros) $18. 91 Editors' Choice *—S.H. (12/15/2002)*

Beaulieu Vineyard 1999 Chardonnay (Carneros) $18. 86 *—S.H. (8/1/2001)*

Beaulieu Vineyard 2000 Coastal Chardonnay (California) $11. 85 *—S.H. (12/31/2001)*

Beaulieu Vineyard 1999 Coastal Chardonnay (California) $10. 83 *—S.H. (8/1/2001)*

Beaulieu Vineyard 2003 Coastal Estates Chardonnay (California) $11. 85 *—S.H. (12/1/2005)*

Beaulieu Vineyard 2004 Reserve Chardonnay (Carneros) $33. Nice and dry, with smoky oak framing tropical fruit and peach flavors, finishing with Asian spices. With its crisp acids and rich fruitiness, it's a natural for shellfish or creamed chicken. **92** *—S.H. (8/1/2007)*

Beaulieu Vineyard 2003 Reserve Chardonnay (Carneros) $28. 90 *—S.H. (12/15/2005)*

Beaulieu Vineyard 1999 Reserve Chardonnay (Carneros) $30. 87 *(7/1/2001)*

Beaulieu Vineyard 1997 Reserve Chardonnay (Carneros) $24. 87 *(6/1/2000)*

Beaulieu Vineyard 1996 Merlot (Napa Valley) $16. 86 *—J.C. (7/1/2000)*

Beaulieu Vineyard 2003 Merlot (Napa Valley) $18. 87 *—S.H. (7/1/2006)*

Beaulieu Vineyard 2002 Merlot (Napa Valley) $18. 87 *—S.H. (12/1/2005)*

Beaulieu Vineyard 2001 Merlot (Napa Valley) $17. 90 *—S.H. (5/1/2005)*

Beaulieu Vineyard 2000 Merlot (Napa-Carneros) $17. 85 *—S.H. (6/1/2004)*

Beaulieu Vineyard 1999 Merlot (Napa Valley) $18. 90 *— (11/15/2002)*

Beaulieu Vineyard 1998 Merlot (Napa Valley) $17. 85 *—S.H. (8/1/2001)*

Beaulieu Vineyard 1999 Coastal Merlot (California) $12. 88 Best Buy *—S.H. (12/31/2001)*

Beaulieu Vineyard 1998 Coastal Merlot (California) $12. 83 *—S.H. (8/1/2001)*

Beaulieu Vineyard 2004 Maestro Collection Pinot Gris (Carneros) $17. 86 *—S.H. (2/1/2006)*

Beaulieu Vineyard 2005 Pinot Noir (Carneros) $17. Good enough for its dryness and silky crispness and Pinot-esque character of cherries, cola and oak. But I wish the wine had more concentration. **84** *—S.H. (9/1/2007)*

Beaulieu Vineyard 2003 Pinot Noir (Carneros) $18. 87 *—S.H. (6/1/2005)*

Beaulieu Vineyard 2002 Pinot Noir (Carneros) $18. 85 *(11/1/2004)*

Beaulieu Vineyard 2000 Pinot Noir (Carneros) $18. 83 *(10/1/2002)*

Beaulieu Vineyard 1999 Pinot Noir (Carneros) $18. 86 *(10/1/2002)*

Beaulieu Vineyard 1997 Carneros Pinot Noir (Carneros) $16. 87 *(11/15/1999)*

Beaulieu Vineyard 2001 Coastal Pinot Noir (California) $11. 85 *—S.H. (7/1/2003)*

Beaulieu Vineyard 2000 Coastal Pinot Noir (California) $11. 86 Best Buy *—S.H. (12/15/2001)*

Beaulieu Vineyard 2004 Coastal Estates Pinot Noir (California) $11. 81 *—S.H. (12/1/2005)*

Beaulieu Vineyard 2000 Maestro-Signet Collection Pinot Noir (Carneros) $100. 87 *(10/1/2002)*

Beaulieu Vineyard 2004 Reserve Pinot Noir (Carneros) $40. On a par with Beaulieu's reserve Pinots of the last several years, maybe a touch riper. Dry, round and supple, this well-oaked wine has cherry and cola flavors with hints of sautéed mushrooms and a dash of balsamic. Should hold for five years. **90** *—S.H. (9/1/2007)*

Beaulieu Vineyard 2003 Reserve Pinot Noir (Carneros) $39. 87 *—S.H. (12/15/2005)*

Beaulieu Vineyard 2002 Reserve Pinot Noir (Carneros) $35. 86 *(11/1/2004)*

Beaulieu Vineyard 2000 Reserve Pinot Noir (Carneros) $32. 87 *(10/1/2002)*

Beaulieu Vineyard 1999 Reserve Pinot Noir (Carneros) $35. 92 *—S.H. (12/15/2001)*

Beaulieu Vineyard 1997 Reserve Carneros Pinot Noir (Carneros) $30. 90 *(10/1/1999)*

Beaulieu Vineyard 2005 Beauzeaux Red Wine Red Blend (California) $10. Rushed to market, this is almost like Beaujolais Nouveau, so fresh in acids and primary jammy fruit. A blend of Zin, Syrah, Charbono and five other Mediterranean reds, it's dark, bone dry, tannic, and perfect for steak fajitas. **84** *—S.H. (2/1/2007)*

Beaulieu Vineyard 2003 Dulcet Reserve Red Blend (Napa Valley) $40. Dulcet is Beaulieu's Super-Rhone blend, or whatever the term is, with Cabernet Sauvignon and Syrah. It's a very rich wine, deep and long in cherries, blackberries and chocolate. The flavors are very nice, yet the wine is sugary on the finish, which with the hard tannins makes it unbalanced. **84** *—S.H. (2/1/2007)*

Beaulieu Vineyard 2002 Reserve Dulcet Red Blend (Napa Valley) $40. 89 *—S.H. (12/1/2005)*

Beaulieu Vineyard 1999 Reserve Tapestry Red Blend (Napa Valley) $50. 89 *—M.S. (3/1/2003)*

Beaulieu Vineyard 2000 Tapestry Reserve Red Blend (Napa Valley) $40. 91 *(2/1/2004)*

Beaulieu Vineyard 1997 Signet Collection Beauzeaux Rhône Red Blend (California) $20. 88 *—J.C. (11/1/1999)*

Beaulieu Vineyard 2000 Signet Collection Ensemble Rhône Red Blend (California) $25. 86 *—S.H. (6/1/2003)*

Beaulieu Vineyard 1996 Signet Collection Ensemble Rhône Red Blend (California) $25. 86 *—J.C. (11/1/1999)*

Beaulieu Vineyard 1997 Signet Collection Sangiovese (Napa Valley) $20. 87 *—S.H. (12/15/1999)*

Beaulieu Vineyard 1996 Signet Collection Sangiovese (Napa Valley) $16. 86 *(10/1/1999)*

Beaulieu Vineyard 1997 Coastal Estates Sauvignon Blanc (California) $9. 83 *(3/1/2000)*

Beaulieu Vineyard 2004 Coastal Estates Sauvignon Blanc (California) $11. 84 *—S.H. (12/1/2005)*

Beaulieu Vineyard 2002 Coastal Estates Private Cellars Shiraz (California) $11. 82 *(9/1/2005)*

Beaulieu Vineyard 2003 Syrah (Napa Valley) $15. 85 *(9/1/2005)*

Beaulieu Vineyard 2000 Syrah (California) $15. 85 *—S.H. (6/1/2003)*

Beaulieu Vineyard 1999 Syrah (California) $15. 85 *—S.H. (10/1/2001)*

Beaulieu Vineyard 1999 Signet Syrah (Napa County) $25. 83 *(11/1/2001)*

Beaulieu Vineyard 1996 Signet Collection Syrah (North Coast) $25. 87 *—J.C. (11/1/1999)*

Beaulieu Vineyard 1998 Winemaker's Collection Syrah (North Coast) $25. 91 Editors' Choice *(8/1/2001)*

Beaulieu Vineyard 1997 Signet Collection Tocai (Monterey County) $15. 80 *—J.C. (11/1/1999)*

Beaulieu Vineyard 1997 Viognier (Napa Valley) $17. 88 *—S.H. (6/1/1999)*

Beaulieu Vineyard 2001 Signet Collection Viognier (Carneros) $17. 87 *—M.S. (3/1/2003)*

Beaulieu Vineyard 1997 Signet Collection Viognier (Napa Valley) $16. 84 *—J.C. (11/1/1999)*

Beaulieu Vineyard 1996 Zinfandel (Napa Valley) $16. 87 *—S.H. (5/1/2000)*

Beaulieu Vineyard 2003 Zinfandel (Napa Valley) $14. 86 *—S.H. (12/1/2005)*

Beaulieu Vineyard 2002 Zinfandel (Napa Valley) $14. 86 *—S.H. (5/1/2005)*

Beaulieu Vineyard 2001 Zinfandel (Napa Valley) $14. 88 *(11/1/2003)*

Beaulieu Vineyard 2000 Zinfandel (Napa Valley) $15. 90 Best Buy *—S.H. (11/1/2002)*

Beaulieu Vineyard 1999 Zinfandel (Napa Valley) $14. 85 *—S.H. (8/1/2001)*

Beaulieu Vineyard 1997 Zinfandel (Napa Valley) $16. 88 *—P.G. (3/1/2001)*

Beaulieu Vineyard 1998 Coastal Zinfandel (California) $NA. 82 *—D.T. (3/1/2002)*

Beaulieu Vineyard 1997 Coastal Zinfandel (California) $10. 88 Best Buy *—P.G. (11/15/1999)*

Beaulieu Vineyard 2003 Coastal Estates Zinfandel (California) $11. 84 *—S.H. (12/1/2005)*

Beaulieu Vineyard 1999 Signet Collection Zinfandel (Napa Valley) $28. 85 *—D.T. (3/1/2002)*

BEAUREGARD

Beauregard 2003 Beauregard Ranch Vineyard Cabernet Sauvignon (Ben Lomond Mountain) $45. Firmly tannic and very dry, this young Cab needs time or decanting to soften it. But it's a fine wine, with a complex array of blackberry, sweet cured tobacco, tangerine and smoky oak flavors, and should develop well through the next six years. 88 *—S.H. (7/1/2007)*

Beauregard 2002 Beauregard Ranch Vineyard Cabernet Sauvignon (Ben Lomond Mountain) $45. This Cab is from the Santa Cruz Mountains, but is a real disappointment. It's vegetal, with only modest cherry flavors and a sandpapery mouthfeel. 83 *—S.H. (7/1/2007)*

Beauregard 2005 Chardonnay (Russian River Valley) $25. With ripe green apple, pineapple and oak flavors and crisp acidity, this shows good varietal character. The big problem is an apricot sweetness in the finish that tastes like botrytis, and makes the wine distasteful. 82 *—S.H. (7/1/2007)*

Beauregard 2002 Bald Mountain Vineyard Chardonnay (Santa Cruz Mountains) $20. 88 *—S.H. (2/1/2005)*

Beauregard 2004 Beauregard Ranch Vineyard Chardonnay (Ben Lomond Mountain) $40. There's a firm minerality and an acidic mouthfeel to this that suggests some cellaring. The oak dominates, all smoky vanillins and wood-sweet, but the underlying fruit is enormously ripe. Give it a year or so to knit together. 87 *—S.H. (7/1/2007)*

Beauregard 2002 Beauregard Ranch Vineyard Chardonnay (Santa Cruz Mountains) $25. 87 *—S.H. (2/1/2005)*

Beauregard 2005 Trout Gulch Vineyard Chardonnay (Santa Cruz Mountains) $25. Tastes firmly acidic and young. There's tightness and minerality to the citrus, pineapple sorbet and oaky flavors that finish dry. Don't serve too cold. 89 *—S.H. (7/1/2007)*

Beauregard 2003 Fambrini Vineyard Merlot (Ben Lomond Mountain) $45. With its firm, dry tannins and crisp acids, this is not one of those soft, fruit-driven Merlots, but an earthy one. It shows tobacco, sage and wintergreen flavors, with a suggestion of red cherries and sweet oak. It's a nice delineation of a drier, more structured style of Merlot. 87 *—S.H. (7/1/2007)*

Beauregard 2002 Hirsch Vineyard Pinot Noir (Sonoma Coast) $35. 86 *—S.H. (2/1/2005)*

Beauregard 2004 Trout Gulch Vineyard Pinot Noir (Santa Cruz Mountains) $45. Not a successful Pinot. It's simply too ripe, with stewed cherry and raisin flavors. The silky texture, crisp acids and gentle tannins all are fine, but that overripeness lowers the quality. 84 *—S.H. (7/1/2007)*

Beauregard 2005 Syrah (Santa Cruz Mountains) $25. This is a junior version of the winery's Nelson Vineyard bottling, showing many of the same qualities, although it's thinner. Dry and fairly tannic, the wine has blackberry, smoked meat, coffee and carob flavors, and is full-bodied and balanced. Drink now. 87 *—S.H. (7/1/2007)*

Beauregard 2005 Nelson Family Vineyard Syrah (Santa Cruz Mountains) $45. Very dry and dramatically tannic now, this is a young Syrah in need of time. It opens with the most classic spray of white pepper and bacon fat, and has impressively deep blackberry, coffee, leather, tar, dark bitter chocolate and spice flavors. Drink 2012–2015. 92 Cellar Selection *—S.H. (7/1/2007)*

Beauregard 2004 Zayante Vineyard Syrah (Santa Cruz Mountains) $45. Dry and tannic, this single-vineyard Syrah has a deep core of blackberry, coffee, tobacco, dark chocolate and spicy flavor. It's a little acidically sharp on the finish, which limits ageability. Drink now. 88 *—S.H. (7/1/2007)*

Beauregard 2004 Beauregard Ranch Vineyard Zinfandel (Ben Lomond Mountain) $45. The product of a warm vintage in a cool-climate region, this is a very good Zin. It achieves interest and complexity. Structured like a good Cab Sauvignon, it has impressively deep blue and black wild berry and stone fruit, coffee, dried herb and spice flavors, wrapped into firm, dusty tannins. 94 Editors' Choice *—S.H. (7/1/2007)*

Beauregard 2002 Beauregard Ranch Vineayrd Zinfandel (Santa Cruz Mountains) $25. 85 *—S.H. (2/1/2005)*

Beauregard 2005 Primitivo Clone Zinfandel (Lake County) $18. This is a Zin to drink with BBQ ribs and not get all bent out of shape that it's a little hot and rustic. It's a solidly country wine, dry and earthy-fruity, with good tannins and acids to cut through greasy fats. 85 *—S.H. (7/1/2007)*

BEAUX FRERES

Beaux Freres 1997 Pinot Noir (Yamhill County) $50. 88 *(11/15/1999)*

Beaux Freres 2000 Pinot Noir (Willamette Valley) $75. 92 Cellar Selection *(10/1/2002)*

Beaux Freres 2004 Estate Pinot Noir (Willamette Valley) $73. Though it was the most expensive bottle on the table, it was also one of the lightest. Elegance and restraint are virtues to be sure, and this is a lovely, harmonious wine, lightly dappled with cinnamon and herb. But at this price, from this producer, you want to be dazzled. 88 *—P.G. (7/1/2007)*

Beaux Freres 1999 Belles-Soeurs Shea Vineyard Pinot Noir (Yamhill County) $50. 93 Cellar Selection *—P.G. (11/1/2001)*

BECKMEN

Beckmen 1997 Atelier Bordeaux Blend (Santa Barbara County) $20. 91 *(3/1/2000)*

Beckmen 1996 Cabernet Sauvignon (Santa Barbara County) $20. 92 *—M.S. (7/1/2000)*

Beckmen 1999 Cabernet Sauvignon (Santa Barbara County) $24. 85 *—S.H. (11/15/2002)*

Beckmen 1998 Chardonnay (Santa Barbara County) $16. 91 *(6/1/2000)*

Beckmen 2001 Purisima Mountain Vineyard Grenache (Santa Ynez Valley) $14. 86 *—S.H. (9/1/2003)*

Beckmen 2000 Purisima Mountain Vineyard Grenache (Santa Ynez Valley) $24. 88 *—S.H. (12/1/2002)*

Beckmen 2002 Purisima Mountain Vineyard Marsanne (Santa Ynez Valley) $16. 85 *—S.H. (3/1/2004)*

Beckmen 2001 Purisima Mountain Vineyard Marsanne (Santa Ynez Valley) $16. 85 *—S.H. (12/15/2002)*

Beckmen 1998 Purisima Mountain Vineyard Marsanne (Santa Ynez Valley) $14. 90 *—S.H. (10/1/1999)*

Beckmen 1999 Atelier Red Blend (Santa Ynez Valley) $22. 84 *—S.H. (11/15/2002)*

Beckmen 2000 Cuvée Le Bec Red Blend (Santa Barbara County) $14. 84 *—S.H. (12/1/2002)*

Beckmen 2001 Cuvée Le Bec Rhône Red Blend (Santa Ynez Valley) $14. 90 Best Buy *—S.H. (12/1/2003)*

Beckmen 2002 Purisima Mountain Vineyard Roussanne (Santa Ynez Valley) $16. 85 *—S.H. (3/1/2004)*

Beckmen 2001 Estate Sauvignon Blanc (Santa Ynez Valley) $12. 87 *—S.H. (9/1/2003)*

Beckmen 2001 Purisima Mountain Vineyard Sauvignon Blanc (Santa Ynez Valley) $20. 87 *—S.H. (12/15/2003)*

Beckmen 1999 Purisima Mountain Vineyard Sauvignon Blanc (Santa Ynez Valley) $20. 86 *(8/1/2002)*

Beckmen 2000 Syrah (Santa Ynez Valley) $24. 88 *—S.H. (12/1/2002)*

Beckmen 1999 Syrah (Santa Barbara County) $24. 88 *(11/1/2001)*

Beckmen 1997 Syrah (Santa Barbara County) $20. 92 *(3/1/2000)*

Beckmen 2003 Estate Syrah (Santa Ynez Valley) $22. 85 *(9/1/2005)*

Beckmen 2001 Estate Syrah (Santa Ynez Valley) $22. 91 Editors' Choice —*S.H. (12/1/2003)*

Beckmen 2003 Purisima Mountain Vineyard Syrah (Santa Ynez Valley) $38. 88 *(9/1/2005)*

Beckmen 2001 Purisima Mountain Vineyard Syrah (Santa Ynez Valley) $38. 94 —*S.H. (12/1/2003)*

Beckmen 1999 Purisima Mountain Vineyard Syrah (Santa Ynez Valley) $35. 90 *(11/1/2001)*

Beckmen 2003 Purisima Mountain Vineyard Block Six Syrah (Santa Ynez Valley) $42. 89 *(9/1/2005)*

Beckmen 2002 Purisima Mountain Vineyard Clone #1 Syrah (Santa Ynez Valley) $40. 85 —*S.H. (5/1/2005)*

Beckmen 2001 Purisima Mountain Vineyard Clone #1 Syrah (Santa Ynez Valley) $40. 95 Editors' Choice —*S.H. (12/1/2003)*

BEDELL

Bedell 2002 Cupola Bordeaux Blend (North Fork of Long Island) $30. A blend of Merlot, Cabernet, Cabernet Franc and Petit Verdot, this wine (predominantly Cabernet) has a spicy, full-bodied fruit nose followed by an overabundance of tannic, peppery flavors. It's a little hard to move beyond the wall of chew to the fruit beyond, but pleasing nuances of toasted oak and cinnamon prevail. Needs a softer edge to really showcase the grapes. **82** —*S.K. (2/1/2007)*

Bedell 2001 Cupola Bordeaux Blend (North Fork of Long Island) $NA. 87 —*J.C. (10/2/2004)*

Bedell 1997 Cabernet Sauvignon (North Fork of Long Island) $25. 87 —*J.C. (4/1/2001)*

Bedell 1997 Reserve Chardonnay (North Fork of Long Island) $15. 86 —*J.C. (4/1/2001)*

Bedell 1998 Gewürztraminer (North Fork of Long Island) $13. 83 —*J.C. (4/1/2001)*

Bedell 2002 Merlot (North Fork of Long Island) $18. 88 Editors' Choice —*M.D. (12/1/2006)*

Bedell 2000 Merlot (North Fork of Long Island) $21. 84 —*J.C. (10/2/2004)*

Bedell 1997 Merlot (North Fork of Long Island) $18. 86 —*J.C. (4/1/2001)*

Bedell 2000 C-Block South Merlot (North Fork of Long Island) $39. 82 —*J.C. (10/2/2004)*

Bedell 2002 Reserve Merlot (North Fork of Long Island) $30. 86 —*M.D. (12/1/2006)*

Bedell NV Main Road Red Merlot-Cabernet Sauvignon (North Fork of Long Island) $14. 80 —*J.C. (10/2/2004)*

Bedell 1998 Cupola Red Blend (North Fork of Long Island) $30. 87 —*J.C. (4/1/2001)*

Bedell 2004 Taste Red Red Blend (North Fork of Long Island) $25. Aromas of bright cherry and spice paired with flavors of pepper and plum marry well here, despite a somewhat heavy toasted oak quality. **86** —*S.K (2/1/2007)*

Bedell 2001 Late Harvest Riesling Riesling (North Fork of Long Island) $35. 88 —*J.C. (8/1/2003)*

Bedell 2005 Taste White White Blend (North Fork of Long Island) $25. Bright, vibrant but with a little oak to keep it balanced, this enjoyable white will please fans of the drier style of white wines. There's citrus in the nose and floral notes on the palate, and the wine finishes clean. Not terribly complex, but overall, a pleasing, food-friendly offering. **84** —*S.K. (5/1/2007)*

Bedell 1999 Viognier (North Fork of Long Island) $18. 85 —*J.C. (4/1/2001)*

BEDFORD THOMPSON

Bedford Thompson 2000 Thompson Vineyard Cabernet Franc (Santa Barbara County) $20. 85 —*S.H. (12/15/2004)*

Bedford Thompson 1998 Chardonnay (Santa Barbara County) $18. 84 *(6/1/2000)*

Bedford Thompson 2002 Thompson Vineyard Chardonnay (Santa Barbara County) $20. 84 —*S.H. (12/15/2004)*

Bedford Thompson 1997 Gewürztraminer (Santa Barbara County) $12. 90 —*S.H. (9/1/1999)*

Bedford Thompson 2000 Thompson Vineyard Grenache (Santa Barbara County) $20. 83 —*S.H. (3/1/2004)*

Bedford Thompson 2000 Thompson Vineyard Mourvèdre (Santa Barbara County) $20. 87 —*S.H. (12/1/2003)*

Bedford Thompson 2001 Thompson Vineyard Petite Sirah (Santa Barbara County) $45. 84 —*S.H. (12/15/2004)*

Bedford Thompson 1998 Syrah (Santa Barbara County) $20. 81 *(10/1/2001)*

Bedford Thompson 2000 Thompson Vineyard Syrah (Santa Barbara County) $22. 88 —*S.H. (12/1/2003)*

BEHRENS & HITCHCOCK

Behrens & Hitchcock 2002 Beckstoffer Tokalon Vineyard Cabernet Sauvignon (Oakville) $75. 84 —*S.H. (6/1/2005)*

Behrens & Hitchcock 2001 Beckstoffer Tokalon Vineyard Cabernet Sauvignon (Napa Valley) $65. 85 —*S.H. (6/1/2005)*

Behrens & Hitchcock 1999 Beckstoffer Vineyards Cabernet Sauvignon (Oakville) $NA. 83 —*S.H. (6/1/2005)*

Bel Arbor 1999 Cabernet Sauvignon (California) $6. 86 Best Buy —*S.H. (12/15/2000)*

BEL ARBOR

Bel Arbor 1998 Chardonnay (California) $6. 82 —*S.H. (7/1/1999)*

Bel Arbor 2000 Chardonnay (Mendocino County) $6. 84 —*S.H. (5/1/2002)*

Bel Arbor 1999 Chardonnay (California) $6. 82 —*S.H. (11/15/2000)*

Bel Arbor 2000 Merlot (Mendocino County) $6. 83 —*S.H. (7/1/2002)*

Bel Arbor 1999 Merlot (California) $6. 86 Best Buy —*S.H. (11/15/2000)*

BEL GLOS

Bel Glos 2000 Pinot Noir (Santa Maria Valley) $30. 88 —*J.M. (2/1/2003)*

BELFORD SPRINGS

Belford Springs 2000 Chardonnay (California) $8. 86 —*S.H. (12/15/2002)*

Belford Springs 2000 Pinot Noir (California) $8. 84 —*S.H. (4/1/2003)*

Belford Springs 2001 Sauvignon Blanc (California) $8. 86 —*S.H. (9/1/2003)*

Belford Springs 2001 Zinfandel (California) $6. 85 Best Buy *(11/1/2003)*

Belford Springs 1999 Zinfandel (California) $8. 83 —*S.H. (12/1/2002)*

BELL

Bell 2003 Claret Bordeaux Blend (Napa Valley) $30. 88 —*S.H. (12/1/2006)*

Bell 2003 Cabernet Sauvignon (Napa Valley) $40. The grapes come from the best communes of south-central Napa, and most of the barrels were new French oak. The Cabernet is blended with a little Petit Verdot, Cab Franc and Merlot. The wine itself is soft and plush, with a velvety mouthfeel framing dry, ripe blackberry, cherry and cocoa flavors. Drink now. **88** —*S.H. (2/1/2007)*

Bell 2003 Cabernet Sauvignon (Napa Valley) $40. 84 —*S.H. (12/1/2006)*

Bell 2000 Cabernet Sauvignon (Napa Valley) $35. 85 —*S.H. (11/15/2003)*

Bell 1999 Cabernet Sauvignon (Napa Valley) $35. 85 —*S.H. (5/1/2003)*

Bell 1999 Baritelle Vineyard Cabernet Sauvignon (Rutherford) $60. 92 Editors' Choice —*S.H. (12/31/2002)*

Bell 2000 Baritelle Vineyard-Jackson Clone Cabernet Sauvignon (Rutherford) $65. 87 —*S.H. (6/1/2004)*

Bell 1998 Baritelle Vineyard-Jackson Clone Cabernet Sauvignon (Rutherford) $55. 93 —*S.H. (6/1/2002)*

Bell 1996 Baritelle Vineyard Jackson Clo Cabernet Sauvignon (Rutherford) $50. 89 —*M.S. (9/1/2000)*

Bell 1997 Baritelle Vineyard Cabernet Sauvignon (Rutherford) $60. 90 *(11/1/2000)*

Bell 2002 Clone Six Cabernet Sauvignon (Rutherford) $65. 87 —*S.H. (12/15/2005)*

Bell 1999 Talianna Cabernet Sauvignon (Rutherford) $35. 92 —*S.H. (6/1/2002)*

Bell 1999 Talianna Cabernet Sauvignon-Syrah (Rutherford) $35. 92 —*S.H. (6/1/2002)*

Bell 2005 Chardonnay (Napa Valley) $26. Earthy and dry, with a dusty feeling, this pleasant Chard has apple and peach flavors enhanced with winemaker bells and whistles, like partial malo and partial oak. Still, it has a certain one-dimensionality of fruit. **85** —*S.H. (2/1/2007)*

Bell 2005 Chardonnay (Napa Valley) $25. 85 —*S.H. (12/1/2006)*

Bell 1998 Aleta's Vineyard Chardonnay (Yountville) $24. 82 *(6/1/2000)*

Bell 2003 Merlot (Napa Valley) $30. There's a sharpness, a cutting acidity to this wine that hits you immediately and makes everything else hard to appreciate. Too bad, because the tannins are lush and the fruit and oak seem to be very nice. **82** —*S.H. (2/1/2007)*

Bell 2003 Merlot (Napa Valley) $30. 83 —*S.H. (12/1/2006)*

Bell 2000 Merlot (Yountville) $30. 85 —*S.H. (8/1/2003)*

Bell 1999 Aleta's Vineyard Merlot (Yountville) $35. 88 —*S.H. (6/1/2002)*

Bell 1996 Aleta's Vineyard Merlot (Napa Valley) $28. 85 —*J.C. (7/1/2000)*

Bell 2003 Claret Red Blend (Napa Valley) $30. The difference between Bell's Cabernet and its Claret seems to be the addition of a dash of Syrah to the Bordeaux grapes in the latter. Otherwise the two wines are pretty similar. The Claret is a little fuller-bodied, with a tarry undertow to the blackberry and cassis. **87** *—S.H. (2/1/2007)*

Bell 2004 Canterbury Vineyard Syrah (Sierra Foothills) $26. The wine tastes like it comes from hot country, as indeed this 2,200-foot high vineyard is during the summer. It's too soft in both acids and tannins, but makes up for it with deliciously sweet, but dry, chocolate-covered cherry and blackberry flavors that have quite a bit of sophistication. **86** *—S.H. (2/1/2007)*

Bell 2004 Canterbury Vineyard Syrah (Sierra Foothills) $25. 87 *—S.H. (12/1/2006)*

Bell 2003 Canterbury Vineyard Syrah (Sierra Foothills) $24. 87 *(9/1/2005)*

Bell 2000 Canterbury Vineyard Syrah (Sierra Foothills) $28. 84 *—S.H. (6/1/2003)*

Bell 1999 Canterbury Vineyard Syrah (Sierra Foothills) $28. 88 *(11/1/2001)*

Bell 1997 Canterbury Vineyard Syrah (Sierra Foothills) $28. 88 *(5/1/2000)*

Bell 2000 T&A Vineyard Viognier (Santa Cruz County) $28. 88 *—J.M. (12/15/2002)*

BELLA

Bella 2006 Rosé Rosé Blend (Dry Creek Valley) $20. Too sweet by far for a good recommendation. Tastes like sugared cherry and raspberry juice. Zinfandel and Syrah. **82** *—S.H. (7/1/2007)*

Bella 2002 Big River Ranch Syrah (Alexander Valley) $38. 89 *—S.H. (11/1/2005)*

Bella 2004 Lily Hill Estate Syrah (Dry Creek Valley) $38. I loved the winery's '04 Lily Hill Zin, but not this wine, because Zin can tolerate heat a lot better than Syrah. This wine is stewed and soft, with coffee flavors that taste artificially sweetened. **82** *—S.H. (6/1/2007)*

Bella 2002 Lily Hill Estate Syrah (Dry Creek Valley) $34. 88 *—S.H. (11/1/2005)*

Bella 2001 Zinfandel (Dry Creek Valley) $24. 88 *(11/1/2003)*

Bella 2004 Belle Canyon Zinfandel (Dry Creek Valley) $32. A lovely Zin; superdrinkable by itself for the exuberance of its fruit, yet dry enough to accompany grills. Massive in chocolate, cassis, cherry jam and peppery spice flavors, it's balanced by smooth tannins and fine acidity. **88** *—S.H. (6/1/2007)*

Bella 2002 Belle Canyon Estate Zinfandel (Dry Creek Valley) $30. 90 *—S.H. (11/1/2005)*

Bella 2001 Belle Canyon Estate Zinfandel (Dry Creek Valley) $28. 89 *(11/1/2003)*

Bella 2004 Big River Ranch Zinfandel (Alexander Valley) $34. Great Zin. From this hot vintage, it's thick, soft and almost sweet, but the deliciousness factor is high, and the finish is entirely dry. That comes at the cost of fairly high alcohol, but the cassis, cherry, mocha and cola flavors, with their spicy finish, define Alexander Valley Zin. **90** *—S.H. (6/1/2007)*

Bella 2003 Big River Ranch Zinfandel (Alexander Valley) $34. 87 *—S.H. (7/1/2006)*

Bella 2002 Big River Ranch Zinfandel (Alexander Valley) $34. 88 *—S.H. (10/1/2005)*

Bella 2001 Big River Ranch Zinfandel (Alexander Valley) $32. 89 *(11/1/2003)*

Bella 2002 Estate Zinfandel (Dry Creek Valley) $24. 87 *—S.H. (11/1/2005)*

Bella 2004 Lily Hill Estate Zinfandel (Dry Creek Valley) $34. Picture-perfect Dry Creek Zin, rich in wild berry, tobacco, coffee and spice flavors, just nudging into superripe chocolate-covered raisins. The tannins are sweetly ripe and gentle. With its edge of rustic charm and balancing acidity, it's just delicious. **89** *—S.H. (6/1/2007)*

Bella 2002 Lily Hill Estate Zinfandel (Dry Creek Valley) $30. 85 *—S.H. (10/1/2005)*

Bella 2001 Lily Hill Estate Zinfandel (Dry Creek Valley) $28. 86 *(11/1/2003)*

Bella 2003 Lily Hill Vineyard Zinfandel (Dry Creek Valley) $30. 92 Editors' Choice *—S.H. (7/1/2006)*

BELLA VIGNA

Bella Vigna 1998 Costa Vineyard Zinfandel (Lodi) $16. 82 *—P.G. (3/1/2001)*

BELLE GLOS

Belle Glos 2001 Pinot Noir (Santa Maria Valley) $30. 90 *—S.H. (7/1/2003)*

Belle Glos 2005 Clark & Telephone Vineyard Pinot Noir (Santa Maria Valley) $38. Just luscious, such a good, complete wine. Perfectly structured, its intricate acid-tannin-oak architecture captures delicate cherry, plum, pomegranate and cola flavors. Not a power-packed ager, just a gorgeous Pinot to drink now. **92** *—S.H. (11/1/2007)*

Belle Glos 2004 Clark & Telephone Vineyard Pinot Noir (Santa Maria Valley) $38. 84 *—S.H. (10/1/2006)*

Belle Glos 2003 Clark & Telephone Vineyard Pinot Noir (Santa Maria Valley) $38. 94 Cellar Selection *—S.H. (12/1/2005)*

Belle Glos 2002 Clark & Telephone Vineyard Pinot Noir (Santa Maria Valley) $38. 95 *—S.H. (5/1/2005)*

Belle Glos 2005 Las Alturas Vineyard Pinot Noir (Santa Lucia Highlands) $50. Like most Pinots from this Monterey appellation, this is a big wine, the kind that garners high scores from critics for its Rubensesque stature. It's probably ageworthy, given the depth of raspberry and cassis and rich tannins, but it's a little thick and heavy now. Give it five years. **87** *—S.H. (11/1/2007)*

Belle Glos 2004 Las Alturas Vineyard Pinot Noir (Santa Lucia Highlands) $48. 88 *—S.H. (10/1/2006)*

Belle Glos 2006 Oeil de Perdrix Pinot Noir Blanc Pinot Noir (Yorkville Highlands) $22. Good dry rosé that shows some real complexity. The dryness and acidity are the best parts, making the mouthfeel racy. The subtle flavors of raspberries, gingerbread, cola and peppery cinnamon finish long and clean. From Caymus. **89** *—S.H. (11/1/2007)*

Belle Glos 2005 Taylor Lane Vineyard Pinot Noir (Sonoma Coast) $50. One sip, and all you want to do is sit back and reflect on this beautiful Pinot Noir. It's so dry and elegant, with crisp acids providing a silky balance to the wealth of cherry, pomegranate, tea, cola, mushroom, spice and balsam flavors. Great now and should develop for at least six years. **94** *—S.H. (11/1/2007)*

Belle Glos 2004 Taylor Lane Vineyard Pinot Noir (Sonoma Coast) $50. 85 *—S.H. (10/1/2006)*

Belle Glos 2003 Taylor Lane Vineyard Pinot Noir (Sonoma Coast) $50. 91 Editors' Choice *—S.H. (12/1/2005)*

Belle Glos 2002 Taylor Lane Vineyard Pinot Noir (Sonoma Coast) $50. 87 *—S.H. (4/1/2005)*

BELLE VALLÉE

Belle Vallée 2004 Cabernet Sauvignon (Rogue Valley) $25. Despite its hefty 14.9% alcohol, this still carries distinct scents of pickle barrel, dill herb and a bit of canned bean. Somewhere in there is some reasonably ripe, cherry-flavored fruit, but then it hits a wall of thick, chalky tannins. It's just not very well balanced. **84** *—P.G. (7/1/2007)*

Belle Vallée 2004 Merlot (Rogue Valley) $25. A big bruiser, somewhat of a surprise for a Rogue Valley bottling. The alcohol is at 15.2%, and the fruit is quite ripe, extracted, plummy and lush. There's nothing subtle going on here, but the fruit stands up to the alcohol and the tannins, and in a rough and tumble way the wine delivers the goods. No wimpy wines indeed! **87** *—P.G. (7/1/2007)*

Belle Vallée 2004 Pinot Gris (Willamette Valley) $13. 88 *—P.G. (2/1/2006)*

Belle Vallée 2005 Pinot Noir (Willamette Valley) $22. This is the least expensive of Belle Vallée's current Pinot Noirs, and far and away the best value. It's bright and spicy, fragrant with sweet-smelling berries, cherries and grapes. Forward and fruity, it is a fine choice for sipping on the deck. **86** *—P.G. (7/1/2007)*

Belle Vallée 2004 Pinot Noir (Willamette Valley) $20. 86 *—P.G. (5/1/2006)*

Belle Vallée 2002 Pinot Noir (Oregon) $20. 86 *(11/1/2004)*

Belle Vallée 2005 Grand Cuvée Pinot Noir (Willamette Valley) $55. Apart from its impenetrable faux "wax" capsule, this top shelf offering from Belle Vallée is difficult to distinguish from the winery's Willamette Valley cuvée, except for its lofty price. It's light, insubstantial and one dimensional, pleasant to drink but without the depth or detail that you would expect from a prestige bottling. **85** *—P.G. (7/1/2007)*

Belle Vallée 2004 Grand Cuvée Pinot Noir (Willamette Valley) $49. 87 *—P.G. (5/1/2006)*

Belle Vallée 2005 Reserve Pinot Noir (Willamette Valley) $35. The winery's reserve Pinot Noir is of a piece with its other two offerings. Light, tart, cranberry-flavored red fruit, lots of acid, lots of tannin and not much in the way of extract. The wine disappears quickly once it hits the palate. **86** *—P.G. (7/1/2007)*

Belle Vallée 2004 Reserve Pinot Noir (Willamette Valley) $30. 86 *—P.G. (5/1/2006)*

Belle Vallée 2002 Reserve Pinot Noir (Oregon) $30. 86 *(11/1/2004)*

Belle Vallée 2004 Whole Cluster Pinot Noir (Willamette Valley) $15. 84 *—P.G. (5/1/2006)*

Belle Vallée 2002 Whole Cluster Pinot Noir (Willamette Valley) $15. 86 *(11/1/2004)*

BELO

Belo 1999 Muscat Gris Muscat (California) $16. 89 *—S.H. (9/1/2003)*

Belo 1999 Sousao Port Port (California) $15. 86 *—S.H. (12/1/2002)*

Belo 1999 Touriga Nacional Vintage Reserve Port (Napa Valley) $40. 96 Cellar Selection *—S.H. (12/1/2002)*

Belo 1999 Dessert Wine Sauvignon Blanc (Napa Valley) $25. 87 *—S.H. (9/1/2003)*

BELVEDERE

Belvedere 2000 Healdsburg Ranches Cabernet Sauvignon (Sonoma County) $26. 86 *—S.H. (7/1/2006)*

Belvedere 1998 Chardonnay (Russian River Valley) $18. 89 *(6/1/2000)*

Belvedere 1998 Chardonnay (Sonoma County) $18. 89 *(6/1/2000)*

Belvedere 2004 Chardonnay (Russian River Valley) $20. 85 *—S.H. (12/1/2006)*

Belvedere 2002 Chardonnay (Russian River Valley) $20. 88 *—S.H. (8/1/2005)*

Belvedere 2000 Chardonnay (Russian River Valley) $20. 90 *—J.M. (12/15/2002)*

Belvedere 2004 Healdsburg Ranches Chardonnay (Sonoma County) $14. 84 *—S.H. (12/1/2006)*

Belvedere 2003 Healdsburg Ranches Chardonnay (Sonoma County) $14. 88 *—S.H. (8/1/2005)*

Belvedere 2000 Healdsburg Ranches Chardonnay (Sonoma County) $14. 88 Best Buy *—J.M. (12/15/2002)*

Belvedere 2002 Healdsburg Ranches Merlot (Sonoma County) $19. 85 *—S.H. (12/1/2006)*

Belvedere 2005 Pinot Noir (Russian River Valley) $29. This is a good Pinot Noir with some real complexity. It shows the way Russian River ripens the grapes to satisfying cola, cherry and pomegranate flavors, while preserving vital acidity. Drink this dry wine now for its delicate elegance. 88 *—S.H. (11/1/2007)*

Belvedere 2004 Pinot Noir (Russian River Valley) $28. 90 *—S.H. (12/1/2006)*

Belvedere 2001 Pinot Noir (Russian River Valley) $28. 91 Editors' Choice *—S.H. (7/1/2006)*

Belvedere 2000 Pinot Noir (Russian River Valley) $30. 91 *—S.H. (5/1/2002)*

Belvedere 1997 Floodgate Vineyard Pinot Noir (Anderson Valley) $20. 89 *—M.S. (10/1/2000)*

Belvedere 2005 Sauvignon Blanc (Dry Creek Valley) $18. 86 *—S.H. (11/15/2006)*

Belvedere 1998 Syrah (Dry Creek Valley) $22. 87 *(11/1/2001)*

Belvedere 1999 Healdsburg Ranches Syrah (Sonoma County) $26. 92 Editors' Choice *—S.H. (9/1/2002)*

Belvedere 1999 Zinfandel (Dry Creek Valley) $NA. 89 *—D.T. (3/1/2002)*

Belvedere 2001 Healdsburg Ranches Zinfandel (Sonoma County) $24. 90 *(11/1/2003)*

BENESSERE

Benessere 2006 Pinot Grigio (Napa Valley) $25. There's a reason PG has become so popular in America, and this new one from Napa-based Benessere shows why. It's as dry and bright in acidity as a fine Sauvignon Blanc, yet with the rich fruit American wine drinkers love. Those flavors range from peaches and nectarines to Meyer lemons and pineapples, with honeysuckle and spice nuances. 90 *—S.H. (12/15/2007)*

Benessere 2005 Pinot Grigio (Carneros) $24. 88 *—S.H. (12/15/2006)*

Benessere 2003 Pinot Grigio (Carneros) $22. 88 *—J.M. (10/1/2004)*

Benessere 2002 Pinot Grigio (Napa-Carneros) $22. 90 *—J.M. (2/1/2004)*

Benessere 2000 Pinot Grigio (Napa Valley) $20. 88 *—J.M. (11/15/2001)*

Benessere 2004 Costa del Sol Red Blend (Napa Valley) $15. This affordable blend of Sangiovese, Zinfandel and Merlot is a serious red wine. Showing layers of blackberries, mocha, herbs, spices and smoke, with a complex acid-tannin structure that will stand up well alongside dry reds costing much more. 89 Editors' Choice *—S.H. (12/31/2007)*

Benessere 2002 Phenomenon Red Blend (Napa Valley) $60. 85 *—S.H. (3/1/2006)*

Benessere 1997 Sangiovese (Napa Valley) $26. 88 *—S.H. (9/1/2000)*

Benessere 1996 Sangiovese (Napa Valley) $25. 87 *—M.S. (6/1/1999)*

Benessere 2002 Sangiovese (Napa Valley) $28. 86 *—S.H. (3/1/2006)*

Benessere 2001 Sangiovese (Napa Valley) $28. 88 *—S.H. (3/1/2005)*

Benessere 2000 Sangiovese (Napa Valley) $25. 87 *—J.M. (4/1/2004)*

Benessere 1999 Sangiovese (Napa Valley) $29. 91 Editors' Choice *—J.M. (12/1/2002)*

Benessere 1998 Sangiovese (Napa Valley) $28. 92 Editors' Choice *—J.M. (12/1/2001)*

Benessere 2004 Estate Sangiovese (St. Helena) $32. This is one of Benessere's more promising efforts with Sangiovese. It's a bone-dry, crisply acidic, not too alcoholic wine, with dusty tannins. It rewards with a wealth of refined cherry flavors, and retains the stylish elegance of a fine table wine. Drink now–2008. 90 Editors' Choice *—S.H. (7/1/2007)*

Benessere 2003 Syrah (Napa Valley) $40. 89 *(9/1/2005)*

Benessere 1999 Estate Syrah (Napa Valley) $38. 92 *—J.M. (12/1/2002)*

Benessere 1999 Benessere Estate Black Glass Vineyard Zinfandel (Napa Valley) $35. 92 Editors' Choice *—J.M. (12/15/2001)*

Benessere 2004 BK Collins Old Vines Zinfandel (Napa Valley) $35. You can do better for the price. The wine is soft and hot, with peppery flavors of stewed fruits, but it offers plenty of rustic Zin personality. 85 *—S.H. (4/1/2007)*

Benessere 2001 BK Collins, Old Vines Zinfandel (Napa Valley) $28. 89 *—J.M. (11/1/2003)*

Benessere 2004 Black Glass Vineyard Zinfandel (Napa Valley) $40. The heat of the vintage is vividly displayed in the superripe, almost stewed cherry and blackberry-pie filling flavors and soft mouthfeel of this dry wine. The best thing about it is the tannins, so smooth and finely ground. 86 *—S.H. (4/1/2007)*

Benessere 2001 Black Glass Vineyard Zinfandel (Napa Valley) $35. 91 *(11/1/2003)*

Benessere 1999 Black Glass Vineyard Zinfandel (Napa Valley) $35. 92 Editors' Choice *—J.M. (12/15/2001)*

BENJAMIN SILVER

Benjamin Silver 2003 Julia's Vineyard Pinot Noir (Santa Barbara County) $45. The vineyard is in Santa Maria Valley, a cool area, but this is an exceedingly ripe Pinot. The flavors are of cherry pie filling, raspberry-infused chocolate truffle and cola, made spicier by toasty oak. Fortunately, the wine has a silky elegance. The French will scratch their heads, but it's a polished, delicious New World Pinot. 88 *—S.H. (4/1/2007)*

BENMARL

Benmarl 2004 Pinot Grigio (Oregon) $18. 81 *(2/1/2006)*

BENNETT LANE

Bennett Lane 2002 Maximus Cabernet Blend (Napa Valley) $28. 87 *—S.H. (10/1/2005)*

Bennett Lane 2004 Cabernet Sauvignon (Napa Valley) $55. Pretty generic Napa Cab, ripe in jammy cherry and blackberry fruit and well-oaked, with vanilla and caramel char. There's a little too much sugary sweetness to qualify for dryness. 84 *—S.H. (10/1/2007)*

Bennett Lane 2002 Cabernet Sauvignon (Napa Valley) $45. 88 *—S.H. (10/1/2005)*

Bennett Lane 2006 Maximus White Feasting Wine White Blend (Napa Valley) $28. A few drops of Chard and Muscat help to add richer, more honeyed floral notes, but this dry wine is mainly Sauv Blanc, and that variety dominates, with tart citrus, gooseberry and cat pee notes. 84 *—S.H. (11/1/2007)*

BENSON FERRY

Benson Ferry 2001 Select Chardonnay (North Coast) $9. 86 Best Buy *—S.H. (6/1/2003)*

Benson Ferry 2001 Syrah (Lodi) $NA. 83 *—S.H. (9/1/2003)*

Benson Ferry 2001 Old Vines Zinfandel (Lodi) $13. 88 *(11/1/2003)*

BENT CREEK

Bent Creek 2000 Cabernet Sauvignon (Livermore Valley) $20. 82 *—S.H. (11/15/2003)*

BENTON-LANE

Benton-Lane 2006 Pinot Gris (Willamette Valley) $16. Stainless steel fermented, this bright, juicy PG did not go through malolactic fermentation. The crisp acids add definition and lift, the flavors a generous mix of pear, apple and tropical fruits. Tasted just a few months after harvest, it's a great wine for summer enjoyment while the young fruit flavors are in full bloom. 88 *—P.G. (7/1/2007)*

Benton-Lane 2004 Pinot Gris (Oregon) $15. 85 *(2/1/2006)*

Benton-Lane 2002 Pinot Noir (Willamette Valley) $21. 84 *(11/1/2004)*

Benton-Lane 2000 Pinot Noir (Oregon) $18. 83 *(10/1/2002)*

Benton-Lane 1998 Pinot Noir (Willamette Valley) $17. 82 *—M.S. (12/1/2000)*

Benton-Lane 2005 Estate Pinot Noir (Willamette Valley) $25. Benton-Lane makes a significant amount of this moderately priced Pinot, and in the right years it is one of the better Oregon values. The 2005 offers sweet, pleasing strawberry fruit and earthy streaks of wild herb. The tannins, at least at the moment, are still rough and taste of green tea. Time may smooth it out so that the finish is less rugged. 85 *—P.G. (7/1/2007)*

Benton-Lane 2002 First Class Pinot Noir (Willamette Valley) $35. 84 *(11/1/2004)*

Benton-Lane 1999 Reserve Pinot Noir (Oregon) $30. 89 *—P.G. (12/31/2001)*

Benton-Lane 1998 Reserve Pinot Noir (Willamette Valley) $30. 84 *—M.S. (12/1/2000)*

Benton-Lane 1999 Sunnymount Cuvée Pinot Noir (Willamette Valley) $65. 91 Cellar Selection *—P.G. (2/1/2004)*

Benton-Lane 1998 Sunnymount Cuvée Pinot Noir (Willamette Valley) $50. 85 *—J.C. (12/1/2000)*

Benton-Lane 1998 Sunnymount Cuvée Pinot Noir (Oregon) $50. 88 *—P.G. (12/31/2001)*

BENZIGER

Benziger 2002 Tribute Cabernet Blend (Sonoma Mountain) $65. 94 Editors' Choice *—S.H. (12/1/2005)*

Benziger 2004 Cabernet Sauvignon (Sonoma County) $19. Even with a drop of Merlot and Malbec added, this still is a fairly simple wine, flavor-wise. It satisfies for basic dryness and tannic structure, with a bit of cherry-blackberry fruit. 84 *—S.H. (11/1/2007)*

Benziger 2001 Cabernet Sauvignon (Sonoma County) $19. 89 *—S.H. (6/1/2004)*

Benziger 2000 Cabernet Sauvignon (Sonoma County) $19. 89 *—S.H. (10/1/2003)*

Benziger 1999 Cabernet Sauvignon (Sonoma County) $19. 86 *—S.H. (12/15/2003)*

Benziger 1999 Cabernet Sauvignon (Sonoma County) $19. 90 *—S.H. (7/1/2002)*

Benziger 1997 Blue Rock Vineyards Cabernet Sauvignon (Alexander Valley) $50. 90 *—S.H. (12/31/2001)*

Benziger 1996 Blue Rock Vineyard Cabernet Sauvignon (Sonoma) $30. 91 *—M.S. (7/1/1999)*

Benziger 1998 Estate Cabernet Sauvignon (Sonoma Mountain) $60. 88 *—S.H. (12/31/2001)*

Benziger 1996 Rancho Salinas Vineyard Cabernet Sauvignon (Sonoma) $30. 87 *—J.C. (7/1/1999)*

Benziger 2002 Reserve Cabernet Sauvignon (Sonoma County) $45. This is really a first-class Cabernet showing not only the beauty of the vintage but the blender's craft. Drinkable now for its finely grained tannins and refined black currant and cassis flavors, it has the dry balance for the cellar. Elegant and sophisticated, it's best now through 2008. 92 *—S.H. (4/1/2007)*

Benziger 2001 Reserve Cabernet Sauvignon (Sonoma County) $42. 89 *—S.H. (3/1/2005)*

Benziger 2000 Reserve Cabernet Sauvignon (Sonoma County) $42. 90 *—S.H. (6/1/2004)*

Benziger 1998 Reserve Cabernet Sauvignon (Sonoma County) $45. 91 *—S.H. (12/1/2001)*

Benziger 1997 Reserve Cabernet Sauvignon (Sonoma County) $45. 90 *(11/1/2000)*

Benziger 2001 Stone Farm Vineyard Cabernet Sauvignon (Sonoma Valley) $27. 91 *—S.H. (3/1/2005)*

Benziger 2005 Chardonnay (Carneros) $16. A bit on the weedy, sharp side, with some prickly acids. Has just enough peaches and cream flavor to satisfy Chard lovers. 83 *—S.H. (9/1/2007)*

Benziger 2003 Chardonnay (Carneros) $16. 85 *—S.H. (8/1/2005)*

Benziger 2002 Chardonnay (Carneros) $16. 87 *—S.H. (11/15/2004)*

Benziger 2001 Chardonnay (Carneros) $16. 88 *—S.H. (12/15/2003)*

Benziger 2000 Chardonnay (Carneros) $16. 86 *—S.H. (5/1/2002)*

Benziger 1999 Chardonnay (Carneros) $16. 88 *—S.H. (11/15/2001)*

Benziger 2002 Reserve Chardonnay (Carneros) $27. 87 *—S.H. (3/1/2005)*

Benziger 1998 Reserve Chardonnay (Carneros) $25. 85 *(6/1/2000)*

Benziger 2002 Ricci Vineyard Chardonnay (Carneros) $25. 86 *—S.H. (3/1/2005)*

Benziger 1998 Sangiacomo Vineyards Chardonnay (Carneros) $25. 88 *—S.H. (5/1/2002)*

Benziger 2001 Sangiacomo Vineyards Reserve Chardonnay (Carneros) $27. 92 *—S.H. (12/15/2003)*

Benziger 1998 Yamakawa Vineyards Chardonnay (Carneros) $25. 86 *(6/1/2000)*

Benziger 2003 Fumé Blanc (North Coast) $13. 84 *—S.H. (3/1/2005)*

Benziger 2002 Fumé Blanc (North Coast) $13. 84 *—S.H. (2/1/2004)*

Benziger 2003 Merlot (Sonoma County) $19. They held this Merlot back almost four years, a long time for a relatively inexpensive wine. Hard to say why, for the tannins are still aggressive, and the wine feels tough and dryly gritty. 82 *—S.H. (11/1/2007)*

Benziger 2001 Merlot (Sonoma County) $19. 88 *—S.H. (6/1/2004)*

Benziger 2000 Merlot (Sonoma County) $19. 85 *—S.H. (12/1/2003)*

Benziger 1999 Merlot (Sonoma County) $19. 91 *—S.H. (7/1/2002)*

Benziger 1999 Merlot (Sonoma County) $19. 85 *—S.H. (8/1/2003)*

Benziger 2000 Blue Rock Vineyard Merlot (Alexander Valley) $30. 91 *—S.H. (4/1/2004)*

Benziger 1998 McNab Ranch Merlot (Mendocino County) $35. 90 *—S.H. (12/31/2001)*

Benziger 2000 Reserve Merlot (Sonoma County) $42. 90 *—S.H. (8/1/2005)*

Benziger 1998 Reserve Merlot (Sonoma County) $42. 90 *—S.H. (12/31/2001)*

Benziger 1997 Reserve Merlot (Sonoma County) $41. 91 *(6/1/2001)*

Benziger 2000 McNab Ranch Petite Sirah (Mendocino) $27. 90 *—S.H. (11/15/2004)*

Benziger 1999 McNab Ranch Petite Sirah (Mendocino County) $21. 83 *(4/1/2003)*

Benziger 2000 Pinot Gris (Oregon) $20. 85 *—S.H. (8/1/2002)*

Benziger 2005 Pinot Noir (Sonoma Coast) $25. With some Carneros fruit blended in, this Sonoma Coast Pinot is a very nice example of cool-climate Sonoma County Pinot Noir. It has good enough acidity to balance the rich, exotic cherry, raspberry, cola, pomegranate, tea and cinnamon clove flavors that are enriched with the vanilla and caramel of oak. 90 *—S.H. (11/1/2007)*

Benziger 2004 Pinot Noir (Sonoma Coast) $25. Superextracted, with jammy cherry, cola, raspberry pie filling, chocolate and spicy gingerbread flavors. Almost sweet in fruity concentration, but it's pretty dry. Ripeness was no problem in this warm vintage. Elegance is the challenge. 86 *—S.H. (4/1/2007)*

Benziger 2001 Pinot Noir (Sonoma County) $22. 86 *—S.H. (12/15/2004)*

Benziger 2000 Pinot Noir (Sonoma County) $21. 86 *—S.H. (7/1/2003)*

Benziger 1999 Pinot Noir (Sonoma County) $21. 85 *(10/1/2002)*

Benziger 1997 Pinot Noir (California) $15. 87 *(11/15/1999)*

Benziger 1999 Bien Nacido Pinot Noir (Santa Maria Valley) $33. 86 *(10/1/2002)*

Benziger 2001 Bien Nacido Vineyard Pinot Noir (Santa Maria Valley) $33. 87 *—S.H. (12/1/2004)*

Benziger 2000 Bien Nacido Vineyard Pinot Noir (Santa Maria Valley) $33. 87 *—S.H. (7/1/2003)*

Benziger 1999 Reserve Pinot Noir (Sonoma County) $43. 88 *(10/1/2002)*

Benziger 1997 Reserve Pinot Noir (California) $40. 90 *—S.H. (12/15/2001)*

Benziger 2000 Reserve Santa Barbara-Sonoma Pinot Noir (California) $42. 83 *—S.H. (8/1/2005)*

Benziger 2001 Tribute Red Blend (Sonoma Mountain) $65. 94 Cellar Selection *(4/1/2005)*

Benziger 2005 Sauvignon Blanc (North Coast) $13. 86 *—S.H. (11/15/2006)*

Benziger 2000 Estate Sauvignon Blanc (Sonoma Mountain) $22. 90 *(8/1/2002)*

Benziger 2005 Paradiso de Maria Sauvignon Blanc (Sonoma Mountain) $29. 92 *—S.H. (9/1/2006)*

Benziger 2004 Paradiso de Maria Sauvignon Blanc (Sonoma Mountain) $27. 91 Editors' Choice *—S.H. (12/1/2005)*

Benziger 2004 Shone Farm Sauvignon Blanc (Russian River Valley) $27. 94 Editors' Choice *—S.H. (8/1/2006)*

Benziger 1996 Syrah (Central Coast) $18. 90 *—S.H. (6/1/1999)*

Benziger 2000 Syrah (California) $22. 85 *—S.H. (10/1/2003)*

Benziger 2000 Bien Nacido Vineyard Syrah (Santa Maria Valley) $35. 91 —*S.H. (10/1/2003)*

Benziger 1998 Bien Nacido Vineyard Syrah (Santa Maria Valley) $24. 90 —*S.H. (7/1/2002)*

Benziger 2002 Bien Nacido Vineyards Syrah (Santa Maria Valley) $35. 85 *(9/1/2005)*

Benziger 1997 Viognier (Sonoma County) $18. 89 —*S.H. (6/1/1999)*

Benziger 2000 Carreras Vineyard Zinfandel (Dry Creek Valley) $35. 90 —*S.H. (3/1/2004)*

BERAN

Beran 2002 Pinot Noir (Willamette Valley) $30. 86 *(11/1/2004)*

Beran 1998 Pinot Noir (Willamette Valley) $28. 83 —*M.S. (12/1/2000)*

BERESAN

Beresan 2004 Cabernet Franc (Walla Walla (WA)) $25. Pure Cab Franc entirely from Walla Walla Valley fruit; in fact this is the winery's only Walla Walla Valley wine of the vintage. It's a good effort under the difficult growing conditions of the vintage, in which all the estate fruit was from secondary buds. Flavors of bell pepper, toast and coffee dominate; this will benefit from a year or two more in bottle. **87** —*P.G. (3/1/2007)*

Beresan 2004 Cabernet Sauvignon (Columbia Valley (WA)) $29. This Cabernet from the estate's Waliser and Yellow Jacket vineyards has been blended with about 7% Pepper Bridge Malbec. As with Beresan's other 2004 releases, this is well made but significantly lighter than previous vintages. The fruit tastes of pretty strawberry and cherry with a hint of bell pepper; the oak adds a dusty cinnamon and mocha note to it. It's all proportionate and very well made, just not showing the customary depth and detail. **87** —*P.G. (3/1/2007)*

Beresan 2003 Cabernet Sauvignon (Walla Walla (WA)) $25. 92 —*P.G. (4/1/2006)*

Beresan 2002 Cabernet Sauvignon (Walla Walla (WA)) $25. 90 —*P.G. (4/1/2005)*

Beresan 2004 Merlot (Columbia Valley (WA)) $29. Pure Merlot, this shows just a touch of leather in the nose, though nothing overpowering. The fruit is solid, unspectacular but well defined and balanced. The use of the new oak (about 35%) is tasteful and tasty. The wine is forward and immediately delicious, then tails off in the finish. **89** —*P.G. (3/1/2007)*

Beresan 2003 Merlot (Walla Walla (WA)) $25. 91 —*P.G. (4/1/2006)*

Beresan 2002 Merlot (Walla Walla (WA)) $25. 91 Editors' Choice —*P.G. (4/1/2005)*

Beresan 2004 Stone River Red Blend (Columbia Valley (WA)) $35. In 2004 the estate fruit was severely damaged by the freeze, so the blend includes a fair amount from Columbia Valley vineyards. It's very well made, fragrant and smooth, ready to drink and tasting very good. The flavors are nicely melded and show the mix of primary red fruits but also a bit of spice and a hint of caramel. Though considerably lighter than previous vintages, this is still an excellent effort. **90** —*P.G. (3/1/2007)*

Beresan 2003 Stone River Red Red Blend (Walla Walla (WA)) $35. 94 —*P.G. (4/1/2006)*

Beresan 2002 Stone River Red Wine Red Blend (Walla Walla (WA)) $28. 95 Editors' Choice —*P.G. (11/15/2004)*

Beresan 2004 Syrah (Columbia Valley (WA)) $29. This is 100% Syrah sourced from Candy Mountain, Stone Tree and Kestrel View. Substantial, chewy, ripe and bracing, it's the best of the 2004 lineup from Beresan. You get saturated color, a lush, fragrant nose, and spicy, peppery cherry fruit with some pretty tobacco accents. In the mouth it's just plain delicious. There's a perfect streak of vanilla/coffee/Kahlùa running through the spine, and the wine unfolds in a long, seamless finish. **91** —*P.G. (3/1/2007)*

Beresan 2003 Syrah (Walla Walla (WA)) $25. 90 —*P.G. (4/1/2006)*

Beresan 2002 Syrah (Walla Walla (WA)) $30. 90 —*P.G. (4/1/2005)*

BERGEVIN LANE

Bergevin Lane 2003 Intuition Reserve Bordeaux Blend (Columbia Valley (WA)) $45. 92 —*P.G. (4/1/2006)*

Bergevin Lane 2004 Cabernet Franc (Columbia Valley (WA)) $30. 86 —*P.G. (12/31/2006)*

Bergevin Lane 2003 Cabernet Sauvignon (Columbia Valley (WA)) $25. 90 —*P.G. (4/1/2006)*

Bergevin Lane 2002 Cabernet Sauvignon (Columbia Valley (WA)) $25. 86 —*P.G. (4/1/2005)*

Bergevin Lane 2004 Alder Ridge Vineyard Cabernet Sauvignon (Horse Heaven Hills) $30. Tight and tannic, this is a Bordeaux blend which leans to the herbal side of the line. It's got interesting aromas, a mix of leaf, soil and herb, and there is a solid red currant base to it. I suspect this will open up and smooth out in a few more years; right now it's a bit chewy. **89** —*P.G. (11/1/2007)*

Bergevin Lane 2004 Merlot (Columbia Valley (WA)) $25. 88 —*P.G. (12/31/2006)*

Bergevin Lane 2002 Merlot (Walla Walla (WA)) $30. 91 —*P.G. (4/1/2005)*

Bergevin Lane 2005 Calico Red Blend (Columbia Valley (WA)) $19. This classy mutt wine mixes Cab Sauvignon, Syrah, Merlot and a dollop each of Zin and Cab Franc. It's quite substantial, showing muscle and nerve along with a strong streak of licorice right through the heart of the cherry-flavored fruit. They've upped the price, but this is bigger, richer and more structured than ever. **89** —*P.G. (11/1/2007)*

Bergevin Lane 2004 Calico Red Red Blend (Columbia Valley (WA)) $18. 87 —*P.G. (4/1/2006)*

Bergevin Lane 2003 Calico Red Red Blend (Columbia Valley (WA)) $16. 90 —*P.G. (6/1/2005)*

Bergevin Lane 2003 Sémillon (Columbia Valley (WA)) $19. 89 —*P.G. (6/1/2005)*

Bergevin Lane 2004 Syrah (Columbia Valley (WA)) $25. This is tart, high-acid Syrah, with strong green tea tannins under tangy wild berries. Light streaks of earth and pepper add some interest, but this feels as though it didn't quite fully ripen, and may not lose its aggressive herbaceousness. **86** —*P.G. (11/1/2007)*

Bergevin Lane 2003 Syrah (Columbia Valley (WA)) $25. 88 *(9/1/2005)*

Bergevin Lane 2002 Syrah (Walla Walla (WA)) $30. 88 —*P.G. (4/1/2005)*

Bergevin Lane 2003 Jaden's Reserve Syrah (Columbia Valley (WA)) $55. 93 —*P.G. (8/1/2006)*

Bergevin Lane 2004 Oui Deux Syrah (Wahluke Slope) $30. A soft and spicy Syrah, with the defining Wahluke appellation characteristic of citrus, here expressed as a flavor of bitter rind. The grapefruity note is persistent, perhaps due to 11% Viognier co-fermentation. The wine at this stage seems to be disconnected from itself; the two grapes are competing rather than blending. The Syrah, smoky and peppery, may reassert itself with a bit more bottle age. **88** —*P.G. (3/1/2007)*

Bergevin Lane 2004 Viognier (Columbia Valley (WA)) $25. 90 —*P.G. (12/15/2005)*

Bergevin Lane 2006 Viognier (Columbia Valley (WA)) $25. Bergevin Lane has a fine track record with their Viogniers. This new vintage includes grapes from Willow Crest and Lonesome Spring, two excellent growers, and incorporates 11% Roussanne in the final blend. The oak influence is subtle and appropriate, lending a light streak of butterscotch to the finish. There's an elegant spicy note and overall, it's a sophisticated, understated, most enjoyable wine. **89** —*P.G. (11/1/2007)*

Bergevin Lane 2003 Viognier (Columbia Valley (WA)) $25. 89 —*P.G. (9/1/2004)*

Bergevin Lane 2006 Calico White Blend (Columbia Valley (WA)) $15. This is two thirds Chardonnay, one third Viognier, melded into a very crisp, leesy and refreshing wine. There's a nice orange peel aroma leading off; and once in the mouth the wine has a brisk insouciance that invites sip after sip. **88 Best Buy** —*P.G. (11/1/2007)*

Bergevin Lane 2003 375ml Zinfandel (Horse Heaven Hills) $19. 87 —*P.G. (12/31/2006)*

BERGSTRÖM

Bergström 2001 Chardonnay (Willamette Valley) $28. 90 —*S.H. (9/1/2003)*

Bergström 2000 Chardonnay (Willamette Valley) $28. 88 —*S.H. (8/1/2002)*

Bergström 2000 Pinot Gris (Willamette Valley) $16. 87 —*S.H. (8/1/2002)*

Bergström 2001 Pinot Noir (Willamette Valley) $18. 90 Editors' Choice —*S.H. (12/1/2003)*

Bergström 2000 Pinot Noir (Willamette Valley) $35. 91 —*S.H. (12/31/2002)*

Bergström 2000 Arcus Pinot Noir (Willamette Valley) $50. 95 Editors' Choice *(10/1/2002)*

Bergström 2001 Arcus Vineyard Pinot Noir (Willamette Valley) $50. 93 Cellar Selection —*S.H. (12/1/2003)*

Bergström 2001 Cumberland Reserve Pinot Noir (Willamette Valley) $30. 91 —*S.H. (12/1/2003)*

BERINGER

Beringer 2000 Alluvium Bordeaux Blend (Knights Valley) $30. 90 —*S.H. (12/1/2004)*

Beringer 1996 Alluvium Bordeaux Blend (Knights Valley) $30. 87 *(3/1/2000)*

Beringer 2002 Alluvium Red Table Wine Bordeaux Blend (Knights Valley) $30. 87 —*S.H. (12/15/2006)*

Beringer 2001 Alluvium Red Table Wine Bordeaux Blend (Knights Valley) $30. 86 *—S.H. (12/15/2005)*

Beringer 1996 Cabernet Sauvignon (Knights Valley) $25. 87 *—L.W. (12/31/1999)*

Beringer 2002 Cabernet Sauvignon (Knights Valley) $27. 86 *—S.H. (12/15/2006)*

Beringer 2001 Cabernet Sauvignon (Napa Valley) $35. 90 *—S.H. (3/1/2005)*

Beringer 2000 Cabernet Sauvignon (Knights Valley) $26. 85 *—S.H. (11/15/2003)*

Beringer 1999 Cabernet Sauvignon (Knights Valley) $26. 87 *—S.H. (2/1/2003)*

Beringer 1998 Cabernet Sauvignon (Knights Valley) $25. 87 *—S.H. (7/1/2002)*

Beringer 1999 Appellation Collection Reserve Cabernet Sauvignon (Knights Valley) $50. 84 *—S.H. (12/15/2003)*

Beringer 2001 Bancroft Ranch Cabernet Sauvignon (Howell Mountain) $90. 93 Cellar Selection *—S.H. (9/1/2006)*

Beringer 1998 Bancroft Ranch Cabernet Sauvignon (Howell Mountain) $80. 89 *—S.H. (11/15/2003)*

Beringer 2001 Chabot Vineyard Cabernet Sauvignon (St. Helena) $90. 89 *—S.H. (8/1/2006)*

Beringer 1998 Chabot Vineyard Cabernet Sauvignon (St. Helena) $80. 91 *—S.H. (11/15/2003)*

Beringer 2003 Founders' Estate Cabernet Sauvignon (California) $11. 86 Best Buy *—S.H. (4/1/2006)*

Beringer 2001 Founders' Estate Cabernet Sauvignon (California) $12. 86 *—S.H. (10/1/2004)*

Beringer 2000 Founders' Estate Cabernet Sauvignon (California) $12. 85 *—S.H. (3/1/2003)*

Beringer 1999 Founders' Estate Cabernet Sauvignon (California) $12. 84 *—S.H. (12/31/2001)*

Beringer 1997 Founders' Estate Cabernet Sauvignon (California) $11. 87 *(11/15/1999)*

Beringer 2001 Marston Vineyard Cabernet Sauvignon (Spring Mountain) $90. 92 Cellar Selection *—S.H. (9/1/2006)*

Beringer 1998 Marston Vineyard Cabernet Sauvignon (Spring Mountain) $80. 91 *—S.H. (11/15/2003)*

Beringer 2002 Private Reserve Cabernet Sauvignon (Napa Valley) $116. 90 *—S.H. (9/1/2006)*

Beringer 2000 Private Reserve Cabernet Sauvignon (Napa Valley) $100. 86 *—S.H. (5/1/2005)*

Beringer 1999 Private Reserve Cabernet Sauvignon (Napa Valley) $75. 91 *(8/1/2003)*

Beringer 1997 Private Reserve Cabernet Sauvignon (Napa Valley) $100. 93 *—S.H. (12/31/2001)*

Beringer 1996 Private Reserve Cabernet Sauvignon (Napa Valley) $100. 95 *—S.H. (2/1/2001)*

Beringer 1995 Private Reserve Cabernet Sauvignon (Napa Valley) $75. 95 *—S.H. (7/1/2000)*

Beringer 2001 Quarry Vineyard Cabernet Sauvignon (Rutherford) $90. 92 Cellar Selection *—S.H. (9/1/2006)*

Beringer 1998 Quarry Vineyard Cabernet Sauvignon (Rutherford) $80. 91 *—S.H. (11/15/2003)*

Beringer 2001 Rancho del Oso Vineyard Cabernet Sauvignon (Howell Mountain) $90. 92 Cellar Selection *—S.H. (9/1/2006)*

Beringer 2001 St. Helena Home Vineyard Cabernet Sauvignon (St. Helena) $90. 92 Cellar Selection *—S.H. (9/1/2006)*

Beringer 1998 St. Helena Home Vineyard Cabernet Sauvignon (St. Helena) $80. 92 *—S.H. (11/15/2003)*

Beringer 1998 State Lane Cabernet Sauvignon (Napa Valley) $80. 91 *—S.H. (11/15/2003)*

Beringer 2001 Steinhauer Ranch Cabernet Sauvignon (Howell Mountain) $90. 92 Cellar Selection *—S.H. (9/1/2006)*

Beringer 1998 Tre Colline Cabernet Sauvignon (Howell Mountain) $80. 91 *—S.H. (11/15/2003)*

Beringer 2004 Third Century Cabernet Sauvignon (North Coast) $14. Here's an everyday style Cab, with decent varietal character. It's totally dry, with some scoury tannins and earthy, herbaceous flavors of red currants and cedar. 84 *—S.H. (11/1/2007)*

Beringer 1999 Alluvium Cabernet Sauvignon-Merlot (Knights Valley) $30. 87 *—S.H. (3/1/2004)*

Beringer 2005 Chardonnay (Napa Valley) $16. Simple and thin in fruit, with modest pineapple and peach flavors and an awkward overlay of sweet oak. 83 *—S.H. (7/1/2007)*

Beringer 2004 Chardonnay (Napa Valley) $16. 84 *—S.H. (8/1/2006)*

Beringer 2003 Chardonnay (Napa Valley) $16. 84 *—S.H. (10/1/2005)*

Beringer 2002 Chardonnay (Napa Valley) $16. 86 *—S.H. (3/1/2005)*

Beringer 2001 Chardonnay (Napa Valley) $16. 86 *—S.H. (12/15/2003)*

Beringer 1998 Chardonnay (Napa Valley) $16. 86 *(6/1/2000)*

Beringer 2000 Appellation Collection Chardonnay (Napa Valley) $16. 92 *—S.H. (12/15/2002)*

Beringer 2005 Founders' Estate Chardonnay (California) $11. 83 *—S.H. (12/31/2006)*

Beringer 2002 Founders' Estate Chardonnay (California) $12. 87 *—S.H. (8/1/2004)*

Beringer 2001 Founders' Estate Chardonnay (California) $12. 85 *—S.H. (6/1/2003)*

Beringer 2000 Founders' Estate Chardonnay (California) $12. 85 *—S.H. (9/1/2002)*

Beringer 2005 Private Reserve Chardonnay (Napa Valley) $35. The underlying wine in Beringer's '05 Reserve is a rich blend of tropical fruit, peach, pear and apple flavors. But the wine is overoaked, with 75% new wood in the barrel fermentation. Anyone sensitive to the taste of new oak will instantly recognize the immense cosmetic of smoky char, sweet vanilla, buttered toast and spicy, sappy wood essence, which seems excessive and not really needed. 87 *—S.H. (11/1/2007)*

Beringer 2004 Private Reserve Chardonnay (Napa Valley) $35. 90 *—S.H. (8/1/2006)*

Beringer 2002 Private Reserve Chardonnay (Napa Valley) $35. 91 *—S.H. (12/15/2004)*

Beringer 2001 Private Reserve Chardonnay (Napa Valley) $35. 93 Editors' Choice *—S.H. (2/1/2004)*

Beringer 2000 Private Reserve Chardonnay (Napa Valley) $35. 91 *—S.H. (5/1/2003)*

Beringer 1999 Private Reserve Chardonnay (Napa Valley) $35. 90 *(7/1/2001)*

Beringer 1998 Private Reserve Chardonnay (Napa Valley) $36. 89 *(10/1/2000)*

Beringer 2005 Sbragia Limited Release Chardonnay (Napa Valley) $40. The only criticism I have is excessive new oak. In this case, it's 100%, and the sweet char, smoky vanilla and brûléed butterscotch flavors completely dominate. Good as Beringer's top Chards are, they're not Montrachet, and the wine simply cannot shoulder that burden of wood. Having said that, it's still an elegant wine, and oak devotees will love it. 89 *—S.H. (11/1/2007)*

Beringer 2000 Sbragia-Limited Release Chardonnay (Napa Valley) $40. 92 *—J.M. (12/15/2002)*

Beringer 2001 Sbragia Limited Release Chardonnay (Napa Valley) $40. 92 *—S.H. (12/1/2003)*

Beringer 1997 Sbragia Limited Release Chardonnay (Napa Valley) $40. 94 *—M.M. (11/15/1999)*

Beringer 1999 Sbragia-Limited Release Chardonnay (Napa Valley) $40. 91 *(7/1/2001)*

Beringer 2005 Stanly Ranch Chardonnay (Carneros) $20. Stanly Ranch is one of the great historic vineyards of Carneros, but this wine is not a good expression of it. It's thin and watery, with a touch of peaches, tangerines and oak. Not a bad wine, but a disappointing one given its origin. 84 *—S.H. (7/1/2007)*

Beringer 2005 Third Century Chardonnay (Central Coast) $14. Thin to the point of watery. It has extremely modest fruit, but a lot of toasted, sweet oak. 82 *—S.H. (11/1/2007)*

Beringer 2003 Chenin Blanc (California) $6. 83 *—S.H. (10/1/2004)*

Beringer 2002 Chenin Blanc (California) $6. 83 *—S.H. (12/15/2003)*

Beringer 2003 Gewürztraminer (California) $8. 83 *—S.H. (10/1/2004)*

Beringer 2002 Gewürztraminer (California) $6. 84 *—S.H. (12/31/2003)*

Beringer 2003 Johannisberg Riesling (California) $8. 83 *—S.H. (10/1/2004)*

Beringer 2002 Johannisberg Riesling (California) $6. 85 Best Buy *—S.H. (12/31/2003)*

Beringer 1998 Special Late Harvest Johannisberg Riesling (California) $20. 94 *—S.H. (9/1/2004)*

Beringer 2005 Merlot (Napa Valley) $20. Simple and soft, this is one to drink now. It rewards for the wealth of cherry, blackberry, licorice and cocoa flavors that finish dry and clean. **84** *—S.H. (12/31/2007)*

Beringer 2001 Merlot (Napa Valley) $19. 83 *—S.H. (11/15/2005)*

Beringer 2000 Appellation Collection Merlot (Napa Valley) $19. 85 *—S.H. (2/1/2004)*

Beringer 1997 Bancroft Ranch Merlot (Howell Mountain) $75. 89 *(6/1/2001)*

Beringer 1996 Bancroft Ranch Merlot (Howell Mountain) $75. 92 *(3/1/2000)*

Beringer 2003 Founders' Estate Merlot (California) $11. 85 *—S.H. (12/31/2006)*

Beringer 2002 Founders' Estate Merlot (California) $11. 83 *—S.H. (11/15/2005)*

Beringer 2001 Founders' Estate Merlot (California) $12. 85 *—S.H. (9/1/2004)*

Beringer 2000 Founders' Estate Merlot (California) $12. 87 Best Buy *—S.H. (10/1/2003)*

Beringer 1999 Founders' Estate Merlot (California) $12. 85 Best Buy *—S.H. (12/31/2001)*

Beringer 2000 Private Reserve Howell Mountain Merlot (Napa Valley) $50. 86 *—S.H. (5/1/2005)*

Beringer 2004 Third Century Merlot (North Coast) $14. This rustic wine is sharp, with green, minty flavors and astringent tannins, although with airing, a core of cherries emerges, and the finish is dry. **83** *—S.H. (11/1/2007)*

Beringer 1998 Hayne Vineyard Petite Sirah (St. Helena) $35. 82 *(4/1/2003)*

Beringer 2003 Pinot Grigio (California) $7. 83 *—S.H. (10/1/2004)*

Beringer 2005 Founders' Estate Pinot Grigio (California) $11. 84 *—S.H. (12/31/2006)*

Beringer 2004 Founders' Estate Pinot Grigio (California) $11. 86 Best Buy *—S.H. (11/15/2005)*

Beringer 2004 Premier Vineyard Selection Pinot Grigio (California) $6. 84 Best Buy *—S.H. (2/1/2006)*

Beringer 2003 Stone Cellars Pinot Grigio (California) $8. 84 *—S.H. (2/1/2006)*

Beringer 2006 Pinot Noir (Napa Valley) $20. The grapes come from the cooler Oak Knoll area of Napa Valley, yet this wine is very soft and melted, without much acidity to provoke and enliven the ripe cherry, vanilla and sassafras flavors. It does show Pinot's silkiness, and is easy to drink. **84** *—S.H. (12/31/2007)*

Beringer 2004 Pinot Noir (Napa Valley) $16. 84 *—S.H. (11/15/2005)*

Beringer 2003 Pinot Noir (Napa Valley) $16. 84 *—S.H. (6/1/2005)*

Beringer 2002 Pinot Noir (Carneros) $16. 87 *(11/1/2004)*

Beringer 2000 Pinot Noir (Carneros) $16. 84 *(10/1/2002)*

Beringer 1999 Pinot Noir (North Coast) $16. 83 *(10/1/2002)*

Beringer 2005 Founders' Estate Pinot Noir (California) $12. 85 *—S.H. (12/31/2006)*

Beringer 2002 Founders' Estate Pinot Noir (California) $12. 85 *—S.H. (11/1/2004)*

Beringer 2001 Founders' Estate Pinot Noir (California) $12. 86 Best Buy *—S.H. (12/1/2003)*

Beringer 2000 Founders' Estate Pinot Noir (California) $12. 84 Best Buy *(10/1/2002)*

Beringer 2002 Stanly Ranch Pinot Noir (Carneros) $30. 92 Editors' Choice *—S.H. (11/1/2004)*

Beringer 2000 Stanly Ranch Pinot Noir (Carneros) $30. 91 *—S.H. (12/1/2003)*

Beringer 1999 Stanly Ranch Pinot Noir (Napa Valley) $30. 92 Editors' Choice *(10/1/2002)*

Beringer 2005 Third Century Pinot Noir (Central Coast) $14. Although this is a fairly one-dimensional wine, it does show real Pinot character, with a silky texture, modest cherry and cola flavors, crispness and dry finish. It's a great wine for those who want to try Pinot without breaking the bank. **85** *—S.H. (11/1/2007)*

Beringer 1999 Port of Cabernet Sauvignon Port (Napa Valley) $20. 86 *—S.H. (7/1/2005)*

Beringer 1998 Alluvium Red Blend (Knights Valley) $30. 88 *—J.M. (11/15/2002)*

Beringer 2001 Nouveau Red Blend (California) $8. 86 *—S.H. (9/1/2002)*

Beringer 2002 Riesling (Napa Valley) $16. 87 *—S.H. (9/1/2004)*

Beringer 1997 Johannisberg Riesling (Napa Valley) $8. 85 *—M.S. (6/1/1999)*

Beringer 1998 Rose de Saignee Rosé Blend (California) $16. 86 *—J.C. (8/1/2000)*

Beringer 2006 Sauvignon Blanc (Napa Valley) $16. Tangy acidity is the star here. It gives structure and backbone to the lemon, lime, pineapple and fig flavors, and makes the wine a great cocktail sipper. **85** *—S.H. (12/31/2007)*

Beringer 2004 Sauvignon Blanc (Napa Valley) $12. 83 *—S.H. (11/15/2005)*

Beringer 2003 Sauvignon Blanc (Napa Valley) $12. 85 *—S.H. (12/15/2004)*

Beringer 2002 Sauvignon Blanc (Napa Valley) $12. 85 *—S.H. (12/31/2003)*

Beringer 1998 Sauvignon Blanc (Napa Valley) $12. 87 *—S.H. (5/1/2000)*

Beringer 2004 Founders' Estate Sauvignon Blanc (California) $11. 85 *—S.H. (11/15/2005)*

Beringer 2002 Founders' Estate Sauvignon Blanc (California) $11. 85 *—S.H. (8/1/2004)*

Beringer 2001 Founders' Estate Sauvignon Blanc (California) $11. 86 *—S.H. (3/1/2003)*

Beringer 2000 Founders' Estate Sauvignon Blanc (California) $11. 84 *—S.H. (12/15/2001)*

Beringer 2003 Alluvium Blanc Sauvignon Blanc-Sémillon (Knights Valley) $16. 85 *—S.H. (11/15/2005)*

Beringer 2001 Alluvium Blanc Sémillon-Sauvignon Blanc (Knights Valley) $16. 84 *—S.H. (7/1/2003)*

Beringer 2003 Nightingale Semillon-Sauvignon Blanc (Napa Valley) $40. The warm vintage rewarded this dessert wine, yielding incredibly ripe fruit. Barrel-fermented, this blend of Sémillon and Sauvignon Blanc was picked at 35% of sugar, and has a residual sweetness of 12.1 grams. The wine is tremendous in apricot jam, pineapple tart, vanilla custard and crème brûlée flavors, with gorgeously balancing, clean acids and a rich, honeyed finish. **97** *—S.H. (6/1/2007)*

Beringer 2001 Nightingale Sémillon-Sauvignon Blanc (Napa Valley) $30. 89 *—S.H. (4/1/2004)*

Beringer 2000 Nightingale Sémillon-Sauvignon Blanc (Napa Valley) $35. 86 *—S.H. (12/1/2003)*

Beringer 1998 Nightingale Sémillon-Sauvignon Blanc (Napa Valley) $30. 94 Cellar Selection *—S.H. (12/1/2002)*

Beringer 2002 Nightingale Private Reserve Sémillon-Sauvignon Blanc (Napa Valley) $30. 90 *—S.H. (5/1/2006)*

Beringer 2003 Founders' Estate Shiraz (California) $11. 85 *(9/1/2005)*

Beringer 1999 Founders' Estate Shiraz (California) $11. 86 *(10/1/2001)*

Beringer 2001 Marston Vineyard Syrah (Spring Mountain) $35. 89 *(9/1/2005)*

Beringer 1997 Viognier (Napa Valley) $20. 91 *—S.H. (10/1/1999)*

Beringer 2004 Viognier (Napa Valley) $16. 84 *—S.H. (11/15/2005)*

Beringer 2003 Viognier (Napa Valley) $16. 88 *—S.H. (12/15/2004)*

Beringer 2002 Viognier (Napa Valley) $16. 85 *—S.H. (9/1/2004)*

Beringer 2004 Alluvium Blanc White Blend (Knights Valley) $16. 88 *—S.H. (12/15/2006)*

Beringer 2002 Alluvium Blanc White Blend (Knights Valley) $16. 89 *—S.H. (12/15/2004)*

Beringer 2000 Alluvium Blanc White Blend (Knights Valley) $16. 87 *—J.M. (12/15/2002)*

Beringer 1999 Alluvium Blanc White Blend (Knights Valley) $16. 85 *—S.H. (9/1/2002)*

Beringer 1998 Alluvium Blanc White Blend (Knights Valley) $16. 89 *—S.H. (5/1/2001)*

Beringer 1997 Alluvium Blanc White Blend (Knights Valley) $16. 89 *—M.S. (8/1/2000)*

Beringer 1996 Nightingale White Blend (North Coast) $30. 93 *—S.H. (12/31/2000)*

Beringer 1996 Zinfandel (North Coast) $13. 88 Best Buy *—M.S. (9/1/1999)*

Beringer 2001 Zinfandel (California) $12. 82 *(11/1/2003)*

Beringer 1998 Zinfandel (Clear Lake) $14. 86 *—S.H. (11/1/2002)*

Beringer 1999 Appelation Collection Zinfandel (Clear Lake) $14. 81 *—S.H. (3/1/2004)*

Beringer 1999 Founders' Estate Zinfandel (California) $12. 86 *—S.H. (2/1/2003)*

Beringer 2004 Founders' Estate Old Vine Zinfandel (California) $11. 84 *—S.H. (12/31/2006)*

Beringer 2003 Founders' Estate Old Vine Zinfandel (California) $11. 85 —*S.H. (11/15/2005)*

BERNARDUS

Bernardus 2003 Marinus Bordeaux Blend (Carmel Valley) $40. Not quite on a par with the '01 or '02, this is more like the 2000 Marinus. Made mainly of Cabernet Sauvignon, with the other four Bordeaux varieties, it's dry and gentle in tannins, with very ripe flavors of blackberry jam, cassis, cocoa, licorice and smoky oak. Elegant, but not an ager; drink now. 87 —*S.H. (12/1/2007)*

Bernardus 2000 Marinus Bordeaux Blend (Carmel Valley) $46. 87 —*S.H. (10/1/2004)*

Bernardus 2002 Marinus Cabernet Blend (Carmel Valley) $44. 90 —*S.H. (9/1/2006)*

Bernardus 2001 Marinus Cabernet Sauvignon (Carmel Valley) $46. 90 —*S.H. (4/1/2005)*

Bernardus 2005 Chardonnay (Monterey County) $20. As is usually the case, Bernardus's regular Monterey Chard offers lots of bang for the buck. Dry and crisp in citrusy acids, it has complex flavors of pineapple, grapefruit, kiwi, lime and spicy coconut macaroon, with delicious oak influence. 90 —*S.H. (8/1/2007)*

Bernardus 2004 Chardonnay (Monterey County) $20. 87 —*S.H. (10/1/2006)*

Bernardus 2003 Chardonnay (Monterey) $20. 91 Editors' Choice —*S.H. (11/1/2005)*

Bernardus 2002 Chardonnay (Monterey County) $20. 92 —*S.H. (12/15/2004)*

Bernardus 2001 Chardonnay (Monterey County) $20. 90 Editors' Choice —*S.H. (8/1/2003)*

Bernardus 2000 Chardonnay (Monterey County) $20. 88 —*S.H. (2/1/2003)*

Bernardus 1996 Bien Nacido Reserve Chardonnay (Santa Barbara County) $32. 84 *(7/1/2001)*

Bernardus 1997 Chardonnay (Monterey County) $18. 90 *(11/15/1999)*

Bernardus 2002 Cypress Vineyard Chardonnay (Monterey County) $50. 87 —*S.H. (6/1/2006)*

Bernardus 2001 Griva Vineyard Chardonnay (Monterey County) $38. 91 —*S.H. (8/1/2003)*

Bernardus 2002 Rosella's Vineyard Chardonnay (Santa Lucia Highlands) $40. 90 —*S.H. (6/1/2006)*

Bernardus 1996 Sangiacomo Vineyards Reserve Chardonnay (Sonoma County) $30. 87 *(7/1/2001)*

Bernardus 1999 Marinus Estate Grown & Estate Bottled Meritage (Carmel Valley) $50. 85 —*S.H. (8/1/2003)*

Bernardus 1996 Merlot (Carmel Valley) $30. 89 —*J.C. (7/1/2000)*

Bernardus 2000 Pinot Noir (Santa Barbara County) $28. 85 —*S.H. (8/1/2003)*

Bernardus 2004 Bien Nacido Vineyard Pinot Noir (Santa Maria Valley) $34. 84 —*S.H. (12/31/2006)*

Bernardus 2002 Bien Nacido Vineyard Pinot Noir (Santa Maria Valley) $34. 82 —*S.H. (3/1/2006)*

Bernardus 2000 Bien Nacido Vineyard Pinot Noir (Santa Barbara County) $48. 87 —*S.H. (12/1/2003)*

Bernardus 2005 Rosella's Pinot Noir (Santa Lucia Highlands) $50. Showing classic Santa Lucia highlights of enormously ripe cherries, Asian spices and acidity, this wine flatters the palate with the sheer force of its fruit and new oak. It's a young, fresh, vibrant wine that's at its best now. 90 —*S.H. (12/15/2007)*

Bernardus 2004 Rosella's Pinot Noir (Santa Lucia Highlands) $50. How come Bernardus doesn't do a better job with Pinot? They get their grapes from the best vineyards, but the wines seem stuck in the mid-80s, score-wise. This one is very nice, dry, tannic and fruity, but it feels like it wants to be better than it is, and should be, at this price. 87 —*S.H. (2/1/2007)*

Bernardus 2003 Rosella's Vineyard Pinot Noir (Santa Lucia Highlands) $50. 87 —*S.H. (3/1/2006)*

Bernardus 2006 Sauvignon Blanc (Carmel Valley) $15. For those who like their Sauvignon Blancs bone dry, high in acidity and with nervy gooseberry and juniper berry flavors. It really gets those tastebuds flowing. 86 —*S.H. (11/15/2007)*

Bernardus 2005 Sauvignon Blanc (Monterey County) $15. 83 —*S.H. (12/1/2006)*

Bernardus 2004 Sauvignon Blanc (Monterey County) $15. 88 —*S.H. (11/1/2005)*

Bernardus 2003 Sauvignon Blanc (Monterey County) $15. 85 —*S.H. (5/1/2005)*

Bernardus 2001 Sauvignon Blanc (Monterey County) $15. 89 —*S.H. (7/1/2003)*

Bernardus 2000 Sauvignon Blanc (Monterey) $15. 89 Best Buy *(8/1/2002)*

Bernardus 1998 Sauvignon Blanc (Monterey County) $14. 87 —*S.H. (11/1/1999)*

Bernardus 2006 Griva Vineyard Sauvignon Blanc (Arroyo Seco) $20. Bernardus has been doing a great job with this bottling, while keeping the price affordable. It's an upscale, vibrant wine of great charm and elegance. Showing keen Arroyo Seco acidity, it offers a powerhouse punch of figs, dates, pineapples, Meyer lemons, honseysuckle and peppery spice. 88 Editors' Choice —*S.H. (11/15/2007)*

Bernardus 2005 Griva Vineyard Sauvignon Blanc (Arroyo Seco) $20. 84 —*S.H. (12/1/2006)*

Bernardus 2004 Griva Vineyard Sauvignon Blanc (Arroyo Seco) $20. 90 —*S.H. (11/1/2005)*

Bernardus 2003 Griva Vineyard Sauvignon Blanc (Arroyo Seco) $20. 86 *(7/1/2005)*

Bernardus 2001 Griva Vineyard Sauvignon Blanc (Arroyo Seco) $20. 89 —*S.H. (10/1/2003)*

BETHEL HEIGHTS

Bethel Heights 2001 Chardonnay (Willamette Valley) $15. 88 —*P.G. (12/1/2003)*

Bethel Heights 1999 Estate Grown Chardonnay (Willamette Valley) $15. 89 Best Buy —*P.G. (4/1/2002)*

Bethel Heights 1998 Pinot Blanc (Willamette Valley) $12. 88 —*L.W. (12/31/1999)*

Bethel Heights 2002 Pinot Blanc (Willamette Valley) $12. 88 Best Buy —*P.G. (12/1/2003)*

Bethel Heights 2000 Reserve Pinot Blanc (Willamette Valley) $12. 87 —*M.M. (11/1/2001)*

Bethel Heights 2004 Pinot Gris (Oregon) $15. 90 Best Buy —*P.G. (2/1/2006)*

Bethel Heights 2000 Pinot Gris (Willamette Valley) $12. 86 —*P.G. (4/1/2002)*

Bethel Heights 1998 Pinot Gris (Willamette Valley) $12. 87 *(8/1/1999)*

Bethel Heights 1997 Pinot Noir (Willamette Valley) $15. 84 *(11/15/1999)*

Bethel Heights 2002 Pinot Noir (Willamette Valley) $15. 84 *(11/1/2004)*

Bethel Heights 2001 Pinot Noir (Willamette Valley) $25. 87 —*P.G. (12/1/2003)*

Bethel Heights 2000 Pinot Noir (Willamette Valley) $25. 86 *(10/1/2002)*

Bethel Heights 2002 Casteel Reserve Pinot Noir (Willamette Valley) $40. 86 *(11/1/2004)*

Bethel Heights 1999 Estate Grown Pinot Noir (Willamette Valley) $25. 88 —*P.G. (4/1/2002)*

Bethel Heights 2002 Flat Block Reserve Pinot Noir (Willamette Valley) $38. 85 *(11/1/2004)*

Bethel Heights 2001 Flat Block Reserve Pinot Noir (Willamette Valley) $38. 88 —*P.G. (12/1/2003)*

Bethel Heights 2000 Flat Block Reserve Pinot Noir (Willamette Valley) $35. 87 *(10/1/2002)*

Bethel Heights 1999 Flat Block Reserve Pinot Noir (Willamette Valley) $35. 91 Editors' Choice —*P.G. (4/1/2002)*

Bethel Heights 2002 Freedom Hill Vineyard Pinot Noir (Willamette Valley) $30. 86 *(11/1/2004)*

Bethel Heights 2001 Freedom Hill Vineyard Pinot Noir (Willamette Valley) $30. 89 —*P.G. (12/1/2003)*

Bethel Heights 1998 Freedom Hill Vineyard Pinot Noir (Willamette Valley) $30. 89 —*M.M. (12/1/2000)*

Bethel Heights 1998 Lewman Vineyard Pinot Noir (Willamette Valley) $25. 85 —*M.S. (12/1/2000)*

Bethel Heights 2002 Nysa Vineyard Pinot Noir (Willamette Valley) $30. 86 *(11/1/2004)*

Bethel Heights 2001 Nysa Vineyard Pinot Noir (Willamette Valley) $30. 88 —*P.G. (12/1/2003)*

Bethel Heights 2000 Nysa Vineyard Pinot Noir (Willamette Valley) $30. 87 *(10/1/2002)*

Bethel Heights 1999 Nysa Vineyard Pinot Noir (Willamette Valley) $30. 89 —*P.G. (4/1/2002)*

Bethel Heights 1998 Nysa Vineyard Pinot Noir (Willamette Valley) $25. 87 —*M.S. (12/1/2000)*

Bethel Heights 2002 SE Block Reserve Pinot Noir (Willamette Valley) $38. 86 *(11/1/2004)*

Bethel Heights 2002 Seven Springs Vineyard Pinot Noir (Willamette Valley) $38. 87 *(11/1/2004)*

Bethel Heights 2001 Southeast Block Reserve Pinot Noir (Willamette Valley) $38. 88 *—P.G. (12/1/2003)*

Bethel Heights 2000 Southeast Block Reserve Pinot Noir (Willamette Valley) $40. 87 *(10/1/2002)*

Bethel Heights 1999 Southeast Block Reserve Pinot Noir (Willamette Valley) $40. 89 *—P.G. (4/1/2002)*

Bethel Heights 1998 Southeast Block Reserve Pinot Noir (Willamette Valley) $35. 90 *—M.S. (12/1/2000)*

Bethel Heights 1998 Wadenswil Block Reserve Pinot Noir (Willamette Valley) $35. 89 *—M.S. (12/1/2000)*

Bethel Heights 1999 Wädenswil Block Reserve Pinot Noir (Willamette Valley) $35. 89 *—M.M. (11/1/2001)*

Bethel Heights 2001 West Block Reserve Pinot Noir (Willamette Valley) $38. 88 *—P.G. (12/1/2003)*

Bethel Heights 2000 West Block Reserve Pinot Noir (Willamette Valley) $35. 88 *(10/1/2002)*

BETZ FAMILY WINERY

Betz Family Winery 2002 Clos de Betz Bordeaux Blend (Columbia Valley (WA)) $29. 93 Editors' Choice *—P.G. (6/1/2005)*

Betz Family Winery 2003 Père de Famille Cabernet Sauvignon (Columbia Valley (WA)) $45. 95 Editors' Choice *—P.G. (6/1/2006)*

Betz Family Winery 2002 Père de Famille Cabernet Sauvignon (Columbia Valley (WA)) $45. 93 *—P.G. (6/1/2005)*

Betz Family Winery 2003 Bésolei Grenache (Columbia Valley (WA)) $35. 91 *—P.G. (12/15/2005)*

Betz Family Winery 2004 Bésoleil Red Blend (Columbia Valley (WA)) $40. This is the second vintage for this very limited (165 cases) Grenache-based red wine. In 2004 the blend includes 19% Mourvèdre and 12% Syrah. Though winemaker Bob Betz says he is "still struggling between size and elegance," this is not a wine you must struggle to enjoy. Bright and spicy, it attacks the palate with the Grenache's powerfully concentrated raspberry fruit. Added weight and mass come from the other two grapes; all beautifully proportioned and blended. Notes of pepper, sweet cinnamon and even a whiff of toast come into play in the creamy finish. **92** *—P.G. (3/1/2007)*

Betz Family Winery 2003 Clos de Betz Red Blend (Columbia Valley (WA)) $32. 93 *—P.G. (6/1/2006)*

Betz Family Winery 2004 La Cote Rousse Syrah (Red Mountain) $45. This Côte Rousse has really pulled itself together. It's a subtle wine but offers perfectly ripened, silky, beautifully proportioned flavors of mixed fruits, highlighted with Rhône-like notes of mineral, forest floor, truffle and smoke. This is the good funk—the exotic nuances that come only from the most sensitive winemaking. A vin de garde, this should evolve over the next decade or more. **94 Cellar Selection** *—P.G. (3/1/2007)*

Betz Family Winery 2003 La Cote Rousse Syrah (Red Mountain) $44. 93 *—P.G. (12/15/2005)*

Betz Family Winery 2002 La Cote Rousse Syrah (Red Mountain) $41. 92 *—P.G. (12/15/2004)*

Betz Family Winery 2004 La Serenne Syrah (Columbia Valley (WA)) $45. The Boushey Vineyard is the source for this Syrah, which once again delivers complex aromas and flavors whose ebullient mix includes wild herb, citrus, spiced plum, posh cherry and luscious vanilla cream. It's killer juice, thick with tar, smoke and bacon fat; but its vivid citrus peel acidity lifts it until it soars. This is seamless, sensuous and thrilling Syrah. **93** *—P.G. (3/1/2007)*

Betz Family Winery 2003 La Serenne Syrah (Columbia Valley (WA)) $44. 91 *—P.G. (12/15/2005)*

Betz Family Winery 2002 La Serenne Syrah (Columbia Valley (WA)) $41. 94 *—P.G. (12/15/2004)*

BIANCHI

Bianchi 2004 Signature Selection Cabernet Franc (Paso Robles) $24. Tannic and gritty, with sweetened cherry and blackberry LifeSaver flavors. **82** *—S.H. (12/1/2007)*

Bianchi 2004 Jack Ranch Signature Selection Chardonnay (Edna Valley) $20. 90 *—S.H. (12/31/2005)*

Bianchi 2005 Signature Selection Chardonnay (Edna Valley) $18. A little on the light side, fruit-wise, this Chard has brisk acidity and clean, but slight, flavors of kiwi. The oak tends to dominate. **84** *—S.H. (12/1/2007)*

Bianchi 2004 Signature Selection Merlot (Paso Robles) $18. Soft, dry and tannic, this Merlot has warm-climate flavors of cherries and blackberries that taste slightly stewed or plumped. **83** *—S.H. (12/1/2007)*

Bianchi 2004 Signature Selection Petite Sirah (Paso Robles) $24. Will have its fans, but despite the Porty aroma, the wine is just too dry and acid-sharp, and lacks fruity substance. **82** *—S.H. (12/15/2007)*

Bianchi 2005 Signature Selection Pinot Grigio (Arroyo Grande Valley) $19. Semisweet and simple, the best thing about this wine is acidity. It's crisp and cleansing, balancing out the guava, peach, citrus and honeysuckle flavors. **83** *—S.H. (5/1/2007)*

Bianchi 2004 Signature Selection Pinot Grigio (Arroyo Grande Valley) $25. 83 *—S.H. (2/1/2006)*

Bianchi 2004 Signature Selection Pinot Noir (Paso Robles) $25. 82 *—S.H. (12/15/2006)*

Bianchi 2005 Signature Selection Sauvignon Blanc (Monterey) $14. From the warmer southern part of the county, the grapes got nice and ripe during this long hangtime vintage. They developed citrus, melon, guava and passionfruit flavors, with absolutely no grassiness. Crisp acidity makes the wine balanced and clean, and the finish is basically, but not totally, dry. **84** *—S.H. (5/1/2007)*

Bianchi 2004 Signature Selection Sauvignon Blanc (Central Coast) $16. 84 *—S.H. (12/31/2005)*

Bianchi 2004 Signature Selection Syrah (Paso Robles) $21. This Syrah does what Paso does so well with big reds. It's soft and lusciously fruity and almost decadent. Of course, the alcohol is high, but those caramelized blackberry and cherry pie, crème de cassis, and raspberry-filled chocolate bonbon flavors are irresistable. **88** *—S.H. (12/1/2007)*

Bianchi 2001 Zen Ranch Zinfandel (Paso Robles) $18. 86 *(11/1/2003)*

BIG ASS

Big Ass 2005 Cabernet Sauvignon (Napa Valley) $15. The name is apropos, for this is a big, fleshy wine, almost like one of those Aussie Shirazes in jammy fruit, although it's Cabernet all the way with blackberries and currants. With fine tannins and a smooth finish, it shows quite a bit of sophistication. **87** *—S.H. (11/15/2007)*

Big Ass 2005 Chardonnay (Napa Valley) $15. With jammy apple and pineapple flavors, this wine's oaky edge adds enough richness to satisfy your basic Chardonnay needs. The finish is simple and sweet. **83** *—S.H. (11/15/2007)*

Big Ass 2005 Syrah (Napa Valley) $15. Pretty good price for a Napa Syrah of this quality. It's a pleasantly fruity sipper, immediately appealing for its ripe, fresh blackberry, cherry and leather flavors. Has a level of dry elegance and tannic complexity that lifts it above the ordinary. **87** *—S.H. (11/15/2007)*

Big Ass 2004 Zinfandel (Sonoma County) $15. This is a seriously good Zinfandel, both for what it is and what it isn't. It's dry, grippy in dusty tannins and complex, with earthy flavors of coffee, cherries, tobacco, blackberries and Asian spices. What it is not is overly alcoholic and sweet, as so many Zins are. The alcohol is a modest 13.9%. The wine has true balance and finesse, and is a great buy in Sonoma Zin. **91 Best Buy** *—S.H. (11/15/2007)*

BIG BASIN

Big Basin 2004 Mandala Syrah (Santa Cruz County) $42. 89 *—S.H. (11/15/2006)*

Big Basin 2004 Rattlesnake Rock Syrah (Santa Cruz Mountains) $55. 94 Editors' Choice *—S.H. (11/15/2006)*

BIG FIRE

Big Fire 2004 Pinot Gris (Oregon) $18. 89 *—P.G. (2/1/2006)*

Big Fire 2001 Pinot Gris (Oregon) $14. 88 *—P.G. (12/31/2002)*

BIG HOUSE

Big House 2005 Red Red Blend (California) $10. Simple and gluey-soft, this blend of at least 10 varieties finishes medicinally sweet. **81** *—S.H. (11/15/2007)*

Big House 2006 White Blend (California) $10. A fruity, charming white wine. It's juicy in pineapples, pears, apples, honeysuckle flowers and vanilla. Chenin Blanc, Sauvignon Blanc, Viognier and several others. **84** *—S.H. (11/15/2007)*

BIG YELLOW

Big Yellow 2003 Cabernet Sauvignon (North Coast) $11. 84 *—S.H. (12/15/2005)*

Big Yellow 2004 Cab Cabernet Sauvignon (Mendocino County) $11. It's a bit raw and slightly sweet. Still, it offers acceptable cassis fruity flavors. **80** *—S.H. (11/1/2007)*

BIGHORN

Bighorn 2001 Cabernet Sauvignon (Napa Valley) $29. 86 *—S.H. (11/1/2005)*

Bighorn 2003 Broken Rock Vineyard Cabernet Sauvignon (Napa Valley) $40. A shade off the '02, offering riper, more decadent flavors at the expense of subtlety and structure. Floods the mouth with blackberry jam, cherry marmalade, crème de cassis and Kahlúa deliciousness, wrapped into a soft, melted texture. **87** *—S.H. (10/1/2007)*

Bighorn 2002 Broken Rock Vineyard Cabernet Sauvignon (Napa Valley) $36. 92 *—S.H. (12/1/2006)*

Bighorn 2003 Coombsville Vineyard Cabernet Sauvignon (Napa Valley) $40. Made solidly in the Californian style, a ripe, soft, direct wine that attempts to seduce the palate with big fruit and oak and a velvety smooth mouthfeel. The blackberry jam, cherry cola and toasty flavors are tasty. Drink now. **86** *—S.H. (10/1/2007)*

Bighorn 2001 Coombsville Cabernet Sauvignon (Napa Valley) $39. 83 *—S.H. (11/1/2005)*

Bighorn 2002 Coombsville Vineyard Cabernet Sauvignon (Napa Valley) $36. 87 *—S.H. (12/1/2006)*

Bighorn 2000 Coombsville Vineyard Cabernet Sauvignon (Napa Valley) $30. 88 *—S.H. (6/1/2004)*

Bighorn 1998 Coombsville Cabernet Sauvignon (Napa Valley) $39. 93 *—S.H. (11/15/2002)*

Bighorn 2001 Grand Reserve Cabernet Sauvignon (Napa Valley) $36. 82 *—S.H. (5/1/2006)*

Bighorn 2000 Grand Reserve Cabernet Sauvignon (Napa Valley) $49. 83 *—S.H. (11/1/2005)*

Bighorn 1998 Soda Canyon Cabernet Sauvignon (Napa Valley) $19. 85 *—S.H. (11/15/2002)*

Bighorn 2002 Chardonnay (Napa Valley) $16. 84 *—S.H. (6/1/2004)*

Bighorn 2002 Chardonnay (Carneros) $18. 83 *—S.H. (6/1/2004)*

Bighorn 2001 Chardonnay (Carneros) $17. 89 *—S.H. (12/15/2004)*

Bighorn 1999 Camelback Chardonnay (Carneros) $16. 91 *—S.H. (12/15/2002)*

Bighorn 2005 Camelback Vineyard Chardonnay (Carneros) $25. Shows the dried hay and light tobacco herbalness that sometimes accompany Carneros Chards, with riper notes of pineapples. When the oak kicks it, it brings smoke, buttered toast, toasted coconut and vanilla. This is a very dry wine to have with a wide range of foods. **88** *—S.H. (10/1/2007)*

Bighorn 2004 Camelback Vineyard Chardonnay (Carneros) $22. 91 *—S.H. (12/1/2006)*

Bighorn 2001 Coombsville Vineyard Chardonnay (Napa Valley) $15. 93 Best Buy *—S.H. (12/15/2004)*

Bighorn 1999 Grand Reserve Chardonnay (Napa Valley) $24. 92 *—S.H. (12/15/2002)*

Bighorn 2003 Broken Rock Vineyard Merlot (Napa Valley) $30. 87 *—S.H. (12/15/2005)*

Bighorn 2005 Amity Hills Vineyard Pinot Noir (Eola-Amity Hills) $45. Dark and smelling largely of barrel toast, this lightly fruity Pinot from the Amity Hills vineyard has a juicy tartness to it. Simple, fruity and clean. **86** *—P.G. (11/15/2007)*

Bighorn 2004 Sugarloaf Mountain Vineyard Syrah (Napa Valley) $30. Not as good as the 2003, probably due to excessive ripeness. Tastes soft and melted, lacking the structure to balance an almost dessert level of jammy sweet raspberries, cola, vanilla fudge and peppermint. **84** *—S.H. (10/1/2007)*

Bighorn 2003 Sugerloaf Mountain Vineyard Syrah (Napa Valley) $30. 90 *—S.H. (12/15/2005)*

BINK

Bink 2004 Hawks Butte Vineyard Merlot (Yorkville Highlands) $35. Not a success. The wine is semisweet, almost insipid, with jammy fruit flavors. Save your money. **81** *—S.H. (5/1/2007)*

Bink 2004 Weir Vineyard Pinot Noir (Yorkville Highlands) $40. The vineyard is a well-regarded source of a Williams Selyem bottling, from this hilly region midway between Anderson Valley and inland Mendocino County. The Pinots always seem to have a more rustic quality than, say, Russian River to the south, although in this hot vintage, the wine is extraordinarily sweet and soft. It has lip-smacking flavors of raspberry jam, cinnamon spice and melted cherry-vanilla ice cream, although it's actually dry. **90** *—S.H. (6/1/2007)*

Bink 2005 Randle Hill Vineyard Sauvignon Blanc (Yorkville Highlands) $20. This unoaked, stainless steel-fermented wine shows that this hilly appellation of Mendocino County can produce an exceptionally nice Sauvignon Blanc. It reminds me of Lake County, with its crispness and varietal purity. The flavors are of Meyer lemons, figs and yellow apricots. **89 Editors' Choice** *—S.H. (5/1/2007)*

Bink 2002 Hawks Butte Vineyard Syrah (Mendocino) $40. 87 *(9/1/2005)*

BIONDI

Biondi 2003 Cabernet Sauvignon (North Coast) $14. 83 *—S.H. (4/1/2006)*

Biondi 2004 Chardonnay (North Coast) $13. 82 *—S.H. (4/1/2006)*

Biondi NV Red Table Wine Red Blend (California) $11. 85 *—S.H. (4/1/2006)*

Biondi 2004 Sauvignon Blanc (Mendocino County) $11. 83 *—S.H. (4/1/2006)*

Biondi 2004 Viognier (Mendocino) $13. 84 *—S.H. (4/1/2006)*

BISHOP CREEK

Bishop Creek 2002 Barrel Selection Pinot Noir (Yamhill County) $25. 85 *(11/1/2004)*

Bishop Creek 2005 Valois Reserve Pinot Noir (Yamhill-Carlton District) $40. The Valois reserve makes its debut with this 2005 bottling. It is a blend of the winery's five best barrels, and was given the all-star treatment. It's still pulling itself together; somewhat muddy in color, with a soft, plummy nose of primary fruits. A strongly acidic component left a chalky impression in the mouth, further suggesting that this needs more time to integrate. **87** *—P.G. (7/1/2007)*

BISHOP'S PEAK

Bishop's Peak 2005 Cabernet Sauvignon (Paso Robles) $18. This dry, country-style Cab has some sharp, green tannins that bring astringency to the blackberry, cherry and cola flavors. Will go fine with a cheeseburger. **84** *—S.H. (12/31/2007)*

Bishop's Peak 2002 Cabernet Sauvignon (Paso Robles) $16. 83 *—S.H. (10/1/2005)*

Bishop's Peak 2001 Cabernet Sauvignon (Paso Robles) $15. 84 *—S.H. (6/1/2004)*

Bishop's Peak 2005 Chardonnay (Edna Valley) $14. Simple and a little obvious in its appeal, this Chard offers ripe tropical fruit, apricot, peach and sweet oak flavors that have a tart, raw edge. **83** *—S.H. (12/31/2007)*

Bishop's Peak 2004 Chardonnay (Edna Valley) $14. 85 *—S.H. (11/1/2006)*

Bishop's Peak 2003 Chardonnay (Edna Valley) $14. 84 *—S.H. (10/1/2005)*

Bishop's Peak 2001 Chardonnay (Central Coast) $13. 85 *—S.H. (6/1/2004)*

Bishop's Peak 2000 Chardonnay (Central Coast) $13. 85 *—S.H. (2/1/2003)*

Bishop's Peak 2002 Pinot Noir (Central Coast) $16. 86 *—S.H. (10/1/2005)*

Bishop's Peak 2001 Pinot Noir (Central Coast) $16. 84 *—S.H. (6/1/2004)*

Bishop's Peak 2004 Rock Solid Red Red Blend (Paso Robles) $12. 86 *—S.H. (9/1/2006)*

Bishop's Peak 2004 Syrah (Edna Valley) $16. There's a reason why Syrah is on a roll in America, and it's wines like this that make the case. Soft and juicy, it's a mellow, sensual wine, with a taffeta mouthfeel that carries rich flavors of cherry-pie filling, red licorice and vanilla oak that are delicious and worthy of a second glass. **87** *—S.H. (12/31/2007)*

Bishop's Peak 2003 Syrah (Edna Valley) $16. 85 *—S.H. (11/1/2006)*

Bishop's Peak 2002 Syrah (Edna Valley) $16. 89 Editors' Choice *(9/1/2005)*

Bishop's Peak 2001 Syrah (Edna Valley) $15. 89 *—S.H. (12/1/2004)*

Bishop's Peak 2000 Syrah (Central Coast) $15. 85 *—S.H. (2/1/2003)*

Bishop's Peak 2001 Zinfandel (Paso Robles) $14. 84 *—S.H. (6/1/2004)*

BJORNSTAD

Bjornstad 2005 Porter-Bass Vineyard Chardonnay (Sonoma Coast) $50. Here's a young, powerful wine that captures the essence of cool-climate Chardonnay. The vineyard is where Russian River Valley meets Sonoma Coast, south and west of Rochioli, and the wine is similar, in both tart green apples and acidity, with richer notes of tangerine, peach and papaya. Buttered toast, butterscotch and smoky vanilla are oak's contributions, in this brilliant, suave Chard. **93** *—S.H. (10/1/2007)*

Bjornstad 2005 Ritchie Vineyard Chardonnay (Russian River Valley) $50. Great Chardonnay, exotically rich and complex. With the crisp, zesty acidity of Russian River in a cool vintage, the wine is impressively balanced despite its powerhouse flavors. Pineapples, mangoes, papayas, new oak, minerals and Asian spices mingle together, leading to a long finish. **93** *—S.H. (12/31/2007)*

Bjornstad 2005 Hellenthal Vineyard Pinot Noir (Sonoma Coast) $50. This Pinot, from former Tandem partner Greg Bjornstad, defines an exotic, almost feral style of Pinot. There's a raw meat, bloody quality to the wild cherry, blackberry, forest floor and cola flavors that finish in a wild dusting of black pepper and Indian spices. Absolutely unique Pinot Noir, tight, minerally and tannic now, but endlessly fascinating. Has the stuff for 8–10 years. **96** *—S.H. (10/1/2007)*

Bjornstad 2005 Van der Kamp Vineyard Pinot Noir (Sonoma Mountain) $50. Brilliant; defines cool-climate terroir. Hard to exaggerate the deliciousness of the cherries, raspberries, cola, licorice, gingersnap cookie, sweet oak, vanilla and spice flavors. The near-perfect alignment of acids, tannins and tasteful new oak make this dry, elegant, single-vineyard Pinot gorgeous now, and terrifically versatile with food. **93** *—S.H. (10/1/2007)*

BLACK BART

Black Bart 2005 Stagecoach Vineyard Syrah (Napa Valley) $65. The vineyard has had a mixed record of producing reds, usually expensive, not always great. This Syrah is too sugary sweet, with jammy berry and fruit flavors and lots of caramelly oak. **83** *—S.H. (12/15/2007)*

BLACK BART'S BRIDE

Black Bart's Bride 2006 White Blend (Napa Valley) $50. A composite of Marsanne, Viognier and Chardonnay, with lots of new oak, this blend is heavy, soft and sugary sweet, with jellied apricot, pineapple and vanilla flavors. **82** *—S.H. (12/15/2007)*

BLACK BOX

Black Box 2003 Cabernet Sauvignon (Paso Robles) $18. 86 *—S.H. (11/15/2004)*

Black Box 2004 Cabernet Sauvignon (Paso Robles) $18. 85 Best Buy *—S.H. (9/1/2006)*

Black Box 2002 Cabernet Sauvignon (Paso Robles) $20. 82 *—S.H. (8/1/2004)*

Black Box 2002 Chardonnay (Napa Valley) $22. 84 *—S.H. (12/31/2004)*

Black Box 2004 Chardonnay (Monterey County) $22. 83 Best Buy *—S.H. (7/1/2006)*

Black Box 2004 Chardonnay (Napa Valley) $24. 84 Best Buy *—S.H. (9/1/2006)*

Black Box 2003 Chardonnay (Monterey County) $20. 86 Best Buy *—S.H. (8/1/2004)*

Black Box 2001 Merlot (Sonoma County) $24. 86 *—S.H. (12/31/2004)*

Black Box 2003 Merlot (California) $22. 84 Best Buy *—S.H. (7/1/2006)*

Black Box NV 3L Merlot (Sonoma County) $24. 84 Best Buy *—S.H. (9/1/2006)*

BLACK COYOTE

Black Coyote 2004 Bates Creek Vineyard Cabernet Sauvignon (Stags Leap District) $40. Ripe to the point of jammy, this Cab was blended with some Merlot, and also shows quite a bit of new oak. It's a direct, fruity wine, appealing for its blackberry, cherry and plumped raisin flavors. **85** *—S.H. (12/15/2007)*

Black Coyote 2002 Bates Creek Vineyard Cabernet Sauvignon (Napa Valley) $30. 85 *—S.H. (11/1/2005)*

Black Coyote 2000 Bates Creek Vineyard Cabernet Sauvignon (Napa Valley) $25. 84 *—S.H. (4/1/2004)*

BLACK CREEK

Black Creek 2000 Bates Creek Vineyard Cabernet Sauvignon (Napa Valley) $25. 84 *—S.H. (2/1/2004)*

Black Kite 2005 Pinot Noir (Anderson Valley) $35. Made in an alluring, voluptuous style, with soft acids and tannins framing lush cherry, raspberry, cola, red currant and vanilla flavors, this refreshing Pinot is beautiful now. It's a real crowd-pleaser. **90** *—S.H. (11/1/2007)*

Black Kite 2005 Redwoods' Edge Pinot Noir (Anderson Valley) $40. Opens with a burst of red cherry, plum and pomegranate aromas, and a smoky scent of charred meat bone that offers hints of bacon fat. Tastes beautifully ripe and supple, with complex fruit, spice and oak flavors that are supported by an intricate acid-tannin structure. A terrific wine, but I encountered some bottle variation in various tastings. **91** *—S.H. (10/1/2007)*

Black Kite 2005 Stony Terrace Pinot Noir (Anderson Valley) $48. The biggest of the winery's three '05s, this starts to approach Grenache in its voluptuousness and rich mouthfeel of cherries and cocoa. This is tricky territory to navigate, but the wine pulls back into Pinot land with a dry silkiness and acidity. **91** *—S.H. (10/1/2007)*

BLACK SHEEP

Black Sheep 2001 Cinsault (Calaveras County) $18. 86 *—S.H. (3/1/2005)*

Black Sheep 2002 Sémillon (Calaveras County) $13. 84 *—S.H. (3/1/2005)*

Black Sheep 2001 Shiraz (Calaveras County) $16. 85 *—S.H. (3/1/2005)*

Black Sheep 1997 Zinfandel (Amador County) $14. 87 Best Buy *—S.H. (5/1/2000)*

Black Sheep 2001 Clockspring Vineyard Zinfandel (Amador County) $16. 81 *(11/1/2003)*

BLACKBIRD VINEYARDS

Blackbird Vineyards 2003 Merlot (Oak Knoll) $70. 90 *—S.H. (12/15/2006)*

Blackbird Vineyards 2004 Proprietary Red Wine Bordeaux Blend (Oak Knoll) $80. Nearly all Merlot, with just 5% Cab Sauvignon, this Bordeaux blend is from a vineyard in the cooler, southern part of Napa Valley, influenced by Carneros breezes. Yet in this hot-hot vintage, it's too ripe in jammy cherry and blackberry flavors, and the tannic structure has a rustic edge. Drink now. **85** *—S.H. (11/1/2007)*

BLACKJACK

Blackjack 1997 Harmonie Bordeaux Blend (Santa Barbara County) $32. 91 *(11/1/2000)*

Blackjack 1998 Laetitia Vineyard Pinot Noir (San Luis Obispo County) $32. 84 *—M.S. (10/1/2000)*

BLACKRIDGE CANYON

Blackridge Canyon 2001 Pinot Noir (Napa Valley) $20. 87 *—S.H. (8/1/2005)*

BLACKSTONE

Blackstone 2004 Sonoma Reserve Meritage Bordeaux Blend (Sonoma County) $17. Softly elegant and dry, this is a lovely Bordeaux blend to pair with a wide variety of meats and cheeses. Structure is the star, with grapeskin and oak barrel tannins framing delicate cherry, herb and earth flavors. **87** *—S.H. (10/1/2007)*

Blackstone 2003 Cabernet Sauvignon (Napa Valley) $12. 87 *—S.H. (12/31/2006)*

Blackstone 2003 Cabernet Sauvignon (California) $12. 82 *—S.H. (4/1/2006)*

Blackstone 2002 Cabernet Sauvignon (Sonoma County) $15. 83 *—S.H. (10/1/2005)*

Blackstone 2002 Cabernet Sauvignon (California) $12. 83 *(6/1/2004)*

Blackstone 1998 Cabernet Sauvignon (California) $10. 84 *—S.H. (11/15/2001)*

Blackstone 2002 Reserve Cabernet Sauvignon (Dry Creek Valley) $28. 85 *—S.H. (10/1/2005)*

Blackstone 1997 Chardonnay (California) $10. 84 *—L.W. (7/1/1999)*

Blackstone 2005 Chardonnay (Monterey County) $12. 85 *—S.H. (10/1/2006)*

Blackstone 2004 Chardonnay (Monterey County) $11. 84 *—S.H. (12/31/2005)*

Blackstone 2004 Chardonnay (Sonoma County) $16. 86 *—S.H. (12/15/2006)*

Blackstone 2003 Chardonnay (Monterey County) $10. 85 Best Buy *—S.H. (10/1/2005)*

Blackstone 2003 Chardonnay (Sonoma County) $16. 85 *—S.H. (7/1/2005)*

Blackstone 2002 Chardonnay (Sonoma County) $16. 84 *(6/1/2004)*

Blackstone 2000 Chardonnay (Monterey County) $10. 83 *—S.H. (12/31/2001)*

Blackstone 1999 Chardonnay (Monterey County) $10. 82 *—S.H. (5/1/2001)*

Blackstone 2002 Reserve Chardonnay (Santa Lucia Highlands) $26. 86 *(6/1/2004)*

Blackstone 2005 Sonoma Reserve Chardonnay (Sonoma County) $17. Lots of rich, ripe, forward fruit in this well-oaked wine, with tart green apple, pineapple, lime and kiwi flavors. It's stylishly dry, with a nice, creamy finish. **87** *—S.H. (10/1/2007)*

Blackstone 2005 Gewürztraminer (Monterey County) $12. 84 *—S.H. (12/31/2006)*

Blackstone 2004 Gewürztraminer (Monterey County) $11. 84 *—S.H. (10/1/2005)*

Blackstone 1997 Merlot (Napa Valley) $13. 86 *(11/15/1999)*

Blackstone 2003 Merlot (Napa Valley) $18. 86 *—S.H. (4/1/2006)*

Blackstone 2003 Merlot (Sonoma County) $16. 85 *—S.H. (7/1/2005)*

Blackstone 2003 Merlot (California) $12. 84 *—S.H. (12/15/2005)*

Blackstone 2002 Merlot (Monterey County) $17. 84 *—S.H. (12/31/2004)*

Blackstone 2002 Merlot (Sonoma County) $16. 87 *—S.H. (10/1/2005)*

Blackstone 2002 Merlot (Napa Valley) $17. 83 *—S.H. (5/1/2005)*

Blackstone 2002 Merlot (California) $12. 84 *(6/1/2004)*

Blackstone 2001 Merlot (Sonoma County) $16. 86 *(6/1/2004)*

Blackstone 1999 Merlot (Napa Valley) $16. 86 *—S.H. (11/15/2001)*

Blackstone 1999 Merlot (California) $10. 84 *—S.H. (11/15/2001)*

Blackstone 1998 Merlot (Napa Valley) $18. 89 *—S.H. (5/1/2001)*

Blackstone 2001 Reserve Merlot (Napa Valley) $28. 86 *—S.H. (2/1/2005)*

Blackstone 2000 Reserve Merlot (Napa Valley) $28. 85 *(6/1/2004)*

Blackstone 2005 Sonoma Reserve Merlot (Sonoma County) $17. This is a nice, smooth and fairly sophisticated Merlot for immediate drinking. It's totally dry, with young tannins to cut through rich meats, and the cherry-blackberry fruit is balanced with an earthy, bitter coffee edge that gets the mouth watering. **87** *—S.H. (10/1/2007)*

Blackstone 2005 Pinot Grigio (California) $11. With a touch of residual sugar, this PG benefits from zesty acidity and appealingly forward lemon, peach, honeysuckle and vanilla flavors. It's a delightful wine that makes you think of summer days on the beach. **84** *—S.H. (10/1/2007)*

Blackstone 2005 Pinot Grigio (Monterey County) $12. 85 *—S.H. (10/1/2006)*

Blackstone 2004 Pinot Noir (Monterey County) $12. 84 *—S.H. (12/15/2005)*

Blackstone 2003 Pinot Noir (Monterey County) $12. 85 *—S.H. (5/1/2005)*

Blackstone 2002 Pinot Noir (Monterey County) $12. 85 *(11/1/2004)*

Blackstone 2001 Pinot Noir (Monterey County) $12. 83 *—S.H. (9/1/2004)*

Blackstone 2002 Reserve Pinot Noir (Santa Lucia Highlands) $28. 85 *—S.H. (11/1/2004)*

Blackstone 2002 Reserve Pinot Noir (Santa Lucia Highlands) $28. 86 *(6/1/2004)*

Blackstone 2005 Sonoma Reserve Pinot Noir (Sonoma County) $17. Blackstone's been working hard on their Pinot, and with this new Sonoma Reserve line, they've produced their best ever. It's a rich, dry wine that seems to have both cool- and warm-climate notes. Shows cherry pie, cola, blackberry tart and spice flavors, although it's a bit on the soft side. **88** *—S.H. (10/1/2007)*

Blackstone 2005 Riesling (Monterey County) $12. 83 *—S.H. (10/1/2006)*

Blackstone 2004 Riesling (Monterey County) $11. 84 *—S.H. (10/1/2005)*

Blackstone 2004 Cole Ranch Riesling (Mendocino County) $16. A bit off-dry, with excellent acidity, this German-style Riesling is clean and vibrant, with characteristic notes of petrol, peaches and wildflowers and a long, persistently spicy finish. Nice for an apéritif quaffer. **85** *—S.H. (9/1/2007)*

Blackstone 2004 Sauvignon Blanc (Monterey County) $10. 85 **Best Buy** *—S.H. (10/1/2005)*

Blackstone 2003 Sauvignon Blanc (Monterey County) $10. 84 *(6/1/2004)*

Blackstone 2002 Syrah (Sonoma County) $16. 86 *(9/1/2005)*

Blackstone 2002 Syrah (California) $16. 86 *—S.H. (7/1/2005)*

Blackstone 2001 Syrah (California) $12. 83 *(6/1/2004)*

Blackstone 2002 Hamilton Vineyards Reserve Syrah (Dry Creek Valley) $28. 82 *—S.H. (12/31/2005)*

Blackstone 2002 Reserve Syrah (Dry Creek Valley) $28. 86 *(9/1/2005)*

Blackstone 2003 Zinfandel (Sonoma County) $16. 86 *—S.H. (12/15/2005)*

Blackstone 2003 Zinfandel (California) $12. 82 *—S.H. (10/1/2006)*

Blackstone 2002 Zinfandel (Sonoma County) $16. 87 *(6/1/2004)*

Blackstone 2002 Zinfandel (California) $12. 82 *—S.H. (8/1/2005)*

Blackstone 2002 Reserve Zinfandel (Dry Creek Valley) $28. 90 **Editors' Choice** *—S.H. (12/15/2005)*

BLANKIET

Blankiet 2004 Cabernet Sauvignon (Napa Valley) $150. Starts out black and inky, with the ashy, charry aroma that 100% new French oak brings to the tease of blackberry fruit. In the mouth, this is a very soft, almost sweet Cab, with the flavors of candied blackberries, caramelly peanut brittle, chocolate fudge and crème de cassis. It's so rich and exotic, it's almost obvious. Made by Helen Turley in the international style, huge and seductive. The estate vineyard is in Yountville, next to Dominus. **93** *—S.H. (3/1/2007)*

Blankiet 2004 Merlot (Napa Valley) $100. This is a stunning Merlot, impossibly rich. Saturated and opaque in color, it tastes fat and flashy, with masses of cherry and blackberry jam, anise, chocolate and Provençal herb flavors. Yet this opulently soft wine has a classic structure, backed up with firm tannins. This is a profound Merlot. **95** *—S.H. (3/1/2007)*

BLISS

Bliss 2004 Heritage Series Cabernet Sauvignon (Mendocino) $12. Although this is fully dry and has some good cassis and black cherry fruit, it's just a little too rugged in the texture of the tannins, and the finish turns syrupy. **83** *—S.H. (11/15/2007)*

Bliss 2002 Heritage Series Cabernet Sauvignon (Mendocino) $11. 80 *—S.H. (12/15/2005)*

Bliss 2005 Heritage Series Chardonnay (Mendocino) $12. 83 *—S.H. (12/15/2006)*

Bliss 2004 Heritage Series Chardonnay (Mendocino) $11. 81 *—S.H. (12/15/2005)*

Bliss 2004 Heritage Series Merlot (Mendocino) $12. 82 *—S.H. (12/15/2006)*

Bliss 2002 Heritage Series Merlot (Mendocino) $25. 83 *—S.H. (12/15/2005)*

Bliss 2002 Pinot Noir (Mendocino) $11. 82 *—S.H. (12/15/2005)*

BLOCKHEADIA RINGNOSII

Blockheadia Ringnosii 2006 All Tank Rosé Rosé Blend (California) $17. It's a Rhône blend of Cinsault, Mourvedre, Grenache and Syrah, entirely made in stainless steel, and it's as fresh as a berry plucked off the bush. Entirely dry, with crisp acidity, the flavors are of mildly tannic red cherryskins, with a sprinkle of vanilla and cinnamon. Earns extra points for finesse. From Cosentino. **87** *—S.H. (7/1/2007)*

Blockheadia Ringnosii 2001 Zinfandel (Mendocino) $24. 90 *(11/1/2003)*

Blockheadia Ringnosii 2001 Zinfandel (Napa Valley) $24. 91 **Editors' Choice** *(11/1/2003)*

BLUE MOON

Blue Moon 2004 Pinot Gris (Oregon) $11. 83 *—P.G. (2/1/2006)*

BLUE ROCK

Blue Rock 2003 Cabernet Sauvignon (Alexander Valley) $45. 89 *—S.H. (12/15/2006)*

Blue Rock 2003 Best Barrel Malbec (Alexander Valley) $75. 92 *—S.H. (12/15/2006)*

Blue Rock 2003 Syrah (Alexander Valley) $36. 85 *—S.H. (12/15/2006)*

BLUE TEAL

Blue Teal 2006 White Merlot (New Mexico) $8. There's curiosity in the concept of a white Merlot, but once you move beyond the appealing citrus nose and into the very sweet flavors of this New Mexico offering, there's question as to whether this actually works. Sweetness overpowers the fruit, and the wine wants balance. **82** *—S.K. (7/1/2007)*

Blue Teal 2005 Riesling (New Mexico) $9. Honey, pineapple and pear on the nose are continued on the palate. The flavors are quite pretty but the overall structure of the wine tends toward watery; could use more acid and strength. Still, enjoy it chilled on a patio or in a hammock and you'll find it an enjoyable, affordable warm-weather choice. **82** *—S.K. (9/1/2007)*

Blue Teal 2004 Shiraz (New Mexico) $9. Clove and cherry lead the wine but on the palate, there's too much of a tart, fruit juice blast. There's some spice and heft in the finish but overall, the flavors are one-dimensional. **83** *—S.K. (2/1/2007)*

BLUENOSE

Bluenose 2004 Zinfandel (Dry Creek Valley) $25. This is a new winery to me, and it's off to a good start with this Zinfandel, which contains grapes from some 80-year-old vines and from the Rockpile appellation. It's classic Dry Creek Zin, dense, full-bodied and dry, with beautiful tannins and impressive flavors of wild blackberries, wild mountain thyme and lavender, and a bitter chocolate, coffee earthiness. At its best now. **91** *—S.H. (3/1/2007)*

BOCAGE

Bocage 2006 Chardonnay (California) $13. This Chardonnay has all the highlights of Central Coast white wines. It's dry, acidic, pure and clean in varietal character, which in this case means pineapples, golden mangoes and white peaches. There's something so vanilla rich, you'd swear there was new oak, but there isn't. This is an entirely unwooded wine. **87 Editors' Choice** *—S.H. (11/15/2007)*

Bocage 2001 Chardonnay (Monterey) $11. 86 *—S.H. (12/15/2002)*

Bocage 2005 Unoaked Chardonnay (Monterey) $13. 86 *—S.H. (12/1/2006)*

Bocage 2004 Unoaked Chardonnay (Monterey) $11. 87 **Best Buy** *—S.H. (12/15/2005)*

Bocage 2003 Unoaked Chardonnay (Monterey) $11. 85 *—S.H. (3/1/2005)*

Bocage 2005 Merlot (Monterey) $13. Soft and fruity, with cherry, raspberry and melted chocolate flavors that finish dry and spicy. This easy wine will pair well with an upscale cheeseburger made with blue cheese. **84** *—S.H. (11/15/2007)*

Bocage 2004 Merlot (Monterey) $13. 82 *—S.H. (12/15/2006)*

Bocage 2003 Merlot (Monterey) $11. 84 *—S.H. (9/1/2006)*

Bocage 2002 Merlot (Monterey) $11. 85 *—S.H. (3/1/2005)*

BOCCE

Bocce 2004 Pinot Grigio (California) $10. 84 *—S.H. (2/1/2006)*

Bocce 2001 Rosso Red Blend (California) $6. 84 Best Buy *—S.H. (3/1/2005)*

BOEDECKER CELLARS

Boedecker Cellars 2004 Athena Pinot Noir (Willamette Valley) $28. The Athena blend is a deceptively simple wine, showing juicy, tart pomegranate and cranberry fruit flavors. The tannins are clean and well-managed, the flavors light and crisply delineated. 87 *—P.G. (4/1/2007)*

Boedecker Cellars 2004 Momtazi Vineyard Pinot Noir (Willamette Valley) $40. This is an elegant style, light and pretty. The cherry fruit is spiced with cinnamon and licorice candy. Very clean. 88 *—P.G. (4/1/2007)*

Boedecker Cellars 2004 Shea Vineyard Pinot Noir (Willamette Valley) $40. A good effort built upon firm black cherry with berry and citrus. There's a light whiff of the barnyard that adds some interest without detracting from the overall quality. 89 *—P.G. (4/1/2007)*

Boedecker Cellars 2004 Stewart Pinot Noir (Willamette Valley) $28. A blend of three vineyards—Maresh, Anderson Family and Stoller—this appealing Pinot wraps its raspberry fruit in streaks of cola and cocoa. The herbal, earthy tannins come in later, adding more depth and weight. 88 *—P.G. (4/1/2007)*

Boedecker Cellars 2004 Stoller Vineyard Pinot Noir (Willamette Valley) $40. Tart fruit suggests red currants and sour cherry, along with flavors of earth and soil. Hints of soy and iron filings add texture to the tannins, and the finish has a spicy lift. 89 *—P.G. (4/1/2007)*

BOEGER

Boeger 2001 Barbera (El Dorado) $15. 84 *—S.H. (12/1/2003)*

Boeger 1998 Barbera (El Dorado) $14. 89 *—S.H. (8/1/2001)*

Boeger 1996 Bordeaux Blend (El Dorado County) $18. 88 *—L.W. (12/31/1999)*

Boeger 1999 Reserve Petite Sirah (El Dorado) $25. 85 *(4/1/2003)*

Boeger 1997 Pinot Noir (El Dorado) $20. 88 *—L.W. (5/1/2000)*

Boeger 1999 Reserve Pinot Noir (El Dorado) $25. 85 *—S.H. (2/1/2003)*

Boeger 1998 Sauvignon Blanc (El Dorado County) $13. 87 *—L.W. (3/1/2000)*

Boeger 1998 Reserve Tempranillo (El Dorado) $25. 86 *—S.H. (5/1/2002)*

Boeger 2001 Zinfandel (El Dorado) $15. 84 *(11/1/2003)*

Boeger 1997 Estate Zinfandel (El Dorado) $15. 87 *—P.G. (3/1/2001)*

Boeger 2001 Walker Vineyard Zinfandel (El Dorado) $18. 84 *(11/1/2003)*

Boeger 1998 Walker Vineyard Zinfandel (El Dorado County) $18. 86 *—S.H. (5/1/2000)*

Boeger 1997 Walker Vineyard Zinfandel (El Dorado) $18. 85 *—P.G. (3/1/2001)*

BOGLE

Bogle 2004 Cabernet Sauvignon (California) $11. A bit raw and rustic, with a sharp, acidic finish, but saved by modest cherry fruit and softening oak influences, this Cab is okay for everyday purposes. 83 *—S.H. (3/1/2007)*

Bogle 2003 Cabernet Sauvignon (California) $11. 85 *—S.H. (11/1/2006)*

Bogle 2002 Cabernet Sauvignon (California) $12. 83 *—S.H. (10/1/2005)*

Bogle 1998 Chardonnay (California) $9. 86 Best Buy *—L.W. (12/31/1999)*

Bogle 2005 Chardonnay (California) $9. 83 *—S.H. (12/1/2006)*

Bogle 2004 Chardonnay (California) $9. 83 *—S.H. (11/1/2005)*

Bogle 2000 Chardonnay (Clarksburg) $9. 85 *—J.M. (11/15/2001)*

Bogle 1998 Colby Ranch Reserve Chardonnay (Clarksburg) $18. 86 *(6/1/2000)*

Bogle 2005 Chenin Blanc (California) $9. 84 *—S.H. (12/1/2006)*

Bogle 2004 Chenin Blanc (Clarksburg) $7. 84 *—S.H. (8/1/2005)*

Bogle 2003 Chenin Blanc (Clarksburg) $7. 86 Best Buy *—S.H. (7/1/2005)*

Bogle 2005 Merlot (California) $9. The alcohol is nice and low on this soft, likeable Merlot, grown in Clarksburg and Lodi. The cherry, blackberry, chocolate and mint flavors are pleasant, and the price for everyday drinking is just fine. 84 *—S.H. (11/15/2007)*

Bogle 2004 Merlot (California) $11. 80 *—S.H. (12/1/2006)*

Bogle 2003 Merlot (California) $9. 84 Best Buy *—S.H. (10/1/2005)*

Bogle 2005 Petite Sirah (California) $11. Dry, dusty and tannic, this wine shows a rustic nature. The berry and coffee flavors have edges of vegetables such as asparagus. 82 *—S.H. (12/31/2007)*

Bogle 2003 Petite Sirah (California) $10. 87 Best Buy *—S.H. (11/1/2005)*

Bogle 2001 Petite Sirah (California) $10. 84 *(4/1/2003)*

Bogle 2000 Petite Sirah (California) $10. 84 *(4/1/2003)*

Bogle 1998 Petite Sirah (California) $10. 87 *—J.C. (11/15/1999)*

Bogle 2004 Pinot Noir (Russian River Valley) $13. Simple and harsh, with weedy, peppery flavors that only faintly suggest cherries, cola and rhubarb. Not a bad wine, just a one-dimensional one. 82 *—S.H. (5/1/2007)*

Bogle 2003 Phantom Red Blend (California) $16. 87 *—S.H. (12/1/2006)*

Bogle 2006 Sauvignon Blanc (California) $9. A good example of a California Sauvignon Blanc, this white shows citrus, hay, fig and spicy green-melon flavors. It's dry and crisp, making it balanced, and a good accompaniment to food. 85 Best Buy *—S.H. (11/15/2007)*

Bogle 2005 Sauvignon Blanc (California) $9. 85 Best Buy *—S.H. (11/15/2006)*

Bogle 2004 Sauvignon Blanc (California) $8. 83 *—S.H. (11/1/2005)*

Bogle 1998 Sauvignon Blanc (California) $7. 85 Best Buy *—L.W. (3/1/2000)*

Bogle 2005 Old Vine Zinfandel (California) $11. Simple, semisweet and harsh, with a peppery sting, this Zin gains a point for its rich berry flavors. Sourced from Lodi, Amador and Fiddletown. 83 *—S.H. (11/15/2007)*

Bogle 2004 Old Vine Zinfandel (California) $12. Way too sweet, with sugared blackberry tea flavors and not enough acidity, which makes the wine insipid. 81 *—S.H. (4/1/2007)*

Bogle 2003 Old Vine Zinfandel (California) $11. 83 *—S.H. (10/1/2005)*

Bogle 2001 Old Vine Zinfandel (California) $11. 89 Best Buy *(11/1/2003)*

Bogle 1997 Old Vine Cuvée Zinfandel (California) $10. 90 Best Buy *—P.G. (11/15/1999)*

BOITANO

Boitano 2002 Barbera (Shenandoah Valley (CA)) $18. 85 *—S.H. (3/1/2005)*

Boitano 2002 Port (Sierra Foothills) $14. 86 *—S.H. (2/1/2005)*

Boitano 2002 Sapore di Cielo Red Blend (Sierra Foothills) $25. 83 *—S.H. (2/1/2005)*

Boitano 2002 Mokelumne Hill Sangiovese (Calaveras County) $24. 84 *—S.H. (3/1/2005)*

BOKISCH

Bokisch 2005 Albariño (Lodi) $16. Looking for something different? Try this very dry, crisp, minerally wine, made from a grape popular in Spain and Portugal. It's really wonderful, with lemony, flowery flavors and an edge of peach custard. The acidity is terrific. 88 *—S.H. (2/1/2007)*

Bokisch 2004 Albariño (Lodi) $16. 89 *—S.H. (12/31/2005)*

Bokisch 2002 Albariño (Lodi) $16. 88 *—S.H. (2/1/2004)*

Bokisch 2005 Garnacha (Lodi) $18. Dry, tannic and one-dimensional, this wine shows cherry flavors and alcohol, with oaky vanilla notes and a cinnamon-spice finish. Drink now. 84 *—S.H. (2/1/2007)*

Bokisch 2004 Garnacha (Lodi) $18. 85 *—S.H. (12/31/2005)*

Bokisch 2004 Graciano (Lodi) $26. Whatever the future of this Spanish variety is in California, this wine isn't it. It's overtly sweet and flabbily soft, lacking the acidity that's so sorely needed for balance. 82 *—S.H. (3/1/2007)*

Bokisch 2003 Graciano (Lodi) $26. 84 *—S.H. (12/31/2005)*

Bokisch 2001 Graciano (Lodi) $19. 88 *—S.H. (4/1/2004)*

Bokisch 2004 Tempranillo (Lodi) $21. Bokisch has struggled for years to overcome rusticity in Temp, and this vintage does not advance the cause. It's dry, acidic and tannic, with an unrewarding mouthfeel despite the wealth of cherry flavor. 83 *—S.H. (2/1/2007)*

Bokisch 2003 Tempranillo (Lodi) $21. 84 *—S.H. (12/31/2005)*

Bokisch 2001 Tempranillo (Lodi) $19. 86 *—S.H. (4/1/2004)*

BONACCORSI

Bonaccorsi 2003 Sanford & Benedict Vineyard Pinot Noir (Santa Rita Hills) $42. 92 *—S.H. (6/1/2005)*

Bonaccorsi 2001 Syrah (Central Coast) $32. 89 *—S.H. (12/1/2003)*

Bonaccorsi 2003 Bien Nacido Vineyard Syrah (Santa Maria Valley) $50. 93 Cellar Selection *—S.H. (8/1/2006)*

BONAIR

Bonair 2004 Cabernet Sauvignon (Yakima Valley) $10. The blend includes 5% Merlot and 20% Cabernet Franc. Though not as appealing as the 2003, it's a firm, solid effort, an example of plain, no-frills Yakima Valley winemaking. The fruit includes lightly herbal/bell peppery notes, and the wine is balanced and clean. **87 Best Buy** *—P.G. (3/1/2007)*

Bonair 2003 Cabernet Sauvignon (Yakima Valley) $16. 88 *—P.G. (6/1/2006)*

Bonair 2002 Chateau Puryear Estate Reserve Cabernet Sauvignon (Yakima Valley) $26. The extra time in bottle hasn't hurt this reserve bottling, but it doesn't seem to have added much either. It is a bit more concentrated than the 2004 regular Cabernet, otherwise quite similar in character, and a bit monolithic. The tannins still retain some coarseness, and there are no leavening nuances of new oak. The fruit, ripened from a single site, strikes its single note well. 87 *—P.G. (3/1/2007)*

Bonair 2002 Morrison Vineyard Cabernet Sauvignon (Yakima Valley) $21. 88 *—P.G. (6/1/2006)*

Bonair 2004 Chardonnay (Yakima Valley) $13. 87 *—P.G. (6/1/2006)*

Bonair 2003 Château Puryear Vineyard Reserve Chardonnay (Yakima Valley) $21. 88 *—P.G. (6/1/2006)*

Bonair 2005 Dry Gewürztraminer (Yakima Valley) $9. This is a very well-made, bone-dry Gewürz, textural and fresh. The flavors are a perfect blend of grapefruit and floral notes, without becoming overly perfumy. Good concentration and length. **90 Best Buy** *—P.G. (3/1/2007)*

Bonair 2004 Port Gewürztraminer (Yakima Valley) $21. 90 *—P.G. (6/1/2006)*

Bonair 1998 Merlot (Yakima Valley) $18. 89 *—P.G. (9/1/2002)*

Bonair 2001 Riesling (Yakima Valley) $10. 90 *—P.G. (9/1/2002)*

Bonair 2005 Ice Wine Riesling (Yakima Valley) $35. Already a deep amber, though not even a year old, this is ready to drink right now. It is quite ripe and unctuous, without being syrupy, and the fruit flavors move beyond simple peach and apricot into a more interesting blend that includes citrus and tropical candied fruit flavors. The acid keeps it lively and the length is impressive. 91 *—P.G. (3/1/2007)*

BOND

BOND 2004 Melbury Bordeaux Blend (Napa Valley) $210. A dark, rich wine, this opens with ripe, sweet aromas of fresh blackberries, cedar, cigar box, pencil lead and cinnamon. Brings to mind a classified Pauillac, rather hard and tannic now, but sweetly ripe and refined, and very rich in mulberries, cherries, licorice and mocha. A magnificent young wine. Best now, with decanting, through 2012, at least. **94 Cellar Selection** *—S.H. (12/1/2007)*

BOND 2004 Pluribus Bordeaux Blend (Napa Valley) $210. In the Bond stable, Pluribus marches to a different beat. There's something of a baked pastry quality, with scents of marzipan, blackstrap molasses, and blackberry-cherry pie filling. This is the rawest Bond wine, the most tannic and least approachable. It's almost rustic in heft, like an Amador Zinfandel. Best to cellar for a few years, and could go the long haul. 91 *—S.H. (12/1/2007)*

BOND 2004 St. Eden Bordeaux Blend (Napa Valley) $210. Brilliant aromatics here, just stupendously attractive. Among the sweetest and most approachable of Harlan's current stable, it's also complex and ageworthy. Fairly tannic now, with a refined sandpapery grittiness coating pure flavors of ripe cherries, plums and blackberries and their associated liqueurs. The finish is so long, balanced and harmonious. It's hard to imagine that this won't be one to age 12–15 years. 96 *—S.H. (12/1/2007)*

Bond 2000 Vecina Bordeaux Blend (Napa Valley) $150. 89 *—S.H. (12/1/2004)*

Bond 2003 Melbury Cabernet Blend (Napa Valley) $230. Fairly high in alcohol, this sumptuous red wine is almost sweet in fudgy, macaroon, cherry pie filling and chocolate truffle flavors, with a candied opulence all the way through. Yet it's dry. The 100% new oak adds to the caramelly, meringue taste. Elegant and voluptuous, it's an unabashed beauty, firmly in the Harlan style. 94 *—S.H. (2/1/2007)*

Bond 2002 Melbury Cabernet Blend (Napa Valley) $225. 95 *—S.H. (9/1/2006)*

Bond 2001 Melbury Cabernet Blend (Napa Valley) $210. 95 *—S.H. (6/1/2005)*

Bond 2003 Pluribus Cabernet Blend (Napa Valley) $230. From Spring Mountain, a new Bond single-vineyard bottling. It's a big wine, a bit obvious and, for me, the least of the current batch. It's so big it's almost cumbersome, and lacks the breed and elegance of its sister wines. Toasty caramel overpowers, while the wine is as gooey-sweet as melted chocolate. It's a controversial wine, made from very young vines. Could be an ager. 90 *—S.H. (2/1/2007)*

Bond 2003 St. Eden Cabernet Blend (Napa Valley) $230. Tasted alongside the Melbury, St. Eden is richer, more layered and complex. The jammy cherry and chocolate flavors here possess deeper notes of blue and purple fruits, with a brooding, mulchy depth that grounds the wine. The texture is gorgeous, with perfectly ripe, sweet tannins. Despite the wine's power, it has an airy, cloud-like quality, surely the mark of a great wine. 96 *—S.H. (2/1/2007)*

Bond 2002 St. Eden Cabernet Blend (Napa Valley) $225. More structured than the Melbury, with deeper, firmer tannins: but it's certainly not a tannic, hard wine. It's the quality of the tannins, fine, ripely sweet, intricate. The flavors are enormously rich in blue and black berries, as well as chocolate. Magnificent wine, fleshy, fat, opulent. As delicious as it is now, should age well through 2020. 96 *—S.H. (9/1/2006)*

Bond 2001 St. Eden Cabernet Blend (Napa Valley) $210. 95 *—S.H. (6/1/2005)*

Bond 2003 Vecina Cabernet Blend (Napa Valley) $230. From a vineyard just adjacent to the Oakville estate comes this wonderfully earth-scented wine. Deep and brooding, the aromas bring to mind a walk through a forest. Now a whiff of bay laurel, then pine cone and a rich, mulchy humus, and hovering over all are ripe blackberries and oodles of caramelized new oak. Much more open at this point in its life than the '02, but should live for many years. 96 *—S.H. (2/1/2007)*

Bond 2002 Vecina Cabernet Blend (Napa Valley) $225. **95 Cellar Selection** *—S.H. (9/1/2006)*

Bond 2001 Vecina Cabernet Blend (Napa Valley) $210. **96 Cellar Selection** *—S.H. (6/1/2005)*

Bond 2000 Melbury Red Blend (Napa Valley) $150. 89 *—S.H. (11/15/2004)*

Bond 1999 Melbury Red Blend (Napa Valley) $150. 94 *—J.M. (7/1/2003)*

Bond 1999 Vecina Red Blend (Napa Valley) $150. 93 *—J.M. (7/1/2003)*

BONNEAU

Bonneau 2004 Cabernet Sauvignon (Sonoma County) $34. This is a very good, somewhat complex Sonoma County blend. It's soft and dry, with upfront, accessible berry, cherry, herb and oak flavors, and smooth tannins. Balanced and restrained, it's a nice partner for steak. Drink now. 88 *—S.H. (12/1/2007)*

Bonneau 2003 Cabernet Sauvignon (Napa Valley) $42. A little rustic for Napa, but solid in blackberry, cherry, cassis and plum fruit that has a stewed, pie-filling taste. The tannins are gorgeous, so soft and plump. 84 *—S.H. (5/1/2007)*

Bonneau 2005 Catherine's Vineyard Chardonnay (Carneros) $28. This is too oaky. The wine is just overwhelmed by charry toast and strong, spicy oak wood flavors. Some people confuse the taste of Chardonnay with the taste of oak, but they are not the same. 83 *—S.H. (12/1/2007)*

Bonneau 2004 Catherine's Vineyard Chardonnay (Los Carneros) $28. This is a very oaky wine, and you have to wonder why they plastered it on so thick, because underneath all that sweet, toasty, caramelized woodsap is a nice, fruity Chardonnay. I've seen other reviews that praised the oak, but I can't go there. 84 *—S.H. (5/1/2007)*

Bonneau 2003 Private Reserve Chardonnay (Carneros) $22. 89 *—S.H. (11/1/2005)*

Bonneau 2005 Zinfandel (Shenandoah Valley (CA)) $28. Bonneau's '05 is a really nice mountain Zin. It stays true to the wild, rustic character of the variety, with an explosion of leathery forest berries, coffee and herbs. But it retains balance and elegance. 87 *—S.H. (12/1/2007)*

Bonneau 2004 Zinfandel (Shenandoah Valley (CA)) $28. Nice everyday Zin, a little one-dimensional, but polished and varietal, just the ticket with barbecued or smoked meat, or a good smoked cheese like gouda. It's basically dry, but with a sweet, plumped raisin edge to the cherry, raspberry, cocoa, leather and plum flavors. 86 *—S.H. (5/1/2007)*

BONNY DOON

Bonny Doon 2001 Freisa (Monterey County) $18. 84 *—S.H. (11/15/2004)*

Bonny Doon 2004 Clos de Gilroy Grenache (California) $12. 84 *—S.H. (6/1/2005)*

Bonny Doon 2003 Clos de Gilroy Grenache (California) $12. 86 *—S.H. (10/1/2004)*

Bonny Doon 2002 Old Telegram Mourvèdre (California) $32. 86 *—S.H. (10/1/2005)*

Bonny Doon 2001 Vin de Glacière Muscat (California) $17. 92 *—S.H. (6/1/2004)*

Bonny Doon NV Angelica Red Blend (California) $18. **90 Editors' Choice** *—S.H. (12/31/2005)*

Bonny Doon 2003 Barbera Arneis Red Blend (Monterey County) $18. 84 *—S.H. (11/1/2005)*

Bonny Doon 2004 Big House Red Red Blend (California) $10. **90 Best Buy** *—S.H. (10/1/2006)*

Bonny Doon NV Framboise Red Blend (California) $11. 92 *—S.H. (8/1/2004)*

Bonny Doon NV Framboise Red Blend (California) $12. 86 *—S.H. (12/1/2002)*

Bonny Doon 2001 Le Cigare Volant Red Blend (California) $32. 91 *—S.H. (4/1/2004)*

Bonny Doon 2000 Le Cigare Volant Red Blend (California) $32. 91 *—S.H. (12/1/2002)*

Bonny Doon 1996 Le Cigare Volant Red Blend (California) $25. 88 *(11/1/1999)*

Bonny Doon 1995 Le Cigare Volant Red Blend (California) $20. 90 *—M.S. (6/1/1999)*

Bonny Doon 2003 Le Cigare Volant Rhône Red Blend (California) $30. I don't always give high scores to Cigare, but it's almost always an interesting wine that marches to its own beat. The '03 is really good. Syrah gives sturdy tannins and full body. Grenache adds a wealth of cherry and raspberry flavors. It's hard to say what Mourvèdre brings, perhaps a chocolaty richness. The result is a soft, appealing and complex Rhône-style red. 90 *—S.H. (6/1/2007)*

Bonny Doon NV Le Cigare Volant Riserva Triperfecto Red Blend (California) $32. 89 *—S.H. (11/15/2004)*

Bonny Doon 2002 Le Cigare Volant Rhône Red Blend (California) $32. 86 *—S.H. (8/1/2005)*

Bonny Doon 1999 Le Cigare Volant Rhône Red Blend (California) $30. 91 *—S.H. (9/1/2002)*

Bonny Doon 2004 Le Cigare Blanc Rhône White Blend (California) $20. This is the white equivalent to Bonny Doon's successful red Rhône blend, Cigare Volant. A blend of Roussanne, Grenache Blanc and Marsanne, it shows Randall Grahm's touch in the way the richness has balance and complexity, going well beyond well-ripened peach, melon and spicy apricot fruit. There's a stony minerality, a tangy taste of stone, that makes this wine distinctive and compelling. 92 *—S.H. (6/1/2007)*

Bonny Doon 1998 Dry Pacific Rim Riesling (California-Washington) $10. 90 Best Buy *—M.S. (11/15/1999)*

Bonny Doon 1997 Dry Pacific Rim Riesling (California-Washington) $9. 90 Best Buy *—M.S. (9/1/1999)*

Bonny Doon 2002 Pacific Rim Riesling (America) $10. 86 *—S.H. (2/1/2004)*

Bonny Doon 1999 Pacific Rim Dry Riesling (California-Washington) $10. 89 Best Buy *—S.H. (5/1/2001)*

Bonny Doon 2003 The Heart Has Its Rieslings Riesling (Washington) $15. 84 *—S.H. (11/15/2004)*

Bonny Doon 2002 The Heart Has Its Rieslings Riesling (California) $15. 86 *—S.H. (12/31/2003)*

USA

Bonny Doon 2006 Vin Gris de Cigare Rosé Blend (California) $14. A Rhône blend based on Cinsault and Grenache, this is a bright, crisp rosé brimming with tea and raspberry flavors. It's dry and balanced, and is a good accompaniment to a wide variety of food. 85 *—S.H. (11/15/2007)*

Bonny Doon 2005 Vin Gris de Cigare Rosé Blend (California) $12. 83 *—S.H. (10/1/2006)*

Bonny Doon 2004 Vin Gris de Cigare Rosé Blend (California) $11. 90 Best Buy *—S.H. (11/15/2005)*

Bonny Doon 2003 Vin Gris de Cigare Rosé Blend (California) $11. 85 *—S.H. (10/1/2004)*

Bonny Doon 2002 Vin Gris de Cigare Rosé Blend (California) $10. 89 Best Buy *—S.H. (11/15/2003)*

Bonny Doon 2000 Vin Gris de Cigare Rosé Blend (California) $9. 90 *—S.H. (11/15/2001)*

Bonny Doon 2006 Le Vol des Anges Beeswax Vineyard Roussanne (Arroyo Seco) $30. This is a new dessert wine from Bonny Doon, from the Arroyo Seco region which is such a great source of whites. With 11% residual sugar, it's quite sweet. The apricot, peach, pear and lime flavors have a honeyed, botrytised richness. 87 *—S.H. (12/31/2007)*

Bonny Doon 2001 Syrah (California) $18. 91 Editors' Choice *—S.H. (6/1/2004)*

Bonny Doon 2004 Le Pousseur Syrah (Central Coast) $16. Here's a dry, big, bold, but soft Syrah, packed with jammy cherry, cassis and raspberry fruit, with interesting notes of soil, leather, grilled meat bone and oak. It's a blend of Bien Nacido fruit and a Paso Robles vineyard and tastes like a Northern Rhône, except for the softness, which limits aging; drink this polished wine now. Great food wine. 88 *—S.H. (6/1/2007)*

Bonny Doon 2003 Le Pousseur Syrah (Central Coast) $16. 85 *(9/1/2005)*

Bonny Doon 2002 Le Pousseur Syrah (California) $15. 83 *(9/1/2005)*

Bonny Doon 2003 Doux Viognier (Paso Robles) $18. 89 *—S.H. (10/1/2004)*

Bonny Doon 2002 Viognier Doux Viognier (Paso Robles) $18. 89 *—S.H. (6/1/2004)*

Bonny Doon 2004 Big House White White Blend (California) $10. 90 Best Buy *—S.H. (10/1/2006)*

Bonny Doon 2001 Big House White White Blend (California) $10. 86 Best Buy *—S.H. (12/15/2002)*

Bonny Doon 2005 Le Cigar Blanc White Blend (California) $20. The grapes were grown on the Central Coast, mostly in Arroyo Grande, and the wine is characterized by vibrant acidity. There is an intense taste of raspberries, more usually found in a red variety like Grenache than a white wine, but Grenache Blanc consitutes nearly half the blend, along with Roussanne. 87 *—S.H. (12/15/2007)*

Bonny Doon 2003 Le Cigare Blanc White Blend (California) $20. 91 *—S.H. (8/1/2005)*

Bonny Doon 2003 Cardinal Zin Zinfandel (California) $20. 85 *—S.H. (10/1/2005)*

Bonny Doon 2000 Cardinal Zin Zinfandel (California) $20. 86 *—S.H. (12/15/2001)*

Bonny Doon 2002 Cardinal Zin Beastly Old Vines Zinfandel (California) $20. 86 *—S.H. (4/1/2004)*

Bonny Doon 2001 Cardinal Zin/Beastly Old Vines Zinfandel (California) $20. 87 *—J.M. (11/1/2003)*

BONTERRA

Bonterra 2005 Cabernet Sauvignon (Mendocino County) $15. This wine is okay. It has a dry sharpness, a green chlorophyll mintiness, that suggests unripe fruit mixed in with the riper grapes that give blackberries. There's lots of new oak. 83 *—S.H. (11/15/2007)*

Bonterra 2004 Cabernet Sauvignon (Mendocino County) $15. Bonterra has been a champion of organic grapegrowing, and their wines have always been classic expressions of varietal character. So it is with this inexpensive Cabernet. It's dry, richly tannic and flavorful in blackberries and cherries, with a ripe edge of cocoa. Fully drinkable now, it has real elegance and class. 87 *—S.H. (2/1/2007)*

Bonterra 2003 Cabernet Sauvignon (Mendocino County) $15. 87 *—S.H. (7/1/2006)*

Bonterra 2002 Cabernet Sauvignon (North Coast) $15. 89 *—S.H. (12/15/2005)*

Bonterra 1999 Chardonnay (Mendocino County) $12. 87 Best Buy *—P.G. (10/1/2000)*

Bonterra 1998 Chardonnay (Mendocino) $12. 90 Best Buy *—S.H. (3/1/2000)*

Bonterra 1997 Chardonnay (Mendocino County) $11. 89 Best Buy *—S.H. (10/1/1999)*

Bonterra 2005 Chardonnay (Mendocino County) $13. 85 *—S.H. (12/31/2006)*

Bonterra 2004 Chardonnay (Mendocino County) $13. 89 Best Buy *—S.H. (12/31/2005)*

Bonterra 2000 Chardonnay (Mendocino County) $15. 88 *—S.H. (5/1/2002)*

Bonterra 1999 Lakeview Vineyards Marsanne (Mendocino County) $19. 85 *—S.H. (8/1/2001)*

Bonterra 2004 Merlot (Mendocino County) $15. 87 *—S.H. (12/31/2006)*

Bonterra 2003 Merlot (Mendocino County) $15. 90 Best Buy *—S.H. (5/1/2006)*

Bonterra 2002 Merlot (Mendocino County) $15. 90 Best Buy *—S.H. (12/15/2005)*

Bonterra 2000 Merlot (Paso Robles) $15. 84 *—S.H. (12/15/2003)*

Bonterra 1998 Merlot (Mendocino County) $16. 85 *—S.H. (5/1/2002)*

Bonterra 1997 Merlot (Mendocino County) $19. 86 *(6/1/2001)*

Bonterra 2005 Bartolucci Vineyard Muscat (Lake County) $16. 86 *—S.H. (11/1/2006)*

Bonterra 2004 Bartolucci Vineyard Muscat (Lake County) $16. 84 *—S.H. (4/1/2006)*

Bonterra 2003 The McNab Red Blend (Mendocino County) $45. With half Merlot, and the rest Cabernet Sauvignon and old-vine Petite Sirah, this is a gorgeously smooth wine, absolutely dry and sturdily tannic. The tannins are ripe and sweet, framing pure, complex flavors of cherries and raspberries, rhubarb-pie filling, cola and cocoa-infused coffee drinks, liberally spinkled with cinnamon and nutmeg. Worthy of careful attention. Certified biodynamically. 92 *—S.H. (10/1/2007)*

Bonterra 2002 The McNab Red Blend (Mendocino) $45. This is the best Bonterra wine, and easily the best red they've ever produced. A Bordeaux blend with some Petite Sirah, it's wonderfully lush and complex, offering ever-changing blackberry, coffee, plum, cocoa, licorice, spice and oaky flavors that finish soft and dry. Made entirely by biodynamic growing methods, it's really versatile with a wide range of foods. **92** *—S.H. (2/1/2007)*

Bonterra 2005 Roussanne (Mendocino County) $18. Made from organic grapes, this is a very clean, purely flavored wine, dry and buttery, with flavors of kiwis, limes, pineapples and honeysuckle flowers. There's a rich, oily nuttiness, like cashews. With some new French oak, it's an offbeat alternative to Chardonnay. **88** *—S.H. (5/1/2007)*

Bonterra 2004 Roussanne (Mendocino County) $18. 88 *—S.H. (12/15/2005)*

Bonterra 1997 Roussanne (Mendocino) $17. 91 *—L.W. (10/1/1999)*

Bonterra 1999 Lakeview Vineyards Roussanne (Mendocino County) $19. 87 *—S.H. (8/1/2001)*

Bonterra 2004 Syrah (Mendocino County) $15. A little one-dimensional, this is a simple country wine. On the plus side, it's balanced, clean and dry, with good varietal character. But it's thin, and would benefit from greater depth of fruit. The vines seem severely stretched. **84** *—S.H. (7/1/2007)*

Bonterra 2003 Syrah (Mendocino County) $15. 87 *—S.H. (11/1/2006)*

Bonterra 2002 Syrah (Mendocino County) $15. 83 *—S.H. (3/1/2006)*

Bonterra 2001 Syrah (Mendocino County) $17. 85 *(9/1/2005)*

Bonterra 1998 Syrah (Mendocino) $19. 89 Editors' Choice *(10/1/2001)*

Bonterra 2006 Viognier (Lake County-Mendocino County) $18. Bonterra's wines are always so crisp in acidity and so clean. Maybe that's because of their intense organic and biodynamic practices. This Viognier has the variety's exotic wildflower and fruit flair, but is grounded with a mineral chalk and gunmetal taste. **89 Editors' Choice** *—S.H. (12/15/2007)*

Bonterra 2005 Viognier (Mendocino County) $18. 88 *—S.H. (11/1/2006)*

Bonterra 2004 Viognier (Mendocino County) $18. 85 *—S.H. (12/15/2005)*

Bonterra 2000 Viognier (Mendocino County) $18. 88 *—S.H. (5/1/2002)*

Bonterra 1999 Viognier (Mendocino County) $19. 88 Editors' Choice *(8/1/2001)*

Bonterra 1997 Viognier (North Coast) $17. 91 *—S.H. (10/1/1999)*

Bonterra 2005 Zinfandel (Mendocino County) $15. Rustically tannic and a little on the thin side, but rewards for wild berry and tobacco flavors and a dry, spicy finish. This is a Zin to gulp with hard cheeses. **85** *—S.H. (10/1/2007)*

Bonterra 2004 Zinfandel (Mendocino County) $15. A little on the sweet side, a little rustic, but this is a pleasant Zin, and you can easily imagine drinking it on some terrace in wine country, as the sun goes down. If that's not an option, try barbecued steak or pork chops, and decant for a few hours. **85** *—S.H. (4/1/2007)*

BOOKWALTER

Bookwalter 2004 Cabernet Sauvignon (Columbia Valley (WA)) $38. Rich, ripe and fruit-powered, this retains more of the high tones (and citrus) than the Merlot. It's powerful and young, smooth but a bit chalky on the finish. It's not yet knit together, and I wonder if and when it will do so. **88** *—P.G. (12/1/2007)*

Bookwalter 2000 Cabernet Sauvignon (Columbia Valley (WA)) $28. 93 Cellar Selection *—P.G. (1/1/2004)*

Bookwalter 1998 Cabernet Sauvignon (Columbia Valley (WA)) $35. 87 *—P.G. (6/1/2001)*

Bookwalter 1999 Chardonnay (Columbia Valley (WA)) $18. 87 *—P.G. (11/15/2000)*

Bookwalter 1997 Vintner's Select Chardonnay (Washington) $20. 88 *—P.G. (11/15/2000)*

Bookwalter 2002 Johannisberg Riesling (Columbia Valley (WA)) $8. 89 *—P.G. (8/1/2003)*

Bookwalter 2005 Merlot (Columbia Valley (WA)) $36. The 2005 continues along the established path of this rising star winery. It's big, no holds barred, rich and jammy, and just a bit warm at 14.8% alcohol. The fruit is nicely woven together, brambly and dark, and coated with clean barrel flavors of coffee and chocolate. Everything is balanced and forward, but you get the sense that this wine is holding something back for the future. **91** *—P.G. (12/1/2007)*

Bookwalter 2001 Merlot (Columbia Valley (WA)) $NA. 91 Cellar Selection *—P.G. (1/1/2004)*

Bookwalter NV Lot 14 Red Wine Red Blend (Columbia Valley (WA)) $NA. 88 Best Buy *—P.G. (1/1/2004)*

BOTASEA

Botasea 2005 Rosato di Palmina Rosé Blend (Santa Barbara County) $18. They blended the Italian varieties of Dolcetto, Nebbiolo and Barbera, but these heavy, tannic varieties just don't lend themselves to rosé. Although the wine is dry and clean, it's dense and clumsy. **82** *—S.H. (7/1/2007)*

BOUCHAINE

Bouchaine 2005 Chardonnay (Carneros) $30. Nice, dry and complex, a crisp wine with quite a bit of minerality undergirding the fruit and oak. Feels fine and balanced in the mouth, and should take a couple years in the cellar. **90** *—S.H. (9/1/2007)*

Bouchaine 2004 Chardonnay (Carneros) $28. 85 *—S.H. (7/1/2006)*

Bouchaine 2003 Chardonnay (Carneros) $25. 87 *—S.H. (10/1/2005)*

Bouchaine 2001 Chardonnay (Carneros) $18. 88 *—S.H. (6/1/2003)*

Bouchaine 1999 Chardonnay (Carneros) $25. 90 *—S.H. (5/1/2002)*

Bouchaine 1998 Chardonnay (Carneros) $20. 89 *(6/1/2000)*

Bouchaine 1999 B Chardonnay (Napa Valley) $13. 82 *—S.H. (9/1/2002)*

Bouchaine 2002 Buchli Station Chardonnay (California) $12. 85 *—S.H. (6/1/2004)*

Bouchaine 2005 Pinot Noir (Carneros) $30. A very pretty Pinot, and while it's not terribly complicated or ageworthy, it's one of those wines that goes gently with almost anything you serve it with. Dry and elegant, its flavors veer toward cherries, tobacco and herbs. **87** *—S.H. (9/1/2007)*

Bouchaine 2004 Pinot Noir (Carneros) $28. 83 *—S.H. (12/1/2006)*

Bouchaine 2003 Pinot Noir (Carneros) $25. 85 *—S.H. (10/1/2005)*

Bouchaine 2002 Pinot Noir (Carneros) $23. 89 *(11/1/2004)*

Bouchaine 2000 Pinot Noir (Carneros) $18. 84 *—S.H. (7/1/2003)*

Bouchaine 1999 Pinot Noir (Carneros) $34. 86 *(10/1/2002)*

Bouchaine 1999 20th Anniversary Gee Vineyard Pinot Noir (Carneros) $50. 86 *(10/1/2002)*

Bouchaine 2000 B Pinot Noir (California) $15. 82 *(10/1/2002)*

Bouchaine 2002 Buchli Station Pinot Noir (California) $11. 84 *—S.H. (6/1/2004)*

Bouchaine 2005 Estate Vineyard Pinot Noir (Carneros) $45. Here's a very elegant, balanced Pinot that shows classic Carneros character. It's a vibrant, likeable wine, silky and dry, with pleasurable flavors of cherries, cola, herbs and spices. The finish is especially rewarding, lasting through a long, spicy aftertaste. Drink now. **89** *—S.H. (12/1/2007)*

Bouchaine 2003 Estate Vineyard Pinot Noir (Carneros) $35. 87 *—S.H. (10/1/2005)*

Bouchaine 2002 Gee Vineyard Pinot Noir (Carneros) $40. 85 *(11/1/2004)*

BOUDREAUX CELLARS

Boudreaux Cellars 2003 Cabernet Sauvignon (Washington) $40. 88 *—P.G. (6/1/2006)*

Boudreaux Cellars 2002 Cabernet Sauvignon (Walla Walla (WA)) $40. 89 *—P.G. (4/1/2005)*

Boudreaux Cellars 2001 Seven Hills Vineyard Cabernet Sauvignon (Walla Walla (WA)) $30. 87 *—P.G. (11/15/2004)*

Boudreaux Cellars 2004 Chardonnay (Columbia Valley (WA)) $26. 89 *—P.G. (6/1/2006)*

Boudreaux Cellars 2002 Chardonnay (Washington) $20. 88 *—P.G. (11/15/2004)*

Boudreaux Cellars 2003 Merlot (Washington) $40. 88 *—P.G. (6/1/2006)*

Boudreaux Cellars 2001 Pepper Bridge Vineyard Merlot (Walla Walla (WA)) $25. 87 *—P.G. (11/15/2004)*

Boudreaux Cellars 2002 Syrah (Walla Walla (WA)) $32. 91 *—P.G. (4/1/2005)*

Boudreaux Cellars 2003 Pepper Bridge Vineyard Syrah (Walla Walla (WA)) $40. 87 *(9/1/2005)*

BOURASSA VINEYARDS

Bourassa Vineyards 2002 Harmony 3 Bordeaux Blend (Napa Valley) $52. 86 *—S.H. (5/1/2005)*

Bourassa Vineyards 2001 Block 42 Cabernet Franc (Napa Valley) $29. 84 *—S.H. (5/1/2005)*

Bourassa Vineyards 2004 Symphony 3 Proprietors Reserve Cabernet Sauvignon (Napa Valley) $50. Shows the ripeness and soft tannins of Napa Cabernet, but also firmer acidity than many, which gives it a good grip that's food-friendly. The flavors of cherries, blackberries, currants, cassis and dark chocolate are accented by oak. This stylish young Cab will be best over the next five years. **88** *—S.H. (11/1/2007)*

Bourassa Vineyards NV Solera3 Port (Napa Valley) $60. 84 *—S.H. (12/1/2006)*

Bourassa Vineyards 2003 Sauvignon Blanc (Napa Valley) $16. 87 —*S.H. (12/31/2004)*

Bourassa Vineyards 2004 Rhapsody 3 Syrah (Napa Valley) $30. 86 —*S.H. (12/1/2006)*

Bourassa Vineyards 2003 Rhapsody 3 Syrah (Napa Valley) $32. 86 *(9/1/2005)*

Bourassa Vineyards 2003 Viognier (Napa Valley) $24. 85 —*S.H. (12/31/2004)*

Bourassa Vineyards 2003 Odyssey 3 Zinfandel (Napa Valley) $32. 80 —*S.H. (6/1/2005)*

BOYER

Boyer 2004 Riesling (Monterey) $14. 89 Best Buy —*S.H. (12/1/2005)*

BRADFORD MOUNTAIN

Bradford Mountain 1998 Block One Zinfandel (Dry Creek Valley) $36. 85 —*D.T. (3/1/2002)*

Bradford Mountain 1999 Grist Vineyard Zinfandel (Dry Creek Valley) $30. 89 —*T.H. (3/1/2002)*

Bradford Mountain 1998 Grist Vineyard Zinfandel (Dry Creek Valley) $24. 87 —*D.T. (3/1/2002)*

BRANDBORG

Brandborg 2005 Gewürztraminer (Umpqua Valley) $17. 88 —*P.G. (12/1/2006)*

Brandborg 2004 Gewürztraminer (Umpqua Valley) $14. 82 —*P.G. (5/1/2006)*

Brandborg 2004 Pinot Gris (Umpqua Valley) $17. 86 —*P.G. (12/1/2006)*

Brandborg 2003 Pinot Gris (Umpqua Valley) $14. 86 —*P.G. (2/1/2006)*

Brandborg 2001 Pinot Noir (Anderson Valley) $23. 85 —*S.H. (4/1/2004)*

Brandborg 2004 Benchlands Pinot Noir (Umpqua Valley) $21. 87 —*P.G. (12/1/2006)*

Brandborg 2002 Benchlands Pinot Noir (Umpqua Valley) $18. 87 *(11/1/2004)*

Brandborg 2003 Northern Reach Pinot Noir (Umpqua Valley) $27. 87 —*P.G. (12/1/2006)*

Brandborg 2002 Northern Reach Pinot Noir (Umpqua Valley) $23. 87 *(11/1/2004)*

Brandborg 2005 Riesling (Umpqua Valley) $19. 85 —*P.G. (12/1/2006)*

Brandborg 2004 Riesling (Umpqua Valley) $14. 80 —*P.G. (5/1/2006)*

Brandborg 2001 Sangiovese (Russian River Valley) $18. 86 —*S.H. (4/1/2004)*

Brandborg 2004 Syrah (Umpqua Valley) $29. 86 —*P.G. (12/1/2006)*

Brandborg 2003 Syrah (Umpqua Valley) $25. 84 *(9/1/2005)*

BRANDER

Brander 2004 Bouchet Bordeaux Blend (Santa Ynez Valley) $32. 90 —*S.H. (7/1/2006)*

Brander 2005 Bouchet (Santa Ynez Valley) $32. A blend of the two Cabs, this is less ripe and lower in alcohol than most Cabs from, say, Napa or Paso Robles. It has a minty, green olive taste to the cherries and cassis, and is very soft and drinkable. 86 —*S.H. (7/1/2007)*

Brander 2002 Bouchet (Santa Ynez Valley) $30. 88 —*S.H. (9/1/2004)*

Brander 2001 Bouchet (Santa Ynez Valley) $30. 86 —*S.H. (12/31/2003)*

Brander 2003 Bouchet Cabernet Blend (Santa Ynez Valley) $30. 88 —*S.H. (12/1/2005)*

Brander 2005 Cabernet Sauvignon (Santa Ynez Valley) $25. 83 —*S.H. (12/1/2006)*

Brander 2004 Cabernet Sauvignon (Santa Ynez Valley) $20. 87 —*S.H. (5/1/2006)*

Brander 2003 Cabernet Sauvignon (Santa Ynez Valley) $20. 83 —*S.H. (12/1/2005)*

Brander 2002 Cabernet Sauvignon (Santa Ynez Valley) $18. 84 —*S.H. (5/1/2005)*

Brander 2004 Reserve Cabernet Sauvignon (Santa Ynez Valley) $50. 83 —*S.H. (12/31/2006)*

Brander 2002 Reserve Cabernet Sauvignon (Santa Ynez Valley) $45. 84 —*S.H. (12/1/2005)*

Brander 2000 Reserve Cabernet Sauvignon (Santa Ynez Valley) $45. 87 —*S.H. (11/15/2003)*

Brander 2003 Vogelzang Vineyard Cabernet Sauvignon (Santa Ynez Valley) $30. 87 —*S.H. (5/1/2006)*

Brander 2004 Merlot (Santa Ynez Valley) $20. 87 —*S.H. (5/1/2006)*

Brander 2003 Merlot (Santa Ynez Valley) $20. 86 —*S.H. (10/1/2005)*

Brander 2002 Merlot (Santa Ynez Valley) $20. 84 —*S.H. (12/15/2004)*

Brander 1999 Merlot (Santa Ynez Valley) $18. 85 —*S.H. (5/1/2001)*

Brander 2005 Château Neuf du Pink Rosé Blend (Santa Ynez Valley) $13. 86 —*S.H. (12/1/2006)*

Brander 2006 Sauvignon Blanc (Santa Ynez Valley) $15. This has a little barrel fermentation, lending a creaminess. But it has the same fizziness of a young white just months out of the fermenter. It's also delicious. 88 —*S.H. (8/1/2007)*

Brander 2005 Sauvignon Blanc (Santa Ynez Valley) $13. 87 —*S.H. (7/1/2006)*

Brander 2004 Sauvignon Blanc (Santa Ynez Valley) $12. 85 —*S.H. (10/1/2005)*

Brander 2003 Sauvignon Blanc (Santa Ynez Valley) $12. 87 —*J.M. (8/1/2004)*

Brander 1999 Sauvignon Blanc (Santa Ynez Valley) $12. 86 —*S.H. (5/1/2001)*

Brander 2005 Au Naturel Sauvignon Blanc (Santa Ynez Valley) $30. 93 Editors' Choice —*S.H. (11/15/2006)*

Brander 2004 Au Naturel Sauvignon Blanc (Santa Ynez Valley) $30. 92 Editors' Choice —*S.H. (5/1/2006)*

Brander 2003 Au Naturel Sauvignon Blanc (Santa Ynez Valley) $30. 89 *(7/1/2005)*

Brander 2002 Au Naturel Sauvignon Blanc (Santa Ynez Valley) $30. 91 —*J.M. (8/1/2004)*

Brander 2004 Cuvée Natalie Sauvignon Blanc (Santa Ynez Valley) $16. 84 —*S.H. (10/1/2005)*

Brander 1999 Cuvée Natalie Sauvignon Blanc (Santa Ynez Valley) $15. 90 Editors' Choice —*S.H. (5/1/2001)*

Brander 2006 Cuvée Nicolas Sauvignon Blanc (Santa Ynez Valley) $25. This is Brander's barrel-fermented, new oaky Sauvignon Blanc. You can taste the creaminess and smokiness imparted by the wood. It marries nicely with the grape's citrus and fig flavors and zippy acids. 90 —*S.H. (12/1/2007)*

Brander 2005 Cuvée Nicolas Sauvignon Blanc (Santa Ynez Valley) $25. 90 —*S.H. (11/15/2006)*

Brander 2004 Cuvée Nicolas Sauvignon Blanc (Santa Ynez Valley) $26. 92 Editors' Choice —*S.H. (12/1/2005)*

Brander 2002 Cuvée Nicolas Sauvignon Blanc (Santa Ynez Valley) $25. 89 —*J.M. (8/1/2004)*

Brander 2006 Early Release Sauvignon Blanc (Santa Ynez Valley) $14. It tastes like it's still fermenting, with the fizzy feeling the French call pettilant, while the flavors are of gooseberries, lemongrass, pineapple juice and vanilla. Finishes slightly sweet. 86 —*S.H. (7/1/2007)*

Brander 2005 Early Release Sauvignon Blanc (Santa Ynez Valley) $12. 87 Best Buy —*S.H. (5/1/2006)*

Brander 2004 Early Release Sauvignon Blanc (Santa Ynez Valley) $12. 87 Best Buy —*S.H. (5/1/2005)*

Brander 2006 Purisima Mountain Vineyard Sauvignon Blanc (Santa Ynez Valley) $25. Rich and layered, this wine expresses the essence of its vineyard's fruit. Smacks of tangy citrus, lime blossom, lemon curd, peach and yellow apricot flavors that flood the palate and finish long and spicy. It's a very big wine, but balanced and elegant. 91 —*S.H. (12/1/2007)*

Brander 2005 Purisima Mountain Sauvignon Blanc (Santa Ynez Valley) $25. 92 Editors' Choice —*S.H. (12/1/2006)*

Brander 2004 Purisima Mountain Vineyard Sauvignon Blanc (Santa Ynez Valley) $22. 87 —*S.H. (12/1/2005)*

Brander 2001 Sauvignon au Naturel Sauvignon Blanc (Santa Ynez Valley) $30. 91 —*S.H. (10/1/2003)*

Brander 2003 Cuvée Nicolas Sauvignon Blanc-Sémillon (Santa Ynez Valley) $25. 86 *(7/1/2005)*

Brander 2005 Syrah (Santa Ynez Valley) $25. A little rough around the edges, but flavorful in ripe cherries, black raspberries and chocolate. Finishes dry and crisp, with loads of Asian spices. 85 —*S.H. (7/1/2007)*

Brander 2005 Cuvée Natalie White Blend (Santa Ynez Valley) $18. 85 —*S.H. (11/15/2006)*

Brander 2003 Cuvée Natalie White Blend (Santa Ynez Valley) $16. 86 —*S.H. (12/1/2004)*

Brander 2006 Uno Mas White Blend (Santa Ynez Valley) $22. Right up there with last year's bottling, this Grenache Blanc-Sauvignon Blanc blend is unoaked, offering pure flavors of terroir-inspired fruit. High acidity backs up the lemongrass, pineapple, peach and honeysuckle flavors that finish so dry and spicy. **90 Editors' Choice** —*S.H. (12/1/2007)*

Brander 2005 Uno Mas White Blend (Santa Ynez Valley) $25. 91 Editors' Choice —*S.H. (12/31/2006)*

BRAREN PAULI

Braren Pauli 1999 Frost Reserve Cabernet Sauvignon (Mendocino) $16. 83 —*S.H. (5/1/2002)*

Braren Pauli 1999 Busch Creek Vineyard Chardonnay (Mendocino County) $12. 83 —*S.H. (5/1/2002)*

Braren Pauli 1998 Merlot (Redwood Valley) $14. 82 —*S.H. (5/1/2002)*

Braren Pauli 1999 Roar Vineyard Pinot Noir (Mendocino) $14. 85 —*S.H. (5/1/2002)*

BRASSFIELD

Brassfield 2003 Monte Sereno Vineyard Cabernet Sauvignon (High Valley) $40. 85 —*S.H. (12/31/2006)*

Brassfield 2003 High Serenity Ranch Merlot (High Valley) $19. 91 Editors' Choice —*S.H. (12/31/2006)*

Brassfield 2004 Pinot Grigio (Clear Lake) $15. 86 —*S.H. (12/15/2005)*

Brassfield 2003 Pinot Grigio (Clear Lake) $16. 85 —*S.H. (3/1/2005)*

Brassfield 2005 High Serenity Ranch Pinot Grigio (High Valley) $15. 88 Editors' Choice —*S.H. (12/31/2006)*

Brassfield 2006 High Serenity Ranch Dry Riesling (High Valley) $16. Although it says dry, there's a honeyed edge of sweetness to this crisp, delicate wine. The acidity is a welcome balance to the flowery citrus, apricot and mango flavors. 87 —*S.H. (9/1/2007)*

Brassfield 2005 Susan's Passion Late Harvest Riesling (High Valley) $25. 90 —*S.H. (12/31/2006)*

Brassfield 2004 Sauvignon Blanc (Clear Lake) $15. 83 —*S.H. (12/15/2005)*

Brassfield 2003 Sauvignon Blanc (Clear Lake) $15. 84 —*S.H. (8/1/2005)*

Brassfield 2005 High Serenity Ranch Sauvignon Blanc (High Valley) $15. 91 Best Buy —*S.H. (12/31/2006)*

Brassfield 2002 Syrah (Clear Lake) $24. 86 —*S.H. (3/1/2005)*

Brassfield 2003 Monte Sereno Vineyard Syrah (High Valley) $30. 91 —*S.H. (12/31/2006)*

Brassfield 2003 Round Mountain Vineyard Syrah (Clear Lake) $23. 85 —*S.H. (12/31/2006)*

Brassfield 2005 High Serenity Ranch Serenity White Table Wine White Blend (High Valley) $15. 83 —*S.H. (12/31/2006)*

Brassfield 2004 Serenity White Blend (Clear Lake) $15. 83 —*S.H. (12/15/2005)*

Brassfield 2001 High Valley Zinfandel (Lake County) $19. 86 *(11/1/2003)*

Brassfield 2003 Round Mountain Vineyard Zinfandel (Clear Lake) $19. 86 —*S.H. (12/31/2006)*

BRAVANTE

Bravante 2003 Cabernet Sauvignon (Howell Mountain) $45. 87 —*S.H. (12/31/2006)*

Bravante 2003 Merlot (Howell Mountain) $34. If it wasn't for the overripeness in this wine, it would be a fantastic Merlot. But there it is, raisins and heat from 15-plus alcohol. If you can get around that, it's soft, smooth and voluptuous, dry and rich in black and red cherry pie, violet, mocha and spicy flavors. Best now. 87 —*S.H. (3/1/2007)*

Bravante 2001 Merlot (Howell Mountain) $35. 85 —*S.H. (8/1/2005)*

BRAY

Bray 2002 Zinfandel (Shenandoah Valley (CA)) $16. 81 —*S.H. (3/1/2005)*

BREGGO

Breggo 2005 Pinot Noir (Anderson Valley) $35. Simple and a little sweet in raspberry and red cherry jam flavors, this Pinot has too much oak, or too much toast, for the underlying wine. 86 —*S.H. (11/1/2007)*

Breggo 2005 Ferrington Vineyard Pinot Noir (Anderson Valley) $50. Made in a sweetly ripe, approachable style, this Pinot exudes raspberry, cherry, vanilla and spicy oak flavors. It's a hedonistic wine that's showing well now. 89 —*S.H. (11/1/2007)*

Breggo 2005 Savoy Vineyard Pinot Noir (Anderson Valley) $50. Fine and supple, this Pinot combines grace and power with plenty of flavor. It's forward in jammy cherry, raspberry, rose, lavender and cola, and the finish is long and sweet. The wine is balanced with firm tannins and crisp acidity. 90 —*S.H. (11/1/2007)*

BREWER-CLIFTON

Brewer-Clifton 2004 Ashleys Chardonnay (Santa Rita Hills) $60. 93 —*S.H. (3/1/2006)*

Brewer-Clifton 2004 Clos Pepe Chardonnay (Santa Rita Hills) $40. 92 —*S.H. (8/1/2006)*

Brewer-Clifton 2004 Melville Chardonnay (Santa Rita Hills) $46. 93 —*S.H. (8/1/2006)*

Brewer-Clifton 2005 Mt. Carmel Chardonnay (Santa Rita Hills) $52. This Chard shows the immaculate purity of SRH Chard, that intensely pure lemon drop and pineapple taste, while oak adds exotic layers of custard and buttercream. High acidity adds the perfect finishing touch, making all this richness bright. 93 —*S.H. (4/1/2007)*

Brewer-Clifton 2004 Mount Carmel Chardonnay (Santa Rita Hills) $52. 95 Editors' Choice —*S.H. (3/1/2006)*

Brewer-Clifton 2004 Rancho Santa Rosa Chardonnay (Santa Rita Hills) $46. 93 —*S.H. (8/1/2006)*

Brewer-Clifton 2005 Seasmoke Chardonnay (Santa Rita Hills) $48. This is a big, rich wine, huge in fruit of the tropical-pie flavors. Huge in alcohol, it wears its weight well. The wine, from this venerable vineyard, feels honeyed, opulent, massive, and is almost better by itself than with food. 93 —*S.H. (4/1/2007)*

Brewer-Clifton 2005 Sweeney Canyon Chardonnay (Santa Rita Hills) $56. From some of the oldest Chard vines in the area comes this dramatically rich wine. Bursting with lemon drop, Meyer lemon mousse, peach pulp and toasty new oak, this is a very ripe wine whose high alcohol, 16.4%, shows only as a dusting of white pepper and spicy clove that makes the finish piquant. 93 —*S.H. (4/1/2007)*

Brewer-Clifton 2005 Ashley's Pinot Noir (Santa Rita Hills) $48. This Pinot shows a gamey, truffly aroma that may come from the Pommard clone, although Dijons add their usual fresh cherries and raspberries. There's a chewy bunch of Provençal herbs somewhere in there, too. B-C uses stems in the fermentation, which makes for an earthier, or "grounded" wine, in Steve Clifton's words, and one he believes will age. 91 —*S.H. (4/1/2007)*

Brewer-Clifton 2004 Ashley's Pinot Noir (Santa Rita Hills) $50. 91 —*S.H. (3/1/2006)*

Brewer-Clifton 2005 Cargasacchi Pinot Noir (Santa Rita Hills) $56. This is among my favorites of the '05 B-C Pinots. The stems make the wine earthier and more tannic than most other SRH Pinot Noirs, in a way, more old-fashioned. The wine needs time, but the massive heart of cola, black cherry, plum and coffee flavors, not to mention the brisk acidity, suggests greater drinkability by 2008. This is a classy, exotic and complex young wine. **93 Cellar Selection** —*S.H. (4/1/2007)*

Brewer-Clifton 2004 Cargasacchi Pinot Noir (Santa Rita Hills) $64. 93 —*S.H. (3/1/2006)*

Brewer-Clifton 2004 Melville Pinot Noir (Santa Rita Hills) $64. 86 —*S.H. (8/1/2006)*

Brewer-Clifton 2005 Mt. Carmel Pinot Noir (Santa Rita Hills) $60. The complex aromaa of this dramatic young wine is of mushrooms and wet tree bark, wintergreen, cloves, nutmeg and anise, and fruitier notes of cherries, cola and pomegranates. The mouth is very complex, too, with a finish of intensely pure cherries. But the wine is young and tannic. It will be best after 2008, and should drink well for at least another five years. **94 Cellar Selection** —*S.H. (4/1/2007)*

Brewer-Clifton 2004 Mount Carmel Pinot Noir (Santa Rita Hills) $72. 92 —*S.H. (8/1/2006)*

Brewer-Clifton 2004 Rancho Santa Rosa Pinot Noir (Santa Rita Hills) $56. 93 —*S.H. (8/1/2006)*

BRIAN CARTER CELLARS

Brian Carter Cellars 2003 L'Etalon Bordeaux Blend (Yakima Valley) $30. This Bordeaux blend sends up lovely, mixed scents of perfectly blended fruits, light toast, light herb and earth. The oak is a nice accent to the firm, well-structured core. It's still youthful and tight, and will require some decanting and breathing time to reveal itself fully. The blend is slightly more than half Cabernet Sauvignon, the rest Merlot, Cab Franc and a splash of Petit Verdot. 89 —*P.G. (5/1/2007)*

Brian Carter Cellars 2002 L'Etalon Bordeaux Blend (Yakima Valley) $30. 90 —*P.G. (6/1/2006)*

Brian Carter Cellars 2002 Byzance Grenache-Shiraz (Yakima Valley) $30. 89 —*P.G. (6/1/2006)*

Brian Carter Cellars 2003 Abracadabra Red Red Blend (Columbia Valley (WA)) $16. 87 —*P.G. (6/1/2006)*

Brian Carter Cellars 2003 Tuttorosso Red Blend (Yakima Valley) $30. This super Tuscan styled Tuttorosso includes 27% Cabernet Sauvignon and 9% Syrah. It captures the Sangio character, the tangy acids, the plummy fruit, the hints of leaf and fennel, and beefs up the natural thinness of the grape with the Cab and Syrah. So the wine gains some weight and muscle, keeps its balance, and checks in at just 13.7% alcohol. It's a lovely effort. **90** —*P.G. (5/1/2007)*

Brian Carter Cellars 2003 Byzance Rhône Red Blend (Yakima Valley) $30. This is Brian Carter's southern Rhône blend, two-thirds Syrah and one third Grenache. A lovely, dark, plummy purple, intensely fragrant with fresh berries, plums, whiffs of cocoa and sandalwood, a wine to sniff with contemplative pleasure. I love the details, and how the flavors follow the appealing nose with graceful harmony. Carter keeps the alcohol at 13.3% without sacrificing a bit of flavor or ripeness. **91 Editors' Choice** —*P.G. (5/1/2007)*

Brian Carter Cellars 2002 Tuttorosso Sangiovese (Yakima Valley) $30. 88 —*P.G. (6/1/2006)*

Brian Carter Cellars 2005 Oriana White Blend (Yakima Valley) $24. What makes this Roussanne/Viognier blend really clever is the addition of 25% Riesling, which enhances the aromas and cuts through some of the heaviness and heat of the two Rhône grapes. This follow up to the excellent 2004 Oriana is just as good, with lovely scents of fruit and flower, and flavors of citrus rind and ripe stone fruits. There's just enough residual sugar (.6%) to plump it up and round out the acids. **90** —*P.G. (5/1/2007)*

Brian Carter Cellars 2004 Oriana White Blend White Blend (Yakima Valley) $24. 90 —*P.G. (6/1/2006)*

BRICE STATION

Brice Station 2003 Gold Rush Cabernet Franc (Calaveras County) $18. 86 —*S.H. (3/1/2005)*

Brice Station 2002 Gold Rush Cabernet Sauvignon (Calaveras County) $16. 83 —*S.H. (3/1/2005)*

Brice Station 2003 Chardonnay (California) $17. 83 —*S.H. (2/1/2005)*

BRICELAND

Briceland 2000 Elk Prairie Vineyard Pinot Noir (Humboldt County) $24. 84 —*S.H. (4/1/2003)*

Briceland 2000 Phelps Vineyard Pinot Noir (Humboldt County) $22. 83 —*S.H. (2/1/2003)*

BRICK HOUSE

Brick House 2005 Chardonnay (Willamette Valley) $27. Done in a full, round, slightly oxidative style, this 100% Dijon clone Chard is a deep yellow straw color. Strong hints of banana and other tropical fruit claim the nose. The acids are up just enough to keep it from tipping over into a world of mushy banana flavors. Along with banana are ripe apple and pear. **88** —*P.G. (7/1/2007)*

Brick House 2002 Pinot Noir (Willamette Valley) $26. ı**84** *(11/1/2004)*

Brick House 2002 Clos Ladybug Pinot Noir (Willamette Valley) $20. 86 *(11/1/2004)*

Brick House 1997 Cuvée du Tonnelier Pinot Noir (Willamette Valley) $36. 87 *(10/1/1999)*

Brick House 2005 Evelyn's Pinot Noir (Willamette Valley) $50. The fruit remains a bit subdued, the tannins tasting of green tea and black coffee. There is a strong, concentrated center, and a finish with grip and authority. This wine needs to breathe, and it will require some serious time before it will unwrap itself. **92** —*P.G. (7/1/2007)*

Brick House 2002 Evelyn's Pinot Noir (Willamette Valley) $40. 87 *(11/1/2004)*

Brick House 2005 Les Dijonnais Pinot Noir (Willamette Valley) $45. Les Dijonnais distinguishes itself by being a bit tighter, with more pungent herbaceousness, more precision, more verticality. It has extra concentration and power, but remains consistent to the house style. Those who follow biodynamic wines will enjoy the typical notes of herb, leaf and silage. **91** —*P.G. (7/1/2007)*

Brick House 2002 Les Dijonnais Pinot Noir (Willamette Valley) $40. 90 *(11/1/2004)*

Brick House 2005 Select Pinot Noir (Willamette Valley) $35. Round and loose-knit, this opens with warm, accessible flavors that include wet earth, leaf and herb. It lasts into a finish that keeps moving, adding nuances of sun- dried tomato, pie cherry and rhubarb. All in all it's an interesting, flavorful, well-made and well-rounded Pinot. **89** —*P.G. (7/1/2007)*

BRIDGEVIEW

Bridgeview 2003 Cabernet Sauvignon-Merlot (Southern Oregon) $10. 83 —*P.G. (9/1/2006)*

Bridgeview 2001 Cabernet Sauvignon-Merlot (Oregon) $10. 84 —*P.G. (8/1/2002)*

Bridgeview 2000 Chardonnay (Oregon) $7. 88 Best Buy —*P.G. (8/1/2002)*

Bridgeview 1999 Chardonnay (Oregon) $7. 85 Best Buy —*P.G. (11/1/2001)*

Bridgeview 2003 Blue Moon Chardonnay (Oregon) $10. 82 —*P.G. (9/1/2006)*

Bridgeview 2000 Blue Moon Chardonnay (Oregon) $10. 88 Best Buy —*P.G. (8/1/2002)*

Bridgeview 1999 Blue Moon Chardonnay (Oregon) $10. 86 —*P.G. (11/1/2001)*

Bridgeview 2000 Gewürztraminer (Oregon) $10. 86 —*P.G. (4/1/2002)*

Bridgeview 2003 Merlot (Southern Oregon) $10. 84 —*P.G. (9/1/2006)*

Bridgeview 2000 Merlot (Oregon) $10. 85 —*P.G. (8/1/2002)*

Bridgeview 1999 Black Beauty Merlot (Oregon) $15. 80 —*P.G. (4/1/2002)*

Bridgeview 1997 Black Beauty Merlot (Oregon) $15. 83 —*P.G. (11/1/2001)*

Bridgeview 2000 Pinot Gris (Oregon) $11. 84 —*P.G. (2/1/2002)*

Bridgeview 2000 Reserve Pinot Gris (Oregon) $16. 89 Editors' Choice —*P.G. (8/1/2002)*

Bridgeview 2004 Pinot Noir (Southern Oregon) $13. 84 —*P.G. (9/1/2006)*

Bridgeview 2000 Pinot Noir (Oregon) $12. 87 Best Buy *(10/1/2002)*

Bridgeview 1999 Pinot Noir (Oregon) $12. 84 —*P.G. (11/1/2001)*

Bridgeview 2004 Blue Moon Pinot Noir (Oregon) $18. 84 —*P.G. (9/1/2006)*

Bridgeview 2002 Blue Moon Pinot Noir (Oregon) $15. 85 *(11/1/2004)*

Bridgeview 2000 Blue Moon Pinot Noir (Oregon) $15. 84 *(10/1/2002)*

Bridgeview 1998 Blue Moon Pinot Noir (Oregon) $15. 90 Best Buy —*M.S. (12/1/2000)*

Bridgeview 1998 Oregon Pinot Noir (Oregon) $11. 88 Best Buy *(11/15/1999)*

Bridgeview 1998 Red Cedar Pinot Noir (Rogue Valley) $30. 84 —*P.G. (12/1/2003)*

Bridgeview 2000 Reserve Pinot Noir (Southern Oregon) $20. 85 —*P.G. (9/1/2006)*

Bridgeview 1999 Reserve Pinot Noir (Rogue Valley) $18. 87 —*P.G. (8/1/2002)*

Bridgeview 1998 Reserve Pinot Noir (Rogue Valley) $20. 87 —*J.C. (12/1/2000)*

Bridgeview 2006 Blue Moon Riesling (Oregon) $10. The blue bottle with the banana-colored cork is almost iconic in Oregon. The wine, as always, is far less flashy but perfectly serviceable. It gives fair flavor for your 10 bucks, keeping it simple, sweet and slightly tropical. Don't look for complexity, but if you want a decent, tasting room Riesling, this does the job nicely. **85** —*P.G. (11/15/2007)*

Bridgeview 2005 Blue Moon Riesling (Oregon) $10. 84 —*P.G. (9/1/2006)*

Bridgeview 2002 Blue Moon Riesling (Oregon) $8. 87 —*P.G. (8/1/2003)*

Bridgeview 2001 Blue Moon Riesling (Oregon) $7. 82 —*J.C. (8/1/2003)*

Bridgeview 2000 Blue Moon Riesling (Oregon) $7. 86 Best Buy —*P.G. (11/1/2001)*

BRIDGEWAY

Bridgeway 2003 Cabernet Sauvignon (Napa Valley) $20. Seems a bit pricey for what you get: a ripe, forward but ultimately simple Cab-based red. It's candied in cherry-mocha flavors, with raw tannins. **83** —*S.H. (10/1/2007)*

Bridgeway 2003 Syrah (Central Coast) $16. 84 *(9/1/2005)*

Bridgeway 2003 Zinfandel (Sonoma County) $18. Good, everyday red for those who like their Zins briary, brambly and rustic. It's a soul food wine, whose berry-cherry flavors are just short of of raisiny. Not without its faults, but easy and gulpable. **85** —*S.H. (9/1/2007)*

BRIDGMAN

Bridgman 2002 Chardonnay (Columbia Valley (WA)) $10. 87 —*P.G. (9/1/2004)*

Bridgman 2000 Chardonnay (Columbia Valley (WA)) $11. 86 —*P.G. (7/1/2002)*

Bridgman 1999 Merlot (Columbia Valley (WA)) $17. 84 —*P.G. (6/1/2002)*

Bridgman 2002 Roussanne (Yakima Valley) $13. 86 —*P.G. (9/1/2004)*

Bridgman 2000 Sauvignon Blanc (Yakima Valley) $11. 85 —*P.G. (6/1/2002)*

Bridgman 1998 Syrah (Columbia Valley (WA)) $18. 81 —*S.H. (9/1/2000)*

Bridgman 2001 Syrah (Yakima Valley) $13. 86 —*P.G. (9/1/2004)*

Bridgman 2000 Syrah (Yakima Valley) $17. 83 —*P.G. (12/31/2002)*

Bridgman 1999 Syrah (Yakima Valley) $18. 85 *(10/1/2001)*

Bridgman 2000 Viognier (Yakima Valley) $17. 84 —*P.G. (6/1/2002)*

BRIDLEWOOD

Bridlewood 1997 Cabernet Franc (Central Coast) $28. 88 —*S.H. (7/1/2000)*

Bridlewood 1997 Chardonnay (Central Coast) $18. 86 *(6/1/2000)*

Bridlewood 2000 Chardonnay (Edna Valley) $16. 81 *—S.H. (9/1/2003)*

Bridlewood 1999 Chardonnay (Santa Barbara County) $18. 84 *—S.H. (12/31/2001)*

Bridlewood 1998 Chenin Blanc (Santa Barbara County) $10. 86 *—J.C. (10/14/2003)*

Bridlewood 1997 Merlot (Santa Barbara County) $22. 88 *(7/1/2000)*

Bridlewood 1999 Merlot (Central Coast) $22. 84 *—S.H. (8/1/2003)*

Bridlewood 1998 Arabesque Red Blend (California) $14. 86 *—S.H. (11/15/2000)*

Bridlewood 2004 Arabesque Rhône Red Blend (Central Coast) $24. This is a blend of six Rhône varieties, and it's clean, but not very rewarding. It's too thin, and the absence of fruit just makes the acidity and tannins stick out. **83** *—S.H. (4/1/2007)*

Bridlewood 1999 Arabesque Rhône Red Blend (California) $14. 85 *—S.H. (12/15/2001)*

Bridlewood 1998 Ranger Red Rhône Red Blend (California) $12. 85 *—S.H. (2/1/2000)*

Bridlewood 1998 Saddlesore Rosé Rhône Red Blend (California) $12. 85 *—M.S. (8/1/2000)*

Bridlewood 1998 Sauvignon Blanc (Santa Barbara County) $14. 87 *—S.H. (2/1/2000)*

Bridlewood 2000 Sauvignon Blanc (Santa Ynez Valley) $12. 87 *—S.H. (7/1/2003)*

Bridlewood 1999 Sauvignon Blanc (Santa Barbara County) $12. 84 *—S.H. (12/15/2001)*

Bridlewood 2004 Syrah (Central Coast) $0. This dry, full-bodied red wine is a little rustic, but the structure is great, and the blackberry, plum, coffee and herb flavors work just fine. **84** *—S.H. (4/1/2007)*

Bridlewood 2003 Syrah (Central Coast) $8. 84 Best Buy *—S.H. (12/31/2006)*

Bridlewood 2001 Syrah (Central Coast) $20. 83 *(9/1/2005)*

Bridlewood 2000 Syrah (Central Coast) $19. 90 Editors' Choice *—S.H. (6/1/2003)*

Bridlewood 1999 Syrah (Central Coast) $20. 89 *(10/1/2001)*

Bridlewood 1998 Syrah (Paso Robles) $18. 89 *—S.H. (11/15/2000)*

Bridlewood 2003 Estate Syrah (Santa Ynez Valley) $40. A very fine wine that shows the ability of warmish Santa Ynez to ripen the variety, while still preserving vital acidity and that classic, Northern Rhône peppery note. It's a dark, full-bodied wine that contains a drop of Petite Sirah, and while it's tannic and young, it's delicious now. Perfect with grilled meats. **93** *—S.H. (4/1/2007)*

Bridlewood 2002 Estate Syrah (Santa Ynez Valley) $40. 85 *—S.H. (10/1/2006)*

Bridlewood 2003 Reserve Syrah (Central Coast) $24. 84 *—S.H. (10/1/2006)*

Bridlewood 1998 Winners Circle Syrah (Central Coast) $25. 90 *—S.H. (11/15/2000)*

Bridlewood 1999 Winners Circle Selection Syrah (San Luis Obispo County) $24. 89 *(11/1/2001)*

Bridlewood 2004 Viognier (Central Coast) $24. 90 *—S.H. (9/1/2006)*

Bridlewood 2006 Reserve Viognier (Central Coast) $24. Does a good job of bringing controlled elegance to a variety that can be exotically over-the-top. You'll find the array of tropical fruits, wildflowers and spices Viognier is known for, in a balanced, crisply dry texture. **87** *—S.H. (12/15/2007)*

Bridlewood 2005 Reserve Viognier (Central Coast) $20. 86 *—S.H. (12/15/2006)*

Bridlewood 2001 Estate Reserve Zinfandel (Santa Ynez Valley) $24. 90 Editors' Choice *(11/1/2003)*

Bridlewood 1998 French Camp Zinfandel (Paso Robles) $16. 83 *—S.H. (5/1/2000)*

BROADFIELDS

Broadfields 2001 Merlot (North Fork of Long Island) $NA. 86 *—J.C. (10/2/2004)*

BROADLEY

Broadley 2005 Bergström Vineyard Pinot Noir (Willamette Valley) $36. Showing some adolescent awkwardness. The young, primary fruit flavors lead into a disjointed palate that shows increasing scents of funk and fish as it opens. A late-breaking streak of coffee syrup does set in, and it is entirely possible that it will knit together in time, but it shows the difficulties consumers face when wines are released so young. **86** *—P.G. (7/1/2007)*

Broadley 1997 Reserve Pinot Noir (Willamette Valley) $23. 82 *(11/15/1999)*

BROCHELLE VINEYARDS

Brochelle Vineyards 2001 Zinfandel (Paso Robles) $30. 83 *(11/1/2003)*

BROLL MOUNTAIN VINEYARDS

Broll Mountain Vineyards 2002 Merlot (Calaveras County) $32. 85 *—S.H. (2/1/2005)*

Broll Mountain Vineyards 2003 Syrah (Calaveras County) $32. 86 *—S.H. (12/31/2005)*

Broll Mountain Vineyards 2002 Syrah (Calaveras County) $31. 89 *—S.H. (7/1/2005)*

Broll Mountain Vineyards 2001 Syrah (Calaveras County) $31. 88 *—S.H. (2/1/2005)*

BROMAN

Broman 2002 Cabernet Sauvignon (Napa Valley) $48. Held back for nearly five years, this Cab is still pretty tannic and acidic. It has a deep core of black cherry, cassis, raspberry and coffee flavors, but seems at its peak, so drink up. **87** *—S.H. (12/15/2007)*

Broman 1999 Cabernet Sauvignon (Napa Valley) $54. 83 *—S.H. (10/1/2004)*

Broman 2005 Sauvignon Blanc (Napa Valley) $16. I might have thought there was oak on this wine, it's so rich and vanilla-smoky, but there isn't. Just goes to show. It's dramatic in rich peach, fig, date and ripe green melon, but where does all that butterscotch and crème brûlée come from? The grapes come from a single Beckstoffer-owned vineyard in Rutherford. **90** *—S.H. (12/15/2007)*

Broman 2002 Sauvignon Blanc (Napa Valley) $16. 85 *—J.M. (9/1/2004)*

BROOKDALE VINEYARDS

Brookdale Vineyards 2003 Cabernet Sauvignon (Napa Valley) $45. The winery has made a name for itself with fresh, young Cabs that are rich and balanced and ageable. The '03 shows tough tannins framing blackberry, cherry, cola and oak flavors, and is thoroughly dry. Should develop well over the next 10 years. **92** *—S.H. (4/1/2007)*

Brookdale Vineyards 2002 Cabernet Sauvignon (Napa Valley) $52. 90 *—S.H. (12/15/2005)*

Brookdale Vineyards 2001 Cabernet Sauvignon (Napa Valley) $52. 91 *—J.M. (6/1/2004)*

Brookdale Vineyards 2000 Cabernet Sauvignon (Napa Valley) $48. 91 *—J.M. (6/1/2003)*

BROOKS

Brooks 2002 Pinot Noir (Oregon) $20. 85 *(11/1/2004)*

Brooks 2002 Pinot Noir (Oregon) $20. 88 *(11/1/2004)*

Brooks 2002 Janus Pinot Noir (Oregon) $29. 88 *(11/1/2004)*

Brooks 2002 Amycas White White Blend (Willamette Valley) $13. 90 Best Buy *—P.G. (12/1/2003)*

BROPHY CLARK

Brophy Clark 2004 Pinot Noir (Santa Rita Hills) $24. 89 *—S.H. (12/31/2006)*

Brophy Clark 2001 Pinot Noir (Santa Maria Valley) $20. 84 *—S.H. (12/1/2004)*

Brophy Clark 2000 Pinot Noir (Santa Maria Valley) $22. 86 *(10/1/2002)*

Brophy Clark 1999 Pinot Noir (Santa Maria Valley) $22. 88 *(10/1/2002)*

Brophy Clark 1998 Pinot Noir (Santa Maria Valley) $20. 85 *—M.M. (12/15/2000)*

Brophy Clark 1998 Pinot Noir (Arroyo Grande Valley) $18. 89 *—J.C. (12/15/2000)*

Brophy Clark 2005 Ashley's Vineyard Pinot Noir (Santa Rita Hills) $26. Easy and varietally correct, this is elegantly structured. It has flavors of tart cherryskins, blackberries and cola, with crisp acidity and a dry finish. Drink now. **85** *—S.H. (11/1/2007)*

Brophy Clark 2001 Ashley's Vineyard Pinot Noir (Santa Rita Hills) $24. 87 *—S.H. (12/1/2004)*

Brophy Clark 2004 Sauvignon Blanc (Santa Ynez Valley) $13. 87 *—S.H. (12/31/2006)*

Brophy Clark 2000 Valley View Sauvignon Blanc (Santa Ynez Valley) $14. 88 *—S.H. (7/1/2003)*

Brophy Clark 2005 Valley View Vineyard Sauvignon Blanc (Santa Ynez Valley) $13. Shows how well this inland Santa Barbara County appellation ripens Sauvignon Blanc to perfection while maintaining the vital acidity the variety needs for balance. This charming wine brims with citrus, fig, green melon and sweet lemongrass flavors, and finishes dry, with a tart, juicy bite. Great value. **88 Best Buy** *—S.H. (11/1/2007)*

Brophy Clark 2002 Valley View Vineyard Sauvignon Blanc (Santa Ynez Valley) $13. 85 *—S.H. (9/1/2004)*

Brophy Clark 2001 Syrah (Santa Ynez Valley) $18. 85 *—S.H. (9/1/2004)*

Brophy Clark 1999 Syrah (Santa Ynez Valley) $18. 83 *(10/1/2001)*

Brophy Clark 1999 Edna Ranch Syrah (Edna Valley) $22. 87 *(11/1/2001)*

Brophy Clark 2005 Fess Parker Vineyards Syrah (Santa Ynez Valley) $20. What makes this Syrah difficult is the thin, weedy fruit, which accentuates both the acids and aggressive tannins. With peppery herb flavors and just a hint of cherried cassis, the wine is hard and unsatisfying, and is unlikely to age out. **83** *—S.H. (11/1/2007)*

Brophy Clark 2003 Rodney Shull Vineyard Syrah (Santa Ynez Valley) $18. 86 *—S.H. (12/31/2006)*

Brophy Clark 2002 Rodney Shull Vineyard Syrah (Santa Ynez Valley) $18. 86 *(9/1/2005)*

Brophy Clark 2000 Rodney's Vineyard Syrah (Santa Ynez Valley) $21. 85 *—S.H. (12/1/2002)*

Brophy Clark 2005 Zinfandel (Paso Robles) $18. You want brawny and brambly and briary? Take this Zin. With wildly mouthfilling berry, raisin, cranberry, coffee and peppery spice flavors, it finishes dry and clean. The alcohol is high, but in this case, it's exactly what a wine of this power requires. **89** *—S.H. (11/1/2007)*

Brophy Clark 2001 Lone Oak Vineyard Zinfandel (Paso Robles) $17. 85 *(11/1/2003)*

Brophy Clark 2000 Lone Oak Vineyard Zinfandel (Paso Robles) $17. 85 *—M.S. (9/1/2003)*

BROSSEAU

Brosseau 2005 Brosseau Vineyard Chardonnay (Chalone) $26. Bill Brosseau is Testarossa's winemaker and now he has his own brand, from his vineyard up in the Gavilan mountains. It's a very good Chard, a little tight in minerals and acidity, but oak adds richness to the tropical fruit and apricot flavors. It's delicious and a pretty good value. **90** *—S.H. (7/1/2007)*

Brosseau 2005 Cuvée Kilene Syrah (Chalone) $38. This Syrah is so good, it makes you wonder if the Chalone appellation isn't more Rhône than Burgundy. The vines were incredibly low-yielding, giving only 1.2 tons to the acre, and the flavors are intensely concentrated in cassis, black cherry, blueberry jam and vanilla mocha. Soft and gentle, the wine seems best now for its voluptuous fruit. **92** *—S.H. (10/1/2007)*

BROTHERHOOD

Brotherhood 2006 Riesling (New York) $11. With its faintly floral and citric nose and dry, almost tart flavors, this Riesling may be a touch austere for fans of a fruitier style. Flavors of lemon and spice are appealing but the wine lacks some complexity. **83** *—S.K. (2/1/2007)*

Brotherhood NV Blush Chablis Rosé Blend (New York) $7. Heavy apple aromas followed by a fresh, fruity flavor make this affordable blush an easy choice for a hot summer day on the patio. Pair with seafood or chicken salads. **83** *—S.K. (7/1/2007)*

Brotherhood NV Harvest Blush Catawba Rosé Blend (New York) $7. Semisweet with flavors of baked apple and honey, this blush wine is made from Catawba, a hybrid of Labrusca and other native species. In general, its character is quite sweet, but the winemakers at Brotherhood have counteracted that with good acidity. The wine has a strong character and is more in the dessert wine sphere, but the flavors are good and the finish appealing. **84 Best Buy** *—S.K. (7/1/2007)*

Brotherhood NV White Zinfandel (New York) $8. Light, floral aromas mingled with strawberry lead into a pretty, flavorful wine that's sweet but not cloying. A honeyed mouthfeel and clean finish, along with the affordable pricetag, make it an attractive selection for everyday quaffing. **84 Best Buy** *—S.K. (7/1/2007)*

BROWN ESTATE

Brown Estate 2001 Zinfandel (Napa Valley) $32. 92 *—J.M. (3/1/2004)*

BRUTOCAO

Brutocao 2005 Feliz Vineyard Barbera (Mendocino) $18. Has a sweaty aroma that's that's hard to get past. In the mouth, the wine is simple, sweet and sharp, with raspberry-mint jelly flavors. **80** *—S.H. (12/1/2007)*

Brutocao 2003 Cabernet Sauvignon (Mendocino) $20. 87 *—S.H. (12/15/2006)*

Brutocao 1996 Bliss Vineyard Cabernet Sauvignon (Mendocino) $16. 87 *—S.H. (3/1/2000)*

Brutocao 1997 Brutocao Vineyards Cabernet Sauvignon (Mendocino) $18. 88 *—P.G. (12/15/2000)*

Brutocao 2001 Estate Bottled Cabernet Sauvignon (Mendocino) $20. 83 *—S.H. (12/15/2005)*

Brutocao 2004 Reserve Cabernet Sauvignon (Mendocino) $36. Intensely flavored in blackberries, cherries, raspberries, cola and spicy oak, this has a simple structure, and finishes a little sweet. **84** *—S.H. (12/15/2007)*

Brutocao 2003 Riserva d'Argento Cabernet Sauvignon (Mendocino) $34. The sulfur was slow to blow off, but eventually a nice Cab emerged. Soft and gentle in texture, it has rich flavors of chocolate-covered cherries, black currants and spicy oak, with nice crunchy tannins. Drink now. **87** *—S.H. (7/1/2007)*

Brutocao 2002 Riserva d'Argento Cabernet Sauvignon (Mendocino) $34. 88 *—S.H. (11/1/2005)*

Brutocao 1999 Riserva d'Argento Cabernet Sauvignon (Mendocino) $32. 86 *—S.H. (5/1/2002)*

Brutocao 2002 Vineyard Select Cabernet Sauvignon (Mendocino) $25. 85 *—S.H. (11/1/2005)*

Brutocao 2005 Bliss Vineyard Chardonnay (Mendocino) $16. Hot and rustic, with the flavor of stewed peaches and apricots. Lacks the cool, creamy elegance you want in a nice Chard. **82** *—S.H. (5/1/2007)*

Brutocao 1998 Bliss Vineyard Chardonnay (Mendocino County) $15. 84 *(6/1/2000)*

Brutocao 1997 Bliss Vineyard Reserve Chardonnay (Mendocino) $23. 86 *—P.G. (10/1/2000)*

Brutocao 1999 Riserva d'Argento Chardonnay (Mendocino) $24. 90 *—S.H. (5/1/2002)*

Brutocao 2005 Feliz Vineyard Dolcetto (Mendocino) $18. Soft, simple and fairly sweet in fruity ripeness, this rustic wine has red cherry, leather and milk chocolate flavors, with a plumskin and sugar-cured tobacco edge. It's all wrapped into firm tannins. **84** *—S.H. (7/1/2007)*

Brutocao 2004 Feliz Vineyard Dolcetto (Mendocino) $18. 83 *—S.H. (12/15/2005)*

Brutocao 2002 Bliss Vineyard Select Merlot (Mendocino) $20. 84 *—S.H. (12/15/2005)*

Brutocao 2004 Bliss Vineyards Merlot (Mendocino) $20. This is a nice, smooth Merlot whose distinguishing feature is its structure. Keen acids and dusty tannins frame the fruit, coffee and tobacco flavors, and the finish is totally dry. Food-friendly, it just shows you don't need super-ripeness to make a good bottle of red wine. **88** *—S.H. (7/1/2007)*

Brutocao 2003 Bliss Vineyards Merlot (Mendocino) $20. 86 *—S.H. (12/15/2006)*

Brutocao 1996 Brutocao Vineyards Merlot (Mendocino) $18. 90 *—S.H. (3/1/2000)*

Brutocao 2004 Reserve Merlot (Mendocino) $34. A little on the sweet side, with cherry-berry, licorice, rum and coke, plum and new oak flavors and a superripe taste of raisins in the finish. Drink now. **84** *—S.H. (12/15/2007)*

Brutocao 2003 Riserva d'Argento Merlot (Mendocino) $34. 90 *—S.H. (12/15/2006)*

Brutocao 2002 Riserva d'Argento Merlot (Mendocino) $34. 84 *—S.H. (12/15/2005)*

Brutocao 1998 Riserva d'Argento Merlot (Mendocino) $32. 90 *—S.H. (5/1/2002)*

Brutocao 2005 Pinot Noir (Anderson Valley) $24. There could have been a very good wine here, but the fruit has a baked cherry pie flavor, like the gooey filling that drips out and gets caramelized in the oven, or maybe it's some kind of extra-charred oak. Whatever, it's a little too much of a good thing. **84** *—S.H. (6/1/2007)*

Brutocao 2004 Pinot Noir (Anderson Valley) $24. 87 *—S.H. (7/1/2006)*

Brutocao 1998 Feliz Vineyard Pinot Noir (Mendocino) $24. 87 *—P.G. (12/15/2000)*

Brutocao 2003 Riserva d'Argento Pinot Noir (Anderson Valley) $32. 91 *—S.H. (11/1/2005)*

Brutocao NV Bliss Vineyard Tawny Port Port (Mendocino) $26. Pretty good Port-like dessert wine, with tons of honeyed, brown sugar sweetness framing blackberry, cherry, chocolate truffle and coffee flavors. Not designed to age, it's best now with anything chocolaty. **87** *—S.H. (5/1/2007)*

Brutocao 2004 Feliz #62 Zinfandel Port (Mendocino) $32. 85 *—S.H. (7/1/2006)*

Brutocao 2004 Contento Vineyard Primitivo (Mendocino) $20. Soft and rustic, this Zin-like wine has spicy cassis and black cherry flavors veering all the way into chocolate-covered raisins. It's a succulent, country-style sipper, and the slightly caramelized sweetness suggests pairing with a sugar-cured baked ham. **87** *—S.H. (7/1/2007)*

Brutocao 2003 Contento Vineyard Primitivo (Mendocino) $18. 82 *—S.H. (11/1/2005)*

Brutocao 2002 Contento Vineyard Primitivo (Mendocino) $18. 86 *—J.M. (10/1/2004)*

Brutocao 2001 Coro Mendocino Red Blend (Mendocino) $35. 85 *—J.M. (9/1/2004)*

Brutocao 2003 Hopland Ranches Quadriga Red Blend (Mendocino) $24. 81 *—S.H. (11/15/2006)*

Brutocao 2004 Quadriga Red Blend (Mendocino) $24. Ripe and juicy, a deliciously balanced wine. It's an Italian Mediterranean blend of Sangiovese, Primitivo, Barbera and Dolcetto, one of the only ones of its type I know of in California. There should be more. **89** *—S.H. (7/1/2007)*

Brutocao 2001 Sauvignon Blanc (Mendocino County) $12. 84 *—J.M. (10/1/2003)*

Brutocao 1997 Bliss Vineyard Sauvignon Blanc (Mendocino) $15. 87 *—S.H. (3/1/2000)*

Brutocao 2003 Bliss Vineyards Sauvignon Blanc (Mendocino) $12. 84 *—J.M. (10/1/2004)*

Brutocao 2006 Feliz Vineyard Sauvignon Blanc (Mendocino) $14. Here's a crisp, refreshing SB that shows real elegance. It's dry and brisk in acids, with pleasant flavors of pineapples, dates, mangoes, vanilla and spices. **87** *—S.H. (11/15/2007)*

Brutocao 2005 Feliz Vineyard Sauvignon Blanc (Mendocino) $14. 85 *—S.H. (11/15/2006)*

Brutocao 2004 Feliz Vineyard Sauvignon Blanc (Mendocino) $12. 83 *—S.H. (11/1/2005)*

Brutocao 2004 Feliz Vineyard Syrah (Mendocino) $25. Shows a burnt edge that's either from the wood or from berries that baked under the sun; probably both. There's a charred, overripe raisin taste. This country-style wine lacks elegance and balance. **82** *—S.H. (6/1/2007)*

Brutocao 2003 Feliz Vineyard Select Syrah (Mendocino) $25. 86 *(9/1/2005)*

Brutocao 2002 Zinfandel (Mendocino) $20. 84 *—J.M. (10/1/2004)*

Brutocao 2001 Zinfandel (Mendocino) $18. 80 *(11/1/2003)*

Brutocao 2002 Bliss #3 Vineyard Zinfandel (Mendocino) $20. 88 *—J.M. (10/1/2004)*

Brutocao 1996 Bliss Vineyard Zinfandel (Mendocino) $15. 87 *—J.C. (5/1/2000)*

Brutocao 1999 Brutocao Vineyards Zinfandel (Mendocino) $16. 86 *—S.H. (5/1/2002)*

Brutocao 1998 Brutocao Vineyards Zinfandel (Mendocino) $18. 85 *—P.G. (3/1/2001)*

Brutocao 2003 Estate Zinfandel (Mendocino) $20. 81 *—S.H. (12/15/2005)*

Brutocao 2005 Hopland Ranches Zinfandel (Mendocino) $22. With overripe raisin flavors, this Zin has a stewed fruit flavor. In its favor is dryness and smooth tannins. But it really finishes hot, with an alcohol level of 15.2%. **83** *—S.H. (12/15/2007)*

Brutocao 2004 Hopland Ranches Zinfandel (Mendocino) $22. Brutocao's Zins always seem rustic to me, with the slightly sweet, Porty edge of a homemade wine. Nothing wrong with that, if it's your style, but it's not mine. If you like that sugary finish, it's a clean, fruity wine. **83** *—S.H. (5/1/2007)*

BUCKLIN

Bucklin 2005 Old Hill Ranch Vineyard Cabernet Sauvignon (Sonoma Valley) $30. There's a ton of Cabernet flavor here. The California sunshine of this warm appellation ripened the grapes to cassis and black cherry perfection. The oak and tannin structure is polished and fine, but acidity is a little low, so it's not an ager. Drink now through 2009 for its sheer lusciousness. **87** *—S.H. (12/15/2007)*

Bucklin 2005 Compagni Portis Vineyard Gewürztraminer (Sonoma Valley) $20. 90 *—S.H. (12/15/2006)*

Bucklin 2005 Old Hill Ranch Zinfandel (Sonoma Valley) $34. With the '05, Bucklin is getting a handle on this old-vine field blend of two dozen varieties, which seems to do best in cooler years. It's a rustic-chic wine, with a brawny muscularity tamed by extreme dryness, and even though the alcohol is 15.6%, it doesn't feel too hot. **87** *—S.H. (12/15/2007)*

Bucklin 2004 Old Hill Ranch Zinfandel (Sonoma Valley) $34. 86 *—S.H. (12/15/2006)*

Bucklin 2001 Old Hill Ranch Zinfandel (Sonoma Valley) $30. 88 *(11/1/2003)*

BUEHLER

Buehler 2002 Chardonnay (Russian River Valley) $10. 81 *—S.H. (12/15/2005)*

Buehler 2000 Reserve Chardonnay (Russian River Valley) $30. 86 *—S.H. (2/1/2003)*

Buehler 2001 Zinfandel (Napa Valley) $14. 88 *—J.M. (9/1/2004)*

Buehler 1997 Estate Zinfandel (Napa Valley) $18. 89 *—P.G. (11/15/1999)*

BUENA VISTA

Buena Vista 2000 Cabernet Sauvignon (Carneros) $20. 87 *—S.H. (4/1/2003)*

Buena Vista 2000 Cabernet Sauvignon (California) $9. 85 Best Buy *—S.H. (11/15/2002)*

Buena Vista 1998 Cabernet Sauvignon (Carneros) $17. 90 Editors' Choice *—S.H. (11/15/2001)*

Buena Vista 1997 Cabernet Sauvignon (Carneros) $18. 90 Editors' Choice *—S.H. (5/1/2001)*

Buena Vista 1996 Cabernet Sauvignon (Carneros) $18. 88 *—M.M. (6/1/1999)*

Buena Vista 1995 Grand Reserve Cabernet Sauvignon (Carneros) $27. 90 *—M.M. (6/1/1999)*

Buena Vista 2005 Chardonnay (Carneros) $19. Shows the bright acidity of Carneros, which seems even brighter this cool vintage. That accentuates the lush flavors of puréed pineapples, guavas, nectarines, butterscotch and honey, leading to a long, spicy, rewarding finish. Easy to find, with more than 16,000 cases produced. **90 Editors' Choice** *—S.H. (11/1/2007)*

Buena Vista 2004 Chardonnay (Carneros) $20. 87 *(10/1/2006)*

Buena Vista 2000 Chardonnay (California) $8. 86 Best Buy *—S.H. (12/15/2002)*

Buena Vista 1999 Chardonnay (Carneros) $18. 88 *—S.H. (2/1/2003)*

Buena Vista 1998 Chardonnay (Carneros) $14. 88 Best Buy *—S.H. (12/31/2001)*

Buena Vista 1997 Chardonnay (Carneros) $15. 89 Best Buy *—S.H. (6/1/2000)*

Buena Vista 1996 Estate Chardonnay (Carneros) $14. 87 *—M.M. (6/1/1999)*

Buena Vista 1997 Grand Reserve Chardonnay (Carneros) $28. 89 *(6/1/2000)*

Buena Vista 1996 Grand Reserve Chardonnay (Carneros) $26. 91 *—M.M. (6/1/1999)*

Buena Vista 2004 Ramal Vineyard Chardonnay (Carneros) $34. 90 *(10/1/2006)*

Buena Vista 2003 Ramal Vineyard Chardonnay (Carneros) $32. 89 *—S.H. (12/15/2005)*

Buena Vista 2004 Ramal Vineyard Clone 17RY Chardonnay (Carneros) $34. 94 Editors' Choice *—S.H. (8/3/2006)*

Buena Vista 2003 Ramal Vineyard Clone 17RY Chardonnay (Carneros) $32. 92 *—S.H. (12/15/2005)*

Buena Vista 2003 Ramal Vineyard Clone 96 Chardonnay (Carneros) $32. 92 *—S.H. (12/15/2005)*

Buena Vista 2004 Ramal Vineyard Dijon Clones Chardonnay (Carneros) $34. 93 *—S.H. (8/3/2006)*

Buena Vista 2004 Merlot (Carneros) $21. There are some problems here, beginning with a vegetal, asparagus smell and ending with a soft, simple syrup finish. In between are some decent cherry flavors wrapped into harsh tannins. **82** *—S.H. (12/1/2007)*

Buena Vista 2003 Merlot (Carneros) $25. 86 *(10/1/2006)*

Buena Vista 2000 Merlot (California) $9. 88 Best Buy *—S.H. (11/15/2002)*

Buena Vista 1999 Merlot (Carneros) $22. 86 *—S.H. (2/1/2003)*

Buena Vista 1998 Merlot (Carneros) $18. 89 Editors' Choice *—S.H. (11/15/2001)*

Buena Vista 1998 Merlot (California) $10. 86 Best Buy *—S.H. (5/1/2001)*

Buena Vista 1996 Estate Merlot (Carneros) $19. 85 *—M.M. (6/1/1999)*

Buena Vista 2004 Pinot Noir (Carneros) $22. 87 *(10/1/2006)*

Buena Vista 2000 Pinot Noir (Carneros) $22. 86 *—S.H. (2/1/2003)*

Buena Vista 1999 Pinot Noir (Carneros) $17. 91 Best Buy *—S.H. (12/15/2001)*

Buena Vista 1998 Pinot Noir (Carneros) $17. 89 *—S.H. (5/1/2001)*

Buena Vista 1996 Estate Pinot Noir (Carneros) $16. 87 *—M.M. (6/1/1999)*

Buena Vista 1996 Grand Reserve Pinot Noir (Carneros) $26. 92 *—M.M. (6/1/1999)*

Buena Vista 2004 Ramal Vineyard Pinot Noir (Carneros) $38. 89 *(10/1/2006)*

Buena Vista 2003 Ramal Vineyard Pinot Noir (Carneros) $38. 85 *—S.H. (12/15/2005)*

Buena Vista 2004 Ramal Vineyard Dijon Clones Pinot Noir (Carneros) $NA. 92 *—S.H. (8/3/2006)*

Buena Vista 2003 Ramal Vineyard Pommard Clone 5 Pinot Noir (Carneros) $38. 89 *—S.H. (12/15/2005)*

Buena Vista 2004 Ramal Vineyard Swan Selection Pinot Noir (Carneros) $NA. 92 Cellar Selection *—S.H. (8/3/2006)*

Buena Vista 2002 Reserve Pinot Noir (Carneros) $15. 86 *(11/1/2004)*

Buena Vista 2001 Sauvignon Blanc (Lake County) $7. 90 *—S.H. (9/1/2003)*

Buena Vista 2000 Sauvignon Blanc (California) $8. 86 Best Buy *—S.H. (11/15/2001)*

Buena Vista 1999 Sauvignon Blanc (California) $9. 87 Best Buy *—S.H. (5/1/2001)*

Buena Vista 2004 Syrah (Carneros) $25. 86 *(10/1/2006)*

Buena Vista 2004 Ramal Vineyard Syrah (Carneros) $38. 89 *(10/1/2006)*

Buena Vista 1998 Harazsthy Collection White Blend (Carneros) $25. 88 *—S.H. (8/1/2001)*

Buena Vista 2001 Zinfandel (California) $9. 87 Best Buy *(11/1/2003)*

Buena Vista 2000 Zinfandel (California) $9. 90 Best Buy *—S.H. (12/1/2002)*

BUFFALO RIDGE

Buffalo Ridge 1999 French Camp Vineyard Chardonnay (Central Coast) $13. 87 *—S.H. (11/15/2001)*

Buffalo Ridge 1999 Reserve-Bien Nacido Vineyard Chardonnay (Central Coast) $20. 88 *—S.H. (11/15/2001)*

Buffalo Ridge 1999 French Camp Vineyard Syrah (Central Coast) $12. 83 *(10/1/2001)*

Buffalo Ridge 1998 French Camp Zinfandel (Central Coast) $12. 82 *—P.G. (3/1/2001)*

Buffalo Ridge 1999 French Camp Vineyard Zinfandel (Central Coast) $12. 84 *—D.T. (3/1/2002)*

BUGAY

Bugay 2003 Cabernet Sauvignon (Sonoma County) $58. 90 *—S.H. (7/1/2006)*

Bugay 2004 Sauvignon Blanc (Dry Creek Valley) $22. 90 *—S.H. (7/1/2006)*

Bugay 2003 Syrah (Sonoma County) $48. 92 *—S.H. (7/1/2006)*

BULLY HILL

Bully Hill 2002 Cabernet Franc (New York) $10. Tea, cigar and cedar on the nose lead into a very dry, tannic blend of pepper and spice on this Cabernet Franc from historic Bully Hill. There's no dimension here, and there's a lack of the bright raspberry, plum and cherry flavors that balance out the heft in this varietal. 80 *—S.K. (2/1/2007)*

Bully Hill NV Elise Chardonnay (North Fork of Long Island) $8. This offering from North Fork veteran Bully Hill is more about nostalgia than true Chardonnay character, whether your taste runs dry or unoaked. Bright fruit aromas are roadblocked by an angular mouthfeel and one-dimensional flavors—there is a hint of citrus but it fizzles fast on the palate and there is little trace of the oak that purports to be in the mix. 80 *—S.K. (2/1/2007)*

Bully Hill 2003 Merlot (New York) $10. 80 *—M.D. (12/1/2006)*

Bully Hill 2003 Pinot Noir (New York) $10. 84 *—M.D. (12/1/2006)*

Bully Hill 2002 Riesling (New York) $9. 86 *—J.C. (7/15/2003)*

BUNNELL FAMILY CELLAR

Bunnell Family Cellar 2005 Northridge Vineyard Mourvèdre (Wahluke Slope) $38. Scents of roses and white pepper are wrapped into a dark, tannic, sturdy red that opens out and miraculously expresses itself with a strong floral component despite its muscularity. This is unique, distinctive and delicious, with tight spice. It has a big front and a quick finish. 91 *—P.G. (11/1/2007)*

Bunnell Family Cellar 2005 Stonetree Vineyard à pic Red Blend (Wahluke Slope) $28. This Rhône-style picnic red is a blend of 47% Syrah, 29% Grenache, 12% Cinsault and 12% Mourvèdre. Scented with the spicy authority of the Syrah, the other grapes add meat and muscle and spread the flavors broadly out across the palate. It's got a good mix of smoke, spicy fruit, meat and sage. The name means "at the moment" and the moment is still a ways away, so air this one out. 90 *—P.G. (11/1/2007)*

Bunnell Family Cellar 2005 vif Red Blend (Columbia Valley (WA)) $28. Bright and snappy, this blend of three quarters Syrah and one quarter Mourvèdre sports lots of cranberry and rhubarb fruit flavors; there's plenty of zip to it. The cool climate Syrah piles on plenty of herb and spice, and there is a strong herbal underpinning throughout, but the wine remains lively and tart. 89 *—P.G. (11/1/2007)*

Bunnell Family Cellar NV Vif Red Wine Red Blend (Columbia Valley (WA)) $25. 89 *—P.G. (10/1/2006)*

Bunnell Family Cellar 2004 Syrah (Horse Heaven Hills) $40. 91 *—P.G. (11/15/2006)*

Bunnell Family Cellar 2005 Boushey-McPherson Vineyard Syrah (Yakima Valley) $38. This is Washington Cote Rôtie; smoky, meaty and dense. It is very tart, with cranberry fruit packed with dense layers of dried herbs and smoked meats. Extremely young, sharp, edgy and herbal, it needs a lot more time. But it's got the kind of organic, lightly funky detail that you see in Cayuse, the kind of detail that promises greatness in the future. 93 *—P.G. (11/1/2007)*

Bunnell Family Cellar 2004 Boushey-McPherson Vineyard Syrah (Yakima Valley) $35. 92 *—P.G. (10/1/2006)*

Bunnell Family Cellar 2005 Clifton Hill Vineyard Syrah (Wahluke Slope) $38. Spicy, sharp and tight, this is packed with compact herbs, spicy fruit, smoke and black tar. Tannins remain sharp-edged and a bit unforgiving for now. Very young, herbal and aggressive, this is a wine that has the structure and power to develop complex, unique flavors in the bottle. Definitely needs more time. 91 *—P.G. (11/1/2007)*

Bunnell Family Cellar 2004 Clifton Hill Vineyard Syrah (Wahluke Slope) $37. 90 *—P.G. (10/1/2006)*

Bunnell Family Cellar 2006 Talcott Vineyard Viognier (Columbia Valley (WA)) $20. Stainless fermented, finished in neutral barrels. Talcott is a warm site, which produces a completely different expression of the grape from the winery's other Viognier. In fact, this is more like a ripe, rich Chardonnay, buttery and round, with toast and butterscotch flavors supporting the tight, citrus (lime, grapefruit) edge. 88 *—P.G. (11/1/2007)*

BURFORD & BROWN

Burford & Brown 2002 Barbera (Dry Creek Valley) $15. 86 *—S.H. (9/1/2004)*

Burford & Brown 2005 The Crusader Syrah (Amador County) $20. A honeyed, velvety-smooth wine. It's ultrarich in cherry pie, raspberry cream and white chocolate truffle flavors, although it's technically dry. The soft tannins, glycerine and high alcohol add to the perception of sweetness. 86 *—S.H. (10/1/2007)*

BURGESS

Burgess 2000 Enveiere Bordeaux Blend (Napa Valley) $48. This is Burgess's Bordeaux blend, typically held back far longer than any wine in California I know of. But time has not done the 2000 much good. The wine is dry and vegetal, and not going anywhere. 82 *—S.H. (7/1/2007)*

Burgess 1999 Enveiere Bordeaux Blend (Napa Valley) $70. 91 *—S.H. (10/1/2003)*

Burgess 2004 Cabernet Sauvignon (Napa Valley) $30. Simple, easy and balanced, this crowd-pleasing Cab will satisfy for its wealth of ripe fruit and oak flavors. Floods the mouth with cassis, licorice and melted milk chocolate, wrapped in smooth, gentle tannins. 86 *—S.H. (12/1/2007)*

Burgess 2003 Cabernet Sauvignon (Napa Valley) $30. This basic Cab from Burgess is rich and ripe, with slightly sweet cherry, blackberry and oaky flavors. It's a little simple, but well-structured. Drink now. 86 *—S.H. (4/1/2007)*

Burgess 1997 Cabernet Sauvignon (Napa Valley) $33. 88 *(11/1/2000)*

Burgess 1999 Cabernet Sauvignon (Napa Valley) $38. 90 *—S.H. (2/1/2003)*

Burgess 1998 Enveiere Cabernet Sauvignon (Napa Valley) $75. 90 *—D.T. (6/1/2002)*

Burgess 2002 Vintage Selection Cabernet Sauvignon (Napa Valley) $36. 83 *—S.H. (5/1/2006)*

Burgess 2001 Vintage Selection Cabernet Sauvignon (Napa Valley) $36. 89 *—S.H. (7/1/2005)*

Burgess 2000 Vintage Selection Cabernet Sauvignon (Napa Valley) $39. 85 *—S.H. (11/15/2003)*

Burgess 1998 Vintage Selection Cabernet Sauvignon (Napa Valley) $35. 89 *—S.H. (9/12/2002)*

Burgess 1998 Chardonnay (Napa Valley) $18. 91 *(6/1/2000)*

Burgess 2000 Triere Estate Vineyard Chardonnay (Napa Valley) $22. 86 *—S.H. (2/1/2003)*

Burgess 2003 Merlot (Napa Valley) $22. 83 *—S.H. (5/1/2006)*

Burgess 2004 Merlot (Howell Mountain) $22. Feels hot, soft and thin in the mouth, a real disappointment from a winery that could do better. The absence of fruit just exaggerrates the alcohol and tannins. 82 *—S.H. (11/1/2007)*

Burgess 2002 Merlot (Napa Valley) $20. 88 *—S.H. (7/1/2005)*

Burgess 2000 Merlot (Napa Valley) $25. 87 *—S.H. (8/1/2003)*

Burgess 1999 Merlot (Napa Valley) $28. 91 *—S.H. (9/12/2002)*

Burgess 1998 Merlot (Napa Valley) $28. 88 *—S.H. (6/1/2001)*

Burgess 2004 Syrah (Napa Valley) $22. There's a touch of raisiny over-ripeness in this dry Syrah, not a lot, but just enough to confuse the palate. Other than that, the wine is as smooth as can be, with a chocolate and bitter cherry finish. 87 *—S.H. (12/1/2007)*

Burgess 2003 Syrah (Napa Valley) $22. Here's a very ripe Syrah, deep in chocolate, blackberry, currant, licorice and leather flavors. It's smooth and polished now, and should be opened in the next year or two. 85 *—S.H. (5/1/2007)*

Burgess 2001 Syrah (Lake County) $19. 85 *(9/1/2005)*

Burgess 2001 Syrah (Napa Valley) $22. 86 *(9/1/2005)*

Burgess 2000 Syrah (Lake County) $22. 87 *—S.H. (10/1/2003)*

Burgess 2000 Syrah (Napa Valley) $22. 86 *—S.H. (2/1/2003)*

Burgess 1997 Zinfandel (Napa Valley) $16. 86 *—S.H. (5/1/2000)*

Burgess 2000 Zinfandel (Napa Valley) $22. 90 Editors' Choice *—S.H. (9/1/2003)*

Burgess 1999 Zinfandel (Napa Valley) $22. 90 *—S.H. (9/12/2002)*

Burgess 1998 Zinfandel (Russian River Valley) $18. 83 *—D.T. (3/1/2002)*

BURRELL SCHOOL VINEYARDS

Burrell School Vineyards 2002 Valedictorian Cabernet Blend (Santa Cruz Mountains) $50. 87 *—S.H. (10/1/2005)*

Burrell School Vineyards 2002 Estate Pichon Voneyard Cabernet Franc (Santa Cruz Mountains) $30. 87 *—S.H. (7/1/2005)*

Burrell School Vineyards 2001 Ryan Oaks Vineyard Zinfandel (Amador County) $20. 83 *(11/1/2003)*

BUSH-FIELD

Bush-Field 2005 Sonoma Mountain-Top Vineyards Pinot Noir (Sonoma Valley) $54. Awkward. Despite some cherry jam and candied licorice flavors, accented by quite a bit of oak, there's a semisweet sharpness in the finish reminiscent of cough medicine, and a touch of sweaty funk. 83 *—S.H. (10/1/2007)*

BUTTERFIELD STATION

Butterfield Station 2000 Cabernet Sauvignon (California) $7. 82 *—S.H. (12/31/2002)*

Butterfield Station 2001 Chardonnay (California) $7. 84 *—S.H. (12/15/2002)*

Butterfield Station 2000 Chardonnay (California) $8. 81 *—J.M. (12/15/2002)*

Butterfield Station 2000 Merlot (California) $8. 81 *—S.H. (12/31/2002)*

Butterfield Station 2000 Syrah (California) $7. 86 Best Buy *—S.H. (12/1/2002)*

BUTTONWOOD FARM

Buttonwood Farm 1997 Trevin Bordeaux Blend (Santa Ynez Valley) $30. 87 *—S.H. (4/1/2003)*

Buttonwood Farm 1996 Trevin Bordeaux Blend (Santa Ynez Valley) $26. 84 *—S.H. (12/31/2001)*

Buttonwood Farm 1999 Cabernet Franc (Santa Ynez Valley) $18. 85 *—S.H. (5/1/2003)*

Buttonwood Farm 1998 Cabernet Franc (Santa Ynez Valley) $18. 84 *—S.H. (9/1/2002)*

Buttonwood Farm 1995 Cabernet Franc (Santa Ynez Valley) $18. 84 *—S.H. (9/1/1999)*

Buttonwood Farm 1995 Cabernet Sauvignon (Santa Ynez Valley) $18. 84 *—S.H. (7/1/1999)*

Buttonwood Farm 2000 Cabernet Sauvignon (Santa Ynez Valley) $24. 85 *—S.H. (11/15/2004)*

Buttonwood Farm 1998 Cabernet Sauvignon (Santa Ynez Valley) $18. 85 *—S.H. (6/1/2002)*

Buttonwood Farm 1997 Cabernet Sauvignon (Santa Ynez Valley) $18. 86 *—S.H. (12/15/2000)*

Buttonwood Farm 1997 Marsanne (Santa Ynez Valley) $12. 88 *—S.H. (10/1/1999)*

Buttonwood Farm 2002 Marsanne (Santa Ynez Valley) $12. 86 *—S.H. (12/15/2004)*

Buttonwood Farm 1999 Marsanne (Santa Ynez Valley) $12. 85 *—S.H. (8/1/2001)*

Buttonwood Farm 1998 Marsanne (Santa Ynez Valley) $12. 87 *—S.H. (11/15/2000)*

Buttonwood Farm 1996 Merlot (Santa Ynez Valley) $18. 90 *—S.H. (12/31/1999)*

Buttonwood Farm 1995 Merlot (Santa Ynez Valley) $18. 88 *—S.H. (9/1/1999)*

Buttonwood Farm 2001 Merlot (Santa Ynez Valley) $18. 86 *—S.H. (12/15/2004)*

Buttonwood Farm 2000 Merlot (Santa Ynez Valley) $18. 88 *—S.H. (9/1/2004)*

Buttonwood Farm 1999 Merlot (Santa Ynez Valley) $18. 86 *—S.H. (4/1/2003)*

Buttonwood Farm 1998 Merlot (Santa Ynez Valley) $18. 88 *—S.H. (6/1/2002)*

Buttonwood Farm 1997 Merlot (Santa Ynez Valley) $18. 82 *—S.H. (11/15/2000)*

Buttonwood Farm 1999 Trevin Merlot (Santa Ynez Valley) $30. 88 *—J.M. (4/1/2004)*

Buttonwood Farm 2001 Devin Pinot Noir (Santa Ynez Valley) $16. 87 *—S.H. (4/1/2004)*

Buttonwood Farm 1998 Sauvignon Blanc (Santa Ynez Valley) $12. 86 *—S.H. (9/1/1999)*

Buttonwood Farm 2004 Sauvignon Blanc (Santa Ynez Valley) $14. 89 Best Buy *—S.H. (2/1/2006)*

Buttonwood Farm 2003 Sauvignon Blanc (Santa Ynez Valley) $14. 86 *—S.H. (10/1/2005)*

Buttonwood Farm 2002 Sauvignon Blanc (Santa Ynez Valley) $14. 90 *—S.H. (9/1/2004)*

Buttonwood Farm 2001 Sauvignon Blanc (Santa Ynez Valley) $12. 86 *—S.H. (3/1/2003)*

Buttonwood Farm 2000 Sauvignon Blanc (Santa Ynez Valley) $12. 86 *—S.H. (12/15/2001)*

Buttonwood Farm 1999 Sauvignon Blanc (Santa Ynez Valley) $12. 87 *—S.H. (11/15/2000)*

Buttonwood Farm 2001 Devin Sauvignon Blanc-Sémillon (Santa Ynez Valley) $16. 86 *—J.M. (6/1/2004)*

Buttonwood Farm 2000 Devin Sémillon-Sauvignon Blanc (Santa Ynez Valley) $16. 89 *—S.H. (7/1/2003)*

Buttonwood Farm 2001 Syrah (Santa Ynez Valley) $22. 85 *—S.H. (12/15/2004)*

Buttonwood Farm 1998 Syrah (Santa Ynez Valley) $22. 87 *(11/1/2001)*

Buttonwood Farm 2003 Rosé Syrah (Santa Ynez Valley) $16. 86 *—S.H. (12/15/2004)*

Buttonwood Farm 1997 Syrah-Cabernet (Santa Ynez Valley) $30. 92 Editors' Choice *—S.H. (8/1/2001)*

Buttonwood Farm 1999 Devin White Blend (Santa Ynez Valley) $16. 88 *—S.H. (12/15/2001)*

Buttonwood Farm 1997 Devin White Blend (Santa Ynez Valley) $16. 88 *—S.H. (9/1/1999)*

BUTY

Buty 2003 Columbia Rediviva Cabernet Sauvignon-Syrah (Columbia Valley (WA)) $40. The grapes —57% Cabernet Sauvignon and 43% Syrah—come from Champoux and Cailloux, and the wine is bursting at the seams with bright berry flavors, quite young and still tart and tight. It needs to be aired out to release the compact, powerful fruit and smooth the tannins, but despite its edgy acidity it shows a bounty of spice, moist earth and ripe tannins balanced against the sweet-tart blackberry juice. 91 *—P.G. (3/1/2007)*

Buty 2002 Columbia Rediviva Cabernet Sauvignon-Syrah (Columbia Valley (WA)) $40. 91 *—P.G. (4/1/2006)*

Buty 2001 Columbia Rediviva Cabernet Sauvignon-Syrah (Columbia Valley (WA)) $40. 87 *—P.G. (6/1/2005)*

Buty 2002 Conner Lee Chardonnay (Columbia Valley (WA)) $25. 89 *—P.G. (11/15/2004)*

Buty 2005 Conner Lee Vineyard Chardonnay (Columbia Valley (WA)) $30. Rich, lush and creamy, this barrel fermented (in 1–4 year-old Burgundy barrels) Chardonnay has brilliant fruit flavors of apples and white peaches, shot through with butterscotch and caramel. The finish, though not exactly sweet, has a pleasing candy quality. This is distinctive and delicious, never palate-fatiguing, and beautifully balanced. 93 *—P.G. (3/1/2007)*

Buty 2004 Conner Lee Vineyard Chardonnay (Columbia Valley (WA)) $28. 91 —*P.G. (4/1/2006)*

Buty 2002 Roza Bergé Chardonnay (Yakima Valley) $25. 89 —*P.G. (11/15/2004)*

Buty 2005 Merlot-Cabernet Franc (Columbia Valley (WA)) $35. The final blend was done right before bottling, and this young wine is still knitting itself together. The Cab Franc contributes a lovely, graceful aromatic layer with pretty strawberry and brioche; while the Merlot is the dark fruit foundation, with nicely-applied cinnamon spice. A floral quality emerges as the wine breathes. **92** —*P.G. (8/1/2007)*

Buty 2002 Merlot-Cabernet Franc (Columbia Valley (WA)) $35. 90 —*P.G. (11/15/2004)*

Buty 2003 Merlot-Cabernet Franc Red Blend (Columbia Valley (WA)) $35. 91 —*P.G. (12/15/2005)*

Buty 2004 Rediviva of the Stones Red Blend (Walla Walla (WA)) $40. This 72% Syrah/ 28% Cab Sauvignon blend, from the biodynamic Cailloux vineyard, displays characteristic aromas that mix silage, moist earth, resin, green tea and mixed herbal aromatics. The base flavor is bready, yeasty, leesy; the fruits are compact and hinting at pomegranate, strawberry and red plum. The Cab adds a pleasing minerality to the finish. Cellar Candidate (up to 10 years). **94** —*P.G. (8/1/2007)*

Buty 2005 Semillon-Sauvignon Blanc (Columbia Valley (WA)) $21. This outstanding Bordeaux blanc-style wine is consistent with recent vintages, which is to say very smooth, round, rich and toasty. Still young, it is showing a lot of pretty new oak toast, and somewhat waxy peach and fig fruit.The Semillon comprises 73% of the blend, within a percentage of the '04, and has been crushed and then fermented and matured in neutral Burgundy barrels. The SB has been tank-fermented. Very tasty, with potential to improve still further over the next couple of years. **92** —*P.G. (3/1/2007)*

Buty 2004 Sémillon-Sauvignon Blanc (Columbia Valley (WA)) $21. 93 Editors' Choice —*P.G. (4/1/2006)*

Buty 2002 Sémillon-Sauvignon Blanc (Columbia Valley (WA)) $18. 88 —*P.G. (11/15/2004)*

Buty 2002 Rediviva of the Stones Syrah (Walla Walla (WA)) $40. 85 *(9/1/2005)*

Buty 2001 Rediviva of the Stones Syrah-Cabernet (Walla Walla (WA)) $35. 90 Editors' Choice —*P.G. (11/15/2004)*

Buty 2000 Sémillon-Sauvignon Blanc White Blend (Columbia Valley (WA)) $18. 88 —*P.G. (9/1/2002)*

BYINGTON

Byington 2003 Alliage Cabernet Sauvignon (Paso Robles) $26. Soft and somewhat simple, with lots of liqueur-like cherry, cassis, chocolate, coffee, spice and oak flavors, but not much structure. Best now. **86** —*S.H. (9/1/2007)*

Byington 2003 Bates Ranch Vineyard Cabernet Sauvignon (Santa Cruz Mountains) $35. Soft and ripe, this Cab has polished cherry, blackberry and black raspberry flavors, enriched with spicy, toasty oak. Seems to typify a well-grown, well-made California Cabernet that got plenty of heat during the growing season. Drink now. **87** —*S.H. (9/1/2007)*

Byington 2004 Cerro Prieto Cabernet Sauvignon (Paso Robles) $32. I like this wine for the way it mimics Napa cult Cab, yet carves out a distinct identity. Like Napa, it's dry, soft and ripely opulent, with rich blackberry, cassis, cherry, cocoa and oak flavors, housed in sweet, finely ground tannins. Yet there's an earthy, tobacco and sassafras quality that suggests real terroir. Showing its best now. **91** —*S.H. (9/1/2007)*

Byington 1995 Santa Cruz Mountains Cabernet Sauvignon (Santa Cruz County) $23. 91 —*S.H. (7/1/1999)*

Byington 2003 Signature Cabernet Sauvignon (Paso Robles) $45. There are some pretty features to this wine, namely the lovely tannins and rich fruit, but it's just too soft and sweet. Tastes like blackberry jam, with extra white sugar spinkled on top. **83** —*S.H. (9/1/2007)*

Byington 2001 Smith-Riechel Vineyard Cabernet Sauvignon (Alexander Valley) $29. 86 —*S.H. (10/1/2004)*

Byington 1998 Chardonnay (Santa Cruz Mountains) $20. 87 *(6/1/2000)*

Byington 1997 Chardonnay (Santa Cruz Mountains) $17. 83 —*L.W. (11/15/1999)*

Byington 2002 Chardonnay (Santa Cruz Mountains) $22. 90 —*S.H. (12/1/2004)*

Byington 2002 Chardonnay (Sonoma County) $22. 86 —*S.H. (12/1/2004)*

Byington 2004 Quenneville Vineyard Chardonnay (Santa Cruz Mountains) $35. Here's a dry Chardonnay, notable for its firm structure. Acidity and oak tannins provide the framework for the candied Meyer lemon, mango, floral, mineral and buttered toast flavors. There's a touch of bitterness in the finish that suggests very modest aging. Drink now through 2008. **90** —*S.H. (8/1/2007)*

Byington 1997 Santa Cruz Mountains Chardonnay (Santa Cruz Mountains) $20. 90 —*S.H. (7/1/1999)*

Byington 2004 Estate Pinot Noir (Santa Cruz Mountains) $35. Opens with pleasant aromas of cherry and raspberry purée, cola, Asian spice, vanilla and toasted marshmallow, then turns opulently fruity and dry in the mouth. It's not light-bodied, though; shows a weight of tannic density that suggests serious pairings, such as lamb and steak. **89** —*S.H. (8/1/2007)*

Byington 2002 Hastings Ranch Pinot Noir (Paso Robles) $24. 81 *(11/1/2004)*

Byington 2002 Van der Kamp Vineyard Pinot Noir (Sonoma Mountain) $30. 84 *(11/1/2004)*

Byington 2002 Alliage Red Blend (Sonoma County) $24. 87 —*S.H. (12/1/2005)*

Byington 2002 Hastings Ranch Zinfandel (Paso Robles) $24. 85 —*S.H. (12/15/2004)*

BYRON

Byron 1998 Chardonnay (Santa Maria Valley) $20. 87 *(6/1/2000)*

Byron 1997 Chardonnay (Santa Maria Valley) $19. 91 —*L.W. (11/15/1999)*

Byron 2003 Chardonnay (Santa Maria Valley) $25. 88 —*S.H. (5/1/2006)*

Byron 2002 Chardonnay (Santa Maria Valley) $25. 90 —*S.H. (12/15/2004)*

Byron 2001 Chardonnay (Santa Maria Valley) $24. 89 —*S.H. (12/15/2003)*

Byron 1997 Byron Vineyard Chardonnay (Santa Maria Valley) $32. 90 —*S.H. (2/1/2001)*

Byron 1996 Estate Chardonnay (Santa Maria Valley) $32. 91 —*S.H. (7/1/1999)*

Byron 1999 Nielson Vineyard Chardonnay (Santa Maria Valley) $40. 93 —*S.H. (12/15/2002)*

Byron 1998 Nielson Historic Vines Chardonnay (Santa Maria Valley) $75. 91 *(7/1/2001)*

Byron 2002 Nielson Vineyard Chardonnay (Santa Maria Valley) $35. 92 Cellar Selection —*S.H. (5/1/2006)*

Byron 2001 Nielson Vineyard Chardonnay (Santa Maria Valley) $30. 92 —*S.H. (2/1/2005)*

Byron 2000 Nielson Vineyard Chardonnay (Santa Maria Valley) $30. 90 —*S.H. (12/31/2003)*

Byron 1998 Nielson Vineyard Chardonnay (Santa Maria Valley) $35. 90 *(7/1/2001)*

Byron 1996 Reserve Chardonnay (Santa Maria Valley) $24. 90 —*S.H. (7/1/1999)*

Byron 2000 Sierra Madre Chardonnay (Santa Maria Valley) $30. 91 —*S.H. (9/1/2004)*

Byron 1998 Sierra Madre Chardonnay (Santa Maria Valley) $35. 92 —*S.H. (9/1/2002)*

Byron 1999 Sierra Madre Vineyard Chardonnay (Santa Maria Valley) $35. 93 —*S.H. (12/15/2002)*

Byron 1997 Pinot Blanc (Santa Maria Valley) $16. 88 —*S.H. (9/1/1999)*

Byron 2004 Pinot Blanc (Santa Maria Valley) $20. 89 —*S.H. (7/1/2006)*

Byron 2004 Pinot Noir (Santa Maria Valley) $25. 90 Editors' Choice —*S.H. (11/1/2006)*

Byron 2003 Pinot Noir (Santa Maria Valley) $25. 89 —*S.H. (12/15/2005)*

Byron 2002 Pinot Noir (Santa Maria Valley) $25. 89 *(11/1/2004)*

Byron 2000 Pinot Noir (Santa Maria Valley) $25. 83 *(10/1/2002)*

Byron 1998 Pinot Noir (Santa Maria Valley) $25. 89 —*S.H. (7/1/2002)*

Byron 1997 Pinot Noir (Santa Maria Valley) $20. 88 *(10/1/1999)*

Byron 2002 Bien Nacido Vineyard Pinot Noir (Santa Maria Valley) $40. 89 *(11/1/2004)*

Byron 1996 Byron Estate Vineyard Pinot Noir (Santa Maria Valley) $40. 89 *(10/1/1999)*

Byron 2003 Nielson Vineyard Pinot Noir (Santa Maria Valley) $40. 92 —*S.H. (7/1/2006)*

Byron 2002 Nielson Vineyard Pinot Noir (Santa Maria Valley) $40. 94 Editors' Choice —*S.H. (12/15/2005)*

Byron 2001 Nielson Vineyard Pinot Noir (Santa Maria Valley) $40. 93 —*S.H. (12/15/2004)*

Byron 2000 Nielson Vineyard Pinot Noir (Santa Maria Valley) $40. 89 —*S.H. (12/1/2004)*

Byron 1999 Nielson Vineyard Pinot Noir (Santa Maria Valley) $45. 90 *(10/1/2002)*

Byron 1999 Sierra Madre Pinot Noir (Santa Maria Valley) $45. 88 *(10/1/2002)*

Byron 1997 Sierra Madre Vineyard Pinot Noir (Santa Maria Valley) $32. 90 *—S.H. (12/15/2000)*

Byron 1999 IO Red Blend (Santa Barbara County) $60. 92 *—S.H. (12/1/2002)*

C. BECK

C. Beck 2004 Petite Sirah (Napa Valley) $35. From a Calistoga vineyard, this is a wine Pet fans will celebrate. Inky black and concentrated, it's lush in pastry-filling blackberry, cherry, plum, chocolate and coffee flavors, and with twenty months in French oak, there's tons of vanilla, caramel char and sweet oak tannins. 87 *—S.H. (10/1/2007)*

C.G. DI ARIE

C.G. di Arie 2005 Estate Grown Petite Sirah (Shenandoah Valley (CA)) $25. My bottle never quite overcame a sulfury smell; excessively soft with candied chocolate-raspberry sweetness. 80 *—S.H. (12/31/2007)*

C.G. di Arie 2004 Rosé Blend (Sierra Foothills) $13. 83 *—S.H. (12/1/2005)*

C.G. di Arie 2004 Syrah (Sierra Foothills) $30. Smells sulfury and candied, a soft, melted wine with sweet flavors of raspberry jam and milk chocolate. 80 *—S.H. (12/31/2007)*

C.G. di Arie 2003 Syrah (Sierra Foothills) $30. 80 *—S.H. (12/1/2005)*

C.G. di Arie 2002 Syrah (Sierra Foothills) $25. 82 *—S.H. (4/1/2005)*

C.G. di Arie 2004 Southern Exposure Syrah (Fair Play) $35. Soft and easy, with upfront cherry, raspberry, cola, chocolate and smoky oak flavors. The wine is tasty, but lacks the tannins and acids to give it structure. 84 *—S.H. (12/31/2007)*

C.G. di Arie 2003 Zinfandel (Shenandoah Valley (CA)) $25. 83 *—S.H. (6/1/2006)*

C.G. di Arie 2002 Zinfandel (Shenandoah Valley (CA)) $25. 83 *—S.H. (4/1/2005)*

C.G. di Arie 2002 Zinfandel (Shenandoah Valley (CA)) $25. 87 *—S.H. (8/1/2005)*

C.G. di Arie 2001 Zinfandel (Shenandoah Valley (CA)) $25. 90 *—S.H. (12/15/2004)*

C.G. di Arie 2005 Southern Exposure Zinfandel (Shenandoah Valley (CA)) $35. Okay for everyday drinking, this simple Zin is soft, smooth and one-dimensional. It's enormously ripe, with sweet black cherry, raspberry and chocolate flavors. 84 *—S.H. (12/31/2007)*

C.G. di Arie 2003 Southern Exposure Zinfandel (Sierra Foothills) $30. 86 *—S.H. (12/1/2005)*

C.R. SANDIDGE

C.R. Sandidge 2003 Tri*Umph Bordeaux Blend (Yakima Valley) $50. A blend of 53% Cabernet, 28% Malbec and 19% Merlot. Rich, lush and chocolaty, it's a very appealing wine from start to finish. Ripe fruit flavors include blueberry and blackberry jam, pie cherry and mincemeat. The acids keep it lively and suggest some years of further development ahead. 90 *—P.G. (5/1/2007)*

C.R. Sandidge 2002 Tri*Umph Red Wine Bordeaux Blend (Yamhill County) $39. 89 *—P.G. (12/1/2006)*

C.R. Sandidge 2002 Boushey Vineyard Syrah (Yakima Valley) $18. 87 *—P.G. (12/31/2006)*

C.R. Sandidge 2002 Klingele Vineyard Syrah (Yakima Valley) $28. 89 *—P.G. (10/1/2006)*

C.R. Sandidge 2000 Klingele Vineyard Syrah (Yakima Valley) $28. 87 *—P.G. (12/31/2002)*

C.R. Sandidge 2003 Minick Vineyard Syrah (Yamhill County) $18. The 2003 is comparable to the Willow Crest from the same vineyard, with somewhat less concentration. Pleasing berry flavors are lightly touched with smoke and coffee, with some chalky, ashy tannins. 88 *—P.G. (2/1/2007)*

C.R. Sandidge 2002 Minick Vineyard Syrah (Yamhill County) $20. This has dark fruits, leaning toward mulberry and plum, and moves grudgingly through the midpalate wall of tannins into a finish of lightly buttery chocolate. But it moves, and it shows a confident, stylish winemaker at the helm. 88 *—P.G. (2/1/2007)*

C.R. Sandidge 2000 Minick Vineyard Syrah (Yakima Valley) $28. 89 *—P.G. (12/31/2002)*

C.R. Sandidge 2004 Stone Tree Red Syrah-Grenache (Columbia Valley (WA)) $34. 90 *—P.G. (10/1/2006)*

C.R. Sandidge 2005 Viognier (Columbia Valley (WA)) $21. Clean, fresh fruit captures crisp apples, nectarines and Meyer lemon. The wine shows more elegance and delicate floral notes than most Viognier from warmer sites, and it has none of the bitterness or heat that can spoil the finish on these wines. Bone dry, it's a lovely food wine. 90 *—P.G. (5/1/2007)*

C.R. Sandidge 2004 Viognier (Yakima Valley) $19. 89 *—P.G. (10/1/2006)*

C5

C5 2005 Zinfandel (Dry Creek Valley) $30. Fire up the barbie and load it up. This lusty wine will stand up to grilled stuff, no matter how rich the BBQ sauce. The jammy berry and spice flavors are kicked up with firm tannins and just a touch of sweetness. 87 *—S.H. (12/15/2007)*

CA' DEL SOLO

Ca' del Solo 2004 Albariño (Monterey County) $15. 86 *—S.H. (11/15/2005)*

Ca' del Solo 2006 Ca' del Solo Vineyard Albariño (Monterey County) $18. Even by Albariño standards, this is a particularly dry, acidic wine. It's what you look for, and what you get, in this wine from Bonny Doon's Randall Grahm. From the east side of Salinas Valley, the wine brims with tart lime zest and tangerine fruit, with a pungently peppery edge of nasturtium flower. 87 *—S.H. (11/1/2007)*

Ca' del Solo 2002 Barbera (Monterey) $15. 85 *—S.H. (10/1/2004)*

Ca' del Solo 2001 Fresia Frizzante Champagne Blend (Monterey County) $15. 85 *—K.F. (12/1/2002)*

Ca' del Solo 2001 La Farfalla Charbono (California) $15. 88 *—S.H. (6/1/2004)*

Ca' del Solo 1997 La Farfalla Charbono (California) $15. 86 *—J.C. (10/1/1999)*

Ca' del Solo 2000 Freisa (Frizzante) Freisa (Monterey County) $15. 87 **Editors' Choice** *—M.M. (12/1/2001)*

Ca' del Solo 2003 Malvasia Bianca (Monterey) $13. 85 *—S.H. (10/1/2004)*

Ca' del Solo 2002 Malvasia Bianca (Monterey) $13. 88 *—S.H. (3/1/2004)*

Ca' del Solo 2000 Malvasia Bianca (Monterey) $12. 88 **Best Buy** *—S.H. (6/1/2002)*

Ca' del Solo 2005 Malvasia Bianca Malvasia Bianca (Central Coast) $13. 88 **Best Buy** *—S.H. (10/1/2006)*

Ca' del Solo 2006 Ca' del Solo Vineyard Muscat (Monterey County) $15. With 1% residual sugar, this Muscat straddles the line between a table and a dessert wine. I'm classifying it as the former, because it's crisp and minerally, but you could certainly enjoy it with a fruit tart. With flavors of peaches, pineapples, limes, papayas and wildflowers, it's a beautiful wine whose purity is sculpted with acidity. 87 *—S.H. (11/1/2007)*

Ca' del Solo 2004 San Bernabe Vineyard (Monterey) $13. 89 *—S.H. (11/15/2005)*

Ca' del Solo 2000 Moscato del Solo Moscato (Monterey County) $15. 86 *—S.H. (12/1/2001)*

Ca' del Solo 2003 Big House Red Red Blend (California) $10. 85 *—S.H. (11/15/2005)*

Ca' del Solo 2003 Big House Red Red Blend (California) $10. 85 **Best Buy** *—S.H. (10/1/2005)*

Ca' del Solo 2002 Big House Red Red Blend (California) $10. 88 **Best Buy** *—S.H. (5/1/2004)*

Ca' del Solo 2001 Big House Red Red Blend (Santa Cruz County) $10. 90 **Best Buy** *—S.H. (11/15/2002)*

Ca' del Solo 2000 Big House Red Red Blend (California) $10. 89 **Best Buy** *—S.H. (9/1/2002)*

Ca' del Solo 1999 Big House Red Red Blend (California) $10. 86 *—D.T. (11/15/2001)*

Ca' del Solo 2004 Big House Pink Rosé Blend (California) $10. 90 **Best Buy** *—S.H. (10/1/2006)*

Ca' del Solo 2003 Big House Pink Rosé Blend (California) $10. 83 *—S.H. (10/1/2004)*

Ca' del Solo 2002 Big House Pink Rosé Blend (California) $10. 84 *—S.H. (11/15/2005)*

Ca' del Solo 2005 Sangiovese (San Benito County) $15. Shows the bright, forward cherry flavors and zingy acidity of the variety, in a rustic package that's a little sharp on the finish. Okay for rich, everyday fare. 84 *—S.H. (11/1/2007)*

Ca' del Solo 2003 Sangiovese (Monterey) $15. 81 *—S.H. (10/1/2005)*

Ca' del Solo 2002 Il Fiasco Sangiovese (Monterey) $15. 86 *—S.H. (10/1/2004)*

Ca' del Solo 1997 Il Fiasco Sangiovese (California) $15. 87 *—M.S. (10/1/1999)*

Ca' del Solo 2003 White Blend (Monterey County) $18. 86 —*S.H. (12/1/2004)*

Ca' del Solo 2003 Big House White White Blend (California) $10. 87 Best Buy —*S.H. (10/1/2005)*

Ca' del Solo 2003 Big House White White Blend (California) $10. 84 —*S.H. (11/15/2005)*

Ca' del Solo 2002 Big House White White Blend (California) $10. 87 —*S.H. (2/1/2004)*

Ca' del Solo NV Club Montonico White Blend (California) $12. 84 —*J.C. (12/31/1999)*

CA'BELLA

Ca'Bella 2004 Pinot Grigio (Willamette Valley) $17. 85 —*P.G. (2/1/2006)*

CA'NA

Ca'Na 2002 Tamayo Family Vineyard Cabernet Sauvignon (Contra Costa County) $15. Contra Costa, "opposite coast," is a county across the Bay from San Francisco. Warm and sunny, its climate is like Napa's. This polished wine shows warm-coastal character in the smooth tannins and ripe cassis fruit. Not a blockbuster, but a very nice wine for the money. 86 —*S.H. (4/1/2007)*

Ca'Na 2005 Celebration Rose Rosé Blend (Contra Costa County) $14. Made from Cabernet Sauvignon, this is a full-bodied and rather rustic pink-hued wine, with earthy peach and spice flavors. If you tasted it blind, you might even think it was Chardonnay. 85 —*S.H. (4/1/2007)*

Ca'Na 2001 Syrah (Contra Costa County) $30. 82 *(9/1/2005)*

Ca'Na 2000 Syrah (Contra Costa County) $29. 86 —*S.H. (12/15/2003)*

Ca'Na 1999 Syrah (Contra Costa County) $21. 86 *(11/1/2001)*

Ca'Na 2002 Tamayo Family Vineyards Syrah (Contra Costa County) $15. Harsh and raw and unrelieved by much fruit, this Syrah from the suburbs of San Francisco has tobacco and dried herb flavors. 81 —*S.H. (4/1/2007)*

CADENCE

Cadence 2004 Bel Canto Bordeaux Blend (Red Mountain) $50. This is wonderfully fragrant, lush, plush and enveloping—it almost suffocates you with aromas of fruit and barrel and nicely-rendered spice. The fruit is pure and ripe, but the acids are preserved and the tannins are ripe, though still a bit chewy. 92 —*P.G. (3/1/2007)*

Cadence 2002 Bel Canto Bordeaux Blend (Red Mountain) $60. 90 —*P.G. (12/15/2005)*

Cadence 2001 Bel Canto Bordeaux Blend (Red Mountain) $50. 92 —*P.G. (5/1/2004)*

Cadence 2003 Coda Bordeaux Blend (Columbia Valley (WA)) $22. 89 —*P.G. (12/15/2005)*

Cadence 2004 Klipsun Vineyard Bordeaux Blend (Red Mountain) $38. From the exceptional Klipsun vineyard, this blend of two thirds Merlot and one third Cabernet Sauvignon delivers beautifully softened and ripened tannins. This is a great effort; it clearly shows why Washington is the place for that grape, and the Cabernet filling in the spine. The oak (40% new, all French) is matched to the weight of the fruit, and used properly, as a spice, not an event unto itself. This is as good as Klipsun gets, with the acid still there, no roasted flavors, no heat and no rough tannins. 92 —*P.G. (3/1/2007)*

Cadence 2004 Taptiel Vineyard Bordeaux Blend (Red Mountain) $38. Soft, spicy and complex, but also muscular; this Cabernet-driven Bordeaux blend may be the most complex of Cadence's three vineyard-designates. The wine has more heat and power than the other two, and I love the way the spice kicks in. There is considerable toasty and coffee flavor in it as well; all wrapped into a lush and harmonious, smooth and contiguous whole. 93 —*P.G. (3/1/2007)*

Cadence 2004 Camerata Cabernet Sauvignon (Red Mountain) $50. This is a special wine, a beautiful rendition of pure Cab from a single Red Mountain vineyard—Tapteil. It shows the power of the grape, the structural verticality, the austerity, but it is also ripe enough to stand alone and shine all by itself. This is a perfectly sculpted wine, elegant and fine, sleek and muscular. It needs time, no doubt, but it's delicious right now as well. I just love pure Cabernet. It's like a Zen wine. 95 Editors' Choice —*P.G. (3/1/2007)*

Cadence 2003 Bel Canto Red Blend (Red Mountain) $50. 94 —*P.G. (4/1/2006)*

Cadence 2001 Camerata Red Blend (Red Mountain) $50. 89 —*P.G. (5/1/2004)*

Cadence 2004 Ciel du Cheval Vineyard Red Blend (Red Mountain) $38. Here is another stellar effort from Cadence, with the control and precision that begins to show why Washington should emulate France more than California. This does not have the sheer weight and tannin of the Klipsun, but it compensates with an underlying minerality and a sinuous core of ripe but not too ripe red fruits. Complex and understated, this is a wine for fans of subtlety and elegance. 91 —*P.G. (3/1/2007)*

Cadence 2003 Ciel du Cheval Vineyard Red Blend (Red Mountain) $38. 94 —*P.G. (4/1/2006)*

Cadence 2001 Ciel du Cheval Vineyard Red Blend (Red Mountain) $35. 91 —*P.G. (5/1/2004)*

Cadence 2002 Ciel du Cheval Vineyard Red Wine Red Blend (Red Mountain) $37. 92 —*P.G. (12/15/2005)*

Cadence 2004 Coda Red Blend (Columbia Valley (WA)) $22. This mostly Cabernet Franc red blend is drinking beautifully right now, but it's got some real stuffing. The fruit is polished, plummy, and evolved; there are nice toasty hightlights and even hints of tobacco if you look. It drinks like a much pricier wine. 89 —*P.G. (3/1/2007)*

Cadence 2003 Klipsun Red Blend (Red Mountain) $35. 90 —*P.G. (4/1/2006)*

Cadence 2001 Klipsun Vineyard Red Blend (Red Mountain) $35. 90 —*P.G. (5/1/2004)*

Cadence 2003 Tapteil Vineyard Red Blend (Red Mountain) $38. 92 —*P.G. (4/1/2006)*

Cadence 2001 Tapteil Vineyard Red Blend (Red Mountain) $38. 89 —*P.G. (5/1/2004)*

Cadence 2002 Tapteil Vineyard Red Wine Red Blend (Red Mountain) $37. 88 —*P.G. (12/15/2005)*

CAERNARVON CELLARS

Caernarvon Cellars 1999 Pinot Noir (San Lucas) $26. 89 —*J.M. (7/1/2003)*

Caernarvon Cellars 2002 Rio San Lucas Vineyard Pinot Noir (San Lucas) $25. 86 —*S.H. (6/1/2005)*

Caernarvon Cellars 2001 Rio San Lucas Vineyard Pinot Noir (San Lucas) $25. 83 —*S.H. (10/1/2004)*

Caernarvon Cellars 1999 Cuvée Frank Zinfandel (Monterey) $23. 85 —*J.M. (2/1/2003)*

Caernarvon Cellars 2002 Cuvée Frank Zinfandel (Paso Robles) $20. 87 —*S.H. (10/1/2005)*

Caernarvon Cellars 2001 Cuvée Frank Zlahtina Zinfandel (Paso Robles) $NA. 88 —*J.M. (10/1/2004)*

CAFARO

Cafaro 1997 Cabernet Sauvignon (Napa Valley) $39. 92 *(11/1/2000)*

Cafaro 2000 Syrah (Napa Valley) $32. 85 —*S.H. (12/1/2002)*

CAIN

Cain 1997 Cain Five Bordeaux Blend (Napa Valley) $75. 91 *(11/1/2000)*

Cain 2001 Concept Bordeaux Blend (Napa Valley) $46. 89 —*S.H. (5/1/2005)*

Cain 1997 Concept Bordeaux Blend (Napa Valley) $42. 89 *(11/1/2000)*

Cain NV Cuvée NVO Bordeaux Blend (Napa Valley) $24. 84 —*S.H. (10/1/2004)*

Cain 2001 Cain Five Cabernet Blend (Napa Valley) $90. 92 Cellar Selection —*S.H. (10/1/2005)*

Cain 1999 Cain Five Cabernet Blend (Napa Valley) $85. 88 —*S.H. (5/1/2003)*

Cain 2003 Concept - The Benchland Cabernet Blend (Napa Valley) $54. You might call this Cain's junior version of their famous Cain Five Bordeaux blend. This one's blended from up and down the valley, and it's exceptionally fine. Dry and smooth, with richly textured tannins, it shows ripe cherries, plums and currants, with a spicy, earthy finish. Best now through 2013. 92 —*S.H. (2/1/2007)*

Cain 2002 Concept Cabernet Blend (Napa Valley) $50. 82 —*S.H. (2/1/2006)*

Cain 2001 Five Cabernet Blend (Napa Valley) $90. 89 —*S.H. (11/1/2005)*

Cain 1999 Concept Cabernet Sauvignon (Napa Valley) $46. 88 —*S.H. (11/15/2002)*

Cain 1996 Cuvée Cabernet Sauvignon (Napa Valley) $24. 89 —*L.W. (7/1/1999)*

Cain 2002 Ventana Vineyard Musqué Sauvignon Blanc (Arroyo Seco) $23. 91 —*S.H. (6/1/2005)*

Cain 2001 Ventana Vineyard Musqué Sauvignon Blanc (Arroyo Seco) $23. 92 —*S.H. (9/1/2003)*

Cain 1998 Ventana Vineyards Musqué Sauvignon Blanc (Monterey County) $20. 89 —*M.S. (2/1/2000)*

Cain 1997 Ventana Vineyards Musqué Sauvignon Blanc (Monterey) $20. 90 —*L.W. (9/1/1999)*

CAKEBREAD

Cakebread 2002 Cabernet Sauvignon (Napa Valley) $55. 85 —*S.H. (6/1/2006)*

Cakebread 1997 Cabernet Sauvignon (Napa Valley) $37. 93 *(11/1/2000)*

Cakebread 2001 Benchland Select Cabernet Sauvignon (Napa Valley) $95. 92 —*S.H. (11/15/2005)*

Cakebread 2000 Benchland Select Cabernet Sauvignon (Napa Valley) $90. 88 —*S.H. (11/15/2004)*

Cakebread 1999 Benchland Select Cabernet Sauvignon (Napa Valley) $90. 92 —*J.M. (2/1/2003)*

Cakebread 1999 Three Sisters Cabernet Sauvignon (Napa Valley) $90. 92 —*J.M. (2/1/2003)*

Cakebread 1999 Vine Hill Ranch Cabernet Sauvignon (Napa Valley) $90. 82 —*S.H. (4/1/2004)*

Cakebread 1997 Vine Hill Ranch Cabernet Sauvignon (Napa Valley) $70. 90 —*J.M. (9/10/2003)*

Cakebread 1999 Chardonnay (Russian River Valley) $32.91 *(7/1/2001)*

Cakebread 1996 Merlot (Napa Valley) $35. 87 *(3/1/2000)*

Cakebread 2002 Merlot (Napa Valley) $48. 91 —*S.H. (11/15/2005)*

Cakebread 2002 Pinot Noir (Carneros) $44. 88 *(11/1/2004)*

Cakebread 1998 Sauvignon Blanc (Napa Valley) $16. 86 *(3/1/2000)*

Cakebread 2004 Sauvignon Blanc (Napa Valley) $21. 89 —*S.H. (6/1/2006)*

Cakebread 2003 Sauvignon Blanc (Napa Valley) $22. 85 *(7/1/2005)*

Cakebread 2002 Sauvignon Blanc (Napa Valley) $17. 86 —*S.H. (12/15/2003)*

Cakebread 2002 Syrah (Carneros) $43. 88 *(9/1/2005)*

Cakebread 2000 Syrah (Carneros) $45. 92 —*J.M. (2/1/2003)*

Cakebread 1998 Syrah (Napa Valley) $40. 83 *(11/1/2001)*

CALAFIA

Calafia 2003 Meritage (Napa Valley) $38. 87 —*S.H. (12/15/2006)*

CALCAREOUS

Calcareous 2003 Cabernet Sauvignon (York Mountain) $26. 88 —*S.H. (12/15/2006)*

Calcareous 2002 Cabernet Sauvignon (Paso Robles) $24. 90 Editors' Choice —*S.H. (8/1/2005)*

Calcareous 2002 Reserve Cabernet Sauvignon (Paso Robles) $28. 87 —*S.H. (12/31/2005)*

Calcareous 2004 Chardonnay (York Mountain) $24. The winery's name comes from the limestone that is found in this part of San Luis Obispo, and you can indeed detect a chalky minerality, not to mention high acidity that makes the fruit clean and bright. Shows tart green apple and peach flavors, and lots of Asian spice. 88 —*S.H. (4/1/2007)*

Calcareous 2004 Pinot Noir (York Mountain) $28. 85 —*S.H. (12/1/2006)*

Calcareous 2004 Tré Violet Rhône Red Blend (Paso Robles) $28. Tons of fruit in this soft, ripe Rhône blend, ranging from blackberry marmalade, cherry cola, Kona coffee and milk chocolate truffle to spiced plums and pomegranates. Yet it's dry. Syrah, Mourvèdre and Grenache. 86 —*S.H. (4/1/2007)*

Calcareous 2004 Roussanne (Paso Robles) $24. 88 —*S.H. (12/1/2006)*

Calcareous 2003 Syrah (Paso Robles) $24. 87 —*S.H. (12/31/2005)*

Calcareous 2002 Syrah (Paso Robles) $24. 88 *(9/1/2005)*

Calcareous 2004 Viognier (Paso Robles) $24. 87 —*S.H. (12/31/2005)*

Calcareous 2002 Zinfandel (Paso Robles) $24. 85 —*S.H. (8/1/2005)*

CALE

Cale 1998 Sangiacomo Vineyards Chardonnay (Carneros) $24. 88 *(6/1/2000)*

Cale 1997 Vintner's Reserve Merlot (Sonoma Valley) $NA. 89 Best Buy *(12/31/1999)*

CALERA

Calera 2005 Chardonnay (Mount Harlan) $25. If you like oak, you'll love the toast, caramel, butterscotch and crème brûlée flavors in this Chard. There's apricot and pineapple fruit, too, but that oak is the dominant taste. 85 —*S.H. (12/15/2007)*

Calera 2004 Chardonnay (Mt. Harlan) $25. Minerals, acidity and sweet green argula give a tangy tinge to the underlying citrus fruit in this dry, structured wine. Fans of big, fat Chards will find it austere, but those valuing elegance will call it Chablisian. 90 —*S.H. (11/1/2007)*

Calera 2004 Chardonnay (Central Coast) $15. 86 —*S.H. (12/31/2006)*

Calera 2003 Chardonnay (Central Coast) $14. 86 —*S.H. (7/1/2006)*

Calera 2003 Chardonnay (Mt. Harlan) $25. Calera Chard, a tightly wound wine that's the opposite of a fruit bomb. It's marked by mineral, dried herb and oak flavors, and what fruit there is veers toward mangoes and pineapples. The acidity makes it mouthwateringly clean. The model is Chablis, and the wine will age well for 10 years. 90 —*S.H. (6/1/2007)*

Calera 2002 Chardonnay (Mt. Harlan) $34. 87 —*S.H. (12/31/2006)*

Calera 2002 Chardonnay (Central Coast) $14. 86 —*S.H. (12/15/2005)*

Calera 2001 Chardonnay (Central Coast) $14. 85 —*S.H. (12/15/2004)*

Calera 2000 Chardonnay (Central Coast) $18. 82 —*S.H. (10/1/2004)*

Calera 2000 Chardonnay (Mount Harlan) $34. 89 —*S.H. (12/15/2005)*

Calera 1999 Chardonnay (Mount Harlan) $34. 83 —*S.H. (11/15/2004)*

Calera 1999 Chardonnay (Central Coast) $22. 86 —*S.H. (12/1/2001)*

Calera 1997 Chardonnay (Mount Harlan) $38. 89 *(7/1/2001)*

Calera 1996 Chardonnay (Mount Harlan) $38. 93 —*S.H. (10/1/1999)*

Calera 2005 Pinot Noir (Central Coast) $23. 85 —*S.H. (12/31/2006)*

Calera 2003 Pinot Noir (Central Coast) $21. 88 —*S.H. (7/1/2006)*

Calera 2002 Pinot Noir (Central Coast) $20. 89 —*S.H. (12/15/2005)*

Calera 2001 Pinot Noir (Central Coast) $20. 84 —*S.H. (12/1/2004)*

Calera 2000 Pinot Noir (Central Coast) $24. 80 *(10/1/2002)*

Calera 1999 Pinot Noir (Central Coast) $20. 87 —*S.H. (7/1/2002)*

Calera 2004 Jensen Vineyard Pinot Noir (Mount Harlan) $60. If only this wine had greater structure, it would earn a higher score, but as it is, it's too soft and sugary, which makes it taste like the filling of a pie or tart. Raspberries, cherries and figs are the flavors, with the smoke and caramel of oak. Drink now. 85 —*S.H. (12/15/2007)*

Calera 2003 Jensen Pinot Noir (Mt. Harlan) $55. The '02 was one of the greatest Caleras I've ever had, and this isn't far behind. It's soft, rich and enormously appealing right now, for its fabulous array of raspberry purée, cherry jam, mocha and Asian spice flavors that are so complex and layered. The texture is so soft, it's like drinking taffeta. For all the approachability, this is a serious cellar candidate, if you can keep your hands off it over the next eight years. 93 —*S.H. (6/1/2007)*

Calera 2002 Jensen Vineyard Pinot Noir (Mt. Harlan) $53. 95 Editors' Choice —*S.H. (7/1/2006)*

Calera 2001 Jensen Vineyard Pinot Noir (Mt. Harlan) $50. 89 —*S.H. (8/1/2005)*

Calera 2000 Jensen Vineyard Pinot Noir (Mount Harlan) $50. 84 —*S.H. (12/1/2004)*

Calera 1999 Jensen Vineyard Pinot Noir (Mt. Harlan) $50. 89 —*M.S. (12/1/2003)*

Calera 1997 Mélange Pinot Noir (Mount Harlan) $40. 90 —*S.H. (7/1/2002)*

Calera 2004 Mills Vineyard Pinot Noir (Mount Harlan) $45. The heat of the vintage took its toll, giving us a soft, melted wine whose deficit of acidity makes the superripe cherry and raspberry flavors taste syrupy sweet. There's no getting around this problem, even though the wine is not without its charms. Drink now. 85 —*S.H. (12/15/2007)*

Calera 2003 Mills Pinot Noir (Mt. Harlan) $45. With some firm tannins, this is a wine to decant for a few hours or age for up to eight years before it starts to lose its luscious fruit. The flavors are expansive, ranging from cherries and raspberries to cola, tamari and cinnamon spice. With its silky texture and long, spicy finish, this is a top-notch Pinot. Best now–2010. 92 —*S.H. (6/1/2007)*

Calera 2002 Mills Vineyard Pinot Noir (Mt. Harlan) $43. 92 —*S.H. (12/1/2006)*

Calera 2001 Mills Vineyard Pinot Noir (Mount Harlan) $40. 90 —*S.H. (12/15/2005)*

Calera 2000 Mills Pinot Noir (Mt. Harlan) $40. 91 —*S.H. (12/15/2004)*

Calera 1997 Mills Vineyard Pinot Noir (Mount Harlan) $55. 91 —*S.H. (7/1/2002)*

Calera 2004 Mt. Harlan Cuvée Pinot Noir (Mt. Harlan) $28. This seems to be a blend of lesser barrels from the estate vineyard, and the wine is gently tasty and dry, but not particularly complex. It has a rich array of cherry, raspberry, cola, clove and tamari flavors, with a touch of smoky oak. 86 —*S.H. (11/1/2007)*

Calera 2002 Mt. Harlan Cuvée Pinot Noir (Mt. Harlan) $28. 88 —*S.H. (12/31/2006)*

Calera 2004 Reed Vineyard Pinot Noir (Mount Harlan) $50. Shows the earthiness that often marks young Calera Pinot, which makes it less flashy but more elegant and food-friendly than many more expensive wines. The herb-infused cherry, raspberry and cola flavors are ripe and succulent, but acidity is a little deficient, so this may not be the most ageable wine. **88** —*S.H. (12/15/2007)*

Calera 2003 Reed Pinot Noir (Mt. Harlan) $50. On a par with the excellent '02, the '03 Reed is warmly ripe and delicious. It's drinkable now for the softness and forward cherry, pomegranate, rhubarb and root beer flavors, with a vanilla and toasted oak edge, but has the balance and complexity to age for a good 10 years. This is seriously fine, white tablecloth Pinot Noir. **92** —*S.H. (6/1/2007)*

Calera 2002 Reed Vineyard Pinot Noir (Mt. Harlan) $48. 93 Cellar Selection —*S.H. (7/1/2006)*

Calera 2001 Reed Vineyard Pinot Noir (Mt. Harlan) $45. 88 —*S.H. (8/1/2005)*

Calera 2000 Reed Vineyard Pinot Noir (Mount Harlan) $45. 86 —*S.H. (12/1/2004)*

Calera 1999 Reed Vineyard Pinot Noir (Mt. Harlan) $45. 91 —*M.S. (12/1/2003)*

Calera 2004 Ryan Pinot Noir (Mt. Harlan) $40. This is the ripest, softest, most immediately accessible Ryan in years. It instantly appeals for the opulent cherry, raspberry, orange rind, root beer, Asian spice, vanilla and toast flavors that just sing on the palate. The tannins and acids are on the soft, low side, but adequate to balance this early-drinking Pinot Noir. **89** —*S.H. (11/1/2007)*

Calera 2003 Ryan Vineyard Pinot Noir (Mt. Harlan) $40. 92 Cellar Selection —*S.H. (7/1/2006)*

Calera 2002 Ryan Vineyard Pinot Noir (Mount Harlan) $40. 90 —*S.H. (12/15/2005)*

Calera 2004 Selleck Vineyard Pinot Noir (Mount Harlan) $75. This wine is too soft, which makes the ripe cherry and raspberry flavors taste syrupy and in fact sweet, although it may be technically dry. **86** —*S.H. (12/15/2007)*

Calera 2003 Selleck Pinot Noir (Mt. Harlan) $60. You'll fall in love with this Pinot right away for its softly luscious flavors and balanced harmony. The cherries and raspberries taste like they came from gorgeously ripe fruit, baked into a delicious pie. Yet somehow the wine stays dry and elegant, due in part to its acidity. Tastes completely young and fresh now, and should develop bottle complexity through 2012. **93** —*S.H. (6/1/2007)*

Calera 2002 Selleck Vineyard Pinot Noir (Mt. Harlan) $58. 93 Cellar Selection —*S.H. (12/1/2006)*

Calera 2001 Selleck Vineyard Pinot Noir (Mount Harlan) $55. 91 —*S.H. (12/15/2005)*

Calera 2000 Selleck Pinot Noir (Mt. Harlan) $55. 88 —*S.H. (12/15/2004)*

Calera 1996 Selleck Vineyard Pinot Noir (Mount Harlan) $80. 91 *(10/1/1999)*

Calera 2005 Thirtieth Anniversary Vintage Mt. Harlan Cuvée Pinot Noir (Mount Harlan) $30. The winery celebrates with this dry, rich Pinot, apparently made from grapes that didn't go into the single-vineyard bottlings. Nonetheless it shows the estate's balance and integrity, and is helped by coming from a cool vintage. Drink now. **87** —*S.H. (12/15/2007)*

Calera 2006 Vin Gris of Pinot Noir Pinot Noir (Central Coast) $16. Smell this blind and you might just mistake it for a regular Pinot. It's that strong in cherries, raspberries, cola and spice. Feels a little heavy for a rosé, but it's dry and crisp. **85** —*S.H. (7/1/2007)*

Calera 2005 Vin Gris of Pinot Noir Pinot Noir (Central Coast) $14. 87 —*S.H. (6/21/2006)*

Calera 1997 Viognier (Mount Harlan) $30. 93 —*S.H. (10/1/1999)*

Calera 2003 Viognier (Mt. Harlan) $36. 91 —*S.H. (8/1/2005)*

Calera 2001 Mt. Harlan Estate Viognier (Mt. Harlan) $36. 89 —*J.M. (12/15/2002)*

Calera 2005 Thirtieth Anniversary Vintage Viognier (Mt. Harlan) $28. Calera's was the first California Viognier I ever fell in love with, years ago. It hasn't changed much. Still loaded with exotic fruits, it's an opulent wine that manages to be elegant and charming despite the size. Guavas, nectarines, peaches, lemon mousse, honeysuckle and crème brûlée begin to suggest the range of flavor sensations. **91** —*S.H. (6/1/2007)*

Calera 2005 Thirtieth Anniversary Vintage Dessert Viognier (Mt. Harlan) $30. 87 —*S.H. (12/1/2006)*

CALISTOGA CELLARS

Calistoga Cellars 2003 Cabernet Sauvignon (Napa Valley) $34. 84 —*S.H. (12/15/2006)*

Calistoga Cellars 2002 Cabernet Sauvignon (Napa Valley) $30. 86 —*S.H. (6/1/2005)*

Calistoga Cellars 2000 Louer Family Vineyard Cabernet Sauvignon (St. Helena) $26. 91 Editors' Choice —*S.H. (11/15/2003)*

Calistoga Cellars 2005 Chardonnay (Napa Valley) $20. This is a light-bodied, elegant Chard meant to satisfy America's appetite for the variety. It shows very ripe tropical fruit and date flavors, but for me is far too oaky, with a toothpicky, caramelly taste. **83** —*S.H. (5/1/2007)*

Calistoga Cellars 2004 Chardonnay (Napa Valley) $22. 85 —*S.H. (5/1/2006)*

Calistoga Cellars 2004 Merlot (Napa Valley) $29. This is for you if you like your Merlots soft, gentle and ripe almost to the point of sweetness. It's a one-dimensional wine, rich in fudgy chocolate, blackberry tart and sweetened rosehip tea flavors. **84** —*S.H. (3/1/2007)*

Calistoga Cellars 2003 Merlot (Napa Valley) $29. 84 —*S.H. (5/1/2006)*

Calistoga Cellars 2002 Merlot (Napa Valley) $26. 85 —*S.H. (6/1/2005)*

Calistoga Cellars 2005 Sauvignon Blanc (Napa Valley) $18. 83 —*S.H. (12/15/2006)*

Calistoga Cellars 2004 Blossom Creek Vineyard Sauvignon Blanc (Napa Valley) $17. 85 —*S.H. (5/1/2006)*

Calistoga Cellars 2004 Zinfandel (Napa Valley) $27. Very ripe, almost a dessert wine, except it's dry. The acids and tannins are soft and melted, and the flavors are as forward as modern viticulture achieves. Milk chocolate, cassis, black cherry pie, macaroon, and pecan pie; it's just delicious. What do you drink such a wine with? Almost anything that wants a big red. **88** —*S.H. (6/1/2007)*

Calistoga Cellars 2003 Zinfandel (Napa Valley) $26. 87 —*S.H. (5/1/2006)*

Calistoga Cellars 2002 Zinfandel (Napa Valley) $22. 91 —*S.H. (6/1/2005)*

Calistoga Cellars 2001 Zinfandel (Napa Valley) $22. 90 Editors' Choice *(11/1/2003)*

CALIX

Calix 2004 Masked Man Vineyard Cabernet Sauvignon (Napa Valley) $60. Made in the Napa cult Cab style, this soft, gentle wine is enormous in cassis, blackberry essence, cherry purée, vanilla and toast flavors that sink deep into the palate and last through a spicy finish. Not for the long haul, so drink now though 2010. **92** —*S.H. (10/1/2007)*

Calix 2004 Masked Man Vineyard Syrah (Napa Valley) $35. Tastes like one of those long hangtime wines where the grapes got superripe. The result is enormous flavors, stupendous really, of melted chocolate, raspberry and cherry purée, gingerbread, chocolate chip cookie, crème de cassis, licorice; the list goes on and on. Yet the wine is fundamentally dry, with balancing acids and tannins. Drink now. **91** —*S.H. (9/1/2007)*

Calix 2003 Masked Man Vineyard Syrah (Napa Valley) $33. 87 —*S.H. (12/31/2005)*

Calix 2003 Parmalee-Hill Vineyard Syrah (Sonoma County) $33. 92 —*S.H. (12/31/2005)*

CALLAGHAN VINEYARDS

Callaghan Vineyards 2004 Buena Suerte Cuvee Cabernet Sauvignon-Merlot (Sonoita) $25. Fruit fanatics take notice—this wine is all about a berry blast. These Merlot and Cabernet grapes are grown in the red, iron- and calcium-rich clays of Callaghan's Buena Suerte Vineyard in Arizona and while not as complex as advertised, the wine is flavorful and easy to drink. Various vintages of this wine have been served at the White House. **83** —*S.K. (2/1/2007)*

CALLAWAY

Callaway 1997 Cabernet Sauvignon (California) $10. 85 Best Buy *(12/31/1999)*

Callaway 1999 Coastal Cabernet Sauvignon (California) $11. 84 —*S.H. (11/15/2001)*

Callaway 1998 Coastal Cabernet Sauvignon (California) $10. 84 —*S.H. (12/15/2000)*

Callaway 2000 Coastal Winemaker's Reserve Cabernet Sauvignon (Paso Robles) $35. 83 —*S.H. (11/15/2003)*

Callaway 1998 Chardonnay (Temecula) $10. 84 —*L.W. (12/31/1999)*

Callaway 2000 Coastal Chardonnay (California) $11. 86 Best Buy —*S.H. (12/15/2002)*

Callaway 1999 Coastal Chardonnay (California) $10. 86 —*S.H. (2/1/2001)*

Callaway 2000 Coastal Reserve Chardonnay (Santa Maria Valley) $16. 85 —*S.H. (5/1/2003)*

Callaway 1999 Reserve Coastal Chardonnay (California) $15. 87 —*S.H. (5/1/2001)*

Callaway 1998 Chenin Blanc (California) $8. 86 Best Buy —*S.H. (9/1/1999)*

Callaway 2001 Coastal Chenin Blanc (California) $7. 86 —*S.H. (9/1/2003)*

Callaway 2000 Coastal Chenin Blanc (California) $8. 83 —*S.H. (11/15/2001)*

Callaway 1996 Dolcetto (Temecula) $11. 88 Best Buy *—S.H. (10/1/1999)*

Callaway 1997 Special Collection Dolcetto (Temecula) $15. 85 *(11/1/1999)*

Callaway 1997 Merlot (California) $13. 86 *—L.C. (12/31/1999)*

Callaway 1999 Coastal Merlot (California) $11. 85 *—S.H. (11/15/2001)*

Callaway 1998 Coastal Merlot (California) $10. 82 *(2/1/2001)*

Callaway 1999 Coastal Reserve Merlot (California) $16. 84 *—S.H. (9/1/2003)*

Callaway 1998 Reserve Coastal Merlot (California) $15. 83 *—S.H. (5/1/2001)*

Callaway 1998 Special Collection Pinot Gris (Temecula) $14. 86 *—S.H. (3/1/2000)*

Callaway 1998 Sauvignon Blanc (Temecula) $9. 85 *—L.W. (9/1/1999)*

Callaway 2000 Coastal Sauvignon Blanc (California) $8. 86 *—S.H. (9/1/2003)*

Callaway 1999 Coastal Sauvignon Blanc (California) $9. 85 Best Buy *— S.H. (8/1/2001)*

Callaway 1999 Coastal Syrah (California) $12. 84 *(10/1/2001)*

Callaway 1999 Coastal Reserve Syrah (San Luis Obispo) $16. 87 *—S.H. (12/1/2002)*

Callaway 2000 Coastal-Reserve Viognier (California) $15. 85 *—S.H. (11/15/2001)*

Callaway 2001 Coastal Reserve Viognier (California) $15. 85 *—S.H. (3/1/2003)*

Callaway 1998 Special Collection Viognier (Temecula) $15. 85 *—S.H. (11/1/1999)*

CAMARADERIE CELLARS

Camaraderie Cellars 2001 Grace Bordeaux Blend (Columbia Valley (WA)) $32. 90 *—P.G. (12/31/2003)*

Camaraderie Cellars 2003 Cabernet Franc (Washington) $25. 91 Editors' Choice *—P.G. (11/15/2006)*

Camaraderie Cellars 2001 Cabernet Sauvignon (Columbia Valley (WA)) $25. 92 Cellar Selection *—P.G. (12/31/2003)*

Camaraderie Cellars 1999 Cabernet Sauvignon (Washington) $22. 91 Cellar Selection *—P.G. (6/1/2002)*

Camaraderie Cellars 2001 Merlot (Columbia Valley (WA)) $25. 89 *—P.G. (12/31/2003)*

Camaraderie Cellars 1998 Grace Red Blend (Washington) $22. 91 Cellar Selection *—P.G. (6/1/2002)*

Camaraderie Cellars 2002 Sauvignon Blanc (Washington) $10. 87 Best Buy *—P.G. (12/31/2003)*

Camaraderie Cellars 2000 Sauvignon Blanc (Washington) $12. 90 Best Buy *—P.G. (6/1/2002)*

CAMBIATA

Cambiata 2005 Estate Albariño (Monterey) $24. Albariño's natural acidity is amplified in this wine, which comes from one of California's chilliest growing regions and the coolest vintage in years. Consumed on its own, the acidity is so high, it's almost sour. But this is a food wine if ever there was one. With salty tapas, it will be perfect. 87 *—S.H. (11/1/2007)*

Cambiata 2004 Estate Bottled Tannat (Monterey) $32. The variety is best known in the French appellation of Madiran, where the wines are inky, tannic and long-lived. Here, California terroir has produced a soft red, in the manner of Napa Cabs, with similar flavors, except for a wild edge of violets and Provençal herbs. An impressive debut. 90 *—S.H. (10/1/2007)*

CAMBRIA

Cambria 2000 Bench Break Vineyard Chardonnay (Santa Maria Valley) $25. 87 *—S.H. (8/1/2003)*

Cambria 1999 Bench Break Vineyard Chardonnay (Santa Maria Valley) $30. 91 Best Buy *(7/1/2001)*

Cambria 1999 Experimental Clone 4 Chardonnay (Santa Maria Valley) $40. 91 *(10/1/2002)*

Cambria 2001 Katherine's Estate Bottled Chardonnay (Santa Maria Valley) $22. 89 *—S.H. (8/1/2003)*

Cambria 2004 Katherine's Vineyard Chardonnay (Santa Maria Valley) $16. 88 *—S.H. (12/1/2006)*

Cambria 1999 Katherine's Vineyard Chardonnay (Santa Maria Valley) $22. 87 *(10/1/2002)*

Cambria 1998 Katherine's Vineyard Chardonnay (Santa Maria Valley) $21. 84 *(6/1/2000)*

Cambria 1997 Katherine's Vineyard Chardonnay (Santa Maria Valley) $20. 91 *—S.H. (7/1/1999)*

Cambria 2000 Rae's Chardonnay (Santa Maria Valley) $44. 90 *—S.H. (8/1/2003)*

Cambria 1999 Rae's Chardonnay (Santa Maria Valley) $41. 91 *(7/1/2001)*

Cambria 1995 Reserve Chardonnay (Santa Maria Valley) $32. 92 *—S.H. (7/1/1999)*

Cambria 2002 Tepusquet Vineyard Pinot Gris (Santa Maria Valley) $16. 90 *—S.H. (2/1/2006)*

Cambria 1999 Bench Break Vineyard Pinot Noir (Santa Maria Valley) $42. 86 *(10/1/2002)*

Cambria 1999 Experimental 4-2A-115 Pinot Noir (Santa Maria Valley) $50. 90 *(10/1/2002)*

Cambria 2000 Experimental Clone 115 Pinot Noir (Santa Maria Valley) $50. 93 *(10/1/2002)*

Cambria 2004 Clone 23 Pinot Noir (Santa Maria Valley) $48. What a wonderful Pinot Noir. I tasted this with a range of other good coastal Pinots and it stood out for the depth and complexity. You'll find the silkiness, acidity and ripe cherries and blackberries in many other Pinots, but also a richly earthy, grilled Portobello, miso and tannin quality. There's a ton of new oak, but it's totally appropriate. 94 Editors' Choice *—S.H. (2/1/2007)*

Cambria 2000 Experimental Clone 23 Pinot Noir (Santa Maria Valley) $50. 92 *(10/1/2002)*

Cambria 2004 Clone 2A Pinot Noir (Santa Maria Valley) $48. How pale this wine pours. Don't be deceived! It's an enormous Pinot Noir, almost too big for its own good, explosive in ripe cherries, raspberries, chocolate and especially new French oak that just floods the palate with vanilla-infused smoky char. It's so big, it's hard to figure out what to drink it with, except simple fare, like a grilled steak or even carpaccio of beef tenderloin. 92 *— S.H. (2/1/2007)*

Cambria 2000 Experimental Clone 2A Pinot Noir (Santa Maria Valley) $50. 92 *(10/1/2002)*

Cambria 2000 Julia's Pinot Noir (Santa Maria Valley) $22. 87 *—S.H. (8/1/2003)*

Cambria 1999 Julia's Pinot Noir (Santa Maria Valley) $26. 83 *(10/1/2002)*

Cambria 2004 Julia's Vineyard Pinot Noir (Santa Maria Valley) $19. 87 *— S.H. (12/1/2006)*

Cambria 1999 Rae's Pinot Noir (Santa Maria Valley) $50. 87 *(10/1/2002)*

Cambria 2000 Rae's Estate Bottled Pinot Noir (Santa Maria Valley) $50. 92 *—S.H. (12/1/2003)*

Cambria 2002 Tepusquet Vineyard Syrah (Santa Maria Valley) $20. 87 *(9/1/2005)*

Cambria 1999 Tepusquet Vineyard Syrah (Santa Maria Valley) $22. 87 *(11/1/2001)*

Cambria 1999 Tepusquet Vineyard Syrah (Santa Maria Valley) $50. 87 *(10/1/2002)*

Cambria 1997 Tepusquet Vineyard Syrah (Santa Maria Valley) $22. 89 *— L.W. (2/1/2000)*

Cambria 2000 Tepusquet Vineyard Viognier (Santa Maria Valley) $16. 85 *(10/1/2002)*

Cambria 1997 Tepusquet Vineyard Viognier (Santa Maria Valley) $16. 91 Best Buy *—S.H. (6/1/1999)*

CAMELLIA

Camellia 2000 Lencioni Vineyard Cabernet Sauvignon (Dry Creek Valley) $40. 82 *S.H. (8/1/2004)*

Camellia 1999 Lencioni Vineyard Cabernet Sauvignon (Dry Creek Valley) $45. 81 *—S.H. (11/15/2002)*

Camellia 1998 Lencioni Vineyard Cabernet Sauvignon (Dry Creek Valley) $35. 87 *—S.H. (12/31/2001)*

Camellia 2001 Diamo Grazie Red Wine Cabernet Sauvignon-Sangiovese (Dry Creek Valley) $42. 82 *—S.H. (8/1/2004)*

Camellia 1999 Diamo Grazie Red Table Wine Red Blend (Dry Creek Valley) $42. 87 *—S.H. (12/15/2001)*

Camellia 2001 Merlo Vineyards Sangiovese (Dry Creek Valley) $24. 81 *— S.H. (8/1/2004)*

Camellia 2000 Merlo Vineyards Sangiovese (Dry Creek Valley) $28. 84 *— S.H. (12/1/2002)*

Camellia 1999 Merlo Vineyards Sangiovese (Dry Creek Valley) $28. 86 *— S.H. (12/15/2001)*

Camellia 2001 Lencioni Vineyard Zinfandel (Dry Creek Valley) $22. 82 *— S.H. (8/1/2004)*

USA

Camellia 1999 Lencioni Vineyard Zinfandel (Dry Creek Valley) $22. 86 —*S.H. (12/15/2001)*

CAMELOT

Camelot 2002 Cabernet Sauvignon (California) $8. 85 Best Buy —*S.H. (12/1/2005)*

Camelot 2001 Cabernet Sauvignon (California) $7. 84 —*S.H. (10/1/2004)*

Camelot 1999 Cabernet Sauvignon (California) $10. 85 —*S.H. (6/1/2002)*

Camelot 1997 Chardonnay (California) $13. 87 —*L.W. (10/1/1999)*

Camelot 2003 Chardonnay (California) $7. 84 Best Buy —*S.H. (6/1/2005)*

Camelot 2000 Chardonnay (California) $10. 82 —*S.H. (5/1/2002)*

Camelot 1996 Merlot (California) $13. 85 *(3/1/2000)*

Camelot 2001 Merlot (California) $7. 85 Best Buy —*S.H. (12/15/2004)*

Camelot 1998 Merlot (California) $10. 82 —*S.H. (12/31/2001)*

Camelot 1997 Merlot (California) $10. 82 *(2/1/2001)*

Camelot 2003 Pinot Noir (California) $7. 82 —*S.H. (6/1/2005)*

Camelot 2002 Pinot Noir (California) $7. 84 Best Buy *(11/1/2004)*

Camelot 2001 Pinot Noir (California) $10. 83 —*M.S. (12/1/2003)*

Camelot 2000 Pinot Noir (California) $10. 84 —*S.H. (12/15/2001)*

Camelot 1997 Pinot Noir (California) $10. 82 —*S.H. (2/1/2001)*

Camelot 2004 Sauvignon Blanc (California) $8. 85 Best Buy —*S.H. (12/1/2005)*

Camelot 2003 Sauvignon Blanc (California) $7. 85 Best Buy —*S.H. (6/1/2005)*

Camelot 2002 Shiraz (California) $7. 86 Best Buy —*S.H. (6/1/2005)*

Camelot 1999 Syrah (California) $9. 83 *(10/1/2001)*

Camelot 2002 Zinfandel (California) $7. 83 —*S.H. (6/1/2005)*

CAMERON

Cameron 2003 Red Wine Cabernet Blend (Napa Valley) $50. 91 —*S.H. (9/1/2006)*

Cameron 1997 Clos Electrique Chardonnay (Willamette Valley) $35. 92 *(11/15/1999)*

CAMERON HUGHES

Cameron Hughes 2004 Lot 17 Barbera (Sierra Foothills) $14. If you like old-fashioned Barbera, this one's for you. Dry, tannic and thick in dark fruit and berry flavors, it also has high acidity, the kind that calls for cheese, duck, lamb, anything larded with fat. 86 —*S.H. (4/1/2007)*

Cameron Hughes 2002 Lot 23 Meritage Bordeaux Blend (Sonoma-Napa) $10. Made from all five Bordeaux reds, based on Merlot, this is rich and soft. You get plenty of blackberry, cherry, plum, milk chocolate and spicy, oaky flavors, and a dry finish. Drink now. 86 Best Buy —*S.H. (7/1/2007)*

Cameron Hughes 2003 Lot 15 Cabernet Sauvignon (Napa Valley) $15. 86 —*S.H. (12/31/2006)*

Cameron Hughes 2004 Lot 16 Cabernet Sauvignon (Stags Leap District) $16. 86 —*S.H. (12/31/2006)*

Cameron Hughes 2002 Lot 7 Cabernet Sauvignon (Knights Valley) $10. 85 Best Buy —*S.H. (5/1/2006)*

Cameron Hughes 2005 Chardonnay (Edna Valley) $10. Good value from this dependable nègociant. It shows typical Edna Valley acidity, like the fresh juice from a ripe lime. The flavors veer toward limes, clover honey and vanilla, although the finish is dry and clean. 84 —*S.H. (4/1/2007)*

Cameron Hughes 2005 Chardonnay (Russian River Valley) $11. Simple and fruity, with very ripe pineapple, peach and green apple flavors. The wine finishes crisply. 83 —*S.H. (4/1/2007)*

Cameron Hughes 2005 Lot 20 Chardonnay (Russian River Valley) $11. Only 20% new oak on this wine, but it sure does stand out, dominating the modest fruit with a smoky, charry taste. Hard to like this toothpicky Chard. 82 —*S.H. (11/1/2007)*

Cameron Hughes 2005 Lot 22 Chardonnay (Edna Valley) $8. No oak on this stainless steel-fermented wine, so that the Edna Valley character shines. Brims with lemon and lime, kiwi and vanilla flavors, with clean acidity. 86 Best Buy —*S.H. (7/1/2007)*

Cameron Hughes 2003 Lot 8 Pinot Noir (Monterey County) $10. 82 —*S.H. (5/1/2006)*

Cameron Hughes 1998 Lot 25 Sparkling Wine Sparkling Blend (Carneros) $18. This is quite a good sparkler; a great price especially for a Chard-Pinot Noir blend from a major appellation that has spent eight years on the lees. Dry and creamy, it has mouthfilling, yeasty, raspberry-strawberry and vanilla-spice flavors, boosted with a honeyed dosage. 90 Editors' Choice —*S.H. (7/1/2007)*

Cameron Hughes 2005 Lot 24 Syrah (Sonoma County) $12. Very soft, almost melted is the texture on this wine. Soft in both tannins and acids, which leaves the fruit and alcohol to star. The flavors, of blackberries, cherries, milk chocolate, plums and coffee, are rich, but the wine could use greater structure. 84 —*S.H. (9/1/2007)*

Cameron Hughes 2005 Lot 27 Syrah (Russian River Valley) $12. Here's a tasty little country wine, rich in berry-cherry fruit and chocolate chip cookies. It's soft in tannins, and dry. 84 —*S.H. (9/1/2007)*

Cameron Hughes 2004 Lot 21 Zinfandel (California) $11. What a great job this winery is doing at giving the public sound varietal wines at everyday prices. Bravo. This Zin is especially succulent. It's dry and balanced and rich in blackberry, cherry, carob, sweet tobacco and exotic spice flavors. Perfect for roast chicken, lasagna or grilled meats. 86 Best Buy —*S.H. (7/1/2007)*

CAMPION

Campion 2001 Pinot Noir (Edna Valley) $35. 87 —*S.H. (3/1/2004)*

Campion 2000 Pinot Noir (Santa Lucia Highlands) $32. 86 —*S.H. (4/1/2004)*

Campion 2000 Pinot Noir (Carneros) $32. 86 —*S.H. (4/1/2004)*

Campion 2001 Firepeak Vineyard Pinot Noir (Edna Valley) $45. 88 —*S.H. (4/1/2004)*

CAMPUS OAKS

Campus Oaks 1998 Cabernet Sauvignon (Mendocino) $12. 82 —*S.H. (6/1/2002)*

Campus Oaks 2002 Chardonnay (California) $7. 82 —*S.H. (5/1/2004)*

Campus Oaks 1999 Chardonnay (California) $8. 83 —*S.H. (5/1/2002)*

Campus Oaks 2001 Merlot (California) $9. 85 —*S.H. (5/1/2004)*

Campus Oaks 1998 Merlot (California) $9. 84 —*S.H. (6/1/2002)*

Campus Oaks 2001 Pinot Noir (Mendocino County) $9. 84 —*S.H. (5/1/2004)*

Campus Oaks 1999 Syrah (California) $9. 82 *(10/1/2001)*

Campus Oaks 2001 Old Vine Zinfandel (Lodi) $15. 85 —*S.H. (5/1/2004)*

Campus Oaks 1999 Old Vine Zinfandel (California) $10. 84 —*S.H. (7/1/2002)*

CANA'S FEAST

Cana's Feast 1999 Bordeaux Blend (Red Mountain) $30. 90 —*M.S. (6/1/2003)*

Cana's Feast 2000 Del Rio Vineyard Bordeaux Blend (Rogue Valley) $30. 89 —*M.S. (8/1/2003)*

Cana's Feast 1999 Cuvée G Pinot Noir (Willamette Valley) $30. 90 —*M.S. (9/1/2003)*

Cana's Feast 2002 Meredith Mitchell Vineyard Pinot Noir (Willamette Valley) $40. 87 *(11/1/2004)*

CANEPA

Canepa 1998 Gauer Vineyard Chardonnay (Sonoma County) $30. 89 *(7/1/2001)*

CANOE RIDGE

Canoe Ridge 2003 Cabernet Sauvignon (Columbia Valley (WA)) $20. 87 —*P.G. (4/1/2006)*

Canoe Ridge 2001 Cabernet Sauvignon (Columbia Valley (WA)) $20. 87 —*P.G. (7/1/2004)*

Canoe Ridge 1999 Cabernet Sauvignon (Columbia Valley (WA)) $28. 88 Editors' Choice —*P.G. (5/1/2002)*

Canoe Ridge 1998 Cabernet Sauvignon (Columbia Valley (WA)) $25. 89 —*P.G. (6/1/2001)*

Canoe Ridge 1997 Cabernet Sauvignon (Columbia Valley (WA)) $25. 87 —*P.G. (11/15/2000)*

Canoe Ridge 1996 Cabernet Sauvignon (Columbia Valley (WA)) $25. 91 —*S.H. (7/1/1999)*

Canoe Ridge 2004 Block 1 Reserve Cabernet Sauvignon (Columbia Valley (WA)) $45. This is a fine bottle of wine—presumably all Cabernet—with a good mix of black cherry, fig and plum; rounding into chocolate and clove, and finishing up with a firm minerally stoniness. Classy, full and ripe. 91 —*P.G. (11/1/2007)*

Canoe Ridge 2005 Chardonnay (Columbia Valley (WA)) $15. Christophe Paubert brings a distinctly French palate to these grapes, and he knows how to bring out the elegance that is too often buried in buttery oak. Here the fruit stands out, crisply defined, clean and extremely fresh. Only 20% was put through malo, and fully 85% was fermented in stainless steel. This is a fine effort, and a terrific value. 88 —*P.G. (11/1/2007)*

Canoe Ridge 2002 Chardonnay (Columbia Valley (WA)) $19. 87 *—P.G. (5/1/2004)*

Canoe Ridge 2001 Chardonnay (Columbia Valley (WA)) $19. 87 *—M.S. (6/1/2003)*

Canoe Ridge 2000 Chardonnay (Columbia Valley (WA)) $18. 90 *—P.G. (2/1/2002)*

Canoe Ridge 2000 Chardonnay (Columbia Valley (WA)) $19. 86 *—J.M. (5/1/2002)*

Canoe Ridge 2000 Oak Ridge Gewürztraminer (Washington) $12. 88 *—P.G. (12/31/2001)*

Canoe Ridge 2002 Oak Ridge Vineyard Gewürztraminer (Washington) $13. 90 Best Buy *—P.G. (5/1/2004)*

Canoe Ridge 1999 Oak Ridge Vineyard Gewürztraminer (Washington) $12. 90 Best Buy *—P.G. (11/15/2000)*

Canoe Ridge 2006 Snipes Vineyard Gewürztraminer (Columbia Valley (WA)) $16. This is a mirror image of the winery's Riesling, which provides 10% of the blend. Fragrant rose petal and toasted nut aromas mingle, creating a sensuous effect. It's quite dry, fresh and youthful, capturing the intensity of Washington fruit and the elegance of an Alsatian Gewürztraminer. This should make an excellent cellar wine, but there's no reason it can't be enjoyed immediately. **90** *—P.G. (11/1/2007)*

Canoe Ridge 2003 Merlot (Columbia Valley (WA)) $20. 87 *—P.G. (4/1/2006)*

Canoe Ridge 2001 Merlot (Columbia Valley (WA)) $15. 88 *—P.G. (9/1/2004)*

Canoe Ridge 1999 Merlot (Columbia Valley (WA)) $14. 86 *—C.S. (12/31/2002)*

Canoe Ridge 1999 Merlot (Columbia Valley (WA)) $25. 89 *—P.G. (12/31/2001)*

Canoe Ridge 1998 Merlot (Columbia Valley (WA)) $25. 88 *—P.G. (11/15/2000)*

Canoe Ridge 1997 Merlot (Columbia Valley (WA)) $19. 90 *—S.H. (11/1/1999)*

Canoe Ridge 2003 Block 13 Reserve Merlot (Columbia Valley (WA)) $45. Tart and smoky, showing some brick around the edges and a bit of volatility in the nose and mouth. This does not have the depth of fruit to support the oak and acid; it's chalky and tart at the same time. Though not a bad wine by any means, it is not really living up to its reserve status. **87** *—P.G. (11/1/2007)*

Canoe Ridge 1998 Reserve Merlot (Columbia Valley (WA)) $45. 90 *—P.G. (11/15/2000)*

Canoe Ridge 1999 Reserve-Lot No. 10 Merlot (Columbia Valley (WA)) $45. 91 *—P.G. (6/1/2002)*

Canoe Ridge 1998 Reserve Lot No. 16 Merlot (Columbia Valley (WA)) $45. 93 Cellar Selection *—P.G. (12/31/2001)*

Canoe Ridge 1998 Red Table Wine Merlot-Cabernet Sauvignon (Columbia Valley (WA)) $14. 87 *—P.G. (11/15/2000)*

Canoe Ridge 2000 Red Table Wine Red Blend (Columbia Valley (WA)) $14. 86 *—M.S. (6/1/2003)*

CANON DE SOL

Canon de Sol 2000 Meritage (Columbia Valley (WA)) $28. 88 *—P.G. (9/1/2003)*

Canon de Sol 2000 Merlot (Columbia Valley (WA)) $24. 87 *—P.G. (9/1/2003)*

Canon de Sol 1999 Merlot (Columbia Valley (WA)) $24. 86 *—P.G. (9/1/2003)*

CANTIGA WINEWORKS

Cantiga Wineworks 2000 Cabernet Sauvignon (El Dorado) $18. 84 *—S.H. (3/1/2005)*

Cantiga Wineworks 2000 Cabernet Sauvignon-Shiraz (Central Coast) $18. 84 *—J.M. (4/1/2003)*

Cantiga Wineworks 2000 Chardonnay (Monterey) $20. 89 *—J.M. (2/1/2003)*

Cantiga Wineworks 2000 Oakless Chardonnay (Monterey) $20. 85 *—J.M. (2/1/2003)*

Cantiga Wineworks 2001 Shiraz (Monterey) $24.84 *—S.H. (3/1/2005)*

Cantiga Wineworks 2000 Shiraz (Monterey) $24. 86 *—J.M. (2/1/2003)*

Cantiga Wineworks 2001 Ryan Oaks Vineyard Zinfandel (Sierra Foothills) $16. 84 *—S.H. (3/1/2005)*

CANYON ROAD

Canyon Road 2004 Cabernet Sauvignon (California) $9. Consumers looking to this winery to supply varietally true, inexpensive wines won't be disappointed. This has real Cabernet character, in the cherry-berry flavors, dryness and sturdy tannins. **84** *—S.H. (2/1/2007)*

Canyon Road 2003 Cabernet Sauvignon (California) $9. 85 Best Buy *—S.H. (10/1/2005)*

Canyon Road 2002 Cabernet Sauvignon (California) $10. 84 *—S.H. (12/31/2004)*

Canyon Road 2001 Cabernet Sauvignon (California) $10. 83 *—S.H. (6/1/2004)*

Canyon Road 2000 Cabernet Sauvignon (California) $10. 87 Best Buy *—S.H. (6/1/2002)*

Canyon Road 1998 Cabernet Sauvignon (California) $8. 87 *(11/15/1999)*

Canyon Road 2005 Chardonnay (California) $9. The winemaker says the majority of grapes come from the North Coast and Central Coast, which are cooler areas, and it's easy to believe. The wine brims with bright acidity. That makes the green apple and pink grapefruit flavors zesty and clean. An enriching touch of oak makes the wine a good value. **84** *—S.H. (2/1/2007)*

Canyon Road 2004 Chardonnay (California) $8. 7 Best Buy *—S.H. (11/15/2005)*

Canyon Road 2003 Chardonnay (California) $10. 84 *—S.H. (12/31/2004)*

Canyon Road 2002 Chardonnay (California) $10. 85 *—S.H. (6/1/2004)*

Canyon Road 2001 Chardonnay (California) $9. 86 *—S.H. (12/15/2002)*

Canyon Road 1999 Chardonnay (California) $8. 84 *—S.H. (10/1/2000)*

Canyon Road 1998 Chardonnay (California) $8. 84 Best Buy *—J.C. (10/1/1999)*

Canyon Road 2004 Merlot (California) $10. A dry, balanced wine with ripe cherry and blackberry flavors, and a nice edge of tannins to cut through beef and cheese. Great for inexpensive entertaining. **85 Best Buy** *—S.H. (2/1/2007)*

Canyon Road 2003 Merlot (California) $9. 85 Best Buy *—S.H. (10/1/2005)*

Canyon Road 2002 Merlot (California) $10. 85 *—S.H. (9/1/2004)*

Canyon Road 2001 Merlot (California) $10. 85 *—S.H. (12/1/2003)*

Canyon Road 2000 Merlot (California) $10. 86 Best Buy *—S.H. (6/1/2002)*

Canyon Road 1999 Merlot (California) $8. 83 *—J.C. (6/1/2001)*

Canyon Road 1998 Merlot (California) $8. 81 *—S.H. (12/31/1999)*

Canyon Road 2005 Sauvignon Blanc (California) $8. Canyon Road established their formula for Sauvignon Blanc years ago and hasn't budged. The wine remains a fair-priced source of very dry, light-bodied, tart wine, with lemon juice, lime zest and green grass flavors. **85 Best Buy** *—S.H. (2/1/2007)*

Canyon Road 2004 Sauvignon Blanc (California) $8. 86 Best Buy *—S.H. (10/1/2005)*

Canyon Road 2003 Sauvignon Blanc (Alexander Valley) $9. 84 *—S.H. (9/1/2004)*

Canyon Road 2002 Sauvignon Blanc (California) $9. 85 *—S.H. (7/1/2003)*

Canyon Road 2001 Sauvignon Blanc (California) $9. 86 Best Buy *—S.H. (9/1/2002)*

Canyon Road 2000 Sauvignon Blanc (California) $8. 88 *—M.N. (11/15/2001)*

Canyon Road 1999 Sauvignon Blanc (California) $8. 86 *—S.H. (9/1/2000)*

Canyon Road 1998 Sauvignon Blanc (California) $NA. 84 *—S.H. (9/1/1999)*

Canyon Road 2002 Shiraz (California) $10. 84 *—S.H. (12/31/2004)*

Canyon Road 2001 Shiraz (California) $10. 83 *—S.H. (6/1/2004)*

Canyon Road 2000 Shiraz (California) $10. 85 *—S.H. (9/1/2002)*

Canyon Road 2001 Zinfandel (California) $10. 86 *(11/1/2003)*

CANYON WIND

Canyon Wind 2001 Cabernet Sauvignon (Grand Valley) $20. An impressive product from Colorado winery Canyon Wind. Deep and dark aromas of plums, grilled meat and chocolate are followed by an elegant blend of dark cherry, clove and coffee flavors. Balanced nicely, this wine has some heft but is smooth and easy to drink. **86** *—S.K. (2/1/2007)*

Canyon Wind 2004 Chardonnay (Grand Valley) $15. Kudos to Colorado winemaker Canyon Wind Cellars for making wine in an area not known for grapes, and on first pass, this seems a rather friendly, accessible Chardonnay. A floral nose of pear and apricot is followed by spice and lemon on the palate. There is also oak to weigh down the zip. But it's a bit wiry and lacks dimension. **84** *—S.K. (2/1/2007)*

Canyon Wind 2002 Merlot (Grand Valley) $18. An appealing smoked sausage and clove spice nose on this wine leads to a flavorful, though slightly dry, array of berries, plum and smoke on the palate. Impressive structure and complexity but the wine should probably age 2–5 years for maximum enjoyment and to take off that tannic edge. **85** —*S.K. (5/1/2007)*

Canyon Wind 2005 Desert Rosé Rosé Blend (Grand Valley) $13. Lovely floral scents mingle with fruit flavors of strawberry, peach and honey in this rose from Colorado producer Canyon Wind. It's a bit on the sweet side which overpowers some of the more delicate flavors, but a hearty dose of acidity cuts some of the candy. The wine would pair well with lobster or oysters. **83** —*S.K. (2/1/2007)*

Canyon Wind 2006 Sauvignon Blanc (Grand Valley) $15. Pleasant aromas and flavors of grass, grapefruit and flowers recommend this likeable wine from the Grand Valley appellation of Colorado. Paired with seafood or Asian cuisine, the wine is an interesting alternative for everyday sipping. **83** —*S.K. (10/1/2007)*

CAPAROSO

Caparoso 2001 Cabernet Sauvignon (Central Coast) $10. 86 —*S.H. (11/15/2003)*

Caparoso 2001 Pinot Noir (San Luis Obispo) $17. 89 —*S.H. (12/1/2003)*

CAPAY VALLEY

Capay Valley 2000 Syrah (California) $16. 83 —*S.H. (12/1/2004)*

Capay Valley 1999 Syrah (California) $21. 88 *(11/1/2001)*

Capay Valley 2002 Tempranillo (California) $15. 82 —*S.H. (12/15/2004)*

Capay Valley 2004 Viognier (Capay Valley) $15. 83 —*S.H. (10/1/2005)*

Capay Valley 2003 Viognier (California) $15. 84 —*S.H. (11/15/2004)*

CAPELLO

Capello 1999 Cabernet Sauvignon (California) $9. 84 —*S.H. (6/1/2003)*

Capello 1999 Chardonnay (California) $9. 84 —*S.H. (6/1/2003)*

Capello 1999 Merlot (California) $9. 84 —*S.H. (9/1/2003)*

CAPE MAY

Cape May 2005 Cabernet Sauvignon (New Jersey) $18. Cinnamon, clove and plum on the nose are followed by like flavors of plum and spice, with a touch of vanilla. Approachable now, and good with sharp cheeses. **83** —*S.K. (10/1/2007)*

Cape May 2006 Riesling (New Jersey) $17. This is rife with earthy spice on the nose and on the palate, some of that lively spice continues. But there's a lack of dimension and finesse here that would make this stand out. The intentions are good, but there's not enough here to support them. **82** —*S.K. (9/1/2007)*

CAPIAUX

Capiaux 2000 Pisoni Vineyard Pinot Noir (Santa Lucia Highlands) $45. 90 *(10/1/2002)*

Capiaux 2000 Widdoes Vineyard Pinot Noir (Russian River Valley) $36. 88 *(10/1/2002)*

Capiaux 2006 Swink Rosé Blend (California) $14. It tastes of raspberry juice with a healthy spoonful of white sugar. The fundamentals are there, though. Makes you wish it were dry, like table wine ought to be. **82** —*S.H. (7/1/2007)*

CAPOLAN

Capolan 2004 Merlot (Sonoma County) $10. Simple and rustic, with a soft texture framing cherry and raspberry LifeSaver flavors. **82** —*S.H. (10/1/2007)*

CARABELLA

Carabella 2005 Dijon 76 Chardonnay (Willamette Valley) $28. This 100% barrel-fermented Chardonnay leads you seductively with a softly fruity approach, filling out throughout the midpalate with a lovely blend of stone fruits. Layers of sweet cream, spicy, pepper and hazelnuts keep it interesting right into a lingering finish. The length and texture really set this wine apart from the pack. **91 Editors' Choice** —*P.G. (11/15/2007)*

Carabella 2004 Dijon 76 Chardonnay (Willamette Valley) $26. Nicely crafted, with the crisp, focused flavors of the Dijon clone. The wine opens prettily with fragrant aromas of citrus rind. It's concentrated and firm, a mix of lime, pineapple and citrus. French oak aged in a mix of neutral, used and new barrels, it wears its butterscotch lightly and goes out with a hint of resin. Very polished effort. **91** —*P.G. (4/1/2007)*

Carabella 2002 Dijon 76 Clone Chardonnay (Willamette Valley) $23. 85 —*P.G. (2/1/2005)*

Carabella 2006 Pinot Gris (Chehalem Mountain) $16. This is one of the first wines to put the new Chehalem Mountains AVA on the label. This is home turf for the estate vineyard. This is great fruit, fully ripe and simply packed with luscious flavor. The winemaking pushes it a bit, and there are hints of volatility, but it pulls itself together into a truly delicious midpalate loaded with fruits, nuts and butterscotch. Dense and resonant, this is a wine that keeps on going, and you can't help yourself—you want another glass. **90** —*P.G. (11/15/2007)*

Carabella 2003 Pinot Gris (Willamette Valley) $14. 87 —*P.G. (2/1/2006)*

Carabella 2003 Pinot Gris (Willamette Valley) $14. 87 —*P.G. (2/1/2005)*

Carabella 2002 Pinot Gris (Willamette Valley) $14. 87 Best Buy —*P.G. (2/1/2004)*

Carabella 2000 Pinot Gris (Willamette Valley) $14. 86 —*P.G. (2/1/2002)*

Carabella 2002 Pinot Noir (Willamette Valley) $35. 86 —*P.G. (2/1/2005)*

Carabella 2001 Pinot Noir (Willamette Valley) $33. 88 —*P.G. (2/1/2004)*

Carabella 1999 Pinot Noir (Willamette Valley) $33. 86 —*P.G. (12/31/2001)*

Carabella 1998 Pinot Noir (Willamette Valley) $30. 87 —*M.S. (12/1/2000)*

Carabella 2004 Estate Pinot Noir (Willamette Valley) $39. The Carabella vineyard shows its best stuff in 2004. Lovely aromas of fruit, cola, herb and cedar waft from the glass. Classic Pinot, elegant and complex right off the bat. Beautifully structured and harmonious, this wine is a lovely example of how the best Oregon wines straddle the line between the succulent fruit of California and the acid-driven structure of premier cru Burgundy. **92** —*P.G. (4/1/2007)*

Carabella 2001 Les Meres Pinot Noir (Willamette Valley) $19. 87 —*P.G. (2/1/2004)*

CARDINALE

Cardinale 1997 Cabernet Sauvignon (Mount Veeder) $125. 95 *(11/1/2000)*

Cardinale 2000 Cabernet Sauvignon (Napa-Sonoma) $120. 89 —*S.H. (12/31/2003)*

CARHARTT CELLARS

Carhartt Cellars 2001 Merlot (Santa Ynez Valley) $30. 86 —*S.H. (2/1/2004)*

CARHARTT VINEYARD

Carhartt Vineyard 2002 Estate Merlot (Santa Ynez Valley) $29. 84 —*S.H. (6/1/2005)*

Carhartt Vineyard 2003 Syrah (Santa Ynez Valley) $28. 86 *(9/1/2005)*

Carhartt Vineyard 2001 Syrah (Santa Ynez Valley) $30. 90 —*S.H. (3/1/2004)*

Carhartt Vineyard 2002 Estate Syrah (Santa Ynez Valley) $29. 84 —*S.H. (6/1/2005)*

CARICA

Carica 2005 Kick Ranch Sauvignon Blanc (Sonoma County) $19. Dry and crisply acidic, with the gooseberry flavors from 40% Musque clone, this wine was grown northeast of Santa Rosa, which would put it near Chalk Hill. Mainly stainless steel fermented, with a touch of new French oak, it shows elegance and finesse. **87** —*S.H. (7/1/2007)*

CARINA CELLARS

Carina Cellars 2001 Syrah (Santa Barbara County) $16. 89 Editors' Choice —*S.H. (10/1/2003)*

Carina Cellars 2004 Viognier (Santa Barbara County) $18. 82 —*S.H. (7/1/2006)*

Carina Cellars 2001 Viognier (Santa Barbara County) $16. 85 —*S.H. (6/1/2003)*

CARLISLE

Carlisle 2001 Petite Sirah (Dry Creek Valley) $36. 89 *(4/1/2003)*

Carlisle 2002 Two Acres Red Blend (Russian River Valley) $36. 87 —*S.H. (8/1/2005)*

Carlisle 2001 Two Acres Red Blend (Russian River Valley) $36. 93 —*S.H. (12/31/2003)*

Carlisle 2000 Two Acres Red Blend (Russian River Valley) $36. 96 Cellar Selection —*S.H. (11/15/2002)*

Carlisle 2001 Three Birds Rhône Red Blend (Sonoma County) $23. 89 —*S.H. (12/1/2003)*

Carlisle 2001 Syrah (Dry Creek Valley) $40. 91 —*S.H. (12/1/2003)*

Carlisle 2000 Syrah (Dry Creek Valley) $40. 93 Editors' Choice —*S.H. (6/1/2003)*

Carlisle 2000 Syrah (Dry Creek Valley) $46. 95 —*S.H. (12/1/2002)*

Carlisle 2001 Zinfandel (Sonoma County) $23. 88 *(11/1/2003)*

Carlisle 2002 Carlisle Vineyard Zinfandel (Russian River Valley) $36. 86 —*S.H. (8/1/2005)*

Carlisle 2001 Carlisle Vineyard Zinfandel (Russian River Valley) $35. 89 *(11/1/2003)*

CARMEL

Carmel 2002 Cabernet Sauvignon (Monterey County) $40. 82 *—S.H. (3/1/2006)*

Carmel 2003 Vintner's Selection Chardonnay (Monterey County) $23. 90 *—S.H. (5/1/2006)*

CARMEL ROAD

Carmel Road 2004 Chardonnay (Monterey) $16. 82 *—S.H. (10/1/2006)*

Carmel Road 1999 Chardonnay (Monterey) $50. 91 *(7/1/2001)*

Carmel Road 2004 Pinot Noir (Monterey) $20. 90 Editors' Choice *—S.H. (10/1/2006)*

Carmel Road 2003 Pinot Noir (Arroyo Seco) $35. 92 *—S.H. (10/1/2006)*

CARMENET

Carmenet 1995 Moon Mountain Estate Reserve Bordeaux Blend (Sonoma) $40. 89 *—S.H. (7/1/1999)*

Carmenet 2000 Cabernet Franc (Sonoma Valley) $18. 84 *—S.H. (5/1/2004)*

Carmenet 2001 Cabernet Sauvignon (Lake County) $18. 84 *—S.H. (5/1/2004)*

Carmenet 2001 Cellar Selection Cabernet Sauvignon (California) $9. 84 *—S.H. (6/1/2004)*

Carmenet 2000 Cellar Selection Cabernet Sauvignon (California) $8. 84 *—S.H. (11/15/2003)*

Carmenet 1998 Dynamite Cabernet Sauvignon (North Coast) $20. 86 *—S.H. (9/1/2000)*

Carmenet 1997 Dynamite Cabernet Sauvignon (North Coast) $20. 88 *—S.H. (7/1/1999)*

Carmenet 1999 Moon Mountain Reserve Cabernet Sauvignon (Sonoma Valley) $65. 89 *—J.M. (5/1/2002)*

Carmenet 1997 Moon Mountain Reserve Cabernet Sauvignon (Sonoma Valley) $48. 93 *(11/1/2000)*

Carmenet 1996 Moon Mountain Reserve Cabernet Sauvignon (Sonoma Valley) $40. 90 *(11/1/1999)*

Carmenet 2002 Chardonnay (Napa Valley) $16. 84 *—S.H. (2/1/2004)*

Carmenet 2002 Cellar Selection Chardonnay (California) $9. 85 *—S.H. (6/1/2004)*

Carmenet 2001 Cellar Selection Chardonnay (California) $8. 84 *—S.H. (12/1/2003)*

Carmenet 1997 Sangiacomo Vineyard Chardonnay (Carneros) $18. 87 *—S.H. (10/1/1999)*

Carmenet 2001 Merlot (Sonoma County) $20. 87 *—S.H. (5/1/2004)*

Carmenet 2001 Cellar Selection Merlot (California) $9. 85 *—S.H. (6/1/2004)*

Carmenet 2000 Cellar Selection Merlot (California) $8. 85 Best Buy *—S.H. (12/31/2003)*

Carmenet 2002 Pinot Noir (Sonoma County) $20. 88 *(11/1/2004)*

Carmenet 2002 Cellar Selection Sauvignon Blanc (California) $8. 86 Best Buy *—S.H. (10/1/2003)*

Carmenet 2002 Hanson Vineyard Sauvignon Blanc (Lake County) $17. 87 *—S.H. (4/1/2004)*

Carmenet 1999 Paragon Vineyard Reserve Sauvignon Blanc (Edna Valley) $16. 88 *—S.H. (8/1/2001)*

Carmenet 1997 Paragon Vineyard-Reserve Sauvignon Blanc (Edna Valley) $16. 82 *—M.M. (9/1/1999)*

Carmenet 1999 Evangelho Vineyard Zinfandel (Contra Costa County) $25. 90 *—S.H. (9/1/2002)*

Carmenet 2001 Evangelho Vineyard Old Vine Zinfandel (Contra Costa County) $20. 89 *—S.H. (5/1/2004)*

Carmenet 1997 Evangelho Vineyard Old Vines Zinfandel (Contra Costa County) $17. 85 *—S.H. (5/1/2000)*

CARMICHAEL

Carmichael 2000 Sa Vini Red Blend (Monterey County) $18. 84 *—S.H. (4/1/2005)*

Carmichael 2002 Sur le Pont Rhône Red Blend (Monterey County) $18. 86 *—S.H. (2/1/2005)*

Carmichael 2005 Grigio e Bianco White Table Wine White Blend (Monterey County) $14. 89 Best Buy *—S.H. (12/1/2006)*

Carmichael 2003 Grigio e Bianco White Table Wine White Blend (Monterey County) $15. 89 *—S.H. (12/1/2005)*

CARMODY MCKNIGHT

Carmody McKnight 1997 Chardonnay (Paso Robles) $15. 85 *(6/1/2000)*

Carmody McKnight 1998 Millennium Celebration Chardonnay (Paso Robles) $17. 86 *(6/1/2000)*

CARNEROS CREEK

Carneros Creek 2001 Gavin Vineyard Chardonnay (Carneros) $20. 84 *—S.H. (12/31/2003)*

Carneros Creek 1997 Palombo Vineyard Chardonnay (Carneros) $18. 81 *(6/1/2000)*

Carneros Creek 2000 Pinot Noir (Carneros) $24. 90 Editors' Choice *(10/1/2002)*

Carneros Creek 2002 Carneros Signature Reserve Pinot Noir (Carneros) $20. 84 *—S.H. (11/1/2004)*

Carneros Creek 2000 Cote de Carneros Pinot Noir (Carneros) $17. 87 Best Buy *(10/1/2002)*

Carneros Creek 1997 Estate Grown Pinot Noir (Carneros) $18. 87 *(5/1/2000)*

Carneros Creek 2002 Grail Pinot Noir (Carneros) $40. 86 *—S.H. (10/1/2005)*

Carneros Creek 2001 Las Brisas Vineyard Pinot Noir (Carneros) $40. 89 *—S.H. (2/1/2004)*

Carneros Creek 2002 Los Carneros Reserve Pinot Noir (Carneros) $25. 85 *—S.H. (11/1/2004)*

Carneros Creek 2001 Los Carneros Reserve Pinot Noir (Carneros) $25. 90 *—S.H. (3/1/2004)*

Carneros Creek 2001 Mahoney Vineyard Pinot Noir (Carneros) $40. 90 *—S.H. (2/1/2004)*

Carneros Creek 2004 Reserve Pinot Noir (Carneros) $25. Very good and savory, athough it's a bit heavy for a Pinot Noir, with a soft, thick texture and ultraripe chocolate, cherry liqueur and cappuccino flavors. Who wouldn't like that? But the wine could be crisper, more delicate and refined. 87 *—S.H. (5/1/2007)*

Carneros Creek 1999 Signature Reserve Pinot Noir (Carneros) $48. 89 *(10/1/2002)*

CARNEROS DELLA NOTTE

Carneros della Notte 2003 Pinot Noir (Carneros) $48. There are admirable qualities of dryness, crispness and true varietal silkiness, with good cola, blackberry, spicy coffee and unsweetened chocolate flavors. But there's something bitter, astringent and heavy that puts me off. Could do something in time, but it's already nearly four years old. 85 *—S.H. (10/1/2007)*

Carneros della Notte 2005 Eclipse Late Harvest Pinot Noir (Carneros) $60. Few wineries in California make Pinot Noir into a dessert wine, and there may be a good reason for that. This one's heavy and simple, despite loads of sweet raspberry jam and sugared tea flavors. 84 *—S.H. (10/1/2007)*

Carneros della Notte 2005 Solstice Late Harvest Riesling (San Francisco Bay) $40. Made in the sweet, German style, this dessert Riesling opens with honeyed apricot, tangerine and vanilla aromas, then turns soft, sweet and a little one-dimensional. The flavors follow the aromas. 85 *—S.H. (9/1/2007)*

CAROL SHELTON

Carol Shelton 2006 Rendezvous Rosé Rosé Blend (Mendocino) $15. According to the paperwork, it's made from Carignan, and the wine shows that variety's rustic, wild berry nature. It's not terribly complex, but there's something about the savory fruit, silky texture and dry acidity that captures the essence of rosé. 86 *—S.H. (7/1/2007)*

Carol Shelton 2004 Cox Vineyard Wild Thing Zinfandel (Mendocino County) $28. Carol Shelton's Zins are indeed wild. They have a wild berry character, a briary taste like freshly-picked black raspberries right off the bush. This one has a milk chocolate and white pepper edge, but it's dry and feels balanced despite enormously high alcohol. 87 *—S.H. (2/1/2007)*

Carol Shelton 2002 Cox Vineyard Old Vines Wild Thing Zinfandel (Mendocino County) $28. 90 *—S.H. (12/31/2004)*

Carol Shelton 2001 KarmaZin, Old Vines Zinfandel (Russian River Valley) $30. 89 *(11/1/2003)*

Carol Shelton 2002 Lopez Vineyard Old Vines MongaZin Zinfandel (Cucamonga Valley) $24. 87 *—S.H. (12/31/2004)*

Carol Shelton 2004 Maple Zin Old Vine Zinfandel (Dry Creek Valley) $33. They say the vines are 75 years old, head-trained and dry-farmed. That's winespeak for intensity, which this Zin has plenty of. The concentrated cherry, raspberry, blackberry, root beer and chocolate flavors are wrapped

USA

into a soft, velvety mouthfeel that finishes somewhere between dry and just off-dry. **88** *—S.H. (2/1/2007)*

Carol Shelton 2004 Monga Zin Lopez Vineyard Old Vines Zinfandel (Cucamonga Valley) $22. Made in an old-fashioned, rustic style, the kind of Zin you used to be able to buy in jugs straight from the winery. It's acidic, harsh and raisiny. **81** *—S.H. (3/1/2007)*

Carol Shelton 2001 MongaZin, Lopez Vineyard Zinfandel (Cucamonga Valley) $24. 90 Editors' Choice *(11/1/2003)*

Carol Shelton 2002 Rock Pile Ridge Vineyard Rocky Reserve Zinfandel (Dry Creek Valley) $32. 88 *—S.H. (12/31/2004)*

Carol Shelton 2004 Rocky Reserve Zinfandel (Dry Creek Valley) $33. I've liked this wine over the years because of the Bordeaux-like elegance it achieves without losing Zin's wild, briary side. Here, the wine is softer and a little sweeter than in the past, given the hot vintage, but it's still balanced and rich in true Dry Creek Zinny character. **87** *—S.H. (2/1/2007)*

Carol Shelton 2001 Rocky Reserve, Rockpile Ridge Vineyard Zinfandel (Dry Creek Valley) $32. 91 *(11/1/2003)*

Carol Shelton 2004 Rue Vineyard Old Vines Karma Zinfandel (Russian River Valley) $33. More tannic, drier than in the past, this single-vineyard Zin, made from century-old field blended grapes, is tough right now. But it has a wealth of ripe blackberry and cherry jam fruit. The tannins really need rich, fatty meats and cheeses. Slow-cooked short ribs of beef will be perfect. **86** *—S.H. (2/1/2007)*

Carol Shelton 2002 Rue Vineyard Old Vines KarmaZin Zinfandel (Russian River Valley) $30. 89 *—S.H. (12/31/2004)*

Carol Shelton 2001 Wild Thing, Old Vines Zinfandel (Mendocino County) $28. 90 *(11/1/2003)*

CARPE DIEM

Carpe Diem 2005 Cabernet Sauvignon (Napa Valley) $22. Better known for Edna Valley Pinot Noir and Chardonnay, Carpe Diem now turns to Napa Cab. Although it's a clean Cab with some elegance, it's lean and herbal, lacking the opulence Napa Cab ought to have. **84** *—S.H. (10/1/2007)*

Carpe Diem 2004 Chardonnay (Edna Valley) $26. 90 *—S.H. (11/1/2006)*

Carpe Diem 2005 Firepeak Vineyard Chardonnay (Edna Valley) $28. From a cool appellation in a cool vintage, a balanced, drily crisp Chardonnay. Oak dominates, with toast, butterscotch and vanilla notes riding high over underlying green apple and kiwi fruit. **87** *—S.H. (10/1/2007)*

Carpe Diem 2003 Firepeak Vineyard Chardonnay (Edna Valley) $26. 90 *—S.H. (10/1/2006)*

Carpe Diem 2002 Firepeak Vineyard Chardonnay (Edna Valley) $25. 87 *—S.H. (8/1/2004)*

Carpe Diem 2001 Firepeak Vineyard Chardonnay (Edna Valley) $25. 85 *—S.H. (8/1/2003)*

Carpe Diem 2000 Firepeak Vineyard Chardonnay (Edna Valley) $25. 92 Editors' Choice *—S.H. (12/15/2002)*

Carpe Diem 2005 Firepeak Vineyard Pinot Noir (Edna Valley) $28. The '05, as befits the cool vintage, is very dry and crisply elegant, with crushed cherry, raspberry and root beer flavors boosted by a squirt of lime juice, enriched by sweet vanilla and oak. Best now–2008. **89** *—S.H. (10/1/2007)*

Carpe Diem 2004 Firepeak Vineyard Pinot Noir (Edna Valley) $31. 88 *—S.H. (11/15/2006)*

Carpe Diem 2002 Firepeak Vineyard Pinot Noir (Edna Valley) $29. 86 *—S.H. (11/1/2004)*

Carpe Diem 2001 Firepeak Vineyard Pinot Noir (Edna Valley) $31. 90 *—S.H. (3/1/2004)*

Carpe Diem 2000 Firepeak Vineyard Pinot Noir (Edna Valley) $23. 87 *(10/1/2002)*

CARPENTER CREEK

Carpenter Creek 2002 Chardonnay (Washington) $14. 83 *—P.G. (1/1/2004)*

Carpenter Creek 2002 Riesling (Washington) $10. 80 *—P.G. (1/1/2004)*

Carpenter Creek 2002 Sauvignon Blanc (Washington) $13. 83 *—P.G. (1/1/2004)*

Carpenter Creek 2002 Syrah (Washington) $38. 81 *—P.G. (11/15/2004)*

Carpenter Creek 2002 Signature Series Syrah (Yakima Valley) $38. 82 *(9/1/2005)*

CARR

Carr 2004 Pinot Grigio (Santa Rita Hills) $18. 86 *—S.H. (2/1/2006)*

Carr 2005 Turner Vineyard Pinot Gris (Santa Rita Hills) $18. 90 *—S.H. (11/15/2006)*

Carr 2004 Ashley's Vineyard Pinot Noir (Santa Rita Hills) $30. 85 *—S.H. (7/1/2006)*

Carr 2003 Ashley's Vineyard Pinot Noir (Santa Rita Hills) $35. 90 *—S.H. (10/1/2005)*

Carr 2002 Ashley's Vineyard Pinot Noir (Santa Rita Hills) $NA. 87 *(11/1/2004)*

Carr 2004 Clos Pepe Vineyard Pinot Noir (Santa Rita Hills) $40. 82 *—S.H. (7/1/2006)*

Carr 2005 Three Vineyards Pinot Noir (Santa Rita Hills) $30. Carr's 2005 Turner Vineyard was a very exciting discovery for me, and while their Three Vineyards isn't quite in the same league, it's still a seriously good wine. Shows full-throttle Santa Rita atttibutes of crisp balance, intensely ripe fruit, great mouthfeel and limited ageability. The palate loves the cherries, raspberries, cola, spicy vanilla and smoky flavors. The wine comes from some of the best vineyards: Ashley's, Clos Pepe and Turner. **91 Editors' Choice** *—S.H. (7/1/2007)*

Carr 2003 Three Vineyards Pinot Noir (Santa Rita Hills) $40. 92 *—S.H. (10/1/2005)*

Carr 2005 Turner Vineyard Pinot Noir (Santa Rita Hills) $35. This wine is a blend of Dijon clones, which bring pure, jammy fruit. Paired with the older Pommard, the result is a meaty, full-bodied Pinot. There's an earthiness to the cherries and berries, and the wine is complex and probably ageworthy for 6–8 years. This polished wine exemplifies the art of blending, although it's a single-vineyard wine that vividly captures a sense of place. **94** *—S.H. (4/1/2007)*

Carr 2004 Turner Vineyard Pinot Noir (Santa Rita Hills) $35. 88 *—S.H. (7/1/2006)*

Carr 2006 Turner Vineyard Pinot Rosé Rosé Blend (Santa Rita Hills) $20. This is full-bodied and weighty compared to most of the California rosés in this tasting. If not for the pinkish color, you might think it was a full-fledged Pinot Noir. It has an ample feeling of raspberries and cola, with a scour of tannins. But it's dry and balanced. **85** *—S.H. (7/1/2007)*

CARREFOUR

Carrefour 2003 Cabernet Franc (Napa Valley) $30. 86 *—S.H. (12/15/2006)*

Carrefour 2003 Cabernet Sauvignon (Napa Valley) $40. 86 *—S.H. (12/15/2006)*

Carrefour 2003 Merlot (Napa Valley) $25. 86 *—S.H. (12/15/2006)*

Carrefour 2003 Pinot Noir (Carneros) $28. 87 *—S.H. (12/15/2006)*

Carrefour 2005 Sauvignon Blanc (Napa Valley) $18. 84 *—S.H. (12/15/2006)*

CARTER

Carter 2002 Beckstoffer To Kalon Vineyard Cabernet Sauvignon (Oakville) $75. 90 *—S.H. (2/1/2006)*

Carter 2001 Beckstoffer Vineyards Cabernet Sauvignon (Oakville) $75. 93 *—S.H. (8/1/2005)*

Carter 1998 Coliseum Block Cabernet Sauvignon (Napa Valley) $50. 92 *—J.M. (12/31/2001)*

Carter 1999 Fortuna Block Cabernet Sauvignon (Napa Valley) $60. 92 *—J.M. (11/15/2002)*

Carter 2004 Truchard Vineyards Merlot (Napa Valley) $75. The grapes are from Carneros; the winemaker is the veteran Nils Venge. The wine is big and complex. Right now it's heavy, almost ponderous, a mixture of direct primary cherry, plum, coffee and oak flavors and sturdy tannins. But it's very balanced and elegant, and should begin to unfold its riches after 2007 and hang in there for a few years. **90** *—S.H. (5/1/2007)*

Carter 2002 Truchard Vineyards Merlot (Carneros) $45. 90 *—S.H. (8/1/2005)*

Carter 2001 Truchard Vineyards Merlot (Napa Valley) $38. 90 *—J.M. (8/1/2004)*

CARTLIDGE & BROWNE

Cartlidge & Browne 2005 Cabernet Sauvignon (California) $12. Raw and minty green, with herbal flavors and an overlay of oak. **82** *—S.H. (10/1/2007)*

Cartlidge & Browne 2004 Cabernet Sauvignon (California) $13. 83 *—S.H. (12/31/2006)*

Cartlidge & Browne 2000 Cabernet Sauvignon (California) $10. 83 *—S.H. (11/15/2002)*

Cartlidge & Browne 2000 Chardonnay (California) $10. 85 *—S.H. (12/15/2002)*

Cartlidge & Browne 2004 Merlot (California) $13. 85 *—S.H. (12/31/2006)*

Cartlidge & Browne 2001 Merlot (California) $10. 86 Best Buy *—S.H. (10/1/2003)*

Cartlidge & Browne 2000 Merlot (California) $10. 86 Best Buy *—S.H. (12/31/2002)*

Cartlidge & Browne 2005 Pinot Noir (California) $13. 86 *—S.H. (12/31/2006)*

Cartlidge & Browne 2005 Pinot Noir Rosé Pinot Noir (Sonoma County) $13. 88 Best Buy *—S.H. (11/15/2006)*

Cartlidge & Browne 2001 Syrah (California) $10. 85 *—S.H. (12/15/2003)*

Cartlidge & Browne 2001 Zinfandel (California) $10. 85 *(11/1/2003)*

Cartlidge & Browne 1998 Zinfandel (California) $10. 87 Best Buy *—P.G. (3/1/2001)*

CARVALHO

Carvalho 2003 Chardonnay (Clarksburg) $18. 82 *—S.H. (3/1/2006)*

Carvalho 2004 Late Harvest Chenin Blanc (Clarksburg) $12. 82 *—S.H. (3/1/2006)*

Carvalho 2003 Pinot Noir (Clarksburg) $22. 83 *—S.H. (3/1/2006)*

Carvalho 2004 Dantone Vineyards Sauvignon Blanc (Clarksburg) $15. 82 *—S.H. (3/1/2006)*

Carvalho 2002 Old Vine Zinfandel (Dry Creek Valley) $22. 82 *—S.H. (3/1/2006)*

CARVER SUTRO

Carver Sutro 1999 Palisades Vineyard Petite Sirah (Napa Valley) $92. 82 *(12/31/2003)*

Carver Sutro 2000 Palisades Vineyards Petite Sirah (Napa Valley) $38. 87 *(4/1/2003)*

CASA BARRANCA

Casa Barranca 2003 Craftsman Red Cabernet Sauvignon (Central Coast) $15. 83 *—S.H. (12/1/2005)*

Casa Barranca 2004 Chardonnay (Santa Rita Hills) $20. 87 *—S.H. (7/1/2006)*

Casa Barranca 2004 Pinot Noir (Santa Rita Hills) $20. 91 Editors' Choice *—S.H. (7/1/2006)*

Casa Barranca 2003 Pinot Noir (Arroyo Grande Valley) $25. 82 *—S.H. (12/1/2005)*

Casa Barranca 2005 La Encantada Vineyard Pinot Noir (Santa Rita Hills) $33. This is an okay Pinot Noir. On the plus side is the silky texture and rich flavors of cherries, cola and oak-infused vanilla. On the minus is a certain simple one-dimensionality. 86 *—S.H. (11/1/2007)*

Casa Barranca 2003 Bungalow Red Syrah-Grenache Rhône Red Blend (Santa Barbara County) $15. 83 *—S.H. (12/1/2005)*

Casa Barranca 2003 Reserve Sémillon (Santa Barbara County) $15. 83 *—S.H. (12/1/2005)*

Casa Barranca 2004 Syrah (Santa Barbara County) $22. Well-structured and dry, this Syrah shows flavors of dried plums, cherries, herbs and tobacco, and is firm in tannins. Finishes with a scour of white pepper. 85 *—S.H. (11/1/2007)*

Casa Barranca 2003 Barrel Select Syrah (Central Coast) $15. 85 *—S.H. (7/1/2006)*

Casa Barranca 2003 Reserve Syrah (Santa Barbara County) $19. 83 *—S.H. (12/1/2005)*

Casa Barranca 2004 Bungalow Red Syrah-Grenache (Santa Barbara County) $15. 84 *—S.H. (8/1/2006)*

Casa Barranca 2006 Wulf Vineyard Viognier (Madera) $22. Flavor is what it's all about in this exuberant Viognier, which comes from the Central Valley. Peaches, pineapples, nectarines, kumquats, kiwi fruit, spicy mango, even a note of butter-sautéed bananas and a splash of rum and cola. Brisk acidity adds balance to this attractively dry wine. 87 *—S.H. (11/1/2007)*

CASA CARNEROS

Casa Carneros 2001 Pinot Noir (Carneros) $30. 86 *—S.H. (12/1/2004)*

CASA CASSARA

Casa Cassara 2001 Burning Creek Vineyard Pinot Noir (Santa Rita Hills) $46. 85 *—S.H. (12/1/2004)*

Casa Cassara 2005 Estate Pinot Noir (Santa Rita Hills) $34. Here's a lighter-bodied Pinot that appeals for its direct cherry, cola, root beer and spicy flavors. It's silky, with a briny finish. Drink now. 86 *—S.H. (4/1/2007)*

Casa Cassara 2001 Estate Pinot Noir (Santa Rita Hills) $28. 85 *—S.H. (12/1/2004)*

Casa Cassara 2001 Syrah (Santa Ynez Valley) $24. 86 *—S.H. (12/1/2004)*

CASA DE CABALLOS

Casa de Caballos 2000 Forgetmenot Cabernet Blend (Paso Robles) $24. 82 *—S.H. (11/15/2003)*

Casa de Caballos 2002 Choclate Lily Cabernet Sauvignon (Paso Robles) $30. 82 *—S.H. (2/1/2005)*

Casa de Caballos 2002 Forgetmenot Cabernet Sauvignon-Merlot (Paso Robles) $30. 82 *—S.H. (12/31/2004)*

Casa de Caballos 2002 Ultra Violet Merlot (Paso Robles) $26. 83 *—S.H. (2/1/2005)*

Casa de Caballos 2000 Ultra Violet Merlot (Paso Robles) $24. 83 *—S.H. (8/1/2003)*

Casa de Caballos 2000 Maggie May El Nino Red Pinot Noir (Paso Robles) $17. 82 *(10/1/2002)*

Casa de Caballos 2000 Periwinkle Pinot Noir (Paso Robles) $20. 84 *(10/1/2002)*

CASA LARGA

Casa Larga 2005 Fiori delle Stelle Limited Release Ice Wine Vidal Blanc (Finger Lakes) $35. This friendly icewine shows flavors of orange, tropical fruit, honey and maple. Definitely on the sweet side, it will appeal to sweet tooths and fans of a heavier dessert wine. 84 *—S.K. (12/1/2007)*

CASA NUESTRA

Casa Nuestra 2004 Meritage Bordeaux Blend (Napa Valley) $45. This Merlot-based blend, with equal parts of the two Cabs, is soft and luscious. It has dramatically ripe cherry and blackberry fruit, with a chocolaty edge, yet never loses balance and harmony. Best now—2012. 92 *—S.H. (4/1/2007)*

Casa Nuestra 2004 Cabernet Franc (Napa Valley) $38. Cab Franc should be lighter in structure and body than Cab Sauvignon, and this wine succeeds perfectly. It's very dry, with finely ripe, dusty tannins, and offers a wealth of cherry and herb flavors that finish long and complex. Could even pick up additional nuance with five or six years in the bottle. 92 *—S.H. (4/1/2007)*

Casa Nuestra 2004 Cabernet Sauvignon (Napa Valley) $55. Rich and balanced, made from the winery's estate in St. Helena. It's not your typically super ripe, opulent Napa Cab, but an elegant, almost understated wine, designed for the table. Dry, with herb-infused blackberry fruit, this 100% Cab has 50% new oak, which adds a toasty edge. Drink now–2014. 92 *—S.H. (4/1/2007)*

Casa Nuestra 2006 Old Vines Dry Chenin Blanc (Napa Valley) $24. This is one of the better Chenin Blancs, without the sharp medicinal flavor the variety sometimes shows. Very dry, the wine has citrus, flower and spicy melon flavors that are enriched with a touch of new oak. 87 *—S.H. (12/1/2007)*

Casa Nuestra 2005 Old Vines Home Vineyard Dry Chenin Blanc (Napa Valley) $24. The wine is amazing, although if you don't like Chenin Blanc, it's not for you. It's high in acid, almost sour, which makes it a beautiful wine for food, a connoisseur's wine, a sommelier's dream. The flavors run toward lemon drop, wild flowers and elemental things like wax and steel. Should do all sorts of interesting things as it ages. Editors' Choice. 93 Editors' Choice *—S.H. (4/1/2007)*

Casa Nuestra 2000 Reserve Chenin Blanc (Napa Valley) $22. 88 *—S.H. (9/1/2002)*

Casa Nuestra 2004 Merlot (Napa Valley) $35. This is one of the most interesting Merlots I've tasted lately, mainly due to the compelling balance. It's very ripe in cherry, blackberry and mocha flavors, with a dash of cinnamon, nutmeg and vanilla. The balance comes from the wonderfully smooth tannins, crisp acids and deft way the new oak integrates with everything else. Now through 2010. 93 *—S.H. (3/1/2007)*

Casa Nuestra 1999 Merlot (Napa Valley) $38. 90 *—S.H. (9/1/2002)*

Casa Nuestra 2006 Rosado Rosé Blend (Napa Valley) $23. A little heavy but nonetheless pleasing, this Merlot-Cab Franc blend is dry and full-bodied for a rosé. The cherry-berry and spice flavors are offset by crisp acids and even a dusting of tannins. 85 *—S.H. (7/1/2007)*

CASA RONDEÑA WINERY

Casa Rondeña Winery 2004 Meritage Bordeaux Blend (New Mexico) $23. A blend of 40% Merlot, 40% Cabernet Franc and 20% Cabernet Sauvignon, this Bordeaux-style red is rich but not overpowering, with aromas and flavors of cedar, toast, tobacco and red berry. Tannins are gentle and the finish lingering. Not much flavor unfolding but still a good effort that will pair nicely with red meat and roasted chicken. 83 *—S.K. (12/1/2007)*

Casa Rondeña Winery 2005 Calvin Clarion Red Blend (New Mexico) $28. A pretty floral nose and appetizing, juicy flavors of jammy fruit should recommend this wine, but there's a bitterness on the midplate and finish that make the wine a touch too angular. Pair with food to even it out. **82** —*S.K. (12/1/2007)*

Casa Rondeña Winery 2006 Meritage White Sauvignon Blanc (New Mexico) $16. This blend of Semillon and Sauvignon Blanc tends on the sweet side, but it offers appealing flavors of vanilla and tropical fruit. An enjoyable, approachable wine. **82** —*S.K. (10/1/2007)*

CASS

Cass 2005 Cabernet Franc (Paso Robles) $42. Here's a soft, fruity Cab Franc rich in cherry and blackberry flavors. It has good balance and a posh mouthfeel, and finishes dry. Something about it suggests a juicy, flame-broiled steak. **87** —*S.H. (12/15/2007)*

Cass 2005 Estate Grenache (Paso Robles) $28. With 15% Mourvèdre, this pale-colored Paso red is soft and dry, with earthy, fruity flavors suggesting cherries, tobacco, cola, carob and spices. **84** —*S.H. (12/1/2007)*

Cass 2004 Rockin' One Grenache-Syrah (Paso Robles) $34. Grenache stars, offering oodles of ripe cherry liqueur flavor, while a dash of Syrah brings a deeper touch of blackberry and licorice. It's a deft combination. The wine is distinctly Paso Robles in the soft acidity and gentle tannins. It melts in the mouth like a chocolate truffle, yet finishes dry. **88** —*S.H. (6/1/2007)*

Cass 2005 Hacienda Mourvèdre (Paso Robles) $34. Smells vegetal and inert and tastes slightly sweet, with cherry cough medicine flavors. Gets slightly better as it breathes. **82** —*S.H. (11/1/2007)*

Cass 2005 Rockin' One Rhône Red Blend (Paso Robles) $42. A blend of Syrah, Mourvèdre and Grenache, this has a chocolate mint edge to the sugary sweet LifeSaver candy blackberries and cherries. The tannins and acids are good, though, and the wine would score higher if it were drier. **84** —*S.H. (12/31/2007)*

Cass 2004 Rockin' One Rhône Red Blend (Paso Robles) $34. **87** —*S.H. (12/15/2006)*

Cass 2006 Estate Cuvée Rhône White Blend (Paso Robles) $28. This easy, simple white-Rhône blend of Marsanne, Viognier and Roussanne is soft and fruity, and finishes a little sweet. It has LifeSaver candy flavors of lemons, limes and oranges. **84** —*S.H. (10/1/2007)*

Cass 2004 Estate Syrah (Paso Robles) $36. Soft and sharp, this rustic wine has simple cherry, blackberry, leather, coffee and wintergreen mint flavors. It finishes with a touch of sweetened coffee. Might get better after a year or so in the bottle. **84** —*S.H. (8/1/2007)*

Cass 2006 Viognier (Paso Robles) $24. Sweet and smooth, this Viognier has honeyed flavors of peaches, vanilla and wildflowers, offset by a tingle of acidity. **84** —*S.H. (12/1/2007)*

Cass 2005 Viognier (Paso Robles) $24. **83** —*S.H. (12/15/2006)*

USA

CASTALIA

Castalia 2004 Rochioli Vineyard Pinot Noir (Russian River Valley) $45. A difficult wine made problematic by the vintage. The cherry fruit tastes overtly sweet, and I suspect there's some residual sugar, the tradeoff for keeping alcohol moderate. Most unfortunate, because everything else works. **83** —*S.H. (8/1/2007)*

Castalia 2003 Rochioli Vineyard Pinot Noir (Russian River Valley) $45. **90** —*S.H. (12/1/2005)*

CASTELLETTO

Castelletto 2000 Cortese (Temecula) $18. **87** —*S.H. (4/1/2002)*

Castelletto 1997 Trovato Red Blend (Temecula) $15. **90 Best Buy** —*S.H. (11/15/2001)*

Castelletto 1999 Sangiovese (Temecula) $16. **87** —*S.H. (12/1/2002)*

Castelletto 1999 Trovato Sangiovese (Temecula) $15. **90** —*S.H. (4/1/2002)*

CASTELLO DA VINCI

Castello Da Vinci 2003 Cabernet Sauvignon (Napa Valley) $25. **90** —*S.H. (5/1/2006)*

CASTELLO DI BORGHESE

Castello di Borghese 2000 Meritage Bordeaux Blend (North Fork of Long Island) $48. **84** —*J.C. (10/2/2004)*

Castello di Borghese 2001 Ovation Private Reserve Bordeaux Blend (North Fork of Long Island) $75. **82** —*J.C. (10/2/2004)*

Castello di Borghese NV Petit Château Bordeaux Blend (North Fork of Long Island) $10. **83** —*J.C. (4/1/2001)*

Castello di Borghese 1998 Hargrave Vineyard Cabernet Franc (North Fork of Long Island) $17. **85** —*J.C. (4/1/2001)*

Castello di Borghese 1998 Hargrave Vineyard Reserve Cabernet Franc (North Fork of Long Island) $22. **88** —*J.C. (4/1/2001)*

Castello di Borghese 1998 Hargrave Vineyard Reserve Cabernet Sauvignon (North Fork of Long Island) $32. **86** —*J.C. (4/1/2001)*

Castello di Borghese 2002 Reserve Cabernet Franc (North Fork of Long Island) $32. It's not the most thought-provoking Cab Franc on the market, but there's a nice array of bright berry flavors like plum and cherry here, and a smooth balance of fruit and spice. The finish is slightly weak, but this is overall an easy-drinking, accessible wine. **83** —*S.K. (2/1/2007)*

Castello di Borghese 1998 Hargrave Vineyard Chardonnay (North Fork of Long Island) $14. **82** —*J.C. (4/1/2001)*

Castello di Borghese 2001 Hargrave Vineyard Barrel Fermented Chardonnay (North Fork of Long Island) $22. **83** —*J.C. (10/2/2004)*

Castello di Borghese 2000 Hargrave Vineyard Barrel Fermented Chardonnay (North Fork of Long Island) $22. **88** —*J.C. (3/1/2002)*

Castello di Borghese 1998 Hargrave Vineyard Reserve Chardonnay (North Fork of Long Island) $18. **88** —*J.C. (4/1/2001)*

Castello di Borghese 1998 Meritage (North Fork of Long Island) $45. **80** —*M.S. (3/1/2003)*

Castello di Borghese 2001 Hargrave Vineyard Reserve Merlot (North Fork of Long Island) $29. There are some enticing aromas of pepper and spiced meat on the nose, but on the palate, this wine has a tannic, bitter edge to it that will surprise fans of luxuriant, supple Merlot. One-dimensional and lean, this wine lacks elegance. **81** —*S.K. (2/1/2007)*

Castello di Borghese 2001 Hargrave Vineyard Merlot (North Fork of Long Island) $20. **83** —*M.D. (12/1/2006)*

Castello di Borghese 2000 Hargrave Vineyard Merlot (North Fork of Long Island) $19. **81** —*J.C. (10/2/2004)*

Castello di Borghese 1998 Hargrave Vineyard Merlot (North Fork of Long Island) $18. **82** —*J.C. (4/1/2001)*

Castello di Borghese 2000 Hargrave Vineyard Reserve Merlot (North Fork of Long Island) $25. **84** —*M.S. (1/1/2004)*

Castello di Borghese 1998 Hargrave Vineyard Reserve Merlot (North Fork of Long Island) $25. **88** —*J.C. (4/1/2001)*

Castello di Borghese 1999 Hargrave Vineyard Pinot Blanc (North Fork of Long Island) $10. **82** —*J.C. (4/1/2001)*

Castello di Borghese 2003 Barrel Fermented Pinot Noir (North Fork of Long Island) $38. Tea leaves and cranberry lead in this barrel fermented Pinot. The berry flavors are ripe but there's little happening here beyond the initial, quiet fruit presence. Needs more complexity and elegance. **82** —*S.K. (5/1/2007)*

Castello di Borghese NV Fleurette Pinot Noir (North Fork of Long Island) $10. **83** —*J.C. (4/1/2001)*

Castello di Borghese 1998 Hargrave Vineyard Pinot Noir (North Fork of Long Island) $35. **84** —*J.C. (4/1/2001)*

Castello di Borghese 2002 Hargrave Vineyard Reserve Pinot Noir (North Fork of Long Island) $38. **84** —*M.D. (12/1/2006)*

Castello di Borghese 2005 Fleurette Rosé Blend (North Fork of Long Island) $10. For fans of sweet wine, this sugary rose will please, but fans of drier rose will find this to be a bit of a candy bomb. A blend of chardonnay (around 75%) and merlot (around 25%), it has aromas of peach and strawberry, and those flavors, combined with a bit of acidity, are playful on the palate. It's a basic wine but pleasant. **83** —*S.K. (2/1/2007)*

Castello di Borghese 1999 Hargrave Vineyard Sauvignon Blanc (North Fork of Long Island) $11. **85** —*J.C. (4/1/2001)*

Castello di Borghese NV Chardonette White Blend (North Fork of Long Island) $7. **83** —*J.C. (4/1/2001)*

CASTLE

Castle 1998 Cabernet Sauvignon (Sonoma Valley) $25. **86** —*S.H. (12/31/2001)*

Castle 2005 Chardonnay (Sonoma Valley) $24. Simple and fruity, this everyday Chard has peach, pineapple and spice flavors. The taste of smoky oak shows up on the finish. **83** —*S.H. (12/15/2007)*

Castle 1998 Chardonnay (Sonoma Valley) $18. **84** *(6/1/2000)*

Castle 1998 Chardonnay (Carneros) $22. **88** *(6/1/2000)*

Castle 1999 Chardonnay (Sonoma Valley) $17. **89 Best Buy** —*S.H. (12/31/2001)*

Castle 1999 Chardonnay (Carneros) $20. **87** —*S.H. (12/31/2001)*

Castle 2000 Merlot (Sonoma Valley) $20. **82** —*S.H. (5/1/2005)*

Castle 1999 Merlot (Sonoma Valley) $17. **87** —*S.H. (12/15/2004)*

Castle 1998 Merlot (Sonoma Valley) $20. **90** —*S.H. (12/31/2001)*

Castle 1998 Merlot (Sonoma Valley) $20. **90** —*S.H. (12/31/2001)*

Castle 1999 Sangiacomo Vineyard Merlot (Carneros) $24. **82** —*S.H. (5/1/2005)*

Castle 1997 Sangiacomo Vineyard Donnel Ranch Merlot (Carneros) $25. 90 Editors' Choice *(8/1/2001)*

Castle 2005 Pinot Noir (Carneros) $23. Soft and gentle, with pleasant raspberry, cherry, cola and spice flavors, this Pinot offers lots of immediate pleasure. It's a dry, balanced wine that will pair well with lamb and beef. **87** *—S.H. (12/15/2007)*

Castle 2005 Pinot Noir (Sonoma Coast) $30. A lovely young Pinot, filled with fresh fruits and spices, wrapped into a fine, silky texture. The flavors of raspberries, cherries and cola have a rich, meaty, leathery edge that adds complexity and earthiness. Good now, and should hold for several years. **89** *—S.H. (12/15/2007)*

Castle 2004 Pinot Noir (Carneros) $23. Soft and simple, with a white sugar edge to the cherry fruit, this is just too sweet. **82** *—S.H. (12/15/2007)*

Castle 2001 Pinot Noir (Carneros) $24. 85 *—S.H. (5/1/2005)*

Castle 2000 Pinot Noir (Carneros) $24. 85 *—S.H. (8/1/2004)*

Castle 1999 Pinot Noir (Carneros) $24. 86 *—S.H. (12/15/2001)*

Castle 1999 Durell Vineyard Pinot Noir (Carneros) $35. 89 *(10/1/2002)*

Castle 1997 Durell Vineyard Pinot Noir (Carneros) $30. 90 *(10/1/1999)*

Castle 2005 Estate Pinot Noir (Carneros) $30. A little sweet for a table wine, with jellied raspberry and cherry flavors. Too bad, because the texture is silky, the tannins are fine, and the acidity is bright. **85** *—S.H. (12/15/2007)*

Castle 2004 Estate Pinot Noir (Carneros) $28. You can taste the warmth of the vintage in the ripeness of the wine. It just explodes with jammy cherry, raspberry, red currant, milk chocolate and vanilla flavors. Soft and easy, it's at its best now. **88** *—S.H. (12/15/2007)*

Castle 2001 Estate Pinot Noir (Carneros) $32. 86 *—S.H. (5/1/2005)*

Castle 2005 Sangiacomo Vineyards Pinot Noir (Carneros) $32. There's a sweetmeat, salty leatheriness to this Pinot, like beef jerky. Give it a year or so to mellow out and let the smoky oak integrate with the ripe cherry, cola and raspberry flavors. Decant for an hour or two if you pop it open now. **87** *—S.H. (12/15/2007)*

Castle 1999 Sangiacomo Vineyard Pinot Noir (Carneros) $30. 90 Editors' Choice *(10/1/2002)*

Castle 1997 Sangiacomo Vineyard Pinot Noir (Carneros) $30. 90 *(10/1/1999)*

Castle 2006 La Belle Rosé Annadel Estate Rhône Red Blend (Sonoma Valley) $20. A Rhône blend with Provençal aspirations, this blush is overtly sweet, with sugary raspberry flavors. **82** *—S.H. (12/15/2007)*

Castle 2001 Syrah (Sonoma Valley) $24. 89 *—S.H. (8/1/2004)*

Castle 1999 Syrah (Sonoma Valley) $22. 90 *(11/1/2001)*

Castle 2001 Port Syrah (Carneros) $28. 83 *—S.H. (5/1/2005)*

Castle 2002 Viognier (California) $16. 84 *—S.H. (8/1/2004)*

Castle 2000 Viognier (California) $19. 86 *—S.H. (12/15/2001)*

Castle 2005 Landa Vineyards Viognier (Sonoma Valley) $28. With sweet-and-sour flavors, this Viognier has jammy apricot and pineapple flavors with some vinegar in the finish. **82** *—S.H. (12/15/2007)*

Castle 2002 Ripkin Vineyards Late Harvest Viognier (Lodi) $20. 85 *—S.H. (5/1/2005)*

Castle 2001 Zinfandel (Sonoma Valley) $19. 88 *—J.M. (11/1/2003)*

Castle 1999 Zinfandel (Sonoma Valley) $19. 90 Editors' Choice *—S.H. (12/15/2001)*

Castle 1998 Zinfandel (Sonoma Valley) $19. 89 *—P.G. (3/1/2001)*

Castle 1998 Zinfandel (Russian River Valley) $16. 85 *—P.G. (3/1/2001)*

Castle 1997 Zinfandel (Sonoma Valley) $18. 90 *—S.H. (5/1/2000)*

Castle 2001 Parmelee-Hill Vineyards Zinfandel (Sonoma County) $25. 82 *—J.M. (11/1/2003)*

CASTLE ROCK

Castle Rock 2005 Cabernet Sauvignon (Napa Valley) $12. Tannic and sharp, this dry wine has a tough, astringent mouthfeel that makes it hard to appreciate the blackberry and cherry flavors. It's not the kind of wine that ages, so drink now. **84** *—S.H. (11/15/2007)*

Castle Rock 2005 Cabernet Sauvignon (Paso Robles) $10. This is typical of the appellation, a soft, gentle wine, with polished berry-cherry flavors. It's also dry, balanced and modest in alcohol, at a good price. **85 Best Buy** *—S.H. (9/1/2007)*

Castle Rock 2004 Cabernet Sauvignon (Alexander Valley) $11. A bit hot and raisiny, although on the plus side, the wine is dry and the tannins are smooth and ripe. There are some pretty nice cherry jam, blueberry and tobacco flavors. **84** *—S.H. (4/1/2007)*

Castle Rock 2003 Cabernet Sauvignon (Columbia Valley (WA)) $11. 88 Best Buy *—P.G. (4/1/2006)*

Castle Rock 2002 Cabernet Sauvignon (Sonoma County) $11. 84 *—S.H. (8/1/2005)*

Castle Rock 2002 Cabernet Sauvignon (Napa Valley) $11. 84 *—S.H. (2/1/2005)*

Castle Rock 2000 Cabernet Sauvignon (Columbia Valley (WA)) $10. 87 Best Buy *—D.T. (12/31/2002)*

Castle Rock 2004 Reserve Cabernet Sauvignon (Napa Valley) $18. 85 *—S.H. (12/15/2006)*

Castle Rock 2003 Reserve Cabernet Sauvignon (Napa Valley) $15. 86 *—S.H. (8/1/2005)*

Castle Rock 2006 Chardonnay (Central Coast) $12. This is a sound, everyday Chard, barrel-fermented and dry. The peaches-and-cream flavor has a bubble gum edge. **84** *—S.H. (11/15/2007)*

Castle Rock 2005 Chardonnay (Edna Valley) $11. Dry and brightly crisp, with the pineapple tart, vanilla-flecked kiwi and lime custard flavors that are so typical of the appellation. **86 Best Buy** *—S.H. (2/1/2007)*

Castle Rock 2005 Reserve Chardonnay (Russian River Valley) $15. This is really a nice Chardonnay especially at this price. From the appealing tropical fruit pie filling, tart green apple, kumquat, pear sorbet and sweet toasty oak flavors to the buttery, creamy texture, you'd guess it cost a lot more. **89** *—S.H. (2/1/2007)*

Castle Rock 2003 Reserve Chardonnay (Napa Valley) $15. 84 *—S.H. (8/1/2005)*

Castle Rock 2004 Merlot (Napa Valley) $10. Smells so nice and pretty, just like a young Merlot should, but that white sugary edge to the cherries really detracts. **83** *—S.H. (7/1/2007)*

Castle Rock 2003 Merlot (Napa County) $11. Good price for a nicely dry, fruity Merlot that offers rich, ripe tannins that frame cherry, blackberry and spice flavors. For an everyday wine, it shows lots of elegance and finesse. **85** *—S.H. (2/1/2007)*

Castle Rock 2002 Merlot (Napa Valley) $11. 85 *—S.H. (2/1/2005)*

Castle Rock 2005 Petite Sirah (Russian River Valley) $12. Good evocation of a cool-climate Petite Sirah, in all its fruity glory. Dry, crisp and dense in tannins, the flavors are of jammy blackberries, tobacco and plums, with a spicy finish. **87 Best Buy** *—S.H. (11/15/2007)*

Castle Rock 2003 Reserve Petite Sirah (Napa Valley) $15. 87 *—S.H. (8/1/2005)*

Castle Rock 2006 Pinot Noir (Mendocino County) $12. Tastes like an ordinary inexpensive Pinot Noir, namely a somewhat harsh, semisweet wine, with jellied raspberry and mint flavors. More than 100,000 cases produced. **82** *—S.H. (11/15/2007)*

Castle Rock 2006 Pinot Noir (Monterey County) $12. Like a photocopy of a photocopy, this thinned-down Pinot Noir contains only a suggestion of the real thing. It's dry, but watery in cherry cola flavors. **82** *—S.H. (11/15/2007)*

Castle Rock 2005 Pinot Noir (Mendocino County) $12. Nicely silky and dry, and the everyday price makes it a relative value for Pinot lovers. But purists will find it a little rugged, with some overripe, stewed prune flavors. **83** *—S.H. (5/1/2007)*

Castle Rock 2005 Pinot Noir (Monterey County) $12. Overplanting of coastal Pinot Noir has now led to prices on decent wines that, just a few years ago, would have seemed unbelievable. The market is crowded with wines like this. It's a good expression of the variety, dry and silky and fruity, with a mushroomy earthiness. Your basic Intro to Pinot 101. **84** *—S.H. (5/1/2007)*

Castle Rock 2005 Pinot Noir (Sonoma County) $13. An everyday Pinot, true to the variety. Shows cherry and cola flavors in a delicately-structured Pinot. With 30,000 cases, there's a lot of Sonoma Pinot looking for a home. **85** *—S.H. (4/1/2007)*

Castle Rock 2003 Pinot Noir (Mendocino County) $11. 82 *—S.H. (2/1/2005)*

Castle Rock 2003 Pinot Noir (Carneros) $11. 84 *—S.H. (2/1/2005)*

Castle Rock 2002 Pinot Noir (Russian River Valley) $11. 84 *(11/1/2004)*

Castle Rock 2002 Pinot Noir (Napa Valley) $11. 82 *—S.H. (2/1/2005)*

Castle Rock 2002 Pinot Noir (Sonoma Coast) $11. 87 Best Buy *—S.H. (10/1/2005)*

Castle Rock 2001 Pinot Noir (Russian River Valley) $10. 87 *—M.S. (12/1/2003)*

Castle Rock 2005 Reserve Pinot Noir (Edna Valley) $18. Sharp, raw and palate-scouring, this thin wine has a harsh texture and green fruit. Not opulent, but it's a clean, technically correct Pinot Noir. **82** *—S.H. (5/1/2007)*

Castle Rock 2003 Sauvignon Blanc (Napa Valley) $9. 86 Best Buy —*S.H. (11/15/2004)*

Castle Rock 2004 Syrah (Alexander Valley) $11. This is a great price for a full-bodied, rich, dry red wine that's fancy enough to stand up to steak, chops, ribs. The blackberries are joined by cola and spice flavors, and the mouthfeel is lush and tannic. A great value. **86 Best Buy** —*S.H. (3/1/2007)*

Castle Rock 2003 Syrah (Central Coast) $9. 87 Best Buy —*S.H. (8/1/2005)*

Castle Rock 1998 Syrah (California) $10. 87 *(6/1/2003)*

Castle Rock 1999 California Cuvée Syrah (California) $10. 82 *(10/1/2001)*

Castle Rock 2005 Zinfandel (Mendocino County) $11. Here's a rustic, soft, country-style wine. It's a little sweet in the finish, with some unresolved grape sugar but crisp acids, and very rich flavors of blackberry jam, cherry pie filling and chocolate candy, with a spicy edge. **84** —*S.H. (2/1/2007)*

Castle Rock 2003 Zinfandel (Dry Creek Valley) $9. 84 —*S.H. (8/1/2005)*

Castle Rock 1999 California Cuvée Zinfandel (California) $10. 83 —*D.T. (3/1/2002)*

CASTORO

Castoro 2002 Ventuno Anni Bordeaux Blend (Paso Robles) $22. 87 —*S.H. (2/1/2005)*

Castoro 2003 Cabernet Blend (Paso Robles) $26. 86 —*S.H. (12/31/2006)*

Castoro 2003 Cabernet Sauvignon (Paso Robles) $15. 85 —*S.H. (12/1/2005)*

Castoro 2002 Cabernet Sauvignon (Paso Robles) $15. 87 —*S.H. (4/1/2005)*

Castoro 2000 Cabernet Sauvignon (Paso Robles) $14. 85 —*S.H. (6/1/2003)*

Castoro 2004 Chardonnay (Central Coast) $13. 85 —*S.H. (12/1/2005)*

Castoro 2003 Chardonnay (Central Coast) $13. 85 —*S.H. (2/1/2005)*

Castoro 2005 Reserve Chardonnay (Central Coast) $20. Soft, ripe and oaky, this Chard is a blend of Monterey, Paso Robles and Santa Barbara fruit. It's jammy and forward in apricot and peach flavors. **84** —*S.H. (5/1/2007)*

Castoro 2005 Fumé Blanc (Paso Robles) $10. 85 Best Buy —*S.H. (7/1/2006)*

Castoro 2004 Fumé Blanc (Paso Robles) $9. 84 —*S.H. (11/15/2005)*

Castoro 2005 Gewürztraminer (Paso Robles) $16. 85 —*S.H. (12/15/2006)*

Castoro 2001 Due Mila Tre Meritage (Paso Robles) $33. 82 —*S.H. (5/1/2005)*

Castoro 1997 Merlot (Paso Robles) $15. 83 —*J.C. (7/1/2000)*

Castoro 2002 Merlot (Paso Robles) $14. 85 —*S.H. (12/15/2004)*

Castoro 2000 Merlot (Paso Robles) $13. 84 —*S.H. (12/15/2003)*

Castoro 2003 Late Harvest Muscat Canelli (Paso Robles) $17. 85 —*S.H. (12/1/2005)*

Castoro 2003 Reserve Petite Sirah (Paso Robles) $18. 87 —*S.H. (12/31/2006)*

Castoro 1999 Reserve Petite Sirah (Paso Robles) $16. 85 *(4/1/2003)*

Castoro 2002 Stone's Throw Reserve Petite Sirah (Paso Robles) $18. 80 —*S.H. (5/1/2005)*

Castoro 2004 Oakenshield Wineworks Pinot Grigio (Paso Robles) $20. 84 —*S.H. (2/1/2006)*

Castoro 2004 Bien Nacido Vineyard Pinot Noir (Santa Barbara County) $20. 87 —*S.H. (11/15/2006)*

Castoro 2002 Reserve Pinot Noir (Central Coast) $18. 87 —*S.H. (2/1/2005)*

Castoro 2000 Reserve Pinot Noir (Central Coast) $18. 82 *(10/1/2002)*

Castoro 2000 Reserve-Blind Faith Vineyard Pinot Noir (Central Coast) $18. 85 *(10/1/2002)*

Castoro 2003 Venti Due Anni Red Blend (Paso Robles) $27. 88 —*S.H. (5/1/2006)*

Castoro 2005 Rosato di Paso Rosé Blend (Paso Robles) $20. 86 —*S.H. (12/31/2006)*

Castoro 2004 Rosato di Syrah Rosé Blend (Paso Robles) $20. 87 —*S.H. (6/1/2006)*

Castoro 2000 Syrah (Paso Robles) $18. 84 —*S.H. (6/1/2003)*

Castoro 2004 Reserve Syrah (Paso Robles) $18. 84 —*S.H. (12/31/2006)*

Castoro 2003 Reserve Syrah (Paso Robles) $18. 90 —*S.H. (5/1/2006)*

Castoro 2002 Reserve Syrah (Paso Robles) $18. 85 *(9/1/2005)*

Castoro 2001 Reserve Syrah (Paso Robles) $18. 84 —*S.H. (5/1/2005)*

Castoro 1999 Reserve Syrah (Paso Robles) $18. 87 *(10/1/2001)*

Castoro 2004 Reserve Tempranillo (California) $20. 85 —*S.H. (11/15/2006)*

Castoro 2002 Reserve Tempranillo (California) $16. 87 —*S.H. (4/1/2005)*

Castoro 2003 Viognier (Paso Robles) $18. 87 —*S.H. (12/15/2004)*

Castoro 2006 Reserve Viognier (Central Coast) $18. Sweet and simple, with an array of Lifesaver candy flavors. **82** —*S.H. (11/1/2007)*

Castoro 2004 Stone's Throw Vineyard Viognier (Paso Robles) $18. 85 —*S.H. (12/1/2005)*

Castoro 2005 Tango White Blend (Central Coast) $20. 83 —*S.H. (12/31/2006)*

Castoro 2002 Zinfandel (Paso Robles) $14. 84 —*S.H. (2/1/2005)*

Castoro 2001 Zinfandel (Paso Robles) $14. 87 —*S.H. (4/1/2004)*

Castoro 2000 Zinfandel (Paso Robles) $14. 85 —*S.H. (9/1/2003)*

Castoro 2004 Cobble Creek Zinfandel (Paso Robles) $25. 82 —*S.H. (11/15/2006)*

Castoro 2001 Cobble Creek Zinfandel (Paso Robles) $20. 82 —*J.M. (11/1/2003)*

Castoro 2003 Cobble Creek Vineyard Zinfandel (Paso Robles) $25. 80 —*S.H. (12/1/2005)*

Castoro 2000 Giubbine Zinfandel (Paso Robles) $18. 85 —*S.H. (4/1/2004)*

Castoro 2001 Giubbini Zinfandel (Paso Robles) $19. 87 *(11/1/2003)*

Castoro 2001 Late Harvest Zinfandel (Paso Robles) $16. 85 —*S.H. (12/1/2003)*

Castoro 2004 Oakenshield Wineworks Zinfandel (Paso Robles) $20. 81 —*S.H. (12/31/2006)*

Castoro 2005 Reserve Zinfusion Zinfandel (Paso Robles) $22. Dry and tannic, with stewed berry, tobacco and coffee flavors, this is a Zin to wash down barbecue and not worry about the aesthetic details. **83** —*S.H. (11/1/2007)*

Castoro 2002 Reserve Zinfusion Zinfandel (Paso Robles) $19. 83 —*S.H. (5/1/2005)*

Castoro 2001 Vineyard Tribute Zinfandel (Paso Robles) $19. 86 *(11/1/2003)*

Castoro 1998 Vineyard Tribute Zinfandel (Paso Robles) $18. 89 —*P.G. (3/1/2001)*

Castoro 2005 Whale Rock Zinfandel (Paso Robles) $30. Soft in acids, with stewed or raisiny cherry and blackberry flavors, this is thick and sticky in tannins. It really needs rich, greasy fare to resolve it. Try with ribs. **85** —*S.H. (11/1/2007)*

Castoro 2004 Zinfusion Zinfandel (Paso Robles) $19. 86 —*S.H. (12/15/2006)*

Castoro 2003 Zinfusion Reserve Zinfandel (Paso Robles) $19. 83 —*S.H. (12/1/2005)*

CATACULA

Catacula 2003 Cabernet Sauvignon (Napa Valley) $34. 81 —*S.H. (12/31/2006)*

Catacula 2002 Cabernet Sauvignon (Napa Valley) $22. 83 —*S.H. (12/15/2005)*

Catacula 2001 Napa Valley Cabernet Sauvignon (Napa Valley) $19. 88 —*S.H. (10/1/2004)*

Catacula 2000 Rancho Cuvée Cabernet Sauvignon-Merlot (Napa Valley) $19. 86 —*S.H. (11/15/2003)*

Catacula 2005 Sauvignon Blanc (Napa Valley) $14. 84 —*S.H. (12/31/2006)*

Catacula 2004 Sauvignon Blanc (Napa Valley) $12. 83 —*S.H. (12/15/2005)*

Catacula 2001 Sauvignon Blanc (Napa Valley) $11. 88 —*S.H. (9/1/2004)*

Catacula 2000 Sauvignon Blanc (Napa Valley) $11. 86 —*S.H. (7/1/2003)*

Catacula 2003 Late Harvest Sauvignon Blanc (Napa Valley) $25. 85 —*S.H. (12/15/2005)*

Catacula 2001 Zinfandel (Napa Valley) $15. 85 —*S.H. (9/1/2004)*

Catacula 2000 Zinfandel (Napa Valley) $15. 82 *S.H. (9/1/2003)*

Catacula 2004 Estate Old Vine Zinfandel (Napa Valley) $22. 83 —*S.H. (12/31/2006)*

CATANA

Catana NV Reserve Quintetta Port (California) $26. 91 —*S.H. (12/1/2004)*

CATERINA

Caterina 1999 Cabernet Sauvignon (Columbia Valley (WA)) $20. 88 —*P.G. (12/31/2002)*

Caterina 1998 Cabernet Sauvignon (Washington) $24. 87 —*P.G. (10/1/2001)*

Caterina 1997 Cabernet Sauvignon (Columbia Valley (WA)) $19. 84 *—S.H. (11/15/2000)*

Caterina 1999 DuBrul Vineyard Cabernet Sauvignon (Yakima Valley) $28. 89 *—P.G. (12/31/2002)*

Caterina 1999 Willard Family Vineyard Cabernet Sauvignon (Yakima Valley) $28. 91 *—P.G. (12/31/2002)*

Caterina 1998 Willard Family Vineyard Cabernet Sauvignon (Columbia Valley (WA)) $30. 90 *—P.G. (10/1/2001)*

Caterina 2000 Chardonnay (Columbia Valley (WA)) $13. 88 Best Buy *—P.G. (7/1/2002)*

Caterina 1999 Merlot (Columbia Valley (WA)) $20. 88 *—P.G. (12/31/2002)*

Caterina 1998 Merlot (Columbia Valley (WA)) $24. 87 *—P.G. (10/1/2001)*

Caterina 1997 Merlot (Columbia Valley (WA)) $19. 86 *—S.H. (11/15/2000)*

Caterina 1999 DuBrul Vineyard Merlot (Yakima Valley) $30. 91 *—P.G. (9/1/2002)*

Caterina 1999 Willard Family Vineyard Merlot (Yakima Valley) $28. 89 *—P.G. (12/31/2002)*

Caterina 1998 Willard Family Vineyard Merlot (Columbia Valley (WA)) $30. 90 *—P.G. (10/1/2001)*

Caterina 1999 Rosso Red Blend (Washington) $15. 88 *—P.G. (6/1/2002)*

Caterina 2002 Sauvignon Blanc (Columbia Valley (WA)) $15. 89 *—P.G. (4/1/2006)*

Caterina 2001 Sauvignon Blanc (Columbia Valley (WA)) $10. 88 Best Buy *—P.G. (12/31/2002)*

Caterina 2000 Sauvignon Blanc (Columbia Valley (WA)) $10. 88 Best Buy *—P.G. (6/1/2002)*

Caterina 2003 Willard Family Vineyard Viognier (Washington) $20. 90 *—P.G. (4/1/2006)*

CATHY MACGREGOR

Cathy MacGregor 1998 MacGregor Vineyard Chardonnay (Edna Valley) $30. 88 *(7/1/2001)*

Cathy MacGregor 1998 Benito Dusi Vineyard Zinfandel (Paso Robles) $26. 84 *—D.T. (3/1/2002)*

CAVE B

Cave B 2003 Cuvée du Soleil Bordeaux Blend (Columbia Valley (WA)) $40. Earthy and lightly leathery, this concentrated, chewy wine skates along the borders of volatility and a bit too much leathery character, but ultimately it keeps itself together with a core of dense black cherry, plum and and prune fruit. **89** *—P.G. (3/1/2007)*

Cave B 2002 Famiglia Vineyards Cabernet Sauvignon (Columbia Valley (WA)) $30. 85 *—P.G. (12/15/2005)*

Cave B 2004 Chardonnay (Columbia Valley (WA)) $16. Deep green-gold, this buttery, slightly oxidized wine veers toward flavors of banana and has been given the heavy American oak treatment. The flavors have not entirely knit together and may not have a lot of time left to do so. **86** *—P.G. (3/1/2007)*

Cave B 2003 Janine's Vineyard Chardonnay (Columbia Valley (WA)) $20. 87 *—P.G. (12/15/2005)*

Cave B 2001 Janine's Vineyard Chardonnay (Columbia Valley (WA)) $30. 85 *—P.G. (1/1/2004)*

Cave B 2002 Famiglia Vineyards Merlot (Columbia Valley (WA)) $30. 85 *—P.G. (12/15/2005)*

Cave B 2000 Jersey's Vineyard Merlot (Columbia Valley (WA)) $45. 85 *—P.G. (1/1/2004)*

Cave B 2002 Cuvée du Soleil Red Blend (Columbia Valley (WA)) $35. 88 *—P.G. (12/15/2005)*

Cave B 2003 Kimberley's Vineyard Sémillon (Columbia Valley (WA)) $25. 87 *—P.G. (12/15/2005)*

Cave B 2001 Kimberley's Vineyard Sémillon (Columbia Valley (WA)) $35. 85 *—P.G. (1/1/2004)*

Cave B 2004 Syrah (Columbia Valley (WA)) $35. This is the winery's first vintage of Syrah from estate fruit. It tastes of red licorice, cranberries and raspberries; there's a whiff of white pepper and some well-managed tea-flavored tannins. Clearly young wine from young vines. **88** *—P.G. (3/1/2007)*

CAYALLA

Cayalla 2005 RTW Red Blend (Columbia Valley (WA)) $13. Cab Sauvignon, Merlot and Syrah from both Washington and Oregon vineyards are mixed into Cayalla, a tart, supple, somewhat chalky red wine. It's light and elegant, balanced and clean, and the fruit flavors are of wild strawberry, raspberry and rhubarb. It's just 13% alcohol, and will please those consumers who are looking for a wine to enjoy with meals, and one that won't tire the palate or dull the brain. **87 Best Buy** *—P.G. (11/1/2007)*

Cayalla 2004 RTW Red Blend (Columbia Valley (WA)) $13. 88 Best Buy *—P.G. (6/1/2006)*

CAYMUS

Caymus 2004 Cabernet Sauvignon (Napa Valley) $70. Here's an extraordinary wine to add to your cellar collection. It's a guaranteed ager. Supported by rich, sturdy tannins, it shows a firm, dry mouthfeel and deep flavors of blackberries, with a seamless hem of toasty oak. So balanced, so powerful and elegant, it's at the top of its class, and proves that the floor of the Napa Valley can produce great Cabernet. Drink now–2020. **95 Cellar Selection** *—S.H. (2/1/2007)*

Caymus 2003 Cabernet Sauvignon (Napa Valley) $70. 94 Cellar Selection *—S.H. (6/1/2006)*

Caymus 2002 Cabernet Sauvignon (Napa Valley) $70. 90 *—S.H. (3/1/2005)*

Caymus 2000 Cabernet Sauvignon (Napa Valley) $70. 91 *—J.M. (4/1/2003)*

Caymus 1999 Cabernet Sauvignon (Napa Valley) $70. 93 *—M.S. (11/15/2002)*

Caymus 1998 Cabernet Sauvignon (Napa Valley) $70. 89 *(6/26/2002)*

Caymus 1997 Cabernet Sauvignon (Napa Valley) $70. 91 *(11/1/2000)*

Caymus 2004 Special Selection Cabernet Sauvignon (Napa Valley) $136. Beautiful wine, lush and soft in the style of this warm vintage. It's immediately enjoyable for the wealth of cherries, blackberries and raspberries, with a decadent edge of melted milk chocolate. Oak adds extra dimensions of smoky vanilla, caramel, butterscotch and gingerbread. Those who think they don't like red wine will enjoy. Hard to tell if it has the stuffing for the long haul, but it's gorgeous now and for the next six years. **97 Editors' Choice** *—S.H. (8/1/2007)*

Caymus 2003 Special Selection Cabernet Sauvignon (Napa Valley) $136. 93 Cellar Selection *—S.H. (9/1/2006)*

Caymus 2002 Special Selection Cabernet Sauvignon (Napa Valley) $136. 91 *—S.H. (10/1/2005)*

Caymus 2001 Special Selection Cabernet Sauvignon (Napa Valley) $136. 93 *—J.M. (12/31/2004)*

Caymus 2000 Special Selection Cabernet Sauvignon (Napa Valley) $136. 93 *—J.M. (12/15/2003)*

Caymus 2003 Conundrum White Blend (California) $24. 85 *—S.H. (10/1/2005)*

Caymus 2001 Conundrum White Blend (California) $24. 89 *—J.M. (2/1/2003)*

CAYUSE

Cayuse 2003 Camaspelo Bordeaux Blend (Walla Walla (WA)) $55. 92 *—P.G. (4/1/2006)*

Cayuse 1999 Syrah (Walla Walla (WA)) $40. 85 *(11/1/2001)*

Cayuse 2003 Armada Syrah (Walla Walla (WA)) $65. A truly stunning wine of amazing complexity. It has layers of depth rarely found in any Washington wines, beginning with dense black fruits, black licorice, smoke, pepper and charcoal. The trademark Cayuse herbal/green tea elements are there also, more as hints than as layers. The aging in big neutral barriques has buffed it out; as it breathes in the glass the wine opens beautifully, gaining flesh and density. A genuine tour de force, deeply aromatic and fascinating. **97** *—P.G. (3/1/2007)*

Cayuse 2004 Bionic Frog Syrah (Walla Walla (WA)) $75. Smooth, supple and full-flavored, The Bionic Frog shows the characteristic uber-funk that it is known for. But in this new vintage it seems to be a bit less in-your-face than previously. There's plenty of wild herb, beef blood and silage to go around; but the flavors are already fully integrated, the wine viscous and plush with an intensely spicy quality. This is beautiful, thick and meaty yet still lifted through the finish, which keeps adding new scents and flavors as it sails along—vanilla, clove and baking spices. **96** *—P.G. (3/1/2007)*

Cayuse 2003 Cailloux Vineyard Syrah (Walla Walla (WA)) $55. 95 Cellar Selection *—P.G. (4/1/2006)*

Cayuse 2002 Cailloux Vineyard Syrah (Walla Walla (WA)) $55. 85 *(9/1/2005)*

Cayuse 2004 En Cerise Syrah (Walla Walla (WA)) $60. Here's a strong whiff of what Cayuse's Christophe Baron calls the "good funk," augmented with a blast of black pepper, meat and blood. There's wild herb lurking in the background also, and as the Syrah opens up slowly in the glass it develops a powerful green tea scent. But what a glorious, pungent, earthy and sensuous mix of flavors, wild, organic and fascinating. **92** *—P.G. (3/1/2007)*

Cayuse 2003 En Cerise Vineyard Syrah (Walla Walla (WA)) $55. 93 Editors' Choice *—P.G. (4/1/2006)*

Cayuse 2002 En Cerise Vineyard Syrah (Walla Walla (WA)) $55. 88 *(9/1/2005)*

Cayuse 2000 Cailloux Vineyard Viognier (Walla Walla (WA)) $28. 92 —*P.G. (10/1/2001)*

Cayuse 2004 Cailloux Vineyard Viognier Viognier (Walla Walla (WA)) $21. 93 Editors' Choice —*P.G. (4/1/2006)*

CE2V

CE2V 2001 Meritage Cabernet Blend (Napa Valley) $75. 90 —*S.H. (8/1/2005)*

CE2V 2000 Meritage (Napa Valley) $75. 88 —*J.C. (5/1/2004)*

CE2V 2000 Estate Bottled Sangiovese (Napa Valley) $30. 84 —*S.H. (9/1/2003)*

CE2V 2000 Sauvignon Blanc (Napa Valley) $25. 87 —*S.H. (12/1/2001)*

CE2V 2001 Estate Bottled Sauvignon Blanc (Napa Valley) $25. 84 —*S.H. (7/1/2003)*

CEAGO VINEGARDEN

Ceago Vinegarden 2001 Camp Masut Cabernet Sauvignon (Mendocino) $32. 84 —*S.H. (12/15/2005)*

Ceago Vinegarden 2000 Clone 337 Cabernet Sauvignon (Mendocino) $38. 88 —*S.H. (11/15/2003)*

Ceago Vinegarden 2005 Del Lago Chardonnay (Mendocino) $18. 84 —*S.H. (12/1/2006)*

Ceago Vinegarden 2004 Jeriko Vineyard Chardonnay (Mendocino) $18. 87 —*S.H. (12/15/2005)*

Ceago Vinegarden 2000 Camp Lema Merlot (Mendocino County) $30. 88 —*S.H. (2/1/2004)*

Ceago Vinegarden 2001 Camp Masut Merlot (Mendocino) $25. 84 —*S.H. (12/15/2005)*

Ceago Vinegarden 1999 McNab Ranch Merlot (Mendocino County) $39. 91 —*S.H. (8/1/2003)*

Ceago Vinegarden 2005 Del Lago Muscat Canelli (Clear Lake) $22. 87 —*S.H. (12/1/2006)*

Ceago Vinegarden 2000 Petite Sirah (Mendocino County) $30. 92 —*S.H. (12/31/2003)*

Ceago Vinegarden 2005 Kathleen's Vineyard Sauvignon Blanc (Clear Lake) $18. 86 —*S.H. (12/1/2006)*

Ceago Vinegarden 2002 Kathleen's Vineyard Sauvignon Blanc (Mendocino County) $17. 85 —*S.H. (12/1/2003)*

Ceago Vinegarden 2001 Kathleen's Vineyard Sauvignon Blanc (Mendocino County) $19. 88 —*S.H. (7/1/2003)*

Ceago Vinegarden 2006 Del Lago Syrah Rosé Syrah (Clear Lake) $18. A really nice blush wine from this pretty property up in Lake County. Shows its Syrah parentage and extreme youth in the fresh-picked cherry and raspberry flavors, boosted by keen acidity, and it's totally dry despite relatively low alcohol. Defines a fulller, bigger style of rosé. **88** —*S.H. (7/1/2007)*

Ceago Vinegarden 2005 Del Lago Syrah Rosé Syrah (Clear Lake) $18. 83 —*S.H. (12/1/2006)*

CECCHETTI SEBASTIANI CELLAR

Cecchetti Sebastiani Cellar 2000 Pinot Noir (Central Coast) $14. 81 *(10/1/2002)*

Cecchetti Sebastiani Cellar 1999 Pinot Noir (Central Coast) $14. 82 *(10/1/2002)*

Cecchetti Sebastiani Cellar 2000 Viognier (North Coast) $14. 85 —*J.M. (12/15/2002)*

CEDAR KNOLL

Cedar Knoll 2004 Cabernet Sauvignon (Napa Valley) $35. This is a second wine from Palmaz. It's a big Cabernet, dry and full-bodied, with extravagant cassis, cherry and oak flavors that contain riper notes of red currants and licorice. Gets better as it sits in the glass and breathes, and could benefit from up to five years in the cellar. **89,**—*S.H. (12/31/2007)*

CEDERGREEN CELLARS

Cedergreen Cellars 2006 Riesling (Columbia Valley (WA)) $17. From Evergreen vineyards. This is all stainless and rather sweet, touching 4% residual sugar. Despite that, the underlying acids keep the wine reasonably crisp and buoyant. Flavors of cotton candy, strawberry lollipop and sweet watermelon make this a perfect summer sipper. **86** —*P.G. (9/1/2007)*

CEDAR MOUNTAIN

Cedar Mountain 1997 Duet Bordeaux Blend (Livermore Valley) $22. 86 —*M.S. (9/1/2000)*

Cedar Mountain 1998 Blanche's Vineyard Reserve Cabernet Sauvignon (Livermore Valley) $50. 83 —*S.H. (9/1/2003)*

Cedar Mountain 1999 Blanches Vineyard Cabernet Sauvignon (Livermore Valley) $22. 81 —*S.H. (11/15/2003)*

Cedar Mountain 1998 Cabernet Royale Cabernet Sauvignon (Livermore Valley) $25. 87 —*S.H. (11/15/2003)*

Cedar Mountain 1999 Estate Reserve Blanches Vineyard Cabernet Sauvignon (Livermore Valley) $50. 82 —*S.H. (11/15/2003)*

Cedar Mountain 2000 Blanche's Vineyard Chardonnay (Livermore Valley) $18. 82 —*S.H. (8/1/2003)*

Cedar Mountain 1998 Blanches Vineyard Chardonnay (Livermore Valley) $18. 84 *(6/1/2000)*

Cedar Mountain 1998 Chardonnay del Sol Chardonnay (Livermore Valley) $25. 88 —*S.H. (6/1/2003)*

Cedar Mountain 1997 One Oak Vineyard Merlot (Livermore Valley) $21. 84 —*S.H. (8/1/2003)*

Cedar Mountain 2004 Del Arroyo Vineyard Pinot Grigio (Livermore Valley) $11. 87 Best Buy —*S.H. (7/1/2005)*

Cedar Mountain 1997 Vintage Port (Amador County) $21. 87 —*S.H. (9/1/2003)*

Cedar Mountain 1998 Port Royale Red Blend (California) $35. 83 —*S.H. (12/15/2003)*

Cedar Mountain 2004 Del Arroyo Vineyard Sauvignon Blanc (Livermore Valley) $12. 84 —*S.H. (8/1/2005)*

Cedar Mountain 2003 Del Arroyo Vineyard Sauvignon Blanc (Livermore Valley) $18. 83 —*S.H. (8/1/2005)*

Cedar Mountain 1999 Zinfandel (Amador County) $18. 83 —*S.H. (9/1/2003)*

CEDARVILLE

Cedarville 2001 Viognier (El Dorado) $20. 85 —*S.H. (5/1/2003)*

Cedarville 2001 Zinfandel (El Dorado) $22. 82 *(11/1/2003)*

Cedarville 2000 Zinfandel (El Dorado) $22. 85 —*S.H. (9/1/2003)*

CEDARVILLE VINEYARD

Cedarville Vineyard 2002 Estate Syrah (El Dorado) $25. 85 *(9/1/2005)*

CEJA

Ceja 2000 Merlot (Carneros) $32. 83 —*S.H. (3/1/2005)*

Ceja 2002 Syrah (Sonoma Coast) $28. 87 *(9/1/2005)*

Ceja 2001 Syrah (Sonoma County) $28. 86 —*S.H. (3/1/2005)*

CELADON TV

Celadon TV 2002 Esperanza Vineyard Grenache (Clarksburg) $20. 90 —*J.C. (10/1/2004)*

CELLAR NO. 8

Cellar No. 8 2003 Cabernet Sauvignon (California) $10. 87 Best Buy —*S.H. (12/31/2006)*

Cellar No. 8 2002 Cabernet Sauvignon (California) $10. 81 —*S.H. (4/1/2006)*

Cellar No. 8 2001 Cabernet Sauvignon (North Coast) $14. 86 —*S.H. (5/1/2004)*

Cellar No. 8 2004 Merlot (California) $10. 84 —*S.H. (12/31/2006)*

Cellar No. 8 2003 Merlot (California) $10. 84 —*S.H. (3/1/2006)*

Cellar No. 8 2001 Merlot (North Coast) $14. 85 —*S.H. (5/1/2004)*

Cellar No. 8 2004 Zinfandel (California) $10. 82 —*S.H. (12/31/2006)*

Cellar No. 8 2003 Zinfandel (California) $10. 80 —*S.H. (10/1/2006)*

Cellar No. 8 2002 Zinfandel (North Coast) $14. 83 —*S.H. (10/1/2005)*

Cellar No. 8 2001 Zinfandel (North Coast) $14. 89 Best Buy —*S.H. (5/1/2004)*

CENAY

Cenay 2001 Blue Tooth Vineyard Cabernet Sauvignon (Napa Valley) $30. 91 Editors' Choice —*S.H. (10/1/2004)*

Cenay 2000 Blue Tooth Vineyard Cabernet Sauvignon (Napa Valley) $30. 89 —*S.H. (12/15/2003)*

Cenay 1999 Blue Tooth Vineyard Cabernet Sauvignon (Napa Valley) $30. 93 —*S.H. (6/1/2002)*

Cenay 2000 Rodger's Vineyard Pinot Noir (Napa Valley) $26. 88 *(10/1/2002)*

Cenay 2002 Rodgers Vineyard Pinot Noir (Napa Valley) $34. 87 *(11/1/2004)*

Cenay 2001 Rodgers Vineyard Pinot Noir (Napa Valley) $26. 84 —*S.H. (7/1/2003)*

Cenay 1999 Rodgers Vineyard Pinot Noir (Napa Valley) $26. 85 *(10/1/2002)*

CENTURY OAK

Century Oak 2002 Cabernet Sauvignon (Lodi) $13. 83 —*S.H. (12/31/2005)*

Century Oak 2002 Reserve Cabernet Sauvignon (Lodi) $20. 81 —*S.H. (12/31/2005)*

Century Oak 2001 Reserve Cabernet Sauvignon (Lodi) $20. 84 —*S.H. (3/1/2005)*

Century Oak 2002 Old Vine Zinfandel (Lodi) $13. 82 —*S.H. (12/31/2005)*

CERRO CALIENTE

Cerro Caliente 2001 Cabernet Sauvignon (Paso Robles) $19. 83 —*S.H. (12/15/2003)*

Cerro Caliente 2002 White Cabernet Sauvignon (Paso Robles) $12. 83 —*S.H. (11/15/2003)*

Cerro Caliente 2004 Chardonnay (Edna Valley) $20. 83 —*S.H. (10/1/2006)*

Cerro Caliente 2001 Chardonnay (Edna Valley) $18. 83 —*S.H. (10/1/2003)*

Cerro Caliente 1999 Barrel Reserve Merlot (Paso Robles) $25. 80 —*S.H. (12/15/2003)*

Cerro Caliente 2005 Pinot Grigio (Edna Valley) $20. 85 —*S.H. (10/1/2006)*

Cerro Caliente 2002 Pinot Grigio (Edna Valley) $16. 84 —*S.H. (12/1/2003)*

Cerro Caliente 2004 Dixon Ranch Vineyard Pinot Noir (Edna Valley) $24. 87 —*S.H. (11/1/2006)*

Cerro Caliente 2001 Syrah (Edna Valley) $23. 84 —*S.H. (12/15/2003)*

Cerro Caliente 2003 Dixon Ranch Vineyard Syrah (Edna Valley) $24. 91 —*S.H. (11/1/2006)*

CHADDSFORD

Chaddsford 2002 Merican Bordeaux Blend (Pennsylvania) $40. An enticing nose of smoky spice and herbed sausage leads into flavors of dark fruit and wood on the palate with this Cabernet Sauvignon, Merlot, Cabernet Franc and Petit Verdot blend. Good structure and length. Pair with creamy cheeses or grilled lamb. 84 —*S.K. (12/1/2007)*

Chaddsford 2001 Merican Bordeaux Blend (Pennsylvania) $40. 86 —*M.D. (8/1/2006)*

Chaddsford 2001 Cabernet/Chambourcin Cabernet Blend (Pennsylvania) $15. 83 —*M.S. (3/1/2003)*

Chaddsford 1997 Cabernet Franc (Pennsylvania) $13. 87 —*J.C. (8/1/1999)*

Chaddsford 1999 Cabernet Franc (Pennsylvania) $14. 80 —*J.C. (1/1/2004)*

Chaddsford 2003 Cabernet Sauvignon (Pennsylvania) $15. 80 —*M.D. (8/1/2006)*

Chaddsford 1999 Cabernet Sauvignon (Pennsylvania) $17. 81 —*J.C. (1/1/2004)*

Chaddsford 1998 Seven Valleys Vineyard Chambourcin (Pennsylvania) $16. 83 —*J.C. (8/1/1999)*

Chaddsford 2005 Miller Estate Vineyard Chambourcin (Pennsylvania) $25. Tobacco and spice aromas lead into flavors of jammy fruit and vanilla. A touch smoky on the finish, with pretty aromatics typical of the grape. Pair with lamb or grilled meats. 83 —*S.K. (12/1/2007)*

Chaddsford 1999 Barrel Select Chardonnay (Pennsylvania) $NA. 84 —*J.C. (1/1/2004)*

Chaddsford 2004 Miller Estate Vineyard Chardonnay (Pennsylvania) $21. Sweet flavors and aromas of pineapple, vanilla and candied spice give this a fruitcake feel, which could be considered appealing or odd, depending on your taste. The character is slightly muddled, but the wine finishes long and assertively. 82 —*S.K. (7/1/2007)*

Chaddsford 2005 Naked Chardonnay (Pennsylvania) $15. An unusual, slightly skunky nose leads to an angular wine with lots of acidic, citric notes. Some balance and weight is lacking here, but the wine will likely pair well with seafood and salads. 82 —*S.K. (5/1/2007)*

Chaddsford 2000 Philip Roth Vineyard Chardonnay (Pennsylvania) $33. 91 —*J.C. (7/1/2002)*

Chaddsford 1997 Philip Roth Vineyard Chardonnay (Pennsylvania) $30. 84 —*J.C. (8/1/1999)*

Chaddsford 2004 Merlot (Pennsylvania) $17. Impressive, enticing aromas of chocolate, tobacco, mint and spice mingle with flavors of berries and tea. There's more spice than fruit here, though, and the wine lacks balance. 83 —*S.K. (7/1/2007)*

Chaddsford 2003 Merlot (Pennsylvania) $19. 80 —*M.D. (8/1/2006)*

Chaddsford 2005 Pinot Grigio (New York) $17. An approachable, food-friendly wine with an earthy character and subtle, soft flavors. Fans of a plumper PG will enjoy this offering. 84 —*S.K. (7/1/2007)*

Chaddsford 2004 Pinot Grigio (New York) $16. 83 —*J.C. (2/1/2006)*

Chaddsford 1998 Pinot Grigio (Pennsylvania) $15. 87 *(8/1/1999)*

Chaddsford 2005 Pinot Noir (Pennsylvania) $17. Black cherry, spice and smoke comprise this Pinot. There's decent structure and roundness on the palate and a flavorful mingling of fruit and spice, but the wine is not very complex. Some aging may remedy this. Overall, the wine is good and accessible. 84 —*S.K. (5/1/2007)*

Chaddsford 2000 Pinot Noir (Pennsylvania) $16. 80 *(10/1/2002)*

Chaddsford 2002 Barrel Select Pinot Noir (Pennsylvania) $25. 84 *(11/1/2004)*

Chaddsford 2002 Miller Estate Vineyard Pinot Noir (Pennsylvania) $35. 85 *(11/1/2004)*

Chaddsford 1999 Merican Red Blend (Pennsylvania) $35. 85 —*M.S. (3/1/2003)*

Chaddsford 1997 Proprietors Reserve Red Blend (Pennsylvania) $11. 82 —*J.C. (8/1/1999)*

Chaddsford 2000 Proprietor's Reserve White Blend (Pennsylvania) $10. 80 —*J.C. (1/1/2004)*

Chaddsford 1997 Proprietors Reserve White Blend (Pennsylvania) $9. 85 —*J.C. (8/1/1999)*

Chaddsford 1998 Spring Wine White Blend (Pennsylvania) $9. 83 —*J.C. (8/1/1999)*

CHALEUR ESTATE

Chaleur Estate 2004 Blanc Bordeaux White Blend (Columbia Valley (WA)) $31. 91 —*P.G. (12/15/2005)*

CHALK HILL

Chalk Hill 2001 Cabernet Sauvignon (Chalk Hill) $66. 90 —*S.H. (12/1/2005)*

Chalk Hill 2000 Cabernet Sauvignon (Chalk Hill) $54. 91 —*S.H. (6/1/2004)*

Chalk Hill 1999 Cabernet Sauvignon (Chalk Hill) $64. 90 —*S.H. (2/1/2003)*

Chalk Hill 2003 Estate Bottled Cabernet Sauvignon (Chalk Hill) $64. 94 Editors' Choice —*S.H. (12/15/2006)*

Chalk Hill 1997 Estate Bottled Cabernet Sauvignon (Chalk Hill) $50. 90 *(11/1/2000)*

Chalk Hill 2004 Chairman's Club Cabernet Sauvignon-Carmenère (Chalk Hill) $85. Made with 82% Cabernet, this interesting wine is showing all kinds of possibilities. It's a good red now, sturdily dry and tannic, with red cherry, pomegranate, sweet tobacco and allspice flavors. But it's a little juvenile. I would decant it as long as possible, and it should enjoy a cellar life of up to 10 years. 91 —*S.H. (8/1/2007)*

Chalk Hill 2002 Chardonnay (Chalk Hill) $36. 86 —*S.H. (12/1/2005)*

Chalk Hill 2000 Chardonnay (Chalk Hill) $42. 90 —*S.H. (12/31/2003)*

Chalk Hill 2004 Chairman's Club Chardonnay (Chalk Hill) $75. Everything you look for in a Burgundian Chard is here. It's dramatically rich in tropical fruit and Meyer lemon flavors, with crisp natural acidity. Lots of new toasty oak, sur lies aging and malolactic fermentation add integrated dimensions of flavor and texture. A sensational wine, dense and complex, and should develop well for five years. Only 45 cases produced. 95 —*S.H. (4/1/2007)*

Chalk Hill 2004 Estate Chardonnay (Chalk Hill) $40. With its array of ripe peach, lemon drop, guava and nectarine fruit and bright acidity, this Chard's complexity is boosted by fine new oak and a steely minerality that makes the wine clean and vibrant. It's balanced, elegant and enjoyable to drink. Best now–2007. 91 —*S.H. (4/1/2007)*

Chalk Hill 2003 Estate Chardonnay (Chalk Hill) $42. 93 Editors' Choice —*S.H. (11/15/2006)*

Chalk Hill 1999 Estate Bottled Chardonnay (Chalk Hill) $42. 92 —*S.H. (12/1/2001)*

Chalk Hill 1998 Estate Bottled Chardonnay (Chalk Hill) $40. 91 *(7/1/2001)*

Chalk Hill 2002 Estate Vineyard Selection Chardonnay (Chalk Hill) $67. 90 —*S.H. (12/1/2005)*

Chalk Hill 1999 Estate Vineyard Selection Chardonnay (Chalk Hill) $67. 94 Cellar Selection —*S.H. (12/15/2002)*

Chalk Hill 2004 Oak Hill Block B Chardonnay (Russian River Valley) $NA. Intense and concentrated in cooked guava, papaya and pineapple fruit, this well-oaked wine is brightened with crisp acidity. It's a big, bold Chardonnay that trades subtlety for in-your-face voluptuousness, but could do with a little more of the former. 87 —*S.H. (4/1/2007)*

Chalk Hill 2005 Unfined & Unfiltered Estate Chardonnay (Chalk Hill) $45. They pulled out all the stops on this white Burgundy-inspired Chard. It tastes quite leesy, with a Champagne-like yeastiness riding over the tropical fruit and oaky, caramelized flavors. Complex and intriguing, this unfined, unfiltered Chard should drink well for the next few years. **90** —*S.H. (12/15/2007)*

Chalk Hill 2005 Unfined & Unfiltered Founder's Block Chardonnay (Chalk Hill) $85. The block is the oldest on the estate, with extremely low-yielding vines, and the wine is not produced every year. The resulting Chard is very concentrated and dense. Everything about it is big: the apricot and peach fruit, the smoky oak, the yeasty lees. Tasted in August 2007, the wine was a little disconnected, like the parts of an enormous machine that has not yet been put together. Give this ambitious young wine a year or so to come together. **92** —*S.H. (12/15/2007)*

Chalk Hill 2004 Chairman's Club Malbec (Chalk Hill) $85. With Malbec so popular these days, I guess Chalk Hill decided to weigh in. The wine is inky black and bone dry, earthy, supertannic and not very interesting. It's also seriously overpriced. **83** —*S.H. (8/1/2007)*

Chalk Hill 2000 Merlot (Chalk Hill) $43. 89 —*S.H. (12/15/2004)*

Chalk Hill 1999 Merlot (Chalk Hill) $51. 90 —*S.H. (2/1/2003)*

Chalk Hill 1998 Adele's Merlot (Chalk Hill) $100. 86 —*S.H. (11/15/2002)*

Chalk Hill 2003 Estate Merlot (Chalk Hill) $68. A letdown after the recent string of good vintages, the '03 Merlot has an edge of overripe raisins side by side with a vegetal taste. It's a strange, discombobulated wine, whose new oak seems out of place. **82** —*S.H. (12/15/2007)*

Chalk Hill 2001 Estate Merlot (Chalk Hill) $43. 89 —*S.H. (12/1/2005)*

Chalk Hill 2002 Estate Bottled Merlot (Chalk Hill) $43. 92 —*S.H. (12/15/2006)*

Chalk Hill 2005 Estate North Slope Pinot Gris (Chalk Hill) $40. Fruit and acidity star in this wine; aging in neutral oak barrels has given it just a little softness and creaminess. With no malolactic fermentation, the acidity is quite crisp and stimulating, just what you want in a wine of this dryness. It scores high on the deliciousness scale, with pineapple, lime and apricot flavors. **88** —*S.H. (12/15/2007)*

Chalk Hill 2002 Estate Vineyard Selection Pinot Gris (Chalk Hill) $40. 92 —*S.H. (2/1/2006)*

Chalk Hill 2000 Estate Vineyard Selection Pinot Gris (Chalk Hill) $40. 86 —*S.H. (9/1/2003)*

Chalk Hill 2003 North Slope Pinot Gris (Chalk Hill) $40. Chalk Hill is attempting to create a world-class PG, full-throttle with ripe fruit and sur lies, produced from selected blocks in the estate vineyard. But at three-plus years, the wine is losing the charm and vibrancy of its fruit, and is picking up the brittle, decaying character of a white wine that's too old. **84** —*S.H. (4/1/2007)*

USA

Chalk Hill 2005 Sauvignon Blanc (Chalk Hill) $28. Even in a warm year, like '04, Chalk Hill's estate Sauvignon teeters on the brink of unripeness. In this cool '05 vintage, it's dominated by cat pee aromas and flavors. Aging on the lees, a dash of Sémillon and some new French oak lend softening nuances. **87** —*S.H. (4/1/2007)*

Chalk Hill 2004 Sauvignon Blanc (Chalk Hill) $25. 91 —*S.H. (8/1/2006)*

Chalk Hill 2003 Sauvignon Blanc (Chalk Hill) $25. 87 *(7/1/2005)*

Chalk Hill 2001 Sauvignon Blanc (Chalk Hill) $24. 90 —*S.H. (10/1/2003)*

Chalk Hill 1999 Sauvignon Blanc (Chalk Hill) $29. 85 *(8/1/2002)*

Chalk Hill 2003 Estate Sauvignon Blanc (Chalk Hill) $25. 88 —*S.H. (12/1/2005)*

Chalk Hill 2000 Estate Bottled Sauvignon Blanc (Sonoma County) $29. 91 —*S.H. (9/1/2003)*

Chalk Hill 2005 Botrytised Sémillon (Chalk Hill) $55. This is one of the sweetest white California dessert wines out there. It's addictively decadent, like an upscale Sauternes. Barrel fermentation in new French oak gives an opulent, palate-flattering honeyed vanilla richness to the apricot, peach, pineapple and crème brûlée flavors that are so rich and refined. Crisp acidity provide clean, vibrant balance. Just gorgeous, and worth the price. **95** —*S.H. (12/31/2007)*

CHALONE

Chalone 2005 Chardonnay (Chalone) $25. Ripe and oaky, with juicy pineapple marmalade and butterscotch flavors balanced with crisp acidity, and a dry finish. Easy to like this creamy Chard. **86** —*S.H. (8/1/2007)*

Chalone 2005 Chardonnay (Monterey County) $10. Gets the job done; a simple, easy wine, showing tons of ripe, candied peach, pineapple and cotton candy flavors. The finish is sugary. **83** —*S.H. (5/1/2007)*

Chalone 2004 Chardonnay (Monterey County) $12. 84 —*S.H. (3/1/2006)*

Chalone 2003 Chardonnay (Chalone) $30. 88 —*S.H. (12/1/2005)*

Chalone 2002 Chardonnay (Chalone) $25. 91 Editors' Choice —*S.H. (12/1/2004)*

Chalone 2001 Chardonnay (Chalone) $25. 91 —*S.H. (12/1/2003)*

Chalone 2000 Chardonnay (Chalone) $28. 88 —*J.M. (12/15/2002)*

Chalone 1998 Chardonnay (Chalone) $31. 90 —*S.H. (10/1/2000)*

Chalone 1997 Chardonnay (Chalone) $31. 94 —*L.W. (7/1/1999)*

Chalone 2004 Estate Chardonnay (Chalone) $26. 86 —*S.H. (11/15/2006)*

Chalone 2005 Chenin Blanc (Chalone) $22. Interesting; it's dry, refreshingly crisp and aromatic, with citrus and floral flavors. Try as a Sauvignon Blanc alternative. **86** —*S.H. (8/1/2007)*

Chalone 2004 Chenin Blanc (Chalone) $22. 87 —*S.H. (2/1/2006)*

Chalone 2003 Chenin Blanc (Chalone) $22. 86 —*S.H. (7/1/2005)*

Chalone 2002 Chenin Blanc (Chalone) $22. 89 —*S.H. (12/1/2004)*

Chalone 2000 Chalone Chenin Blanc (Chalone) $22. 93 —*J.M. (9/1/2003)*

Chalone 2001 Estate Grown Chenin Blanc (Chalone) $22. 92 Editors' Choice —*J.M. (5/1/2003)*

Chalone 2003 Grenache (Chalone) $22. 88 —*S.H. (8/1/2005)*

Chalone 2004 Merlot (Monterey County) $15. 85 —*S.H. (12/15/2006)*

Chalone 2004 Pinot Blanc (Chalone) $22. 87 —*S.H. (2/1/2006)*

Chalone 2002 Pinot Blanc (Chalone) $22. 90 —*S.H. (12/1/2004)*

Chalone 2001 Pinot Blanc (Chalone) $22. 89 —*S.H. (2/1/2004)*

Chalone 2000 Pinot Blanc (Monterey) $24. 91 —*J.M. (9/1/2003)*

Chalone 1999 Pinot Blanc (Chalone) $24. 91 —*S.H. (2/1/2001)*

Chalone 2003 Estate Pinot Blanc (Chalone) $22. 84 —*S.H. (10/1/2005)*

Chalone 1997 Reserve Pinot Blanc (Monterey County) $22. 92 —*L.W. (3/1/2000)*

Chalone 2005 Pinot Noir (Monterey County) $14. Everyday Pinot, a one-dimensional wine with pleasant cherry, raspberry and cocoa flavors finished with a touch of smoky oak. At this price, it's a good buy for consumers who are curious about Pinot but don't want to drop a bundle. **84** —*S.H. (5/1/2007)*

Chalone 2004 Pinot Noir (Chalone) $35. 90 —*S.H. (11/15/2006)*

Chalone 2003 Pinot Noir (Chalone) $25. 86 —*S.H. (12/1/2005)*

Chalone 2001 Pinot Noir (Chalone) $25. 86 —*S.H. (2/1/2004)*

Chalone 2000 Pinot Noir (Chalone) $30. 88 *(10/1/2002)*

Chalone 1998 Pinot Noir (Chalone) $35. 85 —*S.H. (10/1/2000)*

Chalone 1997 Pinot Noir (Chalone) $31. 90 *(10/1/1999)*

Chalone 2005 Estate Grown Pinot Noir (Chalone) $35. This may do something down the line, but who knows? It's okay, with sweet-and-sour cherry, herb and oak flavors, and a soft, one-dimensional feeling. **84** —*S.H. (8/1/2007)*

Chalone 2001 Gavilan Rhône Red Blend (Chalone) $30. 84 —*S.H. (12/1/2003)*

Chalone 2003 Syrah (Chalone) $25. 85 *(9/1/2005)*

Chalone 2002 Syrah (Chalone) $25. 88 —*S.H. (12/31/2004)*

Chalone 2001 Syrah (Chalone) $25. 90 —*S.H. (12/1/2003)*

Chalone 2000 Syrah (Chalone) $30. 91 —*J.M. (12/1/2002)*

CHAMELEON

Chameleon 1998 Barbera (Amador County) $17. 86 *(9/1/2000)*

Chameleon 2002 Barbera (Lake County) $15. 84 —*S.H. (8/1/2005)*

Chameleon 1998 Sangiovese (North Coast) $19. 86 —*J.C. (9/1/2000)*

Chameleon 1997 Sangiovese (North Coast) $18. 86 —*J.C. (10/1/1999)*

Chameleon 2003 Syrah (North Coast) $16. 85 *(9/1/2005)*

Chameleon 2002 Syrah (Napa Valley) $25. 89 *(9/1/2005)*

Chameleon 1999 Syrah (Napa Valley) $31. 90 *(11/1/2001)*

CHANDLER REACH

Chandler Reach 2000 Monte Regale Bordeaux Blend (Yakima Valley) $22. 86 —*P.G. (9/1/2003)*

Chandler Reach 2003 Parris Cabernet Franc (Yakima Valley) $38. This is 100% Cab Franc. Chandler Reach has made another terrific example, saturated and lush with sweet, ripe black cherry fruit. There is a hint of leather, plenty of snappy acid, well-modulated tannins and behind the tangy fruit a wine with pleasing texture and balance. It's muscular without steroids, a fine follow up to the excellent 2002. **91** —*P.G. (5/1/2007)*

Chandler Reach 2002 Parris Cabernet Franc (Yakima Valley) $38. 91 —*P.G. (6/1/2006)*

Chandler Reach 2003 Parris Cabernet Sauvignon (Yakima Valley) $42. The Parris wines are the estate-grown reserves, and as the vineyard matures, the wines should gain in concentration and complexity. As before, the Cabernet shows clean, ripe but still young fruit, sweet and plump. Subtle notes are your reward if you are willing to give it some extra attention—finishing streaks of black tea, ground coffee, toffee, pepper and herb. Though 60% new French oak was used, the wine has adjusted well and kept its elegant balance. **91** *—P.G. (5/1/2007)*

Chandler Reach 2002 Parris Cabernet Sauvignon (Yakima Valley) $42. 90 *—P.G. (12/15/2005)*

Chandler Reach 2004 Merlot (Yakima Valley) $16. A luscious, velvety, 100% Merlot—how many places in the world can you make Merlot this tasty for this price? It shows why Washington Merlot stands apart from the crowd—it's full-flavored, full-figured and delicious in a ripe, forward, fruit-and-chocolate explosion. **90** *—P.G. (5/1/2007)*

Chandler Reach 2005 36 Red Blend (Yakima Valley) $12. A budget blend of four fifths Cabernet and a mix of Cab Franc, Merlot and Syrah for the balance. This is what Washington needs more of—bright, full-bodied, everyday reds at everyday prices. There's good grip here and more substantial fruit than you'll find elsewhere for the price. This needs just a bit of breathing time to turbocharge the fruit. **88 Best Buy** *—P.G. (5/1/2007)*

Chandler Reach 2004 Corella Red Blend (Yakima Valley) $16. Corella is the winery's Sangiovese/Cabernet/Syrah blend—a super-Yakiman? This is the best version they've made yet, as the tart, astringent berry flavors of the Sangiovese are beautifully set up against the stiffer tannins and deeper black fruit components from the Cab, with just a hint of peppery smoke from the Syrah. It's a wonderful balance of flavors, with surprising depth and substance. **90** *—P.G. (5/1/2007)*

Chandler Reach 2003 Monte Regalo Red Blend (Yakima Valley) $22. 92 *—P.G. (6/1/2006)*

Chandler Reach 2003 Syrah (Yakima Valley) $26. 88 *—P.G. (6/1/2006)*

Chandler Reach 2001 Syrah (Yakima Valley) $26. 89 *—P.G. (9/1/2003)*

CHANGALA

Changala 1999 Syrah (Paso Robles) $16. 86 *—S.H. (12/1/2002)*

CHANNING DAUGHTERS

Channing Daughters 1999 Brick Kiln Chardonnay (Long Island) $17. 86 *—J.C. (4/1/2001)*

Channing Daughters 1999 Scuttlehole Chardonnay (Long Island) $13. 84 *—J.C. (4/1/2001)*

Channing Daughters 1998 Sculpture Garden Merlot (Long Island) $19. 83 *—J.C. (4/1/2001)*

Channing Daughters 1999 Fresh Red Red Blend (Long Island) $15. 84 *—J.C. (4/1/2001)*

CHANNING PERRINE

Channing Perrine 1998 Mudd Vineyard Cabernet Sauvignon (Long Island) $19. 82 *—J.C. (4/1/2001)*

Channing Perrine 1999 Mudd Vineyard Fleur de Terre Merlot (North Fork of Long Island) $16. 83 *—J.C. (4/1/2001)*

Channing Perrine 1998 Oregon Road Riesling (Long Island) $13. 83 *—J.C. (4/1/2001)*

CHANTICLEER

Chanticleer 2001 Cabernet Sauvignon (Napa Valley) $45. 91 *—J.M. (12/31/2004)*

CHAPPELLET

Chappellet 2003 Mountain Cuvée Bordeaux Blend (Napa Valley) $26. 90 *—S.H. (10/1/2006)*

Chappellet 1996 Cabernet Franc (Napa Valley) $24. 87 *—M.S. (6/1/1999)*

Chappellet 2002 Pritchard Hill Estate Vineyard Cabernet Sauvignon (Napa Valley) $120. 95 *—S.H. (12/15/2005)*

Chappellet 2001 Pritchard Hill Estate Vineyard Cabernet Sauvignon (Napa Valley) $110. 94 Cellar Selection *—S.H. (12/31/2004)*

Chappellet 1999 Pritchard Hill Estate Vineyard Cabernet Sauvignon (Napa Valley) $110. 92 Cellar Selection *(8/1/2003)*

Chappellet 2004 Signature Cabernet Sauvignon (Napa Valley) $46. This is one of the softer Chappellet Cabs, and whether it's because of the hot vintage or a change in winemaking, it's not in the same league as the '02 and '03. Tastes like a melted chocolate bar, with a squeeze of crème de cassis and licorice, and of course new toasted oak. Just too soft. Drink now. **86** *—S.H. (9/1/2007)*

Chappellet 2003 Signature Cabernet Sauvignon (Napa Valley) $44. 94 Cellar Selection *—S.H. (10/1/2006)*

Chappellet 2001 Signature Cabernet Sauvignon (Napa Valley) $42. 91 Cellar Selection *—S.H. (10/1/2004)*

Chappellet 1997 Signature Cabernet Sauvignon (Napa Valley) $35. 90 *(11/1/2000)*

Chappellet 2005 Chardonnay (Napa Valley) $29. Ripe in pineapples and pears, creamy and well-oaked, this is a pretty good Chard, with a dried herb edge to the fruit. It finishes with a soft, peaty earthiness. **86** *—S.H. (7/1/2007)*

Chappellet 2004 Chardonnay (Napa Valley) $28. 92 *—S.H. (2/1/2006)*

Chappellet 2003 Chardonnay (Napa Valley) $28. 90 *—S.H. (5/1/2005)*

Chappellet 1998 Chardonnay (Napa Valley) $20. 89 *(6/1/2000)*

Chappellet 1997 Chardonnay (Napa Valley) $17. 87 *—J.C. (10/1/1999)*

Chappellet 2000 Signature Chardonnay (Napa Valley) $35. 90 *—S.H. (2/1/2003)*

Chappellet 1999 Signature Chardonnay (Napa Valley) $35. 91 *(7/1/2001)*

Chappellet 2003 Dry Chenin Blanc (Napa Valley) $15. 87 *—S.H. (12/15/2005)*

Chappellet 1997 Moelleux Chenin Blanc (Napa Valley) $40. 91 *—J.C. (12/31/1999)*

Chappellet 1997 Old Vine Cuvée Chenin Blanc (Napa Valley) $14. 92 Best Buy *—M.S. (12/15/2003)*

Chappellet 2004 Merlot (Napa Valley) $32. Coming off a string of great vintages, Chappellet's '04 Merlot isn't quite in the same league, and the reason has got to be the heat of the vintage, which caused an unusually early harvest. The wine is fruit-forward in cherries and blackberries, very soft and a little simple, but quite delicious and dry. Drink now. **86** *—S.H. (7/1/2007)*

Chappellet 2004 Merlot (Napa Valley) $32. I've scored Chappellet's Merlots over 90 points for the last four years. They're doing a great job, vintage after vintage, getting the fruit nice and ripe in cherries, blackberries and carob, while keeping the wine elegantly balanced. This is a beautiful, upscale Merlot now, and is best consumed over the next five years. **90** *—S.H. (3/1/2007)*

Chappellet 2003 Merlot (Napa Valley) $30. 93 *—S.H. (10/1/2006)*

Chappellet 2002 Merlot (Napa Valley) $30. 90 *—S.H. (5/1/2005)*

Chappellet 2001 Merlot (Napa Valley) $28. 90 *—S.H. (12/15/2004)*

Chappellet 1997 Sangiovese (Napa Valley) $24. 87 *—S.H. (12/15/1999)*

Chappellet 1996 Sangiovese (Napa Valley) $23. 91 *—S.H. (11/1/1999)*

CHARIOT

Chariot 2000 Dolcetto (Central Coast) $18. 90 *—J.M. (5/1/2002)*

Chariot 2000 Sangiovese (Central Coast) $15. 88 *—J.M. (5/1/2002)*

CHARLES B. MITCHELL

Charles B. Mitchell 2006 Riesling (Fair Play) $15. Made in an off-dry style, with honeyed tastes of yellow flowers, peaches, kumquats, nougat, vanilla and cinnamon spice. Notable for its crisp spine of acidity, which makes the wine clean and balanced. **86** *—S.H. (9/1/2007)*

CHARLES CREEK

Charles Creek 2001 La Sonrisa del Tecolote Cabernet Sauvignon (Napa Valley) $26. 92 *—S.H. (5/1/2004)*

Charles Creek 2001 Hawk Hill Vineyard Chardonnay (Russian River Valley) $22. 85 *—S.H. (6/1/2003)*

Charles Creek 2002 La Sorpresa Chardonnay (Carneros) $25. 85 *—S.H. (8/1/2004)*

Charles Creek 2003 Las Abuelas Hyde Vineyard Chardonnay (Carneros) $39. 92 *—S.H. (6/1/2005)*

Charles Creek 2002 Las Patolitas Chardonnay (Sonoma County) $20. 88 *—S.H. (2/1/2004)*

Charles Creek 2002 Vista del Halcon Chardonnay (Russian River Valley) $22. 83 *—S.H. (6/1/2004)*

Charles Creek 2002 Miradero Merlot (Napa-Sonoma) $24. 84 *—S.H. (4/1/2005)*

Charles Creek 2001 Miradero Merlot (Sonoma-Napa) $22. 90 *—S.H. (12/31/2003)*

Charles Creek 2000 Miradero Merlot (Sonoma County) $18. 87 *—S.H. (6/1/2003)*

CHARLES KRUG

Charles Krug 1996 Generations Bordeaux Blend (Napa Valley) $34. 89 *(4/1/2001)*

Charles Krug 1997 Generations-Reserve Bordeaux Blend (Napa Valley) $34. 92 Editors' Choice *—S.H. (12/1/2001)*

Charles Krug 2002 Family Reserve Generations Cabernet Blend (Napa Valley) $42. 89 *—S.H. (11/15/2005)*

Charles Krug 2002 Limited Release Cabernet Franc (Napa Valley) $60. 91 *(4/12/2006)*

Charles Krug 2004 Cabernet Sauvignon (Yountville) $26. There are so many good qualities to this wine that I wish it were more concentrated. With a very high production, the vines must have been stretched. Too bad, because it shows gorgeous structure of acids and tannins, the kind of Cabernet only Napa Valley can produce. Still, it rewards for elegance and modest blackberry and oak flavors. 85 *—S.H. (9/1/2007)*

Charles Krug 1997 Cabernet Sauvignon (Napa Valley) $17. 87 *(12/15/1999)*

Charles Krug 2002 Limited Release Cabernet Sauvignon (Napa Valley) $70. 92 *(4/12/2006)*

Charles Krug 2002 Limited Release IX Clones Cabernet Sauvignon (Napa Valley) $80. 93 Cellar Selection *(4/12/2006)*

Charles Krug 2002 Peter Mondavi Family Cabernet Sauvignon (Napa Valley) $24. 88 *—S.H. (11/15/2005)*

Charles Krug 1999 Peter Mondavi Family Cabernet Sauvignon (Napa Valley) $21. 87 *—S.H. (11/15/2002)*

Charles Krug 1996 Peter Mondavi Family Cabernet Sauvignon (Napa Valley) $16. 86 *—S.H. (9/1/1999)*

Charles Krug 1996 Vintage Select Cabernet Sauvignon (Napa Valley) $50. 90 Cellar Selection *(4/1/2001)*

Charles Krug 2002 Vintage Selection Cabernet Sauvignon (Napa Valley) $51. 92 Cellar Selection *—S.H. (11/15/2005)*

Charles Krug 1997 Vintage Selection Cabernet Sauvignon (Napa Valley) $50. 93 *—S.H. (11/15/2002)*

Charles Krug 1995 Vintage Selection Cabernet Sauvignon (Napa Valley) $47. 89 *(12/15/1999)*

Charles Krug 1998 Chardonnay (Napa Valley) $15. 85 *(12/15/1999)*

Charles Krug 2001 Chardonnay (Napa Valley) $17. 88 *—S.H. (6/1/2003)*

Charles Krug 2003 Family Reserve Chardonnay (Napa Valley) $24. 90 *—S.H. (11/15/2005)*

Charles Krug 1999 Family reserve Chardonnay (Napa Valley) $21. 88 *—S.H. (12/1/2001)*

Charles Krug 1999 Family Reserve Chardonnay (Carneros) $21. 88 *—S.H. (12/1/2001)*

Charles Krug 2002 Peter Mondavi Family Chardonnay (Napa Valley) $17. 85 *—S.H. (2/1/2004)*

Charles Krug 2000 Peter Mondavi Family Reserve Chardonnay (Carneros) $21. 88 *—S.H. (12/15/2002)*

Charles Krug 1999 Family Reserve Generations Meritage (Napa Valley) $35. 91 *—S.H. (3/1/2003)*

Charles Krug 2004 Merlot (Napa Valley) $22. Better known for Cabernet Sauvignon, Charles Krug has a good track record for Merlot, too, and their '04 is quite a rich wine. Dry and balanced, it offers a wealth of black cherry, black currant and mocha flavors, and is soft and lingering on the finish. 88 *—S.H. (12/31/2007)*

Charles Krug 1999 Merlot (Napa Valley) $21. 90 Editors' Choice *—S.H. (8/1/2003)*

Charles Krug 1997 Merlot (Napa Valley) $17. 90 *(12/15/1999)*

Charles Krug 2002 Family Reserve Merlot (Napa Valley) $36. 85 *—S.H. (11/15/2005)*

Charles Krug 1997 P.Mondavi Family Reserve Merlot (Napa Valley) $25. 91 Editors' Choice *(6/1/2001)*

Charles Krug 1997 Reserve Merlot (Napa Valley) $28. 92 *(12/15/1999)*

Charles Krug 1996 Pinot Noir (Carneros) $16. 90 Best Buy *—S.H. (6/1/1999)*

Charles Krug 2000 Pinot Noir (Carneros) $19. 85 *—S.H. (7/1/2003)*

Charles Krug 1999 Pinot Noir (Carneros) $18. 88 *(10/1/2002)*

Charles Krug 1998 Pinot Noir (Napa Valley) $16. 88 *(4/1/2001)*

Charles Krug 1998 Peter Mondavi Family Pinot Noir (Napa Valley) $17. 87 *—S.H. (11/15/2001)*

Charles Krug 2003 Peter Mondavi Family Pinot Noir (Carneros) $20. 87 *—S.H. (11/15/2005)*

Charles Krug 2002 Peter Mondavi Family Pinot Noir (Carneros) $20. 85 *—S.H. (2/1/2005)*

Charles Krug 2001 Peter Mondavi Family Pinot Noir (Carneros) $20. 83 *—S.H. (5/1/2004)*

Charles Krug 1999 Family Reserve Sangiovese (Napa Valley) $20. 90 Editors' Choice *—S.H. (12/1/2002)*

Charles Krug 1998 Reserve Sangiovese (Napa Valley) $18. 89 Editors' Choice *(4/1/2001)*

Charles Krug 2006 Sauvignon Blanc (Napa Valley) $18. Crisp and refreshing, this Sauvignon Blanc has ripe flavors of lemons, limes and pineapples, with flowery notes of jasmine and honeysuckle. It finishes slightly sweet. 84 *—S.H. (8/1/2007)*

Charles Krug 2000 Sauvignon Blanc (Napa Valley) $14. 88 *—S.H. (11/15/2001)*

Charles Krug 1999 Sauvignon Blanc (Napa Valley) $13. 86 *(4/1/2001)*

Charles Krug 1998 Sauvignon Blanc (Napa Valley) $13. 88 *—M.S. (11/15/1999)*

Charles Krug 2004 Peter Mondavi Family Sauvignon Blanc (Napa Valley) $16. 87 *(12/15/2005)*

Charles Krug 2003 Peter Mondavi Family Sauvignon Blanc (Napa Valley) $16. 86 *—S.H. (10/1/2004)*

Charles Krug 2002 Limited Release Syrah (Napa Valley) $50. 90 *(4/12/2006)*

Charles Krug 1996 Zinfandel (Napa Valley) $11. 84 *—L.W. (9/1/1999)*

Charles Krug 2001 Zinfandel (Napa Valley) $15. 88 *(11/1/2003)*

Charles Krug 1999 Zinfandel (Napa Valley) $15. 87 Best Buy *—S.H. (12/1/2002)*

Charles Krug 1998 Zinfandel (Napa Valley) $12. 87 *(4/1/2001)*

Charles Krug 1998 Zinfandel (Alexander Valley) $12. 89 Best Buy *(4/1/2001)*

Charles Krug 2003 Peter Mondavi Family Zinfandel (Napa Valley) $20. 87 *—S.H. (11/15/2005)*

Charles Krug 2001 Peter Mondavi Family Zinfandel (Napa Valley) $14. 84 *—S.H. (2/1/2005)*

Charles Krug 2000 Peter Mondavi Family Zinfandel (Napa Valley) $15. 82 *—S.H. (5/1/2004)*

CHÂTEAU BENOIT

Château Benoit 2000 Chardonnay (Willamette Valley) $16. 84 *—M.S. (9/1/2003)*

Château Benoit 2000 Pinot Noir (Oregon) $18. 83 *(10/1/2002)*

Château Benoit 2000 Doe Ridge Vineyard Pinot Noir (Willamette Valley) $40. 86 *(10/1/2002)*

Château Benoit 2000 Kestrel Vineyard Pinot Noir (Willamette Valley) $40. 87 *(10/1/2002)*

Château Benoit 2000 Yamhill Springs Vineyard Pinot Noir (Willamette Valley) $40. 87 *(10/1/2002)*

CHÂTEAU BIANCA

Château Bianca 2000 Barrel Fermented Chardonnay (Willamette Valley) $10. 81 *—P.G. (8/1/2003)*

Château Bianca 1998 Barrel Fermented Chardonnay (Willamette Valley) $9. 83 *—P.G. (11/1/2001)*

Château Bianca 2001 Estate Reserve Chardonnay (Willamette Valley) $20. 83 *—P.G. (10/1/2004)*

Château Bianca 1999 Reserve Chardonnay (Willamette Valley) $20. 86 Best Buy *—P.G. (2/1/2002)*

Château Bianca 2000 Winery Estate Reserve Chardonnay (Willamette Valley) $20. 81 *—P.G. (8/1/2003)*

Château Bianca 2006 Gewürztraminer (Willamette Valley) $10. Spicy and dry, this is done to a wickedly tart finish; the flavors are set up beautifully to accompany food. The floral and rose petal scents of the grape are nicely rendered but not overwhelming, and the 1% RS residual sugar is almost invisible, given the juicy fruit and acids. 88 Best Buy *—P.G. (11/15/2007)*

Château Bianca 1999 Gewürztraminer (Willamette Valley) $9. 84 *—P.G. (11/1/2001)*

Château Bianca 2001 Estate Bottled Gewürztraminer (Willamette Valley) $9. 83 *—P.G. (12/31/2002)*

Château Bianca 2006 Wetzel Estate Gewürztraminer (Willamette Valley) $16. This has similar, spicy fruit flavors as the winery's regular Gewürztraminer, but here the sugar comes in at just .08% so the wine feels much more dry. The rich, textural palate adds wet stone to the mix. The alcohol reaches a healthy 14.3% but is not intrusive. 89 *—P.G. (11/15/2007)*

Château Bianca 1999 Pinot Blanc (Willamette Valley) $12. 85 *—P.G. (11/1/2001)*

Château Bianca 2002 Estate Pinot Blanc (Willamette Valley) $12. 88 Best Buy *—P.G. (10/1/2004)*

Château Bianca 2000 Estate Bottled Pinot Blanc (Oregon) $12. 82 *—P.G. (4/1/2002)*

Château Bianca 2001 Wetzel Family Estate Pinot Blanc (Willamette Valley) $18. 85 *—P.G. (8/1/2003)*

Château Bianca 2001 Wetzel Family Estate-Single Cluster Pinot Blanc (Willamette Valley) $18. 85 *—P.G. (12/31/2002)*

Château Bianca 2006 Pinot Gris (Willamette Valley) $12. Finished with 1% RS, this is a wine that has a bit of an identity crisis. It's an odd, orange blush color and tastes very much like a white. Not what you are looking for in an Oregon Pinot Gris. 82 *—P.G. (11/15/2007)*

Château Bianca 2004 Pinot Gris (Willamette Valley) $12. 89 Best Buy *—P.G. (2/1/2006)*

Château Bianca 2002 Pinot Gris (Willamette Valley) $10. 88 Best Buy *—P.G. (10/1/2004)*

Château Bianca 2001 Pinot Gris (Willamette Valley) $10. 85 Best Buy *—P.G. (12/31/2002)*

Château Bianca 2005 Cellar Select Pinot Noir (Willamette Valley) $20. This brings a lot of flavor to the table for its relatively modest price. Round and spicy, it leads with juicy strawberry, cherry and apple pie fruit flavors. Hints of cinnamon wind through the finish, and overall the impression is of a pretty, lively and slightly sweet wine without pretense. 88 Editors' Choice *—P.G. (11/15/2007)*

Château Bianca 2001 Pinot Noir (Willamette Valley) $12. 85 *—P.G. (10/1/2004)*

Château Bianca 2000 Pinot Noir (Willamette Valley) $12. 88 Best Buy *(10/1/2002)*

Château Bianca 1999 Pinot Noir (Oregon) $10. 83 *—P.G. (4/1/2002)*

Château Bianca 1998 Pinot Noir (Willamette Valley) $10. 84 *—P.G. (11/1/2001)*

Château Bianca 2001 Cellar Select Pinot Noir (Willamette Valley) $16. 87 *—P.G. (10/1/2004)*

Château Bianca 1999 Estate Reserve Pinot Noir (Willamette Valley) $29. 84 *—P.G. (4/1/2002)*

Château Bianca 1997 Estate Reserve Pinot Noir (Willamette Valley) $25. 85 *—P.G. (11/1/2001)*

Château Bianca 2005 Wetzel Estate Reserve Pinot Noir (Willamette Valley) $28. This seems at first to be a bit tough and chewy. It's dense and herbal, but does not quite pack the pleasure. In fact, it feels a bit stripped, with tannins out in front of the fruit. It's a bit of a mystery at the moment. 86 *—P.G. (11/15/2007)*

Château Bianca 2000 Winery Estate Reserve Pinot Noir (Willamette Valley) $28. 84 *—P.G. (4/1/2003)*

Château Bianca 2006 Riesling (Willamette Valley) $10. This is a light, pretty, pear-flavored Riesling, with orange blossom aromas inviting you to sip away. Elegant and fresh, it is finished at 12.5% alcohol and 2.5% residual sugar. 87 Best Buy *—P.G. (11/15/2007)*

Château Bianca 2003 Riesling (Willamette Valley) $9. 89 Best Buy *—P.G. (10/1/2004)*

Château Bianca 1999 Riesling (Willamette Valley) $9. 84 *—P.G. (11/1/2001)*

Château Bianca 2006 Wetzel Estate Riesling (Willamette Valley) $15. This Riesling has more structure and less residual sugar than the winery's regular bottling, and the pretty, pear-laden fruit falls across the palate with a pleasing stiffness. Lean, textural and layered, the mix of apple, pear and apricot fruit gives it a lightly tropical character. Given its quality, it would behoove the winery to give it a classy screwcap seal and lose the nubby plastic cork. 89 *—P.G. (11/15/2007)*

CHÂTEAU BOSWELL

Château Boswell 2003 Estate Cabernet Sauvignon (St. Helena) $94. 86 *—S.H. (8/1/2006)*

CHÂTEAU CHANTAL

Château Chantal 2005 Proprietor's Reserve Trio Bordeaux Blend (Old Mission Peninsula) $20. This Bordeaux blend falls flat with a weak, vanilla-laden nose and flavors that tend toward watery. There's some berry in the beginning but little beyond. 81 *—S.K. (5/1/2007)*

Château Chantal 2005 Proprietor's Reserve Pinot Noir (Old Mission Peninsula) $20. Berry and spice meet in a delicate combination in this Michigan Pinot, but the overall character is edgy and acidic with a forward tartness. The wine has promise but lacks integration and style. 83 *—S.K. (5/1/2007)*

CHÂTEAU CHEVALIER

Château Chevalier 2003 Cabernet Sauvignon (Spring Mountain) $30. 89 *—S.H. (12/15/2006)*

Château Chevalier 2005 Sauvignon Blanc (Spring Mountain) $24. 84 *—S.H. (12/15/2006)*

CHÂTEAU DE DEIGHTON

Château de Deighton 2004 Pink Nun Rosé Blend (Central Coast) $10. This is a controversial wine that some will like, but not me. Mostly Chardonnay, with some Pinot Noir, it has a bizarre orange color, and a burnt, stewed fruit taste that's like a Fig Newton. 82 *—S.H. (4/1/2007)*

Château de Deighton 2004 Cuvee Blanc White Blend (Central Coast) $10. Dry, watery and a little veggie. A blend of Semillon and Sauvignon Blanc. 81 *—S.H. (4/1/2007)*

Château de Deighton 2004 Purple Haze Zinfandel (Paso Robles) $15. Speaking of Jimi Hendrix, I guess if you were on acid you might like this wine. Or, it could make you jump out of the window. Sweet and rustic and barely drinkable. 82 *—S.H. (4/1/2007)*

CHÂTEAU FAIRE LE PONT

Château Faire Le Pont 2005 Pinot Noir (Washington) $27. Light and forward, this has a slightly cooked, raisiny character, along with chewy tannins. It does lack the elegance and grace that should characterize Pinot Noir. The tannins are too rough for the fruit. 84 *—P.G. (11/1/2007)*

Château Faire Le Pont 2004 Provence Red Blend (Washington) $29. Despite excellent vineyard sources, this is overripe for my palate, with flavors that are pruny and soft, and lacking definition and authority. It's soft and mysteriously weightless, with figgy fruit and a quick finish. 85 *—P.G. (11/1/2007)*

CHÂTEAU FELICE

Château Felice 2002 Acier Chardonnay (Russian River Valley) $16. 84 *—S.H. (12/1/2003)*

Château Felice 2001 Estate Chardonnay (Chalk Hill) $20. 84 *—S.H. (2/1/2004)*

Château Felice 2001 Syrah (Chalk Hill) $22. 82 *—S.H. (12/1/2003)*

Château Felice 2001 Mill Road Vineyard Syrah (Paso Robles) $30. 86 *—S.H. (2/1/2004)*

Château Felice 2001 Zinfandel (Chalk Hill) $16. 83 *(11/1/2003)*

CHÂTEAU FRANK

Château Frank 1996 Champagne Blend (Finger Lakes) $20. 85 *—S.H. (12/31/2000)*

Château Frank 1995 Blanc de Blancs Champagne Blend (Finger Lakes) $25. 83 *—P.G. (6/1/2001)*

Château Frank NV Célébre Crémant Champagne Blend (New York) $15. 84 *(12/31/2000)*

Château Frank 1996 Blanc de Noirs Red Blend (Finger Lakes) $25. 87 *—M.M. (12/1/2001)*

CHÂTEAU JULIEN

Château Julien 2004 Bravura Bordeaux Blend (Monterey County) $85. A 50-50 blend of Merlot and Malbec, this is the most expensive wine the chateau has ever produced, a commemoration of their 25th anniversary. It commands attention for dryness and complexity. The usual Bordeaux flavors of blackberries, plums and mocha are weaved into earthier tastes of salty, cured-olive tapenade and sweet miso, enhanced with smoky new oak. This is a very important release from the winery, one worthy of follow up. 94 *—S.H. (11/1/2007)*

Château Julien 2003 Cabernet Sauvignon (Monterey County) $10. Defines country style, with its raw mouthfeel and jagged tannins, but give it this. It has ripe, New World-style cherries and blackberries, and that kind of fruit goes a long way. 83 *—S.H. (7/1/2007)*

Château Julien 2001 Cabernet Sauvignon (Monterey County) $10. 84 *—S.H. (10/1/2004)*

Château Julien 1999 Cabernet Sauvignon (Monterey County) $10. 80 *—S.H. (9/12/2002)*

Château Julien 2005 Barrel Aged Cabernet Sauvignon (Monterey County) $10. Pretty basic Cab. Simple and soft, with blackberry and cherry flavors and a hit of oak. 82 *—S.H. (11/15/2007)*

Château Julien 2002 Barrel Aged Cabernet Sauvignon (Monterey County) $10. 84 *—S.H. (4/1/2006)*

Château Julien 2000 Barrel Aged Cabernet Sauvignon (Monterey County) $10. 86 Best Buy *—S.H. (10/1/2003)*

Château Julien 1998 Barrel Aged Cabernet Sauvignon (Monterey County) $10. 87 Best Buy *—S.H. (5/1/2001)*

Château Julien 1999 Estate Cabernet Sauvignon (Monterey County) $22. 88 *—S.H. (11/15/2002)*

Château Julien 1998 Estate Vineyard Cabernet Sauvignon (Monterey County) $22. 86 *—S.H. (12/1/2001)*

Château Julien 1996 Grand Reserve Cabernet Sauvignon (Monterey) $9. 84 *—M.S. (7/1/1999)*

Château Julien 2001 Private Reserve Cabernet Sauvignon (Monterey County) $36. 85 *—S.H. (12/1/2005)*

Château Julien 2000 Private Reserve Cabernet Sauvignon (Monterey County) $36. 86 *—S.H. (11/15/2004)*

Château Julien 1999 Private Reserve Cabernet Sauvignon (Monterey County) $36. 87 *—S.H. (10/1/2003)*

Château Julien 1998 Private Reserve Cabernet Sauvignon (Monterey County) $36. 84 *—S.H. (11/15/2002)*

Château Julien 1996 Private Reserve Cabernet Sauvignon (Monterey County) $28. 87 *(2/1/2000)*

Château Julien 2005 Chardonnay (Monterey County) $10. A great buy at this price, with juicy fruit and a rich mouthfeel. Apricot, peach, pineapple, vanilla and buttercream flavors mingle into a spicy finish. **85 Best Buy** *—S.H. (7/1/2007)*

Château Julien 2002 Chardonnay (Monterey County) $10. 85 Best Buy *—S.H. (12/15/2004)*

Château Julien 2001 Chardonnay (Monterey County) $10. 85 *—S.H. (2/1/2003)*

Château Julien 2006 Barrel Fermented Chardonnay (Monterey County) $10. The wine is soft, simple and sweet, with flavors of canned peaches and pears. **82** *—S.H. (11/15/2007)*

Château Julien 1998 Barrel Fermented Chardonnay (Monterey County) $10. 85 *(2/1/2000)*

Château Julien 2000 Estate Chardonnay (Monterey County) $22. 89 *—S.H. (12/15/2002)*

Château Julien 2001 Estate Vineyard Chardonnay (Monterey County) $22. 83 *—S.H. (3/1/2004)*

Château Julien 1999 Estate Vineyard Chardonnay (Monterey County) $22. 88 *(8/1/2001)*

Château Julien 2001 Private Reserve Sur Lie Chardonnay (Monterey County) $30. 85 *—S.H. (2/1/2004)*

Château Julien 2000 Private Reserve Sur Lie Chardonnay (Monterey County) $30. 86 *—S.H. (2/1/2003)*

Château Julien 1998 Private Reserve Sur Lie Chardonnay (Monterey County) $20. 86 *(6/1/2000)*

Château Julien 1997 Private Reserve Sur Lie Chardonnay (Monterey County) $20. 91 Editors' Choice *(2/1/2000)*

Château Julien 2003 Merlot (Monterey County) $10. Yes, the price is right, but it's simple and thin, dry and soft, with modest cherry-berry flavors. **82** *—S.H. (7/1/2007)*

Château Julien 1999 Merlot (Monterey County) $10. 83 *—S.H. (9/12/2002)*

Château Julien 2005 Barrel Aged Merlot (Monterey County) $10. Dry and simple, this Merlot tastes weirdly soft and sharp at the same time, suggesting unevenly ripened grapes went into the high-production blend. The flavors are of cherries and green stalky mint. **82** *—S.H. (11/15/2007)*

Château Julien 2001 Barrel Aged Merlot (Monterey County) $10. 82 *—S.H. (3/1/2005)*

Château Julien 2000 Barrel Aged Merlot (Monterey County) $10. 85 *—S.H. (12/1/2003)*

Château Julien 1998 Barrel Aged Merlot (Monterey County) $10. 85 Best Buy *—S.H. (5/1/2001)*

Château Julien 1997 Barrel Aged Merlot (Monterey County) $10. 86 *(2/1/2000)*

Château Julien 1999 Estate Merlot (Monterey County) $22. 85 *—S.H. (11/15/2002)*

Château Julien 2000 Estate Bottled Merlot (Monterey County) $22. 82 *—S.H. (2/1/2004)*

Château Julien 2002 Estate Vineyard Merlot (Monterey County) $20. 81 *—S.H. (11/1/2006)*

Château Julien 2001 Estate Vineyard Merlot (Monterey County) $22. 84 *S.H. (3/1/2005)*

Château Julien 1998 Estate Vineyard Merlot (Monterey County) $22. 86 *S.H. (12/1/2001)*

Château Julien 2001 Private Reserve Merlot (Monterey County) $36. 82 *—S.H. (12/1/2005)*

Château Julien 2000 Private Reserve Merlot (Monterey County) $30. 82 *—S.H. (3/1/2005)*

Château Julien 1999 Private Reserve Merlot (Monterey County) $30. 86 *—S.H. (12/31/2003)*

Château Julien 1998 Private Reserve Merlot (Monterey County) $30. 85 *(11/15/2002)*

Château Julien 1997 Private Reserve Merlot (Monterey County) $20. 86 *—S.H. (5/1/2001)*

Château Julien 1996 Private Reserve Merlot (Monterey County) $20. 87 *(2/1/2000)*

Château Julien 2005 Pinot Grigio (Monterey County) $10. There's no one who won't like this wine. It's dryish, crisply tart and clean, with creamy lemongrass, pineapple and vanilla custard flavors. What a great value! **86 Best Buy** *—S.H. (7/1/2007)*

Château Julien 2004 Pinot Grigio (Monterey County) $10. 85 Best Buy *—S.H. (2/1/2006)*

Château Julien 2003 Pinot Grigio (Monterey County) $10. 84 *—S.H. (12/15/2004)*

Château Julien 2000 Pinot Grigio (Monterey County) $10. 83 *—S.H. (11/15/2001)*

Château Julien 2002 Barrel Aged Pinot Grigio (Monterey County) $10. 85 *—S.H. (2/1/2004)*

Château Julien 2001 Barrel Aged Pinot Grigio (Monterey County) $10. 84 *—S.H. (9/1/2003)*

Château Julien 1997 Sangiovese (California) $13. 87 *(2/1/2000)*

Château Julien 1999 Sangiovese (Monterey County) $10. 84 *—S.H. (11/15/2001)*

Château Julien 2001 Barrel Aged Sangiovese (Monterey County) $10. 85 *—S.H. (3/1/2004)*

Château Julien 2000 Barrel Aged Sangiovese (Monterey County) $10. 86 *—S.H. (12/1/2002)*

Château Julien 2001 Sauvignon Blanc (Monterey County) $9. 84 *—S.H. (9/1/2003)*

Château Julien 2000 Sauvignon Blanc (Monterey County) $9. 83 *—S.H. (11/15/2001)*

Château Julien 1998 Barrel Aged Sauvignon Blanc (Monterey County) $8. 84 *(2/1/2000)*

Château Julien 2002 Barrel Fermented Sauvignon Blanc (Monterey County) $9. 83 *—S.H. (12/31/2003)*

Château Julien 2002 Syrah (Monterey County) $22. 89 *—S.H. (10/1/2004)*

Château Julien 2000 Syrah (Monterey County) $10. 88 Best Buy *—S.H. (12/1/2002)*

Château Julien 1999 Syrah (Monterey County) $15. 85 *(10/1/2001)*

Château Julien 2003 Estate Vineyard Syrah (Monterey County) $22. 84 *—S.H. (3/1/2006)*

Château Julien 2001 Estate Vineyard Syrah (Monterey County) $22. 87 *—S.H. (2/1/2004)*

Château Julien 2005 Private Reserve Syrah (Monterey County) $36. If you're looking for a soft, sweetish wine, here's one. It has flavors of ripe red and black cherries, currants, dark chocolate, root beer and licorice, and tastes like a fruit and honey energy bar. **84** *—S.H. (12/1/2007)*

Château Julien 2000 Barrel Aged Zinfandel (Monterey County) $10. 85 *(11/1/2003)*

Château Julien 1999 Barrel Aged Zinfandel (Monterey County) $10. 83 *—S.H. (11/1/2002)*

Château Julien 2003 Private Reserve Zinfandel (Monterey County) $36. 87 *—S.H. (6/1/2006)*

CHÂTEAU LAFAYETTE RENEAU

Château Lafayette Reneau 2002 Cabernet Sauvignon (Finger Lakes) $NA. 82 *—M.D. (8/1/2006)*

Château Lafayette Reneau 1999 Owner's Reserve Cabernet Sauvignon (Finger Lakes) $45. 86 *—M.S. (3/1/2003)*

Château Lafayette Reneau 1997 Blanc de Blancs Champagne Blend (Finger Lakes) $30. 87 *—M.M. (12/1/2000)*

Château Lafayette Reneau 2000 Barrel Fermented Chardonnay (Finger Lakes) $13. 84 *—J.M. (1/1/2003)*

Château Lafayette Reneau 2000 Proprietor's Reserve-Barrel Fermented Chardonnay (Finger Lakes) $19. 89 *—J.M. (1/1/2003)*

Château Lafayette Reneau 2005 Johannisberg Riesling (Finger Lakes) $15. 83 *—M.D. (8/1/2006)*

Château Lafayette Reneau 2001 Johannisberg Riesling (Finger Lakes) $12. 85 *—J.C. (8/1/2003)*

Château Lafayette Reneau 2006 Estate Bottled Johannisberg Riesling (Finger Lakes) $15. A sweet but spicy nose of honeysuckle and pear, and a flavor profile of tropical fruit and honey, make this Riesling an attractive wine to pair with food or enjoy on it own. There's sweetness but it's well-balanced with a minerality and acid that gives it lift. Good weight but a pretty touch. 86 *—S.K. (9/1/2007)*

Château Lafayette Reneau 2006 Estate Bottled Dry Riesling (Finger Lakes) $15. Delicious aromas of peach, tropical fruit and spice lead this spirited wine from consistently good Chateau Lafayette, located on New York's Seneca Lake. There's a bright, zippy, and eaysgoing character of citrus and fruit on the palate that recommends this wine for food pairing and just sipping out on the deck. It's not terribly complex but it doesn't need to be—it's delivering everything in an elegant, approachable package and at a good price. 88 *—S.K. (9/1/2007)*

Château Lafayette Reneau 2002 Pinot Noir (Finger Lakes) $20. 84 *—M.D. (12/1/2006)*

Château Lafayette Reneau 2001 Cuvée Rouge Red Blend (Finger Lakes) $9. 80 *—J.M. (3/1/2003)*

Château Lafayette Reneau 2005 Dry Riesling (Finger Lakes) $15. 86 *—M.D. (8/1/2006)*

CHÂTEAU MONTELENA

Château Montelena 2003 Cabernet Sauvignon (Napa Valley) $40. 90 Cellar Selection *—S.H. (12/1/2006)*

Château Montelena 2002 Montelena Estate Cabernet Sauvignon (Napa Valley) $95. 93 Cellar Selection *—J.C. (9/1/2006)*

Château Montelena 1998 Chardonnay (Napa Valley) $30. 87 *(7/1/2001)*

Château Montelena 1997 Chardonnay (Napa Valley) $29. 86 *(6/1/2000)*

Château Montelena 1996 Chardonnay (Napa Valley) $29. 90 *—S.H. (6/1/1999)*

Château Montelena 2001 Riesling (Potter Valley) $15. 85 *—S.H. (12/31/2003)*

Château Montelena 2000 Zinfandel (Napa Valley) $25. 87 *—S.H. (9/1/2003)*

CHÂTEAU MORRISETTE

Château Morrisette 2004 Chardonnay (Virginia) $16. Aromas of apple and tropical fruit on this rich Chardonnay lead into vanilla and honey on the palate. The wine is full and opulent in the mouth but not overwrought. Good balance and a lingering finish add to the appeal. 86 *—S.K. (10/1/2007)*

Château Morrisette 2002 Chardonnay (Virginia) $16. 83 *—J.C. (9/1/2005)*

Château Morrisette NV Angel Chardonnay (Virginia) $10. Tropical fruit and citrus flavors mingle with a touch of earthy toast in this Chardonnay made in the Blue Ridge region of Virginia. The feel of this wine is light but there's a lingering acidity and assertive fruit character that make it memorable. Pair it with lighter seafood dishes or enjoy on its own. 85 *—S.K. (7/1/2007)*

Château Morrisette NV Liberty Service Dog Red Red Blend (Virginia) $12. Made from three of the prominent grapes grown in Virginia—Chambourcin, Cabernet Franc and Petit Verdot—this dry, spicy red blend is energetic and packed with red cherry, pepper and cinnamon. Friendly and accessible, it's a great everyday sip. The wine pays tribute to service dogs and their work with disabled people. 84 *—S.K. (12/1/2007)*

Château Morrisette 2006 Vidal Blanc (Virginia) $10. This Vidal Blanc offers tropical fruit flavors of peach and pineapple and a playful, lively acidity. Balanced and bold, the wine has enough personality to sip on it own. A fun white wine alternative at a nice price. 86 Best Buy *—S.K. (10/1/2007)*

Château Morrisette 2005 Viognier (Virginia) $19. Château Morrisette hits the mark again with this fragrant, floral wine. Round and full on the mouth, the wine has ample acidity to keep the honeyed, tropical fruit flavors from overpowering. A lovely effort with real class. 86 *—S.K. (10/1/2007)*

CHÂTEAU POTELLE

Château Potelle 2004 VGS Cabernet Sauvignon (Mount Veeder) $60. Here's one for the cellar, not just because the tannins are so aggressive, but because the wine is so balanced. With alcohol only 13.8%, it's dry and rich in black currant fruit, almost a throwback to the Napa Cabernets of old that aged so well. It possesses a dry, elegant sophistication that stands in deliberate contrast to today's gooey, sweet style. Best 2009–2015, if not longer, with proper cellaring. 92 Cellar Selection *—S.H. (12/15/2007)*

Château Potelle 2001 VGS Cabernet Sauvignon (Mount Veeder) $60. 90 Cellar Selection *—S.H. (9/1/2006)*

Château Potelle 2000 VGS Cabernet Sauvignon (Mount Veeder) $40. 86 *—S.H. (2/1/2005)*

Château Potelle 1997 VGS Cabernet Sauvignon (Mount Veeder) $63. 92 *(11/1/2000)*

Château Potelle 2005 VGS Chardonnay (Mount Veeder) $45. Made from the estate vineyard high up on Mount Veeder, the wine has a brilliant intensity and near-perfect balance. It's big, but not in the usual California style. Rather, it maintains an elegantly supple and wonderfully balanced character. The taste is of mineral-inspired tropical fruits, complexed with Burgundian technique. 94 Editors' Choice *—S.H. (12/15/2007)*

Château Potelle 2002 VGS Chardonnay (Mount Veeder) $35. 93 *—S.H. (5/1/2005)*

Château Potelle 1999 VGS Chardonnay (Mount Veeder) $39. 93 *—S.H. (5/1/2003)*

Château Potelle 1998 VGS Chardonnay (Mount Veeder) $39. 94 *—S.H. (9/1/2002)*

Château Potelle 1997 VGS Chardonnay (Mount Veeder) $45. 87 *(7/1/2001)*

Château Potelle 2002 Riviera Red Blend (Paso Robles) $15. 85 *—S.H. (11/15/2003)*

Château Potelle 2001 Riviera Red Blend (Paso Robles) $16. 86 *—S.H. (9/1/2003)*

Château Potelle 2006 Sauvignon Blanc (Mendocino) $15. Napa-based Potelle reaches into Mendocino for Sauvignon Blanc, with good results. The wine has rich flavors of citrus fruits and figs, balanced with crisp, palate-stimulating acidity. Partial barrel fermentation and lees aging add richer notes of cream to this dry, complex wine. 89 *—S.H. (11/15/2007)*

Château Potelle 2004 Sauvignon Blanc (Mendocino) $15. 87 *—S.H. (12/1/2006)*

Château Potelle 2001 Sauvignon Blanc (Napa Valley) $15. 90 Best Buy *—S.H. (10/1/2003)*

Château Potelle 2000 Sauvignon Blanc (Napa Valley) $15. 86 *—S.H. (9/1/2003)*

Château Potelle 2001 Syrah (Paso Robles) $24. 88 *(9/1/2005)*

Château Potelle 2004 VGS Syrah (Mount Veeder) $75. This is the best Potelle Syrah I've ever had, but be forewarned: It's an extraordinarily tannic wine that shows its 1,800-foot mountain origins. It clocks in at 13.9% alcohol, yet it's bone dry. The fruit is powerfully concentrated in blackberries enhanced with sweet, smoky oak. If ever there was a Syrah for the cellar, this is it. Best now (if you like young tannic wines, but please decant) and for at least eight years, as it gradually mellows. 93 Cellar Selection *—S.H. (12/15/2007)*

Château Potelle 2002 VGS Syrah (Mount Veeder) $75. 87 *(9/1/2005)*

Château Potelle 2001 Zinfandel (Paso Robles) $22. 90 Editors' Choice *(11/1/2003)*

Château Potelle 2000 Zinfandel (Paso Robles) $22. 85 *—S.H. (12/1/2002)*

Château Potelle 2004 Mount Veeder Estate Zinfandel (Napa Valley) $55. 90 *—S.H. (11/15/2003)*

CHÂTEAU SOUVERAIN

Château Souverain 2003 Cabernet Sauvignon (Alexander Valley) $22. Needs a little airing to come around, but when it does, it's nice. Dry and balanced, it shows cherry, black raspberry and oak flavors that are wrapped in a medium-bodied, smooth, dry wine. Finishes soft and polished. Drink now–2007. 84 *—S.H. (3/1/2007)*

Château Souverain 1997 Winemaker's Reserve Cabernet Sauvignon (Alexander Valley) $35. 92 Editors' Choice *—S.H. (12/1/2001)*

Château Souverain 1996 Winemaker's Reserve Cabernet Sauvignon (Sonoma County) $35. 88 *—S.H. (12/15/2000)*

Château Souverain 2004 Chardonnay (Sonoma County) $17. 85 *—S.H. (3/1/2006)*

Château Souverain 2003 Chardonnay (Sonoma County) $14. 86 *—S.H. (3/1/2005)*

Château Souverain 2002 Chardonnay (Sonoma County) $14. 89 Best Buy *—S.H. (2/1/2004)*

Château Souverain 2001 Chardonnay (Sonoma County) $14. 86 *—S.H. (6/1/2003)*

Château Souverain 2000 Chardonnay (Sonoma County) $14. 91 *—S.H. (5/1/2002)*

Château Souverain 1999 Chardonnay (Sonoma County) $14. 85 *—S.H. (5/1/2001)*

Château Souverain 1997 Reserve Chardonnay (Russian River Valley) $25. 88 *(6/1/2000)*

Château Souverain 2005 Winemaker's Reserve Chardonnay (Russian River Valley) $30. Here's a pull out all the stops, bells-and-whistles Chard that aims to compete at a high level. Barrel fermented in 80% new oak, aged on the lees and put through full malolactic fermentation, it's rich, creamy, buttery and exotically flavored in opulent toasted barrel and tropical fruits. I personally like this style, but others might find it too oaky. **89** —*S.H. (10/1/2007)*

Château Souverain 2004 Winemaker's Reserve Chardonnay (Russian River Valley) $30. The winery continues to struggle for elegance in this superoaky Chardonnay. The wood almost drowns out the fruit. The wine also is on the sweet side, which will make it appeal to lots of consumers, but keeps it from being truly competitive at a global level. **84** —*S.H. (3/1/2007)*

Château Souverain 2003 Winemaker's Reserve Chardonnay (Russian River Valley) $30. 82 —*S.H. (11/15/2005)*

Château Souverain 2001 Winemaker's Reserve Chardonnay (Russian River Valley) $25. 90 *(12/31/2003)*

Château Souverain 2000 Winemaker's Reserve Chardonnay (Alexander Valley) $25. 87 —*J.M. (12/15/2002)*

Château Souverain 1999 Winemaker's Reserve Chardonnay (Russian River Valley) $25. 86 —*S.H. (12/1/2001)*

Château Souverain 1997 Merlot (Sonoma County) $17.87 —*J.C. (7/1/2000)*

Château Souverain 2002 Merlot (Alexander Valley) $18. 87 —*S.H. (6/1/2005)*

Château Souverain 2000 Merlot (Alexander Valley) $18. 89 —*S.H. (8/1/2003)*

Château Souverain 1999 Merlot (Alexander Valley) $17. 89 —*S.H. (9/1/2002)*

Château Souverain 2006 Sauvignon Blanc (Alexander Valley) $15. Lots of stimulating gooseberry, lemongrass and honeysuckle flavors in this crisp, rich wine. There's a touch of cat pee and a slight, spearmint gum sugariness on the finish. **84** —*S.H. (11/15/2007)*

Château Souverain 2005 Sauvignon Blanc (Alexander Valley) $14. 84 —*S.H. (12/1/2006)*

Château Souverain 2004 Sauvignon Blanc (Alexander Valley) $14. 85 —*S.H. (11/15/2005)*

Château Souverain 2002 Sauvignon Blanc (Alexander Valley) $14. 87 —*S.H. (2/1/2004)*

Château Souverain 2001 Sauvignon Blanc (Alexander Valley) $12. 87 —*J.M. (9/1/2003)*

Château Souverain 2000 Sauvignon Blanc (Sonoma County) $12. 84 —*S.H. (11/15/2001)*

Château Souverain 1997 Sauvignon Blanc (Sonoma County) $9. 87 Best Buy —*S.H. (9/1/1999)*

Château Souverain 2002 Syrah (Alexander Valley) $20. 87 —*S.H. (6/1/2005)*

Château Souverain 2000 Syrah (Alexander Valley) $20. 87 —*S.H. (2/1/2003)*

Château Souverain 1999 Syrah (Sonoma County) $20. 86 *(10/1/2001)*

Château Souverain 1997 Zinfandel (Dry Creek Valley) $13. 86 —*J.C. (5/1/2000)*

Château Souverain 2002 Zinfandel (Dry Creek Valley) $18. 88 —*S.H. (4/1/2005)*

Château Souverain 2001 Zinfandel (Dry Creek Valley) $18. 87 *(11/1/2003)*

Château Souverain 1999 Zinfandel (Dry Creek Valley) $13. 84 —*S.H. (11/15/2001)*

Château Souverain 1998 Winemaker's Reserve Zinfandel (Dry Creek Valley) $25. 89 —*P.G. (3/1/2001)*

CHÂTEAU ST. CROIX

Château St. Croix 2004 Three Barrel Reserve Red Blend (California) $65. Made from mainly Lodi-grown Cabernet, Merlot and Petite Sirah, this is a tart, minty young wine, with a chlorophyl-like greenness to the modest cherry and cocoa flavors. The texture is smooth and polished, but it sure is pricy for what you get. **84** —*S.H. (7/1/2007)*

CHÂTEAU ST. JEAN

Château St. Jean 1998 Cinq Cepages Cabernet Blend (Sonoma County) $70. 90 —*D.T. (6/1/2002)*

Château St. Jean 2001 Estate Vineyard Cabernet Franc (Sonoma Valley) $50. 88 —*S.H. (3/1/2005)*

Château St. Jean 2003 St. Jean Estate Cabernet Franc (Sonoma Valley) $50. This lovely wine's flavors are of red and black cherries, with overtones of blueberries, violets, carob and smoky oak. It's hard to describe the succulence. It's so smooth and velvety, yet so complex, and changes with every sniff and sip. Best now, though, for freshness. **91** —*S.H. (7/1/2007)*

Château St. Jean 2002 St. Jean Estate Vineyard Cabernet Franc (Sonoma Valley) $50. 87 —*S.H. (4/1/2006)*

Château St. Jean 2004 Cabernet Sauvignon (Sonoma County) $27. Dry and balanced, it shows the deft hand of the winery, a softly delicious Bordeaux-style wine with lushly ripe cherry, cassis and spicy oak flavors, and a long, smooth, elegant finish. **91 Editors' Choice** —*S.H. (7/1/2007)*

Château St. Jean 2003 Cabernet Sauvignon (Sonoma County) $27. 89 —*S.H. (11/15/2006)*

Château St. Jean 2003 Cabernet Sauvignon (California) $15. 85 —*S.H. (12/15/2005)*

Château St. Jean 2002 Cabernet Sauvignon (Sonoma County) $27. 84 —*S.H. (12/31/2005)*

Château St. Jean 2002 Cabernet Sauvignon (California) $15. 84 —*S.H. (2/1/2005)*

Château St. Jean 2001 Cabernet Sauvignon (Sonoma County) $27. 89 —*S.H. (8/1/2004)*

Château St. Jean 2000 Cabernet Sauvignon (Sonoma County) $27. 87 —*M.S. (11/15/2003)*

Château St. Jean 2003 Cinq Cepages Cabernet Sauvignon (Sonoma County) $75. Smooth and complex, with 78% Cab Sauvignon contributing the firm tannic backbone that gives this such excellent structure. The other four Bordeaux varieties are here as well. The flavors are so interesting: black cherries, blackberry jam, plum sauce, coffee, root beer and new oak. There's an acidic vibrancy as well. Just beautiful California claret. Drink now–2010. **94** —*S.H. (7/1/2007)*

Château St. Jean 2002 Cinq Cepages Cabernet Sauvignon (Sonoma County) $75. 90 Cellar Selection —*S.H. (4/1/2006)*

Château St. Jean 2001 Cinq Cepages Cabernet Sauvignon (Sonoma County) $75. 93 —*S.H. (3/1/2005)*

Château St. Jean 2000 Cinq Cepages Cabernet Sauvignon (Sonoma County) $70. 90 —*S.H. (5/1/2004)*

Château St. Jean 1999 Cinq Cepages Cabernet Sauvignon (Sonoma County) $70. 88 —*M.S. (3/1/2003)*

Château St. Jean 1998 Cinq Cepages Cabernet Sauvignon (Sonoma Valley) $70. 90 *(6/1/2002)*

Château St. Jean 1996 Cinq Cepages Cabernet Sauvignon (Sonoma County) $33. 92 —*J.C. (2/1/2000)*

Château St. Jean 2002 Reserve Cabernet Sauvignon (Sonoma County) $90. This small-production reserve Cab from one of Sonoma's premier wineries is notable for its power. The tannins are quite firm, giving an astringent bite, while the fruity-oaky flavors are massive. Cherries, blackberries, raspberries, spicy plums, vanilla, cocoa and char just explode, yet the wine maintains balance. Good as it is, it's a young wine that will benefit from several years in the bottle. **90** —*S.H. (11/1/2007)*

Château St. Jean 2001 Reserve Cabernet Sauvignon (Sonoma County) $90. 93 Cellar Selection —*S.H. (12/1/2006)*

Château St. Jean 2000 Reserve Cabernet Sauvignon (Sonoma County) $90. 88 —*S.H. (10/1/2005)*

Château St. Jean 1999 Reserve Cabernet Sauvignon (Sonoma Valley) $90. 90 —*S.H. (11/15/2004)*

Château St. Jean 1995 Reserve Cabernet Sauvignon (Sonoma County) $70. 89 —*M.S. (9/1/2000)*

Château St. Jean 2005 Chardonnay (Sonoma County) $14. Lots of oak here, with toast, butter and caramelly vanilla riding over underlying peach and tropical fruit flavors. The texture is creamy smooth and rich. Nice Chardonnay at a decent price. **85** —*S.H. (2/1/2007)*

Château St. Jean 2004 Chardonnay (Sonoma County) $14. 85 —*S.H. (12/1/2005)*

Château St. Jean 2003 Chardonnay (Sonoma County) $14. 86 —*S.H. (5/1/2005)*

Château St. Jean 2001 Chardonnay (Sonoma County) $16. 88 —*S.H. (6/1/2003)*

Château St. Jean 2000 Chardonnay (Sonoma County) $14. 87 —*J.M. (12/15/2002)*

Château St. Jean 1998 Chardonnay (Sonoma County) $12. 88 —*L.W. (3/1/2000)*

Château St. Jean 2005 Belle Terre Vineyard Chardonnay (Alexander Valley) $22. Here's your basic straightforward upscale California Chard. It's forward in tropical fruit and oaky butterscotch and vanilla char flavors, wrapped into a creamy texture. There's a touch of green in the finish, though. **86** —*S.H. (10/1/2007)*

Château St. Jean 2002 Belle Terre Vineyard Chardonnay (Alexander Valley) $22. 89 *—S.H. (12/1/2005)*

Château St. Jean 2001 Belle Terre Vineyard Chardonnay (Alexander Valley) $24. 90 *—S.H. (2/1/2004)*

Château St. Jean 2000 Belle Terre Vineyard Chardonnay (Alexander Valley) $22. 91 Editors' Choice *—J.M. (12/15/2002)*

Château St. Jean 1999 Belle Terre Vineyard Chardonnay (Alexander Valley) $22. 89 *—S.H. (12/1/2001)*

Château St. Jean 2000 Durell Vineyard Chardonnay (Carneros) $25. 91 *—J.M. (12/15/2002)*

Château St. Jean 1997 Durell Vineyard Chardonnay (Carneros) $24. 89 *—L.W. (11/1/1999)*

Château St. Jean 2004 Reserve Chardonnay (Sonoma County) $45. Chateau St. Jean continues to teach Chard wannabes how the game is played. This is a huge wine, but one of extraordinary finesse and interest. One reason is winemaker Margo van Staaveren's instinct for controlled tension. Another is the winery's access to fruit from throughout the county. Rich and opulent and powerful, this Chardonnay is, in a word, great. **95** *—S.H. (11/1/2007)*

Château St. Jean 2003 Reserve Chardonnay (Sonoma County) $45. 96 Editors' Choice *—S.H. (12/1/2006)*

Château St. Jean 2001 Reserve Chardonnay (Sonoma County) $45. 93 *—S.H. (9/1/2004)*

Château St. Jean 1998 Reserve Chardonnay (Sonoma County) $45. 91 *(7/1/2001)*

Château St. Jean 2004 Robert Young Vineyard Chardonnay (Alexander Valley) $25. 90 *—S.H. (12/31/2006)*

Château St. Jean 2002 Robert Young Vineyard Chardonnay (Alexander Valley) $25. 90 Editors' Choice *—S.H. (12/1/2005)*

Château St. Jean 2001 Robert Young Vineyard Chardonnay (Alexander Valley) $25. 92 *—S.H. (12/15/2004)*

Château St. Jean 2000 Robert Young Vineyard Chardonnay (Alexander Valley) $25. 90 *—S.H. (10/1/2003)*

Château St. Jean 1999 Robert Young Vineyard Chardonnay (Alexander Valley) $25. 90 *—J.M. (12/15/2002)*

Château St. Jean 1997 Robert Young Vineyard Chardonnay (Sonoma County) $24. 90 *(6/1/2000)*

Château St. Jean 1996 Robert Young Vineyard Reserve Chardonnay (Sonoma County) $24. 88 *(6/1/2000)*

Château St. Jean 2006 Fumé Blanc (Sonoma County) $13. You get a big mouthful of wine for the price of this crisp, fruity white. It's bright and zesty in acidity, with balanced citrus, fig, melon and spice flavors, and the finish is long and rich. **86** *—S.H. (11/15/2007)*

Château St. Jean 2005 Fumé Blanc (Sonoma County) $13. A little sugary, but the fine acidity provides balance, and then there's the fruit, which really flatters. It's an explosion of pineapples, figs, apricots, limes, kiwis and vanilla, rich and complex. I had this with pea soup with pancetta. Fantastic echoing of flavors. **87** *—S.H. (2/1/2007)*

Château St. Jean 2004 Fumé Blanc (Sonoma County) $13. 85 *—S.H. (12/1/2005)*

Château St. Jean 2003 Fumé Blanc (Sonoma County) $13. 87 *—S.H. (5/1/2005)*

Château St. Jean 2002 Fumé Blanc (Sonoma County) $13. 85 *—S.H. (2/1/2004)*

Château St. Jean 2001 Fumé Blanc (Sonoma County) $13. 87 *—J.M. (7/1/2003)*

Château St. Jean 2005 La Petite Etoile Vineyard Fumé Blanc (Russian River Valley) $20. This is a very concentrated and intense young Sauvignon Blanc. With 43% new oak, it shows a rich creaminess riding over the laser-like gooseberry, grapefruit and lime flavors. It's also extremely crisp in acidity, since malolactic fermentation was entirely prevented. **89** *—S.H. (10/1/2007)*

Château St. Jean 2004 La Petite Etoile Vineyard Fumé Blanc (Russian River Valley) $20. 92 Editors' Choice *—S.H. (8/1/2006)*

Château St. Jean 2003 La Petite Etoile Vineyard Fumé Blanc (Russian River Valley) $20. 87 *(7/1/2005)*

Château St. Jean 2002 La Petite Etoile Vineyard Fumé Blanc (Russian River Valley) $20. 92 *—S.H. (12/15/2004)*

Château St. Jean 2001 La Petite Etoile Fumé Blanc (Russian River Valley) $20. 88 *—S.H. (2/1/2004)*

Château St. Jean 2000 La Petite Etoile Vineyard Fumé Blanc (Russian River Valley) $20. 84 *(8/1/2002)*

Château St. Jean 2005 Gewürztraminer (Sonoma County) $15. 86 Editors' Choice *—S.H. (12/1/2006)*

Château St. Jean 2004 Gewürztraminer (Sonoma County) $15. 83 *—S.H. (12/1/2005)*

Château St. Jean 2003 Gewürztraminer (Sonoma County) $15. 84 *—S.H. (10/1/2004)*

Château St. Jean 2000 Gewürztraminer (Sonoma County) $15. 90 *—J.M. (9/1/2003)*

Château St. Jean 2001 Estate Vineyard Malbec (Sonoma Valley) $50. 90 *—S.H. (3/1/2005)*

Château St. Jean 2003 St. Jean Estate Vineyard Malbec (Sonoma Valley) $50. The '03 is a dark, soft, intense wine, with blackberry jam , spiced coffee and rum and cola flavors, but beyond color and fruit, it's a little simple. **85** *—S.H. (7/1/2007)*

Château St. Jean 2002 Reserve Malbec (Sonoma County) $60. 92 *—S.H. (12/1/2006)*

Château St. Jean 2001 Reserve Malbec (Sonoma County) $55. 83 *—S.H. (7/1/2005)*

Château St. Jean 2002 St. Jean Estate Vineyard Malbec (Sonoma Valley) $50. 90 Cellar Selection *—S.H. (4/1/2006)*

Château St. Jean 2004 Merlot (Sonoma County) $25. Nice everyday Merlot. The cassis, cherry liqueur and blueberry flavors are finished with smoky oak, and it is totally dry and balanced in smooth tannins and brisk coastal acidity. Drink now. **87** *—S.H. (7/1/2007)*

Château St. Jean 2003 Merlot (Sonoma County) $25. 87 *—S.H. (11/15/2006)*

Château St. Jean 2003 Merlot (California) $15. 86 *—S.H. (12/15/2005)*

Château St. Jean 2002 Merlot (Sonoma County) $25. 85 *—S.H. (12/31/2005)*

Château St. Jean 2002 Merlot (California) $15. 85 *—S.H. (2/1/2005)*

Château St. Jean 2001 Merlot (Sonoma County) $25. 88 *—S.H. (8/1/2004)*

Château St. Jean 1999 Merlot (Sonoma County) $25. 92 Editors' Choice *—S.H. (12/1/2001)*

Château St. Jean 1997 Merlot (Sonoma County) $18. 92 *(11/15/1999)*

Château St. Jean 2001 Estate Vineyard Merlot (Sonoma Valley) $50. 91 *—S.H. (3/1/2005)*

Château St. Jean 2002 Reserve Merlot (Sonoma County) $90. At about five years of age, this dramatic Merlot is just coming into its own, and there aren't many Merlots you can say that about. Its tannins are just beginning to melt. As that astringent tide recedes, a beach of pure cherries and blackberries emerges, deep and dry and spicy. Probably at its best now and for a year or two. **93** *—S.H. (11/1/2007)*

Château St. Jean 2001 Reserve Merlot (Sonoma County) $90. 93 *—S.H. (12/1/2006)*

Château St. Jean 2000 Reserve Merlot (Sonoma County) $90. 89 *—S.H. (10/1/2005)*

Château St. Jean 1999 Reserve Merlot (Sonoma County) $90. 93 *—S.H. (9/1/2004)*

Château St. Jean 1997 Reserve Merlot (Sonoma County) $100. 93 Cellar Selection *—J.M. (11/15/2002)*

Château St. Jean 2003 St. Jean Estate Vineyard Merlot (Sonoma Valley) $50. A nice, smooth Merlot, maybe a little obvious in fruit and structure, but with a clean elegance. The cherry, blackberry, blueberry, cola, coffee and oak flavors are balanced with sweet, dusty tannins and good acidity. Drink now. **89** *—S.H. (7/1/2007)*

Château St. Jean 2002 St. Jean Estate Merlot (Sonoma Valley) $50. 88 *—S.H. (4/1/2006)*

Château St. Jean 2005 Pinot Noir (Sonoma County) $20. The perfect restaurant by-the-glass wine, and not only because it's relatively affordable by today's Pinot standards. Crisp, light-bodied and elegant, it's totally dry, with a pleasant array of ripe cherry, cherryskin, raspberry, cola and dusty spice flavors. Easy to find, with almost 20,000 cases produced. **87 Editors' Choice** *—S.H. (7/1/2007)*

Château St. Jean 2004 Pinot Noir (Sonoma County) $22. 87 *—S.H. (11/15/2006)*

Château St. Jean 2003 Pinot Noir (Sonoma County) $19. 85 *—S.H. (5/1/2005)*

Château St. Jean 2002 Pinot Noir (Sonoma County) $19. 88 *—S.H. (11/1/2004)*

Château St. Jean 2000 Pinot Noir (Sonoma County) $19. 86 *(10/1/2002)*

Château St. Jean 2002 Durell Vineyard Pinot Noir (Sonoma Valley) $45. 88 *(11/1/2004)*

Château St. Jean 2000 Durell Vineyard Pinot Noir (Carneros) $38. 88 *(10/1/2002)*

Château St. Jean 1999 Durell Vineyard Pinot Noir (Carneros) $38. 87 *(10/1/2002)*

Château St. Jean 1997 Durrell Vineyard Pinot Noir (Carneros) $30. 90 *(10/1/1999)*

Château St. Jean 2005 Riesling (Sonoma County) $15. 83 *—S.H. (12/1/2006)*

Château St. Jean 2004 Johannisberg Riesling (Sonoma County) $15. 81 *—S.H. (12/1/2005)*

Château St. Jean 2003 Johannisberg Riesling (Sonoma County) $15. 84 *—S.H. (10/1/2004)*

Château St. Jean 2002 Johannisberg Riesling (Sonoma County) $15. 87 *—J.C. (8/1/2003)*

Château St. Jean 2001 Johannisberg Riesling (Sonoma County) $15. 87 *—J.M. (9/1/2003)*

Château St. Jean 1995 Belle Terre Vineyards Special Selec Johannisberg Riesling (Sonoma County) $30. 90 *—J.C. (12/31/1999)*

Château St. Jean 1997 La Petite Etoile Sauvignon Blanc (Sonoma) $13. 84 *—M.M. (9/1/1999)*

CHÂTEAU STE. MICHELLE

Château Ste. Michelle 1996 Cold Creek Vineyard Cabernet Franc (Columbia Valley (WA)) $28. 82 *—J.C. (4/1/2000)*

Château Ste. Michelle 2003 Cabernet Sauvignon (Columbia Valley (WA)) $16. 87 *—P.G. (10/1/2006)*

Château Ste. Michelle 2002 Cabernet Sauvignon (Columbia Valley (WA)) $16. 84 *—P.G. (12/15/2005)*

Château Ste. Michelle 2001 Cabernet Sauvignon (Columbia Valley (WA)) $16. 88 *—P.G. (7/1/2004)*

Château Ste. Michelle 1999 Cabernet Sauvignon (Columbia Valley (WA)) $15. 87 *—P.G. (6/1/2002)*

Château Ste. Michelle 1998 Cabernet Sauvignon (Columbia Valley (WA)) $15. 88 **Best Buy** *—P.G. (10/1/2001)*

Château Ste. Michelle 2002 Canoe Ridge Cabernet Sauvignon (Columbia Valley (WA)) $22. 85 *—P.G. (12/15/2005)*

Château Ste. Michelle 2004 Canoe Ridge Estate Cabernet Sauvignon (Horse Heaven Hills) $24. Ripe and fruity, loaded with soft, plush, blackberry/black cherry fruit. This is a sweet, soft, open and forward style—a rather dramatic shift in style that was sparked, no doubt, by newly-installed, California-trained winemaker Bob Bertheau, who guided this vintage from the start. Though delicious and ripe, it could stand to be tightened up a bit. **88** *—P.G. (8/1/2007)*

Château Ste. Michelle 2003 Canoe Ridge Estate Cabernet Sauvignon (Columbia Valley (WA)) $22. 87 *—P.G. (10/1/2006)*

Château Ste. Michelle 2001 Canoe Ridge Estate Cabernet Sauvignon (Columbia Valley (WA)) $24. 86 *—P.G. (12/15/2004)*

Château Ste. Michelle 2000 Canoe Ridge Estate Vineyard Cabernet Sauvignon (Columbia Valley (WA)) $24. 89 *—P.G. (12/31/2003)*

Château Ste. Michelle 1998 Canoe Ridge Estate Vineyard Cabernet Sauvignon (Columbia Valley (WA)) $24. 91 *(10/1/2001)*

Château Ste. Michelle 1999 Canoe Ridge Estates Cabernet Sauvignon (Columbia Valley (WA)) $24. 90 *—P.G. (9/1/2002)*

Château Ste. Michelle 2004 Cold Creek Vineyard Cabernet Sauvignon (Columbia Valley (WA)) $26. This is pure Cabernet from one of Washington's oldest vineyards. Cold Creek is a hot site, and its grapes are scattered throughout many of the Ste. Michelle brands, often providing the core fruit. Here is the essence, a wine that opens a bit grudgingly, but has structure and concentration if you take the time to let it blossom. Dense cherry and cassis fruit is tightly wound with balancing acids. The use of new oak is restrained, but sufficient, and this is a wine that should age nicely for many years. **91 Cellar Selection** *—P.G. (12/31/2007)*

Château Ste. Michelle 2003 Cold Creek Vineyard Cabernet Sauvignon (Columbia Valley (WA)) $25. 88 *—P.G. (10/1/2006)*

Château Ste. Michelle 2002 Cold Creek Vineyard Cabernet Sauvignon (Columbia Valley (WA)) $25. 85 *—P.G. (12/15/2005)*

Château Ste. Michelle 2001 Cold Creek Vineyard Cabernet Sauvignon (Columbia Valley (WA)) $29. 91 **Cellar Selection** *—P.G. (12/15/2004)*

Château Ste. Michelle 2000 Cold Creek Vineyard Cabernet Sauvignon (Columbia Valley (WA)) $29. 89 **Cellar Selection** *—P.G. (12/31/2003)*

Château Ste. Michelle 1999 Cold Creek Vineyard Cabernet Sauvignon (Columbia Valley (WA)) $29. 88 *—P.G. (12/31/2002)*

Château Ste. Michelle 1998 Cold Creek Vineyard Cabernet Sauvignon (Columbia Valley (WA)) $32. 92 *—P.G. (12/31/2001)*

Château Ste. Michelle 1996 Cold Creek Vineyard Cabernet Sauvignon (Columbia Valley (WA)) $25. 91 *—L.W. (2/1/2000)*

Château Ste. Michelle 2004 Indian Wells Cabernet Sauvignon (Columbia Valley (WA)) $17. Here at last are the flavors that have been missing from Ste. Michelle Cabs for some time. This is crisply structured, varietally spot-on Cabernet. The ripe—but not jammy—fruit flavors of blackberry and black plum are amplified with spicy cinnamon from aging in American oak. There is a hint of chalkiness in the way the acids hit the palate, but otherwise this is picture-perfect, with well-delineated tannins and some delicious Asian spices on the finish. **89** *—P.G. (8/1/2007)*

Château Ste. Michelle 2003 Indian Wells Cabernet Sauvignon (Columbia Valley (WA)) $17. 85 *—P.G. (6/1/2006)*

Château Ste. Michelle 2002 Reserve Cabernet Sauvignon (Columbia Valley (WA)) $36. 88 *—P.G. (12/15/2005)*

Château Ste. Michelle 2001 Reserve Cabernet Sauvignon (Columbia Valley (WA)) $33. 86 *—P.G. (4/1/2005)*

Château Ste. Michelle 1998 Reserve Cabernet Sauvignon (Columbia Valley (WA)) $33. 90 *—P.G. (6/1/2002)*

Château Ste. Michelle 2005 Chardonnay (Columbia Valley (WA)) $13. Soft and creamy, this is consistent with the previous vintage and sets the stage for the winery's bigger, oakier single-vineyard Chardonnays. Mixed stone fruits, pineapple and an elegant, full-bodied mouthfeel make this particularly appealing for the price. It uses the oak judiciously, and avoids the overdone vanilla flavors that many inexpensive New World Chardonnays rely on. **88 Best Buy** *—P.G. (8/1/2007)*

Château Ste. Michelle 2004 Chardonnay (Columbia Valley (WA)) $13. 87 *—P.G. (8/1/2006)*

Château Ste. Michelle 2003 Chardonnay (Columbia Valley (WA)) $12. 88 **Best Buy** *—P.G. (11/15/2005)*

Château Ste. Michelle 2002 Chardonnay (Columbia Valley (WA)) $13. 87 *—P.G. (7/1/2004)*

Château Ste. Michelle 2000 Chardonnay (Columbia Valley (WA)) $13. 89 **Best Buy** *—P.G. (7/1/2002)*

Château Ste. Michelle 1998 Chardonnay (Columbia Valley (WA)) $13. 86 *—P.G. (11/15/2000)*

Château Ste. Michelle 1999 Barrel Fermented Chardonnay (Columbia Valley (WA)) $13. 90 **Best Buy** *—P.G. (6/1/2001)*

Château Ste. Michelle 1997 Barrel Fermented Chardonnay (Columbia Valley (WA)) $13. 87 *(2/1/2000)*

Château Ste. Michelle 2005 Canoe Ridge Estate Chardonnay (Horse Heaven Hills) $20. A smashing success, this exceptional value is loaded with the typical fruit flavors of cut green apple, pineapple and melon. The fruit is set in a creamy frame and finished with beautifully restrained oak accents that support it without burying it. **91** *—P.G. (8/1/2007)*

Château Ste. Michelle 2004 Canoe Ridge Estate Chardonnay (Columbia Valley (WA)) $20. 89 *—P.G. (8/1/2006)*

Château Ste. Michelle 2003 Canoe Ridge Estate Chardonnay (Columbia Valley (WA)) $20. 92 **Editors' Choice** *—P.G. (12/15/2005)*

Château Ste. Michelle 2000 Canoe Ridge Estate Chardonnay (Washington) $20. 91 *—P.G. (9/1/2002)*

Château Ste. Michelle 1999 Canoe Ridge Estate Vineyard Chardonnay (Columbia Valley (WA)) $20. 87 *—P.G. (6/1/2001)*

Château Ste. Michelle 2005 Cold Creek Vineyard Chardonnay (Columbia Valley (WA)) $20. The hot climate of the Cold Creek Vineyard sharpens up the contours of this Chardonnay, which shows more of a classic Washington character. Bright fruit, a mix of apples and peaches and pears, is shot through with streaks of butterscotch from fermentation in new French oak. It's been through 100% malolactic, yet retains some crispness. Polished and full-bodied. **89** *—P.G. (12/1/2007)*

Château Ste. Michelle 2004 Cold Creek Chardonnay (Columbia Valley (WA)) $22. 90 *—P.G. (6/1/2006)*

Château Ste. Michelle 2003 Cold Creek Chardonnay (Columbia Valley (WA)) $22. 93 **Editors' Choice** *—P.G. (12/15/2005)*

Château Ste. Michelle 2001 Cold Creek Vineyard Chardonnay (Columbia Valley (WA)) $26. 91 *—P.G. (12/31/2003)*

Château Ste. Michelle 2000 Cold Creek Vineyard Chardonnay (Columbia Valley (WA)) $28. 90 *—P.G. (12/31/2002)*

Château Ste. Michelle 1998 Cold Creek Vineyard Chardonnay (Columbia Valley (WA)) $25. 91 *—P.G. (10/1/2001)*

Château Ste. Michelle 2005 Ethos Chardonnay (Columbia Valley (WA)) $30. This is a very rich, with quite ripe, banana and tropical fruits. Barrel fermentation brings more richness to the palate: buttered nuts, caramel and crème brûlée. For its over-the-top style, it's been done very well, but it tires the palate rather quickly. **88** *—P.G. (12/1/2007)*

Château Ste. Michelle 2004 Ethos Chardonnay (Columbia Valley (WA)) $30. 91 *—P.G. (6/1/2006)*

Château Ste. Michelle 2003 Ethos Chardonnay (Columbia Valley (WA)) $30. 94 *—P.G. (8/1/2005)*

Château Ste. Michelle 2005 Indian Wells Chardonnay (Columbia Valley (WA)) $17. This is yet another superripe, rich and luscious Chardonnay from Chateau Ste. Michelle. It's a tropical fruit-flavored California take on Washington terroir. Plush, smooth and plump, it nonetheless carries its weight well, with an especially fine, lingering finish. **89** *—P.G. (8/1/2007)*

Château Ste. Michelle 2004 Indian Wells Chardonnay (Columbia Valley (WA)) $17. 89 *—P.G. (8/1/2006)*

Château Ste. Michelle 2003 Indian Wells Chardonnay (Columbia Valley (WA)) $17. 89 *—P.G. (12/15/2005)*

Château Ste. Michelle 2000 Indian Wells Vineyard Chardonnay (Columbia Valley (WA)) $21. 91 Editors' Choice *—P.G. (12/31/2002)*

Château Ste. Michelle 1999 Indian Wells Vineyard Chardonnay (Columbia Valley (WA)) $22. 88 *—P.G. (10/1/2001)*

Château Ste. Michelle 2002 Reserve Chardonnay (Columbia Valley (WA)) $30. 93 *—P.G. (4/1/2005)*

Château Ste. Michelle 2001 Reserve Chardonnay (Columbia Valley (WA)) $29. 89 *—P.G. (5/1/2004)*

Château Ste. Michelle 1999 Reserve Chardonnay (Columbia Valley (WA)) $31. 90 *—P.G. (7/1/2002)*

Château Ste. Michelle 1997 Reserve Chardonnay (Columbia Valley (WA)) $29. 87 *(4/1/2000)*

Château Ste. Michelle 2006 Gewürztraminer (Columbia Valley (WA)) $10. Simple, off-dry, and very much in the style of the Riesling. The blend includes 9% Muscat Canelli. It's basically a fruity, somewhat sweet tasting room wine. **87 Best Buy** *—P.G. (8/1/2007)*

Château Ste. Michelle 2003 Gewürztraminer (Columbia Valley (WA)) $9. 87 *—P.G. (9/1/2004)*

Château Ste. Michelle 2001 Gewürztraminer (Columbia Valley (WA)) $8. 87 *—P.G. (9/1/2002)*

Château Ste. Michelle 1997 Merlot (Columbia Valley (WA)) $18. 87 *(4/1/2000)*

Château Ste. Michelle 1996 Merlot (Columbia Valley (WA)) $16. 89 *(11/15/1999)*

Château Ste. Michelle 2002 Merlot (Columbia Valley (WA)) $16. 84 *—P.G. (12/15/2005)*

Château Ste. Michelle 2001 Merlot (Columbia Valley (WA)) $16. 87 *—P.G. (7/1/2004)*

Château Ste. Michelle 2000 Merlot (Columbia Valley (WA)) $16. 88 *—P.G. (12/31/2003)*

Château Ste. Michelle 1999 Merlot (Columbia Valley (WA)) $18. 88 *—P.G. (6/1/2002)*

Château Ste. Michelle 2004 Canoe Ridge Estate Merlot (Horse Heaven Hills) $22. This is a wonderful Merlot, dark and plummy. The nose introduces a round, warm entrance, with hints of leather, wood, herb and spice. The soft, ripe fruit tastes of black cherries, with dusty, silky tannins. Smooth to a fault, and quite delicious. **89** *—P.G. (8/1/2007)*

Château Ste. Michelle 2002 Canoe Ridge Estate Merlot (Columbia Valley (WA)) $24. 87 *—P.G. (4/1/2005)*

Château Ste. Michelle 2001 Canoe Ridge Estate Merlot (Columbia Valley (WA)) $24. 88 *—P.G. (5/1/2004)*

Château Ste. Michelle 1999 Canoe Ridge Estate Merlot (Columbia Valley (WA)) $23. 90 *—P.G. (6/1/2002)*

Château Ste. Michelle 1998 Canoe Ridge Estate Vineyard Merlot (Columbia Valley (WA)) $22. 87 *—P.G. (10/1/2001)*

Château Ste. Michelle 1996 Canoe Ridge Estate Vineyard Merlot (Columbia Valley (WA)) $32. 89 *—L.W. (9/1/1999)*

Château Ste. Michelle 2001 Cold Creek Merlot (Columbia Valley (WA)) $33. 90 *—P.G. (5/1/2004)*

Château Ste. Michelle 2002 Cold Creek Vineyard Merlot (Columbia Valley (WA)) $33. 85 *—P.G. (4/1/2005)*

Château Ste. Michelle 1999 Cold Creek Vineyard Merlot (Columbia Valley (WA)) $32. 88 *—P.G. (6/1/2002)*

Château Ste. Michelle 1998 Cold Creek Vineyard Merlot (Columbia Valley (WA)) $32. 91 *—P.G. (12/31/2001)*

Château Ste. Michelle 2002 Indian Wells Merlot (Columbia Valley (WA)) $17. 87 *—P.G. (4/1/2005)*

Château Ste. Michelle 2001 Indian Wells Merlot (Columbia Valley (WA)) $18. 87 *—P.G. (5/1/2004)*

Château Ste. Michelle 1999 Indian Wells Vineyard Merlot (Columbia Valley (WA)) $32. 88 *—P.G. (6/1/2002)*

Château Ste. Michelle 1998 Indian Wells Vineyard Merlot (Columbia Valley (WA)) $31. 90 *—P.G. (10/1/2001)*

Château Ste. Michelle 2002 Reserve Merlot (Columbia Valley (WA)) $36. 86 *—P.G. (12/15/2005)*

Château Ste. Michelle 2001 Reserve Merlot (Columbia Valley (WA)) $37. 87 *—P.G. (12/15/2004)*

Château Ste. Michelle 2000 Reserve Merlot (Columbia Valley (WA)) $37. 90 *—P.G. (12/31/2003)*

Château Ste. Michelle 1999 Reserve Merlot (Columbia Valley (WA)) $37. 92 Cellar Selection *—P.G. (9/1/2002)*

Château Ste. Michelle 1998 Reserve Merlot (Columbia Valley (WA)) $37. 91 *(10/1/2001)*

Château Ste. Michelle 2006 Pinot Gris (Columbia Valley (WA)) $13. This is very fresh and crisp, mingling light citrus and green apple fruit with interesting herbal enticements of white pepper and tarragon. Just a touch (6%) of Viognier in the blend adds to the citrus and floral highlights. It seems as if a distinct Washington Pinot Gris style, quite different from Oregon, is beginning to emerge. **89 Best Buy** *—P.G. (8/1/2007)*

Château Ste. Michelle 2004 Pinot Gris (Columbia Valley (WA)) $9. 86 *—P.G. (2/1/2006)*

Château Ste. Michelle 2003 Pinot Gris (Columbia Valley (WA)) $13. 88 Best Buy *—P.G. (9/1/2004)*

Château Ste. Michelle 2001 Pinot Gris (Columbia Valley (WA)) $13. 89 *—P.G. (9/1/2002)*

Château Ste. Michelle 2004 Artist Series Meritage Red Blend (Columbia Valley (WA)) $48. This Bordeaux blend has a different artist's label every year but otherwise has no identity of its own. This new release is tight, hot and shows signs of reduction; it's got a burnt rubber scent underlying the ultraripe, almost pruny fruit. It's just not a compelling wine; it hasn't jelled and it doesn't seem as if it will. There is concentration and power to be sure, but pleasure is in short supply. **85** *—P.G. (12/31/2007)*

Château Ste. Michelle 2003 Artist Series Meritage Red Blend (Columbia Valley (WA)) $48. 86 *—P.G. (10/1/2006)*

Château Ste. Michelle 2002 Artist Series Meritage Red Blend (Columbia Valley (WA)) $48. 88 *—P.G. (12/15/2005)*

Château Ste. Michelle 2001 Artist Series Meritage Meritage Red Blend (Columbia Valley (WA)) $48. 86 *—P.G. (4/1/2005)*

Château Ste. Michelle 2000 Artist Series Meritage Red Blend (Columbia Valley (WA)) $48. 89 *—P.G. (12/31/2003)*

Château Ste. Michelle 1998 Artist Series Meritage Red Blend (Columbia Valley (WA)) $50. 91 *—P.G. (12/31/2001)*

Château Ste. Michelle 2005 Riesling (Columbia Valley (WA)) $8. 89 Best Buy *—P.G. (8/1/2006)*

Château Ste. Michelle 2000 Cold Creek Riesling (Columbia Valley (WA)) $14. 89 Best Buy *—P.G. (6/1/2002)*

Château Ste. Michelle 2003 Cold Creek Vineyard Riesling (Columbia Valley (WA)) $14. 91 *—P.G. (9/1/2004)*

Château Ste. Michelle 2002 Cold Creek Vineyard Riesling (Columbia Valley (WA)) $11. 89 *—R.V. (8/1/2003)*

Château Ste. Michelle 2001 Cold Creek Vineyard Riesling (Columbia Valley (WA)) $14. 90 Best Buy *—P.G. (12/31/2002)*

Château Ste. Michelle 1998 Cold Creek Vineyard Riesling (Columbia Valley (WA)) $12. 86 *(2/1/2000)*

Château Ste. Michelle 2001 Dr. Loosen Eroica Riesling (Columbia Valley (WA)) $20. 92 Cellar Selection *—P.G. (9/1/2002)*

Château Ste. Michelle 2003 Dry Riesling (Columbia Valley (WA)) $8. 87 *—P.G. (9/1/2004)*

Château Ste. Michelle 2001 Dry Riesling (Columbia Valley (WA)) $8. 90 *—P.G. (9/1/2002)*

Château Ste. Michelle 2005 Eroica Riesling (Columbia Valley (WA)) $22. 92 Editors' Choice *—P.G. (8/1/2006)*

Château Ste. Michelle 2003 Eroica Riesling (Columbia Valley (WA)) $20. 89 *—P.G. (9/1/2004)*

Château Ste. Michelle 2002 Eroica Riesling (Columbia Valley (WA)) $20. 91 *—P.G. (12/31/2003)*

Château Ste. Michelle 2005 Indian Wells Riesling (Columbia Valley (WA)) $17. 90 *—P.G. (8/1/2006)*

Château Ste. Michelle 2003 Johannisberg Riesling (Columbia Valley (WA)) $9. 88 Best Buy *—P.G. (9/1/2004)*

Château Ste. Michelle 2001 Johannisberg Riesling (Columbia Valley (WA)) $8. 85 *—M.S. (12/31/2003)*

Château Ste. Michelle 2005 Sauvignon Blanc (Columbia Valley (WA)) $15. A blast of SO2 quickly blows off after pulling the cork, revealing a lovely mix of fruit and a more authentic, varietal herbaceous character. Clean and detailed, with citrus, dried herbs and no new oak, it leaves you with a hint of flint and an urge to pour another glass. **88** *—P.G. (8/1/2007)*

Château Ste. Michelle 2004 Sauvignon Blanc (Columbia Valley (WA)) $15. 89 *—P.G. (12/31/2006)*

Château Ste. Michelle 2003 Sauvignon Blanc (Columbia Valley (WA)) $10. 88 Best Buy *—P.G. (12/15/2005)*

Château Ste. Michelle 2002 Sauvignon Blanc (Columbia Valley (WA)) $10. 86 *—P.G. (7/1/2004)*

Château Ste. Michelle 2000 Sauvignon Blanc (Columbia Valley (WA)) $10. 85 *—S.H. (9/12/2002)*

Château Ste. Michelle 1998 Sauvignon Blanc (Columbia Valley (WA)) $10. 87 *—P.G. (4/1/2000)*

Château Ste. Michelle 1997 Sauvignon Blanc (Columbia Valley (WA)) $10. 88 Best Buy *—L.W. (9/1/1999)*

Château Ste. Michelle 2005 Horse Heaven Vineyard Sauvignon Blanc (Horse Heaven Hills) $15. This is an excellent vintage in Washington, and Bob Bertheau has made a soft, smooth, well-crafted Sauvignon Blanc. Just a bit more than one third was barrel fermented, and the blend is 100% varietal. It's a fruity, polished effort with citrusy highlights, but I'd love to see the winemaker veer a bit more towards a Washington State-style that includes some sweet grassiness in the finish. **88** *—P.G. (8/1/2007)*

Château Ste. Michelle 2004 Horse Heaven Vineyard Sauvignon Blanc (Columbia Valley (WA)) $15. 87 *—P.G. (12/31/2006)*

Château Ste. Michelle 2003 Horse Heaven Vineyard Sauvignon Blanc (Columbia Valley (WA)) $15. 88 *—P.G. (12/15/2005)*

Château Ste. Michelle 2002 Horse Heaven Vineyard Sauvignon Blanc (Columbia Valley (WA)) $15. 87 *—P.G. (5/1/2004)*

Château Ste. Michelle 2000 Horse Heaven Vineyard Sauvignon Blanc (Columbia Valley (WA)) $14. 90 *—P.G. (2/1/2002)*

Château Ste. Michelle 1999 Horse Heaven Vineyard Sauvignon Blanc (Columbia Valley (WA)) $14. 92 Best Buy *—P.G. (6/1/2001)*

Château Ste. Michelle 1997 Horse Heaven Vineyard Sauvignon Blanc (Columbia Valley (WA)) $14. 88 *—L.W. (9/1/1999)*

Château Ste. Michelle 2005 Sémillon (Columbia Valley (WA)) $9. Sémillon, sadly, is getting pulled out and replanted all over Washington, despite the fact that it makes a fine stable mate to the state's better-known Sauvignon Blancs. This includes 22% Sauv Blanc in the blend, a delivers flavors of fig and melon along with fresh grain and a bit of spice. It's balanced and crisp; a good summer sip. **86 Best Buy** *—P.G. (8/1/2007)*

Château Ste. Michelle 2003 Sémillon (Columbia Valley (WA)) $9. 87 Best Buy *—P.G. (12/15/2005)*

Château Ste. Michelle 2002 Sémillon (Columbia Valley (WA)) $9. 87 Best Buy *—P.G. (7/1/2004)*

Château Ste. Michelle 1998 Sémillon (Columbia Valley (WA)) $8. 85 *—P.G. (11/15/2000)*

Château Ste. Michelle 1997 Sémillon (Columbia Valley (WA)) $10. 86 *—L.W. (9/1/1999)*

Château Ste. Michelle 1997 Late Harvest Sémillon (Columbia Valley (WA)) $23. 90 *—P.G. (11/15/2000)*

Château Ste. Michelle 2002 Syrah (Columbia Valley (WA)) $15. 84 *(9/1/2005)*

Château Ste. Michelle 2001 Syrah (Columbia Valley (WA)) $13. 88 Best Buy *—P.G. (12/31/2003)*

Château Ste. Michelle 2000 Syrah (Columbia Valley (WA)) $15. 88 Best Buy *—P.G. (12/31/2002)*

Château Ste. Michelle 2003 Ethos Syrah (Columbia Valley (WA)) $29. 94 *—P.G. (6/1/2006)*

Château Ste. Michelle 2003 Ethos Syrah (Columbia Valley (WA)) $29. 94 *—P.G. (12/31/2006)*

Château Ste. Michelle 2002 Reserve Syrah (Columbia Valley (WA)) $29. 88 *(9/1/2005)*

Château Ste. Michelle 2001 Reserve Syrah (Columbia Valley (WA)) $29. 89 *—P.G. (12/15/2004)*

Château Ste. Michelle 2000 Reserve Syrah (Columbia Valley (WA)) $29. 90 *—P.G. (12/31/2003)*

Château Ste. Michelle 1999 Reserve Syrah (Columbia Valley (WA)) $29. 90 *—P.G. (9/1/2002)*

Château Ste. Michelle 1998 Reserve Syrah (Columbia Valley (WA)) $29. 87 *(11/1/2001)*

CHÂTEAU WOLTNER

Château Woltner 1997 Private Reserve Bordeaux Blend (Howell Mountain) $50. 85 *(11/1/2000)*

CHATFIELD

Chatfield 1998 Clements Vineyards Chardonnay (California) $15. 85 *(6/1/2000)*

CHATOM

Chatom 1999 Cabernet Sauvignon (Calaveras County) $18. 83 *(9/1/2002)*

Chatom 2005 Chardonnay (Calaveras County) $16. Good everyday Chard, a little minty, but rewards for its upfront pineapple pie, peaches and cream and vanilla smoke flavors. The tart acidity actually works to balance out the richness. **84** *—S.H. (10/1/2007)*

Chatom 2003 Chardonnay (Calaveras County) $14. 88 *—S.H. (3/1/2005)*

Chatom 2002 Chardonnay (Calaveras County) $14. 84 *—S.H. (12/1/2003)*

Chatom 2002 Gitano Sangiovese (Calaveras County) $12. 84 *—S.H. (9/1/2003)*

Chatom 2005 Sauvignon Blanc (Calaveras County) $18. Simple and fruity, with straightforward lemonade, wildflower, sweet vanilla and spice flavors. There may be some residual sugar, for the wine straddles the dry-off dry line. **83** *—S.H. (10/1/2007)*

Chatom 2003 Sauvignon Blanc (Calaveras County) $18. 87 *—S.H. (2/1/2005)*

Chatom 2002 Sauvignon Blanc (Calaveras County) $14. 83 *—S.H. (12/15/2003)*

Chatom 2002 Sémillon (Calaveras County) $11. 84 *—S.H. (12/1/2003)*

Chatom 2002 Syrah (Calaveras County) $22. 86 *—S.H. (8/1/2005)*

Chatom 2001 Syrah (Calaveras County) $23. 85 *—S.H. (12/1/2003)*

Chatom 1999 Syrah (Calaveras County) $18. 88 *(10/1/2001)*

Chatom 2002 Esmeralda Syrah (Calaveras County) $34. 85 *(9/1/2005)*

Chatom 2001 Esmeralda Syrah (Calaveras County) $28. 87 *—S.H. (2/1/2005)*

Chatom 2004 Zinfandel (Calaveras County) $16. Hot, dry and Porty; the thinness of fruit merely accentuates the heat. **81** *—S.H. (11/1/2007)*

Chatom 2002 Zinfandel (Calaveras County) $16. 84 *—S.H. (8/1/2005)*

Chatom 2001 Zinfandel (Calaveras County) $16. 84 *(11/1/2003)*

Chatom 2000 Zinfandel (Calaveras County) $16. 85 *—S.H. (9/1/2003)*

CHATTER CREEK

Chatter Creek 2002 Bordeaux Blend (Columbia Valley (WA)) $16. 87 *—P.G. (6/1/2005)*

Chatter Creek 2005 Alder Ridge Vineyard Cabernet Franc (Horse Heaven Hills) $24. Three quarters Cabernet Franc with Cabernet Sauvignon and Merlot filling in the rest, the Horse Heaven Hills fruit mixes strawberry, black cherry with tart cranberry flavors. It looks a little murky in the glass (unfiltered perhaps?) but the flavors are fresh enough, and the wine holds your attention for quite a long while. Needs a bit more definition on the finish. **87** *—P.G. (11/1/2007)*

Chatter Creek 2004 Alder Ridge Vineyard Cabernet Franc (Horse Heaven Hills) $20. Good winemaking is evident in this tight, polished wine. The fruit leans strongly toward tart cranberry flavors, with an imposing streak of fresh basil and hints of mint. For those who like a cool-climate style, reminiscent of Bordeaux, this will be a very good choice. It is still young and knitting together, but it's well-structured for aging. **88** *—P.G. (5/1/2007)*

Chatter Creek 2003 Alder Ridge Vineyard Cabernet Franc (Columbia Valley (WA)) $20. 88 *—P.G. (6/1/2005)*

Chatter Creek 2002 Alder Ridge Vineyard Cabernet Franc (Columbia Valley (WA)) $20. 87 *—P.G. (6/1/2005)*

Chatter Creek 2000 Alder Ridge Vineyard Cabernet Franc (Washington) $18. 86 *—P.G. (6/1/2002)*

Chatter Creek 1998 Cabernet Sauvignon (Washington) $20. 87 *—P.G. (10/1/2001)*

Chatter Creek 2002 Alder Ridge Vineyard Cabernet Sauvignon (Columbia Valley (WA)) $30. 89 *—P.G. (8/1/2006)*

Chatter Creek 1999 Alder Ridge Vineyard Cabernet Sauvignon (Washington) $20. 88 *—P.G. (10/1/2001)*

Chatter Creek 2001 Alder Ridge Vineyard Cabernet Sauvignon-Merlot (Columbia Valley (WA)) $22. 88 *—P.G. (6/1/2005)*

Chatter Creek 2006 Pinot Gris (Columbia Valley (WA)) $16. Young, fresh and still yeasty, this shows lightly ripened fruit flavors of white peach, melon, green apple and pineapple. It retains a pretty floral quality in the nose. No malolactic fermentation here; it's done in a crisp, lean and lively style. **87** *—P.G. (11/1/2007)*

Chatter Creek 2003 Pinot Gris (Columbia Valley (WA)) $12. 87 *—P.G. (6/1/2005)*

Chatter Creek 2000 Pinot Gris (Washington) $12. 86 *—P.G. (10/1/2001)*

Chatter Creek 2004 Blend 105 Red Blend (Columbia Valley (WA)) $22. This is done in a nice, fruity style that tastes like a bowl full of berries, cherries and plums, then misted with lemon juice. It's a bright, palate-cleaning wine, fresh and youthful, with no big ambitions. Drink up. **88** *—P.G. (5/1/2007)*

Chatter Creek 2004 Clifton Hill Vineyard Syrah (Wahluke Slope) $30. Clifton Hill has established itself as a premier source for Washington Syrah. One look at the glass shows you why: it's as black as the night sky, with only the rim showing purple/garnet. Concentrated but not fat or jammy, it frames its black fruits with barrel fat and hints of pineapple. Young as it is, the wine has smoothed out nicely, and washes into a soft finish with all of its fruits wrapped in a lick of butterscotch. **90** *—P.G. (11/1/2007)*

Chatter Creek 2002 Clifton Hill Vineyard Syrah (Columbia Valley (WA)) $30. 91 *—P.G. (6/1/2005)*

Chatter Creek 2003 Jack Jones Vineyard Syrah (Columbia Valley (WA)) $22. 88 *—P.G. (6/1/2005)*

Chatter Creek 2000 Jack Jones Vineyard Syrah (Washington) $20. 89 *—P.G. (6/1/2002)*

Chatter Creek 2005 Lonesome Spring Ranch Syrah (Yakima Valley) $28. Pure Syrah and 100% single vineyard, this young, tight wine is already beginning to reveal a fragrant side, suggesting black fruits, aromatic herbs and smoky pepper. Dark and spicy, the acids jut out a bit, showing a tart, lemony edge. This will need another year or two to develop and flesh out, but all the right components are here. **88** *—P.G. (11/1/2007)*

Chatter Creek 2003 Lonesome Spring Ranch Syrah (Yakima Valley) $22. 88 *—P.G. (6/1/2005)*

Chatter Creek 2000 Lonesome Spring Ranch Syrah (Yakima Valley) $20. 91 Editors' Choice *—P.G. (6/1/2002)*

Chatter Creek 2006 Viognier (Columbia Valley (WA)) $24. As before, the new vintage of Chatter Creek Viognier treats you immediately to bracingly fresh scents of peach, apricot and ripe melon. Tart and leesy, immaculately clean, it starts with crisp, slightly bitter notes of lime and citrus, then fans out, adding a creamy texture to the midpalate. This is a moderate 13.5% alcohol, rare in Washington Viognier. **90** *—P.G. (11/1/2007)*

Chatter Creek 2004 Viognier (Columbia Valley (WA)) $20. 88 *—P.G. (4/1/2006)*

Chatter Creek 2003 Viognier (Yakima Valley) $15. 87 *—P.G. (6/1/2005)*

CHEAPSKATE

CheapSkate 2003 Miser Cabernet Blend (California) $8. 84 Best Buy *—S.H. (11/1/2005)*

CheapSkate 2003 Cabernet Sauvignon (California) $8. 84 Best Buy *—S.H. (11/1/2005)*

CheapSkate 2002 Pinot Noir (California) $8. 82 *—S.H. (11/1/2005)*

CheapSkate 2005 SkinFlint Rosé Table Wine Rosé Blend (California) $8. Soft and simple, with semisweet root beer and vanilla flavors. The absence of balancing acidity gives this wine a medicinal feel. **81** *—S.H. (7/1/2007)*

CheapSkate 2004 SkinFlint Rosé Blend (California) $8. 84 Best Buy *—S.H. (11/1/2005)*

CHEHALEM

Chehalem 2000 Chardonnay (Willamette Valley) $19. 90 *(8/1/2002)*

Chehalem 2000 Ian's Reserve Chardonnay (Willamette Valley) $32. 91 *—P.G. (7/1/2002)*

Chehalem 1999 Ian's Reserve Chardonnay (Willamette Valley) $32. 89 *—P.G. (2/1/2002)*

Chehalem 2004 INOX Chardonnay (Willamette Valley) $17. 90 *—P.G. (5/1/2006)*

Chehalem 2003 Pinot Gris (Willamette Valley) $16. 89 *—P.G. (12/15/2004)*

Chehalem 2001 Pinot Gris (Willamette Valley) $15. 89 Best Buy *—P.G. (12/31/2002)*

Chehalem 2000 Pinot Gris (Willamette Valley) $15. 88 *—P.G. (2/1/2002)*

Chehalem 1997 Pinot Gris (Willamette Valley) $19. 80 *(8/1/1999)*

Chehalem 2004 Reserve Pinot Gris (Willamette Valley) $21. 90 *—P.G. (2/1/2006)*

Chehalem 2003 3 Vineyard Pinot Noir (Willamette Valley) $25. 90 Editors' Choice *—P.G. (5/1/2006)*

Chehalem 2000 3 Vineyard Pinot Noir (Willamette Valley) $25. 88 *(10/1/2002)*

Chehalem 1998 3 Vineyard Pinot Noir (Willamette Valley) $25. 90 *—M.S. (12/1/2000)*

Chehalem 2000 Corral Creek Pinot Noir (Willamette Valley) $39. 88 *(10/1/2002)*

Chehalem 2002 Corral Creek Vineyard Pinot Noir (Willamette Valley) $39. 84 *(11/1/2004)*

Chehalem 1998 Corral Creek Vineyards Pinot Noir (Willamette Valley) $39. 93 *—M.S. (12/1/2000)*

Chehalem 2002 Reserve Pinot Noir (Willamette Valley) $50. 84 *(11/1/2004)*

Chehalem 2002 Ridgecrest Vineyard Pinot Noir (Willamette Valley) $39. 87 *(11/1/2004)*

Chehalem 2000 Ridgecrest Vineyards Pinot Noir (Willamette Valley) $39. 87 *(10/1/2002)*

Chehalem 1999 Ridgecrest Vineyards Pinot Noir (Willamette Valley) $39. 86 *(10/1/2002)*

Chehalem 2000 Rion Reserve Pinot Noir (Willamette Valley) $50. 92 Editors' Choice *(10/1/2002)*

Chehalem 1999 Rion Reserve Pinot Noir (Willamette Valley) $50. 89 *(10/1/2002)*

Chehalem 2002 Stoller Vineyard Pinot Noir (Dundee Hills) $39. 85 *(11/1/2004)*

Chehalem 2000 Stoller Vineyards Pinot Noir (Willamette Valley) $39. 85 *(10/1/2002)*

Chehalem 1997 Stoller Vineyards Pinot Noir (Willamette Valley) $28. 86 *(10/1/1999)*

Chehalem 2002 Three Vineyards Pinot Noir (Willamette Valley) $39. 88 *(11/1/2004)*

Chehalem 1997 Three Vineyards Pinot Noir (Willamette Valley) $18. 90 *(10/1/1999)*

Chehalem 2001 Corral Creek Reserve Dry Riesling (Willamette Valley) $19. 90 *—P.G. (12/31/2002)*

Chehalem 2004 Reserve Dry Riesling (Willamette Valley) $21. 89 *—P.G. (5/1/2006)*

CHELAN ESTATE

Chelan Estate 2002 Cabernet Sauvignon (Columbia Valley (WA)) $25. 87 *—P.G. (9/1/2004)*

Chelan Estate 2004 Chardonnay-Viognier (Columbia Valley (WA)) $16. 88 *—P.G. (4/1/2006)*

CHERRY HILL ESTATE

Cherry Hill Estate 2006 Poverty Road Pinot Gris (Willamette Valley) $16. This is a very light, generic, almost watery white wine. There is absolutely nothing wrong with it, but it is so ephemeral as to be ghostlike. **83** *—P.G. (11/15/2007)*

Cherry Hill Estate 2002 Pinot Noir (Willamette Valley) $27. 87 *(11/1/2004)*

Cherry Hill Estate 2005 Estate Pinot Noir (Willamette Valley) $29. Pungent with aromas of resin, tomato leaf and sour cherry, this thin, acidic wine is fairly typical of Oregon fruit. It does not seem to have the ripeness to carry the tannins, and the lingering impression is tart and chalky, like a sour cherry candy. **84** *—P.G. (11/15/2007)*

Cherry Hill Estate 2005 Papillon Estate Pinot Noir (Willamette Valley) $22. This is a sturdy, tannic wine, with a pleasing softness upon entry, but that turns leafy and tannic. The fruit is austere and the dominant flavors are herb and leaf. Tannins are hard and taste of earth and rock. The label features a picture of a big-eared dog. **85** *—P.G. (11/15/2007)*

Cherry Hill Estate 2006 Vonda Rosé Blend (Willamette Valley) $16. Pale and simple, with light strawberry fruit and no complexity or weight. **82** *—P.G. (11/15/2007)*

CHESLER

Chesler 2004 Red Wine Bordeaux Blend (Napa Valley) $70. Quite delicious, a modern-style wine with soft richness, with enough tannin-acid balance to counterpoise the enormously ripe blackberry, cherry, cassis, chocolate, Kahlúa and new oaky, cedar-spice flavors. Probably not an ager. **93** *—S.H. (10/1/2007)*

CHESTER KIDDER

Chester Kidder 2003 Red Blend (Columbia Valley (WA)) $50. The second vintage of Chester Kidder is quite a different blend from the 2002—38% Cabernet Sauvignon, 29% Syrah, 14% Merlot, 12% Cab Franc, 5% Malbec, 2% Petit Verdot. Yet despite the obvious effort to craft a vinous all-star, to me it remains somewhat amorphous and a bit over-driven by the barrels. The dominant flavors are all barrel-derived—mocha, coffee grounds, toast—and the fruit, though sleek and polished, stands well in the background. Notes of berry are most prevalent; seamless but a bit anonymous—this wine is still looking for a unique identity. **89** *—P.G. (3/1/2007)*

Chester Kidder 2002 Red Blend (Columbia Valley (WA)) $50. 88 —P.G. (4/1/2006)

CHEVAL SAUVAGE

Cheval Sauvage 2002 Ashley Vineyard Pinot Noir (Santa Rita Hills) $50. 90 *(10/1/2005)*

CHEYANNA

Cheyanna 2004 Zinfandel (Napa Valley) $15. 82 *—S.H. (12/31/2006)*

CHIARELLO FAMILY VINEYARDS

Chiarello Family Vineyards 2002 Felicia Old Vine Zinfandel (Napa Valley) $45. 93 *—J.M. (10/1/2004)*

CHIMERE

Chimere 2002 Angelica Orange Muscat (Santa Barbara County) $14. 92 *—S.H. (3/1/2005)*

Chimere 1996 Pinot Noir (Edna Valley) $23. 89 *(11/15/1999)*

Chimere 2002 Paragon Vineyard Pinot Noir (Edna Valley) $30. Smells Porty and caramelized, and drinks hot and dry. **82** *—S.H. (3/1/2005)*

Chimere 1999 Paragon Vineyard Pinot Noir (Edna Valley) $22. 85 *(10/1/2002)*

Chimere 1997 Paragon Vineyard Pinot Noir (Edna Valley) $22. 84 *—J.C. (12/15/2000)*

Chimere 1999 Santa Maria Hill Vineyard Pinot Noir (Santa Barbara County) $26. 87 *(10/1/2002)*

CHIMNEY ROCK

Chimney Rock 2004 Elevage Bordeaux Blend (Stags Leap District) $78. A Cabernet-based blend, with Merlot and Petit Verdot, this is a fruit-driven wine with masses of ripe black cherries, blackberries and raspberries, whose sweetness is boosted by fancy toasted oak. It shows a much-needed youthful grip of tannins that balances out the honeyed sweetness and grounds it. **89** *—S.H. (11/1/2007)*

Chimney Rock 2003 Elevage Bordeaux Blend (Stags Leap District) $75. 91 *(9/1/2006)*

Chimney Rock 1997 Elevage Bordeaux Blend (Stags Leap District) $52. 89 *(11/1/2000)*

Chimney Rock 1998 Dionysus Cabernet Blend (Stags Leap District) $74. 90 *—D.T. (6/1/2002)*

Chimney Rock 2002 Elevage Cabernet Blend (Stags Leap District) $76. 92 *—S.H. (12/1/2005)*

Chimney Rock 2003 Rosé Cabernet Franc (Stags Leap District) $21. 88 *—S.H. (12/15/2004)*

Chimney Rock 2005 Rosé of Cabernet Franc Cabernet Franc (Stags Leap District) $21. 85 *—S.H. (11/15/2006)*

Chimney Rock 2004 Rosé of Cabernet Franc Cabernet Franc (Stags Leap District) $21. 89 *—S.H. (12/1/2005)*

Chimney Rock 2004 Cabernet Sauvignon (Stags Leap District) $54. Off a bit from the last few vintages but nonetheless smooth and ripe with lots of fruity power. Tastes exceptionally ripe in effusive blackberry, cassis, licorice, mushu plum sauce and oak flavors, but could use a more structure and restraint. **89** *—S.H. (11/1/2007)*

Chimney Rock 2003 Cabernet Sauvignon (Stags Leap District) $52. 90 *(9/1/2006)*

Chimney Rock 2003 Cabernet Sauvignon (Stags Leap District) $52. 90 *—S.H. (9/1/2006)*

Chimney Rock 2002 Cabernet Sauvignon (Stags Leap District) $49. 87 *—S.H. (11/15/2005)*

Chimney Rock 2002 Cabernet Sauvignon (Napa Valley) $49. 87 *—S.H. (10/1/2005)*

Chimney Rock 2001 Cabernet Sauvignon (Stags Leap District) $49. 93 *—S.H. (10/1/2004)*

Chimney Rock 2000 Cabernet Sauvignon (Stags Leap District) $45. 86 *—S.H. (11/15/2003)*

Chimney Rock 1999 Cabernet Sauvignon (Stags Leap District) $45. 88 *—C.S. (11/15/2002)*

Chimney Rock 1997 Cabernet Sauvignon (Napa Valley) $40. 91 *(11/1/2000)*

Chimney Rock 1996 Cabernet Sauvignon (Napa Valley) $30. 90 *—M.S. (6/1/1999)*

Chimney Rock 2004 Reserve Cabernet Sauvignon (Stags Leap District) $107. Chimney Rock had three Bordeaux-style wines from the '04 vintage, and this reserve is not only the priciest, but the best. It shows the appealing blackberry, cherry and chocolate fruit and oak of the Elevage bottling, but also is tannicly balanced enough for the cellar. Good now for its complexity, but should peak around 2010, then hold through 2015. **91** *—S.H. (12/15/2007)*

Chimney Rock 2002 Reserve Cabernet Sauvignon (Stags Leap District) $100. 93 Editors' Choice *—S.H. (12/1/2005)*

Chimney Rock 2001 Reserve Cabernet Sauvignon (Stags Leap District) $107. 93 *—S.H. (7/1/2005)*

Chimney Rock 1999 Reserve Cabernet Sauvignon (Stags Leap District) $90. 88 *—M.S. (11/15/2002)*

Chimney Rock 1997 Reserve Cabernet Sauvignon (Stags Leap District) $80. 88 *(11/1/2000)*

Chimney Rock 2003 Fumé Blanc (Napa Valley) $20. 86 *—S.H. (12/15/2004)*

Chimney Rock 2000 Fumé Blanc (Napa Valley) $18. 85 *(8/1/2002)*

Chimney Rock 2001 Elevage Red Blend (Stags Leap District) $72. 91 *—S.H. (4/1/2005)*

Chimney Rock 2000 Elevage Red Blend (Stags Leap District) $60. 88 *—S.H. (11/15/2003)*

Chimney Rock 1998 Elevage Red Blend (Stags Leap District) $60. 89 *—D.T. (6/1/2002)*

Chimney Rock 2005 Elevage Blanc Bordeaux White Blend (Stags Leap District) $39. Lots to like in this dry, elegant wine, which is a Graves-style blend of Sauvignon Blanc and Sémillon. The flavors are quite complex, with nectarine, peach, pineapple and flowery buttercup accented with a nutty, cashew-rich oiliness. All that richness is perfectly balanced with crisp acidity. **92** *—S.H. (11/1/2007)*

Chimney Rock 2004 Elevage Blanc White Blend (Napa Valley) $36. 88 *(9/1/2006)*

CHINOOK

Chinook 2003 Cabernet Franc (Yakima Valley) $20. 89 *—P.G. (6/1/2006)*

Chinook 2003 Chardonnay (Yakima Valley) $17. 88 *—P.G. (12/15/2005)*

Chinook 1998 Merlot (Yakima Valley) $28. 90 *—P.G. (9/1/2002)*

Chinook 2005 Sauvignon Blanc (Yakima Valley) $17. 88 *—P.G. (12/31/2006)*

Chinook 2000 Sauvignon Blanc (Yakima Valley) $15. 90 *—P.G. (9/1/2002)*

Chinook 2004 Sémillon (Yakima Valley) $17. 90 *—P.G. (6/1/2006)*

Chinook 2000 Sémillon (Yakima Valley) $14. 88 *—P.G. (9/1/2002)*

CHOUINARD

Chouinard 2001 Joan's Vineyard Orange Muscat Ice Wine (Paso Robles) $16. 93 Best Buy *—S.H. (12/1/2003)*

Chouinard NV Brut Sparkling Blend (California) $13. 84 *—S.H. (12/1/2003)*

CHRISTIAN LAZO

Christian Lazo 2005 Barbera (Paso Robles) $25. Nice and smooth for this sometimes boring variety, with a lush texture and appealingly dry flavors of blackberries, violets, mocha and coconut macaroon cookie, and an almond skin bitterness in the finish. The tannins are there, rich and sturdy, offering a firm counterbalance to the ripeness. **90** *—S.H. (10/1/2007)*

Christian Lazo 2005 Petite Sirah (Paso Robles) $25. One-dimensional and harsh, with medicinal, sweet-and-sour fruit sauce flavors. **81** *—S.H. (10/1/2007)*

Christian Lazo 2005 Zinfandel (Paso Robles) $20. Soft and simple and as sweet as something you'd pour over ice cream. The flavors are terrifically ripe—cherries, raspberries, dates, vanilla fudge, butterscotch. And look at that alcohol, 16.6%! **82** *—S.H. (10/1/2007)*

CHRISTINE ANDREW

Christine Andrew 2005 Cabernet Sauvignon (Sonoma County) $15. Dry, a little unripe and rustic, with mint, herb and cherry flavors, this Cab gets the job done. A new brand from Ironstone. **83** *—S.H. (10/1/2007)*

Christine Andrew 2005 Chardonnay (Sonoma County) $13. Juicy and crisp, with green apple, lime and cinnamon granola flavors. Finishes clean and spicy. **86** *—S.H. (11/1/2007)*

Christine Andrew 2004 Malbec (Lodi) $15. Absolutely dry, this full-bodied red has coffee, cherryskin and dried herb flavors. It's also very tart and tannic, almost to the point of bitterness, but it has great structure, and the total absence of fruity sweetness makes it versatile with food. **87** *—S.H. (10/1/2007)*

Christine Andrew 2005 Merlot (Sonoma County) $15. Pretty good country-type Merlot, bone dry and tannic, with herb, coffee and tobacco flavors and a dusting of cherry fruit. **84** *—S.H. (10/1/2007)*

Christine Andrew 2004 Petite Sirah (Lodi) $15. Dull and heavy, with medicinal LifeSaver candy and cola flavors, this wine has a sugary finish. **82** *—S.H. (11/1/2007)*

Christine Andrew 2005 Viognier (California) $13. Very high in acidity, almost sour, with sweetened flavors of canned peaches and vanilla. **82** *—S.H. (10/1/2007)*

Christine Andrew 2005 Old Vine Zinfandel (Lodi) $15. Spicy, peppery briary flavors of wild, freshly-picked red and black berries star in this wine. It has its faults, namely deficient acidity, but possesses an honest rusticity, a sense of place, that make it appealing. Best with barbecue with a rich, sweet, fruity tomato sauce. **86** *—S.H. (11/1/2007)*

CHRISTINE WOODS

Christine Woods NV Pinot Noir (Anderson Valley) $20. 85 *—S.H. (5/1/2002)*

CHRISTOPHE

Christophe 2000 Pinot Noir (Monterey) $10. 82 *(10/1/2002)*

CHRISTOPHER CREEK

Christopher Creek 1999 Petite Sirah (Russian River Valley) $28. 84 *(4/1/2003)*

Christopher Creek 2001 Zinfandel (Dry Creek Valley) $22. 84 *(11/1/2003)*

CHUMEIA

Chumeia 2002 Partridge-Leigh Vineyard Barbera (Paso Robles) $25. 85 *—S.H. (6/1/2006)*

Chumeia 2003 Cabernet Sauvignon (California) $13. 83 *—S.H. (12/31/2005)*

Chumeia 2002 Cabernet Sauvignon (California) $12. 81 *—S.H. (2/1/2005)*

Chumeia 2000 Cabernet Sauvignon (Central Coast) $25. 85 *—S.H. (8/1/2003)*

Chumeia 2000 Cabernet Sauvignon (California) $10. 85 Best Buy *—S.H. (8/1/2003)*

Chumeia 2000 Chardonnay (Central Coast) $16. 84 *—S.H. (6/1/2003)*

Chumeia 2004 Simpson Vineyard Chardonnay (Madera) $11. 82 *—S.H. (12/31/2005)*

Chumeia 2003 Simpson Vineyard Chardonnay (California) $10. 83 *—S.H. (2/1/2005)*

Chumeia 2001 Simpson Vineyard Chardonnay (California) $10. 85 *—S.H. (6/1/2003)*

Chumeia 2003 Merlot (California) $13. 80 *—S.H. (12/31/2005)*

Chumeia 2002 Simpson Vineyard Merlot (California) $12. 86 Best Buy *—S.H. (12/31/2004)*

Chumeia 2001 Pinot Blanc (Monterey County) $14. 82 *—S.H. (3/1/2005)*

Chumeia 2000 Pinot Blanc (Monterey County) $14. 84 *—S.H. (3/1/2004)*

Chumeia 2003 Pinot Noir (Central Coast) $16. 83 *—S.H. (2/1/2006)*

Chumeia 2002 Pinot Noir (Central Coast) $16. 86 *—S.H. (2/1/2005)*

Chumeia 2001 Pinot Noir (Santa Lucia Highlands) $28. 84 *—S.H. (2/1/2005)*

Chumeia 2000 Pinot Noir (Santa Lucia Highlands) $28. 85 *(10/1/2002)*

Chumeia 2003 Silver Nectar Muscat-French Columbard Red Blend (California) $10. 84 *—S.H. (2/1/2005)*

Chumeia 2000 Simpson Vineyard Syrah (California) $10. 84 *—S.H. (12/15/2003)*

Chumeia 2000 Viognier (California) $10. 83 *—S.H. (5/1/2003)*

Chumeia 2000 Zinfandel (Paso Robles) $22. 87 *—S.H. (9/1/2003)*

Chumeia 2001 Dante Dusi Vineyard Zinfandel (Paso Robles) $22. 89 *—J.M. (11/1/2003)*

CHURCHILL

Churchill 2004 Pinot Noir (Russian River Valley) $35. 87 *—S.H. (12/31/2006)*

Churchill 2004 Bella Luna Vineyard Pinot Noir (Russian River Valley) $39. 87 *—S.H. (12/31/2006)*

CILURZO

Cilurzo 1998 Barrel Fermented Chardonnay (Temecula) $16. 81 *(6/1/2000)*

CINERGI

Cinergi 2000 Red Blend (Napa Valley) $18. 86 *—S.H. (12/1/2002)*

CINNABAR

Cinnabar 2004 Mercury Rising Bordeaux Blend (California) $19. They make this Bordeaux blend from grapes grown in Lodi, Monterey, Paso Robles and Sonoma, and it does taste like a warm-climate wine, with its soft acids and tannins and easy, slightly sweet cherry-berry flavors. Drink soon. **84** *—S.H. (5/1/2007)*

Cinnabar 2001 Mercury Rising Bordeaux Blend (California) $18. 90 Editors' Choice *—S.H. (12/1/2004)*

Cinnabar 2000 Mercury Rising Bordeaux Blend (California) $17. 88 *—S.H. (8/1/2003)*

Cinnabar 2003 Mercury Rising Cabernet Blend (California) $18. 87 *—S.H. (11/1/2006)*

Cinnabar 2002 Mercury Rising Cabernet Blend (California) $18. 84 *—S.H. (11/1/2005)*

Cinnabar 2001 Estate Cabernet Sauvignon (Santa Cruz Mountains) $40. 90 *—S.H. (2/1/2005)*

Cinnabar 2005 Chardonnay (Monterey) $18. A little simple, but rich and forward in ripe fruit flavors, this zesty Chard offers a wealth of apricot, pineapple and peach jam flavors. Oak adds complexities of buttered toast and caramel. **85** *—S.H. (5/1/2007)*

Cinnabar 2003 Chardonnay (Monterey) $18. 86 *—S.H. (2/1/2005)*

Cinnabar 2002 Chardonnay (Santa Cruz Mountains) $25. 90 Editors' Choice *—S.H. (11/1/2005)*

Cinnabar 2001 Chardonnay (Santa Cruz Mountains) $25. 86 *—S.H. (8/1/2004)*

Cinnabar 1999 Chardonnay (Santa Cruz Mountains) $25. 90 *—S.H. (9/1/2002)*

Cinnabar 1998 Chardonnay (Central Coast) $17.85 *(6/1/2000)*

Cinnabar 1999 Quicksilver Chardonnay (Central Coast) $18. 89 *—S.H. (5/1/2001)*

Cinnabar 1997 Saratoga Vineyard Chardonnay (Santa Cruz Mountains) $25. 84 *(6/1/2000)*

Cinnabar 2000 Sleepy Hollow Vineyard Chardonnay (Santa Lucia Highlands) $25. 92 *—S.H. (8/1/2003)*

Cinnabar 2004 Merlot (Paso Robles) $20. Shows the soft fruitiness you usually find in Paso Robles reds, with low acids and easy tannins framing ripe cherry liqueur and blackberry jam flavors complexed with a rich, leathery earthiness. There's nothing like this in Napa-Sonoma, and it's wines like this that have made Paso such a nice alternative. **90 Editors' Choice** *—S.H. (3/1/2007)*

Cinnabar 2003 Merlot (Paso Robles) $20. 86 *—S.H. (10/1/2006)*

Cinnabar 2002 Merlot (Paso Robles) $19. 84 *—S.H. (2/1/2005)*

Cinnabar 2001 Merlot (Paso Robles) $19. 87 *—S.H. (12/1/2003)*

Cinnabar 2005 Pinot Noir (Central Coast) $25. A blend of Santa Cruz Mountains, Santa Lucia Highlands and Edna Valley, this is a tasty, easy-drinking Pinot. It's soft, with cola, cherry, raspberry, tea, licorice and cinnamon spice flavors, and finishes dry. **86** *—S.H. (11/1/2007)*

Cinnabar 2003 Pinot Noir (Santa Cruz Mountains) $35. 87 *—S.H. (11/1/2005)*

Cinnabar 1999 Pinot Noir (Santa Cruz Mountains) $38. 89 *—S.H. (9/1/2002)*

Cinnabar 1999 Gary's Vineyard Pinot Noir (Santa Lucia Highlands) $42. 86 *(10/1/2002)*

Cinnabar 1999 Watts-Borden Ranch Syrah (Lodi) $17. 91 *—S.H. (11/15/2001)*

Cinnabar 2005 Mercury Rising Blanc Rhône White Blend (California) $18. This is an unusual blend of Sauvignon Blanc, Viognier and Sémillon, and it just shows what an interesting wine you can make with exotic combinations. Sauvignon brings citrus and acidity, while Viognier contributes flowers and passionfruit. **87** *—S.H. (5/1/2007)*

CIRCLES EDGE

Circles Edge 2005 Circle's Edge Cabernet Sauvignon (Lodi) $17. With sugary blackberry and cherry tart flavors side by side with bitter rhubarbs, and green, raw acidity, this is a simple, country wine, with notable defects. **81** *—S.H. (9/1/2007)*

Circles Edge 2005 Chardonnay (California) $17. Awkward and overoaked, with apricot flavors and deficient acidity, which mars the slight sweetness. **81** *—S.H. (9/1/2007)*

Circles Edge 2005 Merlot (California) $17. Fire up the barbie and don't worry about the wine. This one's dry and clean, with a smear of blackberries, and just enough tannins to chew through meats. **84** *—S.H. (9/1/2007)*

CIVELLO

Civello 2005 Pinot Gris (California) $14. With no oak, the fruit stars in this simple, refreshingly dry wine. Lemons and limes, apples and figs predominate, with a spicy, peppery edge leading to a tart finish. **84** *—S.H. (4/1/2007)*

CK MONDAVI

CK Mondavi 1998 Cabernet Sauvignon (California) $8. 86 Best Buy *—S.H. (5/1/2001)*

CK Mondavi 2002 Wildcreek Canyon Cabernet Sauvignon (California) $10. 84 *—S.H. (11/15/2004)*

CK Mondavi 2003 Chardonnay (California) $6. 84 Best Buy *—S.H. (10/1/2004)*

CK Mondavi 1999 Chardonnay (California) $8. 84 *—S.H. (5/1/2001)*

CK Mondavi 1997 Merlot (California) $9. 81 *—J.C. (7/1/2000)*

CK Mondavi 1999 Merlot (California) $9. 84 *—S.H. (5/1/2001)*

CK Mondavi 2002 Wildcreek Canyon Merlot (California) $10. 85 Best Buy *—S.H. (12/15/2004)*

CK Mondavi 2001 Merlot-Cabernet Sauvignon (California) $8. 86 Best Buy *—S.H. (5/1/2003)*

CK Mondavi 2002 Wildcreek Canyon Merlot-Cabernet Sauvignon (California) $10. 84 *—S.H. (11/15/2004)*

CK Mondavi 2003 Sauvignon Blanc (California) $6. 82 *—S.H. (10/1/2004)*

CK Mondavi 1998 Shiraz (California) $8. 83 *(10/1/2001)*

CK Mondavi 2001 Zinfandel (California) $7. 86 *—S.H. (9/1/2003)*

CK Mondavi 2003 White Zinfandel (California) $7. 84 *—S.H. (11/15/2004)*

CK Mondavi 2002 Wildcreek Canyon Zinfandel (California) $10. 82 *—S.H. (12/15/2004)*

CL

CL 2000 Madonna Vineyard Gewürztraminer (Carneros) $15. 90 *—S.H. (9/1/2003)*

CL 2000 Armagh Vineyard Pinot Noir (Sonoma Coast) $35. 90 *—S.H. (2/1/2003)*

CL 2000 Kanzler Vineyard Pinot Noir (Sonoma Coast) $40. 90 *—S.H. (2/1/2003)*

CLAAR

Claar 1999 White Bluffs Estate Grown & Bottled Cabernet Sauvignon (Columbia Valley (WA)) $21. 82 *—M.S. (8/1/2003)*

Claar 2002 Corneauxcopia Red Blend (Columbia Valley (WA)) $35. This is Claar's Bordeaux blend. Despite the extra bottle age, the wine is still stiff and tannic. The fruit verges on the vegetal, and there is a bitter, medicinal flavor that dominates the midpalate and extends right through the finish. **82** *—P.G. (12/31/2007)*

Claar 2006 Riesling (Columbia Valley (WA)) $12. This is a bit stinky right out of the bottle, with some sour, rotten egg aromas. Ultimately they blow off, but there's still a palate impression of sulfur and burnt match. The net effect is to put a damper on the fruit, which pokes through the sulfurous fog tasting rather soapy and limpid. **82** *—P.G. (12/1/2007)*

Claar 2003 Sangiovese (Columbia Valley (WA)) $15. This is Sangiovese stretched to the max, with raisiny, pruny fruit flavors that lead into smoke, burnt rubber and tar. Rough and tumble stuff. **81** *—P.G. (12/31/2007)*

Claar 2006 Sauvignon Blanc (Columbia Valley (WA)) $12. Traces of kerosene and candle wax are threaded into the strongly herbaceous Sauvignon Blanc scents. In the mouth this is austere and grassy, on the green side of just ripe. There is a hint of sweetness in the finish. **84** *—P.G. (12/1/2007)*

CLAIBORNE & CHURCHILL

Claiborne & Churchill 2005 Dry Gewürztraminer (Central Coast) $18. Gewurz fans will exult in this Alsatian-style wine. It's basically dry, although low in alcohol (by California standards), and provides an array of papayas, citrus fruits, lichee, honeysuckle, tangerine zest and those wonderful Gewurz spices. If more Gewurz was like this, more people would drink it. **87** *—S.H. (2/1/2007)*

Claiborne & Churchill 2002 Dry Gewürztraminer (Central Coast) $14. 87 *—S.H. (2/1/2004)*

Claiborne & Churchill 2000 Dry Gewürztraminer (Central Coast) $14. 88 *—S.H. (9/1/2003)*

Claiborne & Churchill 2005 Pinot Gris (Arroyo Grande Valley) $18. Try this next time you're looking for something rich like a Chardonnay, streamlined like a Sauvignon Blanc, but different. It has the creamy opulence of Chard, with honeyed melon, pineapple and peach custard flavors. Yet there's firm acidity and a minerally core that gives the wine backbone. **90** *—S.H. (2/1/2007)*

Claiborne & Churchill 2000 Pinot Gris (Edna Valley) $18. 86 *—S.H. (9/1/2003)*

Claiborne & Churchill 2005 Alsatian Style Pinot Gris (Arroyo Grande Valley) $18. 87 *—S.H. (10/1/2006)*

Claiborne & Churchill 2004 Pinot Noir (Edna Valley) $18. 82 *—S.H. (11/1/2006)*

Claiborne & Churchill 2002 Pinot Noir (Edna Valley) $16. 90 *(11/1/2004)*

Claiborne & Churchill 2000 Pinot Noir (Edna Valley) $20. 88 *(10/1/2002)*

Claiborne & Churchill 2000 Runestone Pinot Noir (Edna Valley) $29. 82 *(10/1/2002)*

Claiborne & Churchill 1999 Runestone Pinot Noir (Edna Valley) $29. 86 *(10/1/2002)*

Claiborne & Churchill 2002 Runestone Barrel Select Pinot Noir (Edna Valley) $26. 86 *(11/1/2004)*

Claiborne & Churchill 2003 Twin Creeks Pinot Noir (Edna Valley) $30. 83 *—S.H. (11/1/2006)*

Claiborne & Churchill 2002 Twin Creeks Pinot Noir (Edna Valley) $33. 90 *(11/1/2004)*

Claiborne & Churchill 2005 Dry Riesling (Central Coast) $18. Dry like the label says, and crisply acidic, with pleasant peach and wildflower flavors. Would score a lot higher if the fruit was more concentrated, because it's a little on the watery side. **84** *—S.H. (2/1/2007)*

Claiborne & Churchill 2002 Dry Riesling (Central Coast) $14. 87 *—S.H. (2/1/2004)*

Claiborne & Churchill 2000 Dry Riesling (Central Coast) $14. 87 *—S.H. (9/1/2003)*

CLARK-CLAUDEN

Clark-Clauden 2003 Ten-Year Anniversary Cabernet Sauvignon (Napa Valley) $90. 86 *—S.H. (9/1/2006)*

Clark-Claudon 1997 Cabernet Sauvignon (Napa Valley) $78. 92 *(11/1/2000)*

Clark-Claudon 2002 Cabernet Sauvignon (Napa Valley) $90. 91 Cellar Selection *—S.H. (8/1/2006)*

CLARY RANCH

Clary Ranch 2004 Grower's Reserve Pinot Noir (Sonoma Coast) $50. This is a new winery for me, and one to keep an eye on. They say the vineyard is 11 miles from Tomales Bay, which would put it close enough to the Pacific to get chilly winds and fog. In this hot vintage, the wine sure did get ripe, with cherry liqueur, raspberry jam, white chocolate and cola flavors, but is harmoniously dry, with crisp, balancing acidity and a rewardingly silky texture. **92** *—S.H. (5/1/2007)*

CLAUDIA SPRINGS

Claudia Springs 2000 Pinot Gris (Anderson Valley) $14. 83 *—S.H. (5/1/2002)*

Claudia Springs 2004 Klindt Vineyard Pinot Gris (Anderson Valley) $17. 90 *—S.H. (2/1/2006)*

Claudia Springs 1999 Pinot Noir (Anderson Valley) $25. 87 *—S.H. (5/1/2002)*

Claudia Springs 1998 Pinot Noir (Mendocino) $18. 91 *—P.G. (12/15/2000)*

Claudia Springs 1998 Clone 115 Vidmar Vineyard Pinot Noir (Mendocino) $25. 90 *—P.G. (12/15/2000)*

Claudia Springs 2004 Klindt Vineyard Pinot Noir (Anderson Valley) $28. There's a funky, leathery taste in this single-vineyard Pinot that calls to mind beef jerky, but there's also plenty of red plum and cherry fruit, so the funk is just one element. The finish is dry, and the wine is tannic enough to suggest a good 4-6 years of useful life. **87** *—S.H. (11/1/2007)*

Claudia Springs 2001 Syrah (Mendocino) $20. 89 *(9/1/2005)*

Claudia Springs 2000 Lolonis Vineyard Viognier (Redwood Valley) $24. 93 *—P.G. (5/1/2002)*

Claudia Springs 1998 Eagle Point Ranch Zinfandel (Mendocino) $20. 93 Editors' Choice *—P.G. (3/1/2001)*

Claudia Springs 2000 Eaglepoint Ranch Zinfandel (Mendocino) $20. 88 *(11/1/2003)*

USA

Claudia Springs 2000 Rhodes Vineyard Zinfandel (Redwood Valley) $26. 86 *(11/1/2003)*

Claudia Springs 1999 Rhodes Vineyard Zinfandel (Redwood Valley) $26. 86 *—S.H. (5/1/2002)*

Claudia Springs 1998 Rhodes Vineyard Zinfandel (Redwood Valley) $24. 93 *—P.G. (3/1/2001)*

Claudia Springs 1997 Rhodes Vineyard Zinfandel (Redwood Valley) $24. 86 *—S.H. (5/1/2000)*

Claudia Springs 1999 Vassar Vineyard Zinfandel (Redwood Valley) $20. 88 *—S.H. (5/1/2002)*

CLAUTIERE

Clautiere 2004 Estate Cabernet Sauvignon (Paso Robles) $28. Shows its warm country terroir nicely in the well-ripened, jammy cherry, blackberry and mocha fruit flavors and soft texture. Beautiful now, this is one for the near term for its youthful lushness. 87 *—S.H. (6/1/2007)*

Clautiere 2004 Grenache (Paso Robles) $26. Almost as sweet as a dessert wine, this Grenache is rich in cherry liqueur flavor, with a finish of melted milk chocolate and root beer. It's a soft, easy gulper. 83 *—S.H. (6/1/2007)*

Clautiere 2004 Estate Mourvèdre (Paso Robles) $23. Soft, ripe and rustic, with cherry, cola and chocolate flavors that finish with a medicinal, sugary sweetness. 82 *—S.H. (6/1/2007)*

Clautiere 2004 Estate Port (Paso Robles) $69. Made with original Port varieties, this is a very sweet wine, with a rich array of milk chocolate, blackberry jam, cassis, cherry pie, butterscotch and vanilla caramel flavors. It's not an ager, so drink now. 90 *—S.H. (6/1/2007)*

Clautiere 2004 Estate Grand Rouge Red Blend (Paso Robles) $33. An ambitious Rhône blend, with Cabernet Sauvignon and Viognier, the wine is soft and simple. It has stewed fruit flavors, and rough-hewn tannins. 83 *—S.H. (6/1/2007)*

Clautiere 2004 Mon Rouge Red Blend (Paso Robles) $30. This is a blend of Syrah and Cab Sauvignon. It's very fruity, soft in acidity and slightly sweet, with candied blackberry, cherry and cocoa flavors. 84 *—S.H. (6/1/2007)*

Clautiere 2004 Mon Beau Rouge Rhône Red Blend (Paso Robles) $29. A Southern Rhône blend of Syrah, Counoise, Grenache and Mourvèdre, this wine is as soft as a melted chocolate candy bar, with blackberry and cherry flavors. It's a little cloying on the finish. 83 *—S.H. (6/1/2007)*

Clautiere 2005 Roussanne (Paso Robles) $20. This is quite a distinctive wine, not quite like anything else out there, which makes you think about it. Dry and creamy, it shows the flavors of dried fruits, such as apricots and peaches, with a streak of fresh green herbs, and a stony, metallic taste, like white chalk. Really notable for its uniqueness. 89 *—S.H. (6/1/2007)*

Clautiere 2004 Estate Syrah (Paso Robles) $24. This soft, simple wine has modest chocolate, cherry-berry and coffee flavors, straddling the border of dry and off-dry. 83 *—S.H. (6/1/2007)*

Clautiere 2005 Estate Viognier (Paso Robles) $21. With all the lush, exotic tropical fruit, vanilla cream and butterscotch flavors, and a honeyed sweetness in the finish, this wine could use more acidity. The lack of it makes it a little cloying. 83 *—S.H. (6/1/2007)*

CLAY STATION

Clay Station 2003 Malbec (Lodi) $13. 83 *—S.H. (12/15/2005)*

Clay Station 2002 Malbec (Lodi) $13. 83 *—S.H. (12/15/2004)*

Clay Station 2004 Petite Sirah (Lodi) $13. 83 *—S.H. (12/31/2006)*

Clay Station 2005 Pinot Gris (Lodi) $13. 84 *—S.H. (12/1/2006)*

Clay Station 2004 Pinot Gris (Lodi) $13. 84 *—S.H. (2/1/2006)*

Clay Station 2001 Cabernet-Petite Sirah Red Blend (Lodi) $13. 84 *—S.H. (12/15/2004)*

Clay Station 2003 Shiraz (Lodi) $13. 85 *—S.H. (3/1/2005)*

Clay Station 2005 Viognier (Lodi) $13. 83 *—S.H. (12/15/2006)*

Clay Station 2004 Viognier (Lodi) $13. 86 *(8/1/2006)*

Clay Station 2004 Viognier (Lodi) $13. 83 *—S.H. (12/15/2005)*

Clay Station 2003 Viognier (Lodi) $13. 84 *—S.H. (12/15/2004)*

Clay Station 2004 Old Vine Zinfandel (Lodi) $13. 85 *—S.H. (12/15/2005)*

Clay Station 2004 Old Vine Zinfandel (Lodi) $12. 86 *(8/1/2006)*

CLAYHOUSE

Clayhouse 2004 Hillside Cuvée Bordeaux Blend (Paso Robles) $32. Lots to like in this 59% Cab, 41% Petite Verdot blend, but not without its problems. On the plus side is a lush texture, with fine tannins and a rich layer of oak. You'll find rich blackberry and cherry flavors, but there's also a touch of green unripeness, suggesting asparagus. 84 *—S.H. (12/1/2007)*

Clayhouse 2005 Cabernet Sauvignon (Paso Robles) $14. Even at this price, this isn't a very good buy. It's soft and clumsy, with medicinal cherry lozenge flavors. It will do in a pinch. 81 *—S.H. (11/15/2007)*

Clayhouse 2004 Petite Sirah (Paso Robles) $23. Brawny and fruity, this wine has a hot mouthfeel from high alcohol, accentuating the tannins. The blackberry and cherry flavors taste stewed. But the finish is dry. 83 *—S.H. (12/15/2007)*

Clayhouse 2003 Estate Petite Sirah (Paso Robles) $20. 83 *—S.H. (12/31/2005)*

Clayhouse 2004 Estate Cuvée Rhône Red Blend (Paso Robles) $28. A Rhône blend of Syrah, Petite Sirah and Grenache, this wine is dry and tannic, with jammy and roasted fruit cherry-berry, spice and smoky oak flavors. 84 *—S.H. (12/15/2007)*

Clayhouse 2006 Sauvignon Blanc (Paso Robles) $13. The cool vintage was of special benefit down in Paso Robles, where the usual heat was mitigated, allowing this wine to ripen at lower sugars and still retain good acidity. The flavors are of citrus fruits, figs, dates, spicy green melons and white pepper. 86 *—S.H. (11/15/2007)*

Clayhouse 2004 Sauvignon Blanc (Paso Robles) $12. 84 *—S.H. (12/31/2005)*

Clayhouse 2003 Syrah (Paso Robles) $13. 83 *—S.H. (12/31/2005)*

CLAYTON

Clayton 1999 Estate Vineyard Old Vine Petite Sirah (Lodi) $29. 89 *(4/1/2003)*

Clayton 1999 Estate Vineyard Old Vine Block SC Petite Sirah (Lodi) $29. 86 *(4/1/2003)*

Clayton 2000 Zinfandel (Lodi) $19. 91 Editors' Choice *—J.M. (9/1/2003)*

CLEMENTS HILLS

Clements Hills 2002 Syrah (Lodi) $12. 85 *(9/1/2005)*

CLIFF CREEK WINERY

Cliff Creek Winery 2003 Claret Red Blend (Southern Oregon) $30. This classy claret puts a sophisticated spin on southern Oregon Bordeaux-blends. The roughly equal mix of Cabernet Sauvignon, Merlot and Cabernet Franc has a supple power. Aromatic and sexy with scents of berry and plum, it slides into a silky, seductive midpalate and continues seamlessly through a finish that is both spicy and shows a touch of new oak. 89 *—P.G. (11/15/2007)*

Cliff Creek Winery 2004 Syrah (Southern Oregon) $35. This is estate-grown and nicely ripened, showing sweet scents and flavors of blackberry compote. Though it trends toward a jammy, high-alcohol profile, it keeps itself firm with solid, smooth tannins and enough acid to provide support. It's more California than Oregon, with the sweet fruit and high alcohol backed with a liquor-barrel finish. 88 *—P.G. (11/15/2007)*

CLIFF LEDE

Cliff Lede 2002 Claret Bordeaux Blend (Stags Leap District) $32. 90 *—S.H. (12/15/2005)*

Cliff Lede 2002 Cabernet Sauvignon (Stags Leap District) $50. 93 *—S.H. (12/15/2005)*

Cliff Lede 2001 Cabernet Sauvignon (Stags Leap District) $50. 92 *—S.H. (10/3/2004)*

Cliff Lede 2004 *Barrel Sample* Cabernet Sauvignon (Stags Leap District) $NA. 92 *—S.H. (8/1/2004)*

Cliff Lede 2001 Poetry Cabernet Sauvignon (Stags Leap District) $100. 94 *—S.H. (10/1/2004)*

Cliff Lede 2001 Merlot (Stags Leap District) $38. 90 *—S.H. (12/15/2004)*

Cliff Lede 2004 Sauvignon Blanc (Napa Valley) $18. 90 *—S.H. (12/15/2005)*

Cliff Lede 2003 Sauvignon Blanc (Napa Valley) $18. 90 *—S.H. (12/15/2004)*

CLINE

Cline 2005 Ancient Vines Carignan (Contra Costa County) $16. 85 *—S.H. (12/15/2006)*

Cline 1998 Marsanne (Carneros) $18. 89 *—S.H. (6/1/1999)*

Cline 2004 Ancient Vines Mourvèdre (Contra Costa County) $15. 87 *—S.H. (12/31/2006)*

Cline 2003 Ancient Vines Mourvèdre (Contra Costa County) $18. 84 *—S.H. (4/1/2005)*

Cline 1997 Ancient Vines Mourvèdre (Contra Costa County) $18. 87 *—S.H. (10/1/1999)*

Cline 2006 Mourvedre Rosé Mourvèdre (Contra Costa County) $16. With its pretty pink color and inviting raspberry sorbet flavor, this is very drinkable. It's light in body and delicately structured, with some slight sweetness in the finish. **85** *—S.H. (7/1/2007)*

Cline 2003 Small Berry Mourvèdre (Contra Costa County) $35. 89 *—S.H. (11/1/2005)*

Cline 1997 Small Berry Mourvèdre (Contra Costa County) $24. 91 *—S.H. (10/1/1999)*

Cline 2004 Pinot Grigio-Chardonnay (California) $10. 84 Best Buy *—S.H. (11/1/2005)*

Cline 2003 fiveREDS Red Blend (California) $9. 85 Best Buy *—S.H. (12/15/2006)*

Cline 2002 Oakley Five Reds Red Blend (California) $11. 86 Best Buy *—S.H. (4/1/2005)*

Cline 1998 Roussanne (Carneros) $18. 89 *—S.H. (6/1/1999)*

Cline 2005 Syrah (California) $10. Clumsy and awkward, with candied LifeSaver flavors and a sour finish. **80** *—S.H. (11/15/2007)*

Cline 2004 Syrah (California) $10. 84 *—S.H. (12/15/2006)*

Cline 2003 Syrah (California) $10. 86 Best Buy *—S.H. (12/31/2005)*

Cline 2002 Syrah (California) $11. 85 *—S.H. (4/1/2005)*

Cline 2002 Syrah (Carneros) $20. 87 *—S.H. (6/1/2004)*

Cline 2001 Syrah (Sonoma County) $14. 87 *—S.H. (6/1/2004)*

Cline 2001 Syrah (California) $10. 86 Best Buy *—S.H. (6/1/2004)*

Cline 2000 Syrah (Sonoma County) $15. 87 *—S.H. (12/1/2002)*

Cline 2000 Syrah (California) $8. 83 *—S.H. (12/1/2002)*

Cline 2000 Syrah (Carneros) $22. 90 *—S.H. (12/1/2002)*

Cline 1999 Syrah (California) $10. 85 *(10/1/2001)*

Cline 1997 Syrah (Carneros) $20. 88 *—S.H. (6/1/1999)*

Cline 2004 Cool Climate Syrah (Sonoma Coast) $16. 84 *—S.H. (12/15/2006)*

Cline 1999 Los Carneros Syrah (Carneros) $23. 88 *(11/1/2001)*

Cline 2006 Viognier (California) $12. Sweet and simple, with jellied apricot, peach and vanilla flavors, and a honeysuckle finish. **82** *—S.H. (11/15/2007)*

Cline 2004 Viognier (Sonoma County) $10. 85 Best Buy *—S.H. (11/1/2005)*

Cline 2001 Viognier (Sonoma County) $16. 84 *—S.H. (5/1/2003)*

Cline 2000 Viognier (Sonoma County) $18. 80 *—J.M. (12/15/2002)*

Cline 1998 Viognier (Carneros) $18. 89 *—S.H. (6/1/1999)*

Cline 2002 Four Whites White Blend (California) $11. 85 *—S.H. (2/1/2005)*

Cline 2000 Oakley Vin Blanc White Blend (California) $9. 84 *—J.M. (11/15/2001)*

Cline 2006 Zinfandel (California) $10. This Zin tastes sweet, with white sugared blackberry and cherry juice and green mint jelly flavors. **82** *—S.H. (11/15/2007)*

Cline 2003 Zinfandel (California) $10. 86 Best Buy *—S.H. (11/1/2005)*

Cline 2001 Zinfandel (California) $10. 86 Best Buy *(11/1/2003)*

Cline 1999 Zinfandel (California) $10. 87 Best Buy *(3/1/2001)*

Cline 2006 Ancient Vines Zinfandel (Contra Costa County) $18. Too sweet and simple, this wine has sugary flavors of blackberry, cherry and raspberry jam. **86** *—S.H. (12/1/2007)*

Cline 2005 Ancient Vines Zinfandel (Contra Costa County) $16. 85 *—S.H. (12/15/2006)*

Cline 2004 Ancient Vines Zinfandel (California) $18. 90 *—S.H. (11/1/2005)*

Cline 2003 Ancient Vines Zinfandel (California) $18. 87 *—S.H. (4/1/2005)*

Cline 1999 Ancient Vines Zinfandel (California) $23. 84 *—D.T. (3/1/2002)*

Cline 1998 Ancient Vines Zinfandel (California) $23. 89 *—P.G. (3/1/2001)*

Cline 1997 Ancient Vines Zinfandel (Contra Costa County) $18. 89 *—S.H. (9/1/1999)*

Cline 2003 Big Break Zinfandel (Contra Costa County) $25. 83 *—S.H. (11/1/2005)*

Cline 2001 Big Break Zinfandel (Contra Costa County) $28. 88 *(11/1/2003)*

Cline 1998 Big Break Vineyard Zinfandel (Contra Costa County) $28. 93 *—P.G. (3/1/2001)*

Cline 1997 Big Break Zinfandel (Contra Costa County) $25. 90 *—S.H. (9/1/1999)*

Cline 2003 Bridgehead Zinfandel (Contra Costa County) $25. 86 *—S.H. (11/1/2005)*

Cline 2001 Bridgehead Zinfandel (Contra Costa County) $28. 90 *(11/1/2003)*

Cline 1999 Bridgehead Vineyard Zinfandel (Contra Costa County) $28. 86 *—D.T. (3/1/2002)*

Cline 1999 Fulton Road Vineyard Zinfandel (Russian River Valley) $28. 87 *—D.T. (3/1/2002)*

Cline 2003 Live Oak Zinfandel (Contra Costa County) $25. 83 *—S.H. (11/1/2005)*

Cline 2001 Live Oak Zinfandel (Contra Costa County) $28. 89 *(11/1/2003)*

Cline 1999 Live Oak Zinfandel (Contra Costa County) $28. 90 *—D.T. (3/1/2002)*

Cline 1998 Live Oak Vineyard Zinfandel (Contra Costa County) $28. 93 *—P.G. (3/1/2001)*

Cline 1997 Live Oak Vineyard Zinfandel (Contra Costa County) $28. 92 *—S.H. (5/1/2000)*

CLINTON

Clinton 1999 Seyval Blanc (Hudson River Region) $13. 83 *—J.C. (1/1/2004)*

Clinton NV Jubilee Seyval Blanc (Hudson River Region) $30. 83 *—J.C. (12/1/2001)*

CLOCKSPRING

Clockspring 2003 Zinfandel (Amador County) $8. 84 Best Buy *—S.H. (3/1/2006)*

CLONINGER

Cloninger 1998 Quinn Vineyard Cabernet Sauvignon (Carmel Valley) $18. 86 *—S.H. (5/1/2001)*

Cloninger 1999 Chardonnay (Santa Lucia Highlands) $16. 87 *—S.H. (5/1/2001)*

Cloninger 2000 Estate Grown Chardonnay (Santa Lucia Highlands) $16. 88 *—S.H. (5/1/2003)*

Cloninger 1999 Pinot Noir (Monterey) $23. 87 *(10/1/2002)*

Cloninger 1997 Jardini Vineyard. Pinot Noir (Monterey County) $22. 81 *(10/1/1999)*

CLOS DU BOIS

Clos du Bois 1999 Marlstone Bordeaux Blend (Alexander Valley) $39. 91 *—S.H. (10/1/2003)*

Clos du Bois 1996 Marlstone Vineyard Bordeaux Blend (Sonoma County) $30. 84 *(7/1/2000)*

Clos du Bois 2003 Marlstone Cabernet Blend (Alexander Valley) $50. 85 *—S.H. (12/15/2006)*

Clos du Bois 2002 Marlstone Cabernet Blend (Alexander Valley) $50. 83 *—S.H. (12/1/2005)*

Clos du Bois 2001 Marlstone Cabernet Blend (Alexander Valley) $50. 87 *(6/1/2005)*

Clos du Bois 2003 Cabernet Sauvignon (Sonoma County) $18. Tough, dry and rustic, a difficult wine that's flat and raisiny. **81** *—S.H. (2/1/2007)*

Clos du Bois 2001 Cabernet Sauvignon (Sonoma County) $17. 84 *—S.H. (6/1/2005)*

Clos du Bois 2000 Cabernet Sauvignon (Sonoma County) $17. 85 *—S.H. (4/1/2003)*

Clos du Bois 1999 Cabernet Sauvignon (Sonoma County) $17. 84 *—S.H. (12/31/2001)*

Clos du Bois 1996 Cabernet Sauvignon (Sonoma County) $15. 83 *—S.H. (7/1/1999)*

Clos du Bois 2003 Briarcrest Cabernet Sauvignon (Alexander Valley) $40. Seems stretched of late, the blackberry fruit thinned down with herbs and green mint. While the wine has a lovely, polished texture, the lack of concentration disappoints. **84** *—S.H. (4/1/2007)*

Clos du Bois 2002 Briarcrest Cabernet Sauvignon (Alexander Valley) $36. 83 *—S.H. (12/1/2005)*

Clos du Bois 2001 Briarcrest Cabernet Sauvignon (Alexander Valley) $40. 89 *(6/1/2005)*

Clos du Bois 1999 Briarcrest Cabernet Sauvignon (Alexander Valley) $36. 89 *—S.H. (10/1/2003)*

Clos du Bois 2002 Reserve Cabernet Sauvignon (Alexander Valley) $22. 90 *—S.H. (12/1/2005)*

Clos du Bois 1999 Reserve Cabernet Sauvignon (Alexander Valley) $22. 88 *—S.H. (6/1/2002)*

Clos du Bois 1997 Reserve Cabernet Sauvignon (Sonoma County) $20. 87 *—S.H. (2/1/2000)*

Clos du Bois 1997 Winemaker's Reserve Cabernet Sauvignon (Alexander Valley) $50. 87 *—S.H. (12/1/2001)*

Clos du Bois 1995 Winemaker's Reserve Cabernet Sauvignon (Sonoma County) $50. 88 *—J.C. (7/1/1999)*

Clos du Bois 2005 Chardonnay (North Coast) $14. Pretty good everyday Chard, with a lemon twist and date nut bread edge to the peaches and cream flavors. Finishes with a touch of honeyed sweetness. 84 *—S.H. (6/1/2007)*

Clos du Bois 2004 Chardonnay (North Coast) $12. 83 *—S.H. (12/1/2005)*

Clos du Bois 2003 Chardonnay (North Coast) $12. 85 *—S.H. (5/1/2005)*

Clos du Bois 2002 Chardonnay (Sonoma County) $14. 87 *—S.H. (12/15/2003)*

Clos du Bois 2001 Chardonnay (Sonoma County) $14. 86 *—S.H. (12/15/2002)*

Clos du Bois 2000 Chardonnay (Sonoma County) $14. 86 *—S.H. (11/15/2001)*

Clos du Bois 1999 Chardonnay (Sonoma County) $14. 86 *—S.H. (11/15/2000)*

Clos du Bois 1998 Chardonnay (Sonoma County) $14. 86 *—S.H. (12/31/1999)*

Clos du Bois 1998 Chardonnay (Sonoma County) $16. 87 *—L.W. (12/31/1999)*

Clos du Bois 2005 Calcaire Chardonnay (Russian River Valley) $30. This is not the Calcaire that was so famous years ago. It feels stretched and pulled and thin, like a Chard one third its price. Barrel fermentation and sur lies aging are all very nice, but the fruit just isn't there to justify this price. 84 *—S.H. (9/1/2007)*

Clos du Bois 2003 Calcaire Chardonnay (Russian River Valley) $22. 89 *—S.H. (12/1/2005)*

Clos du Bois 2000 Calcaire Chardonnay (Alexander Valley) $22. 90 *—S.H. (2/1/2003)*

Clos du Bois 1998 Calcaire Vineyard Chardonnay (Sonoma County) $20. 87 *(6/1/2000)*

Clos du Bois 1999 Flintwood Chardonnay (Dry Creek Valley) $22. 91 **Editors' Choice** *—S.H. (2/1/2003)*

Clos du Bois 1997 Flintwood Vineyard Chardonnay (Dry Creek Valley) $22. 86 *(6/1/2000)*

Clos du Bois 2005 Reserve Chardonnay (Russian River Valley) $17. Decent everyday Chard, but disappointingly thin, especially for a reserve. All the parts are here, from the creamy mouthfeel and oak to the pineapple and nectarine flavors, but it's like a photocopy of a photocopy. 84 *—S.H. (9/1/2007)*

Clos du Bois 2004 Reserve Chardonnay (Russian River Valley) $20. 87 *—S.H. (12/1/2006)*

Clos du Bois 2003 Reserve Chardonnay (Russian River Valley) $16. 87 *(6/1/2005)*

Clos du Bois 2000 Reserve Chardonnay (Alexander Valley) $16. 88 *—S.H. (9/1/2002)*

Clos du Bois 1999 Reserve Chardonnay (Sonoma County) $16. 84 *—S.H. (2/1/2001)*

Clos du Bois 1998 Reserve Chardonnay (Sonoma County) $16. 85 *—S.H. (2/1/2000)*

Clos du Bois 2004 Merlot (North Coast) $18. Here's a nice drinking young wine that's dry, fruity and soft. It has cherry-berry flavors, with a streak of herbs, mint and a touch of oak. 84 *—S.H. (6/1/2007)*

Clos du Bois 2003 Merlot (Sonoma County) $18. There's some ripe, forward blackberry and cherry jam and chocolate flavors here, and the wine is fully dry. But it has a sharpness, a raw, green minty acidity, that detracts, making the wine a bit pricy for what you get. 83 *—S.H. (2/1/2007)*

Clos du Bois 2000 Merlot (Sonoma County) $18. 87 *—S.H. (4/1/2003)*

Clos du Bois 1999 Merlot (Sonoma County) $18. 82 *—S.H. (7/1/2002)*

Clos du Bois 1998 Merlot (Sonoma County) $17. 84 *—J.C. (6/1/2001)*

Clos du Bois 1997 Merlot (Sonoma County) $17. 83 *(3/1/2000)*

Clos du Bois 2004 Reserve Merlot (Alexander Valley) $22. There is lots to like in this dry, complex young Merlot. It's as fresh as can be in just-picked red and black cherries and juicy blueberries and blackberries, with a dusting of cocoa and cinnamon. It's too forward for aging, but is a lovely sipper now. 87 *—S.H. (6/1/2007)*

Clos du Bois 2003 Reserve Merlot (Alexander Valley) $22. Clos du Bois over the years has not produced great Merlot, but that may be changing, to judge from this wine, their best Merlot ever. It's lush and dry, with ripe blackberry and cherry pie filling and dark chocolate flavors. Yet it's not simple, offering layers of herbs, spices and oak and a good interplay of acids and tannins. 90 *—S.H. (2/1/2007)*

Clos du Bois 2002 Reserve Merlot (Alexander Valley) $22. 87 *(6/1/2005)*

Clos du Bois 1998 Reserve Merlot (Sonoma County) $22. 89 *—S.H. (6/1/2001)*

Clos du Bois 1997 Reserve Merlot (Sonoma County) $22. 85 *—S.H. (3/1/2000)*

Clos du Bois 2006 Pinot Grigio (California) $14. With no oak, you get PG's crisp acids and pure citrus and honeysuckle flavors in a clean wine that finishes with a touch of sweetness. The acids testify to the wine's coastal origins. 85 *—S.H. (11/15/2007)*

Clos du Bois 2005 Pinot Grigio (California) $14. 85 *—S.H. (11/1/2006)*

Clos du Bois 2004 Pinot Grigio (California) $12. 85 *(6/1/2005)*

Clos du Bois 2004 Pinot Noir (Sonoma County) $16. This is a good starter Pinot for those curious about the variety and don't wish to spend a lot. The wine shows a very nice character, with cherry, cola, coffee and herb flavors and a dry, silky mouthfeel. 85 *—S.H. (3/1/2007)*

Clos du Bois 2003 Pinot Noir (Sonoma County) $16. 85 *(6/1/2005)*

Clos du Bois 2001 Pinot Noir (Sonoma County) $17. 84 *—S.H. (7/1/2003)*

Clos du Bois 2000 Pinot Noir (Sonoma County) $17. 86 *—S.H. (12/15/2001)*

Clos du Bois 1999 Pinot Noir (Sonoma County) $17. 86 *—S.H. (5/1/2001)*

Clos du Bois 2004 Appellation Reserve Series Reserve Pinot Noir (Sonoma Coast) $22. Last year's bottling was wonderfully rich. The '04 is more streamlined and minerally, and drier, too. The cherries, cola and rhubarb are there, and the finish is elegant and dry, but the wine is on the lean side. Just shows the importance of vintage in Pinot Noir. 87 *—S.H. (2/1/2007)*

Clos du Bois 2005 Reserve Pinot Noir (Sonoma Coast) $24. Decent Pinot-esque wine, with good coastal acidity and a silky delicacy to the mouthfeel, but needs richer flavors. Shows suggestions of cherries, pomegranates and cola that are disappointingly thin. 84 *—S.H. (9/1/2007)*

Clos du Bois 2003 Reserve Pinot Noir (Sonoma Coast) $22. 88 *(6/1/2005)*

Clos du Bois 2006 Riesling (California) $12. Plays it right down the middle for your standard everyday German-style Riesling. With crisp acids framing apple and honeysuckle flavors, it finishes just off-dry, and very, very clean. Mainly from Monterey fruit. 84 *—S.H. (9/1/2007)*

Clos du Bois 2006 Rosé Blend (Sonoma County) $12. This Syrah and Bordeaux blend is crisp and dry, with modest cherry, watermelon and raspberry flavors. A punch of spice on the finish adds complexity. 84 *—S.H. (11/15/2007)*

Clos du Bois 2005 Sauvignon Blanc (North Coast) $14. Most of the grapes are from Sonoma County, but a portion are from neighboring Lake, and you can taste that deeply figgy, spiced cantaloupe, zingy fruit. The acidity is refreshing, and there's a touch of creamy oak in the finish. 85 *—S.H. (2/1/2007)*

Clos du Bois 2003 Sauvignon Blanc (North Coast) $12. 84 *(6/1/2005)*

Clos du Bois 2001 Sauvignon Blanc (North Coast) $10. 85 *—S.H. (3/1/2003)*

Clos du Bois 2000 Sauvignon Blanc (North Coast) $10. 85 *—S.H. (11/15/2001)*

Clos du Bois 1998 Sauvignon Blanc (Sonoma County) $9. 84 *—S.H. (9/1/1999)*

Clos du Bois 2003 Shiraz (Sonoma County) $14. Not much going on with this dry, sharp, weedy wine. It shows modest cherry flavors, but is mostly thin and tart. 82 *—S.H. (2/1/2007)*

Clos du Bois 2003 Shiraz (Sonoma County) $15. 85 *(9/1/2005)*

Clos du Bois 2002 Shiraz (Sonoma County) $12. 85 *(9/1/2005)*

Clos du Bois 1996 Shiraz (Sonoma County) $16. 87 *—S.H. (6/1/1999)*

Clos du Bois 1998 Reserve Shiraz (Sonoma County) $16. 85 *(10/1/2001)*

Clos du Bois 1997 Reserve Shiraz (Sonoma County) $16. 88 *—S.H. (2/1/2000)*

Clos du Bois 2004 Reserve Tempranillo (Alexander Valley) $23. Clos du Bois is one of the few wineries that's trying to figure out Tempranillo. Nobody really knows what this Spanish variety is capable of in California. This wine is soft, dry and fairly simple, with upfront cherry liqueur flavors. 86 *—S.H. (10/1/2007)*

Clos du Bois 2003 Reserve Tempranillo (Alexander Valley) $23. Clos du Bois has been quietly working on this Spanish variety for years now, and the wine is showing results. It's a light-bodied, dry, soft wine, with cherry flavors and an earthy undertow of mushrooms and chocolate. The next step is greater complexity and depth. 86 *—S.H. (2/1/2007)*

Clos du Bois 2002 Reserve Tempranillo (Alexander Valley) $22. 88 *(6/1/2005)*

Clos du Bois 2004 Zinfandel (North Coast) $14. A good everyday Zin, with lots of fresh, ripe cherry, raspberry and blackberry fruit accented with a generous dusting of spice. Finishes dry and clean. **86** —*S.H. (6/1/2007)*

Clos du Bois 1999 Zinfandel (Sonoma County) $14. 84 —*S.H. (7/1/2002)*

Clos du Bois 1997 Zinfandel (Sonoma County) $14. 84 *(2/1/2000)*

Clos du Bois 2004 Reserve Zinfandel (Dry Creek Valley) $22. Tames Zin's wild, briary side without restraining its exuberance. Shows the variety's ripe cherry-berry, cola, cocoa, coffee and spice flavors, wrapped into an elegantly dry texture, finished with a clean scour of fresh, fruity acidity. **88** —*S.H. (6/1/2007)*

Clos du Bois 2000 Reserve Zinfandel (Dry Creek Valley) $22. 90 —*S.H. (2/1/2003)*

Clos du Bois 1999 Reserve Zinfandel (Dry Creek Valley) $22. 90 —*S.H. (7/1/2002)*

CLOS DU LAC

Clos du Lac 2001 Estate Petite Verdot (Amador County) $20. 84 —*S.H. (10/1/2004)*

Clos du Lac 2001 Sangiovese (Amador County) $14. 83 —*S.H. (12/15/2004)*

Clos du Lac 2001 Sauvignon Blanc (Amador County) $20. 85 —*S.H. (10/1/2003)*

Clos du Lac 1997 Syrah (California) $12. 88 Best Buy *(5/1/2000)*

Clos du Lac 2001 Syrah (Amador County) $12. 84 —*S.H. (12/15/2004)*

Clos du Lac 2001 Ghirardelli Vineyard Zinfandel (Calaveras County) $20. 87 —*S.H. (12/15/2004)*

Clos du Lac 2001 Kane Vineyard Zinfandel (Amador County) $20. 86 —*S.H. (3/1/2004)*

Clos du Lac 2002 Potter Vineyard Zinfandel (Shenandoah Valley (CA)) $20. 84 —*S.H. (3/1/2005)*

Clos du Lac 1998 Potter Vineyard Zinfandel (Shenandoah Valley (CA)) $18. 89 —*P.G. (3/1/2001)*

Clos du Lac 2001 Reserve Blend Zinfandel (Amador County) $16. 87 —*S.H. (12/15/2004)*

USA

CLOS DU VAL

Clos du Val 2001 Ariadne Bordeaux Blend (Napa Valley) $32. 91 —*S.H. (10/1/2003)*

Clos du Val 2001 Reserve Cabernet Franc (Stags Leap District) $85. 89 —*S.H. (12/31/2004)*

Clos du Val 2004 Cabernet Sauvignon (Napa Valley) $32. Tastes sweet and jammy in fruit, with cherry-blackberry, cocoa and cedar flavors and satin-smooth tannins. Finishes with a bite of tartness. Could age for 6–8 years. 34,000 cases produced. **87** —*S.H. (7/1/2007)*

Clos du Val 2003 Cabernet Sauvignon (Napa Valley) $30. 87 —*S.H. (11/1/2006)*

Clos du Val 2002 Cabernet Sauvignon (Napa Valley) $28. 85 —*S.H. (10/1/2005)*

Clos du Val 2001 Cabernet Sauvignon (Napa Valley) $28. 90 —*S.H. (11/15/2004)*

Clos du Val 2000 Cabernet Sauvignon (Napa Valley) $28. 89 —*S.H. (8/1/2003)*

Clos du Val 1999 Cabernet Sauvignon (Napa Valley) $29. 88 —*J.M. (6/1/2002)*

Clos du Val 1998 Cabernet Sauvignon (Stags Leap District) $55. 90 —*S.H. (12/1/2001)*

Clos du Val 1997 Cabernet Sauvignon (Stags Leap District) $48. 90 *(11/1/2000)*

Clos du Val 1995 Cabernet Sauvignon (Napa Valley) $24. 85 —*S.H. (6/1/1999)*

Clos du Val 2003 Oak Vineyard Cabernet Sauvignon (Stags Leap District) $62. Here's one for the cellar. Still youthful, the wine brims with fresh acids and dry tannins that leave behind an astringent finish. Clos du Val Cabernets age well over decades, and this one stays true to the winery's Médoc-oriented vision, marching to its own beat in an age of drink-me-now wines. Stash until 2009, at least. **90 Cellar Selection** —*S.H. (12/1/2007)*

Clos du Val 2002 Oak Vineyard Cabernet Sauvignon (Stags Leap District) $62. 85 *(9/1/2006)*

Clos du Val 2001 Oak Vineyard Cabernet Sauvignon (Stags Leap District) $62. 91 —*S.H. (10/3/2004)*

Clos du Val 2000 Oak Vineyard Cabernet Sauvignon (Stags Leap District) $62. 91 —*S.H. (11/15/2003)*

Clos du Val 1999 Palisade Vineyard Cabernet Sauvignon (Stags Leap District) $62. 92 —*C.S. (11/15/2002)*

Clos du Val 2002 Reserve Cabernet Sauvignon (Napa Valley) $95. 92 Cellar Selection —*S.H. (12/15/2006)*

Clos du Val 2001 Reserve Cabernet Sauvignon (Napa Valley) $95. 90 Cellar Selection —*S.H. (12/15/2005)*

Clos du Val 2000 Reserve Cabernet Sauvignon (Napa Valley) $95. 91 —*S.H. (12/31/2004)*

Clos du Val 1999 Reserve Cabernet Sauvignon (Napa Valley) $95. 94 Editors' Choice —*S.H. (11/15/2003)*

Clos du Val 1998 Reserve Cabernet Sauvignon (Napa Valley) $95. 91 —*S.H. (11/15/2002)*

Clos du Val 1997 Reserve Cabernet Sauvignon (Napa Valley) $90. 92 —*S.H. (3/1/2003)*

Clos du Val 1995 Reserve Cabernet Sauvignon (Napa Valley) $65. 92 —*L.W. (10/1/1999)*

Clos du Val 1998 Vineyard Georges III Cabernet Sauvignon (Rutherford) $55. 94 —*S.H. (12/1/2001)*

Clos du Val 1997 Vineyard Georges III Cabernet Sauvignon (Rutherford) $48. 94 *(11/1/2000)*

Clos du Val 2005 Chardonnay (Napa Valley) $22. Dull and soft, dominated by charry oak that covers simple peach and pear syrup flavors. 13,000 cases produced. **82** —*S.H. (7/1/2007)*

Clos du Val 2004 Chardonnay (Napa Valley) $22. 84 —*S.H. (11/1/2006)*

Clos du Val 2003 Chardonnay (Napa Valley) $21. 91 Editors' Choice —*S.H. (10/1/2005)*

Clos du Val 2002 Chardonnay (Napa Valley) $21. 85 —*S.H. (11/15/2004)*

Clos du Val 2001 Chardonnay (Napa Valley) $21. 88 —*S.H. (6/1/2003)*

Clos du Val 2000 Chardonnay (Napa Valley) $23. 88 —*J.M. (5/1/2002)*

Clos du Val 2001 Carneros Vineyard Reserve Chardonnay (Carneros) $46. 87 —*S.H. (12/15/2003)*

Clos du Val 2005 Reserve Chardonnay (Napa Valley) $42. This big Chardonnay, which was entirely barrel fermented, is tasting a bit too oaky. It was sourced from the winery's estate Carneros vineyard and shows that appellation's crisp acids, along with bright tropical fruit and spice flavors. But the sweet, charry vanilla and caramel from barrels tends to dominate. **88** —*S.H. (12/15/2007)*

Clos du Val 2004 Reserve Chardonnay (Carneros) $42. 87 —*S.H. (12/15/2006)*

Clos du Val 2000 Reserve Chardonnay (Carneros) $39. M92 —*S.H. (12/15/2002)*

Clos du Val 1998 Single Vineyard Chardonnay (Carneros) $21. 88 *(6/1/2000)*

Clos du Val 2004 Merlot (Napa Valley) $26. Shows fine qualities, from the balanced, rich mouthfeel to the cherry, violet and cocoa flavors to the long, spicy finish. Plenty of restrained elegance and finesse in this dry, polished Merlot. Drink now. **88** —*S.H. (7/1/2007)*

Clos du Val 2003 Merlot (Napa Valley) $25. 90 —*S.H. (11/1/2006)*

Clos du Val 2002 Merlot (Napa Valley) $25. 88 —*S.H. (10/1/2005)*

Clos du Val 2001 Merlot (Napa Valley) $25. 90 —*S.H. (12/15/2004)*

Clos du Val 2000 Merlot (Napa Valley) $25. 88 —*S.H. (8/1/2003)*

Clos du Val 1999 Merlot (Napa Valley) $25. 87 —*J.M. (6/1/2002)*

Clos du Val 2005 Pinot Noir (Carneros) $28. Despite some good cherry-cola fruit and an overlay of vanilla and toast from new oak, this is fairly one-dimensional. It's easy, gentle, silky and proper, but is fundamentally an everyday wine. **85** —*S.H. (7/1/2007)*

Clos du Val 2004 Pinot Noir (Carneros) $24. 82 —*S.H. (11/1/2006)*

Clos du Val 2003 Pinot Noir (Napa Valley) $24. 84 —*S.H. (10/1/2005)*

Clos du Val 2002 Pinot Noir (Napa Valley) $24. 86 —*S.H. (11/1/2004)*

Clos du Val 2002 Pinot Noir (Carneros) $24. 86 *(11/1/2004)*

Clos du Val 2000 Pinot Noir (Carneros) $38. 91 Editors' Choice *(10/1/2002)*

Clos du Val 2001 Carneros Vineyard Pinot Noir (Napa Valley) $38. 86 —*S.H. (2/1/2004)*

Clos du Val 2004 Reserve Pinot Noir (Carneros) $46. The '04 is close to the '03 in quality, but falls off in structure, no doubt due to the hot vintage. It's a little too soft to balance the cola and cherry pie-filling flavors. Still, it's elegant. **87** —*S.H. (12/15/2007)*

Clos du Val 2003 Reserve Pinot Noir (Carneros) $42. 92 —*S.H. (12/15/2006)*

Clos du Val 1998 Single Vineyard Pinot Noir (Carneros) $26. 89 *—M.M. (12/15/2000)*

Clos du Val 2002 Ariadne Sémillon-Sauvignon Blanc (Napa Valley) $32. 89 *—J.M. (10/1/2004)*

Clos du Val 1999 White Blend (Napa Valley) $25. 87 *—S.H. (12/1/2001)*

Clos du Val 2000 Ariadne White Blend (Napa Valley) $32. 90 *—S.H. (12/15/2002)*

Clos du Val 1997 Zinfandel (Napa Valley) $17. 84 *—M.S. (5/1/2000)*

Clos du Val 1999 Palisade Vineyard Zinfandel (Stags Leap District) $28. 88 *—S.H. (12/15/2001)*

Clos du Val 1998 Palisade Vineyard Zinfandel (Stags Leap District) $25. 87 *—S.H. (12/1/2000)*

Clos du Val 1997 Palisade Vineyard Zinfandel (Stags Leap District) $17. 80 *—P.G. (11/15/1999)*

Clos du Val 2001 Reserve Zinfandel (Stags Leap District) $55. 87 *(11/1/2003)*

CLOS LA CHANCE

Clos La Chance 2000 Cabernet Franc (Central Coast) $35. 86 *—S.H. (11/15/2003)*

Clos La Chance 1997 Cabernet Franc (Santa Cruz Mountains) $32. 85 *—S.H. (2/1/2001)*

Clos La Chance 2004 Estate Cabernet Franc (Central Coast) $35. Dry and balanced, but with a tough, raw streak that seems to come from unripe grapes. You want a soft opulence in Cab Franc, and even with some modest cherry flavors, this one doesn't have it. 84 *—S.H. (5/1/2007)*

Clos La Chance 2002 Cabernet Sauvignon (Napa Valley) $25. 85 *—S.H. (5/1/2005)*

Clos La Chance 2001 Cabernet Sauvignon (Napa Valley) $25. 84 *—S.H. (6/1/2004)*

Clos La Chance 2000 Cabernet Sauvignon (Napa Valley) $23. 86 *—S.H. (4/1/2003)*

Clos La Chance 1997 Cabernet Sauvignon (Santa Cruz Mountains) $21. 91 *—S.H. (7/1/2000)*

Clos La Chance 2005 Ruby-Throated Cabernet Sauvignon (Central Coast) $18. This easy-drinking Cab from the southern Salinas Valley comes down on the ripely fruity side, with upfront blackberry, cola and cherry flavors that finish in a swirl of spice. Has a firm grip of sandpapery tannins that calls for roasts, grilled meats and similar fare. 85 *—S.H. (11/1/2007)*

Clos La Chance 2004 Ruby-Throated Cabernet Sauvignon (Central Coast) $18. There's nothing hummingbirdy about this big, full-bodied, superripe wine. It trades elegance for sheer size, with fruit that veers into raisins, and a semisweet, medicinal finish. 82 *—S.H. (2/1/2007)*

Clos La Chance 2003 Ruby-Throated Cabernet Sauvignon (Central Coast) $17. 85 *—S.H. (3/1/2006)*

Clos La Chance 2005 Chardonnay (Santa Cruz Mountains) $18. Made in a leaner, crisper style, this Chard has citrus, floral and tart green apple flavors with a steely minerality. It's a very balanced wine that won't overshadow cracked crab or roasted chicken with rice. 86 *—S.H. (5/1/2007)*

Clos La Chance 2004 Chardonnay (Santa Cruz Mountains) $18. 84 *—S.H. (11/1/2006)*

Clos La Chance 2003 Chardonnay (Santa Cruz Mountains) $19. 85 *—S.H. (11/15/2005)*

Clos La Chance 2002 Chardonnay (Santa Cruz Mountains) $18. 86 *—S.H. (6/1/2004)*

Clos La Chance 2001 Chardonnay (Santa Cruz Mountains) $18. 91 Editors' Choice *—S.H. (10/1/2003)*

Clos La Chance 2000 Chardonnay (Santa Cruz Mountains) $19. 90 Editors' Choice *—S.H. (5/1/2003)*

Clos La Chance 2000 Chardonnay (Napa Valley) $18. 90 Editors' Choice *—S.H. (12/15/2002)*

Clos La Chance 1998 Chardonnay (Santa Cruz Mountains) $19. 87 *(6/1/2000)*

Clos La Chance 1998 Chardonnay (Napa Valley) $18. 88 *(6/1/2000)*

Clos La Chance 1997 Chardonnay (Santa Cruz Mountains) $19. 90 *—J.C. (11/15/1999)*

Clos La Chance 1997 Chardonnay (Napa Valley) $18. 90 *—J.C. (11/15/1999)*

Clos La Chance NV Amber's Cuvée Chardonnay (Santa Cruz Mountains) $30. 90 *—S.H. (12/1/2002)*

Clos La Chance 2004 Biagini Vineyard Chardonnay (Santa Cruz Mountains) $35. There's a rich, deep earthiness flowing underneath the fruit that's reminiscent of cured tobacco, a sweetly resinous note that complexes the pineapples and guavas. Add oaky creaminess and char, and you've got a really good Chardonnay. 90 *—S.H. (2/1/2007)*

Clos La Chance 2006 Glittering-Throated Emerald Chardonnay (Central Coast) $15. Shows what is becoming the classic profile of unoaked, cool-climate Chard. Clean, crisp and minerally, the wine shows high-toned flavors of ripe kiwis, limes, passionfruit, pineapples, green apples, vanilla and cinnamon-spice. A match for scallops with mango salsa. 87 *—S.H. (10/1/2007)*

Clos La Chance 2005 Glittering Throated Emerald Chardonnay (Monterey County) $15. 83 *—S.H. (11/15/2006)*

Clos La Chance 2004 Liebler Vineyard Chardonnay (Santa Cruz Mountains) $35. Really rich; a big, oaky Chardonnay that works because it's so balanced. Reams of ripe tropical fruits, gingerbread, vanilla custard, buttered toast, the works, and it's all framed in fine, citrusy acids. 90 *—S.H. (2/1/2007)*

Clos La Chance 2002 Vanumanutagi Vineyard Chardonnay (Santa Cruz County) $30. 87 *—S.H. (6/1/2004)*

Clos La Chance 2001 Vanumanutagi Vineyard Chardonnay (Santa Cruz Mountains) $30. 92 *—S.H. (6/1/2003)*

Clos La Chance 1999 Vanumanutagi Vineyard Chardonnay (Santa Cruz Mountains) $30. 89 *—J.M. (5/1/2002)*

Clos La Chance 2000 Vanumanutagi Vineyards Chardonnay (Santa Cruz Mountains) $30. 86 *—J.C. (9/1/2002)*

Clos La Chance 2003 Grenache (Central Coast) $29. 86 *—S.H. (12/31/2005)*

Clos La Chance 2002 Grenache (Central Coast) $20. 85 *—S.H. (3/1/2005)*

Clos La Chance 2004 Estate Grenache (Central Coast) $35. This is the winery's best Grenache ever. It's just enormous in the sweet, red fruit essence of cherries, with a raspberry and cocoa edge, but it's soundly dry. Shows that delicate, exciting dance between sheer power and elegance that defines great wine. 91 *—S.H. (5/1/2007)*

Clos La Chance 1997 Merlot (Central Coast) $17. 88 *—M.M. (3/1/2000)*

Clos La Chance 2002 Merlot (Central Coast) $18. 84 *—S.H. (6/1/2004)*

Clos La Chance 2001 Merlot (Central Coast) $18. 91 Editors' Choice *—S.H. (10/1/2003)*

Clos La Chance 2000 Merlot (Central Coast) $18. 86 *—S.H. (11/15/2002)*

Clos La Chance 2004 Violet-Crowned Merlot (Central Coast) $18. From a winery that names their wines after hummingbirds comes this Merlot. Hard to imagine a red wine getting fruitier and still remaining technically dry. Floods the mouth in melted cherry jam, blackberry marmalade, milk chocolate, blueberry and licorice flavors. Could use greater acidity, though, because it's a little flat. 85 *—S.H. (10/1/2007)*

Clos La Chance 2003 Violet-Crowned Merlot (Central Coast) $17. 86 *—S.H. (3/1/2006)*

Clos La Chance 2003 Petite Sirah (Central Coast) $35. 88 *—S.H. (12/31/2005)*

Clos La Chance 2005 Pinot Noir (Santa Cruz Mountains) $30. Starts out very light in mouthfeel, almost delicately simple, with such a dry, wispy texture that it feels almost inconsequential. Then you notice the flavors of cola, tart cherryskin, ripe rhubarb, coffee, Asian spices and caramelized oak. They mingle together in a complex swirl that makes you want another sip. 89 *—S.H. (11/1/2007)*

Clos La Chance 2004 Pinot Noir (Santa Cruz Mountains) $25. Nice, dry Pinot, a little thin but elegant enough with the silky texture and bright, crisp cool-climate acids. The flavors are of cola and rhubarb. Would score much higher if there was more there. 84 *—S.H. (2/1/2007)*

Clos La Chance 2002 Pinot Noir (Santa Cruz Mountains) $25. 87 *—S.H. (2/1/2005)*

Clos La Chance 2001 Pinot Noir (Santa Cruz County) $28. 88 *—S.H. (7/1/2003)*

Clos La Chance 1999 Pinot Noir (Santa Cruz Mountains) $28. 86 *(10/1/2002)*

Clos La Chance 1997 Pinot Noir (Santa Cruz Mountains) $24. 93 *(10/1/1999)*

Clos La Chance 2004 Biagini Vineyard Pinot Noir (Santa Cruz Mountains) $40. I love this Pinot. Just love it. It's so soft and sensual, so silky and velvety, and so balanced and dry. With a wealth of cola, pomegranate, persimmon, cherry, tea and spicy oak flavors, it's complex and delicious, a wine that reveals layer after layer. 92 *—S.H. (5/1/2007)*

Clos La Chance 2002 Biagini Vineyard Pinot Noir (Santa Cruz Mountains) $35. 88 *—S.H. (11/15/2005)*

Clos La Chance 2001 Erwin Vineyard Pinot Noir (Santa Cruz Mountains) $35. 89 *—S.H. (2/1/2005)*

Clos La Chance 1997 Erwin Vineyard Pinot Noir (Santa Cruz Mountains) $50. 89 *(10/1/2000)*

Clos La Chance 2005 Pink-Throated Brilliant Rosé Wine Rosé Blend (Central Coast) $14. 85 *—S.H. (11/1/2006)*

Clos La Chance 2004 Rose Wine Rosé Blend (Central Coast) $14. 85 *—S.H. (11/15/2005)*

Clos La Chance 2003 Sauvignon Blanc (Central Coast) $16. 84 *—S.H. (2/1/2005)*

Clos La Chance 2006 Estate Sauvignon Blanc (Central Coast) $16. I'd like to like this wine more than I do, because the acidity is brilliantly clean and scouring, which is a good thing, and the citrus, gooseberry, fig and wildflower flavors are very Marlborough-like. But the sugary finish is a letdown. **84** *—S.H. (10/1/2007)*

Clos La Chance 2005 Estate Sauvignon Blanc (Central Coast) $16. 83 *—S.H. (11/15/2006)*

Clos La Chance 2004 Estate Sauvignon Blanc (Central Coast) $16. 87 *—S.H. (11/15/2005)*

Clos La Chance 2002 Syrah (Central Coast) $18. 85 *—S.H. (2/1/2005)*

Clos La Chance 2001 Syrah (Central Coast) $20. 85 *—S.H. (12/15/2003)*

Clos La Chance 2000 Syrah (Paso Robles) $20. 90 Editors' Choice *—S.H. (12/1/2002)*

Clos La Chance 2004 Black-Chinned Syrah (Central Coast) $18. Rich and fruity, this Syrah, blended with some Grenache, offers palate-appealing cherry, chocolate, blackberry, blueberry, licorice and coffee flavors wrapped in a softly ripe package. It's not especially complex, but offers plenty of elegant deliciousness. **86** *—S.H. (5/1/2007)*

Clos La Chance 2003 Black-Chinned Syrah (Central Coast) $17. 83 *—S.H. (3/1/2006)*

Clos La Chance 2003 Viognier (Central Coast) $18. 85 *—S.H. (8/1/2005)*

Clos La Chance 2006 Estate Viognier (Central Coast) $20. The wine was half cool-fermented in steel, half in neutral barrels, a nice combination that lets the pure fruit flavors star, while juicing them with a tiny boost of smoke. Viognier's exotic style is emphasized, with rich tropical fruit and honeysuckle flavors, but the finish tastes like there's some residual sugar. **85** *—S.H. (10/1/2007)*

Clos La Chance 2005 Estate Viognier (Central Coast) $19. 83 *—S.H. (11/15/2006)*

Clos La Chance 2004 Estate Viognier (Central Coast) $18. 86 *—S.H. (11/15/2005)*

Clos La Chance 2002 Zinfandel (El Dorado County) $18. 87 *—S.H. (5/1/2005)*

Clos La Chance 2001 Zinfandel (El Dorado County) $20. 82 *(11/1/2003)*

Clos La Chance 1997 Zinfandel (El Dorado County) $17. 88 *(5/1/2000)*

Clos La Chance 2004 Buff-Bellied Zinfandel (Central Coast) $18. I didn't like the '03 or the '04 because they were too Porty. It smells and tastes like Port, with raisiny, stewed prune and fudgy flavors that flirt with sweetness. **82** *—S.H. (5/1/2007)*

Clos La Chance 2003 Buff-Bellied Zinfandel (Central Coast) $17. 82 *—S.H. (3/1/2006)*

Clos La Chance 2000 Twin Rivers Zinfandel (El Dorado County) $20. 89 *—S.H. (11/1/2002)*

CLOS MIMI

Clos Mimi 2001 Bunny Slope Vineyard Syrah (Paso Robles) $50. 83 *(9/1/2005)*

Clos Mimi 2000 Bunny Slope Vineyard Syrah (Paso Robles) $50. 90 *—S.H. (12/1/2003)*

Clos Mimi NV Nini Syrah (California) $13. 83 *—S.H. (3/1/2006)*

Clos Mimi 2004 Petite Rousse Syrah (Paso Robles) $18. Excessive sweetness in the finish mars this otherwise fine wine, with its plum, cherry and leather flavors and rich, sticky tannins. **82** *—S.H. (3/1/2006)*

Clos Mimi 2003 Petite Rousse Syrah (Paso Robles) $17. 85 *(9/1/2005)*

Clos Mimi 2002 Petite Rousse Red Wine Syrah (Paso Robles) $16. 91 *—S.H. (4/1/2004)*

CLOS PEGASE

Clos Pegase 2003 Cabernet Sauvignon (Napa Valley) $33. Tastes frankly sweet in sugary blackberry and cherry pie and chocolate fudge flavors that are framed in sweetly ripe, soft tannins. Kind of one-dimensional, it's a pretty, polished Cab for early drinking. **85** *—S.H. (5/1/2007)*

Clos Pegase 2002 Cabernet Sauvignon (Napa Valley) $33. 87 *—S.H. (5/1/2006)*

Clos Pegase 2001 Cabernet Sauvignon (Napa Valley) $32. 91 *—S.H. (3/1/2005)*

Clos Pegase 1999 Cabernet Sauvignon (Napa Valley) $33. 89 *—S.H. (6/1/2003)*

Clos Pegase 1997 Cabernet Sauvignon (Napa Valley) $30. 90 *(11/1/2000)*

Clos Pegase 1996 Cabernet Sauvignon (Napa Valley) $30. 88 *—M.M. (10/1/1999)*

Clos Pegase 2002 Graveyard Hill Vineyard Cabernet Sauvignon (Carneros) $60. This shows crisp acids and fine balance. It's huge in blackberry and cherry fruit, but has the structural integrity and finesse that, quite simply, make it a very great Cabernet Sauvignon. Drink now–2015. **96 Editors' Choice** *—S.H. (5/1/2007)*

Clos Pegase 2001 Graveyard Hill Cabernet Sauvignon (Carneros) $60. 91 Cellar Selection *—S.H. (12/15/2006)*

Clos Pegase 2000 Graveyard Hill Cabernet Sauvignon (Carneros) $60. 92 *—S.H. (3/1/2005)*

Clos Pegase 1999 Graveyard Hill Cabernet Sauvignon (Carneros) $60. 92 Cellar Selection *—S.H. (5/1/2003)*

Clos Pegase 2003 Hommage Cabernet Sauvignon (Napa Valley) $75. Fully dry and almost promiscuous in charry, sweet new oak, it has soft but complex tannins framing blackberry and cassis flavors. Elegant, but a little thin, so drink now. **89** *—S.H. (10/1/2007)*

Clos Pegase 2002 Hommage Cabernet Sauvignon (Napa Valley) $75. 91 *—S.H. (12/15/2006)*

Clos Pegase 2001 Hommage Cabernet Sauvignon (Napa Valley) $75. 91 *—S.H. (11/15/2005)*

Clos Pegase 1998 Hommage Cabernet Sauvignon (Napa Valley) $75. 84 *—D.T. (6/1/2002)*

Clos Pegase 2002 Palisades Vineyard Cabernet Sauvignon (Napa Valley) $60. One of the later-released Cabs from the excellent '02 vintage, this 100% Cabernet bottling, which comes from the winery's vineyard near Calistoga, is ultraripe, yet firm and balanced. It's showing beautifully now, with its wealth of blackberry, cherry, mushu sauce and cocoa flavors, but has the inherent balance for moderate, and possibly longterm, aging. **93 Cellar Selection** *—S.H. (5/1/2007)*

Clos Pegase 2001 Palisades Vineyard Cabernet Sauvignon (Napa Valley) $60. 94 Editors' Choice *—S.H. (12/15/2006)*

Clos Pegase 1999 Palisades Vineyard Cabernet Sauvignon (Napa Valley) $60. 91 *—S.H. (6/1/2003)*

Clos Pegase 2003 Artist Series Reserve Mitsuko's Vineyard Chardonnay (Napa-Carneros) $36. 92 *—S.H. (7/1/2006)*

Clos Pegase 1999 Hommage Artist Series Reserve Mitsuko's Chardonnay (Carneros) $36. 94 Editors' Choice *—S.H. (12/15/2002)*

Clos Pegase 2004 Hommage Mitsuko's Vineyard Chardonnay (Carneros) $40. This Hommage upholds the tradition for its ripe fruit and firm, dry structure. Tropical fruits, nectarines, apricots, peaches and toasty oak lead to a long, spicy, complex finish. **91** *—S.H. (5/1/2007)*

Clos Pegase 2001 Hommage Mitsuko's Vineyard Chardonnay (Carneros) $36. 92 *—S.H. (3/1/2005)*

Clos Pegase 2005 Mitsuko's Vineyard Chardonnay (Carneros) $24. A beautiful Chardonnay with powerful tropical fruit, lime, nectarine, apricot and new oak flavors. Firmer acidity than you usually get from Carneros. This is a sleek, elegant wine, with a bracing streak of steely minerality. Kudos to owner Jan Shrem for putting it into a screwcap. **90** *—S.H. (5/1/2007)*

Clos Pegase 2004 Mitsuko's Vineyard Chardonnay (Carneros) $21. 84 *—S.H. (5/1/2006)*

Clos Pegase 2003 Mitsuko's Vineyard Chardonnay (Carneros) $21. 90 *—S.H. (12/31/2005)*

Clos Pegase 2002 Mitsuko's Vineyard Chardonnay (Carneros) $21. 88 *—S.H. (4/1/2004)*

Clos Pegase 1997 Mitsuko's Vineyard Chardonnay (Carneros) $19. 91 *—S.H. (11/15/1999)*

Clos Pegase 2002 Mitsuko's Vineyard Hommage Chardonnay (Carneros) $36. 92 *—S.H. (12/15/2005)*

Clos Pegase 1998 Mitsuko's Vineyard Chardonnay (Carneros) $19. 86 *(6/1/2000)*

Clos Pegase 2003 Mitsuko's Vineyard Merlot (Carneros) $25. I like the dry balance, with its well-crafted tannins, brisk acidity and gentle touch of oak. But the taste is disappointingly thin, showing herb-dominated dill and tobacco, with just a splash of cherry fruit. **84** *—S.H. (10/1/2007)*

Clos Pegase 2002 Mitsuko's Vineyard Merlot (Carneros) $25. 86 *—S.H. (12/15/2006)*

Clos Pegase 2001 Mitsuko's Vineyard Merlot (Carneros) $25. 87 *—S.H. (12/15/2005)*

Clos Pegase 1999 Mitsuko's Vineyard Merlot (Carneros) $25. 94 Editors' Choice *—S.H. (11/15/2002)*

Clos Pegase 2000 Mitsuko's Vineyard Merlot (Carneros) $25. 85 *—S.H. (5/1/2004)*

Clos Pegase 2005 Mitsuko's Vineyard Pinot Noir (Carneros) $35. Pinots from this vineyard have been variable, but the '05 is one of the best in years. The long, cool vintage yielded exceptionally ripe grapes, rich in cherries, pomegranates, cola and root beer flavor, yet the wine maintains a delicately dry, crisp silkiness. With quite a bit of new oak, this is a delicious Pinot best enjoyed in the next few years. **91** *—S.H. (5/1/2007)*

Clos Pegase 2004 Mitsuko's Vineyard Pinot Noir (Carneros) $30. 85 *—S.H. (11/1/2006)*

Clos Pegase 2003 Mitsuko's Vineyard Pinot Noir (Carneros) $30. 89 *—S.H. (5/1/2006)*

Clos Pegase 2002 Mitsuko's Vineyard Pinot Noir (Carneros) $30. 86 *—S.H. (12/15/2005)*

Clos Pegase 2001 Mitsuko's Vineyard Pinot Noir (Carneros) $30. 92 *—S.H. (3/1/2005)*

Clos Pegase 2001 Mitsuko's Q Block Sauvignon Blanc (Carneros) $18. 88 *—S.H. (9/1/2003)*

Clos Pegase 2006 Mitsuko's Vineyard Sauvignon Blanc (Carneros) $20. This is one of the drier Sauvignon Blancs on the market, showing palate-cleansing acidity and citrus flavors that make it extremely drinkable. Modest oak aging adds a touch of creamy smoke to the pink grapefruit, lemongrass, lime and fig flavors. Made from the Musque clone, it's a truly elegant, sophisticated white wine. **90 Editors' Choice** *—S.H. (12/15/2007)*

Clos Pegase 2005 Mitsuko's Vineyard Sauvignon Blanc (Carneros) $19. 87 *—S.H. (12/15/2006)*

Clos Pegase 2004 Mitsuko's Vineyard Sauvignon Blanc (Carneros) $19. 90 *—S.H. (12/31/2005)*

Clos Pegase 2003 Mitsuko's Vineyard Sauvignon Blanc (Napa-Carneros) $19. 88 *—S.H. (5/1/2005)*

Clos Pegase 2002 Mitsuko's Vineyard Sauvignon Blanc (Carneros) $18. 88 *—S.H. (2/1/2004)*

CLOS PEPE

Clos Pepe 2001 Estate Barrel Fermented Chardonnay (Santa Rita Hills) $20. 89 *—S.H. (4/1/2004)*

Clos Pepe 2002 Homage to Chablis Chardonnay (Santa Rita Hills) $25. 91 *—S.H. (9/1/2004)*

Clos Pepe 2004 Pinot Noir (Santa Rita Hills) $45. Here's a very pure, expressive young Pinot, rich and tangy in forward cherry, cola, cranberry, herb tea and pomegranate flavors. It's likeable for its dryness and supple, silky mouthfeel. Drink this high-quality Pinot now–2010. **91** *—S.H. (6/1/2007)*

Clos Pepe 2002 Pinot Noir (Santa Rita Hills) $35. 85 *(11/1/2004)*

Clos Pepe 2000 Pinot Noir (Santa Rita Hills) $35. 89 *(10/1/2002)*

CLOS TITA

Clos Tita 1997 Cabernet Sauvignon (Santa Cruz Mountains) $22. 91 *—S.H. (2/1/2000)*

CLOUD 9

Cloud 9 2001 Composition Red Blend (California) $35. 91 *—S.H. (11/15/2005)*

Cloud 9 2000 Composition Tempranillo Blend (California) $65. 86 *—S.H. (12/15/2004)*

Cloud 9 2003 Seity Zinfandel (Amador County) $35. 90 *—S.H. (12/31/2005)*

Cloud 9 2001 Seity Zinfandel (Amador County) $35. 88 *—S.H. (12/15/2004)*

CLOUD VIEW

Cloud View 2001 Red Wine Bordeaux Blend (Napa Valley) $60. 91 *(6/6/2005)*

Cloud View 2002 Estate Red Blend (Napa Valley) $60. 87 *—S.H. (12/31/2005)*

COASTAL RIDGE

Coastal Ridge 2003 Cabernet Sauvignon (California) $7. 82 *—S.H. (9/1/2006)*

Coastal Ridge 2001 Cabernet Sauvignon (California) $7. 84 Best Buy *—S.H. (4/1/2005)*

Coastal Ridge 2000 Cabernet Sauvignon (California) $7. 86 Best Buy *—S.H. (11/15/2003)*

Coastal Ridge 1999 Cabernet Sauvignon (California) $7. 85 Best Buy *—S.H. (6/1/2002)*

Coastal Ridge 1998 Cabernet Sauvignon (California) $7. 81 *—S.H. (5/1/2001)*

Coastal Ridge 2005 Chardonnay (California) $7. Basic Chard, if thin, with just enough peaches and cream, vanilla and toast flavors to satisfy. **83** *—S.H. (10/1/2007)*

Coastal Ridge 2004 Chardonnay (California) $7. 83 *—S.H. (8/1/2006)*

Coastal Ridge 2002 Chardonnay (California) $7. 83 *—S.H. (11/15/2004)*

Coastal Ridge 1999 Chardonnay (California) $6. 85 Best Buy *—S.H. (5/1/2001)*

Coastal Ridge 2000 Barrel Aged Chardonnay (Napa County) $7. 84 *—S.H. (12/15/2002)*

Coastal Ridge 2004 Gewürztraminer (California) $7. 84 Best Buy *—S.H. (12/1/2005)*

Coastal Ridge 2004 Johannisberg Riesling (California) $7. 83 Best Buy *—S.H. (12/1/2005)*

Coastal Ridge 2003 Merlot (California) $7. 84 Best Buy *—S.H. (10/1/2005)*

Coastal Ridge 2002 Merlot (California) $7. 83 *—S.H. (4/1/2005)*

Coastal Ridge 2001 Merlot (Napa Valley) $7. 86 Best Buy *—S.H. (12/1/2003)*

Coastal Ridge 1998 Merlot (California) $7. 84 Best Buy *—S.H. (5/1/2001)*

Coastal Ridge 2004 Pinot Grigio (California) $7. 83 *—S.H. (7/1/2005)*

Coastal Ridge 2003 Pinot Noir (California) $7. 84 Best Buy *—S.H. (12/31/2005)*

Coastal Ridge 2005 Shiraz (California) $7. Tons of bottles of this easy, polished Syrah will wash down huge quantities of burgers, hot dogs and pizzas, and will make millions of people happy for the wine's cherry, cocoa and spice flavors and gentle tannins. **83** *—S.H. (10/1/2007)*

Coastal Ridge 2003 Shiraz (California) $7. 85 Best Buy *(9/1/2005)*

Coastal Ridge 2001 Shiraz (California) $7. 83 *—S.H. (12/1/2004)*

Coastal Ridge 2000 Shiraz (California) $7. 84 Best Buy *—S.H. (9/1/2002)*

Coastal Ridge 1999 Shiraz (California) $7. 83 *(10/1/2001)*

COBBLESTONE

Cobblestone 2003 Cabernet Sauvignon (Napa Valley) $39. The grapes are from Atlas Peak; this may be the ripest Cab I've ever had from that mountain. It's rich and deep in blackberry, cherry, blueberry and chocolate pie filling, and is very soft and luscious. Complex now, it should hold for 5–7 years. **90** *—S.H. (4/1/2007)*

Cobblestone 2002 Cabernet Sauvignon (Napa Valley) $39. 90 *—S.H. (6/1/2006)*

Cobblestone 2001 Cabernet Sauvignon (Napa Valley) $65. 84 *—S.H. (10/1/2004)*

Cobblestone 2003 Reserve Cabernet Sauvignon (Napa Valley) $69. I liked Cobblestone's regular Cab; at nearly half the price, it's better. Like that one, this is very ripe and rich in jammy blackberry, cassis, cherry and milk chocolate flavors, but seems oakier and riper, which intensifies the sweet flavors almost beyond table wine levels. **87** *—S.H. (9/1/2007)*

Cobblestone 2005 Chardonnay (Arroyo Seco) $29. Tastes superoaky, with a heavy layer of wood spice and butterscotchy char, but the underlying fruit is powerful enough to support it. The pineapple tart, peach custard and cinnamon flavors are crisp and juicy with acidity. **90** *—S.H. (4/1/2007)*

Cobblestone 2004 Chardonnay (Arroyo Seco) $29. 88 *—S.H. (6/1/2006)*

Cobblestone 2003 Chardonnay (Arroyo Seco) $34. 85 *—S.H. (2/1/2005)*

Cobblestone 1999 Chardonnay (Arroyo Seco) $22. 87 *—S.H. (12/31/2001)*

Cobblestone 1998 Chardonnay (Arroyo Seco) $23. 86 *—S.H. (11/15/2000)*

Cobblestone 1997 Chardonnay (Arroyo Seco) $23. 87 *(6/1/2000)*

CODORNÍU NAPA

Codorníu Napa NV Grand Reserve Sparkling Blend (Carneros) $45. 87 *—S.H. (6/1/2006)*

COELHO

Coelho 2005 Paciência Pinot Noir (Oregon) $25. Assertive and spicy, this interesting bottling, from Amity vineyard estate grapes, shows that even at just 13% alcohol Oregon Pinot can cut it. Made in a distinctive style that is clearly neither California nor Burgundy, this herbal, intense, wine puts the focus on the aromas, a beguiling mix of pine and herb. But the fruit is there right behind, tart and sassy, with cola and root beer notes sliding into a well-modulated but tannic finish. **88** *—P.G. (11/15/2007)*

COEUR D'ALENE CELLARS

Coeur d'Alene Cellars 2005 Chardonnay (Washington) $18. Crisply defined and built upon a core of lime and pineapple, this is dappled with toasty spice and balanced perfectly. No rough edges, no hurtful oak, no blowsy fruit salad; it's elegant and stylish, detailed and textural, and fills the mouth with perfectly defined varietal fruit. **90** *—P.G. (5/1/2007)*

Coeur d'Alene Cellars 2003 Syrah (Washington) $28. 90 *—P.G. (6/1/2006)*

Coeur d'Alene Cellars 2002 Syrah (Washington) $25. 90 Editors' Choice *(9/1/2005)*

Coeur d'Alene Cellars 2004 Boushey Vineyard Syrah (Washington) $36. I quickly run out of superlatives for this spectacular wine. It is satiny and saturated with pure, clean Syrah flavors, the fruit dancing from plum to mulberry to pie cherry, laced with smoke and white pepper. Fine grained tannins ride the finish, which continues to send up little spice flares as it lingers in the back of the throat. This is a wine anyone would be proud to call their own. **94 Editors' Choice** *—P.G. (5/1/2007)*

Coeur d'Alene Cellars 2004 Opulence Syrah (Washington) $40. An excellent Syrah. It's opulent almost to a fault, the fruit thick as a brick and ripe to the point of raisiny. It's buoyed with firm acidity and loads of black pepper and pencil lead. The wine is still a bit of a monster at 15.5% alcohol, but it's a loveable monster for sure. **91** *—P.G. (5/1/2007)*

Coeur d'Alene Cellars 2005 Viognier (Washington) $18. Grapes are sourced from top vineyards such as Elerding and Milbrandt, and the wine is given 100% barrel fermentation. This is a rich, ripe, almost unctuous style of Viognier, and it is impossible to resist. Lush, creamy and loaded with tropical fruits, it fills the mouth with warm, round fruit, and sails into a lingering finish of bananas and cream. **92** *—P.G. (5/1/2007)*

Coeur d'Alene Cellars 2004 Viognier (Washington) $18. 90 *—P.G. (6/1/2006)*

Coeur d'Alene Cellars 2005 L'Artiste Viognier (Washington) $24. This 100% Viognier is given a no-malo, 100% stainless steel regimen, which produces an elegant and steely style of Viognier. **88** *—P.G. (5/1/2007)*

Coeur d'Alene Cellars 2004 Sarah's Cuvée Viognier (Washington) $22. 89 *—P.G. (6/1/2006)*

COL SOLARE

Col Solare 2004 Red Table Wine Bordeaux Blend (Columbia Valley (WA)) $75. Tasted right after bottling, this new release from the high-profile Ste. Michelle/Antinori Red Mountain project may be the finest Col Solare to date. The blend is 80% Cabernet Sauvignon, 17% Merlot, and a splash each of Cabernet Franc and Petite Verdot. Half is Horse Heaven Hills fruit, one quarter Cold Creek and one quarter Wahluke Slope. This is a chewy, muscular wine, dense with plummy fruit, and layered with flavors of earth, soy and black tea. There is a hint of baked, pruny flavor that is restrained enough to add interest rather than detract. **92 Editors' Choice** *—P.G. (8/1/2007)*

Col Solare 2003 Red Table Wine Bordeaux Blend (Columbia Valley (WA)) $70. 89 *—P.G. (12/31/2006)*

Col Solare 1999 Red Blend (Columbia Valley (WA)) $70. 92 Editors' Choice *—C.S. (12/31/2002)*

COLD HEAVEN

Cold Heaven 2001 Le Bon Climate Viognier (Santa Barbara County) $25. 81 *—S.H. (8/1/2005)*

Cold Heaven 2005 Sanford & Benedict Vineyard Viognier (Santa Barbara County) $35. 90 *—S.H. (11/15/2006)*

Cold Heaven 2002 Sanford & Benedict Vineyard Viognier (Santa Barbara County) $NA. 86 *(11/15/2004)*

Cold Heaven 2000 Sanford & Benedict Vineyard Viognier (Santa Ynez Valley) $25. 88 *—J.M. (12/15/2002)*

Cold Heaven 2002 Young Vine Sanford & Benedict Vineyard Viognier (Santa Rita Hills) $18. 87 *(11/15/2004)*

COLE BAILEY

Cole Bailey 2004 Sesquipedalian Cabernet Sauvignon (Mendocino) $30. Ripe in cherries and blackberries, generously oaked, with firmer tannins and acids than most anything you'd get from Napa, which is the inevitable comparison. A minor quibble is the taste of raisins, the result of overripeness in the grapes. **86** *—S.H. (7/1/2007)*

Cole Bailey 2003 Sesquipedalian Cabernet Sauvignon (Mendocino) $30. 89 *—S.H. (3/1/2006)*

Cole Bailey 2005 Sesquipedalian Sauvignon Blanc (Mendocino) $18. Cole Bailey has SB nailed down. Dry, ultracrisp in acids and elegant, it's vibrant in lemongrass, fig, date, melon and spice flavors, with a brisk, minerally finish. **89** *—S.H. (7/1/2007)*

Cole Bailey 2004 Sesquipedalian Sauvignon Blanc (Mendocino) $18. 90 *—S.H. (3/1/2006)*

COLEMAN

Coleman 2004 Pinot Gris (Willamette Valley) $14. 88 *—P.G. (2/1/2006)*

Coleman 2002 Estate Pinot Noir (Willamette Valley) $19. 87 *(11/1/2004)*

Coleman 2002 Estate Reserve Pinot Noir (Willamette Valley) $32. 86 *(11/1/2004)*

COLGIN

Colgin 2003 Cariad Bordeaux Blend (Napa Valley) $225. 95 *—S.H. (9/1/2006)*

Colgin 2003 IX Estate Red Wine Bordeaux Blend (Napa Valley) $175. 98 Cellar Selection *—S.H. (9/1/2006)*

Colgin 2003 Herb Lamb Vineyard Cabernet Sauvignon (Napa Valley) $225. 95 *—S.H. (9/1/2006)*

Colgin 1999 Herb Lamb Vineyard Cabernet Sauvignon (Napa Valley) $150. 96 *—J.M. (6/1/2002)*

Colgin 2003 Tychson Hill Vineyard Cabernet Sauvignon (Napa Valley) $250. 93 Cellar Selection *—S.H. (9/1/2006)*

Colgin 2003 IX Estate Syrah (Napa Valley) $125. 92 *—S.H. (11/15/2006)*

Colgin 2002 IX Estate Syrah (Napa Valley) $125. 91 *(9/1/2005)*

COLLEGE CELLARS

College Cellars 2003 Minick Vineyards Syrah (Yakima Valley) $18. 85 *(9/1/2005)*

COLLIER FALLS

Collier Falls 2002 Hillside Estate Cabernet Sauvignon (Dry Creek Valley) $36. There's a weedy grassiness, a green chlorophyll bitterness, that plagues the wine. Although there are some decent cherry flavors, the acids and tannins dominate, and aging will not help. Decant. **83** *—S.H. (2/1/2007)*

Collier Falls 2001 Hillside Estate Cabernet Sauvignon (Dry Creek Valley) $36. 88 *—S.H. (10/1/2004)*

Collier Falls 2000 Hillside Estate Cabernet Sauvignon (Dry Creek Valley) $36. 89 *—S.H. (12/31/2003)*

Collier Falls 2004 Hillside Estate Petite Sirah (Dry Creek Valley) $30. If you're a fan of Petite Sirah, you'll like this one. It's inky dark, totally dry, tannic, acidic and rich in extracted berry, coffee and bitter chocolate flavors. It's obviously young now, calling for something oily like lamb, but should age for 10 or 20 years. **87** *—S.H. (2/1/2007)*

Collier Falls 2002 Zinfandel (Dry Creek Valley) $26. 87 *—S.H. (11/1/2005)*

Collier Falls 2002 Zinfandel (Dry Creek Valley) $26. 89 *—S.H. (12/31/2004)*

Collier Falls 2000 Zinfandel (Dry Creek Valley) $26. 86 *—S.H. (11/1/2002)*

Collier Falls 2003 Private Reserve Zinfandel (Dry Creek Valley) $26. It may be a reserve, but this Zin is pretty common, with a rustic mouthfeel and overripe flavors. It's dry, at the price of very high, hot alcohol. Still, the enormous fruit saves it. **83** *—S.H. (2/1/2007)*

Collier Falls 2001 Private Reserve Zinfandel (Dry Creek Valley) $28. 83 *(11/1/2003)*

Collier Falls 2000 Private Reserve Zinfandel (Dry Creek Valley) $26. 89 *—S.H. (9/1/2003)*

Collier Falls 1998 Private Reserve Zinfandel (Dry Creek Valley) $21. 91 Editors' Choice *—P.G. (3/1/2001)*

COLUMBIA CREST

Columbia Crest 1996 Reserve Bordeaux Blend (Columbia Valley (WA)) $25. 90 *—P.G. (6/1/2000)*

Columbia Crest 2001 Walter Clore Reserve Red Bordeaux Blend (Columbia Valley (WA)) $35. 90 *—P.G. (4/1/2005)*

Columbia Crest 2000 Reserve Cabernet Blend (Columbia Valley (WA)) $30. 88 *—P.G. (1/1/2004)*

Columbia Crest 1997 Cabernet Sauvignon (Columbia Valley (WA)) $9. 88 Best Buy *—P.G. (6/1/2000)*

Columbia Crest 1996 Cabernet Sauvignon (Columbia Valley (WA)) $11. 89 *(11/15/1999)*

Columbia Crest 1996 Estate Series Cabernet Sauvignon (Columbia Valley (WA)) $15. 88 *—P.G. (6/1/2000)*

Columbia Crest 2004 Grand Estates Cabernet Sauvignon (Columbia Valley (WA)) $11. This follows along the same track as the 2003—moderately ripe with lightly herbal fruit mixing plum, blueberry and cherry. The tannins have a rough edge and a rather sharp bite; this will smooth out if you decant it an hour or so. **87 Best Buy** *—P.G. (8/1/2007)*

Columbia Crest 2003 Grand Estates Cabernet Sauvignon (Columbia Valley (WA)) $11. 87 *—P.G. (12/31/2006)*

Columbia Crest 2002 Grand Estates Cabernet Sauvignon (Columbia Valley (WA)) $11. 89 **Best Buy** *—P.G. (4/1/2005)*

Columbia Crest 2001 Grand Estates Cabernet Sauvignon (Columbia Valley (WA)) $11. 87 *—P.G. (7/1/2004)*

Columbia Crest 1999 Grand Estates Cabernet Sauvignon (Columbia Valley (WA)) $11. 89 **Best Buy** *—P.G. (9/1/2002)*

Columbia Crest 2003 Reserve Cabernet Sauvignon (Columbia Valley (WA)) $30. 89 *—P.G. (12/31/2006)*

Columbia Crest 2002 Reserve Cabernet Sauvignon (Columbia Valley (WA)) $30. 89 *—P.G. (12/15/2005)*

Columbia Crest 2001 Reserve Cabernet Sauvignon (Columbia Valley (WA)) $30. 91 *—P.G. (4/1/2005)*

Columbia Crest 1999 Reserve Cabernet Sauvignon (Columbia Valley (WA)) $28. 92 *—P.G. (9/1/2002)*

Columbia Crest 1998 Reserve Cabernet Sauvignon (Columbia Valley (WA)) $28. 91 *—P.G. (12/31/2001)*

Columbia Crest 2004 Two Vines Cabernet Sauvignon (Columbia Valley (WA)) $8. This is a solid effort in a very difficult vintage. A freeze took out a lot of Washington grapevines in 2004, and it probably impacted the quality of the fruit available for this budget blend. The 2004 carries far more of the green bean and herbal qualities than recent vintages, but the tannins are softened and for the price it seems honest and well made. **85 Best Buy** *—P.G. (8/1/2007)*

Columbia Crest 2003 Two Vines Cabernet Sauvignon (Columbia Valley (WA)) $8. **88 Best Buy** *—P.G. (6/1/2006)*

Columbia Crest 2002 Two Vines Cabernet Sauvignon (Columbia Valley (WA)) $8. **88 Best Buy** *—P.G. (4/1/2005)*

Columbia Crest 2001 Two Vines Cabernet Sauvignon (Columbia Valley (WA)) $8. **86 Best Buy** *—P.G. (7/1/2004)*

Columbia Crest 1999 Cabernet Sauvignon-Merlot (Columbia Valley (WA)) $30. 92 *—P.G. (9/1/2002)*

Columbia Crest 2000 Walter Clore Private Reserve Red Cabernet Sauvignon-Merlot (Columbia Valley (WA)) $35. 89 *—P.G. (1/1/2004)*

Columbia Crest 2000 Chardonnay (Columbia Valley (WA)) $8. 87 *—P.G. (2/1/2002)*

Columbia Crest 1999 Chardonnay (Columbia Valley (WA)) $12. 86 *(6/1/2001)*

Columbia Crest 1998 Chardonnay (Columbia Valley (WA)) $8. **87 Best Buy** *—P.G. (6/1/2000)*

Columbia Crest 2005 Grand Estates Chardonnay (Columbia Valley (WA)) $11. Big, bold, and buttery, with plenty of oaky micro-popcorn flavors. Don't look for subtlety, but you get plenty of flavor. **86 Best Buy** *—P.G. (12/1/2007)*

Columbia Crest 2004 Grand Estates Chardonnay (Columbia Valley (WA)) $11. Chardonnay is the sweet spot in the white wine lineup (along with Riesling, of course). Big, bright and buttery, with plenty of legit oak highlights—none of this fake vanilla or microwave popcorn excess. Bacon fat, smoke and toast match the big, round, rich fruit. **88 Best Buy** *—P.G. (8/1/2007)*

Columbia Crest 2003 Grand Estates Chardonnay (Columbia Valley (WA)) $12. **88 Best Buy** *—P.G. (6/1/2006)*

Columbia Crest 2002 Grand Estates Chardonnay (Columbia Valley (WA)) $11. 87 *—P.G. (7/1/2004)*

Columbia Crest 2002 Grand Estates Chardonnay (Columbia Valley (WA)) $11. **90 Best Buy** *—P.G. (4/1/2005)*

Columbia Crest 2000 Grand Estates Chardonnay (Columbia Valley (WA)) $11. **89 Best Buy** *—P.G. (2/1/2002)*

Columbia Crest 1999 Grand Estates Chardonnay (Columbia Valley (WA)) $13. **89 Best Buy** *—P.G. (6/1/2001)*

Columbia Crest 2004 Reserve Chardonnay (Horse Heaven Hills) $30. 89 *—P.G. (12/31/2006)*

Columbia Crest 2003 Reserve Chardonnay (Columbia Valley (WA)) $30. 88 *—P.G. (12/15/2005)*

Columbia Crest 2002 Reserve Chardonnay (Columbia Valley (WA)) $30. 90 *—P.G. (4/1/2005)*

Columbia Crest 1998 Reserve Chardonnay (Columbia Valley (WA)) $18. 90 **Editors' Choice** *—P.G. (6/1/2001)*

Columbia Crest 1997 Reserve Chardonnay (Columbia Valley (WA)) $18. 88 *—P.G. (6/1/2000)*

Columbia Crest 2003 Two Vines Chardonnay (Columbia Valley (WA)) $8. **88 Best Buy** *—P.G. (6/1/2006)*

Columbia Crest 2002 Two Vines Chardonnay (Columbia Valley (WA)) $9. **88 Best Buy** *—P.G. (5/1/2004)*

Columbia Crest 2002 Two Vines Chardonnay (Columbia Valley (WA)) $8. **88 Best Buy** *—P.G. (4/1/2005)*

Columbia Crest 2002 Two Vines Chardonnay (Columbia Valley (WA)) $8. **87 Best Buy** *—P.G. (7/1/2004)*

Columbia Crest 2000 Gewürztraminer (Columbia Valley (WA)) $8. 87 *—P.G. (12/31/2001)*

Columbia Crest 1999 Gewürztraminer (Columbia Valley (WA)) $8. **86 Best Buy** *—P.G. (11/15/2000)*

Columbia Crest 2004 Two Vines Gewürztraminer (Columbia Valley (WA)) $8. **86 Best Buy** *—P.G. (6/1/2006)*

Columbia Crest 2003 Two Vines Gewürztraminer (Columbia Valley (WA)) $8. **88 Best Buy** *—P.G. (6/1/2005)*

Columbia Crest 1997 Merlot (Columbia Valley (WA)) $11. **88 Best Buy** *—P.G. (6/1/2000)*

Columbia Crest 1998 Merlot (Columbia Valley (WA)) $11. **89 Best Buy** *—S.H. (12/31/2003)*

Columbia Crest 1996 Estate Series Merlot (Columbia Valley (WA)) $16. 87 *—P.G. (8/19/2003)*

Columbia Crest 2004 Grand Estates Merlot (Columbia Valley (WA)) $11. Roughly 140,000 cases were produced, making this (along with the Two Vines) the benchmark budget Merlot for the state, if not the country. These wines are given plenty of cellaring, which helps to soften them up. The style is wide open and flavorful, with broad cherry and berry fruit set against very smooth, chocolatey tannins. The Grand Estates has thicker, more substantial weight and a silky, milk chocolaty finish. **88 Best Buy** *—P.G. (8/1/2007)*

Columbia Crest 2003 Grand Estates Merlot (Columbia Valley (WA)) $11. **86 Best Buy** *—P.G. (12/15/2005)*

Columbia Crest 2001 Grand Estates Merlot (Columbia Valley (WA)) $11. **89 Best Buy** *—P.G. (4/1/2005)*

Columbia Crest 2000 Grand Estates Merlot (Columbia Valley (WA)) $11. **87 Best Buy** *—P.G. (1/1/2004)*

Columbia Crest 1999 Grand Estates Merlot (Columbia Valley (WA)) $11. **87 Best Buy** *—P.G. (9/1/2002)*

Columbia Crest 2003 Reserve Merlot (Columbia Valley (WA)) $30. 88 *—P.G. (12/31/2006)*

Columbia Crest 2002 Reserve Merlot (Columbia Valley (WA)) $30. 90 *—P.G. (12/15/2005)*

Columbia Crest 2001 Reserve Merlot (Columbia Valley (WA)) $30. 91 *—P.G. (4/1/2005)*

Columbia Crest 2000 Reserve Merlot (Columbia Valley (WA)) $30. 88 *—P.G. (1/1/2004)*

Columbia Crest 1999 Reserve Merlot (Columbia Valley (WA)) $28. 90 *—P.G. (9/1/2002)*

Columbia Crest 2003 Two Vines Merlot (Columbia Valley (WA)) $8. Though perhaps just a notch below the 2002 version, this remains the Merlot to beat in the budget bottle sweepstakes. Bright berry fruit is married to smooth chocolate, without appearing over-manipulated or laced with fake vanilla. Creamy and consistent, it's widely available at a great price. Over 172,000 cases were produced. **87 Best Buy** *—P.G. (8/1/2007)*

Columbia Crest 2002 Two Vines Merlot (Columbia Valley (WA)) $8. **88 Best Buy** *—P.G. (6/1/2006)*

Columbia Crest 2001 Two Vines Merlot (Columbia Valley (WA)) $8. **88 Best Buy** *—P.G. (12/15/2004)*

Columbia Crest 1999 Merlot-Cabernet Sauvignon (Columbia Valley (WA)) $10. **87 Best Buy** *—P.G. (6/1/2002)*

Columbia Crest 2003 Two Vines Merlot-Cabernet Sauvignon (Columbia Valley (WA)) $8. The Two Vines lineup consistently offers some of the best value wines made in Washington, but this is not their best effort. It's thin to the point of watery, with rather sharp, acidic fruit tasting mildly of cherry candy. There's no weight beyond that; it's clean and one-dimensional, a one-note red wine. **83** *—P.G. (12/31/2007)*

Columbia Crest 2002 Two Vines Merlot-Cabernet Sauvignon (Columbia Valley (WA)) $8. **88 Best Buy** *—P.G. (11/15/2006)*

Columbia Crest 2001 Two Vines Merlot-Cabernet Sauvignon (Columbia Valley (WA)) $8. 85 *—P.G. (7/1/2004)*

Columbia Crest 2006 Grand Estates Pinot Grigio (Columbia Valley (WA)) $11. Here again the Grand Estates bottling shows a softer, gentler side of the fruit; the acids seem to have been smoothed over. The fruit is ripe and clean, suggesting white peaches and green apples, but there isn't much depth to it. **85** —*P.G. (12/1/2007)*

Columbia Crest 2005 Grand Estates Pinot Grigio (Columbia Valley (WA)) $11. 87 —*P.G. (12/31/2006)*

Columbia Crest 1997 Reserve Red Blend (Columbia Valley (WA)) $24. 90 —*P.G. (6/1/2001)*

Columbia Crest 1998 Reserve Red Wine Red Blend (Columbia Valley (WA)) $32. 92 Editors' Choice —*P.G. (12/31/2001)*

Columbia Crest 2003 Walter Clore Private Reserve Red Blend (Columbia Valley (WA)) $35. 88 —*P.G. (12/31/2006)*

Columbia Crest 2002 Walter Clore Reserve Red Red Blend (Columbia Valley (WA)) $35. 88 —*P.G. (12/15/2005)*

Columbia Crest 2005 Grand Estates Riesling (Columbia Valley (WA)) $11. 89 Best Buy —*P.G. (12/31/2006)*

Columbia Crest 2001 Johannisberg Riesling (Columbia Valley (WA)) $7. 87 Best Buy —*P.G. (9/1/2002)*

Columbia Crest 2005 Two Vines Riesling (Columbia Valley (WA)) $8. 87 Best Buy —*P.G. (10/1/2006)*

Columbia Crest 2004 Two Vines Riesling (Columbia Valley (WA)) $8. 86 —*P.G. (6/1/2005)*

Columbia Crest 2003 Two Vines Riesling (Columbia Valley (WA)) $8. 89 Best Buy —*P.G. (7/1/2004)*

Columbia Crest 1998 Sauvignon Blanc (Columbia Valley (WA)) $6. 88 Best Buy —*P.G. (6/1/2000)*

Columbia Crest 2006 Grand Estates Sauvignon Blanc (Columbia Valley (WA)) $11. This is a waxy, rather soft rendition of Sauvignon Blanc, and the pretty fruit flavors mix grapefruit, citrus and pineapple. There is very little suggestion of Sauvignon Blanc's herbal or grassy side; the grapes seem to have been ripened past that point, though not all the way to California-style, tropical fruit flavors. All in all this is a well-crafted, smooth and flavorful wine, with a portion barrel-aged for extra complexity. **87 Best Buy** —*P.G. (12/1/2007)*

Columbia Crest 2005 Grand Estates Sauvignon Blanc (Columbia Valley (WA)) $11. 88 Best Buy —*P.G. (12/31/2006)*

Columbia Crest 2005 Two Vines Sauvignon Blanc (Columbia Valley (WA)) $8. Here is another gem from the Two Vines lineup. Clean, fresh-tasting, varietal flavors show grapefruit and melon front and center. A hint of residual sugar (less than 1%) thickens the midpalate and softens the acids. The wine retains its herbaceous, penetrating, vivacious character. **87 Best Buy** —*P.G. (8/1/2007)*

Columbia Crest 2004 Two Vines Sauvignon Blanc (Columbia Valley (WA)) $8. 88 Best Buy —*P.G. (6/1/2006)*

Columbia Crest 2002 Two Vines Sauvignon Blanc (Columbia Valley (WA)) $8. 87 Best Buy —*P.G. (4/1/2005)*

Columbia Crest 1999 Sémillon (Columbia Valley (WA)) $9. 86 —*P.G. (6/1/2001)*

Columbia Crest 1998 Reserve Ice Wine Sémillon (Columbia Valley (WA)) $28. 92 —*P.G. (6/1/2000)*

Columbia Crest 1997 Reserve Late Harvest Sémillon (Columbia Valley (WA)) $23. 84 —*P.G. (6/1/2000)*

Columbia Crest 2000 Sémillon-Chardonnay (Columbia Valley (WA)) $6. 87 —*P.G. (2/1/2002)*

Columbia Crest 2002 Two Vines Sémillon-Chardonnay (Columbia Valley (WA)) $8. 87 Best Buy —*P.G. (12/15/2005)*

Columbia Crest 2003 Grand Estates Shiraz (Columbia Valley (WA)) $11. This is a clear step up from the excellent Two Vines Shiraz, and worth the extra couple of bucks. Wild berry flavors and varietal spice are given a somewhat tannic, earthy frame. Flavors suggest graphite, moist soil and some textural, grainy tannins. It's substantial, not just simple and fruity, and offers a lot of depth for the price. **88 Best Buy** —*P.G. (8/1/2007)*

Columbia Crest 2002 Grand Estates Shiraz (Columbia Valley (WA)) $11. 90 Best Buy —*P.G. (10/1/2006)*

Columbia Crest 2003 Two Vines Shiraz (Columbia Valley (WA)) $8. 85 Best Buy *(9/1/2005)*

Columbia Crest 2002 Two Vines Shiraz (Columbia Valley (WA)) $8. 88 Best Buy —*P.G. (4/1/2005)*

Columbia Crest 2002 Grand Estates Syrah (Columbia Valley (WA)) $11. 88 Best Buy —*P.G. (4/1/2005)*

Columbia Crest 2001 Grand Estates Syrah (Columbia Valley (WA)) $11. 88 Best Buy —*P.G. (5/1/2004)*

Columbia Crest 2004 Reserve Syrah (Columbia Valley (WA)) $30. 87 —*P.G. (12/31/2006)*

Columbia Crest 2003 Reserve Syrah (Columbia Valley (WA)) $30. 87 —*P.G. (12/15/2005)*

Columbia Crest 2002 Reserve Syrah (Columbia Valley (WA)) $30. 91 —*P.G. (4/1/2005)*

Columbia Crest 2001 Reserve Syrah (Columbia Valley (WA)) $30. 90 Editors' Choice —*P.G. (1/1/2004)*

Columbia Crest 2000 Reserve Syrah (Columbia Valley (WA)) $28. 89 —*P.G. (9/1/2002)*

Columbia Crest 1999 Reserve Syrah (Columbia Valley (WA)) $28. 89 —*P.G. (6/1/2002)*

Columbia Crest 1998 Reserve Syrah (Columbia Valley (WA)) $28. 91 Editors' Choice *(11/1/2001)*

Columbia Crest 1997 Reserve Syrah (Columbia Valley (WA)) $25. 80 —*P.G. (9/1/2000)*

Columbia Crest 1996 Reserve Syrah (Columbia Valley (WA)) $20. 92 —*P.G. (9/1/2000)*

Columbia Crest 2004 Two Vines Shiraz (Columbia Valley (WA)) $8. A good effort, with plenty of snap and sizzle for an eight dollar wine. You get juicy berry fruit, some clean spice and suggestions of white pepper, fine acids and decent length. It says Shiraz but it's less of an Aussie style and more of a snappy, acid-driven Washington take. **87 Best Buy** —*P.G. (5/1/2007)*

Columbia Crest 1998 White Blend (Columbia Valley (WA)) $8. 85 —*P.G. (11/15/2000)*

COLUMBIA WINERY

Columbia Winery 2001 Alder Ridge Barbera (Washington) $20. 88 *(1/1/2004)*

Columbia Winery 1996 Millennium Bordeaux Blend (Columbia Valley (WA)) $75. 89 *(4/1/2000)*

Columbia Winery 1997 Peninsula Bordeaux Blend (Yakima Valley) $60. 88 —*P.G. (12/31/2003)*

Columbia Winery 2001 Red Willow Cabernet Franc (Yakima Valley) $23. 85 —*P.G. (12/31/2003)*

Columbia Winery 1999 Red Willow Vineyard Cabernet Franc (Yakima Valley) $23. 86 —*P.G. (12/31/2002)*

Columbia Winery 1997 Red Willow Vineyard Cabernet Franc (Yakima Valley) $24. 88 —*P.G. (6/1/2001)*

Columbia Winery 1996 Red Willow Vineyard Cabernet Franc (Yakima Valley) $22. 87 —*J.C. (9/1/1999)*

Columbia Winery 1998 Signature Series Red Willow Vineyard Cabernet Franc (Columbia Valley (WA)) $22. 89 —*P.G. (12/31/2001)*

Columbia Winery 2001 Cabernet Sauvignon (Columbia Valley (WA)) $15. 89 —*P.G. (4/1/2005)*

Columbia Winery 2000 Cabernet Sauvignon (Columbia Valley (WA)) $15. 87 —*P.G. (12/31/2003)*

Columbia Winery 1999 Cabernet Sauvignon (Columbia Valley (WA)) $15. 88 —*P.G. (9/1/2002)*

Columbia Winery 1998 Cabernet Sauvignon (Columbia Valley (WA)) $15. 85 —*P.G. (10/1/2001)*

Columbia Winery 2000 Otis Vineyard Cabernet Sauvignon (Yakima Valley) $25. 89 —*P.G. (12/15/2005)*

Columbia Winery 1999 Otis Vineyard Cabernet Sauvignon (Yakima Valley) $23. 91 Cellar Selection —*P.G. (4/1/2005)*

Columbia Winery 1998 Otis Cabernet Sauvignon (Yakima Valley) $29. 89 —*P.G. (12/31/2003)*

Columbia Winery 1997 Otis Vineyard Cabernet Sauvignon (Yakima Valley) $26. 89 —*P.G. (12/31/2002)*

Columbia Winery 1996 Otis Vineyard Cabernet Sauvignon (Yakima Valley) $29. 88 —*P.G. (6/1/2002)*

Columbia Winery 1998 Red Willow Cabernet Sauvignon (Yakima Valley) $29. 90 Cellar Selection —*P.G. (12/31/2003)*

Columbia Winery 1997 Red Willow Cabernet Sauvignon (Yakima Valley) $29. 89 *(1/1/2004)*

Columbia Winery 2000 Red Willow Vineyard Cabernet Sauvignon (Yakima Valley) $23. 91 Cellar Selection —*P.G. (4/1/2005)*

Columbia Winery 1996 Red Willow Vineyard Cabernet Sauvignon (Yakima Valley) $29. 87 —*P.G. (6/1/2002)*

Columbia Winery 1999 Sagemoor Vineyard Cabernet Sauvignon (Columbia Valley (WA)) $29. 89 —*P.G. (6/1/2002)*

Columbia Winery 1998 Sagemoor Vineyard Cabernet Sauvignon (Columbia Valley (WA)) $29. 88 —*P.G. (12/31/2003)*

Columbia Winery 1997 Sagemoor Vineyard Cabernet Sauvignon (Columbia Valley (WA)) $29. 89 —*P.G. (6/1/2002)*

Columbia Winery 1996 Sagemoor Vineyard Cabernet Sauvignon (Columbia Valley (WA)) $24. 89 —*P.G. (4/1/2000)*

Columbia Winery 1999 Otis Vineyard Chardonnay (Yakima Valley) $24. 88 —*P.G. (10/1/2001)*

Columbia Winery 1998 Otis Vineyard Chardonnay (Yakima Valley) $50. 89 —*P.G. (11/15/2000)*

Columbia Winery 1999 Otis Vineyard Block 6 Chardonnay (Columbia Valley (WA)) $40. 89 —*P.G. (7/1/2002)*

Columbia Winery 2001 Otis Vineyard Block 6 Chardonnay (Yakima Valley) $40. 88 —*P.G. (9/1/2004)*

Columbia Winery 1999 Woodburne Cuvée Chardonnay (Columbia Valley (WA)) $14. 86 —*P.G. (6/1/2001)*

Columbia Winery 1997 Woodburne Cuvée Chardonnay (Columbia Valley (WA)) $14. 86 —*M.M. (11/1/1999)*

Columbia Winery 2003 Wyckoff Vineyard Chardonnay (Yakima Valley) $19. 89 —*P.G. (12/15/2005)*

Columbia Winery 2002 Wyckoff Vineyard Chardonnay (Yakima Valley) $19. 90 —*P.G. (4/1/2005)*

Columbia Winery 2001 Wyckoff Vineyard Chardonnay (Yakima Valley) $19. 87 —*P.G. (9/1/2004)*

Columbia Winery 2000 Wyckoff Chardonnay (Yakima Valley) $19. 87 *(1/1/2004)*

Columbia Winery 1999 Wyckoff Vineyard Chardonnay (Yakima Valley) $19. 88 —*P.G. (12/31/2002)*

Columbia Winery 1998 Wyckoff Vineyard Chardonnay (Yakima Valley) $19. 89 *(10/1/2001)*

Columbia Winery 1997 Wyckoff Vineyard Chardonnay (Yakima Valley) $21. 88 —*P.G. (4/1/2000)*

Columbia Winery 2005 Gewürztraminer (Columbia Valley (WA)) $8. 90 Best Buy —*P.G. (11/15/2006)*

Columbia Winery 2004 Gewürztraminer (Columbia Valley (WA)) $9. 90 Best Buy —*P.G. (12/15/2005)*

Columbia Winery 2003 Gewürztraminer (Columbia Valley (WA)) $9. 90 Best Buy —*P.G. (4/1/2005)*

Columbia Winery 2001 Gewürztraminer (Columbia Valley (WA)) $7. 87 —*P.G. (9/1/2002)*

Columbia Winery 2000 Merlot (Columbia Valley (WA)) $15. 87 —*P.G. (12/31/2003)*

Columbia Winery 1999 Merlot (Columbia Valley (WA)) $15. 87 —*P.G. (9/1/2002)*

Columbia Winery 1998 Merlot (Columbia Valley (WA)) $15. 84 —*P.G. (10/1/2001)*

Columbia Winery 1997 Merlot (Columbia Valley (WA)) $15. 88 —*P.G. (4/1/2000)*

Columbia Winery 1999 Red Willow Milestone Merlot (Yakima Valley) $29. 89 —*P.G. (12/31/2003)*

Columbia Winery 1997 Red Willow Vineyard Milestone Merlot (Yakima Valley) $24. 89 —*P.G. (10/1/2001)*

Columbia Winery 2004 Pinot Gris (Columbia Valley (WA)) $10. 86 —*P.G. (2/1/2006)*

Columbia Winery 2002 Pinot Gris (Yakima Valley) $10. 86 Best Buy —*P.G. (12/1/2004)*

Columbia Winery 2000 Pinot Gris (Yakima Valley) $10. 86 —*P.G. (9/1/2002)*

Columbia Winery 1998 Pinot Gris (Yakima Valley) $9. 84 —*P.G. (11/15/2000)*

Columbia Winery 2000 Cellarmaster's Riesling (Columbia Valley (WA)) $7. 82 —*M.S. (8/19/2003)*

Columbia Winery 2002 Red Willow Vineyard Sangiovese (Yakima Valley) $25. 90 —*P.G. (12/1/2004)*

Columbia Winery 2001 Red Willow Vineyard Sangiovese (Yakima Valley) $20. 84 —*P.G. (12/31/2003)*

Columbia Winery 1999 Red Willow Vineyard Sangiovese (Yakima Valley) $25. 88 —*P.G. (6/1/2002)*

Columbia Winery 1998 Red Willow Vineyard Sangiovese (Yakima Valley) $18. 90 —*P.G. (11/15/2000)*

Columbia Winery 2001 Sémillon (Columbia Valley (WA)) $8. 90 Best Buy —*P.G. (12/31/2003)*

Columbia Winery 1998 Sémillon (Columbia Valley (WA)) $7. 86 Best Buy —*P.G. (11/15/2000)*

Columbia Winery 1997 Syrah (Yakima Valley) $14. 90 —*P.G. (4/1/2000)*

Columbia Winery 2004 Syrah (Columbia Valley (WA)) $13. 89 Best Buy —*P.G. (11/15/2006)*

Columbia Winery 2001 Syrah (Columbia Valley (WA)) $15. 90 Best Buy —*P.G. (4/1/2005)*

Columbia Winery 2000 Syrah (Columbia Valley (WA)) $15. 88 Best Buy —*P.G. (12/31/2002)*

Columbia Winery 1999 Syrah (Columbia Valley (WA)) $18. 87 *(10/1/2001)*

Columbia Winery 1998 Syrah (Yakima Valley) $15.88 —*P.G. (11/15/2000)*

Columbia Winery 1999 Red Willow Syrah (Yakima Valley) $35. 90 *(1/1/2004)*

Columbia Winery 2000 Red Willow South Chapel Block Syrah (Yakima Valley) $50. 89 —*P.G. (12/31/2003)*

Columbia Winery 2000 Red Willow Vineyard Syrah (Yakima Valley) $35. 88 Cellar Selection —*P.G. (9/1/2004)*

Columbia Winery 1998 Red Willow Vineyard Syrah (Yakima Valley) $35. 86 *(11/1/2001)*

Columbia Winery 1996 Red Willow Vineyard Syrah (Yakima Valley) $29. 87 —*S.H. (11/1/1999)*

Columbia Winery 1997 Reserve Syrah (Columbia Valley (WA)) $32. 92 —*S.H. (11/1/1999)*

Columbia Winery 2001 Red Willow Viognier (Yakima Valley) $40. 88 —*P.G. (12/31/2002)*

Columbia Winery 2000 Red Willow Viognier (Yakima Valley) $23. 85 —*P.G. (12/31/2001)*

Columbia Winery 2001 Alder Ridge Vineyard Zinfandel (Columbia Valley (WA)) $20. 87 —*J.M. (11/1/2003)*

COLVIN VINEYARDS

Colvin Vineyards 2001 Allégresse Bordeaux Blend (Walla Walla (WA)) $36. 85 —*P.G. (12/1/2004)*

Colvin Vineyards 2002 Cabernet Sauvignon (Walla Walla (WA)) $26. 89 —*P.G. (4/1/2006)*

Colvin Vineyards 2002 Patina Vineyard Syrah (Walla Walla (WA)) $23. 90 —*P.G. (6/1/2005)*

Colvin Vineyards 2003 Spofford Station Vineyard Syrah (Walla Walla (WA)) $23. 88 —*P.G. (4/1/2006)*

COM E BELLA

Com e Bella 2000 Cabernet Sauvignon (Calaveras County) $30. 82 —*S.H. (3/1/2005)*

Com e Bella 2001 Cabernet Sauvignon-Syrah (Calaveras County) $24. 84 —*S.H. (3/1/2005)*

COMPASS

Compass 2000 Merlot (Napa Valley) $12. 86 —*S.H. (12/31/2003)*

Compass 1998 Merlot (California) $10. 84 —*S.H. (2/1/2001)*

COMTESSE THÉRÈSE

Comtesse Thérèse 2002 Cabernet Sauvignon (North Fork of Long Island) $25. 82 —*M.D. (8/1/2006)*

Comtesse Thérèse 2004 Russian Oak Chardonnay (North Fork of Long Island) $18. 86 —*J.C. (3/1/2006)*

Comtesse Thérèse 2001 Chateau Reserve Merlot (North Fork of Long Island) $25. 88 —*J.C. (10/2/2004)*

Comtesse Thérèse 2003 Hungarian Oak Merlot (North Fork of Long Island) $17. 82 —*J.C. (3/1/2006)*

Comtesse Thérèse 2003 Traditional Merlot (North Fork of Long Island) $18. 82 —*M.D. (8/1/2006)*

Comtesse Thérèse 2001 Traditional Merlot (North Fork of Long Island) $18. 84 —*J.C. (10/2/2004)*

CONCANNON

Concannon 2002 Reserve Assemblage Red Cabernet Blend (Livermore Valley) $24. 84 —*S.H. (6/1/2005)*

Concannon 2004 Limited Release Assemblage Cabernet Sauvignon (Central Coast) $14. Firm and crisp, with a slightly herbal edge, this hits winemaker Adam Richardson's goal of "food friendly." The tart blackberry and cassis flavors would be helped by a hunk of rare beef. **86** —*J.C. (6/1/2007)*

Concannon 2003 Limited Release Assemblage Cabernet Sauvignon (Central Coast) $14. 83 —*S.H. (3/1/2006)*

Concannon 2003 Reserve Cabernet Sauvignon (Livermore Valley) $24. 80 —*S.H. (9/1/2006)*

Concannon 2001 Reserve Cabernet Sauvignon (Livermore Valley) $24. 87 —*S.H. (12/31/2004)*

Concannon 2000 Reserve Limited Release Cabernet Sauvignon (Livermore Valley) $24. 88 —*S.H. (6/1/2004)*

Concannon 2004 Selected Vineyards Cabernet Sauvignon (Central Coast) $10. Decent everyday Cab, fully dry and balanced. It's on the light side, weight-wise and fruit-wise, but has enough cherry-berry stuff going on to satisfy at this price. **84 Best Buy** —*S.H. (3/1/2007)*

Concannon 2003 Selected Vineyards Cabernet Sauvignon (Central Coast) $10. 84 —*S.H. (12/31/2005)*

Concannon 2002 Selected Vineyards Cabernet Sauvignon (Central Coast) $12. 81 —*S.H. (12/1/2005)*

Concannon 2001 Selected Vineyards Cabernet Sauvignon (Central Coast) $12. 85 —*S.H. (10/1/2004)*

Concannon 2005 Reserve Chardonnay (Livermore Valley) $18. Tastes like oak. Pure and simple, it's about vanilla, spice, char, woodsap, caramel and buttered toast. The fruit is pretty thin, suggesting apricots and citrus. Fans of oaky Chards will like it. **83** —*S.H. (4/1/2007)*

Concannon 2004 Reserve Chardonnay (Edna Valley) $18. 83 *(6/1/2000)*

Concannon 1996 Reserve Chardonnay (Livermore Valley) $19. 84 —*M.S. (10/1/1999)*

Concannon 2002 Reserve Limited Release Chardonnay (Edna Valley) $18. 86 —*S.H. (6/1/2004)*

Concannon 2005 Selected Vineyards Chardonnay (Central Coast) $10. Like the Pinot Gris, this is fairly weighty, with ample concentration and richness at its price point. Pear and melon flavors easily carry the light touches of spicy oak. Drink now. **85 Best Buy** —*J.C. (6/1/2007)*

Concannon 2004 Selected Vineyards Chardonnay (Central Coast) $10. 82 —*S.H. (11/15/2006)*

Concannon 2003 Selected Vineyards Chardonnay (Central Coast) $12. 86 —*S.H. (2/1/2005)*

Concannon 2002 Selected Vineyards Chardonnay (Central Coast) $12. 85 —*S.H. (12/1/2004)*

Concannon 2004 Reserve Merlot (Livermore Valley) $24. Nice and smooth, dry and plump in fruit. The vintage was warm in this hot region and the grapes are perfectly ripe, with Merlot's sometimes earthiness eliminated in favor of cherries and blackberries. Finishes with real elegance. **88** —*S.H. (3/1/2007)*

Concannon 2003 Reserve Merlot (Livermore Valley) $24. 85 —*S.H. (5/1/2006)*

Concannon 2002 Reserve Merlot (Livermore Valley) $24. 83 —*S.H. (12/31/2004)*

Concannon 2001 Reserve Limited Release Merlot (Livermore Valley) $24. 91 —*S.H. (6/1/2004)*

Concannon 2004 Selected Vineyards Merlot (Central Coast) $10. An easy-drinking Merlot priced right for restaurants seeking a by-the-glass wine, this is smooth and soft, with hints of red raspberry and herbs complemented by vanilla and caramel. **86 Best Buy** —*J.C. (6/1/2007)*

Concannon 2004 Selected Vineyards Merlot (Central Coast) $10. Tastes unripe, with a disagreeably green, minty streak, and although the wine is fully dry, it's just too tough and lean to recommend. **81** —*S.H. (3/1/2007)*

Concannon 2003 Selected Vineyards Merlot (Central Coast) $10. 85 Best Buy —*S.H. (12/31/2005)*

Concannon 2002 Selected Vineyards Merlot (Central Coast) $12. 84 —*S.H. (12/31/2004)*

Concannon 2001 Selected Vineyards Merlot (Central Coast) $12. 88 Best Buy —*S.H. (12/15/2004)*

Concannon 2000 Petite Sirah (Central Coast) $12. 86 *(4/1/2003)*

Concannon 1997 Petite Sirah (Central Coast) $24. 86 —*S.H. (12/1/2001)*

Concannon 2004 Heritage Petite Sirah (Livermore Valley) $50. The flagship Petite Sirah from the winery's own vineyards in the Livermore Valley is the biggest and richest wine in the lineup. The nose is filled with intense blueberries, but also picks up hints of licorice, flowers and grilled meat, while the flavors feature lush fruit and spice. Full-bodied and richly tannic, this should evolve well for years to come. **90 Cellar Selection** —*J.C. (6/1/2007)*

Concannon 2001 Heritage Petite Sirah (Livermore Valley) $40. 92 Cellar Selection —*S.H. (12/1/2005)*

Concannon 2000 Heritage Petite Sirah (Livermore Valley) $36. 84 —*S.H. (2/1/2005)*

Concannon 2004 Limited Release Petite Sirah (Central Coast) $14. The winery's signature bottling remains a staple for PS lovers. Dark berry flavors pick up hints of spice and herb on the tannic finish. It's reasonably full-bodied, but it does have a slightly tart, constricted feel to the finish. Drink now or hold 3–5 years. **87** —*J.C. (6/1/2007)*

Concannon 2003 Reserve Petite Sirah (Livermore Valley) $24. 88 —*S.H. (11/15/2006)*

Concannon 2002 Reserve Petite Sirah (Livermore Valley) $30. 90 —*S.H. (6/1/2005)*

Concannon 1999 Reserve Petite Sirah (Livermore Valley) $25. 86 *(4/1/2003)*

Concannon 1995 Reserve Petite Sirah (Central Coast) $23. 90 —*J.C. (11/1/1999)*

Concannon 2000 Reserve Limited Release Petite Sirah (Livermore Valley) $24. 91 —*S.H. (12/31/2003)*

Concannon 2002 Selected Vineyard Petite Sirah (Central Coast) $12. 88 Best Buy —*S.H. (11/15/2004)*

Concannon 2003 Selected Vineyards Petite Sirah (Central Coast) $12. 83 —*S.H. (2/1/2005)*

Concannon 2005 Limited Release Pinot Gris (Central Coast) $14. This carries a touch of copper to its color courtesy of some skin contact, and maybe that accounts for the hints of berries found in its aromas as well. This is a slightly thick-textured Pinot Gris, with flashy almond, apple, citrus and melon flavors. Drink now. **86** —*J.C. (6/1/2007)*

Concannon 2005 Limited Release Pinot Gris (Central Coast) $14. 87 —*S.H. (12/31/2006)*

Concannon 2005 Limited Release Pinot Noir (Central Coast) $14. Inexpensive Central Coast Pinots are usually thin, which is why Concannon blended 15% Petite Sirah and Grenache. The wine is like a Pinot Noir with its light color and silkiness, but it offers plenty of cherry candy and blueberry flavors. Fully dry, this high-production Pinot is a good value. **86** —*S.H. (2/1/2007)*

Concannon 2004 Limited Release Pinot Noir (Central Coast) $14. 85 —*S.H. (11/15/2006)*

Concannon 2002 Limited Release Pinot Noir (Edna Valley) $24. 82 —*S.H. (6/1/2005)*

Concannon 2002 Selected Vineyards Pinot Noir (Central Coast) $12. 85 *(11/1/2004)*

Concannon 2004 Limited Release Assemblage Red Wine Red Blend (Central Coast) $14. 81 —*S.H. (12/31/2006)*

Concannon 2002 Stampmaker's Red Wine Rhône Red Blend (Livermore Valley) $24. 84 —*S.H. (6/1/2005)*

Concannon 2003 Limited Release Sauvignon Blanc (Monterey) $18. 86 —*S.H. (6/1/2005)*

Concannon 2004 Limited Release Assemblage White Wine Sauvignon Blanc (Central Coast) $15. 87 —*S.H. (12/15/2005)*

Concannon 2005 Reserve Sauvignon Blanc (Monterey County) $18. 85 —*S.H. (12/1/2006)*

Concannon 2004 Reserve Sauvignon Blanc (Monterey County) $18. 90 —*S.H. (12/1/2005)*

Concannon 2002 Reserve Limited Release Sauvignon Blanc (Monterey) $18. 89 —*S.H. (12/1/2003)*

Concannon 2006 Selected Vineyards Sauvignon Blanc (Central Coast) $10. On the sweet side, tasting almost like a peach and pineapple sports drink. If you like sugar in your white wines, you'll appreciate this one. **83** —*S.H. (11/15/2007)*

Concannon 2004 Selected Vineyards Sauvignon Blanc (Central Coast) $10. 86 Best Buy —*S.H. (12/15/2005)*

Concannon 2003 Selected Vineyards Sauvignon Blanc (Central Coast) $12. 85 Best Buy —*S.H. (2/1/2005)*

Concannon 2002 Selected Vineyards Sauvignon Blanc (Central Coast) $12. 85 —*S.H. (12/1/2004)*

Concannon 1997 Syrah (Livermore Valley) $20. 86 *(10/1/2001)*

Concannon 2004 Limited Release Stepmaker's Syrah (Central Coast) $14. Has true varietal spice, something we don't always see in bargain-priced Syrah. White pepper notes lead, backed by superripe blueberries and dried spices. Does seem a wee bit tart. **87** —*J.C. (6/1/2007)*

Concannon 2004 Limited Release Stampmaker's Syrah (Central Coast) $14. 81 —*S.H. (12/31/2006)*

Concannon 2003 Limited Release Stampmaker's Syrah (Central Coast) $14. 82 —*S.H. (3/1/2006)*

Concannon 2004 Reserve Syrah (Livermore Valley) $24. Impresses for its depth of fruit and overall dry balance, and the way the wine feels sumptuous and classy in the mouth. It's a small-production Syrah, rich in plummy blackberry, pepper and mocha flavors and softly tannic and complex, like a good Saint-Joseph from the Rhône. **90** *—S.H. (4/1/2007)*

Concannon 2003 Reserve Syrah (Livermore Valley) $24. **89** *—S.H. (5/1/2006)*

Concannon 2001 Reserve Syrah (Livermore Valley) $24. **83** *—S.H. (2/1/2005)*

Concannon 2005 Selected Vineyard Syrah (Central Coast) $10. For 10 bucks, you get a dry, balanced, wonderfully food-friendly Syrah. The blackberry, mulberry and black cherry flavors have a rich streak of tobacco and nutmeg, with a bitter, espresso finish that grounds the wine. Small percentages of Petite Sirah and Malbec add flavor and structural complexity. **87 Best Buy** *—S.H. (11/15/2007)*

Concannon 2003 Selected Vineyard Syrah (Central Coast) $10. **84** *—S.H. (12/31/2005)*

Concannon 2002 Selected Vineyard Syrah (Central Coast) $12. **89 Best Buy** *—S.H. (12/1/2005)*

Concannon 2001 Selected Vineyard Syrah (Central Coast) $12. **85** *—S.H. (12/1/2004)*

Concannon 1999 Viognier (Central Coast) $15. **85** *—S.H. (11/15/2001)*

Concannon 2004 Limited Release Stampmaker's Viognier (Central Coast) $15. **87** *—S.H. (12/15/2005)*

Concannon 2003 Stampmaker's White Wine White Blend (Central Coast) $18. **85** *—S.H. (6/1/2005)*

CONIGLIO

Coniglio 2003 Cabernet Franc (Napa Valley) $35. Not as good as the '02, this '03 is dry and elegant, with polished cherry and oak flavors and rich tannins. Finishes just a bit thin, with a minty note. **86** *—S.H. (9/1/2007)*

Coniglio 2002 Cabernet Franc (Napa Valley) $35. **91** *—S.H. (6/1/2006)*

Coniglio 2003 Cabernet Sauvignon (Spring Mountain) $45. Difficult now for its extreme toughness. The wine is muted in aroma, except for new oak and a tease of blackberry, and hits the mouth with astringent tannins. The fruit seems too thin to age. **84** *—S.H. (9/1/2007)*

Coniglio 2003 Cabernet Sauvignon (Atlas Peak) $45. Tannins and acids mark this wine, even at nearly four years. Remember, it's from an appellation with a tendency for toughness. Yet the blackberry, black cherry and chocolate-mint flavors are delicious. Shows Atlas Peak Cab at its complex, food-loving best. Drink now through 2009. **92** *—S.H. (9/1/2007)*

Coniglio 2002 Cabernet Sauvignon (Atlas Peak) $45. **91** *—S.H. (6/1/2006)*

Coniglio 2005 Leola Sauvignon Blanc (Napa Valley) $22. Dry, crisp and elegant, but too watery-thin in flavor. The palate struggles to savor the modest citrus flavors. **83** *—S.H. (9/1/2007)*

CONN CREEK

Conn Creek 2003 Anthology Bordeaux Blend (Napa Valley) $54. A blend of all five Bordeaux reds, this is a very ripe, soft wine, brimming with cherry, chocolate, pecan pie and oak flavors. It doesn't seem like an ager, but rewards now for its lushness. **87** *—S.H. (6/1/2007)*

Conn Creek 1996 Anthology Bordeaux Blend (Napa Valley) $44. **91** *(7/1/2000)*

Conn Creek 2002 Anthology Cabernet Blend (Napa Valley) $54. **83** *—S.H. (7/1/2006)*

Conn Creek 2001 Anthology Cabernet Blend (Napa Valley) $54. **88** *—S.H. (12/1/2005)*

Conn Creek 2000 Anthology Cabernet Blend (Napa Valley) $54. **92** *—S.H. (6/1/2004)*

Conn Creek 2002 Limited Release Cabernet Franc (Napa Valley) $28. **87** *—S.H. (6/1/2006)*

Conn Creek 2001 Limited Release Cabernet Franc (Napa Valley) $28. **88** *—S.H. (5/1/2005)*

Conn Creek 1999 Limited Release Cabernet Franc (Napa Valley) $25. **93 Editors' Choice** *—S.H. (9/1/2002)*

Conn Creek 2003 Collins Vineyard Cabernet Sauvignon (St. Helena) $45. Tasted with Conn Creek's Yountville Cab, this is the lesser bottling, probably due to the vintage. It was warm to hot, and this Cab has notes of overripe chocolate-covered raisins and Port. The difference of a few degrees seem to have made this one ponderous, giving the nod to the cooler Cab from the south. **86** *—S.H. (6/1/2007)*

Conn Creek 2003 Herrick Vineyard Cabernet Sauvignon (Yountville) $45. This is a young, immature wine, but a charming one with a good future. It's showing cassis and cherry flavors, with a rich French cured olive and toasty oak edge, and is also firm in tannins. Should soften up in a few years. If you open it now, decant. **90** *—S.H. (6/1/2007)*

Conn Creek 2002 Hozhoni Vineyard Cabernet Sauvignon (Rutherford) $60. **91** *—S.H. (12/15/2005)*

Conn Creek 2004 Limited Release Cabernet Sauvignon (Napa Valley) $28. Thin and raw, and slightly sweet, this is not a very satisfying Cab. It tastes like candied blackberry and cherry LifeSavers. **82** *—S.H. (12/31/2007)*

Conn Creek 2003 Limited Release Cabernet Sauvignon (Napa Valley) $28. Shows lots of class and polish in a Cab with real Napa character. Everything is so ripe and sunny, from the sweet nutty tannins to the blackberry, coffee and cassis flavors, yet there's a balance of crisp acids. Doesn't seem like an ager, so drink up. **88** *—S.H. (2/1/2007)*

Conn Creek 2002 Limited Release Cabernet Sauvignon (Napa Valley) $28. **86** *—S.H. (6/1/2006)*

Conn Creek 2001 Limited Release Cabernet Sauvignon (Napa Valley) $28. **87** *—S.H. (10/1/2005)*

Conn Creek 2000 Limited Release Cabernet Sauvignon (Napa Valley) $28. **87** *—S.H. (6/1/2004)*

Conn Creek 1998 Limited Release Cabernet Sauvignon (Napa Valley) $25. **90** *—S.H. (6/1/2002)*

Conn Creek 2001 Limited Release Merlot (Napa Valley) $28. **91 Editors' Choice** *—S.H. (6/1/2004)*

Conn Creek 1999 Limited Release Merlot (Napa Valley) $25. **91** *—S.H. (6/1/2002)*

CONN VALLEY

Conn Valley 1997 Eloge Bordeaux Blend (Napa Valley) $80. **89** *(11/1/2000)*

Conn Valley 1997 Estate Reserve Cabernet Sauvignon (Napa Valley) $55. **90** *(11/1/2000)*

Conn Valley 1998 Fournier Vineyard Chardonnay (Carneros) $40. **85** *(7/1/2001)*

Conn Valley 1999 Dutton Ranch Pinot Noir (Russian River Valley) $48. **83** *(10/1/2002)*

Conn Valley 1999 Valhalla Pinot Noir (Napa Valley) $60. **86** *(10/1/2002)*

Conn Valley 1997 Valhalla Vineyard Pinot Noir (Napa Valley) $45. **87** *(10/1/1999)*

CONSILIENCE

Consilience 2001 Petite Sirah (Santa Barbara County) $22. **90** *—J.M. (10/1/2004)*

Consilience 2000 Petite Sirah (Santa Barbara County) $21. **86** *(4/1/2003)*

Consilience 2001 Pinot Noir (Santa Barbara County) $30. **90** *—S.H. (12/1/2004)*

Consilience 2003 Ashleys Vineyard Pinot Noir (Santa Rita Hills) $39. **87** *—S.H. (3/1/2006)*

Consilience 2002 Roussanne (Santa Barbara County) $22. **86** *—S.H. (5/1/2005)*

Consilience 2002 Syrah (Santa Barbara County) $19. **85** *(9/1/2005)*

Consilience 2001 Syrah (Santa Barbara County) $17. **91** *—S.H. (9/1/2004)*

Consilience 1998 Syrah (Santa Barbara County) $19. **88** *(10/1/2001)*

Consilience 2002 Great Oaks Vineyard Syrah (Santa Barbara County) $28. **86** *(9/1/2005)*

Consilience 2002 Hampton Vineyard Syrah (Santa Barbara County) $38. **88** *(9/1/2005)*

Consilience 2001 Rodney Shull Vineyard Syrah (Santa Barbara County) $24. **82** *(9/1/2005)*

Consilience 2000 Rodney's Vineyard Syrah (Santa Barbara County) $22. **92** *—S.H. (9/1/2004)*

Consilience 2000 Rodney's Vineyard Syrah (Santa Barbara County) $30. **90** *—S.H. (2/1/2004)*

Consilience 2002 Star Lane Vineyard Syrah (Santa Barbara County) $36. **82** *(9/1/2005)*

Consilience 2002 Viognier (Santa Barbara County) $21. **84** *—S.H. (5/1/2005)*

Consilience 2001 Viognier (Santa Barbara County) $21. **88** *—S.H. (12/31/2003)*

Consilience 2000 Viognier (Santa Barbara County) $21. **90** *—J.M. (12/15/2002)*

Consilience 2002 Rhodes Vineyard Zinfandel (Redwood Valley) $30. **84** *—S.H. (5/1/2005)*

Consilience 1999 Rhodes Vineyard Zinfandel (Redwood Valley) $30. **84** *—D.T. (3/1/2002)*

Consilience 1998 Rhodes Vineyard Zinfandel (Redwood Valley) $27. **88** *(3/1/2001)*

CONSTANT

Constant 2002 Claret Bordeaux Blend (Diamond Mountain) $50. 92 *—S.H. (7/1/2006)*

Constant 2004 Cabernet Franc (Napa Valley) $75. A gentle, tasty Cab Franc that shows the variety's pure, clean cherry and cassis personality. It's really luscious at the flavor level. It's not particularly complex, though, and finishes a little obvious in sweet oaky caramel. **87** *—S.H. (12/1/2007)*

Constant 2001 Diamond Mountain Vineyard Cabernet Franc (Napa Valley) $45. 90 *—S.H. (12/15/2004)*

Constant 2004 Cabernet Sauvignon (Napa Valley) $85. Nice and fairly complex, showing ripe cherry, blueberry and cassis fruit, well-oaked, this is backed up by rich tannins that can be described as mountain-style. But they're new-style tannins, silky and refined, so the wine is drinkable now. Will develop for up to five years. **88** *—S.H. (12/1/2007)*

Constant 2003 Diamond Mountain Vineyard Cabernet Sauvignon (Napa Valley) $85. Not as rich and opulent as the great '02, the '03 nonetheless is elegant, showing true mountain character. It's dry and tannic, with blackberry, currant, plum and cherry flavors. Should hold for five years, but it's not for the long haul. **88** *—S.H. (10/1/2007)*

Constant 2002 Diamond Mountain Vineyard Cabernet Sauvignon (Diamond Mountain) $85. 94 Cellar Selection *—S.H. (7/1/2006)*

Constant 2000 Diamond Mountain Vineyard Cabernet Sauvignon (Napa Valley) $75. 90 *—S.H. (11/15/2004)*

Constant 2001 Estate Cabernet Sauvignon (Napa Valley) $85. 89 *—S.H. (10/1/2004)*

Constant 2004 Syrah (Northern Sonoma) $65. This wine is soft both in acidity and tannins, and simple and semisweet, with sugared raspberry tea and cola flavors, and isn't going anywhere. **83** *—S.H. (12/1/2007)*

Constant 2002 Diamond Mountain Vineyard Syrah (Sonoma County) $48. 92 Cellar Selection *(9/1/2005)*

Constant 2003 Queen of Diamonds Estate Diamond Mountain Vineyard Syrah (Northern Sonoma) $60. A high-altitude wine from the Sonoma side of Diamond Mountain, this Syrah's main ingredient is tannin, the big, tough kind that dries out the palate. Will it age? My best guess is, not for the long term. There's good cherry-blackberry fruit but the telltale finish is short. **87** *—S.H. (10/1/2007)*

CONTRADA

Contrada 2003 Cabernet Sauvignon (Napa Valley) $16. 86 *—S.H. (4/1/2006)*

Contrada 2004 Sauvignon Blanc (Napa Valley) $12. 84 *—S.H. (4/1/2006)*

COOK'S

Cook's NV Blush Champagne Blend (California) $7. 82 *—S.H. (12/15/1999)*

Cook's NV Brut Champagne Blend (California) $7. 82 *—S.H. (12/15/1999)*

Cook's NV Brut Champagne Blend (California) $7. 82 *—J.M. (12/1/2002)*

Cook's 2000 Collector's Series Brut Champagne Blend (California) $7. 84 *(6/1/2001)*

Cook's NV Grand Spumante Champagne Blend (California) $7. 84 *—J.M. (12/1/2002)*

Cook's NV Grand Spumante Champagne Blend (California) $7. 84 Best Buy *—J.M. (11/15/2002)*

Cook's NV Spumante Champagne Blend (California) $7. 84 *—S.H. (6/1/2001)*

Cook's NV White Zinfandel Rosé Blend (California) $7. 80 *—J.M. (12/1/2002)*

COOKE CELLARS

Cooke Cellars 2000 Sangiovese (Paso Robles) $24. 82 *—S.H. (2/1/2003)*

COOPER

Cooper 2001 Zinfandel (Lodi) $20. 89 *—S.H. (3/1/2005)*

COOPER MOUNTAIN

Cooper Mountain 1999 Chardonnay (Willamette Valley) $12. 88 Best Buy *—P.G. (4/1/2002)*

Cooper Mountain 2005 Old Vines Chardonnay (Willamette Valley) $25. Funky and disjointed. This is cracking up, cumbersome and just not a very pleasant wine to drink. Bitter on the finish, simple in the fruit. **83** *—P.G. (7/1/2007)*

Cooper Mountain 1999 Estate Bottled Pinot Blanc (Willamette Valley) $14. 82 *—D.T. (11/1/2001)*

Cooper Mountain 2004 Cooper Hill Pinot Gris (Willamette Valley) $10. 84 *(2/1/2006)*

Cooper Mountain 2000 Estate Bottled Pinot Gris (Willamette Valley) $15. 87 *—P.G. (4/1/2002)*

Cooper Mountain 2004 Reserve Pinot Gris (Willamette Valley) $14. 86 *(2/1/2006)*

Cooper Mountain 1999 Pinot Noir (Willamette Valley) $17. 86 *—P.G. (4/1/2002)*

Cooper Mountain 1998 20th Anniversary Pinot Noir (Willamette Valley) $25. 88 *—M.S. (12/1/2000)*

Cooper Mountain 2005 Meadowlark Pinot Noir (Willamette Valley) $30. The fruits are slightly deeper in this "Five Elements Wine." The fruit flavors are austere, with wild berries, dry tannins and a somewhat metallic finish. It needs more time to pull together. **87** *—P.G. (7/1/2007)*

Cooper Mountain 2002 Meadowlark Vineyard Pinot Noir (Willamette Valley) $27. 89 *(11/1/2004)*

Cooper Mountain 2005 Mountain Terroir Pinot Noir (Willamette Valley) $40. One of the "Five Elements Series" Pinots, the Mountain Terroir has good color, slightly more pronounced fruit than the winery's Reserve, and plenty of acid. There could be more sweetness to the fruit, but this is still young and pulling itself together, and probably will be better in two or three years. **87** *—P.G. (7/1/2007)*

Cooper Mountain 2005 Old Vines Pinot Noir (Willamette Valley) $40. This wine comes from the original estate plantings dating to 1978. It's got more expressive aromas than its stable mates, with nuances of barnyard, cola and black cherry. It's tight and austere, a bit chewy and high in acid. Clean and fresh. **88** *—P.G. (7/1/2007)*

Cooper Mountain 2005 Reserve Pinot Noir (Willamette Valley) $20. Reserve seems an odd designation for this inexpensive wine, but whatever you call it's a very drinkable, light and balanced, with some interesting highlights. Organically grown grapes—really biodynamic—show some lightly earthy notes. The fruit tails off quickly and the acids take over. Nice quaffer. **86** *—P.G. (7/1/2007)*

Cooper Mountain 2002 Reserve Pinot Noir (Willamette Valley) $18. 84 *(11/1/2004)*

COOPER-GARROD

Cooper-Garrod 1996 Cabernet Franc (Santa Cruz Mountains) $18. 89 *—S.H. (2/1/2000)*

Cooper-Garrod 1995 Cabernet Sauvignon (Santa Cruz Mountains) $28. 92 *—S.H. (2/1/2000)*

Cooper-Garrod 1997 Gravel Ridge Vineyard Chardonnay (Santa Cruz Mountains) $20. 92 *—S.H. (2/1/2000)*

COPAIN WINES

Copain Wines 2004 Hacienda-Secoya Pinot Noir (Anderson Valley) $45. Tastes a little on the tannic side for an '04 Pinot, with an astringency that locks down the fruit. But there's a good core of sweet cherry and cranberry. Might soften by 2008. **88** *—S.H. (11/1/2007)*

Copain Wines 2004 Hein Family Pinot Noir (Anderson Valley) $50. Generous in ripe red cherry, plum, carob and anise flavors, this very dry Pinot has a unique touch of tangerine. Tasted spring of 2007, this showed firm, slightly hard tannins, suggesting a period in the cellar is warranted. Better after winter '07, or decant for a bit if opening now. **89** *—S.H. (11/1/2007)*

Copain Wines 2004 Kiser En Bas Pinot Noir (Anderson Valley) $50. The most complete and rewarding of Copain's '04 Pinots, the Kiser En Bas shows the vintner's propensity for tannins, but offers a great wealth of cherries, raspberries, red currants, vanilla, lavender and cedar flavors that mitigate the slight astringency. Beautiful now, with decanting, and should develop over the next 3–5 years. **91** *—S.H. (11/1/2007)*

Copain Wines 2001 Eaglepoint Ranch Syrah (Mendocino County) $35. 93 Editors' Choice *—S.H. (12/1/2003)*

COPELAND CREEK

Copeland Creek 2002 Chardonnay (Sonoma Coast) $18. 84 *—S.H. (3/1/2006)*

Copeland Creek 2001 Meritage (Sonoma Coast) $30. 81 *—S.H. (3/1/2006)*

Copeland Creek 2002 Pinot Noir (Sonoma Coast) $30. 87 *—S.H. (11/1/2004)*

Copeland Creek 2001 Pinot Noir (Sonoma Coast) $30. 81 *—S.H. (2/1/2005)*

CORAL MUSTANG

Coral Mustang 2004 Tempranillo (Paso Robles) $28. Soft and gluey, a one-dimensional wine with cherry flavors. Finishes dryish to off-dry. **82** *—S.H. (3/1/2007)*

Coral Mustang 2005 Tempranillo Rose Tempranillo (Paso Robles) $15. Nice and dry, with good acidity, but the flavors are a little one-dimensional and thin. You'll find very modest cherries and spices. **83** *—S.H. (3/1/2007)*

CORBETT CANYON

Corbett Canyon 1997 Cabernet Sauvignon (Napa Valley) $10. 81 *—S.H. (9/1/1999)*

Corbett Canyon 1997 Reserve Chardonnay (Santa Barbara County) $10. 84 *(10/1/2000)*

Corbett Canyon 1999 Reserve Merlot (California) $7. 83 *—S.H. (7/1/2002)*

Corbett Canyon 1997 Reserve Merlot (North Coast) $10. 84 *(11/15/2000)*

Corbett Canyon 1999 Reserve Syrah (California) $7. 84 *—S.H. (7/1/2002)*

CORE WINERY

Core Winery 2001 Rhône Red Blend (Santa Barbara County) $24. 90 *—S.H. (3/1/2004)*

COREY CREEK

Corey Creek 2004 Chardonnay (North Fork of Long Island) $18. Inviting lemon, vanilla and honey aromas introduce a wine with pleasant toasted oak flavors, but there's little heft beyond the initial wash of warmth that hits the palate. Some citric pop to the finish which helps balance the honey and oak. The overall impression is positive and flavors are within the right realm, but the lack of depth leaves you wanting more. **84** *—S.K. (2/1/2007)*

Corey Creek 2001 Chardonnay (North Fork of Long Island) $16. 83 *—J.C. (10/2/2004)*

Corey Creek 1999 Chardonnay (North Fork of Long Island) $15. 85 *—J.C. (1/1/2004)*

Corey Creek 1998 Chardonnay (North Fork of Long Island) $15. 85 *—J.C. (4/1/2001)*

Corey Creek 2001 Reserve Chardonnay (North Fork of Long Island) $21. 87 *—J.C. (10/2/2004)*

Corey Creek 1999 Reserve Chardonnay (North Fork of Long Island) $18. 82 *—J.C. (1/1/2004)*

Corey Creek 2002 Gewürztraminer (North Fork of Long Island) $23. 83 *—J.C. (10/2/2004)*

Corey Creek 1998 Merlot (North Fork of Long Island) $18. 87 *—J.C. (4/1/2001)*

Corey Creek 1998 Rosé Blend (North Fork of Long Island) $11. 83 *—J.C. (4/1/2001)*

CORISON

Corison 1997 Cabernet Sauvignon (Napa Valley) $50. 93 *(11/1/2000)*

Corison 1996 Cabernet Sauvignon (Napa Valley) $45.94 *—S.H. (2/1/2000)*

Corison 2003 Cabernet Sauvignon (Napa Valley) $65. 89 *—S.H. (12/15/2006)*

Corison 2002 Cabernet Sauvignon (Napa Valley) $60. 88 *—S.H. (3/1/2006)*

Corison 2001 Cabernet Sauvignon (Napa Valley) $58. 91 *—S.H. (12/1/2005)*

Corison 2002 Kronos Vineyard Cabernet Sauvignon (Napa Valley) $100. 90 *—S.H. (12/15/2006)*

Corison 2001 Kronos Vineyard Cabernet Sauvignon (Napa Valley) $90. 94 *—S.H. (12/1/2005)*

CORLEY

Corley 2003 Proprietary Red Wine Bordeaux Blend (Napa Valley) $50. 92 *—S.H. (12/15/2006)*

Corley 2002 Proprietary Red Wine Bordeaux Blend (Napa Valley) $50. 92 *—S.H. (12/15/2005)*

Corley 2004 Proprietary Red Wine Cabernet Blend (Oak Knoll) $55. Soft and fruity, this Bordeaux blend has a splash of Syrah. It's dry and grippy in tannins, and there's a dried herb edge to the blackberry fruit. Finishes polished and elegant, but the softness suggests early drinking. **87** *—S.H. (12/15/2007)*

Corley Reserve 2002 Cabernet Sauvignon (Napa Valley) $65. 94 Editors' Choice *—S.H. (12/15/2005)*

Corley Reserve 2003 Estate Grown Chardonnay (Oak Knoll) $50. 87 *—S.H. (12/15/2005)*

Corley 2005 Reserve Estate Chardonnay (Oak Knoll) $40. There's a lot going on in this young Chard, suggesting moderate aging to let all the parts meld. The wine, from a southern appellation close to Carneros, is dry and crisp in acids, with peach, green apple and dried herb flavors enhanced by smoky, vanilla-tinged oak. Give it through 2007, and should hold for another five years. **88** *—S.H. (12/15/2007)*

CORNERSTONE

Cornerstone 2002 Cabernet Sauvignon (Howell Mountain) $80. 82 *—S.H. (5/1/2006)*

Cornerstone 2002 Cabernet Sauvignon (Napa Valley) $60. 82 *—S.H. (12/31/2005)*

COSENTINO

Cosentino 2003 CE2V Meritage Red Wine Bordeaux Blend (Napa Valley) $100. With one third of Merlot and Cab Franc, it's wildly rich in blackberry, currant, blueberry, cherry and milk chocolate, but is no mere fruit bomb. Possesses the gorgeously ripe tannins and overall balance you expect from a Cab of this pedigree and price. Drink now, and should hold and improve for 10 years. **93** *—S.H. (5/1/2007)*

Cosentino 2006 The Novelist Meritage Bordeaux White Blend (California) $18. This is mainly Sauvignon Blanc, with some Sémillon. It's a dry wine with decent acidity. The fig, citrus, green melon and licorice flavors go down nice and easy. **85** *—S.H. (12/31/2007)*

Cosentino 2005 The Novelist Meritage White Bordeaux White Blend (California) $18. 86 *—S.H. (12/15/2006)*

Cosentino 2003 The Poet Meritage Red Wine Cabernet Blend (Napa Valley) $65. 90 *—S.H. (12/31/2006)*

Cosentino 2002 Reserve Cabernet Franc (St. Helena) $45. 91 *—S.H. (10/1/2006)*

Cosentino 2003 Cabernet Sauvignon (Napa Valley) $45. 86 *—S.H. (10/1/2006)*

Cosentino 2005 Crystal Valley Cellars Franc Cabernet Franc (California) $22. A pretty basic but good red wine. It's dry, fruity, softly tannic and ready to drink now. The cherry flavors have a spicy, smoky oak edge. **85** *—S.H. (12/31/2007)*

Cosentino 2003 Reserve Cabernet Franc (Napa Valley) $45. You never quite know what to expect from a Cab Franc, but Napa red wine specialist Mitch Cosentino has produced one of the more definitive bottlings. It's softer and plumper than Cab Sauvignon, with a silky texture and lush cherry fruit that's been well-oaked. From a St. Helena vineyard. **90** *—S.H. (5/1/2007)*

Cosentino 2005 Crystal Valley Cellars The Cab Cabernet Sauvignon (California) $18. A rustic, brawny wine made for barbecued steak, this Cab has pronounced tannins balanced by lots of sweet, ripe fruit. The cherry, blackberry, plum and unsweetened chocolate flavors have a spicy, peppery finish. **86** *—S.H. (12/31/2007)*

Cosentino 2003 Hoopes Ranch Cabernet Sauvignon (Oakville) $75. Cosentino has a lot of Napa Bordeaux reds out there: the M. Coz, Legends and Poet, among others. This is not his finest wine from the vintage, but it's a very good wine. Polished and refined, it has black currant and oak flavors and is dry. But there's some thinness. Drink now–2009. **89** *—S.H. (4/1/2007)*

Cosentino 2004 Legends Cabernet Sauvignon (Sonoma County) $28. This is a wine Cosentino has negotiated with the basketball legend, Larry Bird, hence its name, and to my knowledge, it's the first time the winery has ventured to Sonoma for Cabernet. It's a good wine, not great. Savory in plum, black currant, cocoa and coffee flavors, it's dry and full-bodied, and should hold for a couple years. **87** *—S.H. (5/1/2007)*

Cosentino 2005 Chardonnay (Napa Valley) $28. Soft and dry, with stewed peach, pineapple, apricot and pear flavors, this Chard, from the Oak Knoll District, is liberally oaked. Drink now. **84** *—S.H. (4/1/2007)*

Cosentino 2005 CE2V Chardonnay (Napa Valley) $40. This high-end wine shows the dusting of thyme and sweet tobacco that often complexes Napa Chard. It's also fruited in pineapple and spicy melon, with a rich coating of smoky oak. Notable for balance and dry elegance. **91** *—S.H. (5/1/2007)*

Cosentino 2005 Crystal Valley The Chard Chardonnay (California) $16. A pretty nice everyday Chard. A little soft and simple, but rich in apricot, stewed peach and buttered toast flavors. The grapes are from Napa, Sonoma and Solano counties. **84** *—S.H. (5/1/2007)*

Cosentino 2004 Gewürztraminer (Yountville) $22. 87 *—S.H. (12/15/2006)*

Cosentino 2002 Reserve Merlot (Napa Valley) $42. 90 *—S.H. (10/1/2006)*

Cosentino 2005 Kirschenmann Vineyard Pinot Grigio (Lodi) $18. 84 *—S.H. (11/1/2006)*

Cosentino 2004 Il Chiaretto Sangiovese (California) $18. 81 *—S.H. (11/15/2006)*

Cosentino 2003 Crystal Valley Syrah (California) $18. Easy and likeable for its wealth of cherry, blackberry, currant, chocolate and spice flavors, this ripe Syrah is dry and gentle in tannins. It has some complexity and will play well against rich meats. **86** *—S.H. (5/1/2007)*

Cosentino 2005 Crystal Valley Cellars CigarZin Zinfandel (California) $30. Maybe a cigar will improve this Zin. It's hot and soft, with unbalanced, sweet cherry-jelly and green-mint flavors, and the sweetness makes the tannins astringent. 82 *—S.H. (12/31/2007)*

Cosentino 2005 Crystal Valley Cellars The Zin Zinfandel (California) $30. Lots of people will like this sweet young Lodi Zin for its jammy raspberry, cherry and cola flavors, and its tannins will cut through a sugary barbecue sauce. But if you're looking for something dry, go elsewhere. 83 *—S.H. (12/31/2007)*

COSMOS

Cosmos NV Orpheus III Bordeaux Blend (Napa Valley) $40. Mainly Cab Sauvignon, unusually blended with some Argentine Malbec, this is a dark, full-bodied, dry wine, rich and long in fruit. Blackberries, plums, smoky leather, sweet tobacco, cedar and spice flavors fill the mouth, leading to a complex, sharp finish. Best now–2010. 89 *—S.H. (8/1/2007)*

COSTA DE ORO

Costa de Oro 1998 Reserva Dorada Cold Coast Vineyard Chardonnay (Santa Maria Valley) $30. 89 *(6/1/2000)*

Costa de Oro 1999 Reserva Dorada Gold Coast Vineyard Chardonnay (Santa Maria Valley) $30. 89 *(7/1/2001)*

COSTA DEL SOL

Costa del Sol 2003 Red Wine Red Blend (Napa Valley) $15. 88 *—S.H. (12/1/2006)*

Costa del Sol 2001 Red Wine Red Blend (Napa Valley) $15. 88 *—J.M. (10/1/2004)*

COTTONWOOD CANYON

Cottonwood Canyon 2001 Chardonnay (Santa Maria Valley) $24. Lots of oak on this dry wine, which is clean despite its age. Crisp acidity frames tropical fruit flavors, wrapped into a creamy texture. Drink now. 87 *—S.H. (7/1/2007)*

Cottonwood Canyon 2001 Barrel Select Chardonnay (Santa Maria Valley) $39. Oaky and leesy, this is a pretty good Chardonnay whose main attributes are dryness and acidity. Toast and smoke dominate the tropical fruit flavors. 86 *—S.H. (7/1/2007)*

Cottonwood Canyon NV Bistro Classic Chardonnay (Santa Barbara County) $19. Tasted alongside the winery's more expensive vintage bottlings, this one's so close, you can hardly tell the difference. It's very dry and oaky, with a bracing minerality to the kumquat and pineapple flavors. 86 *—S.H. (7/1/2007)*

Cottonwood Canyon 2000 Bistro Classic Chardonnay (Santa Maria Valley) $20. 86 *—J.M. (12/15/2002)*

Cottonwood Canyon 2001 Pinot Noir (Santa Maria Valley) $39. Getting old and pale, but there's good, crisp acidity, and the wine is clean and vibrant. Although it's a bit thin, the flavors, of dried raspberries and cherries, sweet leather and anise, are interesting. 86 *—S.H. (7/1/2007)*

Cottonwood Canyon 2000 Pinot Noir (Santa Maria Valley) $36. 86 *—S.H. (8/1/2004)*

Cottonwood Canyon 2001 Elizabeth's Vista Pinot Noir (Santa Maria Valley) $48. At nearly six years old, this Pinot is losing fruit and getting tired. Pale in color, turning brown and soft, it shows dried cherry and cola flavors. 84 *—S.H. (7/1/2007)*

Cottonwood Canyon 1999 Estate Pinot Noir (Santa Maria Valley) $32. 86 *(10/1/2002)*

Cottonwood Canyon 2000 Sharon's Vineyard Barrel Select Pinot Noir (Santa Maria Valley) $64. 89 *—S.H. (8/1/2004)*

Cottonwood Canyon 2000 Blanc de Blanc Sparkling Blend (Santa Maria Valley) $48. 90 *—S.H. (12/31/2006)*

Cottonwood Canyon 2001 Blanc de Noir Sparkling Blend (Santa Maria Valley) $48. 90 *—S.H. (12/31/2006)*

Cottonwood Canyon 2001 Syroir Red Blend (Central Coast) $38. This Syrah-Pinot Noir blend shows elements of both. It's interesting, a work in progress, with the silky, light body and cherry cola flavors of a coastal Pinot, and a grippy edge of tannin. Good structure, with some complexity. Drink now. 86 *—S.H. (7/1/2007)*

Cottonwood Canyon NV Bistro Classic Syrah (Central Coast) $28. A pretty simple wine. Dry and rough, it has green, minty flavors and disagreeable acidity. 81 *—S.H. (7/1/2007)*

Cottonwood Canyon 2003 Bistro Classic Zinfandel (Paso Robles) $19. On the sharp, green, minty side, which makes it problematic, although there's just enough cherry flavor for salvage. Finishes totally dry. 83 *—S.H. (7/1/2007)*

COTURRI WINERY

Coturri Winery 2001 Zinfandel (Sonoma Mountain) $20. 82 *(11/1/2003)*

COUGAR CREST

Cougar Crest 2001 Hangartown Select Merlot (Walla Walla (WA)) $26. 87 *—P.G. (9/1/2003)*

Cougar Crest 2001 Syrah (Walla Walla (WA)) $30. 87 *—P.G. (9/1/2003)*

Cougar Crest 2002 Stellar Vineyard Reserve Syrah (Walla Walla (WA)) $45. 86 *—P.G. (12/15/2005)*

COUGAR RIDGE

Cougar Ridge 1999 Cabernet Sauvignon (Paso Robles) $18. 82 *—S.H. (4/1/2003)*

Cougar Ridge 1999 Chardonnay (Central Coast) $13. 84 *—S.H. (2/1/2003)*

Cougar Ridge 1999 Merlot (Paso Robles) $18. 83 *—S.H. (4/1/2003)*

COULSON ELDORADO

Coulson Eldorado 2000 Kipp Vineyard Mataro (El Dorado) $15. 85 *—S.H. (9/1/2002)*

Coulson Eldorado 2001 Koel Vineyard Mataro Mourvèdre (El Dorado) $15. 85 *—S.H. (12/1/2003)*

Coulson Eldorado 2000 Vintners Blend Red Blend (El Dorado) $16. 82 *—S.H. (5/1/2002)*

Coulson Eldorado 1999 Johnson Vineyard Syrah (El Dorado County) $16. 81 *(10/1/2001)*

Coulson Eldorado 2000 Safari Vineyard Zinfandel (El Dorado) $18. 83 *—S.H. (11/1/2002)*

COUNTY LINE

County Line 2006 Rosé Pinot Noir (Anderson Valley) $20. Whole cluster pressing has given this pale-colored wine a rich earthiness, even some tannins. It's also bone dry, with subtle cherryskin, herb tea and tobacco flavors. Shows quite a bit of sophistication and polish. 89 *—S.H. (7/1/2007)*

COUP DE FOUDRE

Coup de Foudre 2004 Cabernet Sauvignon (Napa Valley) $75. This wine is from John Schwartz, who partners with Heidi Peterson Barrett to make Amuse Bouche. For Coup de Foudre, he has paired with Danielle Price, MS, and wine director at Wynn Las Vegas, to produce this stunning Cabernet, which contains 12% Syrah. Grown in a 5-acre Stags Leap District vineyard, it shows stunning levels of blackberry and chocolate fruit enhanced with waves of smoky oak. Yet somehow, for all the opulence and power, there's an almost weightless elegance to the wine. Sometimes cult Cabs can lack restraint, be too obvious. This one teases with richness, then pulls back under a velvety cover of tannin. A major debut. 98 Editors' Choice *—S.H. (5/1/2007)*

COURTNEY BENHAM

Courtney Benham 2002 Cabernet Sauvignon (Sonoma County) $25. 87 *—S.H. (12/31/2005)*

Courtney Benham 2002 Cabernet Sauvignon (Napa Valley) $25. 85 *—S.H. (5/1/2005)*

Courtney Benham 2005 Chardonnay (Napa Valley) $16. 84 *—S.H. (12/15/2006)*

Courtney Benham 2005 Sauvignon Blanc (Napa Valley) $12. 85 *—S.H. (12/15/2006)*

Courtney Benham 2004 Sauvignon Blanc (Napa Valley) $14. 84 *—S.H. (7/1/2006)*

Courtney Benham 2003 Sauvignon Blanc (Napa Valley) $14. 85 *—S.H. (6/1/2005)*

Courtney Benham 2005 Zinfandel (Dry Creek Valley) $20. Deliciously showcases the variety in a pure, classic way, while retaining the elegant balance of a light Pinot. With its silky mouthfeel, the complex flavors are all Zin, showing wild berries, gingersnap cookie, cocoa and vanilla, and a rich array of pepper, cinnamon and other spices. Great job from this second label of Martin Ray. 90 Editors' Choice *—S.H. (12/1/2007)*

Courtney Benham 2004 Zinfandel (Stags Leap District) $25. 84 *—S.H. (12/1/2006)*

COUVILLION WINERY

Couvillion Winery 2004 Cabernet Sauvignon (Columbia Valley (WA)) $25. This is pure Cabernet from the Dionysus vineyard, and is meant to become this new winery's flagship wine. It's a standout debut that captures the herb, the dust and the mixed wild berries of the grape, presented in a graceful, harmonious and flavorful package. 90 *—P.G. (3/1/2007)*

Couvillion Winery 2004 Merlot (Columbia Valley (WA)) $15. This new winery has fashioned a tight, slightly tarry, nicely balanced wine. Though it's not a big wine, it elegantly wraps together varietal flavors of blackberry and cassis with accents of earth and tar. 88 *—P.G. (3/1/2007)*

COVEY RUN

Covey Run 1997 Newhouse Vineyard Aligoté (Yakima Valley) $14. 88 —*M.S. (11/1/1999)*

Covey Run 2003 Cabernet Sauvignon (Columbia Valley (WA)) $9. 86 Best Buy —*P.G. (4/1/2006)*

Covey Run 2002 Cabernet Sauvignon (Washington) $9. 89 Best Buy —*P.G. (11/15/2004)*

Covey Run 2001 Cabernet Sauvignon (Washington) $9. 88 Best Buy —*P.G. (9/1/2004)*

Covey Run 1999 Cabernet Sauvignon (Washington) $9. 86 —*P.G. (9/1/2002)*

Covey Run 1997 Cabernet Sauvignon (Washington) $13. 83 —*P.G. (11/15/2000)*

Covey Run 1998 Barrel Select Cabernet Sauvignon (Yakima Valley) $15. 85 —*P.G. (12/31/2001)*

Covey Run 2004 Quail Series Cabernet Sauvignon (Columbia Valley (WA)) $9. Herbal and tannic, this won't be mistaken for a cult Cab, but in its price range it offers authentic Cabernet flavors. The fruit is lean and the tannins slightly green, and the herbal side of the grape is much in evidence. But everything is in balance, and it avoids the watery soda pop flavors of most cheap Cabs. **85 Best Buy** —*P.G. (8/1/2007)*

Covey Run 1996 Whiskey Canyon Vineyard Cabernet Sauvignon (Yakima Valley) $29. 84 —*P.G. (11/15/2000)*

Covey Run 2002 Winemaker's Collection Cabernet Sauvignon (Columbia Valley (WA)) $13. 87 —*P.G. (12/15/2005)*

Covey Run 1997 Cabernet Sauvignon-Merlot (Washington) $8. 87 —*J.C. (11/15/1999)*

Covey Run 2002 Cabernet Sauvignon-Merlot (Columbia Valley (WA)) $9. 86 Best Buy —*P.G. (12/15/2005)*

Covey Run 2001 Cabernet Sauvignon-Merlot (Washington) $9. 87 Best Buy —*P.G. (12/31/2003)*

Covey Run 2000 Cabernet Sauvignon-Merlot (Washington) $9. 85 —*P.G. (9/1/2002)*

Covey Run 1999 Cabernet Sauvignon-Merlot (Washington) $11. 87 Best Buy *(5/1/2002)*

Covey Run 1997 Chardonnay (Washington) $10. Best Buy —*M.M. (11/1/1999)*

Covey Run 2004 Chardonnay (Columbia Valley (WA)) $9. 87 Best Buy —*P.G. (10/1/2006)*

Covey Run 2003 Chardonnay (Columbia Valley (WA)) $9. 86 Best Buy —*P.G. (12/15/2005)*

Covey Run 2002 Chardonnay (Washington) $9. 88 Best Buy —*P.G. (11/15/2004)*

Covey Run 2001 Chardonnay (Yakima Valley) $9. 85 —*P.G. (5/1/2004)*

Covey Run 2000 Chardonnay (Washington) $9. 86 Best Buy —*P.G. (12/31/2003)*

Covey Run 1999 Chardonnay (Columbia Valley (WA)) $12. 87 *(5/1/2002)*

Covey Run 1998 Chardonnay (Columbia Valley (WA)) $10. 88 Best Buy —*P.G. (11/15/2000)*

Covey Run 2000 Barrel Select Chardonnay (Yakima Valley) $13. 86 —*P.G. (12/31/2003)*

Covey Run 2005 Quail Series Chardonnay (Columbia Valley (WA)) $9. Light and fruity with pineapple, melon and apple. This fruit forward, food-friendly wine has natural acids and a delicate balance. For the money it is a fine choice to accompany seafood, poultry and pasta salads. **85** —*P.G. (12/31/2007)*

Covey Run 2003 Reserve Chardonnay (Columbia Valley (WA)) $22. 89 —*P.G. (10/1/2006)*

Covey Run 2002 Reserve Chardonnay (Yakima Valley) $22. 88 —*P.G. (9/1/2004)*

Covey Run 1998 Reserve Chardonnay (Yakima Valley) $15. 87 —*P.G. (10/1/2001)*

Covey Run 2004 Winemaker's Collection Chardonnay (Columbia Valley (WA)) $13. 88 Best Buy —*P.G. (12/15/2005)*

Covey Run 2004 Chenin Blanc (Columbia Valley (WA)) $8. 89 Best Buy —*P.G. (12/15/2005)*

Covey Run 2002 Chenin Blanc (Washington) $7. 86 Best Buy —*P.G. (12/31/2003)*

Covey Run 2000 Chenin Blanc (Washington) $7. 85 —*P.G. (8/20/2003)*

Covey Run 2005 Quail Series Chenin Blanc (Columbia Valley (WA)) $8. Not too many wineries bother with Chenin any more; a shame, since it grows so well in Washington's desert climate. Covey's off-dry version retains the honeyed floral characteristics of Loire Valley versions, but beefs up the fruit with juicy flavors of melon, sweet pear and honeysuckle. **88 Best Buy** —*P.G. (8/1/2007)*

Covey Run 2002 Fumé Blanc (Washington) $9. 85 —*P.G. (5/1/2004)*

Covey Run 2001 Fumé Blanc (Washington) $9. 85 —*P.G. (12/31/2003)*

Covey Run 2000 Fumé Blanc (Washington) $12. 86 *(5/1/2002)*

Covey Run 1997 Fumé Blanc (Washington) $7. 89 Best Buy —*M.S. (9/1/1999)*

Covey Run 1998 Gewürztraminer (Washington) $7. 80 *(4/1/2000)*

Covey Run 2004 Gewürztraminer (Columbia Valley (WA)) $7. 90 Best Buy —*P.G. (12/15/2005)*

Covey Run 2003 Gewürztraminer (Washington) $7. 86 —*P.G. (7/1/2004)*

Covey Run 2002 Gewürztraminer (Washington) $7. 88 Best Buy —*P.G. (12/31/2003)*

Covey Run 2000 Gewürztraminer (Columbia Valley (WA)) $8. 86 *(5/1/2002)*

Covey Run 2005 Quail Series Gewürztraminer (Columbia Valley (WA)) $8. 87 Best Buy —*P.G. (12/31/2006)*

Covey Run 2002 Lemberger (Washington) $7. 87 Best Buy —*P.G. (12/31/2003)*

Covey Run 2000 Lemberger (Yakima Valley) $7. 87 Best Buy —*P.G. (9/1/2002)*

Covey Run 1999 Lemberger (Yakima Valley) $7. 85 Best Buy *(6/1/2001)*

Covey Run 2004 Quail Series Lemberger (Columbia Valley (WA)) $7. Covey's much-loved Lemberger is a nod to Washington's early days, when the rustic red was considered to be the state's finest effort. These days it's just another light, grapy, innocuous party wine, but at least the rasty tannins have been smoothed out. **84 Best Buy** —*P.G. (8/1/2007)*

Covey Run 2003 Merlot (Columbia Valley (WA)) $9. 87 Best Buy —*P.G. (10/1/2006)*

Covey Run 2002 Merlot (Columbia Valley (WA)) $9. 87 Best Buy —*P.G. (6/1/2005)*

Covey Run 2001 Merlot (Washington) $9. 86 —*P.G. (9/1/2004)*

Covey Run 1999 Merlot (Washington) $9. 88 Best Buy —*P.G. (9/1/2002)*

Covey Run 2001 Barrel Select Merlot (Columbia Valley (WA)) $13. 83 —*P.G. (6/1/2005)*

Covey Run 2000 Barrel Select Merlot (Washington) $13. 87 —*P.G. (9/1/2004)*

Covey Run 1998 Barrel Select Merlot (Columbia Valley (WA)) $15. 85 —*P.G. (10/1/2001)*

Covey Run 2004 Quail Series Merlot (Columbia Valley (WA)) $9. This is bone dry, light as a feather and as simple and basic as only Merlot can be. It hints at flavors of rhubarb and bark, with all its components balanced out, but offers no depth or nuance. **83** —*P.G. (12/31/2007)*

Covey Run 2001 Reserve Merlot (Columbia Valley (WA)) $22. 88 —*P.G. (9/1/2004)*

Covey Run 2002 Winemaker's Collection Merlot (Columbia Valley (WA)) $13. 88 Best Buy —*P.G. (12/15/2005)*

Covey Run 2002 Morio Muskat (Washington) $7. 85 —*P.G. (9/1/2004)*

Covey Run 1999 Morio Muskat (Yakima Valley) $18. 84 —*P.G. (11/15/2000)*

Covey Run 2004 Pinot Grigio (Columbia Valley (WA)) $7. 88 Best Buy —*P.G. (2/1/2006)*

Covey Run 2005 Quail Series Pinot Grigio (Columbia Valley (WA)) $9. They've upped the price, but Covey still makes the best under-$10 Pinot Grigio in the land. Prickly acids prop up moderately ripe flavors of stone fruits, pear, pineapple and green apple. This has punch and grip, and the persistent, palate-refreshing tartness takes away any undue sweetness. **87 Best Buy** —*P.G. (8/1/2007)*

Covey Run 2004 Riesling (Columbia Valley (WA)) $7. 89 Best Buy —*P.G. (11/15/2005)*

Covey Run 2003 Riesling (Washington) $7. 88 Best Buy —*P.G. (9/1/2004)*

Covey Run 2000 Riesling (Washington) $7. 89 Best Buy —*P.G. (12/31/2001)*

Covey Run 1999 Riesling (Washington) $7. 85 —*P.G. (11/15/2000)*

Covey Run 2004 Dry Riesling (Columbia Valley (WA)) $7. 88 Best Buy —*P.G. (12/15/2005)*

Covey Run 2003 Dry Riesling (Washington) $7. 87 —*P.G. (9/1/2004)*

Covey Run 2002 Dry Riesling (Washington) $7. 88 Best Buy —*P.G. (12/31/2003)*

Covey Run 1998 Ice Wine Riesling (Yakima Valley) $22. 89 *(5/1/2002)*

Covey Run 2003 Late Harvest Riesling (Washington) $9. 87 Best Buy —*P.G. (11/15/2004)*

Covey Run 2002 Late Harvest Riesling (Yakima Valley) $9. 87 —*P.G. (8/1/2003)*

Covey Run 2005 Quail Series Riesling (Columbia Valley (WA)) $8. 86 —*P.G. (12/31/2006)*

Covey Run 2005 Quail Series Dry Riesling (Columbia Valley (WA)) $8. 85 —*P.G. (12/31/2006)*

Covey Run 2004 Winemaker's Collection Late Harvest Riesling (Columbia Valley (WA)) $13. 88 Best Buy —*P.G. (12/15/2005)*

Covey Run 2004 Sauvignon Blanc (Columbia Valley (WA)) $8. 87 Best Buy —*P.G. (6/1/2006)*

Covey Run 2003 Sauvignon Blanc (Washington) $9. 88 Best Buy —*P.G. (11/15/2004)*

Covey Run 2005 Quail Series Sauvignon Blanc (Columbia Valley (WA)) $9. Light, tart and mildly grassy. The herbal notes underscore citrus fruit flavors cutting across the borders of Mandarin orange, lime, grapefruit and pineapple. There's a pleasing snap to the crisp, authoritative finish. 87 Best Buy —*P.G. (8/1/2007)*

Covey Run 2002 Sémillon-Chardonnay (Washington) $7. 85 —*P.G. (9/1/2004)*

Covey Run 2000 Sémillon-Chardonnay (Washington) $7. 86 —*P.G. (9/1/2002)*

Covey Run 2003 Syrah (Columbia Valley (WA)) $9. 83 *(9/1/2005)*

Covey Run 2002 Syrah (Washington) $9. 89 Best Buy —*P.G. (11/15/2004)*

Covey Run 2001 Barrel Select Syrah (Columbia Valley (WA)) $13. 85 —*P.G. (7/1/2004)*

Covey Run 2000 Barrel Select Syrah (Columbia Valley (WA)) $13. 85 —*P.G. (12/31/2003)*

Covey Run 1998 Barrel Select Syrah (Yakima Valley) $15. 89 Best Buy *(5/1/2002)*

Covey Run 1998 Barrel Select Syrah (Yakima Valley) $15. 84 *(10/1/2001)*

Covey Run 2004 Quail Series Syrah (Columbia Valley (WA)) $9. This budget-priced Syrah offers hints of why the grape does so well in Washington. It has a bit of peppery bite, some very tart cranberry fruit, crisp acids and a lifted, citrusy finish. Clean and varietal, it's a good everyday effort. 84 —*P.G. (12/31/2007)*

Covey Run 2003 Winemaker's Collection Syrah (Columbia Valley (WA)) $13. This limited-production (2,000 cases) reserve is a fitting companion to Covey's amazingly good every day Syrah. It's very clean, well-balanced and solidly varietal. The bacon fat barrel flavors are welcome accents, as are the hints of citrus peel and smoke. Tart berry fruit and polished, lightly herbal tannins flesh it out. 88 Best Buy —*P.G. (8/1/2007)*

Covey Run 2002 Winemaker's Collection Syrah (Columbia Valley (WA)) $13. 88 Best Buy —*P.G. (12/15/2005)*

Covey Run 1998 White Blend (Columbia Valley (WA)) $7.83 —*P.G. (11/15/2000)*

COVINGTON CELLARS

Covington Cellars 2005 Sangiovese (Columbia Valley (WA)) $29. Hard and tannic, this doesn't show much in the way of varietal character. There's a hint of red fruit, some tar and rubber, and a thin, somewhat stemmy finish. 82 —*P.G. (12/31/2007)*

Covington Cellars 2003 Tuscan Red Sangiovese (Walla Walla (WA)) $28. 86 —*P.G. (6/1/2006)*

Covington Cellars 2003 Starr Syrah (Walla Walla (WA)) $25. 86 —*P.G. (6/1/2006)*

Covington Cellars 2006 Sémillon (Columbia Valley (WA)) $24. The wine is almost honey-colored, and scented with sweet hay and clover. That impression of sweet grass carries over into the mouth, and it adds life and lift to the rather rich and heavy fruit. Don't look for it to improve or to age beyond a year or two. The blend includes 7% Sauvignon Blanc. 87 —*P.G. (12/1/2007)*

Covington Cellars 2006 Viognier (Columbia Valley (WA)) $19. The emphasis here is squarely on the fruit, which is fresh and varietal, carrying flavors of apricot, peach and apple. Pleasing aromas support the impression of ripe stone fruit, with moderate alcohol and none of the bitterness that Viognier can show in the finish. 87 —*P.G. (12/1/2007)*

COYOTE CANYON

Coyote Canyon 2002 Chenin Blanc (Santa Lucia Highlands) $15. 84 —*S.H. (12/31/2004)*

Coyote Canyon 2001 Chenin Blanc (Santa Lucia Highlands) $21. 87 —*S.H. (12/15/2003)*

Coyote Canyon 2002 Pinot Noir (Santa Lucia Highlands) $18. 87 —*S.H. (11/1/2004)*

Coyote Canyon 1999 Garys' Vineyard Pinot Noir (Santa Lucia Highlands) $55. 88 —*S.H. (8/1/2003)*

Coyote Canyon 2002 Reserve Pinot Noir (Santa Cruz Mountains) $32. 87 —*S.H. (11/1/2004)*

Coyote Canyon 2001 The Big Pond Pinot Noir (Santa Lucia Highlands) $42. 91 —*S.H. (12/1/2004)*

Coyote Canyon 2001 Sangiovese (Russian River Valley) $30. 90 —*S.H. (9/1/2003)*

Coyote Canyon 2002 Syrah (Arroyo Seco) $32. 85 —*S.H. (12/31/2004)*

COYOTE CREEK

Coyote Creek 1999 Syrah (Paso Robles) $17. 81 *(10/1/2001)*

Coyote Creek 1999 Zinfandel (Paso Robles) $19. 84 —*D.T. (3/1/2002)*

CRANE BROTHERS

Crane Brothers 2004 Crane Ranch Vineyard Hillside Block Cabernet Sauvignon (Napa Valley) $44. What's so nice about this Cab is that it's the opposite of today's cult Cab style, which is soft and gooey. Instead, it's tannic and acidic and not ashamed of presenting these food-worthy aspects of its personality. Tastes like a young, ageable Third or Fourth Growth Bordeaux, with a good core of black currants and cedar. Put it in the cellar until 2009 or so, and it should hold and improve for another five years. 90 —*S.H. (11/1/2007)*

Crane Brothers 2004 Crane Ranch Vineyard Merlot (Napa Valley) $30. Steaks, chops and grilled mushrooms will love this dry, tannic wine. It's old-style, a term that is not meant to be derogatory, but instead recalls a time when wine was made to be had with food. Similar to a good Bordeaux, it has richly earthy flavors of blackberries, mocha and cedar. Drink now through 2008. 91 Editors' Choice —*S.H. (11/1/2007)*

Crane Brothers 2004 Brodacious Red Blend (Napa Valley) $36. Another winery owns the rights to the word Bodacious, so this Bordeaux-Syrah blend adds an "r" to the proprietary name. It's on the rustic side, but elegantly so, with ragged tannins framing savory flavors of ripe cherry juice, black currants and Chinese green tea. 86 —*S.H. (11/1/2007)*

Crane Brothers 2002 Syrah (Napa Valley) $40. 86 *(9/1/2005)*

Crane Brothers 2004 Crane Ranch Vineyard Syrah (Napa Valley) $36. This is quite a good Syrah from a small vineyard in the Oak Knoll area of the southern valley. Alcohol is very high (15.5%) but the wine wears it well due to the size of its fruit. Dried blackberries and pomegranates, sweet leather, violets and toasty new oak flavors comprise the flavors, and the finish is tannic and distinguished. This elegant wine is one to watch. 92 —*S.H. (11/1/2007)*

CRANE FAMILY

Crane Family 1999 Merlot (Napa Valley) $37. 87 —*S.H. (12/31/2001)*

Crane Family 2000 Don Raffaele Estate Merlot (Napa Valley) $39. 86 —*S.H. (8/1/2003)*

Crane Family 2000 Hilltop Selection Merlot (Napa Valley) $52. 89 —*S.H. (8/1/2003)*

CRANE LAKE

Crane Lake 2003 Chardonnay (California) $5. 84 Best Buy —*S.H. (12/15/2004)*

Crane Lake 2004 Merlot (California) $5. 82 —*S.H. (4/1/2006)*

Crane Lake 2003 Merlot (California) $5. 84 Best Buy —*S.H. (8/1/2005)*

Crane Lake 2004 Pinot Grigio (California) $5. 84 Best Buy —*S.H. (11/15/2006)*

Crane Lake 2005 Sauvignon Blanc (California) $5. 82 —*S.H. (11/1/2006)*

Crane Lake 2004 Sauvignon Blanc (California) $5. 83 Best Buy —*S.H. (3/1/2006)*

Crane Lake 2004 Shiraz (California) $5. 84 Best Buy —*S.H. (11/15/2006)*

CRAUFORD

Crauford 2004 Maroon Vineyard Tattoo Cabernet Sauvignon (Napa Valley) $38. Ripe to the point of mushy with hugely oaked, cooked, black currant and baked cherry-pie flavors. Needs more balance, elegance and harmony. 84 —*S.H. (12/1/2007)*

Crauford 2006 Maroon Vineyard Highlander Sauvignon Blanc (Napa Valley) $16. There's lots to like in this dry wine layered with fruit. Clean and pure, with little or no oak influence, it shows rich, fruity flavors of lemons, limes and peaches, with a pleasant honeysuckle complexity. 90 —*S.H. (12/1/2007)*

Crauford 2005 Kilt Lifter Brown Vineyard Zinfandel (Napa Valley) $32. A great Zin from Napa, this shows the classic structure of a claret, but with Zin's distinctive personality. Briary, brambly wild berries, mocha and masses of white pepper are the aromas and flavors. **91** *—S.H. (12/1/2007)*

CRAWFORD

Crawford 2003 Sauvignon Blanc (Napa Valley) $22. **88** *—J.M. (10/1/2005)*

CRICHTON HALL

Crichton Hall 2003 Chardonnay (Napa Valley) $28. **84** *—S.H. (3/1/2006)*

Crichton Hall 2001 Chardonnay (Napa Valley) $28. **85** *—S.H. (11/15/2004)*

Crichton Hall 1998 Chardonnay (Napa Valley) $26. **88** *(6/1/2000)*

Crichton Hall 1997 Chardonnay (Napa Valley) $22. **91** *—M.S. (6/1/1999)*

Crichton Hall 1996 Chardonnay (Napa Valley) $22. **91** *—M.S. (6/1/1999)*

Crichton Hall 2001 Merlot (Napa Valley) $32. **87** *—S.H. (12/15/2004)*

Crichton Hall 1996 Merlot (Napa Valley) $26. **90** *—M.S. (6/1/1999)*

Crichton Hall 1995 Merlot (Napa Valley) $26. **93** *—M.S. (6/1/1999)*

Crichton Hall 2001 Reflexion Merlot-Cabernet Sauvignon (Napa Valley) $75. **93** *—S.H. (11/15/2004)*

Crichton Hall 2000 Pinot Noir (Carneros) $32. **89** *(10/1/2002)*

Crichton Hall 1996 Pinot Noir (Napa Valley) $26. **89** *—M.S. (6/1/1999)*

Crichton Hall 1995 Pinot Noir (Napa Valley) $26. **88** *—M.S. (6/1/1999)*

Crichton Hall 2003 Truchard Vineyard Pinot Noir (Carneros) $32. **89** *—S.H. (3/1/2006)*

Crichton Hall 2001 Truchard Vineyard Pinot Noir (Carneros) $32. **89** *—S.H. (12/1/2004)*

CRINELLA

Crinella 2005 Marino Vineyard Sauvignon Blanc (Russian River Valley) $22. Has dryness and structure, with excellent acidity marking citrus and fig flavors. Spicy finish. There's a little dip in concentration in the middle palate, but it's really a wine to watch. **88** *—S.H. (7/1/2007)*

Crinella 2004 Marino Vineyard Sauvignon Blanc (Russian River Valley) $22. **84** *—S.H. (10/1/2006)*

CRISTOM

Cristom 2003 Pinot Gris (Willamette Valley) $16. **87** *—P.G. (2/1/2005)*

Cristom 2004 Estate Pinot Gris (Willamette Valley) $17. **92 Editors' Choice** *—P.G. (2/1/2006)*

Cristom 1998 Oregon/Washington Pinot Gris (Oregon) $15. **92 Editors' Choice** *—P.G. (11/1/2001)*

Cristom 2004 Eileen Vineyard Pinot Noir (Willamette Valley) $47. In 2004 the Eileen bottling seems to have retained a bit more freshness and sweetness to the fruit, but despite that it carries a dominant impression of rough, chalky tannins and earth. It's chewy, tannic and a bit rough in the finish. **86** *—P.G. (4/1/2007)*

Cristom 2003 Eileen Vineyard Pinot Noir (Willamette Valley) $45. **89** *—P.G. (5/1/2006)*

Cristom 2002 Eileen Vineyard Pinot Noir (Willamette Valley) $45. **90** *—P.G. (2/1/2005)*

Cristom 2000 Eileen Vineyard Pinot Noir (Willamette Valley) $39. **86** *(10/1/2002)*

Cristom 2004 Jessie Vineyard Pinot Noir (Willamette Valley) $47. Past vintages of Jessie have been big, brawny wines, but in '04 this too seems to be a bit tired and dried out. The herbal flavors dominate; in truth, it is difficult to distinguish this as different from the Sommers Reserve. **87** *—P.G. (4/1/2007)***91** *—P.G. (5/1/2006)*

Cristom 2000 Jessie Vineyard Pinot Noir (Willamette Valley) $39. **89** *(10/1/2002)*

Cristom 2000 Louise Vineyard Pinot Noir (Willamette Valley) $39. **91 Editors' Choice** *(10/1/2002)*

Cristom 1998 Louise Vineyard Pinot Noir (Willamette Valley) $39. **88** *(12/1/2000)*

Cristom 1997 Louise Vineyard Pinot Noir (Willamette Valley) $32. **90** *(10/1/1999)*

Cristom 2003 Marjorie Vineyard Pinot Noir (Willamette Valley) $45. **90** *—P.G. (5/1/2006)*

Cristom 2000 Marjorie Vineyard Pinot Noir (Willamette Valley) $39. **89** *(10/1/2002)*

Cristom 1997 Marjorie Vineyard Pinot Noir (Willamette Valley) $32. **89** *—P.G. (9/1/2000)*

Cristom 1998 Marjorie Vineyards Pinot Noir (Willamette Valley) $39. **92** *—M.S. (12/1/2000)*

Cristom 2004 Mt. Jefferson Cuvée Pinot Noir (Willamette Valley) $30. Light and showing signs of oxidation (possibly an off bottle), this wine is already drying out. Aromas are of cooked strawberries, tannins are quite dry, and the finish is earthy and has lost its freshness. **86** *—P.G. (4/1/2007)*

Cristom 2003 Mt. Jefferson Cuvée Pinot Noir (Willamette Valley) $25. **91 Editors' Choice** *—P.G. (5/1/2006)*

Cristom 2002 Mt. Jefferson Cuvée Pinot Noir (Willamette Valley) $25. **89** *—P.G. (2/1/2005)*

Cristom 2000 Mt. Jefferson Cuvée Pinot Noir (Willamette Valley) $24. **83** *— (10/1/2002)*

Cristom 1998 Mt. Jefferson Cuvée Pinot Noir (Willamette Valley) $25. **87** *(12/1/2000)*

Cristom 1997 Mt. Jefferson Cuvée Pinot Noir (Willamette Valley) $20. **82** *(10/1/1999)*

Cristom 2003 Reserve Pinot Noir (Willamette Valley) $35. **92** *—P.G. (5/1/2006)*

Cristom 2002 Reserve Pinot Noir (Willamette Valley) $35. **91** *—P.G. (2/1/2005)*

Cristom 2000 Reserve Pinot Noir (Willamette Valley) $39. **89** *(10/1/2002)*

Cristom 1998 Reserve Pinot Noir (Willamette Valley) $36. **91** *(12/1/2000)*

Cristom 1997 Reserve Pinot Noir (Willamette Valley) $30. **88** *—P.G. (9/1/2000)*

Cristom 2004 Sommers Reserve Pinot Noir (Willamette Valley) $42. The reserve is strongly herbal, with the tomato leaf character often found in Oregon Pinots. It's tannic and strong, with a finish that puts the accent squarely on dried herb, leaf and bark, somewhat to the detriment of the fruit. **87** *—P.G. (4/1/2007)*

Cristom 2004 Estate Syrah (Willamette Valley) $30. Most Oregon Syrah is grown in the south and trucked up to Willamette Valley wineries, but Cristom grows its own. Admirable effort, but it falls a bit short on flavor. Tannins dominate and the fruit fails to gather itself into any identifiable varietal shape. It's a gentle, generic red. **85** *—P.G. (4/1/2007)*

Cristom 2003 Viognier (Willamette Valley) $25. **88** *—P.G. (2/1/2005)*

Cristom 2005 Estate Viognier (Willamette Valley) $27. This is solid, juicy viognier, with pleasing texture and plenty of spice. The fruit is thick and mixes pear, apple and pineapple with hints of lime. Some heat can be felt in the finish—this is not a shy wine—but the winery has done an excellent job with the fruit. **88** *—P.G. (4/1/2007)*

CRISTOPHE

Cristophe 2000 Pinot Noir (Monterey) $10. **82** *(10/1/2002)*

CROCKER & STARR

Crocker & Starr 2003 Stone Place Bordeaux Blend (Napa Valley) $65. Showing an earthiness to the cherries, plums and black currants, with a rich array of fresh thyme and sage, this wine, mainly Cabernet, is young and closed now, with solid tannins. But it's polished and elegant and balanced, and the fruit is there for modest aging. Best 2007–2012. **88** *—S.H. (4/1/2007)*

Crocker & Starr 2003 Sauvignon Blanc (Napa Valley) $23. **89** *(7/1/2005)*

CROOKED VINE

Crooked Vine 2001 Chardonnay (Livermore Valley) $30. **85** *—S.H. (12/15/2003)*

Crooked Vine 2001 Sangiovese (Livermore Valley) $30. **85** *—S.H. (12/1/2003)*

CROSSPOINT

Crosspoint 2001 Cabernet Sauvignon (Paso Robles) $12. **84** *—S.H. (12/31/2003)*

Crosspoint 2002 Pinot Noir (Monterey County) $12. **88 Best Buy** *(11/1/2004)*

CROZE

Croze 1999 Cabernet Sauvignon (Napa Valley) $35. **82** *—S.H. (11/15/2002)*

Croze 2004 Rosé of Cabernet Sauvignon (Suisun Valley) $14. **85** *—S.H. (11/1/2005)*

Croze 2005 Vin d'Une Nuit Rosé of Cabernet Sauvignon (Suisun Valley) $14. Sweet, with cooked pie filling cherry and raspberry flavors and a slight vegginess. Soft acidity adds to the mouthfeel of flabbiness. **82** *—S.H. (7/1/2007)*

Croze 2001 Sweetwater Ranch Cabernet Sauvignon (Oak Knoll) $28. **89** *—S.H. (11/1/2005)*

CRUSH

Crush 2004 Proprietary Red Bordeaux Blend (Dry Creek Valley) $11. A Cab-Merlot blend, this scores high on the deliciousness factor. It's lush in ripe blackberry and cherry flavors, with sweet, refined tannins. The alcohol is on the high side, but there's no heat, just a nice, smooth roundness. Great price for such a nice Bordeaux-style wine. **88 Best Buy** *—S.H. (11/15/2007)*

CRYSTAL BASIN CELLARS

Crystal Basin Cellars 2001 Reserve Mourvèdre (El Dorado) $25. 90 *—S.H. (12/1/2003)*

Crystal Basin Cellars 2001 Reserve Syrah (El Dorado) $22. 88 *—S.H. (12/1/2003)*

CRYSTAL VALLEY CELLARS

Crystal Valley Cellars 2003 Cabernet Franc (California) $18. 83 *—S.H. (7/1/2006)*

Crystal Valley Cellars 2002 Cabernet Sauvignon (California) $16. 88 *—S.H. (10/1/2005)*

Crystal Valley Cellars 2000 Cabernet Sauvignon (Yountville) $16. 91 *—S.H. (12/31/2002)*

Crystal Valley Cellars 2002 Chardonnay (California) $14. 84 *—S.H. (8/1/2004)*

Crystal Valley Cellars 2001 Chardonnay (California) $14. 81 *—S.H. (10/1/2003)*

Crystal Valley Cellars 2000 Chardonnay (California) $14. 87 *—S.H. (11/15/2001)*

Crystal Valley Cellars 2000 Reserve Chardonnay (California) $16. 85 *—S.H. (12/31/2001)*

Crystal Valley Cellars 2004 The Chard Chardonnay (California) $16. 85 *—S.H. (12/15/2005)*

Crystal Valley Cellars 2003 Merlot (California) $18. 87 *—S.H. (3/1/2006)*

Crystal Valley Cellars 2002 Reserve Merlot (California) $16. 86 *—S.H. (10/1/2005)*

Crystal Valley Cellars 2001 Reserve Merlot (California) $16. 84 *—S.H. (12/31/2003)*

Crystal Valley Cellars 2000 Reserve Merlot (California) $16. 90 *—S.H. (11/15/2002)*

Crystal Valley Cellars 1999 Reserve Merlot (California) $18. 84 *—S.H. (12/31/2001)*

Crystal Valley Cellars 2001 Pinot Noir (California) $16. 82 *—S.H. (7/1/2003)*

Crystal Valley Cellars 2000 Pinot Noir (California) $16. 84 *(10/1/2002)*

Crystal Valley Cellars 2002 Sauvignon Blanc (California) $14. 86 *—S.H. (8/1/2004)*

Crystal Valley Cellars 2000 Mohr-Fry Ranch Sauvignon Blanc (California) $13. 86 *—S.H. (11/15/2001)*

Crystal Valley Cellars 2001 Mohr-Fry Vineyards Sauvignon Blanc (Lodi) $14. 85 *—S.H. (7/1/2003)*

Crystal Valley Cellars 2002 Syrah (Lodi) $16. 82 *—S.H. (9/1/2005)*

Crystal Valley Cellars 2001 Syrah (California) $16. 86 *—S.H. (12/1/2003)*

Crystal Valley Cellars 2000 Syrah (California) $16. 91 Best Buy *—S.H. (12/1/2002)*

Crystal Valley Cellars 1999 Syrah (California) $15. 85 *(10/1/2001)*

Crystal Valley Cellars 2004 Cigar Zin Zinfandel (California) $27. 83 *—S.H. (12/15/2005)*

CUILLIN HILLS

Cuillin Hills 2005 Claret Bordeaux Blend (Columbia Valley (WA)) $23. This new winery does some very cool labels, but the wine—50% Merlot, 40% Cabernet Sauvignon and 10% Cabernet Franc—hasn't quite come together. The fruit is okay, with some lightly volatile lift and chocolate notes from the barrel. The wine is smooth enough, but the fruit component does not have the cut, the texture or the weight to keep it interesting. **86** *—P.G. (11/1/2007)*

Cuillin Hills 2005 Syrah (Walla Walla (WA)) $32. This classy Walla Walla Syrah is nicely rendered, firm and toasty, with crisp acids that lend a lemony touch to the bright berry fruit. There's a delicate floral quality to this wine, a high-toned lift, and it runs through the midpalate with verve and nerve and plenty of acid. The oak adds chocolate and smooth mass to the finish. **90** *—P.G. (11/1/2007)*

Cuillin Hills 2005 The Dungeon Syrah (Washington) $27. This is smooth and full, and has got the requisite black cherry fruit, some lemon rind and pineapple peeking through the acids. In the finish are suggestions, just a lick, of tobacco, wild cherry, maybe sweet ham. Gets interesting in the end, though it remains very tart and acidic. **88** *—P.G. (11/1/2007)*

CUNEO

Cuneo 1999 Cabernet Sauvignon-Merlot-Cabernet Franc Bordeaux Blend (Columbia Valley (WA)) $15. 88 Editors' Choice *—M.S. (6/1/2003)*

Cuneo 2001 Two Rivers Bordeaux Blend (Washington) $25. 85 *—P.G. (9/1/2004)*

Cuneo 2000 Two Rivers Bordeaux Blend (Oregon) $18. 90 Best Buy *—M.S. (8/1/2003)*

Cuneo 2003 Pinot Noir (Willamette Valley) $25. 88 *—P.G. (5/1/2006)*

Cuneo 2002 Pinot Noir (Willamette Valley) $25. 87 *(11/1/2004)*

Cuneo 2000 Pinot Noir (Willamette Valley) $15. 89 Best Buy *—M.S. (9/1/2003)*

Cuneo 2000 Ciel du Cheval Vineyard Sangiovese (Red Mountain) $30. 82 *—M.S. (6/1/2003)*

Cuneo 2001 Del Rio Vineyard Syrah (Rogue Valley) $25. 86 *—M.S. (9/1/2003)*

CUPCAKE

Cupcake 2005 Chardonnay (Central Coast) $10. Clumsy, with a vegetal edge to the syrupy pineapple flavors. Finishes sweet enough to suspect some residual sugar. **81** *—S.H. (11/15/2007)*

CURTIS

Curtis 2004 The Crossroad Grenache-Syrah (Santa Ynez Valley) $22. A blend of Grenache and Syrah, this wine is dry and softly balanced. It has pleasant flavors of cherries, raspberries, cola and spice, with a wild edge of thyme and lavender. A simple country wine, it's showing its best now. **84** *—S.H. (8/1/2007)*

Curtis 2004 Heritage Cuvée Rhône Red Blend (Santa Barbara County) $18. It's hard to like this blend of four red Rhône varieties. It's tough in tannins and acids, and the slight cherry fruit has a dominantly green, herbal, minty quality. **82** *—S.H. (8/1/2007)*

Curtis 2003 Heritage Cuvée Rhône Red Blend (Santa Barbara County) $14. 89 Best Buy *—S.H. (6/1/2006)*

Curtis 2002 Heritage Cuvée Rhône Red Blend (Santa Barbara County) $14. 84 *—S.H. (10/1/2005)*

Curtis 2001 Heritage Cuvée Rhône Red Blend (Santa Barbara County) $12. 90 Best Buy *—S.H. (12/1/2004)*

Curtis 2000 Heritage Cuvée Rhône Red Blend (Central Coast) $14. 88 *—S.H. (6/1/2003)*

Curtis 1999 Heritage Cuvée Rhône Red Blend (Central Coast) $12. 84 *—S.H. (9/1/2002)*

Curtis 2003 Heritage Cuvée Rhône Red Blend (Santa Barbara County) $14. 89 Best Buy *—S.H. (6/1/2006)*

Curtis 2003 The Crossroads Rhône Red Blend (Santa Barbara County) $20. 90 *—S.H. (6/1/2006)*

Curtis 2005 Heritage Blanc Rhône White Blend (Santa Barbara County) $14. 85 *—S.H. (11/15/2006)*

Curtis 2001 Heritage Blanc Rhône White Blend (Santa Barbara County) $14. 86 *—S.H. (2/1/2004)*

Curtis 2003 Roussanne (Santa Barbara County) $18. 84 *—S.H. (10/1/2005)*

Curtis 2004 Ambassador's Vineyard Syrah (Santa Ynez Valley) $24. Dry and rasping, with sandpapery tannins, this Zin has berry flavors. What it needs is brighter acidity and more focused, concentrated fruit. **83** *—S.H. (11/1/2007)*

Curtis 2003 Ambassador's Vineyard Syrah (Santa Barbara County) $25. 84 *—S.H. (10/1/2006)*

Curtis 2002 Ambassador's Vineyard Syrah (Santa Barbara County) $25. 85 *(9/1/2005)*

Curtis 1999 Ambassador's Vineyard Syrah (California) $22. 87 *—J.M. (12/1/2002)*

Curtis 1998 Ambassador's Vineyard Syrah (Santa Barbara County) $20. 87 *(10/1/2001)*

Curtis 2004 Crossroads Vineyard Syrah (Santa Ynez Valley) $28. Soft and dry, with baked flavors of cherries and cola, this high alcohol wine finishes with a tannic scour of red currants. **83** *—S.H. (11/1/2007)*

Curtis 2003 Crossroads Vineyard Syrah (Santa Barbara County) $30. 85 *—S.H. (10/1/2006)*

Curtis 2002 Crossroads Vineyard Syrah (Santa Barbara County) $30. 85 *(9/1/2005)*

Curtis 2000 Crossroads Vineyard Syrah (Santa Ynez Valley) $32. 87 *—S.H. (6/1/2003)*

Curtis 1998 Reserve Syrah (Santa Ynez Valley) $30. 84 *(11/1/2001)*

Curtis 2004 Vogelzang Vineyard Syrah (Santa Ynez Valley) $24. Rustic to the point of barely acceptable, with semisweet LifeSaver candy flavors and a hot, Port-y finish. 80 *—S.H. (11/1/2007)*

Curtis 2000 Vogelzang Vineyard Syrah (Santa Ynez Valley) $18. 86 *—S.H. (6/1/2003)*

Curtis 2005 Viognier (Santa Ynez Valley) $20. 84 *—S.H. (12/1/2006)*

Curtis 2003 Viognier (Santa Barbara County) $18. 84 *—S.H. (10/1/2005)*

Curtis 2002 Viognier (Santa Barbara County) $18. 87 *—S.H. (11/15/2004)*

Curtis 2001 Viognier (Santa Barbara County) $18. 85 *—S.H. (6/1/2003)*

Curtis 2000 Viognier (Santa Barbara County) $18. 87 *—J.M. (12/15/2002)*

Curtis 1997 Viognier (Santa Ynez Valley) $18. 87 *—S.H. (10/1/1999)*

CUVAISON

Cuvaison 2004 Cabernet Sauvignon (Mount Veeder) $45. The wine, from a warm vintage, bursts with fruity charm, but this is a mountain Cab, and while acids are low, you'll find strong tannins. The combination of black currant, cherry, red plum and cocoa flavors with firm, sandpapery tannins is charming and complex. Finishes with a bit of high-alcohol sweetness. 91 *—S.H. (8/1/2007)*

Cuvaison 2003 Cabernet Sauvignon (Mount Veeder) $38. 90 *—S.H. (12/31/2006)*

Cuvaison 2002 Cabernet Sauvignon (Mount Veeder) $40. 92 *—S.H. (11/1/2006)*

Cuvaison 2001 Cabernet Sauvignon (Napa Valley) $38. 93 Editors' Choice *—S.H. (12/15/2005)*

Cuvaison 1999 Cabernet Sauvignon (Napa Valley) $40. 90 *—S.H. (8/1/2003)*

Cuvaison 1997 Cabernet Sauvignon (Napa Valley) $32. 91 *(6/1/2000)*

Cuvaison 2004 Chardonnay (Carneros) $25. 84 *—S.H. (11/15/2006)*

Cuvaison 2003 Chardonnay (Carneros) $22. 92 Editors' Choice *—S.H. (12/1/2005)*

Cuvaison 2002 Chardonnay (Carneros) $24. 91 *—S.H. (8/1/2004)*

Cuvaison 2001 Chardonnay (Carneros) $22. 91 *—S.H. (6/1/2003)*

Cuvaison 2000 Chardonnay (Napa Valley) $20. 90 *—J.M. (5/1/2002)*

Cuvaison 1998 Chardonnay (Carneros) $19. 88 *(6/1/2000)*

Cuvaison 1997 Chardonnay (Carneros) $17. 93 *—S.H. (12/31/1999)*

Cuvaison 2002 ATS Chardonnay (Carneros) $50. 87 *—S.H. (12/1/2005)*

Cuvaison 1996 ATS Selection Chardonnay (Carneros) $43. 93 *—S.H. (6/1/1999)*

Cuvaison 1999 Carneros Reserve Chardonnay (Napa Valley) $32. 89 *(7/1/2001)*

Cuvaison 2005 Estate Chardonnay (Carneros) $25. Here's a polished, delicate wine that shows the poise and elegance that Carneros Chard can achieve. It's varietally pure, with pineapple, mineral and toast flavors that finish dry, a wine meant to enjoy with food, rather than star on its own. Easy to find, with 31,000 cases produced. 90 Editors' Choice *—S.H. (9/1/2007)*

Cuvaison 2004 Estate Selection Chardonnay (Carneros) $36. 86 *—S.H. (11/15/2006)*

Cuvaison 2000 Estate Selection Chardonnay (Carneros) $34. 88 *—J.M. (12/15/2002)*

Cuvaison 1998 Reserve Chardonnay (Carneros) $32. 90 *(6/1/2000)*

Cuvaison 2004 Merlot (Carneros) $32. Rich and dry, with a wealth of blackberry and cherry tart flavors, straight from the oven with the smoky-sweet, cinnamon and burnt butter tang of the crust. You'll notice the tannins, which lend a stimulating structure. This isn't one of those blockbuster cult Merlots, just a red wine of impeccable proportions that yearns to wash down elegant fare. 91 *—S.H. (9/1/2007)*

Cuvaison 2003 Merlot (Carneros) $31. 87 *—S.H. (12/31/2006)*

Cuvaison 2001 Merlot (Carneros) $32. 91 *—S.H. (12/15/2004)*

Cuvaison 2000 Merlot (Carneros) $29. 86 *—S.H. (12/15/2003)*

Cuvaison 1997 Merlot (Napa Valley) $32. 90 *(6/1/2000)*

Cuvaison 2005 Pinot Noir (Carneros) $31. After their disastrous 2004 Pinots, Cuvaison returns to form with this light, easy wine. It's dry and soft, with cola, cherry, root beer, licorice, peppery spice and vanilla oak flavors, and will be versatile at the table. 86 *—S.H. (9/1/2007)*

Cuvaison 2003 Pinot Noir (Carneros) $25. 85 *—S.H. (12/15/2005)*

Cuvaison 2002 Pinot Noir (Carneros) $25. 85 *(11/1/2004)*

Cuvaison 2001 Pinot Noir (Carneros) $29. 89 *—S.H. (7/1/2003)*

Cuvaison 2000 Pinot Noir (Carneros) $29. 87 *(10/1/2002)*

Cuvaison 1998 Eris Vineyard Pinot Noir (Carneros) $20. 90 *(6/1/2000)*

Cuvaison 2003 Estate Selection Pinot Noir (Carneros) $42. 86 *—S.H. (12/15/2005)*

Cuvaison 2002 Estate Selection Pinot Noir (Carneros) $42. 84 *(11/1/2004)*

Cuvaison 2003 Mariafeld Pinot Noir (Carneros) $28. 84 *—S.H. (12/1/2005)*

Cuvaison 2004 Sauvignon Blanc (Carneros) $19. 88 *—S.H. (12/1/2005)*

Cuvaison 2003 Syrah (Carneros) $30. 91 Editors' Choice *(11/8/2006)*

Cuvaison 2002 Syrah (Carneros) $28. 88 *(9/1/2005)*

Cuvaison 2001 Syrah (Carneros) $29. 91 *—S.H. (8/1/2004)*

Cuvaison 2004 Estate Syrah (Carneros) $30. Cuvaison does another good job of producing a fine Syrah from their Carneros vineyard. Despite the heat of the vintage, the wine is balanced by bracing acidity that makes the blackberry and cherry-pie filling flavors lively. Drink now for its youthful vivacity. 88 *—S.H. (9/1/2007)*

CUVÉE LUCIA

Cuvée Lucia 2005 Cabernet Sauvignon (Washington) $25. Here you have more of the stiffer qualities of herb, leaf, earth and stem. Good concentration and length, with a full midpalate. The blend includes 8% Cabernet Franc. 89 *—P.G. (12/1/2007)*

Cuvée Lucia 2004 Merlot (Washington) $25. The tannins are still showing some edgy roughness, green tea and composty streaks. But the fruit is balanced nicely between clean and ripe, while retaining the herbal character that makes it distinctly Washington. 88 *—P.G. (12/1/2007)*

Cuvée Lucia 2006 Celilo Vineyard Pinot Gris (Washington) $15. Forward and ripe, with flavors of tangerine, lemongrass and light herb. The elegant, nicely textured midpalate is extended and still a bit tight. There is a delicacy to this fruit that rewards those who prize nuance. Lightly touched with cinnamon and sweet spice, flavors linger pleasantly with hints of wet stone. 90 Best Buy *—P.G. (12/1/2007)*

CYCLES GLADIATOR

Cycles Gladiator 2005 Cabernet Sauvignon (Central Coast) $10. It's not quite a cult Napa Cab, but you'd be surprised how close the profile fits with this soft, sumptuous wine. Like its competitors costing 10 times as much, it's velvety smooth, with enormously ripe cassis, milk chocolate, cherry pie, vanilla and cinnamon spice flavors. At this price, it's a steal, and easy to find, with 15,000 cases produced. 89 Best Buy *—S.H. (7/1/2007)*

Cycles Gladiator 2004 Cabernet Sauvignon (Central Coast) $10. 84 *—S.H. (11/15/2006)*

Cycles Gladiator 2005 Chardonnay (Central Coast) $10. This isn't the most sophisticated wine out there, but at this price, it's not bad. Semi-dry and smooth in texture, it has modest peach and smoky oak flavors that will satisfy Chard fans. 83 *—S.H. (6/1/2007)*

Cycles Gladiator 2004 Chardonnay (Central Coast) $10. 83 *—S.H. (11/15/2006)*

Cycles Gladiator 2005 Merlot (Central Coast) $10. What an interesting wine this is. Classic California Merlot, soft and rich, with a burst of cherry, raspberry and mocha flavors, and spicy, smoky vanilla from considerable new oak. But the addition of Petite Sirah, Syrah and Cab Sauvignon give it added depth, texture and nuance. At this price, stock up by the case. 88 Best Buy *—S.H. (7/1/2007)*

Cycles Gladiator 2004 Merlot (Central Coast) $10. 81 *—S.H. (11/15/2006)*

Cycles Gladiator 2005 Pinot Grigio (California) $11. 83 *—S.H. (11/15/2006)*

Cycles Gladiator 2005 Pinot Noir (Central Coast) $14. This is the first Cycles Pinot I've had, and it's solidly in line with their philosophy of value. It shows good cool climate character, with crisp acids and a silky texture framing cherry, black raspberry, cola and oaky spice flavors. This is a great everyday introduction to the seductive mysteries of Pinot Noir. 87 *—S.H. (6/1/2007)*

Cycles Gladiator 2005 Syrah (Central Coast) $10. If you like your big reds in the New World style, this one's for you. It's soft, creamy and voluptuous, almost sweet in milk chocolate, black cherry-pie filling, cassis and spicy vanilla flavors. With 65% new French oak, this is really a great price for this kind of wine. 88 Best Buy *—S.H. (7/1/2007)*

Cycles Gladiator 2004 Syrah (Central Coast) $10. 83 *—S.H. (11/15/2006)*

CYPRESS

Cypress 2002 Cabernet Sauvignon (California) $10. 84 *—S.H. (3/1/2005)*

Cypress 2001 Cabernet Sauvignon (California) $10. 84 *—S.H. (12/31/2003)*

Cypress 2003 Chardonnay (California) $10. 84 *—S.H. (3/1/2005)*

Cypress 2002 Merlot (California) $10. 82 *—S.H. (3/1/2005)*

Cypress 2003 Sauvignon Blanc (California) $10. 83 *—S.H. (3/1/2005)*

Cypress 2002 Shiraz (California) $10. 85 Best Buy *—S.H. (4/1/2005)*

CYRUS

Cyrus 1995 Bordeaux Blend (Sonoma County) $35. 84 *—L.W. (12/31/1999)*

Cyrus 1998 Bordeaux Blend (Alexander Valley) $50. 91 *—J.M. (6/1/2002)*

Cyrus 1999 Wetzel Family Estate Bordeaux Blend (Alexander Valley) $50. 92 *—S.H. (8/1/2003)*

D'ANBINO

D'Anbino 2002 Syrah (Paso Robles) $24. 90 *—S.H. (12/1/2004)*

D'ARGENZIO

D'Argenzio 2002 Merlot (Napa Valley) $38. 86 *—S.H. (8/1/2005)*

D'Argenzio 2002 Pinot Noir (Russian River Valley) $32. 86 *—S.H. (8/1/2005)*

D'Argenzio 2001 Pinot Noir (Russian River Valley) $29. 90 *—S.H. (8/1/2005)*

D'Argenzio 2001 Dutton Ranch Pinot Noir (Russian River Valley) $30. 86 *—S.H. (12/1/2004)*

D-CUBED CELLARS

D-Cubed Cellars 2001 Zinfandel (Napa Valley) $25. 88 *(11/1/2003)*

D-Cubed Cellars 2001 Zinfandel (Howell Mountain) $35. 91 *(11/1/2003)*

D-Cubed Cellars 2001 Black Sears Vineyard Zinfandel (Howell Mountain) $45. 90 *(11/1/2003)*

D.R. STEPHENS

D.R. Stephens 2000 Moose Valley Cabernet Sauvignon (Napa Valley) $90. 90 *—S.H. (11/15/2004)*

D.R. Stephens 2003 Moose Valley Estate Cabernet Sauvignon (Napa Valley) $100. 87 *—S.H. (8/1/2006)*

D.R. Stephens 2000 Walther River Block Cabernet Sauvignon (Napa Valley) $75. 88 *—S.H. (11/15/2004)*

DAEDALUS

Daedalus 2004 Pinot Gris (Oregon) $16. 90 *—P.G. (2/1/2006)*

Daedalus 2004 Pinot Noir (Willamette Valley) $25. Daedalus Cellars winemaker Aron Hess purchases fruit from a wide range of vineyards and here mixes fruit, clone and fermentation practices with exceptional skill. This is a tightly wound young wine, showing a solid core of sweet cherry fruit. Rather than broaden out into a lazy fatness, as so many California Pinots do, this resonates with lingering grace notes and firm acids through an extended finish. 89 *—P.G. (2/1/2007)*

Daedalus 2003 Pinot Noir (Willamette Valley) $24. 90 Editors' Choice *—P.G. (5/1/2006)*

Daedalus 2004 Labyrinth Pinot Noir (Willamette Valley) $40. The Labyrinth bottling is thicker and somewhat more tannic that the winery's 'regular' Pinot. Superb vineyard sources (Seven Springs, Carabella, Momtazi) comprise the blend, and the wine gets plenty of skin contact while awaiting spontaneous fermentation. It's saturated with color and redolent of herb and earth, bark and root, while the fruit, for the moment, takes a back seat. This is a wine that will benefit from extended breathing time and/or cellaring. 89 *—P.G. (2/1/2007)*

Daedalus 2003 Labyrinth Pinot Noir (Willamette Valley) $39. 90 *—P.G. (5/1/2006)*

Daedalus 2006 Maresh Vineyard Riesling (Willamette Valley) $21. This wine, from a 30-year-old Riesling vineyard, will appeal especially to those who prefer a steely, austere style. Sleek and slightly metallic, it has plenty of acid and tart citrus flavor, but tails off into a finish that feels just a bit too sour. With the right food—oysters anyone?—it could be magic. 88 *—P.G. (11/15/2007)*

Daedalus 2003 Syrah (Columbia Valley (OR)) $24. 91 Editors' Choice *—P.G. (5/1/2006)*

DALLA VALLE

Dalla Valle 2001 Cabernet Sauvignon (Oakville) $100. 94 *—S.H. (11/1/2005)*

Dalla Valle 1999 Cabernet Sauvignon (Napa Valley) $100. 94 *—J.M. (6/1/2002)*

Dalla Valle 1999 Maya Red Blend (Napa Valley) $120. 96 *—J.M. (6/1/2002)*

Dalla Valle 1997 Pietre Rosse Sangiovese (Napa Valley) $30. 93 *—L.W. (10/1/1999)*

DALLA VINA

Dalla Vina 2005 Pinot Noir (Willamette Valley) $25. Tart and herbal upon entry, this modest Pinot brings a bit of spicy varietal character with it upon entry. It seems more promising than it ultimately shows, as the finish gets flat and flabby in a hurry. The fruit tails off into a thin, watery pale red. 85 *—P.G. (7/1/2007)*

DALTON

Dalton 2004 Martin Vineyard Pinot Noir (Carneros) $25. Carneros Pinot near its best. Crisply soft and balanced, it's simply delicious; a silky, velvety wine with a mouthwatering wealth of cherry pie filling, cola, mocha, cinnamon spice and toasty oak flavors that go on and on, and finish long and intense. Best now–2008. 92 *—S.H. (4/1/2007)*

Dalton 2003 Martin Vineyard Pinot Noir (Carneros) $25. Showing its age, with the mouthfeel softening and the fruit slowly turning dry and brittle. But it's an interesting, complex wine, and the flavors, of Chinese black tea and cherry-teased cola, are classic older Pinot. Drink now. 90 *—S.H. (4/1/2007)*

DAMA

Dama 2006 Riesling (Columbia Valley (WA)) $16. Here is yet another Washington Riesling that shows how good these wines can be. This is well beyond the sweet and fruity style of the tasting room wines; here are layers of stone fruits, density and weight, length and detail. Once in the mouth this explodes with flavor and keeps bringing the oranges, peaches, apricots, nectarines and apples to the table. 90 Editors' Choice *—P.G. (12/31/2007)*

DAMIAN RAE

Damian Rae 2005 White Hawk Syrah (Santa Barbara County) $48. Dry enough, but the fruit has a baked, raisiny taste, suggesting that some of the grapes got by the sorting table in a shriveled condition. The finish is tannic and rich in blackberries and spices, but the wine is not an ager. 84 *—S.H. (12/15/2007)*

DANCING BEAR CELLARS

Dancing Bear Cellars 2004 Pinot Noir (Los Carneros) $18. A silky, delicate, almost lightweight Pinot Noir, this is a pretty wine, the antithesis of full-bodied and lusty. Yet it still packs in plenty of flavor and complexity, ranging from cola and sassafras to cherries, mushrooms, brown sugar and earth. Drink now. 88 *(10/1/2007)*

Dancing Bear Cellars 2005 Sauvignon Blanc (Columbia Valley (WA)) $0. Combines stone fruit and slight grassiness in a medium-bodied wine Munson calls "extra crispy." It's made all in stainless steel to accentuate the fruit. 85 *(10/1/2007)*

Dancing Bear Cellars 2005 Zinfandel (Dry Creek Valley) $17. This easy-drinking Zinfandel starts off with heady, almost Port-like aromas of berries and spice, then continues that theme on the palate, but with reasonable alcohol levels and moderate body. Chocolate, mixed berry and spice flavors trail away on the finish. 87 *(10/1/2007)*

DANCING BULL

Dancing Bull 2003 Cabernet Sauvignon (California) $12. 82 *—S.H. (11/15/2006)*

Dancing Bull 2004 Chardonnay (California) $12. 82 *—S.H. (12/1/2006)*

Dancing Bull 2004 Merlot (California) $10. 85 Best Buy *—S.H. (11/15/2006)*

Dancing Bull 2006 Sauvignon Blanc (California) $12. A very well-behaved and drinkable Sauvignon Blanc, showing honeyed pineapple, fig, green apple and spice flavors. The crisp acidity makes it especially clean. 85 *—S.H. (11/15/2007)*

Dancing Bull 2005 Sauvignon Blanc (California) $12. Most of the grapes come from the Central Coast, and that explains the juicy acidity that makes the wine so clean and bright. It's also very ripe, with pineapple, grapefuit and spicy cantaloupe flavors that finish with a honeyed semi-sweetness. 85 *—S.H. (2/1/2007)*

Dancing Bull 2004 Zinfandel (California) $12. Juicy and chockful of fruity flavor, this is a nice, inexpensive Zin for ribs, chicken, even a steak. Berries, cherries, cola, coffee, chocolate and spices all mingle into a richly tannic finish. The wine is fully dry and moderate in alcohol. 85 *—S.H. (2/1/2007)*

DANCING COYOTE

Dancing Coyote 2005 Albariño (Clarksburg) $10. This is a really nice wine to pair with fish, poultry or pork. With high acidity, it cleanses the palate, and leaves behind a long, rich finish. With a little Pinot Grigio and Orange Muscat, it has lime, tangerine, green apple, floral and spice flavors. Sommeliers should line up to snag it by the case. 88 Best Buy *—S.H. (4/1/2007)*

Dancing Coyote 2004 Chenin Blanc (Clarksburg) $10. The best features of this Chenin are the dryness and mouthwatering acidity. With subtle citrus, green bean and green apple flavors, this will complement food, rather than taking center stage on the table. **87 Best Buy** —*S.H. (4/1/2007)*

Dancing Coyote 2004 Petite Sirah (Clarksburg) $12. It's awfully hard to train Petite Sirah into elegance, but Dancing Coyote has done it. The wine has the mouthfeel of a Merlot, soft, gentle and medium-bodied, but with Petite Sirah's spicy, cherry jam, blackberry and mocha-choca flavors. **86 Best Buy** —*S.H. (4/1/2007)*

Dancing Coyote 2005 Verdelho (Clarksburg) $10. Lovely and aromatic, perfumed with summer daisy flowers, night-blooming jasmine, pineapples, apricots and vanilla flavors. With crisp, balancing acidity, it's a great alternative to Sauvignon Blanc. **86 Best Buy** —*S.H. (4/1/2007)*

DANIEL GEHRS

Daniel Gehrs 2005 Cabernet Sauvignon (Paso Robles) $16. Tastes like it just came out of the fermenter, with grapy flavors and bright, young acidity. Makes you wonder why they didn't hold it back a little longer, but you can do that on your own. **85** —*S.H. (4/1/2007)*

Daniel Gehrs 2004 Cabernet Sauvignon (Santa Ynez Valley) $28. I haven't been a fan of Santa Ynez Cabs for the simple reason that they're so seldom ripe. You get this green, herb and mint streak that's not flattering to Cab's tannins. This wine is in that vein. **82** —*S.H. (4/1/2007)*

Daniel Gehrs 2000 Cabernet Sauvignon (Santa Ynez Valley) $24. 85 —*S.H. (11/15/2003)*

Daniel Gehrs 2005 Unoaked Chardonnay (Santa Barbara County) $15. Riding the unoaked Chardonnay train is Daniel Gehrs, not really known for this variety. The wine is brisk, fruity and clean, bursting with tropical fruit and spice flavors and finishing long and clean. **85** —*S.H. (4/1/2007)*

Daniel Gehrs 2005 Pinnacles Chenin Blanc (Monterey County) $12. Chenin is a high acid wine, and there's a tartness in the finish here that some will find sour. But that makes the wine a natural for chewing through butter, oil, cheese. Coming from the Pinnacles region, in the eastern hills of the Salinas Valley, the wine displays citrus, apricot and peach flavors. **87 Best Buy** —*S.H. (4/1/2007)*

Daniel Gehrs 2000 Pinnacles Chenin Blanc (Monterey County) $13. 87 —*S.H. (11/15/2001)*

Daniel Gehrs 2005 Gewürztraminer (Central Coast) $15. Here's one of the better Gewürzes at this price point. It shows the variety's flowery, spicy personality, with citrus and honeysuckle flavors and dusty crushed nutmeg, cinnamon and Chinese five spice. Finishes nice and dry, in the Alsatian style. Its low alcohol content makes it easy to toss back a few glasses. **86** —*S.H. (4/1/2007)*

Daniel Gehrs 2004 Gewürztraminer (Central Coast) $15. 87 —*S.H. (3/1/2006)*

Daniel Gehrs 2005 Merlot (Santa Barbara County) $25. Almost as sweet as a Port, this has sugary flavors of very ripe blackberries and cassis. Nothing wrong with that, except that it's not really a dry table wine. If the sweetness doesn't bother you, the wine is rich and voluptuous, with smooth tannins. **85** —*S.H. (12/1/2007)*

Daniel Gehrs 1999 Merlot (Santa Ynez Valley) $20. 90 Editors' Choice —*S.H. (11/15/2001)*

Daniel Gehrs 2001 Pinot Noir (Santa Barbara County) $20. 86 —*S.H. (2/1/2004)*

Daniel Gehrs 2004 Careaga Pinot Noir (Santa Barbara County) $32. There are two kinds of good Pinot in California, the rich, full-bodied ones and the silkier, more accessible Pinots. This is the latter type. It's not an ager, but has a delicate elegance, and easy but complex flavors of cherries, cola, herb tea and Asian spices. **87** —*S.H. (4/1/2007)*

Daniel Gehrs 2000 Careaga Pinot Noir (Santa Barbara County) $25. 86 *(10/1/2002)*

Daniel Gehrs 1999 Careaga Pinot Noir (Santa Barbara County) $26. 83 *(10/1/2002)*

Daniel Gehrs 2000 Goodfellow Pinot Noir (Santa Maria Valley) $25. 87 *(10/1/2002)*

Daniel Gehrs 2004 Fireside Port (Amador County) $31. Made with Portuguese varieties, this is a real Port-like wine. It's supersweet, just fabulously rich in blackberry, chocolate, coffee and vanilla flavors, and all that richness is beautifully balanced with crisp acids and smooth, succulently ripe tannins. The finish goes on. A great price. **94 Editors' Choice** —*S.H. (12/1/2007)*

Daniel Gehrs 2004 Ozymandias Red Wine Red Blend (Santa Barbara County) $36. The Syrah that comprises half the blend is soft, ripe and voluptuous, with polished cherry flavors. The rest is Cab, lean, tart, and unripe, dragging the wine way down. **83** —*S.H. (4/1/2007)*

Daniel Gehrs 2006 Riesling (Central Coast) $19. Daniel Gehrs brings his balanced touch to this off-dry Riesling, whose residual sugar is 2.8%. Acidity makes it bright and clean, adding zest to the extremely ripe pineapple tart, orange meringue and honeysuckle flavors. **87** —*S.H. (9/1/2007)*

Daniel Gehrs 2005 Riesling (Santa Barbara County) $15. I'm not a fan of California Rieslings, but this is one of the better ones of late. It has real richness, showing a broad spectrum of honeyed wildflower, peach and apple flavors. Not exactly dry, with 2.25% residual sugar, but crisp acidity makes it clean and balanced. **87** —*S.H. (4/1/2007)*

Daniel Gehrs 2004 Dry Riesling (Central Coast) $15. 85 —*S.H. (3/1/2006)*

Daniel Gehrs 2005 Late Harvest Sauvignon Blanc (Santa Barbara County) $18. This dessert wine is sweetly complex, with apricot jam, peach pie, honeysuckle, vanilla fudge and smoky butterscotch flavors. Fortunately, the acidity is fine and crisp, providing a clean balance to the sweetness. **90** —*S.H. (12/1/2007)*

Daniel Gehrs 2001 Shiraz (Santa Ynez Valley) $20. 89 *(9/1/2005)*

Daniel Gehrs 2005 Syrah (Paso Robles) $16. Too young to drink now; it's almost still fermenting. Why did they release it so soon after the vintage? But it's a good wine with fine blackberry, cherry and peppery spice flavors. Best 2007–2010. **86** —*S.H. (4/1/2007)*

Daniel Gehrs 2001 Syrah (Paso Robles) $20. 88 —*S.H. (5/1/2004)*

Daniel Gehrs 2001 Syrah (Santa Barbara County) $25. 88 —*S.H. (5/1/2004)*

Daniel Gehrs 1999 Syrah (Paso Robles) $20. 89 *(10/1/2001)*

Daniel Gehrs 1999 Syrah (Santa Ynez Valley) $25. 90 *(11/1/2001)*

Daniel Gehrs 2001 Harmon Syrah (Santa Ynez Valley) $25. 85 *(9/1/2005)*

Daniel Gehrs 2000 Harmon Syrah (Santa Ynez Valley) $25. 89 —*S.H. (3/1/2004)*

Daniel Gehrs 2000 Viognier (Santa Ynez Valley) $18. 88 —*J.M. (11/15/2001)*

Daniel Gehrs 1998 Stolpman Vineyard Viognier (Santa Barbara County) $19. 90 —*S.H. (10/1/1999)*

Daniel Gehrs 2005 Eleganza White Blend (Santa Barbara County) $28. Unoaked Chard and barrel-fermented Viognier comprise the blend on this aromatically fruity dry wine. Brims with floral, citrus, peach and apple flavors. It's fun to drink, but shows real complexity and style. Try with Asian food, or arugula and citrus fruit salads. **88** —*S.H. (4/1/2007)*

Daniel Gehrs 2005 Zinfandel (Santa Ynez Valley) $22. This isn't nearly as ripe as most North Coast Zins. You get a hit of cherries, but then a follow-up of wintergreen. Brisk acidity and dryness emphasize the minty quality, making the wine somewhat tart and rustic. **83** —*S.H. (4/1/2007)*

DARCIE KENT VINEYARDS

Darcie Kent Vineyards 2001 Merlot (Livermore Valley) $18. 84 —*S.H. (2/1/2004)*

DARIOUSH

Darioush 2000 Signature Cabernet Sauvignon (Napa Valley) $64. 94 —*J.M. (6/1/2003)*

Darioush 1999 Chardonnay (Napa Valley) $34. 93 Editors' Choice *(7/1/2001)*

Darioush 2001 Signature Chardonnay (Napa Valley) $38. 90 —*J.M. (6/1/2003)*

Darioush 2000 Merlot (Napa Valley) $44. 91 —*J.M. (6/1/2003)*

Darioush 2000 Shiraz (Napa Valley) $64. 92 —*J.M. (6/1/2003)*

Darioush 2002 Signature Shiraz (Napa Valley) $64. 86 *(9/1/2005)*

Darioush 2001 Viognier (Napa Valley) $28. 89 —*S.H. (12/1/2003)*

DARK STAR

Dark Star 2001 Ricordati Cabernet Blend (Paso Robles) $20. 84 —*S.H. (6/1/2005)*

Dark Star 2001 Cabernet Sauvignon (Paso Robles) $20. 83 —*S.H. (6/1/2005)*

Dark Star 1997 Cabernet Sauvignon (Paso Robles) $20. 87 —*S.H. (7/1/2000)*

Dark Star 1999 Ricordati Cabernet Sauvignon (Paso Robles) $24. 83 —*S.H. (9/12/2002)*

Dark Star 2001 Anderson Road Cabernet Sauvignon-Syrah (Paso Robles) $15. 86 —*S.H. (6/1/2005)*

Dark Star 2001 Merlot (Paso Robles) $18. 83 —*S.H. (6/1/2005)*

Dark Star 1999 Merlot (Paso Robles) $18. 84 —*S.H. (9/12/2002)*

Dark Star 1997 Merlot (Paso Robles) $18. 83 —*S.H. (7/1/2000)*

Dark Star 1997 Ricordati Red Blend (Paso Robles) $24. 83 —*S.H. (7/1/2000)*

Dark Star 2001 Meeker Vineyard Syrah (Paso Robles) $10. 80 *—S.H. (6/1/2005)*

Dark Star 1999 Meeker Vineyard Syrah (Paso Robles) $22. 84 *—S.H. (9/12/2002)*

Dark Star 2001 Zinfandel (Paso Robles) $18. 84 *—S.H. (6/1/2005)*

Dark Star 1997 Zinfandel (Paso Robles) $19. 86 *—S.H. (10/1/2000)*

DASHE CELLARS

Dashe Cellars 2003 Cabernet Sauvignon (Alexander Valley) $38. Dashe is a solid Zin producer, and this is the first Cabernet from them that I've reviewed, so it's nice to report how good it is. It's a dry, soft, earthy wine, with lots of new oak, and it's also young. The tannins and acids are a bit strong right now. Give it a few years, and it will come around. **87** *—S.H. (5/1/2007)*

Dashe Cellars 2000 Merlot (Potter Valley) $26. 91 Editors' Choice *—S.H. (4/1/2003)*

Dashe Cellars 2003 Iron Oak Vineyard Merlot (Potter Valley) $26. 83 *—S.H. (12/1/2006)*

Dashe Cellars 2006 McFadden Farms Dry Riesling (Potter Valley) $20. Give this Mendocino-grown Riesling a bit more flavorful concentration, and it would be in the top ranks. As it is, it's still refreshing, a bone dry, crisp white with peach and honeysuckle flavors. **86** *—S.H. (9/1/2007)*

Dashe Cellars 1999 Sangiovese (Sonoma County) $18. 87 *—S.H. (2/1/2003)*

Dashe Cellars 2005 Zinfandel (Dry Creek Valley) $22. In a good vintage, which '05 was, Dashe's Dry Creek Zin defines the appellation's style. Very dry, tannic and acidic, the wine offers a rich array of wild blackberries and cherries, peppery spices, and earthy, savory notes of tabasco, root beer, sautéed Portobellos splashed with balsamic vinegar and espresso. Will develop over the next five years. **89** *—S.H. (10/1/2007)*

Dashe Cellars 2004 Zinfandel (Dry Creek Valley) $22. In this scorching vintage, getting the grapes ripe was no problem, but Dashe has done an admirable job at maintaining balance and elegance. It's a big, expressive Zin, stuffed with cherry and blackberry jam, prune preserves, datenut bread, chocolate fudge and spicy rum punch flavors, but they've kept it almost dry, with just a trace of honey. Delicious. **90** *—S.H. (5/1/2007)*

Dashe Cellars 2003 Zinfandel (Dry Creek Valley) $22. 83 *(12/18/2006)*

Dashe Cellars 2002 Zinfandel (Dry Creek Valley) $22. 87 *—S.H. (11/1/2005)*

Dashe Cellars 2001 Zinfandel (Dry Creek Valley) $20. 89 *(11/1/2003)*

Dashe Cellars 2000 Zinfandel (Dry Creek Valley) $20. 86 *—S.H. (2/1/2003)*

Dashe Cellars 1999 Zinfandel (Dry Creek Valley) $20. 89 *—P.G. (3/1/2002)*

Dashe Cellars 2003 Big River Ranch Zinfandel (Alexander Valley) $28. 84 Cellar Selection *(12/18/2006)*

Dashe Cellars 2001 Big River Vineyard Zinfandel (Alexander Valley) $28. 90 *(11/1/2003)*

Dashe Cellars 2004 Louvau Vineyard Old Vines Zinfandel (Dry Creek Valley) $28. They say the vines are 68 years old, and they certainly produced a dense, concentrated young Zin. It's like the liquid essence of raspberries, cherries and blackberries, enriched with a dusting of cinnamon, cocoa, coffee and nutmeg. The finish is completely dry. One problem: acidity is very low, making the wine soft and a little medicinal. **86** *—S.H. (10/1/2007)*

Dashe Cellars 2003 Louvau Vineyard Old Vines Zinfandel (Dry Creek Valley) $28. 80 *(12/18/2006)*

Dashe Cellars 2001 Louvau Vineyard, Old Vines Zinfandel (Dry Creek Valley) $28. 89 *(11/1/2003)*

Dashe Cellars 2001 Todd Brothers Ranch Zinfandel (Alexander Valley) $25. 90 *(11/1/2003)*

Dashe Cellars 2000 Todd Brothers Ranch Zinfandel (Alexander Valley) $25. 92 Editors' Choice *—S.H. (2/1/2003)*

Dashe Cellars 1999 Todd Brothers Ranch Zinfandel (Alexander Valley) $25. 91 *—P.G. (3/1/2002)*

Dashe Cellars 1998 Todd Brothers Ranch Zinfandel (Alexander Valley) $25. 91 *—P.G. (3/1/2002)*

Dashe Cellars 2004 Todd Brothers Ranch Old Vines Zinfandel (Alexander Valley) $28. One of the richest Zins on the market now. Enormous in blackberry, cherry, raspberry, blueberry and every other kind of berry flavors, with a coating of melted milk chocolate, sweet red licorice and Fig Newton. If that sounds sweet, it tastes that way, too, although the rich tannin-acid balance pushes everything toward table wine dryness. **88** *—S.H. (10/1/2007)*

Dashe Cellars 2003 Todd Brothers Ranch Old Vines Zinfandel (Alexander Valley) $28. 83 *(12/18/2006)*

DAVID BRUCE

David Bruce 2001 Petite Sirah (Central Coast) $18. 86 *(4/1/2003)*

David Bruce 1997 Pinot Noir (Chalone) $35. 88 *(11/15/1999)*

David Bruce 2000 Pinot Noir (Central Coast) $20. 86 *(10/1/2002)*

David Bruce 2000 Pinot Noir (Santa Cruz Mountains) $35. 89 *(10/1/2002)*

David Bruce 2000 Pinot Noir (Russian River Valley) $35. 90 *(10/1/2002)*

David Bruce 2000 Pinot Noir (Sonoma) $25. 83 *(10/1/2002)*

David Bruce 1997 Pinot Noir (Santa Cruz Mountains) $35. 90 *(10/1/1999)*

David Bruce 1997 Pinot Noir (Sonoma County) $24. 91 *(10/1/1999)*

David Bruce 2000 Truchard Vineyard Pinot Noir (Carneros) $35. 88 *(10/1/2002)*

DAVID COFFARO

David Coffaro 2001 Zinfandel (Dry Creek Valley) $22. 85 *(11/1/2003)*

David Coffaro 2003 Bernier's Zinfandel (Dry Creek Valley) $22. 85 *—S.H. (11/1/2005)*

David Coffaro 2003 My Zin Zinfandel (Dry Creek Valley) $22. 87 *—S.H. (11/1/2005)*

DAVID GIRARD

David Girard 2004 Grenache (El Dorado) $16. 90 Editors' Choice *—S.H. (12/15/2006)*

David Girard 2004 Couer du Terroir Rouge Rhône Red Blend (El Dorado) $30. The words "country style" apply perfectly to this Rhône blend based on Mourvèdre. It's soft and simple and dry, with pleasant cherry, blackberry and Kahlúa flavors. **85** *—S.H. (9/1/2007)*

David Girard 2005 Coeur du Terroir Blanc Rhône White Blend (El Dorado) $22. 90 *—S.H. (12/15/2006)*

David Girard 2002 Viognier-Roussanne Rhône White Blend (California) $18. 84 *—S.H. (12/15/2005)*

David Girard 2006 Rosé Blend (El Dorado) $16. Pale in color and light in body, this blush also is light in flavor. It shows modest citrus fruit, with a strong edge of feline essence, and finishes dry and crisply acidic. **82** *—S.H. (7/1/2007)*

David Girard 2004 Syrah (El Dorado) $32. Solid Syrah, round, smooth and fruity, with a nice bite of tannins and acids for balance. The blackberries, cassis, coffee, carob, cola, tobacco and peppery spice flavors finish impressively long. **88** *—S.H. (9/1/2007)*

David Girard 2003 Syrah (El Dorado) $28. 88 *—S.H. (12/15/2005)*

DAVID HILL

David Hill 2005 Chardonnay (Willamette Valley) $12. This inexpensive bottling offers up round, soft, pleasant fruit flavors with a tilt toward papaya and banana. It was aged in mostly neutral oak, and it has some musty bitterness at the very end. But in this price range, for those who simply want a glass of ripe fruit, it works just fine. Drink it cold. **86** *—P.G. (11/15/2007)*

David Hill 2001 Chardonnay (Willamette Valley) $15. 84 *—P.G. (12/1/2003)*

David Hill 2002 Gewürztraminer (Willamette Valley) $12. 81 *—P.G. (12/1/2003)*

David Hill 2006 Estate Gewürztraminer (Willamette Valley) $15. This is finished dry, at 13.3% alcohol, and puts the emphasis on citrus and grass, cracker and grain. There is a smidgeon of varietal perfume—a whiff of rose petal—but overall it's trending more toward Sauvignon Blanc than most Gewürztraminer. Nonetheless there is an impression of sweetness on the palate, from the nicely ripened fruit. **88** *—P.G. (11/15/2007)*

David Hill 2002 Estate Port Muscat (Oregon) $42. 90 *—P.G. (11/15/2005)*

David Hill 2002 Pinot Gris (Willamette Valley) $12. 85 *—P.G. (12/1/2003)*

David Hill 2006 Estate Pinot Gris (Willamette Valley) $12. This has a definite blush color—a pretty pale copper—and intense aromas of tropical fruits and apple cider. It's off-dry—1.6% residual sugar—and finishes with a sugary sweetness. If this is the style you seek, it's done well enough, but it seems to lose focus quickly and the sugar has rounded it off to such a degree that it almost feels nubby. **85** *—P.G. (11/15/2007)*

David Hill 2005 Pinot Noir (Willamette Valley) $14. This is a substantial effort for the price. It's got an Oregon spin to the varietal, which is to say that it has more than a hint of tomato leaf, and a somewhat resinous character. But the sharp, acidic fruit comes through with authority, and it will give you more meat and muscle than almost anything else under $20. **86** *—P.G. (11/15/2007)*

David Hill 2001 Pinot Noir (Willamette Valley) $16. 84 *—P.G. (12/1/2003)*

David Hill 2002 Cuvée Anna-Lara Pinot Noir (Willamette Valley) $18. 83 *(11/1/2004)*

David Hill 2002 Estate Pinot Noir (Willamette Valley) $15. 83 *(11/1/2004)*

David Hill 2002 Estate Reserve Pinot Noir (Willamette Valley) $30. 84 *(11/1/2004)*

David Hill NV Estate Tawny Port (Oregon) $42. 86 *—P.G. (11/15/2005)*

David Hill 2006 Estate Riesling (Willamette Valley) $12. The winery notes that these are the oldest commercial Riesling vines in Oregon, planted in 1965. This has a succulent core of sweet apple-flavored fruit, quite rich and delicious. It dries out a little toward the back, but continues with excellent length and more of that crystal clear fresh red apple flavor. It's got enough textural interest to keep it from feeling one-dimensional. 90 Best Buy *—P.G. (11/15/2007)*

David Hill 2002 Late Harvest Riesling (Willamette Valley) $15. 85 *—P.G. (12/1/2003)*

David Hill 1992 Brut Sparkling Blend (Oregon) $14. 87 Best Buy *—P.G. (12/1/2003)*

DAVID NOYES

David Noyes 2005 Pinot Noir (Sonoma County) $24. As often happens, the winery's "regular" Pinot is better than their more expensive vineyard-designated bottling, released at the same time. Silky and expansive in cherries, pomegranates and new oak flavors, the wine is dry and elegant. 87 *—S.H. (6/1/2007)*

David Noyes 2004 Dutton Ranch Pinot Noir (Russian River Valley) $34. Ripe and jammy in cherry, raspberry and cola fruit, but there's a stewed prune quality, and the wine feels unsatisfyingly simple. 83 *—S.H. (6/1/2007)*

David Noyes 2005 Pagani Vineyard Tocai Friulano (North Coast) $15. Not much of this Italian variety in California, but there should be. Almost totally from Sonoma Valley, with a few drops from Mendocino, the wine is bone dry and crisp in acidity, with Meyer lemon, buttercup flower and cardamom spice flavors. Sort of a cross between Pinot Grigio and Viognier. 87 *—S.H. (6/1/2007)*

DAVIS BYNUM

Davis Bynum 1997 Hedin Vineyard Cabernet Sauvignon (Russian River Valley) $30. 92 *(11/1/2000)*

Davis Bynum 1999 Chardonnay (Russian River Valley) $25. 92 *—J.M. (12/31/2001)*

Davis Bynum 1998 Limited Edition Chardonnay (Russian River Valley) $25. 90 *(6/1/2000)*

Davis Bynum 2004 Fumé Blanc (Russian River Valley) $15. 81 *—S.H. (12/15/2005)*

Davis Bynum 1999 Westside Road Meritage (Sonoma County) $35. 87 *—S.H. (11/15/2003)*

Davis Bynum 1999 Laureles Merlot (Russian River Valley) $28. 91 Editors' Choice *—S.H. (2/1/2003)*

Davis Bynum 1997 Laureles Merlot (Russian River Valley) $28. 89 *—S.H. (6/1/2001)*

Davis Bynum 2002 Pinot Noir (Russian River Valley) $28. 85 *—S.H. (12/15/2005)*

Davis Bynum 2001 Pinot Noir (Russian River Valley) $28. 86 *—S.H. (10/1/2004)*

Davis Bynum 2000 Pinot Noir (Russian River Valley) $30. 90 Editors' Choice *(10/1/2002)*

Davis Bynum 2001 3 Vineyards Pinot Noir (Russian River Valley) $50. 86 *—S.H. (10/1/2004)*

Davis Bynum 2000 Allen Pinot Noir (Russian River Valley) $45. 92 *(10/1/2002)*

Davis Bynum 2001 Allen Vineyard Pinot Noir (Russian River Valley) $50. 88 *—S.H. (10/1/2004)*

Davis Bynum 2001 Bynum & Moshin Vineyards Pinot Noir (Russian River Valley) $50. 87 *—S.H. (10/1/2004)*

Davis Bynum 1999 Bynum & Moshin Vineyards Pinot Noir (Russian River Valley) $45. 91 *(10/1/2002)*

Davis Bynum 1999 Le Pinot Rochioli Vineyard Pinot Noir (Russian River Valley) $75. 86 *(10/1/2002)*

Davis Bynum 2002 Lindley's Knoll Pinot Noir (Russian River Valley) $55. 85 *—S.H. (12/15/2006)*

Davis Bynum 2001 Lindley's Knoll Pinot Noir (Russian River Valley) $50. 87 *—S.H. (10/1/2004)*

Davis Bynum 2000 Lindley's Knoll Pinot Noir (Russian River Valley) $45. 87 *—S.H. (4/1/2003)*

Davis Bynum 1999 Lindleys' Knoll Pinot Noir (Russian River Valley) $45. 90 *—J.M. (5/1/2002)*

Davis Bynum 1999 Lindley's Knoll Best 4 Barrels Pinot Noir (Russian River Valley) $90. 91 *(10/1/2002)*

Davis Bynum 2001 Rochioli Vineyard Le Pinot Pinot Noir (Russian River Valley) $80. 89 *—S.H. (6/1/2005)*

Davis Bynum 2000 Rochioli Vineyard Le Pinot Pinot Noir (Russian River Valley) $NA. 87 *—S.H. (6/1/2005)*

Davis Bynum 1999 Rochioli Vineyard Le Pinot Pinot Noir (Russian River Valley) $NA. 86 *—S.H. (6/1/2005)*

Davis Bynum 2004 Rosé Blend (Russian River Valley) $15. 83 *—S.H. (12/15/2005)*

DAVIS FAMILY

Davis Family 2001 Cabernet Sauvignon (Napa Valley) $40. 89 *—S.H. (8/1/2005)*

Davis Family 2003 Dutton Ranch Chardonnay (Russian River Valley) $35. 91 *—S.H. (12/15/2005)*

Davis Family 2002 Dutton Ranch Chardonnay (Russian River Valley) $30. 87 *—S.H. (8/1/2005)*

Davis Family 2004 Pinot Noir (Russian River Valley) $38. 88 *—S.H. (12/1/2006)*

Davis Family 2002 Pinot Noir (Russian River Valley) $30. 91 *(11/1/2004)*

Davis Family 2001 Zinfandel (Russian River Valley) $25. 88 *(11/1/2003)*

DAYDREAM

Daydream 2005 Sauvignon Blanc (Napa Valley) $17. 83 *—S.H. (5/1/2007)*

DE LA MONTANYA

De La Montanya 2003 Syrah (Russian River Valley) $32. 88 *(9/1/2005)*

DE LOACH

De Loach 1998 Los Amigos Ranch Cabernet Sauvignon (Russian River Valley) $22. 87 *—S.H. (9/1/2003)*

De Loach 2003 O.F.S. Cabernet Sauvignon (Russian River Valley) $30. 90 *—S.H. (10/1/2006)*

De Loach 2000 O.F.S. Cabernet Sauvignon (Russian River Valley) $30. 87 *—S.H. (11/15/2004)*

De Loach 1998 O.F.S. Cabernet Sauvignon (Russian River Valley) $50. 87 *—S.H. (8/1/2003)*

De Loach 1997 O.F.S. Cabernet Sauvignon (Russian River Valley) $40. 90 *(11/1/2000)*

De Loach 2006 Chardonnay (Russian River Valley) $16. There's lots of acidity in this young wine, which gives it a slightly minty, prickly feeling that actually adds to its food-friendliness. With pineapple, green apple, spice and smoky oak flavors, it finishes thoroughly dry. Easy to find, with 30,000 case production. 88 *—S.H. (12/15/2007)*

De Loach 2005 Chardonnay (Russian River Valley) $16. Good everyday Chard, with direct flavors of pineapples and kiwis, and the buttercream and smoky vanillins that oak barrels contribute. Finishes dry and crisp. 86 *—S.H. (10/1/2007)*

De Loach 2004 Chardonnay (Russian River Valley) $16. 82 *—S.H. (10/1/2006)*

De Loach 2002 Chardonnay (Russian River Valley) $16. 86 *(8/1/2005)*

De Loach 2001 Chardonnay (Russian River Valley) $16. 85 *—S.H. (12/1/2004)*

De Loach 2000 Chardonnay (Russian River Valley) $18. 86 *—S.H. (12/15/2002)*

De Loach 1999 Chardonnay (Russian River Valley) $21. 87 *(8/1/2001)*

De Loach 1998 Chardonnay (Russian River Valley) $18. 91 *—S.H. (2/1/2000)*

De Loach 1997 Chardonnay (Russian River Valley) $18. 92 *—S.H. (11/1/1999)*

De Loach 2005 Durell Vineyard Chardonnay (Sonoma County) $32. Couldn't be riper or more powerful in flavor, a Chard that just detonates with explosive pineapple tart filling, honey, vanilla and crème brûlée. Could use a bit of subtlety, but fans of pure Chardonnay flavor will be delighted. 89 *—S.H. (10/1/2007)*

De Loach 2005 O.F.S. Chardonnay (Russian River Valley) $30. Almost sweet in pineapple custard, marzipan and butterscotch flavors, and there may even be a bit of residual sugar in this honey-rich Chard. Saved by a crisp backbone of acidity. 87 *—S.H. (10/1/2007)*

De Loach 2004 O.F.S. Chardonnay (Russian River Valley) $30. 88 *—S.H. (5/1/2006)*

De Loach 2003 O.F.S. Chardonnay (Russian River Valley) $26. 89 *(8/1/2005)*

De Loach 1998 O.F.S. Chardonnay (Russian River Valley) $30. 89 *(7/1/2001)*

De Loach 1999 Olivet Ranch Chardonnay (Russian River Valley) $22. 90 —*S.H. (12/15/2002)*

De Loach 1998 Olivet Ranch Chardonnay (Russian River Valley) $20. 89 *(6/1/2000)*

De Loach 2000 Fumé Blanc (Russian River Valley) $14. 87 —*S.H. (9/1/2003)*

De Loach 2004 Early Harvest Gewürztraminer (Russian River Valley) $14. 87 —*S.H. (12/1/2005)*

De Loach 2000 Early Harvest Gewürztraminer (Russian River Valley) $14. 86 —*J.M. (6/1/2002)*

De Loach 2002 Merlot (Russian River Valley) $19. 87 —*S.H. (5/1/2005)*

De Loach 1999 Estate Bottled Merlot (Russian River Valley) $20. 89 —*S.H. (11/15/2002)*

De Loach 1997 Estate-Bottled Merlot (Russian River Valley) $19. 89 *(11/15/1999)*

De Loach 2001 Pinot Gris (Sonoma County) $14. 87 —*S.H. (9/1/2003)*

De Loach 2006 Pinot Noir (California) $12. It's really not a very interesting Pinot Noir, showing simple candied cherry flavors. Production was 16,800 cases. 83 —*S.H. (11/15/2007)*

De Loach 2006 Pinot Noir (Russian River Valley) $20. Weirdly medicinal, with cherry cough syrup flavors and a gooey texture. This is a huge disappointment. Tasted twice. 81 —*S.H. (12/15/2007)*

De Loach 2005 Pinot Noir (Russian River Valley) $20. Shows the balance and harmony of RRV Pinot, at a fair price. Dry and silky, bursting with cherry, raspberry, cola, pomegranate and cinnamon spice flavors that are enriched with sweet vanilla from oak barrels. Easy to find, with more than 17,000 cases produced. 87 —*S.H. (10/1/2007)*

De Loach 2005 Pinot Noir (California) $12. Of all varieties, Pinot is the most price sensitive, but this is a good wine for $12. Seems to have quite a bit of coastal fruit. It's dry and silky and clean, with cherry, tea, cola and spice flavors, and even a bit of fanciness. 85 —*S.H. (3/1/2007)*

De Loach 2005 Pinot Noir (Green Valley) $45. I would have held this wine back longer, as it's still rich in sugary flavors that will slowly go away. For whatever reason De Loach pushed it into market so early, it's a very good wine, showing typical Green Valley character of well-ripened fruit and crisp acidity, enhanced by fine, smoky oak. Best 2007 through 2010. 88 —*S.H. (3/1/2007)*

De Loach 2004 Pinot Noir (Russian River Valley) $18. 88 —*S.H. (10/1/2006)*

De Loach 2002 Pinot Noir (Sonoma County) $18. 85 *(8/1/2005)*

De Loach 2000 Pinot Noir (Russian River Valley) $18. 87 *(10/1/2002)*

De Loach 2004 30th Anniversary Cuvée Pinot Noir (Russian River Valley) $45. 96 Editors' Choice —*S.H. (8/1/2006)*

De Loach 2000 Balletto Ranch Pinot Noir (Russian River Valley) $25. 88 —*S.H. (8/1/2003)*

De Loach 2005 Durell Vineyard Pinot Noir (Sonoma County) $45. A delicious Pinot, but not particularly complex. With direct, primary cherry marmalade and jellied mint flavors, accented with a bit of oak, it's dry and crisp. Drink now. 87 —*S.H. (10/1/2007)*

De Loach 2001 Estate Pinot Noir (Russian River Valley) $18. 86 —*S.H. (12/1/2004)*

De Loach 1999 Estate Bottled Pinot Noir (Russian River Valley) $21. 87 Editors' Choice *(8/1/2001)*

De Loach 2005 Maborishi Vineyard Pinot Noir (Russian River Valley) $42. A bit on the hot, unbalanced side. Despite dryness, ripe cherry pie, cola, cinnamon and sweet vanilla flavors and a gentle, silky texture, there's some burn, and not a lot of depth. Drink now. 86 —*S.H. (10/1/2007)*

De Loach 2005 O.F.S. Pinot Noir (Russian River Valley) $38. This is the winery's top Pinot, Our Finest Stuff. It's nice and dry, with crisp acidity and firm tannins framing cherry cola flavors, but it's not particularly complex or ageworthy. Needs greater force, power and concentration for a reserve bottling. 87 —*S.H. (11/1/2007)*

De Loach 2003 O.F.S. Pinot Noir (Russian River Valley) $29. 90 *(8/1/2005)*

De Loach 2002 O.F.S. Pinot Noir (Russian River Valley) $29. 85 —*S.H. (5/1/2005)*

De Loach 2000 O.F.S. Pinot Noir (Russian River Valley) $50. 85 *(10/1/2002)*

De Loach 1999 O.F.S. Pinot Noir (Russian River Valley) $44. 88 *(8/1/2001)*

De Loach 1997 O.F.S Pinot Noir (Russian River Valley) $32. 87 *(11/15/1999)*

De Loach 2005 Sonoma Stage Vineyard Pinot Noir (Sonoma Coast) $85. There's no doubting this is a rich wine. It's flamboyant in jammy cherry, boysenberry and cola flavors, while oak adds pronounced char and vanilla. It's the most expensive wine ever released by the winery, but tasty as it is, it's sweet and simple. Tasted four times. 86 —*S.H. (12/15/2007)*

De Loach 1998 Splendo Blendo 1 Red Blend (Russian River Valley) $80. 89 *(8/1/2001)*

De Loach 2000 Los Amigos Ranch Sangiovese (Russian River Valley) $28. 87 —*S.H. (12/1/2002)*

De Loach 2006 Sauvignon Blanc (Russian River Valley) $14. A great food wine. Bone dry and very crisp. This has deep, appealing flavors of citrus fruits, figs and white peppery spices. Would go great with savory dishes like roast chicken and mushroom tarts. 89 Best Buy —*S.H. (11/15/2007)*

De Loach 2003 Sauvignon Blanc (Russian River Valley) $16. 85 —*S.H. (5/1/2005)*

De Loach 2006 O.F.S. Sauvignon Blanc (Russian River Valley) $22. This shows the combo of a cool vintage and deft winemaking. It's impressively deep in citrus, fig and pepper flavors, with just a touch of oak that adds a nice, smoky edge. With high acidity, it really gets those tastebuds whistling. Best of all, the wine achieves the Holy Grail: low alcohol, only 13%, and bone dryness. 92 Editors' Choice —*S.H. (12/15/2007)*

De Loach 2004 O.F.S. Sauvignon Blanc (Russian River Valley) $20. 91 Editors' Choice —*S.H. (5/1/2006)*

De Loach 2001 Viognier (Russian River Valley) $20. 88 —*S.H. (3/1/2003)*

De Loach 2003 Zinfandel (Russian River Valley) $18. 88 —*S.H. (10/1/2006)*

De Loach 2002 Zinfandel (Russian River Valley) $18. 85 *(8/1/2005)*

De Loach 2001 Zinfandel (Russian River Valley) $20. 86 *(11/1/2003)*

De Loach 2000 Zinfandel (Russian River Valley) $20. 84 —*S.H. (11/1/2002)*

De Loach 1999 Zinfandel (Russian River Valley) $20. 90 Editors' Choice —*S.H. (11/15/2001)*

De Loach 1999 Zinfandel (California) $13. 85 *(8/1/2001)*

De Loach 2001 Barbieri Ranch Zinfandel (Russian River Valley) $25. 92 —*S.H. (3/1/2004)*

De Loach 2000 Barbieri Ranch Zinfandel (Russian River Valley) $28. 92 Editors' Choice —*S.H. (11/1/2002)*

De Loach 1999 Barbieri Ranch Zinfandel (Russian River Valley) $30. 90 Editors' Choice *(8/1/2001)*

De Loach 1998 Barbieri Ranch Zinfandel (Russian River Valley) $22. 93 —*S.H. (2/1/2000)*

De Loach 1997 Barbieri Ranch Zinfandel (Russian River Valley) $20. 88 —*P.G. (11/15/1999)*

De Loach 2000 Doe Mill Ranch Zinfandel (Sierra Foothills) $28. 85 —*S.H. (11/1/2002)*

De Loach 1997 Estate Zinfandel (Russian River Valley) $18. 87 —*P.G. (11/15/1999)*

De Loach 1999 Estate Bottled Zinfandel (Russian River Valley) $21. 88 *(8/1/2001)*

De Loach 1998 Estate Bottled Zinfandel (Russian River Valley) $18. 90 —*S.H. (2/1/2000)*

De Loach 2005 Forgotten Vines Zinfandel (Sonoma County) $32. Just about the most perfect Sonoma Zin from a typicity point of view. It's gorgeously balanced, offering polished wild cherry, cassis, cola, lavender and white peppery spice flavors in an opulent, smooth texture. The finish is richly dry and crisp. 92 —*S.H. (11/1/2007)*

De Loach 2003 Gambogi Ranch Zinfandel (Russian River Valley) $27. 88 *(8/1/2005)*

De Loach 2001 Gambogi Ranch Zinfandel (Russian River Valley) $25. 92 —*S.H. (3/1/2004)*

De Loach 2000 Gambogi Ranch Zinfandel (Russian River Valley) $28. 89 —*S.H. (11/1/2002)*

De Loach 1999 Gambogi Ranch Zinfandel (Russian River Valley) $30. 88 *(8/1/2001)*

De Loach 1998 Gambogi Ranch Zinfandel (Russian River Valley) $22. 88 —*S.H. (2/1/2000)*

De Loach 1997 Gambogi Ranch Zinfandel (Russian River Valley) $20. 89 —*P.G. (11/15/1999)*

De Loach 2005 Nova Vineyard Zinfandel (Lake County) $32. A bit too hot and heavy for real balance. The wine has a stewed blackberry and cherry taste that accentuates the astringent tannins. **84** *—S.H. (11/1/2007)*

De Loach 2001 O.F.S. Zinfandel (Russian River Valley) $40. 85 *(11/1/2003)*

De Loach 1998 O.F.S. Zinfandel (Russian River Valley) $35. 93 *—S.H. (2/1/2000)*

De Loach 2003 O.F.S. Zinfandel (Russian River Valley) $29. 89 *(8/1/2005)*

De Loach 2000 O.F.S. Zinfandel (Russian River Valley) $50. 87 *—S.H. (9/1/2003)*

De Loach 1999 O.F.S. Zinfandel (Russian River Valley) $44. 90 *(8/1/2001)*

De Loach 2001 Papera Ranch Zinfandel (Russian River Valley) $25. 90 *—S.H. (3/1/2004)*

De Loach 2000 Papera Ranch Zinfandel (Russian River Valley) $28. 87 *—S.H. (11/1/2002)*

De Loach 1999 Papera Ranch Zinfandel (Russian River Valley) $30. 88 *(8/1/2001)*

De Loach 1998 Papera Ranch Zinfandel (Russian River Valley) $22. 90 *—S.H. (2/1/2000)*

De Loach 2000 Pelletti Ranch Zinfandel (Russian River Valley) $28. 91 *—S.H. (11/1/2002)*

De Loach 1999 Pelletti Ranch Zinfandel (Russian River Valley) $30. 91 Cellar Selection *(8/1/2001)*

De Loach 1998 Pelletti Ranch Zinfandel (Russian River Valley) $22. 91 *—S.H. (2/1/2000)*

De Loach 1997 Pelletti Ranch Zinfandel (Russian River Valley) $20. 92 *—P.G. (11/15/1999)*

De Loach 2001 Saitone Ranch Zinfandel (Russian River Valley) $25. 93 Editors' Choice *—S.H. (3/1/2004)*

De Loach 2000 Saitone Ranch Zinfandel (Russian River Valley) $28. 86 *—S.H. (11/1/2002)*

De Loach 1999 Saitone Ranch Zinfandel (Russian River Valley) $30. 88 *(8/1/2001)*

De Loach 1998 Saitone Ranch Zinfandel (Russian River Valley) $22. 87 *—S.H. (2/1/2000)*

De Loach 1997 Saitone Ranch Zinfandel (Russian River Valley) $20. 90 *—P.G. (11/15/1999)*

DE PONTE CELLARS

De Ponte Cellars 2004 Pinot Noir (Dundee Hills) $34. This is an intriguing mix of herb, leaf, root and fruit. The nose opens with plenty of that classic Oregon tomato leaf character, followed with beet root and bark. But there's also sweet plum and currant, cherry and berry. It's big, potent, flavorful and still coming together, but all the components are there for an ageworthy, detailed wine. **88** *—P.G. (2/1/2007)*

De Ponte Cellars 2002 Pinot Noir (Willamette Valley) $28. 88 *(11/1/2004)*

DE SANTE

De Sante 2001 Calder Cabernet Sauvignon (Napa Valley) $40. 87 *—S.H. (5/1/2005)*

De Sante 2004 Sauvignon Blanc (Napa Valley) $20. 87 *—S.H. (5/1/2005)*

De Sante 2001 Sauvignon Blanc (Napa Valley) $18. 90 *—S.H. (10/1/2003)*

DE TIERRA

De Tierra 2005 Chardonnay (Santa Lucia Highlands) $20. From the large Vinco vineyard, in the middle of the appellation right on the River Road wine trail, comes this brisk, refreshing Chard. It's zippy in acids and very ripe, with apricot and nectarine flavors. The wine has had no malo, and the oak is fairly neutral. **87** *—S.H. (7/1/2007)*

De Tierra 2005 Coast View Vineyard Chardonnay (Monterey) $30. The wine is intense, with firm acids and a chalkiness to the peach, guava and nectarine flavors. This is an elegant wine that will last and improve over six years. **90** *—S.H. (7/1/2007)*

De Tierra 2003 Merlot (Monterey) $25. There's an explosion of ripe fruit in this dry wine—blackberries, cherries, raspberries and milk chocolate. It's basically a fruit bomb, though, with just enough acids and tannins to make it balanced. **84** *—S.H. (7/1/2007)*

De Tierra 2003 Merlot (Monterey) $30. 83 *—S.H. (12/1/2006)*

De Tierra 2005 Pinot Noir (Monterey) $22. Not bad, but comes off harsh, with its stewed cherry flavors and hot mouthfeel. A common, regional-style wine with a dry finish. **83** *—S.H. (7/1/2007)*

De Tierra 2005 Silacci Vineyard Pinot Noir (Monterey) $40. Made from the fanciest clones, this wine tastes a bit stewed, although it has Pinot's silky texture and forward cherry, pomegranate and vanilla oak flavors. Hard to say what went wrong in this cool vintage. **84** *—S.H. (7/1/2007)*

De Tierra 2005 Tondre Grapefield Pinot Noir (Monterey) $35. From the Santa Lucia Highlands, this is a dry, crisp Pinot, with a stony minerality to the intensely ripe cherry and root beer flavors. It feels upscale in the balance of acids, tannins and oak. Drink now. **88** *—S.H. (7/1/2007)*

De Tierra 2005 EKEM Sauvignon Blanc Musqué Sauvignon Musqué (Monterey) $50. Named after Yquem (get it?), this is a very sweet but fairly simple dessert wine with 15.2% residual sugar and 12.3% alcohol. It has flavors of apricot jam and vanilla bean, and is pretty soft. Easy to like because of the clean sweetness. **86** *—S.H. (7/1/2007)*

De Tierra 2004 Syrah (Monterey) $25. Sharp and overripe, with annoyingly tart, medicinal cherry flavors. **80** *—S.H. (7/1/2007)*

De Tierra Vineyards 2002 Syrah (Monterey) $NA. 82 *—S.H. (6/1/2005)*

DEAVER

Deaver 2002 Zinfandel (Amador County) $25. 92 *—S.H. (3/1/2005)*

DEBONNÉ

Debonné 2005 Ice Wine Vidal Blanc (Grand River Valley) $30. This sweet surprise from Ohio offers delicate citrus and apricot notes on the nose and a honeyed but lively flavor profile of tropical fruit on the palate. Pretty but complex enough to offer unfolding layers of fruit and some spice, the wine proves that lesser-known winemaking regions like Ohio can make wines that play well with the big boys. **88** *—S.K. (12/1/2007)*

DECOY

Decoy 2005 Bordeaux Blend (Napa Valley) $28. From Duckhorn's second label, this Bordeaux blend is based on Cabernet and Merlot. At less than half the price of Duckhorn's main Cabs and Merlots, it's a very good buy, showing richness, balance and complexity. The blackberry and cherry fruit has been tastefully enhanced with smoky oak. A great food wine. **90 Editors' Choice** *—S.H. (12/31/2007)*

Decoy 2004 Bordeaux Blend (Napa Valley) $28. Decoy is Duckhorn's second wine. This wine is a Bordeaux blend based on not quite half Cabernet Sauvignon, made from vineyards throughout Napa Valley. My main quibble is that it's sweet, with a white sugar tinge to the cherries and blackberries. **84** *—S.H. (4/1/2007)*

Decoy 2003 Red Blend (Napa Valley) $28. 89 *—S.H. (2/1/2006)*

DEERFIELD RANCH

Deerfield Ranch 2001 Cabernet Sauvignon (North Coast) $30. 87 *—S.H. (8/1/2005)*

Deerfield Ranch 2000 Cabernet Sauvignon (Napa Valley) $50. 87 *—S.H. (11/15/2004)*

Deerfield Ranch 2000 Cabernet Sauvignon (Sonoma County) $35. 90 *—S.H. (4/1/2004)*

Deerfield Ranch 2003 Los Chamasal Vineyard Cabernet Sauvignon (Sonoma Valley) $45. Just too sweet for a dry table wine. The first sip puts the palate on sugar alert. Although the tannins and acids are a good expression of Sonoma Valley, that cherry LifeSaver sweetness lowers the score. **84** *—S.H. (7/1/2007)*

Deerfield Ranch 2002 Chardonnay (Sonoma Valley) $25. 84 *—S.H. (8/1/2005)*

Deerfield Ranch 2001 Chardonnay (Carneros) $20. 87 *—S.H. (4/1/2004)*

Deerfield Ranch 1999 Labbe Vineyard Chardonnay Chardonnay (Sonoma Valley) $30. 91 *—S.H. (9/1/2002)*

Deerfield Ranch 2000 Begin Vineyard Gewürztraminer (California) $16. 85 *—S.H. (6/1/2002)*

Deerfield Ranch 1999 DRX Meritage (North Coast) $100. 85 *—S.H. (11/15/2003)*

Deerfield Ranch 2000 Ladi's Vineyard Meritage (Sonoma County) $75. 86 *—S.H. (11/15/2004)*

Deerfield Ranch 2003 Merlot Cuvee Merlot (North Coast) $24. Except for some sweetness, this is pretty good. It has plush cherry, blackberry, milk chocolate, tobacco and sweet herb flavors, wrapped into ripe, polished tannins. Would be better if not for that sugary aftertaste. A blend of Merlot, Cab, Malbec and Sangiovese. **84** *—S.H. (7/1/2007)*

Deerfield Ranch 2000 Roumiguiere Vineyard Merlot (Clear Lake) $24. 87 *—S.H. (9/1/2003)*

Deerfield Ranch 2000 Russian River Vineyards Merlot (Russian River Valley) $30. 85 *—S.H. (12/15/2004)*

Deerfield Ranch 1999 Russian River Vineyards Merlot (Russian River Valley) $32. 90 *—S.H. (9/1/2002)*

Deerfield Ranch 2001 Pinot Noir (Sonoma Valley) $30. 85 *—S.H. (4/1/2004)*

Deerfield Ranch 2001 Pinot Noir (Carneros) $25. 85 *—S.H. (4/1/2004)*

Deerfield Ranch 2002 Cohn Vineyard Pinot Noir (Russian River Valley) $48. 87 *(11/1/2004)*

Deerfield Ranch 2000 Cohn Vineyard Pinot Noir (Russian River Valley) $48. 86 *—S.H. (2/1/2003)*

Deerfield Ranch 2002 Jemrose Vineyard Pinot Noir (Bennett Valley) $40. 87 *(11/1/2004)*

Deerfield Ranch 2002 Jemrose Vineyard Pinot Noir (Bennett Valley) $25. 86 *—S.H. (8/1/2005)*

Deerfield Ranch 2003 Red Rex Red Blend (Sonoma County) $20. This is sort of an old-fashioned field blend, a mixture of Cabernet, Syrah, Sangiovese and a bunch of other varieties. It's easy to drink and dryish, with upfront cherry-berry and chocolate flavors. 85 *—S.H. (7/1/2007)*

Deerfield Ranch 2001 Super Rex Red Blend (North Coast) $40. 85 *—S.H. (12/31/2003)*

Deerfield Ranch 2002 Super T Red Blend (North Coast) $40. 84 *—S.H. (8/1/2005)*

Deerfield Ranch 1999 Gold Orion Vineyard Late Harvest Botrytis Riesling (Napa Valley) $50. 92 *—S.H. (9/1/2002)*

Deerfield Ranch 2001 Roumiguiere Vineyard Sangiovese (Clear Lake) $22. 84 *—S.H. (8/1/2005)*

Deerfield Ranch 1999 Roumiguiere Vineyard Sangiovese (Lake County) $22. 89 *—S.H. (9/1/2002)*

Deerfield Ranch 2002 Sauvignon Blanc (North Coast) $18. 85 *—S.H. (4/1/2004)*

Deerfield Ranch 2003 Peterson Vineyard Sauvignon Blanc (Sonoma Valley) $20. 87 *(7/1/2005)*

Deerfield Ranch 2001 Peterson Vineyard Sauvignon Blanc (Sonoma Valley) $18. 89 *—S.H. (7/1/2003)*

Deerfield Ranch 2000 Peterson Vineyard Sauvignon Blanc (Sonoma Valley) $18. 88 *—S.H. (9/1/2002)*

Deerfield Ranch 2002 Ladi's Vineyard Syrah (Sonoma County) $40. 82 *(9/1/2005)*

Deerfield Ranch 2001 Ladi's Vineyard Syrah (Sonoma County) $40. 91 *—S.H. (4/1/2004)*

Deerfield Ranch 2000 Ladi's Vineyard Syrah (Sonoma County) $40. 94 *—S.H. (9/1/2002)*

Deerfield Ranch 2001 Buchignani Vineyard Old Vine Zinfandel (Dry Creek Valley) $40. 93 *—S.H. (1/1/2004)*

Deerfield Ranch 2000 Old Vine Buchignani Vineyard Zinfandel (Dry Creek Valley) $40. 91 *—S.H. (9/1/2003)*

Deerfield Ranch 1999 Old Vine Buchignani Vineyard Zinfandel (Sonoma County) $40. 91 *— (11/1/2002)*

DEHLINGER

Dehlinger 1998 Chardonnay (Russian River Valley) $30. 92 Top Value *(7/1/2001)*

Dehlinger 1997 Chardonnay (Russian River Valley) $26. 91 *—J.C. (11/1/1999)*

Dehlinger 1999 Goldridge Vineyard Pinot Noir (Russian River Valley) $40. 89 *(10/1/2002)*

Dehlinger 1997 Goldridge Vineyard Pinot Noir (Russian River Valley) $35. 89 *(10/1/1999)*

Dehlinger 1998 Syrah (Russian River Valley) $35. 94 Editors' Choice *(11/1/2001)*

DEL BONDIO

Del Bondio 1999 Cabernet Sauvignon (Rutherford) $38. 90 *—S.H. (11/15/2003)*

DEL RIO

Del Rio 2005 Pinot Gris (Rogue Valley) $16. Here there is about 8% Viognier added to the blend; presumably to up the aromas. It's an uneasy alliance; the Pinot Gris tastes tart and grassy; the Viognier adds some orange peel and a little bitterness in the finish, but neither really connects with the other. 85 *—P.G. (11/15/2007)*

Del Rio 2005 Viognier (Rogue Valley) $20. Sharp and bitter, this is an edgy version of Viognier. Citrus peel leads into a thin middle and a finish that seems tannic and hard. 85 *—P.G. (11/15/2007)*

DELECTUS

Delectus 2000 Stanton Vineyard Merlot (Oakville) $42. 86 *—S.H. (5/1/2004)*

Delectus 2000 Petite Sirah (Napa Valley) $45. 91 *—J.M. (12/31/2003)*

Delectus 2000 Argentum Red Blend (Napa Valley) $20. 84 *—S.H. (6/1/2004)*

Delectus 2001 Terra Alta Vineyard Syrah (Lodi) $25. 86 *—S.H. (5/1/2004)*

Delectus 1999 Terra Alta Vineyard Syrah (California) $29. 87 *(11/1/2001)*

DELICATO

Delicato 2004 Cabernet Sauvignon (California) $7. 82 *—S.H. (12/15/2006)*

Delicato 2001 Vine Select Monte Rosso Vineyard Cabernet Sauvignon (Sonoma County) $70. 87 *(8/1/2006)*

Delicato 2005 Chardonnay (California) $7. 85 Best Buy *—S.H. (11/15/2006)*

Delicato 2003 Chardonnay (California) $7. 85 Best Buy *—S.H. (3/1/2005)*

Delicato 1998 Chardonnay (California) $6. 84 Best Buy *(9/1/2000)*

Delicato 2005 Merlot (California) $7. 80 *—S.H. (12/15/2006)*

Delicato 2004 Merlot (California) $6. 84 Best Buy *(8/1/2006)*

Delicato 2004 Merlot (California) $7. 86 Best Buy *—S.H. (11/15/2005)*

Delicato 2003 Merlot (California) $7. 83 *—S.H. (3/1/2005)*

Delicato 2002 Merlot (California) $18. 86 *—S.H. (5/1/2004)*

Delicato 1998 Merlot (California) $6. 83 *(9/1/2000)*

Delicato 2003 3 Liter Merlot (California) $18. 84 Best Buy *—S.H. (3/1/2005)*

Delicato 2001 Monterey Vine Select San Bernabe Vineyard Merlot (Monterey) $30. 87 *(8/1/2006)*

Delicato 2001 San Bernabe Vineyard Monterey Vine Select Merlot (Monterey County) $25. 86 *—S.H. (11/15/2005)*

Delicato 2004 Pinot Grigio (California) $7. 86 Best Buy *—S.H. (2/1/2006)*

Delicato 1998 Sauvignon Blanc (California) $5. 81 *(9/1/1999)*

Delicato 2005 Shiraz (California) $7. 84 Best Buy *—S.H. (12/31/2006)*

Delicato 2004 Shiraz (California) $7. 85 Best Buy *(9/1/2005)*

Delicato 2004 Shiraz (California) $6. 84 Best Buy *(8/1/2006)*

Delicato 2003 Shiraz (California) $7. 84 Best Buy *—S.H. (12/15/2004)*

Delicato 2002 Shiraz (California) $6. 90 Best Buy *—S.H. (11/15/2003)*

Delicato 2001 Shiraz (California) $8. 85 Best Buy *(12/1/2002)*

Delicato 2003 3 Liter Shiraz (California) $18. 85 Best Buy *—S.H. (3/1/2005)*

Delicato 2000 Syrah (California) $8. 87 Best Buy *(10/1/2001)*

Delicato 1998 Syrah (California) $6. 84 Best Buy *(2/1/2000)*

DELICATO MONTEREY VINE SELECT

Delicato Monterey Vine Select 1998 San Bernabe Vineyard Chardonnay (Monterey) $35. 89 *(9/1/2000)*

Delicato Monterey Vine Select 1998 San Bernabe Vineyard Merlot (Monterey) $40. 88 *(9/1/2000)*

Delicato Monterey Vine Select 1998 San Bernabe Vineyard Petite Sirah (Monterey) $40. 86 *(9/1/2000)*

Delicato Monterey Vine Select 1998 San Bernbe Vineyard Syrah (Monterey) $40. 89 *(9/1/2000)*

DELILLE CELLARS

DeLille Cellars 2004 Chaleur Estate Bordeaux Blend (Yakima Valley) $70. This is a similar blend to DeLille's Harrison Hill bottling, but these grapes are largely from Red Mountain. Chaleur Estate is a very site-specific wine, and it has a strong component of mineral, granite or pencil lead. Dense, well-articulated flavors of very tart, precise red fruits, blue fruits, black fruits almost overwhelms; this is a wine to savor and one that requires a lot of airtime. The only cautionary note is the high alcohol (15.2%), which may shorten its lifespan. 93 *—P.G. (3/1/2007)*

DeLille Cellars 2002 Chaleur Estate Bordeaux Blend (Columbia Valley (WA)) $29. 90 *—P.G. (7/1/2004)*

DeLille Cellars 2001 Chaleur Estate Bordeaux Blend (Red Mountain) $60. 92 *—P.G. (9/1/2004)*

DeLille Cellars 1997 Chaleur Estate Bordeaux Blend (Yakima Valley) $40. 93 *(6/1/2000)*

DeLille Cellars 2004 D2 Bordeaux Blend (Columbia Valley (WA)) $35. An extraordinary, effusive nose, smooth and voluptuous, with spectacular focus and concentration, opens this wine. There is an herbal underpinning, and just a bit of tannic roughness, but it's nothing that won't soften up with time. This, along with Quilceda's second-tier red, is the best red wine value in the state. Still showing youthful tart, tight acid; it's chewy but focused. Good flavors of very tart cherry, plum and even red apple, leading into hints of menthol, cigar box, pepper and slate. **91 Editors' Choice** *—P.G. (3/1/2007)*

DeLille Cellars 2001 D2 Bordeaux Blend (Yakima Valley) $32. 90 *—P.G. (7/1/2004)*

DeLille Cellars 1997 D2 Bordeaux Blend (Yakima Valley) $25. 88 *—P.G. (6/1/2000)*

DeLille Cellars 2004 Doyenne Aix Bordeaux Blend (Columbia Valley (WA)) $37. A blend of two thirds Sagemoor old vine Cab; the rest Red Mountain Cab and Syrah. This is dark, toasty, loaded with dark flavors of chocolate and coffee grounds; a succulent and delicious, oak-driven red. If you like smoke, oak and toast barrel flavors riding on top of tangy, spicy red fruit, this is your wine. 89 *—P.G. (3/1/2007)*

DeLille Cellars 2004 Harrison Hill Bordeaux Blend (Yakima Valley) $70. Sour cherry, rock and an almost delicate earthy quality define the entry. In the mouth it has a pleasing granularity, warmed by soft, sweet fruit, and it sits on its mid-palate flavors for a long, long time. Then, slowly, it fades into a tart, somewhat high-toned finish; hinting at wild berry, spicy plum and even a bit of tobacco. 92 *—P.G. (3/1/2007)*

DeLille Cellars 2005 Chaleur Estate Blanc Bordeaux White Blend (Columbia Valley (WA)) $33. A rich, golden, toasty, hedonistic wine. Ripe and loaded with gorgeous fruit: sweet citrus, pineapple, grapefruit, peach and stone fruit. As it moves through the palate it's laced with smoke and toast, while the fruit core expands into marmalade and tupelo honey, and the wine grows unctuous and creamy. Doesn't taste like a young wine, but it certainly will continue to round out and develop further in the bottle. 94 *—P.G. (3/1/2007)*

DeLille Cellars 1997 Harrison Hill Bordeaux Blend (Yakima Valley) $40. 92 *—P.G. (6/1/2000)*

DeLille Cellars 2003 Chaleur Estate Bordeaux White Blend (Columbia Valley (WA)) $31. 91 *—P.G. (6/1/2005)*

DeLille Cellars 2003 Doyenne Aix Cabernet Sauvignon-Syrah (Columbia Valley (WA)) $35. 89 *—P.G. (4/1/2006)*

DeLille Cellars 2002 D2 Merlot (Columbia Valley (WA)) $36. 89 *—P.G. (6/1/2005)*

DeLille Cellars 2003 Chaleur Estate Red Blend (Columbia Valley (WA)) $68. 92 *—P.G. (8/1/2006)*

DeLille Cellars 1999 Chaleur Estate Red Blend (Yakima Valley) $55. 91 **Cellar Selection** *—P.G. (6/1/2002)*

DeLille Cellars 1998 Chaleur Estate Red Blend (Yakima Valley) $45. 91 *—P.G. (6/1/2001)*

DeLille Cellars 2003 D2 Red Blend (Columbia Valley (WA)) $35. 90 *—P.G. (4/1/2006)*

DeLille Cellars 1999 D2 Red Blend (Yakima Valley) $32. 89 *—P.G. (6/1/2002)*

DeLille Cellars 1998 D2 Red Blend (Yakima Valley) $30. 89 *—P.G. (6/1/2001)*

DeLille Cellars 1992 D2 Red Blend (Yakima Valley) $32. 89 *—P.G. (6/1/2002)*

DeLille Cellars 2003 Harrison Hill Red Blend (Yakima Valley) $68. 93 *—P.G. (8/1/2006)*

DeLille Cellars 2001 Harrison Hill Red Blend (Yakima Valley) $60. 91 *—P.G. (9/1/2004)*

DeLille Cellars 1999 Harrison Hill Red Blend (Yakima Valley) $55. 90 *—P.G. (6/1/2002)*

DeLille Cellars 1998 Harrison Hill Red Blend (Yakima Valley) $45. 90 *—P.G. (6/1/2001)*

DeLille Cellars 2005 Doyenne Roussanne (Columbia Valley (WA)) $31. Pure Roussanne, all Ciel du Cheval fruit; supremely fresh, juicy and ripe. This is absolutely delicious fruit, ripe and bursting with all the flavors you could hope to find in the grape and the vineyard. The floral/citrus highlights are there, along with honeysuckle and lime. They lead gracefully into rich stone fruits, buttressed with tangy acids. Then into a sweetly peachy, creamy, lightly vanilla-flavored finish. This is the best Roussanne yet from Doyenne. 91 *—P.G. (3/1/2007)*

DeLille Cellars 2004 Doyenne Roussanne (Columbia Valley (WA)) $26. 90 *—P.G. (4/1/2006)*

DeLille Cellars 2004 Doyenne Syrah (Yakima Valley) $48. Fragrant, tight, spicy, focused. This is pure cranberry and cherry, underscored by a slightly chalky minerality. There's a great acid base, great concentration and beautifully ripened fruit that captures both the floral elegance and pure fruit power of Washington Syrah. This extremely youthful, tight wine will surely expand and improve over the next few years. 90 *—P.G. (3/1/2007)*

DeLille Cellars 2003 Doyenne Syrah (Columbia Valley (WA)) $46. 90 *—P.G. (4/1/2006)*

DeLille Cellars 2002 Doyenne Syrah (Columbia Valley (WA)) $46. 88 *—P.G. (6/1/2005)*

DeLille Cellars 2001 Doyenne Syrah (Yakima Valley) $40. 92 *—P.G. (7/1/2004)*

DeLille Cellars 1999 Doyenne Syrah (Yakima Valley) $38. **93 Editors' Choice** *—P.G. (6/1/2002)*

DeLille Cellars 1998 Doyenne Syrah (Yakima Valley) $38. 93 *—P.G. (6/1/2001)*

DeLille Cellars 1997 Doyenne Syrah (Yakima Valley) $28. 89 *(6/1/2000)*

DeLille Cellars 2000 Chaleur Estate White Blend (Columbia Valley (WA)) $25. **92 Editors' Choice** *—P.G. (6/1/2002)*

DeLille Cellars 1999 Chaleur Estate White Blend (Columbia Valley (WA)) $28. 93 *—P.G. (6/1/2001)*

DeLille Cellars 1998 Chaleur Estate White Blend (Columbia Valley (WA)) $23. 91 *(6/1/2000)*

DeLille Cellars 2005 Doyenne Métier Blanc White Blend (Columbia Valley (WA)) $31. This is a lovely blend of floral and citrus, two thirds Viognier and the rest Chardonnay. The Chard thickens it up, adding flesh, but the floral aspect of the Viognier remains dominant. It's bright, tight, tart, loaded with crisp citrus and penetrating lemon rind. In sum, this is a vibrant, sharp, juicy, lingering, delicious white wine. 91 *—P.G. (3/1/2007)*

DELORIMIER

DeLorimier 1999 Mosaic Bordeaux Blend (Alexander Valley) $30. 91 *—S.H. (11/15/2002)*

DeLorimier 2002 Mosaic Meritage Bordeaux Blend (Alexander Valley) $40. Tastes salty, soft and sweet-sour, with berry and tangerine flavors that are very acidic. A blend of Cab, Merlot and Malbec, it should be better, and is not likely to improve. 83 *—S.H. (6/1/2007)*

DeLorimier 2001 Mosaic Meritage Cabernet Blend (Alexander Valley) $35. 88 *—S.H. (10/1/2005)*

DeLorimier 2005 Chardonnay (Alexander Valley) $17. A sweet edge of sugar lines the fruit on this Chard, making the tangerine, peach, pineapple and oak flavors taste more like a dessert wine than of a dry table wine. In its favor, the wine is crisp and clean. 82 *—S.H. (6/1/2007)*

DeLorimier 2003 Chardonnay (Alexander Valley) $16. 84 *—S.H. (11/1/2005)*

DeLorimier 2002 Clonal Select Chardonnay (Alexander Valley) $24. **90 Editors' Choice** *—S.H. (11/1/2005)*

DeLorimier 2000 Malbec (Alexander Valley) $20. 87 *—S.H. (8/1/2003)*

DeLorimier 2000 Mosaic Meritage (Alexander Valley) $30. 85 *—S.H. (11/15/2003)*

DeLorimier 2003 Merlot (Alexander Valley) $23. DeLorimier's reds all have tasted sugary-sweet to me lately, which has got to be a conscious decision by management. It's baffling, because the estate fruit is good, and Alexander Valley is capable of producing superb reds that are fully dry. So what's going on? 83 *—S.H. (6/1/2007)*

DeLorimier 2001 Merlot (Alexander Valley) $20. 83 *—S.H. (8/1/2005)*

DeLorimier 2000 Merlot (Alexander Valley) $20. **91 Editors' Choice** *—S.H. (12/15/2003)*

DeLorimier 2005 Lace Late Harvest Muscat Blanc (Alexander Valley) $23. Soft and fairly, but not intensely, sweet, this polished wine has orange and tangerine, apricot, honeysuckle and vanilla cream flavors that are balanced with decent acids. It's a simple, likeable dessert wine. 85 *—S.H. (7/1/2007)*

DeLorimier 2005 Sauvignon Blanc (Alexander Valley) $14. This is a crisp, clean wine, with ultraripe flavors of apricots, grapefruits, lemongrass and flowers. It is overtly sweet, though, which limits its appeal. 83 *—S.H. (6/1/2007)*

DeLorimier 2003 Sauvignon Blanc (Alexander Valley) $10. 84 *—S.H. (8/1/2005)*

DeLorimier 2002 Sauvignon Blanc (Alexander Valley) $10. 85 *—S.H. (6/1/2004)*

DeLorimier 2001 Sauvignon Blanc (Alexander Valley) $10. 84 *—S.H. (10/1/2003)*

DeLorimier 2002 Lace Sauvignon Blanc (Alexander Valley) $20. 89 *—S.H. (6/1/2004)*

DeLorimier 2003 Spectrum Reserve Sauvignon Blanc (Alexander Valley) $20. This wine is getting tired. The citrus and oak flavors are just beginning to wilt and decay on the finish. It's pleasant now, but the lifespan of this wine is short. Drink now. With 10% Sémillon. 85 *—S.H. (6/1/2007)*

DeLorimier 2001 Spectrum Reserve Sauvignon Blanc (Alexander Valley) $16. 85 *—S.H. (2/1/2005)*

DeLorimier 2000 Spectrum Reserve Sauvignon Blanc (Alexander Valley) $16. 85 *—S.H. (10/1/2003)*

DEMETRIA

Demetria 2005 Gaia Vineyard Chardonnay (Santa Rita Hills) $27. The vineyard is the farthest west in the appellation, and the resulting wine is a high-acid thriller. It's 100% barrel fermented, the wine has Meyer lemon, crème brûlée and char flavors, backed by a firm minerality. Sleek and refined, this is the winery's first-ever Chard, and one to watch. **93** *—S.H. (4/1/2007)*

Demetria 2005 Gaia Vineyard Pinot Blanc (Santa Rita Hills) $30. The winery's flagship white wine is among the greatest California PBs I've ever tasted. Made Alsatian-style, it's tremendous in tangerine, kumquat, apricot, honeysuckle, buttercream, cinnamon-clove and vanilla aromas. In the mouth, it turns rich and opulent, and while the wine is dry, it has a dessert pastry taste, like coconut cream pie, Key lime pie and tangerine custard. Absolutely world-class wine. **94 Editors' Choice** *—S.H. (4/1/2007)*

Demetria 2005 Cuvée Sandra Pinot Noir (Santa Rita Hills) $55. From the former Ashley's Vineyard, one of the best-known in the AVA, comes this very ripe, extracted Pinot Noir. Tastes like it had a long hangtime, getting ripe to the point of baked pie-filling cherries and puréed, smoky, almost raisined blackberries. The tradeoff for all this richness is softness and a resulting one-dimensionality. **86** *—S.H. (12/1/2007)*

Demetria 2005 Jours de Bonheur Pinot Noir (Santa Rita Hills) $35. Made in a nice, light style, this is Demetria's least costly of the three latest Pinots, but it's also the most charming, with appealing cherry, cola and spice flavors. **87** *—S.H. (12/1/2007)*

Demetria 2005 Le Bélier Pinot Noir (Santa Rita Hills) $45. Definitely on the ripe, rich side, almost like a Grenache with thick flavors of cherry purée, mashed red raspberries and cola, enriched with toasty cedar. Very succulent, although a little obvious in broad palate appeal. **88** *—S.H. (12/1/2007)*

DEMUTH

Demuth 2002 Chardonnay (Anderson Valley) $32. 87 *—S.H. (12/31/2004)*

Demuth 2002 Pinot Noir (Anderson Valley) $40. 90 *—S.H. (5/1/2005)*

DEROSE

DeRose 2002 Special Reserve Cardillo Vineyard Cabernet Franc (Cienega Valley) $19. 84 *—S.H. (11/15/2004)*

DeRose 2002 Vintner's Reserve Merlot (Livermore Valley) $23. 83 *—S.H. (10/1/2004)*

DeRose 2001 Negrette (Cienega Valley) $20. 83 *—S.H. (8/1/2003)*

DeRose 2002 Miller Family Vineyard Negrette (Cienega Valley) $23. 84 *—S.H. (11/15/2004)*

DeRose 1995 Port (Cienega Valley) $26. 85 *—S.H. (12/1/2004)*

DeRose NV Hollywood Red Red Blend (Cienega Valley) $18. 83 *—S.H. (12/15/2004)*

DeRose NV Hollywood Red Red Blend (Cienega Valley) $16. 81 *—S.H. (5/1/2003)*

DeRose 2002 Al DeRose Vineyard Viognier (Cienega Valley) $26. 88 *—S.H. (11/15/2004)*

DeRose 2002 Cedolini Family Vineyard Zinfandel (Cienega Valley) $24. 85 *—S.H. (11/15/2004)*

DeRose 2002 Nick DeRose Sr. Vineyard Zinfandel (Cienega Valley) $21. 84 *—S.H. (11/15/2004)*

DES VOIGNE

Des Voigne 2005 The Emcee Merlot (Columbia Valley (WA)) $26. Soft and plush, this is a sweetly plummy, cherry pie-flavored Merlot that does for a meal what a pillow does for a bed. Lay down and enjoy the lush cherry fruit, the sandalwood scents and the spice. This is a drink-now wine that should win a lot of favorable consumer comments. **89** *—P.G. (12/31/2007)*

Des Voigne 2005 Solea Red Blend (Columbia Valley (WA)) $28. What we have here is really a Cabernet-based blend, or a Meritage-style blend if you wish. It shows good structure, a stiff spine, some barrelly chocolate and caramel flavors, and a slight burst of heat in the finish. **86** *—P.G. (12/31/2007)*

Des Voigne 2005 The Duke Red Blend (Walla Walla (WA)) $26. Here's an interesting blend: 71% Zinfandel, 21% Cabernet Sauvignon and the rest a split between Merlot and Cab Franc—all of it Walla Walla Valley fruit. It jumps out with a spicy hit of barrel, a little rough but quickly smothered in cherry-flavored fruit and chocolaty tannins. It's got a little bit of wild herb as well, and it's a crafty mix that never falls back into neutral. **87** *—P.G. (12/31/2007)*

Des Voigne 2005 San Remo Seven Hills Vineyard Sangiovese (Walla Walla (WA)) $25. Pure Sangio, has soft, seductive fruit and meat flavors. As it sits in the glass scents of tobacco and rose petals come into play, but in the mouth it's all about butterscotch and strawberries. Nicely done. **88** *—P.G. (12/31/2007)*

Des Voigne 2005 Montreux Syrah (Columbia Valley (WA)) $27. Here's Washington Syrah in the flesh, unadulterated, unblended, blasting out aromas of wild berries, spicy cranberry and rhubarb. It leads into a tart and peppery wine with whiffs of smoke and herb; young, wild and just slightly raw. A flavor parade for your mouth. **90** *—P.G. (12/31/2007)*

DESERT WIND

Desert Wind 1997 Ruah Bordeaux Blend (Columbia Valley (WA)) $50. 86 *—P.G. (12/31/2001)*

Desert Wind 2004 Cabernet Sauvignon (Wahluke Slope) $15. 80 *—P.G. (6/1/2006)*

Desert Wind 1999 Cabernet Sauvignon (Columbia Valley (WA)) $13. 84 *—P.G. (9/1/2004)*

Desert Wind 1998 Desert Wind Vineyard Cabernet Sauvignon (Columbia Valley (WA)) $20. 85 *—P.G. (12/31/2001)*

Desert Wind 2004 Bare Naked Chardonnay (Wahluke Slope) $15. 84 *—P.G. (6/1/2006)*

Desert Wind 2004 Merlot (Wahluke Slope) $15. 80 *—P.G. (6/1/2006)*

Desert Wind 1999 Desert Wind Vineyard Merlot (Columbia Valley (WA)) $20. 85 *—P.G. (12/31/2001)*

Desert Wind 2002 Sémillon (Columbia Valley (WA)) $13. 84 *—P.G. (9/1/2004)*

Desert Wind 2000 Desert Wind Vineyard Sémillon (Columbia Valley (WA)) $20. 83 *—P.G. (12/31/2001)*

Desert Wind 2005 Bare Naked Viognier (Wahluke Slope) $15. 82 *—P.G. (6/1/2006)*

DESOLATION FLATS

Desolation Flats 2000 Cabernet Sauvignon (San Lucas) $17. 84 *—S.H. (7/1/2005)*

DESPERATE RED

Desperate Red 2003 Cabernet Sauvignon (Napa Valley) $20. Decent Cab; a little harsh in tannins, with some astringency throughout, but you'll find notes of cassis and oak, and the finish is dry. Might soften with two or three years in the cellar. **84** *—S.H. (9/1/2007)*

DESPERATE WHITE

Desperate White 2005 Sauvignon Blanc (Alexander Valley) $20. Hits the palate with acidity so high, it's almost searing. Not unpleasant, but certainly calls for the softening effects of food. Pleasant flavors, too, of ripe passionfruit, zesty pineapple, crisp green apple and honeysuckle, and a finish of real complexity. **87** *—S.H. (9/1/2007)*

DETERT FAMILY VINEYARDS

Detert Family Vineyards 2002 Cabernet Franc (Oakville) $35. 92 *—S.H. (11/15/2004)*

Detert Family Vineyards 2000 Cabernet Franc (Oakville) $30. 87 *—J.M. (12/1/2002)*

Detert Family Vineyards 2002 Cabernet Sauvignon (Oakville) $45. 92 *—S.H. (11/15/2004)*

DEUX AMIS

Deux Amis 2002 Vyborny Vineyards Petite Sirah (Alexander Valley) $25. 88 *—S.H. (12/31/2005)*

Deux Amis 2002 Zinfandel (Sonoma County) $19. 88 *—S.H. (12/31/2005)*

Deux Amis 2001 Zinfandel (Sonoma County) $21. 86 *(11/1/2003)*

Deux Amis 1999 Zinfandel (Sonoma County) $19. 86 *—S.H. (7/1/2002)*

Deux Amis 2002 Belle Canyon Vineyards Zinfandel (Dry Creek Valley) $25. 89 *—S.H. (12/31/2005)*

Deux Amis 2002 Halling Vineyard Zinfandel (Dry Creek Valley) $25. 90 *—S.H. (12/31/2005)*

Deux Amis 2001 Rued Vineyard Zinfandel (Dry Creek Valley) $20. 89 *(11/1/2003)*

Deux Amis 1998 Rued Vineyard Zinfandel (Dry Creek Valley) $24. 85 *—S.H. (7/1/2002)*

Deux Amis 1997 Rued Vineyards Zinfandel (Dry Creek Valley) $24. 90 *—P.G. (11/15/1999)*

DI FRONZO

Di Fronzo 2003 Syrah (Arroyo Grande Valley) $42. 87 *—S.H. (12/1/2006)*

DI STEFANO

Di Stefano 1998 Sogno Cabernet Franc (Columbia Valley (WA)) $25. 88 —*J.C. (6/1/2001)*

Di Stefano 1999 Cabernet Sauvignon (Columbia Valley (WA)) $NA. 88 —*P.G. (9/1/2004)*

Di Stefano 1999 Cabernet Sauvignon (Columbia Valley (WA)) $25. 85 —*P.G. (12/31/2002)*

Di Stefano 1998 Cabernet Sauvignon (Columbia Valley (WA)) $25. 87 —*J.C. (6/1/2001)*

Di Stefano 2003 Sogno Cabernet Sauvignon (Columbia Valley (WA)) $36. This is 96% Cabernet Franc, and why the winery doesn't just call a spade a spade is beyond me. But that quibble aside, there is much to recommend here. The fruit is plenty ripe and tastes of strawberry, raspberry and cherry preserves. The oak flavors bring on the smoke and toast, and the natural tendency of Cab Franc to impart green coffee bean notes is also much in evidence. The tannins have been softened up, but still leave a lingering green tea impression in the back of the throat. **87** —*P.G. (8/1/2007)*

Di Stefano 2000 Merlot (Columbia Valley (WA)) $NA. 86 —*P.G. (9/1/2004)*

Di Stefano 1999 Merlot (Columbia Valley (WA)) $28. 85 —*P.G. (12/31/2002)*

Di Stefano 1998 Merlot (Columbia Valley (WA)) $25. 88 —*J.C. (6/1/2001)*

Di Stefano 2003 Domenica Red Table Wine Red Blend (Columbia Valley (WA)) $25. This blend of Merlot and Cabernet Sauvignon does not bear the usual DiStefano label; rather it is a simple design with plain text and the winery's name in small type at the bottom. Apparently meant to emulate a homemade Zinfandel, it actually comes pretty close, although there isn't a drop of Zin in the blend. But it's sharp and spicy, tannic with a hint of green stem, and just the sort of wine that would slide down well with a slice of pizza. **84** —*P.G. (12/31/2007)*

Di Stefano 2004 Meritage Red Blend (Columbia Valley (WA)) $25. This is solidly made, with rough, chewy tannins and hard fruit flavors that show concentrated plum and cassis. Everything is in good proportion, although the acids are a bit chalky and the high alcohol (just under 15%) takes it away from classic Bordeaux flavors. It would be nice to see the ripeness ramped down a notch, because the mix of grapes is right and there's good fruit here. It just has been ripened to the point where the alcohol takes over. **86** —*P.G. (12/31/2007)*

Di Stefano 2000 Meritage Red Blend (Columbia Valley (WA)) $NA. 86 —*P.G. (9/1/2004)*

Di Stefano 2006 Sauvignon Blanc (Columbia Valley (WA)) $15. There is nothing shy here at 14.7% alcohol, but the impressive bouquet mixes together orange blossoms, citrus rind, powdered sugar and baking spices. It plays out broadly across the palate, with ripe, lightly tropical fruits and a dusting of spice. The only fall-off is right at the end, but the last impression is of a sweet lick of honey. **88** —*P.G. (12/1/2007)*

Di Stefano 2005 Sauvignon Blanc (Columbia Valley (WA)) $15. Slightly soapy and pungent, the aromas do not immediately suggest Sauvignon Blanc fruit. There's a pine resin undertone, but once in the mouth the wine asserts itself and tastes of ripe citrus and fresh herb. It's fairly soft and lush for Sauv Blanc. **86** —*P.G. (8/1/2007)*

Di Stefano 2003 Sauvignon Blanc (Columbia Valley (WA)) $10. 91 Best Buy —*P.G. (12/1/2004)*

Di Stefano 2000 Sauvignon Blanc (Columbia Valley (WA)) $12. 87 —*P.G. (12/31/2002)*

Di Stefano 2002 Syrah (Columbia Valley (WA)) $28. 86 *(9/1/2005)*

Di Stefano 2004 R Syrah (Columbia Valley (WA)) $29. This has a moderately strong streak of funk, barnyard, leather, whatever you want to call it, wrapped around sweet boysenberry fruit. It's not an immaculate conception of a wine, but it packs plenty of flavor, and the fruit has the kind of snap and tang that makes Washington Syrah stand out from the New World pack. **86** —*P.G. (12/31/2007)*

Di Stefano 2002 R Syrah (Columbia Valley (WA)) $32. 87 *(9/1/2005)*

Di Stefano 2005 Viognier (Columbia Valley (WA)) $19. This opens with a very pretty nose composed of rose petals, pear, orange peel and orange liqueur. Soft and pretty, it shows the feminine side of Viognier, avoids the bitterness and excessive alcohol that can detract from its elegance. A lovely springtime apéritif. **88** —*P.G. (8/1/2007)*

DIABLO CREEK

Diablo Creek 2001 Cabernet Sauvignon (California) $10. 85 —*S.H. (5/1/2004)*

Diablo Creek 2002 Chardonnay (California) $10. 83 —*S.H. (2/1/2004)*

Diablo Creek 2001 Merlot (California) $10. 84 —*S.H. (5/1/2004)*

DIAMOND CREEK

Diamond Creek 2002 Gravelly Meadow Cabernet Sauvignon (Napa Valley) $175. 93 —*S.H. (8/1/2006)*

Diamond Creek 2000 Gravelly Meadow Cabernet Sauvignon (Napa Valley) $175. 93 —*J.M. (4/1/2004)*

Diamond Creek 2002 Red Rock Terrace Cabernet Sauvignon (Napa Valley) $175. 97 Cellar Selection —*S.H. (8/1/2006)*

Diamond Creek 2000 Red Rock Terrace Cabernet Sauvignon (Napa Valley) $175. 92 —*J.M. (4/1/2004)*

Diamond Creek 2002 Volcanic Hill Cabernet Sauvignon (Napa Valley) $175. 95 Cellar Selection —*S.H. (8/1/2006)*

Diamond Creek 2000 Volcanic Hill Cabernet Sauvignon (Napa Valley) $175. 94 —*J.M. (4/1/2004)*

Diamond Creek 2004 Volcanic Hill *Barrel Sample* Cabernet Sauvignon (Napa Valley) $NA. 94 —*S.H. (8/1/2004)*

DIAMOND OAKS

Diamond Oaks 2002 Pinot Noir (Carneros) $21. 87 *(11/1/2004)*

DIAMOND OAKS DE MANIAR

Diamond Oaks de Maniar 2001 Chardonnay (Chalk Hill) $32. 87 —*S.H. (12/15/2003)*

Diamond Oaks de Maniar 2001 Chardonnay (Carneros) $14. 85 —*S.H. (12/15/2003)*

Diamond Oaks de Maniar 2000 Reserve Chardonnay (Carneros) $47. 88 —*S.H. (12/15/2003)*

Diamond Oaks de Maniar 2002 Merlot (Carneros) $19. 83 —*S.H. (5/1/2005)*

Diamond Oaks de Maniar 2002 Hira Ranch Merlot (Carneros) $35. 83 —*S.H. (5/1/2005)*

DIAMOND RIDGE

Diamond Ridge 2000 Merlot (Russian River Valley) $20. 85 —*S.H. (11/15/2002)*

DIAMOND TERRACE

Diamond Terrace 2002 Cabernet Sauvignon (Diamond Mountain) $55. 83 —*S.H. (12/1/2005)*

Diamond Terrace 2001 Cabernet Sauvignon (Diamond Mountain) $50. 91 Cellar Selection —*S.H. (10/1/2004)*

DIATOM

Diatom 2005 Huber Chardonnay (Santa Rita Hills) $42. Whatever your feelings on the 16.2% alcohol might be, this wine is an achievement. Compared to Diatom's Clos Pepe bottling, this one's more citrusy, and certainly more acidic, which helps balance the alcohol. The lemon drop flavor detonates on the palate with an almost searing intensity that stimulates the salivary glands, and while the finish is bone dry, it has a honey-rich opulence. **94** —*S.H. (4/1/2007)*

DICKERSON

Dickerson 1999 Limited Release Reserve Zinfandel (Napa Valley) $30. 93 —*S.H. (9/1/2002)*

DIERBERG

Dierberg 2004 Pinot Noir (Santa Maria Valley) $38. 93 —*S.H. (12/15/2006)*

Dierberg 2002 Pinot Noir (Santa Maria Valley) $33. 87 *(11/1/2004)*

DILIBERTO

Diliberto 2002 Tre Bordeaux Blend (North Fork of Long Island) $25. 85 —*M.D. (12/1/2006)*

DILLIAN

Dillian 2001 Zinfandel (Shenandoah Valley (CA)) $22. 90 —*S.H. (3/1/2005)*

DILLON

Dillon 2005 Barrel Fermented Chardonnay (Yountville) $23. The oak is sweet and upfront but well-proportioned to the size of the fruit in this luscious Chardonnay, which comes from a cooler part of Napa Valley. There's Carneros-like acidity and very ripe, forward pear, peach, pineapple and date nut bread flavors. **91** —*S.H. (11/1/2007)*

Dillon 2005 Stainless Steel Fermented Chardonnay (Yountville) $23. The honeyed richness just oozes out from this dry wine. You can almost picture the freshly crushed grapes in their steel fermenters, it's that fresh and keen in pineapple, tangerine, kiwi, guava and other spicy, acid-rich tropical fruits. Absolutely luscious, a complex, fruit-driven wine of great sophistication and elegance. **89** *—S.H. (11/1/2007)*

DIVAS UNCORKED

Divas Uncorked 2005 Chardonnay (Mendocino County) $13. These divas are some winemaking women, and they've produced a Chard of style and elegance. It's long on crisp green apples, with richer notes of pineapple marmalade and butterscotch, and is completely dry. Very nice for the price. **86** *—S.H. (6/1/2007)*

DOBBES FAMILY ESTATE

Dobbes Family Estate 2005 Vanjohn Vineyard Pinot Gris (Willamette Valley) $18. This is quite tart, tasting much like fresh pears drenched in lemon juice. That said, it is clean, crisp and varietal. With the right food (possibly even oysters) it could cut through nicely; but as a stand-alone Pinot Gris it lacks flesh and depth. **86** *—P.G. (7/1/2007)*

Dobbes Family Estate 2005 Pinot Noir (Oregon) $18. Ten different vineyards scattered from the Willamette on down to the Rogue valley are sourced for the Wine by Joe, the budget bottling from Dobbes Family Estate. This is a fine effort for the price, crisp and fruity with plenty of cool climate citrus character. Tart red fruits lead into a tight, hard finish, but there is none of the weedy, stemmy flavor that cheap Oregon Pinot can acquire. **87** *—P.G. (4/1/2007)*

Dobbes Family Estate 2002 Black Label Pinot Noir (Willamette Valley) $50. **90** *(11/1/2004)*

Dobbes Family Estate 2005 Cuvée Noir Pinot Noir (Willamette Valley) $50. This wine offers barnyard scents: saddle leather and silage, compost and herb. It's got the sort of aromas that are found in some biodynamic wines, smells of moist earth and what one winemaker calls the good funk. But it doesn't follow through in the mouth. It offers no depth and little weight, leaving an astringent, earthy impression. Maybe with time it will show more flesh. **87** *—P.G. (11/15/2007)*

Dobbes Family Estate 2004 Cuvée Noir Pinot Noir (Willamette Valley) $50. Joe Dobbes makes this top-tier Pinot Noir in a full-on, fleshy, ripe style. It's lush but nicely proportioned, featuring generous, velvety fruit flavors and restrained notes of leaf, herb and root. **90** *—P.G. (7/1/2007)*

Dobbes Family Estate 2005 Grande Assemblage Pinot Noir (Oregon) $24. The name Grande Assemblage suggests a more imposing blend than this wine, which occupies the lowest rung on the Dobbes Family Pinot ladder. Herbal and lightly spicy, it is a tart, simple wine which would fit comfortably alongside the most generic Bourgogne. **85** *—P.G. (11/15/2007)*

Dobbes Family Estate 2004 Grande Assemblage Pinot Noir (Oregon) $24. The Grande Assemblage is a six-vineyard blend displaying mixed red fruits tending toward the lean currant/rhubarb flavors. The acids cut through and the tannins take over quickly, leaving the thin fruit in the background. The wine needs airing and food. **86** *—P.G. (4/1/2007)*

Dobbes Family Estate 2002 Grand Assemblage Cuvée Pinot Noir (Oregon) $22. **83** *(11/1/2004)*

Dobbes Family Estate 2003 Griffin's Cuvée Pinot Noir (Willamette Valley) $45. Note that this is an older vintage than the winery's other current releases. From a ripe, hot year this is a typical effort, with more color, alcohol and tannin than the creamy '04s or elegant '05s, but less finesse. Thick, tight and chewy, it's got plenty of chunky fruit, hard tannins, and chalky acids. Perhaps some years in the cellar will soften it up a bit, but right now it's one tough Pinot. **87** *—P.G. (4/1/2007)*

Dobbes Family Estate 2005 Meyer Vineyard Pinot Noir (Dundee Hills) $65. Tart, acidic red fruit—pomegranate, sour raspberry—is given some sweet spice and sandalwood from barrel aging. The all-too-typical earthy/herbal aromas that plague so many Oregon Pinots are out in force. The wine sits in the mouth, sour and tight, without enough weight or texture to hint at future pleasure. **86** *—P.G. (11/15/2007)*

Dobbes Family Estate 2004 Quailhurst Estate Pinot Noir (Willamette Valley) $65. Quailhurst is the first single vineyard bottling ever done for Dobbes, though it's not the winery's estate vineyard. This is dark, smoky, fragrant and immediately seductive juice. But along with the obvious power and weight comes fruit that is just a bit syrupy, and far too much of the vanilla extract flavors for my palate. Maybe the barrel influence will fade with time. **88** *—P.G. (4/1/2007)*

Dobbes Family Estate 2005 Quailhurst Vineyard Pinot Noir (Willamette Valley) $65. This has some pretty black cherry fruit, a dusting of cinnamon spice and a bit of the Oregon herb. But there is nothing to suggest why it is worthy of single-vineyard status; it's a light, pleasant and quaffable everyday Pinot, at a special occasion price. **86** *—P.G. (11/15/2007)*

Dobbes Family Estate 2004 Skipper's Cuvée Pinot Noir (Rogue Valley) $28. This is one of the best Rogue Valley Pinots I've ever tasted. Quite lovely right from the start, with scents of spicy berries and cherries. The fruit is clearly defined, and lit up with nuances of clove, cinnamon stick and sandalwood. Smooth and creamy in the mouth, with buttered nuts, mocha and caramel as it weaves its way down the throat. Tannins are smooth and supple, and everything is in proportion. **90** *—P.G. (4/1/2007)*

Dobbes Family Estate 2002 Skipper's Cuvée Pinot Noir (Rogue Valley) $35. **88** *(11/1/2004)*

Dobbes Family Estate 2004 Fortmiller Vineyard Syrah (Rogue Valley) $45. I've really been enthusiastic about this wine in the past, but the 2004 seemed to be missing the richness of 2002 and 2003. Where rough tannins were the challenge in the past, here it's the fruit that has gone into hiding. Fairly generic red fruit flavors, lightly edged with citrus oil, lead into light, slightly chalky tannins. **86** *—P.G. (7/1/2007)*

Dobbes Family Estate 2003 Fortmiller Vineyard Syrah (Rogue Valley) $45. **88** *—P.G. (9/1/2006)*

Dobbes Family Estate 2002 Fortmiller Vineyard Syrah (Rogue Valley) $45. **90** *—P.G. (8/1/2005)*

Dobbes Family Estate 2004 Grande Assemblage Syrah (Rogue Valley) $24. This seems just a bit lighter than in previous vintages. It's well-made but it lacks power and definition. Light flavors of blackberry lead into restrained tannins. Lacking is the peppery spice of Syrah, or even some of the citrusy edge that some of the Washington Syrahs bring to the table. **86** *—P.G. (7/1/2007)*

Dobbes Family Estate 2003 Grande Assemblage Syrah (Rogue Valley) $24. **87** *—P.G. (9/1/2006)*

Dobbes Family Estate 2002 Grande Assemblage Syrah (Rogue Valley) $26. **88** *—P.G. (8/1/2005)*

Dobbes Family Estate 2004 Sundown Vineyard Syrah (Rogue Valley) $50. There are just two barrels (50 cases) of the Sundown Syrah in 2004, but it's a big boy. Dark and sappy, it clocks in with 15% alcohol and compact, dense flavors that start with blackberry and black cherry and run to graphite and smoke. It shows some leafy undertones, along with a bit of heat in the finish. **88** *—P.G. (7/1/2007)*

Dobbes Family Estate 2003 Sundown Vineyard Syrah (Rogue Valley) $48. **88** *—P.G. (9/1/2006)*

Dobbes Family Estate 2002 Sundown Vineyard Syrah (Rogue Valley) $48. **89** *—P.G. (8/1/2005)*

Dobbes Family Estate 2004 Viognier (Rogue Valley) $20. Hits the nose with sharp, penetrating, spicy aromas that indicate a lively and authoritative wine. It doesn't disappoint, delivering a flavorful mix of tropical and citrus fruits, highlighted with grapefruit peel and light herb. **89** *—P.G. (7/1/2007)*

DOCE ROBLES

Doce Robles 1999 Syrah (Paso Robles) $20. **83** *—S.H. (12/1/2002)*

DOG HOUSE

Dog House 2002 Checker's Cab Cabernet Sauvignon (California) $9. **84** *—S.H. (11/15/2005)*

Dog House 2004 Charlie's Chard Chardonnay (California) $9. **86 Best Buy** *—S.H. (11/15/2005)*

Dog House 2002 Maxie's Merlot Merlot (California) $9. **86 Best Buy** *—S.H. (11/15/2005)*

DOG TAIL

Dog Tail 2005 Cabernet Sauvignon (California) $9. **83** *—S.H. (12/15/2006)*

Dog Tail 2005 Chardonnay (California) $9. **86 Best Buy** *—S.H. (12/15/2006)*

Dog Tail 2005 Merlot (California) $9. **84 Best Buy** *—S.H. (12/15/2006)*

Dog Tail NV Fire Hydrant Red Red Blend (California) $9. **83** *—S.H. (12/15/2006)*

Dog Tail 2005 Watchdog White White Blend (California) $9. **85 Best Buy** *—S.H. (12/15/2006)*

DOGWOOD

Dogwood 2003 Meritage Bordeaux Blend (Mendocino County) $38. **84** *—S.H. (12/31/2006)*

Dogwood 2003 Cabernet Sauvignon (Mendocino) $36. **84** *—S.H. (12/31/2006)*

Dogwood 2004 Zinfandel (Mendocino County) $28. **82** *—S.H. (12/31/2006)*

Dogwood 2003 Zinfandel (Mendocino) $28. **86** *—S.H. (12/15/2005)*

DOLCE

Dolce 2003 Semillon-Sauvignon Blanc (Napa Valley) $85. This is not the best Dolce over the last five years, but having said that, it's still a wonderful dessert wine. Rich in apricot, orange, pineapple tart, caramel and vanilla crème brûlée flavors, and with residual sugar of 10.4%, it seduces the palate with zesty sweetness. As delicious as it is, it just lacks that extra punch of intensity. **89** *—S.H. (10/1/2007)*

Dolce 2002 Late Harvest Wine Sémillon-Sauvignon Blanc (Napa Valley) $80. 96 Editors' Choice *—S.H. (12/15/2006)*

Dolce 1998 White Blend (Napa Valley) $75. 93 *(2/1/2001)*

Dolce 2001 Late Harvest White Blend (Oakville) $75. 93 *—S.H. (10/1/2005)*

Dolce 1999 Late Harvest Table Wine White Blend (Napa Valley) $75. 97 Editors' Choice *—S.H. (12/1/2003)*

Dolce 2000 Late Harvest Wine White Blend (Napa Valley) $75. 96 Editors' Choice *—S.H. (2/1/2005)*

DOMAINE ALFRED

Domaine Alfred 2005 Chamisal Vineyards Chardonnay (Edna Valley) $24. Lots of acidity in this crunchy wine; this is so tart it's almost like fresh-squeezed lime juice. Fortunately, creamy lees and plenty of new oak add softer, sweeter notes of buttered toast and vanilla. **88** *—S.H. (8/1/2007)*

Domaine Alfred 2004 Chamisal Vineyards Chardonnay (Edna Valley) $24. 88 *—S.H. (11/1/2006)*

Domaine Alfred 2003 Chamisal Vineyards Chardonnay (Edna Valley) $24. 91 *—S.H. (11/15/2005)*

Domaine Alfred 2004 Chamisal Vineyards Califa Chardonnay (Edna Valley) $38. 92 *—S.H. (7/1/2006)*

Domaine Alfred 2003 Chamisal Vineyards Califa Chardonnay (Edna Valley) $38. 89 *—S.H. (11/15/2005)*

Domaine Alfred 2000 Chamisal Vineyards Estate Bottled Chardonnay (Edna Valley) $22. 85 *—S.H. (6/1/2003)*

Domaine Alfred 2005 Chamisal Vineyards Pinot Gris (Edna Valley) $25. 86 *—S.H. (11/1/2006)*

Domaine Alfred 2005 Califa Pinot Noir (Edna Valley) $60. Represents a big improvement over last year's Califa; this one returns to dryness thanks to the cool vintage. Edna Valley acidity brightens cherry, root beer, vanilla bean and oak flavors. Dry and complex now, the wine should peak in a year or so, then hold through 2010. **88** *—S.H. (12/15/2007)*

Domaine Alfred 2002 Califa Chamisal Vineyard Estate Bottled Pinot Noir (Edna Valley) $48. 91 *—S.H. (8/1/2005)*

Domaine Alfred 2000 Califa Chamisal Vineyards Pinot Noir (Edna Valley) $42. 88 *(10/1/2002)*

Domaine Alfred 1999 Chamisal Pinot Noir (Edna Valley) $28. 89 *(10/1/2002)*

Domaine Alfred 2005 Chamisal Vineyards Pinot Noir (Edna Valley) $38. A little rugged in tannins, but rewarding for its wealth of cherries, cola, licorice, spice and sweet oak. Finishes dry and quite long. Could pick up some nuance in a few years. **88** *—S.H. (10/1/2007)*

Domaine Alfred 2003 Chamisal Vineyard Pinot Noir (Edna Valley) $28. 86 *—S.H. (11/15/2005)*

Domaine Alfred 2000 Chamisal Vineyard Pinot Noir (Edna Valley) $28. 87 *(10/1/2002)*

Domaine Alfred 2003 Chamisal Vineyards Califa Pinot Noir (Edna Valley) $48. 92 *—S.H. (11/15/2005)*

Domaine Alfred 1999 Chamisal Vineyards Califa Pinot Noir (Edna Valley) $42. 91 Editors' Choice *(10/1/2002)*

Domaine Alfred 2002 Chamisal Vineyards Estate Bottled Pinot Noir (Edna Valley) $28. 89 *—S.H. (8/1/2005)*

Domaine Alfred 2004 Da Red Red Blend (Edna Valley) $18. 88 *—S.H. (6/1/2006)*

Domaine Alfred 2003 Da Red Red Blend (Edna Valley) $18. 86 *—S.H. (11/15/2005)*

Domaine Alfred 2005 Chamisal Vineyards Rosé Rosé Blend (Edna Valley) $22. 85 *—S.H. (11/1/2006)*

Domaine Alfred 2005 Chamisal Vineyards Vin Gris Rosé Blend (Edna Valley) $22. 88 *—S.H. (11/1/2006)*

Domaine Alfred 2004 Chamisal Vineyards Syrah (Edna Valley) $28. I've always enjoyed this bottling for its exuberant white pepper opening and dry, tannic structure, and the '04 continues that tradition. It has black cherry and coffee flavors, and the 40% new oak shows up in the touch of smoke. **87** *—S.H. (8/1/2007)*

Domaine Alfred 2003 Chamisal Vineyard Syrah (Edna Valley) $28. 92 Editors' Choice *—S.H. (4/1/2006)*

Domaine Alfred 2004 Chamisal Vineyards Califa Syrah (Edna Valley) $42. Califa is the winery's highest designation, kind of a reserve, and this Syrah is oakier and riper than the regular Chamisal bottling, although fully as dry. Marked with high, minty acidity and firm tannins. But there's huge red and black cherry fruit, courtesy of one of the hottest vintages in Edna Valley history. Elegant and intense, it's ready now. **89** *—S.H. (8/1/2007)*

Domaine Alfred 2003 Chamisal Vineyard Califa Syrah (Edna Valley) $42. 90 *—S.H. (4/1/2006)*

Domaine Alfred 2002 Chamisal Vineyards Estate Bottled Syrah (Edna Valley) $28. 88 *—S.H. (8/1/2005)*

Domaine Alfred 2004 Chamisal Vineyards Rosé of Syrah (Edna Valley) $24. 85 *—S.H. (11/15/2005)*

DOMAINE BECQUET

Domaine Becquet 2002 Cabernet Sauvignon-Shiraz (Lodi) $22. 87 *—S.H. (3/1/2005)*

DOMAINE CARNEROS

Domaine Carneros 1999 Brut Champagne Blend (Carneros) $24. 88 *—M.S. (6/1/2003)*

Domaine Carneros 1997 Brut Champagne Blend (Napa Valley) $22. 89 *—S.H. (6/1/2001)*

Domaine Carneros 1994 Brut Champagne Blend (Carneros) $20. 90 Best Buy *—J.C. (12/1/1999)*

Domaine Carneros 1998 Brut Cuvée Champagne Blend (Carneros) $23. 87 *—S.H. (12/1/2002)*

Domaine Carneros 1995 Brut Cuvée Champagne Blend (Napa Valley) $20. 89 *—S.H. (12/15/1999)*

Domaine Carneros NV Frivolites Champagne Blend (Carneros) $90. 90 *—J.M. (2/1/2003)*

Domaine Carneros 1996 La Reve Champagne Blend (Carneros) $55. 89 *—S.H. (12/1/2002)*

Domaine Carneros 1994 La Rêve Brut Champagne Blend (Napa Valley) $55. 86 *—S.H. (12/1/2000)*

Domaine Carneros 1993 Le Rêve Champagne Blend (Carneros) $55. 91 *—S.H. (12/15/1999)*

Domaine Carneros 2004 Pinot Noir (Carneros) $28. The '04 is right up there with the last several vintages. It's dry and silky, with cherry cola flavors grounded with an earthy edge of tea, herbs and balsamic-splashed Portobello. Comes down in favor of elegance rather than heavy opulence, a balanced wine made for a wide selection of food. **89** *—S.H. (5/1/2007)*

Domaine Carneros 2003 Pinot Noir (Carneros) $28. 90 *—S.H. (12/15/2005)*

Domaine Carneros 2001 Pinot Noir (Carneros) $27. 86 *—S.H. (4/1/2004)*

Domaine Carneros 2000 Pinot Noir (Carneros) $34. 85 *—K.F. (2/1/2003)*

Domaine Carneros 1999 Pinot Noir (Carneros) $34. 87 *(10/1/2002)*

Domaine Carneros 1997 Pinot Noir (Carneros) $35. 90 *(10/1/1999)*

Domaine Carneros 2002 Avant Garde Pinot Noir (Carneros) $18. 84 *(11/1/2004)*

Domaine Carneros 2000 Avant Garde Pinot Noir (Carneros) $18. 88 *(10/1/2002)*

Domaine Carneros 2001 The Famous Gate Pinot Noir (Carneros) $50. 91 *—S.H. (12/1/2004)*

Domaine Carneros 2000 The Famous Gate Pinot Noir (Carneros) $45. 88 *(10/1/2002)*

Domaine Carneros 2004 Brut Sparkling Blend (Carneros) $25. The vintage was a very ripe one, and the heat shows. It's very forward, almost jammy, in sweet strawberry and peach flavors. This robs the wine of some elegance and finesse, but it's still an attractive sipper. **85** *—S.H. (12/31/2007)*

Domaine Carneros 2003 Brut Cuvée Sparkling Blend (Carneros) $25. The winery's brut has been a remarkably consistent wine over many years, offering plenty of real Champagne quality at a relatively affordable price. The '03 is dry, crisp and clean, with a fine, silky mouthfeel. It's also subtle, with suggestions of limes, cherries, brioche and toast. **90** *—S.H. (6/1/2007)*

Domaine Carneros 2002 Brut Cuvée Sparkling Blend (Carneros) $25. 85 *—S.H. (12/31/2005)*

Domaine Carneros 2000 Brut Cuvée Sparkling Blend (Carneros) $24. 90 *—J.M. (12/1/2003)*

Domaine Carneros NV Brut Rosé Cuvee de la Pompadour Sparkling Blend (Carneros) $35. Slightly sweet in dosage, with a distinct finish of sugar, this Pinot Noir and Chardonnay sparkler is crisp in acidity and very clean. It has forward flavors of strawberries, raspberries, brioche, toast, vanilla and cinnamon spice. **85** *—S.H. (6/1/2007)*

Domaine Carneros NV Brut Rosé Cuvée de la Pompadour Sparkling Blend (Carneros) $35. Not the winery's best bubbly, as it's on the rough, sandpapery side. A blend of Chardonnay and Pinot Noir, it has cherry, yeast and smoky vanilla flavors, and finishes dry. **84** *—S.H. (7/1/2007)*

Domaine Carneros NV Brut Rosé Cuvée de la Pompadour Sparkling Blend (Carneros) $34. 88 *—J.M. (12/1/2003)*

Domaine Carneros NV Brut Rosé Cuvée de la Pompadour Sparkling Blend (Carneros) $34. 86 *—S.H. (12/31/2004)*

Domaine Carneros 2000 Le Rêve Sparkling Blend (Carneros) $65. Almost 100% Chardonnay, this bubbly shows a gorgeous elegance and dry sophistication. It's all taffeta and silk, so light and airy, so drinkable. With subtle hints of lime custard, bread dough, lees and vanilla, it's one of the best blanc de blancs of this year. Drink now through 2010. 93 *—S.H. (6/1/2007)*

Domaine Carneros 2001 Le Rêve Blanc de Blancs Sparkling Blend (Carneros) $75. A delicious sparkler; shows the delicacy and elegance of a blanc de blancs at its California best. The Chardonnay contributes subtle peach and citrus flavors, and the mousse, or bubbly mouthfeel, is very refined. Should age well. Drink now–2009, at least. 92 *—S.H. (12/31/2007)*

Domaine Carneros 1999 La Reve Blanc de Blancs Sparkling Blend (Carneros) $59. 90 *—S.H. (12/31/2005)*

Domaine Carneros 1996 Le Reve Sparkling Blend (Carneros) $55. 91 *—J.M. (12/1/2003)*

Domaine Carneros 1997 Le Rêve Brut Sparkling Blend (Carneros) $55. 92 *—S.H. (12/31/2004)*

DOMAINE CHANDON

Domaine Chandon NV 396 Champagne Blend (Carneros) $15. 91 Best Buy *—S.H. (12/15/1999)*

Domaine Chandon NV Blanc de Noirs Champagne Blend (California) $17. 86 *—S.H. (12/1/2002)*

Domaine Chandon NV Blanc de Noirs Champagne Blend (California) $17. 86 *—S.H. (12/31/2004)*

Domaine Chandon NV Brut Classic Champagne Blend (California) $17. 87 *—S.H. (12/31/2004)*

Domaine Chandon NV Brut Classic 196 Champagne Blend (Carneros) $15. 89 Best Buy *—S.H. (12/15/1999)*

Domaine Chandon NV Brut Classic 198 Champagne Blend (California) $16. 87 *—D.T. (12/1/2001)*

Domaine Chandon NV Brut Classic 198 Champagne Blend (California) $16. 86 *—J.M. (12/1/2002)*

Domaine Chandon NV Etoile Champagne Blend (Napa County) $35. 85 *—S.H. (12/1/2002)*

Domaine Chandon NV Etoile Champagne Blend (Napa-Sonoma) $35. 88 *(12/1/2001)*

Domaine Chandon NV Étoile Brut Champagne Blend (Napa County) $35. 88 *(12/1/2001)*

Domaine Chandon NV Étoile Brut Champagne Blend (California) $35. 93 *—S.H. (12/1/2000)*

Domaine Chandon NV étoile Brut Sur Lees 1999 Champagne Blend (Napa-Sonoma) $35. 90 *—S.H. (12/31/2004)*

Domaine Chandon NV Étoile Rosé Champagne Blend (Napa Valley) $40. 90 *—J.M. (2/1/2003)*

Domaine Chandon NV Étoile Rosé Champagne Blend (California) $40.92 *—S.H. (12/1/2000)*

Domaine Chandon NV Étoile Rosé Champagne Blend (California) $40. 85 *—J.C. (12/1/2001)*

Domaine Chandon 2000 Étoile Rosé Champagne Blend (Mendocino-Napa-Sonoma) $45. 88 *—S.H. (12/31/2005)*

Domaine Chandon 1999 Étoile Rosé Champagne Blend (Napa-Sonoma) $40. 90 *—S.H. (12/31/2004)*

Domaine Chandon NV Extra-Dry Riche Champagne Blend (California) $17. 87 *—S.H. (12/1/2002)*

Domaine Chandon NV Reserve Blanc de Noirs Champagne Blend (Sonoma-Napa) $24. 87 *—S.H. (12/31/2004)*

Domaine Chandon NV Reserve Brut Champagne Blend (Napa County) $24. 89 *—S.H. (12/1/2000)*

Domaine Chandon NV Reserve Brut Champagne Blend (California) $24. 85 *(12/1/2001)*

Domaine Chandon NV Reserve Brut Champagne Blend (Napa-Sonoma) $24. 92 Editors' Choice *—S.H. (12/31/2004)*

Domaine Chandon NV Reserve Brut Champagne Blend (Sonoma-Napa) $24. 87 *—S.H. (12/1/2002)*

Domaine Chandon 1996 Vintage Brut Champagne Blend (Sonoma-Napa) $50. 88 *—S.H. (12/31/2004)*

Domaine Chandon 1995 Vintage Brut Champagne Blend (California) $50. 86 *(12/1/2001)*

Domaine Chandon 2005 Chardonnay (Carneros) $24. A little weedy, despite lots of flashy oak. The pineapples and peaches have notes of dried dill and thyme, and the finish is dry and crisp. Nice with broiled halibut in a thyme-butter sauce. 86 *—S.H. (12/1/2007)*

Domaine Chandon 2004 Chardonnay (Carneros) $18. 85 *—S.H. (10/1/2006)*

Domaine Chandon 2003 Chardonnay (Carneros) $19. 90 *—S.H. (12/15/2005)*

Domaine Chandon 2002 Chardonnay (Carneros) $19. 87 *—S.H. (12/31/2004)*

Domaine Chandon 2001 Chardonnay (Carneros) $19. 87 *—S.H. (5/1/2004)*

Domaine Chandon 2000 Chardonnay (Carneros) $19. 87 *— (9/1/2002)*

Domaine Chandon 2001 Brut Chardonnay (Mount Veeder) $30. Beautiful young bubbly, light and elegant, with Chardonnay flavors of peaches and limes, enriched with leesy dough and smoky spice. The texture is ultra-refined, with a very fine mousse. This is one of the best, most complex Chandon bruts in a long time. 91 *—S.H. (12/1/2007)*

Domaine Chandon 2006 Unoaked Chardonnay (Sonoma County) $20. With no oak influences at all, this Chard is on the acidic side, with bright, clean flavors of green grapes, yellow apricots and fresh pineapples. It's dry, but rich in fruity essence. 85 *—S.H. (12/1/2007)*

Domaine Chandon 1996 Blanc de Blancs Mt. Veeder Ranch Chardonnay (Mount Veeder) $60. 88 *(12/1/2001)*

Domaine Chandon 2005 Pinot Meunier (Carneros) $35. This variety is commonly used in Champagne but rarely vinified on its own. This wine shows why. It's like Pinot Noir in the silky texture, but feels jagged and harsh, and the fruit tastes a little baked and sugary. 84 *—S.H. (12/1/2007)*

Domaine Chandon 2003 Pinot Meunier (Carneros) $29. 87 *—S.H. (12/15/2005)*

Domaine Chandon 2002 Pinot Meunier (Carneros) $29. 87 *(11/1/2004)*

Domaine Chandon 2001 Pinot Meunier (Carneros) $29. 86 *—S.H. (5/1/2004)*

Domaine Chandon 2000 Pinot Meunier (Carneros) $29. 89 *— (9/1/2002)*

Domaine Chandon 2005 Pinot Noir (Carneros) $35. This winery's Pinots rarely rise to the top, but are almost always soundly made, very good wines, with extra points for complexity. The '05 is directly on par with previous vintages, a silky, dry wine showing rich flavors of cherries, cola, pomegranates and spices. It's the kind of Pinot that pairs well with foods without taking center stage. 89 *—S.H. (12/1/2007)*

Domaine Chandon 2002 Pinot Noir (Carneros) $29. 89 *(11/1/2004)*

Domaine Chandon 2000 Pinot Noir (Carneros) $29. 89 *— (9/1/2002)*

Domaine Chandon NV Blanc de Noirs 398 Pinot Noir (Carneros) $15. 85 *(12/1/2001)*

Domaine Chandon NV Brut Pinot Noir (Napa-Sonoma) $30. Just delicious, a fascinating counterpoint to the winery's '01 Brut Chardonnay, with which it was coreleased. Shows a beautiful Pinotesque weight, with a cherried edge to the lime and yeast flavors. With a grand cru texture, this is really one of the best Chandon bubblies of recent memory. 93 Editors' Choice *—S.H. (12/1/2007)*

Domaine Chandon 2006 Unoaked Pinot Noir Rosé Rosé Blend (Carneros) $20. With no wood, the flavors of the grape star in this dry, crisp blush. The cherry, lime and apricot fruit is complexed with dried herbs and intense Asian spices, while the bitter finish cries out for food. Great with tempura and a splash of soy, or a simple roasted chicken. 86 *—S.H. (12/15/2007)*

Domaine Chandon 2003 Ramal Road Reserve Pinot Noir (Carneros) $45. 92 *—S.H. (12/15/2005)*

Domaine Chandon 2002 Ramal Road Reserve Pinot Noir (Carneros) $45. 87 *(11/1/2004)*

Domaine Chandon NV Blanc de Noirs Sparkling Blend (California) $18. 89 *—S.H. (12/31/2006)*

Domaine Chandon NV Blanc de Noirs Sparkling Blend (California) $18. 85 *—S.H. (12/31/2005)*

Domaine Chandon NV Blanc de Noirs Sparkling Blend (California) $17. 88 *—S.H. (12/1/2003)*

Domaine Chandon NV Brut Classic Sparkling Blend (California) $17. 88 *—S.H. (12/1/2003)*

Domaine Chandon NV Brut Classic Sparkling Blend (California) $18. 90 Editors' Choice *—S.H. (12/31/2006)*

Domaine Chandon NV Brut Classic Sparkling Blend (California) $18. 86 *—S.H. (12/31/2005)*

Domaine Chandon NV Etoile Sparkling Blend (Napa-Sonoma) $35. 90 *—S.H. (12/1/2003)*

Domaine Chandon 2000 Etoile Sparkling Blend (Napa-Sonoma) $29. 90 —*S.H. (12/31/2006)*

Domaine Chandon NV Etoile Rosé Sparkling Blend (Napa-Sonoma) $40. 91 —*J.M. (12/1/2003)*

Domaine Chandon 2001 Etoile Rosé Sparkling Blend (Mendocino-Napa-Sonoma) $34. 92 —*S.H. (12/31/2006)*

Domaine Chandon NV Extra-Dry Riche Sparkling Blend (California) $17. 87 —*S.H. (12/1/2003)*

Domaine Chandon 1999 L'Etoile Brut Sparkling Blend (Napa-Sonoma) $37. 87 —*S.H. (12/31/2005)*

Domaine Chandon 2000 Mt. Veeder Single Vineyard Blanc de Blancs Sparkling Blend (Mount Veeder) $45. 92 Editors' Choice —*S.H. (12/31/2005)*

Domaine Chandon NV Red Sparkling Blend (California) $19. 86 —*S.H. (12/31/2004)*

Domaine Chandon NV Reserve Sparkling Blend (Sonoma-Napa) $24. 91 Editors' Choice —*S.H. (12/1/2003)*

Domaine Chandon NV Reserve Brut Sparkling Blend (Napa-Sonoma) $25. 86 —*S.H. (12/31/2006)*

Domaine Chandon NV Reserve Brut Sparkling Blend (Napa-Sonoma) $25. 87 —*S.H. (12/31/2005)*

Domaine Chandon NV Riche Sparkling Blend (California) $17. 85 —*S.H. (12/31/2004)*

Domaine Chandon NV Riche Extra Dry Sparkling Blend (California) $18. 85 —*S.H. (12/31/2006)*

Domaine Chandon 1997 Vintage Brut Sparkling Blend (Napa-Sonoma) $50. 91 Cellar Selection —*S.H. (12/31/2005)*

DOMAINE COTEAU

Domaine Coteau 2002 Pinot Noir (Yamhill County) $27. 84 *(11/1/2004)*

Domaine Coteau 2005 Reserve Pinot Noir (Eola-Amity Hills) $29. Unfined and unfiltered. this is dark, earthy and richly endowed with scents and flavors of organic matter, mushroom, compost and coffee grounds. There's fruit in there also, but it really captures the earthy, broadly aromatic side of the grape. About one third new French oak was used, to good effect. **90** —*P.G. (7/1/2007)*

Domaine Coteau 2002 Reserve Pinot Noir (Yamhill County) $34. 87 *(11/1/2004)*

DOMAINE DANICA

Domaine Danica 2000 Chardonnay (Anderson Valley) $28. 91 —*J.M. (12/15/2002)*

Domaine Danica 2002 Heintz Ranch Chardonnay (Sonoma Coast) $25. 83 —*S.H. (3/1/2006)*

Domaine Danica 1999 Pinot Noir (Carneros) $32. 85 —*S.H. (7/1/2003)*

Domaine Danica 1999 Zinfandel (Sonoma County) $33. 89 —*D.T. (3/1/2002)*

Domaine Danica 2000 Salzgeber Vineyard Zinfandel (Russian River Valley) $32. 84 —*S.H. (7/1/2003)*

DOMAINE DE LA TERRE ROUGE

Domaine de la Terre Rouge 2004 Mourvèdre (Sierra Foothills) $22. Dry and smooth as satin, this Mourvèdre satisfies for its lush texture and complex flavors. Cherry, blackberry and smoky plum fruit is balanced with earthier tones of mushrooms, game and leather, leading to a long, spicy finish. **87** —*S.H. (6/1/2007)*

Domaine de la Terre Rouge 2003 Mourvèdre (Sierra Foothills) $22. 84 —*S.H. (6/1/2006)*

Domaine de la Terre Rouge 2002 Mourvèdre (Sierra Foothills) $22. 87 —*S.H. (8/1/2005)*

Domaine de la Terre Rouge 2000 Mourvèdre (Sierra Foothills) $20. 86 —*S.H. (5/1/2003)*

Domaine de la Terre Rouge 1996 Mourvèdre (Amador County) $16. 87 —*S.H. (6/1/1999)*

Domaine de la Terre Rouge 2000 Muscat a Petits Grains Muscat (Shenandoah Valley (CA)) $15. 87 —*S.H. (12/1/2002)*

Domaine de la Terre Rouge 2004 Muscat-a-Petits Grains Vin Doux Naturel Muscat (Shenandoah Valley (CA)) $15. 92 Best Buy —*S.H. (6/1/2006)*

Domaine de la Terre Rouge 2001 Noir Rhône Red Blend (Sierra Foothills) $25. 84 —*S.H. (6/1/2006)*

Domaine de la Terre Rouge 2000 Noir Rhône Red Blend (Sierra Foothills) $25. 89 —*S.H. (8/1/2005)*

Domaine de la Terre Rouge 1998 Noir Rhône Red Blend (Sierra Foothills) $22. 87 —*S.H. (6/1/2003)*

Domaine de la Terre Rouge 1999 Noir Grande Annee Rhône Red Blend (Sierra Foothills) $25. 88 —*S.H. (6/1/2004)*

Domaine de la Terre Rouge 1995 Noir Grande Année Rhône Red Blend (Sierra Foothills) $20. 91 —*S.H. (10/1/1999)*

Domaine de la Terre Rouge 2004 Tete-a-Tete Rhône Red Blend (Sierra Foothills) $14. Bandol is the model for this dry, likeable blend of Mourvèdre, Grenache and Syrah. It's a complex wine, with layers of smoky plum, blackberry tea, carob, heirloom tomato and cedar. Finishes a little aggressively in texture, but it's a good value. **86** —*S.H. (6/1/2007)*

Domaine de la Terre Rouge 2003 Tete-a-Tete Rhône Red Blend (Sierra Foothills) $13. 83 —*S.H. (6/1/2006)*

Domaine de la Terre Rouge 2002 Tete-a-Tete Rhône Red Blend (Sierra Foothills) $13. 88 Best Buy —*S.H. (8/1/2005)*

Domaine de la Terre Rouge 2001 Tete-a-Tete Rhône Red Blend (Sierra Foothills) $13. 86 Best Buy —*S.H. (6/1/2003)*

Domaine de la Terre Rouge 2005 Enigma Rhône White Blend (Sierra Foothills) $22. A blend of Marsanne, Viognier and Roussanne, this wine, which was grown at 3,000 feet, has a rustic feeling. Acidity controls the palate, making the ripe peach, green apple, pineapple and wildflower flavors finish tart. Might pick up bottle complexity in five or six years. **85** —*S.H. (6/1/2007)*

Domaine de la Terre Rouge 2004 Enigma Rhône White Blend (Sierra Foothills) $20. 90 Editors' Choice —*S.H. (6/1/2006)*

Domaine de la Terre Rouge 2001 Enigma Rhône White Blend (Sierra Foothills) $20. 85 —*S.H. (9/1/2003)*

Domaine de la Terre Rouge 2005 Vin Gris d'Amador Rosé Blend (Sierra Foothills) $14. Mourvèdre, Grenache and Syrah constitute the blend in this simple blush wine. It's tart in acids and a little off-dry, with rosehip tea, raspberry, cola, mineral and spice flavors. **84** —*S.H. (6/1/2007)*

Domaine de la Terre Rouge 2004 Vin Gris d'Amador Rosé Blend (Sierra Foothills) $13. 88 Best Buy —*S.H. (6/1/2006)*

Domaine de la Terre Rouge 2003 Vin Gris d'Amador Rosé Blend (Sierra Foothills) $13. 85 —*S.H. (8/1/2005)*

Domaine de la Terre Rouge 2001 Vin Gris d'Amador Rosé Blend (Sierra Foothills) $12. 88 —*S.H. (9/1/2003)*

Domaine de la Terre Rouge 2005 Roussanne (Sierra Foothills) $22. Tastes like a pineapple-flavored Chinese sweet and sour sauce, with sugary fruit and tart acidity. The texture is rich and buttercreamy. **84** —*S.H. (6/1/2007)*

Domaine de la Terre Rouge 2004 Roussanne (Sierra Foothills) $22. 90 —*S.H. (6/1/2006)*

Domaine de la Terre Rouge 2001 Roussanne (Sierra Foothills) $22. 87 —*S.H. (6/1/2003)*

Domaine de la Terre Rouge 2004 Syrah (Sierra Foothills) $24. Rustic and fruity, with considerable new oak, this wine is fully dry. It offers a wealth of blackberry, cola, coffee and dark bitter chocolate flavors, with a peppery finish. Best now and for a few years. **85** —*S.H. (6/1/2007)*

Domaine de la Terre Rouge 2002 Syrah (Sierra Foothills) $24. 88 —*S.H. (8/1/2005)*

Domaine de la Terre Rouge 2000 Syrah (Sierra Foothills) $24. 90 —*S.H. (6/1/2003)*

Domaine de la Terre Rouge 2004 Ascent Syrah (Sierra Foothills) $80. This is almost always the winery's richest, ripest, oakiest Syrah, and usually the best. The '04 is definitely a ripe wine, with huge blackberry, cherry and raspberry jam flavors complexed with coffee, cola, milk chocolate, macaroon and rhubarb flavors. But it's very young, dominated by juicy, juvenile tannins and fresh, tart acidity. If you drink it now, decant. Otherwise, hold for at least five years. **92** —*S.H. (6/1/2007)*

Domaine de la Terre Rouge 2003 Ascent Syrah (Sierra Foothills) $75. 87 —*S.H. (6/1/2006)*

Domaine de la Terre Rouge 2002 Ascent Syrah (Sierra Foothills) $75. 92 —*S.H. (8/1/2005)*

Domaine de la Terre Rouge 2000 Ascent Syrah (Sierra Foothills) $75. 94 Cellar Selection —*S.H. (6/1/2003)*

Domaine de la Terre Rouge 2004 High Slopes Syrah (Sierra Foothills) $35. This is a tannic, full-bodied Syrah. With fleshy blackberry, cola, chocolate and coffee flavors, it has a rustic mouthfeel and a dry astringency. This might age to greater softness and complexity in a few years. **87** —*S.H. (6/1/2007)*

Domaine de la Terre Rouge 2003 High Slopes Syrah (Sierra Foothills) $35. 84 —*S.H. (6/1/2006)*

Domaine de la Terre Rouge 2002 High Slopes Hautes Cotes Syrah (Sierra Foothills) $35. 90 —*S.H. (8/1/2005)*

Domaine de la Terre Rouge 2004 Les Cotes de l'Ouest Syrah (California) $15. This is the winery's least expensive Syrah, but it's right up there with some of the more costly ones, which makes it a relative value. Dry and soft, it has furry tannins that frame ripe blackberry, cherry, cola, chocolate and white pepper. **85** *—S.H. (6/1/2007)*

Domaine de la Terre Rouge 2003 Les Cotes de L'Ouest Syrah (California) $15. **85** *(9/1/2005)*

Domaine de la Terre Rouge 2002 Les Cotes de L'Ouest Syrah (California) $15. **93** *—S.H. (8/1/2005)*

Domaine de la Terre Rouge 2001 Les Cotes de l'Ouest Syrah (California) $15. **84** *—S.H. (12/15/2003)*

Domaine de la Terre Rouge 2004 Sentinel Oak Vineyard Pyramid Block Syrah (Shenandoah Valley (CA)) $35. Rich and unctuous, this wine is made from the oldest Syrah vineyard in the Sierra Foothills, and you can taste the concentration in the intense blackberry, cherry, blueberry and chocolate flavors. Fortunately the wine is not only fruity, but balanced in crisp acidity and firm tannins, while new French oak adds an overlay of vanilla and toast. Delicious now, it will develop bottle complexity over the next eight years. **93 Editors' Choice** *—S.H. (6/1/2007)*

Domaine de la Terre Rouge 2003 Sentinel Oak Vineyard Pyramid Block Syrah (Shenandoah Valley (CA)) $35. **84** *—S.H. (6/1/2006)*

Domaine de la Terre Rouge 2002 Sentinel Oak Vineyard Pyramid Block Syrah (Shenandoah Valley (CA)) $35. **86** *—S.H. (8/1/2005)*

Domaine de la Terre Rouge 2001 Sentinel Oak Vineyard Pyramid Block Syrah (Sierra Foothills) $35. **93** *—S.H. (3/1/2006)*

Domaine de la Terre Rouge 2000 Sentinel Oak Vineyard Pyramid Block Syrah (Shenandoah Valley (CA)) $35. **92 Editors' Choice** *—S.H. (6/1/2003)*

Domaine de la Terre Rouge 2005 Viognier (Amador County) $24. This is a 100% varietal that has been barrel fermented in French oak. It underwent full malolactic fermentation, which may explain the soft, buttery mouthfeel. The flavors are of apricots, peaches and honeysuckle, with a sugary finish. **84** *—S.H. (6/1/2007)*

Domaine de la Terre Rouge 2004 Viognier (Amador County) $30. **90** *—S.H. (6/1/2006)*

Domaine de la Terre Rouge 2003 Viognier (Shenandoah Valley (CA)) $30. **88** *—S.H. (8/1/2005)*

Domaine de la Terre Rouge 2001 Viognier (Shenandoah Valley (CA)) $28. **86** *—S.H. (6/1/2003)*

Domaine de la Terre Rouge 1997 Viognier (Shenandoah Valley (CA)) $25. **90** *—S.H. (6/1/1999)*

Domaine de la Terre Rouge 2003 Enigma White Blend (Sierra Foothills) $20. **87** *—S.H. (8/1/2005)*

Domaine de la Terre Rouge 1997 Enigma White Blend (Sierra Foothills) $16. **89** *—S.H. (6/1/1999)*

Domaine de la Terre Rouge 1996 Vin Gris d'Amado White Blend (California) $9. **88** *—S.H. (6/1/1999)*

USA

DOMAINE DES MONDES

Domaine des Mondes 2005 Sanford & Benedict Vineyard Saints and Sinners Viognier (Santa Barbara County) $30. **93 Editors' Choice** *—S.H. (11/15/2006)*

DOMAINE DROUHIN

Domaine Drouhin 2000 Chardonnay (Oregon) $40. **92** *—P.G. (7/1/2002)*

Domaine Drouhin 2005 Arthur Chardonnay (Willamette Valley) $30. Veronique Drouhin makes this estate Chardonnay as she would make it in her native Burgundy. It's a wine of breed and finesse, with crisp, detailed aromas that reward your attention with nuances of flowers, stone fruit, melon and spice. Precisely-detailed, sculpted and elegant, it is still rather young and unyielding. Unlike most New World white wines, this one definitely needs more years in the bottle. **89** *—P.G. (2/1/2007)*

Domaine Drouhin 2004 Arthur Chardonnay (Willamette Valley) $27. **92 Editors' Choice** *—P.G. (5/1/2006)*

Domaine Drouhin 2002 Pinot Noir (Willamette Valley) $40. **86** *(11/1/2004)*

Domaine Drouhin 2000 Pinot Noir (Willamette Valley) $40. **84** *(10/1/2002)*

Domaine Drouhin 1999 Pinot Noir (Oregon) $45. **90** *—P.G. (12/31/2001)*

Domaine Drouhin 2003 Laurene Pinot Noir (Willamette Valley) $65. The Laurene bottling has long been DDO's reserve Pinot. In recent years, as the densely-planted estate vineyards have gained maturity, the wine seems to have become more austere. Although it is already three years past the harvest, it remains tight and unyielding, lightly herbal, perhaps a bit tannic and earthy. Hints of clay and mineral come through in the finish, and there is sharp-edged raspberry/cranberry fruit. **89** *—P.G. (2/1/2007)*

Domaine Drouhin 2002 Laurene Pinot Noir (Oregon) $55. **85** *(11/1/2004)*

Domaine Drouhin 2000 Laurene Pinot Noir (Oregon) $55. **89** *—P.G. (2/1/2004)*

Domaine Drouhin 1999 Laurene Pinot Noir (Willamette Valley) $55. **88** *(10/1/2002)*

Domaine Drouhin 1998 Laurene Pinot Noir (Oregon) $50. **88** *—P.G. (12/31/2001)*

Domaine Drouhin 1996 Laurene Pinot Noir (Willamette Valley) $45. **85** *(10/1/1999)*

Domaine Drouhin 1999 Louise Drouhin Pinot Noir (Oregon) $45. **95 Cellar Selection** *—P.G. (8/1/2002)*

Domaine Drouhin 2004 Oregon Pinot Noir (Willamette Valley) $45. This is the best regular bottling of DDO Pinot Noir since 2001: It's a nicely ripened, forward, juicy wine that puts the fruit front and center. Scented with cherry candy, cola and sweet brown sugar, it shows a sturdy core that goes well beyond the sweet strawberry flavors into tart berry, herb and a finish built upon beautiful, fine-grained tannins. Give this plenty of breathing time, and watch it blossom. **90** *—P.G. (7/1/2007)*

DOMAINE LAURIER

Domaine Laurier 2001 Reserve Pinot Noir (Sonoma County) $13. **86** *—S.H. (12/1/2004)*

DOMAINE M

Domaine M 2001 Cabernet Sauvignon (Napa Valley) $25. **85** *—S.H. (8/1/2005)*

DOMAINE MERIWETHER

Domaine Meriwether 1998 Captain Wm Clark Cuvée Brut Champagne Blend (Oregon) $25. **90 Editors' Choice** *—P.G. (12/1/2001)*

Domaine Meriwether 2002 Pinot Noir (Willamette Valley) $28. **88** *(11/1/2004)*

Domaine Meriwether NV Discovery Cuvée Sparkling Blend (Oregon) $16. **84** *—J.C. (8/1/2003)*

Domaine Meriwether 1998 Fort Clatsop Cuvée Blanc de Blancs Sparkling Blend (Oregon) $25. **81** *—J.C. (12/1/2003)*

Domaine Meriwether 1998 Olivia's Cuvée Brut Rose Sparkling Blend (Oregon) $27. **84** *—J.C. (12/1/2003)*

DOMAINE SAINT GREGORY

Domaine Saint Gregory 1999 Pinot Blanc (Mendocino) $13. **83** *—S.H. (5/1/2002)*

Domaine Saint Gregory 1997 Pinot Noir (Mendocino) $18. **90** *—J.C. (5/1/2000)*

Domaine Saint Gregory 1999 Pinot Noir (Mendocino) $18. **84** *—S.H. (5/1/2002)*

Domaine Saint Gregory 1999 Reserve Pinot Noir (Redwood Valley) $28. **82** *—S.H. (5/1/2002)*

Domaine Saint Gregory 1998 Reserve Pinot Noir (Anderson Valley) $28. **85** *—P.G. (12/15/2000)*

DOMAINE SANTA BARBARA

Domaine Santa Barbara 2005 Chardonnay (Santa Barbara County) $15. **85** *—S.H. (11/15/2006)*

Domaine Santa Barbara 2004 Chardonnay (Santa Barbara County) $15. **85** *—S.H. (12/1/2005)*

Domaine Santa Barbara 2002 Chardonnay (Santa Barbara County) $15. Simple and one-dimensional, this Chard offers sweet fruit flavors. Finishes rough. **82** *—S.H. (5/1/2005)*

Domaine Santa Barbara 1999 Chardonnay (Santa Barbara) $15. **88** *—S.H. (5/1/2001)*

Domaine Santa Barbara 2002 Pinot Gris (Santa Barbara County) $12. **87** *—S.H. (9/1/2004)*

Domaine Santa Barbara 1999 Pinot Gris (Santa Barbara County) $16. **86** *—S.H. (5/1/2001)*

Domaine Santa Barbara 1999 Pinot Noir (Santa Barbara County) $17. **83** *(10/1/2002)*

Domaine Santa Barbara 1998 Pinot Noir (Santa Barbara County) $17. **85** *—S.H. (5/1/2001)*

Domaine Santa Barbara 2003 Great Oaks Ranch Syrah (Santa Barbara County) $25. **84** *—S.H. (5/1/2005)*

Domaine Santa Barbara 2002 Great Oaks Ranch Syrah (Santa Barbara County) $25. **87** *—S.H. (8/1/2004)*

DOMAINE SERENE

Domaine Serene 2003 Clos du Soleil Vineyard Chardonnay (Willamette Valley) $40. **90** *—P.G. (5/1/2006)*

Domaine Serene 2000 Clos du Soleil Vineyard Chardonnay (Willamette Valley) $35. **88** *—P.G. (8/1/2002)*

Domaine Serene 1999 Clos du Soleil Vineyard Chardonnay (Willamette Valley) $35. 86 *—P.G. (8/1/2002)*

Domaine Serene 2004 Cote Sud Vineyard Chardonnay (Willamette Valley) $45. From Dijon clones, this is oaked-up big time in the winery style; the fruit is tightly wound and apple-flavored, but the oak really is the whole story here. To my taste it has a bitter edge; I would give it plenty of breathing time to try to soften it up. 86 *—P.G. (11/15/2007)*

Domaine Serene 2000 Cote Sud Chardonnay (Willamette Valley) $38. 87 *—P.G. (12/1/2003)*

Domaine Serene 1999 Cote Sud Vineyard Chardonnay (Willamette Valley) $35. 87 *—P.G. (8/1/2002)*

Domaine Serene 2004 Etoile Vineyard Chardonnay (Willamette Valley) $40. Made from Dijon clones, this immediately hits the palate with broad, buttery, oaky flavors that seem over the top for the fruit. But give it a couple of hours to breathe and the fruit flows back into it, bringing ripe, tangy apple, lemon, pineapple and tropical flavors to bear. 90 *—P.G. (7/1/2007)*

Domaine Serene 2004 Evenstad Reserve Pinot Noir (Willamette Valley) $52. This vintage is a step or two lighter than the 2003 Evenstad Reserve, medium in color and weight. It's done in Domaine Serene's typical style, emphasizing sweet, soft, pretty fruit backed with buttery oak. 88 *—P.G. (7/1/2007)*

Domaine Serene 2003 Evenstad Reserve Pinot Noir (Willamette Valley) $52. 91 *—P.G. (9/1/2006)*

Domaine Serene 2000 Evenstad Reserve Pinot Noir (Willamette Valley) $47. 88 *—P.G. (12/1/2003)*

Domaine Serene 1999 Evenstad Reserve Pinot Noir (Willamette Valley) $47. 87 *(10/1/2002)*

Domaine Serene 2003 Fleur de Lis Vineyard Pinot Noir (Dundee Hills) $75. 89 *—P.G. (9/1/2006)*

Domaine Serene 2002 Fleur de Lis Vineyard Pinot Noir (Willamette Valley) $47. 88 *(11/1/2004)*

Domaine Serene 2004 Grace Vineyard Pinot Noir (Willamette Valley) $90. The Grace Vineyard bottling has a devoted following, and always stands out among its Oregon peers for being exceedingly Californian in style. That is to say it's ripe, sweet, forward, round and buttery. This is Pinot Noir done up in a supremely fruity and accessible style. It's plenty ripe, sweet and fruity, but it doesn't go past that into something more textural and complex. 89 *—P.G. (7/1/2007)*

Domaine Serene 2003 Grace Vineyard Pinot Noir (Willamette Valley) $90. 93 *—P.G. (9/1/2006)*

Domaine Serene 1999 Grace Vineyard Pinot Noir (Willamette Valley) $75. 88 *(10/1/2002)*

Domaine Serene 2004 Jerusalem Hill Vineyard Pinot Noir (Willamette Valley) $75. Soft and rich, with appealing flavors of chocolate, cherry and butterscotch, this is a seductive wine. It is ripe but not hot, and the chocolaty richness wraps around the sweet cherry fruit but retains just enough of the leafy quality that defines it as Oregon. Nice balance and structure too. 90 *—P.G. (11/15/2007)*

Domaine Serene 2003 Jerusalem Hill Vineyard Pinot Noir (Willamette Valley) $75. 91 *—P.G. (9/1/2006)*

Domaine Serene 1999 Mark Bradford Vineyard Pinot Noir (Willamette Valley) $75. 90 Cellar Selection *(10/1/2002)*

Domaine Serene 2004 Winery Hill Vineyard Pinot Noir (Dundee Hills) $75. Very much a crowd-pleaser, this begins with full, in-your-face aromas of vanilla and ripe fruits. It's supremely smooth, supple and polished—no rough edges here. The fruit is a forward, lovely mix of berries, dried cherries and light spice. The barrel flavors deliver a delicious mix of vanilla, mocha and toast. 90 *—P.G. (2/1/2007)*

Domaine Serene 2003 Winery Hill Vineyard Pinot Noir (Willamette Valley) $75. 90 *—P.G. (9/1/2006)*

Domaine Serene 2000 Yamhill Cuvée Pinot Noir (Willamette Valley) $30. 88 *(10/1/2002)*

Domaine Serene 2002 Yamhill Cuvée Pinot Noir (Willamette Valley) $33. 85 *(11/1/2004)*

DOMAINE ST. GEORGE

Domaine St. George 2001 Cabernet Sauvignon (Sonoma County) $10. 83 *—S.H. (5/1/2004)*

Domaine St. George 2001 Barrel Reserve Cabernet Sauvignon (Sonoma County) $10. 84 *—S.H. (6/1/2004)*

Domaine St. George 2001 Coastal Cabernet Sauvignon (California) $8. 83 *—S.H. (10/1/2004)*

Domaine St. George 2000 Coastal Cabernet Sauvignon (California) $7. 83 *—S.H. (3/1/2004)*

Domaine St. George 2001 Wells Vineyard Cabernet Sauvignon (Dry Creek Valley) $15. 85 *—S.H. (5/1/2004)*

Domaine St. George 2000 Chardonnay (Chalk Hill) $14. 82 *—S.H. (5/1/2004)*

Domaine St. George 2001 Barrel Reserve Barrel Aged Chardonnay (Sonoma Valley) $10. 82 *—S.H. (9/1/2003)*

Domaine St. George 2003 Coastal Chardonnay (California) $8. 81 *—S.H. (6/1/2005)*

Domaine St. George 2001 Coastal Chardonnay (California) $8. 84 *—S.H. (2/1/2004)*

Domaine St. George 2000 Coastal Chardonnay (California) $7. 81 *—S.H. (6/1/2003)*

Domaine St. George 2003 Merlot (Sonoma County) $10. 86 Best Buy *—S.H. (12/1/2005)*

Domaine St. George 2001 Merlot (Sonoma County) $10. 84 *—S.H. (5/1/2004)*

Domaine St. George 1999 Merlot (California) $13. 83 *—S.H. (7/1/2002)*

Domaine St. George 2001 Coastal Merlot (California) $8. 84 *—S.H. (6/1/2004)*

Domaine St. George 2000 Coastal Merlot (California-Washington) $7. 85 *—S.H. (3/1/2004)*

Domaine St. George 2002 Sauvignon Blanc (California) $6. 81 *—S.H. (5/1/2004)*

Domaine St. George 2001 Coastal Syrah (California) $8. 84 *—S.H. (5/1/2004)*

Domaine St. George 2002 White Zinfandel Zinfandel (California) $5. 83 *—S.H. (5/1/2004)*

DOMAINE STE MICHELLE

Domaine Ste Michelle NV Champagne Blend (Columbia Valley (WA)) $11. 83 *(12/15/1999)*

Domaine Ste Michelle NV Blanc de Blanc Champagne Blend (Columbia Valley (WA)) $11. 86 Best Buy *—P.G. (12/1/2001)*

Domaine Ste Michelle NV Blanc de Blancs Champagne Blend (Columbia Valley (WA)) $11. 87 Best Buy *—S.H. (12/1/2002)*

Domaine Ste Michelle NV Blanc de Noir Champagne Blend (Columbia Valley (WA)) $11. 86 Best Buy *(12/1/2001)*

Domaine Ste Michelle NV Cuvée Brut Champagne Blend (Columbia Valley (WA)) $11. 90 Best Buy *—S.H. (12/1/2002)*

Domaine Ste Michelle NV Cuvée Brut Champagne Blend (Columbia Valley (WA)) $11. 82 *(12/15/1999)*

Domaine Ste Michelle NV Cuvée Brut Champagne Blend (Columbia Valley (WA)) $11. 86 Best Buy *(12/1/2001)*

Domaine Ste Michelle NV Cuvée Brut Champagne Blend (Columbia Valley (WA)) $12. 86 *—P.G. (12/31/2004)*

Domaine Ste Michelle NV Extra Dry Champagne Blend (Columbia Valley (WA)) $12. 85 *—P.G. (12/31/2004)*

Domaine Ste Michelle NV Extra Dry Champagne Blend (Columbia Valley (WA)) $11. 82 *(12/15/1999)*

Domaine Ste Michelle NV Extra Dry Champagne Blend (Columbia Valley (WA)) $11. 88 Best Buy *—S.H. (12/1/2002)*

Domaine Ste Michelle NV Blanc de Blancs Chardonnay (Columbia Valley (WA)) $12. 86 *—P.G. (12/31/2004)*

Domaine Ste Michelle 1998 Luxe Chardonnay (Columbia Valley (WA)) $23. 89 *—P.G. (12/31/2004)*

Domaine Ste Michelle NV Blanc de Noirs Pinot Noir (Columbia Valley (WA)) $12. 85 *—P.G. (11/15/2005)*

Domaine Ste Michelle NV Blanc de Noirs Pinot Noir (Columbia Valley (WA)) $12. 87 Best Buy *—P.G. (12/31/2004)*

Domaine Ste Michelle NV Blanc de Blanc Sparkling Blend (Columbia Valley (WA)) $11. 84 *—J.C. (12/1/2003)*

Domaine Ste Michelle NV Cuvée Brut Sparkling Blend (Columbia Valley (WA)) $11. 83 *—J.C. (12/1/2003)*

Domaine Ste Michelle NV Extra Dry Sparkling Blend (Columbia Valley (WA)) $11. 83 *—J.C. (12/1/2003)*

DOMENICO

Domenico 2004 Cabernet Franc (Amador County) $22. 83 *—S.H. (12/15/2006)*

Domenico 2004 Cabernet Sauvignon (Napa Valley) $35. 83 *—S.H. (12/15/2006)*

Domenico 2004 Merlot (Napa Valley) $28. Drinks too hot for balance at the table, a dry wine with a jalapeño pepper edge to the blackberry jam and mocha flavors. It's not a bad wine, but this was a very hot vintage and things evidently got out of control. **83** —*S.H. (3/1/2007)*

Domenico 2004 Syrah (Amador County) $30. 83 —*S.H. (12/15/2006)*

DOMINARI

Dominari 2002 Cabernet Sauvignon (Napa Valley) $75. 86 —*S.H. (12/31/2005)*

Dominari 2001 Cabernet Sauvignon (Napa Valley) $75. 88 —*S.H. (10/1/2004)*

Dominari 2002 Merlot (Napa Valley) $45. 82 —*S.H. (12/31/2005)*

Dominari 2001 Merlot (Napa Valley) $45. 92 —*S.H. (9/1/2004)*

DOMINUS

Dominus 2003 Bordeaux Blend (Napa Valley) $109. 87 —*S.H. (9/1/2006)*

Dominus 2002 Estate Bordeaux Blend (Napa Valley) $109. 89 —*S.H. (12/15/2005)*

Dominus 2001 Estate Bottled Bordeaux Blend (Napa Valley) $109. 94 Cellar Selection —*S.H. (10/1/2004)*

Dominus 1997 Estate Bottled Bordeaux Blend (Napa Valley) $100. 93 *(11/1/2000)*

Dominus 2000 Estate Bottled Red Wine Bordeaux Blend (Napa Valley) $95. 90 —*S.H. (12/10/2003)*

Dominus 2000 Napanook Bordeaux Blend (Napa Valley) $39. 85 —*S.H. (11/15/2003)*

Dominus 1996 Napanook Bordeaux Blend (Napa Valley) $30. 91 —*L.W. (7/1/1999)*

Dominus 1997 Napanook Vineyard Bordeaux Blend (Napa Valley) $30. 90 *(11/1/2000)*

Dominus 2002 Napanook Cabernet Blend (Napa Valley) $39. 85 —*S.H. (12/31/2005)*

Dominus 2001 Napanook Cabernet Sauvignon (Napa Valley) $39. 91 —*S.H. (10/1/2004)*

Dominus 1999 Red Blend (Napa Valley) $117. 91 —*S.H. (11/15/2002)*

Dominus 1999 Napanook Red Blend (Napa Valley) $42. 91 —*S.H. (11/15/2002)*

DON ERNESTO

Don Ernesto 2006 Vin Gris Rosé Pinot Noir (Napa Valley) $13. Soft, simple and slightly sweet, this easy-sipping blush has raspberry, cherry, rose petal, herb tea, vanilla and cinnamon spice flavors. It's from Hagafen. **84** —*S.H. (7/1/2007)*

Don Ernesto 2005 Vin Gris Rosé Pinot Noir (Napa Valley) $0. Here's a simple, sugary rosé wine. Appeals for raspberry, cherry and vanilla flavors, and crisp acids, and the alcohol is nice and low. Great with fried chicken, fruit salad, ham. **84** —*S.H. (7/1/2007)*

DOÑA SOL

Doña Sol 2002 Cabernet Sauvignon (California) $5. 84 Best Buy —*S.H. (6/1/2006)*

Doña Sol 2001 Cabernet Sauvignon (California) $5. 84 Best Buy —*S.H. (10/1/2004)*

DONEDEI

Donedei 2003 Cabernet Sauvignon (Columbia Valley (WA)) $35. Though this is three quarters Cabernet Sauvignon, it's hard to distinguish it from the Merlot. Both are ripe, pruney, chalky and fully mature. The acids have a volatile edge to them. This one really piles on the barrel flavors of chocolate. **87** —*P.G. (11/1/2007)*

Donedei 2003 Merlot (Columbia Valley (WA)) $35. This is about as thick and pruney, dense and chalky as Merlot can be. It will have much appeal to some palates. The fruit is ripe, raisiny and mature, wrapped with layers of leaf and chocolate. It's a drink-now wine; not likely to improve with further cellaring. **88** —*P.G. (11/1/2007)*

Donedei 2000 Merlot (Columbia Valley (WA)) $37. 86 —*P.G. (9/1/2003)*

DONUM ESTATE

Donum Estate 2004 Pinot Noir (Carneros) $60. This is classic Carneros from a ripe vintage, with zesty acidity balancing cherry, black raspberry, cassis, cola, sweet beetroot and smoky vanilla flavors that are as rich and ripe as Pinot gets. Yet the wine finishes fully dry. **90** —*S.H. (10/1/2007)*

Donum Estate 2002 Pinot Noir (Carneros) $60. 88 —*S.H. (6/1/2004)*

Donum Estate 2003 Estate Grown Pinot Noir (Carneros) $60. 86 —*S.H. (12/15/2006)*

DOS CABEZAS

Dos Cabezas 2005 El Norte Red Blend (Cochise County) $20. This Mourvèdre/Grenache/Petite Sirah blend offers appealing aromas and flavors of spicy berry and smoke, with good structure and length. The smoky character borders on excessive, though, so pair it with some grilled, spicy ribs or kebabs for the best experience. **82** —*S.K. (12/1/2007)*

Dos Cabezas 2005 La Montaña Red Blend (Cochise County) $30. Anise, blackberry and heady spice on the nose and palate make this 80% Petite Sirah, 18% Merlot, 2% Cabernet Sauvignon an appealing choice for a cold winter's night. The wine has ample structure, but is gentle on the palate, with an elegant, long finish and overall balanced, integrated character. **85** —*S.K. (12/1/2007)*

DOUGLAS HILL

Douglas Hill 1997 Chardonnay (Napa Valley) $17. 84 *(6/1/2000)*

Douglas Hill 1997 Chardonnay (Napa Valley) $16. 82 —*M.S. (10/1/1999)*

DOVER CANYON

Dover Canyon 2001 Bone Blend Rhône Red Blend (Paso Robles) $24. 84 —*S.H. (11/15/2002)*

Dover Canyon 1998 Chequera Vineyard Roussanne (Central Coast) $19. 83 —*S.H. (10/1/1999)*

Dover Canyon 1999 Fralich Vineyard Cuvée Syrah (Paso Robles) $28. 88 *(6/1/2003)*

Dover Canyon 1999 Reserve Syrah (Paso Robles) $35. 85 *(11/1/2001)*

DOWNING FAMILY

Downing Family 1999 Cabernet Sauvignon (Napa Valley) $38. 91 —*J.M. (2/1/2003)*

Downing Family 2001 Zinfandel (Oakville) $30. 90 *(11/1/2003)*

DR. KONSTANTIN FRANK

Dr. Konstantin Frank 1999 Limited Release Cabernet Franc (Finger Lakes) $25. 85 —*J.C. (1/1/2004)*

Dr. Konstantin Frank 1999 Reserve Cabernet Sauvignon (Finger Lakes) $40. 83 —*M.S. (3/1/2003)*

Dr. Konstantin Frank 1999 Chardonnay (Finger Lakes) $13. 90 Best Buy —*J.M. (7/1/2002)*

Dr. Konstantin Frank 2001 Gewürztraminer (Finger Lakes) $16. 86 —*J.M. (1/1/2003)*

Dr. Konstantin Frank 1999 Limited Release Merlot (Finger Lakes) $20. 84 —*J.C. (3/1/2002)*

Dr. Konstantin Frank 1999 Reserve Merlot (New York) $35. 84 —*M.S. (1/1/2004)*

Dr. Konstantin Frank NV Fleur de Pinot Noir Pinot Noir (Finger Lakes) $12. 84 —*J.C. (3/1/2002)*

Dr. Konstantin Frank 1999 Old Vines Pinot Noir (Finger Lakes) $25. 85 —*J.C. (1/1/2004)*

Dr. Konstantin Frank 1996 Old Vines Pinot Noir (Finger Lakes) $19. 82 *(10/1/1999)*

Dr. Konstantin Frank 2006 Dry Riesling (Finger Lakes) $18. Crisp acidity and minerality make this wine a great food cohort and attractive to anyone who favors a drier, more delicate style of Riesling. Apple, pear and spice come together in layers, and while refreshing, the wine also contains a lovely creaminess on the palate. A fruity, lingering aftertaste seals the deal. **89** —*S.K. (9/1/2007)*

Dr. Konstantin Frank 2001 Dry Johannisberg Riesling (Finger Lakes) $13. 84 —*J.C. (8/1/2003)*

Dr. Konstantin Frank 2000 Dry Johannisberg Riesling (Finger Lakes) $12. 83 —*J.C. (3/1/2002)*

Dr. Konstantin Frank 2005 Reserve Riesling (Finger Lakes) $30. Strong floral and fruit aromas of apple, pear and apricot, followed by crisp and minerally flavors, typify this Riesling. The wine could use a touch more dimension but the clean, dry flavors will pair very nicely with various dishes—primarily seafood and poultry. There's also a nice spicy spin on the finish that adds to the appeal. **85** —*S.K. (9/1/2007)*

Dr. Konstantin Frank 2001 Reserve Johannisberg Riesling (Finger Lakes) $25. 81 —*J.C. (8/1/2003)*

Dr. Konstantin Frank 2006 Semi Dry Riesling (Finger Lakes) $16. Ripe fruit balanced with a zingy backbone make this semi-dry Riesling from Dr. Frank an overall winner for varied palates. Melon, pear and a hint of exotic floral flavors set the wine aside from standard whites of this type, and its structure—balanced and substantial without being heavy—further recommend it. Chilled and in an elegant glass, this is a fun and affordable wine with character. **88** —*S.K. (9/1/2007)*

Dr. Konstantin Frank 2001 Semi Dry Johannisberg Riesling (Finger Lakes) $13. 83 *—J.C. (8/1/2003)*

Dr. Konstantin Frank 2000 Semi Dry Johannisberg Riesling (Finger Lakes) $12. 82 *—J.C. (3/1/2002)*

Dr. Konstantin Frank 2001 Rkatsiteli (Finger Lakes) $19. 86 *—J.M. (1/1/2003)*

Dr. Konstantin Frank 2000 Limited Release Rkatsiteli (Finger Lakes) $15. 86 *—J.C. (3/1/2002)*

DREW

Drew 2005 Fog-Eater Pinot Noir (Anderson Valley) $35. Really just about the perfect Anderson Valley Pinot in terms of the beautifully crisp acidity, and the way the wine blasts pure flavors of red cherries, cassis and raspberries across the palate. With 30% new French oak, this opulence is made more exotic with notes of caramel, butterscotch, vanilla and toast. Combines all this massive power with elegant finesse in an effortless way. **95 Editors' Choice** *—S.H. (10/1/2007)*

Drew 2004 Gatekeepers Pinot Noir (Santa Rita Hills) $36. 88 *—S.H. (3/1/2006)*

Drew 2003 Rio Vista Vineyard Pinot Noir (Santa Rita Hills) $32. 87 *—S.H. (3/1/2006)*

Drew 2003 Hearthstone Vineyard Syrah (Paso Robles) $35. 86 *(9/1/2005)*

Drew 2003 Morehouse Vineyard Syrah (Santa Ynez Valley) $40. 87 *(9/1/2005)*

Drew 2003 Old Westy-Alisos Vineyard Syrah (Santa Barbara County) $30. **90 Editors' Choice** *(9/1/2005)*

Drew 2003 Rodney's and Larner Vineyards Syrah (Santa Ynez Valley) $32. 88 *(9/1/2005)*

Drew 2003 Six-Sense Syrah (Santa Barbara County) $27. 88 *(9/1/2005)*

DREYER SONOMA

Dreyer Sonoma 1998 Cabernet Sauvignon (Sonoma County) $14. **88 Best Buy** *—S.H. (12/15/2000)*

Dreyer Sonoma 1998 Chardonnay (Sonoma County) $10. 84 *(10/1/2000)*

Dreyer Sonoma 2001 Chardonnay (Sonoma County) $10. **89 Best Buy** *—S.H. (12/1/2003)*

Dreyer Sonoma 2000 Chardonnay (Sonoma County) $10. 87 *—S.H. (5/1/2002)*

Dreyer Sonoma 1999 Chardonnay (Sonoma County) $10. 86 *—S.H. (2/1/2001)*

DRY CREEK VINEYARD

Dry Creek Vineyard 1997 Bordeaux Blend (Sonoma County) $25. 90 *—S.H. (11/1/1999)*

Dry Creek Vineyard 2003 Meritage Bordeaux Blend (Dry Creek Valley) $28. A good wine, with tons of ripe, jammy cherry, blackberry and carob flavors, but a little on the sugary sweet, soft side. Drink now. 84 *—S.H. (5/1/2007)*

Dry Creek Vineyard 1998 Meritage Bordeaux Blend (Sonoma County) $28. 90 *—S.H. (2/1/2001)*

Dry Creek Vineyard 2002 Meritage Cabernet Blend (Dry Creek Valley) $28. 84 *—S.H. (7/1/2006)*

Dry Creek Vineyard 2004 Cabernet Sauvignon (Dry Creek Valley) $22. The tannins are quite hard and dry, giving an astringency to this young Cab, but it's so rich in fruit, so long in the finish, that it will make a great partner with certain rich foods, especially lamb and grilled steak. There's a deep core of ripe blackberries, currants, dark unsweetened chocolate and pepper deep down inside this complex wine. Should develop through 2010. 90 *—S.H. (12/15/2007)*

Dry Creek Vineyard 2003 Cabernet Sauvignon (Dry Creek Valley) $21. **90 Editors' Choice** *—S.H. (11/15/2006)*

Dry Creek Vineyard 2002 Cabernet Sauvignon (Dry Creek Valley) $19. 91 *—S.H. (11/15/2005)*

Dry Creek Vineyard 2000 Cabernet Sauvignon (Sonoma County) $21. **90 Editors' Choice** *—S.H. (11/15/2003)*

Dry Creek Vineyard 1999 Cabernet Sauvignon (Sonoma County) $21. 87 *—S.H. (11/15/2002)*

Dry Creek Vineyard 1997 Cabernet Sauvignon (Sonoma County) $20. 88 *—S.H. (2/1/2000)*

Dry Creek Vineyard 2002 Endeavor Cabernet Sauvignon (Dry Creek Valley) $55. 89 *—S.H. (12/15/2006)*

Dry Creek Vineyard 1999 Endeavour Cabernet Sauvignon (Dry Creek Valley) $55. 86 *—S.H. (3/1/2005)*

Dry Creek Vineyard 1998 Endeavour Cabernet Sauvignon (Dry Creek Valley) $50. 91 *(12/31/2003)*

Dry Creek Vineyard 1997 Endeavour Cabernet Sauvignon (Dry Creek Valley) $50. 90 *—S.H. (12/31/2002)*

Dry Creek Vineyard 1997 Epoch II Millenium Cuvée Cabernet Sauvignon (Dry Creek Valley) $60. 87 *—S.H. (2/1/2001)*

Dry Creek Vineyard 1999 Reserve Cabernet Sauvignon (Dry Creek Valley) $35. **92 Editors' Choice** *—S.H. (10/1/2003)*

Dry Creek Vineyard 1998 Reserve Cabernet Sauvignon (Dry Creek Valley) $35. 88 *—S.H. (7/1/2002)*

Dry Creek Vineyard 1997 Reserve Cabernet Sauvignon (Dry Creek Valley) $35.89 *(11/1/2000)*

Dry Creek Vineyard 2005 Chardonnay (Russian River Valley) $20. Lots of ripe tropical fruit in this wine, with pastry-filling pineapple, peach, butterscotch and vanilla spice flavors. Although technically dry, it has a richly honeyed finish. 87 *—S.H. (9/1/2007)*

Dry Creek Vineyard 2004 Chardonnay (Russian River Valley) $18. 85 *—S.H. (7/1/2006)*

Dry Creek Vineyard 2003 Chardonnay (Russian River Valley) $16. 84 *—S.H. (12/1/2005)*

Dry Creek Vineyard 2001 Chardonnay (Sonoma County) $16. 85 *—S.H. (12/15/2003)*

Dry Creek Vineyard 2000 Chardonnay (Sonoma County) $16. 86 *—S.H. (12/15/2002)*

Dry Creek Vineyard 1999 Chardonnay (Sonoma County) $16. 85 *—S.H. (5/1/2001)*

Dry Creek Vineyard 1998 Barrel Fermented Chardonnay (Sonoma County) $16. 87 *(6/1/2000)*

Dry Creek Vineyard 2000 DCV4 Chardonnay (Dry Creek Valley) $22. 87 *—S.H. (5/1/2003)*

Dry Creek Vineyard 2000 Reserve Chardonnay (Russian River Valley) $22. 87 *—S.H. (12/15/2003)*

Dry Creek Vineyard 1999 Reserve Chardonnay (Dry Creek Valley) $22. 88 *—S.H. (12/15/2002)*

Dry Creek Vineyard 1998 Reserve Chardonnay (Dry Creek Valley) $22. 89 *(6/1/2000)*

Dry Creek Vineyard 2003 Saralee's Vineyard Chardonnay (Russian River Valley) $30. 87 *—S.H. (12/1/2005)*

Dry Creek Vineyard 2002 Saralee's Vineyard Chardonnay (Russian River Valley) $25. 89 *—S.H. (12/31/2004)*

Dry Creek Vineyard 2006 Dry Chenin Blanc (Clarksburg) $11. The winery has made a specialty of this variety for years, always taking care to keep prices low, and consumers are the beneficiaries. The '06 is bright and zesty, with intense flavors of fresh-picked green apples and white pepper. Nice as an apéritif, or an alternative to Sauvignon Blanc or Pinot Grigio. **86 Best Buy** *—S.H. (9/1/2007)*

Dry Creek Vineyard 2005 Dry Chenin Blanc (Clarksburg) $11. **86 Best Buy** *—S.H. (7/1/2006)*

Dry Creek Vineyard 2004 Dry Chenin Blanc (Clarksburg) $10. **87 Best Buy** *—S.H. (7/1/2005)*

Dry Creek Vineyard 2003 Dry Chenin Blanc (Clarksburg) $9. **85 Best Buy** *—S.H. (10/1/2004)*

Dry Creek Vineyard 2002 Dry Chenin Blanc (Clarksburg) $9. 85 *—S.H. (12/15/2003)*

Dry Creek Vineyard 2001 Dry Chenin Blanc (Clarksburg) $9. 85 *—S.H. (9/1/2003)*

Dry Creek Vineyard 1998 Dry Chenin Blanc (Clarksburg) $9. 82 *—L.W. (11/1/1999)*

Dry Creek Vineyard 2005 Fumé Blanc (Sonoma County) $13. This is Dry Creek Vineyard's basic SB, fermented in stainless steel and rushed onto the market to preserve freshness. It could be richer in fruit, as it's a little watery, but the crisp dryness is nice and elegant. 84 *—S.H. (3/1/2007)*

Dry Creek Vineyard 2004 Fumé Blanc (Sonoma County) $13. 86 *—S.H. (4/1/2006)*

Dry Creek Vineyard 2003 Fumé Blanc (Sonoma County) $13. 85 *—S.H. (5/1/2005)*

Dry Creek Vineyard 2003 Fumé Blanc (Sonoma County) $13. 84 *—S.H. (10/1/2005)*

Dry Creek Vineyard 2002 Fumé Blanc (Sonoma County) $13. 86 *—S.H. (12/15/2003)*

Dry Creek Vineyard 2001 Fumé Blanc (Green Valley) $13. **89 Best Buy** *—S.H. (11/15/2002)*

Dry Creek Vineyard 1999 Fumé Blanc (Sonoma County) $12. 84 *—S.H. (11/15/2000)*

Dry Creek Vineyard 2003 DCV3 Fumé Blanc (Dry Creek Valley) $25. 87 *(7/1/2005)*

Dry Creek Vineyard 2002 DCV3 Fumé Blanc (Dry Creek Valley) $18. 86 *(12/31/2003)*

Dry Creek Vineyard 2001 DCV3 Fumé Blanc (Dry Creek Valley) $18. 90 *—S.H. (3/1/2003)*

Dry Creek Vineyard 2004 DCV3 Estate Fumé Blanc (Dry Creek Valley) $25. 84 *—S.H. (12/15/2006)*

Dry Creek Vineyard 1998 Limited Edition -DCV3 Fumé Blanc (Dry Creek Valley) $16. 90 *(2/1/2000)*

Dry Creek Vineyard 2000 Limited Edition DCVIII Fumé Blanc (Dry Creek Valley) $18. 86 *(8/1/2002)*

Dry Creek Vineyard 2001 Reserve Fumé Blanc (Dry Creek Valley) $18. 88 *(12/31/2003)*

Dry Creek Vineyard 2000 Reserve Fumé Blanc (Dry Creek Valley) $18. 86 *—S.H. (3/1/2003)*

Dry Creek Vineyard 1999 Reserve Fumé Blanc (Dry Creek Valley) $18. 82 *(8/1/2002)*

Dry Creek Vineyard 1998 Reserve Fumé Blanc (Dry Creek Valley) $18. 88 *—S.H. (11/15/2000)*

Dry Creek Vineyard 1997 Reserve Fumé Blanc (Dry Creek Valley) $16. 90 *—L.W. (2/1/2000)*

Dry Creek Vineyard 2000 Meritage (Dry Creek Valley) $26. 89 *(12/31/2003)*

Dry Creek Vineyard 1999 Meritage (Sonoma County) $28. 90 *—S.H. (11/15/2002)*

Dry Creek Vineyard 2004 Merlot (Dry Creek Valley) $19. Back in the '80s Dry Creek Valley had a reputation for Merlot that seems to have been forgotten but shouldn't be, to judge by this fine, soft bottling. It's rich and forward in raspberry and cherry jam, mocha-choca and cola flavors, with a long, spicy, dry and very elegant finish. 88 *—S.H. (3/1/2007)*

Dry Creek Vineyard 2003 Merlot (Dry Creek Valley) $18. 88 *—S.H. (7/1/2006)*

Dry Creek Vineyard 2002 Merlot (Sonoma County) $19. 87 *—S.H. (12/15/2005)*

Dry Creek Vineyard 1999 Merlot (Sonoma County) $19. 84 *—S.H. (12/31/2002)*

Dry Creek Vineyard 1998 Merlot (Sonoma County) $21. 85 *—S.H. (2/1/2001)*

Dry Creek Vineyard 1997 Merlot (Sonoma County) $20. 85 *(3/1/1999)*

Dry Creek Vineyard 1999 Reserve Merlot (Dry Creek Valley) $30. 91 *—S.H. (2/1/2004)*

Dry Creek Vineyard 1998 Reserve Cuvée Merlot (Dry Creek Valley) $35. 84 *— (11/15/2002)*

Dry Creek Vineyard 2000 Limited Bottling Petite Sirah (Dry Creek Valley) $21. 86 *(4/1/2003)*

Dry Creek Vineyard 1999 Pinot Noir (California) $20. 86 *—S.H. (5/1/2001)*

Dry Creek Vineyard 1997 Pinot Noir (Sonoma Valley) $24. 90 *(10/1/1999)*

Dry Creek Vineyard 2003 Soleil Late Harvest Sauvignon Blanc (Sonoma County) $25. 87 *—S.H. (5/1/2006)*

Dry Creek Vineyard 2000 Soleil—Limited Edition Sauvignon Blanc (Sonoma County) $20. 86 *—S.H. (9/1/2002)*

Dry Creek Vineyard 2005 Taylor's Vineyard Musqué Sauvignon Blanc (Dry Creek Valley) $25. With bright kiwi, pineapple, lime zest, gooseberry and vanilla flavors, and a great big burst of acidity, this wine is just delicious to savor. It's dry and clean, with a long finish that reprises the fruit. 89 *—S.H. (9/1/2007)*

Dry Creek Vineyard 2004 Taylor's Vineyard Musqué Sauvignon Blanc (Dry Creek Valley) $25. 88 *—S.H. (12/15/2006)*

Dry Creek Vineyard 2003 Taylor's Vineyard Musqué Sauvignon Blanc (Dry Creek Valley) $25. 86 *(7/1/2005)*

Dry Creek Vineyard 1998 Vintner's Selection Syrah (Dry Creek Valley) $25. 86 *(11/1/2001)*

Dry Creek Vineyard 2004 Beeson Ranch Zinfandel (Dry Creek Valley) $30. Finally, a Zin that bursts with ripe, rich fruit, but isn't high in alcohol or sugary sweet. After the assault of raspberry and cherry-pie filling, cola, cocoa and spice flavors, the wine shows a balance of acids and tannins that's Bordeaux-like in elegance. Drink now. 90 *—S.H. (9/1/2007)*

Dry Creek Vineyard 2003 Beeson Ranch Zinfandel (Dry Creek Valley) $30. 89 *—S.H. (12/15/2006)*

Dry Creek Vineyard 2002 Beeson Ranch Zinfandel (Dry Creek Valley) $30. 89 *—S.H. (10/1/2005)*

Dry Creek Vineyard 2001 Beeson Ranch Zinfandel (Dry Creek Valley) $30. 89 *(12/31/2003)*

Dry Creek Vineyard 2005 Heritage Zinfandel (Sonoma County) $16. These are supposedly old clones, hence the name. The wine is sharp in acidity and jammy, with pungent cherry-blackberry fruit that tastes like it's just out of the fermenting tank. 84 *—S.H. (9/1/2007)*

Dry Creek Vineyard 2004 Heritage Zinfandel (Sonoma County) $15. Lots to like in this slightly rustic red, which has some Petite Sirah. It's authentic old-style Sonoma Zin, very dry, lusty in tannins, and fruity, with a coffee and tobacco undertone to the cherries and blackberries. Practically begs for lamb chops or bacon-wrapped grilled shrimp. 87 *—S.H. (3/1/2007)*

Dry Creek Vineyard 2003 Heritage Zinfandel (Sonoma County) $15. 87 *—S.H. (12/31/2005)*

Dry Creek Vineyard 2001 Heritage Clone Zinfandel (Sonoma County) $15. 88 *(11/1/2003)*

Dry Creek Vineyard 2000 Heritage Clone Zinfandel (Sonoma County) $15. 86 *—S.H. (11/1/2002)*

Dry Creek Vineyard 1999 Heritage Clone Zinfandel (Sonoma County) $15. 86 *—S.H. (11/15/2001)*

Dry Creek Vineyard 1998 Heritage Clone Zinfandel (Sonoma County) $15. 85 *—S.H. (12/1/2000)*

Dry Creek Vineyard 1997 Heritage Clone Zinfandel (Sonoma County) $15. 90 *—P.G. (11/15/1999)*

Dry Creek Vineyard 2003 Late Harvest Zinfandel (Dry Creek Valley) $30. 83 *—S.H. (5/1/2006)*

Dry Creek Vineyard 1999 Limited Edition Late Harvest Zinfandel (Dry Creek Valley) $NA. 83 *—S.H. (9/12/2002)*

Dry Creek Vineyard 2004 Old Vine Zinfandel (Sonoma County) $25. Dark and dramatically rich, with blackberry jam, cherry-pie filling, milk chocolate and cinnamon spice flavors, this polished wine has gorgeously fine tannins. It could use greater acidity for structure, though, because it's very soft and melted, which makes all that fruit taste sugary sweet. 87 *—S.H. (9/1/2007)*

Dry Creek Vineyard 2003 Old Vine Zinfandel (Sonoma County) $25. 93 **Editors' Choice** *—S.H. (11/15/2006)*

Dry Creek Vineyard 2002 Old Vine Zinfandel (Sonoma County) $25. 90 *—S.H. (11/15/2005)*

Dry Creek Vineyard 2001 Old Vines Zinfandel (Sonoma County) $21. 88 *(11/1/2003)*

Dry Creek Vineyard 2000 Old Vines Zinfandel (Sonoma County) $21. 87 *—S.H. (2/1/2003)*

Dry Creek Vineyard 1999 Old Vines Zinfandel (Sonoma County) $21. 91 *—S.H. (3/1/2002)*

Dry Creek Vineyard 1998 Old Vines Zinfandel (Sonoma County) $19. 86 *—S.H. (12/1/2000)*

Dry Creek Vineyard 1997 Old Vines Zinfandel (Sonoma County) $18. 88 *—J.C. (5/1/2000)*

Dry Creek Vineyard 1999 Reserve Zinfandel (Dry Creek Valley) $30. 90 *—S.H. (3/1/2004)*

Dry Creek Vineyard 1998 Reserve Zinfandel (Dry Creek Valley) $30. 90 *—S.H. (12/15/2001)*

Dry Creek Vineyard 1997 Reserve Zinfandel (Dry Creek Valley) $30. 90 *—P.G. (3/1/2001)*

Dry Creek Vineyard 2004 Somers Ranch Zinfandel (Dry Creek Valley) $30. After a couple of off years, this bottling is back on form. The Port-y edge is gone, and in its place is a gorgeously ripe wine with full control over the fruit. Raspberries, cherries, cassis, pecan pie, pumpkin pie, cocoa, gingerbread, cola, vanilla, Asian spice; the list goes on and on. Meanwhile the mouthfeel is pure velvet, the finish long-lasting. This is Dry Creek Valley Zin at its best. 93 **Editors' Choice** *—S.H. (9/1/2007)*

Dry Creek Vineyard 2003 Somers Ranch Zinfandel (Dry Creek Valley) $30. 83 *—S.H. (12/15/2006)*

Dry Creek Vineyard 2002 Somers Ranch Zinfandel (Dry Creek Valley) $30. 86 *—S.H. (10/1/2005)*

Dry Creek Vineyard 2001 Somers Ranch Zinfandel (Dry Creek Valley) $30. 90 *(12/31/2003)*

DRYTOWN

Drytown 2002 Zinfandel (Sierra Foothills) $15. 85 *—S.H. (3/1/2005)*

DUCK POND

Duck Pond 1997 Cabernet Franc (Columbia Valley (WA)) $95. 90 *—S.H. (12/31/2003)*

Duck Pond 1997 Cabernet Sauvignon (Columbia Valley (WA)) $12. 85 *—P.G. (6/1/2000)*

Duck Pond 2002 Cabernet Sauvignon (Columbia Valley (WA)) $12. 83 *—P.G. (6/1/2006)*

Duck Pond 2000 Cabernet Sauvignon (Columbia Valley (OR)) $12. 83 *—P.G. (12/1/2003)*

Duck Pond 2004 Chardonnay (Columbia Valley (WA)) $10. 83 *—P.G. (6/1/2006)*

Duck Pond 2000 Chardonnay (Willamette Valley) $8. 86 *—S.H. (12/31/2002)*

Duck Pond 1998 Chardonnay (Oregon) $10. 87 Best Buy *—S.H. (9/1/2000)*

Duck Pond 1999 Fries' Desert Wind Vineyard/Wahluke Chardonnay (Columbia Valley (WA)) $9. 81 *—P.G. (2/1/2002)*

Duck Pond 1997 Merlot (Columbia Valley (WA)) $12. 82 *—P.G. (6/1/2000)*

Duck Pond 1998 Fries' Desert Wind Vineyard Merlot (Columbia Valley (WA)) $11. 87 Best Buy *—P.G. (6/1/2001)*

Duck Pond 1997 Pinot Grigio (Oregon) $9. 85 *(8/1/1999)*

Duck Pond 2005 Pinot Gris (Willamette Valley) $12. 87 Best Buy *—P.G. (11/15/2006)*

Duck Pond 2003 Pinot Gris (Oregon) $12. 82 *—P.G. (10/1/2004)*

Duck Pond 2002 Pinot Gris (Oregon) $12. 86 *—P.G. (12/1/2003)*

Duck Pond 2000 Pinot Gris (Willamette Valley) $9. 82 *—P.G. (2/1/2002)*

Duck Pond 2003 Pinot Noir (Oregon) $12. 83 *—P.G. (10/1/2004)*

Duck Pond 2002 Pinot Noir (Willamette Valley) $9. 86 Best Buy *—P.G. (12/1/2003)*

Duck Pond 1998 Pinot Noir (Willamette Valley) $9. 83 *—J.C. (12/1/2000)*

Duck Pond 1997 Syrah (Columbia Valley (WA)) $15. 82 *—P.G. (9/1/2000)*

Duck Pond 2003 Syrah (Columbia Valley (WA)) $12. 83 *—P.G. (6/1/2006)*

Duck Pond 2002 Syrah (Columbia Valley (WA)) $12. 88 Best Buy *—P.G. (11/15/2004)*

Duck Pond 2001 Syrah (Columbia Valley (WA)) $35. 82 *—P.G. (9/1/2004)*

Duck Pond 2002 Desert Wind Vineyard Syrah (Columbia Valley (WA)) $35. 81 *—P.G. (6/1/2006)*

Duck Pond 1999 Fries' Desert Wind Vineyard Syrah (Columbia Valley (WA)) $35. 85 *(11/1/2001)*

Duck Pond 1998 Wahluke Slope Frei's Desert Wi Syrah (Columbia Valley (WA)) $22. 84 *—P.G. (9/1/2000)*

DUCK WALK

Duck Walk 1997 Cabernet Sauvignon (North Fork of Long Island) $19. 85 *—J.C. (4/1/2001)*

Duck Walk 1997 Reserve Cabernet Sauvignon (North Fork of Long Island) $29. 87 *—J.C. (4/1/2001)*

Duck Walk 1997 Reserve Chardonnay (Long Island) $13. 87 Best Buy *—J.C. (4/1/2001)*

Duck Walk 1998 Aphrodite Late Harvest Gewürztraminer (North Fork of Long Island) $15. 86 *—J.C. (4/1/2001)*

Duck Walk 1997 Reserve Merlot (North Fork of Long Island) $19. 86 *—J.C. (4/1/2001)*

Duck Walk 1998 Pinot Grigio (The Hamptons, Long Island) $15. 87 *—J.C. (4/1/2001)*

Duck Walk 1997 Pinot Meunier (The Hamptons, Long Island) $9. 87 Best Buy *—J.C. (4/1/2001)*

DUCKHORN

Duckhorn 2004 Cabernet Sauvignon (Napa Valley) $60. Although it's a very good wine, this is just a little too ripe. The blackberry and cherry flavors are almost raisined, especially on the finish, due to the extreme heat of the vintage. Duckhorn managed it better than many, but despite an official alcohol of just 14.5%, the wine has a burnt jam taste. Drink now. **87** *—S.H. (12/31/2007)*

Duckhorn 2003 Cabernet Sauvignon (Napa Valley) $90. As always, Duckhorn's Cab this year is a very tannic wine. But it's a very fine wine, packed with ripe black currant and cassis fruit, and coated with spicy, toasty oak. This firm wine needs long decanting, and should develop well through 2012 or so. **92 Cellar Selection** *—S.H. (4/1/2007)*

Duckhorn 2003 Cabernet Sauvignon (Napa Valley) $60. 87 *—S.H. (9/1/2006)*

Duckhorn 2002 Cabernet Sauvignon (Napa Valley) $60. 84 *—S.H. (12/1/2005)*

Duckhorn 2000 Cabernet Sauvignon (Napa Valley) $55. 87 *—S.H. (8/1/2004)*

Duckhorn 1999 Est Grown Cabernet Sauvignon (Napa Valley) $80. 91 *—S.H. (11/15/2002)*

Duckhorn 2001 Estate Cabernet Sauvignon (Napa Valley) $85. 92 *—S.H. (5/1/2005)*

Duckhorn 2002 Estate Grown Cabernet Sauvignon (Napa Valley) $90. 89 *—S.H. (2/1/2006)*

Duckhorn 2000 Estate Grown Cabernet Sauvignon (Napa Valley) $80. 90 *—S.H. (8/1/2004)*

Duckhorn 1998 Estate Grown Cabernet Sauvignon (Napa Valley) $80. 89 *(6/1/2002)*

Duckhorn 2003 Monitor Ledge Vineyard Cabernet Sauvignon (Napa Valley) $95. So tannic, it's hard to drink now, with the way it puckers the palate. So will it age? One hundred percent Cab, it's balanced and dry, with flashy oak and a good depth of cassis, orange marmalade and roasted coffee bean. Delicious and complex, but those tannins really stick out. Best 2007–2012. **91 Cellar Selection** *—S.H. (4/1/2007)*

Duckhorn 2002 Monitor Ledge Vineyard Cabernet Sauvignon (Napa Valley) $95. 90 *—S.H. (2/1/2006)*

Duckhorn 2001 Monitor Ledge Vineyard Cabernet Sauvignon (Napa Valley) $90. 93 *—S.H. (5/1/2005)*

Duckhorn 2000 Monitor Ledge Vineyard Cabernet Sauvignon (Napa Valley) $90. 92 *—S.H. (8/1/2004)*

Duckhorn 1999 Monitor Ledge Vineyard Est Grown Cabernet Sauvignon (Napa Valley) $90. 91 *(2/1/2003)*

Duckhorn 2003 Patzimaro Vineyard Cabernet Sauvignon (Napa Valley) $95. This Cab, with a little Cab Franc and Merlot, is more accessible than Duckhorn's other '03 single vineyard Cabs, but it's still tough in sticky, sandpapery tannins. But there's some lovely cherry, tangerine custard, blueberry and gingerbread fruit flavor, and the wine should be perfect with a grilled steak. **92** *—S.H. (4/1/2007)*

Duckhorn 2001 Patzimaro Vineyard Cabernet Sauvignon (Napa Valley) $90. 92 *—S.H. (5/1/2005)*

Duckhorn 2000 Patzimaro Vineyard Cabernet Sauvignon (St. Helena) $90. 91 *—S.H. (8/1/2004)*

Duckhorn 1999 Patzimaro Vineyard Est Grown St. Helena Cabernet Sauvignon (Napa Valley) $90. 90 *(2/1/2003)*

Duckhorn 2003 Rector Creek Vineyard Cabernet Sauvignon (Napa Valley) $95. The vineyard is north of Yountville, on the Silverado Trail. The wine is extremely dry and very tannic, too astringent now, although decanting and airing will help. There's some deeply polished cassis fruit way down that suggests midterm aging. **89** *—S.H. (4/1/2007)*

Duckhorn 2001 Stout Vineyard Cabernet Sauvignon (Napa Valley) $90. 92 *—S.H. (5/1/2005)*

Duckhorn 2004 Merlot (Napa Valley) $50. There's a beautiful Merlot in here but you're going to have to paddle against the powerful tannins to find it. It brings to mind the old Duckhorn Three Palms Merlots, which were similarly tough and tannic in youth, but aged well. This wine is ripe in chocolate, blackberry, cassis, coconut macaroon and plum sauce flavors, but needs four or five years to begin to come around. **90 Cellar Selection** *—S.H. (3/1/2007)*

Duckhorn 2003 Merlot (Howell Mountain) $70. Those notorious mountain tannins have largely melted, making the wine drinkable now, although it will hold for a decade with proper cellaring. Lush and velvety, with a drop of Cabernet Franc, this is voluptuous in cherries, black currants and fine, toasty oak. **94** *—S.H. (12/31/2007)*

Duckhorn 2003 Merlot (Napa Valley) $50. 92 *—S.H. (2/1/2006)*

Duckhorn 2002 Merlot (Howell Mountain) $70. 92 *—S.H. (12/1/2006)*

Duckhorn 2001 Merlot (Howell Mountain) $70. 93 Editors' Choice *—S.H. (12/1/2005)*

Duckhorn 2001 Merlot (Napa Valley) $48. 92 *—S.H. (8/1/2004)*

Duckhorn 2000 Merlot (Napa Valley) $46. 90 *—K.F. (4/1/2003)*

Duckhorn 1997 Merlot (Napa Valley) $36. 90 *(3/1/2000)*

Duckhorn 1995 Merlot (Howell Mountain) $42. 92 *(3/1/2000)*

Duckhorn 2002 25th Harvest Merlot (Napa Valley) $48. 94 Cellar Selection *—S.H. (5/1/2005)*

Duckhorn 2001 Estate Merlot (Napa Valley) $82. 94 *—S.H. (8/1/2004)*

Duckhorn 1996 Estate Merlot (Napa Valley) $53. 93 *(3/1/2000)*

Duckhorn 2004 Estate Grown Merlot (Napa Valley) $85. A blend of four vineyards, this is an extremely impressive Merlot. It dazzles with rich, ripe black currant, cherry liqueur, raspberry, milk chocolate, smoky oak and spice flavors that are complex and go on and on through the finish. Beyond that is the texture, so refined and elegant, combining power and subtle elegance. Just a gorgeous, sensual Merlot. Drink now–2010. **95** —*S.H. (12/31/2007)*

Duckhorn 2003 Estate Grown Merlot (Napa Valley) $85. 87 —*S.H. (12/1/2006)*

Duckhorn 2002 Estate Grown Merlot (Napa Valley) $85. 84 —*S.H. (3/1/2006)*

Duckhorn 2000 Estate Grown Merlot (Napa Valley) $80. 90 Cellar Selection *(5/1/2004)*

Duckhorn 1999 Estate Grown Merlot (Napa Valley) $80. 91 —*K.F. (4/1/2003)*

Duckhorn 1997 Estate Grown Merlot (Napa Valley) $65. 89 —*J.C. (6/1/2001)*

Duckhorn 1999 Howell Mountain Merlot (Howell Mountain) $65. 93 —*S.H. (8/1/2004)*

Duckhorn 1998 Howell Mountain Merlot (Napa Valley) $50. 89 —*K.F. (4/1/2003)*

Duckhorn 1996 Howell Mountain Merlot (Napa Valley) $50. 92 Cellar Selection *(6/1/2001)*

Duckhorn 2004 Three Palms Vineyard Merlot (Napa Valley) $85. This is Duckhorn's signature vineyard for Merlot, located off the Silverado Trail below Calistoga. It's also the winery's most variable Merlot, showing distinct vintage variation. The 2004 was a warm vintage, and the wine is soft and voluptuous in pie-filling cherry, raspberry and blackberry flavors. But it doesn't have the tough tannins that cooler vintages show. **88** —*S.H. (12/31/2007)*

Duckhorn 2003 Three Palms Vineyard Merlot (Napa Valley) $80. 88 —*S.H. (12/1/2006)*

Duckhorn 2002 Three Palms Vineyard Merlot (Napa Valley) $80. 84 —*S.H. (12/1/2005)*

Duckhorn 2001 Three Palms Vineyard Merlot (Napa Valley) $77. 93 —*S.H. (8/1/2004)*

Duckhorn 2000 Three Palms Vineyard Merlot (Napa Valley) $75. 90 *(5/1/2004)*

Duckhorn 1999 Three Palms Vineyard Merlot (Napa Valley) $70. 92 —*K.F. (4/1/2003)*

Duckhorn 1997 Three Palms Vineyard Merlot (Napa Valley) $60. 88 —*J.C. (6/1/2001)*

Duckhorn 1996 Three Palms Vineyard Merlot (Napa Valley) $47. 91 —*M.S. (3/1/2000)*

Duckhorn 2001 Decoy Red Blend (Napa Valley) $26. 88 —*S.H. (5/1/2005)*

Duckhorn 2006 Sauvignon Blanc (Napa Valley) $25. With 20% Semillon, this is a very rich wine, partly barrel-fermented and aged on the lees. It's packed with ripe, fruity peaches, pineapples, green apples, melons, figs and dates. It's a little sweet, but zesty acidity comes to the rescue to provide balance and elegance. **88** —*S.H. (12/31/2007)*

Duckhorn 2005 Sauvignon Blanc (Napa Valley) $25. 91 Editors' Choice —*S.H. (12/1/2006)*

Duckhorn 2004 Sauvignon Blanc (Napa Valley) $25. 88 —*S.H. (2/1/2006)*

Duckhorn 2003 Sauvignon Blanc (Napa Valley) $23. 89 —*S.H. (5/1/2005)*

Duckhorn 2002 Sauvignon Blanc (Napa Valley) $22. 88 —*S.H. (8/1/2004)*

Duckhorn 2000 Sauvignon Blanc (Napa Valley) $21. 88 *(8/1/2002)*

DUKE

DUKE 2001 Merlot (California) $9. 85 Best Buy —*S.H. (12/31/2003)*

DUKE 2001 Shiraz (California) $9. 85 Best Buy —*S.H. (2/1/2004)*

DUNCAN PEAK

Duncan Peak 2002 Cabernet Sauvignon (Mendocino County) $25. 85 —*S.H. (10/1/2006)*

Duncan Peak 1998 Cabernet Sauvignon (Mendocino County) $35. 90 —*S.H. (6/1/2002)*

Duncan Peak 2001 Reserve Cabernet Sauvignon (Mendocino County) $35. 89 —*S.H. (10/1/2006)*

Duncan Peak 2003 Petite Sirah (Mendocino County) $25. 90 —*S.H. (10/1/2006)*

DUNDEE SPRINGS

Dundee Springs 1999 Pinot Blanc (Oregon) $16. 86 —*S.H. (8/1/2002)*

Dundee Springs 1999 Pinot Gris (Oregon) $12. 85 —*P.G. (8/1/2002)*

DUNHAM

Dunham 2004 Trutina Bordeaux Blend (Columbia Valley (WA)) $24. Trutina, Dunham's Bordeaux blend, has long been the value wine in the Walla Walla superstar's portfolio. The 2004 is no exception, a seamless, silk-on-steel compendium of Merlot and Cabernet Sauvignon. The wild card in '04 is the addition of 3% Syrah. It opens the wine up a bit, adding some spice and mint to the sweet cherry Merlot fruit. There's also an interesting grace note reminiscent of caraway cutting through. **91** —*P.G. (5/1/2007)*

Dunham 2001 Trutina Bordeaux Blend (Columbia Valley (WA)) $28. 88 —*P.G. (12/15/2004)*

Dunham 1999 Cabernet Sauvignon (Columbia Valley (WA)) $45. 88 —*C.S. (12/31/2002)*

Dunham 2003 IX Cabernet Sauvignon (Columbia Valley (WA)) $45. 100% Cabernet, it is sappy, supple, silky and filled with ripe blackberry flavor. The berries and cherries lead into a super smooth and liquorous finish. The oak is well-integrated, lending sweet caramel notes and a lick of licorice and mocha. Blending pure Cabernet from the right mix of sites to fill it out is the real art; that's what Dunham does especially well. **91** —*P.G. (3/1/2007)*

Dunham 2004 Lewis Vineyard Cabernet Sauvignon (Columbia Valley (WA)) $75. This is glorious stuff. Dunham's first vineyard designated Cab is an absolute home run. Pure, dense Cabernet flavors fill the glass, at once forward and open, yet firm and concentrated. The lush black fruits roll through followed with lacy layers of smoke, tea, earth and tobacco. This wine just keeps on going; cellar it if you can keep your hands off it, or treat yourself and drink it today. **94 Editors' Choice** —*P.G. (8/1/2007)*

Dunham 2002 Lewis Vineyard Cabernet Sauvignon (Columbia Valley (WA)) $75. 93 —*P.G. (4/1/2006)*

Dunham 2001 VII Cabernet Sauvignon (Columbia Valley (WA)) $45. 91 Cellar Selection —*P.G. (12/15/2004)*

Dunham 2002 VIII Cabernet Sauvignon (Columbia Valley (WA)) $45. 92 —*P.G. (4/1/2006)*

Dunham 2005 Lewis Estate "Shirley Mays" Chardonnay (Columbia Valley (WA)) $35. 91 —*P.G. (10/1/2006)*

Dunham 2004 Lewis Vineyard Merlot (Columbia Valley (WA)) $75. This is Eric Dunham's first Lewis Merlot, although he's made vineyard-designated Syrah and Cab from the same site. This is satiny smooth and shows a cherry cola character unique to the site; it's chocolaty and rich, but not hot or raisiny. Dunham's reds have seamless, full-throttle flavors; this is right there. **90** —*P.G. (3/1/2007)*

Dunham 2003 Shirley Mays Sémillon (Walla Walla (WA)) $35. 91 —*P.G. (11/15/2004)*

Dunham 2004 Syrah (Columbia Valley (WA)) $45. Pure Syrah from Columbia Valley vineyards, it's a saturated and dense purple/black, with a firm core of spicy and penetrating fruit. A juicy wine, with some mint and herb underlying the tart blueberry and black cherry flavors. **89** —*P.G. (3/1/2007)*

Dunham 2003 Syrah (Columbia Valley (WA)) $45. 84 *(9/1/2005)*

Dunham 2002 Syrah (Columbia Valley (WA)) $45. 92 —*P.G. (11/15/2004)*

Dunham 2001 Syrah (Columbia Valley (WA)) $45. 91 —*P.G. (11/15/2004)*

Dunham 2000 Syrah (Columbia Valley (WA)) $45. 92 —*P.G. (9/1/2002)*

Dunham 2004 Lewis Vineyard Syrah (Columbia Valley (WA)) $75. 94 —*P.G. (11/15/2006)*

Dunham 2002 Lewis Vineyard Syrah (Columbia Valley (WA)) $60. 93 —*P.G. (11/15/2004)*

Dunham 1999 Lewis Vineyard Syrah (Columbia Valley (WA)) $45. 92 Cellar Selection *(11/1/2001)*

DUNNEWOOD

Dunnewood 2000 Cabernet Sauvignon (Mendocino County) $9. 85 Best Buy —*S.H. (10/1/2003)*

Dunnewood 1998 Cabernet Sauvignon (North Coast) $8. 83 —*S.H. (5/1/2001)*

Dunnewood 1995 Dry Silk Reserve Seven Arches Cabernet Sauvignon (Sonoma County) $13. 86 *(7/1/2000)*

Dunnewood 1996 Dry Silk Seven Arches Vineyard Rese Cabernet Sauvignon (Sonoma County) $13. 86 *(7/1/2000)*

Dunnewood 1998 Signature Clara's Vineyard Cabernet Sauvignon (Mendocino County) $15. 87 —*S.H. (8/1/2003)*

Dunnewood 1997 Signature Clara's Vineyards Cabernet Sauvignon (Mendocino) $13. 89 Best Buy —*S.H. (5/1/2001)*

Dunnewood 1995 Dry Silk Reserve Charbono (Napa Valley) $14. 86 *(7/1/2000)*

Dunnewood 2001 Chardonnay (Mendocino County) $9. 84 *—S.H. (6/1/2003)*

Dunnewood 2000 Chardonnay (Mendocino County) $9. 82 *—S.H. (5/1/2002)*

Dunnewood 1998 Chardonnay (North Coast) $8. 83 Best Buy *—S.H. (7/1/2000)*

Dunnewood 2002 Signature Chardonnay (Anderson Valley) $13. 86 *—S.H. (12/15/2004)*

Dunnewood 2000 Signature Chardonnay (Carneros) $13. 84 *—S.H. (6/1/2003)*

Dunnewood 1997 Dry Silk Reserve Dolcetto (Napa Valley) $14. 85 *(7/1/2000)*

Dunnewood 1999 Merlot (Mendocino County) $9. 84 *—S.H. (5/1/2002)*

Dunnewood 1998 Merlot (North Coast) $8. 84 *—S.H. (5/1/2001)*

Dunnewood 1997 Reserve Merlot (Napa Valley) $13. 84 *(7/1/2000)*

Dunnewood 2000 Pinot Noir (Mendocino County) $9. 82 *—S.H. (7/1/2003)*

Dunnewood 1999 Pinot Noir (North Coast) $9. 80 *(10/1/2002)*

Dunnewood 1998 Pinot Noir (North Coast) $8. 86 Best Buy *—S.H. (5/1/2001)*

Dunnewood 1997 Barrel Select Coastal Series Pinot Noir (North Coast) $9. 84 Best Buy *(7/1/2000)*

Dunnewood 2002 Signature Pinot Noir (Mendocino County) $9. 86 *(11/1/2004)*

Dunnewood 1997 Reserve Sangiovese (Mendocino County) $14. 84 *(7/1/2000)*

Dunnewood 1999 Signature Mendocino Sangiovese (Mendocino County) $13. 84 *—S.H. (5/1/2002)*

Dunnewood 2000 Sauvignon Blanc (Mendocino County) $7. 84 *—S.H. (5/1/2002)*

Dunnewood 1999 Sauvignon Blanc (Mendocino) $7. 87 Best Buy *—S.H. (5/1/2001)*

Dunnewood 1998 Vintner's Select Coastal Serie Sauvignon Blanc (Mendocino County) $8. 83 *(7/1/2000)*

Dunnewood 2002 Syrah (Mendocino County) $9. 85 Best Buy *—S.H. (12/15/2004)*

Dunnewood 2002 Zinfandel (Mendocino County) $9. 85 Best Buy *—S.H. (2/1/2005)*

Dunnewood 2001 Zinfandel (Mendocino County) $9. 80 *(11/1/2003)*

Dunnewood 1998 Zinfandel (Mendocino County) $9. 85 *—S.H. (5/1/2002)*

DUNNING VINEYARDS

Dunning Vineyards 2004 Private Reserve Cabernet Franc (Paso Robles) $38. Sweet, simple and raw in primary fruit acid, with ripely forward cherry and raspberry fruit. This is a decent country wine. Drink now. 83 *—S.H. (5/1/2007)*

Dunning Vineyards 2004 Private Reserve Cabernet Sauvignon (Paso Robles) $45. Pretty much near the top for warm-climate Paso Cabernet, with its sweet, pretty tannins, soft acidity and well-ripened fruit. The flavors, of blackberries, cola, sassafras and spicy plums, last deep and long. Drink now for freshness. 87 *—S.H. (5/1/2007)*

Dunning Vineyards 2003 Westside Cabernet Sauvignon (Paso Robles) $24. 87 *—S.H. (7/1/2006)*

Dunning Vineyards 2005 Westside Chardonnay (Paso Robles) $18. Decent country-style Chard, a little rough and ready around the edges, but with good, upfront fruit. Will benefit from some decanting. 83 *—S.H. (5/1/2007)*

Dunning Vineyards 2004 Westside Chardonnay (Paso Robles) $16. 84 *—S.H. (7/1/2006)*

Dunning Vineyards 2004 Westside Merlot (Paso Robles) $24. Soft, fruity, simple and on the sweet, desserty side, with pie filling cherry, raspberry and sugared coffee flavors. 82 *—S.H. (3/1/2007)*

Dunning Vineyards 2003 Westside Merlot (Paso Robles) $24. 84 *—S.H. (7/1/2006)*

Dunning Vineyards 2004 Private Reserve Syrah (Paso Robles) $32. Soft and sugary, this is a simple wine, with appealing cherry marmalade and sugared herb tea flavors. It has good acids and tannins, but that sweetness is a turnoff. 83 *—S.H. (5/1/2007)*

Dunning Vineyards 2003 Westside Syrah (Paso Robles) $28. 82 *(9/1/2005)*

Dunning Vineyards 2002 Westside Syrah (Paso Robles) $24. 87 *—S.H. (12/1/2004)*

Dunning Vineyards 2003 Westside Zinfandel (Paso Robles) $32. 84 *—S.H. (7/1/2006)*

Dunning Vineyards 2001 Westside Zinfandel (Paso Robles) $24. 85 *(11/1/2003)*

DURNEY

Durney 1993 Estate Bottled Cabernet Sauvignon (Carmel Valley) $25. 85 *—S.H. (7/1/1999)*

Durney 1996 Estate Bottled Chardonnay (Carmel Valley) $23. 86 *(6/1/2000)*

Durney 1998 Heller Estate Merlot (Carmel Valley) $26. 86 *—J.C. (6/1/2001)*

DUSTED VALLEY

Dusted Valley 2004 BFM Bordeaux Blend (Columbia Valley (WA)) $32. BFM stands for Blow Your Freakin' Mind, say the winemakers, whose marketing spin is to aggressively position their wines as ready to party. Nonetheless this four grape Bordeaux blend is priced to compete with serious and substantial wines from around the world, and in terms of flavor it does so competently. Though no Sangiovese is listed in the blend, it shows some of the high-acid and tobacco leaf qualities of that grape, and has a good mix of leafy herb, light red fruits, hints of leather and grippy acid throughout. 88 *—P.G. (8/1/2007)*

Dusted Valley 2004 Barrel Thief Cabernet Sauvignon (Columbia Valley (WA)) $24. Past vintages of Barrel Thief have been red blends, but in 2004 it's labeled Cabernet Sauvignon. The rest of the blend is Cab Franc and Merlot, so the Thief has gone a bit upscale, with visions of Bordeaux dancing in its head. Screwcapped and high-toned, there's nothing shy about this wine. It hits you head-on, dumps its plain fruit flavors and runs off, leaving a bit of volatile heat in the back of your mouth. 86 *—P.G. (8/1/2007)*

Dusted Valley 2003 Stomp! Cabernet Sauvignon (Columbia Valley (WA)) $15. Stomp! Cab is a year older than Stomp! Merlot and shows more bourbon barrel flavor. Tannins are softened up, and the fruit is fading. This is pleasant sipping wine, undemanding and approachable, with a clean finish. 85 *—P.G. (8/1/2007)*

Dusted Valley 2005 Chardonnay (Columbia Valley (WA)) $20. This is a deep gold, scented with cooked apple and pear, and showing some soft, oxidative character from extended barrel fermentation. It is quite accessible, soft and forward, with light hints of tropical fruits leading into a smooth, lightly toasty finish. Definitely a drink-now Chardonnay. 88 *—P.G. (8/1/2007)*

Dusted Valley 2005 Birch Creek Vineyard Chardonnay (Walla Walla (WA)) $28. A very limited production wine from a new Walla Walla vineyard, this was barrel fermented in neutral oak and softened up with partial malo. It leans a bit more toward the citrus/pineapple flavor side than does the winery's regular Chardonnay bottling. This is a bit crisper, with subtle grassy highlights adding some lift and interest. 88 *—P.G. (8/1/2007)*

Dusted Valley 2004 Old Vine Chardonnay (Yakima Valley) $20. 89 *—P.G. (4/1/2006)*

Dusted Valley 2003 Old Vine Chardonnay (Columbia Valley (WA)) $20. 87 *—P.G. (11/15/2004)*

Dusted Valley 2004 Stomp! Merlot (Columbia Valley (WA)) $15. Stomp! is a second label for Dusted Valley, with colorful graphics and a bit of 'tude ("Don't worry, we keep our gnarly, fungus ridden toes away from the grapes" reads the back label.) As an everyday red it gets the job done, with simple red fruit flavors and a light touch with the tannins. 85 *—P.G. (8/1/2007)*

Dusted Valley 2003 Barrel Thief Red Red Blend (Columbia Valley (WA)) $20. 86 *—P.G. (4/1/2006)*

Dusted Valley 2004 Reserve Syrah (Columbia Valley (WA)) $32. 89 *—P.G. (4/1/2006)*

Dusted Valley 2004 Stained Tooth Syrah (Columbia Valley (WA)) $24. 87 *—P.G. (4/1/2006)*

Dusted Valley 2005 Viognier (Yakima Valley) $20. Spicy and packed with mixed citrus peel, tangerine, white peach, stone fruit, mineral and licorice. This really delivers the full complement of varietal flavors, in a well-structured, tartly crisp wine. 90 *—P.G. (8/1/2007)*

Dusted Valley 2004 Viognier (Yakima Valley) $20. 88 *—P.G. (4/1/2006)*

Dusted Valley 2003 Viognier (Columbia Valley (WA)) $20. 88 *—P.G. (11/15/2004)*

DUTCH HENRY WINERY

Dutch Henry Winery 2001 Chafen Vineyards Cabernet Sauvignon (Napa Valley) $42. 87 *—S.H. (10/3/2004)*

Dutch Henry Winery 2001 Argos Meritage (Napa Valley) $38. 85 *—S.H. (10/3/2004)*

DUTCHER CROSSING

Dutcher Crossing 2002 Nevins Vineyard Cabernet Sauvignon (Alexander Valley) $32. 86 *—S.H. (8/1/2005)*

Dutcher Crossing 2003 Chardonnay (Russian River Valley) $22. 85 *—S.H. (8/1/2005)*

Dutcher Crossing 2003 Stuhlmuller Vineyard Chardonnay (Alexander Valley) $30. 88 *—S.H. (8/1/2005)*

DUTTON ESTATE

Dutton Estate 2004 Dutton Palms Vineyard Chardonnay (Russian River Valley) $45. 94 Editors' Choice *—S.H. (7/1/2006)*

Dutton Estate 2002 Dutton Palms Vineyard Chardonnay (Russian River Valley) $40. 91 *—S.H. (12/31/2004)*

Dutton Estate 2004 Dutton Ranch Chardonnay (Russian River Valley) $35. 93 Editors' Choice *—S.H. (12/31/2006)*

Dutton Estate 2005 Dutton Ranch Dutton Palms Vineyard Chardonnay (Russian River Valley) $42. Like the winery's other 2005 Chardonnays, this one, tasted in March, is tightly wound and minerally. The aroma will show little if the wine is too cold. Flavor-wise, hints of tart tangerines, lemongrass, green apples, candied ginger and vanilla cream swirl into a smoky oak, spicy finish. This is a Chardonnay that needs some time in the bottle. Drink now and for a couple of years. **93** *—S.H. (9/1/2007)*

Dutton Estate 2005 Dutton Ranch Kyndall's Reserve Chardonnay (Russian River Valley) $36. Charry, smoky oak stars in this young, well-structured wine, leading to powerhouse peach pie (with the crust), lemon mousse and buttered toast flavors that finish long and spicy. Acidity is high, and gives a tangy minerality that adds complexity. **92** *—S.H. (9/1/2007)*

Dutton Estate 2004 Devil's Gulch Vineyard Pinot Noir (Marin County) $52. Marin, just over the Golden Gate Bridge from San Francisco, is a rare origin for wine grapes, and for good reason. It's too cold. This Pinot shows its origins in the acidic, green minty streak that pervades it. There's lots of delicious cherry and raspberry fruit, but that wintergreen dominates, to the wine's detriment. **86** *—S.H. (2/1/2007)*

Dutton Estate 2004 Dutton Ranch Pinot Noir (Russian River Valley) $35. 87 *—S.H. (7/1/2006)*

Dutton Estate 2004 Dutton Ranch Sanchietti Vineyard Pinot Noir (Russian River Valley) $55. Getting Pinot ripe in the Green Valley is always the challenge. This is a wine made by the finest viticulture and enology. It's dry, lush, classically structured and silky, with beautiful cherry and blueberry flavors. Still, there's a green mint streak that's fine in a cough drop but bothersome in Pinot Noir. **87** *—S.H. (2/1/2007)*

Dutton Estate 2005 Dutton Thomas Road Vineyard Pinot Noir (Russian River Valley) $48. An interesting wine that makes you think. Straddles the border between minty wintergreen unripeness and cherry cola ripeness, coming down in favor of the latter. Streamlined and elegant, it's good now for the dry crispness, but not an ager. Drink soon. **89** *—S.H. (9/1/2007)*

Dutton Estate 2004 Dutton-Thomas Road Vineyard Pinot Noir (Russian River Valley) $45. 90 *—S.H. (12/31/2006)*

Dutton Estate 2004 Jewell Block Vineyard Pinot Noir (Russian River Valley) $52. 88 *—S.H. (12/31/2006)*

Dutton Estate 2005 Manzana Vineyard Pinot Noir (Russian River Valley) $45. From the translucent, see-through ruby color to the intricate cola, cherry and toasted coconut flavors, this delicately powerful in a Burgundian way. Feels silky and light-bodied in the mouth, but there's nothing scanty about the wine's powerful intensity of fruit, spice and oak. Best now and for a couple of years. **92** *—S.H. (8/1/2007)*

Dutton Estate 2003 Thomas Road Pinot Noir (Russian River Valley) $40. 93 Editors' Choice *—S.H. (12/1/2005)*

Dutton Estate 2006 Dutton Ranch Cohen Vineyard Sauvignon Blanc (Russian River Valley) $18. Pretty good Sauv Blanc, a little one-dimensional, but satisfies for its flowery, citrus blossom and passionfruit flavors that finish in a swirl of palate-stimulating spices. **87** *—S.H. (9/1/2007)*

Dutton Estate 2005 Dutton Ranch Cohen Vineyard Sauvignon Blanc (Russian River Valley) $35. 93 Editors' Choice *—S.H. (8/1/2006)*

Dutton Estate 2004 Dutton Ranch Cherry Ridge Vineyard Syrah (Russian River Valley) $34. Superripe in black cherry, cola and mocha flavors enhanced with smoky oak, this is soft, but quite elegant. It's not an ager, but has a full-bodied richness that suggests steaks and chops. **88** *—S.H. (8/1/2007)*

Dutton Estate 2003 Cherry Ridge Vineyard Syrah (Russian River Valley) $34. 86 *(9/1/2005)*

Dutton Estate 2003 Gail Ann's Vineyard Syrah (Russian River Valley) $35. 85 *—S.H. (12/31/2006)*

Dutton Estate 2002 Gail Ann's Vineyard Syrah (Russian River Valley) $34. 82 *(9/1/2005)*

DUTTON-GOLDFIELD

Dutton-Goldfield 2005 Dutton Ranch Chardonnay (Russian River Valley) $35. This wine has much in common with the winery's '05 Dutton Ranch Sauvignon Blanc. It's a tight, high-acid, lean wine, with mineral and citrus flavors enriched with a touch of honeysuckle and oak. More notable for structure than opulence, it will finely support food, and should develop bottle complexity over the next five years. **89** *—S.H. (6/1/2007)*

Dutton-Goldfield 2004 Dutton Ranch Chardonnay (Russian River Valley) $35. 94 Editors' Choice *—S.H. (6/1/2006)*

Dutton-Goldfield 2003 Dutton Ranch Chardonnay (Russian River Valley) $30. 91 Editors' Choice *—S.H. (10/1/2005)*

Dutton-Goldfield 2002 Dutton Ranch Chardonnay (Russian River Valley) $30. 87 *—S.H. (10/1/2004)*

Dutton-Goldfield 2001 Dutton Ranch Chardonnay (Russian River Valley) $30. 86 *—S.H. (12/15/2003)*

Dutton-Goldfield 2000 Dutton Ranch Chardonnay (Russian River Valley) $35. 87 *—S.H. (12/15/2002)*

Dutton-Goldfield 1998 Dutton Ranch Chardonnay (Russian River Valley) $28. 87 *(3/1/2000)*

Dutton-Goldfield 2005 Dutton Ranch Rued Vineyard Chardonnay (Russian River Valley) $45. A very fine Chard, complex and layered, and quite dry. Acidity makes the tangerine, kumquat, ripe yellow pear, roasted pineapple and oaky, crème brûlée flavors really come alive. After you swallow, the wine leaves behind a delicious impression. **95 Editors' Choice** *—S.H. (12/1/2007)*

Dutton-Goldfield 2004 Dutton Ranch Rued Vineyard Chardonnay (Russian River Valley) $45. 95 Editors' Choice *—S.H. (12/15/2006)*

Dutton-Goldfield 2002 Dutton Ranch Rued Vineyard Chardonnay (Russian River Valley) $40. 88 *—S.H. (10/1/2004)*

Dutton-Goldfield 2000 Rued Vineyard Chardonnay (Russian River Valley) $45. 90 *—S.H. (12/15/2002)*

Dutton-Goldfield 2003 Rued Vineyard Dutton Ranch Chardonnay (Russian River Valley) $40. 92 *—S.H. (12/15/2005)*

Dutton-Goldfield 2001 Rued Vineyard Dutton Ranch Chardonnay (Russian River Valley) $40. 91 *—S.H. (12/15/2003)*

Dutton-Goldfield 2000 Devil's Gulch Pinot Noir (Marin County) $50. 89 *(10/1/2002)*

Dutton-Goldfield 2002 Devil's Gulch Ranch Pinot Noir (Marin County) $48. 90 *(11/1/2004)*

Dutton-Goldfield 2003 Devil's Gulch Vineyard Pinot Noir (Marin County) $48. 86 *—S.H. (2/1/2006)*

Dutton-Goldfield 2001 Devil's Gulch Ranch Pinot Noir (Marin County) $48. 87 *—S.H. (2/1/2004)*

Dutton-Goldfield 2005 Dutton Ranch Pinot Noir (Russian River Valley) $35. There's something sharp and minty green, the result either of overcropped vines or, more likely, a too-cool vintage in which the grapes didn't fully ripen. You can taste the pedigree of the structure, but this lacks the opulence you expect. **84** *—S.H. (7/1/2007)*

Dutton-Goldfield 2004 Dutton Ranch Pinot Noir (Russian River Valley) $35. 92 *—S.H. (10/1/2006)*

Dutton-Goldfield 2003 Dutton Ranch Pinot Noir (Russian River Valley) $35. 86 *—S.H. (12/15/2005)*

Dutton-Goldfield 2002 Dutton Ranch Pinot Noir (Russian River Valley) $35. 90 *(11/1/2004)*

Dutton-Goldfield 2001 Dutton Ranch Pinot Noir (Russian River Valley) $35. 91 *—S.H. (4/1/2004)*

Dutton-Goldfield 2000 Dutton Ranch Pinot Noir (Russian River Valley) $40. 87 *(10/1/2002)*

Dutton-Goldfield 1999 Dutton Ranch Pinot Noir (Russian River Valley) $40. 93 *—S.H. (7/1/2002)*

Dutton-Goldfield 1998 Dutton Ranch Pinot Noir (Russian River Valley) $33. 90 *—M.S. (5/1/2000)*

Dutton-Goldfield 2005 Dutton Ranch Freestone Hill Vineyard Pinot Noir (Russian River Valley) $58. This is ageable and enormously complex, and should do very interesting things over the next six years. Right now it is tight and fresh in primary fruits and acidity. It's an enormously rich wine, vast in black cherries, pomegranates, cola, red plums, balsam and sautéed mushroom flavors, with a gamy, forest-floor earthiness. Time in the bottle can only improve it through 2011. **96** *—S.H. (12/1/2007)*

Dutton-Goldfield 2000 Dutton Ranch Maurice Galante Vineyard Pinot Noir (Russian River Valley) $55. 90 *(10/1/2002)*

Dutton-Goldfield 2004 Dutton Ranch Sanchietti Vineyard Pinot Noir (Russian River Valley) $55. 90 Cellar Selection *—S.H. (12/15/2006)*

Dutton-Goldfield 2000 Dutton-Freestone Hill Pinot Noir (Russian River Valley) $55. 89 *(10/1/2002)*

Dutton-Goldfield 1999 Freestone Hill Vineyard Pinot Noir (Russian River Valley) $55. 92 *—S.H. (7/1/2002)*

Dutton-Goldfield 2004 McDougall Vineyard Pinot Noir (Sonoma Coast) $52. 95 Editors' Choice *—S.H. (12/15/2006)*

Dutton-Goldfield 2002 McDougall Vineyard Pinot Noir (Sonoma Coast) $48. 89 *(11/1/2004)*

Dutton-Goldfield 2002 Sanchietti Vineyard Pinot Noir (Russian River Valley) $52. 90 *(11/1/2004)*

Dutton-Goldfield 2003 Sanchietti Vineyard Dutton Ranch Pinot Noir (Russian River Valley) $52. 89 *—S.H. (2/1/2006)*

Dutton-Goldfield 2004 Cherry Ridge Vineyard Syrah (Russian River Valley) $35. This is a good vineyard but I think Dan Goldfield met his match with the hot weather that plagued the harvest. The wine, which has 40% new oak, is ripe and forward in cherry pie, chocolate and cassis flavors. This is initially delicious, but not particularly complex; it's just too soft. The winemaker suggests pairing with Gouda and Gruyère. **87** *—S.H. (6/1/2007)*

Dutton-Goldfield 2003 Cherry Ridge Vineyard Syrah (Russian River Valley) $35. 89 *—S.H. (2/1/2006)*

Dutton-Goldfield 2002 Cherry Ridge Vineyard Syrah (Russian River Valley) $35. 91 *—S.H. (3/1/2005)*

Dutton-Goldfield 2001 Dutton Ranch Cherry Ridge Vineyard Syrah (Russian River Valley) $35. 93 Editors' Choice *—S.H. (6/1/2004)*

Dutton-Goldfield 2000 Dutton Ranch Cherry Ridge Vineyard Syrah (Russian River Valley) $35. 92 Editors' Choice *—S.H. (2/1/2003)*

Dutton-Goldfield 2005 Zinfandel (Russian River Valley) $30. Although there's lots to like in this Zin, it's just too sweet. On the plus side are rich, complex flavors of cherry pie, raspberry tart, cassis, cocoa and mushu plum sauce, accented by peppery spices and a bit of wood. Also nice are the dense but ripe tannins. But then there's that sugary, brownie taste that's inappropriate in a table wine. **84** *—S.H. (10/1/2007)*

Dutton-Goldfield 2004 Zinfandel (Russian River Valley) $30. 85 *—S.H. (10/1/2006)*

Dutton-Goldfield 2005 Dutton Ranch Morelli Lane Vineyard Zinfandel (Russian River Valley) $40. Midnight black and drily astringent, this is not a wine to pop open tonight. But it's extraordinarily ripe and deep in black currants, with all kinds of earthy cocoa, balsamic, basil, Portobello, coffee and spice flavors. It will blossom and knit together with some time in the bottle. Best 2008–2011, at least. **91** *—S.H. (8/1/2007)*

Dutton-Goldfield 2004 Dutton Ranch Morelli Lane Vineyard Zinfandel (Russian River Valley) $40. 90 *—S.H. (6/1/2006)*

Dutton-Goldfield 2002 Dutton Ranch Morelli Lane Vineyard Zinfandel (Russian River Valley) $35. 91 *—J.M. (12/31/2004)*

Dutton-Goldfield 2001 Dutton Ranch/Morelli Lane Vineyard Zinfandel (Russian River Valley) $35. 90 *(11/1/2003)*

Dutton-Goldfield 2000 Morelli Lane Vineyard Zinfandel (Russian River Valley) $35. 94 Cellar Selection *—S.H. (12/1/2002)*

DUXOUP

Duxoup 2002 Syrah (Dry Creek Valley) $19. 86 *—S.H. (11/1/2005)*

DYNAMITE VINEYARDS

Dynamite Vineyards 2002 Cabernet Sauvignon (North Coast) $17. 85 *—S.H. (2/1/2005)*

Dynamite Vineyards 2001 Cabernet Sauvignon (North Coast) $17. 84 *—S.H. (5/1/2004)*

Dynamite Vineyards 2000 Red Hills Cabernet Sauvignon (Lake County) $25. 87 *—S.H. (12/31/2003)*

Dynamite Vineyards 2004 Chardonnay (Mendocino County) $15. 82 *—S.H. (3/1/2006)*

Dynamite Vineyards 2002 Merlot (North Coast) $17. 89 *—S.H. (10/1/2005)*

Dynamite Vineyards 2001 Merlot (North Coast) $17. 87 *—S.H. (5/1/2004)*

Dynamite Vineyards 2000 Merlot (North Coast) $18. 86 *—J.M. (11/15/2002)*

Dynamite Vineyards 2005 Sauvignon Blanc (Lake County) $13. 84 *—S.H. (12/15/2006)*

Dynamite Vineyards 2002 Sauvignon Blanc (Lake County) $11. 84 *—J.M. (4/1/2004)*

Dynamite Vineyards 2004 Kelsey Creek Sauvignon Blanc (Lake County) $11. 85 *—S.H. (3/1/2006)*

Dynamite Vineyards 2003 Kelsey Creek Sauvignon Blanc (Lake County) $11. 83 *—S.H. (10/1/2005)*

Dynamite Vineyards 2004 Zinfandel (Mendocino County) $17. 86 *—S.H. (12/15/2006)*

Dynamite Vineyards 2003 Zinfandel (Mendocino County) $17. 88 *—S.H. (10/1/2005)*

E & J GALLO

E & J Gallo 1999 Barelli Creek Vineyard Barbera (Sonoma County) $19. 86 *(7/1/2001)*

E & J Gallo 1998 Estate Chardonnay (Northern Sonoma) $50. 92 *(7/1/2001)*

E B FOOTE

E B Foote 1997 Bordeaux Blend (Columbia Valley (WA)) $18. 83 *—P.G. (6/1/2000)*

E B Foote 2004 Perfect à Trois Bordeaux Blend (Columbia Valley (WA)) $25. The Perfect à Trois is 70% Cab Sauvignon, 15% Merlot and 15% Cab Franc. It shows more new oak—particularly vanilla and toasted coconut flavors—but the fruit is substantial and carries through. There is a volatile lift to the flavors that some will object to, but others will find quite refreshing. All in all it's very nicely done. **89** *—P.G. (5/1/2007)*

E B Foote 2003 Cabernet Sauvignon (Columbia Valley (WA)) $18. Dense and concentrated, this wine looks serious from the get-go. The scents are smoky, earthy and rich, a sensual mix of fruit, leather and wood. There is plenty of acid behind the tannin, and the modest (13.1%) alcohol sends it squarely into the Bordeaux camp. You can pick up hints of dried herb, mushroom and leaf; an intriguing, well-made wine. **87** *—P.G. (5/1/2007)*

E B Foote 1999 Cabernet Sauvignon (Columbia Valley (WA)) $16. 84 *—D.T. (12/31/2002)*

E B Foote 1998 Cellar Reserve Cabernet Sauvignon (Columbia Valley (WA)) $32. 82 *—P.G. (6/1/2002)*

E B Foote 2004 Cabernet Sauvignon-Merlot (Columbia Valley (WA)) $18. This is the sort of rustic, earthy wine that should be served from a carafe and accompanied with hearty country cooking. There is nothing fancy here, but the fruit is plump and round, and the flavors seem more evolved than the vintage would suggest. It's a wine to enjoy right now, with no worries about cellaring or when it will be ready. It's ready. **87** *—P.G. (5/1/2007)*

E B Foote 1998 Chardonnay (Columbia Valley (WA)) $12. 85 *—P.G. (6/1/2000)*

E B Foote 2001 Chardonnay (Columbia Valley (WA)) $12. 86 *—M.S. (6/1/2003)*

E B Foote 1999 Chardonnay (Columbia Valley (WA)) $12. 82 *—P.G. (7/1/2002)*

E B Foote 2003 Merlot (Columbia Valley (WA)) $18. This is Wahluke Slope fruit, which means a hot climate, high alcohol, nothing-shy-about-it red wine. The Merlot is buttressed with 11% Cab Franc, which gives a tannic underpinning and a hint of green tea in the finishing tannins. Substantial and thick, it's definitely a hearty wine for meaty, midwinter dishes. **88** *—P.G. (5/1/2007)*

E B Foote 2000 Merlot (Columbia Valley (WA)) $16. 84 *—M.S. (6/1/2003)*

E B Foote 1998 Merlot (Columbia Valley (WA)) $16. 87 *—P.G. (6/1/2001)*

E B Foote 2001 Pinot Gris (Columbia Valley (WA)) $10. 80 *—M.S. (1/1/2004)*

E B Foote 2001 Syrah (Columbia Valley (WA)) $18. 82 *—M.S. (6/1/2003)*

E B Foote 2000 Syrah (Columbia Valley (WA)) $18. 88 *(10/1/2001)*

E. B. Foote 2003 Syrah (Columbia Valley (WA)) $16. 86 *(9/1/2005)*

E B Foote NV Rainy Day Red III Syrah (Columbia Valley (WA)) $18. The Rainy Day Red is really a Syrah, with just 13% Cab in the blend. High-toned and floral, it opens with scents of citrus rind, blossom, black cherry and spice. The fruit is tart and bracing. This is a high-acid style of Syrah, which keeps it lifted and makes it particularly good for pairing with rich foods. **88** *—P.G. (5/1/2007)*

E B Foote 2005 Milbrandt Vineyards Zinfandel (Columbia Valley (WA)) $18. This has the racy authority of Dry Creek Zins, with splendid, high acid raspberry flavors, and holds its alcohol (15.6%) well, without cutting out the grace notes of flower and citrus. It's a Rosenblum style of Zin, and the fact that it was made in Washington shows that there is real potential for this grape in a state where it was barely a curiosity a decade ago. **89** *—P.G. (5/1/2007)*

EAGLE & ROSE ESTATE

Eagle & Rose Estate 1999 Cabernet Sauvignon (Napa Valley) $34. 86 *—S.H. (11/15/2002)*

Eagle & Rose Estate 1998 Cabernet Sauvignon (Napa Valley) $NA. 84 *—S.H. (12/1/2001)*

Eagle & Rose Estate 2000 Merlot (Napa Valley) $24. 85 *—S.H. (12/15/2004)*

Eagle & Rose Estate 1999 Merlot (Napa Valley) $24. 87 *—S.H. (11/15/2002)*

Eagle & Rose Estate 1998 Merlot (Napa Valley) $24. 85 *—S.H. (12/1/2001)*

Eagle & Rose Estate 1999 Sangiovese (Napa Valley) $24. 81 *—S.H. (11/15/2002)*

Eagle & Rose Estate 1998 Sangiovese (Napa Valley) $24. 87 *—S.H. (12/1/2001)*

Eagle & Rose Estate 2000 Sauvignon Blanc (Napa Valley) $16. 84 *—S.H. (9/1/2003)*

Eagle & Rose Estate 1999 Sauvignon Blanc (Napa Valley) $16. 84 *—S.H. (11/15/2001)*

Eagle & Rose Estate 1998 Sauvignon Blanc (Napa Valley) $16. 88 *—S.H. (11/15/2000)*

EAGLE'S DOMAIN

Eagle's Domain 2000 Reserve Chardonnay (Napa Valley) $7. 86 Best Buy *—S.H. (11/15/2004)*

EAGLEPOINT RANCH

Eaglepoint Ranch 2006 Grenache (Mendocino County) $20. A little on the simple side, this wine's most appealing trait is straightforward cherry flavor. It has a pleasant structure, but could use more depth and complexity. **84** *—S.H. (12/31/2007)*

Eaglepoint Ranch 2004 Grenache (Mendocino County) $18. 87 *—S.H. (12/31/2005)*

Eaglepoint Ranch 2003 Grenache (Mendocino) $16. 90 *—S.H. (3/1/2005)*

Eaglepoint Ranch 2001 Grenache (Mendocino County) $14. 86 *—S.H. (5/1/2004)*

Eaglepoint Ranch 2005 Petite Sirah (Mendocino County) $26. One of the best Petite Sirahs of the vintage, this rich wine shows an impeccable balance rare in this variety. Everything's just right, from the smooth dryness and furry tannins to the succulent blackberry fruit to the long, cherried finish. Really a nice, full-bodied red wine. If you're into cellaring, this should remain viable for at least 10 years. **93 Editors' Choice** *—S.H. (12/31/2007)*

Eaglepoint Ranch 2003 Petite Sirah (Mendocino County) $26. 91 Cellar Selection *—S.H. (12/31/2005)*

Eaglepoint Ranch 2002 Petite Sirah (Mendocino County) $24. 87 *—S.H. (3/1/2005)*

Eaglepoint Ranch 2001 Petite Sirah (Mendocino County) $24. 88 *—S.H. (5/1/2004)*

Eaglepoint Ranch 2001 Coro Mendocino Red Blend (Mendocino) $35. 89 *—J.M. (9/1/2004)*

Eaglepoint Ranch 1999 Sangiovese (Mendocino County) $18. 86 *—S.H. (5/1/2002)*

Eaglepoint Ranch 2005 Syrah (Mendocino County) $22. Rugged tannins are front and center in this youthful wine. There's a wealth of complex wild blackberry, licorice, grilled meat, sage and white-pepper flavor, and the wine is impeccably balanced. With alcohol a relatively modest 14.4%, this powerful Syrah will reward cellaring. Best 2008–2012. **92 Cellar Selection** *—S.H. (12/31/2007)*

Eaglepoint Ranch 2000 Syrah (Mendocino) $22. 88 *—S.H. (12/1/2003)*

Eaglepoint Ranch 1999 Syrah (Mendocino) $24. 94 *—S.H. (5/1/2002)*

EAGLES LANDING

Eagles Landing 2004 Private Reserve Chardonnay (Russian River Valley) $25. At three-plus years, this Chard tastes soft and candied, with pineapple LifeSaver flavors. **83** *—S.H. (12/1/2007)*

Eagles Landing 2004 Syrah (Edna Valley) $25. Coming from cool Edna Valley, the acidity is here, even in this hot vintage, and so is the clean, long hangtime fruit. The wine bursts with blackberries, cherries, plums and wilder notes of unidentified forest berries and sweet, smoky leather. Drink now, for its complex, juicy youthfulness. **89** *—S.H. (12/1/2007)*

EARTHQUAKE

Earthquake 2003 Cabernet Sauvignon (Lodi) $28. 83 *—S.H. (7/1/2006)*

Earthquake 2004 Petite Sirah (Lodi) $28. 83 *—S.H. (7/1/2006)*

Earthquake 2004 Syrah (Lodi) $28. 89 *—S.H. (12/31/2006)*

Earthquake 2003 Syrah (Lodi) $25. 87 *(9/1/2005)*

Earthquake 2005 Zinfandel (Lodi) $28. Hot and clumsy. The huge alcohol really sticks out, making the wine Port-like, with a caramelly, chocolate fudge finish to the blackberry fruit. If you like this style, and lots of people do, it's for you. **83** *—S.H. (3/1/2007)*

EAST VALLEY

East Valley 2002 Cabernet Sauvignon (Santa Ynez Valley) $33. 89 *—S.H. (11/1/2006)*

East Valley 2004 Pinot Noir (Santa Barbara County) $36. 83 *—S.H. (10/1/2006)*

East Valley 2003 Sangiovese (Santa Barbara County) $26. 82 *—S.H. (10/1/2006)*

East Valley 2002 Syrah (Edna Valley) $22. 85 *—S.H. (10/1/2006)*

EASTON

Easton 2004 Barbera (Shenandoah Valley (CA)) $22. Nature seems to have condemned California Barbera to be a rustic, hard wine, at best and this is a prime example of the species. Black in color and very tannic, it shows ripe berry and coffee flavors accented with peppery spice. These wines live forever, without gaining much complexity, so best now through 2020. **85** *—S.H. (6/1/2007)*

Easton 2003 Barbera (Shenandoah Valley (CA)) $22. 88 *—S.H. (6/1/2006)*

Easton 2002 Barbera (Shenandoah Valley (CA)) $20. 83 *—S.H. (8/1/2005)*

Easton 2001 Barbera (Shenandoah Valley (CA)) $20. 86 *—S.H. (6/1/2004)*

Easton 2000 Barbera (Shenandoah Valley (CA)) $20. 87 *—S.H. (5/1/2003)*

Easton 2000 Cabernet Sauvignon (California) $15. 90 Best Buy *—S.H. (6/1/2003)*

Easton 2003 Estate Bottled Cabernet Sauvignon (Shenandoah Valley (CA)) $30. An interesting Cab that's taking the lead in this variety up in the Foothills. From 30-plus year old, low-yielding vines, and aged in considerable new French oak, it's made along Bordeaux lines. Better structured than your typical Napa Cab, it has ripe varietal flavors. This is a wine of charm and elegance. **90** *—S.H. (6/1/2007)*

Easton 2002 Estate Cabernet Sauvignon (Shenandoah Valley (CA)) $30. 88 *—S.H. (6/1/2006)*

Easton 2001 Estate Bottled Cabernet Sauvignon (Shenandoah Valley (CA)) $30. 89 *—S.H. (8/1/2005)*

Easton 2005 Sauvignon Blanc (Sierra Foothills) $16. A little sweet for my taste, with pineapple and peach flavors that taste sugary, but the acidity is bright and crisp. With just a touch of oak, it's a pleasant everyday wine. **84** *—S.H. (6/1/2007)*

Easton 2004 Sauvignon Blanc (Sierra Foothills) $16. 83 *—S.H. (6/1/2006)*

Easton 2003 Sauvignon Blanc (Sierra Foothills) $16. 85 *—S.H. (8/1/2005)*

Easton 2005 Zinfandel (Amador County) $14. A good, basic, everyday Zin, with a rich harvest of wild berry jam, chocolate and peppery spice flavors. The wine is dry, with balancing acidity and firm tannins. **84** *—S.H. (6/1/2007)*

Easton 2004 Zinfandel (Amador County) $13. 86 *—S.H. (6/1/2006)*

Easton 2003 Zinfandel (Amador County) $13. 85 *—S.H. (4/1/2005)*

Easton 2002 Zinfandel (Amador County) $13. 85 *—S.H. (6/1/2004)*

Easton 2002 Zinfandel (Fiddletown) $25. 89 *—S.H. (8/1/2005)*

Easton 2001 Zinfandel (Fiddletown) $25. 90 *—S.H. (6/1/2004)*

Easton 2001 Zinfandel (Amador County) $13. 84 *—S.H. (9/1/2003)*

Easton 2001 Zinfandel (Shenandoah Valley (CA)) $30. 90 *—S.H. (6/1/2004)*

Easton 2000 Zinfandel (Shenandoah Valley (CA)) $30. 93 Editors' Choice *—S.H. (9/1/2003)*

Easton 2000 Zinfandel (Shenandoah Valley (CA)) $22. 88 *—S.H. (9/1/2003)*

Easton 2000 Zinfandel (Amador County) $13. 89 Best Buy *—S.H. (3/1/2002)*

Easton 2000 Zinfandel (Fiddletown) $25. 84 *—S.H. (9/1/2003)*

Easton 1999 Zinfandel (Fiddletown) $25. 91 *—S.H. (3/1/2002)*

Easton 1999 Zinfandel (Shenandoah Valley (CA)) $30. 83 *—S.H. (3/1/2002)*

Easton 1997 Zinfandel (Shenandoah Valley (CA)) $20. 87 *—P.G. (3/1/2001)*

Easton 2004 Estate Bottled Zinfandel (Shenandoah Valley (CA)) $30. I like this wine even though it has overripe raisin flavors, which usually turn me off. In this case, it's like the raisins are part of a rum-soaked Christmas fruit cake, a piquant flavor along with blackberries, cherries, tangerines, pineapples and apricots. Soft and intricate, this is a special wine that's best now and for a couple more years. **92** *—S.H. (6/1/2007)*

Easton 2003 Estate Bottled Zinfandel (Shenandoah Valley (CA)) $30. 86 *—S.H. (6/1/2006)*

Easton 2002 Estate Bottled Zinfandel (Shenandoah Valley (CA)) $30. 90 *—S.H. (8/1/2005)*

Easton 2002 Late Harvest Zinfandel (El Dorado) $18. 84 *—S.H. (8/1/2005)*

Easton 2004 Old Vine Zinfandel (Fiddletown) $25. It's from a vineyard in this Amador County high valley, and vine yield is very low, resulting in a concentrated wine. This may sound weird, but it's like Pinot Noir in the silky, racy mouthfeel and elegant structure. But it's distinctly Zin, with explosive cherry pie, carob, cola and cinnamon spice flavors. 90 *—S.H. (6/1/2007)*

Easton 2003 Old Vine Zinfandel (Fiddletown) $25. 88 *—S.H. (6/1/2006)*

EASTON HOUSE

Easton House NV Lot No. 0102 Red Blend (California) $10. 84 *—S.H. (8/1/2005)*

EASTWOOD

Eastwood 2004 Cabernet Sauvignon (California) $9. 84 *—S.H. (6/1/2006)*

Eastwood 2004 Chardonnay (California) $9. 84 *—S.H. (6/1/2006)*

Eastwood 2004 Merlot (California) $9. 84 *—S.H. (6/1/2006)*

EBERLE

Eberle 2002 Sauret & Steinbeck Vineyards Barbera (Paso Robles) $18. 86 *—S.H. (12/15/2004)*

Eberle 2001 Sauret Vineyard Barbera (Paso Robles) $18. 86 *—S.H. (12/1/2003)*

Eberle 2004 Steinbeck and Sauret Vineyards Barbera (Paso Robles) $20. 88 *—S.H. (11/15/2006)*

Eberle 2003 Steinbeck and Sauret Vineyards Barbera (Paso Robles) $18. 84 *—S.H. (11/15/2005)*

Eberle 2000 Cabernet Sauvignon (Paso Robles) $23. 85 *—S.H. (11/15/2003)*

Eberle 1999 Cabernet Sauvignon (Paso Robles) $28. 91 *—S.H. (7/1/2002)*

Eberle 2002 Estate Cabernet Sauvignon (Paso Robles) $27. 91 *—S.H. (11/15/2005)*

Eberle 2001 Estate Cabernet Sauvignon (Paso Robles) $25. 86 *—S.H. (10/1/2004)*

Eberle 2003 Estate Bottled Cabernet Sauvignon (Paso Robles) $29. 90 *—S.H. (11/15/2006)*

Eberle 1997 Estate Bottled Cabernet Sauvignon (Paso Robles) $30. 86 *(11/1/2000)*

Eberle 2001 Estate Bottled Reserve Cabernet Sauvignon (Paso Robles) $65. 88 *—S.H. (9/1/2006)*

Eberle 1999 Reserve Cabernet Sauvignon (Paso Robles) $75. 90 *—S.H. (11/15/2004)*

Eberle 2003 Vineyard Selection Cabernet Sauvignon (Paso Robles) $17. 87 *—S.H. (11/15/2006)*

Eberle 2002 Vineyard Selection Cabernet Sauvignon (Paso Robles) $17. 86 *—S.H. (11/15/2005)*

Eberle 2001 Vineyard Selection Cabernet Sauvignon (Paso Robles) $17. 88 *—S.H. (10/1/2004)*

Eberle 2002 Cabernet Sauvignon-Syrah (Paso Robles) $24. 91 *—S.H. (12/15/2004)*

Eberle 2001 Cabernet Sauvignon-Syrah (Paso Robles) $24. 85 *—S.H. (11/15/2003)*

Eberle 2004 Chardonnay (Paso Robles) $16. 90 *—S.H. (11/15/2005)*

Eberle 2002 Chardonnay (Paso Robles) $16. 85 *—S.H. (12/1/2003)*

Eberle 2003 Estate Chardonnay (Paso Robles) $16. 87 *—S.H. (12/15/2004)*

Eberle 1998 Estate Chardonnay (Paso Robles) $15. 85 *(6/1/2000)*

Eberle 2005 Estate Bottled Chardonnay (Paso Robles) $18. 85 *—S.H. (11/15/2006)*

Eberle 2005 Muscat Canelli (Paso Robles) $14. 84 *—S.H. (12/1/2006)*

Eberle 2004 Muscat Canelli (Paso Robles) $12. 87 **Best Buy** *—S.H. (11/15/2005)*

Eberle 2003 Muscat Canelli (Paso Robles) $12. 87 *—S.H. (12/15/2004)*

Eberle 2003 Vintage Port (Paso Robles) $55. With cherry, raspberry, chocolate, coffee and vanilla flavors, this Port-style wine is very sweet, and has enough acidity for balance. Drink now. 85 *—S.H. (7/1/2007)*

Eberle 2003 Cabernet Sauvignon-Syrah Red Blend (Paso Robles) $24. 88 *—S.H. (11/15/2005)*

Eberle 1997 Cotes-du-Robles Red Blend (Paso Robles) $14. 88 **Best Buy** *—S.H. (6/1/1999)*

Eberle 2003 Roussanne (Paso Robles) $22. 87 *—S.H. (12/15/2004)*

Eberle 2005 Cass Vineyards Roussanne (Paso Robles) $22. 85 *—S.H. (11/15/2006)*

Eberle 2004 Cass Vineyards Roussanne (Paso Robles) $22. 86 *—S.H. (11/15/2005)*

Eberle 2003 Sangiovese (Paso Robles) $16. 85 *—S.H. (11/15/2005)*

Eberle 2002 Sangiovese (Paso Robles) $16. 85 *—S.H. (12/15/2004)*

Eberle 2001 Filipponi & Thompson Vineyard Sangiovese (Paso Robles) $16. 84 *—S.H. (12/1/2003)*

Eberle 2002 Lonesome Oak Vineyard Syrah (Paso Robles) $16. 87 *—S.H. (12/15/2004)*

Eberle 2001 Reid Vineyard Syrah (Paso Robles) $20. 85 *—S.H. (2/1/2004)*

Eberle 1999 Reid Vineyard Syrah (Paso Robles) $20. 85 *(10/1/2001)*

Eberle 1997 Reid Vineyard Syrah (Paso Robles) $18. 88 *—S.H. (6/1/1999)*

Eberle 2003 Rose Syrah (Paso Robles) $14. 86 *—S.H. (12/15/2004)*

Eberle 2002 Rosé Syrah (Paso Robles) $14. 85 *—S.H. (3/1/2004)*

Eberle 2004 Rose of Syrah (Paso Robles) $14. 86 *—S.H. (11/15/2005)*

Eberle 2003 Steinbeck Vineyard Syrah (Paso Robles) $24. 84 *—S.H. (11/15/2005)*

Eberle 2002 Steinbeck Vineyard Syrah (Paso Robles) $20. 87 *—S.H. (12/15/2004)*

Eberle 2001 Steinbeck Vineyard Syrah (Paso Robles) $20. 87 *(2/1/2004)*

Eberle 1997 Steinbeck Vineyard Syrah (Paso Robles) $18. 87 *—S.H. (6/1/1999)*

Eberle 2002 Steinbeck Vineyard Reserve Syrah (Paso Robles) $45. 84 *—S.H. (11/15/2005)*

Eberle 2005 Syrah Rosé Syrah (Paso Robles) $16. 87 *—S.H. (11/15/2006)*

Eberle 2002 Glenrose Vineyard Viognier (Paso Robles) $22. 87 *—S.H. (12/1/2003)*

Eberle 1998 Glenrose Vineyard Viognier (Paso Robles) $20. 87 *—S.H. (10/1/1999)*

Eberle 2004 Mill Road Viognier (Paso Robles) $18. 89 *—S.H. (11/15/2005)*

Eberle 2005 Mill Road Vineyard Viognier (Paso Robles) $20. 85 *—S.H. (11/15/2006)*

Eberle 2003 Mill Road Vineyard Viognier (Paso Robles) $18. 85 *—S.H. (12/15/2004)*

Eberle 2002 Mill Road Vineyard Viognier (Paso Robles) $18. 89 *—S.H. (12/1/2003)*

Eberle 2001 Mill Road Vineyard Viognier (Paso Robles) $18. 90 *—J.M. (12/15/2002)*

Eberle 2003 Zinfandel (Paso Robles) $16. 87 *—S.H. (11/15/2005)*

Eberle 2004 Remo Belli Vineyard Zinfandel (Paso Robles) $22. 87 *—S.H. (12/1/2006)*

Eberle 2003 Remo Belli Vineyard Zinfandel (Paso Robles) $22. 84 *—S.H. (11/15/2005)*

Eberle 2002 Remo Belli Vineyard Zinfandel (Paso Robles) $18. 88 *—J.M. (12/31/2004)*

Eberle 2001 Remo Belli Vineyard Zinfandel (Paso Robles) $18. 88 *(11/1/2003)*

Eberle 1997 Sauret Vineyard Zinfandel (Paso Robles) $20. 91 *—J.C. (9/1/1999)*

Eberle 2004 Steinbeck Vineyard Zinfandel (Paso Robles) $18. 85 *—S.H. (11/15/2006)*

Eberle 2002 Steinbeck Vineyard Zinfandel (Paso Robles) $16. 90 *—S.H. (12/15/2004)*

Eberle 1997 Steinbeck Vineyard Zinfandel (Paso Robles) $16. 87 *—J.C. (9/1/1999)*

ECHELON

Echelon 2003 Cabernet Sauvignon (Hames Valley) $13. 84 *—S.H. (5/1/2006)*

Echelon 2002 Cabernet Sauvignon (Hames Valley) $12. 84 *—S.H. (8/1/2005)*

Echelon 2001 Cabernet Sauvignon (California) $12. 84 *—S.H. (11/15/2003)*

Echelon 2000 Cabernet Sauvignon (California) $13. 83 *—J.M. (12/31/2002)*

Echelon 1998 Chardonnay (Central Coast) $15. 85 *(6/1/2000)*

Echelon 2003 Chardonnay (Central Coast) $12. 81 *—S.H. (12/1/2005)*

Echelon 2002 Chardonnay (Central Coast) $10. 86 *—S.H. (5/1/2004)*

Echelon 1997 Merlot (Central Coast) $15. 84 *—S.H. (7/1/2000)*

Echelon 2002 Merlot (Central Coast) $12. 84 *—S.H. (8/1/2005)*

Echelon 2001 Merlot (Central Coast) $12. 84 *—S.H. (2/1/2004)*

Echelon 1999 Merlot (California) $13. 85 *—S.H. (5/1/2001)*

Echelon 2001 Pinot Grigio (Central Coast) $11. 84 *—J.M. (9/1/2003)*

Echelon 2004 Esperanza Vineyard Pinot Grigio (Clarksburg) $10. 83 *—S.H. (2/1/2006)*

Echelon 2003 Esperanza Vineyard Pinot Grigio (Clarksburg) $11. 84 *—S.H. (9/1/2004)*

Echelon 2004 Pinot Noir (Central Coast) $13. 85 *—S.H. (5/1/2006)*

Echelon 2003 Pinot Noir (Central Coast) $10. 86 Best Buy *—R.V. (11/15/2004)*

Echelon 2002 Pinot Noir (Central Coast) $10. 85 Best Buy *—S.H. (5/1/2004)*

Echelon 2001 Pinot Noir (Central Coast) $12. 84 *—M.S. (12/1/2003)*

Echelon 2000 Pinot Noir (Central Coast) $14. 87 *—J.M. (5/1/2002)*

Echelon 1997 Pinot Noir (Central Coast) $NA. 83 *— (10/1/1999)*

Echelon 2003 Shiraz (Central Coast) $12. 84 *—S.H. (5/1/2006)*

Echelon 1999 Syrah (California) $14. 86 *(10/1/2001)*

Echelon 2002 Esperanza Vineyard Syrah (Clarksburg) $10. 85 Best Buy *— S.H. (4/1/2005)*

Echelon 2001 Esperanza Vineyard Syrah (Clarksburg) $10. 85 *—S.H. (2/1/2004)*

Echelon 2000 Esperanza Vineyard Syrah (Clarksburg) $10. 84 Best Buy *— J.M. (11/15/2002)*

Echelon 2001 Esperanza Vineyard Viognier (Clarksburg) $13. 85 *—J.M. (9/1/2003)*

Echelon 2003 Driving Range Vineyard Zinfandel (Contra Costa County) $13. 82 *—S.H. (8/1/2005)*

ECKERT

Eckert 2000 Eckert Acres Cabernet Sauvignon (Livermore Valley) $18. 85 *—S.H. (11/15/2003)*

Eckert 2000 Petite Sirah (Lodi) $18. 83 *—S.H. (3/1/2004)*

EDEN CANYON

Eden Canyon 2002 Cabernet Sauvignon (Paso Robles) $25. 87 *—S.H. (12/31/2006)*

Eden Canyon 2003 Estate Cabernet Sauvignon (Paso Robles) $30. 88 *— S.H. (12/31/2006)*

EDEN CREST

Eden Crest 2004 Cabernet Sauvignon (Red Hills Lake County) $20. This 2,200-foot high appellation has a real future for red wines, but it's subject to true vintage variation. There are a lot of distinguishing features here, from the blackberry-cherry fruit to the smooth, complex tannins, but the wine is too ripe in this ultrahot year. Drink now. **85** *—S.H. (7/1/2007)*

EDGEFIELD

Edgefield 2002 Chukar Ridge Vineyard Syrah (Columbia Valley (WA)) $22. 86 *(9/1/2005)*

Edgefield 1998 Chukar Ridge Vineyard Syrah (Columbia Valley (WA)) $11. 88 Best Buy *(10/1/2001)*

EDGEWOOD

Edgewood 2000 Tradition Bordeaux Blend (Napa Valley) $35. 88 *—S.H. (5/1/2004)*

Edgewood 1995 Tradition Bordeaux Blend (Napa Valley) $30. 88 *(3/1/2000)*

Edgewood 2001 Cabernet Sauvignon (Napa Valley) $26. 88 *—S.H. (11/15/2004)*

Edgewood 2000 Cabernet Sauvignon (Napa Valley) $24. 88 *—S.H. (2/1/2004)*

Edgewood 2000 Estate Vineyard Cabernet Sauvignon (Napa Valley) $35. 90 *—S.H. (12/31/2003)*

Edgewood 2000 Frediani Vineyard Cabernet Sauvignon (Napa Valley) $40. 90 *—S.H. (2/1/2004)*

Edgewood 2000 Lewelling Vineyard Cabernet Sauvignon (Napa Valley) $35. 88 *—S.H. (12/31/2003)*

Edgewood 2000 Reserve Cabernet Sauvignon (Napa Valley) $50. 91 *—S.H. (5/1/2004)*

Edgewood 1999 Reserve Cabernet Sauvignon (Napa Valley) $50. 89 *—S.H. (2/1/2004)*

Edgewood 2002 Chardonnay (Napa-Sonoma) $20. 89 *—S.H. (2/1/2004)*

Edgewood 2000 Chardonnay (Napa Valley) $24. 88 *—J.M. (5/1/2002)*

Edgewood 2001 Malbec (Napa Valley) $20. 86 *—S.H. (9/1/2004)*

Edgewood 2000 Malbec (Napa Valley) $20. 87 *—S.H. (3/1/2004)*

Edgewood 2000 Emmolo Vineyard Malbec (Napa Valley) $40. 91 *—S.H. (3/1/2004)*

Edgewood 2000 Reserve Malbec (Napa Valley) $50. 88 *—S.H. (5/1/2004)*

Edgewood 1999 Reserve Malbec (Napa Valley) $50. 86 *—S.H. (3/1/2004)*

Edgewood 1998 Reserve Malbec (Napa Valley) $65. 93 Editors' Choice *— S.H. (12/1/2002)*

Edgewood 1996 Merlot (Napa Valley) $20. 88 *—M.S. (3/1/2000)*

Edgewood 2001 Merlot (Napa Valley) $26. 91 *—S.H. (9/1/2004)*

Edgewood 2000 Merlot (Napa Valley) $24. 91 *(2/1/2004)*

Edgewood 1999 Merlot (Napa Valley) $24. 86 *—S.H. (12/15/2003)*

Edgewood 2000 Nepenthes Vineyard Merlot (Napa Valley) $40. 93 *—S.H. (2/1/2004)*

Edgewood 2001 Pinot Noir (Carneros) $24. 80 *—S.H. (7/1/2003)*

Edgewood 1999 Tradition Red Blend (Napa Valley) $35. 92 *—S.H. (12/31/2003)*

Edgewood 2003 Sauvignon Blanc (Napa Valley) $15. 89 *—S.H. (12/1/2004)*

Edgewood 2002 Sauvignon Blanc (Napa Valley) $15. 86 *—S.H. (12/15/2003)*

Edgewood 2001 Sauvignon Blanc (Napa Valley) $20. 89 *—S.H. (9/1/2003)*

Edgewood 2000 Sauvignon Blanc (Napa Valley) $20. 81 *(8/1/2002)*

Edgewood 2001 Syrah (Napa Valley) $20. 84 *—S.H. (12/15/2003)*

Edgewood 1996 Zinfandel (Napa Valley) $14. 87 Best Buy *—J.C. (5/1/2000)*

Edgewood 2001 Zinfandel (Napa Valley) $20. 89 *—S.H. (5/1/2004)*

Edgewood 2000 Zinfandel (Napa Valley) $20. 82 *—S.H. (9/1/2003)*

Edgewood 2001 Butala Vineyard Zinfandel (Napa Valley) $35. 91 *—S.H. (5/1/2004)*

EDIZIONE PENNINO

Edizione Pennino 2003 Zinfandel (Rutherford) $38. 87 *—S.H. (6/1/2006)*

EDMEADES

Edmeades 2000 Chardonnay (Anderson Valley) $18. 91 *—S.H. (5/1/2002)*

Edmeades 1999 Eaglepoint Ranch Petite Sirah (Mendocino) $25. 90 *— S.H. (5/1/2002)*

Edmeades 1996 Eaglepoint Vineyard Petite Sirah (Mendocino) $20. 89 *— S.H. (5/1/2000)*

Edmeades 1997 Pinot Noir (Anderson Valley) $20. 89 *—J.C. (5/1/2000)*

Edmeades 2000 Pinot Noir (Anderson Valley) $20. 87 *—S.H. (3/1/2004)*

Edmeades 1999 Pinot Noir (Anderson Valley) $20. 90 *—S.H. (5/1/2002)*

Edmeades 1998 Pinot Noir (Anderson Valley) $16. 83 *—S.H. (2/1/2001)*

Edmeades 2003 Zinfandel (Mendocino) $19. 88 *—S.H. (8/1/2005)*

Edmeades 2001 Zinfandel (Mendocino) $19. 87 *—S.H. (11/15/2004)*

Edmeades 2000 Zinfandel (Mendocino) $19. 86 *—S.H. (3/1/2004)*

Edmeades 1999 Zinfandel (Mendocino Ridge) $25. 90 *—S.H. (11/1/2002)*

Edmeades 1998 Zinfandel (Mendocino Ridge) $25. 90 *—P.G. (3/1/2001)*

Edmeades 1996 Zinfandel (Mendocino) $18. 85 *—S.H. (5/1/2000)*

Edmeades 1999 Alden Ranch Zinfandel (Mendocino Ridge) $25. 85 *—S.H. (5/1/2002)*

Edmeades 2003 Alden Vineyard Late Harvest Zinfandel (Mendocino Ridge) $12. The winemaker chose to allow the wine to get to 16.1% alcohol instead of keeping lots of sugar. The result is an interesting, very good wine, although it's tough to figure out when to drink it, and with what. Dry to off-dry, it has raspberry, cherry, cola and spice flavors, and is very balanced. **87** *—S.H. (7/1/2007)*

Edmeades 2002 Alden Vineyard Late Harvest Zinfandel (Mendocino) $16. 85 *—S.H. (11/15/2004)*

Edmeades 2000 Alden Vineyard-Late Harvest Zinfandel (Mendocino Ridge) $25. 84 *—S.H. (5/1/2002)*

Edmeades 2005 Chase Vineyard Zinfandel (Redwood Valley) $30. Edmeades' longtime winemaker is Van Williamson, nicknamed "Vanimal," and he makes big, bold reds. This may be his highest-alcohol ever. At 17%, it's dry and velvety, with fresh, fruity flavors of blackberries, cherries and vanilla-chocolate. There's no denying its deliciousness, but you'll have to decide if this heady, only-in-California wine suits you. **88** *—S.H. (12/15/2007)*

Edmeades 2004 Ciapusci Vineyard Zinfandel (Mendocino Ridge) $25. A briary, brambly texture and wild berry and spice flavors. Veering on the edge of raisiny overripeness, the wine, which is fairly oaky for a Zin, stays just this side of balanced. Drink now. **87** *—S.H. (7/1/2007)*

Edmeades 2002 Ciapusci Vineyard Zinfandel (Mendocino Ridge) $29. 86 *—S.H. (11/15/2004)*

Edmeades 2001 Ciapusci Vineyard Zinfandel (Mendocino Ridge) $25. 84 *(11/1/2003)*

Edmeades 1999 Ciapusci Vineyard Zinfandel (Mendocino Ridge) $25. 92 *—S.H. (11/1/2002)*

Edmeades 1998 Ciapusci Vineyard Zinfandel (Mendocino Ridge) $25. 92 *—P.G. (3/1/2001)*

Edmeades 1997 Ciapusci Vineyard Zinfandel (Mendocino Ridge) $36. 88 *—S.H. (5/1/2000)*

Edmeades 1999 Eaglepoint Ranch Zinfandel (Mendocino) $25. 86 *—S.H. (11/1/2002)*

Edmeades 1998 Eaglepoint Ranch Zinfandel (Mendocino) $24. 92 *—P.G. (3/1/2001)*

Edmeades 2004 Perli Vineyard Zinfandel (Mendocino Ridge) $25. Edmeades, a true Mendocino pioneer, has crafted an enormously likeable Zin, deeply flavored in black currant, cherry and black raspberry-pie filling and chocolaty, spicy deliciousness. But for all its size and high alcohol, the wine retains a silky, elegant mouthfeel. **90 Editors' Choice** *—S.H. (7/1/2007)*

Edmeades 2004 Piffero Vineyard Zinfandel (Mendocino) $25. From the interior Redwood Valley appellation comes this slightly stewed Zin, with flavors of cherry and raspberry-pie filling. It's totally dry, and the high alcohol is a fundamental part of the Zin experience. **86** *—S.H. (7/1/2007)*

Edmeades 2002 Piffero Vineyard Zinfandel (Mendocino) $29. 85 *—S.H. (11/15/2004)*

Edmeades 2001 Piffero Vineyard Zinfandel (Mendocino) $25. 84 *(11/1/2003)*

Edmeades 1998 Zeni Zinfandel (Mendocino Ridge) $30. 86 *—P.G. (3/1/2001)*

Edmeades 2002 Zeni Vineyard Zinfandel (Mendocino Ridge) $29. 86 *—S.H. (11/15/2004)*

Edmeades 2001 Zeni Vineyard Zinfandel (Mendocino Ridge) $25. 86 *(11/1/2003)*

Edmeades 1999 Zeni Vineyard Zinfandel (Mendocino Ridge) $25. 93 Editors' Choice *—S.H. (11/1/2002)*

Edmeades 1996 Zeni Vineyard Zinfandel (Mendocino) $25. 92 *—S.H. (9/1/1999)*

EDMUNDS ST JOHN

Edmunds St John 2000 Los Robles Viejos Rozet Red Blend (Paso Robles) $28. 87 *—S.H. (11/15/2002)*

Edmunds St John 1997 Rocks and Gravel Red Blend (California) $18. 90 *—S.H. (6/1/1999)*

Edmunds St John 1996 Durell Vineyard Syrah (Sonoma Valley) $25. 91 *—S.H. (6/1/1999)*

Edmunds St John 1997 Fenaughty Vineyard Syrah (El Dorado County) $30. 93 *—S.H. (6/1/1999)*

Edmunds St John 1999 Wylie-Fenaughty Syrah (El Dorado) $32. 84 *(11/1/2001)*

Edmunds St John 1997 Alban-Durell Vineyards Viognier (California) $20. 87 *—S.H. (6/1/1999)*

Edmunds St John 1998 Alban/Durell Vineyards Viognier (California) $20. 93 *—S.H. (10/1/1999)*

Edmunds St John 2000 Los Robles Viejos Rozet White Blend (Paso Robles) $24. 87 *—S.H. (12/15/2002)*

EDNA VALLEY VINEYARD

Edna Valley Vineyard 2005 Paragon Chardonnay (Edna Valley) $12. Pretty good price for a Chardonnay of this cool-climate quality. Boosted by crisp acids, it shows pineapple, lime and kiwi flavors, and finishes dry and savory. Easy to find, with nearly a quarter-million cases produced. **84** *—S.H. (5/1/2007)*

Edna Valley Vineyard 2004 Paragon Chardonnay (Edna Valley) $15. 85 *—S.H. (12/1/2005)*

Edna Valley Vineyard 2003 Paragon Chardonnay (Edna Valley) $14. 85 *—S.H. (4/1/2005)*

Edna Valley Vineyard 2002 Paragon Chardonnay (Edna Valley) $14. 89 Best Buy *—S.H. (6/1/2004)*

Edna Valley Vineyard 2001 Paragon Chardonnay (Edna Valley) $13. 85 *—S.H. (12/15/2003)*

Edna Valley Vineyard 2000 Paragon Chardonnay (Edna Valley) $17. 86 *—S.H. (6/1/2003)*

Edna Valley Vineyard 1998 Paragon Chardonnay (Edna Valley) $19. 90 *(12/31/1999)*

Edna Valley Vineyard 1997 Paragon Vineyard Chardonnay (Edna Valley) $17. 92 *—L.W. (7/1/1999)*

Edna Valley Vineyard 2004 Paragon Reserve Chardonnay (Edna Valley) $30. Rewards for its rich, spicy oak, flamboyant flavors, and the crisp, juicy acidity that characterizes this cool coastal appellation. Pineapples, guavas, kiwis, limes and ripe peaches flood the mouth, leading to a dry, clean finish. **87** *—S.H. (8/1/2007)*

Edna Valley Vineyard 2004 Merlot (San Luis Obispo County) $15. 86 *—S.H. (12/15/2006)*

Edna Valley Vineyard 2004 Paragon Pinot Gris (Edna Valley) $18. 88 *—S.H. (2/1/2006)*

Edna Valley Vineyard 2003 Paragon Pinot Gris (Edna Valley) $18. 89 *—S.H. (10/1/2004)*

Edna Valley Vineyard 2005 Paragon Pinot Noir (Edna Valley) $15. If you're looking for an everyday, affordable wine with real Pinot character, try this. It shows the silky texture, dryness and polished cherry, root beer, spice and oaky flavors that characterize the variety, but is not a simple wine, offering layers of complexity and satisfaction. **87** *—S.H. (5/1/2007)*

Edna Valley Vineyard 2004 Paragon Pinot Noir (Edna Valley) $20. 90 Editors' Choice *—S.H. (10/1/2006)*

Edna Valley Vineyard 2003 Paragon Pinot Noir (Edna Valley) $20. 87 *—S.H. (10/1/2005)*

Edna Valley Vineyard 2002 Paragon Pinot Noir (Edna Valley) $15. 87 *—S.H. (6/1/2004)*

Edna Valley Vineyard 2000 Paragon Pinot Noir (Edna Valley) $23. 89 *—J.M. (5/1/2002)*

Edna Valley Vineyard 1998 Paragon Pinot Noir (Edna Valley) $19. 86 *—S.H. (10/1/2000)*

Edna Valley Vineyard 1997 Paragon Pinot Noir (Central Coast) $20. 86 *(11/15/1999)*

Edna Valley Vineyard 2005 Paragon Sauvignon Blanc (Edna Valley) $15. Like your whites superdry, crisp and grassy? This one's for you. From the cool Edna Valley comes this sleek wine, with lemongrass, passionfruit and lime flavors, and just a touch of that notorious cat pee. Turns rich and spicy on the finish. **85** *—S.H. (5/1/2007)*

Edna Valley Vineyard 2004 Paragon Sauvignon Blanc (Edna Valley) $14. 89 *—S.H. (3/1/2006)*

Edna Valley Vineyard 2003 Paragon Sauvignon Blanc (Edna Valley) $14. 90 Best Buy *—S.H. (2/1/2005)*

Edna Valley Vineyard 2002 Paragon Sauvignon Blanc (Edna Valley) $14. 89 *—J.M. (9/1/2004)*

Edna Valley Vineyard 2003 Paragon Syrah (Central Coast) $14. 82 *(9/1/2005)*

Edna Valley Vineyard 2001 Paragon Syrah (Central Coast) $14. 84 *—S.H. (6/1/2004)*

Edna Valley Vineyard 1999 Paragon Syrah (Central Coast) $17. 88 Editors' Choice *(10/1/2001)*

Edna Valley Vineyard 1998 Fralich Vineyard Viognier (Paso Robles) $18. 88 *—S.H. (10/1/1999)*

EDWARDS SELLERS

Edward Sellers 2004 Cognito Red Blend (Paso Robles) $26. Here's a blend of traditional red Rhône varieties with Zinfandel. It's a great concept, but the problem is that the wine is too sweet, and tastes artificially acidified. **83** *—S.H. (5/1/2007)*

Edward Sellers 2004 Cuvee des Cinq Rhône Red Blend (Paso Robles) $42. This is a Châteauneuf-style blend of Rhône varieties, a soft, simple and slightly sweet red. It brims with ripe black cherry, raspberry, mocha-choca, cola, rum punch and licorice flavors. **84** *—S.H. (5/1/2007)*

Edward Sellers 2005 Blanc du Rhone Rhône White Blend (Paso Robles) $32. Tastes like there's quite a bit of unresolved sugar in this blend of Roussanne, Marsanne and Viognier, even if there officially isn't. To this palate, that's a major flaw in a table wine that's supposed to be dry. **82** *—S.H. (5/1/2007)*

Edward Sellers 2005 Roussanne (Paso Robles) $26. A bit cloying for me, although lovers of semisweet wines will like it for its jellied apricot, peach and honeysuckle flavors. Fortunately, there's good acidity. **83** *—S.H. (5/1/2007)*

Edward Sellers 2004 Syrah (Paso Robles) $30. The high alcohol gives this wine heat, a chili pepper kind of burn that isn't exactly unpleasant. It seasons the rich blackberry and black cherry flavors, and causes the tastebuds to crave the alleviating effects of food. Grilled lamb would be perfect.

Finishes sweet, which for me reduces the score a point. **86** *—S.H. (5/1/2007)*

EGRET

Egret 2005 Chardonnay (Carneros) $15. This is a pretty good price for a nice, clean Chardonnay from Carneros. The wine is dry and crisp, with green apple, peach and pineapple flavors, as well as the buttered toast from aging in oak barrels. **86** *—S.H. (5/1/2007)*

EHLERS ESTATE

Ehlers Estate 2003 Cabernet Franc (Napa Valley) $33. 91 *—S.H. (8/1/2006)*

Ehlers Estate 2003 Cabernet Sauvignon (Napa Valley) $33. 90 *—S.H. (12/1/2006)*

Ehlers Estate 2001 Cabernet Sauvignon (Napa Valley) $28. 85 *—S.H. (10/1/2004)*

Ehlers Estate 2000 Cabernet Sauvignon (Napa Valley) $28. 87 *—J.M. (4/1/2004)*

Ehlers Estate 2003 1886 Estate Cabernet Sauvignon (St. Helena) $75. 94 Editors' Choice *—S.H. (8/1/2006)*

Ehlers Estate 2003 Merlot (Napa Valley) $30. 89 *—S.H. (8/1/2006)*

Ehlers Estate 2001 Merlot (Napa Valley) $25. 85 *—S.H. (10/1/2004)*

Ehlers Estate 2005 Sauvignon Blanc (Napa Valley) $20. 89 *—S.H. (12/1/2006)*

EHLERS GROVE

Ehlers Grove 1998 Chardonnay (Carneros) $30. 88 *(6/1/2000)*

Ehlers Grove 1998 Dutton Ranch Chardonnay (Russian River Valley) $25. 88 *(6/1/2000)*

EL ALACRAN

El Alacran 2002 Mourvèdre (Amador County) $34. 83 *—S.H. (4/1/2005)*

EL MIRADOR

El Mirador 2000 Merlot (Walla Walla (WA)) $20. 86 *—P.G. (9/1/2004)*

EL MOLINO

El Molino 2005 Chardonnay (Rutherford) $45. They didn't let any malolactic fermentation into this wine, a wise decision because you wouldn't want it to be any softer. Still, there's a prettiness to the ripe green apple, honey and toast flavors, which are complexed with layers of tropical fruits, spices and lees. **90** *—S.H. (9/1/2007)*

El Molino 2004 Chardonnay (Rutherford) $42. 92 *—S.H. (6/1/2006)*

El Molino 2003 Chardonnay (Rutherford) $40. 89 *—S.H. (12/15/2005)*

El Molino 2002 Chardonnay (Rutherford) $40. 87 *—S.H. (4/1/2005)*

El Molino 1999 Chardonnay (Rutherford) $40. 90 *(7/1/2001)*

El Molino 2004 Pinot Noir (Rutherford) $55. This is soft, dry and a little heavy. They must have kept yields really low, because the cherry and raspberry fruit is really concentrated and liqueur-like. Plenty of toasty new oak adds to the impression of opulence. **87** *—S.H. (9/1/2007)*

El Molino 2003 Pinot Noir (Rutherford) $52. 84 *—S.H. (5/1/2006)*

El Molino 2002 Pinot Noir (Rutherford) $52. 83 *—S.H. (2/1/2006)*

El Molino 2001 Pinot Noir (Napa Valley) $51. 87 *—S.H. (4/1/2005)*

El Molino 1999 Pinot Noir (Napa Valley) $51. 87 *(10/1/2002)*

ELAINE MARIA

Elaine Maria 2002 Merlot (Alexander Valley) $19. 85 *—S.H. (5/1/2005)*

Elaine Maria 2002 Reserve Merlot (Alexander Valley) $28. 88 *—S.H. (5/1/2005)*

Elaine Maria 2003 Sauvignon Blanc (Alexander Valley) $16. 87 *—S.H. (5/1/2005)*

ELAN

Elan 1997 Cabernet Sauvignon (Atlas Peak) $45. 88 *(11/1/2000)*

Elan 2002 Cabernet Sauvignon (Atlas Peak) $47. 92 *—S.H. (3/1/2006)*

Elan 2001 Cabernet Sauvignon (Atlas Peak) $45. 83 *—S.H. (12/31/2004)*

Elan 2000 Cabernet Sauvignon (Atlas Peak) $42. 88 *—S.H. (11/15/2004)*

Elan 1999 Cabernet Sauvignon (Atlas Peak) $45. 91 *—S.H. (11/15/2002)*

ELARA

Elara 2000 Tollini Vineyard Petite Sirah (Mendocino County) $27. 89 *—S.H. (12/31/2003)*

Elara 2000 Sherwin Vineyard Sangiovese (Mendocino County) $24. 84 *—S.H. (9/1/2003)*

Elara 2000 Syrah (McDowell Valley) $32. 87 *—S.H. (12/15/2003)*

ELEMENTAL CELLARS

Elemental Cellars 2004 Croft Vineyard Pinot Gris (Willamette Valley) $15. 91 *—P.G. (2/1/2006)*

ELEVEN

eleven 2003 Cowan Vineyard Cabernet Sauvignon (Yakima Valley) $21. 87 *—P.G. (10/1/2006)*

ELIAS

Elias 2000 Pinot Noir (Russian River Valley) $40. 89 *—S.H. (5/1/2002)*

ELIZABETH

Elizabeth 1998 Sauvignon Blanc (Redwood Valley) $14. 87 *—S.H. (5/1/2000)*

Elizabeth 1998 Zinfandel (Redwood Valley) $18. 85 *—S.H. (5/1/2000)*

Elizabeth 1997 Zinfandel (Redwood Valley) $18. 81 *P.G. (11/15/1999)*

ELK COVE

Elk Cove 2005 Pinot Blanc (Willamette Valley) $18. 89 *—P.G. (9/1/2006)*

Elk Cove 2004 Pinot Blanc (Willamette Valley) $17. 89 *—P.G. (8/1/2005)*

Elk Cove 2006 Pinot Gris (Willamette Valley) $19. This is an elegant, refreshing style scented with a lush nose that cleverly blends cut fruit, blossom, citrus and a hint of mineral. The mixed fruit flavors continue on the palate—pear, melon, peach and spice, perfectly balanced and ripe. **91 Editors' Choice** *—P.G. (11/15/2007)*

Elk Cove 2005 Pinot Gris (Willamette Valley) $18. 91 Editors' Choice *—P.G. (9/1/2006)*

Elk Cove 2004 Pinot Gris (Willamette Valley) $17. 86 *—P.G. (8/1/2005)*

Elk Cove 2002 Pinot Gris (Willamette Valley) $15. 91 Best Buy *—P.G. (12/1/2003)*

Elk Cove 2001 Pinot Gris (Willamette Valley) $15. 91 Editors' Choice *—P.G. (8/1/2003)*

Elk Cove 2000 Pinot Gris (Willamette Valley) $15. 86 *—P.G. (2/1/2002)*

Elk Cove 1998 Pinot Gris (Willamette Valley) $15. 88 Editors' Choice *(8/1/1999)*

Elk Cove 2005 Pinot Noir (Willamette Valley) $26. Good winemaking is evident here. This is clean and fresh, with light, appealing flavors of berry, cola and chocolate-covered espresso bean. The wine has a smooth, silky texture, and feels substantial without being fat or hot. It is certainly age-worthy and it wouldn't surprise me if it lasted a decade or more. But tough to keep your hands off it right now. **90** *—P.G. (4/1/2007)*

Elk Cove 2004 Pinot Noir (Willamette Valley) $25. 89 *—P.G. (9/1/2006)*

Elk Cove 2003 Pinot Noir (Willamette Valley) $24. 88 *—P.G. (8/1/2005)*

Elk Cove 2002 Pinot Noir (Willamette Valley) $24. 86 *(11/1/2004)*

Elk Cove 2001 Pinot Noir (Willamette Valley) $20. 89 *—M.S. (9/1/2003)*

Elk Cove 2000 Pinot Noir (Willamette Valley) $20. 89 *—P.G. (4/1/2003)*

Elk Cove 1999 Pinot Noir (Willamette Valley) $18. 85 *—P.G. (4/1/2002)*

Elk Cove 1998 Pinot Noir (Willamette Valley) $18. 90 Best Buy *—M.S. (12/1/2000)*

Elk Cove 2005 La Bohème Pinot Noir (Willamette Valley) $38. Elk Cove has kept a lid on the prices of its best Pinots, despite the inflation that has crept in elsewhere and without a surcharge for old vine fruit and superior winemaking. La Bohème wines always seem to be buttoned up upon release, but reward cellaring and demand attention. I find a little bit of leathery funk in this new release, but along with that is finely sculpted, tart and tangy red fruit, and a wine that is proportionate and detailed. **89** *—P.G. (11/15/2007)*

Elk Cove 2002 La Bohéme Pinot Noir (Willamette Valley) $36. 86 *(11/1/2004)*

Elk Cove 2001 La Bohéme Pinot Noir (Willamette Valley) $32. 90 *—P.G. (12/1/2003)*

Elk Cove 2000 La Bohéme Pinot Noir (Oregon) $34. 88 *—P.G. (4/1/2003)*

Elk Cove 1998 La Bohéme Pinot Noir (Willamette Valley) $28. 89 *—M.S. (12/1/2000)*

Elk Cove 2005 Mount Richmond Pinot Noir (Willamette Valley) $38. Cuttings from the winery's Roosevelt vineyard were used to plant the Mount Richmond site in 1996. This is a tight, crisp, elegant wine. Aromas suggest coffee grounds, and the fruit is tart and compact—rhubarb and strawberry. But the wine has what the Brits call breed—a somewhat indefinable quality of finesse and elegance, and for a cooler site it has ripened sufficiently to warrant an excellent score. **90** *—P.G. (4/1/2007)*

Elk Cove 2004 Mount Richmond Pinot Noir (Willamette Valley) $36. 88 *—P.G. (9/1/2006)*

Elk Cove 2003 Mount Richmond Pinot Noir (Willamette Valley) $36. 89 —*P.G. (8/1/2005)*

Elk Cove 2002 Reserve Pinot Noir (Willamette Valley) $60. 90 *(11/1/2004)*

Elk Cove 2004 Roosevelt Pinot Noir (Willamette Valley) $52. Elk Cove's cool-climate Pinots require some study, and time to relax, and reward the patient taster. The tart fruit found here is lightly nuanced with barnyard funk, but is never overpowering. It works in a French manner, adding aromatic interest, while the textural, tannic body of the wine takes its time to open. This is supple and muscular, and will certainly reward some further years in bottle. **90** —*P.G. (7/1/2007)*

Elk Cove 2002 Roosevelt Pinot Noir (Willamette Valley) $48. 88 *(11/1/2004)*

Elk Cove 2001 Roosevelt Pinot Noir (Willamette Valley) $32. 90 —*P.G. (12/1/2003)*

Elk Cove 2000 Roosevelt Pinot Noir (Oregon) $48. 90 —*P.G. (4/1/2003)*

Elk Cove 1999 Roosevelt Pinot Noir (Oregon) $48. 89 —*P.G. (4/1/2002)*

Elk Cove 1998 Roosevelt Pinot Noir (Willamette Valley) $48. 89 —*J.C. (12/1/2000)*

Elk Cove 2003 Shea Pinot Noir (Willamette Valley) $36. 88 —*P.G. (8/1/2005)*

Elk Cove 2005 Windhill Pinot Noir (Willamette Valley) $38. Pinot from this 30-year-old vineyard is spicy and fragrant, with overtones of pine needle and camphor. It's very distinctive, elegant and stylish. It does not try to be either California Pinot or Burgundy; it is in some sense uniquely Oregonian. Aromas and fruit flavors are nicely threaded together, cherry and cranberry, pine and tomato leaf. **89** —*P.G. (11/15/2007)*

Elk Cove 2004 Windhill Pinot Noir (Willamette Valley) $38. 88 —*P.G. (9/1/2006)*

Elk Cove 2003 Windhill Pinot Noir (Willamette Valley) $36. 90 —*P.G. (8/1/2005)*

Elk Cove 2002 Windhill Pinot Noir (Willamette Valley) $30. 88 —*P.G. (2/1/2005)*

Elk Cove 2001 Windhill Pinot Noir (Willamette Valley) $32. 91 —*M.S. (9/1/2003)*

Elk Cove 2000 Windhill Pinot Noir (Oregon) $34. 89 —*P.G. (4/1/2003)*

Elk Cove 1998 Windhill Pinot Noir (Willamette Valley) $28. 88 —*M.S. (12/1/2000)*

Elk Cove 1997 Windhill Pinot Noir (Willamette Valley) $28. 86 *(11/15/1999)*

Elk Cove 2004 Riesling (Willamette Valley) $17. 90 —*P.G. (8/1/2005)*

Elk Cove 2001 Riesling (Willamette Valley) $12. 86 —*J.C. (8/1/2003)*

Elk Cove 2006 Estate Riesling (Willamette Valley) $19. A fine effort from Elk Cove, this authoritative, bone-dry Riesling is laced with lovely streaks of licorice, and built upon sturdy acids and crisp green apple fruit. The wine is impeccably balanced, so that the flavors do not tire the palate or feel one-dimensional. It picks up interesting grace notes of citrus oil, tea and grapefruit as it winds through a long finish. **91** —*P.G. (11/15/2007)*

Elk Cove 2000 Estate Riesling (Willamette Valley) $18. 84 —*J.C. (8/1/2003)*

Elk Cove 1999 Brut Sparkling Blend (Oregon) $22. 89 —*M.S. (6/1/2003)*

Elk Cove 2001 Del Rio Vineyard Syrah (Rogue Valley) $28. 87 —*P.G. (12/1/2003)*

Elk Cove 2001 Del Rio Viognier (Rogue Valley) $22. 88 —*M.S. (8/1/2003)*

ELKE

Elke 2000 Donnelly Creek Vineyard Pinot Noir (Anderson Valley) $24. 80 *(10/1/2002)*

Elke 1997 Donnelly Creek Vineyard Pinot Noir (Anderson Valley) $24. 89 *(10/1/2000)*

Elke 1999 Donnelly Vineyards Pinot Noir (Anderson Valley) $24. 87 —*S.H. (5/1/2002)*

ELKHORN PEAK

Elkhorn Peak 2000 Fagan Creek Merlot (Napa Valley) $18. 85 —*S.H. (11/15/2004)*

Elkhorn Peak 2002 Fagan Creek Vineyard Pinot Noir (Napa Valley) $30. 83 —*S.H. (10/1/2005)*

Elkhorn Peak 1999 Fagan Creek Vineyard Pinot Noir (Napa Valley) $30. 83 —*S.H. (8/1/2005)*

ELKHORN RIDGE

Elkhorn Ridge 2005 777 Pinot Noir (Willamette Valley) $30. The number refers to the particular clone of Pinot Noir. It's a tightly wound effort, showing wild berry and black cherry fruit, annotated with black licorice and herb. Straight-ahead, some muscular fruit, it finishes with a streak of vanilla. **87** —*P.G. (7/1/2007)*

Elkhorn Ridge 2005 Le Terre Foss Pinot Noir (Willamette Valley) $35. This is the winery's reserve, and it shows more tannin, earthy herb, grip and funk than the '777' bottling. It's a flavorful wine, pungently aromatic, and it begins with more complexity than it shows in the back half. It may well soften up and smooth out with another few years in the bottle; hard to tell at this point. **88** —*P.G. (7/1/2007)*

ELLISTON

Elliston 1998 Cabernet Sauvignon (Livermore Valley) $30. 84 —*S.H. (11/15/2003)*

Elliston 1997 Sunol Valley Vineyard Pinot Grigio (Central Coast) $10. 87 Best Buy *(8/1/1999)*

ELVENGLADE

ElvenGlade 2004 Pinot Gris (Yamhill County) $15. 91 Best Buy —*P.G. (2/1/2006)*

ELYSE

Elyse 2001 Morisoli Vineyard Cabernet Sauvignon (Rutherford) $65. 89 —*S.H. (10/1/2005)*

Elyse 1999 Morisoli Vineyard Cabernet Sauvignon (Napa Valley) $57. 89 —*J.M. (2/1/2003)*

Elyse 2004 Tietjen Vineyard Cabernet Sauvignon (Rutherford) $80. Ripe and expressive, with a gentle, velvety mouthfeel, this is marked by some firm, dry tannins that suggest moderate aging. There's some good spicy cherry and blackberry flavor, along with the sweet vanilla and cedar from considerable new oak. **89** —*S.H. (12/15/2007)*

Elyse 2003 Tietjen Vineyard Cabernet Sauvignon (Napa Valley) $65. 89 —*S.H. (12/15/2006)*

Elyse 2002 Tietjen Vineyard Cabernet Sauvignon (Rutherford) $65. 85 —*S.H. (12/15/2005)*

Elyse 2001 Tietjen Vineyard Cabernet Sauvignon (Napa Valley) $65. 86 —*S.H. (5/1/2005)*

Elyse 2000 Tietjen Vineyard Cabernet Sauvignon (Napa Valley) $57. 90 —*S.H. (2/1/2004)*

Elyse 2003 Petite Sirah (Rutherford) $36. 92 —*S.H. (10/1/2005)*

Elyse 2003 Nero Misto Red Blend (California) $26. 83 —*S.H. (10/1/2005)*

Elyse 2002 D'Adventure Rhône Red Blend (California) $25. 85 —*S.H. (5/1/2005)*

Elyse 2001 Syrah (Napa Valley) $32. 85 —*S.H. (5/1/2005)*

Elyse 1999 Syrah (Napa Valley) $35. 87 —*J.M. (2/1/2003)*

Elyse 2003 Korte Ranch Zinfandel (Napa Valley) $28. 84 —*S.H. (10/1/2005)*

Elyse 2002 Morisoli Vineyard Zinfandel (Napa Valley) $35. 85 —*S.H. (5/1/2005)*

Elyse 2000 Morisoli Vineyard Zinfandel (Napa Valley) $32. 88 —*J.M. (2/1/2003)*

EMERALD BAY

Emerald Bay 1997 Cabernet Sauvignon (California) $7. 83 *(2/1/2000)*

Emerald Bay 1997 Chardonnay (Central Coast) $7. 84 *(2/1/2000)*

Emerald Bay 1997 Merlot (California) $7. 85 Best Buy *(2/1/2000)*

EMERIL'S

Emeril's 2000 Classics Red Blend (California) $13. 86 —*S.H. (12/1/2002)*

EMERITUS

Emeritus 2005 Pinot Noir (Russian River Valley) $32. Really balanced and elegant, with such bracing acidity. Shows pure flavors of cherries and cassis, with earthy, forest floor notes and a touch of cherry tomato and beetroot. Only moderately oaked, just enough to add a smoky edge. Very young and minerally now, this should hold and improve for 5–8 years. **91** —*S.H. (10/1/2007)*

Emeritus 2005 William Wesley Pinot Noir (Sonoma Coast) $50. Tasted alongside its Russian River Valley sister bottling, released at the same time, this new wine from Sonoma-Cutrer founder Brice Jones shows far greater power. Just erupts with masses of sweet cherries and raspberries with a liqueur richness, and nuances of forest floor, pine needles and smoky oak. Really notable for balance. Citrusy acids and firm, sweet tannins give this Pinot, from way out on the Far Sonoma Coast, a brilliant structure. Beautiful now and for the next 10 years. **95** —*S.H. (10/1/2007)*

EMILIO'S TERRACE

Emilio's Terrace 2004 Cabernet Sauvignon (Oakville) $50. I really liked the past releases of this wine, but the '04 is not in the same league. It's a hot wine, with baked or stewed fruit flavors, and finishes with prickly, drily astringent tannins. Not going anywhere, so drink now. **83** *—S.H. (12/15/2007)*

Emilio's Terrace 1999 Estate Cabernet Sauvignon (Napa Valley) $45. 93 Editors' Choice *—J.M. (2/1/2003)*

Emilio's Terrace 2003 Reserve Cabernet Sauvignon (Oakville) $50. You want a dramatic young, ageworthy Cab? Here it is. Totally immature, because of the tight tannins. Completely dry. Lots of fresh sweet oak. Not drinkable at all now, but what a core of fruit. Huge blackberry, cherry and cassis flavors, just waiting to emerge, and they will. Hold until 2010, then drink for a decade. **92 Cellar Selection** *—S.H. (2/1/2007)*

Emilio's Terrace 2002 Reserve Cabernet Sauvignon (Oakville) $50. 91 Cellar Selection *—S.H. (8/1/2006)*

Emilio's Terrace 2001 Reserve Cabernet Sauvignon (Napa Valley) $50. 91 *—S.H. (5/1/2005)*

EMMOLO

Emmolo 2000 Rutherford Sauvignon Blanc (Napa Valley) $16. 85 *(8/1/2002)*

Emmolo 2006 South 40 Ranch Rosé Syrah (Napa Valley) $14. This is the palest rosé I've ever seen. It's straw colored, with just a hint of ochre. It also has strong tastes, but they're almost exactly like Sauvignon Blanc, with those infamous feline scents and gooseberry flavors. Did they bottle the wrong wine? **82** *—S.H. (7/1/2007)*

ENCORE

Encore 2004 San Bernabe Vineyard White Medley White Blend (Monterey County) $18. 84 *—S.H. (12/1/2005)*

Encore 2002 San Bernabe Vineyard White Medley White Blend (Monterey) $18. 87 *—S.H. (12/15/2004)*

ENGELMANN

Engelmann 2000 Cabernet Sauvignon-Shiraz (California) $16. 82 *—S.H. (12/1/2002)*

Engelmann 2000 Sangiovese (California) $12. 81 *—S.H. (12/1/2002)*

Engelmann 2000 Very Old Vine Zinfandel (California) $12. 82 *—S.H. (12/1/2002)*

ENJOIE

Enjoie 2005 Dry Rose Wine Rosé Blend (California) $13. 83 *—S.H. (12/1/2006)*

ENLACE

Enlace 2002 Cabernet Sauvignon (Napa Valley) $26. 90 *—S.H. (3/1/2006)*

Enlace 2002 Merlot (Napa Valley) $25. 89 *—S.H. (3/1/2006)*

Enlace 2004 Sauvignon Blanc (North Coast) $15. 90 Best Buy *—S.H. (4/1/2006)*

ENO

Eno 2005 Eaglepoint Ranch Grenache (Mendocino County) $25. Peppery and tannic, this Grenache hails from a vineyard that long has been the source of muscular reds. The taste is cherries, pure, intense and concentrated, along with the smoke and caramel of oak barrels. Could develop over the next 10 years. **88** *—S.H. (12/15/2007)*

Eno 2005 Fairview Road Ranch Pinot Noir (Santa Lucia Highlands) $38. Vibrant in candied cherry-raspberry and cola fruit, this Pinot is also very spicy. It finishes a little simple and sugary. Drink now. **84** *—S.H. (12/15/2007)*

Eno 2005 Las Madres Vineyard Syrah (Carneros) $35. Give this lush young wine a year or two to come around. That should give all the elements time to meld. It's a juicy, ripe wine, bursting with jammy cherry and cassis flavors, with a strong note of white pepper and clove that dissolves into a tannic finish. **88** *—S.H. (12/15/2007)*

Eno 2005 Teldeschi Vineyard Old Vine Zinfandel (Dry Creek Valley) $25. This wine might be the poster child for the raging debate over high alcohol. With 15.7%, it certainly qualifies in that category. But it's also quite good, and has its place. It is dry and exuberant, with cherry, plum, currant and spice flavors, and as heady as it is, it will be fantastic with barbecue. **88** *—S.H. (12/15/2007)*

ENOTRIA

Enotria 1999 Arneis (Mendocino) $14. 84 *—S.H. (8/1/2001)*

Enotria 1999 Arneis (Mendocino) $15. 85 *—S.H. (5/1/2002)*

Enotria 1999 Barbera (Mendocino) $13. 81 *—S.H. (5/1/2002)*

Enotria 1998 Riserva Barbera (Mendocino) $NA. 85 *—S.H. (12/1/2001)*

Enotria 1999 Dolcetto (Mendocino) $16. 84 *—S.H. (5/1/2002)*

Enotria 1998 Dolcetto (Mendocino) $16. 84 *—S.H. (8/1/2001)*

ENSEMBLE

Ensemble NV Release Number Two Red Blend (Washington) $48. This unusual project, a single Bordeaux blend from a mix of vintages, has put out its second wine. It is, as you would expect, rounder and more advanced than the usual new releases, with melded flavors and softened tannins. Yet it retains a fair amount of youthful spice and a sharp edge to the acids, lifting it and giving definition to the midpalate. **89** *—P.G. (11/1/2007)*

ENZO

Enzo 2003 Cabernet Sauvignon (Oakville) $70. At four-plus years, this Oakville Cab is still fairly tannic and hard, with a gritty astringency to the blackberry and oak flavors. A taste of raisins and bell peppers argues against ageability, but it could improve over the next year or so. **84** *—S.H. (12/15/2007)*

EOLA HILLS

Eola Hills 2005 Cabernet Sauvignon (Oregon) $12. Rough and chewy, to be sure, but it's got flavor in spades. Firm and tannic, this herbal take on Oregon Cabernet would match up quite nicely with skirt steak or anything off the grill. **86 Best Buy** *—P.G. (11/15/2007)*

Eola Hills 2004 Cabernet Sauvignon (Oregon) $10. Granted, Oregon is not the first place you look for when you want a decent $10 Cabernet, but here it is. Stiff and tannic—make that "Bordeaux-like"—the most appealing feature of this budget bottle is its sweet core of grapey cherry fruit. The candy quality is really quite pleasant, and has enough substance behind it to elevate it well above the Kool-Aid category. **87 Best Buy** *—P.G. (4/1/2007)*

Eola Hills 1998 LBV Port Style Cabernet Sauvignon (Oregon) $18. 86 *—J.M. (12/1/2002)*

Eola Hills 2005 Chardonnay (Oregon) $10. Another fruit-driven success for this winery's Chard program. This opens with generous plump and tangy pineapple, pink grapefruit and Meyer lemon, succulent and crisp. The fruit continues along without any off notes through a satisfying finish. Not sure if this is "unwooded" or not, but if so it can stand quite comfortably alongside most of its more expensive peers. **87 Best Buy** *—P.G. (4/1/2007)*

Eola Hills 2000 Chardonnay (Oregon) $10. 88 Best Buy *—P.G. (4/1/2002)*

Eola Hills $10 Chardonnay (Oregon) $10. This is graceful and surprisingly dense, with a mix of tropical fruit flavors and a midpalate thickness tasting a bit like ripe bananas. In this price range it's a pleasure to find a Chardonnay with some meat on its bones, and if there was some oak chip treatment (not sure that there was) it's been done with some restraint. **86 Best Buy** *—P.G. (11/15/2007)*

Eola Hills 2005 La Creole Reserve Chardonnay (Oregon) $15. The reserve Chardonnay from Eola Hills gets an extra year in bottle, and it has a more elegant, vertical structure, with the fruit framed in toasty oak flavors and some tarragon spice. It's persistent as well; the flavors seem to gather strength in the midpalate and continue through a strong and moderately complex finish. **88** *—P.G. (11/15/2007)*

Eola Hills 2003 Reserve Chardonnay (Oregon) $15. Here's a real tropical fruit salad of a Chardonnay, ripe and lightly toasty and simply loaded with rich fruit flavor. The only off notes are some slightly bitter phenolics, but the big, juicy fruit more than compensates, especially as it drives through a long and powerful finish. **88** *—P.G. (4/1/2007)*

Eola Hills 1998 Merlot (Oregon) $12. 85 *—C.S. (12/31/2002)*

Eola Hills 2004 Pinot Gris (Oregon) $10. 88 Best Buy *—P.G. (2/1/2006)*

Eola Hills 1997 Pinot Gris (Oregon) $10. 83 *(8/1/1999)*

Eola Hills 2006 Pinot Noir (Oregon) $12. Where else in this country can you find $12 Pinot with actual varietal character? Yes, it's quite young, light, lean, tart and even simple, but it does taste like the grape it's made from, and avoids the vegetal and the overtly leathery qualities of many of its rivals. Gentle flavors of raspberry and cherry are supported with juicy acids and hints of spice. This would be a lovely companion to a simple roast chicken. **87 Best Buy** *—P.G. (11/15/2007)*

Eola Hills 2005 Pinot Noir (Oregon) $12. It would be hard to find a better Oregon Pinot at this price. Clean, tart and nicely defined, the cherry and raspberry fruit shows some polish and sweetness at its core. Tannins are firm and a bit too big for the delicate fruit, but that's a minor quibble. **86** *—P.G. (4/1/2007)*

Eola Hills 1999 Pinot Noir (Oregon) $12. 84 Best Buy *(10/1/2002)*

Eola Hills 2001 La Creole Pinot Noir (Oregon) $20. 86 *—P.G. (10/1/2004)*

Eola Hills 2005 La Creole Reserve Pinot Noir (Oregon) $24. Eola Hills designates this one of their reserve Pinot Noirs, and it delivers a lot of flavor for the price, as do all of their wines. The entry is lovely, silky and seductive, spiced up with cinnamon and clove. It resonates through the mid-palate, never changing but not fading either, and there is none of the rough herbaceousness of most inexpensive Oregon Pinots. There's a pleasing smoky quality running gently through the finish, and the tannins are managed softly. **88 Editors' Choice** —*P.G. (11/15/2007)*

Eola Hills 1999 La Creole Reserve Pinot Noir (Oregon) $25. 81 *(10/1/2002)*

Eola Hills 1998 La Creole Reserve Pinot Noir (Oregon) $25. 89 —*J.C. (12/1/2000)*

Eola Hills 2002 La Creole Vineyard Pinot Noir (Eola Hills) $20. 84 *(11/1/2004)*

Eola Hills 2002 Oak Grove Pinot Noir (Oregon) $13. 84 *(11/1/2004)*

Eola Hills 2004 Reserve Pinot Noir (Oregon) $24. The winery's reserve Pinot is a substantial wine that clearly stands apart from its well-made budget bottle. (It should also be noted that, to the winery's credit, their reserve costs about what most Oregon budget bottles go for). This is vertically structured with mixed red fruits and nicely detailed whiffs and streaks of bark, earth, pepper and iron filings. It carries its compact flavors through a crisp and extended finish. 89 —*P.G. (4/1/2007)*

Eola Hills 2001 Wolf Hill Vineyard Pinot Noir (Oregon) $40. 87 —*P.G. (10/1/2004)*

Eola Hills 2005 Wolf Hill 667 Reserve Pinot Noir (Oregon) $50. Sometimes winery prices can be baffling. Here's a value producer, with excellent wines at a $12 and $24 price point, and they tag this one with the big 50. It sets up certain expectations. The justification seems to be the wine's extra-strong concentration, the alcohol topping out at 15.5%, and a strong streak of vanilla. If that's your style, go for it. 86 —*P.G. (11/15/2007)*

Eola Hills 2002 Wolf Hill Vineyard Reserve Pinot Noir (Oregon) $40. 87 *(11/1/2004)*

Eola Hills 1999 Wolf Hill Vineyard Reserve Pinot Noir (Oregon) $40. 88 *(10/1/2002)*

Eola Hills 2000 Sauvignon Blanc (Applegate Valley) $10. 81 —*M.S. (8/1/2003)*

Eola Hills 2000 Syrah (Oregon) $12. 85 —*R.V. (12/31/2002)*

Eola Hills 1999 Applegate Valley Syrah (Oregon) $20. 88 —*C.S. (12/31/2002)*

Eola Hills 2000 Reserve Syrah (Columbia Valley (OR)) $20. 85 *(9/1/2005)*

Eola Hills 1998 Reserve Syrah (Applegate Valley) $18. 85 *(10/1/2001)*

Eola Hills 1999 Old Vines Zinfandel (Lodi) $25. 86 —*D.T. (3/1/2002)*

EOS

EOS 2004 French Connection Bordeaux Blend (Paso Robles) $25. This is EOS's Bordeaux blend. The '04 is mainly Cabernet, with a little Petite Sirah, a good move that adds deep plummy flavors and textural tannins to the cherries and blackberries. It's a sophisticated Cab. 88 —*S.H. (12/31/2007)*

EOS 2002 French Connection Bordeaux Blend (Paso Robles) $20. 83 —*S.H. (11/1/2005)*

EOS 2000 French Connection Cabernet Blend (Paso Robles) $20. 86 —*S.H. (5/1/2003)*

EOS 1999 French Connection Cabernet Blend (Paso Robles) $20. 88 —*M.M. (4/1/2002)*

EOS 2004 Cabernet Sauvignon (Paso Robles) $18. EOS isn't known for its Cabs. The wines, like this one, have been hot and rustic and bordering on sweet. This one has all five Bordeaux varieties, with some new oak. 82 —*S.H. (5/1/2007)*

EOS 2002 Cabernet Sauvignon (Paso Robles) $14. 83 —*S.H. (3/1/2006)*

EOS 2001 Cabernet Sauvignon (Paso Robles) $18. 89 —*S.H. (2/1/2004)*

EOS 2000 Cabernet Sauvignon (Paso Robles) $18. 87 —*S.H. (11/15/2002)*

EOS 1999 Cabernet Sauvignon (Paso Robles) $15. 88 —*M.M. (4/1/2002)*

EOS 1996 Hyperion Vineyard Cabernet Sauvignon (Paso Robles) $16. 89 *(11/15/1999)*

EOS 1999 Reserve Cabernet Sauvignon (Paso Robles) $24. 89 —*M.M. (4/1/2002)*

EOS 2005 Chardonnay (Paso Robles) $13. You can taste how extremely ripe the grapes got under the summer sun with every sip. Explosive in nectarine, peach, lime, green apple and pineapple flavors, this Chard has a nice balance of acidity and oak. 84 —*S.H. (5/1/2007)*

EOS 2003 Chardonnay (Paso Robles) $12. 83 —*S.H. (11/1/2005)*

EOS 2002 Chardonnay (Paso Robles) $15. 84 —*S.H. (6/1/2004)*

EOS 2001 Chardonnay (Paso Robles) $15. 84 —*S.H. (12/15/2002)*

EOS 2000 Chardonnay (Paso Robles) $14. 85 —*M.M. (4/1/2002)*

EOS 1998 Chardonnay (Paso Robles) $15. 88 *(6/1/2000)*

EOS 1997 Chardonnay (Paso Robles) $15. 88 *(11/15/1999)*

EOS 2002 Cupa Grandis Chardonnay (Paso Robles) $40. 86 —*S.H. (6/1/2004)*

EOS 2003 Cupa Grandis Grand Barrel Reserve Chardonnay (Paso Robles) $40. 89 —*S.H. (11/1/2005)*

EOS 2003 Reserve Chardonnay (Paso Robles) $20. 87 —*S.H. (11/1/2005)*

EOS 1999 Reserve Chardonnay (Paso Robles) $24. 87 —*M.M. (4/1/2002)*

EOS 2002 Fumé Blanc (Paso Robles) $18. 90 —*J.M. (6/1/2004)*

EOS 2003 Brothers Ranch Vineyard 4, Block 8 Fumé Blanc (Paso Robles) $20. 86 *(7/1/2005)*

EOS 2001 Reserve Fumé Blanc (Paso Robles) $18. 89 —*S.H. (9/1/2003)*

EOS 2000 Reserve Fumé Blanc (Paso Robles) $19. 88 *(8/1/2002)*

EOS 2002 Merlot (Paso Robles) $15. 80 —*S.H. (11/1/2005)*

EOS 2000 Merlot (Paso Robles) $18. 87 —*S.H. (11/15/2002)*

EOS 1999 Merlot (Paso Robles) $22. 85 —*M.M. (4/1/2002)*

EOS 2005 Tears of Dew Late Harvest Moscato (Paso Robles) $22. Tears of Dew has established itself as one of the leading white dessert wines in California, and the '05 is nobly in that tradition, although it's not quite up to the astonishing opulence of '04. Very sweet and well acidified, it has delicious apricot liqueur, orange marmalade and vanilla cream flavors and a long, complex finish. Just gorgeous. **93 Editors' Choice** —*S.H. (5/1/2007)*

EOS 2000 Tears of Dew Late Harvest Moscato (Paso Robles) $20. 90 —*S.H. (12/1/2002)*

EOS 1999 Tears of Dew Late Harvest Moscato (Paso Robles) $17. 86 —*M.M. (4/1/2002)*

EOS 2001 Tears of Dew Late Harvest Moscato (Paso Robles) $20. 93 —*S.H. (12/1/2003)*

EOS 1997 Tears of Dew Late Harvest Moscato (Paso Robles) $15. **91 Best Buy** *(11/15/1999)*

EOS 2004 Tears of Dew Late Harvest 375ml Moscato (Paso Robles) $22. **95 Editors' Choice** —*S.H. (12/1/2006)*

EOS 2003 Tears of Dew Late Harvest Moscato Muscat Canelli (Paso Robles) $20. **93 Editors' Choice** —*S.H. (11/1/2005)*

EOS 2004 Petite Sirah (Paso Robles) $18. Sweet and sharp in green chlorophyll, this tastes of cherry cough drops. 81 —*S.H. (12/31/2007)*

EOS 2003 Petite Sirah (Paso Robles) $18. Your basic California warm country Petite Sirah: soft, tannic, a little sweet in plumped raisins, and lusty. It's a wine to gulp with barbecue. 83 —*S.H. (5/1/2007)*

EOS 2002 Petite Sirah (Paso Robles) $13. 83 —*S.H. (3/1/2006)*

EOS 2003 Cupa Grandis Petite Sirah (Paso Robles) $55. Cupa Grandis is EOS's highest expression of Petite Sirah and also its priciest. I gave the '01 and '02 high scores, and while '03 is a good wine, it's not in their league, probably because of the vintage's heat. The wine is rich and velvety and dry, but has more than a touch of warmth and raisined fruit. 88 —*S.H. (5/1/2007)*

EOS 2002 Cupa Grandis Grand Barrel Reserve Petite Sirah (Paso Robles) $40. 92 —*S.H. (11/1/2005)*

EOS 2001 Cupa Grandis Peck Ranch Vineyard Block P7 Petite Sirah (Paso Robles) $40. 92 —*J.M. (6/1/2004)*

EOS 2001 Peck Ranch Vineyard Reserve Petite Sirah (Paso Robles) $20. 80 —*S.H. (11/1/2005)*

EOS 2004 Reserve Petite Sirah (Paso Robles) $24. This tastes like blackberry wine made with white sugar. The tannins and acids are fine, but that sweetness is unbalanced in a table wine. 82 —*S.H. (12/31/2007)*

EOS 2003 Reserve Petite Sirah (Paso Robles) $25. EOS's reserve Petite kicks the regular '03 up several notches in richness and overall impressiveness. The fruit is kick-butt, all blackberry jam, root beer, cola, cherry pie and gingerbread, but for all that, the wine is dry. It's also soft in acids, and the tannins cry out for marbled beef. 88 —*S.H. (5/1/2007)*

EOS 2000 Reserve Petite Sirah (Paso Robles) $25. 85 *(4/1/2003)*

EOS 1999 Reserve Petite Sirah (Paso Robles) $22. **90 Editors' Choice** —*M.M. (4/1/2002)*

EOS 1996 Zephyrus Vineyard Petite Sirah (Paso Robles) $17. 88 *(11/15/1999)*

EOS 2001 French Connection Red Blend (Paso Robles) $20. 90 —*S.H. (12/31/2003)*

EOS 1999 Torre del Gobbo Red Blend (Paso Robles) $22. 86 —*M.M. (4/1/2002)*

EOS 2006 Sauvignon Blanc (Paso Robles) $14. Pair this dry, spicy wine with everything from roast chicken to hummus, or drink as a refreshing cocktail sipper. It's really interesting and fairly complex, providing a balance of citrus and fig flavors with a tangy minerality that seems to show off the wine's terroir. **88 Editors' Choice** *—S.H. (11/15/2007)*

EOS 2002 Sauvignon Blanc (Paso Robles) $15. 88 *—J.M. (6/1/2004)*

EOS 2001 Sauvignon Blanc (Paso Robles) $15. 85 *—S.H. (3/1/2003)*

EOS 1997 Sauvignon Blanc (Paso Robles) $14. 87 *(11/15/1999)*

EOS 2000 Estate Bottled Sauvignon Blanc (Paso Robles) $14. 87 *—M.M. (4/1/2002)*

EOS 2004 Zinfandel (Paso Robles) $18. Soft and simple, with pleasant raspberry, cherry, mocha and vanilla flavors that finish just this side of dry. You can taste the superripe flavor of red currants in the long aftertaste. **84** *—S.H. (12/31/2007)*

EOS 2003 Zinfandel (Paso Robles) $18. 84 *—S.H. (12/1/2006)*

EOS 2002 Zinfandel (Paso Robles) $15. 82 *—S.H. (11/1/2005)*

EOS 2001 Zinfandel (Paso Robles) $16. 88 *—J.M. (2/1/2004)*

EOS 2000 Zinfandel (Paso Robles) $16. 86 *—S.H. (12/1/2002)*

EOS 1997 Zinfandel (Paso Robles) $16. 89 *(11/15/1999)*

EOS 2002 Brothers Ranch Vineyard 5 Block 5A Late Harvest Zinfandel (Paso Robles) $20. 82 *—S.H. (11/1/2005)*

EOS 1999 Estate Bottled Zinfandel (Paso Robles) $15. 87 *—D.T. (3/1/2002)*

EOS 2003 Port Zinfandel (Paso Robles) $30. I want to like this wine more than I do, because it starts off so sweet and ripe in chocolate-infused blackberry jam and cassis flavors. Yet it turns thin from the middle through the finish. Everything just sort of falls apart. **84** *—S.H. (5/1/2007)*

EOS 2001 Port Zinfandel (Paso Robles) $28. 90 *—J.M. (6/1/2004)*

EOS 1999 Port Zinfandel (Paso Robles) $27. 88 *—M.M. (4/1/2002)*

EPIPHANY

Epiphany 1999 Chardonnay (Santa Barbara County) $19. 90 *—S.H. (12/15/2002)*

Epiphany 2004 Grenache (Santa Barbara County) $30. Simple and fruity, this ultraripe cherry- and chocolate-flavored wine also has a dry grip of tannins. It finishes in a peppery swirl of cherry liqueur. **85** *—S.H. (12/1/2007)*

Epiphany 2006 Camp Four Vineyard Grenache Blanc (Santa Barbara County) $23. With peach, citrus and flower flavors and a dry, creamy texture, this has the richness of an oaky Chardonnay and the acidity of Pinot Grigio. An interesting wine, one you might want to try with Thai or Vietnamese food. **87** *—S.H. (12/1/2007)*

Epiphany 2005 Camp 4 Vineyard Grenache Blanc (Santa Barbara County) $18. 86 *—S.H. (12/15/2006)*

Epiphany 2006 Rosé Grenache Blend (Santa Barbara County) $14. Dark in color and full-bodied for a rosé, this dry wine is enormously concentrated in the ripest, sweetest red and black cherries. Turns increasingly complex in the mouth, showing layers of anise, vanilla and spice. **90 Best Buy** *—S.H. (10/1/2007)*

Epiphany 2005 Rosé Grenache (Santa Barbara County) $14. 86 *—S.H. (12/15/2006)*

Epiphany 2004 Rodney's Vineyard Petite Sirah (Santa Barbara County) $30. Pet fans will like it. Fans of delicacy and elegance may shake their heads at the alcohol level—early 16%—and almost Port-like flavors. But the wine is fully dry. **83** *—S.H. (10/1/2007)*

Epiphany 2003 Rodney's Vineyard Petite Sirah (Santa Barbara County) $24. 88 *—S.H. (11/15/2006)*

Epiphany 2002 Rodney's Vineyard Petite Sirah (Santa Barbara County) $25. 87 *—S.H. (11/1/2005)*

Epiphany 1999 Pinot Blanc (Santa Barbara County) $19. 88 *—S.H. (2/1/2003)*

Epiphany 1999 Pinot Gris (Santa Barbara County) $18. 87 *—S.H. (9/1/2003)***90** *—S.H. (2/1/2006)*

Epiphany 2006 Goodchild Vineyard Pinot Gris (Santa Maria Valley) $18. With the racy acidity this variety is known for when grown in a cool place, this is a good palate cleanser. It's a little on the candied side, with candied pineapple flavors, but that zestiness is really nice. **85** *—S.H. (12/1/2007)*

Epiphany 2005 Goodchild Vineyard Pinot Gris (Santa Maria Valley) $18. 90 *—S.H. (12/15/2006)*

Epiphany 2002 Revelation Red Blend (Santa Barbara County) $34. 83 *—S.H. (11/1/2005)*

Epiphany 2004 Gypsy Rhône Red Blend (Santa Barbara County) $25. Epiphany's varietal '04s weren't very good, so how could this Mourvèdre, Grenache and Syrah blend be? It's dry, tannic and dull, with thin, barely ripe flavors. **82** *—S.H. (12/1/2007)*

Epiphany 2004 Revelation Rhône Red Blend (Santa Barbara County) $35. Soft and syrupy, with tons of oaky spice framing blackberry, cherry, raspberry and chocolate liqueur flavors, this high-alcohol blend of Syrah, Grenache and Petite Sirah tastes sweet and simple. **82** *—S.H. (10/1/2007)*

Epiphany 2003 Revelation Red Rhône Red Blend (Santa Barbara County) $32. 89 *—S.H. (12/15/2006)*

Epiphany 1999 Rodney's Rhône Red Blend (Santa Barbara County) $36. 85 *—S.H. (9/1/2003)*

Epiphany 2004 Camp 4 Vineyard Roussanne (Santa Ynez Valley) $18. 89 *—S.H. (5/1/2006)*

Epiphany 2004 Block 2 Camp Four Vineyard Syrah (Santa Barbara County) $45. Why are all of Epiphany's '04 Syrahs so high in alcohol? This one is 16%. Granted, the vintage was a scorcher, but others in Santa Barbara managed to produce beautiful, balanced Syrahs in '04. Not this one, which is hot and simple. **82** *—S.H. (10/1/2007)*

Epiphany 2004 F Block Rodney's Vineyard Syrah (Santa Barbara County) $45. Really not a very likeable Syrah despite some tasty cherry fruit flavors. The problem is enormously high alcohol, 15.9%, that makes the wine hot, and a near absence of acidity, which makes it cloying. The imbalance makes the tannins astringent. **82** *—S.H. (10/1/2007)*

Epiphany 2004 Hampton Syrah (Santa Barbara County) $35. Way too hot for a table wine, with prickly, unpleasant heat, the result of 16.1% alcohol and insufficient fruit. **81** *—S.H. (10/1/2007)*

Epiphany 2003 Hampton Vineyard Syrah (Santa Barbara County) $35. 90 *—S.H. (12/15/2006)*

Epiphany 2002 Hampton Vineyard Syrah (Santa Barbara County) $35. 89 *(9/1/2005)*

Epiphany 2004 Paradise Road Vineyard Syrah (Santa Barbara County) $45. The problem with Epiphany's Syrahs over the years has been excessively high alcohol, which seems to be a deliberate decision. This one clocks in at 15.9%, which gives it the blackberry, cherry and cola flavors a dessert sweet taste and a hot, chili pepper finish. **85** *—S.H. (11/1/2007)*

Epiphany 2003 Starlane Vineyard Syrah (Santa Barbara County) $35. 82 *—S.H. (11/15/2006)*

Epiphany 1999 Stonewall Vineyard Syrah (California) $45. 89 *(11/1/2001)*

EPONYMOUS

Eponymous 2004 Red Wine Bordeaux Blend (Sonoma Valley) $45. A Cabernet-based Bordeaux blend that shows lots of fruity character and real elegance. Dry and soft, the blackberry, cassis, cherry and sweet oak flavors are delicious. Drink now. **88** *—S.H. (9/1/2007)*

Eponymous 2003 Cabernet Sauvignon (Napa Valley) $58. Not as rich as the last few vintages, showing a tougher, leaner but possibly more ageworthy profile. There's some green, minty stuff going on, but also a wealth of blackberries and cherries. Try after 2007. **87** *—S.H. (4/1/2007)*

Eponymous 2002 Cabernet Sauvignon (Napa Valley) $50. 92 Cellar Selection *—S.H. (3/1/2006)*

Eponymous 2001 Cabernet Sauvignon-Merlot (Napa Valley) $50. 88 *—S.H. (2/1/2005)*

Eponymous 2000 Red Wine Cabernet Sauvignon-Merlot (Napa Valley) $50. 90 *—S.H. (10/1/2004)*

EQUINOX

Equinox 2002 Merlot (Oakville) $75. 92 *—S.H. (3/1/2005)*

EQUUS

Equus 1999 James Berry Vineyard Grenache (Paso Robles) $18. 86 *—S.H. (2/1/2003)*

Equus 1999 Mourvèdre (Paso Robles) $18. 85 *—S.H. (5/1/2003)*

Equus 2000 Roussanne (Paso Robles) $16. 85 *—S.H. (3/1/2003)*

Equus 1999 Syrah (Paso Robles) $18. 90 *—S.H. (2/1/2003)*

Equus 1998 Syrah (Paso Robles) $22. 86 *(11/1/2001)*

Equus 2000 Viognier (Central Coast) $16. 86 *—S.H. (3/1/2003)*

ERATH

Erath 1997 Niederberger Vineyard Reserve Chardonnay (Willamette Valley) $35. 91 *—S.H. (12/31/1999)*

Erath 1998 Pinot Blanc (Willamette Valley) $12. 87 *—S.H. (12/31/1999)*

Erath 2005 Pinot Blanc (Willamette Valley) $14. 84 *—P.G. (12/1/2006)*

Erath 2003 Pinot Blanc (Willamette Valley) $13. 88 Best Buy *—P.G. (2/1/2005)*

Erath 2006 Pinot Gris (Oregon) $14. Now part of the Ste. Michelle Wine Estates portfolio, this pioneering Oregon winery seems to be holding firm to a clean, simple style of winemaking, as exemplified by this fresh and lightly fruity Pinot Gris. Lemony and tart, it's the sort of pleasantly generic white wine that one might expect to find from Italy. **86** *—P.G. (11/15/2007)*

Erath 2005 Pinot Gris (Oregon) $13. 86 Best Buy *—P.G. (11/15/2006)*

Erath 2004 Pinot Gris (Oregon) $14. 88 *—P.G. (2/1/2006)*

Erath 2003 Pinot Gris (Oregon) $13. 85 *—P.G. (2/1/2005)*

Erath 2000 Pinot Gris (Oregon) $12. 88 Best Buy *—P.G. (4/1/2002)*

Erath 1998 Pinot Gris (Willamette Valley) $13. 85 *—S.H. (12/31/1999)*

Erath 2002 Pinot Noir (Oregon) $16. 87 *(11/1/2004)*

Erath 2001 Pinot Noir (Oregon) $15. 87 Best Buy *—P.G. (12/1/2003)*

Erath 2000 Pinot Noir (Oregon) $15. 86 Best Buy *(10/1/2002)*

Erath 1999 Pinot Noir (Willamette Valley) $24. 82 *(10/1/2002)*

Erath 1998 Pinot Noir (Willamette Valley) $16. 87 Best Buy *—M.S. (12/1/2000)*

Erath 2000 30th Anniversary Reserve Pinot Noir (Oregon) $30. 88 *—P.G. (12/1/2003)*

Erath 2005 Estate Selection Pinot Noir (Dundee Hills) $30. This is a blend of five different Dundee Hills sites, and as is often the case in Oregon, delivers more accessible and complete flavors than some of the winery's individual vineyard-designated wines. It's herbal and spicy, with strong scents of tomato leaf and root beer. The fruit is tart and clean, and the wine comes out swinging, but then it falls away in the back end, adding just a lick of vanilla as a sweet coda. **88** *—P.G. (11/15/2007)*

Erath 2004 Estate Selection Pinot Noir (Dundee Hills) $30. 90 Cellar Selection *—P.G. (12/1/2006)*

Erath 2002 Estate Selection Pinot Noir (Willamette Valley) $30. 87 *(11/1/2004)*

Erath 2004 Fuqua Pinot Noir (Dundee Hills) $40. Pronounced FOO-kway, this is the highest in alcohol but the lowest in flavor of the Erath line up. The first bottle tasted flat, leafy and dull, but a second bottle was significantly improved. Nonetheless it appears to be aging quickly, with an astringent, tannic finish. **85** *—P.G. (11/15/2007)*

Erath 2005 Juliard Pinot Noir (Dundee Hills) $40. This seems very dry, thin, leafy and tannic, upon entry. It tastes like green tea, with cranberry and wild cherry fruit. It's not a simple wine by any means, and it will probably flesh out with some bottle age, for the complexity is there in the aromas and in the length. The 12.5% alcohol is quite unusual by New World standards. **88** *—P.G. (11/15/2007)*

Erath 2002 Leland Pinot Noir (Willamette Valley) $40. 83 *(11/1/2004)*

Erath 1999 Leland Pinot Noir (Willamette Valley) $45. 89 *(10/1/2002)*

Erath 2005 Niederberger Pinot Noir (Dundee Hills) $40. This is a bit softer than the other single-vineyard bottlings, with an impression of sweet cherry fruit. But it's lighter as well, and lacks the detail and depth of the others. It's a gentle, pleasant quaffer. **86** *—P.G. (11/15/2007)*

Erath 2005 Prince Hill Pinot Noir (Dundee Hills) $40. This is a thin, hard and tight version of the estate wine. It shows a bit more depth, but it's compact and slow to unravel. The oak is delivering butterscotch and vanilla, laid on as a buttery finish. This is too young to drink right now. **89** *—P.G. (11/15/2007)*

Erath 2002 Prince Hill Pinot Noir (Willamette Valley) $40. 86 *(11/1/2004)*

Erath 1996 Prince Hill Pinot Noir (Willamette Valley) $35. 85 *(10/1/1999)*

Erath 1999 Reserve Pinot Noir (Yamhill County) $25. 84 *(10/1/2002)*

Erath 1998 Reserve Pinot Noir (Willamette Valley) $34. 89 *—J.C. (12/1/2000)*

Erath 1998 Vintage Select Pinot Noir (Willamette Valley) $24. 89 *—M.S. (12/1/2000)*

ERBA

Erba 2003 Mountainside Vineyards Cabernet Sauvignon (Napa Valley) $50. The vineyard is on Atlas Peak. Modern winemaking has softened the tannins, while long hangtime steers the fruit towards ultraripe cherries and chocolate. It's a flashy wine with lots of new French oak, meant to impress, but it may pall after a few sips. **87** *—S.H. (6/1/2007)*

Erba 2004 Mountainside Vineyards Merlot (Napa Valley) $35. Dense, balanced and young, this is an impressive Merlot that satisfies for its wealth of fruit. Explosive in cherry jam, cassis and rum-soaked chocolate cake, it's dry and soft and complicated, a wine very much in the expensive Napa style of modern red wines. **89** *—S.H. (6/1/2007)*

Erba 2003 Mountainside Vineyards Merlot (Napa Valley) $35. Shows the earthiness that always characterized Atlas Peak Bordeaux reds, but today's riper approach gives the wine impossibly rich cherry jam, crème de cassis and milk chocolate flavors, wrapped into the softest, sweetest tannins. It's almost like a dessert wine, except it's dry and balanced. **90** *—S.H. (6/1/2007)*

Erba 2003 Mountainside Vineyards Syrah (Napa Valley) $40. Like the winery's Cabernet and Merlot—grown in the same Atlas Peak estate vineyard—this is a soft, voluptuous wine, made in the modern style. It's as rich as a dessert, with cherry, cassis, chocolate, plum pudding, pumpkin pie and datenut bread flavors, although it's totally dry. It takes a lot of effort and expense to make a wine this deliciously balanced. Drink now. **91** *—S.H. (6/1/2007)*

ERIC ROSS

Eric Ross 1999 Klapp Pinot Noir (Russian River Valley) $40. 85 *(10/1/2002)*

Eric Ross 2004 Poule d'Or Pinot Noir (Russian River Valley) $35. 90 *—S.H. (12/1/2006)*

ERRAZURIZ

Errazuriz 1999 La Nuit Magique Pinot Noir (Willamette Valley) $60. 86 *(10/1/2002)*

ESHCOL RANCH

Eshcol Ranch 2001 Cabernet Sauvignon (California) $10. 84 *—S.H. (12/15/2005)*

ESSER CELLARS

Esser Cellars 2003 Cabernet Sauvignon (California) $9. 83 *—S.H. (6/1/2005)*

Esser Cellars 2001 Cabernet Sauvignon (California) $8. 87 Best Buy *—S.H. (6/1/2003)*

Esser Cellars 2005 Chardonnay (California) $10. 85 Best Buy *—S.H. (11/15/2006)*

Esser Cellars 2003 Chardonnay (California) $9. 82 *—S.H. (6/1/2005)*

Esser Cellars 2002 Chardonnay (California) $9. 82 *—S.H. (12/31/2003)*

Esser Cellars 2001 Chardonnay (California) $8. 90 Best Buy *—S.H. (6/1/2003)*

Esser Cellars 2005 Merlot (California) $10. 84 *—S.H. (12/31/2006)*

Esser Cellars 2001 Merlot (California) $8. 85 *—S.H. (4/1/2004)*

Esser Cellars 2002 Pinot Noir (California) $12. 84 *—S.H. (6/1/2005)*

ESTANCIA

Estancia 2004 Meritage Bordeaux Blend (Paso Robles) $33. Soft and tannic, this Cabernet-based blend has cherry, blackberry and cola flavors, with an edge of dried herbs. Despite the tannins, it doesn't have the balance for aging, so drink now. **85** *—S.H. (12/15/2007)***86** *—S.H. (12/15/2006)*

Estancia 2002 Red Meritage Cabernet Blend (Paso Robles) $35. 84 *—S.H. (5/1/2006)*

Estancia 1997 Cabernet Sauvignon (California) $15. 84 *—S.H. (7/1/2000)*

Estancia 2002 Cabernet Sauvignon (Paso Robles) $15. 86 *—S.H. (12/31/2004)*

Estancia 2002 Keyes Canyon Ranches Cabernet Sauvignon (Paso Robles) $16. 86 *—S.H. (8/1/2005)*

Estancia 2001 Paso Robles Cabernet Sauvignon (Paso Robles) $15. 85 *—S.H. (10/1/2004)*

Estancia 2002 Pinnacles Chardonnay (Monterey) $12. 84 *—S.H. (11/15/2004)*

Estancia 2000 Pinnacles Chardonnay (Monterey) $13. 88 *—J.M. (5/1/2002)*

Estancia 1998 Pinnacles Chardonnay (Monterey County) $12. 89 Best Buy *—S.H. (5/1/2000)*

Estancia 2006 Pinnacles Ranches Chardonnay (Monterey County) $12. High, brisk acidity is the star in this Central Coast Chard. It gives a good kick to the ripe guava, nectarine, mineral and vanilla flavors. Good value, and very versatile with food. **85** *—S.H. (11/15/2007)*

Estancia 2005 Pinnacles Ranches Chardonnay (Monterey) $12. From the east side of Salinas Valley, this Chard hows great Central Coast Chard character, with crisp, clean acidity brightening the kiwi and lime flavors. Some new oak adds welcome buttered toast and smoky vanilla complexities. Restaurateurs should scoop this up. **87 Best Buy** *—S.H. (7/1/2007)*

Estancia 2004 Pinnacles Ranches Chardonnay (Monterey) $12. 81 *—S.H. (10/1/2006)*

Estancia 2003 Pinnacles Ranches Chardonnay (Monterey) $12. 86 *—S.H. (12/1/2005)*

Estancia 1998 Single Vineyard Reserve Chardonnay (Monterey County) $20. 87 *(6/1/2000)*

Estancia 2001 Meritage (Alexander Valley) $35. 86 *—S.H. (8/1/2005)*

Estancia 2000 Red Meritage Meritage (Alexander Valley) $35. 90 *—S.H. (1/1/2005)*

Estancia 2000 Merlot (California) $16. 85 *—S.H. (4/1/2003)*

Estancia 2006 Pinot Grigio (California) $12. Nice for an everyday sipper and especially for a cocktail style wine. Crisp acids undergird the structure, making the citrus, fig and vanilla bean flavors come alive. 84 *—S.H. (11/15/2007)*

Estancia 2004 Pinot Grigio (California) $15. 84 *—S.H. (7/1/2005)*

Estancia 2003 Pinot Grigio (California) $15. 85 *—S.H. (11/15/2004)*

Estancia 2002 Pinot Grigio (California) $15. 87 *—S.H. (2/1/2004)*

Estancia 2001 Pinnacles Pinot Noir (Monterey) $15. 86 *—S.H. (4/1/2004)*

Estancia 2000 Pinnacles Pinot Noir (Monterey) $16. 87 *—J.M. (5/1/2002)*

Estancia 1997 Pinnacles Pinot Noir (Monterey County) $14. 88 *(11/15/1999)*

Estancia 2003 Pinnacles Ranches Pinot Noir (Monterey) $15. 86 *—S.H. (12/1/2005)*

Estancia 2002 Pinnacles Ranches Pinot Noir (Monterey) $15. 87 *(11/1/2004)*

Estancia 2000 Proprietor's Selection Pinot Noir (Monterey) $10. 87 Best Buy *—S.H. (11/15/2004)*

Estancia 1997 Reserve Pinot Noir (Monterey County) $22. 89 *—J.C. (5/1/2000)*

Estancia 2005 Stonewall Vineyard Pinot Noir (Santa Lucia Highlands) $25. This is a very good Pinot Noir that shows how well the appellation can balance the variety. It has lush cherry, blackberry, tea, cola and cocoa flavors, and a rich, silky texture. Could develop bottle complexity over the next six years. 88 *—S.H. (12/15/2007)*

Estancia 2004 Stonewall Vineyard Pinot Noir (Santa Lucia Highlands) $25. This limited production wine comes from Estancia's vineyard in the red-hot Santa Lucia appellation. Like most Pinots from there, it's a big wine; gutsy with real acidity and tannins, but very ripe fruit. It's brawny now, but should be smoother in four or five years. 89 *—S.H. (4/1/2007)*

Estancia 2003 Stonewall Vineyard Pinot Noir (Santa Lucia Highlands) $25. 85 *—S.H. (12/1/2005)*

Estancia 2002 Stonewall Vineyard Reserve Pinot Noir (Santa Lucia Highlands) $22. 88 Editors' Choice *—S.H. (8/1/2005)*

Estancia 2002 Stonewall Vineyard Reserve Pinot Noir (Santa Lucia Highlands) $25. 86 *(11/1/2004)*

Estancia 1997 Duo Sangiovese (Sonoma County) $22. 88 *—S.H. (9/1/2000)*

Estancia 1996 Duo Sangiovese (Sonoma County) $22. 90 *—S.H. (11/1/1999)*

Estancia 2004 Syrah (Central Coast) $16. 85 *—S.H. (12/31/2006)*

Estancia 2003 Lucia Range Ranches Syrah (Central Coast) $15. 84 *—S.H. (10/1/2006)*

Estancia 2002 Keyes Canyon Ranches Zinfandel (Paso Robles) $12. 88 Best Buy *—S.H. (8/1/2005)*

ESTATE RAFFAELE

Estate Raffaele 2002 Clareta Red Blend (California) $22. 84 *—S.H. (10/1/2005)*

Estate Raffaele 2004 Century Old Vines Zinfandel (California) $NA. 82 *—S.H. (11/15/2006)*

ESTERLINA

Esterlina 2000 Cabernet Sauvignon (Alexander Valley) $35. 87 *—S.H. (10/1/2004)*

Esterlina 1999 Chardonnay (Anderson Valley) $20. 87 *—S.H. (5/1/2002)*

Esterlina 2003 Tres Appellations Chardonnay (Anderson Valley, Sonoma County, Cole Ranch) $18. 87 *—S.H. (12/1/2005)*

Esterlina 2001 Merlot (Cole Ranch) $18. 85 *—S.H. (10/1/2004)*

Esterlina 2001 Pinot Noir (Anderson Valley) $35. 85 *—S.H. (10/1/2004)*

Esterlina 1998 Pinot Noir (Anderson Valley) $35. 85 *—S.H. (5/1/2002)*

Esterlina 2002 Estate Pinot Noir (Anderson Valley) $35. 82 *—S.H. (12/1/2005)*

Esterlina 2004 Riesling (Cole Ranch) $16. 86 *—S.H. (12/1/2005)*

Esterlina 2002 Riesling (Cole Ranch) $16. 85 *—S.H. (10/1/2004)*

Esterlina 1999 Ferrington Vineyards Sauvignon Blanc (Anderson Valley) $18. 84 *—S.H. (5/1/2002)*

Esterlina 2003 Janian Vineyard Syrah (Sonoma Mountain) $25. 92 *—S.H. (12/1/2005)*

Esterlina 1999 White Riesling (Mendocino) $13. 90 *—S.H. (5/1/2002)*

ESTRELLA

Estrella 2002 Proprietor's Reserve Shiraz (California) $6. 85 Best Buy *(9/1/2005)*

ETUDE

Etude 2004 Cabernet Sauvignon (Napa Valley) $90. A lush Cabernet that feels soft and delicious right now, but has layers of complexity that make it a cellar candidate. Dry and oaky, the wine is enormously rich in blackberry, cassis, cocoa and cedar flavors, with considerable tannins. The wine is wonderfully balanced. Drink now through 2010, at least. 93 *—S.H. (12/15/2007)*

Etude 2003 Cabernet Sauvignon (Napa Valley) $90. A little off the pace of previous vintages, although it shows that Soter elegance and Napa pedigree. It's tremendously concentrated in black currant and cherry fruit, almost with the superintensity of a wine reduction sauce, and you'll also find significant new French oak. A blend of the major township communes along Highway 29, it's a beautifully lush Cab, but doesn't seem like an ager. 87 *—S.H. (5/1/2007)*

Etude 2003 Cabernet Sauvignon (Rutherford) $100. Practically overflows with lush, ripe fruit—mainly cassis—but that richness is kept in classic balance by the dusty tannins on the finish. This is fuller and creamier than the also impressive St. Helena bottling. 125 cases produced. Drink now–2015. 93 *(9/1/2007)*

Etude 2003 Cabernet Sauvignon (St. Helena) $100. Like the Rutherford bottling, this is a strictly limited-production item, with only 125 cases produced. Some mint overtones give the raspberry and cassis fruit a sense of lightness, an impression bolstered by the wine's silky tannins and long finish. Drink now–2015. 91 *(9/1/2007)*

Etude 2002 Cabernet Sauvignon (Napa Valley) $90. 93 *—S.H. (12/1/2005)*

Etude 2001 Cabernet Sauvignon (Napa Valley) $90. 95 *—S.H. (5/1/2005)*

Etude 2000 Cabernet Sauvignon (Napa Valley) $80. 90 *—S.H. (6/1/2004)*

Etude 1999 Cabernet Sauvignon (Napa Valley) $80. 90 *(2/1/2003)*

Etude 2002 Merlot (Napa Valley) $48. 95 Editors' Choice *—S.H. (4/1/2006)*

Etude 1998 Pinot Blanc (Carneros) $25. 91 *—S.H. (2/1/2001)*

Etude 2005 Pinot Gris (Carneros) $24. 91 *—S.H. (12/1/2006)*

Etude 2004 Pinot Gris (Carneros) $24. 91 Editors' Choice *—S.H. (2/1/2006)*

Etude 2005 Pinot Noir (Carneros) $42. The blended Pinot is lighter in body and lower in alcohol than the special bottlings, but still features a wonderful sense of balance and plenty of complexity. Chocolate, cinnamon and black cherry scents mark the nose, while the flavors add briary, herbal hints. Well-structured, with some slightly dusty tannins on the finish. Drink now–2015. 89 *(9/1/2007)*

Etude 2003 Pinot Noir (Carneros) $40. 93 Editors' Choice *—S.H. (12/1/2005)*

Etude 2002 Pinot Noir (Carneros) $40. 89 *(11/1/2004)*

Etude 2001 Pinot Noir (Carneros) $40. 90 *—S.H. (5/1/2004)*

Etude 2000 Pinot Noir (Carneros) $40. 90 *—M.S. (12/1/2003)*

Etude 2004 Deer Camp Estate Pinot Noir (Carneros) $60. This is the first release of this designation. The vintage was warm and ripe, and the vineyard is hard by the Sonoma border but in Napa. It's an interesting wine. It shows the power and intensity of low-yielding vines, with explosive blackberry and cherry flavors, but maintains the silky elegance you want in Pinot. 93 *—S.H. (5/1/2007)*

Etude 2004 Estate Pinot Noir (Carneros) $42. 91 *—S.H. (12/1/2006)*

Etude 2004 Heirloom Pinot Noir (Carneros) $80. A big, rich, almost chocolaty Pinot, with some of those darker flavors offset by brighter cherry notes. There's also a slightly herbal, spicy character to the bouquet, which adds a welcome note of complexity. Powerful and long. Drink now–2012. 91 *(9/1/2007)*

Etude 2002 Heirloom Pinot Noir (Carneros) $80. 95 Editors' Choice *—S.H. (12/1/2005)*

Etude 2001 Heirloom Pinot Noir (Carneros) $80. 92 *—S.H. (12/1/2004)*

Etude 2000 Heirloom Pinot Noir (Carneros) $80. 94 *—M.S. (12/1/2003)*

Etude 2005 Rosé Pinot Noir (Carneros) $20. 88 *—S.H. (12/1/2006)*

EUGENE WINE CELLARS

Eugene Wine Cellars 1999 Melon (Oregon) $14. 85 *—P.G. (11/1/2001)*

Eugene Wine Cellars 1999 Pinot Gris (Oregon) $14. 85 *—P.G. (11/1/2001)*

Eugene Wine Cellars 1999 Pinot Noir (Oregon) $15. 82 *—P.G. (11/1/2001)*

Eugene Wine Cellars 1999 Syrah (Oregon) $23. 83 *—P.G. (11/1/2001)*

Eugene Wine Cellars 1999 Viognier (Oregon) $18. 84 *—P.G. (11/1/2001)*

EVERETT RIDGE

Everett Ridge 1997 Cabernet Sauvignon (Dry Creek Valley) $22. 86 *—S.H. (12/31/1999)*

Everett Ridge 1999 Cabernet Sauvignon (Dry Creek Valley) $28. 84 *—S.H. (12/15/2003)*

Everett Ridge 2002 Pinot Noir (Russian River Valley) $30. 87 *(11/1/2004)*

Everett Ridge 2004 Sauvignon Blanc (Dry Creek Valley) $15. 87 *—S.H. (8/1/2006)*

Everett Ridge 2003 Powerhouse Vineyard Sauvignon Blanc (Mendocino County) $15. 86 *—S.H. (12/15/2004)*

Everett Ridge 2002 Powerhouse Vineyard Sauvignon Blanc (Mendocino County) $14. 82 *—S.H. (3/1/2004)*

Everett Ridge 2000 Powerhouse Vineyard Sauvignon Blanc (Mendocino) $13. 85 *(9/1/2003)*

Everett Ridge 2002 Nuns Canyon Vineyard Syrah (Sonoma Valley) $24. 87 *(9/1/2005)*

Everett Ridge 2001 Nuns Canyon Vineyard Syrah (Sonoma Valley) $28. 85 *—S.H. (12/15/2004)*

Everett Ridge 2000 Nuns Canyon Vineyard Syrah (Sonoma Valley) $26. 88 *—S.H. (12/15/2003)*

Everett Ridge 1999 Nuns Canyon Vineyard Syrah (Sonoma Valley) $26. 89 *(11/1/2001)*

Everett Ridge 2001 Zinfandel (Dry Creek Valley) $28. 90 *(11/1/2003)*

Everett Ridge 2000 Zinfandel (Dry Creek Valley) $28. 83 *—S.H. (9/1/2003)*

Everett Ridge 2002 Estate Zinfandel (Dry Creek Valley) $22. 87 *—S.H. (10/1/2006)*

Everett Ridge 1998 Old Vines Zinfandel (Dry Creek Valley) $22. 90 *—P.G. (3/1/2001)*

Everett Ridge 1997 Old Vines Zinfandel (Dry Creek Valley) $20. 89 *—S.H. (2/1/2000)*

EVESHAM WOOD

Evesham Wood 1998 Pinot Noir (Willamette Valley) $15. 87 Best Buy *—J.C. (12/1/2000)*

Evesham Wood 2004 Cuvée J Pinot Noir (Willamette Valley) $38. The 2004 vintage produced a forward, fruity Cuvée J, sporting pretty scents of cherry cola. Light in color, it's fresh, fruit-driven and carries a streak of vanilla from still-unresolved oak. If there is a quibble, it's that the finish has some heat in it, and the fruit, though sweet and pretty, brings along no extra measure of extract or texture, things you look for in a top-end Pinot. 87 *—P.G. (7/1/2007)*

Evesham Wood 1997 Estate Vineyard Pinot Noir (Willamette Valley) $21. 84 *(10/1/1999)*

Evesham Wood 1998 Le Puits Sec Cuvée J Pinot Noir (Willamette Valley) $36. 86 *—M.S. (12/1/2000)*

Evesham Wood 1997 Shea Vineyard Cuvée 'J' Pinot Noir (Willamette Valley) $27.5. 86 *(10/1/1999)*

Evesham Wood 1998 Temperance Hill Vineyard Pinot Noir (Willamette Valley) $24. 89 *—M.M. (12/1/2000)*

EXP

EXP 2000 Syrah (Dunnigan Hills) $14. 83 *—S.H. (12/1/2002)*

EXP 1999 Syrah (Dunnigan Hills) $14. 85 *(10/1/2001)*

EXP 1999 Tempranillo (Dunnigan Hills) $25. 88 *—S.H. (12/1/2002)*

EXP 2002 Viognier (Dunnigan Hills) $14. 87 *—S.H. (6/1/2004)*

EXP 2001 Viognier (Dunnigan Hills) $14. 82 *—S.H. (12/15/2002)*

EXP 2003 Estate Bottled Viognier (Dunnigan Hills) $14. 84 *—S.H. (8/1/2005)*

EYRIE

Eyrie 2003 Pinot Gris (Willamette Valley) $16. 89 *—P.G. (2/1/2006)*

FAGAN CREEK

Fagan Creek 2002 Horsley Vineyards Syrah (Dunnigan Hills) $16. 88 *(9/1/2005)*

FAILLA

Failla 2003 Estate Vineyard Syrah (Sonoma Coast) $48. 92 Editors' Choice *(9/1/2005)*

Failla 2003 Phoenix Ranch Syrah (Napa Valley) $38. 90 *(9/1/2005)*

FAILLA JORDAN

Failla Jordan 2000 Keefer Ranch Chardonnay (Russian River Valley) $32. 93 Editors' Choice *—S.H. (7/1/2003)*

Failla Jordan 2001 Hirsch Vineyard Pinot Noir (Sonoma Coast) $48. 91 *—S.H. (7/1/2003)*

Failla Jordan 2001 Keefer Ranch Pinot Noir (Russian River Valley) $38. 90 *—S.H. (7/1/2003)*

Failla Jordan 2000 Estate Syrah (Sonoma Coast) $48. 92 Editors' Choice *—J.M. (12/1/2002)*

Failla Jordan 2000 Que Syrah Vineyard Syrah (Sonoma Coast) $45. 90 *—J.M. (12/1/2002)*

FALCONE

Falcone 2005 Cabernet Sauvignon (Paso Robles) $28. Soft and generous in fruit, this wine needs a good steak to show its stuff. It's dry, with a gentle scour of tannins framing earthy blackberry, cherry, blueberry, orange zest and oak flavors, and a dustiness that calls Rutherford to mind. Grows in the glass. 90 *—S.H. (9/1/2007)*

Falcone 2005 Syrah (Paso Robles) $28. Shows the better side of Paso Syrah, with a white pepper and sweet leather note to the cherry, blackberry and black raspberry fruit. The wine is soft and dry, with just enough acidity and tannins for structure, and a very long, persistent finish. Drink now. 90 *—S.H. (9/1/2007)*

Falcone 2002 Mia's Vineyard Syrah (Paso Robles) $28. 85 *(9/1/2005)*

FALCONER

Falconer 1997 Late Disgorged Blanc de Noir Champagne Blend (Sonoma) $22. 83 *—S.H. (12/1/2002)*

FALCOR

Falcor 2002 Le Bijou Bordeaux Blend (Napa Valley) $38. 92 *—S.H. (12/31/2006)*

Falcor 2003 Cabernet Franc (Napa Valley) $38. Lots to like in this wine, with plush, smoky oak framing luscious red and black cherry and chocolate flavors, and the finish is smooth and dry. The major flaw is an excessive softness that makes the wine lack balance. 87 *—S.H. (12/15/2007)*

Falcor 2002 Cabernet Sauvignon (Napa Valley) $48. 93 *—S.H. (12/31/2006)*

Falcor 2001 Chardonnay (Napa Valley) $35. 85 *—S.H. (5/1/2005)*

Falcor 2004 Bacigalupi Vineyard Chardonnay (Russian River Valley) $38. There's a decent wine here, crisp and ripe in pineapple flavor, but it's been buried under so much oak, it's practically invisible. The wine reeks of woodsap and charred barrels, dominated by a sweet vanilla taste. 83 *—S.H. (12/15/2007)*

Falcor 2003 Bacigalupi Vineyard Chardonnay (Russian River Valley) $38. 86 *—S.H. (12/31/2006)*

Falcor 2004 Durell Vineyard Chardonnay (Sonoma Valley) $42. The idea here was to make a white Burgundy-style Chardonnay with lots of oak. But the new oak is so strong that it overshadows what's actually a pretty nice wine underneath. You have to dive down through an ocean of smoky char, woody vanilla and sweet woodsap to find the basic peach and pineapple flavors. 84 *—S.H. (12/15/2007)*

Falcor 2003 Genny's Vineyard Chardonnay (Napa Valley) $35. 86 *—S.H. (12/31/2006)*

Falcor 2001 Merlot (Napa Valley) $32. 84 *—S.H. (5/1/2005)*

Falcor 2005 Rosé Rosé Blend (California) $15. 83 *—S.H. (12/31/2006)*

Falcor 2004 Sangiovese (Napa Valley) $32. Falcor's previous Sangioveses both seemed underripe. This one's just the opposite, a soft, jammy wine with sweetened cherry and raspberry candy flavors. 83 *—S.H. (12/15/2007)*

Falcor 2003 Sangiovese (Napa Valley) $29. 82 *—S.H. (12/31/2006)*

Falcor 2004 Syrah (Napa Valley) $32. This is quite a good Syrah that impresses all the way through. The first sniff is of a burst of white pepper, while the first sip assaults the palate, in a good way, with ripe blackberry, plum, mulberry and roasted meat flavors, and a sprinkling of cloves and anise. It's an upscale wine, but softness will limit ageability, so drink now through 2008. 91 *—S.H. (12/15/2007)*

Falcor 2004 Zinfandel (Sonoma County) $34. From grapes in the Russian River and Dry Creek valleys, this Zin, which has a fine, complex tannic structure, shows a raisiny, sweet edge that was a result of the searing vintage. Overripe fruit gives a taste of sugared blackberry juice. 86 *—S.H. (12/15/2007)*

FALKNER

Falkner 2000 Chardonnay (South Coast) $8. 80 *—S.H. (10/1/2003)*

Falkner 2000 Reserve Chardonnay (South Coast) $18. 81 *—S.H. (8/1/2003)*

Falkner 2002 Meritage (Temecula) $30. 83 *—S.H. (12/15/2005)*

Falkner 2002 Merlot (Temecula) $20. 87 *—S.H. (12/15/2005)*

Falkner 2000 Muscat Canelli (South Coast) $12. 85 *—S.H. (12/15/2003)*

Falkner 2002 Amante Red Blend (South Coast) $25. 86 *—S.H. (12/15/2005)*

Falkner 2001 Riesling (Temecula) $13. 84 *—S.H. (12/31/2003)*

Falkner 1999 Amante Sangiovese (South Coast) $16. 93 Editors' Choice *—S.H. (4/1/2002)*

Falkner 2001 Sauvignon Blanc (Temecula) $11. 81 *(10/1/2003)*

Falkner 2000 Sauvignon Blanc (South Coast) $10. 86 *—S.H. (4/1/2002)*

Falkner 2001 Viognier (Temecula) $13. 82 *—S.H. (12/1/2003)*

FALL CREEK VINEYARD

Fall Creek Vineyard 2002 Meritus Cabernet Sauvignon (Texas) $30. 84 *—J.C. (9/1/2005)*

FALL LINE

Fall Line 2004 Bordeaux Blend (Red Mountain) $30. A blend of 45% Merlot, 45% Cab Franc and the rest Cab. The wine is compact and tannic, but not over-built or chalky. It clearly demonstrates the underlying iron and mineral character of Red Mountain, and despite its youth it drinks well with a bit of breathing time. This is a wine that should continue to evolve nicely in bottle for up to a decade. 92 *—P.G. (5/1/2007)*

Fall Line 2004 Bordeaux Blend (Horse Heaven Hills) $30. A seductive, creamy and mouthfilling Bordeaux blend. The buttery, caramel flavors pour over the ripe, cherry-flavored fruit like butterscotch on pie. It's a ripe, open style that may well be the consumer favorite of this excellent trio of releases from a very promising new winery. 90 *—P.G. (5/1/2007)*

Fall Line 2004 Cabernet Sauvignon (Columbia Valley (WA)) $30. This 100% Cab inverts the formula of the winery's other two reds, blending vineyards rather than varieties. About 45% comes from Boushey in the Yakima Valley, another 45% from Artz on Red Mountain, and the rest from Destiny Ridge in the Horse Heaven Hills. It is the most fruit-driven and forward of the three, and the well-matched vineyard blend puts the focus on the varietal character of the grape, using the different terroirs to create a complete wine. Very sophisticated handling of the different lots creates a whole that is worthy of its parts. 91 *—P.G. (5/1/2007)*

FALLBROOK

Fallbrook 2001 Reserve Cabernet Sauvignon (California) $16. 83 *—S.H. (10/1/2005)*

Fallbrook 2002 Special Selection Cabernet Sauvignon (South Coast) $25. 83 *—S.H. (10/1/2005)*

Fallbrook 2000 Special Selection Cabernet Sauvignon (California) $25. 84 *—S.H. (10/1/2005)*

Fallbrook 2005 Reserve Chardonnay (California) $14. Not much to like in this semisweet, soft Chard. It tastes like the syrup from canned peaches and pears. 80 *—S.H. (11/15/2007)*

Fallbrook 2002 Chardonnay (California) $14. 84 *—S.H. (10/1/2005)*

Fallbrook 2002 Sleepy Hollow Vineyard Chardonnay (Monterey) $20. 87 *—S.H. (10/1/2005)*

Fallbrook 2004 Reserve Sleepy Hollow Vineyard Chardonnay (Monterey County) $25. Oak dominates, with a powerful taste of caramel and char flattening the underlying fruit. The basic wine seems to be pretty good, with crisp acidity and mineral and pineapple flavors. But all that oak is heavy-handed and unnecessary. 83 *—S.H. (12/1/2007)*

Fallbrook 2005 Reserve Merlot (California) $16. Soft and semisweet, this simple wine has sugary cherry juice flavors. It contains 18% Syrah. 81 *—S.H. (12/1/2007)*

Fallbrook 2002 Reserve Merlot (California) $16. 84 *—S.H. (10/1/2005)*

Fallbrook 2000 Special Selection Merlot (California) $25. 86 *—S.H. (10/1/2005)*

Fallbrook 2006 Reserve Yakut Vineyard Sauvignon Blanc (South Coast) $14. The acidity is just fine, a racy .7g/L, which makes for a clean stimulation that gets the tastebuds going. But the wine is simply too sweet; it tastes like sugary lemonade. 82 *—S.H. (11/15/2007)*

Fallbrook 2004 Yakut Vineyard Sauvignon Blanc (South Coast) $12. 84 *—S.H. (10/1/2005)*

Fallbrook 2004 Special Selection Syrah (Central Coast) $30. There's nothing special about this Syrah. It's not only soft and semisweet, it's thin in fruit, with watered-down blackberry jelly flavors. 80 *—S.H. (12/1/2007)*

FANTESCA

Fantesca 2002 Cabernet Sauvignon (Spring Mountain) $60. 92 Editors' Choice *—S.H. (12/15/2005)*

FANUCCHI

Fanucchi 2005 Wood Road Vineyard Trousseau Gris (Russian River Valley) $19. Smells honeyed and tastes like one of those fruity bottled sodas. It's a riot of peaches, pears and vanilla cream, with a honey-sweet finish. 84 *—S.H. (12/1/2007)*

Fanucchi 2003 Trousseau Gris (Russian River Valley) $15. 84 *—S.H. (10/1/2004)*

Fanucchi 2004 Old Vine Zinfandel (Russian River Valley) $45. This is a hot, sweet Zinfandel, with an alcohol level of 15.4%. It's very ripe and forward in jammy cherry-berry fruit, with a spicy edge of cola and mocha. It contains some Petite Sirah and Alicante, like an old-fashioned field blend. 83 *—S.H. (12/15/2007)*

Fanucchi 2001 Old Vine Zinfandel (Russian River Valley) $29. 87 *(11/1/2003)*

Fanucchi 2000 Old Vine Zinfandel (Russian River Valley) $29. 85 *—S.H. (12/15/2004)*

Fanucchi 1998 Old Vine Zinfandel (Russian River Valley) $29. 88 *—S.H. (12/1/2002)*

Fanucchi 1997 Old Vine Zinfandel (Russian River Valley) $24.90 *—S.H. (5/1/2000)*

Fanucchi 1996 Old Vine Zinfandel (Russian River Valley) $35. 91 *—S.H. (9/1/1999)*

FAR NIENTE

Far Niente 2003 Cabernet Sauvignon (Oakville) $115. 94 *—S.H. (12/15/2006)*

Far Niente 2001 Cabernet Sauvignon (Oakville) $100. 91 *—S.H. (10/1/2004)*

Far Niente 1997 Cabernet Sauvignon (Napa Valley) $100. 93 *(11/1/2000)*

Far Niente 2002 Estate Cabernet Sauvignon (Oakville) $110. 92 *—S.H. (10/1/2005)*

Far Niente 1998 Chardonnay (Napa Valley) $44. 91 *—S.H. (2/1/2000)*

Far Niente 1997 Chardonnay (Napa Valley) $44. 90 *—S.H. (10/1/1999)*

Far Niente 2002 Chardonnay (Napa Valley) $52. 91 *—S.H. (11/15/2004)*

Far Niente 2000 Estate Bottled Chardonnay (Napa Valley) $52. 89 *—S.H. (9/1/2002)*

Far Niente 1999 Estate Bottled Chardonnay (Napa Valley) $52. 90 *(7/1/2001)*

FARALLON

Farallon 1997 Merlot (North Coast) $10. 84 Best Buy *—J.C. (7/1/2000)*

FARELLA

Farella 2001 Alta Cabernet Sauvignon-Merlot (Napa Valley) $50. One of the last released 2001 Cabs. At five years, the wine is good, but tannic, acidic and hot. From such a great vintage, you have to wonder why. Was it picked too early? It might go somewhere, because there's some fruit down in there, but for now, it's way too expensive for what you get. 84 *—S.H. (3/1/2007)*

FARELLA-PARK

Farella-Park 2002 Cabernet Sauvignon (Napa Valley) $32. Grown in the cooler, southeastern Coombsville section of the valley, this 100% Cab is big, rich and dry. It fills the mouth with ripe blackberry and cherry flavors that are jammy and oaky. Finishing a bit sharp, it should mellow for a few more years. 85 *—S.H. (3/1/2007)*

Farella-Park 1997 Cabernet Sauvignon (Napa Valley) $32. 91 *(11/1/2000)*

Farella-Park 1996 Cabernet Sauvignon (Napa Valley) $32. 91 *—S.H. (7/1/2000)*

Farella-Park 1996 Merlot (Napa Valley) $24. 90 *—S.H. (7/1/2000)*

Farella-Park 2005 Sauvignon Blanc (Napa Valley) $14. Sits right on the border of everday and fancy, one of those wines that's not so impressive on its own, but can rise to the occasion with the right food. Quite crisp, with minerally, citrus rind, melon and date flavors. Versatile with food. 86 *—S.H. (3/1/2007)*

FARM BOY

Farm Boy 2005 Red Table Wine Red Blend (Yakima Valley) $18. Roughly two-thirds Cabernet Sauvignon and one-third Syrah, this soft, dark and fruity wine offers surprisingly deep and luscious flavors of sweet boysenberry and black cherry. The star of the Farm Boy lineup by a wide margin, it has a lively snap to the fruit and a pleasing sweet/tart finish. **88** *—P.G. (12/31/2007)*

Farm Boy 2006 Riesling (Yakima Valley) $12. Very sharp and acidic, this is dominated by a pine-scented diesel note. It has plenty of bite and intensity, but a harsh, hot finish. **83** *—P.G. (12/1/2007)*

Farm Boy 2006 Rosé Blend (Columbia Valley (WA)) $0. This Sangiovese and Cabernet Franc-based rosé is the pale color of Pinot Noir. Scents offer up rhubarb and sour plum; and the finishing hits a strong sour note. **82** *—P.G. (12/1/2007)*

FAT CAT

Fat Cat 2005 Chardonnay (California) $10. 80 *—S.H. (12/31/2006)*

Fat Cat 2004 Merlot (California) $10. 83 *—S.H. (12/31/2006)*

FATTORIA ENOTRIA

Fattoria Enotria 1997 Dolcetto (Mendocino) $16. 84 *(9/1/2000)*

FEATHER

Feather 2004 Cabernet Sauvignon (Columbia Valley (WA)) $55. This is 100% Cabernet from a mix of vineyards scattered across the state. Lovely aromatics, impressive purity, a confident attack and fine-tuned flavors—blueberry and boysenberry and black cherry—are well matched to oak and acid. **92** *—P.G. (8/1/2007)*

Feather 2003 Cabernet Sauvignon (Columbia Valley (WA)) $55. 91 *—P.G. (6/1/2006)*

FENESTRA

Fenestra 2003 Silvaspoons Vineyard Alvarelhão (Lodi) $18. 84 *—S.H. (12/1/2006)*

Fenestra 2001 Chardonnay (Contra Costa County) $14. 81 *—S.H. (4/1/2004)*

Fenestra 2001 Chardonnay (Livermore Valley) $16. 81 *—S.H. (4/1/2004)*

Fenestra 2000 Merlot (Livermore Valley) $19. 84 *—S.H. (6/1/2004)*

Fenestra 2000 Merlot (Santa Lucia Highlands) $17. 81 *—S.H. (6/1/2004)*

Fenestra 2003 Estate Mourvèdre (Livermore Valley) $17. 83 *—S.H. (12/1/2006)*

Fenestra 1999 Petite Sirah (Lodi) $17. 86 *(4/1/2003)*

Fenestra 2003 Pinot Noir (Livermore Valley) $22. 86 *—S.H. (12/1/2006)*

Fenestra 2002 Silvaspoons Vineyard Port Port (Lodi) $17. 90 *—S.H. (12/1/2006)*

Fenestra NV True Red Lot 16 Rhône Red Blend (Lodi) $9. 83 *—S.H. (6/1/2004)*

Fenestra 2002 Dry Rose Rosé Blend (California) $8. 83 *—S.H. (6/1/2004)*

Fenestra 2000 Sangiovese (Lodi) $14. 82 *—S.H. (6/1/2004)*

Fenestra 2002 Sauvignon Blanc (Livermore Valley) $16. 81 *—S.H. (3/1/2004)*

Fenestra 2002 Sémillon (Livermore Valley) $9. 82 *—S.H. (3/1/2004)*

Fenestra 2002 Semonnay Sémillon-Chardonnay (Livermore Valley) $13. 81 *—S.H. (3/1/2004)*

Fenestra 1999 Syrah (Livermore Valley) $20. 85 *—S.H. (2/1/2004)*

Fenestra 2000 Estate Syrah (Livermore Valley) $15. 88 Editors' Choice *(9/1/2005)*

Fenestra 2000 Reserve Syrah (Livermore Valley) $18. 87 *(9/1/2005)*

Fenestra 2003 Silvaspoons Vineyard Tempranillo (Lodi) $19. 85 *—S.H. (12/1/2006)*

Fenestra 2003 Silvaspoons Vineyard Touriga Franca (Lodi) $22. 85 *—S.H. (12/1/2006)*

Fenestra 2002 Viognier (Contra Costa County) $17. 85 *—S.H. (6/1/2004)*

Fenestra 1999 Zinfandel (Livermore Valley) $17. 87 *—S.H. (3/1/2004)*

FERNWOOD

Fernwood 2002 Redwood Retreat Vineyards Cabernet Sauvignon (Santa Cruz Mountains) $40. 82 *—S.H. (4/1/2006)*

Fernwood 2005 Vanumanutagi Vineyard Chardonnay (Santa Cruz Mountains) $30. With too much oak and too sweet fruit, the result is an unbalanced Chardonnay. It tastes like LifeSaver lemon candies cooked into a baked Alaska dessert. **82** *—S.H. (6/1/2007)*

Fernwood 2005 Machado Creek Vineyards Petite Sirah (Central Coast) $30. This is a very good Petite Sirah. It's dark and inky and tannic, as you'd expect, and ultrajuicy in blackberries, plums, black cherries, moo shu pork sauce, dark chocolate truffle, balsamic and white pepper flavors. Sure is good now. **92** *—S.H. (6/1/2007)*

Fernwood 2003 Redwood Retreat Vineyards Syrah (Santa Cruz Mountains) $33. 90 *—S.H. (4/1/2006)*

Fernwood 2002 Zinfandel (El Dorado) $27. 82 *—S.H. (2/1/2005)*

Fernwood 2002 Redwood Retreat Vineyards Zinfandel (Santa Cruz Mountains) $27. 82 *—S.H. (2/1/2005)*

FERRARI-CARANO

Ferrari-Carano 2000 Eldorado Noir Black Muscat (Russian River Valley) $25. 86 *(11/1/2002)*

Ferrari-Carano 2004 Trésor Bordeaux Blend (Sonoma County) $55. It has been some years since I last tasted this proprietary Bordeaux blend, and it's nice to see it's a very good wine. A little hard and unresolved now, it shows a wealth of oak-infused blackberry, cherry, olive and cocoa flavors, and an acid-tannin balance that will help it age. Best 2008–2010 or so. **90** *—S.H. (12/1/2007)*

Ferrari-Carano 1999 Trésor Bordeaux Blend (Sonoma County) $45. 90 *—S.H. (8/1/2004)*

Ferrari-Carano 1999 Trésor Red Table Wine Bordeaux Blend (Sonoma County) $32. 92 *—S.H. (12/1/2004)*

Ferrari-Carano 1994 Tresor Reserve Bordeaux Blend (Sonoma County) $65. 87 *—S.H. (3/1/2000)*

Ferrari-Carano 2001 Trésor Cabernet Blend (Alexander Valley) $45. 86 *—S.H. (12/1/2005)*

Ferrari-Carano 2004 Cabernet Sauvignon (Alexander Valley) $34. Smells just gorgeous and tastes the same way. This is a Cab to savor. It's pure Alexander Valley, soft, dry and complex, with rich cherry and vanilla fruit, accented by smoky oak. The tannins are gentle and finely grained. **90** *—S.H. (9/1/2007)*

Ferrari-Carano 2003 Cabernet Sauvignon (Alexander Valley) $30. 88 *—S.H. (12/31/2006)*

Ferrari-Carano 2002 Cabernet Sauvignon (Alexander Valley) $34. 84 *—S.H. (12/1/2005)*

Ferrari-Carano 2001 Cabernet Sauvignon (Sonoma County) $28. 91 *—S.H. (8/1/2004)*

Ferrari-Carano 1999 TreMonte Cabernet Sauvignon (Alexander Valley) $38. 86 *—J.M. (11/15/2002)*

Ferrari-Carano 1998 Tremonte Cabernet Sauvignon (Alexander Valley) $38. 86 *(11/1/2002)*

Ferrari-Carano 1998 Chardonnay (Sonoma County) $25. 87 *(6/1/2000)*

Ferrari-Carano 1997 Chardonnay (Sonoma County) $22. 92 *—M.S. (7/1/1999)*

Ferrari-Carano 2004 Chardonnay (Alexander Valley) $28. 83 *—S.H. (12/31/2006)*

Ferrari-Carano 2003 Chardonnay (Alexander Valley) $28. 90 *—S.H. (12/1/2005)*

Ferrari-Carano 2001 Chardonnay (Alexander Valley) $23. 86 *—S.H. (8/1/2004)*

Ferrari-Carano 2000 Chardonnay (Alexander Valley) $25. 87 *(11/1/2002)*

Ferrari-Carano 2005 Dominique Chardonnay (Russian River Valley) $38. Tastes of new oak and is also acidic, a combo that makes the mouthfeel rather harsh and salty, despite obviously well-ripened fruit. May settle down and show softer, lusher notes in a year or so. **87** *—S.H. (10/1/2007)*

Ferrari-Carano 2005 Emelia's Cuvée Chardonnay (Russian River Valley) $36. Rich and appealing, a new bottling from the winery. All the parts have yet to knit together, but they're all good, and the wine should drink well by winter 2007. New oak frames tart green apple, pineapple, kumquat and cinnamon spice flavors that are heightened by bright, zesty acidity. **90** *—S.H. (10/1/2007)*

Ferrari-Carano 2005 Fiorella Chardonnay (Russian River Valley) $36. There's a minerality to this pleasantly dry Chard, a stony tang that dominates, although you'll find pineapple underpinnings. It's a leaner, more elegant style, and the winemaker has tried to enrich it with oak, sur lie aging and 50% malolactic fermentation. **87** *—S.H. (10/1/2007)*

Ferrari-Carano 2003 Reserve Chardonnay (Napa-Sonoma) $42. 89 *—S.H. (12/1/2005)*

Ferrari-Carano 2001 Reserve Chardonnay (Carneros) $32. 92 *—S.H. (6/1/2004)*

Ferrari-Carano 2001 Reserve Chardonnay (Carneros) $32. 89 *—S.H. (8/1/2004)*

Ferrari-Carano 2000 Reserve Chardonnay (Carneros) $32. 89 *—J.M. (12/15/2002)*

Ferrari-Carano 1999 Reserve Chardonnay (Napa County) $32. 89 *(7/1/2001)*

Ferrari-Carano 2005 Tré Terre Chardonnay (Russian River Valley) $36. This is a new, reserve-style wine from veteran Ferrari-Carano. It shows its cool-climate origins in the brisk acidity that boosts well-ripened pineapple tart, green apple sauce, and Key lime pie flavors. It's also extremely oaky, and would be a better wine if it had less barrel influence. **87** —*S.H.* *(10/1/2007)*

Ferrari-Carano 2004 Tre Terre Chardonnay (Russian River Valley) $34. 84 —*S.H. (12/31/2006)*

Ferrari-Carano 2000 TreMonte Chardonnay (Alexander Valley) $32. 87 *(11/1/2002)*

Ferrari-Carano 2006 Fumé Blanc (Sonoma County) $17. This 100% Sauv is delicately structured and dry and crisp in acidity. While it has a touch of oak, the fruit has been allowed to star. Lemon, lime, green apple, fig, honeydew and vanilla all come together in this pure, fresh wine. **87** —*S.H.* *(10/1/2007)*

Ferrari-Carano 2005 Fumé Blanc (Sonoma County) $16. 85 —*S.H.* *(12/31/2006)*

Ferrari-Carano 2004 Fumé Blanc (Sonoma County) $16. 84 —*S.H.* *(12/1/2005)*

Ferrari-Carano 2003 Fumé Blanc (Sonoma County) $15. 89 —*S.H.* *(12/31/2004)*

Ferrari-Carano 2002 Fumé Blanc (Sonoma County) $15. 85 —*S.H.* *(7/1/2003)*

Ferrari-Carano 2001 Fumé Blanc (Sonoma County) $15. 88 Best Buy *(11/1/2002)*

Ferrari-Carano 2000 Fumé Blanc (Sonoma County) $15. 87 —*J.M.* *(11/15/2001)*

Ferrari-Carano 1998 Fumé Blanc (Sonoma County) $12. 89 Best Buy —*S.H. (3/1/2000)*

Ferrari-Carano 1996 Fumé Blanc (Sonoma County) $11. 88 Best Buy —*S.H. (9/1/1999)*

Ferrari-Carano 1998 Reserve Fumé Blanc (Sonoma County) $18. 89 —*S.H.* *(3/1/2000)*

Ferrari-Carano 2004 Merlot (Sonoma County) $25. The winery did a nice job with this high production (19,000 cases) Merlot, which was assembled from various parts of the county. The wine is dry and spicy, with scoury tannins that frame cherry, tobacco, thyme and dill flavors. Drink now. **87** —*S.H. (12/15/2007)*

Ferrari-Carano 2003 Merlot (Sonoma County) $25. 87 —*S.H. (12/31/2006)*

Ferrari-Carano 2002 Merlot (Sonoma County) $25. 91 —*S.H. (12/1/2005)*

Ferrari-Carano 2001 Merlot (Sonoma County) $25. 86 —*S.H. (12/31/2004)*

Ferrari-Carano 1999 Merlot (Sonoma County) $23. 87 *(11/1/2002)*

Ferrari-Carano 1999 TreMonte Merlot (Alexander Valley) $32. 86 *(11/1/2002)*

Ferrari-Carano 1997 Vineyards of TreMonte Merlot (Sonoma County) $28. 86 —*J.C. (6/1/2001)*

Ferrari-Carano 2005 Siena Red Blend (Sonoma County) $24. This is the winery's Sangiovese-based blend, with small amounts of Malbec and Zinfandel. It's a rustic, lusty wine, with hard acids and sturdy tannins framing dry flavors of blackberry tea and raspberry jam. Drink now, with big, rich fare. **86** —*S.H. (12/15/2007)*

Ferrari-Carano 2000 Siena Red Blend (Sonoma County) $24. 92 Editors' Choice —*S.H. (11/15/2003)*

Ferrari-Carano 1999 Siena Red Blend (Sonoma County) $28. 91 *(11/1/2002)*

Ferrari-Carano 1997 Tresor Reserve Red Blend (Sonoma County) $45. 86 *(11/1/2002)*

Ferrari-Carano 1996 Siena Sangiovese (Sonoma County) $28. 90 *(10/1/1999)*

Ferrari-Carano 1997 Vineyards of Tremonte Sangiovese (Alexander Valley) $28. 88 —*S.H. (12/1/2001)*

Ferrari-Carano 1996 Vineyards of TreMonte Sangiovese (Sonoma County) $35. 87 —*M.S. (10/1/1999)*

Ferrari-Carano 1998 Storey Creek Vineyard Sauvignon Blanc (Russian River Valley) $15. 90 —*S.H. (3/1/2000)*

Ferrari-Carano 1997 TreMonte Syrah (Sonoma County) $32. 86 *(11/1/2001)*

Ferrari-Carano 2005 Zinfandel (Dry Creek Valley) $30. With small amounts of Carignane and Petite Sirah, this hails from the winery's estate vineyard in Dry Creek Valley, one of the great sources of Zinfandel in California. It is a very fine Zin, showing near perfect balance. Tannic and dry, the blackberry, blueberry, cherry, chocolate, sweet leather and spice flavors are enriched with the vanilla and smoky char of oak. **92 Editors' Choice** —*S.H. (12/15/2007)*

Ferrari-Carano 2004 Zinfandel (Dry Creek Valley) $26. Tastes unevenly ripened, with a thyme and peppermint jelly green quality side by side with blackberry jam and blueberry pie filling. The wine also straddles the border of dry and raisiny, Port-y sweet. In its own curious way, it's complex. **87** —*S.H. (11/1/2007)*

Ferrari-Carano 1996 Zinfandel (Sonoma) $16. 88 —*S.H. (9/1/1999)*

FESS PARKER

Fess Parker 2005 Chardonnay (Santa Barbara County) $18. Ripe in fruit, oaky and spicy, with a creamy texture. All the parts are there, it just feels one-dimensional. **83** —*S.H. (7/1/2007)*

Fess Parker 2004 Chardonnay (Santa Barbara County) $18. 85 —*S.H. (5/1/2006)*

Fess Parker 2001 Chardonnay (Santa Barbara County) $18. 86 —*S.H. (12/15/2002)*

Fess Parker 1998 Chardonnay (Santa Barbara County) $16. 87 *(6/1/2000)*

Fess Parker 1996 American Tradition Reserve Chardonnay (Santa Barbara County) $22. 91 —*S.H. (7/1/1999)*

Fess Parker 2005 Ashley's Vineyard Chardonnay (Santa Rita Hills) $28. This is a bold, oaky Chardonnay. Toasty roasted-nut aromas lead the charge, followed by hints of peach and melon, while a strong vanilla component comes forward on the palate. Finishes warm, with prominent oak spice. **89** —*S.H. (12/31/2007)*

Fess Parker 2004 Ashley's Vineyard Chardonnay (Santa Rita Hills) $28. 93 Editors' Choice —*S.H. (10/1/2006)*

Fess Parker 2003 Ashley's Vineyard Chardonnay (Santa Rita Hills) $26. 93 Editors' Choice —*S.H. (11/1/2005)*

Fess Parker 1997 Santa Barbara County Chardonnay (Santa Barbara County) $15. 89 —*S.H. (7/1/1999)*

Fess Parker 2005 Pinot Noir (Santa Barbara County) $25. The winery's vineyard-designated '05 Pinots have been so good, it's a disappointment to find this one so common. The burnt, ashy taste here seems to be from well-toasted oak meant to make up for thin fruit. **83** —*S.H. (7/1/2007)*

Fess Parker 2004 Pinot Noir (Santa Barbara County) $25. 83 —*S.H. (5/1/2006)*

Fess Parker 2002 Pinot Noir (Santa Barbara County) $22. 85 —*S.H. (11/1/2004)*

Fess Parker 2000 Pinot Noir (Santa Barbara County) $20. 86 —*S.H. (2/1/2003)*

Fess Parker 1999 Pinot Noir (Santa Barbara County) $18. 88 Best Buy —*S.H. (12/15/2001)*

Fess Parker 2000 American Tradition Reserve Pinot Noir (Santa Barbara) $45. 85 *(10/1/2002)*

Fess Parker 1999 American Tradition Reserve Pinot Noir (Santa Barbara County) $32. 92 —*S.H. (12/15/2001)*

Fess Parker 2005 Ashley's Vineyard Pinot Noir (Santa Rita Hills) $52. Ashley's, sold recently by the Parkers and now renamed Gaia, is a fabulous vineyard on the coolest western edge of the appellation. In this long hangtime vintage, the grapes achieved spectacularly ripe, fruity flavors, of cherries, raspberry purée and sweet, oak-infused cola. But this is no mere fruit bomb. The acid-tannin balance is amazing, and the wine has a deeply impressive, long-lasting appeal. **94** —*S.H. (4/1/2007)*

Fess Parker 2004 Ashley's Vineyard Pinot Noir (Santa Rita Hills) $50. 84 —*S.H. (10/1/2006)*

Fess Parker 2003 Ashley's Vineyard Pinot Noir (Santa Rita Hills) $45. 94 Editors' Choice —*S.H. (11/1/2005)*

Fess Parker 2002 Ashley's Vineyard Pinot Noir (Santa Rita Hills) $45. 90 —*S.H. (11/1/2004)*

Fess Parker 2001 Ashley's Vineyard Pinot Noir (Santa Barbara County) $45. 93 —*S.H. (3/1/2004)*

Fess Parker 2005 Ashley's Vineyard Clone 115 Pinot Noir (Santa Rita Hills) $50. This single-clone barrel selection takes the essence of the gorgeous, regular '05 Ashley's and concentrates it. Brims with sautéed Portobello mushroom, tamari, tangerine zest and black cherry preserves, leading to an immaculately rich, delicately silky, nuanced and enormously complicated Pinot. Hard to exaggerate the purity and finesse. Drink now–2012, before the lush fruit fades. **96** —*S.H. (4/1/2007)*

Fess Parker 2005 Bien Nacido Vineyard Pinot Noir (Santa Barbara County) $50. Full-bodied, round and creamy in the mouth, this is a big Pinot, weighing in at 15.5% alcohol. Lush cola, plum and spice flavors are delicious, but warm on the finish. **87** *(7/1/2007)*

Fess Parker 2004 Bien Nacido Vineyard Pinot Noir (Santa Barbara County) $50. 88 —*S.H. (12/1/2006)*

Fess Parker 2002 Bien Nacido Vineyard Pinot Noir (Santa Barbara County) $45. 88 *—S.H. (11/1/2004)*

Fess Parker 2000 Bien Nacido Vineyard Pinot Noir (Santa Barbara County) $45. 85 *(10/1/2002)*

Fess Parker 1999 Bien Nacido Vineyard Pinot Noir (Santa Barbara County) $45. 93 *—S.H. (12/15/2001)*

Fess Parker 2000 Dierberg Vineyard Pinot Noir (Santa Barbara) $45. 85 *(10/1/2002)*

Fess Parker 2002 Marcella's Vineyard Pinot Noir (Santa Barbara County) $45. 88 *—S.H. (11/1/2004)*

Fess Parker 2000 Marcella's Vineyard Pinot Noir (Santa Barbara County) $45. 88 *(10/1/2002)*

Fess Parker 1999 Marcella's Vineyard Pinot Noir (Santa Barbara County) $45. 94 Editors' Choice *—S.H. (12/15/2001)*

Fess Parker 2005 Pommard Clone Pinot Noir (Santa Barbara County) $50. A blend of lots from Bien Nacido Vineyard and Ashley's Vineyard, this full-bodied Pinot features cola, mushroom and plum aromas, backed by similar flavors. It's crisper than the winery's other Pinot offerings, with an earthier component to its flavors. 88 *(7/1/2007)*

Fess Parker 1997 Santa Barbara County Pinot Noir (Santa Maria Valley) $18. 90 *(10/1/1999)*

Fess Parker NV Lot 22 Frontier Red Rhône Red Blend (California) $10. 87 Best Buy *—S.H. (5/1/2003)*

Fess Parker NV Lot 71 Frontier Red Blend (California) $10. A very nice everyday red—dry, soft and warming. The blend is of at least eight varieties, and the flavors range from ripe cherries and raspberries to gingerbread, oatmeal cookies, peppermint pattie and licorice, with a finish of Asian spices. 85 Best Buy *—S.H. (10/1/2007)*

Fess Parker 1997 Syrah (Santa Barbara County) $18. 89 *—S.H. (10/1/1999)*

Fess Parker 1996 Syrah (Santa Barbara County) $17. 92 *—S.H. (10/1/1999)*

Fess Parker 2002 Syrah (Santa Barbara County) $18. 84 *(9/1/2005)*

Fess Parker 2000 Syrah (Santa Barbara County) $20. 85 *—S.H. (12/1/2002)*

Fess Parker 1999 Syrah (Santa Barbara County) $20. 87 *—S.H. (7/1/2002)*

Fess Parker 2002 American Tradition Reserve Syrah (Santa Barbara County) $30. 83 *(9/1/2005)*

Fess Parker 2000 American Tradition Reserve Syrah (Santa Barbara County) $32. 88 *—S.H. (10/1/2003)*

Fess Parker 2000 Mackie's Blend Syrah (Central Coast) $13. 84 *—S.H. (12/15/2003)*

Fess Parker 2004 Rodney's Vineyard Syrah (Santa Barbara County) $40. Perhaps it's Fox's previous role as Rhône winemaker, but the Syrahs seem more complex and better balanced than the winery's Pinots, better able to handle the heady alcohol levels. This is a rich, syrupy wine, with concentrated fruit based on blackberries and spice, made more complex by hints of coffee, earth and grilled meat. 91 *(7/1/2007)*

Fess Parker 2002 Rodney's Vineyard Syrah (Santa Barbara County) $36. 86 *(9/1/2005)*

Fess Parker 2000 Rodney's Vineyard Syrah (Santa Barbara County) $36. 90 *—S.H. (3/1/2004)*

Fess Parker 1999 Rodney's Vineyard Syrah (Santa Barbara County) $30. 89 *(11/1/2001)*

Fess Parker 2004 The Big Easy Syrah (Santa Barbara County) $40. Slightly more peppery and herbal than the winery's Rodney's Vineyard Syrah, this has a rich, creamy texture and brighter fruit—more in the raspberry family than blackberry. Long on the finish, with attractively dusty tannins. 91 *7/1/2007)*

Fess Parker 2003 The Big Easy Syrah (Santa Barbara County) $35. 93 Editors' Choice *—S.H. (12/1/2006)*

Fess Parker 2002 The Big Easy Syrah (Santa Barbara County) $36. 85 *(9/1/2005)*

Fess Parker 2005 Viognier (Santa Barbara County) $22. This is a round, buxom Viognier, flashy and obvious, with upfront aromas of flowers, honey and spice backed by fruit-forward flavors of apricot and melon. Shows a touch of warmth on the finish. 87 *(7/1/2007)*

Fess Parker 1997 Viognier (Santa Barbara) $18. 91 *—S.H. (6/1/1999)*

Fess Parker 2004 Viognier (Santa Barbara County) $22. 90 *—S.H. (5/1/2006)*

Fess Parker 2001 Viognier (Santa Barbara County) $20. 88 *—S.H. (5/1/2003)*

Fess Parker 2000 Viognier (Santa Barbara County) $20. 90 Editors' Choice *—S.H. (11/15/2001)*

Fess Parker 1997 Melange du Rhône White Blend (Santa Barbara County) $15. 91 *—S.H. (6/1/1999)*

Fess Parker 2001 White Riesling (Santa Barbara County) $12. 85 *—S.H. (9/1/2003)*

FETZER

Fetzer 1998 Barrel Select Cabernet Sauvignon (North Coast) $17. 87 *—S.H. (9/5/2002)*

Fetzer 1997 Barrel Select Cabernet Sauvignon (North Coast) $15. 88 Best Buy *—P.G. (12/15/2000)*

Fetzer 1996 Barrel Select Cabernet Sauvignon (North Coast) $15. 88 *—S.H. (2/1/2000)*

Fetzer 1999 Five Rivers Ranch Cabernet Sauvignon (Central Coast) $13. 87 *(11/15/2001)*

Fetzer 1999 Reserve Cabernet Sauvignon (Napa Valley) $30. 90 *(5/1/2001)*

Fetzer 1998 Reserve Cabernet Sauvignon (Napa Valley) $40. 87 *—(11/15/2002)*

Fetzer 1996 Reserve Cabernet Sauvignon (Napa Valley) $30. 88 *—P.G. (12/15/2000)*

Fetzer 2004 Valley Oaks Cabernet Sauvignon (California) $9. 83 *—S.H. (5/1/2006)*

Fetzer 2003 Valley Oaks Cabernet Sauvignon (California) $9. 85 Best Buy *—S.H. (12/15/2005)*

Fetzer 1999 Valley Oaks Cabernet Sauvignon (California) $10. 86 Best Buy *—S.H. (6/1/2002)*

Fetzer 1998 Valley Oaks Cabernet Sauvignon (California) $13. 83 *(5/1/2001)*

Fetzer 1997 Valley Oaks Cabernet Sauvignon (California) $10. 87 *(11/15/1999)*

Fetzer 2000 Barrel Select Chardonnay (Mendocino County) $13. 84 *—S.H. (5/1/2002)*

Fetzer 1999 Barrel Select Chardonnay (Mendocino County) $14. 85 *(5/1/2001)*

Fetzer 2003 Five Rivers Ranch Chardonnay (Monterey County) $13. 82 *—S.H. (5/1/2005)*

Fetzer 2000 Five Rivers Ranch Chardonnay (Mendocino County) $14. 85 *(11/15/2001)*

Fetzer 1999 Sundial Chardonnay (California) $9. 81 *—S.H. (10/1/2000)*

Fetzer 1998 Sundial Chardonnay (California) $9. 86 Best Buy *—M.S. (10/1/1999)*

Fetzer 2006 Valley Oaks Chardonnay (California) $9. Like the '05, the '06 Valley Oaks Chard is another Best Buy. It's fruity, spicy and creamy, with a rich coating of oaky vanilla and a honeyed finish. Easy to find, with production of 650,000 cases. 84 Best Buy *—S.H. (11/15/2007)*

Fetzer 2005 Valley Oaks Chardonnay (California) $9. 85 Best Buy *—S.H. (11/15/2006)*

Fetzer 2004 Valley Oaks Chardonnay (California) $9. 87 Best Buy *—S.H. (12/1/2005)*

Fetzer 1998 Gewürztraminer (California) $8. 80 *—J.C. (11/1/1999)*

Fetzer 2001 Echo Ridge Gewürztraminer (California) $8. 87 *—S.H. (9/1/2003)*

Fetzer 2000 Echo Ridge Gewürztraminer (California) $10. 84 *(5/1/2001)*

Fetzer 2005 Valley Oaks Gewürztraminer (California) $9. 85 Best Buy *—S.H. (7/1/2006)*

Fetzer 2004 Valley Oaks Gewürztraminer (California) $9. 83 *—S.H. (12/1/2005)*

Fetzer 1998 Johannisberg Riesling (California) $8. 83 *—J.C. (11/1/1999)*

Fetzer 2002 Echo Ridge Johannisberg Riesling (California) $6. 87 Best Buy *—S.H. (11/15/2003)*

Fetzer 2001 Echo Ridge Johannisberg Riesling (California) $8. 85 *—S.H. (12/31/2003)*

Fetzer 1999 Echo Ridge Johannisberg Riesling (California) $10. 82 *(5/1/2001)*

Fetzer 2003 Merlot (California) $9. 84 *—S.H. (12/15/2005)*

Fetzer 2001 Barrel Select Merlot (Sonoma County) $14. 85 *—S.H. (4/1/2004)*

Fetzer 1999 Barrel Select Merlot (Sonoma County) $13. 88 *—S.H. (9/1/2003)*

Fetzer 1998 Barrel Select Merlot (Sonoma County) $13. 85 *—J.C. (6/1/2001)*

Fetzer 1997 Barrel Select Merlot (Sonoma County) $15. 86 *—J.C. (3/1/2000)*

Fetzer 2000 Eagle Peak Merlot (California) $9. 86 Best Buy *—S.H. (6/1/2002)*

Fetzer 1999 Eagle Peak Merlot (California) $13. 84 *(5/1/2001)*

Fetzer 1998 Eagle Peak Merlot (California) $9. 82 *—S.H. (7/1/2000)*

Fetzer 1999 Five Rivers Ranch Merlot (Central Coast) $13. 86 *(11/15/2001)*

Fetzer 2005 Valley Oaks Merlot (California) $9. Kind of sharp, in the way of a young, rustic wine, but pleases for the ripe cherry, blackberry, cola and spice flavors. You might even stash this one away for six months to let it soften and smooth out. **85 Best Buy** *—S.H. (3/1/2007)*

Fetzer 2004 Valley Oaks Merlot (California) $9. 85 Best Buy *—S.H. (11/15/2006)*

Fetzer 2003 Valley Oaks Merlot (California) $9. 85 Best Buy *—S.H. (12/31/2005)*

Fetzer 2000 Reserve Petite Sirah (Spring Mountain) $30. 82 *(4/1/2003)*

Fetzer 2006 Pinot Grigio (California) $9. Clean and zesty, this is a nice cocktail sipper, with rich flavors of green apples, pineapples, peaches, apricots, vanilla and spice. The honeyed finish is brightened with crisp acidity. **85 Best Buy** *—S.H. (12/31/2007)*

Fetzer 2004 Pinot Grigio (California) $9. 84 *—S.H. (2/1/2006)*

Fetzer 2006 Valley Oaks Pinot Grigio (California) $9. Clean and zesty, this is a nice cocktail sipper, with rich flavors of green apples, pineapples, peaches, apricots, vanilla and spice. The honeyed finish is brightened with crisp acidity. **85 Best Buy** *—S.H. (11/15/2007)*

Fetzer 2005 Valley Oaks Pinot Grigio (California) $9. 86 Best Buy *—S.H. (7/1/2006)*

Fetzer 2000 Barrel Select Pinot Noir (Sonoma County) $15. 81 *(10/1/2002)*

Fetzer 1999 Barrel Select Pinot Noir (California) $19. 86 *(5/1/2001)*

Fetzer 1998 Barrel Select Pinot Noir (California) $15. 87 *—P.G. (12/15/2000)*

Fetzer 1997 Barrel Select Pinot Noir (California) $15. 85 *(11/15/1999)*

Fetzer 1999 Bien Nacido Reserve Pinot Noir (Santa Barbara County) $28. 91 *—S.H. (12/15/2001)*

Fetzer 2000 Bien Nacido Vineyard Pinot Noir (Santa Maria Valley) $40. 88 *(10/1/2002)*

Fetzer 2000 Bien Nacido Vineyard Blocks G + Q Winemaker's Reserve Pinot Noir (Santa Maria Valley) $40. 89 *(10/1/2002)*

Fetzer 1998 Bien Nacido Vineyard Reserve Pinot Noir (Santa Barbara County) $28. 87 *—S.H. (12/15/2000)*

Fetzer 2001 Five Rivers Ranch Pinot Noir (Santa Barbara County) $7. 85 Best Buy *—S.H. (2/1/2004)*

Fetzer 2000 Five Rivers Ranch Pinot Noir (Santa Maria Valley) $13. 87 Best Buy *(11/15/2001)*

Fetzer 2000 Five Rivers Ranch Pinot Noir (Central Coast) $14. 84 *(10/1/2002)*

Fetzer 2004 Coro Mendocino Red Blend (Mendocino County) $35. The Mendocino winemaker, Dennis Patton, who's a real veteran, made this extraordinary wine. A blend of Zinfandel, Petite Sirah, Grenache and Syrah, it's one of the best Rhône-style, field blend-type wines of the vintage, showing lush raspberry, cherry, cassis, gingerbread and herb flavors. A tannic taste of bitter almondskin rounds out the finish. **92** *—S.H. (12/31/2007)*

Fetzer 2002 Coro Mendocino Red Blend (Mendocino County) $35. 90 Cellar Selection *—S.H. (2/1/2006)*

Fetzer 2001 Coro Mendocino Red Blend (Mendocino) $35. 89 *—J.M. (9/1/2004)*

Fetzer 2005 Valley Oaks Riesling (California) $9. 84 *—S.H. (7/1/2006)*

Fetzer 2004 Valley Oaks Riesling (California) $9. 82 *—S.H. (12/1/2005)*

Fetzer 2001 Echo Ridge Sauvignon Blanc (California) $8. 84 *—S.H. (9/1/2003)*

Fetzer 1999 Echo Ridge Sauvignon Blanc (California) $10. 85 *(5/1/2001)*

Fetzer 1998 Echo Ridge Sauvignon Blanc (California) $8. 86 *(3/1/2000)*

Fetzer 2006 Valley Oaks Sauvignon Blanc (California) $9. Only a wise old company like Fetzer, with vast access to good vineyards and decades of winemaking experience, could produce such a nice Sauvignon Blanc in such huge quantities. The wine is dry and crisp, with rewarding flavors of green apples, pink grapefruits and figs. It tastes smoky and full of vanilla, even though it has no oak. **85 Best Buy** *—S.H. (11/15/2007)*

Fetzer 2005 Valley Oaks Sauvignon Blanc (California) $9. 86 Best Buy *—S.H. (7/1/2006)*

Fetzer 2004 Valley Oaks Sauvignon Blanc (California) $9. 85 Best Buy *—S.H. (12/1/2005)*

Fetzer 2004 Shiraz (California) $9. With burgers, dogs and the like, this is a nice red wine, gutsy and full-bodied, with cherry and blackberry flavors and the acidity to stand up to ketchup. **84** *—S.H. (4/1/2007)*

Fetzer 2003 Shiraz (California) $9. 83 *—S.H. (12/31/2005)*

Fetzer 2001 Valley Oaks Shiraz (California) $9. 85 Best Buy *(9/1/2005)*

Fetzer 1999 Barrel Select Syrah (Mendocino County) $20. 92 *—S.H. (5/1/2002)*

Fetzer 1999 Valley Oaks Syrah (California) $9. 86 Best Buy *—S.H. (9/1/2002)*

Fetzer 1998 Valley Oaks Syrah (California) $11. 84 *(5/1/2001)*

Fetzer 2004 Valley Oaks Rosé Syrah (California) $9. 86 Best Buy *—S.H. (12/1/2005)*

Fetzer 2002 Winemaker's Reserve Syrah (Mendocino) $25. 85 *(9/1/2005)*

Fetzer 2001 Barrel Select Zinfandel (Mendocino County) $14. 87 *—J.M. (11/1/2003)*

Fetzer 1999 Barrel Select Zinfandel (Mendocino County) $12. 86 *—S.H. (11/1/2002)*

Fetzer 1998 Barrel Select Zinfandel (Mendocino County) $12. 90 *—S.H. (5/1/2002)*

Fetzer 1997 Barrel Select Zinfandel (Mendocino County) $14. 88 *—S.H. (12/1/2000)*

Fetzer 1999 Echo Ridge Zinfandel (California) $7. 82 *(5/1/2001)*

Fetzer 1997 Home Ranch Zinfandel (California) $9. 82 *—S.H. (12/1/2000)*

Fetzer 1996 Home Ranch Zinfandel (California) $8. 83 *—S.H. (9/1/1999)*

Fetzer 2005 Valley Oaks Zinfandel (California) $9. A bit sharp and minty, but with its base of raspberries, cherries and crisp acids It's okay for everyday purposes. **83** *—S.H. (11/15/2007)*

Fetzer 2004 Valley Oaks Zinfandel (California) $9. 84 *—S.H. (11/15/2006)*

Fetzer 2003 Valley Oaks Zinfandel (California) $9. 84 *—S.H. (12/31/2005)*

Fetzer 2002 Valley Oaks Zinfandel (California) $9. 83 *—S.H. (10/1/2005)*

Fetzer 1999 Valley Oaks Zinfandel (California) $10. 86 Best Buy *—S.H. (7/1/2002)*

Fetzer 1998 Valley Oaks Zinfandel (California) $11. 81 *(5/1/2001)*

FIDDLEHEAD

Fiddlehead 2000 Pinot Noir (Santa Barbara) $50. 92 Editors' Choice *—S.H. (12/31/2002)*

Fiddlehead 1998 Pinot Noir (Willamette Valley) $36. 87 *—S.H. (12/31/2002)*

Fiddlehead 2001 Fiddlestix Seven Twenty Eight Pinot Noir (Santa Ynez Valley) $38. 93 *—S.H. (5/1/2005)*

Fiddlehead 2004 Fiddlestix Vineyard Lollapalloza Pinot Noir (Santa Rita Hills) $50. 94 *—S.H. (11/15/2006)*

Fiddlehead 2005 Lollapalooza Pinot Noir (Santa Rita Hills) $50. This is beautiful, dark and powerful, but refined and elegant. Packed with red and dark cherry stone fruit flavors, it has an excitingly smooth, silky texture, and finishes with an explosion of spice. **94 Editors' Choice** *—S.H. (4/1/2007)*

Fiddlehead 2001 Lollapalooza Fiddlestix Pinot Noir (Santa Ynez Valley) $50. 92 *—S.H. (3/1/2004)*

Fiddlehead 1999 Oldsville Reserve Pinot Noir (Willamette Valley) $40. 91 *—S.H. (12/31/2002)*

Fiddlehead 2005 Pink Fiddle Rosé Pinot Noir (Santa Rita Hills) $15. 91 *—S.H. (11/15/2006)*

Fiddlehead 2003 Seven Twenty Eight Pinot Noir (Santa Rita Hills) $38. Slightly earthy and angular, with some sharp tannins and a streak of wintergreen, this Pinot has a clean, silky mouthfeel. The solid core of cherries makes it appealing. Drink now. **87** *—S.H. (6/1/2007)*

Fiddlehead 2000 Sauvignon Blanc (Santa Ynez Valley) $22. 88 *—S.H. (9/1/2003)*

FIDDLEHEAD CELLARS

Fiddlehead Cellars 2003 Goosebury Sauvignon Blanc (Santa Ynez Valley) $32. 87 *(7/1/2005)*

Fiddlehead Cellars 2002 Happy Canyon Sauvignon Blanc (Santa Ynez Valley) $22. 81 *(7/1/2005)*

Fiddlehead Cellars 2001 Honeysuckle Sauvignon Blanc (Santa Ynez Valley) $22. 88 *(7/1/2005)*

FIDELITAS

Fidelitas 2003 Optu Bordeaux Blend (Columbia Valley (WA)) $40. 90 *—P.G. (12/31/2006)*

Fidelitas 2003 Cabernet Sauvignon (Walla Walla (WA)) $40. 89 *—P.G. (12/31/2006)*

Fidelitas 2003 Cabernet Sauvignon (Columbia Valley (WA)) $30. 90 *—P.G. (12/15/2005)*

Fidelitas 2003 Champoux Vineyard Cabernet Sauvignon (Columbia Valley (WA)) $55. 91 *—P.G. (12/31/2006)*

Fidelitas 2002 Red Table Wine Cabernet Sauvignon-Merlot (Columbia Valley (WA)) $18. 88 *—P.G. (12/15/2004)*

Fidelitas 2001 Meritage (Columbia Valley (WA)) $35. 89 *—P.G. (12/15/2004)*

Fidelitas 2000 Meritage (Columbia Valley (WA)) $40. 90 *—P.G. (11/20/2003)*

Fidelitas 2003 Merlot (Columbia Valley (WA)) $25. 88 *—P.G. (12/15/2005)*

Fidelitas 2002 Optu Red Blend (Columbia Valley (WA)) $35. 89 *—P.G. (12/15/2005)*

Fidelitas 2005 Sémillon (Columbia Valley (WA)) $20. 89 *—P.G. (12/31/2006)*

Fidelitas 2004 Sémillon (Columbia Valley (WA)) $18. 89 *—P.G. (12/15/2005)*

Fidelitas 2003 Sémillon (Columbia Valley (WA)) $15. 92 Best Buy *—P.G. (12/15/2004)*

Fidelitas 2003 Syrah (Columbia Valley (WA)) $35. 89 *—P.G. (12/15/2005)*

Fidelitas 2002 Syrah (Columbia Valley (WA)) $40. 90 *—P.G. (12/15/2004)*

Fidelitas 2001 Syrah (Yakima Valley) $35. 91 *—P.G. (11/20/2003)*

FIELD

Field 2003 Katarina Cabernet Sauvignon (Alexander Valley) $39. 84 *—S.H. (12/31/2005)*

FIELD STONE

Field Stone 2003 Cabernet Sauvignon (Alexander Valley) $24. 82 *—S.H. (12/1/2006)*

Field Stone 2000 Cabernet Sauvignon (Alexander Valley) $22. 82 *—S.H. (5/1/2004)*

Field Stone 2002 Staten Family Reserve Cabernet Sauvignon (Alexander Valley) $40. 90 Cellar Selection *—S.H. (12/1/2006)*

Field Stone 1997 Staten Family Reserve Cabernet Sauvignon (Sonoma County) $38. 93 *(11/1/2000)*

Field Stone 1998 Chardonnay (Sonoma County) $16. 86 *(6/1/2000)*

Field Stone 2000 Staten Family Reserve Chardonnay (Russian River Valley) $22. 89 *—S.H. (5/1/2003)*

Field Stone 2003 Merlot (Alexander Valley) $20. 82 *—S.H. (12/15/2006)*

Field Stone 1999 Staten Family Reserve Petite Sirah (Alexander Valley) $30. 84 *(4/1/2003)*

Field Stone 2005 Sauvignon Blanc (Alexander Valley) $16. 85 *—S.H. (12/1/2006)*

Field Stone 2002 Sauvignon Blanc (Alexander Valley) $14. 86 *—S.H. (2/1/2004)*

Field Stone 2003 Syrah (Alexander Valley) $22. 86 *(9/1/2005)*

FIELDING HILLS

Fielding Hills 2004 Cabernet Franc (Wahluke Slope) $28. 91 *—P.G. (12/31/2006)*

Fielding Hills 2003 Cabernet Franc (Columbia Valley (WA)) $26. 94 Editors' Choice *—P.G. (12/15/2005)*

Fielding Hills 2004 Cabernet Sauvignon (Wahluke Slope) $30. 95 *—P.G. (12/31/2006)*

Fielding Hills 2003 Cabernet Sauvignon (Columbia Valley (WA)) $30. 93 Editors' Choice *—P.G. (12/15/2005)*

Fielding Hills 2002 Cabernet Sauvignon (Columbia Valley (WA)) $28. 90 *—P.G. (6/1/2005)*

Fielding Hills 2002 Cabernet Sauvignon-Syrah (Columbia Valley (WA)) $28. 88 *—P.G. (11/1/2005)*

Fielding Hills 2004 Merlot (Wahluke Slope) $32. 94 *—P.G. (12/31/2006)*

Fielding Hills 2003 Merlot (Columbia Valley (WA)) $28. 95 Editors' Choice *—P.G. (12/15/2005)*

Fielding Hills 2002 Merlot (Columbia Valley (WA)) $28. 91 *—P.G. (6/1/2005)*

Fielding Hills 2004 RiverBend Red Blend (Wahluke Slope) $28. 93 *—P.G. (12/31/2006)*

Fielding Hills 2003 Riverbend Red Red Blend (Columbia Valley (WA)) $28. 93 Editors' Choice *—P.G. (12/15/2005)*

Fielding Hills 2002 Riverbend Red Red Blend (Columbia Valley (WA)) $28. 90 *—P.G. (6/1/2005)*

Fielding Hills 2004 Syrah (Columbia Valley (WA)) $32. 94 *—P.G. (12/31/2006)*

Fielding Hills 2003 Syrah (Columbia Valley (WA)) $32. 94 Editors' Choice *—P.G. (12/15/2005)*

FIFE

Fife 1997 Cabernet Sauvignon (Napa Valley) $30. 88 *(11/1/2000)*

Fife 2000 Cabernet Sauvignon (Napa Valley) $37. 85 *—S.H. (12/15/2003)*

Fife 2001 10th Anniversary Reserve Cabernet Sauvignon (Napa Valley) $32. 92 Cellar Selection *—S.H. (11/15/2006)*

Fife 1999 Reserve Cabernet Sauvignon (Spring Mountain) $45. 91 *—S.H. (10/1/2005)*

Fife 1997 Reserve Cabernet Sauvignon (Spring Mountain) $45. 91 *(11/1/2000)*

Fife 1997 Redhead Vineyard Carignane (Redwood Valley) $19. 90 *—S.H. (3/1/2000)*

Fife 2000 Petite Sirah (Mendocino) $20. 85 *(4/1/2003)*

Fife 1997 Redhead Petite Sirah (Redwood Valley) $24. 89 *—S.H. (10/1/1999)*

Fife 2002 Redhead Vineyard Petite Sirah (Redwood Valley) $24. 92 *—S.H. (11/1/2006)*

Fife 2000 Redhead Vineyard Petite Sirah (Redwood Valley) $24. 83 *(4/1/2003)*

Fife NV 3&4 Max Cuvée Red Blend (Napa Valley) $38. This is a combination of 2003 Petite Sirah, as well as Syrah from both 2001 and 2004. Vineyards from Spring Mountain comprise a majority of the blend. The multi-vintage approach works well, for the wine has the softness and bouquet of an older wine, with the fresh, ripe fruit and acidity of a young one. Raspberries, cherries, blueberries, plums and sweet leather and Asian spices are the main flavors. 91 *—S.H. (12/15/2007)*

Fife 2000 L'Attitude Rhône Red Blend (Mendocino) $20. 86 *—S.H. (12/1/2003)*

Fife 1999 L'Attitude Rhône Red Blend (Mendocino) $20. 94 Cellar Selection *—S.H. (5/1/2002)*

Fife 1997 L'Attitude Rhône Red Blend (Mendocino) $18. 93 *—S.H. (3/1/2000)*

Fife 2004 L'Attitude 39 Rhône Red Blend (Mendocino) $18. L'Attitude needs a warm vintage to succeed, and it got one in '04. The wine, a blend of Carignane, Syrah and other Rhône reds, is dry and complicated, offering rich, earthy, Provençal herb flavors with fruitier tastes of cherries, blackberries and cola. Notable for balance, elegance and power. Drink now through 2010. 93 *—S.H. (12/15/2007)*

Fife 2001 L'Attitude 39 Rhône Red Blend (Mendocino) $18. 93 Editors' Choice *—S.H. (11/1/2006)*

Fife 2001 Max Cuvée Rhône Red Blend (Napa Valley) $38. 93 Cellar Selection *—S.H. (11/1/2006)*

Fife 2002 Redhead Red Rhône Red Blend (Mendocino) $12. 87 Best Buy *—S.H. (11/1/2006)*

Fife 2005 Redhead Rosé Blend (Mendocino) $12. 86 *—S.H. (11/1/2006)*

Fife 2000 Redhead Rosé Blend (Redwood Valley) $14. 87 *—J.M. (11/15/2001)*

Fife 2002 Syrah (Mendocino) $20. 83 *(9/1/2005)*

Fife 2002 Syrah (Mendocino) $18. 87 *—S.H. (11/1/2006)*

Fife 2001 Syrah (Mendocino) $20. 88 *—S.H. (12/1/2004)*

Fife 2001 Max Vineyard Syrah (Napa Valley) $32. 91 *—S.H. (11/1/2006)*

Fife 1999 Max Vineyard Syrah (Napa Valley) $35. 89 *—S.H. (12/1/2004)*

Fife 1999 Old Yokayo Ranch Vineyard Syrah (Mendocino) $35. 95 Editors' Choice *—S.H. (5/1/2002)*

Fife 2004 Old Yokayo Vineyard Syrah (Mendocino) $24. The vineyard, in interior Mendocino, has produced a lush, compelling Syrah in this warm vintage. The fruit is perfectly ripe, bringing cherries and blackberries to the edge of liqueur, while maintaining complete dryness, with no trace of raisins and relatively modest alcohol. Combines weight with elegance to produce an upscale Syrah. 92 *—S.H. (12/15/2007)*

Fife 2002 Old Yokayo Rancho Vineyard Syrah (Mendocino) $24. 85 *—S.H. (11/1/2006)*

Fife 2000 Old Yokayo Rancho Vineyard Syrah (Mendocino) $30. 86 *—S.H. (12/1/2004)*

Fife 1997 Old Yokayo Rancho Vineyard Syrah (Mendocino) $40. 87 *(11/1/2001)*

Fife 2003 Mendocino Uplands Zinfandel (Mendocino) $18. 86 *—S.H. (11/1/2006)*

Fife 2001 Mendocino Uplands Zinfandel (Mendocino) $17. 89 *(11/1/2003)*

Fife 2003 Old Vines Zinfandel (Napa Valley) $24. 88 *—S.H. (11/1/2006)*

Fife 2003 Redhead Vineyard Zinfandel (Redwood Valley) $24. 91 *—S.H. (11/1/2006)*

Fife 2001 Redhead Vineyard Zinfandel (Redwood Valley) $24. 87 *(11/1/2003)*

Fife 1997 Redhead Vineyard Zinfandel (Redwood Valley) $24. 91 *—S.H. (5/1/2000)*

Fife 2000 Uplands Zinfandel (Mendocino) $17. 92 *—S.H. (5/1/2002)*

Fife 2000 Whaler Vineyard Zinfandel (Mendocino County) $20. 92 *—S.H. (5/1/2002)*

FIGGE

Figge 2005 La Reina Vineyard Chardonnay (Santa Lucia Highlands) $25. Big and bold, a Chard that shows off its terroir in the crisp, citrusy acidity and clean purity of fruit. The flavors veer toward pineapples and green tropical fruits. Oak plays a very prominent role, perhaps a little too much so, in this dry wine. 86 *—S.H. (12/1/2007)*

Figge 2005 Paraiso Vineyard Pinot Noir (Santa Lucia Highlands) $35. A bit brittle for a Pinot from this fine vineyard at the southeastern end of the appellation. This is dry, with candied raspberry flavors and a scour of acidity. Might soften and fatten by the end of 2007. 86 *—S.H. (12/1/2007)*

Figge 2005 Syrah (Arroyo Seco) $30. A vibrantly refreshing, juicy Syrah that flatters with tons of fruit. Cherries, cassis, raspberries, plums, mocha, licorice—that just begins to describe the palate. Balance comes from dryness and a nice structure of acids and tannins. 88 *—S.H. (12/1/2007)*

FILSINGER

Filsinger 2000 Special Reserve Chardonnay (Temecula) $10. 87 Best Buy *—S.H. (4/1/2002)*

Filsinger 1999 Fumé Blanc (Temecula) $7. 83 *—S.H. (4/1/2002)*

FIORE D'ARANCIO

Fiore d'Arancio NV Late Harvest Orange Muscat (California) $15. With residual sugar of 15.2%, this is a very sweet wine, but crisp acidity gives it complete balance. The flavors are direct and appealing and, as the variety suggests, powerful in tangerines and honeyed oranges. 87 *—S.H. (12/31/2007)*

FIRE STATION RED

Fire Station Red 2003 Shiraz (California) $15. 82 *—S.H. (11/15/2006)*

FIREFALL

Firefall 2000 Lone Meadow Vineyard Rosato di Sangiovese Sangiovese (Fair Play) $10. 85 *—S.H. (9/1/2002)*

Firefall 1999 Lone Meadow Vineyard Syrah (El Dorado) $20. 90 *—S.H. (12/1/2002)*

Firefall 1998 Lone Meadow Vineyard Syrah (El Dorado) $20. 85 *—S.H. (7/1/2002)*

FIRESTEED

Firesteed 2004 Pinot Gris (Oregon) $14. 86 *—P.G. (2/1/2006)*

Firesteed 2003 Pinot Gris (Oregon) $10. 88 Best Buy *—P.G. (11/15/2005)*

Firesteed 2000 Pinot Gris (Oregon) $11. 88 Best Buy *—P.G. (2/1/2002)*

Firesteed 2005 Pinot Noir (Oregon) $14. A bright cherry-red color, this lively, sweet-scented wine proves that Oregon can still make a Pinot Noir in a lighter style without having it turn vegetal. Despite a citrusy snap to the palate, it feels smooth and even a bit satiny, and the pretty cranberry/cherry fruit is annotated with cinnamon and light toast. A superb value. 87 *—P.G. (11/15/2007)*

Firesteed 2003 Pinot Noir (Oregon) $10. 87 Best Buy *—P.G. (8/1/2005)*

Firesteed 2003 Pinot Noir (Willamette Valley) $29. The 2003, though still just 13% alcohol, seems to have more stiffness to the structure, more tannin and more density than the 2002. It's harder, chewier, less open and more challenging. It may also age more slowly. Right now there is a certain stemminess and bitterness to the tannins that keeps the fruit at bay, though the aromas seem to promise more. It may profit from an hour or two of breathing. 87 *—P.G. (11/15/2007)*

Firesteed 2002 Pinot Noir (Oregon) $18. 86 *(11/1/2004)*

Firesteed 2002 Pinot Noir (Willamette Valley) $29. Firesteed gives even its modestly-priced mid-tier Pinot extra time in bottle, which smoothes out the leafy flavors and softens up the tannins. It holds onto secondary fruit flavors of cooked rhubarb and strawberry, adding in hints of resin, herb and lemon oil. 88 *—P.G. (11/15/2007)*

Firesteed 2001 Pinot Noir (Oregon) $10. 87 Best Buy *—P.G. (4/1/2003)*

Firesteed 2001 Pinot Noir (Willamette Valley) $19. 88 *—P.G. (8/1/2005)*

Firesteed 1999 Pinot Noir (Oregon) $10. 84 *—S.H. (8/1/2002)*

Firesteed 1998 Pinot Noir (Oregon) $10. 83 *—M.S. (12/1/2000)*

FIRESTONE

Firestone 2002 Vintage Reserve Bordeaux Blend (Santa Ynez Valley) $32. 82 *—S.H. (12/31/2005)*

Firestone 2001 Vintage Reserve Bordeaux Blend (Santa Ynez Valley) $30. 90 *—S.H. (10/1/2004)*

Firestone 2003 Cabernet Sauvignon (Santa Ynez Valley) $18. 86 *—S.H. (12/1/2006)*

Firestone 2002 Cabernet Sauvignon (Santa Ynez Valley) $18. 84 *—S.H. (11/1/2005)*

Firestone 2001 Cabernet Sauvignon (Santa Ynez Valley) $18. 86 *—S.H. (11/15/2004)*

Firestone 2000 Cabernet Sauvignon (Santa Ynez Valley) $18. 83 *—S.H. (8/1/2003)*

Firestone 2001 Chardonnay (Santa Barbara County) $16. 86 *—S.H. (10/1/2003)*

Firestone 2000 Chardonnay (Santa Barbara) $16. 87 *—J.M. (12/15/2002)*

Firestone 2002 Reserve Chardonnay (Santa Ynez Valley) $25. 89 *—S.H. (12/15/2004)*

Firestone 2002 Santa Barbara Chardonnay (Santa Barbara County) $16. 85 *—S.H. (8/1/2004)*

Firestone 1997 Santa Ynez Valley Chardonnay (Santa Ynez Valley) $12. 87 Best Buy *—S.H. (7/1/1999)*

Firestone 2004 Gewürztraminer (Santa Barbara County) $11. 85 *—S.H. (11/1/2005)*

Firestone 2003 Gewürztraminer (Santa Ynez Valley) $10. 85 *—S.H. (9/1/2004)*

Firestone 2001 Gewürztraminer (Santa Barbara) $9. 87 Best Buy *—J.M. (11/15/2002)*

Firestone 2000 Gewürztraminer (Santa Barbara County) $8. 88 *—S.H. (11/15/2001)*

Firestone 2006 Carranza Mesa Vineyard Gewürztraminer (Santa Ynez Valley) $13. Vaguely Gewürz-like, this dry wine is too thin and watery in flavor to merit a higher score. If you concentrate, you can find the flowers and famed spices the variety is noted for. 82 *—S.H. (11/15/2007)*

Firestone 2005 Carranza Mesa Vineyard Gewürztraminer (Santa Ynez Valley) $12. 82 *—S.H. (10/1/2006)*

Firestone 2002 Estate Bottled Gewürztraminer (Santa Ynez Valley) $9. 82 *—S.H. (3/1/2004)*

Firestone 2003 Merlot (Santa Ynez Valley) $18. 86 *—S.H. (12/1/2006)*

Firestone 2001 Merlot (Santa Ynez Valley) $18. 85 *—S.H. (12/15/2004)*

Firestone 2000 Merlot (Santa Ynez Valley) $18. 85 *—S.H. (8/1/2003)*

Firestone 2001 Reserve Merlot (Santa Ynez Valley) $30. 90 *—S.H. (12/15/2004)*

Firestone 1997 Winemaker's Reserve Merlot (Santa Ynez Valley) $25. 84 *—J.C. (7/1/2000)*

Firestone 1997 Riesling (Santa Barbara County) $7. 86 Best Buy *—S.H. (9/1/1999)*

Firestone 2002 Riesling (Central Coast) $8. 86 Best Buy *—J.M. (8/1/2003)*

Firestone 2001 Late Harvest Riesling (Santa Barbara) $13. 88 Best Buy *—C.S. (11/15/2002)*

Firestone 2006 Vineyard Select Riesling (Central Coast) $12. Not much going on in this simple, semisweet white, with its weak flavors of apricots, citrus and honey. 82 *—S.H. (11/15/2007)*

Firestone 2005 Vineyard Select Riesling (Central Coast) $10. 83 *—S.H. (10/1/2006)*

Firestone 2004 Vineyard Select Riesling (Central Coast) $10. 84 *—S.H. (10/1/2005)*

Firestone 2006 Sauvignon Blanc (Santa Ynez Valley) $14. Explosive in hay, gooseberry and citrus, but also pretty strong in cat pee and Band-Aid aromas, which may turn some off. Finshes bone dry and tart. **84** *—S.H. (11/15/2007)*

Firestone 2005 Sauvignon Blanc (Santa Ynez Valley) $13. 82 *—S.H. (10/1/2006)*

Firestone 2004 Sauvignon Blanc (Santa Ynez Valley) $12. 84 *—S.H. (11/1/2005)*

Firestone 2003 Sauvignon Blanc (Santa Ynez Valley) $12. 87 *—J.M. (9/1/2004)*

Firestone 2002 Sauvignon Blanc (Santa Ynez Valley) $12. 83 *—S.H. (12/15/2003)*

Firestone 2001 Sauvignon Blanc (Santa Ynez Valley) $12. 87 *—J.M. (9/1/2003)*

Firestone 2000 Sauvignon Blanc (Santa Barbara County) $10. 85 *—S.H. (11/15/2001)*

Firestone 1997 Sauvignon Blanc (Santa Ynez Valley) $8. 87 Best Buy *—S.H. (9/1/1999)*

Firestone 2003 Reserve Sauvignon Blanc (Santa Ynez Valley) $25. 87 *(7/1/2005)*

Firestone 2004 Syrah (Santa Ynez Valley) $20. Soft and simple, this dry Syrah has a light, silky texture, with polished cherry, spice, root beer and sweet oak flavors. Finishes pleasantly balanced. Drink now. **84** *—S.H. (8/1/2007)*

Firestone 2003 Syrah (Santa Ynez Valley) $18. 83 *—S.H. (7/1/2006)*

Firestone 2002 Syrah (Santa Ynez Valley) $18. 85 *(9/1/2005)*

Firestone 2001 Syrah (Santa Ynez Valley) $18. 90 *—S.H. (2/1/2004)*

Firestone 2000 Syrah (Santa Ynez Valley) $18. 88 Best Buy *—J.M. (11/15/2002)*

FISHER

Fisher 2002 Cameron Bordeaux Blend (Napa Valley) $50. 84 *—S.H. (5/1/2005)*

Fisher 2003 Coach Insignia Cabernet Sauvignon (Napa Valley) $70. Fisher's been on a roll with this wine. While the '03 could use greater structure in terms of acids and tannins, it has that plush, opulent Napa feel of world-class Cabernet, with its succulent cassis and chocolate flavors and sweet oak. Drink through 2008 for freshness. **90** *—S.H. (6/1/2007)*

Fisher 2002 Coach Insignia Cabernet Sauvignon (Napa Valley) $70. 94 Cellar Selection *—S.H. (12/15/2006)*

Fisher 2001 Coach Insignia Cabernet Sauvignon (Napa Valley) $65. 90 *—S.H. (5/1/2005)*

Fisher 2000 Coach Insignia Cabernet Sauvignon (Napa Valley) $75. 90 *—S.H. (4/1/2004)*

Fisher 2001 Coach Insignia Chardonnay (Sonoma County) $32. 93 *—S.H. (4/1/2004)*

Fisher 1998 Coach Insignia Chardonnay (Sonoma County) $25. 88 *(6/1/2000)*

Fisher 1997 Coach Insignia Chardonnay (Sonoma County) $25. 89 *—S.H. (11/15/1999)*

Fisher 2003 Mountain Estate Chardonnay (Sonoma County) $45. 84 *—S.H. (11/1/2005)*

Fisher 2004 Mountain Estate Vineyard Chardonnay (Sonoma County) $56. 92 *—S.H. (11/1/2006)*

Fisher 1999 Paladini Vineyards Chardonnay (Carneros) $45. 92 *(7/1/2001)*

Fisher 1997 Whitney's Vineyard Chardonnay (Sonoma County) $45. 88 *(7/1/2001)*

Fisher 1997 RCF Merlot (Napa Valley) $28. 89 *—S.H. (12/31/1999)*

Fisher 1996 Coach Insignia Red Blend (Napa County) $30.90 *—S.H. (2/1/2000)*

FISHEYE

Fisheye 2004 Cabernet Sauvignon (California) $8. 84 *—S.H. (12/1/2006)*

Fisheye 2005 Pinot Grigio (California) $8. 84 Best Buy *—S.H. (12/1/2006)*

Fisheye 2005 Sauvignon Blanc (California) $8. 84 Best Buy *—S.H. (12/1/2006)*

Fisheye 2004 Shiraz (California) $8. 83 *—S.H. (12/1/2006)*

FITZPATRICK

Fitzpatrick 1999 Grenache (El Dorado County) $17. 85 *—S.H. (12/15/2001)*

Fitzpatrick 1999 Tir Na Nog Red Blend (El Dorado) $20. 81 *—S.H. (5/1/2002)*

Fitzpatrick 2000 Syrah (Fair Play) $20. 85 *—S.H. (6/1/2003)*

Fitzpatrick 2001 Zinfandel (Fair Play) $21. 87 *(11/1/2003)*

FIVE RIVERS

Five Rivers 2004 Cabernet Sauvignon (Paso Robles) $10. This Cab is soft and plump, with blackberry, cherry jam and cola flavors grounded in a rich earthiness. Finishes completely dry. **84** *—S.H. (4/1/2007)*

Five Rivers 2003 Cabernet Sauvignon (Paso Robles) $10. 84 *—S.H. (3/1/2006)*

Five Rivers 2002 Cabernet Sauvignon (Paso Robles) $10. 85 Best Buy *—S.H. (12/1/2005)*

Five Rivers 2001 Cabernet Sauvignon (Central Coast) $10. 85 Best Buy *(12/16/2005)*

Five Rivers 2005 Chardonnay (Monterey County) $11. Vaguely Chard-like, with some peach and oak flavors, this wine gets the job done. It's clean, but not very interesting. **82** *—S.H. (4/1/2007)*

Five Rivers 2004 Chardonnay (Monterey County) $10. 82 *—S.H. (12/1/2005)*

Five Rivers 2003 Chardonnay (Monterey County) $10. 85 Best Buy *—S.H. (10/1/2005)*

Five Rivers 2003 Merlot (Central Coast) $10. 84 *—S.H. (4/1/2006)*

Five Rivers 2002 Merlot (Central Coast) $10. 83 *—S.H. (12/1/2005)*

Five Rivers 2005 Pinot Grigio (Monterey County) $10. 84 *—S.H. (8/1/2006)*

Five Rivers 2005 Pinot Noir (Central Coast) $13. 82 *—S.H. (12/31/2006)*

Five Rivers 2004 Pinot Noir (Santa Barbara County) $11. 83 *—S.H. (12/1/2005)*

Five Rivers 2003 Pinot Noir (Santa Barbara County) $10. 83 *—S.H. (10/1/2005)*

FIVE STAR CELLARS

Five Star Cellars 2003 Syrah (Walla Walla (WA)) $28. 84 *(9/1/2005)*

FLEMING JENKINS

Fleming Jenkins 2006 Victories Rosé Wine Rosé Blend (California) $20. The majority Pinot Noir in the blend brings its typical light body and delicate structure, along with bright, brisk cherry, cola, vanilla and tangerine notes. Thirty percent Syrah adds a little depth, maybe a hint of cassis, to this pale, lovely, elegant rosé. **90** *—S.H. (7/1/2007)*

Fleming Jenkins 2005 Victories Rose Wine Rosé Blend (San Francisco Bay) $20. 86 *—S.H. (12/1/2006)*

Fleming Jenkins 2005 Syrah Rosé Syrah (San Francisco Bay) $17. 85 *—S.H. (12/1/2006)*

FLEUR DE CALIFORNIA

Fleur de California 2006 Vin Gris Pinot Noir (Carneros) $13. From Carneros Creek, although you won't see it on the label (why not?). Pretty good dry blush, a little bitter and thin, but crisply acidic, with decent cherry skin, pomegranate and vanilla spice flavors. **84** *—S.H. (7/1/2007)*

FLOODGATE

Floodgate 2000 Pinot Noir (Anderson Valley) $30. 87 *(10/1/2002)*

FLORA SPRINGS

Flora Springs 2004 Trilogy Bordeaux Blend (Napa Valley) $65. A blend of the two Cabernets and Merlot, the '04 Trilogy shows the wine's traditional elegance. The flavors are extremely ripe, suggesting blackberries, cherries and cocoa, with a sugared finish. Fully drinkable now due to the softness of the tannins. **88** *—S.H. (12/15/2007)*

Flora Springs 1997 Trilogy Bordeaux Blend (Napa Valley) $45. 93 *(11/1/2000)*

Flora Springs 2003 Trilogy Cabernet Blend (Napa Valley) $60. 91 Cellar Selection *—S.H. (9/1/2006)*

Flora Springs 2002 Trilogy Cabernet Blend (Napa Valley) $60. 91 *—S.H. (12/1/2005)*

Flora Springs 2003 Cabernet Sauvignon (Napa Valley) $30. 87 *—S.H. (12/15/2006)*

Flora Springs 2002 Cabernet Sauvignon (Napa Valley) $30. 84 *—S.H. (12/1/2005)*

Flora Springs 2001 Cabernet Sauvignon (Napa Valley) $30. 86 *—S.H. (10/1/2004)*

Flora Springs 2000 Cabernet Sauvignon (Napa Valley) $30. 85 *—S.H. (11/15/2003)*

Flora Springs 2002 25th Anniversary Cabernet Sauvignon (Napa Valley) $150. 87 *—S.H. (12/31/2005)*

Flora Springs 2000 25th Anniversary Celebration Cabernet Sauvignon (Napa Valley) $300. 85 *—S.H. (12/15/2003)*

Flora Springs 2003 Club Selection Cabernet Sauvignon (Napa Valley) $35. I like this 100% Cab a lot for its distinguished mouthfeel. Classy and refined, with the balance of a great wine region. The grapes come from the winery's vineyards across the valley, and show the blender's art in the refined tannins and seamless integration of fruit and oak. Deeply flavored, it will hold for a decade. Available only through the winery's Wine Club. **92** *—S.H. (4/1/2007)*

Flora Springs 2004 Hillside Reserve Cabernet Sauvignon (Rutherford) $108. The vineyard is source of high-quality fruit, but also intense mountain tannins that require time to melt. Under those tannins is dramatically rich black currant and carob fruit flavor, easily big enough to sustain 100% new French oak. By 2009 this 100% Cab should begin to soften and sweeten, and it will drink beautifully for at least six more years. **93 Cellar Selection** *—S.H. (12/15/2007)*

Flora Springs 2004 Holy Smoke Cabernet Sauvignon (Oakville) $85. The least successful of this bottling in some years. The wine is just too ripe and raisiny-sweet, with a white sugar edge to the cherries, cassis and blackberries that's almost like a dessert wine. **84** *—S.H. (12/15/2007)*

Flora Springs 2002 Holy Smoke Vineyard Cabernet Sauvignon (Napa Valley) $85. 91 *—S.H. (10/1/2005)*

Flora Springs 2001 Holy Smoke Vineyard Cabernet Sauvignon (Napa Valley) $85.91 *—S.H. (10/1/2004)*

Flora Springs 2004 Out-of-Sight Cabernet Sauvignon (Oak Knoll) $85. With powerful cassis flavors that approach raisins and red licorice candy, this Cab, which hails from a vineyard off the Silverado Trail, shows the extraordinary heat of the vintage. It's a good, even a delicious wine, but not an ager, one to enjoy now while your '02s and '03s are in the cellar. **87** *—S.H. (12/15/2007)*

Flora Springs 2002 Out-of-Sight Vineyard Cabernet Sauvignon (Napa Valley) $85. 88 *—S.H. (10/1/2005)*

Flora Springs 2001 Out-of-Sight Vineyard Cabernet Sauvignon (Napa Valley) $85. 89 *—S.H. (10/1/2004)*

Flora Springs 2002 Rutherford Hillside Reserve Cabernet Sauvignon (Napa Valley) $100. 94 *—S.H. (10/1/2005)*

Flora Springs 2001 Rutherford Hillside Reserve Cabernet Sauvignon (Napa Valley) $100. 94 *—S.H. (10/1/2004)*

Flora Springs 1999 Rutherford Hillside Reserve Cabernet Sauvignon (Napa Valley) $100. 87 *—S.H. (12/31/2002)*

Flora Springs 1997 Rutherford Hillside Reserve Cabernet Sauvignon (Napa Valley) $65. 89 *(11/1/2000)*

Flora Springs 1996 Trilogy Cabernet Sauvignon (Napa Valley) $45. 94 *(11/15/1999)*

Flora Springs 2002 Wild Boar Vineyard Cabernet Sauvignon (Napa Valley) $85. 92 *—S.H. (10/1/2005)*

Flora Springs 1999 Wild Boar Vineyard Cabernet Sauvignon (Napa Valley) $60. 87 *—S.H. (11/15/2002)*

Flora Springs 1998 Wild Boar Vineyard Cabernet Sauvignon (Napa Valley) $60. 89 *—S.H. (6/1/2002)*

Flora Springs 1996 Wild Boar Vineyard Cabernet Sauvignon (Napa Valley) $40. 89 *(9/1/2000)*

Flora Springs 2001 Wild Boar Wineyard Cabernet Sauvignon (Napa Valley) $85. 91 *—S.H. (10/1/2004)*

Flora Springs 2000 Poggio del Papa Cabernet Sauvignon-Sangiovese (Napa Valley) $35. 88 *—S.H. (5/1/2003)*

Flora Springs 2002 Chardonnay (Carneros) $25. 88 *—S.H. (12/15/2004)*

Flora Springs 2006 Barrel Fermented Chardonnay (Napa Valley) $26. Has all your basic barrel-fermented Chardonnay character without being particularly complex. The wine is slightly sweet and oaky-creamy, with apricot, pineapple, peach and spicy mango flavors. **86** *—S.H. (12/31/2007)*

Flora Springs 2005 Barrel Fermented Chardonnay (Napa Valley) $25. Flora Springs' BF Chardonnay was a famous wine in the eighties, one of the first to alert consumers to the beauties of true barrel fermentation. It's still a great wine, although the price is higher now. Rich and creamy, it shows ripe tropical fruit and vanilla caramel flavors, with a smoky edge of oak. **91** *—S.H. (2/1/2007)*

Flora Springs 2004 Barrel Fermented Chardonnay (Napa Valley) $25. 87 *—S.H. (7/1/2006)*

Flora Springs 2003 Barrel Fermented Chardonnay (Napa Valley) $22. 85 *—S.H. (10/1/2005)*

Flora Springs 2001 Barrel Fermented Reserve Chardonnay (Napa Valley) $26. 90 *—S.H. (12/15/2002)*

Flora Springs 2000 Barrel Fermented Reserve Chardonnay (Napa Valley) $25. 92 *—S.H. (5/1/2002)*

Flora Springs 1998 Barrel Fermented Reserve Chardonnay (Napa Valley) $23. 85 *(6/1/2000)*

Flora Springs 1998 Lavender Hill Vineyard Chardonnay (Napa Valley) $30. 85 *(6/1/2000)*

Flora Springs 2002 Select Cuvée Chardonnay (Napa Valley) $35. 90 *—S.H. (5/1/2004)*

Flora Springs 2003 Select Cuvée Chardonnay (Napa Valley) $35. 91 *—S.H. (10/1/2005)*

Flora Springs 2000 Trilogy Meritage (Napa Valley) $60. 91 *—S.H. (11/15/2003)*

Flora Springs 2005 Merlot (Napa Valley) $24. So forward and appealing right now, it's hard to resist, but this could gain a little traction with a two or three years of age. It's polished in cherry jam and blackberry-pie filling, with earthy tones of coffee, figs, sage and cedar. The intricate tannins play nicely against the acidity, which gives it an upscale feeling. **91** *—S.H. (12/31/2007)*

Flora Springs 2004 Merlot (Napa Valley) $24. A little light, but shows real elegance and class in the smoothly ripe tannins, soft, expressive acidity that boosts the fruit just enough, and succulent oak regimen. If the cherry and black raspberry fruit was more concentrated, the score would soar. **86** *—S.H. (2/1/2007)*

Flora Springs 2003 Merlot (Napa Valley) $25. 86 *—S.H. (12/1/2005)*

Flora Springs 2002 Merlot (Napa Valley) $25. 87 *—S.H. (9/1/2004)*

Flora Springs 2001 Merlot (Napa Valley) $22. 86 *—S.H. (12/1/2003)*

Flora Springs 2000 Merlot (Napa Valley) $22. 91 *—S.H. (11/15/2002)*

Flora Springs 1999 Windfall Vineyard Merlot (Napa Valley) $50. 91 *—S.H. (6/1/2002)*

Flora Springs 2001 Pinot Grigio (Napa Valley) $12. 85 *—S.H. (9/1/2003)*

Flora Springs 2000 Pinot Grigio (Napa Valley) $12. 85 *—S.H. (11/15/2001)*

Flora Springs 2000 Lavender Hill Pinot Noir (Napa Valley) $35. 87 *(10/1/2002)*

Flora Springs 1998 Lavender Hill Pinot Noir (Napa Valley) $33. 87 *(10/1/2000)*

Flora Springs 1999 Lavender Hill Vineyard Pinot Noir (Napa Valley) $33. 88 *—S.H. (2/1/2001)*

Flora Springs 2001 Trilogy Red Blend (Napa Valley) $60. 90 *—S.H. (9/1/2004)*

Flora Springs 1999 Trilogy Red Blend (Napa Valley) $60. 92 *—S.H. (11/15/2002)*

Flora Springs 1998 Sangiovese (Napa Valley) $17. 90 *—S.H. (12/15/1999)*

Flora Springs 1999 Sangiovese (Napa Valley) $16. 90 *—S.H. (7/1/2002)*

Flora Springs 1999 Poggio del Papa Sangiovese (Napa Valley) $35. 91 *—S.H. (7/1/2002)*

Flora Springs 1998 Sauvignon Blanc (Napa Valley) $12. 89 *—S.H. (3/1/2000)*

Flora Springs 2006 Soliloquy Sauvignon Blanc (Oakville) $25. A deliciously vibrant wine, with oak-inspired citrus peel, peach, fig and creamy honey-vanilla flavors. However, as succulent as it is, from such a great winery, it could be far better. **91** *—S.H. (12/31/2007)*

Flora Springs 2005 Soliloquy Sauvignon Blanc (Oakville) $25. Soliloquy's always a good wine. In recent years, it's better than ever. The grapes on the 2005, sourced from Oakville, are 100% Sauvignon Blanc. The Musqué clone gives an exotic lemongrass mousse taste. While the wine is fully dry, it has a rich, honeyed finish, like vanilla sorbet. **90** *—S.H. (2/1/2007)*

Flora Springs 2004 Soliloquy Sauvignon Blanc (Oakville) $25. 93 Editors' Choice *—S.H. (7/1/2006)*

Flora Springs 2003 Soliloquy Sauvignon Blanc (Napa Valley) $25. 88 *(7/1/2005)*

Flora Springs 2002 Soliloquy Sauvignon Blanc (Napa Valley) $25. 88 *—J.M. (9/1/2004)*

Flora Springs 2001 Soliloquy Sauvignon Blanc (Napa Valley) $25. 88 *—S.H. (10/1/2003)*

Flora Springs 2000 Soliloquy Sauvignon Blanc (Napa Valley) $22. 90 *—S.H. (9/1/2003)*

Flora Springs 1999 Soliloquy Sauvignon Musqué (Napa Valley) $18. 87 *(8/1/2002)*

FLOWERS

Flowers 2002 Andreen-Gale Cuvée Chardonnay (Sonoma County) $44. 90 *—S.H. (5/1/2005)*

Flowers 2001 Andreen-Gale Cuvée Chardonnay (Sonoma Coast) $44. 94 *—S.H. (8/1/2004)*

Flowers 2002 Andreen-Gale Cuvée Pinot Noir (Sonoma Coast) $49. 87 —*S.H. (5/1/2005)*

Flowers 2001 Andreen-Gale Cuvée Pinot Noir (Sonoma Coast) $48. 92 —*S.H. (8/1/2004)*

Flowers 1999 Camp Meeting Ridge Pinot Noir (Sonoma Coast) $50. 91 *(10/1/2002)*

Flowers 2000 Keefer Ranch Pinot Noir (Green Valley) $44. 92 Cellar Selection *(10/1/2002)*

FLYING GOAT CELLARS

Flying Goat Cellars 2000 Pinot Noir (Santa Maria Valley) $30. 88 —*J.M. (6/1/2004)*

Flying Goat Cellars 2003 Dierberg Vineyard Pinot Noir (Santa Maria Valley) $34. 84 —*S.H. (8/1/2005)*

Flying Goat Cellars 2005 Rancho Santa Rosa Vineyard Pinot Noir (Sta. Rita Hills) $44. This one is a blend of Dijon clone blocks, and is very forward and jammy in raspberry, cherry, blueberry and tangerine zest. It's a bit one-dimensional, but crisp and dry, and will be luscious with grilled meats or salmon. **87** —*S.H. (4/1/2007)*

Flying Goat Cellars 2004 Rancho Santa Rosa Vineyard Pinot Noir (Santa Rita Hills) $40. 87 —*S.H. (11/1/2006)*

Flying Goat Cellars 2003 Rancho Santa Rosa Vineyard Pinot Noir (Santa Rita Hills) $36. 87 —*S.H. (8/1/2005)*

Flying Goat Cellars 2004 Rio Vista Vineyard Pinot Noir (Santa Rita Hills) $42. 84 —*S.H. (11/1/2006)*

Flying Goat Cellars 2003 Rio Vista Vineyard Pinot Noir (Santa Rita Hills) $38. 84 —*S.H. (8/1/2005)*

Flying Goat Cellars 2004 Rio Vista Vineyard 2A Pinot Noir (Santa Rita Hills) $38. 84 —*S.H. (11/1/2006)*

FLYNN

Flynn 1998 Pinot Noir (Willamette Valley) $16. 83 —*M.S. (12/1/2000)*

Flynn 1998 Cellar Select Clos d'Or Pinot Noir (Oregon) $10. 81 —*M.S. (12/1/2000)*

FOG MOUNTAIN

Fog Mountain 2000 Chardonnay (California) $8. 86 Best Buy —*S.H. (5/1/2003)*

FOLEY

Foley 2001 Chardonnay (Santa Maria Valley) $35. 88 —*J.M. (2/1/2004)*

Foley 2004 Barrel Select Chardonnay (Santa Rita Hills) $38. 91 —*S.H. (11/1/2006)*

Foley 1999 Barrel Select Chardonnay (Santa Barbara County) $38. 91 *(7/1/2001)*

Foley 2000 Barrel Select Bien Nacido Vineyard Chardonnay (Santa Barbara County) $27. 89 —*S.H. (12/1/2003)*

Foley 1999 Bien Nacido Vineyard Chardonnay (Santa Maria Valley) $35. 91 *(7/1/2001)*

Foley 2004 Clone 76 Chardonnay (Santa Rita Hills) $35. 90 —*S.H. (11/1/2006)*

Foley 1999 Dierberg Vineyard Chardonnay (Santa Maria Valley) $35. 87 *(7/1/2001)*

Foley 2005 Rancho Santa Rosa Chardonnay (Santa Rita Hills) $30. Opens with powerful lemon drop, lemon peel and toast aromas that turn firm and minerally in the mouth, almost hard, with a steely, gun-flint edge to the lemon custard flavors. With very high acidity, this polished Chard finishes dry and classy. **89** —*S.H. (4/1/2007)*

Foley 2004 Rancho Santa Rosa Chardonnay (Santa Rita Hills) $30. 90 —*S.H. (10/1/2006)*

Foley 2003 Rancho Santa Rosa Chardonnay (Santa Rita Hills) $30. 94 Editors' Choice —*S.H. (12/15/2005)*

Foley 2002 Rancho Santa Rosa Chardonnay (Santa Rita Hills) $30. 88 —*S.H. (5/1/2005)*

Foley 2005 Rancho Santa Rosa Barrel Select Chardonnay (Santa Rita Hills) $38. Beautiful and young, rewarding in every aspect. It shows bright, ripe Meyer lemon marmalade, apricot preserve, nectarine butter and guava flavors, with an exotic array of tropical spices and an elaborate coating of caramelized, vanilla-infused oak. It's also clean in citrusy acids. A bit tight now, so decant, and don't serve too cold. Best now–2010. **94 Editors' Choice** —*S.H. (4/1/2007)*

Foley 2005 Rancho Santa Rosa Clone 76 Chardonnay (Santa Rita Hills) $35. It must be the clone that lends a slightly heavy, earthy weight and flavor to this Chard, which is softer and more rustic than Foley's other '05s. The pineapple, lemon, guava and nectarine have a stewed or baked pie-filling quality. Quite good, but not really my favorite of the lineup. **88** —*S.H. (4/1/2007)*

Foley 2005 Rancho Santa Rosa Clone 96 Chardonnay (Santa Rita Hills) $35. Shows the intense, focused lemon drop and minerality of the estate and indeed of the appellation, with an additional high-toned floral honeysuckle quality and almost a honeyed touch of botrytis. Very rich, very pure in lemon candy, guava and pineapple, with firm acidity and a steely, stony feel in the finish. This is really an elegant, complex white wine. **94 Editors' Choice** —*S.H. (4/1/2007)*

Foley 2001 Pinot Noir (Santa Maria Valley) $38. 92 —*S.H. (5/1/2005)*

Foley 2004 Barrel Select Pinot Noir (Santa Rita Hills) $50. There's an aroma leading into this Pinot that seems bretty and leathery. In the mouth, it turns dry and complex, with a silky texture framing complex cherry, cola, pomegranate and rhubarb flavors that testify to its cool-climate origins. The finish is dry and balanced. Best to decant for a few hours to let the off aromas blow away. **90** —*S.H. (2/1/2007)*

Foley 2004 Dijon Clone 667 Pinot Noir (Santa Rita Hills) $45. Foley, one of Santa Rita Hills' leading wineries, is having fun with Pinot, releasing various bottlings that reflect terroir and clones. Their 667 bottling is a terrific wine. It shows the cleanness and purity of this Dijon clone, with the appellation's ability to ripen fruit to cherried richness while maintaining dryness. **90** —*S.H. (2/1/2007)*

Foley 2005 Rancho Santa Rosa Pinot Noir (Santa Rita Hills) $38. Right up there with Foley's clonal bottlings, this wine shows a classic Pinot profile. Exceptionally balanced and drinkable, it's a silky wine, instantly appealing for its delicate texture and pure flavors of cherries, cola, cloves, cinnamon and toasty oak. Drink now. **90** —*S.H. (4/1/2007)*

Foley 2004 Rancho Santa Rosa Pinot Noir (Santa Rita Hills) $38. 91 —*S.H. (11/1/2006)*

Foley 2003 Rancho Santa Rosa Pinot Noir (Santa Rita Hills) $38. 87 —*S.H. (12/15/2005)*

Foley 2002 Rancho Santa Rosa Pinot Noir (Santa Rita Hills) $38. 85 —*S.H. (5/1/2005)*

Foley 2005 Rancho Santa Rosa Barrel Select Pinot Noir (Santa Rita Hills) $50. Foley's Barrel Select is a kind of reserve bottling and is always worthy of the designation. This is a gorgeous wine that showcases the qualities of vineyard and vintage. Ripe and polished in cherry pie, pomegranate, cola and spice flavors, it has a perfect acid-tannin balance, all wrapped in a taffeta mouthfeel. It's a big wine, but never loses sight of balance and harmony. Brilliant, pedigreed Pinot, and one that should last for a decade. **94** —*S.H. (4/1/2007)*

Foley 2003 Rancho Santa Rosa Barrel Select Pinot Noir (Santa Rita Hills) $50. 93 —*S.H. (12/15/2005)*

Foley 2002 Rancho Santa Rosa Barrel Select Pinot Noir (Santa Rita Hills) $50. 90 —*S.H. (5/1/2005)*

Foley 2003 Rancho Santa Rosa Block 4A Clone 2A Pinot Noir (Santa Rita Hills) $45. 93 —*S.H. (12/15/2005)*

Foley 2003 Rancho Santa Rosa Block 4D Pommard Clone Pinot Noir (Santa Rita Hills) $45. 92 —*S.H. (12/15/2005)*

Foley 2002 Rancho Santa Rosa Block 4D Pommard Clone Pinot Noir (Santa Rita Hills) $45. 94 —*S.H. (5/1/2005)*

Foley 2003 Rancho Santa Rosa Block 5C Dijon Clone Pinot Noir (Santa Rita Hills) $45. 95 Editors' Choice —*S.H. (12/15/2005)*

Foley 2002 Rancho Santa Rosa Block 5C Dijon Clone 667 Pinot Noir (Santa Rita Hills) $45. 92 —*S.H. (5/1/2005)*

Foley 2005 Rancho Santa Rosa Clone 115 Pinot Noir (Santa Rita Hills) $45. Call it Burgundian, with its feral leather and mushroom edge to the well-ripened cherries. A big wine, penetrating in cherry, with an enormously complicated finish of cola and spicebox. But it's young, with fresh acids and primary fruit tang. Give this classy wine some time. Best 2008–2012. **93** —*S.H. (4/1/2007)*

Foley 2005 Rancho Santa Rosa Clone 2A Pinot Noir (Santa Rita Hills) $45. An aromatic young wine, yielding fresh primary fruit red cherries, pomegranates and spicy cola scents, with hints of violets and milk chocolate. Drinking very dry and forward now, it's a fat, opulent wine with delicious cherry, Bay leaf, spice and toast flavors. Should hold and improve for up to six years. **93** —*S.H. (4/1/2007)*

Foley 2004 Rancho Santa Rosa Clone 2A Pinot Noir (Santa Rita Hills) $45. 87 —*S.H. (11/1/2006)*

Foley 2005 Rancho Santa Rosa Dijon Clone 667 Pinot Noir (Santa Rita Hills) $45. Exotic, showing ripe, forward red cherry, raspberry and cola spice flavors, with hints of tangerine peel, white chocolate truffle, candied ginger and licorice. And that's just for starters. Complex and rich, with a wonderfully silky texture, this wine has the rich tannins and zesty acids for midterm cellaring. Drink now–2011. **94 Cellar Selection** —*S.H. (4/1/2007)*

Foley 2005 Rancho Santa Rosa Pommard Clone Pinot Noir (Santa Rita Hills) $45. Pommard is one of the old, pre-Dijon clones in California, and here, it yields a slightly rustic wine, with wild berry, pepper, rhubarb, coffee and earthy flavors, edged with new oak. It's dry and young now, but the fruity core is dramatically rich in cherries, and the acid-tannin balance is perfect. All it needs is 2–5 years to come around. **91** —*S.H. (4/1/2007)*

Foley 2004 Rancho Santa Rosa Pommard Clone Pinot Noir (Santa Rita Hills) $45. 89 —*S.H. (11/1/2006)*

Foley 2000 Santa Maria Hills Pinot Noir (Santa Maria Valley) $31. 91 —*S.H. (2/1/2004)*

Foley 2003 Sauvignon Blanc (Santa Barbara County) $16. 90 Editors' Choice —*S.H. (5/1/2005)*

Foley 2000 Sauvignon Blanc (Santa Barbara) $17. 89 *(8/1/2002)*

Foley 2005 Rancho Santa Rosa Syrah (Santa Rita Hills) $30. Not quite as opulent as the '04, but rich and softly appealing in blackberry, cherry, raspberry, mocha, lavender and peppery spice flavors. Drink now and through 2008 for its youthful fruitiness. **90** —*S.H. (12/31/2007)*

Foley 2004 Rancho Santa Rosa Syrah (Santa Rita Hills) $30. Inky dark and saturated, with scads of glycerine, a serious young wine. Erupts with cascades of white pepper, violets, cassis, plum pudding, rum, molasses, sweet kid leather, root beer and more. In the mouth, the primary fruit is black cherries and kirsch, while the new oak and glycerine makes for a rich, honeyed, almost unguent mouthfeel. Decant if you open it now; should gain additional complexities in the next eight years. **95 Editors' Choice** —*S.H. (4/1/2007)*

Foley 2003 Rancho Santa Rosa Syrah (Santa Rita Hills) $30. 88 *(9/1/2005)*

Foley 2002 Rancho Santa Rosa Syrah (Santa Rita Hills) $30. 84 —*S.H. (5/1/2005)*

FOLEY & PHILLIPS

Foley & Phillips 2006 Rosé Wine Rosé Blend (Santa Ynez Valley) $15. For the second vintage in a row, this is one of the best rosés in California, and it's not all that expensive. Made from Grenache, Syrah and Cinsault, the wine shows the elements of cool-climate Santa Barbara. Dry and crisp, it has subtle flavors of cherries and spices. **90 Best Buy** —*S.H. (7/1/2007)*

Foley & Phillips 2005 Rose Wine Rosé Blend (Santa Ynez Valley) $12. 90 Best Buy —*S.H. (11/1/2006)*

USA

FOLIE A DEUX

Folie a Deux 1999 Harvey Vineyard Barbera (Amador County) $8. 88 —*S.H. (12/15/2001)*

Folie a Deux 1997 Cabernet Sauvignon (Napa Valley) $24. 89 —*S.H. (7/1/2000)*

Folie a Deux 2000 Cabernet Sauvignon (Napa Valley) $26. 90 —*S.H. (11/15/2003)*

Folie a Deux 2000 Cabernet Sauvignon (Napa Valley) $26. 83 —*S.H. (2/1/2005)*

Folie a Deux 1999 Cabernet Sauvignon (Napa Valley) $26. 91 —*S.H. (11/15/2002)*

Folie a Deux 1998 Cabernet Sauvignon (Napa Valley) $24. 83 —*S.H. (12/15/2000)*

Folie a Deux 2000 Private Reserve Cabernet Sauvignon (Napa Valley) $45. 84 —*S.H. (2/1/2005)*

Folie a Deux 1999 Private Reserve Cabernet Sauvignon (Napa Valley) $40. 94 Editors' Choice —*S.H. (11/15/2003)*

Folie a Deux 1998 Reserve Cabernet Sauvignon (Napa Valley) $36. 84 —*S.H. (12/15/2000)*

Folie a Deux 1997 Reserve Cabernet Sauvignon (Napa Valley) $36. 87 *(11/1/2000)*

Folie a Deux 1997 Champagne Blend (Napa Valley) $18. 88 —*S.H. (9/1/2000)*

Folie a Deux 1995 Brut Champagne Blend (Napa Valley) $18. 90 Best Buy —*S.H. (12/15/1999)*

Folie a Deux 1997 Chardonnay (Napa Valley) $18.84 *(6/1/2000)*

Folie a Deux 2000 Chardonnay (Napa Valley) $22. 87 —*S.H. (12/15/2002)*

Folie a Deux 2001 Chenin Blanc (Napa County) $18. 86 —*S.H. (9/1/2003)*

Folie a Deux 1999 Frost Glacon du Raison Gewürztraminer (Mendocino) $31. 91 —*J.M. (12/1/2002)*

Folie a Deux 1997 Merlot (Napa Valley) $24. 88 —*S.H. (7/1/2000)*

Folie a Deux 2003 Menage à Trois Red Blend (California) $12. 86 Best Buy —*S.H. (12/31/2004)*

Folie à Deux 2005 Ménage à Trois Rosé Table Wine Rosé Blend (California) $12. Here's one of your darker, fuller-bodied, stronger rosés. A blend of Merlot, Syrah and Gewürztraminer, it's powerful in cherries and plums, but is a little over-bearing, and Gewürz's floweriness seems inappropriate. **83** —*S.H. (7/1/2007)*

Folie a Deux 1999 Sangiovese (Napa Valley) $18. 86 —*S.H. (12/15/2001)*

Folie a Deux 2001 Sémillon (Amador County) $18. 85 —*S.H. (12/15/2002)*

Folie a Deux 1999 Lani's Vineyard Syrah (Amador County) $26. 88 *(11/1/2001)*

Folie à Deux 2006 Ménage à Trois White Table Wine White Blend (California) $10. Soft and honeyed, with vanilla-tinged flavors of all sorts of tropical fruits that finish with a spicy hit of butterscotch. A blend of Chardonnay, Muscat and Chenin Blanc. **86** —*S.H. (11/15/2007)*

Folie a Deux 2003 Menage à Trois White Blend (California) $12. 86 Best Buy —*S.H. (12/31/2004)*

Folie a Deux 1997 Zinfandel (Amador County) $18. 87 *(9/1/1999)*

Folie a Deux 2001 Zinfandel (Amador County) $17. 86 —*S.H. (2/1/2005)*

Folie a Deux 2000 Zinfandel (Amador County) $18. 88 —*S.H. (9/1/2003)*

Folie a Deux 1999 Bowman Zinfandel (Amador County) $26. 91 —*S.H. (11/1/2002)*

Folie a Deux 1999 Bowman Vineyard Zinfandel (Amador County) $26. 94 —*S.H. (3/1/2004)*

Folie a Deux 1997 Bowman Vineyard Zinfandel (Amador County) $24.88 *(9/1/1999)*

Folie a Deux 1998 D'Agostini Vineyard Old Vine Zinfandel (Amador County) $22. 90 —*P.G. (3/1/2001)*

Folie a Deux 1997 D'Agostini Vineyard Old-Vine Zinfandel (Amador County) $20. 86 *(9/1/1999)*

Folie a Deux 1999 DeMille Vineyard Old Vine Zinfandel (Amador County) $24. 90 —*S.H. (12/15/2001)*

Folie a Deux 1998 Eschen Vineyard Old Vine Zinfandel (Fiddletown) $24. 84 —*S.H. (8/1/2001)*

Folie a Deux 1997 Eschen Vineyard Old Vine Zinfandel (Fiddletown) $22. 88 *(9/1/1999)*

Folie a Deux 1997 Harvey-Binz Vineyard Zinfandel (Amador County) $28. 90 —*S.H. (9/1/2000)*

Folie a Deux 1998 La Grande Folie Old Vine Zinfandel (Amador County) $44. 87 —*P.G. (3/1/2001)*

Folie a Deux 2000 The Wild Bunch Vineyard Old Vine Zinfandel (Amador County) $22. 93 —*S.H. (3/1/2004)*

Folie à Deux 2004 Ménage à Trois Rosé Blend (California) $12. 85 —*S.H. (11/1/2005)*

Folie à Deux 2004 Ménage à Trois White Blend (California) $12. 84 —*S.H. (11/1/2005)*

FOPPIANO

Foppiano 2001 Cabernet Sauvignon (Russian River Valley) $17. 86 —*S.H. (5/1/2005)*

Foppiano 2000 Cabernet Sauvignon (Russian River Valley) $17. 89 —*S.H. (11/15/2002)*

Foppiano 2004 Estate Cabernet Sauvignon (Russian River Valley) $17. Shows a distinctly rustic note in the jagged tannins, green acids and somewhat thin blackberry fruit that's stretched with dill and mint. Sweet oak helps to fatten it up. **83** —*S.H. (10/1/2007)*

Foppiano 2001 Riverside Collection Cabernet Sauvignon (California) $7. 82 —*S.H. (10/1/2004)*

Foppiano 2003 Riverside Collection Chardonnay (California) $7. 84 —*S.H. (10/1/2004)*

Foppiano 2001 Merlot (Russian River Valley) $15. 84 —*S.H. (5/1/2005)*

Foppiano 1999 Merlot (Russian River Valley) $17. 85 *(8/1/2002)*

Foppiano 2004 Estate Merlot (Russian River Valley) $15. Merlot is tricky under the best circumstances, and this one is adequate, at best. Dry and fairly tannic, it shows modest, somewhat overripe blackberry flavors. **83** —*S.H. (10/1/2007)*

Foppiano 1997 Petite Sirah (Sonoma County) $17. 91 —*M.S. (5/1/2000)*

Foppiano 2003 Petite Sirah (Russian River Valley) $18. 87 —*S.H. (3/1/2006)*

Foppiano 2001 Petite Sirah (Paso Robles) $15. 86 *(4/1/2003)*

Foppiano 2000 Petite Sirah (Sonoma County) $23. 90 —*S.H. (12/1/2002)*

Foppiano 2003 Bacigalupi Vineyard Petite Sirah (Russian River Valley) $17. 91 Editors' Choice —*S.H. (12/15/2005)*

Foppiano 2002 Bacigalupi Vineyard Petite Sirah (Russian River Valley) $17. 87 —*S.H. (8/1/2004)*

Foppiano 2001 Bacigalupi Vineyards Petite Sirah (Russian River Valley) $18. 83 *(4/1/2003)*

Foppiano 2004 Estate Petite Sirah (Russian River Valley) $23. No winery has associated itself more with Petite Sirah than Foppiano. That understanding shows in this wine, which wrestles the variety's rustically wild nature into something resembling submission. Still, it retains its dry, tannic edge, with all sorts of forest berry and herb flavors. Will live for many years, gradually softening. **88** *—S.H. (10/1/2007)*

Foppiano 2002 Estate Petite Sirah (Russian River Valley) $23. 90 *—S.H. (8/1/2005)*

Foppiano 2000 Estate Millenium Selection Reserve Petite Sirah (Russian River Valley) $48. 87 *(4/1/2003)*

Foppiano 2004 Pinot Noir (Russian River Valley) $23. 82 *—S.H. (11/15/2006)*

Foppiano 2002 Pinot Noir (Russian River Valley) $23. 90 *—S.H. (12/15/2005)*

Foppiano 2000 Pinot Noir (Russian River Valley) $23. 85 *—S.H. (6/1/2004)*

Foppiano 2005 Estate Pinot Noir (Russian River Valley) $23. Raw and hot, with a burnt cherry pie taste and a dry, tannic finish. **82** *—S.H. (10/1/2007)*

Foppiano NV Lot 96 Bin 001 Red Blend (Sonoma County) $10. Savor this blend of Zin, Sangiovese and Petite Sirah with anything calling for an easy, full-bodied red wine. It's fruity and spicy, with berry-cherry flavors and a smooth, rich balance of acids and tannins. **85 Best Buy** *—S.H. (12/31/2007)*

Foppiano 2002 Sangiovese (Alexander Valley) $17. 86 *—S.H. (8/1/2005)*

Foppiano 2001 Sangiovese (Alexander Valley) $18. 87 *(8/1/2003)*

Foppiano 2002 Zinfandel (Dry Creek Valley) $15. 84 *—S.H. (8/1/2005)*

Foppiano 2001 Zinfandel (Dry Creek Valley) $15. 86 *—J.M. (4/1/2004)*

Foppiano 2000 Zinfandel (Dry Creek Valley) $15. 86 *—S.H. (12/1/2002)*

Foppiano 1998 Zinfandel (Dry Creek Valley) $15. 84 *—P.G. (3/1/2001)*

FORCHINI

Forchini 2004 Proprietor's Reserve Pinot Noir (Russian River Valley) $26. 83 *—S.H. (12/1/2006)*

Forchini 2000 Proprietor's Reserve Pinot Noir (Russian River Valley) $24. 86 *(10/1/2002)*

Forchini 1998 Papa Nonno Old Vine Clone Zinfandel (Dry Creek Valley) $20. 93 *—S.H. (5/1/2000)*

Forchini 2001 Proprietor's Reserve Zinfandel (Dry Creek Valley) $24. 82 *(11/1/2003)*

FOREFATHER'S

Forefather's (CA) 1999 Cabernet Sauvignon (Alexander Valley) $35. 86 *—J.M. (2/1/2003)*

FOREFATHERS

Forefathers 2003 Cabernet Sauvignon (Alexander Valley) $40. Very ripe and forward, with flashy cherry, blackberry and cocoa flavors that lead to a long, spicy finish. It's a soft, slightly earthy wine, rich and balanced, with lots of layered complexity. **90** *—S.H. (2/1/2007)*

Forefathers 2000 Cabernet Sauvignon (Alexander Valley) $32. 92 Editors' Choice *—S.H. (11/15/2003)*

FOREST GLEN

Forest Glen 2003 Cabernet Franc (California) $10. There's a touch of the cherries you want in a Cab Franc, but the wine succombs to a rustic harshness, although it is dry. **82** *—S.H. (2/1/2007)*

Forest Glen 1998 Cabernet Sauvignon (California) $10. 82 *—S.H. (5/1/2001)*

Forest Glen 2002 Oak Barrel Selection Cabernet Sauvignon (California) $10. 85 Best Buy *—S.H. (6/1/2005)*

Forest Glen 1999 Oak Barrel Selection Cabernet Sauvignon (Sonoma) $10. 84 *—S.H. (3/1/2003)*

Forest Glen 2001 Reserve Cabernet Sauvignon (Sonoma County) $34. 82 *—S.H. (11/15/2005)*

Forest Glen 2001 Chardonnay (Sonoma) $12. 84 *—S.H. (9/1/2003)*

Forest Glen 2000 Chardonnay (California) $10. 84 *—S.H. (12/15/2002)*

Forest Glen 1999 Chardonnay (California) $11. 82 *—S.H. (8/1/2001)*

Forest Glen 1999 Forest Fire Chardonnay (California) $8. 84 *—S.H. (2/1/2001)*

Forest Glen 2004 Oak Barrel Fermented Chardonnay (California) $10. 83 *—S.H. (11/15/2006)*

Forest Glen 2003 Oak Barrel Fermented Chardonnay (California) $10. 87 Best Buy *—S.H. (10/1/2005)*

Forest Glen 2002 Oak Barrel Fermented Chardonnay (California) $10. 84 *—S.H. (6/1/2004)*

Forest Glen 2001 Oak Barrel Fermented Chardonnay (California) $10. 84 *—S.H. (6/1/2003)*

Forest Glen 1999 Oak Barrel Fermented Chardonnay (California) $10. 82 *—S.H. (5/1/2001)*

Forest Glen 2002 Reserve Chardonnay (Sonoma County) $22. 89 *—S.H. (11/15/2005)*

Forest Glen 2000 Merlot (California) $10. 84 *—S.H. (8/1/2003)*

Forest Glen 1999 Merlot (California) $11. 86 Best Buy *—S.H. (8/1/2001)*

Forest Glen 1998 Merlot (California) $10. 83 *—S.H. (11/15/2000)*

Forest Glen 2004 Oak Barrel Selection Merlot (California) $10. 83 *—S.H. (11/15/2006)*

Forest Glen 2003 Oak Barrel Selection Merlot (California) $10. 83 *—S.H. (6/1/2005)*

Forest Glen 2002 Oak Barrel Selection Merlot (California) $10. 85 *—S.H. (6/1/2004)*

Forest Glen 2001 Oak Barrel Selection Merlot (California) $10. 84 *—S.H. (12/15/2003)*

Forest Glen 2004 White Merlot (California) $10. 84 *—S.H. (11/15/2005)*

Forest Glen 2005 Pinot Grigio (California) $10. 84 *—S.H. (12/15/2006)*

Forest Glen 2002 Pinot Grigio (California) $10. 84 *—S.H. (12/1/2003)*

Forest Glen 2001 Pinot Grigio (Sonoma) $10. 84 *—S.H. (9/1/2003)*

Forest Glen 2000 Pinot Grigio (California) $10. 83 *—S.H. (9/1/2002)*

Forest Glen 1999 Pinot Grigio (California) $11. 84 *—S.H. (8/1/2001)*

Forest Glen 2003 Oak Barrel Selection Sangiovese (California) $10. 85 Best Buy *—S.H. (6/1/2006)*

Forest Glen 1999 Shiraz (California) $11. 84 *—S.H. (10/1/2001)*

Forest Glen 2002 Oak Barrel Selection Shiraz (California) $10. 84 *(9/1/2005)*

Forest Glen 2000 Oak Barrel Selection Shiraz (California) $10. 84 *—S.H. (2/1/2003)*

Forest Glen 2005 White Zinfandel Zinfandel (California) $10. 84 *—S.H. (12/15/2006)*

FORESTVILLE

ForestVille 1999 Cabernet Sauvignon (California) $6. 84 *—S.H. (11/15/2002)*

ForestVille 2000 Sonoma Reserve Cabernet Sauvignon (Alexander Valley) $12. 85 *—S.H. (6/1/2003)*

ForestVille 2002 Chardonnay (Sonoma County) $6. 81 *—S.H. (11/15/2004)*

ForestVille 2000 Chardonnay (California) $6. 83 *—S.H. (12/15/2002)*

ForestVille 1997 Chardonnay (California) $6. 81 *—J.C. (10/1/1999)*

ForestVille 2002 Sonoma Reserve Chardonnay (Russian River Valley) $12. 85 *—S.H. (12/15/2004)*

ForestVille 2003 Gewürztraminer (California) $6. 85 Best Buy *—S.H. (10/1/2005)*

ForestVille 2003 Merlot (California) $6. 84 Best Buy *—S.H. (12/1/2005)*

ForestVille 2000 Merlot (California) $6. 84 *—S.H. (11/15/2002)*

FORESTVILLE

ForestVille 2000 Sonoma Reserve Merlot (Alexander Valley) $12. 85 *—S.H. (8/1/2003)*

ForestVille 2004 Pinot Grigio (California) $6. 84 Best Buy *—S.H. (7/1/2006)*

ForestVille 2003 Reserve Pinot Noir (Sonoma County) $16. 85 *—S.H. (5/1/2005)*

ForestVille 2004 Sauvignon Blanc (California) $6. 85 Best Buy *—S.H. (10/1/2005)*

ForestVille 1997 Sauvignon Blanc (California) $8. 82 *(3/1/2000)*

ForestVille 2003 Shiraz (California) $6. 85 Best Buy *(9/1/2005)*

ForestVille 2002 Shiraz (Sonoma County) $6. 84 Best Buy *—S.H. (12/1/2004)*

ForestVille 2000 Shiraz (California) $6. 83 *—S.H. (10/1/2003)*

ForestVille 1999 Shiraz (California) $6. 83 *(10/1/2001)*

ForestVille 2003 Zinfandel (California) $6. 83 Best Buy *—S.H. (8/1/2005)*

ForestVille 2002 Zinfandel (California) $6. 83 *—S.H. (10/1/2004)*

ForestVille 2001 Zinfandel (California) $6. 83 *(11/1/2003)*

FORGERON

Forgeron 2002 Cabernet Sauvignon (Columbia Valley (WA)) $30. 84 *—P.G. (12/15/2005)*

Forgeron 2001 Cabernet Sauvignon (Columbia Valley (WA)) $29. 90 *—P.G. (9/1/2004)*

Forgeron 2005 Chardonnay (Columbia Valley (WA)) $25. This is quite consistent with the 2004 in terms of style, showing lots of vanilla-laced bourbon barrel, spice and buttered nuts in a tight, stylish frame. The alcohol is just over 14%; the wine is ripe, full, with a mix of citrus and green apple flavors, fresh, crisp and penetrating. It could age for another 5–6 years, as per a good village Burgundy. 90 *—P.G. (11/1/2007)*

Forgeron 2004 Chardonnay (Columbia Valley (WA)) $22. 90 *—P.G. (4/1/2006)*

Forgeron 2003 Chardonnay (Columbia Valley (WA)) $19. 88 *—P.G. (6/1/2005)*

Forgeron 2002 Merlot (Columbia Valley (WA)) $27. This is nicely evolved, dark and generous, with rich aromas of berry, baking spice, dust, cocoa, cinnamon. It's drinking beautifully right now, and 2002 is still the current release. It's not a big wine, but nicely ripened, rounded and showing pleasing, sweet fruit and baking spice. 88 *—P.G. (11/1/2007)*

Forgeron 2004 Boushey Merlot (Columbia Valley (WA)) $46. This is very pretty and lightly floral, with lilac, sweet cream and bourbon barrel scents mixed in with the sweet cherry fruit. Right now the barrel flavors tend to overpower the fruit, giving the finish a hard, slightly alcoholic edge. With more time, fruit will re-emerge—it's quite pretty cherry flavored; clean and precise, polished but not at all fat or jammy. 89 *—P.G. (11/1/2007)*

Forgeron 2002 Vinfinity Red Blend (Columbia Valley (WA)) $46. 86 *—P.G. (4/1/2006)*

Forgeron 2003 Syrah (Columbia Valley (WA)) $30. This is 100% Syrah, delicious, fragrant and loaded with spice. It's a blend from several different Washington AVAs, and has just the right mix of citrus, pepper, smoke, spice, acid, toast and tannin, bringing in elements from all of them. The fruit is sweet and brambly; the herbal elements are just right, adding notes of leaf and tobacco. There is a whiff of smoke and bacon fat, and the citrus/acid component lifts it nicely. 91 *—P.G. (11/1/2007)*

Forgeron 2002 Syrah (Columbia Valley (WA)) $30. 86 *(9/1/2005)*

Forgeron 2001 Syrah (Columbia Valley (WA)) $29. 91 *—P.G. (9/1/2004)*

Forgeron 2001 Zinfandel (Columbia Valley (WA)) $25. 88 *—P.G. (1/1/2004)*

Forgeron 2003 Alder Ridge Zinfandel (Columbia Valley (WA)) $27. 87 *—P.G. (4/1/2006)*

FORIS

Foris 2000 Chardonnay (Rogue Valley) $11. 86 *—P.G. (8/1/2002)*

Foris 1996 Siskiyou Terrace Chardonnay (Rogue Valley) $20. 87 *—L.W. (12/31/1999)*

Foris 2000 Gewürztraminer (Rogue Valley) $11. 91 Best Buy *—P.G. (4/1/2002)*

Foris 1997 Klipsun Meritage (Washington) $29. 88 *—P.G. (4/1/2002)*

Foris 1998 Merlot (Rogue Valley) $18. 85 *—P.G. (4/1/2002)*

Foris 1998 Pinot Blanc (Rogue Valley) $11. 89 Best Buy *—L.W. (12/31/1999)*

Foris 2000 Pinot Blanc (Rogue Valley) $13. 87 *—P.G. (4/1/2002)*

Foris 2004 Pinot Gris (Rogue Valley) $12. 85 *—P.G. (2/1/2006)*

Foris 2000 Pinot Gris (Rogue Valley) $13. 91 Best Buy *—P.G. (2/1/2002)*

Foris 1999 Pinot Noir (Rogue Valley) $16. 87 *—P.G. (4/1/2002)*

Foris 1998 Maple Ranch Pinot Noir (Rogue Valley) $30. 87 *—P.G. (4/1/2002)*

FORT ROSS VINEYARD

Fort Ross Vineyard 2002 Chardonnay (Sonoma Coast) $32. 91 *—S.H. (5/1/2005)*

Fort Ross Vineyard 2002 Reserve Chardonnay (Sonoma Coast) $40. 93 *—S.H. (5/1/2005)*

Fort Ross Vineyard 2001 Pinot Noir (Sonoma Coast) $34. 92 *—S.H. (5/1/2005)*

Fort Ross Vineyard 2001 Reserve Pinot Noir (Sonoma Coast) $39. 94 Editors' Choice *—S.H. (5/1/2005)*

FORTH

Forth 2002 Cabernet Sauvignon (Dry Creek Valley) $28. 88 *—S.H. (5/1/2006)*

Forth 2001 Cabernet Sauvignon (Dry Creek Valley) $30. 87 *—S.H. (10/1/2005)*

Forth 2000 Cabernet Sauvignon (Dry Creek Valley) $28. 82 *—S.H. (11/15/2003)*

Forth 2003 All Boys Cabernet Sauvignon (Dry Creek Valley) $18. 82 *—S.H. (5/1/2006)*

Forth 2002 All Boys Cabernet Sauvignon (Dry Creek Valley) $18. 90 *—S.H. (10/1/2005)*

Forth 2006 Rosé of Syrah Syrah (Dry Creek Valley) $12. Simple and easy, with raspberry-cherry, tea and spice flavors. The best parts are dryness and acidity. This is a balanced young wine that will go well with a variety of foods, and the price is fair. 85 *—S.H. (7/1/2007)*

Forth 2004 Sauvignon Blanc (Mendocino) $14. 84 *—S.H. (10/1/2005)*

Forth 2002 Syrah (Dry Creek Valley) $25. 87 *—S.H. (9/1/2005)*

Forth 2001 Syrah (Dry Creek Valley) $25. 88 *—S.H. (5/31/2005)*

FORTITUDE

Fortitude 2004 Frediani Field Blend Red Blend (Napa Valley) $28. Fortitude is a new brand produced at the Etude winery aimed at expressing the grape growers' original intentions. This is an old-style field blend of Charbono, Zinfandel, Carignane and Petite Sirah grown up-valley, near Calistoga. Lovely dark fruit and spice aromas include a few turns of cracked black pepper, then the palate adds some crisp acids to pull everything together. It's a wine with bold fruit, low tannins and food-friendly acids, probably best consumed young. 87 *(9/1/2007)*

Fortitude 2004 Frediani Field Blend Red Blend (Napa Valley) $28. This is an inaugural wine from Tony Soter, of Etude. The wine comes from a 70-year old vineyard in Calistoga, a mixture of Charbono, Zinfandel, Carignane and Petite Sirah, hence the term field blend. It's dry, layered and complex, and also tannic and acidic, a wine that surely will develop bottle complexity over the next 10 years. 88 *—S.H. (2/1/2007)*

Fortitude 2005 Rosé Wine Rosé Blend (Napa Valley) $18. The variety is Valdiguié, from old vines grown in Calistoga, with smaller amounts of Barbera, Tempranillo, Primitivo and Syrah from elsewhere, which makes it sound like the modern equivalent of an old field blend. It's a wonderful rosé, bone dry and so high in acidity it's a little sour, with subtle, complex herb, strawberry, dried flower and tobacco flavors. 87 *—S.H. (2/1/2007)*

Fortitude 2005 Sémillon (Napa Valley) $18. Fortitude is a new brand from Tony Soter, of Etude fame. The grapes for this wine come from a Calistoga vineyard. It's very dry, quite tart in acids, and minerally-citrusy, without the buttery, nutty quality of California Semillon, but it's a very elegant wine. Think of a cross between Albariño and Pinot Grigio. Sommeliers: Great by-the-glass wine. 87 *—S.H. (2/1/2007)*

FORTRESS

Fortress 2005 Sauvignon Blanc (Red Hills Lake County) $20. I loved the '04 for its big, bright bold fruit, and this '05 is nearly as good, even though the winery dropped the price by a buck. Could be a little drier, but the incredible acidity, so racy and zesty, keeps the citrus, spearmint and peach fruit clean. A 100% Musque clone. 87 *—S.H. (4/1/2007)*

Fortress 2004 Musqué Clone Sauvignon Blanc (Lake County) $21. 90 *—S.H. (11/1/2005)*

FOUNDRY VINEYARDS

Foundry Vineyards 2003 Cabernet Sauvignon (Walla Walla (WA)) $30. A dry, somewhat metallic, austere mouthfeel marks the entrance of this Cabernet. It has an Old World touch of musty dryness throughout, and the black cherry fruit seems to be drying out already. Flavors are succinct and contained. No blend is given, but it feels like a mix of grapes rather than just Cabernet Sauvignon. There's a slight herbal, spicy edge to the finish. 86 *—P.G. (8/1/2007)*

FOUNTAIN GROVE

Fountain Grove 1997 Cabernet Sauvignon (California) $10. 84 *—L.W. (12/31/1999)*

Fountain Grove 1998 Chardonnay (California) $10. 83 *—L.W. (12/31/1999)*

Fountain Grove 1997 Merlot (California) $10. 84 *—L.W. (12/31/1999)*

Fountain Grove 1998 Sauvignon Blanc (North Coast) $10. 86 *—L.W. (5/1/2000)*

FOUNTAINHEAD

Fountainhead 2003 Morisoli Borges Vineyard Cabernet Sauvignon (Rutherford) $45. 89 *—S.H. (12/15/2006)*

FOUR SONS

Four Sons 2002 Cabernet Sauvignon (Stags Leap District) $30 86 *—S.H. (12/15/2005)*

Four Sons 2002 Merlot (Carneros) $25. 84 *—S.H. (12/15/2005)*

USA

FOUR VINES

Four Vines 2002 Bailey Vineyard Syrah (Amador County) $25. 84 —*S.H. (12/1/2004)*

Four Vines 2002 Old Vine Cuvée Zinfandel (California) $10. 83 —*S.H. (12/15/2005)*

FOX BROOK

Fox Brook 1998 Ceãga Vinegarden Merlot (Mendocino) $32. 88 *(8/1/2001)*

FOX CREEK

Fox Creek 1997 Ceago Vinegarden Chardonnay (Santa Ynez Valley) $35. 88 —*M.M. (10/1/1999)*

FOX RUN

Fox Run 1997 Cabernet Franc (Finger Lakes) $13. 88 Best Buy —*L.W. (12/1/1999)*

Fox Run 1999 Cabernet Franc (Finger Lakes) $20. 83 —*J.C. (1/1/2004)*

Fox Run NV Blanc de Blancs Champagne Blend (Finger Lakes) $14. 88 *(11/15/1999)*

Fox Run 1999 Chardonnay (Finger Lakes) $9. 87 Best Buy —*J.C. (7/1/2002)*

Fox Run 2000 Reserve Seneca Lake Estate Grown Chardonnay (Finger Lakes) $13. 88 Best Buy —*J.M. (1/1/2003)*

Fox Run 2002 Pinot Noir (Finger Lakes) $15. 86 *(11/1/2004)*

Fox Run 1999 Pinot Noir (Finger Lakes) $12. 81 —*J.C. (1/1/2004)*

Fox Run 1997 Estate-grown Reserve Pinot Noir (Finger Lakes) $20. 85 *(10/1/1999)*

Fox Run 2002 Reserve Pinot Noir (Finger Lakes) $25. 83 *(11/1/2004)*

Fox Run 2000 Sable Seneca Lake Estate Grown Red Blend (Finger Lakes) $13. 85 —*J.M. (3/1/2003)*

Fox Run 2002 Riesling (Finger Lakes) $10. 85 —*J.C. (8/1/2003)*

Fox Run 1999 Riesling (Finger Lakes) $9. 86 *(11/15/2001)*

Fox Run 2001 Dry Riesling (Finger Lakes) $10. 84 —*J.C. (8/1/2003)*

Fox Run 2005 Reserve Riesling (Seneca Lake) $30. There's an unusual aroma but the flavors of mango and lime are bright and fresh. The wine is simple and the mouthfeel tends to be overly acidic, but fans of New World-style whites will enjoy its clean and lively character. It would also pair well with spicy Asian dishes and bold seafood flavors. 84 —*S.K. (5/1/2007)*

FOXEN

Foxen 1998 Chardonnay (Santa Maria Valley) $20. 92 *(6/1/2000)*

Foxen 1997 Chardonnay (Santa Maria Valley) $20. 85 —*S.H. (7/1/1999)*

Foxen 2006 Bien Nacido Vineyard Block UU Chardonnay (Santa Maria Valley) $32. This wine starts out so acidic, it's almost sour. Then the intense lemondrop flavors kick in, followed by the lush vanilla-accented smoky new oak, and the chalky minerals on the finish, and suddenly, the acidity makes sense. It's Chablisian, built for the cellar. By sometime in 2008, everything should start to meld together, and this block selection could do amazing things over the next 4–6 years. 92 Cellar Selection —*S.H. (12/31/2007)*

Foxen 2006 Tinaquaic Vineyard Chardonnay (Santa Maria Valley) $34. This single-vineyard wine from Foxen's estate is a little too sweet. It seems to contain residual sugar, to judge by the jellied pineapple and apricot flavors. If you don't mind that, you'll find a crisply acidic, clean wine, with oak and lees complexities. 86 —*S.H. (12/31/2007)*

Foxen 2003 Tinaquaic Vineyard Chardonnay (Santa Maria Valley) $24. 93 Editors' Choice —*S.H. (12/15/2005)*

Foxen 1998 Tinaquaic Vineyard Chardonnay (Santa Maria Valley) $30. 86 *(7/1/2001)*

Foxen 1997 Tinaquaic Vineyard Chardonnay (Santa Maria Valley) $30. 90 *(6/1/2000)*

Foxen 2005 Tinaquiac Vineyard Chardonnay (Santa Maria Valley) $28. 93 Editors' Choice —*S.H. (12/31/2006)*

Foxen 1996 Tinaquiac Vineyard Chardonnay (Santa Maria Valley) $30. 89 —*S.H. (7/1/1999)*

Foxen 1999 Chenin Blanc (Santa Barbara County) $14. 86 —*S.H. (5/1/2001)*

Foxen 2004 Ernesto Wickenden Vineyard Chenin Blanc (Santa Maria Valley) $18. 93 Editors' Choice —*S.H. (12/31/2006)*

Foxen 2006 Ernesto Wickenden Vineyard Old Vines Chenin Blanc (Santa Maria Valley) $20. Fresh and tart in acidity, this is a clean, savory evocation of a variety that few Californians manage to produce this well. It's rich in apple, citrus, peach and floral flavors, with a lychee, spicy complexity that makes it a natural for Asian fare. 88 —*S.H. (12/31/2007)*

Foxen 2005 Ernesto Wickenden Vineyard Old Vines Chenin Blanc (Santa Maria Valley) $20. The 2005 has been co-released with the 2006. The '05 is a better wine, probably due in part to the extra year of age, which has allowed the parts to come together harmoniously. It continues a multiyear streak of being one of the top Chenin Blancs in California. The main feature is dry acidity. It frames apple, citrus, peach and flower flavors, with a nutty, slightly bitter finish. Try as an interesting alternative to Sauv Blanc. 92 —*S.H. (12/31/2007)*

Foxen 2003 Ernesto Wickenden Vineyard Old Vines Chenin Blanc (Santa Maria Valley) $18. 93 Editors' Choice —*S.H. (8/1/2006)*

Foxen 1998 Mourvèdre (Santa Ynez Valley) $25. V92 —*S.H. (10/1/1999)*

Foxen 2000 Pinot Noir (Santa Maria Valley) $24. 90 Editors' Choice *(10/1/2002)*

Foxen 2000 Bien Nacido Vineyard Pinot Noir (Santa Maria Valley) $40. 84 *(10/1/2002)*

Foxen 1997 Bien Nacido Vineyard Pinot Noir (Santa Maria Valley) $30. 89 *(10/1/1999)*

Foxen 2003 Bien Nacido Vineyard Block 8 Pinot Noir (Santa Maria Valley) $42. 88 —*S.H. (12/15/2005)*

Foxen 2004 Bien Nacido Vineyard Block Eight Pinot Noir (Santa Maria Valley) $42. 90 —*S.H. (11/15/2006)*

Foxen 2004 Julia's Vineyard Pinot Noir (Santa Maria Valley) $42. 85 —*S.H. (11/15/2006)*

Foxen 2003 Julia's Vineyard Pinot Noir (Santa Maria Valley) $42. 90 —*S.H. (12/15/2005)*

Foxen 2000 Julia's Vineyard Pinot Noir (Santa Maria Valley) $40. 89 *(10/1/2002)*

Foxen 1997 Julia's Vineyard Pinot Noir (Santa Maria Valley) $30. 91 *(10/1/1999)*

Foxen 1997 Sanford & Benedict Vineyard Pinot Noir (Santa Ynez Valley) $30. 90 *(10/1/1999)*

Foxen 1994 Sanford & Benedict Vineyard Pinot Noir (Santa Ynez Valley) $NA. 94 Editors' Choice —*S.H. (6/1/2005)*

Foxen 1993 Sanford & Benedict Vineyard Pinot Noir (Santa Ynez Valley) $NA. 91 —*S.H. (6/1/2005)*

Foxen 2003 Sea Smoke Pinot Noir (Santa Rita Hills) $60. 89 —*S.H. (3/1/2006)*

Foxen 2004 Sea Smoke Vineyard Pinot Noir (Santa Rita Hills) $62. 82 —*S.H. (11/15/2006)*

Foxen 2003 Sea Smoke Vineyard Pinot Noir (Santa Rita Hills) $60. 92 —*S.H. (12/15/2005)*

Foxen 2003 Cuvée Jean Marie Red Table Wine Red Blend (Santa Ynez Valley) $30. 86 —*S.H. (3/1/2006)*

Foxen 2000 Foothills Reserve Red Blend (Santa Ynez Valley) $40. 86 —*S.H. (11/15/2003)*

Foxen 2004 Williamson-Dore Vineyard Cuvée Jeanne Marie Rhône Red Blend (Santa Ynez Valley) $34. 83 —*S.H. (12/1/2006)*

Foxen 2000 Carhartt Vineyard Syrah (Santa Ynez Valley) $30. 88 —*S.H. (3/1/2004)*

Foxen 2002 Cuvée Jeanne Marie Syrah (Santa Ynez Valley) $35. 85 *(9/1/2005)*

Foxen 1999 Morehouse Vineyard Syrah (Santa Ynez Valley) $35. 81 *(11/1/2001)*

Foxen 1997 Morehouse Vineyard Syrah (Santa Ynez Valley) $35. 91 —*S.H. (10/1/1999)*

Foxen 2002 Tianquaic Vineyard Syrah (Santa Maria Valley) $30. 84 —*S.H. (12/1/2004)*

Foxen 2004 Tianquiac Vineyard Syrah (Santa Maria Valley) $42. 84 —*S.H. (12/1/2006)* 93 Editors' Choice —*S.H. (3/1/2006)*

Foxen 2003 Williamson Dore Vineyard Syrah (Santa Ynez Valley) $30. 90 —*S.H. (3/1/2006)*

Foxen 2004 Williamson-Dore Vineyard Syrah (Santa Ynez Valley) $40. 85 —*S.H. (12/1/2006)*

Foxen 2002 Williamson-Dore Vineyard Syrah (Santa Ynez Valley) $35. 93 —*S.H. (6/1/2005)*

Foxen 2000 Williamson-Dore Vineyard Syrah (Santa Ynez Valley) $30. 89 —*S.H. (3/1/2004)*

Foxen 1997 Rothberg Vineyard Viognier (Santa Ynez Valley) $25. 87 —*S.H. (6/1/1999)*

FOXGLOVE

Foxglove 2001 Chardonnay (Edna Valley) $13. 84 *—S.H. (6/1/2003)*

FOXRIDGE

FoxRidge 1997 Chardonnay (Carneros) $12. 82 *—M.S. (10/1/1999)*

FoxRidge 1997 Merlot (Northern Sonoma) $11. 84 *—J.C. (7/1/2000)*

FoxRidge 1997 Merlot (Northern Sonoma) $11. 84 *—J.C. (7/1/2000)*

FRALICH

Fralich 2003 Harry's Concierge Port (Paso Robles) $25. Sweet, with an intense sugary edge to the cherry and cassis flavors, this Zin-Syrah blend has a simple finish. 84 *—S.H. (12/15/2007)*

Fralich 2004 Harry's Cuvée Red Blend (Paso Robles) $42. A blend of Syrah and Zinfandel, this is a sharp, Port-y wine with flavors of raisins and caramelized blackberries. It's semisweet and sharp on the finish. 83 *—S.H. (12/15/2007)*

Fralich 2004 Harry's Me'Lange du Rouge Red Blend (Paso Robles) $38. Soft and simple, this blend of Cab, Petite Verdot and Syrah has stewed fruit and chocolate flavors that finish with candied sweetness. 82 *—S.H. (12/15/2007)*

Fralich 2004 Harry's Patio Red Red Blend (Paso Robles) $25. A blend of Zinfadel, Syrah and Viognier, this will appeal to those who like their reds full of fruit, soft and sweet. Tastes like a spicy mix of blackberry, raspberry, milk chocolate and mint jelly. 84 *—S.H. (12/15/2007)*

Fralich 2002 Harry's Patio Red Blend (Paso Robles) $15. 83 *—S.H. (8/1/2005)*

Fralich 2003 Claret of Syrah Rosé Blend (Paso Robles) $16. 84 *—S.H. (8/1/2005)*

Fralich 2004 Harry's Billabong Red Shiraz (Paso Robles) $36. It's excessively soft and melted, with oaky flavors of blackberry and cherry jam, coffee and peppery spices that finish dry. Mostly Syrah with 15% Cab. 84 *—S.H. (12/15/2007)*

Fralich 2003 Harry's Walkabout Shiraz (Paso Robles) $42. With 4% Cab, this is a dry, tannic wine that tastes hot even though the official alcohol is 14.4%. The flavors are of raisins and stewed blackberries and cherries. 84 *—S.H. (12/15/2007)*

Fralich 2004 Harry's Red Passion Syrah (Paso Robles) $36. Harry's passion evidently is for sweet, soft, simple wines, to judge by this one. Almost totally devoid of balancing crispness and vitality, it has syrupy flavors of blackberry jam and melted chocolate. 83 *—S.H. (12/15/2007)*

Fralich 2003 Fralich Vineyard Viognier (Paso Robles) $22. 85 *—S.H. (8/1/2005)*

Fralich 2003 Harry's Menage à Trois White Blend (Paso Robles) $18. 87 *—S.H. (8/1/2005)*

USA

FRANCIS COPPOLA

Francis Coppola 1998 Black Label Bordeaux Blend (California) $17. 82 *—S.H. (7/1/2000)*

Francis Coppola 2000 Diamond Series Black Label Claret Cabernet Sauvignon (California) $17. 90 *—S.H. (11/15/2002)*

Francis Coppola 2000 Director's Reserve Cabernet Sauvignon (Napa Valley) $30. 86 *—S.H. (12/31/2002)*

Francis Coppola 2002 Sofia Blanc de Blancs Champagne Blend (California) $19. 86 *—S.H. (12/1/2002)*

Francis Coppola 1998 Diamond Series Chardonnay (California) $15. 88 *(6/1/2000)*

Francis Coppola 2000 Diamond Series Blue Label Merlot (California) $17. 84 *—S.H. (11/15/2002)*

Francis Coppola 2001 Rosso Red Blend (California) $9. 89 **Best Buy** *—S.H. (11/15/2003)*

Francis Coppola 2004 Diamond Collection Yellow Label Sauvignon Blanc (Napa Valley) $16. 85 *—S.H. (10/1/2005)*

Francis Coppola 2001 Director's Reserve Sauvignon Blanc (Napa Valley) $18. 88 *—S.H. (10/1/2003)*

Francis Coppola 2004 Rosso Shiraz (California) $11. 84 *—S.H. (12/1/2006)*

Francis Coppola 2003 Rosso Shiraz (California) $11. 84 *—S.H. (12/31/2004)*

Francis Coppola 2003 Diamond Collection Green Label Syrah-Shiraz Syrah (California) $16. 85 *(9/1/2005)*

Francis Coppola 1999 Diamond Series Green Label Syrah (California) $17. 86 *(10/1/2001)*

Francis Coppola 2004 Diamond Collection Red Label Zinfandel (California) $16. 84 *—S.H. (12/15/2006)*

Francis Coppola 1997 Diamond Series Zinfandel (California) $14. 82 *—J.C. (2/1/2000)*

FRANCIS FORD COPPOLA PRESENTS

Francis Ford Coppola Presents 2005 Director's Cut Chardonnay (Russian River Valley) $20. A little on the thin side, this wine has modest green apple, pink grapefruit and vanilla char flavors. It's bone dry and crisp, with a fast finish. 84 *—S.H. (9/1/2007)*

Francis Ford Coppola Presents 2005 Director's Cut Pinot Noir (Sonoma Coast) $24. Although it's forward in cherry, raspberry, cola and spice flavors, it's a balanced, polished wine, with nice coastal acidity and a touch of tannins. Drink now. 87 *—S.H. (9/1/2007)*

Francis Ford Coppola Presents 2005 Director's Cut Zinfandel (Dry Creek Valley) $22. The latest from Coppola, as he moves into Sonoma County from Napa. It's one of those old-fashioned, rustic Zins, ripe and sweet in jammy, spicy flavors. Pair with roast chicken. 85 *—S.H. (10/1/2007)*

FRANCISCAN

Franciscan 2003 Oakville Estate Magnificat Cabernet Blend (Napa Valley) $45. 92 *—S.H. (12/15/2006)*

Franciscan 2001 Cabernet Sauvignon (Napa Valley) $27. 85 *—S.H. (10/3/2004)*

Franciscan 1998 Cabernet Sauvignon (Napa Valley) $25. 86 *—J.M. (12/31/2001)*

Franciscan 2003 Oakville Estate Cabernet Sauvignon (Napa Valley) $28. 84 *—S.H. (7/1/2006)*

Franciscan 2002 Oakville Estate Cabernet Sauvignon (Napa Valley) $27. 91 **Editors' Choice** *—S.H. (12/1/2005)*

Franciscan 2002 Oakville Estate Cabernet Sauvignon (Napa Valley) $25. 91 *—S.H. (8/1/2005)*

Franciscan 2005 Cuvée Sauvage Chardonnay (Carneros) $35. Franciscan helped pioneer the use of wild or indigenous yeasts years ago, hence the name, and whether that technique makes better wines is debatable. Still, the level of Cuvée Sauvage has been generally high. The '05 reflects the cool balance of the vintage, with ripe peach, pear, mango and oaky-butterscotch flavors accompanied by crisp balancing acidity. 89 *—S.H. (12/1/2007)*

Franciscan 2001 Cuvée Sauvage Chardonnay (Carneros) $35. 88 *—S.H. (12/15/2003)*

Franciscan 1999 Cuvée Sauvage Chardonnay (Napa Valley) $35. 91 *—J.M. (5/1/2002)*

Franciscan 1996 Cuvée Sauvage Chardonnay (Napa Valley) $35. 89 *—L.W. (10/1/1999)*

Franciscan 2003 Oakville Estate Chardonnay (Napa Valley) $17. 84 *—S.H. (12/1/2005)*

Franciscan 2002 Oakville Estate Chardonnay (Napa Valley) $16. 85 *—S.H. (11/15/2004)*

Franciscan 1999 Oakville Estate Chardonnay (Napa Valley) $18. 87 *—J.M. (5/1/2002)*

Franciscan 1998 Oakville Estate Chardonnay (Napa Valley) $18. 90 *(6/1/2000)*

Franciscan 1997 Oakville Estate Chardonnay (Napa Valley) $17. 91 *—L.W. (6/1/2003)*

Franciscan 1996 Oakville Estate Chardonnay (Napa Valley) $18. 88 *—M.S. (6/1/1999)*

Franciscan 2000 Oakville Estate Cuvée Sauvage Chardonnay (Carneros) $35. 92 *—S.H. (2/1/2003)*

Franciscan 2000 Oakville Estates Chardonnay (Napa Valley) $17. 91 **Cellar Selection** *—J.M. (5/1/2002)*

Franciscan 2001 Merlot (Napa Valley) $22. 87 *—S.H. (12/15/2004)*

Franciscan 1997 Oakville Esate Merlot (Napa Valley) $18. 91 *(11/15/1999)*

Franciscan 2003 Oakville Estate Merlot (Napa Valley) $22. 84 *—S.H. (12/1/2006)*

Franciscan 2002 Oakville Estate Merlot (Napa Valley) $22. 88 *—S.H. (8/1/2005)*

Franciscan 2000 Oakville Estate Merlot (Napa Valley) $22. 85 *—S.H. (4/1/2003)*

Franciscan 1999 Oakville Estate Merlot (Napa Valley) $22. 92 *—J.M. (5/1/2002)*

Franciscan 2001 Magnificat Red Blend (Napa Valley) $45. 90 *—S.H. (3/1/2005)*

FRANK FAMILY

Frank Family 2002 Cabernet Sauvignon (Napa Valley) $40. 90 *—S.H. (9/1/2006)*

Frank Family 2001 Cabernet Sauvignon (Rutherford) $65. 90 *—S.H. (10/1/2004)*

Frank Family 2004 Reserve Cabernet Sauvignon (Rutherford) $95. Ripe and fleshy in young fruit, this Cab, with minor amounts of Cab Franc and Merlot, shows black currant, plum, cherry and cedar flavors, with a dry-sweet dusting of crushed brown herbs and spices. Fairly tannic and tight now, it's balanced enough for mid-term aging. Best 2008–2012. 89 *—S.H. (12/15/2007)*

Frank Family 2003 Reserve Cabernet Sauvignon (Rutherford) $70. 92 *—S.H. (12/15/2006)*

Frank Family 2002 Reserve Cabernet Sauvignon (Rutherford) $70. 92 *—S.H. (9/1/2006)*

Frank Family 2000 Reserve Cabernet Sauvignon (Rutherford) $65. 90 *—S.H. (2/1/2004)*

Frank Family 1999 Reserve Cabernet Sauvignon (Rutherford) $65. 94 Cellar Selection *—S.H. (12/31/2002)*

Frank Family 1998 Reserve Cabernet Sauvignon (Rutherford) $65. 85 *—S.H. (6/1/2002)*

Frank Family 2004 Chardonnay (Napa Valley) $32. 85 *—S.H. (3/1/2006)*

Frank Family 2000 Chardonnay (Napa Valley) $29. 90 *—S.H. (9/1/2002)*

Frank Family 2004 Zinfandel (Napa Valley) $35. 87 *—S.H. (12/1/2006)*

Frank Family 2003 Zinfandel (Napa Valley) $35. 87 *—S.H. (3/1/2006)*

FRANUS

Franus 2000 Cabernet Sauvignon (Napa Valley) $25. 86 *—S.H. (5/1/2004)*

Franus 1999 Rancho Chimiles Cabernet Sauvignon (Napa Valley) $40. 89 *—S.H. (5/1/2004)*

Franus 2002 Brandlin Vineyard Zinfandel (Mount Veeder) $32. 93 Cellar Selection *—S.H. (5/1/2005)*

Franus 2001 Brandlin Vineyard Zinfandel (Mount Veeder) $22. 88 *—J.M. (4/1/2004)*

Franus 2001 Planchon Vineyard Zinfandel (Contra Costa County) $18. 86 *—J.M. (4/1/2004)*

FRAZIER

Frazier 2003 Cabernet Sauvignon (Napa Valley) $55. 90 *—S.H. (9/1/2006)*

Frazier 1999 Lupine Hill Vineyard Cabernet Sauvignon (Napa Valley) $45. 86 *—S.H. (11/15/2002)*

Frazier 1997 Lupine Hill Vineyard Cabernet Sauvignon (Napa Valley) $45. 90 *(11/1/2000)*

Frazier 1996 Lupine Hill Vineyard Cabernet Sauvignon (Napa Valley) $36. 86 *—M.S. (12/31/1999)*

Frazier 2000 Memento Cabernet Sauvignon (Napa Valley) $75. 92 *—S.H. (2/1/2004)*

Frazier 2003 Merlot (Napa Valley) $40. 88 *—S.H. (12/1/2006)*

Frazier 2004 Estate Merlot (Napa Valley) $40. Just a bit too ripe and hot, which gives it a superficial deliciousness of fruit, but the underlying structure prevents complexity and longevity. The flavors are of cooked blackberries and cherries, with an edge of Port. 84 *—S.H. (8/1/2007)*

Frazier 1999 Lupine Hill Merlot (Napa Valley) $35. 93 *—S.H. (11/15/2002)*

Frazier 1997 Lupine Hill Vineyard Merlot (Napa Valley) $35. 87 *—J.C. (7/1/2000)*

FREEMAN

Freeman 2004 Pinot Noir (Russian River Valley) $35. 91 *—S.H. (12/1/2006)*

Freemark Abbey 1996 Cabernet Sauvignon (Napa Valley) $27. 85 *—S.H. (7/1/2000)*

Freemark Abbey 1995 Cabernet Sauvignon (Napa Valley) $23. 88 *—S.H. (6/1/1999)*

FREEMARK ABBEY

Freemark Abbey 2002 Cabernet Sauvignon (Napa Valley) $35. 87 *—S.H. (12/15/2006)*

Freemark Abbey 2001 Cabernet Sauvignon (Napa Valley) $35. 89 *—S.H. (3/1/2005)*

Freemark Abbey 2000 Cabernet Sauvignon (Napa Valley) $34. 90 *—S.H. (5/1/2004)*

Freemark Abbey 2002 Bosché Cabernet Sauvignon (Napa Valley) $65. 94 Cellar Selection *—S.H. (12/15/2006)*

Freemark Abbey 2001 Bosché Cabernet Sauvignon (Napa Valley) $65. 96 Editors' Choice *—S.H. (12/15/2005)*

Freemark Abbey 2000 Bosché Cabernet Sauvignon (Napa Valley) $68. 87 *—S.H. (8/1/2005)*

Freemark Abbey 1997 Bosché Cabernet Sauvignon (Napa Valley) $68. 90 *(6/1/2003)*

Freemark Abbey 1999 Estate Bottled Cabernet Sauvignon (Napa Valley) $34. 87 *(6/1/2003)*

Freemark Abbey 2003 Sycamore Vineyards Cabernet Sauvignon (Napa Valley) $55. 87 *—S.H. (12/31/2006)*

Freemark Abbey 2002 Sycamore Vineyards Cabernet Sauvignon (Napa Valley) $60. 87 *—S.H. (12/15/2006)*

Freemark Abbey 2001 Sycamore Vineyards Cabernet Sauvignon (Rutherford) $55. 87 *—S.H. (10/1/2004)*

Freemark Abbey 2000 Sycamore Vineyards Cabernet Sauvignon (Napa Valley) $60. 84 *—S.H. (8/1/2005)*

Freemark Abbey 1997 Sycamore Vineyards Cabernet Sauvignon (Napa Valley) $59. 91 Cellar Selection *(6/1/2003)*

Freemark Abbey 1994 Sycamore Vineyards Cabernet Sauvignon (Napa Valley) $39. 93 *(11/15/1999)*

Freemark Abbey 1993 Sycamore Vineyards Cabernet Sauvignon (Napa Valley) $35. 94 *—S.H. (6/1/1999)*

Freemark Abbey 1992 Sycamore Vineyards Cabernet Sauvignon (Napa Valley) $85. 90 *(6/1/2003)*

Freemark Abbey 2004 Chardonnay (Napa Valley) $20. The grapes are from all parts of the valley, cool as well as warm, and the wine shows a complex structure and rich fruity flavors. The tiers of pineapples, tangerines, sautéed bananas, green apples and butterscotch have a honeyed, botrytisy richness, although the finish is thoroughly dry. 90 *—S.H. (12/1/2007)*

Freemark Abbey 2003 Chardonnay (Rutherford) $20. 90 *—S.H. (3/1/2005)*

Freemark Abbey 1998 Chardonnay (Napa Valley) $19. 84 *(6/1/2000)*

Freemark Abbey 1997 Carpy Ranch Chardonnay (Napa Valley) $26. 85 *(6/1/2000)*

Freemark Abbey 2001 Estate Bottled Chardonnay (Rutherford) $18. 87 *(6/1/2003)*

Freemark Abbey 1997 Napa Valley Chardonnay (Napa Valley) $18. 87 *—S.H. (6/1/1999)*

Freemark Abbey 1997 Merlot (Napa Valley) $28. 87 *—S.H. (7/1/2000)*

Freemark Abbey 1996 Merlot (Napa Valley) $23. 89 *—S.H. (6/1/1999)*

Freemark Abbey 2002 Merlot (Napa Valley) $24. 84 *—S.H. (12/31/2005)*

Freemark Abbey 2001 Merlot (Rutherford) $27. 91 *—S.H. (3/1/2005)*

Freemark Abbey 2000 Merlot (Rutherford) $25. 86 *—S.H. (5/1/2004)*

Freemark Abbey 1999 Merlot (Rutherford) $25. 85 *(6/1/2003)*

Freemark Abbey 2000 Petite Sirah (Rutherford) $28. 82 *(4/1/2003)*

Freemark Abbey 2004 Viognier (Rutherford) $27. 93 Editors' Choice *—S.H. (12/15/2006)*

Freemark Abbey 2003 Viognier (Rutherford) $24. 92 *—S.H. (12/15/2004)*

Freemark Abbey 2002 Carpy Ranch Viognier (Rutherford) $20. 85 *—S.H. (5/1/2004)*

Freemark Abbey 2000 Carpy Ranch Viognier (Napa Valley) $25. 87 *—J.M. (12/15/2002)*

Freemark Abbey 1997 Edelwein Gold White Blend (Napa Valley) $40. 91 *—S.H. (6/1/1999)*

FREESTONE

Freestone 1997 Merlot (Napa Valley) $18. 87 *—J.C. (7/1/2000)*

FREI BROTHERS

Frei Brothers 2000 Cabernet Sauvignon (Alexander Valley) $24. 85 *—S.H. (10/1/2003)*

Frei Brothers 2000 Redwood Creek Cabernet Sauvignon (California) $8. 87 Best Buy *—S.H. (3/1/2003)*

Frei Brothers 2003 Reserve Cabernet Sauvignon (Alexander Valley) $24. Shows the delicate softness of Alexander Valley Cabernet, with the elegance that good viticulture and winemaking can bring to wine. This is a really drinkable Cabernet, but it's not a simple one. Shows layers of complexity in the way the ripe fruit, oak, tannins and acids all play off each other. 90 *—S.H. (2/1/2007)*

Frei Brothers 2002 Reserve Cabernet Sauvignon (Alexander Valley) $24. 82 *—S.H. (12/1/2005)*

Frei Brothers 1999 Reserve Cabernet Sauvignon (Alexander Valley) $24. 86 —*S.H. (12/31/2002)*

Frei Brothers 2001 Chardonnay (Russian River Valley) $20. 91 Editors' Choice —*S.H. (5/1/2003)*

Frei Brothers 2005 Reserve Chardonnay (Russian River Valley) $20. Polished and sophisticated, with lush green apple, pineapple, buttered toast and cinnamon flavors. Likeable for its balance and sheer drinkability. 88 —*S.H. (12/15/2007)*

Frei Brothers 2004 Reserve Chardonnay (Russian River Valley) $20. 83 —*S.H. (3/1/2006)*

Frei Brothers 2003 Reserve Chardonnay (Russian River Valley) $20. 89 —*S.H. (12/1/2005)*

Frei Brothers 2000 Reserve Chardonnay (Russian River Valley) $17. 86 —*J.M. (12/15/2002)*

Frei Brothers 2004 Redwood Creek Merlot (California) $8. Surprisingly polished and refined for a statewide Merlot, much less at this price and high case production. The wine is soft, with a rich array of cherries, blackberries, mocha, cola and dried herb flavors. Great by-the-glass wine for restaurants. 85 Best Buy —*S.H. (3/1/2007)*

Frei Brothers 2001 Redwood Creek Merlot (California) $7. 86 —*S.H. (4/1/2004)*

Frei Brothers 2005 Reserve Merlot (Dry Creek Valley) $20. Shows off the reasons why Dry Creek has achieved a good reputation for this finicky variety, Merlot. The wine isn't made big, gooey Napa-style. Instead, there's an herbal earthiness to the cherry-berry fruit, and the dry tannins suggest pairing with rich fare. 87 —*S.H. (12/15/2007)*

Frei Brothers 2004 Reserve Merlot (Dry Creek Valley) $20. Pretty nice Merlot, dry and smooth. There's a little green vegetalness going on, as if the vines were overcropped, but there's enough cherry fruit to satisfy. 85 —*S.H. (3/1/2007)*

Frei Brothers 2003 Reserve Merlot (Dry Creek Valley) $20. 88 —*S.H. (12/1/2005)*

Frei Brothers 2001 Reserve Merlot (Dry Creek Valley) $20. 85 —*S.H. (12/1/2003)*

Frei Brothers 2001 Pinot Noir (Russian River Valley) $24. 87 —*S.H. (7/1/2003)*

Frei Brothers 2003 Reserve Pinot Noir (Russian River Valley) $24. 84 —*S.H. (10/1/2005)*

Frei Brothers 2000 Reserve Pinot Noir (Russian River Valley) $24. 88 *(10/1/2002)*

Frei Brothers 2001 Redwood Creek Sauvignon Blanc (California) $8. 85 —*S.H. (3/1/2003)*

Frei Brothers 2005 Reserve Syrah (Russian River Valley) $24. Not only extremely drinkable, but shows real varietal elegance and class. Dry and fairly tannic, the wine brims with flavors of blackberries, blueberries, chocolate, sweet leather and Provençal herbs, with good acidity for balance. Best now. 89 —*S.H. (12/15/2007)*

Frei Brothers 2003 Reserve Syrah (Russian River Valley) $24. 84 —*S.H. (6/1/2006)*

Frei Brothers 2002 Reserve Syrah (Russian River Valley) $24. 83 *(9/1/2005)*

FRENCH HILL

French Hill 2002 Barbera (Sierra Foothills) $39. 92 —*S.H. (3/1/2005)*

French Hill 2004 Grand Reserve Barbera (Sierra Foothills) $39. I've given mixed reviews to this winery's Barberas. Sometimes they seem rustic, sometimes they show promise. This one's on the rustic side. It's kind of sweet and raw, in a young Port way, and the high alcohol adds to the impression of sweetness. 84 —*S.H. (6/1/2007)*

French Hill 2003 Grand Reserve Barbera (Sierra Foothills) $39. 82 —*S.H. (12/1/2005)*

French Hill 2001 Grand Reserve Barbera (El Dorado) $39. 85 —*S.H. (12/1/2003)*

French Hill 2004 Cabernet Franc (Sierra Foothills) $30. Cab Franc seems to produce an interesting wine in these foothills, where it shows intense cherry flavors while maintaining good acidic balance and dryness. French Hill's is typical of the better class, showing nuances of carob, lavender and spice. Drink now. 86 —*S.H. (6/1/2007)*

French Hill 2005 Premium Select Grenache (California) $24. Nice, fairly elegant red wine, gently structured and dry, with a silky texture and bursting with the most intense cherry liqueur flavor. It's a bit of a fruit bomb, though, and could use greater complexity. 84 —*S.H. (6/1/2007)*

French Hill 2004 Grand Reserve Pinotage (Amador County) $32. This is a grape no one really knows how to deal with, and the learning curve is steep. With the warm '04 vintage, the winery has achieved enormous ripeness. Cherries, cassis and milk chocolate star, but don't look for the balance of a South African Pinotage. This softly tannic wine retains the stubborn rusticity of the Sierra Foothills. 84 —*S.H. (6/1/2007)*

French Hill 2003 Grand Reserve Pinotage (Amador County) $32. 80 —*S.H. (12/1/2005)*

French Hill 2002 Grand Reserve Pinotage (Amador County) $32. 87 —*S.H. (3/1/2005)*

French Hill 2004 Sangiovese (Sierra Foothills) $24. Black and red cherries are the flavors of this wine, which shows the problems of growing Sangiovese in hot California. Not only is the wine enormously high in alcohol—16.5%—but the variety's acidity remains. The result is a hot, tart and rustic wine, but one not without a certain country charm. 84 —*S.H. (6/1/2007)*

French Hill 2004 Winemaker's Selection Tempranillo (California) $35. I've had some good Tempranillos from California, but this is not one of them. The wine is sweet, soft and simple, and while it has delicious cherry and chocolate flavors, it's simply too rustic and raw to merit a better score. 83 —*S.H. (6/1/2007)*

FREY

Frey 2000 Merlot (Redwood Valley) $15. 84 —*S.H. (5/1/2002)*

Frey 2000 Petite Sirah (Mendocino) $12. 82 —*S.H. (5/1/2002)*

Frey 2000 Syrah (Redwood Valley) $11. 82 —*S.H. (5/1/2002)*

Frey 1999 Butow Vineyards Syrah (Redwood Valley) $11. 88 Best Buy *(10/1/2001)*

Frey 2000 Zinfandel (Mendocino) $11. 82 —*S.H. (5/1/2002)*

FRIAS

Frias 2004 Cabernet Sauvignon (Spring Mountain) $65. Good Cabernet from this mountain-based winery. The warm vintage has made it juicy and ripe, a wine for immediate consumption. With its melted chocolate, cherry and cassis flavors and lusciously soft texture, it's a real crowd pleaser. 87 —*S.H. (7/1/2007)*

Frias 2002 Cabernet Sauvignon (Spring Mountain) $65. 89 —*S.H. (10/1/2005)*

Frias 2001 Cabernet Sauvignon (Spring Mountain) $65. 92 —*S.H. (10/1/2005)*

Frias 1998 Private Reserve Cabernet Sauvignon (Napa Valley) $50. 83 —*S.H. (11/15/2002)*

Frias 1999 Spring Mountain Cabernet Sauvignon (Napa Valley) $60. 84 —*S.H. (11/15/2002)*

FRICK

Frick 2004 Carignane (Mendocino County) $19. Like an old-time California wine grown in the backyard and vinified in the basement, this is a rustic, berry-filled red, tannic and cheerful and made for homemade pasta and tomato sauce. The tannins will let it age for a long time. It's a little sweet toward the finish. 85 —*S.H. (4/1/2007)*

Frick 2004 Cinsault (Dry Creek Valley) $21. Cinsault is a minor French variety, grown in the Rhône and the southwest of France. It typically produces a ripe, full-bodied red wine, as it has here, brimming with dry cherry and blackberry flavors and a rich, pastry taste suggesting chocolate coconut cream pie. Very nice, but drink now. 87 —*S.H. (5/1/2007)*

Frick 1995 Cinsault (Dry Creek Valley) $15. 85 —*M.S. (6/1/1999)*

Frick 2003 C2 Rhône Red Blend (North Coast) $18. A blend of Carignane and Cinsault is fruity and rich in red and black cherry flavors with a streak of Provençal lavender, rosemary and thyme. It's dry and robust, with balancing acids and tannins that will pair nicely with beef stew, lamb or veal. 85 —*S.H. (5/1/2007)*

Frick 1996 Syrah (Dry Creek Valley) $24. 91 —*M.S. (6/1/1999)*

Frick 1998 Syrah (Dry Creek Valley) $21. 88 *(11/1/2001)*

Frick 2000 Owl Hill Vineyard Syrah (Dry Creek Valley) $23. 83 *(9/1/2005)*

FRITZ

Fritz 2004 Cabernet Sauvignon (Dry Creek Valley) $35. Ripe, with tons of juicy cherry, blackberry, mocha and woody spice flavors, but fully dry. There's good acids and tannins, so it's all balanced and harmonious. It's not an ager, but is lovely and fairly complex. 88 —*S.H. (8/1/2007)*

Fritz 2003 Cabernet Sauvignon (Dry Creek Valley) $35. 90 —*S.H. (12/31/2006)*

Fritz 2000 Cabernet Sauvignon (Sonoma County) $29. 84 —*S.H. (11/15/2004)*

Fritz 2005 Chardonnay (Russian River Valley) $25. From a winery that's sometimes overlooked comes this finely crafted Chard. It's a nice balance of crisp acids, butterscotchy oak and polished green apple, kiwi and Key lime pie flavors, and finishes with elegant length. 89 —*S.H. (3/1/2007)*

Fritz 2002 Chardonnay (Russian River Valley) $20. 89 *—S.H. (10/1/2004)*

Fritz 2001 Dutton Ranch Chardonnay (Russian River Valley) $20. 89 *—S.H. (6/1/2004)*

Fritz 2000 Dutton Ranch Chardonnay (Russian River Valley) $22. 88 *—J.C. (9/1/2002)*

Fritz 1997 Dutton Ranch Chardonnay (Russian River Valley) $20. 92 *—S.H. (11/1/1999)*

Fritz 1997 Dutton Ranch Shop Block Chardonnay (Russian River Valley) $30. 86 *—L.W. (12/31/1999)*

Fritz 1998 Dutton Vineyard Chardonnay (Russian River Valley) $22. 87 *—S.H. (2/1/2001)*

Fritz 1997 Poplar Vineyard Dutton Ranch Chardonnay (Russian River Valley) $22. 85 *—S.H. (2/1/2000)*

Fritz 2005 Reserve Chardonnay (Russian River Valley) $45. At first this Chard struck me as austere, but as it aired and warmed in the glass, all kinds of minerally complexities emerged. Decant this one, and don't serve it too cold, to appreciate the gunmetal and leesy complexities, with hints of white peaches, vanilla custard and buttered toast. 91 *—S.H. (3/1/2007)*

Fritz 1998 Ruxton Vineyard Chardonnay (Russian River Valley) $27. 89 *—S.H. (2/1/2001)*

Fritz 1997 Ruxton Vineyard Dutton Ranch Chardonnay (Russian River Valley) $26. 90 *—S.H. (10/1/2000)*

Fritz 2000 Shop Block Dutton Ranch Chardonnay (Russian River Valley) $22. 90 *—S.H. (12/31/2003)*

Fritz 1998 Shop Block Vineyard Dutton Ranch Chardonnay (Russian River Valley) $30. 91 *—S.H. (2/1/2001)*

Fritz 1997 Merlot (Dry Creek Valley) $18. 85 *—L.W. (12/31/1999)*

Fritz 2004 Pinot Noir (Russian River Valley) $30. 89 *—S.H. (12/1/2006)*

Fritz 2002 Pinot Noir (Russian River Valley) $29. 88 *(11/1/2004)*

Fritz 2000 Dutton Ranch Pinot Noir (Russian River Valley) $29. 85 *(10/1/2002)*

Fritz 2006 Rosé Blend (Russian River Valley) $16. One of the palest rosés of the year in color, this blush isn't shy in flavor. It offers a sunburst of lemon chiffon pie, strawberry, raspberry and chutney flavors, and finishes thoroughly dry and crisp. This is a really excellent wine. **90 Editors' Choice** *—S.H. (11/1/2007)*

Fritz 2005 Sauvignon Blanc (Russian River Valley) $18. 84 *—S.H. (12/1/2006)*

Fritz 2002 Estate Sauvignon Blanc (Dry Creek Valley) $16. 87 *—S.H. (12/1/2004)*

Fritz 1998 Jenner Vineyard Sauvignon Blanc (Dry Creek Valley) $12. 87 *—S.H. (3/1/2000)*

Fritz 1998 Poplar Vineyard Sauvignon Blanc (Russian River Valley) $15. 88 *—S.H. (8/1/2001)*

Fritz 2002 Zinfandel (Dry Creek Valley) $23. 87 *—S.H. (10/1/2004)*

Fritz 2004 Estate Zinfandel (Dry Creek Valley) $25. Unfiltered, to judge from the heavy sediment, but don't worry about it, it's a good sign, not a bad one. It's a huge Zin, not at all like those superripe soft ones with residual sugar. The tannins stick out, and so does acidity, but it's a structurally elegant wine, built along Cab lines. 87 *—S.H. (3/1/2007)*

Fritz 2001 Old Vine Zinfandel (Dry Creek Valley) $24. 88 *—S.H. (6/1/2004)*

Fritz 1999 Old Vine Zinfandel (Dry Creek Valley) $25. 87 *—J.M. (3/1/2002)*

Fritz 1997 Old Vine Zinfandel (Dry Creek Valley) $20. 92 *—S.H. (11/1/1999)*

Fritz 1997 Roger's Reserve Zinfandel (Dry Creek Valley) $30. 88 3 *—L.W. (2/1/2000)*

FROG POND

Frog Pond 2001 Fralich Vineyard Syrah (Paso Robles) $NA. 86 *—S.H. (12/1/2004)*

FROG'S LEAP

Frog's Leap 2000 Rutherford Cabernet Blend (Napa Valley) $65. 93 *—S.H. (11/15/2003)*

Frog's Leap 1999 Rutherford Cabernet Blend (Napa Valley) $65. 92 *—J.M. (2/1/2003)*

Frog's Leap 2004 Cabernet Sauvignon (Napa Valley) $39. What a fine, elegant Cab. It's not a blockbuster, the kind of Cab designed to impress through sheer size, but one designed for the upscale table. Elegant and refined, it shows ripe currant, carob and oak flavors wrapped in soft, intricate tannins. Drink now–2012. 92 *—S.H. (5/1/2007)*

Frog's Leap 2004 Cabernet Sauvignon (Rutherford) $75. Tasted in a flight of other '04 Rutherford Cabs, this one was a little leaner and greener. There's a pepperminty sharpness alongside the cherry and cedar flavors. Best now and for a few years. 88 *—S.H. (12/15/2007)*

Frog's Leap 2003 Cabernet Sauvignon (Napa Valley) $39. 84 *—S.H. (3/1/2006)*

Frog's Leap 2003 Cabernet Sauvignon (Rutherford) $75. 91 *—S.H. (12/15/2006)*

Frog's Leap 2002 Cabernet Sauvignon (Rutherford) $65. 85 *—S.H. (12/15/2005)*

Frog's Leap 2002 Cabernet Sauvignon (Napa Valley) $39. 86 *—S.H. (5/1/2005)*

Frog's Leap 2001 Cabernet Sauvignon (Rutherford) $65. 94 *—S.H. (10/1/2004)*

Frog's Leap 1999 Cabernet Sauvignon (Napa Valley) $35. 90 *—M.S. (11/15/2002)*

Frog's Leap 1997 Cabernet Sauvignon (Napa Valley) $30. 91 *(11/1/2000)*

Frog's Leap 2005 Chardonnay (Napa Valley) $24. There's an earthy quality to this Chard, with herbal sage, dill and Bay laurel flavors to the underlying peach and apricot flavors. It's also a little on the soft side. Will benefit from decanting for a few hours, to take the edge off and let it breathe. 85 *—S.H. (5/1/2007)*

Frog's Leap 2003 Chardonnay (Napa Valley) $24. 85 *—S.H. (5/1/2005)*

Frog's Leap 2001 Chardonnay (Napa Valley) $22. 84 *—S.H. (12/15/2003)*

Frog's Leap 2000 Chardonnay (Napa Valley) $22. 88 *—J.M. (5/1/2002)*

Frog's Leap 1998 Chardonnay (Napa Valley) $22. 83 *(6/1/2000)*

Frog's Leap 2004 Merlot (Napa Valley) $34. There's an ashy, sage and thyme edge to this ripe young Merlot that actually adds interest to the cherry, blackberry and cranberry aromas and flavors. The wine is voluptuously rich, almost decadent, so ripe is the fruit and so fine are the tannins, but it never loses its dry sense of balance. Very Bordeaux-like in elegance. 91 *—S.H. (3/1/2007)*

Frog's Leap 2003 Merlot (Napa Valley) $34. 87 *—S.H. (3/1/2006)*

Frog's Leap 2002 Merlot (Napa Valley) $34. 87 *—S.H. (3/1/2005)*

Frog's Leap 1998 Merlot (Napa Valley) $28. 86 *—J.C. (6/1/2001)*

Frog's Leap 2006 La Grenouille Rouganté Pink Vin Rosé Rosé Blend (Napa Valley) $12. There's lots of stimulating acidity in this wine, which is mostly from the Valdiguie grape, otherwise known as Napa Gamay. It shows good cherry and spice flavors and is on the dry side, making it a good palate cleaner. Great with sushi. 86 *—S.H. (11/1/2007)*

Frog's Leap 2004 La Grenouille Rougante Pink Rosé Blend (Napa Valley) $12. **85 Best Buy** *—S.H. (10/1/2005)*

Frog's Leap 2006 Sauvignon Blanc (Napa Valley) $18. They kept the alcohol nice and low, only 12.7%, resulting in a light-bodied, Sancerre-style wine of delicacy and finesse. It's also very dry, allowing the acidity and savory citrus fruit and wildflower flavors to shine. What a versatile white wine this is. 88 *—S.H. (10/1/2007)*

Frog's Leap 2005 Sauvignon Blanc (Rutherford) $16. 87 *—S.H. (12/1/2006)*

Frog's Leap 2004 Sauvignon Blanc (Rutherford) $16. **90 Editors' Choice** *—S.H. (11/1/2005)*

Frog's Leap 2003 Sauvignon Blanc (Rutherford) $17. 87 *—J.M. (10/1/2004)*

Frog's Leap 2001 Sauvignon Blanc (Napa Valley) $16. 88 *(8/1/2002)*

Frog's Leap 2002 Syrah (Napa Valley) $25. 89 *—S.H. (12/31/2004)*

Frog's Leap 2004 Leapfrogmilch White Blend (Napa Valley) $14. 82 *—S.H. (10/1/2005)*

Frog's Leap 2005 Zinfandel (Napa Valley) $25. Beautiful young Zin, built along balanced, Napa Cab lines. Thick, rich, dusty tannins and upfront acidity frame exuberant wild berry, tobacco, balsamic, cola, espresso and spice flavors that finish long and dry. Those tannins will protect this as it ages over the next 10 years. 88 *—S.H. (10/1/2007)*

Frog's Leap 2004 Zinfandel (Napa Valley) $25. 84 *—S.H. (12/1/2006)*

Frog's Leap 2003 Zinfandel (Napa Valley) $25. **91 Editors' Choice** *—S.H. (11/1/2005)*

Frog's Leap 2002 Zinfandel (Napa Valley) $23. 87 *—J.M. (10/1/2004)*

Frog's Leap 2001 Zinfandel (Rutherford) $22. 86 *(11/1/2003)*

Frog's Leap 2000 Zinfandel (Napa Valley) $22. 86 *—M.S. (11/1/2002)*

Frog's Leap 1999 Zinfandel (Napa Valley) $22. 85 *—D.T. (3/1/2002)*

Frog's Leap 1997 Zinfandel (Napa Valley) $18. 86 *—P.G. (11/15/1999)*

FRONTIER RED

Frontier Red 2004 Lot 51 California Red Wine Red Blend (California) $10. **85 Best Buy** —*S.H. (5/1/2006)*

Frontier Red NV Rhône Red Blend (California) $10. **83** —*S.H. (12/31/2006)*

FROSTWATCH

Frostwatch 2004 Chardonnay (Bennett Valley) $27. **89** —*S.H. (7/1/2006)*

Frostwatch 2004 Merlot (Bennett Valley) $28. This is a wonderfully rewarding wine, rich, dry, soft and complex. The cherry, blackberry and mocha-vanilla oak flavors are deep and long, and the wine is totally beautiful now. **90** —*S.H. (3/1/2007)*

FULKERSON

Fulkerson 2005 Cabernet Sauvignon (Finger Lakes) $16. Leather and tobacco on the nose and a tart, oaky spicy flavor profile make this Finger Lakes Cab a little tough to tame, but paired with a sharp cheese or heartier fare, it will round out nicely. Fruit-forward and assertive; needs time to aerate before drinking. **83** —*S.K. (10/1/2007)*

Fulkerson 2005 Pinot Noir (Finger Lakes) $20. Buttery, spiced aromas mingled with berry start this Pinot from Finger Lakes producer Fulkerson. Cherry, plum and smoke are present on the palate, and the wine has a soft, elegant character, but the body is weak and watery. There's just not enough personality here to make an impact, despite the pleasant flavors. **83** —*S.K. (5/1/2007)*

Fulkerson 2005 Dry Riesling (Finger Lakes) $13. A clean, minerally, citric nose with a touch of flowers leads into flavors of melon, lemon and lime with this dry Riesling. The wine is refreshing and lively but there's ample structure, too. The finish is a bit thin but the wine will pair well with a variety of foods, especially cheeses and seafood. **86** —*S.K. (5/1/2007)*

Fulkerson 2005 Semi-Dry Riesling (Finger Lakes) $13. Intense tropical aromas are the hallmark of this semi-dry (Johannisberg) Riesling from New York's Fulkerson. The flavors—lemon, apricot, apple—are intense but not heavy, and the wine strikes a good balance of acidity and sweetness. It's not the most elegant or integrated of wines but it's an excellent wine for food pairing and hot summer days. **85** —*S.K. (5/1/2007)*

Fulkerson 2006 Traminette (Finger Lakes) $12. A beautiful nose of delicate white flowers entices with this Traminette from New York. On the palate, the wine offers a combination of citrus and pear which is both elegant and an interesting match to myriad foods. Very pretty and a good price. **87 Best Buy** —*S.K. (10/1/2007)*

Fulkerson 2005 Traminette (Finger Lakes) $12. Orange citrus and flowers lead the nose, and on the palate exhibits lime, apple and spice. It's a touch sweet but overall, enjoyable and unique. **84** —*S.K. (10/1/2007)*

Fulkerson 2004 Iced Wine Vidal Blanc (Finger Lakes) $24. This opulent, golden icewine displays rich aromas and flavors of peach, honey, apple and spice, with a soft edge that gives it an elegant overall character. Perfect for the end of the meal and on its own. **86** —*S.K. (7/1/2007)*

FULL CIRCLE

Full Circle 2002 Cabernet Sauvignon (California) $8. **86 Best Buy** —*S.H. (3/1/2005)*

Full Circle 2003 Chardonnay (California) $8. **85 Best Buy** —*S.H. (3/1/2005)*

Full Circle 2003 Merlot (California) $8. **85 Best Buy** —*S.H. (3/1/2005)*

FUSÉE

Fusée 2003 Cabernet Sauvignon (California) $6. **85 Best Buy** —*S.H. (11/15/2005)*

Fusée 2002 Cabernet Sauvignon (California) $6. **84 Best Buy** —*S.H. (4/1/2005)*

Fusée 2005 Chardonnay (California) $6. **83 Best Buy** —*S.H. (12/1/2006)*

Fusée 2004 Chardonnay (California) $6. **84 Best Buy** —*S.H. (4/1/2006)*

Fusée 2003 Chardonnay (California) $6. **84 Best Buy** —*S.H. (4/1/2005)*

Fusée 2004 Merlot (California) $6. **83 Best Buy** —*S.H. (11/1/2006)*

Fusée 2003 Merlot (California) $6. **87 Best Buy** —*S.H. (11/15/2005)*

Fusée 2002 Merlot (California) $6. **86 Best Buy** —*S.H. (4/1/2005)*

Fusée 2003 Syrah (California) $6. **86 Best Buy** *(9/1/2005)*

Fusée 2002 Syrah (California) $6. **85 Best Buy** —*S.H. (12/31/2004)*

Fusée 2001 Syrah (California) $6. **84** —*S.H. (9/1/2004)*

Fusée 2000 Syrah (California) $5. **90 Best Buy** —*S.H. (11/15/2003)*

Fusée 2004 White Zinfandel (California) $6. **84 Best Buy** —*S.H. (11/15/2005)*

GABRIELLI

Gabrielli 2001 Coro Mednocino Red Blend (Mendocino) $35. **85** —*J.M. (9/1/2004)*

Gabrielli 1999 Sangiovese (Redwood Valley) $NA. **85** —*S.H. (5/1/2002)*

Gabrielli 2000 Rosato Sangiovese (Redwood Valley) $28. **85** —*S.H. (5/1/2002)*

Gabrielli 1997 Syrah (Redwood Valley) $18. **85** *(10/1/2001)*

Gabrielli 1999 Zinfandel (Redwood Valley) $18. **84** —*S.H. (11/1/2002)*

Gabrielli 1998 Goforth Vineyard Zinfandel (Redwood Valley) $18. **83** —*S.H. (11/1/2002)*

Gabrielli 1997 Goforth Vineyard Zinfandel (Redwood Valley) $20. **87** —*S.H. (5/1/2000)*

GAINEY

Gainey 2005 Chardonnay (Santa Rita Hills) $20. Wow, what a good value! This is a Chard that shows tremendous authority and power, not to mention that cool-climate character of Santa Rita Hills. Bursts with bright Meyer lemondrop, Key-lime pie, vanilla custard and smoky oak aromas, with similar flavors that are heightened by crisp, clean acidity. **90 Editors' Choice** —*S.H. (7/1/2007)*

Gainey 2004 Chardonnay (Santa Rita Hills) $19. **87** —*S.H. (11/15/2006)*

Gainey 2003 Chardonnay (Santa Barbara County) $19. **83** —*S.H. (12/31/2005)*

Gainey 2002 Chardonnay (Santa Barbara County) $18. **86** —*S.H. (11/15/2004)*

Gainey 2001 Chardonnay (Santa Rita Hills) $32. **91** —*S.H. (10/1/2003)*

Gainey 2000 Chardonnay (Santa Barbara County) $18. **90** —*S.H. (12/15/2002)*

Gainey 2005 Limited Selection Chardonnay (Santa Rita Hills) $32. This five-vineyard blend of Chard has superripe, possibly botrytised, flavors of apricots and new oak. It's almost late-harvest in style, although it's fully dry. A disappointment. **84** —*S.H. (12/31/2007)*

Gainey 2004 Limited Selection Chardonnay (Santa Rita Hills) $32. Gainey's Limited Selection Chard has been a remarkably consistent wine, hanging onto its minerally rich Santa Rita character through vintage variations. The '04 retains the wine's sleek elegance, rich without being heavy, offering a wealth of tropical fruit, limestone and new oak flavors. **91** —*S.H. (5/1/2007)*

Gainey 2003 Limited Selection Chardonnay (Santa Rita Hills) $32. **92** —*S.H. (3/1/2006)*

Gainey 2001 Limited Selection Chardonnay (Santa Barbara County) $31. **91** —*S.H. (11/15/2004)*

Gainey 1999 Limited Selection Chardonnay (Santa Barbara County) $28. **92** —*S.H. (12/15/2002)*

Gainey 1997 Limited Selection Chardonnay (Santa Barbara County) $28. **91** *(6/1/2000)*

Gainey 1997 Triada Grenache (Santa Ynez Valley) $16. **90** —*S.H. (10/1/1999)*

Gainey 2004 Merlot (Santa Ynez Valley) $24. Smooth as velvet, with a good balance of cherries, blackberries, violets and new, toasty oak, this is a luscious Merlot, dry and balanced. The alcohol is below 14%, so it's not one of those chocolaty confections. But it is an elegant, sophisticated table wine that drinks well now and will hold for a couple years. **89** —*S.H. (9/1/2007)*

Gainey 2003 Merlot (Santa Ynez Valley) $20. **88** —*S.H. (12/15/2006)*

Gainey 2002 Merlot (Santa Ynez Valley) $19. **88** —*S.H. (10/1/2005)*

Gainey 2001 Merlot (Santa Ynez Valley) $19. **90** —*S.H. (3/1/2005)*

Gainey 1999 Merlot (Santa Ynez Valley) $20. **92** —*S.H. (11/15/2002)*

Gainey 2004 Limited Selection Merlot (Santa Ynez Valley) $35. Always among the top Santa Barbara Merlots, the '04 is the ripest Gainey I've ever had. It's a burst of chocolate-covered raspberries and cherries, with a rich smoky veneer of sweet oak. If this were any sweeter on the palate, it would be flawed, but it has just enough tannins and acids to keep it balanced. **87** —*S.H. (10/1/2007)*

Gainey 2002 Limited Selection Merlot (Santa Ynez Valley) $34. **90** —*S.H. (10/1/2005)*

Gainey 1999 Limited Selection Merlot (Santa Ynez Valley) $35. **91** —*S.H. (10/1/2003)*

Gainey 1998 Limited Selection Merlot (Santa Ynez Valley) $35. **88** —*J.M. (7/1/2002)*

Gainey 1996 Limited Selection Merlot (Santa Ynez Valley) $25. **95** —*S.H. (9/1/1999)*

Gainey 2005 Pinot Noir (Santa Rita Hills) $30. This is Gainey's basic '05 Pinot, and it shows the quality of the vintage. The wine is dry, crisp in acidity and under 14% in alcohol, with dramatic cherry and boysenberry fruit complexed with leather, cola, Chinese five spice and balsamic notes. Fairly tannic, it's best now and for a few years. **92** *—S.H. (12/15/2007)*

Gainey 2005 Limited Selection Pinot Noir (Santa Rita Hills) $44. Gainey's regular '05 was a beautiful wine. This is more full-bodied, richer and higher in alcohol, and merits its reserve status. It's a young wine, opulent in cherries and raspberries that have a baked pie-filling warmth, and complexed with cola, sweet leather, figs, pomegranates and dusty Asian spices. Very delicious now, it should develop additional complexities over the next six years. **93** *—S.H. (12/31/2007)*

Gainey 2004 Limited Selection Pinot Noir (Santa Rita Hills) $48. Here's a dark, young Pinot that needs a little time to come around. It's fresh and pert in primary blackberry and cherry fruit, with smoky oak that hasn't quite integrated yet. You could drink it now with decanting, but it really wants a couple of years to knit together and become softer and more gracious. **91** *—S.H. (5/1/2007)*

Gainey 2003 Limited Selection Pinot Noir (Santa Rita Hills) $48. 92 *—S.H. (3/1/2006)*

Gainey 2001 Limited Selection Pinot Noir (Santa Barbara County) $35. 93 Editors' Choice *—S.H. (7/1/2003)*

Gainey 2006 Riesling (Santa Ynez Valley) $13. Much like Gainey's past Rieslings, this one's simple and easy, with pleasant fruit and spice, but of no particular distinction. **84** *—S.H. (11/15/2007)*

Gainey 2005 Riesling (Santa Ynez Valley) $13. 85 *—S.H. (12/1/2006)*

Gainey 2003 Riesling (Santa Barbara County) $13. 86 *—S.H. (2/1/2005)*

Gainey 2000 Riesling (Santa Ynez Valley) $12. 84 *—S.H. (11/15/2001)*

Gainey 1998 Limited Selection Late Harvest Riesling (Santa Ynez Valley) $20. 90 *—S.H. (12/31/2000)*

Gainey 2005 Sauvignon Blanc (Santa Ynez Valley) $13. This is a good price for a wine of this complexity, depth and overall interest. It's crisp and citrusy, with lemongrass and pineapple flavors enriched with one-fifth Sémillon, which brings a nutty, buttery nuance, and it's hard to believe there's no oak at all, because of all the cream. Grown entirely at Gainey's Home Ranch, in one of the best Sauvignon Blanc areas of California. **88 Best Buy** *—S.H. (5/1/2007)*

Gainey 2004 Sauvignon Blanc (Santa Ynez Valley) $13. 86 *—S.H. (7/1/2006)*

Gainey 2003 Sauvignon Blanc (Santa Ynez Valley) $14. 86 *—S.H. (12/15/2005)*

Gainey 2002 Sauvignon Blanc (Santa Ynez Valley) $13. 88 Best Buy *—S.H. (2/1/2005)*

Gainey 2006 Limited Selection Sauvignon Blanc (Santa Ynez Valley) $20. Slightly sweet, with spearmint, fig, lime and vanilla oak flavors balanced with crisp acids, this Sauvignon Blanc comes from the winery's estate vineyard in the warmer eastern valley. Very good, and would be even better if it finished drier. **89** *—S.H. (12/31/2007)*

Gainey 2005 Limited Selection Sauvignon Blanc (Santa Ynez Valley) $20. Another beautiful wine from Gainey, a great producer whose Sauvignon Blanc comes from one of the best terroirs for that variety in California. The aroma is so invitingly rich in lemongrass, pineapple zest, Key lime pie and coconut macaroon that you almost fear it won't follow up in the mouth, but it does. Bone dry, rich, zesty and clean, it seems to have benefited from the coolness of the vintage, in the way the beautifully ripe fruit is accented by crisp, flinty acidity. This is gorgeous, world-class Sauvignon Blanc. **93 Editors' Choice** *—S.H. (5/1/2007)*

Gainey 2004 Limited Selection Sauvignon Blanc (Santa Ynez Valley) $20. 92 Editors' Choice *—S.H. (7/1/2006)*

Gainey 2003 Limited Selection Sauvignon Blanc (Santa Ynez Valley) $19. 90 Editors' Choice *—S.H. (10/1/2005)*

Gainey 2002 Limited Sauvignon Blanc (Santa Ynez Valley) $30. 91 *—S.H. (2/1/2005)*

Gainey 2001 Limited Selection Sauvignon Blanc (Santa Ynez Valley) $21. 87 *—S.H. (10/1/2003)*

Gainey 2000 Limited Selection Sauvignon Blanc (Santa Ynez Valley) $20. 90 *—S.H. (9/1/2003)*

Gainey 1998 Limited Selection Sauvignon Blanc (Santa Ynez Valley) $20. 90 *—S.H. (11/15/2000)*

Gainey 1997 Limited Selection Sauvignon Blanc (Santa Ynez Valley) $18. 90 *—S.H. (9/1/1999)*

Gainey 2004 Limited Selection Syrah (Santa Ynez Valley) $38. The grapes actually are from an estate vineyard in the warmer eastern Santa Rita Hills, with 12% from Santa Ynez Valley, which makes it more or less a blend of warm and cool climates. This pretty Syrah shows a varietal purity and structural integrity that make it great. Smooth and long in the finish, it's a tour de force of black currants, licorice, cola, cedar, carob and smoky leather. Best now through 2010. **94** *—S.H. (6/1/2007)*

Gainey 2002 Limited Selection Syrah (Santa Barbara County) $35. 85 *—S.H. (9/1/2005)*

Gainey 2000 Limited Selection Syrah (Santa Barbara County) $32. 92 *—S.H. (3/1/2004)*

GALANTE

Galante 2003 Blackjack Pasture Cabernet Sauvignon (Carmel Valley) $60. 85 *—S.H. (12/15/2006)*

Galante 2002 Blackjack Pasture Cabernet Sauvignon (Carmel Valley) $60. 91 Cellar Selection *—S.H. (7/1/2006)*

Galante 2001 Blackjack Pasture Cabernet Sauvignon (Carmel Valley) $60. 92 Cellar Selection *—S.H. (10/1/2004)*

Galante 2000 Blackjack Pasture Cabernet Sauvignon (Carmel Valley) $50. 93 *—S.H. (11/15/2003)*

Galante 1997 Blackjack Pasture Cabernet Sauvignon (Carmel Valley) $40. 93 *—S.H. (2/1/2000)*

Galante 2003 Rancho Galante Cabernet Sauvignon (Carmel Valley) $20. 87 *—S.H. (7/1/2006)*

Galante 2001 Rancho Galante Cabernet Sauvignon (Carmel Valley) $20. 86 *—S.H. (10/1/2004)*

Galante 2000 Rancho Galante Cabernet Sauvignon (Carmel Valley) $20. 90 Editors' Choice *—S.H. (11/15/2003)*

Galante 1997 Rancho Galante Cabernet Sauvignon (Carmel Valley) $18. 89 *—S.H. (2/1/2000)*

Galante 2002 Red Rose Hill Cabernet Sauvignon (Carmel Valley) $30. 88 *—S.H. (7/1/2006)*

Galante 2001 Red Rose Hill Cabernet Sauvignon (Carmel Valley) $30. 90 *—S.H. (10/1/2004)*

Galante 2000 Red Rose Hill Cabernet Sauvignon (Carmel Valley) $30. 92 *—S.H. (11/15/2003)*

Galante 1997 Red Rose Hill Cabernet Sauvignon (Carmel Valley) $28. 91 *—S.H. (2/1/2000)*

Galante 2003 Estate Merlot (Carmel Valley) $35. 80 *—S.H. (7/1/2006)*

Galante 2004 Estate Pinot Noir (Carmel Valley) $30. 84 *—S.H. (7/1/2006)*

Galante 2000 Sauvignon Blanc (Carmel Valley) $22. 87 *—S.H. (12/1/2003)*

GALLEANO

Galleano 1999 Dos Rancheros Zinfandel (Cucamonga Valley) $18. 87 *—S.H. (4/1/2002)*

Galleano 2001 Dos Rancheros Old Vines Zinfandel (Cucamonga Valley) $18. 82 *—S.H. (3/1/2004)*

Galleano NV Old Vines Zinfandel (Cucamonga Valley) $6. 81 *—S.H. (3/1/2004)*

Galleano 2000 Old Vines Zinfandel Port Zinfandel (Cucamonga Valley) $20. 93 Editors' Choice *—S.H. (9/1/2003)*

Galleano 2001 Pioneers Legendary Old Vines Zinfandel (Cucamonga Valley) $16. 80 *—S.H. (3/1/2004)*

GALLERON

Galleron 2000 Cabernet Sauvignon (Napa Valley) $45. 92 *—S.H. (2/1/2005)*

Galleron 2004 Generation Series Cabernet Sauvignon (Rutherford) $40. Made from 100% Cabernet, this young wine was showing some tough, hard tannins in July 2007. It's clean and dry, but doesn't quite have the fruity stuffing for the long haul. Drink now. **85** *—S.H. (12/15/2007)*

Galleron 2001 Morisoli Vineyard Cabernet Sauvignon (Rutherford) $100. 90 *—S.H. (10/1/2004)*

Galleron 2000 Morisoli Vineyard Cabernet Sauvignon (Napa Valley) $100. 90 *—S.H. (2/1/2005)*

Galleron 1999 Morisoli Vineyard Cabernet Sauvignon (Napa Valley) $100. 95 *—S.H. (12/31/2002)*

Galleron 1999 Trio Vineyard Chardonnay (Napa Valley) $40. 87 *(7/1/2001)*

Galleron 2000 Jaeger Vineyard Merlot (Napa Valley) $32. 85 *—S.H. (2/1/2005)*

Galleron 2001 Branham Rockpile Zinfandel (Sonoma County) $32. 84 *—S.H. (2/1/2005)*

GALLERON LAINE

Galleron Laine 1998 Lo Vecchio Estate Vineyard Chardonnay (Napa Valley) $35. 88 *(7/1/2001)*

Galleron Laine 1997 Merlot (Napa Valley) $35. 84 —*J.C. (6/1/2001)*

GALLO FAMILY VINEYARDS

Gallo Family Vineyards 2003 Estate Cabernet Sauvignon (Northern Sonoma) $75. 92 —*S.H. (9/1/2006)*

Gallo Family Vineyards 2003 Reserve Cabernet Sauvignon (Sonoma County) $15. 87 *(5/1/2006)*

Gallo Family Vineyards 2004 Laguna Vineyard Chardonnay (Russian River Valley) $28. An interesting and complex Chard marked by intense minerality. Calls to mind Chablis in the acidity, dryness and racy taste of cold steel. Also in the flavor mix are tart green apples, pineapples, limes, cinnamon spice and creamy lees. 91 —*S.H. (12/15/2007)*

Gallo Family Vineyards NV Twin Valley Cabernet Sauvignon (California) $5. 85 **Best Buy** —*S.H. (12/15/2006)*

Gallo Family Vineyards NV Twin Valley Chardonnay (California) $5. 84 **Best Buy** —*S.H. (12/15/2006)*

Gallo Family Vineyards NV Merlot (California) $5. 83 **Best Buy** —*S.H. (12/15/2006)*

Gallo Family Vineyards 2003 Reserve Merlot (Sonoma County) $13. 87 *(5/1/2006)*

Gallo Family Vineyards NV Twin Valley Merlot (California) $5. This is the best five-dollar Merlot on the market. Heck, maybe even the best six-dollar Merlot. It's dry and smooth and even stylish, with solid cherry, blackberry and herb flavors. 84 —*S.H. (3/1/2007)*

Gallo Family Vineyards NV Twin Valley Moscato (California) $5. Very sweet in orange marmalade flavors, just like those little jelly containers they serve you with your toast, this wine fortunately has juicy acidity for balance. It's a really nice everyday dessert wine. 84 **Best Buy** —*S.H. (2/1/2007)*

Gallo Family Vineyards 2005 Reserve Pinot Gris (Sonoma County) $15. There's little or no oak on this wine to mask the pure fruit flavors that are boosted by succulent acidity. It's an explosion of pineapples, tart green apples, figs, spicy melons and kiwi fruit, with a tangy, white peppery finish. Easy to enjoy, yet fancy enough for that white tablecloth. 86 —*S.H. (2/1/2007)*

Gallo Family Vineyards 2006 Sonoma Reserve Pinot Gris (Sonoma County) $15. Crisp, juicy acidity and tangy flavors of Meyer lemons and limes make this wine immediately appealing. Partial barrel fermentation adds a touch of toast and cream, but a keen racy freshness really is the hallmark. 87 **Editors' Choice** —*S.H. (11/15/2007)*

Gallo Family Vineyards 2004 Reserve Pinot Noir (Sonoma County) $15. 87 *(5/1/2006)*

Gallo Family Vineyards NV Hearty Burgundy Red Blend (California) $5. 84 **Best Buy** —*S.H. (12/15/2006)*

Gallo Family Vineyards NV Twin Valley Sauvignon Blanc (California) $5. 84 **Best Buy** —*S.H. (12/15/2006)*

Gallo Family Vineyards 2004 Reserve Zinfandel (Sonoma County) $13. 88 **Best Buy** —*S.H. (10/1/2006)*

Gallo Family Vineyards NV Twin Valley White Zinfandel (California) $5. 83 **Best Buy** —*S.H. (12/15/2006)*

Gallo Family Vineyards NV Twin Valley White Zinfandel (California) $6. 82 —*S.H. (7/1/2006)*

GALLO OF SONOMA

Gallo of Sonoma 2000 Barrelli Creek Vineyard Barbera (Alexander Valley) $24. 88 —*S.H. (2/1/2003)*

Gallo of Sonoma 1999 Cabernet Sauvignon (Sonoma County) $13. 87 **Best Buy** —*S.H. (11/15/2002)*

Gallo of Sonoma 1999 Barelli Creek Cabernet Sauvignon (Alexander Valley) $32. 88 —*S.H. (8/1/2003)*

Gallo of Sonoma 1997 Barelli Creek Cabernet Sauvignon (Sonoma County) $28. 91 *(7/1/2001)*

Gallo of Sonoma 1994 Barrelli Creek Cabernet Sauvignon (Sonoma County) $18. 88 —*S.H. (11/1/1999)*

Gallo of Sonoma 1998 Estate Cabernet Sauvignon (Northern Sonoma) $75. 90 *(3/1/2003)*

Gallo of Sonoma 1998 Frei Ranch Vineyard Cabernet Sauvignon (Dry Creek Valley) $30. 90 —*S.H. (8/1/2003)*

Gallo of Sonoma 1997 Frei Vineyard Cabernet Sauvignon (Dry Creek Valley) $26. 87 —*S.H. (9/1/2002)*

Gallo of Sonoma 2000 Reserve Cabernet Sauvignon (Sonoma County) $13. 89 —*S.H. (3/1/2003)*

Gallo of Sonoma 1995 Sonoma County Cabernet Sauvignon (Sonoma County) $11. 90 **Best Buy** —*L.W. (7/1/1999)*

Gallo of Sonoma 1998 Stefani Vineyard Cabernet Sauvignon (Dry Creek Valley) $30. 91 **Editors' Choice** —*S.H. (5/1/2003)*

Gallo of Sonoma 1997 Stefani Vineyard Cabernet Sauvignon (Dry Creek Valley) $28. 91 *(7/1/2001)*

Gallo of Sonoma 2001 Chardonnay (Sonoma County) $11. 86 **Best Buy** —*S.H. (6/1/2003)*

Gallo of Sonoma 2000 Estate Chardonnay (Northern Sonoma) $45. 92 —*S.H. (3/1/2006)*

Gallo of Sonoma 2002 Laguna Ranch Vineyard Chardonnay (Russian River Valley) $22. 87 —*S.H. (10/1/2005)*

Gallo of Sonoma 2003 Laguna Vineyard Chardonnay (Russian River Valley) $24. 83 —*S.H. (3/1/2006)*

Gallo of Sonoma 2000 Laguna Vineyard Chardonnay (Russian River Valley) $24. 90 —*S.H. (12/15/2002)*

Gallo of Sonoma 1999 Laguna Vineyard Chardonnay (Russian River Valley) $23. 87 —*J.C. (9/1/2002)*

Gallo of Sonoma 2004 Reserve Chardonnay (Sonoma County) $13. 89 **Best Buy** —*S.H. (3/1/2006)*

Gallo of Sonoma 2000 Reserve Chardonnay (Sonoma County) $11. 87 **Best Buy** —*S.H. (12/15/2002)*

Gallo of Sonoma 1997 Russian River Valley Chardonnay (Russian River Valley) $10. 87 *(11/15/1999)*

Gallo of Sonoma 1999 Stefani Vineyard Chardonnay (Dry Creek Valley) $23. 91 —*S.H. (2/1/2003)*

Gallo of Sonoma 1997 Stefani Vineyard Chardonnay (Dry Creek Valley) $20. 88 —*M.S. (10/1/2000)*

Gallo of Sonoma 2001 Two Rock Vineyard Chardonnay (Sonoma Coast) $28. 88 —*J.M. (6/1/2003)*

Gallo of Sonoma 2002 Merlot (Sonoma County) $11. 87 **Best Buy** —*S.H. (12/1/2005)*

Gallo of Sonoma 2000 Merlot (Sonoma County) $11. 86 —*S.H. (11/15/2002)*

Gallo of Sonoma 1997 Merlot (Sonoma County) $11. 89 *(11/15/1999)*

Gallo of Sonoma 2001 Reserve Merlot (Sonoma County) $11. 89 —*S.H. (4/1/2004)*

Gallo of Sonoma 2004 Pinot Gris (Sonoma County) $13. 87 —*S.H. (2/1/2006)*

Gallo of Sonoma 2001 Pinot Gris (Sonoma Coast) $13. 86 —*S.H. (9/1/2003)*

Gallo of Sonoma 1997 Pinot Noir (Russian River Valley) $12. 87 *(11/15/1999)*

Gallo of Sonoma 2000 Pinot Noir (Sonoma County) $13. 87 **Best Buy** —*S.H. (2/1/2003)*

Gallo of Sonoma 1999 Pinot Noir (Sonoma County) $13. 85 *(10/1/2002)*

Gallo of Sonoma 1998 Pinot Noir (Sonoma County) $13. 88 *(7/1/2001)*

Gallo of Sonoma 2003 Reserve Pinot Noir (Sonoma Coast) $13. 89 **Best Buy** —*S.H. (10/1/2005)*

Gallo of Sonoma 2001 Reserve Pinot Noir (Sonoma Coast) $8. 90 **Best Buy** —*S.H. (11/15/2003)*

Gallo of Sonoma 2000 Reserve Pinot Noir (Sonoma County) $13. 81 —*M.S. (12/1/2003)*

Gallo of Sonoma 2001 Two Rock Vineyard Pinot Noir (Sonoma Coast) $28. 87 —*S.H. (12/15/2004)*

Gallo of Sonoma 1997 Sangiovese (Sonoma County) $11. 87 **Best Buy** —*S.H. (12/15/1999)*

Gallo of Sonoma 1998 Sangiovese (Sonoma County) $13. 89 *(7/1/2001)*

Gallo of Sonoma 1999 Barrel Aged Sangiovese (Alexander Valley) $13. 87 —*S.H. (12/1/2002)*

Gallo of Sonoma 2003 Reserve Syrah (Sonoma County) $13. 87 **Best Buy** *(9/1/2005)*

Gallo of Sonoma 1996 Zinfandel (Dry Creek Valley) $11. 86 **Best Buy** —*M.S. (9/1/1999)*

Gallo of Sonoma 1996 Barrelli Creek Zinfandel (Sonoma County) $20. 91 —*S.H. (11/1/1999)*

Gallo of Sonoma 1999 Barrelli Creek Vineyard Zinfandel (Alexander Valley) $22. 88 —*S.H. (2/1/2003)*

Gallo of Sonoma 1996 Chiotti Vineyard Zinfandel (Dry Creek Valley) $18. 86 —*J.C. (9/1/1999)*

Gallo of Sonoma 1999 Frei Ranch Vineyard Zinfandel (Dry Creek Valley) $22. 91 —*S.H. (2/1/2003)*

Gallo of Sonoma 1998 Frei Vineyard Zinfandel (Dry Creek Valley) $20. 83 —*D.T. (3/1/2002)*

Gallo of Sonoma 1997 Frei Vineyard Zinfandel (Dry Creek Valley) $19. 84 *(3/1/2001)*

Gallo of Sonoma 2003 Reserve Zinfandel (Sonoma County) $13. 84 —*S.H. (12/1/2005)*

GALLUCIO FAMILY WINERIES

Gallucio Family Wineries 2002 Barile Dolce Chardonnay (North Fork of Long Island) $35. 82 —*J.C. (10/2/2004)*

Gallucio Family Wineries 2001 Cru George Allaire Chardonnay (North Fork of Long Island) $22. 80 —*J.C. (10/2/2004)*

GAMACHE

Gamache 2004 Estate Cabernet Sauvignon (Columbia Valley (WA)) $28. Consistent with the rather lean house style this opens with herbal aromas set against firm, varietal cassis and blue plum fruit. The grapes come from a block planted in 1985. Some barrel spice adds cinnamon to the nose, and there's a touch of Cab Franc (6%) in the blend, which stiffens up the tannins. Retasting this wine after it has spent a few extra months in bottle, it's smoothed out a bit, and the sweet black- cherry fruit has moved forward. This should age really well. 89 Cellar Selection —*P.G. (12/31/2007)*

Gamache 2004 GV Reserve Gamache - Champoux Vineyard Select Cabernet Sauvignon (Columbia Valley (WA)) $40. This 50-50 blend from two well-established vineyards is 100% Cabernet Sauvignon. Young and stiff and still quite tannic, it shows compact cassis and blackberry fruit with an earthy underpinning, a hint of stem that adds some bite to the tannins. As time smoothes it and softens the tannins, more of the concentrated fruit should emerge; it's well-made and balanced; a fine example of Washington Cabernet Sauvignon done in a classic Bordeaux style. 89 —*P.G. (12/31/2007)*

Gamache 2003 GV Reserve Gamache–Champoux Vineyard Select Cabernet Sauvignon (Columbia Valley (WA)) $40. 90 —*P.G. (11/15/2006)*

Gamache 2005 Estate Malbec (Columbia Valley (WA)) $28. Ten acres of Malbec was planted at Gamache in 2003; this is the first vintage to be released. It's off to a promising start, although the fruit thins out quickly. There are nicely managed tannins, earthy and herbal, tasting of green tea and displaying lovely aromatics. Scents of rose petals mingle with black tea, and in the mouth it is balanced and complex, with sweet blueberry and candy apple fruit, lightly dusted with cinnamon spice. 88 —*P.G. (12/31/2007)*

Gamache 2005 Estate Merlot (Columbia Valley (WA)) $24. This is a tight, rather austere style of Merlot, but has muscle and nerve. Winemaker Charlie Hoppes has kept a slightly green edge to the tannins, which are well-managed and taste good, while adding length and firmness to the back end. 88 —*P.G. (12/31/2007)*

Gamache 2005 Boulder Red Blend (Columbia Valley (WA)) $18. The Gamache brothers call this blend, which is half Cabernet Franc, one quarter Merlot, and the rest split between Malbec and Syrah, a happy accident—the result of having a shortage of Cabernet Sauvignon for blending. The Franc is a great base wine, a little rough and green, but packed with firm, cool-site red grape flavors. Aromatic and tasting of mixed fruits, it's blended just ahead of bottling, so the juice gets the same care as the pricier varietal wines. 87 —*P.G. (12/31/2007)*

Gamache 2003 Syrah (Columbia Valley (WA)) $28. 84 *(9/1/2005)*

Gamache 2004 Estate Syrah (Columbia Valley (WA)) $28. This is young, tangy, juicy and sweet, with ripe but quite tart fruit, showing plenty of acid and citrus rind. The toasty oak flavors are front and center, and delicious. All the Gamache red wines will benefit from additional bottle age, which will soften and meld the bacon fat, herb and sharp spice flavors. There is a lot of potential here for further development. 90 Editors' Choice —*P.G. (12/31/2007)*

Gamache 2006 Velida Estate Viognier (Columbia Valley (WA)) $18. This meaty, substantial wine was barrel fermented in neutral oak and hints at oxidation, particularly in terms of its dusty, tawny color. Clocking in at 14.9% alcohol, it definitely shows some heat on the finish. But it's a full-bodied style with immediate appeal, lush with candied fruit flavors, streaks of butter and toasted nuts. Its weight and mouthfeel are very much like a ripe Chardonnay, but with added perfume and precision. 88 —*P.G. (12/31/2007)*

GAMBA VINEYARDS & WINERY

Gamba Vineyards & Winery 2001 Old Vine Zinfandel (Sonoma County) $40. 89 *(11/1/2003)*

GAN EDEN

Gan Eden 1994 Chardonnay (Sonoma County) $13. 82 *(4/1/2001)*

GANN

Gann 2004 Spring Hill Vineyard Sauvignon Blanc (Alexander Valley) $18. 80 —*S.H. (5/1/2006)*

GARDEN CREEK

Garden Creek 2002 Tesserae Bordeaux Blend (Alexander Valley) $65. Dramatically structured, this is a firm, full-bodied young Cab that needs time. Shows slightly astringent tannins at the moment, with Bordeaux-like acidity and a dry, spicy finish. Give it a few years to let the cassis, herb and cedar flavors emerge. Mainly Cab Sauv, with some Cab Franc and Merlot. 93 Cellar Selection —*S.H. (10/1/2007)*

GARFIELD ESTATES

Garfield Estates 2006 Vin Rosé Rosé Blend (Grand Valley) $12. Strawberry and melon on the nose of this Colorado rosé are followed by like flavors of freshness and elegance on the palate. The wine still has some complexity but could use a touch more acidity to add cleaner edge. Overall, a friendly wine for summer suppers and patio lounging. 84 —*S.K. (7/1/2007)*

Garfield Estates 2005 Syrah (Grand Valley) $21. Colorado producer Garfield Estates offers a Shiraz with ripe fruit flavors and a dash of pepper. It's drinkable but very lean on character and balance. 82 —*S.K. (5/1/2007)*

Garfield Estates 2004 Syrah (Grand Valley) $21. Approachable with a smooth balance of oak and fruit, this wine has a cherry and floral character with hints of cinnamon. The grapes are grown in a scenic spot—at the foot of Mt. Garfield in Grand Valley, Colorado, in the midst of a brugeoning wine country. It's not complex by any means—neither on the nose or on the palate—nor is it unique. But with a good piece of steak, it would do nicely. 83 —*S.K. (2/1/2007)*

GARGIULO

Gargiulo 2002 Money Road Ranch Cabernet Sauvignon (Oakville) $55. 87 —*S.H. (11/1/2005)*

Gargiulo 2002 Money Road Ranch Merlot (Oakville) $35. 88 —*S.H. (11/1/2005)*

Gargiulo 2004 Pinot Grigio (Oakville) $25. 83 —*S.H. (2/1/2006)*

Gargiulo 2002 Aprile Red Blend (Oakville) $28. 86 —*S.H. (11/1/2005)*

Gargiulo 2000 Aprile Sangiovese (Napa Valley) $25. 88 —*J.M. (9/1/2003)*

Gargiulo 2006 Money Road Ranch Rosato di Sangiovese Sangiovese (Oakville) $20. Pretty good, satisfying for dryness, upfront cherry and spice fruit, and the crisp acidity that makes it clean. But there's some bitterness throughout, with a green streak of stalky chlorophyll. 84 —*S.H. (7/1/2007)*

Gargiulo 2000 Rosato di Sangiovese Sangiovese (Oakville) $13. 87 —*J.M. (9/1/2002)*

GARRETSON

Garretson 2003 The Spainnéach Grenache (Paso Robles) $28. 88 —*S.H. (10/1/2005)*

Garretson 2002 Hastings Ranch "The Graosta" Mourvèdre (Paso Robles) $25. 82 —*S.H. (12/31/2004)*

Garretson 2003 The Graosta Mourvèdre (Paso Robles) $28. 89 —*S.H. (10/1/2005)*

Garretson NV Glimigrim Red Blend (Paso Robles) $12. 86 *(5/1/2000)*

Garretson 2003 G Red Rhône Red Blend (Central Coast) $20. 87 —*S.H. (10/1/2005)*

Garretson 1998 The Celeidh Rhône Red Blend (Central Coast) $16. 88 —*J.C. (8/1/2000)*

Garretson 2004 G White Rhône White Blend (Central Coast) $18. 87 —*S.H. (10/1/2005)*

Garretson 2004 The Chumhra Rhône White Blend (Central Coast) $20. 83 —*S.H. (10/1/2005)*

Garretson 2003 "The Celeidh" Rosé Blend (Paso Robles) $18. 86 —*S.H. (12/31/2004)*

Garretson 2004 The Celeidh Rosé Blend (Paso Robles) $18. 87 —*S.H. (10/1/2005)*

Garretson 2001 "The Aisling" Syrah (Paso Robles) $30. 91 —*S.H. (12/31/2004)*

Garretson 2002 "The Craic" Syrah (Central Coast) $30. 89 —*S.H. (12/31/2004)*

Garretson 1999 Alban Vineyard The Finné Syrah (Edna Valley) $60. 91 *(11/1/2001)*

Garretson 2001 Hoage Vineyard "The Bulladoir" Syrah (Paso Robles) $45. 87 —*S.H. (12/31/2004)*

Garretson 2003 Mon Amie Bassetti Vineyard Syrah (San Luis Obispo County) $50. 82 *(9/1/2005)*

Garretson 2001 Rozet Vineyard "The Lusacain" Syrah (Paso Robles) $45. 90 *—S.H. (12/31/2004)*

Garretson 2003 The Aisling Syrah (Paso Robles) $30. 83 *(9/1/2005)*

Garretson 1997 The Aisling Syrah (Paso Robles) $25. 87 *—J.C. (2/1/2000)*

Garretson 2003 The Bulladoir Syrah (Paso Robles) $65. 80 *(9/1/2005)*

Garretson 1999 The Corcairghorm Fralich Vineyard Syrah (Paso Robles) $30. 88 *—S.H. (7/1/2002)*

Garretson 2003 The Craic Syrah (Central Coast) $30. 83 *(9/1/2005)*

Garretson 2003 The Luascain Syrah (Paso Robles) $45. 83 *(9/1/2005)*

Garretson 2001 Viognier (Santa Ynez Valley) $30. 91 *—J.M. (12/15/2002)*

Garretson 2004 The Saothar Viognier (Paso Robles) $30. 85 *—S.H. (10/1/2005)*

GARY FARRELL

Gary Farrell 2002 Encounter Proprietary Red Wine Bordeaux Blend (Sonoma County) $65. A fairly tough wine in youth, although the fine '02 vintage brings a wealth of cherries, orange marmalade, gingersnap cookie and mocha cinnamon flavors, it's also a tannic wine, dry and acidic. But all indications are that it should cellar well. Best now, with decanting, and through 2012. 90 *—S.H. (4/1/2007)*

Gary Farrell 1998 Encounter Bordeaux Blend (Sonoma County) $60. 90 *—D.T. (6/1/2002)*

Gary Farrell 1997 Encounter Pine Mountain Bordeaux Blend (Sonoma County) $42. 92 *(11/1/2000)*

Gary Farrell 1996 Encounter Pine Mountain Bordeaux Blend (Pine Mountain) $42. 89 *—J.C. (11/1/1999)*

Gary Farrell 2001 Encounter Cabernet Blend (Sonoma County) $60. 88 *—S.H. (11/1/2005)*

Gary Farrell 2000 Cabernet Sauvignon (Sonoma County) $34. 88 *—S.H. (11/15/2004)*

Gary Farrell 2000 Bradford Mountain Cabernet Sauvignon (Dry Creek Valley) $40. 89 *—S.H. (11/15/2004)*

Gary Farrell 1999 Hillside Vineyard Selection Cabernet Sauvignon (Sonoma County) $34. 92 *—M.S. (11/15/2002)*

Gary Farrell 2002 Sonoma County Selection Cabernet Sauvignon (Sonoma County) $34. You don't think of Gary Farrell as a Cabernet producer, but here he is, and it's a good wine. Its tannicly tough and acidic, not your soft, chocolaty Cab but one of structure and a certain austerity you could call elegant. The wine is totally dry and should age well. Drink now–2016. 89 *—S.H. (2/1/2007)*

Gary Farrell 2002 Chardonnay (Russian River Valley) $30. 89 *—S.H. (11/15/2004)*

Gary Farrell 1999 Chardonnay (Russian River Valley) $30. 88 *(7/1/2001)*

Gary Farrell 2002 Bien Nacido Vineyard Chardonnay (Santa Barbara County) $34. 89 *—S.H. (10/1/2004)*

Gary Farrell 1999 Bien Nacido Vineyard Chardonnay (Santa Barbara County) $30. 85 *(7/1/2001)*

Gary Farrell 1998 Bien Nacido Vineyard Chardonnay (Santa Barbara County) $28. 89 *(6/1/2000)*

Gary Farrell 2004 Cresta Ridge Vineyard Chardonnay (Russian River Valley) $38. 92 *—S.H. (12/1/2006)*

Gary Farrell 2003 Cresta Ridge Vineyard Chardonnay (Russian River Valley) $38. 88 *—S.H. (11/1/2005)*

Gary Farrell 1998 Rochioli Vineyard Chardonnay (Russian River Valley) $34. 87 *(7/1/2001)*

Gary Farrell 2002 Rochioli-Allen Vineyards Chardonnay (Russian River Valley) $38. 90 *—S.H. (11/15/2004)*

Gary Farrell 2004 Russian River Selection Chardonnay (Russian River Valley) $32. 90 *—S.H. (12/1/2006)*

Gary Farrell 2003 Russian River Selection Chardonnay (Russian River Valley) $32. 86 *—S.H. (11/1/2005)*

Gary Farrell 2004 Starr Ridge Vineyard Chardonnay (Russian River Valley) $38. A finely structured Chard. It has the citrusy acidity you get only from the coolest areas, providing a bracing, steely quality to the green apple, quince and oaky flavors. Just feels elegant and opulent all the way, a true California first growth that should pick up additional complexities for four or five years before slowly expiring. =94 **Editors' Choice** *—S.H. (4/1/2007)*

Gary Farrell 2003 Starr Ridge Vineyard Chardonnay (Russian River Valley) $38. 91 *—S.H. (12/1/2005)*

Gary Farrell 2004 Westside Farms Chardonnay (Russian River Valley) $38. Shows the lean, structural approach Farrell famously takes toward his wines. It's almost an austere Chard. You get dryness, acidity, alcohol, oak, lees, and citrusy, flowery fruit. This is not one of your big, fat Chards, but it is a complex wine that will benefit from four or five years of cellaring. 90 *—S.H. (2/1/2007)*

Gary Farrell 2003 Westside Farms Chardonnay (Russian River Valley) $38. 86 *—S.H. (12/1/2005)*

Gary Farrell 2002 Westside Farms Chardonnay (Russian River Valley) $34. 91 *—S.H. (5/1/2005)*

Gary Farrell 2000 Westside Farms Chardonnay (Russian River Valley) $34. 93 **Editors' Choice** *—S.H. (2/1/2003)*

Gary Farrell 1997 Calypso Vineyard Merlot (Russian River Valley) $32. 88 *—J.C. (7/1/2000)*

Gary Farrell 1997 Ladi's Vineyard Merlot (Sonoma County) $30. 87 *—J.C. (6/1/2001)*

Gary Farrell 1998 Pinot Noir (Russian River Valley) $30. 89 *(10/1/2000)*

Gary Farrell 1997 Pinot Noir (Russian River Valley) $24. 86 *— (10/1/1999)*

Gary Farrell 2002 Pinot Noir (Russian River Valley) $32. 86 *(11/1/2004)*

Gary Farrell 2000 Pinot Noir (Russian River Valley) $34. 83 *(10/1/2002)*

Gary Farrell 1999 Pinot Noir (Russian River Valley) $34. 89 *(10/1/2002)*

Gary Farrell 1999 Allen Vineyard Pinot Noir (Russian River Valley) $NA. 87 *—S.H. (6/1/2005)*

Gary Farrell 1999 Allen Vineyard Pinot Noir (Russian River Valley) $50. 89 *(10/1/2002)*

Gary Farrell 1997 Allen Vineyard Pinot Noir (Russian River Valley) $NA. 88 *—S.H. (6/1/2005)*

Gary Farrell 1997 Allen Vineyard Pinot Noir (Russian River Valley) $40. 88 *(11/15/1999)*

Gary Farrell 1994 Allen Vineyard Pinot Noir (Russian River Valley) $NA. 87 *—S.H. (6/1/2005)*

Gary Farrell 2004 Allen Vineyard Hillside Blocks Pinot Noir (Russian River Valley) $60. An opulent Pinot, and despite the volume, it never loses elegance. Rich in cherry pie, cola, pomegranate and oak flavors, backed up by firm tannins and acids, it's ripe to the point of supermaturity, with an edge of raisins. Should develop well over five years. 91 *—S.H. (4/1/2007)*

Gary Farrell 2003 Allen Vineyard Hillside Blocks Pinot Noir (Russian River Valley) $60. 92 *—S.H. (8/1/2006)*

Gary Farrell 2002 Allen Vineyard Hillside Blocks Pinot Noir (Russian River Valley) $50. 94 *—S.H. (5/1/2005)*

Gary Farrell 1997 Bien Nacido Vineyard. Pinot Noir (Santa Barbara County) $30. 88 *— (10/1/1999)*

Gary Farrell 2003 Jack Hill Vineyard Pinot Noir (Russian River Valley) $45. 84 *—S.H. (12/1/2006)*

Gary Farrell 2000 Olivet Lane Vineyards Pinot Noir (Russian River Valley) $38. 87 *(10/1/2002)*

Gary Farrell 2004 Rochioli Vineyard Pinot Noir (Russian River Valley) $60. The challenge in the warm Middle Reach, where Rochioli is ideally situated, is to achieve elegance, especially in a hot vintage like '04. That's a challenge Farrell rises to. His penchant for bone dry, crisply structured wines is nowhere more evident than here, in this high acid Pinot with its wealthy core of cherry and cola flavors. Great now, it should develop bottle complexity for 10 years. 93 **Cellar Selection** *—S.H. (2/1/2007)*

Gary Farrell 2003 Rochioli Vineyard Pinot Noir (Russian River Valley) $38. 84 *—S.H. (12/1/2005)*

Gary Farrell 2002 Rochioli Vineyard Pinot Noir (Russian River Valley) $50. 91 *—S.H. (11/1/2004)*

Gary Farrell 1999 Rochioli Vineyard Pinot Noir (Russian River Valley) $60. 88 *(10/1/2002)*

Gary Farrell 1997 Rochioli Vineyard Pinot Noir (Russian River Valley) $50. 91 *(10/1/1999)*

Gary Farrell 2004 Rochioli-Allen Vineyards Pinot Noir (Russian River Valley) $65. These vineyards are, of course, very famous, among the oldest and more respected in Russian River. Gary Farrell has long had access to their coveted fruit and 2004 is one of his greatest bottlings ever. It may be due to the warm vintage, but the fruit is spectacular, not in your face at the expense of balance, and rich in cherries, cola and cinnamon-infused rum punch. This is a young, vibrant, crisp Pinot Noir, with a good life ahead for the next 10 years. 95 *—S.H. (4/1/2007)*

Gary Farrell 2003 Rochioli-Allen Vineyard Pinot Noir (Russian River Valley) $65. 92 *—S.H. (7/1/2006)*

Gary Farrell 2000 Rochioli-Allen Vineyard Pinot Noir (Russian River Valley) $60. 90 *—S.H. (7/1/2003)*

Gary Farrell 2002 Rochioli-Allen Vineyards Pinot Noir (Russian River Valley) $60. 90 *—S.H. (5/1/2005)*

Gary Farrell 2002 Rochioli-Allen Vineyards Pinot Noir (Russian River Valley) $60. 92 *—S.H. (6/1/2005)*

Gary Farrell 2004 Russian River Selection Pinot Noir (Russian River Valley) $42. 86 *—S.H. (12/1/2006)*

Gary Farrell 2003 Russian River Selection Pinot Noir (Russian River Valley) $34. 85 *—S.H. (11/1/2005)*

Gary Farrell 2000 Starr Ridge Pinot Noir (Russian River Valley) $38. 88 *(10/1/2002)*

Gary Farrell 2004 Starr Ridge Vineyard Pinot Noir (Russian River Valley) $50. This vineyard needs heat to ripen. In a cool vintage like 2000, it can be tart. But 2004 was a very warm year, and the wine shows unctuous cherry pie, cola, rhubarb and spiced rum punch flavors balanced by dependably crisp acidity. It's a very dry wine, and should hold and improve for five years. 90 *—S.H. (2/1/2007)*

Gary Farrell 2003 Starr Ridge Vineyard Pinot Noir (Russian River Valley) $45. 90 *—S.H. (11/1/2005)*

Gary Farrell 1997 Stiling Vineyard Pinot Noir (Russian River Valley) $30. 84 *(10/1/1999)*

Gary Farrell 2000 Encounter Red Blend (Sonoma County) $60. 90 *—S.H. (9/1/2004)*

Gary Farrell 1999 Encounter Red Blend (Sonoma County) $60. 91 *—M.S. (11/15/2002)*

Gary Farrell 2005 Redwood Ranch Sauvignon Blanc (Sonoma County) $20. 90 *—S.H. (12/1/2006)*

Gary Farrell 2004 Redwood Ranch Sauvignon Blanc (Sonoma County) $24. 85 *—S.H. (11/1/2005)*

Gary Farrell 2003 Redwood Ranch Sauvignon Blanc (Sonoma County) $20. 90 Editors' Choice *—S.H. (12/1/2004)*

Gary Farrell 2001 Redwood Ranch Sauvignon Blanc (Sonoma County) $20. 87 *(8/1/2002)*

Gary Farrell 1998 Syrah (Russian River Valley) $32. 90 *(11/1/2001)*

Gary Farrell 2002 Zinfandel (Dry Creek Valley) $24. 86 *—S.H. (10/1/2004)*

Gary Farrell 2004 Bradford Mountain Zinfandel (Dry Creek Valley) $36. Peppery and acidic and dry. That's the first impression you get of this wine. Then the tannins lock in. Last but not least is the raspberry and cherry fruit, with tobacco and wild herb complexities. It's the Cabernet of Zinfandels, elegant and rich and complex, a real white tablecloth red wine, and it should age well for five years. 91 *—S.H. (2/1/2007)*

Gary Farrell 1997 Bradford Mountain Zinfandel (Dry Creek Valley) $30. 87 *—J.C. (11/1/1999)*

Gary Farrell 2000 Bradford Mountain Vineyard Zinfandel (Dry Creek Valley) $36. 89 *—M.S. (11/1/2002)*

Gary Farrell 2003 Bradford Mountain Vineyards Zinfandel (Dry Creek Valley) $36. 80 *—S.H. (7/1/2006)*

Gary Farrell 2004 Dry Creek Selection Zinfandel (Dry Creek Valley) $26. Textbook Dry Creek Zin. The wine is dry, ripe and tannic, with briary, wild raspberry and cherry flavors and an earthy herb quality with suggestions of espresso, thyme, lavender, soy, balsamic and smoky leather. It's one of the most elegant Zins out there, although it never loses Zin's basically rustic nature. 90 *—S.H. (2/1/2007)*

Gary Farrell 2000 Dry Creek Valley Zinfandel (Sonoma County) $24. 90 *—M.S. (11/1/2002)*

Gary Farrell 1999 Maple Vineyard Zinfandel (Dry Creek Valley) $30. 88 *—D.T. (3/1/2002)*

Gary Farrell 1997 Maple Vineyard Zinfandel (Dry Creek Valley) $30. 86 *—J.C. (11/1/1999)*

Gary Farrell 2003 Maple Vineyard Tina's Block Zinfandel (Dry Creek Valley) $36. 86 *—S.H. (7/1/2006)*

Gary Farrell 2002 Maple Vineyard Tina's Block Zinfandel (Dry Creek Valley) $36. 89 *—S.H. (10/1/2004)*

Gary Farrell 1997 Old Vine Selection Zinfandel (Sonoma) $24. 89 *—J.C. (11/1/1999)*

Gary Farrell 2000 Rice Vineyard Zinfandel (Russian River Valley) $27. 87 *—M.S. (11/1/2002)*

GELFAND

Gelfand 2004 Petite Sirah (Paso Robles) $30. 90 *—S.H. (12/15/2006)*

Gelfand 2004 Cabyrah Red Blend (Paso Robles) $28. 87 *—S.H. (12/15/2006)*

Gelfand 2004 Quixotic Red Blend (Paso Robles) $35. 85 *—S.H. (12/15/2006)*

GENERATIONS OF SONOMA

Generations of Sonoma 2005 Serres Ranch Late Harvest Aleatico (Sonoma Valley) $30. 80 *—S.H. (12/1/2006)*

GENNAIO

Gennaio 2002 Sangiovese (Dry Creek Valley) $19. 86 *—S.H. (11/1/2005)*

GEORIS WINERY

Georis Winery 2000 Cabernet Sauvignon (Carmel Valley) $34. 85 *—S.H. (5/1/2004)*

Georis Winery 2002 Sauvignon Blanc (Monterey) $21. 86 *—S.H. (2/1/2004)*

GEYSER PEAK

Geyser Peak 2003 Reserve Alexandre Bordeaux Blend (Alexander Valley) $55. This is the winery's Meritage, and the '03 has all five Bordeaux varieties, led by Cabernet Sauvignon. It's a fairly standard Alexander Valley Cab, dry and herbal, soft in tannins and ageworthy, and, in this case, complex and elegant. Drink now through 2015. 89 *—S.H. (4/1/2007)*

Geyser Peak 2004 Reserve Alexandre Meritage Bordeaux Blend (Alexander Valley) $56. Reserve Alexandre is always a really nice, interesting wine, but with recent price increases, consumers should be wary. The '04 shows classic Alexander Valley softness and herbs, along with cherries, blackberries and oak, and it's an elegantly balanced wine. But it doesn't seem to be an ager, as it's a little thin on the finish, so drink now. 87 *—S.H. (12/31/2007)*

Geyser Peak 2002 Reserve Alexandre Meritage Bordeaux Blend (Alexander Valley) $49. 88 *—S.H. (5/1/2006)*

Geyser Peak 1998 Reserve Alexandre Cabernet Blend (Alexander Valley) $45. 90 *—S.H. (9/1/2002)*

Geyser Peak 1999 Reserve Alexandre Meritage Cabernet Blend (Alexander Valley) $45. 93 Editors' Choice *—S.H. (5/1/2003)*

Geyser Peak 1997 Cabernet Franc (Sonoma County) $20. 92 *—S.H. (7/1/2000)*

Geyser Peak 2004 Cabernet Sauvignon (Alexander Valley) $18. Soft and supple, with a gentle, velvety mouthfeel. Black currants, cherries, chocolate, spicy rum, cola and coffee fill the mouth, finishing dry and sweet-oaky. Shows great texture and verve. 87 *—S.H. (7/1/2007)*

Geyser Peak 2003 Cabernet Sauvignon (Alexander Valley) $18. 91 Editors' Choice *—S.H. (7/1/2006)*

Geyser Peak 2002 Cabernet Sauvignon (Alexander Valley) $18. 85 *—S.H. (12/31/2005)*

Geyser Peak 2001 Cabernet Sauvignon (Alexander Valley) $18. 89 *—S.H. (11/15/2004)*

Geyser Peak 2000 Cabernet Sauvignon (Sonoma County) $17. 86 *—S.H. (11/1/2003)*

Geyser Peak 1999 Cabernet Sauvignon (Sonoma County) $17. 90 *—S.H. (6/1/2002)*

Geyser Peak 1996 Cabernet Sauvignon (Sonoma County) $16. 89 *—M.S. (10/1/1999)*

Geyser Peak 2003 Block Collection Ascentia Estate Vineyard Cabernet Sauvignon (Alexander Valley) $47. You won't find tannins like this in many Napa Cabs, especially the cults. In that sense, it's a throwback. But how refreshing to find something with structure that won't overwhelm food. It's a beautiful wine, ageworthy to judge from the dryness and tannins and huge core of fruit. 92 *—S.H. (2/1/2007)*

Geyser Peak 2003 Block Collection Kuimelis Vineyard Cabernet Sauvignon (Alexander Valley) $47. I've always felt this is one of the best ageworthy Cabs from Sonoma County. This year it's dependably dry and tannic, but those tannins can't entirely keep the briary blackberry and cherry fruit from bursting through. This is a complex, beautiful wine now, with proper decanting, but it should be better beyond 2010. 91 *—S.H. (2/1/2007)*

Geyser Peak 2001 Block Collection Kuimelis Vineyard Cabernet Sauvignon (Alexander Valley) $32. 90 *—S.H. (11/15/2004)*

Geyser Peak 2000 Block Collection Kuimelis Vineyard Cabernet Sauvignon (Alexander Valley) $26. 90 Editors' Choice *(11/1/2003)*

Geyser Peak 1999 Block Collection Kuimelis Vineyard Cabernet Sauvignon (Alexander Valley) $26. 91 *—S.H. (11/15/2002)*

Geyser Peak 1999 Block Collection, Vallerga Vineyard Cabernet Sauvignon (Yountville) $36. 89 *—S.H. (10/1/2004)*

Geyser Peak 2003 Block Collection Walking Tree Vineyard Cabernet Sauvignon (Alexander Valley) $47. An interesting, ageworthy wine that's textbook Alexander Valley. The cherry fruit is accented by sage, thyme, dill, that sort of leafy green herb thing, and the softness is from low acidity, although the tannins are rich and sturdy. This is the anti-Napa Cab, so balanced and dry, it won't overwhelm food. 92 *—S.H. (2/1/2007)*

Geyser Peak 1998 Kuimelis Vineyard Cabernet Sauvignon (Alexander Valley) $28. 88 *—S.H. (7/1/2002)*

Geyser Peak 1997 Kuimelis Vineyards Cabernet Sauvignon (Sonoma County) $27. 91 *(1/1/2000)*

Geyser Peak 2002 Kumelis Vineyard Cabernet Sauvignon (Alexander Valley) $42. 92 Cellar Selection *—S.H. (11/1/2005)*

Geyser Peak 2002 Reserve Cabernet Sauvignon (Alexander Valley) $46. 86 *—S.H. (5/1/2006)*

Geyser Peak 2001 Reserve Cabernet Sauvignon (Alexander Valley) $46. 90 Cellar Selection *—S.H. (10/1/2005)*

Geyser Peak 2000 Reserve Cabernet Sauvignon (Sonoma County) $40. 91 *(11/1/2003)*

Geyser Peak 1999 Reserve Cabernet Sauvignon (Sonoma County) $40. 88 *—S.H. (6/1/2002)*

Geyser Peak 1997 Reserve Cabernet Sauvignon (Sonoma County) $40. 91 *—S.H. (12/15/2000)*

Geyser Peak 1996 Reserve Cabernet Sauvignon (Sonoma County) $32. 88 *—S.H. (11/1/1999)*

Geyser Peak 1998 Vallerga Vineyard Cabernet Sauvignon (Napa Valley) $35. 86 *—S.H. (6/1/2002)*

Geyser Peak 1997 Vallerga Vineyards Cabernet Sauvignon (Napa Valley) $27. 90 *(1/1/2000)*

Geyser Peak 2004 Walking Tree Vineyard Cabernet Sauvignon (Alexander Valley) $47. A lovely, balanced, elegant young Cab. We're not in Napa Valley anymore, for the wine has a dried cherry herbaceousness and different tannin structure, but it defines the style that made Alexander Valley famous for Cabernet Sauvignon. For all those who complain that Cab isn't food-friendly, this one is. Ageability is almost guaranteed. Best now through 2014, with proper cellaring. 92 Cellar Selection *—S.H. (11/1/2007)*

Geyser Peak 2005 Chardonnay (Alexander Valley) $13. Tasted in a flight of far more expensive Chards, this one held its own. Creamy, with apple and peach flavors and a touch of oak and lees, it will satisfy your basic Chardonnay instincts at a good price. 87 *—S.H. (4/1/2007)*

Geyser Peak 2004 Chardonnay (Alexander Valley) $14. 89 Best Buy *—S.H. (12/31/2005)*

Geyser Peak 2003 Chardonnay (Russian River Valley) $19. 85 *—S.H. (10/1/2005)*

Geyser Peak 2003 Chardonnay (Alexander Valley) $19. 84 *—S.H. (5/1/2005)*

Geyser Peak 2002 Chardonnay (Sonoma County) $12. 85 *—S.H. (10/1/2004)*

Geyser Peak 2001 Chardonnay (Sonoma County) $12. 88 Best Buy *—S.H. (2/1/2003)*

Geyser Peak 2000 Chardonnay (Russian River Valley) $16. 83 *—S.H. (5/1/2002)*

Geyser Peak 2000 Chardonnay (Sonoma County) $12. 84 *—S.H. (5/1/2002)*

Geyser Peak 1998 Chardonnay (Russian River Valley) $20. 88 *(1/1/2000)*

Geyser Peak 1998 Chardonnay (Sonoma County) $12. 86 *—L.W. (3/1/2000)*

Geyser Peak 1998 Block Collection Big River Ranch Chardonnay (Russian River Valley) $23. 88 *—S.H. (11/15/2000)*

Geyser Peak 2001 Block Collection Ricci Vineyard Chardonnay (Carneros) $21. 89 *—S.H. (6/1/2003)*

Geyser Peak 1999 Block Collection Ricci Vnyd. Chardonnay (Carneros) $20. 91 Editors' Choice *—S.H. (5/1/2001)*

Geyser Peak 2005 Reserve Chardonnay (Alexander Valley) $23. Geyser Peak's Reserve Chards have been pretty good lately, as they learn how to bring balance to grapes that ripen so easily. The '05 is plenty ripe, packed with jammy apricot, tangerine and oaky vanilla custard and butterscotch flavors. It's a rich, exotic wine, with good enough acidity for balance. 88 *—S.H. (10/1/2007)*

Geyser Peak 2003 Reserve Chardonnay (Alexander Valley) $25. 90 Editors' Choice *—S.H. (10/1/2005)*

Geyser Peak 2002 Reserve Chardonnay (Alexander Valley) $24. 88 *—S.H. (11/15/2004)*

Geyser Peak 2001 Reserve Chardonnay (Alexander Valley) $23. 87 *(11/1/2003)*

Geyser Peak 2000 Reserve Chardonnay (Alexander Valley) $23. 86 *—S.H. (5/1/2002)*

Geyser Peak 1997 Reserve Chardonnay (Sonoma County) $23. 87 *(1/1/2000)*

Geyser Peak 1996 Reserve Chardonnay (Sonoma County) $20. 88 *—J.C. (11/1/1999)*

Geyser Peak 2003 Ricci Vineyard Chardonnay (Carneros) $23. 91 Editors' Choice *—S.H. (11/1/2005)*

Geyser Peak 2000 Ricci Vineyard Chardonnay (Carneros) $21. 89 *—J.M. (12/15/2002)*

Geyser Peak 1997 Sonoma Valley Chardonnay (Sonoma Valley) $14. 87 Best Buy *—S.H. (7/1/1999)*

Geyser Peak 2001 Gewürztraminer (California) $9. 86 Best Buy *—J.M. (6/1/2002)*

Geyser Peak 1998 Johannisberg Riesling (California) $8. 85 Best Buy *—S.H. (9/1/1999)*

Geyser Peak 2000 Reserve Alexandre Meritage (Alexander Valley) $45. 88 *—S.H. (10/1/2004)*

Geyser Peak 2001 Reserve Alexandre Meritage Meritage (Alexander Valley) $49. 90 *—S.H. (11/1/2005)*

Geyser Peak 2004 Merlot (Alexander Valley) $19. This isn't a very complex Merlot, but it is textbook if you're looking for soft fruitiness. It has oak-influenced cherry and blackberry flavors, with hints of violets and fruit tea, and is dry and dusty in tannins. Give it more concentration and it would be a star. 87 *—S.H. (12/31/2007)*

Geyser Peak 2003 Merlot (Alexander Valley) $19. Not the richest Merlot Geyser Peak has ever made. The wine is totally dry and fairly tannic, with dried herb, licorice and cherry flavors. Best thing about it is the structural elegance. 85 *—S.H. (10/1/2007)*

Geyser Peak 2002 Merlot (Alexander Valley) $19. 81 *—S.H. (11/1/2005)*

Geyser Peak 2001 Merlot (Sonoma County) $18. 87 *—S.H. (12/15/2004)*

Geyser Peak 2000 Merlot (Sonoma County) $17. 85 *—S.H. (8/1/2003)*

Geyser Peak 1998 Merlot (Sonoma County) $17. 82 *—J.C. (6/1/2001)*

Geyser Peak 1997 Merlot (Sonoma County) $16. 86 *—L.W. (12/31/1999)*

Geyser Peak 1997 Merlot (Sonoma County) $16. 84 *(3/1/2000)*

Geyser Peak 1997 Merlot (Sonoma) $16. 84 *(3/1/2000)*

Geyser Peak 1999 Block Collection Shorenstein Vineyard Merlot (Sonoma Valley) $26. 87 *—S.H. (11/15/2002)*

Geyser Peak 1998 Block Collection Shorenstein Vineyard Merlot (Sonoma Valley) $26. 85 *—S.H. (6/1/2001)*

Geyser Peak 2001 Block Collection Shorenstein Vineyard Merlot (Sonoma Valley) $26. 87 *—S.H. (11/1/2005)*

Geyser Peak 2000 Block Collection Shorenstein Vineyard Merlot (Sonoma Valley) $26. 87 *—S.H. (12/31/2004)*

Geyser Peak 2001 Reserve Merlot (Knights Valley) $40. 82 *—S.H. (11/1/2005)*

Geyser Peak 2000 Reserve Merlot (Alexander Valley) $39. 86 *—S.H. (12/15/2004)*

Geyser Peak 1999 Reserve Merlot (Sonoma County) $40. 93 *—S.H. (11/15/2002)*

Geyser Peak 1998 Reserve Merlot (Alexander Valley) $40. 90 *—S.H. (12/1/2001)*

Geyser Peak 1997 Reserve Merlot (Sonoma County) $32. 88 *—S.H. (7/1/2000)*

Geyser Peak 2001 Riesling (California) $9. 86 Best Buy *—S.H. (6/1/2002)*

Geyser Peak 2000 Late Harvest Reserve Riesling (Mendocino) $19. 88 *—J.M. (12/1/2002)*

Geyser Peak 1998 Reserve Late Harvest Riesling (Dry Creek Valley) $19. 86 *—S.H. (12/31/2000)*

Geyser Peak 2005 Sauvignon Blanc (California) $12. 84 *—S.H. (7/1/2006)*

Geyser Peak 2004 Sauvignon Blanc (California) $12. 84 *—S.H. (12/31/2005)*

Geyser Peak 2003 Sauvignon Blanc (Sonoma County) $12. 85 *—S.H. (10/1/2004)*

Geyser Peak 2002 Sauvignon Blanc (Russian River Valley) $20. 90 Editors' Choice *(11/1/2003)*

Geyser Peak 2002 Sauvignon Blanc (California) $10. 86 Best Buy *(11/1/2003)*

Geyser Peak 2001 Sauvignon Blanc (California) $10. 86 *—S.H. (9/1/2002)*

Geyser Peak 2000 Sauvignon Blanc (Sonoma County) $9. 88 Best Buy *—J.M. (11/15/2001)*

Geyser Peak 1999 Sauvignon Blanc (Sonoma County) $9. 84 *—S.H. (5/1/2000)*

Geyser Peak 1998 Sauvignon Blanc (Sonoma County) $9. 82 *—S.H. (9/1/1999)*

Geyser Peak 2005 Block Collection River Road Ranch Sauvignon Blanc (Russian River Valley) $21. 84 *—S.H. (12/31/2006)*

Geyser Peak 2004 Block Collection River Road Ranch Sauvignon Blanc (Russian River Valley) $21. 90 Editors' Choice *(7/1/2005)*

Geyser Peak 2003 Block Collection River Road Ranch Sauvignon Blanc (Russian River Valley) $19. 88 *—S.H. (12/1/2004)*

Geyser Peak 1997 Shiraz (Sonoma County) $16. 88 *—S.H. (5/1/2000)*

Geyser Peak 2002 Shiraz (Sonoma County) $17. 85 *(9/1/2005)*

Geyser Peak 2001 Shiraz (Sonoma County) $18. 85 *—S.H. (12/1/2004)*

Geyser Peak 2000 Shiraz (Sonoma County) $17. 88 *—S.H. (2/1/2003)*

Geyser Peak 1999 Shiraz (Sonoma County) $17. 82 *(10/1/2001)*

Geyser Peak 1995 Bin 1 Shiraz (Sonoma County) $100. 92 *(1/1/2000)*

Geyser Peak 2000 Reserve Shiraz (Sonoma County) $46. 86 *(9/1/2005)*

Geyser Peak 1999 Reserve Shiraz (Sonoma County) $45. 89 *—S.H. (12/1/2004)*

Geyser Peak 1998 Reserve Shiraz (Sonoma County) $40. 86 *(11/1/2001)*

Geyser Peak 1997 Sparkling Shiraz (Sonoma County) $30. 90 *—J.M. (12/1/2003)*

Geyser Peak 2003 Block Collection Preston Vineyard Viognier (Dry Creek Valley) $19. 90 *—S.H. (11/15/2004)*

Geyser Peak 2002 Block Collection Preston Vineyard Viognier (Dry Creek Valley) $19. 88 *—S.H. (12/31/2003)*

Geyser Peak 2000 Block Collection Sonoma Moment Viognier (Alexander Valley) $19. 90 *—J.M. (12/15/2002)*

Geyser Peak 2004 Preston Vineyard Viognier (Dry Creek Valley) $19. 91 Editors' Choice *—S.H. (11/1/2005)*

Geyser Peak 1997 Zinfandel (Sonoma County) $16. 84 *(5/1/2000)*

Geyser Peak 2000 Zinfandel (Sonoma County) $17. 88 *—S.H. (11/1/2002)*

Geyser Peak 1996 Zinfandel (Sonoma County) $20. 86 *(1/1/2000)*

Geyser Peak 1999 Block Collection Zinfandel (Cucamonga Valley) $23. 87 *—S.H. (9/12/2002)*

Geyser Peak 2002 Block Collection Lopez Vineyard Zinfandel (Cucamonga Valley) $30. 86 *—S.H. (12/15/2004)*

Geyser Peak 2002 Block Collection Sandy Lane Vineyard Zinfandel (Contra Costa County) $30. 90 *—S.H. (12/31/2004)*

Geyser Peak 2001 Block Collection, Sandy Lane Vineyard Zinfandel (Contra Costa County) $30. 88 *(11/1/2003)*

Geyser Peak 1999 De Ambrogio Ranch Zinfandel (Cucamonga Valley) $28. 85 *—S.H. (7/1/2002)*

Geyser Peak 1997 Winemaker's Selection Zinfandel (Cucamonga Valley) $30. 89 *(1/1/2000)*

Geyser Peak 1997 Winemaker's Selection Zinfandel (Cucamonga Valley) $26. 88 *—P.G. (11/15/1999)*

GHOST BLOCK

Ghost Block 2004 Estate Cabernet Sauvignon (Oakville) $55. This is an enormously ripe, sumptuous Cabernet Sauvignon. It has all the hallmarks of the modern cult style, from focused blackberry, cassis and spicy chocolate flavors and profoundly ripe, sweet tannins to the balancing acidity and oak elaboration that adds that extra touch of richness. This elegant wine is at its best now and for five years. 92 *—S.H. (12/1/2007)*

GIACINTO

Giacinto 1999 Red Blend (Sonoma County) $30. 86 *—S.H. (12/1/2002)*

GIFFORD HIRLINGER

Gifford Hirlinger 2004 -18° Below Bordeaux Blend (Columbia Valley (WA)) $25. Named for the big freeze, this 70-30 blend of Cabernet Sauvignon and Merlot was sourced from Canoe Ridge Vineyard. It shows a good mix of purple and blue fruits, spicy notes of licorice and vanilla bean, and it makes a lively palate impression. The balance is just right, and the half-and-half mix of neutral and new oak adds pleasing toast and vanilla to the finish. 88 *—P.G. (3/1/2007)*

GINA

Gina 2003 Chardonnay (Napa Valley) $10. 86 Best Buy *—S.H. (11/15/2004)*

GINO DA PINOT

Gino da Pinot 2005 Pinot Noir (Monterey) $16. 84 *—S.H. (12/1/2006)*

GIRARD

Girard 1999 Bordeaux Blend (Napa Valley) $40. 92 Editors' Choice *—S.H. (11/15/2002)*

Girard 2004 Artistry Bordeaux Blend (Napa Valley) $40. A blend of all five Bordeaux varieties, the is a rich, soft wine that appeals immediately for its wealth of flavor and overall balance. Cabernet dominates, bringing oak-influenced cassis flavors that finish with a flourish of cherries, Asian spice and smoke. The firmly tannic finish suggests midterm aging. Drink now through 2012. 91 *—S.H. (12/15/2007)*

Girard 1998 Cabernet Blend (Napa Valley) $40. 90 *—J.M. (5/1/2002)*

Girard 2003 Artistry Red Wine Cabernet Blend (Napa Valley) $40. This is Girard's Meritage, based on Cabernet but with the other four varieties. The grapes come from St. Helena and Oakville. The wine is young, tannic and dry now, with great complexity, a Bordeaux-style blend of endless fascination and pleasure. Should drink well for 10 years or more. 92 *—S.H. (2/1/2007)*

Girard 2003 Cabernet Franc (Napa Valley) $40. 90 *—S.H. (12/15/2006)*

Girard 2002 Cabernet Franc (Napa Valley) $40. 91 *—S.H. (7/1/2005)*

Girard 2004 Estate Cabernet Sauvignon (Napa Valley) $75. From the knoll on the eastern side of the Silverado Trail known as Pritchard Hill comes this sophisticated Cab. With a softly gentle mouthfeel comprised of rich, sweetly ripe tannins, blackberry and blueberry fruit and oak, it finishes completely dry. Drink now. 87 *—S.H. (10/1/2007)*

Girard 2002 Estate Cabernet Sauvignon (Napa Valley) $60. 90 Cellar Selection *—S.H. (12/15/2005)*

Girard 1997 Chardonnay (Napa Valley) $28. 86 *(6/1/2000)*

Girard 2005 Chardonnay (Russian River Valley) $22. Crispness and minerals are the key to understanding this elegant wine. It has peaches, apples, mangoes and plenty of charry oak, but so do many California Chards. What makes it special is the bright, steely hardness, a flinty character that cries out for food, such as ahi tuna tartare on a buttery, garlicky crostini. 90 *—S.H. (2/1/2007)*

Girard 2004 Chardonnay (Russian River Valley) $20. 89 *—S.H. (5/1/2006)*

Girard 2002 Chardonnay (Russian River Valley) $20. 90 *—S.H. (6/1/2004)*

Girard 2000 Chardonnay (Russian River Valley) $24. 89 *—J.M. (5/1/2002)*

Girard 2000 Meritage (Napa Valley) $40. 91 *—S.H. (4/1/2004)*

Girard 2005 Petite Sirah (Napa Valley) $28. Brings a boutique touch to this often rustic variety, with a classic structure, although no Petite Sirah can ever quite escape its brawny bulk. Nor should it want to. Blackberries, black currants, loganberries, plums, cherries, dark unsweetened chocolate, leather, coffee, violets—they all come together in this dry, fresh young wine. Will easily hold for a decade or two, gradually getting softer and sweeter. 92 *—S.H. (10/1/2007)*

Girard 2004 Petite Sirah (Napa Valley) $24. 85 *—S.H. (12/31/2006)*

Girard 2003 Petite Sirah (Napa Valley) $24. 92 Cellar Selection *—S.H. (12/1/2005)*

Girard 2002 Petite Sirah (Napa Valley) $24. 0 *—S.H. (11/15/2004)*

Girard 2000 Petite Sirah (Napa Valley) $24. 87 *—S.H. (12/1/2002)*

Girard 1999 Petite Sirah (Napa Valley) $24. 91 *—J.M. (5/1/2002)*

Girard 2002 Napa Valley Red Wine Red Blend (Napa Valley) $40. 86 *—S.H. (12/31/2005)*

Girard 2006 Sauvignon Blanc (Napa Valley) $16. Made New Zealand style, with no oak to influence the gooseberry, grapefruit, lime, green grass and vanilla flavors. Brisk acidity and a clean, stony mouthfeel make this wine elegant and food-friendly. Easy to find, with more than 15,000 cases produced. 88 *—S.H. (9/1/2007)*

Girard 2005 Sauvignon Blanc (Napa Valley) $15. 87 *—S.H. (7/1/2006)*

Girard 2004 Sauvignon Blanc (Napa Valley) $15. 87 *—S.H. (10/1/2005)*

Girard 2003 Sauvignon Blanc (Napa Valley) $15. 88 *—S.H. (12/1/2004)*

Girard 2001 Sauvignon Blanc (Napa Valley) $15. 84 *—S.H. (9/1/2003)*

Girard 2000 Sauvignon Blanc (Napa Valley) $15. 90 *—J.C. (5/1/2002)*

Girard 2005 Zinfandel (Napa Valley) $24. From warm, dry vineyards in the eastern Vaca mountains, this Zin, which is one quarter Petite Sirah, is ultrarich and smooth in blackberry, cassis, raspberry and mocha flavors, with a complex dash of Provençal herbs. It's quite a good Zin, made in the style of a dry, balanced Cab or Merlot. 90 *—S.H. (10/1/2007)*

Girard 2002 Zinfandel (Napa Valley) $24. 92 Editors' Choice *—S.H. (11/15/2004)*

Girard 2001 Zinfandel (Napa Valley) $24. 91 Editors' Choice *(11/1/2003)*

Girard 2004 Late Harvest Zinfandel (Napa Valley) $27. 81 *—S.H. (3/1/2006)*

Girard 2004 Old Vine Zinfandel (Napa Valley) $24. 85 *—S.H. (12/15/2006)*

Girard 2003 Old Vine Zinfandel (Napa Valley) $24. 90 *—S.H. (2/1/2006)*

GIRARDET

Girardet 2005 Baco Noir (Umpqua Valley) $25. The world of Baco Noir producers is rather limited, at least here on the west coast, but Girardet has been a leader for decades. This 2005 edition brings red currant and very tart berry fruit with it, and it somehow seems wrapped in pastry dough. The structure on the palate is a bit like Sangiovese, acidic and light, but clean and showing some staying power once you get past the hole in the midpalate. 86 *—P.G. (11/15/2007)*

Girardet 2000 Reserve Baco Noir (Umpqua Valley) $35. 87 *—P.G. (8/1/2002)*

Girardet 1999 Reserve Baco Noir (Umpqua Valley) $32. 85 *—P.G. (4/1/2002)*

Girardet 2000 Chardonnay (Umpqua Valley) $12. 86 *—P.G. (8/1/2002)*

Girardet 2006 Pinot Gris (Umpqua Valley) $16. Girardet farms its vineyards organically, does not irrigate, and ferments this wine in stainless steel. The result is a solidly made Pinot Gris, offering lush scents and tastes of ripe pear. Good texture and balance keep it from feeling one dimensional; puts the fruit front and center. 88 *—P.G. (11/15/2007)*

Girardet 2000 Pinot Gris (Umpqua Valley) $12. 85 *—P.G. (8/1/2002)*

Girardet 2000 Barrel Select Pinot Noir (Umpqua Valley) $17. 87 *—P.G. (12/31/2002)*

Girardet 1998 Barrel Select Pinot Noir (Umpqua Valley) $16. 82 *—M.S. (12/1/2000)*

Girardet 2000 Petite Cuvée Pinot Noir (Umpqua Valley) $12. 87 Best Buy *—P.G. (12/31/2002)*

Girardet 1999 Premiere Cuvée Pinot Noir (Umpqua Valley) $59. 87 *—P.G. (8/1/2002)*

Girardet 1999 Reserve Pinot Noir (Umpqua Valley) $35. 88 *—P.G. (8/1/2002)*

Girardet 1998 Reserve Pinot Noir (Umpqua Valley) $35. 88 *—J.C. (12/1/2000)*

Girardet 2005 Grand Rouge Red Blend (Umpqua Valley) $14. The winery rather coyly refuses to divulge the blend here, saying only that it is a "secret recipe" that contains 14 different Rhône grapes. Whatever. If you are expecting a true grand rouge you are going to be disappointed, for it's more like a rosé, just a bit darker in color. Dry and tart, with fruit flavors of the sort that come with a rosé of Sangiovese for example. Serve well chilled. 85 *—P.G. (11/15/2007)*

Girardet 1999 Marechal Foch Red Blend (Umpqua Valley) $15. 86 *—P.G. (8/1/2002)*

Girardet 2001 Estate Riesling (Umpqua Valley) $8. 87 Best Buy *—P.G. (8/1/2002)*

GLACIER'S END

Glacier's End NV Chardonnay (North Fork of Long Island) $10. 85 *—J.C. (3/1/2002)*

Glacier's End NV Merlot (North Fork of Long Island) $10. 85 Best Buy *—J.C. (3/1/2002)*

GLASS MOUNTAIN

Glass Mountain 2001 Cabernet Sauvignon (California) $8. 83 *—S.H. (8/1/2005)*

Glass Mountain 1999 Cabernet Sauvignon (California) $10. 87 Best Buy *—C.S. (11/15/2002)*

Glass Mountain 2001 Syrah (California) $8. 84 Best Buy *—S.H. (8/1/2005)*

Glass Mountain 1999 Syrah (California) $10. 87 *—J.C. (9/1/2002)*

GLEN ELLEN

Glen Ellen 1999 Reserve Cabernet Sauvignon (Sonoma) $7. 85 *—S.H. (9/12/2002)*

Glen Ellen 1998 Reserve Cabernet Sauvignon (California) $7. 83 *—S.H. (12/15/2000)*

Glen Ellen 1998 Reserve Chardonnay (California) $7. 82 *—S.H. (11/15/2000)*

Glen Ellen 2000 Proprietor's Reserve Gamay (Sonoma) $NA. 82 *—S.H. (9/1/2002)*

Glen Ellen 1999 Reserve Merlot (California) $7. 83 *—S.H. (9/12/2002)*

Glen Ellen 1998 Reserve Merlot (California) $7. 83 *(6/1/2001)*

Glen Ellen 2000 Reserve Sauvignon Blanc (Sonoma) $NA. 84 *—S.H. (9/12/2002)*

Glen Ellen 1998 Reserve White Zinfandel (California) $7. 83 *—S.H. (2/1/2001)*

GLEN FIONA

Glen Fiona 2001 Cuvée Parallel 46 Red Blend (Walla Walla (WA)) $25. 86 *—P.G. (7/1/2004)*

Glen Fiona 1998 Syrah (Walla Walla (WA)) $40. 88 *—P.G. (9/1/2000)*

Glen Fiona 2001 Syrah (Walla Walla (WA)) $20. 88 *—P.G. (7/1/2004)*

Glen Fiona 2000 Bacchus Vineyard Syrah (Columbia Valley (WA)) $20. 84 *(10/1/2001)*

Glen Fiona 1999 Bacchus Vineyard Syrah (Columbia Valley (WA)) $24. 82 *—P.G. (9/1/2000)*

Glen Fiona 2004 Basket Press Reserve Syrah (Columbia Valley (WA)) $30. In 2004 new winemaker William Ammons began at Glen Fiona, and this is the first of his wines to be released. This is spicy with pepper and herb, both in the nose and in the mouth. The fruit is quite tart and tastes of rhubarb and cranberry. 86 *—P.G. (12/31/2007)*

Glen Fiona 1997 Basket Press Reserve Syrah (Walla Walla (WA)) $55. 93 *—P.G. (11/15/2000)*

Glen Fiona 2001 Basket Press Reserve Cuvée Lot 57 Syrah (Walla Walla (WA)) $40. 88 *—P.G. (7/1/2004)*

Glen Fiona 1999 Puncheon Aged Syrah (Walla Walla (WA)) $40. 86 *(11/1/2001)*

GLENORA

Glenora 1996 25th Anniversary Cuvée Champagne Blend (New York) $25. 87 *—J.M. (12/1/2002)*

Glenora 1998 Brut Champagne Blend (Finger Lakes) $15. 86 *—J.M. (12/1/2002)*

Glenora 1999 Barrel Fermented Chardonnay (Finger Lakes) $12. 87 Best Buy *—J.M. (1/1/2003)*

Glenora 2002 Riesling (Finger Lakes) $21. 85 *—J.C. (8/1/2003)*

Glenora 2000 Riesling (Finger Lakes) $9. 81 *—J.C. (3/1/2002)*

Glenora 2002 Dry Riesling (Finger Lakes) $10. 86 *—J.C. (8/1/2003)*

Glenora 2001 Dry Riesling (Finger Lakes) $10. 82 *—J.C. (8/1/2003)*

Glenora 2000 Dry Riesling (Finger Lakes) $9. 84 *—J.C. (6/19/2003)*

Glenora 2001 Vintner's Select Riesling (Finger Lakes) $15. 83 *—J.C. (8/1/2003)*

Glenora 2000 Vintner's Select Riesling (Finger Lakes) $15. 87 *—J.C. (1/1/2004)*

GLORIA FERRER

Gloria Ferrer NV Champagne Blend (Sonoma County) $17. 89 Best Buy *—S.H. (12/15/1999)*

Gloria Ferrer NV Champagne Blend (Carneros) $35. 88 *—J.M. (12/1/2002)*

Gloria Ferrer NV Blanc de Blancs Champagne Blend (Carneros) $22. 86 *—S.H. (12/1/2002)*

Gloria Ferrer 2001 Blanc de Blancs Champagne Blend (Carneros) $24. 90 *—S.H. (12/31/2004)*

Gloria Ferrer NV Blanc de Noirs Champagne Blend (Sonoma County) $18. 84 *(12/1/2000)*

Gloria Ferrer NV Blanc de Noirs Champagne Blend (Sonoma County) $18. 83 *—J.C. (12/1/2001)*

Gloria Ferrer NV Brut Champagne Blend (Sonoma County) $17. 86 *—S.H. (12/15/2000)*

Gloria Ferrer NV Brut Champagne Blend (Sonoma County) $18. 86 *—S.H. (12/1/2001)*

Gloria Ferrer NV Brut Champagne Blend (Sonoma Valley) $18. 87 *—S.H. (12/1/2002)*

Gloria Ferrer NV Brut Rosé Champagne Blend (Carneros) $35. 88 *—J.M. (12/1/2002)*

Gloria Ferrer 1991 Carneros Cuvée Brut LD Champagne Blend (Carneros) $32. 90 *—P.G. (12/15/2000)*

Gloria Ferrer 1990 Carneros Cuvée Brut LD Champagne Blend (Carneros) $32. 88 *—S.H. (12/15/1999)*

Gloria Ferrer 1992 Late Disgorged Carneros Cuvée Brut Champagne Blend (Carneros) $32. 91 Cellar Selection *—J.M. (12/1/2002)*

Gloria Ferrer 1991 Royal Cuvée Champagne Blend (Carneros) $20. 89 *—J.C. (12/1/1999)*

Gloria Ferrer 1993 Royal Cuvée Brut Champagne Blend (Carneros) $22. 91 Editors' Choice *—J.C. (12/1/2001)*

Gloria Ferrer 1992 Royal Cuvée Brut Champagne Blend (Carneros) $22. 88 *—S.H. (12/1/2000)*

Gloria Ferrer 1994 Vintage Reserve-Brut-Royal Cuvée Champagne Blend (Carneros) $22. 89 *—S.H. (12/1/2002)*

Gloria Ferrer 2005 Chardonnay (Carneros) $18. Dry and crisp, this Chard, which was 100% barrel fermented, has complex flavors of flowers, minerals and citrus fruits, with a rich vein of toasty oak. It's quite elegant and a great food wine. Easy to find, with 19,000 cases produced. **90 Editors' Choice** *—S.H. (11/1/2007)*

Gloria Ferrer 2003 Chardonnay (Carneros) $18. 88 *—S.H. (12/15/2006)*

Gloria Ferrer 2001 Chardonnay (Carneros) $18. 89 *—S.H. (12/1/2003)*

Gloria Ferrer 2000 Chardonnay (Carneros) $20. 90 *—S.H. (12/15/2002)*

Gloria Ferrer 1998 Chardonnay (Carneros) $20. 88 *(6/1/2000)*

Gloria Ferrer 1997 Chardonnay (Carneros) $20. 91 *—L.W. (11/15/1999)*

Gloria Ferrer 2004 Estate Chardonnay (Carneros) $18. If you've never seen the winery's estate, it's wide open to the fog and winds of San Francisco/San Pablo Bay, so even in a hot vintage like this, their Chards possess keen acidity that gives them a steely minerality. It's not a particularly ripe wine, but shows tart citrus flavors, while new French oak adds a much-needed creamy richness. This is a terrific food Chardonnay, not one that needs to be appreciated by itself. 87 *—S.H. (5/1/2007)*

Gloria Ferrer 2003 Merlot (Carneros) $19. Cool Carneros struggled to ripen the fruit this vintage, with the result that acidity is firm, and there's a grape-skin tannic tartness to the underlying blackberry, plum, root beer and cherry flavors. The wine is strangely attractive. It's not a hedonistic seducer, nor a cellar candidate, but a complex, dry red that will rise to the occasion while playing modest second fiddle to the food. 88 *—S.H. (3/1/2007)*

Gloria Ferrer 1998 Merlot (Carneros) $23. 81 *—J.M. (12/1/2001)*

Gloria Ferrer 2005 Pinot Noir (Carneros) $28. Made from a selection of clones from the winery's large estate vineyard, this polished, very pretty wine is a classic Carneros Pinot. Dry and elegant, it has an herbal, tobacco edge to the cherry, rhubarb and spiced plum flavors. Very rewarding. Easy to find, with 17,000 cases produced. Drink now–2009. 89 *—S.H. (12/15/2007)*

Gloria Ferrer 2004 Pinot Noir (Carneros) $28. 85 *—S.H. (12/15/2006)*

Gloria Ferrer 2002 Pinot Noir (Carneros) $26. 84 *(11/1/2004)*

Gloria Ferrer 2000 Pinot Noir (Carneros) $24. 85 *(10/1/2002)*

Gloria Ferrer 1999 Pinot Noir (Carneros) $24. 84 *(10/1/2002)*

Gloria Ferrer 1997 Pinot Noir (Carneros) $20. 85 *(11/15/1999)*

Gloria Ferrer NV Blanc De Noirs Pinot Noir (Sonoma County) $18. 89 *—J.M. (12/1/2002)*

Gloria Ferrer 2002 Etesian Pinot Noir (Sonoma County) $12. 85 *(11/1/2004)*

Gloria Ferrer 2002 Gravel Knob Pinot Noir (Carneros) $40. 86 *—S.H. (12/15/2006)*

Gloria Ferrer 2000 Gravel Knob Vineyard Pinot Noir (Carneros) $40. 91 *—S.H. (2/1/2004)*

Gloria Ferrer 2003 Jose S. Ferrer Selection Pinot Noir (Carneros) $35. Gloria continues to figure out how to make Pinot, after starting life as a sparkling wine house. This Pinot is dry and elegantly silky, with subtle complexities. It's a delicious wine to drink now for its spicy cherry and smoky oak flavors. 87 *—S.H. (5/1/2007)*

Gloria Ferrer 2002 Jose S. Ferrer Selection Pinot Noir (Carneros) $35. 87 *—S.H. (12/15/2006)*

Gloria Ferrer 2002 Rust Rock Terrace Pinot Noir (Carneros) $40. 85 *—S.H. (12/15/2006)*

Gloria Ferrer 2000 Rust Rock Terrace Vineyard Pinot Noir (Carneros) $40. 93 *—S.H. (3/1/2004)*

Gloria Ferrer 2003 Blanc de Blancs Sparkling Blend (Carneros) $24. Made entirely from Chardonnay, this is the most elegant and delicate of the winery's current bubblies. It's a dry, sophisticated wine, with subtle citrus, peach, apple and yeast flavors. If you've never cellared a sparkling wine, try stashing this away for up to a decade. 90 *—S.H. (12/31/2007)*

Gloria Ferrer NV Blanc de Blancs Sparkling Blend (Carneros) $24. 87 *—S.H. (12/31/2006)*

Gloria Ferrer 2002 Blanc de Blancs Sparkling Blend (Carneros) $24. 82 *—S.H. (12/31/2005)*

Gloria Ferrer 2000 Blanc de Blancs Sparkling Blend (Carneros) $22. 90 *—S.H. (12/1/2003)*

Gloria Ferrer NV Blanc de Noirs Sparkling Blend (Sonoma County) $20. This bubbly charms with cherry and raspberry flavors and a touch of limes and vanilla. It's nice and smooth in the mouth, with a creamy mousse. Showing real finesse and elegance, this sparkler will be delicious with raw tuna. 91 *—S.H. (12/31/2007)*

Gloria Ferrer NV Blanc de Noirs Sparkling Blend (Sonoma County) $18. 87 *—S.H. (12/1/2003)*

Gloria Ferrer NV Blanc de Noirs Sparkling Blend (Sonoma County) $18. 86 *—S.H. (12/31/2004)*

Gloria Ferrer NV Blanc de Noirs Sparkling Blend (Sonoma County) $18. 86 *—S.H. (12/31/2005)*

Gloria Ferrer NV Blanc de Noirs Sparkling Blend (Sonoma County) $18. 87 *—S.H. (12/31/2006)*

Gloria Ferrer NV Brut Sparkling Blend (Sonoma County) $18. 87 *—S.H. (12/1/2003)*

Gloria Ferrer NV Brut Sparkling Blend (Sonoma County) $18. 85 *—S.H. (12/31/2006)*

Gloria Ferrer 2004 Brut Rosé Sparkling Blend (Carneros) $42. Made primarily from Pinot Noir with a little Chardonnay, this has a subtle color of the first blush on a peach, and is fragrant and delicious. The fruit flavors of raspberries and cherries have a lime tinge, and the finish is dry and impressively long. Really easy to like, just filled with charm and finesse. 92 *—S.H. (12/31/2007)*

Gloria Ferrer NV Brut Rosé Sparkling Blend (Carneros) $35. 90 *—S.H. (12/1/2003)*

Gloria Ferrer NV Brut Rosé Sparkling Blend (Carneros) $35. 88 *—S.H. (12/31/2004)*

Gloria Ferrer NV Brut Rosé Sparkling Blend (Carneros) $35. 92 *—S.H. (12/31/2005)*

Gloria Ferrer 2003 Brut Rosé Sparkling Blend (Carneros) $35. 91 *—S.H. (12/31/2006)*

Gloria Ferrer 1997 Carneros Cuvée Sparkling Blend (Carneros) $50. This is the winery's most expensive bottling, a late disgorged bubbly that has now seen a decade of age. It shows the elegant polish of the '97 Royal Cuvée, but is superior even to it in richness. The creamy smoothness is the star attraction, but so are the subtle citrus, raspberry, brioche and vanilla flavors. Impeccably dry balance guarantees that this beautiful brut will age effortlessly for 10 years, if not longer. **95 Editors' Choice** *—S.H. (12/31/2007)*

Gloria Ferrer 1995 Carneros Cuvée Sparkling Blend (Carneros) $50. 91 *—S.H. (12/31/2004)*

Gloria Ferrer 1996 Late Disgorged Brut Carneros Cuvée Sparkling Blend (Carneros) $50. 94 *—S.H. (12/31/2005)*

Gloria Ferrer 2000 Royal Cuvée Brut Sparkling Blend (Carneros) $28. Royal Cuvée has turned into one of the most consistent buys in an upscale California bubbly, mainly due to the elegance that always marks the wine. The 2000, which is a classic blend of Pinot Noir and Chardonnay, shows the smoothness and complexity that mark fine sparkling wine, with subtle citrus, peach, raspberry, brioche and smoky vanilla flavors. 93 *—S.H. (12/31/2007)*

Gloria Ferrer 1997 Royal Cuvée Brut Sparkling Blend (Carneros) $28. **92 Editors' Choice** *—S.H. (12/31/2006)*

Gloria Ferrer 1996 Royal Cuvée Brut Sparkling Blend (Carneros) $24. 89 *—S.H. (12/31/2004)*

Gloria Ferrer 1995 Royal Cuvée Brut Sparkling Blend (Carneros) $22. **92 Editors' Choice** *—S.H. (12/1/2003)*

Gloria Ferrer NV Sonoma Brut Sparkling Blend (Sonoma County) $20. This bubbly is rich in cherry and raspberry fruit, in addition to the usual sparkling wine notes of bread dough and smoke. It's a little sweet and scoury on the palate, but a fairly polished sparkler for this price. 86 *—S.H. (12/31/2007)*

Gloria Ferrer NV Sonoma Brut Sparkling Blend (Sonoma County) $18. 86 *—S.H. (12/31/2004)*

Gloria Ferrer NV Sonoma Brut Sparkling Blend (Sonoma County) $18. 85 *—S.H. (12/31/2005)*

Gloria Ferrer 2001 Syrah (Carneros) $22. 85 *(9/1/2005)*

Gloria Ferrer 2002 Estate Syrah (Carneros) $19. Carneros' cool climate gives this fine Syrah a fresh cut of acidity, firm but ripe tannins, and a complex leathery, mushroomy angle to the blackberry, cherry and carob fruit that warm climates routinely deliver. Bottom line: This is a really fine, upscale Syrah. 89 *—S.H. (5/1/2007)*

GNARLY HEAD

Gnarly Head 2005 Old Vine Zinfandel (Lodi) $12. 83 *—S.H. (12/1/2006)*

Gnarly Head 2004 Old Vine Zinfandel (Lodi) $11. **86 Best Buy** *(8/1/2006)*

GNEISS

Gneiss 2000 Cabernet Sauvignon (Napa Valley) $25. 85 *—S.H. (11/15/2003)*

Gneiss 2000 Reserve Cabernet Sauvignon (Napa Valley) $39. 87 *—S.H. (11/15/2003)*

GNEKOW

Gnekow 2000 Nies Old Vine Carignane (Lodi) $14. 91 Editors' Choice *—S.H. (12/1/2002)*

Gnekow 2004 Campus Oaks Old Vine Zinfandel (Lodi) $12. This Zin is off-dry to sweet, with a taste like sugared Lipton tea. Soft and simple. 81 *—S.H. (11/15/2007)*

GODSPEED

Godspeed 1999 Cabernet Sauvignon (Mount Veeder) $31. 85 *—S.H. (5/1/2005)*

Godspeed 2001 Chardonnay (Mount Veeder) $20. 87 *—S.H. (5/1/2005)*

GODWIN

Godwin 2005 Floral Clone Chardonnay (Russian River Valley) $28. Enormous in jammy apricot, peach, pineapple, Asian spice and sweet charred oak vanillins, this Burgundy-inspired Chard is a little sweet. But it provides enough acidity for balanced structure. 87 *—S.H. (12/15/2007)*

Godwin 2004 Floral Clone Chardonnay (Russian River Valley) $28. 91 *—S.H. (12/15/2006)*

Godwin 2001 Merlot (Alexander Valley) $35. 87 *—S.H. (5/1/2006)*

Godwin 2000 Moss Oak Vineyard Merlot (Alexander Valley) $35. 86 *—S.H. (12/31/2004)*

Godwin 1999 Moss Oak Vineyard Merlot (Alexander Valley) $35. 84 *—J.M. (11/15/2002)*

GOLD DIGGER CELLARS

Gold Digger Cellars 2000 Chardonnay (Washington) $15. 82 *—P.G. (2/1/2002)*

Gold Digger Cellars 2000 Gewürztraminer (Washington) $12. 86 *—P.G. (2/1/2002)*

GOLD HILL

Gold Hill 1999 Cabernet Sauvignon (El Dorado) $25. 86 *—S.H. (9/1/2002)*

Golden 2001 Coro Mendocino Red Blend (Mendocino) $35. 86 *—J.M. (9/1/2004)*

GOLDEN VALLEY

Golden Valley 1997 St. Herman's Vineyard Chardonnay (Willamette Valley) $15. 88 *—P.G. (9/1/2000)*

GOLDENEYE

Goldeneye 2004 Pinot Noir (Anderson Valley) $52. Goldeneye is a real vintage-dominated wine, and as delicious as the '04 is, it suffered from this hot harvest. The grapes got superripe in cassis and cherry flavors before the tannins resolved, leaving a hard mouthfeel. But there's no denying the deliciousness and Pinotesque silkiness. Drink now. 89 *—S.H. (11/1/2007)*

Goldeneye 2003 Pinot Noir (Anderson Valley) $52. 93 Editors' Choice *—S.H. (12/1/2006)*

Goldeneye 2002 Pinot Noir (Anderson Valley) $52. 85 *—S.H. (11/1/2005)*

Goldeneye 2001 Pinot Noir (Anderson Valley) $48. 92 *—S.H. (8/1/2004)*

Goldeneye 2000 Pinot Noir (Anderson Valley) $48. 87 *—M.S. (12/1/2003)*

Goldeneye 1999 Pinot Noir (Anderson Valley) $45. 93 *—S.H. (5/1/2002)*

Goldeneye 2004 Confluence Vineyard Pinot Noir (Anderson Valley) $70. The wine is a beauty. Dry, silky and pure in red cherry, raspberry, red currant and cola flavors, it was aged 16 months in 100% new French oak barrels, which give an appropriate measure of smoky caramel. With a sturdy acid-tannin structure, this supple Pinot classically exhibits the best of Anderson Valley terroir. Drink this in its flashy youth, over the next five years. 94 *—S.H. (12/15/2007)*

Goldeneye 2001 Migration Pinot Noir (Anderson Valley) $26. 87 *—S.H. (3/1/2004)*

Goldeneye 2004 The Narrows Vineyard Pinot Noir (Anderson Valley) $70. This luscious Pinot shows the appellation's ability to perfectly ripen the fruit while maintaining complete balance. The flavors are of cherries, raspberries, currants and cola, with nuances of licorice and gingerbread, yet for all that the finish is totally dry. So powerful is the wine in itself that it easily shoulders the 100% new French oak, which pushes the richness into a smoky, ne plus ultra territory. As for the mouthfeel, it's silky, racy, voluptuous and delicate at the same time, the hallmarks of the very finest California Pinot Noirs. 96 *—S.H. (12/15/2007)*

GOLDSCHMIDT

Goldschmidt 2004 Game Ranch Cabernet Sauvignon (Oakville) $65. You'll want to cellar this, although I won't guarantee results because the combination of hard tannins and superripe fruit is unusual. Those lockdown tannins limit pleasure now, while the fruit stretches from blackberries all the way to raisins. Yet the wine is dry and complex, and could surprise. 87 *—S.H. (2/1/2007)*

Goldschmidt 2001 Game Ranch Cabernet Sauvignon (Oakville) $65. 91 *—S.H. (12/15/2005)*

Goldschmidt 2004 Vyborny Vineyard Cabernet Sauvignon (Alexander Valley) $65. This single-vineyard Cab, from the personal label of the head winemaker at giant Beam Wines, is a very good example of Alexander Valley. It's rich, soft, earthy and complex, a wine to lay down for 10 years or to open now. It shows ripe cherry-berry flavors that veer into chocolate and coconut pie, but is dry and balanced. 92 *—S.H. (2/1/2007)*

Goldschmidt 2001 Vyborny Vineyard Cabernet Sauvignon (Alexander Valley) $65. 90 *—S.H. (12/15/2005)*

Goldschmidt 2000 Vyborny Vineyard Cabernet Sauvignon (Alexander Valley) $65. 90 *—S.H. (2/1/2004)*

GOOSE RIDGE

Goose Ridge 2004 Cabernet Sauvignon (Columbia Valley (WA)) $25. This wine lacks definition and focus, despite being pure Cabernet Sauvignon. The fruit is very light and thin; the smoky, oaky barrel flavors almost overwhelm it. The finish is tart and slightly green, without any weight or varietal power. 85 *—P.G. (3/1/2007)*

Goose Ridge 2002 Cabernet Sauvignon (Columbia Valley (WA)) $40. 86 *—P.G. (6/1/2006)*

Goose Ridge 2001 Cabernet Sauvignon (Columbia Valley (WA)) $27. 87 *—P.G. (11/15/2004)*

Goose Ridge 2003 Reserve Cabernet Sauvignon (Columbia Valley (WA)) $27. 90 *—P.G. (6/1/2006)*

Goose Ridge 1999 Cabernet Sauvignon-Merlot (Columbia Valley (WA)) $39. 86 *—C.S. (12/31/2002)*

Goose Ridge 2000 Meritage Red Wine Cabernet Sauvignon-Merlot (Columbia Valley (WA)) $28. 87 *—P.G. (9/1/2004)*

Goose Ridge 2005 Chardonnay (Columbia Valley (WA)) $18. Ripe, juicy and packed with banana, citrus oil and light tropical fruit flavors. This is Chard done in a broad, lush, generous style, meant for immediate enjoyment. 88 *—P.G. (3/1/2007)*

Goose Ridge 2002 Chardonnay (Columbia Valley (WA)) $21. 85 *—P.G. (11/15/2004)*

Goose Ridge 2001 Chardonnay (Columbia Valley (WA)) $20. 90 *—P.G. (1/1/2004)*

Goose Ridge 2001 Chardonnay (Columbia Valley (WA)) $18. 88 *—P.G. (9/1/2004)*

Goose Ridge 2000 Meritage Red Wine Meritage (Columbia Valley (WA)) $28.88 *—P.G. (1/1/2004)*

Goose Ridge 2004 Merlot (Columbia Valley (WA)) $25. The same exact blend as the Estate Red, this offers slightly more generous fruit flavors, and shows more of the barrel toast as well. This must be the barrel selection of the riper lots, as it seems to have shed much of the stemminess that characterizes the Estate Red. 86 *—P.G. (3/1/2007)*

Goose Ridge 2002 Merlot (Columbia Valley (WA)) $40. 89 *—P.G. (6/1/2006)*

Goose Ridge 2004 Estate Red Blend (Columbia Valley (WA)) $15. The blend is 78% Merlot, 11% Cabernet Sauvignon and 11% Malbec. The fruit carries a strong component of green, unripe herbs, along with some stemmy tannins. It could be perfectly enjoyable with a grilled steak, comparable to a rather ordinary Bordeaux. 85 *—P.G. (3/1/2007)*

Goose Ridge 2001 Vireo Red Wine Red Blend (Columbia Valley (WA)) $30. 85 *—P.G. (11/15/2004)*

Goose Ridge 2000 Vireo Red Wine Red Blend (Columbia Valley (WA)) $30. 87 *—P.G. (1/1/2004)*

Goose Ridge 2003 Syrah (Columbia Valley (WA)) $25. A bit volatile when first opened, the aromas carry sharp, vinegary scents along with plenty of new oak. Caught in the backwash, the light fruit does not show much varietal character; there's no density, simply not much flavor there. 84 *—P.G. (3/1/2007)*

Goose Ridge 2002 Syrah (Columbia Valley (WA)) $25. 88 *(9/1/2005)*

Goose Ridge 2001 Syrah (Columbia Valley (WA)) $25. 86 *—P.G. (11/15/2004)*

Goose Ridge 2000 Syrah (Columbia Valley (WA)) $26. 91 Editors' Choice *—P.G. (1/1/2004)*

Goose Ridge 2004 Reserve Syrah (Columbia Valley (WA)) $40. 89 *—P.G. (6/1/2006)*

Goose Ridge 2005 Viognier (Columbia Valley (WA)) $25. Thick and fleshy, with ripe flavors of fig, pear and baked apple, with exceptional balance for its weight. The spice is lightly sensed, as is the toasty influence of the barrel fermentation. It's a complex, creamy take on Viognier, and clearly the best wine this winery makes. **91** *—P.G. (3/1/2007)*

Goose Ridge 2002 Viognier (Columbia Valley (WA)) $21. 86 *—P.G. (9/1/2004)*

GOOSECROSS

Goosecross 1998 Chardonnay (Napa Valley) $22. 88 *(6/1/2000)*

Goosecross 2002 Syrah (South Coast) $25. 87 *(9/1/2005)*

Goosecross 1999 Syrah (California) $25. 85 *(11/1/2001)*

GORDON BROTHERS

Gordon Brothers 2005 Cabernet Sauvignon (Columbia Valley (WA)) $22. This estate-grown Cabernet shows good concentration and a stylish mix of fruit, leaf and herb across the palate. There are subtle notes of tomato leaf, bark and earth, along with black currant and blackberry fruit. The tannins are smoky and substantial, with a green tea edge to them. The wine is finished at under 14% alcohol, and it captures the sort of varietal character that cannot be found in superripe, superhot New World wines. **88** *—P.G. (12/31/2007)*

Gordon Brothers 2001 Cabernet Sauvignon (Columbia Valley (WA)) $17. 87 *—P.G. (11/15/2004)*

Gordon Brothers 1999 Cabernet Sauvignon (Columbia Valley (WA)) $22. 87 *—P.G. (9/1/2002)*

Gordon Brothers 2006 Chardonnay (Columbia Valley (WA)) $15. Lovely scents of apple blossoms lead into a fine, textural wine that proves you can put the focus on the fruit without sacrificing complexity. Drinking this is like biting into a bowl of mixed apples, with a delightful fruit salad effect. It's lightly dusted with cinnamon accents, which linger in an elegantly toasty finish. The wine keeps its balance and its delicacy throughout. **90 Best Buy** *—P.G. (12/1/2007)*

Gordon Brothers 2004 Chardonnay (Columbia Valley (WA)) $13. 86 *—P.G. (6/1/2006)*

Gordon Brothers 2000 Chardonnay (Columbia Valley (WA)) $16. 87 *—P.G. (9/1/2002)*

Gordon Brothers 1999 Estate Grown Chardonnay (Columbia Valley (WA)) $20. 88 *—P.G. (7/1/2002)*

Gordon Brothers 1999 Merlot (Columbia Valley (WA)) $20. 86 *—P.G. (9/1/2002)*

Gordon Brothers 2001 Tradition Red Blend (Columbia Valley (WA)) $40. A late release, this mature blend of Cabernet, Merlot and Syrah is quite delicious, with a smoothness acquired by all the extra time in bottle. The flavors have moved into secondary fruits, and the tannins are softened by time. You'll taste a pleasing mix fruit pastry, jam and brioche as the wine slides into a pillow-soft finale. It's not a blockbuster, but it's drinking at its peak. **89** *—P.G. (5/1/2007)*

Gordon Brothers 1998 Tradition Red Wine Red Blend (Columbia Valley (WA)) $50. 88 *—P.G. (12/31/2001)*

Gordon Brothers 2006 Rosé Blend (Columbia Valley (WA)) $13. This pleasant Cabernet and Merlot mix is estate-grown, tawny colored, scented with rose petals and tastes of rosewater, cocoa and a hint of sweetness. **85** *—P.G. (12/1/2007)*

Gordon Brothers 2006 Sauvignon Blanc (Columbia Valley (WA)) $13. Firm and detailed, this light-on-its-feet Sauvignon Blanc has a wonderful spiciness, as if it's been dappled with sweet pepper. The fruit is just ripe enough to capture the grassy sweetness of the grape, and it holds itself together well into a long and satisfying finish. Elegant and beautifully proportioned, this is a real pleasure to sip. **90 Best Buy** *—P.G. (12/1/2007)*

Gordon Brothers 2001 Katie's Vineyard Sauvignon Blanc (Columbia Valley (WA)) $12. 85 *—P.G. (9/1/2002)*

Gordon Brothers 2002 Syrah (Columbia Valley (WA)) $18. 84 *(9/1/2005)*

Gordon Brothers 2001 Syrah (Columbia Valley (WA)) $17. 86 *—P.G. (11/15/2004)*

Gordon Brothers 1999 Estate Syrah (Columbia Valley (WA)) $30. 82 *(11/1/2001)*

GORMAN WINERY

Gorman Winery 2004 The Bully Cabernet Sauvignon (Columbia Valley (WA)) $35. 93 *—P.G. (12/31/2006)*

Gorman Winery 2003 The Bully Cabernet Sauvignon (Columbia Valley (WA)) $30. 92 *—P.G. (4/1/2006)*

Gorman Winery 2004 The Evil Twin Red Blend (Red Mountain) $50. 94 *—P.G. (12/31/2006)*

Gorman Winery 2004 Zachary's Ladder Red Blend (Columbia Valley (WA)) $25. 91 *—P.G. (12/31/2006)*

Gorman Winery 2002 Zachary's Ladder Red Table Wine Red Blend (Columbia Valley (WA)) $25. 90 Editors' Choice *—P.G. (4/1/2006)*

Gorman Winery 2004 The Pixie Syrah (Red Mountain) $30. 91 *—P.G. (12/31/2006)*

Gorman Winery 2003 The Pixie Syrah (Red Mountain) $30. 89 *—P.G. (4/1/2006)*

Gorman Winery 2003 The Evil Twin Syrah-Cabernet (Red Mountain) $45. 90 *—P.G. (4/1/2006)*

GRAEAGLE

GraEagle 2003 Red Wing Bordeaux Blend (Columbia Valley (WA)) $22. 88 *—P.G. (6/1/2006)*

GRAESER

Graeser 2003 Coeur de Leon Estate Red Wine Bordeaux Blend (Diamond Mountain) $40. A blend of the two Cabernets, Sauvignon and Franc, this is a fruit-driven, simple wine offering tiers of blackberries, cherries, raspberries, milk chocolate and oak. It's a copycat of today's modern cult Cabs, a formulaic approach that's okay, but with no particular identity. **84** *—S.H. (5/1/2007)*

Graeser 2003 Estate Cabernet Franc (Diamond Mountain) $30. An awkward wine, soft, simple and with sweet and sour flavors. It's clean and fruity. Give it a chance. **83** *—S.H. (5/1/2007)*

Graeser 2003 Estate Cabernet Sauvignon (Diamond Mountain) $45. This Cab, grown on Diamond Mountain in the Mayacamas range, is rather dense and rustic. It has an old-fashioned feeling, although the ripe sweetness of the fruit is thoroughly modern. Could improve somewhat with five or so years in the bottle. **84** *—S.H. (5/1/2007)*

Graeser 2004 Sémillon (Napa Valley) $23. Soft and candied, this Sémillon tastes like something from Starbuck's. With vanilla, almond biscotti, mocha and peach custard flavors, it's a little on the sweet side. **84** *—S.H. (5/1/2007)*

GRAND ARCHER

Grand Archer 2005 Chardonnay (Sonoma County) $16. 89 *—S.H. (12/15/2006)*

GRAND CRU

Grand Cru 2000 Gewürztraminer (California) $7. 86 *—S.H. (9/1/2003)*

Grand Cru 2002 Sauvignon Blanc (California) $8. 84 Best Buy *—S.H. (12/15/2003)*

GRANDE FOLIE

Grande Folie 1998 Harvey Vineyard Old Vine Zinfandel (Amador County) $44. 85 *—S.H. (12/15/2001)*

GRANDE RONDE

Grande Ronde 2002 Charlotte's Cuvée Seven Hills Vineyard Bordeaux Blend (Columbia Valley (WA)) $40. 87 *—P.G. (4/1/2006)*

Grande Ronde 2002 Pepper Bridge Vineyard Cabernet Sauvignon (Columbia Valley (WA)) $30. 86 *—P.G. (4/1/2006)*

Grande Ronde 2000 Seven Hills Vineyard Cabernet Sauvignon (Walla Walla (WA)) $40. 86 *—P.G. (12/31/2003)*

Grande Ronde 2002 Chardonnay (Columbia Valley (WA)) $20. 83 *—P.G. (7/1/2004)*

Grande Ronde 1999 Seven Hills Vineyard Merlot (Walla Walla (WA)) $40. 85 *—P.G. (12/31/2003)*

GRANDS AMIS WINERY

Grands Amis Winery 2001 Graffigna Vineyard Zinfandel (Lodi) $18. 88 *(11/1/2003)*

GRANITE SPRINGS

Granite Springs 1999 Petite Sirah (El Dorado) $20. 88 *—S.H. (9/1/2002)*

Granite Springs 2000 Estate Petite Sirah (Fair Play) $30. 82 *(4/1/2003)*

Granite Springs 2000 Syrah (Fair Play) $18. 87 *—S.H. (2/1/2003)*

Granite Springs 1999 Syrah (El Dorado) $16. 86 *—S.H. (7/1/2002)*

Granite Springs 2001 Zinfandel (El Dorado) $30. 84 *(11/1/2003)*

Granite Springs 2000 Zinfandel (Fair Play) $30. 85 *—S.H. (11/1/2002)*

GRANVILLE

Granville 2000 Holstein Vineyard Pinot Gris (Oregon) $16. 80 *—P.G. (2/1/2002)*

Granville 1999 Holstein Vineyard Pinot Noir (Oregon) $30. 86 *—P.G. (12/31/2001)*

GRAVITY HILLS

Gravity Hills 2003 Base Camp Syrah (Paso Robles) $15. 86 *—S.H. (12/31/2006)*

Gravity Hills 2003 Killer Climb Syrah (Paso Robles) $40. Lots to like in this dry, richly layered Syrah, which takes the Northern Rhône for inspiration. It doesn't have the acidity of Hermitage, of course, and is a little soft. But the rich, fine tannins nicely offset delicious currant, blackberry, mocha and cedar flavors. **89** —*S.H. (11/1/2007)*

Gravity Hills 2002 Killer Climb Syrah (Paso Robles) $45. 87 *(9/1/2005)*

Gravity Hills 2002 Westside Syrah (Paso Robles) $15. 83 *(9/1/2005)*

Gravity Hills 2004 Tumbling Tractor Zinfandel (Paso Robles) $15. Lovers of soft, ripe, jammy Zins will exult in this one, a dry wine with plump flavors of blackberries, cherries, raspberries, carob and rum punch. It shows pretty good concentration for the price. **85** —*S.H. (11/1/2007)*

GRAYSON

Grayson 2005 Cabernet Sauvignon (Paso Robles) $10. Classic Paso Cab, very soft, totally ripe and generous, with a plethora of blackberry, cherry and red plum flavors that are almost jammy. Yet the wine is dry, with some real elegance. For early drinking. **84** —*S.H. (6/1/2007)*

Grayson 2004 Cabernet Sauvignon (Paso Robles) $10. 85 Best Buy —*S.H. (10/1/2006)*

Grayson 2003 Cabernet Sauvignon (Paso Robles) $10. 84 —*S.H. (12/1/2005)*

Grayson 2002 Cabernet Sauvignon (Paso Robles) $10. 86 Best Buy —*S.H. (12/1/2005)*

Grayson 2005 Chardonnay (Dry Creek Valley) $10. 86 Best Buy —*S.H. (11/15/2006)*

Grayson 2004 Chardonnay (North Coast) $10. 83 —*S.H. (12/1/2005)*

Grayson 2005 Merlot (Paso Robles) $10. Two Best Buys in a row now for Grayson's Merlot, which constitutes a track record. The wine offers a wealth of ripe, forward blackberry, cherry and mocha flavors that are wrapped in soft, sweet tannins, and the finish is long and dry. **86 Best Buy** —*S.H. (3/1/2007)*

Grayson 2004 Merlot (Paso Robles) $10. 89 Best Buy —*S.H. (12/1/2005)*

Grayson 2005 Zinfandel (Central Coast) $10. Buy this next time you have a big party with barbecue. It's not a great wine, but it's fruity, savory and cheap. **84** —*S.H. (11/15/2007)*

GRAZIANO

Graziano 2001 Coro Mendocino Red Blend (Mendocino) $35. 87 —*J.M. (9/1/2004)*

GREAT WESTERN

Great Western NV Brut Champagne Blend (Finger Lakes) $10. 85 Best Buy *(12/1/2001)*

Great Western NV Brut Champagne Blend (New York) $10. 81 —*S.H. (12/31/2000)*

Great Western NV Extra Dry Champagne Blend (New York) $10. 80 —*S.H. (6/1/2001)*

Great Western NV Extra Dry Champagne Blend (Finger Lakes) $10. 82 *(12/1/2001)*

Great Western NV Chardonnay (Finger Lakes) $10. 84 *(12/1/2001)*

GREEN & RED

Green & Red 1998 Chiles Mill Vineyard Zinfandel (Napa Valley) $22. 89 —*P.G. (2/1/2001)*

GREEN CREEK WINERY

Green Creek Winery 2005 Chardonnay (North Carolina) $16. Delivers a dense, toasty nose and deep color but on the palate, the toast turns to a slighty bitter flavor. Needs balance and more restraint to allow the fruit flavors a presence. **82** —*S.K. (7/1/2007)*

GREENWOOD RIDGE

Greenwood Ridge 2001 Cabernet Sauvignon (Mendocino Ridge) $25. 89 —*S.H. (10/1/2004)*

Greenwood Ridge 1999 Cabernet Sauvignon (Mendocino Ridge) $30. 92 —*S.H. (5/1/2002)*

Greenwood Ridge 1996 Estate Bottled Cabernet Sauvignon (Mendocino Ridge) $24. 88 —*S.H. (2/1/2000)*

Greenwood Ridge 1999 Du Pratt Vineyard Chardonnay (Mendocino Ridge) $24. 90 —*S.H. (5/1/2002)*

Greenwood Ridge 1998 Du Pratt Vineyard Chardonnay (Mendocino County) $24. 88 *(6/1/2000)*

Greenwood Ridge 1997 Merlot (Mendocino Ridge) $24. 90 —*S.H. (3/1/2000)*

Greenwood Ridge 1996 Merlot (Mendocino Ridge) $22. 94 *(11/15/1999)*

Greenwood Ridge 2001 Merlot (Mendocino Ridge) $25. 88 —*S.H. (10/1/2004)*

Greenwood Ridge 1998 Estate Bottled Merlot (Mendocino Ridge) $24. 89 —*S.H. (5/1/2002)*

Greenwood Ridge 2003 Pinot Grigio (Anderson Valley) $16. 87 —*S.H. (10/1/2004)*

Greenwood Ridge 2002 Pinot Grigio (Anderson Valley) $16. 88 —*S.H. (12/1/2003)*

Greenwood Ridge 2006 Pinot Gris (Anderson Valley) $16. There's lots of fresh, green, crunchy fruit and berry flavor in this dry young wine. In this cool vintage, the wine shows zesty flavors of gooseberries, spiced melons and limes, with a touch of feline essence. **86** —*S.H. (12/1/2007)*

Greenwood Ridge 2003 Pinot Noir (Mendocino Ridge) $25. 87 —*S.H. (12/31/2005)*

Greenwood Ridge 2000 Pinot Noir (Mendocino Ridge) $30. 86 —*S.H. (5/1/2002)*

Greenwood Ridge 2000 Pinot Noir (Anderson Valley) $24. 82 *(10/1/2002)*

Greenwood Ridge 1999 Pinot Noir (Anderson Valley) $24. 87 —*S.H. (5/1/2002)*

Greenwood Ridge 2002 Estate Pinot Noir (Mendocino Ridge) $25. 85 —*S.H. (3/1/2005)*

Greenwood Ridge 2001 Eye of the Dragon Pinot Noir (Mendocino Ridge) $25. 90 —*S.H. (12/1/2003)*

Greenwood Ridge 2000 Riesling (Mendocino Ridge) $12. 91 Best Buy —*S.H. (5/1/2002)*

Greenwood Ridge 1999 Late Harvest Riesling (Mendocino Ridge) $24. 93 —*S.H. (5/1/2002)*

Greenwood Ridge 2006 Estate Late Harvest White Riesling (Mendocino Ridge) $25. Bottled at 18% residual sugar, this wine's most delicious quality is its fabulously rich sweetness, almost decadent in pale honey and apricot jam. Acidity is just fine, but what the wine needs is greater depth of fruity flavor. **86** —*S.H. (9/1/2007)*

Greenwood Ridge 2006 Estate White Riesling (Mendocino Ridge) $16. With 2.8% residual sugar, this frankly sweet white is a little soft. The lack of acidity makes the jammy apricot, pineapple and honeysuckle flavors finish a little flat. **84** —*S.H. (9/1/2007)*

Greenwood Ridge 2006 Sauvignon Blanc (Anderson Valley) $16. This is one of the driest, cleanest and most acidic Sauvignon Blancs on the market, and for those reasons, I love it. It's a European-style wine, as fresh and crisp as a young Sancerre, with green grass, grapefruit and lime flavors leading to a clover honey finish. Beautiful as an apéritif sipper. **88 Editors' Choice** —*S.H. (12/1/2007)*

Greenwood Ridge 2004 Sauvignon Blanc (Anderson Valley) $16. 92 Editors' Choice —*S.H. (12/31/2005)*

Greenwood Ridge 2002 Sauvignon Blanc (Anderson Valley) $16. 90 —*S.H. (12/15/2003)*

Greenwood Ridge 2000 Sauvignon Blanc (Anderson Valley) $13. 84 —*S.H. (5/1/2002)*

Greenwood Ridge 1998 Sauvignon Blanc (Anderson Valley) $12. 89 Best Buy —*L.W. (11/1/1999)*

Greenwood Ridge 2004 Sémillon (Anderson Valley) $16. 86 —*S.H. (12/31/2005)*

Greenwood Ridge 2003 White Riesling (Mendocino Ridge) $15. 86 —*S.H. (10/1/2004)*

Greenwood Ridge 2002 White Riesling (Mendocino Ridge) $15. 89 —*S.H. (12/31/2003)*

Greenwood Ridge 2001 Estate Bottled White Riesling (Mendocino Ridge) $12. 88 Best Buy —*J.M. (8/1/2003)*

Greenwood Ridge 1998 Estate Bottled White Riesling (Mendocino County) $NA. 88 *(8/1/2000)*

Greenwood Ridge 2003 Late Harvest White Riesling (Mendocino Ridge) $25. 94 —*S.H. (2/1/2005)*

Greenwood Ridge 1998 Zinfandel (Sonoma County) $21. 90 —*S.H. (2/1/2000)*

Greenwood Ridge 2001 Scherrer Vineyards-Eye of the Dragon Zinfandel (Sonoma County) $25. 90 *(11/1/2003)*

GREY FOX

Grey Fox NV Butte County Cabernet Sauvignon (California) $10. 83 —*S.H. (2/1/2000)*

Grey Fox 1997 Chardonnay (Napa Valley) $10. 86 Best Buy —*S.H. (2/1/2000)*

Grey Fox NV Merlot (Napa Valley) $20. 84 —*S.H. (3/1/2000)*

Grey Fox 2003 Butte County Syrah (California) $16. 84 *(9/1/2005)*

GRGICH HILLS

Grgich Hills 2002 Cabernet Sauvignon (Napa Valley) $58. 87 *—S.H. (9/1/2006)*

Grgich Hills 2001 Cabernet Sauvignon (Napa Valley) $55. 93 *—S.H. (11/15/2005)*

Grgich Hills 2000 Cabernet Sauvignon (Napa Valley) $50. 88 *—S.H. (11/15/2004)*

Grgich Hills 1999 Cabernet Sauvignon (Napa Valley) $50. 92 *—S.H. (5/1/2003)*

Grgich Hills 2003 Estate Cabernet Sauvignon (Napa Valley) $58. I wanted to like this wine more, but it was hard, given the tough, minty green sharpness. Where's the ripe fruit, especially at this price? It's really not very interesting. 83 *—S.H. (6/1/2007)*

Grgich Hills 2002 Yountville Selection Cabernet Sauvignon (Napa Valley) $135. I don't know why this bottling is so variable over the years. The wine has been weedy and thin, and sometimes opulent and ageworthy. This one falls in between. It has harsh tannins and acids and green, minty flavors, but also good cherry and blackberry flavors and lots of new oak. Doesn't seem like an ager. 86 *—S.H. (2/1/2007)*

Grgich Hills 2001 Yountville Selection Cabernet Sauvignon (Napa Valley) $135. 94 Cellar Selection *—S.H. (2/1/2006)*

Grgich Hills 1999 Yountville Selection Cabernet Sauvignon (Napa Valley) $125. 82 *—S.H. (8/1/2005)*

Grgich Hills 1997 Yountville Selection Cabernet Sauvignon (Napa Valley) $95. 84 *—S.H. (2/1/2005)*

Grgich Hills 2004 Chardonnay (Napa Valley) $38. Shows an earthy, dried herb taste that's not unpleasant, but limits the wine's bright fruit purity, and what fruit there is finishes watery thin. What a disappointment. 82 *—S.H. (2/1/2007)*

Grgich Hills 2003 Chardonnay (Napa Valley) $38. 87 *—S.H. (2/1/2006)*

Grgich Hills 2002 Chardonnay (Napa Valley) $35. 85 *—S.H. (6/1/2005)*

Grgich Hills 2001 Chardonnay (Napa Valley) $33. 86 *—S.H. (4/1/2004)*

Grgich Hills 2000 Chardonnay (Napa Valley) $33. 91 *—S.H. (12/15/2002)*

Grgich Hills 1998 Chardonnay (Napa Valley) $30. 87 *(7/1/2001)*

Grgich Hills 1997 Chardonnay (Napa Valley) $30. 87 *(6/1/2000)*

Grgich Hills 2004 30th Anniversary Chardonnay (Carneros) $73. I found the winery's regular '04 disappointing. This commemorative bottling is oakier and much riper in tropical fruit flavors, with non-malolactic crisp acidity and a buttercream texture. Somehow, though, it lacks the power and follow-through a great Chard should have, especially at this price. 87 *—S.H. (10/1/2007)*

Grgich Hills 2001 Carneros Selection Chardonnay (Napa Valley) $58. 93 *—S.H. (12/31/2004)*

Grgich Hills 2005 Estate Chardonnay (Napa Valley) $40. The cool 2005 growing season benefited this wine. It's dry and balanced and quite elegant, with delicious flavors of peaches, buttered popcorn and caramel. 88 *—S.H. (12/1/2007)*

Grgich Hills 2003 Paris Tasting Commemorative Chardonnay (Carneros) $73. This celebrates the 30th anniversary of the famous tasting where Mike Grgich's Chardonnay, from Chateau Montelena, took first place. The wine benefited from a small, warm vintage, and is intensely concentrated in tropical fruit, nectarine, tapioca and crème brûlée flavors that easily handle 100% new French oak. Extraordinarily creamy and rich, with lively balancing acidity. Only 867 cases made. 94 *—S.H. (7/1/2007)*

Grgich Hills 2004 Fumé Blanc (Napa Valley) $24. 89 *—S.H. (11/15/2005)*

Grgich Hills 2006 Dry Fumé Blanc (Napa Valley) $28. Grgich Hills did a good job making this clean and with a kiss of oak, but the feline scent and taste overpower the more pleasant kiwis and grapefruit. 83 *—S.H. (12/1/2007)*

Grgich Hills 2003 Estate Dry Fumé Blanc (Napa Valley) $26. 88 *—S.H. (12/15/2004)*

Grgich Hills 2002 Estate Grown Dry SB Fumé Blanc (Napa Valley) $18. 86 *—S.H. (2/1/2004)*

Grgich Hills 2001 Private Reserve Style Fumé Blanc (Napa Valley) $18. 85 *—S.H. (7/1/2003)*

Grgich Hills 2000 Private Reserve Style Fumé Blanc (Napa Valley) $18. 83 *(8/1/2002)*

Grgich Hills 2002 Merlot (Napa Valley) $38. 83 *—S.H. (4/1/2006)*

Grgich Hills 2001 Merlot (Napa Valley) $46. 91 *—S.H. (12/15/2004)*

Grgich Hills 2000 Merlot (Napa Valley) $38. 86 *—S.H. (4/1/2004)*

Grgich Hills 1999 Merlot (Napa Valley) $38. 89 *—S.H. (8/1/2003)*

Grgich Hills 2003 Estate Merlot (Napa Valley) $38. Pretty good, considering the high production level; nearly 15,000 cases. Very dry, with an elegant structure, the wine shows earthy flavors of blackberries, coffee, tobacco and cedar wrapped into firm tannins. 87 *—S.H. (6/1/2007)*

Grgich Hills 1995 Violetta Riesling (California) $40. 85 *—J.C. (12/31/1999)*

Grgich Hills 2005 Dry Sauvignon Blanc (Napa Valley) $25. 84 *—S.H. (11/15/2006)*

Grgich Hills 2006 Essence Sauvignon Blanc (Napa Valley) $40. This is the first ever release of this reserve-style Sauvignon Blanc from Grgich Hills, but it's not a very good wine. It's semisweet and simple, with sugary LifeSaver candy and green-pea flavors. 82 *—S.H. (12/31/2007)*

Grgich Hills 2000 Violetta-Late Harvest White Blend (Napa Valley) $50. 93 Editors' Choice *—S.H. (12/1/2002)*

Grgich Hills 2003 Violetta Dessert Wine 375mL White Blend (Napa Valley) $75. 95 *—S.H. (11/15/2006)*

Grgich Hills 2002 Late Harvest Violetta White Riesling (Napa Valley) $60. 92 *—S.H. (2/1/2005)*

Grgich Hills 2004 Zinfandel (Napa Valley) $30. This is a difficult Zin to like, because it has a hot, peppery feeling and raisiny taste. Even though the official alcohol is lower than some other Zins, it sticks out. There's not enough fat, fruity richness to offset it. 82 *—S.H. (2/1/2007)*

Grgich Hills 2002 Zinfandel (Napa Valley) $28. 84 *—S.H. (10/1/2005)*

Grgich Hills 2001 Zinfandel (Napa Valley) $29. 87 *—S.H. (2/1/2005)*

Grgich Hills 2000 Zinfandel (Napa Valley) $25. 84 *—S.H. (9/1/2003)*

Grgich Hills 1998 Zinfandel (Sonoma County) $28. 88 *—P.G. (3/1/2001)*

Grgich Hills 1998 Zinfandel (California) $23. 86 *(3/1/2001)*

Grgich Hills 1997 Zinfandel (Sonoma County) $20. 89 *—S.H. (5/1/2000)*

Grgich Hills 1996 Zinfandel (Sonoma) $20. 92 *—M.S. (11/1/1999)*

Grgich Hills 2004 Miljenko's Old Vines Zinfandel (Napa Valley) $69. This suffers from major problems. It has all the faults of a hot Zinfandel: semisweet baked-fruit flavors, a lack of acidity, and a resulting medicinal quality. 80 *—S.H. (12/1/2007)*

GRIFFIN CREEK

Griffin Creek 2000 Cabernet Franc (Rogue Valley) $28. 88 *—M.S. (8/1/2003)*

Griffin Creek 1999 Cabernet Sauvignon (Rogue Valley) $35. 87 *—P.G. (4/1/2002)*

Griffin Creek 1999 Chardonnay (Rogue Valley) $23. 85 *—M.S. (9/1/2003)*

Griffin Creek 2000 Merlot (Rogue Valley) $30. 86 *—P.G. (8/1/2005)*

Griffin Creek 1999 Merlot (Rogue Valley) $35. 86 *—P.G. (4/1/2002)*

Griffin Creek 1998 Merlot (Rogue Valley) $40. 85 *—P.G. (11/1/2001)*

Griffin Creek 2002 Pinot Gris (Rogue Valley) $18. 82 *—P.G. (8/1/2005)*

Griffin Creek 2001 Pinot Gris (Rogue Valley) $18. 81 *—M.S. (12/31/2002)*

Griffin Creek 1999 Pinot Noir (Rogue Valley) $35. 88 *—P.G. (4/1/2002)*

Griffin Creek 1998 Pinot Noir (Rogue Valley) $35. 87 *—M.S. (12/1/2000)*

Griffin Creek 2000 Syrah (Rogue Valley) $33. 86 *—M.S. (9/1/2003)*

Griffin Creek 1999 Syrah (Rogue Valley) $35. 84 *—P.G. (4/1/2002)*

Griffin Creek 1998 Syrah (Rogue Valley) $35. 87 *(11/1/2001)*

Griffin Creek 2002 Lakeside Vineyard Syrah (Rogue Valley) $48. 87 *—P.G. (8/1/2005)*

Griffin Creek 2002 Viognier (Rogue Valley) $25. 88 *—P.G. (2/1/2005)*

Griffin Creek 2000 Viognier (Rogue Valley) $30. 85 *—P.G. (4/1/2002)*

GRISTINA

Gristina 1998 Cabernet Franc (North Fork of Long Island) $22. 85 *—J.C. (4/1/2001)*

Gristina 1998 Cabernet Sauvignon (North Fork of Long Island) $20. 84 *—J.C. (4/1/2001)*

Gristina 1999 Chardonnay (North Fork of Long Island) $20. 85 *—J.C. (4/1/2001)*

Gristina 1999 Andy's Field Chardonnay (North Fork of Long Island) $40. 87 *—J.C. (1/1/2004)*

Gristina 2000 Apaucuck Chardonnay (Long Island) $10. 87 Best Buy *—J.M. (7/1/2002)*

Gristina 1998 Merlot (North Fork of Long Island) $20. 87 *—J.C. (4/1/2001)*

Gristina 1998 Andy's Field Merlot (North Fork of Long Island) $27. 89 *—J.C. (4/1/2001)*

Gristina NV Garnet Red Blend (North Fork of Long Island) $15. 85 *—J.C. (4/1/2001)*

GROTH

Groth 2004 Cabernet Sauvignon (Oakville) $55. I get the concept, which is International Cult Style, but the wine is just taking it to an extreme. Too ripe in jellied blackberries and melted milk chocolate, too soft, without enough tannic backbone, and too oaky. **85** *—S.H. (12/1/2007)*

Groth 2003 Cabernet Sauvignon (Oakville) $55. 84 *—S.H. (9/1/2006)*

Groth 2002 Cabernet Sauvignon (Oakville) $50. 91 *—S.H. (12/1/2005)*

Groth 2001 Cabernet Sauvignon (Oakville) $50. 86 *—S.H. (2/1/2005)*

Groth 1996 Cabernet Sauvignon (Napa Valley) $40. 92 *—L.W. (11/1/1999)*

Groth 1995 Reserve Cabernet Sauvignon (Oakville) $125. 93 *—L.W. (7/1/1999)*

Groth 1998 Sauvignon Blanc (Napa Valley) $14. 90 *—L.W. (11/1/1999)*

Groth 2005 Sauvignon Blanc (Napa Valley) $17. 90 Editors' Choice *—S.H. (11/15/2006)*

GROVE STREET

Grove Street 2001 Cabernet Sauvignon (Sonoma County) $10. 86 *—S.H. (6/1/2004)*

Grove Street 2001 Cabernet Sauvignon (Alexander Valley) $12. 86 *—S.H. (10/1/2004)*

Grove Street 1999 Cabernet Sauvignon (Napa Valley) $50. 88 *—S.H. (11/15/2004)*

Grove Street 2001 Chardonnay (Sonoma County) $7. 84 *—S.H. (6/1/2004)*

Grove Street 1998 Honor Chardonnay (California) $9. 84 *—S.H. (5/1/2000)*

Grove Street 2001 Merlot (Sonoma County) $18. 80 *—S.H. (7/1/2006)*

Grove Street 2004 Pinot Noir (Napa-Carneros) $18. 87 *—S.H. (7/1/2006)*

Grove Street 2001 Pinot Noir (Russian River Valley) $13. 84 *—S.H. (6/1/2004)*

Grove Street 1998 Baker Syrah (California) $9. 86 Best Buy *—S.H. (5/1/2000)*

GRUET

Gruet 1996 Blanc de Blancs Champagne Blend (New Mexico) $22. 88 Editors' Choice *—M.M. (12/1/2001)*

Gruet 1997 Grand Rosé Champagne Blend (New Mexico) $30. 84 *(12/1/2001)*

Gruet 2005 Chardonnay (New Mexico) $13. This well-balanced wine has an appealing citric nose of lemon and orange mingled with oak, and is backed with flavors of apples and toasted vanilla. Sturdy flavors pop and then fizzle a little in the finish, but overall, an impressive selection from an area not known for wine. Good for Chardonnay drinkers who like a little zing with the cream. **87** *—S.K. (2/1/2007)*

Gruet 2005 Barrel Select Unfiltered Chardonnay (New Mexico) $20. Another successful Chard from Gruet. On the nose is a round, creamy wave of toasted oak and hazelnut, followed up by solid flavors of pear and grapefruit. This balances nicely between buttery and dry, offering depth and dimension with a clean character. Pour this with a variety of dishes from poultry to seafood salad—it's flexible and fun. **86** *—S.K. (7/1/2007)*

Gruet 2004 Barrel Select Unfiltered Pinot Noir (New Mexico) $45. 86 *—M.D. (12/1/2006)*

Gruet 2000 Cuvée Gilbert Gruet Pinot Noir (New Mexico) $24. 81 *(10/1/2002)*

Gruet 2004 Cuvée Gilbert Gruet Pinot Noir (New Mexico) $24. 87 *—M.D. (12/1/2006)*

Gruet 2000 Blanc de Blancs Brut Sparkling Blend (New Mexico) $22. 87 *—M.D. (12/31/2006)*

Gruet NV Blanc de Noirs Brut Sparkling Blend (New Mexico) $13. 85 *—M.D. (12/31/2006)*

Gruet NV Brut Sparkling Blend (New Mexico) $13. 83 *—M.D. (12/31/2006)*

Gruet NV Brut Rosé Sparkling Blend (New Mexico) $13. 87 *—M.D. (12/31/2006)*

Gruet 1999 Gilbert Gruet Grande Reserve Sparkling Blend (New Mexico) $45. 90 *—M.D. (12/31/2006)*

Gruet NV Grand Rosé Sparkling Blend (New Mexico) $30. 88 *—M.D. (12/31/2006)*

GRYPHON

Gryphon 2000 Pinot Noir (Anderson Valley) $50. 86 *—S.H. (8/1/2004)*

Gryphon 2000 Reserve Pinot Noir (Anderson Valley) $65. 88 *—S.H. (8/1/2004)*

GUENOC

Guenoc 2000 Victorian Claret Bordeaux Blend (North Coast) $20. 84 *—S.H. (12/1/2005)*

Guenoc 2005 Cabernet Sauvignon (Lake County) $18. Soft and gentle in the mouth, with a silky texture, this very ripe Cab shows jammy blackberry, cherry, vanilla and smoke flavors. This is the best Lake county Cab from Guenoc in years. **87** *—S.H. (12/31/2007)*

Guenoc 2004 Cabernet Sauvignon (California) $9. Lots of ripe blackberry, cherry and mocha fruit here, but a major objection is sharpness. That seems to come from unripe fruit or stems or something green and chlorophylly that gives an unpleasant wintergreen taste. **83** *—S.H. (4/1/2007)*

Guenoc 2004 Cabernet Sauvignon (Lake County) $18. Your basic country Cab, with ripe blackberry fruit accented by oak, and firm tannins. It's a bit on the sweet side. **83** *—S.H. (9/1/2007)*

Guenoc 2003 Cabernet Sauvignon (Lake County) $14. 83 *—S.H. (12/1/2006)*

Guenoc 2002 Cabernet Sauvignon (California) $11. 82 *—S.H. (8/1/2005)*

Guenoc 2001 Cabernet Sauvignon (North Coast) $17. 87 *—S.H. (12/1/2005)*

Guenoc 1999 Beckstoffer IV Cabernet Sauvignon (Napa Valley) $55. 84 *—S.H. (11/15/2003)*

Guenoc 1996 Bella Vista Vineyard Reserve Cabernet Sauvignon (Napa Valley) $41. 92 *—L.W. (3/1/2000)*

Guenoc 1997 Reserve Beckstoffer IV Vineyard Cabernet Sauvignon (Napa Valley) $41. 90 *(11/1/2000)*

Guenoc 1997 Reserve Bella Vista Vineyard Cabernet Sauvignon (Napa Valley) $41. 88 *(11/1/2000)*

Guenoc 1998 Chardonnay (North Coast) $16. 87 *(6/1/2000)*

Guenoc 2005 Chardonnay (Lake County) $12. 84 *—S.H. (12/31/2006)*

Guenoc 2004 Chardonnay (North Coast) $12. 85 *—S.H. (12/1/2006)*

Guenoc 2004 Chardonnay (California) $12. 83 *—S.H. (12/1/2006)*

Guenoc 2003 Chardonnay (California) $11. 83 *—S.H. (8/1/2005)*

Guenoc 1998 Genevieve Magoon Reserve Chardonnay (Guenoc Valley) $30. 86 *(6/1/2000)*

Guenoc 2002 Genevieve Magoon Vineyard Reserve Chardonnay (Guenoc Valley) $26. 87 *—S.H. (3/1/2005)*

Guenoc 1999 Genevieve Magoon Vineyard Reserve Tutu Chardonnay (Guenoc Valley) $40. 91 *(7/1/2001)*

Guenoc 1998 Genevieve Magoon Vineyard Reserve Tutu Unfiltered Chardonnay (Guenoc Valley) $40. 89 *(7/1/2001)*

Guenoc 2004 Merlot (California) $9. 80 *—S.H. (12/1/2006)*

Guenoc 2004 Petite Sirah (Lake County) $20. This is a country-style wine. Dry and satisfying, it shows rich tannins and soft acids framing cherry, blackberry and cola flavors. Easy to sip with burgers or roast chicken. **86** *—S.H. (9/1/2007)*

Guenoc 2003 Petite Sirah (Lake County) $16. 86 *—S.H. (12/31/2006)*

Guenoc 2002 Petite Sirah (Lake County) $16. 87 *—S.H. (12/1/2006)*

Guenoc 2001 Petite Sirah (North Coast) $18. 83 *—S.H. (12/1/2005)*

Guenoc 1999 Petite Sirah (North Coast) $21. 83 *(4/1/2003)*

Guenoc 2000 Serpentine Meadow Petite Sirah (Guenoc Valley) $35. 92 *—S.H. (3/1/2005)*

Guenoc 1999 Serpentine Meadow Reserve Petite Sirah (Guenoc Valley) $40. 85 *(4/1/2003)*

Guenoc 2004 Pinot Grigio (California) $9. 85 Best Buy *—S.H. (12/1/2006)*

Guenoc 2000 Vintage Port (Guenoc Valley) $30. 94 *—S.H. (2/1/2005)*

Guenoc 1998 Sauvignon Blanc (California) $10. 86 *—L.W. (5/1/2000)*

Guenoc 1997 Sauvignon Blanc (North Coast) $13. 85 *—L.W. (9/1/1999)*

Guenoc 2005 Sauvignon Blanc (Lake County) $11. 86 Best Buy *—S.H. (12/31/2006)*

Guenoc 2005 Sauvignon Blanc (Lake County) $12. 86 *—S.H. (11/1/2006)*

Guenoc 2004 Sauvignon Blanc (Lake County) $13. 82 *—S.H. (12/1/2005)*

Guenoc 2000 Estate Selection Sauvignon Blanc (North Coast) $15. 90 Editors' Choice *(8/1/2002)*

Guenoc 2001 Zinfandel (California) $9. 82 *—S.H. (8/1/2005)*

Guenoc 2001 Zinfandel (California) $12. 87 Best Buy *(11/1/2003)*

GUERRERO FERNANDEZ

Guerrero Fernandez 2004 Cabernet Franc (Dry Creek Valley) $28. 80 *—S.H. (6/1/2006)*

Guerrero Fernandez 2004 Merlot (Dry Creek Valley) $28. 81 —*S.H. (6/1/2006)*

Guerrero Fernandez 2004 Pinot Noir (Green Valley) $30. 84 —*S.H. (6/1/2006)*

Guerrero Fernandez 2004 Zinfandel (Dry Creek Valley) $28. 85 —*S.H. (6/1/2006)*

GUILLIAMS

Guilliams 1996 Cabernet Sauvignon (Spring Mountain) $28. 92 —*S.H. (2/1/2000)*

Guilliams 2004 *Barrel Sample* Cabernet Sauvignon (Napa Valley) $NA. 92 —*S.H. (8/1/2004)*

GUISEPPE

Guiseppe 2000 Neese Vineyards Zinfandel (Redwood Valley) $17. 87 —*S.H. (12/15/2001)*

GUNDLACH BUNDSCHU

Gundlach Bundschu 2004 Rhinefarm Vineyard Cabernet Sauvignon (Sonoma Valley) $35. This is one of those Cabs that has the structure and pedigree of a fine appellation, with gorgeously ripe tannins. Yet it also comes from a hot vintage, and the flavors tend toward sweetened pie filling and dessert pastries, which are awkward in a Cabernet. Blackberries and chocolate dominate. 85 —*S.H. (5/1/2007)*

Gundlach Bundschu 2002 Rhinefarm Vineyard Cabernet Sauvignon (Sonoma Valley) $32. 89 —*S.H. (12/1/2005)*

Gundlach Bundschu 2003 Rhinefarm Vineyard Chardonnay (Sonoma Valley) $24. 86 —*S.H. (12/1/2005)*

Gundlach Bundschu 2005 Rhinefarm Vineyard Chardonnay (Sonoma Valley) $25. The vineyard is on the Carneros border, and this Chard has lots of juicy acidity, which may also be due to the winemaker picking the grapes at a relatively low ripeness level. The pepper- and mineral-infused flavors suggest peaches and grapefruits, enriched with new oak and lees. This is an extremely dry, food-friendly wine. 87 —*S.H. (10/1/2007)*

Gundlach Bundschu 1998 Rhinefarm Vineyards Chardonnay (Sonoma Valley) $18. 85 *(6/1/2000)*

Gundlach Bundschu 1998 Sangiacomo Ranch Chardonnay (Sonoma Valley) $16. 87 *(6/1/2000)*

Gundlach Bundschu 2006 Rhinefarm Vineyard Gewürztraminer (Sonoma Valley) $25. Kudos to the winery for picking at low brix and for keeping the residual sugar so low so that the wine is absolutely dry. It lets the palate really appreciate the acid-brightened flavors of exotic fruits, wildflowers, and, especially, Asian spices. The wine could be more concentrated, but it's still a good sipper. 88 —*S.H. (10/1/2007)*

Gundlach Bundschu 2004 Rhinefarm Vineyard Merlot (Sonoma Valley) $29. The vineyard is right on the border of Sonoma Valley and Carneros. Both are good places to grow Merlot, and this wine shows ripe cherry, pomegranate and spice flavors with cool-climate-influenced crisp acidity. It's a rich, sumptuous Merlot that's at its best now. 87 —*S.H. (3/1/2007)*

Gundlach Bundschu 2003 Rhinefarm Vineyard Merlot (Sonoma Valley) $29. 82 —*S.H. (12/31/2006)*

Gundlach Bundschu 1998 Rhinefarm Vineyard Merlot (Sonoma Valley) $26. 85 —*J.M. (12/1/2001)*

Gundlach Bundschu 2000 Rhinefarm Pinot Noir (Sonoma Valley) $28. 86 *(10/1/2002)*

Gundlach Bundschu 2004 Rhinefarm Vineyard Pinot Noir (Sonoma Valley) $32. 90 —*S.H. (12/31/2006)*

Gundlach Bundschu 1999 Rhinefarm Vineyard Pinot Noir (Sonoma Valley) $26. 87 —*S.H. (7/1/2002)*

Gundlach Bundschu 1997 Rhinefarm Vineyards Pinot Noir (Sonoma Valley) $18. 91 *(11/15/1999)*

Gundlach Bundschu 2001 Rhinefarm Vineyard Zinfandel (Sonoma Valley) $32. 90 *(11/1/2003)*

GYPSY CANYON

Gypsy Canyon NV Ancient Vine Angelica 375mL Mission (Santa Rita Hills) $120. 92 —*S.H. (9/1/2006)*

Gypsy Canyon 2004 Pinot Noir (Santa Rita Hills) $75. 89 —*S.H. (3/1/2006)*

Gypsy Canyon 2005 Santa Rita Creek Vineyard Pinot Noir (Santa Rita Hills) $75. Of the scores of Pinots I tasted during my last trip to this region, this was the most exotic yet puzzling one. It's quite pale in color, with a ruby-orange hue, and has a baked fruit, yeast and spice aroma not unlike Madeira. Very delicate and silky in the mouth, it nonetheless bursts with intense cherry and raspberry parfait, tangerine zest, orange Pekoe tea, vanilla and cinnamon spice flavors. Something about it reminds me of certain great Burgundies, yet its future is unknown. 92 —*S.H. (4/1/2007)*

Gypsy Canyon 2004 Dona Marcelina's Vineyard Ancient Vine Angelica White Blend (Santa Rita Hills) $120. This is a rich, hedonistically enjoyable wine, made from the Mission grape planted by the Spanish missionaries. It's very sweet and decadent, with tangerine, pineapple and apricot-infused crème brûlée flavors and a generous coating of spice that finishes in a honey-rich mouthfeel. Whether it's worth the Sauternes-level price is up to you. 92 —*S.H. (4/1/2007)*

GYPSY DANCER

Gypsy Dancer 2006 Christine Lorraine Vineyard Pinot Gris (Oregon) $25. Honeysuckle scents and flavors of pear, papaya and cucumber lead into a fresh and delicate wine, with plenty of acid behind the crisp fruit. 86 —*P.G. (11/15/2007)*

Gypsy Dancer 2005 A&G Estate Vineyard Pinot Noir (Dundee Hills) $60. My favorite of the 2005 releases from Gypsy Dancer, this is a complex wine that seems to be holding back, like a fine race horse at the starting gate. It's got the concentrated core of cherry fruit, which leads into mixed berries, toast, spice and more. A light earthy streak supports notes of root and soil, and the midpalate is a bit subdued, but the flavors come roaring back at the end, gaining strength and suggesting that this is a wine to cellar for some years. 91 Cellar Selection —*P.G. (11/15/2007)*

Gypsy Dancer 2002 A&G Estate Vineyard Pinot Noir (Oregon) $60. 88 *(11/1/2004)*

Gypsy Dancer 2005 Broadley Vineyard Pinot Noir (Dundee Hills) $43. A tart, cranberry- and raspberry-flavored wine, this young, high-acid style of Pinot has a charming, Burgundian feeling to it. The snappy red fruits are underscored with citrus, and the balance is disarmingly light, but not simple or dull. 88 —*P.G. (11/15/2007)*

Gypsy Dancer 2005 Cuvée Romy Pinot Noir (Oregon) $90. A very tight, tart and tannic Pinot Noir, almost impossible to open up despite hours of breathing. Acidic and unyielding, the rating is a compromise between what it is currently showing and what it hints at if you probe deeply enough. 88 —*P.G. (11/15/2007)*

Gypsy Dancer 2005 Gary & Christine's Vineyard Pinot Noir (Oregon) $43. Aromatic with soda pop scents of Dr. Pepper, cola and root beer, this is nonetheless a reasonably substantial wine, not a simple fruit bomb. It's lively and full of interesting flavors that suggest herb, root and spice; the wood remains a background flavor. 88 —*P.G. (11/15/2007)*

Gypsy Dancer 2002 Gary & Christine's Vineyard Pinot Noir (Oregon) $34. 83 *(11/1/2004)*

H. GRAY

H. Gray 2000 Cabernet Sauvignon (Yountville) $34. 85 —*S.H. (5/1/2004)*

H. Gray 1999 Cabernet Sauvignon (Yountville) $25. 92 Editors' Choice —*S.H. (8/1/2003)*

H. Gray 2000 Bad Boy Red Syrah-Cabernet (Yountville) $18. 86 —*S.H. (3/1/2004)*

H. Gray 2001 Bad Boy Zinfandel (Amador County) $20. 82 —*J.M. (4/1/2004)*

HACIENDA

Hacienda 1996 Cabernet Sauvignon (California) $8. 82 *(3/1/2000)*

Hacienda 1999 Clair de Lune Cabernet Sauvignon (California) $7. 83 —*S.H. (11/15/2002)*

Hacienda 2003 Johannisberg Riesling (California) $7. 84 Best Buy —*S.H. (12/31/2004)*

Hacienda 2002 Clair de Lune Merlot (California) $7. 84 Best Buy —*S.H. (12/31/2004)*

Hacienda 2003 Sauvignon Blanc (California) $7. 84 —*S.H. (10/1/2004)*

Hacienda 2002 Clair de Lune Sauvignon Blanc (California) $7. 83 —*S.H. (12/1/2004)*

Hacienda 1999 Clair de Lune Shiraz (California) $7. 85 Best Buy *(10/1/2001)*

HAGAFEN

Hagafen 1999 Cabernet Sauvignon (Napa Valley) $36. 84 —*J.M. (7/1/2002)*

Hagafen 2003 Estate Cabernet Sauvignon (Napa Valley) $40. Tasted against much more expensive young Napa Cabs, this bottling held up well. It shows very ripe cherry pie, blackberry, cassis and smoky oak flavors that are wrapped in sturdy, but softly ripe, tannins, making the wine immediately drinkable. 87 —*S.H. (5/1/2007)*

Hagafen 2002 Estate Cabernet Sauvignon (Napa Valley) $40. 83 —*S.H. (4/1/2005)*

Hagafen 2001 Estate Bottled Cabernet Sauvignon (Napa Valley) $40. 88 —*J.C. (4/1/2005)*

Hagafen NV Brut Cuvée Champagne Blend (Napa Valley) $24. 86 *(4/1/2001)*

Hagafen 2004 Chardonnay (Oak Knoll) $18. 80 *—S.H. (4/1/2006)*

Hagafen 2000 Chardonnay (Napa Valley) $18. 86 *—S.H. (9/1/2002)*

Hagafen 2005 Kosher Chardonnay (Oak Knoll) $21. Here's a rich, complex Chardonnay, made in the full-blown Burgundian way. The fruit itself gives layers of tropical guava, pineapple and nectarine flavors, while finely toasted oak adds caramel, buttered toast and spice flavors. With a creamy texture, it's a delicious wine all the way. **90** *—S.H. (5/1/2007)*

Hagafen 2003 Merlot (Napa Valley) $27. 82 *—S.H. (7/1/2006)*

Hagafen 1999 Merlot (Napa Valley) $27. 87 *—J.M. (6/1/2002)*

Hagafen 2002 Estate Bottled Merlot (Napa Valley) $27. 84 *—J.C. (4/1/2005)*

Hagafen 2005 Estate Pinot Noir (Napa Valley) $32. This is a nice Pinot that shows off the variety's dry silkiness in a showy way. It offers cola, cherry, rhubarb, pomegranate and herb tea flavors, with crisp acidity and enough tannins to accompany steaks and chops. **87** *—S.H. (5/1/2007)*

Hagafen 2004 Estate Pinot Noir (Napa Valley) $32. 83 *—S.H. (4/1/2006)*

Hagafen 2002 Estate Bottled Pinot Noir (Napa Valley) $24. 84 *—J.C. (4/1/2005)*

Hagafen 2004 Fagan Creek Block 38 Reserve Pinot Noir (Napa Valley) $50. 85 *—S.H. (7/1/2006)*

Hagafen 2005 Reserve Fagan Creek Vineyard Block 38 Pinot Noir (Napa Valley) $50. Hagafen has not been known for Pinot Noir, but someone over there is getting serious about it, to judge from this small production wine. It's a dry, ripe Pinot, with jammy kirsch and cassis flavors and a rich coating of oak. Finishes a little heavy, but it's a wine to watch. **89** *—S.H. (5/1/2007)*

Hagafen 2006 Ripken Vineyard Roussanne (Lodi) $18. A fresh, intriguing wine whose balance and depth suggest midterm aging. Golden in color, it's succulent in the flavors of peaches, pineapples, limes, almond biscotti and butterscotch, with fine acidity and a rich, honeyed finish. Give it until sometime in 2008 and for another couple of years. **87** *—S.H. (12/15/2007)*

Hagafen 2005 Sauvignon Blanc (Napa Valley) $15. 84 *—S.H. (7/1/2006)*

Hagafen 2004 Sauvignon Blanc (Napa Valley) $15. 88 *—S.H. (10/1/2005)*

Hagafen 2000 Sauvignon Blanc (Napa Valley) $13. 83 *—M.S. (4/1/2002)*

Hagafen 2001 Brut Cuvée Sparkling Blend (Napa Valley) $30. 86 *—S.H. (12/31/2005)*

Hagafen 2001 Brut Cuvée Late Disgorge Sparkling Blend (Napa Valley) $36. 84 *—S.H. (12/31/2005)*

Hagafen 2001 Syrah (Napa Valley) $27. 85 *—J.C. (4/1/2005)*

Hagafen 2000 Syrah (Napa Valley) $27. 88 *—J.M. (9/1/2002)*

Hagafen 1999 Syrah (Napa Valley) $NA. 90 *(11/1/2001)*

Hagafen 2003 Estate Syrah (Napa Valley) $29. This is an elegant wine, not without its faults, but it benefits from a smooth, plush mouthfeel. The berry-cherry fruit is complexed with various earthy elements, like dried leather, coffee, licorice and a spicy, sweet-and-sour tang that calls to mind tabasco. Best now–2007 for its freshness. **86** *—S.H. (5/1/2007)*

Hagafen 2005 White Riesling (Potter Valley) $16. 82 *—S.H. (7/1/2006)*

Hagafen 2004 White Riesling (Potter Valley) $19. 83 *—S.H. (4/1/2005)*

Hagafen 2005 Estate White Riesling (Napa Valley) $21. 84 *—S.H. (7/1/2006)*

Hagafen 2004 Zinfandel (Napa Valley) $29. This is a Cabernet-like Zin, meaning it has the elegance and balance of a fine red wine. It also means it does not have that overly hot, alcoholic, superripe Portiness that Zin can have, especially in a hot vintage like '04. Nice and dry, with spicy berry flavors, it's a good wine for game. **87** *—S.H. (5/1/2007)*

Hagafen 2004 Reserve Moskowite Ranch Block 61 Zinfandel (Napa Valley) $45. With jammy blackberry, blueberry, chocolate fudge and cassis flavors, this Zin is as rich and thick as a wine reduction sauce, something to pour over a filet of beef or ice cream. On its own, it's a bit simple. **84** *—S.H. (5/1/2007)*

HAGEN HEIGHTS

Hagen Heights 2004 Cabernet Sauvignon (Napa Valley) $48. Here's one for the cellar. You could drink it now, with a little decanting, but such is the structural youth that you'd miss this Bordeaux blend at its best. Rich and savory in spicy black and red currant, cherry and cedar flavors, the wine shows a firm tannic structure, with a crisp bite of acidity. Hold until late 2008; should evolve over the next 6–8 years. **90 Cellar Selection** *—S.H. (12/31/2007)*

Hagen Heights 2003 Cabernet Sauvignon (Napa Valley) $48. A very good Napa Cab. Rich and ripe in blackberry, cassis, cherry and new oak flavors, it's dry and balanced, with firm, sweet tannins and a nice bite of acidity. **91** *—S.H. (7/1/2007)*

Hagen Heights 2002 Cabernet Sauvignon (Napa Valley) $48. 93 Cellar Selection *—S.H. (5/1/2006)*

HAHN

Hahn 2002 Meritage Bordeaux Blend (Central Coast) $20. 88 *—S.H. (6/1/2004)*

Hahn 2003 Meritage Cabernet Blend (Central Coast) $20. 85 *—S.H. (11/1/2005)*

Hahn 2005 Cabernet Franc (Central Coast) $20. Call it country-style, with the minty sharpness and slightly sweet, candied raspberry, cherry and blackberry flavors. The acidity reprises on the finish, accentuating and harshening the tannins. **83** *—S.H. (12/15/2007)*

Hahn 2004 Cabernet Franc (Santa Lucia Highlands) $14. 84 *—S.H. (5/1/2006)*

Hahn 2005 Cabernet Sauvignon (Central Coast) $14. On the semisweet side, this has LifeSaver candy flavors of raspberries, cherries and blackberries, with greener notes of wintergreen and menthol. **82** *—S.H. (11/15/2007)*

Hahn 2004 Cabernet Sauvignon (Central Coast) $14. 84 *—S.H. (5/1/2006)*

Hahn 2003 Cabernet Sauvignon (Central Coast) $14. 83 *—S.H. (11/1/2005)*

Hahn 2002 Cabernet Sauvignon (Central Coast) $14. 83 *—S.H. (10/1/2004)*

Hahn 2001 Cabernet Sauvignon (Central Coast) $12. 84 *—S.H. (6/1/2003)*

Hahn 2005 Chardonnay (Monterey) $14. This is obviously made to appeal to a popular style. It's sharp in acidity, with pineapple, apricot and mineral flavors that are plastered over with caramelized oak. **84** *—S.H. (11/15/2007)*

Hahn 2004 Chardonnay (Monterey) $14. 86 *—S.H. (5/1/2006)*

Hahn 2003 Chardonnay (Monterey) $14. 86 *—S.H. (6/1/2005)*

Hahn 2002 Chardonnay (Monterey) $14. 90 *—S.H. (6/1/2004)*

Hahn 2001 Chardonnay (Monterey) $12. 86 *—S.H. (6/1/2003)*

Hahn 1998 Chardonnay (Monterey County) $12. 84 *—S.H. (10/1/2000)*

Hahn 2005 Meritage (Central Coast) $20. In its youth, this Bordeaux blend is dry and a little harsh, with a green, minty edge to the cherry fruit and oak. The acidity accentuates the tannins, which give the wine a hard finish. Not going anywhere, so drink now. **83** *—S.H. (12/15/2007)*

Hahn 2004 Meritage (Central Coast) $20. 87 *—S.H. (5/1/2006)*

Hahn 2001 Meritage (Central Coast) $18. 86 *—S.H. (8/1/2003)*

Hahn 1999 Meritage (Santa Lucia Highlands) $18. 87 *(9/1/2002)*

Hahn 2005 Merlot (Monterey) $14. Raw in texture, with a harsh, citrus acidity, this bone dry Merlot isn't fully ripe. The cherry flavors coexist with a minty greenness. **82** *—S.H. (11/15/2007)*

Hahn 2004 Merlot (Monterey) $14. 82 *—S.H. (5/1/2006)*

Hahn 2003 Merlot (Monterey) $14. 88 *—S.H. (11/1/2005)*

Hahn 2002 Merlot (Monterey) $14. 83 *—S.H. (10/1/2004)*

Hahn 2001 Merlot (Monterey) $12. 86 *—S.H. (8/1/2003)*

Hahn 1997 Merlot (Santa Lucia Highlands) $12. 86 *—L.W. (12/31/1999)*

Hahn 2005 Pinot Noir (Monterey) $20. Kind of sugary and herbal-minty, this Pinot's best feature is its silky texture. But it feels like the grapes were overcropped. The cherry fruit is pretty thin and green. **83** *—S.H. (12/1/2007)*

Hahn 2004 Pinot Noir (Monterey) $18. 87 *—S.H. (5/1/2006)*

Hahn 2005 Syrah (Central Coast) $15. Syrah-like, with cherry, leather and oaky-spice flavors, this wine is too semisweet and medicinal. **81** *—S.H. (11/15/2007)*

Hahn 2004 Syrah (Central Coast) $14. 83 *—S.H. (5/1/2006)*

Hahn 2003 Syrah (Central Coast) $14. 88 *—S.H. (6/1/2005)*

Hahn 2002 Syrah (Central Coast) $14. 84 *—S.H. (10/1/2004)*

Hahn 2001 Syrah (San Luis Obispo County) $12. 90 Best Buy *—S.H. (6/1/2003)*

HALL

Hall 2004 Cabernet Sauvignon (Napa Valley) $35. This has the plush texture and gorgeously ripe tannins that Napa Cabs specialize in. It's a little on the thin side, fruit-wise, with pleasant blackberry and oak flavors. Drink now. **86** *—S.H. (12/31/2007)*

Hall 2003 Cabernet Sauvignon (Napa Valley) $35. 85 *—S.H. (11/15/2006)*

Hall 2002 Cabernet Sauvignon (Napa Valley) $35. 86 *—S.H. (10/1/2005)*

Hall 2001 Cabernet Sauvignon (Napa Valley) $35. 93 Editors' Choice —*S.H. (10/1/2004)*

Hall 2003 T-bar-T Ranch Cabernet Sauvignon (Alexander Valley) $38.82 —*S.H. (11/15/2006)*

Hall 2004 Merlot (Napa Valley) $28. Overly sweet and sugary, this tastes like raspberry and cherry-pie filling. The 50% new oak, with caramel and butterscotch flavors, doesn't help. **81** —*S.H. (12/15/2007)*

Hall 2003 Merlot (Napa Valley) $28. 83 —*S.H. (11/15/2006)*

Hall 2002 Merlot (Napa Valley) $28. 86 —*S.H. (11/15/2005)*

Hall 2001 Merlot (Napa Valley) $28. 90 —*S.H. (9/1/2004)*

Hall 2004 Napa River Ranch Merlot (Napa Valley) $50. This '04 is off a beat from the '03, showing a tiredness that may be a result of the heat. It's soft, with candied blackberry and cherry flavors that finish dry, and is not ageworthy. **86** —*S.H. (12/15/2007)*

Hall 2003 Napa River Ranch Merlot (Napa Valley) $50. 87 —*S.H. (12/15/2006)*

Hall 2006 Sauvignon Blanc (Napa Valley) $20. A classy wine, made Sancerre-style, with high acidity, a delicate mouthfeel and a dry finish. The acidity energizes the palate, working through lime and mineral flavors, and picking up a rich note of savory figs on the finish. **90** —*S.H. (10/1/2007)*

Hall 2005 Sauvignon Blanc (Napa Valley) $20. 90 —*S.H. (11/1/2006)*

Hall 2004 Sauvignon Blanc (Napa Valley) $20. 86 —*S.H. (11/15/2005)*

Hall 2003 Sauvignon Blanc (Napa Valley) $20. 86 —*S.H. (12/31/2004)*

HALLAUER

Hallauer 2002 Syrah (Santa Ynez Valley) $21. 87 *(9/1/2005)*

HALLCREST VINEYARDS

Hallcrest Vineyards 2001 Clos de Jeannie Red Blend (California) $15. 84 —*S.H. (11/15/2003)*

HALLECK

Halleck 2005 Hallberg Vineyard Pinot Noir (Russian River Valley) $55. This is the most structurally tannic of Halleck's current trio of Pinots, although it's easy enough to drink tonight. Those tannins frame ripe flavors of cherry jam, cola, rhubarb pie, mocha, new oak and Asian spice, and the texture is pure silk and satin. Deliciously gentle, it's a wine that changes in the glass as it airs and warms. **93** —*S.H. (6/1/2007)*

Halleck 2005 The Farm Vineyards Pinot Noir (Russian River Valley) $55. Here's a big, bold Pinot Noir, the kind that's been much discussed in critical circles over the years for not being "typical." No, it's not Burgundy. It could almost be Grenache, it's so rich and ripe in almost sweet cherry-filled chocolate candy flavors. But there's no denying the deliciousness factor, while the acidity is just right to make it clean and balanced. **90** —*S.H. (6/1/2007)*

Halleck 2005 Three Sons Cuvee Pinot Noir (Russian River Valley) $38. Halleck has established itself as a notable Pinot player in the valley, crafting wines made solidly in the New World style of soft, ripe, complicated flavors. Here the fruit brims in cherries, pomegranates, root beer, cola and new oak, wrapped into a classically silky, seductive mouthfeel. Undoubtedly this wine is best in its youth. **90** —*S.H. (6/1/2007)*

Halleck 2005 Little Sister Sauvignon Blanc (Russian River Valley) $28. This is a very fine Sauvignon Blanc. It reminds me of Rochioli's, so ripe and complex in apple, peach, citrus and melon flavors, although this one's sweeter. A touch of oak adds smoky cream and vanilla. For the technically minded, the acidity is 7.7 grams per liter, which is quite high for a California wine. **91 Editors' Choice** —*S.H. (6/1/2007)*

HALO

HaLo 1997 Cabernet Sauvignon (Napa Valley) $125. 93 —*S.H. (12/1/2001)*

HALTER RANCH

Halter Ranch 2004 Estate Cabernet Sauvignon (Paso Robles) $28. This is really a lovely Paso-style Bordeaux blend. With Cab Franc, Malbec and Merlot, it offers delicious cherry, cassis, raspberry, cocoa, vanilla and smoked oak flavors, and while it's soft in acids, the firm tannins provide good structure and grip. Drink now. **87** —*S.H. (9/1/2007)*

Halter Ranch 2004 Estate Syrah (Paso Robles) $28. It's all about fruit and softness in this Syrah, which has a little Mourvèdre, Grenache and Petit Verdot, of all things. Floods the mouth with intense blackberry, black cherry, cappuccino, milk chocolate, spicy vanilla and white pepper flavors, with just enough of a tannic edge for palate-stimulating balance. **88** —*S.H. (9/1/2007)*

HAMACHER

Hamacher 2000 Cuvée Forêts Diverses Chardonnay (Oregon) $25. 91 Editors' Choice —*P.G. (9/1/2003)*

Hamacher 1999 Cuvée Forêts Diverses Chardonnay (Oregon) $25. 89 —*P.G. (8/1/2002)*

Hamacher 2002 Cuvée Forêts Diverses Chardonnay (Willamette Valley) $30. 91 *(9/1/2006)*

Hamacher 1996 Cuvée Forêts Diverses Chardonnay (Willamette Valley) $NA. 88 *(9/1/2006)*

Hamacher 2002 Pinot Noir (Willamette Valley) $40. 92 Editors' Choice *(9/1/2006)*

Hamacher 2001 Pinot Noir (Willamette Valley) $30. 90 *(9/1/2006)*

Hamacher 2000 Pinot Noir (Willamette Valley) $38. 90 —*P.G. (3/11/2003)*

Hamacher 2000 Pinot Noir (Willamette Valley) $NA. 88 *(9/1/2006)*

Hamacher 1999 Pinot Noir (Willamette Valley) $NA. 90 *(9/1/2006)*

Hamacher 1998 Pinot Noir (Willamette Valley) $NA. 90 *(9/1/2006)*

Hamacher 1997 Pinot Noir (Willamette Valley) $NA. 87 *(9/1/2006)*

Hamacher 1996 Pinot Noir (Willamette Valley) $NA. 89 *(9/1/2006)*

Hamacher 1995 Pinot Noir (Willamette Valley) $NA. 92 *(9/1/2006)*

Hamacher 2004 H Pinot Noir (Willamette Valley) $20. 86 —*P.G. (12/1/2006)*

Hamacher 1997 Willamette Valley Pinot Noir (Willamette Valley) $30. 91 *(10/1/1999)*

Hamacher 2006 Pinot Noir Rosé Pinot Noir (Oregon) $17. This is very fresh, with young and pretty flavors of cherry and strawberry. It suggests perfectly picked, immaculately clean fruit was used. The bright, sweet cherry flavors are backed with lightly chocolaty tannins. Immaculate and zesty, this is a real delight. **88** —*P.G. (7/1/2007)*

HAMES VALLEY VINEYARDS

Hames Valley Vineyards 2001 Cabernet Franc (Monterey) $19. 84 —*S.H. (10/1/2004)*

Hames Valley Vineyards 2001 Cabernet Sauvignon (Monterey) $19. 84 —*S.H. (10/1/2004)*

Hames Valley Vineyards 2001 Merlot (Monterey) $19. 84 —*S.H. (10/1/2004)*

Hames Valley Vineyards 2003 Sauvignon Blanc (Monterey) $15. 84 —*S.H. (10/1/2004)*

Hames Valley Vineyards 2000 Syrah (Monterey) $25. 5 —*S.H. (6/1/2005)*

HANDLEY

Handley 1995 Blanc de Blancs Champagne Blend (Anderson Valley) $30. 86 —*S.H. (12/15/2000)*

Handley 1994 Blanc De Blancs Champagne Blend (Anderson Valley) $25. 88 —*S.H. (12/1/2000)*

Handley 1997 Brut Champagne Blend (Anderson Valley) $29. 88 —*S.H. (12/1/2002)*

Handley 1996 Brut Champagne Blend (Anderson Valley) $17. 86 —*S.H. (12/1/2001)*

Handley 1995 Brut Champagne Blend (Anderson Valley) $25. 88 —*S.H. (12/1/2000)*

Handley 1994 Brut Champagne Blend (Anderson Valley) $25. 89 —*L.W. (12/1/1999)*

Handley 1997 Brut Rosé Champagne Blend (Anderson Valley) $28. 89 *(6/1/2001)*

Handley 1996 Brut Rosé Champagne Blend (Anderson Valley) $25. 92 —*S.H. (12/1/2000)*

Handley 1998 Chardonnay (Dry Creek Valley) $20. 85 *(6/1/2000)*

Handley 1997 Chardonnay (Dry Creek Valley) $16. 88 —*S.H. (10/1/1999)*

Handley 2001 Chardonnay (Anderson Valley) $16. 88 —*S.H. (8/1/2003)*

Handley 2001 Chardonnay (Sonoma County) $18. 86 —*S.H. (8/1/2003)*

Handley 1999 Chardonnay (Anderson Valley) $17. 85 —*S.H. (11/15/2001)*

Handley 2005 Estate Chardonnay (Anderson Valley) $20. You can really taste that cool-climate Anderson Valley acidity. There's also a minerality to the citrus and sweet oak flavors. Finishes a little austere, but elegant. Drink now. **85** —*S.H. (12/31/2007)*

Handley 2003 Estate Chardonnay (Anderson Valley) $19. 87 —*S.H. (5/1/2006)*

Handley 2000 Estate Chardonnay (Anderson Valley) $17. 86 —*S.H. (12/15/2002)*

Handley 2005 Handley Vineyard Chardonnay (Dry Creek Valley) $20. Kind of simple and sweet, like oaky apple and pear juice. Needs greater dryness and complexity. **83** —*S.H. (12/31/2007)*

Handley 2004 Handley Vineyard Chardonnay (Dry Creek Valley) $19. 87 —*S.H. (12/15/2006)*

Handley 2003 Handley Vineyard Chardonnay (Dry Creek Valley) $18. 91 —*S.H. (10/1/2005)*

Handley 2000 Handley Vineyard Chardonnay (Dry Creek Valley) $19. 84 —*S.H. (12/15/2002)*

Handley 1999 Handley Vineyard Chardonnay (Dry Creek Valley) $19. 86 —*S.H. (11/15/2001)*

Handley 2006 Gewürztraminer (Anderson Valley) $18. With spicy orange, pineapple, candied ginger and honeysuckle flower flavors, this is a tasty Gewürz. It's not officially sweet, but so soft in acidity that the slight residual sugar is magnified, making it taste almost off-dry. 85 —*S.H. (12/31/2007)*

Handley 2004 Gewürztraminer (Anderson Valley) $16. 83 —*S.H. (12/1/2005)*

Handley 2002 Gewürztraminer (Anderson Valley) $15. 85 —*S.H. (12/31/2003)*

Handley 2001 Gewürztraminer (Anderson Valley) $15. 88 —*S.H. (9/1/2003)*

Handley 2000 Gewürztraminer (Anderson Valley) $14. 85 —*S.H. (11/15/2001)*

Handley 2006 Pinot Gris (Anderson Valley) $18. Crisp and a little sweet, almost off-dry, this has jammy pineapple, peach, apricot and vanilla flavors. The sweetness will nicely balance the spicy heat of Vietnamese fare. 85 —*S.H. (12/31/2007)*

Handley 2004 Pinot Gris (Anderson Valley) $16. 85 —*S.H. (2/1/2006)*

Handley 2002 Pinot Gris (Anderson Valley) $16. 86 —*S.H. (12/1/2003)*

Handley 2001 Pinot Gris (Anderson Valley) $16. 86 —*S.H. (9/1/2003)*

Handley 2000 Pinot Gris (Anderson Valley) $16. 88 —*S.H. (11/15/2001)*

Handley 1999 Pinot Gris (Anderson Valley) $16. 87 —*S.H. (8/1/2001)*

Handley 2000 Pinot Meunier (Anderson Valley) $21. 82 —*S.H. (12/1/2002)*

Handley 1999 Pinot Mystére Pinot Meunier (Anderson Valley) $20. 83 —*S.H. (11/15/2001)*

USA

Handley 2005 Pinot Noir (Anderson Valley) $30. Here's a pretty Pinot that captures the balanced terroir of Anderson Valley. It's not a big, ageworthy wine, more of a village-type, but elegant and savory in cherry, cola and spice flavors. The crispness makes it an exceptionally food-friendly red wine. 88 —*S.H. (12/31/2007)*

Handley 2004 Pinot Noir (Mendocino County) $19. 84 —*S.H. (7/1/2006)*

Handley 2003 Pinot Noir (Mendocino County) $16. 84 —*S.H. (3/1/2006)*

Handley 2003 Pinot Noir (Anderson Valley) $25. 87 —*S.H. (3/1/2006)*

Handley 2002 Pinot Noir (Anderson Valley) $23. 86 —*S.H. (11/1/2004)*

Handley 2002 Pinot Noir (Mendocino County) $18. 85 —*S.H. (11/1/2004)*

Handley 2001 Pinot Noir (Anderson Valley) $25. 87 —*S.H. (4/1/2004)*

Handley 2001 Pinot Noir (Anderson Valley) $13. 85 —*S.H. (9/1/2003)*

Handley 2000 Pinot Noir (Anderson Valley) $25. 89 **Editors' Choice** *(10/1/2002)*

Handley 1999 Pinot Noir (Anderson Valley) $26. 88 —*S.H. (7/1/2002)*

Handley 1998 Brut Rosé Pinot Noir (Anderson Valley) $29. 86 —*S.H. (12/1/2001)*

Handley 2001 Estate Reserve Pinot Noir (Anderson Valley) $23. 89 —*S.H. (12/1/2004)*

Handley 1999 Estate Reserve Pinot Noir (Anderson Valley) $49. 82 *(10/1/2002)*

Handley 1998 Reserve Pinot Noir (Anderson Valley) $48. 88 —*S.H. (12/15/2001)*

Handley 2000 River Road Vineyard Pinot Noir (Santa Lucia Highlands) $21. 85 *(10/1/2002)*

Handley 2003 Rosé Pinot Noir (Mendocino County) $NA. 85 —*S.H. (12/1/2004)*

Handley 2004 Rosé Pinot Noir (Anderson Valley) $16. 84 —*S.H. (12/1/2005)*

Handley 2002 Riesling (Mendocino) $12. 87 —*J.M. (8/1/2003)*

Handley 2006 White Riesling (Mendocino County) $18. This very nice Riesling captures the grape's pure essence. It's very dry and acidic, with a wealth of flower, mineral and yellow apricot flavors. Finishes with balance and elegance. 89 —*S.H. (9/1/2007)*

Handley 2000 Rosé Blend (Anderson Valley) $12. 87 —*S.H. (11/15/2001)*

Handley 2004 Sauvignon Blanc (Dry Creek Valley) $16. 87 —*S.H. (12/15/2006)*

Handley 2001 Ferrington Vineyard Sauvignon Blanc (Anderson Valley) $14. 90 —*S.H. (3/1/2003)*

Handley 2000 Ferrington Vineyard Sauvignon Blanc (Anderson Valley) $15. 86 —*S.H. (9/1/2002)*

Handley 1999 Ferrington Vineyard Sauvignon Blanc (Anderson Valley) $14. 88 —*S.H. (11/15/2001)*

Handley 2006 Handley Vineyard Sauvignon Blanc (Dry Creek Valley) $15. With searing acidity and minerally citrus flavors, this bone dry Sauvignon is a great cocktail sipper with hors d'oeuvres like potstickers or crudité. 87 —*S.H. (11/15/2007)*

Handley 2003 Handley Vineyard Sauvignon Blanc (Dry Creek Valley) $14. 88 —*S.H. (10/1/2005)*

Handley 2002 Handley Vineyard Sauvignon Blanc (Dry Creek Valley) $15. 86 —*S.H. (2/1/2004)*

Handley 2001 Handley Vineyard Sauvignon Blanc (Dry Creek Valley) $14. 87 —*S.H. (3/1/2003)*

Handley 2000 Brut Sparkling Blend (Anderson Valley) $32. 84 —*S.H. (6/1/2006)*

Handley 1998 Brut Sparkling Blend (Anderson Valley) $29. 89 —*S.H. (12/1/2003)*

Handley 2003 Syrah (Mendocino County) $20. 85 —*S.H. (7/1/2006)*

Handley 2002 Syrah (Mendocino County) $20. 85 —*S.H. (2/1/2005)*

Handley 2003 Zinfandel (Mendocino County) $20. 84 —*S.H. (7/1/2006)*

Handley 2002 Zinfandel (Redwood Valley) $20. 86 —*S.H. (2/1/2005)*

Handley 2001 Zinfandel (Redwood Valley) $20. 86 —*S.H. (3/1/2004)*

Handley 2000 Williams Vineyard Zinfandel (Anderson Valley) $26. 86 —*S.H. (5/1/2002)*

HANGTIME

Hangtime 2003 Chardonnay (Edna Valley) $15. 85 —*S.H. (7/1/2006)*

HANNA

Hanna 2001 Two Ranch Red Wine Cabernet Blend (Sonoma County) $22. 84 —*S.H. (8/1/2005)*

Hanna 2004 Cabernet Sauvignon (Alexander Valley) $30. Balance and complexity are the hallmarks of this Cab from veteran producer Hanna. It's deep and long in spicy, oaky blackberry and cherry fruit, while the structure is defined by soft tannins and good acids. Delicious now, and should hold for a decade. 90 —*S.H. (12/15/2007)*

Hanna 2000 Cabernet Sauvignon (Alexander Valley) $26. 86 *(11/15/2003)*

Hanna 1999 Cabernet Sauvignon (Alexander Valley) $25. 86 —*S.H. (6/1/2002)*

Hanna 1998 Cabernet Sauvignon (Alexander Valley) $24. 88 —*J.M. (6/1/2002)*

Hanna 1996 Cabernet Sauvignon (Sonoma County) $21. 90 *(11/15/1999)*

Hanna 2001 Bismark Mountain Vineyard Cabernet Sauvignon (Sonoma Valley) $61. 85 —*S.H. (11/1/2005)*

Hanna 2002 Estate Grown Cabernet Sauvignon (Sonoma County) $31. 84 —*S.H. (10/1/2005)*

Hanna 2001 Estate Grown Cabernet Sauvignon (Sonoma County) $27. 88 —*S.H. (6/1/2004)*

Hanna 1998 Hanna Red Ranch Reserve Cabernet Sauvignon (Alexander Valley) $48. 87 —*S.H. (6/1/2002)*

Hanna 2003 Proprietor Grown Cabernet Sauvignon (Sonoma County) $30. 87 —*S.H. (3/1/2006)*

Hanna 2005 Chardonnay (Russian River Valley) $20. Bright and zesty in acidity, this has ripe tropical fruit and tobacco flavors, with a smoky, caramelized finish. It's a little on the rustic side. Drink now. 84 —*S.H. (7/1/2007)*

Hanna 2004 Chardonnay (Russian River Valley) $19. 88 —*S.H. (3/1/2006)*

Hanna 2001 Chardonnay (Russian River Valley) $18. 87 —*S.H. (12/1/2003)*

Hanna 2000 Chardonnay (Russian River Valley) $19. 87 —*S.H. (5/1/2002)*

Hanna 2002 Estate Grown Chardonnay (Russian River Valley) $18. 89 —*S.H. (6/1/2004)*

Hanna 1998 Proprietor Grown Chardonnay (Russian River Valley) $17. 85 *(6/1/2000)*

Hanna 1999 Merlot (Alexander Valley) $25. 88 —*S.H. (9/1/2002)*

Hanna 1999 Bismark Ranch Merlot (Sonoma County) $50. 88 *(5/1/2004)*

Hanna 1997 Proprietor Grown Merlot (Sonoma County) $22. 84 *—J.C. (6/1/2001)*

Hanna 1999 Pinot Noir (Russian River Valley) $22. 85 *—S.H. (5/1/2002)*

Hanna 2004 Estate Pinot Noir (Russian River Valley) $29. 84 *—S.H. (12/1/2006)*

Hanna 2002 Estate Grown Pinot Noir (Russian River Valley) $27. 85 *(11/1/2004)*

Hanna 1999 Bismark Ranch Sangiovese (Sonoma County) $50. 91 *—D.T. (6/1/2002)*

Hanna 1998 Sauvignon Blanc (Russian River Valley) $12. 85 *—S.H. (11/1/1999)*

Hanna 2004 Sauvignon Blanc (Russian River Valley) $17. 81 *—S.H. (11/1/2005)*

Hanna 1999 Reserve Sauvignon Blanc (Russian River Valley) $24. 88 *—S.H. (9/1/2002)*

Hanna 2005 Slusser Road Vineyard Sauvignon Blanc (Russian River Valley) $17. 88 *—S.H. (7/1/2006)*

Hanna 2002 Slusser Road Vineyard Sauvignon Blanc (Russian River Valley) $16. 87 *—S.H. (6/1/2004)*

Hanna 2001 Slusser Road Vineyard Sauvignon Blanc (Russian River Valley) $16. 85 *—S.H. (9/1/2003)*

Hanna 2000 Slusser Road Vineyard Sauvignon Blanc (Russian River Valley) $16. 88 *—J.M. (11/15/2001)*

Hanna 1999 Bismark Ranch Syrah (Sonoma Valley) $48. 82 *—S.H. (8/1/2005)*

Hanna 2004 Bismark Mountain Vineyard Zinfandel (Sonoma Valley) $51. Way too sweet for a table wine. Hard to tell if it's the 16% alcohol or residual sugar, maybe both. Too soft. **81** *—S.H. (9/1/2007)*

Hanna 2002 Bismark Mountain Vineyard Zinfandel (Sonoma Valley) $51. \86 *—S.H. (7/1/2006)*

Hanna 1999 Bismark Ranch Zinfandel (Sonoma Valley) $49. 92 *—S.H. (7/1/2002)*

Hanna 1997 Bismark Ranch Zinfandel (Sonoma Valley) $45. 88 *—P.G. (3/1/2001)*

Hanna 2003 Proprietor Grown Zinfandel (Alexander Valley) $20. 86 *—S.H. (11/1/2005)*

Hanna 2001 Proprietor Grown Zinfandel (Alexander Valley) $46. 89 *—J.M. (11/1/2003)*

HANS FAHDEN

Hans Fahden 2003 Mountain Cuvee Cabernet Sauvignon (Sonoma County) $28. This is a new winery for me, and it's a promising start. The wine is decadently rich in cassis, cherries, milk chocolate and vanilla flavors, but it has the structural integrity of a fine wine. While acidity is soft, the tannins have the grip of cherry skins, while oak adds its own tannic complexities. **88** *—S.H. (9/1/2007)*

HANZELL

Hanzell 2004 Chardonnay (Sonoma Valley) $65. Massive, complex, with amazing depth, an opulent, voluptuous wine of tremendous power and authority. It's so beautiful now, you almost hesitate to cellar it, but these Hanzell Chards are built for the long haul. Positively volcanic in tropical fruit and toasty new oak, with a honeyed, caramel finish. Absolutely stunning. **96 Editors' Choice** *—S.H. (5/1/2007)*

Hanzell 2003 Chardonnay (Sonoma Valley) $65. 92 *—S.H. (11/15/2006)*

Hanzell 2002 Chardonnay (Sonoma Valley) $55. 90 Cellar Selection *—S.H. (12/15/2005)*

Hanzell 2001 Chardonnay (Sonoma Valley) $55. 94 *—S.H. (12/31/2004)*

Hanzell 1999 Chardonnay (Sonoma Valley) $50. 93 *—S.H. (9/1/2002)*

Hanzell 1997 Chardonnay (Sonoma Valley) $42. 92 *—S.H. (11/15/2000)*

Hanzell 2003 Pinot Noir (Sonoma Valley) $87. It's a solid effort, but finishes a bit thin in cherry and cola fruit. Still, it's an elegant wine, showing typical Hanzell balance of fruit, oak, acids and tannins. Could gain a little complexity over the next five years. **87** *—S.H. (4/1/2007)*

Hanzell 2002 Pinot Noir (Sonoma Valley) $85. 88 *—S.H. (11/15/2006)*

Hanzell 2001 Pinot Noir (Sonoma Valley) $85. 95 Editors' Choice *—S.H. (12/15/2005)*

Hanzell 2000 Pinot Noir (Sonoma Valley) $75. 90 *—S.H. (2/1/2005)*

Hanzell 1998 Pinot Noir (Sonoma Valley) $58. 87 *—S.H. (2/1/2003)*

Hanzell 1997 Pinot Noir (Sonoma Valley) $50. 94 Cellar Selection *—S.H. (12/15/2001)*

HAPPY CAMPER

Happy Camper 2004 Cabernet Sauvignon (California) $9. If you want something properly varietal, fruity and balanced, this Cabernet will pull it off. **84** *—S.H. (3/1/2007)*

Happy Camper 2005 Chardonnay (California) $9. Not the richest wine in history, but fruity enough and dry, this basic Chardonnay has a tease of citrus fruit and vanilla cream. It's perfectly okay for that next big party where no one's overly critical. **84** *—S.H. (3/1/2007)*

Happy Camper 2004 Merlot (California) $9. Decent price for a nice Merlot. It's a little light on cherry-berry fruit, but balanced and clean, with polished tannins and crisp acidity to cut through beef, veal and pork. **84** *—S.H. (3/1/2007)*

HARBINGER

Harbinger 2002 Chardonnay (Napa Valley) $14. 85 *—S.H. (2/1/2004)*

Harbinger 2001 Merlot (Napa Valley) $14. 86 *—S.H. (5/1/2004)*

HARGRAVE

Hargrave 1999 Cabernet Franc (North Fork of Long Island) $17. 81 *—J.C. (1/1/2004)*

Hargrave 1999 Chardonnay (North Fork of Long Island) $14. 83 *—J.C. (1/1/2004)*

Hargrave 1998 Chardonnay (North Fork of Long Island) $14. 82 *—J.C. (4/1/2001)*

Hargrave NV Chardonette/White Blend Chardonnay (North Fork of Long Island) $7. 83 *—J.C. (4/1/2001)*

Hargrave 1998 Reserve Chardonnay (North Fork of Long Island) $18. 88 *—J.C. (4/1/2001)*

Hargrave 1999 Merlot (North Fork of Long Island) $18. 81 *—J.C. (1/1/2004)*

Hargrave 1998 Merlot (North Fork of Long Island) $18. 82 *—J.C. (4/1/2001)*

Hargrave 1998 Pinot Noir (North Fork of Long Island) $35. 84 *—J.C. (4/1/2001)*

Hargrave NV Fleurette Rosé Blend (North Fork of Long Island) $10. 83 *—J.C. (4/1/2001)*

Hargrave 1999 Sauvignon Blanc (North Fork of Long Island) $11. 85 *—J.C. (4/1/2001)*

HARLAN ESTATE

Harlan Estate 2004 Bordeaux Blend (Napa Valley) $350. The price is prerelease; it will soar on the aftermarket. This is very great Harlan. It pours dark and saturated, and the tannins are big and sturdy, not aggressive, but sweet and finely ground. Still, they give a hardness to the immaculately ripe fruit that mandates cellaring. The flavors of currants, blackberries, plums, chocolate and cedar are lush, deep and long-lasting, but just a part of the balanced appeal of this young wine. It really defines the exquisite tension between power and elegance. Best after 2008, then for many years. **98 Cellar Selection** *—S.H. (12/1/2007)*

Harlan Estate 2003 Cabernet Blend (Napa Valley) $265. Another spectacular Harlan hits the market. It shows the earthy quality that marks wines off the estate, with an aroma suggesting a warm bale of hay under the summer sun, a sweet straw and bay laurel scent that adds savory richness to the cherry, blackberry and chocolate flavors. As usual, the tannins are virtual perfection, at once sweet and firm, dense and fine, perfectly in balance with all the fruit and new oak. So young now, a fat little baby of a wine that's irresistible, but will hold and improve well beyond its tenth birthday. **98** *—S.H. (2/1/2007)*

Harlan Estate 2002 Cabernet Blend (Napa Valley) $245. 99 Cellar Selection *—S.H. (9/1/2006)*

Harlan Estate 2000 Cabernet Sauvignon (Napa Valley) $300. 98 Cellar Selection *—S.H. (11/15/2004)*

Harlan Estate 1999 Red Blend (Napa Valley) $200. 96 *—J.M. (7/1/2003)*

HARLEQUIN

Harlequin 2003 Claret Bordeaux Blend (Columbia Valley (WA)) $18. Shows deep color and concentration. The nose carries the strength of the fruity richness, effusive with ripe berry and cherry scents, along with a whiff of chocolate. Everything is balanced—fruit, acid, tannin and oak—and the wine stands up a bit stiffly right now but shows good concentration. Should continue to improve over the next five or six years. Blend of 59% Cab Sauvignon, 35% Merlot, 6% Cab Franc. **88** *—P.G. (3/1/2007)*

Harlequin 2003 Cuvée Alexander Bordeaux Blend (Columbia Valley (WA)) $29. The Cuvée Alexander blend is 36% Cabernet Sauvignon, 55% Merlot and 9% Cab Franc. Dark and roasted, thick and jammy, it bursts with ripe blackberry fruit flavors. This rich, expansive fruit is nicely matched to toasty oak, laced with layers of smoke, coffee grounds and licorice. **90** *—P.G. (3/1/2007)*

Harlequin 2003 Minick Vineyard Syrah (Yakima Valley) $28. 91 *—P.G. (12/15/2005)*

Harlequin 2003 Sundance Vineyard Syrah (Columbia Valley (WA)) $28. 91 *—P.G. (12/15/2005)*

Harlequin 2002 Sundance Vineyard Syrah (Columbia Valley (WA)) $30. 85 *(9/1/2005)*

HARLOW RIDGE

Harlow Ridge 2003 Coastal Vines Cabernet Sauvignon (Lodi) $10. 84 *—S.H. (12/15/2006)*

Harlow Ridge 2005 Chardonnay (Lodi) $10. 83 *—S.H. (12/1/2006)*

Harlow Ridge 2005 Pinot Grigio (Lodi) $10. 85 Best Buy *—S.H. (12/15/2006)*

Harlow Ridge 2005 Pinot Noir (Lodi) $10. 83 *—S.H. (12/1/2006)*

HARMONIQUE

Harmonique 2002 Delicacé Pinot Noir (Anderson Valley) $48. 90 *—S.H. (11/1/2005)*

Harmonique 2004 The Noble One Pinot Noir (Anderson Valley) $50. The near-perfect marriage of acidity and fruit stars in this dramatically structured wine. The flavors, of red cherries and ripe red plums, are pure as can be, and that crispness boosts and brightens them to starburst quality. Lots of oak adds a delicious finish of toast, sweet vanilla and spice. Absolutely gorgeous Pinot Noir. **94** *—S.H. (11/1/2007)*

Harmonique 2002 The Noble One Pinot Noir (Anderson Valley) $48. 92 *—S.H. (11/1/2005)*

HARMONY CELLARS

Harmony Cellars 2002 Diamond Reserve Aria Cabernet Blend (Paso Robles) $38. 80 *—S.H. (7/1/2006)*

Harmony Cellars 2003 Merlot (Paso Robles) $16. 82 *—S.H. (10/1/2006)*

Harmony Cellars 2004 Diamond Reserve Pinot Gris (California) $22. 80 *—S.H. (2/1/2006)*

Harmony Cellars 2002 Zinfandel (Paso Robles) $18. 84 *—S.H. (8/1/2005)*

Harmony Cellars 2001 Zinfandel (Paso Robles) $16. 81 *(11/1/2003)*

HARRINGTON

Harrington 2005 Brosseau Vineyard Pinot Noir (Chalone) $50. Not much going on with this Pinot. Smells thin, tastes thin, with tart acidity that's accentuated by the lack of generosity. Has just enough cherry cola and fruit to score at the bottom of our "good" scale. **83** *—S.H. (9/1/2007)*

Harrington 2005 Galante Vineyard Pinot Noir (Russian River Valley) $35. Too much acidity in this dry, fruity Pinot. Pale in color, it shows silky tannins and nice cherry, cola and spicy oak flavors, but that minty sharpness is awkward. **84** *—S.H. (9/1/2007)*

Harrington 2005 Gap's Crown Pinot Noir (Sonoma Coast) $38. Some Pinots can handle high alcohol. This one feels hot and sweet, not in sugar but in alcohol and glycerine. It merits this score because the tart-like cherry, cocoapuff and cinnamon flavors taste good, but it really needs greater balance. **85** *—S.H. (9/1/2007)*

Harrington 2002 Hirsch Vineyard Pinot Noir (Sonoma Coast) $54. 93 *—S.H. (8/1/2005)*

Harrington 2005 Lund Vineyard Pinot Noir (Carneros) $30. I love the silkiness and delicacy that defines this Pinot's mouthfeel. Also nice is the dryness. Taste-wise, it could use more concentration, as the rhubarbs, pomegranates and cola are a little thin and weedy. **86** *—S.H. (9/1/2007)*

HARRIS

Harris 2003 Jake's Creek Vineyard Cabernet Sauvignon (Napa Valley) $75. 93 *—S.H. (12/31/2006)*

Harris 2003 Treva's Vineyard Cabernet Sauvignon (Napa Valley) $95. 91 Cellar Selection *—S.H. (12/31/2006)*

HARRISON

Harrison 2001 Estate Reserve Cabernet Sauvignon (Napa Valley) $80. 91 Cellar Selection *—S.H. (10/1/2004)*

Harrison 1999 Reserve Cabernet Sauvignon (Napa Valley) $100. 91 *—S.H. (11/15/2003)*

Harrison 1997 Reserve Cabernet Sauvignon (Napa Valley) $100. 94 *(11/1/2000)*

Harrison 2000 Reserve Chardonnay (Napa Valley) $45. 85 *—S.H. (8/1/2004)*

Harrison 1998 Reserve Chardonnay (Napa Valley) $59. 90 *(7/1/2001)*

Harrison 2001 Merlot (Napa Valley) $40. 93 *—S.H. (8/1/2004)*

Harrison 2000 Merlot (Napa Valley) $40. 90 *—S.H. (12/31/2003)*

Harrison 2001 Claret Red Blend (Napa Valley) $37. 89 *—S.H. (3/1/2005)*

Harrison 2000 Claret Red Blend (Napa Valley) $37. 89 *—S.H. (11/15/2003)*

Harrison 2001 Syrah (Napa Valley) $33. 91 *—S.H. (3/1/2005)*

Harrison 2001 Zebra Zinfandel (North Coast) $23. 88 *(11/1/2003)*

HARRISON CLARKE

Harrison Clarke 2005 Grenache (Santa Ynez Valley) $27. This is an extraordinarily lush and complex Syrah, but I have one major objection. From the Ballard Canyon section of the valley, it has 4% Syrah, and a small percentage of new oak that adds a smoky, caramelly richness to the blackberry, cherry and raspberry fruit flavors. My problem is the sweetness. It tastes like there's residual sugar, pushing the wine beyond table status into dessert territory. **85** *—S.H. (12/1/2007)*

HART WINERY

Hart Winery 2002 Syrah (South Coast) $24. 89 *(9/1/2005)*

Hart Winery 1999 Syrah (Temecula) $24. 94 *—S.H. (4/1/2002)*

Hart Winery 1998 Syrah (Temecula) $24. 85 *(11/1/2001)*

Hart Winery 2002 Volcanic Ridge Vineyard Syrah (Temecula) $32. 90 Editors' Choice *(9/1/2005)*

HARTFORD

Hartford 2004 Chardonnay (Sonoma Coast) $25. 92 Editors' Choice *—S.H. (5/1/2006)*

Hartford 2000 Chardonnay (Sonoma Coast) $22. 90 *(7/1/2002)*

Hartford 2000 Laura's Chardonnay (Sonoma Coast) $54. 93 *(8/1/2003)*

Hartford 1999 Laura's Chardonnay (Sonoma Coast) $54. 93 *(7/1/2001)*

Hartford 2000 Seascape Vineyard Chardonnay (Sonoma Coast) $50. 91 *(8/1/2003)*

Hartford 1999 Seascape Vineyard Chardonnay (Sonoma County) $46. 87 *(7/1/2001)*

Hartford 2000 Stone Côte Vineyard Chardonnay (Sonoma Coast) $29. 90 Editors' Choice *(8/1/2003)*

Hartford 1999 Stone Côte Vineyard Chardonnay (Sonoma County) $33. 91 *(7/1/2001)*

Hartford 1999 Three Jacks Vineyard Chardonnay (Russian River Valley) $33. 89 *(7/1/2001)*

Hartford 2004 Pinot Noir (Sonoma Coast) $30. 90 *—S.H. (5/1/2006)*

Hartford 2000 Pinot Noir (Sonoma Coast) $25. 89 *(8/1/2003)*

Hartford 2000 Arrendell Vineyard Pinot Noir (Green Valley) $65. 91 *(8/1/2003)*

Hartford 1999 Arrendell Vineyard Pinot Noir (Russian River Valley) $65. 92 *(7/1/2002)*

Hartford 1999 Dutton Ranch-Sanchietti Vineyard Pinot Noir (Russian River Valley) $50. 94 Editors' Choice *(7/1/2002)*

Hartford 2000 Dutton-Sanchietti Pinot Noir (Russian River Valley) $50. 93 *(8/1/2003)*

Hartford 2004 Hailey's Block Pinot Noir (Russian River Valley) $55. 91 Cellar Selection *—S.H. (12/15/2006)*

Hartford 2000 Marin Pinot Noir (Marin County) $50. 92 Cellar Selection *(8/1/2003)*

Hartford 1999 Marin Pinot Noir (Marin County) $50. 92 Cellar Selection *(7/1/2002)*

Hartford 1999 Sevens Bench Pinot Noir (Carneros) $50. 91 *(7/1/2002)*

Hartford 2000 Sevens Bench Vineyard Pinot Noir (Carneros) $50. 92 Cellar Selection *(8/1/2003)*

Hartford 1999 Velvet Sisters Pinot Noir (Anderson Valley) $50. 90 *(7/1/2002)*

Hartford 2000 Velvet Sisters Vineyard Pinot Noir (Anderson Valley) $50. 91 *(8/1/2003)*

Hartford 2005 Zinfandel (Russian River Valley) $30. Too hot and overripe, with a heavy, baked fruit quality. Although the wine is fully dry, it has a stewed blackberry taste. The alcohol is 15.5%. **83** *—S.H. (11/1/2007)*

Hartford 2001 Zinfandel (Russian River Valley) $25. 90 Editors' Choice *(11/1/2003)*

Hartford 1999 Zinfandel (Russian River Valley) $34. 91 *(7/1/2002)*

Hartford 2001 Dina's Vineyard Zinfandel (Russian River Valley) $34. 91 *(11/1/2003)*

Hartford 2001 Fanucchi-Wood Road Vineyard Zinfandel (Russian River Valley) $34. 92 *(11/1/2003)*

Hartford 2005 Fanucchi-Wood Vineyard Zinfandel (Russian River Valley) $40. Like your Zins high in alcohol and Port-y? Try this one, which comes from low-yielding, century-old vines. It will have its fans, but for this taster, it's hot, dry and raisiny. **84** —*S.H. (11/1/2007)*

Hartford 2001 Hartford Vineyard Zinfandel (Russian River Valley) $34. 93 Editors' Choice *(11/1/2003)*

Hartford 1999 Hartford Vineyard Zinfandel (Russian River Valley) $34. 93 Editors' Choice *(7/1/2002)*

Hartford 2001 Highwire Vineyard Zinfandel (Russian River Valley) $34. 92 *(11/1/2003)*

Hartford 1999 Highwire Vineyard Zinfandel (Russian River Valley) $34. 93 *(7/1/2002)*

HARTFORD COURT

Hartford Court 2005 Four Hearts Vineyards Chardonnay (Russian River Valley) $40. This isn't one of Hartford's single-vineyard Chards, but a blend from around RRV. It's a very elegant, balanced wine, with complexity and charm; 100% barrel fermented, it shows oak-influenced flavors of Meyer lemons, pineapple sorbet and rich Gravenstein apple butter. **91** —*S.H. (4/1/2007)*

Hartford Court 2005 Seascape Vineyard Chardonnay (Sonoma Coast) $60. Seascape is perhaps the winery's coldest vineyard, right in the path of the wind blast coming in off Bodega Bay. You can taste the Pacific chill in the high acidity that makes the fruit so pure and intense. The flavors, of Meyer lemons, lime zest and stony minerals, are bracing, and the finish is absolutely, thoroughly dry. This is a sommelier's dream of a Chardonnay. **93** —*S.H. (11/1/2007)*

Hartford Court 2005 Stone Côte Vineyard Chardonnay (Sonoma Coast) $50. Bone dry, high in acidity, minerally and stony like granite, with the essence of Meyer lemon and green pears, and a leesy, Champagne-like doughiness. There's toasty oak in the background. Elegant and complex now, and should ride out the next decade. **94 Cellar Selection** —*S.H. (11/1/2007)*

Hartford Court 2004 Three Jacks Vineyard Chardonnay (Russian River Valley) $50. This one's a prime example of how fat overripeness is yielding to a leaner balance and elegance. Not that there's anything austere about this luscious Chard, with its white apricot, citron, guava and mineral flavors. It's a terrific wine and showcases Hartford Court at its best. **94** —*S.H. (11/1/2007)*

Hartford Court 2005 Arrendell Vineyard Pinot Noir (Russian River Valley) $75. This is a very serious Pinot Noir, one that will benefit from cellaring despite the drink-me-now deliciousness. It's not just the fruit, which is deeply satisfying in cherries, raspberries, sweet rhubarb pie, blood oranges and juicy pomegranates. It's the structure. Crisp acids and silky tannins create a near-perfect architecture. Elegant and sophisticated, this wine should develop additional complexities for at least six years, with proper cellaring. **95** —*S.H. (11/1/2007)*

Hartford Court 2005 Far Coast Vineyard Pinot Noir (Sonoma Coast) $55. This is from the winery's Annapolis vineyard. It's a very fine and interesting Pinot, showing the acidic, elegant structure of true coast Pinot, and exotic flavors of wild raspberries, red cherries, licorice, sweet leather, tea and Asian spices. All this, in a lightly silky, eminently drinkable texture. **93** —*S.H. (11/1/2007)*

Hartford Court 2005 Hailey's Block Pinot Noir (Green Valley) $55. Showing the beautiful silkiness and delicacy that great Pinot should have, this one also combines immense power. The end result is an important wine of ageworthy proportions. Drinking it now rewards for the wealth of cherry, raspberry, cola, cinnamon spice and oak flavors that are so delicious. But the wine has a fine balance that will allow it to age gracefully for at least six years. **93** —*S.H. (11/1/2007)*

Hartford Court 2005 Jennifer's Pinot Noir (Russian River Valley) $55. From the southern part of the valley, near Sebastopol, comes this young, juicy, crisp Pinot. It's marked by fruit. The freshly crushed flavors of ripe raspberries and cherries are enormously attractive, accented with toasty oak and Asian spices. But the wine has a youthful, acidic tightness that suggests aging. Best now, with decanting, and for six years. **92** —*S.H. (11/1/2007)*

Hartford Court 2005 Land's Edge Vineyards Pinot Noir (Sonoma Coast) $45. Most of the grapes came from the Annapolis Vineyard, with some from Seascape. While the vintage was cool, it gave incredibly long hangtime. Dry, crisp and delicate, the wine has a silky voluptuousness that makes it irresistible, with pie-filling cherry and black raspberry flavors finished with Asian spice. New French oak adds toast and vanilla sweetness. It's expensive, but still a bargain. **96 Editors' Choice** —*S.H. (5/1/2007)*

Hartford Court 2005 Sevens Bench Vineyard Pinot Noir (Carneros) $50. Silky and refined, this pleasant Pinot is light in body, with transparent flavors of cherries, cola, licorice, spices and oak, and a touch of leathery funk. It's young and seems obvious now, but it's hiding its wealth. Give it until 2008 to begin drinking, and should develop through this decade. **89** —*S.H. (11/1/2007)*

Hartford Court 2005 Velvet Sisters Vineyard Pinot Noir (Anderson Valley) $55. The wine comes from a block within the Savoy vineyard, a source of sometimes great Pinot fruit. This wine plays it down the middle. It's good and proper in Pinot-esque qualities, with cherry and cola flavors, a silky texture and a dry, spicy finish. But it's not particularly exciting. **87** —*S.H. (11/1/2007)*

HARTWELL

Hartwell 2002 Cabernet Sauvignon (Stags Leap District) $115. 92 Cellar Selection —*S.H. (10/1/2005)*

Hartwell 2000 Cabernet Sauvignon (Stags Leap District) $100. 93 —*S.H. (11/15/2003)*

Hartwell 1998 Cabernet Sauvignon (Stags Leap District) $100. 90 —*S.H. (6/1/2002)*

Hartwell 2001 Estate Grown Cabernet Sauvignon (Stags Leap District) $115. 93 —*J.C. (10/1/2004)*

Hartwell 1999 Estate Grown Cabernet Sauvignon (Napa Valley) $100. 93 —*J.M. (11/15/2002)*

Hartwell 2004 Estate Reserve Cabernet Sauvignon (Stags Leap District) $115. A delicious Cabernet that managed to finesse the heat of the vintage better than many other wineries. It's much riper than past bottlings, with blackberry, cassis, cherry and chocolate fudge flavors accented by rich, smoky oak. But it's too soft to cellar. Way too soft. Drink now with the best steak you can find. **91** —*S.H. (12/15/2007)*

Hartwell 1997 Sunshine Vineyard Cabernet Sauvignon (Stags Leap District) $95. 93 *(11/1/2000)*

Hartwell 2002 Merlot (Stags Leap District) $65. 92 —*S.H. (8/1/2005)*

Hartwell 2000 Merlot (Stags Leap District) $60. 91 —*J.M. (11/15/2002)*

Hartwell 2001 Estate Grown Merlot (Stags Leap District) $60. 91 —*S.H. (4/1/2004)*

Hartwell 2005 Sauvignon Blanc (Napa Valley) $30. 92 Editors' Choice —*S.H. (12/31/2006)*

Hartwell 2006 Estate Sauvignon Blanc (Carneros) $30. From Carneros, this wine has tangy acidity that balances the sugariness of the tropical fruit and fig flavors. Lots of oak, too, but the wine should be drier. **85** —*S.H. (12/15/2007)*

HARVEST MOON

Harvest Moon 2003 Cabernet Sauvignon (Dry Creek Valley) $32. 88 —*S.H. (12/1/2006)*

Harvest Moon 2005 Estate Dry Gewürztraminer (Russian River Valley) $18. 85 —*S.H. (12/1/2006)*

Harvest Moon 2004 Zinfandel (Russian River Valley) $24. Nasty. Hits the mouth with astringent green flavors and turns harsher and more bitter on the finish. **80** —*S.H. (6/1/2007)*

Harvest Moon 2003 Estate Zinfandel (Russian River Valley) $32. 86 —*S.H. (12/1/2006)*

Harvest Moon 2006 Late Harvest Estate Zinfandel (Russian River Valley) $32. Very fresh in young, tart acidity, this dessert wine has modest cherry and raspberry flavors. It's simple and jammy. **83** —*S.H. (6/1/2007)*

Harvest Moon 2004 Pitts Home Ranch Estate Zinfandel (Russian River Valley) $32. This tastes hot, soft and baked, with stewed berry and dried herb flavors. The finish is tannic and astringent. It's okay for everyday, but a major letdown from the '03. **82** —*S.H. (6/1/2007)*

Harvest Moon 2002 Pitts Home Ranch Zinfandel (Russian River Valley) $28. 93 —*S.H. (8/1/2005)*

HASLEY

Hasley 2004 Meritage Bordeaux Blend (Paso Robles) $25. With two thirds Cabernet and one third Merlot, this is classic Paso Bordeaux, a ripe, fruity wine that's soft in acids and tannins. But it's fully dry, which lets you appreciate the blackberry, cherry and new oak flavors. **87** —*S.H. (9/1/2007)*

HATCHER

Hatcher 2002 Syrah (Calaveras County) $24. 90 —*S.H. (3/1/2005)*

Hatcher 2002 Estate Zinfandel (Calaveras County) $18. 88 —*S.H. (3/1/2005)*

HAUER OF THE DAUEN

Hauer of the Dauen 1998 Pinot Noir (Willamette Valley) $14. 85 —*M.S. (12/1/2000)*

Hauer of the Dauen 1998 Estate Bottled Pinot Noir (Willamette Valley) $14. 81 —*J.C. (12/1/2000)*

HAVENS

Havens 2004 Albariño (Carneros) $24. 90 Editors' Choice *—S.H. (11/1/2005)*

Havens 2003 Albariño (Carneros) $24. 85 *—S.H. (10/1/2004)*

Havens 2001 Bourriquot Cabernet Blend (Carneros) $35. 93 Editors' Choice *—S.H. (11/1/2005)*

Havens 2001 Merlot (Napa Valley) $24. 87 *—S.H. (6/1/2005)*

Havens 2000 Merlot (Napa Valley) $24. 88 *—S.H. (12/31/2003)*

Havens 2000 Reserve Merlot (Carneros) $32. 88 *—S.H. (10/1/2004)*

Havens 2000 Bourriquot Red Blend (Carneros) $35. 86 *—S.H. (10/1/2004)*

Havens 2002 Syrah (Napa Valley) $24. 87 *(9/1/2005)*

Havens 2001 Syrah (Napa Valley) $24. 91 *—S.H. (6/1/2005)*

Havens 2000 Syrah (Napa Valley) $24. 90 *—S.H. (12/1/2003)*

Havens 1999 Syrah (Napa Valley) $26. 91 *S.H. (7/1/2002)*

Havens 1999 Hudson T Reserve Syrah (Napa Valley) $45. 93 *—S.H. (7/1/2002)*

Havens 2001 Hudson Vineyard Syrah (Carneros) $45. 85 *—S.H. (11/1/2005)*

Havens 2000 Hudson Vineyard Syrah (Carneros) $45. 86 *—S.H. (5/1/2004)*

HAWK CREST

Hawk Crest 1997 Cabernet Sauvignon (California) $12. 86 *—S.H. (3/1/2000)*

Hawk Crest 1996 Cabernet Sauvignon (California) $9. 83 *—S.H. (11/1/1999)*

Hawk Crest 2003 Cabernet Sauvignon (California) $14. 83 *—S.H. (10/1/2006)*

Hawk Crest 2001 Cabernet Sauvignon (California) $14. 83 *—S.H. (6/1/2004)*

Hawk Crest 2000 Cabernet Sauvignon (California) $14. 82 *—S.H. (8/1/2003)*

Hawk Crest 1996 Reserve Cabernet Sauvignon (California) $16. 83 *—L.W. (7/1/1999)*

Hawk Crest 2004 Chardonnay (California) $11. 84 *—S.H. (10/1/2006)*

Hawk Crest 2002 Chardonnay (California) $11. 83 *—S.H. (6/1/2004)*

Hawk Crest 2001 Chardonnay (California) $11. 83 *—S.H. (10/1/2003)*

Hawk Crest 1998 Chardonnay (California) $10. 83 *—S.H. (2/1/2001)*

Hawk Crest 1997 Reserve Vineyard Selection Chardonnay (California) $14. 84 *—S.H. (7/1/1999)*

Hawk Crest 1998 Vineyard Selection Chardonnay (California) $15. 88 *(6/1/2000)*

Hawk Crest 1997 Merlot (California) $12. 87 Best Buy *—S.H. (3/1/2000)*

Hawk Crest 2003 Merlot (California) $14. 83 *—S.H. (10/1/2006)*

Hawk Crest 2001 Merlot (California) $14. 85 *—S.H. (6/1/2004)*

Hawk Crest 2000 Merlot (California) $14. 83 *—S.H. (8/1/2003)*

Hawk Crest 1996 Vineyard Select Reserve Merlot (California) $16. 82 *—L.W. (9/1/1999)*

HAWLEY

Hawley 2003 Cabernet Sauvignon (Dry Creek Valley) $28. This was a pretty good vintage, and the wine is balanced and dry, with smooth tannins and cherry-berry flavors. Yet it can't quite overcome that rustic, briary thing that Dry Creek reds often have. 85 *—S.H. (4/1/2007)*

Hawley 2002 Cabernet Sauvignon (Dry Creek Valley) $27. 85 *—S.H. (12/31/2005)*

Hawley 2001 Cabernet Sauvignon (Dry Creek Valley) $28. 84 *—S.H. (5/1/2004)*

Hawley 1999 Cabernet Sauvignon (Dry Creek Valley) $28. 90 *—S.H. (11/15/2002)*

Hawley 2004 Chardonnay (Russian River Valley) $21. 84 *—S.H. (12/31/2005)*

Hawley 2003 Foppoli Ranch Chardonnay (Russian River Valley) $20. 88 *—S.H. (12/15/2004)*

Hawley 2002 Merlot (Dry Creek Valley) $25. Four-plus years have not erased the awkward rusticity and medicinal flavors. The tannins remain, too, sticky and hard. Not going anywhere. 81 *—S.H. (3/1/2007)*

Hawley 2001 Bradford Mountain Merlot (Dry Creek Valley) $26. 86 *—S.H. (11/1/2005)*

Hawley 2000 Bradford Mountain Merlot (Dry Creek Valley) $20. 90 *—S.H. (5/1/2004)*

Hawley 1999 Bradford Mountain Merlot (Dry Creek Valley) $24. 88 *—S.H. (11/15/2002)*

Hawley 2005 Ponzo Vineyard Petite Sirah (Sonoma County) $26. This tannic wine is quintessential North Coast Petite Sirah. The vineyard is where Russian River Valley meets Dry Creek Valley, and the wine is bone dry and astringent. The superextracted cherry and blackberry flavors veer on liqueur, but happily avoid raisins, while cool Sonoma gives the wine an acidic brace. If you like these lusty young reds, you'll happily gulp it down with greasy barbecue and roasts. 88 *—S.H. (12/1/2007)*

Hawley 2004 Pinot Noir (Russian River Valley) $32. Lots going on in this dry, young Pinot. Shows classic cool-climate, RRV character, with a pale color, delicately silky mouthfeel, and powerful cherry, cola, pomegranate, rhubarb, licorice and smoky oak flavors. A lovely wine; should develop over the next six years. 91 *—S.H. (4/1/2007)*

Hawley 2003 Pinot Noir (Russian River Valley) $32. 85 *—S.H. (11/1/2005)*

Hawley 2002 Oehlman Vineyard Pinot Noir (Russian River Valley) $32. 84 *(11/1/2004)*

Hawley 2000 Oehlman Vineyard Pinot Noir (Russian River Valley) $28. 85 *—S.H. (2/1/2003)*

Hawley 2004 Viognier (Placer County) $20. 83 *—S.H. (11/1/2005)*

Hawley 2003 Viognier (Placer County) $20. 85 *—S.H. (12/31/2004)*

Hawley 2001 Viognier (Placer County) $21. 85 *—S.H. (12/15/2002)*

Hawley 2005 Barrel Fermented Viognier (Placer County) $21. Earthy and dry, with ashy aromas and herbal flavors. Doesn't really show much varietal flavor, but it's clean. 83 *—S.H. (4/1/2007)*

Hawley 2005 Old Vine Gaddis Vineyard Zinfandel (Russian River Valley) $28. They say the vines are 85 years old, and I can believe it, because these authentically old Zin vines are intense. It's not just intensity of cherry-berry fruit, but of substances that seem to exist deep in the soil, like stones and minerals and organic matter and decomposing volcanic litter and old compounds washed down from the mountains over time. I like this dry, tannic, complex Zinfandel a lot. 93 Editors' Choice *—S.H. (12/1/2007)*

Hawley 2005 Ponzo Vineyard Zinfandel (Sonoma County) $24. Too sweet and Port-y with sugared, caramelized wild berry flavors, and a pie-filling sweetness made heavy by high alcohol. 83 *—S.H. (12/1/2007)*

HAYES RANCH

Hayes Ranch 2004 In the Saddle Cabernet Sauvignon (Central Coast) $9. This isn't the fruitiest Cab ever, but it does have some decent cherry flavors, and will do if all that's needed is a dry, full-bodied red wine. 83 *—S.H. (4/1/2007)*

Hayes Ranch 2005 Best Foot Forward Chardonnay (Central Coast) $9. One of the best values in Chard of the vintage. It's a rich, dramatically fruity wine, showing oodles of flamboyant pineapple, peach, cantaloupe and smoky, spicy flavors that keep on coming through a long, dry finish. Buy this by the case. 87 Best Buy *—S.H. (4/1/2007)*

Hayes Ranch 2004 Lucky Horseshoe Merlot (Central Coast) $9. Pretty good Merlot, showing cherry and blackberry flavors with a streak of cocoa, and finishes in balance. There are some green, minty notes, probably from overcropped vines, but they add a subtle note of interest. 84 *—S.H. (3/1/2007)*

HAYMAN & HILL

Hayman & Hill 2003 Reserve Selection Cabernet Sauvignon (Napa Valley) $14. 86 *—S.H. (12/15/2005)*

Hayman & Hill 2004 Reserve Selection Chardonnay (Russian River Valley) $14. 85 *—S.H. (12/15/2005)*

Hayman & Hill 2003 Reserve Selection Chardonnay (Russian River Valley) $14. 87 *—S.H. (7/1/2005)*

Hayman & Hill 2003 Reserve Pinot Noir (Edna Valley) $14. 86 *—S.H. (7/1/2005)*

Hayman & Hill 2002 Reserve Selection Shiraz-Viognier (Monterey County) $14. 84 *—S.H. (12/15/2005)*

Hayman & Hill 2002 Reserve Selection Shiraz-Viognier (Monterey County) $14. 86 *S.H. (7/1/2005)*

Hayman & Hill 2003 Reserve Selection Zinfandel (Dry Creek Valley) $14. 83 *—S.H. (12/15/2005)*

Hayman & Hill 2001 Reserve Selection Zinfandel (Dry Creek Valley) $15. 88 *(11/1/2003)*

HAYWOOD

Haywood 1999 Vintner's Select Cabernet Sauvignon (California) $10. 81 *(8/1/2001)*

Haywood 1999 Vintner's Select Chardonnay (California) $10. 82 *—S.H. (8/1/2001)*

Haywood 1999 Vintner's Select Merlot (California) $12. 84 *—S.H. (8/1/2001)*

Haywood 1998 Vintner's Select Merlot (California) $10. 82 *—M.S. (7/1/2000)*

Haywood 1996 Los Chamizal Estate Zinfandel (Sonoma Valley) $16. 91 *—S.H. (11/1/1999)*

Haywood 1996 Los Chamizal Estate Rocky Terrace Zinfandel (Sonoma Valley) $23. 92 *—S.H. (11/1/1999)*

Haywood 2004 Los Chamizal Vineyard Zinfandel (Sonoma Valley) $20. Zinfandel's reputation as a notoriously uneven ripener is exemplified in this wine, which combines blackberry and cherry fruit with harsh minty, green herbaceous notes suggesting dried thyme and dill. The result is uneven. **83** *—S.H. (2/1/2007)*

Haywood 1998 Los Chamizal Vineyard Zinfandel (Sonoma Valley) $20. 88 *(8/1/2001)*

Haywood 1998 Los Chamizal Vineyard Zinfandel (Sonoma County) $20. 88 *—S.H. (8/1/2001)*

Haywood 2004 Los Chamizal Vineyard Rocky Terrace Zinfandel (Sonoma Valley) $35. My scores for Haywood Zins from Los Chamizal have been all over the board over the years, suggesting real vintage differences. In a cool year it can be tough and tannic. In a warm vintage, like this '04, the fruit is showcased, rich in blackberry jam, blueberries and cassis, with a long, dry, spicy finish. **88** *—S.H. (2/1/2007)*

Haywood 1998 Morning Sun Zinfandel (Sonoma County) $30. 86 *—S.H. (8/1/2001)*

Haywood 1998 Rocky Terrace Zinfandel (Sonoma County) $35. 86 *—S.H. (8/1/2001)*

HAZLITT

Hazlitt 1852 Vineyards 2002 Cabernet Sauvignon (Finger Lakes) $16. An overriding element of oak is the central focus; a maple syrup nose and lack of fruit presence fails to deliver the kind of depth a Cab drinker would expect, though some spice on the palate is pleasant. **81** *—S.K. (5/1/2007)*

Hazlitt 1852 Vineyards 2005 Pinot Grigio (Finger Lakes) $18. Floral and delicate with a balanced mouthfeel, this PG from historic Hazlitt 1852 Vineyards offers a rounder mélange of flavors and a creamy finish. Good on its own and even better with food. **84** *—S.K. (7/1/2007)*

Hazlitt 1852 Vineyards 2006 Riesling (Finger Lakes) $12. With its playful balance of sweetness and acid, and its enticing aroma of apples and honey, this offers a pretty, easy-going wine experience. Paired with a chicken salad or a plate of spicy Asian fare, the wine is a great choice and the price is right. Its minerality gives it food-pairing flexibility, so experiment. **84** *—S.K. (9/1/2007)*

Hazlitt 1852 Vineyards 2005 Homestead Reserve Riesling (Finger Lakes) $18. Delicate floral notes of jasmine lead to crisp, zesty flavors of lemon, orange and spice in this crowd-pleasing wine from historic producer Hazlitt 1852. A citric and mineral edge keeps it from being too cloying, but fans of bone dry Riesling may find this a little lush and sweet. Will pair nicely with spicy Thai dishes. **87** *—S.K. (2/1/2007)*

Hazlitt 1852 Vineyards 2006 Sauvignon Blanc (Finger Lakes) $13. This medium-bodied wine is easy to drink and offers citrus and lemongrass flavors. Refreshing and clean, it's a great accompaniment to Indian or Thai. **83** *—S.K. (10/1/2007)*

HDV

HdV 2004 Belle Cousine Bordeaux Blend (Napa Valley) $60. A Merlot-Cabernet blend from the Hyde Vineyard in Carneros, this wine is pretty green for such a ripe vintage as '04. There's a dry tannin, green bean edge to the fruit, and improvement with age doesn't seem likely. **82** *—S.H. (12/15/2007)*

HdV 2003 Napa Valley Red Wine Bordeaux Blend (Carneros) $60. 82 *—S.H. (12/31/2006)*

HdV 2004 Chardonnay (Carneros) $55. 93 *—S.H. (12/31/2006)*

HdV 2003 Chardonnay (Carneros) $55. 89 *—S.H. (12/31/2005)*

HdV 2002 Chardonnay (Carneros) $55. 89 *—S.H. (5/1/2005)*

HdV 2001 Chardonnay (Carneros) $48. 89 *—S.H. (5/1/2004)*

HdV 2001 Red Blend (Carneros) $65. 91 *—S.H. (5/1/2004)*

HdV 2002 Proprietary Red Red Blend (Carneros) $60. 88 *—S.H. (6/1/2005)*

HdV 2004 Syrah (Carneros) $60. 90 *—S.H. (12/31/2006)*

HdV 2002 Syrah (Carneros) $48. 86 *—S.H. (9/1/2004)*

HdV 2001 Syrah (Carneros) $48. 90 *—S.H. (5/1/2005)*

HEALDSBURG

Healdsburg 2001 Cabernet Sauvignon (California) $8. 84 *—S.H. (11/15/2003)*

Healdsburg 2001 Chardonnay (California) $8. 82 *—S.H. (12/1/2003)*

Healdsburg 2001 Merlot (California) $8. 84 *—S.H. (12/1/2003)*

Healdsburg 2001 Shiraz (California) $8. 83 *—S.H. (12/15/2003)*

HEALDSBURG VITICULTURAL SOCIETY

Healdsburg Viticultural Society 2002 Reserve Cabernet Sauvignon (Dry Creek Valley) $13. 88 *—S.H. (11/15/2004)*

HEDGES

Hedges 1998 Bordeaux Blend (Columbia Valley (WA)) $11. 88 Best Buy *(4/1/2000)*

Hedges 2004 Three Vineyards Bordeaux Blend (Red Mountain) $22. Concentrated and showing a whiff of volatility, this is a blend of 62% Merlot, 33% Cabernet Sauvignon and a splash each of Cab Franc and Petit Verdot. Grapes are sourced from three different estate vineyards on Red Mountain. It's acidic and extracted, but opens up with exposure to air into a supple, rich, muscular, raspberry and cherry-flavored red blend. There are hints of rock, fennel and smoke, and a long, concentrated and well-rounded finish. **90** *—P.G. (8/1/2007)*

Hedges 1997 Three Vineyards Bordeaux Blend (Columbia Valley (WA)) $21. 90 *—S.H. (4/1/2000)*

Hedges 1996 Three Vineyards Bordeaux Blend (Columbia Valley (WA)) $20. 90 *(11/15/1999)*

Hedges 1999 Red Mountain Reserve Cabernet Sauvignon (Columbia Valley (WA)) $42. 94 Editors' Choice *—P.G. (6/1/2002)*

Hedges 2002 Two Vineyards Reserve Cabernet Sauvignon (Red Mountain) $52. 88 *—P.G. (4/1/2006)*

Hedges 1997 Red Mountain Reserve Cabernet Sauvignon-Merlot (Columbia Valley (WA)) $45. 92 *—P.G. (11/15/2000)*

Hedges 2001 Three Vineyards Red Wine Cabernet Sauvignon-Merlot (Red Mountain) $18. 90 Best Buy *—P.G. (12/1/2004)*

Hedges 2003 Two Vineyards Cabernet Sauvignon-Syrah (Red Mountain) $40. 91 *—P.G. (4/1/2006)*

Hedges 1999 Fumé Chardonnay (Columbia Valley (WA)) $9. 88 Best Buy *—P.G. (11/15/2000)*

Hedges 1998 Fumé Chardonnay (Columbia Valley (WA)) $9. 88 Best Buy *—S.H. (2/1/2000)*

Hedges 2003 Fumé-Chardonnay (Columbia Valley (WA)) $10. 87 Best Buy *—P.G. (12/1/2004)*

Hedges 2005 CMS Red Blend (Columbia Valley (WA)) $13. For the first time this popular blend contains no Yakima Valley fruit. The savvy blend of Cabernet Sauvignon, Merlot and Syrah works like a charm. Outside of the Ste. Michelle brands, this is probably the most consistent, balanced and expressive red wine blend that is value-priced and widely available from Washington state. It's elegant, somewhat European in style, with light, polished fruit flavors of plum, berry and cherry. **88 Best Buy** *—P.G. (8/1/2007)*

Hedges 2004 CMS Red Blend (Columbia Valley (WA)) $11. 88 Best Buy *—P.G. (10/1/2006)*

Hedges 2002 CMS Red Blend (Columbia Valley (WA)) $12. 89 Best Buy *—P.G. (12/1/2004)*

Hedges 2001 CMS Red Blend (Columbia Valley (WA)) $10. 89 Best Buy *—P.G. (11/15/2003)*

Hedges 2000 CMS Red Blend (Columbia Valley (WA)) $11. 89 Best Buy *—P.G. (6/1/2002)*

Hedges 1999 Columbia Valley Red Blend (Washington) $11. 88 Best Buy *—P.G. (10/1/2001)*

Hedges 1998 Red Mountain Reserve Red Blend (Columbia Valley (WA)) $45. 92 *(10/1/2001)*

Hedges 2003 Three Vineyards Red Blend (Red Mountain) $22. 89 *—P.G. (4/1/2006)*

Hedges 1999 Three Vineyards Red Blend (Red Mountain) $18. 92 *—P.G. (6/1/2002)*

Hedges 1998 Three Vineyards Red Blend (Columbia Valley (WA)) $22. 91 Editors' Choice *(10/1/2001)*

Hedges 2004 Two Vineyards Red Blend (Red Mountain) $38. This limited (350 case) selection tastes strongly of bourbon barrel, with red fruits in a supporting role. Syrah adds some focus and spice; it's a good match. Young, tight and compact, may benefit from additional cellaring. **90** *—P.G. (8/1/2007)*

Hedges 1998 Syrah (Columbia Valley (WA)) $32. 87 —*P.G. (11/15/2000)*

Hedges 2002 Bel Villa Estate North Block Syrah (Red Mountain) $75. 86 *(9/1/2005)*

Hedges 2001 White Blend (Columbia Valley (WA)) $9. 91 Best Buy —*P.G. (6/1/2002)*

Hedges 2000 White Blend (Columbia Valley (WA)) $9. 90 Best Buy —*P.G. (10/1/2001)*

Hedges 2005 CMS White Blend (Columbia Valley (WA)) $11. 88 Best Buy —*P.G. (10/1/2006)*

Hedges 2004 CMS White White Blend (Yakima Valley) $11. 88 —*P.G. (8/1/2005)*

HEITZ

Heitz 2000 Cabernet Sauvignon (Napa Valley) $35. 84 —*S.H. (11/15/2004)*

Heitz 1999 Martha's Vineyard Cabernet Sauvignon (Napa Valley) $120. 94 —*S.H. (11/15/2004)*

Heitz 1994 Trailside Cabernet Sauvignon (Napa Valley) $49. 89 *(3/1/2000)*

HELIX

Helix 2004 Aspersa Chardonnay-Viognier (Columbia Valley (WA)) $16. 90 —*P.G. (6/1/2006)*

Helix 2003 Merlot (Columbia Valley (WA)) $20. 88 —*P.G. (6/1/2006)*

Helix 2004 Syrah (Columbia Valley (WA)) $22. What's not to like? This is just flat-out delicious, dark and spicy with a strong streak of mint and menthol. The fruit is tight, true and tangy, showing a taut mix of berry, cassis and plum. It's hard to believe that Chuck Reininger doesn't slap a "Reserve" label on this and double the price. **90** —*P.G. (3/1/2007)*

Helix 2003 Syrah (Columbia Valley (WA)) $20. 89 —*P.G. (6/1/2006)*

HELLER ESTATE

Heller Estate 2001 Estate Bottled Cabernet Sauvignon (Carmel Valley) $35. 88 —*S.H. (8/1/2005)*

Heller Estate 2003 Estate Chardonnay (Carmel Valley) $22. 85 —*S.H. (11/1/2005)*

Heller Estate 2004 Estate Chenin Blanc (Carmel Valley) $20. 83 —*S.H. (11/1/2005)*

Heller Estate 2002 Toby's Vintage Merlot Port (Carmel Valley) $35. 87 —*S.H. (11/1/2005)*

HELVETIA

Helvetia 1998 Pinot Noir (Willamette Valley) $18. 82 —*M.S. (12/1/2000)*

HENDRY

Hendry 2003 Hendry Vineyard Red Wine Bordeaux Blend (Napa Valley) $33. 88 —*S.H. (7/1/2006)*

Hendry 2001 Red Wine Bordeaux Blend (Napa Valley) $30. 93 —*S.H. (5/1/2004)*

Hendry 2002 Block 8 Cabernet Sauvignon (Napa Valley) $49. 93 —*S.H. (12/15/2006)*

Hendry 2001 Block 8 Cabernet Sauvignon (Napa Valley) $48. 92 —*S.H. (6/1/2006)*

Hendry 2000 Block 8 Cabernet Sauvignon (Napa Valley) $40. 89 —*S.H. (11/15/2004)*

Hendry 1999 Block 8 Cabernet Sauvignon (Napa Valley) $40. 90 —*S.H. (11/15/2003)*

Hendry 1998 Block 8 Cabernet Sauvignon (Napa Valley) $40. 94 Editors' Choice —*S.H. (12/31/2002)*

Hendry 2002 Blocks 19 & 20 Chardonnay (Napa Valley) $25. 85 —*S.H. (12/15/2004)*

Hendry 2001 Blocks 19 & 20 Chardonnay (Napa Valley) $25. 90 —*S.H. (2/1/2004)*

Hendry 2003 Blocks 19 & 20 Dijon Clones Chardonnay (Napa Valley) $25. 89 —*S.H. (5/1/2006)*

Hendry 2000 Blocks 19 and 20 Chardonnay (Napa Valley) $25. 92 —*S.H. (12/15/2002)*

Hendry 2003 Blocks 9 & 21 Chardonnay (Napa Valley) $25. 88 —*S.H. (6/1/2006)*

Hendry 2002 Blocks 9 & 21 Chardonnay (Napa Valley) $25. 89 —*S.H. (4/1/2006)*

Hendry 2001 Blocks 9 & 21 Chardonnay (Napa Valley) $25. 92 Editors' Choice —*S.H. (2/1/2004)*

Hendry 2000 Blocks 9 and 21 Chardonnay (Napa Valley) $25. 91 —*S.H. (12/15/2002)*

Hendry 2005 Unoaked Chardonnay (Napa Valley) $17. 84 —*S.H. (10/1/2006)*

Hendry 2004 Unoaked Chardonnay (Napa Valley) $17. 87 —*S.H. (12/31/2005)*

Hendry 2005 Pinot Gris (Napa Valley) $19. 85 —*S.H. (10/1/2006)*

Hendry 2003 Blocks 4 & 5 Pinot Noir (Napa Valley) $30. 85 —*S.H. (2/1/2006)*

Hendry 2001 Blocks 4 & 5 Pinot Noir (Napa Valley) $27. 86 —*S.H. (4/1/2004)*

Hendry 2002 Hendry Ranch Pinot Noir (Napa Valley) $27. 86 —*S.H. (8/1/2005)*

Hendry 1999 Hendry Vineyard Pinot Noir (Napa Valley) $27. 92 —*S.H. (9/1/2003)*

Hendry 2002 Block 24 Primitivo (Napa Valley) $28. 91 —*S.H. (8/1/2005)*

Hendry 2002 Hendry Ranch Red Blend (Napa Valley) $30. 91 —*S.H. (8/1/2005)*

Hendry 2005 Rosé Blend (Napa Valley) $13. 84 —*S.H. (10/1/2006)*

Hendry 2002 Block 28 Zinfandel (Napa Valley) $31. 88 —*S.H. (5/1/2006)*

Hendry 2001 Block 28 Zinfandel (Napa Valley) $28. 88 —*J.M. (12/31/2004)*

Hendry 2000 Block 28 Zinfandel (Napa Valley) $28. 91 —*S.H. (9/1/2003)*

Hendry 1999 Block 28 Zinfandel (Dry Creek Valley) $28. 92 —*S.H. (12/1/2002)*

Hendry 2004 Block 7 Zinfandel (Napa Valley) $29. 91 —*S.H. (12/15/2006)*

Hendry 2003 Block 7 Zinfandel (Napa Valley) $29. 87 —*S.H. (2/1/2006)*

Hendry 2002 Block 7 Zinfandel (Napa Valley) $27. 90 —*J.M. (12/31/2004)*

Hendry 2001 Block 7 Zinfandel (Napa Valley) $27. 91 *(11/1/2003)*

Hendry 2000 Block 7 Zinfandel (Napa Valley) $20. 91 —*S.H. (9/1/2003)*

Hendry 1999 Block 7 Zinfandel (Napa Valley) $20. 92 —*S.H. (12/1/2002)*

Hendry 1997 Block 7 Zinfandel (Napa Valley) $20. 83 —*P.G. (11/15/1999)*

HENEHAN HILLS

Henehan Hills 2001 Syrah (Dry Creek Valley) $19. 87 —*S.H. (8/1/2005)*

Henehan Hills 2001 Zinfandel (Dry Creek Valley) $19. 84 —*S.H. (8/1/2005)*

HENRY ESTATE

Henry Estate 1998 Barrel Fermented Chardonnay (Umpqua Valley) $15. 84 —*P.G. (11/1/2001)*

Henry Estate 1999 Gewürztraminer (Umpqua Valley) $10. 82 —*P.G. (11/1/2001)*

Henry Estate 1999 Merlot (Oregon) $18. 85 —*P.G. (8/1/2002)*

Henry Estate 2001 Müller-Thurgau (Umpqua Valley) $9. 88 Best Buy —*P.G. (8/1/2002)*

Henry Estate 2004 Pinot Gris (Umpqua Valley) $13. 88 Best Buy —*P.G. (2/1/2006)*

Henry Estate 1999 Pinot Gris (Umpqua Valley) $16. 88 —*P.G. (2/1/2002)*

Henry Estate 2002 Pinot Noir (Umpqua Valley) $18. 83 *(11/1/2004)*

Henry Estate 2000 Pinot Noir (Umpqua Valley) $13. 86 Best Buy —*P.G. (12/31/2002)*

Henry Estate 1999 Pinot Noir (Oregon) $51. 87 *(10/1/2002)*

Henry Estate 2002 Barrel Select Pinot Noir (Umpqua Valley) $28. 84 *(11/1/2004)*

Henry Estate 1998 Barrel Select Pinot Noir (Umpqua Valley) $25. 87 —*P.G. (8/1/2002)*

Henry Estate 1996 Barrel Select Pinot Noir (Umpqua Valley) $20. 87 *(11/15/1999)*

Henry Estate 2001 Umpqua Cuvée Pinot Noir (Umpqua Valley) $39. 82 —*M.S. (8/1/2003)*

Henry Estate 1999 Henry the V Red Blend (Umpqua Valley) $23. 86 —*P.G. (8/1/2002)*

Henry Estate 2000 Muller Thurgau White Blend (Umpqua Valley) $9. 84 —*P.G. (11/1/2001)*

HERINGER

Heringer 2004 Chardonnay (Clarksburg) $13. 84 —*S.H. (7/1/2006)*

Heringer 2003 Petite Sirah (Clarksburg) $21. 83 —*S.H. (7/1/2006)*

HERMAN STORY

Herman Story 2004 Larner Vineyard Grenache (Santa Ynez Valley) $32. 90 —*S.H. (11/15/2006)*

Herman Story 2004 Syrah (San Luis Obispo County) $30. 93 Editors' Choice *—S.H. (11/15/2006)*

Herman Story 2004 Larner Vineyard Syrah (Santa Ynez Valley) $28. 86 *—S.H. (11/15/2006)*

HERMANN J. WIEMER

Hermann J. Wiemer 1997 Cuvée Brut 2000 Champagne Blend (Finger Lakes) $23. 84 *(12/31/2000)*

Hermann J. Wiemer 1997 Chardonnay (Finger Lakes) $12. 88 *(11/15/1999)*

HERMES

Hermes 2006 Estate Bottled Cabernet Sauvignon (Ohio) $15. From winemaker David Kraus, this is simple but enjoyable. Spice, dark berry and blueberry on the nose lead into toasted oak and berry on the palate. A fun sip for fans of offbeat regions, it will pair well with heartier fare like beef and lamb. **83** *—S.K. (10/1/2007)*

Hermes 2006 Estate Bottled Sémillon (Ohio) $15. This Ohio Semillon offers toasted flavors and an overall soft and subtle character. Notes of vanilla and fig, paired with butter, are flavorful, but the wine could use a bit more body. Serve with goat cheese or chicken in a white cream sauce. **82** *—S.K. (10/1/2007)*

Hermes 2006 Estate Bottled Syrah (Ohio) $15. Pronounced aromas and flavors of blackberry and pepper characterize this Syrah from Ohio's Sandusky region. A pleasant sipper but not terribly complex, its pepper will pair well with grilled dishes. **82** *—S.K. (10/1/2007)*

Hermes 2006 Estate Bottled Viognier (Ohio) $15. Typical, elegant flavors of honey, tropical fruit and apricot pervade this wine, which is lead by a full-bodied nose of white flowers. The mouthfeel is measured and not as heavy as some Viogniers, and the finish lingering. **84** *—S.K. (10/1/2007)*

HERON

Heron 2004 Cabernet Sauvignon (California) $12. Sweetly sugary and harsh, with cherry jam flavors doused with bitter coffee. **81** *—S.H. (10/1/2007)*

Heron 2003 Cabernet Sauvignon (California) $12. This is a balanced Cabernet with plenty of true varietal character. The blackberry and cherry flavors are enriched with an edge of smoky oak, and the wine shows smooth polished tannins and a thoroughly dry finish. **85** *—S.H. (2/1/2007)*

Heron 2002 Cabernet Sauvignon (California) $11. 83 *—S.H. (12/15/2005)*

Heron 2001 Cabernet Sauvignon (California) $12. 84 *—S.H. (8/1/2005)*

Heron 2006 Chardonnay (California) $10. Soft and sweet, this Chard has candied flavors of pineapples, peaches and vanilla. The sugary taste makes it finish like soda. **81** *—S.H. (11/15/2007)*

Heron 2005 Chardonnay (California) $11. On the rough and ready side, but this is a good price for an oaky, creamy, fruity Chard of this caliber. It's rich in peaches and cream, tropical fruit and buttered toast flavors. **85** *—S.H. (2/1/2007)*

Heron 2003 Chardonnay (California) $11. 85 Best Buy *—S.H. (8/1/2005)*

Heron 2001 Chardonnay (California) $11. 84 *—S.H. (6/1/2003)*

Heron 2003 Merlot (California) $11. 84 *—S.H. (12/15/2005)*

Heron 2002 Merlot (California) $12. 84 *—S.H. (12/15/2004)*

Heron 1999 Merlot (California) $13. 83 *—D.T. (2/1/2002)*

Heron 2003 Pinot Noir (California) $11. 84 *—S.H. (12/15/2005)*

Heron 2002 Pinot Noir (California) $12. 85 *—S.H. (8/1/2005)*

Heron 2003 Syrah (California) $11. 85 *—S.H. (12/15/2005)*

Heron 2002 Syrah (California) $12. 84 *—S.H. (8/1/2005)*

Heron 1999 Syrah (California) $13. 83 *(10/1/2001)*

HERON HILL

Heron Hill 2003 Ingle Vineyard Johannisberg Riesling (Finger Lakes) $25. 88 *—M.D. (8/1/2006)*

Heron Hill 2003 Icewine Riesling (Finger Lakes) $100. 86 *—M.D. (8/1/2006)*

Heron Hill 2004 Ingle Vineyard Icewine Riesling (Finger Lakes) $50. 88 *—M.D. (8/1/2006)*

Heron Hill 2004 Late Harvest Riesling (Finger Lakes) $36. 86 *—M.D. (8/1/2006)*

Heron Hill 2002 Reserve Riesling (Finger Lakes) $25. 85 *—M.D. (8/1/2006)*

HERRERA

Herrera 2003 Cabernet Sauvignon (Napa Valley) $125. 90 *—S.H. (12/1/2006)*

HERZOG

Herzog 2004 Special Edition Cabernet Sauvignon (Chalk Hill) $75. This bottling has been variable over the years, and the '04 is not showing it at its best. It's a good but not a great Cabernet, ripe and a little sweet in cassis and cherry flavors, backed up with firm, dry tannins. Drink now. **86** *—S.H. (12/31/2007)*

Herzog 2002 Special Edition Warnecke Vineyard Cabernet Sauvignon (Chalk Hill) $70. 86 *—S.H. (12/31/2005)*

Herzog 2000 Special Edition Warnecke Vineyard Cabernet Sauvignon (Chalk Hill) $52. 93 *—S.H. (11/15/2003)*

Herzog 1997 Special Edition Warnecke Vineyard Cabernet Sauvignon (Chalk Hill) $42. 89 *(11/1/2000)*

Herzog 2002 Special Reserve Cabernet Sauvignon (Napa Valley) $34. 82 *—S.H. (12/31/2005)*

Herzog 2000 Special Reserve Cabernet Sauvignon (Napa Valley) $35. 91 Editors' Choice *—S.H. (11/15/2003)*

Herzog 1997 Special Reserve Cabernet Sauvignon (Sonoma County) $32. 86 *(11/1/2000)*

Herzog 2005 Special Reserve Chardonnay (Russian River Valley) $30. There's too much oak for too little fruit in this wine, with the result that it tastes of sappy, smoky toothpicks. Buried under all that wood are modest apricot and pineapple flavors. **83** *—S.H. (12/31/2007)*

Herzog 2004 Special Reserve Chardonnay (Russian River Valley) $30. Besides the smoky new oak and leesy flavors, there's not a whole lot of fruit in this wine. At first, you're tasting apples and peaches, but then the middle falls apart and the finish turns watery. Disappointing. **83** *—S.H. (3/1/2007)*

Herzog 2001 Special Reserve Chardonnay (Russian River Valley) $27. 94 *—S.H. (8/1/2005)*

Herzog 2000 Special Reserve Chardonnay (Russian River Valley) $27. 92 Editors' Choice *—S.H. (12/15/2003)*

Herzog 2003 Late Harvest Chenin Blanc (Clarksburg) $16. 84 *—S.H. (7/1/2005)*

Herzog 2002 Special Reserve Merlot (Alexander Valley) $30. 82 *—S.H. (12/31/2005)*

Herzog 2002 Special Reserve Cabernet/Zinfandel/Syrah Red Blend (California) $40. 87 *—S.H. (8/1/2005)*

Herzog 2003 Special Reserve Syrah (Edna Valley) $30. 92 *—S.H. (12/31/2005)*

Herzog 2002 Special Reserve Syrah (Edna Valley) $30. 91 *—S.H. (8/1/2005)*

Herzog 2001 Special Reserve Syrah (Edna Valley) $30. 94 *—S.H. (1/1/2002)*

Herzog 2003 Late Harvest White Riesling (Monterey) $19. 84 *—S.H. (8/1/2005)*

Herzog 2005 Special Reserve Zinfandel (Lodi) $34. Shows the robust mouthfeel and high alcohol that Lodi Zins usually bring, with a concentration of Zinny essence that must be due to low-yielding vines. The blackberry and cherry jam fruit is tugged earthward by tobacco, coffee, white pepper and Asian spice flavors, giving the wine a dry, rich grounding. **88** *—S.H. (8/1/2007)*

HESS

Hess 2005 Cabernet Sauvignon (California) $15. Simple and a bit harsh in edgy acids and green tannins, this has just enough of a cherry-berry taste to pass. Okay for occasions calling for a decent red. **83** *—S.H. (11/15/2007)*

Hess 2004 Allomi Cabernet Sauvignon (Napa Valley) $25. It is hard to believe that 41,000 cases of this wine were produced because it's so good. Few other wineries could rise to this level at this production. Rich and dry in ripe cherry jam, blackberry pie, cassis, blueberry, smoky oak and spice flavors, it's a complex young wine that approximates the best of Napa Valley. **90** *—S.H. (5/1/2007)*

Hess 2006 Chardonnay (Monterey) $11. There's very little if any oak on this wine, which has a classic Central Coast profile of high acidity and bright, intense fruit. The flavors of limes, kiwis, passionfruit and vanilla finish long and bright. Good value in a classy, superdrinkable Chardonnay. **87 Best Buy** *—S.H. (11/15/2007)*

Hess 2005 Su'skol Vineyard Chardonnay (Napa Valley) $25. Made in the ever-popular style of a fully ripened, fruity Chard, with a good amount of new French oak and a creamy mouthfeel. Gets the job done in a fancy, no-nonsense way. **86** *—S.H. (5/1/2007)*

Hess 2002 Small Block Series Syrah (Napa Valley) $32. 83 *(9/1/2005)*

HESS COLLECTION

Hess Collection 2003 Mountain Cuvée Bordeaux Blend (Mount Veeder) $35. 88 —*S.H. (12/1/2006)*

Hess Collection 2001 Cabernet Blend (Napa Valley) $115. 92 Cellar Selection —*S.H. (12/15/2005)*

Hess Collection 2004 Mountain Cuvée Cabernet Blend (Mount Veeder) $35. A lovely wine, soft, supple and complex. It shows ripe, forward flavors of blackberries, cassis, mushu plum sauce, chocolate and oaky smoke and vanilla, with a sweet, wild edge of lavender and violets. A true Cabernet blend, with a drop of Syrah, it has the tannic structure to improve for five years. **91** —*S.H. (9/1/2007)*

Hess Collection 2002 Cabernet Sauvignon (Mount Veeder) $40. 94 Editors' Choice —*S.H. (3/1/2006)*

Hess Collection 2001 Cabernet Sauvignon (Mount Veeder) $40. 90 Cellar Selection —*S.H. (11/1/2005)*

Hess Collection 1995 Cabernet Sauvignon (Mount Veeder) $27. 87 —*M.M. (6/1/1999)*

Hess Collection 1995 Cabernet Sauvignon (Napa Valley) $25. 91 *(10/1/1999)*

Hess Collection 2004 Estate Grown Cabernet Sauvignon (Mount Veeder) $50. Production was 10,000 cases, amazing when you consider how good this mountain wine is. Immediately drinkable for the soft purity of the tannins and complex cassis, chocolate and oak flavors, it has the sturdy structure to develop for some years, but is best now for its elegant purity. Hess is on a real Cabernet roll, and is one of Napa's overlooked stars. **92** —*S.H. (12/1/2007)*

Hess Collection 2000 Estate Cabernet Sauvignon (Napa Valley) $34. 89 —*S.H. (11/15/2004)*

Hess Collection 1999 Estate Cabernet Sauvignon (Napa Valley) $20. 90 Editors' Choice —*S.H. (11/15/2003)*

Hess Collection 2004 Chardonnay (Napa Valley) $19. 87 —*S.H. (12/1/2006)*

Hess Collection 2003 Chardonnay (Napa Valley) $19. 86 —*S.H. (11/1/2005)*

Hess Collection 2002 Chardonnay (Napa Valley) $18. 87 —*S.H. (11/15/2004)*

Hess Collection 2001 Chardonnay (Napa Valley) $19. 90 —*S.H. (12/1/2003)*

Hess Collection 1997 Chardonnay (Napa Valley) $18. 83 *(6/1/2000)*

Hess Collection 2002 Mountain Cuvée Red Blend (Mount Veeder) $35. 90 —*S.H. (10/1/2005)*

Hess Collection 2001 Zinfandel (Dry Creek Valley) $27. 84 *(11/1/2003)*

Hess Collection 2005 Artezin Zinfandel (California) $18. Like the very nice '03, this multi-county blend is a classic, drink-me-now California Zinfandel. Dry and silky, it has wild berry, tobacco and peppery spice flavors, wrapped into firm but sweet tannins. It's made from Mendocino, Amador and Sonoma fruit. **89** —*S.H. (7/1/2007)*

HESS ESTATE

Hess Estate 2002 Cabernet Sauvignon (Napa Valley) $20. 87 —*S.H. (11/1/2005)*

Hess Estate 2001 Cabernet Sauvignon (Napa Valley) $20. 91 —*S.H. (5/1/2005)*

HESS SELECT

Hess Select 2003 Cabernet Sauvignon (California) $15. 85 —*S.H. (2/1/2006)*

Hess Select 2002 Cabernet Sauvignon (California) $15. 85 —*S.H. (6/1/2005)*

Hess Select 2001 Cabernet Sauvignon (California) $15. 86 —*S.H. (4/1/2004)*

Hess Select 2000 Cabernet Sauvignon (California-Washington) $15. 85 —*S.H. (2/4/2003)*

Hess Select 2004 Chardonnay (California) $10. 85 Best Buy —*S.H. (2/1/2006)*

Hess Select 2003 Chardonnay (California) $10. 84 —*S.H. (6/1/2005)*

Hess Select 1997 Chardonnay (California) $11. 87 *(11/15/1999)*

Hess Select 2003 Syrah (California) $14. 86 *(9/1/2005)*

Hess Select 2002 Syrah (California) $13. 84 —*S.H. (6/1/2005)*

Hess Select 2001 Syrah (California) $13. 85 —*S.H. (3/1/2004)*

Hess Select 1998 Syrah (California) $13. 84 *(10/1/2001)*

HESTIA

Hestia 2004 Red Blend (Columbia Valley (WA)) $20. This debut blend somehow reaches 15% alcohol, not easy to do with Yakima Valley Sangiovese. It's a solid effort, which opens well—supple and polished, with pretty flavors of mixed plum and berry. It's silky, smooth and there's plenty of tangy fruit. The finish gets a little too hot, but that's a minor quibble in a wine that gives you this much flavor at this price. The finish keeps getting more and more interesting, piling on smoked ham and spicy clove as it goes. **90 Editors' Choice** —*P.G. (12/31/2007)*

HEWITT

Hewitt 2002 Cabernet Sauvignon (Rutherford) $75. 92 —*S.H. (12/15/2005)*

Hewitt 2001 Cabernet Sauvignon (Rutherford) $75. 95 Cellar Selection —*S.H. (10/1/2004)*

Hewitt 2003 Estate Grown Cabernet Sauvignon (Rutherford) $80. 91 —*S.H. (12/15/2006)*

Hewitt 2004 Hewitt Vineyard Cabernet Sauvignon (Rutherford) $75. Tasted twice in mid-2007, several months apart. The first time, the wine was tough and astringent. The second tasting showed a fleshy young wine, still with firm tannins, but the cherries and plums were breaking through. This dry young Cab is on a development path. Drink now, with decanting, and through 2012. **90** —*S.H. (12/15/2007)*

HEY MAMBO

Hey Mambo 2004 Red Malbec (Napa Valley) $14. 87 —*S.H. (8/1/2006)*

Hey Mambo 2005 Sultry Red Red Blend (California) $12. This wine has bigtime drinkability. It's rich in berry-cherry, cocoa and spice flavors and totally dry, with the kind of acid-tannin structure made to chew through barbecue and Italian. **85** —*S.H. (10/1/2007)*

Hey Mambo 2006 Swanky White Blend (California) $14. The word for this white is fun. It's filled with apricot, pineapple, peach, green apple, honeysuckle and spice flavors, and is not complicated, but has a fine, crisp structure. The creative blend is Sauvignon Blanc, Viognier, Muscat and Chenin Blanc. **86** —*S.H. (11/15/2007)*

HIDDEN CELLARS

Hidden Cellars 1996 Cabernet Sauvignon (Mendocino) $15. 87 —*S.H. (3/1/2000)*

Hidden Cellars 1998 Eaglepoint Ranch-Mendocino Heritage Petite Sirah (Mendocino) $25. 93 —*S.H. (5/1/2002)*

Hidden Cellars 2002 Alchemy Sauvignon Blanc (Mendocino) $13. 82 —*S.H. (12/1/2004)*

Hidden Cellars 1997 Syrah (Mendocino) $15. 88 —*S.H. (5/1/2000)*

Hidden Cellars 1998 Syrah (Mendocino) $15. 86 *(10/1/2001)*

Hidden Cellars 1997 Deep Valley Zinfandel (Mendocino) $30. 87 —*D.T. (3/1/2002)*

Hidden Cellars 1997 Medocino Heritage Zania-Hitzma Zinfandel (Mendocino County) $28. 90 —*S.H. (9/1/1999)*

Hidden Cellars 1996 Mendocino Heritage Eaglepoint Zinfandel (Mendocino County) $28. 90 —*S.H. (9/1/1999)*

Hidden Cellars 1997 Mendocino Heritage Pacini Vine Zinfandel (Mendocino County) $28. 89 —*S.H. (9/1/1999)*

Hidden Cellars 2000 Old Vines Zinfandel (Mendocino) $13. 84 —*S.H. (9/1/2003)*

Hidden Cellars 1998 Old Vines Zinfandel (Mendocino) $13. 86 —*S.H. (5/1/2002)*

Hidden Cellars 1997 Sorcery Zinfandel (Mendocino) $28. 90 —*S.H. (5/1/2000)*

Hidden Cellars 1996 Sorcery Zinfandel (Mendocino County) $28. 90 —*S.H. (11/1/1999)*

HIDDEN MOUNTAIN RANCH

Hidden Mountain Ranch 1997 Chardonnay (San Luis Obispo) $11. 84 —*S.H. (2/1/2000)*

Hidden Mountain Ranch 1997 Zinfandel (California) $16. 83 —*S.H. (2/1/2000)*

Hidden Mountain Ranch 1998 Dante Dusi Vineyard Zinfandel (Paso Robles) $20. 85 —*S.H. (2/1/2000)*

HIDDEN RIDGE

Hidden Ridge 2003 Cabernet Sauvignon (Sonoma County) $75. This is from a vineyard high in the Mayacamas on the Sonoma side of Diamond Mountain. The wine was made by Marco DiGiulio, a well-known consulting winemaker in Napa Valley. It's a big, thick 100% mountain Cabernet, intense in cassis, dark chocolate and new oak, and an interesting hit of

Provençal herbs. It's also high in alcohol and low in acidity, which may inhibit ageability. **88** —*S.H. (9/1/2007)*

HIGH PASS

High Pass 1998 Pinot Noir (Willamette Valley) $16. 83 —*J.C. (12/1/2000)*

High Pass 1998 Reserve Pinot Noir (Willamette Valley) $25. 87 —*J.C. (12/1/2000)*

HIGH VALLEY

High Valley 2004 Cabernet Sauvignon (High Valley) $25. With a smooth texture, velvety tannins and long finish, there's lots to like in this Cabernet from Lake County. A drawback is that the blackberry and cherry fruit tastes sweetly sugared, which makes the wine rustic. **84** —*S.H. (5/1/2007)*

High Valley 2003 Cabernet Sauvignon (Lake County) $25. 83 —*S.H. (11/1/2005)*

High Valley 2006 Sauvignon Blanc (High Valley) $15. Young and racy, this wine has crisp citrus zest, gooseberry, white pepper and vanilla flavors that finish dry. The mouth-watering acidity scours the palate clean. **85** —*S.H. (8/1/2007)*

High Valley 2005 Sauvignon Blanc (High Valley) $15. Although this wine's chief fault is thinness, probably due to overcropping the vines in this high-yield vintage, it has some really nice attributes. It's clean, bone dry and crisply acidic, with interesting citrus and gooseberry flavors. A little more concentration would make it terrific. **85** —*S.H. (5/1/2007)*

High Valley 2004 Sauvignon Blanc (Lake County) $15. 86 —*S.H. (11/1/2005)*

High Valley 2003 Sauvignon Blanc (Lake County) $18. 84 —*S.H. (12/15/2004)*

HIGHLANDS

Highlands 2002 Beatty Ranch Cabernet Sauvignon (Howell Mountain) $80. 88 —*S.H. (3/1/2006)*

Highlands 2002 Hozhoni Vineyard Syrah (Napa Valley) $30. 80 —*S.H. (3/1/2006)*

Highlands 2002 Zinfandel (Howell Mountain) $30. 85 —*S.H. (3/1/2006)*

Highlands 2002 Beatty Ranch Zinfandel (Howell Mountain) $30. 89 —*S.H. (3/1/2006)*

HIGHTOWER CELLARS

Hightower Cellars 2003 Cabernet Sauvignon (Columbia Valley (WA)) $35. Smooth, rich and chocolaty, it falls into a satiny style that is ripe, but not jammy. It hits your mouth in all the right spots, and certainly brings the tastes that consumers love right to front and center: sweet fruit and rich chocolate. **89** —*P.G. (8/1/2007)*

Hightower Cellars 2003 Cabernet Sauvignon (Red Mountain) $50. 89 —*P.G. (11/15/2006)*

Hightower Cellars 2002 Cabernet Sauvignon (Columbia Valley (WA)) $31. 88 —*P.G. (10/1/2006)*

Hightower Cellars 2001 Cabernet Sauvignon (Columbia Valley (WA)) $28. 88 —*P.G. (11/15/2004)*

Hightower Cellars 2000 Cabernet Sauvignon (Columbia Valley (WA)) $31. 88 —*P.G. (9/1/2004)*

Hightower Cellars 2003 Pepper Bridge Cabernet Sauvignon-Merlot (Walla Walla (WA)) $NA. A 50-50 Cab-Merlot blend from Pepper Bridge, this is quite tight and reductive but grudgingly opens out. It's a stiff, hard wine, layered with blueberry, raspberry and cassis, and annotated with baker's chocolate and anise. Dark and unyielding, it has the muscle and authority to age for another six or eight years. There's a hint of green tea in the chewy tannins. **89** —*P.G. (8/1/2007)*

Hightower Cellars 2003 Pepper Bridge Vineyard Cabernet Sauvignon-Merlot (Walla Walla (WA)) $25. 87 —*P.G. (11/15/2006)*

Hightower Cellars 2004 Merlot (Columbia Valley (WA)) $28. This is a smooth blend of Red Mountain and Horse Heaven Hills Merlot, with a generous (18%) supplement of Cabernet Sauvignon. It's consistent with previous efforts and reminiscent of Reininger—satiny smooth, glossy and somewhat impenetrable. The tightly wound fruits taste of ripe raspberry, and the bright acidity adds intensity to the toasty, coffee-inflected finish. The wine is dense, supple and extracted, with hints of spice, herb, lemon thyme and citrusy high tones. **90** —*P.G. (8/1/2007)*

Hightower Cellars 2003 Merlot (Columbia Valley (WA)) $28. 92 —*P.G. (10/1/2006)*

Hightower Cellars 2001 Merlot (Columbia Valley (WA)) $25. 89 —*P.G. (11/15/2004)*

Hightower Cellars 2000 Merlot (Columbia Valley (WA)) $28. 89 —*P.G. (9/1/2004)*

Hightower Cellars 2004 Red Mountain Red Blend (Red Mountain) $50. Dark, dense, ripe and oaky, this ramps up the oak flavors to higher levels, with rich layers of smoke, cedar, honey and butterscotch wrapped into the spicy, sweet fruit. As the wine ages and opens up the lovely cherry-cassis core fruit should come into the spotlight. Call it a Washington take on ripe, high-octane California reds. **90** —*P.G. (8/1/2007)*

HIGHWAY 12

Highway 12 2004 Serres Ranch Field Blend Bordeaux Blend (Sonoma Valley) $24. 89 —*S.H. (12/1/2006)*

HILL FAMILY ESTATE

Hill Family Estate 2002 Cabernet Sauvignon (Napa Valley) $38. 87 —*S.H. (12/15/2005)*

Hill Family Estate 2001 Origin Cabernet Sauvignon-Merlot (Napa Valley) $38. 91 Editors' Choice —*J.M. (10/1/2004)*

Hill Family Estate 2002 Beau Terre Vineyard Merlot (Napa Valley) $30. 88 —*S.H. (12/15/2005)*

Hill Family Estate 2001 Beau Terre Vineyard Merlot (Napa Valley) $32. 91 —*J.M. (9/1/2004)*

Hill Family Estate 2002 Pinot Noir (Carneros) $38. 84 —*S.H. (12/15/2005)*

HINMAN

Hinman 1999 Chardonnay (Oregon) $10. 82 —*P.G. (4/1/2002)*

Hinman 2001 Pinot Gris (Oregon) $11. 84 —*M.S. (12/31/2002)*

Hinman 1999 Pinot Noir (Oregon) $13. 86 —*P.G. (4/1/2002)*

Hinman 2000 Rogue Red Red Blend (Rogue Valley) $13. 86 —*D.T. (12/31/2002)*

Hinman 2002 Riesling (Oregon) $8. 87 —*P.G. (12/1/2003)*

HIP CHICKS

Hip Chicks 2003 Reserve Pinot Noir (Willamette Valley) $35. 85 —*P.G. (9/1/2006)*

HIP CHICKS DO WINE

Hip Chicks do Wine 2004 Pinot Gris (Willamette Valley) $15. 83 —*P.G. (2/1/2006)*

Hip Chicks do Wine 2002 Pinot Noir (Willamette Valley) $18. 83 *(11/1/2004)*

HITCHING POST

Hitching Post 1988 Benedict Vineyard Pinot Noir (Santa Ynez Valley) $NA. 90 —*S.H. (6/1/2005)*

Hitching Post 2003 Cargasacchi Pinot Noir (Santa Rita Hills) $40. 86 —*S.H. (11/15/2006)*

Hitching Post 2003 Fiddlestix Pinot Noir (Santa Rita Hills) $50. 89 —*S.H. (11/15/2006)*

Hitching Post 2003 Rio Vista Vineyard Pinot Noir (Santa Rita Hills) $40. 87 —*S.H. (11/15/2006)*

Hitching Post 2001 Sanford & Benedict Vineyard Pinot Noir (Santa Rita Hills) $40. 90 —*S.H. (2/1/2004)*

Hitching Post 2001 Santa Rita's Earth Pinot Noir (Santa Rita Hills) $30. 89 —*S.H. (3/1/2004)*

Hitching Post 2000 Purisma Mountain Syrah (Santa Ynez Valley) $25. 92 —*S.H. (3/1/2004)*

HK GENERATIONS

HK Generations 2005 Chardonnay (Russian River Valley) $32. The name comes from Hop Kiln, an old winery now reinventing itself, and this is a good start. Made partly from Dutton fuit, this Chard is dry and crisply acidic, with polished green apple, lime, kiwi and oak flavors. **88** —*S.H. (5/1/2007)*

HK Generations 2004 Pinot Noir (Russian River Valley) $36. Here's a textbook example of a warm vintage Russian River Pinot. It has the appellation's velvety richness and varietal typicity, while the heat made for perfect ripening. Brims with cherry jam, blueberry pie, orange marmalade, date nut bread and oaky flavors, all balanced with juicy acidity, and the finish is dry. At its best now–2008. **93 Editors' Choice** —*S.H. (5/1/2007)*

HOBO

Hobo 2005 Cabernet Sauvignon (Alexander Valley) $20. This is not an ageable Cab, but it is balanced and complex, and has more than $20 worth of elegance. Dry and softly tannic, the Provençal herb, black cherry and oak flavors make you reach for a second glass. **90** —*S.H. (11/1/2007)*

Hobo 2006 Miss Hobo Rosé Blend (Sonoma County) $10. This is one of the zestier, zingier blush wines out there. It attacks the mouth with a lightning blast of acidity that wakes up the tastebuds, and is totally dry. Made from 90% Zinfandel and 10% Pinot Noir, the racy flavors are of slightly underripe raspberries, mint and rosehip tea. **86 Best Buy** —*S.H. (11/1/2007)*

Hobo 2005 Zinfandel (Rockpile) $28. Dry, tannic and concentrated, a fierce, almost feral wine, but it's classic in the way of California mountain Zins. Floods the mouth with blackberry essence, wrapped into strong tannins and finishing with a crisp burst of acidity. Compelling and complex, it cries out for a rustic beef or pork dish, long simmered and well seasoned. **90** —*S.H. (8/1/2007)*

Hobo 2005 Zinfandel (Dry Creek Valley) $20. Nice and balanced, an elegant Zin with classic flavors of wild cherries, cola, herbs and spices, with a delicate mouthfeel that finishes totally dry. A scour of dusty tannins gives it fine structure. Really notable for its silky purity. **90** —*S.H. (11/1/2007)*

HOGUE

Hogue 1998 Bordeaux Blend (Columbia Valley (WA)) $10. 88 Best Buy —*P.G. (6/1/2000)*

Hogue 1997 Genesis Cabernet Franc (Columbia Valley (WA)) $18. 84 —*P.G. (9/1/2000)*

Hogue 2005 Cabernet Sauvignon (Columbia Valley (WA)) $9. Soft and approachable, with 11% Cabernet Franc in the blend. The Franc stiffens up the backside, and adds some interesting aromatics to the front. It's a good ploy. This is a legitimate, no-frills wine. Clean, showing varietal character and well balanced. It bodes well for the future. **87** —*P.G. (11/1/2007)*

Hogue 2004 Cabernet Sauvignon (Columbia Valley (WA)) $9. 85 Best Buy —*P.G. (8/1/2006)*

Hogue 2002 Cabernet Sauvignon (Columbia Valley (WA)) $9. 87 Best Buy —*P.G. (7/1/2004)*

Hogue 1996 Columbia Valley Barrel Select Cabernet Sauvignon (Columbia Valley (WA)) $15. 89 —*L.W. (7/1/1999)*

Hogue 2004 Genesis Cabernet Sauvignon (Columbia Valley (WA)) $16. This is a big step up from recent vintages. Though it still carries an undertone of musty/chalky bark (from overly aggressive maceration?) it doesn't bury the fruit, and actually drinks quite well. 17% Merlot, 3% Syrah, 3% Malbec. **87** —*P.G. (11/1/2007)*

Hogue 2001 Genesis Cabernet Sauvignon (Columbia Valley (WA)) $17. 84 —*P.G. (11/15/2004)*

Hogue 2000 Genesis Cabernet Sauvignon (Columbia Valley (WA)) $16. 91 —*S.H. (1/1/2002)*

Hogue 1999 Genesis Cabernet Sauvignon (Columbia Valley (WA)) $17. 85 —*S.H. (12/31/2002)*

Hogue 2001 Reserve Cabernet Sauvignon (Columbia Valley (WA)) $30. 87 —*P.G. (9/1/2004)*

Hogue 2000 Reserve Cabernet Sauvignon (Columbia Valley (WA)) $30. 93 —*S.H. (1/1/2002)*

Hogue 1996 Reserve Cabernet Sauvignon (Columbia Valley (WA)) $30. 87 —*J.C. (4/1/2000)*

Hogue 1999 Vineyard Selection Cabernet Sauvignon (Columbia Valley (WA)) $17. 87 —*P.G. (6/1/2002)*

Hogue 1998 Vineyard Selection Cabernet Sauvignon (Columbia Valley (WA)) $16. 87 —*P.G. (6/1/2001)*

Hogue 1997 Cabernet Sauvignon-Merlot (Columbia Valley (WA)) $9. 88 Best Buy —*S.H. (7/1/1999)*

Hogue 2000 Cabernet Sauvignon-Merlot (Columbia Valley (WA)) $10. 83 —*P.G. (6/1/2002)*

Hogue 1999 Cabernet Sauvignon-Merlot (Columbia Valley (WA)) $10. 85 —*P.G. (6/1/2001)*

Hogue 2005 Chardonnay (Columbia Valley (WA)) $9. There is nothing especially wrong here, but it is such a predictable, monolithic, corporate wine that it's hard to get very excited. Clean fruit and soft, buttery flavors, along with vanilla and banana, seem calculated rather than crafted. Safe and solid. **85** —*P.G. (11/1/2007)*

Hogue 2002 Chardonnay (Columbia Valley (WA)) $10. 86 —*P.G. (9/1/2004)*

Hogue 2000 Chardonnay (Columbia Valley (WA)) $10. 87 Best Buy —*P.G. (2/1/2002)*

Hogue 1999 Chardonnay (Columbia Valley (WA)) $10. 88 Best Buy —*P.G. (6/1/2001)*

Hogue 1998 Chardonnay (Columbia Valley (WA)) $10. 86 —*P.G. (6/1/2000)*

Hogue 1998 Barrel Select Chardonnay (Columbia Valley (WA)) $15. 87 —*P.G. (6/1/2000)*

Hogue 2002 Genesis Chardonnay (Columbia Valley (WA)) $16. 87 —*P.G. (11/15/2004)*

Hogue 1999 Genesis Chardonnay (Columbia Valley (WA)) $15. 88 Best Buy —*S.H. (12/31/2002)*

Hogue 2002 Reserve Chardonnay (Columbia Valley (WA)) $22. 88 —*P.G. (9/1/2004)*

Hogue 2001 Reserve Chardonnay (Columbia Valley (WA)) $22. 85 —*S.H. (1/1/2002)*

Hogue 1999 Vineyard Selection Chardonnay (Columbia Valley (WA)) $14. 89 —*P.G. (6/1/2001)*

Hogue 1999 Chenin Blanc (Columbia Valley (WA)) $7. 87 Best Buy —*P.G. (8/19/2003)*

Hogue 1998 Fumé Blanc (Columbia Valley (WA)) $8. 88 Best Buy —*L.W. (11/1/1999)*

Hogue 2003 Fumé Blanc (Columbia Valley (WA)) $9. 86 —*P.G. (9/1/2004)*

Hogue 2001 Fumé Blanc (Columbia Valley (WA)) $10. 86 —*S.H. (12/31/2002)*

Hogue 2000 Fumé Blanc (Columbia Valley (WA)) $10. 87 Best Buy —*P.G. (12/31/2001)*

Hogue 1999 Gewürztraminer (Columbia Valley (WA)) $7. 85 —*P.G. (6/1/2000)*

Hogue 1998 Gewürztraminer (Columbia Valley (WA)) $7. 84 *(4/1/2000)*

Hogue 2003 Gewürztraminer (Columbia Valley (WA)) $10. 86 —*P.G. (7/1/2004)*

Hogue 2001 Gewürztraminer (Columbia Valley (WA)) $10. 85 —*P.G. (6/1/2002)*

Hogue 2000 Gewürztraminer (Columbia Valley (WA)) $8. 87 Best Buy —*P.G. (6/1/2001)*

Hogue 1999 Johannisberg Riesling (Columbia Valley (WA)) $7. 87 Best Buy —*P.G. (6/1/2000)*

Hogue 1998 Johannisberg Riesling (Columbia Valley (WA)) $NA. 86 —*L.W. (9/1/1999)*

Hogue 2002 Johannisberg Riesling (Columbia Valley (WA)) $9. 85 —*S.H. (1/1/2002)*

Hogue 2000 Johannisberg Riesling (Columbia Valley (WA)) $8. 86 —*P.G. (6/1/2001)*

Hogue 1997 Genesis Blue Franc Lemberger (Yakima Valley) $14. 85 —*P.G. (9/1/2000)*

Hogue 2001 Terroir Lemberger (Columbia Valley (WA)) $20. 88 —*P.G. (1/1/2004)*

Hogue 2005 Merlot (Columbia Valley (WA)) $9. Simple, clean and rounded out with balanced acids and just enough flesh to fill the midpalate. It's a fair value at this price. A hint of herb and green bean in the finish. **86** —*P.G. (11/1/2007)*

Hogue 2004 Merlot (Columbia Valley (WA)) $9. 86 Best Buy —*P.G. (8/1/2006)*

Hogue 2003 Merlot (Yakima Valley) $10. 87 —*P.G. (8/1/2005)*

Hogue 2002 Merlot (Columbia Valley (WA)) $9. 85 —*P.G. (7/1/2004)*

Hogue 2001 Merlot (Columbia Valley (WA)) $10. 87 Best Buy —*S.H. (12/31/2002)*

Hogue 2000 Merlot (Columbia Valley (WA)) $10. 85 —*P.G. (6/1/2002)*

Hogue 1997 Barrel Select Merlot (Columbia Valley (WA)) $15. 87 —*P.G. (6/1/2000)*

Hogue 2004 Genesis Merlot (Columbia Valley (WA)) $16. Smooth and forward, with high-toned cherry fruit. Oak aging adds notes of vanilla and spice. The alcohol hits a surprising 14.5% but does not feel that substantial in the mouth. **87** —*P.G. (11/1/2007)*

Hogue 2001 Genesis Merlot (Columbia Valley (WA)) $17. 84 —*P.P. (11/15/2004)*

Hogue 1998 Genesis Merlot (Columbia Valley (WA)) $17. 85 —*S.H. (1/1/2002)*

Hogue 2001 Reserve Merlot (Columbia Valley (WA)) $30. 87 —*P.G. (9/1/2004)*

Hogue 1996 Reserve Merlot (Columbia Valley (WA)) $30. 87 —*J.C. (4/1/2000)*

Hogue 1999 Vineyard Selection Merlot (Columbia Valley (WA)) $17. 87 —*P.G. (6/1/2002)*

Hogue 1998 Vineyard Selection Merlot (Columbia Valley (WA)) $16. 87 —*P.G. (6/1/2001)*

Hogue 2006 Pinot Grigio (Columbia Valley (WA)) $9. This is fresh and crisp, with some nice citrus skin flavors under green apple fruit. Nothing too fancy here; but it's clean and sound and perfectly fine served chilled with a seafood salad. **85** —*P.G. (11/1/2007)*

Hogue 2003 Pinot Grigio (Columbia Valley (WA)) $10. 87 —*P.G. (7/1/2004)*

Hogue 1998 Pinot Gris (Columbia Valley (WA)) $8. 86 Best Buy —*S.H. (11/1/1999)*

Hogue 2001 Pinot Gris (Columbia Valley (WA)) $10. 86 Best Buy —*S.H. (12/31/2002)*

Hogue 2000 Pinot Gris (Columbia Valley (WA)) $10. 87 Best Buy —*P.G. (2/1/2002)*

Hogue 1998 Genesis Pinot Gris (Yakima Valley) $13. 89 —*L.W. (2/1/2000)*

Hogue 2006 Riesling (Columbia Valley (WA)) $9. With 14% Gewürztraminer in the blend, and almost 2% residual sugar, this is a popular tasting-room wine. It's got a lightly pleasing streak of tea, and if you like a little lemon in your ice tea you'll like this wine. Clean and showing surprising length, it should be chilled down to boost its backbone. **87** —*P.G. (9/1/2007)*

Hogue 2001 Riesling (Columbia Valley (WA)) $10. 86 Best Buy —*P.G. (6/1/2002)*

Hogue 2006 Genesis Riesling (Washington) $15. Genesis is Hogue's upper tier line, made in much smaller quantities than the regular wines. In effect, it tries to be a sort of reserve, selecting the best lots from the best vineyards. Here it only partially succeeds in eclipsing the much less expensive regular Riesling. This has more mass and concentration, but seems a bit heavy and fat, and loses some of the delicacy in the finish. **87** —*P.G. (9/1/2007)*

Hogue 1997 Genesis Schwartzman Vineyard Riesling (Yakima Valley) $13. 90 —*L.W. (8/19/2003)*

Hogue 2001 Late Harvest Riesling (Columbia Valley (WA)) $12. 88 —*P.G. (6/1/2002)*

Hogue 2002 Terroir Riesling (Columbia Valley (WA)) $13. 88 Best Buy —*P.G. (11/15/2004)*

Hogue 2001 Genesis Sangiovese (Columbia Valley (WA)) $13. 85 —*S.H. (6/1/2003)*

Hogue 2001 Terroir Sangiovese (Columbia Valley (WA)) $25. 87 —*P.G. (9/1/2004)*

Hogue 1998 Genesis Burgess Vineyard Sauvignon Blanc (Columbia Valley (WA)) $15. 88 —*L.W. (2/1/2000)*

Hogue 1998 Sémillon (Columbia Valley (WA)) $7. 86 Best Buy *(2/1/2000)*

Hogue 1999 Sémillon (Columbia Valley (WA)) $8. 88 Best Buy —*P.G. (6/1/2001)*

Hogue 1999 Genesis Sémillon (Columbia Valley (WA)) $13. 85 —*P.G. (12/31/2001)*

Hogue 2005 Shiraz (Columbia Valley (WA)) $9. At this price, this is good stuff. The fruit shows some tangy blackberry and black raspberry crispness; there is plenty of acid, and everything else is in good balance. This seems to be a real step forward for Hogue. **87** —*P.G. (11/1/2007)*

Hogue 2002 Syrah (Columbia Valley (WA)) $9. 87 Best Buy —*P.G. (7/1/2004)*

Hogue 1997 Barrel Select Syrah (Columbia Valley (WA)) $15. 86 —*P.G. (9/1/2000)*

Hogue 1997 Barrel Select Syrah (Columbia Valley (WA)) $15. 87 —*S.H. (11/1/1999)*

Hogue 2004 Genesis Syrah (Columbia Valley (WA)) $16. Firm and lush, the blend also includes 12% Merlot and 2% Cabernet Sauvignon. This is a bigger, more expansive style than the regular Syrah, but still a fine value. Plush flavors of black fruits—blackberry, black cherry and blue plum—linger sensuously and are wrapped into the toasty barrel flavors. **88** —*P.G. (11/1/2007)*

Hogue 2001 Genesis Syrah (Columbia Valley (WA)) $16. 87 *(9/1/2005)*

Hogue 1999 Genesis Syrah (Columbia Valley (WA)) $25. 87 —*P.G. (12/31/2002)*

Hogue 1997 Genesis Syrah (Columbia Valley (WA)) $25. 88 —*P.G. (9/1/2000)*

Hogue 1996 Genesis Syrah (Columbia Valley (WA)) $15. 87 —*P.G. (9/1/2000)*

Hogue 2001 Terroir Syrah (Columbia Valley (WA)) $25. 85 —*P.G. (9/1/2004)*

Hogue 1999 Vineyard Selection Syrah (Columbia Valley (WA)) $18. 86 *(10/1/2001)*

Hogue 2003 Genesis Viognier (Columbia Valley (WA)) $16. 87 —*P.G. (4/1/2005)*

Hogue 2001 Genesis Viognier (Columbia Valley (WA)) $15. 87 —*S.H. (12/31/2002)*

Hogue 2000 Vineyard Selection Viognier (Columbia Valley (WA)) $16. 88 Best Buy —*P.G. (10/1/2001)*

Hogue 2006 Fumé Blanc White Blend (Columbia Valley (WA)) $9. Watery and thin, with only the barest hint of varietal character. This is as innocuous and dull a wine as you could ever hope to find. **83** —*P.G. (11/1/2007)*

HOLBROOK

Holbrook 2003 Syrah (Santa Barbara County) $16. Plenty of juicy berry-cherry and chocolate fruit in this wine, which must have come from the warmer, inland parts of the county. It's smooth in tannins and a little soft, but offers interesting layers of complexity as it warms in the glass. Drink now. **87** —*S.H. (4/1/2007)*

Holbrook 2001 Syrah (Central Coast) $16. 84 —*S.H. (9/1/2005)*

HOLDREDGE

Holdredge 2004 Pinot Noir (Russian River Valley) $32. 82 —*S.H. (7/1/2006)*

Holdredge 2002 Pinot Noir (Russian River Valley) $30. 84 —*S.H. (11/1/2004)*

Holdredge 2004 Wren Hop Vineyard Pinot Noir (Russian River Valley) $36. 88 —*S.H. (7/1/2006)*

Holdredge 2002 Lovers Lane Vineyard Syrah (Russian River Valley) $28. 84 —*S.H. (12/15/2004)*

Holdredge 2004 Zinfandel (Dry Creek Valley) $24. 85 —*S.H. (7/1/2006)*

Holdredge 2004 Zinfandel (Alexander Valley) $24. 80 —*S.H. (7/1/2006)*

HOLLY'S HILL

Holly's Hill 2000 Chardonnay (El Dorado) $15. 85 —*S.H. (12/15/2002)*

Holly's Hill 2003 Grenache (El Dorado) $17. 84 —*S.H. (12/15/2004)*

Holly's Hill 2003 Rosé Traditionnel Grenache (El Dorado) $12. 87 Best Buy —*S.H. (12/15/2004)*

Holly's Hill 2002 Mourvèdre (El Dorado) $18. 82 —*S.H. (12/15/2004)*

Holly's Hill 2004 Patriarche Rhône Red Blend (El Dorado) $30. Simple and likeable, this blend of Mourvèdre, Syrah, Grenache and Counoise brims with cherry, raspberry and cocoa fruit. It seems to have a little residual sugar, to judge by the sugary finish, and though I don't like that, lots of people do. **84** —*S.H. (3/1/2007)*

Holly's Hill 2005 Patriarche Blanc Rhône White Blend (El Dorado) $22. Here's a rich Rhône blend of Roussanne and Viognier. It's big in white and yellow stone fruit flavors, like nectarines, peaches and pineapples, with a tropical wildflower note, and finishes dry and clean. **86** —*S.H. (3/1/2007)*

Holly's Hill 2003 Tranquille Blanc Rhône White Blend (El Dorado) $16. 84 —*S.H. (12/15/2004)*

Holly's Hill 1999 Sangiovese (California) $17. 87 —*S.H. (7/1/2002)*

Holly's Hill 2000 Syrah (El Dorado) $22. 84 —*S.H. (6/1/2003)*

Holly's Hill 1999 Syrah (El Dorado) $20. 85 —*S.H. (7/1/2002)*

Holly's Hill 2002 Wylie-Fenaughty Syrah (El Dorado) $22. 83 —*S.H. (12/15/2004)*

Holly's Hill 2000 Viognier (Amador County) $15. 87 —*J.M. (12/15/2002)*

Holly's Hill 2006 Estate Viognier (El Dorado) $16. Soft, simple and sweet, this easy-drinking wine has ripe, forward flavors of Lifesaver candies, wildflowers, spices and honey. **84** —*S.H. (12/15/2007)*

Holly's Hill 2000 Vin Doux Viognier (California) $18. 82 —*S.H. (12/31/2001)*

Holly's Hill 2001 Zinfandel (Sierra Foothills) $17. 85 *(11/1/2003)*

Holly's Hill 1999 Zinfandel (Amador County) $17. 87 —*S.H. (7/1/2002)*

HOLLYWOOD & VINE

Hollywood & Vine 2000 Cabernet Sauvignon (Napa Valley) $78. 91 Cellar Selection —*J.M. (9/1/2003)*

Hollywood & Vine 1999 Cabernet Sauvignon (Napa Valley) $75. 92 —*J.M. (6/1/2002)*

Hollywood & Vine 2004 2480 Cabernet Sauvignon (Napa Valley) $78. This Cab shows an ultrasoft mouthfeel together with fairly aggressive tannins, suggesting an inherent imbalance. The flavors are complex, with herb- and tobacco-tinged blackberry, mocha and cherry fruit mingled with spicy oak. The tight tannins suggest aging, while the absence of acidity mitigates against it. Probably best now. **85** —*S.H. (11/1/2007)*

Hollywood & Vine 2001 Chardonnay (Napa Valley) $40. 91 —*J.M. (6/1/2003)*

Hollywood & Vine 2006 2480 Chardonnay (Napa Valley) $45. The grapes come from Atlas Peak, and while the wine is dry, it's very soft, which gives the ultraripe apricots and peaches a syrupy taste. The caramelly oak adds to the feeling of heaviness. **83** *—S.H. (11/1/2007)*

HOME HILL

Home Hill 2002 Pinot Noir (Carneros) $30. 84 *—S.H. (4/1/2004)*

HOMEWOOD

Homewood 1997 Merlot (Napa Valley) $25. 84 *—S.H. (12/1/2001)*

Homewood 1997 Kunde Vineyard Zinfandel (Sonoma Valley) $16. 82 *—S.H. (11/15/2001)*

HONIG

Honig 2004 Cabernet Sauvignon (Napa Valley) $35. Balanced and elegant, this is the kind of Cabernet you drink with food where the food, not the wine, takes center stage. It's dry and richly tannic, with complex but never overripe blackberry, cassis, coffee and oak flavors, and the finish is long and satisfying. Drink now–2012. **89** *—S.H. (5/1/2007)*

Honig 2001 Cabernet Sauvignon (Napa Valley) $30. 87 *—S.H. (12/15/2004)*

Honig 1996 Cabernet Sauvignon (Napa Valley) $22. 90 *—M.S. (10/1/1999)*

Honig 2004 Mitchell Vineyard Cabernet Sauvignon (Rutherford) $85. Made in an appealingly ripe, polished style, this 100% Cab has intense flavors of ripe cherries, currants, spices and cedar, with a dusty sprinkle of dried herbs. It shows the elegant balance and ageworthiness of a fine Rutherford Cabernet Sauvignon. Now through 2012, at least. **92** *—S.H. (12/15/2007)*

Honig 2006 Sauvignon Blanc (Napa Valley) $16. Here's a nice cocktail-style wine that pleases for its dryness and crispness. It's basically a simple quaffer, with no oak at all, and rewards for fresh, ripe pineapple, Meyer lemon, fig and date flavors. Try with your best homemade ahi tuna tartare. **86** *—S.H. (9/1/2007)*

Honig 2005 Sauvignon Blanc (Napa Valley) $15. Restaurateurs will be interested in this wine for its food-friendliness and price. All stainless-steel fermented, it's totally dry and very crisp in acidity, with complex lemongrass, gooseberry and vanilla flavors, and a pink grapefruit finish. It's the kind of wine that will go well with almost everything. Great wine, great value. **90 Best Buy** *—S.H. (5/1/2007)*

Honig 2003 Sauvignon Blanc (Rutherford) $20. 87 *(7/1/2005)*

Honig 2001 Sauvignon Blanc (Napa Valley) $14. 90 Best Buy *—J.M. (11/15/2002)*

Honig 1999 Sauvignon Blanc (Napa Valley) $13. 88 *—J.M. (12/15/2001)*

HOODSPORT

Hoodsport 1998 Cabernet Franc (Yakima Valley) $20. 82 *—S.H. (9/1/2000)*

Hoodsport 2005 Cabernet Sauvignon (Columbia Valley (WA)) $17. This starts out with a slightly reduced, tanky smell, then leads into a green, stemmy, tannic wine with a bitter, green tea finish. **81** *—P.G. (12/31/2007)*

Hoodsport 2005 Cabernet - Merlot (Columbia Valley (WA)) $17. Very stiff and tannic, with hard, stemmy flavors and very little evidence of ripe fruit. **82** *—P.G. (12/31/2007)*

Hoodsport 2005 Chardonnay (Columbia Valley (WA)) $14. A simple, plain Jane style, moderately flavorful but quite generic. **83** *—P.G. (12/1/2007)*

Hoodsport 1998 Chardonnay (Yakima Valley) $11. 82 *—S.H. (11/15/2000)*

Hoodsport 1998 Reserve Chardonnay (Yakima Valley) $17. 88 *—S.H. (11/15/2000)*

Hoodsport 1998 Chenin Blanc (Yakima Valley) $9. 81 *—S.H. (11/15/2000)*

Hoodsport 1998 Gewürztraminer (Yakima Valley) $9. 83 *—S.H. (11/15/2000)*

Hoodsport 1998 Lemberger-Cabernet (Yakima Valley) $11. 85 *—S.H. (9/1/2000)*

Hoodsport 2005 Merlot (Columbia Valley (WA)) $17. Light, soda flavors of raspberry and cherry lend modest appeal to this simple Merlot. It's a straightforward style that finishes with a hint of chocolate. **83** *—P.G. (12/31/2007)*

Hoodsport 2002 Pinot Noir (Oregon) $27. 85 *(11/1/2004)*

Hoodsport 1998 Sémillon (Yakima Valley) $9. 81 *—S.H. (11/15/2000)*

Hoodsport 2002 Syrah (Yakima Valley) $27. 88 *(9/1/2005)*

HOOK & LADDER

Hook & Ladder 2003 Third Alarm Reserve Cabernet Sauvignon (Russian River Valley) $30. 86 *—S.H. (12/1/2006)*

Hook & Ladder 2003 Chardonnay (Russian River Valley) $16. 84 *—S.H. (10/1/2005)*

Hook & Ladder 2003 Third Alarm Reserve Chardonnay (Russian River Valley) $25. 81 *—S.H. (12/31/2005)*

Hook & Ladder 2005 Gewürztraminer (Russian River Valley) $12. Simple, fruity-flowery and off-dry, this Gewürz, from the winery's estate vineyard, is forward in peach, honeysuckle, pineapple and kiwi flavors, with a spicy, honeyed finish. **84** *—S.H. (5/1/2007)*

Hook & Ladder 2004 Pinot Noir (Russian River Valley) $20. 88 *—S.H. (3/1/2006)*

Hook & Ladder 2003 The Tillerman Red Blend (Russian River Valley) $16. 83 *—S.H. (11/1/2005)*

Hook & Ladder 2004 Zinfandel (Russian River Valley) $22. 87 *—S.H. (12/1/2006)*

Hook & Ladder 2003 White Zinfandel (Russian River Valley) $8. 83 *—S.H. (10/1/2005)*

HOOPES

Hoopes 2003 Cabernet Sauvignon (Oakville) $60. 90 *—S.H. (9/1/2006)*

Hoopes 2002 Cabernet Sauvignon (Oakville) $60. 94 Editors' Choice *—S.H. (11/1/2005)*

HOP KILN

Hop Kiln 1997 Chardonnay (Russian River Valley) $18. 88 *—S.H. (11/1/1999)*

Hop Kiln NV Big Red Red Blend (California) $13. 85 *—S.H. (11/1/2005)*

Hop Kiln NV Rushin' River Red Red Blend (California) $15. 87 *—S.H. (12/31/2005)*

Hop Kiln 2004 A Thousand Flowers White Blend (North Coast) $12. 84 *—S.H. (11/1/2005)*

Hop Kiln 2005 Thousand Flowers White Blend (California) $14. 84 *—S.H. (11/15/2006)*

Hop Kiln 2004 Old Windmill Zin Zinfandel (Russian River Valley) $22. 82 *—S.H. (11/15/2006)*

Hop Kiln 2001 Turtle Creek Vineyard Zinfandel (Russian River Valley) $16. 84 *(11/1/2003)*

HOPKINS VINEYARD

Hopkins Vineyard 1999 Estate Bottled Cabernet Franc (Western Connecticut Highlands) $16. 83 *—M.S. (3/1/2003)*

Hopkins Vineyard 1999 Estate Bottled Chardonnay (Western Connecticut Highlands) $15. 84 *—J.M. (7/1/2002)*

Hopkins Vineyard 2004 Estate Bottled Ice Wine Vidal Blanc (Western Connecticut Highlands) $40. Estate-bottled with assertive aromas of peach and apricot, this dessert wine tends towards the sweet but is balanced with a good acidity. May still be a tad sweet for fans of an icewine with a more measured touch, but the fruit is fresh and flavorful and the wine has complexity. Will pair well with creamy desserts—think vanilla ice cream or crème brûlée. **84** *—S.K. (7/1/2007)*

HOPPER CREEK

Hopper Creek 2002 Merlot (Napa Valley) $35. 92 *—S.H. (8/1/2006)*

HORAN ESTATES

Horan Estates 2004 CWM Syrah (Columbia Valley (WA)) $28. This is tasty stuff, with plenty of coffee and toast wrapped over and around the medium-weight, sappy red fruit flavors. There's nothing shy here, as the alcohol tops 15%, but the wine carries itself comfortably and the addition of 9% Cabernet Sauvignon adds some muscle to the finish. **88** *—P.G. (3/1/2007)*

HOURGLASS

Hourglass 2003 Cabernet Sauvignon (St. Helena) $115. 93 *—S.H. (8/1/2006)*

Hourglass 2001 Cabernet Sauvignon (St. Helena) $90. 94 *—S.H. (10/1/2004)*

Hourglass 2000 Cabernet Sauvignon (Napa Valley) $85. 95 Editors' Choice *—J.M. (12/15/2003)*

Hourglass 1998 Cabernet Sauvignon (Napa Valley) $75. 95 Cellar Selection *—J.M. (5/1/2002)*

Hourglass 1997 Cabernet Sauvignon (Napa Valley) $125. 95 *—J.M. (12/31/2001)*

HOWELL MOUNTAIN VINEYARDS

Howell Mountain Vineyards 2001 Cabernet Sauvignon (Howell Mountain) $60. 91 *—S.H. (6/1/2005)*

Howell Mountain Vineyards 2000 Cabernet Sauvignon (Napa Valley) $36. 84 *—S.H. (12/15/2003)*

Howell Mountain Vineyards 2001 Beatty Ranch Cabernet Sauvignon (Howell Mountain) $75. 94 *—S.H. (6/1/2005)*

Howell Mountain Vineyards 2001 Black Sears Vineyard Cabernet Sauvignon (Howell Mountain) $75. 93 *—S.H. (6/1/2005)*

Howell Mountain Vineyards 2001 HMV Cabernet Sauvignon (Napa Valley) $36. 89 *—S.H. (10/1/2005)*

Howell Mountain Vineyards 2003 Beatty Ranch Zinfandel (Howell Mountain) $38. 85 *—S.H. (5/1/2006)*

Howell Mountain Vineyards 2002 Beatty Ranch Zinfandel (Howell Mountain) $38. 93 *—S.H. (10/1/2005)*

Howell Mountain Vineyards 2001 Beatty Ranch Zinfandel (Howell Mountain) $34. 90 *(11/1/2003)*

Howell Mountain Vineyards 1997 Beatty Ranch Zinfandel (Howell Mountain) $NA. 90 Best Buy *—S.H. (6/1/1999)*

Howell Mountain Vineyards 2003 Black Sears Vineyard Zinfandel (Howell Mountain) $38. 90 *—S.H. (5/1/2006)*

Howell Mountain Vineyards 2002 Black Sears Vineyard Zinfandel (Howell Mountain) $38. 90 *—S.H. (10/1/2005)*

Howell Mountain Vineyards 2001 Black Sears Vineyard Zinfandel (Napa Valley) $34. 92 *(11/1/2003)*

Howell Mountain Vineyards 1997 Black Sears Vineyards Zinfandel (Howell Mountain) $NA. 88 *—S.H. (6/1/1999)*

Howell Mountain Vineyards 2003 Old Vine Zinfandel (Howell Mountain) $26. 90 *—S.H. (5/1/2006)*

Howell Mountain Vineyards 2001 Old Vine Zinfandel (Howell Mountain) $24. 87 *(11/1/2003)*

Howell Mountain Vineyards 1997 Old Vine Zinfandel (Howell Mountain) $24. 91 *—S.H. (6/1/1999)*

Howell Mountain Vineyards 2002 Old Vines Zinfandel (Howell Mountain) $26. 87 *—S.H. (10/1/2005)*

HRM REX GOLIATH

HRM Rex Goliath NV Cabernet Sauvignon (Central Coast) $9. 83 *—S.H. (6/1/2005)*

HRM Rex Goliath NV Cabernet Sauvignon (Central Coast) $8. 80 *—J.M. (6/1/2003)*

HRM Rex Goliath NV Cabernet Sauvignon (California) $9. 84 *—S.H. (12/15/2005)*

HRM Rex Goliath 2004 Chardonnay (Central Coast) $9. 82 *—S.H. (12/15/2005)*

HRM Rex Goliath 2003 Chardonnay (Central Coast) $9. 83 *—S.H. (6/1/2005)*

HRM Rex Goliath 2001 Free Range Chardonnay (Central Coast) $8. 84 *—S.H. (12/31/2003)*

HRM Rex Goliath NV Merlot (Central Coast) $9. 82 *—S.H. (6/1/2005)*

HRM Rex Goliath NV Merlot (Central Coast) $8. 82 *—J.M. (9/1/2003)*

HRM Rex Goliath NV Merlot (California) $9. 82 *—S.H. (12/15/2005)*

HRM Rex Goliath 2004 Pinot Grigio (California) $9. 85 Best Buy *—S.H. (12/15/2005)*

HRM Rex Goliath NV Pinot Noir (California) $9. 83 *—S.H. (12/15/2005)*

HRM Rex Goliath 2001 Free Range Pinot Noir (Central Coast) $8. 84 *—S.H. (7/1/2003)*

HRM Rex Goliath 2003 Free Range Shiraz (Central Coast) $9. 85 Best Buy *—S.H. (6/1/2005)*

HUBER

Huber 2004 Chardonnay (Santa Rita Hills) $25. 90 *—S.H. (3/1/2006)*

Huber 2005 Estate Chardonnay (Santa Rita Hills) $28. This is everything Huber's previously released unoaked '05 Chard is, but barrel fermentation and partial malo have made it far softer and richer. Strangely, it's not as rewarding, though, as the brilliant purity of fruit and acid have been modified. It's a very good wine, but lacks that je ne sais quoi that makes it stand out from the crowd. **89** *—S.H. (4/1/2007)*

Huber 2005 Estate Grown Chardonnay (Santa Rita Hills) $21. 90 *—S.H. (11/15/2006)*

Huber 2004 Dornfelder (Santa Rita Hills) $25. 89 Cellar Selection *—S.H. (12/1/2006)*

Huber 2005 Estate Dornfelder (Santa Rita Hills) $32. Pours purple-black, with dramatic glycerine streaks that stain the glass. This is obviously a big, bold, intense young wine, grapy to the point of jam in plum and blackberry flavors. It's a big gulp, almost Port-y but staying just this side of dry. **86** *—S.H. (4/1/2007)*

Huber 2004 Pinot Noir (Santa Rita Hills) $34. 88 *—S.H. (3/1/2006)*

Huber 2005 Estate Pinot Noir (Santa Rita Hills) $38. The vineyard, also the source of a Brewer-Clifton bottling, is a top one, and here has produced a luscious wine in this long hangtime vintage. Pinot doesn't get much riper in cherry marmalade, black raspberry and blueberry jam, cola and pomegranate than this and there's a rich, blackstrap molasses undercurrent. For all that, the wine finishes briny-spicy. Has the depth and acid-tannin balance to age gracefully through 2012. **93** *—S.H. (4/1/2007)*

HUDSON SHAH

Hudson Shah 2005 Riesling (Washington) $22. This strong, unusual and quite assertive wine bowls you over with its tutti-frutti flavors of bubble gum, juicy fruit, and so on. It is such a unique style for Riesling that it caught me off guard. Perhaps others will favor the big, heavy, rather clumsy fruit more than I, but to me it seems to be a sort of anti-Riesling. **85** *—P.G. (3/1/2007)*

Hudson Shah 2005 Viognier (Columbia Valley (WA)) $37. Superripe, supersaturated style with rich, thick flavors of pear, peach and papaya, enlivened with cinnamon and toasted coconut spice. This is very well made, and carries its heft with grace and a certain amount of precision. The nose is exceptionally complex, layered with tropical fruits, citrus, mint, exotic spices and more. The finish lingers sensuously. **91** *—P.G. (5/1/2007)*

HUG

Hug 2005 Pinot Noir (Central Coast) $25. Here's a nice Pinot that shows how ripe that sprawling region can get the grapes while still preserving fresh acidity. The raspberries, cherries, cola and rosehip tea are joined by a rich, fudgy coating of almost sweet milk chocolate. Meanwhile, those acids are just perfect, skimming off baby fat and making the wine balanced. **86** *—S.H. (2/1/2007)*

Hug 2005 Cedar Lane Vineyard Pinot Noir (Arroyo Seco) $29. There's not a lot of Pinot grown in this cool Salinas Valley appellation because most of the grapes are white, but judging from this wine, there should be. It has the medium-bodied, silky texture and crisp acids you want in a fine Pinot, as well as flavorful cherry, cola, raspberry, coffee and spice flavors that lead to a dry, polished aftertaste. **90** *—S.H. (2/1/2007)*

Hug 2005 Orchid Hill Vineyard Pinot Noir (Paso Robles) $29. A bit too soft, sweet and thick to be considered a truly coastal Pinot, but the flavors are very tasty. It's the essence of raspberry and cherry jam, with sprinkings of cocoa-dusted cappuccino and cassis. **86** *—S.H. (2/1/2007)*

Hug 2005 Rancho Ontiveros Pinot Noir (Santa Maria Valley) $48. The vineyard is across the road from Bien Nacido, and the wine shows many of the same qualities as that famed property. This Pinot is big, dry and dusty, with some fairly grippy tannins. Yet it has the purity and silky mouthfeel of great Pinot Noir, with a crushed brown spice taste that hovers over ripe cherry-berry, cola and mocha flavors. Decant for a few hours before serving. **93** *—S.H. (2/1/2007)*

Hug 2006 Cedar Lane Vineyard Sauvignon Blanc (Arroyo Seco) $18. Another victim of the cool 2006 vintage, this is unpleasantly loaded with cat pee aromas. **81** *—S.H. (11/1/2007)*

Hug 2005 Syrah (Paso Robles) $29. A little on the soft, one-dimensional side, but very drinkable, with jammy flavors of cherries, blackberries, blueberries and spices, and the leathery, roasted meat taste you sometimes find in Syrah. The gritty tannins will cut through roasts. **86** *—S.H. (11/1/2007)*

Hug 2004 Syrah (Central Coast) $27. Pretty ordinary wine, dry, full-bodied and tannic, with very ripe blackberry fruit veering into chocolate-covered raisins. Seems pricey for what you get. **83** *—S.H. (3/1/2007)*

Hug 2004 Bassetti Vineyard Syrah (San Luis Obispo County) $40. Dry and fruity, this is a softly-structured wine that brims with complex blackberry, plum, coffee, chocolate, soy, balsamic and white pepper flavors. It's a stylish Syrah that's at its best now. **87** *—S.H. (3/1/2007)*

Hug 2003 Bassetti Vineyard Syrah (San Luis Obispo County) $40. 86 *(9/1/2005)*

Hug 2005 Bassetti Vineyard Rena Block Syrah (San Luis Obispo County) $45. This big, ripe, powerful Syrah is potent in everything the grape develops in a cool vintage. The flavors are all about white pepper-accented crushed blackberries and cherries, with a salty, beef jerky savory taste, while the tannins give a sharp, structural edge. There's even an acidic cut. The volume suggests decanting, and it could develop in the bottle over the next few years. **91** *—S.H. (11/1/2007)*

Hug 2005 Cedar Lane Vineyard Syrah (Arroyo Seco) $29. As ripe as the fruit is, and it's very ripe, with showy blackberry, cassis, plum and mocha flavors, this Syrah is dry and balanced, with the acidity and tannic structure that comes from the terroir of this cool Monterey appellation. It's a very interesting wine, with real class and style. **90** *—S.H. (11/1/2007)*

Hug 2005 Zinfandel (Paso Robles) $27. Will have its fans, but for this reviewer, too high in alcohol, with 15.9%, and too soft in acidity. That makes the intensely ripe cherry, raspberry and blackberry flavors syrupy.

Seems more like something you'd pour over pound cake than a table wine. **83** —*S.H. (11/1/2007)*

HUMANITAS

Humanitas 2001 Chardonnay (Edna Valley) $15. 87 —*J.M. (11/15/2003)*

HUNDRED ACRE

Hundred Acre 2000 Cabernet Sauvignon (Napa Valley) $100. 95 Cellar Selection —*J.M. (11/15/2002)*

HUNNICUTT

Hunnicutt 2004 Cabernet Sauvignon (Napa Valley) $45. Although this Cab is incredibly ripe and appealing in cassis, cherry, vanilla and almost white chocolate fudge flavors, somehow it manages to maintain balance and elegance. That's because it's thoroughly dry, and because of those gorgeously ripe Napa tannins, so fine and elegant. **92** —*S.H. (11/1/2007)*

Hunnicutt 2001 Cabernet Sauvignon (Napa Valley) $37. 89 —*S.H. (12/31/2004)*

Hunnicutt 2003 Zinfandel (Napa Valley) $29. 88 —*S.H. (3/1/2006)*

Hunnicutt 2002 Zinfandel (Napa Valley) $28. 91 —*S.H. (12/31/2004)*

HUNT CELLARS

Hunt Cellars 1999 Reserve Rhapsody Meritage Cabernet Blend (Central Coast) $29. 84 —*S.H. (5/1/2003)*

Hunt Cellars 1998 Cabernet Sauvignon (Paso Robles) $40. 84 —*S.H. (5/1/2003)*

Hunt Cellars 2000 Destiny Vineyards Bon Vivant Cabernet Sauvignon (Paso Robles) $34. 86 —*S.H. (10/1/2005)*

Hunt Cellars 2000 Destiny Vineyards Mt. Christo Block Cab-Ovation Cabernet Sauvignon (Paso Robles) $60. 86 —*S.H. (10/1/2005)*

Hunt Cellars 2001 Destiny Vineyards Mt. Christo Block Cab-Ovation Reserve Cabernet Sauvignon (Paso Robles) $48. 83 —*S.H. (12/1/2005)*

Hunt Cellars 2000 Good Vibrations Cabernet Sauvignon (Paso Robles) $50. Like a good tawny Port, this dessert wine has an attractive aroma of caramelized blackberries, roasted nuts, candied tangerine zest and cola. Turns rich and balanced in the mouth, with brisk acidity that makes the sweetness clean. **90** —*S.H. (12/1/2007)*

Hunt Cellars 2000 Moonlight Sonata Chardonnay (Central Coast) $24. 84 —*S.H. (12/15/2002)*

Hunt Cellars 1999 Harmony Reserve Merlot (Central Coast) $27. 86 —*S.H. (12/15/2003)*

Hunt Cellars 1997 Petite Sirah (Central Coast) $35. 90 —*S.H. (12/1/2002)*

Hunt Cellars 2000 Oldie But Goodie Tawny Port (Paso Robles) $70. Really nice California Port-style wine, rich and very sweet, soft and complex, and so easy to drink now. It's a lighter-bodied style, where the tannins don't get in the way, and the milk chocolate, cassis, root beer, cola, caramel, licorice and spicy vanilla flavors are simply delicious. **93** —*S.H. (4/1/2007)*

Hunt Cellars 2001 Zinfandel Port Port (Paso Robles) $45. 88 —*S.H. (12/31/2005)*

Hunt Cellars 2001 Destiny Vineyards Duet Red Blend (Paso Robles) $32. 89 —*S.H. (12/1/2005)*

Hunt Cellars 1997 Rhapsody in Red Red Blend (California) $50. 82 —*S.H. (9/5/2002)*

Hunt Cellars 2002 Destiny Vineyards Rhapsody Reserve Sangiovese (Paso Robles) $28. This simple Sangiovese shows raisiny, stewed cherry and prune flavors. The variety's tannins show through, raw and tough. **82** —*S.H. (4/1/2007)*

Hunt Cellars 2000 Destiny Vineyards Rhapsody Sangiovese (Paso Robles) $20. 84 —*S.H. (9/1/2003)*

Hunt Cellars 2002 Starlight Concerto Destiny Vineyards Sauvignon Blanc (Paso Robles) $34. 80 *(7/1/2005)*

Hunt Cellars 2005 Afternoon Delight Rosé Syrah (Paso Robles) $22. 83 —*S.H. (12/31/2006)*

Hunt Cellars 1997 Calif Syrah (California) $25. 84 *(11/1/2001)*

Hunt Cellars 2001 Destiny Vineyards Hilltop Serenade Reserve Syrah (Paso Robles) $32. 90 Editors' Choice —*S.H. (9/1/2005)*

Hunt Cellars 2003 Raging Bull Vineyards Serenade Reserve Syrah (Paso Robles) $48. Hard to like. Smells raisiny, overripe and herbal, although not at all sweet, and that's the way it tastes, too. The flavors are of shriveled grapes and dried blackberries, with dry, puckery tannins that finish with an astringent rasp. **82** —*S.H. (12/1/2007)*

Hunt Cellars 1999 Serenade Syrah (California) $22. 87 —*S.H. (12/1/2002)*

Hunt Cellars 1998 Zinfandel (Paso Robles) $24. 90 —*S.H. (5/1/2000)*

Hunt Cellars 2001 Old Vines Zinfandel (Paso Robles) $28. 85 *(11/1/2003)*

Hunt Cellars 2001 Outlaw Ridge Vineyard Zinfandel (Paso Robles) $27. 86 —*J.M. (11/1/2003)*

Hunt Cellars 2001 Outlaw Ridge Vineyard, Lower Bench Zinfandel (Paso Robles) $30. 87 —*J.M. (11/1/2003)*

Hunt Cellars 2000 Outlaw Ridge Zinphony #1 Zinfandel (Paso Robles) $30. 85 —*S.H. (9/1/2002)*

Hunt Cellars 2003 Rocket Man Zinfandel (Paso Robles) $38. With 17.5% alcohol, this has much more in common with Port than table wine. Not a bad wine. **83** —*S.H. (11/1/2007)*

Hunt Cellars 1999 Zinphony Zinfandel (Paso Robles) $20. 84 —*S.H. (11/1/2002)*

Hunt Cellars 2000 Zinphony #2 Old Vines Zinfandel (Paso Robles) $28. 92 —*S.H. (9/1/2002)*

Hunt Cellars 1999 Zinphony #2 Reserve Zinfandel (Paso Robles) $24. 91 —*S.H. (9/1/2002)*

HUNT COUNTRY VINEYARDS

Hunt Country Vineyards 2002 Dry Riesling (Finger Lakes) $10.87 Best Buy —*J.C. (8/1/2003)*

Hunt Country Vineyards 2001 Late Harvest Riesling (Finger Lakes) $15. 83 —*J.C. (8/1/2003)*

Hunt Country Vineyards 2002 Semi-Dry Riesling (Finger Lakes) $10. 80 —*J.C. (8/1/2003)*

HUNTER HILL VINEYARD & WINERY

Hunter Hill Vineyard & Winery 2001 Old Vine, Schulenburg Vineyard Zinfandel (Lodi) $17. 81 *(11/1/2003)*

HUNTINGTON

Huntington 2000 Cabernet Franc (Alexander Valley) $18. 87 —*S.H. (6/1/2003)*

Huntington 2003 Cabernet Sauvignon (California) $12. 84 —*S.H. (11/15/2005)*

Huntington 2002 Cabernet Sauvignon (Napa Valley) $20. 85 —*S.H. (11/15/2004)*

Huntington 2001 Cabernet Sauvignon (Napa Valley) $18. 89 —*S.H. (11/15/2003)*

Huntington 2005 Chardonnay (Sonoma County) $14. 85 —*S.H. (12/15/2006)*

Huntington 2004 Chardonnay (Sonoma County) $12. 82 —*S.H. (11/15/2005)*

Huntington 2002 Chardonnay (Russian River Valley) $15. 83 —*S.H. (12/31/2004)*

Huntington 2001 Chardonnay (Russian River Valley) $15. 85 —*S.H. (12/1/2003)*

Huntington 2000 Chardonnay (Russian River Valley) $15. 88 —*S.H. (5/1/2003)*

Huntington 2002 Merlot (California) $12. 84 —*S.H. (11/15/2005)*

Huntington 2005 Petite Sirah (California) $14. Shows the strengths and the weaknesses of Petite Sirah. On the plus side is ripe fruit, firm, classy tannins and an overall balance that suggests this variety is indeed noble. On the minus side is the overripe sweetness that gives a Port-y finish. **84** —*S.H. (5/1/2007)*

Huntington 2006 Sauvignon Blanc (Sonoma County) $14. The grapes are mainly from Dry Creek, with a little Russian River fruit as well, and there's no oak, so it's a really pure expression of Sonoma Sauvignon Blanc. It's dry and briskly clean, with intriguingly complex citrus, apricot, wildflower, fig, white pepper, vanilla and honey flavors. What a nice cocktail wine. **88 Editors' Choice** —*S.H. (11/15/2007)*

Huntington 2005 Sauvignon Blanc (Sonoma County) $14. 85 —*S.H. (12/15/2006)*

Huntington 2004 Earthquake Sauvignon Blanc (Sonoma County) $12. 85 —*S.H. (11/15/2005)*

Huntington 2003 Earthquake Sauvignon Blanc (Sonoma County) $14. 85 —*S.H. (12/1/2004)*

Huntington 2002 Earthquake Sauvignon Blanc (Napa County) $12. 86 —*S.H. (12/15/2003)*

HUSCH

Husch 2003 Cabernet Sauvignon (Mendocino) $21. Husch is one of Anderson Valley's pioneers, but it's too cool for Cab there, so they grow it inland, with good results. The wine, which is moderately oaky, shows good acidity, and very ripe blackberry and cherry flavors that finish dry, with chewy tannins. **87** —*S.H. (2/1/2007)*

Husch 2002 Cabernet Sauvignon (Mendocino) $21. 83 —*S.H. (3/1/2006)*

Husch 2001 Cabernet Sauvignon (Mendocino) $18. 84 *—S.H. (11/1/2005)*

Husch 2000 La Ribera Vineyards Cabernet Sauvignon (Mendocino) $18. 86 *—S.H. (8/1/2004)*

Husch 2002 Old Vines La Ribera Vineyards Carignane (Mendocino) $15. 85 *—S.H. (8/1/2004)*

Husch 2003 Reserve Cabernet Sauvignon (Mendocino) $35. It's hard to find much to like about this overripe wine. It starts with a smell of raisins, then turns raw and peppery in the mouth, with a dry, cooked cherry taste. **82** *—S.H. (5/1/2007)*

Husch 2006 Chardonnay (Mendocino) $15. It's all about acidity and long hangtime with this Chard. The acids come from chilly, foggy nights, the ripeness from long, warm, sunny days. What you get is oodles of bright, pure pineapple, Granny Smith apple, Meyer lemon and spicy clove flavor, with a touch of caramelized oak for richness. **87** *—S.H. (11/15/2007)*

Husch 2005 Chardonnay (Mendocino) $14. I love the purity of this Chardonnay. Even though it was barrel fermented, the oak is hardly noticeable, swamped by the acid-boosted exotic melange of limes, kiwis, pineapples, tangerine, candied ginger and cinnamon. It adds up to a taste treat. **87** *—S.H. (2/1/2007)*

Husch 2004 Chardonnay (Mendocino) $14. 85 *—S.H. (3/1/2006)*

Husch 2004 Chardonnay (Anderson Valley) $18. 88 *—S.H. (3/1/2006)*

Husch 2003 Chardonnay (Mendocino) $14. 87 *—S.H. (11/1/2005)*

Husch 2001 Chardonnay (Mendocino) $14. 85 *—S.H. (6/1/2003)*

Husch 1998 Estate Bottled Chardonnay (Mendocino County) $13. 87 *—S.H. (5/1/2000)*

Husch 2001 La Ribera Vineyards Chardonnay (Mendocino) $18. 90 *—S.H. (8/1/2004)*

Husch 2004 Special Reserve Chardonnay (Mendocino) $25. As of the early Fall of 2006, this was a tight, acidic, dry young Chard, with the bracing quality of minerals and steel of a good Chablis. The winemaking was bells and whistles, with lots of new oak and sur lies aging. I would decant this wine for a few hours, or let it age in the bottle for as long as five years. **89** *—S.H. (2/1/2007)*

Husch 2000 Special Reserve Chardonnay (Anderson Valley) $25. 85 *—S.H. (12/1/2003)*

Husch 1999 Special Reserve Chardonnay (Anderson Valley) $25. 89 *—S.H. (2/1/2003)*

Husch 1998 Special Reserve Chardonnay (Anderson Valley) $25. 85 *—S.H. (5/1/2002)*

Husch 2006 Chenin Blanc (Mendocino) $11. This is quite a distinguished Chenin Blanc, showing an acidic backbone that makes the wine savory. It has appealing apricot, pineapple and honeysuckle flavors, with citrusy crispness. Finishes off-dry, with just a hint of sweetness. **87** *—S.H. (11/15/2007)*

Husch 2005 Chenin Blanc (Mendocino) $11. 86 *—S.H. (12/15/2006)*

Husch 2002 Chenin Blanc (Mendocino) $10. 86 *—S.H. (12/15/2003)*

Husch 2006 Gewürztraminer (Anderson Valley) $14. Wonderfully crisp in juicy acidity, which lends a balanced brightness to the spicy peach, pineapple, green apple, vanilla and honeysuckle flavors. This is a dry, Alsatian-style Gewürz from Anderson Valley, probably the best place in California to grow the variety. **87** *—S.H. (11/15/2007)*

Husch 2005 Gewürztraminer (Anderson Valley) $14. 85 *—S.H. (12/15/2006)*

Husch 2002 Gewürztraminer (Anderson Valley) $12. 85 *—S.H. (12/31/2003)*

Husch 2001 Gewürztraminer (Anderson Valley) $12. 86 *—S.H. (9/1/2003)*

Husch 2000 Gewürztraminer (Anderson Valley) $11. 85 *—S.H. (5/1/2002)*

Husch 2003 Late Harvest Gewürztraminer (Anderson Valley) $18. 85 *—S.H. (11/1/2005)*

Husch 2001 La Ribera Vineyards Merlot (Mendocino) $25. 83 *—S.H. (8/1/2004)*

Husch 2006 Muscat Canelli (Mendocino) $14. This pleasantly fruity wine is a little sweeter than off-dry, with a vanilla and caramelized brown sugar finish to the golden mango, pineapple and tangerine fruit flavors that taste like they were baked into a pie. **84** *—S.H. (11/15/2007)*

Husch 2005 Muscat Canelli (Mendocino) $14. 84 *—S.H. (12/15/2006)*

Husch 1997 Pinot Noir (Anderson Valley) $19. 83 *(11/15/1999)*

Husch 2003 Pinot Noir (Anderson Valley) $21. 90 Editors' Choice *—S.H. (11/1/2005)*

Husch 2001 Pinot Noir (Anderson Valley) $18. 82 *—S.H. (12/15/2004)*

Husch 2000 Pinot Noir (Anderson Valley) $18. 85 *—S.H. (12/1/2003)*

Husch 1999 Pinot Noir (Anderson Valley) $19. 81 *(10/1/2002)*

90 *(10/1/2002)*

Husch 1999 Knoll Vineyard Pinot Noir (Anderson Valley) $35. 85 *(10/1/2002)*

Husch 2006 Vin Gris Pinot Noir (Anderson Valley) $16. You'll find direct Pinot cherry, raspberry and vanilla flavors in this delicate, crisp rosé. It's a fine, silky wine, not especially complicated, but appealingly easy. **85** *—S.H. (12/31/2007)*

Husch 2006 Sauvignon Blanc (Mendocino) $12. There's more than a touch of sugary sweetness in this wine, which fortunately has very crisp acids for balance. The peach, pineapple and smoky vanilla flavors are delicious. If you took away some of the sweetness and steered it more toward dryness, this would be a fabulous wine. **85** *—S.H. (11/15/2007)*

Husch 2005 Sauvignon Blanc (Mendocino) $12. This is one of the best $12 Sauvignon Blancs I've had this year. It's not just the enormous fruit, all figs and pineapples and melons, it's the acidity, which is so bright and mouth-cleansing. A touch of oak adds even richer notes. What a great house white. **86** *—S.H. (2/1/2007)*

Husch 2004 Sauvignon Blanc (Mendocino) $12. 88 Best Buy *—S.H. (3/1/2006)*

Husch 2003 Sauvignon Blanc (Mendocino) $12. 85 *—S.H. (11/1/2005)*

Husch 2002 La Ribera Vineyards Sauvignon Blanc (Mendocino) $12. 87 *—S.H. (8/1/2004)*

Husch 2001 La Ribera Vineyards Sauvignon Blanc (Mendocino) $12. 86 *—S.H. (3/1/2003)*

Husch 1998 La Ribera Vineyards Sauvignon Blanc (Mendocino) $12. 88 Best Buy *—S.H. (5/1/2000)*

Husch 2004 La Ribera Vineyards Renegade Sauvignon Blanc (Mendocino) $18. 84 *—S.H. (3/1/2006)*

Husch 2005 Late Harvest Sauvignon Blanc (Mendocino) $20. 84 *—S.H. (12/15/2006)*

Husch 2005 Renegade Sauvignon Blanc (Mendocino) $18. The name "renegade" refers to the wild yeasts that were allowed to start fermentation. The wine is very similar to Husch's regular Sauvignon Blanc, maybe a little higher in acids, a touch purer and more elegant, but pretty much the same and, like it, is a really good dry white wine. **87** *—S.H. (2/1/2007)*

Husch 2003 Renegade Sauvignon Blanc (Mendocino) $18. 91 Editors' Choice *—S.H. (11/1/2005)*

Husch 2004 Syrah (Mendocino) $28. A rich, dry wine, with that elegantly voluptuous, velvety texture that makes Syrah special. The flavors are pretty good, too, forward in cherry-filled chocolate truffles, with a nice earthy balance of fine herbs, sautéed mushrooms and French roast coffee. A great grilled steak will be a marriage made in heaven. **88** *—S.H. (5/1/2007)*

Husch 2003 Syrah (Mendocino) $28. 85 *—S.H. (3/1/2006)*

Husch 2004 Old Vines Zinfandel (Mendocino) $25. Husch guarantees the vines are 55 years old. The flavors are dry, tannic and concentrated, with a chocolaty licorice and cassis-infused edge to the wild thorn bush berries. This small-production Zin is notable for having the balance and elegance of a fine red wine. **89** *—S.H. (2/1/2007)*

HYATT

Hyatt 1998 Ice Wine Black Muscat (Yakima Valley) $25. 92 *—M.S. (11/15/2000)*

Hyatt 1997 Bordeaux Blend (Yakima Valley) $11. 84 *—P.G. (6/1/2000)*

Hyatt 1997 Cabernet Sauvignon (Yakima Valley) $15. 87 *—P.G. (6/1/2000)*

Hyatt 1997 Reserve Cabernet Sauvignon (Yakima Valley) $25. 88 *—P.G. (6/1/2000)*

Hyatt 1999 Cabernet Sauvignon-Merlot (Yakima Valley) $11. 85 *—P.G. (6/1/2002)*

Hyatt 1998 Chardonnay (Yakima Valley) $11. 89 Best Buy *—P.G. (6/1/2000)*

Hyatt 2000 Chardonnay (Yakima Valley) $10. 83 *—P.G. (9/1/2002)*

Hyatt 1999 Chardonnay (Yakima Valley) $10. 86 *—P.G. (9/1/2002)*

Hyatt 2000 Reserve Chardonnay (Yakima Valley) $18. 87 *—P.G. (9/1/2002)*

Hyatt 1998 Fumé Blanc (Yakima Valley) $11. 87 *—P.G. (6/1/2000)*

Hyatt 1997 Merlot (Yakima Valley) $14. 85 *—P.G. (6/1/2000)*

Hyatt 1999 Merlot (Yakima Valley) $12. 84 *—P.G. (9/1/2002)*

Hyatt 1998 Reserve Merlot (Yakima Valley) $19. 85 *—P.G. (9/1/2002)*

Hyatt 1997 Reserve Merlot (Yakima Valley) $25. 86 *—P.G. (6/1/2000)*

Hyatt 1997 Syrah (Yakima Valley) $20. 87 *—S.H. (9/1/2000)*

Hyatt 2001 Syrah (Yakima Valley) $13. 86 *(9/1/2005)*

Hyatt 1998 Estate Grown Syrah (Yakima Valley) $25. 85 *(11/1/2001)*

Hyatt 2000 Reserve Syrah (Yakima Valley) $18. 83 *—P.G. (9/1/2002)*

HYDE VINEYARD

Hyde Vineyard 2001 Chardonnay (Carneros) $48. 89 *—S.H. (5/1/2004)*

Hyde Vineyard 2001 Merlot-Cabernet Sauvignon (Carneros) $65. 91 *—S.H. (5/1/2004)*

Hyde Vineyard 2001 Syrah (Carneros) $48. 90 *—S.H. (5/1/2004)*

I'M

I'M 2004 Chardonnay (Sonoma County) $17. 86 *—S.H. (11/1/2006)*

I'M 2003 Chardonnay (Sonoma) $17. 84 *—S.H. (3/1/2006)*

I'M 2006 Rosé Blend (Napa Valley) $13. This blush is 100% Cabernet Sauvignon, and may serve as a lesson in why Cab doesn't make great rosé. It's too heavy and full-bodied, with dense cassis flavors that are closer to red wine. But it's clean, balanced and dry. **83** *—S.H. (11/15/2007)*

I'M 2004 Rosé Blend (Napa Valley) $13. 84 *—S.H. (7/1/2006)*

ICARIA CREEK

Icaria Creek 1997 Cabernet Sauvignon (Alexander Valley) $45. 87 *(8/1/2003)*

Icaria Creek 2002 Estate Cabernet Sauvignon (Alexander Valley) $38. 88 *—S.H. (12/15/2005)*

Icaria Creek 2001 Estate Hillside Cabernet Sauvignon (Alexander Valley) $38. 84 *—S.H. (10/1/2004)*

Icaria Creek 1998 Cabernet Sauvignon-Barbera (Alexander Valley) $45. 84 *—S.H. (8/29/2003)*

ICI/LA-BAS

Ici/La-Bas 1998 Philippine Chardonnay (Mendocino County) $35. 89 *(7/1/2001)*

Ici/La-Bas 2004 Les Révelés Pinot Noir (Anderson Valley) $30. A beautifully supple, delicately silky wine. The flavors are of red cherries and hints of clove, vanilla, toasted coconut and bacon. Dry and crisp, this Pinot drinks well now and should remain harmonious through 2009. **92 Editors' Choice** *—S.H. (11/1/2007)*

Ici/La-Bas 1997 Les Revelles-Mendocino Elke Vy Pinot Noir (Anderson Valley) $50. 85 *(10/1/1999)*

Ici/La-Bas 1997 Les Revelles-OR/CA Vineyard Se Pinot Noir (Willamette Valley & Anderson Valley) $35. 88 *(10/1/1999)*

IDYLWOOD

Idylwood 1999 Pinot Noir (Willamette Valley) $14. 84 *(10/1/2002)*

Idylwood 1999 Corral Creek Vineyard Pinot Noir (Willamette Valley) $25. 87 *—P.G. (4/1/2002)*

Idylwood 1998 Founder's Reserve Pinot Noir (Willamette Valley) $25. 86 *—J.C. (12/1/2000)*

IL CUORE

Il Cuore 1996 Rosso Classico Red Blend (California) $11. 85 *—J.C. (10/1/1999)*

Il Cuore 1996 Zinfandel (California) $10. 81 *—J.C. (5/1/2000)*

IL PODERE DELL'OLIVOS

Il Podere Dell'Olivos 1998 Tocai (Central Coast) $12. 88 *—S.H. (12/1/2001)*

Il Ponte 1999 Fra Due Terre Sangiovese (California) $35. 87 *—J.M. (5/1/2002)*

ILONA

Ilona 2002 Red Wine Bordeaux Blend (Howell Mountain) $36. Soft and melted in the modern Napa style, a blend of Merlot and Cab Sauv and Franc. With dry blackberry and oak flavors, the wine represents the triumph of international winemaking over terroir. **86** *—S.H. (11/1/2007)*

Ilona 1999 Meritage (Napa Valley) $70. 92 *—M.M. (11/15/2002)*

ILSLEY

Ilsley 2002 Cabernet Sauvignon (Stags Leap District) $48. 92 Cellar Selection *—S.H. (11/1/2006)*

Ilsley 2003 Single Vineyard Estate Cabernet Sauvignon (Stags Leap District) $50. Pretty good wine, but a little rough right now. May develop, but no guarantees. It has rich chocolate and cassis flavors and plenty of oak, but is also very tannic, leaving a gum-numbing astringency on the slightly sweet finish. Try stashing it for a year or so, then try again. **86** *—S.H. (9/1/2007)*

IMAGERY

Imagery 2003 Artist Collection Barbera (Sonoma Valley) $31. 88 Cellar Selection *—S.H. (6/1/2006)*

Imagery 2001 Artist Collection Barbera (Sonoma Valley) $31. 88 *—S.H. (4/1/2005)*

Imagery 2000 Artist Collection Barbera (Sonoma Valley) $31. 89 *—S.H. (12/1/2003)*

Imagery 1999 Wildwood Vineyard Barbera (Sonoma Valley) $31. 90 *—S.H. (12/1/2001)*

Imagery 1997 Rancho Salina Vineyard Bordeaux Blend (Sonoma Valley) $35. 87 *(11/1/2000)*

Imagery 1996 Cabernet Franc (Sonoma) $22. 88 *—J.C. (6/1/2003)*

Imagery 2002 Artist Collection Cabernet Franc (Sonoma County) $34. 84 *—S.H. (12/15/2005)*

Imagery 1999 Artist Collection Cabernet Franc (Alexander Valley) $27. 87 *—S.H. (11/15/2003)*

Imagery 1998 Artist Collection Cabernet Franc (Sonoma Valley) $27. 85 *—S.H. (12/1/2001)*

Imagery 2001 Ash Creek Vineyard Cabernet Sauvignon (Alexander Valley) $40. 90 *—S.H. (12/15/2005)*

Imagery 1999 Ash Creek Vineyard Cabernet Sauvignon (Alexander Valley) $35. 85 *—S.H. (8/1/2003)*

Imagery 1998 Ash Creek Vineyard Cabernet Sauvignon (Alexander Valley) $50. 87 *(12/1/2001)*

Imagery 1999 Sunny Slope Vineyard Cabernet Sauvignon (Sonoma Valley) $35. 86 *—S.H. (8/1/2003)*

Imagery 1998 Sunny Slope Vineyard Vineyard Collection Cabernet Sauvignon (Sonoma Valley) $50. 85 *(12/1/2001)*

Imagery 2002 Vineyard Collection Ash Creek Vineyard Cabernet Sauvignon (Sonoma Valley) $40. 84 *—S.H. (4/1/2006)*

Imagery 2000 Vineyard Collection Ash Creek Vineyard Cabernet Sauvignon (Alexander Valley) $35. 92 *—S.H. (4/1/2005)*

Imagery 2001 Vineyard Collection Sunny Slope Vineyard Cabernet Sauvignon (Sonoma Valley) $35. 92 *—S.H. (4/1/2005)*

Imagery 1999 Ricci Vineyard Chardonnay (Carneros) $25. 87 *—S.H. (12/1/2001)*

Imagery 2002 Artist Collection Lagrein (Paso Robles) $33. 86 *—S.H. (12/15/2005)*

Imagery 2001 Malbec (North Coast) $33. 86 *—S.H. (10/1/2004)*

Imagery 1999 Malbec (Alexander Valley) $33. 88 *—S.H. (12/1/2001)*

Imagery 2000 Artist Collection Malbec (North Coast) $33. 84 *—S.H. (4/1/2004)*

Imagery 1998 Artist Collection Malbec (Alexander Valley) $33. 87 *—S.H. (12/1/2001)*

Imagery 2002 Sunny Slope Vineyard Merlot (Sonoma Valley) $35. 85 *—S.H. (12/15/2005)*

Imagery 2001 Sunny Slope Vineyard Merlot (Sonoma Valley) $29. 90 *—S.H. (10/1/2004)*

Imagery 1999 Sunny Slope Vineyard Merlot (Sonoma Valley) $29. 85 *—S.H. (8/1/2003)*

Imagery 2000 Vineyard Collection Sunny Slope Vineyard Merlot (Sonoma County) $29. 92 *—S.H. (4/1/2004)*

Imagery 2001 Petite Sirah (Paso Robles) $35. 89 *—S.H. (10/1/2004)*

Imagery 2002 Artist Collection Petite Sirah (Paso Robles) $36. 91 Editors' Choice *—S.H. (10/1/2005)*

Imagery 2000 Artist Collection Petite Sirah (Paso Robles) $35. 86 *—S.H. (8/1/2003)*

Imagery 1998 Artist Collection Petite Sirah (Paso Robles) $32. 87 *—S.H. (12/1/2001)*

Imagery 1999 Shell Creek Petite Sirah (Paso Robles) $35. 90 *—S.H. (12/1/2001)*

Imagery 2001 Petite Verdot (Sonoma County) $33. 85 *—S.H. (12/1/2004)*

Imagery 2003 Artist Collection Petite Verdot (Sonoma Valley) $38. 83 *—S.H. (4/1/2006)*

Imagery 2000 Artist Collection Petite Verdot (Sonoma County) $33. 90 *—S.H. (4/1/2004)*

Imagery 2000 Artist Collection-Bien Nacido Vineyard Pinot Blanc (Santa Maria Valley) $18. 87 *—S.H. (2/1/2004)*

Imagery 1999 Bien Nacido Vineyard Pinot Blanc (Santa Maria Valley) $21. 86 *—S.H. (12/1/2001)*

Imagery 2003 Pinot Noir (Carneros) $25. 85 —*S.H. (12/1/2004)*

Imagery 1999 Rancho Salina Vineyard Red Blend (Sonoma Valley) $29. 85 —*S.H. (12/1/2001)*

Imagery 2001 Sangiovese (Dry Creek Valley) $22. 85 —*S.H. (11/15/2004)*

Imagery 2003 Artist Collection Sangiovese (Dry Creek Valley) $24. 89 —*S.H. (6/1/2006)*

Imagery 2002 Artist Collection Sangiovese (Dry Creek Valley) $24. 82 —*S.H. (10/1/2005)*

Imagery 2000 Artist Collection Sangiovese (Sonoma County) $22. 85 —*S.H. (4/1/2004)*

Imagery 1999 Artist Collection Sangiovese (Sonoma County) $22. 90 Editors' Choice —*S.H. (9/1/2003)*

Imagery 1996 Imagery Series Sangiovese (Dry Creek Valley) $20. 82 —*J.C. (10/1/1999)*

Imagery 1999 Polesky Vineyard-Red Hill Vineyard Sangiovese (Sonoma County) $21. 85 —*S.H. (12/1/2001)*

Imagery 2002 StoneDragon Syrah (Sonoma Valley) $35. 87 *(9/1/2005)*

Imagery 2004 Artist Collection Viognier (Sonoma County) $24. 90 Editors' Choice —*S.H. (12/15/2005)*

Imagery 2002 Artist Collection Viognier (North Coast) $21. 87 —*S.H. (12/31/2003)*

Imagery 1999 Creek Vineyard Viognier (Alexander Valley) $25. 87 —*S.H. (12/1/2001)*

Imagery 1999 Artist Collection White Blend (Napa Valley) $25. 89 Best Buy —*S.H. (12/1/2001)*

Imagery 2000 Artist Collection White Burgundy White Blend (California) $25. 86 —*S.H. (7/1/2003)*

Imagery 2003 White Burgundy White Blend (Carneros) $27. 90 Editors' Choice —*S.H. (10/1/2005)*

Imagery 2002 White Burgundy White Blend (North Coast) $25. 86 —*S.H. (10/1/2004)*

Imagery 1997 White Burgundy White Blend (North Coast) $22. 84 —*J.C. (11/1/1999)*

Imagery 2004 Wow Oui White Burgundy White Blend (Sonoma County) $24. 90 —*S.H. (12/15/2005)*

Imagery 1999 Yountmill Vineyard White Blend (Napa Valley) $25. 86 —*S.H. (12/1/2001)*

Imagery 2002 Taylor Vineyard Zinfandel (Dry Creek Valley) $40. I90 —*S.H. (10/1/2005)*

Imagery 2000 Vineyard Collection-Taylor Vineyard Zinfandel (Alexander Valley) $35. 91 —*S.H. (9/1/2003)*

INCOGNITO

Incognito 2005 Red Blend (Lodi) $19. Soft, fruity, spicy and easy, this is a blend of nine varieties, all of them either Bordeaux or Rhone. Offers a blast of raspberries, cherries, vanilla and spices. 85 —*S.H. (10/1/2007)*

Incognito 2004 Red Blend (Lodi) $19. 87 —*S.H. (12/15/2006)*

Incognito 2006 Pink Wine Rosé Blend (Lodi) $20. This enjoyable wine actually is pink in color. A blend of Cinsault, Grenache and Mourvèdre, it's rich in raspberry essence, vanilla and cinnamon, with a very long, fruity finish. Delicately structured and light in body, it will be great with a bouillabaisse-style fish stew, or little mushroom-filled puff pastries. 87 —*S.H. (7/1/2007)*

Incognito 2006 Viognier (Lodi) $19. Rich, very exotic, decadently drinkable, like an entire fruit store in a glass. Peaches, pears, pineapples, nectarines, mangoes, papayas, they flood the palate, with just enough acidity for balance, and a honeyed finish. Made with a dash of Roussanne and Marsanne. 88 —*S.H. (10/1/2007)*

Incognito 2005 Viognier (Lodi) $19. 90 Editors' Choice —*S.H. (10/1/2006)*

INDIAN SPRINGS

Indian Springs 1997 Cabernet Franc (Nevada County) $15. 90 —*S.H. (2/1/2000)*

Indian Springs 1999 Cabernet Franc (Nevada County) $15. 85 —*S.H. (12/15/2001)*

Indian Springs 1997 Cabernet Sauvignon (Nevada County) $13. 84 —*S.H. (12/31/1999)*

Indian Springs 1998 Chardonnay (Nevada County) $15. 87 *(6/1/2000)*

Indian Springs 2000 Chardonnay (Nevada County) $14. 86 —*S.H. (12/31/2001)*

Indian Springs 2001 Primavera Rossa Red Blend (Nevada County) $16. 81 —*S.H. (5/1/2004)*

Indian Springs 1999 Sangiovese (Nevada County) $16. 85 —*S.H. (9/12/2002)*

Indian Springs 2000 Sauvignon Blanc (Nevada County) $12. 82 —*S.H. (12/15/2001)*

Indian Springs 2000 Sémillon (Nevada County) $10. 83 —*S.H. (9/12/2002)*

Indian Springs 1996 Syrah (Nevada County) $14. 85 —*S.H. (6/1/1999)*

Indian Springs 2001 Syrah (Nevada County) $18. 87 —*S.H. (5/1/2004)*

Indian Springs 1999 Syrah (Nevada County) $16. 86 *(10/1/2001)*

Indian Springs 1997 Viognier (Nevada County) $14. 83 —*S.H. (6/1/1999)*

INDIGO HILLS

Indigo Hills 2000 Cabernet Sauvignon (North Coast) $12. 86 Best Buy —*S.H. (12/31/2002)*

Indigo Hills NV Champagne Blend (North Coast) $12. 86 Best Buy —*S.H. (12/15/1999)*

Indigo Hills 2003 Chardonnay (Sonoma County) $12. 85 —*S.H. (3/1/2006)*

Indigo Hills 2001 Chardonnay (Central Coast) $12. 83 —*S.H. (12/1/2003)*

Indigo Hills 2000 Chardonnay (Central Coast) $12. 83 —*S.H. (5/1/2002)*

Indigo Hills 1997 Merlot (California) $13. 85 Best Buy—*J.C. (7/1/2000)*

Indigo Hills 1999 Pinot Noir (Central Coast) $14. 83 *(10/1/2002)*

INGLESIDE

Ingleside NV Chesapeake Cabernet Sauvignon-Merlot (Virginia) $12. There's a meaty, spicy nose here that promises something good, but on the palate, a tart, bitter character overrides the fruit. This wine has promise but needs integration. 81 —*S.K. (7/1/2007)*

Ingleside 2002 Reserve Merlot (Virginia) $27. A deep and luscious nose of currant, tobacco and spice entices with this reserve selection. In the glass there's body and personality, though the tannins need time to ripen and round, giving the wine an angularity contrary to the desired Merlot balance. With red meat or stews this would be tempered. 83 —*S.K. (7/1/2007)*

Ingleside 2006 Pinot Grigio (Virginia) $16. Good acidity, balance and flavor typifies this elegant Pinot Grigio. Unlike many of the PGs on the market, this one has some depth, but it's still soft enough to appeal to most fans of the variety. The finish lingers, too—another plus in a sea of lean, mean competitors. 84 —*S.K. (7/1/2007)*

INMAN FAMILY

Inman Family 2002 Pinot Gris (Russian River Valley) $24. 87 —*S.H. (12/1/2003)*

INZINERATOR

InZinerator 2003 Zinfandel (California) $15. 86 —*S.H. (11/15/2006)*

IO

Io 2000 Red Blend (Santa Barbara County) $60. 90 —*S.H. (12/31/2003)*

Io 1996 Rhône Red Blend (Santa Barbara County) $40. 90 *(2/1/2000)*

Io 2002 Rhône Red Blend (Santa Barbara County) $30. 86 —*S.H. (11/1/2006)*

Io 2001 Rhône Red Blend (Santa Barbara County) $30. 90 —*S.H. (12/15/2005)*

Io 2000 Rhône Red Blend (Santa Barbara County) $60. 91 —*S.H. (12/1/2004)*

Io 2000 Rhône Red Blend (Santa Barbara County) $30. 85 *(9/1/2005)*

Io 1997 Rhône Red Blend (Santa Barbara County) $40. 94 Editors' Choice —*S.H. (11/15/2000)*

Io 1998 Syrah (Santa Barbara County) $60. 90 *(11/1/2001)*

Io 2002 Ryan Road Vineyard Syrah (San Luis Obispo County) $35. 93 —*S.H. (9/1/2004)*

Io 2001 Ryan Road Vineyard Syrah (San Luis Obispo County) $35. 93 Editors' Choice —*S.H. (10/1/2003)*

Io 2002 Upper Bench Syrah (Santa Maria Valley) $35. 90 —*S.H. (9/1/2004)*

Io 2001 Upper Bench Syrah (Santa Maria Valley) $35. 92 Editors' Choice —*S.H. (10/1/2003)*

IRIS HILL

Iris Hill 2006 Pinot Gris (Oregon) $15. Sharp and spicy, with plenty of acid. The fruit seems underripe and lacks focus. The midpalate is thin and the finish gets a little hot. 84 —*P.G. (11/15/2007)*

Iris Hill 2002 Pinot Noir (Oregon) $16. 90 Best Buy *(11/1/2004)*

Iris Hill 2005 Reserve Pinot Noir (Oregon) $25. Tightly sculpted, and does not try to be bigger than it is. But it captures something elusive, a certain finesse and elegance. Though not a big wine, it wraps itself around the palate in a comforting way and lingers deliciously through the finish. 89 —P.G. (7/1/2007)

IRISH

Irish 2003 Chenin Blanc (Clarksburg) $16. 85 *—S.H. (3/1/2005)*

Irish 2003 Petite Sirah (Lodi) $32. 82 *—S.H. (10/1/2005)*

Irish 2004 Elk Vineyard Petite Sirah (Lodi) $45. 81 *—S.H. (7/1/2006)*

Irish 2003 Late Harvest Petite Sirah (Lodi) $22. 88 *—S.H. (2/1/2005)*

Irish NV Blarny Red Red Blend (California) $18. 80 *—S.H. (7/1/2006)*

Irish 2004 Viognier (California) $14. 83 *—S.H. (7/1/2006)*

Irish 2003 Viognier (California) $14. 85 *—S.H. (2/1/2005)*

IRON HORSE

Iron Horse 1997 T-bar-T Benchmark Bordeaux Blend (Sonoma County) $50. 94 *(11/1/2000)*

Iron Horse 2000 T-bar-T Blend 1 Bordeaux Blend (Alexander Valley) $32. 91 *—S.H. (12/15/2003)*

Iron Horse 2006 T-T Vineyard Cuvée R Bordeaux White Blend (Alexander Valley) $26. This has long been one of the best Sauvignon Blanc-Viognier blends in California, and the '06 continues that tradition. Coming from a cool vintage, it's very dry and racy, with a scour of acidity and stony, minerally flavors, with touches of citrus blossom and wildflower. No, it's not a fruit bomb, but it's a sleek, elegant wine, in the European tradition. 90 *S.H. (11/1/2007)*

Iron Horse 2003 T-bar-T Benchmark Cabernet Blend (Alexander Valley) $70. 96 Editors' Choice *—S.H. (12/15/2006)*

Iron Horse 2002 T-bar-T Benchmark Cabernet Blend (Alexander Valley) $70. 94 Editors' Choice *—S.H. (11/15/2005)*

Iron Horse 1999 T-bar-T Benchmark Cabernet Blend (Alexander Valley) $56. 92 *—S.H. (7/1/2002)*

Iron Horse 1999 T-bar-T Cabernet Franc (Alexander Valley) $26. 86 *—S.H. (9/1/2002)*

Iron Horse 2002 T-bar-T Vineyard Cabernet Franc (Alexander Valley) $30. 92 *—S.H. (11/15/2005)*

Iron Horse 1996 Cabernet Sauvignon (Sonoma County) $23. 91 *(11/1/1999)*

Iron Horse 1997 T-bar-T Cabernet Sauvignon (Sonoma County) $35. 94 *(11/1/2000)*

Iron Horse 2003 T-bar-T Cabernet Sauvignon (Alexander Valley) $35. 93 Editors' Choice *—S.H. (12/15/2006)*

Iron Horse 2001 T-bar-T Proprietor Grown Cabernet Sauvignon (Alexander Valley) $35. 92 *—S.H. (10/1/2004)*

Iron Horse 2002 T-bar-T Vineyard Cabernet Sauvignon (Alexander Valley) $35. 92 *—S.H. (11/15/2005)*

Iron Horse 1991 Champagne Blend (Green Valley) $28. 86 *(12/15/1999)*

Iron Horse 1995 Champagne Blend (Green Valley) $34. 92 *—S.H. (12/31/2004)*

Iron Horse 1993 Blanc de Blancs Champagne Blend (Green Valley) $34. 88 *—S.H. (12/1/2001)*

Iron Horse 1992 Blanc de Blancs Champagne Blend (Sonoma County) $34. 92 *—S.H. (12/1/2000)*

Iron Horse 1994 Brut Classic Vintage Champagne Blend (Green Valley) $25. 85 *(12/15/1999)*

Iron Horse 1991 Brut LD Champagne Blend (Sonoma County) $60. 93 *—S.H. (12/1/2000)*

Iron Horse 1992 Brut LD Champagne Blend (Green Valley) $50. 91 *(12/1/2001)*

Iron Horse 1991 Brut LD Champagne Blend (Green Valley) $50. 91 *—J.C. (12/1/1999)*

Iron Horse 2000 Brut Rosé Champagne Blend (Green Valley) $30. 89 *—S.H. (12/31/2004)*

Iron Horse 1997 Brut Rosé Champagne Blend (Sonoma County) $30. 90 *—P.G. (12/1/2002)*

Iron Horse 1996 Brut Rosé Champagne Blend (Green Valley) $30. 84 *(12/1/2001)*

Iron Horse 1994 Brut Rosé Champagne Blend (Green Valley) $28. 90 *—J.C. (12/1/1999)*

Iron Horse 1995 Brut Rosé Champagne Blend (Sonoma County) $30. 90 *(12/1/2000)*

Iron Horse 1994 Brut Russian Cuvée Champagne Blend (Green Valley) $24. 83 *—J.C. (12/1/1999)*

Iron Horse 1994 Brut Vrais Amis Champagne Blend (Green Valley) $29. 90 *—L.W. (12/1/1999)*

Iron Horse 1996 Brut Wedding Cuvée Champagne Blend (Green Valley) $22. 86 *—J.C. (12/1/1999)*

Iron Horse 1999 Classic Vintage Brut Champagne Blend (Green Valley) $28. 90 *—S.H. (12/31/2004)*

Iron Horse 1997 Classic Vintage Brut Champagne Blend (Sonoma County) $28. 90 *—P.G. (12/1/2002)*

Iron Horse 1996 Classic Vintage Brut Champagne Blend (Green Valley) $28. 87 *—S.H. (12/1/2001)*

Iron Horse 1995 Classic Vintage Brut Champagne Blend (Sonoma County) $26. 89 *—S.H. (12/1/2000)*

Iron Horse 1998 Good Luck Cuvée Champagne Blend (Sonoma County) $24. 86 *—J.M. (12/1/2002)*

Iron Horse 1997 Russian Cuvée Champagne Blend (Sonoma County) $28. 87 *—P.G. (12/1/2002)*

Iron Horse 1996 Russian Cuvée Champagne Blend (Green Valley) $26. 86 *—S.H. (12/1/2001)*

Iron Horse 1995 Russian Cuvée Champagne Blend (Sonoma County) $26. 89 *(12/1/2000)*

Iron Horse 1995 Vrais Amis Champagne Blend (Sonoma County) $26. 90 *(12/1/2000)*

Iron Horse 2000 Wedding Cuvée Champagne Blend (Green Valley) $29. 87 *—S.H. (12/31/2004)*

Iron Horse 1999 Wedding Cuvée Champagne Blend (Sonoma County) $28. 87 *—P.G. (12/1/2002)*

Iron Horse 1998 Wedding Cuvée Champagne Blend (Green Valley) $28. 87 *—S.H. (12/1/2001)*

Iron Horse 1997 Wedding Cuvée Brut Champagne Blend (Green Valley) $28. 90 *—S.H. (12/1/2000)*

Iron Horse 1997 Chardonnay (Green Valley) $22. 92 *—S.H. (7/1/1999)*

Iron Horse 2000 Chardonnay (Green Valley) $26. 92 *—S.H. (12/15/2002)*

Iron Horse 1994 Blanc de Blancs Chardonnay (Sonoma County) $34. 88 *—P.G. (12/1/2002)*

Iron Horse 1993 Blanc De Blancs Chardonnay (Green Valley) $34. 88 *—S.H. (12/1/2001)*

Iron Horse 2005 Corral Vineyard Chardonnay (Green Valley) $38. Like Iron Horse's other '05 Chards, this is a hard, minerally wine. The color is green-tinged, the aroma like lime juice drizzled onto a steel-bladed knife. With lime-grapefruit flavors and high acidity, it's an elegantly structured wine that may surprise with development over the years. 92 *—S.H. (11/1/2007)*

Iron Horse 2003 Corral Vineyard Chardonnay (Green Valley) $35. 93 *—S.H. (2/1/2006)*

Iron Horse 2002 Corral Vineyard Chardonnay (Green Valley) $32. 93 Editors' Choice *—S.H. (7/1/2005)*

Iron Horse 2001 Corral Vineyard Chardonnay (Green Valley) $37. 91 *—S.H. (12/1/2003)*

Iron Horse 1997 Cuvée Joy Chardonnay (Green Valley) $30. 90 *(7/1/2001)*

Iron Horse 1997 Cuvée Joy Chardonnay (Green Valley) $30. 92 *—L.W. (3/1/2000)*

Iron Horse 2005 Estate Chardonnay (Green Valley) $27. Shows the tangy minerality this cool appellation is known for. The pear, green apple, lime and kiwi fruit has a cold metal, almost chalky edge that lends this wine a Chablisian complexity. Bone dry and elegant, it should develop over the next five years. 90 *—S.H. (11/1/2007)*

Iron Horse 2003 Estate Chardonnay (Green Valley) $26. 91 *—S.H. (2/1/2006)*

Iron Horse 2002 Estate Chardonnay (Green Valley) $26. 90 *—S.H. (7/1/2005)*

Iron Horse 2001 Estate Bottled Chardonnay (Green Valley) $26. 90 *—S.H. (6/1/2004)*

Iron Horse 1998 Estate Bottled Chardonnay (Sonoma County) $24. 88 *(6/1/2000)*

Iron Horse 2005 Native Yeast Chardonnay (Green Valley) $38. This is Iron Horse's first foray into native yeast winemaking, and the wine does have a yeasty, leesy quality, in addition to the usual dryness and minerality. In fact, this Chard is a little austere. Try giving it some years in the cellar. 87 *—S.H. (11/1/2007)*

Iron Horse 2005 Rued Clone Chardonnay (Green Valley) $35. With this wine Iron Horse takes a giant step toward great Chablis. By that, I mean the intense dryness and zesty acidity, and the tangy grip of iron and wet stone that undergirds the Meyer lemon, pineapple zest, honeysuckle, apricot, cinnamon spice and new oak flavors. This Chard is all about structural integrity. It should have a useful life of at least six years, gaining momentum and nuance. **94** *—S.H. (8/1/2007)*

Iron Horse 2001 Thomas Road Chardonnay (Green Valley) $37. 91 *—S.H. (12/1/2003)*

Iron Horse 2005 Un-Oaked Chardonnay (Green Valley) $25. Iron Horse joins the unoaked Chard bandwagon with this dry, complex wine. Their estate grapes are so good, the wine doesn't even need all that wood. It's elaborately tailored in pineapple, mango, ripe white peach and spicebox flavors. The vanilla and smoke, which have got to come from the grapes, add extra deliciousness. **91 Editors' Choice** *—S.H. (8/1/2007)*

Iron Horse 1998 T-bar-T Fumé Blanc (Sonoma County) $18. 90 *—S.H. (11/1/1999)*

Iron Horse 2002 T-bar-T Vineyard Merlot (Alexander Valley) $30. 92 *—S.H. (11/15/2005)*

Iron Horse 1998 Pinot Noir (Green Valley) $28. 87 *(10/1/2000)*

Iron Horse 1997 Pinot Noir (Green Valley) $24. 90 *(10/1/1999)*

Iron Horse 2002 Pinot Noir (Green Valley) $30. 87 *—S.H. (11/1/2004)*

Iron Horse 2000 Pinot Noir (Green Valley) $30. 91 Editors' Choice *(10/1/2002)*

Iron Horse 1999 Pinot Noir (Green Valley) $30. 93 Editors' Choice *—S.H. (12/15/2001)*

Iron Horse 2000 Corral Vineyard Pinot Noir (Green Valley) $60. 90 *(10/1/2002)*

Iron Horse 2005 Estate Pinot Noir (Green Valley) $35. This is a really good Pinot, dry and rich, and it shows the balance of power and racy delicacy that Green Valley Pinots, and particularly Iron Horse's, are known for. The cola, cherryskin, rhubarb and pomegranate flavors are quite complex, especially when they create all sorts of waves as they hit the oak. **92** *—S.H. (9/1/2007)*

Iron Horse 2004 Estate Pinot Noir (Green Valley) $35. 90 Cellar Selection *—S.H. (12/15/2006)*

Iron Horse 2003 Estate Pinot Noir (Green Valley) $35. 85 *—S.H. (2/1/2006)*

Iron Horse 2002 Estate Pinot Noir (Green Valley) $30. 88 *—S.H. (10/1/2005)*

Iron Horse 2001 Estate Bottled Pinot Noir (Green Valley) $30. 90 *—S.H. (6/1/2004)*

Iron Horse 2004 Q Pinot Noir (Green Valley) $70. 94 *—S.H. (12/31/2006)*

Iron Horse 2006 Rosé de Pinot Noir (Green Valley) $16. The vintage is looking to be pretty tough in the cooler parts of Sonoma due to the chill and dampness, but it benefits this dry blush wine made from Pinot Noir. It's very dry and firm in acidity, with green tea-accented raspberry and cherry flavors that finish with elegance and flair. **87** *—S.H. (11/1/2007)*

Iron Horse 2005 Rosé de Pinot Noir (Green Valley) $15. 86 *—S.H. (12/1/2006)*

Iron Horse 2002 Rosé de Pinot Noir (Green Valley) $15. 87 *—S.H. (7/1/2003)*

Iron Horse 2005 Thomas Road Pinot Noir (Green Valley) $70. No doubt about it, this is a big, lusty Pinot Noir. From a low-production parcel of the estate, it routinely produces immensely concentrated wines. The winemaker's challenge is to give balance and harmony to grapes of this heft, and here, Iron Horse has it figured out. Dry and enormously ripe in cherries, black raspberries, cocoa and cola, it's good now with lamb chops, grilled steaks and similar upscale fare, and should soften and improve for five years. **95** *—S.H. (9/1/2007)*

Iron Horse 2001 Thomas Road Pinot Noir (Green Valley) $60. 89 *—S.H. (2/1/2004)*

Iron Horse 2000 Thomas Road Pinot Noir (Sonoma County) $60. 90 *(10/1/2002)*

Iron Horse 1998 Thomas Road Vineyard Pinot Noir (Sonoma County) $50. 90*—S.H. (2/1/2001)*

Iron Horse 2004 Rosato di Sangiovese Rosé Blend (Green Valley) $10. 85 *—S.H. (11/15/2005)*

Iron Horse 2004 Rosé de Pinot Noir Rosé Blend (Green Valley) $15. 88 *S.H. (11/15/2005)*

Iron Horse 1997 Sangiovese (Sonoma County) $19. 91 *—S.H. (12/15/1999)*

Iron Horse 1996 Sangiovese (Sonoma County) $22. 91 *—S.H. (10/1/1999)*

Iron Horse 2000 Rosato Sangiovese (Alexander Valley) $15. 86 *—S.H. (11/15/2001)*

Iron Horse 2005 Rosato di Sangiovese (Alexander Valley) $12. 87 Best Buy *—S.H. (12/1/2006)*

Iron Horse 2003 Rosato di Sangiovese (Alexander Valley) $10. 86 Best Buy *—D.T. (11/15/2004)*

Iron Horse 2002 Rosato di Sangiovese (Alexander Valley) $15. 83 *—S.H. (9/1/2003)*

Iron Horse 2006 T-T Vineyard Rosato di Sangiovese (Alexander Valley) $13. Sangiovese can make a great rosé for the same reasons it's tough to perfect as a red wine in California. The acidity works in its favor, making the cherry and spice flavors clean and bright. The wine did not undergo malolactic fermentation, never touched oak and is thoroughly dry. **89 Best Buy** *—S.H. (11/1/2007)*

Iron Horse 1999 T-bar-T Proprietor Grown Sangiovese (Alexander Valley) $24. 87 *S.H. (9/1/2003)*

Iron Horse 2000 T-bar-T Sangiovese (Alexander Valley) $24. 86 *—S.H. (12/15/2004)*

Iron Horse 1997 Cuvée Joy Sauvignon Blanc (Sonoma County) $24. 89 *—S.H. (9/1/2000)*

Iron Horse 1999 T-bar-T Cuvée R Sauvignon Blanc (Alexander Valley) $19. 87 *(8/1/2002)*

Iron Horse 2005 T-bar-T Cuvée R Sauvignon Blanc (Alexander Valley) $24. 93 *—S.H. (10/1/2006)*

Iron Horse 2001 Blanc de Blancs Sparkling Blend (Green Valley) $37. Released after five years on the yeast, this is still a young, tartly aggressive bubbly. It is in fact by far the most acidic of Iron Horse's current stable of superb bubblies. But it's enormously rich, offering a wealth of subtle lime, peach, strawberry, toast and sourdough bread flavors that impress with both depth and length, as well as sheer class. Wonderful now, and should age effortlessly for 6–8 years. **93 Cellar Selection** *—S.H. (12/31/2007)*

Iron Horse 1998 Blanc de Blancs Sparkling Blend (Green Valley) $34. 90 *—S.H. (12/31/2006)*

Iron Horse 1997 Blanc de Blancs Sparkling Blend (Green Valley) $34. 90 Editors' Choice *—S.H. (12/31/2005)*

Iron Horse 1994 Blanc de Blancs Sparkling Blend (Green Valley) $34. 91 *—S.H. (12/1/2003)*

Iron Horse 1996 Blanc de Blancs LD Sparkling Blend (Green Valley) $60. 93 *—S.H. (12/31/2006)*

Iron Horse 1996 Blanc de Blancs LD Sparkling Blend (Green Valley) $60. 93 Cellar Selection *—S.H. (12/31/2005)*

Iron Horse 1996 Brut LD Sparkling Blend (Green Valley) $50. 91 *—S.H. (12/1/2003)*

Iron Horse 1996 Brut LD Sparkling Blend (Green Valley) $50. 93 *—S.H. (12/31/2004)*

Iron Horse 2003 Brut Rosé Sparkling Blend (Green Valley) $50. Iron Horse's Brut Rosé is always a compellingly rich, full-bodied, fun and delicious wine, and the '03 is their best ever. It captivates with raspberry and cherry flavors, slightly liquored, with smoky char and lees nuances, and possesses fresh, vital acids. One fifth Chardonnay adds a citrusy brightness. Try with sushi or ahi tuna tartare. **92** *—S.H. (12/31/2007)*

Iron Horse 1998 Brut Rosé Sparkling Blend (Green Valley) $30. 88 *—S.H. (12/1/2003)*

Iron Horse 1997 Brut Rosé Sparkling Blend (Green Valley) $30. 89 *—J.M. (12/1/2003)*

Iron Horse 2002 Classic Vintage Brut Sparkling Blend (Green Valley) $31. Made with a classic Champagne blend of Pinot Noir and Chardonnay, this is the simplest of Iron Horse's bubblies. It's elegant, and should be consumed in its youth. **87** *—S.H. (12/31/2007)*

Iron Horse 2001 Classic Vintage Brut Sparkling Blend (Green Valley) $30. 88 *—S.H. (12/31/2006)*

Iron Horse 2000 Classic Vintage Brut Sparkling Blend (Green Valley) $30. 87 *—S.H. (12/31/2005)*

Iron Horse 1998 Classic Vintage Brut Sparkling Blend (Green Valley) $28. 87 *—S.H. (12/1/2003)*

Iron Horse 2002 Russian Cuvée Sparkling Blend (Green Valley) $31. For those who like their sparkling wines a little sweet. This Pinot Noir-Chardonnay blend has the highest dose of residual sugar of all Iron Horse's bubblies, and it shows in the jellied flavors of raspberries, strawberries and limes. Very crisp acidity provides needed balance and elegance. **88** *—S.H. (12/31/2007)*

Iron Horse 2001 Russian Cuvée Sparkling Blend (Green Valley) $30. 87 *—S.H. (12/31/2006)*

Iron Horse 2000 Russian Cuvée Sparkling Blend (Green Valley) $30. 87 *—S.H. (12/31/2005)*

Iron Horse 1999 Russian Cuvée Sparkling Blend (Green Valley) $28. 88 *—S.H. (12/31/2004)*

Iron Horse 1998 Russian Cuvée Sparkling Blend (Sonoma County) $28. 87 —*S.H. (12/1/2003)*

Iron Horse 2004 Wedding Cuvée Sparkling Blend (Green Valley) $37. As the name implies, this is an enormously likeable sparkler, based primarily on Pinot Noir and showing that grape's sensual texture. With raspberry, strawberry, lime, vanilla and smoky yeast flavors, it's irresistibly good. **90** —*S.H. (12/31/2007)*

Iron Horse 2002 Wedding Cuvée Sparkling Blend (Green Valley) $34. 91 Editors' Choice —*S.H. (12/31/2005)*

Iron Horse 2003 Wedding Cuvée Sparkling Blend (Green Valley) $34. \92 Editors' Choice —*S.H. (12/31/2006)*

Iron Horse 1999 Wedding Cuvée Sparkling Blend (Green Valley) $28. 87 —*S.H. (12/1/2003)*

Iron Horse 2000 Viognier (Alexander Valley) $17. 90 Editors' Choice —*S.H. (11/15/2001)*

Iron Horse 2000 T-bar-T Viognier (Alexander Valley) $24. 89 —*S.H. (9/1/2002)*

Iron Horse 2005 T-bar-T Viognier (Alexander Valley) $24. \87 —*S.H. (12/15/2006)*

Iron Horse 2002 T-bar-T Viognier (Alexander Valley) $24. 90 —*S.H. (12/1/2003)*

Iron Horse 2004 T-bar-T Late Harvest Viognier (Alexander Valley) $25. \89 —*S.H. (2/1/2006)*

Iron Horse 2001 T-bar-T Proprietor Grown Viognier (Alexander Valley) $24. 87 —*S.H. (3/1/2003)*

Iron Horse 2006 T-T Vineyard Viognier (Alexander Valley) $26. Iron Horse has one of the most consistent Viognier records in California, with a style all their own. From their mountain vineyard in Alexander Valley, the '06 shows tremendous balance, with an exciting tension between dry, minerally acidity and Viognier's exotic fruit and wildflower flavors. The wine was stainless-steel fermented and did not undergo malolactic fermentation, which helps account for the cleanliness. **92** —*S.H. (11/1/2007)*

Iron Horse 2004 T-bar-T Vineyard Viognier (Alexander Valley) $24. 90 —*S.H. (7/1/2006)*

Iron Horse 2001 T-bar-T Cuvée R White Blend (Alexander Valley) $19. 90 Editors' Choice —*S.H. (7/1/2003)*

Iron Horse 2000 T-bar-T Cuvée R White Blend (Alexander Valley) $17. 88 —*S.H. (11/15/2001)*

Iron Horse 2002 T-bar-T Cuvée R White Blend (Alexander Valley) $19. 90 —*S.H. (12/1/2003)*

Iron Horse 2004 T-bar-T Cuvée R White Blend (Alexander Valley) $24. 91 Editors' Choice —*S.H. (7/1/2006)*

USA

IRONSTONE

Ironstone 1994 Crown Jewel Bordeaux Blend (California) $30. 89 *(11/15/1999)*

Ironstone 2003 Reserve Meritage Bordeaux Blend (Calaveras County) $35. This is easily the best Bordeaux red wine Ironstone has ever produced, and it's a welcome addition to their portfolio. Mainly Cabernet, it's absolutely dry and smooth, with dense but finely ground tannins that lend grip and structure to the cassis fruit. Really good now, with its layers of complex interest. **92** —*S.H. (8/1/2007)*

Ironstone 2004 Cabernet Franc (California) $10. The '04 Reserve Cab Franc was a very good wine. This one is much different, rustic and simple, with stewed cherry flavors and a bitter finish. Okay for everyday fare. **84** —*S.H. (9/1/2007)*

Ironstone 2003 Cabernet Franc (California) $10. 84 —*S.H. (11/15/2006)*

Ironstone 1999 Cabernet Franc (California) $10. 83 —*S.H. (12/1/2002)*

Ironstone 1997 Cabernet Franc (California) $11. 88 Best Buy *(11/15/1999)*

Ironstone 2004 Reserve Cabernet Franc (Sierra Foothills) $19. Lots to like in this Cab Franc. Shows ripe, attractive cherry compote, black raspberry purée, cola, cocoa, coffee and spice flavors, with a rich, earthy edge of balsamic, sautéed mushroom and oaky vanilla. Then there are the tannins. They kick in and give the wine a youthful, lively structure. Very nice wine, but be sure to decant it for a few hours. **90** —*S.H. (8/1/2007)*

Ironstone 2003 Reserve Cabernet Franc (Sierra Foothills) $19. Pretty simple fare, a thin, dry wine whose fruit is so watery that the alcohol and tannins dominate. **81** —*S.H. (4/1/2007)*

Ironstone 2002 Reserve Cabernet Franc (Sierra Foothills) $20.87 —*S.H. (6/1/2006)*

Ironstone 1999 Reserve Cabernet Franc (Sierra Foothills) $18. 89 —*S.H. (12/1/2002)*

Ironstone 2004 Cabernet Sauvignon (California) $10. With some Zin and Petite Sirah, this is deeply hued and full-bodied. Soft and gentle, with melted tannins and low acidity that frame earthy blackberry flavors. **85 Best Buy** —*S.H. (7/1/2007)*

Ironstone 2003 Cabernet Sauvignon (California) $10. 86 Best Buy —*S.H. (2/1/2006)*

Ironstone 1999 Cabernet Sauvignon (California) $10. 84 *(11/15/2002)*

Ironstone 1998 Cabernet Sauvignon (California) $9. 86 Best Buy *(8/1/2001)*

Ironstone 2003 Reserve Cabernet Sauvignon (Sierra Foothills) $25. From Calaveras County, this wine shows the ripeness and rusticity of the region. Insistent in blackberries, black currants and chocolate-covered cherries, it shows earthier layers of thyme and pepper, with edgy, slightly green tannins and a bitter finish. Drink now. **85** —*S.H. (9/1/2007)*

Ironstone 2002 Reserve Cabernet Sauvignon (Sierra Foothills) $30. 87 —*S.H. (7/1/2006)*

Ironstone 1999 Reserve Cabernet Sauvignon (Sierra Foothills) $25. 88 *(11/15/2002)*

Ironstone 1997 Reserve Cabernet Sauvignon (Sierra Foothills) $24. 88 *(8/1/2001)*

Ironstone 2005 Chardonnay (Lodi) $10. Tastes too sweet, like the sugared juices of canned apricots and peaches. Fortunately that's offset with very crisp acidity, but the wine finishes simple and disjointed. **82** —*S.H. (5/1/2007)*

Ironstone 2004 Chardonnay (California) $10. 85 Best Buy —*S.H. (2/1/2006)*

Ironstone 2000 Chardonnay (California) $10. 83 —*J.M. (12/15/2002)*

Ironstone 1999 Chardonnay (California) $9. 85 *(8/1/2001)*

Ironstone 1997 Chardonnay (California) $10. 86 *(11/15/1999)*

Ironstone 2005 Reserve Chardonnay (Calaveras County) $15. Ironstone's Reserve Chard has been getting interesting of late, and the '05 is a fascinating study in vintage, contrasted with the '04. The vintage was a cool one, and the wine is loaded with acidity and minerality reminiscent of Chablis. You can taste things like granite and mica that give a rich tang of earth to the underlying pineapple and oak flavors. Finishes long and totally dry. **90 Best Buy** —*S.H. (11/15/2007)*

Ironstone 2004 Reserve Chardonnay (Calaveras County) $15. Held back for an extra year longer than the winery's regular Chard, this bottling shows a smoky richness and fully mature, dried fruit flavors of apricots and pineapples. It's quite a complex wine whose zingy acidity adds balance and life. **87** —*S.H. (2/1/2007)*

Ironstone 2003 Reserve Chardonnay (Sierra Foothills) $18. 85 —*S.H. (2/1/2006)*

Ironstone 2003 Reserve Chardonnay (Sierra Foothills) $18. 83 —*S.H. (3/1/2006)*

Ironstone 1998 Reserve Chardonnay (California) $16. 87 *(8/1/2001)*

Ironstone 2001 Meritage (Sierra Foothills) $35. 90 —*S.H. (2/1/2005)*

Ironstone 2002 Reserve Meritage (Calaveras County) $35. 87 —*S.H. (2/1/2006)*

Ironstone 2000 Merlot (California) $10. 87 Best Buy —*S.H. (11/15/2002)*

Ironstone 1999 Merlot (California) $9. 85 *(8/1/2001)*

Ironstone 1997 Merlot (California) $11. 85 *(11/15/1999)*

Ironstone 2005 Petite Sirah (Lodi) $10. Inky dark, dry and velvety soft, it shows deeply ripe, gooey flavors of blackberry jam, spiced coffee, chocolate, licorice and violets. Great with a cheeseburger or lasagna. **85 Best Buy** —*S.H. (9/1/2007)*

Ironstone 2002 Petite Sirah (California) $10. 86 Best Buy —*S.H. (2/1/2005)*

Ironstone 2005 Expression Red Blend (California) $6. 86 Best Buy —*S.H. (11/15/2006)*

Ironstone 2003 Xpression Red Blend (California) $8. 85 Best Buy —*S.H. (2/1/2005)*

Ironstone 2006 Sauvignon Blanc (Lodi) $10. Thin, dry and citrusy-grassy, with some feline scents. Not much going on, but the price is okay for everyday. **83** —*S.H. (9/1/2007)*

Ironstone 2003 Sauvignon Blanc (California) $10. 87 Best Buy —*S.H. (2/1/2005)*

Ironstone 2005 Shiraz (Lodi) $10. Fast food will find a fast friend with this. It doesn't pretend to be anything more than it is. Dry and simple, it shows cherry and earthy flavors. **83** —*S.H. (9/1/2007)*

Ironstone 2003 Shiraz (California) $10. 84 —*S.H. (2/1/2006)*

Ironstone 2002 Shiraz (California) $10. 85 Best Buy *(9/1/2005)*

Ironstone 2000 Shiraz (California) $10. 84 —*S.H. (12/1/2002)*

Ironstone 1999 Shiraz (California) $9. 86 Best Buy *(8/1/2001)*

Ironstone 2006 Obsession Symphony (California) $8. This dessert wine has been remarkably consistent over the years at a good price. It's an off-dry sipper with crisp acidity, and finishes clean, with a taste of apricots and pineapples. The residual sugar is 2.2%. **85 Best Buy** *—S.H. (11/15/2007)*

Ironstone 2005 Obsession Symphony (California) $8. 84 Best Buy *—S.H. (12/1/2006)*

Ironstone 2003 Obsession Symphony White Blend (California) $8. 85 *—S.H. (6/1/2004)*

Ironstone 2000 Obsession Symphony White Blend (California) $7. 84 *(8/1/2001)*

Ironstone 1998 Obsession Symphony White Blend (California) $8. 85 *(11/15/1999)*

Ironstone 2000 Zinfandel (California) $10. 85 *—D.T. (3/1/2002)*

Ironstone 1999 Zinfandel (California) $9. 86 *(8/1/2001)*

Ironstone 2006 Old Vine Zinfandel (Lodi) $10. This basically dry wine is soft and simple, with cherry, raspberry and mint jelly flavors. Okay with barbecue. **83** *—S.H. (11/15/2007)*

Ironstone 2005 Old Vine Zinfandel (Lodi) $10. 84 *—S.H. (12/15/2006)*

Ironstone 2005 Reserve Old Vine Zinfandel (Lodi) $19. Just too ripe, and although the wine is dry, the stewed fruit and raisin flavors dominate, accentuated by softness. **82** *—S.H. (8/1/2007)*

Ironstone 2004 Reserve Old Vine Zinfandel (Lodi) $19. They say the grapes are a century old. They certainly deliver intense Zinfandel flavors, like the essence of ripened blackberries, cherries and loganberries. The wine is dry, and finishes a little rustic, with a streak of green chlorophyll. **85** *—S.H. (2/1/2007)*

Ironstone 2003 Reserve Old Vine Zinfandel (Lodi) $20. 91 *—S.H. (2/1/2006)*

Ironstone 2000 Reserve Old Vines Zinfandel (Lodi) $18. 87 *—S.H. (11/1/2002)*

IRONY

Irony 2002 Cabernet Sauvignon (Napa Valley) $16. 87 *—S.H. (12/31/2006)*

Irony 2004 Chardonnay (Napa Valley) $14. 82 *—S.H. (12/31/2006)*

Irony 2002 Merlot (Napa Valley) $16. 85 *—S.H. (12/31/2006)*

ISENHOWER CELLARS

Isenhower Cellars 2004 Wild Thyme Bordeaux Blend (Columbia Valley (WA)) $17. Here's another lovely blend from Isenhower, this one with flavors that are dark and roasted, the scents suggesting Syrah rather than what it is—a Merlot-based Bordeaux blend. A pretty wine for the price; firm in the mouth with licorice, blackberry and moist earth flavors. Tannins have been softened a bit but it retains an herbal roughness around the edges. **88** *—P.G. (3/1/2007)*

Isenhower Cellars 2004 Bachelor's Button Cabernet Sauvignon (Columbia Valley (WA)) $32. This is pure Cabernet planted in 1972. There is very little Cab in the country that old, and it's a thrill to taste it. The scents show almost-indefinable old vine character—a kind of brambly, delicate, nuanced mix of herb and fruit that turns up in old vine Zins, but here without the excess alcohol. Beautifully ripe and detailed. **92** *—P.G. (11/1/2007)*

Isenhower Cellars 2003 Bachelor's Button Cabernet Sauvignon (Columbia Valley (WA)) $NA. 88 *—P.G. (4/1/2006)*

Isenhower Cellars 1999 Merlot (Columbia Valley (WA)) $22. 90 *—P.G. (9/1/2002)*

Isenhower Cellars 2003 Red Paintbrush Merlot (Columbia Valley (WA)) $26. 88 *—P.G. (4/1/2006)*

Isenhower Cellars 2001 Red Paintbrush Merlot (Columbia Valley (WA)) $25. 89 *—P.G. (9/1/2004)*

Isenhower Cellars 2005 Red Paintbrush Red Blend (Walla Walla (WA)) $26. 47% Cabernet Sauvignon, 44% Merlot, 6% Cab Franc, 3% Carmenère. Nicely blended scents of red currants and plums lead into a fascinating, sophisticated wine. The Franc and Carmenère are added in small proportions, but stiffen up the tannins and add leafy notes to the fruit. The wine has been given enough barrel time to flesh out the finish with streaks of toffee and vanilla. **89** *—P.G. (11/1/2007)*

Isenhower Cellars 2003 River Beauty Red Blend (Red Mountain) $32. 91 *—P.G. (4/1/2006)*

Isenhower Cellars 2005 Wild Thyme Red Blend (Columbia Valley (WA)) $22. This is a complete switch from the 2004, which had no Syrah; here it is 60% of the blend. Very few wines in this price range have this degree of energy, detail and precision. The mix of fruit, spice, herb, rock, acid, barrel and tannin is delightful. **90** *—P.G. (11/1/2007)*

Isenhower Cellars 2006 Rosé Blend (Horse Heaven Hills) $17. This is a result of the increasing presence of rather rare Rhône valley grapes here in Washington. The blend is 42% Counoise, 41% Mourvèdre and 17% Grenache. This is round, soft, fleshy and forward, an interesting blend to be sure. **87** *—P.G. (7/1/2007)*

Isenhower Cellars 2006 Ciel du Cheval Vineyard Roussanne (Red Mountain) $22. From Tablas Creek cuttings, this outstanding Roussanne is intentionally picked early enough to preserve acidity, minerality and to keep the alcohol at a sensible level. Fragrant with acacia, white peach and pear, this elegant wine skips lightly across the palate, but has a density of flavor that carries well into the lingering finish. **91** *—P.G. (11/1/2007)*

Isenhower Cellars 2006 Snapdragon Roussanne (Horse Heaven Hills) $19. Formerly just labeled Snapdragon White, in 2006 the Roussanne component takes over, relegating the Viognier to 25 percent. As usual, this is a racy, tasty white wine, lightly peppery, with specks of citrus rind and fresh green herb. It's light for Roussanne, but very refreshing. **88** *—P.G. (11/1/2007)*

Isenhower Cellars 2000 Syrah (Columbia Valley (WA)) $25. 91 *—P.G. (9/1/2002)*

Isenhower Cellars 2003 Looking Glass Syrah (Columbia Valley (WA)) $22. 88 *—P.G. (4/1/2006)*

Isenhower Cellars 2003 Looking Glass Syrah (Columbia Valley (WA)) $22. 85 *(9/1/2005)*

Isenhower Cellars 2004 River Beauty Syrah (Horse Heaven Hills) $32. Isenhower changes the vineyard sources for this wine from year to year. This is the first Horse Heaven Hills version I've tasted, and it's right down the heart of the plate as far as Washington Syrah is concerned. The complex mix of spice, herb and wild fruits is bolstered by peppery tannins and lively acids. A truly wonderful wine that seems both poised and racy, wild and refined. The 14.8% alcohol is in no way over the top. **92** *—P.G. (3/1/2007)*

Isenhower Cellars 2002 River Beauty Syrah (Columbia Valley (WA)) $32. 83 *(9/1/2005)*

Isenhower Cellars 2003 Three Dogs Syrah (Columbia Valley (WA)) $20. 88 *—P.G. (4/1/2006)*

Isenhower Cellars 2005 Wild Alfalfa Syrah (Columbia Valley (WA)) $28. Young, tart and tannic, this blend will please those who like a tight, herbal, snappy, peppery, Washington take on Syrah. Tart and extremely young, yet satisfying and seductive, I believe this will age quite nicely for 6–8 years. **90** *—P.G. (11/1/2007)*

Isenhower Cellars 2001 Wild Alfalfa Syrah (Columbia Valley (WA)) $25. 90 Editors' Choice *—P.G. (9/1/2004)*

Isenhower Cellars 2004 Late Harvest White Blend (Columbia Valley (WA)) $22. 90 *—P.G. (4/1/2006)*

Isenhower Cellars 2005 Snapdragon White Blend (Columbia Valley (WA)) $18. This year's Snapdragon is a 55-45 Roussanne/Viognier blend—racier than the '04 but just as tasty, with a mouth-cleaning, yeasty freshness. The fruit is light and interesting, a mix of pink grapefruit, pineapple, green apple and a lick of honey. **90** *—P.G. (3/1/2007)*

Isenhower Cellars 2004 Snapdragon White Blend (Columbia Valley (WA)) $18. 90 *—P.G. (4/1/2006)*

J VINEYARDS & WINERY

J Vineyards & Winery 1998 Champagne Blend (Russian River Valley) $28. 88 *—J.M. (12/1/2002)*

J Vineyards & Winery 1997 Brut Champagne Blend (Russian River Valley) $28. 88 *—M.M. (12/1/2001)*

J Vineyards & Winery 1996 Brut Champagne Blend (Sonoma County) $28. 90 *—S.H. (12/15/1999)*

J Vineyards & Winery 2005 Chardonnay (Russian River Valley) $32. Captures the essence of Russian River Chard with its crisp acids that boost and brighten an explosion of taste. The tropical fruit and spice flavors are enriched by toasty oak, while sur lie aging adds a creaminess to the texture of this deliciously dry wine. **89** *—S.H. (12/15/2007)*

J Vineyards & Winery 2006 Pinot Gris (Russian River Valley) $20. Quite a bit sweeter on the palate than J's Pinot Gris in the past, with a sugary edge to the otherwise pretty pineapple, vanilla and wildflower flavors. Acidity helps to balance, but this is not, strictly speaking, dry. **84** *—S.H. (10/1/2007)*

J Vineyards & Winery 2004 Pinot Gris (Russian River Valley) $18. 85 *—S.H. (7/1/2005)*

J Vineyards & Winery 2002 Pinot Gris (Russian River Valley) $18. 87 *—S.H. (7/1/2003)*

J Vineyards & Winery 2001 Pinot Gris (Russian River Valley) $18. 87 *—S.H. (12/15/2002)*

J Vineyards & Winery 2000 Pinot Gris (Sonoma County) $NA. 88 *—J.M. (9/1/2003)*

J Vineyards & Winery 1998 Pinot Gris (Russian River Valley) $16. 90 —*S.H. (11/1/1999)*

J Vineyards & Winery 2005 Pinot Noir (Russian River Valley) $32. Classic Russian River Pinot, made in a drink-me-now style. Light in body, it's fully dry, with a silky texture framing cherry, cola, pomegranate and sautéed Portobello mushrooms with a splash of balsamic. A hint of oaky toast adds complexity. **88** —*S.H. (11/1/2007)*

J Vineyards & Winery 2002 Pinot Noir (Russian River Valley) $28. 87 —*S.H. (11/1/2004)*

J Vineyards & Winery 2000 Pinot Noir (Russian River Valley) $24. 87 —*S.H. (2/1/2004)*

J Vineyards & Winery 1998 Pinot Noir (Russian River Valley) $20. 88 —*S.H. (11/15/2001)*

J Vineyards & Winery 1999 Estate Bottled Pinot Noir (Russian River Valley) $20. 84 *(10/1/2002)*

J Vineyards & Winery 2005 Nicole's Vineyard Pinot Noir (Russian River Valley) $50. This is a complicated young Pinot; and while the parts are all pretty and polished, they haven't knitted together. Voluptuous flavors of cherries, cola, spices and cedar are wrapped into silky tannins, and the acidity is fine and brisk, but as good as the wine is, it seems unfinished, like the score to a symphony that has yet to be played. Give this until mid-2008, and it should be terrific for the next four years. **92** —*S.H. (12/31/2007)*

J Vineyards & Winery 1999 Nicole's Vineyard Pinot Noir (Russian River Valley) $35. 91 —*S.H. (2/1/2004)*

J Vineyards & Winery 2000 Robert Thomas Vineyard Pinot Noir (Russian River Valley) $40. 89 —*S.H. (4/1/2004)*

J Vineyards & Winery NV Brut Rosé Blend (Russian River Valley) $32. 91 Editors' Choice —*S.H. (6/1/2004)*

J Vineyards & Winery NV Brut Rosé Sparkling Blend (Russian River Valley) $32. With sparkling wine, it's all about finesse. Well, mostly. You want a nice, smooth, silky mouthfeel. This wine doesn't have one. It's all jagged, sharp; it cuts the palate. On the plus side, it's nicely dry, with pronounced strawberry flavors. **85** —*S.H. (3/1/2007)*

J Vineyards & Winery NV Brut Rosé Sparkling Blend (Russian River Valley) $35. The flavors are pure and delicious, suggesting jasmine tea, strawberries, citrus fruits, rose-hip tea, smoky dough and cinnamon. Dry, clean and elegant; the mouthfeel could be a little smoother, though. **87** —*S.H. (12/31/2007)*

J Vineyards & Winery NV Cuvée 20 Brut Sparkling Blend (Russian River Valley) $30. A little rough in texture and sweet on the finish, this pineappley brut is okay for everyday purposes, but the residual sugar is really too high for balance, especially at this price. **84** —*S.H. (12/31/2007)*

J Vineyards & Winery 1997 Late Disgorged Brut Sparkling Blend (Russian River Valley) $100. This has picked up softness and a honeyed mouthfeel, as the chemistry of aging on the lees does its magic. The wine has a plush, creamy feeling, with the silky smoothness of a great sparkling wine. Flavorwise, it's all pears, limes, dough and cinnamon spice. Delicious now, and should hold and improve over the next eight years. **93** —*S.H. (12/31/2007)*

J Vineyards & Winery 2002 Vintage Brut Sparkling Blend (Russian River Valley) $32. Just about half Chardonnay and half Pinot Noir, with a touch of Pinot Meunier, this fruit-forward bubbly tastes sweet, even by California sparkling wine standards. It's almost what the French call demi-sec, with sugared lemon mousse and raspberry-vanilla cream flavors. **84** —*S.H. (10/1/2007)*

J Vineyards & Winery 2001 Vintage Brut Sparkling Blend (Russian River Valley) $32. A blend of Chardonnay and Pinot Noir, with a little Pinot Meunier, this bubbly is really too rough to earn a better score. Instead of a nice, creamy smoothness, it's a jagged, harshly angular wine, but it is dry and clean. **84** —*S.H. (3/1/2007)*

J Vineyards & Winery 1999 Vintage Brut Sparkling Blend (Russian River Valley) $50. A nice bubbly that's mainly Chardonnay and Pinot Noir. It shows Champagne flavors suggesting citrus fruits, pears, strawberries and bread, with crisp acidity making the finish clean. The mouthfeel is a little rough and scoury. **87** —*S.H. (12/31/2007)*

J Vineyards & Winery 1999 Vintage Brut Sparkling Blend (Russian River Valley) $30. 90 —*S.H. (12/31/2004)*

J Vineyards & Winery 2001 Viognier (Alexander Valley) $NA. 84 —*S.H. (9/1/2003)*

J Vineyards & Winery 2002 Hoot Owl Vineyards Viognier (Russian River Valley) $28. 90 —*S.H. (12/31/2003)*

J. BENTON FURROW

J. Benton Furrow 2002 Old Vine Zinfandel (Dry Creek Valley) $20. 83 —*S.H. (5/1/2005)*

J. BOOKWALTER

J. Bookwalter 2002 Cabernet Sauvignon (Columbia Valley (WA)) $38. 91 Cellar Selection —*P.G. (12/15/2005)*

J. Bookwalter 2001 Cabernet Sauvignon (Columbia Valley (WA)) $32. 94 Editors' Choice —*P.G. (11/15/2004)*

J. Bookwalter 2003 Johannisberg Riesling (Columbia Valley (WA)) $12. 93 Best Buy —*P.G. (11/15/2004)*

J. Bookwalter 2002 Chapter One Meritage (Columbia Valley (WA)) $68. 93 —*P.G. (12/15/2005)*

J. Bookwalter 2004 Merlot (Columbia Valley (WA)) $38. 90 —*P.G. (12/31/2006)*

J. Bookwalter 2003 Merlot (Columbia Valley (WA)) $36. 89 —*P.G. (12/15/2005)*

J. Bookwalter 2002 Merlot (Columbia Valley (WA)) $30. 92 Editors' Choice —*P.G. (11/15/2004)*

J. Bookwalter 2006 Riesling (Columbia Valley (WA)) $15. This moderately off-dry (1% residual sugar) Columbia Valley Riesling explodes from the glass with big, round aromas suggestive of ripe melon, tropical fruits and citrus. The balance is perfect, with plenty of natural acidity. The winemaker notes, with unusual aplomb, that "With bottle aging the fermentation aromatics of Bazooka bubblegum will develop into classic, and very subtle petroleum aromas." Who's going to argue with that? **91 Best Buy** —*P.G. (9/1/2007)*

J. Bookwalter 2005 Riesling (Columbia Valley (WA)) $16. 93 —*P.G. (12/31/2006)*

J. Bookwalter 2004 Riesling (Columbia Valley (WA)) $16. 92 Editors' Choice —*P.G. (12/15/2005)*

J. DAVIES

J. Davies 2004 Cabernet Sauvignon (Diamond Mountain) $75. More tannic than in previous vintages, and not as immediately rich, this Cab-dominated Bordeaux blend will benefit from decanting. It needs some air to open up and reveal its heart of cassis. Will develop with six or so years of aging, but doesn't seem like a longterm cellar candidate. **89** —*S.H. (12/15/2007)*

J. Davies 2003 Cabernet Sauvignon (Diamond Mountain) $69. 94 Cellar Selection —*S.H. (12/15/2006)*

J. Davies 2002 Cabernet Sauvignon (Diamond Mountain) $65. 90 Cellar Selection —*S.H. (10/1/2005)*

J. Davies 2001 Cabernet Sauvignon (Diamond Mountain) $65. 92 —*S.H. (12/31/2004)*

J. GARCIA

J. Garcia 2001 Cabernet Sauvignon (Sonoma County) $15. 85 —*S.H. (10/1/2004)*

J. Garcia 2001 Merlot (Sonoma County) $15. 84 —*S.H. (12/15/2004)*

J. Garcia 2001 Zinfandel (Sonoma County) $15. 85 —*S.H. (11/15/2004)*

J. JACAMAN

J. Jacaman 2004 Pinot Noir (Russian River Valley) $40. Jacaman's been doing a good job with their Russian River Pinot. This one's a bit off the pace of the '03, due to the hotter vintage that makes the wine riper and simpler. But it's still a flavorful, dry, silky wine, with a fair degree of complexity. Drink now. **87** —*S.H. (10/1/2007)*

J. Jacaman 2003 Pinot Noir (Russian River Valley) $35. 90 —*S.H. (12/1/2005)*

J. Jacaman 2002 Pinot Noir (Russian River Valley) $35. 88 —*S.H. (3/1/2005)*

J. Jacaman 2004 Toulouse Vineyard Pinot Noir (Anderson Valley) $40. The first Jacaman Pinot I've had from this Mendocino vineyard, and their best Pinot ever. The wine is dry, dense and full-bodied, and complex, with waves of sweet, oak-infused cherries, raspberries, cassis, cola, licorice, mushroom, leather, spice and vanilla flavors washing over the palate. Really impresses all-around as an elegant, fascinating, Burgundian-style Pinot Noir. **93 Editors' Choice** —*S.H. (10/1/2007)*

J. Jacaman 2006 Vin Gris de Pinot Noir (Russian River Valley) $18. Dry and crisp, with subtle herb tea, cherryskin and cola flavors. Lots of acidity gives it a slight bite, which gives this pretty little rosé a nice, clean finish. **86** —*S.H. (7/1/2007)*

J. KIRKWOOD

J. Kirkwood 2002 Merlot (Napa Valley) $30. This is an Oh, wow! wine. It's that good. Ripe in cherry, blackberry and fudgy chocolate flavors, the wine is saved from insipid simpleness by fresh tannins and acids and an earthy, cappuccino darkness that grounds it. Fanatics will delight in knowing that the grapes, which include Cabernet Franc, come from the Truchard, Hyde and Dominus vineyards. **92** *—S.H. (2/1/2007)*

J. LOHR

J. Lohr 2004 Cuvée Pau Bordeaux Blend (Paso Robles) $56. The blend in this Pauillac-inspired cuvée is based on Cabernet Sauvignon, resulting in a wine that's slightly more structured than the others. Tobacco and cassis pick up hints of toffee and brown sugar on the finish. Drink now–2015. **90** *(10/1/2007)*

J. Lohr 2003 Cuvée Pau Bordeaux Blend (Paso Robles) $50. This is the winery's Pauillac-style wine, almost entirely Cab. It's a very good wine, close to a great one. Shows real varietal character with intense cassis aromas and flavors, accented by plenty of oak. The tannins are similar to a Sonoma mountain Cab, firm, dry and dusty, suggesting ageworthiness. Best now through 2012. **92** *—S.H. (11/1/2007)*

J. Lohr 2002 Cuvée Pau Bordeaux Blend (Paso Robles) $50. 91 *—S.H. (9/1/2006)*

J. Lohr 2001 Cuvée Pau Bordeaux Blend (Paso Robles) $50. 91 *—S.H. (4/1/2006)*

J. Lohr 2004 Cuvée Pom Bordeaux Blend (Paso Robles) $56. Merlot is the star in this blend, named for Pomerol. Coffee and carob, tomato leaf and plum all mingle easily, washing the palate with lush, creamy tannins that finish soft. Drink now–2010. **90** *(10/1/2007)*

J. Lohr 2001 Cuvée Pom Bordeaux Blend (Paso Robles) $50. 89 *—S.H. (9/1/2006)*

J. Lohr 2000 Pom Bordeaux Blend (Paso Robles) $50. 88 *—S.H. (11/15/2005)*

J. Lohr 2004 Cuvée St. E Bordeaux Blend (Paso Robles) $56. Our favorite of the three J. Lohr cuvées is this one, based on Cabernet Franc. The variety's floral, herbal notes mark the aromas, then give way on the palate to broad, mouthfilling flavors of brandied cherries and baking spices. It's lush and soft in the style of the winery and the region, but retains a slightly greater sense of focus than the Cuvée Pom. Drink now–2012. **91** *(10/1/2007)*

J. Lohr 2000 Pau Cabernet Blend (Paso Robles) $50. 82 *—S.H. (11/15/2005)*

J. Lohr 2000 St. E Cabernet Blend (Paso Robles) $50. 83 *—S.H. (11/15/2005)*

J. Lohr 2003 Carol's Vineyard Cabernet Sauvignon (Napa Valley) $45. Crisper and a bit leaner than the Paso Robles offerings from J. Lohr, this is a flawlessly made Napa Cab, offering up plenty of smoke- and cedar-accented cassis fruit. With its structure and balance, it should drink well for up to 10 years. **88** *(10/1/2007)*

J. Lohr 2001 Carol's Vineyard Cabernet Sauvignon (Napa Valley) $40. 93 *—S.H. (2/1/2005)*

J. Lohr 2004 Hilltop Vineyard Cabernet Sauvignon (Paso Robles) $32. A lush, sexy wine, this is the next step up the J. Lohr hierarchy from the Seven Oaks line. Smoky, herbal notes on the nose accent the ripe cassis fruit, ending in an avalanche of soft, velvety tannins. **90** *(10/1/2007)*

J. Lohr 2001 Hilltop Vineyard Cabernet Sauvignon (Paso Robles) $32. 88 *—S.H. (4/1/2006)*

J. Lohr 2000 Hilltop Vineyard Cabernet Sauvignon (Paso Robles) $32. H**87** *—S.H. (11/15/2005)*

J. Lohr 1999 Hilltop Vineyard Cabernet Sauvignon (Paso Robles) $32. 90 *—S.H. (11/15/2003)*

J. Lohr 1997 Hilltop Vineyard Cabernet Sauvignon (Paso Robles) $33. 91 *(11/1/2000)*

J. Lohr 2005 Seven Oaks Cabernet Sauvignon (Paso Robles) $17. One of the workhorses on the J. Lohr "farm," the Seven Oaks Cabernet is hugely successful in restaurants because of its accessible pricing and style. Its soft tannins, ripe fruit and slightly herbal edge go perfectly with grilled beef and lamb. **86** *(10/1/2007)*

J. Lohr 2004 Seven Oaks Cabernet Sauvignon (Paso Robles) $17. Sweeter, softer and simpler than in past vintages, the '04 shows the hallmarks of a hot harvest. In its melted structure are ripe blackberries that veer into plumped raisins, and sugared coffee flavors. **83** *—S.H. (7/1/2007)*

J. Lohr 2003 Seven Oaks Cabernet Sauvignon (Paso Robles) $15. 85 *—S.H. (4/1/2006)*

J. Lohr 2002 Seven Oaks Cabernet Sauvignon (Paso Robles) $15. 88 *—S.H. (5/1/2005)*

J. Lohr 2001 Seven Oaks Cabernet Sauvignon (Paso Robles) $15. 87 *(12/1/2003)*

J. Lohr 2005 Arroyo Seco Vineyard Chardonnay (Arroyo Seco) $25. Barrel-fermented and aged on the lees, this Burgundian-style Chard is creamy and rich in ripe tropical fruit flavors and new oak. It's a big wine, forward in pineapple and mango flavors that are honey-ripe and crisp. **88** *—S.H. (12/15/2007)*

J. Lohr 2005 Arroyo Vista Vineyard Chardonnay (Arroyo Seco) $25. A crisp, fresh, medium-bodied Chardonnay, this is toasty and nutty but not overly vanilla-scented. Grilled peach and buttered sweet corn notes pick up citrus overtones that finish long and mouthwatering. **90** *(10/1/2007)*

J. Lohr 2000 Arroyo Vista Chardonnay (Arroyo Seco) $25. 92 *—S.H. (2/1/2004)*

J. Lohr 1999 Arroyo Vista Chardonnay (Arroyo Seco) $25. 89 *—S.H. (12/31/2001)*

J. Lohr 2004 Arroyo Vista Vineyard Chardonnay (Arroyo Seco) $25. 90 *—S.H. (12/31/2006)*

J. Lohr 2003 Arroyo Vista Vineyard Chardonnay (Arroyo Seco) $25. 90 *—S.H. (3/1/2006)*

J. Lohr 2002 Arroyo Vista Vineyard Chardonnay (Arroyo Seco) $25. 90 *—S.H. (5/1/2005)*

J. Lohr 2001 Arroyo Vista Vineyard Chardonnay (Arroyo Seco) $25. 89 *(12/1/2003)*

J. Lohr 1996 Arroyo Vista Vineyard Chardonnay (Monterey) $25. 84 *—L.W. (11/15/1999)*

J. Lohr 2005 October Night Vineyard Chardonnay (Arroyo Seco) $25. Nutty and melon-scented, this is a medium-bodied Chardonnay with distinct tangerine and spice components Lohr attributes to the "Muscat clone" used in this wine. Finishes with a flourish of buttery richness. This would pair beautifully with cold crab. **89** *(10/1/2007)*

J. Lohr 2005 Riverstone Chardonnay (Arroyo Seco) $14. This bottling of Chardonnay, from one of the best white wine sites in Monterey, has kept its quality as well as its price over the years. Dry and zesty in acidity, it has a firm, stony minerality that underlies the apricot, white peach and grapefruit juice flavors. Shows real elegance, at a fair price. **87** *—S.H. (7/1/2007)*

J. Lohr 2004 Riverstone Chardonnay (Arroyo Seco) $14. 88 *—S.H. (3/1/2006)*

J. Lohr 2003 Riverstone Chardonnay (Arroyo Seco) $14. 90 Best Buy *—S.H. (11/15/2005)*

J. Lohr 2001 Riverstone Chardonnay (Arroyo Seco) $14. 87 *—S.H. (2/1/2004)*

J. Lohr 1998 Riverstone Chardonnay (Monterey County) $15. 88 *(6/1/2000)*

J. Lohr 2005 Los Osos Merlot (Paso Robles) $15. New oak gives a smoky edge to the jammy blueberry, cherry, rhubarb and tangerine flavors of this warm-climate Merlot. It's on the sweet, simple side, with a lozenge-candy finish. **84** *—S.H. (11/15/2007)*

J. Lohr 2004 Los Osos Merlot (Paso Robles) $15. An elegantly structured wine with real quality and finesse. It drinks bone dry, with cherry, moo shu plum sauce, mocha and smoky oak flavors wrapped into velvety, firm tannins. Drink now. **87** *—S.H. (7/1/2007)*

J. Lohr 2003 Los Osos Merlot (Paso Robles) $15. 88 *—S.H. (12/1/2006)*

J. Lohr 2002 Los Osos Merlot (Paso Robles) $15. 85 *—S.H. (11/15/2005)*

J. Lohr 2001 Los Osos Merlot (Paso Robles) $15. 86 *(12/1/2003)*

J. Lohr 1999 Cuvée Pau Red Wine Red Blend (Paso Robles) $50. 89 *(12/1/2003)*

J. Lohr 1999 Cuvée Pom Red Wine Red Blend (Paso Robles) $50. 90 *(12/1/2003)*

J. Lohr 1999 Cuvée St. E Red Wine Red Blend (Paso Robles) $50. 91 *(12/1/2003)*

J. Lohr 2003 Wildflower Valdeguie Red Blend (Monterey) $7. 84 Best Buy *—S.H. (5/1/2005)*

J. Lohr 2002 Bay Mist Riesling (Monterey) $8. 86 *—J.M. (8/1/2003)*

J. Lohr 2005 White Riesling (Arroyo Seco) $8. 86 Best Buy *—S.H. (11/15/2006)*

J. Lohr 2006 Late Harvest White Riesling (Arroyo Seco) $25. Sweet enough to be served as a dessert or with cheeses but not with dessert, this is a luscious, fruity wine that simply delicious. A hint of apricot adds dimension to the superripe apple and pineapple flavors. **90** *(10/1/2007)*

J. Lohr 2006 Carol's Vineyard Sauvignon Blanc (Napa Valley) $16. This is ripe to the point of richness, showing broad, mouthfilling flavors of melon and fig and just the merest hint of mint. Drink now. **86** *(10/1/2007)*

J. Lohr 2005 Carol's Vineyard Sauvignon Blanc (Napa Valley) $18. **83** *—S.H. (12/31/2006)*

J. Lohr 2004 Carol's Vineyard Sauvignon Blanc (Napa Valley) $18. 90 *—S.H. (4/1/2006)*

USA

J. Lohr 2003 Carol's Vineyard Sauvignon Blanc (Napa Valley) $18. 87 —*S.H. (2/1/2005)*

J. Lohr 2002 Carol's Vineyard Sauvignon Blanc (Napa Valley) $18. 88 *(12/1/2003)*

J. Lohr 2001 Carol's Vineyard Sauvignon Blanc (Napa Valley) $18. 84 *(8/1/2002)*

J. Lohr 2005 South Ridge Syrah (Paso Robles) $15. Made like an Aussie Shiraz, this is a fresh, young red packed with jammy raspberry, cherry, raw meat and spice flavors. The finish is very dry, with zingy acids and a dusty bite of tannins. **84** —*S.H. (11/15/2007)*

J. Lohr 2004 South Ridge Syrah (Paso Robles) $15. 83 —*S.H. (12/31/2006)*

J. Lohr 2003 South Ridge Syrah (Paso Robles) $15. 84 *(9/1/2005)*

J. Lohr 2001 South Ridge Syrah (Paso Robles) $15. 86 —*S.H. (4/1/2004)*

J. Lohr 1999 South Ridge Syrah (Paso Robles) $15. 87 Editors' Choice *(10/1/2001)*

J. Lohr 1997 South Ridge Syrah (Paso Robles) $14. 90 Best Buy —*S.H. (2/1/2000)*

J. Lohr 2006 Wildflower Valdeguié (Monterey) $8. Give the winery credit for experimenting with this offbeat variety, which was grown in the Arroyo Seco region. Unfortunately, it's far too sweet for a table wine, almost a dessert sipper, with overt sugar marking the berry flavors. **82** —*S.H. (11/15/2007)*

J. Lohr 2004 Wildflower Valdeguié (Arroyo Seco) $8. 86 Best Buy —*S.H. (11/15/2005)*

J. Lohr 2001 Bramblewood Zinfandel (Lodi) $15. 86 *(11/1/2003)*

J. LYNNE

J. Lynne 2005 Chardonnay (Russian River Valley) $19. A very interesting wine that clearly shows its cool-climate origins, with a great big burst of brisk acidity that gets the tastebuds whistling. Underneath are pure flavors of green apples and ripe kiwis. The oak is sizable, but perfect for this formula, adding delicious honey, butterscotch and vanilla flavors. This is the best J. Lynne Chard I've had. **90** —*S.H. (11/1/2007)*

J. Lynne 2003 Chardonnay (Russian River Valley) $23. 84 —*S.H. (10/1/2005)*

J. Lynne 2002 Chardonnay (Russian River Valley) $18. 87 —*S.H. (8/1/2005)*

J. Lynne 2003 Pinot Noir (Russian River Valley) $24. 86 —*S.H. (10/1/2005)*

J. Lynne 2002 Cameron Ranch Vineyard Pinot Noir (Russian River Valley) $22. 84 *(11/1/2004)*

J. WILKES

J. Wilkes 2004 Bien Nacido Vineyard Pinot Blanc (Santa Barbara County) $18. 90 —*S.H. (12/15/2005)*

J. Wilkes 2003 Bien Nacido Vineyard Block Q Pinot Noir (Santa Barbara County) $50. 91 —*S.H. (12/15/2005)*

J. Wilkes 2002 Bien Nacido Vineyard Block Q Pinot Noir (Santa Barbara County) $50. 89 —*S.H. (12/15/2005)*

J. Wilkes 2004 Bien Nacido Vineyard Hillside Pinot Noir (Santa Barbara County) $38. 92 —*S.H. (11/1/2006)*

J. Wilkes 2004 Solomon Hills Vineyards Pinot Noir (Santa Barbara County) $38. 92 —*S.H. (11/15/2006)*

J.C. CELLARS

J.C. Cellars 2005 Preston Vineyard Marsanne (Dry Creek Valley) $32. Dry Creek Valley has a natural affinity for Marsanne, and particularly in this balanced vintage. The grapes got ripe in lemon chiffon, peach and honeysuckle flavors, while a clean crispness and minerality add length and palate interest. Sur lies aging in the barrel brings even richer notes of cream and smoky vanilla. This Marsanne explores the outer reaches of the variety's possibilities in California. **92 Editors' Choice** —*S.H. (8/1/2007)*

J.C. Cellars 1997 St. George Vineyard Petite Sirah (Napa Valley) $35. 84 —*S.H. (6/1/1999)*

J.C. Cellars 2004 A La Cave Syrah (California) $40. Of the winery's current crop of five Syrahs, this is the next most expensive, but it's hard to tell why. Possibly because most of the grapes come from Napa Valley, they paid more for fruit. But that means nothing. The wine is tannic and has a glycerine sweetness to the blackberry and cherry fruit that's almost syrupy. Doesn't seem like an ager. **84** —*S.H. (8/1/2007)*

J.C. Cellars 2004 Californa Cuvee Syrah (California) $25. The sources of this Syrah are all very good, including top vineyards from Santa Barbara, Arroyo Seco, Alexander Valley and Lake County. An example of the art of blending, it's a lovely wine, rich, dry and balanced, with an earthy edge to the ripe cherry and blackberry flavors. **87** —*S.H. (8/1/2007)*

J.C. Cellars 1997 Eaglepoint Vineyard Syrah (Mendocino) $25. 87 —*S.H. (6/1/1999)*

J.C. Cellars 2004 Fess Parker's Vineyard Syrah (Santa Barbara) $29. Dense, dry and young, this is a Syrah for the cellar. With 10% Petite Sirah, it has some fierce tannins, and is a little soft, but possesses the inherent balance to age. Give it two or three years, then enjoy the hearty cherry, cassis, leather, cocoa and balsamic flavors for a couple more years. **89** —*S.H. (8/1/2007)*

J.C. Cellars 1997 Mesa Vineyard Syrah (Santa Barbara County) $20. 89 —*S.H. (6/1/1999)*

J.C. Cellars 2004 Rockpile Vineyard Haley's Reserve Syrah (Rockpile) $50. Rockpile, a mountainy region in Dry Creek Valley, has given in this warm vintage a big young Syrah. Dry and smooth, it bursts with enormously ripe cherry flavors, but also is very tannic. It's high in alcohol, a potential fault, but something in the acid-tannin structure keeps it balanced, and even elegant. Best now and for the next few years. **91** —*S.H. (8/1/2007)*

J.C. Cellars 2003 Ventana Vineyards Syrah (Monterey) $30. Not a bad wine, but too soft-heavy and sweet for my tastes, with cherry flavors that are on the medicinal side due to the very high alcohol. Almost 90% charry new oak doesn't really help. **84** —*S.H. (8/1/2007)*

J.C. Cellars 1999 Ventana Vineyards Syrah (Monterey) $30. 88 *(11/1/2001)*

J.C. Cellars 1998 Alegria Vineyard Zinfandel (Russian River Valley) $30. 90 —*S.H. (5/1/2000)*

J.C. Cellars 2001 Rhodes Vineyard Zinfandel (Redwood Valley) $26. 89 *(11/1/2003)*

J.C. Cellars 1998 Rhodes Vineyard Zinfandel (Redwood Valley) $26. 87 —*S.H. (5/1/2000)*

J.J. MCHALE

J.J. Mchale 1999 Cabernet Franc (Clear Lake) $27. 85 —*S.H. (12/1/2002)*

J.J. Mchale 2000 Lolonis Vineyard Chardonnay (Redwood Valley) $33. 84 —*S.H. (12/15/2002)*

J.J. Mchale 2000 Dorn Vineyard Fumé Blanc (Clear Lake) $18. 86 *(8/1/2002)*

J.J. Mchale 2000 Pinot Noir (Anderson Valley) $33. 86 *(10/1/2002)*

J.J. Mchale 2000 Dorn Vineyard Sauvignon Blanc (Clear Lake) $18. 87 —*S.H. (9/1/2003)*

J.J. Mchale 1999 Syrah (Clear Lake) $29. 86 —*S.H. (12/1/2002)*

J.K. CARRIÈRE

J.K. Carrière 2002 Pinot Noir (Willamette Valley) $36. 87 *(11/1/2004)*

J.K. Carrière 2002 Provocateur Pinot Noir (Willamette Valley) $18. 85 *(11/1/2004)*

JACK WILLIAM

Jack William 2005 Sauvignon Blanc (Alexander Valley) $16. 84 —*S.H. (11/15/2006)*

JADE MOUNTAIN

Jade Mountain 1999 Caldwell Vineyard Merlot (Napa Valley) $38. 89 —*J.M. (11/15/2002)*

Jade Mountain 1997 Caldwell Vineyard Merlot (Napa Valley) $34. 88 —*L.W. (12/31/1999)*

Jade Mountain 1997 Paras Vineyard Merlot (Mount Veeder) $52. 87 *(12/31/1999)*

Jade Mountain 2003 Mourvèdre (Contra Costa County) $18. 87 —*S.H. (11/1/2005)*

Jade Mountain 2002 Mourvèdre (Contra Costa County) $18. 87 —*S.H. (10/1/2004)*

Jade Mountain 2001 Mourvèdre (Contra Costa County) $18. 88 —*J.M. (12/1/2003)*

Jade Mountain 1997 Mourvèdre (California) $20. 84 —*S.H. (10/1/1999)*

Jade Mountain 2004 Evangelho Vineyard Mourvèdre (Contra Costa County) $20. 84 —*S.H. (8/1/2006)*

Jade Mountain 2002 La Provençale Red Blend (California) $16. 88 —*S.H. (10/1/2004)*

Jade Mountain 2001 La Provençale Red Wine Red Blend (California) $16. 88 —*S.H. (4/1/2004)*

Jade Mountain 2003 La Provencale Rhône Red Blend (California) $16. 89 Editors' Choice —*S.H. (11/1/2005)*

Jade Mountain 1997 La Provencale Rhône Red Blend (California) $19. 87 —*M.S. (2/1/2000)*

Jade Mountain 2004 Syrah (Monterey County) $15. 84 —*S.H. (12/1/2006)*

Jade Mountain 2003 Syrah (Monterey County) $15. 83 *(9/1/2005)*

Jade Mountain 2003 Syrah (Napa Valley) $27. 85 *(9/1/2005)*

Jade Mountain 2002 Syrah (Napa Valley) $27. 92 *—S.H. (10/1/2004)*

Jade Mountain 2001 Syrah (Napa Valley) $25. 90 *—S.H. (3/1/2004)*

Jade Mountain 1999 Syrah (Napa Valley) $25. 89 *—J.M. (7/1/2002)*

Jade Mountain 1998 Syrah (Napa Valley) $25. 85 *(11/1/2001)*

Jade Mountain 1997 Hudson Vineyard Syrah (Napa Valley) $32. 90 *(2/1/2000)*

Jade Mountain 2001 Paras Vineyard Syrah (Mount Veeder) $50. 94 *—S.H. (10/1/2004)*

Jade Mountain 2000 Paras Vineyard Syrah (Mount Veeder) $50. 93 *—J.M. (4/1/2004)*

Jade Mountain 1997 Paras Vineyard Syrah (Mount Veeder) $52. 85 *—J.C. (2/1/2000)*

Jade Mountain 2000 Paras Vineyard P-10 Syrah (Mount Veeder) $75. 93 *—S.H. (5/1/2005)*

Jade Mountain 2004 Snows Lake Vineyard Syrah (Red Hills Lake County) $17. 87 *—S.H. (12/1/2006)*

Jade Mountain 2003 Paras Vineyard Viognier (Mount Veeder) $30. 88 *—S.H. (11/1/2005)*

Jade Mountain 2001 Paras Vineyard Viognier (Mount Veeder) $30. 88 *—J.M. (5/1/2003)*

JAFFURS

Jaffurs 2001 Stolpman Vineyard Grenache (Santa Barbara County) $20. 91 *—S.H. (3/1/2004)*

Jaffurs 1997 Mourvèdre (Santa Barbara County) $20. 89 *—S.H. (6/1/1999)*

Jaffurs 1997 Cuvée Red Blend (Santa Barbara County) $19. 90 *—S.H. (6/1/1999)*

Jaffurs 1997 Roussanne (Santa Barbara) $19. 87 *—S.H. (6/1/1999)*

Jaffurs 1997 Syrah (Santa Barbara County) $22. 89 *—S.H. (6/1/1999)*

Jaffurs 2004 Syrah (Santa Barbara County) $23. 87 *—S.H. (12/1/2006)*

Jaffurs 2003 Syrah (Santa Barbara County) $23. 88 *(9/1/2005)*

Jaffurs 2002 Syrah (Santa Barbara County) $23. 89 *—S.H. (5/1/2005)*

Jaffurs 2001 Syrah (Santa Barbara County) $23. 89 *—S.H. (2/1/2004)*

Jaffurs 2004 Ampelos Vineyard Syrah (Santa Barbara County) $42. 91 *—S.H. (11/15/2006)*

Jaffurs 2004 Bien Nacido Vineyard Syrah (Santa Barbara County) $30. 88 *—S.H. (12/1/2006)*

Jaffurs 2003 Bien Nacido Vineyard Syrah (Santa Barbara County) $30. 89 *(9/1/2005)*

Jaffurs 2002 Bien Nacido Vineyard Syrah (Santa Barbara County) $30. 90 *—S.H. (5/1/2005)*

Jaffurs 2001 Bien Nacido Vineyard Syrah (Santa Barbara County) $30. 89 *—S.H. (2/1/2004)*

Jaffurs 1999 Bien Nacido Vineyard Syrah (Santa Barbara County) $30. 86 *—S.H. (7/1/2002)*

Jaffurs 2003 Larner Vineyard Syrah (Santa Barbara County) $34. 85 *(9/1/2005)*

Jaffurs 2003 Melville Vineyard Syrah (Santa Barbara County) $38. 91 **Editors' Choice** *(9/1/2005)*

Jaffurs 2002 Melville Vineyard Syrah (Santa Barbara County) $38. 89 *—S.H. (5/1/2005)*

Jaffurs 2001 Melville Vineyard Syrah (Santa Barbara County) $32. 85 *—S.H. (3/1/2004)*

Jaffurs 2002 Stolpman Vineyard Syrah (Santa Ynez Valley) $38. 87 *—S.H. (5/1/2005)*

Jaffurs 2001 Stolpman Vineyard Syrah (Santa Barbara County) $32. 90 *—S.H. (10/1/2003)*

Jaffurs 1999 Stolpman Vineyard Syrah (Santa Barbara County) $32. 93 *—J.M. (7/1/2002)*

Jaffurs 2004 Thompson Vineyard Syrah (Santa Barbara County) $34. 92 **Cellar Selection** *—S.H. (12/1/2006)*

Jaffurs 2003 Thompson Vineyard Syrah (Santa Barbara County) $34. 89 *(9/1/2005)*

Jaffurs 2002 Thompson Vineyard Syrah (Santa Barbara County) $34. 90 *—S.H. (5/1/2005)*

Jaffurs 2001 Thompson Vineyard Syrah (Santa Barbara County) $34. 91 *—S.H. (2/1/2004)*

Jaffurs 1999 Thompson Vineyard Syrah (Santa Barbara County) $32. 88 *(11/1/2001)*

Jaffurs 2004 Verna's Vineyard Syrah (Santa Barbara County) $38. 88 *—S.H. (12/1/2006)*

Jaffurs 1997 Viognier (Santa Barbara) $22. 87 *—S.H. (6/1/1999)*

Jaffurs 2005 Viognier (Santa Barbara County) $23. 90 *—S.H. (12/1/2006)*

Jaffurs 2003 Viognier (Santa Barbara County) $23. 87 *—S.H. (5/1/2005)*

Jaffurs 2002 Viognier (Santa Barbara County) $23. 91 **Editors' Choice** *—S.H. (12/1/2003)*

JAMES JOHNSON

James Johnson 2002 Bisou Cabernet Sauvignon (Napa Valley) $60. 87 *—S.H. (8/1/2006)*

JAMES LEIGH

James Leigh 2003 Cabernet Sauvignon (Walla Walla (WA)) $28. This is pure Cab from two top Walla Walla vineyards, Spofford Station and Pepper Bridge. It shows polished and sophisticated winemaking, with big, brawny, smoky and edgy flavors. The fruit is spicy and tight, and it is wrapped in ash, graphite and stone. The fruit in this big but focused Cab peeks out from the darker mineral layers, tight and tart and saucy. 91 *—P.G. (3/1/2007)*

James Leigh 2003 Spofford Station Merlot (Walla Walla (WA)) $32. Thick, lush and substantial, this is about as chewy a Merlot as you'll ever find. There's 10% Cabernet in the blend, but it's the Merlot that seems to provide the mass, the weight and the substance—if anything, the Cab thins it out a bit. A very impressive, dense and flavorful wine, it melds black fruits, licorice, graphite and Asian tea into a rich and satisfying whole. 92 *—P.G. (3/1/2007)*

James Leigh 2003 Spofford Station Syrah (Walla Walla (WA)) $32. Dark and smoky, its mouthfeel lifted with citrus scents and juicy acids, this excellent Syrah really delivers the goods. It's packed with zingy fruit, buoyed upon spicy acids, and it sails along, tart and intense, through a very long and detailed finish with a distinct flavor of pineapple. 90 *—P.G. (3/1/2007)*

JAMESPORT

Jamesport 2002 Estate Merlot (North Fork of Long Island) $22. 84 *—M.D. (12/1/2006)*

Jamesport NV East End Series Merlot (North Fork of Long Island) $16. 85 *—M.D. (12/1/2006)*

Jamesport 2001 Reserve Merlot (North Fork of Long Island) $39. 80 *—M.D. (12/1/2006)*

Jamesport 2006 Riesling (North Fork of Long Island) $18. This is a good example of Long Island Riesling from a producer who has a true historic stake in the region. Crisp, lively flavors of apple and melon mingled with a refreshing touch of minerality are light but substantial, and the finish is long and full of fruit flavors. A friendly Riesling that will hold its own against myriad dishes or is is great in the glass alone. 85 *—S.K. (9/1/2007)*

Jamesport 2006 Rosé Blend (North Fork of Long Island) $16. Raspberry and strawberry play on the palate, backed by a good acidity and some weight and complexity on the tongue to balance it out. The finish is good and the overall impression is favorable. 83 *—S.K. (7/1/2007)*

JAMIESON CANYON

Jamieson Canyon 1999 Cabernet Sauvignon (Napa Valley) $20. 91 **Editors' Choice** *—S.H. (8/1/2003)*

Jamieson Canyon 2000 Chardonnay (Napa Valley) $15. 82 *—S.H. (10/1/2003)*

Jamieson Canyon 1999 Merlot (Napa Valley) $17. 90 **Editors' Choice** *—S.H. (8/1/2003)*

JANA

Jana 2003 Cathedral Red Table Wine Cabernet Blend (Napa Valley) $55. This Cab-based Bordeaux blend really surprised me. It's a welcome addition to the mid-priced Napa pantheon. Rich, soft and mouth-filling, it has blackberry and cherry pie filling, cocoa and sweet oak flavors that finish smooth and dry. Drink now–2009. 90 *—S.H. (4/1/2007)*

Jana 2005 Riesling (America) $18. 85 *—S.H. (12/15/2006)*

Jana 2006 Old Vine Riesling (Napa Valley) $20. Not particularly Riesling-like, but it's very dry, nice and crisp in punchy acids, and superclean, with spicy citrus and flower flavors. Pleasant alternative to a good Pinot Gris or Sauvignon Blanc. 86 *—S.H. (12/1/2007)*

Jana 2005 Old Vine Riesling (Napa Valley) $15. 83 *—S.H. (12/15/2006)*

Jana 2005 Old Vine Zinfandel (Napa Valley) $35. The brambly wild berry flavors have an exotic edge of white pepper and Chinese five-spice that's interesting and even complex. But the wine is utterly lacking in acidity, which makes it syrupy even though it's totally dry. **81** —*S.H. (12/1/2007)*

JANKRIS

JanKris 2005 Westside Estate Chardonnay (Paso Robles) $10. 81 —*S.H. (12/31/2006)*

JanKris 2003 Estate Merlot (Paso Robles) $10. 82 —*S.H. (12/31/2006)*

JanKris 2003 Crossfire Red Blend (Paso Robles) $9. 84 —*S.H. (4/1/2005)*

JanKris 2004 Estate Picaro Red Blend (Paso Robles) $10. 82 —*S.H. (12/31/2006)*

JanKris 2003 Riatta Red Blend (Paso Robles) $9. 84 —*S.H. (4/1/2005)*

JanKris 2004 Estate Crossfire Rhône Red Blend (Paso Robles) $10. 85 Best Buy —*S.H. (11/15/2006)*

JanKris 2003 Syrah (Paso Robles) $10. 82 *(9/1/2005)*

JanKris 2002 Tres Ranchos Zinfandel (Paso Robles) $9. 84 —*S.H. (4/1/2005)*

JANUIK WINERY

Januik Winery 2004 Cabernet Sauvignon (Columbia Valley (WA)) $30. The fruit flavors remain primary, and the mouthfeel quite acidic. It tastes like not-quite-ripe blueberries and raspberries. Give it plenty of airing and as it begins to open up it will show additional streaks of flavor—vanilla, tobacco, and even a hint of mint. It's deceptive, a better wine than it first appears, but you have to reach out to it. **89** —*P.G. (11/1/2007)*

Januik Winery 2003 Cabernet Sauvignon (Columbia Valley (WA)) $30. 92 —*P.G. (11/15/2006)*

Januik Winery 2000 Cabernet Sauvignon (Columbia Valley (WA)) $NA. 88 —*P.G. (9/1/2004)*

Januik Winery 2004 Champoux Vineyard Cabernet Sauvignon (Horse Heaven Hills) $40. Initially dark and tannic, it shows some sharp, piercing components with scents of pine and mint. The fruit is sharp and not at all expansive. The color is good, and there's some nicely applied barrel influence, but for a long time it just doesn't go anywhere in the mouth. Finally, after several hours, it begins to flesh out, although the finish remains quite sharp and shows some bite. **89** —*P.G. (11/1/2007)*

Januik Winery 2004 Ciel du Cheval Vineyard Cabernet Sauvignon (Red Mountain) $40. This has a hint of the vineyard's characteristic chalky minerality, but other than that it's tight as a drum, with the same uncompromising, acidic frame, showing compact black cherry fruit and no textural detail. Give it hours of breathing time and it opens up a bit more. **89** —*P.G. (11/1/2007)*

Januik Winery 2003 Seven Hills Vineyard Cabernet Sauvignon (Walla Walla (WA)) $35. 90 —*P.G. (11/15/2006)*

Januik Winery 2005 Cold Creek Vineyard Chardonnay (Columbia Valley (WA)) $30. This is forward, fruity and quite ripe and round, with flavors of peach, pear and apricot. The acid is retained, but this is unusually ripe for the vineyard. The peach flavors dominate, nicely accented with hints of cinnamon and toast. Great fruit, good structure, much less new oak. Still quite young and needing time to add nuance, but plenty of power. **90** —*P.G. (11/1/2007)*

Januik Winery 2004 Cold Creek Vineyard Chardonnay (Columbia Valley (WA)) $30. 90 —*P.G. (10/1/2006)*

Januik Winery 2000 Cold Creek Vineyard Chardonnay (Columbia Valley (WA)) $NA. 91 —*P.G. (9/1/2004)*

Januik Winery 2004 Elerding Vineyard Chardonnay (Columbia Valley (WA)) $25. 89 —*P.G. (10/1/2006)*

Januik Winery 2004 Merlot (Columbia Valley (WA)) $25. This is a pretty, plummy purple color; it smells of cherries and a tease of chocolate. It is drinking well right now, with pie cherry and tart plum fruit. It's relatively high in acid, at least in terms of how it hits the palate, and a bit one-dimensional, lacking in textural interest. **88** —*P.G. (11/1/2007)*

Januik Winery 2003 Merlot (Columbia Valley (WA)) $25. 90 —*P.G. (10/1/2006)*

Januik Winery 2000 Merlot (Columbia Valley (WA)) $NA. 88 —*P.G. (9/1/2004)*

Januik Winery 2004 Ciel du Cheval Vineyard Petite Verdot (Red Mountain) $35. Very young, tart and acidic, this shows the same tight tannins that run through all of the Januik reds. I'd like to see more expansion of these wines, more depth and texture; they are ripe enough, but lack weight through the finish. As with the other reds, this needs hours of decanting before it will begin to open up. **88** —*P.G. (11/1/2007)*

Januik Winery 2003 Syrah (Columbia Valley (WA)) $30.93 Editors' Choice —*P.G. (11/15/2006)*

Januik Winery 2002 Syrah (Columbia Valley (WA)) $30. 87 *(9/1/2005)*

Januik Winery 2000 Syrah (Columbia Valley (WA)) $NA. 88 —*P.G. (9/1/2004)*

Januik Winery 2004 Lewis Vineyard Syrah (Columbia Valley (WA)) $30. Dark, sappy and effusively scented with boysenberry and black cherry. It still has plenty of acid underscoring the fruit, a bit of burn in the back, but great aromas now developing secondary scents of tobacco and spice. Lewis is establishing itself as one of Washington's best Syrah vineyards. **91** —*P.G. (11/1/2007)*

JARVIS

Jarvis 1999 Reserve Chardonnay (Napa Valley) $58. 87 *(7/1/2001)*

Jarvis 1999 Reserve Unfined, Unfiltered Chardonnay (Napa Valley) $58. 91 *(7/1/2001)*

JASON'S VINEYARD

Jason's Vineyard 2002 Cabernet Sauvignon (North Fork of Long Island) $13. There's a one-dimensional tartness and cranberry-like edge to this Long Island Cabernet that's hard to transcend. Notes of spice and plum are faint and there's a slight lingering finish, but in general, the wine needs more heft and integration. **81** —*S.K. (5/1/2007)*

Jason's Vineyard 1999 Merlot (North Fork of Long Island) $NA. To look at the brown color of this wine, you would think it was a lot older than its 1999 vintage. The nose is grassy, herbal, and a bit horsey; on the palate, it's lean and thin, and peters out fast. **81** —*S.K. (2/1/2007)*

JAYSON

Jayson 2005 Pinot Noir (Sonoma Coast) $65. This is the first Pinot from the Napa house of Pahlmeyer, the result of many years of effort in his vineyard in the Fort Ross area of the true Sonoma Coast. The result is rich in cherry pie, raspberry liqueur, cotton candy, licorice, vanilla and cinnamon flavors that captivate from sip one, but there's a certain young vine simple directness that limits the score. As the vines age, the wine is one to watch. **92** —*S.H. (12/1/2007)*

JEAN EDWARDS

Jean Edwards 2004 Stagecoach Vineyard Cabernet Sauvignon (St. Helena) $50. A troubling wine. The vineyard is a good one, but this Cab is hot and overly ripe, with stewed flavors of blackberries and cherries. There's a heaviness that doesn't work, especially at this price. **82** —*S.H. (7/1/2007)*

JEFFERSON VINEYARDS

Jefferson Vineyards 2002 Signature Meritage (Monticello) $24. 82 —*J.C. (9/1/2005)*

Jefferson Vineyards 2002 Estate Reserve Bordeaux Blend (Monticello) $30. 84 —*J.C. (9/1/2005)*

JEKEL

Jekel 2001 Sanctuary Bordeaux Blend (Arroyo Seco) $NA. 89 *(9/2/2004)*

Jekel 1999 Sanctuary Bordeaux Blend (Arroyo Seco) $30. 88 *(9/2/2004)*

Jekel 1995 Sanctuary Estate Reserve Bordeaux Blend (Monterey) $26. 86 —*S.H. (7/1/1999)*

Jekel 1999 Sanctuary Cabernet Blend (Arroyo Seco) $28. 86 —*S.H. (5/1/2003)*

Jekel 1997 Sanctuary Cabernet Blend (Arroyo Seco) $28. 91 Editors' Choice —*S.H. (12/1/2001)*

Jekel 2005 Cabernet Sauvignon (Arroyo Seco) $15. Jekel has long experience with Cabs from Arroyo Seco, a cool region better known for whites. This Bordeaux blend shows the region's classic dryness and acidity, and flavors of blackberries and currants. **85** —*S.H. (12/31/2007)*

Jekel 2004 Cabernet Sauvignon (Central Coast) $15. On the plus side, this Cab is dry and fruity. On the minus, it's raw in acids, with a rustic feeling. Seems pricey for what you get. **83** —*S.H. (4/1/2007)*

Jekel 2003 Cabernet Sauvignon (Central Coast) $15. 83 —*S.H. (7/1/2006)*

Jekel 2002 Cabernet Sauvignon (Central Coast) $15. 82 —*S.H. (12/31/2005)*

Jekel 2004 Chardonnay (Monterey County) $13. 82 —*S.H. (6/1/2006)*

Jekel 1998 F.O.S. Reserve Chardonnay (Monterey) $22. 87 —*S.H. (11/15/2000)*

Jekel 1997 FOS Reserve Chardonnay (Monterey) $21. 88 —*L.W. (11/15/1999)*

Jekel 1999 FOS Reserve Gravelstone Vineyard-Est. Res. Collection Chardonnay (Monterey) $18. 90 Editors' Choice —*S.H. (8/1/2003)*

Jekel 2005 Gravelstone Chardonnay (Monterey) $11. Simple and sweet, with white sugared peach and apricot flavors. It's almost a dessert wine. **82** —*S.H. (5/1/2007)*

Jekel 2003 Gravelstone Chardonnay (Monterey) $11. 84 —*S.H. (5/1/2005)*

Jekel 2002 Gravelstone Chardonnay (Monterey) $14. 86 *(9/2/2004)*

USA

Jekel 2000 Gravelstone Chardonnay (Monterey) $11. 87 —*S.H. (5/1/2002)*

Jekel 1999 Gravelstone Chardonnay (Monterey) $11. 87 Best Buy —*S.H. (11/15/2001)*

Jekel 1998 Gravelstone Chardonnay (Monterey County) $15. 86 *(6/1/2000)*

Jekel 1997 Gravelstone Chardonnay (Monterey) $15. 88 —*S.H. (10/1/1999)*

Jekel 2002 Gravelstone Winemaker's Collection Chardonnay (Monterey) $11. 86 —*S.H. (4/1/2004)*

Jekel 2005 Gewürztraminer (Monterey) $13. 84 —*S.H. (8/1/2006)*

Jekel 2000 Sanctuary Reserve Malbec (Arroyo Seco) $NA. 88 *(9/2/2004)*

Jekel 2003 Merlot (Monterey) $15. 85 —*S.H. (6/1/2006)*

Jekel 2001 Merlot (Monterey) $19. 86 *(9/2/2004)*

Jekel 2002 Winemaker's Collection Merlot (Monterey) $15. 82 —*S.H. (12/31/2005)*

Jekel 2001 Winemaker's Collection Merlot (Monterey) $15. 88 —*S.H. (4/1/2004)*

Jekel 1999 Winemaker's Collection Merlot (Monterey) $15. 84 —*S.H. (6/1/2002)*

Jekel 2005 Pinot Noir (Monterey County) $15. Passes the Pinot test with light-bodied silkiness and cherry cola flavors, but this is a really weak wine. There's just not a lot going on. **82** *S.H. (4/1/2007)*

Jekel 2004 Pinot Noir (Monterey County) $15. 82 —*S.H. (5/1/2006)*

Jekel 2001 Pinot Noir (Monterey) $19. 84 *(9/2/2004)*

Jekel 1999 Pinot Noir (Arroyo Seco) $15. 86 —*S.H. (12/15/2001)*

Jekel 2000 Winemaker's Collection Pinot Noir (Monterey) $15. 83 *(10/1/2002)*

Jekel 1999 Winemaker's Collection Pinot Noir (Monterey) $15. 87 —*S.H. (5/1/2002)*

Jekel 2001 Winemaker's Collection Pinot Noir (Monterey) $19. 90 —*S.H. (12/15/2004)*

Jekel 2005 Riesling (Monterey) $12. 83 —*S.H. (12/1/2006)*

Jekel 2002 Riesling (Monterey) $11. 86 *(9/2/2004)*

Jekel 2001 Riesling (Monterey) $10. 86 Best Buy —*S.H. (8/1/2003)*

Jekel 1999 Riesling (Monterey) $10. 87 *(8/1/2001)*

Jekel 2004 Winemaker's Collection Riesling (Monterey) $10. 84 —*S.H. (12/1/2005)*

Jekel 2002 Winemaker's Collection Riesling (Monterey) $9. 86 —*S.H. (4/1/2004)*

Jekel 2000 Winemaker's Collection Riesling (Monterey) $10. 85 Best Buy —*S.H. (6/1/2002)*

Jekel 2003 Winemaker's Selection Riesling (Monterey) $9. 83 —*S.H. (5/1/2005)*

Jekel 2001 Syrah (Monterey) $15. 85 —*S.H. (6/1/2005)*

Jekel 2000 Syrah (Monterey) $15. 88 Best Buy —*S.H. (10/1/2003)*

Jekel 1999 Winemaker's Collection Syrah (Monterey) $15. 84 —*S.H. (9/1/2002)*

Jekel 1998 Winemaker's Collection Syrah (Monterey) $16. 88 Editors' Choice *(10/1/2001)*

JENICA PEAK

Jenica Peak 2004 Pinot Grigio (California) $10. 83 —*S.H. (2/1/2006)*

Jenica Peak 2003 Coastal Syrah (California) $10. 84 *(9/1/2005)*

JEPSON

Jepson NV Blanc de Blanc Brut Champagne Blend (Mendocino County) $20. 84 —*J.C. (12/1/2001)*

Jepson NV Burnee Hill Vineyard Blanc de Champagne Blend (Mendocino County) $18. 83 —*P.G. (12/1/2000)*

Jepson 1989 Late Disgorged Champagne Blend (Mendocino County) $35. 90 —*L.W. (12/1/1999)*

Jepson 2003 Chardonnay (Mendocino) $15. 82 —*S.H. (12/15/2005)*

Jepson 1999 Estate Select Chardonnay (Mendocino) $16. 91 —*S.H. (5/1/2002)*

Jepson 1998 Estate Select Chardonnay (Mendocino County) $15. 86 *(6/1/2000)*

Jepson 1997 Estate Select Chardonnay (Mendocino) $15. 89 —*L.W. (11/15/1999)*

Jepson 2003 Sauvignon Blanc (Mendocino) $12. 85 —*S.H. (12/15/2005)*

Jepson 2000 Sauvignon Blanc (Mendocino County) $11. 87 —*S.H. (5/1/2002)*

Jepson 1998 Estate Select Sauvignon Blanc (Mendocino County) $11. 88 Best Buy —*L.W. (2/1/2000)*

Jepson 2002 Syrah (Mendocino) $20. 90 —*S.H. (12/15/2005)*

Jepson 2000 Syrah (Mendocino County) $22. 86 —*S.H. (5/1/2002)*

Jepson 2000 Viognier (Mendocino County) $16. 86 —*S.H. (5/1/2002)*

Jepson 1998 Feliz Creek Cuvée White Blend (Mendocino County) $9. 89 Best Buy —*M.S. (11/15/1999)*

Jepson 2000 Feliz Creek Cuvée-Estate Select White Blend (Mendocino County) $9. 86 —*S.H. (5/1/2002)*

Jepson 2001 Poma Ranch Zinfandel (Mendocino) $18. 80 —*J.M. (11/1/2003)*

JERIKO

Jeriko 2005 Chardonnay (Mendocino) $19. Doesn't have the richness or polish of the Reserve, and in fact is pretty ordinary. Shows a creamy mouthfeel and fruity, oaky flavors, with a candied apricot finish. **83** —*S.H. (11/1/2007)*

Jeriko 2000 Chardonnay (Mendocino) $19. 85 —*S.H. (6/1/2003)*

Jeriko 2001 Brut Chardonnay (Mendocino) $50. 93 Editors' Choice —*S.H. (6/1/2006)*

Jeriko 2005 Reserve Chardonnay (Mendocino) $33. Polished and sophisticated Chard, easy to like for its dry crispness, and the way the bright acidity perks up the tropical fruit and mineral flavors. It's 100% barrel-fermented, but the oak feels very natural and seamless. Finishes with real class and elegance. **92** —*S.H. (11/1/2007)*

Jeriko 2005 Pinot Noir (Mendocino) $33. Made from organic grapes, this is a very dry wine. It has the silky delicacy of a fine Pinot, with subtle, complex cola, cherryskin, pomegranate and tea flavors. Those descriptors suggest the tannins, which are dry and sticky. **87** —*S.H. (11/1/2007)*

Jeriko 2006 Estate Rosé Blend (Mendocino) $12. This Provençal-style blend of Syrah and Grenache is clean and brisk in acidity, but a little on the sugary side, which gives the cherry and raspberry flavors a candied finish. **84** —*S.H. (11/1/2007)*

JESSIE'S GROVE

Jessie's Grove 2001 Vintners Choice Zinfandel (Lodi) $15. 87 —*J.M. (3/1/2004)*

Jessie's Grove 2004 Westwind Zinfandel (Lodi) $24. Velvety-smooth in texture, with well-articulated blackberry jam, cherry, cassis and melted dark chocolate flavors, this Zin is a little too dessert-like and Porty for my palate. But lots of people will love this richly superripe style. **86** —*S.H. (12/15/2007)*

Jessie's Grove 2001 Westwind Old Vine Zinfandel (Lodi) $20. 84 *(11/1/2003)*

JESSUP CELLARS

Jessup Cellars 2000 Cabernet Sauvignon (Napa Valley) $45. 84 —*S.H. (10/1/2004)*

Jessup Cellars 1997 Lauer Vineyard Cabernet Sauvignon (Napa Valley) $39. 91 *(11/1/2000)*

Jessup Cellars 2001 Merlot (Mount Veeder) $38. 87 —*S.H. (10/1/2004)*

Jessup Cellars 1999 Port (Napa Valley) $25. 90 —*J.M. (3/1/2004)*

Jessup Cellars 1998 Zinfandel (Dry Creek Valley) $28. 88 —*S.H. (5/1/2000)*

Jessup Cellars 2001 Zinfandel (Napa Valley) $28. 82 —*S.H. (10/1/2004)*

Jessup Cellars 2000 Reserve Zinfandel (Dry Creek Valley) $28. 85 —*J.M. (9/1/2003)*

JEWEL

Jewel 2002 Cabernet Sauvignon (Lodi) $10. 84 —*S.H. (11/1/2005)*

Jewel 2001 Cabernet Sauvignon (California) $10. 85 —*S.H. (10/1/2004)*

Jewel 2000 Firma Cabernet Sauvignon-Sangiovese (California) $NA. 86 —*S.H. (3/1/2004)*

Jewel 2002 Chardonnay (Monterey) $10. 87 Best Buy —*S.H. (12/1/2004)*

Jewel 2005 Un-Oaked Chardonnay (Monterey) $10. Here's the latest entry into the red-hot unoaked Chardonnay category in America, and it's a solid hit. Dry and crisp, it's rich in apricots, pineapples, tangerines and spices. **85 Best Buy** —*S.H. (9/1/2007)*

Jewel 2003 Un-Oaked Chardonnay (Monterey) $10. 87 Best Buy —*S.H. (11/1/2005)*

Jewel 2002 Merlot (California) $10. 84 —*S.H. (12/15/2004)*

Jewel 2004 Petite Sirah (Lodi) $10. A fine everyday wine. With its soft, velvety mouthfeel and luscious fruit, it's a good buy. The blackberry, cassis, plum, coffee, tobacco, leather and cocoa flavors are a little thin, but they finish dry and clean, with a scour of tannins. **85 Best Buy** *—S.H. (9/1/2007)*

Jewel 2002 Petite Sirah (California) $10. 87 Best Buy *—S.H. (12/15/2004)*

Jewel 2001 Petite Sirah (California) $10. 81 *(4/1/2003)*

Jewel 2000 Petite Sirah (California) $10. 81 *(4/1/2003)*

Jewel 2003 Pinot Noir (California) $10. 85 Best Buy *—S.H. (10/1/2005)*

Jewel 2002 Pinot Noir (California) $10. 85 *(11/1/2004)*

Jewel 2003 Firma Red Blend (Lodi) $10. 83 *—S.H. (10/1/2005)*

Jewel 2004 Dry Rosé Blend (Lodi) $10. 87 Best Buy *—S.H. (11/1/2005)*

Jewel 2003 Sauvignon Blanc (Lake County) $10. 86 Best Buy *—S.H. (12/1/2004)*

Jewel 2001 Shiraz (California) $10. 84 *—S.H. (12/15/2004)*

Jewel 1999 Syrah (Lodi) $10. 85 *—S.H. (7/1/2002)*

Jewel 2005 Viognier (California) $10. Inexpensive Viognier is tough to get right. The winemaker has kept this one dry and crisp, with polished pineapple, green apple and spice flavors. Very nice on its own, or as a versatile white. **86 Best Buy** *—S.H. (9/1/2007)*

Jewel 2004 Viognier (California) $10. 85 Best Buy *—S.H. (11/1/2005)*

Jewel 2003 Viognier (California) $10. 85 Best Buy *—S.H. (11/15/2004)*

Jewel 2002 Viognier (California) $10. 86 Best Buy *—S.H. (6/1/2003)*

Jewel 2002 Old Vine Zinfandel (Lodi) $10. 83 *—S.H. (11/1/2005)*

Jewel 2001 Old Vine Zinfandel (Lodi) $10. 86 Best Buy *—S.H. (11/15/2004)*

Jewel 2001 Old Vine Zinfandel (Lodi) $10. 82 *—J.M. (11/1/2003)*

JEZEBEL

Jezebel 2003 Pinot Noir (Willamette Valley) $18. 88 *—P.G. (2/1/2005)*

Jezebel 2003 Syrah (Columbia Valley (OR)) $18. 88 *—P.G. (2/1/2005)*

Jezebel 2003 Blanc White Blend (Willamette Valley) $12. 89 Best Buy *—P.G. (2/1/2005)*

JM CELLARS

JM Cellars 2000 Columbia Valley Cuvée Bordeaux Blend (Columbia Valley (WA)) $21. 90 *—P.G. (9/1/2003)*

JM Cellars 2003 Cuvée Bordeaux Blend (Columbia Valley (WA)) $28. 89 *—P.G. (8/1/2006)*

JM Cellars 2003 Tre Fanciulli Cabernet Blend (Columbia Valley (WA)) $35. 89 *—P.G. (8/1/2006)*

JM Cellars 2003 Cabernet Sauvignon (Red Mountain) $35. 87 *—P.G. (8/1/2006)*

JM Cellars 2000 Cabernet Sauvignon (Red Mountain) $30. 87 *—P.G. (9/1/2003)*

JM Cellars 2003 Merlot (Red Mountain) $32. 88 *—P.G. (8/1/2006)*

JM Cellars 1999 Tre Fancivilli Red Blend (Columbia Valley (WA)) $28. 90 *—C.S. (12/31/2002)*

JM Cellars 2005 Klipsun Vineyard Sauvignon Blanc (Red Mountain) $NA. 88 *—P.G. (12/31/2006)*

JM Cellars 2003 Klipsun Vineyard Sauvignon Blanc (Red Mountain) $18. 89 *—P.G. (12/1/2004)*

JM Cellars 2003 Syrah (Columbia Valley (WA)) $32. 88 *—P.G. (8/1/2006)*

JM Cellars 2005 Viognier (Columbia Valley (WA)) $NA. 89 *—P.G. (12/31/2006)*

JOCELYN

Jocelyn 2002 Cabernet Sauvignon (Napa Valley) $32. 85 *—S.H. (12/15/2005)*

JODAR

Jodar 1999 Cabernet Sauvignon (El Dorado County) $18. 82 *—S.H. (11/15/2003)*

Jodar 1999 2,400 Feet Sangiovese (El Dorado) $26. 81 *—S.H. (5/1/2002)*

JOE BLOW

Joe Blow 2005 Red Blend (California) $12. A mixture of Napa Merlot, Monterey Syrah and Lodi Petite Sirah, this has sharp edges and minty, medicinal flavors of cherries and coffee. **83** *—S.H. (11/15/2007)*

JOEL GOTT

Joel Gott 2005 Blend No. 815 Cabernet Sauvignon (California) $17. A blend of Napa Valley, Lake County and Lodi, this is a somewhat rustic wine, with a minty green, briary edge to the cherry fruit. It's astringently tannic, but appeals for its dry balance. **85** *—S.H. (10/1/2007)*

JOHN ANTHONY

John Anthony 2003 Cabernet Sauvignon (Napa Valley) $55. 92 *—S.H. (9/1/2006)*

John Anthony 2005 Church Vineyard Sauvignon Blanc (Carneros) $19. 92 Editors' Choice *—S.H. (12/1/2006)*

John Anthony 2005 Late Harvest Sauvignon Blanc (Napa Valley) $55. Actually from Carneros, this is a sweet, apricot- and pineapple-infused wine balanced with crisp acidity. It tastes like it has some botrytis, to judge by the honeyed richness. Notable for its crisp, harmonious balance. **91** *—S.H. (5/1/2007)*

John Anthony 2003 Syrah (Napa Valley) $35. 94 Editors' Choice *—S.H. (12/1/2006)*

JOHN ROBERT EPPLER

John Robert Eppler 2004 Cabernet Sauvignon (Rutherford) $65. In a tasting of its 2004 Rutherford peers, this wine did not stand out particularly well. It smelled and tasted porty sweet, with charry oak and syrupy flavors of cherry and blackberry jam. **84** *—S.H. (12/15/2007)*

JOHN TYLER

John Tyler 2003 Bacigalupi Vineyard Pinot Noir (Russian River Valley) $42. The vineyard is in a warm part of the appellation, almost in Dry Creek, and the wine shows a soft, delicate fruitiness that makes it appealing now. It's rich in cherry, cola and spice flavors, with a silky texture and multiple layers of interest. **88** *—S.H. (5/1/2007)*

John Tyler 2003 Bacigalupi Vineyard Zinfandel (Russian River Valley) $36. The vineyard is in the warmest part of Russian River Valley, almost into Dry Creek Valley, and this Zin shows elements of both. It's distinctively varietal in wild berry and peppery spice flavors and rich, fine tannins, but also has a crisp streak of acidity. It will age, but is best in its vibrant, fruity youth. **87** *—S.H. (5/1/2007)*

JOLIESSE

Joliesse 2003 Chardonnay (California) $8. 84 Best Buy *—S.H. (12/15/2004)*

Joliesse 2000 Reserve Chardonnay (California) $7. 83 *—S.H. (6/1/2003)*

Joliesse 2002 Lot 57-Limited Edition Shiraz (California) $9. 85 *—J.C. (7/1/2003)*

Joliesse 2003 Rosé Shiraz (California) $9. 84 *—S.H. (12/15/2004)*

Joliesse 2001 Limited Edition Zinfandel (California) $10. 86 *(11/1/2003)*

JONES FAMILY

Jones Family 1997 Cabernet Sauvignon (Napa Valley) $75. 95 *(11/1/2000)*

Jones Family 1999 Cabernet Sauvignon (Napa Valley) $85. 94 *(11/15/2002)*

JORDAN

Jordan 1999 Cabernet Sauvignon (Sonoma County) $48. 85 *—S.H. (11/15/2003)*

Jordan 1998 Cabernet Sauvignon (Sonoma County) $45. 85 *(11/15/2002)*

Jordan 1997 Cabernet Sauvignon (Sonoma County) $45. 86 *(11/1/2000)*

Jordan 1995 Cabernet Sauvignon (Sonoma County) $38. 91 *—S.H. (11/1/1999)*

Jordan 1998 Chardonnay (Sonoma County) $25. 86 *(6/1/2000)*

Jordan 2000 Chardonnay (Russian River Valley) $26. 91 *—S.H. (2/1/2003)*

JORY

Jory 1998 "El Nino" Chardonnay (Central Coast) $15. 81 *(6/1/2000)*

Jory 1997 Lion Oaks Ranch Sangre De Dono Syrah (Santa Clara Valley) $50. 85 *—J.C. (2/1/2000)*

JOSEPH FILIPPI

Joseph Filippi 2001 Blanc Grenache (Cucamonga Valley) $11. 84 *—S.H. (4/1/2002)*

Joseph Filippi 2001 Zinfandel (Cucamonga Valley) $18. 84 *(11/1/2003)*

JOSEPH PHELPS

Joseph Phelps 2001 Insignia Bordeaux Blend (Napa Valley) $125. 96 *—S.H. (10/1/2004)*

Joseph Phelps 1997 Insignia Bordeaux Blend (Napa Valley) $120. 95 *(11/1/2000)*

Joseph Phelps 2003 Insignia Cabernet Blend (Napa Valley) $165. One of the first, if not the first, of the proprietarily named Napa Bordeaux blends, Phelps Insignia has been one of California's greatest Cabs for decades.

This is their 30th anniversary bottling, and it's worthy of the tradition. Ultrarich and smooth, with a mouthfeel that's pure velvet, it's fairly thick in tannins now, suggesting cellaring. But it's huge in blackberry, dark unsweetened chocolate and spicy plum fruit, and will easily hold for a very long time. Best now, if carefully decanted, and through 2020. **96 Cellar Selection** —*S.H. (3/1/2007)*

Joseph Phelps 2002 Insignia Cabernet Blend (Napa Valley) $142. 92 —*S.H. (12/31/2005)*

Joseph Phelps 1997 Cabernet Sauvignon (Napa Valley) $35. 90 *(11/1/2000)*

Joseph Phelps 2004 Cabernet Sauvignon (Napa Valley) $54. Shows the deft Phelps Cabernet touch, with softly complex tannins that frame ripe blackberry, cherry, spice and new oak flavors. So easy to like, you might not even notice the complexities of structure that keep you reaching for another sip. Drink now. **89** —*S.H. (9/1/2007)*

Joseph Phelps 2003 Cabernet Sauvignon (Napa Valley) $48. 91 —*S.H. (7/1/2006)*

Joseph Phelps 2002 Cabernet Sauvignon (Napa Valley) $48. 87 —*S.H. (10/1/2005)*

Joseph Phelps 2001 Cabernet Sauvignon (Napa Valley) $65. 89 —*S.H. (10/1/2004)*

Joseph Phelps 2000 Cabernet Sauvignon (Napa Valley) $45. 92 Editors' Choice —*S.H. (5/1/2003)*

Joseph Phelps 1999 Cabernet Sauvignon (Napa Valley) $42. 88 —*S.H. (6/1/2002)*

Joseph Phelps 2002 Backus Cabernet Sauvignon (Oakville) $175. 95 —*S.H. (3/1/2005)*

Joseph Phelps 2001 Backus Cabernet Sauvignon (Oakville) $150. 97 Cellar Selection —*S.H. (11/1/2005)*

Joseph Phelps 2000 Backus Vineyard Cabernet Sauvignon (Oakville) $150. 93 Cellar Selection —*D.T. (2/1/2004)*

Joseph Phelps 1999 Backus Vineyard Cabernet Sauvignon (Oakville) $150. 96 Cellar Selection —*J.M. (2/1/2003)*

Joseph Phelps 2000 Insignia Cabernet Sauvignon (Napa Valley) $125. 88 —*S.H. (5/1/2004)*

Joseph Phelps 1998 Chardonnay (Carneros) $22. 90 *(6/1/2000)*

Joseph Phelps 2000 Chardonnay (Carneros) $26. 87 —*S.H. (9/1/2002)*

Joseph Phelps 2004 Ovation Chardonnay (Carneros) $60. Ovation is never a huge, opulent wine, but rather one of control and finesse. It's the kind of Chard that's sometimes called Chablisian because of the firm minerality and streamlined, tightly metallic quality. The '04 is complex and layered, offering fruit pie filling flavors of kiwis, limes and guavas with the caramel and vanilla of well-charred new oak. It's one of the few Chardonnays that will benefit from midterm aging. Drink now—2010. **93** —*S.H. (3/1/2007)*

Joseph Phelps 2002 Ovation Chardonnay (Napa Valley) $44. 94 —*S.H. (12/15/2004)*

Joseph Phelps 2002 Ovation Chardonnay (Napa Valley) $48. 92 —*S.H. (3/1/2005)*

Joseph Phelps 2001 Ovation Chardonnay (Napa Valley) $44. 92 —*S.H. (12/15/2003)*

Joseph Phelps 2000 Ovation Chardonnay (Napa Valley) $44. 92 —*S.H. (2/1/2003)*

Joseph Phelps 1999 Ovation Chardonnay (Napa Valley) $45. 91 *(7/1/2001)*

Joseph Phelps 1998 Ovation Chardonnay (Napa Valley) $44. 92 *(10/1/2000)*

Joseph Phelps 1997 Ovation Chardonnay (Napa Valley) $40. 92 —*L.W. (10/1/1999)*

Joseph Phelps 1997 Merlot (Napa Valley) $35. 87 —*M.S. (7/1/2000)*

Joseph Phelps 2002 Merlot (Napa Valley) $40. 92 —*S.H. (10/1/2005)*

Joseph Phelps 2000 Merlot-Cabernet Sauvignon (Napa Valley) $40. 92 —*S.H. (6/1/2003)*

Joseph Phelps 1999 Le Mistral Red Blend (California) $25. 88 —*S.H. (12/15/2001)*

Joseph Phelps 2005 Le Mistral Rhône Red Blend (Monterey County) $40. Pretty good; a New World-style wine marked by excessive softness and ripeness and delicious, pie-filling flavors, although it's fully dry. Cherries, milk chocolate and root beer dominate, wrapped in soft tannins and acids. Syrah, Grenache, Carignan, Petite Sirah and Alicante Bouschet. **85** —*S.H. (9/1/2007)*

Joseph Phelps 2003 Le Mistral Rhône Red Blend (Monterey County) $30. 88 —*S.H. (12/31/2005)*

Joseph Phelps 2002 Le Mistral Rhône Red Blend (Monterey County) $30. 90 Editors' Choice —*S.H. (10/1/2005)*

Joseph Phelps 2001 Le Mistral Rhône Red Blend (Monterey County) $25. 91 —*S.H. (12/1/2004)*

Joseph Phelps 2000 Le Mistral Rhône Red Blend (California) $25. 91 Editors' Choice —*S.H. (12/1/2003)*

Joseph Phelps 1997 Le Mistral Rhône Red Blend (California) $25. 91 —*M.S. (2/1/2000)*

Joseph Phelps 2005 Sauvignon Blanc (Napa Valley) $30. Napa Valley and Sauvignon Blanc aren't always the best combination, but this is a superior wine that shows how a great winery can perform when it takes things seriously. With 10% Semillon, barrel fermented and aged sur lees, it's a marvelously complicated wine, dry and crisp in acids, with impressive citrus, peach and honeysuckle flavors. **91** —*S.H. (3/1/2007)*

Joseph Phelps 2003 Sauvignon Blanc (Napa Valley) $22. 92 —*S.H. (3/1/2005)*

Joseph Phelps 1998 Sauvignon Blanc (Napa Valley) $15. 81 *(3/1/2000)*

Joseph Phelps 2006 Eisrébe Scheurebe (Napa Valley) $50. The name is a combination of eiswein and Scheurebe, the German variety. The grapes were artificially frozen. The wine is exceptionally sweet, with residual sugar of 21.5%, but balanced by crisp acidity, and the alcohol is amazingly low at 7.6%. Flavorwise, it's all about apricot preserves and vanilla. Hard to imagine anyone not liking this delicious dessert wine. **92** —*S.H. (9/1/2007)*

Joseph Phelps 2004 Syrah (Napa Valley) $40. Shows all the hallmarks of the upscale Cabs the winery is better known for, from the softly sensuous mouthfeel, ripe fruit and judicious use of new French oak, to the long-lasting complexities. Red and black cherry jam, cassis, plum sauce, gingerbread, smoky vanillins, peppery spice, and it's all dry and balanced. What's not to like? Drink now. **92** —*S.H. (9/1/2007)*

Joseph Phelps 2002 Syrah (Napa Valley) $35. 85 *(9/1/2005)*

Joseph Phelps 2000 Syrah (Napa Valley) $40. 92 —*S.H. (4/1/2004)*

Joseph Phelps 1999 Syrah (Napa Valley) $NA. 90 —*S.H. (6/1/2003)*

Joseph Phelps 1998 Syrah (Napa Valley) $37. 86 *(11/1/2001)*

Joseph Phelps 1996 Vin du Mistral Syrah (California) $30. 87 —*L.W (10/1/1999)*

Joseph Phelps 2002 Viognier (Napa Valley) $30. 91 —*S.H. (2/1/2004)*

Joseph Phelps 2001 Viognier (Napa Valley) $35. 90 —*S.H. (3/1/2003)*

Joseph Phelps 2000 Viognier (Napa Valley) $35. 86 —*S.H. (12/15/2001)*

JOSEPH SWAN VINEYARDS

Joseph Swan Vineyards 2000 Cuvée de Trois Pinot Noir (Russian River Valley) $20. 89 Editors' Choice *(10/1/2002)*

Joseph Swan Vineyards 2004 Great Oak Vineyard Pinot Noir (Russian River Valley) $35. Showing quite a bit of tannins and acids, this is a very young wine, of a kind that isn't seen all that much in Russian River Valley these days. Swan makes their Pinots the old-fashioned way, for aging. Dry and astringent, the wine has a deep core of cherry and blackberry fruit, almost like a Merlot, except for the silkiness. Stick this in your cellar until 2008, at least. **90** —*S.H. (8/1/2007)*

Joseph Swan Vineyards 2000 Saralee's Vineyard Pinot Noir (Russian River Valley) $25. 85 *(10/1/2002)*

Joseph Swan Vineyards 1999 Steiner Vineyard Pinot Noir (Sonoma Mountain) $25. 83 *(10/1/2002)*

Joseph Swan Vineyards 2004 Trenton Estate Vineyard Pinot Noir (Russian River Valley) $45. My experience of Swan Pinots is that they've been made the same way for a long time, and require aging. This one shows some hard tannins and even some tough acids, although it's tremendous in cherry-pie filling, black raspberry and blackberry jam flavors. Right now it feels juvenile, rude, even rustic, but 5–8 years in the cellar will reward. **90 Cellar Selection** —*S.H. (8/1/2007)*

Joseph Swan Vineyards 2004 Trenton Estate Pinot Noir (Russian River Valley) $45. 89 Cellar Selection —*S.H. (12/15/2006)*

Joseph Swan Vineyards 1999 Trenton Estate Vineyard Pinot Noir (Russian River Valley) $42. 85 *(10/1/2002)*

Joseph Swan Vineyards 2002 Trenton Estate Vineyard Syrah (Russian River Valley) $25. Nearly five years after it was made, this Syrah remains dark and tannic, but the fruit is starting to make the magical transition from primary to secondary. It's picking up dried blackberry, dessicated blueberry and beef jerky flavors that finish long and spicy. Yet it still has youthful acidity and freshness. This will be a fun wine to follow over the next five years. **92** —*S.H. (9/1/2007)*

Joseph Swan Vineyards 2003 Lone Redwood Ranch Zinfandel (Russian River Valley) $25. Dry and distinctly wild in brambly, briary berry fruit and spice. At first this Zin feels rustic, with a sandpapery grip and fresh, juicy acids. But the brilliant structure of acidity, bracing tannins and caressing mouthfeel reveal how delicate this really is. This is great Zinfandel. **94** —*S.H. (9/1/2007)*

Joseph Swan Vineyards 2003 Mancini Ranch Zinfandel (Russian River Valley) $25. We're almost into Port here, not only in the alcohol level, but the flavors. The blackberries, strawberries, raspberries and cherries are almost raisiny, with that taste of plumped dried fruit, leading to a finish of raspberry liqueur. Yet the wine is dry, as well as tannic. There are certainly few Zinfandels like this anywhere, and you'll either like it or you won't. **89** —*S.H. (9/1/2007)*

Joseph Swan Vineyards 2002 Stellwagen Vineyard Zinfandel (Sonoma Valley) $25. Fully mature now, although it still has a good six years left, this shows why certain Zins benefit from aging. Tight and tannicly dry to begin with, it has aged to something approaching Pinot-like delicacy, although the wild berry, roasted coffee and spice flavors are Zinny, and few Zinfandels will ever have these tannins. **92** —*S.H. (9/1/2007)*

Joseph Swan Vineyards 2002 Zeigler Vineyard Zinfandel (Russian River Valley) $25. If you like a purely California approach to Zin, you'll exult in this one. High in alcohol, almost Port-y, but totally dry, with stewed raspberry, cherry, cola, mocha and spice flavors, it's tough in tannins, and acidic for so ripe a wine. Will do all kinds of interesting things over the next 10 years, without fundamentally changing. **89** —*S.H. (9/1/2007)*

JOSEPH ZAKON

Joseph Zakon NV Kosher Cabernet Sauvignon (America) $9. 85 Best Buy —*J.C. (4/1/2006)*

JOULLIAN

Joullian 2001 Chardonnay (Monterey) $15. 88 —*S.H. (2/1/2004)*

Joullian 2000 Chardonnay (Monterey) $15. 90 Best Buy —*S.H. (2/1/2003)*

Joullian 1999 Chardonnay (Monterey) $15. 85 —*S.H. (12/15/2002)*

Joullian 1996 Family Reserve Chardonnay (Monterey County) $24. 83 *(6/1/2000)*

Joullian 2000 RogerRose Vineyard Chardonnay (Monterey) $23. 87 —*S.H. (12/1/2003)*

Joullian 2000 Sleepy Hollow Vineyard Chardonnay (Monterey) $27. 83 —*S.H. (10/1/2003)*

Joullian 1999 Sleepy Hollow Vineyard Chardonnay (Monterey) $27. 90 —*S.H. (5/1/2002)*

Joullian 1999 Merlot (Carmel Valley) $30. 89 —*S.H. (6/1/2002)*

Joullian 2000 Sauvignon Blanc (Carmel Valley) $14. 88 —*S.H. (9/1/2003)*

Joullian 2003 Family Reserve Sauvignon Blanc (Carmel Valley) $20. 86 *(7/1/2005)*

Joullian 2002 Syrah (Carmel Valley) $30. 88 —*S.H. (6/1/2005)*

Joullian 1997 Zinfandel (Carmel Valley) $20. 83 —*P.G. (3/1/2001)*

Joullian 2002 Sias Cuvée Zinfandel (Carmel Valley) $20. 90 —*S.H. (8/1/2005)*

Joullian 2001 Sias Cuvée Zinfandel (Carmel Valley) $20. 86 —*S.H. (3/1/2004)*

JUDD

Judd 2001 Cranston Vineyard Petite Sirah (California) $26. 85 —*S.H. (6/1/2005)*

Judd 2001 Syrah (Napa Valley) $26. 85 —*S.H. (6/1/2005)*

JUDD'S HILL

Judd's Hill 1999 Estate Cabernet Blend (Napa Valley) $75. 90 —*S.H. (11/15/2003)*

Judd's Hill 2003 Cabernet Sauvignon (Napa Valley) $42. A disappointment from a winery that's earned Cab scores over 90 for so many years. This one's shy of the mark, a bit thin and weedy in fruit, although it has polished tannins and a nice, dry structure. **85** —*S.H. (9/1/2007)*

Judd's Hill 2002 Cabernet Sauvignon (Napa Valley) $40. 92 —*S.H. (5/1/2006)*

Judd's Hill 2001 Cabernet Sauvignon (Napa Valley) $40. 93 —*S.H. (6/1/2005)*

Judd's Hill 1999 Cabernet Sauvignon (Napa Valley) $40. 91 —*S.H. (8/1/2003)*

Judd's Hill 1997 Cabernet Sauvignon (Napa Valley) $45. 93 *(11/1/2000)*

Judd's Hill 1999 Merlot (Napa Valley) $26. 89 —*S.H. (12/1/2003)*

Judd's Hill 1999 Juliana Vineyards Merlot (Napa Valley) $30. 91 —*S.H. (12/1/2003)*

Judd's Hill 1999 Summers Ranch Merlot (Knights Valley) $30. 86 —*S.H. (12/1/2003)*

Judd's Hill 2003 Petite Sirah (Lodi) $28. This is certainly a big, bold Pet wine, the kind lovers of the variety treasure. Dry and tannic, it's explosive in extremely ripe cherry and black raspberry jam flavors, with all kinds of mushroomy, leathery, chocolaty, spicy complexities. As big as the tannins are, they're of the modern, melted kind, making the wine instantly drinkable. **87** —*S.H. (9/1/2007)*

Judd's Hill 2005 Pinot Noir (Napa Valley) $28. Shows the gentle, silky mouthfeel you want in a nice Pinot, and also the variety's array of cherries, cola, tea, cocoa and spice flavors. Feels soft and rustic in the mouth, though. **85** —*S.H. (9/1/2007)*

JUSLYN VINEYARDS

Juslyn Vineyards 2003 Perry's Blend Bordeaux Blend (Napa Valley) $65. A very good wine, rich and packed with flavor. A dry and softly tannic, it floods the mouth with cassis, red currant, blueberry, plum, cocoa and smoky oak flavors. **88** —*S.H. (12/15/2007)*

Juslyn Vineyards 2000 Red Wine Bordeaux Blend (Napa Valley) $50. 84 —*S.H. (12/1/2004)*

Juslyn Vineyards 2002 Estate Red Wine Cabernet Blend (Spring Mountain) $90. 92 —*S.H. (12/15/2006)*

Juslyn Vineyards 2002 Perry's Blend Cabernet Blend (Napa Valley) $60. 91 Cellar Selection —*S.H. (12/15/2006)*

Juslyn Vineyards 2003 Cabernet Sauvignon (Spring Mountain) $95. Showing jammy blackberry and cherry flavors and lots of new smoky oak, this is a young, tannic Cab. It would suggest aging, especially given its mountain origins, except for a streak of green mint that suggests some less than ripe fruit. Best now and for a few years. **87** —*S.H. (12/15/2007)*

Juslyn Vineyards 2001 Cabernet Sauvignon (Napa Valley) $55. 86 —*S.H. (5/1/2005)*

Juslyn Vineyards 2001 Cabernet Sauvignon (Spring Mountain) $85. 90 *(5/1/2005)*

Juslyn Vineyards 2000 Cabernet Sauvignon (Napa Valley) $50. 89 —*S.H. (4/1/2004)*

Juslyn Vineyards 1999 Cabernet Sauvignon (Napa Valley) $60. 92 —*J.M. (2/1/2003)*

Juslyn Vineyards 2000 Estate Cabernet Sauvignon (Spring Mountain) $85. 91 —*S.H. (4/1/2004)*

Juslyn Vineyards 2003 Vineyard Select Cabernet Sauvignon (Napa Valley) $75. Off by a few beats from the '02, the '03 shows red currant, plumped raisin and green mint jelly notes. The flavors are good, but the wine, which is soft in structure, is not an ager. **86** —*S.H. (12/15/2007)*

Juslyn Vineyards 2002 Vineyard Select Cabernet Sauvignon (Napa Valley) $80. 93 Cellar Selection —*S.H. (12/15/2006)*

Juslyn Vineyards 2001 Vineyard Select Cabernet Sauvignon (Napa Valley) $75. 85 —*S.H. (5/1/2005)*

Juslyn Vineyards 2000 Vineyard Select Cabernet Sauvignon (Napa Valley) $75. 90 —*S.H. (4/1/2004)*

Juslyn Vineyards 1999 Vineyard Select Cabernet Sauvignon (Napa Valley) $75. 93 —*J.M. (2/1/2003)*

Juslyn Vineyards 1998 Vineyard Select Cabernet Sauvignon (Napa Valley) $75. 86 —*C.S. (6/1/2002)*

Juslyn Vineyards 2003 Sauvignon Blanc (Napa Valley) $24. 85 —*S.H. (5/1/2005)*

Juslyn Vineyards 2002 Sauvignon Blanc (Napa Valley) $NA. 87 —*S.H. (2/1/2004)*

JUSTIN

Justin 2002 Isosceles Bordeaux Blend (Paso Robles) $55. 87 *(6/1/2006)*

Justin 2001 Isosceles Bordeaux Blend (Paso Robles) $55. 92 —*S.H. (12/31/2004)*

Justin 2004 Justification Bordeaux Blend (Paso Robles) $42. Justin proves that Bordeaux can succeed in western Paso Robles, but interestingly, the wine is Cab Franc and Merlot, with no Sauvignon. Both varieties do well in cooler areas, and this wine does have good acidity and a rich earthiness suggesting butter-sauteed mushrooms with a splash of soy. An interesting, complex wine; a natural beauty to pair with food. **93** —*S.H. (4/1/2007)*

Justin 2003 Justification Bordeaux Blend (Paso Robles) $42. 89 —*S.H. (9/1/2006)*

Justin 1999 Isosceles Cabernet Blend (Paso Robles) $48. 92 —*J.M. (11/15/2002)*

Justin 2005 Obtuse Cabernet Blend (Paso Robles) $24. Mainly Cab, with some of the Portuguese varieties in there. Fairly sweet, with residual sugar of about 12.5%. High alcohol (19%). Not particularly compelling, but clean and balanced. **84** —*S.H. (4/1/2007)*

Justin 2004 Cabernet Sauvignon (Paso Robles) $24. Tastes raisiny and overripe, with a stewed blackberry flavor, and the softness acentuates the tannins, making them seem harsher than they really are. The wine in short is rustic, and unlikely to improve. **83** *—S.H. (4/1/2007)*

Justin 2003 Cabernet Sauvignon (Paso Robles) $25. 82 *—S.H. (9/1/2006)*

Justin 2002 Cabernet Sauvignon (Paso Robles) $22. 81 *—S.H. (6/1/2005)*

Justin 1999 Cabernet Sauvignon (Paso Robles) $23. 89 *—J.M. (11/15/2002)*

Justin 2004 Reserve Cabernet Sauvignon (Paso Robles) $42. This '04 is fairly luscious and rich and soft, but it's thin; needs much greater fruity concentration. **85** *—S.H. (4/1/2007)*

Justin 2002 Reserve Cabernet Sauvignon (Paso Robles) $40. 91 *—S.H. (12/31/2004)*

Justin 2005 Chardonnay (Paso Robles) $20. Fresh and crisp, this Chardonnay has an early-picked quality to it, or maybe the cool vintage is responsible for the citrusy, minerally character, enriched with toasty oak. Either way, it's a refreshing wine, vital in acidity, and a nice presence at the table. **87** *—S.H. (4/1/2007)*

Justin 2000 Chardonnay (Paso Robles) $19. 87 *—J.M. (12/15/2002)*

Justin 1998 Estate Chardonnay (Paso Robles) $19. 88 *(6/1/2000)*

Justin 2003 Reserve Chardonnay (Paso Robles) $22. 84 *—S.H. (7/1/2005)*

Justin 1998 Reserve Chardonnay (Paso Robles) $23. 87 *(6/1/2000)*

Justin 2002 Justification Merlot-Cabernet Franc (Paso Robles) $40. 92 *—S.H. (12/31/2004)*

Justin 2004 Petite Verdot (Paso Robles) $30. There's a fine red Bordeaux wine somewhere in here, and all it needs is a little time to express itself. Right now, it's tannic and tight. But then the enormous core of fruit detonates on the palate, exploding in cherries and blackberries, wrapped into firm, ripe tannins. Should have a nice little window, between 2007–2010. **89** *—S.H. (6/1/2007)*

Justin 2003 Obtuse Port (Paso Robles) $22. 84 *—S.H. (7/1/2005)*

Justin 2004 Savant Red Blend (Paso Robles) $42. Justin's 50-50 Cabernet Sauvignon and Syrah blend has a nicely soft, velvety texture, and some good cherry-berry fruit. It's balanced, with a good coating of oak. Drink now. **85** *—S.H. (4/1/2007)*

Justin 2003 Sauvignon Blanc (Edna Valley) $13. 84 *—S.H. (8/1/2005)*

Justin 2004 Syrah (Paso Robles) $24. This wine has a stewed fruit, raisiny chewiness, and the absolute dryness and tannins make it taste bitterly astringent. Not at all pleasant, and not going anywhere. **81** *—S.H. (2/1/2007)*

Justin 2002 Syrah (Paso Robles) $22. 90 *—S.H. (12/31/2004)*

Justin 2000 Syrah (Paso Robles) $22. 89 *—S.H. (12/15/2003)*

Justin 2000 Halter Vineyard Syrah (Paso Robles) $22. 91 Editors' Choice *—S.H. (12/15/2003)*

Justin 1998 Mac Gillivray Vineyard Syrah (Paso Robles) $23. 84 *(11/1/2001)*

Justin 2002 Reserve Syrah (Paso Robles) $40. 87 *—S.H. (12/31/2004)*

Justin 2004 Reserve Tempranillo (Paso Robles) $32. Dry and acidic, but there is just enough cherry fruit to make it drinkable. **81** *—S.H. (4/1/2007)*

Justin 2002 Reserve Tempranillo (Paso Robles) $30. 83 *—S.H. (8/1/2005)*

Justin 2001 Zinfandel (Paso Robles) $23. 86 *(11/1/2003)*

Justin 1999 Zinfandel (Paso Robles) $23. 85 *—M.S. (11/1/2002)*

K VINTNERS

K Vintners 2003 Ovide–En Cerise Vineyard Red Cabernet Sauvignon-Syrah (Walla Walla (WA)) $55. 94 *—P.G. (12/15/2005)*

K Vintners 2003 Roma–En Chamberlin Vineyard Red Cabernet Sauvignon-Syrah (Walla Walla (WA)) $55. 93 *—P.G. (12/15/2005)*

K Vintners 2003 The Creator Cabernet Sauvignon-Syrah (Walla Walla (WA)) $45. 92 *—P.G. (8/1/2006)*

K Vintners 2003 Guido Red Blend (Walla Walla (WA)) $30. 91 *—P.G. (8/1/2006)*

K Vintners 2005 The Boy Red Blend (Walla Walla (WA)) $40. The Boy is 88% Grenache and 12% Syrah; the Grenache comes from Christophe Baron's biodynamic Armada vineyard. It's got a composty undertone to the fruit, with plenty of spice and earthy elements. There is a citrus component also. It's very smoky, very earthy and gamy. The tannins are smooth, but very earthy and leafy, with some bitterness. An intriguing wine. **89** *—P.G. (11/6/2007)*

K Vintners 2002 The Boy Red Blend (Walla Walla (WA)) $35. 88 *—P.G. (7/1/2004)*

K Vintners 2005 Cougar Hills Syrah (Walla Walla (WA)) $45. A dark, meaty, sappy wine, supple and saturated with gorgeous color and sensuous fruit. The spices are chromatic, and the flavors include charcuterie, wild cherry, smoke, pepper and green tea. The palate is seamless and tightly wrapped, gently unfolding to reveal a lingering finish with the promise of a long cellar life ahead. **93** *—P.G. (11/6/2007)*

K Vintners 2002 Cougar Hills Syrah (Walla Walla (WA)) $35. 91 *—P.G. (7/1/2004)*

K Vintners 2002 End of the Road Syrah (Washington) $28. 90 *—P.G. (7/1/2004)*

K Vintners 2003 Lucky No. 7 Syrah (Walla Walla (WA)) $35. 90 *—P.G. (12/15/2005)*

K Vintners 2005 Milbrandt Syrah (Wahluke Slope) $25. Fruit-forward, spicy and appealing, this is consistent with previous editions of this popular wine. Since 2005 is a particularly good year, this has more concentration and fruit power than usual. The tight blackberry core, wrapped in leaf and showing a lot of earthy flavors is particularly attractive. The oak is folded into the wine; finishes with focus, purity and balance. **90** *—P.G. (11/6/2007)*

K Vintners 2003 Milbrandt Syrah (Columbia Valley (WA)) $24. 88 *—P.G. (12/15/2005)*

K Vintners 2002 Milbrandt Syrah (Wahluke Slope) $25. 91 *—P.G. (7/1/2004)*

K Vintners 2003 Morrison Lane Syrah (Walla Walla (WA)) $45. 89 *—P.G. (12/15/2005)*

K Vintners 2001 Morrison Lane Syrah (Walla Walla (WA)) $45. 91 *—P.G. (5/1/2004)*

K Vintners 2001 Pepper Bridge Syrah (Walla Walla (WA)) $45. 92 *—P.G. (5/1/2004)*

K Vintners 2005 Phil Lane Syrah (Walla Walla (WA)) $70. The wine from this tiny (two-acre) plot is almost jet-black, with a garnet/violet edge. Lavender and violets, black fruit and satiny tannins reveal more of the toasty oak than any other K single-vineyard Syrah. Grainy, textural and lush, with lots of pepper and citrus, this has the most sweetness in the black cherry fruit. Supple, silky, satiny and nicely detailed. **91** *—P.G. (11/6/2007)*

K Vintners 2005 The Beautiful Syrah (Walla Walla (WA)) $50. 'The Beautiful' lives up to its name and reputation. The aromas shoot from the glass; young, herbal and strikingly peppery. This shows a complexity that is rare outside of France. The flavors run through the entire length of the palate, a fascinating mix of herb, leaf, earth, and tightly wound berry fruit. It's young and crunchy, thought not fleshy, a wine that is a unique combination of masculine and feminine qualities. It should age well for at least a decade. **95** *—P.G. (11/6/2007)*

K Vintners 2002 The Beautiful Syrah (Walla Walla (WA)) $30. 93 *—P.G. (7/1/2004)*

K Vintners 2005 Wells Syrah (Walla Walla (WA)) $50. A lot of stems and whole clusters go into the winemaking, adding spice and a chewy earthiness. The nose is scented with camphor, green tea and smoked ham. This is no fruit bomb, rather it's a wine that gathers itself in the midpalate and shows its real strength in the back half, as its layers of earth, soy, tomato leaf and rhubarb mix and mingle. Long, earthy and complex, this is moving closer and closer to a Cayuse style. It finishes with just a little bit of heat. **92** *—P.G. (11/6/2007)*

K Vintners 2003 El Jefe–En Chamberlin Vineyard Red Tempranillo-Cabernet Sauvignon (Walla Walla (WA)) $55. 93 *—P.G. (12/15/2005)*

K Vintners 2006 Viognier (Columbia Valley (WA)) $20. The cool-climate fruit provides the bracing aromas, the lively texture, the crispness without bitterness, and fruit that doesn't veer into overripe peach or apricot. It's got an edge to it, but it's very clean, stylish and polished, with a nice level of intensity that has no bitter, hot or volatile elements. **90** *—P.G. (11/6/2007)*

K Vintners 2004 Viognier (Columbia Valley (WA)) $20. 90 *—P.G. (12/15/2005)*

KAAT

KAAT 1996 Pisoni Vineyard Pinot Noir (Santa Lucia Highlands) $NA. 90 *—S.H. (6/1/2005)*

KAHN

Kahn 2001 Avelina Winery Merlot (Santa Ynez Valley) $15. 84 *—S.H. (12/1/2003)*

Kahn 1999 Cuvée Jacques Red Blend (Santa Barbara County) $20. 83 *—S.H. (11/15/2001)*

Kahn 2003 Sauvignon Blanc (Santa Ynez Valley) $18. 82 *—S.H. (5/1/2005)*

Kahn 2001 Sauvignon Blanc (Santa Ynez Valley) $15. 84 *—S.H. (10/1/2003)*

Kahn 2000 Sauvignon Blanc (Santa Ynez Valley) $16. 82 *(8/1/2002)*

Kahn 2002 Syrah (Santa Ynez Valley) $30. 88 *—S.H. (5/1/2005)*

Kahn 2001 Syrah (Central Coast) $13. 84 *—S.H. (12/15/2003)*

Kahn 2000 Syrah (Santa Ynez Valley) $26. 87 *—S.H. (12/1/2003)*

Kahn 1999 Syrah (Santa Barbara County) $29. 87 *(11/1/2001)*

Kahn 2002 Colson Canyon Vineyard Syrah (Santa Barbara County) $42. 91 *—S.H. (5/1/2005)*

Kahn 2000 Colson Canyon Vineyard Syrah (Santa Barbara County) $38. 89 *—S.H. (12/1/2003)*

Kahn 2002 Susich Vineyard Syrah (Santa Ynez Valley) $42. 84 *(9/1/2005)*

KALAMAR

Kalamar 2002 Syrah (Yakima Valley) $30. 83 *(9/1/2005)*

KALI HART

Kali Hart 2002 Chardonnay (Monterey County) $13. 85 *—S.H. (10/1/2004)*

Kali Hart 2001 Chardonnay (Monterey County) $12. 88 Best Buy *—S.H. (12/1/2003)*

Kali Hart 2001 Pinot Noir (Monterey County) $14. 83 *—S.H. (5/1/2004)*

KALLICK

Kallick 1997 Bien Nacido Vineyard Pinot Noir (Santa Maria Valley) $22. 84 *(10/1/1999)*

KALYRA

Kalyra 1997 Buttonwood Farm Vineyard Cabernet Sauvignon (Santa Ynez Valley) $30. 83 *—S.H. (11/15/2003)*

Kalyra 2001 La Presa Vineyard Chardonnay (Santa Ynez Valley) $20. 84 *—S.H. (12/31/2003)*

Kalyra 2001 Tucker's Run La Presa Vineyard Syrah (Santa Ynez Valley) $20. 85 *—S.H. (3/1/2004)*

KAMEN ESTATE

Kamen Estate 2002 Cabernet Sauvignon (Sonoma Valley) $50. 87 *—S.H. (12/15/2005)*

Kamen Estate 2001 Cabernet Sauvignon (Sonoma Valley) $50. 92 *—S.H. (10/1/2004)*

KAMIAK CELLAR

Kamiak Cellar 2003 Cellar Select Cabernet Sauvignon-Merlot (Columbia Valley (WA)) $10. It's a Cab-Merlot blend, soft and made in a forward, fruit-friendly style. Dark, ripe and flavorful, it is finished with a bit of residual sweetness, welcome in a wine made for early, everyday drinking. The fruit is right up front and quite tasty, and the wine lingers in the back of the palate for a satisfying finish. **87 Best Buy** *—P.G. (5/1/2007)*

Kamiak Cellar 2005 Cellar Select Chardonnay-Sauvignon (Columbia Valley (WA)) $8. This is a pleasant, fairly soft white wine that mixes the herbaceous grassiness of Sauvignon Blanc with some of the plump pleasures of Chardonnay. Forward and agreeable, it offers clean flavors of apple and melon, set against crisp acidity. **86 Best Buy** *—P.G. (5/1/2007)*

KANA

Kana 2004 Barbera (Columbia Valley (WA)) $16. Plastic, Band-Aid® flavors over diminutive fruit flavors. Nothing speaks of Barbera except maybe the high acids. **83** *—P.G. (5/1/2007)*

Kana 2004 Ciel du Cheval Vineyard Bordeaux Blend (Red Mountain) $29. In this Bordeaux blend are some of the sought-after details from this exceptional vineyard—mineral, straw and herb—underlaying the spicy tart fruit that ranges from strawberry through plum. Still, for a wine that hits 15.3% alcohol, it seems to lack concentration and staying power, and the finish has an unappealing plastic ring to it. **85** *—P.G. (5/1/2007)*

Kana 2004 Old Vine Vignes de Marcoux Vineyard Lemberger (Yakima Valley) $16. Pure Lemberger from a vineyard planted almost 30 years ago, this wine is like a time trip back to Washington in the 1980s. Bright, forward, grapy fruit meets dry, astringent tannins. This is straight-on barbecue wine, simple and quaffable. **84** *—P.G. (5/1/2007)*

Kana 2004 Snipes Mountain Vineyard Malbec (Yakima Valley) $18. Kana does a bit better with this concentrated Malbec which shows very tart blackberry, licorice and roasted espresso flavors. There's plenty of acid to balance out the big fruit and alcohol, and the tannins have been well managed. This appears to be a wine that could well improve with up to five years of cellaring. Right now it's very tight. **86** *—P.G. (5/1/2007)*

Kana 2004 Dark Star Red Table Wine Red Blend (Columbia Valley (WA)) $20. The winery has substantially changed the blend and vineyard sources in 2004, and this is a better Dark Star than the last couple of vintages. It's roughly two thirds Syrah, with Mourvèdre and Grenache filling in the final third of the blend. The wine is sappy and strong, packed with flavors of berries, cherries and cassis, and it carries through a medium long finish before resolving into chalky acids and tannins. At 15.6% alcohol it borders on tiring. **87** *—P.G. (5/1/2007)*

Kana 2004 Workingman's Red Red Blend (Columbia Valley (WA)) $15. This unusual blend of Zinfandel, Malbec and Petit Verdot delivers plenty of alcohol (15.3%) and a diffuse mix of fruit flavors that don't add up to much. There is no center or focus here; it's a fruity red with high heat and again some residual plastic/Band-Aid® flavor in the finish. **83** *—P.G. (5/1/2007)*

Kana 2005 Cuvée Le Blanc Reserve Rhône White Blend (Yakima Valley) $18. This "Rhône-style white blend" (53% Viognier/37% Roussanne/10% Marsanne) is heavy, hot (14.8%) and dry. The fruit seems attenuated and the flavors thick and simple. Peaches and apricots rule the fruit, with a plastic edge to the finish. **84** *—P.G. (5/1/2007)*

Kana 2004 Ciel du Cheval Vineyard Syrah (Red Mountain) $29. Despite the ripeness (alcohol clocks in at 15.6%) this wine seems thin and unbalanced. The oak sticks out, and the tart fruit is overwhelmed by flavors of tar and rubber. **83** *—P.G. (5/1/2007)*

KARL LAWRENCE

Karl Lawrence 2004 Cabernet Sauvignon (Napa Valley) $60. This has acids and tannins and plenty of structure. The winemaker is aiming at an age-worthy, more classic wine. It needs time, or at the very least, serious decanting. But the stuffing is there. Hold until 2010. **89** *—S.H. (8/1/2007)*

Karl Lawrence 2001 Cabernet Sauvignon (Napa Valley) $50. 92 Cellar Selection *—S.H. (10/1/2004)*

Karl Lawrence 1997 Cabernet Sauvignon (Napa Valley) $40. 89 *(11/1/2000)*

Karl Lawrence 1996 Cabernet Sauvignon (Napa Valley) $30. 95 *—M.S. (10/1/1999)*

KARLY

Karly 1997 Marsanne (Amador County) $20. 87 *—S.H. (6/1/1999)*

Karly 1996 Syrah (Amador County) $20. 84 *—S.H. (6/1/1999)*

Karly 1997 Buck's Ten Point Zinfandel (Amador County) $15. 88 *—P.G. (11/15/1999)*

Karly 2003 Pokerville Zinfandel (Amador County) $12. 89 Best Buy *—S.H. (3/1/2006)*

Karly 2002 Pokerville Zinfandel (Amador County) $12. 85 *—S.H. (3/1/2005)*

Karly 1998 Sadie Upton Zinfandel (Amador County) $22. 90 *—S.H. (5/1/2000)*

Karly 2003 Warrior Fires Zinfandel (Amador County) $24. 84 *—S.H. (3/1/2006)*

Karly 2002 Warrior Fires Zinfandel (Amador County) $24. 83 *—S.H. (3/1/2005)*

Karly 1997 Warrior Fires Zinfandel (Amador County) $25. 87 *—P.G. (11/15/1999)*

KARMERE

Karmere 2002 Empress Hayley's Zinfandel (Shenandoah Valley (CA)) $12. 83 *—S.H. (3/1/2005)*

KASON

Kason 2002 Barrel Select Pinot Noir (Willamette Valley) $39. 87 *—P.G. (8/1/2005)*

KATHRYN HALL VINEYARDS

Kathryn Hall Vineyards 2003 Sacrashe Vineyard Cabernet Sauvignon (Rutherford) $75. 93 Cellar Selection *—S.H. (12/15/2006)*

Kathryn Hall Vineyards 2002 Sacrashe Vineyard Cabernet Sauvignon (Rutherford) $65. 93 Editors' Choice *—S.H. (12/15/2005)*

Kathryn Hall Vineyards 2001 Sacrashe Vineyard Cabernet Sauvignon (Rutherford) $55. 93 Cellar Selection *—S.H. (10/1/2004)*

Kathryn Hall Vineyards 2000 Sacrashe Vineyard Cabernet Sauvignon (Rutherford) $50. 90 *—S.H. (3/1/2004)*

Kathryn Hall Vineyards 1999 Sacrashe Vineyard Cabernet Sauvignon (Rutherford) $50. 94 Editors' Choice *—S.H. (10/1/2003)*

KATHRYN KENNEDY

Kathryn Kennedy 1997 Cabernet Sauvignon (Santa Cruz Mountains) $120. 90 *(11/1/2000)*

Kathryn Kennedy 1997 Lateral Red Blend (California) $25. 89 *—M.S. (7/1/2000)*

Kathryn Kennedy 2001 Syrah (Santa Cruz County) $36. 87 *—S.H. (12/15/2003)*

Kathryn Kennedy 1997 Maridon Vineyard Syrah (Santa Cruz Mountains) $64. 92 *—S.H. (6/1/1999)*

KAUTZ

Kautz 1997 Library Collection Chardonnay (California) $15. 85 *(6/1/2000)*

KAZMER & BLAISE

Kazmer & Blaise 2002 Primo's Hill Pinot Noir (Carneros) $36. 89 *(11/1/2004)*

Kazmer & Blaise 2001 Primo's Hill Pinot Noir (Carneros) $42. 90 *—S.H. (4/1/2004)*

Kazmer & Blaise 2000 Primo's Hill Pinot Noir (Carneros) $42. 92 *—S.H. (2/1/2003)*

KEEGAN

Keegan 1997 Chardonnay (Knights Valley) $28. 90 *(6/1/2000)*

Keegan 2000 Chardonnay (Russian River Valley) $32. 91 *—S.H. (7/1/2003)*

Keegan 2002 Buena Tierra Vineyard Chardonnay (Russian River Valley) $38. 90 *—S.H. (5/1/2005)*

Keegan 2002 Ritchie Vineyard Chardonnay (Russian River Valley) $38. 91 *—S.H. (5/1/2005)*

Keegan 2002 Pinot Noir (Russian River Valley) $34. 87 *—S.H. (5/1/2005)*

Keegan 1999 Pinot Noir (Russian River Valley) $48. 86 *(10/1/2002)*

Keegan 2002 E Block Pinot Noir (Russian River Valley) $48. 89 *—S.H. (5/1/2005)*

Keegan 1996 Zinfandel (Sonoma County) $24. 93 *—M.S. (9/1/1999)*

KEENAN

Keenan 2003 Mernet Reserve Bordeaux Blend (Spring Mountain) $84. This is the winery's 50-50 blend of Merlot and Cabernet Sauvignon. It's pretty good, but a little unbalanced, with some green tannins that give the cherry-berry flavors a sharp edge. Drink now. **84** *—S.H. (7/1/2007)*

Keenan 2002 Mernet Reserve Bordeaux Blend (Spring Mountain) $79. 84 *—S.H. (7/1/2006)*

Keenan 2002 Cabernet Sauvignon (Napa Valley) $40. 90 *—S.H. (10/1/2006)*

Keenan 2000 Cabernet Sauvignon (Napa Valley) $39. 91 *—S.H. (6/1/2004)*

Keenan 1998 Cabernet Sauvignon (Napa Valley) $40. 88 *—J.M. (6/1/2002)*

Keenan 1997 Cabernet Sauvignon (Napa Valley) $36. 92 *(11/1/2000)*

Keenan 1996 Cabernet Sauvignon (Napa Valley) $36. 87 *—J.M. (12/1/2001)*

Keenan 1995 Cabernet Sauvignon (Napa Valley) $27. 91 *—S.H. (2/1/2000)*

Keenan 2001 25th Anniversary Cabernet Sauvignon (Napa Valley) $39. 88 *—S.H. (11/15/2005)*

Keenan 2002 Reserve Cabernet Sauvignon (Spring Mountain) $89. 85 *—S.H. (12/1/2006)*

Keenan 2005 Chardonnay (Spring Mountain) $27. Napa mountain Chards are curious beasts. Seldom lush on release, at their best they age well, as evidenced by Keenan's '05 bottling. It's a tight, minerally, tart wine, bone dry, with citrus zest flavors. Barrel fermentation and new oak have added richer, creamy notes, but cellar until the end of 2007. **88** *—S.H. (7/1/2007)*

Keenan 2004 Chardonnay (Spring Mountain) $25. 90 Cellar Selection *—S.H. (7/1/2006)*

Keenan 2003 Chardonnay (Spring Mountain) $24. 84 *—S.H. (6/1/2005)*

Keenan 2002 Chardonnay (Napa Valley) $22. 86 *—S.H. (6/1/2004)*

Keenan 1999 Chardonnay (Napa Valley) $22. 87 *—J.M. (11/15/2001)*

Keenan 1998 Chardonnay (Napa Valley) $18. 84 *(6/1/2000)*

Keenan 1997 Chardonnay (Napa Valley) $18. 87 *—S.H. (2/1/2000)*

Keenan 2004 Merlot (Napa Valley) $36. A lovely Merlot, rich and fine, with lots of blackberry and cherry fruit, but also with more complex, earthier notes of olive tapenade, balsamic vinegar and sautéed wild mushrooms. The wine should hold for some years, but is really at its best now. **90** *—S.H. (12/31/2007)*

Keenan 2003 Merlot (Napa Valley) $34. 85 *—S.H. (12/31/2006)*

Keenan 2002 Merlot (Napa Valley) $32. 88 *—S.H. (6/1/2006)*

Keenan 1999 Merlot (Napa Valley) $30. 89 *—J.M. (12/31/2003)*

Keenan 1996 Merlot (Napa Valley) $24. 89 *—S.H. (3/1/2000)*

Keenan 2001 25th Anniversary Merlot (Napa-Carneros) $25. 85 *—S.H. (6/1/2004)*

Keenan 2004 Mailbox Vineyard Reserve Merlot (Spring Mountain) $60. Not many Merlots deserve time in the cellar, but this one does. Such are its mountain tannins that it's in lockdown mode, with a tough, astringent finish. But just below the surface are voluptuously ripe flavors of blackberries, cherries and mulberries. Best to give this young wine at least through mid–2008, and it could improve for another five years. **92** *—S.H. (12/31/2007)*

Keenan 2003 Mailbox Vineyard Reserve Merlot (Spring Mountain) $58. \91 *—S.H. (12/31/2006)*

Keenan 2002 Reserve Merlot (Spring Mountain) $56. \94 Editors' Choice *—S.H. (6/1/2006)*

Keenan 2000 Reserve Merlot (Spring Mountain) $48. 93 *—S.H. (6/1/2004)*

Keenan 1998 Reserve Merlot (Napa Valley) $30. 85 *—J.M. (6/1/2002)*

Keenan 1999 Mernet Merlot-Cabernet Sauvignon (Napa Valley) $75. 91 *—J.M. (11/15/2003)*

Keenan 2000 Reserve Mernet Merlot-Cabernet Sauvignon (Napa Valley) $65. 89 *—S.H. (4/1/2004)*

Keenan 2001 Mernet Reserve Red Blend (Napa Valley) $75. 92 *—S.H. (2/1/2005)*

KEEVER

Keever 2003 Cabernet Sauvignon (Yountville) $60. 90 *—S.H. (8/1/2006)*

KELHAM

Kelham 2000 Cabernet Sauvignon (Oakville) $45. 92 *—S.H. (11/15/2004)*

Kelham 1999 Cabernet Sauvignon (Oakville) $45. 90 *—S.H. (2/1/2003)*

Kelham 2000 Reserve Cabernet Sauvignon (Oakville) $75. 92 *—S.H. (11/1/2005)*

Kelham 1999 Reserve Cabernet Sauvignon (Oakville) $75. 93 *—S.H. (2/1/2003)*

Kelham 2001 Merlot (Oakville) $45. 92 *—S.H. (11/1/2005)*

Kelham 1999 Merlot (Oakville) $45. 93 Editors' Choice *—S.H. (2/1/2003)*

Kelham 2000 Sauvignon Blanc (Oakville) $22. 90 *—S.H. (3/1/2003)*

KELLER

Keller 2004 La Cruz Vineyard Chardonnay (Sonoma Coast) $29. 90 *—S.H. (12/31/2006)*

Keller 2005 Oro de Plata Chardonnay (Sonoma Coast) $22. 88 *—S.H. (12/31/2006)*

KELLER ESTATE

Keller Estate 2006 La Cruz Vineyard Pinot Gris (Sonoma Coast) $20. Expresses the exotic side of Viognier's character, with tropical quince, lychee and pineapple flavors, and a mild sweet-and-sour apricot sauce finish. This rich wine finishes dry. **87** *—S.H. (12/15/2007)*

Keller Estate 2005 La Cruz Vineyard Pinot Noir (Sonoma Coast) $38. Keller enters the big leagues with this marvelously layered Pinot Noir. For starters, it's delicious. Dry and crisp, the flavors are of ripe cherries, raspberries, tangerines, pomegranates and cola, with smoky, spicy complexities from new French oak. The mouthfeel is smooth and velvety, leading to a long, fruity finish. Best now and through 2010. **91** *—S.H. (12/31/2007)*

Keller Estate 2004 La Cruz Vineyard Pinot Noir (Sonoma Coast) $34. Rich and ripe in fruit and oak, this dry Pinot has cherry, cola, plum, balsam and smoky vanilla flavors. It's a little too soft in acidity, though, which makes it feel simple. **85** *—S.H. (12/15/2007)*

Keller Estate 2005 La Cruz Vineyard Syrah (Sonoma Coast) $36. The vineyard is in the Petaluma Gap, a wind tunnel you'll be hearing more about as the source of cool-climate wines. This lusty Syrah is enormously fruit-forward in cherries, blackberries, coffee, beef carpaccio and peppery spice flavors, an exuberant wine balanced with crisp acids. Drink now through 2009. **89** *—S.H. (12/31/2007)*

Keller Estate 2004 La Cruz Vineyard Syrah (Sonoma Coast) $36. Simple and fruity, this Syrah has ripe cherry and chocolate flavors and a layer of caramelized oak. The finish is sugary. **83** *—S.H. (12/15/2007)*

KELTIE BROOK

Keltie Brook 1998 Merlot (California) $13. 87 Best Buy *—J.C. (7/1/2000)*

KEMPTON CLARK

Kempton Clark 2001 Zinfandel (California) $10. 86 Best Buy *(11/1/2003)*

Kempton Clark 1997 Lopez Ranch Zinfandel (Cucamonga Valley) $18. 83 *—P.G. (11/15/1999)*

Kempton Clark 1998 Mad Zin Zinfandel (Dunnigan Hills) $10. 84 *—S.H. (3/1/2002)*

Kempton Clark 1997 Mad Zin Zinfandel (California) $12. 81 *—P.G. (11/15/1999)*

KEN BROWN

Ken Brown 2003 Bien Nacido Vineyard Pinot Noir (Santa Maria Valley) $30. 92 —*S.H. (12/31/2005)*

Ken Brown 2003 Syrah (Santa Barbara County) $28. 87 —*S.H. (12/31/2005)*

KEN WRIGHT

Ken Wright 2004 Celilo Vineyard Chardonnay (Washington) $25. 90 —*P.G. (5/1/2006)*

Ken Wright 2004 Pinot Blanc (Washington) $25. 92 Editors' Choice —*P.G. (5/1/2006)*

Ken Wright 2005 Abbott Claim Pinot Noir (Yamhill-Carlton District) $50. This outstanding vineyard comes through again with a full, fleshy, almost beefy wine. Powerful red fruits are enhanced with subtle flavors of citrus, juniper, pine needle, dried herbs and mint. Elegant and complex, the fruit from these young vines shows power and grace. Most surprisingly, the finish actually gains strength as it lingers. The sweet black cherry flavor seems to last forever. 95 —*P.G. (4/1/2007)*

Ken Wright 2004 Abbott Claim Pinot Noir (Willamette Valley) $50. 94 —*P.G. (5/1/2006)*

Ken Wright 2005 Canary Hill Pinot Noir (Eola-Amity Hills) $50. This is the sort of Pinot that most Oregon vintners would kill for; forward, tart and spicy with scents and flavors of black cherry cola right out front. The tangy red fruit is lifted with light citrus, buttressed with well-modulated tannins, and enhanced with beautiful undertones of moist earth, leaf and spice. Great structure, acidity and persistence. 93 —*P.G. (4/1/2007)*

Ken Wright 2004 Canary Hill Pinot Noir (Willamette Valley) $50. 90 —*P.G. (5/1/2006)*

Ken Wright 2005 Carter Pinot Noir (Eola-Amity Hills) $50. The Carter vineyard, planted in 1983, is close to Canary Hill and carries similar cherry fruit flavors, but in a lighter, softer, much more delicate frame. It's a bit like licking the foam from around the top of a cherry cola sundae – it's that airy and flavorful. Persistent, textural flavors suggest spicy blue plum, cranberry and rhubarb, with a splash of mint in the finish. 90 —*P.G. (4/1/2007)*

Ken Wright 2004 Carter Pinot Noir (Willamette Valley) $50. 91 —*P.G. (5/1/2006)*

Ken Wright 2005 Freedom Hill Pinot Noir (Willamette Valley) $50. The Freedom Hill is once again the most tannic wine in the Ken Wright lineup, even in a vintage that showcases finesse and lightness. Less aromatic than most of the others, this is scented with earth and coffee grounds, and the full-flavored fruit is gutsy and thick. Just the barest hint of volatility strikes the nose, but it has been nicely managed and contained. 91 —*P.G. (4/1/2007)*

Ken Wright 2004 Freedom Hill Pinot Noir (Willamette Valley) $50. 93 —*P.G. (5/1/2006)*

Ken Wright 2005 Guadalupe Pinot Noir (Willamette Valley) $50. This vineyard is still transitioning through a bout of phylloxera, yet still manages to produce a lovely Pinot with rich, fleshy flavors. The balance is perfect, a testament to Ken Wright's exceptional winemaking talent, and the young, spicy fruit is compact and pleasantly herbal. It lacks some of the complexity of the older vine wines, but packs plenty of compressed power. 90 —*P.G. (4/1/2007)*

Ken Wright 2004 Guadalupe Pinot Noir (Willamette Valley) $50. 92 —*P.G. (5/1/2006)*

Ken Wright 2005 McCrone Pinot Noir (Willamette Valley) $50. Violets, sweet candy and Dr. Pepper scents rise from the glass, followed by full, confident fruit flavors, like a bowl of ripe cherries. The vineyard owners spend half the year in New Zealand, where they manage a similar vineyard; this could well pass for a kiwi-style Pinot with its lush, forward, fruit punch style. 92 —*P.G. (4/1/2007)*

Ken Wright 2004 McCrone Pinot Noir (Willamette Valley) $50. 89 —*P.G. (5/1/2006)*

Ken Wright 2005 Nysa Pinot Noir (Dundee Hills) $50. This vineyard is a neighbor of Domaine Drouhin, and its flavors suggest the same fragrant, almost delicate qualities. The vines are on their own rootstock, and the perfumed blue fruits carry whiffs of spice and confectionary candy. It's a very pretty Pinot, textural, supple and tart. The firm acids that carry through the finish promise a long life ahead. 92 —*P.G. (4/1/2007)*

Ken Wright 2004 Nysa Pinot Noir (Willamette Valley) $50. 90 —*P.G. (5/1/2006)*

Ken Wright 2005 Savoya Pinot Noir (Yamhill-Carlton District) $50. It's herbal, spicy, slightly animal and scented with rosemary. As with so many of these '05 Ken Wright Pinots, it is beautifully balanced and elegant, and this, more than any other, could pass for premier cru Burgundy. 93 —*P.G. (4/1/2007)*

USA

Ken Wright 2004 Savoya Pinot Noir (Willamette Valley) $50. 91 —*P.G. (5/1/2006)*

Ken Wright 2005 Shea Pinot Noir (Yamhill-Carlton District) $50. Shea has undergone extensive, phylloxera-driven replanting in recent years, and the new vines do not have the power and complexity of the originals. Nonetheless, the estate's characteristic black cherry fruit core comes through, lightly spiced with notes of cinnamon and hints of herb. It's forward and chunky and shows a slight bit of heat in the finish. A solid effort, just not up to the complexity of the others in the 2005 lineup. 89 —*P.G. (4/1/2007)*

Ken Wright 1999 Shea Vineyard Pinot Noir (Yamhill County) $40. 92 —*P.G. (11/1/2001)*

KENDALL-JACKSON

Kendall-Jackson 2004 Grand Reserve Meritage Bordeaux Blend (Sonoma County) $35. Here's a lush, soft Bordeaux blend, based on Cabernet and blended from vineyards around the county. Showing beautifully now, the wine opens with ripe cherry, blackberry, raspberry and coffee notes, surrounded by elegantly refined tannins. Drink now through 2010 for freshness. 91 —*S.H. (6/1/2007)*

Kendall-Jackson 2002 Stature Bordeaux Blend (Napa Valley) $95. This is a tremendous Cabernet-based wine. A mixture of Atlas Peak, Howell Mountain, Mount Veeder and St. Helena bench grapes, it's a masterpiece of blending. Seductive now for its lush, soft and brilliant cherry, cassis and mocha flavors that are finished with the smoky vanilla and toast of 96% new French oak, the wine is decadently good. 95 —*S.H. (6/1/2007)*

Kendall-Jackson 2001 Stature Bordeaux Blend (Napa Valley) $95. 90 —*S.H. (5/1/2006)*

Kendall-Jackson 2004 Vintner's Reserve Meritage Bordeaux Blend (California) $12. Soft and dull, candied fruit, this Cab-based blend also has a white sugary finish. 82 —*S.H. (11/15/2007)*

Kendall-Jackson 2003 Vintner's Reserve Meritage Bordeaux Blend (California) $12. Not bad, a little sharp and tannic, but it gets the basic Bordeaux job done. With blackberry and tobacco flavors, it's a five-county coastal blend. 83 —*S.H. (11/1/2007)*

Kendall-Jackson 2001 Cabernet Sauvignon (California) $15. 86 —*S.H. (10/1/2004)*

Kendall-Jackson 1997 Buckeye Vineyard Cabernet Sauvignon (Sonoma County) $45. 90 *(11/1/2000)*

Kendall-Jackson 1997 Elite Cabernet Sauvignon (Napa Valley) $100. 91 *(11/1/2000)*

Kendall-Jackson 2004 Grand Reserve Cabernet Sauvignon (Sonoma-Napa) $26. With a little Merlot and Petit Verdot, this is a softly lush, opulent Cab. It shows the intensity of the fruit that comes from mountain viticulture, with concentrated cherry, blackberry and mocha-cola flavors, layered with one third new French oak. The tannins are rich and refined. 89 —*S.H. (6/1/2007)*

Kendall-Jackson 2004 Grand Reserve Cabernet Sauvignon (Sonoma-Napa) $26. Real nice, real smooth Cab. It's almost like a good single-malt scotch, with that light-heavy, rich, velvety mouthfeel and a tangy, iodine and peat tinge to the cherries and oak. Dry and polished. Drink now. 87 —*S.H. (3/1/2007)*

Kendall-Jackson 2001 Grand Reserve Cabernet Sauvignon (California) $26. 90 —*S.H. (6/1/2004)*

Kendall-Jackson 1997 Grand Reserve Cabernet Sauvignon (California) $60. 93 *(11/1/2000)*

Kendall-Jackson 1996 Grand Reserve Cabernet Sauvignon (California) $74. 89 *(2/1/2000)*

Kendall-Jackson 2002 Grand Reserve Sonoma-Napa-Mendocino Counties Cabernet Sauvignon (California) $26. 85 —*S.H. (10/1/2005)*

Kendall-Jackson 1999 Great Estates Cabernet Sauvignon (Napa Valley) $40. 92 —*S.H. (11/15/2003)*

Kendall-Jackson 1999 Great Estates Cabernet Sauvignon (Alexander Valley) $40. 85 —*S.H. (11/15/2003)*

Kendall-Jackson 1998 Great Estates Cabernet Sauvignon (Napa Valley) $49. 90 —*S.H. (12/31/2002)*

Kendall-Jackson 1998 Great Estates Cabernet Sauvignon (Alexander Valley) $49. 88 —*S.H. (12/31/2002)*

Kendall-Jackson 1997 Great Estates Cabernet Sauvignon (Alexander Valley) $45. 92 —*S.H. (12/1/2001)*

Kendall-Jackson 2004 Hawkeye Mountain Estate Cabernet Sauvignon (Alexander Valley) $50. New oak and ripe Cabernet fruit mesh seamlessly in this 100% varietal wine, grown at very high elevations in the Mayacamas Mountains. Full-bodied and lush, it brims with blackberry tart, black cherry jam, mocha, root beer, cola, molasses and sweet vanilla oak. Enormously complex, the wine unfolds in delicious layer after layer. Best opened young to enjoy its voluptuous fruit. 93 —*S.H. (6/1/2007)*

Kendall-Jackson 2003 Hawkeye Mountain Cabernet Sauvignon (Alexander Valley) $50. 93 Cellar Selection —*S.H. (5/1/2006)*

Kendall-Jackson 2002 Hawkeye Mountain Estate Cabernet Sauvignon (Sonoma County) $45. 91 —*S.H. (8/1/2004)*

Kendall-Jackson 2003 Highlands Estate Napa Mountain Cabernet Sauvignon (Mount Veeder) $50. 92 Cellar Selection —*S.H. (5/1/2006)*

Kendall-Jackson 2004 Napa Mountain Estate Cabernet Sauvignon (Mount Veeder) $60. Randy Ullom is crafting some of the best Cabernets in California these days, small-lot releases made from selected mountain vineyards. This one's made in the house style, offering tiers of ripe fruit wrapped into a soft, velvety wine of great style and complexity. Fully dry, this 100% varietal is instantly appealing for its plush cherry, chocolate and blackberry flavors that finish with the smoky sweetness of new oak. 93 —*S.H. (6/1/2007)*

Kendall-Jackson 1999 Stature Cabernet Sauvignon (Napa Valley) $100. 88 *(8/1/2003)*

Kendall-Jackson 2004 Trace Ridge Estate Cabernet Sauvignon (Knights Valley) $55. Tremendous Cab, grown on the high slopes of this appellation where great Bordeaux reds come from. It hits the palate with hugely concentrated Cab flavors, flooding the mouth with black currants, plums, coffee, spices and gorgeously toasty French oak. Feels lavish, powerful, complex and ageworthy. 94 Editors' Choice —*S.H. (6/1/2007)*

Kendall-Jackson 2003 Trace Ridge Cabernet Sauvignon (Knights Valley) $50. 94 Cellar Selection —*S.H. (5/1/2006)*

Kendall-Jackson 2005 Vintner's Reserve Cabernet Sauvignon (California) $18. A little too soft for my taste, this '05 has the benefit of rich tannins and well-ripened cherry-berry fruit. The softness emphasises the sugary sweetness. 83 —*S.H. (12/1/2007)*

Kendall-Jackson 2004 Vintner's Reserve Cabernet Sauvignon (California) $18. Costs a buck or two more than it used to, but the quality of VR has risen, as the winery's grape sources are entirely from estate coastal grapes. This Cab is very ripe and soft, with lavish cherry, cassis and chocolate flavors. The finish is dry and clean. 87 —*S.H. (6/1/2007)*

Kendall-Jackson 2004 Vintner's Reserve Cabernet Sauvignon (California) $18. On the rustic side, with a jagged mouthfeel, a green peppercorn edge to the cherry flavors, and a tart finish, this Cab seems over-priced for what you get. 83 —*S.H. (5/1/2007)*

Kendall-Jackson 2003 Vintner's Reserve Cabernet Sauvignon (Sonoma-Napa-Mendocino) $18. 86 —*S.H. (11/15/2006)*

Kendall-Jackson 2002 Vintner's Reserve Cabernet Sauvignon (Napa-Mendocino-Sonoma) $16. 84 —*S.H. (12/31/2005)*

Kendall-Jackson 2001 Vintner's Reserve Cabernet Sauvignon (California) $16. 84 —*S.H. (10/1/2005)*

Kendall-Jackson 2000 Vintner's Reserve Cabernet Sauvignon (California) $16. 86 —*S.H. (6/1/2004)*

Kendall-Jackson 1997 Vintner's Reserve Cabernet Sauvignon (Calaveras County) $17. 88 —*S.H. (12/15/2000)*

Kendall-Jackson 1996 Vintner's Reserve Cabernet Sauvignon (California) $21. 86 *(2/1/2000)*

Kendall-Jackson 2001 Collage Cabernet Sauvignon-Merlot (California) $10. 84 —*S.H. (6/1/2005)*

Kendall-Jackson 2000 Collage Cabernet Sauvignon-Merlot (California) $9. 84 —*S.H. (6/1/2002)*

Kendall-Jackson 2000 Collage Cabernet Sauvignon-Shiraz (California) $9. 83 —*S.H. (9/1/2002)*

Kendall-Jackson 1999 Collage Cabernet Sauvignon-Shiraz (California) $9. 86 Best Buy —*S.H. (5/1/2001)*

Kendall-Jackson 2001 20th Harvest Release Chardonnay (California) $16. 87 —*S.H. (12/15/2002)*

Kendall-Jackson 2001 Camelot Bench Chardonnay (Santa Maria Valley) $17. 89 —*S.H. (12/1/2003)*

Kendall-Jackson 2005 Camelot Highlands Estate Chardonnay (Santa Maria Valley) $25. This is a great expression of what winemaker Randy Ullom calls the Santa Maria Bench. Full malolactic fermentation has softened the wine, while barrel fermentation adds to the honeyed, creamy texture. Yet there's enough acidity to balance the lush tropical fruit-pie filling, kumquat, pineapple, apricot, vanilla custard and buttered toast richness. 91 —*S.H. (6/1/2007)*

Kendall-Jackson 2002 Camelot Highlands Estate Chardonnay (Santa Barbara County) $25. 90 *(3/1/2004)*

Kendall-Jackson 2002 Camelot Highlands Estate Chardonnay (Santa Barbara County) $25. 91 —*S.H. (8/1/2004)*

Kendall-Jackson 1999 Camelot Vineyard Chardonnay (Santa Maria Valley) $17. 85 —*S.H. (5/1/2001)*

Kendall-Jackson 1998 Camelot Vineyard Chardonnay (Santa Maria Valley) $17. 90 *(6/1/2000)*

Kendall-Jackson 2005 Grand Reserve Chardonnay (Santa Barbara-Monterey) $20. Big, rich and opulent, filled with tropical fruit, lemon mousse, vanilla cream and buttered toast flavors. Really viscous, a soft, honeyed wine of power and charm. Firm acidity balances the richness. 88 —*S.H. (6/1/2007)*

Kendall-Jackson 2005 Grand Reserve Chardonnay (Santa Barbara-Monterey) $20. A little sweet in the K-J tradition, with very ripe tropical fruit, buttercream, vanilla custard and toasty, spicy flavors. Shows real polish and complexity, with fine coastal acidity. 89 —*S.H. (3/1/2007)*

Kendall-Jackson 2004 Grand Reserve Chardonnay (Monterey-Santa Barbara) $20. 90 —*S.H. (4/1/2006)*

Kendall-Jackson 2003 Grand Reserve Chardonnay (California) $20. 85 —*S.H. (10/1/2005)*

Kendall-Jackson 2002 Grand Reserve Chardonnay (California) $20. 89 —*S.H. (6/1/2004)*

Kendall-Jackson 2001 Grand Reserve Chardonnay (California) $20. 91 Editors' Choice —*S.H. (12/1/2003)*

Kendall-Jackson 1999 Grand Reserve Chardonnay (California) $19. 85 —*S.H. (5/1/2001)*

Kendall-Jackson 1998 Grand Reserve Chardonnay (California) $25. 89 *(6/1/2000)*

Kendall-Jackson 1997 Grand Reserve Chardonnay (California) $26. 86 —*S.H. (7/1/1999)*

Kendall-Jackson 2000 Great Estates Chardonnay (Santa Barbara County) $25. 88 —*S.H. (5/1/2003)*

Kendall-Jackson 2000 Great Estates Chardonnay (Monterey County) $25. 89 —*S.H. (5/1/2003)*

Kendall-Jackson 2000 Great Estates Chardonnay (Arroyo Seco) $25. 88 —*S.H. (5/1/2003)*

Kendall-Jackson 1999 Great Estates Chardonnay (Arroyo Seco) $35. 91 *(7/1/2001)*

Kendall-Jackson 1999 Great Estates Chardonnay (Sonoma Coast) $22. 88 —*S.H. (8/1/2003)*

Kendall-Jackson 1999 Great Estates Chardonnay (Sonoma Valley) $35. 90 *(7/1/2001)*

Kendall-Jackson 2004 Highland Estates Camelot Highlands Chardonnay (Santa Maria Valley) $30. 92 —*S.H. (5/1/2006)*

Kendall-Jackson 1997 Paradise Vineyard Chardonnay (Arroyo Seco) $17. 87 *(6/1/2000)*

Kendall-Jackson 2005 Seco Highlands Estate Chardonnay (Arroyo Seco) $30. What a great Chard. Just delicious in palate-filling tropical fruit, buttercream, pineapple jam, honeysuckle, vanilla custard and spice flavors that are so rich and refined. For all the opulence, the wine is dry, with the firm acidity the Arroyo Seco is known for. 92 —*S.H. (6/1/2007)*

Kendall-Jackson 2004 Seco Highlands Estate Chardonnay (Arroyo Seco) $30. 92 —*S.H. (4/1/2006)*

Kendall-Jackson 2001 Stature Chardonnay (Santa Maria Valley) $60. 94 —*S.H. (12/1/2004)*

Kendall-Jackson 1998 Stature Chardonnay (Santa Maria Valley) $60. 90 *(7/1/2001)*

Kendall-Jackson 2005 Vintner's Reserve Chardonnay (California) $12. 85 —*S.H. (12/31/2006)*

Kendall-Jackson 2004 Vintner's Reserve Chardonnay (California) $12. 84 —*S.H. (2/1/2006)*

Kendall-Jackson 2002 Vintner's Reserve Chardonnay (California) $12. 86 *(3/1/2004)*

Kendall-Jackson 2001 Vintner's Reserve Chardonnay (California) $12. 84 —*S.H. (6/1/2003)*

Kendall-Jackson 1999 Vintner's Reserve Chardonnay (California) $11. 84 —*S.H. (5/1/2001)*

Kendall-Jackson 1998 Vintner's Reserve Chardonnay (California) $12. 85 —*S.H. (11/15/2000)*

Kendall-Jackson 2003 Vintner's Reserve Chardonnay (California) $12. 85 *(5/1/2005)*

Kendall-Jackson 2002 Stature Meritage (Napa Valley) $120. 93 *(3/1/2004)*

Kendall-Jackson 2001 Stature Meritage (Napa Valley) $120. 93 Cellar Selection *(3/1/2004)*

Kendall-Jackson 1996 Buckeye Vineyard Merlot (Sonoma County) $33. 86 —*J.C. (7/1/2000)*

Kendall-Jackson 2004 Grand Reserve Merlot (Napa-Sonoma) $26. A serious Merlot. Well-oaked, it shows lots of crowd-pleasing caramel, toast, vanilla and sweet woody flavors, but the fruit, acids and tannins are fully supportive of all that oak. Cherries, black raspberries and mocha flavors are pure and refined, leading to a dry finish. Drink this elegant wine now through 2010. **91** —*S.H. (6/1/2007)*

Kendall-Jackson 2003 Grand Reserve Merlot (Sonoma-Napa) $26. 91 Editors' Choice —*S.H. (4/1/2006)*

Kendall-Jackson 2001 Grand Reserve Merlot (California) $26. 89 —*S.H. (6/1/2004)*

Kendall-Jackson 1995 Grand Reserve Merlot (California) $47. 89 —*S.H. (3/1/2000)*

Kendall-Jackson 2002 Grand Reserve Sonoma-Mendocino-Napa Counties Merlot (California) $26. 84 —*S.H. (10/1/2005)*

Kendall-Jackson 1999 Great Estates Merlot (Sonoma County) $35. 91 —*S.H. (12/31/2002)*

Kendall-Jackson 1998 Great Estates Merlot (Sonoma County) $35. 88 —*S.H. (12/1/2001)*

Kendall-Jackson 1998 Great Estates Merlot (Alexander Valley) $40. 89 —*S.H. (12/1/2001)*

Kendall-Jackson 2003 Highlands Estate Taylor Peak Merlot (Bennett Valley) $40. 92 Editors' Choice —*S.H. (4/1/2006)*

Kendall-Jackson 2002 Piner Hills Estate Merlot (Sonoma County) $35. 90 *(3/1/2004)*

Kendall-Jackson 2002 Sable Mountain Estate Merlot (Mendocino) $25. 87 *(3/1/2004)*

Kendall-Jackson 2000 Stature Merlot (Sonoma County) $60. 86 —*S.H. (12/15/2004)*

Kendall-Jackson 2004 Taylor Peak Estate Merlot (Bennett Valley) $40. Lots of structure in this refined, polished Merlot. The tannins are strong but sweetly ripe, and with the crisp acids, they provide a rich framework to the cherry, cassis, cola and mocha flavors. Dry and elegant, this wine drinks well now and should hold for five years before the fruit fades. **93** —*S.H. (6/1/2007)*

Kendall-Jackson 2002 Taylor Peak Estate Merlot (Sonoma County) $35. 92 —*S.H. (12/15/2004)*

Kendall-Jackson 2002 Taylor Peak Estate Merlot (Bennett Valley) $35. 86 *(3/1/2004)*

Kendall-Jackson 2004 Vintner's Reserve Merlot (California) $18. A rewarding Merlot; polished, supple and dry, that floods the mouth with cherry, blackberry and black raspberry flavors, and a coating of toasty oak. This is really a finely balanced, elegant wine. **88** —*S.H. (6/1/2007)*

Kendall-Jackson 2003 Vintner's Reserve Merlot (Sonoma-Napa-Mendocino) $18. 85 —*S.H. (12/15/2006)*

Kendall-Jackson 2002 Vintner's Reserve Merlot (California) $16. 85 —*S.H. (5/1/2005)*

Kendall-Jackson 2001 Vintner's Reserve Merlot (California) $15. 86 —*S.H. (10/1/2004)*

Kendall-Jackson 2001 Vintner's Reserve Merlot (California) $16. 87 —*S.H. (6/1/2004)*

Kendall-Jackson 2000 Vintner's Reserve Merlot (California) $16. 86 —*S.H. (8/1/2003)*

Kendall-Jackson 1997 Vintner's Reserve Merlot (California) $21. 88 —*S.H. (3/1/2000)*

Kendall-Jackson 1999 Great Estates Pinot Noir (Monterey County) $32. 89 *(10/1/2002)*

Kendall-Jackson 2001 Seco Bench Estate Pinot Noir (Monterey) $35. 90 *(3/1/2004)*

Kendall-Jackson 2005 Seco Highlands Estate Pinot Noir (Arroyo Seco) $35. A beautifully crisp Pinot, dry and silky and loaded with ripe cherry, raspberry, cola and Asian spice flavors. Tastes so opulent in fruit, yet has a subtle complexity leading to a long, spicy finish. This Pinot, from one of Monterey County's top growing areas, is a sommelier's dream. **90** —*S.H. (6/1/2007)*

Kendall-Jackson 2004 Seco Highlands Estate Pinot Noir (Arroyo Seco) $35. 94 Editors' Choice —*S.H. (5/1/2006)*

Kendall-Jackson 2002 Seco Highlands Estate Pinot Noir (Monterey County) $35. 88 —*S.H. (11/1/2004)*

Kendall-Jackson 2005 Vintner's Reserve Pinot Noir (California) $14. 84 —*S.H. (12/1/2006)*

Kendall-Jackson 2004 Vintner's Reserve Pinot Noir (California) $14. 83 —*S.H. (12/31/2005)*

Kendall-Jackson 2003 Vintner's Reserve Pinot Noir (California) $14. 84 —*S.H. (6/1/2005)*

Kendall-Jackson 2002 Vintner's Reserve Pinot Noir (California) $14. 84 —*S.H. (11/1/2004)*

Kendall-Jackson 2001 Vintner's Reserve Pinot Noir (California) $14. 85 —*S.H. (7/1/2003)*

Kendall-Jackson 2000 Vintner's Reserve Pinot Noir (California) $14. 83 *(10/1/2002)*

Kendall-Jackson 1999 Vintner's Reserve Pinot Noir (California) $12. 86 —*S.H. (11/15/2001)*

Kendall-Jackson 1998 Vintner's Reserve Pinot Noir (California) $17. 87 —*S.H. (12/15/2000)*

Kendall-Jackson 1998 Collage Red Blend (California) $9. 84 —*S.H. (5/1/2001)*

Kendall-Jackson 1999 Collage-Zinfandel/Shiraz Red Blend (California) $9. 87 Best Buy —*S.H. (9/1/2002)*

Kendall-Jackson 2002 Collage Zinfandel-Shiraz Red Blend (California) $10. 83 —*S.H. (6/1/2005)*

Kendall-Jackson 2000 Late Harvest Riesling (California) $20. 84 —*J.M. (12/1/2002)*

Kendall-Jackson 2005 Vintner's Reserve Riesling (California) $10. 85 Best Buy —*S.H. (7/1/2006)*

Kendall-Jackson 2004 Vintner's Reserve Riesling (California) $10. 83 —*S.H. (10/1/2005)*

Kendall-Jackson 2000 Vintner's Reserve Riesling (California) $10. 86 —*J.M. (6/1/2002)*

Kendall-Jackson 2006 Grand Reserve Rosé Wine Rosé Blend (Sonoma-Napa) $18. This Merlot-Malbec blend is too sweet for my taste. It's almost a dessert wine, with sugared cherry and raspberry jam flavors. **83** —*S.H. (12/1/2007)*

Kendall-Jackson 1999 Sauvignon Blanc (California) $10. 84 —*S.H. (5/1/2001)*

Kendall-Jackson 2006 Vintner's Reserve Sauvignon Blanc (California) $11. There's a reason K-J's VR wines sell like hotcakes, and this wine is a primo example. It's dry and very crisp and tart, just like a good SB should be. The lemon, lime, grapefruit, and peppery-fig flavors are savory and rich. **86 Best Buy** —*S.H. (10/1/2007)*

Kendall-Jackson 2005 Vintner's Reserve Sauvignon Blanc (California) $11. 84 —*S.H. (11/15/2006)*

Kendall-Jackson 2004 Vintner's Reserve Sauvignon Blanc (California) $10. 85 Best Buy —*S.H. (2/1/2006)*

Kendall-Jackson 2003 Vintner's Reserve Sauvignon Blanc (California) $10. 84 —*S.H. (6/1/2005)*

Kendall-Jackson 2002 Vintner's Reserve Sauvignon Blanc (California) $10. 84 —*S.H. (2/1/2004)*

Kendall-Jackson 2001 Vintner's Reserve Sauvignon Blanc (California) $10. 84 —*S.H. (7/1/2003)*

Kendall-Jackson 2000 Vintner's Reserve Sauvignon Blanc (California) $9. 83 —*S.H. (9/12/2002)*

Kendall-Jackson 1998 Vintner's Reserve Sauvignon Blanc (California) $12. 86 —*S.H. (11/1/1999)*

Kendall-Jackson 1997 Vintner's Reserve Sauvignon Blanc (California) $9. 86 *(9/1/1999)*

Kendall-Jackson 2004 Alisos Hills Estate Syrah (Santa Barbara County) $35. Dark and soft, this Syrah has an enormous depth of fruit. The cherry liqueur and pie filling, mocha, cola, plum and gingerbread flavors finish dry. Loses a few points due to a touch of raisiny, pruny overripeness, which makes the wine heavy. **86** —*S.H. (6/1/2007)*

Kendall-Jackson 2002 Alisos Hills Estate Syrah (Santa Barbara County) $35. 92 —*S.H. (8/1/2004)*

Kendall-Jackson 1999 Grand Reserve Syrah (California) $22. 87 *(11/1/2001)*

Kendall-Jackson 2003 Highlands Estate Alisos Hills Syrah (Santa Barbara County) $30. 93 Editors' Choice —*S.H. (5/1/2006)*

Kendall-Jackson 2005 Vintner's Reserve Syrah (California) $12. This is really quite a successful wine. It shows an array of ripe, juicy blackberry, cherry, plum, coffee and spice flavors that are wrapped in rich tannins, a big wine with some true elegance. **86** —*S.H. (11/1/2007)*

Kendall-Jackson 2004 Vintner's Reserve Syrah (California) $12. Here's a nice alternative to Cabernet in a full-bodied red wine at this price range. It's completely friendly, from the first taste of cherries and chocolate to the softly gentle texture and all the way through the pleasingly spicy finish. **85** *—S.H. (5/1/2007)*

Kendall-Jackson 2003 Vintner's Reserve Syrah (California) $12. 86 *—S.H. (4/1/2006)*

Kendall-Jackson 2002 Vintner's Reserve Syrah (California) $14. 87 *(9/1/2005)*

Kendall-Jackson 2001 Vintner's Reserve Syrah (California) $14. 84 *—S.H. (12/1/2004)*

Kendall-Jackson 1999 Vintner's Reserve Syrah (California) $16. 89 Best Buy *(10/1/2001)*

Kendall-Jackson 1997 Vintner's Reserve Syrah (California) $17. 88 *—S.H. (2/1/2000)*

Kendall-Jackson 1997 Vintner's Reserve Viognier (California) $16. 85 *—S.H. (6/1/1999)*

Kendall-Jackson 2000 Great Estates Zinfandel (Mendocino) $25. 91 *—S.H. (12/1/2002)*

Kendall-Jackson 1999 Great Estates Zinfandel (Dry Creek Valley) $28. 84 *—S.H. (12/15/2001)*

Kendall-Jackson 2005 Vintner's Reserve Zinfandel (California) $12. Good rough-and-ready Zin, with briary, brambly fruit flavors and dry, sturdy tannins. Easy to drink, great with a cheeseburger. **84** *—S.H. (5/1/2007)*

Kendall-Jackson 2004 Vintner's Reserve Zinfandel (California) $12. 84 *—S.H. (12/1/2006)*

Kendall-Jackson 2003 Vintner's Reserve Zinfandel (California) $12. 85 *—S.H. (4/1/2006)*

Kendall-Jackson 2002 Vintner's Reserve Zinfandel (California) $12. 86 *—S.H. (6/1/2005)*

Kendall-Jackson 2001 Vintner's Reserve Zinfandel (California) $12. 86 *(11/1/2003)*

Kendall-Jackson 1997 Vintner's Reserve Zinfandel (California) $17. 83 *—J.C. (2/1/2000)*

KENDRIC

Kendric 2005 Pinot Noir (Marin County) $30. This is a newish producer making Pinot in Marin, the county between San Francisco and Sonoma. The wine is dry, crisp, elegant and medium-bodied, showing cola, cherry liqueur and spicy vanilla flavors. It's a promising Pinot whose next step is to build in additional layers of complexity. **88** *—S.H. (12/31/2007)*

KENNEDY SHAH

Kennedy Shah 2003 Malbec (Columbia Valley (WA)) $24. Herbal and peppery, with wild herb, rosemary and violets lighting up the nose. It's pungent and spicy, and the fruit is lean and scented with herb, earth, bark and mushrooms. This is an interesting wine showcasing a variety just beginning to be explored in Washington. **87** *—P.G. (3/1/2007)*

Kennedy Shah 2002 Syrah (Columbia Valley (WA)) $35. Big, toasty, solid and sturdy, there's smoke and citrus, with hints of meat and plenty of tart berry. Stylish, tilting a bit toward the high tones but it's kept in check. Retains a bit of cool climate green tea and dried herb, which gives it more length, interest and detail than the bigger wines. **89** *—P.G. (5/1/2007)*

KENNETH-CRAWFORD

Kenneth-Crawford 2005 Babcock Vineyard Pinot Noir (Santa Rita Hills) $45. This is lusher, silkier and more immediately appealing than the winery's '04 bottling, but no less complex. It's a Pinot to drink now for its cascades of jammy cherry, raspberry and mocha fruit, but is so classically balanced in firm tannins and crisp acidity that it should ride out the next 6–8 years, gradually fading away. **91** *—S.H. (4/1/2007)*

Kenneth-Crawford 2004 Babcock Vineyard Pinot Noir (Santa Rita Hills) $45. Here's a dense, intricately layered Pinot with an earthy spray of sage, dill and thyme to the cherries, plums, blackberries and coffee-cola fruit. The wine has the weight and texture almost of a heavier Rhône variety, like Grenache. But the silky mouthfeel is all Pinot Noir. Good now–2010. **90** *—S.H. (6/1/2007)*

Kenneth-Crawford 2004 Clos Pepe Vineyard Pinot Noir (Santa Rita Hills) $50. This 100% Clone 115 wine erupts with fresh, ripe kirsch, framboise and tangerine zest flavors, so pure and refined, and finished with vanilla-charred oak. Crisp acidity leads to a clean, bright finish. It's a bit of a fruit bomb, lacking in subtlety but scoring high on the yummy scale. **87** *—S.H. (6/1/2007)*

Kenneth-Crawford 2005 Turner Vineyard Pinot Noir (Santa Rita Hills) $40. In a lineup of 2005 Pinots, this was among the most Burgundian in the mushrooms, sweet kid leather, forest floor and mulch aromas, although it also offers scads of jammy ripe cherry and raspberry fruit. The vineyard is in the heart of the 246 corridor, between Melville and Babcock. **92** *—S.H. (4/1/2007)*

Kenneth-Crawford 2004 Evans Ranch Syrah (Santa Rita Hills) $32. The ranch is in the warmer southeast corner of the AVA, yielding a ripe wine, but the weather still was cool enough for acidity to prosper. The wine is dramatically dark and viscous, erupting with white pepper, smoked meat, sweet kid leather and cherry-cassis aromas. In the mouth, it doesn't disappoint, it's a wine of depth, power and charm. Thoroughly dry, it's best now and through 2010. **91** *—S.H. (6/1/2007)*

Kenneth-Crawford 2004 Lafond Vineyard Syrah (Santa Rita Hills) $32. The vineyard fairly routinely is source to powerful, high-alcohol Syrahs, and this is a great exemplar. Pours an opaque ruby black, staining the glass with glycerine streaks, and leading to a massive wine, with cherry, black pepper, cassis, plum liqueur, milk chocolate and spice flavors, coated with decadent, vanilla-infused oak. Offering endless tiers of flavor and mouthfeel, the wine changes with each sip. Impressive now and for the next eight years. **94 Editors' Choice** *—S.H. (6/1/2007)*

Kenneth-Crawford 2004 Lafond Vineyard Syrah (Santa Rita Hills) $32. 88 *—S.H. (3/1/2006)*

Kenneth-Crawford 2005 Turner Vineyard Syrah (Santa Rita Hills) $40. Young and slightly gawky now in adolescent immaturity, with jammy blackberry, violet and carob flavors, this tannic, single-vineyard Syrah isn't ready yet. But it's so classically proportioned, balanced and refined, it's a natural for mid-term aging. Should start to soften by late 2007 and develop for another 6–8 years. **92 Cellar Selection** *—S.H. (4/1/2007)*

KENT RASMUSSEN

Kent Rasmussen 2002 Cabernet Sauvignon (Napa Valley) $28. 91 Cellar Selection *—S.H. (3/1/2006)*

Kent Rasmussen 2005 Chardonnay (Napa Valley) $28. There's plenty of tropical fruit and peach flavor in this wine, but also a rich, herbal earthiness, not to mention oaky barrel influences. It's a Chard to have with food. **88** *—S.H. (4/1/2007)*

Kent Rasmussen 1997 Chardonnay (Napa Valley) $25. 91 *—M.M. (10/1/1999)*

Kent Rasmussen 1996 Reserve Chardonnay (Napa Valley) $45. 92 *(7/1/2001)*

Kent Rasmussen 2003 Late Harvest Gewürztraminer (Russian River Valley) $16. 94 *—S.H. (3/1/2006)*

Kent Rasmussen 2001 Chavez & Leeds Vineyard Petite Sirah (Rutherford) $30. 91 *—S.H. (12/31/2005)*

Kent Rasmussen 2005 Pinot Noir (Carneros) $35. Nice young Pinot, with a crisp balance that makes you think of rich food, like ahi tuna or a sirloin steak. Shows cherry, black raspberry and cola flavors, with an earthy, soy and balsamic mushroom note. Drink now. **89** *—S.H. (4/1/2007)*

Kent Rasmussen 2003 Pinot Noir (Carneros) $30. 89 *—S.H. (4/1/2006)*

Kent Rasmussen 2001 Pinot Noir (Carneros) $28. 86 *—S.H. (12/1/2004)*

Kent Rasmussen 1996 Pinot Noir (Carneros) $27. 88 *—M.S. (6/1/1999)*

KENWOOD

Kenwood 2004 Cabernet Sauvignon (Sonoma County) $18. This Cab shows restraint that translates into elegance. and it's a wine that's designed to be supportive of the main star at the table, food. Balanced and dry, it shows earthy flavors of blackberries and plums. **88** *—S.H. (12/1/2007)*

Kenwood 2003 Cabernet Sauvignon (Sonoma County) $18. 87 *—S.H. (12/1/2006)*

Kenwood 2002 Cabernet Sauvignon (Sonoma County) $18. 83 *—S.H. (12/15/2005)*

Kenwood 2001 Cabernet Sauvignon (Sonoma County) $18. 88 *—S.H. (12/31/2004)*

Kenwood 2000 Cabernet Sauvignon (Sonoma County) $16. 86 *—S.H. (11/15/2003)*

Kenwood 1999 Cabernet Sauvignon (Sonoma County) $20. 86 *—S.H. (12/31/2002)*

Kenwood 1998 Cabernet Sauvignon (Sonoma County) $22. 86 *—S.H. (12/1/2001)*

Kenwood 1997 Cabernet Sauvignon (Sonoma County) $22. 88 *—S.H. (12/15/2000)*

Kenwood 2002 Artist Series Cabernet Sauvignon (Sonoma County) $70. This bottling, the 28th Artist Series Cabernet, shows ripe, forward blackberry and cherry fruit elaborated with lots of oak. It's young and fresh in acids and tannins, and while drinkable now, should benefit from modest aging. **87** *—S.H. (5/1/2007)*

Kenwood 2001 Artist Series Cabernet Sauvignon (Sonoma County) $70. 84 *—S.H. (6/1/2006)*

Kenwood 1999 Artist Series Cabernet Sauvignon (Sonoma County) $70. 91 *—S.H. (4/1/2004)*

Kenwood 1998 Artist Series Cabernet Sauvignon (Sonoma County) $75. 86 —*S.H. (12/31/2002)*

Kenwood 1997 Artist Series Cabernet Sauvignon (Sonoma County) $75. 93 *(4/1/2002)*

Kenwood 1996 Artist Series Cabernet Sauvignon (Sonoma County) $70. 91 *(4/1/2002)*

Kenwood 1995 Artist Series Cabernet Sauvignon (Sonoma Valley) $65. 92 *(4/1/2002)*

Kenwood 1994 Artist Series Cabernet Sauvignon (Sonoma County) $75. 92 *(4/1/2002)*

Kenwood 1993 Artist Series Cabernet Sauvignon (Sonoma County) $75. 91 *(4/1/2002)*

Kenwood 1992 Artist Series Cabernet Sauvignon (Sonoma County) $75. 91 *(4/1/2002)*

Kenwood 1991 Artist Series Cabernet Sauvignon (Sonoma County) $75. 90 *(4/1/2002)*

Kenwood 1990 Artist Series Cabernet Sauvignon (Sonoma County) $75. 89 *(4/1/2002)*

Kenwood 1989 Artist Series Cabernet Sauvignon (Sonoma County) $75. 87 *(4/1/2002)*

Kenwood 1988 Artist Series Cabernet Sauvignon (Sonoma County) $75. 84 *(4/1/2002)*

Kenwood 1987 Artist Series Cabernet Sauvignon (Sonoma County) $75. 88 *(4/1/2002)*

Kenwood 1986 Artist Series Cabernet Sauvignon (Sonoma County) $75. 90 *(4/1/2002)*

Kenwood 2004 Jack London Vineyard Cabernet Sauvignon (Sonoma Valley) $35. This is a famous single-vineyard Cab that has had ups and downs over the years, and the '04 is a bit of a disappointment. It just tastes too ripe and heavy, with sugary blackberry and cherry jam flavors. 84 —*S.H. (12/1/2007)*

Kenwood 2003 Jack London Vineyard Cabernet Sauvignon (Sonoma Valley) $30. 90 —*S.H. (12/1/2006)*

Kenwood 2002 Jack London Vineyard Cabernet Sauvignon (Sonoma Valley) $30. 89 *(12/15/2005)*

Kenwood 2001 Jack London Vineyard Cabernet Sauvignon (Sonoma Valley) $30. 90 *(12/15/2005)*

Kenwood 2001 Jack London Vineyard Cabernet Sauvignon (Sonoma Valley) $30. 85 —*S.H. (2/1/2005)*

Kenwood 2000 Jack London Vineyard Cabernet Sauvignon (Sonoma Valley) $30. 85 *(12/15/2005)*

Kenwood 1999 Jack London Vineyard Cabernet Sauvignon (Sonoma Valley) $35. 88 —*S.H. (11/15/2002)*

Kenwood 1999 Jack London Vineyard Cabernet Sauvignon (Sonoma Valley) $NA. 87 *(12/15/2005)*

Kenwood 1998 Jack London Vineyard Cabernet Sauvignon (Sonoma Valley) $NA. 83 *(12/15/2005)*

Kenwood 1998 Jack London Vineyard Cabernet Sauvignon (Sonoma Valley) $35. 86 —*J.M. (6/1/2002)*

Kenwood 1997 Jack London Vineyard Cabernet Sauvignon (Sonoma Valley) $NA. 89 *(12/15/2005)*

Kenwood 1996 Jack London Vineyard Cabernet Sauvignon (Sonoma Valley) $NA. 89 *(12/15/2005)*

Kenwood 1995 Jack London Vineyard Cabernet Sauvignon (Sonoma Valley) $NA. 88 *(12/15/2005)*

Kenwood 1994 Jack London Vineyard Cabernet Sauvignon (Sonoma Valley) $NA. 89 *(12/15/2005)*

Kenwood 1993 Jack London Vineyard Cabernet Sauvignon (Sonoma Valley) $NA. 84 *(12/15/2005)*

Kenwood 2000 Jack London Vineyard-25th Anniversary Cabernet Sauvignon (Sonoma Valley) $30. 90 —*S.H. (11/15/2003)*

Kenwood 1997 Jack London Vineyard Cabernet Sauvignon (Sonoma Valley) $35. 91 *(11/1/2000)*

Kenwood 2006 Chardonnay (Sonoma County) $15. A little one-dimensional, but offers enough oak-influenced peach, pineapple, green apple and smoky spice flavors to satisfy. 84 —*S.H. (11/15/2007)*

Kenwood 2005 Chardonnay (Sonoma County) $15. 84 —*S.H. (12/15/2006)*

Kenwood 2004 Chardonnay (Sonoma County) $15. 88 —*S.H. (12/1/2005)*

Kenwood 2003 Chardonnay (Sonoma County) $15. 87 —*S.H. (12/31/2004)*

Kenwood 2001 Chardonnay (Sonoma County) $15. 86 —*S.H. (12/15/2002)*

Kenwood 2000 Chardonnay (Sonoma County) $15. 85 —*S.H. (12/31/2001)*

Kenwood 1999 Chardonnay (Sonoma County) $15. 89 —*S.H. (2/1/2001)*

Kenwood 1998 Chardonnay (Sonoma County) $15. 84 *(6/1/2000)*

Kenwood 2005 Reserve Chardonnay (Russian River Valley) $20. 87 —*S.H. (12/15/2006)*

Kenwood 2004 Reserve Chardonnay (Russian River Valley) $20. 84 —*S.H. (12/1/2005)*

Kenwood 2003 Reserve Chardonnay (Russian River Valley) $20. 84 —*S.H. (6/1/2005)*

Kenwood 2002 Reserve Chardonnay (Russian River Valley) $20. 85 —*S.H. (9/1/2004)*

Kenwood 2001 Reserve Chardonnay (Russian River Valley) $20. 87 —*S.H. (12/15/2002)*

Kenwood 2000 Reserve Chardonnay (Russian River Valley) $20. 88 —*S.H. (12/31/2001)*

Kenwood 1999 Reserve Chardonnay (Sonoma County) $20. 88 —*J.M. (11/15/2001)*

Kenwood 1998 Reserve Chardonnay (Sonoma County) $25. 85 *(6/1/2000)*

Kenwood 2002 Shows Vineyard Pedigree Chardonnay (Sonoma County) $15. 85 —*S.H. (12/1/2003)*

Kenwood 2006 Gewürztraminer (Sonoma County) $11. I like the varietal richness of this Gewürz. It shows powerful, classic tropical fruit and wildflower flavors, with potent cinnamon, nutmeg, ginger and vanilla spices that dominate the finish. A bit soft, but a very nice wine for the price. 85 —*S.H. (10/1/2007)*

Kenwood 2005 Gewürztraminer (Sonoma County) $11. 84 —*S.H. (11/1/2006)*

Kenwood 2001 Gewürztraminer (Sonoma County) $11. 85 —*S.H. (9/1/2003)*

Kenwood 2000 Gewürztraminer (Sonoma County) $11. 84 —*S.H. (11/15/2001)*

Kenwood 2003 Merlot (Sonoma County) $17. 82 —*S.H. (2/1/2006)*

Kenwood 2004 Merlot (Sonoma County) $17. Good and clean, with berry-cherry flavors wrapped into dry, somewhat astringent tannins. Let it breathe for a while to soften and mellow it. 83 —*S.H. (2/1/2007)*

Kenwood 2002 Merlot (Sonoma County) $17. 86 —*S.H. (10/1/2005)*

Kenwood 2000 Merlot (Sonoma County) $17. 87 —*S.H. (9/1/2003)*

Kenwood 1999 Merlot (Sonoma County) $17. 87 —*S.H. (9/12/2002)*

Kenwood 1998 Merlot (Sonoma County) $17. 87 —*S.H. (2/1/2001)*

Kenwood 2004 Jack London Vineyard Merlot (Sonoma Valley) $25. 87 —*S.H. (12/31/2006)*

Kenwood 2003 Jack London Vineyard Merlot (Sonoma Valley) $25. 83 —*S.H. (2/1/2006)*

Kenwood 2002 Jack London Vineyard Merlot (Sonoma Valley) $25. 86 —*S.H. (3/1/2005)*

Kenwood 2001 Jack London Vineyard Merlot (Sonoma Valley) $24. 85 —*S.H. (12/15/2004)*

Kenwood 2000 Jack London Vineyard Merlot (Sonoma Valley) $30. 87 —*S.H. (12/15/2003)*

Kenwood 1999 Jack London Vineyard Merlot (Sonoma Valley) $30. 88 —*J.M. (9/1/2002)*

Kenwood 1998 Jack London Vineyard Merlot (Sonoma Valley) $30. 84 —*J.M. (12/1/2001)*

Kenwood 1998 Massara Merlot (Sonoma Valley) $25. 85 —*S.H. (9/1/2002)*

Kenwood 1997 Massara Vineyard Merlot (Sonoma Valley) $25. 92 —*S.H. (2/1/2001)*

Kenwood 2003 Reserve Merlot (Sonoma County) $25. Plenty of ripe blackberry and coffee flavors in this dry, somewhat rustic wine. It will benefit from a little decanting, as the tannic mouthfeel is on the rough side and air will soften it. 84 —*S.H. (2/1/2007)*

Kenwood 2002 Reserve Merlot (Sonoma Valley) $25. 90 —*S.H. (9/1/2006)*

Kenwood 2001 Reserve Merlot (Sonoma Valley) $25. 86 —*S.H. (10/1/2005)*

Kenwood 2000 Reserve Massara Merlot (Sonoma Valley) $25. 86 —*S.H. (10/1/2004)*

Kenwood 1999 Reserve-Massara Merlot (Sonoma Valley) $25. 89 —*S.H. (10/1/2003)*

Kenwood 2005 Pinot Noir (Russian River Valley) $18. Kenwood has done a very good job crafting a delicate, lighter-bodied Pinot that's rich in real varietal flavor. Polished cherry, cola, pomegranate, coffee, rhubarb and Asian spice flavors, with a balanced finish. 87 —*S.H. (4/1/2007)*

Kenwood 2004 Pinot Noir (Russian River Valley) $18. 85 *—S.H. (5/1/2006)*

Kenwood 2003 Pinot Noir (Russian River Valley) $17. 87 *—S.H. (6/1/2005)*

Kenwood 2002 Pinot Noir (Russian River Valley) $17. 88 *(11/1/2004)*

Kenwood 2001 Pinot Noir (Russian River Valley) $17. 85 *—S.H. (7/1/2003)*

Kenwood 2000 Pinot Noir (Russian River Valley) $17. 85 *(7/1/2003)*

Kenwood 1999 Pinot Noir (Russian River Valley) $17. 86 *—S.H. (5/1/2001)*

Kenwood 2000 Jack London Vineyard Pinot Noir (Sonoma Valley) $20. 80 *(10/1/2002)*

Kenwood 2005 Reserve Pinot Noir (Russian River Valley) $25. A solid effort. Dry, delicately silky and elegant, this polished wine shows flavors of red cherries, raspberries, cola and rosehip tea, with an Asian spice finish. Pair with steak. **87** *—S.H. (9/1/2007)*

Kenwood 2004 Reserve Pinot Noir (Russian River Valley) $25. 90 *—S.H. (9/1/2006)*

Kenwood 2000 Reserve Olivet Pinot Noir (Russian River Valley) $30. 86 *—S.H. (7/1/2003)*

Kenwood 1999 Reserve-Olivet Pinot Noir (Russian River Valley) $30. 89 *(10/1/2002)*

Kenwood 2006 Rosé Pinot Noir (Russian River Valley) $13. Simple and semisweet, this clean blush has cola, raspberry and vanilla spice flavors. It leaves behind a taste of spearmint gum when you swallow. **84** *—S.H. (11/15/2007)*

Kenwood 2005 Rosé Pinot Noir (Russian River Valley) $13. Showcases Pinot Noir's amenability for rosé in the delicate structure, silky mouthfeel, and crisp acidity, not to mention just-right fruit. Not a big or complex wine, but very pleasurable, with cherry, cola, vanilla and cinnamon spice flavors. **86** *—S.H. (7/1/2007)*

Kenwood 2005 Rosé Pinot Noir (Russian River Valley) $15. 86 *—S.H. (12/15/2006)*

Kenwood 2004 Red Table Wine Red Blend (California) $8. This blend of Zin, Petite Sirah and Barbera is rustic and simple, with a harsh mouthfeel and a sweet-sour finish. **82** *—S.H. (11/1/2007)*

Kenwood 2006 Rosé Table Wine Rosé Blend (California) $8. Made from Syrah, Merlot and some other grapes, this is a soft, featureless blush wine, with semisweet medicinal cherry flavors. **82** *—S.H. (11/1/2007)*

Kenwood 2006 Sauvignon Blanc (Sonoma County) $13. I like the light-bodied texture, acidity and delicate mouthfeel of this wine, with its pretty lemonade, honeysuckle and vanilla flavors. But the finish is too sugary sweet. **83** *—S.H. (10/1/2007)*

Kenwood 2005 Sauvignon Blanc (Sonoma County) $13. 85 *—S.H. (11/15/2006)*

Kenwood 2004 Sauvignon Blanc (Sonoma County) $13. 90 Best Buy *—S.H. (12/1/2005)*

Kenwood 2003 Sauvignon Blanc (Sonoma County) $11. 86 Best Buy *—S.H. (12/31/2004)*

Kenwood 2002 Sauvignon Blanc (Sonoma County) $11. 83 *—S.H. (12/31/2003)*

Kenwood 2001 Sauvignon Blanc (Sonoma County) $12. 85 *—S.H. (9/1/2003)*

Kenwood 2000 Sauvignon Blanc (Sonoma County) $13. 88 Best Buy *—J.M. (11/15/2001)*

Kenwood 1999 Sauvignon Blanc (Sonoma County) $12. 85 *—S.H. (11/15/2000)*

Kenwood 1998 Sauvignon Blanc (Sonoma County) $11. 85 *—M.M. (3/1/2000)*

Kenwood 2005 Reserve Sauvignon Blanc (Sonoma County) $15. 84 *—S.H. (12/15/2006)*

Kenwood 2004 Reserve Sauvignon Blanc (Sonoma County) $15. 90 Best Buy *—S.H. (12/1/2005)*

Kenwood 2002 Reserve Sauvignon Blanc (Sonoma County) $15. 86 *—S.H. (2/1/2005)*

Kenwood 2001 Reserve Sauvignon Blanc (Sonoma County) $15. 86 *—S.H. (9/1/2003)*

Kenwood 2000 Reserve Sauvignon Blanc (Sonoma County) $15. 86 *—S.H. (12/15/2001)*

Kenwood 1997 Reserve Sauvignon Blanc (Sonoma County) $16. 87 *—L.W. (9/1/1999)*

Kenwood 2003 Jack London Vineyard Syrah (Sonoma Valley) $30. 86 *—S.H. (12/31/2006)*

Kenwood 2005 White Table Wine White Blend (California) $8. Soft, semisweet and simple, with flavors of canned peaches, pineapples and apricots, this wine is a blend of Chardonnay, Sauvignon Blanc and Muscat Canelli. **83** *—S.H. (11/1/2007)*

Kenwood 2004 Zinfandel (Sonoma County) $16. Enjoyable for its smooth, creamy texture, and the way the ripe fruit plays off against the oak, acids and tannins. Shows slightly sweet chocolate truffle primary flavor, with a follow-up of wild blackberry and cola. One of the more versatile, Merlot-like Zins out there. **85** *—S.H. (4/1/2007)*

Kenwood 2003 Zinfandel (Sonoma County) $16. 87 *—S.H. (3/1/2006)*

Kenwood 2002 Zinfandel (Sonoma County) $16. 86 *—S.H. (10/1/2005)*

Kenwood 2001 Zinfandel (Sonoma County) $16. 87 *(11/1/2003)*

Kenwood 2000 Zinfandel (Sonoma County) $16. 86 *—S.H. (3/1/2003)*

Kenwood 1999 Zinfandel (Sonoma County) $16. 84 *—J.M. (3/1/2002)*

Kenwood 1998 Zinfandel (Sonoma County) $15. 85 *(3/1/2001)*

Kenwood 1997 Zinfandel (Sonoma Valley) $15. 89 *—P.G. (11/15/1999)*

Kenwood 2004 Jack London Vineyard Zinfandel (Sonoma Valley) $23. 87 *—S.H. (12/31/2006)*

Kenwood 2003 Jack London Vineyard Zinfandel (Sonoma Valley) $20. 83 *—S.H. (12/31/2005)*

Kenwood 2002 Jack London Vineyard Zinfandel (Sonoma Valley) $20. 88 *—S.H. (4/1/2005)*

Kenwood 2001 Jack London Vineyard Zinfandel (Sonoma Mountain) $20. 90 *—S.H. (4/1/2004)*

Kenwood 2000 Jack London Vineyard Zinfandel (Sonoma Valley) $20. 86 *—S.H. (3/1/2003)*

Kenwood 1999 Jack London Vineyard Zinfandel (Sonoma Valley) $20. 86 *—J.M. (3/1/2002)*

Kenwood 1998 Jack London Vineyard Zinfandel (Sonoma Valley) $20. 86 *(3/1/2001)*

Kenwood 1997 Jack London Vineyard Zinfandel (Sonoma Valley) $20. 84 *—P.G. (11/15/1999)*

Kenwood 1999 Mazzoni Zinfandel (Sonoma County) $20. 88 *—J.M. (3/1/2002)*

Kenwood 1997 Mazzoni Zinfandel (Sonoma County) $20. 87 *—S.H. (12/1/2000)*

Kenwood 1999 Nuns Canyon Zinfandel (Sonoma Valley) $20. 86 *—J.M. (3/1/2002)*

Kenwood 1997 Nuns Canyon Zinfandel (Sonoma Valley) $20. 88 *—S.H. (12/1/2000)*

Kenwood 1997 Old Vine Zinfandel (California) $16. 85 *—P.G. (11/15/1999)*

Kenwood 2004 Reserve Zinfandel (Sonoma County) $20. Rich and textured, with jammy, spicy blackberry, cherry and chocolate licorice flavors that are deep and long in the finish. Has that extra depth of complexity that makes it classic Sonoma Zin. **88** *—S.H. (4/1/2007)*

Kenwood 2003 Reserve Zinfandel (Sonoma County) $20. 91 Editors' Choice *—S.H. (12/31/2005)*

Kenwood 2002 Reserve Zinfandel (Sonoma County) $20. 85 *—S.H. (2/1/2005)*

Kenwood 2001 Reserve Mazzoni Vineyard Zinfandel (Russian River Valley) $20. 87 *—S.H. (4/1/2004)*

Kenwood 2000 Reserve Mazzoni Vineyard Zinfandel (Sonoma County) $20. 86 *—S.H. (3/1/2003)*

Kenwood 1997 Upper Weise Zinfandel (Sonoma Valley) $15. 87 *—S.H. (12/1/2000)*

Kenwood 1997 Upper Weise Vineyard Zinfandel (Sonoma Valley) $15. 86 *(3/1/2001)*

KESTREL

Kestrel 2004 Cabernet Sauvignon (Yakima Valley) $22. I like this new release far more than the tart and acidic 2003. It's got muscle and sinew, though it is certainly not what you would call a fleshy wine. Lean and tasting of cranberry, pomegranate and wild cherry, it has sharp acids and will stand up to any kind of meat and spice. Pizza anyone? **87** *—P.G. (12/1/2007)*

Kestrel 2003 Cabernet Sauvignon (Yakima Valley) $20. Tart and disjointed, this wine attempts to marry rather thin, acidic fruit with fat, buttery oak, but it doesn't come together. Either ramp up the ripeness or make a leaner, less extracted and tannic wine. As it stands, it's a bit schizophrenic. **83** *—P.G. (5/1/2007)*

Kestrel 2002 Cabernet Sauvignon (Yakima Valley) $20. 83 *—P.G. (12/15/2005)*

Kestrel 1997 Cabernet Sauvignon (Columbia Valley (WA)) $21. 85 *—P.G. (9/1/2002)*

Kestrel 2003 Estate Old Vine Cabernet Sauvignon (Yakima Valley) $50. Though I was not partial to the winery's 2002 Cab, this new vintage is moving in the right direction. It's still a very dry, austere, somewhat chalky enterprise, and the color and mouthfeel suggest that a little less extraction might bring out more of the elegance that is missing. But it is a firm, authoritative Cabernet, with just a splash of Malbec, that offers up everything from violets to black currant, dusted with dried herb. **89** *—P.G. (5/1/2007)*

Kestrel 2002 Estate Old Vine Cabernet Sauvignon (Yakima Valley) $50. 85 *—P.G. (12/15/2005)*

Kestrel 1998 Estate Old Vine Cabernet Sauvignon (Columbia Valley (WA)) $50. 92 *—P.G. (9/1/2002)*

Kestrel 2005 Estate Old Vine Chardonnay (Yakima Valley) $20. Bright yellow-gold in color, this sends out penetrating aromas of pineapple, banana and tropical fruit. From a 35-year-old vineyard, this is a rare example of full-flavored, fully mature Wente clone Chardonnay from the early days of Washington viticulture. Though the winery struggled with this wine in earlier vintages, it is now dialing in what these old grapes have to offer. Broad, fleshy flavors are mitigated with firm acids, and nice grace notes fill out the finish. **88** *—P.G. (5/1/2007)*

Kestrel 2004 Merlot (Yakima Valley) $22. There is just 9% Cabernet in the blend. Smooth and light, with lean flavors showing herb and bark. The tannins have a green edge to them, and perhaps as a result, the vanilla flavors seem to stick out rather awkwardly. **86** *—P.G. (12/1/2007)*

Kestrel 2002 Merlot (Columbia Valley (WA)) $20. 85 *—P.G. (12/15/2005)*

Kestrel 1999 Merlot (Yakima Valley) $20. 88 *—P.G. (12/15/2004)*

Kestrel 2003 Estate Old Vine Merlot (Yakima Valley) $50. These vines, planted in 1972, are among the oldest Merlot in the state, if not the country. It's a pleasure to see the fruit treated so well, unblended, pure and presented in its full glory. Dark, smoky, tight, herbal and quite dense, this offers great concentration and intriguing grace notes of mint, citrus and pine. It's not your standard Merlot by any means, but it is solid, interesting and quite flavorful, with good legs. **89** *—P.G. (5/1/2007)*

Kestrel 2000 Estate Old Vine Merlot (Yakima Valley) $50. 87 *—P.G. (12/15/2004)*

Kestrel 1998 Old Vine Merlot (Yakima Valley) $50. 93 Editors' Choice *—P.G. (9/1/2002)*

Kestrel 2003 Vintners Merlot (Yakima Valley) $20. 89 *—P.G. (6/1/2006)*

Kestrel 2002 Vintners Old Vine Estate Merlot (Yakima Valley) $50. 90 *—P.G. (6/1/2006)*

Kestrel NV Lady In Red Holiday Red Blend (Yakima Valley) $20. This is the second non-vintage holiday edition of Kestrel's popular Marilyn wannabe label. Who can resist a cute girl in a mini-skirted Santa suit? The wine is an all-purpose, sturdy red that could liven up a holiday table and ought to be stellar with turkey. **85** *—P.G. (12/31/2007)*

Kestrel 2006 Rosé Blend (Columbia Valley (WA)) $15. The winery calls it their melting pot wine—a mongrel blend of seven grapes (half Merlot), done as a saignée. The color is pale cherry red, and though finished dry there's a thick, viscous quality that detracts from the elegance and freshness. There's something untoward in the final flavors, an impression of sour, old orange juice. **83** *—P.G. (7/1/2007)*

Kestrel 2006 Rosé Blend (Yakima Valley) $15. Nice spice and strawberry fruit. The blend is a mish-mash—half Merlot, the rest Sangiovese, Cabernet Sauvignon, Syrah, Cab Franc, Viognier and Malbec. Not that it makes a huge difference in a rosé, but it does seem a bit diffuse as a result. Nonetheless, a good sipping wine. **87** *—P.G. (12/1/2007)*

Kestrel 2004 Estate Sangiovese (Yakima Valley) $20. Opening aromas are a bit reductive, with some hints of tar and rubber, but underneath is firm, well-rounded fruit. This is 100% Sangio, rather heavily extracted and hence tannic, with some of the acid knocked down but the distinctive subtlety of the grape not in evidence. It comes across as a sort of younger sibling to Lemberger. **84** *—P.G. (5/1/2007)*

Kestrel 2002 Estate Sangiovese (Yakima Valley) $20. 86 *—P.G. (4/1/2005)*

Kestrel 2000 Syrah (Yakima Valley) $28. 88 *—P.G. (9/1/2002)*

Kestrel 1999 Syrah (Yakima Valley) $28. 87 *(11/1/2001)*

Kestrel 2003 Co-fermented Syrah (Yakima Valley) $38. 93 *—P.G. (6/1/2006)*

Kestrel 2004 Estate Syrah (Yakima Valley) $22. There is a little bit of leathery funk in some of the barrels, but it's subtle enough to be a feature rather than a flaw. Dark, tarry and smoky, this is a firm, bright wine. The addition of 5% Merlot may add a little flesh to its bones, and broaden the palate. **87** *—P.G. (12/1/2007)*

Kestrel 2002 Estate Syrah (Yakima Valley) $20. 83 *(9/1/2005)*

Kestrel 1999 Estate Syrah (Yakima Valley) $50. 89 *—P.G. (9/1/2002)*

Kestrel 2002 Signature Edition Co-Ferment Syrah (Yakima Valley) $38. 85 *(9/1/2005)*

Kestrel 2004 Winemaker's Select Co-ferment Estate Syrah (Yakima Valley) $38. Kestrel remains one of the most enigmatic Washington wineries; brilliant at times, disappointing at others, possessed of excellent old-vine fruit and yet plagued with inconsistency. This Co-ferment Syrah was excellent in 2002 and even better in 2003, but falls a bit short in 2004. It's got the purple-black color but not the density to match; the fruit flavors are chewy and tart, and the wine has an acidic edge that leaves an impression of unripeness. **86** *—P.G. (12/31/2007)*

Kestrel 2004 Viognier (Yakima Valley) $20. Planted in 1999, the estate Viognier is ripening well, and Kestrel doesn't hold back on the winemaking. Barrel fermented and left sur lie for nine months, this is exceptionally rich and buttery. It skates along the edge of volatility, but the intense flavors of lemon, lime, pineapple and tropical fruits make this irresistible. **91** *—P.G. (5/1/2007)*

Kestrel 2006 Estate Viognier (Yakima Valley) $20. Kestrel has Viognier dialed in, and this excellent follow-up to the 2005 is right up the same alley, vibrant with citrus oil, gin and tonic, lime and grapefruit. It's racy and slick, and it slides down quite easily with a finishing kick that invites the next glass. **89** *—P.G. (12/1/2007)*

Kestrel 2005 Estate Viognier (Yakima Valley) $20. The winery does well with this wine, which once again seems to carry all the right stuff, a pleasing mix of lime and grapefruit, Meyer lemon and meringue, nuanced with ginger spice. Full and long-lasting, it is one of the richest Viogniers in the state. **90** *—P.G. (11/1/2007)*

KIDDUSH HASHEM CELLARS

Kiddush Hashem Cellars 2001 Great Oaks Ranch Road Syrah (Santa Barbara County) $29. 89 *—J.M. (4/3/2004)*

KINDRED

Kindred 2005 Amber Ridge Vineyard Pinot Noir (Russian River Valley) $45. Only a fine, cool-climate vineyard could have grown this Pinot. It combines ripe raspberry, cherry and cola flavors with crispness and a delicate, silky mouthfeel. The end result is a dry, complex wine of considerable charm and a drink-me-again deliciousness. **90** *—S.H. (12/31/2007)*

Kindred 2005 Marsanne-Roussanne-Viognier Rhône White Blend (Russian River Valley) $32. This Rhône blend is soft and sugary sweet, with a honeyed, vanilla fudge and smoky oak edge. The underlying wine flavors are of peaches, pineapples and yellow apricots. **85** *—S.H. (12/31/2007)*

KING

King NV Chocolate Harbor Grape Wine with Natural Chocolate Flavor Red Blend (California) $14. The wine is simple and tastes like regular chocolate milk, with a splash of blackberry liqueur. Zinfandel and Petite Sirah. **84** *—S.H. (10/1/2007)*

King 2006 Viognier (Lodi) $15. Oddly sweet and medicinal, with sugary apricot and orange soda flavors and deficient acidity. **80** *—S.H. (9/1/2007)*

KING ESTATE

King Estate 1999 Chardonnay (Oregon) $10. 84 *—S.H. (12/1/2003)*

King Estate 1998 Chardonnay (Oregon) $10. 83 *—S.H. (8/1/2002)*

King Estate 1996 Chardonnay (Oregon) $14. 88 *—M.M. (12/31/1999)*

King Estate 1998 Reserve Chardonnay (Oregon) $20. 87 *—S.H. (8/1/2002)*

King Estate 1997 Reserve Chardonnay (Oregon) $15. 89 *—P.G. (8/1/2003)*

King Estate 2004 Pinot Gris (Oregon) $16. King Estate is certainly the largest producer of Pinot Gris in Oregon, and probably in the country. Unlike the PGs that dominate the market, this is a fleshy wine, with lush flavors of pear and subtle cinnamon scents. All stainless steel fermented, aged sur lie for a bit of creamy texture, it's just slightly over 13% alcohol, making it a terrific oyster wine and flat-out food friendly for all your shellfish and lighter pastas. 64,000 cases. **88** *—P.G. (2/1/2007)*

King Estate 2004 Pinot Gris (Oregon) $15. 85 *(2/1/2006)*

King Estate 2003 Pinot Gris (Oregon) $15. 86 *—P.G. (8/1/2005)*

King Estate 2001 Pinot Gris (Oregon) $15. 84 *—S.H. (12/1/2003)*

King Estate 2000 Pinot Gris (Oregon) $14. 88 Best Buy *(3/1/2002)*

King Estate 1998 Pinot Gris (Oregon) $14. 88 *(3/1/2002)*

King Estate 1997 Pinot Gris (Oregon) $13. 87 Best Buy *(8/1/1999)*

King Estate 2004 Domaine Pinot Gris (Oregon) $25. 91 *—P.G. (2/1/2006)*

King Estate 2003 Domaine Pinot Gris (Oregon) $25. 91 *—P.G. (2/1/2005)*

King Estate 2004 Domaine Vin Glacé Pinot Gris (Oregon) $25. 93 Editors' Choice *(2/1/2006)*

King Estate 2001 Reserve Pinot Gris (Oregon) $20. 86 *—S.H. (8/19/2003)*

King Estate 2000 Reserve Pinot Gris (Oregon) $20. 90 Editors' Choice *(3/1/2002)*

King Estate 1997 Reserve Pinot Gris (Oregon) $18. 87 *(8/1/1999)*

King Estate 2001 Vin Glacé Pinot Gris (Oregon) $18. 86 *—S.H. (12/1/2003)*

King Estate 2004 Vin Glacé Pinot Gris (Oregon) $18. 91 *(2/1/2006)*

King Estate 2000 Vin Glacé Pinot Gris (Oregon) $18. 88 *(3/1/2002)*

King Estate 2004 Pinot Noir (Oregon) $26. This bottling from King is well-made, as always, but doesn't have quite the concentration that has been there in past vintages. The fruit is ripe, without any of the leafy vegetality that can plague Oregon in some vintages, but the wine tails off quickly and loses flavor just as quickly. Still, it might benefit from just another year or two of bottle age. **86** *—P.G. (2/1/2007)*

King Estate 2001 Pinot Noir (Oregon) $22. 84 *—S.H. (12/15/2004)*

King Estate 2000 Pinot Noir (Oregon) $20. 88 *—P.G. (12/15/2002)*

King Estate 1999 Pinot Noir (Oregon) $22. 88 *(10/1/2002)*

King Estate 1998 Pinot Noir (Oregon) $20. 85 *(3/1/2002)*

King Estate 1996 Pinot Noir (Oregon) $18. 84 *(10/1/1999)*

King Estate 1999 Croft Vineyard Pinot Noir (Willamette Valley) $40. 91 *—P.G. (8/1/2002)*

King Estate 2003 Domaine Pinot Noir (Willamette Valley) $50. 90 *—P.G. (9/1/2006)*

King Estate 2002 Domaine Pinot Noir (Oregon) $50. 91 Cellar Selection *—P.G. (11/15/2005)*

King Estate 2001 Domaine Pinot Noir (Oregon) $50. 91 *—P.G. (2/1/2005)*

King Estate 1999 Domaine Pinot Noir (Oregon) $50. 91 Editors' Choice *(10/1/2002)*

King Estate 1998 Domaine Pinot Noir (Oregon) $50. 90 *(3/1/2002)*

King Estate 1999 Pfeiffer Vineyards Pinot Noir (Willamette Valley) $40. 89 *—P.G. (8/1/2002)*

King Estate 1998 Pfeiffer Vineyards Pinot Noir (Willamette Valley) $40. 88 *(3/1/2002)*

King Estate 1999 Reserve Pinot Noir (Oregon) $35. 90 *—P.G. (8/1/2002)*

King Estate 1998 Reserve Pinot Noir (Oregon) $35. 89 *(3/1/2002)*

King Estate 2003 Signature Pinot Noir (Oregon) $25. 89 *—P.G. (5/1/2006)*

King Estate 1998 Late Harvest Riesling (Oregon) $18. 87 *—J.C. (12/31/1999)*

KING FISH

King Fish 2005 Cabernet Sauvignon (California) $6. Showing a minty, green smell and taste to the cherry and blackberry fruit, this wine is very dry, with pronounced tannins and acids. It's a nice little Merlot, and would be a good buy even if it cost a few bucks more. **84 Best Buy** *—S.H. (3/1/2007)*

King Fish 2005 Chardonnay (California) $6. Kind of rustic, with flavors of canned or candied peaches, pears and smoky vanilla, but if you can deal with that, it's a decent little Chard at a low price. **83 Best Buy** *—S.H. (3/1/2007)*

King Fish 2005 Merlot (California) $6. Dry and raw, this Merlot isn't showing much soft fruitiness. It's thin and green. **80** *—S.H. (3/1/2007)*

King Fish NV Pinot Grigio (California) $6. 83 Best Buy *—S.H. (12/1/2006)*

King Fish 2005 Shiraz (California) $6. A wine containing harsh, cola-like acidity. **80** *—S.H. (3/1/2007)*

KINGS RIDGE

Kings Ridge 2006 Pinot Gris (Oregon) $14. From cooler Willamette Valley vineyards, this pleasing Pinot Gris keeps a juicy mix of fresh fruit flavors right up front. Pear, pineapple and grapefruit do a little Snoopy dance in your mouth, buoyed with balanced acidity and a hint of residual sugar. Round and full, it's a generous and quite appealing style. 500 cases were made. **88** *—P.G. (11/15/2007)*

Kings Ridge 2005 Pinot Noir (Oregon) $16. This is a mix of grapes from Willamette and Umpqua Valley vineyards. Light and earthy, it has a classic style that echoes a village Burgundy, only with the distinctive hint of tomato leaf that typifies less expensive Oregon Pinots. There's tart raspberry fruit as well, whiffs of plum and cherry, and overall it packs a lot of interest into its moderately priced frame. **87** *—P.G. (11/15/2007)*

Kings Ridge 2002 Pinot Noir (Oregon) $17. 85 *(11/1/2004)*

Kings Ridge 2000 Pinot Noir (Oregon) $15. 87 Best Buy *—P.G. (4/1/2002)*

Kings Ridge 2006 Riesling (Oregon) $14. This Riesling is right on the borderline of dry/off-dry (just under 1% RS). The fruit, from cooler Willamette Valley vineyard sites, has been fermented in stainless steel and aged on its lees, yielding a wine that is thick, almost meaty. It's as sappy as a fresh peach, and finishes with crisp peach-skin phenolics. All-in-all this is a surprising wine, neither simple nor plain, but full-flavored in the comforting style that seems almost to have vanished from the Northwest. **89 Best Buy** *—P.G. (11/15/2007)*

KINTER COLLINS

Kinter Collins 2005 Chardonnay (Carneros) $22. Thin, dry and acidic, this shows modest peach and citrus flavors. It's a good wine, and elegantly structured, but really should have greater fruity intensity for this price. **83** *—S.H. (8/1/2007)*

Kinter Collins 2004 Pacheco Vineyard Chardonnay (Sonoma Coast) $18. 86 *—S.H. (10/1/2006)*

Kinter Collins 2003 Pacheco Vineyard Chardonnay (Sonoma Coast) $18. 91 Editors' Choice *—S.H. (12/1/2005)*

KIONA

Kiona 2001 Cabernet Sauvignon (Washington) $20. 88 *—P.G. (5/1/2004)*

Kiona 1997 Cabernet Sauvignon (Washington) $20. 87 *—P.G. (11/15/2000)*

Kiona 2001 Estate Bottled Reserve Cabernet Sauvignon (Red Mountain) $32. 90 *—P.G. (5/1/2004)*

Kiona 1997 Reserve Cabernet Sauvignon (Yakima Valley) $30. 87 *—P.G. (11/15/2000)*

Kiona 1998 Cabernet Sauvignon-Merlot (Washington) $10. 85 *—P.G. (11/15/2000)*

Kiona 2002 Chardonnay (Washington) $10. 86 Best Buy *—P.G. (5/1/2004)*

Kiona 1998 Chardonnay (Washington) $10. 85 *—P.G. (11/15/2000)*

Kiona 2000 Estate Bottled Reserve Chardonnay (Red Mountain) $20. 87 *—P.G. (5/1/2004)*

Kiona 1998 Reserve Chardonnay (Columbia Valley (WA)) $18. 86 *—P.G. (11/15/2000)*

Kiona 2003 Chenin Blanc (Columbia Valley (WA)) $8. 87 Best Buy *—P.G. (5/1/2004)*

Kiona 1998 Chenin Blanc (Columbia Valley (WA)) $6. 87 *—P.G. (8/19/2003)*

Kiona 1999 Ice Wine Chenin Blanc (Yakima Valley) $19. 90 *—P.G. (11/15/2000)*

Kiona 2001 Lemberger (Columbia Valley (WA)) $10. 87 Best Buy *—P.G. (5/1/2004)*

Kiona 1998 Lemberger (Washington) $10. 89 *(11/15/1999)*

Kiona 1998 Merlot (Columbia Valley (WA)) $20. 87 *—P.G. (9/1/2002)*

Kiona 1997 Merlot (Washington) $20. 86 *—P.G. (11/15/2000)*

Kiona 2001 Estate Bottled Reserve Merlot (Red Mountain) $30. 87 *—P.G. (5/1/2004)*

Kiona 1999 Late Harvest Muscat (Yakima Valley) $7. 88 Best Buy *—P.G. (11/15/2000)*

Kiona 2003 Dry Riesling (Columbia Valley (WA)) $8. 89 Best Buy *—P.G. (5/1/2004)*

Kiona 2000 Dry White Riesling (Columbia Valley (WA)) $8. 87 *—P.G. (9/1/2002)*

Kiona 2003 White Riesling (Columbia Valley (WA)) $8. 89 Best Buy *—P.G. (5/1/2004)*

Kiona 1999 Rosé Blend (Columbia Valley (WA)) $6. 85 Best Buy *—P.G. (11/15/2000)*

Kiona 1998 Sémillon (Columbia Valley (WA)) $9. 87 Best Buy *—P.G. (11/15/2000)*

Kiona 2002 Syrah (Red Mountain) $25. 86 *(9/1/2005)*

Kiona 1998 Syrah (Yakima Valley) $30. 85 *(11/1/2001)*

Kiona 1997 Syrah (Yakima Valley) $30. 84 *—P.G. (11/15/2000)*

Kiona 1998 White Riesling (Columbia Valley (WA)) $6. 85 *—P.G. (11/15/2000)*

Kiona 1998 Dry White Riesling (Columbia Valley (WA)) $6. 86 Best Buy *—P.G. (11/15/2000)*

Kiona 1998 Late Harvest White Riesling (Yakima Valley) $7. 88 Best Buy *—P.G. (11/15/2000)*

KIRKLAND RANCH

Kirkland Ranch 1998 Cabernet Sauvignon (Napa Valley) $30. 89 *(9/1/2001)*

Kirkland Ranch 1998 Estate Cabernet Sauvignon (Napa Valley) $36. 91 Cellar Selection *(9/1/2001)*

Kirkland Ranch 2000 Chardonnay (Napa Valley) $20. 85 *—S.H. (6/1/2003)*

Kirkland Ranch 1999 Chardonnay (Napa Valley) $20. 88 *(9/1/2001)*

USA

Kirkland Ranch 1999 KRV Block #13 Chardonnay (Napa Valley) $30. 90 *(7/1/2001)*

Kirkland Ranch 1998 Merlot (Napa Valley) $24. 87 *(9/1/2001)*

Kirkland Ranch 1998 Estate Merlot (Napa Valley) $30. 89 *(9/1/2001)*

Kirkland Ranch 2004 Pinot Grigio (Napa Valley) $16. 83 *—S.H. (2/1/2006)*

Kirkland Ranch 2000 Pinot Noir (Napa Valley) $32. 81 *(10/1/2002)*

KIT FOX

Kit Fox 2001 Cabernet Sauvignon (California) $14. 84 *—S.H. (11/15/2003)*

Kit Fox 2002 Sunflower Vineyard Cabernet Sauvignon (California) $14. 82 *—S.H. (5/1/2005)*

Kit Fox 2002 Cabernet Sauvignon-Syrah (California) $14. 82 *—S.H. (5/1/2005)*

Kit Fox 2001 Cabernet Sauvignon-Syrah (California) $14. 83 *—S.H. (11/15/2003)*

Kit Fox 2001 Fumé Blanc (California) $12. 83 *—S.H. (7/1/2003)*

Kit Fox 2002 Syrah (California) $15. 83 *—S.H. (5/1/2005)*

Kit Fox 2001 Syrah (California) $15. 82 *—S.H. (12/15/2003)*

Kit Fox 2005 Chloe's Vineyard Syrah (Salado Creek) $18. Dry, unripe and herbal, with green dill and white pepper flavors and just a trace of cherries. Not much going on in this austere wine. **82** *—S.H. (4/1/2007)*

Kit Fox 2001 Viognier (California) $12. 84 *—S.H. (7/1/2003)*

Kit Fox 2005 Carson's Vineyard Viognier (Salado Creek) $17. A new appellation in Stalislaus County. Rustically easy, with a wide array of fruit, flower and spice flavors that finish with a touch of caramel-like sweetness. **83** *—S.H. (4/1/2007)*

Kit Fox 2005 Foxy White Table Wine White Blend (California) $15. Chenin Blanc, Sauvignon Blanc, Verdelho, Orange Muscat, Riesling and Viognier comprise the blend on this delightful wine. It's a deliciously easy sipper, with all kinds of tree fruit, wildflower and spicy vanilla flavors. **85** *—S.H. (4/1/2007)*

KLINKER BRICK WINERY

Klinker Brick Winery 2004 Old Vine Zinfandel (Lodi) $16. This is not really a dry wine, but it is a very nice one because the acids and tannins make it balanced. The flavors are of mashed ripe cherries and raspberries, sprinkled with cinnamon and powdered cocoa. **85** *—S.H. (12/15/2007)*

Klinker Brick Winery 2001 Old Vine Zinfandel (Lodi) $24. 89 *(11/1/2003)*

KLUGE ESTATE

Kluge Estate 2002 Brut Chardonnay (Albemarle County) $38. 86 *—J.C. (6/1/2005)*

Kluge Estate 2001 Brut Albemarle County Chardonnay (Virginia) $38. 85 *—J.C. (12/31/2004)*

KNAPP

Knapp 2000 Chardonnay (Cayuga Lake) $11. 86 *—J.M. (1/1/2003)*

Knapp 2001 Barrel Reserve Chardonnay (Cayuga Lake) $14. 88 *—J.M. (1/1/2003)*

Knapp 2002 Dry Riesling (Cayuga Lake) $11. 85 *—J.C. (8/1/2003)*

Knapp 2002 Semi-Dry Riesling (Cayuga Lake) $11. 85 *—J.C. (8/1/2003)*

KNIGHTSDALE

Knightsdale 2004 Sir Lancelot du Lac Pinot Noir (Mendocino County) $20. Once you get past the name, you find a pretty good Pinot. It's not a heavy hitter, but shows the elegance and dry silkiness you want in that variety, with pleasant cherry, cola, pomegranate, spice and oak flavors. **86** *—S.H. (5/1/2007)*

KOEHLER

Koehler 2005 Chardonnay (Santa Ynez Valley) $14. Dry, hard and lean, this is a steely, minerally wine with a real bite of acidity. Not showing much fruit, but it's a brisk palate-cleanser. **84** *—S.H. (11/15/2007)*

Koehler 2005 Reserve Chardonnay (Santa Ynez Valley) $30. This wine is very, very dry and minerally lean, with a scour of acidity. The cleansing mouthfeel and the versatility it shows at the table with food are pluses. **85** *—S.H. (12/1/2007)*

Koehler 2005 Pinot Noir (Santa Barbara County) $30. A complicated, satisfying young Pinot. The slight underripeness adds to its mouthfeel, bringing a rhubarb and heirloom tomato contrast to the sweeter cherries, raspberries and cola. With a lightly silky texture and dry finish, it's quite an elegant sipper. **90** *—S.H. (12/1/2007)*

Koehler 2005 Pinot Noir (Santa Rita Hills) $45. Not a success. The wine is thick, heavy and lifeless, with syrupy cherry and cassis flavors that have way too little acidity to perk them up. **83** *—S.H. (12/1/2007)*

Koehler 2005 Estate Magia Nera Red Blend (Santa Ynez Valley) $30. This mix of Sangiovese and Cabernet Sauvignon is sugary and hot. **80** *—S.H. (12/1/2007)*

Koehler 2006 Riesling (Santa Ynez Valley) $14. Softly fruited with peaches, nectarines and honeysuckles, this pleasant sipper has just a touch of sweetness in the background. Best of all is the acidity, which is brisk and mouth-cleansing. **86** *—S.H. (9/1/2007)*

Koehler 2003 Sauvignon Blanc (Santa Ynez Valley) $12. 84 *—S.H. (10/1/2005)*

Koehler 2005 Viognier (Santa Ynez Valley) $18. Dry and acidic, this is a fairly straightforward wine with citrus, spice and mineral flavors. The cleanliness makes it a nicely inexpensive cocktail sipper. **85** *—S.H. (12/1/2007)*

KOENIG VINEYARDS

Koenig Vineyards 2004 Bitner Vineyard Cabernet Sauvignon (Idaho) $20. Black currant and chocolate aromas, paired with well-structured tannins and some oaky smoothness recommend this Idaho Cabernet. I'd like a little more assertiveness of fruit and more complexity, but in general the wine is good and easy to drink. Pair with lamb and grilled beef. **83** *—S.K. (7/1/2007)*

Koenig Vineyards 2003 Cuvée Alden Private Reserve Cabernet Sauvignon-Merlot (Idaho) $50. Cabernet Sauvignon (55%) Merlot (40%) and Cabernet Franc (5%) comprise this red blend from Idaho, named after the winemaker's son. Soft spice and berry on the nose and toast, tobacco and berry on the palate are approachable and pretty. **84** *—S.K. (12/1/2007)*

Koenig Vineyards 2005 Estate Vineyard Merlot (Idaho) $20. Smoke, clove, pepper and mint comprise the aroma, and on the palate, soft tannins and elegant fruit further recommend it. The finish could use a little heft but in general, this is an easy-drinking offering that will appeal to myriad tastes. **84** *—S.K. (7/1/2007)*

Koenig Vineyards 2005 Sunny Slope Cuvée Riesling (Idaho) $12. Honeyed, floral aromas and pretty, delicate flavors make this an interesting and affordable choice for the summer. Think apricot, citrus and a touch of spice. Acidity is good and the finish lovely. **84** *—S.K. (7/1/2007)*

Koenig Vineyards 2005 Windridge Vineyard Ice Wine Riesling (Idaho) $20. Apricot and spicy fig mingle with tropical fruit in this simple but appealing icewine. Balanced on the palate with a clean finish, pair it with a fruit plate or creamy cheese. **83** *—S.K. (12/1/2007)*

Koenig Vineyards 2004 Cuvée Amelia Reserve Syrah (Idaho) $50. There's something more to be found in this than the typical pepper and red berry flavors for which the variety is known. There's depth and complexity to the deep spice and coffee interlaced on the palate, and the finish is lingering and smooth. A very nice Syrah with great food-pairing potential. **85** *—S.K. (10/1/2007)*

Koenig Vineyards 2004 Three Vineyard Cuvée Syrah (Idaho) $20. Friendly and exuberant, exhibiting flavors of red berry, spice and pepper. Balanced but assertive; will pair well with a spicy pizza or pepper steak. **84** *—S.K. (10/1/2007)*

KOKOMO

Kokomo 2005 Cabernet Sauvignon (Dry Creek Valley) $22. Kind of sweet and simple, with jammy blackberry, cherry and raspberry flavors in a soft texture. Drink now. **84** *—S.H. (11/1/2007)*

Kokomo 2005 Petite Sirah (North Coast) $22. Dry, rich, densely tannic and simple, this is Petite Sirah 101. It nicely illustrates the heavy, ripe fruit quality the variety can have, with dark berry fruit and chocolate-tinged flavors. **84** *—S.H. (11/1/2007)*

Kokomo 2005 Winemaker's Reserve Peters Vineyards Pinot Noir (Sonoma Coast) $45. Beautiful Pinot, from this new winery headquartered in Dry Creek Valley. Shows long hangtime cherry, blackberry, blueberry, raspberry and cola flavors, grounded in earthier notes of coffee, rhubarb and wild mushroom, and finishes dry and elegant. Would benefit from higher acidity, which limits its ageability. **90** *—S.H. (11/1/2007)*

Kokomo 2005 Green Pastures Vineyard Syrah (Dry Creek Valley) $22. Soft and simple, this single-vineyard Syrah has raspberry, blackberry, cola and vanilla flavors. It needs greater depth and complexity to truly show its terroir. **84** *—S.H. (11/1/2007)*

Kokomo 2005 Zinfandel (Sonoma County) $18. A little rustic around the edges, with that briary, brambly taste of freshly picked wild berries, this dry Zin hails from a vineyard straddling Dry Creek and Alexander valleys. It's exuberant in spicy flavors of blackberries, blueberries, cherries and cola. **87** *—S.H. (11/1/2007)*

Kokomo 2005 Perotti Vineyards Zinfandel (Dry Creek Valley) $22. Marked by acidity, which gives a tart, hard edge to the fruit, this Zin may benefit from some time in the cellar. The flavors are of wild raspberries, cherries and cola, with an array of Asian spices, and the finish is totally dry. **86** *—S.H. (11/1/2007)*

KONGSGAARD

Kongsgaard 1998 Chardonnay (Oakville) $60. 89 *(7/1/2001)*

KOPRIVA

Kopriva 2005 Cassidy Ranch Chardonnay (Carneros) $14. An unoaked wine that shows you don't need caramel and vanilla to make a good Chard. You get crisp acids and that earthy, mulchy richness that Carneros Chards have underlying the peaches and pineapples. **85** *—S.H. (2/1/2007)*

KORBEL

Korbel NV Blanc de Noirs Champagne Blend (California) $11. 86 Best Buy *—S.H. (12/1/2002)*

Korbel NV Brut Champagne Blend (California) $11. 85 *—S.H. (9/1/2003)*

Korbel NV Brut Champagne Blend (California) $11. 87 Best Buy *—S.H. (12/1/2002)*

Korbel NV Brut Champagne Blend (California) $11. 86 Best Buy *—S.H. (12/31/2004)*

Korbel NV Brut Kosher Champagne Champagne Blend (California) $18. 84 *(12/15/1999)*

Korbel NV Brut Rosé Champagne Blend (California) $13. 87 *—S.H. (6/1/2001)*

Korbel NV Chardonnay Champagne Blend (Russian River Valley) $11. 85 *—S.H. (12/31/2004)*

Korbel NV Extra Dry Champagne Blend (California) $11. 84 *—J.M. (12/1/2002)*

Korbel 1996 Le Premier Reserve Champagne Blend (Russian River Valley) $25. 90 *—S.H. (12/1/2002)*

Korbel 1994 Le Premier Reserve Champagne Blend (Russian River Valley) $22. 90 *—S.H. (12/1/2000)*

Korbel 1997 Master's Reserve Blanc de Noir Champagne Blend (Russian River Valley) $14. 82 *—P.G. (12/31/2000)*

Korbel NV Natural Champagne Blend (Sonoma County) $13. 85 Best Buy *—M.M. (12/1/2001)*

Korbel 2000 Natural Champagne Blend (Russian River Valley) $14. 88 Best Buy *—S.H. (9/1/2003)*

Korbel 1999 Natural Champagne Blend (Sonoma County) $13. 87 *(12/1/2002)*

Korbel 1996 Natural Champagne Blend (Sonoma County) $13. 84 *—L.W. (12/1/1999)*

Korbel 1995 Reserve Le Premier Champagne Blend (Russian River Valley) $22. 87 *(12/1/2001)*

Korbel NV Rouge Champagne Blend (Sonoma County) $13. 80 *—S.H. (12/1/2000)*

Korbel NV Rouge Champagne Blend (Sonoma County) $13. 86 Best Buy *—M.M. (12/1/2001)*

Korbel NV Rouge Champagne Blend (Sonoma County) $13. 85 *—S.H. (12/1/2002)*

Korbel NV Chardonnay (California) $11. 88 Best Buy *—S.H. (12/1/2002)*

Korbel 1998 Chardonnay (Russian River Valley) $18. 88 *(6/1/2000)*

Korbel NV Brut Champagne Chardonnay (California) $18. 85 *(12/15/1999)*

Korbel NV Chardonnay Champagne Chardonnay (California) $11. 85 *—S.H. (12/1/2003)*

Korbel NV Blanc de Noirs Sparkling Blend (California) $12. Lots of Champagne-like richness in this dry blend of Pinot Noir, Gamay, Sangiovese and Zinfandel. Despite these big red varieties, it has subtle, elegant flavors of strawberries, limes, yeast and vanilla. **86** *—S.H. (11/15/2007)*

Korbel NV Blanc de Noirs Sparkling Blend (California) $11. 87 Best Buy *—S.H. (12/31/2004)*

Korbel NV Blanc de Noirs Sparkling Blend (California) $11. 84 *—S.H. (12/31/2005)*

Korbel 1998 Blanc de Noirs-Cuvée Pinot Noir Sparkling Blend (Russian River Valley) $14. 87 *—J.M. (12/1/2003)*

Korbel NV Brut Sparkling Blend (California) $11. 87 Best Buy *—S.H. (12/31/2005)*

Korbel NV Brut Sparkling Blend (California) $11. 87 Best Buy *—S.H. (12/31/2006)*

Korbel NV Brut Rosé Sparkling Blend (California) $11. Another year, another near-perfect brut rosé from Korbel. So dry and balanced, so layered, with yummy raspberry, vanilla, smoke and yeasty dough flavors, it's just irresistible. **90 Best Buy** *—S.H. (7/1/2007)*

Korbel NV Brut Rosé Sparkling Blend (California) $11. 87 Best Buy *—S.H. (6/1/2006)*

Korbel NV Brut Rosé Sparkling Blend (California) $10. 85 *—S.H. (6/1/2005)*

Korbel NV Brut Rosé Sparkling Blend (California) $11. 87 Best Buy *—S.H. (12/31/2004)*

Korbel NV Brut Rosé Sparkling Blend (California) $11. 86 Best Buy *—J.M. (12/1/2003)*

Korbel NV Brut Rosé Sparkling Blend (California) $11. 87 Best Buy *—S.H. (11/15/2006)*

Korbel NV Chardonnay Sparkling Blend (California) $12. Basically a blanc de blancs, and a pretty nice one at that, despite a certain roughness of texture. It's dry and crisp, showing yeasty flavors of peaches, limes and vanilla. **85** *—S.H. (11/15/2007)*

Korbel NV Chardonnay Sparkling Blend (California) $11. 85 *—S.H. (12/31/2005)*

Korbel NV Extra Dry Sparkling Blend (California) $11. 84 *—S.H. (12/31/2005)*

Korbel 1997 Le Premier Sparkling Blend (Russian River Valley) $25. 89 *—J.M. (12/1/2003)*

Korbel 2004 Natural Sparkling Blend (Russian River Valley) $14. 86 *—S.H. (12/31/2006)*

Korbel 2003 Natural Sparkling Blend (Russian River Valley) $14. 85 *—S.H. (12/31/2005)*

Korbel 2002 Natural Sparkling Blend (Russian River Valley) $14. 85 *—S.H. (12/31/2004)*

KOSTA BROWNE

Kosta Browne 2002 Pinot Noir (Sonoma Coast) $28. 83 *(11/1/2004)*

Kosta Browne 2002 Pinot Noir (Russian River Valley) $34. 86 *(11/1/2004)*

Kosta Browne 2002 Cohn Vineyard Pinot Noir (Russian River Valley) $48. 84 *(11/1/2004)*

Kosta Browne 2000 Cohn Vineyard Pinot Noir (Russian River Valley) $48. 92 *—J.M. (7/1/2003)*

Kosta Browne 2002 Kanzler Vineyard Pinot Noir (Sonoma Coast) $48. 86 *(11/1/2004)*

KOVES-NEWLAN

Koves-Newlan 2002 Cabernet Franc (Napa Valley) $30. 84 *—S.H. (7/1/2005)*

Koves-Newlan 1999 Cabernet Sauvignon (Napa Valley) $25. 89 *—S.H. (6/1/2002)*

Koves-Newlan 2002 Estate Cabernet Sauvignon (Oak Knoll) $35. 84 *—S.H. (12/31/2005)*

Koves-Newlan 2001 Estate Cabernet Sauvignon (Napa Valley) $35. 90 *—S.H. (4/1/2005)*

Koves-Newlan 2002 Napa Valley Chardonnay (Napa Valley) $25. 84 *—S.H. (9/1/2004)*

Koves-Newlan 1999 Pinot Noir (Napa Valley) $20. 87 *—S.H. (9/1/2002)*

Koves-Newlan 2003 Estate Pinot Noir (Napa Valley) $26. 83 *—S.H. (11/15/2005)*

Koves-Newlan 2002 Estate Pinot Noir (Oak Knoll) $26. 83 *—S.H. (11/15/2005)*

Koves-Newlan 2001 Estate Pinot Noir (Napa Valley) $26. 85 *—S.H. (4/1/2005)*

Koves-Newlan 2002 Reserve Pinot Noir (Oak Knoll) $30. 83 *—S.H. (12/31/2005)*

Koves-Newlan 1997 Reserve Pinot Noir (Napa Valley) $26. 89 *—S.H. (9/1/2002)*

Koves-Newlan 2001 Zinfandel (Napa Valley) $25. 86 *—S.H. (9/1/2004)*

KRAMER

Kramer 2002 Estate Pinot Noir (Willamette Valley) $20. 84 *(11/1/2004)*

Kramer 2002 Rebecca's Reserve Pinot Noir (Willamette Valley) $35. 85 *(11/1/2004)*

Kramer 2002 Reserve Pinot Noir (Yamhill County) $30. 86 *(11/1/2004)*

KRUTZ

Krutz 2004 Chardonnay (Santa Lucia Highlands) $30. 82 *—S.H. (10/1/2006)*

KULETO ESTATE

Kuleto Estate 2003 Cabernet Sauvignon (Napa Valley) $60. Plays it right down the middle, a food-friendly Cab that doesn't knock you sideways with opulence, just a good, balanced, full-bodied wine. With cassis and oak flavors and a fine acid-tannin balance, it won't compete with food. Best now through 2009. **87** —*S.H. (7/1/2007)*

Kuleto Estate 2002 Cabernet Sauvignon (Napa Valley) $60. 92 —*S.H. (12/15/2005)*

Kuleto Estate 2001 Cabernet Sauvignon (Napa Valley) $50. 87 —*S.H. (4/1/2005)*

Kuleto Estate 2002 Reserve Cabernet Sauvignon (Napa Valley) $85. A good, richly tannic, ripe, balanced wine, impressive for its depth of cassis and cherry fruit and complex finish. It has a good 10-year future ahead. **92** —*S.H. (7/1/2007)*

Kuleto Estate 2002 Pinot Noir (Napa Valley) $40. 87 *(11/1/2004)*

Kuleto Estate 2002 Sangiovese (Napa Valley) $25. 88 —*S.H. (12/15/2005)*

Kuleto Estate 2001 Sangiovese (Napa Valley) $22. 83 —*S.H. (12/1/2005)*

Kuleto Estate 2006 Rosato Sangiovese (Napa Valley) $17. This is a blend of Cabernet, Pinot, Sangiovese, Zin and three other varieties, and it will please fruit-forward fans for its wealth of cherries, raspberries, cola and peppermint candy flavors. **84** —*S.H. (12/15/2007)*

Kuleto Estate 2004 Rosato Sangiovese (Napa Valley) $32. Kuleto has tried their hand at Sangiovese over the years, with little more success than most other California wineries that have tacked this difficult variety. The '04 is dry and one-dimensional, with cherry and herb flavors and sharp acids. **84** —*S.H. (12/15/2007)*

Kuleto Estate 2004 Syrah (Napa Valley) $45. A deeply satisfying Syrah from a hot vintage in a cool climate. You'll find good tannic structure and soft acids backing up the lush, ripe blackberry, cappuccino and melted milk chocolate flavors, and the finish is cinnamon-spicy and dry. But it's not an ager. Drink now or soon. **89** —*S.H. (7/1/2007)*

Kuleto Estate 2002 Estate Syrah (Napa Valley) $40. 86 *(9/1/2005)*

Kuleto Estate 2005 Zinfandel (Napa Valley) $37. Coming from high altitude vines, this Zin defines a certain jammy, hotly ripe style. Although it's basically dry, it has soft, jammy flavors of raspberries, cherries and blackberries, with a licorice and cola finish that reprises the prickly heat from 15.2% of alcohol. **86** —*S.H. (12/15/2007)*

Kuleto Estate 2003 Zinfandel (Napa Valley) $30. 90 —*S.H. (12/1/2005)*

Kuleto Estate 2002 Zinfandel (Napa Valley) $28. 90 —*S.H. (12/15/2004)*

KULETO ESTATE FAMILY VINEYARDS

Kuleto Estate Family Vineyards 2000 Sangiovese (Napa Valley) $24. 86 —*S.H. (5/1/2004)*

Kuleto Estate Family Vineyards 2001 Syrah (Napa Valley) $36. 90 —*S.H. (5/1/2004)*

Kuleto Estate Family Vineyards 2001 Zinfandel (Napa Valley) $28. 90 *(11/1/2003)*

KULETO VILLA

Kuleto Villa 1998 Naitve Son Sangiovese (Napa Valley) $32. 88 —*S.H. (12/1/2001)*

KUNDE

Kunde 2003 Cabernet Sauvignon (Sonoma Valley) $22. Pretty good Cab from this winery; a little thin but rewarding for its soft tannins and good varietal character. The flavors are of blackberries and dried herbs. **85** —*S.H. (10/1/2007)*

Kunde 2001 Cabernet Sauvignon (Sonoma Valley) $21. 90 —*S.H. (12/31/2004)*

Kunde 2000 Cabernet Sauvignon (Sonoma Valley) $21. 86 —*S.H. (11/15/2003)*

Kunde 1998 Cabernet Sauvignon (Sonoma Valley) $20. 87 —*S.H. (11/15/2001)*

Kunde 1997 Cabernet Sauvignon (Sonoma Valley) $20. 90 —*S.H. (7/1/2000)*

Kunde 2000 Drummond Vineyard Cabernet Sauvignon (Sonoma Valley) $45. 88 —*S.H. (11/15/2004)*

Kunde 1999 Drummond Vineyard Cabernet Sauvignon (Sonoma Valley) $30. 84 —*S.H. (5/1/2004)*

Kunde 1997 Drummond Vineyard Cabernet Sauvignon (Sonoma Valley) $25. 87 —*S.H. (7/1/2002)*

Kunde 1996 Drummond Vineyard Cabernet Sauvignon (Sonoma Valley) $24. 87 —*S.H. (12/15/2000)*

Kunde 1998 Drummond Vineyard-Estate Bottled Cabernet Sauvignon (Sonoma Valley) $27. 88 —*S.H. (11/15/2002)*

Kunde 2002 Estate Cabernet Sauvignon (Sonoma Valley) $21.88 —*S.H. (11/1/2006)*

Kunde 2003 Reserve Cabernet Sauvignon (Sonoma Valley) $60. Pretty tannic at this point, which makes for a fairly astringent palate experience despite loads of ripe cherries, blackberries and currants. On the other hand, that grittiness will pair well with steak. Nice now but doesn't have the stuffing for ageability. **88** —*S.H. (12/1/2007)*

Kunde 2002 Reserve Cabernet Sauvignon (Sonoma Valley) $60. 91 —*S.H. (9/1/2006)*

Kunde 2001 Reserve Cabernet Sauvignon (Sonoma Valley) $60. 91 —*S.H. (8/1/2005)*

Kunde 1997 Reserve Cabernet Sauvignon (Sonoma Valley) $40. 93 —*S.H. (12/31/2001)*

Kunde 2004 Chardonnay (Sonoma Valley) $16. 85 —*S.H. (12/31/2005)*

Kunde 2003 Chardonnay (Sonoma Valley) $16. 86 —*S.H. (8/1/2005)*

Kunde 2001 Chardonnay (Sonoma Valley) $16. 87 —*S.H. (12/1/2003)*

Kunde 2000 Chardonnay (Sonoma Valley) $16. 87 —*S.H. (9/1/2002)*

Kunde 1999 Chardonnay (Sonoma Valley) $16. 88 —*S.H. (5/1/2001)*

Kunde 1997 Chardonnay (Sonoma Valley) $15. 88 *(11/1/1999)*

Kunde 1997 C.S. Ridge Chardonnay (Sonoma Valley) $20. 92 *(11/1/1999)*

Kunde 2000 C.S. Ridge Vineyard Chardonnay (Sonoma Valley) $22. 87 —*S.H. (12/15/2002)*

Kunde 1999 C.S. Ridge Vineyard Chardonnay (Sonoma Valley) $22. 90 —*S.H. (5/1/2002)*

Kunde 2002 Estate Grown Chardonnay (Sonoma Valley) $16. 86 —*S.H. (12/15/2004)*

Kunde 2001 Estate Grown, C.S. Ridge Vineyard Chardonnay (Sonoma Valley) $22. 89 —*S.H. (12/15/2004)*

Kunde 2000 Kinneybrook Vineyard Chardonnay (Sonoma Valley) $22. 86 —*S.H. (12/15/2002)*

Kunde 1997 Kinneybrook Vineyard Chardonnay (Sonoma Valley) $20. 92 *(11/1/1999)*

Kunde 2004 Reserve Chardonnay (Sonoma Valley) $35. Three years is an unusually long time to keep a Chardonnay before releasing. There's a prickliness in the mouth that makes the wine fizzy, and gives the lemon drop flavors a weirdly sweet-and-sour finish. **82** —*S.H. (12/1/2007)*

Kunde 2003 Reserve Chardonnay (Sonoma Valley) $35. 87 —*S.H. (11/1/2006)*

Kunde 2002 Reserve Chardonnay (Sonoma Valley) $35. 89 —*S.H. (12/31/2004)*

Kunde 2001 Reserve Chardonnay (Sonoma Valley) $35. 91 —*S.H. (2/1/2004)*

Kunde 2000 Reserve Chardonnay (Sonoma Valley) $35. 91 —*S.H. (6/1/2003)*

Kunde 1999 Reserve Chardonnay (Sonoma Valley) $35. 91 —*S.H. (12/31/2001)*

Kunde 1998 Reserve Chardonnay (Sonoma Valley) $30. 90 —*S.H. (11/15/2000)*

Kunde 1999 Wildwood Vineyard Chardonnay (Sonoma Valley) $22. 93 —*S.H. (5/1/2002)*

Kunde 1997 Wildwood Vineyard Chardonnay (Sonoma Valley) $20. 89 *(11/1/1999)*

Kunde 2000 Wildwood Vineyard-Estate Bottled Chardonnay (Sonoma Valley) $22. 87 —*S.H. (12/15/2002)*

Kunde 1998 Fumé Blanc (Sonoma Valley) $18. 88 —*L.W. (5/1/2000)*

Kunde 1998 Magnolia Lane Vineyard Fumé Blanc (Sonoma Valley) $12. 87 —*L.W. (5/1/2000)*

Kunde 2001 Merlot (Sonoma Valley) $18. 87 —*S.H. (8/1/2005)*

Kunde 2000 Merlot (Sonoma Valley) $18. 87 *(11/15/2002)*

Kunde 1999 Merlot (Sonoma Valley) $18. 83 —*S.H. (11/15/2001)*

Kunde 2003 Block 4SB20 Sauvignon Blanc (Sonoma Valley) $19. 87 —*S.H. (10/1/2005)*

Kunde 2006 Magnolia Lane Sauvignon Blanc (Sonoma Valley) $16. This bottling from Kunde is dependable for its dry, crisp elegance. It always shows bright lemongrass and gooseberry fruit, with more exotic notes of litchi and fig. The trick is to control disagreeable greenness, which pops up here in the finish. **86** —*S.H. (10/1/2007)*

Kunde 2004 Magnolia Lane Sauvignon Blanc (Sonoma Valley) $15. 87 — *S.H. (12/31/2005)*

Kunde 2003 Magnolia Lane Sauvignon Blanc (Sonoma Valley) $15. 88 — *S.H. (12/31/2004)*

Kunde 2002 Magnolia Lane Sauvignon Blanc (Sonoma Valley) $15. 87 — *S.H. (12/15/2003)*

Kunde 2001 Magnolia Lane Sauvignon Blanc (Sonoma Valley) $14. 86 — *S.H. (9/1/2003)*

Kunde 2000 Magnolia Lane Sauvignon Blanc (Sonoma Valley) $14. 86 — *S.H. (11/15/2001)*

Kunde 1999 Magnolia Lane Sauvignon Blanc (Sonoma Valley) $13. 87 Editors' Choice —*S.H. (8/1/2001)*

Kunde 2000 Syrah (Sonoma Valley) $23. 89 —*S.H. (10/1/2003)*

Kunde 1999 Syrah (Sonoma Valley) $23. 87 *(11/1/2001)*

Kunde 1998 Syrah (Sonoma Valley) $20. 86 *(10/1/2001)*

Kunde 2003 Estate Syrah (Sonoma Valley) $22. It's no small feat they were able to hold this sophisticated wine back so long and still sell it for just over $20. The wine is soft, dry and rich in red currant, white pepper, licorice and mocha flavors, and has elegant balance. **92 Editors' Choice** — *S.H. (12/1/2007)*

Kunde 2001 Estate Syrah (Sonoma Valley) $23. 90 —*S.H. (12/15/2004)*

Kunde 1997 Estate Syrah (Sonoma Valley) $20. 90 *(2/1/2000)*

Kunde 2004 Viognier (Sonoma Valley) $24. 83 —*S.H. (12/31/2005)*

Kunde 2003 Viognier (Sonoma Valley) $23. 87 —*S.H. (12/31/2004)*

Kunde 2002 Viognier (Sonoma Valley) $23. 90 —*S.H. (2/1/2004)*

Kunde 2001 Viognier (Sonoma Valley) $23. 88 —*S.H. (9/1/2003)*

Kunde 2000 Viognier (Sonoma Valley) $23. 87 —*J.M. (12/15/2002)*

Kunde 2003 Zinfandel (Sonoma Valley) $18. Rich and spicy, this Zin has waves of cherry jam, raspberry purée, mocha, cinnamon-pepper spice and vanilla oak flavors. It's so fruity, it's almost sweet, an impression heightened by softness. **84** —*S.H. (10/1/2007)*

Kunde 2001 Zinfandel (Sonoma Valley) $16. 83 —*J.M. (11/1/2003)*

Kunde 1999 Zinfandel (Sonoma Valley) $15. 82 —*S.H. (11/15/2001)*

Kunde 1998 Zinfandel (Sonoma Valley) $15. 89 —*P.G. (3/1/2001)*

Kunde 2001 Century Vines Zinfandel (Sonoma Valley) $25. 85 *(11/1/2003)*

Kunde 2000 Century Vines-Shaw Vineyard Zinfandel (Sonoma Valley) $25. 85 —*S.H. (12/1/2002)*

Kunde 2000 Estate Bottled Zinfandel (Sonoma Valley) $16. 85 —*S.H. (11/1/2002)*

Kunde 1997 Estate Bottled Zinfandel (Sonoma Valley) $15. 86 —*P.G. (11/15/1999)*

Kunde 1997 Robusto Zinfandel (Sonoma Valley) $30. 89 —*S.H. (5/1/2000)*

Kunde 2002 Shaw Vineyard Century Vines Zinfandel (Sonoma Valley) $30. 90 —*S.H. (12/31/2005)*

Kunde 1999 Shaw Vineyard Century Vines Zinfandel (Sonoma Valley) $25. 86 —*S.H. (7/1/2002)*

Kunde 1998 Shaw Vineyard Century Vines Zinfandel (Sonoma Valley) $24. 90 —*P.G. (3/1/2001)*

Kunde 1997 Shaw Vineyard Century Vines Zinfandel (Sonoma Valley) $24. 87 —*P.G. (11/15/1999)*

Kunde 2001 Shaw Vineyard, Century Vines Zinfandel (Sonoma Valley) $28. 87 —*J.M. (10/1/2004)*

KUNIN

Kunin 2003 Syrah (Santa Barbara County) $28. 87 *(9/1/2005)*

Kunin 2001 Syrah (Santa Barbara County) $24. 85 —*S.H. (12/1/2003)*

Kunin 2000 Syrah (Santa Maria Valley) $35. 85 —*S.H. (12/1/2002)*

Kunin 2000 Syrah (Santa Rita Hills) $35. 85 —*S.H. (12/1/2002)*

Kunin 2002 Alisos Vineyard Syrah (Santa Barbara County) $35. 86 *(9/1/2005)*

Kunin 2001 Alisos Vineyards Syrah (Santa Barbara County) $30. 89 —*S.H. (2/1/2004)*

Kunin 2000 French Camp Syrah (Paso Robles) $28. 85 —*S.H. (12/1/2002)*

Kunin 1999 French Camp Vineyards Syrah (Paso Robles) $28. 85 —*S.H. (7/1/2002)*

Kunin 2000 Stolpman Vineyard Viognier (Santa Ynez Valley) $28. 91 — *J.M. (12/15/2002)*

KYNSI

Kynsi 2005 Bien Nacido Vineyard Pinot Blanc (Santa Maria Valley) $22. Kynsi is showing a commitment to this variety that is praiseworthy, and consumers should take notice. The wine has the full-bodied creaminess of Chardonnay, but with unique fresh melon, guava and green apple flavors that are deep and long on the finish. **90** —*S.H. (5/1/2007)*

Kynsi 2004 Bien Nacido Vineyard Pinot Blanc (Santa Maria Valley) $22. 90 —*S.H. (12/1/2006)*

Kynsi 2003 Bien Nacido Vineyard Pinot Blanc (Santa Maria Valley) $22. 90 Editors' Choice —*S.H. (10/1/2005)*

Kynsi 2004 Pinot Noir (Edna Valley) $28. Ripe and flavorful, in a direct sort of way, this Pinot offers a mouthful of cherry-pie filling, black raspberry, cola, pomegranate and spicy oak flavors. It's fully dry, with a nice, silky texture, and is best now. **87** —*S.H. (5/1/2007)*

Kynsi 2003 Pinot Noir (Edna Valley) $28. 88 —*S.H. (10/1/2006)*

Kynsi 2002 Pinot Noir (Edna Valley) $28. 85 —*S.H. (10/1/2005)*

Kynsi 2004 Bien Nacido Vineyard Pinot Noir (Santa Maria Valley) $36. Either Kynsi's vines are older, or their learning curve is up, but this is easily their best Bien Nacido Pinot. It's dry and silky, and ultrarich in cherry pie, cola, rhubarb marmalade and rosehip tea flavors, with an enormous Asian spiciness that lasts through a long finish. Very fine, and should hold for five years. **89** —*S.H. (5/1/2007)*

Kynsi 2003 Bien Nacido Vineyard Pinot Noir (Santa Maria Valley) $36. 86 —*S.H. (12/1/2006)*

Kynsi 2002 Bien Nacido Vineyard Pinot Noir (Santa Maria Valley) $36. 85 —*S.H. (10/1/2005)*

Kynsi 2004 Estate Stone Corral Vineyard Pinot Noir (Edna Valley) $45. Riper and more full-bodied than the very good '03, the '04 shows an almost raisiny taste, alongside the cherries and oaky spice. Yet the wine never veers into overripeness, and remains dry and silky. Drink now. **88** —*S.H. (5/1/2007)*

Kynsi 2003 Estate Stone Corral Vineyard Pinot Noir (Edna Valley) $45. 91 —*S.H. (10/1/2006)*

Kynsi 1999 Paragon Vineyard Pinot Noir (Edna Valley) $25. 88 —*R.V. (7/1/2003)*

Kynsi 2004 Bien Nacido Vineyard Syrah (Santa Maria Valley) $22. 87 — *S.H. (12/15/2006)*

Kynsi 2003 Bien Nacido Vineyard Syrah (Santa Maria Valley) $22. 87 — *S.H. (12/15/2006)*

Kynsi 2002 Bien Nacido Vineyard Syrah (Santa Maria Valley) $46. 91 *(9/1/2005)*

Kynsi 2003 Edna Ranch Syrah (Edna Valley) $32. 89 —*S.H. (11/1/2006)*

Kynsi 2002 Edna Ranch Vineyard Syrah (Edna Valley) $28. 92 Editors' Choice *(9/1/2005)*

Kynsi 2003 Kalanna Syrah (Edna Valley) $44. 94 —*S.H. (7/1/2006)*

Kynsi 1999 Paragon Syrah (Edna Valley) $28. 86 —*S.H. (12/1/2002)*

Kynsi 1998 South Ridge Vineyard Syrah (Paso Robles) $25. 83 —*S.H. (7/1/2002)*

Kynsi 2001 Barn Owl Vineyard Zinfandel (Paso Robles) $30. 86 —*S.H. (10/1/2005)*

KYRA

Kyra 2006 Chenin Blanc (Columbia Valley (WA)) $12. Off-dry, with a scent of wheat and cracker mixed with cane sugar. It's simple and sweet, without much character or detail. This does not show what Chenin is capable of; it's sweet white wine, nothing more. **83** —*P.G. (12/1/2007)*

L DE LYETH

L de Lyeth 2003 Cabernet Sauvignon (Sonoma County) $11. 82 —*S.H. (5/1/2006)*

L de Lyeth 2003 Merlot (Sonoma County) $11. 85 —*S.H. (5/1/2006)*

L'AVENTURE

L'Aventure 2002 Cuvée Cote a Cote Red Blend (Paso Robles) $70. 92 — *S.H. (6/1/2005)*

L'Aventure 2002 Estate Cuvée Red Blend (Paso Robles) $80. 93 —*S.H. (6/1/2005)*

L'Aventure 2004 Optimus Red Blend (Paso Robles) $50. A blend of Syrah, Cab and Petit Verdot, the wine flirts with cooked or stewed fruit flavors, and must have presented the winemaker with all kinds of challenges. Drink now. **85** —*S.H. (7/1/2007)*

L'Aventure 2002 Optimus Red Blend (Paso Robles) $50. 94 Editors' Choice —*S.H. (10/1/2005)*

L'Aventure 2001 Optimus Red Blend (Paso Robles) $45. 92 —*S.H. (6/1/2004)*

L'Aventure 2000 Optimus Red Blend (Paso Robles) $45. 93 —*S.H. (11/15/2003)*

L'Aventure 1999 Optimus Red Blend (Paso Robles) $48. 89 —*S.H. (11/15/2002)*

L'Aventure 2006 Rosé Blend (Paso Robles) $15. Nice rosé. Dry, crisp and balanced, it's mainly Syrah, which brings lush cherry and violet flavors. Cabernet Sauvignon adds deeper blackberry flavors, with a touch of cassis. It's pretty full-bodied for rosé, but maintains delicacy and silky lightness, and is totally dry. **87** —*S.H. (7/1/2007)*

L'Aventure 2001 Syrah (Paso Robles) $NA. 91 —*S.H. (6/1/2004)*

L'Aventure 2000 Syrah (Paso Robles) $40. 93 Editors' Choice —*S.H. (12/15/2003)*

L'Aventure 1999 Syrah (Paso Robles) $36. 90 *(11/1/2001)*

L'Aventure 2002 Estate Syrah (Paso Robles) $65. 90 —*S.H. (6/1/2005)*

L'ECOLE NO 41

L'Ecole No 41 1999 Apogee Pepper Bridge Vineyard Bordeaux Blend (Walla Walla (WA)) $42. 90 —*P.G. (6/1/2002)*

L'Ecole No 41 2004 Ferguson Commemorative Reserve Bordeaux Blend (Columbia Valley (WA)) $45. 92 Cellar Selection —*P.G. (12/31/2006)*

L'Ecole No 41 2000 Pepper Bridge Vineyard Bordeaux Blend (Walla Walla (WA)) $42. 86 —*P.G. (9/1/2004)*

L'Ecole No 41 2003 Pepper Bridge Vineyard Apogee Bordeaux Blend (Walla Walla (WA)) $45. 90 —*P.G. (8/1/2006)*

L'Ecole No 41 2002 Pepper Bridge Vineyard Apogee Bordeaux Blend (Walla Walla (WA)) $45. 88 —*P.G. (4/1/2005)*

L'Ecole No 41 2001 Pepper Bridge Vineyard Apogee Bordeaux Blend (Walla Walla (WA)) $42. 87 —*P.G. (7/1/2004)*

L'Ecole No 41 1998 Pepper Bridge Vineyard Apogee Bordeaux Blend (Walla Walla (WA)) $42. 90 —*P.G. (6/1/2001)*

L'Ecole No 41 2003 Seven Hills Vineyard Estate Perigee Bordeaux Blend (Walla Walla (WA)) $45. 90 —*P.G. (8/1/2006)*

L'Ecole No 41 2002 Seven Hills Vineyard Perigee Bordeaux Blend (Walla Walla (WA)) $45. 93 —*P.G. (4/1/2005)*

L'Ecole No 41 2003 Cabernet Sauvignon (Columbia Valley (WA)) $30. 88 —*P.G. (8/1/2006)*

L'Ecole No 41 2003 Cabernet Sauvignon (Walla Walla (WA)) $37. 91 —*P.G. (10/1/2006)*

L'Ecole No 41 2002 Cabernet Sauvignon (Columbia Valley (WA)) $30. 90 Cellar Selection —*P.G. (4/1/2005)*

L'Ecole No 41 2001 Cabernet Sauvignon (Columbia Valley (WA)) $30. 87 —*P.G. (7/1/2004)*

L'Ecole No 41 2000 Cabernet Sauvignon (Columbia Valley (WA)) $30. 87 —*P.G. (9/1/2004)*

L'Ecole No 41 2000 Cabernet Sauvignon (Walla Walla (WA)) $36. 88 —*P.G. (9/1/2004)*

L'Ecole No 41 1999 Cabernet Sauvignon (Walla Walla (WA)) $36. 87 —*P.G. (12/31/2002)*

L'Ecole No 41 1999 Cabernet Sauvignon (Columbia Valley (WA)) $30. 88 —*P.G. (6/1/2002)*

L'Ecole No 41 1998 Cabernet Sauvignon (Walla Walla (WA)) $36. 91 —*P.G. (12/31/2001)*

L'Ecole No 41 1998 Cabernet Sauvignon (Columbia Valley (WA)) $30. 90 —*P.G. (6/1/2001)*

L'Ecole No 41 1997 Cabernet Sauvignon (Walla Walla (WA)) $33. 89 —*J.C. (6/1/2001)*

L'Ecole No. 41 2006 Chardonnay (Columbia Valley (WA)) $22. This is a distinctive Chardonnay, with pea vine and peach, anise and apple mixing it up. It has a lovely, lifted elegance that keeps the flavors intertwined but allows you to experience them separately as well, and it carves a flavor trail through the finish that lingers sensuously. Could be the best CV Chardonnay ever from L'Ecole. **91 Editors' Choice** —*P.G. (12/31/2007)*

L'Ecole No 41 2005 Chardonnay (Columbia Valley (WA)) $20. 90 —*P.G. (12/31/2006)*

L'Ecole No 41 2004 Chardonnay (Columbia Valley (WA)) $20. 89 —*P.G. (8/1/2006)*

L'Ecole No 41 2003 Chardonnay (Columbia Valley (WA)) $20. 87 —*P.G. (4/1/2005)*

L'Ecole No 41 2001 Chardonnay (Columbia Valley (WA)) $20. 87 —*P.G. (9/1/2004)*

L'Ecole No 41 2000 Chardonnay (Columbia Valley (WA)) $19. 88 —*P.G. (2/1/2002)*

L'Ecole No 41 1999 Chardonnay (Columbia Valley (WA)) $20. 88 —*P.G. (6/1/2001)*

L'Ecole No 41 1998 Chardonnay (Columbia Valley (WA)) $20. 90 —*P.G. (6/1/2000)*

L'Ecole No. 41 2006 Walla Voila Chenin Blanc (Washington) $13. Round and varietal, this young and fruity Chenin Blanc captures both the floral and the sweet citrus character of the grape. Finished at just 1% residual sugar, it has bright, clean aromas and a fresh, slightly puckery finish. **87** —*P.G. (11/1/2007)*

L'Ecole No 41 2001 Walla Voila Chenin Blanc (Washington) $12. 89 —*P.G. (9/1/2002)*

L'Ecole No 41 2004 Merlot (Columbia Valley (WA)) $30. 90 —*P.G. (10/1/2006)*

L'Ecole No 41 2000 Merlot (Walla Walla (WA)) $33. 87 —*P.G. (9/1/2004)*

L'Ecole No 41 2000 Merlot (Columbia Valley (WA)) $29. 87 —*P.G. (9/1/2002)*

L'Ecole No 41 1999 Merlot (Columbia Valley (WA)) $30. 86 —*P.G. (12/31/2001)*

L'Ecole No 41 1999 Merlot (Walla Walla (WA)) $36. 92 Cellar Selection —*P.G. (12/31/2001)*

L'Ecole No 41 1998 Merlot (Walla Walla (WA)) $36. 89 —*J.C. (6/1/2001)*

L'Ecole No 41 1998 Merlot (Columbia Valley (WA)) $36. 87 —*P.G. (6/1/2001)*

L'Ecole No. 41 2005 Seven Hills Vineyard Estate Merlot (Walla Walla (WA)) $37. Full, fleshy and ripe, this quite flavorful and fruit-powered Merlot comes from some of the best vines in the valley. In the blend is 12% Cab Sauvignon and 6% Cab Franc, aged 18 months in 60% new oak. It is the fruit that shines through, set against smooth tannins and just a hint of earth. **89** —*P.G. (11/1/2007)*

L'Ecole No 41 2000 Seven Hills Vineyard Merlot (Walla Walla (WA)) $39. 91 —*P.G. (9/1/2002)*

L'Ecole No 41 1999 Seven Hills Vineyard Merlot (Walla Walla (WA)) $40. 91 —*P.G. (12/31/2001)*

L'Ecole No 41 1998 Seven Hills Vineyard Merlot (Walla Walla (WA)) $38. 91 —*P.G. (6/1/2001)*

L'Ecole No. 41 2006 Sémillon (Columbia Valley (WA)) $16. This wine is formulaic in a good way; L'Ecole "owns" Sémillon in Washington, and it is hard to think of any winery in the country that does a better job with the grape. Aged sur lie in neutral oak, blended with 14% Sauvignon Blanc and put through malolactic for added creaminess, this is a delicious, rich and succulent wine that deftly mixes flavors of nettle, lime and melon with vanilla custard and a hint of butterscotch. **90 Editors' Choice** —*P.G. (12/31/2007)*

L'Ecole No 41 2005 Sémillon (Columbia Valley (WA)) $15. 90 —*P.G. (12/31/2006)*

L'Ecole No 41 2004 Barrel-Fermented Sémillon (Columbia Valley (WA)) $15. 91 Best Buy —*P.G. (8/1/2006)*

L'Ecole No 41 2003 Barrel-Fermented Sémillon (Columbia Valley (WA)) $15. 90 Best Buy —*P.G. (4/1/2005)*

L'Ecole No 41 2001 Barrel-Fermented Sémillon (Columbia Valley (WA)) $15. 90 Best Buy —*P.G. (9/1/2004)*

L'Ecole No 41 1999 Barrel-Fermented Sémillon (Columbia Valley (WA)) $15. 89 —*P.G. (6/1/2001)*

L'Ecole No 41 1998 Barrel-Fermented Sémillon (Columbia Valley (WA)) $15. 93 Best Buy —*M.S. (4/1/2000)*

L'Ecole No 41 2000 Barrel-Fermented Sémillon Sémillon (Columbia Valley (WA)) $15. 88 Best Buy —*P.G. (12/31/2001)*

L'Ecole No. 41 2005 Fries Vineyard Sémillon (Wahluke Slope) $20. The third in L'Ecole's stunning triumvirate of Semillons, the Fries, as usual, goes to the head of the glass, with bright, rich and polished fruit tasting of figs, melon and white peaches. Some pleasing hints of herb add interest to the nose; as do the lightly toasty highlights from the barrel fermentation. This is big and full, but not tiring or unbalanced. **91** —*P.G. (3/1/2007)*

L'Ecole No 41 2004 Fries Vineyard Sémillon (Wahluke Slope) $20. 89 —*P.G. (8/1/2006)*

L'Ecole No 41 2003 Fries Vineyard Sémillon (Washington) $20. 93 Editors' Choice —*P.G. (4/1/2005)*

L'Ecole No 41 2001 Fries Vineyard Sémillon (Washington) $20. 93 Editors' Choice —*P.G. (9/1/2004)*

L'Ecole No 41 2000 Fries Vineyard Sémillon (Wahluke Slope) $20. 92 —*P.G. (6/1/2002)*

L'Ecole No 41 1999 Fries Vineyard Sémillon (Wahluke Slope) $22. 92 —*P.G. (6/1/2001)*

L'Ecole No 41 1998 Fries Vineyard Sémillon (Wahluke Slope) $22. 91 *(4/1/2000)*

L'Ecole No 41 2002 Fries Vineyard-Wahluke Slope Sémillon (Washington) $20. 90 —*P.G. (7/1/2004)*

L'Ecole No 41 2003 Seven Hills Vineyard Sémillon (Walla Walla (WA)) $20. 92 Editors' Choice —*P.G. (4/1/2005)*

L'Ecole No 41 2001 Seven Hills Vineyard Sémillon (Walla Walla (WA)) $20. 90 —*P.G. (9/1/2004)*

L'Ecole No 41 2000 Seven Hills Vineyard Sémillon (Walla Walla (WA)) $22. 91 —*P.G. (12/31/2001)*

L'Ecole No 41 1999 Seven Hills Vineyard Sémillon (Walla Walla (WA)) $22. 93 Editors' Choice —*P.G. (6/1/2001)*

L'Ecole No. 41 2006 Seven Hills Vineyard Estate Sémillon (Walla Walla (WA)) $20. The estate bottling is 100% Sémillon and tastes a bit riper and more peachy than the Columbia Valley bottling, though perhaps less nuanced. Barrel fermented in both new and second year French oak, it adds honeysuckle, sweet apple and a hint of mint to the sweet fruit. **91 Editors' Choice** —*P.G. (12/31/2007)*

L'Ecole No 41 2005 Seven Hills Vineyard Estate Sémillon (Walla Walla (WA)) $20. 91 —*P.G. (12/31/2006)*

L'Ecole No 41 2004 Syrah (Columbia Valley (WA)) $25. 91 —*P.G. (12/31/2006)*

L'Ecole No 41 2003 Syrah (Columbia Valley (WA)) $30. 85 *(9/1/2005)*

L'Ecole No 41 2003 Syrah (Columbia Valley (WA)) $25. 89 —*P.G. (8/1/2006)*

L'Ecole No. 41 2005 Seven Hills Vineyard Estate Syrah (Walla Walla (WA)) $37. As usual this is 100% Seven Hills vineyard Syrah, and it delivers lush, tart red fruit flavors, spicy and accented with citrus rind. There is a sharp, high-toned edge to the finish, that gives it definition but needs a bit more time to smooth out. It's substantial and balanced, though a bit monolithic; once in the mouth, it stays put. **88** —*P.G. (11/1/2007)*

L'Ecole No 41 2004 Seven Hills Vineyard Syrah (Walla Walla (WA)) $37. 89 —*P.G. (11/15/2006)*

L'Ecole No 41 2003 Seven Hills Vineyard Syrah (Walla Walla (WA)) $37. 87 *(9/1/2005)*

L'Ecole No 41 2000 Seven Hills Vineyard Syrah (Walla Walla (WA)) $35. 89 —*P.G. (12/31/2002)*

L'Ecole No 41 1999 Seven Hills Vineyard Syrah (Walla Walla (WA)) $34. 92 Editors' Choice *(11/1/2001)*

L'HOMME QUI RIS

L'homme Qui Ris 1998 Sparkling Wine Champagne Blend (Monterey County) $22. 84 —*S.H. (12/31/2006)*

L'UVAGGIO DI GIACOMO

L'Uvaggio di Giacomo 2001 I Colombi Arneis (California) $16. 85 —*S.H. (9/1/2003)*

L'Uvaggio di Giacomo 2000 Il Gufo Barbera (California) $16. 84 —*S.H. (2/1/2003)*

L'Uvaggio di Giacomo 1999 La Pantera Barbera (California) $20. 85 —*S.H. (2/1/2003)*

L'Uvaggio di Giacomo 1999 Il Leopardo Nebbiolo (California) $18. 85 —*S.H. (2/1/2003)*

L'Uvaggio di Giacomo 1999 Il Ponte Sangiovese (California) $32. 86 —*S.H. (2/1/2003)*

L. PRESTON

L. Preston 2000 2000 Red Blend (Dry Creek Valley) $24. 84 —*S.H. (12/1/2002)*

LA BETE

La Bete 2002 Pinot Noir (Willamette Valley) $15. 84 *(11/1/2004)*

La Bete 1998 Knight's Gambit Vineyard Pinot Noir (Willamette Valley) $40. 92 —*M.M. (12/1/2000)*

La Bete 2002 Momtazi Vineyard Pinot Noir (Oregon) $25. 88 *(11/1/2004)*

La Bete 2002 Sélection du Cave Pinot Noir (Oregon) $20. 86 *(11/1/2004)*

La Bete 2002 Stoller Vineyard Pinot Noir (Oregon) $25. 90 *(11/1/2004)*

LA CREMA

La Crema 2005 Chardonnay (Russian River Valley) $27. This is a polished, really likeable Chard. It offers everything the variety should: a rich, creamy texture, brisk acidity, and ripe, delicious flavors of pineapples, apricots, peaches and kiwis coated with vanilla. **90** —*S.H. (12/1/2007)*

La Crema 2004 Chardonnay (Russian River Valley) $24. 89 —*S.H. (11/15/2006)*

La Crema 2001 Chardonnay (Sonoma Coast) $16. 87 —*S.H. (8/1/2003)*

La Crema 2000 Chardonnay (Russian River Valley) $24. 85 —*S.H. (7/1/2003)*

La Crema 2000 Chardonnay (Sonoma Coast) $20. 91 Editors' Choice —*S.H. (12/15/2002)*

La Crema 1999 Chardonnay (Russian River Valley) $30. 90 *(7/1/2001)*

La Crema 1999 Chardonnay (Sonoma Coast) $20. 87 —*J.M. (11/15/2001)*

La Crema 1998 Cold Coast Vineyard Chardonnay (Sonoma Coast) $20. 86 *(6/1/2000)*

La Crema 1997 Cold Coast Vineyards Chardonnay (Sonoma Coast) $16. 90 —*S.H. (11/1/1999)*

La Crema 2003 Nine Barrels Chardonnay (Russian River Valley) $55. 95 Editors' Choice —*S.H. (12/31/2006)*

La Crema 1997 Reserve Chardonnay (Russian River Valley) $27. 90 *(6/1/2000)*

La Crema 1997 Reserve Chardonnay (Russian River Valley) $26. 92 —*S.H. (11/1/1999)*

La Crema 2006 Pinot Gris (Carneros) $20. Brief aging in oak and sur lies aging has given this a much needed creamy richness. Without that, it would be just a crisply acidic, fresh wine, with citrus, apple, peach and honeysuckle flavors. With it, it's elevated. Excessively sweet on the finish. **86** —*S.H. (12/1/2007)*

La Crema 2005 Pinot Noir (Carneros) $34. Soft and hot, almost stewed, the blackberry and cherry fruit tastes like it was mashed and microwaved. On the plus side, the wine is dry. But it's not going anywhere. Disappointing. **84** —*S.H. (12/1/2007)*

La Crema 2005 Pinot Noir (Russian River Valley) $34. On the soft, heavy side, with flavors of baked cherries, blackberries and cola. Satisfies as basic Pinot Noir, but really lacks the substance and quality you want at this price. **84** —*S.H. (12/1/2007)*

La Crema 2005 Pinot Noir (Anderson Valley) $34. This is the most successful of La Crema's three $34 regional Pinots, because it's the fruitiest, most balanced and most satisfying. It shows expressive cherry, pomegranate, cola and spice flavors, but it's a little soft and one-dimensional. **86** —*S.H. (12/1/2007)*

La Crema 2004 Pinot Noir (Anderson Valley) $29. 87 —*S.H. (11/15/2006)*

La Crema 2004 Pinot Noir (Russian River Valley) $29. 88 —*S.H. (11/15/2006)*

La Crema 2004 Pinot Noir (Carneros) $29. 86 —*S.H. (11/15/2006)*

La Crema 2001 Pinot Noir (Sonoma Coast) $18. 84 —*S.H. (8/1/2003)*

La Crema 2000 Pinot Noir (Russian River Valley) $35. 88 *(10/1/2002)*

La Crema 2000 Pinot Noir (Sonoma Coast) $25. 85 *(10/1/2002)*

La Crema 2000 Pinot Noir (Carneros) $26. 90 Editors' Choice *(10/1/2002)*

La Crema 1999 Pinot Noir (Sonoma Coast) $22. 82 —*J.M. (12/15/2001)*

La Crema 1999 Pinot Noir (Carneros) $35. 87 —*S.H. (12/15/2001)*

La Crema 1998 Pinot Noir (Russian River Valley) $35. 87 —*S.H. (12/15/2001)*

La Crema 2003 Nine Barrels Pinot Noir (Russian River Valley) $75. 92 —*S.H. (12/31/2006)*

La Crema 2006 Rosé Pinot Noir (Russian River Valley) $20. I love the aroma on this pale-colored blush. It's so inviting in raspberry, rosehip tea, licorice, fresh rosemary, lavender and vanilla scents. It's a letdown once you sip, though, due to the sugary sweetness, without which it would be a great rosé. **84** —*S.H. (12/1/2007)*

La Crema 2002 Syrah (Sonoma County) $24. 83 *(9/1/2005)*

La Crema 1999 Syrah (Sonoma County) $24. 91 *(11/1/2001)*

La Crema 2006 Viognier (Sonoma County) $20. If you "talk dry and taste sweet," as they say, you'll like this wine. It's not really dry at all. But it's very rich in tropical fruit, wildflower, honey and spice flavors that are balanced out by good enough acidity. **84** —*S.H. (12/1/2007)*

La Crema 2000 Viognier (Sonoma Valley) $24. 84 —*S.H. (12/15/2001)*

La Crema 1998 Zinfandel (Sonoma County) $19. 86 —*P.G. (3/1/2001)*

LA FAMIGLIA DI ROBERT MONDAVI

La Famiglia di Robert Mondavi 1999 Barbera (California) $19. 86 —*S.H. (12/1/2002)*

La Famiglia di Robert Mondavi 1998 Barbera (California) $20. 85 —*S.H. (11/15/2001)*

La Famiglia di Robert Mondavi 1997 Barbera (California) $20. 87 *—S.H. (9/1/2000)*

La Famiglia di Robert Mondavi 2001 Moscato Bianco Moscato (California) $15. 86 *—S.H. (12/1/2003)*

La Famiglia di Robert Mondavi 1999 Moscato Bianco Moscato (California) $11. 90 *—S.H. (12/31/2000)*

La Famiglia di Robert Mondavi 1997 Pinot Grigio (California) $16. 88 *—M.S. (11/15/1999)*

La Famiglia di Robert Mondavi 1997 Pinot Grigio (California) $16. 87 *—S.H. (10/1/1999)*

La Famiglia di Robert Mondavi 2003 Pinot Grigio (Monterey County) $15. 84 *—S.H. (11/15/2004)*

La Famiglia di Robert Mondavi 2002 Pinot Grigio (California) $15. 84 *—S.H. (8/1/2004)*

La Famiglia di Robert Mondavi 2001 Pinot Grigio (California) $18. 85 *—S.H. (9/1/2003)*

La Famiglia di Robert Mondavi 1999 Pinot Gris (Anderson Valley) $16. 86 *—S.H. (8/1/2001)*

La Famiglia di Robert Mondavi 1997 Colmera Red Table Wine Red Blend (Napa Valley) $40. 89 *—S.H. (9/1/2000)*

La Famiglia di Robert Mondavi 1997 Sangiovese (California) $19. 89 *—S.H. (9/1/2000)*

La Famiglia di Robert Mondavi 1996 Sangiovese (California) $22. 88 *—S.H. (10/1/1999)*

La Famiglia di Robert Mondavi 2000 Sangiovese (California) $20. 87 *—S.H. (9/1/2003)*

La Famiglia di Robert Mondavi 1999 Colmera Sangiovese (Napa Valley) $45. 86 *—S.H. (3/1/2004)*

La Famiglia di Robert Mondavi 1998 Colmera Sangiovese (California) $45. 88 *—S.H. (5/1/2002)*

LA FERME MARTIN

La Ferme Martin 1998 Chardonnay (Long Island) $13. 85 *—J.C. (4/1/2001)*

La Ferme Martin 1998 Merlot (Long Island) $14. 85 *—J.C. (4/1/2001)*

LA FILICE

La Filice 2003 Petite Sirah (Hames Valley) $30. 90 *—S.H. (11/15/2006)*

La Filice 2004 Shell Creek Vineyard Petite Sirah (Paso Robles) $26. Making a balanced, delicious Petite Sirah is hard anywhere, much less in a hot place like Paso Robles, but Filice has risen to the challenge. The wine shows Pet's huge, lush blackberry, boysenberry, plum and coffee fruit, complexed with dark chocolate and seasoned with Asian spices. Yet it remains dry and elegant. This is really great Petite Sirah. **93 Editors' Choice** *—S.H. (11/1/2007)*

La Filice 2004 Convivio Red Blend (Paso Robles) $22. Cabernet Sauvignon brings a tough, tannic hardness to the 77% Syrah that is the majority of this blend. That gives a sandpapery astringency to the ripe, forward cassis, licorice and vanilla-oak flavors. **86** *—S.H. (11/1/2007)*

La Filice 2003 Joseph George Cépage Rhône Red Blend (Paso Robles) $30. 90 *—S.H. (11/1/2006)*

La Filice 2003 Syrah (Paso Robles) $20. 87 *—S.H. (11/15/2006)*

La Filice 2004 Watch Hill Vineyard Syrah (Santa Barbara County) $33. Former Tolosa winemaker Ed Filice is off to a good start with his own brand. This northern Rhône-style Syrah opens with a blast of white pepper, then turns softly tannic in the mouth, with a wealth of blackberry, cassis, blueberry and cedar flavors. Shows great sophistication and complexity. **92** *—S.H. (11/1/2007)*

LA GARZA

La Garza 1999 Cabernet Sauvignon (Oregon) $18. 81 *—C.S. (12/31/2002)*

La Garza 1999 Reserve Cabernet Sauvignon (Oregon) $27. 84 *—C.S. (12/31/2002)*

La Garza 1999 Merlot (Umpqua Valley) $25. 86 *—P.G. (4/1/2002)*

LA JOTA VINEYARD

La Jota Vineyard 2001 Cabernet Franc (Howell Mountain) $62. 91 *—S.H. (11/15/2004)*

La Jota Vineyard 2002 Estate Cabernet Franc (Howell Mountain) $60. It's the essence of cherries in this dry, intensely structured mountain wine. They blended it with 15% Cabernet Sauvignon to add tannic structure, but the cherry pie filling shines through, accented by two thirds new French oak, which adds vanilla and sweet woody char. At nearly five years of age, the wine now has a soft, delicious dynamism that's best now and for another year or two. **92** *—S.H. (10/1/2007)*

La Jota Vineyard 2002 Cabernet Sauvignon (Howell Mountain) $50. Classic Napa mountain Cab, intensely concentrated in fruit, richly tannic, and dry, and of course, such a wine needs and deserves the new oak they lavished on it. Flavors and structure perfectly balance, with massive cherry pie, cassis and mocha flavors meshing with sweetly ripe tannins and rich barrel notes of vanilla and char. This is a dramatic, complex young Cab that will hold for six years. **94** *—S.H. (10/1/2007)*

La Jota Vineyard 2001 Cabernet Sauvignon (Howell Mountain) $52. 91 *—S.H. (10/1/2004)*

La Jota Vineyard 2004 *Barrel Sample* Cabernet Sauvignon (Napa Valley) $NA. 93 *—S.H. (8/1/2004)*

La Jota Vineyard 2002 21st Anniversary Release Cabernet Sauvignon (Howell Mountain) $90. Classic Howell Mountain tannins, powerful and focused, but ripely sweet, frame opulent cherry, cassis, plum sauce and new oak flavors, and for all that, there's a crisp edge of acidity that makes everything clean and bright. Drink now through 2012. **96** *—S.H. (10/1/2007)*

La Jota Vineyard 2001 Anniversary Release Cabernet Sauvignon (Howell Mountain) $93. 93 *—S.H. (10/1/2004)*

La Jota Vineyard 2002 Porcini Hill Cabernet Sauvignon (Yountville) $40. This is just coming into its own. It's still pretty tight and astringent in tannins, but has a major league core of cherry and blackberry fruit, and feels elegant and complex. As balanced as it is, it should continue to develop for 6–8 more years. **92** *—S.H. (10/1/2007)*

La Jota Vineyard 2001 Petite Sirah (Howell Mountain) $46. 88 *—S.H. (11/15/2004)*

LA ROCHELLE

La Rochelle 2001 La Rochelle Vineyard Chardonnay (Monterey) $16. 87 *—S.H. (12/15/2003)*

La Rochelle 2004 Pinot Gris (Arroyo Seco) $24. 89 *—S.H. (12/15/2006)*

La Rochelle 2003 Pinot Noir (Monterey) $18. 90 Editors' Choice *—S.H. (12/15/2006)*

La Rochelle 2003 Pinot Noir (Santa Lucia Highlands) $34. 85 *—S.H. (7/1/2006)*

La Rochelle 2001 Pinot Noir (Monterey) $18. 86 *—S.H. (3/1/2004)*

La Rochelle 2005 Classic Clones Pinot Noir (Arroyo Seco) $42. Here's a big, ripe, dry, complex, voluptuous Pinot that comes from a cool Monterey region better known for dry whites. It shows a nice tension between acidity, silky tannins, charred, sweet oak and bright, pure fruit flavors of cherries, cola and raspberries, with a slightly funky, leathery undertow. **90** *—S.H. (10/1/2007)*

La Rochelle 2003 Classic Clones Pinot Noir (Arroyo Seco) $38. 93 Editors' Choice *—S.H. (7/1/2006)*

La Rochelle 2004 Garys' Vineyard Pinot Noir (Santa Lucia Highlands) $75. Like most Garys' Pinots, this is an enormous wine in both fruit and alcohol. It detonates on the palate with mega-flavors of ripe cherries, raspberries and vanilla cola. Yet it maintains a pure, elegant Pinot Noir silkiness. However, there's a funky, sweaty smell that's a turn-off. **84** *—S.H. (10/1/2007)*

La Rochelle 2001 San Vicente Vineyard Pinot Noir (Monterey) $30. 92 *—S.H. (12/15/2004)*

La Rochelle 2003 San vincente Vineyard Pinot Noir (Monterey) $34. 85 *—S.H. (7/1/2006)*

LA SIRENA

La Sirena 2001 Cabernet Sauvignon (Napa Valley) $125. 93 *—S.H. (11/1/2005)*

La Sirena 2004 Moscato Azul Dry Muscat Canelli (Napa Valley) $28. 90 *—S.H. (11/1/2005)*

La Sirena 2002 Syrah (Santa Ynez Valley) $45. 86 *(9/1/2005)*

La Sirena 2002 Syrah (Napa Valley) $55. 90 *(9/1/2005)*

LA STORIA

La Storia 2002 Zinfandel (Alexander Valley) $28. 88 *—S.H. (3/1/2005)*

La Storia 2001 Zinfandel (Alexander Valley) $30. 89 *(11/1/2003)*

LA TOUR

La Tour 2002 Chardonnay (Napa Valley) $18. 91 *—J.M. (10/1/2004)*

LABYRINTH

Labyrinth 2002 Bien Nacido Vineyard Pinot Noir (Santa Maria Valley) $28. 85 *—S.H. (10/1/2005)*

LACHINI

Lachini 2005 Pinot Gris (Oregon) $18. Here's a very seductive Pinot Gris, done in the soft, plush style that Oregon is best at. Smooth and supple, it's got a good mix of apple and pear, the flavors suggesting spicy tart more than fresh cut fruit. Excellent definition and pure pleasure in the mouth. **90** *—P.G. (2/1/2007)*

Lachini 2002 Pinot Noir (Willamette Valley) $30. 88 *(11/1/2004)*

Lachini 2004 Ana Vineyard Pinot Noir (Willamette Valley) $42. This comes from an older vineyard planted to Pommard clone Pinot Noir, and yielded less than a ton an acre in 2004. It is a wine that needs more time to pull itself together; all the right components are there but they are a bit disjointed. The center stage is the sweet, creamy core of the wine—wild berries and vanilla crème. With time it should rope in the still-ragged edges and merit a higher score. **89** *—P.G. (2/1/2007)*

Lachini 2004 Cuvée Giselle Pinot Noir (Willamette Valley) $55. Cuvée Giselle is the top four barrels from the vintage; essentially the winery's reserve. It's not always easy to spot the difference that the winemaker, who tastes the barrels almost daily, has observed. This is an excellent wine, though to my taste the Family Estate bottling showed even more concentration. Here there is more of the pine resin, perhaps more elegance and structure, but less of the sharp acid and pristine fruit. **90** *—P.G. (2/1/2007)*

Lachini 2004 Lachini Vineyards Family Estate Pinot Noir (Willamette Valley) $42. The best wine this estate made in 2004, this is comprised of half Pommard/half Dijon clones, aged a full year in French oak, but only one fifth new. It's quite young and tight, with snappy flavors of bright raspberry and pomegranate. Sharp, etched, almost laser-like in clarity, this beautifully structured and focused effort opens into aromas of wild berry, gravel and earth. Definitely a wine to put away for a few years. **91 Cellar Selection** *—P.G. (2/1/2007)*

Lachini 2002 Lachini Family Estate Pinot Noir (Willamette Valley) $35. 87 *(11/1/2004)*

Lachini 2003 LV Estate Pinot Noir (Willamette Valley) $36. 90 *—P.G. (11/15/2005)*

Lachini 2004 S Pinot Noir (Willamette Valley) $40. Lachini's S is a remarkable wine, broad and lush, heavily extracted, and plump with ripe strawberry fruit. Succulent, thick and chocolaty, it supports its ripe power with underpinnings of tart acid, a combination of voluptuous fruit and snappy acid that really keeps the palate fresh and waiting for the next sip. **90 Editors' Choice** *—P.G. (2/1/2007)*

Lachini 2003 S Pinot Noir (Willamette Valley) $34. 91 Editors' Choice *—P.G. (11/15/2005)*

LADERA

Ladera 2004 Cabernet Sauvignon (Howell Mountain) $70. The elements of great Cab are all here, from the rich, mountain-dense tannins to the gorgeously ripe blackberry, cassis and fig flavors that are enriched by lots of new, flashy oak. But there's a sweaty funk in the aroma that's off-putting, and makes you wonder. **86** *—S.H. (10/1/2007)*

Ladera 2003 Cabernet Sauvignon (Howell Mountain) $68. 87 *—S.H. (12/15/2006)*

Ladera 2003 Cabernet Sauvignon (Napa Valley) $35. 90 *—S.H. (12/15/2006)*

Ladera 2002 Cabernet Sauvignon (Howell Mountain) $65. 92 Cellar Selection *—S.H. (12/1/2005)*

Ladera 2001 Cabernet Sauvignon (Howell Mountain) $65. 92 *—S.H. (3/1/2005)*

Ladera 2003 Lone Canyon Vineyard Cabernet Sauvignon (Napa Valley) $65. Ripe and tasty, with cassis, cherries and sweet new oak flavors. But it has a sweaty, funky smell, and is excessively soft, making the wine melted and flat. **84** *—S.H. (10/1/2007)*

Ladera 2001 Lone Canyon Vineyard Cabernet Sauvignon (Napa Valley) $65. 89 *—S.H. (12/1/2005)*

Ladera 2002 Lone Mountain Vineyard Cabernet Sauvignon (Napa Valley) $65. 93 Cellar Selection *—S.H. (5/1/2006)*

LADY GRACE

Lady Grace 2006 Verdelho (Lodi) $16. On the rustic side, with medicinal lemon cough drop flavors. On the other hand, the dryness and savory crispness argue in its favor. Pretty good, but overpriced for what you get. **84** *—S.H. (9/1/2007)*

LADYBUG

Ladybug NV Red Old Vines Cuvée VI Red Table Wine Red Blend (Redwood Valley) $13. Comprised of Zinfandel, Carignan, Cabernet Sauvignon and Merlot, this is a rustically structured wine whose best features are dryness and fruitiness. Easy and charming for everyday foods. **85** *—S.H. (10/1/2007)*

Ladybug NV Old Vines Cuvée 11 White Table Wine White Blend (Mendocino) $13. 83 *—S.H. (12/1/2006)*

Ladybug NV White Old Vines White Blend (Mendocino) $13. Good everyday dry white, clean and zesty in juicy acids, with citrus fruit and spice flavors and a fine vinosity. An interesting blend of French Columbard, Semillon, Chenin Blanc and Chardonnay. **86** *—S.H. (9/1/2007)*

Ladybug NV White Old Vines White Blend (Mendocino) $13. 84 *—S.H. (12/1/2005)*

LAETITIA

Laetitia NV Brut Cuvée Champagne Blend (Arroyo Grande Valley) $20. 88 Editors' Choice *—M.M. (12/1/2001)*

Laetitia 1997 Brut Rosé Champagne Blend (Arroyo Grande Valley) $28. 90 *—J.M. (12/1/2001)*

Laetitia 1997 Cuvée M Champagne Blend (Arroyo Grande Valley) $28. 88 *—J.M. (12/1/2001)*

Laetitia 1994 Cuvée M Champagne Blend (Arroyo Grande Valley) $30. 86 *(12/31/2000)*

Laetitia 2004 Chardonnay (Arroyo Grande Valley) $16. 92 Editors' Choice *—S.H. (12/31/2005)*

Laetitia 2003 Chardonnay (Arroyo Grande Valley) $16. 88 *—S.H. (2/1/2005)*

Laetitia 2005 Estate Chardonnay (Arroyo Grande Valley) $18. Dry, oaky and tart in citrus and tropical fruits, this Chard teeters on the edge of everyday drinkability and white tablecloth sophistication. The layers of buttercream, crème brûlée and vanilla custard tilt the balance toward elegance. **90** *—S.H. (11/1/2007)*

Laetitia 2001 Estate Chardonnay (Arroyo Grande Valley) $18. 90 Editors' Choice *—S.H. (5/1/2003)*

Laetitia 1998 Estate Chardonnay (Arroyo Grande Valley) $18. 88 *(6/1/2000)*

Laetitia 1997 Estate Reserve Chardonnay (Arroyo Grande Valley) $26. 92 *—L.W. (11/15/1999)*

Laetitia 2000 Reserve Chardonnay (Arroyo Grande Valley) $26. 85 *—S.H. (12/15/2003)*

Laetitia 1998 Reserve Chardonnay (Arroyo Grande Valley) $33. 89 *(7/1/2001)*

Laetitia 1998 Winemaker's Select Chardonnay (Edna Valley) $18. 88 *(6/1/2000)*

Laetitia 2004 Pinot Blanc (Arroyo Grande Valley) $16. 88 *—S.H. (12/31/2005)*

Laetitia 2000 Pinot Blanc (Arroyo Grande Valley) $19. 86 *—S.H. (9/1/2003)*

Laetitia 2005 Estate Pinot Blanc (Arroyo Grande Valley) $16. Feels creamy, full-bodied and rich like Burgundy-inspired Chardonnay, but the flavor profile is different, with a buttery, cashew opulence to the tangerine, nectarine, peach and oak flavors. Try this as a sophisticated alternative to Chard. **89** *—S.H. (11/1/2007)*

Laetitia 1999 Estate Pinot Blanc (Arroyo Grande Valley) $16. 90 Editors' Choice *—S.H. (11/15/2001)*

Laetitia 2001 Pinot Noir (Arroyo Grande Valley) $25. 90 *—S.H. (3/1/2004)*

Laetitia 2000 Pinot Noir (Arroyo Grande Valley) $25. 87 *(10/1/2002)*

Laetitia 1999 Pinot Noir (San Luis Obispo County) $25. 89 *(10/1/2002)*

Laetitia 1999 Pinot Noir (Santa Barbara County) $25. 91 *—J.M. (7/1/2002)*

Laetitia 2003 Estate Pinot Noir (Arroyo Grande Valley) $25. 89 *—S.H. (10/1/2005)*

Laetitia 2002 Estate Pinot Noir (Arroyo Grande Valley) $25. 88 *—S.H. (11/1/2004)*

Laetitia 1997 Estate Pinot Noir (Arroyo Grande Valley) $23. 89 *(11/15/1999)*

Laetitia 2000 Estate Reserve Pinot Noir (Arroyo Grande Valley) $35. 88 *—S.H. (7/1/2003)*

Laetitia 1999 Estate Reserve Pinot Noir (Arroyo Grande Valley) $47. 88 *(10/1/2002)*

Laetitia 1997 Estate Reserve Pinot Noir (Arroyo Grande Valley) $33. 91 *(10/1/1999)*

Laetitia 2004 La Colline Pinot Noir (Arroyo Grande Valley) $60. 96 *—S.H. (7/1/2006)*

Laetitia 2003 La Colline Pinot Noir (Arroyo Grande Valley) $60. 95 Editors' Choice *—S.H. (12/1/2005)*

Laetitia 2002 La Colline Pinot Noir (Arroyo Grande Valley) $60. 92 *—S.H. (2/1/2005)*

Laetitia 2001 La Colline Pinot Noir (Arroyo Grande Valley) $60. 90 *—S.H. (6/1/2004)*

Laetitia 1999 La Colline Pinot Noir (Arroyo Grande Valley) $60. 92 Cellar Selection *(10/1/2002)*

Laetitia 1999 La Colline Pinot Noir (Arroyo Grande Valley) $NA. 89 *—S.H. (9/1/2003)*

Laetitia 2005 Les Galets Pinot Noir (Arroyo Grande Valley) $60. A sensational Pinot Noir for its complexity, ageability and sheer deliciousness. The parts haven't come together yet, but each is great. Smoky new oak dominates, closely followed by enormously ripe crushed cherry, blackberry, pomegranate, cola and mocha flavors. There's a rich tannin-acid structure, and the sweet, spicy oak reprises on the finish. This big, masculine wine needs time to come together. Should open by 2008 and increase in desirability for a number of years. **96 Editors' Choice** *—S.H. (11/1/2007)*

Laetitia 2004 Les Galets Pinot Noir (Arroyo Grande Valley) $60. 93 *—S.H. (11/1/2006)*

Laetitia 2003 Les Galets Pinot Noir (Arroyo Grande Valley) $60. 95 *—S.H. (12/1/2005)*

Laetitia 2002 Les Galets Pinot Noir (Arroyo Grande Valley) $60. 92 *—S.H. (2/1/2005)*

Laetitia 2001 Les Galets Pinot Noir (Arroyo Grande Valley) $60. 92 *—S.H. (6/1/2004)*

Laetitia 2005 Reserve Pinot Noir (Arroyo Grande Valley) $40. This is a big, bold Pinot Noir. It has a weight and density that are almost Rhône-like, with flavors of mashed cherries and blackberries, mixed with cola and sprinkled with cinnamon, cocoa and star anise. It feels luxuriously smooth in the mouth, with an impressively long finish. Best to give this gigantic young wine time in the cellar. Hold until 2008 or 2009, at least. **92 Cellar Selection** *—S.H. (11/1/2007)*

Laetitia 2003 Reserve Pinot Noir (Arroyo Grande Valley) $40. 92 *—S.H. (12/1/2005)*

Laetitia 2002 Reserve Pinot Noir (Arroyo Grande Valley) $40. 90 *—S.H. (2/1/2005)*

Laetitia 2001 Reserve Pinot Noir (Arroyo Grande Valley) $40. 91 *—S.H. (12/15/2004)*

Laetitia 2000 Brut Cocquard Sparkling Blend (Arroyo Grande Valley) $25. 87 *—J.M. (12/1/2003)*

Laetitia 2000 Brut Coquard Sparkling Blend (Arroyo Grande Valley) $25. 90 *—S.H. (5/1/2004)*

Laetitia NV Brut Cuvée Sparkling Blend (San Luis Obispo County) $16. 85 *—S.H. (6/1/2004)*

Laetitia NV Brut Cuvée Sparkling Blend (Arroyo Grande Valley) $18. 86 *—S.H. (12/31/2005)*

Laetitia NV Brut Cuvée Sparkling Blend (Arroyo Grande Valley) $18. 86 *—S.H. (12/31/2006)*

Laetitia NV Brut Cuvée (San Luis Obispo/Santa Barbara Counties) Sparkling Blend (Central Coast) $16. 86 *—J.M. (12/1/2003)*

Laetitia 2002 Brut de Blanc Sparkling Blend (Arroyo Grande Valley) $25. 87 *—S.H. (12/31/2005)*

Laetitia 2003 Brut de Blancs Sparkling Blend (Arroyo Grande Valley) $25. 90 *—S.H. (12/31/2006)*

Laetitia 2001 Brut de Noir Sparkling Blend (Arroyo Grande Valley) $25. 88 *—S.H. (12/31/2005)*

Laetitia NV Brut Rosé Sparkling Blend (Arroyo Grande Valley) $25. Absolutely, compulsively delicious. Totally a California-style bubbly, it's dazzlingly rich in cherry, raspberry, brioche, vanilla and spice flavors, with crisply sharp acids for balance, and a satisfying dosage for softness. Pinot Noir, Chardonnay and Pinot Blanc. **93 Editors' Choice** *—S.H. (7/1/2007)*

Laetitia 2000 Brut Rosé Sparkling Blend (Arroyo Grande Valley) $25. 87 *—J.M. (12/1/2003)*

Laetitia 2002 Cuvée M Sparkling Blend (Arroyo Grande Valley) $30. 92 *—S.H. (12/31/2006)*

Laetitia 2003 Syrah (Arroyo Grande Valley) $25. 92 *—S.H. (12/31/2005)*

Laetitia 2000 Syrah (Santa Barbara County) $25. 85 *—S.H. (3/1/2004)*

LAFOND

Lafond 1998 Lafond Vineyard Chardonnay (Santa Ynez Valley) $30. 87 *(7/1/2001)*

Lafond 1997 Lafond Vineyard Chardonnay (Santa Ynez Valley) $28. 90 *(6/1/2000)*

Lafond 2004 SRH Chardonnay (Santa Rita Hills) $20. 92 Editors' Choice *—S.H. (11/1/2006)*

Lafond 1997 Sweeney Canyon Chardonnay (Santa Ynez Valley) $28. 87 *(6/1/2000)*

Lafond 2000 Sweeny Canyon Vineyard Chardonnay (Santa Ynez Valley) $28. 92 *—S.H. (10/1/2003)*

Lafond 2003 Lafond Vineyard Pinot Noir (Santa Rita Hills) $48. 86 *—S.H. (11/1/2006)*

Lafond 2000 Lafond Vineyard Pinot Noir (Santa Ynez Valley) $35. 86 *—S.H. (2/1/2004)*

Lafond 1999 Lafond Vineyard Pinot Noir (Santa Ynez Valley) $35. 88 *(10/1/2002)*

Lafond 1997 Lafond Vineyard Pinot Noir (Santa Ynez Valley) $35. 82 *—S.H. (2/1/2001)*

Lafond 2004 SRH Pinot Noir (Santa Rita Hills) $24. 84 *—S.H. (11/1/2006)*

Lafond 2000 SRH Pinot Noir (Santa Ynez Valley) $18. 86 *—S.H. (2/1/2003)*

Lafond 2000 Joughin Vineyard Syrah (Santa Ynez Valley) $30. 86 *—S.H. (3/1/2004)*

Lafond 2000 Lafond Vineyard Syrah (Santa Ynez Valley) $30. 86 *—S.H. (3/1/2004)*

Lafond 1998 Lafond Vineyard Syrah (Santa Ynez Valley) $28. 90 *(11/1/2001)*

Lafond 2000 Melville Vineyard Syrah (Santa Ynez Valley) $30. 86 *—S.H. (3/1/2004)*

Lafond 2004 SRH Syrah (Santa Rita Hills) $18. 91 *—S.H. (11/1/2006)*

Lafond 2000 SRH Syrah (Santa Ynez Valley) $18. 89 *—S.H. (12/1/2002)*

Lafond 1998 Stolpman Vineyard Syrah (Santa Ynez Valley) $28. 89 *—S.H. (7/1/2002)*

LAGIER MEREDITH

Lagier Meredith 2000 Syrah (Mount Veeder) $50. 88 *—S.H. (2/1/2004)*

Lagier Meredith 1999 Syrah (Mount Veeder) $50. 93 *—S.H. (12/1/2002)*

LAGO DI MERLO

Lago di Merlo 2001 Sangiovese (Dry Creek Valley) $19. 84 *—S.H. (11/1/2005)*

LAIL

Lail 2004 Blueprint Bordeaux Blend (Napa Valley) $45. This is very good in a Napa-does-Bordeaux style, soft and fruity, with black currant, cherry liqueur and new oak flavors wrapped into brisk tannins. **88** *—S.H. (12/1/2007)*

Lail 1997 J. Daniel Cuvée Bordeaux Blend (Napa Valley) $75. 93 *(11/1/2000)*

Lail 2004 J. Daniel Cuvée Cabernet Sauvignon (Napa Valley) $110. This is what people who pay a hundred bucks for a Napa Cab expect. Soft, ripe and enormously attractive, it seduces the palate with gooey red and black currant, cherry, blueberry, melted Swiss chocolate, anise and cedar flavors that just pile up and up and go on and on. The tannins, needless to say, are the finest money can buy. It's impossible not to be impressed by a wine of this pedigree and accomplishment. Probably at its succulent best now and for the next six years. **94** *—S.H. (8/1/2007)*

Lail 2001 J. Daniel Cuvée Cabernet Sauvignon (Napa Valley) $80. 92 *—S.H. (10/1/2004)*

Lail 2000 J. Daniel Cuvée Cabernet Sauvignon (Napa Valley) $80. 86 *—S.H. (5/1/2004)*

Lail 1999 J. Daniel Cuvée Cabernet Sauvignon (Napa Valley) $80. 95 Editors' Choice *—S.H. (11/15/2002)*

Lail 1998 J. Daniel Cuvée Cabernet Sauvignon (Napa Valley) $75. 93 *—S.H. (6/1/2002)*

Lail 2003 Blueprint Cabernet Sauvignon-Merlot (Napa Valley) $45. 90 *—S.H. (7/1/2006)*

Lail 2002 Blueprint Merlot-Cabernet Sauvignon (Napa Valley) $45. 93 Editors' Choice *—S.H. (11/1/2005)*

Lail 2001 Blueprint Merlot-Cabernet Sauvignon (Napa Valley) $45. 87 *—S.H. (10/1/2004)*

LAIRD

Laird 2000 Cabernet Sauvignon (Napa Valley) $60. 82 *—S.H. (8/1/2005)*

Laird 1999 Laird Family Estate Cabernet Sauvignon (Napa Valley) $65. 88 *—M.S. (11/15/2002)*

Laird 1999 Rutherford Ranch Cabernet Sauvignon (Rutherford) $75. 91 *—D.T. (6/1/2002)*

Laird 2002 Chardonnay (Carneros) $30. 84 *—S.H. (8/1/2005)*

Laird 1999 Chardonnay (Napa Valley) $40. 88 *(7/1/2001)*

Laird 1999 Cold Creek Chardonnay (Carneros) $44. 89 *(7/1/2001)*

Laird 2004 Cold Creek Ranch Pinot Grigio (Carneros) $16. 88 —*S.H. (2/1/2006)*

LAKE MISSOULA

Lake Missoula 2002 Deluge Red Wine Cabernet Blend (Yakima Valley) $40. 92 —*P.G. (8/1/2006)*

Lake Missoula 2003 Deluge Red Blend (Yakima Valley) $40. Kestrel vineyard grapes (75% Cabernet Sauvignon-25% Cabernet Franc) are sourced to make this wine. This follow-up to the inaugral 2002 seems tannic, hard, and volatile. Give it plenty of air and it smoothes out some, but still hits that hard, green, tannic wall. Chewy, highly astringent and disjointed. The plastic cork seems out of place in a wine at this price point. **86** —*P.G. (11/1/2007)*

LAKE SONOMA

Lake Sonoma 2003 Cabernet Sauvignon (Alexander Valley) $22. If you're teaching a course on Alexander Valley Cab, consider this as your textbook example. It's a beautifully drinkable wine, soft and gentle and complex. The blackberry fruit has an herbal, earthy edge, and the wine is very dry. You can even age it for ten years if you want, but it's best now. **89** —*S.H. (3/1/2007)*

Lake Sonoma 2002 Cabernet Sauvignon (Alexander Valley) $22.82 —*S.H. (10/1/2006)*

Lake Sonoma 2001 Cabernet Sauvignon (Alexander Valley) $22. 82 —*S.H. (12/15/2005)*

Lake Sonoma 2000 Cabernet Sauvignon (Alexander Valley) $22. 89 —*S.H. (8/1/2004)*

Lake Sonoma 1999 Cabernet Sauvignon (Alexander Valley) $22. 86 —*S.H. (10/1/2003)*

Lake Sonoma 1998 Cabernet Sauvignon (Alexander Valley) $21. 91 —*S.H. (6/1/2002)*

Lake Sonoma 2006 Chardonnay (Russian River Valley) $18. A little soft and candied in its oaky pineapple, applesauce and buttered-popcorn flavors, but easy to drink. Chardonnay admirers will recognize a distinctively Californian interpretation of the variety. **85** —*S.H. (12/31/2007)*

Lake Sonoma 2005 Chardonnay (Russian River Valley) $16. 85 —*S.H. (12/31/2006)*

Lake Sonoma 2004 Chardonnay (Russian River Valley) $16. 83 —*S.H. (12/15/2005)*

Lake Sonoma 2003 Chardonnay (Russian River Valley) $15. 85 —*S.H. (3/1/2005)*

Lake Sonoma 2002 Chardonnay (Russian River Valley) $15. 86 —*S.H. (6/1/2004)*

Lake Sonoma 2001 Chardonnay (Russian River Valley) $15. 86 —*S.H. (7/1/2003)*

Lake Sonoma 2000 Chardonnay (Russian River Valley) $15. 84 —*J.M. (12/15/2002)*

Lake Sonoma 1999 Chardonnay (Russian River Valley) $15. 87 —*J.M. (11/15/2001)*

Lake Sonoma 1998 Chardonnay (Russian River Valley) $17. 88 *(6/1/2000)*

Lake Sonoma 2000 Heck Family Cellar Selection Chardonnay (Russian River Valley) $11. 86 —*S.H. (5/1/2003)*

Lake Sonoma 2004 Fumé Blanc (Dry Creek Valley) $16. 85 —*S.H. (5/1/2006)*

Lake Sonoma 2003 Fumé Blanc (Dry Creek Valley) $14. 88 Best Buy —*S.H. (3/1/2005)*

Lake Sonoma 2002 Fumé Blanc (Dry Creek Valley) $14. 87 —*S.H. (2/1/2004)*

Lake Sonoma 2006 Sauvignon Blanc (Dry Creek Valley) $15. A fine Sauvignon Blanc, dry and quite crisp, with the kind of acidity that gets your tastebuds zinging. The flavors are very rich, of citrus fruits, gooseberries, dates, green melons and an unusual tang of Chinese five spice. **89** —*S.H. (11/15/2007)*

Lake Sonoma 2005 Sauvignon Blanc (Dry Creek Valley) $16. 85 —*S.H. (12/15/2006)*

Lake Sonoma 2003 Zinfandel (Dry Creek Valley) $18. 88 —*S.H. (7/1/2006)*

Lake Sonoma 2002 Zinfandel (Dry Creek Valley) $16. 84 —*S.H. (10/1/2005)*

Lake Sonoma 2001 Zinfandel (Dry Creek Valley) $17. 87 *(11/1/2003)*

Lake Sonoma 2000 Zinfandel (Russian River Valley) $22. 90 —*S.H. (3/1/2003)*

Lake Sonoma 2000 Zinfandel (Dry Creek Valley) $17. 86 —*S.H. (3/1/2003)*

Lake Sonoma 1999 Zinfandel (Dry Creek Valley) $15. 85 —*J.M. (3/1/2002)*

Lake Sonoma 1998 Zinfandel (Dry Creek Valley) $15. 84 *(3/1/2001)*

Lake Sonoma 1997 Old Vine Zinfandel (Sonoma County) $17. 91 Editors' Choice —*P.G. (3/1/2001)*

Lake Sonoma 2004 Saini Farms Old Vine Zinfandel (Dry Creek Valley) $22. Tasted alongside another 2004 Zin sourced from the same vineyard; that wine was overripe and raisiny. This one isn't. It's certainly a ripe wine, bursting with cherry, blackberry, plum and carob flavors, but has a polished balance. It's a classic Zinfandel, dry, smooth and complex. **88** —*S.H. (6/1/2007)*

Lake Sonoma 2002 Saini Farms Old Vine Zinfandel (Dry Creek Valley) $20. 84 —*S.H. (10/1/2005)*

Lake Sonoma 2001 Saini Farms Old Vine Zinfandel (Dry Creek Valley) $24. 88 *(11/1/2003)*

Lake Sonoma 2000 Saini Farms Old Vine Zinfandel (Dry Creek Valley) $20. 85 —*S.H. (9/1/2003)*

Lake Sonoma 1999 Saini Farms Old Vine Zinfandel (Dry Creek Valley) $20. 89 —*J.M. (11/1/2002)*

Lake Sonoma 1998 Saini Farms Old Vine Zinfandel (Dry Creek Valley) $24. 86 —*J.M. (11/15/2001)*

LAMBERT BRIDGE

Lambert Bridge 1998 Crane Creek Cuvée Bordeaux Blend (Dry Creek Valley) $50. 92 —*S.H. (6/1/2002)*

Lambert Bridge 2002 Crane Creek Cuvée Bordeaux Blend (Dry Creek Valley) $70. 91 —*S.H. (11/1/2005)*

Lambert Bridge 1999 Crane Creek Cuvée Cabernet Blend (Dry Creek Valley) $50. 88 —*S.H. (5/1/2003)*

Lambert Bridge 2002 Chardonnay (Sonoma County) $20. 86 —*S.H. (3/1/2005)*

Lambert Bridge 2001 Chardonnay (Sonoma County) $20. 85 —*S.H. (12/1/2003)*

Lambert Bridge 2000 Chardonnay (Sonoma County) $20. 88 —*J.M. (12/15/2002)*

Lambert Bridge 1999 Chardonnay (Sonoma County) $20. 89 —*J.M. (11/15/2001)*

Lambert Bridge 1998 Chardonnay (Sonoma County) $18. 89 *(6/1/2000)*

Lambert Bridge 1997 Chardonnay (Sonoma County) $18. 87 —*S.H. (2/1/2000)*

Lambert Bridge 1997 Chardonnay (Dry Creek Valley) $24. 90 —*L.W. (10/1/1999)*

Lambert Bridge 2002 Merlot (Sonoma County) $26. 90 —*S.H. (11/1/2005)*

Lambert Bridge 2000 Merlot (Sonoma County) $24. 85 —*S.H. (12/15/2003)*

Lambert Bridge 1999 Merlot (Sonoma County) $24. 92 Editors' Choice —*S.H. (7/1/2002)*

Lambert Bridge 1997 Merlot (Sonoma County) $22. 85 —*S.H. (3/1/2000)*

Lambert Bridge 2000 Old Vine Cuvée, Bacchi Vineyards Red Blend (Russian River Valley) $32. 87 —*J.M. (11/15/2002)*

Lambert Bridge 2003 Sauvignon Blanc (Dry Creek Valley) $16. 87 —*S.H. (11/1/2005)*

Lambert Bridge 2001 Sauvignon Blanc (Dry Creek Valley) $16. 85 —*J.M. (9/1/2003)*

Lambert Bridge 1998 Sauvignon Blanc (Dry Creek Valley) $14. 90 Best Buy *(3/1/1999)*

Lambert Bridge 2000 Dry Creek Sauvignon Blanc (Dry Creek Valley) $16. 85 *(9/1/2003)*

Lambert Bridge 2003 Viognier (Placer County) $20. 87 —*S.H. (12/15/2004)*

Lambert Bridge 2000 Viognier (Placer County) $20. 88 —*J.M. (11/15/2001)*

Lambert Bridge 2001 Damiano Viognier (Sierra Foothills) $20. 87 —*J.M. (12/15/2002)*

Lambert Bridge 2003 Damiano Vineyards Viognier (Placer County) $20. 88 —*S.H. (2/1/2005)*

Lambert Bridge 2001 Zinfandel (Dry Creek Valley) $24. 87 *(11/1/2003)*

Lambert Bridge 2000 Zinfandel (Dry Creek Valley) $24. 84 —*S.H. (11/1/2002)*

Lambert Bridge 1999 Zinfandel (Dry Creek Valley) $22. 88 —*S.H. (12/15/2001)*

Lambert Bridge 1997 Dry Creek Valley Zinfandel (Dry Creek Valley) $22. 91 —*L.W. (9/1/1999)*

LAMBORN FAMILY VINEYARDS

Lamborn Family Vineyards 2001 The Cork Report Zinfandel (Howell Mountain) $30. 90 *(11/1/2003)*

LAMOREAUX LANDING

Lamoreaux Landing NV Pinot Noir (Finger Lakes) $12. 87 *(11/15/1999)*

Lamoreaux Landing 2000 Pinot Noir (Finger Lakes) $15. 84 *(10/1/2002)*

LANCASTER

Lancaster 1999 Estate Bottled Bordeaux Blend (Alexander Valley) $65. 89 *(10/1/2003)*

Lancaster 1997 Reserve Bordeaux Blend (Sonoma County) $65. 92 *(11/1/2000)*

Lancaster 2002 Estate Red Wine Cabernet Blend (Alexander Valley) $70. 90 *—S.H. (12/15/2005)*

Lancaster 2004 Cabernet Sauvignon (Alexander Valley) $65. Lancaster burst on the scene with enormous buzz, perhaps before they had really earned it. Steadily but surely, they've built up the wine, and the '04 is the best ever. It's a gorgeous Cab, softly complex, rich in cassis, cherry, spice and oak flavors anchored with warm, earthy tannins. In fact, the earthiness stands it in good contrast to Napa Valley, making it wholesome and complete. **97 Editors' Choice** *—S.H. (12/1/2007)*

Lancaster 2003 Estate Cabernet Sauvignon (Alexander Valley) $65. A challenging wine, made all the more so because there's a beautiful entry and the wine has truly delicious aspects. It's softly complex and beguiling, with cherry custard, vanilla and smoky oak flavors, and shows real finesse. On the other hand, the short finish suggests it's not going anywhere, so drink up. **89** *—S.H. (8/1/2007)*

Lancaster 2001 Red Blend (Alexander Valley) $65. 89 *—S.H. (5/1/2005)*

LANDMARK

Landmark 2004 Damaris Reserve Chardonnay (Sonoma Valley) $36. 83 *—S.H. (12/31/2006)*

Landmark 2001 Damaris Reserve Chardonnay (Sonoma) $30. 92 Editors' Choice *—S.H. (2/1/2004)*

Landmark 1998 Damaris Reserve Chardonnay (Sonoma County) $32. 86 *(10/1/2000)*

Landmark 1998 Damaris Reserve Chardonnay (California) $32. 89 *(7/1/2001)*

Landmark 2002 Damaris Reserve Bien Nacido Vineyard Chardonnay (Santa Maria Valley) $34. 89 *—S.H. (8/1/2005)*

Landmark 2002 Lorenzo Chardonnay (Russian River Valley) $45. 87 *—S.H. (8/1/2005)*

Landmark 2001 Lorenzo Chardonnay (Russian River Valley) $45. 92 *—S.H. (5/1/2004)*

Landmark 2005 Overlook Chardonnay (Sonoma County-Monterey County-Santa Barbara County) $26. Fruit from more than 20 vineyards went into this three-county blend. The result is a beautiful wine. Dry and spicy, it has lush pineapple, vanilla custard, tapioca, peaches and cream and gingerbread flavors, and a lush, creamy texture. Notable also for the crisp, brisk mouthfeel. **90** *—S.H. (8/1/2007)*

Landmark 2004 Overlook Chardonnay (Sonoma County-Monterey County-Santa Barbara County) $26. 91 Editors' Choice *—S.H. (5/1/2006)*

Landmark 2001 Overlook Chardonnay (Sonoma) $25. 87 *—S.H. (12/15/2003)*

Landmark 2000 Overlook Chardonnay (Sonoma County) $25. 91 *—S.H. (2/1/2003)*

Landmark 1998 Overlook Chardonnay (Sonoma County) $22. 85 *(6/1/2000)*

Landmark 2003 Overlook (Sonoma-Monterey-Santa Barbara) Chardonnay (California) $25. 90 Editors' Choice *—S.H. (8/1/2005)*

Landmark 2005 Grand Detour Pinot Noir (Sonoma Coast) $30. I love this Pinot for its dry silkiness, fruit, and the way it's so complex and ever-changing in the glass. Cherries, raspberries, cola, plum skin, mocha and dusty Asian spice are the elementary flavors, amplified by rich oak, but it's not a fruit bomb. It's elegant and complex, exemplifying cool climate California in a great vintage. **93 Editors' Choice** *—S.H. (8/1/2007)*

Landmark 2001 Grand Detour Van der Kamp Pinot Noir (Sonoma Mountain) $30. 88 *—S.H. (10/1/2005)*

Landmark 1999 Grand Detour Van der Kamp Pinot Noir (Sonoma Mountain) $45. 86 *(10/1/2002)*

Landmark 1997 Grand Detour Van der Kamp Pinot Noir (Sonoma Mountain) $34. 91 *(10/1/1999)*

Landmark 2001 Kastania Pinot Noir (Sonoma Coast) $45. 86 *—S.H. (10/1/2005)*

Landmark 1999 Kastania Vineyard Pinot Noir (Sonoma Coast) $45. 89 *(10/1/2002)*

Landmark 2003 Steel Plow Syrah (Sonoma Valley) $25. 85 *—S.H. (12/31/2006)*

Landmark 2002 Steel Plow Syrah (Sonoma County) $23. 90 Editors' Choice *(9/1/2005)*

LANE TANNER

Lane Tanner 2005 Pinot Noir (Santa Barbara County) $24. The winemaker added a little Syrah "to round it out," and there does seem to be a depth and richness of chocolate and violets to this cherry-flavored wine. It's not a blockbuster or an ager, but a soft, beautifully silky Pinot for immediate enjoyment. **87** *—S.H. (7/1/2007)*

Lane Tanner 2000 Pinot Noir (Santa Maria Valley) $22. 87 *—S.H. (7/1/2003)*

Lane Tanner 2005 Bien Nacido Vineyard Pinot Noir (Santa Maria Valley) $30. Dry and firm in tannins, this is structured, with opulent cherry pie and new smoky oak. It's an early drinker. Best now—2008 for freshness. **91** *—S.H. (7/1/2007)*

Lane Tanner 2002 Bien Nacido Vineyard Pinot Noir (Santa Maria Valley) $28. 88 *—S.H. (10/1/2005)*

Lane Tanner 2000 Bien Nacido Vineyard Pinot Noir (Santa Maria Valley) $28. 91 Editors' Choice *—S.H. (7/1/2003)*

Lane Tanner 1999 Bien Nacido Vineyard Pinot Noir (Santa Maria Valley) $25. 93 *(12/31/2001)*

Lane Tanner 2005 Julia's Vineyard Pinot Noir (Santa Maria Valley) $33. The year 2005 was great for South-Central Coast Pinot. This is what winemaker Tanner calls a "yum-yum" wine. It is indeed yummy in cherry pie, root beer, cola, mocha and woodspice flavors. Drink soon to capture that essential deliciousness. **90** *—S.H. (7/1/2007)*

Lane Tanner 2003 Julia's Vineyard Pinot Noir (Santa Maria Valley) $30. 86 *—S.H. (10/1/2005)*

Lane Tanner 2000 Julia's Vineyard Pinot Noir (Santa Maria Valley) $30. 89 *(10/1/2002)*

Lane Tanner 2002 Melville Vineyard Pinot Noir (Santa Rita Hills) $25. 93 Editors' Choice *—S.H. (10/1/2005)*

Lane Tanner 2000 Melville Vineyard Pinot Noir (Santa Ynez Valley) $25. 90 Editors' Choice *(10/1/2002)*

Lane Tanner 1997 Syrah (San Luis Obispo County) $20. 88 *—S.H. (10/1/1999)*

Lane Tanner 2004 French Camp Vineyard Syrah (San Luis Obispo County) $21. Nice Syrah, dry and fruity, with a peppery edge to the blackberry, raspberry, coffee and roasted meat bone flavors. There's a rusticity to the tannins, which are gritty and chewy. **86** *—S.H. (7/1/2007)*

Lane Tanner 2002 French Camp Vineyard Syrah (San Luis Obispo County) $20. 84 *(9/1/2005)*

Lane Tanner 2000 French Camp Vineyard Syrah (San Luis Obispo County) $20. 89 *—S.H. (9/1/2002)*

Lane Tanner 1997 JK Vineyard Syrah (Santa Ynez Valley) $20. 94 *—S.H. (10/1/1999)*

Lane Tanner 2001 Reserve Syrah (Santa Barbara County) $22. 84 *(9/1/2005)*

LANG

Lang 2005 Zinfandel (Amador County) $17. Pretty good price for a polished, fairly complex Zin. The wine's a little sweet, but with just enough tannins and acids to make it balanced. That lets the palate appreciate the ripe red berry, cocoa, licorice and spice flavors. **86** *—S.H. (11/15/2007)*

LANG & REED

Lang & Reed 2005 Cabernet Franc (North Coast) $22. Shows the dry, lightly elegant mouthfeel that a pure Cab Franc should have, with polished cherry and vanilla flavors. But it struggles to rise beyond country style. **85** *—S.H. (10/1/2007)*

Lang & Reed 2004 Cabernet Franc (Napa Valley) $22. 89 *—S.H. (11/1/2006)*

Lang & Reed 2003 Cabernet Franc (Napa Valley) $22. 88 *—S.H. (12/15/2005)*

Lang & Reed 2000 Cabernet Franc (Napa Valley) $21. 87 *—M.S. (12/1/2002)*

Lang & Reed 2003 Premier Etage Cabernet Franc (Napa Valley) $40. The winery was one of the first to specialize in Cab Franc, and Premier Etage is their reserve-style bottling. The '03 is a very good wine, but misses the richness of the '01 and '02. With its soft, silky, almost Pinot-esque mouthfeel and flavors of cherries and cassis, it possesses great elegance and sophistication. Drink now. **88** *—S.H. (10/1/2007)*

Lang & Reed 2002 Premier Etage Cabernet Franc (Napa Valley) $40. 93 Editors' Choice —*S.H. (12/31/2006)*

Lang & Reed 2001 Premier Etage Cabernet Franc (Napa Valley) $36. 92 Editors' Choice —*S.H. (12/15/2005)*

Lang & Reed 2000 Wild Hare Cabernet Franc (Rutherford) $15. 84 —*J.M. (11/15/2001)*

LANGE

Lange 2004 Pinot Gris (Willamette Valley) $16. 83 —*P.G. (2/1/2006)*

Lange 2005 Dundee Hills Estate Pinot Noir (Dundee Hills) $60. This is a 2005 vintage Pinot; released quite young. The wine is still knitting itself together, still showing very youthful flavors. The fruit runs to light red berries with some cherry tomato tartness; the 13 months in French oak, just a third of it new, adds smooth vanilla and light chocolate to the finish. Another six or 12 months should pull this together. **87** —*P.G. (2/1/2007)*

Lange 2005 Freedom Hill Vineyard Pinot Noir (Willamette Valley) $60. This young wine is quite tight, sharp and edgy, but promises good things to come. Spicy plum up front quickly goes to bark and earth with the grainy tannins. There is some tasty caramel running through the finish; it's still quite compact. **88** —*P.G. (4/1/2007)*

Lange 2005 Reserve Pinot Noir (Willamette Valley) $30. This young wine opens with a distinctive spicy scent suggesting caraway, then black pepper. That peppery streak runs straight through it, inspiring hope but ultimately leading into a tight, earthy wine whose flavors quickly dry up. Might it evolve? Yes, but after an hour or two in the glass it seemed to be going backwards, at least for the time being. **87** —*P.G. (7/1/2007)*

LANGETWINS

Langetwins 2005 Cabernet Sauvignon (Lodi) $15. A country wine, with rustic blackberry and grapy flavors. It's a dry, balanced sipper whose charm is hard to describe. But it's there. **85** —*S.H. (9/1/2007)*

Langetwins 2005 Midnight Reserve Bordeaux Blend (Lodi) $30. Soft and simple, with blackberry syrup flavors and a sweetish finish. Mostly Cabernet Sauvignon and Malbec. **82** —*S.H. (12/31/2007)*

Langetwins 2005 Chardonnay (California) $15. Rustic, soft and sweet, with apricot and oak flavors. Gets the Chard job done in a simple way. **82** —*S.H. (9/1/2007)*

Langetwins 2005 Merlot (California) $15. Drink with everyday fare. Dry and tannic, with earthy, blackberry and coffee flavors. **84** —*S.H. (9/1/2007)*

Langetwins 2006 Sauvignon Blanc (Lodi) $11. A little sweet in honey, this Musque-clone Sauvignon Blanc has ripe flavors of citrus fruits, figs and dates. It was aged on the lees, which adds extra richness, but the best part is brisk acidity. **86 Best Buy** —*S.H. (11/15/2007)*

LANGTRY

Langtry 1998 Bordeaux Blend (Guenoc Valley) $23. 84 —*L.W. (3/1/2000)*

Langtry 1996 Bordeaux Blend (Napa Valley) $48. 87 —*L.W. (11/1/1999)*

Langtry 1997 Meritage Bordeaux Blend (North Coast) $50. 91 *(11/1/2000)*

Langtry 2004 Serpentine Meadow Petite Sirah (Guenoc Valley) $40. Hard to like with its sugary sweet medicinal flavors that taste like cough medicine. **80** —*S.H. (12/15/2007)*

Langtry 2000 Meritage Red Blend (North Coast) $40. 84 —*S.H. (12/31/2004)*

Langtry 2006 Lillie Sauvignon Blanc (Lake County) $25. This is a vineyard selection from the winery's estate, and it's a nicely drinkable Sauvignon Blanc, showing how well the variety does in Lake County. Fresh and juicy, the pineapple and fig flavors finish with a honeyed richness. **86** —*S.H. (12/15/2007)*

Langtry 2002 Meritage White Blend (Guenoc Valley) $20. 85 —*S.H. (12/31/2004)*

LAPIS LUNA

Lapis Luna 2000 Chardonnay (California) $10. 85 —*J.M. (11/15/2003)*

Lapis Luna 2000 Merlot (California) $10. 86 Best Buy —*S.H. (12/15/2004)*

LARAINE

Laraine 2001 Gerber Vineyards Chardonnay (Sierra Foothills) $14. 89 Best Buy —*S.H. (2/1/2005)*

Laraine 2002 Gerber Vineyards Syrah (Sierra Foothills) $22. 84 —*S.H. (2/1/2005)*

LARKMEAD

Larkmead 2001 Cabernet Sauvignon (Napa Valley) $45. 85 —*S.H. (10/3/2004)*

Larkmead 2001 Merlot (Napa Valley) $35. 85 —*S.H. (12/15/2004)*

LATAH CREEK

Latah Creek 2001 Cabernet Sauvignon-Merlot (Washington) $20. 89 Cellar Selection —*P.G. (12/31/2003)*

Latah Creek 2005 Cabernet-Syrah (Washington) $20. This 50-50 blend brings a bowl full of sweet cherry fruit to the nose; it's hard to resist after the first sniff. There's plenty of glycerin and a lushness to the mouthfeel, and the fruit flavors pile on sweet streaks of cherry, plum and raisin. Much of the pleasure is right up front, and the wine turns a bit stiff and stemmy as it heads down the back stretch. **87** —*P.G. (12/31/2007)*

Latah Creek 2004 Chardonnay (Washington) $11. 85 —*P.G. (4/1/2006)*

Latah Creek 2002 Chardonnay (Washington) $11. 88 Best Buy —*P.G. (12/31/2003)*

Latah Creek 2002 Quilomene Hills Vineyard Johannisberg Riesling (Washington) $7. 88 Best Buy —*P.G. (12/31/2003)*

Latah Creek 2002 Moscato d'Latah Moscato (Washington) $14. 86 —*P.G. (12/31/2003)*

Latah Creek 2004 Muscat Canelli (Washington) $10. 88 —*P.G. (4/1/2006)*

Latah Creek 2004 Johannisberg Riesling (Washington) $7. 90 Best Buy —*P.G. (4/1/2006)*

Latah Creek 1999 Syrah (Washington) $19. 83 *(10/1/2001)*

LATCHAM

Latcham 2000 Sauvignon Blanc (El Dorado) $12. 89 Best Buy —*S.H. (9/1/2002)*

Latcham 1999 Zinfandel (El Dorado) $18. 87 —*S.H. (11/1/2002)*

Latcham 2001 Special Reserve Zinfandel (El Dorado) $25. 86 *(11/1/2003)*

Latcham 2000 Special Reserve Zinfandel (Fair Play) $25. 84 —*S.H. (11/1/2002)*

LATITUDE 46° N

Latitude 46° N 2004 Katherine Leone Merlot (Wahluke Slope) $25. It begins with a pleasant nut rind aroma, then adds a bit of herb and leaf, and finally hits the center with ripe, chunky cherry fruit. This has the big, broad shoulders of fully ripened Washington Merlot, with flesh and interesting herbal/spice notes. Unusual because of the herb accents, it shows some lightly stemmy tannins, so it may not please everyone. But it certainly delivers lots of flavor. **88** —*P.G. (3/1/2007)*

Latitude 46° N 2004 Syrah (Columbia Valley (WA)) $28. 92 —*P.G. (6/1/2006)*

Latitude 46° N 2004 Clifton Cuvée Red Wine Syrah (Columbia Valley (WA)) $18. 83 *(9/1/2005)*

Latitude 46° N 2005 The Power and the Glory Syrah (Columbia Valley (WA)) $28. Blended with 5% Grenache and 6% Mourvèdre. Raspberry and cherry and tart red fruits jump out; and the tannins remain young, hard and abrasive. This definitely needs some more bottle age; but it already shows fine fruit flavors that persist right through the young tannins. **89** —*P.G. (3/1/2007)*

Latitude 46° N 2003 The Power and the Glory Syrah (Columbia Valley (WA)) $28. 86 *(9/1/2005)*

LATOUR

LaTour 2003 Chardonnay (Napa Valley) $39. 84 —*S.H. (10/1/2005)*

LAURA ZAHTILA

Laura Zahtila 2004 Beckstoffer Vineyard Georges III Cabernet Sauvignon (Rutherford) $55. A wonderfully opulent wine, so succulent and rich, it's almost decadent. But it stays smooth, polished and dry. The warm vintage yielded perfectly ripe cherry, plum and carob flavors accented by 20 months in 40% new French oak. Fully ready now, and should drink well through 2012. **91** —*S.H. (12/15/2007)*

LAUREL GLEN

Laurel Glen 2003 Cabernet Sauvignon (Sonoma Mountain) $55. This is one of the ripest Laurel Glens in years, and it's sumptuous now. With gigantic cherry, blackberry, black raspberry, cassis, root beer and cinnamon-anise flavors wrapped into a softly tannic texture. Seems at its best now and for four or five more years. **89** —*S.H. (11/1/2007)*

Laurel Glen 2002 Cabernet Sauvignon (Sonoma Mountain) $55. 95 —*S.H. (9/1/2006)*

Laurel Glen 2001 Cabernet Sauvignon (Sonoma Mountain) $50. 92 Cellar Selection —*S.H. (10/1/2004)*

Laurel Glen 2000 Cabernet Sauvignon (Mendocino County) $10. 87 —*S.H. (6/1/2003)*

Laurel Glen 2000 Cabernet Sauvignon (Sonoma Mountain) $50. 87 —*S.H. (10/1/2004)*

Laurel Glen 1999 Cabernet Sauvignon (Sonoma Mountain) $50. 92 —*S.H. (11/15/2002)*

Laurel Glen 1997 Cabernet Sauvignon (Sonoma Mountain) $50. 89 —*S.H. (12/1/2001)*

Laurel Glen 2002 Counterpoint Cabernet Sauvignon (Sonoma Mountain) $30. 91 —*S.H. (11/15/2006)*

Laurel Glen 2001 Counterpoint Cabernet Sauvignon (Sonoma Mountain) $25. 87 —*S.H. (12/15/2004)*

Laurel Glen 2000 Counterpoint Cabernet Sauvignon (Sonoma Mountain) $25. 91 Editors' Choice —*S.H. (11/15/2003)*

Laurel Glen 1999 Counterpoint Cabernet Sauvignon (Sonoma Mountain) $25. 91 —*S.H. (9/12/2002)*

Laurel Glen 1999 Reserve Cabernet Sauvignon (Sonoma Mountain) $75. 94 Cellar Selection —*S.H. (11/15/2003)*

Laurel Glen 1999 Red Blend (California) $9. 86 Best Buy —*S.H. (7/1/2002)*

Laurel Glen 2004 Reds Red Blend (Lodi) $10. 86 Best Buy —*S.H. (7/1/2006)*

Laurel Glen 2002 Reds Red Blend (Lodi) $9. 89 Editors' Choice —*S.H. (3/1/2005)*

Laurel Glen 2001 Reds Red Blend (California) $8. 84 —*S.H. (9/1/2004)*

Laurel Glen 2000 Reds Red Blend (California) $8. 87 Best Buy —*S.H. (12/1/2002)*

Laurel Glen 1999 Old Vine Za Zin Zinfandel (California) $18. 90 —*S.H. (7/1/2002)*

Laurel Glen 2002 Old Vine Za-Zin Zinfandel (Lodi) $15. 85 —*S.H. (3/1/2004)*

Laurel Glen 2000 Za Zin Zinfandel (Lodi) $15. 85 —*S.H. (11/1/2002)*

Laurel Glen 2004 Za Zin Old Vine Zinfandel (Lodi) $15. 82 —*S.H. (7/1/2006)*

LAUREL LAKE

Laurel Lake 1999 Cabernet Sauvignon (North Fork of Long Island) $15. 85 —*J.C. (1/1/2004)*

Laurel Lake 1998 Reserve Cabernet Sauvignon (North Fork of Long Island) $18. 82 —*J.C. (4/1/2001)*

Laurel Lake 2001 Reserve Chardonnay (North Fork of Long Island) $18. 87 —*J.C. (10/2/2004)*

Laurel Lake 1999 Reserve Chardonnay (North Fork of Long Island) $15. 87 —*J.C. (1/1/2004)*

Laurel Lake 1998 Reserve Chardonnay (North Fork of Long Island) $18. 80 —*J.C. (4/1/2001)*

Laurel Lake 2000 Merlot (North Fork of Long Island) $14. 82 —*J.C. (10/2/2004)*

Laurel Lake 2002 Syrah (North Fork of Long Island) $20. 85 *(9/1/2005)*

LAURIER

Laurier 2000 Chardonnay (Carneros) $15. 86 —*S.H. (6/1/2003)*

Laurier 1996 Barrel-Fermented Chardonnay (Sonoma County) $19. 84 *(6/1/2000)*

Laurier 2000 Merlot (Dry Creek Valley) $15. 85 —*S.H. (10/1/2004)*

Laurier 2003 Pinot Noir (Carneros) $15. 83 —*S.H. (5/1/2005)*

LAUTERBACH

Lauterbach 2001 Pinot Noir (Russian River Valley) $32. 87 —*S.H. (12/1/2004)*

Lauterbach 2001 Syrah (Russian River Valley) $38. 87 —*S.H. (9/1/2004)*

LAVA CAP

Lava Cap 2000 Granite Hill Reserve Petite Sirah (El Dorado) $30. 83 *(4/1/2003)*

Lava Cap 2000 Sémillon (El Dorado) $18. 82 —*S.H. (9/1/2002)*

Lava Cap 2001 Reserve Syrah (El Dorado) $20. 84 *(9/1/2005)*

Lava Cap 1999 Reserve Syrah (El Dorado) $40. 93 Editors' Choice —*S.H. (6/1/2003)*

Lava Cap 1998 Reserve Syrah (El Dorado) $20. 89 *(10/1/2001)*

LAVELLE

LaVelle 2004 Vintage Select Pinot Noir (Willamette Valley) $18. 84 —*P.G. (12/1/2006)*

LaVelle 2005 Riesling (Willamette Valley) $14. 86 —*P.G. (12/1/2006)*

LaVelle 2006 Estate Riesling (Willamette Valley) $15. Looking for a stylish, elegant, low-alcohol, off-dry Riesling? Here it is. Under 11% alcohol, this floral, almost delicate wine is a breath of sweet air. A perfect mix of honeydew, Asian pear and ripe apple, it holds down center court with a delicious liveliness. Flavors extend, lightly kissed with honey, into a lingering, clean and sweetly fresh finish. **91 Best Buy** —*P.G. (11/15/2007)*

LAVENDER RIDGE

Lavender Ridge 2002 Syrah (Sierra Foothills) $28. 85 *(9/1/2005)*

LAWRENCE J. BARGETTO

Lawrence J. Bargetto 1998 Chardonnay (Santa Cruz Mountains) $20. 89 *(6/1/2000)*

Lawrence J. Bargetto 1998 Pinot Grigio (California) $15. 87 *(8/1/1999)*

LAWSON RANCH

Lawson Ranch 2002 Lockwood Vineyard Chardonnay (Monterey County) $8. 84 Best Buy —*S.H. (7/1/2005)*

LAZY CREEK

Lazy Creek 2000 Chardonnay (Anderson Valley) $16. 86 —*S.H. (5/1/2002)*

Lazy Creek 2000 Gewürztraminer (Anderson Valley) $16. 89 —*S.H. (5/1/2002)*

Lazy Creek 1999 Gewürztraminer (Anderson Valley) $12. 87 —*S.H. (11/15/2001)*

Lazy Creek 1999 Barrel #9 Gewürztraminer (Anderson Valley) $27. 87 —*S.H. (5/1/2002)*

Lazy Creek 2000 Pinot Noir (Anderson Valley) $32. 90 *(10/1/2002)*

Lazy Creek 1999 Pinot Noir (Anderson Valley) $26. 94 —*S.H. (5/1/2002)*

Lazy Creek 2000 Puncheon #3 Pinot Noir (Anderson Valley) $62. 87 —*S.H. (4/1/2003)*

LAZY RIVER

Lazy River 2006 Private Lumpkin Riesling (Yamhill-Carlton District) $18. This is made by Eric Hamacher (Carlton Winemakers Studio) and mixes dried herb, tea, honeysuckle and green apple in a convivial style. Round and fruity, it's dry without being stiff or steely. Very drinkable. **88** —*P.G. (11/15/2007)*

LE BON VIN DE LA NAPA VALLEY

Le Bon Vin de la Napa Valley 2003 Cabernet Sauvignon (Napa Valley) $10. 85 Best Buy —*S.H. (12/31/2005)*

Le Bon Vin de la Napa Valley 2004 Chardonnay (Napa Valley) $10. 85 Best Buy —*S.H. (12/31/2005)*

Le Bon Vin de la Napa Valley 2004 Merlot (Napa Valley) $14. 87 —*S.H. (11/15/2006)*

LE CADEAU VINEYARD

Le Cadeau Vineyard 2003 Pinot Noir (Willamette Valley) $40. 95 Editors' Choice —*P.G. (9/1/2006)*

Le Cadeau Vineyard 2004 Cote Est Pinot Noir (Willamette Valley) $45. This concentrated, stiff young wine is scented strongly with herb and earth. The fruit is packed tight, and flavors show as much spice and herb as they do sweet fruit. Dense and unyielding, it suggests more than shows its textural complexity at the moment. Give this a lot of breathing time. **91** —*P.G. (4/1/2007)*

Le Cadeau Vineyard 2004 Diversité Pinot Noir (Willamette Valley) $45. Not as successful as the winery's other releases, the Diversité Pinot Noir has aromas that suggest less than perfect fruit. Tough and earthy, it's a bit ungenerous. The finish carries a hint of mint. **85** —*P.G. (4/1/2007)*

Le Cadeau Vineyard 2004 Rocheux Pinot Noir (Willamette Valley) $45. There is plenty of herb evident in this wine, along with an underlying minerality. This is an almost textbook example of a particular Oregon style, quite different from the broad, sweet flavors of California Pinot Noir. Here you'll find plenty of earthy texture and flavors of leaf, stem and soil. **89** —*P.G. (4/1/2007)*

LE CUVIER

Le Cuvier 1999 Zinfandel (San Luis Obispo County) $30. 88 —*J.M. (2/1/2003)*

LE VIN

Le Vin 2000 Cabernet Sauvignon (Mendocino County) $36. 92 —*S.H. (11/15/2003)*

Le Vin 2000 Chardonnay (Russian River Valley) $19. 88 —*S.H. (8/1/2003)*

Le Vin 2000 Merlot (Mendocino County) $28. 91 —*S.H. (12/31/2003)*

LEAL VINEYARDS

Leal Vineyards 2004 Carnaval Meritage Bordeaux Blend (San Benito County) $24. Way too sweet for my palate, a sugary confection of blackberry and cherry puree made for pie filling. Will have its fans, but it really tastes too sweet for balance. **82** *—S.H. (2/1/2007)*

Leal Vineyards 2003 Estate Carnaval Cabernet Blend (San Benito County) $24. 87 *—S.H. (6/1/2006)*

Leal Vineyards 2005 Williams Vineyard Cabernet Franc (San Benito County) $28. Very rich, almost decadent in cherry liqueur, cassis and dark chocolate flavors, but saved from collapse by acidity and tannins that give vital structure to the massive richness. **89** *—S.H. (12/1/2007)*

Leal Vineyards 2001 Cabernet Sauvignon (San Benito County) $24. 84 *—S.H. (10/1/2005)*

Leal Vineyards 2004 Estate Cabernet Sauvignon (San Benito County) $24. Tastes a bit on the sugary-sweet side, with a brown sugar edge to the blackberry and cherry flavors. The tannins are rich and fine, the acidity crisp and balancing. If only the wine tasted drier. **84** *—S.H. (2/1/2007)*

Leal Vineyards 2005 Estate Chardonnay (San Benito County) $24. There's good structure in this dry Chard, which has good acids and a nice creamy texture. The drawback is that it could use greater fruity concentration, as it's dominated by alcohol and sweet oak. **83** *—S.H. (2/1/2007)*

Leal Vineyards 2004 Estate Chardonnay (San Benito County) $24. 85 *—S.H. (12/1/2006)*

Leal Vineyards 2003 Estate Chardonnay (San Benito County) $24. 83 *—S.H. (11/15/2005)*

Leal Vineyards 2005 Malbec (San Benito County) $28. This is a bit flat and one-dimensional. The cherry and raspberry flavors would benefit from greater vitality and a drier finish. But it's okay for an everyday red. **85** *—S.H. (12/1/2007)*

Leal Vineyards 2001 Carnivàl Meritage (San Benito County) $24. 81 *—S.H. (11/15/2005)*

Leal Vineyards 2003 Estate Merlot (San Benito County) $24. 83 *—S.H. (11/15/2005)*

Leal Vineyards 2005 MacWilliamson Vineyard Petite Sirah (San Benito County) $28. Oodles of rich, ripe fruit in this soft, gently structured wine. The blackberries, cherries, plums, chocolate and spiced coffee finish with evident sweetness. **86** *—S.H. (12/1/2007)*

Leal Vineyards 2003 Estate Grown Threesome Rhône Style Blend Rhône Red Blend (San Benito County) $24. 83 *—S.H. (12/31/2005)*

Leal Vineyards 2004 Threesome Rhône Red Blend (San Benito County) $24. 82 *—S.H. (12/1/2006)*

Leal Vineyards 2005 Sauvignon Blanc (Lake County) $24. Textbook Lake Sauvignon, basically dry (maybe there's a touch of sweetness), well acidified and rich in figgy, citrus and tropical fruit flavors. The acidity is really what makes the wine work. **86** *—S.H. (2/1/2007)*

Leal Vineyards 2003 Estate Syrah (San Benito County) $24. 84 *—S.H. (11/15/2005)*

Leal Vineyards 2002 Estate Grown Syrah (San Benito County) $24. 86 *(9/1/2005)*

LEAPING HORSE

Leaping Horse 2000 Cabernet Sauvignon (Lodi) $5. 85 Best Buy *—S.H. (2/1/2003)*

Leaping Horse 2005 Chardonnay (Lodi) $6. Not bad for an everyday Chard at this price. You'll be surprised by how much real varietal character there is, from the tangerine and apple flavors to the creamy, smoky texture to the spicy, clean finish. **84 Best Buy** *—S.H. (2/1/2007)*

Leaping Horse 2004 Chardonnay (Lodi) $6. 82 *—S.H. (2/1/2006)*

Leaping Horse 2001 Chardonnay (Lodi) $5. 84 *—S.H. (2/1/2003)*

Leaping Horse 2005 Merlot (Lodi) $6. So what do you get for the price? A nice little country wine, dry and balanced, with upfront cherry pie filling and cinnamon-spice flavors, and even a touch of smoky oak. Good, and easy to find, with 80,000 cases produced. **83 Best Buy** *—S.H. (7/1/2007)*

Leaping Horse 2000 Merlot (Lodi) $5. 85 Best Buy *—S.H. (2/1/2003)*

Leaping Horse 2005 Shiraz (Lodi) $NA. 84 *—S.H. (12/1/2006)*

Leaping Horse 2003 Shiraz (Lodi) $5. 84 Best Buy *—S.H. (8/1/2005)*

Leaping Horse 2001 Shiraz (Lodi) $5. 82 *—S.H. (12/1/2004)*

LEAPING LIZARD

Leaping Lizard 2004 Cabernet Sauvignon (Napa Valley) $12. Here's a solid value that shows true Napa style. Dry and balanced, it offers up rich flavors of cherries, blackberries and spice, wrapped into smooth tannins. **86** *—S.H. (11/15/2007)*

Leaping Lizard 2005 Chardonnay (Napa Valley) $12. Simple and sweet, with orange marmalade and green mint jelly flavors. The oak tastes like vanilla pudding. **82** *—S.H. (11/15/2007)*

Leaping Lizard 2003 Chardonnay (Napa Valley) $10. 85 Best Buy *—S.H. (11/15/2005)*

Leaping Lizard 2004 Merlot (Napa Valley) $12. Good value in an everyday Merlot. Smooth and plush in texture, the ripe flavors include cherries, blackberries, mocha, dried herbs and peppery spices, with a touch of toasty oak. **87 Best Buy** *—S.H. (11/15/2007)*

Leaping Lizard 2003 Pinot Noir (Carneros) $10. 85 Best Buy *—S.H. (11/15/2005)*

Leaping Lizard 2005 Sauvignon Blanc (Napa Valley) $12. Leaping Lizard is turning out good value wines that show true varietal character. This Sauvignon Blanc, which doesn't seem to have any oak, shows crisp, bright flavors of pineapples, apricots and spices. It's a bit on the sweet side, but with good balancing acidity. **85** *—S.H. (11/15/2007)*

Leaping Lizard 2004 Zinfandel (Sonoma County) $12. What a great success. It brings to mind that old saying, less is more. This a wonderfully balanced wine with tons of Zin-y flavor. Wild black, blue and red berries, sweet cocoa, root beer and all kinds of dusty Asian spices spread over the palate, leading to a dry, satisfying aftertaste. Buy this one by the case. **90 Best Buy** *—S.H. (11/15/2007)*

LEDGEWOOD CREEK

Ledgewood Creek 2004 Cabernet Sauvignon (Napa Valley) $16. 84 *—S.H. (12/31/2006)*

Ledgewood Creek 2004 Chardonnay (Suisun Valley) $14. 83 *—S.H. (12/31/2006)*

Ledgewood Creek 2002 Limited Reserve Suisun Valley Chardonnay (North Coast) $18. 85 *—S.H. (6/1/2004)*

Ledgewood Creek 2002 Suisun Valley Chardonnay (North Coast) $13. 84 *—S.H. (6/1/2004)*

Ledgewood Creek 2001 Suisun Valley Chardonnay (North Coast) $13. 83 *—S.H. (10/1/2003)*

Ledgewood Creek 2005 Picnique Fumé Blanc (Suisun Valley) $9. 84 *—S.H. (12/31/2006)*

Ledgewood Creek 2001 Suisun Valley Merlot (North Coast) $15. 84 *—S.H. (6/1/2004)*

Ledgewood Creek 2005 Sauvignon Blanc (Suisun Valley) $12. 85 *—S.H. (12/31/2006)*

Ledgewood Creek 2004 Estate Grown Syrah (Suisun Valley) $12. 83 *—S.H. (12/31/2006)*

LEDSON

Ledson 2004 Cabernet Franc (Alexander Valley) $48. There are some exquisite flavors in this Cab Franc: cassis, cherries, raspberries, cocoa, smoky oak and a rich array of dusty crushed brown spices. The wine is fully dry, with finely meshed tannins, but the main quibble is that it's too soft to be completely balanced. **88** *—S.H. (12/31/2007)*

Ledson 2002 Cabernet Franc (Alexander Valley) $48. 86 *—S.H. (7/1/2005)*

Ledson 2002 Cabernet Sauvignon (Alexander Valley) $90. 91 *—S.H. (10/1/2005)*

Ledson 2004 Reserve Cabernet Sauvignon (Knights Valley) $95. Give this Cab extra points for the dazzle factor. It shows the most beautifully ripe flavors of blackberries and cassis, and a powerful but tasty coating of smoky oak. The tannins are so sweet and fine, but the excessive softness robs the wine of structure. **88** *—S.H. (12/31/2007)*

Ledson 2002 Reserve Cabernet Sauvignon (Alexander Valley) $110. 82 *—S.H. (12/31/2005)*

Ledson 2004 Chardonnay (Carneros) $36. 87 *—S.H. (12/31/2005)*

Ledson 2002 Chardonnay (Russian River Valley) $24. 87 *—S.H. (8/1/2004)*

Ledson 2001 Chardonnay (Russian River Valley) $24. 90 Editors' Choice *—S.H. (7/1/2003)*

Ledson 2000 Chardonnay (Arroyo Seco) $20. 86 *—S.H. (5/1/2003)*

Ledson 2000 Chardonnay (Russian River Valley) $24. 89 *—S.H. (2/1/2003)*

Ledson 1999 Reserve Chardonnay (Russian River Valley) $32. 88 *(7/1/2001)*

Ledson 1998 Reserve Chardonnay (Sonoma County) $32. 91 *(7/1/2001)*

Ledson 2000 Johannisberg Riesling (Monterey) $16. 87 *—S.H. (6/1/2002)*

Ledson 2000 Harmony Collection Jeff Bridges Be Here Soon Meritage (Napa Valley) $125. 84 *—S.H. (2/1/2006)*

Ledson 1999 Merlot (Sonoma Valley) $36. 91 *—S.H. (8/1/2003)*

Ledson 1998 Merlot (Sonoma Valley) $34. 93 *—S.H. (7/1/2002)*

Ledson 2002 Estate Merlot (Sonoma Valley) $38. 87 *—S.H. (10/1/2005)*

Ledson 2003 Petite Sirah (Contra Costa County) $34. 88 *—S.H. (11/15/2006)*

Ledson 2002 Pinot Noir (Russian River Valley) $36. 85 —*S.H. (11/1/2004)*

Ledson 2003 Primitivo (Napa Valley) $36. 83 —*S.H. (11/15/2006)*

Ledson 1999 Legend Red Blend (Sonoma County) $36. 91 —*S.H. (7/1/2002)*

Ledson 2003 Mes Trois Amours Red Wine Rhône Red Blend (California) $30. 90 —*S.H. (11/15/2006)*

Ledson 2000 Rosé Blend (California) $14. 87 —*S.H. (9/10/2002)*

Ledson 2003 Sangiovese (Alexander Valley) $34. 83 —*S.H. (11/15/2006)*

Ledson 2002 Sangiovese (Alexander Valley) $34. 86 —*S.H. (10/1/2005)*

Ledson 2006 Sauvignon Blanc (Napa Valley) $26. With a strong dose of cat pee and bell pepper, this Sauvignon Blanc tastes like it just didn't get ripe enough. Grapefruit is the only fruit in evidence, and the acidity makes it slightly sour on the finish. **81** —*S.H. (11/1/2007)*

Ledson 2006 Sauvignon Blanc (Russian River Valley) $26. A nice, crisp Sauvignon Blanc that rewards for the array of spearmint, lemon, lime and fig newton flavors. With a rich bite of citrusy acidity, it finishes with a dusting of Asian spices. **87** —*S.H. (11/1/2007)*

Ledson 2003 Sauvignon Blanc (Russian River Valley) $20. 85 —*S.H. (12/15/2004)*

Ledson 2001 Sauvignon Blanc (Napa Valley) $20. 87 —*S.H. (10/1/2003)*

Ledson 2000 Sauvignon Blanc (Napa Valley) $18. 87 *(8/1/2002)*

Ledson 2000 Michele's Cuvée White Blend (California) $20. 88 —*S.H. (6/1/2002)*

Ledson 2003 Bacigalupi Vineyard Zinfandel (Russian River Valley) $40. 90 —*S.H. (11/15/2006)*

Ledson 2004 Baldoochi Old Vine Zinfandel (Russian River Valley) $36. There's more than a little residual sugar in this soft, sensual Zin, but the wine handles its sweetness well. It's terrifically ripe in blackberry, mulberry, boysenberry and other rustic berry flavors, with lots of spices and vanilla. Drink now. **87** —*S.H. (12/31/2007)*

Ledson 2002 Century Vine Zinfandel (Russian River Valley) $46. 90 —*S.H. (10/1/2005)*

Ledson 2002 Old Vine Zinfandel (Russian River Valley) $36. 84 —*S.H. (10/1/2005)*

Ledson 2001 Old Vine Zinfandel (Russian River Valley) $30. 89 —*S.H. (12/31/2004)*

Ledson 2001 Old Vine Zinfandel (Dry Creek Valley) $36. 90 —*S.H. (8/1/2004)*

Ledson 1999 Old Vine Zinfandel (Dry Creek Valley) $28. 87 —*S.H. (7/1/2002)*

Ledson 2000 Old Vines Zinfandel (Lodi) $28. 88 —*S.H. (3/1/2004)*

Ledson 1999 Old Vines Zinfandel (Russian River Valley) $36. 88 —*S.H. (7/1/2002)*

LEEWARD

Leeward 1996 Edna Valley Reserve Chardonnay (Edna Valley) $16. 85 —*M.S. (10/1/1999)*

Leeward 1998 Reserve Chardonnay (Edna Valley) $16. 85 *(6/1/2000)*

Leeward 1996 Merlot (Napa Valley) $24. 91 —*M.S. (6/1/1999)*

Leeward 1997 Bien Nacido Vineyard Pinot Noir (Santa Barbara County) $20. 86 *(11/15/1999)*

LEGACY

Legacy 1997 Estate Bottled Bordeaux Blend (Sonoma County) $90. 88 *(11/1/2000)*

LEHRER

Lehrer 2002 Syrah (Contra Costa County) $34. 84 *(9/1/2005)*

LEMELSON

Lemelson 2000 Chardonnay (Willamette Valley) $20. 89 —*P.G. (9/1/2003)*

Lemelson 2000 Wascher Vineyard Chardonnay (Willamette Valley) $26. 90 —*P.G. (9/1/2003)*

Lemelson 1999 Wascher Vineyard Chardonnay (Willamette Valley) $26. 88 —*P.G. (2/1/2002)*

Lemelson 1999 Pinot Gris (Oregon) $18. 88 —*P.G. (2/1/2002)*

Lemelson 2000 Tikka's Run Pinot Gris (Willamette Valley) $18. 90 Editors' Choice —*P.G. (8/1/2003)*

Lemelson 2001 Pinot Noir (Oregon) $13. 88 —*P.G. (4/1/2003)*

Lemelson 2003 Chestnut Hill Vineyard Pinot Noir (Willamette Valley) $38. 92 —*P.G. (5/1/2006)*

Lemelson 2002 Chestnut Hill Vineyard Pinot Noir (Willamette Valley) $33. 87 *(11/1/2004)*

Lemelson 2005 Jerome Reserve Pinot Noir (Willamette Valley) $50. This low-yield (1.33 tons/acre average) mix of clones and vineyards, from Red Hills, WillaKenzie and Jory soils, yields a more textural wine with subtle layers of flavor. As with the winery's other releases, it enters the palate quite softly and leaves rather quickly, giving the impression that (especially noting the 13.8% alcohol) some manipulative technology has been used. Some details of herb, tobacco leaf and citrus do add interesting detail to the blackberry fruit. **89** —*P.G. (11/15/2007)*

Lemelson 2003 Jerome Reserve Pinot Noir (Willamette Valley) $44. 89 —*P.G. (5/1/2006)*

Lemelson 2002 Jerome Reserve Pinot Noir (Willamette Valley) $44. 90 *(11/1/2004)*

Lemelson 2000 Jerome Reserve Pinot Noir (Willamette Valley) $44. 91 Cellar Selection —*P.G. (4/1/2003)*

Lemelson 1999 Jerome Reserve Pinot Noir (Willamette Valley) $44. 91 —*P.G. (12/31/2001)*

Lemelson 2005 Meyer Vineyard Pinot Noir (Willamette Valley) $42. It opens with sweet/tart raspberry fruit, a streamlined, well-defined wine underscored by tart, citrusy acids. It does not show the harmonious complexity of the blends, but it is a very pleasant wine, soft and approachable, sweet and smooth. A bit one-dimensional; it begins with fresh berry fruit, tosses in a hint of cherry tobacco, and leaves a slightly earthy impression in the finish, but fails to move in the mouth. **87** —*P.G. (11/15/2007)*

Lemelson 2000 Reed & Reynolds Vineyard Pinot Noir (Willamette Valley) $38. 91 —*P.G. (4/1/2003)*

Lemelson 2003 Resonance Vineyard Pinot Noir (Willamette Valley) $38. 93 —*P.G. (5/1/2006)*

Lemelson 2002 Resonance Vineyard Pinot Noir (Willamette Valley) $38. 88 *(11/1/2004)*

Lemelson 2005 Stermer Vineyard Pinot Noir (Willamette Valley) $42. The Stermer, which I have enjoyed in previous vintages, gets kudos for achieving an alcohol level at a moderate 13.5% despite being harvested at less than two tons/acre. Tight, spicy and astringent, it falls quite short in the mouth, resisting efforts to open it up with additional breathing time. It is more of a component than a full-flavored, full-bodied finished wine. **86** —*P.G. (11/15/2007)*

Lemelson 2003 Stermer Vineyard Pinot Noir (Willamette Valley) $38. 91 —*P.G. (5/1/2006)*

Lemelson 2002 Stermer Vineyard Pinot Noir (Willamette Valley) $38. 90 *(11/1/2004)*

Lemelson 2000 Stermer Vineyard Pinot Noir (Willamette Valley) $38. 89 —*P.G. (4/1/2003)*

Lemelson 1999 Stermer Vineyard Pinot Noir (Willamette Valley) $38. 90 —*P.G. (12/31/2001)*

Lemelson 2005 Thea's Selection Pinot Noir (Willamette Valley) $32. Thea's Selection book-ends the single-vineyard wines and is the winery's lower-priced, multi-vineyard blend. As with the Jerome, the flavors are more complex and woven than in the single-vineyard bottlings; with cherry and berry fruit, fresh herb and streaks of bitter chocolate. It's a complete, supple wine, with no holes, moderately ripe fruit, and just a hint of heat in the finish. **88** —*P.G. (11/15/2007)*

Lemelson 2002 Thea's Selection Pinot Noir (Willamette Valley) $29. 88 *(11/1/2004)*

Lemelson 2000 Thea's Selection Pinot Noir (Willamette Valley) $29. 88 —*P.G. (4/1/2003)*

Lemelson 1999 Thea's Selection Pinot Noir (Willamette Valley) $29. 89 —*P.G. (12/31/2001)*

Lemelson 2001 Adria Vineyard-Dry Riesling Riesling (Willamette Valley) $19. 83 —*J.C. (8/1/2003)*

LENZ

Lenz 1997 Cabernet Sauvignon (North Fork of Long Island) $30. 88 —*J.C. (4/1/2001)*

Lenz 1994 Cuvée Champagne Blend (North Fork of Long Island) $30. 90 Editors' Choice —*J.C. (4/1/2001)*

Lenz 1998 Gold Label Chardonnay (North Fork of Long Island) $25. 87 —*J.C. (4/1/2001)*

Lenz 1998 White Label Chardonnay (North Fork of Long Island) $11. 86 Best Buy —*J.C. (4/1/2001)*

Lenz 1998 Gewürztraminer (North Fork of Long Island) $12. 87 Best Buy —*J.C. (4/1/2001)*

Lenz 1997 Merlot (North Fork of Long Island) $25. 89 —*J.C. (4/1/2001)*

Lenz 1997 Estate Bottled Merlot (North Fork of Long Island) $55. 91 Cellar Selection *—J.C. (4/1/2001)*

Lenz 1998 Pinot Gris (North Fork of Long Island) $20. 85 *—J.C. (4/1/2001)*

LEONARDO FAMILY VINEYARDS

Leonardo Family Vineyards 2001 Cabernet Sauvignon (Lodi) $12. 85 *—S.H. (8/1/2003)*

Leonardo Family Vineyards 2001 Cabernet Sauvignon-Syrah (Lodi) $14. 85 *—S.H. (8/1/2003)*

Leonardo Family Vineyards 2002 Pinot Grigio (California) $10. 85 *—S.H. (12/1/2003)*

LEONESSE CELLARS

Leonesse Cellars 2004 Merlot (Temecula) $32. Dark and dry, this softly tannic, fruity wine has some sharp acids that make the cherry and berry flavors finish with a bite. **84** *—S.H. (11/1/2007)*

Leonesse Cellars 2006 White Merlot (Temecula) $16. Very pale, with sugared orange tea flavors and a touch of grapeskin tannin. Simple and enjoyable as a quaffer. **83** *—S.H. (7/1/2007)*

Leonesse Cellars 2005 Limited Selection Four Red Blend (California) $40. On the sugary, jammy side, this Cabernet Sauvignon and Zinfandel blend offers forward cherry, raspberry, blackberry, blueberry and chocolate flavors, with some raisiny notes. It's very soft and melted. **84** *—S.H. (12/15/2007)*

Leonesse Cellars 2004 Melange de Rêves Red Table Wine Red Blend (Temecula) $28. Smells a little indistinct, tastes soft and simple, with candied cherry, blackberry and licorice flavors that finish dry. Syrah, Cinsault, Grenache and Petit Verdot. **83** *—S.H. (11/1/2007)*

Leonesse Cellars 2004 Vista del Monte Vineyard Syrah (Temecula) $44. Deeply flavored, this impressive Syrah advances the red wine cause in Temecula. It's a big, powerful wine, rich in blackberry, currant and new oak flavors, with a peppery, chocolate, anise and grilled meat finish. Really fine now, but also packed with young, astringent tannins, it's a wine to decant, or cellar for up to five years. **90** *—S.H. (12/15/2007)*

Leonesse Cellars 2004 Syrah-Cabernet (Temecula) $34. Pretty good flavors in this dry Bordeaux-Rhône blend, with blackberries, coffee, tobacco and grilled meat, and the tannins are firmly complex. Loses a few points for excessive softness and a watery finish. **84** *—S.H. (11/1/2007)*

Leonesse Cellars 2006 Viognier (Temecula) $20. A bit on the soft, sweet side, with jammy flavors of apricots, pineapples and vanilla, this wine never saw any wood. **84** *—S.H. (12/15/2007)*

LEONETTI CELLAR

Leonetti Cellar 2003 Reserve Bordeaux Blend (Walla Walla (WA)) $100. 95 *—P.G. (10/1/2006)*

Leonetti Cellar 2002 Reserve Bordeaux Blend (Walla Walla (WA)) $95. 95 *—P.G. (12/15/2005)*

Leonetti Cellar 2001 Reserve Bordeaux Blend (Walla Walla (WA)) $95. 94 *—P.G. (11/15/2004)*

Leonetti Cellar 2000 Reserve Bordeaux Blend (Walla Walla (WA)) $95. 94 *—P.G. (9/1/2003)*

Leonetti Cellar 2004 Reserve Cabernet Blend (Walla Walla (WA)) $110. 100% estate grown, this truly exceptional Cabernet, Merlot and Petit Verdot blend opens with angular, vertical fruit flavors, stacked tightly and detailed with citrus, graphite and chalk. The layered midpalate mixes grape, berry, cherry and plum, sweet and dense. The oak is applied moderately, not dominating as in past Leonetti reserves. It's a profound wine with a gorgeous, entrancing structure that is barely beginning its evolution. Flavors emerge in surprising succession, like spring wildflowers that pop up overnight. A remarkable achievement, and quite possibly the best wine ever made by Leonetti. **97** *—P.G. (11/1/2007)*

Leonetti Cellar 2004 Cabernet Sauvignon (Walla Walla (WA)) $75. Though most Walla Walla vineyards got wiped out in 2004, Leonetti was able to keep its best Cabernet from the higher elevation sites. This reflects the tight, somewhat herbal aspect of the vintage, and is still showing a bit of a raw edge to the tannins. But the fruit is sweet and ripe, and the balance impeccable. The flavors mix fresh herb (basil, oregano) and tangy fruit (berry, cherry) with pleasing flashes of leaf and bark. The wine is nervy, compact and refined; the flavors linger and the aromas slowly unwind. This is a wine that I believe will age beautifully. **94** *—P.G. (11/1/2007)*

Leonetti Cellar 2003 Cabernet Sauvignon (Walla Walla (WA)) $70. 94 *—P.G. (11/15/2006)*

Leonetti Cellar 2002 Cabernet Sauvignon (Walla Walla (WA)) $65. 94 *—P.G. (12/15/2005)*

Leonetti Cellar 2001 Cabernet Sauvignon (Walla Walla (WA)) $65. 91 *—P.G. (11/15/2004)*

Leonetti Cellar 2000 Cabernet Sauvignon (Walla Walla (WA)) $65. 93 *—P.G. (9/1/2003)*

Leonetti Cellar 1999 Cabernet Sauvignon (Walla Walla (WA)) $60. 92 *—P.G. (9/1/2002)*

Leonetti Cellar 1998 Cabernet Sauvignon (Columbia Valley (WA)) $60. 95 *—P.G. (10/1/2001)*

Leonetti Cellar 1997 Cabernet Sauvignon (Columbia Valley (WA)) $55. 93 *—P.G. (11/15/2000)*

Leonetti Cellar 1998 Reserve Cabernet Sauvignon (Walla Walla (WA)) $95. 96 *—P.G. (10/1/2001)*

Leonetti Cellar 2005 Merlot (Columbia Valley (WA)) $65. Bright, saturated, and deeply colored, this poster child Merlot proves that there is no other place in the world that can do Merlot in this style. Magnificent in color, aroma, depth and texture; it is polished, elegant, firm and confident. Blossom, fruit, herb and barrel aromas are beautifully interwoven. The tightly packed fruit has it all, from red, blue and black berries on to cherry and cassis. The midpalate, though quite full, is fleshy and tight. The acids are firm but not sour, the tannins fine and smooth and ripe. The finish, still young and compact, hints at an almost existential longevity. **95** *—P.G. (11/1/2007)*

Leonetti Cellar 2004 Merlot (Columbia Valley (WA)) $60. 92 *—P.G. (10/1/2006)*

Leonetti Cellar 2003 Merlot (Columbia Valley (WA)) $55. 93 *—P.G. (12/15/2005)*

Leonetti Cellar 2002 Merlot (Columbia Valley (WA)) $55. 92 Editors' Choice *—P.G. (11/15/2004)*

Leonetti Cellar 2001 Merlot (Columbia Valley (WA)) $55. 92 *—P.G. (12/31/2003)*

Leonetti Cellar 2000 Merlot (Columbia Valley (WA)) $55. 91 *—P.G. (9/1/2002)*

Leonetti Cellar 1999 Merlot (Columbia Valley (WA)) $55. 94 *—P.G. (10/1/2001)*

Leonetti Cellar 1998 Merlot (Columbia Valley (WA)) $50. 94 *—P.G. (11/15/2000)*

Leonetti Cellar 2005 Sangiovese (Walla Walla (WA)) $55. This is just three quarters Sangiovese, with 13% Syrah and 11% Cabernet Sauvignon (the most ever) added. Dark, silky, young and tart, it is packed with berries, cranberries, pie cherries and a dark streak mixing coffee and black pepper. This is quite young, tight and yet polished. **91** *—P.G. (11/1/2007)*

Leonetti Cellar 2004 Sangiovese (Walla Walla (WA)) $50. 91 *—P.G. (10/1/2006)*

Leonetti Cellar 2003 Sangiovese (Walla Walla (WA)) $50. 89 *—P.G. (12/15/2005)*

Leonetti Cellar 2002 Sangiovese (Walla Walla (WA)) $50. 91 *—P.G. (11/15/2004)*

Leonetti Cellar 2001 Sangiovese (Walla Walla (WA)) $50. 89 *—P.G. (9/1/2003)*

Leonetti Cellar 2000 Sangiovese (Walla Walla (WA)) $50. 91 *—P.G. (9/1/2002)*

Leonetti Cellar 1999 Sangiovese (Walla Walla (WA)) $50. 91 *—P.G. (10/1/2001)*

Leonetti Cellar 1998 Sangiovese (Walla Walla (WA)) $50. 91 *—P.G. (11/15/2000)*

LEUCADIA

Leucadia 2006 Chenin Blanc (Paso Robles) $12. Barrel fermented in older oak, this has a fine dryness and crispness, with stimulating flavors of lime, grapefruit, honeysuckle and white pepper. A good bargain. **86** *—S.H. (11/1/2007)*

Leucadia 2005 Rooftop Red Blend (Paso Robles) $9. Just about half and half Cab Sauvignon and Petite Sirah, this red smells Port-y, with caramelized, brown sugar aromas. Tastes semisweet, too, with chocolate fudge, cherry jam and cassis flavors. What are we to make of it? It's all wrong for a table wine, but it's so yummy. **85 Best Buy** *—S.H. (11/1/2007)*

LEVERONI

Leveroni 2004 Chardonnay (Carneros) $16. 84 *—S.H. (12/15/2005)*

Leveroni 2003 Chardonnay (Carneros) $16. 85 *—S.H. (4/1/2005)*

Leveroni 2003 Merlot (Sonoma Valley) $18. 86 *—S.H. (12/15/2005)*

Leveroni 2002 Merlot (Sonoma Valley) $18. 90 *—S.H. (4/1/2005)*

Leveroni 2001 Merlot (Sonoma Valley) $18. 89 *—S.H. (6/1/2004)*

Leveroni 2004 Pinot Noir (Sonoma Valley) $18. 83 *—S.H. (12/15/2005)*

Leveroni 2002 Pinot Noir (Sonoma Valley) $15. 85 *—S.H. (11/1/2004)*

Leveroni 2003 Syrah (Sonoma Valley) $18. 83 —*S.H. (12/15/2005)*

Leveroni 2002 Syrah (Sonoma Valley) $18. 84 —*S.H. (6/1/2004)*

LEWLLING

Lewelling 2003 Cabernet Sauvignon (St. Helena) $50. Rough and ready Napa Cab, with sturdy tannins and a rustic texture that really need food to show their best. This has cherry fruit, coffee and earthy, herbal flavors with a touch of oak. 85 —*S.H. (6/1/2007)*

Lewelling 2003 Wight Vineyard Cabernet Sauvignon (St. Helena) $75. A single-vineyard Cab that's so ripe, it's like a spoonful of jam. Cherries, blackberries, raspberries, carob, coffee and new oak are the flavors, in a full-bodied wine where the tannins are firm. 87 —*S.H. (6/1/2007)*

LEWIS

Lewis 1997 Reserve Cabernet Sauvignon (Napa Valley) $60. 96 Cellar Selection *(11/1/2000)*

Lewis 1999 Reserve Chardonnay (Napa Valley) $48. 90 *(7/1/2001)*

Lewis 2002 Syrah (Napa Valley) $60. 90 *(9/1/2005)*

Lewis 1999 Syrah (Napa Valley) $NA. 91 *(11/1/2001)*

LIBERTY SCHOOL

Liberty School 2005 Cabernet Sauvignon (Paso Robles) $14. Always a pretty dependable Cab at around this price, the '05 is soft and basically dry, with very ripe flavors of cherry jam and blackberry preserves, and rich, dusty tannins to bite through barbecue. 85 —*S.H. (11/15/2007)*

Liberty School 2004 Cabernet Sauvignon (Paso Robles) $14. 89 Best Buy —*S.H. (12/15/2006)*

Liberty School 2003 Cabernet Sauvignon (California) $12. 87 Best Buy —*S.H. (12/15/2005)*

Liberty School 2002 Cabernet Sauvignon (California) $13. 86 —*S.H. (11/15/2004)*

Liberty School 2005 Chardonnay (Central Coast) $13. A little heavy in oak, this Chard has rich, long hangtime flavors of apricot jam and pineapples, wrapped in a creamy texture. It finishes dry and spicy. 85 —*S.H. (11/15/2007)*

Liberty School 2004 Chardonnay (Central Coast) $13. 84 —*S.H. (12/15/2006)*

Liberty School 2003 Chardonnay (Central Coast) $12. 82 —*S.H. (12/15/2005)*

Liberty School 2002 Chardonnay (Central Coast) $13. 85 —*S.H. (12/15/2004)*

Liberty School 2000 Chardonnay (Central Coast) $14. 82 —*S.H. (9/1/2003)*

Liberty School 2004 Syrah (Central Coast) $13. 86 —*S.H. (12/15/2006)*

Liberty School 2003 Syrah (California) $12. 85 —*S.H. (12/31/2005)*

USA

LIEB

Lieb 1993 Champagne Blend (North Fork of Long Island) $20. 86 —*J.C. (4/1/2001)*

Lieb 1999 Chardonnay (North Fork of Long Island) $15. 86 —*J.C. (4/1/2001)*

Lieb 2002 Merlot (North Fork of Long Island) $24. 86 —*M.D. (12/1/2006)*

Lieb 1997 Reserve Merlot (North Fork of Long Island) $20. 88 —*J.C. (4/1/2001)*

Lieb 1998 Pinot Blanc (North Fork of Long Island) $15. 84 —*J.C. (4/1/2001)*

LIGHTHOUSE

Lighthouse 2002 Crescendo Chardonnay (Central Coast) $15. 87 —*S.H. (7/1/2005)*

Lighthouse 2002 Cachet Merlot (Central Coast) $16. 90 Editors' Choice —*S.H. (7/1/2005)*

LILY

Lily 2002 Chardonnay (Sonoma County) $16. 83 —*S.H. (8/1/2005)*

Lily 2002 Pinot Noir (Sonoma Coast) $18. 86 —*S.H. (8/1/2005)*

LIMERICK LANE

Limerick Lane 2003 Collins Vineyard Syrah (Russian River Valley) $28. 89 *(9/1/2005)*

Limerick Lane 2002 Collins Vineyard Syrah (Russian River Valley) $28. 87 —*S.H. (12/15/2004)*

Limerick Lane 1999 Collins Vineyard Syrah (Russian River Valley) $36. 90 *(11/1/2001)*

Limerick Lane 2002 Collins Vineyard Zinfandel (Russian River Valley) $26. 92 —*S.H. (12/15/2004)*

Limerick Lane 2001 Collins Vineyard Zinfandel (Russian River Valley) $26. 86 *(11/1/2003)*

Limerick Lane 1999 Collins Vineyard Zinfandel (Russian River Valley) $26. 91 —*D.T. (3/1/2002)*

Limerick Lane 1998 Collins Vineyard Zinfandel (Russian River Valley) $26. 90 *(3/1/2001)*

Limerick Lane 2001 Collins Vineyard, Old Vine Zinfandel (Russian River Valley) $26. 89 *(11/1/2003)*

LINCOURT

Lincourt 2002 La Cuesta Vineyard Cabernet Sauvignon (Santa Ynez Valley) $35. 88 —*S.H. (11/1/2006)*

Lincourt 2005 Chardonnay (Santa Barbara County) $15. Lincourt is the second label of Foley, a major force in Santa Rita Hills, and this county-wide bottling shows a lot of class and finesse. It's a Chablis-type Chard, totally dry, high in acidity, with a mineral, metallic quality to the peach flavors. The finish is so rich and complex. What a great food wine. 90 Best Buy —*S.H. (2/1/2007)*

Lincourt 2004 Chardonnay (Santa Barbara County) $18. 85 —*S.H. (11/1/2006)*

Lincourt 2002 Chardonnay (Santa Barbara County) $18. 87 —*S.H. (5/1/2005)*

Lincourt 2005 Pinot Noir (Santa Rita Hills) $30. This is another brand from the well regarded Foley. Starts off with invitingly pure aromas of cola, rhubarb, Bay leaf, beetroot, pomegranate, spicy cherry pie and cinnamon stick, leading to a supple, silky, delicately powerful mouthfeel. Really lovely now and for the next few years. 89 —*S.H. (4/1/2007)*

Lincourt 2004 Pinot Noir (Santa Rita Hills) $30. Foley, whose second label this is, has been one of the most consistent Pinot producers in Santa Barbara, and their various tiers offer good value. This Santa Rita Pinot is dry and silky, an elegant wine with cherry, cola and oak flavors and a greal deal of polished complexity. 88 —*S.H. (2/1/2007)*

Lincourt 2004 Pinot Noir (Santa Barbara County) $22. 85 —*S.H. (11/1/2006)*

Lincourt 2002 Pinot Noir (Santa Barbara County) $22. 86 —*S.H. (5/1/2005)*

Lincourt 2001 Pinot Noir (Santa Barbara County) $22. 87 —*S.H. (5/1/2005)*

Lincourt 2000 Pinot Noir (Santa Barbara County) $31. 88 *(10/1/2002)*

Lincourt 2005 Sauvignon Blanc (Santa Ynez Valley) $16. Shows the dry, zesty Santa Ynez character of Sauvignon Blanc, with citrus, fig, melon and tobacco flavors that are rich and complex. Great acidity, bright and juicy, balances it all. This is a sophisticated white wine that sommeliers will love. From Foley. 88 —*S.H. (2/1/2007)*

Lincourt 2004 Sauvignon Blanc (Santa Ynez Valley) $16. 89 —*S.H. (11/1/2006)*

Lincourt 2005 Syrah (Santa Barbara County) $20. A solid, middle-of-the-road Syrah, with a gently tannic structure framing blackberry, cherry and blueberry jam, mocha, fig, leather, dried herb and spice flavors. 86 —*S.H. (12/31/2007)*

Lincourt 2004 Syrah (Santa Barbara County) $20. 87 —*S.H. (11/1/2006)*

Lincourt 2003 Syrah (Santa Barbara County) $20. 89 *(9/1/2005)*

Lincourt 2002 Syrah (Santa Barbara County) $20. 86 —*S.H. (5/1/2005)*

LINDEN

Linden 2001 Glen Manor Bordeaux Blend (Virginia) $29. 83 —*J.C. (9/1/2005)*

Linden 2001 Hardscrabble Bordeaux Blend (Virginia) $32. 85 —*M.D. (8/1/2006)*

Linden 1998 Hardscrabble Red Bordeaux Blend (Virginia) $24. 83 —*J.C. (1/1/2004)*

Linden 1997 Reserve Red Bordeaux Blend (Virginia) $28. 83 —*J.C. (1/1/2004)*

Linden 2001 Hardscrabble Chardonnay (Virginia) $22. 85 —*M.D. (8/1/2006)*

Linden 1998 Hardscrabble Chardonnay (Virginia) $20. 84 —*J.C. (1/1/2004)*

Linden 2002 Petite Verdot (Virginia) $24. 83 —*M.D. (8/1/2006)*

Linden 1999 Glen Manor Red Blend (Virginia) $23. 84 —*M.S. (3/1/2003)*

Linden 1999 Hardscrabble Red Blend (Virginia) $28. 84 —*M.S. (3/1/2003)*

Linden 2000 Vidal Blanc (Virginia) $22. 89 —*J.M. (1/1/2003)*

Linden 2003 Late Harvest Vidal Blanc (Virginia) $23. 89 —*J.C. (9/1/2005)*

LINNE CALODO

Linne Calodo 2003 Nemesis Rhône Red Blend (Paso Robles) $60. 94 Editors' Choice —*S.H. (10/1/2005)*

Linne Calodo 2003 Rising Tides Rhône Red Blend (Paso Robles) $42. 93 Editors' Choice —*S.H. (10/1/2005)*

Linne Calodo 2003 Sticks and Stones Rhône Red Blend (Paso Robles) $60. 92 Editors' Choice —*S.H. (10/1/2005)*

Linne Calodo 2005 Contrarian Rhône White Blend (Paso Robles) $36. 94 Editors' Choice —*S.H. (12/1/2006)*

Linne Calodo 2004 Contrarian Rhône White Blend (Paso Robles) $36. 92 —*S.H. (10/1/2005)*

LION VALLEY

Lion Valley 1999 Reserve Chardonnay (Willamette Valley) $16. 83 —*S.H. (4/1/2002)*

Lion Valley 1999 Estate Pinot Gris (Willamette Valley) $14. 83 —*S.H. (8/1/2002)*

LIPARITA

Liparita 2001 Cabernet Sauvignon (Napa Valley) $38. 92 —*S.H. (5/1/2005)*

Liparita 1999 Cabernet Sauvignon (Napa Valley) $36. 93 Editors' Choice —*S.H. (11/15/2003)*

Liparita 1997 Cabernet Sauvignon (Napa Valley) $45. 92 *(11/1/2000)*

Liparita 2003 Vineyard Reserve Cabernet Sauvignon (Napa Valley) $65. 89 —*S.H. (9/1/2006)*

Liparita 1999 Vineyard Reserve Cabernet Sauvignon (Napa Valley) $50. 95 Cellar Selection —*S.H. (11/15/2003)*

Liparita 1997 Vineyard Reserve Cabernet Sauvignon (Napa Valley) $65. 88 *(11/1/2000)*

Liparita 2000 Chardonnay (Carneros) $24. 87 —*J.M. (10/1/2003)*

Liparita 1998 Chardonnay (Carneros) $33. 88 *(7/1/2001)*

Liparita 2001 Merlot (Napa Valley) $29. 87 —*S.H. (5/1/2005)*

Liparita 1999 Sauvignon Blanc (Napa Valley) $18. 91 Editors' Choice —*S.H. (5/1/2001)*

Liparita 2000 Oakville Sauvignon Blanc (Napa Valley) $18. 85 *(8/1/2002)*

LITTLE VALLEY

Little Valley 1999 White Rabbit Cabernet Sauvignon (San Francisco Bay) $18. 83 —*S.H. (11/15/2003)*

Little Valley 2001 White Rabbit Chardonnay (San Francisco Bay) $13. 84 —*S.H. (3/1/2004)*

LIVINGSTON

Livingston 1996 Moffett Vineyard Cabernet Sauvignon (Napa Valley) $50. 88 *(3/1/2000)*

Livingston 1997 Mitchell Vineyard Syrah (Napa Valley) $35. 91 *(3/1/2000)*

LIVINGSTON MOFFETT

Livingston Moffett 2004 20th Anniversary Vintage Cabernet Sauvignon (Rutherford) $95. They pulled out their best for their birthday, and the result is a spectacular wine. Dense and concentrated in enormously complex cassis, black currant, cherry pie and cedar, it shows the dryness and firm tannins of a fine young Cabernet. Easy to predict a good lifetime ahead. Give it a year to resolve, and then should develop slowly for another 6–8 years, at least. 94 —*S.H. (9/1/2007)*

Livingston Moffett 2002 Mitchell Vineyard Syrah (Napa Valley) $27. 87 *(9/1/2005)*

Livingston Moffett 2004 Parkinson Vineyard Syrah (Oak Knoll) $45. Co-fermented with 3% Viognier, this single-vineyard Syrah aims at the Northern Rhône. It's very dry and tannic, with a crunch of acidity, and there are powerfully ripe, deep flavors of blackberries, cherries, carob, leather and plums. Reminds me of a young Qupe Bien Nacido. Tight and closed now, with lots of astringency, but should develop over the next 5–7 years. 90 Cellar Selection —*S.H. (9/1/2007)*

Livingston Moffett 2002 Parkinson Vineyard Syrah (Napa Valley) $45. 85 *(9/1/2005)*

Livingston Moffett 1997 Gemstone Vineyard Bordeaux Blend (Napa Valley) $75. 90 *(11/1/2000)*

Livingston Moffett 1999 Chardonnay (Napa Valley) $40. 88 *(7/1/2001)*

Livingston Moffett 1999 Mitchell Vineyard Syrah (Napa Valley) $35. 89 *(11/1/2001)*

LLANO

Llano 1997 Signature Bordeaux Blend (Texas) $9. 91 *(11/15/1999)*

LLANO ESTACADO

Llano Estacado 1998 Celler Select Cabernet Sauvignon (Texas) $18. 90 —*S.H. (5/1/2001)*

Llano Estacado 2000 Chardonnay (Texas) $12. 88 —*S.H. (5/1/2001)*

Llano Estacado 2000 Cellar Select Chardonnay (Texas) $18. 90 —*S.H. (5/1/2001)*

Llano Estacado 1999 Signature Red Red Blend (Texas) $9. 88 —*S.H. (5/1/2001)*

Llano Estacado 1999 Passionelle Rhône Red Blend (Texas) $9. 84 —*S.H. (5/1/2001)*

Llano Estacado 2000 Sauvignon Blanc (Texas) $8. 86 —*S.H. (5/1/2001)*

LOCAL WINE COMPANY

Local Wine Company 2006 Murphy's Law Rosé Blend (Columbia Valley (WA)) $12. A blend of Sangiovese, Grenache and Syrah, this Washington-grown, Oregon-produced rosé is thick and juicy, with flavors of stone fruits, and a bit of cherry. It's full in the mouth, but turns a little flabby, and finishes with a tight, reduced quality. 85 —*P.G. (7/1/2007)*

LOCKWOOD

Lockwood 2004 Partner's Reserve Bordeaux Blend (Monterey) $20. Mostly Cab, with Malbec, this Bordeaux blend is dry and not quite ripe despite the hot vintage. It has weedy, minty flavors and harsh acidity. 82 —*S.H. (12/15/2007)*

Lockwood 2005 Cabernet Sauvignon (Monterey) $13. Harsh, tannic and unripe, this simply structured Cab has a green minty flavor, with a suggestion of cherries. Drink now. 82 —*S.H. (11/15/2007)*

Lockwood 2004 Estate Cabernet Sauvignon (Monterey) $13. 83 —*S.H. (12/15/2006)*

Lockwood 2001 Estate Cabernet Sauvignon (Monterey County) $12. 85 —*S.H. (7/1/2005)*

Lockwood 1997 Estate Grown & Bottled Cabernet Sauvignon (Monterey) $16. 88 *(6/1/2001)*

Lockwood 1999 Estate Grown & Estate Bottled Cabernet Sauvignon (Monterey) $15. 86 *(11/15/2002)*

Lockwood 2005 Chardonnay (Monterey County) $11. Oaky and simple, with apricot and tropical fruit flavors and a creamy texture brightened with clean acidity. This is a pretty good price for a fresh Monterey Chard. 84 —*S.H. (7/1/2007)*

Lockwood 2004 Chardonnay (Monterey) $11. 82 —*S.H. (12/15/2006)*

Lockwood 1998 Chardonnay (Monterey County) $16. 87 Best Buy *(6/1/2001)*

Lockwood 2000 Estate Grown & Bottled Chardonnay (Monterey) $15. 86 —*S.H. (2/1/2003)*

Lockwood 1998 Estate Grown & Bottled Chardonnay (Monterey County) $16. 86 *(6/1/2000)*

Lockwood 1998 VSR Chardonnay (Monterey) $35. 90 *(7/1/2001)*

Lockwood 1997 VSR Chardonnay (Monterey) $30. 89 *(6/1/2001)*

Lockwood 1997 VSR Meritage (Monterey County) $45. 92 Editors' Choice *(6/1/2001)*

Lockwood 2005 Merlot (Monterey) $13. A little sharp and pepperminty, but with enough cherry, blackberry and spice flavors to make it an easy quaffer with burgers and tacos. 83 —*S.H. (11/15/2007)*

Lockwood 2002 Merlot (Monterey) $13. 84 —*S.H. (12/15/2006)*

Lockwood 2000 Merlot (Monterey) $12. 84 —*S.H. (5/1/2004)*

Lockwood 1997 Merlot (Monterey County) $18. 88 Best Buy *(6/1/2001)*

Lockwood 2001 Estate Merlot (Monterey County) $12. 85 —*S.H. (7/1/2005)*

Lockwood 1999 Estate Grown & Estate Bottled Merlot (Monterey) $15. 86 *(11/15/2002)*

Lockwood 1997 VSR Merlot (Monterey) $45. 91 *(6/1/2001)*

Lockwood 1998 Pinot Blanc (Monterey) $12. 85 *(6/1/2001)*

Lockwood 2004 Block 7 Pinot Noir (Monterey) $20. 88 —*S.H. (12/15/2006)*

Lockwood 2005 Sauvignon Blanc (Monterey) $11. 84 —*S.H. (12/15/2006)*

Lockwood 2001 Sauvignon Blanc (Monterey) $9. 85 —*S.H. (5/1/2004)*

Lockwood 1999 Sauvignon Blanc (Monterey County) $12. 87 Best Buy *(6/1/2001)*

Lockwood 2004 Estate Sauvignon Blanc (Monterey) $10. 86 Best Buy —*S.H. (12/1/2005)*

Lockwood 1998 Estate Grown Sauvignon Blanc (Monterey) $11. 87 —*L.W. (5/1/2000)*

Lockwood 2000 Estate Grown & Bottled Sauvignon Blanc (Monterey County) $11. 87 —*S.H. (7/1/2003)*

Lockwood 2005 Syrah (Monterey) $13. A little rustic, but not bad for the price. This rugged wine brims with cherries, blackberries, spices and herbs, and will happily wash down barbecue. **83** *—S.H. (11/15/2007)*

Lockwood 2001 Syrah (Monterey) $14. 86 *—S.H. (6/1/2005)*

Lockwood 1999 Syrah (Monterey) $16. 85 *—S.H. (12/1/2002)*

Lockwood 1996 Syrah (Monterey County) $15. 87 *—L.W. (2/1/2000)*

Lockwood 2001 Estate Syrah (Monterey County) $11. 85 *—S.H. (7/1/2005)*

Lockwood 2002 Shale Ridge Syrah (Monterey) $8. 84 *—S.H. (4/1/2004)*

LOGAN

Logan 2002 Sleepy Hollow Vineyard Chardonnay (Monterey County) $18. 86 *—S.H. (10/1/2004)*

Logan 2001 Sleepy Hollow Vineyard Chardonnay (Monterey County) $18. 87 *—S.H. (2/1/2004)*

Logan 1998 Sleepy Hollow Vineyard Chardonnay (Monterey County) $17. 88 *(6/1/2000)*

Logan 2000 Pinot Noir (Monterey County) $18. 85 *—S.H. (10/1/2004)*

Logan 2002 Sleepy Hollow Vineyard Pinot Noir (Monterey County) $18. 86 *—S.H. (12/15/2005)*

Logan 1999 Sleepy Hollow Vineyard Pinot Noir (Monterey County) $20. 86 *—S.H. (2/1/2004)*

LOGAN RIDGE

Logan Ridge 2002 Riesling (Finger Lakes) $9. 87 Best Buy *—J.C. (8/1/2003)*

LOKOYA

Lokoya 2002 Cabernet Sauvignon (Mount Veeder) $120. 94 Cellar Selection *—S.H. (5/1/2005)*

LOLONIS

Lolonis 2004 Cabernet Sauvignon (Redwood Valley) $20. It's hot up there in Redwood Valley, and this wine, even from a coolish vintage, is soft and cooked in fruit, although fortunately it's fully dry. It has stewed cherry and blackberry flavors, with a touch of raisins. **84** *—S.H. (9/1/2007)*

Lolonis 2002 Cabernet Sauvignon (Redwood Valley) $22. 85 *—S.H. (8/1/2005)*

Lolonis 2001 Cabernet Sauvignon (Redwood Valley) $22. 87 *—S.H. (10/1/2004)*

Lolonis 2000 Cabernet Sauvignon (Redwood Valley) $22. 82 *—S.H. (11/15/2003)*

Lolonis 1999 Private Reserve Cabernet Sauvignon (Redwood Valley) $35. 85 *—S.H. (3/1/2004)*

Lolonis 1997 Private Reserve Cabernet Sauvignon (Redwood Valley) $30. 89 *(11/1/2000)*

Lolonis 2002 Winegrower Selection Cabernet Sauvignon (Redwood Valley) $32. 84 *—S.H. (3/1/2006)*

Lolonis 2001 Winegrower Selection Cabernet Sauvignon (Redwood Valley) $32. 84 *—S.H. (10/1/2004)*

Lolonis 2002 Winegrowers Selection Castenon Vineyard Cabernet Sauvignon (Redwood Valley) $32. 88 *—S.H. (8/1/2005)*

Lolonis NV Carignane (Redwood Valley) $14. 86 *—S.H. (5/1/2002)*

Lolonis 2005 Chardonnay (Redwood Valley) $20. A little one-dimensional and on the soft side, but enormously rich in apple butter, pineapple custard, apricot jam, gingerbread, vanilla honey and sweet oak flavors. **87** *—S.H. (9/1/2007)*

Lolonis 2004 Chardonnay (Redwood Valley) $17. 84 *—S.H. (2/1/2006)*

Lolonis 2000 Chardonnay (Redwood Valley) $17. 84 *—S.H. (6/1/2003)*

Lolonis 1998 Chardonnay (Redwood Valley) $16. 86 *(6/1/2000)*

Lolonis 1997 Chardonnay (Redwood Valley) $21. 86 *—S.H. (3/1/2000)*

Lolonis 2002 Antigone Late Harvest Chardonnay (Redwood Valley) $24. 88 *—S.H. (2/1/2006)*

Lolonis 1997 Late Harvest Chardonnay (Redwood Valley) $35. 88 *—S.H. (6/1/2003)*

Lolonis 2000 Private Reserve Chardonnay (Redwood Valley) $30. 86 *—S.H. (6/1/2003)*

Lolonis 2005 Fumé Blanc (Redwood Valley) $14. A little bit sweet, but the acidity is so bright that it balances everything out. Just delicious, with juicy citrus, spearmint, gingersnap and peach custard flavors, finished with cinnamon and nutmeg. **86** *—S.H. (4/1/2007)*

Lolonis 2003 Fumé Blanc (Redwood Valley) $13. 85 *—S.H. (12/1/2004)*

Lolonis 2001 Fumé Blanc (Redwood Valley) $14. 87 *—S.H. (7/1/2003)*

Lolonis 2000 Fumé Blanc (Redwood Valley) $14. 87 *—S.H. (5/1/2002)*

Lolonis 2004 Merlot (Redwood Valley) $18. From this warm, interior Mendocino appellation comes this slightly cooked Merlot. It has stewed cherry and blackberry flavors, but is dry and clean, with oak and herb complexities. **85** *—S.H. (11/1/2007)*

Lolonis 2001 Merlot (Redwood Valley) $22. 85 *—S.H. (6/1/2004)*

Lolonis 1997 Merlot (Redwood Valley) $21. 85 *—S.H. (3/1/2000)*

Lolonis 2002 Heritage Vineyards Petros Merlot (Redwood Valley) $40. 85 *—S.H. (12/15/2006)*

Lolonis 2001 Petros Heritage Vineyards Merlot (Redwood Valley) $65. 90 *—S.H. (10/1/2004)*

Lolonis 1999 Private Reserve Merlot (Redwood Valley) $28. 88 *—S.H. (8/1/2003)*

Lolonis 1998 Private Reserve Merlot (Redwood Valley) $28. 82 *—S.H. (5/1/2002)*

Lolonis 1997 Private Reserve Merlot (Redwood Valley) $28. 88 *(6/1/2001)*

Lolonis 2000 Petros Merlot-Syrah (Redwood Valley) $70. 84 *—S.H. (5/1/2004)*

Lolonis 1996 Orpheus Private Reserve Petite Sirah (Redwood Valley) $20. 89 *—M.S. (3/1/2000)*

Lolonis 1999 Orpheus-Private Reserve Petite Sirah (Redwood Valley) $35. 84 *(4/1/2003)*

Lolonis NV Ladybug Red Cuvée III Red Blend (Redwood Valley) $13. 85 *—S.H. (12/15/2004)*

Lolonis 2001 Ladybug Red Old Vines Red Wine Red Blend (Redwood Valley) $13. 85 *—S.H. (6/1/2004)*

Lolonis 2000 Old Vines Ladybug Red Blend (Redwood Valley) $12. 87 *—S.H. (5/1/2004)*

Lolonis NV Old Vines Ladybug Red Cuvée V Red Blend (Redwood Valley) $13. 83 *—S.H. (3/1/2006)*

Lolonis 1998 Petros Red Blend (Redwood Valley) $70. 90 *—S.H. (5/1/2002)*

Lolonis 2002 Eugenia Late Harvest Heritage Vineyard Sauvignon Blanc (Redwood Valley) $32. 90 *—S.H. (2/1/2006)*

Lolonis 1998 Fumé Blanc Sauvignon Blanc (Redwood Valley) $12. 86 *—S.H. (5/1/2000)*

Lolonis 2002 Winegrower Selection Syrah (Redwood Valley) $32. 86 *—S.H. (12/1/2005)*

Lolonis 1997 Zinfandel (Redwood Valley) $20. 87 *—J.C. (5/1/2000)*

Lolonis 2003 Zinfandel (Redwood Valley) $20. 85 *—S.H. (12/1/2005)*

Lolonis 2002 Zinfandel (Redwood Valley) $18. 84 *—S.H. (8/1/2005)*

Lolonis 2001 Zinfandel (Redwood Valley) $18. 90 Editors' Choice *(11/1/2003)*

Lolonis 2000 Zinfandel (Redwood Valley) $18. 87 *—S.H. (9/1/2003)*

Lolonis 1999 Zinfandel (Redwood Valley) $20. 84 *—S.H. (5/1/2002)*

Lolonis 1998 Zinfandel (Redwood Valley) $20. 88 *—P.G. (3/1/2001)*

Lolonis 1999 Beaucage Vineyard Zinfandel (Redwood Valley) $30. 83 *—S.H. (5/1/2002)*

Lolonis 2003 Late Harvest Zinfandel Port Zinfandel (Redwood Valley) $32. 92 *—S.H. (5/1/2006)*

Lolonis 1998 Private Reserve Zinfandel (Redwood Valley) $30. 82 *—D.T. (3/1/2002)*

Lolonis 1996 Private Reserve Zinfandel (Redwood Valley) $25. 88 *—J.C. (9/1/1999)*

Lolonis 2000 Tollini Vineyard Zinfandel (Redwood Valley) $32. 86 *—J.M. (9/1/2003)*

Lolonis 1998 Tollini Vineyard Zinfandel (Redwood Valley) $28. 87 *—P.G. (3/1/2001)*

Lolonis 2001 Winegrower Selection Zinfandel (Redwood Valley) $32. 87 *—S.H. (6/1/2004)*

Lolonis 2002 Winegrowers Selection Tollini Vineyard Zinfandel (Redwood Valley) $32. 86 *—S.H. (8/1/2005)*

LONDER

Londer 2003 Kent Ritchie Vineyard Chardonnay (Sonoma Coast) $36. 90 *—S.H. (8/1/2005)*

Londer 2002 Kent Ritchie Vineyard Chardonnay (Sonoma Coast) $35. 90 *—S.H. (6/1/2004)*

Londer 2003 Dry Gewürztraminer (Anderson Valley) $20. 86 —*S.H. (3/1/2005)*

Londer 2002 Dry Gewürztraminer (Anderson Valley) $20. 85 —*S.H. (6/1/2004)*

Londer 2004 Pinot Noir (Anderson Valley) $30. 84 —*S.H. (11/1/2006)*

Londer 2002 Pinot Noir (Anderson Valley) $28. 87 —*S.H. (2/1/2005)*

Londer 2001 Pinot Noir (Anderson Valley) $28. 85 —*S.H. (6/1/2004)*

Londer 2004 Keefer Ranch Pinot Noir (Green Valley) $42. 86 —*S.H. (11/1/2006)*

Londer 2004 Londer Estate Grown Pinot Noir (Anderson Valley) $46. 85 —*S.H. (11/1/2006)*

Londer 2004 Paraboll Pinot Noir (Anderson Valley) $52. 89 —*S.H. (11/1/2006)*

Londer 2002 Paraboll Pinot Noir (Anderson Valley) $45. 88 —*S.H. (2/1/2005)*

Londer 2001 Paraboll Pinot Noir (Anderson Valley) $42. 86 —*S.H. (6/1/2004)*

Londer 2001 Van Der Kamp Vineyard Pinot Noir (Sonoma Mountain) $35. 88 —*S.H. (6/1/2004)*

LONE CANARY

Lone Canary 2005 Barbera (Columbia Valley (WA)) $15. Lone Canary's Mike Scott has found some at the Milbrandt Vineyards, and this well-crafted bottle shows that the grape has some potential in Washington. Tart, sour cherry flavors are right up front in this young wine, which doesn't hide its sharp acids. Balanced with flavors of cherry and strawberry and no significant impact from the oak barrels, it's a good choice for those who like their wines racy and tart. **86** —*P.G. (3/1/2007)*

Lone Canary NV Red Bordeaux Blend (Yakima Valley) $13. 88 Best Buy —*P.G. (9/1/2004)*

Lone Canary 2003 Rouge Bordeaux Blend (Columbia Valley (WA)) $20. 87 —*P.G. (6/1/2006)*

Lone Canary 2002 Rouge Bordeaux Blend (Yakima Valley) $20. 89 —*P.G. (9/1/2004)*

Lone Canary 2004 Cabernet Franc (Columbia Valley (WA)) $20. This is dark and slightly murky, with sweet scents of cooked fruits and baking spices. Somehow it keeps the alcohol levels well down (13%) but the fruit flavors are ultraripe, pruny, and deep. There is a good long finish that delves into soy, earth, baking chocolate, vanilla and clove, and is undeniably fascinating. This is not a wine that will ring everyone's bell, but it offers a lot of flavor. **86** —*P.G. (8/1/2007)*

Lone Canary NV Red Blend (Yakima Valley) $13. 85 —*P.G. (12/31/2003)*

Lone Canary 2003 Rosso Red Blend (Columbia Valley (WA)) $15. 89 —*P.G. (4/1/2006)*

Lone Canary 2002 Rosso Red Blend (Yakima Valley) $17. 88 —*P.G. (9/1/2004)*

Lone Canary 2004 Sangiovese (Wahluke Slope) $18. This Sangiovese-based blend, which also includes 10% Merlot and a bit of the two Cabs, used to be labeled "Rosso." It is quite ripe, almost cooked, and its flavors are round, sweet, warm, soft and almost tropical. This is not your typical Sangio, what with its flavors of bananas and cherries, and just a hint of tobacco. **86** —*P.G. (8/1/2007)*

Lone Canary 2006 Sauvignon Blanc (Columbia Valley (WA)) $10. I like Mike Scott's Sauv Blancs for their pungent, grassy aromas, and their piercingly tart acids. The spiky fruit flavors combine pear and pineapple, gooseberry and lime—think New Zealand without the asparagus. This is really a lovely bottle, ripe and round, lush and perfectly balanced between tart and fruity. **89 Best Buy** —*P.G. (8/1/2007)*

Lone Canary 2005 Sauvignon Blanc (Yakima Valley) $10. 88 Best Buy —*P.G. (6/1/2006)*

Lone Canary 2003 Sauvignon Blanc (Yakima Valley) $10. 88 Best Buy —*P.G. (9/1/2004)*

Lone Canary 2002 Sauvignon Blanc (Yakima Valley) $10. 88 Best Buy —*P.G. (12/31/2003)*

LONETREE

Lonetree 1997 Sangiovese (Mendocino) $17. 89 —*S.H. (9/1/2000)*

Lonetree 1998 Syrah (Mendocino County) $20. 85 —*S.H. (11/15/2001)*

Lonetree 1998 Eaglepoint Ranch Syrah (Mendocino) $20. 87 *(10/1/2001)*

Lonetree 1997 Eaglepoint Ranch Syrah (Mendocino County) $19. 91 *(5/1/2000)*

Lonetree 1996 Zinfandel (Mendocino) $16. 88 —*S.H. (5/1/2000)*

LONG

Long 1998 Seghesio Vineyard Sangiovese (Sonoma County) $25. 90 —*S.H. (12/15/1999)*

LONG MEADOW RANCH

Long Meadow Ranch 1997 Cabernet Sauvignon (Napa Valley) $50. 90 *(11/1/2000)*

Long Meadow Ranch 1996 Cabernet Sauvignon (Napa Valley) $59. 92 —*M.S. (12/31/1999)*

Long Meadow Ranch 2001 Cabernet Sauvignon (Napa Valley) $55. 90 —*S.H. (5/1/2005)*

Long Meadow Ranch 1999 Cabernet Sauvignon (Napa Valley) $60. 91 —*S.H. (11/15/2002)*

Long Meadow Ranch 1998 Cabernet Sauvignon (Napa Valley) $57. 87 —*S.H. (11/15/2002)*

LONG RIDGE GROVE VINEYARDS

Long Ridge Grove Vineyards 2001 Cabernet Sauvignon (Central Coast) $10. 81 —*S.H. (6/1/2004)*

Long Ridge Grove Vineyards 2002 Chardonnay (California) $10. 84 —*S.H. (6/1/2004)*

Long Ridge Grove Vineyards 2001 Merlot (Central Coast) $10. 83 —*S.H. (6/1/2004)*

LONG VINEYARDS

Long Vineyards 1998 Cabernet Sauvignon (Napa Valley) $60. 92 —*J.M. (12/1/2001)*

Long Vineyards 1998 Chardonnay (Napa Valley) $40. 93 Cellar Selection —*J.M. (12/1/2001)*

Long Vineyards 2002 Laird Family Vineyard Pinot Grigio (Carneros) $18. 86 —*S.H. (2/1/2004)*

Long Vineyards 2000 Laird Family Vineyard Pinot Grigio (Carneros) $20. 88 —*J.M. (11/15/2001)*

Long Vineyards 1999 Seghesio Vineyards Sangiovese (Sonoma County) $25. 85 —*J.M. (12/1/2001)*

LONGBOARD

Longboard 2003 Redgrav Vineyard Cabernet Sauvignon (Alexander Valley) $50. 89 —*S.H. (12/15/2006)*

Longboard 2003 Rochioli Vineyard Cabernet Sauvignon (Russian River Valley) $50. 88 —*S.H. (12/15/2006)*

Longboard 2001 Rochioli Vineyard Cabernet Sauvignon (Russian River Valley) $42. 90 —*S.H. (11/15/2003)*

Longboard 1999 Rochioli Vineyard Cabernet Sauvignon (Russian River Valley) $50. 93 Editors' Choice —*S.H. (11/15/2002)*

Longboard 2005 DaKine Vineyard Merlot (Russian River Valley) $24. This is a new wine from Longboard. The vineyard is on Westside Road, in the Middle Reach area that is prime Pinot country. But somehow, Merlot loves it. Softly lush and complex, with blackberry, blueberry, cherry, cola and spiced coffee flavors, finishing with new oaky vanillins. Really notable for its balance and harmony. **92** —*S.H. (9/1/2007)*

Longboard 2006 Sauvignon Blanc (Russian River Valley) $24. This cool vintage wine, with almost no oak, is crisp and young in acids, with gooseberry flavors and a touch of feline influence. It's simple and dry. **84** —*S.H. (7/1/2007)*

Longboard 2005 Sauvignon Blanc (Russian River Valley) $24. 89 —*S.H. (12/15/2006)*

Longboard 2003 Syrah (Russian River Valley) $32. 88 *(9/1/2005)*

Longboard 2003 Syrah (Russian River Valley) $32. 86 —*S.H. (12/15/2006)*

Longboard 2002 Syrah (Russian River Valley) $33. 91 —*S.H. (12/31/2004)*

Longboard 2001 Syrah (Russian River Valley) $29. 87 —*S.H. (2/1/2004)*

Longboard 2000 Syrah (Russian River Valley) $29. 91 —*S.H. (12/1/2002)*

Longboard 1999 Syrah (Russian River Valley) $27. 90 —*S.H. (12/1/2002)*

Longboard 2002 Dakine Syrah (Russian River Valley) $47. 90 —*S.H. (12/31/2004)*

Longboard 2003 Dakine Vineyard Syrah (Russian River Valley) $45. 90 —*S.H. (12/15/2006)*

Longboard 2003 Dakine Vineyard Syrah (Russian River Valley) $47. 85 *(9/1/2005)*

LONGFELLOW

Longfellow 2002 Cabernet Sauvignon (Napa Valley) $50. 83 —*S.H. (9/1/2006)*

Longfellow 2001 Cabernet Sauvignon (Napa Valley) $50. 83 *—S.H. (5/1/2005)*

Longfellow 2003 Pinot Noir (Sonoma Coast) $35. 87 *—S.H. (11/1/2006)*

Longfellow 2002 Pinot Noir (Sonoma Coast) $35. 90 *—S.H. (5/1/2005)*

Longfellow 2001 Pinot Noir (Los Carneros) $36. 89 *—J.C. (3/1/2004)*

Longfellow 2003 Syrah (Dry Creek Valley) $32. 93 Editors' Choice *—S.H. (11/1/2006)*

Longfellow 2002 Syrah (Dry Creek Valley) $32. 89 *—S.H. (5/1/2005)*

Longfellow 2001 Syrah (Dry Creek Valley) $29. 87 *—S.H. (2/1/2004)*

LONGORIA

Longoria 2005 Clover Creek Vineyard Albariño (Santa Ynez Valley) $26. 93 Editors' Choice *—S.H. (12/15/2006)*

Longoria 2000 Evidence Bordeaux Blend (Santa Barbara County) $35. 89 *—S.H. (11/15/2003)*

Longoria 2003 Evidence Red Wine Bordeaux Blend (Santa Barbara County) $42. 87 *—S.H. (12/15/2006)*

Longoria 2000 Blues Cuvée Cabernet Franc (Santa Ynez Valley) $25. 87 *—S.H. (6/1/2003)*

Longoria 2005 Chardonnay (Santa Rita Hills) $28. A blend of the Foley and Sweeney vineyards, both of them top estates, this Chard has rich lemon drop and mineral flavors, with a subtle coat of toasty oak. It's crisp and clean and very fine. **90** *—S.H. (4/1/2007)*

Longoria 2001 Chardonnay (Santa Rita Hills) $25. 92 Editors' Choice *—S.H. (12/15/2003)*

Longoria 2000 Clos Pepe Vineyard Chardonnay (Santa Barbara) $32. 90 *—S.H. (12/15/2002)*

Longoria 2005 Cuvee Diana Chardonnay (Santa Rita Hills) $40. The volume on this wine is kicked way up over Longoria's regular '05. It's a voluptuous blend of two old-vine vineyards, Sanford & Benedict and Sweeney. The wine possesses a weight and density that impress, with a rich, exotic array of flavors: Key lime pie, pineapple custard, candied ginger, macaroon, honey and buttered toast, with a finish of mineral and steel. Completely balanced, this gorgeous Chard will hold for many years. **95 Editors' Choice** *—S.H. (4/1/2007)*

USA

Longoria 2004 Cuvée Diana Chardonnay (Santa Rita Hills) $36. 93 *—S.H. (11/15/2006)*

Longoria 2002 Cuvée Diana Chardonnay (Santa Rita Hills) $32. 92 *—S.H. (2/1/2005)*

Longoria 1999 Huber Vineyard Chardonnay (Santa Ynez Valley) $32. 86 *(7/1/2001)*

Longoria 2000 Mt. Carmel Vineyard Chardonnay (Santa Barbara County) $36. 92 *—S.H. (12/15/2002)*

Longoria 1999 Mt. Carmel Vineyard Chardonnay (Santa Ynez Valley) $60. 88 *(7/1/2001)*

Longoria 1998 Sanford & Benedict Vineyard Chardonnay (Santa Ynez Valley) $28. 88 *(6/1/2000)*

Longoria 1998 Santa Rita Cuvée Chardonnay (Santa Ynez Valley) $25. 87 *(6/1/2000)*

Longoria 1997 Santa Rita Cuvée Chardonnay (Santa Ynez Valley) $25. 89 *—S.H. (7/1/1999)*

Longoria 2000 Santa Rita Hills Chardonnay (Santa Barbara County) $25. 92 *—S.H. (9/1/2002)*

Longoria 2004 Alisos Vineyard Grenache (Santa Barbara County) $22. 87 *—S.H. (12/15/2006)*

Longoria 1996 Merlot (Santa Ynez Valley) $23. 89 *—S.H. (9/1/1999)*

Longoria 1999 Merlot (Santa Barbara County) $28. 87 *—S.H. (4/1/2003)*

Longoria 1998 Merlot (Santa Barbara County) $28. 85 *—J.C. (6/1/2001)*

Longoria 2005 Pinot Grigio (Santa Barbara County) $19. 85 *—S.H. (12/1/2006)*

Longoria 2004 Pinot Grigio (Santa Barbara County) $19. 84 *—S.H. (2/1/2006)*

Longoria 2002 Pinot Grigio (Santa Barbara County) $18. 88 *—S.H. (12/1/2003)*

Longoria 2005 Pinot Noir (Santa Rita Hills) $32. What a beautiful translucent ruby color, so clean and pure! The wine itself is direct in raspberry, cherry and cola flavors, but it's not simple. Shows layers of spice, leather, Provençal herbs and fine oak, with a silky mouthfeel. A real sommeliers' wine, it's a blend of Longoria's Fe Ciega vineyard and the Foley estate. **92** *—S.H. (4/1/2007)*

Longoria 2003 Bien Nacido Vineyard Pinot Noir (Santa Maria Valley) $42. 94 Editors' Choice *—S.H. (8/1/2006)*

Longoria 2002 Bien Nacido Vineyard Pinot Noir (Santa Maria Valley) $NA. 84 *(11/1/2004)*

Longoria 2001 Bien Nacido Vineyard Pinot Noir (Santa Maria Valley) $36. 85 *—S.H. (7/1/2003)*

Longoria 1999 Bien Nacido Vineyard Pinot Noir (Santa Maria Valley) $36. 89 *(10/1/2002)*

Longoria 2005 Fe Ciega Vineyard Pinot Noir (Santa Rita Hills) $48. You'd never guess the power from the pale color. A multi-clone blend, it impresses from the first sniff, all puréed ripe cherries and strawberries, leading to a dramatically fruited, fresh, pure and vibrant mouthfeel. Should hold and improve for a decade. **95 Editors' Choice** *—S.H. (4/1/2007)*

Longoria 2004 Fe Ciega Vineyard Pinot Noir (Santa Rita Hills) $43. 95 Editors' Choice *—S.H. (11/15/2006)*

Longoria 2002 Fe Ciega Vineyard Pinot Noir (Santa Rita Hills) $40. 91 Editors' Choice *—S.H. (11/1/2004)*

Longoria 2001 Fe Cienaga Pinot Noir (Santa Rita Hills) $36. 94 *—S.H. (3/1/2004)*

Longoria 2004 Mt. Carmel Vineyard Pinot Noir (Santa Rita Hills) $85. 96 Editors' Choice *—S.H. (3/1/2006)*

Longoria 2002 Mt. Carmel Vineyard Pinot Noir (Santa Rita Hills) $50. 94 *—S.H. (11/1/2004)*

Longoria 2001 Mt. Carmel Vineyard Pinot Noir (Santa Rita Hills) $50. 92 *—S.H. (10/1/2003)*

Longoria 2000 Mt. Carmel Vineyard Pinot Noir (Santa Barbara County) $50. 88 *(10/1/2002)*

Longoria 2005 Rancho Santa Rosa Vineyard Pinot Noir (Santa Rita Hills) $45. Made from the Pommard clone grown at the Foley estate vineyard, near the eastern edge of the appellation, this Pinot is tremendously aromatic. It's slightly rustic and backward now, with rhubarb, mushroom, cherry jam and Asian spice flavors. Shows gobs of complexity and is rich and balanced, but will benefit from short-term aging. Give it four years in the bottle. **93 Cellar Selection** *—S.H. (4/1/2007)*

Longoria 2005 Sanford & Benedict Vineyard Pinot Noir (Santa Rita Hills) $42. Classic S&B Pinot, young and grapy now, and a little sharp in acids, this wine's aristocratic rusticity calls for time in the cellar. Shows primary fruit cherries and black raspberries, with earthy, forest floor Portobello mushroom notes and distinctive tannins. Made from the oldest vines in the vineyard, it's a wine that should ease into its own by 2009, and hold for another five years. **94** *—S.H. (4/1/2007)*

Longoria 2002 Sanford & Benedict Vineyard Pinot Noir (Santa Rita Hills) $42. 91 *—S.H. (11/1/2004)*

Longoria 2001 Syrah (Santa Barbara County) $22. 92 Editors' Choice *—S.H. (2/1/2004)*

Longoria 2000 Syrah (Santa Barbara County) $22. 86 *—S.H. (12/1/2002)*

Longoria 2003 Alisos Vineyard Syrah (Santa Barbara County) $32. 92 Editors' Choice *—S.H. (12/1/2006)*

Longoria 2001 Alisos Vineyard Syrah (Santa Barbara County) $22. 93 *—S.H. (2/1/2004)*

LOOKOUT RIDGE

Lookout Ridge 2000 Chardonnay (Sonoma Coast) $35. 90 *—S.H. (6/1/2005)*

Lookout Ridge 2001 Keefer Ranch Pinot Noir (Sonoma Coast) $45. 88 *—S.H. (6/1/2005)*

Lookout Ridge 2001 Alta Coma Sangiovese (Mendocino) $40. 88 *—S.H. (6/1/2005)*

LORANE VALLEY

Lorane Valley 1996 Chardonnay (Oregon) $10. 86 *—M.M. (12/31/1999)*

LORCA

Lorca 2004 Pinot Gris (Monterey County) $14. 86 *—S.H. (2/1/2006)*

LORING WINE COMPANY

Loring Wine Company 2004 Brosseau Vineyard Pinot Noir (Chalone) $48. 90 Cellar Selection *—S.H. (5/1/2006)*

Loring Wine Company 2002 Brosseau Vineyard Pinot Noir (Chalone) $46. 88 *—S.H. (11/1/2004)*

Loring Wine Company 2004 Cargasacchi Vineyard Pinot Noir (Santa Rita Hills) $48. 91 *—S.H. (5/1/2006)*

Loring Wine Company 2000 Clos Pepe Pinot Noir (Santa Lucia Highlands) $40. 91 Editors' Choice *(10/1/2002)*

Loring Wine Company 2004 Clos Pepe Vineyard Pinot Noir (Santa Rita Hills) $48. 88 *—S.H. (5/1/2006)*

Loring Wine Company 2002 Clos Pepe Vineyard Pinot Noir (Santa Rita Hills) $46. 87 *—S.H. (11/1/2004)*

Loring Wine Company 2004 Durrell Vineyard Pinot Noir (Sonoma Coast) $48. 91 *—S.H. (5/1/2006)*

Loring Wine Company 2004 Garys' Vineyard Pinot Noir (Santa Lucia Highlands) $48. 94 Editors' Choice *—S.H. (5/1/2006)*

Loring Wine Company 2003 Garys' Vineyard Pinot Noir (Santa Lucia Highlands) $46. 90 *—S.H. (7/1/2005)*

Loring Wine Company 2002 Garys' Vineyard Pinot Noir (Santa Lucia Highlands) $46. 87 *—S.H. (11/1/2004)*

Loring Wine Company 2000 Garys' Vineyard Pinot Noir (Santa Lucia Highlands) $40. 92 Editors' Choice *(10/1/2002)*

Loring Wine Company 2004 Keefer Ranch Vineyard Pinot Noir (Green Valley) $48. 86 *—S.H. (5/1/2006)*

Loring Wine Company 2004 Llama Farm Pinot Noir (California) $48. 88 *—S.H. (5/1/2006)*

Loring Wine Company 2004 Naylor Dry Hole Vineyard Pinot Noir (Chalone) $48. 89 *—S.H. (5/1/2006)*

Loring Wine Company 2004 Rancho Ontiveros Vineyard Pinot Noir (Santa Maria Valley) $48. 89 *—S.H. (5/1/2006)*

Loring Wine Company 2002 Rancho Ontiveros Vineyard Pinot Noir (Santa Maria Valley) $46. 85 *—S.H. (11/1/2004)*

Loring Wine Company 2004 Rosella's Vineyard Pinot Noir (Santa Lucia Highlands) $48. 93 *—S.H. (5/1/2006)*

Loring Wine Company 2002 Rosella's Vineyard Pinot Noir (Santa Lucia Highlands) $46. 85 *—S.H. (11/1/2004)*

LOST CANYON

Lost Canyon 2001 Pinot Noir (Carneros) $38. 86 *—S.H. (7/1/2003)*

Lost Canyon 2005 Dutton Ranch Morelli Lane Vineyard Pinot Noir (Russian River Valley) $40. Big, juicy Pinot, dry and fruity, with layers of flavor that change with every sip. Black cherries, cola, rhubarbs, pomegranates, coffee, sweet tobacco, spice and oak all mingle in a myriad of sensations, finishing long and intense. Good now, but tannicly closed enough to warrant cellaring beyond 2007. 91 *—S.H. (8/1/2007)*

Lost Canyon 2004 Dutton Ranch Morelli Lane Vineyard Pinot Noir (Russian River Valley) $40. 92 *—S.H. (9/1/2006)*

Lost Canyon 2003 Dutton Ranch Morelli Lane Vineyard Pinot Noir (Russian River Valley) $38. 84 *—S.H. (10/1/2005)*

Lost Canyon 2002 Dutton Ranch Morelli Lane Vineyard Pinot Noir (Russian River Valley) $38. 85 *—S.H. (11/1/2004)*

Lost Canyon 2005 Las Brisas Vineyard Pinot Noir (Carneros) $40. This is so big, it's almost Rhône-like. With its full-bodied richness, tannins and voluminous cherry, currant and leather flavors, you might think it was Grenache. Not varietally correct, but still a tasty wine. 87 *—S.H. (8/1/2007)*

Lost Canyon 2004 Las Brisas Vineyard Pinot Noir (Los Carneros) $40. 91 *—S.H. (9/1/2006)*

Lost Canyon 2003 Las Brisas Vineyard Pinot Noir (Carneros) $38. 83 *—S.H. (10/1/2005)*

Lost Canyon 2002 Las Brisas Vineyard Pinot Noir (Carneros) $38. 87 *—S.H. (11/1/2004)*

Lost Canyon 2005 Saralee's Vineyard Pinot Noir (Russian River Valley) $40. Straddles the line between villages-type and premier cru Pinot. Light in color and body, one minute it seems simple and fruity, the next, it shows the complex dimensions of a fine young Burgundy. Hard to tell where it's headed, but it's a dry, crisp, silky wine, with lip-smacking cherry, cola and oak flavors. 90 *—S.H. (8/1/2007)*

Lost Canyon 2004 Saralee's Vineyard Pinot Noir (Russian River Valley) $40. 93 Editors' Choice *—S.H. (9/1/2006)*

Lost Canyon 2003 Saralee's Vineyard Pinot Noir (Russian River Valley) $38. 82 *—S.H. (10/1/2005)*

Lost Canyon 2002 Saralee's Vineyard Pinot Noir (Russian River Valley) $36. 84 *—S.H. (11/1/2004)*

Lost Canyon 2005 Alegria Vineyard Syrah (Russian River Valley) $35. Very dry, high in acidity and with a minty edge to the cherries and blackberries, this wine tastes young and raspingly tart right now. It's elegant enough in structure, but wants opulence. Hard to tell if it will go anywhere. 86 *—S.H. (8/1/2007)*

Lost Canyon 2003 Alegria Vineyard Syrah (Russian River Valley) $33. 87 *(9/1/2005)*

Lost Canyon 2002 Alegria Vineyard Syrah (Russian River Valley) $32. 86 *—S.H. (12/1/2004)*

Lost Canyon 2005 Stagecoach Vineyard Syrah (Sonoma Coast) $35. Bone dry, firm in tannins and tartly acidic, this wine feels hard in the mouth. It shows flavors of cherries and cola, with a leathery finish. Elegant in structure, it may soften and sweeten over the next five years. 87 *—S.H. (8/1/2007)*

Lost Canyon 2004 Stage Gulch Vineyard Syrah (Sonoma Coast) $35. 88 *—S.H. (10/1/2006)*

Lost Canyon 2003 Stage Gulch Vineyard Syrah (Sonoma Coast) $33. 88 *(9/1/2005)*

Lost Canyon 2002 Stage Gulch Vineyard Syrah (Sonoma Coast) $32. 90 *—S.H. (12/1/2004)*

Lost Canyon 2001 Stage Gulch Vineyard Syrah (Sonoma Coast) $33. 87 *—S.H. (12/15/2003)*

Lost Canyon 2005 Trenton Station Vineyard Syrah (Russian River Valley) $35. Shows a beautiful balance of all its parts. The fruit is forwardly ripe, showing cherries, blackberries and rich dark chocolate. But the tannins are firm and supportive, and there's gorgeous acidity that makes the tastebuds sing. This is a really delicious young Syrah for the most upscale foods, and it's at its best now. 92 *—S.H. (8/1/2007)*

Lost Canyon 2004 Trenton Station Vineyard Syrah (Russian River Valley) $35. 93 Editors' Choice *—S.H. (10/1/2006)*

Lost Canyon 2003 Trenton Station Vineyard Syrah (Russian River Valley) $35. 88 *(9/1/2005)*

Lost Canyon 2006 Catie's Corner Vineyard Viognier (Russian River Valley) $25. This is the first Viognier from Lost Canyon I've had, and it's very good. An early release from last year's vintage, it's supercrisp in fresh young acidity, with the long hangtime fruit of a cool harvest. Marked by intense tropical fruit, wildflower, vanilla and spice flavors. 87 *—S.H. (8/1/2007)*

LOST RIVER

Lost River 2003 Cabernet Sauvignon (Columbia Valley (WA)) $23. 86 *—P.G. (6/1/2006)*

Lost River 2002 Cabernet Sauvignon (Columbia Valley (WA)) $23. 88 *—P.G. (4/1/2005)*

Lost River 2002 Merlot (Columbia Valley (WA)) $21. 91 Editors' Choice *—P.G. (12/1/2004)*

Lost River 2005 Pinot Gris (Columbia Valley (WA)) $14. Cool fermented in stainless steel and whole cluster pressed, this lively take on Pinot Gris offers rich pear fruit flavors, succulent and fresh. It's a big, ripe, solid effort, with a lovely juicy quality that fills the mouth with a burst of just-picked flavor. 88 *—P.G. (12/31/2007)*

Lost River 2003 Sémillon (Columbia Valley (WA)) $14. 92 Best Buy *—P.G. (12/1/2004)*

Lost River 2004 Wallula Vineyard Syrah (Horse Heaven Hills) $22. The Wallula vineyard, set high atop a bluff overlooking the Columbia river, gives grapes that bring dark, roasted flavors to the large-scale wine. The fruit tastes as if it has been pushed, perhaps a bit too far, and the impression it leaves tilts toward the raisiny side. It's a wine that could go in a positive direction with cellar time, but it is impossible to tell right now, as it cuts off quickly once in the mouth. 86 *—P.G. (12/31/2007)*

LOST RIVER WINERY

Lost River Winery 2003 Syrah (Walla Walla (WA)) $21. 87 *(9/1/2005)*

LOUIS M. MARTINI

Louis M. Martini 1995 Barbera (Lake County) $12. 87 Best Buy *—M.S. (9/1/2000)*

Louis M. Martini 2004 Cabernet Sauvignon (Alexander Valley) $35. Shows a soft, sugary quality to the raspberry, cherry and blackberry fruit that makes it jammy and simple. This is not the drily ageable Martini reserve of yesteryear. 84 *—S.H. (12/15/2007)*

Louis M. Martini 2004 Cabernet Sauvignon (Sonoma County) $17. Rich and dry, with a smooth, tannic structure framing ripe flavors of blackberries, cherries, smoky oak and dusty Asian spices. Shows lots of class for this price. 87 *—S.H. (12/15/2007)*

Louis M. Martini 2003 Cabernet Sauvignon (Sonoma County) $17. 84 *—S.H. (11/1/2006)*

Louis M. Martini 2002 Cabernet Sauvignon (Sonoma County) $15. 86 *(9/1/2005)*

Louis M. Martini 2002 Cabernet Sauvignon (Napa Valley) $24. 85 *—S.H. (12/1/2005)*

Louis M. Martini 2001 Cabernet Sauvignon (Sonoma County) $17. 85 *—S.H. (2/1/2004)*

Louis M. Martini 2000 Cabernet Sauvignon (Napa Valley) $24. 84 *—S.H. (2/1/2004)*

Louis M. Martini 1997 Family Vineyard Selection Ghost Pines Vineyard Cabernet Sauvignon (Chiles Valley) $30. 87 *(8/1/2001)*

Louis M. Martini 1999 Ghost Pines Vineyard-Family Vineyard Selection Cabernet Sauvignon (Chiles Valley) $30. 84 *—S.H. (11/15/2003)*

Louis M. Martini 2003 Lot No. 1 Cabernet Sauvignon (Napa Valley) $100. 89 *—S.H. (9/1/2006)*

Louis M. Martini 2002 Monte Rosso Vineyard Cabernet Sauvignon (Sonoma Valley) $85. 90 *—S.H. (9/1/2006)*

Louis M. Martini 2001 Monte Rosso Vineyard Cabernet Sauvignon (Sonoma Valley) $50. 91 *(9/1/2005)*

Louis M. Martini 2000 Monte Rosso Vineyard Cabernet Sauvignon (Sonoma Valley) $55. 88 *(9/1/2005)*

Louis M. Martini 2000 Monte Rosso Vineyard Cabernet Sauvignon (Sonoma Valley) $55. 92 Cellar Selection *—S.H. (12/31/2003)*

Louis M. Martini 1999 Monte Rosso Vineyard Cabernet Sauvignon (Sonoma Valley) $50. 88 *—J.M. (11/15/2002)*

Louis M. Martini 1999 Monte Rosso Vineyard Cabernet Sauvignon (Sonoma Valley) $65. 88 *(9/1/2005)*

Louis M. Martini 1998 Monte Rosso Vineyard Cabernet Sauvignon (Sonoma Valley) $65. 85 *(9/1/2005)*

Louis M. Martini 1998 Monte Rosso Vineyard Cabernet Sauvignon (Sonoma Valley) $50. 93 Cellar Selection *—S.H. (12/1/2001)*

Louis M. Martini 1997 Monte Rosso Vineyard Cabernet Sauvignon (Sonoma Valley) $40. 93 *(11/1/2000)*

Louis M. Martini 1996 Monte Rosso Vineyard Selection Cabernet Sauvignon (Sonoma Valley) $35. 88 *—L.W. (10/1/1999)*

Louis M. Martini 2003 Reserve Cabernet Sauvignon (Alexander Valley) $35. For years Martini's best Cabernet has been from Monte Rosso, but it's ironic that this Napa Valley icon's second best Cab is the Alexander Valley Reserve. The wine is beautifully soft and rich, with ripe black currant, cherry and chocolate flavors that are perfectly drinkable now. **90** *—S.H. (2/1/2007)*

Louis M. Martini 2003 Reserve Cabernet Sauvignon (Napa Valley) $24. 85 *—S.H. (11/15/2006)*

Louis M. Martini 2002 Reserve Cabernet Sauvignon (Napa Valley) $24. 87 *—S.H. (7/1/2006)*

Louis M. Martini 2001 Reserve Cabernet Sauvignon (Napa Valley) $25. 87 *—S.H. (5/1/2005)*

Louis M. Martini 2001 Reserve Cabernet Sauvignon (Alexander Valley) $35. 89 *(9/1/2005)*

Louis M. Martini 2000 Reserve Cabernet Sauvignon (Alexander Valley) $35. 91 *—S.H. (2/1/2004)*

Louis M. Martini 2000 Del Rio Vineyard Chardonnay (Russian River Valley) $22. 85 *—S.H. (9/1/2002)*

Louis M. Martini NV Family Vineyard Selection Del Rio Vineyard Chardonnay (Russian River Valley) $21. 84 *S.H. (8/1/2001)*

Louis M. Martini 1997 Reserve Chardonnay (Russian River Valley) $18. 85 *(6/1/2000)*

Louis M. Martini 2001 Monte Rosso Vineyard Folle Blanche (Sonoma Valley) $18. 87 *—J.M. (9/1/2003)*

Louis M. Martini 2000 Monte Rosso Vineyard Folle Blanche (Sonoma Valley) $17. 84 *—S.H. (12/15/2002)*

Louis M. Martini 2000 Del Rio Vineyard Gewürztraminer (Russian River Valley) $18. 88 *—S.H. (6/1/2002)*

Louis M. Martini 2002 Del Rio Vineyard-5 Nail Selection Gewürztraminer (Russian River Valley) $16. 85 *—S.H. (12/31/2003)*

Louis M. Martini 1997 Merlot (Chiles Valley) $25. 90 *—S.H. (11/15/2000)*

Louis M. Martini 1999 Del Rio Vineyard Merlot (Russian River Valley) $22. 90 Editors' Choice *S.H. (9/1/2002)*

Louis M. Martini 1999 Ghost Pines Vineyard-Family Vineyard Selection Merlot (Chiles Valley) $27. 83 *—S.H. (12/1/2003)*

Louis M. Martini 1997 Sangiovese (Dunnigan Hills) $14. 83 *(10/1/1999)*

Louis M. Martini 2001 Monte Rosso Vineyard Sémillon (Sonoma Valley) $18. 87 *—S.H. (12/15/2002)*

Louis M. Martini 1996 Zinfandel (Sonoma County) $12. 85 *—P.G. (11/15/1999)*

Louis M. Martini 1999 Gnarly Vine-Monte Rosso Vineyard Zinfandel (Sonoma Valley) $40. 87 *—J.M. (12/1/2002)*

Louis M. Martini 1997 Gnarly Vine Monte Rosso Vineyard Zinfandel (Sonoma Valley) $40. 86 *—S.H. (12/1/2000)*

Louis M. Martini 2001 Monte Rosso Vineyard Zinfandel (Sonoma Valley) $20. 84 *(11/1/2003)*

Louis M. Martini 2000 Monte Rosso Vineyard Zinfandel (Sonoma Valley) $20. 92 Editors' Choice *—S.H. (12/1/2002)*

Louis M. Martini 1999 Monte Rosso Vineyard Zinfandel (Sonoma Valley) $30. 90 *—S.H. (12/15/2001)*

Louis M. Martini 2004 Monte Rosso Vineyard Gnarly Vine Zinfandel (Sonoma Valley) $50. Pretty much a copy of the '03, which I found too ripe and Port-y. Although the wine is dry, it has raisiny flavors, with a stewed fruit, prune and chocolate pie crust quality. Actually tastes hotter than the official alcohol reading of 14.5%. **84** *—S.H. (8/1/2007)*

Louis M. Martini 2003 Monte Rosso Vineyard Gnarly Vine Zinfandel (Sonoma Valley) $50. The '03, despite 15.6% residual sugar, tastes sugary sweet in cherries, almost Port-y, like something you cooked up for Sunday crepes. **84** *—S.H. (7/1/2007)*

Louis M. Martini 2002 Monte Rosso Vineyard Gnarly Vine Zinfandel (Sonoma Valley) $35. 90 *(9/1/2005)*

Louis M. Martini 1998 Monte Rosso Vineyard Gnarly Vine Zinfandel (Sonoma Valley) $40. 91 *—S.H. (12/15/2001)*

LOXTON

Loxton 2002 Reserve Syrah (Sonoma County) $30. 85 *(9/1/2005)*

Loxton 2002 Sonoma Hillside Vineyards Syrah (Sonoma County) $24. 86 *(9/1/2005)*

Loxton 1999 Timbervine Ranch Syrah (Russian River Valley) $26. 90 *—S.H. (7/1/2002)*

LOWDEN HILLS

Lowden Hills 2003 Birch Creel Cabernet Sauvignon (Walla Walla (WA)) $26. From an Oregon vineyard, this also contains a splash of Syrah and Cab Franc in the blend. Spicy and soft, this wine could best be described as pretty. Its light fruit flavors suggest mulberry and strawberry preserves; the alcohol is a modest 13.8%. **86** *—P.G. (3/1/2007)*

Lowden Hills 2003 Pepper Bridge Cabernet Sauvignon (Walla Walla (WA)) $27. This is a good representation of Pepper Bridge fruit, with a satiny, polished mouthfeel and broad, forward flavors. It's been aged in one quarter new American oak, three quarters used French. Here the flavors of coffee and clove add an extra dimension. **87** *—P.G. (3/1/2007)*

Lowden Hills 2003 Win Chester Merlot (Walla Walla (WA)) $24. This is the estate vineyard, located in the flat, dry western end of the Walla Walla Valley. It's 95% Merlot with a splash of Syrah and Cab Franc, and it is dark, tannic and straightforward. What's missing is the extra detail and complexity that would add interest to the roasty-toasty tannins. **86** *—P.G. (3/1/2007)*

Lowden Hills 2003 Merlin Winemaker's Reserve Red Blend (Walla Walla (WA)) $40. The cluttered label, featuring a dog, seems out of character with the reserve designation and hefty price. It's a Cabernet with small amounts of Merlot, Franc and Syrah; and it has spent more time in oak than the winery's other Cabs. Hence, more extract, more tannin, more chocolaty flavor, all of which pushes it into an overdone, somewhat rough and scrappy style. **86** *—P.G. (3/1/2007)*

Lowden Hills 2004 Boushey Syrah (Yakima Valley) $28. Pure Syrah from the great Boushey Vineyard. The fruit has a young vine character; bright and tangy, with added layers of coffee and peppery toast. **87** *—P.G. (3/1/2007)*

LUCAS & LEWELLEN

Lucas & Lewellen 2001 Cabernet Franc (Santa Barbara County) $22. 83 *—S.H. (7/1/2005)*

Lucas & Lewellen 2000 Valley View Vineyard Cabernet Franc (Santa Barbara County) $25. 91 *—S.H. (10/1/2003)*

Lucas & Lewellen 2001 Cote del Sol Cabernet Sauvignon (Santa Barbara County) $32. 80 *—S.H. (8/1/2005)*

Lucas & Lewellen 2000 Cote del Sol Valley View Vineyard Cabernet Sauvignon (Santa Barbara County) $32. 89 *—S.H. (11/15/2003)*

Lucas & Lewellen 2003 Valley View Vineyard Cabernet Sauvignon (Santa Barbara County) $25. I'm not sure why they held this Cab back a full four years, but it's smooth and rich and drinkable now. With chocolate-infused cherry-cassis flavors, the wine is soft and gentle, with a finish of licorice and cinnamon spice. **85** *—S.H. (10/1/2007)*

Lucas & Lewellen 2002 Valley View Vineyard Cabernet Sauvignon (Santa Barbara County) $25. 83 *—S.H. (9/1/2006)*

Lucas & Lewellen 2001 Valley View Vineyard Cabernet Sauvignon (Santa Barbara County) $25. 81 *—S.H. (8/1/2005)*

Lucas & Lewellen 2000 Valley View Vineyard Cabernet Sauvignon (Santa Barbara County) $23. 87 *—S.H. (11/15/2003)*

Lucas & Lewellen 2005 Chardonnay (Santa Barbara County) $15. Soft and flabby, especially on the entry, without the acidity to balance the very ripe pineapple, guava and vanilla-oak flavors. A wine this flavorful desperately needs crispness. **83** *—S.H. (10/1/2007)*

Lucas & Lewellen 2004 Chardonnay (Santa Barbara County) $15. 84 *—S.H. (12/1/2006)*

Lucas & Lewellen 2003 Chardonnay (Santa Barbara County) $15. 83 *—S.H. (8/1/2005)*

Lucas & Lewellen 2005 Goodchild Vineyard Chardonnay (Santa Barbara County) $22. Many wineries have taken fruit from this vineyard, generally with good results. The '05 Lucas & Lewellen shows its terroir, with a cool-climate crispness backing up ripe pineapple tart, nectarine and papaya flavors. But the oak-inspired caramel, char and butterscotch is a bit heavy-handed. **86** *—S.H. (10/1/2007)*

Lucas & Lewellen 2004 Goodchild Vineyard Chardonnay (Santa Barbara County) $22. 88 *—S.H. (12/1/2006)*

Lucas & Lewellen 2003 Goodchild Vineyard Chardonnay (Santa Barbara County) $22. 84 *—S.H. (8/1/2005)*

Lucas & Lewellen 2000 Goodchild Vineyard Chardonnay (Santa Barbara County) $20. 89 *—S.H. (12/15/2003)*

Lucas & Lewellen 2000 Goodchild Vineyard Chardonnay (Santa Barbara County) $20. 84 *—S.H. (12/31/2003)*

Lucas & Lewellen 2004 Merlot (Santa Barbara County) $25. A bit hot and rugged, this Merlot has flavors of baked cherries, coffee, plums and spicy cola. It's dry on the finish. Earns extra points for balance and interest value. **84** *—S.H. (10/1/2007)*

Lucas & Lewellen 2003 Merlot (Santa Barbara County) $21. 82 *—S.H. (12/1/2006)*

Lucas & Lewellen 2001 Merlot (Santa Barbara County) $21. 81 *—S.H. (8/1/2005)*

Lucas & Lewellen 2000 Merlot (Santa Barbara County) $18. 87 *—S.H. (3/1/2004)*

Lucas & Lewellen 2002 Petite Sirah (Santa Barbara County) $26. 84 *—S.H. (8/1/2005)*

Lucas & Lewellen 2005 Pinot Noir (Santa Barbara County) $20. This is recognizably Pinot-esque with its silky mouthfeel and flavors of cherries and cola, but beyond that, all similarities stop. It's slightly sweet and too soft. **82** *—S.H. (10/1/2007)*

Lucas & Lewellen 2005 Hilltop Pinot Noir (Santa Barbara County) $30. The '04 was so much better, maybe because of vintage or sourcing differences. This is sharp in green, minty tastes, and the cherry and cola flavors finish simple and thin. Earns an extra point for a rich spiciness. **83** *—S.H. (10/1/2007)*

Lucas & Lewellen 2004 Hilltop Pinot Noir (Santa Barbara County) $26. 89 *—S.H. (12/1/2006)*

Lucas & Lewellen 2001 Vin Gris Pinot Noir (Santa Barbara County) $12. 87 *—S.H. (10/1/2003)*

Lucas & Lewellen 2003 Sauvignon Blanc (Santa Barbara County) $18. 84 *—S.H. (8/1/2005)*

Lucas & Lewellen 2001 Sauvignon Blanc (Santa Barbara County) $12. 86 *—S.H. (12/31/2003)*

Lucas & Lewellen 2005 Late Harvest Sauvignon Blanc (Santa Barbara County) $19. There's a weird discrepancy between the aroma, which is watery, and the flavor, which is very sweet and rich in apricot honey, marzipan, butterscotch and vanilla fudge. If flavor's all you need, this is a satisfying dessert wine. **85** *—S.H. (10/1/2007)*

Lucas & Lewellen 2005 Valley View Vineyard Sauvignon Blanc (Santa Barbara County) $18. Tastes overtly sweet, like lemonade and honey. Sauvignon Blanc should be dry unless it's late harvest. **82** *—S.H. (10/1/2007)*

Lucas & Lewellen 2004 Syrah (Santa Barbara County) $26. Has a stubborn, funky smell that didn't blow off. Below that, the wine is tough and tannic, with muted coffee and cherry flavors. **82** *—S.H. (10/1/2007)*

Lucas & Lewellen 2003 Syrah (Santa Barbara County) $24. 84 *—S.H. (12/1/2006)*

Lucas & Lewellen 2002 Syrah (Santa Barbara County) $20. 85 *(9/1/2005)*

LUCAS VINEYARDS

Lucas Vineyards NV Lucas Blanc de Blancs Chardonnay (Finger Lakes) $15. 82 *—J.C. (12/1/2003)*

Lucas Vineyards 2001 Dry Riesling (Finger Lakes) $10. 85 *—J.C. (8/1/2003)*

Lucas Vineyards 2002 Semi-Dry Riesling (Finger Lakes) $10. 86 *—J.C. (8/1/2003)*

Lucas Vineyards NV Lucas Extra Dry Sparkling Blend (Finger Lakes) $12. 86 Best Buy *—J.C. (12/1/2003)*

LUCCA

Lucca NV Vino Rosso di Santa Barbara Red Wine Sangiovese (California) $10. 86 Best Buy *—S.H. (3/1/2005)*

LUCIA

Lucia 2004 Chardonnay (Santa Lucia Highlands) $35. 87 *—S.H. (8/1/2006)*

Lucia 2004 Garys' Vineyard Pinot Noir (Santa Lucia Highlands) $45. 91 *—S.H. (8/1/2006)*

Lucia 2002 Garys' Vineyard Syrah (Santa Lucia Highlands) $38. 89 *—S.H. (7/1/2005)*

LUCY

Lucy 2006 Rosé of Pinot Noir (Santa Lucia Highlands) $18. I love this wine. It's more like a Provençal rosé than almost anything out there, even though it's made from Pinot Noir. Dry, crisp and silky, it has interesting waves of cherryskin, rosehip tea, tobacco, vanilla and peppery spice flavors, and finishes impressively long. **91 Editors' Choice** *—S.H. (7/1/2007)*

Lucy 2005 Rosé of Pinot Noir Rosé Blend (Santa Lucia Highlands) $18. 85 *—S.H. (6/21/2006)*

LUNA

Luna 2004 Cabernet Sauvignon (Napa Valley) $80. A nice, rich Cab that shows off its Napa pedigree. It's a little soft and not an ager, but lush in black currant, blackberry tart, cherry pie, chocolate, vanilla, smoky oak and spice flavors that are delicious. The tannins are thick, but so ripe and sweet, you can drink it right now. **92** *—S.H. (9/1/2007)*

Luna 2004 Reserve Cabernet Sauvignon (Napa Valley) $100. The difference from Luna's regular '04 Cab is in the increased alcohol, nearly 1% higher, and greater tannic structure. There's probably more new oak, too, which is in proportion to the massive blackcurrant and cherry fruit. As young as it is, it's fully drinkable now, but should hold and improve for 6–8 years. **93** *—S.H. (10/1/2007)*

Luna 2004 Merlot (Howell Mountain) $75. I'm not sure Howell Mountain is the best place for Merlot, because the dry, rugged terrain imparts strong tannins that seem weird in this supposedly gentle red variety. This 100% Merlot has big cherry, blackberry, cocoa and sweet new oak flavors wrapped in a firmly astringent, sandpapery texture. Decanting will help. So will a rich, fatty steak. **88** *—S.H. (10/1/2007)*

Luna 2003 Merlot (Napa Valley) $40. At about four years, this Merlot, from the southerly Oak Knoll region of the valley, is overtly sweet, possibly from high alcohol. The official reading is 15.3%. There's no doubting the wealth of cherry-cassis fruit and fine, vanilla-scented oak, but the sweetness is off-putting, and so is the heat on the finish. **84** *—S.H. (10/1/2007)*

Luna 1999 Merlot (Napa Valley) $32. 88 *—S.H. (9/12/2002)*

Luna 2005 Pinot Grigio (Napa County) $18. Barrel-fermented, this wine shows a rich creaminess akin to Chard. But it's strictly PG, with crisp acidity and tart flavors of green apples, limes, pineapples, wildflowers and minerals. Finishes with a distinctly sugary taste. **84** *—S.H. (10/1/2007)*

Luna 2004 Pinot Grigio (Napa County) $18. 86 *—S.H. (2/1/2006)*

Luna 1999 Canto Red Blend (Napa Valley) $60. 95 *—S.H. (9/1/2002)*

Luna 2003 Sangiovese (Napa Valley) $18. 84 *—S.H. (5/1/2006)*

Luna 2002 Sangiovese (Napa Valley) $18. 82 *—S.H. (12/15/2005)*

Luna 2000 Sangiovese (Napa Valley) $18. 90 *—S.H. (12/1/2002)*

Luna 1999 Reserve Sangiovese (Napa Valley) $50. 88 *—S.H. (5/1/2002)*

Luna 2005 Freakout White Wine White Blend (Napa Valley) $25. From Luna Vineyards, better known for reds (which is perhaps why the front label says only Freakout), comes this interesting Sauvignon Blanc, Chardonnay, Pinot Grigio and Tocai Friulano blend. It's crisp and fruity, with citrus, wildflower, honey and vanilla flavors that finish with a touch of mineral. **85** *—S.H. (9/1/2007)*

LYETH

Lyeth 1996 Bordeaux Blend (Napa County) $14. 88 *—M.S. (10/1/1999)*

Lyeth 2003 Meritage Cabernet Blend (Sonoma County) $15. 84 *—S.H. (5/1/2006)*

Lyeth 2002 L de Lyeth Cabernet Sauvignon (Sonoma County) $11. 83 *—S.H. (10/1/2004)*

Lyeth 2001 Reserve Cabernet Sauvignon-Merlot (Alexander Valley) $32. 88 *—S.H. (2/1/2005)*

Lyeth 2002 Meritage (Sonoma County) $15. 86 *—S.H. (2/1/2005)*

Lyeth 2001 Meritage (Sonoma County) $15. 84 *—S.H. (5/1/2004)*

Lyeth 2002 L de Lyeth Merlot (Sonoma County) $11. 85 *—S.H. (10/1/2004)*

Lyeth 2002 L de Lyeth Sauvignon Blanc (Sonoma County) $11. 86 —*S.H. (10/1/2004)*

LYNCH

Lynch 2002 Cabernet Sauvignon (Napa Valley) $60. 92 —*S.H. (7/1/2005)*

Lynch 2002 Canis Major, Unti Vineyard Syrah (Dry Creek Valley) $25. 90 —*J.M. (9/1/2004)*

Lynch 2002 Lynch Knoll Vineyard Syrah (Spring Mountain) $65. 90 —*S.H. (7/1/2005)*

Lynch 2002 Canis Major Zinfandel (Dry Creek Valley) $24. 91 —*J.M. (9/1/2004)*

LYNMAR

Lynmar 2005 Chardonnay (Russian River Valley) $30. Really classic Russian River Chard, so elegantly structured and sleek, yet so flavorful. A wonderful structure of bright acidity and fine, toasty oak frames succulent flavors of pineapples, tangerines, green apples pears and minerals, leading to a long, richly spicy finish. **92** —*S.H. (10/1/2007)*

Lynmar 2004 Chardonnay (Russian River Valley) $27. 89 *(6/1/2006)*

Lynmar 2003 Chardonnay (Russian River Valley) $22. 84 —*S.H. (5/1/2005)*

Lynmar 2000 Chardonnay (Russian River Valley) $24. 92 —*S.H. (12/15/2002)*

Lynmar 2002 Quail Cuvée Chardonnay (Russian River Valley) $30. 85 —*S.H. (5/1/2005)*

Lynmar 1999 Quail Cuvée Chardonnay (Russian River Valley) $30. 89 —*S.H. (12/15/2002)*

Lynmar 2004 Quail Hill Vineyard Chardonnay (Russian River Valley) $40. Richer and more interesting than the '03, but pretty much built along the same lines. The wine is oaky and leesy, with tart flavors of grapefruit juice, apricots and minerals. if you like your Chards more austere and compact, you'll enjoy this one. Might develop over the midterm. **89** —*S.H. (3/1/2007)*

Lynmar 2003 Quail Hill Vineyard Chardonnay (Russian River Valley) $38. 91 *(6/1/2006)*

Lynmar 2004 Pinot Noir (Russian River Valley) $36. Lynmar's basic Russian River is lighter than its more expensive designation bottlings, but it's right up there, which makes it a relative value. Shows the same dry, crisp varietal richness and finesse, with cherry, cola and oak flavors. Balanced, and entirely ready now. **89** —*S.H. (3/1/2007)*

Lynmar 2003 Pinot Noir (Russian River Valley) $32. 88 *(6/1/2006)*

Lynmar 1999 Pinot Noir (Russian River Valley) $28. 86 —*S.H. (2/1/2003)*

Lynmar 2004 Estate Grown Quail Hill Vineyard Pinot Noir (Russian River Valley) $50. Dark, rich, young and dramatic, with a sappy young Pinot taste that's all jammy black cherries and cola, this is a wine that needs bottle age. From Lynmar's estate, in the southern Russian River Valley, the wine is dry and complex, and shows Pinot's silky elegance. Drink now with decanting and through 2012. **91** —*S.H. (3/1/2007)*

Lynmar 2004 Five Sisters Pinot Noir (Russian River Valley) $80. 90 —*S.H. (12/1/2006)*

Lynmar 1997 Five Sisters Pinot Noir (Russian River Valley) $NA. 89 *(6/1/2006)*

Lynmar 2003 Quail Hill Vineyard Pinot Noir (Russian River Valley) $45. 90 *(6/1/2006)*

Lynmar 2002 Quail Hill Vineyard Pinot Noir (Russian River Valley) $30. 90 —*S.H. (6/1/2005)*

Lynmar 1994 Quail Hill Vineyard Pinot Noir (Russian River Valley) $NA. 87 *(6/1/2006)*

Lynmar 2001 Quail Hill Vineyard Quail Cuvée Pinot Noir (Russian River Valley) $35. 93 —*S.H. (12/15/2004)*

Lynmar 2002 Quail Hill Vineyard Quail Cuvée Pinot Noir (Russian River Valley) $40. 92 —*S.H. (6/1/2005)*

Lynmar 1999 Reserve Pinot Noir (Russian River Valley) $50. 88 —*S.H. (2/1/2003)*

Lynmar 1996 Reserve Pinot Noir (Russian River Valley) $NA. 89 *(6/1/2006)*

Lynmar 2006 Vin Gris Rosé of Pinot Noir (Russian River Valley) $20. This is one of the best rosés in California. It's totally dry, crisply acidic and delicately structured, with subtle, complex flavors that run from cherries, cranberries and rose petals to dried herbs and peppery Asian spice. Hats off to consulting winemaker Paul Hobbs for mastering the essence of rosé. **91 Editors' Choice** —*S.H. (10/1/2007)*

Lynmar 2005 Vin Gris of Pinot Noir (Russian River Valley) $24. 90 —*S.H. (12/15/2006)*

M2

M2 2004 Soucie Vineyard Old Vine Zinfandel (Lodi) $22. This wine has a ridiculous alcohol of 16.3%, which makes it prickly, and the dryness makes it taste even hotter, since there's no sugar to balance and soften. It's got extremely ripe blackberry pie flavors. Be careful if you drink this; a little goes a long way. **83** —*S.H. (12/15/2007)*

M. COSENTINO

M. Cosentino 1999 CE2V Bordeaux Blend (Napa Valley) $75. 90 —*S.H. (11/15/2002)*

M. Cosentino 1997 M. Coz Bordeaux Blend (Napa Valley) $100. 88 *(11/1/2000)*

M. Cosentino 1996 M. Coz Bordeaux Blend (Napa Valley) $80. 86 *(3/1/2000)*

M. Cosentino 1998 The Poet Bordeaux Blend (Napa Valley) $65. 88 —*J.M. (6/1/2002)*

M. Cosentino 1997 The Poet Bordeaux Blend (Napa Valley) $65. 94 *(11/1/2000)*

M. Cosentino 1996 The Poet Bordeaux Blend (Napa Valley) $40. 87 *(2/1/2000)*

M. Cosentino 2002 CE2V Meritage Cabernet Blend (Napa Valley) $100. 94 —*S.H. (7/1/2006)*

M. Cosentino 2001 Cabernet Franc (Lodi) $28. 83 —*S.H. (10/1/2004)*

M. Cosentino 2001 Cabernet Franc (St. Helena) $34. 90 —*S.H. (3/1/2005)*

M. Cosentino 2000 Cabernet Franc (Napa Valley) $34. 86 —*S.H. (6/1/2003)*

M. Cosentino 1999 Cabernet Franc (Napa Valley) $34. 84 —*S.H. (9/1/2002)*

M. Cosentino 1997 Cabernet Sauvignon (Napa Valley) $28. 88 *(3/1/2000)*

M. Cosentino 2002 Cabernet Sauvignon (Napa Valley) $45. 90 —*S.H. (11/1/2005)*

M. Cosentino 2001 Cabernet Sauvignon (Napa Valley) $38. 92 Cellar Selection —*S.H. (10/1/2004)*

M. Cosentino 2000 Cabernet Sauvignon (Napa Valley) $34. 85 —*S.H. (12/31/2003)*

M. Cosentino 1999 Cabernet Sauvignon (Napa Valley) $34. 85 —*S.H. (9/12/2002)*

M. Cosentino 2002 Hoopes Ranch Cabernet Sauvignon (Oakville) $75. 94 Cellar Selection —*S.H. (11/1/2005)*

M. Cosentino 2001 Hoopes Ranch Cabernet Sauvignon (Oakville) $65. 93 —*S.H. (10/1/2004)*

M. Cosentino 2001 Reserve Cabernet Sauvignon (Napa Valley) $80. 90 —*S.H. (4/1/2005)*

M. Cosentino 2000 Reserve Cabernet Sauvignon (Napa Valley) $80. 86 —*S.H. (11/15/2003)*

M. Cosentino 1999 Reserve Cabernet Sauvignon (Yountville) $80. 87 —*S.H. (11/15/2002)*

M. Cosentino 1997 Reserve Cabernet Sauvignon (Napa Valley) $80. 90 —*S.H. (8/1/2001)*

M. Cosentino 2000 Charbono (Napa Valley) $25. 84 —*S.H. (10/1/2005)*

M. Cosentino 2004 Chardonnay (Napa Valley) $28. 84 —*S.H. (6/1/2006)*

M. Cosentino 2003 Chardonnay (Napa Valley) $22. 88 —*S.H. (10/1/2005)*

M. Cosentino 2002 Chardonnay (Napa Valley) $30. 92 —*S.H. (9/1/2004)*

M. Cosentino 2002 Chardonnay (Napa Valley) $25. 88 —*S.H. (12/1/2004)*

M. Cosentino 2001 Chardonnay (Napa Valley) $22. 84 —*S.H. (12/31/2003)*

M. Cosentino 2000 Chardonnay (Napa County) $22. 87 —*S.H. (5/1/2002)*

M. Cosentino 1999 Chardonnay (Napa Valley) $22. 90 —*S.H. (8/1/2001)*

M. Cosentino 1999 Chardonnay (California) $18. 86 —*S.H. (8/1/2001)*

M. Cosentino 1998 Barrel-Fermented Chardonnay (California) $20. 86 *(6/1/2000)*

M. Cosentino 2004 CE2V Chardonnay (Napa Valley) $40. 85 —*S.H. (7/1/2006)*

M. Cosentino 2003 CE2V Chardonnay (Napa Valley) $40. 88 —*S.H. (8/1/2005)*

M. Cosentino 2002 CE2V Chardonnay (Napa Valley) $28. 90 —*S.H. (8/1/2004)*

M. Cosentino 2000 CE2V Chardonnay (Napa Valley) $28. 93 —*S.H. (12/31/2001)*

M. Cosentino 2005 Legends Chardonnay (California) $25. 83 —*S.H. (12/31/2006)*

M. Cosentino 2001 The Sculptor Reserve Chardonnay (Napa Valley) $30. 89 *—S.H. (2/1/2004)*

M. Cosentino 2000 The Sculptor Reserve Chardonnay (Napa Valley) $30. 89 *—S.H. (6/1/2003)*

M. Cosentino 1999 The Sculptor Reserve Chardonnay (Napa Valley) $34. 85 *(7/1/2001)*

M. Cosentino 2003 Dolcetto (Lodi) $18. 84 *—S.H. (5/1/2005)*

M. Cosentino 2002 Dolcetto (Lodi) $18. 84 *—S.H. (11/15/2004)*

M. Cosentino 2001 Celle Vineyard Dolcetto (California) $18. 88 *—S.H. (3/1/2004)*

M. Cosentino 2002 Gewürztraminer (Yountville) $22. 88 *—S.H. (10/1/2005)*

M. Cosentino 2001 Gewürztraminer (Yountville) $22. 91 *—S.H. (6/1/2004)*

M. Cosentino 2000 Gewürztraminer (Yountville) $22. 86 *—S.H. (6/1/2002)*

M. Cosentino 1999 Gewürztraminer (Yountville) $22. 87 *—S.H. (12/1/2001)*

M. Cosentino 1998 Estate Yountville Gewürztraminer (Napa Valley) $22. 87 *—L.W. (9/1/1999)*

M. Cosentino 2003 Legends Meritage (Napa Valley) $80. 93 *—S.H. (9/1/2006)*

M. Cosentino 2000 M Coz Meritage (Napa Valley) $100. 91 *—S.H. (3/1/2004)*

M. Cosentino 2002 M. Coz Meritage (Napa Valley) $125. 92 Cellar Selection *—S.H. (12/31/2005)*

M. Cosentino 2001 M. Coz Meritage (Napa Valley) $120. 95 *—S.H. (10/1/2004)*

M. Cosentino 1999 M. Coz Meritage (Napa Valley) $100. 92 *—S.H. (11/15/2002)*

M. Cosentino 1999 The Novelist Meritage (California) $16. 89 *—S.H. (12/15/2001)*

M. Cosentino 2000 The Poet Meritage (Napa Valley) $65. 87 *—S.H. (5/1/2004)*

M. Cosentino 1999 The Poet Meritage (Napa Valley) $65. 85 *—S.H. (11/15/2003)*

M. Cosentino 1997 Merlot (California) $20. 86 *(3/1/2000)*

M. Cosentino 2002 Merlot (Napa Valley) $34. 85 *—S.H. (11/1/2005)*

M. Cosentino 2002 Merlot (Oakville) $90. 92 *—S.H. (11/1/2005)*

M. Cosentino 2001 Merlot (Oakville) $75. 88 *—S.H. (6/1/2004)*

M. Cosentino 2001 Merlot (Napa Valley) $38. 92 *—S.H. (9/1/2004)*

M. Cosentino 2002 Estate Merlot (Oakville) $75. 85 *—S.H. (12/31/2005)*

M. Cosentino 1999 Estate Merlot (Oakville) $90. 93 *—S.H. (9/12/2002)*

M. Cosentino 2004 Legends Merlot (Napa County) $28. 83 *—S.H. (12/31/2006)*

M. Cosentino 1997 Oakville Estate Merlot (Napa Valley) $75. 91 *(12/31/1999)*

M. Cosentino 2000 Reserve Merlot (Napa Valley) $38. 90 *—S.H. (4/1/2004)*

M. Cosentino 1999 Reserve Merlot (Napa Valley) $38. 87 *—S.H. (12/31/2001)*

M. Cosentino 2001 Sonoma Valley Nebbiolo (Sonoma Valley) $28. 90 *—S.H. (9/1/2004)*

M. Cosentino 2002 Petite Sirah (Lodi) $27. 90 *—S.H. (5/1/2005)*

M. Cosentino 2003 Knoll Family Vineyard Petite Sirah (Lodi) $27. 90 *—S.H. (6/1/2006)*

M. Cosentino 2001 Knoll Family Vineyard Petite Sirah (Lodi) $24. 80 *(4/1/2003)*

M. Cosentino 2004 Pinot Grigio (Lodi) $18. 84 *—S.H. (2/1/2006)*

M. Cosentino 2002 Pinot Grigio (Solano County) $18. 87 *—S.H. (11/15/2004)*

M. Cosentino 2001 Pinot Grigio (California) $18. 84 *—S.H. (9/1/2003)*

M. Cosentino 2000 Pinot Grigio (Yountville) $16. 84 *—S.H. (11/15/2001)*

M. Cosentino 2005 Stewart Vineyard Pinot Grigio (Solano County) $18. 84 *—S.H. (11/15/2006)*

M. Cosentino 2002 Pinot Noir (Russian River Valley) $35. 85 *—S.H. (11/1/2005)*

M. Cosentino 2001 Pinot Noir (Russian River Valley) $25. 89 *—S.H. (2/1/2004)*

M. Cosentino 2001 Pinot Noir (Yountville) $34. 92 Editors' Choice *—S.H. (5/1/2004)*

M. Cosentino 2000 Pinot Noir (Carneros) $30. 88 *(10/1/2002)*

M. Cosentino 2000 Pinot Noir (Yountville) $30. 87 *(10/1/2002)*

M. Cosentino 1999 Pinot Noir (Yountville) $34. 93 Editors' Choice *—S.H. (12/15/2001)*

M. Cosentino 1999 Il Chiaretto Red Blend (Yountville) $20. 88 *—S.H. (11/15/2001)*

M. Cosentino 2003 Med Red Red Blend (Lodi) $16. 86 *—S.H. (5/1/2005)*

M. Cosentino 2002 Med Red Red Blend (Lodi) $12. 84 *—S.H. (6/1/2004)*

M. Cosentino NV Ol' Red Red Blend (California) $12. 88 Best Buy *—S.H. (5/1/2006)*

M. Cosentino 2000 Tenero Rosso Red Blend (Lodi) $18. 82 *—S.H. (12/1/2002)*

M. Cosentino 2001 CE2V Sangiovese (Napa Valley) $30. 90 *—S.H. (8/1/2005)*

M. Cosentino 2001 Il Chiaretto Sangiovese (California) $16. 83 *—S.H. (8/1/2004)*

M. Cosentino 2003 Il Chiaretto Sangiovese (California) $18. 82 *—S.H. (12/15/2005)*

M. Cosentino 2002 Il Chiaretto Sangiovese (California) $18. 82 *—S.H. (5/1/2005)*

M. Cosentino 2000 Il Chiaretto Sangiovese (California) $20. 90 Editors' Choice *—S.H. (9/1/2003)*

M. Cosentino 1997 Il Chiaretto Sangiovese (California) $18. 88 *—J.C. (10/1/1999)*

M. Cosentino 2002 CE2V Sauvignon Blanc (Napa Valley) $25. 87 *(7/1/2005)*

M. Cosentino 2000 The Sem Sémillon (Napa Valley) $18. 90 Editors' Choice *—S.H. (12/1/2003)*

M. Cosentino 1998 The Sem Sémillon (Napa Valley) $22. 86 *—L.W. (9/1/1999)*

M. Cosentino 2000 The Novelist Meritage Sémillon-Sauvignon Blanc (California) $16. 89 *—S.H. (7/1/2003)*

M. Cosentino 2003 Syrah (California) $18. 87 *—S.H. (5/1/2006)*

M. Cosentino 2002 The Temp Tempranillo (Lodi) $18. 84 *—S.H. (8/1/2004)*

M. Cosentino 2000 Viognier (California) $22. 87 *—S.H. (12/15/2002)*

M. Cosentino 2000 Vin Doux Viognier Kay Viognier (California) $30. 88 *—S.H. (9/1/2002)*

M. Cosentino 2002 White Blend (California) $12. 87 *—S.H. (5/1/2005)*

M. Cosentino 2001 Avant et apres White Blend (California) $16. 84 *—S.H. (6/1/2004)*

M. Cosentino 2001 The Novelist White Meritage White Blend (California) $16. 85 *—S.H. (2/1/2004)*

M. Cosentino 2002 Cigar Zinfandel (Lodi) $27. 84 *—S.H. (10/1/2004)*

M. Cosentino 2000 Cigar Zin Zinfandel (Lodi) $27. 86 *—S.H. (7/1/2002)*

M. Cosentino 1998 Cigar Zin Zinfandel (California) $22. 92 *—P.G. (11/15/1999)*

M. Cosentino 2001 Cigar Zin Zinfandel (Lodi) $27. 89 *(11/1/2003)*

M. Cosentino 2004 The Zin Zinfandel (Lodi) $30. 84 *—S.H. (3/1/2006)*

M. Cosentino 2003 The Zin Zinfandel (California) $30. 84 *—S.H. (10/1/2005)*

M. Cosentino 2002 The Zin Zinfandel (Lodi) $30. 86 *—S.H. (2/1/2005)*

M. Cosentino 2001 The Zin Zinfandel (Lodi) $30. 87 *(11/1/2003)*

M. Cosentino 2000 The Zin Zinfandel (Lodi) $30. 87 *—S.H. (7/1/2002)*

M. Cosentino 1997 The Zin Zinfandel (California) $22. 93 *—P.G. (11/15/1999)*

M. TRINCHERO

M. Trinchero 1996 Coastal Selection Cabernet Sauvignon (California) $13. 85 *—S.H. (2/1/2000)*

M. Trinchero 1997 Family Selection Cabernet Sauvignon (Santa Barbara County) $13. 86 Best Buy *—S.H. (12/15/2000)*

M. Trinchero 1997 Founder's Estate Cabernet Sauvignon (Napa Valley) $40. 89 *(11/1/2000)*

M. Trinchero 1998 Coastal Selection Chardonnay (California) $12. 86 *—S.H. (12/31/1999)*

M. Trinchero 1998 Founder's Estate Chardonnay (Napa Valley) $25. 90 *(6/1/2000)*

M. Trinchero 1999 Marios Reserve Chardonnay (Napa Valley) $30. 92 *(7/1/2001)*

M. Trinchero 1997 Coastal Selection Merlot (California) $12. 84 *—S.H. (3/1/2000)*

M. Trinchero 1998 Family Selection Merlot (California) $12. 87 Best Buy *—S.H. (5/1/2001)*

M. Trinchero 2000 Mary's Vineyard Sauvignon Blanc (Napa Valley) $19. 84 *(8/1/2002)*

M.G. VALLEJO

M.G. Vallejo 2000 Pinot Noir (Sonoma) $11. 83 *(10/1/2002)*

M.G. Vallejo 1996 Red Blend (Sonoma County) $7. 84 *(11/15/1999)*

MACARI

Macari 2000 Alexandra Bordeaux Blend (North Fork of Long Island) $65. 87 *—J.C. (10/2/2004)*

Macari 2004 Bergen Road Bordeaux Blend (North Fork of Long Island) $43. This medium-bodied Bordeaux blend features deep spice, pepper and red cherry flavors. It's a soft wine with gentle tannins and a subtle overall character. 82 *—S.K. (12/1/2007)*

Macari 2001 Bergen Road Bordeaux Blend (North Fork of Long Island) $40. This Meritage is a blend of 75% Merlot, 23% Cabernet Sauvignon and 2% Malbec. Cherry, toasted spice, tobacco and sweet vanilla notes are followed by a robust mingling of chocolate, raspberry and deep berry flavors on the palate. The finish is soft but the wine is a bit tannic right now—it needs aging. Overall an impressive wine from a consistently good producer. 84 *—S.K. (5/1/2007)*

Macari 2000 Bergen Road Bordeaux Blend (North Fork of Long Island) $36. 85 *—J.C. (10/2/2004)*

Macari 1997 Bergen Road Bordeaux Blend (North Fork of Long Island) $32.87 *—J.C. (4/1/2001)*

Macari 1997 Estate Bottled Cabernet Franc (North Fork of Long Island) $19. 80 *—J.C. (4/1/2001)*

Macari 2003 Unfiltered Cabernet Franc (North Fork of Long Island) $24. 80 *—M.D. (8/1/2006)*

USA

Macari NV Brut Champagne Blend (North Fork of Long Island) $21. 84 *—D.T. (12/1/2001)*

Macari 2000 Chardonnay (North Fork of Long Island) $15. 84 *—J.C. (3/1/2002)*

Macari 2003 Early Wine Chardonnay (North Fork of Long Island) $12. 84 *—J.C. (10/2/2004)*

Macari 1998 Estate Bottled Chardonnay (North Fork of Long Island) $15. 83 *—J.C. (4/1/2001)*

Macari 1998 Reserve Chardonnay (North Fork of Long Island) $22. 85 *—J.C. (4/1/2001)*

Macari 1998 Merlot (North Fork of Long Island) $24. 88 *—J.C. (2/1/2002)*

Macari 2002 Estate Merlot (North Fork of Long Island) $15. 84 *—J.C. (3/1/2006)*

Macari 2001 Reserve Merlot (North Fork of Long Island) $35. 83 *—J.C. (10/2/2004)*

Macari 2003 Unfiltered Estate Merlot (North Fork of Long Island) $15. A delicious nose of chocolate, spice and berry is followed by an elegant, slightly soft wine on the palate. Plum and blackberry flavors are smooth and well balanced. Not terribly complex, but easy to drink. 84 *—S.K. (2/1/2007)*

Macari 2004 Unfiltered Reserve Merlot (North Fork of Long Island) $36. A dark garnet color entices with this approachable Merlot, a consistently good producer. Merlot is Long Island's forté and this wine, with its nose of clove, game and minerality, and its smoke, berry and spicy flavors, is an example of the impressive things that can be done there. Integrated and flavorful, it finishes nicely and with elegance. 84 *—S.K. (7/1/2007)*

Macari 2004 Rosé Blend (North Fork of Long Island) $NA. This is a delightful wine, with unique aromas of pomegranate, neroli and strawberry. In the mouth, it's a successful balance of clean acidity and more complex body than is typical in a rose. Great with medium-bodied cheeses or seafood dishes, this wine is also good enough (and has enough character) to just enjoy on its own. 86 *—S.K. (2/1/2007)*

Macari 2004 Sauvignon Blanc (North Fork of Long Island) $16. 80 *—M.D. (8/1/2006)*

Macari 1999 Estate Bottled Sauvignon Blanc (North Fork of Long Island) $10. 85 Best Buy *—J.C. (4/1/2001)*

Macari 2006 Katherine's Field Sauvignon Blanc (North Fork of Long Island) $19. With its aromas of lemon and grapefruit and tangy, refreshing citrus flavors, this is an excellent cohort to delicate Asian dishes or enjoyed on its own. Good acidity, balanced, minerally flavors and a lively finish add to the wine's character. 86 *—S.K. (10/1/2007)*

Macari 2005 Syrah (North Fork of Long Island) $22. Rose petals and leathery spice on the nose are intriguing, while the palate combines red fruit and assertive tannins. Pepper and spice give it a dry edge but the finish has a nice touch of tobacco and cherry. 83 *—S.K. (10/1/2007)*

Macari 2002 Block E White Blend (North Fork of Long Island) $36. 82 *—J.C. (10/2/2004)*

Macari 2000 Essencia White Blend (North Fork of Long Island) $35. 90 *—J.M. (12/1/2002)*

MACCALLUM

MacCallum 2002 DJ Red Cabernet Sauvignon-Syrah (Yakima Valley) $28. 93 *—P.G. (12/15/2004)*

MacCallum 2003 Shannon's Reserve Malbec (Columbia Valley (WA)) $28. 90 *—P.G. (10/1/2006)*

MacCallum 2003 Pinot Noir (Willamette Valley) $35. 92 *—P.G. (9/1/2006)*

MacCallum 2002 Syrah (Yakima Valley) $25. 93 *—P.G. (12/15/2004)*

MACCHIA

Macchia 2001 Barbero Vineyard, Voluptuous Zinfandel (Lodi) $18. 87 *(11/1/2003)*

Macchia 2001 Clock Spring Vineyard Zinfandel (Amador County) $16. 86 *(11/1/2003)*

Macchia 2001 Generous Zinfandel (Lodi) $16. 86 *(11/1/2003)*

Macchia 2001 Linsteadt Vineyard Zinfandel (Amador County) $20. 85 *(11/1/2003)*

Macchia 2005 Mischievous Old Vine Zinfandel (Lodi) $18. Soft, semi-sweet and simple, with jellied raspberry, cherry and blackberry flavors, this high-alcohol (15.7%) wine has a problematic vegetal taste throughout. 80 *—S.H. (12/15/2007)*

Macchia 2005 Soucie Vineyard Generous Old Vine Zinfandel (Lodi) $22. With 16% alcohol, this wine has a vegetal edge to the sugary-sweet chocolate and raspberry flavors. They say the vines are 90 years old. 80 *—S.H. (12/15/2007)*

MACLEAN

Maclean 2002 Cabernet Sauvignon (Napa Valley) $45. 85 *—S.H. (12/1/2005)*

Maclean 2001 Cabernet Sauvignon (Napa Valley) $50. 82 *—S.H. (9/1/2005)*

Maclean 2003 Sauvignon Blanc (Napa Valley) $18. 84 *—S.H. (11/1/2005)*

MACMURRAY RANCH

MacMurray Ranch 2005 Pinot Gris (Sonoma Coast) $20. One thing about PG is that, no matter whether it's oaked or not, the best ones need a cool climate. That's just what the grapes got here. The racy acidity is preserved, while long hang time gives ripe fruit and spice flavors. In this case, there's a touch of oak and lees, which adds layers to this delicious, complex white wine. 90 *—S.H. (2/1/2007)*

MacMurray Ranch 2004 Pinot Gris (Russian River Valley) $20. 87 *(11/1/2005)*

MacMurray Ranch 2003 Pinot Gris (Russian River Valley) $20. 87 *—S.H. (5/1/2005)*

MacMurray Ranch 2002 Pinot Gris (Russian River Valley) $23. 87 *—S.H. (2/1/2004)*

MacMurray Ranch 2001 Pinot Gris (Russian River Valley) $23. 86 *—S.H. (9/1/2003)*

MacMurray Ranch 2004 Pinot Noir (Santa Rita Hills) $35. A nice, crisp Pinot. It's not the best of the appellation, but then again, it's not as expensive either. Shows the acidity of the region, with black cherry, blackberry tea, tobacco, cola and spice flavors that finish very dry. Best now. 86 *—S.H. (7/1/2007)*

MacMurray Ranch 2003 Pinot Noir (Sonoma Coast) $20. 87 *(11/1/2005)*

MacMurray Ranch 2003 Pinot Noir (Russian River Valley) $35. 87 *(11/1/2005)*

MacMurray Ranch 2002 Pinot Noir (Sonoma Coast) $15. 85 *—S.H. (11/1/2004)*

MacMurray Ranch 2001 Pinot Noir (Sonoma Coast) $15. 83 *—S.H. (7/1/2003)*

MacMurray Ranch 2000 Pinot Noir (Russian River Valley) $32. 87 *(10/1/2002)*

MacMurray Ranch 2003 River Cuvée Pinot Noir Pinot Noir (Russian River Valley) $60. 89 *(11/1/2005)*

MacMurray Ranch 2003 Winemaker's Block Selection Pinot Noir (Russian River Valley) $50. 83 —*S.H. (5/1/2006)*

MACPHAIL

MacPhail 2004 Pinot Noir (Sonoma Coast) $40. 90 —*S.H. (9/1/2006)*

MacPhail 2003 Pinot Noir (Russian River Valley) $40. 91 —*S.H. (12/15/2005)*

MacPhail 2002 Pinot Noir (Russian River Valley) $40. 86 *(11/1/2004)*

MacPhail 2005 Ferrington Vineyard Pinot Noir (Anderson Valley) $48. It's a little heavy and soft, but there's no denying the basic deliciousness. Floods the mouth with cherry, blackberry and raspberry jam and cocoa flavors, and is dry with a silky in texture. Needs more acidic punch. 89 —*S.H. (9/1/2007)*

MacPhail 2004 Goodin Vineyard Pinot Noir (Sonoma Coast) $54. 92 —*S.H. (9/1/2006)*

MacPhail 2005 Pratt Vineyard Pinot Noir (Sonoma Coast) $56. Tastes like cherry-pie filling that got a little caramelized in the oven, giving it a Rhône-type note. Maybe charred oak contributes to the smoky heaviness. Either way, it's a distraction from the delicate, sensual silkiness we all want from Pinot Noir. 87 —*S.H. (9/1/2007)*

MacPhail 2004 Pratt Vineyard Pinot Noir (Sonoma Coast) $56. 92 —*S.H. (9/1/2006)*

MacPhail 2005 Sangiacomo Vineyard Pinot Noir (Sonoma Coast) $52. After missing a beat in '04, the '05 reverts to the high quality of the '03. Made from Dijon clones, the wine shows a brilliant purity of cherry fruit, with rich, earthy complexities of mushrooms, forest floor, cola and balsam. Bone dry, it has an elegantly silky quality that cries out for the best foods. Best now and for the next four years. 93 —*S.H. (9/1/2007)*

MacPhail 2004 Sangiacomo Vineyard Pinot Noir (Sonoma Coast) $58. 87 —*S.H. (9/1/2006)*

MacPhail 2003 Sangiacomo Vineyard Pinot Noir (Sonoma Coast) $40. 94 Editors' Choice —*S.H. (12/15/2005)*

MacPhail 2005 Toulouse Vineyard Pinot Noir (Anderson Valley) $40. I have not been impressed by this bottling in past vintages, but the '05 establishes a new benchmark. Just exactly why is hard to say. Yields were exceptionally low in this long, cool vintage, and lots of new French oak frames dramatically rich, ripe flavors of mashed cherries and raspberries, sprinkled with cinnamon, a drop of crème de cassis, and a pinch of white pepper. The depth and length are beautiful. 94 Editors' Choice —*S.H. (9/1/2007)*

MacPhail 2004 Toulouse Vineyard Pinot Noir (Anderson Valley) $37. 86 —*S.H. (9/1/2006)*

MacPhail 2003 Toulouse Vineyard Pinot Noir (Anderson Valley) $35. 87 —*S.H. (12/15/2005)*

MacPhail 2002 Toulouse Vineyard Pinot Noir (Anderson Valley) $35. 84 *(11/1/2004)*

MACROSTIE

MacRostie 2005 Chardonnay (Carneros) $22. Over the years, this has been a remarkably consistent wine, and the '05 is right up there in quality. Elegant and dry, it shows Carneros Chardonnay at its best, with forward tropical fruit, pear and peach flavors, and a gorgeously acidic, creamy structure. 90 —*S.H. (5/1/2007)*

MacRostie 2004 Chardonnay (Carneros) $22. 89 —*S.H. (7/1/2006)*

MacRostie 2003 Chardonnay (Carneros) $20. 90 Editors' Choice —*S.H. (10/1/2005)*

MacRostie 2002 Chardonnay (Carneros) $20. 90 —*S.H. (11/15/2004)*

MacRostie 1998 Chardonnay (Carneros) $19. 86 *(6/1/2000)*

MacRostie 2000 Reserve Chardonnay (Carneros) $25. 90 —*S.H. (2/1/2004)*

MacRostie 1998 Reserve Chardonnay (Carneros) $33. 88 *(7/1/2001)*

MacRostie 2003 Wildcat Mountain Vineyard Chardonnay (Carneros) $30. 90 —*S.H. (11/1/2005)*

MacRostie 2001 Wildcat Mountain Vineyard Chardonnay (Carneros) $30. 89 —*S.H. (11/15/2004)*

MacRostie 2002 Merlot (Carneros) $26. 90 —*S.H. (12/1/2006)*

MacRostie 2001 Merlot (Carneros) $26. 90 —*S.H. (10/1/2004)*

MacRostie 1996 Merlot (Carneros) $26. 87 —*M.S. (6/1/1999)*

MacRostie 2004 Pinot Noir (Carneros) $28. Easily as good as the '03, this shows well-ripened cherry, cola, coffee and oak flavors, with a rich, kid leather quality and the fine, swift finish of expresso. Crafted from both the Napa and Sonoma sides of the appellation, it's a complex young Pinot that's showing really well now. 91 —*S.H. (4/1/2007)*

MacRostie 2003 Pinot Noir (Carneros) $26. 90 —*S.H. (5/1/2006)*

MacRostie 2002 Pinot Noir (Carneros) $24. 86 —*S.H. (4/1/2005)*

MacRostie 2001 Pinot Noir (Carneros) $24. 85 —*S.H. (5/1/2004)*

MacRostie 2001 Beresini Vineyard Reserve Pinot Noir (Carneros) $27. 87 —*S.H. (12/1/2004)*

MacRostie 2004 Wildcat Mountain Vineyard Pinot Noir (Sonoma Coast) $42. I love this wine. The vineyard is in one of the coolest parts of Carneros, where the maritime influence has given crisp acidity boosting long hangtime fruit. The cherry, raspberry and cola flavors are gorgeous, while the earthier pomegranates and rhubarb are elevated to pie-filling sweetness. Yet the wine is entirely dry. What a beauty. 95 Editors' Choice —*S.H. (7/1/2007)*

MacRostie 2003 Wildcat Mountain Vineyard Syrah (Carneros) $32. Wildcat is a great vineyard, to judge by the wines it's produced over the years, and this Syrah is right up there. It's intense, balanced, clean and dry, with rich blueberry, blackberry jam, smoky leather, plum, tobacco and Asian spice flavors. For all the complexity, it remains elegant. 90 —*S.H. (5/1/2007)*

MacRostie 2002 Wildcat Mountain Vineyard Syrah (Carneros) $32. 92 Editors' Choice *(9/1/2005)*

MacRostie 2001 Wildcat Mountain Vineyard Syrah (Carneros) $39. 93 Editors' Choice —*S.H. (5/1/2004)*

MADDALENA

Maddalena 2003 Cabernet Sauvignon (Paso Robles) $14. 85 —*S.H. (12/31/2006)*

Maddalena 2002 Cabernet Sauvignon (Paso Robles) $13. 83 —*S.H. (7/1/2006)*

Maddalena 2001 Cabernet Sauvignon (Paso Robles) $17. 84 —*S.H. (10/1/2004)*

Maddalena 1999 Cabernet Sauvignon (Central Coast) $13. 84 —*S.H. (5/1/2003)*

Maddalena 2005 Chardonnay (Monterey) $13. Basically dry but a little raisined, this has apricot jam and lemon candy flavors. Although the new oak is modest, it seems to dominate, with a woody, toothpicky heaviness. 83 —*S.H. (12/31/2007)*

Maddalena 2004 Chardonnay (Monterey) $12. 85 —*S.H. (11/15/2006)*

Maddalena 2003 Chardonnay (Monterey) $12. 82 —*S.H. (12/1/2005)*

Maddalena 2002 Chardonnay (Monterey) $10. 86 Best Buy —*S.H. (11/15/2004)*

Maddalena 2001 Chardonnay (Monterey) $10. 84 —*S.H. (8/1/2003)*

Maddalena 2000 Chardonnay (Monterey) $10. 85 —*S.H. (6/1/2003)*

Maddalena 2003 Merlot (Paso Robles) $14. A little salty and soft, but saved by blackberry, cherry, blueberry and mocha flavors. There's a rich texture and a nice coating of oak in this decent everyday Merlot. 84 —*S.H. (6/1/2007)*

Maddalena 2002 Merlot (Paso Robles) $13. 83 —*S.H. (7/1/2006)*

Maddalena 2000 Merlot (Central Coast) $12. 85 —*S.H. (8/1/2003)*

Maddalena 2003 Muscat Canelli (Paso Robles) $10. 85 Best Buy —*S.H. (5/1/2005)*

Maddalena 2006 Pinot Grigio (Monterey) $14. Give credit to cool Monterey for yielding a wine that's this dry, with acidic long hangtime fruit. It's this type of PG that has made the variety an overnight success. The acids perk up the palate, making the pineapple, peach, fig and wildflower flavors bright and tangy. 87 —*S.H. (12/31/2007)*

Maddalena 2005 Pinot Grigio (Monterey) $12. 83 —*S.H. (11/15/2006)*

Maddalena 2004 Pinot Grigio (Paso Robles) $12. 84 —*S.H. (2/1/2006)*

Maddalena 2003 Pinot Grigio (Monterey) $11. 85 —*S.H. (12/15/2004)*

Maddalena 2002 Pinot Grigio (Monterey) $11. 85 —*S.H. (12/1/2003)*

Maddalena 1999 Pinot Grigio (Arroyo Seco) $10. 87 Best Buy —*S.H. (12/15/2001)*

Maddalena 1998 Loma Vista Vineyard Pinot Grigio (Arroyo Seco) $9. 86 Best Buy *(8/1/1999)*

Maddalena 2006 Riesling (Monterey) $13. Maddelena has cornered the market on this style of Riesling. It's crisp, bright and pure in the way of Monterey whites, with peach, pineapple, honeysuckle and apricot flavors, and with 4.5% residual sugar, sweet enough to enjoy on its own, with fresh fruit or even a fruit tart. 85 —*S.H. (12/31/2007)*

Maddalena 2005 Riesling (Monterey) $12. 84 —*S.H. (11/1/2006)*

Maddalena 2004 Riesling (Monterey) $11. 82 —*S.H. (12/1/2005)*

Maddalena 2003 Riesling (Monterey) $10. 85 Best Buy —*S.H. (12/1/2004)*

Maddalena 2002 Riesling (Monterey) $10. 87 Best Buy —*J.M. (8/1/2003)*

Maddalena 2006 Sauvignon Blanc (Paso Robles) $13. Like its vintage predecessors, this seems to have some residual sugar, which gives a honeyed sweetness to the peach, pear, fig and honeysuckle flavors. But it has a very crisp, pleasant acidity that keeps the wine lively. **85** —*S.H. (12/31/2007)*

Maddalena 2005 Sauvignon Blanc (Paso Robles) $12. 84 —*S.H. (12/31/2006)*

Maddalena 2004 Sauvignon Blanc (Paso Robles) $12. 83 —*S.H. (12/1/2005)*

Maddalena 2002 Sauvignon Blanc (Paso Robles) $10. 85 —*S.H. (12/15/2003)*

Maddalena 2002 Syrah (Central Coast) $13. 84 —*S.H. (12/31/2005)*

Maddalena 1997 Loma Vista Vineyard Syrah (Arroyo Seco) $15. 86 —*L.W. (2/1/2000)*

Maddalena 2005 Syrah Rosé Syrah (Paso Robles) $12. 83 —*S.H. (11/15/2006)*

MADEMOISELLE VINEYARDS

Mademoiselle Vineyards NV Blush Rosé Blend (New Mexico) $6. This semisweet blush has light aromas of strawberry with a touch of minerality, and is an easy food pairing alternative when exotic, spicy dishes are on the menu. Nothing blockbuster here, but the flavors are pretty good. **82** —*S.K. (7/1/2007)*

MADISON

Madison 2003 Cabernet Sauvignon (Paso Robles) $25. Shows the semi-sweet, sugary quality of so many Paso reds, with a jellied taste to the cherry and blackberry fruit. If you can get past that, the wine is smooth and velvety. **83** —*S.H. (5/1/2007)*

Madison 2003 Syrah (Paso Robles) $25. Sweet, soft and simple, with candied flavors like a chocolate truffle with a cherry liqueur core and a tart, acidic quality. **83** —*S.H. (5/1/2007)*

MADONNA

Madonna 2004 Mont. St. John Pinot Grigio (Carneros) $26. 91 —*S.H. (2/1/2006)*

Madonna 2001 Due Ragazzi Reserve Pinot Noir (Carneros) $55. 86 —*S.H. (12/1/2004)*

MADONNA ESTATE

Madonna Estate 2002 Madonna Estate Pinot Noir (Carneros) $20. 85 *(11/1/2004)*

Madonna Estate-Mont St. John 2000 Chardonnay (Carneros) $16. 85—*S.H. (6/1/2003)*

MADRIGAL

Madrigal 1997 Merlot (Napa Valley) $24. 82 —*J.C. (7/1/2000)*

Madrigal 1996 Petite Sirah (Napa Valley) $24. 84 —*M.S. (6/1/1999)*

Madrigal 2001 Petite Sirah (Napa Valley) $35. 93 —*J.M. (9/1/2004)*

Madrigal 2000 Petite Sirah (Napa Valley) $33. 88 *(4/1/2003)*

Madrigal 1999 Petite Sirah (Napa Valley) $30. 91 Editors' Choice —*J.M. (12/1/2002)*

Madrigal 2001 Zinfandel (Napa Valley) $26. 91 —*J.M. (8/1/2004)*

MADRONA

Madrona 2000 Gewürztraminer (El Dorado) $10. 84 —*S.H. (9/1/2003)*

Madrona 2002 Malbec (El Dorado) $27. 90 —*S.H. (7/1/2005)*

Madrona 1999 Marsanne (El Dorado) $15. 84 —*S.H. (12/15/2001)*

Madrona 2002 New-World Port (El Dorado) $24. 84 —*S.H. (7/1/2005)*

Madrona 2003 Melange de Trois Rhône White Blend (El Dorado) $16. 85 —*S.H. (10/1/2005)*

Madrona 2001 Riesling (El Dorado) $10. 82 —*J.M. (8/1/2003)*

Madrona 2000 Dry Riesling (El Dorado County) $12. 87 Best Buy —*S.H. (6/1/2002)*

Madrona 1999 Dry Riesling (El Dorado) $14. 85 —*S.H. (8/1/2001)*

Madrona 2002 Shiraz-Cabernet Sauvignon (El Dorado) $16. 84 —*S.H. (10/1/2005)*

Madrona 1999 Reserve Syrah (El Dorado) $20. 87 —*S.H. (2/1/2003)*

Madrona 1998 Zinfandel (El Dorado County) $12. 86 —*S.H. (5/1/2000)*

Madrona 2003 Zinfandel (El Dorado) $15. 87 —*S.H. (10/1/2005)*

Madrona 2000 Zinfandel (El Dorado) $14. 87 —*S.H. (11/1/2002)*

Madrona 2003 30th Anniversary Zinfandel (El Dorado) $38. 92 Editors' Choice —*S.H. (7/1/2006)*

Madrona 1997 Late Harvest Zinfandel (El Dorado) $16. 84 —*S.H. (5/1/2000)*

Madrona 1998 Reserve Zinfandel (El Dorado) $18. 87 —*P.G. (3/1/2001)*

Madrona 1997 Reserve Zinfandel (Paso Robles) $18. 89 —*S.H. (5/1/2000)*

MAFFEY

Maffey 2000 Zinfandel (California) $24. 87 —*S.H. (12/1/2002)*

MAGITO

Magito 2005 The Highlands Bordeaux Blend (Sonoma County) $18. Not quite enough Cabernet Sauvignon in this wine to varietally label it, and kudos to the winemaker for blending in Merlot and Cab Franc, which increases complexity. Fully ready to drink now, the wine is dry and succulent in cherries, blackberries, cocoa and new oaky flavors, with a rich tug of tannins. **89** —*S.H. (9/1/2007)*

Magito 2006 Rivertrace Sauvignon Blanc (North Coast) $18. This is quite an interesting wine, and it just shows how a little creative blending can lift an ordinary wine up. The dominant Sauvignon Blanc brings the usual citrus and grassy acidity, while 8% of Viognier adds flowery perfume, and 10% Verdelho brings more acidity and a lemongrass and green apple edge. Terrific, versatile food wine. **90 Editors' Choice** —*S.H. (9/1/2007)*

Magito 2005 Panorama Zinfandel (California) $18. A little overripe, with some stewed cherry and raisin flavors and richer notes of chocolate and vanilla. But it's dry and not too alcoholic, with a good structure of rich tannins and acidity. Contains some Cabernet, Syrah, Sangiovese, Merlot and Petite Sirah. **84** —*S.H. (9/1/2007)*

MAGNIFICENT WINE COMPANY

Magnificent Wine Company 2006 Chardonnay (Columbia Valley (WA)) $10. Mixed into the blend are smallish proportions of Muscat, Pinot Grigio, Riesling and Gewürztraminer, and this is not really trying to be Chardonnay. It's a dry, tart, all-purpose, everyday white wine, which you can serve with confidence and almost any style of white-wine food you can cook up. **87 Best Buy** —*P.G. (12/1/2007)*

MAHONEY

Mahoney 2005 Gavin Vineyard Chardonnay (Carneros) $20. Earthy and rich, with a good swirl of ripe white peach, buttery sauteed banana and sweet apricot flavors with an edge of fresh green herbs. Seems a little caramel sweet on the finish. **84** —*S.H. (2/1/2007)*

Mahoney 2004 Pinot Noir (Carneros) $24. Francis Mahoney has crafted a young, expressive Pinot Noir, and while it's not particularly complex, it shows real Carneros terroir. Dry and balanced, the wine has cherry, mushroom and earthy flavors, balanced with rich acids and a dusting of tannins. Drink now. **87** —*S.H. (12/1/2007)*

Mahoney 2003 Pinot Noir (Carneros) $24. Shows lots of elegant, cool climate Pinot character in the silky texture, crisp acids and extremely ripe cherry, raspberry, root beer and Asian spice flavors that finish long. Delicious with grilled salmon or lamb chops. **90** —*S.H. (2/1/2007)*

Mahoney 2004 Las Brisas Vineyard Pinot Noir (Carneros) $36. Not only silky and fruity, but with all kinds of complexities, this is a great example of Carneros Pinot at its best. It's dry and crisp, with a myriad of cherry, raspberry, cola, vanilla, oaky char and Asian spice flavors all mingling into a complicated finish. **92** —*S.H. (2/1/2007)*

Mahoney 2004 Mahoney Ranch Pinot Noir (Carneros) $36. Just what you look for in Carneros Pinot, or any cool climate Pinot: an elegant mouthfeel, silky texture and ripe fruit accented by toasty oak. In this case the fruit is raspberries and cherries, bright and pure through the finish. Defines elegance and complexity. **92** —*S.H. (2/1/2007)*

Mahoney 2002 Mahoney Vineyard Pinot Noir (Carneros) $36. 86 —*S.H. (11/1/2004)*

Mahoney 2006 Vermentino (Carneros) $14. If you know how dry Albariño can get, then you know what to expect from this Italian variety. Dry, acidic and elegant, with grapefruit zest and tangy mineral flavors, it's a welcome addition to the California pantheon. **89 Best Buy** —*S.H. (11/15/2007)*

MAISON BASQUE

Maison Basque 1997 Black Zinfandel Zinfandel (California) $24. 82 —*P.G. (3/1/2001)*

MAKOR

Makor 2001 Zinfandel (Arroyo Grande Valley) $12. 87 *(11/1/2003)*

MALIBU

Malibu 2004 Bordeaux Blend (California) $40. 82 —*S.H. (12/1/2006)*

Malibu 2004 Cabernet Franc (California) $30. 86 —*S.H. (12/1/2006)*

Malibu 2005 Cabernet Sauvignon-Cabernet Franc (California) $40. Malibu is considerably colder than Napa Valley, at least during the growing season, and this wine, from a cool vintage, shows high acidity and a minty, green edge. Drink now. **84** —*S.H. (8/1/2007)*

Malibu 2004 Syrah (California) $30. 82 —*S.H. (12/1/2006)*

MALM

Malm 2006 Pinot Noir (Anderson Valley) $26. Made in a nice, light style, this gentle Pinot has flavors of cherries, cola, vanilla and spices. It finishes on a dry, pleasant note. **86** —*S.H. (11/1/2007)*

MALVOLIO

Malvolio 2002 Laetitia Vineyard Block A Pinot Noir (Arroyo Grande Valley) $56. 92 *(11/1/2004)*

Malvolio 2001 Laetitia Vineyard Block A Pinot Noir (Arroyo Grande Valley) $48. 92 —*S.H. (10/1/2004)*

Malvolio 2001 Laetitia Vineyard Block F Pinot Noir (Arroyo Grande Valley) $48. 91 —*S.H. (10/1/2004)*

Malvolio 2001 Laetitia Vineyard Block I Pinot Noir (Arroyo Grande Valley) $48. 93 —*S.H. (10/1/2004)*

Malvolio 2002 Laetitia Vineyard Clone 115 Pinot Noir (Arroyo Grande Valley) $48. 92 *(11/1/2004)*

Malvolio 2003 Laetitia Vineyard Clone 667 Pinot Noir (Arroyo Grande Valley) $48. 92 —*S.H. (10/1/2006)*

Malvolio 2002 Laetitia Vineyard Clone 667 Pinot Noir (Arroyo Grande Valley) $48. 89 *(11/1/2004)*

Malvolio 2003 Laetitia Vineyard Clone 777 Pinot Noir (Arroyo Grande Valley) $48. 92 —*S.H. (7/1/2006)*

MANDOLIN

Mandolin 2005 Chardonnay (Monterey) $10. Pretty good wine for $10. It's dry and crisp, in the Monterey style, with good citrus fruit and mineral flavors that are accented by sweet oak. **85 Best Buy** —*S.H. (10/1/2007)*

Mandolin 2004 Merlot (Central Coast) $10. Hot, harsh, dry and raw, this doesn't offer much pleasure. It has a green, minty streak and is very tannic and astringent. **82** —*S.H. (3/1/2007)*

Mandolin 2005 Pinot Noir (Monterey) $12. At $12 you don't expect great Pinot, but this is a pretty good approximation of the real thing. It's silky, with cherry, cola and pomegranate flavors, and a touch of cedary oak. Not bad for everyday purposes. **85 Best Buy** —*S.H. (4/1/2007)*

Mandolin 2005 Riesling (Monterey) $10. I dislike sweetness in Sauvignon Blanc, Pinot Grigio and other whites that should be dry, but there's something about Riesling that makes it work. This one is perceptibly sweet, yet it's luscious. Acidity helps balance, and the flower blossom, green apple, peach, mineral and petrol flavors love that honeyed edge. Just lovely, and a great buy. **88 Best Buy** —*S.H. (9/1/2007)*

Mandolin 2004 Riesling (Monterey) $10. With crisp acidity and some residual sugar that makes it off-dry, this unoaked Riesling is like a good Kabinett. It's rich and intense in slate, green apple, peach and gardenia flower flavors, and is one of the best interpretations of German-style Riesling in California. **90 Best Buy** —*S.H. (5/1/2007)*

Mandolin 2002 Syrah (Central Coast) $10. Harsh in texture, though there's some good cherry-berry fruit. The wine feels rustic and clumsy. **83** —*S.H. (4/1/2007)*

Mandolin 2003 Old Vines Zinfandel (Lodi) $10. While this will have its fans, it is too ripe and hot for me. The official alcohol is only 14.5%, but it has that heated, Port-like taste, with a raisiny, stewed prune and bitter chocolate finish. **82** —*S.H. (4/1/2007)*

MANDOLINA

Mandolina 2001 Dolcetto (Santa Barbara County) $12. 86 —*S.H. (3/1/2004)*

Mandolina 2002 Nebbiolo (Santa Barbara County) $24. A funny wine, maybe going through an awkward stage. It's pale, light-bodied, silky, acidic and bone dry, with cherry, orange zest, root beer, kid leather and vanilla spice flavors. Resembles a decent Barbaresco at a young age. Seems a bit simple now, but could develop bottle complexity over the next five years. **87** —*S.H. (10/1/2007)*

Mandolina 2005 Pinot Grigio (Santa Barbara County) $14. 84 —*S.H. (12/1/2006)*

Mandolina 2004 Pinot Grigio (Santa Barbara County) $14. 84 —*S.H. (2/1/2006)*

Mandolina 2003 Toccata Classico Red Blend (Santa Barbara County) $18. A Cal-Ital blend of mostly Sangiovese and Bordeaux reds, this rustic country wine is forward in sweet cherry jam, sugared orange tea and vanilla flavors. **83** —*S.H. (10/1/2007)*

Mandolina 2003 Toccata Riserva Red Blend (Santa Barbara County) $32. 82 —*S.H. (12/1/2006)*

Mandolina 2002 Rosato Rosé Blend (Santa Barbara County) $12. 85 —*S.H. (3/1/2004)*

MANNING ESTATES

Manning Estates 2001 Cabernet Sauvignon (Central Coast) $8. 83 —*S.H. (11/15/2003)*

Manning Estates 2002 Chardonnay (Central Coast) $8. 84 —*S.H. (12/31/2003)*

Manning Estates 2001 Merlot (Central Coast) $8. 83 —*S.H. (2/1/2004)*

MANZANITA CREEK

Manzanita Creek 2003 Irene's Vineyard Pinot Noir (Sonoma Coast) $55. What this wine needs is more acidic crispness. The flavors are totally delicious, the texture is elegant, the finish is totally dry, but the superripe cherries, raspberries, cocoa and cola just sort of melt into the palate, then fade away. **86** —*S.H. (9/1/2007)*

Manzanita Creek 2003 Reserve Pinot Noir (Russian River Valley) $45. Very fruity, in fact superfruity, this wine attacks with ripe pie-filling raspberries, red cherries, pomegranates, cola and vanilla-cocoa flavors that flood the mouth, lasting through a long, spicy finish. All that fruit is balanced with crisp acids, while a touch of dusty tannins adds to the fullness. Drink now. **89** —*S.H. (12/31/2007)*

Manzanita Creek 2004 Benediction Syrah (Dry Creek Valley) $32. There's a savage quality to this Syrah, suggesting fresh wild berries growing in fields of lavender, rosemary and pepper tree, and something animal, like roasted meat bone. Under all that it erupts with intense cherry and blackberry fruit, and the sizable tannins make for a puckery feeling. This is quite an interesting Syrah that will gain in complexity over the next five years. **91** —*S.H. (9/1/2007)*

Manzanita Creek 2003 Carreras Ranch Zinfandel (Dry Creek Valley) $36. There's a lot of sugary sweetness in this wine, which tastes like the blackberry and cherry filling of those pop-up toaster tarts. Fortunately, it has the acidity and tannic richness to balance. But it's not really a table wine. More like dessert. **84** —*S.H. (9/1/2007)*

Manzanita Creek 2003 Three Vines Zinfandel (Dry Creek Valley) $28. Hot in alcohol, with sweetened blackberry and raisin flavors. A good example of a Port-like table wine. **83** —*S.H. (9/1/2007)*

MANZONI

Manzoni 2005 Lucia Highland Vineyard Chardonnay (Santa Lucia Highlands) $28. Okay Chard, but pretty thin, especially for this prestige appellation. The plaster of oak is too strong for the fruit. The flavors are of lemon candy and oak. **84** —*S.H. (9/1/2007)*

Manzoni 2004 Family Estate Vineyard Pinot Noir (Santa Lucia Highlands) $23. 88 —*S.H. (12/1/2006)*

Manzoni 2005 Paraiso Vineyard Syrah (Santa Lucia Highlands) $35. The vineyard has been the source of great Syrah, and while this is a good wine, it's not without flaws. Brilliantly ripe in black currants, cherries, cassis, chocolate, sweet leather and spices, it's dry and finely structured. But there's a scour of acid that disturbs its equilibrium. **85** —*S.H. (9/1/2007)*

MARA

Mara 2004 Dolinsek Ranch Reserve Zinfandel (Russian River Valley) $40. 82 —*S.H. (12/15/2006)*

MARAMONTE

Maramonte 2002 Syrage Premium Red Table Wine Red Blend (California) $12. 88 Best Buy —*S.H. (12/31/2006)*

MARCELINA

Marcelina 1998 Cabernet Sauvignon (Napa Valley) $30. 87 —*S.H. (6/1/2002)*

Marcelina 1995 Cabernet Sauvignon (Napa Valley) $25. 87 —*L.W. (11/1/1999)*

Marcelina 2003 Chardonnay (Carneros) $24. 86 —*S.H. (10/1/2005)*

Marcelina 2001 Chardonnay (Carneros) $25. 89 —*S.H. (5/1/2003)*

Marcelina 1997 Chardonnay (Napa Valley) $22. 88 *(6/1/2000)*

Marcelina 2000 Pinot Noir (Carneros) $32. 87 *(10/1/2002)*

MARGUERITE-RYAN

Marguerite-Ryan 2000 Pisoni Vineyards Pinot Noir (Santa Lucia Highlands) $48. 92 —*J.M. (7/1/2003)*

Marguerite-Ryan 2000 Sara Jean's Vineyard Pinot Noir (Santa Lucia Highlands) $45. 90 —*J.M. (7/1/2003)*

MARIAH

Mariah 1999 Merlot (Mendocino Ridge) $30. 93 —*S.H. (5/1/2002)*

Mariah 1998 Merlot (Mendocino Ridge) $28. 93 —*S.H. (5/1/2002)*

Mariah 1999 Syrah (Mendocino Ridge) $30. 85 —*S.H. (5/1/2002)*

Mariah 1999 Syrah (Mendocino Ridge) $30. 85 —*S.H. (5/1/2002)*

Mariah 2003 Zinfandel (Mendocino Ridge) $25. 90 *—S.H. (11/15/2006)*

Mariah 2004 Zinfandel (Mendocino County) $24. The Mariah model of Zin always has been elegant, Bordeaux-style Zins like this. It has the silky body almost of a Pinot Noir, with rich raspberry, cherry, carob and spice flavors, and is soft and dry. There's some notable sweaty funk in the aroma, though, that lowers the score. **86** *—S.H. (11/1/2007)*

Mariah 2002 Zinfandel (Mendocino Ridge) $35. 90 *—S.H. (5/1/2006)*

Mariah 2001 Zinfandel (Mendocino Ridge) $30. 93 Editors' Choice *—S.H. (2/1/2005)*

Mariah 2000 Zinfandel (Mendocino Ridge) $30. 90 *—S.H. (2/1/2005)*

Mariah 1999 Zinfandel (Mendocino Ridge) $31. 90 *—S.H. (5/1/2002)*

Mariah 2001 Poor Ranch Vineyard Zinfandel (Mendocino) $35. 90 *—S.H. (2/1/2005)*

MARICOPA

Maricopa 1999 Shiraz (California) $8. 87 Best Buy *(10/1/2001)*

MARILYN MERLOT

Marilyn Merlot 2005 Merlot (Napa Valley) $27. Can't miss this bottle on the shelf, with La Monroe herself giving that come-hither look. The wine too is soft and fleshy. With 12% Cabernet Sauvignon to give some punch, it has uplifted blackberry, cherry, dark chocolate and smoke flavors, and is totally dry. **87** *—S.H. (12/15/2007)*

MARILYN REMARK

Marilyn Remark 2003 Grenache (Monterey County) $45. 87 *—S.H. (12/1/2005)*

Marilyn Remark 2002 Wild Horse Road Vineyard Grenache (Monterey County) $45. 88 *—S.H. (12/31/2004)*

Marilyn Remark 2001 Wild Horse Road Vineyard Grenache (Monterey County) $45. 92 *—S.H. (5/1/2004)*

Marilyn Remark 2004 Loma Pacific Vineyard Marsanne (Monterey County) $30. 86 *—S.H. (12/1/2005)*

Marilyn Remark 2003 Loma Pacific Vineyard Marsanne (Monterey County) $30. 89 *—S.H. (12/31/2004)*

Marilyn Remark 2002 Loma Pacific Vineyard Marsanne (Monterey County) $28. 91 *—S.H. (2/1/2004)*

Marilyn Remark 2003 Petite Sirah (California) $26. 90 *—S.H. (12/1/2005)*

Marilyn Remark 2004 Rosé de Saignee Rosé Blend (Monterey County) $22. 87 *—S.H. (12/1/2005)*

Marilyn Remark 2004 Lockwood Valley Vineyard Roussanne (Monterey County) $25. 85 *—S.H. (12/1/2005)*

Marilyn Remark 2003 Arroyo Loma Vineyard Syrah (Monterey County) $35. 82 *(9/1/2005)*

Marilyn Remark 2002 Arroyo Loma Vineyard Syrah (Monterey County) $35. 88 *—S.H. (12/31/2004)*

MARIMAR ESTATE

Marimar Estate 2005 Don Miguel Vineyard Chardonnay (Russian River Valley) $32. An acidic, minerally Chardonnay showing structure, cleanliness and elegance. Richness comes by way of intense limes, as well as the usual complexities of new oak and lees aging, and there is not the slightest suggestion of sweetness. This is a very pure, Zen-like expression of cool-climate California Chardonnay. **91** *—S.H. (12/1/2007)*

Marimar Estate 2004 Don Miguel Vineyard Chardonnay (Russian River Valley) $28. Oaky and ripe, with powerful tropical pineapple, kumquat, mineral and floral aromas and flavors. New oak adds smoke, vanilla and char. The bottom line is of a flavorful, acidic and elegant Chard with a lingering, spicy finish. **90** *—S.H. (10/1/2007)*

Marimar Estate 2003 Don Miguel Vineyard Chardonnay (Russian River Valley) $28. 92 *—S.H. (12/1/2006)*

Marimar Estate 2002 Don Miguel Vineyard Chardonnay (Russian River Valley) $28. 93 Editors' Choice *—S.H. (11/15/2005)*

Marimar Estate 2006 Don Miguel Vineyard Acero Chardonnay (Russian River Valley) $26. This unoaked Chard is bright and exuberant in ripe green fruits, such as Granny Smith apples, kiwis, limes, table grapes and mangoes. Acidity in this cool vintage is very high, and when I tasted it, it still had some fizzy fermentation. Technically this is a flaw, but it didn't interfere with my enjoyment. **87** *—S.H. (12/1/2007)*

Marimar Estate 2005 Don Miguel Vineyard Acero Chardonnay (Russian River Valley) $25. 91 *—S.H. (12/31/2006)*

Marimar Estate 2004 Don Miguel Vineyard Dobles Lías Chardonnay (Russian River Valley) $40. Dobles lías means double lees. Extended lees contact has given this Chard great creaminess in the mouth, a smooth impression that is heightened by malolatic fermentation. Beyond that, the wine is fully dry, balanced in alcohol, and lush in flavor. Pineapple custard and charred meringue take center stage, but there's a complex cast of Key lime pie, peach preserves, butterscotch, cinnamon and vanilla. Compelling and authoritative. **94** *—S.H. (10/1/2007)*

Marimar Estate 2003 Don Miguel Vineyard Dobles Lias Chardonnay (Russian River Valley) $40. 92 *—S.H. (7/1/2006)*

Marimar Estate 2002 Don Miguel Vineyard Dobles Lias Estate Chardonnay (Russian River Valley) $40. 92 *—S.H. (10/1/2005)*

Marimar Estate 2004 Don Miguel Vineyard Pinot Noir (Russian River Valley) $39. A bit soft and semisweet, this seems to be the victim of an overly hot vintage. It has candied flavors of cherry and blackberry jam and, while a pleasant sipper, isn't really very interesting, although it does show Pinot-esque silkiness. **85** *—S.H. (12/1/2007)*

Marimar Estate 2003 Don Miguel Vineyard Pinot Noir (Russian River Valley) $35. 91 *—S.H. (12/1/2006)*

Marimar Estate 2002 Don Miguel Vineyard Pinot Noir (Russian River Valley) $35. 86 *(11/1/2004)*

Marimar Estate 2004 Don Miguel Vineyard Cristina Pinot Noir (Russian River Valley) $47. This is a small production barrel selection from the estate vineyard in Green Valley. It's very rich and quite young, too primary and tannic to drink now, but extraordinarily rich in the cherries, blackberries, blueberries and Asian spices that characterize the estate. Best 2008–2012. **95 Editors' Choice** *—S.H. (12/1/2007)*

Marimar Estate 2003 Don Miguel Vineyard Cristina Selection Pinot Noir (Russian River Valley) $47. 86 *—S.H. (12/1/2006)*

Marimar Estate 2002 Don Miguel Vineyard Cristina Selection Pinot Noir (Russian River Valley) $45. 85 *(11/1/2004)*

Marimar Estate 2004 Don Miguel Vineyard Earthquake Pinot Noir (Russian River Valley) $47. 94 *—S.H. (12/31/2006)*

Marimar Estate 2003 Don Miguel Vineyard Earthquake Block Pinot Noir (Russian River Valley) $42. 93 *—S.H. (11/15/2005)*

Marimar Estate 2005 Doña Margarita Vineyard Pinot Noir (Sonoma Coast) $45. I love this wine for its balance and dryness. The texture is velvety-silky and gently tannic, while the flavors are complex, suggesting red cherries with the astringent skins, mashed black raspberries, tangerines, cola, root beer, dark unsweetened chocolate, a touch of cassis liqueur, and something earthy, like Portobello mushrooms. This is really a gorgeous Pinot Noir that will develop over the next five years or so. **96 Editors' Choice** *—S.H. (12/1/2007)*

Marimar Estate 2004 Doña Margarita Vineyard Pinot Noir (Sonoma Coast) $45. 90 *—S.H. (12/1/2006)*

MARIMAR TORRES

Marimar Torres 2001 Dobles Lias Chardonnay (Russian River Valley) $40. 88 *—S.H. (12/15/2003)*

Marimar Torres 2000 Don Miguel-Dobles Lias Chardonnay (Russian River Valley) $40. 92 *—S.H. (12/15/2002)*

Marimar Torres 2001 Don Miguel Vineyard Chardonnay (Russian River Valley) $28. 90 *—S.H. (11/15/2004)*

Marimar Torres 2000 Don Miguel Vineyard Chardonnay (Russian River Valley) $26. 92 *—S.H. (5/1/2003)*

Marimar Torres 1998 Don Miguel Vineyard Chardonnay (Russian River Valley) $25. 86 *—S.H. (11/15/2000)*

Marimar Torres 1997 Don Miguel Vineyard Chardonnay (Russian River Valley) $25. 85 *(6/1/2000)*

Marimar Torres 1998 Don Miguel Vineyard Dobles Lías Chardonnay (Russian River Valley) $45. 90 *(7/1/2001)*

Marimar Torres 2001 Don Miguel Vineyard Pinot Noir (Russian River Valley) $35. 88 *—S.H. (12/1/2004)*

Marimar Torres 2000 Don Miguel Vineyard Pinot Noir (Russian River Valley) $32. 88 *(10/1/2002)*

Marimar Torres 1999 Don Miguel Vineyard Pinot Noir (Russian River Valley) $32. 89 *(10/1/2002)*

Marimar Torres 1998 Don Miguel Vineyard Pinot Noir (Russian River Valley) $30. 91 *—S.H. (12/15/2000)*

MARIO PERELLI-MINETTI

Mario Perelli-Minetti 2001 Cabernet Sauvignon (Napa Valley) $21. 84 *—S.H. (10/1/2005)*

Mario Perelli-Minetti 2000 Miriam Reserve Cabernet Sauvignon (Napa Valley) $75. 93 *—S.H. (10/1/2005)*

MARK RIDGE

Mark Ridge 2000 Merlot (California) $9. 86 Best Buy *—S.H. (11/15/2002)*

MARK RYAN

Mark Ryan 2001 Ciel du Cheval Vineyard "Dead Horse" Bordeaux Blend (Red Mountain) $35. 93 —*P.P. (12/1/2004)*

Mark Ryan 2003 Gun Metal Red Bordeaux Blend (Columbia Valley (WA)) $35. 90 —*P.G. (12/15/2005)*

Mark Ryan 2001 Long Haul Red Bordeaux Blend (Columbia Valley (WA)) $35. 90 —*P.G. (12/1/2004)*

Mark Ryan 2005 Chardonnay (Columbia Valley (WA)) $35. 91 —*P.G. (12/31/2006)*

Mark Ryan 2003 Bad Lands Red Red Blend (Red Mountain) $45. 89 —*P.G. (12/15/2005)*

Mark Ryan 2004 Dead Horse Ciel du Cheval Vineyard Red Blend (Red Mountain) $42. 94 —*P.G. (12/31/2006)*

Mark Ryan 2003 Dead Horse Red Red Blend (Red Mountain) $39. 93 Editors' Choice —*P.G. (12/15/2005)*

Mark Ryan 2004 Long Haul Ciel du Cheval Vineyard Red Blend (Red Mountain) $39. 93 —*P.G. (12/31/2006)*

Mark Ryan 2003 Long Haul Red Red Blend (Red Mountain) $37. 92 —*P.G. (12/15/2005)*

Mark Ryan 2004 The Dissident Red Blend (Washington) $25. 89 —*P.G. (12/31/2006)*

Mark Ryan 2004 Wild Eyed Syrah (Red Mountain) $35. 92 —*P.G. (12/31/2006)*

Mark Ryan 2005 Viognier (Red Mountain) $25. 93 —*P.G. (12/31/2006)*

MARK WEST

Mark West 1997 Chardonnay (Russian River Valley) $14. 88 —*S.H. (11/1/1999)*

Mark West 1999 Gewürztraminer (Sonoma County) $12. 87 —*S.H. (5/1/2001)*

Mark West 1996 Godwin Family Reserve Merlot (Sonoma County) $NA. 81 —*L.W. (12/31/1999)*

Mark West 2004 Pinot Noir (Central Coast) $9. 84 —*S.H. (12/15/2005)*

Mark West 1999 Pinot Noir (Sonoma County) $18. 85 —*S.H. (5/1/2001)*

MARKHAM

Markham 2002 Cabernet Sauvignon (Napa Valley) $30. 83 —*S.H. (9/1/2006)*

Markham 2001 Cabernet Sauvignon (Napa Valley) $27. 81 —*S.H. (12/1/2005)*

Markham 1996 Cabernet Sauvignon (Napa Valley) $22. 89 —*S.H. (2/1/2000)*

Markham 2005 Chardonnay (Napa Valley) $21. Dry and thin, with modest fruit flavors, this comes down on the earthy, dried herbal side, with tobacco and dill flavors. There's some green bitterness on the finish. **83** —*S.H. (7/1/2007)*

Markham 2004 Chardonnay (Napa Valley) $18. 83 —*S.H. (11/15/2006)*

Markham 2002 Chardonnay (Napa Valley) $19. 86 —*S.H. (12/1/2004)*

Markham 2000 Chardonnay (Napa Valley) $17. 86 —*J.M. (12/15/2002)*

Markham 1999 Chardonnay (Napa Valley) $17. 82 —*J.M. (12/15/2002)*

Markham 1999 Reserve Chardonnay (Napa Valley) $31. 89 *(6/1/2003)*

Markham 1997 Reserve Chardonnay (Napa Valley) $28. 91 —*L.W. (11/15/1999)*

Markham 2004 Merlot (Napa Valley) $26. A few years in the bottle have nicely mellowed this wine, giving it a soft, smooth mouthfeel. The flavors are of cherries, red and black, perfectly ripe, seasoned with cassis and smoky new oak. Dry and elegant, this Merlot should hold well for five years. **88** —*S.H. (12/15/2007)*

Markham 2002 Merlot (Napa Valley) $22. 88 —*S.H. (8/1/2005)*

Markham 1997 Merlot (Napa Valley) $19. 85 —*S.H. (7/1/2000)*

Markham 2000 Reserve Merlot (Napa Valley) $42. 92 —*S.H. (8/1/2005)*

Markham 1998 Reserve Merlot (Napa Valley) $38. 85 —*J.M. (11/15/2002)*

Markham 1997 Reserve Merlot (Napa Valley) $35. 92 Editors' Choice —*S.H. (6/1/2001)*

Markham 1996 Reserve Merlot (Napa Valley) $35. 92 —*M.S. (3/1/2000)*

Markham 1999 Petite Sirah (Napa Valley) $24. 83 *(4/1/2003)*

Markham 1998 Petite Sirah (Napa Valley) $24. 88 —*J.C. (9/1/2002)*

Markham 2005 Sauvignon Blanc (Napa Valley) $16. Crisp, fruity and simple, a pleasantly dry sipper whose bright acids boost citrus, fig, melon and spearmint flavors. **84** —*S.H. (7/1/2007)*

Markham 2004 Sauvignon Blanc (Napa Valley) $14. 85 —*S.H. (11/15/2005)*

Markham 2003 Sauvignon Blanc (Napa Valley) $14. 84 —*S.H. (12/1/2004)*

Markham 2001 Sauvignon Blanc (Napa Valley) $13. 88 *(9/1/2003)*

Markham 1999 Sauvignon Blanc (Napa Valley) $10. 84 —*S.H. (5/1/2001)*

Markham 1998 Sauvignon Blanc (Napa Valley) $10. 87 Best Buy *(3/1/2000)*

Markham 2002 Zinfandel (Napa Valley) $20. 85 —*S.H. (12/1/2005)*

Markham 2001 Zinfandel (Napa Valley) $17. 85 *(11/1/2003)*

Markham 1999 Zinfandel (Napa Valley) $17. 85 —*P.G. (3/1/2002)*

MARR

Marr 2002 Cuvée Selena Grenache (California) $18. 85 —*S.H. (12/1/2006)*

Marr 2003 Petite Sirah (Tehema Foothills) $27. 86 —*S.H. (12/1/2006)*

Marr 2002 Petite Sirah (Tehema Foothills) $27. 86 —*S.H. (12/1/2006)*

Marr 2001 Petite Sirah (Tehema Foothills) $24. 86 *(4/1/2003)*

Marr 2004 Shannon Ranch Petite Sirah (Lake County) $25. Fans of Petite Sirah will exult. This darkly brooding wine is heavy, tannic and fully dry, although at the cost of very high alcohol. The flavors, of extraordinarily ripe red and black cherries, currants, espresso, sweet leather and mushu plum sauce, finish with an unsweetened dark chocolate bitterness. It's a wine that will evolve over a decade. **90** —*S.H. (8/1/2007)*

Marr 2003 Cuvée Patrick Reserve Rhône Red Blend (California) $22. 86 —*S.H. (12/1/2006)*

Marr 2004 Syrah (California) $19. The wine is mostly from a place called Tehama Foothills, which is a Sierra Mountain region about which little is known, wine-wise. It has a drop of Viognier and 30% new oak. Ripeness was not a problem, with a sunburst of cherry jam flavors, and the wine is balanced, although rustic. **85** —*S.H. (8/1/2007)*

Marr 1999 Vine Hill Syrah (Russian River Valley) $25. 85 —*S.H. (12/1/2002)*

Marr 2003 Zinfandel (Sonoma County) $26. 88 —*S.H. (12/1/2006)*

Marr 2004 Mattern Ranch Old Vine Zinfandel (Mendocino County) $23. A disappointment after the fine '03. Was it the heat? There's an overripe, rustic taste of cooked blackberry and cherry pie filling, and it finishes a little sweet. Still, it's pretty good California Coastal Zin. **84** —*S.H. (8/1/2007)*

Marr 2003 Mattern Ranch Old Vine Zinfandel (Mendocino County) $23. 89 —*S.H. (12/1/2006)*

MARSHALL

Marshall 2004 Duarte Vineyard Barbera (Placer County) $13. 84 —*S.H. (11/1/2005)*

Marshall 2001 Cabernet Franc (Napa Valley) $28. 81 —*S.H. (11/1/2005)*

Marshall 2003 Pinot Noir (Carneros) $28. 87 —*S.H. (11/1/2005)*

MARSHALL FAMILY WINES

Marshall Family Wines 2003 Syrah (Napa Valley) $26. 83 *(9/1/2005)*

MARSTON FAMILY

Marston Family 2004 Cabernet Sauvignon (Spring Mountain) $90. The vineyard, on Spring Mountain, has been the source of very good Cabs from both Marston and Beringer, and the '04 continues that tradition. Made in the modern style, this is soft and very ripe to the point of sweetness. But it pulls back at the last minute, allowing the cassis, chocolate and red cherry flavors to finish dry. Best with something simple, like a grilled steak. **91** —*S.H. (12/1/2007)*

Marston Family 2001 Cabernet Sauvignon (Spring Mountain) $65. 93 Cellar Selection —*S.H. (10/1/2004)*

Marston Family 2000 Cabernet Sauvignon (Spring Mountain) $60. 88 —*J.M. (2/1/2004)*

Marston Family 1999 Cabernet Sauvignon (Spring Mountain) $60. 87 —*S.H. (2/1/2003)*

Marston Family 2002 Proprietor Grown Cabernet Sauvignon (Spring Mountain) $80. 86 —*S.H. (11/15/2005)*

MARTELLA

Martella 2004 Oleta Vineyard Grenache (Fiddletown) $26. 86 —*S.H. (10/1/2006)*

Martella 2003 Heart Arrow Ranch Petite Sirah (Mendocino) $35. 82 —*S.H. (10/1/2006)*

Martella 2003 Camel Hill Syrah (Santa Cruz Mountains) $55. 88 —*S.H. (10/1/2006)*

Martella 2002 Camel Hill Vineyard Syrah (Santa Cruz Mountains) $55. 87 *(9/1/2005)*

Martella 2003 Fairbairn Ranch Syrah (Mendocino) $45. 88 *(9/1/2005)*

Martella 2003 Hammer Syrah (California) $24. 83 *—S.H. (10/1/2006)*

Martella 2002 Hammer Syrah (California) $24. 86 *(9/1/2005)*

Martella 2000 Hammer Syrah (California) $23. 87 *—S.H. (12/1/2002)*

Martella 1999 Hammer Syrah (California) $NA. 91 *(11/1/2001)*

Martella 2004 Zinfandel (Fiddletown) $26. 84 *—S.H. (10/1/2006)*

MARTHA CLARA

Martha Clara 2000 6025 Bordeaux Blend (North Fork of Long Island) $NA. 84 *—J.C. (10/2/2004)*

Martha Clara 2003 Estate Reserve Cabernet Sauvignon (North Fork of Long Island) $30. There's black pepper, leather, roasted meat and spice on the palate of this Long Island Cabernet, but the mouthfeel is watery, and overall the wine lacks depth or roundness. **83** *—S.K. (5/1/2007)*

Martha Clara 2000 Chardonnay (North Fork of Long Island) $14. 82 *—J.C. (3/1/2002)*

Martha Clara 1999 Chardonnay (North Fork of Long Island) $10. 83 *—J.C. (4/1/2001)*

Martha Clara 2000 Estate Reserve Chardonnay (North Fork of Long Island) $18. 90 Editors' Choice *—J.M. (4/1/2003)*

Martha Clara 1999 Estate Reserve Chardonnay (North Fork of Long Island) $17. 87 *—J.M. (7/1/2002)*

Martha Clara 2004 Gewürztraminer (North Fork of Long Island) $16. 84 *—M.D. (8/1/2006)*

Martha Clara 2001 Gewürztraminer (North Fork of Long Island) $15. 87 *—J.M. (1/1/2003)*

Martha Clara 2000 Gewürztraminer (North Fork of Long Island) $15. 85 *—J.C. (3/1/2002)*

Martha Clara 2002 Merlot (North Fork of Long Island) $16. A good example of what Long Island Merlot can be. The nose is full of classic spicy, earthy varietal aromas, and the delicate flavors of cherry and toasted oak offer appealing flavor and body. The tannins are soft and the fruit distinctive. Would be great with seared duck. **84** *—S.K. (7/1/2007)*

Martha Clara 2000 Merlot (North Fork of Long Island) $16. 84 *—J.C. (10/2/2004)*

Martha Clara 2001 Estate Reserve Merlot (North Fork of Long Island) $25. Soft and elegant Merlot aromas of cigarbox, pepper and game waft from the glass, followed by sturdy flavors of cherry and spice. The elements need a little more integration, and the finish cuts off too soon, but overall the wine is good and can be drunk now. **83** *—S.K. (7/1/2007)*

Martha Clara 2004 Pinot Grigio (North Fork of Long Island) $16. 83 *—J.C. (2/1/2006)*

Martha Clara 2002 Five-O Red Blend (North Fork of Long Island) $25. 84 *—M.D. (8/1/2006)*

Martha Clara 2005 Riesling (North Fork of Long Island) $18. This is a delicious, German-style Riesling that balances rich, ripe fruit flavors with crisp, citric acidity. First, there are the aromas of honey, flowers and lemon, and then rich, elegant flavors of apricot and tropical fruit that finish clean and bright. The intensity of the wine means it could age, but it's great to drink now. **88** *—S.K. (5/1/2007)*

Martha Clara 2004 Riesling (North Fork of Long Island) $15. 80 *—M.D. (8/1/2006)*

Martha Clara 2000 Riesling (North Fork of Long Island) $15. 87 *—J.C. (1/1/2004)*

Martha Clara 2004 Sauvignon Blanc (North Fork of Long Island) $16. 85 *—J.C. (3/1/2006)*

Martha Clara 2003 Estate Reserve Sauvignon Blanc (North Fork of Long Island) $21. 85 *(7/1/2005)*

Martha Clara 1999 Sémillon-Chardonnay (North Fork of Long Island) $15. 84 *—J.C. (4/1/2001)*

Martha Clara NV Brut Methode Sparkling Blend (North Fork of Long Island) $18. 84 *—J.C. (12/1/2003)*

Martha Clara 1999 Viognier (North Fork of Long Island) $15. 81 *—J.C. (4/1/2001)*

Martha Clara 2000 Ciel White Blend (North Fork of Long Island) $26. 88 *—J.M. (12/1/2002)*

MARTIN & WEYRICH

Martin & Weyrich 2003 Cabernet Sauvignon (Paso Robles) $35. Not very successful, especially at this price. It's showing the weaknesses of Paso Cabernet. Although there's obviously ripe fruit, the wine has an awkward mouthfeel, with semisweet fruit flavors that finish with a green, peppermint jelly note. **84** *—S.H. (12/1/2007)*

Martin & Weyrich 2001 Cabernet Sauvignon (Paso Robles) $40. 86 *—S.H. (10/1/2004)*

Martin & Weyrich 2003 Etrusco Cabernet Sauvignon (Paso Robles) $22. This is the winery's super-Tuscan blend, with 15% Sangiovese. It's soft, simple and kind of sweet in LifeSaver cherry flavors. **82** *—S.H. (7/1/2007)*

Martin & Weyrich 2001 Etrusco Cabernet Sauvignon (Paso Robles) $22. 86 *—S.H. (10/1/2004)*

Martin & Weyrich 2000 Etrusco Cabernet Sauvignon (Paso Robles) $22. 86 *—S.H. (10/1/2004)*

Martin & Weyrich 1997 Etrusco Cabernet Sauvignon (Paso Robles) $18. 84 *—S.H. (7/1/2000)*

Martin & Weyrich 2003 Chardonnay (Edna Valley) $18. 90 *—S.H. (6/1/2006)*

Martin & Weyrich 1999 Chardonnay (Edna Valley) $18. 90 Editors' Choice *—S.H. (9/1/2002)*

Martin & Weyrich 1998 Chardonnay (Edna Valley) $18. 86 *(6/1/2000)*

Martin & Weyrich 1998 Hidden Valley Chardonnay (Paso Robles) $13. 88 Best Buy *—S.H. (5/1/2000)*

Martin & Weyrich 2005 Jack Ranch Chardonnay (Edna Valley) $18. There's too much oak on this wine for the fruit. The oak provides luscious toast and vanilla caramel, but the pineapples, pears and mangoes can't stand up to all that wood. As a result, the wine is unbalanced. **84** *—S.H. (12/15/2007)*

Martin & Weyrich 2004 Jack Ranch Chardonnay (Edna Valley) $18. With its rich kiwi, Key lime pie and roasted hazelnut flavors and creamy texture, this Chard packs plenty of pleasure. Crisp acidity makes the finish clean and zesty. **86** *—S.H. (7/1/2007)*

Martin & Weyrich 1999 Reserve Chardonnay (Edna Valley) $24. 92 *—S.H. (9/1/2002)*

Martin & Weyrich 1998 Reserve Chardonnay (Edna Valley) $28. 88 *(6/1/2000)*

Martin & Weyrich 2006 Unwooded Chardonnay (Central Coast) $14. As much as I enjoy acidity in a wine, this is one of the rare ones that has too much. It's so prickly sharp, it's almost still fermenting, while the flavors are grape and apple-like. Tasted in July 2007, it may settle down eventually. **83** *—S.H. (11/15/2007)*

Martin & Weyrich 2006 Moscato Allegro Muscat Canelli (Paso Robles) $12. The sweetness from the 10.5% residual sugar is the main thing this has going for it. The orange and vanilla flavors should be more concentrated, but it's a clean, crisp dessert wine at a fair price. **85** *—S.H. (11/15/2007)*

Martin & Weyrich 2005 Moscato Allegro Muscat Canelli (California) $12. 85 *—S.H. (4/1/2006)*

Martin & Weyrich 1999 Moscato Allegro Muscat Canelli (California) $12. 88 *—S.H. (12/31/2000)*

Martin & Weyrich 2002 Nebbiolo (Paso Robles) $15. Just beyond rose in the color department, this dry wine's chief problem is high and palate-searing acidity. It also finishes on the sweet side. **83** *—S.H. (8/1/2007)*

Martin & Weyrich 1999 Nebbiolo (Paso Robles) $15. 86 *—S.H. (12/1/2001)*

Martin & Weyrich 2003 Il Vecchio Nebbiolo (Paso Robles) $22. Simple and sweet, with LifeSaver candy flavors of raspberries and cherries. Lacks acidity and zest. **82** *—S.H. (12/1/2007)*

Martin & Weyrich 2002 Il Vecchio Reserve Nebbiolo (Paso Robles) $19. 86 *—S.H. (6/1/2006)*

Martin & Weyrich 2006 Pinot Grigio (Central Coast) $15. This wine is a combo of Paso Robles and Edna Valley. The Paso fruit brings slightly cooked, jammy pear and apricot flavors, while the San Luis Obispo grapes provide balancing acidity and a keen lime edge. The result is dry and easy. **86** *—S.H. (11/15/2007)*

Martin & Weyrich 2000 Pinot Grigio (Central Coast) $13. 85 *—S.H. (11/15/2001)*

Martin & Weyrich 2003 Flamenco Rojo Red Blend (Napa Valley) $35. 89 *—S.H. (5/1/2006)*

Martin & Weyrich 2002 Flamenco Rojo Red Blend (Napa Valley) $35. 90 *—S.H. (5/1/2006)*

Martin & Weyrich 2001 Flamenco Rojo Red Blend (Napa Valley) $35. 87 *—S.H. (5/1/2006)*

Martin & Weyrich 2003 Insieme Red Blend (Paso Robles) $16. With at least six reds in here, including Barbera and Sangiovese, this blend is rustic and sweet. It's almost a dessert wine, with cherry jelly flavors, but it's good and clean. **83** *—S.H. (8/1/2007)*

Martin & Weyrich 2002 Insieme Red Blend (Paso Robles) $18. 85 *—S.H. (6/1/2006)*

Martin & Weyrich 1999 Insieme Red Blend (Paso Robles) $16. 86 *—S.H. (11/15/2002)*

Martin & Weyrich 2005 Matador Rosé Blend (Central Coast) $12. 85 *—S.H. (12/1/2006)*

Martin & Weyrich 2003 Il Palio Sangiovese (Paso Robles) $16. Dry, acidic and direct, this warm climate Sangiovese appeals for its cherry flavors and dusty tannins. It really needs rich, oily meats and cheeses to open up and show its sweet core of fruit. **84** *—S.H. (8/1/2007)*

Martin & Weyrich 2002 Il Palio Sangiovese (Paso Robles) $15. 86 *—S.H. (6/1/2006)*

Martin & Weyrich 1999 Il Palio Sangiovese (Paso Robles) $16. 84 *—S.H. (11/15/2001)*

Martin & Weyrich 2001 Syrah (York Mountain) $25. 88 *—S.H. (12/1/2004)*

Martin & Weyrich 2006 Matador Rosé Tempranillo (Central Coast) $13. Nice and dry and crisp, and while the fruit is thin, it has a lightness of body and a palate-stimulating vivacity that make it a good quaffer. This is not a wine to ponder over, but to enjoy with food. Restaurateurs should take note, if they can keep the glass price below nine bucks. **86** *—S.H. (7/1/2007)*

Martin & Weyrich 2003 Dante Dusi Vineyard Zinfandel (Paso Robles) $30. This is a pretty famous vineyard in Paso and other wineries have made good Zin from it, but this one from Martin & Weyrich tastes as sweet as a dessert pastry, with chocolate fudge, cassis, rum, cola, caramel and peppery spice flavors. But there's something to be said for the intensity and the acidity from these 60-year-old vines. **85** *—S.H. (12/1/2007)*

Martin & Weyrich 2002 Dante Dusi Vineyard Zinfandel (Paso Robles) $25. 91 *—S.H. (6/1/2006)*

Martin & Weyrich 1997 Dante Dusi Vineyard Reserve Zinfandel (Paso Robles) $22. 85 *—P.G. (3/1/2001)*

Martin & Weyrich 2004 La Primitiva Zinfandel (Paso Robles) $14. 83 *—S.H. (6/1/2006)*

Martin & Weyrich 1997 Ueberroth Vineyard Zinfandel (Paso Robles) $22. 87 *—P.G. (3/1/2001)*

MARTIN ALFARO

Martin Alfaro 2005 Chardonnay (Santa Cruz Mountains) $23. Oak stars in this Chard—too much oak, in fact. Vanilla, char, wood sap, woody spice and smoke tastes dominate the tropical fruit, peach and citrus flavors. **84** *—S.H. (10/1/2007)*

Martin Alfaro 2005 Sleepy Hollow Vineyard Chardonnay (Santa Lucia Highlands) $25. A little on the thin side, fruit-wise, although there's a wealth of toasty oak, and the wine possesses that bright acidity so associated with the vineyard and appellation. The flavors veer toward apricots and papayas. While official alcohol is only 14.5%, the finish is chili pepper hot. **85** *—S.H. (10/1/2007)*

Martin Alfaro 2005 Alfaro Family Vineyard Pinot Noir (Santa Cruz Mountains) $30. A little too soft, despite nice, dry varietal flavors. The cola, cherry, rhubarb and oak woodspice flavors just lack the acidity to come alive, much less last in the bottle. **84** *—S.H. (10/1/2007)*

Martin Alfaro 2005 Deer Park Vineyard Pinot Noir (Santa Cruz Mountains) $33. Nice and varietally correct, with an herbal, mushroomy undertow to the cherry, cola and pomegranate flavors. It's a little soft, but dry and silky, in the way of coastal Pinot Noir. **86** *—S.H. (10/1/2007)*

Martin Alfaro 2005 Gary's Vineyard Pinot Noir (Santa Lucia Highlands) $42. Tastes soft and direct, with very ripe, accessible cherry, raspberry, cola, gingerbread, mocha, cinnamon spice and smoky oak flavors. Fairly one-dimensional, but a pretty Pinot Noir. **86** *—S.H. (10/1/2007)*

Martin Alfaro 2005 Schultze Family Vineyard Pinot Noir (Santa Cruz Mountains) $33. Unattractive, with funky, medicinal cherry flavors and a soft, collapsed texture. The oak sticks way out. **80** *—S.H. (10/1/2007)*

Martin Alfaro 2005 Sleepy Hollow Vineyard Pinot Noir (Santa Lucia Highlands) $33. Disappointing for this legendary vineyard; a soft, medicinal Pinot with funky, mushroomy cherry flavors. **82** *—S.H. (10/1/2007)*

MARTIN BROTHERS

Martin Brothers 1998 Moscato Allegro Muscat Canelli (Paso Robles) $12. 86 *—J.C. (12/31/1999)*

MARTIN ESTATE

Martin Estate 2004 Cabernet Sauvignon (Rutherford) $70. A bit raisiny and harsh in tannins, with stewed berry and dark baker's chocolate flavors. Finishes dry and a bit hot. Drink now. **84** *—S.H. (12/15/2007)*

Martin Estate 2003 Collector's Reserve Cabernet Sauvignon (Rutherford) $110. 90 Cellar Selection *—S.H. (12/15/2006)*

Martin Estate 2002 Collector's Reserve Cabernet Sauvignon (Rutherford) $100. 85 *—S.H. (12/15/2005)*

MARTIN FAMILY VINEYARDS

Martin Family Vineyards 1999 Cabernet Sauvignon (Napa Valley) $44. 87 *—J.M. (12/15/2003)*

Martin Family Vineyards 2001 Pinot Noir (Russian River Valley) $35. 83 *—J.M. (7/1/2003)*

Martin Family Vineyards 1999 Syrah (Alexander Valley) $32. 85 *—J.M. (12/15/2003)*

Martin Family Vineyards 2001 Crazy Horse Zinfandel (Dry Creek Valley) $32. 85 *—J.M. (3/1/2004)*

Martin Family Vineyards 2001 Rattlesnake Rock Zinfandel (Russian River Valley) $32. 87 *—J.M. (3/1/2004)*

Martin Family Vineyards 2001 Red Rooster Zinfandel (Dry Creek Valley) $28. 80 *(11/1/2003)*

Martin Family Vineyards 2001 The Rooster Zinfandel (Dry Creek Valley) $32. 87 *—J.M. (3/1/2004)*

MARTIN RANCH

Martin Ranch 2003 Cabernet Sauvignon (Santa Clara Valley) $25. This valley is known as Silicon Valley, but before the suburbs overran the vineyards, it was one of the most famous sources of Cabernet in California. Although this wine is a little overripe, it shows the lost promise of the valley, in the beautiful tannins and overall balance. **86** *—S.H. (4/1/2007)*

Martin Ranch 2003 Reserve Cabernet Sauvignon (Santa Cruz Mountains) $40. Lush and elegant, showing its mountain origins in the dusty tannins. A really beautiful wine, with perfectly ripened blackberry, plum, cola, coffee and spicy oak flavors, and those tannins are rich, ripe and refined. Buy by the case, then open one bottle a year as it slowly evolves. **93 Cellar Selection** *—S.H. (4/1/2007)*

Martin Ranch 2004 Thérese Vineyards Estate Cabernet Sauvignon (Santa Cruz Mountains) $50. This winery seems to be trying to find an identity. The Cabs are vintage-driven, and do better in cool years, which 2004 wasn't. This wine is a little soft and direct, but delicious enough, with ripe, pastry-filling blackberry, cherry, boysenberry and chocolate flavors. You can taste high-char oak on the finish. **86** *—S.H. (12/1/2007)*

Martin Ranch 2004 J.D. Hurley Merlot (Santa Clara Valley) $20. Definitely on the ripe, hot side, with blackberry flavors veering all the way into shriveled raisins. With lots of new oak, the wine is fully dry, but at the cost of very high alcohol, 15.6%, which gives the palate a Port-like burn. **83** *—S.H. (9/1/2007)*

Martin Ranch 2004 Thérese Vineyards Syrah (Santa Clara Valley) $27. The valley is today's modern Silicon Valley, but used to be one of the most famous placenames in California wine. This Syrah is dry and classy, with a Côtes-du-Rhône berried deliciousness and a soft, immediate appeal. **88** *—S.H. (10/1/2007)*

MARTIN RAY

Martin Ray 1997 Synthesis Diamond Mountain Vineyard Bordeaux Blend (Napa Valley) $50. 91 *(11/1/2000)*

Martin Ray 2003 Cabernet Sauvignon (Napa Valley) $20. Here's a rich, opulent Cab that brims with the special balance that Napa brings. Dry and smoothly tannic, it shows lush flavors of blackberries, cassis, raspberries and oak. Doesn't seem to be an ager, but it's awfully good now. **87** *—S.H. (11/1/2007)*

Martin Ray 2003 Cabernet Sauvignon (Sonoma Mountain) $55. Of the winery's three new mountain Cabs, this is the least successful, because it's hot and stewed. Has cooked berry flavors, stickily dry tannins and an overall astringent mouthfeel that won't age away. **83** *—S.H. (2/1/2007)*

Martin Ray 2003 Cabernet Sauvignon (Santa Cruz Mountains) $60. I love this Cab for its dryness, richness and balance. It's a lovely wine, poised between thick tannins, crisp acids, ripe blackberry fruit and ample new oak, but it is young. As polished as it is now, it should soften and sweeten with a few years of bottle age. Best 2007–2010. **93** *—S.H. (2/1/2007)*

Martin Ray 2002 Cabernet Sauvignon (Napa-Mendocino-Santa Clara Counties) $20. 84 *—S.H. (12/15/2006)*

Martin Ray 2001 Cabernet Sauvignon (Diamond Mountain) $50. 94 Cellar Selection *—S.H. (4/1/2006)*

Martin Ray 2001 Cabernet Sauvignon (Santa Cruz Mountains) $50. 93 *—S.H. (5/1/2005)*

Martin Ray 2004 Angeline Cabernet Sauvignon (Sonoma County) $14. 84 *—S.H. (9/1/2006)*

Martin Ray 2003 Angeline Cabernet Sauvignon (Sonoma County) $14. 85 *—S.H. (7/1/2006)*

Martin Ray 2002 Angeline Cabernet Sauvignon (Sonoma County) $10. 82 *—S.H. (11/1/2005)*

Martin Ray 2001 Napa, Sonoma & Mendocino Counties Cabernet Sauvignon (California) $16. 87 *—S.H. (10/1/2005)*

Martin Ray 2004 Reserve Cabernet Sauvignon (Stags Leap District) $40. This is the first Stags Leap wine I've ever had from Martin Ray, who's been making Cabs from many other appellations for years. It's also one of the best Cabs the winery has ever produced. Exceptionally ripe and well-oaked to surround blackberry, blueberry, cherry and currant pie filling flavors, it's a softly beautiful, complex wine that's gorgeous now, and should age well for a decade. 93 *—S.H. (11/1/2007)*

Martin Ray 2003 Reserve Cabernet Sauvignon (Diamond Mountain) $60. Soft and lush enough to drink now, but such is the balance that it's also a good cellar candidate. The tannins are there, but they're the finely meshed, velvety kind. The flavors are an intricate blend of ripe blackberry and cherry fruit and new, smoky oak. This is really a polished, elegant Cabernet. 88 *—S.H. (2/1/2007)*

Martin Ray 2002 Reserve Cabernet Sauvignon (Santa Cruz Mountains) $60. 93 Cellar Selection *—S.H. (9/1/2006)*

Martin Ray 2002 Reserve Cabernet Sauvignon (Diamond Mountain) $60. 93 Cellar Selection *—S.H. (9/1/2006)*

Martin Ray 2002 Reserve Cabernet Sauvignon (Sonoma Mountain) $60. 91 Cellar Selection *—S.H. (9/1/2006)*

Martin Ray 2001 Reserve Cabernet Sauvignon (Napa Valley) $25. 90 *—S.H. (12/31/2004)*

Martin Ray 2005 Chardonnay (Russian River Valley) $20. 86 *—S.H. (12/15/2006)*

Martin Ray 2004 Chardonnay (Russian River Valley) $16. 83 *—S.H. (12/31/2005)*

Martin Ray 2003 Chardonnay (Russian River Valley) $16. 83 *—S.H. (11/1/2005)*

Martin Ray 2004 Angeline Chardonnay (Russian River Valley) $10. 83 *—S.H. (12/31/2005)*

Martin Ray 1999 Mariage Chardonnay (Russian River Valley) $20. 91 Editors' Choice *—S.H. (5/1/2001)*

Martin Ray 1998 Mariage Chardonnay (California) $18. 86 *(6/1/2000)*

Martin Ray 1997 Mariage Chardonnay (California) $20. 90 *—S.H. (10/1/1999)*

Martin Ray 2000 Miriage Chardonnay (Russian River Valley) $16. 86 *—S.H. (5/1/2003)*

Martin Ray 2005 Reserve Chardonnay (Yountville) $25. Oaky and a little earthy, with an array of peach, pineapple, gingerbread and buttered toast flavors. Don't over chill. 88 *—S.H. (7/1/2007)*

Martin Ray 2005 Angeline Gewürztraminer (Mendocino County) $14. 89 Best Buy *—S.H. (11/15/2006)*

Martin Ray 2004 Angeline Gewürztraminer (Mendocino County) $10. 84 *—S.H. (10/1/2005)*

Martin Ray 2004 Merlot (Napa Valley) $20. The '04 is considerably better than the '03, probably because the warmer vintage ripened the fruit and did away with the minty greenness. No unripeness here. It's all deliciously jammy blackberry, cherry and chocolate fruit, with an sweet, oaky finish. 84 *—S.H. (12/1/2007)*

Martin Ray 2003 Merlot (Napa Valley) $20. Tough and unbalanced, with some raisiny flavors as well as greener, minty ones that are accompanied by harsh tannins and burning acids. Twenty bucks is a high price to pay for this wine. 81 *—S.H. (2/1/2007)*

Martin Ray 2002 Merlot (Napa Valley) $16. 83 *—S.H. (11/1/2005)*

Martin Ray 2004 Angeline Merlot (Sonoma County) $14. 81 *—S.H. (7/1/2006)*

Martin Ray 2002 Angeline Merlot (Sonoma County) $10. 82 *—S.H. (11/1/2005)*

Martin Ray 2001 Diamond Mountain Merlot (Napa Valley) $40. 92 *—S.H. (5/1/2005)*

Martin Ray 1997 Diamond Mountain Vineyard Merlot (Napa Valley) $50. 86 *—M.S. (3/1/2000)*

Martin Ray 2006 Pinot Gris (Mendocino County) $20. Beautiful PG, one of the better ones out there, and the kind of wine that's driving the category through the roof. Absolutely dry, elegantly crisp and minerally-fruity, it defines elegance. The flavors veer toward limes and grapefruits and riper, lusher tropical fruits and white flowers. 90 Editors' Choice *—S.H. (10/1/2007)*

Martin Ray 2005 Pinot Noir (Santa Barbara County) $25. This is not an especially complex Pinot, but it is a satisfying one. They got everything right, from the balanced cherry, cola and blueberry flavors to the delicate structure, fine acidity and deft touch of oak. Should be easy to find, with 11,000 cases produced. 86 *—S.H. (5/1/2007)*

Martin Ray 1997 Pinot Noir (Russian River Valley) $40. 88 *—M.S. (5/1/2000)*

Martin Ray 2004 Angeline Pinot Noir (Russian River Valley) $10. 85 Best Buy *—S.H. (4/1/2006)*

Martin Ray 2004 Angeline Pinot Noir (Sonoma Coast) $10. 83 *—S.H. (12/31/2005)*

Martin Ray 2003 Angeline Pinot Noir (Russian River Valley) $10. 86 Best Buy *—S.H. (6/1/2005)*

Martin Ray 2004 Reserve Pinot Noir (Russian River Valley) $40. 92 *—S.H. (11/1/2006)*

Martin Ray 2001 **1 Liter Red Blend (Central Coast) $15.** 83 *—S.H. (11/1/2005)*

Martin Ray 2005 Angeline Riesling (Mendocino County) $14. 89 Best Buy *—S.H. (11/15/2006)*

Martin Ray 2006 Sauvignon Blanc (Napa Valley) $20. Finally, a completely dry, tart young wine that's loaded with fruit, but is neither candy-sweet nor cat-pee unripe. Floods the mouth with spearmint, pineapple and vanilla flavors that finish long, clean and spicy. 89 *—S.H. (12/1/2007)*

Martin Ray 2006 Angeline Sauvignon Blanc (Russian River Valley) $14. With apricot, pineapple, rice wine vinegar and white sugar flavors, this wine tastes like a sweet-and-sour sauce in a Chinese restaurant. The acidity is emphasized on the prickly finish. 83 *—S.H. (10/1/2007)*

Martin Ray 2004 Angeline Syrah (Dry Creek Valley) $14. 85 *—S.H. (8/1/2006)*

Martin Ray 2004 Angeline Zinfandel (Dry Creek Valley) $14. 84 *—S.H. (10/1/2006)*

MARTINE'S

Martine's 2000 Syrah (California) $17. 86 *(10/1/2003)*

Martine's 2001 Viognier (California) $15. 85 *(10/1/2003)*

MARTINI & PRATI

Martini & Prati 1999 Tower Hill Pinot Noir (California) $14. 80 *(10/1/2002)*

MARYHILL

Maryhill 2003 Proprietor's Reserve Serendipity Bordeaux Blend (Washington) $40. 88 *—P.G. (6/1/2006)*

Maryhill 2004 Proprietor's Reserve Cabernet Franc (Columbia Valley (WA)) $30. I really liked the winery's 2003 Cab Franc, for its dark, black fruits laced with licorice and streaks of tarry tannin. What's missing here is that defining structure; they've slipped this one into the soft, smooth, generic red category. Sweet fruit, some smoke and a bit more stiffness to the tannins still make this wine a relative standout, but it's lost its edge. 87 *—P.G. (8/1/2007)*

Maryhill 2003 Proprietor's Reserve Cabernet Franc (Columbia Valley (WA)) $32. 90 *—P.G. (6/1/2006)*

Maryhill 2002 Cabernet Sauvignon (Columbia Valley (WA)) $20. 87 *—P.G. (6/1/2006)*

Maryhill 2004 Proprietor's Reserve Cabernet Sauvignon (Columbia Valley (WA)) $30. Maryhill, frustrating as many of their wines may be, does well by their Cabernets. This is not in the same class as the exceptional 2003, but offers ripe red fruits highlighted with smooth tannins and traces of black tea wrapped around black cherry and blackberry fruit. Ultimately, it falls into the same soft sweet red category as the winery's other wines, but with a bit more definition, snap and style. 87 *—P.G. (8/1/2007)*

Maryhill 2003 Proprietor's Reserve Cabernet Sauvignon (Columbia Valley (WA)) $34. 90 *—P.G. (6/1/2006)*

Maryhill 2003 Proprietor's Reserve Chardonnay (Columbia Valley (WA)) $18. 87 *—P.G. (6/1/2006)*

Maryhill 2006 Gewürztraminer (Columbia Valley (WA)) $14. Though Washington is rarely recognized for its Gewürztraminers, the grape does exceptionally well here, and Celilo in particular has become a treasured hunting ground for winemakers specializing in the grape. This one is a gem: spicy and off-dry, it expands across the palate with authority and precision. Rather than sweetly floral, it leans toward flavors that are sweetly grassy, but lets pretty rose petal highlights fill in the back of the palate. 89 Best Buy *—P.G. (12/1/2007)*

Maryhill 2002 Grenache (Columbia Valley (WA)) $24. 86 *—P.G. (9/1/2004)*

Maryhill 2004 Proprietor's Reserve Grenache (Columbia Valley (WA)) $30. Though I applaud and encourage the re-discovery of Grenache in Washington state, this oxidized, flat-tasting wine does little to encourage me. There is no trace of varietal character, just a soft, meek and generic red wine quickly going over the edge. A sweet, vinegary flavor ramps up in the finish. 82 *—P.G. (8/1/2007)*

Maryhill 2004 Merlot (Columbia Valley (WA)) $15. This is a cheerful, agreeable wine, with loose-knit fruit flavors of strawberry and sweet cranberry, interwoven with generous streaks of butter and toast. Drink up. **86** —*P.G. (8/1/2007)*

Maryhill 2004 Proprietor's Reserve Merlot (Columbia Valley (WA)) $28. The reserve Merlot lacks the smooth, buttery softness of the regular bottling, substituting stiffer tannins, deeper color and a definite herbal component. Perhaps the thinking is that this will age longer, but for sheer pleasure it does not measure up to its less expensive sibling. **85** —*P.G. (8/1/2007)*

Maryhill 2006 Pinot Gris (Columbia Valley (WA)) $16. Sappy with flavors of ripe Macintosh apples, this snappy, juicy wine brings a lively lushness to this versatile grape. The mix of fruit and acid is just right, and it keeps its balance all through the finish. Almost bone dry. **88 Editors' Choice** —*P.G. (12/1/2007)*

Maryhill 2003 Pinot Gris (Willamette Valley) $13. 85 —*P.G. (10/1/2004)*

Maryhill 2002 Pinot Noir (Willamette Valley) $18. 87 —*P.G. (11/1/2004)*

Maryhill 2005 Winemaker's Blend Red Blend (Columbia Valley (WA)) $10. For my money, this is the most authentic wine that Maryhill makes. It has not been softened, oaked, sweetened and vanilla'd up—it just shows the great fruit and the verticality of nicely ripened grapes. Composed of 40% Merlot, 32% Cabernet, 22% Syrah, 6% Cab Franc and 13.9% alcohol. **88 Best Buy** —*P.G. (8/1/2007)*

Maryhill 2004 Sangiovese (Columbia Valley (WA)) $15. This is already quite soft, oxidized and mature. It's a pleasant take on Sangiovese, absolutely ready to drink and approachable with warm, raisiny fruit flavors. There's a soft, chocolaty landing that keeps the tannins easy also. But there's not much character and no real stuffing here. **85** —*P.G. (8/1/2007)*

Maryhill 2002 Sangiovese (Columbia Valley (WA)) $16. 86 —*P.G. (9/1/2004)*

Maryhill 2004 Proprietor's Reserve Sangiovese (Columbia Valley (WA)) $24. Maryhill's Proprietor's Reserve bottling features heavy barrel toast and more extraction than the regular Sangiovese. It is very soft, very approachable, smooth and sweet, with a finish that tastes of strawberries and cream. Definitely a consumer-pleasing style. **86** —*P.G. (8/1/2007)*

Maryhill 2002 Proprietor's Reserve Sangiovese (Columbia Valley (WA)) $26. 87 —*P.G. (9/1/2004)*

Maryhill 2005 Rosé of Sangiovese (Yakima Valley) $14. This is not a truly dry style; the relatively low (11.6%) alcohol is backed with a palate impression that is a bit sweet, but the wine retains enough acid to provide balance. It's a forward, fruity, round and flavorful, consumer-friendly style. It would work well with spicy food if served chilled. **86** —*P.G. (7/1/2007)*

Maryhill 2006 Sauvignon Blanc (Columbia Valley (WA)) $12. There is a fair amount of sweetness in this wine, keeping the alcohol at 12.5% but filling in the midpalate with grainy sugar. It is not a style that will hold much appeal for lovers of this grassy grape; the sweetness obliterates much of the natural character. **84** —*P.G. (12/1/2007)*

Maryhill 2004 Syrah (Columbia Valley (WA)) $18. Lush and fruity, this has a raisiny, cooked prune quality to its fruit. It's sweet and roasted, easy-going, and fits in neatly with the winery's lineup of ripe, soft reds. But it could be almost anything in that lineup; it doesn't have any of the particular character that makes Washington Syrah so distinctive. **85** —*P.G. (8/1/2007)*

Maryhill 2003 Syrah (Columbia Valley (WA)) $16. 89 Editors' Choice *(9/1/2005)*

Maryhill 2001 Syrah (Columbia Valley (WA)) $18. 87 —*P.G. (9/1/2004)*

Maryhill 2004 Proprietor's Reserve Syrah (Columbia Valley (WA)) $32. Here's a well-made wine that shows that this important producer can rise to the challenge when it retains its focus on varietal character. This authoritative, smoky wine smells like Syrah and it follows through with firm, supple, rich flavors. The floral and citrus notes, the herbal/olive underpinnings, the ripe—not roasted—fruit all hit the mark. **89** —*P.G. (8/1/2007)*

Maryhill 2003 Proprietor's Reserve Syrah (Washington) $36. 85 —*P.G. (6/1/2006)*

Maryhill 2001 Reserve Syrah (Columbia Valley (WA)) $28. 90 Editors' Choice —*P.G. (9/1/2004)*

Maryhill 2006 Viognier (Columbia Valley (WA)) $18. Here is an interesting take on Viognier, relatively low in alcohol (13%) but quite sweet, at almost 2% residual sugar. The sweetness takes away a fair amount of the interesting citrus character of the grape, and seems to dumb it down a bit, but it might fit in well with spicy Asian dishes. **86** —*P.G. (12/1/2007)*

Maryhill 2003 Viognier (Columbia Valley (WA)) $15. 86 —*P.G. (9/1/2004)*

Maryhill 2006 Winemaker's White Blend (Columbia Valley (WA)) $14. This Chardonnay, Sémillon, Sauvignon Blanc and Viognier blend is a good, all-purpose white wine but lacks focus. **85** —*P.G. (12/1/2007)*

Maryhill 2002 Zinfandel (Columbia Valley (WA)) $22. 87 —*P.G. (9/1/2004)*

Maryhill 2002 Proprietor's Reserve Zinfandel (Columbia Valley (WA)) $32. 88 —*P.G. (9/1/2004)*

MASON CELLARS

Mason Cellars 2005 Sauvignon Blanc (Napa Valley) $16. Nicely dry and crisp, with polished lemongrass and vanilla flavors, but a feline smell shows up throughout. **84** —*S.H. (9/1/2007)*

Mason Cellars 2004 Sauvignon Blanc (Napa Valley) $16. 91 —*S.H. (3/1/2006)*

MASSET WINERY

Masset Winery 2000 Cabernet Sauvignon (Yakima Valley) $20. 83 —*P.G. (1/1/2004)*

Masset Winery 1999 Cabernet Sauvignon (Yakima Valley) $20. 82 —*P.G. (1/1/2004)*

MASUT

Masut 2003 Pinot Noir (Redwood Valley) $30. 86 —S.H. (10/1/2005)

Masut 2002 Pinot Noir (Redwood Valley) $30. 84 —*S.H. (11/1/2004)*

Masut 2001 Pinot Noir (Redwood Valley) $30. 88 —*S.H. (7/1/2003)*

Masut 2003 Block 7 Pinot Noir (Redwood Valley) $50. 90 —*S.H. (10/1/2005)*

MATANZAS CREEK

Matanzas Creek 2000 Cabernet Sauvignon (Sonoma County) $35. 86 —*M.S. (11/15/2003)*

Matanzas Creek 2005 Chardonnay (Sonoma Valley) $29. This is a wine that does best in cool vintages, which '05 was. A blend of Carneros and Bennett Valley, the wine shows Burgundian character, with apple butter, pineapple custard and lemon zest flavors undergirded by a rich, stony minerality, and a long, rewarding, spicy finish. Very nice now, and should develop for five years. **90** —*S.H. (7/1/2007)*

Matanzas Creek 1998 Chardonnay (Sonoma County) $33. 87 *(7/1/2001)*

Matanzas Creek 1997 Chardonnay (Sonoma Valley) $31. 91 —*L.W. (11/1/1999)*

Matanzas Creek 1996 Sonoma County Chardonnay (Sonoma County) $30. 86 —*S.H. (7/1/1999)*

Matanzas Creek 2000 Merlot (Sonoma County) $30. 85 *(1/21/2004)*

Matanzas Creek 1997 Merlot (Sonoma Valley) $56. 91 —*J.M. (12/1/2001)*

Matanzas Creek NV Rosé Wine of Merlot (Sonoma County) $17. Dry and full-bodied, this polished wine shows pronounced fruit. Bursts with ripe cherry compote, raspberry tea and spice flavors, with an exotic note of candied ginger. One of the better Merlot rosés out there. **86** —*S.H. (7/1/2007)*

Matanzas Creek 2005 Sauvignon Blanc (Sonoma County) $22. Made in the slightly sweet lemongrass and fig style that's so popular nowadays, this wine, with some of the Musqué clone, has very crisp acidity that balances out the ripeness. Great with a salad of mixed greens with chevre, grapefruit and roasted peppers. **87** —*S.H. (5/1/2007)*

Matanzas Creek 2000 Sauvignon Blanc (Sonoma County) $22. 89 *(8/1/2002)*

Matanzas Creek 2002 Syrah (Sonoma County) $25. 85 *(9/1/2005)*

MATCH

Match 2003 Butterdragon Hill Cabernet Sauvignon (Napa Valley) $72. The '03 thankfully is drier and more balanced than the inaugural '02, which shows a learning curve. It's made in the classic Napa mode, with rich, thick tannins supporting blackberry, olive tapenade and sweet oak flavors. Gracious now, the wine should age well for a decade. **90 Cellar Selection** —*S.H. (5/1/2007)*

Match 2002 Butterdragon Hill Cabernet Sauvignon (St. Helena) $72. 85 —*S.H. (7/1/2006)*

MATCHBOOK

Matchbook 2004 Syrah (Dunnigan Hills) $16. From the San Francisco Delta, inland but cooled by coastal breezes, comes this dryish, balanced Syrah. It's a nice everyday sipper, with berry-cherry flavors and nicely ripe tannins. **84** —*S.H. (5/1/2007)*

MATRIARCH

Matriarch 2004 Bordeaux Blend (Napa Valley) $85. This lower end wine from Harlan's stable is as good as most Napa wineries' best. It's beautiful to drink right now, showing class and distinction. Tasted alone, its burst of black currants and cherries is rich, without any trace of overripeness. **92** —*S.H. (12/1/2007)*

MATTHEWS

Matthews 2001 Bordeaux Blend (Columbia Valley (WA)) $50. 90 —*P.G. (6/1/2005)*

Matthews 2003 Conner Lee Vineyard Reserve Cabernet Franc (Columbia Valley (WA)) $110. This is surely the most ambitious Cabernet Franc/Conner Lee wine ever made, and it's priced accordingly. I love the purity, the focus and the way it plays across the palate; it's a real high-wire act. Cab Franc does not lend itself to either elegance or completeness as a varietal grape, which is why it is almost always blended. But here it is the whole show, and it's razzle dazzle all the way. Ripe blackberry and black cherry fruit is framed in spice and tannin, with a sweetness rarely found. The finishing notes of fresh roasted coffee and mocha linger sensuously in the back of the mouth. A rare mix of delicacy and power. **94** —*P.G. (12/1/2007)*

Matthews 2001 Elerding Vineyard Reserve Cabernet Sauvignon (Yakima Valley) $60. 93 —*P.G. (11/15/2004)*

Matthews 2003 Red Blend (Columbia Valley (WA)) $60. This has rich tannins, dense fruit and overall deep flavors. This is a dark wine, just this side of brooding, with ripe blueberry and cherry fruit, softly chalky tannins, whiffs of smoke and splashes of pepper. The dark fruit flavors are bold and seamless, melded with smoke and chocolate, dotted with ground espresso, and finished with a nice lift. This probably needs another five years to really show all of its complexity. **93** —*P.G. (12/1/2007)*

Matthews 2002 Red Blend (Columbia Valley (WA)) $50. 94 —*P.G. (12/15/2005)*

Matthews 2004 Claret Red Blend (Columbia Valley (WA)) $30. Because he blends shortly after fermentation, Matt Loso's wines attain a seamless complexity early on; it's a hallmark of the winery. This beautifully crafted Claret has no rough edges; in fact, no edges at all. It is a supple, elegant wine, loaded with fruit flavors that run from berry to cherry to plum, while the oak gently adds spice and toast. **91** —*P.G. (12/1/2007)*

Matthews 2004 Klipsun Sauvignon Blanc (Red Mountain) $18. 90 —*P.G. (12/15/2005)*

Matthews 2003 Hedges Estate Vineyard Syrah (Red Mountain) $50. 89 *(9/1/2005)*

Matthews 2004 Hedges Vineyard Syrah (Red Mountain) $50. 94 Editors' Choice —*P.G. (11/15/2006)*

MAURITSON

Mauritson 2005 Sauvignon Blanc (Dry Creek Valley) $16. 90 Editors' Choice —*S.H. (12/15/2006)*

Mauritson 2004 Sauvignon Blanc (Dry Creek Valley) $16. 91 Editors' Choice —*S.H. (8/1/2006)*

Mauritson 2003 Sauvignon Blanc (Dry Creek Valley) $16. 88 —*S.H. (11/1/2005)*

Mauritson 2004 Zinfandel (Dry Creek Valley) $24. 86 —*S.H. (12/15/2006)*

Mauritson 2002 Zinfandel (Dry Creek Valley) $24. 90 Editors' Choice —*S.H. (11/1/2005)*

Mauritson 2001 Zinfandel (Dry Creek Valley) $24. 85 *(11/1/2003)*

Mauritson 2001 Growers Reserve Zinfandel (Dry Creek Valley) $33. 91 —*S.H. (11/1/2005)*

MAYACAMAS

Mayacamas 1999 Chardonnay (Napa Valley) $32. 87 —*S.H. (12/15/2002)*

Mayacamas 2002 Sauvignon Blanc (Napa Valley) $20. 93 —*S.H. (12/15/2004)*

MAYO

Mayo 2002 The Libertine Bordeaux Blend (Sonoma County) $15. 84 —*S.H. (6/1/2004)*

Mayo 2000 Los Chamizal Vineyard Cabernet Sauvignon (Sonoma Valley) $35. 87 —*S.H. (4/1/2003)*

Mayo 1997 Los Chamizal Vineyard Cabernet Sauvignon (Sonoma Valley) $35. 89 *(11/1/2000)*

Mayo 2001 Napa River Ranch Vineyard Cabernet Sauvignon (Napa Valley) $35. 90 —*S.H. (6/1/2004)*

Mayo 1998 Barrel Select Chardonnay (Sonoma Valley) $25. 87 *(6/1/2000)*

Mayo 2002 Laurel Hill Vineyard Chardonnay (Sonoma Valley) $20. 87 —*S.H. (6/1/2004)*

Mayo 2004 Balletto Vineyards Unwooded Pinot Gris (Sonoma Coast) $20. 90 Editors' Choice —*S.H. (12/15/2005)*

Mayo 2002 Piner Ranch Vineyard Pinot Noir (Russian River Valley) $30. 89 —*S.H. (11/1/2004)*

Mayo 2001 Piner Ranch Vineyard Pinot Noir (Russian River Valley) $30. 91 —*S.H. (7/1/2003)*

Mayo 1998 Piner Ranch Vineyard Pinot Noir (Russian River Valley) $35. 91 —*J.C. (12/15/2000)*

Mayo 2000 Sangiacomo Vineyard Pinot Noir (Carneros) $35. 85 —*S.H. (7/1/2003)*

Mayo 1998 Sangiacomo Vineyards Pinot Noir (Carneros) $35. 87 —*J.C. (12/15/2000)*

Mayo 2004 Emma's Vineyard Unwooded Sauvignon Blanc (Napa Valley) $20. 89 —*S.H. (12/15/2005)*

Mayo 2001 Unwooded Emma's Vineyard Sauvignon Blanc (Napa Valley) $20. 86 —*S.H. (9/1/2003)*

Mayo 2002 Page-Nord Vineyard Syrah (Sonoma Valley) $30. 89 —*S.H. (6/1/2004)*

Mayo 2001 Page-Nord Vineyard Syrah (Napa Valley) $30. 85 —*S.H. (12/15/2003)*

Mayo 2002 Ricci Vineyard Zinfandel (Russian River Valley) $25. 86 —*S.H. (6/1/2004)*

Mayo 2000 Ricci Vineyard-Old Vine Zinfandel (Russian River Valley) $25. 83 —*S.H. (11/1/2002)*

Mayo 2000 Ricci Vineyard-Reserve-Old Vine Zinfandel (Russian River Valley) $35. 83 —*S.H. (11/1/2002)*

Mayo 2001 Ricci Vineyard Old Vines Zinfandel (Russian River Valley) $25. 91 Editors' Choice *(11/1/2003)*

Mayo 2000 Ricci Vineyard Unfiltered Zinfandel Port Zinfandel (Russian River Valley) $30. 87 —*S.H. (9/1/2002)*

Mayo 2001 Ricci Vineyard, Reserve, Old Vines Zinfandel (Russian River Valley) $38. 89 *(11/1/2003)*

Mayo 1998 Ricci Vineyard Zinfandel (Russian River Valley) $25. 85 *(3/1/2001)*

MAYO FAMILY

Mayo Family 2003 Laurel Hill Vineyard Unwooded Chardonnay (Sonoma Valley) $15. 85 —*S.H. (4/1/2005)*

Mayo Family 2003 Emma's Vineyard Unwooded Sauvignon Blanc (Napa Valley) $20. 88 —*S.H. (4/1/2005)*

MAYRO-MURDICK

Mayro-Murdick 2005 Pinot Noir (Carneros) $35. Lots of zesty Carneros acidity in this young Pinot that impresses for its silkiness and ripe fruit flavors. Cherries, raspberries, cola, vanilla and mint, finely etched and pure, are the flavors, with a dry, spicy finish. Drink now–2008. **88** —*S.H. (12/31/2007)*

MAYSARA

Maysara 2006 Pinot Gris (Willamette Valley) $18. This has a sugary sweetness to the fruit; it may be as high as 1.5 or 2% residual sugar. Sweet pear and baked apple dominate, so serve it cold. It could be a fine accompaniment to sweet/spicy Southeast Asian cuisine. Simple, fruity, but appealing to many palates. **86** —*P.G. (7/1/2007)*

Maysara 2003 Pinot Gris (Willamette Valley) $15. 88 —*P.G. (2/1/2005)*

Maysara 2001 Pinot Gris (Willamette Valley) $15. 89 —*P.G. (12/1/2003)*

Maysara 2002 Delara Pinot Noir (Willamette Valley) $45. 89 —*P.G. (2/1/2005)*

Maysara 2002 Delara Pinot Noir (Willamette Valley) $45. 86 *(11/1/2004)*

Maysara 2004 Estate Cuvée Pinot Noir (McMinnville) $32. Also biodynamically farmed and certified, the estate cuvée is scented with rose petals and mint, which deepens into sweet and tangy black fruits and spice. It's got good depth and some interesting details suggesting forest floor and dried leaves. No velvet or silk here, but if you can take some roughness it's got some sturdy flavor. **88** —*P.G. (7/1/2007)*

Maysara 2002 Estate Cuvée Pinot Noir (Willamette Valley) $32. 90 —*P.G. (2/1/2005)*

Maysara 2002 Estate Cuvée Pinot Noir (Willamette Valley) $32. 89 *(11/1/2004)*

Maysara 2001 Estate Cuvée Pinot Noir (Willamette Valley) $32. 89 Cellar Selection —*P.G. (12/1/2003)*

Maysara 2005 Jamsheed Pinot Noir (McMinnville) $25. Biodynamically farmed and certified, this is a warm, round wine with an engaging entry. It hits the palate with sweet but contained berry flavors, round and pretty, then tails off. I love the way it starts, but it doesn't carry through. A pretty wine and fine quaffer in a sensible screwcapped package. **87** —*P.G. (7/1/2007)*

Maysara 2003 Reserve Pinot Noir (Willamette Valley) $22. 88 —*P.G. (2/1/2005)*

Maysara 2001 Reserve Pinot Noir (Willamette Valley) $22. 89 Editors' Choice *—P.G. (12/1/2003)*

Maysara 2002 Willamette Reserve Pinot Noir (Willamette Valley) $22. 85 *(11/1/2004)*

Maysara 2006 Roseena Rosé Blend (Willamette Valley) $16. This is 50-50 Pinot Blanc and Pinot Noir, made in an off-dry style. The color is light onion, and in terms of flavor it's just a small step up from a "white Pinot." **84** *—P.G. (7/1/2007)*

MAZZOCCO

Mazzocco 1999 Matrix Bordeaux Blend (Dry Creek Valley) $40. 87 *—S.H. (12/1/2004)*

Mazzocco 1995 Matrix Bordeaux Blend (Dry Creek Valley) $30. 86 *(12/31/1999)*

Mazzocco 1995 Cabernet Sauvignon (Sonoma County) $18. 88 *—L.W. (12/31/1999)*

Mazzocco 2000 Cabernet Sauvignon (Sonoma County) $20. 87 *—S.H. (4/1/2004)*

Mazzocco 1999 Reserve Cabernet Sauvignon (Dry Creek Valley) $50. 87 *—S.H. (12/31/2004)*

Mazzocco 1997 Stone Ranch-Old Vine Carignane (Sonoma County) $14. 88 *—L.W. (11/1/1999)*

Mazzocco 2004 Reserve Chardonnay (Sonoma County) $28. Not much going on fruit-wise in this lean, but clean, brisk wine. Oak stars, with charry caramel and vanilla overpowering the modest peach and apricot flavors. **83** *—S.H. (6/1/2007)*

Mazzocco 1998 River Lane Chardonnay (Sonoma County) $15. 87 *(12/31/1999)*

Mazzocco 2001 River Lane Vineyards Chardonnay (Sonoma County) $15. 87 *—S.H. (2/1/2004)*

Mazzocco 2000 River Lane Vineyards Chardonnay (Sonoma County) $18. 86 *—S.H. (6/1/2003)*

Mazzocco 1997 Winemaker's Select Chardonnay (Sonoma County) $20. 90 *—L.W. (12/31/1999)*

Mazzocco 1996 Merlot (Dry Creek Valley) $20. 83 *(12/31/1999)*

Mazzocco 2001 Pinot Noir (Russian River Valley) $28. 84 *—S.H. (12/31/2004)*

Mazzocco 2002 Sauvignon Blanc (Russian River Valley) $14. 87 *—S.H. (2/1/2005)*

Mazzocco 1997 Viognier (Dry Creek Valley) $24. 88 *—L.W. (10/1/1999)*

Mazzocco 2001 Bevill Vineyards Viognier (Dry Creek Valley) $24. 86 *—S.H. (2/1/2005)*

Mazzocco 1997 Bevill Vineyards Viognier (Dry Creek Valley) $24. 90 *—S.H. (11/1/1999)*

Mazzocco 1996 Zinfandel (Dry Creek Valley) $18. 88 *—L.W. (9/1/1999)*

Mazzocco 1995 Zinfandel (Sonoma County) $22. 90 *—L.W. (9/1/1999)*

Mazzocco 2001 Zinfandel (Dry Creek Valley) $16. 86 *(11/1/2003)*

Mazzocco 1997 Zinfandel (Dry Creek Valley) $16. 89 *—P.G. (3/1/2001)*

Mazzocco 2001 Cuneo & Saini Zinfandel (Dry Creek Valley) $22. 87 *(11/1/2003)*

Mazzocco 2004 Cuneo & Saini Vineyards Zinfandel (Dry Creek Valley) $24. The grapes got a little too ripe, getting away from the winemaker's control. There's lots of deliciousness, but that supermature edge of raisins, excessive softness and touch of Port make the wine unbalanced, despite the excellence of its vineyard sources. **85** *—S.H. (6/1/2007)*

Mazzocco 2001 Cuneo & Saini Vineyard Zinfandel (Dry Creek Valley) $22. 84 *—S.H. (10/1/2005)*

Mazzocco 1997 Cuneo & Saini Vineyard Zinfandel (Dry Creek Valley) $22. 89 *—D.T. (3/1/2002)*

Mazzocco 1995 Cuneo Sani Vineyard Zinfandel (Dry Creek Valley) $22. 87 *—L.W. (9/1/1999)*

Mazzocco 2004 Home Ranch Zinfandel (Dry Creek Valley) $27. Superripeness defines this wine. It's responsible for the high alcohol, incredibly rich flavors of cherry liqueur-infused chocolate candy and raspberry gumdrop, and the low acidity, so soft it's like butter. But Zin's natural tannins survive, giving structural integrity to this dry, opulent wine. **89** *—S.H. (6/1/2007)*

Mazzocco 2004 Quinn Vineyard Zinfandel (Dry Creek Valley) $24. This lusciously ripe Zin classically defines Dry Creek Valley. Dry and exuberant in wild blueberry, cherry, coffee, carob and spice, it tames Zin's feral side, making the wine elegant. **88** *—S.H. (6/1/2007)*

Mazzocco 2001 Quinn Vineyard Zinfandel (Dry Creek Valley) $22. 85 *(11/1/2003)*

Mazzocco 2001 Quinn Vineyard Zinfandel (Dry Creek Valley) $22. 84 *—S.H. (10/1/2005)*

Mazzocco 1997 Quinn Vineyard Zinfandel (Dry Creek Valley) $22. 91 *—D.T. (3/1/2002)*

Mazzocco 2001 Somers Vineyard Zinfandel (Dry Creek Valley) $22. 83 *—S.H. (10/1/2005)*

Mazzocco 2004 Stone Ranch Zinfandel (Alexander Valley) $24. The Stone Ranch Zins I've had over the years have generally been very good, but this is the best in many years. Probably the warm vintage was responsible. It coaxed fabulously rich flavors from the 80-year-old vines, from chocolate, blueberry pie and blackberry jam to espresso, sweet leather and cinnamon. The wine is soft, dry and warming, a perfect elaboration of ripe Alexander Valley Zin. **92** *—S.H. (6/1/2007)*

Mazzocco 2001 Stone Ranch Zinfandel (Alexander Valley) $22. 85 *—S.H. (10/1/2005)*

Mazzocco 1999 Stone Ranch Vineyard Zinfandel (Alexander Valley) $22. 92 *—S.H. (11/15/2004)*

MCCRAY RIDGE

McCray Ridge 2000 Two Moon Vineyard Merlot (Dry Creek Valley) $30. 89 *—S.H. (9/1/2004)*

McCray Ridge 1999 Two Moon Vineyard Merlot (Dry Creek Valley) $29. 93 *—S.H. (9/1/2002)*

McCray Ridge 2000 Two Moon Vineyard Luna Miel Merlot-Cabernet Sauvignon (Dry Creek Valley) $32. 84 *—S.H. (11/15/2004)*

MCCREA

McCrea 2001 Elerding Vineyard Chardonnay (Yakima Valley) $32. 88 *—P.G. (12/31/2003)*

McCrea 2000 Elerding Vineyard Chardonnay (Yakima Valley) $30. 90 *—P.G. (7/1/2002)*

McCrea 1998 Elerding Vineyard Chardonnay (Yakima Valley) $28. 92 *—P.G. (6/1/2000)*

McCrea 2004 Ciel du Cheval Counoise (Red Mountain) $32. 90 *—P.G. (10/1/2006)*

McCrea 2005 Grenache (Washington) $32. Just when you thought Doug McCrea could not make a better Grenache, he has. This year's blend, which includes 17% Syrah, simply has more muscle and more grip than ever before. The wine is loaded with concentrated berry preserves, then spiced up with pepper and minerality. Just the right amount of chocolate fills in the back end. **92** *—P.G. (5/1/2007)*

McCrea 2004 Grenache (Washington) $32. 90 *—P.G. (10/1/2006)*

McCrea 2005 Ciel du Cheval Vineyard Mourvèdre (Red Mountain) $32. This Mourvèdre (with 8% Syrah) is still coming together, but all the right pieces are in place. Young, tight and compact, it opens with tart berry and currant fruit, then shows a distinctive, earthy underpinning. As it unwinds it shows wet earth, graphite, pepper and truffle, balanced and layered but still a bit shut down. Give it a lot of breathing time, or put it away for a couple of years. **90** *—P.G. (5/1/2007)*

McCrea 2004 Ciel du Cheval Mourvèdre (Red Mountain) $32. 92 *—P.G. (10/1/2006)*

McCrea 2004 Sirocco Rhône Red Blend (Washington) $35. 91 *—P.G. (12/31/2006)*

McCrea 2005 Ciel du Cheval Vineyard Roussanne (Red Mountain) $25. 88 *—P.G. (12/31/2006)*

McCrea 2004 Syrah (Washington) $28. 88 *—P.G. (12/31/2006)*

McCrea 2000 Syrah (Yakima Valley) $35. 88 *—P.G. (9/1/2002)*

McCrea 1999 Syrah (Yakima Valley) $35. 87 *—S.H. (6/1/2002)*

McCrea 1998 Syrah (Yakima Valley) $28. 90 *—P.G. (6/1/2000)*

McCrea 2004 Amerique Syrah (Yakima Valley) $45. 89 *—P.G. (12/31/2006)*

McCrea 2001 Amerique Syrah (Yakima Valley) $40. 87 *—P.G. (12/31/2003)*

McCrea 2000 Amerique Syrah (Yakima Valley) $40. 90 *—P.G. (9/1/2002)*

McCrea 2004 Boushey Grande Côte Vineyard Syrah (Yakima Valley) $52. This wine is jam-packed with flavors and scents of smoked meat, cured ham, black truffle, charcoal, pencil lead, toasted nuts. It's a powerhouse that fascinates and resonates, sailing into a lingering finish that keeps all the various components in play. A perfect mix of fruit and barrel, not to be missed. **94 Editors' Choice** *—P.G. (5/1/2007)*

McCrea 2001 Boushey Grand Cote Syrah (Yakima Valley) $45. 90 *—P.G. (12/31/2003)*

McCrea 1999 Boushey Grande Cote Vineyard Syrah (Yakima Valley) $42. 91 *—S.H. (6/1/2002)*

McCrea 2003 Boushey Vineyard Syrah (Yakima Valley) $52. 94 Editors' Choice —*P.G. (11/15/2006)*

McCrea 2002 Boushey Vineyard Syrah (Yakima Valley) $55. 87 *(9/1/2005)*

McCrea 1998 Boushley Vineyards Syrah (Yakima Valley) $35. 90 —*P.G. (9/1/2000)*

McCrea 2003 Ciel du Cheval Syrah (Red Mountain) $52. 93 Editors' Choice —*P.G. (11/15/2006)*

McCrea 2001 Ciel du Cheval Syrah (Yakima Valley) $45. 91 Cellar Selection —*P.G. (12/31/2003)*

McCrea 2002 Ciel du Cheval Vineyard Syrah (Red Mountain) $55. 89 *(9/1/2005)*

McCrea 1998 Ciel du Cheval Vineyard Syrah (Yakima Valley) $35. 90 —*P.G. (9/1/2000)*

McCrea 1999 Ciel du Cheval Vineyard Syrah (Yakima Valley) $45. 86 *(11/1/2001)*

McCrea 1999 Cuvée Orleans Syrah (Yakima Valley) $50. 92 —*P.G. (9/1/2002)*

McCrea 2003 Cuvée Orleans Syrah (Yakima Valley) $60. 91 —*P.G. (11/15/2006)*

McCrea 2002 Cuvée Orleans Syrah (Yakima Valley) $60. 87 *(9/1/2005)*

McCrea 2000 Cuvée Orleans Syrah (Yakima Valley) $50. 91 —*P.G. (12/31/2003)*

McCrea 2001 Yakima Valley Syrah Syrah (Yakima Valley) $38. 88 —*P.G. (12/31/2003)*

McCrea 2001 Viognier (Yakima Valley) $22. 92 Editors' Choice —*P.G. (12/31/2003)*

McCrea 2000 Viognier (Yakima Valley) $23. 91 —*P.G. (9/1/2002)*

McCrea 1998 Viognier (Yakima Valley) $20. 89 —*P.G. (6/1/2000)*

McCrea 2005 Ciel du Cheval Vineyard Viognier (Red Mountain) $25. 90 —*P.G. (12/31/2006)*

McCrea 2000 La Mer White Blend (Yakima Valley) $18. 89 —*P.G. (9/1/2002)*

MCDOWELL

McDowell 2003 Grenache (McDowell Valley) $12. 82 —*S.H. (6/1/2005)*

McDowell 2000 Rosé Grenache (California) $9. 86 —*S.H. (9/1/2002)*

McDowell 1997 Rosé Grenache (Mendocino) $9. 88 Best Buy —*S.H. (6/1/1999)*

McDowell 2006 Grenache Rosé Blend (McDowell Valley) $12. Blended with 5% Syrah, presumably for body and depth, this is really a nice rosé. It's very dry and balanced in acidity, with succulent flavors of cherries, berries and gingery spices. Finishes with an earthy, tea-like grip of tannin. **87 Best Buy** —*S.H. (11/15/2007)*

McDowell 2001 Marsanne (Mendocino) $16. 85 —*S.H. (6/1/2003)*

McDowell 1997 Marsanne (Mendocino) $16. 87 —*S.H. (6/1/1999)*

McDowell 2000 Reserve Petite Sirah (Mendocino) $20. 83 *(4/1/2003)*

McDowell 2002 Syrah (Mendocino County) $25. 85 —*S.H. (6/1/2005)*

McDowell 2000 Syrah (Mendocino County) $12. 85 —*S.H. (12/1/2002)*

McDowell 1999 Syrah (Mendocino) $14. 80 *(10/1/2001)*

McDowell 1997 Syrah (Mendocino) $12. 88 —*M.G. (11/15/1999)*

McDowell 1997 Mendocino Estate Syrah (Mendocino) $22. 89 —*S.H. (6/1/1999)*

McDowell 1999 Reserve-McDowell Valley Syrah (Mendocino) $24. 90 *(11/1/2001)*

McDowell 2003 Viognier (Mendocino County) $16. 87 —*S.H. (6/1/2005)*

McDowell 2000 Viognier (Mendocino) $16. 87 —*S.H. (5/1/2002)*

McDowell 1997 Viognier (Mendocino) $16. 90 Best Buy —*S.H. (6/1/1999)*

MCILROY

McIlroy 1999 Salzgeber Vineyard Cabernet Franc (Russian River Valley) $24. 83 —*S.H. (9/1/2002)*

McIlroy 2000 Aquarius Ranch Chardonnay (Russian River Valley) $21. 87 —*S.H. (9/1/2002)*

McIlroy 2000 Aquarius Ranch Late Harvest Gewürztraminer (Russian River Valley) $13. 89 Best Buy —*S.H. (9/1/2002)*

McIlroy 1999 Aquarius Ranch Merlot (Russian River Valley) $21.87 —*S.H. (9/1/2002)*

McIlroy 1999 Aquarius Ranch Pinot Noir (Russian River Valley) $24. 86 —*S.H. (9/1/2002)*

McIlroy 1998 Porter-Bass Vineyard Zinfandel (Russian River Valley) $18. 88 —*S.H. (11/1/2002)*

MCINTYRE VINEYARDS

McIntyre Vineyards 2003 Chardonnay (Monterey County) $13. 82 —*S.H. (12/1/2005)*

McIntyre Vineyards 2002 Force Canyon Vineyard Pinot Noir (Monterey County) $31. 92 Editors' Choice —*S.H. (12/1/2005)*

McIntyre Vineyards 1998 L'Homme Qui Ris Sparkling Blend (Monterey County) $22. 84 —*J.C. (12/1/2003)*

MCKENZIE-MUELLER

McKenzie-Mueller 2001 Cabernet Franc (Napa Valley) $28. 86 —*S.H. (7/1/2005)*

McKenzie-Mueller 2001 Cabernet Sauvignon (Napa Valley) $40. 83 —*S.H. (7/1/2005)*

McKenzie-Mueller 2002 Malbec (Carneros) $30. 83 —*S.H. (7/1/2005)*

McKenzie-Mueller 2001 Merlot (Carneros) $28. 84 —*S.H. (7/1/2005)*

McKenzie-Mueller 2003 Pinot Grigio (Carneros) $16. 84 —*S.H. (7/1/2005)*

McKenzie-Mueller 2004 Reserve Pinot Grigio (Carneros) $16. 87 —*S.H. (2/1/2006)*

McKenzie-Mueller 2001 Pinot Noir (Carneros) $28. 82 —*S.H. (7/1/2005)*

McKenzie-Mueller 2001 Reserve Pinot Noir (Carneros) $35. 82 —*S.H. (7/1/2005)*

MCKINLEY SPRINGS

McKinley Springs 2004 Syrah (Horse Heaven Hills) $25. Deep, spicy and heavily extracted, this estate-grown Syrah is an excellent expression of a clear-cut Washington approach to the grape. The tangy blue fruit is etched in citrus rind, especially grapefruit, which gives it a marvelous acidic lift throughout the palate. Tight, young, sharp and focused, it promises good development over the next decade. **88** —*P.G. (5/1/2007)*

McKinley Springs 2002 Syrah (Columbia Valley (WA)) $24. 86 —*P.G. (12/15/2004)*

MCMANIS

McManis 2006 Cabernet Sauvignon (California) $10. Pretty good for a $10 red, this has proper varietal flavors of blackberries, cherries and oak, and is fullbodied and tannic. There's a rustic edge, but it will do fine with roast chicken or even macaroni and cheese. **84** —*S.H. (12/31/2007)*

McManis 2005 Cabernet Sauvignon (California) $10. 84 Best Buy —*S.H. (12/31/2006)*

McManis 2004 Cabernet Sauvignon (California) $10. 84 —*S.H. (12/31/2005)*

McManis 2003 Cabernet Sauvignon (California) $10. 84 —*S.H. (12/31/2004)*

McManis 2002 Cabernet Sauvignon (California) $10. 84 —*S.H. (2/1/2004)*

McManis 2001 Cabernet Sauvignon (California) $9. 82 —*S.H. (12/31/2002)*

McManis 2000 Cabernet Sauvignon (California) $10. 80 —*S.H. (11/15/2002)*

McManis 2006 Chardonnay (California) $10. A little soft and dull, but with enough Chard-like character to satisfy diehard fans who don't want to spend a lot. Has apple, peach and pear flavors with a candied taste of oak. **82** —*S.H. (11/15/2007)*

McManis 2005 Chardonnay (River Junction) $10. 85 Best Buy —*S.H. (12/1/2006)*

McManis 2004 Chardonnay (River Junction) $10. 84 —*S.H. (11/15/2005)*

McManis 2001 Chardonnay (California) $9. 84 —*S.H. (12/15/2002)*

McManis 2000 Chardonnay (California) $9. 84 —*S.H. (5/1/2002)*

McManis 2003 River Junction Chardonnay (Central Coast) $10. 84 —*S.H. (12/1/2004)*

McManis 2006 Merlot (California) $10. Not a success due to excessive sharpness. Other than that, you'll find mint and cherry flavors. **81** —*S.H. (12/31/2007)*

McManis 2005 Merlot (California) $10. 84 Best Buy —*S.H. (12/31/2006)*

McManis 2004 Merlot (California) $10. 83 —*S.H. (5/1/2006)*

McManis 2003 Merlot (California) $10. 82 —*S.H. (12/15/2004)*

McManis 2002 Merlot (California) $10. 90 Best Buy —*S.H. (2/1/2004)*

McManis 2001 Merlot (California) $9. 85 —*S.H. (12/31/2002)*

McManis 2000 Merlot (California) $9. 81 —*S.H. (11/15/2002)*

McManis 2006 Petite Sirah (California) $11. Harsh and raisiny, with baked flavors of prunes. The finish is dry and tannic. **80** —*S.H. (12/31/2007)*

McManis 2004 Petite Sirah (California) $11. 83 *—S.H. (12/31/2005)*

McManis 2003 Petite Sirah (California) $10. 84 *—S.H. (12/31/2004)*

McManis 2006 Pinot Grigio (California) $10. On the sweet side, but balanced with fresh acidity that makes the wine brisk and clean. The polished flavors are of citrus, apricots, peaches, nectarines and spicy apple sauce. **85 Best Buy** *—S.H. (9/1/2007)*

McManis 2005 Pinot Grigio (California) $10. 86 Best Buy *—S.H. (10/1/2006)*

McManis 2004 Pinot Grigio (California) $10. 84 *—S.H. (7/1/2005)*

McManis 2003 River Junction Pinot Grigio (Central Coast) $10. 83 *—S.H. (11/15/2004)*

McManis 2006 Pinot Noir (California) $10. For $10, this is a fine Pinot. It's dry and silky, with cherry, cola and spice flavors. **85 Best Buy** *—S.H. (11/15/2007)*

McManis 2006 Syrah (California) $10. Here's a soft, easy Syrah, with a peppermint edge to the blackberries, cherries, carob, white pepper and leather flavors. The tannins are firm but gentle, lending a nice backbone to the structure. **85 Best Buy** *—S.H. (12/31/2007)*

McManis 2005 Syrah (California) $10. 83 *—S.H. (12/31/2006)*

McManis 2004 Syrah (California) $10. 81 *—S.H. (6/1/2006)*

McManis 2003 Syrah (California) $10. 84 *—S.H. (12/31/2004)*

McManis 2002 Syrah (California) $10. 86 Best Buy *—S.H. (2/1/2004)*

McManis 2001 Syrah (California) $9. 84 *—S.H. (12/1/2002)*

McManis 2006 Viognier (California) $10. Lots of acidity in this fruity wine, which gives a tart, biting quality to the exotic tropical fruit, wildflower and lime flavors. The finish is dry. **84** *—S.H. (11/1/2007)*

McManis 2005 Viognier (California) $10. 85 Best Buy *—S.H. (10/1/2006)*

McManis 2004 Viognier (California) $10. 86 Best Buy *—S.H. (10/1/2005)*

McManis 2003 Viognier (California) $10. 88 Best Buy *—S.H. (12/15/2004)*

McManis 2006 Zinfandel (California) $11. Okay in a pinch, but a pretty rugged wine. It has raisin and prune flavors that have a medicinal, tannic finish. **80** *—S.H. (12/31/2007)*

McManis 2005 Zinfandel (California) $10. Soft and rustic, with some green, minty notes side by side with riper cherries and chocolate. At this price, it's good with pizza and similar simple fare. **83** *—S.H. (2/1/2007)*

MCNAB RIDGE

McNab Ridge 1997 Reserve Cabernet Sauvignon (Mendocino County) $18. 85 *—S.H. (5/1/2002)*

McNab Ridge 2000 Meritage (Mendocino County) $20. 90 *—S.H. (11/15/2004)*

McNab Ridge 1999 John H. Parducci Signature Series Mendotage Meritage (Mendocino) $35. 87 *—C.S. (5/1/2002)*

McNab Ridge 1998 Merlot (Mendocino County) $15. 84 *—S.H. (5/1/2002)*

McNab Ridge 1999 Muscat Canelli (Mendocino County) $12. 89 *—S.H. (5/1/2002)*

McNab Ridge 2000 Petite Sirah (Mendocino County) $18. 81 *(4/1/2003)*

McNab Ridge 2002 Napoli Vineyard Pinotage (Mendocino) $18. 84 *—S.H. (12/15/2004)*

McNab Ridge 2004 Sauvignon Blanc (Mendocino) $12. 85 *—S.H. (4/1/2006)*

McNab Ridge 2003 Sauvignon Blanc (Mendocino) $12. 85 *—S.H. (12/15/2004)*

McNab Ridge 2003 Zinfandel (Mendocino) $18. 83 *—S.H. (4/1/2006)*

McNab Ridge 2002 Zinfandel (Mendocino) $18. 83 *—S.H. (12/15/2004)*

MCPRICE MYERS

McPrice Myers 2002 Larner Vineyard Syrah (Santa Ynez Valley) $25. 92 *—S.H. (12/1/2004)*

MEADOR

Meador 2000 Maverick Syrah (Arroyo Seco) $50. 92 *—S.H. (9/1/2004)*

Meador 1998 Maverick Syrah (Arroyo Seco) $50. 83 *(11/1/2001)*

Meador Estate 2003 Block 9 Chardonnay (Arroyo Seco) $30. 84 *—S.H. (12/15/2006)*

Meador Estate 2001 Maverick Syrah (Arroyo Seco) $50. 90 *—S.H. (6/1/2005)*

MEANDER

Meander 2003 Cabernet Sauvignon (Napa Valley) $65. 84 *—S.H. (12/31/2005)*

MEDLOCK AMES

Medlock Ames 2002 Bell Mountain Ranch Red Bordeaux Blend (Alexander Valley) $25. 91 *—S.H. (12/15/2006)*

Medlock Ames 2002 Bell Mountain Vineyard Cabernet Sauvignon (Alexander Valley) $42 92 *—S.H (12/15/2006)*

Medlock Ames 2004 Bell Mountain Vineyard Chardonnay (Alexander Valley) $20. 92 *—S.H. (10/1/2006)*

Medlock Ames 2001 Bell Mountain Vineyard Merlot (Alexander Valley) $35. 87 *—S.H. (12/15/2006)*

MEDOLLA

Medolla 2002 Merlot (North Fork of Long Island) $23. Tobacco and mint aromas and raspberry and cherry flavors are the hallmarks of this medium-bodied selection. There's a good, long finish and an overall smooth character typical of this region's Merlot. **83** *—S.K. (7/1/2007)*

MEDUSA

Medusa 2004 Old Vine Creekside Block Bar 49 Vineyard Zinfandel (Napa Valley) $35. A new brand that has just released three new Zins. This one is not the best. It's hot and soft, with syrupy cherry and blackberry flavors. **84** *—S.H. (10/1/2007)*

Medusa 2004 Old Vine Lover's Lane Vineyard Zinfandel (Mendocino) $35. An awkward wine. High alcohol can work in Zin, but not in this one. It has hot, jalapeño pepper flavors along with cherry and blackberry, and even though the official reading is 15.6%, there seems to be residual sugar and deficient acidity. **82** *—S.H. (10/1/2007)*

Medusa 2004 Old Vine Pig Pen Vineyard Deaver Ranch Zinfandel (Amador County) $35. Very good, savory Amador Zin, exuberantly rich in briary mountain wild blackberry, blueberry and loganberry flavors, with a huge dusting of spice: white pepper, black pepper, nutmeg, cinnamon, allspice, and, for the finale, a sweet dose of crème de cassis-laced cola. Yet the wine is thoroughly dry. Shows Zin's ability to combine rusticity with elegance. **91** *—S.H. (10/1/2007)*

MEEKER

Meeker 1997 Eighth Rack Zinfandel (Sonoma County) $14. 86 *—P.G. (3/1/2001)*

Meeker 1997 Gold Leaf Cuvée Zinfandel (Dry Creek Valley) $18. 82 *—P.G. (3/1/2001)*

MELANTO TERRACE

Melanto Terrace 2006 Sauvignon Blanc (North Coast) $10. With a greenish tinge to the straw color, this is an ultradry, very crisp wine, especially notable for terrifically clean vibrancy. Blended with 5% Verdelho, it shows strong lemongrass, grapefruit, wildflower, candied ginger, spice and mineral flavors that finish impressively long. Easily one of the best $10 wines of the year. **90 Best Buy** *—S.H. (9/1/2007)*

Melanto Terrace 2005 Zinfandel (Amador County) $12. Too soft and too sweet, with sugared cherry, raspberry, blackberry and chocolate flavors. Okay and clean, but with this inherent sweetness, the wine could use more balancing acids and tannins. **83** *—S.H. (9/1/2007)*

MELROSE

Melrose 2005 Chardonnay (Umpqua Valley) $15. This is soft and almost weightless, with no aromas and a midpalate that drops into a black hole. It's not that there are any off flavors; just that the search for flavor is, to put it bluntly, fruitless. Rare to find a wine with such a gaping hole in the middle. **81** *—P.G. (11/15/2007)*

Melrose 2004 Merlot (Umpqua Valley) $20. Light, grapy and fruity, this might be a nouveau wine or a Grenache. But it's southern Oregon Merlot, so the tannins are substantial, and far outrace the fruit. Some sweaty aromas compete with the tannins and herbal notes. **81** *—P.G. (11/15/2007)*

Melrose 2002 Parker's Pinot Noir (Umpqua Valley) $24. 89 *(11/1/2004)*

Melrose 2002 Reserve Pinot Noir (Umpqua Valley) $26. 88 *(11/1/2004)*

Melrose 2006 Viognier (Umpqua Valley) $18. This is a light, spritzy wine; it could almost qualify as frizzante. The light citrus flavors start out fine, then become rough and vegetal. **82** *—P.G. (11/15/2007)*

MELVILLE

Melville 2000 Chardonnay (Santa Rita Hills) $20. 86 *—S.H. (12/15/2002)*

Melville 2005 Clone 76 Inox Chardonnay (Santa Rita Hills) $30. Pretty much as flashy as California Chard gets. Huge in exotic tropical fruit and spice, all tarted up with crème brûlée and baked meringue, it finishes with a sweetly decadent touch of pineapple-vanilla truffle. **94** *—S.H. (4/1/2007)*

Melville 2002 Clone 76 Inox Chardonnay (Santa Rita Hills) $28. 86 *—S.H. (12/15/2003)*

Melville 2005 Estate Chardonnay (Santa Rita Hills) $26. Big, ripe, in-your-face Chard here, as gooey as a fruity custard. Almost a dessert wine, it stays just this side of dry, offering huge flavors of lemon drop mousse, pineapple jam, guava, papaya, golden mango and spicy oak. This is a dramatic, show-me-off Chardonnay. **93** *—S.H. (4/1/2007)*

Melville 2004 Estate Chardonnay (Santa Rita Hills) $26. 88 *—S.H. (3/1/2006)*

Melville 1999 Pinot Noir (Santa Rita Hills) $24. 89 *—S.H. (2/1/2003)*

Melville 2001 Carrie's Pinot Noir (Santa Rita Hills) $40. 90 *—S.H. (10/1/2003)*

Melville 2005 Estate Pinot Noir (Santa Rita Hills) $28. Despite a hefty alcohol of 15.4%, this Pinot feels lilting and charming, a wine of early drinkability. Rich in gentle cherry, black raspberry and cinnamon-clove flavors, it shows the winemakers' liking for stem inclusion in the earthy, sage-and herb notes, and a salty, peat moss quality in the finish, like a fine single-malt Scotch. Thoroughly enjoyable now. **89** *—S.H. (4/1/2007)*

Melville 2001 Estate Pinot Noir (Santa Rita Hills) $25. 89 *—S.H. (3/1/2004)*

Melville 2000 Syrah (Santa Rita Hills) $24. 86 *—S.H. (12/1/2002)*

Melville 2004 Donna's Syrah (Santa Rita Hills) $36. Made more in a Côtes-du-Rhône style than Northern Rhône, even though it's all Syrah, this wine is medium-bodied and gentle, with approachable blackberry, cherry, cedar and milk chocolate flavors. It's almost jammy, but rich tannins and brisk acidity make it a serious red wine. **90** *—S.H. (6/1/2007)*

Melville 2004 Donna's Syrah (Santa Rita Hills) $30. 92 *—S.H. (11/15/2006)*

Melville 2003 Estate Syrah (Santa Barbara County) $20. 89 *—S.H. (11/15/2006)*

Melville 2005 Verna's Viognier (Santa Barbara County) $18. 88 *—S.H. (11/15/2006)*

MENDELSON

Mendelson 1999 Muscat Canelli (Mendocino County) $35. 87 *—J.M. (12/1/2002)*

Mendelson 1999 Dessert Wine Pinot Gris (Napa Valley) $35. 85 *—J.M. (12/1/2002)*

Mendelson 2002 Pinot Noir (Santa Lucia Highlands) $38. 82 *(11/1/2004)*

Mendelson 2001 Pinot Noir (Santa Lucia Highlands) $38. 89 *—J.M. (2/1/2004)*

MENDOCINO COLLECTION

Mendocino Collection 1997 SketchBook Collection Merlot (Mendocino) $23. 84 *(11/1/1999)*

MENDOCINO GOLD

Mendocino Gold 2000 Cabernet Sauvignon (Mendocino County) $12. 86 *—S.H. (8/1/2003)*

Mendocino Gold 2001 Chardonnay (Mendocino County) $10. 86 Best Buy *—S.H. (6/1/2003)*

MENDOCINO HILL

Mendocino Hill 1999 Sangiovese (Mendocino County) $18. 89 *—S.H. (5/1/2002)*

Mendocino Hill 1999 Syrah (Mendocino County) $20. 88 *—S.H. (5/1/2002)*

MEOLA VINEYARDS

Meola Vineyards 2003 Cabernet Sauvignon (Alexander Valley) $55. This Cab shows ripe, crushed fruit flavors of cherries, blackberries and blueberries, with a green mint jelly note that adds acidic richness. It has a certain fatty succulence now that should hold for several years. **86** *—S.H. (11/1/2007)*

Meola Vineyards 2002 Unfiltered Cabernet Sauvignon (Alexander Valley) $60. 89 *—S.H. (12/15/2005)*

Meola Vineyards 2002 Venezia Cabernet Sauvignon (Alexander Valley) $60. 85 *—S.H. (12/15/2005)*

Meola Vineyards 2003 Venezia Reserve Cabernet Sauvignon (Alexander Valley) $55. Rustic and common despite the reserve designation and price, this shows simple cherry and blackberry flavors that combine overripe, plumped raisin tastes with underripe herbal ones. **83** *—S.H. (11/1/2007)*

MER SOLEIL

Mer Soleil 2005 Chardonnay (Central Coast) $42. Mer Soleil Chards seem to get bigger, riper and oakier every year. Of course, this is the winery's style, and when it works, the results can be fabulously rich, but this caramelized wine seems a little top-heavy. **86** *—S.H. (12/1/2007)*

Mer Soleil 2004 Chardonnay (Central Coast) $42. This shows the ripe tropical fruit of a fine vintage, yet maintains the keen citrusy acidity that makes this vineyard's Chards so balanced and ageworthy. Beneath the pineapple marmalade, apricot and caramelly oak flavors is a rich, flinty minerality that cries out for lobster. **92** *—S.H. (5/1/2007)*

Mer Soleil 2003 Chardonnay (Central Coast) $42. 90 Cellar Selection *—S.H. (6/1/2006)*

Mer Soleil 2002 Chardonnay (Central Coast) $42. 92 *—S.H. (5/1/2005)*

Mer Soleil 2001 Chardonnay (Central Coast) $42. 92 *—S.H. (2/1/2004)*

Mer Soleil 2000 Chardonnay (Central Coast) $42. 93 *—S.H. (2/1/2003)*

Mer Soleil 1999 Chardonnay (Central Coast) $40. 93 *—J.M. (12/15/2002)*

Mer Soleil 1998 Chardonnay (Central Coast) $40. 90 *(7/1/2001)*

Mer Soleil 2000 Late Harvest White Wine White Blend (Santa Lucia Highlands) $36. 92 *—J.M. (9/1/2003)*

MERIDIAN

Meridian 2003 Cabernet Sauvignon (California) $10. 82 *—S.H. (5/1/2006)*

Meridian 1996 Coastal Reserve Cabernet Sauvignon (California) $22. 83 *—S.H. (12/15/2000)*

Meridian 2005 Chardonnay (Santa Barbara County) $10. 83 *—S.H. (11/15/2006)*

Meridian 2004 Chardonnay (Santa Barbara County) $10. 87 Best Buy *—S.H. (12/31/2005)*

Meridian 2003 Chardonnay (Santa Barbara County) $10. 86 Best Buy *—S.H. (11/15/2005)*

Meridian 2002 Chardonnay (Santa Barbara) $10. 83 *—S.H. (2/1/2005)*

Meridian 2001 Chardonnay (Santa Barbara County) $11. 84 *—S.H. (6/1/2003)*

Meridian 2000 Chardonnay (Santa Barbara County) $11. 87 Best Buy *—S.H. (12/31/2001)*

Meridian 1998 Chardonnay (Santa Barbara County) $10. 89 Best Buy *—M.M. (11/15/1999)*

Meridian 1999 Limited Release Chardonnay (Santa Barbara County) $22. 89 *—S.H. (12/15/2002)*

Meridian 2002 Reserve Chardonnay (Santa Barbara County) $16. 84 *—S.H. (11/15/2004)*

Meridian 1999 Reserve Chardonnay (Edna Valley) $14. 88 Best Buy *—S.H. (12/15/2002)*

Meridian 1998 Reserve Chardonnay (Edna Valley) $15. 89 *(6/1/2000)*

Meridian 2002 Gewürztraminer (Santa Barbara County) $8. 85 *—S.H. (12/31/2003)*

Meridian 1999 Limited Release Petite Sirah (Paso Robles) $18. 84 *(4/1/2003)*

Meridian 2005 Pinot Grigio (California) $10. 85 Best Buy *—S.H. (10/1/2006)*

Meridian 2004 Pinot Grigio (California) $10. 90 Best Buy *—S.H. (2/1/2006)*

Meridian 2003 Pinot Grigio (California) $11. 85 *—S.H. (7/1/2005)*

Meridian 2002 Pinot Grigio (California) $11. 85 *—S.H. (2/1/2004)*

Meridian 2005 Pinot Noir (Central Coast) $11. 84 *—S.H. (11/15/2006)*

Meridian 2004 Pinot Noir (Central Coast) $10. 86 Best Buy *—S.H. (5/1/2006)*

Meridian 2003 Pinot Noir (Central Coast) $11. 83 *—S.H. (7/1/2005)*

Meridian 2000 Pinot Noir (Santa Barbara County) $12. 82 *(10/1/2002)*

Meridian 1999 Pinot Noir (Santa Barbara County) $11. 86 Best Buy *—S.H. (12/15/2001)*

Meridian 1998 Pinot Noir (Santa Barbara County) $13. 86 *—S.H. (5/1/2001)*

Meridian 1996 Coastal Reserve Pinot Noir (Santa Barbara County) $22. 90 *(10/1/1999)*

Meridian 2002 Reserve Pinot Noir (Santa Barbara County) $16. 84 *—S.H. (11/1/2004)*

Meridian 1998 Reserve Pinot Noir (Santa Barbara County) $22. 88 *—S.H. (12/15/2000)*

Meridian 2005 Sauvignon Blanc (Central Coast) $10. 84 *—S.H. (10/1/2006)*

Meridian 2004 Sauvignon Blanc (Central Coast) $10. 85 Best Buy *—S.H. (5/1/2006)*

Meridian 2002 Sauvignon Blanc (Central Coast) $8. 83 *—S.H. (12/31/2003)*

Meridian 2000 Sauvignon Blanc (California) $8. 86 *—S.H. (9/12/2002)*

Meridian 1998 Syrah (Paso Robles) $15. 87 Editors' Choice *(10/1/2001)*

Meridian 2002 Reserve Syrah (Santa Barbara County) $16. 86 *—S.H. (12/1/2004)*

MERRIAM VINEYARDS

Merriam Vineyards 2003 Jones Vineyard Cabernet Franc (Dry Creek Valley) $35. 88 —*S.H. (3/1/2006)*

Merriam Vineyards 2003 Cabernet Sauvignon (Dry Creek Valley) $35. 86 —*S.H. (12/15/2006)*

Merriam Vineyards 2001 Cabernet Sauvignon (Sonoma County) $35. 85 —*S.H. (10/1/2005)*

Merriam Vineyards 2000 Cabernet Sauvignon (Dry Creek Valley) $35. 86 —*S.H. (6/1/2004)*

Merriam Vineyards 2002 Windacre Merlot (Russian River Valley) $35. 80 —*S.H. (10/1/2005)*

Merriam Vineyards 2001 Windacre Merlot (Russian River Valley) $35. 93 —*S.H. (12/15/2004)*

Merriam Vineyards 2000 Windacre Vineyard Merlot (Russian River Valley) $34. 88 —*S.H. (7/1/2003)*

MERRY CELLARS

Merry Cellars 2005 Carmenère (Walla Walla (WA)) $32. It's Seven Hills fruit and it carries some of the lushness and also the green flavors (tea and bark) of the vineyard. Light in the mouth, balanced and well made with those flavors of bark and tea mixed in with tart cranberry/strawberry fruit. The oak is just right. 88 —*P.G. (12/1/2007)*

Merry Cellars 2005 Twilight Hills Red Red Blend (Washington) $30. Not a shy wine, but quite lively on the palate, loaded with high-toned fruits and bright acids. This is an interesting flavor mix, not jammy despite the high alcohol. The mainly red fruits are a bit jumbled together, and hints of leaf and fresh herb are scattered throughout. It's interesting and complex; a little on the green side. 87 —*P.G. (12/1/2007)*

Merry Cellars 2006 Sauvignon Blanc (Columbia Valley (WA)) $14. This shows interesting fragrances that mix fresh grain, grass and leaf. It's pumped up with plush fruit; the wine is 100% varietal and 100% stainless-steel fermented. A confident hand is at the winemaking helm here; this nicely matches up the varietal character, the ripeness, the acids and the alcohol, keeping it all in balance. The wine is seamless and variegated, with a smooth, lingering finish. 89 —*P.G. (12/1/2007)*

Merry Cellars 2006 Stillwater Creek Vineyard Sémillon (Columbia Valley (WA)) $18. This wine carries a whiff of honeyed fig, which opens out into a luscious, rich, satisfying, full-bodied Sémillon. It's a complete wine, which seems to run through a lifetime's evolution in the mouth, finishing with a creamy, plush mix of fruit and barrel. Long, seamless and delicious. 91 —*P.G. (12/1/2007)*

MERRY EDWARDS

Merry Edwards 2004 Pinot Noir (Russian River Valley) $36. Without the bright acidity of Merry's '04 Sonoma Coast Pinot, this is a less interesting wine. It has rich flavors of cola, cherries, plums and earth, but is a little on the soft side. In a hot vintage like 2004, the cooler Coast does better than the warmer Russian River. And vice versa in a cool year. Drink now. 87 —*S.H. (3/1/2007)*

Merry Edwards 2004 Pinot Noir (Sonoma Coast) $30. What a roll Merry Edwards is on. This is a basic, appellation series Pinot, but it's as good or better as most other wineries' single-vineyard bottlings, showing a dry, rich, acidic, earthy character in its youth. But there's enough cherry cola fruit to drink now, if you decant. Chewy and complex, it should improve for five years and hold for another five. 93 Editors' Choice —*S.H. (3/1/2007)*

Merry Edwards 2003 Pinot Noir (Sonoma Coast) $29. 87 —*S.H. (12/1/2005)*

Merry Edwards 2002 Pinot Noir (Sonoma Coast) $27. 88 *(11/1/2004)*

Merry Edwards 2002 Pinot Noir (Russian River Valley) $32. 86 —*S.H. (4/1/2005)*

Merry Edwards 2001 Pinot Noir (Russian River Valley) $32. 87 —*S.H. (6/1/2004)*

Merry Edwards 2001 Pinot Noir (Sonoma Coast) $27. 91 —*S.H. (4/1/2004)*

Merry Edwards 2000 Pinot Noir (Russian River Valley) $32. 93 Editors' Choice —*S.H. (2/1/2003)*

Merry Edwards 2003 Klopp Ranch Pinot Noir (Russian River Valley) $48. 93 —*S.H. (7/1/2006)*

Merry Edwards 2002 Klopp Ranch Pinot Noir (Russian River Valley) $48. 89 —*S.H. (4/1/2005)*

Merry Edwards 2001 Klopp Ranch Pinot Noir (Russian River Valley) $48. 92 —*S.H. (6/1/2004)*

Merry Edwards 2000 Klopp Ranch Pinot Noir (Russian River Valley) $48. 92 —*S.H. (2/1/2003)*

Merry Edwards 2003 Meredith Estate Pinot Noir (Sonoma Coast) $48. 91 —*S.H. (7/1/2006)*

Merry Edwards 2001 Meredith Estate Pinot Noir (Sonoma Coast) $45. 91 —*S.H. (6/1/2004)*

Merry Edwards 2000 Meredith Estate Pinot Noir (Sonoma Coast) $45. 91 —*S.H. (2/1/2003)*

Merry Edwards 2004 Olivet Lane Pinot Noir (Russian River Valley) $57. 94 —*S.H. (12/15/2006)*

Merry Edwards 2001 Olivet Lane Pinot Noir (Russian River Valley) $48. 89 —*J.M. (4/1/2004)*

Merry Edwards 2000 Olivet Lane Pinot Noir (Russian River Valley) $48. 94 —*S.H. (2/1/2003)*

Merry Edwards 2003 Olivet Lane Methode a L'Ancienne Pinot Noir (Russian River Valley) $54. 90 —*S.H. (12/1/2005)*

Merry Edwards 2002 Olivet Lane Methode a la Ancienne Pinot Noir (Russian River Valley) $51. 86 *(11/1/2004)*

Merry Edwards 2003 Windsor Gardens Pinot Noir (Russian River Valley) $57. 89 Cellar Selection —*S.H. (12/1/2005)*

Merry Edwards 2000 Windsor Gardens Pinot Noir (Russian River Valley) $54. 92 —*S.H. (2/1/2003)*

Merry Edwards 2001 Windsor Gardens Methode a l'Ancienne Pinot Noir (Russian River Valley) $54. 92 —*S.H. (4/1/2004)*

Merry Edwards 2005 Sauvignon Blanc (Russian River Valley) $27. Made from Musque clone, and completely barrel fermented with sur lie aging in partial new oak, this is a good wine that can't quite overcome its feline character. Minor feline essence notes in a symphony of lemongrass, pineapple, fig and honeydew. 87 —*S.H. (7/1/2007)*

MERRYVALE

Merryvale 1997 Beckstoffer Vineyard Bordeaux Blend (Napa Valley) $45. 93 *(11/1/2000)*

Merryvale 2003 Profile Bordeaux Blend (Napa Valley) $95. Merryvale's Profile has been one of the most reliable Bordeaux blends for a long time, and the '03, which is mainly Cab Sauvignon, is a very fine expression of the house style. A blend of impressive vineyards, it's opulent in black currant flavors, and is most notable for its softly elegant balance. It's the kind of wine that will dazzle even people who say they don't like reds. Best now–2011 or so. 93 —*S.H. (5/1/2007)*

Merryvale 2000 Profile Bordeaux Blend (Napa Valley) $79. 87 —*S.H. (3/1/2004)*

Merryvale 1998 Profile Bordeaux Blend (Napa Valley) $90. 96 Cellar Selection —*J.M. (12/1/2001)*

Merryvale 1997 Profile Bordeaux Blend (Napa Valley) $85. 92 —*S.H. (12/15/2000)*

Merryvale 1996 Profile Bordeaux Blend (Napa Valley) $75. 86 *(7/1/2000)*

Merryvale 1997 Cabernet Sauvignon (Napa Valley) $20. 90 —*M.S. (2/1/2000)*

Merryvale 1999 Cabernet Sauvignon (Napa Valley) $26. 88 —*S.H. (6/1/2002)*

Merryvale 1998 Cabernet Sauvignon (Napa Valley) $25. 87 —*S.H. (12/15/2000)*

Merryvale 2002 Beckstoffer-Clone Six Cabernet Sauvignon (Rutherford) $88. 90 —*S.H. (12/15/2005)*

Merryvale 2001 Beckstoffer Clone Six Cabernet Sauvignon (Rutherford) $90. 91 *(7/1/2005)*

Merryvale 2003 Beckstoffer Vineyard Clone Six Cabernet Sauvignon (Rutherford) $95. 94 —*S.H. (12/15/2006)*

Merryvale 2002 Beckstoffer Vineyard X Cabernet Sauvignon (Oakville) $75. 91 Cellar Selection —*S.H. (8/1/2006)*

Merryvale 2001 Beckstoffer Vineyard X Cabernet Sauvignon (Oakville) $75. 90 *(7/1/2005)*

Merryvale 2001 Beckstoffer Vineyards Clone Six Cabernet Sauvignon (Rutherford) $88. 90 —*S.H. (10/1/2004)*

Merryvale 2000 Beckstoffer Vineyards Clone Six Cabernet Sauvignon (Rutherford) $75. 91 —*S.H. (11/15/2003)*

Merryvale 2001 Beckstoffer Vineyards Vineyard X Cabernet Sauvignon (Oakville) $75. 91 —*S.H. (10/1/2004)*

Merryvale 2000 Beckstoffer-Vineyard X Cabernet Sauvignon (Oakville) $75. 92 —*J.M. (12/15/2003)*

Merryvale 2003 Reserve Cabernet Sauvignon (Napa Valley) $39. Merryvale's '03 Reserve doesn't quite show the complexity of the Clone Six or Vineyard X bottlings, but then again, it's nowhere near the price. And as rich as it is, it's a comparative bargain. With luxuriously soft tannins, it's opulent in black currant, cocoa and new oak flavors that finish long and smooth. **90** —*S.H. (5/1/2007)*

Merryvale 2002 Reserve Cabernet Sauvignon (Napa Valley) $40. 86 —*S.H. (5/1/2006)*

Merryvale 2001 Reserve Cabernet Sauvignon (Napa Valley) $35. 91 —*S.H. (2/1/2005)*

Merryvale 2000 Reserve Cabernet Sauvignon (Napa Valley) $35. 86 —*S.H. (12/31/2003)*

Merryvale 1999 Reserve Cabernet Sauvignon (Napa Valley) $39. 92 —*S.H. (11/15/2002)*

Merryvale 1998 Reserve Cabernet Sauvignon (Napa Valley) $39. 88 —*J.M. (12/1/2001)*

Merryvale 1997 Reserve Cabernet Sauvignon (Napa Valley) $39. 89 *(11/1/2000)*

Merryvale 2004 Starmont Cabernet Sauvignon (Napa Valley) $27. The Starmont designation is sort of a junior version of Merryvale's more expensive wines and is often a solid value. So it is with this Cab, whose grapes come from some prestigious vineyards. It's dry, rich and complex, with a classic Napa balance of firm, sweet tannins, acidity and cassis and cherry fruit. Beautiful now, and should hold well for six years. **91 Editors' Choice** —*S.H. (11/1/2007)*

Merryvale 2003 Starmont Cabernet Sauvignon (Napa Valley) $27. You might almost think this was from Paso Robles, it's so soft, ripe, superma-ture and almost sweet. The finely grained tannins frame pie-fillng blackberry and cassis flavors that are well-oaked. **84** —*S.H. (5/1/2007)*

Merryvale 2002 Starmont Cabernet Sauvignon (Napa Valley) $25. 85 —*S.H. (8/1/2006)*

Merryvale 2001 Starmont Cabernet Sauvignon (Napa Valley) $24. 91 Editors' Choice —*S.H. (6/1/2004)*

Merryvale 2000 Starmont Cabernet Sauvignon (Napa Valley) $25. 86 —*S.H. (10/1/2003)*

Merryvale 2003 Vineyard X Cabernet Sauvignon (Oakville) $75. So rich, so opulent in primary fruit extract and new oak that it just demands time in the bottle to calm down. Explodes in cassis flavors spiced up with sweet, charry oak, and the tannins are fresh, young and vibrant, the kind that will usher this wine through a long lifetime. Best 2007–2012, or decant to let it breathe. **92** —*S.H. (5/1/2007)*

Merryvale 2001 Dutton Ranch Chardonnay (Russian River Valley) $29. 91 —*S.H. (2/1/2004)*

Merryvale 2000 Dutton Ranch Chardonnay (Russian River Valley) $29. 90 —*J.M. (7/1/2003)*

Merryvale 1999 Dutton Ranch Chardonnay (Russian River Valley) $35. 91 —*J.M. (12/15/2002)*

Merryvale 1998 Dutton Ranch Chardonnay (Russian River Valley) $35. 88 —*S.H. (11/15/2000)*

Merryvale 2004 Reserve Chardonnay (Carneros) $29. Here's a seriously good Chardonnay that fruit lovers will covet, but it's also enormously oaky. I like all that new French wood because the caramelly, smoky vanil-la and buttered toast, which is boosted by total malolactic fermentation, works so well with the mangoes, papayas and pineapples. But I know peo-ple who would call this Chard toothpicky. **92 Editors' Choice** —*S.H. (5/1/2007)*

Merryvale 2003 Reserve Chardonnay (Carneros) $29. 88 —*S.H. (5/1/2006)*

Merryvale 2002 Reserve Chardonnay (Carneros) $30. 90 *(7/1/2005)*

Merryvale 2001 Reserve Chardonnay (Carneros) $29. 90 —*S.H. (10/1/2004)*

Merryvale 2000 Reserve Chardonnay (Carneros) $29. 86 —*S.H. (6/1/2003)*

Merryvale 1999 Reserve Chardonnay (Napa Valley) $35. 93 —*J.M. (12/1/2001)*

Merryvale 2003 Silhouette Chardonnay (Napa Valley) $45. Silhouette typi-cally is held back a little longer than most Chards, which seems to soften it slightly. Still, the '03 is as fresh and pure in fruit as a young wine. It brims with ripe green apple butter, pineapple custard, butterscotch and spicy rum flavors that are well-oaked, and has none of the herbaceousness that often marks Napa Valley Chardonnay. Drink now–2009. **93 Editors' Choice** —*S.H. (5/1/2007)*

Merryvale 2002 Silhouette Chardonnay (Napa Valley) $50. 88 —*S.H. (8/1/2006)*

Merryvale 2001 Silhouette Chardonnay (Napa Valley) $45. 92 —*S.H. (12/31/2004)*

Merryvale 2000 Silhouette Chardonnay (Napa Valley) $45. 88 —*S.H. (6/1/2003)*

Merryvale 1999 Silhouette Chardonnay (Napa Valley) $49. 93 —*S.H. (5/1/2002)*

USA

Merryvale 1997 Silhouette Chardonnay (Napa Valley) $48. 89 *(10/1/2000)*

Merryvale 2005 Starmont Chardonnay (Napa Valley) $20. Shows a deft touch with the varietal, with lusciously ripe apricot purée, green apple and tropical fruit flavors that are layered with spicy oak. Notable for its bal-ance, and the fresh acidity that makes the finish so clean and lively. **86** —*S.H. (5/1/2007)*

Merryvale 2002 Starmont Chardonnay (Napa Valley) $19. 87 —*S.H. (6/1/2004)*

Merryvale 2001 Starmont Chardonnay (Napa Valley) $19. 92 Editors' Choice —*S.H. (12/1/2003)*

Merryvale 2000 Starmont Chardonnay (Napa Valley) $20. 86 —*S.H. (5/1/2002)*

Merryvale 1999 Starmont Chardonnay (Napa Valley) $20. 90 Editors' Choice —*S.H. (5/1/2001)*

Merryvale 1998 Starmont Chardonnay (Napa Valley) $20. 89 *(6/1/2000)*

Merryvale 2004 Merlot (Napa Valley) $24. Good price for a Napa Merlot of this quality. It's not a big, ageable wine, but shows plenty of fleshy pleas-ure now, with a rich array of plums, cassis and raspberries, and smoky char influences of oak. Merryvale packed a lot of elegant sophistication into this one. **89** —*S.H. (11/1/2007)*

Merryvale 2003 Beckstoffer Las Amigas Vineyard Merlot (Carneros) $39. This is an enormously complex and appealing Merlot that's offering its best fruit now and for the next three or four years. It's fresh and lively in oak-enhanced blackberry jam, cassis, blueberry, licorice, mushu plum sauce and coffee flavors that last for a full minute into the finish. Shows the elegant balance and finesse of a great Napa red. **91** —*S.H. (3/1/2007)*

Merryvale 2001 Beckstoffer Las Amigas Vineyard Merlot (Carneros) $35. 87 *(7/1/2005)*

Merryvale 2002 Beckstoffer Las Amigas Vineyard Merlot (Carneros) $43. 84 —*S.H. (8/1/2006)*

Merryvale 2001 Beckstoffer Las Amigas Vineyard Merlot (Carneros) $39. 85 —*S.H. (12/15/2004)*

Merryvale 2000 Los Amigos Vineyard Merlot (Carneros) $39. 90 —*J.M. (12/1/2003)*

Merryvale 2003 Reserve Merlot (Napa Valley) $35. The winery has clever-ly and properly positioned this in price between its Starmont and Las Amigas Merlots, and you get exactly what you pay for. It's a rich, sumptu-ous wine, with lush berry, carob, coffee and cinnamon spice flavors. Dry and refined, it may improve for a couple years. **89** —*S.H. (3/1/2007)*

Merryvale 2001 Reserve Merlot (Napa Valley) $32. 88 —*S.H. (2/1/2005)*

Merryvale 2000 Reserve Merlot (Napa Valley) $32. 87 —*S.H. (2/1/2004)*

Merryvale 1999 Reserve Merlot (Napa Valley) $39. 92 —*S.H. (11/15/2002)*

Merryvale 1998 Reserve Merlot (Napa Valley) $39. 91 —*J.M. (12/1/2001)*

Merryvale 2003 Starmont Merlot (Napa Valley) $24. There's lots to like in this Merlot, which is Merryvale's lowest priced bottling that shares much in common with its expensive ones. It has the upscale elegance of a fine Napa red, with gorgeous tannins and refined cherry marmalade, blackber-ry, cola, violet and earthy flavors. Drink now. **87** —*S.H. (3/1/2007)*

Merryvale 2002 Starmont Merlot (Napa Valley) $24. 86 —*M.S. (12/31/2006)*

Merryvale 2001 Starmont Merlot (Napa Valley) $22. 90 —*S.H. (6/1/2004)*

Merryvale 2000 Starmont Merlot (Napa Valley) $29. 86 —*S.H. (4/1/2003)*

Merryvale 1998 Beckstoffer Vineyard Merlot-Cabernet Sauvignon (Napa Valley) $60. 92 —*J.M. (12/1/2001)*

Merryvale NV Antigua Muscat Canelli (California) $30. 91 —*J.C. (12/31/1999)*

Merryvale 2005 Pinot Noir (Carneros) $35. Here's a fruit-forward Pinot with all the silky pleasure you could want. It's nice and dry, with rich, ripe cherry, cola, raspberry and white chocolate flavors, enhanced with layers of smoky oak. **87** —*S.H. (5/1/2007)*

Merryvale 2003 Pinot Noir (Carneros) $40. 89 *(7/1/2005)*

Merryvale 2002 Pinot Noir (Carneros) $29. 90 —*S.H. (11/1/2004)*

Merryvale 2000 Pinot Noir (Sonoma Coast) $44. 92 —*S.H. (2/1/2003)*

Merryvale 2001 Profile Red Blend (Napa Valley) $85. 93 —*S.H. (12/31/2004)*

Merryvale 1999 Profile Red Blend (Napa Valley) $90. 90 —*S.H. (12/31/2002)*

Merryvale 2000 Sauvignon Blanc (Napa Valley) $17. 88 —*J.M. (11/15/2001)*

Merryvale 2005 Juliana Vineyards Sauvignon Blanc (Napa Valley) $22. The grapes are from Pope Valley, a warmer, more inland section of Napa Valley, but the vintage was cool, and this barrel-fermented wine shows crisp acidity and polished flavors of citrus fruits, hay, figs and melons. With a dash of Sémillon, it's a sophisticated, dry white wine. **88** *—S.H. (5/1/2007)*

Merryvale 2004 Juliana Vineyard Sauvignon Blanc (Napa Valley) $22. 87 *—S.H. (5/1/2006)*

Merryvale 2003 Juliana Vineyards Sauvignon Blanc (Napa Valley) $22. 90 Editors' Choice *(7/1/2005)*

Merryvale 1999 Juliana Vineyard Sauvignon Blanc (Napa Valley) $22. 87 *—S.H. (11/15/2000)*

Merryvale 1998 Reserve Sauvignon Blanc (Napa Valley) $22. 86 *(3/1/2000)*

Merryvale 2006 Starmont Sauvignon Blanc (Napa Valley) $18. Merryvale, as usual, was able to find success in the cold '06 vintage with Sauvignon Blanc. This wine is as dry as can be and high in acidity, and since the winemaker held off on malolactic fermentation, it's very crisp. That gives the lime, gooseberry and lemongrass flavors a great bite. **88 Editors' Choice** *—S.H. (11/1/2007)*

Merryvale 2005 Starmont Sauvignon Blanc (Napa Valley) $18. A little on the green, feline side, but saved by enough figgy date and cantaloupe flavors to rescue it. The wine is totally dry and crisp in acids. **84** *—S.H. (5/1/2007)*

Merryvale 2003 Starmont Sauvignon Blanc (Napa Valley) $15. 91 *—S.H. (10/1/2004)*

Merryvale 2002 Starmont Sauvignon Blanc (Napa Valley) $16. 87 *—J.M. (2/1/2004)*

Merryvale 2001 Starmont Sauvignon Blanc (Napa Valley) $17. 88 *—S.H. (9/1/2003)*

Merryvale 2002 Syrah (Napa Valley) $30. 85 *(9/1/2005)*

MESSINA HOF

Messina Hof 2005 Barrel Reserve Cabernet Sauvignon (Texas) $11. With its ruby purple color and deep, plummy aromas, this Cab from respected winery Messina Hof is likeable from the start. On the palate, the tannins are good and the fruit and spice integrated. Can hold its own against beef or hearty dishes. **84** *—S.K. (7/1/2007)*

Messina Hof 2004 Barrel Reserve Merlot (Texas) $11. Toasted oak and spice dominate the nose of this Merlot from Texas, and those flavors carry through on the palate. The wine has structure but is a bit tannic and tart, lacking the smooth integration and elegance Merlot drinkers typically seek. **82** *—S.K. (5/1/2007)*

Messina Hof 2000 Angel Johannisberg Riesling (Texas) $15. 81 *—J.C. (8/1/2003)*

Messina Hof 2005 Angel Late Harvest Riesling (Texas) $16. For fans of sweet wines, this dessert Riesling offers layers of tropical fruit and some lemon that will pair well with Asian cuisine and is tasty on its own. Despite the floral and more opulent fruit, there's a minerality here, too, which anchors the wine. **83** *—S.K. (9/1/2007)*

Messina Hof 2006 Angel Late Harvest Merril's Vineyard Riesling (Texas) $17. Bright floral and tropical flavors are enveloped in a lush sweetness, creating an overall character that is not complex, but is appealing. Could use a little acid to tighten and lighten the structure and cut the heavy-handed sweetness, but the wine will pair nicely with a spicy Asian salad or a salty cheese. **83** *—S.K. (9/1/2007)*

Messina Hof 2006 Father and Son Cuvée Riesling (Texas) $9. Delicate apple flavors dominate this enjoyable but simple wine, which still has enough body to hold its own against a spicy Asian dish or a platter of robust seafood. Good acids and a pretty finish round out the deal. **82** *—S.K. (9/1/2007)*

Messina Hof 2005 Barrel Reserve Shiraz (Texas) $11. Tea, tobacco and a blast of bright fruit waft from this wine, but on the palate, there's little beyond oak and a tart, lean fruit flavor. Needs balance and elegance. **82** *—S.K. (5/1/2007)*

METHVEN FAMILY

Methven Family 2004 Pinot Gris (Willamette Valley) $23. 86 *—P.G. (12/1/2006)*

Methven Family 2004 Pinot Noir (Willamette Valley) $33. 86 *—P.G. (12/1/2006)*

Methven Family 2004 Reserve Pinot Noir (Willamette Valley) $55. 88 *—P.G. (12/1/2006)*

Methven Family 2004 Riesling (Willamette Valley) $21. 87 *—P.G. (12/1/2006)*

METTLER FAMILY VINEYARDS

Mettler Family Vineyards 2002 Cabernet Sauvignon (Lodi) $25. 83 *—S.H. (11/1/2005)*

Mettler Family Vineyards 2001 Cabernet Sauvignon (Lodi) $26. 85 *—S.H. (6/1/2004)*

Mettler Family Vineyards 2000 Cabernet Sauvignon (Lodi) $24. 87 *—M.S. (11/15/2003)*

Mettler Family Vineyards 2004 Petite Sirah (Lodi) $25. This very dry Petite Sirah has a wealth of cherry, cola, mulberry and spice flavors wrapped into sturdy tannins and acids. It's rustic, in the way of country wines, but will nicely accompany simple fare, especially barbecue with a rich tomato sauce. **86** *—S.H. (12/15/2007)*

Mettler Family Vineyards 2003 Petite Sirah (Lodi) $25. 90 Editors' Choice *—S.H. (5/1/2006)*

Mettler Family Vineyards 2002 Petite Sirah (Lodi) $25. 82 *—S.H. (11/1/2005)*

Mettler Family Vineyards 2001 Petite Sirah (Lodi) $26. 85 *—S.H. (6/1/2004)*

MI SUEÑO

Mi Sueño 2003 Cabernet Sauvignon (Napa Valley) $60. 92 *—S.H. (12/1/2006)*

Mi Sueño 2004 Chardonnay (Carneros) $35. 89 *—S.H. (12/1/2006)*

Mi Sueño 2004 Pugash Vineyard Chardonnay (Sonoma Mountain) $45. 92 *—S.H. (12/1/2006)*

Mi Sueño 2004 Ulises Valdez Vineyard Chardonnay (Russian River Valley) $38. 90 *—S.H. (10/1/2006)*

Mi Sueño 2004 Ulises Valdez Vineyard Pinot Noir (Russian River Valley) $42. 85 *—S.H. (10/1/2006)*

Mi Sueño 2003 El Llano Red Wine Red Blend (Napa Valley) $35. 89 *—S.H. (12/1/2006)*

Mi Sueño 2003 Syrah (Napa Valley) $40. 89 *—S.H. (12/1/2006)*

MIA'S PLAYGROUND

Mia's Playground 2003 Cabernet Sauvignon (Alexander Valley) $16. 86 *—S.H. (12/1/2005)*

Mia's Playground 2002 Cabernet Sauvignon (Alexander Valley) $16. 83 *—S.H. (5/1/2005)*

Mia's Playground 2005 Chardonnay (Russian River Valley) $16. Rich, creamy and fruity, with a blast of pineapple, peach pie, green apple butter and Asian spice flavors, it's dry, with refreshing cool climate acidity. **86** *—S.H. (4/1/2007)*

Mia's Playground 2003 Chardonnay (Russian River Valley) $16. 85 *—S.H. (5/1/2005)*

Mia's Playground 2002 Merlot (Dry Creek Valley) $16. 83 *—S.H. (12/1/2005)*

Mia's Playground 2005 Pinot Noir (Russian River Valley) $16. Thin, with cola and root beer flavors and a richer dash of cherries. It's clean enough, just one-dimensional. **83** *—S.H. (4/1/2007)*

Mia's Playground 2002 Pinot Noir (Sonoma Coast) $16. 84 *—S.H. (12/31/2004)*

Mia's Playground 2003 Zinfandel (Dry Creek Valley) $16. 85 *—S.H. (12/1/2005)*

Mia's Playground 2002 Zinfandel (Dry Creek Valley) $16. 87 *—S.H. (12/31/2004)*

Mia's Playground 2005 Old Vine Zinfandel (Dry Creek Valley) $16. This is a very fruity, dynamic Zin with concentrated cherry, raspberry, blackberry and cola flavors, generously spiced. It has the dryness and tannic structure you want in a nice Zin, with a touch of oak. **86** *—S.H. (8/1/2007)*

MICHAEL CHIARELLO

Michael Chiarello 2000 Eileen Cabernet Sauvignon (Napa Valley) $45. 87 *—S.H. (5/1/2004)*

Michael Chiarello 2000 Petite Sirah (Napa Valley) $45. 91 *—J.M. (12/31/2003)*

Michael Chiarello 2001 Roux Old Vine Petite Sirah (Napa Valley) $45. 88 *—S.H. (5/1/2004)*

Michael Chiarello 2000 Zinfandel (Napa Valley) $45. 90 *—J.M. (9/1/2003)*

Michael Chiarello 2001 Felicia Old Vine Zinfandel (Napa Valley) $50. 92 *—J.M. (9/1/2004)*

Michael Chiarello 2000 Giana Young Vines Zinfandel (Napa Valley) $28. 89 *—J.M. (9/1/2003)*

Michael Chiarello 2001 Giana Zinfandel (Napa Valley) $30. 90 *—J.M. (9/1/2004)*

MICHAEL DAVID

Michael David 2003 Rapture Cabernet Sauvignon (Lodi) $59. Classic Lodi Cab, from a vintage that wasn't too hot or too cool. The wine is soft and lush, with milk chocolate and cassis flavors and the vanillins and sweet char of oak. Easy and delicious, it's a wine to drink now. **88** *—S.H. (8/1/2007)*

Michael David 2005 Petite Petit Red Blend (Lodi) $22. A blend of Petite Sirah and Petit Verdot, this is a clumsy wine. It's soft and overripe, and the oaky overlay doesn't do anything to improve the situation. **80** *—S.H. (12/1/2007)*

Michael David 2005 Lust Zinfandel (Lodi) $49. I think by "lust" they mean something like a decadent chocolate truffle with a gooey cherry liqueur filling. That's what this sweetish wine, which has 15.9% alcohol, tastes like. It is awfully tasty, but it's hard to imagine what you'd drink it with, except, well, a chocolate truffle. **84** *—S.H. (12/15/2007)*

Michael David 2004 Lust Zinfandel (Lodi) $49. This is an expensive wine, by Lodi or any standards, but it's also a really good one. Blended with Petite Sirah, it has a soft texture and decadent mouthfeel, and the flavors are of creme de cassis, caramel cream, melted milk chocolate, tangerine zest and cinnamon-spiced gingerbread. It's certainly not an ager, so drink up. **91** *—S.H. (8/1/2007)*

MICHAEL POZZAN

Michael Pozzan 2002 Annabella Special Selection Cabernet Sauvignon (Napa Valley) $15. 87 *—S.H. (3/1/2005)*

Michael Pozzan 2003 Annabella Special Selection Chardonnay (Napa Valley) $12. 84 *—S.H. (3/1/2005)*

Michael Pozzan 2002 Annabella Special Selection Merlot (Napa Valley) $14. 84 *—S.H. (3/1/2005)*

Michael Pozzan 1997 Reserve Red Blend (Napa Valley) $13. 88 *(11/15/1999)*

Michael Pozzan 2005 Sawyer Vineyards Sauvignon Blanc (Lake County) $10. 87 Best Buy *—S.H. (11/15/2006)*

Michael Pozzan 2003 Special Reserve Sauvignon Blanc (Napa Valley) $9. 87 Best Buy *—S.H. (11/15/2004)*

MICHAEL SULLBERG

Michael Sullberg 2001 Cabernet Sauvignon (California) $9. 85 *—S.H. (11/15/2003)*

Michael Sullberg 2001 Merlot (California) $9. 85 *—S.H. (12/31/2003)*

MICHAEL-SCOTT

Michael-Scott 2001 Balliet Vineyard Cabernet Sauvignon (Napa Valley) $35. 85 *—S.H. (6/1/2004)*

Michael-Scott 2001 Zinfandel (Sonoma County) $24. 89 *—S.H. (6/1/2004)*

Michael-Scott 2001 Stagnaro Vineyard Zinfandel (Napa Valley) $22. 87 *(11/1/2003)*

MICHAUD

Michaud 2000 Chardonnay (Chalone) $40. 90 *—S.H. (5/1/2003)*

Michaud 2002 The Pinnacles Chardonnay (Chalone) $35. 88 *—S.H. (12/1/2006)*

Michaud 2000 Pinot Noir (Chalone) $45. 85 *—S.H. (7/1/2003)*

Michaud 2000 Sangiovese (Chalone) $25. 86 *—S.H. (9/1/2003)*

Michaud 2000 Syrah (Chalone) $35. 92 Cellar Selection *—S.H. (10/1/2003)*

MICHEL LAROCHE

Michel Laroche at Rutherford Hill 1999 Chardonnay (Napa Valley) $50. 89 *(12/1/2001)*

MICHEL-SCHLUMBERGER

Michel-Schlumberger 2001 Cabernet Sauvignon (Dry Creek Valley) $32. 91 *—S.H. (12/31/2004)*

Michel-Schlumberger 1998 Cabernet Sauvignon (Dry Creek Valley) $27. 85 *—S.H. (12/1/2001)*

Michel-Schlumberger 1997 Benchland Cabernet Sauvignon (Dry Creek Valley) $27. 87 *—S.H. (9/1/2000)*

Michel-Schlumberger 1997 Reserve Cabernet Sauvignon (Dry Creek Valley) $62. 89 *—S.H. (12/1/2001)*

Michel-Schlumberger 1997 Chardonnay (Dry Creek Valley) $20. 92 *—S.H. (11/1/1999)*

Michel-Schlumberger 2000 Chardonnay (Dry Creek Valley) $23. 86 *—S.H. (5/1/2003)*

Michel-Schlumberger 1999 Chardonnay (Dry Creek Valley) $20. 86 *—S.H. (11/15/2001)*

Michel-Schlumberger 2001 La Brume Chardonnay (Dry Creek Valley) $30. 87 *—S.H. (8/1/2003)*

Michel-Schlumberger 1998 Merlot (Dry Creek Valley) $21. 89 *—S.H. (12/1/2001)*

Michel-Schlumberger 1997 Benchland Merlot (Dry Creek Valley) $27. 87 *—S.H. (11/15/2000)*

Michel-Schlumberger 2003 Pinot Blanc (Dry Creek Valley) $21. 87 *—S.H. (12/1/2004)*

Michel-Schlumberger 1999 Benchland Wine Syrah (North Coast) $20. 86 *(10/1/2001)*

MIDLIFE CRISIS

Midlife Crisis 2004 Pinot Grigio (Paso Robles) $16. 82 *—S.H. (2/1/2006)*

MIDNIGHT CELLARS

Midnight Cellars 2003 Mare Nectaris Bordeaux Blend (Paso Robles) $40. This is Midnight's most expensive red, a blend of all five Bordeaux reds. Like its other '04 reds, it shows great poise and balance, with very ripe fruit in equilibrium with strong tannins, new oak and just-so acidity. The result is just fine. Midnight has quietly been working at its reds for years, and it shows. **90** *—S.H. (11/1/2007)*

Midnight Cellars 2000 Mare Nectaris Reserve Bordeaux Blend (Paso Robles) $35. 88 *—S.H. (2/1/2005)*

Midnight Cellars 1997 Mare Nectarus Reserve Bordeaux Blend (Paso Robles) $31. 90 *—S.H. (8/1/2001)*

Midnight Cellars 1999 Mare Nectaris Cabernet Blend (Paso Robles) $35. 88 *—M.S. (5/1/2003)*

Midnight Cellars 1998 Mare Nectaris Reserve Cabernet Blend (Paso Robles) $34. 88 *(9/1/2002)*

Midnight Cellars 2001 Mare Nectaris Reserve Red Wine Cabernet Blend (Paso Robles) $38. 84 *—S.H. (2/1/2006)*

Midnight Cellars 2004 Moonlight Cabernet Franc (Paso Robles) $26. Bright and forward in Cab Franc cherry fruit, this dry wine shows plenty of polish and sophistication. Besides the cherry flavors, the other notable feature here is tannins. They're of the sticky, astringent kind, but by no means unpleasant. This is a wine that simply calls for very rich steak, to break down and soften it. **87** *—S.H. (11/1/2007)*

Midnight Cellars 2001 Moonlight Cabernet Franc (Paso Robles) $22. 83 *—S.H. (5/1/2005)*

Midnight Cellars 2001 Estate Cabernet Sauvignon (Paso Robles) $28. 82 *—S.H. (5/1/2005)*

Midnight Cellars 2004 Nebula Cabernet Sauvignon (Paso Robles) $21. It's easy to imagine drinking this Cab at one of Paso's good restaurants, on a summer evening outside, accompanied by a grilled steak. This is quite tannic, but richly dry and succulent in black currant flavors. It really defines Paso Robles Cab. **89** *—S.H. (11/1/2007)*

Midnight Cellars 2001 Nebula Cabernet Sauvignon (Paso Robles) $19. 81 *—S.H. (5/1/2005)*

Midnight Cellars 1999 Nebula Cabernet Sauvignon (Paso Robles) $22. 83 *(9/1/2002)*

Midnight Cellars 1997 Nebula Cabernet Sauvignon (Paso Robles) $22. 88 *—S.H. (8/1/2001)*

Midnight Cellars 2000 Capriccio Italien Cabernet Sauvignon-Sangiovese (Paso Robles) $30. 85 *—S.H. (5/1/2003)*

Midnight Cellars 1997 Chardonnay (Paso Robles) $18. 84 *(6/1/2000)*

Midnight Cellars 2004 Equinox Chardonnay (Central Coast) $16. 85 *—S.H. (4/1/2006)*

Midnight Cellars 2000 Equinox Chardonnay (Paso Robles) $18. 86 *—S.H. (12/15/2002)*

Midnight Cellars 1999 Equinox Chardonnay (Paso Robles) $18. 86 *—S.H. (11/15/2001)*

Midnight Cellars 1997 Capricorn Merlot (Paso Robles) $22. 88 *—J.C. (7/1/2000)*

Midnight Cellars 1999 Eclipse Merlot (Paso Robles) $22. 86 *—S.H. (12/1/2001)*

Midnight Cellars 2004 Estate Merlot (Paso Robles) $21. Just too raisiny and stewed for real satisfaction. The extreme dryness and shriveled fruit taste accentuates the alcohol and tannins, making the wine hot and astringent. **83** *—S.H. (12/1/2007)*

Midnight Cellars 2001 Estate Merlot (Paso Robles) $18. 83 *—S.H. (5/1/2005)*

Midnight Cellars 1999 Estate Merlot (Paso Robles) $23. 84 *—S.H. (12/1/2001)*

Midnight Cellars NV Gemini Port (Paso Robles) $23. 84 *—S.H. (2/1/2005)*

Midnight Cellars 2000 Full Moon Red Blend (Paso Robles) $10. 83 *—S.H. (11/15/2002)*

Midnight Cellars 2001 Full Moon Red Wine Red Blend (Paso Robles) $13. 84 *—S.H. (3/1/2005)*

Midnight Cellars 2004 Gemini Red Blend (Paso Robles) $35. A 50-50 Zin and Syrah, this is classic Paso Robles rustic-chic red wine. It's dry and soft in acidity, with a slightly rough mouthfeel framing intensely ripe berry, cherry and tobacco fruit. If the flavor was more concentrated, the score would rise dramatically. **87** *—S.H. (11/1/2007)*

Midnight Cellars 2002 Gemini Red Blend (Paso Robles) $32. 84 *—S.H. (4/1/2005)*

Midnight Cellars 2000 Starlight Sangiovese (Dry Creek Valley) $19. 87 *—M.S. (5/1/2003)*

Midnight Cellars 1999 Starlight Sangiovese (Paso Robles) $22. 85 *—S.H. (9/1/2002)*

Midnight Cellars 2001 Starlight Reba Sangiovese (Paso Robles) $19. 80 *—S.H. (2/1/2006)*

Midnight Cellars 2000 Starlight Reba Sangiovese (Dry Creek Valley) $19. 82 *—S.H. (4/1/2005)*

Midnight Cellars 2002 Nocturne Syrah (Paso Robles) $19. 85 *—S.H. (12/1/2005)*

Midnight Cellars 2001 Nocturne Syrah (Paso Robles) $24. 85 *—S.H. (3/1/2005)*

Midnight Cellars 2000 Nocturne Syrah (Paso Robles) $26. 85 *—S.H. (12/1/2002)*

Midnight Cellars 1999 Nocturne Syrah (Paso Robles) $24. 90 *(11/1/2001)*

Midnight Cellars 2001 Vineyard Select Syrah (Paso Robles) $48. 83 *—S.H. (3/1/2005)*

Midnight Cellars 2001 Zinfandel (Paso Robles) $18. 88 *—J.M. (11/1/2003)*

Midnight Cellars 2000 Zinfandel (Paso Robles) $18. 83 *—M.S. (9/1/2003)*

Midnight Cellars 1998 Zinfandel (Paso Robles) $21. 90 *—P.G. (3/1/2001)*

Midnight Cellars 2003 Crescent Zinfandel (Paso Robles) $26. 82 *—S.H. (2/1/2006)*

Midnight Cellars 1999 Crescent Zinfandel (Paso Robles) $22. 87 *—D.T. (3/1/2002)*

Midnight Cellars 2005 Estate Zinfandel (Paso Robles) $28. Soft and hot, with nearly 16% alcohol, this Zin has the benefit of dryness. But the alcohol gives it a prickly feel, and the flavors are of raisins and prunes. **82** *—S.H. (10/1/2007)*

Midnight Cellars 2002 Estate Zinfandel (Paso Robles) $24. 85 *—S.H. (3/1/2005)*

Midnight Cellars 1999 Estate Zinfandel (Paso Robles) $26. 88 *—D.T. (3/1/2002)*

Midnight Cellars 1999 Reserve Zinfandel (Paso Robles) $28. 85 *—S.H. (12/15/2001)*

MIDSUMMER CELLARS

Midsummer Cellars 2004 Cañon Creek Vineyard Cabernet Sauvignon (Napa Valley) $48. Made in a riper style, with fruit pushed to the brink just before it turns raisiny, this single-vineyard Cab also is soft. It's immediately drinkable and is enjoyable in a rustically upscale way. **86** *—S.H. (2/1/2007)*

Midsummer Cellars 2003 Cañon Creek Vineyard Cabernet Sauvignon (Napa Valley) $45. 90 Cellar Selection *—S.H. (4/1/2006)*

Midsummer Cellars 2003 Mann Vineyard Cabernet Sauvignon (Napa Valley) $35. 91 Cellar Selection *—S.H. (4/1/2006)*

Midsummer Cellars 2001 Hickok Traulsen Zinfandel (Napa Valley) $22. 85 *(11/1/2003)*

MIGRATION

Migration 2005 Pinot Noir (Anderson Valley) $32. This is the second wine of Duckhorn-owned Goldeneye, comprised of lots that don't make the main blend. It shows the power and acidity of the main wine, with rich cherry, cassis, cola and vanilla flavors, but not quite the same finesse. Drink this polished, elegant Pinot now. **88** *—S.H. (11/1/2007)*

Migration 2004 Pinot Noir (Anderson Valley) $30. 88 *—S.H. (12/1/2006)*

Migration 2003 Pinot Noir (Anderson Valley) $28. 85 *—S.H. (12/1/2005)*

Migration 2002 Pinot Noir (Anderson Valley) $26. 87 *(11/1/2004)*

Migration 2006 Vin Gris of Pinot Noir (Anderson Valley) $20. I love everything about this blush. It's the pretty color of a peach whose gold is turning rosy pink, and the rich flavors are of raspberries, strawberries, cherries and vanilla, all balanced with a crisp streak of acidity. Fun and serious at the same time, it will go with everything from salmon to vanilla ice cream. **90** *—S.H. (12/15/2007)*

MILBRANDT

Milbrandt 2005 Legacy Cabernet Sauvignon (Washington) $25. This is really solidly made and appealing wine, which nicely combines lush, chocolaty barrel flavors with penetrating Cabernet fruit. Cassis, cherry and sweet plum create a substantial fruit center, and it's swathed in a roasted coffee and mocha wrapping. Try it with a grilled steak, or better yet, a rich molé sauce. **90 Editors' Choice** *—P.G. (12/31/2007)*

Milbrandt 2006 Legacy Evergreen Vineyard Chardonnay (Washington) $23. Concentrated, beautifully defined flavors of pear, apple and ripe pineapple drive a stake through the heart of this wine, blazing a trail across the palate with tongue-thrashing acids and bracing minerality. As it slowly unwinds, it reveals a finish of banana caramel tart, luscious and long. **90 Editors' Choice** *—P.G. (12/31/2007)*

Milbrandt 2006 Legacy Sundance Vineyard Chardonnay (Washington) $20. This is the oldest of the Milbrandt vineyards, planted in 1997. Though a bit riper than the Evergreen vineyard bottling, this Chardonnay feels lighter, with less density. It's balanced and complete, and the flavors of green apple and Asian pear offer a fine rendition of well-ripened Washington fruit. **88** *—P.G. (12/31/2007)*

Milbrandt 2006 Traditions Chardonnay (Washington) $15. Made in a fresh, clean, lighthearted style, this immaculate Chardonnay shows no signs of new oak. The fruit is crisp apple, the acids bracing and lightly mineral, and it's a palate-cleaning wine that should be served chilled for maximum refreshment. **87** *—P.G. (12/1/2007)*

Milbrandt 2005 Legacy Merlot (Washington) $25. There's a ton of dark, chocolaty toast atop the succulent fruit in this tasty Merlot. The spicy plum and black cherry flavors carry hints of sweet tobacco and chocolate cake. Though not a massive wine, its broad flavors are full and engaging. **89** *—P.G. (12/31/2007)*

Milbrandt 2006 Traditions Riesling (Washington) $12. An off-dry, leesy, delicately floral Riesling, this elegantly captures the floral and mineral qualities that make the grape so exceptional. The wine doesn't push too hard, but it persists, mixing white peach and papaya with citrus blossom, rosewater and body powder. Exotic and delightful. **90 Best Buy** *—P.G. (12/1/2007)*

Milbrandt 2005 Legacy Syrah (Washington) $25. Many winemakers use Milbrandt fruit for their Syrahs, so it's no surprise that the brothers' own winery has a Syrah that stands at the top of the product line. There is precision and power here, with deep cherry and boysenberry fruit, tart acids that hint at lemon rind, a sharp peppery streak and a finish that somehow suggests chocolate and pineapple candy. Complex, muscular and delicious. **91 Editors' Choice** *—P.G. (12/31/2007)*

MILES

Miles 1999 Pinot Noir (Finger Lakes) $16. 84 *—J.C. (3/1/2002)*

MILL CREEK

Mill Creek 2005 Kreck Family Vineyards Cabernet Sauvignon (Sonoma County) $25. Soft and ripe in extracted cherry and blackberry jam fruit, this also has some heat on the palate, the result of 15% alcohol. It feels a little simple, and the heat is off-putting. **84** *—S.H. (12/31/2007)*

Mill Creek 2002 Kreck Family Vineyards Cabernet Sauvignon (Sonoma County) $25. 85 *—S.H. (12/1/2006)*

Mill Creek 2005 Estate Chardonnay (Dry Creek Valley) $16. 86 *—S.H. (12/1/2006)*

Mill Creek 2006 Estate Gewürztraminer (Dry Creek Valley) $16. All stainless steel fermentation allows the natural flavor to shine in this dry, friendly Gewürz. It shows pleasantly varietal flavors of tropical fruits, wildflowers and Asian spices, and finishes dry and clean. **85** *—S.H. (7/1/2007)*

Mill Creek 2005 Estate Gewürztraminer (Dry Creek Valley) $14. 86 *—S.H. (12/1/2006)*

Mill Creek 2002 Estate Merlot (Dry Creek Valley) $20. 84 *—S.H. (12/1/2006)*

Mill Creek 2006 Estate Sauvignon Blanc (Dry Creek Valley) $16. If you like your white wines with a white sugary finish, this is for you. Tastes like apricot, pineapple, peach and apple jelly. **82** *—S.H. (12/31/2007)*

Mill Creek 2005 Estate Sauvignon Blanc (Dry Creek Valley) $16. 85 *—S.H. (12/1/2006)*

Mill Creek 2004 Estate Syrah (Dry Creek Valley) $27. A little heavy and soft, but with a nice grilled steak, it has enough waves of complexity to stand out. The ripe blackberry, root beer, mocha and sweet oak flavors are wrapped into rich, dusty tannins, and the finish is smooth and long. Drink now. **88** *—S.H. (7/1/2007)*

Mill Creek 2005 Zinfandel (Dry Creek Valley) $30. Unacceptably high in alcohol, nearly 16%, this Zin is overwhelmed with heat. It's almost Port, without the luscious fruit, and burns the palate. **80** *—S.H. (12/31/2007)*

Mill Creek 2001 Zinfandel (Russian River Valley) $22. 89 *—J.M. (11/1/2003)*

Mill Creek 1998 Zinfandel (Dry Creek Valley) $18. 83 *—P.G. (3/1/2001)*

MILLBROOK

Millbrook 2004 Cabernet Franc (New York) $20. Cassis and spice lead this medium-bodied, garnet-red selection from Hudson Valley's Millbrook. There's some depth and backbone on the palate, with a touch of lightly oaky vanilla, plum and blueberry to add to the mix, but the finish is lean and overall, the wine's impression is somewhat fleeting. Nonetheless, would pair well with roasted meats and poultry dishes. **84** *—S.K. (2/1/2007)*

Millbrook 2000 Cabernet Franc (New York) $18. 83 *—M.S. (2/27/2003)*

Millbrook 2000 Chardonnay (New York) $14. 81 *—J.M. (2/27/2003)*

Millbrook 1999 Proprietor's Special Reserve Chardonnay (Hudson River Region) $16. 85 *—J.M. (2/27/2003)*

Millbrook 2004 Pinot Noir (New York) $20. 81 *—M.D. (12/1/2006)*

Millbrook 2001 Tocai Friulano Estate Bottled Tocai (Hudson River Region) $12. 88 Best Buy *—J.M. (2/27/2003)*

MILLIAIRE

Milliaire 1997 Clairmont Cabernet Sauvignon (Sierra Foothills) $22. 87 *—S.H. (8/1/2001)*

Milliaire 2002 Eagle's Nest Petite Sirah (Lodi) $18. 84 *—S.H. (2/1/2005)*

Milliaire 2001 Syrah (Sierra Foothills) $20. 85 *—S.H. (2/1/2005)*

Milliaire 2001 Clockspring Zinfandel (Sierra Foothills) $18. 91 Editors' Choice *—S.H. (2/1/2005)*

Milliaire 1997 Clockspring Zinfandel (Sierra Foothills) $18. 90 *—P.G. (3/1/2001)*

Milliaire 2001 Ghirardelli Zinfandel (Sierra Foothills) $18. 90 *—S.H. (2/1/2005)*

Milliaire 1997 Ghirardelli Zinfandel (Sierra Foothills) $18. 89 *—P.G. (3/1/2002)*

MILONE

Milone 1996 Bells Echo Vineyard Echo Bordeaux Blend (Mendocino) $25. 91 *—S.H. (3/1/2000)*

Milone 1997 Sanel Valley Vineyard Sanel Bordeaux Blend (Mendocino County) $48. 85 *—S.H. (5/1/2002)*

Milone 1997 Hopland Cuvée Chardonnay (Mendocino) $10. 88 Best Buy *—S.H. (3/1/2000)*

Milone 1999 Sanel Valley Vineyard Chardonnay (Mendocino) $18. 85 *—S.H. (5/1/2002)*

Milone 1997 Bells Echo Vineyards Echo Red Blend (Mendocino County) $30. 83 *—S.H. (5/1/2002*

Milone 1999 Sanel Valley Vineyard Zinfandel (Mendocino County) $15. 83 *—S.H. (5/1/2002)*

Milone 1997 Sanel Valley Vineyard Zinfandel (Mendocino County) $15. 88 *(5/1/2000)*

MINASSIAN-YOUNG

Minassian-Young 2004 Cabernet Sauvignon (Paso Robles) $18. This Cab has 20% Mourvèdre in it, which adds an exotic chocolaty and mulberry note to the blackberries and cherries. It's a full-bodied, fairly tannic wine, and nicely dry, but there's a taste of shriveled berries or raisins that makes for some bitterness. **85** *—S.H. (12/31/2007)*

Minassian-Young 2004 Rhône Red Blend (Paso Robles) $18. Just delicious, a blend of Syrah, Mourvedre and Grenache that shows how well Paso Robles can make these Rhône reds. The wine is soft and voluptuous, with complex flavors of blackberries, cherries, raspberries, milk chocolate, licorice and cinnamon spice. Finishes long and rewardingly dry. **91 Editors' Choice** *—S.H. (12/31/2007)*

Minassian-Young 2005 Estate Zinfandel (Paso Robles) $20. What a great Zinfandel this is. It's lusty and hearty, just the way you want a Zin to wash down barbecue, but it also has balance and even elegance, despite the high alcohol. The ripe blackberry and cherry flavors are jammy, complexed with spicy tobacco and chocolate, and a pure finish of cassis. **90** *—S.H. (12/31/2007)*

MINER

Miner 2004 The Oracle Bordeaux Blend (Napa Valley) $70. This Cab-based Bordeaux blend has sizable amounts of Merlot and Cab Franc. It's quite a distinguished wine, classic in the modern Napa sense of softness and ripeness to the point of decadent drinkability. There's a sweet olive tapenade edge to the blackberry, cassis and cherry flavors. The finish, believe it or not, suggests blueberry pie, fresh from the oven. **91** *—S.H. (12/31/2007)*

Miner 2002 The Oracle Cabernet Blend (Napa Valley) $50. 85 *—S.H. (12/15/2005)*

Miner 2004 Cabernet Sauvignon (Oakville) $65. The opening scent of funky, sweaty leather is not promising, and indeed, it tastes overly soft and muted. You can sense some good fruit in there, but it's tamped down. The tannins stick out, making the wine awkward and common. **84** *—S.H. (12/15/2007)*

Miner 2003 Cabernet Sauvignon (Oakville) $54. 88 *—S.H. (7/1/2006)*

Miner 2002 Cabernet Sauvignon (Oakville) $50. 85 *—S.H. (12/15/2005)*

Miner 2001 Cabernet Sauvignon (Oakville) $50. 93 *—S.H. (12/31/2004)*

Miner 2000 Cabernet Sauvignon (Oakville) $50. 87 *—S.H. (11/15/2003)*

Miner 1999 Cabernet Sauvignon (Oakville) $60. 92 *—C.S. (11/15/2002)*

Miner 1997 Cabernet Sauvignon (Oakville) $60. 86 *(11/1/2000)*

Miner 2005 Chardonnay (Napa Valley) $30. Miner has been doing one of the better jobs at non-Carneros Napa Chardonnay, and this pleasant wine continues that ride. It's a bit soft and earthy, but has rich pear and peach flavors and lots of toasty new oak. **87** *—S.H. (3/1/2007)*

Miner 2004 Chardonnay (Napa Valley) $30. 88 *—S.H. (3/1/2006)*

Miner 2003 Chardonnay (Napa Valley) $28. 87 *—S.H. (7/1/2005)*

Miner 2002 Chardonnay (Napa Valley) $25. 90 *—S.H. (11/15/2004)*

Miner 2000 Chardonnay (Napa Valley) $30. 85 *—S.H. (6/1/2003)*

Miner 1998 Chardonnay (Napa Valley) $28. 87 *(6/1/2000)*

Miner 2000 Oakville Ranch Chardonnay (Napa Valley) $35. 90 *—J.M. (2/1/2003)*

Miner 2004 Wild Yeast Chardonnay (Napa Valley) $50. 84 *—S.H. (11/15/2006)*

Miner 2002 Wild Yeast Chardonnay (Napa Valley) $50. 86 *—S.H. (7/1/2005)*

Miner 2002 Merlot (Napa Valley) $30. 90 *—S.H. (4/1/2006)*

Miner 2001 Oakville Ranch Vineyard Merlot (Oakville) $28. 88 *—S.H. (12/15/2004)*

Miner 2004 Stagecoach Vineyard Merlot (Napa Valley) $35. Smells a little herbal-weedy, tastes a little semisweet and soft, with raisiny blackberry and cherry flavors. Ready now. **84** *—S.H. (12/1/2007)*

Miner 2003 Stagecoach Vineyard Merlot (Napa Valley) $35. 91 *—S.H. (11/15/2006)*

Miner 2001 Stagecoach Vineyard Merlot (Napa Valley) $28. 84 *—S.H. (12/1/2005)*

Miner 2001 Stagecoach Vineyard Merlot (Napa Valley) $28. 92 *—S.H. (12/15/2004)*

Miner 2000 Stagecoach Vineyard Merlot (Napa Valley) $35. 93 Editors' Choice *—S.H. (12/1/2003)*

Miner 2002 Petite Sirah (Napa Valley) $40. 92 *—S.H. (8/1/2005)*

Miner 2005 Garys' Vineyard Pinot Noir (Santa Lucia Highlands) $60. Soft and lush, the flavors are just delicious, ranging from cherries and cassis to cola, cocoa, gingersnap cookie, rose petal tea and Asian spices. With every sip, you find something new. The wine would benefit from a firmer texture, though, as it's on the soft, one-dimensional side. **87** *—S.H. (12/1/2007)*

Miner 2004 Garys' Vineyard Pinot Noir (Santa Lucia Highlands) $50. 86 *—S.H. (11/15/2006)*

Miner 2002 Garys' Vineyard Pinot Noir (Santa Lucia Highlands) $50. 93 *—S.H. (11/1/2004)*

Miner 2000 Garys' Vineyard Pinot Noir (Santa Lucia Highlands) $50. 90 *(10/1/2002)*

Miner 2005 Rosella's Vineyard Pinot Noir (Santa Lucia Highlands) $60. This is a terrific vineyard. Miner's '05 Rosella's is a deliciously compelling wine, dry and complex. With its gently polished tannins and adequate acidity, the blackberry, cherry, cola and cinnamon spice flavors are wrapped into a beautiful texture. Drink now through 2009. **90** *—S.H. (12/1/2007)*

Miner 2004 Rosella's Vineyard Pinot Noir (Santa Lucia Highlands) $50. 92 *—S.H. (10/1/2006)*

Miner 2002 Rosella's Vineyard Pinot Noir (Santa Lucia Highlands) $50. 92 *—S.H. (11/1/2004)*

Miner 2004 Rosato Rosé Blend (Mendocino) $15. 83 *—S.H. (12/1/2005)*

Miner 2000 Rosato Rosé Blend (Mendocino) $13. 87 *—J.M. (11/15/2001)*

USA

Miner 1997 Sangiovese (Mendocino County) $20. 89 *—S.H. (12/15/1999)*

Miner 2003 Syrah (Napa Valley) $30. A disappointment from a good winery. The wine is soft and cough-medicinal sweet, a rustic creation despite coming from Napa vineyards. 82 *—S.H. (4/1/2007)*

Miner 2002 Syrah (Napa Valley) $28. 84 *(9/1/2005)*

Miner 2001 Syrah (Napa Valley) $28. 92 *—S.H. (12/15/2004)*

Miner 2004 Simpson Vineyard Viognier (California) $20. 84 *—S.H. (12/1/2005)*

Miner 2003 Simpson Vineyard Viognier (California) $20. 85 *—S.H. (11/15/2004)*

Miner 2002 Simpson Vineyard Viognier (California) $20. 84 *—S.H. (12/1/2003)*

Miner 2002 Zinfandel (Napa Valley) $28. 86 *—S.H. (8/1/2005)*

MIRABELLE

Mirabelle NV Brut Champagne Blend (North Coast) $16. 85 *—D.T. (12/1/2001)*

Mirabelle NV Brut Champagne Blend (North Coast) $16. 87 *—J.M. (12/1/2002)*

MIRAMONT

Miramont 2002 Celestial Cabernet Sauvignon (Lodi) $19. 86 *—S.H. (4/1/2006)*

Miramont 2005 Celestial White Cabernet Sauvignon (Lodi) $14. Full-bodied for a rosé, with black cherry and vanilla flavors, this blush is dry and simple. Nice for everyday. 83 *—S.H. (7/1/2007)*

Miramont 2003 Vintners Reserve Celestial Cabernet Sauvignon (Lodi) $25. Sharp in acids, dry and rustic, this country wine offers earthy straw flavors, with a medicinal cherry finish. It's also very tannic. 82 *—S.H. (8/1/2007)*

Miramont 2002 Vintners Reserve Celestial Cabernet Sauvignon (Lodi) $25. 87 *—S.H. (4/1/2006)*

MIRASSOU

Mirassou 2004 Cabernet Sauvignon (California) $12. Sometimes, all you need is a dry, full-bodied red wine that's honest and has no faults. That's what you get with this fruity, spicy wine. It's a fine example of a California-appellated Cabernet Sauvignon. 84 *—S.H. (11/15/2007)*

Mirassou 2003 Cabernet Sauvignon (California) $10. 83 *—S.H. (11/1/2006)*

Mirassou 2002 Cabernet Sauvignon (California) $10. 82 *—S.H. (11/1/2005)*

Mirassou 2001 Cabernet Sauvignon (California) $10. 85 **Best Buy** *(11/15/2004)*

Mirassou 1999 Coastal Selection Cabernet Sauvignon (Central Coast) $11. 87 **Best Buy** *—S.H. (11/15/2002)*

Mirassou 2005 Chardonnay (Monterey County) $12. This is not a very good Chardonnay. It's thin and simple, with syrupy flavors and a heavy hand of oak. 82 *—S.H. (10/1/2007)*

Mirassou 2004 Chardonnay (Monterey County) $11. 83 *—S.H. (9/1/2006)*

Mirassou 2003 Chardonnay (Central Coast) $11. 84 *—S.H. (4/1/2005)*

Mirassou 2002 Chardonnay (California) $10. 84 *(11/15/2004)*

Mirassou 2000 Coastal Selection Chardonnay (Monterey) $11. 88 **Best Buy** *—S.H. (12/15/2002)*

Mirassou 1999 Coastal Selection Chardonnay (Monterey County) $13. 85 *—S.H. (11/15/2001)*

Mirassou 1998 Coastal Selection Chardonnay (Monterey County) $12. 83 *—S.H. (10/1/2000)*

Mirassou 1998 Harvest Reserve Chardonnay (Monterey County) $16. 88 *(6/1/2000)*

Mirassou 1996 Harvest Reserve Chardonnay (Monterey County) $16. 87 *—S.H. (7/1/1999)*

Mirassou 1998 Mission Vineyard Chardonnay (Monterey County) $24. 91 *—S.H. (2/1/2000)*

Mirassou 1998 San Vicente Vineyard Chardonnay (Monterey County) $24. 88 *(6/1/2000)*

Mirassou 1999 Showcase Selection Chardonnay (Monterey County) $30. 89 *(7/1/2001)*

Mirassou 1998 Showcase Selection Chardonnay (Monterey County) $30. 85 *(6/1/2000)*

Mirassou 2002 Merlot (California) $10. 82 *—S.H. (11/1/2005)*

Mirassou 2001 Merlot (California) $10. 83 *(11/15/2004)*

Mirassou 1999 Coastal Selection Merlot (Monterey) $11. 84 *(11/15/2002)*

Mirassou 1997 Coastal Selection Merlot (Monterey County) $13. 81 *—S.H. (11/15/2000)*

Mirassou 1998 Harvest Reserve Merlot (Monterey County) $18. 85 *—S.H. (7/1/2002)*

Mirassou 1996 Limited Bottling Merlot (Monterey County) $18. 85 *—J.C. (7/1/2000)*

Mirassou 1999 Mirassou Harvest Reserve Merlot (Monterey County) $18. 85 *—S.H. (11/15/2002)*

Mirassou 1997 Harvest Reserve Dedication Bot Petite Sirah (Monterey County) $18. 89 *(11/1/1999)*

Mirassou 2000 Coastal Selection Pinot Blanc (Monterey County) $12. 88 *—S.H. (9/1/2003)*

Mirassou 1999 Coastal Selection White Burgundy Pinot Blanc (Monterey County) $12. 84 *—S.H. (12/15/2001)*

Mirassou 1997 Limited Bottling Fifth Generat Pinot Blanc (Monterey County) $16. 87 *—S.H. (9/1/1999)*

Mirassou 2000 Mirassou Mission Vineyard Pinot Blanc (Monterey County) $22. 87 *—S.H. (9/1/2003)*

Mirassou 1999 Mission Vineyard Pinot Blanc (Arroyo Seco) $24. 85 *—S.H. (12/15/2001)*

Mirassou 1997 White Burgundy Pinot Blanc (Monterey County) $9. 82 *—M.S. (9/1/1999)*

Mirassou 1997 Pinot Noir (Monterey County) $11. 84 *(11/15/1999)*

Mirassou 2002 Pinot Noir (Central Coast) $10. 85 **Best Buy** *(11/15/2004)*

Mirassou 1999 Coastal Selection Pinot Noir (Central Coast) $13. 82 *—S.H. (12/15/2001)*

Mirassou 1999 Coastal Selection Pinot Noir (Monterey County) $10. 86 **Best Buy** *(10/1/2002)*

Mirassou 1998 Coastal Selection Pinot Noir (Monterey County) $14. 83 *—S.H. (11/15/2001)*

Mirassou 1999 Harvest Reserve Pinot Noir (Monterey County) $15. 88 **Best Buy** *(10/1/2002)*

Mirassou 1997 Harvest Reserve Pinot Noir (Monterey County) $16. 86 *(12/15/1999)*

Mirassou 1997 Limited Bottling Pinot Noir (Monterey County) $18. 86 *(12/15/1999)*

Mirassou 1999 Showcase Selection Pinot Noir (Monterey County) $30. 89 *(10/1/2002)*

Mirassou 1997 Showcase Selection Pinot Noir (Monterey County) $30. 91 *(10/1/1999)*

Mirassou 2005 Riesling (Monterey County) $12. Simple and fruity, with crisp Monterey acids framing pleasant citrus, peach, wildflower and mineral flavors. The wine finishes off-dry and firm. 83 *—S.H. (2/1/2007)*

Mirassou 2004 Riesling (Monterey County) $11. 84 *—S.H. (10/1/2006)*

Mirassou 2004 Riesling (Monterey) $10. 83 *—S.H. (12/1/2005)*

Mirassou 2001 Coastal Selection Riesling (Monterey) $7. 86 *—J.M. (6/1/2002)*

Mirassou 2000 Coastal Selection Riesling (Monterey County) $8. 85 *—S.H. (6/1/2002)*

Mirassou 1998 Family Selection Riesling (Monterey) $8. 86 **Best Buy** *—S.H. (9/1/1999)*

Mirassou 2003 Sauvignon Blanc (Calaveras County) $10. 85 **Best Buy** *(11/15/2004)*

Mirassou 1999 Harvest Reserve Syrah (Monterey County) $18. 83 *—S.H. (12/1/2002)*

MIRO

Miro 2004 Coyote Ridge Vineyard Petite Sirah (Dry Creek Valley) $30. 90 *—S.H. (12/31/2006)*

Miro 2001 Coyote Ridge Vineyard Petite Sirah (Dry Creek Valley) $35. 92 *—S.H. (3/1/2005)*

MISSION MEADOW

Mission Meadow 2000 Merlot (Santa Barbara County) $25. 85 *—S.H. (2/1/2004)*

MISSION PARK

Mission Park NV Artist Series Red Cuvée Red Blend (Central Coast) $8. 86 **Best Buy** *—S.H. (9/1/2006)*

MITCHELL

Mitchell 1999 Reserve Malbec (El Dorado) $21. 82 *—S.H. (5/1/2002)*

MITCHELL KATZ WINERY

Mitchell Katz Winery 2000 JK's Cabernet Sauvignon (Livermore Valley) $24. 90 Editors' Choice *—S.H. (11/15/2003)*

Mitchell Katz Winery 2001 Crackerbox Vineyards Sangiovese (Livermore Valley) $22. 82 *—S.H. (12/1/2003)*

MIXED BAG

Mixed Bag 2002 Red Wine Red Blend (California) $10. 85 Best Buy *—S.H. (5/1/2005)*

Mixed Bag 2002 White Wine White Blend (California) $10. 83 *—S.H. (5/1/2005)*

MOKELUMNE GLEN

Mokelumne Glen 2001 Kerner (Lodi) $12. 83 *—S.H. (3/1/2004)*

Mokelumne Glen 2004 Lemberger (Lodi) $14. 80 *—S.H. (4/1/2006)*

Mokelumne Glen 2004 Select Late Harvest Dreirebe White Blend (Lodi) $20. 87 *—S.H. (4/1/2006)*

Mokelumne Glen 2001 Zinfandel (Lodi) $12. 88 Best Buy *(11/1/2003)*

MOLNAR FAMILY

Molnar Family 2005 Poseidon's Vineyard Chardonnay (Carneros) $22. Made by Michael Terrien, the winemaker at Hanzell, this is a vivid interpretation of a Carneros Chard. It's bone-dry, crisp in acids, and has an earthy, dried herb edge to the citrus, green apple, white peach and spicy oak flavors, with a mineral, wet stone quality. Finishes balanced and elegantly complex. **91 Editors' Choice** *—S.H. (4/1/2007)*

Molnar Family 2004 Poseidon's Vineyard Pinot Noir (Carneros) $25. There's a soft richness to this wine, almost a dessert pastry quality, like a cherry-filled bonbon that melted and then was splashed with licorice, cola and fennel. It's really delicious, a bit one-dimensional, but crisp and dry. **88** *—S.H. (4/1/2007)*

MONT PELLIER

Mont Pellier 2000 Syrah (California) $7. 84 *—S.H. (12/15/2003)*

Mont Pellier 2000 Viognier (California) $7. 85 Best Buy *—S.H. (12/15/2002)*

MONTAGE

Montage 2004 Cabernet Sauvignon (California) $11. An excellent Cab for this price. You get a richly ripe wine with polished tannins framing blackberry, cassis and cherry flavors. There's citrus too, with a crisp tangerine brightness. The alcohol is a modest 13.8%. **87 Best Buy** *—S.H. (11/15/2007)*

Montage 2003 Cabernet Sauvignon (California) $11. 86 Best Buy *—S.H. (6/1/2006)*

Montage 2002 Cabernet Sauvignon (California) $12. 84 *—S.H. (11/15/2005)*

Montage 2005 Chardonnay (California) $11. There's no lack of fruit in this ripe, jammy wine. It bursts with pineapple and mango flavors, with the vanilla and caramel of oak, from whatever source, and it may or may not be barrels. **83** *—S.H. (11/15/2007)*

Montage 2003 Chardonnay (California) $11. 86 Best Buy *—S.H. (5/1/2006)*

MONTE LAGO

Monte Lago 2000 Single Vineyard Sauvignon Blanc (Clear Lake) $20. 86 *(8/1/2002)*

MONTE VOLPE

Monte Volpe 1996 Barbera (California) $11. 86 *(11/15/1999)*

Monte Volpe 1999 Montepulciano (Mendocino) $14. 84 *—S.H. (5/1/2002)*

Monte Volpe 1997 Pinot Grigio (Mendocino) $12. 87 Best Buy *(8/1/1999)*

Monte Volpe 2000 Pinot Grigio (Mendocino) $13. 85 *—S.H. (5/1/2002)*

Monte Volpe 1999 Pinot Grigio (Mendocino) $12. 84 *—S.H. (8/1/2001)*

Monte Volpe 1997 Sangiovese (Mendocino) $16. 88 *—M.S. (9/1/2000)*

MONTELLE

Montelle 2005 Dry Vignoles (Missouri) $10. This dry Vignoles offers pineapple and grapefruit flavors and a pretty floral and spiced nose. Clean and delicate on the palate, it's a good cheese-pairing wine and has a balanced but expressive overall character. **83** *—S.K. (10/1/2007)*

MONTEMAGGIORE

Montemaggiore 2002 Superiore Red Blend (Dry Creek Valley) $40. 89 *—S.H. (10/1/2005)*

Montemaggiore 2003 Paolo's Vineyard Syrah (Dry Creek Valley) $32. 84 *—S.H. (7/1/2006)*

Montemaggiore 2002 Paolo's Vineyard Syrah (Dry Creek Valley) $32. 88 *(9/1/2005)*

MONTEREY PENINSULA

Monterey Peninsula 1997 Sleepy Hollow Vineyardd-Doctor's Rese Pinot Noir (Monterey County) $22. 90 *(10/1/1999)*

MONTEREY VINEYARD

Monterey Vineyard 1998 Cabernet Sauvignon (Monterey County) $7. 83 *—S.H. (12/15/2000)*

Monterey Vineyard 1998 Chardonnay (Monterey County) $7. 83 *—S.H. (5/1/2000)*

Monterey Vineyard 1997 Merlot (California) $7. 82 *—J.C. (7/1/2000)*

Monterey Vineyard 1997 Pinot Noir (California) $8. 82 *(10/1/1999)*

Monterey Vineyard 1999 Pinot Noir (Central Coast) $7. 81 *—S.H. (12/15/2000)*

MONTERRA

Monterra 2000 Encore San Bernabe Vineyard Red Medley Cabernet Blend (Monterey County) $18. 87 *—S.H. (6/1/2004)*

Monterra 2000 Cabernet Sauvignon (Monterey County) $13. 84 *(12/1/2002)*

Monterra 2001 Chardonnay (Monterey County) $10. 85 *(12/1/2002)*

Monterra 1998 Chardonnay (Monterey) $9. 87 Best Buy *(9/1/2000)*

Monterra 2001 Merlot (Monterey County) $10. 84 *—S.H. (12/15/2004)*

Monterra 2000 Merlot (Monterey County) $13. 86 *(12/1/2002)*

Monterra 1997 Merlot (Monterey) $9. 85 Best Buy *(9/1/2000)*

Monterra 1996 Promise Merlot (Monterey) $10. 87 *(11/15/1999)*

Monterra 1999 Encore Red Blend (Monterey County) $20. 85 *(12/1/2002)*

Monterra 2001 Encore Rosé Blend (Monterey County) $18. 85 *(12/1/2002)*

Monterra 2002 Encore Dry Rosé Medley Rosé Blend (Monterey County) $18. 84 *—S.H. (6/1/2004)*

Monterra 1998 Sangiovese (Monterey) $9. 83 *(9/1/2000)*

Monterra 2004 Shiraz (Monterey County) $9. 84 *(9/1/2005)*

Monterra 2001 Syrah (Monterey County) $10. 83 *—S.H. (12/15/2004)*

Monterra 2000 Syrah (Monterey County) $13. 86 *(12/1/2002)*

Monterra 1998 Syrah (Monterey) $13. 84 *(10/1/2001)*

Monterra 1997 Syrah (Monterey) $9. 86 Best Buy *(9/1/2000)*

Monterra 2000 Encore White Blend (Monterey County) $18. 85 *(12/1/2002)*

Monterra 2002 San Bernabe Vineyard White Medley White Blend (Monterey County) $18. 85 *—S.H. (6/1/2004)*

Monterra 1998 Zinfandel (Monterey) $9. 82 *(9/1/2000)*

MONTES

Montes 1999 Montes Alpha Merlot (Santa Cruz County) $16. 85 *—D.T. (7/1/2002)*

MONTEVINA

Montevina 2003 Barbera (Amador County) $10. 83 *—S.H. (12/1/2005)*

Montevina 2001 Barbera (Amador County) $11. 88 Best Buy *—S.H. (6/1/2004)*

Montevina 1998 Barbera (Amador County) $12. 87 *—S.H. (11/15/2001)*

Montevina 1999 Terra d'Oro Barbera (Amador County) $18. 90 *—S.H. (2/1/2003)*

Montevina 1996 Terra d'Oro Barbera (Amador County) $18. 84 *—S.H. (10/1/1999)*

Montevina 2000 Terra d'Oro Barbera (Amador County) $15. 89 Editors' Choice *—S.H. (6/1/2004)*

Montevina 2000 Fumé Blanc (California) $7. 85 Best Buy *(8/1/2001)*

Montevina 2005 Terra d'Oro Moscato (California) $18. 85 *—S.H. (11/15/2006)*

Montevina 2000 Rosato Nebbiolo (Sierra Foothills) $8. 84 *—S.H. (11/15/2001)*

Montevina 2004 Pinot Grigio (California) $10. 84 Best Buy *—S.H. (12/1/2005)*

Montevina 2002 Pinot Grigio (California) $10. 85 *—M.S. (12/1/2003)*

Montevina 2001 Pinot Grigio (California) $10. 83 *—S.H. (9/1/2003)*

Montevina 2000 Pinot Grigio (California) $10. 86 *(8/1/2001)*

Montevina 2005 Terra d'Oro Pinot Grigio (Santa Barbara County) $18. 87 *—S.H. (11/1/2006)*

Montevina 2001 Freisa Red Blend (Amador County) $13. 86 —*S.H. (6/1/2004)*

Montevina 2005 Sierra Sunrise Rosé Blend (Amador County) $10. Dry and light-bodied, with a pleasant array of raspberry, tea and dried herb flavors. A little bitterness in the finish is a minor defect. **83** —*S.H. (7/1/2007)*

Montevina 1998 Sangiovese (Amador County) $12. 85 —*S.H. (9/1/2003)*

Montevina 1997 Sangiovese (Amador County) $12. 85 —*S.H. (11/1/1999)*

Montevina 2002 Terra d'Oro Sangiovese (Amador County) $NA. 83 —*S.H. (3/1/2006)*

Montevina 1998 Terra d'Oro Sangiovese (Amador County) $18. 83 —*S.H. (11/15/2001)*

Montevina 1996 Terra d'Oro Sangiovese (Amador County) $16. 86 —*S.H. (10/1/1999)*

Montevina 2001 Sauvignon Blanc (California) $10. 85 Best Buy —*S.H. (3/1/2003)*

Montevina 2002 Syrah (Amador County) $12. 85 *(9/1/2005)*

Montevina 2000 Syrah (Amador County) $10. 84 —*S.H. (6/1/2003)*

Montevina 1998 Syrah (Sierra Foothills) $18. 87 Editors' Choice *(8/1/2001)*

Montevina 2002 Terra d'Oro Syrah (Amador County) $20. 83 *(9/1/2005)*

Montevina 2000 Terra d'Oro Syrah (Amador County) $18. 85 —*S.H. (2/1/2004)*

Montevina 2001 Terra d'Oro Syrah (Amador County) $15. 89 —*S.H. (6/1/2004)*

Montevina 2002 Teroldego (Amador County) $16. 84 —*S.H. (4/1/2005)*

Montevina NV Zinfandel (Amador County) $15. 86 —*S.H. (9/12/2002)*

Montevina 2002 Zinfandel (Sierra Foothills) $10. 84 Best Buy —*S.H. (12/1/2005)*

Montevina 2001 Zinfandel (Sierra Foothills) $11. 86 —*S.H. (6/1/2004)*

Montevina 1999 Zinfandel (Amador County) $12. 88 Best Buy —*S.H. (11/15/2001)*

Montevina 1998 Zinfandel (Sierra Foothills) $10. 84 —*S.H. (12/1/2000)*

Montevina 1997 Zinfandel (Amador County) $10. 86 —*P.G. (11/15/1999)*

Montevina 2003 Deaver Vineyard 100 Year Old Vines Zinfandel (Amador County) $28. 90 —*S.H. (3/1/2006)*

Montevina 1998 SHR Field Blend Zinfandel (Sierra Foothills) $14. 87 *(8/1/2001)*

Montevina 2003 Terra d'Oro Zinfandel (Amador County) $18. 88 —*S.H. (3/1/2006)*

Montevina 2002 Terra d'Oro Zinfandel (Amador County) $18. 91 —*S.H. (3/1/2005)*

Montevina 1999 Terra d'Oro Zinfandel (Amador County) $18. 89 —*S.H. (2/1/2003)*

Montevina 1997 Terra d'Oro Zinfandel (Amador County) $16. 87 —*S.H. (12/1/2000)*

Montevina 1996 Terra d'Oro Zinfandel (Amador County) $16. 86 —*S.H. (9/1/1999)*

Montevina 2002 Terra d'Oro Deaver Vineyard 100 Year Old Vines Zinfandel (Amador County) $28. 90 —*S.H. (4/1/2005)*

Montevina 2003 Terra d'Oro Home Vineyard Zinfandel (Amador County) $25. 87 —*S.H. (6/1/2006)*

Montevina 2002 Terra d'Oro Home Vineyard Zinfandel (Amador County) $24. 85 —*S.H. (4/1/2005)*

Montevina 2001 Terra d'Oro Zinfandel (Amador County) $15. 84 —*S.H. (6/1/2004)*

Montevina 2001 Terra d'Oro Deaver Vineyard Old Vine Zinfandel (Amador County) $21. 89 —*S.H. (6/1/2004)*

Montevina 2000 Terra d'Oro School House Road Zinfandel (Amador County) $21. 90 —*S.H. (6/1/2004)*

Montevina 2000 Terra d'Oro Schook House Road Field Blend (Amador County) $24. 90 —*S.H. (3/1/2005)*

Montevina 1999 White Zinfandel (Amador County) $7. 83 —*S.H. (2/1/2001)*

MONTHAVEN

Monthaven 2001 Cabernet Sauvignon (Central Coast) $12. 84 —*S.H. (3/1/2004)*

Monthaven 2001 Coastal Merlot (Central Coast) $12. 84 —*S.H. (2/1/2004)*

Monthaven 2000 Pinot Noir (California) $10. 84 —*S.H. (7/1/2003)*

Monthaven 2000 Syrah (California) $10. 84 —*S.H. (12/15/2003)*

Monthaven 2000 Zinfandel (California) $10. 83 —*S.H. (9/1/2003)*

Monthaven 2001 Coastal Zinfandel (Central Coast) $8. 86 Best Buy *(11/1/2003)*

MONTICELLO

Monticello 2004 Tietjen Vineyard Cabernet Sauvignon (Napa Valley) $58. The Rutherford vineyard has been the source of well-regarded Cabs for Monticello and the '04 is the latest. Compact and ageworthy, it shows well-ripened blackberry, cherry and cola flavors that have been generously oaked. The tannins are firm and sticky now, suggesting development. Best 2008–2012. **92** —*S.H. (12/15/2007)*

Monticello 2003 Tietjen Vineyard Cabernet Sauvignon (Rutherford) $45. 90 —*S.H. (12/15/2006)*

Monticello 2005 Estate Chardonnay (Oak Knoll) $26. The '05 is a good wine, a little thin in peach and pineapple fruit, with a strong overlay of toasty, spice oak and a vanilla cream mouthfeel. **86** —*S.H. (7/1/2007)*

Monticello 2005 Estate Syrah (Oak Knoll) $38. For the past several years, Monticello has been quietly producing deliciously drinkable Syrahs. The '05 is rich in cassis, cherry, mocha, violet, leather and spicy flavors, wrapped into a smooth, velvety texture. **90** —*S.H. (12/15/2007)*

Monticello 2004 Estate Grown Syrah (Oak Knoll) $34. 91 —*S.H. (12/15/2006)*

MONTICELLO VINEYARDS

Monticello Vineyards 2000 Proprietary Bordeaux Blend (Napa Valley) $50. 91 —*S.H. (8/1/2003)*

Monticello Vineyards 1999 Corley Reserve Cabernet Sauvignon (Napa Valley) $85. 91 —*S.H. (2/1/2003)*

Monticello Vineyards 1997 Corley Reserve Cabernet Sauvignon (Napa Valley) $65. 91 *(11/1/2000)*

Monticello Vineyards 2001 Jefferson Cuvée Cabernet Sauvignon (Napa Valley) $34. 91 —*S.H. (2/1/2005)*

Monticello Vineyards 1999 Jefferson Cuvée Cabernet Sauvignon (Napa Valley) $34. 90 —*S.H. (2/1/2003)*

Monticello Vineyards 2002 Jefferson Cuvée Cabernet Sauvignon (Napa Valley) $34. 87 —*S.H. (12/15/2005)*

Monticello Vineyards 2001 Reserve Cabernet Sauvignon (Napa Valley) $75. 92 —*S.H. (2/1/2005)*

Monticello Vineyards 2002 Tietjen Vineyard Cabernet Sauvignon (Rutherford) $45. 90 —*S.H. (12/15/2005)*

Monticello Vineyards 2001 Tietjen Vineyard Cabernet Sauvignon (Rutherford) $45. 91 —*S.H. (10/1/2004)*

Monticello Vineyards 2000 Tietjen Vineyard Cabernet Sauvignon (Napa Valley) $50. 86 —*S.H. (2/1/2004)*

Monticello Vineyards 1999 Tietjen Vineyard Cabernet Sauvignon (Napa Valley) $55. 89 —*S.H. (12/31/2002)*

Monticello Vineyards 2001 Corley Reserve Chardonnay (Napa Valley) $50. 93 —*S.H. (8/1/2003)*

Monticello Vineyards 1999 Corley Reserve Chardonnay (Napa Valley) $40. 89 *(7/1/2001)*

Monticello Vineyards 1997 Corley Reserve Chardonnay (Napa Valley) $30. 88 *(6/1/2000)*

Monticello Vineyards 2003 Estate Chardonnay (Napa Valley) $26. 85 *(5/1/2005)*

Monticello Vineyards 2001 Home Ranch Vineyard Chardonnay (Napa Valley) $45. 92 —*S.H. (8/1/2003)*

Monticello Vineyards 1999 Merlot (Napa Valley) $30. 93 Editors' Choice —*S.H. (2/1/2003)*

Monticello Vineyards 2002 Estate Merlot (Napa Valley) $30. 85 —*S.H. (3/1/2005)*

Monticello Vineyards 1997 Corley Family Vineyards Pinot Noir (Napa Valley) $24. 87 *(12/15/1999)*

Monticello Vineyards 2002 Estate Pinot Noir (Napa Valley) $34. 90 —*S.H. (3/1/2005)*

Monticello Vineyards 2004 Estate Grown Pinot Noir (Oak Knoll) $34. 87 —*S.H. (12/1/2006)*

Monticello Vineyards 2003 Estate Grown Pinot Noir (Oak Knoll) $34. 86 —*S.H. (12/15/2005)*

Monticello Vineyards 2001 Proprietary Red Blend (Napa Valley) $50. 93 —*S.H. (2/1/2005)*

MONTINORE

Montinore 1999 Winemaker's Reserve Chardonnay (Willamette Valley) $18. 83 —*P.G. (2/1/2002)*

Montinore 2005 Gewürztraminer (Willamette Valley) $14. 85 —*P.G. (9/1/2006)*

Montinore 2004 Gewürztraminer (Willamette Valley) $9. 88 Best Buy —*P.G. (11/15/2005)*

Montinore 2003 Gewürztraminer (Willamette Valley) $9. 87 Best Buy —*P.G. (10/1/2004)*

Montinore 2000 Gewürztraminer (Willamette Valley) $9. 87 Best Buy —*P.G. (4/1/2002)*

Montinore 2001 Late Harvest Estate Bottled Gewürztraminer (Willamette Valley) $9. 87 Best Buy —*M.S. (8/1/2003)*

Montinore 2003 Müller-Thurgau (Willamette Valley) $12. 83 —*P.G. (11/15/2005)*

Montinore 2000 Müller-Thurgau (Willamette Valley) $7. 80 —*M.S. (8/1/2003)*

Montinore 2005 Pinot Gris (Willamette Valley) $14. 84 —*P.G. (9/1/2006)*

Montinore 2004 Pinot Gris (Willamette Valley) $10. 82 —*P.G. (11/15/2005)*

Montinore 2003 Pinot Gris (Willamette Valley) $10. 85 —*P.G. (10/1/2004)*

Montinore 2002 Pinot Gris (Willamette Valley) $10. 88 Best Buy —*P.G. (12/1/2003)*

Montinore 2001 Pinot Gris (Willamette Valley) $10. 88 Best Buy —*M.S. (8/1/2003)*

Montinore 2000 Pinot Gris (Willamette Valley) $10. 84 —*P.G. (4/1/2002)*

Montinore 2002 Entre Deux Pinot Gris (Willamette Valley) $14. 86 —*P.G. (12/1/2003)*

Montinore 2003 Pinot Noir (Willamette Valley) $14. 84 —*P.G. (11/15/2005)*

Montinore 2002 Pinot Noir (Willamette Valley) $13. 84 *(11/1/2004)*

Montinore 2001 Pinot Noir (Willamette Valley) $13. 86 —*P.G. (12/1/2003)*

Montinore 2000 Pinot Noir (Willamette Valley) $12. 82 *(10/1/2002)*

Montinore 1999 Pinot Noir (Willamette Valley) $13. 83 —*P.G. (4/1/2002)*

Montinore 2004 Graham's Block 7 Pinot Noir (Willamette Valley) $32. Funky, animal smells greet you, followed by bark, stem and root. Not a pretty nose by any means. The wine follows hard, tough, stemmy and chewy. It's hard to imagine a more charmless bottle in this price range. 83 —*P.G. (4/1/2007)*

Montinore 2003 Graham's Block 7 Pinot Noir (Willamette Valley) $32. 86 —*P.G. (12/1/2006)*

Montinore 2000 Graham's Block 7 Pinot Noir (Willamette Valley) $30. 89 —*P.G. (12/31/2002)*

Montinore 1999 Graham's Block 7 Pinot Noir (Willamette Valley) $30. 90 Cellar Selection —*P.G. (12/31/2001)*

Montinore 2004 Parson's Ridge Pinot Noir (Willamette Valley) $32. Many Oregon wineries made elegant, appealing wines in 2004, but the estate's unusual location does better in warmer years. This Parson's Ridge bottling is full of the dried herb and leaf scents that can dominate Oregon's less-fortunate vineyards, with some relief provided by the cinnamon and cocoa flavors from the barrel aging. But where's the fruit? 85 —*P.G. (4/1/2007)*

Montinore 2003 Parson's Ridge Pinot Noir (Willamette Valley) $32. 87 —*P.G. (12/1/2006)*

Montinore 2000 Parson's Ridge Vineyard Pinot Noir (Willamette Valley) $30. 87 —*P.G. (12/31/2002)*

Montinore 1999 Parson's Ridge Vineyard Pinot Noir (Willamette Valley) $30. 89 —*P.G. (12/31/2001)*

Montinore 1998 Pierce's Elbow Single Vineyard Pinot Noir (Willamette Valley) $35. 91 —*M.M. (11/1/2001)*

Montinore 2000 Pierce's Elbow Vineyard Pinot Noir (Willamette Valley) $30. 87 —*P.G. (12/31/2002)*

Montinore 1999 Pierce's Elbow Vineyard Pinot Noir (Willamette Valley) $30. 88 —*P.G. (12/31/2001)*

Montinore 2004 Winemaker's Reserve Pinot Noir (Willamette Valley) $21. 84 —*P.G. (12/1/2006)*

Montinore 2000 Winemaker's Reserve Pinot Noir (Willamette Valley) $19. 88 —*P.G. (12/31/2002)*

Montinore 1999 Winemaker's Reserve Pinot Noir (Willamette Valley) $19. 87 —*P.G. (12/31/2001)*

Montinore 2002 Winemaker's Reserve Pinot Noir (Willamette Valley) $19. 83 —*P.G. (11/15/2005)*

Montinore 2001 Late Harvest Riesling (Willamette Valley) $10. 87 —*J.C. (9/1/2003)*

Montinore 2005 Semi-Dry Riesling (Willamette Valley) $10. 87 Best Buy —*P.G. (9/1/2006)*

Montinore 2004 Semi-Dry Riesling (Willamette Valley) $9. 83 —*P.G. (11/15/2005)*

Montinore 2003 Semi-Dry Riesling (Willamette Valley) $9. 86 Best Buy —*P.G. (10/1/2004)*

Montinore 2001 Semi-Dry Estate Bottled Riesling (Willamette Valley) $9. 85 —*K.F. (12/31/2002)*

MONTONA

Montona 2000 Reserve Cabernet Sauvignon (Napa Valley) $50. 91 —*S.H. (5/1/2004)*

Montona 2000 Reserve Cabernet Sauvignon (Napa Valley) $50. 83 —*S.H. (12/1/2005)*

Montona 2002 Chardonnay (Napa Valley) $30. 87 —*S.H. (2/1/2004)*

Montona 2002 Chardonnay (Napa Valley) $30. 88 —*S.H. (12/1/2005)*

Montona 2001 Merlot (Napa Valley) $40. 83 —*S.H. (12/1/2005)*

Montona 2001 Merlot (Napa Valley) $40. 92 —*S.H. (5/1/2004)*

MONTPELLIER

Montpellier 2003 Merlot (California) $7. 84 Best Buy —*S.H. (12/1/2005)*

Montpellier 2001 Merlot (California) $7. 86 —*S.H. (9/1/2004)*

Montpellier 1997 Pinot Noir (California) $8. 83 *(5/1/2000)*

Montpellier 1999 Pinot Noir (California) $8. 83 *(10/1/2002)*

Montpellier 2003 Syrah (California) $7. 84 Best Buy *(9/1/2005)*

Montpellier 1999 Syrah (California) $7. 86 Best Buy *(10/1/2001)*

Montpellier 2002 Viognier (California) $7. 83 —*S.H. (10/1/2004)*

MOON MOUNTAIN VINEYARD

Moon Mountain Vineyard 2000 Cabernet Franc (Sonoma Valley) $30. 90 —*S.H. (5/1/2004)*

Moon Mountain Vineyard 2004 Cabernet Sauvignon (Sonoma County) $16. A nice, rich Cab that's a little jagged around the edges, but with rewarding fruit and a dry, complex finish. The blackberry, cherry, plum, coffee, licorice, soy and smoky vanilla flavors are deep and long. 87 —*S.H. (6/1/2007)*

Moon Mountain Vineyard 2003 Cabernet Sauvignon (Sonoma County) $16. 89 —*S.H. (4/1/2006)*

Moon Mountain Vineyard 2002 Reserve Cabernet Sauvignon (Sonoma Valley) $35. 92 Cellar Selection —*S.H. (4/1/2006)*

Moon Mountain Vineyard 2001 Reserve Cabernet Sauvignon (Sonoma Valley) $30. 84 —*S.H. (10/1/2005)*

Moon Mountain Vineyard 2000 Reserve Cabernet Sauvignon (Sonoma Valley) $40. 86 —*S.H. (5/1/2004)*

Moon Mountain Vineyard 2004 Chardonnay (Sonoma County) $13. 88 Best Buy —*S.H. (4/1/2006)*

Moon Mountain Vineyard 2005 Sauvignon Blanc (Sonoma County) $12. Made slightly sweet, this wine shows fresh, ripe citrus, melon and floral flavors that are offset by crisp, coastal-cool acidity, thanks to arresting malolactic fermentation. A touch of oak adds barrel complexities. 86 —*S.H. (6/1/2007)*

Moon Mountain Vineyard 2004 Sauvignon Blanc (Sonoma County) $13. 85 —*S.H. (3/1/2006)*

Moon Mountain Vineyard 2003 Vadasz Vineyard Sauvignon Blanc (Sonoma Valley) $20. 87 *(7/1/2005)*

Moon Mountain Vineyard 2002 Vadasz Vineyard Sauvignon Blanc (Sonoma Valley) $20. 87 —*S.H. (5/1/2004)*

Moon Mountain Vineyard 2002 Reserve Sémillon-Sauvignon Blanc (Edna Valley) $16. 84 —*S.H. (5/1/2004)*

Moon Mountain Vineyard 2003 Syrah (Sonoma Valley) $40. Easy to imagine drinking this with a really nice lamb dish or grilled steak. It has an upscale feeling, with a complex interplay of tannins and oak, and the flavors are long, lush and liqueur-like. However, it's soft, and not ageable. 90 —*S.H. (9/1/2007)*

Moon Mountain Vineyard 2005 Zinfandel (Dry Creek Valley) $30. The official alcohol is 14.9%, but the wine smells and tastes like a young harsh Port. In the mouth, it has a tight, sweet acid feel, rather medicinal. Not going anywhere, so drink up. 82 —*S.H. (9/1/2007)*

Moon Mountain Vineyard 2002 Monte Rosso Zinfandel (Sonoma Valley) $30. 92 —*S.H. (6/1/2004)*

MOOREWOOD

Moorewood 2001 Syrah (Monterey County) $19. 90 Editors' Choice —*S.H. (6/1/2004)*

MORGAN

Morgan 2004 Chardonnay (Monterey) $20. 87 —*S.H. (12/31/2005)*

Morgan 2003 Chardonnay (Monterey) $20. 90 —*S.H. (11/15/2005)*

Morgan 2002 Chardonnay (Monterey) $20. 84 —*S.H. (12/15/2004)*

Morgan 2000 Chardonnay (Monterey) $20. 88 —*J.M. (5/1/2002)*

Morgan 1999 Chardonnay (Monterey) $20. 89 —*S.H. (11/15/2001)*

Morgan 1998 Chardonnay (Monterey County) $20. 87 *(6/1/2000)*

Morgan 2001 Barrel Fermented Chardonnay (Monterey) $20. 90 Editors' Choice —*S.H. (2/1/2004)*

Morgan 2004 Double L Vineyard Chardonnay (Santa Lucia Highlands) $35. 92 —*S.H. (4/1/2006)*

Morgan 2003 Double L Vineyard Chardonnay (Santa Lucia Highlands) $35. 91 Cellar Selection —*S.H. (12/15/2005)*

Morgan 2002 Double L Vineyard Chardonnay (Santa Lucia Highlands) $34. 92 Editors' Choice —*S.H. (3/1/2005)*

Morgan 2001 Double L Vineyard Chardonnay (Santa Lucia Highlands) $30. 90 —*S.H. (2/1/2004)*

Morgan 2004 Double L Vineyard Hat Trick Chardonnay (Santa Lucia Highlands) $65. 95 Editors' Choice —*S.H. (12/1/2006)*

Morgan 2000 Double L Vineyard Chardonnay (Santa Lucia Highlands) $36. 88 —*J.M. (12/15/2002)*

Morgan 2003 Hat Trick Double L Vineyard Chardonnay (Santa Lucia Highlands) $50. 92 —*S.H. (12/15/2005)*

Morgan 2002 Hat Trick Double L Vineyard Chardonnay (Santa Lucia Highlands) $50. 96 Editors' Choice —*S.H. (5/1/2005)*

Morgan 2005 Highland Chardonnay (Santa Lucia Highlands) $25. This is a new bottling from Morgan, a junior version of their great Hat Trick Chardonnay. Most of the grapes come from the winery's Double L estate. The wine is bone dry, high in acidity, and compellingly complex. The dryness makes the lime zest and kiwi flavors star on their own, while new French oak adds a gorgeous layer of toasty cream. **92** —*S.H. (2/1/2007)*

Morgan 2006 Metallico Chardonnay (Monterey) $22. Juicy acids and rich flavors of limes, green melons, kiwi and papayas star in this dry, unoaked Chard. The acidity gives the wine an exceptionally clean, vibrant mouthfeel. **89** —*S.H. (12/15/2007)*

Morgan 2005 Metallico Chardonnay (Monterey) $20. 90 —*S.H. (11/15/2006)*

Morgan 2004 Metallico Chardonnay (Monterey) $20. 90 —*S.H. (11/15/2005)*

Morgan 2003 Metallico Chardonnay (Santa Lucia Highlands) $20. 86 —*S.H. (12/1/2004)*

Morgan 2002 Metallico Chardonnay (Santa Lucia Highlands) $20. 83 —*S.H. (12/1/2003)*

Morgan 2001 Metallico Chardonnay (Santa Lucia Highlands) $20. 87 —*S.H. (12/15/2002)*

Morgan 1999 Reserve Chardonnay (Monterey) $30. 86 *(7/1/2001)*

Morgan 1998 Reserve Chardonnay (Monterey) $30. 90 *(6/1/2000)*

Morgan 2004 Rosella's Vineyard Chardonnay (Santa Lucia Highlands) $35. 95 Editors' Choice —*S.H. (4/1/2006)*

Morgan 2003 Rosella's Vineyard Chardonnay (Santa Lucia Highlands) $35. 91 —*S.H. (12/15/2005)*

Morgan 2001 Rosella's Vineyard Chardonnay (Santa Lucia Highlands) $34. 91 —*S.H. (2/1/2004)*

Morgan 2000 Rosella's Vineyard Chardonnay (Santa Lucia Highlands) $34. 88 —*J.M. (12/15/2002)*

Morgan 2002 Rosella's Vineyard Chardonnay (Santa Lucia Highlands) $34. 91 —*S.H. (3/1/2005)*

Morgan 1998 Pinot Gris (Monterey) $18. 87 —*M.S. (3/1/2000)*

Morgan 2006 R&D Franscioni Vineyard Pinot Gris (Santa Lucia Highlands) $18. A example of a dry, crisp PG, this great white from Monterey pioneer Morgan bursts with juicy flavors of papayas, honeysuckle flowers, limes and pink grapefruits. High acidity makes the wine bright and zesty in the mouth. **89** —*S.H. (12/15/2007)*

Morgan 2005 R&D Franscioni Vineyard Pinot Gris (Santa Lucia Highlands) $16. 91 Editors' Choice —*S.H. (11/15/2006)*

Morgan 2004 R&D Franscioni Vineyard Pinot Gris (Santa Lucia Highlands) $16. 88 —*S.H. (11/15/2005)*

Morgan 2003 R&D Franscioni Vineyard Pinot Gris (Santa Lucia Highlands) $16. 85 —*S.H. (11/15/2004)*

Morgan 2002 R&D Franscioni Vineyard Pinot Gris (Santa Lucia Highlands) $16. 84 —*S.H. (12/1/2003)*

Morgan 2001 R&D Franscioni Vineyards Pinot Gris (Santa Lucia Highlands) $15. 84 —*S.H. (9/1/2003)*

Morgan 1997 Pinot Noir (Monterey County) $20. 84 *(11/15/1999)*

Morgan 2001 Pinot Noir (Santa Lucia Highlands) $22. 87 —*S.H. (4/1/2004)*

Morgan 2000 Pinot Noir (Santa Lucia Highlands) $22. 90 Editors' Choice —*S.H. (2/1/2003)*

Morgan 1999 Pinot Noir (Santa Lucia Highlands) $38. 88 —*J.M. (12/15/2001)*

Morgan 1999 Pinot Noir (Monterey) $24. 88 —*S.H. (12/15/2001)*

Morgan 1998 Pinot Noir (Monterey County) $21. 88 —*M.S. (5/1/2000)*

Morgan 2005 Double L Vineyard Pinot Noir (Santa Lucia Highlands) $55. From Dan Lee's personal vineyard, one of the coolest and most northerly in the appellation. Concentrated and intense, a dry, crisp wine of great depth and balance. The flavors of cherries, cranberries, raspberries, cola, root beer, red currants and spices detonate on the palate; the finish is fabulously long. **94** —*S.H. (10/1/2007)*

Morgan 2004 Double L Vineyard Pinot Noir (Santa Lucia Highlands) $55. 93 —*S.H. (8/1/2006)*

Morgan 2003 Double L Vineyard Pinot Noir (Santa Lucia Highlands) $50. 94 Editors' Choice —*S.H. (12/15/2005)*

Morgan 2002 Double L Vineyard Pinot Noir (Santa Lucia Highlands) $45. 92 —*S.H. (3/1/2005)*

Morgan 2001 Double L Vineyard Pinot Noir (Santa Lucia Highlands) $42. 92 —*S.H. (8/1/2004)*

Morgan 2000 Double L Vineyard Pinot Noir (Santa Lucia Highlands) $42. 92 Cellar Selection —*S.H. (7/1/2003)*

Morgan 2005 Garys' Vineyard Pinot Noir (Santa Lucia Highlands) $55. Located in the middle of the appellation, Garys' Vineyard wines often show a cool-warm combination of acidity and fruit-forwardness. This '05, from Pinot master Dan Morgan Lee, shows brisk, zesty, squeezed-from-the-lime acids that boost exceptionally ripe cherry, strawberry and cola flavors that finish utterly dry and spicy. It will probably hang in there for a decade, but seems best for its fresh youthfulness. **93** —*S.H. (10/1/2007)*

Morgan 2004 Garys' Vineyard Pinot Noir (Santa Lucia Highlands) $50. 92 —*S.H. (8/1/2006)*

Morgan 2003 Garys' Vineyard Pinot Noir (Santa Lucia Highlands) $45. 93 Editors' Choice—*S.H. (12/15/2005)*

Morgan 2002 Garys' Vineyard Pinot Noir (Santa Lucia Highlands) $38. 89 —*S.H. (3/1/2005)*

Morgan 2001 Garys' Vineyard Pinot Noir (Santa Lucia Highlands) $35. 93 —*S.H. (8/1/2004)*

Morgan 2000 Garys' Vineyard Pinot Noir (Santa Lucia Highlands) $38. 91 —*S.H. (7/1/2003)*

Morgan 1999 Reserve Pinot Noir (Santa Lucia Highlands) $38. 89 —*S.H. (12/15/2001)*

Morgan 2005 Rosella's Vineyard Pinot Noir (Santa Lucia Highlands) $55. Morgan's '05 Rosella's is a very fine and enjoyable Pinot, but it has a brittle, slightly unripe sharpness that defines its limits. The cherry, raspberry and mocha-cola flavors finish with an edge of spearmint. Drink now through 2009. **90** —*S.H. (10/1/2007)*

Morgan 2004 Rosella's Vineyard Pinot Noir (Santa Lucia Highlands) $50. 93 —*S.H. (8/1/2006)*

Morgan 2003 Rosella's Vineyard Pinot Noir (Santa Lucia Highlands) $45. 86 —*S.H. (12/15/2005)*

Morgan 2002 Rosella's Vineyard Pinot Noir (Santa Lucia Highlands) $38. 91 —*S.H. (3/1/2005)*

Morgan 2001 Rosella's Vineyard Pinot Noir (Santa Lucia Highlands) $35. 91 —*S.H. (8/1/2004)*

Morgan 2000 Rosella's Vineyard Pinot Noir (Santa Lucia Highlands) $38. 91 —*S.H. (7/1/2003)*

Morgan 2005 Tondré's Grapefield Pinot Noir (Santa Lucia Highlands) $55. This is not as good a Pinot as Morgan's Garys' Vineyard. The main problem is overripe fruit. The wine has a baked, almost burnt pie-filling quality. Hard to say why two Pinots grown so close together are so different, but that's terroir for you. **86** —*S.H. (10/1/2007)*

Morgan 2005 Twelve Clones Pinot Noir (Santa Lucia Highlands) $30. Kind of on the light side, but it shows the Highlands character of crispness, elegance, dryness and varietal purity. With its thinned-down cherry, cola and pomegranate flavors, it lets you put a Morgan Pinot Noir on your table for less than any of its other bottlings. **86** —*S.H. (9/1/2007)*

Morgan 2004 Twelve Clones Pinot Noir (Santa Lucia Highlands) $30. 91 —*S.H. (4/1/2006)*

Morgan 2003 Twelve Clones Pinot Noir (Santa Lucia Highlands) $25. 87 —*S.H. (11/15/2005)*

Morgan 2002 Twelve Clones Pinot Noir (Santa Lucia Highlands) $22. 87 *(11/1/2004)*

Morgan 2005 Cotes du Crow's Rhône Red Blend (Monterey) $18. This is Morgan's everyday, southern Rhône-style blend. Quality has varied over the years. The '05 is Grenache and Syrah. It's dry, full-bodied and simple, with cherry, blackberry and loganberry flavors that finish with a scour of astringent tannins. **84** —*S.H. (9/1/2007)*

Morgan 2001 Cotes du Crow's Red Blend (Monterey) $13. 85 —*S.H. (3/1/2004)*

Morgan 2004 Cotes du Crow's Rhône Red Blend (Monterey) $18. 84 —*S.H. (12/15/2006)*

Morgan 2003 Cotes du Crow's Rhône Red Blend (Monterey) $22. 89 Best Buy —*S.H. (11/15/2005)*

Morgan 2000 Cotes du Crow's Rhône Red Blend (California) $14. 86 —*S.H. (9/1/2002)*

Morgan 2006 Sauvignon Blanc (Monterey) $16. This Sauvignon Blanc comes from two areas, the Arroyo Seco, which is such a great home to dry whites, and the warmer San Lucas appellation. Blended with small amounts of the Musqué clone and Semillon, the wine is bone dry, refreshingly crisp, and a close approximation of the famous wines of New Zealand's Marlborough. The flavors, of gooseberries, limes, Meyer lemons, figs and wildflowers, are deep and impressively long-lasting. **90 Editors' Choice** —*S.H. (12/15/2007)*

Morgan 2005 Sauvignon Blanc (Monterey) $16. 85 —*S.H. (12/1/2006)*

Morgan 2004 Sauvignon Blanc (Monterey) $15. 87 —*S.H. (12/31/2005)*

Morgan 2003 Sauvignon Blanc (Monterey) $14. 89 Best Buy —*S.H. (11/15/2005)*

Morgan 2002 Sauvignon Blanc (Monterey County) $14. 87 —*J.M. (10/1/2004)*

Morgan 2001 Sauvignon Blanc (Monterey) $14. 88 —*S.H. (3/1/2003)*

Morgan 2000 Sauvignon Blanc (California) $15. 85 —*S.H. (11/15/2001)*

Morgan 1998 Sauvignon Blanc (California) $12. 88 —*M.S. (11/15/1999)*

Morgan 2005 Syrah (Monterey) $24. This is very good wine, showing total dryness, richness of tannins and herb-laden blackberry fruit. The tannins impress with their dry astringency, but the fruit is so rich and intense, the wine so balanced with acidity, that mid-term cellaring seems a good bet. Drink 2008–2011. **89** —*S.H. (12/15/2007)*

Morgan 2003 Syrah (Monterey) $22. 87 —*S.H. (11/15/2006)*

Morgan 2002 Syrah (Monterey) $22. 87 *(9/1/2005)*

Morgan 2001 Syrah (Monterey) $22. 85 —*S.H. (12/1/2004)*

Morgan 2000 Syrah (Monterey) $20. 87 —*S.H. (2/1/2003)*

Morgan 1997 Syrah (Monterey) $15. 87 —*S.H. (6/1/1999)*

Morgan 2004 Tierra Mar Syrah (Santa Lucia Highlands) $40. A big, thick, dry, tannic wine that suggests a young Saint-Joseph, without the acidity. There's a strong white pepper edge to the cassis, but the tannins are big-time. Give it until 2008, then drink in a narrow, two-year window. **90** —*S.H. (12/1/2007)*

Morgan 2003 Tierra Mar Syrah (Monterey County) $40. 87 —*S.H. (12/15/2006)*

Morgan 2002 Tierra Mar Syrah (Monterey County) $35. 89 *(9/1/2005)*

Morgan 2001 Tierra Mar Syrah (Santa Lucia Highlands) $35. 93 —*S.H. (7/1/2005)*

Morgan 2000 Tierra Mar Syrah (Santa Lucia Highlands) $35. 94 Editors' Choice —*S.H. (12/1/2003)*

Morgan 1999 Tierra Mar Syrah (Monterey) $52. 89 *(11/1/2001)*

MORRISON LANE

Morrison Lane 2003 Barbera (Walla Walla (WA)) $24. 90 —*P.G. (10/1/2006)*

Morrison Lane 2003 Cinsault (Walla Walla (WA)) $27. 88 —*P.G. (10/1/2006)*

Morrison Lane 2003 Counoise (Walla Walla (WA)) $33. 90 —*P.G. (10/1/2006)*

Morrison Lane 2003 33 1/3 Red Blend (Walla Walla (WA)) $33. 90 —*P.G. (10/1/2006)*

Morrison Lane 2003 Sangiovese (Walla Walla (WA)) $24. 88 —*P.G. (10/1/2006)*

Morrison Lane 2002 Syrah (Walla Walla (WA)) $NA. 86 *(9/1/2005)*

Morrison Lane 2002 Reserve Syrah (Walla Walla (WA)) $29. 86 *(9/1/2005)*

Morrison Lane 2002 Reserve Syrah (Walla Walla (WA)) $50. 90 —*P.G. (11/15/2006)*

MOSAIC

Mosaic 2002 Meritage Red Wine Cabernet Blend (Alexander Valley) $40. 84 —*S.H. (12/15/2006)*

Mosaic 2003 Reserve Cabernet Sauvignon (Alexander Valley) $40. 88 —*S.H. (12/15/2006)*

Mosaic 2004 Chardonnay (Sonoma County) $16. 86 —*S.H. (12/15/2006)*

Mosaic 2002 Reserve Chardonnay (Alexander Valley) $28. 90 —*S.H. (12/15/2006)*

Mosaic 2004 Malbec (Alexander Valley) $25. 90 —*S.H. (12/15/2006)*

Mosaic 2002 Merlot (Sonoma County) $20. 85 —*S.H. (12/15/2006)*

Mosaic 2004 Sauvignon Blanc (Sonoma County) $12. 86 —*S.H. (12/15/2006)*

Mosaic 2004 Reserve Sauvignon Blanc (Alexander Valley) $20. 88 —*S.H. (12/15/2006)*

MOSBY

Mosby 1997 Santa Barbara County Chardonnay (Santa Barbara County) $10. 85 —*S.H. (7/1/1999)*

Mosby 2006 Cortese (Santa Barbara County) $18. Crisp and fruity, this has fig, citrus, apricot and honeysuckle flavors. It seems sweeter than in the past, with a sugary finish, but the acidity helps a great deal to balance that out. **85** —*S.H. (12/31/2007)*

Mosby 2004 Cortese (Santa Barbara County) $16. 88 —*S.H. (5/1/2006)*

Mosby 2003 Cortese (Santa Barbara County) $14. 84 —*S.H. (12/1/2005)*

Mosby 2002 Cortese (Santa Barbara County) $14. 85 —*S.H. (3/1/2004)*

Mosby 2004 Stelline di Cortese Cortese (Santa Barbara County) $16. 82 —*S.H. (4/1/2006)*

Mosby 2005 Dolcetto (Santa Barbara County) $20. This is one of Mosby's specialties. As in previous years, it's rustic, showing high acidity behind the cherry and red licorice flavors, as well as a sugary sweetness on the finish. **83** —*S.H. (12/31/2007)*

Mosby 2004 Dolcetto (Santa Barbara County) $18. Smells inviting, with a lush, drink-me cherry, blackberry and spice richness, but then turns harsh in the mouth, with high acidity and a dry herbal quality. Cheese, olive oil and beef will soften and sweeten it. **84** —*S.H. (3/1/2007)*

Mosby 2002 Dolcetto (Santa Barbara County) $16. 85 —*S.H. (12/1/2005)*

Mosby 2002 La Seduzione Lagrein (California) $26. 86 —*S.H. (10/1/2005)*

Mosby 1994 Rosso di Nebbiolo Nebbiolo (Santa Barbara County) $10. 86 Best Buy —*S.H. (10/1/1999)*

Mosby 2006 Pinot Grigio (Santa Barbara County) $18. Dry and acidic, this has thin flavors of pink grapefruit juice and limes. It's not terribly complicated, but it's a clean, refreshing cocktail-style wine. Nice with grilled veggies or garlicky bruschetta with olive tapenade. **84** —*S.H. (11/1/2007)*

Mosby 2005 Pinot Grigio (Santa Barbara) $14. 85 —*S.H. (12/1/2006)*

Mosby 2004 Pinot Grigio (Santa Barbara County) $14. 82 —*S.H. (2/1/2006)*

Mosby 2003 Pinot Grigio (Santa Barbara County) $14. 84 —*S.H. (11/15/2004)*

Mosby 2002 Pinot Grigio (Santa Barbara County) $14. 84 —*S.H. (12/1/2003)*

Mosby 1998 Pinot Grigio (Santa Barbara County) $14. 83 —*S.H. (3/1/2000)*

Mosby 1997 Pinot Grigio (Santa Barbara County) $10. 88 Best Buy —*S.H. (10/1/1999)*

Mosby 2003 Primitivo (Monterey County) $20. 82 —*S.H. (12/1/2005)*

Mosby 2003 La Seduzione French Camp Vineyard Red Blend (California) $26. The variety is Lagrein, an Italian grape. The wine tastes "Italian" in the sense of having very high acidity and extreme dryness. There are cherries, but earthier: balsamic-splashed grilled Portebellos and a hint of tamari. This is a good, interesting wine that needs good food. **88** —*S.H. (3/1/2007)*

Mosby NV Lucca Red Wine Red Blend (California) $10. 83 —*S.H. (10/1/2006)*

Mosby NV Roc Michel Fremir Vineyards Rhone Varietal Blend Rhône Red Blend (Monterey County) $22. So soft and ripe; tastes as sweet as a raspberry tart, with melted milk chocolate, a splash of cassis and dusting of toasted coconut and cinnamon sugar. Tastes great, though not really a dry table wine in the classic sense. Syrah and Mourvèdre. **85** —*S.H. (7/1/2007)*

Mosby 2001 Roc Michel Red Blend (Monterey County) $18. 82 —*S.H. (3/1/2005)*

Mosby 2000 Roc Michel Fremir Rhône Red Blend (Monterey County) $18. 87 —*S.H. (3/1/2004)*

Mosby 2003 Sangiovese (Santa Barbara County) $22. 82 —*S.H. (12/1/2005)*

Mosby 1995 Sangiovese (Santa Barbara County) $16. 90 —*S.H. (10/1/1999)*

Mosby 2005 Rosato di Sangiovese (Santa Barbara County) $18. 86 —*S.H. (12/1/2006)*

Mosby 2004 Rosato di Sangiovese Sangiovese (Santa Barbara County) $14. 85 —*S.H. (10/1/2005)*

Mosby 2004 Vigna Della Casa Vecchia Sangiovese (Santa Barbara County) $26. Tough and common, with rasping acidity and sandpapery tannins framing cherry flavors. Drink now. **84** —*S.H. (11/1/2007)*

Mosby 1996 Vigna della Casa Vecchia Sangiovese (Santa Barbara County) $18. 88 —*S.H. (12/15/1999)*

Mosby 2005 Teroldego (Santa Barbara County) $30. Dark, bone dry, and acidic, although not particularly tannic, with bitter cherry and blackberry flavors. **84** —*S.H. (11/1/2007)*

Mosby 2004 Teroldego (Santa Barbara County) $26. 81 —*S.H. (4/1/2006)*

Mosby 2003 Teroldego (Santa Barbara County) $26. 86 —*S.H. (10/1/2005)*

Mosby 2002 Teroldego (Santa Barbara County) $24. 82 —*S.H. (3/1/2005)*

Mosby 2005 Traminer (Santa Barbara County) $18. 82 —*S.H. (10/1/2006)*

Mosby 2004 Traminer (Santa Barbara County) $18. 82 *S.H. (12/1/2005)*

Mosby 2003 Traminer (Santa Barbara County) $16. 85 —*S.H. (12/1/2004)*

Mosby 2002 Traminer (Santa Barbara County) $16. 86 —*S.H. (2/1/2004)*

MOSER SCHARDING

Moser Scharding 2004 Pinot Noir (Sonoma Valley) $35. Delicate and sweet, with candied cherry, raspberry and carob flavors. Tasty enough, but seriously lacks the acidity to make this fruity wine come alive. From Cartlidge & Browne. **83** —*S.H. (10/1/2007)*

MOSHIN

Moshin 2004 Clone 115 Pinot Noir (Russian River Valley) $45. 87 —*S.H. (12/1/2006)*

Moshin 2005 Estate Pinot Noir (Russian River Valley) $30. Kind of harsh, with green, searing acidity. The wine is fully dry and silky, with decent cherry and spice flavors, but it has that cutting quality. **83** —*S.H. (8/1/2007)*

Moshin 2005 Lot 4 Selection Pinot Noir (Russian River Valley) $38. Really young now, this vineyard block bottling needs a little time to come into its own. Tasted in February, a combination of acidity and bottle shock has made it brittle. But it's a very good wine, deliciously flavored, with a medium-bodied silkiness and Pinot's exotic sensuality. **88** —*S.H. (8/1/2007)*

MOTIF

Motif NV Classic Champagne Blend (California) $8. 83 —*S.H. (6/1/2001)*

MOUNT AUKUM

Mount Aukum 2003 Syrah (El Dorado) $16. 85 *(9/1/2005)*

Mount Aukum 2003 Syrah (Fair Play) $26. 85 *(9/1/2005)*

MOUNT EDEN

Mount Eden 2000 Cabernet Sauvignon (Santa Cruz Mountains) $30. 87 —*S.H. (8/1/2003)*

Mount Eden 2002 Cuvée Saratoga Cabernet Sauvignon (Santa Cruz Mountains) $24. 87 —*S.H. (9/1/2006)*

Mount Eden 2002 Estate Cabernet Sauvignon (Santa Cruz Mountains) $37. **93 Editors' Choice** —*S.H. (9/1/2006)*

Mount Eden 2001 Estate Cabernet Sauvignon (Santa Cruz Mountains) $35. 90 —*S.H. (6/1/2005)*

Mount Eden 2000 Old Vine Reserve Cabernet Sauvignon (Santa Cruz Mountains) $55. 91 —*S.H. (5/1/2004)*

Mount Eden 1999 Old Vine Reserve Cabernet Sauvignon (Santa Cruz Mountains) $55. **92 Cellar Selection** —*S.H. (8/1/2003)*

Mount Eden 2002 Chardonnay (Santa Cruz Mountains) $35. 90 —*S.H. (9/1/2006)*

Mount Eden 2001 Chardonnay (Santa Cruz Mountains) $35. 90 —*S.H. (9/1/2006)*

Mount Eden 2000 Chardonnay (Santa Cruz Mountains) $45. 92 —*S.H. (5/1/2004)*

Mount Eden 1999 Chardonnay (Santa Cruz Mountains) $45. **94 Editors' Choice** —*S.H. (2/1/2003)*

Mount Eden 1998 Cottonwood Canyon Vineyard Chardonnay (Santa Maria Valley) $18. 90 *(6/1/2000)*

Mount Eden 2003 Estate Bottled Chardonnay (Santa Cruz Mountains) $38. The mountain vineyard somehow manages not only to beautifully ripen the grapes to a great expression of fruit, but also preserves vital acidity and lends a firm layer of minerality. The result is a big, powerful wine that easily absorbs its lavish coat of new oak. The flavors are of candied pineapple tart, Meyer lemon mousse and vanilla custard, with a finish of sweet, crushed Asian spices. Perfect now, and just beginning to gather momentum. Drink through 2011, at least, with proper cellaring. **95 Editors' Choice** —*S.H. (10/1/2007)*

Mount Eden 1998 Mac Gregor Vineyard Chardonnay (Edna Valley) $18. 87 *(6/1/2000)*

Mount Eden 2001 MacGregor Vineyard Chardonnay (Edna Valley) $16. 85 —*S.H. (5/1/2004)*

Mount Eden 2000 MacGregor Vineyard Chardonnay (Edna Valley) $18. 91 —*S.H. (2/1/2003)*

Mount Eden 2001 West Slope Edna Ranch Chardonnay (Edna Valley) $12. **87 Best Buy** —*S.H. (9/1/2003)*

Mount Eden 2005 Wolff Vineyard Chardonnay (Edna Valley) $18. Brisk and ripe, this Chard, from a cool region on San Luis Obispo, shows a classic profile of pure kiwi and lime fruit flavor. A layer of oak adds caramel, butterscotch and vanilla flavors. It all finishes in a long, spicy swirl of orange blossom honey. **88** —*S.H. (10/1/2007)*

Mount Eden 2004 Wolff Vineyard Chardonnay (Edna Valley) $17. This deeply-flavored Chard comes from one of the coolest growing areas in California, and in this warm vintage, the grapes are perfectly ripe. They brim with white peach, pineapple, vanilla custard, tangerine and kiwi flavors, heightened and brightened with crisp acidity. **88** —*S.H. (4/1/2007)*

Mount Eden 2003 Wolff Vineyard Chardonnay (Edna Valley) $17. 86 —*S.H. (8/1/2006)*

Mount Eden 2002 Wolff Vineyard Chardonnay (Edna Valley) $17. 82 —*S.H. (6/1/2005)*

Mount Eden 2002 Pinot Noir (Santa Cruz Mountains) $35. **91 Cellar Selection** —*S.H. (9/1/2006)*

Mount Eden 2001 Pinot Noir (Santa Cruz Mountains) $35. 90 —*S.H. (6/1/2005)*

Mount Eden 1999 Pinot Noir (Santa Cruz Mountains) $45. **92 Editors' Choice** *(10/1/2002)*

Mount Eden 2003 Estate Pinot Noir (Santa Cruz Mountains) $35. Even though this is really good now, it's an ager. It has that raw grapesap, acidic, too-young quality that makes it mere potential. But what potential! With loads of cherries and black raspberries, terrific balance and dryness, and a gorgeously silky texture, it should open by mid-2007 and drink well through 2010. **92 Cellar Selection** —*S.H. (4/1/2007)*

Mount Eden 2000 Estate Pinot Noir (Santa Cruz Mountains) $45. 85 —*S.H. (5/1/2004)*

MOUNT PALOMAR

Mount Palomar 1999 Meritage (Temecula) $18. 89 —*S.H. (11/15/2002)*

Mount Palomar 1997 Meritage (Temecula) $16. 90 —*S.H. (4/1/2002)*

Mount Palomar NV Limited Reserve Port (California) $28. 90 —*S.H. (9/12/2002)*

Mount Palomar 2000 Shorty's Bistro Red Red Blend (Temecula) $12. **86 Best Buy** —*S.H. (12/1/2002)*

Mount Palomar 2001 Riesling (Temecula) $9. 83 —*S.H. (12/31/2003)*

Mount Palomar 1999 Syrah (Temecula) $16. 84 —*S.H. (7/1/2002)*

MOUNT PLEASANT WINERY

Mount Pleasant Winery 2004 Church Vineyard Cabernet Sauvignon (Augusta) $40. Bluffs along the Missouri River help to create a more temperate climate for the three valleys that comprise the Augusta appellation—this wine's home. It has a heady nose of cedar, cherry, tobacco and mint, and there's a berry balance on the palate, but the flavors do not extend much beyond the cherry blast. **82** —*S.K. (2/1/2007)*

Mount Pleasant Winery NV Bartolucci Vineyard Chardonnay (Augusta) $20. Can a wine have a personality complex? Citrus and cream duke it out with this Chardonnay from Missouri, and while there's an appealing nose of toasted oak, on the palate, the Chardonnay is angular and lacks body. Despite the lack of balance, elements of the wine are appealing and it will be enjoyable if paired with chicken or fish. **83** —*S.K. (7/1/2007)*

Mount Pleasant Winery 2004 Merlot (Augusta) $30. This oak-driven selection from Missouri producer Mount Pleasant is comprised of bare-bones Merlot flavors—plum, clove, coffee—but a bland character and weak structure do little to make an impact. There's no backbone here, and the oak overrides any attribute. **81** —*S.K. (2/1/2007)*

Mount Pleasant Winery 2003 Brut Imperial Sparkling Blend (Augusta) $16. 83 —*J.C. (6/1/2005)*

MOUNT ST. HELENA

Mount St. Helena 2003 Cabernet Sauvignon (Napa Valley) $25. This is a tough wine to love. It's dry and tannic and there's a gritty, jagged mouthfeel, the kind of old-fashioned Cab that used to be undrinkable without time in the cellar. But this doesn't seem to be ageable. **83** —*S.H. (4/1/2007)*

Mount St. Helena 2002 Cabernet Sauvignon (Napa Valley) $25. 85 —*S.H. (8/1/2005)*

Mount St. Helena 2003 Rose of Charbono (Napa Valley) $16. 81 —*S.H. (11/1/2005)*

Mount St. Helena 2003 Sauvignon Blanc (Napa Valley) $16. 88 —*S.H. (10/1/2005)*

Mount St. Helena 2003 Sauvignon Blanc (Napa Valley) $16. 84 —*S.H. (11/1/2005)*

MOUNT TAMALPAIS

Mount Tamalpais 2004 Merlot (Marin County) $25. Tannic, dry and rustic, this Merlot offers simple grapy, berry flavors. It's from the county just north of the Golden Gate that's making a name for Burgundian and Alsatian varieties, but not for Bordeaux. **83** —*S.H. (12/1/2007)*

Mount Tamalpais 1999 Merlot (Marin County) $23. 88 —*J.M. (7/1/2002)*

Mount Tamalpais 2006 Vin Gris Rosé Blend (Marin County) $18. This is a very interesting rosé from just north of the Golden Gate. It smells as candy-jammy as a pack of LifeSavers, then turns acidically tart in the mouth, with bright, juicy flavors of fresh raspberries and cherries. Loads of fun on its own, or with bouillabaisse, baked ham, gravlax. **90 Editors' Choice** —*S.H. (11/1/2007)*

MOUNT VEEDER

Mount Veeder 2003 Reserve Bordeaux Blend (Napa Valley) $80. As good as the winery's '03 Cab was, this is even better. It's almost all Cabernet Sauvignon, with a few drops of other Bordeaux varieties, and is so long, rich and deep in flavor, it just has to cellar well. The tannins currently star, and they're tough and gritty, but six or more years will start to melt them, leaving behind pure, sweet black fruit. **94 Cellar Selection** —*S.H. (7/1/2007)*

Mount Veeder 1995 Reserve Bordeaux Blend (Mount Veeder) $50. 92 *(11/1/1999)*

Mount Veeder 2002 Reserve Cabernet Blend (Napa Valley) $80. 84 —*S.H. (7/1/2006)*

Mount Veeder 2001 Reserve Cabernet Blend (Mount Veeder) $80. 95 Cellar Selection —*S.H. (10/1/2005)*

Mount Veeder 2004 Cabernet Sauvignon (Napa Valley) $40. Shows a finely tannic and crisply acidic mouthfeel that brings great structure, and very ripe black currant, cassis and cherry flavors. But the drawback is a jellied sweetness that leaves behind a sugary aftertaste. **84** —*S.H. (12/1/2007)*

Mount Veeder 2003 Cabernet Sauvignon (Napa Valley) $40. 91 —*S.H. (12/15/2006)*

Mount Veeder 2001 Cabernet Sauvignon (Napa Valley) $40. 91 —*S.H. (10/1/2004)*

Mount Veeder 2000 Cabernet Sauvignon (Napa Valley) $40. 89 —*S.H. (11/15/2003)*

MOUNTAIN DOME

Mountain Dome NV Brut Champagne Blend (Columbia Valley (OR)) $15. 86 —*P.G. (12/31/2004)*

Mountain Dome NV Brut Sparkling Blend (Washington) $16. 87 —*P.G. (4/1/2006)*

Mountain Dome 1998 Brut Sparkling Blend (Washington) $20. 88 —*P.G. (4/1/2006)*

Mountain Dome 1997 Brut Sparkling Blend (Washington) $26. 84 —*P.G. (12/1/2003)*

Mountain Dome NV Brut Rosé Sparkling Blend (Washington) $26. 86 —*P.G. (12/1/2003)*

Mountain Dome NV Cuvée Forté Sparkling Blend (Washington) $30. 90 —*P.G. (4/1/2006)*

Mountain Dome NV Rosé Sparkling Blend (Washington) $24. 88 —*P.G. (4/1/2006)*

MOUNTAIN GATE

Mountain Gate NV Red Wine Red Blend (Lodi) $22. 83 —*S.H. (3/1/2005)*

MOUNTAIN VIEW

Mountain View 2004 Chardonnay (Monterey) $7. 85 Best Buy —*S.H. (3/1/2006)*

Mountain View 1997 Pinot Noir (California) $8. 83 *(11/15/1999)*

Mountain View 1996 Zinfandel (California) $7. 82 —*J.C. (5/1/2000)*

Mountain View 2002 Clockspring Vineyard Zinfandel (Amador County) $10. 84 —*S.H. (3/1/2006)*

MT. VERNON

Mt. Vernon 2000 Cabernet Sauvignon (Sierra Foothills) $28. 84 —*S.H. (8/1/2003)*

MUELLER

Mueller 2004 Emily's Cuvée Pinot Noir (Russian River Valley) $38. 88 —*S.H. (12/1/2006)*

MUIRWOOD

Muirwood 2001 Syrah (Monterey) $11. 85 —*S.H. (6/1/2005)*

MUMM CUVÉE NAPA

Mumm Cuvée Napa NV Blanc de Blancs Champagne Blend (Napa Valley) $22. 86 —*S.H. (12/15/2000)*

Mumm Cuvée Napa 1997 Blanc de Blancs Champagne Blend (Napa Valley) $22. 88 —*S.H. (12/1/2002)*

Mumm Cuvée Napa NV Blanc de Noirs Champagne Blend (Napa Valley) $18. 89 —*S.H. (12/31/2004)*

Mumm Cuvée Napa NV Brut Prestige Champagne Blend (Napa Valley) $18. 87 —*S.H. (12/31/2004)*

Mumm Cuvée Napa NV Cuvée M Champagne Blend (Napa Valley) $18. 87 —*S.H. (12/31/2004)*

Mumm Cuvée Napa 1998 DVX Champagne Blend (Napa Valley) $45. 92 —*S.H. (12/31/2004)*

Mumm Cuvée Napa 1996 DVX Champagne Blend (Napa Valley) $50. 89 —*P.G. (12/15/2000)*

Mumm Cuvée Napa NV XXV Anniversary Reserve Brut Champagne Blend (Napa Valley) $25. 87 —*S.H. (12/31/2004)*

Mumm Cuvée Napa 1998 Blanc de Blancs Champagne Blend (Napa Valley) $22. 85 —*S.H. (12/1/2003)*

Mumm Cuvée Napa NV Blanc de Noirs Champagne Blend (Napa Valley) $18. 87 —*S.H. (12/31/2005)*

Mumm Cuvée Napa NV Brut Prestige Champagne Blend (Napa Valley) $18. 86 —*S.H. (12/31/2005)*

Mumm Cuvée Napa NV Cuvée M Champagne Blend (Napa Valley) $18. 87 —*S.H. (12/31/2005)*

Mumm Cuvée Napa 1997 DVX Champagne Blend (Napa Valley) $45. 91 —*S.H. (12/1/2003)*

Mumm Cuvée Napa NV Reserve Brut Champagne Blend (Napa Valley) $25. 89 —*S.H. (12/31/2005)*

MUMM NAPA

Mumm Napa 2002 Blanc de Blancs Sparkling Blend (Napa Valley) $26. Made from Chardonnay and Pinot Gris, this is fine and delicate, with citrus, flower, vanilla, smoke and doughy yeast flavors that finish crisp and dry. Drink now. **87** —*S.H. (12/31/2007)*

Mumm Napa 2001 Blanc de Blancs Sparkling Blend (Napa Valley) $25. 92 Editors' Choice —*S.H. (12/31/2006)*

Mumm Napa NV Blanc de Noirs Sparkling Blend (Napa Valley) $19. Mostly Pinot Noir with some Chardonnay, this bubbly shows the pedigree of these two noble varieties in its balance and elegance. It has rich Champagne-like flavors of smoke, brioche, raspberry, lime and vanilla, and finishes dry and polished. This is a great price for a sparkling wine of this quality and sophistication. **90 Editors' Choice** —*S.H. (12/31/2007)*

Mumm Napa NV Blanc de Noirs Sparkling Blend (Napa Valley) $19. Mainly Pinot Noir, with 15% Chardonnay, this pale pink bubbly is impressive for ripe raspberry-cherry flavors, with a polished edge of bread dough and smoky vanilla. It's quite a delicious rosé sparkler, finishing dry and elegant. **89** —*S.H. (7/1/2007)*

Mumm Napa NV Blanc de Noirs Sparkling Blend (Napa Valley) $18. 87 —*S.H. (12/31/2006)*

Mumm Napa NV Brut Prestige Sparkling Blend (Napa Valley) $19. A solid brut from Mumm Napa, this Pinot-Chardonnay blend is a little rough around the edges, but has the dry, bubbly finesse of a true Champagne-style wine. It shows peach, lime and strawberry flavors. **87** —*S.H. (12/31/2007)*

Mumm Napa NV Brut Prestige Sparkling Blend (Napa Valley) $18. 87 —*S.H. (12/31/2006)*

Mumm Napa NV Cuvée M Sparkling Blend (Napa Valley) $15. This is the winery's sweet sparkling wine. It has the elegant structure, fine acidity and forward raspberry, strawberry, lime, vanilla and smoke flavors of the dry bruts, with a sugary finish, for those who like their bubblies on the sweet side. 86 —*S.H. (12/31/2007)*

Mumm Napa NV Cuvée M Sparkling Blend (Napa Valley) $18. 84 —*S.H. (12/31/2006)*

Mumm Napa 2000 DVX Sparkling Blend (Napa Valley) $55. An hommage to the winery's late, great winemaker, Guy Devaux, Mumm's vintage-dated DVX is their tête de cuvée, a selection of the finest lots of grapes which are then given white glove treatment. The 2000 is a worthy successor to its predecessors, rich, smooth and dramatic. It has the silky finesse of great Champagne, with charming lime, raspberry, vanilla and smoky dough flavors. Should age well. Drink now–2010. 94 —*S.H. (12/31/2007)*

Mumm Napa 1999 DVX Sparkling Blend (Napa Valley) $45. 93 —*S.H. (12/31/2006)*

Mumm Napa 2001 DVX Rosé Sparkling Blend (Napa Valley) $65. Delicious sparkling wine, dry, crisp and elegant. The bubbles are really tiny, giving the wine a silky mouthfeel, while the flavors are forward in raspberries and cherries, with a yeasty tang. As dry as the wine is, it shows a rich vein of honey on the finish. Drink now through 2010. 94 Editors' Choice —*S.H. (10/1/2007)*

Mumm Napa 2001 Grand Année Sparkling Blend (Napa Valley) $30. A brut-style Pinot Noir and Chardonnay blend, this sparkler is really good, and easily worth its relatively modest cost. It drinks rich and fine, with an elegant, dry structure framing complex, honeyed flavors of strawberries, limes, vanilla, leesy yeast and smoke. Will easily stand aging through 2010. 92 Editors' Choice —*S.H. (12/31/2007)*

Mumm Napa NV Reserve Brut Sparkling Blend (Napa Valley) $26. Rewards for its rich Champagne personality and California expression of fruity flavor. Although the texture could be a bit smoother, the wine has a fine mousse, with complex, subtle flavors of strawberries, limes, vanilla, yeasty dough and wood smoke. 90 —*S.H. (12/31/2007)*

Mumm Napa NV Reserve Brut Sparkling Blend (Napa Valley) $25. 91 —*S.H. (12/31/2006)*

MURPHY-GOODE

Murphy-Goode 2002 Wild Card Claret Bordeaux Blend (Alexander Valley) $19. 85 —*S.H. (2/1/2005)*

Murphy-Goode 2001 Wild Card Claret Bordeaux Blend (Alexander Valley) $19. 86 —*S.H. (8/1/2004)*

Murphy-Goode 2000 Wild Card Claret Bordeaux Blend (Alexander Valley) $19. 90 —*S.H. (11/15/2002)*

Murphy-Goode 2003 All In Claret Cabernet Blend (Alexander Valley) $45. 80 —*S.H. (7/1/2006)*

Murphy-Goode 2003 Wild Card Claret Cabernet Blend (Alexander Valley) $20. 81 —*S.H. (7/1/2006)*

Murphy-Goode 2003 Cabernet Sauvignon (Alexander Valley) $24. This is a good, regional Cabernet, juicy in blackberry and cherry flavors, with a nice little kiss of oak. It's not complicated and doesn't pretend to be. 84 —*S.H. (7/1/2007)*

Murphy-Goode 2002 Cabernet Sauvignon (Alexander Valley) $24. 83 —*S.H. (2/1/2006)*

Murphy-Goode 2001 Cabernet Sauvignon (Alexander Valley) $22. 85 —*S.H. (8/1/2004)*

Murphy-Goode 2000 Cabernet Sauvignon (Alexander Valley) $22. 91 Editors' Choice —*S.H. (8/1/2003)*

Murphy-Goode 1999 Cabernet Sauvignon (Alexander Valley) $22. 90 Editors' Choice —*S.H. (12/1/2001)*

Murphy-Goode 2002 Adams Knoll Cabernet Sauvignon (Alexander Valley) $35. 90 Cellar Selection —*S.H. (3/1/2006)*

Murphy-Goode 1998 Brenda Block Reserve Cabernet Sauvignon (Alexander Valley) $55. 87 —*J.M. (12/1/2001)*

Murphy-Goode 1999 Goode-Ready Cabernet Sauvignon (Alexander Valley) $18. 85 —*S.H. (11/15/2001)*

Murphy-Goode 2002 Sarah Block Murphy Ranch Cabernet Sauvignon (Alexander Valley) $35. 87 —*S.H. (3/1/2006)*

Murphy-Goode 2001 Sarah Block Murphy Ranch Cabernet Sauvignon (Alexander Valley) $40. 87 *(10/1/2005)*

Murphy-Goode 1997 Sarah Block Swan Song Reserve Cabernet Sauvignon (Sonoma County) $39. 90 *(11/1/2000)*

Murphy-Goode 2002 Terra A Lago #4 Cabernet Sauvignon (Alexander Valley) $45. 92 Cellar Selection —*S.H. (3/1/2006)*

Murphy-Goode 2005 Chardonnay (Sonoma County) $15. Good everyday Chard, a little rustic and sweet, but with pleasant apricot, pineapple zest, peaches and cream and spicy flavors. 84 —*S.H. (7/1/2007)*

Murphy-Goode 2002 Chardonnay (Sonoma County) $15. 90 Best Buy —*S.H. (11/1/2005)*

Murphy-Goode 2001 Chardonnay (Sonoma County) $15. 87 —*S.H. (5/1/2004)*

Murphy-Goode 2000 Chardonnay (Sonoma County) $15. 86 —*J.M. (5/1/2002)*

Murphy-Goode 1999 Chardonnay (Sonoma County) $15. 88 Best Buy —*J.M. (11/15/2001)*

Murphy-Goode 1998 Barrel-Fermented Chardonnay (Sonoma County) $15. 89 *(6/1/2000)*

Murphy-Goode 2005 Island Block Chardonnay (Alexander Valley) $24. There's something about this single-vineyard Chard that almost always satisfies in every vintage. It's so balanced, with dependably ripe fruit offset by crisp acidity, and the oak seems just right. The '05 is deeply flavored in pineapple, peach, mango and butterscotch, with a long, spicy finish. 89 —*S.H. (7/1/2007)*

Murphy-Goode 2003 Island Block Chardonnay (Alexander Valley) $19. 91 Editors' Choice —*S.H. (7/1/2006)*

Murphy-Goode 2002 Island Block Chardonnay (Alexander Valley) $19. 87 —*S.H. (11/1/2005)*

Murphy-Goode 2000 Island Block Estate Chardonnay (Alexander Valley) $21. 86 —*S.H. (6/1/2003)*

Murphy-Goode 1999 Island Block Reserve Chardonnay (Alexander Valley) $21. 87 —*J.M. (12/1/2001)*

Murphy-Goode 2002 Fumé Blanc (Sonoma County) $12. 84 —*S.H. (12/1/2004)*

Murphy-Goode 2001 Fumé Blanc (Sonoma County) $13. 86 —*S.H. (7/1/2003)*

Murphy-Goode 2000 Fumé Blanc (Sonoma County) $13. 86 —*J.M. (11/15/2001)*

Murphy-Goode 1997 Reserve Fumé Blanc (Sonoma County) $24. 91 —*S.H. (9/1/1999)*

Murphy-Goode 2003 Merlot (Alexander Valley) $20. 83 —*S.H. (2/1/2006)*

Murphy-Goode 2002 Merlot (Alexander Valley) $19. 89 —*S.H. (12/15/2004)*

Murphy-Goode 2001 Merlot (Alexander Valley) $19. 88 —*S.H. (5/1/2004)*

Murphy-Goode 2000 Merlot (Alexander Valley) $19. 90 Editors' Choice —*S.H. (5/1/2003)*

Murphy-Goode 1999 Merlot (Alexander Valley) $19. 89 —*J.M. (7/1/2002)*

Murphy-Goode 1998 Merlot (Sonoma County) $19. 86 —*J.M. (11/15/2001)*

Murphy-Goode 1999 Reserve Robert Young Vineyards Merlot (Alexander Valley) $45. 92 —*S.H. (2/1/2003)*

Murphy-Goode 2001 Robert Young Vineyard Reserve Merlot (Alexander Valley) $45. 90 —*S.H. (10/1/2005)*

Murphy-Goode 2000 Robert Young Vineyards Reserve Merlot (Alexander Valley) $45. 93 —*S.H. (8/1/2004)*

Murphy-Goode 1999 Petite Verdot (Alexander Valley) $32. 88 *(12/15/2001)*

Murphy-Goode 2001 Murphy Ranch Petite Verdot (Alexander Valley) $35. 90 —*S.H. (10/1/2005)*

Murphy-Goode 2002 Pinot Noir (Russian River Valley) $30. 87 —*S.H. (3/1/2005)*

Murphy-Goode 1999 Pinot Noir (Russian River Valley) $35. 87 *(12/15/2001)*

Murphy-Goode 1997 Pinot Noir (Russian River Valley) $30. 91 —*M.S. (5/1/2000)*

Murphy-Goode 2000 J&K Vineyard Pinot Noir (Russian River Valley) $35. 87 *(10/1/2002)*

Murphy-Goode 2001 Sauvignon Blanc (Alexander Valley) $18. 88 —*J.M. (10/1/2004)*

Murphy-Goode 1999 Fumé II The Deuce Sauvignon Blanc (Sonoma County) $24. 86 *(8/1/2002)*

Murphy-Goode 2000 Reserve Fumé Sauvignon Blanc (Alexander Valley) $17. 88 —*S.H. (7/1/2003)*

Murphy-Goode 2002 Reserve Fumé Sauvignon Blanc (Alexander Valley) $17. 83 —*S.H. (2/1/2006)*

Murphy-Goode 1999 Reserve Fumé Sauvignon Blanc (Sonoma County) $17. 88 —*J.M. (11/15/2001)*

Murphy-Goode 2001 Reserve Fumé Sauvignon Blanc (Alexander Valley) $17. 88 *—J.M. (2/1/2004)*

Murphy-Goode 2000 The Deuce Sauvignon Blanc (Alexander Valley) $24. 87 *—S.H. (10/1/2003)*

Murphy-Goode 2004 Liar's Dice Zinfandel (Sonoma County) $20. Ripe to the point of overripeness and soft, this Zin, which, for some reason, contains a little Carignane, is pretty sweet in Port, chocolate and raisin flavors. **84** *—S.H. (7/1/2007)*

Murphy-Goode 2003 Liar's Dice Zinfandel (Sonoma County) $20. 86 *—S.H. (11/1/2005)*

Murphy-Goode 2000 Liar's Dice Zinfandel (Sonoma County) $20. 87 *—J.M. (11/1/2002)*

Murphy-Goode 1999 Liar's Dice Zinfandel (Sonoma County) $19. 89 Editors' Choice *—S.H. (11/15/2001)*

Murphy-Goode 1998 Liar's Dice Zinfandel (Sonoma County) $17. 91 Editors' Choice *—P.G. (3/1/2001)*

Murphy-Goode 1997 Liar's Dice Zinfandel (Sonoma County) $16. 83 *—P.G. (11/15/1999)*

Murphy-Goode 2001 Liar's Dice, TJM Zinfandel (Sonoma County) $20. 88 *(11/1/2003)*

Murphy-Goode 2002 Liar's Dice Zinfandel (Sonoma County) $19. 86 *—S.H. (11/15/2004)*

Murphy-Goode 2000 Snake Eyes Zinfandel (Alexander Valley) $35. 90 *—S.H. (2/1/2003)*

Murphy-Goode 2001 Snake Eyes Ellis Ranch Zinfandel (Alexander Valley) $35. 90 *(11/1/2003)*

Murphy-Goode 2002 Snake Eyes Ellis Ranch Reserve Zinfandel (Alexander Valley) $35. 92 *—S.H. (3/1/2005)*

MURRIETA'S WELL

Murrieta's Well 2003 Meritage Bordeaux Blend (Livermore Valley) $36. Disappointingly thin and acidic, with weedy, herbal flavors and a stubborn streak of stalky green mint to the cherries and berries. Not likely to do anything with age, so drink up. **83** *—S.H. (4/1/2007)*

Murrieta's Well 2001 Vendimia Bordeaux Blend (Livermore Valley) $30. 92 Editors' Choice *—S.H. (11/15/2003)*

Murrieta's Well 1999 Vendimia Red Wine Bordeaux Blend (Livermore Valley) $35. 87 *—S.H. (3/1/2004)*

Murrieta's Well 2004 Meritage Bordeaux White Blend (Livermore Valley) $23. Not too many Semillon-Sauvignon Blanc blends call themselves Meritage anymore, but here's one, and it's a nice wine. Semillon fattens the wine out, adding a rich, nutty oiliness to Sauvignon's lean citrus and grass flavors. The result is balanced and elegant. **89** *—S.H. (4/1/2007)*

Murrieta's Well 2001 White Vendimia Bordeaux Blend (Livermore Valley) $21. 90 Editors' Choice *—S.H. (11/15/2003)*

Murrieta's Well 2003 Zarzuela Red Wine Red Blend (Livermore Valley) $30. I admire this blend. It took real courage to work with the Spanish varieties of Touriga, Tempranillo and Souzao. The wine is soft and rich, with spicy flavors veering toward cherry kirsch, and a veneer of smoky oak. One can only hope that the winery continues working at it. Could be a real breakthrough. **88** *—S.H. (4/1/2007)*

Murrieta's Well 2005 Los Tesoros de Joaquin Sauvignon Blanc (Livermore Valley) $28. There are numerous historical references in the titles of this wine, but what consumers need to know is that it's crisp, with citrus and green grass flavors, and if you don't care for the feline essence, don't buy it. **85** *—S.H. (4/1/2007)*

Murrieta's Well 1998 Vendimia Sémillon-Sauvignon Blanc (Livermore Valley) $20. 86 *—S.H. (11/15/2001)*

Murrieta's Well 2004 Los Tesoros de Joaquin Touriga Franca (Livermore Valley) $60. I've long felt that the Portuguese Port varieties would do well as dry table wines when grown in the hotter parts of California, except that no one wanted to make them. Now, someone does. The wine is pretty good, not great, but shows promise. Soft and full-bodied, it has cherry pie, Kahlúa and licorice flavors. **86** *—S.H. (4/1/2007)*

Murrieta's Well 1998 Zinfandel (Livermore Valley) $27. 91 *—S.H. (3/1/2004)*

Murrieta's Well 1997 Zinfandel (Livermore Valley) $29. 88 *—S.H. (12/15/2001)*

MUSCARDINI

Muscardini 2005 Tesoro Red Wine Red Blend (Sonoma County) $38. A rewarding wine. A blend of Sangiovese, Syrah and Cabernet Sauvignon, it offers a profusion of berry and cherry flavors wrapped in rich, ripe tannins. Probably best now and for a short while, to take advantage of the upfront fruit. **89** *—S.H. (5/1/2007)*

Muscardini 2005 Merlo Vineyards Sangiovese (Dry Creek Valley) $32. You never quite know what California Sangiovese is going to give you. Here, it's a high-acid wine, very ripe in pie filling cherry and raspberry flavors, and a bit sweet and simple. **84** *—S.H. (5/1/2007)*

Muscardini 2006 Merlo Vineyards Rosato di Sangiovese (Dry Creek Valley) $17. A little sweet and rustic, with baked pie filling flavors of cherries, raspberries, Asian spice and toast. Okay with easy fare, like chicken, ham, burgers. **84** *—S.H. (7/1/2007)*

Muscardini 2005 Unti Vineyards Syrah (Dry Creek Valley) $36. Unti is a well-known vineyard in central Dry Creek that's the source of well-regarded Syrah, and here, the winemaker justifies the fruit. The wine is dry, rich and complex in berry flavors, with interesting leather, soy, cocoa and cola layers, and an enormously spicy tang. It might age for five years, but is best soon for its vibrancy. **87** *—S.H. (5/1/2007)*

MUTT LYNCH

Mutt Lynch 2002 Merlot Over and Play Dead Merlot (Livermore Valley) $20. 89 *—J.M. (9/1/2004)*

Mutt Lynch 1999 Merlot Over and Play Dead Merlot (Livermore Valley) $20. 90 *—J.M. (12/31/2001)*

Mutt Lynch 2001 Canis Major, Perotti Vineyard Zinfandel (Dry Creek Valley) $23. 88 *(11/1/2003)*

Mutt Lynch 1999 Domaine du Bone Zinfandel (Dry Creek Valley) $20. 88 *—J.M. (12/15/2001)*

Mutt Lynch 2002 Portrait of a Mutt Zinfandel (Sonoma County) $15. 88 *—J.M. (9/1/2004)*

Mutt Lynch 2001 Portrait of a Mutt Zinfandel (Sonoma County) $15. 88 *(11/1/2003)*

MYSTIC CLIFFS

Mystic Cliffs 1997 Cabernet Sauvignon (California) $7. 84 *—S.H. (5/1/2001)*

Mystic Cliffs 1999 Chardonnay (California) $7. 84 Best Buy *—S.H. (5/1/2001)*

Mystic Cliffs 1997 Merlot (California) $7. 85 Best Buy *—S.H. (5/1/2001)*

Mystic Cliffs 1997 Winemaker's Select Merlot (Monterey County) $11. 83 *(3/1/2000)*

MYSTIC WINES

Mystic Wines 1999 McDuffee Vineyard Cabernet Sauvignon (Columbia Valley (OR)) $28. 83 *—P.G. (2/1/2004)*

Mystic Wines 1999 Hillside Vineyard Merlot (Columbia Valley (OR)) $24. 83 *—P.G. (2/1/2004)*

Mystic Wines 2002 Temperance Hill Vineyard Pinot Noir (Willamette Valley) $24. 88 *(11/1/2004)*

Mystic Wines 2001 Syrah (Columbia Valley (OR)) $20. 87 *—P.G. (2/1/2004)*

Mystic Wines 2001 Hillside Vineyard Zinfandel (Columbia Valley (OR)) $20. 83 *—P.G. (2/1/2004)*

NACHES HEIGHTS

Naches Heights 2006 Pinot Gris (Columbia Valley (WA)) $16. A flat tasting, slightly sweet, generic white wine. **81** *—P.G. (12/1/2007)*

Naches Heights 2006 Riesling (Columbia Valley (WA)) $16. Flat, fruity and lacking in complexity. **82** *—P.G. (12/1/2007)*

Naches Heights 2005 Syrah (Columbia Valley (WA)) $18. From a very high altitude vineyard, this solidly built Syrah is soft and saturated with dark fruits. It has an earthy base and a broad midpalate, that lasts well but could use just a bit more focus. This is the first Syrah from this young vineyard, and it's definitely headed in the right direction. **87** *—P.G. (12/31/2007)*

NADEAU FAMILY VINTNERS

Nadeau Family Vintners 2002 Critical Mass Zinfandel (Paso Robles) $28. 88 *—S.H. (11/1/2005)*

Nadeau Family Vintners 2002 Home Ranch Zinfandel (Paso Robles) $25. 86 *—S.H. (11/1/2005)*

Nadeau Family Vintners 2001 Mooney Homestead Zinfandel (Paso Robles) $28. 88 *(11/1/2003)*

Nadeau Family Vintners 2002 The Bouncer Zinfandel (Paso Robles) $25. 86 *—S.H. (11/1/2005)*

NADIA

Nadia 2004 Santa Barbara Highlands Vineyard Bordeaux Blend (Santa Barbara County) $50. This ambitious launch is from the owner of Laetitia. The grapes are from the Sierra Madre Mountains of eastern Santa Barbara County. Almost totally Cabernet Sauvignon, the wine is clean, balanced and dry, with an elegant structure. It's rather like a good Third or Fourth

Growth. The next step is to build in layers of depth and complexity. **88** —*S.H. (11/1/2007)*

Nadia 2006 Rhône White Blend (Santa Barbara County) $30. A blend of Viognier, Roussanne and Grenache Blanc, this wine is slightly sweet and simple, despite high acidity. There's a firm minerality to the honeysuckle, pineapple and oak flavors. The challenge for the winemaker is to make the wine drier. **86** —*S.H. (12/31/2007)*

NAGGIAR

Naggiar 2003 Sangiovese (Sierra Foothills) $19. 84 —*S.H. (12/1/2006)*

Naggiar 2003 Syrah (Sierra Foothills) $22. 86 —*S.H. (12/1/2006)*

NALLE

Nalle 2003 Hopkins Vineyard Pinot Noir (Russian River Valley) $38. 90 Cellar Selection —*S.H. (11/1/2005)*

Nalle 2003 Zinfandel (Dry Creek Valley) $26. 90 —*S.H. (11/1/2005)*

Nalle 1999 Zinfandel (Sonoma County) $28. 88 —*J.M. (3/1/2002)*

NAPA CELLARS

Napa Cellars 2004 Cabernet Sauvignon (Napa County) $25. Dry and tannic, this tastes rustically overripe, with a slightly cooked quality to the blackberry, licorice and raisin flavors. **83** —*S.H. (12/1/2007)*

Napa Cellars 2005 Chardonnay (Napa County) $24. Taste more like a white Rhône wine than Chard, so loses a point or two for lack of typicity, but it's a flavorful sipper. With rich flavors of honeysuckle and tropical fruit, the mouthfeel is soft and barrel-creamy. **86** —*S.H. (11/1/2007)*

Napa Cellars 1998 Chardonnay (Napa Valley) $22. 83 *(6/1/2000)*

Napa Cellars 2004 Zinfandel (Napa County) $20. Hot and semisweet, with candied cherry flavors, this is a superripe, almost dessert-style Zinfandel. **82** —*S.H. (12/1/2007)*

NAPA CREEK

Napa Creek 2000 Cabernet Sauvignon (Napa Valley) $12. 85 —*S.H. (6/1/2004)*

Napa Creek 1996 Chardonnay (Napa Valley) $16. 87 *(6/1/2000)*

Napa Creek 2002 Chardonnay (Napa Valley) $12. 87 —*S.H. (6/1/2004)*

Napa Creek 2000 Merlot (Napa Valley) $12. 84 —*S.H. (6/1/2004)*

NAPA DAN

Napa Dan 2003 Cabernet Sauvignon (Napa Valley) $30. 87 —*S.H. (7/1/2005)*

Napa Dan 2003 Pool Yard Chardonnay (Napa Valley) $18. 84 —*S.H. (7/1/2005)*

NAPA REDWOODS ESTATE

Napa Redwoods Estate 2000 Alden Perry Reserve Castle Rock Vineyard Red Wine Bordeaux Blend (Mount Veeder) $48. 89 —*S.H. (5/1/2004)*

Napa Redwoods Estate 1999 Castle Rock Vineyard Alden Perry Reserve Bordeaux Blend (Mount Veeder) $56. 92 —*S.H. (10/1/2003)*

Napa Redwoods Estate 2004 Yates Family Vineyard Cabernet Franc (Mount Veeder) $45. Softer and gentler than a Cabernet Sauvignon, this wine, from one of the best but least known of Napa's mountain appellations, offers a wealth of oak-influenced cherry flavors. It finishes dry and spicy and complex. **89** —*S.H. (12/15/2007)*

Napa Redwoods Estate 2004 Yates Family Vineyard Cabernet Sauvignon (Mount Veeder) $60. Made very much in the modern cult style, this is an enormously rich, soft, immediately delicious wine, with a milk chocolate edge to the blackberry, cherry and new oak flavors. It's not an ager; drink now. **89** —*S.H. (12/15/2007)*

Napa Redwoods Estate 2001 Castle Rock Vineyard Merlot (Mount Veeder) $38. 90 —*S.H. (5/1/2004)*

Napa Redwoods Estate 1999 Castle Rock Vineyard Merlot (Mount Veeder) $42. 92 —*S.H. (10/1/2003)*

Napa Redwoods Estate 2004 Yates Family Vineyard Merlot (Mount Veeder) $45. Soft and direct, this Merlot has cooked or jellied flavors of raspberries, cherries, blackberries and milk chocolate. Finishes a little sweet in toasty, new oak vanilla. Drink now. **85** —*S.H. (12/15/2007)*

Napa Redwoods Estate 2001 Alden Perry Reserve Red Blend (Mount Veeder) $48. 87 —*S.H. (11/15/2004)*

NAPA RIDGE

Napa Ridge 2003 Cabernet Sauvignon (Napa Valley) $12. 83 —*S.H. (4/1/2006)*

Napa Ridge 2000 Cabernet Sauvignon (Napa Valley) $12. 85 —*S.H. (11/15/2004)*

Napa Ridge 2000 Cabernet Sauvignon (Lodi) $10. 84 —*S.H. (4/1/2003)*

Napa Ridge 1999 Cabernet Sauvignon (Napa Valley) $12. 85 —*S.H. (11/15/2002)*

Napa Ridge 1997 Coastal Vines Cabernet Sauvignon (Central Coast) $11. 87 *(11/15/1999)*

Napa Ridge 2003 Reserve Cabernet Sauvignon (Napa Valley) $20. The winery's reserve is soft and simple, but rewards with a wealth of flavor. Blackberries, cherries, milk chocolate, cinnamon-spiced cappuccino and caramelly oak flood the mouth. The finish is soft and long in fruit and spice. **85** —*S.H. (6/1/2007)*

Napa Ridge 1997 Reserve Cabernet Sauvignon (Napa Valley) $20. 88 —*C.S. (11/15/2002)*

Napa Ridge 2003 Chardonnay (Napa Valley) $12. 84 —*S.H. (7/1/2005)*

Napa Ridge 2000 Chardonnay (Napa Valley) $12. 84 —*S.H. (12/15/2002)*

Napa Ridge 1998 Chardonnay (North Coast) $10. 83 —*S.H. (8/1/2001)*

Napa Ridge 2003 Coastal Vines Chardonnay (North Coast) $10. 84 —*S.H. (12/31/2005)*

Napa Ridge 1996 Reserve Chardonnay (North Coast) $17. 87 —*J.C. (10/1/1999)*

Napa Ridge 2003 Merlot (Napa Valley) $12. 83 —*S.H. (4/1/2006)*

Napa Ridge 2000 Merlot (Napa Valley) $11. 84 —*C.S. (11/15/2002)*

Napa Ridge 2003 Coastal Ridge Merlot (California) $7. 84 Best Buy —*S.H. (11/1/2005)*

Napa Ridge 2002 Coastal Vines Merlot (Lodi) $10. 84 —*S.H. (12/15/2004)*

Napa Ridge 1998 Coastal Vines Merlot (California) $10. 81 —*S.H. (8/1/2001)*

Napa Ridge 2003 Reserve Merlot (Napa Valley) $20. This gets the job done with direct cherry, chocolate and root beer flavors and a veneer of smoky oak. Finishing soft and a little sweet, this Merlot straddles the line between everyday and fancy. **84** —*S.H. (6/1/2007)*

Napa Ridge 1997 Reserve Merlot (Napa Valley) $20. 84 —*S.H. (6/1/2001)*

Napa Ridge 1999 Pinot Grigio (California) $10. 84 —*S.H. (8/1/2001)*

Napa Ridge 2004 Coastal Ridge Pinot Grigio (California) $7. 83 —*S.H. (7/1/2005)*

Napa Ridge 2001 Pinot Noir (North Coast) $10. 84 —*S.H. (7/1/2003)*

Napa Ridge 2003 Coastal Vines Pinot Noir (North Coast) $10. 82 —*S.H. (12/31/2005)*

Napa Ridge 2005 Sauvignon Blanc (Napa Valley) $12. Feline scents dominate this wine, both in the aroma and flavor. There's some grapefruit fruit, and crisp, minty acidity. **83** —*S.H. (4/1/2007)*

Napa Ridge 1998 Shiraz (Stanislaus County) $10. 85 —*S.H. (10/1/2001)*

Napa Ridge 2003 Coastal Vines Shiraz (Lodi) $10. 84 —*S.H. (7/1/2005)*

Napa Ridge 2003 Syrah (Napa Valley) $12. Kind of a generic red wine, but smooth and polished, with some cherry fruit. It's also balanced, a perfectly good sipper for burgers, steaks, or chicken at a fair price. **84** —*S.H. (4/1/2007)*

Napa Ridge 1998 Triad White Blend (North Coast) $9. 85 —*S.H. (8/1/2001)*

Napa Ridge 2005 Zinfandel (Napa Valley) $12. Pretty good everyday Zin, the kind of spicy wine that makes you think of burgers, lasagna and roast chicken. Offers plenty of cherry-berry flavors and rich tannins. **84** —*S.H. (4/1/2007)*

Napa Ridge 1996 Coastal Zinfandel (North Coast) $9. 86 Best Buy —*L.W. (11/1/1999)*

NAPA VALLEY VINEYARDS

Napa Valley Vineyards 2002 Reserve Cabernet Sauvignon (Napa Valley) $17. 80 —*S.H. (7/1/2006)*

Napa Valley Vineyards 2003 Chardonnay (Napa Valley) $15. 81 —*S.H. (10/1/2005)*

Napa Valley Vineyards 2004 Reserve Chardonnay (Napa Valley) $15. 85 —*S.H. (7/1/2006)*

Napa Valley Vineyards 2004 Reserve Chardonnay (Napa Valley) $18. 84 —*S.H. (3/1/2006)*

Napa Valley Vineyards 2002 Reserve Merlot (Napa Valley) $15. 83 —*S.H. (7/1/2006)*

NAPA WINE CO.

Napa Wine Co. 1997 Cabernet Sauvignon (Napa Valley) $32. 90 *(11/1/2000)*

Napa Wine Co. 2001 Cabernet Sauvignon (Napa Valley) $32. 91 —*S.H. (3/1/2005)*

Napa Wine Co. 2000 Cabernet Sauvignon (Napa Valley) $32. 90 —*S.H. (6/1/2004)*

Napa Wine Co. 1999 Cabernet Sauvignon (Napa Valley) $32. 92 *—J.M. (2/1/2003)*

Napa Wine Co. 1998 Cabernet Sauvignon (Napa Valley) $32. 91 *—J.M. (12/1/2001)*

Napa Wine Co. 1999 Pinot Blanc (Napa Valley) $18. 88 *—J.M. (11/15/2001)*

Napa Wine Co. 1998 Pinot Blanc (Napa Valley) $18. 85 *—L.W. (3/1/2000)*

Napa Wine Co. 1998 Sauvignon Blanc (Napa Valley) $18. 89 *—L.W. (3/1/2000)*

Napa Wine Co. 2003 Sauvignon Blanc (Yountville) $14. 90 Best Buy *—S.H. (10/1/2004)*

Napa Wine Co. 2001 Sauvignon Blanc (Oakville) $18. 85 *(8/1/2002)*

Napa Wine Co. 2000 Sauvignon Blanc (Yountville) $18. 88 *—J.M. (11/15/2001)*

Napa Wine Co. 2001 Zinfandel (Napa Valley) $20. 89 *(11/1/2003)*

NAVARRO

Navarro 1994 Cabernet Sauvignon (Mendocino County) $24. 89 *—L.W. (11/1/1999)*

Navarro 1997 Cabernet Sauvignon (Mendocino) $25. 91 *—S.H. (5/1/2002)*

Navarro 1997 Chardonnay (Anderson Valley) $13. 89 Best Buy *—L.W. (11/15/1999)*

Navarro 2001 Chardonnay (Anderson Valley) $18. 92 Editors' Choice *—S.H. (12/1/2003)*

Navarro 2001 Chardonnay (Mendocino) $13. 88 Best Buy *—S.H. (12/1/2003)*

Navarro 1999 Chardonnay (Mendocino) $13. 86 *—S.H. (12/31/2001)*

Navarro 2002 Premiere Reserve Chardonnay (Anderson Valley) $19. 90 *—S.H. (12/31/2004)*

Navarro 1999 Premiere Reserve Chardonnay (Anderson Valley) $18. 87 *—S.H. (12/31/2001)*

Navarro 1997 Gewürztraminer (Anderson Valley) $14. 89 *—L.W. (9/1/1999)*

Navarro 2002 Gewürztraminer (Anderson Valley) $16. 87 *—S.H. (6/1/2004)*

Navarro 2000 Gewürztraminer (Anderson Valley) $14. 84 *—S.H. (12/15/2001)*

Navarro 2002 Cluster Select Late Harvest Gewürztraminer (Anderson Valley) $25. 93 *—S.H. (6/1/2004)*

Navarro 1998 Late Harvest Gewürztraminer (Anderson Valley) $12. 90 Best Buy *—S.H. (12/31/2000)*

Navarro 1997 Late Harvest Gewürztraminer (Anderson Valley) $45. 92 *—L.W. (9/1/1999)*

Navarro 2000 Vintage Select Late Harvest Gewürztraminer (Anderson Valley) $25. 90 *—S.H. (12/31/2001)*

Navarro 1999 Mourvèdre (Mendocino) $19. 89 *—S.H. (5/1/2002)*

Navarro 2001 Dry Blanc Muscat (Anderson Valley) $14. 87 *—S.H. (3/1/2004)*

Navarro 1999 Dry Muscat Blanc Muscat (Anderson Valley) $18. 86 *—S.H. (12/15/2001)*

Navarro 1998 Petite Sirah (Mendocino) $19. 91 *—S.H. (5/1/2002)*

Navarro 2002 Pinot Gris (Anderson Valley) $16. 88 *—S.H. (6/1/2004)*

Navarro 2000 Pinot Gris (Anderson Valley) $16. 87 *—S.H. (12/15/2001)*

Navarro 2001 Pinot Noir (Mendocino) $14. 88 *—S.H. (2/1/2004)*

Navarro 2000 Deep End Pinot Noir (Anderson Valley) $38. 90 *—S.H. (5/1/2002)*

Navarro 1999 Methode a l'Ancienne Pinot Noir (Anderson Valley) $19. 87 *—S.H. (12/15/2001)*

Navarro 2001 Methode a l'Ancienne Pinot Noir (Anderson Valley) $20. 86 *—S.H. (6/1/2004)*

Navarro 2000 Navarrouge Red Blend (Mendocino) $9. 86 Best Buy *—S.H. (5/1/2002)*

Navarro 2002 White Riesling (Anderson Valley) $15. 86 *—S.H. (12/31/2004)*

Navarro 2002 Rosé Blend (Mendocino) $13. 88 *—S.H. (3/1/2004)*

Navarro 2003 Old Vine Cuvée Rosé Blend (Mendocino) $13. 84 *—S.H. (12/31/2004)*

Navarro 2002 Cuvée 128 Sauvignon Blanc (Mendocino) $14. 87 *—S.H. (6/1/2004)*

Navarro 2000 Cuvée 128 Sauvignon Blanc (Anderson Valley) $14. 84 *—S.H. (12/15/2001)*

Navarro 1998 Cuvée 128 Sauvignon Blanc (Mendocino) $13. 91 Best Buy *—S.H. (9/1/2000)*

Navarro 2001 White Riesling (Anderson Valley) $14. 85 *—S.H. (12/31/2003)*

Navarro 2000 White Riesling (Anderson Valley) $14. 88 *—S.H. (5/1/2002)*

Navarro 1997 Late Harvest Cluster Select White Riesling (Anderson Valley) $25. 94 *—S.H. (12/31/2000)*

Navarro 2001 Zinfandel (Mendocino) $19. 87 *—S.H. (6/1/2004)*

Navarro 2000 Old Vine Zinfandel (Mendocino) $25. 89 *—S.H. (5/1/2002)*

NEESE

Neese 2000 Nonno Guiseppe Zinfandel (Redwood Valley) $17. 87 *—S.H. (9/12/2002)*

NEFARIOUS

Nefarious 2006 Stone's Throw Vineyard Riesling (Columbia Valley (WA)) $18. From estate-grown fruit, this is fragrant and off-dry, showing honeysuckle, Meyer lemon, tangerine and grapefruit in the mix of scents and flavors. It's a fine example of what Washington can do with Riesling, bringing bright, sappy fruit flavors to vibrant acidity, complex sugars and a lingering liveliness on the palate. If this is any indication of what this vineyard (and Chelan in general) is capable of producing, Washington has found its next great Riesling appellation. 92 *—P.G. (9/1/2007)*

NELMS ROAD

Nelms Road 2005 Cabernet Sauvignon (Columbia Valley (WA)) $20. Another lovely effort from Nelms Road. This is firm and loaded with dense black fruits, the long midpalate spreading deliciously into a full, rich, earthy finish. Forest floor, earth, hints of leather and barnyard, and lovely fruit all mingle to create a rich and sexy wine. 90 *—P.G. (12/1/2007)*

Nelms Road 2000 Cabernet Sauvignon (Columbia Valley (WA)) $25. 87 *—P.G. (6/1/2002)*

Nelms Road 2000 Cabernet Sauvignon (Columbia Valley (WA)) $19. 87 *—P.G. (9/1/2003)*

Nelms Road 2005 Merlot (Columbia Valley (WA)) $20. This blend of Merlot, Cabernet, Barbera and Syrah has become a popular glass pour around the country. It's easy to understand the appeal; it's very soft, lush and fruity, yet has a richness that speaks of nicely ripened grapes. The fruit tastes like ripe cherries—young, bright and fresh—and plums. Extra time brings in hints of cut tobacco, fresh hay and earth. 89 *—P.G. (12/1/2007)*

Nelms Road 2001 Merlot (Columbia Valley (WA)) $19. 88 *—P.G. (9/1/2003)*

Nelms Road 2000 Merlot (Columbia Valley (WA)) $20. 87 *—P.G. (6/1/2002)*

NELSON

Nelson 1998 Cabernet Franc (Sonoma Valley) $32. 87 *—S.H. (12/1/2001)*

Nelson 1997 Cabernet Franc (Sonoma Valley) $24. 84 *—S.H. (2/1/2001)*

Nelson 1999 Pinot Noir (Russian River Valley) $28. 86 *—S.H. (12/15/2001)*

NERELLI

Nerelli 2004 After Hours Proprietor's Choice Bien Nacido Vineyard White Blend (Santa Maria Valley) $40. 91 *—S.H. (8/1/2006)*

NEVADA CITY

Nevada City 2001 Vin Cinq Bordeaux Blend (Sierra Foothills) $16. 84 *—S.H. (6/1/2004)*

Nevada City 2001 Cabernet Franc (Sierra Foothills) $17. 84 *—S.H. (6/1/2004)*

Nevada City 2000 Cabernet Sauvignon (Sierra Foothills) $16. 83 *—S.H. (6/1/2004)*

Nevada City 1999 Cabernet Sauvignon (Sierra Foothills) $16. 84 *—S.H. (11/15/2002)*

Nevada City 2000 Petite Sirah (Sierra Foothills) $28. 85 *(4/1/2003)*

Nevada City NV Rough and Ready Red Cask 202 Lirac Red Blend (California) $10. 84 *—S.H. (6/1/2004)*

Nevada City 2001 Syrah (Sierra Foothills) $20. 85 *—S.H. (6/1/2004)*

Nevada City 2000 Syrah (Sierra Foothills) $18. 85 *—S.H. (12/1/2002)*

Nevada City 2000 Zinfandel (Sierra Foothills) $15. 85 *—S.H. (6/1/2004)*

Nevada City 1999 Zinfandel (Sierra Foothills) $15. 86 *—S.H. (11/1/2002)*

NEVEU

Neveu 2003 Pinot Gris (Siskiyou County) $13. 82 *—S.H. (5/1/2005)*

Neveu 2002 Pinot Noir (Siskiyou County) $15. 81 *—S.H. (7/1/2005)*

NEWELL

Newell 2003 Para Dois Petite Sirah (Monterey County) $36. 89 —*S.H. (12/1/2006)*

NEWLAN

Newlan 2000 Cabernet Sauvignon (Napa Valley) $30. 90 —*S.H. (12/31/2003)*

Newlan 1998 Chardonnay (Napa Valley) $16. 88 *(6/1/2000)*

Newlan 2000 Chardonnay (Napa Valley) $17. 87 —*S.H. (12/15/2002)*

Newlan 1999 Chardonnay (Napa Valley) $18. 86 —*S.H. (11/15/2001)*

Newlan 1999 Merlot (Napa Valley) $20. 90 Editors' Choice —*S.H. (8/1/2003)*

Newlan 1998 Merlot (Napa Valley) $20. 85 —*S.H. (2/1/2001)*

Newlan 2000 Pinot Noir (Napa Valley) $24. 87 —*S.H. (12/1/2004)*

Newlan 1999 Pinot Noir (Napa Valley) $20. 87 —*S.H. (9/1/2002)*

Newlan 1996 Reserve Pinot Noir (Napa Valley) $25. 85 —*S.H. (12/15/2000)*

Newlan 1997 Reseve Pinot Noir (Napa Valley) $26. 89 —*S.H. (9/1/2002)*

Newlan 1999 Late Harvest White Riesling (Napa Valley) $25. 91 —*S.H. (12/1/2001)*

Newlan 1997 Zinfandel (Sonoma County) $20. 86 —*S.H. (5/1/2000)*

Newlan 2000 Zinfandel (Napa Valley) $22. 86 —*S.H. (11/1/2002)*

Newlan 1998 Zinfandel (Napa Valley) $22. 87 —*P.G. (3/1/2001)*

Newlan 1997 Zinfandel (Napa Valley) $20. 88 —*S.H. (5/1/2000)*

Newlan 1997 Wallstrum Family Zinfandel (Sonoma County) $20. 83 —*P.G. (3/1/2001)*

NEWSOME-HARLOW

Newsome-Harlow 2001 Meritage (Calaveras County) $28. 88 —*S.H. (2/1/2005)*

Newsome-Harlow 2004 Big John's Zinfandel (Calaveras County) $25. 85 —*S.H. (12/1/2006)*

Newsome-Harlow 2003 Big John's Vineyard Zinfandel (Calaveras County) $24. 89 —*S.H. (10/1/2005)*

Newsome-Harlow 2001 Big John's Vineyard Zinfandel (Calaveras County) $24. 84 —*S.H. (2/1/2005)*

Newsome-Harlow 2002 Big John's Vineyard Zinfandel (Calaveras County) $24. 84 —*S.H. (5/1/2005)*

NEWTON

Newton 2003 Claret Bordeaux Blend (Napa Valley) $25. This Merlot-based blend of Bordeaux varieties is pretty good, with minor drawbacks including excessive softness and an overripe edge to the cherries and mocha. It's elegant and clean. Drink now. **84** —*S.H. (7/1/2007)*

Newton 2002 The Puzzle Bordeaux Blend (Spring Mountain) $70. Deliciously complex, and made solidly in the soft, ripe modern style. It's the kind of Bordeaux blend that immediately dazzles, with its wealth of cherries, blackberries, tobacco, carob and peppery spice. Seems too soft for aging, so drink now. **90** —*S.H. (7/1/2007)*

Newton 2000 Le Puzzle Cabernet Sauvignon (Spring Mountain) $45. 89 —*S.H. (11/15/2003)*

Newton 2002 Unfiltered Cabernet Sauvignon (Napa Valley) $55. Balance is the key here. Acids and tannins get equal billing with fruit, but there's no shortage of blackberries and cassis, not to mention oak. The result is polished and elegant, a gorgeous food wine. **92** —*S.H. (7/1/2007)*

Newton 2000 Unfiltered Cabernet Sauvignon (Napa Valley) $41. 88 —*S.H. (11/15/2003)*

Newton 2005 Chardonnay (Napa-Sonoma) $25. Smells like canned fruits and tastes flat and semisweet, lacking the vibrancy of acidity. A plaster of sweet oak just adds to the texture and taste of butterscotch pudding. **83** —*S.H. (12/1/2007)*

Newton 2004 Chardonnay (Napa-Sonoma) $25. Ripe and oaky, this multi-county Chard has apricot and tangerine flavors, and is dry. It's a little hollow in the middle before finishing with a swirl of spicy toast. **85** —*S.H. (7/1/2007)*

Newton 2002 Chardonnay (Napa-Sonoma) $24. 88 —*S.H. (8/1/2005)*

Newton 1998 Naturally Fermented Chardonnay (Sonoma County) $23. 86 *(6/1/2000)*

Newton 2004 Unfiltered Chardonnay (Napa Valley) $55. The '04 is rich and savory in tropical fruit, apricot, butterscotch and vanilla flavors, with a dry, balanced finish. **91** —*S.H. (7/1/2007)*

Newton 2002 Unfiltered Chardonnay (Napa Valley) $56. 94 —*S.H. (8/1/2005)*

Newton 2000 Unfiltered Chardonnay (Napa Valley) $42. 90 —*S.H. (12/1/2003)*

Newton 2000 Epic Merlot (Napa Valley) $42. 93 —*S.H. (12/31/2003)*

Newton 2002 Unfiltered Merlot (Napa Valley) $55. I wish there were more fruity concentration here, because the individual parts are quite good. There's beautifully ripe, sweet tannins, fine acidity, polished smoky oak, and pretty cherry, plum and violet flavors that could use a boost in the midpalate through the finish. **86** —*S.H. (7/1/2007)*

Newton 2000 Unfiltered Merlot (Spring Mountain) $NA. 91 —*S.H. (12/31/2003)*

Newton 2000 Special Cuvée Pinot Noir (Sonoma) $66. 90 *(10/1/2002)*

NEYERS

Neyers 2001 Cuvée d'Honeur Syrah (Napa Valley) $45. 94 Editors' Choice —*S.H. (11/1/2003)*

Neyers 2001 Pato Vineyard Zinfandel (Contra Costa County) $30. 90 *(11/1/2003)*

Neyers 2001 Tofanelli Vineyard Zinfandel (Napa Valley) $35. 91 *(11/1/2003)*

NICHOLAS COLE CELLARS

Nicholas Cole Cellars 2004 Camille Bordeaux Blend (Columbia Valley (WA)) $48. Soft aromas with a mix of plum, berry, melon and smooth mocha. The scents envelop you and the flavors follow, good, still tight, still firm, still showing a little bit of green tea in the tannins. It's structured well, with a forward, lush, roundness from the Merlot, backed with more assertive tannins and some moist earth flavors from the Cab Franc. Just a hint of coffee comes through at the end. **92** —*P.G. (8/1/2007)*

Nicholas Cole Cellars 2003 Camille Bordeaux Blend (Columbia Valley (WA)) $48. 91 —*P.G. (10/1/2006)*

Nicholas Cole Cellars 2002 Camille Bordeaux Blend (Columbia Valley (WA)) $48. 91 —*P.G. (4/1/2005)*

Nicholas Cole Cellars 2001 Claret Bordeaux Blend (Columbia Valley (WA)) $46. 93 —*P.G. (4/1/2005)*

Nicholas Cole Cellars 2004 GraEagle Red Wing Red Bordeaux Blend (Columbia Valley (WA)) $25. Nicholas Cole Cellars is the winery, and the grapes are sourced from top vineyards such as Klipsun, Champoux, DuBrul, Alder Ridge and Canoe Ridge. This is a straightforward Bordeaux blend—Cabernet, Merlot and Cab Franc—soft and spicy with a sensuous cooked-plum flavor. It's already showing a bit of a Port-like or pruny edge and mature flavors suggesting cooked fruits, cola and confectionary spice. **88** —*P.G. (5/1/2007)*

NICHOLS

Nichols 1997 Central Coast Blend Chardonnay (Central Coast) $30. 88 —*J.C. (3/1/2000)*

NICHOLSON RANCH

Nicholson Ranch 2005 Chardonnay (Sonoma Valley) $28. Simple and too oaky, with peach, pineapple, vanilla cream and buttered toast flavors. The toast overwhelms everything. **83** —*S.H. (12/15/2007)*

Nicholson Ranch 2005 Pinot Noir (Sonoma Valley) $32. The winery says this was the longest hangtime vintage in their history. The fruit is extraordinarily ripe in blackberries and cherries, with a rich coating of smoky oak, but retains a nice tannin-acid balance. Scads of Asian spices make the finish exotic. Drink now. **88** —*S.H. (12/15/2007)*

Nicholson Ranch 2006 Ramona Pinot Noir Rosé Rosé Blend (Sonoma Valley) $20. A little heavy and soft, with jelled raspberry, cola and vanilla flavors. The finish turns sugary. **83** —*S.H. (12/15/2007)*

NICKEL & NICKEL

Nickel & Nickel 2002 Branding Iron Cabernet Sauvignon (Oakville) $75. 90 —*S.H. (12/1/2005)*

Nickel & Nickel 1997 Carpenter Vineyard Cabernet Sauvignon (Napa Valley) $75. 92 *(11/1/2000)*

Nickel & Nickel 2002 Dragonfly Vineyard Cabernet Sauvignon (St. Helena) $90. 94 —*S.H. (12/1/2005)*

Nickel & Nickel 1999 Dragonfly Vineyard Cabernet Sauvignon (Napa Valley) $90. 92 Cellar Selection —*M.S. (5/1/2003)*

Nickel & Nickel 2002 John C. Sullenger Vineyard Cabernet Sauvignon (Oakville) $75. 88 —*S.H. (12/1/2005)*

Nickel & Nickel 2001 John C. Sullenger Vineyard Cabernet Sauvignon (Oakville) $75. 94 —*S.H. (10/1/2004)*

Nickel & Nickel 1999 John C. Sullenger Vineyard Cabernet Sauvignon (Oakville) $75. 90 —*M.S. (5/1/2003)*

Nickel & Nickel 1998 John C. Sullenger Vineyard Cabernet Sauvignon (Oakville) $75. 87 *—J.M. (12/31/2001)*

Nickel & Nickel 1997 John C. Sullenger Vineyard Cabernet Sauvignon (Oakville) $65. 92 *(11/1/2000)*

Nickel & Nickel 1997 Rock Cairn Cabernet Sauvignon (Oakville) $75. 90 *(11/1/2000)*

Nickel & Nickel 2001 Rock Cairn Vineyard Cabernet Sauvignon (Oakville) $75. 93 *—S.H. (10/1/2004)*

Nickel & Nickel 2002 Stelling Vineyard Cabernet Sauvignon (Oakville) $130. 92 *—S.H. (12/1/2005)*

Nickel & Nickel 2001 Stelling Vineyard Cabernet Sauvignon (Oakville) $125. 93 *—S.H. (10/1/2004)*

Nickel & Nickel 1999 Stelling Vineyard Cabernet Sauvignon (Oakville) $125. 91 *—J.C. (6/1/2003)*

Nickel & Nickel 1998 Stelling Vineyard Cabernet Sauvignon (Oakville) $100. 91 *—S.H. (12/31/2001)*

Nickel & Nickel 1997 Stelling Vineyard Cabernet Sauvignon (Oakville) $95. 93 *(11/1/2000)*

Nickel & Nickel 1999 Tench Vineyard Cabernet Sauvignon (Oakville) $65. 89 *—J.C. (6/1/2003)*

Nickel & Nickel 2002 Vogt Vineyard Cabernet Sauvignon (Howell Mountain) $75. 85 *—S.H. (12/1/2005)*

Nickel & Nickel 2001 Vogt Vineyard Cabernet Sauvignon (Howell Mountain) $75. 93 *—S.H. (10/1/2004)*

Nickel & Nickel 2000 John's Creek Chardonnay (Napa Valley) $50. 87 *—J.M. (12/15/2002)*

Nickel & Nickel 2003 John's Creek Vineyard Chardonnay (Napa Valley) $50. 88 *—S.H. (10/1/2005)*

Nickel & Nickel 1999 John's Creek Chardonnay (Napa Valley) $50. 89 *(7/1/2001)*

Nickel & Nickel 2005 Medina Vineyard Chardonnay (Russian River Valley) $43. Fairly soft for an '05 Russian River Chard, this is very well-oaked and bone dry. The mouthfilling fruit has a spicy pie filling quality, and ranges from green apple and pineapple to honeydew and kumquat. 92 *—S.H. (7/1/2007)*

Nickel & Nickel 2005 Searby Vineyard Chardonnay (Russian River Valley) $43. This Chard has been variable over the years, and I'm not sure why. This one plays it straight down the middle. The winemaker says it has "Muscat" flavors, which it does, but that makes the wine floral, while acidity gives it an almost chlorophyll taste. But it's dry and zesty. 86 *—S.H. (7/1/2007)*

Nickel & Nickel 2004 Searby Vineyard Chardonnay (Russian River Valley) $40. 85 *—S.H. (10/1/2006)*

Nickel & Nickel 2003 Searby Vineyard Chardonnay (Russian River Valley) $38. 90 *—S.H. (10/1/2005)*

Nickel & Nickel 2002 Searby Vineyard Chardonnay (Russian River Valley) $35. 92 *—S.H. (9/1/2004)*

Nickel & Nickel 2005 Truchard Vineyard Chardonnay (Carneros) $43. The vineyard has been a reliable source of Chardonnays that display a good Carneros character. Acidity is never a problem, and the wines often have a Chablis-like minerality. Ripeness varies by vintage; this wine is from a cooler season, and shows lime zest and tart green apple flavors that new oak has made creamy and rich. 90 *—S.H. (5/1/2007)*

Nickel & Nickel 2004 Truchard Vineyard Chardonnay (Carneros) $40. 85 *—S.H. (10/1/2006)*

Nickel & Nickel 2003 Truchard Vineyard Chardonnay (Carneros) $38. 89 *—S.H. (10/1/2005)*

Nickel & Nickel 2002 Truchard Vineyard Chardonnay (Carneros) $35. 90 *—S.H. (9/1/2004)*

Nickel & Nickel 2001 Truchard Vineyard Chardonnay (Carneros) $35. 89 *—S.H. (12/1/2003)*

Nickel & Nickel 2000 Truchard Vineyard Chardonnay (Carneros) $35. 89 *—J.M. (12/15/2002)*

Nickel & Nickel 2004 Harris Vineyard Merlot (Oakville) $48. Although in this hot vintage it explodes in cherries, blackberries, milk chocolate and new oak flavors, it's far more tannic than most Napa Valley wines. The combination of toughness and almost sweet ripeness makes for strange bedfellows. 87 *—S.H. (7/1/2007)*

Nickel & Nickel 2002 Harris Vineyard Merlot (Oakville) $40. 90 *—S.H. (10/1/2005)*

Nickel & Nickel 2001 Harris Vineyard Merlot (Oakville) $40. 91 *—S.H. (12/15/2004)*

Nickel & Nickel 2000 Harris Vineyard Merlot (Oakville) $40. 93 *—S.H. (12/31/2003)*

Nickel & Nickel 2002 Sori Bricco Vineyard Merlot (Diamond Mountain) $40. 82 *—S.H. (12/1/2005)*

Nickel & Nickel 2001 Sori Bricco Vineyard Merlot (Diamond Mountain) $40. 92 Cellar Selection *—S.H. (12/15/2004)*

Nickel & Nickel 2004 Suscol Ranch Merlot (Napa Valley) $55. A powerfully ripe 100% Merlot, explosive in cherry flavors. Has tannic structure and an edge of ripe black currants, along with new French oak. The tannins are strong and pronounced, but sweet. Not likely to age, so drink now through 2010. 91 *—S.H. (7/1/2007)*

Nickel & Nickel 2003 Suscol Ranch Merlot (Napa Valley) $55. 86 *—S.H. (10/1/2006)*

Nickel & Nickel 2002 Suscol Ranch Merlot (Napa Valley) $50. 93 *—S.H. (10/1/2005)*

Nickel & Nickel 2001 Suscol Ranch Merlot (Napa Valley) $50. 93 *—S.H. (12/15/2004)*

Nickel & Nickel 2002 Darien Vineyard Syrah (Russian River Valley) $40. 87 *(9/1/2005)*

Nickel & Nickel 2002 Dyer Vineyard Syrah (Carneros) $35. 89 *(9/1/2005)*

Nickel & Nickel 2001 Dyer Vineyard Syrah (Carneros) $35. 91 *—S.H. (12/1/2004)*

Nickel & Nickel 2000 Ponzo Vineyard Zinfandel (Russian River Valley) $45. 87 *—S.H. (3/1/2004)*

Nickel & Nickel 1998 Ponzo Vineyard Zinfandel (Russian River Valley) $45. 88 *—D.T. (3/1/2002)*

NIEBAUM-COPPOLA

Niebaum-Coppola 1999 Rubicon Bordeaux Blend (Rutherford) $100. 94 *(8/1/2003)*

Niebaum-Coppola 1996 Rubicon Bordeaux Blend (Rutherford) $90. 87 *—S.H. (9/1/2006)*

Niebaum-Coppola 2001 Rubicon Cabernet Blend (Rutherford) $100. 90 *—S.H. (10/1/2005)*

Niebaum-Coppola 2002 Cabernet Franc (Rutherford) $44. 94 *—S.H. (4/1/2005)*

Niebaum-Coppola 2001 Cabernet Franc (Rutherford) $44. 86 *—S.H. (5/1/2004)*

Niebaum-Coppola 2000 Cabernet Franc (Rutherford) $44. 86 *—S.H. (6/1/2003)*

Niebaum-Coppola 2002 Cask Cabernet Sauvignon (Rutherford) $65. 93 Cellar Selection *—S.H. (12/15/2005)*

Niebaum-Coppola 2000 Cask Cabernet Sauvignon (Rutherford) $65. 86 *—S.H. (5/1/2004)*

Niebaum-Coppola 1999 Cask Cabernet Cabernet Sauvignon (Rutherford) $65. 93 *—S.H. (2/1/2003)*

Niebaum-Coppola 1998 Cask Cabernet Cabernet Sauvignon (Rutherford) $65. 89 *—S.H. (6/1/2002)*

Niebaum-Coppola 2001 Estate Cask Cabernet Sauvignon (Rutherford) $110. 93 *—S.H. (10/1/2004)*

Niebaum-Coppola 2002 Blancaneaux Marsanne (Napa Valley) $30. 88 *—J.M. (9/1/2004)*

Niebaum-Coppola 1997 Merlot (Napa Valley) $40. 89 *—S.H. (7/1/2000)*

Niebaum-Coppola 2000 Merlot (Rutherford) $44. 91 Cellar Selection *—S.H. (12/15/2003)*

Niebaum-Coppola 1999 Merlot (Rutherford) $44. 90 *—S.H. (6/1/2002)*

Niebaum-Coppola 2000 Dolcetto Red Blend (Napa Valley) $28. 87 *—S.H. (12/1/2002)*

Niebaum-Coppola 2000 Rubicon Red Blend (Rutherford) $100. 90 *—S.H. (11/15/2003)*

Niebaum-Coppola 1997 Rubicon Red Blend (Rutherford) $100. 97 Cellar Selection *—S.H. (9/1/2006)*

Niebaum-Coppola 2003 Blancaneaux Rhône White Blend (Rutherford) $40. 86 *—S.H. (10/1/2005)*

Niebaum-Coppola 2002 Blancaneax Rhône White Blend (Rutherford) $30. 89 *—S.H. (9/1/2004)*

Niebaum-Coppola 2002 RC Reserve Syrah (Rutherford) $46. 90 *(9/1/2005)*

Niebaum-Coppola 2000 RC Reserve Syrah (Rutherford) $56. 94 Editors' Choice *—S.H. (12/1/2003)*

Niebaum-Coppola 2001 Edizione Pennino Zinfandel (Rutherford) $35. 87 *—J.M. (4/1/2004)*

Niebaum-Coppola 2000 Edizione Pennino Zinfandel (Rutherford) $44. 88 *—S.H. (2/1/2003)*

Niebaum-Coppola 1999 Edizione Pennino Zinfandel (Rutherford) $40. 89 *—D.T. (4/1/2002)*

Niebaum-Coppola 1998 Edizione Pennino Zinfandel (Napa Valley) $40. 89 *—D.T. (3/1/2002)*

NIGHT HARVEST BY R.H. PHILLIPS

Night Harvest by R.H. Phillips 2005 Chardonnay (California) $9. A little raw, with a touch of green asparagus, but saved by just enough peaches-and-cream and oak flavors to satisfy as a party Chard. **83** *—S.H. (11/15/2007)*

Night Harvest by R.H. Phillips 2004 Merlot (California) $9. Even at this price, the wine is just too soft and gluey to merit a higher score. The flavors are sweet, like sugary cherry jelly. **82** *—S.H. (11/15/2007)*

Night Harvest by R.H. Phillips 2005 Sauvignon Blanc (California) $9. Don't be too fussy with this one. Good for casual get-togethers where they're munching on appetizers, and something dry and fruity is needed to wash it all down. **83** *—S.H. (11/15/2007)*

Night Harvest by R.H. Phillips 2004 Shiraz (California) $9. Sharp and pepperminty, with jammy blackberry, cherry and cocoa flavors, this sprightly young Syrah is rich and juicy enough to drown the perfect cheeseburger. **84** *—S.H. (11/15/2007)*

Night Harvest by R.H. Phillips 2006 White Zinfandel (California) $9. Simple and sweet, like a cup of raspberry herb tea with a spoonful of white sugar. **81** *—S.H. (11/15/2007)*

NIGHT OWL

Night Owl 2004 San Bernabe Vineyard Chardonnay (Monterey County) $12. 83 *—S.H. (12/15/2005)*

Night Owl 2003 San Bernabe Vineyard Pinot Noir (Monterey County) $14. 86 *—S.H. (12/15/2005)*

Night Owl 2005 San Bernabe Vineyard Riesling (Monterey County) $12. 84 *—S.H. (12/15/2006)*

Night Owl 2004 San Bernabe Vineyard Shiraz (Monterey County) $12. 84 *—S.H. (12/31/2006)*

Night Owl 2004 San Bernabe Vineyard Shiraz (Monterey) $12. 86 *(8/1/2006)*

Night Owl 2003 San Bernabe Vineyard Shiraz (Monterey County) $12. 88 Best Buy *(9/1/2005)*

NINE GABLES

Nine Gables 2001 Pifari Cedar Vista Vineyard Zinfandel (Shenandoah Valley (CA)) $20. 81 *—S.H. (3/1/2005)*

NO

No 2006 Sauvignon Blanc (Lake County) $10. Way too sweet. The alcohol is nice and low, but this lemonade and sugared mint tea-tasting wine is not dry. **82** *—S.H. (11/15/2007)*

No 2005 Sauvignon Blanc (Lake County) $10. 85 Best Buy *—S.H. (12/1/2006)*

NOAH

Noah 2002 Merlot (Yountville) $25. 92 *—S.H. (8/1/2006)*

Noah 2001 Los Chamizal Vineyards Zinfandel (Sonoma Valley) $20. 86 *—S.H. (12/15/2004)*

NOCETO

Noceto 1997 Sangiovese (Shenandoah Valley (CA)) $13. 90 Best Buy *—S.H. (12/15/1999)*

Noceto 1998 Riserva Sangiovese (Shenandoah Valley (CA)) $22. 87 *—S.H. (12/1/2001)*

Noceto 1998 Riserva Sangiovese (Shenandoah Valley (CA)) $22. 87 *—S.H. (12/1/2001)*

Noceto 2002 Ferrero Ranch Zinfandel (Shenandoah Valley (CA)) $16. 85 *—S.H. (3/1/2005)*

NONNE GIUSEPPE

Nonne Giuseppe 2001 Neese Vineyards Zinfandel (Redwood Valley) $15. 84 *—S.H. (12/31/2004)*

NONNO ZITO

Nonno Zito 2001 Carmela-Katie Bien Nacidio Vineyards Barbera (Santa Maria Valley) $30. This is the most New World, California Cabernet-inspired Barbera I've ever had. You might almost think it was a Bordeaux variety, with its blackberry jam and chocolate flavors. Soft and unctuous, it's deliciously forward now. Don't even think about aging it for 10 or 20 years, the way the old-style Barberas required. **90** *—S.H. (5/1/2007)*

Nonno Zito 2001 Carmela-Katie Bien Nacidio Vineyards Barbera (Santa Maria Valley) $30. This is the most New World, California Cabernet-inspired Barbera I've ever had. You might almost think it was a Bordeaux variety, with its blackberry jam and chocolate flavors. Soft and unctuous, it's deliciously forward now. From Ambullneo. **90** *—S.H. (5/1/2007)*

Nonno Zito 2002 Carmela-Katie Bien Nacidio Vineyards Merlot (Santa Maria Valley) $30. Shows rich, ripe, Cabernet-style cassis and chocolate fruit and softly ripe, sweet tannins. The fresh acidity gives it an extra boost. Give it time. Best 2007–2012. **92** *—S.H. (5/1/2007)*

Nonno Zito 2002 Giovanna-Jeanette Bien Nacido Vineyards Nebbiolo (Santa Maria Valley) $80. Fresh in primary fruit, jammy blackberry and cherry flavors, with a keen streak of acidity, and an overall sense of balance and complexity. Although this wine has no history of aging, it seems to have everything it needs to develop. Try from 2008–2014. **92 Cellar Selection** *—S.H. (5/1/2007)*

Nonno Zito 2001 Giovanna-Jeanette Bien Nacido Vineyards Nebbiolo (Santa Maria Valley) $80. Held back an extra year and co-released with the '02, this is the best California Nebbiolo I've ever had. There haven't been many serious competitors, but here is a producer that takes the variety seriously. It's made in the style of a Napa Cab, soft and ripe, with intricately layered cherry, plum, minty chocolate and new oak flavors that finish dry and spicy. You can open it now, but it has the tannic depth for 10–15 years in the cellar. **94 Cellar Selection** *—S.H. (6/1/2007)*

NORD ESTATE

Nord Estate 2002 Red Wine Cuvée Bordeaux Blend (Napa Valley) $45. 92 *—S.H. (3/1/2006)*

Nord Estate 2003 Page Nord Vineyard Cabernet Sauvignon (Napa Valley) $42. 88 *—S.H. (3/1/2006)*

Nord Estate 2003 Page Nord Vineyard Cabernet Sauvignon (Napa Valley) $42. 87 *—S.H. (8/1/2006)*

Nord Estate 2002 Chardonnay (Napa Valley) $24. 84 *—S.H. (3/1/2006)*

Nord Estate 2002 Trio Merlot (Yountville) $30. 84 *—S.H. (3/1/2006)*

Nord Estate 2003 Green Island Vineyards Pinot Noir (Napa Valley) $24. 86 *—S.H. (3/1/2006)*

Nord Estate 2001 Diversity Syrah (Napa Valley) $85. 85 *—S.H. (3/1/2006)*

NORMAN

Norman 2002 Conquest Cabernet Sauvignon (Paso Robles) $20. 85 *—S.H. (8/1/2005)*

Norman 2003 Reserve Cabernet Sauvignon (Paso Robles) $36. 85 *—S.H. (12/15/2006)*

Norman 2004 Pinot Grigio (Paso Robles) $15. 83 *—S.H. (2/1/2006)*

Norman 2003 The Vocation Rhône Red Blend (Paso Robles) $32. 85 *—S.H. (12/15/2006)*

Norman 2003 Vino Rosado Dry Rosé Blend (Paso Robles) $15. 86 *—S.H. (12/1/2004)*

Norman 2003 Syrah (Paso Robles) $20. 84 *(9/1/2005)*

Norman 2002 Syrah (Paso Robles) $20. 85 *—S.H. (12/15/2004)*

Norman 2002 The Vocation Syrah (Paso Robles) $32. 85 *(9/1/2005)*

Norman 1998 The Monster Zinfandel (Paso Robles) $18. 85 *—P.G. (3/1/2001)*

Norman 2002 Old Vine Zinfandel (Cucamonga Valley) $19. 83 *—S.H. (11/15/2004)*

Norman 2000 Old Vine Zinfandel Port Zinfandel (Cucamonga Valley) $20. 86 *—S.H. (12/15/2004)*

Norman 2002 The Classic Zinfandel (Paso Robles) $12. 84 *—S.H. (11/15/2004)*

Norman 2002 The Monster Zinfandel (Paso Robles) $20. 85 *—S.H. (11/15/2004)*

Norman 1997 The Monster Zinfandel (Paso Robles) $18. 84 *—P.G. (11/15/1999)*

NORTHSTAR

Northstar 2004 Cabernet Franc (Walla Walla (WA)) $40. Quite roasty-toasty, this is heavily scented with coffee and smoke. Smooth tannins surround plummy fruit, and there is enough concentration for a good, long finish. The blend includes 8% Cab Sauvignon, 4% Petit Verdot and a splash of Merlot. Just 150 cases were made. **91** *—P.G. (12/1/2007)*

Northstar 2004 Merlot (Columbia Valley (WA)) $41. In the blend of this intensely fragrant young wine is 14% Cabernet Sauvignon and 10% Petit Verdot. I like the complexity, the way the primary fruits mix in unusual notes of pineapple along with the black cherry. It's resonant and tangy, with good, long flavors and lots of new oak. This was a year of winemaker transition, and may be the last of the real chocolaty wines from Northstar.

Give this plenty of airing, or cellar it for another 3–4 years. **92** *—P.G. (12/1/2007)*

Northstar 2003 Merlot (Walla Walla (WA)) $60. 87 *—P.G. (11/15/2006)*

Northstar 2003 Merlot (Columbia Valley (WA)) $52. 88 *—P.G. (11/15/2006)*

Northstar 2002 Merlot (Walla Walla (WA)) $60. 88 *—P.G. (12/15/2005)*

Northstar 2002 Merlot (Columbia Valley (WA)) $52. 87 *—P.G. (12/15/2005)*

Northstar 2001 Merlot (Walla Walla (WA)) $60. 90 *—P.G. (7/1/2004)*

Northstar 2001 Merlot (Columbia Valley (WA)) $52. 88 *—P.G. (4/1/2005)*

Northstar 1999 Merlot (Columbia Valley (WA)) $50. 94 Editors' Choice *—P.G. (9/1/2002)*

Northstar 1998 Merlot (Columbia Valley (WA)) $50. 93 Editors' Choice *(10/1/2001)*

Northstar 2003 Syrah (Columbia Valley (WA)) $40. 91 *—P.G. (6/1/2006)*

NOTA BENE CELLARS

Nota Bene Cellars 2004 Abbinare Bordeaux Blend (Washington) $27. Cheval and Champoux. Snappy and crisply defined, this sharp-edged wine opens with tight berry flavors, some chalky acids, and grainy, stony tannins. It shows less flesh than the other reds, more acid, and a stiffness to the tannins. After extensive airing the vanilla flavors come out, along with an interesting spice. The fruit is clean and ripe, and the balance, except possibly for the chalky acids, is right on. **88** *—P.G. (8/1/2007)*

Nota Bene Cellars 2003 Abbinare Bordeaux Blend (Washington) $25. Basically it's the same mix of grapes as the Miscela, but from different vineyard sources. There is a bit of leather and tack room in the nose, but it does not completely submerge the soft, pretty cherry fruit, which finishes with flavors of cut tobacco leaf. This wine is perhaps more approachable and a bit funkier than the Miscela, without the classic structure. **87** *—P.G. (3/1/2007)*

Nota Bene Cellars 2004 Ciel du Cheval Vineyard Bordeaux Blend (Red Mountain) $27. The blend is 47% Cabernet Sauvignon, 24% Merlot, 24% Cabernet Franc, 5% Petit Verdot. Another fine effort from this young winery. Here is classic styling from a great vineyard source, with beautiful definition, and gorgeous, refined and sculpted fruit framed in concise, molded, firm tannins. The tart red fruit is wrapped in crisp acids and finished with tight, hard, slightly bitter tannins. The penetration and elegance of this wine are what stand out; it's young and compact and suggests a long life ahead. **91** *—P.G. (8/1/2007)*

USA

Nota Bene Cellars 2003 Ciel du Cheval Vineyard Bordeaux Blend (Red Mountain) $27. A Bordeaux blend, roughly one third each Cab Sauvignon and Merlot, and the rest split between Cab Franc and Petit Verdot. It says something about the quality of winemaker Tim Narby's efforts that he has access to this fruit, which goes to many of the state's best wineries. He has made an exceptionally fragrant wine, mixing leather, violets and sweet cherry—unusual yet beguiling. In the mouth the wine cuts through, with assertive flavors of cherry, pomegranate, leather, cocoa and coffee. The tannins carry a sense of mineral and earth, as is usually true with Ciel du Cheval fruit. **90** *—P.G. (3/1/2007)*

Nota Bene Cellars 2004 Miscela Bordeaux Blend (Washington) $28. The blend is 40% Merlot, 36% Cab Sauvignon and 24% Cab Franc. Full and fleshy, with broad flavors of black cherry and blackberry. Though plenty ripe and round, the fruit is punctuated with some grainy, dusty, smoky tannins. It's a nice combination, the fruit opening up the wine and the tannins giving it authority. The finish is light but pretty, with hints of oaky butter and cinnamon. **89** *—P.G. (8/1/2007)*

Nota Bene Cellars 2003 Miscela Bordeaux Blend (Washington) $26. This is the winery's Merlot-dominated Bordeaux blend, crafted from a who's who of excellent vineyard sources. It's a step up from the 2002; more structured, more vertical, more confident all around. The fruit is a precision mix of blueberry, blackberry and black cherry; with oak-infused tannins that carry streaks of stone, coffee, vanilla and caramel. This is a young, firm wine, with real muscle. **91** *—P.G. (3/1/2007)*

Nota Bene Cellars 2004 Kestrel View Estates Red Blend (Yakima Valley) $28. This vineyard-designate was first made in 2001, and not since. The tangy fruit shows red berry flavors, cranberry sauce, and some flatness in the midpalate. There is a slightly bitter, slightly medicinal note on the finish. **86** *—P.G. (8/1/2007)*

Nota Bene Cellars 2004 Syrah (Washington) $28. Lush, thick and chewy, with rich purple and black fruits, pepper and a finish of vanilla cream. The tannins are substantial but not intrusive; they carry a sensation of rock and graphite. Flavors extend themselves gracefully; the ripe fruit remains front and center, but it finishes with plenty of nuanced rock and spice and hints of herb. An exceptional effort. **92** *—P.G. (8/1/2007)*

Nota Bene Cellars 2003 Syrah (Washington) $26. It's an interesting experiment—basically a Syrah-dominated Bordeaux blend—but it does not entirely knit together. The Syrah is up front, toasty and peppery, and the Bordeaux grapes lay back, adding weight to the tannins and a sense, more than a flavor, of herb. But there's a disconnect between the two components. As with previous vintages, this wine opens with breathing time, adding smoke and spice to the finish. **88** *—P.G. (3/1/2007)*

Nota Bene Cellars 2002 Syrah (Washington) $22. 84 *(9/1/2005)*

NOVELLA

Novella 2004 Cabernet Sauvignon (Paso Robles) $12. Pretty nice country-style Cabernet, a little hot and peppery, but dry, with the smooth, polished tannins you want in a red table wine. The flavors are of currants, herbs and oak, and at this price, you get lots of style. **85** *—S.H. (5/1/2007)*

Novella 2001 Brothers Vineyard 6, Block 5 Cabernet Sauvignon (Paso Robles) $11. 84 *—S.H. (6/1/2004)*

Novella 2005 Chardonnay (Paso Robles) $10. 85 Best Buy *—S.H. (12/1/2006)*

Novella 2001 Chardonnay (Paso Robles) $11. 84 *—S.H. (6/1/2004)*

Novella 2002 Merlot (Paso Robles) $10. 83 *—S.H. (11/1/2005)*

Novella 2000 Merlot (California) $11. 80 *—S.H. (6/1/2004)*

Novella 2002 Moscato (Paso Robles) $11. 85 *—S.H. (6/1/2004)*

Novella 2003 Muscat Canelli (Paso Robles) $10. 94 Best Buy *—S.H. (11/1/2005)*

Novella 2005 Rayons de Soleil Muscat Canelli (Paso Robles) $12. Lovers of inexpensive sweet white wines have lots to enjoy with this one. It's sweet and fruity in pineapple, apricot, tangerine, vanilla and cinnamon spice flavors, balanced with crisp acids. **85** *—S.H. (5/1/2007)*

Novella 2003 Petite Sirah (Paso Robles) $12. Novella's best wine has been Petite Sirah, which thrives in the dry heat of Paso Robles. With a little Zinfandel and Sangiovese for complexity, this is a very dry, crisp wine, with deep flavors of cherries, plums, dark unsweetened chocolate, espresso and peppery spices. Should hold for at least 10 years. **88** *—S.H. (5/1/2007)*

Novella 2000 Petite Sirah (Paso Robles) $13. 88 Best Buy *(4/1/2003)*

Novella 2002 Brothers Ranch Vineyard Pinot Grigio (Paso Robles) $13. 84 *—S.H. (6/1/2004)*

Novella 2003 Synergy Red Blend (Paso Robles) $14. A blend of Petite Sirah, Zinfandel and Sangiovese, the '03 Synergy is quite a nice wine. It's dry and balanced. You notice the cut of acidity that makes the tastebuds whistle and get ready for food. Then the supporting cast of cherries and herbs steps in. Good food wine, fair price. **85** *—S.H. (5/1/2007)*

Novella 2002 Synergy Red Blend (Paso Robles) $12. 83 *—S.H. (11/1/2005)*

Novella 1999 Synergy Red Blend (Paso Robles) $11. 90 Best Buy *—M.M. (4/1/2002)*

Novella 2005 Sauvignon Blanc (Paso Robles) $10. 84 *—S.H. (12/1/2006)*

Novella 2002 Brothers Vineyard 6, Block 4 Sauvignon Blanc (Paso Robles) $11. 85 *—J.M. (6/1/2004)*

NOVELTY HILL

Novelty Hill 2004 Cabernet Sauvignon (Columbia Valley (WA)) $28. A dark and spicy wine, with streaks of mineral and herb buried within very tart, acidic black fruit. This is complex, quite youthful and tightly woven. I think it will require some years to pull itself together, but the balance is here, in a medium-bodied style, showing some herb, some citrus and plenty of muscle. Tasted over many hours after being decanted, it showed itself to be a wonderful wine that developed multiple layers of flavor. **93** *—P.G. (12/1/2007)*

Novelty Hill 2003 Cabernet Sauvignon (Columbia Valley (WA)) $25. 90 *—P.G. (11/15/2006)*

Novelty Hill 2001 Cabernet Sauvignon (Columbia Valley (WA)) $20. 86 *—P.G. (12/15/2004)*

Novelty Hill 2002 Conner Lee Vineyard Chardonnay (Columbia Valley (WA)) $20. 87 *—P.G. (12/15/2004)*

Novelty Hill 2001 Conner Lee Vineyard Chardonnay (Columbia Valley (WA)) $22. 91 Editors' Choice *—P.G. (9/1/2004)*

Novelty Hill 2005 Stillwater Creek Vineyard Chardonnay (Columbia Valley (WA)) $20. Rich, creamy and lush, this is right up to the very high standard set by the rest of Novelty Hill's white wines. It's rare to taste an American Chardonnay with this mix of exotically ripe fruit, baking spices and crisp natural acids. It just hits every base square on, and takes its time rounding third and heading for a home plate finish. A very impressive effort. **93 Editors' Choice** *—P.G. (11/1/2007)*

Novelty Hill 2004 Merlot (Columbia Valley (WA)) $20. Lovely aromas greet you straight from the glass, as this young, juicy Columbia Valley Merlot brings its bright cherry-berry fruit right up front. There are intimations of chocolate— nothing too heavy—and a clean finish with a lick of stems in the tannin. **88** *—P.G. (12/1/2007)*

Novelty Hill 2003 Merlot (Columbia Valley (WA)) $25. 89 *—P.G. (10/1/2006)*

Novelty Hill 2001 Merlot (Columbia Valley (WA)) $18. 86 *—P.G. (12/15/2004)*

Novelty Hill 2000 Merlot (Columbia Valley (WA)) $25. 89 *—P.G. (9/1/2004)*

Novelty Hill 2004 Stillwater Creek Vineyard Merlot (Columbia Valley (WA)) $25. This wine has a firm, authoritative spine, lending stiff support to the black cherry and blackberry fruit flavors. The tart acids and fine-grained tannins are modulated and in fine form, and the wine sets up nicely in midpalate. Young and compact, it has a good 6-8 years of life ahead. **90** *—P.G. (12/1/2007)*

Novelty Hill 2003 Stillwater Creek Merlot (Columbia Valley (WA)) $25. 91 *—P.G. (10/1/2006)*

Novelty Hill 2003 Klipsun Vineyard Sauvignon Blanc (Red Mountain) $18. 88 *—P.G. (12/1/2004)*

Novelty Hill 2000 Klipsun Vineyard Sauvignon Blanc (Red Mountain) $19. 92 *—P.G. (9/1/2002)*

Novelty Hill 2005 Stillwater Creek Vineyard Sauvignon Blanc (Columbia Valley (WA)) $18. This is top drawer—elegant, detailed and richly varietal. The fruit is tart and tangy but not sour or thin. Mixed green fruits, apple, citrus, and a lightly toasty nose set up a wine with impressive length. The midpalate richness includes ripe melon, butterscotch and cinnamon spice. It's all barrel-fermented in neutral oak. This is a real strength of the brand. **91** *—P.G. (12/1/2007)*

Novelty Hill 2004 Stillwater Creek Sauvignon Blanc (Columbia Valley (WA)) $25. 90 *—P.G. (10/1/2006)*

Novelty Hill 2005 Stillwater Creek Vineyard Sémillon (Columbia Valley (WA)) $16. This is just about perfect Sémillon— the gorgeous fruit has more flesh and breadth with flavors suggesting ripe fig, melon and citrus. The use of oak is judicious and thoughtful; it adds grace notes without dominating. You can't help but wonder why this grape remains such a novelty (except, ironically, at Novelty Hill!). It's seductive, delicious and unique. **92** *—P.G. (12/1/2007)*

Novelty Hill 2003 Syrah (Columbia Valley (WA)) $20. 92 Editors' Choice *—P.G. (10/1/2006)*

Novelty Hill 2002 Syrah (Columbia Valley (WA)) $20. 87 *(9/1/2005)*

Novelty Hill 2004 Stillwater Creek Vineyard Syrah (Columbia Valley (WA)) $28. I can see why so many of Washington's winemakers love this young vineyard. It is already expressing the sort of subtleties that most viticulturalists would kill for. The fruit is ripe but not too sweet or jammy. It is annotated with citrus, leaf and stem, along with streaks of smoke and herb and mineral. It's all mixed together seamlessly and focused into a firm, almost muscular style with real authority. **91** *—P.G. (12/1/2007)*

Novelty Hill 2002 Stillwater Creek Vineyard Syrah (Columbia Valley (WA)) $28. 83 *(9/1/2005)*

NOVY CELLARS

Novy Cellars 2002 Meritage (Mendocino County) $19. 88 *—S.H. (2/1/2005)*

Novy Cellars 2000 Syrah (Napa Valley) $22. 92 *—S.H. (12/1/2002)*

Novy Cellars 2003 Christensen Family Vineyard Syrah (Russian River Valley) $32. 88 *(9/1/2005)*

Novy Cellars 2000 Gary's Syrah (Santa Lucia Highlands) $35. 90 *—S.H. (12/1/2002)*

Novy Cellars 2003 Gary's Vineyard Syrah (Santa Lucia Highlands) $32. 85 *(9/1/2005)*

Novy Cellars 2003 Judge Family Vineyard Syrah (Bennett Valley) $32. 84 *(9/1/2005)*

Novy Cellars 2000 Page-Nord Syrah (Napa Valley) $26. 94 Cellar Selection *—S.H. (12/1/2002)*

Novy Cellars 2002 Page-Nord Vineyard Syrah (Napa Valley) $30. 90 *—S.H. (3/1/2005)*

Novy Cellars 1999 Page-Nord Vineyard Syrah (Napa Valley) $34. 87 *(11/1/2001)*

Novy Cellars 2002 Rosella's Vineyard Syrah (Santa Lucia Highlands) $30. 92 *—S.H. (3/1/2005)*

O'BRIEN

O'Brien 2004 Seduction Bordeaux Blend (Napa Valley) $36. A Bordeaux blend based on Cabernet Sauvignon, this is a beautifully structured, opulent red wine, rich in blackberry, cherry, rum, chocolate and coffee flavors. It shows the firm tannins and clean acids of a young wine, and while it will be beautiful with a grilled steak now, it has the stuffing to last for 10 years. **92** *—S.H. (4/1/2007)*

O'Brien 2005 Chardonnay (Napa Valley) $24. Actually from the cooler Oak Knoll area, this is crisp and earthy. It has rich peach, pear and pineapple fruit, with hints of thyme and rosemary, and a pronounced coating of oak. **86** *—S.H. (4/1/2007)*

O'Brien 2003 Chardonnay (Napa Valley) $18. 84 *—S.H. (5/1/2005)*

O'Brien 2003 Merlot (Napa Valley) $30. Bright and juicy in the mouth, a big, fruity wine that erupts with black cherry, chocolate, orange marmalade, cinnamon, pepper spice and toasted oak flavors. It's a little obvious, but dry and classy. From the cooler Oak Knoll District. **87** *—S.H. (3/1/2007)*

O'Brien 2001 Estate Merlot (Napa Valley) $36. 86 *—S.H. (5/1/2005)*

O'Brien 2002 Seduction Red Blend (Napa Valley) $25. 84 *—S.H. (5/1/2005)*

O'REILLY'S

O'Reilly's 2005 Pinot Gris (Oregon) $13. 88 Best Buy *—P.G. (12/1/2006)*

O'Reilly's 2004 Pinot Gris (Willamette Valley) $12. 91 Best Buy *—P.G. (2/1/2006)*

O'Reilly's 2005 Pinot Noir (Oregon) $15. 86 *—P.G. (12/1/2006)*

O'SHAUGHNESSY

O'Shaughnessy 2001 Cabernet Sauvignon (Howell Mountain) $54. 94 Editors' Choice *—S.H. (10/1/2005)*

OAK HOLLOW WINERY

Oak Hollow Winery 2001 Zinfandel (California) $5. 80 *(11/1/2003)*

OAK KNOLL

Oak Knoll 2004 Pinot Gris (Willamette Valley) $11. 87 Best Buy *—P.G. (2/1/2006)*

Oak Knoll 2000 Pinot Gris (Willamette Valley) $13. 87 *—P.G. (8/1/2002)*

Oak Knoll 2002 Willamette Valley Pinot Gris (Willamette Valley) $11. 86 *—S.H. (8/1/2004)*

Oak Knoll 1999 Pinot Noir (Willamette Valley) $15. 82 *(10/1/2002)*

Oak Knoll 1998 Five Mountains Pinot Noir (Willamette Valley) $40. 86 *—M.S. (12/1/2000)*

Oak Knoll 1999 Five Mountains Vineyard Pinot Noir (Willamette Valley) $30. 83 *(10/1/2002)*

Oak Knoll 1999 Vintage Reserve Pinot Noir (Willamette Valley) $25. 88 *(10/1/2002)*

Oak Knoll 1998 Vintage Reserve Pinot Noir (Willamette Valley) $38. 83 *—J.C. (12/1/2000)*

Oak Knoll 2000 Willamette Valley Pinot Noir (Willamette Valley) $NA. 84 *—S.H. (8/1/2004)*

OAKFORD

Oakford 1996 Cabernet Sauvignon (Oakville) $75. 92 *(12/31/1999)*

Oakford 1995 Cabernet Sauvignon (Oakville) $60. 95 *—S.H. (6/1/1999)*

Oakford 2001 Cabernet Sauvignon (Oakville) $85. 93 Cellar Selection *—S.H. (11/1/2005)*

Oakford 1998 Cabernet Sauvignon (Oakville) $100. 95 Cellar Selection *—S.H. (8/1/2001)*

Oakford 1997 Estate Grown Cabernet Sauvignon (Oakville) $85. 90 *(11/1/2000)*

OAKSTONE

Oakstone 1999 Estate De Cascabel Vineyard Cabernet Sauvignon (Fair Play) $18. 82 *—S.H. (9/1/2002)*

OAKVILLE RANCH

Oakville Ranch 2002 Robert's Blend Bordeaux Blend (Napa Valley) $80. Based on Cab Franc, with some Cab Sauvignon, this wine is marked by huge blackberry and cherry fruit. It's not particularly elegant right now, with green sharpness throughout. Will benefit from decanting; might age well, but it's a gamble. **86** *—S.H. (4/1/2007)*

Oakville Ranch 2001 Estate Robert's Blend Bordeaux Blend (Oakville) $75. 88 *—S.H. (12/15/2005)*

Oakville Ranch 2003 Cabernet Sauvignon (Napa Valley) $60. Ripe, dry and immature, this 100% Cab comes from a vineyard in the Vaca Mountains east of the Silverado Trail. It's quite tight and tannic now, but shows a rich heart of blue and black stone fruits and berries. Seems to have the balance to age, and should improve after 2008. **88** *—S.H. (4/1/2007)*

Oakville Ranch 2001 Cabernet Sauvignon (Oakville) $50. 93 Cellar Selection *—S.H. (11/15/2005)*

Oakville Ranch 2000 Cabernet Sauvignon (Oakville) $42. 85 *—S.H. (3/1/2005)*

Oakville Ranch 2000 Reserve Cabernet Sauvignon (Oakville) $101. 82 —*S.H. (8/1/2005)*

Oakville Ranch 2000 Robert's Blend Cabernet Sauvignon-Cabernet Franc (Oakville) $75. 84 —*S.H. (8/1/2005)*

Oakville Ranch 2004 Chardonnay (Oakville) $35. 87 —*S.H. (7/1/2006)*

Oakville Ranch 2003 Chardonnay (Oakville) $35. 82 —*S.H. (12/15/2005)*

Oakville Ranch 2001 Vista Vineyard Chardonnay (Oakville) $30. 85 —*S.H. (3/1/2005)*

Oakville Ranch 2000 Merlot (Oakville) $33. 82 —*S.H. (3/1/2005)*

Oakville Ranch 2003 Field Blend Red Blend (Napa Valley) $30. 86 —*S.H. (7/1/2006)*

Oakville Ranch 2002 Field Blend Red Blend (Oakville) $30. 88 —*S.H. (12/15/2005)*

Oakville Ranch 2001 Field Blend Red Blend (Oakville) $30. 88 —*S.H. (3/1/2005)*

OASIS

Oasis 1998 Dry Gewürztraminer (Virginia) $18. 81 —*J.C. (8/1/1999)*

Oasis 2004 Pinot Noir (Santa Barbara County) $22. 90 —*S.H. (3/1/2006)*

Oasis NV Dogwood Blush Rosé Blend (Virginia) $10. 80 —*J.C. (8/1/1999)*

OBSIDIAN

Obsidian 2002 Obsidian Ridge Vineyard Cabernet Sauvignon (Lake County) $25. 90 —*S.H. (11/15/2004)*

Obsidian 2004 Obsidian Ridge Vineyard Syrah (Red Hills Lake County) $25. This needs work, but it's promising for several reasons. The fruit is tremendous in sappy blackberry jam, blueberries and roasted coffee bean. The tannins are huge, but smooth and ripe. The oak is clunky, but this is definitely a Syrah to watch. 86 —*S.H. (4/1/2007)*

Obsidian 2003 Obsidian Ridge Vineyard Syrah (Red Hills Lake County) $25. 85 *(9/1/2005)*

OBSIDIAN RIDGE

Obsidian Ridge 2004 Obsidian Ridge Vineyard Cabernet Sauvignon (Red Hills Lake County) $25. I understand what they're trying to do in Red Hills, a potentially exciting appellation of Lake County. But it's a hot climate and 2004 was a hot year, resulting in a Cab that is sweet, soft and high in alcohol. The best feature is the rich blackberry fruit. Drink now. 84 —*S.H. (4/1/2007)*

ODISEA

Odisea 2006 Muse Rosé Rosé Blend (California) $15. Simple, crisp and enjoyable, with watermelon, raspberry, rose petal and spice flavors that finish dry. Grenache, Mourvèdre, Tempranillo and Viognier. 84 —*S.H. (7/1/2007)*

OJAI

Ojai 2004 Bien Nacido Vineyard Chardonnay (Santa Maria Valley) $28. 92 —*S.H. (8/1/2006)*

Ojai 2002 Bien Nacido Vineyard Syrah (Santa Barbara County) $40. 92 Cellar Selection —*S.H. (8/1/2006)*

OKANAGAN ESTATE

Okanagan Estate 2004 Pinot Grigio (Washington) $NA. 89 —*P.G. (2/1/2006)*

OLD BROOKVILLE

Old Brookville 2000 Gold Coast Reserve Chardonnay (Long Island) $14. 81 —*J.M. (9/10/2002)*

OLDE LOCKFORD

Olde Lockford 2005 Old Vine Zinfandel (Lodi) $16. Too soft in structure, too simple in flavor to earn a better score, but if you're not fussy, the wine will get you through a hamburger. 82 —*S.H. (12/15/2007)*

OLIVET LANE

Olivet Lane 1997 Pinot Noir (Russian River Valley) $20. 87 *(12/15/1999)*

OLSON OGDEN

Olson Ogden 2003 Syrah (Sonoma County) $22. 87 *(9/1/2005)*

Olson Ogden 2004 Unti Vineyard Syrah (Dry Creek Valley) $33. Richly fruity and ripe, almost sweet in plum sauce, espresso and pomegranate flavors, this is a young wine. It has fresh, firm tannins and a citrusy cut of acidity. A little immature right now; should hold and improve by early 2007, and drink well for a year or two. 87 —*S.H. (5/1/2007)*

Olson Ogden 2003 Unti Vineyard Syrah (Dry Creek Valley) $29. 83 *(9/1/2005)*

Olson Ogden 2002 Unti Vineyard Syrah (Dry Creek Valley) $29. 89 —*S.H. (5/1/2005)*

OPOLO

Opolo 2000 Cabernet Sauvignon (Paso Robles) $32. 89 —*S.H. (8/1/2003)*

Opolo 2001 Estate Cabernet Sauvignon (Paso Robles) $30. 82 —*S.H. (5/1/2005)*

Opolo 2002 Rhapsody Meritage (Paso Robles) $45. 85 —*S.H. (5/1/2005)*

Opolo 2002 Merlot (Paso Robles) $26. 84 —*S.H. (5/1/2005)*

Opolo 2000 Merlot (Paso Robles) $26. 88 —*S.H. (12/15/2003)*

Opolo 2002 Pinot Noir (Paso Robles) $24. 84 —*S.H. (5/1/2005)*

Opolo 2000 Pinot Noir (Central Coast) $32. 87 —*S.H. (7/1/2003)*

Opolo 2003 Roussanne (Central Coast) $20. 84 —*S.H. (5/1/2005)*

Opolo 2000 Syrah (Paso Robles) $28. 87 —*S.H. (12/1/2002)*

Opolo 2001 Estate Syrah (Paso Robles) $24. 90 —*S.H. (5/1/2005)*

Opolo 2003 Viognier (Central Coast) $22. 84 —*S.H. (5/1/2005)*

Opolo 2003 Mountain Zinfandel (Paso Robles) $24. 83 —*S.H. (5/1/2005)*

Opolo 2003 Reserve Zinfandel (Paso Robles) $32. 87 —*S.H. (5/1/2005)*

Opolo 2003 Summit Creek Zinfandel (Paso Robles) $18. 85 —*S.H. (5/1/2005)*

OPTIMA

Optima 2001 Cabernet Sauvignon (Alexander Valley) $40. 90 —*S.H. (11/15/2005)*

Optima 2003 Rosé of Cabernet Sauvignon (Alexander Valley) $13. 83 —*S.H. (10/1/2004)*

Optima 2003 Zinfandel (Dry Creek Valley) $25. 92 Editors' Choice —*S.H. (11/15/2005)*

OPUS ONE

Opus One 2000 Bordeaux Blend (Napa Valley) $125. 92 —*S.H. (12/1/2004)*

Opus One 2001 Cabernet Blend (Napa Valley) $160. 95 Cellar Selection —*S.H. (11/1/2005)*

ORBIS

Orbis 2000 Chardonnay (Carneros) $19. 91 Editors' Choice —*S.H. (12/15/2002)*

OREANA

Oreana 2005 Sauvignon Blanc (California) $18. 88 —*S.H. (11/1/2006)*

Oreana 2005 Verdelho (California) $22. 84 —*S.H. (11/1/2006)*

ORCHID HILL

Orchid Hill 2004 Pinot Noir (Paso Robles) $27. Feels a bit hot and sweet for a Pinot, although there are some pretty blackberry, cherry, cola and spice flavors. It may come from a cool part of Paso, but this Central Coast appellation is just too hot for Pinot. 84 —*S.H. (2/1/2007)*

Orchid Hill 2005 Viognier (Paso Robles) $21. An awkward wine. The alcohol is very high and hot and the wine is a little sweet, with Lifesaver candy flavors. 82 —*S.H. (2/1/2007)*

Orchid Hill 2004 Zinfandel Primi Zinfandel (Paso Robles) $22. Nice everyday Zin for its upfront fruit and rich tannins. Floods the mouth with blackberries, chocolate and spicy flavors that are as ripe as pie filling, but the wine stays dry. 83 —*S.H. (2/1/2007)*

OREANA

Oreana 2005 ? Red Table Wine Red Blend (California) $9. There's a big, orange question mark on the front label—that's all there is—so it's easy to recognize this Cabernet and Syrah blend on the shelf. The wine is so-so, sharp and raw in green-tinged cherry flavors. 83 —*S.H. (8/1/2007)*

ORFILA

Orfila 1997 Ambassador's Reserve Limited B Chardonnay (San Diego County) $15. 87 *(6/1/2000)*

Orfila 2003 Ambassador's Reserve Merlot (San Diego County) $28. 85 —*S.H. (12/15/2006)*

Orfila 1997 Ambassador's Reserve Limited B Merlot (San Diego County) $25. 81 —*J.C. (7/1/2000)*

Orfila 2000 Limited Bottling Ambassador's Reserve Merlot (San Diego County) $28. 84 —*S.H. (12/15/2003)*

Orfila 2001 Pinot Noir (Edna Valley) $41. 87 —*S.H. (12/15/2006)*

Orfila 1999 Pinot Noir (Edna Valley) $35. 84 —*S.H. (2/1/2003)*

Orfila 1997 Limited Bottling Pinot Noir (Arroyo Grande Valley) $30. 84 —*J.C. (5/1/2000)*

Orfila NV Lotus Cuvée Lot #123 Rhône White Blend (San Pasqual) $28. 86 —*S.H. (5/1/2005)*

Orfila NV Lotus Lot #45 Rhône White Blend (San Pasqual) $28. 87 —*S.H. (12/15/2006)*

Orfila 1998 Sangiovese (San Pasqual) $20. 82 —*S.H. (12/1/2002)*

Orfila 2003 Di Collina Sangiovese (San Pasqual) $20. 85 —*S.H. (12/15/2006)*

Orfila 2001 Di Collina Sangiovese (San Pasqual) $20. 83 —*S.H. (5/1/2005)*

Orfila 1999 Syrah (San Pasqual) $24. 84 —*S.H. (12/1/2002)*

Orfila 1999 Limited Bottling Val de la Mer Syrah (San Pasqual) $25. 85 —*S.H. (12/15/2003)*

Orfila 2003 Val de la Mer Syrah (San Pasqual) $25. 80 —*S.H. (12/15/2006)*

Orfila 1998 Val de la Mer Estate Syrah (San Pasqual) $24. 88 *(11/1/2001)*

Orfila 1998 Lotus Cuvée Viognier (San Pasqual) $28. 89 —*S.H. (4/1/2002)*

Orfila NV Lotus White Blend (San Pasqual) $28. 85 —*S.H. (12/15/2002)*

Orfila 2004 Gold Rush Zinfandel (California) $24. 86 —*S.H. (12/15/2006)*

Orfila 2002 Gold Rush Old Vines Zinfandel (California) $24. 82 —*S.H. (5/1/2005)*

Orfila 2001 Gold Rush, Old Vines Zinfandel (California) $22. 83 *(11/1/2003)*

ORGANIC VINTNERS

Organic Vintners 2003 California Collection Vegan Cabernet Sauvignon (Mendocino) $15. 85 —*S.H. (8/1/2005)*

Organic Vintners 2003 Vegan Pinot Noir (Mendocino) $15. 84 —*S.H. (12/1/2005)*

ORIEL

Oriel 2002 Midnight Rambler Cabernet Sauvignon (Rutherford) $30. 87 —*S.H. (11/1/2005)*

Oriel 2003 Dylan Chardonnay (Russian River Valley) $25. 82 —*S.H. (11/1/2005)*

Oriel 2003 Jasper Pinot Noir (Russian River Valley) $25. 85 —*S.H. (11/1/2005)*

ORIGIN

Origin 2002 Paramount Cabernet Blend (Napa Valley) $65. 91 —*S.H. (10/1/2005)*

Origin 2002 Family Home Cabernet Sauvignon (Napa Valley) $55. 88 —*S.H. (10/1/2005)*

Origin 2002 Heritage Sites Red Blend (Napa Valley) $35. 87 —*S.H. (10/1/2005)*

ORIGIN NAPA

Origin Napa 2003 Gamble Vineyard Sauvignon Blanc (Napa Valley) $27. 86 *(7/1/2005)*

Origin Napa 2001 Gamble Vineyard Sauvignon Blanc (Napa Valley) $23. 85 —*S.H. (10/1/2003)*

Origin Napa 2002 Heart Block Sauvignon Blanc (Napa Valley) $50. 90 —*S.H. (12/15/2004)*

OROGENY

Orogeny 2005 Chardonnay (Green Valley) $25. From this little RRV subregion, this is a superdrinkable Chard with lots of interesting characteristics. It has a soft-sharp feeling, a buttery crispness, and the flavors, while on the modest side, are rewarding in tropical fruits and apricots. Finishes dry and complex. 88 —*S.H. (8/1/2007)*

Orogeny 2005 Pinot Noir (Green Valley) $35. Good everyday Pinot, showing the racy acidity and silk-and-taffeta mouthfeel of the appellation and vintage. Bone dry and a little thin in cherry fruit, its tartness calls for food. Ahi tuna tartare will be nice. 85 —*S.H. (8/1/2007)*

Orogeny 2004 Pinot Noir (Green Valley) $30. 88 —*S.H. (11/15/2006)*

Orogeny 2003 Pinot Noir (Green Valley) $30. 87 —*S.H. (12/1/2005)*

Orogeny 2002 Pinot Noir (Green Valley) $25. 85 *(11/1/2004)*

Orogeny 2005 Fox Den Vineyard Pinot Noir (Green Valley) $50. Shows the clear, fine color, silky mouthfeel and crisp acidity that characterize a fine, cool climate Pinot Noir, but I wish the fruit were a little more concentrated. It's fine in cola, red cherry, pomegranate and rhubarb, but the middle is thin and the finish is quick. Drink now. 86 —*S.H. (8/1/2007)*

ORTMAN FAMILY

Ortman Family 2002 Cabernet Sauvignon (Napa Valley) $35. 85 —*S.H. (4/1/2006)*

Ortman Family 2001 Cabernet Sauvignon (Napa Valley) $45. 87 —*S.H. (3/1/2005)*

Ortman Family 2000 Cabernet Sauvignon (Napa Valley) $50. 91 —*S.H. (5/1/2004)*

Ortman Family 2005 Chardonnay (Edna Valley) $25. The best thing about this Chard is that refreshing Edna Valley backbone of acidity. Otherwise, it's just another ripe, oaky California Chard, with the usual tropical fruit and buttered toast flavors. But those juicy acids make it keen and vital. 87 —*S.H. (3/1/2007)*

Ortman Family 2004 Chardonnay (Edna Valley) $25. 87 —*S.H. (10/1/2006)*

Ortman Family 2003 Chardonnay (Edna Valley) $24. 89 —*S.H. (12/1/2005)*

Ortman Family 2002 Chardonnay (Edna Valley) $25. 87 —*S.H. (6/1/2005)*

Ortman Family 2001 Chardonnay (Edna Valley) $28. 90 —*S.H. (5/1/2004)*

Ortman Family 2005 Pinot Noir (Santa Rita Hills) $35. This is Ortman's best Pinot since 2002, perhaps because of the vintage's relative coolness. It's dry, silky and balanced, and shows a really nice coastal character. Pop this open now and enjoy the elaborate cherry, raspberry, orange Pekoe tea, root beer, gingerbread and licorice spice flavors. 88 —*S.H. (12/1/2007)*

Ortman Family 2004 Pinot Noir (Santa Rita Hills) $30. 87 —*S.H. (11/15/2006)*

Ortman Family 2003 Pinot Noir (Willamette Valley) $30. 84 —*S.H. (12/1/2005)*

Ortman Family 2003 Pinot Noir (Santa Rita Hills) $30. 84 —*S.H. (12/1/2005)*

Ortman Family 2002 Pinot Noir (Santa Barbara County) $34. 90 —*S.H. (11/1/2004)*

Ortman Family 2001 Pinot Noir (Santa Barbara County) $34. 87 —*S.H. (5/1/2004)*

Ortman Family 2004 Fiddlestix Vineyard Pinot Noir (Santa Rita Hills) $40. 90 —*S.H. (12/15/2006)*

Ortman Family 2003 Fiddlestix Vineyard Pinot Noir (Santa Rita Hills) $40. 85 —*S.H. (12/1/2005)*

Ortman Family 2005 Syrah Rosé Blend (Paso Robles) $16. 83 —*S.H. (11/1/2006)*

Ortman Family 2002 Sangiovese (Paso Robles) $20. 85 —*S.H. (11/15/2004)*

Ortman Family 2004 Syrah (Paso Robles) $20. After a shaky start, Ortman is beginning to get its Syrah act together. It's not easy making a high-quality Syrah for this price, but this one manages to do it. Dry, soft and lush, it shows opulent blackberry, cherry, plum, coffee and chocolate flavors, with a spicy finish. Drink now. 89 —*S.H. (9/1/2007)*

Ortman Family 2003 Syrah (San Luis Obispo County) $25. 86 *(9/1/2005)*

Ortman Family 2002 Syrah (San Luis Obispo County) $25. 86 —*S.H. (6/1/2005)*

Ortman Family 2001 Syrah (San Luis Obispo County) $25. 86 —*S.H. (5/1/2004)*

Ortman Family 2006 Syrah Rosé Syrah (Paso Robles) $16. Brings to mind Beaujolais Nouveau, with that fresh, vinous, slightly gassy, high acid fruit that tastes like it's right out of the fermenting tank. With 7% Viognier, the wine is dry and brisk in cherries, raspberries, lime, root beer and vanilla spices. 85 —*S.H. (7/1/2007)*

OS WINERY

OS Winery 2004 Bordeaux Blend (Washington) $22. 88 —*P.G. (10/1/2006)*

OS Winery 2003 Champoux Vineyard Bordeaux Blend (Columbia Valley (WA)) $30. 88 —*P.G. (12/15/2005)*

OS Winery 2004 Champoux Vineyard Cabernet Franc (Horse Heaven Hills) $30. OS consistently makes one of the best Cab Francs in the state—for me it is always their best wine. Here again the flavors are a powerful mix of ripe berries, cherries, strawberry jam and streaks of coffee and tobacco. Firm and confident, drinks well right now. 91 —*P.G. (3/1/2007)*

OS Winery 2004 Meek Vineyard Petite Verdot (Yakima Valley) $42. 89 —*P.G. (10/1/2006)*

OS Winery 2003 Red Blend (Columbia Valley (WA)) $20. 88 —*P.G. (12/15/2005)*

OS Winery 2004 R3 Red Blend (Columbia Valley (WA)) $35. "My basic idea," says winemaker Bill Owen, "is Catherine Deneuve; if it reminds me of her in Belle du Jour, I'm happy. She's my inspiration; taste the wine." Okay! This is the winery's softer, most detailed wine, done in a lighter, more elegantly feminine style. A lovely wine, with no harsh edges. 88 —*P.G. (3/1/2007)*

OS Winery 2004 Sheridan Vineyard Ulysses Red Blend (Yakima Valley) $50. 87 —*P.G. (10/1/2006)*

OS Winery 2003 Sheridan Vineyard Ulysses Red Blend (Yakima Valley) $50. 93 *—P.G. (12/15/2005)*

OS Winery 2006 Champoux Vineyard Riesling (Horse Heaven Hills) $22. A good follow-up to the 2005, though not as ripe and rich. The lemon drop flavors are thinned out, and the 3% residual sugar is down by a full percentage point. This is firm, tangy and crisp, but does not have the concentration to carry it to the next level. It seems to hit a plateau and sit there through the finish. **87** *—P.G. (9/1/2007)*

OS Winery 2005 Champoux Vineyard Riesling (Horse Heaven Hills) $22. 90 *—P.G. (10/1/2006)*

OS Winery 2004 Dineen Vineyard Syrah (Yakima Valley) $42. 89 *—P.G. (11/15/2006)*

OSPREY'S DOMINION

Osprey's Dominion 2002 Cabernet Franc (North Fork of Long Island) $22. 84 *—M.D. (8/1/2006)*

Osprey's Dominion 2001 Cabernet Franc (North Fork of Long Island) $18. 87 *—M.D. (8/1/2006)*

Osprey's Dominion 2002 Flight Meritage (North Fork of Long Island) $35. 87 *—M.D. (8/1/2006)*

Osprey's Dominion 2001 Flight Meritage (North Fork of Long Island) $35. 85 *—M.D. (8/1/2006)*

Osprey's Dominion 2000 Flight Meritage (North Fork of Long Island) $35. 80 *—M.D. (8/1/2006)*

Osprey's Dominion 2002 Merlot (North Fork of Long Island) $18. 87 *—M.D. (8/1/2006)*

Osprey's Dominion 2001 Merlot (North Fork of Long Island) $18. 85 *—J.C. (3/1/2006)*

Osprey's Dominion 2000 Merlot (North Fork of Long Island) $18. 84 *—J.C. (10/2/2004)*

Osprey's Dominion 2002 Reserve Merlot (North Fork of Long Island) $35. 85 *—M.D. (8/1/2006)*

OTIS KENYON

Otis Kenyon 2004 Cabernet Sauvignon (Walla Walla (WA)) $28. The fruit, from Panorama vineyards, is one of the few Walla Walla Valley wines made in 2004, the year of a major freeze. I like this winery's debut effort very much; it's lush, toasty and smoky, firm in the mouth and structured around solid cassis and black cherry fruit. The oak is a presence, adding a nice smoky thread to the long, coffee-flavored finish. **89** *—P.G. (3/1/2007)*

OTTIMINO VINEYARDS

Ottimino Vineyards 2001 Von Weidlich Vineyard Zinfandel (Russian River Valley) $36. 89 *(11/1/2003)*

OUTPOST

Outpost 2000 Pringle Family Vineyard Zinfandel (Howell Mountain) $45. 94 *—C.S. (11/1/2002)*

OVENE

Ovene 2004 The Puzzle Grenache (Central Coast) $25. Has the color, weight and silky texture of Pinot Noir, with a nice acidity for balance. Unfortunately, the flavors are not as good. There's a vegetal aspect to the raspberries and cherries that lowers the score. **84** *—S.H. (12/1/2007)*

Ovene 2005 Pinot Noir (Santa Rita Hills) $45. Don't look to this expensive Pinot as a prime example of Santa Rita Hills. It's too soft and simple in oak-influenced raspberry and cherry jam. **84** *—S.H. (12/1/2007)*

Ovene 2005 Solomon Hills Vineyard Pinot Noir (Santa Maria Valley) $40. The vineyard is new, within sight of the Pacific and is owned by the family that controls Bien Nacido. This Pinot shows its promise. It has a young-vine simplicity, with ripe raspberry, cherry, root beer and spice flavors, and is ready to drink now. But the tannic-acid structure is such that this is a wine to watch. **88** *—S.H. (12/1/2007)*

Ovene 2005 The Puzzle Pinot Noir (San Luis Obispo County) $30. Soft, semisweet and simple, this has flavors of mashed, very ripe cherries and raspberries, with vanilla and caramel oak influences. **84** *—S.H. (12/1/2007)*

Ovene 2004 The Puzzle Syrah (Central Coast) $25. This is a new winery for me. It was started by a veteran of the wine industry on the business side. Not clear exactly where the grapes come from along the sprawling Central Coast, but they're quite ripe in blackberry jam and licorice flavors, although there's a bite of acidity and tannins for balance. Appeals for its directness. Drink now. **86** *—S.H. (12/1/2007)*

OWEN ROE

Owen Roe 2004 Rosa Mystica Cabernet Franc (Columbia Valley (WA)) $36. 88 *—P.G. (8/1/2006)*

Owen Roe 2003 DuBrul Vineyard Cabernet Sauvignon (Yakima Valley) $60. 90 *—P.G. (8/1/2006)*

Owen Roe 2004 DuBrul Vineyard Merlot (Yakima Valley) $45. 90 *—P.G. (8/1/2006)*

Owen Roe 2004 Pinot Gris (Willamette Valley) $20. 91 *—P.G. (2/1/2006)*

Owen Roe 2004 Red Blend (Yakima Valley) $42. 91 *—P.G. (8/1/2006)*

Owen Roe 2004 Lady Rosa Syrah (Columbia Valley (WA)) $45. 89 *—P.G. (8/1/2006)*

OWEN-SULLIVAN

Owen-Sullivan 2004 BSH Bordeaux Blend (Columbia Valley (WA)) $35. The BSH blend is two thirds Cabernet Sauvignon, the rest a mix of Bordeaux blend grapes. The Cab is definitely in the driver's seat, pushing out flavors of cherry/berry and whiffs of straw and cooked plum. It's consistent with the ripe, somewhat volatile house style, but offering smooth, well-integrated flavors and subtle use of new oak. **88** *—P.G. (3/1/2007)*

Owen-Sullivan 2002 BSH Bordeaux Blend (Washington) $35. 87 *—P.G. (6/1/2005)*

Owen-Sullivan 2000 Champoux Vineyard Cabernet Franc (Columbia Valley (WA)) $25. 88 *—P.G. (6/1/2002)*

Owen-Sullivan 2000 Klipsun Vineyard Merlot (Red Mountain) $25. 87 *—P.G. (6/1/2002)*

Owen-Sullivan 2002 Ulysses Merlot-Cabernet Sauvignon (Yakima Valley) $50. 87 *—P.G. (6/1/2005)*

OWL RIDGE

Owl Ridge 2003 Brigden Vineyard Cabernet Sauvignon (Sonoma County) $50. 93 Cellar Selection *—S.H. (9/1/2006)*

Owl Ridge 2003 T.R. Passalacqua Vineyard Cabernet Sauvignon (Dry Creek Valley) $48. The 40% new French oak dominates right now, releasing refined aromas of char, cedar, cigar box and vanilla. Below that are profoundly ripe scents of cassis, black currants, mocha, herbs and minerals. Quite dry and tannic, but so powerful are the flavors and so balanced is the wine that it should easily negotiate the next 10 years. Decant now and serve with roasts, grills. **92** *—S.H. (10/1/2007)*

Owl Ridge 2004 Vineyard Select Cabernet Sauvignon (Sonoma County) $38. 86 *—S.H. (12/31/2006)*

Owl Ridge 2004 Vineyard Select Chardonnay (Sonoma Coast) $32. 86 *—S.H. (12/31/2006)*

PACIFIC ECHO

Pacific Echo 1996 Champagne Blend (Anderson Valley) $27. 85 *(12/15/1999)*

Pacific Echo 1995 Blanc de Blancs Champagne Blend (Anderson Valley) $27. 89 *(12/31/2000)*

Pacific Echo NV Brut Champagne Blend (Mendocino County) $22. 87 *—P.G. (12/31/2000)*

Pacific Echo NV Brut Champagne Blend (Mendocino County) $22. 88 *—J.M. (12/1/2002)*

Pacific Echo 1995 Brut Champagne Blend (Anderson Valley) $33. 93 *—S.H. (6/1/2001)*

Pacific Echo 1997 Brut Rosé Champagne Blend (Mendocino County) $27. 90 *—S.H. (6/1/2001)*

Pacific Echo NV Crémant Champagne Blend (Anderson Valley) $23. 87 *—S.H. (12/31/2000)*

Pacific Echo 1995 Private Reserve Brut Champagne Blend (Anderson Valley) $31. 88 *—M.M. (12/31/2000)*

Pacific Echo 1992 Private Reserve Brut Champagne Blend (Anderson Valley) $32. 91 *—M.S. (12/1/2000)*

Pacific Echo 1996 Blanc de Blancs Sparkling Blend (Anderson Valley) $27. 91 *—J.M. (12/1/2003)*

Pacific Echo 1998 Brut Sparkling Blend (Anderson Valley) $22. 88 *—J.M. (12/1/2003)*

Pacific Echo 1998 Brut Rosé Sparkling Blend (Anderson Valley) $24. 91 Editors' Choice *—J.M. (12/1/2003)*

Pacific Echo NV Cramant Sparkling Blend (Anderson Valley) $22. 84 *—J.M. (12/1/2003)*

PACIFIC OASIS

Pacific Oasis 2005 Pinot Noir (Santa Barbara County) $25. The wine is a blend of Santa Maria Valley and Los Alamos Valley. It's more of a textbook Pinot than a thrilling one, with good cherry-spice flavors. **85** *—S.H. (7/1/2007)*

Pacific Oasis 2005 Syrah (Santa Barbara County) $14. Dry, crisp in acids and earthy, this has a dash of Viognier, which brightens what otherwise might be a heavy wine. It has flavors of coffee, blackberries and cherryskins. **84** *—S.H. (7/1/2007)*

PACIFIC RIDGE

Pacific Ridge 2004 Grace Bordeaux Blend (Napa Valley) $55. This is a Merlot-Cabernet blend from St. Helena and Oakville. It's pretty good, dry and rich in black currants, cherries and oak. The tannins are stronger than on your average gooey cult Cab, with a peppery astringency suggesting modest aging. Try after 2008. **91** *—S.H. (12/15/2007)*

PACIFIC STAR

Pacific Star 1996 Venturi Vineyard Charbono (Mendocino County) $32. 89 *—S.H. (12/1/2001)*

Pacific Star 2000 Pamela's Vineyard Chardonnay (Mendocino County) $NA. 84 *—S.H. (6/1/2003)*

Pacific Star 1999 Liebelt Vineyards Merlot (Lodi) $20. 83 *—S.H. (7/1/2002)*

Pacific Star 1997 Reserve Merlot (Mendocino County) $22. 84 *—S.H. (12/1/2001)*

Pacific Star 1999 Meadows Vineyard Mourvèdre (Contra Costa County) $20. 84 *—S.H. (11/15/2001)*

Pacific Star 2000 Petite Sirah (Mendocino County) $26. 82 *(4/1/2003)*

Pacific Star 1999 Reserve Petite Sirah (Mendocino County) $26. 86 *—S.H. (9/1/2003)*

Pacific Star 2001 Coro Mendocino Red Blend (Mendocino) $35. 84 *—J.M. (9/1/2004)*

Pacific Star 1999 Dad's Daily Red Red Blend (California) $12. 83 *—S.H. (11/15/2002)*

Pacific Star 2000 Viognier (California) $16. 82 *—S.H. (12/15/2001)*

Pacific Star 1999 Zinfandel (Mendocino County) $14. 82 *—S.H. (12/15/2001)*

Pacific Star 1999 B-Bar-X Ranch Reserve Zinfandel (Mendocino County) $24. 83 *—S.H. (12/15/2001)*

PAEONIA

Paeonia 2003 Late Harvest Bien Nacido Vineyard Pinot Blanc (Santa Maria Valley) $30. 88 *—S.H. (8/1/2006)*

PAGE

Page 1999 Bordeaux Blend (Napa Valley) $58. 93 Cellar Selection *—J.M. (5/1/2003)*

PAGE CELLARS

Page Cellars 2001 Preface Red Wine Bordeaux Blend (Red Mountain) $37. 88 *—P.G. (9/1/2004)*

Page Cellars 2002 Preface Cabernet Sauvignon-Cabernet Franc (Red Mountain) $37. 85 *—P.G. (6/1/2006)*

Page Cellars 2002 Syrah (Columbia Valley (WA)) $37. 85 *—P.G. (11/15/2004)*

PAGOR

Pagor 2001 Tempranillo (California) $11. 86 *—J.M. (11/15/2003)*

PAIGE 23

Paige 23 2000 Syrah (Santa Barbara County) $21. 93 Editors' Choice *—S.H. (12/1/2002)*

PAINTER BRIDGE

Painter Bridge 2003 Chardonnay (California) $7. 82 *—S.H. (5/1/2005)*

Painter Bridge 2001 Chardonnay (California) $7. 87 Best Buy *—S.H. (2/1/2003)*

Painter Bridge 2002 Zinfandel (California) $7. 83 *—S.H. (5/1/2005)*

PALMAZ

Palmaz 2004 Cabernet Sauvignon (Napa Valley) $100. Few Cabs on earth are riper than this, with its enormous flavors of black currants, cherry-pie filling, plum jam and chocolate that overwhelm the mouth with decadence. It's modern in tannins, which are soft and finely ground, and opulent in smoky, spicy new oak. It is, in short, the very model of a Napa cult Cab. **92** *—S.H. (12/31/2007)*

Palmaz 2002 Cabernet Sauvignon (Napa Valley) $100. 88 *—S.H. (5/1/2006)*

Palmaz 2001 Cabernet Sauvignon (Napa Valley) $100. 90 *—S.H. (5/1/2005)*

PALMER

Palmer 1997 Select Reserve Bordeaux Blend (North Fork of Long Island) $25. 87 *(4/1/2001)*

Palmer 1995 Select Reserve Bordeaux Blend (North Fork of Long Island) $25. 84 *—J.C. (12/1/1999)*

Palmer 2002 Proprietor's Reserve Cabernet Franc (North Fork of Long Island) $19. 80 *—M.D. (8/1/2005)*

Palmer 1998 Proprietor's Reserve Cabernet Franc (North Fork of Long Island) $18. 88 Editors' Choice *—J.C. (4/1/2001)*

Palmer 1997 Proprietor's Reserve Cabernet Franc (North Fork of Long Island) $18. 88 *—J.C. (12/1/1999)*

Palmer 1998 Cabernet Sauvignon (North Fork of Long Island) $15. 83 *—J.C. (4/1/2001)*

Palmer 2002 Proprietors Reserve Cabernet Sauvignon (North Fork of Long Island) $NA. 80 *—M.D. (8/1/2006)*

Palmer 2003 5 Acre Block Chardonnay (North Fork of Long Island) $NA. 81 *—J.C. (3/1/2006)*

Palmer 1995 Barrel-Fermented Chardonnay (North Fork of Long Island) $17. 81 *—J.C. (8/1/2000)*

Palmer 1998 Estate Chardonnay (North Fork of Long Island) $12. 84 *—J.C. (4/1/2001)*

Palmer 1997 Estate Chardonnay (North Fork of Long Island) $12. 84 *—J.C. (8/1/1999)*

Palmer 1998 Reserve Chardonnay (North Fork of Long Island) $15. 86 *—J.C. (4/1/2001)*

Palmer 1999 Gewürztraminer (North Fork of Long Island) $15. 84 *—J.C. (4/1/2001)*

Palmer 1999 Select Harvest Gewürztraminer (North Fork of Long Island) $30. 89 *—J.C. (4/1/2001)*

Palmer 2003 Merlot (North Fork of Long Island) $NA. A smoked oak treatment in the barrels lends a unique nose to this plum and berry-forward wine. On the palate, the taste of that oak wanders into the realm of roasted, though the ripeness of the fruit helps to balance. Not much dimension. Pair with pork or red meat. **82** *—S.K. (2/1/2007)*

Palmer 1997 Merlot (North Fork of Long Island) $18. 83 *—J.C. (4/1/2001)*

Palmer 2002 Reserve Merlot (North Fork of Long Island) $30. 81 *—M.D. (12/1/2006)*

Palmer 1997 Reserve Merlot (North Fork of Long Island) $30. 86 *—J.C. (4/1/2001)*

Palmer 1998 Vintner's Cuvée Merlot (North Fork of Long Island) $10. 83 *—J.C. (1/1/2004)*

Palmer 1998 Estate Pinot Blanc (North Fork of Long Island) $13. 83 *—J.C. (4/1/2001)*

Palmer 1997 Lieb Vineyards Pinot Blanc (North Fork of Long Island) $13. 86 *—J.C. (8/1/1999)*

Palmer 2001 White Riesling (North Fork of Long Island) $14. 85 *—J.C. (8/1/2003)*

Palmer 1998 Select Reserve White Blend (North Fork of Long Island) $14. 86 *—J.C. (4/1/2001)*

Palmer 2000 White Riesling (North Fork of Long Island) $13. 85 *—J.C. (3/1/2002)*

PALMERI

Palmeri 2004 Stagecoach Vineyard Syrah (Napa Valley) $51. The most important aspect of this wine is acidity. Without it, it would be just another mushy, chocolate- and blackberry-flavored wine. With the crispness, it achieves real balance, and lets the palate discover additional complexities of sweet, smoky leather, moo shu plum sauce and a salty tang of blood. **93** *—S.H. (9/1/2007)*

Palmeri 2002 Stagecoach Vineyard Syrah (Napa Valley) $47. 89 *(9/1/2005)*

Palmeri 2003 Van Ness Vineyard Syrah (Alexander Valley) $47. 93 *—S.H. (2/1/2006)*

PALMINA

Palmina 2004 Alisos Vineyard Pinot Grigio (Santa Barbara County) $22. 85 *—S.H. (3/1/2006)*

PALOMA

Paloma 2004 Merlot (Napa Valley) $54. Grown on Spring Mountain, this is front-loaded in young, primary fruit character, and shows firm, fresh tannins that require aging. There aren't many Merlots that will benefit from four to eight years in the cellar like this one. It's stuffed with vibrant black cherry, blackberry and spicy cola flavors, and has the balanced integrity of a fine, ageworthy Napa red. **92 Cellar Selection** *—S.H. (3/1/2007)*

Paloma 2002 Merlot (Spring Mountain) $51. 94 Cellar Selection *—S.H. (10/1/2005)*

Paloma 1999 Syrah (Spring Mountain) $36. 90 *(11/1/2001)*

PALOTAI

Palotai 2002 Pinot Noir (Umpqua Valley) $18. 85 *(11/1/2004)*

PALUMBO FAMILY VINEYARDS

Palumbo Family Vineyards 2000 Tre Fratelli Bordeaux Blend (Temecula) $28. 82 *—S.H. (4/1/2004)*

PANTHER CREEK

Panther Creek 1993 Brut Champagne Blend (Willamette Valley) $50. 86 *—K.F. (12/1/2002)*

Panther Creek 2004 Melrose Vineyard Pinot Gris (Oregon) $18. 89 *—P.G. (2/1/2006)*

Panther Creek 2003 Anden Vineyard Pinot Noir (Willamette Valley) $40. Reasonably firm and concentrated up front, the wine continues with generic fruit flavors that fail to show much Pinot character. Flavors tail off quickly, leaving rough tannins and a watery finish. **86** *—P.G. (4/1/2007)*

Panther Creek 2000 Arcus Pinot Noir (Willamette Valley) $60. 91 Cellar Selection *(10/1/2002)*

Panther Creek 1999 Arcus Estate Pinot Noir (Willamette Valley) $60. 92 *—S.H. (11/1/2001)*

Panther Creek 2000 Bednarik Vineyard Pinot Noir (Willamette Valley) $48. 86 *(10/1/2002)*

Panther Creek 1998 Bednarik Vineyard Pinot Noir (Willamette Valley) $48. 92 *—J.C. (12/1/2000)*

Panther Creek 2003 Freedom Hill Vineyard Pinot Noir (Willamette Valley) $40. This excellent vineyard does not show its best stuff here. There's good color, and a whiff of pleasant spice in the nose, but the back half is watery and carries an off, resiny character. **85** *—P.G. (4/1/2007)*

Panther Creek 2000 Freedom Hill Pinot Noir (Willamette Valley) $48. 86 *(10/1/2002)*

Panther Creek 1999 Freedom Hill Pinot Noir (Willamette Valley) $49. 90 *—S.H. (11/1/2001)*

Panther Creek 1998 Freedom Hill Vineyard Pinot Noir (Willamette Valley) $48. 91 *—J.C. (12/1/2000)*

Panther Creek 2003 Nysa Vineyard Pinot Noir (Willamette Valley) $40. A pretty nose is the whole story here; once in the mouth the wine is light and watery, with a chalky finish. It seems a bit odd that in such a hot, ripe vintage, all these Panther Creek Pinots are so watery and posted at just 13% alcohol. **86** *—P.G. (4/1/2007)*

Panther Creek 2002 Nysa Vineyard Pinot Noir (Willamette Valley) $40. 85 *(11/1/2004)*

Panther Creek 2000 Nysa Vineyard Pinot Noir (Willamette Valley) $48. 84 *(10/1/2002)*

Panther Creek 1999 Nysa Vineyard Pinot Noir (Willamette Valley) $49. 88 *—J.C. (11/1/2001)*

Panther Creek 1998 Nysa Vineyard Pinot Noir (Willamette Valley) $48. 90 *—M.S. (12/1/2000)*

Panther Creek 2000 Red Hills Pinot Noir (Willamette Valley) $60. 87 *(10/1/2002)*

Panther Creek 1999 Red Hills Estate Pinot Noir (Willamette Valley) $60. 87 *—S.H. (11/1/2001)*

Panther Creek 1999 Reserve Pinot Noir (Willamette Valley) $40. 87 *(11/1/2001)*

Panther Creek 1998 Reserve Pinot Noir (Willamette Valley) $36. 91 *—M.S. (12/1/2000)*

Panther Creek 2003 Shea Vineyard Pinot Noir (Willamette Valley) $40. Stiff, chalky tannins take over quickly, after a light, slightly spicy entry. Like the rest of the '03 lineup the wine seems thin and watery, and the mouthfeel a bit stressed. The vineyard is capable of much more. **86** *—P.G. (4/1/2007)*

Panther Creek 2002 Shea Vineyard Pinot Noir (Willamette Valley) $40. 88 *(11/1/2004)*

Panther Creek 2000 Shea Vineyard Pinot Noir (Willamette Valley) $48. 88 *(10/1/2002)*

Panther Creek 1999 Shea Vineyard Pinot Noir (Willamette Valley) $49. 89 *(11/1/2001)*

Panther Creek 2003 Temperance Hill Vineyard Pinot Noir (Willamette Valley) $40. Another thin, watery effort. Despite the excellent vineyard source and the hot vintage, this awkward wine gives back very little except its dark color and stemmy tannins. **85** *—P.G. (4/1/2007)*

Panther Creek 2002 Temperance Hill Vineyard Pinot Noir (Willamette Valley) $40. 85 *(11/1/2004)*

Panther Creek 2000 Winemaker's Cuvee Pinot Noir (Oregon) $35. 87 *(10/1/2002)*

Panther Creek 2003 Winemaker's Cuvée Pinot Noir (Willamette Valley) $20. 85 *—P.G. (11/15/2005)*

Panther Creek 2002 Winemaker's Cuvée Pinot Noir (Oregon) $25. 86 *(11/1/2004)*

Panther Creek 2000 Youngberg Pinot Noir (Willamette Valley) $48. 92 Editors' Choice *(10/1/2002)*

PANTHER HILLS

Panther Hills 2004 Shiraz (Oklahoma) $9. There's not much beyond the earthy nose on this Shiraz from Oklahoma producer Panther Hills. The color is brown, and the fruit tired and watery, leaving just a hint of leather and oak on the palate. The finish is weak. **80** *—S.K. (2/1/2007)*

Panther Hills 2004 Shiraz (Oklahoma) $9. There's not much beyond the earthy nose on this Shiraz from Oklahoma producer Panther Hills. The color is brown, and the fruit tired and watery, leaving just a hint of leather and oak on the palate. The finish is weak. **80** *—S.K. (2/1/2007)*

PANZA

Panza 2000 Stag's Leap Ranch Petite Sirah (Napa Valley) $NA. 88 *(4/1/2003)*

PAOLETTI

Paoletti 1997 Cabernet Sauvignon (Napa Valley) $48. 87 *(11/1/2000)*

Paoletti 1997 Non Plus Ultra Cabernet Sauvignon (Napa Valley) $110. 90 *(11/1/2000)*

PAPAPIETRO PERRY

Papapietro Perry 2003 Pinot Noir (Russian River Valley) $38. 85 *—S.H. (3/1/2006)*

Papapietro Perry 2002 Pinot Noir (Russian River Valley) $38. 87 *—S.H. (3/1/2005)*

Papapietro Perry 2003 Leras Family Vineyards Pinot Noir (Russian River Valley) $45. 86 *—S.H. (3/1/2006)*

Papapietro Perry 2004 Peters Vineyard Pinot Noir (Sonoma Coast) $45. This is from the cool Sonoma Coast, but 2004 was a blistering vintage and the heat struck at harvest. The result is that this Pinot has a cooked berry taste, like cherry pie filling that leaked from the crust in the oven and partly caramelized. Still, the wine is dry, silky and elegant. **86** *—S.H. (5/1/2007)*

Papapietro Perry 2003 Peters Vineyard Pinot Noir (Sonoma Coast) $45. 85 *—S.H. (3/1/2006)*

Papapietro Perry 2002 Peters Vineyard Pinot Noir (Sonoma Coast) $42. 90 *—S.H. (3/1/2005)*

Papapietro Perry 2003 Pommard Clones Pinot Noir (Sonoma Coast) $58. 85 *—S.H. (3/1/2006)*

Papapietro Perry 2004 Zinfandel (Russian River Valley) $33. Classic California Zin, with cherry, blackberry and loganberry flavors and that briary, brambly edge of freshly picked wild fruit. You'll also find loads of spices and fresh green thyme and sage. Finishes with a slight sweetness, although it's basically a dry wine, with some elegance and finesse. **88** *—S.H. (5/1/2007)*

Papapietro Perry 2003 Zinfandel (Russian River Valley) $30. 93 *—S.H. (3/1/2006)*

PAPIO

Papio 2004 Cabernet Sauvignon (California) $6. 83 Best Buy *—S.H. (12/31/2005)*

Papio 2004 Chardonnay (California) $6. 84 Best Buy *—S.H. (12/31/2005)*

Papio 2004 Merlot (California) $6. 82 *—S.H. (12/31/2005)*

PARADIGM

Paradigm 2002 Cabernet Sauvignon (Oakville) $53. 92 *—S.H. (7/1/2006)*

Paradigm 2001 Cabernet Sauvignon (Oakville) $53. 91 *—S.H. (11/1/2005)*

Paradigm 1997 Estate Bottled Cabernet Sauvignon (Napa Valley) $48. 92 *(11/1/2000)*

PARADIS

Paradis 1997 Woodbridge Ranch Cabernet Sauvignon (California) $12. 80 *—S.H. (11/15/2001)*

Paradis 1999 Woodbridge Ranch Chardonnay (California) $10. 81 *—S.H. (11/15/2001)*

Paradis 1997 Woodbridge Ranch Merlot (California) $10. 85 Best Buy *—J.C. (6/1/2001)*

Paradis 2001 Cask Reserve/Old Vine Zinfandel (Lodi) $12. 87 Best Buy *—J.M. (11/1/2003)*

PARADISE RANCH

Paradise Ranch 2002 Rockpile Vineyard Cabernet Sauvignon (Sonoma County) $35. 84 *—S.H. (12/1/2006)*

PARADISE RIDGE

Paradise Ridge 2000 Cabernet Sauvignon (Sonoma County) $28. 85 *—S.H. (10/1/2003)*

Paradise Ridge 1999 Cabernet Sauvignon (Sonoma County) $25. 83 *—S.H. (7/1/2002)*

Paradise Ridge 1998 Cabernet Sauvignon (Sonoma County) $22. 82 *—S.H. (12/1/2001)*

Paradise Ridge 2001 Elevation Rockpile Vineyard Cabernet Sauvignon (Sonoma County) $36. 87 *—S.H. (10/1/2004)*

Paradise Ridge 2003 Ladi's Vineyard Cabernet Sauvignon (Sonoma County) $28. Soft and dull, with blackberry and cherry jam and sweet vanilla flavors. The tannins and acids both are low. Not going anywhere. 82 *—S.H. (12/1/2007)*

Paradise Ridge 2002 Ladi's Vineyard Cabernet Sauvignon (Sonoma County) $27. 84 *—S.H. (12/1/2006)*

Paradise Ridge 2001 Ladi's Vineyard Cabernet Sauvignon (Sonoma County) $29. 85 *—S.H. (2/1/2005)*

Paradise Ridge 2003 Rockpile Vineyard Cabernet Sauvignon (Sonoma County) $38. Tastes more like a Zin than a Cab, with rustic tannins and a peppery, briary flavor of wild berries. The wine is dry, but way too soft for any development, so drink now. 84 *—S.H. (12/1/2007)*

Paradise Ridge 1997 Barrel Select Nagasawa Vineyard Chardonnay (Sonoma County) $18. 82 *(6/1/2000)*

Paradise Ridge 2002 Nagasawa Vineyard Chardonnay (Sonoma County) $22. 87 *—S.H. (2/1/2005)*

Paradise Ridge 2001 Nagasawa Vineyard Chardonnay (Sonoma County) $19. 84 *—S.H. (6/1/2003)*

Paradise Ridge 2000 Nagasawa Vineyard Chardonnay (Sonoma County) $18. 87 *—S.H. (12/31/2001)*

Paradise Ridge 1998 Nagasawa Vineyard Chardonnay (Sonoma County) $16. 80 *—S.H. (11/15/2001)*

Paradise Ridge 2003 Merlot (Sonoma County) $20. This is a very dark Syrah. It may be unfiltered; when I popped the cork, it left an inky residue on my palm. Don't let it bother you. There are some fierce tannins now that hide the fruit, but the core of blackberries and chocolate suggests midterm aging. Best 2007-2010. 87 *—S.H. (2/1/2007)*

Paradise Ridge 2001 Merlot (Sonoma County) $28. 86 *—S.H. (12/1/2005)*

Paradise Ridge 2000 Ladi's Vineyard Merlot (Sonoma County) $25. 84 *—S.H. (12/15/2003)*

Paradise Ridge 1999 Ladi's Vineyard Merlot (Sonoma County) $23. 84 *—S.H. (7/1/2002)*

Paradise Ridge 1998 Ladi's Vineyard Merlot (Sonoma County) $22. 84 *—S.H. (12/1/2001)*

Paradise Ridge 2003 Rockpile Vineyard Merlot (Sonoma County) $32. Smells and tastes vegetal; this is not a successful wine. 82 *—S.H. (12/1/2007)*

Paradise Ridge 2002 Rockpile Vineyard Merlot (Sonoma County) $30. 85 *—S.H. (12/1/2006)*

Paradise Ridge 2002 Pinot Noir (Russian River Valley) $29. 86 *(11/1/2004)*

Paradise Ridge 2004 Elizabeth & Henry's Vineyard Pinot Noir (Russian River Valley) $32. Nicely ripe, smooth, textbook Russian River Pinot. It rewards for its silky texture and ripe cherry pie filling, chocolate and spice flavors, balanced with good acidity. Not a complicated ager, it's fine now and for a couple years. 87 *—S.H. (7/1/2007)*

Paradise Ridge 2003 Elizabeth and Henry's Vineyard Pinot Noir (Sonoma Coast) $32. 82 *—S.H. (12/31/2005)*

Paradise Ridge 2002 Elizabeth and Henry's Vineyard Pinot Noir (Russian River Valley) $29. 87 *(11/1/2004)*

Paradise Ridge 2006 Grandview Vineyard Sauvignon Blanc (Russian River Valley) $17. My bottle still had some spritz going on. It finished with a treacly flavor of pineapple custard that's on the semisweet side. The spritz will go away, but sweetness won't. 84 *—S.H. (12/1/2007)*

Paradise Ridge 2005 Grandview Vineyard Sauvignon Blanc (Russian River Valley) $16. With no oak or malo — an increasingly popular style in whites — the fruit stars here. Tart green apples, grapefruits, limes, kiwis, persimmons and figs mingle and swirl into a long, clean and nicely dry finish. 87 *—S.H. (2/1/2007)*

Paradise Ridge 2003 Grandview Vineyard Sauvignon Blanc (Sonoma County) $15. 86 *—S.H. (2/1/2005)*

Paradise Ridge 2001 Grandview Vineyard Sauvignon Blanc (Sonoma County) $14. 87 *—S.H. (9/1/2003)*

Paradise Ridge 2000 Grandview Vineyard Sauvignon Blanc (Sonoma County) $14. 87 *—S.H. (12/15/2001)*

Paradise Ridge 1999 Grandview Vineyard Sauvignon Blanc (Sonoma County) $14. 82 *—S.H. (11/15/2001)*

Paradise Ridge 2003 Garrod Ranch Syrah (Santa Cruz Mountains) $30. An awkward wine. While it's very ripe, the raspberry, cherry and blackberry flavors are simple and jammy, and there's a sweet-sour taste that's accompanied by gritty tannins. 83 *—S.H. (12/1/2007)*

Paradise Ridge 2002 Garrod Ranch Syrah (Santa Cruz Mountains) $29. 86 *—S.H. (2/1/2005)*

Paradise Ridge 2001 Hoenselaars Vineyard Upper Block Syrah (Sonoma County) $32. 90 *—S.H. (12/15/2003)*

Paradise Ridge 2002 Ladi's Vineyard Syrah (Sonoma County) $28. 87 *—S.H. (12/1/2005)*

Paradise Ridge 2001 Ladi's Vineyard Syrah (Sonoma County) $28. 87 *—S.H. (12/1/2004)*

Paradise Ridge 2000 Ladi's Vineyard Syrah (Sonoma County) $27. 87 *—S.H. (12/1/2002)*

Paradise Ridge 1999 Ladi's Vineyard Syrah (Sonoma County) $25. 84 *—S.H. (7/1/2002)*

Paradise Ridge 2005 Hoenselaars Vineyard Zinfandel (Russian River Valley) $32. An unbalanced wine, at once overripe with hot, raisiny flavors, and underripe with sage and wintergreen. But then, Zinfandel is notorious as an uneven ripener. Okay as an everyday Zin, but drink now. 84 *—S.H. (12/1/2007)*

Paradise Ridge 2004 Hoenselaars Vineyard Zinfandel (Russian River Valley) $30. This is a very rich, flavorful Zin, strong in fruits and spices. It calls for equally powerfully flavored foods. With its array of blackberries, cherries, mocha, rum punch and macaroon flavors and thick tannins, it will be good with a broiled steak in a wine reduction sauce. 88 *—S.H. (2/1/2007)*

Paradise Ridge 2003 Hoenselaars Vineyard Zinfandel (Russian River Valley) $30. 82 *—S.H. (12/31/2005)*

Paradise Ridge 2001 Hoenselaars Vineyard Lower Block Zinfandel (Sonoma County) $25. 90 *—S.H. (3/1/2004)*

Paradise Ridge 2002 Hoenselaars Vineyard Upper Block Zinfandel (Sonoma County) $27. 87 *—S.H. (11/15/2004)*

PARADUXX

Paraduxx 2002 Red Blend (Napa Valley) $43. 87 *—S.H. (8/1/2005)*

Paraduxx 1999 Red Blend (Napa Valley) $40. 89 *—C.S. (12/1/2002)*

Paraduxx 2002 Paraduxx Red Blend (Napa Valley) $43. 84 *—S.H. (12/1/2005)*

Paraduxx 2004 Red Wine Red Blend (Napa Valley) $45. This year the blend is Zinfandel, Cabernet Sauvignon and Merlot. As always, the wine is rich, complex, ageable, and unique among California reds. Zin brings its distinctly briary, wild berry taste to the pedigree of the Bordeaux varieties. The result is a balanced, elegant and refined wine that will stand 5-8 years of age. A great accomplishment, with nearly 13,000 cases produced. 91 *—S.H. (10/1/2007)*

Paraduxx 2003 Red Wine Red Blend (Napa Valley) $45. 89 *—S.H. (12/1/2006)*

Paraduxx 2001 Red Wine Red Blend (Napa Valley) $43. 88 *—S.H. (8/1/2004)*

PARAISO VINEYARDS

Paraiso Vineyards 2005 Chardonnay (Santa Lucia Highlands) $18. Here's a nice, everyday Chard that shows the pedigree of its appellation in the balance of crisp acidity and ripe fruit. Shows peach, apple, apricot and smoky vanilla flavors that finish with a dusting of Asian spice. 85 *—S.H. (12/15/2007)*

Paraiso Vineyards 2004 Chardonnay (Santa Lucia Highlands) $16. 84 *—S.H. (10/1/2006)*

Paraiso Vineyards 2003 Chardonnay (Santa Lucia Highlands) $18. 86 *—S.H. (12/1/2005)*

Paraiso Vineyards 2002 Chardonnay (Monterey County) $18. 83 —*S.H. (5/1/2005)*

Paraiso Vineyards 2001 Chardonnay (Santa Lucia Highlands) $16. 86 *(10/1/2003)*

Paraiso Vineyards 2000 Chardonnay (Santa Lucia Highlands) $16. 85 —*S.H. (6/1/2003)*

Paraiso Vineyards 1999 Chardonnay (Monterey County) $16. 89 —*S.H. (5/1/2001)*

Paraiso Vineyards 1998 Chardonnay (Santa Lucia Highlands) $16. 86 —*S.H. (11/15/2000)*

Paraiso Vineyards 1997 Chardonnay (Santa Lucia Highlands) $16. 85 —*L.W. (7/1/1999)*

Paraiso Vineyards 2004 Eagles' Perch Chardonnay (Santa Lucia Highlands) $35. Classic cool climate Chard, with brisk, keen acidity framing bright, pure kiwi, Key lime pie and vanilla flavors. Shows an elegant balance that makes it a great apéritif wine, but also a natural for the table. 250 cases produced. **91** —*S.H. (5/1/2007)*

Paraiso Vineyards 2003 Eagles' Perch Chardonnay (Santa Lucia Highlands) $30. 91 Cellar Selection —*S.H. (12/1/2006)*

Paraiso Vineyards 1999 Pinot Blanc (Santa Lucia Highlands) $13. 87 —*S.H. (5/1/2001)*

Paraiso Vineyards 1998 Pinot Blanc (Santa Lucia Highlands) $13. 86 *(3/1/2000)*

Paraiso Vineyards 1997 Pinot Blanc (Monterey County) $13. 83 —*J.C. (11/1/1999)*

Paraiso Vineyards 1997 Reserve Pinot Blanc (Santa Lucia Highlands) $23. 87 —*J.C. (11/1/1999)*

Paraiso Vineyards 2005 Pinot Noir (Santa Lucia Highlands) $25. Simple, earthy, with modest cherry flavors breaking through the mushrooms and dried herbs. On the plus side, it's dry, silky and balanced. Drink now. **84** —*S.H. (7/1/2007)*

Paraiso Vineyards 2004 Pinot Noir (Santa Lucia Highlands) $20. This is Paraiso's basic Pinot, and it's okay, a good expression of the variety at a decent price. It's clean, crisp and dry, with a silky texture framing cherry, root beer, cola and cinnamon spice flavors. **86** —*S.H. (7/1/2007)*

Paraiso Vineyards 2003 Pinot Noir (Santa Lucia Highlands) $22. 87 —*S.H. (12/1/2005)*

Paraiso Vineyards 2002 Pinot Noir (Monterey County) $20. 83 —*S.H. (5/1/2005)*

Paraiso Vineyards 2001 Pinot Noir (Santa Lucia Highlands) $20. 86 *(10/1/2003)*

Paraiso Vineyards 2000 Pinot Noir (Santa Lucia Highlands) $16. 83 *(10/1/2002)*

Paraiso Vineyards 1999 Pinot Noir (Monterey) $16. 84 *(10/1/2002)*

Paraiso Vineyards 2006 Rosé of Pinot Noir (Santa Lucia Highlands) $14. A little sweet for my taste, but the acidity is here for balance, the texture delicate and sensual, and the cherry, root beer and spicy flavors are quite tasty. **85** —*S.H. (9/1/2007)*

Paraiso Vineyards 2005 West Terrace Pinot Noir (Santa Lucia Highlands) $40. This is Paraiso's most expensive Pinot, a block selection from their estate vineyard in the southern part of the Highlands. The wine is very good, although for some reason not quite up there with the 2001 or 2003. The fruity ripeness shows in the forward cherry, raspberry and cola-root beer flavors, and and wine is fully dry. Drink now. **88** —*S.H. (12/31/2007)*

Paraiso Vineyards 2003 West Terrace Pinot Noir (Santa Lucia Highlands) $40. 91 —*S.H. (11/15/2006)*

Paraiso Vineyards 2002 West Terrace Pinot Noir (Santa Lucia Highlands) $40. 86 —*S.H. (12/1/2005)*

Paraiso Vineyards 2001 West Terrace Pinot Noir (Santa Lucia Highlands) $40. 92 —*S.H. (12/15/2004)*

Paraiso Vineyards 2000 West Terrace Pinot Noir (Santa Lucia Highlands) $32. 88 *(10/1/2003)*

Paraiso Vineyards 2006 Riesling (Santa Lucia Highlands) $14. Made in the slightly sweet German style, this Riesling shows crisp, high acidity that gives the sugary peach, pineapple, green apple and honeysuckle flavors a simple balance and harmony. **86** —*S.H. (12/31/2007)*

Paraiso Vineyards 2005 Riesling (Santa Lucia Highlands) $14. 84 —*S.H. (12/15/2006)*

Paraiso Vineyards 2004 Riesling (Santa Lucia Highlands) $14. 89 Best Buy —*S.H. (12/1/2005)*

Paraiso Vineyards 2001 Riesling (Monterey County) $14. 85 —*S.H. (9/1/2003)*

Paraiso Vineyards 2001 Riesling (Santa Lucia Highlands) $13. 85 —*S.H. (9/1/2003)*

Paraiso Vineyards 1999 Riesling (Monterey County) $10. 88 Best Buy —*S.H. (5/1/2001)*

Paraiso Vineyards 1998 Riesling (Santa Lucia Highlands) $9. 87 Best Buy —*L.W. (9/1/1999)*

Paraiso Vineyards 2002 Syrah (Santa Lucia Highlands) $20. 87 *(9/1/2005)*

Paraiso Vineyards 2001 Syrah (Santa Lucia Highlands) $20. 88 *(10/1/2003)*

Paraiso Vineyards 2000 Syrah (Santa Lucia Highlands) $24. 86 —*S.H. (6/1/2003)*

Paraiso Vineyards 1999 Syrah (Santa Lucia Highlands) $24. 88 *(11/1/2001)*

Paraiso Vineyards 1997 Syrah (Santa Lucia Highlands) $23. 91 *(11/1/1999)*

Paraiso Vineyards 2003 Wedding Hill Syrah (Santa Lucia Highlands) $45. This low-production Syrah is one of the more interesting in California. This year, it's fairly tannic, with a fascinating interplay between the tannins, acids, oak and flavors. The tastes range from blackberries and pomegranates through coffee and cola to violets, and the finish is dry, with no residual sugar. Best now through 2010. **91** —*S.H. (2/1/2007)*

Paraiso Vineyards 2001 Wedding Hill Syrah (Santa Lucia Highlands) $45. 95 —*S.H. (12/15/2004)*

Paraiso Vineyards 2000 Wedding Hill Syrah (Santa Lucia Highlands) $40. 89 *(10/1/2003)*

PARDUCCI

Parducci 2002 Cabernet Sauvignon (Mendocino County) $10. 83 —*S.H. (12/31/2004)*

Parducci 2001 Cabernet Sauvignon (California) $10. 85 —*S.H. (5/1/2004)*

Parducci 2000 Cabernet Sauvignon (Mendocino) $9. 84 —*S.H. (8/1/2003)*

Parducci 1999 Cabernet Sauvignon (Mendocino) $9. 88 —*S.H. (5/1/2002)*

Parducci 1997 Reserve Cabernet Sauvignon (Mendocino) $14. 85 —*S.H. (4/1/2004)*

Parducci 2002 Chardonnay (Mendocino County) $10. 82 —*S.H. (10/1/2004)*

Parducci 2001 Chardonnay (Mendocino) $9. 84 —*S.H. (8/1/2003)*

Parducci 2000 Chardonnay (Mendocino) $9. 87 —*S.H. (5/1/2002)*

Parducci 1998 Largo Ranch Reserve Chardonnay (Mendocino County) $20. 84 *(6/1/2000)*

Parducci 1998 Reserve Chardonnay (Mendocino County) $16. 81 *(6/1/2000)*

Parducci 2003 Vintage White Chardonnay-Sauvignon (North Coast) $4. 85 Best Buy —*S.H. (12/1/2004)*

Parducci 2001 Merlot (California) $9. 85 —*S.H. (12/1/2003)*

Parducci 1999 Merlot (Mendocino) $10. 89 —*S.H. (5/1/2002)*

Parducci 2000 Petite Sirah (California) $10. 85 —*S.H. (12/31/2003)*

Parducci 1998 Reserve Petite Sirah (Mendocino) $14. 88 —*S.H. (12/31/2003)*

Parducci 2003 True Grit Petite Sirah (Mendocino) $25. Parducci is proud of their history with Petite Sirah. The name "True Grit" seems to suggest their own stick-to-itiveness, and the wine's gutsy personality. It shows massive cherry, blackberry, plum, cocoa, tobacco, balsamic, soy, coffee and Asian spice flavors, and will probably age forever. Good now with grilled meats. **92** —*S.H. (3/1/2007)*

Parducci 2004 Pinot Grigio (California) $10. 84 —*S.H. (2/1/2006)*

Parducci 2002 Pinot Noir (Mendocino County) $10. 83 —*S.H. (11/1/2004)*

Parducci 2001 Pinot Noir (Willamette Valley) $9. 84 —*S.H. (8/1/2003)*

Parducci 2001 Pinot Noir (Mendocino) $9. 83 —*S.H. (12/1/2003)*

Parducci 2000 Pinot Noir (Mendocino) $9. 80 *(10/1/2002)*

Parducci 1999 Red Blend (Mendocino) $5. 83 —*S.H. (11/15/2003)*

Parducci 2001 Coro Mendocino Red Blend (Mendocino) $35. 86 —*J.M. (9/1/2004)*

Parducci 1997 Sangiovese (Mendocino County) $10. 87 Best Buy —*S.H. (12/15/1999)*

Parducci 2003 Sauvignon Blanc (Lake County) $8. 83 —*S.H. (12/1/2004)*

Parducci 2002 Sauvignon Blanc (Lake County) $8. 84 Best Buy —*S.H. (10/1/2003)*

Parducci 1998 Reserve Syrah (Mendocino) $14. 84 —*S.H. (10/1/2003)*

Parducci 2001 White Blend (North Coast) $5. 83 —*S.H. (7/1/2003)*

Parducci 2000 Zinfandel (Mendocino) $9. 85 Best Buy —*S.H. (9/1/2003)*

Parducci 1997 Vineyard Select Zinfandel (Mendocino) $10. 83 —*P.G. (11/15/1999)*

Parducci 2003 White Zinfandel (Mendocino County) $5. 83 *—S.H. (11/15/2004)*

Parducci 2002 White Zinfandel (California) $5. 84 *—S.H. (3/1/2004)*

PARKER STATION

Parker Station 2003 Chardonnay (Santa Barbara County) $12. 83 *—S.H. (5/1/2006)*

Parker Station 2001 Pinot Noir (Santa Barbara County) $12. 84 *—S.H. (4/1/2004)*

Parker Station 2003 Syrah (Santa Barbara County) $12. 87 Best Buy *—S.H. (5/1/2006)*

PARKERS ESTATE

Parkers Estate 2003 Private Reserve Old Vine Street Cabernet Sauvignon (Sonoma County) $15. 83 *—S.H. (2/1/2006)*

Parkers Estate 2004 Private Reserve Blue Ash Road Chardonnay (Sonoma County) $15. 85 *—S.H. (2/1/2006)*

Parkers Estate 2002 Private Reserve North Peyton Block Merlot (Sonoma County) $15. 82 *—S.H. (2/1/2006)*

Parkers Estate 2003 Private Reserve Dillon Ranch Zinfandel (Sonoma County) $15. 87 *—S.H. (4/1/2006)*

PARKMON

Parkmon 2005 White Hawk Vineyard Syrah (Santa Barbara County) $30. The problem with this wine is it's too sweet and hot. It goes beyond rich, ripe fruit into frankly jellied flavors of blackberries, cherries and vanilla, with a Port-y finish. The alcohol is 15.4%. 83 *—S.H. (12/31/2007)*

Parkmon 2006 Marsha's Vineyard Viognier (Russian River Valley) $22. There's lots of exotic Viognier character packed into this fruity, slightly sweet wine. It's powerful in peach and pineapple flavors that are so ripe, they taste like melted jelly, with a hit of alcohol. 84 *—S.H. (12/31/2007)*

Parkmon 2005 Evangelho Vineyard Ancient Vines Zinfandel (Contra Costa County) $24. Too sweet and sugary. The relatively low alcohol (13.7%) seems to have been accomplished at the cost of residual sugar, making the cherry and blackberry fruit taste like a dessert wine. 81 *—S.H. (12/31/2007)*

PARRY CELLARS

Parry Cellars 2002 Cabernet Sauvignon (St. Helena) $48. 84 *—S.H. (4/1/2006)*

Parry Cellars 2001 Cabernet Sauvignon (Napa Valley) $46. 90 *—S.H. (10/3/2004)*

Parry Cellars 2000 Cabernet Sauvignon (Napa Valley) $40. 85 *—S.H. (4/1/2004)*

PARSONAGE VILLAGE

Parsonage Village 2001 Cabernet Sauvignon (Carmel Valley) $42. 82 *—S.H. (8/1/2004)*

Parsonage Village 2001 Reserve Cabernet Sauvignon (Carmel Valley) $54. 84 *—S.H. (8/1/2004)*

Parsonage Village 2001 Chardonnay (Carmel Valley) $36. 86 *—S.H. (9/1/2004)*

Parsonage Village 2001 Syrah (Carmel Valley) $36. 86 *—S.H. (8/1/2004)*

Parsonage Village 2001 Carmelstone Reserve Syrah (Carmel Valley) $54. 91 *—S.H. (8/1/2004)*

PASCHAL

Paschal 2000 Quartet Red Wine Bordeaux Blend (Applegate Valley) $25. 86 *—P.G. (8/1/2002)*

Paschal 1998 Cabernet Sauvignon (Applegate Valley) $28. 87 *—P.G. (4/1/2002)*

Paschal 2000 Reserve Cabernet Sauvignon (Rogue Valley) $28. 89 *—M.S. (8/1/2003)*

Paschal 1999 Chardonnay (Rogue Valley) $16. 88 *—P.G. (8/1/2002)*

Paschal 2000 Estate Chardonnay (Rogue Valley) $18. 88 *—P.G. (8/1/2002)*

Paschal 2001 Estate Grown Chardonnay (Rogue Valley) $18. 85 *—M.S. (9/1/2003)*

Paschal 2000 Merlot (Applegate Valley) $25. 87 *—P.G. (8/1/2002)*

Paschal 2000 Pinot Blanc (Rogue Valley) $16. 90 Editors' Choice *—P.G. (8/1/2002)*

Paschal 2001 Pinot Gris (Rogue Valley) $18. 80 *—M.S. (8/1/2003)*

Paschal 1999 Pinot Gris (Rogue Valley) $18. 82 *—P.G. (2/1/2002)*

Paschal 2000 Estate Pinot Noir (Rogue Valley) $24. 86 *—P.G. (8/1/2002)*

Paschal 2001 Syrah (Rogue Valley) $26. 85 *—M.S. (9/1/2003)*

Paschal 1998 Syrah-Cabernet (Oregon) $24. 85 *—P.G. (8/1/2002)*

PASSALACQUA

Passalacqua 2004 Gia Domella Zinfandel (Russian River Valley) $24. There's an old fashioned quality to this Zin, good for washing down sausages, lamb, char-broiled beef, a savory roast chicken. There's some overripeness, in the raisins and chocolaty Port, but in this case, it's fine, just a quirky part of the wine's likeable personality. 86 *—S.H. (2/1/2007)*

PATIANNA ORGANIC VINEYARDS

Patianna Organic Vineyards 2005 Sauvignon Blanc (Mendocino County) $18. 91 Editors' Choice *—S.H. (12/31/2006)*

Patianna Organic Vineyards 2004 Sauvignon Blanc (Mendocino County) $16. 87 *—S.H. (12/15/2005)*

Patianna Organic Vineyards 2003 Estate Grown Sauvignon Blanc (Mendocino) $16. 90 Best Buy *—S.H. (12/31/2004)*

Patianna Organic Vineyards 2003 Fairbairn Ranch Syrah (Mendocino County) $30. 90 *—S.H. (11/15/2005)*

PATIT CREEK CELLARS

Patit Creek Cellars 2003 Cabernet Sauvignon (Walla Walla (WA)) $35. Despite its excellent fruit sources (Les Collines, Pepper Bridge and Seven Hills), this fails to stand out from the pack. Flavors are generic and already feeling a bit tired, with mixed red fruits, raisins and baking spice. The tannins carry a bit of roughness through the finish. 86 *—P.G. (3/1/2007)*

Patit Creek Cellars 2001 Cabernet Sauvignon (Walla Walla (WA)) $35. 86 *—P.G. (4/1/2005)*

Patit Creek Cellars 2004 Merlot (Columbia Valley (WA)) $26. This is their fifth vintage of merlot (started in 2000, but the '04 has been sourced from Columbia valley vineyards due to the freeze. The fruit carries blackberry jam into the strong, bourbon-barrel flavors of oak, although it was mostly French, rather than American. The tannins are chewy and the wine has a blocky construction, simple and hard in the mouth. 86 *—P.G. (8/1/2007)*

Patit Creek Cellars 2003 Merlot (Walla Walla (WA)) $32. 88 *—P.G. (6/1/2006)*

Patit Creek Cellars 2000 Merlot (Walla Walla (WA)) $32. 88 *—P.G. (9/1/2003)*

PATRICK M. PAUL

Patrick M. Paul 2000 Merlot (Columbia Valley (WA)) $28. 85 *—P.G. (9/1/2002)*

PATTON VALLEY VINEYARD

Patton Valley Vineyard 2004 Pinot Noir (Willamette Valley) $30. The screwcap tells you that this is a wine for near-term, everyday enjoyment, and its unpretentious flavors will work in a variety of food settings. It's a bit weedy, showing the more herbal/stemmy side of Oregon fruit, but there are also flavors of cola, wild berry and buttercream, this last softening the finish and cutting the acidity. 87 *—P.G. (2/1/2007)*

Patton Valley Vineyard 2002 Pinot Noir (Willamette Valley) $30. 91 *—P.G. (8/1/2005)*

Patton Valley Vineyard 2002 Pinot Noir (Willamette Valley) $30. 86 *(11/1/2004)*

Patton Valley Vineyard 2000 Pinot Noir (Oregon) $28. 88 *—P.G. (12/31/2002)*

PATZ & HALL

Patz & Hall 2005 Chardonnay (Napa Valley) $36. Dry and crisp and with some complexity. The oak is 50% new and very evident in the smoky caramel, while the fruit veers toward peaches and pineapples. As is often the case with Napa Chard, there's a sweet, herbal quality. Drink now through 2009. 89 *—S.H. (12/15/2007)*

Patz & Hall 2002 Chardonnay (Napa Valley) $33. 87 *—S.H. (4/1/2004)*

Patz & Hall 2002 Durell Vineyard Chardonnay (Sonoma Valley) $38. 86 *—S.H. (4/1/2004)*

Patz & Hall 2005 Dutton Ranch Chardonnay (Russian River Valley) $39. Patz & Hall has captured the cool-climate essence of southern Sonoma Chard with this dry, crisply acidic, and vibrantly fruity young wine. Might have benefited from less new oak though, because the caramel and toast seem a little excessive. 86 *—S.H. (12/15/2007)*

Patz & Hall 2002 Woolsey Road Vineyard Chardonnay (Russian River Valley) $38. 91 *—S.H. (4/1/2004)*

Patz & Hall 1999 Woolsey Road Vineyard Chardonnay (Russian River Valley) $37. 92 Cellar Selection *(7/1/2001)*

Patz & Hall 2005 Zio Tony Ranch Chardonnay (Russian River Valley) $55. The vineyard is on Frei Road, which is in the cooler, southern part of the appellation, and this wine shows how well a good vintage can ripen the grapes into tropical fruit directions while still maintaining vibrant acidity. But the oak drowns the terroir in caramelly, butterscotchy sweetness. **86** —*S.H. (12/15/2007)*

Patz & Hall 2002 Pinot Noir (Sonoma Coast) $33. 87 *(11/1/2004)*

Patz & Hall 2002 Alder Springs Vineyard Pinot Noir (Mendocino County) $50. 90 *(11/1/2004)*

Patz & Hall 2001 Alder Springs Vineyard Pinot Noir (Mendocino County) $50. 87 —*S.H. (4/1/2004)*

Patz & Hall 2005 Chenoweth Ranch Pinot Noir (Russian River Valley) $55. This is one of the most successful Pinots the winery has produced, and I have no doubt it's because the vintage was so cool. The wine is absolutely dry and has bracing acidity, with extraordinarily long, deep flavors of grapes that achieved maximum ripeness but remain balanced. Cherries, raspberries and blackberries flood the palate, enriched with earthier notes of balsam, cola, soy, licorice and spice. Drink now through 2011. **93** *S.H. (12/15/2007)*

Patz & Hall 2002 Hyde Vineyard Pinot Noir (Carneros) $50. 86 *(11/1/2004)*

Patz & Hall 2002 Pisoni Vineyard Pinot Noir (Santa Lucia Highlands) $65. 91 *(11/1/2004)*

Patz & Hall 2001 Pisoni Vineyard Pinot Noir (Santa Lucia Highlands) $70. 93 —*S.H. (4/1/2004)*

PAUL HOBBS

Paul Hobbs 2002 Beckstoffer Tokalon Vineyard Cabernet Sauvignon (Oakville) $NA. 92 Cellar Selection —*S.H. (6/1/2005)*

Paul Hobbs 2000 Beckstoffer Tokalon Vineyard Cabernet Sauvignon (Napa Valley) $NA. 85 —*S.H. (6/1/2005)*

Paul Hobbs 2001 Beckstoffer-Tokalon Vineyard Cabernet Sauvignon (Oakville) $185. 94 Cellar Selection —*S.H. (6/1/2005)*

Paul Hobbs 1999 Chardonnay (Russian River Valley) $38. 91 *(7/1/2001)*

Paul Hobbs 1999 Richard Dinner Vineyard Chardonnay (Sonoma Mountain) $47. 90 *(7/1/2001)*

PAUL MATTHEW

Paul Matthew 2002 Pinot Noir (Russian River Valley) $25. 85 *(11/1/2004)*

PAUL THOMAS

Paul Thomas 1997 Bordeaux Blend (Washington) $9. 83 —*J.C. (11/1/1999)*

Paul Thomas 1999 Cabernet Sauvignon (Washington) $8. 84 —*P.G. (6/1/2002)*

Paul Thomas 1999 Cabernet Sauvignon-Merlot (Washington) $8. 83 —*P.G. (10/1/2001)*

Paul Thomas 1997 Chardonnay (Washington) $7. 83 —*J.C. (11/1/1999)*

Paul Thomas 1999 Chardonnay (Washington) $8. 84 —*P.G. (7/1/2002)*

Paul Thomas 1997 Reserve Chardonnay (Columbia Valley (WA)) $11. 91 Best Buy —*M.M. (11/1/1999)*

Paul Thomas 1999 Merlot (Washington) $8. 83 —*P.G. (6/1/2002)*

PAUMANOK

Paumanok 2002 Assemblage Bordeaux Blend (North Fork of Long Island) $36. 88 —*M.D. (12/1/2006)*

Paumanok 2000 Assemblage Bordeaux Blend (North Fork of Long Island) $36. 86 —*J.C. (10/2/2004)*

Paumanok 1998 Cabernet Franc (North Fork of Long Island) $18. 88 Editors' Choice —*J.C. (4/1/2001)*

Paumanok 1998 Cabernet Sauvignon (North Fork of Long Island) $18. 84 —*J.C. (4/1/2001)*

Paumanok 2001 Barrel-Fermented Chardonnay (North Fork of Long Island) $18. 82 —*J.C. (10/2/2004)*

Paumanok 1999 Barrel-Fermented Chardonnay (North Fork of Long Island) $17. 85 —*J.C. (4/1/2001)*

Paumanok NV Festival Chardonnay (North Fork of Long Island) $10. 84 —*J.C. (4/1/2001)*

Paumanok 2003 Festival Chardonnay (North Fork of Long Island) $10. 83 —*J.C. (10/2/2004)*

Paumanok 2000 Dry Chenin Blanc (North Fork of Long Island) $15. 86 —*J.C. (4/1/2001)*

Paumanok 2002 Merlot (North Fork of Long Island) $18. 84 —*M.D. (12/1/2006)*

Paumanok 2002 Grand Vintage Merlot (North Fork of Long Island) $36. 85 —*M.D. (12/1/2006)*

Paumanok 2000 Grand Vintage Merlot (North Fork of Long Island) $36. 83 —*J.C. (10/2/2004)*

Paumanok 2003 Dry Riesling (North Fork of Long Island) $18. 85 —*J.C. (10/2/2004)*

Paumanok 2000 Dry Riesling (North Fork of Long Island) $15. 87 —*J.C. (4/1/2001)*

Paumanok 2002 Late Harvest Riesling (North Fork of Long Island) $27. 84 —*J.C. (10/2/2004)*

Paumanok 1998 Late Harvest Riesling (North Fork of Long Island) $27. 87 —*J.C. (4/1/2001)*

Paumanok 2003 Semi Dry Riesling (North Fork of Long Island) $18. 85 —*J.C. (10/2/2004)*

Paumanok 2000 Semi Dry Riesling (North Fork of Long Island) $15. 83 —*J.C. (4/1/2001)*

Paumanok 2004 Sauvignon Blanc (North Fork of Long Island) $20. 87 *(7/1/2005)*

PAVILION

Pavilion 2005 Cabernet Sauvignon (Napa Valley) $12. Pavilion's price and quality have not varied in years, making it one of the more dependable Cabs. As always, it's ripe and juicy in forwardly sweet blackberry, cherry, toffee and vanilla flavors that finish with a swirl of toast. **86** —*S.H. (11/1/2007)*

Pavilion 2004 Cabernet Sauvignon (Napa Valley) $12. This is an awfully good price for such a nice Cabernet. It's well-structured and ripe, with a good acid-tannin balance and forward blackberry and cherry flavors. You'll be surprised at how much elegance there is. **86** —*S.H. (5/1/2007)*

Pavilion 2003 Cabernet Sauvignon (Napa Valley) $12. 85 —*S.H. (9/1/2006)*

Pavilion 2002 Cabernet Sauvignon (Napa Valley) $12. 84 —*S.H. (5/1/2005)*

Pavilion 2001 Cabernet Sauvignon (Napa Valley) $11. 86 —*S.H. (10/1/2004)*

Pavilion 2005 Chardonnay (Yountville) $10. 86 Best Buy —*S.H. (11/15/2006)*

Pavilion 2004 Chardonnay (Napa Valley) $10. 86 Best Buy —*S.H. (9/1/2006)*

Pavilion 2003 Chardonnay (Napa Valley) $11. 86 —*S.H. (10/1/2004)*

Pavilion 2005 Merlot (Napa Valley) $12. Here's a decent inexpensive Merlot, a little rustic in the way the tannic structure rubs with raw elbows, but otherwise dry and fruity. Pleases for its oaky cherry, blackberry and raspberry flavors. **85** —*S.H. (11/15/2007)*

Pavilion 2004 Merlot (Napa Valley) $12. Dry and rich in tannins, with some good berry fruit, but if you're a perfectionist, marred by an unripe, herbal quality of green mint. For a big, happy party, it's fine. **83** —*S.H. (2/1/2007)*

Pavilion 2003 Merlot (Napa Valley) $12. 85 —*S.H. (10/1/2006)*

Pavilion 2002 Merlot (Napa Valley) $12. 85 —*S.H. (10/1/2004)*

Pavilion 2005 Sauvignon Blanc (Napa Valley) $10. 83 —*S.H. (11/1/2006)*

Pavilion 2004 Syrah (Napa Valley) $12. A good Syrah at a good price. It's fully dry and quite balanced, with a nice tension between the dusty tannins, acids, oak and the earthy, blackberry fruit. That feeling of elegant complexity lasts through the finish. Nice job. **87 Best Buy** —*S.H. (2/1/2007)*

Pavilion 2003 Syrah (Napa Valley) $12. 80 —*S.H. (7/1/2006)*

PAVIN & RILEY

Pavin & Riley 2001 Merlot (Columbia Valley (WA)) $12. 86 —*P.G. (12/31/2003)*

PAVONA

Pavona 2001 Chardonnay Blanc Chardonnay (Monterey County) $18. 85 —*S.H. (9/1/2004)*

Pavona 1997 Paraiso Springs Pinot Blanc (Santa Lucia Highlands) $13. 90 —*L.W. (3/1/2000)*

Pavona 1997 Pinot Noir (Monterey County) $18. 85 *(11/15/1999)*

Pavona 1999 Pinot Noir (Monterey County) $18. 88 —*S.H. (11/15/2001)*

Pavona 2001 Coastal Selection Pinot Noir (Monterey County) $20. 85 —*S.H. (12/1/2004)*

Pavona 1999 Peacock Blue Ltd. Release Syrah (California) $21. 85 *(11/1/2001)*

Pavona 1999 Purple Peacock Syrah (California) $18. 81 *(10/1/2001)*

Pavona 1999 Purple Peacock Syrah (Lodi) $18. 85 —*S.H. (9/1/2004)*

Pavona 1999 Old Vine Zinfandel (Lodi) $18. 86 —*S.H. (11/15/2001)*

PEACHY CANYON

Peachy Canyon 2004 Para Siempre Bordeaux Blend (Paso Robles) $40. Smooth and ripe, this Bordeaux blend pleases for its rich array of blackberry, cherry and spicy plum flavors. The texture is soft and chocolaty. Loses a point or two for the sugary finish, though. Drink now. **85** —*S.H. (12/1/2007)*

Peachy Canyon 2000 Para Siempre Bordeaux Blend (Paso Robles) $38. 86 —*S.H. (11/15/2003)*

Peachy Canyon 1999 Para Siempre Bordeaux Blend (Paso Robles) $38. 89 —*S.H. (9/1/2002)*

Peachy Canyon 2003 Para Siempre Cabernet Blend (Paso Robles) $38. 86 —*S.H. (12/15/2006)*

Peachy Canyon 2002 Para Siempre Cabernet Blend (Paso Robles) $38. 86 —*S.H. (12/1/2006)*

Peachy Canyon 2001 Para Siempre Cabernet Blend (Paso Robles) $38. 86 —*S.H. (7/1/2005)*

Peachy Canyon 2002 Cabernet Sauvignon (Paso Robles) $38. 87 —*S.H. (12/15/2006)*

Peachy Canyon 2000 Cabernet Sauvignon (Paso Robles) $25. 85 —*S.H. (11/15/2003)*

Peachy Canyon 2004 De Vine Cabernet Sauvignon (Paso Robles) $40. I wanted to like this wine more, but the sugary sweetness is just a turn-off. Too bad, because the fruit is beautifully ripe, the mouthfeel is soft and lush, and acidity is just right. **84** —*S.H. (12/1/2007)*

Peachy Canyon 2000 De Vine Cabernet Sauvignon (Paso Robles) $30. 85 —*S.H. (11/15/2003)*

Peachy Canyon 2003 Devine Cabernet Sauvignon (Paso Robles) $38. 87 —*S.H. (12/15/2006)*

Peachy Canyon 2001 DeVine Cabernet Sauvignon (Paso Robles) $50. 88 —*S.H. (7/1/2005)*

Peachy Canyon 2000 DeVine Cabernet Sauvignon (Paso Robles) $50. 83 —*S.H. (12/31/2004)*

Peachy Canyon 2003 Old School House Cabernet Sauvignon (Paso Robles) $25. 87 —*S.H. (12/15/2006)*

Peachy Canyon 1999 West Side Cabernet Sauvignon (Paso Robles) $25. 88 —*S.H. (9/1/2002)*

Peachy Canyon 2001 Merlot (Paso Robles) $23. 86 —*S.H. (7/1/2005)*

Peachy Canyon 2000 Merlot (Paso Robles) $23. 85 —*S.H. (12/31/2003)*

Peachy Canyon 1999 Merlot (Paso Robles) $23. 86 —*S.H. (6/1/2002)*

Peachy Canyon 2003 Mr. Wilson's Vineyard Merlot (Paso Robles) $23. 82 —*S.H. (12/15/2006)*

Peachy Canyon 2002 Petite Sirah (Paso Robles) $22. 88 —*S.H. (10/1/2005)*

Peachy Canyon 2001 Petite Sirah (Paso Robles) $22. 90 —*S.H. (11/15/2004)*

Peachy Canyon NV Zinfandel Port III Port (Paso Robles) $25. 81 —*S.H. (7/1/2005)*

Peachy Canyon 2000 Para Seimpre Red Blend (Paso Robles) $38. 82 —*S.H. (12/31/2004)*

Peachy Canyon 1999 Syrah (California) $19. 84 *(10/1/2001)*

Peachy Canyon 2006 Viognier (Paso Robles) $25. So sugary sweet, it's basically a dessert wine, and a nice one, at that. The peach and pineapple fruit flavors have a caramelized, tart-filling taste. Not really a table wine, though. **85** —*S.H. (12/1/2007)*

Peachy Canyon 1999 Zinfandel (Paso Robles) $15. 89 Best Buy —*S.H. (12/15/2001)*

Peachy Canyon 1998 Zinfandel (Paso Robles) $17. 87 —*D.T. (9/1/2003)*

Peachy Canyon 1999 Benito Dusi Ranch Zinfandel (Paso Robles) $26. 91 Editors' Choice —*S.H. (12/15/2001)*

Peachy Canyon 1998 Benito Dusi Ranch Zinfandel (Paso Robles) $26. 89 —*S.H. (5/1/2000)*

Peachy Canyon 2005 BFD Zinfandel (Paso Robles) $36. With its hot, sugary finish, this will appeal only to those who like an overripe style; sweet as raspberry jam. **83** —*S.H. (12/1/2007)*

Peachy Canyon 1997 Dusi Ranch Zinfandel (Paso Robles) $26. 89 —*P.G. (11/15/1999)*

Peachy Canyon 2000 Eastside Zinfandel (Paso Robles) $15. 86 —*S.H. (2/1/2003)*

Peachy Canyon 1997 Eastside Zinfandel (Paso Robles) $15. 85 —*P.G. (11/15/1999)*

Peachy Canyon 2005 Especial Zinfandel (Paso Robles) $40. This is quite a fine Zinfandel that shows the benefits of a relatively cool vintage in Paso Robles. The fruit is entirely ripe, but without the Port-y sweetness that can mar Paso reds in a hot year. Although there's a caramelly edge, it's not over the top, lending a soupçon of honey to the blackberry and spice flavors. **88** —*S.H. (12/1/2007)*

Peachy Canyon 2004 Especial Zinfandel (Paso Robles) $36. 88 —*S.H. (12/1/2006)*

Peachy Canyon 2003 Especial Zinfandel (Paso Robles) $30. 84 —*S.H. (12/1/2005)*

Peachy Canyon 2001 Especial Zinfandel (Paso Robles) $30. 91 *(11/1/2003)*

Peachy Canyon 2000 Especial Zinfandel (Paso Robles) $30. 86 —*S.H. (2/1/2003)*

Peachy Canyon 1997 Especial Zinfandel (Paso Robles) $28. 86 —*P.G. (11/15/1999)*

Peachy Canyon 1999 Estate Bottled Zinfandel (Paso Robles) $30. 90 —*S.H. (12/15/2001)*

Peachy Canyon 1998 Estate Bottled Zinfandel (Paso Robles) $30. 89 —*P.G. (3/1/2001)*

Peachy Canyon 2005 Incredible Red Zinfandel (Paso Robles) $12. Peachy Canyon's least expensive wine is a soft, simple, and rather sweet with candied raspberry and cherry flavors. **82** —*S.H. (11/15/2007)*

Peachy Canyon 1999 Incredible Red Bin 110 Zinfandel (California) $NA. 86 —*J.M. (11/15/2001)*

Peachy Canyon 2002 Incredible Red Bin 114 Zinfandel (Paso Robles) $12. 86 —*S.H. (11/15/2004)*

Peachy Canyon 2003 Incredible Red Bin 116 Zinfandel (Paso Robles) $12. 85 —*S.H. (12/1/2005)*

Peachy Canyon 2004 Incredible Red Bin 119 Zinfandel (California) $12. 86 —*S.H. (12/1/2006)*

Peachy Canyon 2001 Incredible Red, Bin 113 Zinfandel (Paso Robles) $12. 80 *(11/1/2003)*

Peachy Canyon 1997 Lakeview Zinfandel (Paso Robles) $21. 85 —*P.G. (11/15/1999)*

Peachy Canyon 2001 Mr. Wilson's Vineyard Zinfandel (Paso Robles) $26. 88 *(11/1/2003)*

Peachy Canyon 2005 Mustang Springs Zinfandel (Paso Robles) $36. An interesting Zin that attracts for its range of sweet fruit and dried herb flavors. The cherries, blackberries and raspberries have complex interweavings of thyme and lavender, leaving the palate to discover new sensations with every sip. Finishes dry and smoothly tannic. **90** —*S.H. (12/1/2007)*

Peachy Canyon 2004 Mustang Springs Zinfandel (Paso Robles) $30. 92 —*S.H. (12/1/2006)*

Peachy Canyon 2000 Mustang Springs Zinfandel (Paso Robles) $26. 86 —*S.H. (2/1/2003)*

Peachy Canyon 1999 Mustang Springs Zinfandel (Paso Robles) $26. 90 —*S.H. (12/15/2001)*

Peachy Canyon 1998 Mustang Springs Zinfandel (Paso Robles) $26. 86 —*P.G. (3/1/2001)*

Peachy Canyon NV Mustang Springs Port Zinfandel (Paso Robles) $NA. 86 —*S.H. (11/15/2001)*

Peachy Canyon 2003 Mustang Springs Ranch Zinfandel (Paso Robles) $26. 88 —*S.H. (12/1/2005)*

Peachy Canyon NV Mustang Springs Ranch Port Zinfandel (Paso Robles) $40. 85 —*S.H. (9/1/2002)*

Peachy Canyon 2005 Old School House Zinfandel (Paso Robles) $36. There's a sweet herbal quality to this Zin, bringing to mind fresh green thyme, rosemary and lavender. It undergirds the ripe raspberry, cherry and cassis fruit flavors of this interesting young wine, giving it an earthy grounding of complexity. **88** —*S.H. (12/1/2007)*

Peachy Canyon 2004 Old School House Zinfandel (Paso Robles) $30. 91 —*S.H. (12/1/2006)*

Peachy Canyon 2003 Old School House Zinfandel (Paso Robles) $26. 86 —*S.H. (12/1/2005)*

Peachy Canyon 2001 Old School House Zinfandel (Paso Robles) $26. 90 *(11/1/2003)*

Peachy Canyon 2000 Old School House Zinfandel (Paso Robles) $26. 87 —*S.H. (2/1/2003)*

Peachy Canyon 2005 Snow Vineyard Zinfandel (Paso Robles) $36. There's heat in this high alcohol wine, but it's okay, a chili pepper burn that works with the fruity, herbal flavors the way a hit of jalapeño heightens a mango salsa. Although the wine is a bit sweet in the finish, it's a natural for barbecue. **87** *—S.H. (12/1/2007)*

Peachy Canyon 2004 Snow Vineyard Zinfandel (Paso Robles) $30. 88 *—S.H. (12/1/2006)*

Peachy Canyon 2003 Snow Vineyard Zinfandel (Paso Robles) $26. 83 *—S.H. (12/1/2005)*

Peachy Canyon 2004 Westside Zinfandel (Paso Robles) $20. 90 Editors' Choice *—S.H. (12/1/2006)*

Peachy Canyon 2003 Westside Zinfandel (Paso Robles) $19. 86 *—S.H. (12/1/2005)*

Peachy Canyon 2001 Westside Zinfandel (Paso Robles) $19. 90 Editors' Choice *(11/1/2003)*

Peachy Canyon 2000 Westside Zinfandel (Paso Robles) $19. 89 *—S.H. (2/1/2003)*

Peachy Canyon 1999 Westside Zinfandel (Paso Robles) $19. 87 *—S.H. (12/15/2001)*

Peachy Canyon 1998 Westside Zinfandel (Paso Robles) $19. 89 *—P.G. (3/1/200*

PEACOCK FAMILY VINEYARD

Peacock Family Vineyard 2001 Cabernet Sauvignon (Spring Mountain) $60. 84 *—S.H. (12/1/2005)*

PECONIC BAY WINERY

Peconic Bay Winery 2002 Cabernet Franc (North Fork of Long Island) $22. 82 *—M.D. (8/1/2006)*

Peconic Bay Winery 2003 La Barrique Chardonnay (North Fork of Long Island) $17. 83 *—J.C. (3/1/2006)*

Peconic Bay Winery 2001 La Barrique Chardonnay (North Fork of Long Island) $17. 84 *—J.C. (10/2/2004)*

Peconic Bay Winery 2003 Steel-Fermented Chardonnay (North Fork of Long Island) $13. 84 *—M.D. (8/1/2006)*

Peconic Bay Winery 2002 Steel-Fermented Chardonnay (North Fork of Long Island) $13. 84 *—J.C. (10/2/2004)*

USA

Peconic Bay Winery 2001 Merlot (North Fork of Long Island) $24. 81 *—J.C. (10/2/2004)*

Peconic Bay Winery NV Local Flavor Merlot (North Fork of Long Island) $18. There are some beguiling notes of grilled meat, blackberry and spices on the nose, but in the mouth, this wine has a one-dimensional feel to it. The fruit and oak come together in a nice balance, and there's structure, too, but it's somewhat innocuous. Would pair well with dry sausage or cheeses. **82** *—S.K. (2/1/2007)*

Peconic Bay Winery 2004 Riesling (North Fork of Long Island) $13. 87 *—M.D. (8/1/2006)*

Peconic Bay Winery 2003 Riesling (North Fork of Long Island) $13. 83 *—J.C. (10/2/2004)*

Peconic Bay Winery NV Polaris Riesling (North Fork of Long Island) $35. 83 *—M.D. (8/1/2006)*

Peconic Bay Winery 2003 Polaris Ice Wine Riesling (North Fork of Long Island) $35. 85 *—J.C. (10/2/2004)*

PEDESTAL

Pedestal 2004 Merlot (Columbia Valley (WA)) $55. Michel Rolland consults on this exceptional Merlot. The blend is 77% Merlot, 16% Cabernet Sauvignon, 5% Cabernet Franc and 2% Petit Verdot. Though not quite as supremely dark, dense and concentrated as the immense '03, this silky wine is more elegant, with grace notes of licorice, citrus, coffee and plenty of tart strawberry and raspberry fruit. **91** *—P.G. (8/1/2007)*

Pedestal 2003 Merlot (Columbia Valley (WA)) $55. 93 Editors' Choice *—P.G. (6/1/2006)*

PEDRONCELLI

Pedroncelli 2003 Three Vineyards Cabernet Sauvignon (Dry Creek Valley) $14. 86 *—S.H. (12/1/2006)*

Pedroncelli 2005 Vintage Selection Chardonnay (Dry Creek Valley) $12. Like a fruit basket in a glass, this easy-drinking Chard explodes with orange popsicle, pineapple jam, lemon meringue pie, peach custard and vanilla aromas and flavors. It's creamy-smooth and a little sweet. **84** *—S.H. (4/1/2007)*

Pedroncelli 1997 Fumé Blanc (Dry Creek Valley) $9. 80 *—M.M. (9/1/1999)*

Pedroncelli 2002 Bench Vineyards Merlot (Dry Creek Valley) $14. 84 *—S.H. (3/1/2006)*

Pedroncelli 2002 Petite Sirah (Dry Creek Valley) $14. 86 *—S.H. (12/1/2006)*

Pedroncelli 2000 Petite Sirah (Dry Creek Valley) $15. 85 *(4/1/2003)*

Pedroncelli 2002 F. Johnson Vineyard Pinot Noir (Sonoma County) $15. 86 *(11/1/2004)*

Pedroncelli 2000 F. Johnson Vineyard Pinot Noir (Russian River Valley) $NA. 88 Best Buy *(10/1/2002)*

Pedroncelli 2006 East Side Vineyards Sauvignon Blanc (Dry Creek Valley) $10. Sauvignon Blanc is the white wine that made Dry Creek Valley famous, and this is a classic example. It's a deliciously light-bodied wine, with a delicate, crisp mouthfeel framing citrus fruit, melon and fig flavors that finish dry. **86 Best Buy** *—S.H. (11/1/2007)*

Pedroncelli 2004 East Side Vineyards Sauvignon Blanc (Dry Creek Valley) $10. 86 Best Buy *—S.H. (3/1/2006)*

Pedroncelli 1997 Zinfandel (Dry Creek Valley) $9. 85 *—M.S. (11/1/1999)*

Pedroncelli 2004 Mother Clone Zinfandel (Dry Creek Valley) $14. Big, juicy, ripe and tannic. From the crushed wild berry, pepper and nettle aromas to the blast of smoky, raisin-tinged raspberries, cherries and blackberries, it expresses its terroir perfectly. Great price for a Zin of such textbook authority. **89 Best Buy** *—S.H. (11/1/2007)*

Pedroncelli 2003 Mother Clone Zinfandel (Dry Creek Valley) $14. Brings a classic, Bordeaux-like control and polish to Zinfandel's wild and woolly side. The flavors are briary and brambly, with wild berries, dusty spices, cherries and chili peppers, and the finish is dry and interesting. The spices suggest spicy foods. **87** *—S.H. (4/1/2007)*

Pedroncelli 2002 Mother Clone Zinfandel (Dry Creek Valley) $14. 83 *—S.H. (3/1/2006)*

Pedroncelli 2001 Mother Clone Zinfandel (Dry Creek Valley) $14. 80 *—J.M. (11/1/2003)*

Pedroncelli 1997 Mother Clone Special Vineyard Sele Zinfandel (Dry Creek Valley) $13. 87 *—J.C. (5/1/2000)*

Pedroncelli 2002 Pedroni-Bushnell Vineyard Zinfandel (Dry Creek Valley) $16. Held back for four years, it cannot have been very tough even at release. Today, it's really soft, with extremely ripe wild blueberry, boysenberry, loganberry and crab apple flavors that seem to have just been picked. Classic Sonoma Zin, for barbecued or braised beef. **87** *—S.H. (4/1/2007)*

Pedroncelli 1996 Pedroni-Bushnell Zinfandel (Dry Creek Valley) $14. 84 *—P.G. (11/15/1999)*

Pedroncelli 2006 Zinfandel Rosé Zinfandel (Dry Creek Valley) $10. Rosé doesn't get more aromatic than this, which opens with a burst of ripe, freshly crushed red cherries. Those are the flavors, too, along with raspberries, root beer and vanilla. This is a refreshing blush, at a good everyday price. **84 Best Buy** *—S.H. (11/1/2007)*

Pedroncelli 2005 Zinfandel Rosé Zinfandel (Dry Creek Valley) $10. 83 *—S.H. (12/1/2006)*

PEIRANO

Peirano 2003 The Heritage Collection Barbera (Lodi) $12. 84 *—S.H. (6/1/2006)*

Peirano 2002 The Heritage Collection Barbera (Lodi) $13. 84 *—S.H. (11/15/2004)*

Peirano 2002 Cabernet Sauvignon (Lodi) $10. 84 *—S.H. (11/15/2004)*

Peirano 1999 Cabernet Sauvignon (Lodi) $10. 87 Best Buy *—S.H. (9/1/2002)*

Peirano 2004 Autumn's Blush Cabernet Sauvignon (Lodi) $5. 84 Best Buy *—S.H. (5/1/2006)*

Peirano 2001 Autumn's Blush Cabernet Sauvignon (Lodi) $9. 82 *—S.H. (2/1/2004)*

Peirano 2001 Heritage Collection Cabernet Sauvignon (Lodi) $18. 84 *—S.H. (11/15/2003)*

Peirano 2004 The Heritage Collection Cabernet Sauvignon (Lodi) $12. 88 Best Buy *—S.H. (5/1/2006)*

Peirano 1999 Chardonnay (Lodi) $11. 86 *—S.H. (12/15/2002)*

Peirano 1998 Chardonnay (Lodi) $10. 84 *—S.H. (5/1/2002)*

Peirano 2001 The Heritage Collection Chardonnay (Lodi) $15. 83 *—S.H. (4/1/2004)*

Peirano 1999 Six Clones Merlot (Lodi) $12. 80 *—S.H. (11/15/2002)*

Peirano 1998 Six Clones Merlot (Lodi) $10. 86 Best Buy *—S.H. (6/1/2002)*

Peirano 2001 The Heritage Collection Six Clones Merlot (Lodi) $17. 86 *—S.H. (2/1/2004)*

Peirano 2004 The Heritage Collection Petite Sirah (Lodi) $14. Robust and bone dry, with palate-coating tannins, this full-bodied young wine is rich in blackberry, coffee and dried herb flavors, with a very long finish. It's a big, tough wine that calls for big, rich meats. **84** *—S.H. (5/1/2007)*

Peirano 2002 The Heritage Collection Petite Sirah (Lodi) $18. 84 *—S.H.*

(11/15/2004)

Peirano NV The Other Red Blend (Lodi) $14. 83 —*S.H. (5/1/2006)*

Peirano 1999 Sauvignon Blanc (Lodi) $9. 87 Best Buy —*S.H. (9/1/2002)*

Peirano 2004 Heritage Collection Sauvignon Blanc (Lodi) $12. 84 —*S.H. (4/1/2006)*

Peirano 2002 The Heritage Collection Sauvignon Blanc (Lodi) $12. 87 Best Buy —*S.H. (12/1/2004)*

Peirano 1998 Shiraz (Lodi) $10. 87 Best Buy —*S.H. (9/1/2002)*

Peirano 2002 The Heritage Collection Shiraz (Lodi) $13. 83 —*S.H. (5/1/2006)*

Peirano 1999 The Heritage Collection Shiraz (Lodi) $17. 89 —*S.H. (3/1/2004)*

Peirano 1999 Viognier (Lodi) $12. 84 —*S.H. (11/15/2001)*

Peirano 2004 Heritage Collection Viognier (Lodi) $12. 86 —*S.H. (4/1/2006)*

Peirano 2001 The Heritage Collection Viognier (Lodi) $15. 83 —*S.H. (12/31/2003)*

Peirano 2004 Heritage Collection The Other White Blend (Lodi) $12. 86 —*S.H. (4/1/2006)*

Peirano 1999 Old Vine Zinfandel (Lodi) $10. 80 —*S.H. (4/1/2006)*

Peirano 1998 Old Vine Zinfandel (Lodi) $14. 85 —*S.H. (11/1/2002)*

Peirano 1997 Old Vine Zinfandel (Lodi) $10. 91 —*S.H. (9/1/2002)*

Peirano 1998 Primo Zinfandel (Lodi) $11. 82 —*S.H. (11/1/2002)*

PEJU

Peju 2001 Cabernet Franc (Rutherford) $65. 93 —*S.H. (8/1/2004)*

Peju 2000 Cabernet Franc (Napa Valley) $30. 88 —*S.H. (6/1/2003)*

Peju 1999 Cabernet Franc (Napa Valley) $30. 85 —*S.H. (12/1/2002)*

Peju 2002 Estate Cabernet Franc (Napa Valley) $40. 90 —*S.H. (7/1/2005)*

Peju 2002 Reserve Cabernet Franc (Rutherford) $90. 90 —*S.H. (11/1/2005)*

Peju 1997 Cabernet Sauvignon (Napa Valley) $45. 91 *(11/1/2000)*

Peju 1999 Cabernet Sauvignon (Napa Valley) $48. 92 —*S.H. (11/15/2002)*

Peju 1998 Cabernet Sauvignon (Sonoma County) $38. 85 —*S.H. (6/1/2002)*

Peju 2003 Estate Cabernet Sauvignon (Napa Valley) $40. 82 —*S.H. (12/31/2006)*

Peju 2001 Estate Cabernet Sauvignon (Napa Valley) $38. 91 —*S.H. (11/1/2005)*

Peju 2000 Estate Cabernet Sauvignon (Napa Valley) $38. 84 —*S.H. (8/1/2004)*

Peju 2002 Estate Bottled Cabernet Sauvignon (Napa Valley) $38. 92 —*S.H. (7/1/2006)*

Peju 1997 Estate Bottled Reserve Cabernet Sauvignon (Rutherford) $95. 90 *(11/1/2000)*

Peju 2003 H.B. Vineyard Cabernet Sauvignon (Napa Valley) $150. Here's the most expensive wine from Peju ever. Is it worth it? You decide. This is a magnificent wine. It's as ripely gorgeous as anything out there, with tons of black and red cherry, plum, chocolate and 100% new oak flavors. But it has a dense, sandpapery overlay of tannins. You can drink it now with decanting, but it will soften and improve over a decade. 94 —*S.H. (7/1/2007)*

Peju 2004 Reserve Cabernet Sauvignon (Rutherford) $105. Made in a very ripe style, this Cab-based Bordeaux blend is fat and rich in cherries, blackberries, chocolate, cola and cedar flavors. The soft density is partly the result of relatively high alcohol, but the wine wears it well. Shows a good balance of alcohol, acids, fruit, oak and firm, dusty tannins, and should age well through 2012. 93 —*S.H. (12/15/2007)*

Peju 2003 Reserve Cabernet Sauvignon (Rutherford) $105. 90 —*S.H. (12/15/2006)*

Peju 2002 Reserve Cabernet Sauvignon (Rutherford) $125. 93 Cellar Selection —*S.H. (12/31/2005)*

Peju 2000 Reserve Cabernet Sauvignon (Rutherford) $85. 85 —*S.H. (8/1/2004)*

Peju 1999 Reserve Cabernet Sauvignon (Rutherford) $95. 94 —*S.H. (11/15/2002)*

Peju 1998 Reserve Cabernet Sauvignon (Rutherford) $85. 87 —*S.H. (6/1/2002)*

Peju 2005 Chardonnay (Napa Valley) $28. After variable experience with Chardonnay, Peju is getting a grip. This wine, with nearly two thirds new French oak, is fruity and crisp, with smooth, long pineapple and peaches-and-cream flavors. 87 —*S.H. (7/1/2007)*

Peju 2001 Chardonnay (Napa Valley) $22. 84 —*S.H. (6/1/2003)*

Peju 1998 Chardonnay (Napa Valley) $22. 84 *(6/1/2000)*

Peju 1998 H.B. Vineyard Chardonnay (Napa Valley) $28. 84 *(6/1/2000)*

Peju 2002 Lianna Late Harvest Chardonnay (Napa Valley) $45. 90 —*S.H. (8/1/2004)*

Peju 2001 Carnival French Columbard (California) $12. 84 —*S.H. (3/1/2004)*

Peju 2001 Merlot (Napa Valley) $35. 84 —*S.H. (8/1/2004)*

Peju 2000 Merlot (Napa Valley) $35. 92 —*S.H. (10/1/2003)*

Peju 2002 Estate Merlot (Napa Valley) $35. 87 —*S.H. (11/1/2005)*

Peju 2002 Petite Verdot (Napa Valley) $35. 89 —*S.H. (5/1/2006)*

Peju 2001 Rosé Blend (California) $18. 88 —*S.H. (3/1/2004)*

Peju NV Provance Rosé Blend (California) $22. I've seen red wines that are paler in color than this heavy, soft, slightly sweet blend of five varieties, including Chardonnay and Cabernet Sauvignon. It has cherry pie filling, caramel and vanilla flavors. 83 —*S.H. (7/1/2007)*

Peju NV Provence Rosé Blend (California) $18. 84 —*S.H. (12/31/2005)*

Peju 2001 Sauvignon Blanc (Napa Valley) $16. 87 —*S.H. (3/1/2003)*

Peju 2000 Sauvignon Blanc (Napa Valley) $22. 82 —*S.H. (9/1/2002)*

Peju 2004 Estate Sauvignon Blanc (Napa Valley) $16. 83 —*S.H. (12/31/2005)*

Peju 2005 Estate Bottled Sauvignon Blanc (Napa Valley) $18. 83 —*S.H. (12/31/2006)*

Peju 2004 Syrah (Napa Valley) $32. Peju, which does such a good job with Bordeaux reds, continues to struggle with Syrah. Hard to say why, but the hot '04 vintage didn't help. The wine is overly soft, with a Port-y, raisiny edge to the cherry and cocoa flavors. 84 —*S.H. (7/1/2007)*

Peju 1999 Syrah (Napa Valley) $65. 84 —*S.H. (12/1/2002)*

Peju 2004 Zinfandel (Napa Valley) $25. Delicious Zin, ripe and rich in flavor. It floods the palate with milk chocolate, blackberry, cherry and spicy tobacco flavors. While it's a little simple, it rewards for its immediate appeal. 85 —*S.H. (7/1/2007)*

Peju 2003 Zinfandel Port Zinfandel (Napa Valley) $38. Nice after-dinner sipper, a very sweet wine with chocolaty blackberry and coffee flavors that are balanced with a crisp edge of acidity. It has a wonderfully smooth, velvety texture. 87 —*S.H. (7/1/2007)*

PEJU PROVINCE

Peju Province 2001 Cabernet Franc (Napa Valley) $35. 91 —*S.H. (3/1/2005)*

Peju Province 2001 Reserve Cabernet Sauvignon (Rutherford) $85. 92 —*S.H. (10/1/2004)*

Peju Province 2002 Syrah (Napa Valley) $32. 85 *(9/1/2005)*

Peju Province 2001 Estate Syrah (Napa Valley) $32. 88 —*S.H. (3/1/2005)*

Peju Province 2002 Zinfandel (Napa Valley) $25. 91 —*S.H. (3/1/2005)*

Peju Province 2002 Reserve Zinfandel (Napa Valley) $45. 92 —*S.H. (3/1/2005)*

PELLEGRINI

Pellegrini 1995 Encore Red Table Wine Bordeaux Blend (North Fork of Long Island) $24. 86 —*J.C. (8/1/1999)*

Pellegrini 1997 Vintner's Pride Encore Bordeaux Blend (North Fork of Long Island) $29. 88 —*J.C. (4/1/2001)*

Pellegrini 1997 Cabernet Sauvignon (North Fork of Long Island) $17. 87 —*J.C. (4/1/2001)*

Pellegrini 1995 Cabernet Sauvignon (North Fork of Long Island) $35. 87 —*J.C. (4/1/2001)*

Pellegrini 2004 Cloverdale Ranch Cabernet Sauvignon (Alexander Valley) $24. Pellegrini's Cabs always seem to have a rustic edge, meaning the sharp-elbowed tannins, and the green, dried herb flavors that dominate. The wine's structure is great, but it would really benefit from more fruity richness. 84 —*S.H. (10/1/2007)*

Pellegrini 2003 Cloverdale Ranch Cabernet Sauvignon (Alexander Valley) $22. 87 —*S.H. (9/1/2006)*

Pellegrini 1998 Estate Bottled Unfiltered Cabernet Sauvignon (North Fork of Long Island) $17. 84 —*M.S. (3/1/2003)*

Pellegrini 2005 Old Vines Carignan (Redwood Valley) $18. From a variety with a reputation for rusticity, this Carignan is from a vineyard interspersed with Zinfandel, Barbera, and perhaps other varieties. It's nice that Pellegrini is treating it with dignity, but the limitation is in the grapes themselves. The wine is ripe and juicy, but overly soft, with rustic tannins. 84 —*S.H. (10/1/2007)*

Pellegrini 2004 Old Vines Carignan (Redwood Valley) $18. 82 —*S.H. (11/15/2006)*

Pellegrini 2003 Old Vine Carignane (Redwood Valley) $16. 84 —*S.H. (3/1/2005)*

Pellegrini 1996 Chardonnay (North Fork of Long Island) $13. 83 —*J.C. (8/1/1999)*

Pellegrini 2001 Chardonnay (Russian River Valley) $10. 85 —*S.H. (6/1/2003)*

Pellegrini 2001 Chardonnay (North Fork of Long Island) $13. 82 —*J.C. (10/2/2004)*

Pellegrini 1998 Chardonnay (North Fork of Long Island) $13. 86 —*J.C. (4/1/2001)*

Pellegrini 2005 Olivet Lane Vineyard Chardonnay (Russian River Valley) $22. Nice and oaky and rich, from a vineyard in the heart of the cool-climate southern part of Russian River Valley. Acidity stars, giving zesty balance to the ripe pineapple, green apple, Key lime pie and pear flavors. New oak, to the tune of 40%, adds an opulent touch. **90** —*S.H. (10/1/2007)*

Pellegrini 2004 Olivet Lane Chardonnay (Russian River Valley) $24. 88 —*S.H. (11/15/2006)*

Pellegrini 2006 Unoaked Chardonnay (Russian River Valley) $16. A dry, and elegant fruit-forward wine. It was harvested relatively early, at lower brix, resulting in crisp acidity and succulent flavors of tart green apples and kiwis, with a tang of pepper and cinnamon. Delicious. **88** —*S.H. (10/1/2007)*

Pellegrini 2005 Unoaked Chardonnay (Russian River Valley) $16. 89 —*S.H. (11/15/2006)*

Pellegrini 2000 Merlot (North Fork of Long Island) $18. 84 —*J.C. (10/2/2004)*

Pellegrini 1997 Merlot (North Fork of Long Island) $17. 87 —*J.C. (4/1/2001)*

Pellegrini 2004 Cloverdale Ranch Merlot (Alexander Valley) $22. Tough, dry and weedy, with astringent tannins. Clean, but not going anywhere. **82** —*S.H. (10/1/2007)*

Pellegrini 2003 Cloverdale Ranch Merlot (Alexander Valley) $21. 88 —*S.H. (11/15/2006)*

Pellegrini 2001 East End Select Merlot (North Fork of Long Island) $13. 80 —*J.C. (10/2/2004)*

Pellegrini 1999 East End Select Merlot (North Fork of Long Island) $12. 84 —*J.C. (4/1/2001)*

Pellegrini 1998 Estate Bottled Unfiltered Merlot (North Fork of Long Island) $17. 82 —*J.M. (3/1/2003)*

Pellegrini 2001 Unfiltered Merlot (North Fork of Long Island) $NA. A little young and not terribly complex, this wine still has pleasing flavors of plum, blueberry, and cherry that come through. Could use a little more heft with herbal or spice flavors, as the fruit is overpowering here. Decent balance, but the finish is a little short and edgy. **83** —*S.K. (2/1/2007)*

Pellegrini 2005 Olivet Lane Vineyard Pinot Noir (Russian River Valley) $30. Another successful Pinot, similar to the '04— may be a bit crisper and more elegant, but with the same lovely cola, cherry, strawberry, root beer, dusty spice and vanilla-oak flavors. Probably offering its most exuberant side now and for a year or two. **89** —*S.H. (10/1/2007)*

Pellegrini 2004 Olivet Lane Vineyard Pinot Noir (Russian River Valley) $24. 89 —*S.H. (11/15/2006)*

Pellegrini 2005 Cuvée 107 Red Blend (Sonoma County) $14. A blend of Zin, Merlot, Syrah, Carignan and several others, this is the anti-Napa red wine. It has an austerity, acidity and dryness that will elegantly show off complex food without dominating it. A very nice effort from Pellegrini. **88** —*S.H. (10/1/2007)*

Pellegrini 2000 Frank's Steak House Red Unfiltered Red Blend (North Fork of Long Island) $NA. 84 —*J.C. (10/2/2004)*

Pellegrini 1998 Vintner's Pride Encore Unfiltered Estate Grown Red Blend (North Fork of Long Island) $29. 86 —*J.M. (3/1/2003)*

Pellegrini 2005 Rosato Rosé Blend (Redwood Valley) $14. 83 —*S.H. (11/15/2006)*

Pellegrini 2006 Leveroni Vineyard Sauvignon Blanc (Lake County) $14. Dry, crisp and elegantly structured, which are the best features of Lake County Sauvignon Blanc. But there's just too much feline essence and asparagus, and it's pretty aggressive. **83** —*S.H. (10/1/2007)*

Pellegrini 2005 Leveroni Vineyard Sauvignon Blanc (Lake County) $14. 88 —*S.H. (11/15/2006)*

Pellegrini 1996 Finale White Dessert Wine White Blend (North Fork of Long Island) $25. 80 —*J.C. (8/1/1999)*

Pellegrini 2005 Eight Cousins Vineyard Zinfandel (Russian River Valley) $24. Great Zin. It's robust and brawny, in the way of Zin, with the rustic wild berry, nettle, chamomile and spice flavors you expect from the variety, but shows good control in the smooth tannins and modulated alcohol. Picks up extra points for sheer deliciousness. **89** —*S.H. (10/1/2007)*

Pellegrini 2004 Eight Cousins Vineyard Zinfandel (Russian River Valley) $24. 90 —*S.H. (11/15/2006)*

Pellegrini 2003 Eight Cousins Vineyard Zinfandel (Sonoma County) $24. 85 —*S.H. (2/1/2005)*

PELTON HOUSE

Pelton House 2004 Cabernet Sauvignon (Knights Valley) $40. Like many of Jess Jackson's high mountain Cabs, this is extremely tannic and dry, at least by Napa standards. So is it ageable? Probably, given the rich heart of blackberry, cherry, violet flower and coffee flavors. But it's a new brand, unproven. Give it until 2009, then try again. **88** —*S.H. (10/1/2007)*

Pelton House 2004 Merlot (Knights Valley) $35. This is a new brand from Jess Jackson. The wine is quite interesting—absolutely dry, very tannic, acidic and austere, with a bitterness to the cherryskin flavors. Yet it possesses polish and elegance. Work is needed, but this is a Merlot to watch. **88** —*S.H. (10/1/2007)*

PEND D'OREILLE

Pend d'Oreille 2001 L'Oeuvre Reserve Red Table Wine Bordeaux Blend (Columbia Valley (WA)) $25. 87 —*P.G. (9/1/2004)*

Pend d'Oreille 2001 Cabernet Sauvignon (Columbia Valley (WA)) $16. 87 —*P.G. (6/1/2005)*

Pend d'Oreille 2000 Cabernet Sauvignon (Columbia Valley (WA)) $16. 84 —*P.G. (9/1/2004)*

Pend d'Oreille 1998 Cabernet Sauvignon (Columbia Valley (WA)) $16. 85 —*D.T. (12/31/2002)*

Pend d'Oreille 1999 Bistro Rouge Cabernet Sauvignon-Merlot (Washington) $11. 87 Best Buy —*C.S. (12/31/2002)*

Pend d'Oreille 2000 Bistro Blanc Chardonnay (Washington) $11. 86 —*M.S. (6/1/2003)*

Pend d'Oreille 2002 Merlot (Columbia Valley (WA)) $20. 88 —*P.G. (6/1/2005)*

Pend d'Oreille 2001 Merlot (Columbia Valley (WA)) $20. 84 —*P.G. (9/1/2004)*

Pend d'Oreille 1999 Merlot (Columbia Valley (WA)) $20. 84 —*C.S. (12/31/2002)*

Pend d'Oreille 2002 Sauvignon Blanc (Washington) $8. 86 —*P.G. (9/1/2004)*

Pend d'Oreille 2000 Syrah (Columbia Valley (WA)) $23. 90 —*C.S. (12/31/2002)*

PENDLETON

Pendleton 2004 Lockwood Oaks Vineyard Reserve Cabernet Sauvignon (Monterey County) $38. A bite of green peppercorn sits right next to riper tastes of blackberries, currants and dark bitter chocolate in this wine grown in the far southern Salinas Valley, just north of Paso Robles. Has good structure, with finely meshed, sweet tannins. **87** —*S.H. (9/1/2007)*

Pendleton 2005 Paraiso Vineyards Reserve Chardonnay (Santa Lucia Highlands) $36. Lots of oak on this fresh, young Chard. It's a bit too heavy on the char, toast, vanilla, and woodsap, and not enough about the peaches, pears and pineapples. **86** —*S.H. (12/1/2007)*

Pendleton 2004 Reserve Chardonnay (Santa Lucia Highlands) $35. 92 —*S.H. (12/15/2006)*

PENDULUM

Pendulum 2004 Red Blend (Columbia Valley (WA)) $25. This is a collaboration between Long Shadows and Precept Brands. Half Cabernet and the rest an unusual mix of Merlot, Syrah, Cab Franc and Barbera, it's a kitchen sink compendium of grapes from a dozen vineyards scattered across the state. Predictably, it's a diffuse, unfocused red blend, which does not express grape or region in any identifiable way. A good quaffer. **86** —*P.G. (5/1/2007)*

Pendulum 2003 Red Blend (Columbia Valley (WA)) $25. 87 —*P.G. (12/15/2005)*

PENNER-ASH

Penner-Ash 2000 Pinot Noir (Willamette Valley) $45. 90 *(10/1/2002)*

Penner-Ash 1999 Pinot Noir (Willamette Valley) $49. 88 *(10/1/2002)*

PEPI

Pepi 2000 Barbera (California) $14. 86 —*S.H. (12/1/2002)*

Pepi 2004 Chardonnay (California) $9. 84 —*S.H. (11/15/2005)*

Pepi 2003 Chardonnay (Napa Valley) $8. 83 *—S.H. (12/1/2004)*

Pepi 2002 Chardonnay (Napa Valley) $14. 85 *—S.H. (2/1/2004)*

Pepi 2001 Chardonnay (Napa Valley) $14. 88 Best Buy *—S.H. (12/15/2002)*

Pepi 2002 Merlot (Calaveras County) $8. 84 *—S.H. (12/15/2004)*

Pepi 2002 Merlot (California) $8. 84 *—S.H. (10/1/2004)*

Pepi 2004 Pinot Grigio (California) $11. 86 Best Buy *—S.H. (11/15/2005)*

Pepi 2003 Pinot Grigio (Oregon) $11. 85 *—S.H. (12/15/2004)*

Pepi 2001 Pinot Grigio (Willamette Valley) $11. 85 *—M.S. (8/1/2003)*

Pepi 2000 Pinot Grigio (Willamette Valley) $12. 84 *—S.H. (8/1/2002)*

Pepi 1998 Colline di Sassi Red Blend (Alexander Valley) $25. 92 Editors' Choice *—S.H. (12/15/2001)*

Pepi 2003 Sangiovese (California) $11. 84 *—S.H. (6/1/2005)*

Pepi 1999 Sangiovese (California) $14. 90 Best Buy *—S.H. (12/1/2002)*

Pepi 1998 Two Heart Sangiovese (California) $14. 84 *—S.H. (12/15/2001)*

Pepi 1997 Two Heart Canopy Sangiovese (California) $17. 87 *—S.H. (12/15/1999)*

Pepi 2004 Sauvignon Blanc (California) $9. 84 *—S.H. (11/15/2005)*

Pepi 2003 Sauvignon Blanc (California) $8. 84 Best Buy *—S.H. (12/1/2004)*

Pepi 2002 Sauvignon Blanc (California) $13. 85 *—S.H. (2/1/2004)*

Pepi 1999 Two Heart Canopy Sauvignon Blanc (California) $12. 84 *—S.H. (12/15/2001)*

Pepi 2000 Two Heart Canopy Sauvignon Blanc (California) $11. 88 *—S.H. (9/1/2003)*

Pepi 2002 Shiraz (California) $8. 86 Best Buy *—S.H. (12/1/2004)*

PEPPER BRIDGE

Pepper Bridge 2003 Cabernet Sauvignon (Walla Walla (WA)) $50. Tight, elegant and showing less of the Merlot's broad, up front fruit flavor, but it's very well structured. The winery's barrel regimen adds a lot of coffee grounds and dark chocolate. In a riper year such as this, the vineyard loses the herbal character; here the fruit is tight and acidic, clean and tasting of ripe berry and plum. **91** *—P.G. (5/1/2007)*

Pepper Bridge 2002 Cabernet Sauvignon (Walla Walla (WA)) $50. 87 *—P.G. (6/1/2006)*

Pepper Bridge 2001 Cabernet Sauvignon (Walla Walla (WA)) $50. 89 *—P.G. (11/15/2004)*

Pepper Bridge 1999 Cabernet Sauvignon (Walla Walla (WA)) $50. 90 *—P.G. (6/1/2002)*

Pepper Bridge 2004 Merlot (Columbia Valley (WA)) $45. This is a fine effort. The fruit is laid out right up front, big and dense, with a rich mouthfeel and very silky tannins. Flavors of black fruits, smoke and chocolate, thick and supple, are beautifully integrated, textural and complete. This is an especially good effort in a difficult year. Aging in 100% French oak adds coffee-mocha flavors to the lingering finish. **90** *—P.G. (5/1/2007)*

Pepper Bridge 2002 Merlot (Walla Walla (WA)) $45. 90 *—P.G. (12/15/2005)*

Pepper Bridge 2001 Merlot (Walla Walla (WA)) $45. 88 *—P.G. (7/1/2004)*

Pepper Bridge 1999 Merlot (Walla Walla (WA)) $45. 88 *—P.G. (6/1/2002)*

Pepper Bridge 2003 Seven Hills Vineyard Reserve Red Blend (Walla Walla (WA)) $50. 90 *—P.G. (8/1/2006)*

Pepper Bridge 2002 Seven Hills Vineyard Reserve Red Blend (Walla Walla (WA)) $50. 90 *—P.G. (12/15/2005)*

PEPPERWOOD GROVE

Pepperwood Grove 1997 Cabernet Franc (California) $7. 85 Best Buy *—S.H. (7/1/2000)*

Pepperwood Grove 2005 Cabernet Sauvignon (California) $8. Sharp and green, with an unripe minty note, but at the same time, the wine is too sweet. Rescued from oblivion by some nice cherry flavor. **82** *—S.H. (2/1/2007)*

Pepperwood Grove 2003 Cabernet Sauvignon (California) $8. 82 *—S.H. (11/15/2005)*

Pepperwood Grove 2002 Cabernet Sauvignon (California) $9. 85 Best Buy *—S.H. (5/1/2005)*

Pepperwood Grove 2005 Chardonnay (California) $8. You won't believe how good this wine is at this price, how rich in true Chardonnay taste and mouthfeel. The peaches-and-cream, nectarine, tangerine and pineapple fruit are accented with smoky, vanilla-custard oak and creamy lees. An incredible bargain. **88 Best Buy** *—S.H. (2/1/2007)*

Pepperwood Grove 2003 Chardonnay (California) $9. 84 *—S.H. (3/1/2005)*

Pepperwood Grove 1998 Chardonnay (California) $7. 84 *—S.H. (5/1/2000)*

Pepperwood Grove 2004 Merlot (California) $8. 85 Best Buy *—S.H. (5/1/2006)*

Pepperwood Grove 2003 Merlot (California) $9. 85 Best Buy *—S.H. (6/1/2005)*

Pepperwood Grove 2001 Merlot (California) $8. 88 *—S.H. (3/1/2004)*

Pepperwood Grove 2004 Pinot Grigio (California) $8. 85 Best Buy *—S.H. (11/15/2005)*

Pepperwood Grove 1997 Pinot Noir (California) $7. 85 *(5/1/2000)*

Pepperwood Grove 2003 Pinot Noir (California) $9. 85 *—S.H. (3/1/2005)*

Pepperwood Grove 2002 Pinot Noir (California) $9. 86 Best Buy *(11/1/2004)*

Pepperwood Grove 2000 Pinot Noir (California) $9. 84 Best Buy *(10/1/2002)*

Pepperwood Grove 2005 Sauvignon Blanc (California) $8. Here's a good buy in a nice, dry, crisp young Sauvignon Blanc. It has subtle green grass, citrus and vanilla flavors, and finishes clean and zesty. **85** *—S.H. (8/1/2007)*

Pepperwood Grove 2004 Syrah (California) $8. 84 Best Buy *—S.H. (11/15/2006)*

Pepperwood Grove 2002 Syrah (California) $9. 86 Best Buy *—S.H. (6/1/2005)*

Pepperwood Grove 2002 Syrah (California) $9. 89 *—S.H. (6/1/2004)*

Pepperwood Grove 1999 Syrah (California) $7. 83 *(10/1/2001)*

Pepperwood Grove 2005 Viognier (California) $8. 84 Best Buy *—S.H. (12/1/2006)*

Pepperwood Grove 2004 Viognier (California) $8. 84 Best Buy *—S.H. (11/15/2005)*

Pepperwood Grove 2003 Viognier (California) $9. 86 Best Buy *—S.H. (8/1/2005)*

Pepperwood Grove 2002 Viognier (California) $9. 84 *—S.H. (12/31/2003)*

Pepperwood Grove 2001 Viognier (California) $9. 83 *—S.H. (7/1/2003)*

Pepperwood Grove 1997 Zinfandel (California) $7. 83 *—S.H. (5/1/2000)*

Pepperwood Grove 2004 Zinfandel (California) $8. 83 *—S.H. (11/1/2006)*

Pepperwood Grove 2003 Zinfandel (California) $8. 84 *—S.H. (11/15/2005)*

Pepperwood Grove 1999 California Cuvée Zinfandel (California) $7. 83 *—D.T. (3/1/2002)*

Pepperwood Grove 2005 Old Vine Zinfandel (California) $8. Dry and punchy in cherry-berry and spice flavors, with rich acids and spices that will cut perfectly through mayo, mustard, relish, ketchup and fatty meats and cheeses. A perfect barbecue wine. **85 Best Buy** *—S.H. (8/1/2007)*

PER SEMPRE

Per Sempre 1997 Select Reserve Cabernet Sauvignon (Napa Valley) $66. 91 *(11/1/2000)*

Per Sempre 1999 The Lisa Shiraz (Napa Valley) $60. 85 *(11/1/2001)*

Per Sempre 1998 Wirth Ranch Vineyard Zinfandel (Solano County) $30. 87 *(3/1/2001)*

PERALTA

Peralta 2001 Cabernet Sauvignon (Central Coast) $10. 84 *—S.H. (10/1/2004)*

Peralta 2002 Chardonnay (Santa Barbara County) $10. 84 *—S.H. (12/1/2004)*

Peralta 2003 Sauvignon Blanc (Paso Robles) $8. 81 *—S.H. (12/1/2004)*

Peralta 2001 Syrah (California) $8. 85 Best Buy *(9/1/2005)*

PERBACCO CELLARS

Perbacco Cellars 2005 Chardonnay (Edna Valley) $32. Here's a big, bright Chard notable for the purity of its acid-driven fruit. Kiwis, limes, pineapples, sweet lemongrass and peach are enriched by lees aging in new oak, leading to an impressively rich, dry finish. **90** *—S.H. (2/1/2007)*

Perbacco Cellars 2003 Chardonnay (Edna Valley) $22. 85 *—S.H. (10/1/2006)*

Perbacco Cellars 2001 Chardonnay (Edna Valley) $20. 82 *—S.H. (6/1/2005)*

Perbacco Cellars 2000 La Linda Vineyard Chardonnay (Edna Valley) $18. 90 Editors' Choice *—S.H. (5/1/2003)*

Perbacco Cellars 2004 Petite Sirah (Paso Robles) $25. Smells sharp and piquant, with mint and currant aromas, and the flavors join peppermint with cassis and chocolate. This wine defines a certain hot climate, countrified style. On the plus side, it finishes dry. 85 *—S.H. (12/15/2007)*

Perbacco Cellars 2006 Laetitia Vineyard Pinot Grigio (Arroyo Grande Valley) $19. The vineyard is the source of often very great wines along the Central Coast. It's a cool place, in sight of the Pacific, that in this case ripened the grapes perfectly while preserving vital acidity. That makes the citrus, fig and spicy vanilla flavors finish brilliantly clean and vibrant. 87 *—S.H. (12/15/2007)*

Perbacco Cellars 2005 Laetitia Vineyard Pinot Grigio (Arroyo Grande Valley) $19. 87 *—S.H. (12/31/2006)*

Perbacco Cellars 2004 Laetitia Vineyard Pinot Grigio (Arroyo Grande Valley) $18. 90 Editors' Choice *—S.H. (10/1/2006)*

Perbacco Cellars 2004 Laetitia Vineyard Pinot Grigio (Arroyo Grande Valley) $14. 90 Best Buy *—S.H. (2/1/2006)*

Perbacco Cellars 2005 Pinot Noir (Arroyo Grande Valley) $32. I like this for its dryness and silky texture, which of course are what you look for in a good Pinot Noir. It has somewhat simple cherry, cola and sassafras flavors, and isn't an ager, but it's an elegant example of a well-made, cool climate Pinot. 87 *—S.H. (12/15/2007)*

Perbacco Cellars 2004 Pinot Noir (Arroyo Grande Valley) $28. 84 *—S.H. (11/1/2006)*

Perbacco Cellars 2002 Pinot Noir (Arroyo Grande Valley) $25. 87 *—S.H. (6/1/2005)*

Perbacco Cellars 2005 Dionysus Pinot Noir (Arroyo Grande Valley) $55. Far richer and more concentrated than the winery's regular '05 Pinot, this is a true reserve. It shows the same dryness and silky texture, but the spicy fruit is more intense in cherries and black raspberries, veering into cassis and anisette. Drink now for its extravagent flavors. 90 *—S.H. (12/15/2007)*

Perbacco Cellars 2003 Dionysus Pinot Noir (Arroyo Grande Valley) $45. 90 *—S.H. (11/1/2006)*

Perbacco Cellars 2006 Chiaretto Rosé Wine Rosé Blend (Arroyo Grande Valley) $18. Made from Pinot Noir, this is a dry, crisp young blush wine of some real interest and complexity. It has flavors of unsweetened orange Pekoe tea, tangerine zest and vanilla, with a scour of dusty tannins. 86 *—S.H. (12/15/2007)*

Perbacco Cellars 2005 Syrah (San Luis Obispo County) $32. Too soft and simple, this bone dry Syrah tastes syrupy, with flavors of ripe blackberries, coffee, herbs and dark unsweetened chocolate. 84 *—S.H. (12/15/2007)*

Perbacco Cellars 2003 Passito Zinfandel (Paso Robles) $28. This Zin comes in a half-bottle, and the alcohol is a Port-like 18.5%. It's a sweet wine, with sugary flavors of cherry pie filling, raspberry tart, chocolate and cassis-infused crème brûlée, finished with a crisp dose of acidity. Likeable for its balance, it makes a nice after-dinner or late night conclusion to a long, hard day. 87 *—S.H. (12/15/2007)*

PEREGRINE HILL

Peregrine Hill 2005 Cabernet Sauvignon (Texas) $8. Sweet tobacco, oak and spice on the nose show promise, and in the glass the sturdy tannins and tobacco flavors show that the winemakers meant business. The wine feels heavy and the parts somewhat disparate, though—it needs more balance and heft. Still, interesting flavors are part of the package. 82 *—S.K. (7/1/2007)*

Peregrine Hill 2003 Cabernet Sauvignon (Texas) $8. 83 *—J.C. (9/1/2005)*

Peregrine Hill 2005 Chardonnay (Texas) $8. A creamy, toasty nose is followed by crisp flavors of tropical fruit and apple. Friendly, but there's a watery feel to the flavors, leaving the wine in need of additional dimension. That said, the finish has some depth and the flavors make for a refreshing warm weather sip. 82 *—S.K. (7/1/2007)*

PERFECT 10

Perfect 10 2003 Blonde Chardonnay (Monterey) $10. 85 Best Buy *—M.S. (11/1/2005)*

PERISCOPE

Periscope 2005 Petite Verdot (Lodi) $18. Harsh in texture, this simple wine has sweet-and-sour cherry, blackberry and tangerine flavors. 81 *—S.H. (12/15/2007)*

Periscope 2005 Syrah (Dry Creek Valley) $20. Simple, hot and sweet-and-sour, this is not a success. 80 *—S.H. (12/15/2007)*

PERRY CREEK

Perry Creek 1996 Cabernet Sauvignon (El Dorado) $12. 88 *—S.H. (7/1/1999)*

Perry Creek 1999 Estate Bottled Cabernet Sauvignon (El Dorado) $14. 82 *—S.H. (11/15/2002)*

Perry Creek 1999 Estate Bottled Cellar Select Cabernet Sauvignon (El Dorado County) $28. 84 *—S.H. (12/15/2003)*

Perry Creek 2002 Chardonnay (El Dorado) $14. 84 *—S.H. (10/1/2004)*

Perry Creek 2001 Chardonnay (El Dorado County) $14. 86 *—S.H. (8/1/2003)*

Perry Creek 2000 Estate Bottled Merlot (El Dorado) $12. 85 *—S.H. (11/15/2002)*

Perry Creek 1999 Mourvèdre (El Dorado) $16. 84 *—S.H. (9/1/2002)*

Perry Creek 2003 Estate Bottled Muscat Canelli (El Dorado) $10. 84 *—S.H. (10/1/2004)*

Perry Creek 2000 Cellar Select Petite Sirah (El Dorado) $28. 84 *(4/1/2003)*

Perry Creek 1996 Syrah (El Dorado) $15. 90 *—S.H. (10/1/1999)*

Perry Creek 2002 Syrah (El Dorado) $15. 83 *(9/1/2005)*

Perry Creek 1999 Syrah (El Dorado) $16. 85 *—S.H. (6/1/2003)*

Perry Creek 1999 Cellar Select Syrah (El Dorado) $24. 90 *(11/1/2001)*

Perry Creek 1998 Estate Bottled Syrah (El Dorado) $16. 85 *(10/1/2001)*

Perry Creek 2000 Estate Bottled Cellar Select Syrah (El Dorado County) $28. 85 *—S.H. (12/15/2003)*

Perry Creek 2002 Wild Turkey Ridge Cellar Select Syrah (El Dorado) $28. 85 *(9/1/2005)*

Perry Creek 2002 Viognier (El Dorado) $18. 84 *—S.H. (10/1/2004)*

Perry Creek 2000 Viognier (El Dorado) $16. 86 *—S.H. (12/15/2002)*

Perry Creek 1999 Viognier (El Dorado) $16. 84 *—S.H. (12/15/2001)*

Perry Creek 2001 Estate Bottled Viognier (El Dorado) $16. 83 *—S.H. (12/15/2002)*

Perry Creek 2002 La Vie Sur Mars White Blend (El Dorado) $16. 84 *—S.H. (12/15/2004)*

Perry Creek 2001 Zinfandel (El Dorado) $12. 87 *(11/1/2003)*

Perry Creek 2000 Cellar Select Zinfandel (El Dorado) $24. 84 *—S.H. (11/1/2002)*

Perry Creek 2000 Cellar Select Spanish Creek Ranch Zinfandel (El Dorado) $24. 84 *—S.H. (11/1/2002)*

Perry Creek 2004 Cellar Select Potter Vineyards Zinfandel (Amador County) $28. 82 *—S.H. (12/1/2006)*

Perry Creek 2001 Spanish Creek Ranch Zinfandel (El Dorado) $24. 86 *(11/1/2003)*

Perry Creek 2004 Zin Man Zinfandel (Sierra Foothills) $14. 85 *—S.H. (12/1/2006)*

Perry Creek 2001 Zin Man Zinfandel (Sierra Foothills) $12. 84 *(11/1/2003)*

Perry Creek 2000 Zin Man Zinfandel (Sierra Foothills) $12. 82 *—S.H. (11/1/2002)*

Perry Creek 1998 Zin Man Zinfandel (Sierra Foothills) $12. 83 *—P.G. (3/1/2001)*

Perry Creek 1997 Zin Man Zinfandel (Sierra Foothills) $12. 88 Best Buy *—S.H. (9/1/1999)*

PESSAGNO

Pessagno 2001 Sleepy Hollow Vineyard Chardonnay (Santa Lucia Highlands) $25. 93 Editors' Choice *—J.M. (6/1/2004)*

Pessagno 2000 Sleepy Hollow Vineyard Chardonnay (Santa Lucia Highlands) $30. 92 *—J.M. (5/1/2003)*

Pessagno 1999 Sleepy Hollow Vineyard Chardonnay (Santa Lucia Highlands) $35. 92 *—J.M. (12/1/2001)*

Pessagno 2001 Central Avenue Vineyard Pinot Noir (Monterey) $18. 87 *—S.H. (12/15/2004)*

Pessagno 2000 Central Avenue Vineyard Pinot Noir (Monterey) $25. 85 *(10/1/2002)*

Pessagno 1999 Central Avenue Vineyard Pinot Noir (Monterey) $65. 90 *—J.M. (12/15/2001)*

Pessagno 2001 Gary's Vineyard Pinot Noir (Santa Lucia Highlands) $50. 92 *—J.M. (6/1/2004)*

Pessagno 2000 Gary's Vineyard Pinot Noir (Santa Lucia Highlands) $55. 93 Editors' Choice *(10/1/2002)*

Pessagno 1999 Gary's Vineyard Pinot Noir (Santa Lucia Highlands) $50. 92 *—J.M. (12/15/2001)*

Pessagno 2000 Spring Grove Vineyard Pinot Noir (San Benito County) $28. 84 *(10/1/2002)*

Pessagno 2001 Spring Grove Vineyards Pinot Noir (San Benito County) $25. 90 *—J.M. (6/1/2004)*

Pessagno 2000 Hames Valley Vineyard Port (Monterey) $33. 92 *—J.M.*

(6/1/2004)

Pessagno 2001 Idyll Times Vineyard Zinfandel (San Benito County) $21. 89 —*J.M. (11/1/2003)*

Pessagno 2000 Idyll Times Vineyard Zinfandel (San Benito County) $21. 89 —*J.M. (11/1/2002)*

PETER CELLARS

Peter Cellars 2003 Cabernet Sauvignon (Sonoma Valley) $28. The grapes come from the Kenwood area, a warm region of the valley. A very ripe Cab with a little Merlot and Syrah, this is well-structured, with a fine North Coast acid-tannin balance. There's a raisiny taste that suggests the wine is not ageable, but it's pretty now. **86** —*S.H. (6/1/2007)*

Peter Cellars 2005 Pinot Noir (Sonoma Coast) $32. This is a soft, simple wine, sweet in LifeSaver candy raspberry and cherry flavors. Lots of new oak only adds a plaster of melted vanilla ice cream. **83** —*S.H. (12/1/2007)*

Peter Cellars 2004 Pinot Noir (Sonoma Coast) $29. This is an okay wine, dry and silky, but it's just too cooked or stewed. Even out on the coast, the vintage was brutally hot, and you can taste how those grapes shriveled into raisins. There should be better results in '05 and '06. **84** —*S.H. (6/1/2007)*

Peter Cellars 2004 Syrah (Sonoma Valley) $27. The aromas of white pepper, blackberries grilled meat bone and smoke promise a classy, Hermitage-like Syrah, but it's not the Northern Rhône at all. Definitely California, with its soft tannins and acids and almost sweet berry pie filling flavors. Drink soon. **87** —*S.H. (6/1/2007)*

PETER MCCOY

Peter McCoy 1997 Clos des Pierres Reserve Chardonnay (Knights Valley) $45. 85 *(7/1/2001)*

PETER MICHAEL WINERY

Peter Michael Winery 2003 Les Pavots Cabernet Blend (Knights Valley) $150. 93 Cellar Selection —*S.H. (9/1/2006)*

Peter Michael Winery 2000 Les Pavots Cabernet Blend (Knights Valley) $110. 93 —*S.H. (5/1/2004)*

Peter Michael Winery 2001 Belle Cote Chardonnay (Sonoma County) $60. 92 —*S.H. (2/1/2004)*

Peter Michael Winery 1999 Belle Côte Chardonnay (Sonoma County) $60. 90 *(7/1/2001)*

Peter Michael Winery 1999 Cuvée Indigene Chardonnay (Sonoma County) $85. 92 Cellar Selection *(7/1/2001)*

Peter Michael Winery 2001 La Carriere Chardonnay (Sonoma County) $60. 93 —*S.H. (2/1/2004)*

Peter Michael Winery 1999 La Carriere Chardonnay (Sonoma County) $60. 90 *(7/1/2001)*

Peter Michael Winery 2002 Ma Belle-Fille Chardonnay (Sonoma County) $75. 93 —*S.H. (5/1/2005)*

Peter Michael Winery 2001 Mon Plaisir Chardonnay (Sonoma County) $60. 91 —*S.H. (2/1/2004)*

Peter Michael Winery 1999 Mon Plaisir Chardonnay (Sonoma County) $60. 90 *(7/1/2001)*

Peter Michael Winery 2001 L'Apres Midi Sauvignon Blanc (Sonoma County) $38. 86 —*S.H. (2/1/2004)*

Peter Michael Winery 2004 L'Apres-Midi Sauvignon Blanc (Knights Valley) $42. 94 Editors' Choice —*S.H. (8/1/2006)*

Peter Michael Winery 2003 L'Apres Midi Sauvignon Blanc (Sonoma County) $42. 86 *(7/1/2005)*

PETER PAUL WINES

Peter Paul Wines 2001 Merlot (Napa Valley) $39. 84 —*S.H. (10/1/2005)*

PETERS FAMILY

Peters Family 2002 Meritage Cabernet Blend (California) $25. 91 —*S.H. (12/1/2005)*

Peters Family 2002 Gardner Vineyard Cabernet Sauvignon (Sierra Foothills) $34. 84 —*S.H. (12/1/2005)*

Peters Family 2001 Gardner Vineyard Cabernet Sauvignon (Sierra Foothills) $40. 86 —*S.H. (10/1/2004)*

Peters Family 2004 Sangiacomo Vineyard Chardonnay (Carneros) $36. 91 —*S.H. (11/15/2006)*

Peters Family 2003 Sangiacomo Vineyard Chardonnay (Carneros) $30. 90 —*S.H. (12/1/2005)*

Peters Family 2002 Sangiacomo Vineyard Chardonnay (Carneros) $32. 88 —*S.H. (12/15/2004)*

Peters Family 2005 Sonoma Stage Vineyard Chardonnay (Sonoma Coast) $36. Lots going on in this complex young Chard. It shows crisp, zippy acidity and a firm, steely minerality that marries well with the oak and lees to produce a coconut cream pie, macaroon richness. That's on top of the tropical fruit. Delicious now, and should hang in there for four years or so. **91** —*S.H. (11/1/2007)*

Peters Family 2001 Meritage (California) $25. 88 —*S.H. (10/1/2004)*

Peters Family 2004 Dunah Vineyard Pinot Noir (Sonoma Coast) $42. 92 —*S.H. (11/15/2006)*

Peters Family 2005 Sonoma Stage Vineyard Pinot Noir (Sonoma Coast) $44. My bottle started out with a funky, disagreeably cheesy odor that gradually led to a dry, spicy Pinot Noir, rich in cherry and cola flavors, and well-acidified. But that bretty smell never entirely disappeared. **84** —*S.H. (11/1/2007)*

Peters Family 2002 Clements Ridge Vineyard Syrah (Lodi) $25. 85 —*S.H. (12/1/2005)*

PETERSON

Peterson 1998 Agraria Big Barn Red Cabernet Blend (Dry Creek Valley) $52. 86 —*S.H. (5/1/2003)*

Peterson 1999 Bradford Mountain Cabernet Sauvignon (Dry Creek Valley) $28. 89 —*S.H. (6/1/2003)*

Peterson 2000 Bradford Mountain Vineyard Cabernet Sauvignon (Dry Creek Valley) $29. 85 —*S.H. (10/1/2004)*

Peterson 1999 Merlot (Dry Creek Valley) $24. 90 —*S.H. (7/1/2002)*

Peterson 1999 Floodgate Vineyard Pinot Noir (Anderson Valley) $28. 88 —*S.H. (7/1/2002)*

Peterson 1997 Zinfandel (Dry Creek Valley) $18. 82 —*P.G. (11/15/1999)*

Peterson 1998 Zinfandel (Dry Creek Valley) $18. 87 —*P.G. (3/1/2001)*

Peterson 2000 Bradford Mountain Zinfandel (Dry Creek Valley) $25. 85 —*S.H. (10/1/2004)*

Peterson 1997 Bradford Mountain Zinfandel (Dry Creek Valley) $21. 91 Editors' Choice —*P.G. (3/1/2001)*

PETRONI

Petroni 2000 Cabernet Sauvignon (Sonoma Valley) $55. 84 —*S.H. (12/31/2004)*

Petroni 2005 Chardonnay (Napa Valley) $30. Very dry and a little earthy, with a dusty hay or dried straw quality to the tangerine, sweet lime, lychee, peaches and cream flavors. An interesting, crisp Chard with plenty of nuanced complexity. **91** —*S.H. (8/1/2007)*

Petroni 2002 Poggio Alla Pietra Brunello di Sonoma Sangiovese (Sonoma Valley) $60. A controversial wine. On the plus side are dryness and silky elegance, courtesy of finely ground tannins and crisp acidity, while the cherry and earthy tobacco and truffle flavors are restrained and complex. But then there's the price, which seems excessive. You decide. **87** —*S.H. (8/1/2007)*

Petroni 2000 Poggio Alla Pietra Sangiovese (Sonoma Valley) $55. 84 —*S.H. (12/31/2004)*

PEY-MARIN

Pey-Marin 2005 Trois Filles Pinot Noir (Marin County) $39. You're going to be hearing a lot more about Pinots from Marin County, which is between Sonoma and San Francisco. It's cool climate, as witnessed by the crunchy acidity that accompanies the cola, cherry and blackberry flavors of this three-vineyard wine. There's a lot of oak, but it works well. Shows the leaner, more elegant side of Pinot. **91** —*S.H. (10/1/2007)*

Pey-Marin 2006 The Shell Mound Riesling (Marin County) $22. The grapes barely got ripe in this vineyard in chilly Marin, just north of the Golden Gate. The numbers tell the story. Acidity is .082 grams, alcohol is 11.8%, there's no oak, and the wine was stirred on the lees for five months. The result is an impressive Riesling, one of the driest on the market, a wine of great delicacy and subtlety. Fruit isn't the star here; minerals are. This is a wine to watch. **91** —*S.H. (9/1/2007)*

PEZZI KING

Pezzi King 2000 Cabernet Sauvignon (Sonoma County) $25. 89 —*S.H. (6/1/2004)*

Pezzi King 1998 Chardonnay (Sonoma County) $17. 86 *(6/1/2000)*

Pezzi King 1997 Susie's Reserve Merlot (Dry Creek Valley) $26. 91 *(3/1/2000)*

Pezzi King 2000 Pinot Noir (Russian River Valley) $30. 88 *(10/1/2002)*

Pezzi King 1999 Pinot Noir (Russian River Valley) $30. 87 *(10/1/2002)*

Pezzi King 2003 Jane's Reserve Sauvignon Blanc (Mendocino County) $27. 87 *(7/1/2005)*

Pezzi King 1999 Syrah (Dry Creek Valley) $27. 87 *(11/1/2001)*

Pezzi King 1997 Estate Zinfandel (Dry Creek Valley) $26. 87 *—P.G. (11/15/1999)*

Pezzi King 2001 Old Vines Zinfandel (Dry Creek Valley) $25. 87 *—J.M. (8/1/2004)*

Pezzi King 2000 Old Vines Zinfandel (Dry Creek Valley) $25. 88 *—J.M. (6/11/2004)*

Pezzi King 1997 SLR Zinfandel (Dry Creek Valley) $24. 88 *—P.G. (11/15/1999)*

PHARAOHMOANS

PharaohMoans 2005 Westside Syrah (Paso Robles) $95. The name is a play on "pheromones." The wine itself is dense and dry. Soft in the manner of Paso Robles, it has a deep core of blackberries, coffee and violets, assisted by oak. The tannins are really hard now, and it's difficult to tell where the wine is going. But it's one to watch. **89** *—S.H. (6/1/2007)*

PHEASANT VALLEY

Pheasant Valley 2003 Celilo Vineyard Chardonnay (Washington) $15. 90 *—P.G. (6/1/2005)*

PHELAN VINEYARD

Phelan Vineyard 2000 Cabernet Sauvignon (Napa Valley) $75. 91 *—J.M. (12/15/2003)*

PHELPS CREEK VINEYARDS

Phelps Creek Vineyards 2004 Chardonnay (Columbia Gorge) $17. It's rather odd to see a winery release its chardonnay a year later than its pinot noir, but this estate-grown Columbia Gorge wine seems to have benefited from the extra time in bottle. It's a spicy wine, showing baked apple pie flavors and a lovely mix of fruits in the mouth. Forward and juicy and truly ready to drink right now. **89** *—P.G. (2/1/2007)*

Phelps Creek Vineyards 2005 Unoaked Chardonnay (Columbia Gorge) $15. Unoaked is the buzzword in the Chardonnay world at the moment, and here you see it done especially well. The wine is bursting with fruit, lively with zippy acids and flavors of fresh pineapple and citrus. Crisp and fruity, forward and fresh; what's not to like? **88** *—P.G. (2/1/2007)*

Phelps Creek Vineyards 2005 Becky's Cuvée Pinot Noir (Columbia Gorge) $24. A light Pinot from the Columbia Gorge (Oregon side). This is well-crafted (by Sineann's Peter Rosback) but simple; a straight-ahead style which fades quickly. The vintage is looking this way in Oregon; early releases of Pinot Noir have been unusually light, at least by recent standards, and this is no exception. **85** *—P.G. (2/1/2007)*

Phelps Creek Vineyards 2005 Judith's Reserve Pinot Noir (Columbia Gorge) $39. Here is an elegant, almost demure Pinot Noir, released very young. Pinot at this early stage can be a bit flirty; perhaps this one is playing hide-and-seek. Wild raspberry and sour cherry flavors define the midpalate; but overall it is compact, closed and subdued. **87** *—P.G. (2/1/2007)*

PHILIP STALEY

Philip Staley 1999 Chardonnay (Russian River Valley) $15. 87 *—S.H. (5/1/2001)*

Philip Staley 2000 Staley Vineyard Grenache (Russian River Valley) $18. 88 *—S.H. (12/1/2002)*

Philip Staley 1999 Staley Vineyard Grenache (Russian River Valley) $18. 89 *—S.H. (7/1/2002)*

Philip Staley 1996 Staley Vineyard Grenache (Russian River Valley) $13. 89 *—L.W. (6/1/1999)*

Philip Staley 1998 Mourvèdre (Russian River Valley) $16. 87 *—S.H. (7/1/2002)*

Philip Staley 1995 Staley Vineyard Mourvèdre (Russian River Valley) $15. 90 *—L.W. (6/1/1999)*

Philip Staley 2000 Somers Vineyard Petite Sirah (Dry Creek Valley) $24. 86 *(4/1/2003)*

Philip Staley 1999 Somers Vineyard Petite Sirah (Dry Creek Valley) $21. 89 *—S.H. (12/1/2002)*

Philip Staley NV The Coat of the Roan Foal 1 Rhône Red Blend (California) $12. 89 *—S.H. (8/1/2004)*

Philip Staley 2002 Duet Sauvignon Blanc-Sémillon (Sonoma County) $16. 90 *—S.H. (8/1/2004)*

Philip Staley 1998 Syrah (Russian River Valley) $18. 86 *—S.H. (7/1/2002)*

Philip Staley 1999 Staley Vineyard Syrah (Russian River Valley) $21. 90 *—S.H. (12/1/2002)*

Philip Staley 2002 Staley Vineyard Viognier (Russian River Valley) $22. 89 *—S.H. (8/1/2004)*

Philip Staley 2001 Staley Vineyard Viognier (Russian River Valley) $23. 88 *—S.H. (12/1/2003)*

Philip Staley 2000 Staley Vineyard Viognier (Russian River Valley) $21. 83 *—S.H. (9/1/2003)*

Philip Staley 1997 Staley Vineyard Viognier (Russian River Valley) $16. 88 *—L.W. (6/1/1999)*

Philip Staley 2001 Duet White Blend (Sonoma County) $17. 90 *—S.H. (12/15/2002)*

Philip Staley 1998 Zinfandel (Dry Creek Valley) $18. 89 *—S.H. (7/1/2002)*

PHILIPPE-LORRAINE

Philippe-Lorraine 1998 Chardonnay (Napa Valley) $18. 87 *(6/1/2000)*

Philippe-Lorraine 1999 Chardonnay (Napa Valley) $16. 88 *—S.H. (11/15/2001)*

Philippe-Lorraine 1998 Merlot (Napa Valley) $23. 88 *—S.H. (12/1/2001)*

PHILLIPS

Phillips 1999 Reserve Chardonnay (Lodi) $20. 80 *—S.H. (12/31/2001)*

Phillips 1997 Reserve Merlot (California) $15. 87 *—J.C. (3/1/2000)*

Phillips 1999 Syrah (California) $16. 87 *(10/1/2001)*

Phillips 1999 Old Vine Zinfandel (Lodi) $20. 83 *—D.T. (3/1/2002)*

PHILLIPS HILL

Phillips Hill 2005 Oppenlander Vineyard Pinot Noir (Anderson Valley) $42. Made in a very ripe, fruit-driven, jammy style, this Pinot is lush in rhubarb pie, sweet cherry tart, cola, pomegranate and spice flavors. Could use a little more restraint and elegance, but it's a pretty good wine. **88** *—S.H. (11/1/2007)*

Phillips Hill 2005 Toulouse Vineyard Pinot Noir (Anderson Valley) $40. A luscious young Pinot, made in an instantly appealing style. It shows ripe, sweet cherry, raspberry, framboise, red currant and spicy vanilla and oak flavors that finish long and balanced. This is a voluptuous wine, almost decadent. **91** *—S.H. (11/1/2007)*

PHILO RIDGE

Philo Ridge 2004 Pinot Noir (Anderson Valley) $28. This balanced Pinot is easy to like. Made in a lighter-bodied style, it's fragrant in red cherry, cola, tangerine and root beer. Finishes with a nice, food-friendly bite of acidity, and should hold well for several years. **90** *—S.H. (11/1/2007)*

Philo Ridge 2002 Syrah (Sonoma County) $18. 88 *(9/1/2005)*

PHIPPS

Phipps 2005 Sonoma County Ranches Zinfandel (Sonoma County) $36. With 10% Petite Sirah, which seems to give it a tannic essence of dark fruit intensity, this Zin is enormous in jammy blackberry and cherry fruit, with cola and caramel notes. It's full-bodied and dry and, once again, those tannins are center stage. **87** *—S.H. (12/1/2007)*

Phipps 2004 Sonoma County Ranches Zinfandel (Sonoma County) $36. This is a new winery for me, and they're off to a promising start. The grapes come from well-regarded vineyards in Russian River and Dry Creek, and the wine displays classic Sonoma features of dryness and richness, with Zin's typical wild, briary, brambly character. **89** *—S.H. (2/1/2007)*

PHOENIX

Phoenix 2000 Cabernet Sauvignon (Napa Valley) $28. 92 Editors' Choice *—S.H. (11/15/2003)*

Phoenix 2000 Reserve Chardonnay (Napa Valley) $19. 85 *—S.H. (9/12/2002)*

Phoenix 2000 Reserve Pinot Noir (Napa Valley) $23. 87 *—S.H. (12/1/2003)*

Phoenix 2000 Blood of Jupiter Sangiovese (Napa Valley) $20. 85 *—S.H. (9/1/2003)*

Phoenix 1999 Blood of Jupitor Sangiovese (Napa Valley) $20. 84 *—S.H. (9/12/2002)*

PIANETTA

Pianetta 2004 Cabernet Sauvignon (Monterey) $28. Just barely acceptable, this soft, semisweet Cab has Lifesaver candy flavors of cherries and raspberries. **80** *—S.H. (12/1/2007)*

Pianetta 2003 Estate Cabernet Sauvignon (Monterey) $28. 84 *—S.H. (3/1/2006)*

Pianetta 2003 Estate Shiraz-Cabernet Sauvignon (Monterey) $24. 88 *—S.H. (4/1/2006)*

Pianetta 2004 Syrah (Monterey) $28. This superripe wine is a blast of blackberry, cherry and blueberry fruit, puréed in the blender and then sprinkled with a dusting of cocoa and white pepper. But it's too sweet by far, and too soft, lacking the structure for balance. **83** *—S.H. (12/1/2007)*

Pianetta 2003 Estate Syrah (Monterey) $28. 86 *—S.H. (4/1/2006)*

PIEDRA CREEK

Piedra Hill 2004 Cabernet Sauvignon (Howell Mountain) $42. Following on the heels of the fine, ageable '03 comes this softer bottling. The tannins aren't as hard, although they're there, framing ripe blackberry and cassis flavors that finish with a swirl of dark unsweetened chocolate and cappuccino. This lovely young Cab drinks beautifully now, and will hold for a good eight years. **90** —*S.H. (5/1/2007)*

Piedra Hill 2004 Purple Label Cabernet Sauvignon (Howell Mountain) $54. The wine is owned by the Smiths, who started La Jota and know from Howell Mountain Cabernet. Judging from the last few bottlings, it's off to a promising start. Dry, rich and balanced, fruit is the star here, with explosive blackberries and cherries, while 100% new oak adds lush layers of cedar and smoke. Fully enjoyable now, with decanting; it should enjoy a long life for at least 10 years. **94** —*S.H. (8/1/2007)*

Pietra Santa 2001 Sassolino Red Wine Super Tuscan Style Cabernet Blend (Cienega Valley) $18. They held this Cab-Sangiovese blend back, but it's still awkward. It's clean and fruity, but way too sugary sweet for a dry table wine. **82** —*S.H. (6/1/2007)*

Piedra Creek 2004 San Floriano Vineyard Pinot Noir (Edna Valley) $22. 83 —*S.H. (9/1/2006)*

Piedra Creek 2004 San Floriano Red Blend (San Luis Obispo) $22. 85 —*S.H. (10/1/2006)*

Piedra Creek 2001 Benito Dusi Vineyard Zinfandel (Paso Robles) $24. 90 —*S.H. (4/1/2004)*

PIEDRA HILL

Piedra Hill 2003 Cabernet Sauvignon (Howell Mountain) $40. 91 Cellar Selection —*S.H. (10/1/2006)*

PIETRA SANTA

Pietra Santa 2002 Cabernet Sauvignon (Cienega Valley) $24. Suffers from a burnt taste and an overall rustic mouthfeel, neither of which will age away. Although the wine is dry, it's hot and clumsy. **82** —*S.H. (6/1/2007)*

Pietra Santa 2002 Vache Cabernet Sauvignon (Cienega Valley) $40. If your standard for Cab is Napa, and mine is, this wine is more tannic, acidic and grippy. It does show similar flavors, of enormously ripe, chocolate-tinged blackberry, cassis, cherry and soy-tabasco flavors, but then there's that ruggedness. It may be one for the cellar, but it's hard to tell. I'm giving it the benefit of a doubt. **88** —*S.H. (6/1/2007)*

Pietra Santa 2005 Chardonnay (Central Coast) $15. Simple and citrusy, this high-acid (7.2 grams) Chard has slightly sweet Meyer lemon, pink grapefruit, green pear and vanilla flavors. It's a clean, easy to like wine. **85** —*S.H. (6/1/2007)*

Pietra Santa 2002 Chardonnay (California) $14. 86 —*S.H. (12/15/2004)*

Pietra Santa 2001 Chardonnay (Cienega Valley) $13. 88 Best Buy —*J.M. (6/1/2003)*

Pietra Santa 2004 Vache Chardonnay (Cienega Valley) $35. There's an ashy, burnt aspect of this wine that's probably from overly toasted wood, and it dominates the aroma and taste. It's not a bad wine, and has no technical defects, but it's like drinking toothpicks. **83** —*S.H. (6/1/2007)*

Pietra Santa 2001 Dolcetto (Cienega Valley) $18. After five-plus years, this is not a very likeable wine. It's heavy and harsh, with a jagged mouthfeel framing sweet-and-sour cherry LifeSaver candy flavors. **82** —*S.H. (6/1/2007)*

Pietra Santa 2000 Dolcetto (Cienega Valley) $25. 83 —*S.H. (6/1/2005)*

Pietra Santa 2006 Gewürztraminer (Cienega Valley) $15. The acidity is fine and crisp, but the wine lacks concentration. The apricot, peach and pineapple flavors are on the thin side, letting the alcohol show through. But it shows good Gewürz personality for this price. **85** —*S.H. (11/15/2007)*

Pietra Santa 2003 Merlot (Cienega Valley) $15. Dry, rustic and harsh, with a sandpapery texture, although the fruit itself is polished and fine. The flavors are of cherries, blackberries and root beer. **83** —*S.H. (6/1/2007)*

Pietra Santa 2001 Merlot (Cienega Valley) $18. 83 —*S.H. (6/1/2005)*

Pietra Santa 2000 Merlot (Cienega Valley) $18. 84 —*S.H. (12/15/2004)*

Pietra Santa 1999 Merlot (Cienega Valley) $13. 86 —*J.M. (12/1/2003)*

Pietra Santa 2002 Vache Merlot (Cienega Valley) $40. There can't be too many 2002 Merlots yet to be released. Here's one; it's as tannic and berry fresh as a younger wine. Flooded with cherry jam, cassis and spice flavors, it's fairly tough and gritty. It could age out in a couple years, but it's far from guaranteed. **84** —*S.H. (6/1/2007)*

Pietra Santa 2002 Pinot Grigio (California) $14. 86 —*S.H. (12/15/2004)*

Pietra Santa 2006 Amore Pinot Grigio (Cienega Valley) $20. The appellation is in San Benito County, a terroir that has plenty of coastal influence. Acidity and ripeness are the stars in this bright, expressive, dry but fruity wine, with pineapple, lime and honeysuckle flavors. Try as an interesting alternative to Sauvignon Blanc or Viognier. **87** —*S.H. (12/31/2007)*

Pietra Santa 2005 Amore Pinot Grigio (Cienega Valley) $20. Simple, soft and a little cloying, this wine has off-dry citrus and fig flavors; finishes with honeysuckle sweetness. **82** —*S.H. (6/1/2007)*

Pietra Santa 2005 Pinot Noir (Central Coast) $18. A bit raw, but dry and crisp, with a pleasantly silky mouthfeel. The cherry, cola and wintergreen flavors finish with a bite of acidic sharpness. **83** —*S.H. (9/1/2007)*

Pietra Santa 2001 Sacred Stone Red Blend (California) $14. 85 —*S.H. (12/15/2004)*

Pietra Santa NV Sacred Stone Old World Style Red Wine Red Blend (Cienega Valley) $100. Made from Merlot, Sangiovese and others, this wine indeed is "Old World Style," if by that you mean a rustic, sturdy wine. It's not particularly sophisticated, but will do with pizza, burgers, that sort of fare. **83** —*S.H. (6/1/2007)*

Pietra Santa 2000 Sasso Rosso Red Blend (California) $14. 84 —*S.H. (12/15/2004)*

Pietra Santa 1999 Sasso Rosso Red Blend (Cienega Valley) $12. 82 —*S.H. (6/1/2005)*

Pietra Santa 1998 Sasso Rosso Red Blend (California) $13. 87 —*J.C. (12/1/2001)*

Pietra Santa 2005 Rosato Rosé Blend (Cienega Valley) $14. Made from Sangiovese, this pale wine has orange soda flavors with a splash of pineapple juice. It's overtly sweet. **83** —*S.H. (7/1/2007)*

Pietra Santa 2001 Sangiovese (Cienega Valley) $24. 84 —*S.H. (6/1/2005)*

Pietra Santa 2000 Sangiovese (Cienega Valley) $24. 84 —*S.H. (12/31/2004)*

Pietra Santa 2006 Rosato Sangiovese (Cienega Valley) $14. Made from Sangiovese, this is a lightly delicate rosé with appealing cherry and vanilla flavors. There's a honey taste on the finish, although the wine is basically dry. **84** —*S.H. (11/15/2007)*

Pietra Santa 2000 Sassolino Sangiovese (Cienega Valley) $25. 85 —*S.H. (12/15/2004)*

Pietra Santa 2002 Zinfandel (Cienega Valley) $15. Soft and simple, with sweetened cherry candy flavors. The finish is hot in alcohol. **82** —*S.H. (6/1/2007)*

Pietra Santa 2000 Zinfandel (Cienega Valley) $20. 82 —*S.H. (12/31/2004)*

PIÑA

Piña 2000 Cabernet Sauvignon (Howell Mountain) $48. 90 —*S.H. (11/15/2004)*

Piña 2001 Estate Cabernet Sauvignon (Howell Mountain) $54. 94 Editors' Choice —*S.H. (11/1/2005)*

PINDAR VINEYARDS

Pindar Vineyards NV Pythagoras Bordeaux Blend (North Fork of Long Island) $13. This non-vintage, Bordeaux-style blend of Cabernet Sauvignon, Cabernet Franc, Merlot, Petit Verdot and Malbec has a fruity, subtle bouquet with hints of cherry, tea leaves and flowers. On the palate, it's slightly bitter—the raspberry tea prevailing—and dry, but there are some hints of complexity and earthiness. **82** —*S.K. (2/1/2007)*

Pindar Vineyards 1997 Reserve Cabernet Sauvignon (North Fork of Long Island) $19. 84 —*J.C. (4/1/2001)*

Pindar Vineyards 1995 Cuvée Rare Chardonnay (Long Island) $28. 86 —*J.C. (4/1/2001)*

Pindar Vineyards 1998 Peacock Chardonnay (Long Island) $9. 84 —*J.C. (4/1/2001)*

Pindar Vineyards 1998 Reserve Chardonnay (Long Island) $13. 86 —*J.C. (4/1/2001)*

Pindar Vineyards 1998 Sunflower Chardonnay (Long Island) $18. 88 —*J.C. (4/1/2001)*

Pindar Vineyards 1999 Ice Wine Johannisberg Riesling (Long Island) $35. 90 —*J.C. (4/1/2001)*

Pindar Vineyards 1997 Mythology Merlot (North Fork of Long Island) $28. 90 —*J.C. (4/1/2001)*

Pindar Vineyards 2003 Reserve Barrel Select Merlot (North Fork of Long Island) $19. 86 —*M.D. (12/1/2006)*

Pindar Vineyards 1997 Port (Long Island) $25. 86 —*J.C. (4/1/2001)*

Pindar Vineyards NV Pythagoras Red Blend (North Fork of Long Island) $11. 83 —*J.C. (4/1/2001)*

Pindar Vineyards 1997 Syrah (Long Island) $25. 87 —*J.C. (4/1/2001)*

Pindar Vineyards 1998 Viognier (Long Island) $23. 85 —*J.C. (4/1/2001)*

PINE & POST

Pine & Post 2005 Chardonnay (Washington) $6. Don't look for richness at this price, but you will find a clean, straightforward wine, with supple, ripe fruit flavors and surprising midpalate weight. There's nothing flabby, watery, thin or fake about it. **87 Best Buy** —*P.G. (12/1/2007)*

Pine & Post 2004 Chardonnay (Columbia Valley (WA)) $5. 87 Best Buy —*P.G. (4/1/2006)*

Pine & Post 2004 Merlot (Columbia Valley (WA)) $5. 87 Best Buy —*P.G. (4/1/2006)*

PINE RIDGE

Pine Ridge 1999 Andrus Reserve Bordeaux Blend (Napa Valley) $135. 90 —*J.C. (6/1/2003)*

Pine Ridge 2002 Charmstone Bordeaux Blend (Napa Valley) $30. 82 —*S.H. (11/15/2006)*

Pine Ridge 2002 Onyx Bordeaux Blend (Napa Valley) $55. 92 —*S.H. (9/1/2006)*

Pine Ridge 2002 Red Wine Cabernet Blend (Oakville) $60. 83 —*S.H. (10/1/2005)*

Pine Ridge 2004 Cabernet Sauvignon (Oakville) $75. There's a sweat smell that dominates this Cab, and it's too bad, because there's a beautiful wine beneath the funk. Decant it, and the wine improves. Tasted three times. **83** —*S.H. (10/1/2007)*

Pine Ridge 2004 Cabernet Sauvignon (Rutherford) $48. Smells funky, sweaty and leathery, and while the oaky fruit flavors are ripe and the tannic structure fine, the wine seems flat and stale. Tasted three times. **81** —*S.H. (10/1/2007)*

Pine Ridge 2003 Cabernet Sauvignon (Stags Leap District) $75. Shows the gorgeous tannins of this appellation, all firm but pliant velvet, with nicely balanced blackberry and cassis flavors. Yet there's a stubborn note of mustiness, an earthy, funky flatness that stamps the fruit down. Tasted three times. **84** —*S.H. (10/1/2007)*

Pine Ridge 2003 Cabernet Sauvignon (Howell Mountain) $80. 95 Cellar Selection —*S.H. (12/31/2006)*

Pine Ridge 2003 Cabernet Sauvignon (Rutherford) $40. 94 Editors' Choice —*S.H. (12/15/2006)*

Pine Ridge 2003 Cabernet Sauvignon (Oakville) $75. 92 Cellar Selection —*S.H. (12/31/2006)*

Pine Ridge 2002 Cabernet Sauvignon (Rutherford) $39. 90 —*S.H. (10/1/2005)*

Pine Ridge 2002 Cabernet Sauvignon (Stags Leap District) $75. 93 Cellar Selection —*S.H. (8/1/2006)*

Pine Ridge 2001 Cabernet Sauvignon (Howell Mountain) $70. 92 Cellar Selection —*S.H. (10/1/2004)*

Pine Ridge 2001 Cabernet Sauvignon (Stags Leap District) $70. 94 Cellar Selection —*S.H. (10/1/2004)*

Pine Ridge 2001 Cabernet Sauvignon (Rutherford) $37. 91 —*S.H. (10/1/2004)*

Pine Ridge 2001 Cabernet Sauvignon (Oakville) $55. 89 —*S.H. (10/1/2004)*

Pine Ridge 2000 Cabernet Sauvignon (Rutherford) $37. 87 —*J.M. (8/1/2003)*

Pine Ridge 1999 Cabernet Sauvignon (Howell Mountain) $50. 92 —*S.H. (11/15/2002)*

Pine Ridge 1999 Chardonnay (Stags Leap District) $40. 87 *(7/1/2001)*

Pine Ridge 1997 Cabernet Sauvignon (Howell Mountain) $50. 89 *(11/1/2000)*

Pine Ridge 1997 Cabernet Sauvignon (Rutherford) $26. 85 *(3/1/2000)*

Pine Ridge 1997 Cabernet Sauvignon (Stags Leap District) $50. 95 *(11/1/2000)*

Pine Ridge 2005 Dijon Clones Chardonnay (Carneros) $33. Better known for Cabernet, Pine Ridge has been doing an interesting job with Chardonnay. Every vintage is different, but usually worth a peek. The '05, from a cool year, is high in acidity, which gives the long hangtime peach, apricot and nectarine fruit a tart, jam-like boost. **87** —*S.H. (5/1/2007)*

Pine Ridge 2004 Dijon Clones Chardonnay (Carneros) $33. 90 —*S.H. (8/1/2006)*

Pine Ridge 2003 Dijon Clones Chardonnay (Carneros) $27. 84 —*S.H. (10/1/2005)*

Pine Ridge 2001 Dijon Clones Chardonnay (Carneros) $25. 89 —*J.M. (8/1/2003)*

Pine Ridge 2000 Dijon Clones Chardonnay (Napa Valley) $25. 91 —*J.M. (5/1/2002)*

Pine Ridge 1998 Dijon Clones Chardonnay (Carneros) $25. 88 *(6/1/2000)*

Pine Ridge 2005 Epitome Chardonnay (Carneros) $60. This immature Chard needs some time in the bottle for the rich acids and forward oak to knit together with the tremendous wealth of tropical fruit. Give it until 2008, by which time it should provide opulent pleasure. **90** —*S.H. (11/1/2007)*

Pine Ridge 2002 Le Petit Clos Chardonnay (Stags Leap District) $50. 95 —*S.H. (12/31/2004)*

Pine Ridge 2001 Onyx Malbec (Napa Valley) $50. 91 —*S.H. (12/31/2004)*

Pine Ridge 2004 Crimson Creek Merlot (Napa Valley) $27. A very nice, casual Merlot that has layers of complex elegance beyond just the fruit. And what fruit it is, ripe and sweet in cherry pie, raspberry cream, cola and vanilla, with a splash of cassis. Fortunately, there's enough acidity and tannin for balance. **88** —*S.H. (10/1/2007)*

Pine Ridge 2003 Crimson Creek Merlot (Napa Valley) $27. This is a blend of grapes from Carneros, Rutherford, Oakville and Stags Leap. One thing it offers is fruit. Red and black cherries and blackberries, to be exact, on the jammy side, with a spicy lift of new oak. It's not a complex ager, but it does show real white-tablecloth fanciness. **87** —*S.H. (3/1/2007)*

Pine Ridge 2002 Crimson Creek Merlot (Napa Valley) $27. 84 —*S.H. (8/1/2006)*

Pine Ridge 1997 Crimson Creek Merlot (Napa Valley) $22. 93 *(11/15/1999)*

Pine Ridge 2004 Onyx Red Blend (Napa Valley) $50. The concept is interesting: Create an imaginative blend of Tannat, Malbec, Merlot, Petit Verdot and Cabernet. The wine, however, has major problems. It opens with a sweaty, cheesy smell, then turns harshly tannic. Not going anywhere. **82** —*S.H. (11/1/2007)*

Pine Ridge 1998 White Blend (California) $11. 89 —*M.S. (11/1/1999)*

Pine Ridge 2006 Chenin Blanc-Viognier White Blend (Clarksburg) $13. Has the feline scent, as well as zesty acidity, but if you can get past that, it's dry, and there's a wealth of ripe citrus and tropical fruits. **84** —*S.H. (10/1/2007)*

Pine Ridge 2005 Chenin Blanc - Viognier White Blend (Clarksburg) $13. From grapes grown in the windy, warmish Delta comes this unusual Loire-Rhône blend, and it's a really nice wine at a good price. Brimming with citrus, peach, wildflower and brine flavors, it's quite tart in acidity, a wine that needs food. Try with oysters or clams, or as a refreshing appetizer. **86** —*S.H. (5/1/2007)*

Pine Ridge 2004 Chenin Blanc-Viognier White Blend (Clarksburg) $14. 84 —*S.H. (11/15/2006)*

PINK UMBRELLA

Pink Umbrella 2005 Pink Pinot Grigio (California) $10. I like everything about this wine except the thinness. The peach blush color is pretty, the wine is totally dry and crisp, and it's nice and delicate in the mouth. But it's watered down, with almost no flavor. **82** —*S.H. (7/1/2007)*

PINOT EVIL

Pinot Evil 2004 Reserve Pinot Noir (Edna Valley) $15. 85 —*S.H. (9/1/2006)*

PIPER SONOMA

Piper Sonoma NV Blanc de Noir Champagne Blend (Sonoma County) $19. 87 *(12/1/2001)*

Piper Sonoma NV Brut Champagne Blend (Sonoma County) $19. 85 *(12/1/2001)*

Piper Sonoma NV Blanc de Noir Pinot Noir (Sonoma County) $20. 88 —*S.H. (12/31/2004)*

Piper Sonoma NV Blanc de Noir Sparkling Blend (California) $18. 85 —*J.C. (12/1/2003)*

Piper Sonoma NV Brut Sparkling Blend (Sonoma County) $20. 87 —*S.H. (12/31/2004)*

Piper Sonoma NV Brut Sparkling Blend (California) $18. 88 —*J.C. (12/1/2003)*

Piper Sonoma NV Select Cuvée Brut Sparkling Blend (Sonoma County) $15. This has subtle flavors of strawberries, limes, dough and vanilla smoke. It's a little rough in the mouth, with a scoury texture, but it's a good buy at this price. **86** —*S.H. (12/31/2007)*

PIPESTONE VINEYARDS

Pipestone Vineyards 2001 Zinfandel (Paso Robles) $22. 85 *(11/1/2003)*

PIROUETTE

Pirouette 2004 Red Blend (Columbia Valley (WA)) $55. Long Shadows Pirouette is made by Agustin Huneeus and Philippe Melka; it's 49% Cabernet Sauvignon, 27% Merlot, 11% Syrah and 13% Petit Verdot. Aromatic and seductive, it sends waves of perfumed fruit, dusty cocoa, bright espresso and toasted grain from the glass, leading into a soft, smooth and seamless palate. This rich and luscious wine could easily pass for a much pricier Napa Valley blend. 91 *—P.G. (8/1/2007)*

Pirouette 2003 Red Blend (Columbia Valley (WA)) $55. 90 *—P.G. (4/1/2006)*

PISONI

Pisoni 1996 Pinot Noir (Santa Lucia Highlands) $NA. 92 *—S.H. (6/1/2005)*

Pisoni 1994 Pinot Noir (Santa Lucia Highlands) $NA. 91 *—S.H. (6/1/2005)*

Pisoni 2002 Pinot Noir (Santa Lucia Highlands) $60. 92 *—S.H. (11/1/2004)*

Pisoni 2001 Estate Pinot Noir (Santa Lucia Highlands) $NA. 93 *—S.H. (6/1/2005)*

Pisoni 2000 Estate Pinot Noir (Santa Lucia Highlands) $NA. 90 *—S.H. (6/1/2005)*

Pisoni 1999 Estate Pinot Noir (Santa Lucia Highlands) $NA. 95 *—S.H. (6/1/2005)*

Pisoni 1998 Estate Pinot Noir (Santa Lucia Highlands) $NA. 93 *—S.H. (6/1/2005)*

Pisoni 2002 Garys' Vineyard Pinot Noir (Santa Lucia Highlands) $38. 86 *—S.H. (11/1/2004)*

PIZIALI

Piziali 2004 Late Harvest 375 mL Sauvignon Blanc (Lake County) $32. 90 *—S.H. (10/1/2006)*

PLUMPJACK

Plumpjack 2004 Cabernet Sauvignon (Oakville) $72. This is the winery's regular estate Cab, and it's good, elegant wine. Dry and balanced, it shows blackberry, cassis and new oaky, smoky flavors; it's rich in smooth, ripe, dense tannins. It's a masculine wine in need of some time in the cellar, though not one of PlumpJack's greater Cabernets, marked as it is by some sharpness. Drink now through 2010. 89 *—S.H. (7/1/2007)*

Plumpjack 2001 Cabernet Sauvignon (Oakville) $58. 95 *—S.H. (10/1/2004)*

Plumpjack 1997 Cabernet Sauvignon (Oakville) $44. 94 *—S.H. (2/1/2000)*

Plumpjack 2003 Estate Cabernet Sauvignon (Oakville) $68. 86 *—S.H. (9/1/2006)*

Plumpjack 2002 Estate Cabernet Sauvignon (Oakville) $62. 90 *—S.H. (10/1/2005)*

Plumpjack 1999 Reserve Cabernet Sauvignon (Napa Valley) $155. 93 *—J.M. (2/1/2003)*

Plumpjack 1999 Reserve Chardonnay (Napa Valley) $40. 86 *(7/1/2001)*

PLUNGERHEAD

Plungerhead 2005 Zinfandel (Dry Creek Valley) $19. What an easy-drinking Zin, and it has real complexity, too. The flavors are of rich, chocolaty cherry, raspberry and blackberry flavors, with Zinny spices, while firm tannins and good acidity provide a rich structural balance. This is a lip-smackingly good Zinfandel. 88 *—S.H. (10/1/2007)*

Plungerhead 2005 Zinfandel (Lodi) $14. Pure Lodi, very soft, very ripe and slightly sweet. With syrupy flavors of raspberries, cherries, plumped raisins, milk chocolate and licorice, it's balanced with grainy tannins. 84 *—S.H. (10/1/2007)*

Plungerhead 2004 Zinfandel (Sierra Foothills) $16. Nice, rugged mountain Zin, with the briary, brambly tannins and peppery taste of wild berries freshly picked off the vine. Alcohol adds heat and structure, and time in the barrel has softened the tannins. This might just be the perfect backyard barbecue red wine. 86 *—S.H. (10/1/2007)*

Plungerhead 2004 Zinfandel (Dry Creek Valley) $14. 85 *—S.H. (7/1/2006)*

POET'S LEAP

Poet's Leap 2005 Riesling (Columbia Valley (WA)) $20. Poet's Leap was the first wine to be released under the Long Shadows portfolio, and this 2005 is clearly its best yet. Old-vine Riesling from Dionysus and Weinbau form the core of the wine, which is immaculate, rich and generous. The fruits sound like a county fair in summer—melon, stone fruits, citrus, honey—and the mix of residual sugar (about 1.6%) and racy acids is thrillingly on target. 93 Editors' Choice *—P.G. (5/1/2007)*

Poet's Leap 2004 Riesling (Columbia Valley (WA)) $22. 90 *—P.G. (4/1/2006)*

Poet's Leap 2003 Riesling (Columbia Valley (WA)) $22. 89 *—P.G. (11/15/2004)*

POINT CONCEPCIÓN

Point Concepción 2005 Esplandia Syrah Rosé Syrah (Paso Robles) $14. Full-bodied and fruity, this wine could use greater polish and discretion. It's big and ripe in black cherry and smoky, spicy vanilla, with almost the weight of a red wine. It also finishes sugary sweet. 83 *—S.H. (7/1/2007)*

POMELO

Pomelo 2006 Sauvignon Blanc (California) $10. Way too much cat pee in the aroma of this wine. There's a big difference between gooseberries and that feline smell, and you don't have to be a chemist to discern it. 82 *—S.H. (9/1/2007)*

PONTIN DEL ROZA

Pontin del Roza 1999 Cabernet Sauvignon (Yakima Valley) $18. 87 *—P.G. (9/1/2002)*

Pontin del Roza 2000 Chenin Blanc (Yakima Valley) $7. 87 *—P.G. (9/1/2002)*

Pontin del Roza 2003 Pinot Grigio (Yakima Valley) $15. 88 *—P.G. (2/1/2006)*

Pontin del Roza 2000 Pinot Grigio (Yakima Valley) $12. 85 *—P.G. (9/1/2002)*

Pontin del Roza 2000 White Riesling (Yakima Valley) $8. 87 *—P.G. (9/1/2002)*

Pontin del Roza 2000 Sangiovese (Yakima Valley) $23. 84 *—P.G. (9/1/2002)*

PONZI

Ponzi 2004 Arneis (Willamette Valley) $20. 88 *—P.G. (11/15/2005)*

Ponzi 1998 Arneis (Willamette Valley) $18. 90 *—M.S. (4/1/2000)*

Ponzi 2005 Chardonnay (Willamette Valley) $20. A big wine, round and ripe with luscious flavors of peach, pineapple and citrus fruits, layered into plenty of toasty oak. It's smooth and seductive, and the finish, which tastes like a dessert of toasty hazelnuts and cream, is especially enticing. Just a bit of heat runs through it. 90 *—P.G. (11/15/2007)*

Ponzi 1997 Chardonnay (Willamette Valley) $18. 87 *—S.H. (12/31/1999)*

Ponzi 1997 Clonal Chardonnay (Willamette Valley) $22. 89 *—S.H. (12/31/1999)*

Ponzi 2004 Reserve Chardonnay (Willamette Valley) $30. Tawny gold in color, this wine's flavors can only be described as autumnal. It's a bit one dimensional – tart apple, tasting a bit like a hard cider, dusted with cinnamon and quite juicy. Definitely a wine for acid lovers, and a wine that will match up well to foods that need some acid to cut through. Despite 100% malolactic fermentation and extended lees contact, the acids reign supreme. 87 *—P.G. (2/1/2007)*

Ponzi 2003 Reserve Chardonnay (Willamette Valley) $30. 88 *—P.G. (5/1/2006)*

Ponzi 2002 Reserve Chardonnay (Willamette Valley) $30. 90 *—P.G. (8/1/2005)*

Ponzi 1999 Reserve Chardonnay (Willamette Valley) $25. 92 Editors' Choice *—P.G. (8/1/2002)*

Ponzi 1998 Reserve Chardonnay (Willamette Valley) $27. 87 *—P.G. (2/1/2002)*

Ponzi 2006 Pinot Blanc (Willamette Valley) $17. Ponzi's white wines go from strength to strength, an extremely luscious and fruit-driven lineup that is almost irresistible. Ripe pear flavors are lightly wrapped in clean citrus and green apple, with a bit more of the tart apple showing than in the heavier Pinot Gris. Elegant and yet full-flavored, this could become your go-to wine for almost any seafood. 88 *—P.G. (11/15/2007)*

Ponzi 2005 Pinot Blanc (Willamette Valley) $17. 88 *—P.G. (12/1/2006)*

Ponzi 2001 Pinot Blanc (Willamette Valley) $15. 89 Best Buy *—M.S. (12/31/2002)*

Ponzi 2006 Pinot Gris (Willamette Valley) $17. This has lovely complexity, suggesting everything from sweet honeysuckle to ripe fig to citrusy lime and of course the classic varietal pear fruit. It couldn't be any fresher, and beautifully balanced as well, with plenty of acid to clean the palate. A delicious wine made for near-term enjoyment. 88 *—P.G. (11/15/2007)*

Ponzi 2005 Pinot Gris (Willamette Valley) $17. 90 Editors' Choice *—P.G. (12/1/2006)*

Ponzi 2004 Pinot Gris (Willamette Valley) $17. 87 *—P.G. (11/15/2005)*

Ponzi 2001 Pinot Gris (Willamette Valley) $12. 86 Best Buy *—M.S. (12/31/2002)*

Ponzi 2004 Pinot Noir (Willamette Valley) $35. 89 *—P.G. (12/1/2006)*

Ponzi 2003 Pinot Noir (Willamette Valley) $30. 88 *—P.G. (11/15/2005)*

Ponzi 2002 Pinot Noir (Willamette Valley) $30. 85 *(11/1/2004)*

Ponzi 1998 Pinot Noir (Willamette Valley) $25. 92 *—M.S. (12/1/2000)*

Ponzi 2006 Pinot Noir Rosato Pinot Noir (Oregon) $17. The color is a pretty, pale coppery salmon, the nose laden with fresh strawberries. Persistent on the palate, the wine displays pleasing details of peach, red apple and grapefruit, good length and an extremely clean, fresh finish. **89** —*P.G. (7/1/2007)*

Ponzi 2004 Reserve Pinot Noir (Willamette Valley) $50. At the moment this newly released Pinot rests a bit uneasy; its fruit seems both overripe and underripe, and there is a bit of a hole in the middle palate. The flavors of green apple and rhubarb, combined with sharp acids, create a youthful wine which will certainly last a number of years. How it will develop is uncertain. For the moment, a few hours breathing time are in order. **87** —*P.G. (2/1/2007)*

Ponzi 2003 Reserve Pinot Noir (Willamette Valley) $50. 90 —*P.G. (5/1/2006)*

Ponzi 2002 Reserve Pinot Noir (Willamette Valley) $50. 88 —*P.G. (8/1/2005)*

Ponzi 2005 Tavola Pinot Noir (Willamette Valley) $23. A marvelous value, the Tavola brings bright raspberry fruit, spicy black tea and Dr. Pepper flavors to the fore. Details include streaks of licorice and baking chocolate; it's got great complexity for a wine in this price range, and steers clear of the vegetal/leafy stuff that plagues a lot of Oregon Pinot. This is complex and almost satiny as it swoops through the finish. **90** —*P.G. (4/1/2007)*

Ponzi 2003 Tavola Pinot Noir (Willamette Valley) $20. 88 —*P.G. (11/15/2005)*

Ponzi 2005 Riesling (Willamette Valley) $25. 92 —*P.G. (12/1/2006)*

Ponzi 2006 Rosato Rosé Blend (Willamette Valley) $17. Bright and colorful, somewhere between a salmon pink and a light copper, this fresh rosé tastes of strawberries and wild raspberries. The finish is lightly spicy and showing just a hint of milk chocolate. **86** —*P.G. (11/15/2007)*

POPE VALLEY WINERY

Pope Valley Winery 2003 Eakle Ranch Reserve Cabernet Sauvignon (Napa Valley) $24. More tannic than the usual Napa Cab, drier and earthier too, but it's nice to have something different. In fact, the balance and harmony are positively Bordeaux-esque. This is a Cabernet that won't swamp food and won't pall after two sips. **90** —*S.H. (2/1/2007)*

Pope Valley Winery 2001 Chenin Blanc (Napa Valley) $16. 88 —*J.M. (12/15/2003)*

Pope Valley Winery 2005 Old Vine Meyercamp Ranch Chenin Blanc (Napa Valley) $12. Not much going on in this dry, watery wine. It has weak citrus flavors. **81** —*S.H. (2/1/2007)*

Pope Valley Winery 2003 Old Vine Meyercamp Ranch Chenin Blanc (Napa Valley) $10. 86 Best Buy —*S.H. (6/1/2005)*

Pope Valley Winery 2004 Eakle Ranch Merlot (Napa Valley) $20. Dry and tart in acids, with herb, blackberry and bitter dark chocolate flavors that finish with a tannic scour. More Bordeaux-like than Californian in the earthiness, but it's a polished wine. Decanting and food will soften and sweeten it. **86** —*S.H. (2/1/2007)*

Pope Valley Winery 2005 Bella Rosa Sangiovese (Napa Valley) $10. This is dark in color for a blush, almost a red wine, but it's better treated as a rose and chilled. It shows a vibrant freshness and Sangiovese's cherry flavors that are set off by crisp acids and a fruity, dry finish. **85 Best Buy** —*S.H. (2/1/2007)*

Pope Valley Winery 2003 Reserve Syrah (Napa Valley) $20. A little sweet and overly-extracted for balance, this Syrah has cola, stewed blackberry and persimmon flavors. It's okay, in a rustic way. Drink now. **83** —*S.H. (3/1/2007)*

Pope Valley Winery 2001 Zinfandel Port Zinfandel (Napa Valley) $35. 84 —*S.H. (6/1/2005)*

Pope Valley Winery 2004 Eakle Ranch Zinfandel (Napa Valley) $18. Dry and country-style, with a jagged mouthfeel that lets the tannins star, this Zin has modest berry flavors and a cooked, stewed quality. **82** —*S.H. (2/1/2007)*

PORTER CREEK

Porter Creek 2002 Timbervine Ranch Syrah (Russian River Valley) $36. 87 *(9/1/2005)*

POWERS

Powers 2001 Bordeaux Blend (Columbia Valley (WA)) $30. 88 —*P.G. (4/1/2006)*

Powers 2004 Cabernet Sauvignon (Columbia Valley (WA)) $15. Some interesting tobacco scents open up the nose. In the mouth the wine is very tart, showing cool-climate flavors of plum, cassis and berry. There is a hint of leather but not enough to dampen the fruit. This is varietal and solid in a basic, blocky style. **85** —*P.G. (12/31/2007)*

Powers 2004 Chardonnay (Columbia Valley (WA)) $10. 82 —*P.G. (4/1/2006)*

Powers 1999 Chardonnay (Columbia Valley (WA)) $10. 85 —*P.G. (2/1/2002)*

Powers 2004 Merlot (Columbia Valley (WA)) $15. Strongly herbal, this leathery wine occasionally hints at black cherry fruit, but it's pretty well buried under flavors and aromas that often accompany spoilage yeast. Tannic and hard through the finish. **81** —*P.G. (12/31/2007)*

Powers 2004 Pinot Grigio (Columbia Valley (WA)) $12. 82 —*P.G. (2/1/2006)*

Powers 1999 Pinot Noir (Columbia Valley (WA)) $10. 83 —*P.G. (12/31/2001)*

Powers 1998 Parallel 46 Red Blend (Columbia Valley (WA)) $30. 88 —*P.G. (12/31/2001)*

Powers 2004 Riesling (Columbia Valley (WA)) $10. 86 —*P.G. (4/1/2006)*

Powers 2004 Syrah (Columbia Valley (WA)) $15. Slightly stewed fruit scents suggest cooked prunes, and lead into a pretty hard, tannic red wine. It has leafy, somewhat underripe flavors, lots of tannin and a generic red wine flavor; it could be almost anything. **82** —*P.G. (12/31/2007)*

Powers 1999 Syrah (Columbia Valley (WA)) $16. 86 *(10/1/2001)*

PRAGER

Prager NV Noble Companion Tawny Port Cabernet Sauvignon (Napa Valley) $45. 93 —*S.H. (12/1/2003)*

Prager 1999 Aria White Port Chardonnay (Napa Valley) $45. 89 —*S.H. (12/1/2003)*

Prager 2003 Petite Sirah (Napa Valley) $38. Pretty pricey for a Petite Sirah, but this is actually one of the more interesting ones out there. It's very dry, and shows the balance you expect from a Napa red. There's an earthy, cappuccino edge to the blackberry, cherry and cola flavors, and the wine has the variety's rich, mouth-coating tannins. Drink now through 2020. **87** —*S.H. (4/1/2007)*

Prager 1999 Port Petite Sirah (California) $32. 93 Editors' Choice —*S.H. (12/1/2003)*

Prager 2001 Royal Escort Paladini Vineyard LBV Port Petite Sirah (Napa Valley) $65. 93 —*S.H. (12/15/2004)*

Prager 2001 Aria White Port (Napa Valley) $48. 87 —*S.H. (3/1/2006)*

Prager 2000 Aria White Port (Napa Valley) $48. 83 —*S.H. (12/15/2004)*

Prager NV Noble Companion Tawny Port (Napa Valley) $50. Made from 100% Cabernet Sauvignon grapes, this Port-style wine has very sweet flavors of blackberry jam, creme de cassis, tangerine zest and vanilla wafer candy. Bright, citrusy acidity provides needed balance. This is tawny Port, California-style, and a very nice, satisfying after-dinner sipper. **89** —*S.H. (11/1/2007)*

Prager NV Noble Companion Tawny Port (Napa Valley) $45. 92 —*S.H. (12/15/2004)*

Prager 2004 Royal Escort Paladini Vineyard Port (Napa Valley) $65. Made from Petite Sirah, with residual sugar of 8.5%, this wine's sweetness is pleasing, expressed through cassis, chocolate and raspberry fruit flavors. It's a simple wine, though, whose sugar hides some faults, mainly a lack of depth. **85** —*S.H. (12/15/2007)*

Prager 2003 Royal Escort Paladini Vineyard Vintage Port (Napa Valley) $80. This is the first Port in six years that Prager declared a vintage, so you know they think highly of it. It's pretty good, not great, but nicely sweet in blackberry and chocolate fudge flavors, with a good edge of acidity. **86** —*S.H. (2/1/2007)*

Prager 2004 Tomás Port (Napa Valley) $48. Made from native Port varieties, this dessert wine is sweet and simple, with pleasant chocolate fudge, cassis and licorice-spice flavors. **84** —*S.H. (11/1/2007)*

Prager 2003 White Port (Napa Valley) $48. Not too many Port-style wines are made from Chardonnay, as this one is. The residual sugar is 6%, but it's not a very good wine. Tastes cooked or stewed in pineapple, and the high alcohol makes for a burnt feeling. **83** —*S.H. (12/15/2007)*

Prager 2001 Sweet Clair Late Harvest Riesling (Napa Valley) $27. 85 —*S.H. (12/1/2003)*

Prager 2002 Sweet Claire Riesling (Central Coast) $38. 90 —*S.H. (12/15/2004)*

PRAXIS

Praxis 2005 Merlot (Alexander Valley) $15. From warm Alexander Valley comes this superripe young Merlot. It's fresh and vibrant in jammy cherry, blackberry and wintergeen flavors, with a keen sharpness of acidity. **84** —*S.H. (11/15/2007)*

Praxis 2004 Merlot (Alexander Valley) $15. 87 —*S.H. (12/15/2006)*

Praxis 2006 Pinot Noir (Monterey County) $18. Soft and one-dimensional, with a silky texture and modest flavors of cherries, cola, sassafras and spices. **83** —*S.H. (12/31/2007)*

Praxis 2003 Pinot Noir (Monterey) $15. 84 —*S.H. (12/15/2004)*

Praxis 2005 Sauvignon Blanc (Sonoma County) $15. 85 —*S.H.*

(12/15/2006)

Praxis 2003 Syrah (Dry Creek Valley) $14. 85 *(9/1/2005)*

Praxis 2006 Viognier (Lodi) $15. This unoaked Viognier is crisp and balanced, with flashy tropical fruit, wildflower and spice flavors. It's a pleasant sipper, with some exotic complexity. 84 *—S.H. (11/15/2007)*

Praxis 2002 Viognier (Lodi) $15. 86 *—J.M. (4/1/2004)*

PREJEAN

Prejean 2001 Dry Riesling (Finger Lakes) $9. 83 *—J.C. (8/1/2003)*

Prejean 2001 Semi-Dry Riesling (Finger Lakes) $9. 84 *—J.C. (8/1/2003)*

PRESIDIO

Presidio 1997 Chardonnay (Santa Barbara County) $12. 86 *—S.H. (7/1/1999)*

Presidio 1999 Merlot (Santa Barbara County) $18. 87 *—S.H. (3/1/2004)*

PRESTON

Preston 1995 Platinum Red Bordeaux Blend (Columbia Valley (WA)) $17. 81 *—S.H. (9/1/2000)*

Preston 1998 Cabernet Sauvignon (Columbia Valley (WA)) $12. 83 *—P.G. (6/1/2002)*

Preston 1997 Cabernet Sauvignon (Columbia Valley (WA)) $12. 85 *—P.G. (6/1/2001)*

Preston 1998 Chardonnay (Columbia Valley (WA)) $10. 81 *—P.G. (6/1/2000)*

Preston 1998 Reserve Chardonnay (Columbia Valley (WA)) $16. 82 *—P.G. (6/1/2000)*

Preston 1998 Beaujolais Rose Gamay (Columbia Valley (WA)) $10. 82 *—P.G. (6/1/2000)*

Preston 1998 Merlot (Columbia Valley (WA)) $12. 82 *—P.G. (6/1/2002)*

Preston 1997 Merlot (Columbia Valley (WA)) $12. 86 *—P.G. (6/1/2001)*

Preston 1999 Reserve Merlot (Columbia Valley (WA)) $22. 89 *—C.S. (12/31/2002)*

Preston 1998 Sauvignon Blanc (Columbia Valley (WA)) $8. 80 *—P.G. (6/1/2000)*

Preston 2002 Preston Vineyard Syrah (Columbia Valley (WA)) $23. 84 *(9/1/2005)*

PRESTON OF DRY CREEK

Preston 2003 Cavallo Barbera (Dry Creek Valley) $25. 89 *—S.H. (11/1/2005)*

Preston 1999 Carignane (Dry Creek Valley) $20. 86 *—S.H. (9/1/2002)*

Preston 1998 Marsanne (Dry Creek Valley) $13. 92 Best Buy *—L.W. (5/1/2000)*

Preston 1999 Mourvèdre (Dry Creek Valley) $22. 87 *—S.H. (9/1/2002)*

Preston 1997 Mourvèdre (Dry Creek Valley) $16. 90 *—S.H. (2/1/2000)*

Preston 1997 Mas Viejo Mourvèdre (Dry Creek Valley) $16. 85 *—S.H. (10/1/1999)*

Preston 1996 Vineyard Select Mourvèdre (Dry Creek Valley) $20. 86 *—S.H. (6/1/1999)*

Preston 1997 Faux Red Red Blend (Dry Creek Valley) $11. 86 *—S.H. (6/1/1999)*

Preston 2002 L. Preston Red Blend (Dry Creek Valley) $25. 88 *—S.H. (11/1/2005)*

Preston 1997 Cuvée de Fumé Sauvignon Blanc (Dry Creek Valley) $12. 89 Best Buy *—S.H. (9/1/1999)*

Preston 2001 Hartsock Sauvignon Blanc (Dry Creek Valley) $18. 86 *—S.H. (9/1/2003)*

Preston 1998 Syrah (Dry Creek Valley) $18. 90 *—S.H. (2/1/2000)*

Preston 1997 Syrah (Dry Creek Valley) $18. 87 *—J.C. (11/1/1999)*

Preston 1997 Estate Grown Syrah (Dry Creek Valley) $18. 86 *(6/1/1999)*

Preston 1997 Estate Reserve Vogensen Bench Syrah (Dry Creek Valley) $28. 89 *(11/1/2001)*

Preston 1998 Viognier (Dry Creek Valley) $20. 89 *—J.C. (10/1/1999)*

Preston 2000 Old Vine / Old Clone Zinfandel (Dry Creek Valley) $20. 93 *—S.H. (12/1/2002)*

Preston 2003 Old Vines Old Clones Zinfandel (Dry Creek Valley) $25. 85 *—S.H. (11/1/2005)*

Preston 1997 Old Vines/Old Clones Zinfandel (Dry Creek Valley) $15. 89 *—P.G. (11/15/1999)*

Preston of Dry Creek 2001 Cavallo Block Barbera (Dry Creek Valley) $25. 86 *—S.H. (5/1/2003)*

Preston of Dry Creek 2002 Cinsault (Dry Creek Valley) $20. 83 *—S.H. (10/1/2004)*

Preston of Dry Creek 1999 Petite Sirah (Dry Creek Valley) $36. 87 *—S.H. (9/1/2003)*

Preston of Dry Creek 2002 Vogensen Bench Syrah-Sirah Red Blend (Dry Creek Valley) $20. 86 *(9/1/2005)*

Preston of Dry Creek 2003 Vin Gris Rosé Blend (Dry Creek Valley) $15. 85 *—S.H. (10/1/2004)*

Preston of Dry Creek 2000 Vin Gris Rosé Blend (Dry Creek Valley) $11. 87 Best Buy *—S.H. (11/15/2001)*

Preston of Dry Creek 2003 Hartsock Sauvignon Blanc (Dry Creek Valley) $16. 85 *—S.H. (10/1/2004)*

Preston of Dry Creek 2000 Hartsock Estate Reserve Sauvignon Blanc (Dry Creek Valley) $16. 87 *—S.H. (11/15/2001)*

Preston of Dry Creek 2000 Late Harvest Sémillon (Dry Creek Valley) $28. 89 *—S.H. (12/15/2003)*

Preston of Dry Creek 1999 Estate Syrah (Dry Creek Valley) $20. 89 *(10/1/2001)*

Preston of Dry Creek 2001 Vogensen Bench Syrah (Dry Creek Valley) $18. 86 *—S.H. (10/1/2004)*

Preston of Dry Creek 2000 Vogensen Bench Syrah (Dry Creek Valley) $22. 87 *—S.H. (12/15/2003)*

Preston of Dry Creek 2003 Viognier (Dry Creek Valley) $25. 86 *—S.H. (10/1/2004)*

Preston of Dry Creek 2002 Viognier (Dry Creek Valley) $25. 87 *—S.H. (6/1/2003)*

Preston of Dry Creek 2000 Viognier (Dry Creek Valley) $18. 87 *—S.H. (11/15/2001)*

Preston of Dry Creek 2002 Old Vines/ Old Clones Zinfandel (Dry Creek Valley) $24. 85 *—J.M. (10/1/2004)*

Preston of Dry Creek 2001 Old Vines/Old Clones Zinfandel (Dry Creek Valley) $20. 85 *(11/1/2003)*

PRETTY-SMITH

Pretty-Smith 2000 Palette de Rouge Red Wine Bordeaux Blend (Paso Robles) $26. This has got to be the last 2000 wine to be released. It's pretty good, a dry, soft Bordeaux blend based on Cab Franc. Shows cherry and oak flavors, in a light- to medium-bodied texture, and is just beginning to develop the character of an aged Bordeaux. 86 *—S.H. (4/1/2007)*

Pretty-Smith 2000 Cabernet Franc (Paso Robles) $22. The cherry fruit is becoming desiccated, like the dried cherries you buy in health food stores, but it still feels fresh and lively. Acids and tannins are fine, and the wine has delicacy and complexity. But drink soon. 86 *—S.H. (4/1/2007)*

Pretty-Smith 1999 Cabernet Franc (Paso Robles) $18. 85 *—S.H. (9/1/2002)*

Pretty-Smith 2000 Cabernet Sauvignon (Paso Robles) $22. Nice and easy Cab, soft and pleasantly fruity, and you'd never guess its age because it tastes so fresh. Blackberries, cherries, chocolate and licorice, in a smooth, velvety texture. 87 *—S.H. (4/1/2007)*

Pretty-Smith 1999 Cabernet Sauvignon (Paso Robles) $18. 90 *—S.H. (9/12/2002)*

Pretty-Smith 1999 Chardonnay (Paso Robles) $16. 81 *—S.H. (9/12/2002)*

Pretty-Smith 1999 Fumé Blanc (Paso Robles) $13. 85 *—S.H. (9/12/2002)*

Pretty-Smith 1999 Merlot (California) $18. 87 *—S.H. (9/12/2002)*

Pretty-Smith 2005 Sauvignon Blanc (Central Coast) $16. Shows lots of class with crunchy, citrusy acidity brightening and cleansing the upfront fruit. The flavors are of lemons and limes, figs and green melons, drizzled with a splash of wild honey. 85 *—S.H. (4/1/2007)*

Pretty-Smith 2001 Late Harvest Zinfandel (Paso Robles) $16. Plenty of sugar in this sweet wine, but it takes more than sweetness to make a great dessert red wine. There are blackberry, chocolate and coffee flavors, but the wine is sharp, and lacks the smooth, velvety mouthfeel that you want. 83 *—S.H. (4/1/2007)*

Pretty-Smith 1999 Zinfandel Port Zinfandel (Paso Robles) $28. 84 *—S.H. (4/1/2007)*

PREVAIL

PreVail 2003 Back Forty Red Blend (Alexander Valley) $80. 92 *—S.H. (12/31/2006)*

PreVail 2003 West Face Red Blend (Alexander Valley) $50. 92 *—S.H. (12/31/2006)*

PRIDE MOUNTAIN

Pride Mountain 2003 Reserve Claret Bordeaux Blend (Napa-Sonoma) $120. If you're lucky enough to try this with Pride's reserve Cab, which is 100% varietal, you'll find this one fleshier and meatier. Based on Merlot, it shows a voluptuous fatness, a chocolate-covered cherry candy immediacy, that makes it drinkable now. At the same time, it has big, dusty, mouth-coating tannins. Drink now, with decanting, or cellar for 10 years. **95 Editors' Choice** *—S.H. (3/1/2007)*

Pride Mountain 2004 Cabernet Franc (Sonoma County) $60. This is a fun wine, easy to like. It's also a serious wine. That's a hard juggling act, but Pride pulls it off so well. Shows the lighter side of the Cabernet family, with a silky, almost delicate body framing cherry and oak flavors. Yet there's tremendous depth, and the exquisite tension between fruit, acidity, tannins and wood is as intricate as a Cirque du Soleil trapeze act. **93** *—S.H. (3/1/2007)*

Pride Mountain 2002 Cabernet Franc (Sonoma County) $56. 86 *—S.H. (6/1/2005)*

Pride Mountain 2000 Cabernet Franc (Sonoma County) $52. 95 Cellar Selection *—S.H. (12/1/2002)*

Pride Mountain 1999 Cabernet Franc (Sonoma County) $52. 89 *—S.H. (9/1/2002)*

Pride Mountain 2004 Cabernet Sauvignon (Napa-Sonoma) $66. Soft, rich and ripe, this is one of those Cabernets that feels dramatic in the mouth. Partly it's the fruit; complex in cherries, blackberries, mocha and rum and cola. Partly it's the oak and partly it's the fabulous balance of rich, sweet tannins and acidity. Put it all together, and it's irresistible. Best now–2010. **92** *—S.H. (4/1/2007)*

Pride Mountain 2002 Cabernet Sauvignon (Napa Valley) $62. 86 *—S.H. (6/1/2005)*

Pride Mountain 2000 Cabernet Sauvignon (Napa Valley) $56. 93 Editors' Choice *—S.H. (2/1/2003)*

Pride Mountain 1999 Cabernet Sauvignon (Napa Valley) $56. 90 *—S.H. (6/1/2002)*

Pride Mountain 1997 Cabernet Sauvignon (Napa Valley) $36. 92 *(11/1/2000)*

Pride Mountain 1996 Napa Valley Cabernet Sauvignon (Napa Valley) $30. 91 Cellar Selection *—L.W. (7/1/1999)*

Pride Mountain 2003 Reserve Cabernet Sauvignon (Napa-Sonoma) $120. What a wine. Take one of those hugely gooey, famous winemaker Napa Cabs, the kind that melt on your palate like butter on toast or chocolate in a microwave, and add fierce mountain tannins, and this is what you get. A humungous, dry, important Cab, one that desperately needs cellaring. Ten years should do it; 20 might be better. The spicy blackberry and cherry fruit isn't going anywhere. **94 Cellar Selection** *—S.H. (3/1/2007)*

Pride Mountain 2005 Chardonnay (Napa Valley) $37. Rich, ripe and oaky, maybe too oaky, with a mèlange of tropical fruit, peach and pear flavors that are well ripened and a little soft in acidity. The oak takes over in the form of sweet woodsap and vanilla char, through the spicy, oaky finish. **87** *—S.H. (3/1/2007)*

Pride Mountain 2001 Chardonnay (Napa Valley) $35. 92 *—S.H. (2/1/2003)*

Pride Mountain 2000 Chardonnay (Napa Valley) $35. 90 *—S.H. (5/1/2002)*

Pride Mountain 2005 Mountain Top Vineyard Vintner Select Chardonnay (Sonoma County) $47. Big, big, big. Make that huge, huge, huge. This Chard rocks. It's done up in the grand Burgundian way, but all the bells and whistles can't put a dent in the fruit, which is just, well, big and huge. Mangoes, papayas, pineapple custard, peach pie, macaroon, gingersnap cookie, vanilla fudge, buttered toast, all brightened with coastal acidity. Chardonnay just doesn't get any richer than this. **95 Editors' Choice** *—S.H. (3/1/2007)*

Pride Mountain 2001 Vintner's Select Mountain Top Vineyard Chardonnay (Sonoma County) $45. 89 *—S.H. (6/1/2003)*

Pride Mountain 2004 Merlot (Napa-Sonoma) $56. You'll find tannins aplenty in this tightly wound mountain Merlot. That gives it a shut-down, dry astringency. Aging is the obvious solution, and such is the balance, the harmony that 5-10 years should soften and sweeten, letting the blackberry and cherry fruit emerge. **90 Cellar Selection** *—S.H. (3/1/2007)*

Pride Mountain 2002 Merlot (Napa-Sonoma) $52. 93 Editors' Choice *—S.H. (6/1/2005)*

Pride Mountain 2000 Merlot (Napa-Sonoma) $48. 92 *—S.H. (11/15/2002)*

Pride Mountain 1999 Merlot (Napa-Sonoma) $48. 94 Editors' Choice *—S.H. (6/1/2002)*

Pride Mountain 1998 Merlot (Napa-Sonoma) $38. 93 *—J.M. (12/1/2001)*

Pride Mountain 2004 Mountain Top Vineyard Vintner Select Merlot (Sonoma County) $75. Pride's regular '04 Merlot was very good. This one's better. Intensely rich and concentrated in the way of mountain wines, it shows huge, ripe cherry marmalade, black raspberry pie filling, rum and cola, mocha-choca and Asian spice flavors, enriched by smoky oak. Any really ripe wine can do that, but only one from great coastal vineyards can achieve this balance of acids and tannins. Should develop over the next 10 years. **92** *—S.H. (3/1/2007)*

Pride Mountain 2000 Vintner's Select Wind Whistle Vineyard Merlot (Napa County) $65. 91 Cellar Selection *—S.H. (8/1/2003)*

Pride Mountain 2000 Petite Sirah (Napa Valley) $40. 90 *(4/1/2003)*

Pride Mountain 2004 Sangiovese (Sonoma County) $55. Unsuccessful at any price, especially this one. This is a disagreeable wine, acidic and harshly tannic, offering no pleasure and not going anywhere. **81** *—S.H. (3/1/2007)*

Pride Mountain 2004 Syrah (Sonoma County) $57. Tannins play the lead role here, dry, dusty, lockdown. There's plenty of blackberry and spicy plum fruit, but it's buried. What's a consumer to do? Aging is a gamble. How many California Syrahs survive the years? Yet that's your only option, unless you enjoy that astringent, tongue-numbing feeling. **86** *—S.H. (3/1/2007)*

Pride Mountain 2003 Syrah (Sonoma County) $55. 91 Cellar Selection *(9/1/2005)*

Pride Mountain 2005 Viognier (Sonoma County) $42. Shows the exotic side of Viognier, with a cannonade of tropical fruit, exotic spice and wildflower flavors, and is nicely dry. But unusual for Viognier is a tight, minerally intensity, due partly to acids, like putting your tongue on a cold piece of steel. That makes for elegance. One of the more complex Viogniers out there. **92** *—S.H. (3/1/2007)*

Pride Mountain 2003 Viognier (Sonoma County) $40. 92 *—S.H. (6/1/2005)*

Pride Mountain 2001 Viognier (Sonoma County) $40. 90 *—S.H. (6/1/2003)*

Pride Mountain 2000 Viognier (Sonoma County) $40. 93 Editors' Choice *—S.H. (9/1/2002)*

PRIMOS

Primos 2003 Sangiovese (Redwood Valley) $25. 82 *—S.H. (11/1/2005)*

PRINCE MICHEL DE VIRGINIA

Prince Michel de Virginia 1997 Chardonnay (Virginia) $13. 83 *—J.C. (8/1/1999)*

Prince Michel de Virginia 1997 Barrel Select Chardonnay (Virginia) $19. 84 *—J.C. (8/1/1999)*

PRODIGAL

Prodigal 2005 Pinot Noir (Santa Rita Hills) $45. Made in a classic SRH style, a vibrantly fruity, silky young Pinot, front-loaded for early drinking. Shows clean, brightly intense cherry, raspberry, rosehip tea, cola and Asian spicebox flavors, with a long, dry finish. **90** *—S.H. (4/1/2007)*

PROSPERO

Prospero 2002 Cabernet Sauvignon (Sonoma County) $16. Unusual for an inexpensive Cab of this age to hit the market, and it's a pretty good buy. Nothing complicated, but it's soft and smooth, and beginning to show that magical transformation when primary fruit develops bouquet and a dried fruit character. **86** *—S.H. (9/1/2007)*

Prospero 2000 Cabernet Sauvignon (Sonoma County) $15. 82 *—S.H. (12/31/2003)*

Prospero 2001 Chardonnay (Russian River Valley) $18. 83 *—S.H. (4/1/2004)*

Prospero 2002 Merlot (Sonoma County) $16. Tastes flat and simple, with fruit disappearing, although there's a ghost of blackberries that turns a little more intense on the finish. Consume now. **83** *—S.H. (9/1/2007)*

Prospero 2000 Merlot (Sonoma County) $14. 84 *—S.H. (12/31/2003)*

Prospero 1997 Reserve Merlot (Mendocino) $14. 83 *—S.H. (2/1/2004)*

Prospero 2002 Syrah (California) $12. 82 *(9/1/2005)*

PROVENANCE VINEYARDS

Provenance Vineyards 2004 Cabernet Sauvignon (Rutherford) $40. Nice and smooth, this Cab hits the palate with a plush tannic structure and oak-infused cassis and red cherry flavors. It's dry and elegant right now, but not an ager, because it's a bit thin and short in the finish. **87** *—S.H. (8/1/2007)*

Provenance Vineyards 2002 Cabernet Sauvignon (Oakville) $40. 89 *—S.H. (6/1/2005)*

Provenance Vineyards 2002 Cabernet Sauvignon (Rutherford) $35. 88 *—S.H. (6/1/2005)*

Provenance Vineyards 2001 Cabernet Sauvignon (Rutherford) $35. 91 Editors' Choice *—S.H. (10/1/2004)*

Provenance Vineyards 2001 Cabernet Sauvignon (Oakville) $35. 92 *—S.H. (8/1/2004)*

Provenance Vineyards 2000 Cabernet Sauvignon (Rutherford) $35. 87 *—J.M. (6/1/2003)*

Provenance Vineyards 2003 Beckstoffer To Kalon Vineyard Cabernet Sauvignon (Oakville) $50. Provenance has carved out a niche as the affordable upscale Napa wine, and although prices on the Oakville are creeping up, it's still a relative bargain. The wine has that ultra-fancy mouthfeel, as soft as velvet, packed with complex Cabernet fruit and finished with lots of toasty new oak. Too soft for aging, it's beautiful now. **90** *—S.H. (2/1/2007)*

Provenance Vineyards 2001 Beckstoffer Tokalon Vineyard Cabernet Sauvignon (Napa Valley) $NA. 92 *—S.H. (6/1/2005)*

Provenance Vineyards 2004 Merlot (Napa Valley) $35. A little too ripe and raisiny, but not a bad Merlot, with a plush, velvety texture. There's good plum, black currant and smoky oak flavor, and the wine is dry and balanced. Drink now. **86** *—S.H. (8/1/2007)*

Provenance Vineyards 2003 Merlot (Napa Valley) $35. 87 *—S.H. (7/1/2006)*

Provenance Vineyards 2002 Merlot (Carneros) $27. 88 *—S.H. (6/1/2005)*

Provenance Vineyards 2001 Merlot (Carneros) $27. 88 *—S.H. (8/1/2004)*

Provenance Vineyards 2000 Merlot (Carneros) $28. 92 *—J.M. (8/1/2003)*

Provenance Vineyards 2004 Beckstoffer Las Amigas Vineyard Merlot (Carneros) $60. On the plus side is terrifically ripe fruit, a blast of cherries, raspberries and cola, accented by flashy oak. On the minus is a syrupy, sweet-and-sour finish. **84** *—S.H. (11/1/2007)*

Provenance Vineyards 2002 Las Amigas Vineyard Merlot (Carneros) $40. 86 *—S.H. (2/1/2006)*

Provenance Vineyards 2004 Paras Vineyard Merlot (Mount Veeder) $60. Provenance released their regular '04 Merlot a few months ago, and this is a riper, more expensive wine, but it can't quite overcome a certain rusticity. It's a little sweet and cherry cough medicine-like, with sticky tannins. **85** *—S.H. (11/1/2007)*

Provenance Vineyards 2002 Paras Vineyard Merlot (Mount Veeder) $40. 88 *—S.H. (6/1/2005)*

Provenance Vineyards 2005 Sauvignon Blanc (Rutherford) $19. 86 *—S.H. (12/15/2006)*

Provenance Vineyards 2004 Sauvignon Blanc (Napa Valley) $19. 84 *—S.H. (2/1/2006)*

Provenance Vineyards 2003 Sauvignon Blanc (Rutherford) $19. 88 *—S.H. (12/1/2004)*

PROVISOR

Provisor 2004 Syrah (Dry Creek Valley) $31. Loved the '02, didn't care for the '03, but the '04 is a welcome return to form for the softly lush texture and voluptuous fruit. It's so ripe and luscious in cherry marmalade, crème de cassis, melted chocolate truffle and licorice flavors. Serve it with something simple but classy, like a fine grilled steak. **90** *—S.H. (4/1/2007)*

Provisor 2003 Syrah (Dry Creek Valley) $30. 84 *(9/1/2005)*

Provisor 2002 Syrah (Dry Creek Valley) $30. 90 *—S.H. (3/1/2005)*

PUCCIONI

Puccioni 2004 Old Vine Zinfandel (Dry Creek Valley) $28. 90 *—S.H. (12/31/2006)*

Puccioni 2003 Old Vine Zinfandel (Dry Creek Valley) $28. 86 *—S.H. (6/1/2006)*

Q

Q 2002 Syrah (Sonoma County) $16. 86 *(9/1/2005)*

QUADY

Quady 2001 Elysium Black Muscat (California) $10. 89 *—S.H. (11/15/2003)*

Quady 1998 Electra Orange Muscat (California) $NA. 87 *(12/31/1999)*

Quady 1998 Essencia Orange Muscat (California) $18. 81 *—J.C. (12/31/1999)*

QUAIL CREEK

Quail Creek 1999 Cabernet Sauvignon (California) $10. 87 **Best Buy** *—S.H. (8/1/2001)*

Quail Creek 1998 Cabernet Sauvignon (California) $10. 84 *—S.H. (5/1/2001)*

Quail Creek 1999 Chardonnay (California) $10. 84 *—S.H. (5/1/2001)*

Quail Creek 1999 Merlot (California) $10. 85 **Best Buy** *—S.H. (5/1/2001)*

QUAIL RIDGE

Quail Ridge 2001 Cabernet Sauvignon (Napa Valley) $16. 83 *—S.H. (11/1/2005)*

Quail Ridge 1999 Reserve Cabernet Sauvignon (Napa Valley) $50. 91 *—D.T. (6/1/2002)*

Quail Ridge 1997 Volker Eisele Vineyard Reserve Cabernet Sauvignon (Napa Valley) $45. 92 *—S.H. (8/1/2001)*

Quail Ridge 2003 Chardonnay (Napa Valley) $12. 86 *—S.H. (8/1/2005)*

Quail Ridge 2000 Reserve Chardonnay (Mendocino) $24. 86 *—S.H. (10/1/2003)*

Quail Ridge 2002 Merlot (Napa Valley) $14. 85 *—S.H. (11/1/2005)*

Quail Ridge 1998 Volker Eisele Vineyard Merlot (Napa Valley) $40. 91 **Cellar Selection** *—S.H. (8/1/2001)*

Quail Ridge 2000 Sauvignon Blanc (Napa Valley) $14. 85 *(9/1/2003)*

Quail Ridge 1997 Reserve Barrel-Fermented Sauvignon Blanc (Rutherford) $15. 85 *—M.M. (3/1/2000)*

Quail Ridge 1999 Zinfandel (Napa Valley) $23. 80 *—D.T. (3/1/2002)*

QUATRO

Quatro 1997 Cabernet Sauvignon (Sonoma County) $16. 86 *—S.H. (2/1/2000)*

Quatro 2002 Cabernet Sauvignon (Alexander Valley) $15. 85 *—S.H. (11/15/2004)*

Quatro 1997 Merlot (Sonoma County) $16. 84 *(3/1/1999)*

QUEEN OF HEARTS

Queen of Hearts 2002 Cabernet Sauvignon (Santa Barbara County) $12. 82 *—S.H. (9/1/2006)*

Queen of Hearts 2005 Chardonnay (Santa Barbara County) $10. The underlying wine shows real Santa Barbara Chard character of crispness and ripe, juicy fruit, with flavors of pineapples and peaches. But a huge, major flaw is excessive oakiness. All that caramel and butterscotch throws this otherwise likeable wine out of balance. **82** *—S.H. (10/1/2007)*

Queen of Hearts 2004 Chardonnay (Santa Barbara County) $10. 85 **Best Buy** *—S.H. (12/1/2006)*

Queen of Hearts 2004 Merlot (Santa Barbara County) $12. Decent everyday Merlot. Although you can criticize the thinness of fruit, it's got a nice, smooth texture, and is very dry. Shows just enough cherry and mocha fruit to be properly varietal. **84** *—S.H. (10/1/2007)*

Queen of Hearts 2003 Merlot (Santa Barbara County) $12. 84 *—S.H. (12/1/2006)*

Queen of Hearts 2005 Pinot Noir (Santa Barbara County) $12. Smells and tastes raw, weirdly combining green, minty flavors with slightly sweet medicinal ones of cherry cough drops. **81** *—S.H. (10/1/2007)*

Queen of Hearts 2005 Sauvignon Blanc (Santa Barbara County) $10. Thin and sweet, a rustic wine with the flavors of canned pineapples, peaches and apricots. Crisp, balancing acidity helps. **83** *—S.H. (10/1/2007)*

Queen of Hearts 2004 Sauvignon Blanc (Santa Barbara County) $10. 84 *—S.H. (12/1/2006)*

QUILCEDA CREEK

Quilceda Creek 2003 Cabernet Sauvignon (Washington) $95. 97 **Cellar Selection** *—P.G. (10/1/2006)*

Quilceda Creek 2002 Cabernet Sauvignon (Washington) $80. 97 **Cellar Selection** *—P.G. (12/15/2005)*

Quilceda Creek 2001 Cabernet Sauvignon (Washington) $80. 95 **Cellar Selection** *—P.G. (9/1/2004)*

Quilceda Creek 1999 Cabernet Sauvignon (Washington) $60. 93 **Editors' Choice** *—P.G. (6/1/2002)*

Quilceda Creek 1998 Cabernet Sauvignon (Washington) $60. 95 **Editors' Choice** *—P.G. (6/1/2002)*

Quilceda Creek 2003 Merlot (Washington) $65. 95 *—P.G. (11/15/2006)*

Quilceda Creek 2002 Merlot (Washington) $65. 94 **Editors' Choice** *—P.G. (12/15/2005)*

Quilceda Creek 1999 Merlot (Washington) $60. 94 *—P.G. (6/1/2002)*

Quilceda Creek 1998 Merlot (Washington) $60. 92 *—P.G. (6/1/2002)*

Quilceda Creek 2002 Red Blend (Columbia Valley (WA)) $35. 93 *—P.G. (12/15/2005)*

Quilceda Creek 1998 Red Blend (Washington) $40. 89 *—P.G. (6/1/2002)*

Quilceda Creek 2003 Red Red Blend (Columbia Valley (WA)) $35. 93 *—P.G. (10/1/2006)*

Quilceda Creek 2001 Red Wine Red Blend (Columbia Valley (WA)) $35. 92 Editors' Choice —*P.G. (9/1/2004)*

QUILICI

Quilici 2004 Sangiovese (California) $12. 84 —*S.H. (12/31/2006)*

QUINTA DA SONORA

Quinta da Sonora 2000 Verdelho (California) $12.87 —*S.H. (11/15/2001)*

QUINTANA

Quintana 2000 Cabernet Sauvignon (North Coast) $18. 87 —*S.H. (4/1/2003)*

Quintana 1999 Cabernet Sauvignon (North Coast) $18. 88 —*S.H. (9/12/2002)*

QUINTESSA

Quintessa 2004 Bordeaux Blend (Rutherford) $125. A dramatic young wine, fleshy and dazzling now for its lush fruit and oak, although the tannins have a crunchy hardness. But that merely ensures ageability. It's beautiful the way the acid-tannin structure plays against the cherry, cassis and olive fruit, creating an architectural tension. If you open this wine now, decant for a few hours. Otherwise, it should hold for 6–8 years, and develop further bottle complexity afterward. **95** —*S.H. (12/15/2007)*

Quintessa 2002 Bordeaux Blend (Rutherford) $120. 94 Cellar Selection —*S.H. (12/15/2005)*

Quintessa 1999 Bordeaux Blend (Rutherford) $100. 93 —*S.H. (12/31/2002)*

Quintessa 1996 Bordeaux Blend (Rutherford) $90. 90 *(9/1/2000)*

Quintessa 2003 Cabernet Sauvignon (Rutherford) $120. 94 Cellar Selection —*S.H. (12/15/2006)*

Quintessa 2001 Cabernet Sauvignon (Rutherford) $110. 92 —*S.H. (10/1/2004)*

Quintessa 2000 Red Wine Red Blend (Rutherford) $100. 92 Cellar Selection —*S.H. (12/31/2003)*

QUIVIRA

Quivira 2001 Wine Creek Ranch Mourvèdre (Dry Creek Valley) $15. 85 —*S.H. (9/1/2003)*

Quivira 2003 Wine Creek Ranch Mourvèdre (Dry Creek Valley) $14. 85 —*S.H. (10/1/2004)*

Quivira 2004 Wine Creek Ranch Rosé Mourvèdre (Dry Creek Valley) $14. 87 —*S.H. (11/1/2005)*

Quivira 1997 Cuvée Red Blend (Dry Creek Valley) $13. 85 —*L.W. (6/1/1999)*

Quivira 2000 Dry Creek Cuvée Red Blend (Dry Creek Valley) $18. 91 —*S.H. (12/1/2002)*

Quivira 2003 Steelhead Red Blend (Dry Creek Valley) $18. 88 —*S.H. (11/1/2005)*

Quivira 2004 Steelhead Blended Red Wine Red Blend (Dry Creek Valley) $18. 84 —*S.H. (11/15/2006)*

Quivira 1997 Sauvignon Blanc (Dry Creek Valley) $11. 88 Best Buy —*L.W. (9/1/1999)*

Quivira 2004 Fig Tree Vineyard Sauvignon Blanc (Dry Creek Valley) $16. 92 Editors' Choice —*S.H. (7/1/2006)*

Quivira 2003 Fig Tree Vineyard Sauvignon Blanc (Dry Creek Valley) $16. 87 —*S.H. (8/1/2005)*

Quivira 2000 Fig Tree Vineyard Sauvignon Blanc (Dry Creek Valley) $16. 87 —*S.H. (9/1/2003)*

Quivira 1999 Fig Tree Vineyard Sauvignon Blanc (Dry Creek Valley) $18. 87 *(8/1/2002)*

Quivira 1998 Fig Tree Vineyard Sauvignon Blanc (Dry Creek Valley) $14. 89 —*L.W. (2/1/2000)*

Quivira 2002 Wine Creek Ranch Syrah (Dry Creek Valley) $24. 86 *(9/1/2005)*

Quivira 1998 Zinfandel (Dry Creek Valley) $18. 89 —*L.W. (9/1/1999)*

Quivira 2004 Zinfandel (Dry Creek Valley) $20. 91 —*S.H. (11/1/2006)*

Quivira 2003 Zinfandel (Dry Creek Valley) $20. 90 Editors' Choice —*S.H. (11/1/2005)*

Quivira 2001 Zinfandel (Dry Creek Valley) $20. 87 *(11/1/2003)*

Quivira 2000 Zinfandel (Dry Creek Valley) $20. 85 —*S.H. (11/1/2002)*

Quivira 1999 Zinfandel (Dry Creek Valley) $22. 88 —*D.T. (3/1/2002)*

Quivira 2000 Anderson Ranch Zinfandel (Dry Creek Valley) $35. 90 —*S.H. (11/1/2002)*

Quivira 2002 Anderson Road Zinfandel (Dry Creek Valley) $30. 91 —*S.H. (11/1/2005)*

Quivira 1997 Reserve Zinfandel (Dry Creek Valley) $25. 91 —*L.W. (2/1/2000)*

Quivira 2002 Wine Creek Ranch Zinfandel (Dry Creek Valley) $30. 92 —*S.H. (11/1/2005)*

QUPÉ

Qupé 1997 Bien Nacido Cuvée Chardonnay (Santa Barbara County) $16. 87 —*S.H. (9/1/1999)*

Qupé 1999 Bien Nacido Reserve Chardonnay (Santa Barbara County) $30. 91 *(7/1/2001)*

Qupé 1998 Bien Nacido Reserve Chardonnay (Santa Barbara County) $25. 89 *(6/1/2000)*

Qupé 1998 Bien Nacido Vineyard Chardonnay (Santa Barbara County) $18. 87 *(6/1/2000)*

Qupé 2001 Bien Nacido Vineyard Block Eleven Reserve Chardonnay (Santa Maria Valley) $25. 89 —*S.H. (6/1/2004)*

Qupé 1997 Bien Nacido Vineyard Reserve Chardonnay (Santa Barbara County) $25. 92 —*S.H. (7/1/2000)*

Qupé 2002 Bien Nacido Vineyard Y-Block Chardonnay (Santa Maria Valley) $18. 86 —*S.H. (6/1/2004)*

Qupé 1997 Ibarra-Young Vineyard Marsanne (Santa Barbara County) $14. 90 Best Buy —*S.H. (6/1/1999)*

Qupé 1997 Los Olivos Cuvée Red Blend (Santa Barbara County) $18. 90 —*S.H. (10/1/1999)*

Qupé 2001 Los Olivos Cuvée Rhône Red Blend (Santa Ynez Valley) $20. 90 Editors' Choice —*S.H. (6/1/2004)*

Qupé 2001 Alban Vineyard Roussanne (Edna Valley) $25. 88 —*S.H. (6/1/2004)*

Qupé 1997 Alban Vineyard Roussanne (Edna Valley) $25. 91 —*S.H. (10/1/1999)*

Qupé 1996 Alban Vineyard Roussanne (Edna Valley) $25. 91 —*S.H. (6/1/1999)*

Qupé 2003 Syrah (Central Coast) $17. 87 *(9/1/2005)*

Qupé 2002 Bien Nacido Hillside Estate Syrah (Santa Maria Valley) $40. 88 *(9/1/2005)*

Qupé 1997 Bien Nacido Hillside Estate Syrah (Santa Barbara County) $35. 92 —*S.H. (10/1/1999)*

Qupé 1999 Bien Nacido Reserve Syrah (Santa Barbara County) $25. 86 *(11/1/2001)*

Qupé 2003 Bien Nacido Vineyard Syrah (Santa Maria Valley) $28. 84 *(9/1/2005)*

Qupé 2001 Bien Nacido Vineyard Syrah (Santa Maria Valley) $25. 87 —*S.H. (6/1/2004)*

Qupé 2000 Bien Nacido Vineyard Hillside Estate Syrah (Santa Maria Valley) $40. 88 —*S.H. (6/1/2004)*

Qupé 1997 Bien Nacido Vineyard Reserve Syrah (Santa Barbara County) $25. 91 —*S.H. (6/1/1999)*

R & B CELLARS

R & B Cellars 2003 Reserve Cabernet Sauvignon (Napa Valley) $60. The main palate impression is a sharpness that cuts across the incredibly ripe cherry-pie, chocolate and cassis-laced coffee flavors. Other than that, this is a fairly standard ripe, oaky, plush Napa Cab. Drink now. **86** —*S.H. (7/1/2007)*

R & B Cellars 2001 Reserve Cabernet Sauvignon (Napa Valley) $60. Not successful. The wine is sweet and acidic, with a thin, minty edge to the cherry fruit. Shocking, for a wine from this great vintage, at such a high price. **82** —*S.H. (7/1/2007)*

R & B Cellars 1997 Reserve Cabernet Sauvignon (Napa Valley) $74. 90 *(11/1/2000)*

R & B Cellars 2005 Serenade in Blanc Sauvignon Blanc (California) $12. A nice dry white with some real complexity. The RRV fruit was stainless steel fermented; the Napa grapes were barrel fermented. The result? Scads of lemongrass, figs and melons, in a creamy texture. **86** —*S.H. (7/1/2007)*

R & B Cellars 2004 Saxy Syrah (California) $12. Ripe and soft, the kind of wine California's warmer inland regions produce so effortlessly. It's juicy in cherries, blackberries and spicy plums, with an edge of cocoa-dusted cappuccino, and finishes dry. **84** —*S.H. (7/1/2007)*

R & B Cellars 2005 Swingsville Zinfandel (California) $10. From Lodi, a dull, soft, rustic wine. It's fairly dry, but the fruit is thin and watery. **82** —*S.H. (7/1/2007)*

R. MERLO

R. Merlo 2001 Hyampom Valley Ranch Cabernet Sauvignon (Trinity County) $26. 85 —*S.H. (12/31/2006)*

R. Merlo 2002 Hyampom Valley Ranch Merlot (Trinity County) $26. 84 —*S.H. (12/31/2006)*

R. Merlo 2003 Pommard Pinot Noir (Trinity County) $22. 81 —*S.H. (12/31/2006)*

R. Merlo 2004 Syrah (Trinity County) $20. Trinity county is just north of Mendocino, with a hot, inland climate. This wine advances the fine wine cause up there. It's a little soft, but juicy and dry, with ripe cherry, blackberry and cocoa flavors, and a complex note of sweet kid leather. 86 —*S.H. (12/31/2007)*

R. Merlo 2003 Syrah (Trinity County) $20. 85 —*S.H. (12/31/2006)*

R.H. PHILLIPS

R.H. Phillips 2002 Cabernet Sauvignon (Dunnigan Hills) $9. 84 —*S.H. (6/1/2005)*

R.H. Phillips 2000 Cabernet Sauvignon (Dunnigan Hills) $10. 85 —*S.H. (11/15/2002)*

R.H. Phillips 1996 Toasted Head Cabernet Sauvignon (Mendocino) $18. 91 —*S.H. (5/1/2002)*

R.H. Phillips 2001 Chardonnay (Dunnigan Hills) $10. 84 —*S.H. (12/15/2002)*

R.H. Phillips 2000 Chardonnay (Dunnigan Hills) $9. 84 —*S.H. (9/12/2002)*

R.H. Phillips 2003 Toasted Head Chardonnay (California) $14. 87 —*S.H. (8/1/2005)*

R.H. Phillips 2001 Toasted Head Chardonnay (Dunnigan Hills) $16. 86 —*S.H. (12/15/2002)*

R.H. Phillips 2000 Toasted head Chardonnay (Dunnigan Hills) $14. 85 —*S.H. (9/1/2002)*

R.H. Phillips 1999 Toasted Head Chardonnay (Dunnigan Hills) $14. 83 —*S.H. (11/15/2000)*

R.H. Phillips 1997 Toasted Head Chardonnay (Dunnigan Hills) $12. 82 —*J.C. (10/1/1999)*

R.H. Phillips 1999 Toasted Head Giguiere Ranch Chardonnay (Dunnigan Hills) $25. 87 —*S.H. (12/15/2002)*

R.H. Phillips 2002 Merlot (Dunnigan Hills) $9. 84 Best Buy —*S.H. (6/1/2005)*

R.H. Phillips 1998 Merlot (Dunnigan Hills) $9. 82 —*S.H. (11/15/2000)*

R.H. Phillips 2002 Toasted Head Merlot (California) $17. 86 —*S.H. (8/1/2005)*

R.H. Phillips 1997 Toasted Head Merlot (Dunnigan Hills) $17. 86 —*M.S. (3/1/2000)*

R.H. Phillips 2003 Sauvignon Blanc (Dunnigan Hills) $8. 84 —*S.H. (6/1/2005)*

R.H. Phillips 2001 Sauvignon Blanc (Dunnigan Hills) $10. 86 —*S.H. (9/1/2003)*

R.H. Phillips 1999 Night Harvest Sauvignon Blanc (Dunnigan Hills) $10. 83 —*S.H. (8/1/2001)*

R.H. Phillips 1998 Night Harvest Sauvignon Blanc (Dunnigan Hills) $7. 87 Best Buy —*M.M. (9/1/1999)*

R.H. Phillips 2000 Syrah (Dunnigan Hills) $10. 85 —*S.H. (12/1/2002)*

R.H. Phillips 2002 EXP Syrah (Dunnigan Hills) $14. 82 *(9/1/2005)*

R.H. Phillips 1997 EXP Syrah (Dunnigan Hills) $14. 84 —*S.H. (10/1/1999)*

R.H. Phillips 1999 Toasted Head EXP Syrah (Dunnigan Hills) $25. 85 —*S.H. (12/1/2002)*

R.H. Phillips 1999 Estate Bottled Viognier (Dunnigan Hills) $14. 87 —*M.M. (11/21/2000)*

RABBIT RIDGE

Rabbit Ridge 2003 Chardonnay (Paso Robles) $14. 85 —*S.H. (12/15/2004)*

Rabbit Ridge 2002 Merlot (California) $8. 85 Best Buy —*S.H. (12/15/2004)*

Rabbit Ridge 2001 Avventura Reserve Red Blend (California) $25. 85 —*S.H. (12/15/2004)*

Rabbit Ridge 2003 Rabbit Rosé Blend (Paso Robles) $18. 86 —*S.H. (12/15/2004)*

Rabbit Ridge 2001 Brunello Clone Sangiovese (Paso Robles) $14. 84 —*S.H. (12/31/2004)*

Rabbit Ridge 1997 Consiglio Selezione Sangiovese (Sonoma County) $15. 86 —*S.H. (11/1/1999)*

Rabbit Ridge 2002 Syrah (Paso Robles) $18. 87 —*S.H. (12/15/2004)*

Rabbit Ridge 2002 Russell Family Vineyard Reserve Syrah (Paso Robles) $35. 86 —*S.H. (12/31/2004)*

Rabbit Ridge 2003 Westside Viognier (Paso Robles) $18. 88 —*S.H. (12/15/2004)*

Rabbit Ridge 2001 Westside Zinfandel (Paso Robles) $15. 86 *(11/1/2003)*

RABID RED

Rabid Red 2004 Red Blend (California) $15. 83 —*S.H. (12/31/2006)*

RACCHUS

Racchus 2003 Chardonnay (Sonoma County) $10. 84 —*S.H. (12/1/2005)*

Racchus 2003 Red Blend (Alexander Valley) $10. 83 —*S.H. (12/1/2005)*

RADIO-COTEAU

Radio-Coteau 2003 Timbervine Syrah (Russian River Valley) $55. 91 *(9/1/2005)*

RADOG

Radog 2006 Dry Gewürztraminer (Monterey County) $16. I like this wine mainly for its dryness and crispness. It tastes balanced and wholesome, the way a white wine should be. It's not a heavy hitter, but pleases for its spicy fruit, toffee and floral flavors. 86 —*S.H. (12/15/2007)*

Radog 2006 Rosé of Pinot Noir (Arroyo Seco) $16. Simple, with candied flavors of raspberries, cherries and vanilla. Tastes a bit sweet, but the keen acidity provides balance. 84 —*S.H. (12/15/2007)*

Radog 2005 Rose of Pinot Noir Pinot Noir (Monterey County) $16. There's very little flavor in this dry wine. Maybe a dollop of cherries and spices. Needs more concentration. 83 —*S.H. (5/1/2007)*

Radog 2005 Riesling (Santa Lucia Highlands) $17. If you didn't know it was from California, you might think this was a nice German Riesling. Crisp, mouthwatering acidity undergirds the pretty citrus, green apple and honeysuckle flavors, and the wine is off-dry and light-hearted. Great value from this red-hot appellation best known for expensive Pinot Noir. 88 Editors' Choice —*S.H. (5/1/2007)*

Radog 2005 Rose Rosé Blend (Central Coast) $14. A Rhône-style blend of Syrah, Grenache, Mourvèdre and Cinsault, this blush is clean and dry, but suffers from being way too thin. It's like water, with a splash of fruit juice. 83 —*S.H. (5/1/2007)*

Radog 2006 Sauvignon Blanc (Arroyo Seco) $16. The Arroyo Seco is a rocky bench between the Salinas Valley and the Santa Lucia Highlands. It's really great terroir for white wines because the conditions allow for extraordinarily long hangtime, while cool, foggy nights preserve vital acidity. You couldn't ask for a fresher, more vibrant Sauvignon Blanc than this one. It's bone dry and zesty, rich in pineapple, fig and mineral flavors, with a long, spicy finish. 90 Editors' Choice —*S.H. (12/15/2007)*

RAFANELLI

Rafanelli 2002 Cabernet Sauvignon (Dry Creek Valley) $40. 93 Editors' Choice —*S.H. (11/1/2005)*

Rafanelli 2001 Merlot (Dry Creek Valley) $26. 92 Editors' Choice —*S.H. (11/1/2005)*

Rafanelli 2003 Zinfandel (Dry Creek Valley) $30. 90 —*S.H. (11/1/2005)*

RAINBOW RIDGE

Rainbow Ridge 2003 Chardonnay (California) $13. 84 —*S.H. (3/1/2005)*

Rainbow Ridge 2002 Chardonnay (California) $13. 86 —*S.H. (6/1/2004)*

Rainbow Ridge 2003 Avid White Chardonnay (California) $10. 85 Best Buy —*S.H. (12/31/2005)*

Rainbow Ridge 2001 Alicante Bouschet Red Blend (California) $20. 91 —*S.H. (12/31/2003)*

Rainbow Ridge 2003 Flaming Red Red Blend (California) $10. 83 —*S.H. (12/31/2005)*

Rainbow Ridge 2004 Butch Blush Rosé Blend (California) $10. 83 —*S.H. (12/31/2005)*

RAMEY

Ramey 2004 Jericho Canyon Vineyard Cabernet Sauvignon (Napa Valley) $110. The wine shows a soft ripeness and depth of flavor, yet is balanced, with good acidity. Gorgeous structure; it is already forward and fleshy in cassis, raspberry, cherry, milk chocolate and smoky oak flavors. A touch of funky raw meat adds a complexing note. Drink now–2011 or so. 92 —*S.H. (7/1/2007)*

Ramey 2004 Larkmead Vineyard Cabernet Sauvignon (Napa Valley) $75. This may not be especially ageable because it's so soft and forward. But for current drinking and a few years out, it rewards for a wealth of flavor and richness. The wine has the blackberry marmalade, raspberry tart, milk chocolate truffle, cappuccino and new oaky flavors that many very ripe California reds show, but its pedigree is in the tannic structure. Best now through 2010. **89** *—S.H. (7/1/2007)*

Ramey 2004 Pedegral Vineyard Cabernet Sauvignon (Oakville) $140. This is notable for two things: It shows the extreme ripeness of the vintage, and also showcases the way even the ripest Oakville grapes veer toward dark-er-hued stone fruits and berries of balance and finesse. This soft, rich, fat, opulent Cab bursts with cassis, spicy purple plum, black cherry, dark chocolate and sweet licorice flavors, and is best now and for the next 6-8 years, before the fruit fades. **93** *—S.H. (7/1/2007)*

Ramey 1996 Chardonnay (Carneros) $65. 96 *(11/15/1999)*

Ramey 2004 Hudson Vineyard Chardonnay (Carneros) $58. Spectacularly ripe, showing an explosion of near-perfect fruit and smoky oak, balanced by crisply elegant acidity. Among the top ranks of Carneros Chards, the wine comes from manicured, low-yielding vines that, in this warm vintage, offer pineapple custard, lemon meringue, kiwi, crème brûlée and vanilla spice flavors. There's something keenly firm and stony in the finish. **94** *—S.H. (5/1/2007)*

Ramey 1998 Hudson Vineyard Chardonnay (Carneros) $55. 89 *(7/1/2001)*

Ramey 1997 Hudson Vineyard Chardonnay (Carneros) $48. 93 *(5/1/2000)*

Ramey 2004 Hyde Vineyard Chardonnay (Carneros) $58. Tasted alongside Ramey's Hudson bottling, this one's distinctly different, a softer, creamier, fleshier wine, but no less compelling. From the Napa side of the appellation, the wine is fat and oily in peach custard, butter-and-Cognac-sautéed pineapple and vanilla bean flavors, and while the charred oak is notable, it's fully in keeping with the wine's power. **93** *—S.H. (5/1/2007)*

Ramey 1998 Hyde Vineyard Chardonnay (Carneros) $55. 85 *(7/1/2001)*

Ramey 1997 Hyde Vineyard Chardonnay (Carneros) $46. 95 *(5/1/2000)*

Ramey 2001 Hyde Vineyards Chardonnay (Carneros) $56. 93 *—S.H. (11/15/2004)*

Ramey 2004 Ritchie Vineyard Chardonnay (Russian River Valley) $60. There's a bracing, salty tang of the sea in this fog-cooled Chard. It has an almost Islay Scotch quality, although the pineapple, lemon sorbet and new vanilla oak flavors are distinctly varietal. Hard to exaggerate the creamy richness, the way the wine glides across the palate with racy richness. **94** *—S.H. (7/1/2007)*

Ramey 2004 Claret Red Blend (Napa Valley) $38. David Ramey calls this his entry-level Cabernet. It's a blend of all five Bordeaux varieties, with a drop of Syrah, and has softness and immediate appeal. Complex and rich in dark stone fruit, berry, dark chocolate, coffee and spice flavors, it's drinking beautifully now. **90** *—S.H. (7/1/2007)*

Ramey 2004 Syrah (Sonoma Coast) $50. The model is Hermitage, but the wine is distinctly Californian, with its fat, fleshy ripeness and softness. It's very rich in chocolate-covered cherry candy, root beer, tangerine zest and smoky, vanilla bean flavors. A drop or two of Viognier was added and may bring a little brightness that lifts the tone. **90** *—S.H. (7/1/2007)*

RAMSAY

Ramsay 2004 Cabernet Sauvignon (Napa Valley) $16. As good as many Napa Cabs at twice the price. Dry, richly tannic and smooth, with blackberry and cola flavors and a nice streak of fresh green garden herbs. Best now. **89** *—S.H. (4/1/2007)*

Ramsay 2004 Merlot (Napa Valley) $16. Weedy and thin, this Merlot has a stubborn green streak that won't age out. Despite a splash of cherries and oak, that stemmy taste dominates. **83** *—S.H. (3/1/2007)*

Ramsay 1996 Reserve Merlot (Carneros) $26. 86 *—J.C. (7/1/2000)*

RAMSPECK

Ramspeck 2002 Cabernet Sauvignon (North Coast) $17. 84 *—S.H. (11/15/2004)*

Ramspeck 2001 Cabernet Sauvignon (North Coast) $18. 85 *—S.H. (12/15/2003)*

Ramspeck 2002 Pinot Noir (North Coast) $18. 84 *(11/1/2004)*

Ramspeck 2001 Pinot Noir (North Coast) $18. 82 *—S.H. (7/1/2003)*

RANCHO ARROYO GRANDE

Rancho Arroyo Grande 2004 Chardonnay (Arroyo Grande Valley) $15. 85 *—S.H. (12/1/2006)*

Rancho Arroyo Grande 2003 Estate Chardonnay (Arroyo Grande Valley) $15. 88 *—S.H. (12/1/2005)*

Rancho Arroyo Grande 2002 Private Reserve Chardonnay (Arroyo Grande Valley) $15. 86 *—S.H. (9/1/2004)*

Rancho Arroyo Grande 2002 Ian Cuvée Red Blend (Arroyo Grande Valley) $20. 86 *—S.H. (9/1/2004)*

Rancho Arroyo Grande 2003 Ian Cuvée Rhône Red Blend (Arroyo Grande Valley) $20. 86 *—S.H. (12/1/2006)*

Rancho Arroyo Grande 2002 Thereza Cuvée Rhône Red Blend (Arroyo Grande Valley) $20. 85 *—S.H. (12/1/2005)*

Rancho Arroyo Grande 2001 Thereza Cuvée Rhône Red Blend (Arroyo Grande Valley) $28. 86 *—S.H. (12/1/2003)*

Rancho Arroyo Grande 2001 Syrah (Arroyo Grande Valley) $28. 86 *—S.H. (12/15/2003)*

Rancho Arroyo Grande 2002 Private Reserve Syrah (Arroyo Grande Valley) $25. 91 *—S.H. (12/1/2005)*

Rancho Arroyo Grande 2004 Syrah Rosé Syrah (Arroyo Grande Valley) $15. 86 *—S.H. (12/1/2006)*

Rancho Arroyo Grande 2004 Viognier (Arroyo Grande Valley) $20. 87 *—S.H. (12/1/2006)*

Rancho Arroyo Grande 2004 Zinfandel (Arroyo Grande Valley) $15. 87 *—S.H. (12/1/2006)*

Rancho Arroyo Grande 2001 Zinfandel (Arroyo Grande Valley) $18. 87 *(11/1/2003)*

Rancho Arroyo Grande 2002 Dry Farm Zinfandel (Arroyo Grande Valley) $30. 85 *—S.H. (9/1/2004)*

Rancho Arroyo Grande 2003 Estate Zinfandel (Arroyo Grande Valley) $15. 84 *—S.H. (12/1/2005)*

RANCHO NAPA

Rancho Napa 1999 Bordeaux Blend (Napa Valley) $37. 93 Cellar Selection *—S.H. (11/15/2002)*

RANCHO SISQUOC

Rancho Sisquoc 1997 Cabernet Sauvignon (Santa Maria Valley) $22. 81 *—S.H. (9/1/2000)*

Rancho Sisquoc 2001 Flood Family Vineyards Cabernet Sauvignon (Santa Barbara County) $22. 84 *—S.H. (3/1/2005)*

Rancho Sisquoc 1998 Chardonnay (Santa Maria Valley) $18. 84 *—S.H. (10/1/2000)*

Rancho Sisquoc 1996 Chardonnay (Santa Maria Valley) $15. 89 *—S.H. (7/1/1999)*

Rancho Sisquoc 2002 Flood Family Vineyards Chardonnay (Santa Barbara County) $18. 87 *—S.H. (3/1/2005)*

Rancho Sisquoc 2001 Flood Family Vineyards Merlot (Santa Barbara County) $20. 86 *—S.H. (3/1/2005)*

Rancho Sisquoc 1999 Flood Family Vineyard Pinot Noir (Santa Maria Valley) $40. 84 *(10/1/2002)*

Rancho Sisquoc 2002 Flood Family Vineyards Pinot Noir (Santa Barbara County) $30. 87 *—S.H. (3/1/2005)*

Rancho Sisquoc 1998 Sauvignon Blanc (Santa Maria Valley) $14. 83 *—S.H. (9/1/2000)*

Rancho Sisquoc 2002 Flood Family Vineyards Syrah (Santa Barbara County) $30. 91 *—S.H. (3/1/2005)*

RANCHO ZABACO

Rancho Zabaco 2002 Pinot Gris (Sonoma Coast) $20. 88 *—S.H. (12/1/2003)*

Rancho Zabaco 2000 Pinot Gris (Sonoma Coast) $16. 88 Editors' Choice *(7/1/2001)*

Rancho Zabaco 2001 Reserve Pinot Gris (Sonoma County) $18. 87 *(8/1/2002)*

Rancho Zabaco 2002 Sauvignon Blanc (Russian River Valley) $20. 87 *—S.H. (12/1/2003)*

Rancho Zabaco 2001 Sauvignon Blanc (Russian River Valley) $18. 89 *—J.M. (9/1/2003)*

Rancho Zabaco 2000 Sauvignon Blanc (Russian River Valley) $16. 86 *(7/1/2001)*

Rancho Zabaco 2004 Dancing Bull Sauvignon Blanc (California) $10. 85 Best Buy *—S.H. (12/15/2005)*

Rancho Zabaco 2003 Dancing Bull Sauvignon Blanc (California) $10. 87 Best Buy *—S.H. (6/1/2005)*

Rancho Zabaco 2002 Dancing Bull Sauvignon Blanc (California) $10. 84 *—S.H. (12/31/2003)*

Rancho Zabaco 2002 Reserve Sauvignon Blanc (Russian River Valley) $20. 89 *—J.M. (9/1/2004)*

Rancho Zabaco 2001 Reserve Sauvignon Blanc (Sonoma County) $18. 86 *(8/1/2002)*

Rancho Zabaco 1999 Syrah (Sonoma County) $18. 84 *(6/1/2003)*

Rancho Zabaco 2002 Zinfandel (Dry Creek Valley) $18. 86 *—S.H.*

(11/15/2005)

Rancho Zabaco 1999 Zinfandel (Dry Creek Valley) $18. 87 *(8/1/2002)*

Rancho Zabaco 1998 Zinfandel (Dry Creek Valley) $17. 87 *—D.T. (3/1/2002)*

Rancho Zabaco 1997 Zinfandel (Sonoma County) $12. 86 *—L.W. (2/1/2000)*

Rancho Zabaco 2001 Chiotti Vineyard Zinfandel (Dry Creek Valley) $28. 91 *(11/1/2003)*

Rancho Zabaco 2000 Chiotti Vineyard Zinfandel (Dry Creek Valley) $25. 89 *(8/1/2002)*

Rancho Zabaco 1999 Chiotti Vineyard Zinfandel (Dry Creek Valley) $22. 88 *(7/1/2001)*

Rancho Zabaco 2003 Dancing Bull Zinfandel (California) $12. 86 *—S.H. (6/1/2006)*

Rancho Zabaco 2002 Dancing Bull Zinfandel (California) $10. 86 Best Buy *—S.H. (6/1/2005)*

Rancho Zabaco 2001 Dancing Bull Zinfandel (California) $12. 89 Best Buy *—S.H. (11/15/2002)*

Rancho Zabaco 2000 Dancing Bull Zinfandel (California) $12. 84 *(8/1/2002)*

Rancho Zabaco 2003 Monte Rosso Vineyard Zinfandel (Sonoma Valley) $35. 90 *—S.H. (6/1/2006)*

Rancho Zabaco 2003 Monte Rosso Vineyard Toreador Zinfandel (Sonoma Valley) $50. 92 *—S.H. (6/1/2006)*

Rancho Zabaco 2000 Reserve Zinfandel (Dry Creek Valley) $20. 90 *—S.H. (9/1/2003)*

Rancho Zabaco 2003 Sonoma Heritage Vines Zinfandel (Sonoma County) $18. 89 *—S.H. (10/1/2006)*

Rancho Zabaco 2003 Sonoma Heritage Vines Zinfandel (Sonoma County) $18. 90 *—S.H. (12/15/2005)*

Rancho Zabaco 2001 Sonoma Heritage Vines Zinfandel (Sonoma County) $18. 86 *(11/1/2003)*

Rancho Zabaco 2000 Sonoma Heritage Vines Zinfandel (Sonoma County) $16. 85 *(8/1/2002)*

Rancho Zabaco 1999 Stefani Vineyard Zinfandel (Dry Creek Valley) $28. 92 Editors' Choice *—P.G. (3/1/2002)*

RANDALL HARRIS

Randall Harris 2001 Merlot (Washington) $10. 88 *—J.M. (11/15/2003)*

RAPHAEL

Raphael 2002 La Fontana Bordeaux Blend (North Fork of Long Island) $20. 86 *—M.D. (8/1/2006)*

Raphael 2004 Cabernet Franc (North Fork of Long Island) $18. 84 *—M.D. (8/1/2006)*

Raphael 2001 Cabernet Franc (North Fork of Long Island) $40. 83 *—M.D. (8/1/2006)*

Raphael 1999 Merlot (North Fork of Long Island) $38. 84 *—M.S. (1/1/2004)*

Raphael 2003 Estate Merlot (North Fork of Long Island) $15. This 100% merlot is partially aged in older oak for six months and then in stainless steel. It's round and fruity but the chew overpowers a bit here, overcoming the bright, pleasant flavors of plum and toasted oak. The dense mouthfeel and structure add heft. Overall a good wine and may improve with age. **82** *—S.K. (2/1/2007)*

Raphael 2001 Estate Merlot (North Fork of Long Island) $15. 82 *—M.D. (12/1/2006)*

Raphael 2005 Sauvignon Blanc (North Fork of Long Island) $22. 83 *—M.D. (8/1/2006)*

Raphael 2003 Sauvignon Blanc (North Fork of Long Island) $20. 85 *(7/1/2005)*

RAPTOR RIDGE

Raptor Ridge 2004 Pinot Noir (Willamette Valley) $20. 90 Editors' Choice *—P.G. (5/1/2006)*

Raptor Ridge 2003 Coeur de Terre Vineyard Pinot Noir (Willamette Valley) $29. 88 *—P.G. (8/1/2005)*

Raptor Ridge 2003 Harbinger Vineyard Pinot Noir (Willamette Valley) $29. 90 *—P.G. (8/1/2005)*

Raptor Ridge 2005 Meredith Mitchell Vineyard Pinot Noir (Willamette Valley) $39. Pungent with tomato leaf and fresh-turned earth. Young and tight, spicy and earthy, this is a classic example of the Oregon style. The alcohol (presumably ripeness) is significantly lower than in past vintages, and the flavors follow suit. Watch this develop over the next 5–8 years. **91** *—P.G. (7/1/2007)*

Raptor Ridge 2004 Meredith Mitchell Vineyard Pinot Noir (Willamette Valley) $39. 93 Editors' Choice *—P.G. (5/1/2006)*

Raptor Ridge 2003 Meredith Mitchell Vineyard Pinot Noir (Willamette Valley) $29. 93 Editors' Choice *—P.G. (8/1/2005)*

Raptor Ridge 2000 Murto Vineyard Pinot Noir (Willamette Valley) $24. 83 *—M.S. (8/1/2003)*

Raptor Ridge 2005 Reserve Pinot Noir (Willamette Valley) $37. The Raptor Ridge Reserve is an engaging, fruity and tasty wine, immediately showing bright raspberry and bing cherry. The acids prop it up and give it a spicy lift, and the wine sits on the palate with a lively presence, inviting food, another sip, and further exploration. It is not a complex wine, but harmonious and very pleasant, with spicy cinnamon adding interest to the finish. **89** *—P.G. (7/1/2007)*

Raptor Ridge 2004 Reserve Pinot Noir (Willamette Valley) $39. 90 *—P.G. (5/1/2006)*

Raptor Ridge 2003 Reserve Pinot Noir (Willamette Valley) $29. 90 *—P.G. (8/1/2005)*

Raptor Ridge 2005 Rosé Pinot Noir (Willamette Valley) $18. A pale copper, and showing some slight but detectable sweetness, this older rosé still sports pretty rhubarb and strawberry fruit, firm acids and good texture. An elegant wine, nearing the end of its shelf life, it should be served well chilled. **87** *—P.G. (7/1/2007)*

Raptor Ridge 2005 Shea Vineyard Pinot Noir (Willamette Valley) $45. Fragrant and inviting, with rose petals soaked in chocolate, tasted outdoors on a pine-scented evening. It's a beautifully detailed and powerful wine, the classic iron fist in the velvet glove. The cherry fruit is ripe and lively, and there is a slight impression of alcoholic heat in the finish. **90** *—P.G. (7/1/2007)*

Raptor Ridge 2004 Shea Vineyard Pinot Noir (Willamette Valley) $39. 92 *—P.G. (5/1/2006)*

Raptor Ridge 2003 Shea Vineyard Pinot Noir (Willamette Valley) $29. 89 *—P.G. (8/1/2005)*

Raptor Ridge 2000 Shea Vineyard Pinot Noir (Willamette Valley) $35. 86 *—M.S. (7/1/2003)*

Raptor Ridge 2005 Stony Mountain Vineyard Pinot Noir (Willamette Valley) $37. The first bottle was corked, the second shows a soft, somewhat flat center and a flavor of black olive underlying the light, plummy fruit. This is a pleasant, round wine, but it doesn't have the intensity and brilliant definition of previous vintages. **87** *—P.G. (7/1/2007)*

Raptor Ridge 2004 Stony Mountain Vineyard Pinot Noir (Willamette Valley) $39. 92 Editors' Choice *—P.G. (5/1/2006)*

Raptor Ridge 2003 Stony Mountain Vineyard Pinot Noir (Willamette Valley) $29. 91 Editors' Choice *—P.G. (8/1/2005)*

Raptor Ridge 2003 Yamhill County Cuvée Pinot Noir (Willamette Valley) $18. 88 *—P.G. (8/1/2005)*

Raptor Ridge 2005 Yamhill Springs Vineyard Pinot Noir (Willamette Valley) $37. Despite its youth this is already showing a light orange tone and the fruit is round, ripe and quickly maturing. It's drinking well, with forward flavors of berry, plum and leaf. Tannins are tight and hard, ripe but unyielding. **87** *—P.G. (7/1/2007)*

RAVENSWOOD

Ravenswood 2001 Vintner's Blend Cabernet Sauvignon (California) $10. 85 *—S.H. (4/1/2004)*

Ravenswood 2004 Vintners Blend Cabernet Sauvignon (California) $12. 81 *—S.H. (12/15/2006)*

Ravenswood 2003 Vintners Blend Cabernet Sauvignon (California) $10. 84 *—S.H. (12/1/2005)*

Ravenswood 2002 Vintners Blend Cabernet Sauvignon (California) $10. 86 Best Buy *—S.H. (8/1/2005)*

Ravenswood 2003 Vintners Blend Chardonnay (California) $10. 82 *—S.H. (8/1/2005)*

Ravenswood 2002 Vintners Blend Chardonnay (California) $10. 90 Best Buy *—S.H. (9/1/2004)*

Ravenswood 1997 Vintner's Blend Merlot (California) $11. 85 *(11/15/1999)*

Ravenswood 2003 Vintners Blend Merlot (California) $10. 83 *—S.H. (12/1/2005)*

Ravenswood 2002 Vintners Blend Merlot (California) $10. 86 *—S.H. (9/1/2004)*

Ravenswood 2000 Vintners Blend Merlot (California) $10. 86 Best Buy *—S.H. (8/1/2003)*

Ravenswood 1999 Icon Rhône Red Blend (Sonoma County) $20. 84 *—S.H.*

USA

(7/1/2002)

Ravenswood 2001 Zinfandel (Lodi) $15. 87 (11/1/2003)

Ravenswood 2000 Zinfandel (Napa Valley) $17. 87 (5/1/2003)

Ravenswood 2000 Zinfandel (Amador County) $15. 86 —S.H. (5/1/2003)

Ravenswood 2000 Zinfandel (Lodi) $15. 85 —S.H. (5/1/2003)

Ravenswood 1999 Zinfandel (Napa Valley) $15. 88 —D.T. (3/1/2002)

Ravenswood 1999 Zinfandel (Mendocino) $14. 87 —D.T. (3/1/2002)

Ravenswood 1999 Zinfandel (Amador County) $14. 87 —D.T. (3/1/2002)

Ravenswood 1999 Zinfandel (Sonoma County) $15. 86 —S.H. (12/15/2001)

Ravenswood 1999 Zinfandel (Sonoma County) $15. 89 —D.T. (3/1/2002)

Ravenswood 1999 Zinfandel (Lodi) $13. 87 —D.T. (3/1/2002)

Ravenswood 2004 Barricia Zinfandel (Sonoma Valley) $30. One of Ravenswood's most dependable Zins, this contains a good proportion of Petite Sirah, making it ripe and full-bodied. In a warm vintage like '04, the wine is almost Port-y, with strong blackberry, plum, stewed prune, plumped raisin and peppery spice flavors. Yet it remains dry and balanced. Best with rich barbecues and roasts. **87** —S.H. (6/1/2007)

Ravenswood 2002 Barricia Zinfandel (Sonoma Valley) $30. 90 —S.H. (3/1/2005)

Ravenswood 2001 Barricia Zinfandel (Sonoma Valley) $35. 87 (11/1/2003)

Ravenswood 2000 Barricia Zinfandel (Sonoma Valley) $35. 87 (5/1/2003)

Ravenswood 1999 Barricia Zinfandel (Sonoma Valley) $30. 89 —D.T. (3/1/2002)

Ravenswood 2004 Belloni Zinfandel (Russian River Valley) $30. I've never had a less than satisfying Belloni Zin from Ravenswood, but this is certainly the ripest in memory. It's almost a dessert, with melted milk chocolate, cassis, blueberry, red cherry and peppery spice flavors. Yet it remains dry, with the fine acid-tannin balance for which the vineyard is noted. **89** —S.H. (6/1/2007)

Ravenswood 2002 Belloni Zinfandel (Russian River Valley) $30. 91 —S.H. (3/1/2005)

Ravenswood 2001 Belloni Zinfandel (Russian River Valley) $35. 88 (11/1/2003)

Ravenswood 2000 Belloni Zinfandel (Russian River Valley) $35. 89 (5/1/2003)

Ravenswood 2004 Big River Zinfandel (Alexander Valley) $30. Zins from this vineyard are always big, ripe and exuberant. The challenge is to keep the wines elegant. In 2004, Joel Peterson had to struggle, for the grapes were enormously ripe. But he has managed to keep the overall balance, while retaining the vineyard's key traits of gigantic wild berry fruit that fully merits the considerable oak overlay. **87** —S.H. (6/1/2007)

Ravenswood 2002 Big River Zinfandel (Alexander Valley) $30. 86 —S.H. (3/1/2005)

Ravenswood 2001 Big River Zinfandel (Alexander Valley) $30. 89 (11/1/2003)

Ravenswood 2000 Big River Zinfandel (Alexander Valley) $35. 85 —S.H. (5/1/2003)

Ravenswood 1999 Big River Zinfandel (Alexander Valley) $30. 91 —D.T. (3/1/2002)

Ravenswood 2002 Cooke Zinfandel (Sonoma County) $50. 89 —S.H. (3/1/2005)

Ravenswood 2001 Cooke Zinfandel (Sonoma Valley) $28. 88 (11/1/2003)

Ravenswood 1997 Cooke Zinfandel (Sonoma Valley) $28. 89 —S.H. (5/1/2000)

Ravenswood 2002 Dickerson Zinfandel (Napa Valley) $30. 93 —S.H. (3/1/2005)

Ravenswood 2001 Dickerson Zinfandel (Napa Valley) $35. 88 (11/1/2003)

Ravenswood 2000 Dickerson Zinfandel (Napa Valley) $35. 84 —J.M. (9/1/2003)

Ravenswood 1999 Dickerson Zinfandel (Napa Valley) $30. 90 —D.T. (3/1/2002)

Ravenswood 2001 Kunde Zinfandel (Sonoma Valley) $27. 90 (11/1/2003)

Ravenswood 1997 Lodi Zinfandel (Sonoma County) $14. 88 —P.G. (11/15/1999)

Ravenswood 2002 Monte Rosso Zinfandel (Sonoma Valley) $30. 91 —S.H. (3/1/2005)

Ravenswood 2001 Monte Rosso Zinfandel (Sonoma Valley) $35. 86 (11/1/2003)

Ravenswood 2000 Monte Rosso Zinfandel (Sonoma Valley) $35. 92 —S.H. (9/1/2003)

USA

Ravenswood 1999 Monte Rosso Zinfandel (Sonoma Valley) $30. 89 —D.T. (3/1/2002)

Ravenswood 2004 Old Hill Zinfandel (Sonoma Valley) $60. Ravenswood's priciest Zin, Old Hill comes from a field-blended vineyard, containing many varieties other than Zin, that winemaker Joel Peterson says is probably Sonoma's oldest. The '04 is a young wine. It is very rich in slightly stewed blackberry, cherry, plum, pomegranate, prune and raisin flavors, with Zin's distinctively brambly, spicy finish. Fairly tannic, the wine is fully dry. It will age for a long time, gradually losing fruit, and is best enjoyed now–2012. **90** —S.H. (6/1/2007)

Ravenswood 2002 Old Hill Zinfandel (Sonoma Valley) $60. 93 —S.H. (3/1/2005)

Ravenswood 2001 Old Hill Zinfandel (Sonoma Valley) $46. 89 (11/1/2003)

Ravenswood 2000 Old Hill Zinfandel (Sonoma Valley) $46. 90 (5/1/2003)

Ravenswood 1999 Old Hill Zinfandel (Sonoma Valley) $36. 92 —D.T. (3/1/2002)

Ravenswood 2004 Teldeschi Zinfandel (Dry Creek Valley) $30. The hot vintage enormously ripened the grapes, so what you get is a wine that's almost like a fruit reduction sauce. But it's dry and has enough acidity for balance. Really strong in blackberry jam, cassis, cherry and cola flavors, it's a big, bold wine, enriched with a dash of Petite Sirah and Carignane. **87** —S.H. (6/1/2007)

Ravenswood 2002 Teldeschi Zinfandel (Dry Creek Valley) $32. 89 —S.H. (3/1/2005)

Ravenswood 2001 Teldeschi Zinfandel (Dry Creek Valley) $35. 87 (11/1/2003)

Ravenswood 2000 Teldeschi Zinfandel (Dry Creek Valley) $35. 86 (5/1/2003)

Ravenswood 1999 Teldeschi Zinfandel (Dry Creek Valley) $30. 90 —D.T. (3/1/2002)

Ravenswood 1999 Vintners Blend Zinfandel (California) $10. 84 —S.H. (12/15/2001)

Ravenswood 2004 Vintners Blend Zinfandel (California) $10. 84 —S.H. (12/15/2006)

Ravenswood 2003 Vintners Blend Zinfandel (California) $10. 84 —S.H. (12/1/2005)

Ravenswood 2000 Vintners Blend Zinfandel (California) $10. 86 (5/1/2003)

RAVINES

Ravines 2004 Chardonnay (Finger Lakes) $17. Structured, buttery oak flavors comprise this enjoyable wine. Heft from beginning to end and the viscous mouthfeel offers some indulgence, but the wall of oak offers little evidence of the flavors beyond, lending simplicity to a wine that, by variety, has potential to offer something more. **85** —S.K. (2/1/2007)

Ravines 2003 Pinot Noir (Finger Lakes) $20. 83 —M.D. (12/1/2006)

Ravines 2005 Rosé Pinot Noir (Finger Lakes) $13. An alluring perfume of flowers is the hallmark of this amber-hued offering from Finger Lakes producer Ravines, and on the palate, the wine is fresh and full of strawberry notes. It's not the most delicate rose out there, but it's versatile and good with everything from spicy dishes to seafood. **84** —S.K. (7/1/2007)

Ravines 2004 Dry Riesling (Finger Lakes) $16. This firm, Alsatian-style dry Riesling will please fans of more esoteric, terroir driven-wines. Aromas of citrus and peach play on the nose, while a minerally backbone supports elegant flavors of orange and spice. A little oily on the palate and lacking some of the zest of more accessible Rieslings, this wine is still apt to please on many levels. **86** —S.K. (2/1/2007)

Ravines 2005 Dry Riesling (Finger Lakes) $16. **90 Editors' Choice** —M.D. (8/1/2006)

RAY'S STATION VINEYARDS

Ray's Station Vineyards 2004 Cabernet Sauvignon (North Coast) $15. Country-style wine, a rustic, rough-and-ready Cab. It has tough, jagged tannins and blackberry and cherry fruit that finishes fresh and jammy. **83** —S.H. (5/1/2007)

Ray's Station Vineyards 2003 Merlot (Sonoma County) $15. Try sneaking this into your next wine group blind tasting. It might turn some heads. It shows the ripe, polished cherry, plum, sage, carob and licorice flavors of the finest Merlots, with rich, finely ground tannins, and finishes dry. With a drop of Cabs Sauvignon and Franc, it has true complexity. **87 Editors' Choice** —S.H. (12/31/2007)

RAYE'S HILL

Raye's Hill 2003 Red Wine Meritage Bordeaux Blend (Mendocino County) $26. 86 —S.H. (7/1/2006)

Raye's Hill 2000 Merlot (Anderson Valley) $26. 85 —S.H. (6/1/2004)

Raye's Hill 2001 Pinot Blanc (Anderson Valley) $22. 87 —S.H. (6/1/2004)

Raye's Hill 2003 Hein Vineyard Pinot Blanc (Anderson Valley) $18. 84 —*S.H. (12/15/2004)*

Raye's Hill 2003 Pinot Noir (Anderson Valley) $32. 86 —*S.H. (7/1/2006)*

Raye's Hill 2002 Pinot Noir (Anderson Valley) $18. 89 *(11/1/2004)*

Raye's Hill 2001 Pinot Noir (Anderson Valley) $15. 83 —*S.H. (12/15/2004)*

Raye's Hill 1999 Pinot Noir (Anderson Valley) $24. 84 —*S.H. (5/1/2002)*

Raye's Hill 1999 Pinot Noir (Russian River Valley) $20. 84 *(10/1/2002)*

Raye's Hill 1999 Pinot Noir (Russian River Valley) $20. 88 —*S.H. (6/1/2004)*

Raye's Hill 1998 Pinot Noir (Anderson Valley) $24. 88 —*S.H. (5/1/2002)*

Raye's Hill 2002 Estate Bottled Pinot Noir (Anderson Valley) $26. 88 *(11/1/2004)*

Raye's Hill 2004 Wrightman House Vineyard Pinot Noir (Anderson Valley) $30. A bit too ripe, with chocolate-covered raisin flavors and a touch of pruniness in the finish. It's a tasty wine, even a delicious one, and it does the best job it can, but that kind of supermaturity loses points. **87** —*S.H. (5/1/2007)*

Raye's Hill 2002 Wightman House Vineyard Pinot Noir (Anderson Valley) $22. 85 *(11/1/2004)*

RAYMOND

Raymond 2004 Cabernet Sauvignon (Rutherford) $55. This dense, tannic, 100% Cab needs time to come around. It's a masculine wine, with a muscular core of blackberry, plum and cherry fruit, and finishes dry. Should begin to open by 2009, and could really blossom for some years afterward. **92** —*S.H. (12/15/2007)*

Raymond 2003 Cabernet Sauvignon (St. Helena) $50. Oh, what a nice young Cabernet this is. With lots of new French oak, it shows a beautifully balanced, elegant opulence. The fruit is impeccably ripe, all blackberries and cassis, and the all-important tannins are softly ripe and sweet. You could open it now, but it should develop additional bottle complexity after 2007. **92** —*S.H. (5/1/2007)*

Raymond 2003 Cabernet Sauvignon (Rutherford) $50. While this gorgeous Cab shows a ripe approachability that makes it instantly drinkable, it also has a tannicly closed element that suggests aging. A fine steak will pair beautifully with the wine's tannins, acids and blackberry fruit, and you don't want to hang onto it too long. But in the next six years this wine will change in interesting ways. **92** —*S.H. (5/1/2007)*

Raymond 2000 Cabernet Sauvignon (Napa Valley) $18. 89 —*S.H. (10/1/2003)*

Raymond 2001 Amberhill Cabernet Sauvignon (California) $10. 84 —*S.H. (10/1/2004)*

Raymond 2001 Estates Cabernet Sauvignon (California) $15. 87 —*S.H. (10/1/2004)*

Raymond 2002 Estates Cabernet Sauvignon (Napa Valley) $20. 85 —*S.H. (11/1/2005)*

Raymond 2003 Generations Cabernet Sauvignon (Napa Valley) $80. Raymond returns to form with this 100% Cabernet. It's made in the modern cult style, which emphasizes immediate pleasure at the expense of ageability. With rich cherry, cassis and new oak flavors, the wine is soft enough to open now, and should drink well for the next six years. **89** —*S.H. (9/1/2007)*

Raymond 2002 Generations Cabernet Sauvignon (Napa Valley) $75. 84 —*S.H. (9/1/2006)*

Raymond 2001 Generations Cabernet Sauvignon (Napa Valley) $70. 88 —*S.H. (12/31/2005)*

Raymond 1999 Generations Cabernet Sauvignon (Napa Valley) $80. 91 —*J.M. (6/1/2002)*

Raymond 1999 Generations Cabernet Sauvignon (Napa Valley) $65. 89 —*S.H. (8/1/2004)*

Raymond 1998 Generations Cabernet Sauvignon (Napa Valley) $80. 86 —*S.H. (6/1/2002)*

Raymond 1997 Generations Cabernet Sauvignon (Napa Valley) $65. 91 *(11/1/2000)*

Raymond 1996 Generations Cabernet Sauvignon (Napa Valley) $50. 92 —*S.H. (7/1/2000)*

Raymond 2003 R Collection Cabernet Sauvignon (Napa Valley) $19. 84 —*S.H. (10/1/2006)*

Raymond 2003 Reserve Cabernet Sauvignon (Napa Valley) $35. 88 —*S.H. (9/9/1999)*

Raymond 2002 Reserve Cabernet Sauvignon (Napa Valley) $34. 90 —*S.H. (2/1/2006)*

Raymond 2004 Reserve Cabernet Sauvignon (Napa Valley) $35. Here's an intense, nervy young Cab that impresses for its powerful oak and cassis flavors. It's a little sharp now, with an acidic jamminess and tea-like tannic structure that suggests moderate aging capability. Stash it until 2008, then open for a couple of years. **88** —*S.H. (12/31/2007)*

Raymond 2003 Reserve Cabernet Sauvignon (Napa Valley) $35. Classic Raymond, a soft, elegant Cabernet the equal of wines costing much more. With a smooth, velvety mouthfeel, it has flavors of blackberries, coffee, herbs and sweet new oak, and finishes very dry. Keep it for a year or two and it will be better. **90** —*S.H. (2/1/2007)*

Raymond 2002 Reserve Cabernet Sauvignon (Rutherford) $50. 90 —*S.H. (11/1/2005)*

Raymond 2002 Reserve Cabernet Sauvignon (St. Helena) $50. 94 Editors' Choice —*S.H. (7/1/2006)*

Raymond 2001 Reserve Cabernet Sauvignon (Rutherford) $50. 88 —*S.H. (10/1/2004)*

Raymond 2001 Reserve Cabernet Sauvignon (St. Helena) $50. 90 —*S.H. (6/1/2005)*

Raymond 2000 Reserve Cabernet Sauvignon (Napa Valley) $40. 92 Editors' Choice —*S.H. (11/15/2003)*

Raymond 1999 Reserve Cabernet Sauvignon (Napa Valley) $40. 90 —*J.M. (6/1/2002)*

Raymond 1997 Reserve Cabernet Sauvignon (Napa Valley) $23. 90 —*S.H. (3/1/2000)*

Raymond 1996 Reserve Cabernet Sauvignon (Napa Valley) $20. 90 *(11/15/1999)*

Raymond 2003 Chardonnay (Monterey) $13. 88 Best Buy —*S.H. (11/1/2005)*

Raymond 2002 Amberhill Chardonnay (California) $6. 85 —*S.H. (9/1/2004)*

Raymond 2002 Estates Chardonnay (Monterey) $10. 87 Best Buy —*S.H. (12/1/2004)*

Raymond 2001 Estates Chardonnay (Monterey) $11. 83 —*S.H. (8/1/2003)*

Raymond 2000 Estates Chardonnay (Monterey) $12. 86 —*S.H. (9/1/2002)*

Raymond 1999 Estates Chardonnay (Monterey) $10. 87 Best Buy —*S.H. (11/15/2001)*

Raymond 1998 Generations Chardonnay (Napa Valley) $30. 83 *(7/1/2001)*

Raymond 1997 Generations Chardonnay (Napa Valley) $28. 86 *(6/1/2000)*

Raymond 1996 Generations Chardonnay (Napa Valley) $28. 89 *(10/1/1999)*

Raymond 2005 R Collection Chardonnay (Monterey) $13. A Monterey appellation on Chardonnay usually means a crisp, brightly acidic wine, with intense fruit flavors from the long, cool growing season. Here, you get upfront honeydew, apricot, pineapple, white peach, green apple and tangerine flavors wrapped in a creamy texture. Finishes with a softening touch of sweetness. **86** —*S.H. (2/1/2007)*

Raymond 2004 R Collection Chardonnay (Monterey) $13. 84 —*S.H. (10/1/2006)*

Raymond 2005 Reserve Chardonnay (Napa Valley) $20. There's a lot of oak on this wine, or maybe the wood just dominates because the fruit is so thin. Either way, it's clean, lean and dry. **83** —*S.H. (9/1/2007)*

Raymond 2004 Reserve Chardonnay (Napa Valley) $20. 88 —*S.H. (12/1/2006)*

Raymond 2003 Reserve Chardonnay (Napa Valley) $18. 87 —*S.H. (11/1/2005)*

Raymond 2001 Reserve Chardonnay (Napa Valley) $19. 90 —*S.H. (12/1/2003)*

Raymond 2000 Reserve Chardonnay (Napa Valley) $18. 87 —*S.H. (9/1/2002)*

Raymond 1998 Reserve Chardonnay (Napa Valley) $15. 85 *(6/1/2000)*

Raymond 1997 Reserve Chardonnay (Napa Valley) $15. 87 —*S.H. (10/1/1999)*

Raymond 2001 Merlot (California) $10. 84 —*S.H. (12/15/2004)*

Raymond 2000 Merlot (California) $11. 89 Best Buy —*S.H. (12/1/2003)*

Raymond 2000 Amberhill Merlot (California) $9. 85 —*S.H. (12/1/2003)*

Raymond 2002 Estates Merlot (California) $15. 82 —*S.H. (11/1/2005)*

Raymond 2004 R Collection Merlot (California) $14. 83 —*S.H. (12/31/2006)*

Raymond 2003 R Collection Merlot (California) $14. 85 —*S.H. (10/1/2006)*

Raymond 2004 Reserve Merlot (Napa Valley) $24. Rich and forward in cherry, blackberry, coffee and smoky oak flavors, this has ripe and fine polished tannins. It's a nice wine, with some sharpness on the finish. **87** —*S.H. (12/31/2007)*

Raymond 2003 Reserve Merlot (Napa Valley) $24. The most modern tannin management has been applied here, to judge by the mouthfeel, which is as soft and velvety as anything out there. It's a tasty Merlot, but could be more concentrated and intense in fruit. The red and black cherry, black raspberry jam, and blackberry tea flavors are liberally oaked. **87** —*S.H. (2/1/2007)*

Raymond 2002 Reserve Merlot (Napa Valley) $24. 86 —*S.H. (3/1/2006)*

Raymond 2000 Reserve Merlot (Napa Valley) $22. 91 —*S.H. (12/31/2003)*

Raymond 1998 Reserve Merlot (Napa Valley) $22. 89 —*S.H. (6/1/2001)*

Raymond 1997 Reserve Merlot (Napa Valley) $22. 89 —*S.H. (7/1/2000)*

Raymond 1998 Amberhill Sauvignon Blanc (California) $6. 86 Best Buy —*S.H. (9/1/2000)*

Raymond 2006 Reserve Sauvignon Blanc (Napa Valley) $14. Bright, pure lemons, limes and kiwis star in this clean, dry white wine, with overtones of fresh wildflowers and newly mown grass. Stainless steel-fermented, it's a savory and polished sipper with a biting zestiness. **89** —*S.H. (9/1/2007)*

Raymond 2004 Reserve Sauvignon Blanc (Napa Valley) $14. 84 —*S.H. (12/1/2006)*

Raymond 2003 Reserve Sauvignon Blanc (Napa Valley) $12. 83 —*S.H. (11/1/2005)*

Raymond 2002 Reserve Sauvignon Blanc (Napa Valley) $11. 83 —*J.M. (10/1/2004)*

Raymond 2001 Reserve Sauvignon Blanc (Napa Valley) $11. 87 Best Buy —*S.H. (10/1/2003)*

Raymond 2000 Reserve Sauvignon Blanc (Napa Valley) $11. 87 —*J.M. (9/1/2003)*

Raymond 1998 Reserve Sauvignon Blanc (Napa Valley) $11. 86 —*S.H. (9/1/2000)*

Raymond 1999 Reserve Zinfandel (Napa Valley) $22. 87 —*J.M. (11/1/2002)*

Raymond 1998 Reserve Zinfandel (Napa Valley) $16. 81 —*D.T. (3/1/2002)*

RAYMOND BURR

Raymond Burr 2000 Cabernet Franc (Dry Creek Valley) $38. 82 —*S.H. (11/15/2003)*

Raymond Burr 2000 Cabernet Sauvignon (Dry Creek Valley) $38. 84 —*S.H. (11/15/2003)*

Raymond Burr 1999 Cabernet Sauvignon (Dry Creek Valley) $38. 87 —*S.H. (12/15/2003)*

Raymond Burr 1998 Cabernet Sauvignon (Dry Creek Valley) $38. 86 —*J.M. (6/1/2002)*

Raymond Burr 2001 Chardonnay (Dry Creek Valley) $28. 83 —*S.H. (10/1/2003)*

RDLR

RDLR 2002 Syrah (Mendocino County) $24. 86 —*S.H. (9/1/2005)*

RED FLYER

Red Flyer 2003 Red Blend (California) $9. 84 —*S.H. (11/15/2005)*

RED LAVA

Red Lava 2004 Reserve Syrah (Red Hills Lake County) $25. The promise is there in this ripe, plush wine, with its rich tannins and good acidity. It's rewarding in herb-tinged blackberry jam, plum, violet, coffee and chocolate flavors, with a distinct white pepper edge. As good as it is, the next step is to build in extra layers of complexity. **90** —*S.H. (11/1/2007)*

Red Lava 2002 Reserve Syrah (Lake County) $27. Soft and simple, with a rustic nature to the tannins, this estate-grown Syrah, from the promising Red Hills area, has blackberry tea and cherry cola flavors. A first release wine, it has its work cut out. **84** —*S.H. (2/1/2007)*

RED NEWT CELLARS

Red Newt Cellars 2002 Riesling (Finger Lakes) $13. 88 Best Buy —*J.C. (8/1/2003)*

Red Newt Cellars 2006 Dry Riesling (Finger Lakes) $17. Crisp minerality and full fruit flavors of apricot and lemon are the hallmarks of this classic New York Riesling. A plate of freshwater fish or a sampling of cheese and apples would pair perfectly here. **84** —*S.K. (9/1/2007)*

Red Newt Cellars 2001 Reserve Riesling (Finger Lakes) $20. 85 —*J.C. (8/1/2003)*

RED ROVER

Red Rover 2005 Cabernet Sauvignon (Central Coast) $8. Red Rover, a brand from Stevenot, has done a bang-up job with inexpensive varietals. This Cab is a good expression of a rustic, country-style wine that just needs some decent food and a good setting to please. With berries and cherries, it's dry, and has a nice spiciness. **83** —*S.H. (5/1/2007)*

Red Rover 2005 Chardonnay (Central Coast) $8. Good price for an everyday Chard with quite a bit of ripe fruit and what tastes like spicy oak. Finishes clean and long. **83** —*S.H. (4/1/2007)*

Red Rover 2005 Merlot (Central Coast) $8. Here's a new entry in the animal-themed, labels gone wild varietal sweepstakes. For eight bucks, you get a big gulp of cherries and blackberries, in a softly textured, dry package. It's a great deal. **85 Best Buy** —*S.H. (3/1/2007)*

Red Rover 2003 Petite Sirah (Central Coast) $9. A nice wine, full-bodied and gutsy in the style of Pet, with crunchy tannins and upfront currant, coffee, chocolate and herb flavors. There's some raisiny overripeness, but those babybacks won't care. **84 Best Buy** —*S.H. (5/1/2007)*

RED SKY

Red Sky 2003 Bordeaux Blend (Washington) $30. It's 57% Cabernet Sauvignon, one third Merlot and the rest Cab Franc. This wine seems to be less than the sum of its parts, showing volatility on the nose and roughness in the tannins. The mixed flavors include unresolved herb, banana and pickle barrel—and yet these disparate components may well compose themselves with a bit more time. **85** —*P.G. (5/1/2007)*

Red Sky 2002 Bordeaux Blend (Walla Walla (WA)) $30. 89 —*P.G. (6/1/2006)*

Red Sky 2003 Cabernet Franc (Walla Walla (WA)) $20. 90 —*P.G. (6/1/2006)*

Red Sky 2003 Merlot (Washington) $20. A blend of fruit from Conner Lee, Pepper Bridge and Seven Hills vineyards, this ripe (15.3% alcohol) Merlot doesn't show the heat. Rather it delivers intense flavors of black fruits, coffee and nuances of herb and fungus, nicely defined and structured. There is enough backbone for further aging. **89** —*P.G. (5/1/2007)*

Red Sky 2005 Sémillon (Washington) $15. A blend of 90% Sémillon enhanced with 10% Klipsun vineyard Sauvignon Blanc. Golden yellow and softly oxidized, it is made in a fully barrel-fermented style, in 50% new oak, yielding a buttery, toasty wine with details from the extended barrel time. It's undeniably flavorful, but what is sacrificed is fruit freshness and most of the varietal character. **86** —*P.G. (5/1/2007)*

Red Sky 2004 Syrah (Washington) $30. The winery's 2003 Syrah was sourced from Boushey, but in 2004 they switched to Destiny Ridge and Dineen. This is an improvement, perhaps vintage-related, but it shows dark, densely scented black fruits and aromatic hints of leather, cedar and chocolate. It's quite youthful and tangy, with tart, citrusy, racy flavors, and will most certainly continue to add muscle and soften up with a few more years of bottle time. **89** —*P.G. (5/1/2007)*

Red Sky 2002 Syrah (Washington) $25. 87 *(9/1/2005)*

Red Sky 2003 Boushey Vineyard Syrah (Yakima Valley) $30. 88 —*P.G. (6/1/2006)*

Red Sky 2003 Boushey Vineyard Syrah (Washington) $30. 86 *(9/1/2005)*

RED TRUCK

Red Truck 2005 Cabernet Sauvignon (California) $12. Pretty smooth and balanced for such an inexpensive wine, this does a good job of intertwining ripe fruity flavors with earthy, herbal ones, then adding a tasteful level of oak. It finishes dry, with a scour of tannins. **86** —*S.H. (11/1/2007)*

Red Truck 2004 Cabernet Sauvignon (California) $13. 85 —*S.H. (11/15/2006)*

Red Truck 2005 Merlot (California) $12. A little on the harsh, rustic side, but there's enough cherry, vanilla and anise richness to satisfy. Great with a burger. **84** —*S.H. (11/1/2007)*

Red Truck 2004 Merlot (California) $13. 83 —*S.H. (11/15/2006)*

Red Truck 2004 Red Blend (California) $10. 84 —*S.H. (5/1/2006)*

Red Truck 2005 Red Wine Red Blend (California) $10. Made from six varieties, mainly Rhône, this is a soft, simple wine that tastes medicinal. **80** —*S.H. (11/1/2007)*

RED ZEPPELIN

Red Zeppelin 2003 Syrah (Central Coast) $14. 83 —*S.H. (12/1/2005)*

REDBUD

Redbud 2002 Viognier (California) $5. 81 —*S.H. (12/15/2005)*

REDLINE

Redline 2004 Blue Oaks Vineyard Syrah (Paso Robles) $24. 83 —*S.H. (12/31/2006)*

Redline 2004 Cedar Lane Vineyard Syrah (Arroyo Seco) $30. 89 —*S.H. (12/31/2006)*

Redline 2004 Eaglepoint Ranch Syrah (Mendocino) $32. 91 —*S.H. (12/31/2006)*

REDTREE

Redtree 2005 Cabernet Sauvignon (California) $9. Dry and full-bodied, this is the kind of rustic Cab that, at this price, you can serve at your next big condo party or BBQ without breaking the bank. It has leathery flavors of blackberries and cola. 84—*S.H. (11/1/2007)*

Redtree 2005 Petite Sirah (California) $9. The price is good and the wine is totally dry. This is a rugged, country-style wine that's so low in fruit, the alcohol, which is actually pretty low, dominates. 82 —*S.H. (11/1/2007)*

Redtree 2006 Pinot Grigio (California) $9. There's a bit of a vegetal element to this dry, crisp wine that gives a slight asparagus undertow to the citrus and flower flavors. 83 —*S.H. (11/1/2007)*

REDWOOD

Redwood 2004 Select Series Barbera (California) $10. 83 —*S.H. (12/31/2006)*

Redwood 2000 Cabernet Sauvignon (California) $9. 85 Best Buy —*S.H. (6/1/2003)*

Redwood 2001 Chardonnay (California) $9. 84 —*S.H. (6/1/2003)*

Redwood 2000 Merlot (California) $9. 85 Best Buy —*S.H. (8/1/2003)*

Redwood 2001 Rosé Blend (California) $7. 83 —*S.H. (9/1/2003)*

REDWOOD CREEK

Redwood Creek 2004 Cabernet Sauvignon (California) $8. 84 Best Buy —*S.H. (11/15/2006)*

Redwood Creek 2004 Pinot Grigio (California) $8. 85 Best Buy —*S.H. (3/1/2006)*

Redwood Creek 2005 Sauvignon Blanc (California) $8. This is a basic, everyday Sauvignon Blanc, affordably priced and juicy, with semi-sweet tropical fruit, fig, apple and spice flavors. Sourced from the Sacramento Delta and the Central Valley, it's another Gallo brand that delivers value. 84 Best Buy —*S.H. (2/1/2007)*

REED

Reed 2000 Fralich Vineyard Syrah (Paso Robles) $29. 89 —*S.H. (12/1/2002)*

REFLECTIONS

Reflections 2001 Meritage (Alexander Valley) $50. 85 —*S.H. (6/1/2005)*

Reflections 2000 Meritage (Alexander Valley) $55. 84 —*S.H. (6/1/2005)*

REGUSCI

Regusci 2002 Cabernet Sauvignon (Stags Leap District) $48. 92 —*S.H. (10/1/2005)*

Regusci 2002 Merlot (Napa Valley) $40. 91 —*S.H. (10/1/2005)*

REININGER

Reininger 2002 Cabernet Sauvignon (Walla Walla (WA)) $32. 89 —*P.G. (6/1/2006)*

Reininger 1999 Cabernet Sauvignon (Walla Walla (WA)) $35. 92 Editors' Choice —*P.G. (12/31/2001)*

Reininger 2003 Ash Hollow Vineyard Cabernet Sauvignon (Walla Walla (WA)) $32. It's the winemaking that shines here; the fruit is light and leans toward the wild strawberry and fig side. But it is presented as a nicely balanced and harmonious wine, and Chuck Reininger brings out some interesting, lightly applied herb and coffee notes. 89 —*P.G. (3/1/2007)*

Reininger 2003 Carmenère (Walla Walla (WA)) $45. Like Reininger's excellent Malbec, this is 100% varietal, sourced from the Seven Hills Vineyard. Dark, toasty, smooth and delicious, it's got a lot of midpalate power leavened with herbs, cinnamon and black pepper. Give it a bit of extra breathing time and it opens out into a smooth, silky finish. 89 —*P.G. (3/1/2007)*

Reininger 2002 Carmenère (Walla Walla (WA)) $35. 90 —*P.G. (12/15/2005)*

Reininger 2003 Pepper Bridge Vineyard Malbec (Walla Walla (WA)) $45. Pure Malbec, with a tight, tart Bordeaux grape structure amplified with blueberry and black raspberry fruit, then softened with some chocolaty barrel time. This is seductive, assertive, firm and ageworthy; a lovely rendition of the grape with a Washington (high acid) spin. 90 —*P.G. (3/1/2007)*

Reininger 2002 Merlot (Walla Walla (WA)) $30. 90 —*P.G. (6/1/2006)*

Reininger 1999 Merlot (Walla Walla (WA)) $35. 90 —*P.G. (12/31/2001)*

Reininger 1999 Red Table Wine Red Blend (Walla Walla (WA)) $20. 88 —*P.G. (12/31/2001)*

Reininger 2001 Cima Sangiovese (Walla Walla (WA)) $45. 87 —*P.G. (6/1/2006)*

Reininger 2003 Syrah (Walla Walla (WA)) $32. 91 —*P.G. (6/1/2006)*

Reininger 2002 Syrah (Walla Walla (WA)) $32. 83 *(9/1/2005)*

Reininger 1999 Syrah (Walla Walla (WA)) $29. 86 *(11/1/2001)*

RENAISSANCE

Renaissance 1998 Cabernet Sauvignon (North Yuba) $17. 82 —*S.H. (11/15/2001)*

Renaissance 1998 Estate Bottled Chardonnay (North Yuba) $17. 82 *(6/1/2000)*

Renaissance 1997 Première Cuvée Chardonnay (North Yuba) $30. 87 *(6/1/2000)*

Renaissance 1997 Première Cuvée Chardonnay (North Yuba) $35. 85 *(7/1/2001)*

Renaissance 1995 Vendanges Tardives Chardonnay (North Yuba) $25. 81 —*J.C. (12/31/1999)*

Renaissance 1999 Mediterranean Red Red Blend (North Yuba) $21. 81 —*S.H. (12/1/2001)*

Renaissance 2000 Granite Crown Vin de Terroir Red Wine Red Blend (North Yuba) $40. A Rhône-Bordeaux blend of Syrah, Cab Sauvignon, Cab Franc and Merlot. Soft, simple and sweet; tastes like melted milk chocolate infused with blackberry essence, sprinkled with cinnamon sugar and vanilla. 83 —*S.H. (7/1/2007)*

Renaissance 1996 Select Late Harvest Sauvignon Blanc (North Yuba) $35. Intensely sweet, this is honey soft, rich in apricot, gingerbread crumble, crème brûlée and vanilla flavors, and crisp in acidity. The grapes were an astonishing 43% of brix at harvest. 90 —*S.H. (7/1/2007)*

Renaissance 2003 Vin de Terroir Syrah (North Yuba) $35. Thickly soft and rustic, with simple berry-cherry jam flavors that finish with sugary sweetness. Not very sophisticated, but it will appeal to many. 83 —*S.H. (7/1/2007)*

Renaissance 2000 Viognier (North Yuba) $19. 85 —*S.H. (11/15/2001)*

Renaissance 2005 Vin de Terroir Viognier (North Yuba) $30. A clumsy wine. It's semisweet in vanilla and lemon yogurt flavors, and soft, with a funky, soiled finish. 82 —*S.H. (6/1/2007)*

Renaissance 1999 Zinfandel (North Yuba) $19. 81 —*S.H. (11/15/2001)*

RENARD

Renard 2000 Syrah (Santa Rita Hills) $28. 91 —*S.H. (2/1/2004)*

Renard 2000 Arroyo Vineyards Syrah (Napa Valley) $28. 86 —*S.H. (2/1/2004)*

RENWOOD

Renwood 2005 Barbera (Sierra Foothills) $10. Although the alcohol on this wine is a comparatively modest 13.5%, it has a hot, raisiny taste. It's jagged and sharp in the mouth, too. 81 —*S.H. (10/1/2007)*

Renwood 2002 Barbera (Amador County) $20. 85 —*S.H. (5/1/2006)*

Renwood 2001 Barbera (Amador County) $20. 90 Editors' Choice —*S.H. (6/1/2004)*

Renwood 2002 Sierra Series Barbera (Sierra Foothills) $10. 85 —*S.H. (6/1/2004)*

Renwood 2001 Sierra Series Barbera (Sierra Foothills) $12. 86 Best Buy —*S.H. (12/1/2002)*

Renwood 2006 Orange Muscat (Amador County) $11. Fulfills the basic requirement of a sweet white dessert wine, with orange, tangerine and vanilla flavors offset by crisp acidity. This is a pleasant, fairly simple sipper. 84 —*S.H. (11/15/2007)*

Renwood 2005 Orange Muscat (Amador County) $18. Nice and sweet in honeyed orange flavors, with a hit of spice, and acidity gives this dessert wine a crisp balance. It's not particularly intense or complex, though. 85 —*S.H. (9/1/2007)*

Renwood 2005 Orange Muscat (Amador County) $11. 84 —*S.H. (12/31/2006)*

Renwood 2002 Orange Muscat (Amador County) $12. 90 —*S.H. (6/1/2004)*

Renwood 2001 Orange Muscat (Shenandoah Valley (CA)) $12. 87 —*S.H. (12/1/2002)*

Renwood 2005 Pinot Grigio (Lodi) $10. 84 —*S.H. (12/31/2006)*

Renwood 2004 Select Series Pinot Grigio (California) $10. 84 —*S.H. (2/1/2006)*

Renwood 2005 Twin Rivers Vineyard Roberto's Block Pinot Grigio (Sierra Foothills) $25. Here's a nice, easy wine that rewards for upfront pineapple, green apple, apricot and spice flavors. With all that honeyed fruit, it definitely benefits from crisp acidity, and a certain tangy minerality. **85** —*S.H. (9/1/2007)*

Renwood NV Port (Sierra Foothills) $15. 88 —*S.H. (6/1/2004)*

Renwood 1996 Single Harvest Colheita Reserve Port (Shenandoah Valley (CA)) $90. Made from traditional Port varieties, this 11-year-old wine has achieved a soft, nutty silkiness, although it still contains fine, crisp acids and smooth tannins. It's not terribly sweet, with flavors of raspberries, cherries, red currants, chocolate truffle and caramel. Needs more concentration. **89** —*S.H. (12/31/2007)*

Renwood 2003 Vintage Port Port (Amador County) $19. Gets the Port job done with sweet flavors of caramel, blackberry jam, tangerine zest, chocolate, sweetened coffee and licorice flavors, while acidity gives a much-needed crunch. But despite the vintage label, it's not an ager. Made from traditional Port varieties. **87** —*S.H. (9/1/2007)*

Renwood 2003 Vintage Port Port (Sierra Foothills) $15. Made from traditional Port varieties, the wine starts with classic Port aromas of cassis, chocolate and caramel. In the mouth, it doesn't disappoint in sweetness, but turns simple in straightforward fruit pie flavors. **84** —*S.H. (2/1/2007)*

Renwood 1995 Vintage Port (Shenandoah Valley (CA)) $22. 83 —*S.H. (9/1/2003)*

Renwood 2005 Dry Rosé Rosé Blend (Sierra Foothills) $10. Too sweet and rustic for me, dull with sugary LifeSaver candy flavors. **82** —*S.H. (7/1/2007)*

Renwood 2004 Syrah (Sierra Foothills) $10. A good value for dryness and balance, and lots of tasty flavors. Blackberries, currants, cherries, milk chocolate, spice and smoky oak finish with a touch of tannins, suggesting pork or lamb. **85 Best Buy** —*S.H. (9/1/2007)*

Renwood 2000 Syrah (Amador County) $25. 87 —*S.H. (2/1/2003)*

Renwood 1999 Syrah (Amador County) $25. 87 *(11/1/2001)*

Renwood 2003 Select Series Syrah Rosé (California) $9. 83 —*S.H. (10/1/2004)*

Renwood 2004 Select Series Syrah Rosé (California) $12. 82 —*S.H. (12/31/2006)*

Renwood 2002 Sierra Series Syrah (Sierra Foothills) $NA. 85 —*S.H. (6/1/2004)*

Renwood 2001 Sierra Series Syrah (Sierra Foothills) $12. 86 —*S.H. (2/1/2003)*

Renwood 2000 Sierra Series Syrah (California) $13. 85 —*S.H. (12/1/2002)*

Renwood 1999 Sierra Series Syrah (California) $12. 84 *(10/1/2001)*

Renwood 2005 Twin River Vineyard Backside Tempranillo (El Dorado) $40. There's lots to like about this wine, but not enough to justify this price. It's an easy wine, with immediately appealing cherry and cola flavors; soft and silky. **84** —*S.H. (12/1/2007)*

Renwood 2005 Viognier (Lodi) $10. A nice, friendly wine, dry and crisp, with citrus and gooseberry flavors that are more like Sauvignon Blanc than the opulence usually associated with Viognier. If you're not fussy about varietal correctness, it's a good, elegant wine. **85 Best Buy** —*S.H. (9/1/2007)*

Renwood 2002 Viognier (Amador County) $25. 88 —*S.H. (6/1/2004)*

Renwood 2001 Viognier (Shenandoah Valley (CA)) $25. 88 —*S.H. (12/15/2002)*

Renwood 2000 Viognier (Shenandoah Valley (CA)) $25. 90 —*J.M. (12/15/2002)*

Renwood 2002 Select Series Viognier (Lodi) $NA. 83 —*S.H. (6/1/2004)*

Renwood 2001 Select Series Viognier (California) $25. 86 —*S.H. (12/15/2002)*

Renwood 2001 Sierra Series Viognier (California) $12. 85 —*S.H. (5/1/2003)*

Renwood 2000 Sierra Series Viognier (California) $13. 83 —*J.M. (12/15/2002)*

Renwood 2005 Veauta Ranch Vineyard Clos Rene Viognier (Sierra Foothills) $25. Fancy name for a fairly simple wine. Crisp and fruity, it has slightly sweet citrus, honeysuckle and vanilla flavors, with polished acidity for balance. **85** —*S.H. (9/1/2007)*

Renwood 2006 Amador Ice White Blend (Amador County) $35. A little sugar goes a long way. This dessert wine is primarily Ain, with a splash of Muscat and Viognier. It's quite sweet, with apricot, tangerine, peach, honey and dusty spice flavors. This would be a great wine if the flavors were more concentrated. **87** —*S.H. (12/31/2007)*

Renwood 2004 Zinfandel (Fiddletown) $25. The vintage was very hot, and you can taste the blistering sun in the soft, melted cherry and blackberry jam flavors that stop just short of raisins. Still, high alcohol gives it a cooked, Port-y aftertaste. **84** —*S.H. (9/1/2007)*

Renwood 2004 Zinfandel (Sierra Foothills) $10. 81 —*S.H. (12/31/2006)*

Renwood 2003 Zinfandel (Fiddletown) $25. 89 Cellar Selection —*S.H. (5/1/2006)*

Renwood 2002 Zinfandel (Fiddletown) $25. 84 —*S.H. (5/1/2006)*

Renwood 2001 Zinfandel (Fiddletown) $25. 90 —*S.H. (6/1/2004)*

Renwood 2005 Amador Ice Zinfandel (Amador County) $35. Tastes very sweet, with raspberry, cherry and apricot jam flavors that are just delicious, and balanced with just enough acidity to make the finish clean. **86** —*S.H. (9/1/2007)*

Renwood 2005 Amador Ice Zinfandel Zinfandel (Amador County) $35. This dessert wine is left on the vine until it reaches fantastic sugar, then artificially frozen to mimic the conditions of authentic ice wine. With a pale color and strawberry-raspberry flavors, it's enormously sweet and low in alcohol, but not particularly complex. **85** —*S.H. (2/1/2007)*

Renwood 2000 Amador Ice Zinfandel (Shenandoah Valley (CA)) $35. 88 —*S.H. (12/1/2002)*

Renwood 1997 D'Agostini Bros. Zinfandel (Shenandoah Valley (CA)) $30. 87 —*P.G. (11/15/1999)*

Renwood 2000 D'Agostini Bros. Zinfandel (Shenandoah Valley (CA)) $30. 88 —*S.H. (2/1/2003)*

Renwood 1999 D'Agostini Bros. Zinfandel (Amador County) $30. 88 —*D.T. (3/1/2002)*

Renwood 1999 Fiddletown Zinfandel (Amador County) $25. 86 —*D.T. (3/1/2002)*

Renwood 2004 Grandmere Zinfandel (Amador County) $35. If you like your Zins very soft and melted, with gentle cherry and raspberry tart flavors, including the baked, buttery pie crusts, you'll love this one. It's way too soft for aging, so drink now. **85** —*S.H. (9/1/2007)*

Renwood 2002 Grandmère Zinfandel (Amador County) $25. 82 —*S.H. (5/1/2006)*

Renwood 2001 Grandmère Zinfandel (Amador County) $25. 92 —*S.H. (6/1/2004)*

Renwood 2000 Grandmère Zinfandel (Amador County) $25. 86 —*S.H. (2/1/2003)*

Renwood 1999 Grandmère Zinfandel (Amador County) $25. 87 —*D.T. (3/1/2002)*

Renwood 1996 Grandmère Zinfandel (Amador County) $25. 84 —*P.G. (11/15/1999)*

Renwood 2003 Grandmère Zinfandel (Amador County) $25. 92 —*S.H. (5/1/2006)*

Renwood 1997 Grandmère Zinfandel (Amador County) $25. 81 *(3/1/2001)*

Renwood 2004 Grandpere Zinfandel (Amador County) $40. Shows pleasurable cherry, raspberry, blackberry, coffee, cola and dusty spice flavors that are complex in their own way. But the wine is overly soft in both tannins and acids, leaving all that fruit out there to fend for itself, without balancing structure. **84**—*S.H. (9/1/2007)*

Renwood 2002 Grandpère Zinfandel (Amador County) $35. 85 —*S.H. (5/1/2006)*

Renwood 2001 Grandpère Zinfandel (Amador County) $32. 89 —*S.H. (6/1/2004)*

Renwood 2000 Grandpère Zinfandel (Shenandoah Valley (CA)) $32. 86 —*S.H. (2/1/2003)*

Renwood 1999 Grandpère Zinfandel (Amador County) $32. 89 —*D.T. (3/1/2002)*

Renwood 2004 Jack Rabbit Flat Zinfandel (Amador County) $30. Way too hot and high in alcohol. This wine cannot handle the 16%; the fruit isn't here, except for some raisins, leaving behind pure heat. **82** —*S.H. (9/1/2007)*

Renwood 2003 Jack Rabbit Flat Zinfandel (Amador County) $30. 86 —*S.H. (5/1/2006)*

Renwood 2002 Jack Rabbit Flat Zinfandel (Amador County) $30. 82 —*S.H. (5/1/2006)*

Renwood 2001 Jack Rabbit Flat Zinfandel (Amador County) $30. 91 —*S.H. (6/1/2004)*

Renwood 2000 Jack Rabbit Flat Zinfandel (Amador County) $30. 89 —*S.H. (2/1/2003)*

Renwood 1999 Jack Rabbit Flat Zinfandel (Amador County) $30. 86 —*D.T. (3/1/2002)*

Renwood 2004 Old Vine Zinfandel (Amador County) $17. Soft, hot and simple, with thin raspberry and cherry flavors that don't have the concentrated intensity you expect from old Zinfandel vines. **84** —*S.H. (9/1/2007)*

Renwood 2003 Old Vine Zinfandel (Amador County) $20. 90 Editors' Choice

—*S.H.* (5/1/2006)

Renwood 2002 Old Vine Zinfandel (Amador County) $20. 86 —*S.H.* (5/1/2006)

Renwood 2001 Old Vine Zinfandel (Amador County) $20. 88 —*S.H.* (6/1/2004)

Renwood 2000 Old Vine Zinfandel (Amador County) $20. 87 —*S.H.* (12/1/2002)

Renwood 1999 Old Vine Zinfandel (Amador County) $20. 85 —*D.T.* (3/1/2002)

Renwood 2003 Sierra Series Zinfandel (Sierra Foothills) $10. 83 —*S.H.* (5/1/2006)

Renwood 2002 Sierra Series Zinfandel (Sierra Foothills) $10. 85 —*S.H.* (12/15/2004)

Renwood 2001 Sierra Series Zinfandel (Sierra Foothills) $12. 87 Best Buy —*S.H.* (2/1/2003)

RETRO

Retro 2004 Petite Sirah (Howell Mountain) $45. Tannin alert! This is old-fashionedly rustic, a wine for the cellar. Give it 6-8 years to begin to unlock the blackberries; it could live longer that that. **92 Cellar Selection** —*S.H.* (12/1/2007)

Retro 2003 Petite Sirah (Howell Mountain) $40. 92 Cellar Selection —*S.H.* (11/15/2006)

RETZLAFF

Retzlaff 2000 Cabernet Sauvignon-Merlot (Livermore Valley) $38. 83 —*S.H.* (11/15/2003)

Retzlaff 1999 Chardonnay (Livermore Valley) $16. 87 —*S.H.* (12/31/2003)

Retzlaff 1998 Estate Bottled Chardonnay (Livermore Valley) $16. 85 (6/1/2000)

REVANA

Revana 2003 Cabernet Sauvignon (Napa Valley) $90. A beautiful effort from Heidi Barrett, this is a big, ripe, somewhat soft wine, stuffed with blackberry, cherry, coffee and cocoa flavors, and splashed with Provençal herbs. Rich and tannic now, it should age for a decade. **89** —*S.H.* (5/1/2007)

REVERIE

Reverie 2001 Special Reserve Estate Cabernet Blend (Diamond Mountain) $75. 88 —*S.H.* (10/1/2005)

Reverie 2000 Special Reserve Estate Cabernet Blend (Diamond Mountain) $55. 91 —*S.H.* (10/1/2005)

Reverie 2003 Cabernet Franc (Diamond Mountain) $45. 90 —*S.H.* (9/1/2006)

Reverie 2004 Estate Cabernet Franc (Diamond Mountain) $50. If you thought Cab Franc was the soft, early-drinking Cab, reconsider. This is a tough wine, dry and so tannic that it numbs down the palate. But it's huge in sappy red and black cherry fruit, with a chocolate fudge finish, and should develop well. Try holding for three or four years. **90** —*S.H.* (4/1/2007)

Reverie 2001 Estate Cabernet Franc (Diamond Mountain) $42. 86 —*S.H.* (7/1/2005)

Reverie 2002 Cabernet Sauvignon (Diamond Mountain) $55. 90 —*S.H.* (9/1/2006)

Reverie 2004 Estate Cabernet Sauvignon (Diamond Mountain) $60. Here's a ripe, polished Cab, brimming in cherry, plum and new oak flavors. It's soft and gentle enough for immediate drinking, although it has the structure for five or six years in the bottle. **87** —*S.H.* (6/1/2007)

Reverie 2003 Estate Cabernet Sauvignon (Diamond Mountain) $55. There's a nice classic structure to this dry wine, but it's pretty much in lockdown tannin mode now. However, underneath those tannins is a solid core of blackberries and sweet cassis, and one of these days, when the wine has been aged and decanted to rid it of sediment, the sweetness should be gorgeous. Drink 2010–2016. **92 Cellar Selection** —*S.H.* (4/1/2007)

Reverie 2004 Special Reserve Cabernet Sauvignon (Diamond Mountain) $85. This is a big, ripe, soft wine, and flattering in youth. Must be the vintage's heat. The wine is a little raisiny and chocolaty, but quite delicious. Drink this while you're waiting for that '03 to come around. **87** —*S.H.* (4/1/2007)

Reverie 2003 Special Reserve Cabernet Sauvignon (Diamond Mountain) $75. Shows typical Diamond Mountain youthful tannins that are tough and hard, and in this good vintage a dense, vibrant core of cassis and cherry fruit that's jamlike in its richness. Very dry, the wine will benefit from decanting, but it really wants fairly extended cellaring. Hold until 2009, then drink through 2015. **92 Cellar Selection** —*S.H.* (4/1/2007)

Reverie 2002 Special Reserve Cabernet Sauvignon (Diamond Mountain) $75. 84 —*S.H.* (9/1/2006)

Reverie 2003 Merlot (Diamond Mountain) $45. 88 —*S.H.* (8/1/2006)

REX HILL

Rex Hill 1993 Champagne Blend (Oregon) $24. 86 —*P.G.* (12/1/2000)

Rex Hill 2002 Chardonnay (Willamette Valley) $12. 88 —*P.G.* (8/1/2005)

Rex Hill 1999 Chardonnay (Willamette Valley) $17. 88 —*S.H.* (8/1/2002)

Rex Hill 2002 Reserve Chardonnay (Oregon) $24. 90 —*P.G.* (2/1/2005)

Rex Hill 2003 Unwooded Chardonnay (Willamette Valley) $16. 86 —*P.G.* (8/1/2005)

Rex Hill 2002 Unwooded Chardonnay (Willamette Valley) $18. 88 —*P.G.* (2/1/2005)

Rex Hill 2001 Unwooded Chardonnay (Willamette Valley) $17. 87 —*P.G.* (2/1/2004)

Rex Hill 1998 Pinot Blanc (Willamette Valley) $14. 85 —*L.W.* (12/31/1999)

Rex Hill 2003 Pinot Gris (Willamette Valley) $16. 85 —*P.G.* (8/1/2005)

Rex Hill 2001 Pinot Gris (Willamette Valley) $14. 88 Best Buy —*P.G.* (2/1/2004)

Rex Hill 2000 Pinot Gris (Willamette Valley) $14. 83 —*S.H.* (8/1/2002)

Rex Hill 1999 Pinot Gris (Willamette Valley) $14. 84 —*S.H.* (8/1/2002)

Rex Hill 2003 Carabella Vineyard Pinot Gris (Willamette Valley) $24. 91 —*P.G.* (8/1/2005)

Rex Hill 2002 Carabella Vineyard Pinot Gris (Oregon) $28. 90 —*P.G.* (2/1/2004)

Rex Hill 2001 Carabella Vineyard Pinot Gris (Oregon) $24. 89 —*S.H.* (12/31/2002)

Rex Hill 2003 Jacob-Hart Vineyard Pinot Gris (Willamette Valley) $24. 88 —*P.G.* (8/1/2005)

Rex Hill 2002 Jacob-Hart Vineyard Pinot Gris (Oregon) $28. 89 —*P.G.* (2/1/2004)

Rex Hill 1999 Jacob-Hart Vineyard Reserve Pinot Gris (Oregon) $18. 88 —*S.H.* (8/1/2002)

Rex Hill 2005 Reserve Pinot Gris (Oregon) $24. 90 —*P.G.* (12/1/2006)

Rex Hill 2003 Reserve Pinot Gris (Willamette Valley) $21. 87 —*P.G.* (8/1/2005)

Rex Hill 2002 Reserve Pinot Gris (Oregon) $21. 89 —*P.G.* (2/1/2004)

Rex Hill 2001 Reserve Pinot Gris (Oregon) $18. 89 —*S.H.* (12/31/2002)

Rex Hill 2000 Reserve Pinot Gris (Oregon) $18. 90 —*S.H.* (8/1/2002)

Rex Hill 1997 Pinot Noir (Willamette Valley) $18. 87 —*P.G.* (9/1/2000)

Rex Hill 2002 Pinot Noir (Willamette Valley) $24. 84 (11/1/2004)

Rex Hill 2001 Pinot Noir (Willamette Valley) $24. 89 Editors' Choice —*P.G.* (2/1/2004)

Rex Hill 1999 Pinot Noir (Willamette Valley) $24. 85 —*S.H.* (8/1/2002)

Rex Hill 2002 Anden Vineyard Pinot Noir (Oregon) $52. 86 (11/1/2004)

Rex Hill 2003 Carabella Vineyard Pinot Noir (Willamette Valley) $49. 92 —*P.G.* (5/1/2006)

Rex Hill 2002 Carabella Vineyard Pinot Noir (Oregon) $52. 90 (11/1/2004)

Rex Hill 2001 Carabella Vineyard Pinot Noir (Oregon) $52. 89 —*P.G.* (2/1/2004)

Rex Hill 2003 Chehalem Mountains Cuvée Pinot Noir (Willamette Valley) $28. 87 —*P.G.* (5/1/2006)

Rex Hill 2001 Dundee Hills Cuvée Pinot Noir (Oregon) $30. 86 —*P.G.* (2/1/2004)

Rex Hill 2004 Dundee Hills Cuvée Pinot Noir (Dundee Hills) $32. 90 —*P.G.* (12/1/2006)

Rex Hill 2003 Dundee Hills Cuvée Pinot Noir (Dundee Hills) $28. 90 Editors' Choice —*P.G.* (5/1/2006)

Rex Hill 2002 Dundee Hills Cuvée Pinot Noir (Oregon) $29. 89 (11/1/2004)

Rex Hill 2002 Jacob-Hart Vineyard Pinot Noir (Oregon) $52. 84 (11/1/2004)

Rex Hill 2004 Jacob-Hart Vineyard Pinot Noir (Oregon) $49. 92 —*P.G.* (12/1/2006)

Rex Hill 2003 Jacob-Hart Vineyard Pinot Noir (Willamette Valley) $49. 89 —*P.G.* (5/1/2006)

Rex Hill 2001 Jacob-Hart Vineyard Pinot Noir (Oregon) $52. 88 —*P.G.* (2/1/2005)

Rex Hill 1999 Jacob-Hart Vineyard Pinot Noir (Oregon) $52. 90 —*P.G.* (4/1/2002)

Rex Hill 2001 Kings Ridge Pinot Noir (Oregon) $17. 87 *—P.G. (2/1/2005)*

Rex Hill 2004 Maresh Vineyard Pinot Noir (Oregon) $49. 94 *—P.G. (12/1/2006)*

Rex Hill 2003 Maresh Vineyard Pinot Noir (Dundee Hills) $49. 91 *—P.G. (5/1/2006)*

Rex Hill 2002 Maresh Vineyard Pinot Noir (Oregon) $52. 85 *(11/1/2004)*

Rex Hill 2001 Maresh Vineyard Pinot Noir (Oregon) $52. 91 *—P.G. (2/1/2005)*

Rex Hill 1999 Maresh Vineyard Pinot Noir (Oregon) $52. 91 *—P.G. (4/1/2002)*

Rex Hill 2004 Maresh Vineyard Loie's Block Pinot Noir (Oregon) $75. 94 Cellar Selection *—P.G. (12/1/2006)*

Rex Hill 2001 Maresh Vineyard Loie's Block Pinot Noir (Oregon) $75. 90 *—P.G. (2/1/2005)*

Rex Hill 2002 Maresh Vineyard Loie's Block Pinot Noir (Oregon) $75. 90 *(11/1/2004)*

Rex Hill 2001 Melrose Vineyard Pinot Noir (Oregon) $49. 88 *—P.G. (2/1/2005)*

Rex Hill 2000 Melrose Vineyard Pinot Noir (Oregon) $52. 90 *—S.H. (12/31/2002)*

Rex Hill 2004 Reserve Pinot Noir (Oregon) $39. 89 *—P.G. (12/1/2006)*

Rex Hill 2003 Reserve Pinot Noir (Oregon) $39. 88 *—P.G. (5/1/2006)*

Rex Hill 2002 Reserve Pinot Noir (Oregon) $45. 89 *(11/1/2004)*

Rex Hill 2001 Reserve Pinot Noir (Oregon) $45. 90 *—P.G. (2/1/2005)*

Rex Hill 2000 Reserve Pinot Noir (Oregon) $48. 87 *—P.G. (2/1/2004)*

Rex Hill 1999 Reserve Pinot Noir (Oregon) $48. 94 Cellar Selection *—P.G. (4/1/2002)*

Rex Hill 1997 Reserve Pinot Noir (Willamette Valley) $45. 83 *(11/15/1999)*

Rex Hill 2000 Rex Hill Estate Pinot Noir (Oregon) $52. 88 *—S.H. (12/31/2002)*

Rex Hill 2004 Seven Springs Vineyard Pinot Noir (Oregon) $49. 92 *—P.G. (12/1/2006)*

Rex Hill 2003 Seven Springs Vineyard Pinot Noir (Willamette Valley) $49. 88 *—P.G. (5/1/2006)*

Rex Hill 2001 Seven Springs Vineyard Pinot Noir (Oregon) $49. 87 *—P.G. (2/1/2005)*

Rex Hill 2001 Southern Oregon Cuvée Pinot Noir (Oregon) $30. 86 *—P.G. (2/1/2004)*

Rex Hill 2003 Southern Oregon Cuvée Pinot Noir (Southern Oregon) $28. 88 *—P.G. (5/1/2006)*

Rex Hill 2002 Southern Oregon Cuvée Pinot Noir (Oregon) $29. 88 *(11/1/2004)*

Rex Hill 2000 Weber Vineyard Pinot Noir (Oregon) $52. 91 *—S.H. (12/31/2002)*

Rex Hill 2001 Weber Vineyards Pinot Noir (Oregon) $49. 88 *—P.G. (2/1/2005)*

Rex Hill 1999 Weber Vineyards Pinot Noir (Oregon) $52. 89 *—P.G. (4/1/2002)*

Rex Hill 2002 Sauvignon Blanc (Oregon) $15. 89 *—P.G. (2/1/2005)*

Rex Hill 2001 Sauvignon Blanc (Willamette Valley) $14. 87 *—P.G. (2/1/2004)*

Rex Hill 2000 Sauvignon Blanc (Willamette Valley) $12. 88 *—S.H. (12/31/2002)*

REY SOL

Rey Sol 1999 Barbera (South Coast) $15. 90 *—S.H. (4/1/2002)*

Rey Sol 1999 Syrah (South Coast) $18. 86 *—S.H. (4/1/2002)*

REYNOLDS

Reynolds 2002 Estate Cabernet Sauvignon (Napa Valley) $45. 89 *—S.H. (11/15/2005)*

Reynolds 2002 Reserve Cabernet Sauvignon (Stags Leap District) $89. 91 Cellar Selection *—S.H. (11/15/2005)*

Reynolds 2003 Chardonnay (Carneros) $30. 87 *—S.H. (11/15/2005)*

Reynolds 2003 Pinot Noir (Russian River Valley) $45. 86 *—S.H. (11/15/2005)*

REYNOLDS FAMILY WINERY

Reynolds Family Winery 2000 Estate Select Cabernet Sauvignon (Napa Valley) $45. 90 *—S.H. (11/15/2003)*

Reynolds Family Winery 2003 Reserve Cabernet Sauvignon (Stags Leap District) $89. Very fine Cab, young and tight in tannins now, but enormously promising. All the parts have yet to come together, but each part is really good. The flavors are ripe and delicious in cassis, blackberries, cherries, cedar, pencil lead and minerals. The tannins are thick and sweet. Acidity is as fine as Stags Leap gets, and the oak is lavish but tasteful. All it needs is time. Best 2008–2012. **93** *—S.H. (10/1/2007)*

Reynolds Family Winery 2001 Reserve Cabernet Sauvignon (Stags Leap District) $85. 91 *—J.C. (10/1/2004)*

Reynolds Family Winery 2000 Reserve Cabernet Sauvignon (Stags Leap District) $78. 89 *—S.H. (11/15/2003)*

Reynolds Family Winery 2002 Pinot Noir (Russian River Valley) $45. 82 *(11/1/2004)*

Reynolds Family Winery 2002 Pinot Noir (Carneros) $45. 85 *(11/1/2004)*

Reynolds Family Winery 2002 Persistence Red Blend (Napa Valley) $50. 87 *—S.H. (11/15/2005)*

REZONJA

Rezonja 2003 Sky Pine Vineyards Cabernet Sauvignon (Alexander Valley) $32. This is one that needs some age. It shows Alexander's Valley's dry, soft herbal quality, a dusty sweet thyme and sage note to the cherries that's so opposite to Napa's chocolaty opulence, but no less complex. Best now through 2010. **88** *—S.H. (2/1/2007)*

RHR

RHR 2004 Cabernet Sauvignon (Paso Robles) $29. 85 *—S.H. (12/31/2006)*

RHR 2003 Old Bailey Vineyard Cabernet Sauvignon (Paso Robles) $40. 88 *—S.H. (12/31/2006)*

RHR 2004 Pinot Noir (Paso Robles) $28. 87 *—S.H. (12/31/2006)*

RHR 2003 Zinfandel (Paso Robles) $27. 87 *—S.H. (12/31/2006)*

RIBBON RIDGE

Ribbon Ridge 2005 Dewey Kelly Early Muscat (Rogue Valley) $18. From 30-year-old vines, pressed whole cluster and stainless steel fermented. Spritzy and sweet, it smells and tastes quite like orange Pekoe tea, generously infused with sugar. Too sweet, but not enough for dessert, and spritzy but not really frizzante—what exactly do you do with this wine? The winery suggests trying Early Muscat zabaglione, or serve it with lavender butter cookies. **86** *—P.G. (4/1/2007)*

Ribbon Ridge 2004 Pinot Noir (Ribbon Ridge) $32. Ribbon Ridge is the name of the winery, the vineyard and the AVA—one of a half dozen new sub-appellations recently defined in the Willamette Valley. The vineyard was recently planted (1991) but is already delivering thrilling fruit, scented with cherry liqueur, cola syrup, vanilla bean and cocoa. I love the intensity and focus, which conserves the fruit character and does not become heavy or thick. Beautifully structured with acid, spice, confectionery notes and a long, silky finish. **91** *—P.G. (4/1/2007)*

Ribbon Ridge 2005 Dewey Kelly Cuvée M White Blend (Willamette Valley) $20. This fascinating white is two thirds Chardonnay, but the rest is a beguiling blend of Pinot Blanc, Auxerois, Ehrenfelser, Scheurebe, Sylvaner and Ruhlander! Turns out the Alsatian vines were planted by the previous owner 20 years ago as personal vines for his own use. The wine is quite Euro in style, with a tangy, peppery flavor reminiscent of Grüner Veltliner. But along with the spice is some juicy, succulent green and yellow citrus fruit, with persistence and thrilling intensity. **90 Editors' Choice** *—P.G. (4/1/2007)*

RIBOLI

Riboli 2003 Cabernet Sauvignon (Rutherford) $40. L.A.-based Riboli makes Central Coast wines under various labels, reserving the family name for this bottling. It shows a good structure encasing well-oaked currant, herb tapenade and anise flavors, and finishes smooth and dry. **88** *—S.H. (11/1/2007)*

Riboli 2001 Cabernet Sauvignon (Rutherford) $40. 90 *—S.H. (10/1/2004)*

Riboli 1997 Cabernet Sauvignon (Rutherford) $45. 81 *—J.M. (12/1/20010*

RICHARDSON

Richardson 2000 Sangiacomo Vineyard Pinot Noir (Carneros) $16. 88 Best Buy *—S.H. (11/15/2002)*

RIDEAU

Rideau 2004 Reserve Chardonnay (Santa Barbara County) $38. Decent everyday Chard, a little soft and flabby, but with ripe peach, pineapple and apricot flavors. Loses a few points for a stewed fruit quality and oak that's too heavy for what you get. **83** *—S.H. (5/1/2007)*

Rideau 2003 Reserve Chardonnay (Santa Barbara County) $48. 87 *—S.H. (12/31/2005)*

Rideau 2002 Las Presa Vineyards Petite Sirah (Santa Ynez Valley) $52. 90

—*S.H. (12/31/2005)*

Rideau 2004 In-Circle Cellar Club Le Fleur de Lis Rose Pinot Noir (Santa Barbara County) $22. 83 —*S.H. (12/31/2005)*

Rideau 2005 Rancho Santa Rosa Clone 115 Pinot Noir (Santa Rita Hills) $42. Rideau has crafted a very fine Pinot Noir. Bright and polished in cherry, raspberry and spice flavors, it has a darker, earthier note of carob and plum skin tannins. Really impressive; a complex, layered wine. 92 —*S.H. (4/1/2007)*

Rideau 2004 Sanford & Benedict Vineyard Pinot Noir (Santa Rita Hills) $52. 82 —*S.H. (10/1/2006)*

Rideau 2004 Chateau Duplantier Cuvee Red Wine Rhône Red Blend (Santa Barbara County) $52. This Rhône blend of Syrah, Grenache and Mourvèdre is soft and simple, but fans of pure taste will like it for its rich cassis, blackberry and milk chocolate flavors. The lucious tannins are very firm; dusty but sweetly ripe. 85 —*S.H. (6/1/2007)*

Rideau 2003 Château Duplantier Cuvée Red Wine Rhône Red Blend (California) $39. 87 —*S.H. (12/31/2005)*

Rideau 2005 In-Circle Cellar Clujb Fleur Blanche White Wine Rhône White Blend (California) $28. Look at that alcohol, 15.7%. Pretty high. But the heat shows up as a paprika sprinkle to butterscotch and vanilla custard, and the wine actually feels cool and creamy in the mouth. Mainly Viognier, with Roussanne, it's a rich, flamboyantly tropical wine. 88 —*S.H. (5/1/2007)*

Rideau 2006 Riesling (Santa Barbara County) $25. Simple, frankly sweet and way too soft, this tastes like sugared apricot and peach syrup. Would be an interesting wine with a lot more acidity. 82 —*S.H. (9/1/2007)*

Rideau 2004 Riesling (Santa Barbara County) $22. 85 —*S.H. (12/31/2005)*

Rideau 2005 In-Circle Cellar Club Iris Estate Roussanne (Santa Ynez Valley) $48. Heavy, earthy and dull. While there's some decent peaches and cream and honeysuckle flavor, the wine lacks acidity, which makes it flat and charmless. 82 —*S.H. (5/1/2007)*

Rideau 2004 In-Circle Cellar Club Roussanne (Santa Barbara County) $48. 88 —*S.H. (12/31/2005)*

Rideau 2003 Sangiovese (Central Coast) $28. 88 —*S.H. (12/31/2005)*

Rideau 2005 Estate Syrah Rose Syrah (Santa Ynez Valley) $29. Almost as dark and full-bodied as a red wine, this Syrah is also heavy in its texture, with a dull, soft flatness. 82 —*S.H. (5/1/2007)*

Rideau 2004 In-Circle Cellar Club Iris Estate Syrah (Santa Barbara County) $48. This is a smooth, soft and rich Syrah, bursting with intensely ripe blackberry, cherry and cassis flavors that approach chocolate truffles. It's not showing much finesse or complexity, but it's dry. Be warned: The alcohol is a ridiculous 16.8%. 84 —*S.H. (6/1/2007)*

Rideau 2003 In-Circle Cellar Club Iris' Estate Bon Temps Vineyard Syrah (Santa Ynez Valley) $55. 83 *(9/1/2005)*

Rideau 2004 Iris Estate Syrah (Santa Ynez Valley) $58. If anything, this wine is even sweeter and more chocolaty than Rideau's regular Syrah, and that seems to be the point from this winery that likes ripeness to the point of dessert. Soft and gentle, it's easy to drink, with the flashy opulence of one of those cherry liqueur-filled chocolate candies. 86 —*S.H. (6/1/2007)*

Rideau 2003 Iris' Estate Bon Temps Vineyard Syrah (Santa Ynez Valley) $55. 87 *(9/1/2005)*

Rideau 2004 Viognier (Santa Barbara County) $35. 87 —*S.H. (12/31/2005)*

Rideau 2005 In-Circle Cellar Club Estate Viognier (Santa Ynez Valley) $46. Santa Ynez Valley has proven to be a good place to grow Viognier. It's warmish-cool, so the wine gets nice and ripe while preserving vital acidity. This polished wine comes down on the variety's flamboyant side, with lush tropical fruit, honeysuckle and vanilla wafer flavors. 87 —*S.H. (5/1/2007)*

Rideau 2004 Iris Estate Viognier (Santa Ynez Valley) $48. 90 —*S.H. (12/31/2005)*

Rideau 2004 Fleur Blanche White Blend (California) $28. 84 —*S.H. (12/31/2005)*

RIDGE

Ridge 2001 Home Ranch Cabernet Sauvignon-Merlot (Santa Cruz Mountains) $60. 93 Cellar Selection —*S.H. (2/1/2005)*

Ridge 1996 Oat Valley Carignan (Sonoma Valley) $18. 88 —*S.H. (10/1/1999)*

Ridge 1997 Chardonnay (Santa Cruz Mountains) $28. 89 *(6/1/2000)*

Ridge 2001 Chardonnay (Santa Cruz Mountains) $30. 94 —*S.H. (12/15/2004)*

Ridge 1997 Chardonnay (California) $17. 93 —*M.S. (10/1/1999)*

Ridge 2002 Home Ranch Chardonnay (Santa Cruz Mountains) $40. 93 —*S.H. (4/1/2005)*

Ridge 1996 York Creek Petite Sirah (Spring Mountain) $20. 88 —*J.C. (11/1/1999)*

Ridge 2002 Geyserville Red Blend (Sonoma County) $30. 87 —*S.H. (4/1/2005)*

Ridge 1999 Geyserville Red Blend (Sonoma County) $30. 90 —*D.T. (3/1/2002)*

Ridge 1999 Lytton Springs Red Blend (Sonoma County) $30. 91 —*D.T. (3/1/2002)*

Ridge 2001 Monte Bello Red Blend (Santa Cruz Mountains) $120. 97 Cellar Selection —*S.H. (4/1/2005)*

Ridge 1999 Lytton Estate Syrah (Dry Creek Valley) $30. 90 Editors' Choice *(11/1/2001)*

Ridge 1997 Lytton Estate Syrah (Dry Creek Valley) $28. 89 —*S.H. (10/1/1999)*

Ridge 2003 Lytton West Syrah (Dry Creek Valley) $35. 85 *(9/1/2005)*

Ridge 2001 Zinfandel (Paso Robles) $25. 88 *(11/1/2003)*

Ridge 2001 Dusi Ranch Zinfandel (Paso Robles) $22. 89 *(11/1/2003)*

Ridge 1997 Dusi Ranch-Late Picked Zinfandel (Paso Robles) $22. 91 —*J.C. (9/1/1999)*

Ridge 2001 Geyserville Zinfandel (Sonoma County) $30. 89 *(11/1/2003)*

Ridge 1998 Geyserville Zinfandel (Sonoma County) $30. 90 —*P.G. (3/1/2001)*

Ridge 2002 Late Picked Pagani Ranch Zinfandel (Sonoma Valley) $30. 85 —*S.H. (4/1/2005)*

Ridge 2001 Llewelyn Zinfandel (Sonoma County) $22. 90 Editors' Choice *(11/1/2003)*

Ridge 2001 Lytton Springs Zinfandel (Dry Creek Valley) $30. 91 *(11/1/2003)*

Ridge 2000 Lytton Springs Zinfandel (California) $30. 93 —*S.H. (9/1/2002)*

Ridge 1998 Lytton Springs Zinfandel (Dry Creek Valley) $28. 92 —*P.G. (3/1/2001)*

Ridge 1997 Lytton Springs Zinfandel (Dry Creek Valley) $28. 93 —*J.C. (9/1/1999)*

Ridge 1997 Pagani Ranch Zinfandel (California) $28. 92 —*S.H. (2/1/2000)*

Ridge 2001 Sonoma Station Zinfandel (Sonoma County) $18. 88 *(11/1/2003)*

Ridge 1997 Sonoma Station Zinfandel (Sonoma) $18. 88 —*J.C. (9/1/1999)*

Ridge 2002 Spring Mountain District Zinfandel (Napa Valley) $24. 89 —*S.H. (4/1/2005)*

RIDGEFIELD

Ridgefield 2003 Cinnamon Teal Red Cabernet Blend (Columbia Valley (WA)) $10. 86 Best Buy —*P.G. (4/1/2005)*

Ridgefield 2002 Pinot Gris (Red Mountain) $9. 88 Best Buy —*P.G. (9/1/2004)*

RIDGELINE

Ridgeline 2002 Cabernet Sauvignon (Alexander Valley) $40. 85 —*S.H. (12/31/2006)*

RIO DULCE

Rio Dulce NV Sweet Red Wine Red Blend (California) $4. 85 Best Buy —*S.H. (12/31/2004)*

Rio Dulce NV White Red Wine Rosé Blend (California) $4. 84 Best Buy —*S.H. (12/31/2004)*

RIO SECO

Rio Seco 1999 Rio Seco Cabernet Franc (Paso Robles) $24. 85 —*S.H. (12/1/2002)*

Rio Seco 1999 Rio Seco Vineyard Syrah (Paso Robles) $16. 83 —*S.H. (12/1/2002)*

Rio Seco 2001 Zinfandel (Paso Robles) $24. 84 *(11/1/2003)*

Rio Seco 1999 Rio Seco Vineyard Zinfandel (Paso Robles) $24. 82 —*S.H. (11/1/2002)*

RIOS-LOVELL ESTATE WINERY

Rios-Lovell Estate Winery 2000 Cabernet Sauvignon (Livermore Valley) $22. 84 —*S.H. (11/15/2003)*

Rios-Lovell Estate Winery 2000 Petite Sirah (Livermore Valley) $22. 82 —*S.H. (3/1/2004)*

RISTOW ESTATE

Ristow Estate 2003 Quinta de Pedras Vineyard Cabernet Sauvignon (Napa Valley) $59. Smells and tastes a bit baked, with caramelized cherry and blackberry pie filling flavors. Not going anywhere. **84** *—S.H. (10/1/2007)*

Ristow Estate 2002 Quinta de Pedras Vineyard Cabernet Sauvignon (Napa Valley) $64. 93 Cellar Selection *—S.H. (12/15/2005)*

Ristow Estate 2001 Quinta de Pedras Vineyard Cabernet Sauvignon (Napa Valley) $64. 93 *—S.H. (12/31/2005)*

Ristow Estate 1999 Quinta de Pedras Vineyard Cabernet Sauvignon (Napa Valley) $59. 94 *—C.S. (11/15/2002)*

RITCHIE CREEK

Ritchie Creek 1999 Cabernet Sauvignon (Spring Mountain) $58. 87 *—S.H. (11/15/2002)*

Ritchie Creek 2000 Chardonnay (Spring Mountain) $28. 83 *—S.H. (12/15/2002)*

RIVER ROAD VINEYARDS

River Road Vineyards 2004 Hopkins Vineyard Chardonnay (Russian River Valley) $17. 86 *—S.H. (5/1/2006)*

River Road Vineyards 2004 Mills Vineyard Chardonnay (Russian River Valley) $20. 86 *—S.H. (5/1/2006)*

River Road Vineyards 2001 Proprietors Reserve Chardonnay (Russian River Valley) $14. 85 *—S.H. (6/1/2003)*

River Road Vineyards 2001 Pinot Noir (Russian River Valley) $14. 87 *—S.H. (7/1/2003)*

River Road Vineyards 2004 Stephanie's Vineyard Pinot Noir (Russian River Valley) $21. 87 *—S.H. (12/1/2006)*

RIVER'S EDGE

River's Edge 2002 Pinot Noir (Umpqua Valley) $16. 85 *(11/1/2004)*

River's Edge 2000 Pinot Noir (Umpqua Valley) $16. 85 *—P.G. (12/31/2002)*

River's Edge 2002 Barrel Select Pinot Noir (Umpqua Valley) $21. 85 *(11/1/2004)*

River's Edge 2000 Black Oak Vineyard Pinot Noir (Umpqua Valley) $30. 91 *—P.G. (12/31/2002)*

River's Edge 2002 Bradley Vineyard Pinot Noir (Umpqua Valley) $18. 86 *(11/1/2004)*

River's Edge 2000 Bradley Vineyard Pinot Noir (Umpqua Valley) $16. 87 *—P.G. (12/31/2002)*

River's Edge 2000 Elkton Vineyard Pinot Noir (Umpqua Valley) $19. 87 *—P.G. (12/31/2002)*

RIVER STAR

River Star 2004 Cabernet Sauvignon (Paso Robles) $33. Nice structure on this dry, smooth Cab, which is made in the modern cult style of soft, immediate likeability. The blackberry, cassis, cherry and oak flavors are appealing. But at this price, you have a right to demand more depth and complexity. **86** *—S.H. (12/15/2007)*

River Star 2004 Merlot (Paso Robles) $25. I like this Merlot for its plush fruit and soft balance. It's bigtime in chocolate-infused blackberries, plums and cherries, with more exotic notes of Asian spices. Yet the finish is totally dry, and the tannins are rich and ripe. Seems at its best now. **87** *—S.H. (12/15/2007)*

River Star 2004 Syrah (Paso Robles) $30. The dryness hits you first, then the tannins. This is a Syrah that's hard and astringent, almost aggressive. But then the core of blackberries and cherries kicks in, turning spicy and licorice-like on the finish. Suddenly, the wine is interesting. One to watch, if the winemaker can manage those bigtime tannins. **87** *—S.H. (12/15/2007)*

River Star 2003 Syrah (Paso Robles) $24. Young and tannic, with some acidic harshess to the cherry-berry flavors that's unlikely to age out. Drink now, with rich, fatty foods. **83** *—S.H. (4/1/2007)*

RIVERAERIE

RiverAerie 2005 Barbera (Columbia Valley (WA)) $15. Tart and juicy, clean and fresh, with snappy flavors of raspberry and cherry over bright acids. This would make a great picnic wine; it's just like chomping on a big mouthful of fresh-picked raspberries. **87** *—P.G. (11/1/2007)*

RiverAerie 2006 Chardonnay (Columbia Valley (WA)) $10. Another wine done in a fresh, spicy, bright style. Apple and light cinnamon, crisp and clean, make this perfect for summer sipping. **87** *—P.G. (11/1/2007)*

RiverAerie 2005 Malbec (Columbia Valley (WA)) $18. Unusually spicy, purple-toned and lightly herbal, this pure Malbec is not a big, dark, super-tannic wine, but rather a fruit-forward picnic red with a bit of herbal muscle. In the back of the finish you taste some bacon fat and smoked meat. It's well done and interesting, but not quite up to Argentine quality. **88** *—P.G. (11/1/2007)*

RiverAerie 2006 Pinot Gris (Columbia Valley (WA)) $12. From the excellent Evergreen vineyard, this is a soft, appealing mix of melon and apple flavors. A little tight at the moment, but fresh and creamy. **87 Best Buy** *—P.G. (11/1/2007)*

RiverAerie 2005 Fête Red Blend (Columbia Valley (WA)) $20. This blend of 70% Cabernet, 25% Merlot and 5% Petit Verdot is substantial, with more concentration and mass than the other RiverAerie reds. There's a stiff spine and well-built tannins to support tart red fruit. **87** *—P.G. (11/1/2007)*

RiverAerie 2005 Sangiovese (Columbia Valley (WA)) $15. From a 10-year-old Wahluke Slope vineyard comes this impressive Sangio. The blend includes 10% Cabernet Sauvignon. Tasted along with a Sangiovese selling for almost four times the price, it stood up quite well. The wine is a beautiful plummy color, fragrant and fruity, lovely in the mouth, tasting of fresh plums and strawberries. There is good concentration and a tangy snap to the finish. **88** *—P.G. (11/1/2007)*

RiverAerie 2006 Viognier (Columbia Valley (WA)) $15. Liveliest of all the RiverAerie whites, this has been made to maximize the freshness and cleansing acidity. It's crispy crunchy, limned with lime and finishes with wet stone. **88** *—P.G. (11/1/2007)*

RIVERBEND

Riverbend 2001 Coquette White Blend (Humboldt County) $NA. 81 *—S.H. (12/31/2004)*

RIVERSIDE

Riverside 2002 Cabernet Sauvignon (California) $8. 81 *—S.H. (12/15/2005)*

Riverside 2004 Chardonnay (California) $8. 84 Best Buy *—S.H. (12/15/2005)*

Riverside 1997 Syrah (California) $8. 83 *(10/1/2001)*

Riverside NV White Zinfandel (California) $6. 82 *—S.H. (12/15/2005)*

Riverside NV White Zinfandel (California) $6. 83 *—S.H. (10/1/2004)*

Riverside 2004 White Zinfandel (California) $6. 84 Best Buy *—S.H. (12/1/2006)*

RN ESTATE

RN Estate 2004 Cuvee de Trois Cepages Bordeaux Blend (Paso Robles) $35. A Bordeaux blend, this wine shows the softness and ripeness that Paso succeeds at so well with Cabernet and Merlot. It's classic eastside, and in this warm vintage the flavors run toward blackberry marmalade, red cherry jam, milk chocolate, gingerbread and spiced rum. Just delicious. **89** *—S.H. (6/1/2007)*

RN Estate 2004 Westside Cuvee Bordeaux Blend (Paso Robles) $35. A blend of all five Bordeaux varieties, this is an enormously ripe wine, bursting with plum, coffee and cherry-berry flavors that taste well-oaked. It has a rough, sandpapery feeling in the mouth, with a dry, peppery finish. **86** *—S.H. (6/1/2007)*

RN Estate 2004 Cuvee des Artistes Red Blend (Paso Robles) $35. A Syrah-based blend of the two Cabs with Zinfandel, this is a fairly rough-edged, very ripe wine. It's upfront in cherry-berry, cola, leather, chocolate and spice flavors, and finishes dry and tannic. **87** *—S.H. (6/1/2007)*

RN Estate 2003 Syrah Mourvedre Rhône Red Blend (Paso Robles) $35. No fancy name for this two-grape blend, and it's not a fancy wine, either. Direct in berry, earthy coffee, dark bitter chocolate and peppery spice flavors, it's bone dry and tannic. The alcohol is kind of high, and makes for a hot finish, but a good steak will help. **86** *—S.H. (6/1/2007)*

ROANOKE VINEYARDS

Roanoke Vineyards 2003 Blend One Bordeaux Blend (North Fork of Long Island) $30. This 48% Cab Sauvignon, 30% Merlot and 22% Cab Franc blend is an appealing combination of blackberry, spicy pepper and flowers. A touch of oak and a good finish seal the deal. **84** *—S.K. (10/1/2007)*

Roanoke Vineyards 2003 Blend Two Bordeaux Blend (North Fork of Long Island) $36. Lively and bright with vanilla, spice and tart cherries. It's a little spicy and angular for everyday palates, but pair it with a beef stew or grilled steak and it will make a nice addition to the table. **82** *—S.K. (10/1/2007)*

Roanoke Vineyards 2000 Merlot (North Fork of Long Island) $38. Sturdy notes of roasted meat, spice and cherry greet here and lead into a medium-bodied wine that is sure to pair well with roasted game and fowl. There's a little roughness on the palate but the flavors are pleasant—lush berry, mint, pepper—and there's complexity, too. **85** *—S.K. (2/1/2007)*

ROAR

Roar 2003 Pinot Noir (Santa Lucia Highlands) $31. 87 *—S.H. (5/1/2005)*

Roar 2002 Pinot Noir (Santa Lucia Highlands) $31. 86 *(11/1/2004)*

Roar 2001 Pinot Noir (Santa Lucia Highlands) $31. 90 *—S.H. (7/1/2003)*

Roar 2005 Garys' Vineyard Pinot Noir (Santa Lucia Highlands) $50. Delicious in raspberries, cherries, sassafras, cola, orange blossom tea and vanilla, with a beautifully silky texture, this single-vineyard Pinot comes from low-yielding vines in the central part of the appellation. It's a little too soft for cellaring, but offers solid pleasure now. 87 *—S.H. (12/31/2007)*

Roar 2003 Garys Vineyard Pinot Noir (Santa Lucia Highlands) $44. 90 *—S.H. (3/1/2006)*

Roar 2005 Pisoni Vineyard Pinot Noir (Santa Lucia Highlands) $55. This Pinot is pretty extracted, but the flavors are addictively good, offering a cornucopia of raspberries, cherries, blackberries, tangerines and cola, with complex nuances of sassafras, orange Pekoe tea, cola and dusty spices. It's a little soft, but silky and rich in tannins, a classic Pisoni Vineyard Pinot Noir. 91 *—S.H. (12/31/2007)*

Roar 2002 Pisoni Vineyard Pinot Noir (Santa Lucia Highlands) $48. 87 *—S.H. (11/1/2004)*

Roar 2003 Rosella's Vineyard Pinot Noir (Santa Lucia Highlands) $44. 92 *—S.H. (5/1/2005)*

Roar 2002 Rosella's Vineyard Pinot Noir (Santa Lucia Highlands) $44. 88 *(11/1/2004)*

Roar 2001 Rosella's Vineyard Pinot Noir (Santa Lucia Highlands) $44. 93 *—S.H. (7/1/2003)*

Roar 2003 Syrah (Santa Lucia Highlands) $32. 83 *(9/1/2005)*

ROBERT CRAIG

Robert Craig 1999 Affinity Bordeaux Blend (Napa Valley) $48. 90 *(6/1/2002)*

Robert Craig 1997 Affinity Bordeaux Blend (Napa Valley) $44. 92 *(11/1/2000)*

Robert Craig 2002 Affinity Cabernet Blend (Napa Valley) $40. 88 *—S.H. (10/1/2005)*

Robert Craig 1997 Cabernet Sauvignon (Mount Veeder) $44. 91 *(11/1/2000)*

Robert Craig 2004 Cabernet Sauvignon (Mount Veeder) $70. This is a very lush Cab, made in the modern style. All the elements of cult Cab are there: the soft voluptuousness, the finely ground, sweet tannins, the immensely ripe currant, blackberry and cocoa flavors, the coating of fine, smoky oak. I don't think it's an ager because of the softness and ripeness. 92 *—S.H. (12/1/2007)*

Robert Craig 2004 Cabernet Sauvignon (Howell Mountain) $70. The first two things you notice are how delicious the flavors are and how gentle the tannins are. Blackberries, cherries, raspberries and mulberries mingle with 80% new oak to provide a thrill of a palate experience. As for those tannins, they're as ripe and sweet as a hot vintage and modern viticulture can provide, but this wine should do all sort of interesting things over the next 10 years. 94 *—S.H. (12/31/2007)*

Robert Craig 2003 Cabernet Sauvignon (Mount Veeder) $70. 91 *—S.H. (9/1/2006)*

Robert Craig 2003 Cabernet Sauvignon (Howell Mountain) $70. 91 Cellar Selection *—S.H. (9/1/2006)*

Robert Craig 2002 Cabernet Sauvignon (Howell Mountain) $55. 92 *—S.H. (12/1/2005)*

Robert Craig 2002 Cabernet Sauvignon (Mount Veeder) $55. 91 *—S.H. (12/1/2005)*

Robert Craig 2001 Cabernet Sauvignon (Howell Mountain) $50. 92 *—S.H. (10/1/2004)*

Robert Craig 2001 Cabernet Sauvignon (Mount Veeder) $50. 93 Cellar Selection *—S.H. (10/1/2004)*

Robert Craig 2004 Affinity Cabernet Sauvignon (Napa Valley) $45. Raspingly dry and toughly tannic, and the cherry fruit is something your mouth has to struggle to find under all that astringency. It may do something with age, if you feel like rolling the dice. 84 *—S.H. (7/1/2007)*

Robert Craig 1998 Chardonnay (Carneros) $24. 85 *(6/1/2000)*

Robert Craig 1997 Chardonnay (Carneros) $24. 93 *—M.S. (10/1/1999)*

Robert Craig 2002 Chardonnay (Sonoma County) $24. 86 *—S.H. (3/1/2005)*

Robert Craig 2000 Chardonnay (Russian River Valley) $24. 86 *—S.H. (2/1/2003)*

Robert Craig 2003 Durell Vineyard Chardonnay (Sonoma Valley) $38. 89 *—S.H. (10/1/2005)*

Robert Craig 2004 Syrah (Central Coast) $30. Craig has struggled to move this Paso Robles Syrah off-center and into the end zone for years. The fight continues. The wine is just too soft and simple in structure, although it does show pretty pepper-sprinkled black and blue berries and stone fruits. 85 *—S.H. (12/1/2007)*

Robert Craig 2003 Syrah (Central Coast) $30. Made from cool-climate Santa Barbara fruit and warm Paso Robles, this is an easy-drinking Syrah, with some real flair. It's soft and gentle in texture, with a complex and satisfying range of cherry, blackberry jam, dark chocolate, coffee, licorice and spice flavors that finish just a little sweet. 87 *—S.H. (6/1/2007)*

Robert Craig 2002 Syrah (Central Coast) $28. 86 *(9/1/2005)*

Robert Craig 1999 Syrah (Paso Robles) $28. 86 *(11/1/2001)*

Robert Craig 1997 Syrah (Paso Robles) $24. 86 *(3/1/2000)*

Robert Craig 1998 Zinfandel (Amador County) $24. 88 *(3/1/2001)*

ROBERT FOLEY

Robert Foley 2003 Claret Cabernet Blend (Napa Valley) $110. 96 *—S.H. (9/1/2006)*

Robert Foley 2004 Charbono (Napa Valley) $35. 91 Cellar Selection *—S.H. (12/1/2006)*

Robert Foley 2003 Petite Sirah (Napa Valley) $50. 92 Cellar Selection *—S.H. (11/1/2006)*

ROBERT HALL

Robert Hall 2005 Cabernet Sauvignon (Paso Robles) $19. Soft, dry and thin in flavor, except for a splash of cherries and blackberries that disappears rapidly on the finish. 83 *—S.H. (9/1/2007)*

Robert Hall 2004 Cabernet Sauvignon (Paso Robles) $18. 84 *—S.H. (12/1/2006)*

Robert Hall 2003 Cabernet Sauvignon (Paso Robles) $18. 84 *—S.H. (11/1/2005)*

Robert Hall 2000 Cabernet Sauvignon (Paso Robles) $18. 84 *—S.H. (11/15/2002)*

Robert Hall 2006 Chardonnay (Paso Robles) $19. Dry and crisp, with peach and citrus flavors and a touch of oak, this wine benefitted from a cool growing season in usually hot Paso Robles. It has the acidity of a true coastal white wine. 84 *—S.H. (12/1/2007)*

Robert Hall 2005 Chardonnay (Paso Robles) $16. 85 *—S.H. (12/1/2006)*

Robert Hall 2004 Chardonnay (Paso Robles) $16. 84 *—S.H. (11/1/2005)*

Robert Hall 2003 Grenache (Paso Robles) $24. 84 *—S.H. (11/1/2005)*

Robert Hall 2004 Hall Ranch Grenache (Paso Robles) $24. 82 *—S.H. (12/1/2006)*

Robert Hall 2004 Hall Ranch Meritage (Paso Robles) $35. Hall struggles with Bordeaux-style wines, and no more so than in this hot vintage. Although the wine is fully dry, it's harsh, with very little fruit, and a hot, tannic finish. 81 *—S.H. (12/1/2007)*

Robert Hall 2003 Hall Ranch Meritage (Paso Robles) $34. 84 *—S.H. (12/31/2005)*

Robert Hall 2005 Merlot (Paso Robles) $19. Soft and harsh, with dry, earthy, berry flavors and an astringent mouthfeel. 82 *—S.H. (9/1/2007)*

Robert Hall 2004 Merlot (Paso Robles) $18. 80 *—S.H. (12/1/2006)*

Robert Hall 2003 Merlot (Paso Robles) $18. 85 *—S.H. (12/31/2005)*

Robert Hall 2002 Merlot (Paso Robles) $18. 84 *—S.H. (11/1/2005)*

Robert Hall 2000 Merlot (Paso Robles) $18. 85 *—S.H. (11/15/2002)*

Robert Hall 2004 Vintage Port Port (Paso Robles) $28. Made from true Port varieties, this is a totally delicious wine, meant to be opened now. It's tremendous in very sweet blackberry jam, cassis, cherry liqueur, chocolate, vanilla cream and cola flavors, with a fabulous Asian spiciness. Brisk acidity makes all this flavor shine through a long finish. This is a good price for a bottle that will stand for a week without deteriorating. 93 Editors' Choice *—S.H. (6/1/2007)*

Robert Hall 2003 Vintage Port (Paso Robles) $28. 84 *—S.H. (6/1/2006)*

Robert Hall 2005 Rhone de Robles Red Wine Rhône Red Blend (Central Coast) $19. A little thin, but pleasant enough, with cherry, raspberry and cocoa flavors and an edge of smoky leather. A Rhône blend of Grenache, Syrah, Cinsault and Counoise, it's dry and balanced. 85 *—S.H. (7/1/2007)*

Robert Hall 2004 Rhône de Robles Rhône Red Blend (Central Coast) $18. 83 *—S.H. (12/31/2006)*

Robert Hall 2003 Rhône de Robles Rhône Red Blend (Paso Robles) $18. 82 *—S.H. (11/1/2005)*

Robert Hall 2006 Blanc de Robles Rhône White Blend (Paso Robles) $20. Hall hits all the right notes with this unusual white Rhône blend of Grenache Blanc, Roussanne and Piquepol Blanc. It's a fascinating wine, dry and crisp, with honeyed flavors of white peach, nectarine and Meyer lemon. Tastes really good and has that all-important extra touch of complexity. 89 *—S.H. (12/1/2007)*

Robert Hall 2005 Blanc de Robles Rhône White Blend (Paso Robles) $24. 86 *—S.H. (12/1/2006)*

Robert Hall 2004 Rose de Robles Rosé Blend (Paso Robles) $14. **85** —*S.H. (10/1/2005)*

Robert Hall 2006 Hall Ranch Rosé de Robles Rosé Blend (Paso Robles) $15. A Rhône blend of Syrah, Grenache, Mourvèdre and Cinsault, this easy wine has watermelon and raspberry-strawberry flavors. It's a bit sweet on the finish. **84** —*S.H. (7/1/2007)*

Robert Hall 2006 Sauvignon Blanc (Paso Robles) $15. Stylishly dry, with acidic citrus, green grapes skin and lime-zest flavors that are zesty on the palate. Its 20% barrel fermentation and sur lie aging provide a touch of vanilla cream and tastebud-stimulating sourness. A wine that will showcase food without overpowering it. **88** —*S.H. (9/1/2007)*

Robert Hall 2005 Sauvignon Blanc (Paso Robles) $14. **85** —*S.H. (6/1/2006)*

Robert Hall 2004 Sauvignon Blanc (Paso Robles) $14. **85** —*S.H. (11/1/2005)*

Robert Hall 2005 Syrah (Paso Robles) $19. The winery does a good job at presenting Syrah made Paso-style, which is to say soft and ripe and pleasant. The '05 shows cherry, blackberry, cassis, coffee and spice flavors, with hints of toasted oak, and the finish is fully dry. **86** —*S.H. (9/1/2007)*

Robert Hall 2004 Syrah (Paso Robles) $18. **87** —*S.H. (12/1/2006)*

Robert Hall 2003 Syrah (Paso Robles) $18. **84** *(9/1/2005)*

Robert Hall 2002 Syrah (Paso Robles) $18. **85** —*S.H. (12/1/2004)*

Robert Hall 2000 Syrah (Paso Robles) $18. **86** —*S.H. (12/1/2002)*

Robert Hall 2001 Hall Ranch Syrah (Paso Robles) $30. **87** —*S.H. (12/1/2004)*

Robert Hall 2003 Hall Ranch Reserve Syrah (Paso Robles) $34. **85** *S.H. (11/15/2006)*

Robert Hall 2002 Hall Ranch Reserve Syrah (Paso Robles) $34. **84** *(9/1/2005)*

Robert Hall 1999 Huerhuero Creek Syrah (Paso Robles) $26. **84** —*S.H. (12/1/2002)*

Robert Hall 2006 Viognier (Paso Robles) $19. Does a nice job of balancing Viognier's exotic personality with the demands of elegance. The flavors are all here, peaches, pears, pineapples, honey and vanilla, among others. But there's a good bite of acidity, and the finish is absolutely dry. **87** —*S.H. (12/1/2007)*

Robert Hall 2005 Viognier (Paso Robles) $18. **84** —*S.H. (11/15/2006)*

Robert Hall 2001 Zinfandel (Paso Robles) $24. **85** *(11/1/2003)*

Robert Hall 2000 Zinfandel (Paso Robles) $22. **87** *S.H. (11/1/2002)*

ROBERT HUNTER

Robert Hunter 1996 Brut de Noirs Champagne Blend (Sonoma Valley) $38. **90** —*S.H. (12/1/2001)*

Robert Hunter 1994 Brut de Noirs Champagne Blend (Sonoma Valley) $30. **88** —*S.H. (12/1/2000)*

Robert Hunter 2003 Pinot Noir (Sonoma Valley) $35. **87** —*S.H. (11/15/2005)*

Robert Hunter 1997 Brut de Noirs Sparkling Blend (Sonoma Valley) $35. **82** —*S.H. (12/31/2005)*

ROBERT KARL

Robert Karl 2002 Claret Bordeaux Blend (Columbia Valley (WA)) $17. **88** —*P.G. (4/1/2006)*

Robert Karl 2001 Claret Bordeaux Blend (Columbia Valley (WA)) $17. **89** —*P.G. (12/1/2004)*

Robert Karl 2003 Inspiration Reserve Red Bordeaux Blend (Columbia Valley (WA)) $45. **93** —*P.G. (11/15/2006)*

Robert Karl 2003 Cabernet Sauvignon (Columbia Valley (WA)) $33. **91** —*P.G. (10/1/2006)*

Robert Karl 2002 Cabernet Sauvignon (Columbia Valley (WA)) $26. **93** —*P.G. (4/1/2006)*

Robert Karl 2000 Cabernet Sauvignon (Columbia Valley (WA)) $20. **87** —*P.G. (12/31/2003)*

Robert Karl 1999 Cabernet Sauvignon (Columbia Valley (WA)) $29. **87** —*P.G. (12/31/2002)*

Robert Karl 2002 Reserve Cabernet Sauvignon (Columbia Valley (WA)) $33. **92** —*P.G. (4/1/2006)*

Robert Karl 2003 Claret Meritage (Columbia Valley (WA)) $19. **90 Editors' Choice** —*P.G. (10/1/2006)*

Robert Karl 2004 Merlot (Columbia Valley (WA)) $24. **90** —*P.G. (10/1/2006)*

Robert Karl 2002 Sauvignon Blanc (Columbia Valley (WA)) $10. **86** —*P.G. (12/31/2003)*

Robert Karl 2004 Syrah (Columbia Valley (WA)) $29. **90** —*P.G. (11/15/2006)*

ROBERT MONDAVI

Robert Mondavi 2005 Vinetta Bordeaux Blend (California) $11. This Cab-based Bordeaux blend is a little raw, but offers good varietal fruit and spice flavors in a dry package. **84** —*S.H. (11/15/2007)*

Robert Mondavi 2004 Cabernet Sauvignon (Oakville) $45. A Robert Mondavi Cab with an Oakville address has always been a guarantee of quality, but we may have to rethink that equation, to judge by this semi-sweet, soft, simple '04. It tastes like something out of Paso Robles, a melted chocolate and cherry confection. **84** —*S.H. (12/1/2007)*

Robert Mondavi 2004 Cabernet Sauvignon (Napa Valley) $27. Inquiring minds have wondered if the buyout of Mondavi by Constellation would result in diminished wines. So far, so good. This basic Cabernet continues Mondavi's tradition, a dry, balanced and elegant wine, much of which is from ToKalon. It's not a blockbuster, but who needs or can afford blockbusters? **87** —*S.H. (2/1/2007)*

Robert Mondavi 2003 Cabernet Sauvignon (Napa Valley) $25. **86** —*S.H. (4/1/2006)*

Robert Mondavi 2003 Cabernet Sauvignon (Oakville) $40. **90** —*S.H. (12/1/2006)*

Robert Mondavi 2002 Cabernet Sauvignon (Oakville) $45. **91 Cellar Selection** —*S.H. (3/1/2006)*

Robert Mondavi 2001 Cabernet Sauvignon (Napa Valley) $25. **89** —*S.H. (10/1/2004)*

Robert Mondavi 2001 Cabernet Sauvignon (Oakville) $40. **93 Editors' Choice** —*S.H. (10/1/2004)*

Robert Mondavi 2001 Cabernet Sauvignon (Napa Valley) $25. **91 Cellar Selection** —*S.H. (11/15/2005)*

Robert Mondavi 2001 Cabernet Sauvignon (Stags Leap District) $40. **92** —*S.H. (10/1/2004)*

Robert Mondavi 2000 Cabernet Sauvignon (Stags Leap District) $50. **89** —*S.H. (11/15/2003)*

Robert Mondavi 2000 Cabernet Sauvignon (Napa Valley) $30. **92 Editors' Choice** —*S.H. (11/15/2003)*

Robert Mondavi 1999 Cabernet Sauvignon (Oakville) $50. **90** —*S.H. (2/1/2003)*

Robert Mondavi 1998 Cabernet Sauvignon (Oakville) $50. **86** —*S.H. (12/1/2001)*

Robert Mondavi 1998 Cabernet Sauvignon (Napa Valley) $35. **85** —*S.H. (12/1/2001)*

Robert Mondavi 1998 Cabernet Sauvignon (Stags Leap District) $50. **91** —*S.H. (12/1/2001)*

Robert Mondavi 1997 Cabernet Sauvignon (Napa Valley) $29. **90** *(11/1/2000)*

Robert Mondavi 1996 Cabernet Sauvignon (Oakville) $45. **91** —*S.H. (11/1/1999)*

Robert Mondavi 1996 Cabernet Sauvignon (Napa Valley) $26. **91** —*L.W. (10/1/1999)*

Robert Mondavi 1996 Cabernet Sauvignon (Stags Leap District) $45. **86** —*S.H. (9/1/1999)*

Robert Mondavi 1996 30th Anniversary Cabernet Sauvignon (Napa Valley) $150. **95** —*S.H. (7/1/2000)*

Robert Mondavi 1996 30th Anniversary To Kalon Cabernet Sauvignon (Napa Valley) $NA. **89 Cellar Selection** —*S.H. (6/1/2005)*

Robert Mondavi 1998 Coastal Cabernet Sauvignon (North Coast) $13. **83** —*S.H. (12/15/2000)*

Robert Mondavi 1997 Coastal Cabernet Sauvignon (North Coast) $13. **86** —*S.H. (2/1/2000)*

Robert Mondavi 2000 Coastal Private Selection Cabernet Sauvignon (Central Coast) $11. **82** —*S.H. (12/31/2002)*

Robert Mondavi 1998 Equilibrium Cabernet Sauvignon (Stags Leap District) $85. **92** —*S.H. (12/1/2001)*

Robert Mondavi 2001 M-Bar Ranch Cabernet Sauvignon (Oakville) $100. **93** —*S.H. (12/31/2004)*

Robert Mondavi 1998 Marjorie's Sunrise Cabernet Sauvignon (Oakville) $85. **95** —*S.H. (12/1/2001)*

Robert Mondavi 1997 Oakville Cabernet Sauvignon (Oakville) $45. **91** *(11/1/2000)*

Robert Mondavi 2005 Private Selection Cabernet Sauvignon (California) $11. Ripeness was no problem in this fruit-forward wine. It's exuberant in cherries, blackberries, plums and cranberries, with a little dusting of oak, and the finish is totally dry. Gives some real upscale Cab experience, at a decent price. **85** —*S.H. (9/1/2007)*

Robert Mondavi 2003 Private Selection Cabernet Sauvignon (California) $11. 83 —*S.H. (12/15/2005)*

Robert Mondavi 2001 Private Selection Cabernet Sauvignon (Central Coast) $13. 85 —*S.H. (10/1/2004)*

Robert Mondavi 2003 Reserve Cabernet Sauvignon (Napa Valley) $125. 92 Editors' Choice —*S.H. (12/15/2006)*

Robert Mondavi 2002 Reserve Cabernet Sauvignon (Napa Valley) $125. 92 Cellar Selection —*S.H. (3/1/2006)*

Robert Mondavi 2001 Reserve Cabernet Sauvignon (Napa Valley) $125. 94 Cellar Selection —*S.H. (6/1/2005)*

Robert Mondavi 2000 Reserve Cabernet Sauvignon (Napa Valley) $125. 92 —*S.H. (11/15/2003)*

Robert Mondavi 1999 Reserve Cabernet Sauvignon (Napa Valley) $NA. 95 Cellar Selection —*S.H. (6/1/2005)*

Robert Mondavi 1999 Reserve Cabernet Sauvignon (Napa Valley) $125. 96 Editors' Choice —*S.H. (11/15/2002)*

Robert Mondavi 1998 Reserve Cabernet Sauvignon (Napa Valley) $125. 92 —*S.H. (12/1/2001)*

Robert Mondavi 1997 Reserve Cabernet Sauvignon (Napa Valley) $120. 91 *(11/1/2000)*

Robert Mondavi 1991 Reserve Cabernet Sauvignon (Napa Valley) $NA. 90 Cellar Selection —*S.H. (6/1/2005)*

Robert Mondavi 1986 Reserve Cabernet Sauvignon (Napa Valley) $NA. 93 —*S.H. (6/1/2005)*

Robert Mondavi 1978 Reserve Cabernet Sauvignon (Napa Valley) $NA. 94 Editors' Choice —*S.H. (6/1/2005)*

Robert Mondavi 1997 SLD Cabernet Sauvignon (Stags Leap District) $45. 89 *(11/1/2000)*

Robert Mondavi 1999 To Kalon Reserve Cabernet Sauvignon (Oakville) $150. 94 Cellar Selection —*S.H. (2/1/2003)*

Robert Mondavi 2001 To Kalon Vineyard Reserve Cabernet Sauvignon (Napa Valley) $135. 95 Cellar Selection —*S.H. (6/1/2005)*

Robert Mondavi 1999 To Kalon Vineyard Reserve Cabernet Sauvignon (Napa Valley) $NA. 97 Editors' Choice —*S.H. (6/1/2005)*

Robert Mondavi 1998 To Kalon Vineyard Reserve Cabernet Sauvignon (Napa Valley) $NA. 90 —*S.H. (6/1/2005)*

Robert Mondavi 1997 To Kalon Vineyard Reserve Cabernet Sauvignon (Napa Valley) $NA. 92 Cellar Selection —*S.H. (6/1/2005)*

Robert Mondavi 1996 To Kalon Vineyard Reserve Cabernet Sauvignon (Napa Valley) $NA. 96 Cellar Selection —*S.H. (6/1/2005)*

Robert Mondavi 2005 Chardonnay (Napa Valley) $20. What's so nice about this wine is that it has full-throttle Chard personality while keeping everything so balanced that it's also a versatile food wine. You can't say that about a lot of Chardonnays. Mainly it's the acidity, but also the complex, subtle interplay of fruit and oak. A very nice job. **90** —*S.H. (9/1/2007)*

Robert Mondavi 2004 Chardonnay (Carneros) $20. 85 —*S.H. (12/1/2006)*

Robert Mondavi 2003 Chardonnay (Carneros) $18. 87 —*S.H. (3/1/2006)*

Robert Mondavi 2002 Chardonnay (Napa Valley) $18. 85 —*S.H. (12/15/2004)*

Robert Mondavi 2002 Chardonnay (Carneros) $25. 90 —*S.H. (12/15/2004)*

Robert Mondavi 2002 Chardonnay (Carneros) $18. 89 —*S.H. (11/15/2005)*

Robert Mondavi 2001 Chardonnay (Napa Valley) $18. 87 —*S.H. (6/1/2004)*

Robert Mondavi 2001 Chardonnay (Carneros) $25. 87 —*S.H. (12/1/2003)*

Robert Mondavi 1999 Chardonnay (Napa Valley) $22. 86 —*S.H. (12/1/2001)*

Robert Mondavi 1999 Chardonnay (Carneros) $23. 86 —*S.H. (12/1/2001)*

Robert Mondavi 1997 Chardonnay (Napa Valley) $20. 87 *(6/1/2000)*

Robert Mondavi 1997 Carneros District Chardonnay (Carneros) $23. 88 *(6/1/2000)*

Robert Mondavi 2000 Coastal Chardonnay (Central Coast) $11. 84 —*S.H. (5/1/2002)*

Robert Mondavi 1999 Coastal Chardonnay (Central Coast) $NA. 87 Best Buy —*S.H. (5/1/2001)*

Robert Mondavi 1998 Coastal Chardonnay (Central Coast) $12. 86 —*S.H. (11/15/2000)*

Robert Mondavi 2000 Huichica Hills Chardonnay (Carneros) $50. 92 —*S.H. (10/1/2003)*

Robert Mondavi 2002 Huichica Hills Vineyard Reserve Chardonnay (Carneros) $50. 91 —*S.H. (11/15/2005)*

Robert Mondavi 2005 Private Selection Chardonnay (Central Coast) $11. Sweet and soft, with apricot, peach and butterscotch flavors. **82** —*S.H. (9/1/2007)*

Robert Mondavi 2003 Private Selection Chardonnay (Central Coast) $11. 84 —*S.H. (12/15/2005)*

Robert Mondavi 2002 Private Selection Chardonnay (Central Coast) $11. 84 —*S.H. (11/15/2004)*

Robert Mondavi 2001 Private Selection Chardonnay (Central Coast) $11. 83 —*S.H. (8/1/2003)*

Robert Mondavi 2005 Reserve Chardonnay (Napa Valley) $38. Right now my preference between Mondavi's Reserve and regular Chard is the regular. This is a better wine, from a classic Chablisian point of view, but it needs time. It's firm and deep in fruit, with an impressive minerality, and the balance for aging. Lay this Chardonnay down for 2–4 years as it gains some bottle complexity. **92** —*S.H. (9/1/2007)*

Robert Mondavi 2004 Reserve Chardonnay (Carneros) $35. 89 —*S.H. (12/15/2006)*

Robert Mondavi 2003 Reserve Chardonnay (Carneros) $35. 90 —*S.H. (3/1/2006)*

Robert Mondavi 2001 Reserve Chardonnay (Napa Valley) $38. 92 —*S.H. (12/15/2004)*

Robert Mondavi 2000 Reserve Chardonnay (Napa Valley) $38. 91 —*S.H. (8/1/2003)*

Robert Mondavi 1998 Reserve Chardonnay (Napa Valley) $36. 90 *(7/1/2001)*

Robert Mondavi 1997 Reserve Chardonnay (Napa Valley) $36. 90 —*S.H. (12/31/1999)*

Robert Mondavi 2005 Fumé Blanc (Napa Valley) $18. Shows that distinctive Mondavi Fumé quality of extreme dryness, tart acids and gooseberry and spiced melon flavors, in addition to the usual citrus. In fact, there are similarities with Mondavi's famed To Kalon bottling, which vineyard contributed 20% of the grapes to the blend. It's a very good and elegant wine. **89 Editors' Choice** —*S.H. (2/1/2007)*

Robert Mondavi 2004 Fumé Blanc (Napa Valley) $18. 92 Editors' Choice —*S.H. (7/1/2006)*

Robert Mondavi 2002 Fumé Blanc (Napa Valley) $18. 86 —*S.H. (9/1/2004)*

Robert Mondavi 2001 Fumé Blanc (North Coast) $11. 83 —*S.H. (7/1/2003)*

Robert Mondavi 1999 Fumé Blanc (Napa Valley) $18. 86 —*S.H. (11/15/2001)*

Robert Mondavi 1997 Fumé Blanc (Napa Valley) $13. 83 —*M.S. (6/1/1999)*

Robert Mondavi 2000 Coastal Private Selection Fumé Blanc (North Coast) $11. 85 —*S.H. (9/1/2003)*

Robert Mondavi 2005 Private Selection Fumé Blanc (North Coast) $11. Simple and sweet, with sugary pineapple juice and peach pie flavors, right down to the buttery baked pie crust. Not really dry, but tasty. **84** —*S.H. (9/1/2007)*

Robert Mondavi 2003 Private Selection Fumé Blanc (North Coast) $11. 86 Best Buy —*S.H. (12/15/2005)*

Robert Mondavi 1999 Reserve To Kalon Fumé Blanc (Napa Valley) $NA. 94 —*S.H. (6/1/2005)*

Robert Mondavi 1997 Reserve To Kalon Fumé Blanc (Napa Valley) $NA. 84 —*S.H. (6/1/2005)*

Robert Mondavi 1994 Reserve To Kalon Fumé Blanc (Napa Valley) $NA. 95 Editors' Choice —*S.H. (6/1/2005)*

Robert Mondavi 2003 Reserve To Kalon Vineyard Fumé Blanc (Napa Valley) $35. 92 —*S.H. (12/15/2006)*

Robert Mondavi 2002 To Kalon Vineyard I Block Fumé Blanc (Napa Valley) $65. 94 Editors' Choice —*S.H. (6/1/2005)*

Robert Mondavi 2005 To Kalon Vineyard Reserve Fumé Blanc (Oakville) $35. Always one of the best Sauvignon Blancs in California, the '05 is a stunner. It brings new levels of richness and complexity to a variety that can be simple even in the best of hands. With 15% Sémillon, the wine explodes with zesty tangerine, lemon tart, coconut pie and smoky oak flavors, with an edge of wintergreen. The finish is absolutely dry. A triumph. **95 Editors' Choice** —*S.H. (12/1/2007)*

Robert Mondavi 2002 To Kalon Vineyard Reserve Fumé Blanc (Napa Valley) $35. 93 Editors' Choice *(7/1/2005)*

Robert Mondavi 2001 To Kalon Vineyard Reserve Fumé Blanc (Napa Valley) $35. 90 —*S.H. (12/15/2004)*

Robert Mondavi 1997 To Kalon Vineyard I Block Fumé Blanc (Napa Valley) $50. 91 —*J.C. (9/1/1999)*

Robert Mondavi 1998 To Kalon Vineyard Reserve Fumé Blanc (Napa Valley) $28. 88 *—S.H. (11/15/2000)*

Robert Mondavi 1997 To Kalon Vineyard Reserve Fumé Blanc (Napa Valley) $28. 90 *—S.H. (2/1/2000)*

Robert Mondavi 2000 Unfiltered Fumé Blanc (Napa Valley) $19. 89 *(8/1/2002)*

Robert Mondavi 2000 Coastal Johannisberg Riesling (Monterey County) $9. 84 *—S.H. (11/15/2001)*

Robert Mondavi 2001 Coastal Private Selection Johannisberg Riesling (Central Coast) $9. 84 *—S.H. (9/1/2003)*

Robert Mondavi 2004 Private Selection Johannisberg Riesling (Monterey County) $11. 81 *—S.H. (12/15/2005)*

Robert Mondavi 2003 Private Selection Johannisberg Riesling (Central Coast) $11. 83 *—S.H. (9/1/2004)*

Robert Mondavi 2002 Private Selection Johannisberg Riesling (Central Coast) $9. 84 *—J.M. (8/1/2003)*

Robert Mondavi 1998 Malbec (Stags Leap District) $45. 89 *—S.H. (12/1/2001)*

Robert Mondavi 2000 Merlot (Napa Valley) $21. 87 *—S.H. (6/1/2004)*

Robert Mondavi 2000 Merlot (Stags Leap District) $40. 89 *—S.H. (12/1/2003)*

Robert Mondavi 1998 Merlot (Napa Valley) $28. 87 *—S.H. (12/1/2001)*

Robert Mondavi 1998 Merlot (Stags Leap District) $35. 86 *—S.H. (12/1/2001)*

Robert Mondavi 1998 Merlot (Carneros) $35. 83 *—S.H. (12/1/2001)*

Robert Mondavi 1997 Merlot (Carneros) $35. 87 *—S.H. (11/15/2000)*

Robert Mondavi 2000 Coastal Merlot (Central Coast) $11. 85 *—S.H. (6/1/2002)*

Robert Mondavi 1999 Coastal Merlot (Central Coast) $11. 83 *—S.H. (5/1/2001)*

Robert Mondavi 1998 Coastal Merlot (Central Coast) $13. 86 *—S.H. (12/31/1999)*

USA

Robert Mondavi 2005 Private Selection Merlot (California) $11. Merlot remains America's top-selling red wine; wines like this seem to keep the category going. Pretty good for the price, nice and dry with modest cherry-berry flavors and a hit of tannin and acidity. 84 *—S.H. (9/1/2007)*

Robert Mondavi 2003 Private Selection Merlot (California) $11. 83 *—S.H. (12/15/2005)*

Robert Mondavi 2001 Private Selection Merlot (Central Coast) $11. 84 *—S.H. (12/1/2003)*

Robert Mondavi 2004 Moscato d'Oro Moscato (Napa Valley) $20. 86 *—S.H. (3/1/2006)*

Robert Mondavi 2001 Moscato d'Oro Moscato (Napa Valley) $18. 88 *—S.H. (12/1/2003)*

Robert Mondavi 2006 Pinot Grigio (California) $11. They kept this one nice and crisp and basically dry, so it's a fine sipper at a fair price. The juicy flavors star, with spearmint gum, pineapple, lemon and lime fruit. 84 *—S.H. (11/15/2007)*

Robert Mondavi 2005 Pinot Grigio (California) $11. 84 *—S.H. (12/31/2006)*

Robert Mondavi 2003 Pinot Grigio (California) $11. 85 *—S.H. (11/15/2004)*

Robert Mondavi 2004 Private Selection Pinot Grigio (California) $11. 85 *—S.H. (12/15/2005)*

Robert Mondavi 2003 Private Selection Pinot Grigio (California) $11. 85 **Best Buy** *—S.H. (3/1/2005)*

Robert Mondavi 1996 Pinot Noir (Carneros) $24. 88 *—M.S. (6/1/1999)*

Robert Mondavi 2005 Pinot Noir (Central Coast) $11. 81 *—S.H. (12/31/2006)*

Robert Mondavi 2004 Pinot Noir (Carneros) $21. 91 **Editors' Choice** *—S.H. (7/1/2006)*

Robert Mondavi 2003 Pinot Noir (Carneros) $21. 87 *—S.H. (3/1/2006)*

Robert Mondavi 2002 Pinot Noir (Napa Valley) $22. 84 *(11/1/2004)*

Robert Mondavi 2002 Pinot Noir (Carneros) $35. 86 *(11/1/2004)*

Robert Mondavi 2001 Pinot Noir (Napa Valley) $22. 88 *—S.H. (12/1/2004)*

Robert Mondavi 2001 Pinot Noir (Carneros) $40. 88 *—S.H. (12/1/2003)*

Robert Mondavi 2000 Pinot Noir (Carneros) $40. 89 *(10/1/2002)*

Robert Mondavi 1998 Pinot Noir (Carneros) $35. 92 *—S.H. (12/15/2000)*

Robert Mondavi 1999 Coastal Pinot Noir (Central Coast) $12. 83 *—S.H. (12/15/2000)*

Robert Mondavi 1998 Coastal Pinot Noir (Central Coast) $11. 82 *—S.H. (10/1/2000)*

Robert Mondavi 2000 Coastal Private Selection Pinot Noir (Central Coast) $13. 84 *(10/1/2002)*

Robert Mondavi 2002 PNX Pinot Noir (Carneros) $35. 89 *(11/1/2004)*

Robert Mondavi 1999 PNX Pinot Noir (Carneros) $45. 91 *—S.H. (12/15/2001)*

Robert Mondavi 2004 Private Selection Pinot Noir (Central Coast) $11. 84 *—S.H. (12/15/2005)*

Robert Mondavi 2002 Private Selection Pinot Noir (Central Coast) $11. 85 *(11/1/2004)*

Robert Mondavi 2001 Private Selection Pinot Noir (Central Coast) $13. 85 *—S.H. (7/1/2003)*

Robert Mondavi 2002 Reserve Pinot Noir (Napa Valley) $50. 87 *(11/1/2004)*

Robert Mondavi 2001 Reserve Pinot Noir (Napa Valley) $50. 91 *—S.H. (8/1/2003)*

Robert Mondavi 1998 Reserve Pinot Noir (Napa Valley) $50. 93 *—S.H. (12/15/2000)*

Robert Mondavi 1999 Boomerang Red Blend (Oakville) $60. 92 *—S.H. (12/1/2001)*

Robert Mondavi 1997 Sauvignon Blanc (Stags Leap District) $18. 89 *—S.H. (9/1/1999)*

Robert Mondavi 2003 Sauvignon Blanc (Stags Leap District) $23. 88 *(7/1/2005)*

Robert Mondavi 2002 Sauvignon Blanc (Stags Leap District) $23. 86 *—S.H. (12/15/2004)*

Robert Mondavi 2001 Sauvignon Blanc (Stags Leap District) $23. 87 *—S.H. (10/1/2003)*

Robert Mondavi 1999 Sauvignon Blanc (Stags Leap District) $23. 86 *—S.H. (12/1/2001)*

Robert Mondavi 1998 Sauvignon Blanc (Stags Leap District) $18. 89 *—S.H. (11/15/2000)*

Robert Mondavi 1999 Botrytis Sauvignon Blanc (Napa Valley) $50. 90 *—S.H. (12/1/2003)*

Robert Mondavi 2000 Coastal Sauvignon Blanc (Central Coast) $9. 84 *—S.H. (11/15/2001)*

Robert Mondavi 1998 Coastal Sauvignon Blanc (Central Coast) $9. 85 *(3/1/2000)*

Robert Mondavi 2006 Private Selection Sauvignon Blanc (California) $11. A little simple in citrus flavor, but for the price, a pretty nice wine. It's the kind of crisp, dry white I've had many times at gallery openings and such, inexpensive, but with enough panache to satisfy a picky crowd. 85 *—S.H. (11/15/2007)*

Robert Mondavi 2004 Private Selection Sauvignon Blanc (Central Coast) $11. 83 *—S.H. (12/31/2005)*

Robert Mondavi 2003 Private Selection Sauvignon Blanc (Central Coast) $9. 84 *—S.H. (12/15/2004)*

Robert Mondavi 2002 Private Selection Sauvignon Blanc (Central Coast) $9. 82 *—S.H. (9/1/2004)*

Robert Mondavi 2001 Private Selection Sauvignon Blanc (Central Coast) $9. 83 *—S.H. (10/1/2003)*

Robert Mondavi 2000 SLD Sauvignon Blanc (Stags Leap District) $23. 88 *(8/1/2002)*

Robert Mondavi 1999 Coastal Syrah (Central Coast) $14. 83 *(10/1/2001)*

Robert Mondavi 1998 Coastal Syrah (Monterey County) $15. 81 *—L.W. (2/1/2000)*

Robert Mondavi 2000 Coastal Private Selection Syrah (Central Coast) $11. 83 *—S.H. (12/1/2002)*

Robert Mondavi 2005 Private Selection Syrah (Central Coast) $11. Rustic and simple, with a sharpness and modest berry flavors. Okay with fast food. 82 *—S.H. (9/1/2007)*

Robert Mondavi 2002 Private Selection Syrah (Central Coast) $11. 84 *—S.H. (2/1/2005)*

Robert Mondavi 2001 Zinfandel (Napa Valley) $21. 88 *—J.M. (11/1/2003)*

Robert Mondavi 1999 Zinfandel (Napa Valley) $21. 89 *—S.H. (12/15/2001)*

Robert Mondavi 1997 Coastal Zinfandel (North Coast) $12. 84 *—S.H. (2/1/2000)*

Robert Mondavi 2000 Coastal Private Selection Zinfandel (North Coast) $11. 83 *—S.H. (12/1/2002)*

Robert Mondavi 2005 Private Selection Zinfandel (California) $11. Good everyday Zin, a little green, but rich enough in raspberry and cherry flavors with a hit of spice. The dryness and moderate alcohol win extra points. **85** —*S.H. (9/1/2007)*

Robert Mondavi 2003 Private Selection Zinfandel (California) $11. 86 Best Buy —*S.H. (12/15/2005)*

Robert Mondavi 2002 Private Selection Zinfandel (California) $11. 83 —*S.H. (9/1/2004)*

Robert Mondavi 2001 Private Selection Zinfandel (North Coast) $11. 81 *(11/1/2003)*

ROBERT PECOTA

Robert Pecota 1997 Kara's Vineyard Cabernet Sauvignon (Napa Valley) $35. 90 *(11/1/2000)*

Robert Pecota 1997 Steven Andre Vineyard Merlot (Napa Valley) $30. 92 —*S.H. (3/1/2000)*

Robert Pecota 2003 Moscato d'Andrea Muscat Canelli (Napa Valley) $12. A sweet wine, with pleasant apricot and vanilla cream flavors, and perhaps its best quality is the acidity, which makes it so clean. **85** —*S.H. (7/1/2007)*

Robert Pecota 2002 Moscato d'Andrea Muscat Canelli (Napa Valley) $12. 92 —*S.H. (11/15/2006)*

Robert Pecota 2006 L'Artiste Sauvignon Blanc (Napa Valley) $16. Decant this for a little while to let this air out and balance. Then you'll find a flavorful, dry wine, with polished pink grapefruit, fig, vanilla and spice flavors and a crisp bite of citrusy acidity. **85** —*S.H. (10/1/2007)*

Robert Pecota 2005 L'Artiste Sauvignon Blanc (Napa Valley) $15. 85 —*S.H. (8/1/2006)*

Robert Pecota 1997 Syrah (Monterey County) $24. 83 —*M.S. (2/1/2000)*

Robert Pecota 1999 Syrah (Monterey County) $24. 84 *(11/1/2001)*

ROBERT PEPI

Robert Pepi 1996 Sauvignon Blanc (Napa Valley) $15. 90 —*S.H. (6/1/1999)*

ROBERT RUE VINEYARD

Robert Rue Vineyard 2003 Zinfandel (Russian River Valley) $25. 86 —*S.H. (2/1/2006)*

Robert Rue Vineyard 2001 Wood Road Century Old Vines Zinfandel (Russian River Valley) $30. 90 *(11/1/2003)*

Robert Rue Vineyard 2003 Wood Road Reserve Zinfandel (Russian River Valley) $32. 89 —*S.H. (2/1/2006)*

ROBERT SINSKEY

Robert Sinskey 2001 Cabernet Franc (Carneros) $36. 89 —*R.V. (4/1/2005)*

Robert Sinskey 1997 Chardonnay (Carneros) $25. 92 —*S.H. (2/1/2000)*

Robert Sinskey 2001 Three Amigos Vineyard Chardonnay (Carneros) $30. 89 —*R.V. (4/1/2005)*

Robert Sinskey 1995 Reserve Merlot (Carneros) $33. 89 —*S.H. (3/1/2000)*

Robert Sinskey 2003 Pinot Blanc (Carneros) $18. 87 —*R.V. (4/1/2005)*

Robert Sinskey 2001 Four Vineyards Pinot Noir (Carneros) $46. 91 —*R.V. (4/1/2005)*

Robert Sinskey 2000 RSV Four Vineyards Pinot Noir (Carneros) $46. 92 —*S.H. (12/1/2004)*

Robert Sinskey 2001 Three Amigos Vineyard Pinot Noir (Carneros) $46. 89 —*R.V. (4/1/2005)*

Robert Sinskey 2001 Vandal Vineyard Pinot Noir (Carneros) $46. 90 —*R.V. (4/1/2005)*

ROBERT STEMMLER

Robert Stemmler 2004 Estate Grown Chardonnay (Carneros) $34. 84 —*S.H. (12/31/2006)*

Robert Stemmler 2003 Estate Grown Chardonnay (Carneros) $34. 82 —*S.H. (12/31/2006)*

Robert Stemmler 2002 Three Clone Chardonnay (Carneros) $26. 90 —*S.H. (12/15/2005)*

Robert Stemmler 2001 Pinot Noir (Carneros) $32. 87 —*S.H. (6/1/2004)*

Robert Stemmler 2000 Pinot Noir (Carneros) $38. 90 *(10/1/2002)*

Robert Stemmler 2004 Estate Grown Pinot Noir (Carneros) $36. Soft, simple and gentle, with sugary cherry pie and cola flavors. The silky texture and light mouthfeel are wonderful, but the wine would be far better if it finished drier and crisper. **85** —*S.H. (9/1/2007)*

Robert Stemmler 2002 Estate Grown Pinot Noir (Carneros) $32. 86 —*S.H. (12/15/2005)*

Robert Stemmler 2004 Ferguson Block Pinot Noir (Carneros) $44. This is one of those wines where the aroma and flavor disconnect. Smells great, with inviting Pinot-esque scents of ripe raspberries, cherries, root beer, vanilla, cinnamon and smoky oak. But in the mouth, it turns overly soft and sweet. **85** —*S.H. (9/1/2007)*

Robert Stemmler 2003 Ferguson Block Pinot Noir (Carneros) $44. 85 —*S.H. (12/31/2006)*

Robert Stemmler 2002 Ferguson Block Pinot Noir (Carneros) $40. 91 Editors' Choice —*S.H. (12/15/2005)*

Robert Stemmler 2001 Ferguson Block Pinot Noir (Carneros) $40. 89 —*S.H. (6/1/2004)*

Robert Stemmler 2004 Nugent Vineyard Pinot Noir (Russian River Valley) $40. Soft and simple, this is almost a dessert wine—it's that sweet in raspberry-tart filling and cherry jam flavors. Has just enough acidity but the sugary finish is off-putting. **84** —*S.H. (9/1/2007)*

Robert Stemmler 2002 Nugent Vineyard Pinot Noir (Russian River Valley) $32. 88 —*S.H. (12/15/2005)*

Robert Stemmler 2001 Nugent Vineyard Pinot Noir (Russian River Valley) $32. 90 —*S.H. (6/1/2004)*

ROBERT YOUNG

Robert Young 2000 Scion Bordeaux Blend (Alexander Valley) $60. 88 —*S.H. (12/1/2004)*

Robert Young 1997 Scion Bordeaux Blend (Alexander Valley) $50. 97 —*S.H. (6/1/2003)*

Robert Young 2002 Scion Cabernet Blend (Alexander Valley) $54. 95 Editors' Choice —*S.H. (9/1/2006)*

Robert Young 2001 Scion Cabernet Blend (Alexander Valley) $54. 92 *(6/1/2006)*

Robert Young 1999 Scion Cabernet Blend (Alexander Valley) $50. 96 Editors' Choice —*S.H. (11/15/2003)*

Robert Young 1998 Scion Cabernet Sauvignon (Alexander Valley) $50. 94 Editors' Choice —*S.H. (11/15/2002)*

Robert Young 2004 Chardonnay (Alexander Valley) $37. Another beautiful Chardonnay from Robert Young, although it's a step off the pace of recent years. Soft and intricately layered, it has tropical fruit pastry filling flavors accented with lots of toasty new French oak, which seems too strong for the underlying fruit. **87** —*S.H. (4/1/2007)*

Robert Young 2003 Chardonnay (Alexander Valley) $37. 92 —*S.H. (5/1/2006)*

Robert Young 2002 Chardonnay (Alexander Valley) $37. 93 Editors' Choice —*S.H. (8/1/2005)*

Robert Young 2001 Chardonnay (Alexander Valley) $35. 92 —*S.H. (2/1/2004)*

Robert Young 1999 Chardonnay (Alexander Valley) $35. 96 Editors' Choice —*S.H. (12/1/2001)*

Robert Young 2002 Merlot (Alexander Valley) $42. 94 Editors' Choice —*S.H. (6/1/2006)*

ROBIN CREST

Robin Crest 2000 Chardonnay (Sonoma County) $6. 84 —*S.H. (6/1/2003)*

ROBLEDO

Robledo 2000 Pinot Noir (Carneros) $27. 86 —*J.M. (7/1/2003)*

Robledo 2002 The Seven Brothers Sauvignon Blanc (Lake County) $12. 80 —*J.M. (10/1/2004)*

ROCCA

Rocca 2003 Cabernet Sauvignon (Yountville) $55. What's so nice about this Cab is its balance and delicacy, without the heaviness that can mar a more alcoholic wine. It shows polished flavors of cherries, blackberries, cola and cedar, with a long, fine finish of cassis liqueur. Really an elegant sipper, this wine is best now and for a couple years. **90** —*S.H. (12/31/2007)*

Rocca 2001 Cabernet Sauvignon (Yountville) $50. 90 —*S.H. (6/1/2005)*

Rocca 2004 Bad Boy Red Red Blend (Yountville) $29. The winery doesn't disclose the varietals in this wine, but it tastes like Cabernet and shows a fine, southern Napa structure. There's a cut of juicy acidity and dusting of thyme to the complex cassis, mocha and licorice flavors. **90** —*S.H. (4/1/2007)*

Rocca 2003 Syrah (Yountville) $42. This wine has been variable, but the '03 shows lots of varietal distinction. It opens with a burst of white pepper-infused blackberry, chocolate, licorice and oak aromas, and turns rich and soft in the mouth, with similar flavors. The smooth tannins make this immediately drinkable. **90** —*S.H. (12/31/2007)*

Rocca 2002 Syrah (Yountville) $38. 86 *(9/1/2005)*

Rocca 2001 Syrah (Yountville) $38. 90 —*S.H. (6/1/2005)*

Rocca 2000 Syrah (Yountville) $38. 86 *—S.H. (5/1/2004)*

Rocca 1999 Syrah (Yountville) $38. 90 *—S.H. (10/1/2003)*

ROCHE

Roche 2003 Cabernet Sauvignon (Napa Valley) $36. 86 *—S.H. (11/15/2006)*

Roche 1997 Chardonnay (Carneros) $19. 90 *(6/1/2000)*

Roche 1998 Barrel Select Reserve Chardonnay (Carneros) $30. 86 *(6/1/2000)*

Roche 2004 Reserve American Oak Chardonnay (Carneros) $31. 90 *—S.H. (11/15/2006)*

Roche 2004 Reserve French Oak Chardonnay (Carneros) $33. 88 *—S.H. (11/15/2006)*

Roche 2003 Estate Merlot (Carneros) $26. 84 *—S.H. (11/15/2006)*

Roche 2003 Estate Reserve Merlot (Carneros) $33. 91 *—S.H. (11/15/2006)*

Roche 2003 Estate Syrah (Carneros) $26. 83 *—S.H. (11/15/2006)*

ROCHIOLI

Rochioli 2005 Chardonnay (Russian River Valley) $45. Apples, acidity and oak are what this is all about. Green apples, that is, baked into pie, and that includes the buttery, cinnamony, sugary pie crust. The acidity is amazing, but that may partly be due to the cool vintage. Classy, sleek Chard, with quite a bit of elegance. **90** *—S.H. (4/1/2007)*

Rochioli 2005 Estate Chardonnay (Russian River Valley) $34. Classic RRV Chard, showing bright aromas of green apples, pineapples, lemon and lime and roasted coconut, with rich vanilla cream and smoky butter notes, and that lovely, brisk acidity that makes the finish so clean. **89** *—S.H. (7/1/2007)*

Rochioli 1999 Estate Chardonnay (Russian River Valley) $30. 91 Best Buy *(7/1/2001)*

Rochioli 1998 Estate Chardonnay (Russian River Valley) $29. 89 *(6/1/2000)*

Rochioli 1997 Estate Chardonnay (Russian River Valley) $28. 90 *(11/15/1999)*

Rochioli 2001 Estate Grown Chardonnay (Russian River Valley) $37. 93 *—S.H. (7/1/2003)*

Rochioli 2000 Estate Grown Chardonnay (Russian River Valley) $37. 90 *—J.C. (9/1/2002)*

Rochioli 2005 Rachaele's Vineyard Chardonnay (Russian River Valley) $60. From hillier plantings on the steep slopes of the winery's estate vineyard, this is a compact young Chardonnay. It's intense in lemon mousse, green apple, Key lime pie and vanilla caramel, with a minerally, tangy bite of flint or metal. Finishes very dry and crisp. Cellar for up to six years. **94** *—S.H. (7/1/2007)*

Rochioli 2005 River Block Chardonnay (Russian River Valley) $50. This is the lightest of Rochioli's Chards, body-wise, and the softest. It has a melted butter mouthfeel, but it's a very layered, nuanced wine, with intense Meyer lemon, vanilla custard and smoky oak flavors, and has a gorgeous, voluptuous quality. **92** *—S.H. (7/1/2007)*

Rochioli 2005 South River Vineyard Chardonnay (Russian River Valley) $55. An intensely fruity, oaky (40% new) and dramatic Chard. It has pear liqueur, vanilla, butterscotch and crème brûlée aromas, and drinks intensely rich and powerful. Yet it never loses its keen refinement and elegance. Finishes with a bite of crunchy, green apple acidity. **93** *—S.H. (7/1/2007)*

Rochioli 2005 Pinot Noir (Russian River Valley) $42. Starts with a dazzling array of bright, pure aromas of cherries, loganberries and raspberry jam, with intricate complexities of cola, pumpkin pie, nutmeg, cinnamon and smoky oak. The flavors are similar, and the wine is totally dry and elegant. For the winery's village-style Pinot, it's a real beauty. **90** *—S.H. (7/1/2007)*

Rochioli 2004 Pinot Noir (Russian River Valley) $47. 93 *—S.H. (11/1/2006)*

Rochioli 2002 Pinot Noir (Russian River Valley) $40. 84 *(11/1/2004)*

Rochioli 2000 Pinot Noir (Russian River Valley) $40. 90 Editors' Choice *(10/1/2002)*

Rochioli 1999 Pinot Noir (Russian River Valley) $37. 88 *(10/1/2002)*

Rochioli 2005 East Block Pinot Noir (Russian River Valley) $90. From the first Pinot block on the estate (1968), and from an unknown clone sourced from a long-forgotten Napa vineyard. The block is now being replanted. This is the Pinot that established Rochioli's reputation, and the bottling remains a superstar. The '05 is very dry, crisp and full-bodied, with a flood of cherry pie filling, pomegranate, rhubarb, Beefsteak tomato and flashy new oak. It's young and immature in tannins, and needs cellaring. Best after 2009, it will gain complexity through 2015. **95 Cellar Selection** *—S.H. (7/1/2007)*

Rochioli 2003 East Block Pinot Noir (Russian River Valley) $90. 93 Cellar Selection *—S.H. (6/1/2005)*

Rochioli 1999 East Block Pinot Noir (Russian River Valley) $NA. 93 *—S.H. (6/1/2005)*

Rochioli 1997 East Block Pinot Noir (Russian River Valley) $NA. 84 *—S.H. (6/1/2005)*

Rochioli 1994 East Block Reserve Pinot Noir (Russian River Valley) $NA. 90 *—S.H. (6/1/2005)*

Rochioli 2001 Estate Grown Pinot Noir (Russian River Valley) $42. 91 *—S.H. (2/1/2004)*

Rochioli 2005 Little Hill Pinot Noir (Russian River Valley) $65. So young and immature now, but showing tremendous power, this is great Pinot Noir. It's simply not ready yet, a little heavy, with fresh, zingy acidity, firm tannins and primary fruit flavors. There's a tough, lockdown quality, but what a core of fruit. The essence of raspberries, cherries, mint, cola, and such a silky texture. Cries out cellaring until at least 2009. **94** *—S.H. (7/1/2007)*

Rochioli 2000 River Block Pinot Noir (Russian River Valley) $55. 89 *—S.H. (2/1/2003)*

Rochioli 2005 Three Corner Vineyard Pinot Noir (Russian River Valley) $68. Three Corner contains some of the oldest vines on the estate, dating to 1974. Typically, the wines start out almost heavy and dense, but age well. Dry, crisp and jammy now, it has a flood of cherry kirsch, raspberry purée, cola and new oak flavors that finish with great charm and complexity. The '05, from a cool vintage, should hold and improve through 2015. **95** *—S.H. (7/1/2007)*

Rochioli 2003 Three Corner Vineyard Pinot Noir (Russian River Valley) $65. 93 Cellar Selection *—S.H. (6/1/2005)*

Rochioli 1999 Three Corner Vineyard Pinot Noir (Russian River Valley) $NA. 92 *—S.H. (6/1/2005)*

Rochioli 1997 Three Corner Vineyard Pinot Noir (Russian River Valley) $NA. 84 *—S.H. (6/1/2005)*

Rochioli 1994 Three Corner Vineyard Reserve Pinot Noir (Russian River Valley) $NA. 94 *—S.H. (6/1/2005)*

Rochioli 2005 West Block Pinot Noir (Russian River Valley) $80. A big, rich, dense, extracted Pinot. It's tremendously rich in red and black cherry, rhubarb, pomegranate, cola and spice flavors, and feels elegant and balanced. This was a ripe vintage with a long hangtime, yet the wine shows no trace of supermaturity. Silky and crisp, it's young now, with a pucker of cherry-skin tannins. Age this one. Best 2009—2015. **94 Cellar Selection** *—S.H. (7/1/2007)*

Rochioli 2003 West Block Pinot Noir (Russian River Valley) $75. 92 Cellar Selection *—S.H. (6/1/2005)*

Rochioli 2000 West Block Pinot Noir (Russian River Valley) $65. 94 Editors' Choice *—S.H. (2/1/2003)*

Rochioli 1999 West Block Pinot Noir (Russian River Valley) $NA. 91 *—S.H. (6/1/2005)*

Rochioli 1997 West Block Pinot Noir (Russian River Valley) $NA. 84 *—S.H. (6/1/2005)*

Rochioli 1995 West Block Reserve Pinot Noir (Russian River Valley) $NA. 90 *—S.H. (6/1/2005)*

Rochioli 1994 West Block Reserve Pinot Noir (Russian River Valley) $NA. 87 *—S.H. (6/1/2005)*

Rochioli 1992 West Block Reserve Pinot Noir (Russian River Valley) $NA. 90 *—S.H. (6/1/2005)*

Rochioli 2006 Sauvignon Blanc (Russian River Valley) $32. Off a bit from the '05, but still a good wine, this Sauvignon Blanc shows fresh minty lemongrass, melon, green grass and fennel flavors, backed up with firm acids and, as always, very dry. **86** *—S.H. (9/1/2007)*

Rochioli 2005 Sauvignon Blanc (Russian River Valley) $30. 92 Editors' Choice *—S.H. (8/1/2006)*

Rochioli 2004 Sauvignon Blanc (Russian River Valley) $29. 87 *(7/1/2005)*

Rochioli 2003 Sauvignon Blanc (Russian River Valley) $29. 90 *—S.H. (12/1/2004)*

Rochioli 2002 Sauvignon Blanc (Russian River Valley) $24. 92 Editors' Choice *—S.H. (12/1/2003)*

Rochioli 2001 Sauvignon Blanc (Russian River Valley) $24. 90 Editors' Choice *(8/1/2002)*

Rochioli 1998 Sauvignon Blanc (Russian River Valley) $22. 90 *(11/1/1999)*

ROCINANTE

Rocinante 2004 Palindrome Vineyard Syrah (Dry Creek Valley) $35. 88 —*S.H. (12/31/2006)*

ROCK RABBIT

Rock Rabbit 2004 Sauvignon Blanc (Central Coast) $10. 86 Best Buy —*S.H. (12/1/2005)*

Rock Rabbit 2003 Syrah (Central Coast) $10. 84 —*S.H. (12/1/2005)*

Rock Rabbit 2002 Syrah (Central Coast) $10. 89 Best Buy —*S.H. (11/15/2004)*

ROCKBLOCK

Rockblock 2002 Carpenter Hill Vineyard Syrah (Rogue Valley) $40. 90 *(9/1/2005)*

Rockblock 2001 Del Rio Vineyard Syrah (Rogue Valley) $40. 89 *(9/1/2005)*

Rockblock 2000 Del Rio Vineyard Syrah (Rogue Valley) $40. 90 —*P.G. (2/1/2004)*

Rockblock 2002 Seven Hills Vineyard Syrah (Walla Walla (WA)) $40. 87 *(9/1/2005)*

Rockblock 2000 Seven Hills Vineyard Syrah (Walla Walla (OR)) $40. 91 —*P.G. (2/1/2004)*

Rockblock 1999 Seven Hills Vineyard Syrah (Walla Walla (WA)) $40. 90 *(11/1/2001)*

ROCKING HORSE

Rocking Horse 2001 Garvey Family Vineyard Cabernet Sauvignon (Rutherford) $30. 84 —*S.H. (10/1/2005)*

Rocking Horse 2000 Last Call Cabernet Sauvignon (Napa Valley) $24. 82 —*S.H. (10/1/2005)*

Rocking Horse 2000 Merlot (Napa Valley) $20. 83 —*S.H. (10/1/2005)*

Rocking Horse 1998 Garvey Family Vineyard Merlot (Rutherford) $30. 85 —*J.C. (6/1/2001)*

Rocking Horse 2001 Zinfandel (Napa Valley) $18. 87 —*S.H. (10/1/2005)*

Rocking Horse 1999 Zinfandel (Napa Valley) $20. 86 —*D.T. (3/1/2002)*

Rocking Horse 1998 Zinfandel (Napa Valley) $18. 87 *(3/1/2001)*

Rocking Horse 2001 Monte Rosso Vineyard Zinfandel (Sonoma County) $22. 87 —*S.H. (10/1/2005)*

ROCKLAND

Rockland 2000 Petite Sirah (Napa Valley) $30. 90 *(4/1/2003)*

ROCKLEDGE VINEYARDS

Rockledge Vineyards 2003 Cabernet Sauvignon (St. Helena) $25. 90 *S.H. (12/31/2006)*

Rockledge Vineyards 2002 Cabernet Sauvignon (St. Helena) $32. 84 —*S.H. (11/1/2005)*

Rockledge Vineyards 2001 Cabernet Sauvignon (St. Helena) $45. 91 —*J.M. (8/1/2004)*

Rockledge Vineyards 1999 Reserve St. Helena Cabernet Sauvignon (Napa Valley) $50. 90 —*J.M. (11/15/2002)*

Rockledge Vineyards 2004 The Rocks Cabernet Sauvignon (St. Helena) $60. This is very appealing for the soft, sexy texture and drink-me-now black currant flavors, but it's lacking the acid-tannin structure that great Napa Cab needs. Drink now and for a few years. **87** —*S.H. (12/1/2007)*

Rockledge Vineyards 2003 The Rocks Cabernet Sauvignon (St. Helena) $45. 93 Editors' Choice —*S.H. (12/31/2006)*

Rockledge Vineyards 2002 The Rocks Cabernet Sauvignon (St. Helena) $49. 88 —*S.H. (11/1/2005)*

Rockledge Vineyards 2002 Primitivo (Napa Valley) $25. 83 —*S.H. (11/1/2005)*

Rockledge Vineyards 2001 Primitivo (Napa Valley) $24. 90 —*J.M. (8/1/2004)*

Rockledge Vineyards 2000 Primitivo (Napa Valley) $28. 90 —*J.M. (12/1/2002)*

Rockledge Vineyards 2002 Zinfandel (Napa Valley) $22. 84 —*S.H. (11/1/2005)*

Rockledge Vineyards 2001 Zinfandel (Napa Valley) $20. 88 —*J.M. (8/1/2004)*

Rockledge Vineyards 2000 Zinfandel (Napa Valley) $22. 88 —*J.M. (11/1/2002)*

Rockledge Vineyards 1999 Zinfandel (Napa Valley) $22. 87 —*J.M. (11/1/2002)*

ROCKPILE

Rockpile 2004 Cemetary Vineyard Zinfandel (Rockpile) $35. 83 —*S.H. (12/15/2006)*

RODNEY STRONG

Rodney Strong 2000 Symmetry Meritage Cabernet Blend (Alexander Valley) $55. 91 —*S.H. (10/1/2005)*

Rodney Strong 1996 Cabernet Sauvignon (Sonoma County) $16. 86 —*L.W. (9/1/1999)*

Rodney Strong 2003 Cabernet Sauvignon (Sonoma County) $19. 90 Editors' Choice —*S.H. (12/15/2006)*

Rodney Strong 2002 Cabernet Sauvignon (Sonoma County) $19. 87 —*S.H. (11/1/2005)*

Rodney Strong 2001 Cabernet Sauvignon (Sonoma County) $18. 87 —*S.H. (12/31/2004)*

Rodney Strong 2000 Cabernet Sauvignon (Sonoma County) $18. 90 —*S.H. (3/1/2003)*

Rodney Strong 1999 Cabernet Sauvignon (Sonoma County) $18. 87 —*S.H. (11/15/2002)*

Rodney Strong 1998 Cabernet Sauvignon (Sonoma County) $16. 88 —*S.H. (5/1/2001)*

Rodney Strong 1997 Cabernet Sauvignon (Sonoma County) $16. 88 —*S.H. (12/15/2000)*

Rodney Strong 2001 Alden Vineyards Cabernet Sauvignon (Alexander Valley) $30. 91 Cellar Selection —*S.H. (11/1/2005)*

Rodney Strong 1999 Alden Vineyards Cabernet Sauvignon (Alexander Valley) $30. 91 —*S.H. (11/15/2003)*

Rodney Strong 1998 Alden Vineyards Cabernet Sauvignon (Alexander Valley) $30. 84 —*S.H. (11/15/2002)*

Rodney Strong 2001 Alexander's Crown Cabernet Sauvignon (Alexander Valley) $30. 88 —*S.H. (8/1/2005)*

Rodney Strong 2000 Alexander's Crown Cabernet Sauvignon (Alexander Valley) $28. 90 —*S.H. (11/15/2003)*

Rodney Strong 1999 Alexander's Crown Cabernet Sauvignon (Alexander Valley) $28. 92 —*S.H. (3/1/2003)*

Rodney Strong 1998 Alexander's Crown Vineyard Cabernet Sauvignon (Alexander Valley) $28. 86 —*S.H. (8/1/2003)*

Rodney Strong 1997 Alexander's Crown Vineyard Cabernet Sauvignon (Northern Sonoma) $26. 90 *(9/1/2000)*

Rodney Strong 1996 Alexander's Crown Vineyard Cabernet Sauvignon (Northern Sonoma) $25. 86 *(12/31/1999)*

Rodney Strong 2003 Estate Cabernet Sauvignon (Alexander Valley) $25. Well-structured, with firm tannins and acids framing herb, cherry and blond tobacco flavors, with just a touch of smoky oak. The dry finish makes it particularly elegant. **87** —*S.H. (10/1/2007)*

Rodney Strong 2002 Reserve Cabernet Sauvignon (Sonoma County) $40. The winery's reserve Cab has been variable over the years, but this '02 is really a very good wine that will reward cellaring. It's luscious now, but such are the tannins, the dry balance, and the freshness of the blackberry flavors, that time in the bottle is bound to reward. Should open by the end of 2007, and drink well for the next five years. **91 Cellar Selection** —*S.H. (5/1/2007)*

Rodney Strong 2001 Reserve Cabernet Sauvignon (Sonoma County) $40. 88 —*S.H. (12/1/2006)*

Rodney Strong 2000 Reserve Cabernet Sauvignon (Sonoma County) $40. 90 —*S.H. (10/1/2005)*

Rodney Strong 1999 Reserve Cabernet Sauvignon (Sonoma County) $40. 86 —*S.H. (11/15/2003)*

Rodney Strong 1997 Reserve Cabernet Sauvignon (Northern Sonoma) $40. 87 —*S.H. (9/1/2002)*

Rodney Strong 1996 Reserve Cabernet Sauvignon (Northern Sonoma) $40. 92 *(9/1/2000)*

Rodney Strong 1995 Reserve Cabernet Sauvignon (Northern Sonoma) $40. 89 *(11/1/1999)*

Rodney Strong 1999 Symmetry Cabernet Sauvignon (Alexander Valley) $55. 85 —*S.H. (11/15/2004)*

Rodney Strong 2005 Chardonnay (Sonoma County) $15. Made from three prime growing regions, Russian River, Chalk Hill and Sonoma Coast, this Chard offers lots of complexity at a good price. It's a forthright wine, rich in peach pie flavors, including the smoky, buttery pie crust, and is entirely dry. Amazingly good when you consider the massive production: 185,000 cases. **88** —*S.H. (4/1/2007)*

Rodney Strong 2004 Chardonnay (Sonoma County) $15. 85 —*S.H.*

USA

(4/1/2006)

Rodney Strong 2003 Chardonnay (Chalk Hill) $19. 84 *—S.H. (10/1/2005)*

Rodney Strong 2003 Chardonnay (Sonoma County) $15. 89 *—S.H. (11/1/2005)*

Rodney Strong 2002 Chardonnay (Sonoma County) $18. 90 Editors' Choice *—S.H. (6/1/2004)*

Rodney Strong 2002 Chardonnay (Chalk Hill) $18. 88 *—S.H. (11/15/2004)*

Rodney Strong 2001 Chardonnay (Sonoma County) $14. 85 *—S.H. (6/1/2003)*

Rodney Strong 1999 Chardonnay (Sonoma County) $14. 86 *—S.H. (11/15/2000)*

Rodney Strong 1999 Chardonnay (Chalk Hill) $18. 87 *—S.H. (5/1/2001)*

Rodney Strong 2004 Chalk Hill Chardonnay (Sonoma County) $19. 86 *—S.H. (12/1/2006)*

Rodney Strong 2000 Chalk Hill Chardonnay (Sonoma County) $18. 85 *—S.H. (5/1/2002)*

Rodney Strong 1998 Chalk Hill Chardonnay (Chalk Hill) $16. 87 *(6/1/2000)*

Rodney Strong 1997 Chalk Hill Chardonnay (Sonoma County) $14. 88 *(11/15/1999)*

Rodney Strong 1998 Chalk Hill Vineyard Reserve Chardonnay (Northern Sonoma) $30. 89 *(7/1/2001)*

Rodney Strong 1999 Chalk Hill Vineyard Reseve Chardonnay (Sonoma County) $30. 87 *—S.H. (12/15/2002)*

Rodney Strong 2005 Estate Chardonnay (Chalk Hill) $20. Very ripe and oaky, but a little on the obvious side, with flamboyant tropical fruit, honey and buttered toast flavors. Could use greater finesse, subtlety, complexity. 84 *—S.H. (10/1/2007)*

Rodney Strong 2005 Reserve Chardonnay (Sonoma County) $30. This is one of the biggest, richest Chardonnays that Rodney Strong has ever produced, and no wonder, as longtime winemaker Rick Sayre was assisted by David Ramey as a consultant. The wine has Ramey-esque proportions, gigantic in fleshy tropical fruit, caramel, vanilla cream, butterscotch and meringue flavors. It's so softly decadent, it's almost better as a cocktail wine than with food. 91 *—S.H. (12/31/2007)*

Rodney Strong 2003 Reserve Chardonnay (Chalk Hill) $30. 85 *—S.H. (11/1/2005)*

Rodney Strong 1997 Reserve Chalk Hill Vineyard Chardonnay (Northern Sonoma) $30. 92 *—S.H. (11/1/1999)*

Rodney Strong 1997 Symmetry Meritage (Alexander Valley) $55. 91 *—S.H. (7/1/2002)*

Rodney Strong 2001 Symmetry Red Wine Meritage (Alexander Valley) $55. 85 *—S.H. (12/15/2006)*

Rodney Strong 2002 Merlot (Sonoma County) $19. 87 *—S.H. (11/15/2006)*

Rodney Strong 2001 Merlot (Sonoma County) $18. 87 *—S.H. (5/1/2005)*

Rodney Strong 2000 Merlot (Alexander Valley) $26. 87 *—S.H. (12/31/2004)*

Rodney Strong 1999 Merlot (Sonoma County) $18. 89 *—S.H. (7/1/2002)*

Rodney Strong 1999 Merlot (Alexander Valley) $26. 87 *—S.H. (5/1/2004)*

Rodney Strong 1997 Merlot (Sonoma County) $16. 88 *—S.H. (11/15/2000)*

Rodney Strong 1998 Estate Vineyards Merlot (Alexander Valley) $26. 85 *—S.H. (8/1/2003)*

Rodney Strong 2004 Pinot Noir (Russian River Valley) $19. 88 *—S.H. (11/1/2006)*

Rodney Strong 2002 Pinot Noir (Russian River Valley) $19. 89 *—S.H. (8/1/2005)*

Rodney Strong 2000 Pinot Noir (Russian River Valley) $18. 83 *(10/1/2002)*

Rodney Strong 2005 Estate Pinot Noir (Russian River Valley) $20. Strikes the perfect balance between a Pinot that needs aging and one that's perfectly drinkable now. Complex layers of cherries, blackberries, coffee, cola and smoky oak; shows the richness and vivacity of the best of RRV. Best now and for a couple of years. 87 *—S.H. (4/1/2007)*

Rodney Strong 1997 Estate Bottled Pinot Noir (Russian River Valley) $16. 86 *(12/15/1999)*

Rodney Strong 2003 Estate Vineyards Pinot Noir (Russian River Valley) $19. 83 *—S.H. (12/31/2005)*

Rodney Strong 2004 Jane's Vineyard Reserve Pinot Noir (Russian River Valley) $35. The vineyard is in a cool, southerly part of the valley. The wine is classically structured, with crisp acidity and a silky mouthfeel framing rich, dry flavors of cherries, root beer and oaky spices. It's a lovely young Pinot to drink now for its fleshy opulence. 90 *—S.H. (11/1/2007)*

Rodney Strong 2003 Jane's Vineyard Reserve Pinot Noir (Russian River Valley) $35. 88 *—S.H. (12/1/2006)*

Rodney Strong 2002 Jane's Vineyard Reserve Pinot Noir (Russian River Valley) $35. 84 *—S.H. (12/31/2005)*

Rodney Strong 1999 Reserve Pinot Noir (Russian River Valley) $30. 90 Editors' Choice *(10/1/2002)*

Rodney Strong 1998 Reserve Pinot Noir (Northern Sonoma) $30. 87 *—S.H. (12/15/2001)*

Rodney Strong 1999 Russian River Valley Pinot Noir (Russian River Valley) $18. 81 *(10/1/2002)*

Rodney Strong 2006 Charlotte's Home Estate Sauvignon Blanc (Sonoma County) $14. Not a bad price for a Sauvignon Blanc of this interest. You'll find a burst of pineapple, lemongrass, fig and vanilla honey flavors, with the dryness and scoury acidity you want in this variety. Partial barrel fermentation adds a creamy richness to this polished wine. 87 *—S.H. (11/15/2007)*

Rodney Strong 2005 Charlotte's Home Sauvignon Blanc (Sonoma County) $14. 85 *—S.H. (12/15/2006)*

Rodney Strong 2002 Charlotte's Home Sauvignon Blanc (Sonoma Valley) $12. 87 *—S.H. (12/31/2003)*

Rodney Strong 1998 Charlotte's Home Estate Bottle Sauvignon Blanc (Northern Sonoma) $10. 87 *—M.M. (9/1/2003)*

Rodney Strong 2001 Charlotte's Home Vineyard Sauvignon Blanc (Sonoma County) $12. 86 *—S.H. (9/1/2003)*

Rodney Strong 2003 Charlotte's Home Sauvignon Blanc (Sonoma County) $12. 84 *—S.H. (12/31/2004)*

Rodney Strong 2004 Charlotte's Home Sauvignon Blanc (Sonoma County) $14. 85 *—S.H. (3/1/2006)*

Rodney Strong 2004 Knotty Vines Zinfandel (Sonoma County) $20. What a nice Zin this is. Fully dry, it has the full body and dusty tannins to tear into barbecue, with wild berry and cola flavors edged with cocoa and Asian spices, and the balance of a Merlot. They say the wine is based on 100-year-old vines, which may account for its integrity. 90 *—S.H. (5/1/2007)*

Rodney Strong 2003 Knotty Vines Zinfandel (Sonoma County) $19. 90 *—S.H. (11/1/2006)*

Rodney Strong 1999 Knotty Vines Zinfandel (Northern Sonoma) $18. 86 *—S.H. (9/1/2002)*

Rodney Strong 1998 Knotty Vines Zinfandel (Northern Sonoma) $18. 85 *(3/1/2001)*

Rodney Strong 1997 Old Vines Zinfandel (Sonoma County) $18. 87 *—P.G. (3/1/2001)*

Rodney Strong 2004 Reserve Zinfandel (Sonoma County) $30. Beautiful Sonoma Zin, sourced mainly from Alexander Valley. Although the winemaker had to struggle against shriveled, raisiny fruit, the wine shows a soft complexity. Ripe and forward in cherry-berry, tobacco, rum baba, coffee and crushed hard spices, it finishes long and dry. 88 *—S.H. (8/1/2007)*

ROEDERER ESTATE

Roederer Estate 1999 L'Ermitage Champagne Blend (Anderson Valley) $45. 94 *—S.H. (6/1/2005)*

Roederer Estate 1998 L'Ermitage Champagne Blend (Anderson Valley) $45. 93 *—S.H. (12/31/2004)*

Roederer Estate 1997 L'Ermitage Champagne Blend (Anderson Valley) $46. 90 *—S.H. (12/1/2002)*

Roederer Estate 1996 L'Ermitage Champagne Blend (Anderson Valley) $42. 93 *—S.H. (12/15/2001)*

Roederer Estate 1994 L'Ermitage Champagne Blend (Anderson Valley) $43. 88 *(12/31/2000)*

Roederer Estate 1993 L'Ermitage Champagne Blend (Mendocino) $38. 92 *—E.M. (11/15/1999)*

Roederer Estate NV Brut Sparkling Blend (Anderson Valley) $22. This is an absolutely first-rate bubbly, dry, smooth and rich. Has complex flavors of peaches, limes and strawberries, accented by doughy yeast and smoky flavors. Really defines the balanced elegance and pedigree you want in a great sparkler. 92 Editors' Choice *—S.H. (12/31/2007)*

Roederer Estate NV Brut Sparkling Blend (Anderson Valley) $22. 87 *—S.H. (12/1/2003)*

Roederer Estate NV Brut Sparkling Blend (Anderson Valley) $23. 86 *—S.H. (6/1/2006)*

Roederer Estate NV Brut Rosé Sparkling Blend (Anderson Valley) $26. From the pretty pale, amber color to the long, distinguished finish, this is a great rosé sparkler. To begin with, it's dry, a point in its favor, while the flavors are subtle and complex. They suggest pink grapefruits, tangerine zest, a squeeze of white peach, vanilla, and the smoke and dough of oak and lees. With its low alcohol and very low pH, it's a balanced wine of great structural integrity. 91 *—S.H. (12/31/2007)*

Roederer Estate NV Brut Rosé Sparkling Blend (Anderson Valley) $27. 87 —*S.H. (6/1/2006)*

Roederer Estate 2000 L'Ermitage Sparkling Blend (Anderson Valley) $45. Always one of the top sparklers in California, L'Ermitage defines the rigorous selection that marks the best vintage-dated, ageworthy wines. The 2000 is about 50-50 Chardonnay and Pinot, and is very rich and flavorful in yeast, smoke, strawberry, citrus and vanilla flavors, but it's also a very young wine, tight and minerally. It wants bottle age. Should begin to fan-tail out by the end of 2007 and continue to develop for 4-6 years, if not longer. 94 Cellar Selection —*S.H. (12/31/2007)*

Roederer Estate 1999 L'Ermitage Rosé Sparkling Blend (Anderson Valley) $72. 93 —*S.H. (6/1/2005)*

ROESSLER

Roessler 2005 Bluejay Pinot Noir (Anderson Valley) $32. Solid, with ripe, jammy cherry, raspberry, rose petal, tea and cola flavors that are balanced with crisp, tangerine acidity. Drink this dry, flavorful wine now. 89 —*S.H. (10/1/2007)*

Roessler 2004 Dutton Ranch Pinot Noir (Russian River Valley) $38. 85 —*S.H. (10/1/2006)*

Roessler 2005 Hein Family Vineyard Pinot Noir (Anderson Valley) $46. Defines the silky delicacy and balance of Anderson Valley Pinot, a fresh, gently tannic wine of great brightness and approachability. Acidity boosts the purity of the cherries, cassis, tea and cola flavors, making them instantly appealing. Finishes long in cherry cola richness. Drink now–2010. 91 —*S.H. (10/1/2007)*

Roessler 2005 Savoy Pinot Noir (Anderson Valley) $42. From a vineyard in Philo, this shows the grace and elegance of its vineyard's terroir, with crisp, citrusy acids framing remarkably ripe and pure flavors of cherries, raspberries, red plums, gingerbread, vanilla and cinnamon spice. Completely delicious and complex, it will hold for six years or so. 92 —*S.H. (10/1/2007)*

RONAN

Ronan 2003 Lakeview Vineyards Reserve Cabernet Franc (Monterey County) $24. 81 —*S.H. (12/31/2005)*

Ronan 2003 Lakeview Vineyards Cabernet Sauvignon (Monterey County) $24. 83 —*S.H. (12/31/2005)*

Ronan 2003 Lakeview Vineyards Petite Sirah (Monterey County) $26. 83 —*S.H. (12/31/2005)*

Ronan 2003 Lakeview Vineyards Zinfandel (Monterey County) $18. 84 —*S.H. (12/31/2005)*

ROSA D'ORO

Rosa d'Oro 2001 Barbera (Lake County) $17. 82 —*S.H. (5/1/2005)*

Rosa d'Oro 2001 Primitivo (Lake County) $18. 81 —*S.H. (5/1/2005)*

Rosa d'Oro 2002 Syrah (Lake County) $16. 82 —*S.H. (5/1/2005)*

ROSENBLUM

Rosenblum 2004 Holbrook Mitchell Trio Red Wine Bordeaux Blend (Napa Valley) $25. A Bordeaux blend of the two Cabernets plus Merlot, this is a hard wine to like. It feels very hot, with 15.7% of alcohol, and that burn makes the underlying cherry, blackberry and chocolate flavors Port-y and harsh. 82 —*S.H. (11/1/2007)*

Rosenblum 2002 Holbrook Mitchell Trio Red Wine Bordeaux Blend (Napa Valley) $32. 86 —*S.H. (3/1/2006)*

Rosenblum 2001 Holbrook Mitchell Trio Bordeaux Blend (Napa Valley) $36. 92 Editors' Choice —*S.H. (10/3/2004)*

Rosenblum 2000 Holbrook Mitchell Trio Red Wine Cabernet Blend (Napa Valley) $44. 92 —*S.H. (5/1/2003)*

Rosenblum 2003 Kenefick Vineyard Cabernet Franc (Napa Valley) $30. 87 —*S.H. (4/1/2006)*

Rosenblum 2002 Yates Ranch Cabernet Franc (Napa Valley) $28. 86 —*S.H. (12/31/2004)*

Rosenblum 2001 Yates Ranch Cabernet Franc (Napa Valley) $28. 88 —*S.H. (4/1/2004)*

Rosenblum 2000 CRS Yates Ranch Reserve Cabernet Sauvignon (Mount Veeder) $25. 92 —*S.H. (2/1/2004)*

Rosenblum 1997 Holbrook Mitchell Trio Cabernet Sauvignon (Napa Valley) $30. 90 *(11/1/2000)*

Rosenblum 1997 Reserve Cabernet Sauvignon (Napa Valley) $45. 91 *(11/1/2000)*

Rosenblum 1999 Yates Ranch Reserve Cabernet Sauvignon (Mount Veeder) $59. 91 —*S.H. (3/1/2003)*

Rosenblum 1998 Chardonnay (Edna Valley) $19. 87 *(6/1/2000)*

Rosenblum 2002 Lone Oak Vineyard Chardonnay (Russian River Valley) $25. 86 —*S.H. (12/31/2004)*

Rosenblum 2000 Lone Oak Vineyard Chardonnay (Russian River Valley) $35. 86 —*S.H. (5/1/2003)*

Rosenblum 2001 Lone Oak Vineyard Reserve Chardonnay (Russian River Valley) $25. 87 —*S.H. (12/1/2003)*

Rosenblum 1998 Lone Oak Vineyard Reserve Chardonnay (Russian River Valley) $24. 88 *(6/1/2000)*

Rosenblum 2002 Napa Valley Select Chardonnay (Napa Valley) $12. 83 —*S.H. (12/31/2004)*

Rosenblum 2001 Napa Valley Select Chardonnay (Napa Valley) $14. 85 —*S.H. (6/1/2003)*

Rosenblum 2001 RustRidge Chardonnay (Napa Valley) $22. 84 —*S.H. (12/1/2003)*

Rosenblum 2000 RustRidge Vineyard Chardonnay (Napa Valley) $30. 87 —*S.H. (9/1/2003)*

Rosenblum 2003 Marsanne (Dry Creek Valley) $18. 90 Editors' Choice —*S.H. (10/1/2005)*

Rosenblum 2001 Marsanne (Dry Creek Valley) $15. 89 —*S.H. (2/1/2004)*

Rosenblum 2000 Marsanne (Dry Creek Valley) $28. 85 —*S.H. (3/1/2003)*

Rosenblum 2004 Merlot (Russian River Valley) $18. Ripe and plush in the Rosenblum manner, this Merlot shows chocolate, blackberry jam and cherry liqueur flavors. It's easy to understand, an instantly appealing wine that will go nicely with a charred steak. 86 —*S.H. (2/1/2007)*

Rosenblum 2002 Lone Oak Vineyard Merlot (Russian River Valley) $30. 89 —*S.H. (12/31/2004)*

Rosenblum 2001 Lone Oak Vineyard Merlot (Russian River Valley) $21. 90 —*S.H. (5/1/2004)*

Rosenblum 1998 Lone Oak Vineyard Merlot (Russian River Valley) $18. 87 —*J.C. (6/1/2001)*

Rosenblum 2000 Mountain Selection Merlot (Napa Valley) $30. 86 —*S.H. (12/2/2003)*

Rosenblum 1997 Oakville Merlot (Napa Valley) $14. 85 *(11/15/1999)*

Rosenblum 2001 Continente Vineyard Mourvèdre (San Francisco Bay) $16. 85 —*S.H. (5/1/2003)*

Rosenblum 2003 Old Vines Mourvèdre (San Francisco Bay) $25. 88 —*S.H. (4/1/2006)*

Rosenblum 2001 Gallagher Ranch Black Muscat (California) $18. 85 —*S.H. (8/1/2003)*

Rosenblum 2000 Muscat de Glacier Muscat (California) $22. 90 —*S.H. (9/1/2003)*

Rosenblum 2005 Appellation Series Heritage Clones Petite Sirah (San Francisco Bay) $18. Good Petite Sirah that comes down on the chic side of rustic. Shows jiggy-jaggy tannins, wild berry, chocolate and pepper flavors and a high alcohol prickliness, yet it's dry, with that mysterious, drink-me-again quality. 87 —*S.H. (11/1/2007)*

Rosenblum 2004 Heritage Clones Petite Sirah (San Francisco Bay) $20. 87 —*S.H. (11/15/2006)*

Rosenblum 2003 Heritage Clones Petite Sirah (San Francisco Bay) $20. 82 —*S.H. (11/15/2005)*

Rosenblum 2005 Pickett Road Petite Sirah (Napa Valley) $35. Fans of sugar will celebrate this sweet, rich red wine. It smacks of the essence of the most perfectly ripened blackberries, finished with a touch of caramel-ly-oak, then infused with melted chocolate truffle. 87 —*S.H. (12/1/2007)*

Rosenblum 2004 Pickett Road Petite Sirah (Napa Valley) $35. 90 —*S.H. (11/1/2006)*

Rosenblum 2002 Pickett Road Petite Sirah (Napa Valley) $24. 92 —*S.H. (12/15/2004)*

Rosenblum 2001 Pickett Road Petite Sirah (Napa Valley) $22. 90 —*S.H. (12/31/2003)*

Rosenblum 2000 Pickett Road Petite Sirah (Napa Valley) $28. 90 —*S.H. (9/1/2003)*

Rosenblum 2004 Rhodes Vineyard Petite Sirah (Redwood Valley) $25. Petite Sirah can handle high alcohol better than most California reds, and while this one is 15.7% and has a chili pepper heat, its inherent size makes it more or less balanced. The tannins are gigantic, and the fruit is enormous in blackberry jam, black currant, dark chocolate and coffee flavors. Heat actually works as a seasoning, rather than a defect, in such a wine. 90 —*S.H. (11/1/2007)*

Rosenblum 2005 Rockpile Road Vineyard Reserve Petite Sirah (Rockpile) $45. An overly soft, alcoholic wine. It tastes like the blackberry and cola syrup that goes into soda, before the carbonation is added, and finishes prickly hot. 84 —*S.H. (12/15/2007)*

Rosenblum 2004 Rockpile Road Vineyard Petite Sirah (Rockpile) $45. 93 Editors' Choice —*S.H. (12/31/2006)*

Rosenblum 2002 Rockpile Road Vineyard Petite Sirah (Dry Creek Valley) $34. 91 —*S.H. (12/15/2004)*

Rosenblum 2001 Rockpile Road Vineyard Petite Sirah (Dry Creek Valley) $34. 91 —*S.H. (4/1/2004)*

Rosenblum 2000 Rockpile Road Vineyard Petite Sirah (Dry Creek Valley) $35. 87 *(4/1/2003)*

Rosenblum 1999 Rockpile Road Vineyards Petite Sirah (Dry Creek Valley) $25. 89 Cellar Selection —*S.H. (12/1/2001)*

Rosenblum 2006 Chateau La Paws Côte du Bone Blanc Red Blend (California) $14. Made overtly sweet, in the style of some Rosenblum wines, the Viognier, Chardonnay, Sauvignon Blanc and Marsanne blend has sugary flavors of pineapples, peaches and apricots. **83** —*S.H. (12/31/2007)*

Rosenblum 2005 Chateau La Paws Côte du Bone Roan Red Blend (California) $14. A blend of Syrah, Zin and several other Rhône varieties, this is a soft, lusty wine, likeable for its array of ripe, forward fruit flavors. Cherries, blackberries, raspberries and licorice flood the mouth, finishing with a peacock's tail of dusty Asian spices. **87** —*S.H. (12/31/2007)*

Rosenblum 2001 Chateau La Paws Cote du Bone Roan Rhône Red Blend (San Francisco Bay) $16. 87 —*S.H. (6/1/2003)*

Rosenblum 2002 Chateau La Paws Cote du Bone Blanc Rhône White Blend (California) $13. 83 —*S.H. (10/1/2005)*

Rosenblum 2005 Appellation Series Rosé Blend (North Coast) $14. 84 —*S.H. (12/15/2006)*

Rosenblum 2004 Rhodes Vineyard Grenache Rosé Blend (Redwood Valley) $18. 87 —*S.H. (11/15/2005)*

Rosenblum 2003 Fess Parker Vineyard Roussanne (Santa Barbara County) $18. 87 —*S.H. (10/1/2005)*

Rosenblum 2002 Fess Parker Vineyard Roussanne (Santa Barbara County) $18. 84 —*S.H. (12/1/2004)*

Rosenblum 1997 Syrah (Solano County) $18. 83 —*S.H. (6/1/1999)*

Rosenblum 2005 Abba Vineyard Syrah (Lodi) $25. Simple and semisweet, this Syrah has cherry, peppermint and chocolate flavors accented by quite a dose of caramelly oak. Greater acidity would give it balance, but as things stand, it's soft and melted. **83** —*S.H. (12/15/2007)*

Rosenblum 2004 Abba Vineyard Syrah (Lodi) $18. 86 —*S.H. (11/15/2006)*

Rosenblum 2003 Abba Vineyard Syrah (Lodi) $24. 83 *(9/1/2005)*

Rosenblum 2002 Abba Vineyard Syrah (Lodi) $18. 84 —*S.H. (12/1/2004)*

Rosenblum 2001 Abba Vineyard Syrah (Lodi) $18. 84 —*S.H. (12/15/2003)*

Rosenblum 2004 Appellation Series Syrah (Santa Barbara County) $18. Okay if you're looking for something red and fruity, and especially if you want to show the Rosenblum brand. On the other hand the wine has a drily rustic structure despite well-ripened currant, cherry pie and cinnamon chocolate flavors. **84** —*S.H. (2/1/2007)*

Rosenblum 2000 England Shaw Vineyard Syrah (Solano County) $37. 87 —*S.H. (6/1/2003)*

Rosenblum 2002 England-Shaw Vineyard Syrah (Solano County) $30. 87 —*S.H. (12/31/2004)*

Rosenblum 2001 England-Shaw Vineyard Syrah (Solano County) $30. 84 —*S.H. (12/15/2003)*

Rosenblum 2003 England-Shaw Vineyards Syrah (Solano County) $33. 88 *(9/1/2005)*

Rosenblum 1999 England-Shaw Vineyard Syrah (Solano County) $21. 89 *(11/1/2001)*

Rosenblum 2001 Fess Parker Vineyard Syrah (Santa Barbara County) $24. 91 —*S.H. (4/1/2004)*

Rosenblum 2004 Fran's Vineyard Reserve Syrah (Rockpile) $45. Made solidly in the Rosenblum style, namely high alcohol and superripe, but in this case Kent Rosenblum was able to ferment the wine to full dryness, instead of the residual sugar you find in many of his wines. This is a big, dark, rich, tannic Syrah, earthy and cherried. It will last a long time, but is best now. **88** —*S.H. (2/1/2007)*

Rosenblum 2004 Hillside Vineyards Syrah (Sonoma County) $25. 87 —*S.H. (12/15/2006)*

Rosenblum 2003 Hillside Vineyards Syrah (Sonoma County) $28. 88 *(9/1/2005)*

Rosenblum 2002 Hillside Vineyards Syrah (Sonoma County) $26. 87 —*S.H. (12/31/2004)*

Rosenblum 2001 Hillside Vineyards Syrah (Sonoma County) $26. 86 —*S.H. (4/1/2004)*

Rosenblum 2004 Holbrook Mitchell Vineyard Reserve Syrah (Napa Valley) $45. I don't care for this wine. It's too sweet and the underlying fruit, which is on the thin side, really isn't big enough to sustain it. **82** —*S.H. (3/1/2007)*

Rosenblum 2000 Rodney's Vineyard Syrah (Santa Barbara County) $30. 84 —*S.H. (9/1/2003)*

Rosenblum 2005 Rominger Vineyard Syrah (Yolo County) $25. It's pure Rosenblum, as sweet as a confection, as delicious as a filling made from blackberries, cherries, chocolate, licorice, cinnamon, vanilla and white sugar. It's impossible not to be impressed and troubled by a wine such as this. **87** —*S.H. (12/1/2007)*

Rosenblum 2003 Rominger Vineyard Syrah (Yolo County) $26. 91 Editors' Choice *(9/1/2005)*

Rosenblum 2006 Appellation Series Kathy's Cuvée Viognier (California) $18. Frankly sweet in white sugared-flavors of peaches, Meyer lemons, apricots and tangerines, this is more like a dessert wine than a dry table wine. **82** —*S.H. (11/1/2007)*

Rosenblum 2003 Kathy's Cuvée Viognier (Santa Barbara County) $14. 86 —*S.H. (10/1/2005)*

Rosenblum 2005 Kathy's Cuvée Viognier (California) $18. 90 —*S.H. (11/1/2006)*

Rosenblum 2004 Kathy's Cuvée Viognier (California) $16. 87 —*S.H. (3/1/2006)*

Rosenblum 2002 Kathy's Cuvée Viognier (Lodi) $14. 87 —*S.H. (11/15/2004)*

Rosenblum 2001 Late Harvest Ripken Ranch Viognier (Lodi) $19. 85 —*S.H. (12/15/2003)*

Rosenblum 2000 Late Harvest Ripkin Ranch Viognier (Lodi) $22. 86 —*S.H. (5/1/2003)*

Rosenblum 2001 Ripken Vineyard Viognier (Lodi) $19. 85 —*S.H. (3/1/2003)*

Rosenblum 2000 Ripkin Vineyard Viognier (Lodi) $14. 88 Best Buy —*S.H. (11/15/2001)*

Rosenblum 2001 Rodney's Vineyard Viognier (Santa Barbara County) $25. 86 —*S.H. (3/1/2003)*

Rosenblum 2001 Rodney's Vineyard Viognier (Santa Barbara County) $18. 88 —*S.H. (12/1/2003)*

Rosenblum NV Vintners Cuvée Blanc III Vin Blanc Extraordinaire White Blend (California) $11. 84 —*S.H. (7/1/2003)*

Rosenblum 1998 Alegria Zinfandel (Russian River Valley) $26. 91 —*P.G. (3/1/2001)*

Rosenblum 2002 Alegria Vineyard Zinfandel (Russian River Valley) $22. 87 —*S.H. (12/31/2004)*

Rosenblum 2001 Alegria Vineyard Zinfandel (Russian River Valley) $22. 87 *(11/1/2003)*

Rosenblum 2000 Alegria Vineyard Zinfandel (Russian River Valley) $34. 88 —*S.H (5/1/2003)*

Rosenblum 1997 Alegria Vineyard Zinfandel (Russian River Valley) $30. 83 —*J.C. (2/1/2000)*

Rosenblum 2005 Annette's Reserve Zinfandel (Redwood Valley) $35. The vineyard is in a warm, inland section of Mendocino County, and the wine is ripe to the point of super-mature. It lacks the acidity for vibrancy, while the blackberry, coffee and chocolate flavors are Port-y and off-dry. **84** —*S.H. (12/15/2007)*

Rosenblum 2004 Annette's Reserve Zinfandel (Redwood Valley) $35. Rosenblum fans will happily gulp this down. It's made solidly in the winery's style, a big, concentrated, high-alcohol wine dripping with gooey, blackberry pie, chocolate and Port-y flavors. In this case, fortunately, there's no residual sugar. **87** —*S.H. (3/1/2007)*

Rosenblum 2002 Annette's Reserve Zinfandel (Redwood Valley) $28. 90 —*S.H. (3/1/2005)*

Rosenblum 1997 Annette's Reserve Rhodes Viney Zinfandel (Redwood Valley) $26. 89 —*P.G. (11/15/1999)*

Rosenblum 1996 Annette's Reserve Rhodes Viney Zinfandel (Redwood Valley) $26. 89 —*S.H. (9/1/1999)*

Rosenblum 2001 Annette's Reserve Rhodes Vineyard Zinfandel (Redwood Valley) $28. 84 *(11/1/2003)*

Rosenblum 2000 Annette's Reserve Rhodes Vineyard Zinfandel (Redwood Valley) $35. 88 —*S.H. (5/1/2003)*

Rosenblum 1999 Annette's Reserve Rhodes Vineyard Zinfandel (Redwood Valley) $27. 91 Editors' Choice —*S.H. (9/1/2002)*

RRosenblum 2004 Aparicio Vineyard Zinfandel (Amador County) $25. This Zin, with a little Petite Sirah, is a country-style wine, rough and Port-sweet. The winemaker recommends Cajun blackened salmon. **83** —*S.H. (3/1/2007)*

Rosenblum 2003 Aparicio Vineyard Zinfandel (Amador County) $22. 86 *(2/1/2006)*

Rosenblum 2005 Appellation Series Zinfandel (Paso Robles) $18. With its soft, melted mouthfeel and superripe blackberry marmalade, cherry sauce and cherry-chocolate flavors, this Zin exemplifies east side Paso. Many such wines are simple, sweet and rustic, but Kent Rosenblum lifts this one by making it dry, with layers of chewy, herb complexity. **87** —*S.H. (11/1/2007)*

Rosenblum 2005 Appellation Series Zinfandel (San Francisco Bay) $18. With obvious residual sugar, this is more of a dessert than a table wine. It tastes like sugared, stewed blackberries and cherries for pie filling. **82** —*S.H. (11/1/2007)*

Rosenblum 2005 Appellation Series Zinfandel (North Coast) $18. Tastes like an old-fashioned field blend. On the plus side is a wealth of fruit, berry and spice flavors (there's some Carignane and Petite Sirah here), with bigtime but soft tannins that make the wine glide down smooth. On the other hand is a rustic nature and slight sweetness. **84** —*S.H. (2/1/2007)*

Rosenblum 2004 Appellation Series Zinfandel (San Francisco Bay) $18. This has the high alcohol and finishing sweetness of so many Rosenblum red wines, but that's why his customers flock to buy them. For me, it's unbalanced, with its Port-y, chocolate sauce taste. **83** —*S.H. (5/1/2007)*

Rosenblum 2003 Carla's Vineyards Zinfandel (San Francisco Bay) $29. 89 *(2/1/2006)*

Rosenblum 2001 Carla's Vineyards Zinfandel (San Francisco Bay) $23. 91 *(11/1/2003)*

Rosenblum 2000 Carla's Vineyards Zinfandel (San Francisco Bay) $29. 85 —*S.H. (5/1/2003)*

Rosenblum 2002 Carla's Vineyards Zinfandel (San Francisco Bay-Livermore Valley) $24. 87 —*S.H. (11/15/2004)*

Rosenblum 2001 Castanho Vineyard Zinfandel Port Zinfandel (San Francisco Bay) $17. 83 —*S.H. (12/15/2003)*

Rosenblum 2003 Continente Vineyard Zinfandel (San Francisco Bay) $20. 85 —*S.H. (10/1/2005)*

Rosenblum 2002 Continente Vineyard Zinfandel (San Francisco Bay) $18. 85 —*S.H. (12/31/2004)*

Rosenblum 2001 Continente Vineyard Zinfandel (San Francisco Bay) $16. 90 Editors' Choice *(11/1/2003)*

Rosenblum 2000 Continente Vineyard Zinfandel (San Francisco Bay) $20. 88 —*S.H. (5/1/2003)*

Rosenblum 1999 Continente Vineyard Zinfandel (San Francisco Bay) $16. 90 —*M.N. (11/15/2001)*

Rosenblum 1997 Continente Vineyard Zinfandel (Contra Costa County) $19. 90 —*J.C. (9/1/1999)*

Rosenblum 1996 Continente Vineyard Old Old Vine Zinfandel (Contra Costa County) $20. 91 —*J.C. (9/1/1999)*

Rosenblum 2004 Cullinane Reserve Zinfandel (Sonoma Valley) $45. This tastes like the sweetest of Kent Rosenblum's new Zins, which is saying a lot, since they're all as sweet as Port. But here, the sugar seems like it was dumped in by the barrel. It's a delicious wine, chockful of blackberry, cherry, raspberry, blueberry and chocolate flavors, but it really does call for new Federal guidelines on what is a table wine and what is a dessert wine. **86** —*S.H. (2/1/2007)*

Rosenblum 2001 Cullinane Vineyard Zinfandel (Sonoma County) $45. 89 *(11/1/2003)*

Rosenblum NV Cuvée XXV Zinfandel (California) $11. 87 —*M.S. (11/15/2004)*

Rosenblum 2002 Eagle Point Vineyard Zinfandel (Mendocino County) $27. 89 —*S.H. (12/31/2004)*

Rosenblum 2000 Eagle Point Vineyard Zinfandel (Mendocino County) $30. 88 —*S.H. (5/1/2003)*

Rosenblum 2005 Harris Kratka Vineyard Zinfandel (Alexander Valley) $35. Like all Rosenblum Zins, this is a big, tannic wine, with an enormous explosion of fruit. In this case, though, it's dry and balanced. The acidity is low, but the flavors, of crushed ripe blackberries and anisette, are delicious. Cries out for rich meats and cheeses. Drink soon. **88** —*S.H. (12/1/2007)*

Rosenblum 2004 Harris Kratka Vineyard Zinfandel (Alexander Valley) $35. 90 —*S.H. (12/15/2006)*

Rosenblum 2003 Harris Kratka Vineyard Zinfandel (Alexander Valley) $35. 91 *(2/1/2006)*

Rosenblum 2002 Harris Kratka Vineyard Zinfandel (Alexander Valley) $30. 85 —*S.H. (11/15/2004)*

Rosenblum 2001 Harris Kratka Vineyard Zinfandel (Alexander Valley) $30. 88 *(11/1/2003)*

Rosenblum 2004 Hendry Vineyard Zinfandel (Napa Valley) $45. With 17% alcohol, this Zin puzzles me. It is decadently good, soft and gooey as a sauce you'd pour over pie or ice cream. Cherries, chocolate fudge, creme de cassis, raspberry cream liqueur, how delicious is that? More questions: what is the definition of table wine? Am I prejudiced against high alcohol? I welcome reader comments. **85** —*S.H. (2/1/2007)*

Rosenblum 2002 Hendry Vineyard Zinfandel (Napa Valley) $40. 92 —*S.H. (3/1/2005)*

Rosenblum 2001 Hendry Vineyard Zinfandel (Napa Valley) $38. 93 *(11/1/2003)*

Rosenblum 2003 Hendry Vineyard Reserve Zinfandel (Napa Valley) $44. 92 *(2/1/2006)*

Rosenblum 2000 Hendry Vineyard Reserve Zinfandel (Napa Valley) $47. 92 —*S.H. (3/1/2003)*

Rosenblum 1998 Hendry Vineyard Reserve Zinfandel (Napa Valley) $30. 90 —*P.G. (3/1/2001)*

Rosenblum 1997 Hendry Vineyard Reserve Zinfandel (Napa Valley) $30. 86 —*J.C. (2/1/2000)*

Rosenblum 2002 Hillside Vineyards Zinfandel (Sonoma County) $26. 91 —*S.H. (3/1/2005)*

Rosenblum 2005 House Family Vineyards Zinfandel (Sonoma County) $25. This is really one of the least likeable Rosenblum wines I've ever tasted. It smells vegetal and is simple and soft in cherry and blackberry Lifesaver flavors that finish with a sugary sweetness. **80** —*S.H. (12/15/2007)*

Rosenblum 2004 Lyons Reserve Zinfandel (Napa Valley) $45. Kent Rosenblum more than anyone in California is pushing the envelope with high alcohol. This wine, at 16.2%, will fly out the door with his fans. It's as plump and sweet as a cherry-infused chocolate truffle. The fruity intensity comes from the wine's mountain origins. If this is your wine, don't drink and drive. **88** —*S.H. (2/1/2007)*

Rosenblum 2001 Lyons Vineyard 25th Anniversary Zinfandel (Napa Valley) $38. 90 *(11/1/2003)*

Rosenblum 2005 Maggie's Reserve Zinfandel (Sonoma Valley) $45. Another new Rosenblum release and as usual, there is a sweet, sugary edge to the cherries, blackberries and chocolate, although very high acidity helps keep the mouthfeel lively. The official alcohol is 14.8%, but there is something ruby Port-y going on. **86** —*S.H. (12/15/2007)*

Rosenblum 2004 Maggie's Reserve Zinfandel (Sonoma Valley) $45. 89 —*S.H. (12/15/2006)*

Rosenblum 2003 Maggie's Reserve Zinfandel (Sonoma Valley) $46. 91 *(2/1/2006)*

Rosenblum 2005 Monte Rosso Vineyard Reserve Zinfandel (Sonoma Valley) $45. From the pitch-black color you can tell this is an enormously extracted wine. It shows the stuffing of this famous vineyard's Zins, with blackberries, loganberries, cherries, licorice, leather and cocoa-laced coffee, and is quite tannic. But it's diminished by what tastes like notable sugar in the finish, even though the alcohol is over 15%. **84** —*S.H. (12/1/2007)*

Rosenblum 2004 Monte Rosso Vineyard Zinfandel (Sonoma Valley) $45. 93 Editors' Choice —*S.H. (11/1/2006)*

Rosenblum 2002 Monte Rosso Vineyard Zinfandel (Sonoma Valley) $38. 87 —*S.H. (12/15/2004)*

Rosenblum 2001 Monte Rosso Vineyard Zinfandel (Sonoma County) $38. 89 *(11/1/2003)*

Rosenblum 2002 Oakley Vineyards Zinfandel (Contra Costa County) $14. 89 —*S.H. (12/15/2004)*

Rosenblum 2001 Oakley Vineyards Zinfandel (San Francisco Bay) $12. 83 —*S.H. (3/1/2004)*

Rosenblum 2000 Oakley Vineyards Zinfandel (San Francisco Bay) $18. 84 —*S.H. (5/1/2003)*

Rosenblum 2000 Old Vines Zinfandel (Russian River Valley) $18. 89 Editors' Choice —*S.H. (5/1/2003)*

Rosenblum 2000 Pato Vineyard Zinfandel (San Francisco Bay) $26. 84 —*S.H. (5/1/2003)*

Rosenblum 2004 Planchon Vineyard Zinfandel (San Francisco Bay) $25. I like this wine less than the '03, which I criticized for flirting with Portiness. This wine outright marries Port. It has a good deal of residual sugar and is as rich and sweet as a chocolate truffle. That's a good flavor, but at 16.5% alcohol, it's not a dry table wine. **84** —*S.H. (2/1/2007)*

Rosenblum 2003 Planchon Vineyard Zinfandel (San Francisco Bay) $22. 87 —*S.H. (10/1/2005)*

Rosenblum 2002 Planchon Vineyard Zinfandel (San Francisco Bay) $20. 91 *—S.H. (12/15/2004)*

Rosenblum 2001 Planchon Vineyard Zinfandel (San Francisco Bay) $19. 91 **Editors' Choice** *(11/1/2003)*

Rosenblum 2000 Planchon Vineyard Zinfandel (San Francisco Bay) $24. 85 *—S.H. (5/1/2003)*

Rosenblum 2005 Richard Sauret Vineyard Zinfandel (Paso Robles) $25. Hot, soft and uninteresting. It's not a bad wine, being clean and somewhat dry, but that softness results in a serious absence of structure, and there's not enough fruity essence to compensate. 83 *—S.H. (12/1/2007)*

Rosenblum 2002 Richard Sauret Vineyard Zinfandel (Paso Robles) $18. 90 *—S.H. (12/31/2004)*

Rosenblum 2001 Richard Sauret Vineyard Zinfandel (Paso Robles) $19. 91 **Editors' Choice** *(11/1/2003)*

Rosenblum 2000 Richard Sauret Vineyard Zinfandel (Paso Robles) $24. 87 *—S.H. (2/1/2003)*

Rosenblum 1997 Richard Sauret Vineyard Zinfandel (Paso Robles) $22. 88 *—P.G. (11/15/1999)*

Rosenblum 2004 Richard Sauret Vineyards Zinfandel (Paso Robles) $25. 92 **Editors' Choice** *—S.H. (11/1/2006)*

Rosenblum 2003 Richard Sauret Vineyards Zinfandel (Paso Robles) $22. 90 **Editors' Choice** *(2/1/2006)*

Rosenblum 2005 Rockpile Road Vineyard Zinfandel (Rockpile) $35. I love the briary, spicy aroma on this wine. It's so inviting. But then when you taste it, it turns too soft and sweet, like a melted cherry- and cassis-filled chocolate truffle. That's a delicious flavor, but it's not really a dry table wine. 84 *—S.H. (12/15/2007)*

Rosenblum 2001 Rockpile Road Zinfandel (Dry Creek Valley) $26. 86 *(11/1/2003)*

Rosenblum 1998 Rockpile Road Zinfandel (Dry Creek Valley) $19. 90 **Editors' Choice** *—P.G. (3/1/2001)*

Rosenblum 2004 Rockpile Road Vineyard Zinfandel (Rockpile) $35. 92 *—S.H. (12/15/2006)*

Rosenblum 2002 Rockpile Road Vineyard Zinfandel (Dry Creek Valley) $26. 92 *—S.H. (12/15/2004)*

Rosenblum 1999 Rockpile Road Vineyard Zinfandel (Dry Creek Valley) $21. 86 *—S.H. (12/15/2001)*

Rosenblum 1997 Rust Ridge Vineyard Zinfandel (Napa Valley) $22. 88 *—P.G. (11/15/1999)*

Rosenblum 2001 Rust Ridge Vineyard Zinfandel (Napa Valley) $25. 91 *—S.H. (5/1/2004)*

Rosenblum 1998 Rust Ridge Vineyard Zinfandel (Napa Valley) $18. 87 *(3/1/2001)*

Rosenblum 2002 Samsel Vineyard Maggie's Reserve Zinfandel (Sonoma Valley) $42. 87 *—S.H. (12/31/2004)*

Rosenblum 2001 Samsel Vineyard Maggie's Reserve Zinfandel (Sonoma Valley) $42. 90 *(11/1/2000)*

Rosenblum 1997 Samsel Vineyard Maggie's Reserve Zinfandel (Sonoma Valley) $35. 87 *—J.C. (2/1/2000)*

Rosenblum 2004 Snows Lake Zinfandel (Lake County) $35. Solidly in the Rosenblum style, a soft, high-alcohol wine, low in acids and tannins, high in the deliciousness factor. Like a dessert in a glass, it shows flavors of blackberry and cherry pie filling and melted chocolate, drizzled with licorice syrup, then sprinkled with cinnamon, nutmeg and vanilla. Miraculously, the wine is dry. 91 *—S.H. (11/1/2007)*

Rosenblum 2005 Snows Lake Vineyard Zinfandel (Lake County) $35. This is a wine that's soft in structure, and while it's dry, it's hard in tannins and the fruit has a baked taste like shrivelled raisins. Not an ager. 84 *—S.H. (12/1/2007)*

Rosenblum 2004 St. Peter's Church Vineyard Zinfandel (Sonoma County) $55. With 17% alcohol, this Zin still has residual sugar. They must have picked the grapes insanely ripe. It's not a table wine, it's more like Port, but it's not without its pleasures. 80 *—S.H. (11/1/2007)*

Rosenblum 2000 St. Peter's Church Zinfandel (Sonoma County) $50. 86 *—S.H. (5/1/2003)*

Rosenblum 1998 St. Peter's Church Vineyard Zinfandel (Sonoma County) $40. 88 *(3/1/2001)*

Rosenblum NV Vintners Cuvée XXI Zinfandel (California) $10. 88 **Best Buy** *—P.G. (3/1/2001)*

Rosenblum NV Vintners Cuvée Millenium Zinfandel (California) $10. 84 *—J.C. (2/1/2000)*

Rosenblum NV Vintners Cuvée XXIV Zinfandel (California) $11. 84 *—S.H. (3/1/2004)*

USA

Rosenblum 2001 Vintners Cuvée XXV Zinfandel (California) $10. 87 **Best Buy** *(11/1/2003)*

Rosenblum 2002 Vintners Cuvée XXVI Zinfandel (California) $9. 86 **Best Buy** *—S.H. (12/31/2004)*

ROSENTHAL

Rosenthal 1996 The Malibu Estate Cabernet Sauvignon (Malibu-Newton Canyon) $35. 88 *—J.M. (6/1/2002)*

Rosenthal 2000 The Malibu Estate Chardonnay (Malibu-Newton Canyon) $22. 87 *—J.M. (5/1/2002)*

Rosenthal 1997 The Malibu Estate The Devon Vineyard Merlot (Malibu-Newton Canyon) $35. 92 *—J.M. (6/1/2002)*

ROSENTHAL-MALIBU ESTATE

Rosenthal-Malibu Estate 2001 Cabernet Sauvignon (Malibu-Newton Canyon) $35. 81 *—S.H. (12/1/2005)*

Rosenthal-Malibu Estate 1999 Cabernet Sauvignon (Malibu-Newton Canyon) $35. 85 *—S.H. (11/15/2004)*

Rosenthal-Malibu Estate 1999 Founder's Reserve Cabernet Sauvignon (Malibu-Newton Canyon) $70. 90 *—S.H. (11/15/2004)*

Rosenthal-Malibu Estate 2003 Chardonnay (Central Coast) $18. 87 *—S.H. (12/15/2004)*

Rosenthal-Malibu Estate 2001 The Devon Vineyard Merlot (Malibu-Newton Canyon) $25. 83 *—S.H. (12/1/2005)*

Rosenthal-Malibu Estate 1999 The Devon Vineyard Merlot (Malibu-Newton Canyon) $35. 87 *—S.H. (12/15/2004)*

ROSHAMBO

Roshambo 2003 Chardonnay (California) $10. 85 **Best Buy** *—S.H. (10/1/2005)*

Roshambo 2004 Imago Chardonnay (Sonoma County) $18. 85 *—S.H. (12/15/2005)*

Roshambo 2003 Rock Paper Scissors Merlot (California) $10. 85 **Best Buy** *—S.H. (10/1/2005)*

Roshambo 2003 Sauvignon Blanc (Dry Creek Valley) $12. 84 *—S.H. (5/1/2005)*

Roshambo 2005 Imoan Syrah Rosé Syrah (Sonoma County) $16. On the sugary-sweet side, with pastry-filling raspberry flavors generously spiced with cinnamon and vanilla. Finishes simple and fruity. 83 *—S.H. (7/1/2007)*

Roshambo 2002 Justice Syrah (Dry Creek Valley) $21. 87 *—S.H. (12/15/2005)*

Roshambo 2003 Rosé Syrah (Dry Creek Valley) $15. 86 *—S.H. (12/31/2004)*

Roshambo 2004 Think Rosé of Syrah (Sonoma County) $15. 86 *—S.H. (12/15/2005)*

Roshambo 2003 Frank Johnson Vineyards Late Harvest Traminer (Dry Creek Valley) $19. 84 *—S.H. (5/1/2005)*

Roshambo 2001 Zinfandel (Dry Creek Valley) $21. 90 *—S.H. (10/1/2004)*

Roshambo 2001 Zinfandel (Alexander Valley) $18. 88 *—S.H. (10/1/2004)*

Roshambo 2002 The Reverend Zinfandel (Dry Creek Valley) $21. 86 *—S.H. (12/15/2005)*

ROSS VINEYARDS

Ross Vineyards 2000 Sauvignon Blanc (Napa Valley) $18. 90 *—J.M. (9/1/2002)*

ROTH

Roth 2002 Cabernet Sauvignon (Alexander Valley) $40. 88 *—S.H. (5/1/2005)*

Roth 2000 Heritage Red Wine Red Blend (Alexander Valley) $30. 89 *—S.H. (12/31/2003)*

ROTTA

Rotta 2004 Boneso Vineyard Cabernet Franc (Paso Robles) $22. Country-style defines this pale, easy wine, with its softness and earthiness. There's modest cherry flavors, with undertones of pomegranate and rhubarb. Seems pricey for what you get. 83 *—S.H. (7/1/2007)*

Rotta 2003 Black Monukka Dessert Wine Sherry (California) $20. The variety is a table grape grown in California. The winery calls it Sherry, with the qualifier that the barrels were stored in the sun for two years. Not clear if it was invaded with flor, but the wine shows a crisp, Sherried cherry, vanilla and caramel character, sweet and succulent. 88 *—S.H. (7/1/2007)*

Rotta 2004 Estate Giubbini Vineyard Zinfandel (Paso Robles) $25. Shows all the marks of being grown in a hothouse, from the cooked, Port taste with its edge of raisins to the high alcohol. But it's dry. You either like this style, or you don't. 84 —*S.H. (7/1/2007)*

ROUND BARN

Round Barn 2003 Cabernet Franc (Lake Michigan Shore) $45. 84 —*M.D. (8/1/2006)*

Round Barn NV Chardonnay (Lake Michigan Shore) $18. 83 —*M.D. (8/1/2006)*

Round Barn 2003 Pinot Noir (Lake Michigan Shore) $28. 81 —*M.D. (12/1/2006)*

Round Barn NV Vineyard Tears White Blend (Lake Michigan Shore) $15. 82 —*M.D. (8/1/2006)*

ROUND HILL

Round Hill 2000 Cabernet Sauvignon (California) $8. 84 —*S.H. (11/15/2003)*

Round Hill 1999 Cabernet Sauvignon (California) $9. 81 —*S.H. (12/31/2002)*

Round Hill 2003 Chardonnay (California) $9. 83 —*S.H. (10/1/2005)*

Round Hill 2002 Merlot (California) $9. 86 Best Buy —*S.H. (10/1/2005)*

Round Hill 2002 White Zinfandel (California) $4. 82 —*S.H. (3/1/2004)*

Round Hill 2001 White Zinfandel (California) $4. 83 —*S.H. (9/1/2003)*

ROUND POND

Round Pond 2003 Cabernet Sauvignon (Rutherford) $50. 87 —*S.H. (12/15/2006)*

ROW ELEVEN

Row Eleven 2002 Pinot Noir (Santa Maria Valley) $29. 88 —*S.H. (10/1/2005)*

Row Eleven 2002 San Luis Obispo Mendocino Counties Pinot Noir (California) $24. 89 —*S.H. (10/1/2005)*

ROWLAND

Rowland 2001 Mountainside Cabernet Sauvignon (Napa Valley) $27. 90 —*S.H. (10/1/2004)*

Rowland 2000 Red Triangle Cabernet Sauvignon (Napa Valley) $28. 91 Editors' Choice —*S.H. (12/15/2003)*

Rowland 1999 Red Triangle Cabernet Sauvignon (Napa Valley) $28. 92 —*S.H. (6/1/2002)*

Rowland 1997 Red Triangle Cabernet Sauvignon (Napa Valley) $22. 86 —*M.S. (10/1/1999)*

Rowland 1999 Red Triangle Syrah (Napa Valley) $24. 88 *(11/1/2001)*

Rowland 2001 Red Triangle Mountainside Syrah (Napa Valley) $27. 90 —*S.H. (12/1/2004)*

ROY J. MAIER

Roy J. Maier 2003 Sonoma County Mountains Cabernet Sauvignon (Sonoma County) $60. 87 —*S.H. (8/1/2006)*

ROYAL OAKS

Royal Oaks 1999 Aristocrat Bordeaux Blend (Santa Ynez Valley) $18. 89 —*S.H. (4/1/2002)*

Royal Oaks 1999 Westerly Vineyard Reserve Cabernet Franc (Santa Ynez Valley) $30. 86 —*S.H. (4/1/2002)*

Royal Oaks 2000 Chardonnay (Santa Ynez Valley) $16. 85 —*S.H. (4/1/2002)*

Royal Oaks 1999 Chardonnay (Santa Barbara County) $18. 86 —*S.H. (5/1/2001)*

Royal Oaks 1999 Los Alamos Vineyard Reserve Chardonnay (Santa Barbara) $20. 88 —*S.H. (5/1/2001)*

Royal Oaks 2000 White Hawk Vineyard Reserve Chardonnay (Santa Barbara County) $86. 86 —*S.H. (4/1/2002)*

Royal Oaks 1998 Whitegate Vineyard Chardonnay (Santa Ynez Valley) $20. 86 *(6/1/2000)*

Royal Oaks 1999 Merlot (Santa Ynez Valley) $20. 85 —*S.H. (4/1/2002)*

Royal Oaks 1998 Merlot (Santa Ynez Valley) $20. 86 —*S.H. (5/1/2001)*

Royal Oaks 1999 Reserve Merlot (Santa Ynez Valley) $25. 89 —*S.H. (4/1/2002)*

Royal Oaks 2000 Westerly Vineyard Merlot (Santa Ynez Valley) $30. 86 —*S.H. (3/1/2004)*

Royal Oaks 1998 Westerly Vineyard Merlot (Santa Ynez Valley) $25. 87 —*S.H. (6/1/2001)*

Royal Oaks 2000 Pinot Noir (Santa Maria Valley) $22. 88 —*S.H. (4/1/2002)*

Royal Oaks 2000 Sangiovese (Central Coast) $18. 85 —*S.H. (5/1/2002)*

Royal Oaks 2000 Sauvignon Blanc (Santa Barbara County) $15. 85 —*S.H. (4/1/2002)*

Royal Oaks 1999 Sauvignon Blanc (Santa Barbara County) $16. 86 —*S.H. (5/1/2001)*

Royal Oaks 2000 Reserve Sauvignon Blanc (Santa Ynez Valley) $19. 86 —*S.H. (4/1/2002)*

Royal Oaks 1999 Valley View Vineyard Reserve Sauvignon Blanc (Santa Ynez Valley) $18. 85 —*S.H. (5/1/2001)*

Royal Oaks 2001 Westerly Vineyard Sauvignon Blanc (Santa Ynez Valley) $22. 85 —*S.H. (12/31/2003)*

Royal Oaks 2000 Syrah (Central Coast) $20. 85 —*S.H. (9/1/2002)*

Royal Oaks 2001 Westerly Vineyard Viognier (Santa Ynez Valley) $28. 87 —*S.H. (12/31/2003)*

ROZA RIDGE

Roza Ridge 2002 Roza Ridge Vineyard Syrah (Yakima Valley) $14. 84 *(9/1/2005)*

ROZAK

Rozak 2003 Pinot Noir (Santa Rita Hills) $30. 87—*S.H. (3/1/2006)*

RUBICON ESTATE

Rubicon Estate 2003 Bordeaux Blend (Rutherford) $115. This is a lush wine. It's 95% Cabernet, with a few drops of Cab Franc, Merlot and Petit Verdot. Distinctly Californian in the softness of tannins and low acidity, it's ready to drink now. The waves of cassis and notes of licorice, cola and new oak impress with their richness. However, this is the leanest Rubicon in years, missing the qualities of greatness. Drink now. 5,244 cases produced. 89 —*S.H. (12/1/2007)*

Rubicon Estate 2004 Rubicon Bordeaux Blend (Rutherford) $125. At its best Rubicon stuns with power and richness. In lesser vintages (which are usually hotter ones) the wine, which is largely Cabernet Sauvignon, can be raisiny. While 2004 was a warm year, diligent viticulture paid off, resulting in an opulent wine with the purest expression of crushed cherries and blackberries, and oak-inspired hints of nougat and caramel. Fairly aggressive in tannins now, it should begin to open by 2008 and drink well for a decade. 93 —*S.H. (12/15/2007)*

Rubicon Estate 2002 Cabernet Blend (Rutherford) $110. 98 Cellar Selection —*S.H. (9/1/2006)*

Rubicon Estate 2003 Cabernet Franc (Rutherford) $44. 86 —*S.H. (5/1/2006)*

Rubicon Estate 2003 Cask Cabernet Sauvignon (Rutherford) $65. 95 Cellar Selection —*S.H. (12/15/2006)*

Rubicon Estate 2002 Cask Cabernet Cabernet Sauvignon (Rutherford) $65. 90 Cellar Selection —*S.H. (12/15/2005)*

Rubicon Estate 2005 Blancaneaux Rhône White Blend (Rutherford) $40. The '05, as befits a cool vintage, is lean, with the alcohol showing through bare-bones citrus flavors. Even those who like their whites dry and flinty may find this Marsanne, Roussanne and Viognier blend a little thin. 86 —*S.H. (12/1/2007)*

Rubicon Estate 2004 Blancaneaux White Wine Rhône White Blend (Rutherford) $40. 86 —*S.H. (11/15/2006)*

RUBISSOW-SARGENT

Rubissow-Sargent 2003 Trompettes Bordeaux Blend (Mount Veeder) $45. Bone dry and sharp in acids, this is a blend of Cab Franc and Merlot. Lighter in body, with cherry and oak flavors. It's a gamble if it will soften with age. 85 —*S.H. (7/1/2007)*

Rubissow-Sargent 2003 Cabernet Sauvignon (Mount Veeder) $42. You'll want to decant this for a few hours to let it breathe, because it's tight, but it's not an ager. Shows bone dry, jammy, sweet-and-sour cherry and tangerine flavors, wrapped into sturdy mountain tannins. 86 —*S.H. (7/1/2007)*

Rubissow-Sargent 2002 Cabernet Sauvignon (Mount Veeder) $35. The '02 is better than the '03, a ripe, deeply flavored young Cab. Well-oaked, it shows wild blackberry flavors, and finishes dry. Best now–2010. 89 —*S.H. (7/1/2007)*

Rubissow-Sargent 1999 Cabernet Sauvignon (Mount Veeder) $30. 87 —*S.H. (5/1/2005)*

Rubissow-Sargent 2000 Reserve Cabernet Sauvignon (Mount Veeder) $75. 89 Cellar Selection —*S.H. (5/1/2005)*

Rubissow-Sargent 2003 Merlot (Mount Veeder) $32. This is a superripe young wine, brimming with cherry, cocoa, tobacco and oak flavors, with a slightly raisiny finish. The tannins are soft and yielding, but there's a good bite of acidity for balance. Drink now. 86 —*S.H. (7/1/2007)*

RUDD

Rudd 2000 Jericho Canyon Vineyard Red Wine Bordeaux Blend (Napa Valley) $100. 91 —*J.C. (5/1/2004)*

Rudd 2001 Cabernet Sauvignon (Oakville) $75. 94 Cellar Selection —*S.H. (10/1/2004)*

Rudd 2004 *Barrel Sample* Cabernet Sauvignon (Oakville) $NA. 93 —*S.H. (8/1/2004)*

Rudd 2003 Estate Grown Cabernet Sauvignon (Oakville) $125. 92 —*S.H. (9/1/2006)*

Rudd 2002 Oakville Estate Cabernet Sauvignon (Oakville) $90. 96 Cellar Selection —*S.H. (11/1/2005)*

Rudd 1998 Chardonnay (Carneros) $35. 90 *(7/1/2001)*

Rudd 1998 Chardonnay (Russian River Valley) $35. 87 *(7/1/2001)*

Rudd 2000 Estate Red Wine Red Blend (Oakville) $100. 92 —*J.C. (5/1/2004)*

Rudd 2003 Sauvignon Blanc (Napa Valley) $28. 89 *(7/1/2005)*

RULO WINERY

Rulo Winery 2002 Cabernet Sauvignon (Columbia Valley (WA)) $30. 92 —*P.G. (9/1/2004)*

Rulo Winery 2004 Sundance Vineyard Chardonnay (Columbia Valley (WA)) $20. 90 —*P.G. (6/1/2006)*

Rulo Winery 2001 Sundance Vineyard Chardonnay (Columbia Valley (WA)) $23. 90 —*P.G. (9/1/2003)*

Rulo Winery 2003 Vanessa Vineyard Chardonnay (Walla Walla (WA)) $20. 91 —*P.G. (12/15/2005)*

Rulo Winery 2004 Combine Sauvignon Blanc (Columbia Valley (WA)) $15. 91 Best Buy —*P.G. (6/1/2006)*

Rulo Winery 2004 Syrah (Columbia Valley (WA)) $19. 92 Editors' Choice —*P.G. (8/1/2006)*

Rulo Winery 2002 Syrah (Columbia Valley (WA)) $18. 90 —*P.G. (9/1/2004)*

Rulo Winery 2001 Syrah (Columbia Valley (WA)) $18. 89 —*P.G. (9/1/2003)*

Rulo Winery 2002 Silo Syrah (Columbia Valley (WA)) $25. 90 —*P.G. (9/1/2004)*

Rulo Winery 2004 Viognier (Columbia Valley (WA)) $18. 90 —*P.G. (6/1/2006)*

Rulo Winery 2003 Viognier (Walla Walla (WA)) $18. 90 —*P.G. (9/1/2004)*

Rulo Winery 2001 Viognier (Columbia Valley (WA)) $18. 88 —*P.G. (9/1/2003)*

USA

RUSACK

Rusack 2001 Anacapa Bordeaux Blend (Santa Ynez Valley) $38. 90 —*S.H. (10/1/2003)*

Rusack 1997 Anacapa Bordeaux Blend (Santa Ynez Valley) $32. 85 *(11/1/2000)*

Rusack 2002 Anacapa Cabernet Blend (Santa Ynez Valley) $36. 84 —*S.H. (10/1/2005)*

Rusack 2005 Chardonnay (Santa Barbara County) $22. Brisk and dry, this Chard show an acidic brittleness to the tropical fruit, citrus and hay flavors. It makes up for in balance and elegance what it near misses in sheer pizazz. 87 —*S.H. (8/1/2007)*

Rusack 2004 Chardonnay (Santa Barbara County) $20. 88 —*S.H. (8/1/2006)*

Rusack 2003 Chardonnay (Santa Barbara County) $20. 87 —*S.H. (10/1/2005)*

Rusack 2002 Chardonnay (Santa Barbara County) $18. 90 Editors' Choice —*S.H. (6/1/2004)*

Rusack 2001 Chardonnay (Santa Barbara County) $18. 90 Editors' Choice —*S.H. (5/1/2003)*

Rusack 2004 Reserve Chardonnay (Santa Maria Valley) $32. 91 —*S.H. (8/1/2006)*

Rusack 2003 Reserve Chardonnay (Santa Maria Valley) $32. 91 —*S.H. (10/1/2005)*

Rusack 2001 Reserve Chardonnay (Santa Maria Valley) $32. 90 —*S.H. (6/1/2003)*

Rusack 1997 Reserve Chardonnay (Santa Maria Valley) $30. 90 *(6/1/2000)*

Rusack 1998 Reserve Lucas Select Chardonnay (Santa Maria Valley) $35. 88 *(7/1/2001)*

Rusack 1997 Silver Moon Merlot (Santa Ynez Valley) $15. 85 —*J.C. (7/1/2000)*

Rusack 2005 Pinot Noir (Santa Barbara County) $26. Not up there with the winery's Reserve or Rancho Santa Rosa bottlings, but a good, respectable exemplar of terroir. Dry, crisply acidic and balanced, it shows cherry, cola, herb, sweet vanilla and spice flavors wrapped into a silky texture. 86 —*S.H. (8/1/2007)*

Rusack 2004 Pinot Noir (Santa Maria Valley) $30. 90 —*S.H. (8/1/2006)*

Rusack 2002 Pinot Noir (Santa Maria Valley) $25. 89 *(11/1/2004)*

Rusack 2001 Pinot Noir (Santa Maria Valley) $25. 85 —*S.H. (7/1/2003)*

Rusack 2001 Pinot Noir (Santa Barbara County) $18. 85 —*S.H. (7/1/2003)*

Rusack 2000 Pinot Noir (Santa Maria Valley) $28. 84 *(10/1/2002)*

Rusack 2005 Rancho Santa Rosa Pinot Noir (Santa Rita Hills) $45. Young and tight in acidity now, with a bracing mouthfeel, but it's one to cellar for a few years. Dry and elegant, it shows a good balance of sweet cherry and cola fruit with earthier notes of Portobello mushrooms and balsamic. Best after 2008. 90 —*S.H. (7/1/2007)*

Rusack 2005 Reserve Pinot Noir (Santa Rita Hills) $38. This is an opulently layered wine, with vibrantly pure fruit grounded with a touch of sage and sweet thyme. Beautifully balanced and elegant now, it should continue to evolve over the next 6–8 years. 92 —*S.H. (4/1/2007)*

Rusack 2004 Reserve Pinot Noir (Santa Rita Hills) $38. 93 —*S.H. (8/1/2006)*

Rusack 2002 Reserve Pinot Noir (Santa Rita Hills) $32. 87 *(11/1/2004)*

Rusack 2001 Reserve Pinot Noir (Santa Rita Hills) $32. 86 —*S.H. (7/1/2003)*

Rusack 1999 Reserve Lucas Select Pinot Noir (Santa Maria Valley) $35. 86 *(10/1/2002)*

Rusack 2005 Sauvignon Blanc (Santa Ynez Valley) $16. 86 —*S.H. (8/1/2006)*

Rusack 2002 Sauvignon Blanc (Santa Ynez Valley) $15. 87 —*S.H. (12/31/2003)*

Rusack 2003 Syrah (Santa Barbara County) $25. 89 *(9/1/2005)*

Rusack 2001 Syrah (Santa Ynez Valley) $25. 90 —*S.H. (3/1/2004)*

Rusack 2004 Ballard Canyon Reserve Syrah (Santa Barbara County) $36. A great big, oaky wine; it's full-bodied, tannic and incredibly fruity. But the tannins are sweet and softly ripe, and as rich as the fruit is in black cherries, black raspberries, smoky blueberries, moo shu plum sauce and carob, there's good acidity to balance it. It all adds up to a totally delicious wine that's ready to drink now. 93 —*S.H. (8/1/2007)*

Rusack 2003 Ballard Canyon Reserve Syrah (Santa Barbara County) $36. 88 *(9/1/2005)*

Rusack 1999 Estate Vineyard Syrah (Santa Barbara County) $25. 88 *(11/1/2001)*

RUSSELL CREEK

Russell Creek 2002 Tributary Red Wine Bordeaux Blend (Washington) $20. 86 —*P.G. (4/1/2005)*

Russell Creek 2002 Walla Walla Valley & Columbia Valley Cabernet Sauvignon (Washington) $28. 88 —*P.G. (4/1/2005)*

Russell Creek 2002 Winemakers Select Cabernet Sauvignon (Walla Walla (WA)) $38. 88 —*P.G. (4/1/2005)*

Russell Creek 2002 Merlot (Walla Walla (WA)) $26. 87 —*P.G. (4/1/2005)*

Russell Creek 2000 Merlot (Columbia Valley (WA)) $32. 88 —*P.G. (9/1/2002)*

Russell Creek 2002 Winemakers Select Merlot (Walla Walla (WA)) $36. 87 —*P.G. (4/1/2005)*

Russell Creek 2002 Winemakers Select Syrah (Columbia Valley (WA)) $35. 86 —*P.G. (4/1/2005)*

RUSSIAN HILL

Russian Hill 2004 Gail Ann's Vineyard Chardonnay (Russian River Valley) $30. 88 —*S.H. (12/31/2006)*

Russian Hill 2003 Gail Ann's Vineyard Chardonnay (Russian River Valley) $28. 84 —*S.H. (12/15/2005)*

Russian Hill 2002 Gail Ann's Vineyard Chardonnay (Russian River Valley) $30. 87 —*S.H. (3/1/2005)*

Russian Hill 2001 Gail Ann's Vineyard Chardonnay (Russian River Valley) $26. 91 —*S.H. (5/1/2004)*

Russian Hill 2005 Pinot Noir (Russian River Valley) $28. Smells thin and sweaty-funky, with little flavor, except the heat of alcohol. Maybe there's a drop of cherries. 81 —*S.H. (12/1/2007)*

Russian Hill 2003 Pinot Noir (Russian River Valley) $32. 82 —*S.H. (12/15/2005)*

Russian Hill 2002 Pinot Noir (Sonoma Coast) $42. 89 *—S.H. (3/1/2005)*

Russian Hill 2000 Pinot Noir (Russian River Valley) $28. 89 *(10/1/2002)*

Russian Hill 2000 Pinot Noir (Sonoma Coast) $22. 84 *(10/1/2002)*

Russian Hill 1999 Pinot Noir (Russian River Valley) $28. 86 *(10/1/2002)*

Russian Hill 2002 Estate Pinot Noir (Russian River Valley) $33. 87 *—S.H. (3/1/2005)*

Russian Hill 2005 Estate Vineyards Pinot Noir (Russian River Valley) $33. Soft and superripe, although dry, this Pinot certainly floods the mouth with attractively creamy crushed berry, cola, tea and spice flavors. But it's not particularly complex and falls apart on the finish. Drink now. 85 *—S.H. (12/1/2007)*

Russian Hill 2004 Estate Vineyards Pinot Noir (Russian River Valley) $32. 86 *—S.H. (12/31/2006)*

Russian Hill 2004 Leras Vineyard Pinot Noir (Russian River Valley) $40. 91 *—S.H. (12/31/2006)*

Russian Hill 2000 Leras Vineyard Pinot Noir (Russian River Valley) $38. 86 *(10/1/2002)*

Russian Hill 1999 Leras Vineyard Pinot Noir (Russian River Valley) $44. 89 *(10/1/2002)*

Russian Hill 2005 Tara Vineyard Pinot Noir (Russian River Valley) $45. Soft, ripe and thick, this is one of those Rhône-style Pinots that purists will find on the big side for a variety that's supposed to be silky and delicate. On the plus side, it's a dry, rich wine, with oodles of cherries, blackberries and cinnamon-spiced punch. 88 *—S.H. (12/1/2007)*

Russian Hill 2004 Tara Vineyard Pinot Noir (Russian River Valley) $42. 90 *—S.H. (12/1/2006)*

Russian Hill 2003 Tara Vineyard Pinot Noir (Russian River Valley) $47. 81 *—S.H. (12/15/2005)*

Russian Hill 2002 Syrah (Russian River Valley) $22. 88 *(9/1/2005)*

Russian Hill 1999 Syrah (Russian River Valley) $22. 89 *(11/1/2001)*

Russian Hill 2004 Ellen's Block Syrah (Russian River Valley) $30. There's a deep, ultraripe core of cherry and blackberry fruit to this wine that's almost shriveled. You can sense that hint of raisins in the finish, which is very dry and on the astringently tannic side. It's a nicely fashionable wine, but not an ager, so drink now. 87 *—S.H. (12/1/2007)*

Russian Hill 2002 Ellen's Block Syrah (Russian River Valley) $30. 86 *(9/1/2005)*

Russian Hill 2001 Ellen's Block Syrah (Russian River Valley) $30. 91 *(5/1/2004)*

Russian Hill 2004 Top Block Syrah (Russian River Valley) $30. Here's a big, tannic and dry Syrah, the kind that needs either some aging or serious decanting to come around. It's a very fine wine, with a deep, plush core of plums, blackberries and leathery carob flavors, but there's an astringency to the middle through the finish. Air it for a few hours, or wait until after mid-2008. 91 *—S.H. (12/1/2007)*

Russian Hill 2002 Top Block Syrah (Russian River Valley) $30. 85 *(9/1/2005)*

Russian Hill 2001 Top Block Syrah (Russian River Valley) $30. 2 Editors' Choice *(5/1/2004)*

Russian Hill 2001 Windsor Oaks Summit Syrah (Russian River Valley) $40. 90 *(5/1/2004)*

RUSTON

Ruston 2002 La Maestra Red Wine Cabernet Blend (St. Helena) $50. 93 Editors' Choice *—S.H. (8/1/2006)*

Ruston 2000 Merlot (St. Helena) $30. 91 *—J.M. (4/1/2004)*

RUSTRIDGE

RustRidge 1998 Cabernet Sauvignon (Napa Valley) $28. 83 *—S.H. (12/1/2001)*

RustRidge 1997 Reserve Cabernet Sauvignon (Napa Valley) $30. 81 *—S.H. (12/1/2001)*

RustRidge 1999 Chardonnay (Napa Valley) $22. 86 *—S.H. (12/1/2001)*

RustRidge 1998 Estate Bottled Chardonnay (Napa Valley) $25. 83 *(6/1/2000)*

RustRidge 1999 Sauvignon Blanc (Napa Valley) $20. 84 *—S.H. (11/15/2001)*

RustRidge 1999 Zinfandel (Napa Valley) $20. 85 *—S.H. (11/15/2001)*

RustRidge 1997 Zinfandel (Napa Valley) $18. 87 *—P.G. (11/15/1999)*

RUTHERFORD

Rutherford 2001 Cabernet Sauvignon (Napa Valley) $32. 87 *—S.H. (10/1/2004)*

RUTHERFORD GROVE

Rutherford Grove 2001 Cabernet Sauvignon (Napa Valley) $40. 87 *—S.H. (10/1/2005)*

Rutherford Grove 2001 Cabernet Sauvignon (Rutherford) $40. 87 *—S.H. (10/1/2004)*

Rutherford Grove 2004 Estate Reserve Cabernet Sauvignon (Howell Mountain) $65. This is a superior wine. This is big, flashy, dramatic, deeply flavored and ageable. Those legendary Howell Mountain tannins are firm, but can't stop the cassis and mocha flavors from exploding on the palate. Good now, with decanting, and should hold for a good eight years with proper cellaring. 93 *—S.H. (12/1/2007)*

Rutherford Grove 2004 Rutherford Bench Cabernet Sauvignon (Napa Valley) $45. The term "Rutherford Bench" is not a legal one, but colloquially refers to the west side of Highway 29, where the wines, supposedly, are better. And this is quite a good wine. It's fresh and young in sweet tannins and acidity; everything's not quite integrated yet, but it's a big, rich, complexly balanced wine. Should come into its own by 2008, then hold for some years. 91 *—S.H. (12/1/2007)*

Rutherford Grove 2001 Merlot (Napa Valley) $28. 84 *—S.H. (10/1/2005)*

Rutherford Grove 2005 Spring Creek Vineyard Petite Sirah (St. Helena) $37. Fruit stars in this dry, young Petite Sirah. It explodes with jammy flavors of blackberries, cassis, cherries, licorice and plums, with a generous dusting of cinnamon and cocoa. It's distinguished, while holding onto the variety's brawny rusticity. 88 *—S.H. (12/15/2007)*

Rutherford Grove 2001 Spring Creek Vineyard Petite Sirah (St. Helena) $35. 90 *—S.H. (10/1/2004)*

Rutherford Grove 2003 Sauvignon Blanc (Rutherford) $14. 86 *—S.H. (9/1/2004)*

Rutherford Grove 2005 Estate Sauvignon Blanc (Napa Valley) $16. 87 *—S.H. (12/31/2006)*

RUTHERFORD HILL

Rutherford Hill 2004 Cabernet Sauvignon (Napa Valley) $36. Here's a well made, young Cab that's sturdy in tannins, so if you open now, decant for hours, and serve with some big, richly fatty cut of meat. It should age for up to a decade, though, to judge from the overall balance and the rich core of black cherry fruit. 90 *—S.H. (7/1/2007)*

Rutherford Hill 2003 Cabernet Sauvignon (Napa Valley) $35. 83 *—S.H. (11/1/2006)*

Rutherford Hill 2002 Cabernet Sauvignon (Napa Valley) $35. 83 *—S.H. (11/1/2005)*

Rutherford Hill 1999 25th Anniversary Cabernet Sauvignon (Napa Valley) $30. 90 *—C.S. (11/15/2002)*

Rutherford Hill 2005 Chardonnay (Napa Valley) $20. On the earthy, dusty side, this is dry and soft. It appeals for its creamy texture and modest peach and date nut bread flavors. 84 *—S.H. (7/1/2007)*

Rutherford Hill 2004 Chardonnay (Napa Valley) $18. 84 *—S.H. (11/1/2006)*

Rutherford Hill 2002 Chardonnay (Napa Valley) $18. 85 *—S.H. (12/15/2004)*

Rutherford Hill 1998 Chardonnay (Napa Valley) $17. 88 *(11/1/2001)*

Rutherford Hill 2000 26th Anniversary Chardonnay (Napa Valley) $17. 87 *—J.C. (9/1/2002)*

Rutherford Hill 1997 Reserve Chardonnay (Carneros) $28. 88 *(11/1/2001)*

Rutherford Hill 2004 Malbec (Napa Valley) $28. Dark and thick in the way of Malbec, this is big, rich and gooey, powerful in chocolate fudge, blackberry jam, licorice and smoky oak flavors. It's not particularly complicated or ageworthy, but it's softly delicious. 86 *—S.H. (9/1/2007)*

Rutherford Hill 2003 Malbec (Napa Valley) $28. 84 *—S.H. (11/15/2006)*

Rutherford Hill 2002 Malbec (Napa Valley) $26. 84 *—S.H. (11/1/2005)*

Rutherford Hill 2004 Merlot (Napa Valley) $25. Good, dry Merlot, with balanced tannins and oak and ripe blackberry fruit. Those tannins take some getting used to, with an astringent lockdown quality, but this is not an ager. Decant, and drink with steaks and chops. 87 *—S.H. (7/1/2007)*

Rutherford Hill 2003 Merlot (Napa Valley) $25. 84 *—S.H. (11/1/2006)*

Rutherford Hill 2002 Merlot (Napa Valley) $25. 84 *—S.H. (11/1/2005)*

Rutherford Hill 2001 Merlot (Napa Valley) $25. 85 *—S.H. (12/15/2004)*

Rutherford Hill 1999 Merlot (Napa Valley) $24. 87 *(11/1/2001)*

Rutherford Hill 1998 Merlot (Napa Valley) $22. 88 *(11/1/2001)*

Rutherford Hill 1997 Merlot (Napa Valley) $21. 90 *(11/1/2001)*

Rutherford Hill 1996 Merlot (Napa Valley) $21. 88 *(11/1/2001)*

Rutherford Hill 1995 Merlot (Napa Valley) $20. 86 *(11/1/2001)*

Rutherford Hill 1994 Merlot (Napa Valley) $19. 85 *(11/1/2001)*

Rutherford Hill 2004 Reserve Merlot (Napa Valley) $92. Rutherford Hill, a true Merlot pioneer, understands the variety like few others, and when they put their mind to it in a low-production wine like this one, they rock. This Merlot is terrific. It's rich, soft and opulent, with ripe cherry, cassis, milk chocolate, vanilla and new oak flavors. It's at its best now. 91 —*S.H. (7/1/2007)*

Rutherford Hill 2003 Reserve Merlot (Napa Valley) $90. 90 —*S.H. (11/15/2006)*

Rutherford Hill 2002 Reserve Merlot (Napa Valley) $76. 92 Editors' Choice —*S.H. (11/1/2005)*

Rutherford Hill 2001 Reserve Merlot (Napa Valley) $86. 94 —*S.H. (4/1/2005)*

Rutherford Hill 1999 Reserve Merlot (Napa Valley) $70. 90 —*K.F. (4/1/2003)*

Rutherford Hill 1997 Reserve Merlot (Napa Valley) $60. 90 Cellar Selection *(11/1/2001)*

Rutherford Hill 1996 Reserve Merlot (Napa Valley) $50. 88 *(11/1/2001)*

Rutherford Hill 1995 Reserve Merlot (Napa Valley) $47. 87 *(11/1/2001)*

Rutherford Hill 2005 Rosé of Merlot (Napa Valley) $19. 82 —*S.H. (11/15/2006)*

Rutherford Hill 2003 Rosé of Merlot (Napa Valley) $19. 83 —*S.H. (12/15/2004)*

Rutherford Hill 2004 Petite Verdot (Napa Valley) $28. Few make a separate bottling of Petite Verdot, but in the right hands, as it is here, it lends itself to a nice alternative to Cabernet. Dry, full-bodied, tannic and complex, the wine is weightier than Cabernet, with blue and black stone fruit and unsweetened dark chocolate flavors, and a tanned leather animality. But it's soft, so drink now. 88 —*S.H. (9/1/2007)*

Rutherford Hill 2003 Petite Verdot (Napa Valley) $28. 85 —*S.H. (11/15/2006)*

Rutherford Hill 2004 Rose of Merlot Rosé Blend (Napa Valley) $19. 84 —*S.H. (11/1/2005)*

Rutherford Hill 1996 22nd Anniversary Sangiovese (Napa Valley) $30. 88 —*M.S. (9/1/2000)*

Rutherford Hill 2004 Syrah (Napa Valley) $28. A solid effort. Dry and lush, this wine has deliciously forward flavors of cherry liqueur, crème de cassis, milk chocolate, blueberry jam and toasty oak flavors that taste as good as they sound. It's ready now and for the next year or two. 90 —*S.H. (9/1/2007)*

RUTHERFORD OAKS

Rutherford Oaks 1999 Hozhoni Vineyard Cabernet Sauvignon (Rutherford) $50. 90 —*S.H. (11/15/2002)*

Rutherford Oaks 2000 Hozhoni Vineyard Syrah (Rutherford) $30. 88 —*J.M. (6/1/2003)*

Rutherford Oaks 1999 Hozhoni Vineyard Syrah (Rutherford) $38. 90 —*S.H. (12/1/2002)*

RUTHERFORD RANCH

Rutherford Ranch 2005 Cabernet Sauvignon (Napa Valley) $18. A little sharp, but easily the winery's best non-vineyard designated Cab since the '02. Shows a ripeness level that slam dunks cherries, blackberries, cola and oak onto the palate, yet maintains an elegant dryness. 87 —*S.H. (12/31/2007)*

Rutherford Ranch 2004 Cabernet Sauvignon (Napa Valley) $17. Delicious enough, with complex waves of blackberries, cherries, raspberries, root beer, milk chocolate, coffee and cinnamon spice. With a dash of Petite Sirah and Syrah, it's a soft wine that finishes with honeyed sweetness. 85 —*S.H. (10/1/2007)*

Rutherford Ranch 2002 Cabernet Sauvignon (Napa Valley) $16. 86 —*S.H. (5/1/2006)*

Rutherford Ranch 2001 Cabernet Sauvignon (Napa Valley) $15. 83 —*S.H. (10/1/2005)*

Rutherford Ranch 1999 Cabernet Sauvignon (Napa Valley) $14. 84 —*S.H. (12/31/2002)*

Rutherford Ranch 2003 Reserve Cabernet Sauvignon (Napa Valley) $35. Very ripe and soft, almost raisiny but not quite, with the flavor of melted chocolate fudge drizzled with cassis. The alcohol reads below 14%, but there's a heat that's hard to explain. 83 —*S.H. (9/1/2007)*

Rutherford Ranch 2002 Reserve Cabernet Sauvignon (Napa Valley) $30. 91 —*S.H. (8/1/2006)*

Rutherford Ranch 1999 Silverado Trail Vineyard Limited Release Reserve Cabernet Sauvignon (Napa Valley) $35. 89 —*S.H. (5/1/2004)*

Rutherford Ranch 1999 Stagecoach-Krupp Vineyards Limited Release Reserve Cabernet Sauvignon (Napa Valley) $35. 91 —*S.H. (5/1/2004)*

Rutherford Ranch 2003 Chardonnay (Napa Valley) $13. 84 —*S.H. (10/1/2005)*

Rutherford Ranch 2001 Chardonnay (Napa Valley) $12. 84 —*S.H. (12/1/2003)*

Rutherford Ranch 2000 Chardonnay (Napa Valley) $12. 84 —*S.H. (6/1/2003)*

Rutherford Ranch 2002 Merlot (Napa Valley) $13. 87 —*S.H. (10/1/2005)*

Rutherford Ranch 2000 Merlot (Napa Valley) $12. 84 —*S.H. (12/31/2002)*

Rutherford Ranch 2001 Sauvignon Blanc (Napa Valley) $10. 86 —*S.H. (9/1/2003)*

Rutherford Ranch 2005 Zinfandel (Napa Valley) $17. Good, rich Zinfandel that brings a Napa elegance and sophistication to the variety's wild and woolly personality. The briary, brambly thing is all here, with wild berry, cocoa, nutmeg, cinnamon and pepper flavors, and the exuberance is distinctively Zin-y, but the wine has the body and balance of a fine Merlot. 90 Editors' Choice —*S.H. (11/1/2007)*

Rutherford Ranch 2000 Zinfandel (Napa Valley) $14. 87 —*S.H. (3/1/2004)*

RUTHERFORD VINTNERS

Rutherford Vintners 2003 Cabernet Sauvignon (Napa Valley) $16. 82 —*S.H. (7/1/2006)*

Rutherford Vintners 2003 Chardonnay (Napa Valley) $12. 83 —*S.H. (7/1/2006)*

Rutherford Vintners 1997 Barrel Select Fumé Blanc (California) $8. 81 *(3/1/2000)*

Rutherford Vintners 1999 Barrel Select Syrah (Stanislaus County) $9. 83 *(10/1/2001)*

RUTZ

Rutz 2000 Chardonnay (Russian River Valley) $18. 90 —*S.H. (12/1/2003)*

Rutz 1998 Chardonnay (Russian River Valley) $20. 87 —*S.H. (5/1/2001)*

Rutz 2001 Dutton Ranch Chardonnay (Russian River Valley) $38. 89 —*S.H. (8/1/2005)*

Rutz 2000 Dutton Ranch Chardonnay (Russian River Valley) $35. 92 —*S.H. (12/1/2003)*

Rutz 1999 Dutton Ranch Chardonnay (Russian River Valley) $30. 91 —*S.H. (9/1/2002)*

Rutz 2004 Maison Grand Cru Chardonnay (Russian River Valley) $25. This bottling from Rutz has been one of the better Chards you can buy at this price point. It's classic Russian River, dry and crisp in acids, with plush, ripe green apple, pineapple and juicy lemon and lime flavors. Oak, lees and the rest of the Burgundian bells and whistles add all sorts of creamy, textural, spicy complexities. 90 —*S.H. (3/1/2007)*

Rutz 2001 Maison Grand Cru Chardonnay (Russian River Valley) $30. 91 —*S.H. (8/1/2005)*

Rutz 2000 Maison Grand Cru Chardonnay (Russian River Valley) $25. 90 —*S.H. (12/1/2003)*

Rutz 1999 Maison Grand Cru Chardonnay (Russian River Valley) $25. 92 Editors' Choice *(9/1/2002)*

Rutz 2001 Merlot (North Coast) $25. 87 —*S.H. (5/1/2004)*

Rutz 2001 Pinot Noir (Sonoma Coast) $18. 91 Editors' Choice —*S.H. (12/1/2003)*

Rutz 2000 Pinot Noir (Sonoma Coast) $20. 84 *(10/1/2002)*

Rutz 1998 Pinot Noir (Russian River Valley) $20. 87 —*S.H. (5/1/2001)*

Rutz 2002 Burnside Vineyard Reserve Pinot Noir (Russian River Valley) $60. 86 —*S.H. (12/15/2005)*

Rutz 2004 Dutton Ranch Pinot Noir (Russian River Valley) $40. Here's a wine for real Pinot-philes. It's just exquisite, but it's not for neophytes, because it takes an understanding of the variety. Pale in color, silky and delicate in structure, it shows Green Valley's ability to produce great Pinot. There's tremendous oak, but it meshes perfectly with the cola, cherry, rosehip tea and Asian spice flavors. Drink now-2012. 94 —*S.H. (3/1/2007)*

Rutz 2001 Dutton Ranch Pinot Noir (Russian River Valley) $38. 91 —*S.H. (8/1/2005)*

Rutz 1999 Dutton Ranch Pinot Noir (Russian River Valley) $30. 91 Editors' Choice —*S.H. (9/1/2002)*

Rutz 2005 Maison Grand Cru Pinot Noir (Russian River Valley) $30. Almost as rich as Rutz's more expensive Pinots, this is a good showcase for Russian River Pinot, and particularly for the Rutz interpretation of dry, silky elegance. It's a testiment to the art of blending. When you can mix different lots and come up with something this elegant, you're onto something. 90 —*S.H. (3/1/2007)*

Rutz 2001 Maison Grand Cru Pinot Noir (Russian River Valley) $30. 92 Editors' Choice —*S.H. (8/1/2005)*

Rutz 2000 Maison Grand Cru Pinot Noir (Russian River Valley) $25. 93 —*S.H. (12/1/2003)*

Rutz 1999 Maison Grand Cru Pinot Noir (Russian River Valley) $25. 87 —*S.H. (9/1/2002)*

Rutz 2000 Martinelli Vineyard Pinot Noir (Russian River Valley) $35. 90 —*S.H. (12/1/2003)*

Rutz 1999 Martinelli Vineyard Pinot Noir (Russian River Valley) $30. 87 —*S.H. (9/1/2002)*

Rutz 2003 River Road Pinot Noir (Russian River Valley) $40. River Road is where Rochioli and Williams Selyem are located. Good neighborhood. The pale color tells you the body is silky, but there's nothing light about the wine. It's very dry and elegant, with complex layers of cola, cherry, root beer, beetroot and licorice flavors that finish with a tremendous fireworks of spice. Drink now through 2010. **92** —*S.H. (3/1/2007)*

Rutz 1999 Weir Vineyard Pinot Noir (Mendocino) $30. 86 —*S.H. (9/1/2002)*

Rutz 2003 Windsor Gardens Pinot Noir (Russian River Valley) $60. This is the best of Rutz's current releases due to the sheer richness of the wine, which comes from a vineyard made famous by the vintner, Merry Edwards. It's crisp in acidity, and elegantly silky in the mouth, with pomegranate, cola, cherry, rhubarb, rosehip tea and spice flavors. It's very complex now, showing classic Russian River character, and should age well for a decade. **94 Cellar Selection** —*S.H. (3/1/2007)*

Rutz 2002 Windsor Gardens Pinot Noir (Russian River Valley) $60. 85 —*S.H. (12/15/2005)*

RYAN PATRICK

Ryan Patrick 1999 Bordeaux Blend (Columbia Valley (WA)) $29. 92 —*P.G. (9/1/2002)*

Ryan Patrick 2003 Rock Island Bordeaux Blend (Columbia Valley (WA)) $14. 87 —*P.G. (8/1/2006)*

Ryan Patrick 2002 Rock Island Red Bordeaux Blend (Columbia Valley (WA)) $18. 88 —*P.G. (12/1/2004)*

Ryan Patrick 2000 Chardonnay (Columbia Valley (WA)) $15. 89 Best Buy —*P.G. (9/1/2002)*

Ryan Patrick 2004 Estate Chardonnay (Columbia Valley (WA)) $14. 88 —*P.G. (8/1/2006)*

Ryan Patrick 2003 Estate Chardonnay (Columbia Valley (WA)) $18. 89 —*P.G. (12/1/2004)*

Ryan Patrick 2002 Estate Chardonnay (Columbia Valley (WA)) $15. 89 Best Buy —*P.G. (5/1/2004)*

Ryan Patrick 2001 Red Blend (Columbia Valley (WA)) $29. 89 —*P.G. (12/1/2004)*

Ryan Patrick 2003 Reserve Red Blend (Columbia Valley (WA)) $42. 87 —*P.G. (8/1/2006)*

Ryan Patrick 2001 Rock Island Red Red Blend (Columbia Valley (WA)) $15. 87 Best Buy —*P.G. (5/1/2004)*

Ryan Patrick 2004 Sauvignon Blanc (Columbia Valley (WA)) $14. 89 Best Buy —*P.G. (8/1/2006)*

Ryan Patrick 2003 Vin d'Été White Blend (Columbia Valley (WA)) $20. 88 —*P.G. (12/1/2004)*

S. ANDERSON

S. Anderson 1997 Richard Chambers Vineyard Cabernet Sauvignon (Stags Leap District) $75. 93 *(11/1/2000)*

S. Anderson 1994 Blanc de Blanc Champagne Blend (Napa Valley) $46. 90 —*S.H. (12/1/2000)*

S. Anderson 1997 Blanc de Noirs Champagne Blend (Napa Valley) $28. 89 —*J.M. (12/1/2002)*

S. Anderson 1996 Blanc de Noirs Champagne Blend (Napa Valley) $28. 90 —*S.H. (12/1/2000)*

S. Anderson 1997 Brut Champagne Blend (Napa Valley) $28. 88 —*J.M. (12/1/2002)*

S. Anderson 1996 Brut Champagne Blend (Napa Valley) $28. 86 —*S.H. (12/1/2000)*

S. Anderson 1997 Merlot (Stags Leap District) $30. 87 —*J.C. (6/1/2001)*

S. P. DRUMMER

S. P. Drummer 1999 Blair Vineyard Cabernet Blend (Napa Valley) $45. 93 —*J.M. (11/15/2002)*

S. P. Drummer 2004 Cabernet Sauvignon (Oakville) $51. Very ripe, almost jellied in raspberry, cherry and blackberry flavors, this Cab also has a streak of green dill, and finishes with a honeyed sweetness. At its best now and for a year or two. **85** —*S.H. (12/15/2007)*

S. P. Drummer 2003 Blair Vineyard Cabernet Sauvignon-Cabernet Franc (Napa Valley) $48. The vineyard is located between St. Helena and Calistoga, and the blend is just about 50-50 of the two Bordeaux varieties. It's a ripe, fruity, jammy wine with some sharpness in the finish. **86** —*S.H. (12/15/2007)*

S.E. CHASE FAMILY CELLARS

S.E. Chase Family Cellars 2001 Zinfandel (Napa Valley) $36. 93 —*J.M. (4/1/2004)*

S.E. Chase Family Cellars 2000 Zinfandel (Napa Valley) $36. 91 —*J.M. (9/1/2003)*

SABLE RIDGE

Sable Ridge 2000 Petite Sirah (Russian River Valley) $28. 86 *(4/1/2003)*

Sable Ridge 1999 Petite Sirah (Russian River Valley) $28. 92 —*S.H. (9/1/2002)*

Sable Ridge 1999 Hensley-Lauchland Vineyard Old Vine Zinfandel (Lodi) $20. 89 —*S.H. (12/15/2001)*

Sable Ridge 1998 Old Vine Zinfandel (Lodi) $18. 85 —*S.H. (11/15/2001)*

SACRED STONE

Sacred Stone NV Master's Red Blend Rhône Red Blend (California) $9. 84 —*S.H. (5/1/2005)*

SADDLEBACK

Saddleback 2003 Cabernet Sauvignon (Napa Valley) $50. 87 —*S.H. (12/31/2006)*

Saddleback 2000 Cabernet Sauvignon (Napa Valley) $48. 92 —*J.M. (12/31/2003)*

Saddleback 2001 Chardonnay (Napa Valley) $22. 87 —*J.M. (12/15/2003)*

Saddleback 2002 Merlot (Napa Valley) $32. 85 —*S.H. (12/31/2006)*

Saddleback 2001 Merlot (Napa Valley) $36. 87 —*J.M. (12/31/2003)*

Saddleback 2005 Pinot Blanc (Oakville) $18. 86 —*S.H. (12/31/2006)*

Saddleback 2003 Pinot Blanc (Oakville) $18. 85 —*S.H. (3/1/2006)*

Saddleback 2001 Pinot Blanc (Napa Valley) $18. 89 —*J.M. (2/1/2004)*

Saddleback 2005 Pinot Grigio (Oakville) $18. 82 —*S.H. (12/31/2006)*

Saddleback 2001 Pinot Grigio (Napa Valley) $18. 87 —*J.M. (12/1/2003)*

Saddleback 2005 Viognier (Clarksburg) $19. 84 —*S.H. (12/31/2006)*

Saddleback 2003 Viognier (Clarksburg) $19. 84 —*S.H. (3/1/2006)*

Saddleback 2001 Viognier (Napa Valley) $19. 88 —*J.M. (12/1/2003)*

Saddleback 1997 Zinfandel (Napa Valley) $26. 85 —*S.H. (5/1/2000)*

Saddleback 2004 Old Vines Zinfandel (Napa Valley) $36. 92 —*S.H. (12/31/2006)*

Saddleback 2003 Old Vines Zinfandel (Napa Valley) $32. 82 —*S.H. (3/1/2006)*

Saddleback 2001 Old Vines Zinfandel (Napa Valley) $30. 90 *(11/1/2003)*

SADDLEBACK CELLARS

Saddleback Cellars 2004 Pinot Grigio (Oakville) $18. 88 —*S.H. (2/1/2006)*

Saddleback Cellars 2003 Sauvignon Blanc (Napa Valley) $20. 86 *(7/1/2005)*

SAGELANDS

Sagelands 1999 Cabernet Sauvignon (Columbia Valley (WA)) $18. 86 —*P.G. (12/31/2001)*

Sagelands 2004 Andrews Vineyard Cabernet Sauvignon (Horse Heaven Hills) $20. The second release of this vineyard designate. This is several steps up from the generic reds that characterize the lineup. It's got more focus and stuffing, more density and texture, than anything else. There's an interesting mushroom component. The fruit is tight and tart, and the acids a bit flush. This is not a particularly elegant wine, but it hangs in there with extended flavors, finishing with toasted almonds. **88** —*P.G. (12/1/2007)*

Sagelands 2004 Four Corners Cabernet Sauvignon (Columbia Valley (WA)) $16. Price rise. With broad flavors of berry and chocolate, this is pleasant and undistinguished. This does not have the weight or varietal presence of the winery's Merlot. **86** —*P.G. (12/1/2007)*

Sagelands 2001 Four Corners Cabernet Sauvignon (Columbia Valley (WA)) $12. 88 —*S.H. (1/1/2004)*

Sagelands 2004 Malbec (Columbia Valley (WA)) $18. The fruit is juicy, very tart, leaning toward cranberry and pomegranate, maybe some pie cherry too. Tasty, snappy wine, young and acidic, refreshing and clean. Good potential. **88** —*P.G. (12/1/2007)*

Sagelands 2003 Merlot (Columbia Valley (WA)) $13. 91 Best Buy *—P.G. (6/1/2006)*

Sagelands 1999 Merlot (Columbia Valley (WA)) $15. 88 *—P.G. (12/31/2001)*

Sagelands 2004 Four Corners Merlot (Columbia Valley (WA)) $19. This remains one of the better Washington Merlots for lovers of ripe berry and cherry fruits, slathered with a liberal amount of chocolaty oak. Flavors are nicely integrated, with hints of bacon, smoke and ham. A friendly, tasty bottle of wine. 88 *—P.G. (12/1/2007)*

Sagelands 2002 Four Corners Merlot (Washington) $12. 87 Best Buy *—P.G. (4/1/2005)*

Sagelands 2001 Four Corners Merlot (Columbia Valley (WA)) $12. 90 Best Buy *—S.H. (12/31/2003)*

Sagelands 2000 Four Corners Merlot (Columbia Valley (WA)) $15. 86 *—P.G. (9/1/2002)*

Sagelands 2003 Pinot Gris (Oregon) $12. 85 *—S.H. (12/15/2004)*

Sagelands 2006 Riesling (Columbia Valley (WA)) $14. Comes on a bit flat, with a streak of cardboard under the fruit. Not as fresh as it should be, given the vintage. 81 *—P.G. (9/1/2007)*

SAGGI

Saggi 2004 Red Blend (Columbia Valley (WA)) $45. This blend is done along super-Tuscan lines, about one third Sangiovese, one third Cabernet Sauvignon, and the other third Syrah and some not-so-Tuscan Barbera. Smooth, chocolaty and dark, the winemaking is impeccable. But as with some of the other Long Shadows reds, this wine has not completely forged its own identity. The goal is "Tuscan characters showcasing Columbia Valley terroir." The jury is still out on how that will ultimately be accomplished. 90 *—P.G. (5/1/2007)*

SAINT GREGORY

Saint Gregory 1998 Pinot Blanc (Mendocino) $14. 83 *—S.H. (8/1/2001)*

Saint Gregory 1999 Pinot Noir (Mendocino) $19. 84 *(10/1/2002)*

SAINT LAURENT

Saint Laurent 2001 Solé Riché Red Bordeaux Blend (Columbia Valley (WA)) $22. 86 *—P.G. (4/1/2005)*

Saint Laurent 2001 Cabernet Sauvignon (Columbia Valley (WA)) $18. 84 *—P.G. (4/1/2005)*

Saint Laurent 2003 Chardonnay (Columbia Valley (WA)) $15. 85 *—P.G. (4/1/2005)*

Saint Laurent 2001 Merlot (Columbia Valley (WA)) $15. 85 *—P.G. (4/1/2005)*

SAINTSBURY

Saintsbury 2005 Chardonnay (Carneros) $20. This is a pretty good Chard; the grapes come partially from the Upper Barn vineyard, but it's all mountain-grown, showing concentrated pear, pineapple and peach flavors, with a rich, tobacco herbaceousness. 87 *—S.H. (5/1/2007)*

Saintsbury 2001 Chardonnay (Carneros) $20. 88 *—S.H. (8/1/2003)*

Saintsbury 2004 Brown Ranch Chardonnay (Carneros) $40. Here's a young wine that will benefit from decanting. Freshly opened, it's a composite of new oak, citrus and tropical fruit and brisk acidity. Let it breathe and it all mingles together, creating a bright, richly complex Chardonnay. Will hold and improve over the next five years. 90 *—S.H. (5/1/2007)*

Saintsbury 2000 Reserve Chardonnay (Carneros) $35. 85 *—S.H. (8/1/2003)*

Saintsbury 1999 Reserve Chardonnay (Carneros) $35. 87 *(7/1/2001)*

Saintsbury 2005 Pinot Noir (Carneros) $30. With this, their large-production Pinot, Saintsbury has produced a nice villages-style wine, a good introduction to the varietal. It's made for immediate drinking, and is clean and elegant, with dry, crisp cherry, cola and spice flavors. 86 *—S.H. (5/1/2007)*

Saintsbury 2002 Pinot Noir (Carneros) $26. 84 *(11/1/2004)*

Saintsbury 2001 Pinot Noir (Carneros) $26. 85 *—S.H. (7/1/2003)*

Saintsbury 2000 Pinot Noir (Carneros) $24. 86 *(10/1/2002)*

Saintsbury 2005 Brown Ranch Pinot Noir (Carneros) $60. Not as immediately obvious as the beautiful '04, this is a more tannic, structured wine, yet it shows the pedigree of the vineyard. Cherry pie filling, rhubarb, cola and cinnamon spice flavors take over the palate, leaving the impression of balanced, upscale richness in a silky texture. The tannins will be the perfect foil for lamb or veal. 91 *—S.H. (5/1/2007)*

Saintsbury 2004 Brown Ranch Pinot Noir (Carneros) $60. This is one to think about for its complex nature that changes by the moment. On the surface, it's soft and ripe, with an explosion of cherry pie, strawberry, cola and mocha flavors enriched with the vanilla and smoky caramel of new oak. Yet every sip as it warms in the glass reveals another layer. Gorgeously textured, right up there with the best. 94 Editors' Choice *—S.H. (5/1/2007)*

Saintsbury 2000 Brown Ranch Pinot Noir (Carneros) $75. 92 *—S.H. (12/1/2004)*

Saintsbury 1999 Brown Ranch Estate Bottled Pinot Noir (Carneros) $75. 87 *(10/1/2002)*

Saintsbury 2005 Cerise Vineyard Pinot Noir (Anderson Valley) $45. This Mendocino Pinot is delicate and light-bodied. It's definitely not one of those superripe wines, but is a dry, gentle one, silky and crisp in acids. The flavors, cherry, rhubarb, pomegranate, cola and spice, are very supportive of food. 87 *—S.H. (7/1/2007)*

Saintsbury 2001 Garnet Pinot Noir (Carneros) $17. 84 *—S.H. (7/1/2003)*

Saintsbury 2005 Lee Vineyards Pinot Noir (Carneros) $45. Drier and firmer than the '04, this year's Lee shows a slightly dense texture, and even a dusting of tannins that contribute to ageability. The flavors are deep, of red cherries, coffee and smoky oak, with a meaty chewiness. It's a young wine, cellar it for a year before opening, and it should provide elegant drinking through 2011 or so. 90 *—S.H. (5/1/2007)*

Saintsbury 2004 Lee Vineyard Pinot Noir (Carneros) $45. 90 *—S.H. (12/31/2006)*

Saintsbury 2000 Reserve Pinot Noir (Carneros) $50. 90 *(10/1/2002)*

Saintsbury 1999 Reserve Pinot Noir (Carneros) $50. 86 *—S.H. (7/1/2003)*

Saintsbury 2005 Stanly Ranch Pinot Noir (Carneros) $45. This is from a cool part of Carneros, and from this cool vintage, acidity stars in this bone dry wine. It's not the fruitiest Pinot out there, with a wintergreen and white pepper edge to the red cherries and rosehip tea flavors. Elegant and crisp, it's probably at its best now. 88 *—S.H. (5/1/2007)*

Saintsbury 2004 Stanly Ranch Pinot Noir (Carneros) $45. 91 *—S.H. (12/31/2006)*

Saintsbury 2005 Toyon Farm Pinot Noir (Carneros) $45. There's a lilting quality to this Pinot, with its crisp silkiness, and the way the cherry and pomegranate flavors seem to float on the palate, rather than sink into it. Dry and medium-bodied, it has the acids and tannins to improve over the next six years, but if you drink it now, decant for several hours. 90 *—S.H. (5/1/2007)*

Saintsbury 2004 Toyon Farm Pinot Noir (Carneros) $45. 89 *—S.H. (12/31/2006)*

Saintsbury 2006 Vin Gris of Pinot Noir (Carneros) $14. One of the better rosés out there. Pinot Noir seems to lend itself to blush because it's a delicate wine to begin with, as rosé should be. This polished wine is dry and crisp, with sophisticated, complex flavors of berries, spices and earth and a light, airy mouthfeel. 88 *—S.H. (7/1/2007)*

Saintsbury 2004 Syrah (Sonoma Valley) $35. Beautiful Syrah, dry, immensely rich, and fairly tannic. It has a bracing texture framing wild blackberry, carob, cappuccino and dusty spice flavors, enriched with smoky oak. 91 *—S.H. (7/1/2007)*

Saintsbury 2004 Syrah (Carneros) $35. Grown on the Sonoma side of the appellation, in one of the coolest, windiest parts, this is quite simply a delicious Syrah. The grapes achieved perfect ripeness, yielding immense blackberry jam, cherry, chocolate, tangerine zest, coffee and gingersnap cookie flavors. Yet that coastal acidity is there, scrubbing and cleansing the palate. 92 *—S.H. (5/1/2007)*

SAKONNET

Sakonnet 1996 Brut Champagne Blend (Southeastern New England) $30. 87 *—K.F. (12/1/2002)*

Sakonnet 1995 Samson Brut Champagne Blend (Southeastern New England) $25. 90 *(12/15/2000)*

Sakonnet 1999 Chardonnay (Finger Lakes) $15. 89 *—J.C. (7/1/2002)*

Sakonnet 1999 Icewine Vidal Blanc (Southeastern New England) $25. 86 *—J.M. (12/1/2002)*

Sakonnet 2003 Winterwine Vidal Blanc (Southeastern New England) $25. Apricots and honey on the nose lead this rich but balanced dessert wine. Made with the fragrant Vidal Blanc grape, the wine shows an elegant balance of sweetness and fresh acidity. 86 *—S.K. (7/1/2007)*

SALMON CREEK

Salmon Creek 1999 Cabernet Sauvignon (California) $NA. 85 Best Buy *—S.H. (7/1/2002)*

Salmon Creek 1997 Bad Dog Ranch Chardonnay (Carneros) $19. 82 *(6/1/2000)*

SALMON HARBOR

Salmon Harbor 2000 Chardonnay (Washington) $8. 85 *—P.G. (2/1/2002)*

Salmon Harbor 1997 Chardonnay (Central Coast) $10. 85 *—L.W. (7/1/1999)*

Salmon Harbor 2000 Merlot (Washington) $9. 87 *—P.G. (12/31/2001)*

Salmon Harbor 1999 Merlot (Washington) $9. 85 Best Buy *—P.G. (6/1/2001)*

SALMON RUN

Salmon Run 2001 Chardonnay (New York) $10. 82 *—J.M. (1/1/2003)*

Salmon Run 2000 Johannisberg Riesling (New York) $10. 83 *—J.C. (3/1/2002)*

SALVESTRIN

Salvestrin 1999 Cabernet Sauvignon (Napa Valley) $45. 88 *—S.H. (8/1/2003)*

Salvestrin 1997 Cabernet Sauvignon (Napa Valley) $41. 92 *(11/1/2000)*

Salvestrin 2003 Estate Vineyard Cabernet Sauvignon (St. Helena) $49. A solid effort: soft, round and polished, with a classic Cab profile. Cherry, cola, blackberry and cedar aromas and flavors have a delicately earthy edge of fresh Provençal herbs. Rich in ripe tannins, with a splash of Merlot, is beautiful now, and should age well for many years. 94 Editors' Choice *—S.H. (4/1/2007)*

Salvestrin 2001 Estate Vineyard Cabernet Sauvignon (Napa Valley) $45. 90 *—S.H. (8/1/2005)*

Salvestrin 2001 Sangiovese (Napa Valley) $26. 86 *—S.H. (3/1/2004)*

SAN ANTONIO

San Antonio 2002 Heritage Vintage Red Wine Red Blend (Central Coast) $25. This is a Rhône-style blend of Syrah, Petite Sirah, Mourvèdre and Grenache. It's soft, rich, simple and slightly sweet, with cherry pie, cola and cocoa flavors. 84 *—S.H. (5/1/2007)*

SAN JUAN VINEYARDS

San Juan Vineyards 2006 Angevine (Puget Sound) $14. Folks seeking low alcohol wines should be sniffing around San Juan Vineyards; this clocks in at just 11.4% alcohol. Though very light, and very delicate, it is not without interest. These grapes have the sort of ephemeral resonance that you can't get in the eastern Washington desert. Hints of honeycomb, melon and sweet hay combine and cluster in a lingering finish. 88 Best Buy *—P.G. (12/1/2007)*

San Juan Vineyards 2004 Cabernet Blend (Yakima Valley) $15. No stuffing here, just thin berry and cherry fruit and a quick hit of chocolate. 84 *—P.G. (12/1/2007)*

San Juan Vineyards 2003 Cabernet Sauvignon-Merlot (Columbia Valley (WA)) $12. 87 Best Buy *—P.G. (8/1/2006)*

San Juan Vineyards 2004 Celilo Vineyard Chardonnay (Columbia Gorge) $19. 90 *—P.G. (9/1/2006)*

San Juan Vineyards 2001 Reserve Chardonnay (Columbia Valley (WA)) $17. 86 *—P.G. (5/1/2004)*

San Juan Vineyards 2001 Gewürztraminer (Columbia Valley (WA)) $11. 87 Best Buy *—P.G. (5/1/2004)*

San Juan Vineyards 2001 Merlot (Yakima Valley) $23. 86 *—P.G. (5/1/2004)*

San Juan Vineyards 2004 Pinot Gris (Columbia Valley (WA)) $13. 89 Best Buy *—P.G. (8/1/2006)*

San Juan Vineyards 2004 Pinot Gris (Columbia Gorge) $13. 88 Best Buy *—P.G. (2/1/2006)*

San Juan Vineyards 2006 Riesling (Yakima Valley) $14. Off-dry, this has solid flavors suggesting cracker and grain, honey and melon. It's a flavorful, sturdy take on Riesling, but does not have the pretty floral character. 85 *—P.G. (9/1/2007)*

San Juan Vineyards 1999 Sémillon-Chardonnay (Washington) $9. 87 *—P.G. (6/1/2001)*

San Juan Vineyards 2006 Siegerrebe (Puget Sound) $15. Light and tart, mixing grapefruit, lychee, mineral and floral aromas, all evident here. Very spicy, it is a bit like Gewürztraminer without the floral highlights. The Brix (under 20) leads to a thin wine that doesn't quite reach 12% alcohol. 84 *—P.G. (12/1/2007)*

San Juan Vineyards 2004 Syrah (Yakima Valley) $19. From Kestrel View Estates, this is clean and varietal, a bit high-toned, with a citrus underpinning and simple, plain fruit. Tannins are smooth and ripe, and the oak well managed. It's a lighter style, with a bit of heat in the finish. 85 *—P.G. (12/1/2007)*

San Juan Vineyards 2002 Syrah (Columbia Valley (WA)) $23. 86 *(9/1/2005)*

San Juan Vineyards 2001 Syrah (Columbia Valley (WA)) $23. 88 *—P.G. (5/1/2004)*

SAN LUIS CANYON

San Luis Canyon NV Chardonnay (Central Coast) $9. Simple and gluey, with canned tangerine and apricot flavors and an unnatural oaky taste. 82 *—S.H. (10/1/2007)*

SAN MARCOS CREEK

San Marcos Creek 2002 Estate Reserve Cabernet Sauvignon (Paso Robles) $27. 82 *—S.H. (12/1/2006)*

San Marcos Creek 2002 Estate Merlot (Paso Robles) $17. 88 *—S.H. (4/1/2006)*

San Marcos Creek 2002 Epiphany Red Blend (Paso Robles) $30. 86 *—S.H. (9/1/2006)*

San Marcos Creek 2002 Estate Syrah (Paso Robles) $21. 85 *—S.H. (4/1/2006)*

San Marcos Creek 2002 Estate Zinfandel (Paso Robles) $22. 83 *—S.H. (4/1/2006)*

SAN SABA

San Saba 2005 Chardonnay (Monterey) $20. After a very successful '04, San Saba's '05 Chard is a bit of a letdown. It's still very fruity in lemongrass, lime and pineapple fruit, and shows that lovely, crisp Monterey acidity. But it's also too sweet in oaky vanilla, with a sugary, cotton candy finish. 85 *—S.H. (5/1/2007)*

San Saba 2004 Chardonnay (Monterey) $18. 91 Editors' Choice *—S.H. (7/1/2006)*

San Saba 2001 Chardonnay (Monterey) $16. 85 *—S.H. (12/15/2002)*

San Saba 1998 Chardonnay (Central Coast) $20. 88 *(6/1/2000)*

San Saba 1997 Chardonnay (Monterey County) $20. 81 *(6/1/2000)*

San Saba 2004 Merlot (Monterey) $22. 85 *—S.H. (12/15/2006)*

San Saba 2003 Merlot (Monterey) $22. 81 *—S.H. (12/15/2005)*

San Saba 2002 Merlot (Monterey) $22. 84 *—S.H. (5/1/2005)*

San Saba 1996 Merlot (Monterey County) $20. 83 *—J.C. (7/1/2000)*

San Saba 2005 Pinot Noir (Monterey) $28. San Saba has been making a name for itself with mid-priced Monterey wines that show plenty of true varietal character. The price is creeping up, though. This is the most expensive wine from the winery I've ever reviewed. But it's a solid Pinot, dry, silky and crisp, with polished cherry, cola, tea and spice flavors and a sweet, cocoa finish. 87 *—S.H. (5/1/2007)*

San Saba 1999 Pinot Noir (Central Coast) $19. 86 *—S.H. (2/1/2003)*

San Saba 2005 Sauvignon Blanc (Monterey) $15. 85 *—S.H. (12/15/2006)*

SAN SAKANA

San Sakana 2005 Alta Mesa Vineyard Mourvèdre (Santa Barbara County) $40. A little on the rustic side, with pronounced cherry-berry, herb, coffee and spice flavors wrapped into a dry, tannic structure that finishes with some astringency. Drink now. 85 *—S.H. (9/1/2007)*

San Sakana 2005 Las Madres Vineyard Syrah (Carneros) $45. There's a rich, velvety texture here, and it's fully dry, but the fruit has a baked quality, and the burnt char of oak adds to that smoky astringency. Finishes salty. Might simply be going through a clumsy stage. 84 *—S.H. (9/1/2007)*

San Sakana 2005 White Hawk Syrah (Santa Barbara) $52. Dark, dry and rich, this Syrah is tough and astringent now, but it may develop in time. The thick tannins, supporting acidity, and heart of cherry liqueur, blackberry jam, chocolate and sweetly smoked leather strongly suggests aging. Hold until 2008. 90 *—S.H. (9/1/2007)*

San Sakana 2005 Broken Leg Vineyard Viognier (Anderson Valley) $38. Shows crisp, cool-climate acidity framing ripe pineapple, peach, papaya, honeysuckle, vanilla and spice flavors. But the finish is a little salty, which accentuates the inherent fruity sweetness. 85 *—S.H. (12/15/2007)*

SAN SIMEON

San Simeon 2003 Cabernet Sauvignon (Paso Robles) $24. A little on the oaky sweet side, with thick, syrupy cherry, currant, chocolate and anise flavors that finish with a bite of tannin. 84 *—S.H. (11/1/2007)*

San Simeon 2002 Cabernet Sauvignon (Paso Robles) $22. 84 *—S.H. (7/1/2006)*

San Simeon 2001 Cabernet Sauvignon (Paso Robles) $22. 84 *—S.H. (6/1/2005)*

San Simeon 2004 Chardonnay (Monterey) $19. Oaky and direct, this is the kind of Chard that will appeal to lots of people for its spicy, pineapple and papaya fruit flavors and creamy texture. 84 *—S.H. (11/1/2007)*

San Simeon 2003 Chardonnay (Monterey) $19. 84 *—S.H. (11/1/2006)*

San Simeon 2002 Chardonnay (Monterey) $19. 85 *—S.H. (6/1/2005)*

San Simeon 2000 Chardonnay (Monterey) $14. 86 *—S.H. (6/1/2003)*

San Simeon 2003 Merlot (Paso Robles) $24. From Delicato, a Merlot that shows the soft texture of Paso Robles reds with well-ripened blackberry, cherry and carob flavors that last into a long finish. Could use greater structure at this price, though. **84** —*S.H. (11/1/2007)*

San Simeon 2002 Merlot (Paso Robles) $22. 85 —*S.H. (12/1/2005)*

San Simeon 2001 Merlot (Paso Robles) $22. 84 —*S.H. (6/1/2005)*

San Simeon 2003 Petite Sirah (Paso Robles) $22. Shows the Petite Sirah characteristics the public has come to expect from the varietal, namely a dry, tannic mouthfeel and fruitiness. On the other hand, the tannins are numbing, locking down the palate with a dry astringency. If this doesn't bother you, enjoy it with barbecue. **84** —*S.H. (2/1/2007)*

San Simeon 2002 Petite Sirah (Paso Robles) $22. 81 —*S.H. (12/1/2005)*

San Simeon 2001 Petite Sirah (Paso Robles) $18. 82 —*J.M. (9/1/2004)*

San Simeon 2000 100% Petite Sirah (Paso Robles) $22. 85 —*S.H. (9/1/2003)*

San Simeon 2005 Pinot Gris (Monterey) $19. Soft, creamy and a little sweet, this PG is very fruity. It has flavors of peaches, apricots, pineapples, Meyer lemons and green apples that taste like they were baked into a pie. **84** —*S.H. (5/1/2007)*

San Simeon 2004 Pinot Gris (Monterey) $15. 89 —*S.H. (2/1/2006)*

San Simeon 2005 Pinot Noir (Monterey) $24. Here's an easy, delicious Pinot Noir that shows Monterey's ability to ripen fruit while preserving vital acidity. The cherry, cola, spice and vanilla flavors are wrapped into a silky texture that finishes dry and oaky. **87** —*S.H. (11/1/2007)*

San Simeon 2004 Pinot Noir (Monterey) $20. 83 —*S.H. (11/1/2006)*

San Simeon 2003 Pinot Noir (Monterey) $20. 85 —*S.H. (12/1/2005)*

San Simeon 2002 Pinot Noir (Monterey County) $18. 84 *(11/1/2004)*

San Simeon 2000 Pinot Noir (Monterey) $20. 83 *(10/1/2002)*

San Simeon 1999 Pinot Noir (Monterey) $18. 87 —*J.M. (11/15/2001)*

San Simeon 2004 Syrah (Monterey) $22. The winery says the grapes were "focused" in the Arroyo Seco, and while you'd expect something crisper, keep in mind the heat of the vintage. The wine is very soft and chocolaty, with blackberry jam and cola flavors, and the finish is a little sweet. **85** —*S.H. (6/1/2007)*

San Simeon 2003 Syrah (Paso Robles) $24. It's curious that the winery held this back a year longer than their '04 Monterey Syrah, with which it was co-released. But then, this one has a firmer structure, with finer tannins and brighter acidity. It's really a very good wine, showing layers of complexity in the blackberry, cassis, coffee, leather, cocoa and spice flavors. **90** —*S.H. (6/1/2007)*

San Simeon 2002 Syrah (Paso Robles) $22. 87 —*S.H. (12/31/2005)*

San Simeon 2001 Syrah (Monterey) $20. 89 —*S.H. (6/1/2005)*

San Simeon 2000 Syrah (Monterey) $20. 84 —*S.H. (6/1/2003)*

San Simeon 1999 Syrah (Arroyo Seco) $16. 85 —*S.H. (7/1/2002)*

San Simeon 1998 Syrah (Monterey) $15. 87 Editors' Choice *(10/1/2001)*

SANCTUARY

Sanctuary 2003 Usibelli Vineyard Cabernet Sauvignon (Rutherford) $32. 86 —*S.H. (11/15/2006)*

Sanctuary 2005 Bien Nacido Vineyards Pinot Noir (Santa Maria Valley) $36. Dense and closed, this wine needs some cellaring to let it develop. It seems to have everything a young Pinot needs: balanced acids and tannins, a silky texture, dryness, and a hearty core of blackberry and cherry fruit. Let it be through 2007, then open for another five or six years. **90** —*S.H. (7/1/2007)*

Sanctuary 2004 Bien Nacido Vineyards Pinot Noir (Santa Maria Valley) $45. 90 Cellar Selection —*S.H. (11/1/2006)*

SANDHILL

Sandhill 2000 Cabernet Sauvignon (Red Mountain) $25. 85 —*P.G. (1/1/2004)*

Sandhill 1999 Cabernet Sauvignon (Red Mountain) $25. 93 Cellar Selection —*P.G. (9/1/2002)*

Sandhill 2000 Merlot (Red Mountain) $20. 88 —*P.G. (9/1/2004)*

Sandhill 1999 Merlot (Red Mountain) $20. 90 —*P.G. (9/1/2002)*

SANDSTONE

Sandstone Cellars 2004 Syrah (Mason County) $35. Tobacco, chocolate and leather are the aromas on this wine from Texas producer Sandstone Cellars, and in the mouth, the wine is weak and one-dimensional, lacking the fruit and flavor of a good Shiraz. The color seems a little off, too—it's brown and clear at the edges. **81** —*S.K. (5/1/2007)*

SANFORD

Sanford 2005 Chardonnay (Santa Barbara County) $20. Strongly minerally, with a cold metal, chalky tang to the buttery, tropical fruit flavors. With a crisp dose of acidity, this is a dry, elegant Chardonnay that will hold well for five years. **88** —*S.H. (11/1/2007)*

Sanford 2004 Chardonnay (Santa Barbara County) $21. 84 —*S.H. (12/15/2006)*

Sanford 2003 Chardonnay (Santa Barbara County) $21. 88 —*S.H. (12/1/2005)*

Sanford 2002 Chardonnay (Santa Rita Hills) $21. 90 —*S.H. (4/1/2005)*

Sanford 2001 Chardonnay (Santa Rita Hills) $27. 90 —*S.H. (5/1/2004)*

Sanford 2000 Chardonnay (Santa Barbara) $19. 89 —*J.M. (5/1/2002)*

Sanford 1998 Chardonnay (Santa Barbara County) $19. 83 *(6/1/2000)*

Sanford 1999 Barrel Select Chardonnay (Santa Barbara County) $30. 89 *(7/1/2001)*

Sanford 1998 Barrel Select Chardonnay (Santa Barbara County) $30. 85 *(6/1/2000)*

Sanford 2003 La Rinconada Vineyard Chardonnay (Santa Rita Hills) $30. The vineyard is far better known for Pinot Noir. In fact, this is the first Chardonnay I've had from it. It's a very dry, high-acid wine. Compared to lusher Chards, it's a lean wine, streamlined in zingy citrus, wintergreen and mineral flavors, with a richer edge of sweet oak. **87** —*S.H. (6/1/2007)*

Sanford 1997 Sanford & Benedict Vineyard Chardonnay (Santa Ynez Valley) $27. 84 *(6/1/2000)*

Sanford 1997 Santa Barbara County Chardonnay (Santa Barbara County) $18. 89 —*S.H. (7/1/1999)*

Sanford 2005 Pinot Grigio (Santa Barbara County) $19. 86 —*S.H. (12/31/2006)*

Sanford 2004 Pinot Grigio (Santa Barbara County) $18. 89 —*S.H. (2/1/2006)*

Sanford 2005 Pinot Noir (Santa Rita Hills) $31. Smells inert and dull, tastes soft and sugary sweet in cherry pie filling flavor. Production on this is 14,374. **82** —*S.H. (11/1/2007)*

Sanford 2004 Pinot Noir (Santa Rita Hills) $28. 89 —*S.H. (11/1/2006)*

Sanford 2002 Pinot Noir (Santa Rita Hills) $27. 88 —*S.H. (12/31/2005)*

Sanford 2001 Pinot Noir (Santa Rita Hills) $30. 86 —*S.H. (4/1/2005)*

Sanford 2004 La Rinconada Vineyard Pinot Noir (Santa Rita Hills) $40. Not showing all that well now. It has a fat, soft, almost syrupy texture, with cherry, black raspberry and cola flavors that are so ripe, they're almost sweet. Could develop, but doesn't seem to have the balance for the long haul. **85** —*S.H. (5/1/2007)*

Sanford 2002 La Rinconada Vineyard Pinot Noir (Santa Rita Hills) $46. 94 Editors' Choice —*S.H. (12/31/2005)*

Sanford 2001 La Rinconada Pinot Noir (Santa Rita Hills) $50. 88 —*S.H. (3/1/2004)*

Sanford 2000 La Rinconada Pinot Noir (Santa Barbara County) $50. 90 *(10/1/2002)*

Sanford 2004 Sanford & Benedict Vineyard Pinot Noir (Santa Rita Hills) $48. Young, fairly tough in tannins, and with a sappy, grapy taste, this is a wine that badly needs time in the bottle, as do most S&B Pinots. It shows primary fruit flavors of cherries and blackberries, offset by crisp acidity despite full malolactic fermentation. Should begin to come into its own by 2008, improving through 2012 and holding for years afterward. **91 Cellar Selection** —*S.H. (5/1/2007)*

Sanford 2005 Vin Gris Pinot Noir (Santa Rita Hills) $14. 87 —*S.H. (12/15/2006)*

Sanford 2002 Vin Gris Pinot Noir (Santa Rita Hills) $13. 83 —*S.H. (2/1/2004)*

Sanford 2004 Pinot Noir Vin Gris Rosé Blend (Santa Rita Hills) $14. 87 —*S.H. (12/1/2005)*

Sanford 2001 Sauvignon Blanc (Central Coast) $13. 83 —*S.H. (12/1/2003)*

Sanford 1998 Sauvignon Blanc (Central Coast) $15. 88 —*L.W. (3/1/2000)*

Sanford 1997 Sauvignon Blanc (Central Coast) $14. 88 —*S.H. (9/1/1999)*

SANFORD & BENEDICT

Sanford 2002 Sanford & Benedict Vineyard Pinot Noir (Santa Barbara County) $43. 93 Cellar Selection —*S.H. (6/1/2005)*

Sanford 2001 Sanford & Benedict Vineyard Pinot Noir (Santa Rita Hills) $42. 92 —*S.H. (10/1/2003)*

Sanford 2000 Sanford & Benedict Vineyard Pinot Noir (Santa Barbara County) $NA. 91 —*S.H. (6/1/2005)*

Sanford 1999 Sanford & Benedict Vineyard Pinot Noir (Santa Barbara County) $42. 86 *(10/1/2002)*

Sanford 1999 Sanford & Benedict Vineyard Pinot Noir (Santa Barbara County) $NA. 94 Editors' Choice *—S.H. (6/1/2005)*

Sanford 1998 Sanford & Benedict Vineyard Pinot Noir (Santa Barbara County) $NA. 94 Editors' Choice *—S.H. (6/1/2005)*

Sanford 1997 Sanford & Benedict Vineyard Pinot Noir (Santa Barbara County) $23. 87 *(12/15/1999)*

Sanford 1997 Sanford & Benedict Vineyard Pinot Noir (Santa Barbara County) $42. 93 *(10/1/1999)*

Sanford 2000 Sanford & Benedict Vineyard Pinot Noir (Santa Barbara County) $43. 89 *(10/1/2002)*

Sanford & Benedict 1980 Pinot Noir (Santa Ynez Valley) $NA. 92 *—S.H. (6/1/2005)*

SANTA BARBARA WINERY

Santa Barbara Winery 1998 Chardonnay (Santa Barbara County) $16. 89 *(6/1/2000)*

Santa Barbara Winery 1997 Reserve Chardonnay (Santa Ynez Valley) $24. 84 *(6/1/2000)*

Santa Barbara Winery 2000 Pinot Noir (Santa Ynez Valley) $18. 86 *(10/1/2002)*

Santa Barbara Winery 2000 Pinot Noir (Santa Barbara County) $13. 86 Best Buy *(10/1/2002)*

Santa Barbara Winery 2001 Joughin Vineyard Primitivo (Santa Barbara County) $18. 90 Editors' Choice *—J.M. (11/1/2003)*

Santa Barbara Winery 2001 ZCS Red Blend (California) $13. 85 *—J.M. (12/31/2003)*

Santa Barbara Winery 2000 ZCS Red Blend (California) $13. 85 *—S.H. (9/1/2003)*

Santa Barbara Winery 2005 Lafond Vineyard Riesling (Santa Rita Hills) $15. 84 *—S.H. (11/1/2006)*

Santa Barbara Winery 2006 Rosé of Syrah (Santa Rita Hills) $15. Violet-pink in color, this blush has the benefit of extreme dryness, and also shows the high acidity and balance of the appellation. It's not terribly complex or anything, but satisfies for upfront, primary fruit raspberry and cherry flavors. 85 *—S.H. (7/1/2007)*

Santa Barbara Winery 2005 Rosé of Syrah Rosé Blend (Santa Rita Hills) $15. 85 *—S.H. (11/1/2006)*

Santa Barbara Winery 2001 Lafond Vineyard Late Harvest Sauvignon Blanc (Santa Ynez Valley) $16. 95 Editors' Choice *—S.H. (11/1/2006)*

Santa Barbara Winery 1998 Late Harvest Sauvignon Blanc (Santa Ynez Valley) $30. 92 *—J.M. (12/1/2002)*

Santa Barbara Winery 1999 Syrah (Santa Ynez Valley) $22. 89 *(11/1/2001)*

Santa Barbara Winery 2003 Rosé Syrah (Santa Rita Hills) $14. 84 *—S.H. (10/1/2004)*

Santa Barbara Winery 2001 Lafond Vineyard Zinfandel (Santa Rita Hills) $18. 87 *—J.M. (11/1/2003)*

Santa Barbara Winery 2003 Lafond Vineyard Zinfandel Essence Zinfandel (Santa Rita Hills) $34. 81 *—S.H. (11/15/2006)*

SANTINO

Santino 2005 Pinot Grigio (Lodi) $10. 86 Best Buy *—S.H. (12/31/2006)*

Santino 2003 Syrah (Sierra Foothills) $10. 85 Best Buy *—S.H. (12/31/2006)*

Santino 2005 Syrah Rosé Syrah (Sierra Foothills) $10. 86 Best Buy *—S.H. (12/31/2006)*

Santino 2005 Viognier (Lodi) $10. 86 Best Buy *—S.H. (11/15/2006)*

Santino 2003 Zinfandel (Sierra Foothills) $10. 86 Best Buy *—S.H. (12/31/2006)*

Santino 2003 Zinfandel (Fiddletown) $19. 82 *—S.H. (12/31/2006)*

Santino 2003 Old Vine Zinfandel (Amador County) $15. 88 *—S.H. (12/31/2006)*

SANTO STEFANO

Santo Stefano 1997 Cabernet Sauvignon (Sonoma County) $30. 86 *(11/1/2000)*

SAPOLIL CELLARS

Sapolil Cellars 2003 Syrah (Columbia Valley (WA)) $33. 84 *(9/1/2005)*

SAPPHIRE HILL

Sapphire Hill 1998 Chardonnay (Russian River Valley) $22. 84 *(6/1/2000)*

Sapphire Hill 1997 Chardonnay (Russian River Valley) $20. 90 *—S.H. (11/1/1999)*

Sapphire Hill 2004 Sapphire Hill Vineyard Pinot Noir (Russian River Valley) $38. 86 *—S.H. (12/1/2006)*

Sapphire Hill 2000 Winberrie Old Vine Zinfandel (Russian River Valley) $30. 87 *—S.H. (9/1/2002)*

SAPPHIRE MOUNTAIN CELLARS

Sapphire Mountain Cellars 2004 Conner Lee Vineyards Chardonnay (Columbia Valley (WA)) $18. Clean and varietal. The fruit tastes of ripe apples, pears, and maybe a little bit of pineapple, and if there is new oak it has been gracefully melded into the wine so it does not stick out. Just a hint of sweet toast adorns the smooth, lingering finish; then fades with a lick of butterscotch at the tail end. A graceful, elegant debut for this new Walla Walla winery. 90 *—P.G. (8/1/2007)*

SARACINA

Saracina 2001 Sauvignon Blanc (Mendocino County) $24. 84 *—S.H. (7/1/2003)*

SARIAH CELLARS

Sariah Cellars 2000 Syrah (Red Mountain) $25. 87 *—P.G. (9/1/2002)*

SASS

Sass 1998 Dunning Vineyard Chardonnay (Oregon) $12. 88 Best Buy *—S.H. (4/1/2002)*

SATURDAY RED

Saturday Red NV 1 Liter Red Blend (California) $9. 84 *—S.H. (12/15/2005)*

SAUCELITO CANYON

Saucelito Canyon 2004 Cabernet Sauvignon (Arroyo Grande Valley) $20. 83 *—S.H. (11/1/2006)*

Saucelito Canyon 2004 Zinfandel (Arroyo Grande Valley) $20. 83 *—S.H. (11/1/2006)*

Saucelito Canyon 2000 Zinfandel (Arroyo Grande Valley) $20. 90 Editors' Choice *—S.H. (9/1/2003)*

Saucelito Canyon 2004 Dos Ranchos Zinfandel (Arroyo Grande Valley) $30. 83 *—S.H. (11/1/2006)*

Saucelito Canyon 2003 Estate Zinfandel (Arroyo Grande Valley) $18. 82 *—S.H. (10/1/2005)*

Saucelito Canyon 2001 Estate Zinfandel (Arroyo Grande Valley) $17. 90 *—J.M. (4/1/2004)*

Saucelito Canyon 2001 Late Harvest Zinfandel (Arroyo Grande Valley) $20. 91 *—S.H. (3/1/2004)*

Saucelito Canyon 2004 Reserve Zinfandel (Arroyo Grande Valley) $36. 88 *—S.H. (11/1/2006)*

Saucelito Canyon 2001 Reserve Zinfandel (Arroyo Grande Valley) $28. 91 *—J.M. (4/1/2004)*

SAUSAL

Sausal 2003 Cabernet Sauvignon (Alexander Valley) $30. Made in a slightly old-fashioned way, with real tannins of the dusty, dry kind and a rich earthy, mushroomy angle to the blackberry fruit, this is a friendlier food companion than some of those opulent Cabs from "the other side of the hill." 90 *—S.H. (4/1/2007)*

Sausal 2002 Cabernet Sauvignon (Alexander Valley) $30. 84 *—S.H. (11/1/2005)*

Sausal 2001 Cabernet Sauvignon (Alexander Valley) $26. 87 *—S.H. (4/1/2004)*

Sausal 2000 Cabernet Sauvignon (Alexander Valley) $26. 90 *—S.H. (3/1/2003)*

Sausal 2004 Sangiovese (Alexander Valley) $20. 83 *—S.H. (11/15/2006)*

Sausal 2005 Estate Grown Sangiovese (Alexander Valley) $20. Dull and medicinal, with LifeSaver candy cherry and raspberry flavors. 81 *—S.H. (10/1/2007)*

Sausal 2001 Zinfandel (Alexander Valley) $14. 81 *(11/1/2003)*

Sausal 1997 Zinfandel (Sonoma County) $12. 86 Best Buy *—J.C. (5/1/2000)*

Sausal 1996 Alexander Valley Zinfandel (Sonoma County) $12. 86 *(9/1/1999)*

Sausal 2003 Century Vines Zinfandel (Alexander Valley) $30. 82 *—S.H. (11/1/2006)*

Sausal 2002 Century Vines Zinfandel (Alexander Valley) $28. 92 Editors' Choice *—S.H. (11/1/2005)*

Sausal 2001 Century Vines Zinfandel (Alexander Valley) $26. 84 *(11/1/2003)*

Sausal 2000 Century Vines Zinfandel (Alexander Valley) $26. 89 *—S.H. (9/1/2003)*

Sausal 1997 Century Vines Zinfandel (Sonoma County) $22. 90 *—P.G. (3/1/2001)*

Sausal 2004 Old Vine Zinfandel (Alexander Valley) $18. Rugged and lusty, this is an old-fashioned Zin. It's dry and hot, brawny in tannins, wild in briary, brambly, raisiny fruit, and with piercing acidity to cut through olive oil, cheese, and rich, fatty meats. 86 *—S.H. (10/1/2007)*

Sausal 2003 Old Vine Zinfandel (Alexander Valley) $18. 86 *—S.H. (11/1/2006)*

Sausal 2002 Old Vine Zinfandel (Alexander Valley) $18. 86 *—S.H. (8/1/2005)*

Sausal 2000 Old Vine Family Zinfandel (Alexander Valley) $15. 89 *—S.H. (3/1/2003)*

Sausal 2004 Private Reserve Zinfandel (Alexander Valley) $23. 89 *—S.H. (4/1/2007)*

Sausal 2002 Private Reserve Zinfandel (Alexander Valley) $22. 88 *—S.H. (11/1/2005)*

Sausal 2001 Private Reserve Zinfandel (Alexander Valley) $20. 83 *(11/1/2003)*

Sausal 2000 Private Reserve Zinfandel (Alexander Valley) $20. 88 *—S.H. (9/1/2003)*

Sausal 1997 Private Reserve Zinfandel (Sonoma County) $16. 84 *(9/1/1999)*

Sausal 1996 Sogno della Famiglia Zinfandel (Sonoma County) $25. 90 *(9/1/1999)*

SAUVIGNON REPUBLIC

Sauvignon Republic 2006 Sauvignon Blanc (Russian River Valley) $18. Here's a crisp, dry, young Sauvignon Blanc, with a little cat pee, but fortunately it's drowned in a flood of grapefruit, lime, passionfruit and fig flavors. Crisp acidity scours the palate and gets those tastebuds whistling. 85 *—S.H. (10/1/2007)*

Sauvignon Republic 2005 Sauvignon Blanc (Russian River Valley) $18. 86 *—S.H. (10/1/2006)*

Sauvignon Republic 2004 Sauvignon Blanc (Russian River Valley) $18. 87 *—S.H. (12/1/2005)*

Sauvignon Republic 2003 Sauvignon Blanc (Russian River Valley) $16. 82 *—S.H. (5/1/2005)*

SAVANNAH-CHANELLE

Savannah-Chanelle 1998 Estate Bottled Chardonnay (Santa Cruz Mountains) $22. 86 *—S.H. (2/1/2000)*

Savannah-Chanelle 1998 Laetitia Vineyard Pinot Blanc (Arroyo Grande Valley) $16. 88 *—S.H. (3/1/2000)*

Savannah-Chanelle 2002 Pinot Noir (Santa Cruz Mountains) $20. 85 *(11/1/2004)*

Savannah-Chanelle 2002 Pinot Noir (Russian River Valley) $22. 85 *(11/1/2004)*

Savannah-Chanelle 2001 Pinot Noir (Central Coast) $20. 84 *—S.H. (7/1/2003)*

Savannah-Chanelle 2000 Pinot Noir (Central Coast) $20. 85 *—S.H. (5/1/2002)*

Savannah-Chanelle 2000 Pinot Noir (Santa Lucia Highlands) $28. 89 *—S.H. (5/1/2002)*

Savannah-Chanelle 2002 Armagh Vineyard Pinot Noir (Sonoma Coast) $30. 86 *(11/1/2004)*

Savannah-Chanelle 2000 Garys' Vineyard Pinot Noir (Santa Lucia Highlands) $42. 89 *—S.H. (7/1/2003)*

Savannah-Chanelle 2002 Garys' Vineyard Pinot Noir (Santa Lucia Highlands) $35. 88 *(11/1/2004)*

Savannah-Chanelle 2002 Laetitia Vineyard Pinot Noir (Arroyo Grande Valley) $25. 89 *(11/1/2004)*

Savannah-Chanelle 2002 Sleepy Hollow Vineyard Pinot Noir (Santa Lucia Highlands) $25. 85 *(11/1/2004)*

Savannah-Chanelle 2000 Sleepy Hollow Vineyard Pinot Noir (Santa Lucia Highlands) $35. 87 *—S.H. (7/1/2003)*

Savannah-Chanelle 2002 Coast View Vineyard Syrah (Monterey County) $18. 87 *(9/1/2005)*

Savannah-Chanelle 1999 Zinfandel (Santa Cruz Mountains) $36. 91 *—S.H. (7/1/2002)*

Savannah-Chanelle 1998 Zinfandel (Paso Robles) $22. 87 *—P.G. (3/1/2001)*

Savannah-Chanelle 1997 Estate Zinfandel (Santa Cruz Mountains) $36. 84 *—S.H. (5/1/2000)*

Savannah-Chanelle 1997 Westside Zinfandel (Paso Robles) $18. 88 *—S.H. (5/1/2000)*

SAVIAH CELLARS

Saviah Cellars 2004 Big Sky Cuvée Bordeaux Blend (Columbia Valley (WA)) $35. In this lighter vintage, the winery's Merlot-dominated Bordeaux blend is showing sweet red cherry fruit front and center. The acids taste a little chalky in the back of the mouth, and the fruit doesn't carry much weight or authority for a wine in this price range. 86 *—P.G. (3/1/2007)*

Saviah Cellars 2003 Big Sky Cuvée Bordeaux Blend (Columbia Valley (WA)) $35. 89 *—P.G. (6/1/2006)*

Saviah Cellars 2002 Big Sky Cuvée Red Wine Bordeaux Blend (Columbia Valley (WA)) $35. 0 *—P.G. (9/1/2004)*

Saviah Cellars 2004 Laurella Bordeaux Blend (Columbia Valley (WA)) $35. Soft, herbal and showing a streak of sweet baking spice, this unusual red wine immediately sets itself apart from more ordinary Bordeaux blends. Slightly more than half Cabernet, a third Cab Franc and 10% Merlot, this definitely has the pedigreed vineyard fruit. The almost supernal softness of the wine suggests some sort of micro-oxidation, yet it remains sappy and tart. Flavors continue through a myriad of baking spices into a rich and extended finish. The only detriments: the acids are a bit chalky, and the finish lacks finesse. But it's a lovely bottle simply to drink. 89 *—P.G. (8/1/2007)*

Saviah Cellars 2004 Une Vallée Bordeaux Blend (Columbia Valley (WA)) $30. A thoroughly delicious Bordeaux blend, complete and silky smooth. Clear and ripe fruit tastes of a fine mix of plum, spicy cherry and hints of tart cranberry. The subtle use of oak puts a chocolaty coup de grace on top, while hints of tobacco and tea add interest to the lingering finish. 91 *—P.G. (3/1/2007)*

Saviah Cellars 2002 Une Vallée Red Wine Bordeaux Blend (Walla Walla (WA)) $30. 90 *—P.G. (9/1/2004)*

Saviah Cellars 2000 Uné Vallée Bordeaux Blend (Columbia Valley (WA)) $28. 86 *—P.G. (9/1/2003)*

Saviah Cellars 2005 Stillwater Creek Vineyard Chardonnay (Columbia Valley (WA)) $25. This Dijon clone Chard opens with light floral aromas and then fills the palate with rich, mouth-coating fruit; a mix of green apple, melon and white peach. The acids buoy it and continue through a clean finish. At this stage it is not showing the oak influence as much as the previous vintage; this seems lighter, more elegant and quite pretty. 88 *—P.G. (3/1/2007)*

Saviah Cellars 2004 Stillwater Creek Vineyard Chardonnay (Columbia Valley (WA)) $25. 90 *—P.G. (6/1/2006)*

Saviah Cellars 2004 Syrah (Red Mountain) $30. The Red Mountain fruit, from the Ranch at the End of the Road Vineyard, is solid, juicy and spicy with pleasing highlights of citrus and pepper. Fresh and crisp, the snappy mouthfeel sports tart cranberry fruits showing plenty of spice. This is a fine effort, clean and not fussy, with a moderate 14.2% alcohol. 89 *—P.G. (3/1/2007)*

Saviah Cellars 2003 Syrah (Walla Walla (WA)) $28. 88 *(9/1/2005)*

Saviah Cellars 2003 Syrah (Red Mountain) $30. 85 *(9/1/2005)*

Saviah Cellars 2002 Syrah (Red Mountain) $26. 90 *—P.G. (11/15/2004)*

Saviah Cellars 2001 Syrah (Red Mountain) $30. 87 *—P.G. (7/1/2004)*

Saviah Cellars 2000 Syrah (Red Mountain) $30. 87 *—P.G. (9/1/2003)*

Saviah Cellars 2003 Stillwater Creek Vineyard Syrah (Columbia Valley (WA)) $30. 89 *—P.G. (6/1/2006)*

Saviah Cellars 2004 Stillwater Creek Vineyard Syrah (Columbia Valley (WA)) $30. This is bang-on clean and varietal Syrah, with a confident mix of sharp, toasty barrel flavors married to bright, acidic, berry-flavored fruit. Juicy and spicy, it's a great companion to the winery's Red Mountain Syrah, and shows the different character of the varied Washington terroir. It's just 14.2% alcohol, but it has a lot of power and kick to it. 90 *—P.G. (8/1/2007)*

SAVIEZ

Saviez 1998 Zinfandel (Napa Valley) $28. 84 *—P.G. (3/1/2001)*

SAWKAR

Sawkar 2003 Reserve Cabernet Sauvignon (Napa Valley) $42. 88 *—S.H. (3/1/2006)*

Sawkar 2003 Reserve Merlot (Sonoma Mountain) $28. 90 Cellar Selection *—S.H. (3/1/2006)*

Sawkar NV Red Table Wine Red Blend (California) $14. 87 —*S.H. (4/1/2006)*

Sawkar 2003 Reserve Syrah (Sonoma Mountain) $25. 84 —*S.H. (4/1/2006)*

SAWTOOTH

Sawtooth 1999 Merlot (Idaho) $14. 86 —*M.S. (4/1/2003)*

Sawtooth 2002 Syrah (Idaho) $15. 86 *(9/1/2005)*

SAWYER

Sawyer 1999 Bradford Meritage Bordeaux Blend (Napa Valley) $42. 92 —*S.H. (11/15/2002)*

Sawyer 2002 Bradford Meritage Red Table Wine Cabernet Blend (Rutherford) $42. 84 —*S.H. (12/31/2006)*

Sawyer 2004 Cabernet Sauvignon (Rutherford) $46. Likeable for its balance and varietal richness, this 100% Cab is rich in blackberry and cherry fruit, while considerable oak adds a savory jacket of vanilla, toast and cedar-spice. Really defines the elegance and polish of its terroir, and should hold and improve for eight years. **90** —*S.H. (12/15/2007)*

Sawyer 2003 Cabernet Sauvignon (Rutherford) $46. This is a soft, semi-sweet and simple wine, with flavors of cherry cola and milk chocolate. **84** —*S.H. (12/1/2007)*

Sawyer 2002 Cabernet Sauvignon (Rutherford) $46. 90 —*S.H. (12/15/2005)*

Sawyer 2001 Cabernet Sauvignon (Rutherford) $46. 89 —*S.H. (10/1/2004)*

Sawyer 1999 Cabernet Sauvignon (Rutherford) $46. 93 —*S.H. (11/15/2002)*

Sawyer 2000 Bradford Meritage (Rutherford) $42. 91 —*S.H. (6/1/2004)*

Sawyer 2001 Merlot (Rutherford) $37. 87 —*S.H. (12/15/2004)*

Sawyer 1999 Merlot (Rutherford) $34. 93 —*S.H. (11/15/2002)*

Sawyer 2003 Estate Merlot (Rutherford) $38. 83 —*S.H. (12/31/2006)*

Sawyer 2002 Estate Merlot (Rutherford) $38. 85 —*S.H. (12/15/2005)*

Sawyer 2005 Rosé of Merlot (Napa Valley) $14. Ponderous and heavy, this blush has lots of cherry, raspberry, cola and rose petal flavors, but lacks zest and vivacity. Go for it if you like your rosés slightly sweet. **83** —*S.H. (7/1/2007)*

Sawyer 2002 Sauvignon Blanc (Rutherford) $15. 91 Best Buy —*S.H. (12/1/2004)*

Sawyer 2000 Sauvignon Blanc (Rutherford) $18. 90 —*S.H. (6/1/2004)*

Sawyer 2004 Estate Sauvignon Blanc (Rutherford) $17. 84 —*S.H. (12/15/2005)*

SAWYER CELLARS

Sawyer Cellars 2000 Cabernet Sauvignon (Rutherford) $46. 91 —*S.H. (11/15/2003)*

Sawyer Cellars 2000 Merlot (Rutherford) $34. 93 —*S.H. (12/31/2003)*

Sawyer Cellars 2001 Sauvignon Blanc (Rutherford) $15. 87 —*S.H. (10/1/2003)*

SAXON BROWN

Saxon Brown 1999 Pinot Noir (Russian River Valley) $35. 90 —*S.H. (2/1/2003)*

Saxon Brown 2005 Casa Santinamaria Vineyards Sémillon (Sonoma Valley) $30. 86 —*S.H. (12/1/2006)*

Saxon Brown 2002 Casa Santinamaria Vineyards Old Vine Sémillon (Sonoma Valley) $20. 86 —*S.H. (12/1/2003)*

Saxon Brown 2002 Syrah (Napa Valley) $40. 84 *(9/1/2005)*

Saxon Brown 2005 Flora Ranch Syrah Rosé Syrah (Chalk Hill) $20. 84 —*S.H. (12/1/2006)*

Saxon Brown 2003 Parmelee Hill Vineyard Syrah (Sonoma County) $30. 86 *(9/1/2005)*

Saxon Brown 2000 Casa Santinamaria Old Vine Zinfandel (Sonoma Valley) $35. 90 —*S.H. (3/1/2004)*

Saxon Brown 2002 Casa Santinamaria Vineyards Zinfandel (Sonoma Valley) $32. 86 —*S.H. (12/1/2006)*

Saxon Brown 1999 Casa Santinamaria Vineyards Zinfandel (Sonoma Valley) $35. 86 —*S.H. (2/1/2003)*

Saxon Brown 1999 Fighting Brothers Cuvée Zinfandel (Sonoma Valley) $30. 86 —*S.H. (2/1/2003)*

SAXUM

Saxum 2004 Broken Stones Rhône Red Blend (Paso Robles) $38. 90 —*S.H. (12/1/2006)*

Saxum 2004 Heart Stone Vineyard Rhône Red Blend (Paso Robles) $45. 85 —*S.H. (12/1/2006)*

Saxum 2004 James Berry Vineyard Rhône Red Blend (Paso Robles) $45. 84 —*S.H. (12/1/2006)*

Saxum 2004 James Berry Vineyard Bone Rock Rhône Red Blend (Paso Robles) $65. 93 —*S.H. (12/1/2006)*

Saxum 2003 James Berry Vineyard Rocket Block Rhône Red Blend (Paso Robles) $45. 89 —*S.H. (10/1/2005)*

Saxum 2003 Bone Rock Syrah (Paso Robles) $56. 94 Editors' Choice —*S.H. (10/1/2005)*

Saxum 2002 Bone Rock Syrah (Paso Robles) $48. 93 —*S.H. (12/1/2004)*

Saxum 2002 Bone Rock James Berry Vineyard Syrah (Paso Robles) $52. 95 —*S.H. (12/31/2004)*

Saxum 2003 Broken Stones Syrah (Paso Robles) $38. 91 —*S.H. (10/1/2005)*

Saxum 2002 Broken Stones Syrah (Paso Robles) $35. 91 —*S.H. (12/1/2004)*

Saxum 2000 James Berry Bone Rock Syrah (Paso Robles) $50. 92 —*S.H. (12/1/2002)*

SBRAGIA

Sbragia 2004 Andolsen Vineyard Cabernet Sauvignon (Dry Creek Valley) $35. Few Cabs smell more inviting, with come-hither scents of wild blackberries, freshly brewed coffee, raspberry pie and toasted vanilla cream. The wine lives up to its advance, turning voluptuous in all those flavors. It's too soft for aging, though, so drink now. **90** —*S.H. (10/1/2007)*

Sbragia 2003 Monte Rosso Cabernet Sauvignon (Sonoma Valley) $50. This is the second vintage Sbragia has accessed this vineyard. The result is a spectacular 100% Cabernet, stunning now but cellar-worthy. It's a big wine, decadent in cassis and milk chocolate fruit that's massively oaked and ample in tannins, but somehow it all pulls together to make for balance and harmony. Should hold and improve through 2015, at least. **94 Cellar Selection** —*S.H. (5/1/2007)*

Sbragia 2002 Monte Rosso Cabernet Sauvignon (Sonoma Valley) $50. 90 —*S.H. (2/1/2006)*

Sbragia 2003 Rancho Del Oso Cabernet Sauvignon (Howell Mountain) $75. Always decadently opulent in blackberry, currant and chocolate fudge, the '03 seems softer than past vintages, and while it's probably not an ager, it impresses now. It may come from Howell Mountain, but the tannins are as melted as butter on toast. The winemaker suggests steak barbecued in olive oil and rosemary, an assessment I would not argue with. **93** —*S.H. (5/1/2007)*

Sbragia 2002 Rancho del Oso Cabernet Sauvignon (Howell Mountain) $75. 95 Cellar Selection —*S.H. (2/1/2006)*

Sbragia 2001 Rancho Del Oso Cabernet Sauvignon (Howell Mountain) $75. 94 —*S.H. (5/1/2005)*

Sbragia 2004 Gamble Ranch Vineyard Chardonnay (Yountville) $40. This is a gigantic Chardonnay and in my opinion, it's too big for its britches. Everything is so over-sized, especially the oak, that it tastes like a white Burgundy on steroids. A wine like this will have its fans, but it really needs greater control and finesse. **84** —*S.H. (5/1/2007)*

Sbragia 2003 Gamble Ranch Vineyard Chardonnay (Napa Valley) $40. 91 —*S.H. (2/1/2006)*

Sbragia 2002 Gamble Ranch Vineyard Chardonnay (Napa Valley) $40. 90 —*S.H. (4/1/2005)*

Sbragia 2005 Home Ranch Chardonnay (Dry Creek Valley) $25. The underlying fruit smacks of lemon curd, peach pie and kumquats, with a keen, cold minerality. Well-charred oak and lees contribute the richest notes of butterscotch, vanilla and toast. Dry, crisp and elegant, this is one of the best Dry Creek Valley Chards I've ever tasted, but it's still not in the league of the best cool-climate bottlings. **92** —*S.H. (10/1/2007)*

Sbragia 2004 Home Ranch Merlot (Dry Creek Valley) $25. Simple and direct, with cherry-berry and new oak flavors that have an edge of rosemary and thyme. My chief complaint is the apparent sweetness. **84** —*S.H. (10/1/2007)*

Sbragia 2006 Home Ranch Sauvignon Blanc (Dry Creek Valley) $20. I love this Sauvignon Blanc for its dryness and freshness, its acidity that cleanses the mouth so well, and its subtle complexity. The green grass, lime and ruby grapefruit flavors are enriched with dates, vanilla and candied ginger, while the long, spicy finish is just perfect. **91 Editors' Choice** —*S.H. (12/1/2007)*

Sbragia 2004 Gino's Vineyard Zinfandel (Dry Creek Valley) $28. This Zin is so soft, so ripe, so dessert-like, it could come from Paso Robles, Lodi or any other hot climate. Shows honeyed flavors of black cherry preserves, root beer and milk chocolate, with deficient acidity and tannins. Needs greater structure, which the '05 vintage may bring. **85** *—S.H. (10/1/2007)*

SCARECROW

Scarecrow 2003 Cabernet Sauvignon (Rutherford) $100. 91 Cellar Selection *—S.H. (9/1/2006)*

SCHARFFENBERGER

Scharffenberger NV Brut Sparkling Blend (Anderson Valley) $19. This lovely brut offers real Champagne-like finesse. It's rich and dry, with yeasty flavors of pineapples, lemon chiffon and raspberries. The mousse is creamy and smooth. This polished bubbly will develop with five years of cellaring. **90 Editors' Choice** *—S.H. (12/31/2007)*

Scharffenberger NV Brut Sparkling Blend (Mendocino County) $16. 91 *—S.H. (3/1/2006)*

SCHEID VINEYARDS

Scheid Vineyards 2001 Chardonnay (Monterey) $15. 84 *—S.H. (2/1/2004)*

Scheid Vineyards 2001 Riverview Vineyard Pinot Noir (Monterey) $20. 84 *—S.H. (12/15/2004)*

SCHERRER

Scherrer 2002 Cabernet Sauvignon (Alexander Valley) $32. 88 *—S.H. (12/1/2006)*

Scherrer 2001 Cabernet Sauvignon (Alexander Valley) $32. 89 *—S.H. (11/15/2005)*

Scherrer 2001 Scherrer Vineyard Cabernet Sauvignon (Alexander Valley) $42. 93 *—S.H. (11/15/2005)*

Scherrer 2002 Fort Ross Vineyard Chardonnay (Sonoma Coast) $28. 92 *—S.H. (11/15/2005)*

Scherrer 2002 Fort Ross Vineyard Reserve Chardonnay (Sonoma Coast) $28. 92 *—S.H. (11/15/2005)*

Scherrer 2002 Helfer Vineyard Chardonnay (Russian River Valley) $35. 91 *—S.H. (11/15/2005)*

Scherrer 2003 Scherrer Vineyard Chardonnay (Sonoma County) $26. 88 *—S.H. (12/1/2006)*

Scherrer 2002 Scherrer Vineyard Chardonnay (Alexander Valley) $25. 88 *—S.H. (11/15/2005)*

Scherrer 2001 Scherrer Vineyard Chardonnay (Alexander Valley) $25. 90 *—S.H. (11/15/2005)*

Scherrer 2003 Pinot Noir (Russian River Valley) $35. 87 *—S.H. (12/1/2006)*

Scherrer 2002 Pinot Noir (Russian River Valley) $35. 88 *—S.H. (11/15/2005)*

Scherrer 2002 Pinot Noir (Sonoma Coast) $30. 87 *—S.H. (11/15/2005)*

Scherrer 2000 Pinot Noir (Russian River Valley) $35. 87 *(10/1/2002)*

Scherrer 2002 Fort Ross Vineyard Pinot Noir (Sonoma Coast) $38. 93 *—S.H. (11/15/2005)*

Scherrer 2003 Fort Ross Vineyard High Slopes Pinot Noir (Sonoma Coast) $45. 89 *—S.H. (12/1/2006)*

Scherrer 2000 Helfer Pinot Noir (Russian River Valley) $35. 86 *(10/1/2002)*

Scherrer 2000 Hirsch Pinot Noir (Sonoma Coast) $45. 90 *(10/1/2002)*

Scherrer 2002 Laguna Pinot Noir (Russian River Valley) $35. 93 *—S.H. (11/15/2005)*

Scherrer 2004 Dry Rosé Wine Rosé Blend (Sonoma County) $14. 87 *—S.H. (11/15/2005)*

Scherrer 2005 Vin Gris Dry Rosé Wine Rosé Blend (Sonoma County) $14. 87 *—S.H. (12/1/2006)*

Scherrer 1999 Old Mature Vines Zinfandel (Alexander Valley) $28. 92 *—J.M. (3/1/2002)*

Scherrer 2002 Scherrer Old & Mature Vines Zinfandel (Alexander Valley) $28. 86 *—S.H. (11/15/2005)*

Scherrer 2001 Scherrer Old & Mature Vines Zinfandel (Alexander Valley) $28. 91 *(11/1/2003)*

Scherrer 2001 Scherrer Shale Terrace Zinfandel (Alexander Valley) $24. 89 *(11/1/2003)*

Scherrer NV Zinfandoodle Zinfandel (Sonoma County) $16. 83 *—S.H. (12/1/2006)*

SCHNEIDER

Schneider 1998 Cabernet Franc (North Fork of Long Island) $24. 87 *—J.C. (4/1/2001)*

Schneider 1998 Chardonnay (North Fork of Long Island) $19. 85 *—J.C. (4/1/2001)*

USA

SCHRADER

Schrader 2002 Beckstoffer Tokalon Vineyard Cabernet Sauvignon (Oakville) $75. 89 *—S.H. (6/1/2005)*

Schrader 2001 Beckstoffer Tokalon Vineyard Cabernet Sauvignon (Napa Valley) $75. 94 Cellar Selection *—S.H. (6/1/2005)*

Schrader 2000 Beckstoffer Tokalon Vineyard Cabernet Sauvignon (Napa Valley) $75. 85 *—S.H. (6/1/2005)*

Schrader 2004 Double Diamond Beckstoffer Cabernet Sauvignon (Red Hills Lake County) $25. 86 *—S.H. (12/31/2006)*

SCHRAMSBERG

Schramsberg 1999 Blanc de Blancs Champagne Blend (Napa Valley) $30. 91 *—S.H. (12/1/2003)*

Schramsberg 1998 Blanc de Blancs Champagne Blend (California) $30. 86 *—D.T. (12/1/2001)*

Schramsberg 1997 Blanc de Blancs Champagne Blend (Napa Valley) $29. 84 *(12/1/2000)*

Schramsberg 1999 Blanc de Noirs Champagne Blend (California) $31. 91 *—S.H. (6/1/2004)*

Schramsberg 1997 Blanc de Noirs Champagne Blend (Napa Valley) $30. 87 *—J.C. (12/1/2001)*

Schramsberg 1996 Blanc de Noirs Champagne Blend (Napa Valley) $29. 87 *—P.G. (12/31/2000)*

Schramsberg 1996 Brut Champagne Blend (Napa Valley) $27. 86 *—J.C. (12/1/1999)*

Schramsberg 1995 Brut Blanc de Noirs Champagne Blend (Napa Valley) $27. 87 *—J.C. (12/1/1999)*

Schramsberg 1999 Brut Rosé Champagne Blend (California) $33. 89 *—J.M. (12/1/2002)*

Schramsberg 1996 Cuvée de Pinot Brut Rosé Champagne Blend (Napa Valley) $27. 86 *—J.C. (12/1/1999)*

Schramsberg 1998 Cuvée de Pinot Brut Rosé Champagne Blend (Napa County) $30. 87 *—J.C. (12/1/2001)*

Schramsberg 1996 J. Schram Champagne Blend (Napa County) $80. 93 Editors' Choice *—S.H. (12/1/2002)*

Schramsberg 1995 J. Schram Champagne Blend (Napa Valley) $75. 92 *—M.M. (12/1/2001)*

Schramsberg 1993 J. Schram Champagne Blend (Napa Valley) $65. 93 *(12/31/2000)*

Schramsberg 1996 Reserve Champagne Blend (Napa County) $60. 93 Cellar Selection *—S.H. (9/1/2003)*

Schramsberg 1994 Reserve Champagne Blend (Napa Valley) $47. 90 *—S.H. (12/31/2000)*

Schramsberg 1993 Reserve Brut Champagne Blend (Napa Valley) $43. 87 *—J.C. (12/1/1999)*

Schramsberg 1998 Blanc de Noirs Pinot Noir (California) $30. 92 Editors' Choice *—S.H (12/1/2002)*

Schramsberg 1995 Reserve Cuvée Pinot Noir (Napa Valley) $60. 92 *—J.M. (12/1/2002)*

Schramsberg 2004 Blanc de Blancs Sparkling Blend (Napa-Mendocino-Sonoma-Marin) $35. Off a beat from the great '03, closer to the '02, this is an elegant young sparkler, lacking a bit in finesse. This 100% Chardonnay has slightly sweet flavors of lemon candy and yeast. **86** *—S.H. (12/31/2007)*

Schramsberg 2003 Blanc de Blancs Sparkling Blend (North Coast) $35. This 100% Chardonnay is easily the best Schramsberg blanc de blancs to date. It's so rich and luxurious in subtle lime, peach and brioche flavors, and so refined in its beautiful silky mouthfeel, and so long in the finish, you can't help but love it. Gorgeous now, and should hold and even improve for the next 6–8 years. **94 Editors' Choice** *—S.H. (6/1/2007)*

Schramsberg 2002 Blanc de Blancs Sparkling Blend (Napa Valley) $32. 87 *—S.H. (12/31/2006)*

Schramsberg 2000 Blanc de Blancs Sparkling Blend (Napa-Sonoma) $30. 90 *—S.H. (12/31/2004)*

Schramsberg 2001 Blanc de Blancs Brut Sparkling Blend (North Coast) $32. 91 *—S.H. (12/31/2005)*

Schramsberg 1994 Blanc de Blancs Late Disgorged Sparkling Blend (Napa County) $60. 92 *—S.H. (12/31/2005)*

Schramsberg 2004 Blanc de Noirs Sparkling Blend (Napa-Mendocino-Sonoma) $37. Nearly all Pinot Noir, with just 15% Chardonnay, this full-bodied sparkler has raspberry and cherry liqueur flavors that finish with a dose of sweet honey. Very high acidity brings needed balance to this rich wine, but it does seem like it could finish a little drier. 87 *—S.H. (12/31/2007)*

Schramsberg 2003 Blanc de Noirs Sparkling Blend (Napa-Mendocino-Sonoma) $34. 92 *—S.H. (12/31/2006)*

Schramsberg 2002 Blanc de Noirs Sparkling Blend (North Coast) $32. 90 *—S.H. (12/31/2006)*

Schramsberg 2000 Blanc de Noirs Sparkling Blend (Napa-Sonoma) $30. 91 *—S.H. (12/31/2004)*

Schramsberg 2001 Blanc de Noirs Brut Sparkling Blend (North Coast) $30. 89 *—S.H. (12/31/2005)*

Schramsberg 1994 Blanc de Noirs Late Disgorged Sparkling Blend (Napa-Mendocino) $60. 92 Cellar Selection *—S.H. (12/31/2005)*

Schramsberg NV Brut Sparkling Blend (North Coast) $19. If Schramsberg's regular sparkling wines are too pricey for your budget, this second label is a nice alternative. It shows good brut sparkling wine character, with slightly sweet fruity, yeasty flavors and crisp acids that finish with elegance. 86 *—S.H. (12/31/2007)*

Schramsberg 2004 Brut Rosé Sparkling Blend (North Coast) $40. A little sweet, which makes the wine less subtle, this Pinot Noir and Chardonnay blend has jammy raspberry, cherry and vanilla smoke flavors. The finish is very sweet. 85 *—S.H. (12/31/2007)*

Schramsberg 2002 Brut Rosé Sparkling Blend (North Coast) $36. 92 *—S.H. (12/31/2005)*

Schramsberg 2001 Brut Rosé Sparkling Blend (California) $34. 91 *—S.H. (12/31/2004)*

Schramsberg 2000 Brut Rosé Sparkling Blend (California) $33. 92 *—S.H. (12/1/2003)*

Schramsberg 2003 Brut Rosé Sparkling Blend (North Coast) $39. 90 *—S.H. (12/31/2006)*

Schramsberg 2001 Crémant Sparkling Blend (Mendocino) $34. 87 *—S.H. (12/31/2004)*

Schramsberg 2003 Crémant Sparkling Blend (Napa-Mendocino) $34. 87 *—S.H. (12/31/2006)*

Schramsberg 2004 Crémant Demi-sec Sparkling Blend (Napa-Mendocino-Sonoma) $38. This is Schramsberg's sweet sparkler, although it's not terribly sweet; it only suggests a touch of honeyed caramel cream, peach-vanilla frappuccino and gingerbread. Crisp acidity helps to balance. Made mainly from the rare Flora grape, which is a cross between Sémillon and Gewürztraminer. 87 *—S.H. (12/31/2007)*

Schramsberg 2002 Crémant Demi-Sec Sparkling Blend (North Coast) $36. 85 *—S.H. (12/31/2005)*

Schramsberg 2000 Crémant Demi-Sec Sparkling Blend (California) $32. 86 *—S.H. (12/1/2003)*

Schramsberg 2000 J. Schram Sparkling Blend (North Coast) $90. Right up there with the recent string of fabulous têtes de cuvées, the 2000 shows the concentration, power and subtlety of this, the winery's top release. A blend of Chardonnay with 20% Pinot Noir, it shows exotic and complex flavors of tangerines and raspberries, candied ginger, coconut macaroons, baked bread and yeast. It's delicious now, but all the parts haven't come together. Hold until mid-2008 through 2010, but could go well beyond that. 94 *—S.H. (12/31/2007)*

Schramsberg 1999 J. Schram Sparkling Blend (North Coast) $80. 93 Cellar Selection *—S.H. (12/31/2005)*

Schramsberg 1998 J. Schram Sparkling Blend (Napa County) $80. 95 *—S.H. (12/31/2004)*

Schramsberg 1998 J. Schram Sparkling Blend (North Coast) $120. 94 *—S.H. (12/31/2006)*

Schramsberg 1997 J. Schram Sparkling Blend (California) $80. 93 *—S.H. (12/1/2003)*

Schramsberg NV Mirabelle Sparkling Blend (North Coast) $18. 84 *—S.H. (12/31/2004)*

Schramsberg NV Mirabelle Sparkling Blend (California) $17. 84 *—S.H. (12/1/2003)*

Schramsberg NV Mirabelle Brut Sparkling Blend (North Coast) $19. 86 *—S.H. (12/31/2005)*

Schramsberg NV Mirabelle Brut Rosé Sparkling Blend (North Coast) $24. Made in a frankly sweet style, this blend of Pinot Noir and Chardonnay has jellied flavors of raspberries, cherries and toast. It's a little rough in texture. 85 *—S.H. (12/31/2007)*

Schramsberg NV Mirabelle Brut Rosé Sparkling Blend (North Coast) $23. 86 *—S.H. (12/31/2006)*

Schramsberg 2000 Reserve Sparkling Blend (Napa-Mendocino-Sonoma-Marin) $80. 96 Cellar Selection *—S.H. (12/31/2006)*

Schramsberg 1999 Reserve Sparkling Blend (North Coast) $70. 90 Cellar Selection *—S.H. (12/31/2005)*

Schramsberg 1998 Reserve Sparkling Blend (North Coast) $65. 93 Cellar Selection *—S.H. (12/31/2005)*

Schramsberg 1997 Reserve Sparkling Blend (California) $65. 95 *—S.H. (6/1/2004)*

Schramsberg 1997 Reserve Sparkling Blend (California) $60. 91 *—S.H. (12/31/2004)*

Schramsberg 1994 Reserve Late Disgorged Sparkling Blend (Napa Valley) $200. 97 Editors' Choice *(12/31/2005)*

Schramsberg 1999 Crément Demi Sec White Blend (California) $33. 89 *—J.M. (12/1/2002)*

SCHUG

Schug 2005 Cabernet Sauvignon (Sonoma Valley) $26. A very nice Cabernet that's superdrinkable because of its soft, appealing fruit, but also has plenty of complexity. Cherries, blackberries, blueberries and dark chocolate are enriched with spicy oak notes, leading to a long, balanced finish. 89 *—S.H. (12/15/2007)*

Schug 2004 Cabernet Sauvignon (Sonoma Valley) $24. Schug is one of the wineries that sticks in my mind for greatly improving the quality of their Bordeaux reds in recent years. This Cab, with a little Merlot and Cab Franc, is a great value in its price range. It's dry and balanced, with rich, ripe black currant, chocolate and earthy flavors, and will easily stand up to fancy fare at the table. 88 *—S.H. (5/1/2007)*

Schug 2003 Cabernet Sauvignon (Sonoma Valley) $22. 90 *—S.H. (7/1/2006)*

Schug 2001 Cabernet Sauvignon (Sonoma Valley) $20. 88 *(5/1/2004)*

Schug 2000 Cabernet Sauvignon (Sonoma Valley) $20. 87 *—S.H. (11/15/2003)*

Schug 1997 Cabernet Sauvignon (Sonoma Valley) $20. 84 *—S.H. (12/15/2000)*

Schug 2003 Heritage Reserve Cabernet Sauvignon (Sonoma Valley) $50. If you're looking for a Cabernet that has all the hallmarks of California cool-climate ripeness and balance, without demanding to be noticed for itself, try this one. It's dry, elegant and juicy, teasing the palate with fruit, yet wisely pulls back at the last moment, so the food can star. The black currants and smoky oak will perfectly match a charred steak. 92 *—S.H. (5/1/2007)*

Schug 2002 Heritage Reserve Cabernet Sauvignon (Sonoma Valley) $50. 92 *—S.H. (9/1/2006)*

Schug 2001 Heritage Reserve Cabernet Sauvignon (Sonoma Valley) $50. 90 *—S.H. (5/1/2005)*

Schug 2000 Heritage Reserve Cabernet Sauvignon (Sonoma Valley) $50. 89 *(5/1/2004)*

Schug 1999 Heritage Reserve Cabernet Sauvignon (Sonoma Valley) $50. 89 *—S.H. (11/15/2003)*

Schug 1997 Heritage Reserve Cabernet Sauvignon (Sonoma Valley) $40. 94 *(11/1/2000)*

Schug 1996 Heritage Reserve Cabernet Sauvignon (Sonoma Valley) $40. 92 *—S.H. (2/1/2000)*

Schug 2006 Chardonnay (Sonoma Coast) $22. Way too sweet, this tastes like a couple spoons of white sugar were added to a wine that already had good pineapple flavors. 82 *—S.H. (12/15/2007)*

Schug 2005 Chardonnay (Sonoma Coast) $20. Shows rich, racy acidity in a dry wine whose flavors veer toward ripe pineapple-tart filling, cinnamon spice and butterscotch, wrapped in a creamy texture. Would score far higher if the fruit were more concentrated. 87 *—S.H. (8/1/2007)*

Schug 2005 Chardonnay (Carneros) $24. A little light in flavor, but dry, crisp and balanced. The flavors are of pineapples, green apples, nectarines and oaky butterscotch. 86 *—S.H. (8/1/2007)*

Schug 2004 Chardonnay (Carneros) $20. 85 *—S.H. (12/31/2005)*

Schug 2003 Chardonnay (Carneros) $20. 88 *—S.H. (5/1/2005)*

Schug 2001 Chardonnay (Sonoma Valley) $15. 86 *—S.H. (12/1/2003)*

Schug 2001 Chardonnay (Carneros) $20. 88 *—S.H. (12/1/2003)*

Schug 2000 Chardonnay (Sonoma Valley) $15. 85 *—S.H. (5/1/2002)*

Schug 2000 Chardonnay (Carneros) $20. 86 *—S.H. (5/1/2002)*

Schug 1998 Chardonnay (Carneros) $18. 93 *—S.H. (11/15/2000)*

Schug 1998 Chardonnay (Sonoma Valley) $14. 87 *—S.H. (5/1/2000)*

Schug 1997 Chardonnay (Carneros) $18. 88 *—S.H. (6/1/1999)*

Schug 2002 Barrel-Fermented Sur Lie Chardonnay (Carneros) $20. 88 *(5/1/2004)*

Schug 1996 Carneros Reserve Chardonnay (Carneros) $25. 91 *—S.H. (6/1/1999)*

Schug 2005 Heritage Reserve Chardonnay (Carneros) $30. Easily the richest of Schug's current trio of Chards, showing the elegance and crispness of the other bottlings, but with more fruity intensity. It's still a fairly restrained wine, rich in acidity and dry minerality, but rewards with pineapple custard and butterscotch flavors. **90** *—S.H. (8/1/2007)*

Schug 2004 Heritage Reserve Chardonnay (Carneros) $30. 87 *—S.H. (11/1/2006)*

Schug 2003 Heritage Reserve Chardonnay (Carneros) $30. 90 *—S.H. (5/1/2005)*

Schug 2002 Heritage Reserve Chardonnay (Carneros) $30. 89 *(5/1/2004)*

Schug 2001 Heritage Reserve Chardonnay (Carneros) $30. 92 *—S.H. (12/1/2003)*

Schug 2000 Heritage Reserve Chardonnay (Carneros) $30. 87 *—S.H. (5/1/2002)*

Schug 1999 Heritage Reserve Chardonnay (Carneros) $30. 88 *(7/1/2001)*

Schug 1998 Heritage Reserve Chardonnay (Carneros) $25. 88 *(6/1/2000)*

Schug 2005 Merlot (Sonoma Valley) $26. Here's a Merlot that just wants to support the food it's paired with, not dominate it. It's dry and balanced, teasing with cherries, herbs and oak, then pulling back to let the tannins and acids take a bow. Should develop a little complexity by spring 2008, but it's fine now. **87** *—S.H. (12/15/2007)*

Schug 2004 Merlot (Sonoma Valley) $24. This is a really good Merlot. It has an elegance and opulence that make it as good as many that cost more. Floods the palate with cherries, black raspberries, carob, lavender, sweet leather and smoky oak; a dash or two of Cabernet adds firmness and structure. **89** *—S.H. (5/1/2007)*

Schug 2003 Merlot (Sonoma Valley) $22. 91 Editors' Choice *—S.H. (7/1/2006)*

Schug 2001 Merlot (Sonoma Valley) $20. 88 *(5/1/2004)*

Schug 2000 Merlot (Sonoma Valley) $20. 90 *—S.H. (12/31/2003)*

Schug 1997 Merlot (North Coast) $18. 86 *—S.H. (11/15/2000)*

Schug 2003 Heritage Reserve Merlot (Carneros) $35. The vintage was not only a good one for Cabernet, it also made good Merlot in the North Coast. In Carneros, it produced wines that were ripe and opulent, yet balanced and dry, and this one is a winner. Juicy and fruit-forward, it has finely grained tannins that give it structure and finesse. **90** *—S.H. (5/1/2007)*

Schug 2002 Heritage Reserve Merlot (Carneros) $30. 92 *—S.H. (11/1/2006)*

Schug 2001 Heritage Reserve Merlot (Carneros) $30. 85 *—S.H. (5/1/2005)*

Schug 2000 Heritage Reserve Merlot (Carneros) $30. 90 *(5/1/2004)*

Schug 1997 Heritage Reserve Merlot (Carneros) $35. 89 *—S.H. (11/15/2000)*

Schug 2006 Pinot Noir (Sonoma Coast) $22. Schug's regular Pinot, as opposed to their Heritage Reserve, is a dependably village-style expression of easy-drinking, cool-climate Pinot Noir. The '06, like previous vintages, shows a silky, delicate texture framing cherry, raspberry and cola flavors, with a smoky vanilla edge of oak. **87** *—S.H. (12/15/2007)*

Schug 2005 Pinot Noir (Carneros) $24. The best of Schug's three current Pinots, a blend of several vineyards throughout the appellation. The wine is dry, crisp and delicate, with subtle cola, red cherry, dried pomegranate and spice flavors, and a subtle overlay of toast. Drink this polished wine now. **87** *—S.H. (8/1/2007)*

Schug 2005 Pinot Noir (Sonoma Coast) $20. Schug has three new Pinots out. This is the lightest and easiest. It's pale, delicate and silky, with easy cherry, cola, vanilla and spice flavors. Your basic Pinot for beginners. **85** *—S.H. (8/1/2007)*

Schug 2004 Pinot Noir (Sonoma Coast) $16. 86 *—S.H. (3/1/2006)*

Schug 2004 Pinot Noir (Carneros) $22. 90 *—S.H. (3/1/2006)*

Schug 2003 Pinot Noir (Carneros) $20. 84 *—S.H. (5/1/2005)*

Schug 2002 Pinot Noir (Carneros) $20. 87 *(5/1/2004)*

Schug 2001 Pinot Noir (Sonoma Valley) $15. 85 *—S.H. (12/1/2003)*

Schug 2001 Pinot Noir (Carneros) $20. 88 *—S.H. (12/1/2003)*

Schug 2000 Pinot Noir (Sonoma Valley) $15. 88 Best Buy *—S.H. (2/1/2003)*

Schug 2000 Pinot Noir (Carneros) $20. 88 *—S.H. (4/1/2003)*

Schug 1999 Pinot Noir (Sonoma Valley) $15. 90 *—S.H. (2/1/2001)*

Schug 1999 Pinot Noir (Carneros) $20. 83 *(10/1/2002)*

Schug 1998 Pinot Noir (Carneros) $18. 92 *—S.H. (2/1/2001)*

Schug 2005 Heritage Reserve Pinot Noir (Carneros) $35. Simple and likeable in fruity extract, this young Pinot has a silky texture and dry, spicy flavors of cherries, raspberries, cola, leather, tobacco and oak. It seems to be at its juicy best now. **86** *—S.H. (12/1/2007)*

Schug 2004 Heritage Reserve Pinot Noir (Carneros) $30. The biggest, richest, ripest, oakiest of Schug's current trio of Pinots, this wine is gigantic in fruit. It's not quite stewed, but almost, with flavors of sweet tobacco and dried cherries that have been plumped. A little heavy, it may gain elegance with a year or so of bottle age. **86** *—S.H. (8/1/2007)*

Schug 2003 Heritage Reserve Pinot Noir (Carneros) $30. 89 *—S.H. (12/31/2005)*

Schug 2002 Heritage Reserve Pinot Noir (Carneros) $30. 88 *—S.H. (5/1/2005)*

Schug 2001 Heritage Reserve Pinot Noir (Carneros) $30. 91 *—S.H. (4/1/2004)*

Schug 2000 Heritage Reserve Pinot Noir (Carneros) $30. 90 *—S.H. (2/1/2004)*

Schug 1999 Heritage Reserve Pinot Noir (Carneros) $30. 92 Editors' Choice *—S.H. (2/1/2003)*

Schug 1998 Heritage Reserve Pinot Noir (Carneros) $30. 93 *—S.H. (2/1/2001)*

Schug 1997 Heritage Reserve Pinot Noir (Carneros) $30. 86 *(11/15/1999)*

Schug 1998 Rouge de Noirs Pinot Noir (Carneros) $25. 88 *—K.F. (12/1/2002)*

Schug 2006 Sauvignon Blanc (Sonoma County) $18. Let this very young, tart Sauvignon Blanc breathe for a while. That will get rid of most of the feline essence, which are really strong on opening, and let richer notes of figs, melons and citrus fruits emerge. **83** *—S.H. (11/1/2007)*

Schug 2005 Sauvignon Blanc (Sonoma County) $15. 86 *—S.H. (11/1/2006)*

Schug 2004 Sauvignon Blanc (Sonoma County) $15. 86 *—S.H. (8/1/2005)*

Schug 2003 Sauvignon Blanc (Sonoma County) $15. 86 *—S.H. (5/1/2005)*

Schug 2002 Sauvignon Blanc (Sonoma County) $15. 87 *(5/1/2004)*

Schug 2001 Sauvignon Blanc (Sonoma County) $15. 84 *—S.H. (9/1/2003)*

Schug 1998 Sauvignon Blanc (North Coast) $12. 90 Best Buy *(3/1/2000)*

Schug 2000 Brut Rouge de Noirs Sparkling Blend (Carneros) $25. 86 *—S.H. (12/1/2003)*

Schug 2001 Rouge de Noirs Sparkling Blend (Carneros) $25. 90 *—S.H. (6/1/2005)*

Schug 2002 Rouge de Noirs Brut Sparkling Blend (Carneros) $25. 88 *—S.H. (6/1/2006)*

SCHWEIGER

Schweiger 2000 Cabernet Sauvignon (Spring Mountain) $45. 86 *—S.H. (12/31/2003)*

Schweiger 1999 Cabernet Sauvignon (Spring Mountain) $48. 86 *—S.H. (12/15/2003)*

Schweiger 2000 Chardonnay (Spring Mountain) $30. 90 *—S.H. (6/1/2003)*

Schweiger 1999 Merlot (Spring Mountain) $45. 89 *—S.H. (10/1/2003)*

Schweiger NV Port III Port (Spring Mountain) $45. 88 *—J.M. (3/1/2004)*

Schweiger 2000 Dedication Red Blend (Spring Mountain) $65. 88 *—S.H. (12/31/2003)*

Schweiger 2001 Uboldi Vineyard Sauvignon Blanc (Sonoma Valley) $22. 88 *—J.M. (10/1/2003)*

SCOTT

Scott 2005 Pinot Gris (Santa Barbara County) $18. Here's a fruit-forward PG that's like a romp in an orchard. It's got everything from apples and white apricots to peaches, pineapples and pears, with flowery, spicy, honeyed nuances. Juicy acidity provides much-needed balance to this clean, flavorful wine. **87** *—S.H. (11/1/2007)*

Scott 2005 Sharon's Vineyard Pinot Noir (Santa Maria Valley) $26. Enjoyable for its easy flavors of cherries, cola and oaky vanilla, with a sprinkling of crushed hard spices. Seems at its youthful best now for the fresh, juicy fruit; should linger for several years. **85** *—S.H. (11/1/2007)*

Scott 2005 Cuvée J Red Blend (Central Coast) $34. Hot and medicinal, with baked flavors of berries. **80** *—S.H. (11/1/2007)*

SCOTT AARON

Scott Aaron 2003 Integrity Cabernet Blend (Paso Robles) $60. 82 *—S.H. (12/15/2005)*

Scott Aaron 2004 Viognier (Paso Robles) $30. 83 *—S.H. (12/15/2005)*

SCOTT HARVEY

Scott Harvey 2003 Barbera (Amador County) $25. 85 *—S.H. (6/1/2006)*

Scott Harvey 2005 J&S Reserve Barbera (Amador County) $28. This winery has been working for years with Barbera, but it's a tough grape to perfect in California. This shows the variety's rustic side, with briary flavors of wild berries and thick tannins. It's also sweet on the finish, like a simple Port. **83** *—S.H. (12/1/2007)*

Scott Harvey 2004 J&S Reserve Barbera (Amador County) $28. Here's a Barbera that wants to escape its rustic past and turn into a fancy, modern wine. It succeeds, partially. The softness, the round smoothness of the tannins are something new for the variety. The flavors are delicious, cherries and licorice and spices, with a French oak edge. There's still something wildly brawny, but is sure is a nice wine. **87** *—S.H. (2/1/2007)*

Scott Harvey 2004 Syrah (Amador County) $28. Doesn't really taste like Syrah or have the noble richness you'd expect from this variety. More like a Barbera or Petite Sirah, a tannic, dry, heavy wine, with sharp acids and stalky, green flavors. Cheeses, olive oil and hearty meats will soften it. **83** *—S.H. (2/1/2007)*

Scott Harvey 2003 Syrah (Amador County) $25. 84 *—S.H. (4/1/2006)*

Scott Harvey 2003 Mountain Selection Syrah (Amador County) $15. 83 *—S.H. (5/1/2006)*

Scott Harvey 2003 Mountain Selection Zinfandel (Amador County) $13. 83 *—S.H. (6/1/2006)*

Scott Harvey 2004 Old Vine Selection Zinfandel (Amador County) $28. There's lots of ripe, juicy flavor here. Blackberry and cherry jam, cola, mocha-choca with a shake of cinnamon, nutmeg and pepper, it's a classically drinkable, slightly sweet country-style Zin. **84** *—S.H. (7/1/2007)*

Scott Harvey 2003 Old Vine Selection Zinfandel (Amador County) $22. 89 *—S.H. (6/1/2006)*

SCOTT PAUL

Scott Paul 1999 Kent Ritchie Vineyard Chardonnay (Sonoma County) $35. 89 *(7/1/2001)*

Scott Paul 2005 Audrey Pinot Noir (Dundee Hills) $55. Another outstanding Pinot Noir from this rising star winery. The tangy fruit swirls around cranberry, black cherry and plum, with side-car notes of bay leaf and sage. The wine extends itself into a lingering finish, promising further development ahead. It is balanced, textural and complex. **92** *—P.G. (7/1/2007)*

Scott Paul 2004 Audrey Pinot Noir (Willamette Valley) $50. 91 *—P.G. (12/1/2006)*

Scott Paul 2003 Cuvée Martha Pirrie Pinot Noir (Willamette Valley) $20. 89 *—P.G. (8/1/2005)*

Scott Paul 2002 Cuvée Martha Pirrie Pinot Noir (Willamette Valley) $20. 84 *(11/1/2004)*

Scott Paul 2005 La Paulée Pinot Noir (Willamette Valley) $40. An immaculate, fruit-powered Pinot, with a pleasing roundness that is crisply defined and never overblown. Scott Wright practices studiously non-interventionist winemaking, and delivers elegant, beautifully proportioned Pinots. La Paulée is loaded with sweet cherry fruit, cherry candy and spice. **91** *—P.G. (7/1/2007)*

Scott Paul 2004 La Paulée Pinot Noir (Willamette Valley) $35. 90 *—P.G. (12/1/2006)*

Scott Paul 2003 La Paulée Pinot Noir (Willamette Valley) $35. 91 *—P.G. (8/1/2005)*

Scott Paul 2002 La Paulée Pinot Noir (Willamette Valley) $30. 88 *(11/1/2004)*

Scott Paul 2000 Pisoni Vineyard Pinot Noir (Santa Lucia Highlands) $40. 92 Editors' Choice *(10/1/2002)*

Scott Paul 1999 Pisoni Vineyard Pinot Noir (Santa Lucia Highlands) $38. 89 *(10/1/2002)*

SCREAMING EAGLE

Screaming Eagle 2003 Red Wine Cabernet Blend (Oakville) $500. 96 Cellar Selection *—S.H. (9/1/2006)*

Screaming Eagle 2002 Cabernet Sauvignon (Oakville) $300. 92 *—S.H. (11/1/2005)*

Screaming Eagle 2001 Cabernet Sauvignon (Oakville) $250. 91 *—S.H. (10/1/2004)*

SCREAMING JACK

Screaming Jack 2003 Syrah (North Coast) $12. 88 Best Buy *(9/1/2005)*

SCREW KAPPA NAPA

Screw Kappa Napa 2004 Cabernet Sauvignon (Napa Valley) $14. This is a really good Cab: balanced, clean, varietally pure and elegant. It's designed to accompany, rather than overshadow, even the best food. Shows its Napa pedigree in the wonderful interplay of all parts, especially the beautiful tannins and dryness. **87** *—S.H. (4/1/2007)*

Screw Kappa Napa 2003 Cabernet Sauvignon (Napa Valley) $14. 85 *—S.H. (12/1/2006)*

Screw Kappa Napa 2002 Cabernet Sauvignon (Napa Valley) $12. 85 *(12/1/2004)*

Screw Kappa Napa 2002 Cabernet Sauvignon (Napa Valley) $14. 89 Best Buy *—S.H. (11/15/2005)*

Screw Kappa Napa 2005 Chardonnay (Napa Valley) $14. Racy and crisp, this has an earthy quality to it, like herbs that have been scattered onto ripe tangerines, pineapples and mangoes. It's really an interesting wine, and the acidity makes it food-friendly. **86** *—S.H. (4/1/2007)*

Screw Kappa Napa 2004 Chardonnay (Napa Valley) $14. 84 *—S.H. (12/15/2005)*

Screw Kappa Napa 2003 Chardonnay (Napa Valley) $12. 85 *—S.H. (3/1/2005)*

Screw Kappa Napa 2002 Chardonnay (Napa Valley) $12. 84 *(12/1/2004)*

Screw Kappa Napa 2004 Merlot (Napa Valley) $14. SKN has been holding prices steady on its wines for years, and with inflation, they give better value for the money. This Merlot is balanced, with pleasing cherry-berry and herb flavors. It has that extra edge of fanciness that makes it a good buy. **85** *—S.H. (3/1/2007)*

Screw Kappa Napa 2003 Merlot (Napa Valley) $14. 85 *—S.H. (12/15/2005)*

Screw Kappa Napa 2002 Merlot (Napa Valley) $12. 85 *(12/1/2004)*

Screw Kappa Napa 2002 Pinot Noir (Napa Valley) $12. 87 Best Buy *(11/1/2004)*

Screw Kappa Napa 2005 Sauvignon Blanc (Napa Valley) $14. SKN hits the mark again with this crisp, clean, elegantly complex Sauvignon Blanc. It's so food friendly. With its racy acidity and wild berry, citrus and herb flavors, it's a natural for everything from chicken, (fried or roasted) to halibut, to a grapefruit salad with raspberry vinaigrette. **87** *—S.H. (4/1/2007)*

Screw Kappa Napa 2003 Sauvignon Blanc (Napa Valley) $14. 85 *—S.H. (12/15/2005)*

Screw Kappa Napa 2005 Zinfandel (Napa Valley) $14. Likeable for its extreme dryness, smooth tannins and satisfying berry and spice flavors. Fans of vanilla-sweet oak will appreciate that extra edge of richness. **84** *—S.H. (8/1/2007)*

Screw Kappa Napa 2003 Zinfandel (Napa Valley) $14. 84 *—S.H. (12/15/2005)*

SEA SMOKE

Sea Smoke 2005 Botella Pinot Noir (Santa Rita Hills) $40. The lightest of Sea Smoke's trio of Pinots, the '05 Botella starts with ravishing aromas of red fruit confections like cherry pies and raspberry tarts, with notes of gingerbread and cinnamon sugar. Tastes as good as it smells, just a deliciously gentle, pure Pinot Noir. Good now, but the grippy tannins suggest midterm ageability. **90** *—S.H. (12/15/2007)*

Sea Smoke 2002 Botella Pinot Noir (Santa Rita Hills) $25. 89 *(11/1/2004)*

Sea Smoke 2001 Botella Pinot Noir (Santa Rita Hills) $25. 87 *—S.H. (3/1/2004)*

Sea Smoke 2005 Southing Pinot Noir (Santa Rita Hills) $50. The most balanced of Sea Smoke's three new Pinots, Southing was aged in about two thirds new oak, which gives rich caramel, toasted coconut and exotic spice notes to the ripe fruit flavors. The wine explodes with cherries, raspberries, mulberries and even chocolate mint, finishing long and spicy, and leaving the impression of wholesomeness and completeness. Now showing its peak of youthful vivacity, this should develop for an additional six years. **95** *—S.H. (12/15/2007)*

Sea Smoke 2004 Southing Pinot Noir (Santa Rita Hills) $50. Sea Smoke is one of those wineries that sells out immediately and hits the secondary market at astronomical prices, with good reason. The wine is as fine as coastal California Pinot gets, with ripe cherry pie, cola and chocolate macaroon flavors that are captivating in their youthful ebulience. With fine, ripe tannins and mouthwatering cool-climate acidity, this is elegantly balanced, and will hold for a good six years. **93** *—S.H. (4/1/2007)*

Sea Smoke 2002 Southing Pinot Noir (Santa Rita Hills) $45. 87 *(11/1/2004)*

Sea Smoke 2001 Southing Pinot Noir (Santa Rita Hills) $45. 89 *—S.H. (3/1/2004)*

Sea Smoke 2005 Ten Pinot Noir (Santa Rita Hills) $70. Ten is Sea Smoke's biggest Pinot, a barrel selection chosen for sheer volume. It easily handles its 100% new oak coating. Needs decanting; even 15 minutes in the glass brought a unifying process, integrating the cedar and smoke with the explosive blackberry, cherry and chocolate fruit, and revealing the rich, dense, satiny texture. Should age well for up to eight years. **94** *—S.H. (12/15/2007)*

Sea Smoke 2002 Ten Pinot Noir (Santa Rita Hills) $65. 90 *(11/1/2004)*

SEAN THACKREY

Sean Thackrey 2000 Orion Rossi Vineyard Native Red Wine Red Blend (St. Helena) $65. 89 *(4/1/2003)*

SEASIDE

Seaside 2003 Chardonnay (California) $11. 83 *—S.H. (12/31/2005)*

Seaside 2003 Merlot (California) $11. 83 *—S.H. (12/31/2005)*

SEAVEY

Seavey 1997 Cabernet Sauvignon (Napa Valley) $64.92 *(11/1/2000)*

Seavey 2000 Cabernet Sauvignon (Napa Valley) $64. 86 *—S.H. (6/1/2004)*

SEBASTIANI

Sebastiani 2004 Barbera (Sonoma Valley) $24. 87 Cellar Selection *—S.H. (10/1/2006)*

Sebastiani 2000 Appelation Selection Barbera (Sonoma Valley) $18. 89 *—S.H. (12/1/2002)*

Sebastiani 2003 Appellation Selection Barbera (Sonoma Valley) $15. 88 *—S.H. (10/1/2005)*

Sebastiani 2001 Appellation Selection Barbera (Sonoma Valley) $15. 90 Best Buy *—S.H. (11/15/2004)*

Sebastiani 2004 Secolo Red Wine Bordeaux Blend (Sonoma County) $30. Sebastiani scores bigtime with this lush, opulent Cabernet-based blend. It's a joy to drink, offering intensely ripe cherry pie, blackberry, blueberry, orange marmalade, cola, mocha and spice flavors. It feels so smooth in the mouth, with a gorgeous balance of natural and oak-inspired tannins. This is really a special wine, but it is for early consumption. 93 Editors' Choice *—S.H. (6/1/2007)*

Sebastiani 2003 Secolo Red Wine Bordeaux Blend (Sonoma County) $30. 92 Editors' Choice *—S.H. (4/1/2006)*

Sebastiani 2004 Cabernet Sauvignon (Alexander Valley) $30. Fruit is the star in this Bordeaux blend that offers a wealth of date nut raisin bread, cola, milk chocolate, cherry-pie filling and orange marmalade flavors that finish dry and balanced. This is definitely one for early consumption. 86 *—S.H. (6/1/2007)*

USA

Sebastiani 2004 Cabernet Sauvignon (Sonoma County) $18. Another success from Sebastiani. Dry and smooth, this has rich blackberry and oak flavors grounded in earthy tannins, and finishes dry and stylishly elegant. It could be your house Cab without breaking the bank. 87 *—S.H. (10/1/2007)*

Sebastiani 2003 Cabernet Sauvignon (Sonoma County) $17. 87 *—S.H. (10/1/2006)*

Sebastiani 2003 Cabernet Sauvignon (Alexander Valley) $30. 90 *—S.H. (4/1/2006)*

Sebastiani 2002 Cabernet Sauvignon (Sonoma County) $17. 84 *—S.H. (11/1/2005)*

Sebastiani 2001 Cabernet Sauvignon (Sonoma County) $17. 87 *—S.H. (2/1/2005)*

Sebastiani 2000 Cabernet Sauvignon (Sonoma County) $17. 90 Editors' Choice *—S.H. (5/1/2004)*

Sebastiani 1998 Cabernet Sauvignon (Sonoma Valley) $24. 90 *—S.H. (11/15/2002)*

Sebastiani 1998 Cabernet Sauvignon (Sonoma County) $24. 86 *—S.H. (11/15/2002)*

Sebastiani 2002 Appellation Selection Cabernet Sauvignon (Alexander Valley) $28. 4 *—S.H. (10/1/2005)*

Sebastiani 2001 Appellation Selection Cabernet Sauvignon (Alexander Valley) $28. 91 *—S.H. (6/1/2004)*

Sebastiani 1999 Appellation Selection Cabernet Sauvignon (Alexander Valley) $24. 90 *—S.H. (11/15/2002)*

Sebastiani 2001 Cherryblock Cabernet Sauvignon (Sonoma Valley) $70. 90 *(7/1/2003)*

Sebastiani 1999 Cherryblock Cabernet Sauvignon (Sonoma Valley) $70. 91 *—S.H. (11/15/2002)*

Sebastiani 1999 Cherryblock Cabernet Sauvignon (Sonoma Valley) $70. 90 *(7/1/2003)*

Sebastiani 1996 Cherryblock Cabernet Sauvignon (Sonoma Valley) $95. 87 *(7/1/2003)*

Sebastiani 1994 Cherryblock Cabernet Sauvignon (Sonoma Valley) $150. 88 *(7/1/2003)*

Sebastiani 1992 Cherryblock Cabernet Sauvignon (Sonoma Valley) $120. 87 *(7/1/2003)*

Sebastiani 1991 Cherryblock Cabernet Sauvignon (Sonoma Valley) $160. 88 *(7/1/2003)*

Sebastiani 1987 Cherryblock Cabernet Sauvignon (Sonoma Valley) $170. 89 *(7/1/2003)*

Sebastiani 1986 Cherryblock Cabernet Sauvignon (Sonoma Valley) $170. 86 *(7/1/2003)*

Sebastiani 1985 Cherryblock Cabernet Sauvignon (Sonoma Valley) $170. 86 *(7/1/2003)*

Sebastiani 1998 Madrone Ranch Cabernet Sauvignon (Sonoma County) $46. 88 *—S.H. (11/15/2002)*

Sebastiani 1999 Sonoma County Selection Cabernet Sauvignon (Sonoma County) $17. 90 Editors' Choice *—S.H. (3/1/2003)*

Sebastiani 2001 Secolo Sonoma Red Wine Cabernet Sauvignon-Merlot (Sonoma County) $30. 92 Editors' Choice *—S.H. (10/1/2004)*

Sebastiani 2005 Chardonnay (Sonoma County) $13. This is a really nice Chardonnay. Sebastiani knows how to make a balanced varietal wine, and this clean, ripe Chardonnay completely satisfies, with fruity flavors and a rich balance of creamy oak, coastal acidity and spicy oak. 88 Best Buy *—S.H. (10/1/2007)*

Sebastiani 2001 Chardonnay (Sonoma County) $13. 86 *—S.H. (5/1/2004)*

Sebastiani 2000 Chardonnay (Sonoma County) $12. 82 *—S.H. (12/15/2002)*

Sebastiani 1997 Chardonnay (Sonoma County) $13. 87 *—M.S. (10/1/1999)*

Sebastiani 1999 Appellation Selection Chardonnay (Russian River Valley) $20. 91 *—S.H. (5/1/2002)*

Sebastiani 2004 Dutton Ranch Chardonnay (Russian River Valley) $25. 89 *—S.H. (7/1/2006)*

Sebastiani 2001 Dutton Ranch Chardonnay (Russian River Valley) $25. 85 *—S.H. (12/1/2003)*

Sebastiani 1999 Dutton Ranch Chardonnay (Russian River Valley) $35. 89 *—S.H. (5/1/2002)*

Sebastiani 1998 Dutton Ranch Chardonnay (Russian River Valley) $33. 87 *(10/1/2000)*

Sebastiani 1998 Sonoma Cask Chardonnay (Sonoma County) $13. 87 *(10/1/2000)*

Sebastiani 2004 Sonoma County Selection Chardonnay (Sonoma County) $13. 89 Best Buy *—S.H. (4/1/2006)*

Sebastiani 2002 Merlot (Sonoma County) $17. 91 Editors' Choice *—S.H. (10/1/2006)*

Sebastiani 2001 Merlot (Sonoma County) $17. 84 *—S.H. (11/1/2005)*

Sebastiani 2001 Merlot (Alexander Valley) $24. 92 Editors' Choice *—S.H. (5/1/2004)*

Sebastiani 2000 Merlot (Sonoma County) $17. 87 *—S.H. (2/1/2005)*

Sebastiani 1999 Merlot (Sonoma County) $17. 93 Editors' Choice *—S.H. (12/1/2003)*

Sebastiani 1998 Merlot (Sonoma County) $22. 88 *—S.H. (7/1/2002)*

Sebastiani 1996 Merlot (Sonoma County) $16. 90 *(3/1/2000)*

Sebastiani 2003 Appellation Selection Merlot (Alexander Valley) $24. 83 *—S.H. (12/15/2005)*

Sebastiani 1998 Madrone Ranch Merlot (Sonoma Valley) $40. 91 *—S.H. (7/1/2002)*

Sebastiani 2003 Pinot Noir (Sonoma Coast) $15. 87 *—S.H. (10/1/2005)*

Sebastiani 2002 Pinot Noir (Russian River Valley) $25. 87 *(11/1/2004)*

Sebastiani 2002 Pinot Noir (Sonoma Coast) $15. 85 *(11/1/2004)*

Sebastiani 2000 Pinot Noir (Russian River Valley) $22. 86 *(10/1/2002)*

Sebastiani 2000 Pinot Noir (Sonoma Coast) $15. 89 Best Buy *(10/1/2002)*

Sebastiani 1999 Pinot Noir (Russian River Valley) $22. 87 *(10/1/2002)*

Sebastiani 2004 Appellation Selection Pinot Noir (Russian River Valley) $28. 85 *—S.H. (11/15/2006)*

Sebastiani 2001 Appellation Selection Pinot Noir (Russian River Valley) $22. 92 Editors' Choice *—S.H. (12/1/2003)*

Sebastiani 2002 Sonoma County Selection Pinot Noir (Sonoma Coast) $15. 86 *—S.H. (6/1/2004)*

Sebastiani 2001 Sonoma County Selection Pinot Noir (Sonoma Coast) $15. 91 Best Buy *—S.H. (7/1/2003)*

Sebastiani 2002 Secolo Red Blend (Sonoma County) $30. 92 Editors' Choice *—S.H. (11/1/2005)*

Sebastiani 2001 Cohen Vineyard Sauvignon Blanc (Russian River Valley) $18. 90 *—S.H. (9/1/2003)*

Sebastiani 2000 Cohen Vineyard Sauvignon Blanc (Russian River Valley) $18. 86 *(7/1/2003)*

Sebastiani 2005 Zinfandel (Sonoma County) $15. What a great job Sebastiani has done here. It's everything you want in an affordable Sonoma Zin. Soft and rich in blackberry, cherry, cola, vanilla and Asian spice flavors, it's for immediate drinking. 86 *—S.H. (7/1/2007)*

Sebastiani 2004 Zinfandel (Sonoma County) $15. 87 *—S.H. (11/15/2006)*

Sebastiani 2003 Zinfandel (Sonoma County) $13. 86 *—S.H. (4/1/2006)*

Sebastiani 2000 Zinfandel (Sonoma County) $15. 85 *—S.H. (11/1/2002)*

Sebastiani 1999 Domenici Vineyards Zinfandel (Sonoma Valley) $25. 86 *—S.H. (9/1/2002)*

Sebastiani 1997 Domenici Vineyard Old Vines Zinfandel (Sonoma Valley) $24. 89 *—P.G. (11/15/1999)*

Sebastiani 2000 Old Vines Zinfandel (Sonoma Valley) $20. 86 *—S.H. (9/1/2004)*

Sebastiani 1999 Old Vines Zinfandel (Sonoma Valley) $20. 92 *—S.H. (9/12/2002)*

Sebastiani 1998 Old Vines Zinfandel (Sonoma County) $22. 87 *—P.G. (3/1/2001)*

Sebastiani 1997 Old Vines Domenici Vineyard Zinfandel (Sonoma Valley) $24. 89 *—P.G. (11/15/1999)*

SEBASTOPOL

Sebastopol 2001 Dutton Ranch Chardonnay (Russian River Valley) $24. 90 *—S.H. (12/15/2004)*

Sebastopol 1999 Dutton Ranch Chardonnay (Green Valley) $24. 89 *—S.H. (5/1/2002)*

Sebastopol 1998 Dutton Ranch Chardonnay (Russian River Valley) $22. 91 *—S.H. (11/1/1999)*

Sebastopol 2000 Dutton Ranch Dutton Palms Vineyard Chardonnay (Green Valley) $46. 87 *—S.H. (5/1/2003)*

Sebastopol 2001 Dutton Ranch Morelli Lane Vineyard Chardonnay (Russian River Valley) $40. 92 *—S.H. (12/15/2004)*

Sebastopol 2002 Dutton Estate Jewel Block Vineyard Pinot Noir (Russian River Valley) $48. 89 *(11/1/2004)*

Sebastopol 2002 Dutton Estate Thomas Road Vineyard Pinot Noir (Russian River Valley) $40. 87 *(11/1/2004)*

Sebastopol 2001 Dutton Ranch Pinot Noir (Russian River Valley) $20. 86 *—S.H. (2/1/2005)*

Sebastopol 1999 Dutton Ranch Pinot Noir (Green Valley) $30. 93 *—S.H. (7/1/2002)*

Sebastopol 2000 Dutton Ranch Jewell Block Pinot Noir (Russian River Valley) $52. 85 *(10/1/2002)*

Sebastopol 2001 Dutton Ranch Morelli Lane Vineyard Pinot Noir (Russian River Valley) $40. 91 *—S.H. (12/15/2004)*

Sebastopol 2000 Dutton Ranch Morelli Lane Vineyard Pinot Noir (Russian River Valley) $46. 87 *(10/1/2002)*

Sebastopol 2000 Dutton Ranch Morelli Lane Vineyard Pinot Noir (Green Valley) $46. 90 *—S.H. (8/1/2003)*

Sebastopol 2002 Syrah (Russian River Valley) $14. 86 *—S.H. (10/1/2004)*

Sebastopol 1999 Dutton Estate Gail Ann's Vineyard Syrah (Russian River Valley) $24. 84 *(11/1/2001)*

Sebastopol 2002 Dutton Ranch Syrah (Russian River Valley) $30. 84 *(9/1/2005)*

Sebastopol 2000 Dutton Ranch Gail Ann's Vineyard Syrah (Russian River Valley) $32. 94 Editors' Choice *—S.H. (6/24/2003)*

Sebastopol 2001 Gail Ann's Vineyard Syrah (Russian River Valley) $32. 92 *—S.H. (10/1/2004)*

Sebastopol 2004 Three Blocks Syrah (Sonoma County) $25. 87 *—S.H. (11/1/2006)*

SECRET HOUSE

Secret House 1998 Pinot Noir (Willamette Valley) $22. 84 *—M.S. (12/1/2000)*

Secret House 1998 Doerner Vineyard Pinot Noir (Umpqua Valley) $30. 86 *—M.M. (12/1/2000)*

SEGHESIO

Seghesio 2000 Arneis (Russian River Valley) $15. 84 *—S.H. (11/15/2001)*

Seghesio 2001 Barbera (Sonoma County) $25. 89 *—S.H. (12/1/2003)*

Seghesio 2001 San Lorenzo Petite Sirah (Alexander Valley) $30. 89 *(3/1/2004)*

Seghesio 2000 Pinot Grigio (Russian River Valley) $14. 88 *—S.H. (11/15/2001)*

Seghesio 1999 Pinot Noir (Russian River Valley) $25. 88 *—S.H. (12/15/2001)*

Seghesio 2001 Omaggio Red Blend (Sonoma County) $45. 91 *—S.H. (11/15/2003)*

Seghesio 2001 Sangiovese (Alexander Valley) $20. 90 *—S.H. (12/1/2003)*

Seghesio 1998 Sangiovese (Sonoma County) $20. 87 *—S.H. (12/15/1999)*

Seghesio 1999 Chianti Station Sangiovese (Alexander Valley) $32. 89 *—S.H. (4/1/2004)*

Seghesio 2001 Rattlesnake Hill Venom Sangiovese (Alexander Valley) $45. 93 Editors' Choice *—S.H. (12/1/2003)*

Seghesio 2001 Zinfandel (Sonoma County) $19. 88 *(11/1/2003)*

Seghesio 2000 Zinfandel (Sonoma County) $19. 85 *—S.H. (11/1/2002)*

Seghesio 1998 Zinfandel (Sonoma County) $15. 88 *—S.H. (2/1/2000)*

Seghesio 2001 Cortina Zinfandel (Dry Creek Valley) $30. 86 *(11/1/2003)*

Seghesio 2000 Cortina Zinfandel (Dry Creek Valley) $30. 87 *—S.H. (11/1/2002)*

Seghesio 1998 Cortina Zinfandel (Dry Creek Valley) $26. 86 *—P.G. (3/1/2001)*

Seghesio 2001 Home Ranch Zinfandel (Alexander Valley) $30. 87 *(11/1/2003)*

Seghesio 2000 Home Ranch Zinfandel (Alexander Valley) $30. 86 *—S.H. (11/1/2002)*

Seghesio 1998 Home Ranch Zinfandel (Sonoma County) $26. 89 *—P.G. (3/1/2001)*

Seghesio 2001 Old Vine Zinfandel (Sonoma County) $28. 91 *(11/1/2003)*

Seghesio 1998 Old Vine Zinfandel (Sonoma County) $18. 87 *—P.G. (3/1/2001)*

Seghesio 1997 Old Vine Zinfandel (Sonoma County) $25. 89 *—S.H. (2/1/2000)*

Seghesio 1998 San Lorenzo Zinfandel (Sonoma County) $28. 91 *—P.G. (3/1/2001)*

SEIA

Seia 2005 Alder Creek Vineyard Syrah (Horse Heaven Hills) $30. This is very soft upon entry, with remnants of penetrating spicy and herbal flavors that might have punched up the intensity if they hadn't been somehow smoothed over. It's difficult to assess, because many of the right pieces are all here, but somehow they have not jelled. The wine tastes acidic and sharp, with pineapple and citrus dominating, and a chalky, tannic finish. Perhaps it's just a matter of time? 85 *—P.G. (12/31/2007)*

Seia 2005 Clifton Hill Vineyard Syrah (Wahluke Slope) $30. A fine follow-up to Seia's inaugural 2004 Clifton Hill, this again delivers ripe, concentrated flavors of plum and berry, lifted with citrus and finishing with a hint of mint. Despite the high (15.3%) alcohol, it is clean and bracing, with natural acids and very little heat in the finish. As young as it is, it hits a bit of a dead spot in the back, but it has the stuffing (and the pedigree) that would suggest that with a few years of cellaring it will open out and show more of the herb and smoked meat character that is lurking just below the surface. 90 Cellar Selection *—P.G. (12/31/2007)*

Seia 2004 Clifton Hill Vineyard Syrah (Wahluke Slope) $23. 92 Editors' Choice *—P.G. (10/1/2006)*

SELBY

Selby 2001 Cabernet Franc (Alexander Valley) $28. 85 *—S.H. (12/15/2005)*

Selby 1999 Dave Selby Reserve Chardonnay (Sonoma County) $40. 93 *—J.M. (12/1/2001)*

Selby 1998 David Selby Reserve Chardonnay (Sonoma County) $38. 88 *(7/1/2001)*

Selby 2002 Merlot (Sonoma County) $24. 87 *—S.H. (12/15/2005)*

Selby 1999 Merlot (Sonoma County) $24. 91 Editors' Choice *—J.M. (12/1/2001)*

Selby 1999 Syrah (Sonoma County) $24. 84 *(11/1/2001)*

SELENE

Selene 2004 Cabernet Sauvignon (Napa Valley) $70. Napa Cab doesn't get any richer than this. It really sets the New World standard, with almost dessert levels of blackberries, cassis, plums, cherries, chocolate, elaborate new oak, the works. Also in the modern style are the tannins, as ripe, soft and sweet as butter. But it's probably not an ager, and will be problematic at food pairing. From Mia Klein, it's more of a tasting wine. 90 *—S.H. (10/1/2007)*

Selene 2006 Hyde Vineyards Sauvignon Blanc (Carneros) $27. A very fashionable Sauvignon Blanc. It takes the basic architecture of crisp acidity and dry, spicy citrus and fig fruit and boosts it to levels of true elegance and sophistication. Leaves a long, impressive finish that makes you want another sip. **92** —*S.H. (11/1/2007)*

Selene 2005 Hyde Vineyards Sauvignon Blanc (Carneros) $26. 92 Editors' Choice —*S.H. (10/1/2006)*

Selene 2003 Hyde Vineyards Sauvignon Blanc (Carneros) $22. 92 Editors' Choice *(7/1/2005)*

Selene 2000 Hyde Vineyards Sauvignon Blanc (Carneros) $29. 86 *(8/1/2002)*

SENSORIUM

Sensorium 2004 Cabernet Sauvignon (Napa Valley) $40. A pretty nice young Cab, though the weather was too hot and the wine is deficient in acidity. But the flavors of blackberries, cherries, currants and new oak are delicious, and the tannins are smooth and silky. **89** —*S.H. (12/1/2007)*

Sensorium 2005 MdR Vineyard Syrah (Paso Robles) $30. I went back and forth on this wine, hating it, then liking it. It's too soft, but dry. It's candied, but the cherry-berry flavors have a nice edge of spicy cola. The more I sipped it, the better it got. The alcohol is a modest 14.1%. **86** —*S.H. (12/1/2007)*

Sensorium 2006 MdR Vineyard Viognier (Paso Robles) $25. Soft, semi-sweet and medicinal, with candied fruit flavors. **80** —*S.H. (12/1/2007)*

SEQUEL

Sequel 2004 Syrah (Columbia Valley (WA)) $55. Made in a consistent style, this already delivers lush berry, plum, cherry and currant fruit, wrapped in generous new oak (90% of the wine was aged in small French oak barrels). Winemaker John Duval keeps the alcohol at a sensible 14.3%, and adds a small amount of Cabernet Sauvignon to stiffen the spine. **92** —*P.G. (5/1/2007)*

Sequel 2003 Syrah (Columbia Valley (WA)) $55. 88 —*P.G. (4/1/2006)*

SEQUOIA GROVE

Sequoia Grove 2002 Semper V Meritage Bordeaux Blend (Napa Valley) $100. Tannins and acids currently dominate, giving this dry, young wine a bit of a lockdown quality. The winemaker, Michael Trujillo, aims at a more structured style, and he has achieved it here. There's a deep heart of cherries and blackberries, with sweeter oaky notes. This is a wine to lay down for six years or longer. **91** —*S.H. (8/1/2007)*

Sequoia Grove 2004 Cabernet Sauvignon (Napa Valley) $40. Fruity and spicy, with good varietal character to the blackberry, cassis, cocoa and spicy plum flavors, this Cab also has a firm edge of tannins. **86** —*S.H. (12/31/2007)*

Sequoia Grove 2003 Cabernet Sauvignon (Napa Valley) $32. Not quite in the same league as the winery's '03 Morisoli Cab, but at less than half the price, a very good Cabernet. Polished and dry, it's ripe in the modern style, and well-structured in acids and tannins. With true varietal flavors of blackberry jam and cherries, sweetened with smoky cedar, it's beautiful now. **91** —*S.H. (8/1/2007)*

Sequoia Grove 2002 Cabernet Sauvignon (Napa Valley) $32. 91 —*S.H. (12/31/2005)*

Sequoia Grove 1999 Cabernet Sauvignon (Napa Valley) $29. 86 —*S.H. (11/15/2002)*

Sequoia Grove 2003 Morisoli Vineyard Cabernet Sauvignon (Rutherford) $85. 93 —*S.H. (12/31/2006)*

Sequoia Grove 2003 Reserve Cabernet Sauvignon (Napa Valley) $60. Built for the cellar, this Cab is impressively deep in ripe currant, cherry, cocoa, milk chocolate and spice flavors. It's quite tannic, with a brittle astringency, and sweet in oak and fruit on the finish. Best after 2008, and for some years after. **89** —*S.H. (12/31/2007)*

Sequoia Grove 2002 Reserve Cabernet Sauvignon (Rutherford) $57. 93 Cellar Selection —*S.H. (12/31/2005)*

Sequoia Grove 2001 Reserve Cabernet Sauvignon (Rutherford) $55. 93 Editors' Choice *(12/1/2005)*

Sequoia Grove 2000 Reserve Cabernet Sauvignon (Rutherford) $55. 89 —*S.H. (11/15/2003)*

Sequoia Grove 1999 Reserve Cabernet Sauvignon (Rutherford) $55. 94 Editors' Choice —*S.H. (12/31/2002)*

Sequoia Grove 1997 Reserve Cabernet Sauvignon (Napa Valley) $42. 94 *(11/1/2000)*

Sequoia Grove 2004 Rutherford Bench Reserve Cabernet Sauvignon (Rutherford) $55. The term "Rutherford Bench" is not a legal one and refers to vineyards on the west side of Highway 29. The wine contains all five Bordeaux varieties, and is very ripe and oaky, with a fat, fleshy mouthfeel that combines power with elegance. It's bursting with delicious blackberry, plum, cocoa and cedar flavors that should develop for a decade. **93 Editors' Choice** —*S.H. (12/15/2007)*

Sequoia Grove 2005 Chardonnay (Carneros) $18. This is certainly a better Chard than the winery's '04. It's richer and more succulent, overall more rewarding in varietal fruit, including peaches and cream, pineapples, guavas and papayas, with a cinnamon spice finish. The wine also is characterized by crisp, crunchy acidity that makes it racy. **90** —*S.H. (8/1/2007)*

Sequoia Grove 2003 Chardonnay (Carneros) $20. 87 —*S.H. (12/31/2005)*

Sequoia Grove 1997 Chardonnay (Carneros) $16. 84 *(6/1/2000)*

Sequoia Grove 2003 Merlot (Atlas Peak) $48. 90 —*S.H. (7/1/2006)*

Sequoia Grove 2003 Syrah (Atlas Peak) $32. 88 —*S.H. (7/1/2006)*

SEVEN DEADLY ZINS

Seven Deadly Zins 2005 Zinfandel (Lodi) $17. This wine took a bad stumble last year and hasn't recovered. The '05, despite the cooler vintage, has a hot, cooked taste, yet somehow manages to be vegetal at the same time. **81** —*S.H. (4/1/2007)*

Seven Deadly Zins 2001 Zinfandel (Lodi) $16. 89 —*J.M. (11/1/2003)*

Seven Deadly Zins 2004 Old Vine Zinfandel (Lodi) $17. 82 —*S.H. (10/1/2006)*

SEVEN HILLS

Seven Hills 2004 Ciel du Cheval Bordeaux Blend (Red Mountain) $30. A classic Bordeaux blend (about 30% each Cab Sauvignon, Cab Franc and Merlot, the rest Petite Verdot) This wine is still locked up tight upon release. There is metallic minerality underpinning the tart, austere fruit, but there are also surprising high notes of brandied cherries, and a sense of depth missing in more ordinary wines. This is definitely a wine to cellar for up to a decade. As always, this is sensitive, detailed winemaking. **90** —*P.G. (8/1/2007)*

Seven Hills 2003 Pentad Bordeaux Blend (Walla Walla (WA)) $50. 88 —*P.G. (12/31/2006)*

Seven Hills 2004 Cabernet Sauvignon (Walla Walla (WA)) $25. A mix of fruit that survived the big freeze, from Dwelley, Morrison Lane and Minnick vineyards. It's tight, tart and tannic, and showing some pickle barrel notes from time in new American oak. Herbal and compact, this is a wine that should probably be given another year or so in the bottle to smooth itself out. **87** —*P.G. (8/1/2007)*

Seven Hills 2002 Cabernet Sauvignon (Walla Walla (WA)) $30. 89 —*P.G. (12/15/2005)*

Seven Hills 2002 Cabernet Sauvignon (Columbia Valley (WA)) $30. 88 —*P.G. (12/15/2005)*

Seven Hills 1999 Cabernet Sauvignon (Columbia Valley (WA)) $22. 88 —*P.G. (6/1/2002)*

Seven Hills 1998 Cabernet Sauvignon (Columbia Valley (WA)) $20. 90 Editors' Choice —*P.G. (6/1/2001)*

Seven Hills 2003 Klipsun Vineyard Cabernet Sauvignon (Red Mountain) $30. In 2003 the vineyard was going through some changes, and the vintage, the shift in focus and the winemaker's predilection for early picking seemed to conspire to produce a rather thin, austere wine. It's locked up tight, a bit herbal and lean, not yet revealing itself even with aeration. It's one of those mystery wines that you keep coming back to, waiting for the light to blink on. **88** —*P.G. (8/1/2007)*

Seven Hills 1999 Klipsun Vineyard Cabernet Sauvignon (Columbia Valley (WA)) $30. 90 —*P.G. (6/1/2002)*

Seven Hills 1998 Klipsun Vineyard Cabernet Sauvignon (Columbia Valley (WA)) $25. 92 Editors' Choice —*P.G. (6/1/2001)*

Seven Hills 1997 Klipsun Vineyard Cabernet Sauvignon (Columbia Valley (WA)) $25. 90 —*P.G. (11/15/2000)*

Seven Hills 2003 Seven Hills Vineyard Cabernet Sauvignon (Walla Walla (WA)) $30. 88 —*P.G. (12/31/2006)*

Seven Hills 1999 Seven Hills Vineyard Cabernet Sauvignon (Walla Walla (WA)) $30. 91 Editors' Choice —*P.G. (6/1/2002)*

Seven Hills 1998 Seven Hills Vineyard Cabernet Sauvignon (Walla Walla (WA)) $25. 91 —*P.G. (6/1/2001)*

Seven Hills 1997 Seven Hills Vineyard Cabernet Sauvignon (Walla Walla (WA)) $25. 89 —*P.G. (11/15/2000)*

Seven Hills 1997 Seven Hills Vineyard Reserve Cabernet Sauvignon (Walla Walla (WA)) $32. 91 —*P.G. (11/15/2000)*

Seven Hills 1998 Walla Walla Valley Reserve Cabernet Sauvignon (Walla Walla (WA)) $32. 93 —*P.G. (6/1/2001)*

Seven Hills 2004 Merlot (Columbia Valley (WA)) $28. The 2004, like so many Walla Walla wines, was sourced from a different mix of vineyards. In this case the grapes came from Cold Creek, Canoe Ridge, DuBrul and Artz – a very fine group indeed. There's no slip in quality here, just a bit of added richness and darker fruits than in the previous vintage. Blackberry purée laced with coffee liqueur dominates this open, accessible, and thoroughly enjoyable wine. Nicely balanced and showing its youthful freshness in a clean and softly seductive style. 89 —*P.G. (8/1/2007)*

Seven Hills 2003 Merlot (Columbia Valley (WA)) $28. 88 —*P.G. (6/1/2006)*

Seven Hills 1999 Merlot (Columbia Valley (WA)) $35. 88 —*P.G. (6/1/2002)*

Seven Hills 1999 Kilpsun Vineyard Merlot (Columbia Valley (WA)) $28. 91 Cellar Selection —*P.G. (6/1/2002)*

Seven Hills 2001 Klipsun Vineyard Merlot (Columbia Valley (WA)) $28. 89 —*P.G. (7/1/2004)*

Seven Hills 1999 Reserve Merlot (Columbia Valley (WA)) $40. 89 —*P.G. (6/1/2002)*

Seven Hills 2003 Seven Hills Vineyard Merlot (Walla Walla (WA)) $30. Tart, tight, compact and almost dramatically austere when first opened, this estate-grown Merlot unwraps with pretty scents of blueberry pie, followed by clean flavors of blackberry and cassis. The compactness of the wine suggests that it will continue to evolve and merit a higher score in another year or so. For now, you will find intriguing suggestions of gravel and graphite, and the mix of rocks and blue fruits promises more interesting development down the road. Meanwhile, air it out. 88 —*P.G. (3/1/2007)*

Seven Hills 2002 Seven Hills Vineyard Merlot (Walla Walla (WA)) $30. 89 —*P.G. (12/15/2005)*

Seven Hills 2000 Seven Hills Vineyard Merlot (Walla Walla (WA)) $28. 89 —*P.G. (9/1/2002)*

Seven Hills 1999 Seven Hills Vineyard Merlot (Walla Walla (WA)) $28. 88 —*P.G. (6/1/2002)*

Seven Hills 1998 Seven Hills Vineyard Merlot (Columbia Valley (WA)) $25. 89 —*P.G. (6/1/2001)*

Seven Hills 1997 Seven Hills Vineyard Merlot (Walla Walla (WA)) $25. 89 —*P.G. (11/15/2000)*

Seven Hills 1998 Seven Hills Vineyard Reserve Merlot (Walla Walla (WA)) $32. 91 —*P.G. (6/1/2001)*

Seven Hills 1998 Helmick Hill Vineyard Pinot Blanc (Willamette Valley) $10. 86 —*P.G. (11/15/2000)*

Seven Hills 2004 Pinot Gris (Oregon) $15. 90 Best Buy —*P.G. (2/1/2006)*

Seven Hills 1999 Pinot Gris (Willamette Valley) $12. 87 —*P.G. (11/15/2000)*

Seven Hills 1998 Coleman Vineyard Pinot Gris (Willamette Valley) $12. 87 Best Buy *(8/1/1999)*

Seven Hills 2003 Ciel du Cheval Red Blend (Red Mountain) $30. 91 —*P.G. (12/15/2005)*

Seven Hills 2002 Pentad Red Wine Red Blend (Walla Walla (WA)) $50. 89 —*P.G. (6/1/2006)*

Seven Hills 2001 Planing Mill Red Table Wine Red Blend (Columbia Valley (WA)) $16. 89 Best Buy —*P.G. (7/1/2004)*

Seven Hills 2005 Riesling (Columbia Valley (WA)) $12. Exceptionally well-priced, this is the last to come from a vineyard block planted in the Yakima Valley in 1979. It captures the fullness and ripe fruit of such old-style wines, with succulent tangerine and white peach flavors. Big, fruity and forward. 88 Best Buy —*P.G. (8/1/2007)*

Seven Hills 2001 Riesling (Columbia Valley (WA)) $10. 88 —*P.G. (9/1/2002)*

Seven Hills 1999 White Riesling (Columbia Valley (WA)) $8. 88 Best Buy —*P.G. (11/15/2000)*

Seven Hills 2004 Syrah (Walla Walla (WA)) $26. This is a splendid Walla Walla Syrah, co-fermented with Viognier from the Dwelley vineyard. Penetrating and complex, its aromas border on the exotic, and there is so much going in the nose that you almost forget to taste it! It captures the unique, lifted, citrus and spice flavors of great Washington Syrah, adding in tangy cinnamon and spiced plum through a long, silky finish. 92 Editors' Choice —*P.G. (8/1/2007)*

Seven Hills 2003 Syrah (Walla Walla (WA)) $25. 91 —*P.G. (6/1/2006)*

Seven Hills 2002 Syrah (Walla Walla (WA)) $25. 89 *(9/1/2005)*

Seven Hills 1999 Syrah (Walla Walla (WA)) $32. 87 *(11/1/2001)*

Seven Hills 1999 Syrah (Columbia Valley (WA)) $20. 87 *(10/1/2001)*

Seven Hills 1998 Syrah (Walla Walla (WA)) $30. 84 —*P.G. (9/1/2000)*

Seven Hills 2003 Tempranillo (Walla Walla (WA)) $28. 89 —*P.G. (6/1/2006)*

Seven Hills 2006 Viognier (Columbia Valley (WA)) $18. A pleasing rush of peaches, apricots, orange peel and lime greets the palate, as you first taste this young Viognier from the Milbrandt Vineyards in Washington's hot climate Wahluke Slope AVA. This wine has been deftly handled, accenting the lushness of the fruit, minimizing the phenolics, and giving weight and nuance to the midpalate. There's a hint of honey and toast as well, and the 14.2% alcohol feels just right. 90 —*P.G. (12/1/2007)*

SEVEN LIONS WINERY

Seven Lions Winery 2000 Blakeman Vineyard Chardonnay (Anderson Valley) $NA. 88 —*S.H. (2/1/2003)*

Seven Lions Winery 2000 Buena Tierra Vineyards Chardonnay (Russian River Valley) $55. 91 —*J.M. (12/15/2002)*

Seven Lions Winery 2000 Wes Cameron Vineyard 60 Year Old Wente Clone Chardonnay (Russian River Valley) $35. 90 —*J.M. (12/15/2002)*

Seven Lions Winery 2000 Pinot Noir (Russian River Valley) $45. 86 *(10/1/2002)*

Seven Lions Winery 1999 Butch & David's Knoll Pinot Noir (Russian River Valley) $65. 84 *(10/1/2002)*

Seven Lions Winery 2000 Hansen Vineyards Pinot Noir (Russian River Valley) $55. 88 *(10/1/2002)*

Seven Lions Winery 1999 Joe and Emily's Vineyard Zinfandel (Russian River Valley) $65. 88 —*D.T. (3/1/2002)*

Seven Lions Winery 1999 Martinelli & Duckhorn Vineyard Zinfandel (Russian River Valley) $60. 84 —*D.T. (3/1/2002)*

Seven Lions Winery 2000 Poor Man's Flat Vineyards 100 Year Old Vines Zinfandel (Russian River Valley) $30. 86 —*S.H. (9/1/2002)*

Seven Lions Winery 2000 Three Amigos Vineyards Zinfandel (Sonoma County) $38. 96 —*S.H. (9/1/2002)*

SEVEN PEAKS

Seven Peaks 2002 Cabernet Sauvignon (Central Coast) $15. 87 —*S.H. (11/15/2004)*

Seven Peaks 2003 Chardonnay (Arroyo Seco) $16. 87 —*S.H. (12/1/2004)*

Seven Peaks 2000 Chardonnay (Central Coast) $12. 82 —*S.H. (6/1/2003)*

Seven Peaks 1997 Reserve Chardonnay (Edna Valley) $21. 85 *(6/1/2000)*

Seven Peaks 2002 Merlot (Paso Robles) $15. 85 —*S.H. (12/15/2004)*

Seven Peaks 2003 Pinot Noir (Monterey) $16. 85 —*S.H. (12/1/2004)*

Seven Peaks 2002 Shiraz (Paso Robles) $17. 84 —*S.H. (12/1/2004)*

Seven Peaks 1999 Shiraz (Paso Robles) $20. 87 *(10/1/2001)*

SEVENTH MOON

Seventh Moon 2001 Merlot (California) $10. 83 —*S.H. (8/1/2004)*

Seventh Moon 2001 Zinfandel (California) $9. 83 *(11/1/2003)*

SEVENTY-SEVEN DAYS

Seventy-Seven Days 2005 Valois Vineyard Riesling (Seneca Lake) $30. Aromas of citrus and spice fall flat on the palate with this slightly watery, one-dimensional offering from Seneca Lake. There's some heft at midpalate but the character is waterlogged, and it carries on to a finish that lingers off with a wan wave. 83 —*S.K. (2/1/2007)*

SEXTANT

Sextant 2004 Night Watch Red Blend (Paso Robles) $42. 82 —*S.H. (11/15/2006)*

Sextant 2005 Beachcomber Rhône White Blend (Paso Robles) $19. 83 —*S.H. (11/15/2006)*

Sextant 2005 Holystone Zinfandel (Paso Robles) $27. If you don't like high alcohol you might want to stay away from this one, but you'd be missing a classic expression of Paso Robles Zinfandel. It's soft, rich and complex in berry pie, coffee, root beer, tobacco, spice and chocolate flavors; very delicious. I think of drinking this with something off the barbecue, under a warm, starry summer night. 88 —*S.H. (6/1/2007)*

Sextant 2005 Wheelhouse Zinfandel (Paso Robles) $19. Distinctly Zin, with its briary, brambly aromas and flavors of wild berries, freshly picked off thorn bushes in the heat of the summer sun. The freshness perseveres with vibrant cherry, blackberry, loganberry and pepper flavors that finish smooth and dry. Perfect with roasts, barbecue, rich hard cheeses. 89 —*S.H. (6/1/2007)*

SHADOW CANYON

Shadow Canyon 2001 Shadow Canyon Vineyard Cabernet Sauvignon (Yorkville Highlands) $30. 87 —*S.H. (2/4/2003)*

Shadow Canyon 2004 Larner Vineyard Grenache (Santa Ynez Valley) $40. This Grenache smells like Port and tastes hot, with baked blackberry and currant flavors, although it's dry. Finishes with some astringent tannins. 82 —*S.H. (11/1/2007)*

Shadow Canyon 2003 Larner Vineyard Grenache (Santa Ynez Valley) $30. 89 —*S.H. (4/1/2005)*

Shadow Canyon 2002 Paeonia Bien Nacido Vineyard Late Harvest Pinot Blanc (Santa Maria Valley) $45. 94 —*S.H. (12/1/2004)*

Shadow Canyon 2004 Amila Red Wine Rhône Red Blend (Central Coast) $40. A Châteauneuf-style blend of Syrah, Grenache and Viognier, this wine has delicious flavors, but is too soft and hot. Those flavors are of ripe blackberries, cherries and black raspberries, with edges of milk chocolate and licorice. 85 —*S.H. (11/1/2007)*

Shadow Canyon 2005 Rosé Blend (Central Coast) $18. This is one of the more sophisticated rosés I've tasted lately. It has an elegant mouthfeel, dry and silky, and the flavors are complex, although it tamps the fruit down in favor of subtlety. Suggests cherry pulp, sweet vanilla, cinnamon spice and Kir Royale, which is creme de cassis mixed with Champagne or Chardonnay. 90 —*S.H. (7/1/2007)*

Shadow Canyon 2003 Syrah (Santa Barbara County) $25. 89 —*S.H. (4/1/2005)*

Shadow Canyon 2004 Shadow Canyon Vineyard Syrah (Santa Ynez Valley) $40. Soft and a little hot, although the official alcohol is a relatively modest 14.8%. The blackberry, currant, grilled meat and peppery spice flavors are good, but the wine could use extra layers. This is a wine that was a victim of a hard vintage. Drink now. 86 —*S.H. (11/1/2007)*

Shadow Canyon 2003 Shadow Canyon Vineyard Syrah (York Mountain) $38. 90 —*S.H. (12/1/2004)*

Shadow Canyon 2002 Shadow Canyon Vineyard Syrah (York Mountain) $40. 87 —*S.H. (12/31/2004)*

Shadow Canyon 2001 Shadow Canyon Vineyard Syrah (Yorkville Highlands) $40. 92 —*S.H. (3/1/2004)*

Shadow Canyon 2005 Larner Vineyard Viognier (Santa Ynez Valley) $18. Too sweet for me, with overtly sugary flavors. The sweetness may also be a function of high alcohol. The result is almost a dessert wine, with flavors of peach pie filling and pineapple honey. 84 —*S.H. (11/1/2007)*

Shadow Canyon 2002 Larner Vineyard Viognier (Santa Ynez Valley) $22. 85 —*S.H. (12/31/2003)*

USA

SHADOW HILL

Shadow Hill 1998 Cabernet Sauvignon (Washington) $11. 85 —*P.G. (6/1/2001)*

Shadow Hill 1998 Merlot (Columbia Valley (WA)) $11. 82 —*P.G. (6/1/2001)*

SHAFER

Shafer 2003 Cabernet Sauvignon (Napa Valley) $55. 95 Editors' Choice —*S.H. (9/1/2006)*

Shafer 2000 Cabernet Sauvignon (Napa Valley) $48. 93 —*S.H. (8/1/2003)*

Shafer 1999 Cabernet Sauvignon (Napa Valley) $48. 93 —*S.H. (6/1/2002)*

Shafer 1997 Cabernet Sauvignon (Napa Valley) $45. 89 *(11/1/2000)*

Shafer 2002 Hillside Select Cabernet Sauvignon (Stags Leap District) $190. 97 Cellar Selection —*S.H. (9/1/2006)*

Shafer 2001 Hillside Select Cabernet Sauvignon (Stags Leap District) $175. 98 Cellar Selection —*S.H. (12/31/2005)*

Shafer 2000 Hillside Select Cabernet Sauvignon (Stags Leap District) $150. 89 —*S.H. (12/31/2004)*

Shafer 1998 Hillside Select Cabernet Sauvignon (Stags Leap District) $150. 95 Cellar Selection —*S.H. (12/31/2002)*

Shafer 1997 Hillside Select Cabernet Sauvignon (Stags Leap District) $150. 96 —*S.H. (12/31/2001)*

Shafer 1995 Hillside Select Cabernet Sauvignon (Stags Leap District) $110. 94 —*L.W. (12/31/1999)*

Shafer 2001 Napa Valley Cabernet Sauvignon (Napa Valley) $52. 94 —*S.H. (10/1/2004)*

Shafer 2004 One Point Five Cabernet Sauvignon (Stags Leap District) $65. As of this vintage, Shafer has done away with their Napa Valley Cabernet bottling and replaced it with this proprietarily named 100% Cab. It's a junior version of Hillside Select, from different vineyards and not as oaky. But it's nearly as massive in black currants, cherries and carob bean, a dry wine that never loses elegance. Needs a year or so to become less tight and more expressive. 93 —*S.H. (7/1/2007)*

Shafer 2005 Red Shoulder Ranch Chardonnay (Carneros) $45. Shafer's '05 is drier, crisper and more minerally than its predecessors from warmer vintages. You might even call it leaner. But it still shows the elegant balance that always characterizes the wine, with brilliant acidity. 89 —*S.H. (12/1/2007)*

Shafer 2004 Red Shoulder Ranch Chardonnay (Carneros) $43. 94 Editors' Choice —*S.H. (12/1/2006)*

Shafer 2003 Red Shoulder Ranch Chardonnay (Carneros) $40. 93 —*S.H. (10/1/2005)*

Shafer 2002 Red Shoulder Ranch Chardonnay (Carneros) $38. 92 —*S.H. (9/1/2004)*

Shafer 2001 Red Shoulder Ranch Chardonnay (Carneros) $37. 91 —*S.H. (6/1/2003)*

Shafer 2000 Red Shoulder Ranch Chardonnay (Carneros) $37. 93 Editors' Choice —*S.H. (12/15/2002)*

Shafer 1999 Red Shoulder Ranch Chardonnay (Carneros) $37. 89 *(7/1/2001)*

Shafer 1998 Red Shoulder Ranch Chardonnay (Carneros) $35. 91 *(10/1/2000)*

Shafer 1997 Red Shoulder Ranch Chardonnay (Carneros) $35. 93 —*L.W. (6/1/1999)*

Shafer 2004 Merlot (Napa Valley) $45. Others have called this wine sexy and seductive. That's because it's as soft and gooey as a melted chocolate truffle. Throw in some black cherry fruit and smoky new oak, and there you have it. It's rich and ripe and mellow, and while it's very good, the quibble is that it's not particularly complex, and will be difficult to match with food. 87 —*S.H. (2/1/2007)*

Shafer 2003 Merlot (Napa Valley) $44. 92 Editors' Choice —*S.H. (12/31/2005)*

Shafer 2002 Merlot (Napa Valley) $41. 89 —*S.H. (12/31/2004)*

Shafer 2001 Merlot (Napa Valley) $39. 93 —*S.H. (2/1/2004)*

Shafer 2000 Merlot (Napa Valley) $39. 93 —*S.H. (12/31/2002)*

Shafer 1999 Merlot (Napa Valley) $38. 91 —*S.H. (12/31/2001)*

Shafer 1998 Merlot (Napa Valley) $36. 90 —*J.C. (6/1/2001)*

Shafer 1997 Merlot (Napa Valley) $35. 91 —*L.W. (12/31/1999)*

Shafer 2003 Last Chance Firebreak Red Blend (Napa Valley) $42. 93 Editors' Choice —*S.H. (9/1/2006)*

Shafer 2003 Relentless Red Blend (Napa Valley) $63. For some reason theis Syrah and Petite Sirah blend isn't quite as balanced as in previous vintages, but it's still a really good and interesting wine. There's a sharp jamminess here to the cherry, blackberry and fudgy mocha that makes the wine a little rustic. This is a very direct wine and calls for direct food, like a grilled sirloin steak. 89 —*S.H. (2/1/2007)*

Shafer 2000 Relentless Red Blend (Napa Valley) $55. 94 Editors' Choice —*S.H. (12/31/2003)*

Shafer 2002 Firebreak Sangiovese (Napa Valley) $36. 91 —*S.H. (10/1/2005)*

Shafer 2001 Firebreak Sangiovese (Napa Valley) $35. 93 —*S.H. (9/1/2004)*

Shafer 2000 Firebreak Sangiovese (Napa Valley) $33. 93 Editors' Choice —*S.H. (9/1/2003)*

Shafer 1999 Firebreak Sangiovese (Napa Valley) $32. 93 Cellar Selection —*S.H. (12/1/2002)*

Shafer 1996 Firebreak Sangiovese (Stags Leap District) $28. 92 —*L.W. (6/1/1999)*

Shafer 2002 Relentless Syrah (Napa Valley) $62. 91 Cellar Selection *(9/1/2005)*

Shafer 2001 Relentless Syrah (Napa Valley) $60. 93 —*S.H. (12/31/2004)*

Shafer 1999 Relentless Syrah (Napa Valley) $46. 94 Cellar Selection —*J.M. (5/1/2002)*

SHALE RIDGE VINEYARD

Shale Ridge Vineyard 2001 Estate Grown & Bottled Cabernet Sauvignon (Monterey County) $8. 85 Best Buy —*S.H. (11/15/2003)*

Shale Ridge Vineyard 2001 Estate Grown & Estate Bottled Chardonnay (Monterey) $8. 84 —*S.H. (12/1/2003)*

Shale Ridge Vineyard 2002 Lockwood Vineyard Chardonnay (Monterey County) $8. 85 Best Buy —*S.H. (7/1/2005)*

Shale Ridge Vineyard 2001 Estate Grown & Bottled Merlot (Monterey County) $8. 84 —*S.H. (3/1/2004)*

Shale Ridge Vineyard 2001 Estate Grown & Estate Bottled Sauvignon Blanc (Monterey County) $8. 86 Best Buy —*S.H. (10/1/2003)*

Shale Ridge Vineyard 2003 Syrah (Monterey) $8. 86 Best Buy *(9/1/2005)*

Shale Ridge Vineyard 2001 Estate Grown & Bottled Syrah (Monterey County) $8. 87 Best Buy —*S.H. (12/1/2003)*

SHANNON RIDGE

Shannon Ridge 2005 Barbera (High Valley) $19. 86 —*S.H. (12/31/2006)*

Shannon Ridge 2003 Barbera (Lake County) $20. 81 —*S.H. (5/1/2006)*

Shannon Ridge 2003 Cabernet Sauvignon (Lake County) $19. 89 —*S.H. (5/1/2006)*

Shannon Ridge 2002 Cabernet Sauvignon (Lake County) $19. 86 *—S.H. (6/1/2005)*

Shannon Ridge 2003 Petite Sirah (Lake County) $27. 90 Cellar Selection *—S.H. (5/1/2006)*

Shannon Ridge 2002 Petite Sirah (Lake County) $27. 88 *—S.H. (6/1/2005)*

Shannon Ridge 2005 Wrangler Red Red Blend (High Valley) $14. 85 *—S.H. (12/31/2006)*

Shannon Ridge 2006 Sauvignon Blanc (Lake County) $16. Too much feline spray in the aroma. A little goes a long way. Too bad, because the citrus and lemongrass flavors are tasty, and the crisp mouthfeel is a delight. **83** *—S.H. (9/1/2007)*

Shannon Ridge 2005 Sauvignon Blanc (Lake County) $15. 86 *—S.H. (12/31/2006)*

Shannon Ridge 2004 Sauvignon Blanc (Lake County) $15. 84 *—S.H. (5/1/2006)*

Shannon Ridge 2003 Sauvignon Blanc (Lake County) $15. 84 *—S.H. (6/1/2005)*

Shannon Ridge 2005 Syrah (High Valley) $19. 88 *—S.H. (12/31/2006)*

Shannon Ridge 2003 Syrah (Lake County) $30. 85 *(9/1/2005)*

Shannon Ridge 2006 Viognier (Lake County) $18. There's almost nothing here except alcohol, acidity and a drop of citrus. Really a hard wine to find anything nice to say about. **82** *—S.H. (9/1/2007)*

Shannon Ridge 2003 Zinfandel (Lake County) $22. 85 *—S.H. (5/1/2006)*

Shannon Ridge 2002 Zinfandel (Lake County) $22. 84 *—S.H. (6/1/2005)*

SHARK TRUST

Shark Trust 2001 Sixgill Syrah (Lodi) $11. 85 *—S.H. (12/1/2006)*

SHARP CELLARS

Sharp Cellars 2003 Tyla's Point Vineyards Pinot Blanc (Sonoma Valley) $19. 90 Editors' Choice *—S.H. (6/1/2005)*

Sharp Cellars 2001 Hailey's Creek Vineyard, Premices Zinfandel (Sonoma Valley) $45. 81 *(11/1/2003)*

SHEA

Shea 2000 Shea Vineyard Chardonnay (Willamette Valley) $25. 90 *—P.G. (12/31/2002)*

Shea 2002 Block 25 Pinot Noir (Willamette Valley) $48. 88 *(11/1/2004)*

Shea 2002 Block 32 Pinot Noir (Willamette Valley) $48. 86 *(11/1/2004)*

Shea 2000 Shea Vineyard Pinot Noir (Willamette Valley) $42. 87 *(10/1/2002)*

Shea 2002 Shea Vineyard Estate Pinot Noir (Willamette Valley) $35. 84 *(11/1/2004)*

Shea 2002 Shea Vineyard Homer Pinot Noir (Willamette Valley) $65. 88 *(11/1/2004)*

Shea 2002 Shea Vineyard Pommard Clone Pinot Noir (Willamette Valley) $38. 87 *(11/1/2004)*

SHELDON

Sheldon 2004 Unfiltered Chardonnay (Santa Lucia Highlands) $25. 93 Editors' Choice *—S.H. (4/1/2006)*

Sheldon 2005 Ripken Vineyard Petite Sirah (Lodi) $30. Shows the deep, palate-comforting fruit that Lodi reds usually have, offering a broad array of blackberry, cherry and raspberry flavors that are compounded with spicy, dessert-style notes of gingerbread and coconut macaroon. The acidity is soft, of course, given its origin, but there's a dry, dusty coat of tannins that gives all that flavor grip and balance. **88** *—S.H. (12/1/2007)*

Sheldon 2004 Ripken Vineyard Petite Sirah (Lodi) $25. The '03 was a very good wine. This is less so, probably due to the vintage, which simply baked the life out of the grapes. The cherry and blackberry flavors are a little Port-y and hot, although the wine is dry. **84** *—S.H. (6/1/2007)*

Sheldon 2003 Ripken Vineyard Petite Sirah (Lodi) $18. 87 *—S.H. (6/1/2006)*

Sheldon 2003 Vinolocity Red Blend (Santa Barbara County) $28. 82 *—S.H. (6/1/2006)*

Sheldon 2004 Vogelzang Vineyard Vinocity Rhône Red Blend (Santa Ynez Valley) $30. A Grenache-Syrah blend, with 15% new oak, this Rhône-style wine is effusive in cherry liqueur and chocolate flavors, with a rich earthy, mushroom and tobacco undercurrent. It's dry and rustic in the mouth. Drink now. **85** *—S.H. (6/1/2007)*

SHELDRAKE POINT

Sheldrake Point 2002 Cabernet Franc (Finger Lakes) $17. 84 *—M.D. (8/1/2006)*

Sheldrake Point 2002 Barrel Reserve Cabernet Franc (Finger Lakes) $24. 86 *—M.D. (8/1/2006)*

Sheldrake Point 2004 Icewine Cabernet Franc (Finger Lakes) $50. 84 *—S.K. (7/1/2007)*

Sheldrake Point 2001 Barrel Reserve Meritage (Finger Lakes) $24. Full-bodied fruit aromas of raspberry and blackberry are followed by lush blueberry and spice in the mouth. The finish is a little weak and the wine a touch tannic, though. **83** *—S.K. (2/1/2007)*

Sheldrake Point 2005 Riesling (Finger Lakes) $15. 87 *—M.D. (8/1/2006)*

Sheldrake Point 2004 Bunch Select Riesling (Finger Lakes) $20. Apple, honey and flowers on the nose are followed by flavors of baked apple and a raciness that maintains a fine balance between dry and sweet. There are also flashes of lemon here, which keeps the wine clean and exuberant in character. A very good wine that has enough flavor to be enjoyed alone, but will be excellent when paired with seafood. **87** *—S.K. (5/1/2007)*

Sheldrake Point 2001 Bunch Select Riesling (Finger Lakes) $22. 82 *—J.C. (8/1/2003)*

Sheldrake Point 2005 Dry Riesling (Finger Lakes) $15. 89 *—M.D. (8/1/2006)*

Sheldrake Point 2002 Dry Riesling (Finger Lakes) $13. 86 *—J.C. (8/1/2003)*

Sheldrake Point 2003 Reserve Riesling (Finger Lakes) $21. 89 *—M.D. (8/1/2006)*

Sheldrake Point 2001 Semi-Dry Spring Riesling (Finger Lakes) $13. 83 *—J.C. (8/1/2003)*

Sheldrake Point 2004 Petite Dry Rosé Blend (Finger Lakes) $11. Deeper and bolder than your average Finger Lakes rose, this wine is dry and fresh but a little tart on the palate. A good amount of acidity almost balances the fruit-forward, cherry character, but a slightly lighter touch would be more enjoyable. Some oak adds sweetness. A good summer wine. **84** *—S.K. (2/1/2007)*

SHELTON VINEYARDS

Shelton Vineyards 2002 Riesling (North Carolina) $10. 86 *—J.C. (8/1/2003)*

SHENANDOAH

Shenandoah 1997 Barbera (Amador County) $15. 81 *—J.C. (10/1/1999)*

Shenandoah 2004 ReZerve Barbera (Amador County) $24. Even for Barbera, a high acid variety, this is too sharp. With an official total acidity of 7.6, it's almost sour, and especially out of balance with the soft tannins and superripe raisiny, chocolatey fruit. The winemaker recommends Italian fare, which should help. **83** *—S.H. (2/1/2007)*

Shenandoah 2000 Reserve Barbera (Shenandoah Valley (CA)) $24. 87 *—S.H. (12/1/2002)*

Shenandoah 2003 Rezerve Barbera (Shenandoah Valley (CA)) $24. 87 *—S.H. (10/1/2006)*

Shenandoah 2003 Rezerve Barbera (Shenandoah Valley (CA)) $24. 90 Editors' Choice *—S.H. (12/15/2005)*

Shenandoah 2002 Rezerve Barbera (Shenandoah Valley (CA)) $24. 91 *—S.H. (9/1/2004)*

Shenandoah 1999 $13 Black Muscat (Amador County) $7. 84 *—S.H. (12/1/2002)*

Shenandoah 2000 Rezerve Cabernet Sauvignon (Shenandoah Valley (CA)) $24. 85 *—S.H. (11/15/2003)*

Shenandoah 2003 Vintage Port (Amador County) $17. 83 *—S.H. (10/1/2006)*

Shenandoah 2002 Vintage Port (Amador County) $18. 85 *—S.H. (12/1/2004)*

Shenandoah 2004 ReZerve Primitivo (Amador County) $24. If you like your Zins Porty, thick and soft, and lots of people do, you'll love this one. It's a big, rich, chocolaty wine, with primary fruit blackberry syrup and cola overtones, but fortunately it's totally dry. **85** *—S.H. (4/1/2007)*

Shenandoah 2003 Rezerve Primitivo (Shenandoah Valley (CA)) $24. 84 *—S.H. (10/1/2006)*

Shenandoah 2002 Rezerve Primitivo Red Blend (Shenandoah Valley (CA)) $24. 86 *—S.H. (9/1/2004)*

Shenandoah 2001 Sangiovese (Amador County) $14. 85 *—S.H. (9/1/2003)*

Shenandoah 1999 Sangiovese (Amador County) $13. 82 *—S.H. (12/1/2002)*

Shenandoah 2000 Rezerve Sangiovese (Shenandoah Valley (CA)) $24. 82 *—S.H. (9/1/2003)*

Shenandoah 2006 Sauvignon Blanc (Amador County) $11. If you like your whites bone dry, scouringly crisp in acidity and with a touch of tangy min-

USA

erals, you'll like this wine. Seems like a natural for oysters, a Sancerre-like SB with grapefruit and lime flavors and an impressively long, tart finish. **86 Best Buy** *—S.H. (11/1/2007)*

Shenandoah 2005 Sauvignon Blanc (California) $11. There's beautiful apple, citrus and apricot fruit in this clean, zesty wine, which contains a little Viognier and Sémillon. It's on the sweet-tasting side, but the alcohol is refreshingly low. **84** *—S.H. (5/1/2007)*

Shenandoah 2004 Sauvignon Blanc (Amador County) $11. 85 *—S.H. (10/1/2005)*

Shenandoah 2003 Sauvignon Blanc (Amador County) $11. 86 *—S.H. (10/1/2004)*

Shenandoah 2002 Sauvignon Blanc (Amador County) $10. 84 *—S.H. (7/1/2003)*

Shenandoah 2001 Sauvignon Blanc (Amador County) $NA. 82 *—S.H. (9/1/2003)*

Shenandoah 2004 ReZerve Tempranillo (Amador County) $24. The winery has hard work ahead with this Temp, which like so many others from California struggles for identity. The wine is soft and dry, with cherry, raspberry and chocolate flavors that finish with a bit of sweetness. It's a good wine but needs complexity, depth, and interest value, especially at this price. **85** *—S.H. (2/1/2007)*

Shenandoah 2004 Rezerve White Port White Blend (Amador County) $17. 93 *—S.H. (5/1/2006)*

Shenandoah 2002 Rezerve White Port (Shenandoah Valley (CA)) $11. 90 *—S.H. (9/1/2004)*

Shenandoah 2001 Paul's Vineyard Rezerve Zinfandel (Shenandoah Valley (CA)) $24. 88 *(11/1/2003)*

Shenandoah 2002 Rezerve Zinfandel (Shenandoah Valley (CA)) $24. 86 *—S.H. (9/1/2004)*

Shenandoah 2003 Rezerve Paul's Vineyard Zinfandel (Shenandoah Valley (CA)) $24. 87 *—S.H. (5/1/2006)*

Shenandoah 2002 Rezerve Paul's Vineyard Zinfandel (Shenandoah Valley (CA)) $NA. 91 *—S.H. (8/1/2005)*

Shenandoah 2005 Special Reserve Zinfandel (Amador County) $10. You can't beat the price. It's distinctly Amador, with that taste of ripe, briary red and black berries growing on thorn bushes hidden in the mountain scrub. Throw in a chocolaty edge, and total dryness, and you've got a great barbecue wine. **86 Best Buy** *—S.H. (4/1/2007)*

Shenandoah 2004 Special Reserve Zinfandel (Amador County) $10. 85 Best Buy *—S.H. (5/1/2006)*

Shenandoah 2003 Special Reserve Zinfandel (Amador County) $10. 85 Best Buy *—S.H. (10/1/2005)*

Shenandoah 2002 Special Reserve Zinfandel (Amador County) $10. 86 *—S.H. (9/1/2004)*

Shenandoah 2001 Special Reserve Zinfandel (Amador County) $10. 87 Best Buy *(11/1/2003)*

Shenandoah 1998 Special Reserve Zinfandel (Amador County) $10. 87 Best Buy *—P.G. (3/1/2001)*

Shenandoah 1997 Special Reserve Zinfandel (Amador County) $9. 87 Best Buy *—L.W. (9/1/1999)*

Shenandoah 2004 White Zinfandel (Amador County) $6. 82 *—S.H. (10/1/2005)*

Shenandoah 2003 White Zinfandel (Shenandoah Valley (CA)) $6. 83 *—S.H. (9/1/2004)*

Shenandoah VA 1997 Cabernet Sauvignon (Virginia) $NA. 85 *—J.C. (8/1/1999)*

Shenandoah VA 1997 Founder's Reserve Chambourcin (Shenandoah Valley) $17. 86 *—J.C. (8/1/1999)*

Shenandoah VA 1997 Chardonnay (Virginia) $13. 84 *—J.C. (8/1/1999)*

Shenandoah VA 1997 Founder's Reserve Chardonnay (Virginia) $16. 82 *—J.C. (8/1/1999)*

Shenandoah VA NV Lot 95 Merlot (Virginia) $17. 86 *—J.C. (8/1/1999)*

SHERIDAN VINEYARD

Sheridan Vineyard 2003 Cabernet Franc (Yakima Valley) $33. 87 *—P.G. (6/1/2006)*

Sheridan Vineyard 2003 Cabernet Sauvignon (Yakima Valley) $45. 90 *—P.G. (6/1/2006)*

Sheridan Vineyard 2000 Red Blend (Yakima Valley) $30. 86 *—P.G. (9/1/2003)*

Sheridan Vineyard 2003 Kamiakin Red Blend (Yakima Valley) $18. 88 *—P.G. (6/1/2006)*

Sheridan Vineyard 2002 L'Orage Red Blend (Yakima Valley) $35. 93 *—P.G. (12/15/2005)*

Sheridan Vineyard 2003 L'Orage Red Blend (Yakima Valley) $38. 89 *—P.G. (6/1/2006)*

Sheridan Vineyard 2003 Syrah (Yakima Valley) $38. 91 *—P.G. (6/1/2006)*

Sheridan Vineyard 2002 Syrah (Yakima Valley) $36. 88 *(9/1/2005)*

SHERWIN FAMILY

Sherwin Family 1997 Cabernet Sauvignon (Spring Mountain) $65. 94 *(11/1/2000)*

Sherwin Family 1996 Cabernet Sauvignon (Spring Mountain) $52. 92 *—J.C. (7/1/2000)*

SHERWOOD HOUSE VINEYARDS

Sherwood House Vineyards 2001 Proprietor's Reserve Chardonnay (North Fork of Long Island) $23. 84 *—J.C. (10/2/2004)*

Sherwood House Vineyards 2002 Merlot (North Fork of Long Island) $24. 86 *—M.D. (12/1/2006)*

Sherwood House Vineyards 2001 Merlot (North Fork of Long Island) $27. 83 *—J.C. (10/2/2004)*

Sherwood House Vineyards 2002 Oregon Road Merlot (North Fork of Long Island) $16. Vanilla, spice and blackberry flavors meet in this friendly, mellow wine. The structure is soft and bordering on watery, and the finish short, which impedes the impact, but the mouthfeel is velvety and the overall impression favorable. Aged 12 months in older French barrels. Enjoy with duck or red meat. **83** *—S.K. (2/1/2007)*

SHINN ESTATE

Shinn Estate 2004 Wild Boar Doe Bordeaux Blend (North Fork of Long Island) $22. The name of this Meritage wine is a play on the word "Bordeaux," and in style, it is certainly in keeping with that region. Made with 40% Merlot, 23% Cabernet Sauvignon, 17% Malbec, 15% Petit Verdot and 5% Cabernet Franc, the nose vibrant with rosemary, raspberry, pepper and flowers. Red raspberry and oak meet on the palate in a drinkable but not terribly complex union, and the finish is on the flabby side, but overall this wine will please most fans of the blended red. **84** *—S.K. (2/1/2007)*

Shinn Estate 2004 Cabernet Franc (North Fork of Long Island) $38. There are some elegant notes of black fruit and flowers in the nose of this wine, but it disappoints on the palate with its watery lack of dimension. The whole wine is overriden with a tentative structure and it ends with a flimsy finish. **81** *—S.K. (2/1/2007)*

Shinn Estate 2004 Estate Merlot (North Fork of Long Island) $24. Meaty plum, clove and chocolate hit the nose first, followed by flavors of pepper, oak and spice. There's an initial, angular blast of cranberry and some thinness in the mouthfeel, but overall, a pleasant selection that will pair well with duck or lamb. **86** *—S.K. (2/1/2007)*

Shinn Estate 2004 Nine Barrels Reserve Merlot (North Fork of Long Island) $42. 89 *—M.D. (12/1/2006)*

Shinn Estate 2002 Six Barrels Reserve Merlot (North Fork of Long Island) $34. 85 *—J.C. (3/1/2006)*

SHOOTING STAR

Shooting Star 2005 Aligoté (Washington) $12. 88 Best Buy *—P.G. (8/1/2006)*

Shooting Star 2001 Aligoté (Washington) $12. 84 *—M.S. (6/1/2003)*

Shooting Star 2000 Aligoté (Washington) $13. 85 *—P.G. (6/1/2002)*

Shooting Star 2004 Barbera (Lake County) $14. A difficult wine to like, even for Barbera fans, and the main reason is what tastes like quite a bit of residual sugar, which makes the wine insipid, like cough medicine. **82** *—S.H. (4/1/2007)*

Shooting Star 2005 Chardonnay (Sonoma County) $12. With a little neutral oak to give a touch of smoky cream, this everyday wine has good apple and peach fruit, and a nice clean cut of acidity. **85** *—S.H. (4/1/2007)*

Shooting Star 1997 Chardonnay (California) $14. 86 *—L.W. (7/1/1999)*

Shooting Star 2004 Blue Franc Lemberger (Washington) $12. 88 Best Buy *—P.G. (8/1/2006)*

Shooting Star 2001 Blue Franc Lemberger (Washington) $12. 88 Best Buy *—C.S. (12/31/2002)*

Shooting Star 1997 Merlot (Lake County) $15. 89 *(3/1/2000)*

Shooting Star 2000 Pinot Noir (Carneros) $14. 81 *(10/1/2002)*

Shooting Star 1998 Sauvignon Blanc (Lake County) $11. 84 *—M.S. (3/1/2000)*

Shooting Star 2004 Syrah (Lake County) $12. A nice, rich Syrah, if you like full-throttle fruit, and the price ain't bad. Explodes with young, jammy cherry, blackberry, raspberry, tangerine and Fig Newton flavors, with a decadent edge of chocolate fudge. **85** —*S.H. (4/1/2007)*

Shooting Star 1999 Syrah (Lake County) $12. 84 *(10/1/2001)*

Shooting Star 2002 Zinfandel (Lake County) $12. 86 —*S.H. (8/1/2005)*

Shooting Star 1998 Zinfandel (Lake County) $12. 87 —*P.G. (3/1/2001)*

SHOWKET

Showket 2003 Cabernet Sauvignon (Oakville) $75. 94 Cellar Selection —*S.H. (9/1/2006)*

Showket 2002 Cabernet Sauvignon (Oakville) $69. 88 —*S.H. (11/1/2005)*

Showket 2001 Cabernet Sauvignon (Oakville) $75. 92 —*S.H. (10/1/2004)*

Showket 2002 Asante Sana Red Blend (Oakville) $45. 84 —*S.H. (11/1/2005)*

Showket 1997 Sangiovese (Napa Valley) $35. 88 —*S.H. (12/15/1999)*

Showket 2002 Sangiovese (Oakville) $30. 85 —*S.H. (11/1/2005)*

Showket 2001 Sangiovese (Oakville) $30. 89 —*S.H. (10/1/2005)*

SIDURI

Siduri 2005 Pinot Noir (Santa Lucia Highlands) $32. A good example of the principle that you get what you pay for, this regional Pinot is almost as good as Siduri's Rosella's Vineyard botting. It's dry, crisp and silky, with delicious cola, cherry, vanilla and cinnamon spice flavors. It lacks the concentration of the single-vineyard Pinot, but is beautiful now. **88** —*S.H. (8/1/2007)*

Siduri 2005 Pinot Noir (Russian River Valley) $26. A little simple, but pleasant and elegant, with a delicately silky body and cherry, cola, wintergreen, vanilla and oaky flavors. Not going anywhere, so drink up. **86** —*S.H. (5/1/2007)*

Siduri 2005 Pinot Noir (Santa Rita Hills) $29. Shows all the greatness if this appellation, streamlined to its basics. The fundamentals are a crisply acidic, delicately structured wine, with a silky texture and deep flavors of cherries, cola and raspberry purée, with a deeper stream of chocolate, soy and balsamic sautéed Portobello. It's nearly as good as many wines costing twice as much. **90** —*S.H. (4/1/2007)*

Siduri 2004 Pinot Noir (Russian River Valley) $26. 84 —*S.H. (5/1/2006)*

Siduri 2004 Pinot Noir (Santa Rita Hills) $29. 88 —*S.H. (5/1/2006)*

Siduri 2002 Pinot Noir (Central Coast) $25. 85 —*S.H. (5/1/2004)*

Siduri 2002 Pinot Noir (Sonoma County) $25. 86 *(11/1/2004)*

Siduri 2002 Pinot Noir (Santa Lucia Highlands) $35. 85 —*S.H. (5/1/2004)*

Siduri 2001 Pinot Noir (Sonoma Coast) $28. 91 Editors' Choice —*S.H. (7/1/2003)*

Siduri 2001 Pinot Noir (Santa Lucia Highlands) $34. 92 Editors' Choice —*S.H. (7/1/2003)*

Siduri 1999 Pinot Noir (Santa Lucia Highlands) $34. 88 *(10/1/2002)*

Siduri 2000 Cerise Pinot Noir (Anderson Valley) $50. 86 *(10/1/2002)*

Siduri 2005 Clos Pepe Pinot Noir (Santa Rita Hills) $53. This is absolutely classic Santa Rita Pinot, dry, minerally, high in acidity, and ripe in cherries, cola, pomegranates and mocha, offering waves of complexity and interest. The wine also shows distinctly young tannins, which not only will play against a steak but should help this lovely bottle age for five or six years. **93** —*S.H. (4/1/2007)*

Siduri 2005 Ewald Vineyard Pinot Noir (Russian River Valley) $45. This is one of the first important 2005 Russian River Pinots to hit the market, and it's an exciting hint to this eagerly awaited vintage. It was a cool, long hangtime year, and this wine is amazingly rich and deep in chocolaty cherry, black raspberry and cola flavors. For all that, the wine is dry, supple and delicately tannic, and seems to have a fine future. **92** —*S.H. (5/1/2007)*

Siduri 1999 Garys' Vineyard Pinot Noir (Santa Lucia Highlands) $49. 90 *(10/1/2002)*

Siduri 2000 Garys' Pinot Noir (Santa Lucia Highlands) $48. 90 *(10/1/2002)*

Siduri 2001 Garys' Vineyard Pinot Noir (Santa Lucia Highlands) $50. 88 —*S.H. (3/1/2004)*

Siduri 2001 Hirsch Vineyard Pinot Noir (Sonoma Coast) $45. 86 —*S.H. (3/1/2004)*

Siduri 1999 Hirsch Vineyard Pinot Noir (Sonoma County) $49. 90 *(10/1/2002)*

Siduri 1998 Hirsch Vineyard Pinot Noir (Sonoma Coast) $46. 88 *(10/1/2000)*

Siduri 1997 Hirsch Vineyard Pinot Noir (Sonoma Coast) $42. 92 *(10/1/1999)*

Siduri 2005 Keefer Ranch Vineyard Pinot Noir (Russian River Valley) $53. I like the elegance, but it seems like it was rushed to market. It will certainly benefit from cellaring, as it's young and rude in acids right now, and not showing well. But there's something here in the vast heart of cherries and pomegranates and overall balance. Should improve by the end of 2007, and hold for another five years. **91 Cellar Selection** —*S.H. (8/1/2007)*

Siduri 2000 Muirfield Vineyard Pinot Noir (Willamette Valley) $48. 90 *(10/1/2002)*

Siduri 2000 Pisoni Pinot Noir (Santa Lucia Highlands) $50. 93 Editors' Choice *(10/1/2002)*

Siduri 2005 Rosella's Vineyard Pinot Noir (Santa Lucia Highlands) $45. Pale in color and sharp in youthful acids, this Pinot needs time to show its stuff. It tastes good now, with rich cola, cherry, herb tea and cinnamon spice flavors, but the parts desperately need time to knit together. Best beyond 2007, for five years or so. **91 Cellar Selection** —*S.H. (8/1/2007)*

Siduri 2005 Sapphire Hill Vineyard Pinot Noir (Russian River Valley) $42. High in acidity and bone dry, this light-colored Pinot seems a bit one-dimensional right now, but I think it was released too early. It should gain momentum by the end of 2007, when the cherry, rhubarb and cola flavors become more integrated with the tannins and oak. If you have to drink it now, decant for several hours. **89** —*S.H. (8/1/2007)*

Siduri 2000 Sapphire Hill Vineyard Pinot Noir (Russian River Valley) $49. 93 Editors' Choice *(10/1/2002)*

Siduri 2005 Sonatera Vineyard Pinot Noir (Sonoma Coast) $45. Set aside any notions you still have that Sonoma Coast is some kind of cold appellation. Large tracts of it are not, and this wine, which comes from a cool vintage, proves it. Few Pinots could be richer in cherry pie, raspberry purée, chocolate cream and spicy gingerbread cookie flavors that can only come from heat. That said, the wine, delicious as it is, is kind of one-dimensional. **87** —*S.H. (5/1/2007)*

Siduri 2005 Van der Kamp Vineyard Pinot Noir (Sonoma Mountain) $42. This is one of the riper of Siduri's crop of '05 single-vineyard Pinots. It bursts with cherry jam, sweet cola, vanilla and coffee fudge flavors that make it delicious, but it's no mere fruit bomb. The complex of acids, tannins and oak give it dimensions worth pondering. Best now and for five years. **90** —*S.H. (8/1/2007)*

Siduri 2001 Van Der Kamp Vineyard Pinot Noir (Sonoma Mountain) $45. 87 —*S.H. (3/1/2004)*

Siduri 2000 Van Der Kamp Vineyard Pinot Noir (Sonoma Mountain) $48. 83 *(10/1/2002)*

Siduri 1999 Van Der Kamp Vineyard Pinot Noir (Sonoma Mountain) $49. 87 *(10/1/2002)*

Siduri 1997 Van Der Kamp Vineyard Pinot Noir (Sonoma Mountain) $38. 90 *(10/1/1999)*

SIERRA CLUB

Sierra Club 2000 Atira Vineyards Cabernet Sauvignon (Napa Valley) $19. 83 —*S.H. (8/1/2005)*

SIERRA VISTA

Sierra Vista 2005 Unoaked Chardonnay (El Dorado) $13. 83 —*S.H. (11/1/2006)*

Sierra Vista 2002 Unoaked Chardonnay (El Dorado) $12. 82 —*S.H. (10/1/2003)*

Sierra Vista 2005 Fumé Blanc (Sierra Foothills) $13. 90 Best Buy —*S.H. (11/15/2006)*

Sierra Vista 2006 Rosé Grenache (El Dorado) $14. You'll find crisp acidity, total dryness and modest cherry-strawberry fruit and spice in this pink-colored wine. It's a little thin on the finish, but the price isn't bad for a good all-purpose rosé. **84** —*S.H. (7/1/2007)*

Sierra Vista 2001 Belle Rose Rhône Red Blend (El Dorado) $9. 86 —*S.H. (9/1/2003)*

Sierra Vista 2001 Fleur de Montagne Rhône Red Blend (El Dorado) $21. 84 —*S.H. (6/1/2003)*

Sierra Vista 2000 Fleur de Montagne Rhône Red Blend (El Dorado) $21. 85 —*S.H. (5/1/2003)*

Sierra Vista 2005 Belle Rose Rosé Blend (El Dorado) $10. Smells thin, with a trace of cherries, and turns watery in the mouth, reprising the cherry fruit. Decent, clean wine, with some spice in the finish. **83** —*S.H. (7/1/2007)*

Sierra Vista 2004 Syrah (Sierra Foothills) $12. 84 —*S.H. (5/1/2006)*

Sierra Vista 2000 Syrah (Sierra Foothills) $12. 84 —*S.H. (6/1/2003)*

Sierra Vista 1997 Five Star Reserve Syrah (El Dorado County) $60. 90 *(11/1/2001)*

Sierra Vista 2004 La Grande Syrah (Sierra Foothills) $20. 87 —*S.H. (11/15/2006)*

Sierra Vista 2004 Red Rock Ridge Syrah (El Dorado) $25. 84 —*S.H. (11/15/2006)*

Sierra Vista 1999 Red Rock Ridge Syrah (El Dorado) $25. 87 —*S.H. (6/1/2003)*

Sierra Vista 1997 Red Rock Ridge Syrah (El Dorado County) $19. 89 —*S.H. (10/1/1999)*

Sierra Vista 2001 Viognier (El Dorado) $25. 85 —*S.H. (5/1/2003)*

Sierra Vista 1998 Viognier (El Dorado County) $20. 89 —*S.H. (10/1/1999)*

Sierra Vista 2000 Zinfandel (El Dorado) $12. 85 —*S.H. (9/1/2003)*

Sierra Vista 2004 Estate Zinfandel (El Dorado) $12. 86 —*S.H. (5/1/2006)*

Sierra Vista 1999 Reeves Zinfandel (El Dorado) $16. 85 —*S.H. (11/1/2002)*

SIGNORELLO

Signorello 2004 Padrone Bordeaux Blend (Napa Valley) $95. A Bordeaux blend of mainly Cabernet, with Merlot and Cab Franc, the grapes are from the estate, just outside the Stags Leap District on the Silverado Trail. There's a luscious power, as the sweet young fruit hits the palate, supported by firm, lush tannins. But the oak, which is 70% new, really takes center stage, especially on the finish. Some time in the bottle could bring everything together. **89** —*S.H. (11/1/2007)*

Signorello 2000 Padrone Bordeaux Blend (Napa Valley) $75. 93 —*S.H. (4/1/2004)*

Signorello 1997 Padrone Bordeaux Blend (Napa Valley) $125. 92 *(11/1/2000)*

Signorello 2002 Padrone Cabernet Blend (Napa Valley) $95. 95 Cellar Selection —*S.H. (12/1/2005)*

Signorello 2001 Cabernet Sauvignon (Napa Valley) $48. 87 *(6/1/2005)*

Signorello 1999 Cabernet Sauvignon (Napa Valley) $48. 91 —*S.H. (6/1/2002)*

Signorello 1997 Cabernet Sauvignon (Napa Valley) $48. 91 —*S.H. (2/1/2000)*

Signorello 2004 Estate Cabernet Sauvignon (Napa Valley) $40. Very fine and rich, especially the texture, which is as velvety smooth as Napa Cab gets. The tannins are a wonder, perfectly ripe and soft, which gives the wine a feminine mouthfeel. But the oak and fruit are pure power. This is supple and rich, but somehow, it doesn't seem like an ager. Drink now through 2009. **92** —*S.H. (11/1/2007)*

Signorello 2003 Estate Cabernet Sauvignon (Napa Valley) $40. A very good followup to the excellent '02, the '03 is plush and ripe and ageable. With forward cherry, blackberry, cassis and chocolate flavors, it offers plenty of opulence now, but has the tannic backbone to peak and then gradually fade for 10 years. Signorello's estate Cab is really one of the more dependable bottlings in the valley. **92** —*S.H. (5/1/2007)*

Signorello 2002 Estate Cabernet Sauvignon (Napa Valley) $48. 92 Cellar Selection —*S.H. (12/1/2005)*

Signorello 2000 Estate Unfiltered Cabernet Sauvignon (Napa Valley) $48. 89 —*S.H. (6/1/2003)*

Signorello 2000 Chardonnay (Napa Valley) $38. 91 —*J.M. (5/1/2002)*

Signorello 1998 Estate Chardonnay (Napa Valley) $38. 89 —*S.H. (5/1/2000)*

Signorello 1999 Estate Bottled Chardonnay (Napa Valley) $38. 88 *(7/1/2001)*

Signorello 2002 Hope's Cuvée Chardonnay (Napa Valley) $60. 93 —*S.H. (8/1/2004)*

Signorello 2000 Hope's Cuvée Chardonnay (Napa Valley) $60. 91 —*J.M. (5/1/2002)*

Signorello 1999 Hope's Cuvée Chardonnay (Napa Valley) $60. 89 *(7/1/2001)*

Signorello 2005 Veilles Vignes Chardonnay (Napa Valley) $38. From 25-year-old vines, this Burgundian-inspired white wine wisely avoids the herbaceousness that can accompany Napa Valley Chardonnay. It has passion fruit and papaya flavors that could be a little more concentrated, and also possesses a rich coating of caramelized oak. **86** —*S.H. (5/1/2007)*

Signorello 2003 Vielles Vignes Chardonnay (Napa Valley) $38. 88 *(6/1/2005)*

Signorello 2002 Vieilles Vignes Chardonnay (Napa Valley) $38. 91 —*S.H. (8/1/2004)*

Signorello 2001 Vieilles Vignes Chardonnay (Napa Valley) $38. 90 —*S.H. (6/1/2003)*

Signorello 1999 Estate Merlot (Napa Valley) $45. 89 —*S.H. (2/1/2003)*

Signorello 2005 Hudson Vineyard Pinot Noir (Carneros) $50. Fabulous Pinot, about as good as Carneros gets. Sourced from this famous vineyard, it's silky and complex in cherries, sassafras, cola, black raspberry tea, vanilla and cinnamon spices that change and intensify as they roll across the palate. For all that, the finish is dry and balanced in crisp acidity. With just 70 cases produced, it's worth a special search. **94** —*S.H. (11/1/2007)*

Signorello 2005 Las Amigas Vineyard Pinot Noir (Carneros) $38. Defined by tart acids, this shows a balance of cherries and raspberries with drier notes of cola and rhubarb that veer all the way into wintergreen. It's a slightly unripe wine, but dry and elegant, in the way of Carneros Pinot Noir. **87** —*S.H. (11/1/2007)*

Signorello 2004 Las Amigas Vineyard Pinot Noir (Carneros) $38. 92 —*S.H. (11/1/2006)*

Signorello 2002 Las Amigas Vineyard Pinot Noir (Carneros) $32. 90 —*S.H. (11/1/2004)*

Signorello 2001 Las Amigas Vineyard Pinot Noir (Carneros) $32. 93 —*S.H. (4/1/2004)*

Signorello 2000 Las Amigas Vineyard Pinot Noir (Carneros) $32. 89 —*S.H. (7/1/2003)*

Signorello 1999 Las Amigas Vineyard Pinot Noir (Carneros) $50. 89 —*S.H. (9/1/2003)*

Signorello 1998 Las Amigas Vineyard Pinot Noir (Carneros) $50. 91 —*S.H. (9/1/2003)*

Signorello 1997 Las Amigas Vineyard Pinot Noir (Carneros) $45. 90 *(10/1/1999)*

Signorello 2001 Padrone Red Blend (Napa Valley) $110. 86 —*S.H. (6/1/2005)*

Signorello 1998 Barrel-Fermented Sémillon (Napa Valley) $22. 91 Editors' Choice —*S.H. (8/1/2001)*

Signorello 2001 Seta Sémillon-Sauvignon Blanc (Napa Valley) $25. 87 —*S.H. (7/1/2003)*

Signorello 2000 Seta Sémillon-Sauvignon Blanc (Napa Valley) $25. 90 —*S.H. (9/12/2002)*

Signorello 2004 Seta White Wine Sémillon-Sauvignon Blanc (Napa Valley) $25. 89 —*S.H. (11/1/2006)*

Signorello 2003 Seta White Wine Sémillon-Sauvignon Blanc (Napa Valley) $25. 90 —*S.H. (6/1/2005)*

Signorello 2002 Seta White Wine Sémillon-Sauvignon Blanc (Napa Valley) $25. 92 —*S.H. (8/1/2004)*

Signorello 2001 Syrah (Napa Valley) $NA. 94 —*S.H. (5/1/2004)*

Signorello 2005 Estate Syrah (Napa Valley) $36. You don't think of Signorello as a Syrah house, but for years, they've been putting out serious Syrahs, and with the '05 vintage, they certify this tradition. This wine is, in a word, fabulous. It's enormously attractive in well-oaked cassis, plum, leather, cocoa and white pepper aromas and flavors, but that only begins to describe the complexity. The 4% Viognier seems responsible for the bright intrusion of citrusy acidity. As powerful as it is, the wine never loses sight of balance and elegance. **95 Editors' Choice** —*S.H. (11/1/2007)*

Signorello 2004 Estate Syrah (Napa Valley) $36. 88 —*S.H. (11/1/2006)*

Signorello 2002 Estate Syrah (Napa Valley) $32. 91 —*S.H. (6/1/2005)*

Signorello 2000 Estate Bottled Unfiltered Syrah (Napa Valley) $32. 92 —*S.H. (6/1/2003)*

Signorello 2005 Seta Bordeaux White Blend (Napa Valley) $23. A little overworked, with all the barrel fermentation, new French oak and sur lie aging, but this is generally a high-class dry wine made in the manner of a white Graves. It's forward in citrus, green apple and peaches and cream flavors, with a refined mouthfeel. **87** —*S.H. (5/1/2007)*

Signorello 2005 Luvisi Vineyard Zinfandel (Napa Valley) $36. Shows the classic structure and balance of a fine Napa Cabernet, in the interplay of rich, ripe tannins, acidity and fruit. That makes this 100% Zinfandel elegant. It's also delicious, with wild berry, plum, cola, chocolate and peppery spice flavors. **91** —*S.H. (11/1/2007)*

Signorello 2004 Luvisi Vineyard Zinfandel (Napa Valley) $36. 91 —*S.H. (11/15/2006)*

Signorello 2002 Luvisi Vineyard Zinfandel (Napa Valley) $34. 84 —*S.H. (6/1/2005)*

Signorello 2001 Luvisi Vineyard Zinfandel (Napa Valley) $34. 91 —*S.H. (4/1/2004)*

Signorello 2000 Luvisi Vineyard Zinfandel (Napa Valley) $34. 85 —*S.H. (3/1/2003)*

Signorello 1999 Luvisi Vineyard Zinfandel (Napa Valley) $34. 88 —*S.H. (9/12/2002)*

SILK OAK

Silk Oak 1999 Chardonnay (Lodi) $16. 80 —*S.H. (11/15/2001)*

SILVAN RIDGE

Silvan Ridge 2000 Cabernet Sauvignon (Rogue Valley) $26. 88 *—M.S. (8/1/2003)*

Silvan Ridge 1999 Cabernet Sauvignon (Rogue Valley) $26. 84 *—C.S. (12/31/2002)*

Silvan Ridge 2001 Chardonnay (Oregon) $14. 81 *—M.S. (8/1/2003)*

Silvan Ridge 1999 Bing Vineyard Ice Wine Gewürztraminer (Umpqua Valley) $20. 92 *—J.M. (12/1/2002)*

Silvan Ridge 2003 Merlot (Rogue Valley) $19. 86 *—P.G. (9/1/2006)*

Silvan Ridge 1999 Merlot (Rogue Valley) $19. 85 *—C.S. (12/31/2002)*

Silvan Ridge 2004 Reserve Merlot (Rogue Valley) $19. This has more muscle and weight than the winery's '03, but somehow fails to charm. It's dark, chewy, herbal and tight, with some butterfat in the finish, presumably from barrel time. **86** *—P.G. (11/15/2007)*

Silvan Ridge 2002 Early Muscat Semi Sparkling Muscat (Oregon) $14. 85 *—M.S. (8/1/2003)*

Silvan Ridge 2006 Pinot Gris (Oregon) $15. This is a crisp, serviceable Pinot Gris, with sharp green apple and cut pear fruit dominating. It's got plenty of acid underscoring the fruit, and should work well as an all-purpose wine. **87** *—P.G. (11/15/2007)*

Silvan Ridge 2002 Pinot Gris (Oregon) $15. 88 *—P.G. (10/1/2004)*

Silvan Ridge 2001 Pinot Gris (Oregon) $14. 83 *—M.S. (8/1/2003)*

Silvan Ridge 2004 Pinot Noir (Willamette Valley) $19. 86 *—P.G. (9/1/2006)*

Silvan Ridge 2003 Pinot Noir (Willamette Valley) $19. 87 *—P.G. (5/1/2006)*

Silvan Ridge 2002 Pinot Noir (Willamette Valley) $19. 85 *(11/1/2004)*

Silvan Ridge 2000 Pinot Noir (Willamette Valley) $23. 86 *—M.S. (9/1/2003)*

Silvan Ridge 1998 Pinot Noir (Willamette Valley) $22. 87 *—S.H. (8/1/2002)*

Silvan Ridge 2002 Bradshaw Vineyard Pinot Noir (Willamette Valley) $35. 84 *(11/1/2004)*

Silvan Ridge 2005 Reserve Pinot Noir (Willamette Valley) $22. Forward and fruity, this has California-style fruit and sweet, strawberry candy. The difference is that it fills out the middle with some leafy, herbal flavors, nothing too rough, but enough to add some flavor interest. The finish is fat and buttery, showing the influence of oak aging. **88** *—P.G. (11/15/2007)*

Silvan Ridge 2002 Reserve Pinot Noir (Willamette Valley) $35. 84 *(11/1/2004)*

Silvan Ridge 2003 Syrah (Rogue Valley) $20. 87 *—P.G. (9/1/2006)*

Silvan Ridge 2001 Del Rio Vineyard Syrah (Rogue Valley) $20. 87 *—P.G. (10/1/2004)*

Silvan Ridge 2000 Del Rio Vineyard Syrah (Rogue Valley) $26. 87 *—M.S. (9/1/2003)*

Silvan Ridge 2005 Reserve Syrah (Rogue Valley) $20. I sense some sappy black cherry fruit in here, but it's buried in heavily toasted barrels and a reductive, plastic flavor that takes over and won't let go. If you give it plenty of extra air time it smoothes out slightly. **85** *—P.G. (11/15/2007)*

Silvan Ridge 2002 Del Rio Vineyards Viognier (Rogue Valley) $18. 86 *—P.G. (12/1/2003)*

Silvan Ridge 2001 Del Rio Vineyards Viognier (Rogue Valley) $18. 82 *—M.S. (8/1/2003)*

Silvan Ridge 2006 Reserve Viognier (Rogue Valley) $22. This smells exactly as Viognier should: citrus peel, grapefruit and pineapple fruit, lifted with some high tones, and filling out the palate without ever becoming too soft or flabby. It does get a bit diffuse in the back half; still tasty but not quite as sharp and focused. **87** *—P.G. (11/15/2007)*

SILVER

Silver 2000 Cabernet Sauvignon (Santa Barbara County) $30. 88 *—J.M. (12/31/2003)*

Silver 2006 Unoaked Chardonnay (Santa Lucia Highlands) $42. Probably the most expensive unoaked Chard out there, this is a stunning wine, showing the laserlike purity and bright acids that this northwestern part of the Highlands coaxes from the grapes. The brilliantly illuminated flavors range from limes and kiwis to green apples, peaches and guavas. The finish is dry, but with a honeyed unctuousness that could be a touch of botrytis. **92** *—S.H. (12/1/2007)*

Silver 2001 Larner Vineyard Mourvèdre (Santa Barbara County) $20. 90 Editors' Choice *—J.M. (6/1/2004)*

Silver 2000 Nebbiolo (Santa Barbara County) $22. 88 *—J.M. (12/1/2003)*

Silver 2000 Julia's Vineyard Pinot Noir (Santa Barbara County) $45. 87 *—J.M. (7/1/2003)*

Silver 2001 Lake Marie Vineyard Pinot Noir (Santa Barbara County) $40. 90 *—J.M. (12/31/2004)*

Silver 2001 Larner Vineyard Syrah-Mourvèdre Red Blend (Santa Barbara County) $22. 89 *—J.M. (6/1/2004)*

Silver 2002 Syrah & Mourvèdre Rhône Red Blend (Santa Barbara County) $22. 84 *—S.H. (11/15/2006)*

Silver 2000 Sangiovese (Santa Barbara County) $28. 89 *—J.M. (2/1/2003)*

Silver 2003 Vogelzang Vineyard Viognier (Santa Barbara County) $22. 83 *—S.H. (11/15/2006)*

Silver 2002 Vogelzang Vineyard Viognier (Santa Barbara County) $22. 88 *—J.M. (9/1/2004)*

Silver 2001 Vogelzang Vineyard Viognier (Santa Barbara County) $22. 89 *—J.M. (6/1/2003)*

SILVER LAKE

Silver Lake 1998 Cabernet Sauvignon (Columbia Valley (WA)) $14. 87 Best Buy *—D.T. (12/31/2002)*

Silver Lake 1998 Reserve Cabernet Sauvignon (Columbia Valley (WA)) $25. 84 *—C.S. (12/31/2002)*

Silver Lake 1999 Cabernet Sauvignon-Merlot (Columbia Valley (WA)) $7. 82 *—P.G. (6/1/2002)*

Silver Lake 2000 Chardonnay (Columbia Valley (WA)) $12. 85 *—M.S. (6/1/2003)*

Silver Lake 1999 Chardonnay (Columbia Valley (WA)) $7. 84 *—P.G. (7/1/2002)*

Silver Lake 2000 Reserve Chardonnay (Columbia Valley (WA)) $14. 88 *—M.S. (6/1/2003)*

Silver Lake 1998 Reserve Chardonnay (Columbia Valley (WA)) $13. 85 *—P.G. (7/1/2002)*

Silver Lake 2001 Fumé Blanc (Columbia Valley (WA)) $9. 84 *—M.S. (6/1/2003)*

Silver Lake 1998 Merlot (Columbia Valley (WA)) $14. 86 *—P.G. (6/1/2002)*

Silver Lake 1999 Reserve Merlot (Columbia Valley (WA)) $25. 89 *—C.S. (12/31/2002)*

Silver Lake 2001 Roza Hills Vineyard Late Harvest Riesling (Columbia Valley (WA)) $8. 88 *—M.S. (12/1/2003)*

SILVER MOUNTAIN

Silver Mountain 1997 Chardonnay (Santa Cruz Mountains) $18. 85 *(6/1/2000)*

Silver Mountain 2001 Estate Chardonnay (Santa Cruz Mountains) $20. 88 *—S.H. (3/1/2006)*

Silver Mountain 2002 Pinot Noir (Monterey) $28. 88 *—S.H. (3/1/2006)*

SILVER PALM

Silver Palm 2005 Cabernet Sauvignon (North Coast) $30. This wine, which is available only in restaurants, is simple and soft. It has very ripe flavors of blackberry and cherry jam, vanilla and oak. **84** *—S.H. (12/31/2007)*

SILVER PINES

Silver Pines 2004 Sauvignon Blanc (Sonoma Mountain) $32. 88 *(7/1/2005)*

Silver Pines 2003 Sauvignon Blanc (Sonoma Mountain) $35. 90 *—S.H. (12/31/2004)*

SILVER RIDGE

Silver Ridge 1999 Barrel Select Cabernet Sauvignon (California) $10. 84 *—S.H. (11/15/2002)*

Silver Ridge 2003 Chardonnay (California) $10. 84 *—S.H. (8/1/2005)*

Silver Ridge 2003 Merlot (California) $10. 85 Best Buy *—S.H. (12/1/2005)*

Silver Ridge 1999 Barrel Select Syrah (California) $10. 86 *(10/1/2001)*

SILVER RIDGE VINEYARDS

Silver Ridge Vineyards 2003 Barrel Select Syrah (California) $10. 84 *(9/1/2005)*

Silver Ridge Vineyards 2000 Barrel Select Syrah (California) $10. 86 Best Buy *—S.H. (10/1/2003)*

Silver Ridge Vineyards 2000 Barrel Select Viognier (California) $10. 83 *—S.H. (12/1/2003)*

SILVER ROSE CELLARS

Silver Rose Cellars 1999 Chardonnay (Napa Valley) $23. 86 *—J.M. (12/31/2001)*

Silver Rose Cellars 1999 D'argent Chardonnay (Napa Valley) $30. 88 *—J.M. (12/31/2001)*

SILVER SPUR

Silver Spur 2003 Sangiacomo Vineyards Chardonnay (Carneros) $18. 83 —*S.H. (10/1/2005)*

Silver Spur 2002 Casa Carneros Vineyards Pinot Noir (Carneros) $22. 88 —*S.H. (10/1/2005)*

SILVER STAG

Silver Stag 2003 Parsley Family Estates Cabernet Sauvignon (Napa Valley) $75. Tasted alongside the wonderfully rich '02, this Cab is leaner and more tannic. It shows an astringent lockdown, although there's some good blackberry-cherry fruit down below. Lacks a bit of richness, but it's still elegant. From the southerly Tulocay area. **87** —*S.H. (10/1/2007)*

Silver Stag 2002 Parsley Family Estates Cabernet Sauvignon (Napa Valley) $75. From a great vintage, a tight, young Cab just beginning to hit its stride. Grown in the cooler Coombsville area, south of Stags Leap, the wine is bright and brisk in both acids and tannins that give it firm structure. But it's enormously rich in cassis and cherry fruit, and seems to have a good lifespan. Good now, and should live into the next decade. **92** —*S.H. (10/1/2007)*

SILVER STONE WINERY

Silver Stone Winery 2001 Cabernet Sauvignon (California) $9. 5 Best Buy —*S.H. (10/1/2004)*

Silver Stone Winery 2000 Cabernet Sauvignon (California) $9. 84 —*S.H. (5/1/2004)*

Silver Stone Winery 2003 Chardonnay (California) $9. 83 —*S.H. (10/1/2005)*

Silver Stone Winery 2000 Chardonnay (California) $9. 84 —*S.H. (2/1/2004)*

Silver Stone Winery 2003 Bien Nacido Vineyard Chardonnay (Santa Maria Valley) $25. 85 —*S.H. (10/1/2005)*

Silver Stone Winery 2001 Merlot (California) $9. 82 —*S.H. (2/1/2005)*

Silver Stone Winery 1999 Merlot (California) $9. 83 —*S.H. (5/1/2004)*

Silver Stone Winery 2004 Sauvignon Blanc (Arroyo Seco) $15. 83 —*S.H. (10/1/2005)*

Silver Stone Winery 2001 Shiraz (California) $9. 83 —*S.H. (6/1/2004)*

Silver Stone Winery 2003 Syrah (Paso Robles) $33. 83 *(9/1/2005)*

Silver Stone Winery 2002 Hall Ranch Syrah (Paso Robles) $33. 85 *(9/1/2005)*

SILVER THREAD

Silver Thread 1999 Chardonnay (Finger Lakes) $12. 85 —*J.C. (1/1/2004)*

Silver Thread 1999 Reserve Chardonnay (Finger Lakes) $17. 90 Editors' Choice —*J.C. (1/1/2004)*

Silver Thread 1999 Pinot Noir (Finger Lakes) $15. 86 —*J.C. (1/1/2004)*

Silver Thread 2002 Riesling (Finger Lakes) $13. 90 Best Buy —*J.C. (8/1/2003)*

SILVERADO

Silverado 2004 Cabernet Sauvignon (Napa Valley) $43. Silverado flies under the radar, quietly producing opulent and balanced Cabernets while others get their 15 minutes. The '04 is riper and softer than previous vintages, with jammy blackberry, cherry, blueberry and smoky oak flavors, but it maintains balance and elegance. Drink now. **88** —*S.H. (12/15/2007)*

Silverado 2003 Cabernet Sauvignon (Napa Valley) $40. 94 Editors' Choice —*S.H. (12/15/2006)*

Silverado 2002 Cabernet Sauvignon (Napa Valley) $40. 91 —*S.H. (3/1/2006)*

Silverado 2001 Cabernet Sauvignon (Napa Valley) $40. 87 —*S.H. (12/31/2004)*

Silverado 2000 Cabernet Sauvignon (Napa Valley) $35. 90 —*S.H. (5/1/2004)*

Silverado 1999 Cabernet Sauvignon (Napa Valley) $35.88 —*J.M. (11/15/2002)*

Silverado 1999 Cabernet Sauvignon (Stags Leap District) $65. 95 Editors' Choice —*S.H. (11/15/2002)*

Silverado 1998 Cabernet Sauvignon (Stags Leap District) $65. 87 —*J.M. (5/1/2002)*

Silverado 2002 Limited Cabernet Sauvignon (Napa Valley) $100. 91 Cellar Selection —*S.H. (3/1/2006)*

Silverado 2001 Limited Reserve Cabernet Sauvignon (Napa Valley) $100. 94 —*S.H. (12/31/2004)*

Silverado 1999 Limited Reserve Cabernet Sauvignon (Napa Valley) $95. 91 —*S.H. (11/15/2002)*

Silverado 2000 Single-Vineyard Selection Cabernet Sauvignon (Stags Leap District) $65. 90 —*S.H. (11/15/2004)*

Silverado 2004 Solo Cabernet Sauvignon (Stags Leap District) $79. This is 100% Cabernet, hence the name. It's direct in its appeal, with cassis and new oak flavors that are wrapped into significant tannins. It's a nice, rich wine, but not a great one. Despite every effort, the heat has taken its toll, making it overly soft and a little cooked. Drink now. **88** —*S.H. (12/15/2007)*

Silverado 2003 Solo Cabernet Sauvignon (Stags Leap District) $75. Silverado's estate 2003 Cab is a worthy followup to their '02. So classy, only Napa makes Cabs this balanced, rich and ageworthy, and this one from Stags Leap defines Tchelistcheff's description of an iron fist in a velvet glove. Great now, although young, and will age effortlessly for at least 10 years, probably longer. **93 Cellar Selection** —*S.H. (5/1/2007)*

Silverado 2002 Solo Cabernet Sauvignon (Stags Leap District) $75. 93 Cellar Selection —*S.H. (3/1/2006)*

Silverado 2006 Chardonnay (Napa County) $23. Soft, flat and simple, this Chard tastes like tangerine-flavored cola, with some oaky substance added for vanilla. **82** —*S.H. (12/31/2007)*

Silverado 2002 Chardonnay (Napa Valley) $20. 84 —*S.H. (11/15/2004)*

Silverado 2001 Chardonnay (Napa Valley) $20. 87 —*S.H. (6/1/2003)*

Silverado 2000 Chardonnay (Napa Valley) $20. 91 —*S.H. (12/15/2002)*

Silverado 1999 Chardonnay (Napa Valley) $20. 86 —*J.M. (5/1/2002)*

Silverado 1998 Chardonnay (Napa Valley) $19. 83 *(6/1/2000)*

Silverado 1997 Chardonnay (Napa Valley) $21. 90 —*S.H. (11/15/1999)*

Silverado 1997 Limited Reserve Chardonnay (Napa Valley) $40. 91 —*S.H. (11/15/1999)*

Silverado 2005 Vineburg Vineyard Chardonnay (Carneros) $30. Polished and elegant, but a little earthy, with a thyme and sage edge to the fruit, and a soft, oaky finish. Could use more brightness and fruity richness. **85** —*S.H. (5/1/2007)*

Silverado 2004 Vineburg Vineyard Chardonnay (Carneros) $35. 90 —*S.H. (4/1/2006)*

Silverado 2003 Merlot (Napa Valley) $28. A great steak wine. It's so supportive of food, with its sweet, supple tannins and crisp streak of acidity. The flavors are forward but controlled, a complex mèlange of cherries, cola, dark chocolate and smoky, caramelized oak. **91** —*S.H. (3/1/2007)*

Silverado 2002 Merlot (Napa Valley) $28. 83 —*S.H. (3/1/2006)*

Silverado 2000 Merlot (Napa Valley) $25. 90 *(5/1/2004)*

Silverado 1999 Merlot (Napa Valley) $25. 89 —*S.H. (8/1/2003)*

Silverado 1997 Sangiovese (Napa Valley) $20. 88 —*S.H. (12/15/1999)*

Silverado 2000 Sangiovese (Napa Valley) $16. 87 —*S.H. (11/15/2004)*

Silverado 1998 Sangiovese (Napa Valley) $18. 88 —*S.H. (5/1/2002)*

Silverado 2002 Sauvignon Blanc (Napa Valley) $16. 85 —*S.H. (12/1/2004)*

Silverado 2002 Sauvignon Blanc (Napa Valley) $16. 88 —*J.M. (9/1/2004)*

Silverado 2001 Sauvignon Blanc (Napa Valley) $14. 86 —*S.H. (3/1/2003)*

Silverado 2000 Sauvignon Blanc (Napa Valley) $14. 90 Best Buy —*J.M. (9/1/2002)*

Silverado 1998 Sauvignon Blanc (Napa Valley) $15. 89 —*S.H. (2/1/2000)*

Silverado 2006 Miller Ranch Vineyard Sauvignon Blanc (Napa Valley) $18. Not much going on in this flat, candy-sweet wine. It tastes like the liquid in canned peaches and pineapples. **82** —*S.H. (12/31/2007)*

Silverado 2005 Miller Ranch Vineyard Sauvignon Blanc (Napa Valley) $18. This wine is so high-toned in wildflowers you might think it was Alsatian, maybe Pinot Gris, a suspicion the high acidity also supports. But it's Sauvignon Blanc, with a rich core of yellow citrus fruit and papaya and an elegant minerality. This is a classy white wine at a good price. **88** —*S.H. (5/1/2007)*

SILVERSMITH

Silversmith 2000 Petite Sirah (Redwood Valley) $30. 80 *(4/1/2003)*

Silversmith 1998 Zinfandel (Redwood Valley) $25. 84 —*S.H. (5/1/2002)*

SIMI

Simi 2004 Cabernet Sauvignon (Alexander Valley) $26. Soft and polished in cherries, blackberries, cola, tea and oak flavors, this Cab finishes dry. It's got a good, crunchy bite of tannins to work against a grilled steak or chop. **86** —*S.H. (6/1/2007)*

Simi 2002 Cabernet Sauvignon (Alexander Valley) $25. 83 —*S.H. (3/1/2005)*

Simi 1996 Cabernet Sauvignon (Sonoma County) $24. 86 —*L.W. (12/31/1999)*

Simi 1996 Cabernet Sauvignon (Sonoma County) $22. 90 *—S.H. (2/1/2000)*

Simi 2003 Landslide Vineyard Cabernet Sauvignon (Alexander Valley) $33. 92 Editors' Choice *—S.H. (12/15/2006)*

Simi 2001 Landslide Vineyard Cabernet Sauvignon (Alexander Valley) $33. 95 *—S.H. (12/15/2004)*

Simi 2000 Landslide Vineyard Cabernet Sauvignon (Alexander Valley) $40. 90 *—S.H. (4/1/2004)*

Simi 2001 Reserve Cabernet Sauvignon (Alexander Valley) $60. 91 *—S.H. (12/1/2005)*

Simi 1999 Reserve Cabernet Sauvignon (Alexander Valley) $75. 94 Cellar Selection *—S.H. (12/31/2003)*

Simi 1998 Reserve Cabernet Sauvignon (Alexander Valley) $70. 93 *—S.H. (11/15/2002)*

Simi 1995 Reserve Cabernet Sauvignon (Sonoma County) $45. 93 *—L.W. (12/31/1999)*

Simi 2005 Chardonnay (Sonoma County) $17. 86 *—S.H. (12/15/2006)*

Simi 2003 Chardonnay (Sonoma County) $17. 85 *—S.H. (3/1/2005)*

Simi 2000 Chardonnay (Sonoma County) $17. 83 *—J.M. (5/1/2002)*

Simi 1999 Chardonnay (Sonoma County) $21. 88 *—J.M. (12/1/2001)*

Simi 1998 Chardonnay (Sonoma County) $17. 87 *(6/1/2000)*

Simi 1997 Chardonnay (Sonoma County) $19. 89 *—S.H. (10/1/1999)*

Simi 1998 Goldfields Vineyard Reserve Chardonnay (Russian River Valley) $30. 92 Editors' Choice *(7/1/2001)*

Simi 1999 Goldfields Vineyard Reserve Chardonnay (Russian River Valley) $30. 87 *—S.H. (2/1/2003)*

Simi 2004 Reserve Chardonnay (Russian River Valley) $25. 90 *—S.H. (12/15/2006)*

Simi 2003 Reserve Chardonnay (Russian River Valley) $25. 90 *—S.H. (12/1/2005)*

Simi 2002 Reserve Chardonnay (Russian River Valley) $25. 90 *—S.H. (3/1/2005)*

Simi 1998 Reserve Chardonnay (Russian River Valley) $35. 88 *—J.M. (12/1/2001)*

Simi 1996 Reserve Chardonnay (Russian River Valley) $29. 89 *—S.H. (10/1/1999)*

Simi 2002 Sonoma County Chardonnay (Sonoma County) $17. 85 *—S.H. (9/1/2004)*

Simi 2004 Merlot (Sonoma County) $23. Nice and smooth, this Merlot is for early drinking. It's as plump as can be in cherries, cocoa, cola and tobacco, with soft acids and even softer tannins. **85** *—S.H. (6/1/2007)*

Simi 2002 Merlot (Sonoma County) $20. 83 *—S.H. (3/1/2005)*

Simi 2001 Merlot (Alexander Valley) $20. 90 *—S.H. (4/1/2004)*

Simi 2006 Roseto Rosé Blend (Sonoma County) $15. Made from Syrah, this is a heavy, ripe wine. It has decent cherryskin flavors and is dry, but lacks the delicate charm that all rosés should have. **83** *—S.H. (7/1/2007)*

Simi 2006 Sauvignon Blanc (Sonoma County) $15. Easy and tasty, this is a nice everyday wine, with citrus, vanilla and grass flavors, a tangy bite of acid, and a dry, lemon-and-lime finish. **85** *—S.H. (9/1/2007)*

Simi 2005 Sauvignon Blanc (Sonoma County) $14. 85 *—S.H. (12/15/2006)*

Simi 2003 Sauvignon Blanc (Sonoma County) $14. 85 *—S.H. (12/15/2004)*

Simi 2002 Sauvignon Blanc (Sonoma County) $14. 84 *—S.H. (12/15/2003)*

Simi 2001 Sauvignon Blanc (Sonoma County) $14. 86 *—S.H. (3/1/2003)*

Simi 2000 Sauvignon Blanc (Sonoma County) $14. 88 *—J.M. (12/15/2001)*

Simi 1999 Sauvignon Blanc (Sonoma County) $15. 87 *—J.M. (11/15/2001)*

Simi 1997 Sauvignon Blanc (Sonoma County) $13. 84 *—S.H. (9/1/1999)*

Simi 1999 Reserve Sendal Sauvignon Blanc (Sonoma County) $20. 91 *—S.H. (9/1/2002)*

Simi 1998 Sendal Sauvignon Blanc (Sonoma County) $20. 90 *—J.M. (11/15/2001)*

Simi 1996 Sendal Sauvignon Blanc (Sonoma County) $20. 89 *—S.H. (9/1/1999)*

Simi 1999 Shiraz (Sonoma County) $20. 89 *(10/1/2001)*

Simi 1999 Reserve-Sendal White Blend (Sonoma County) $20. 91 Editors' Choice *—S.H. (9/1/2002)*

Simi 2005 Zinfandel (Sonoma County) $16. Made in a lighter style, but with Zin's distinctive wild berry, coffee and peppery spice flavors. The finish flirts with residual sweetness, then pulls back to finish dry and tannic. **85** *—S.H. (11/1/2007)*

Simi 1999 Zinfandel (Dry Creek Valley) $22. 87 *—D.T. (3/1/2002)*

SIMONE

Simone 2004 Reserve Red Table Wine Red Blend (Napa Valley) $75. The wine is a Bordeaux blend with some Zinfandel, and it's made in the cult Cabernet style. That means it's soft in both tannins and acids, with sweet, oak-influenced flavors of ripe blackberries, cherries, raspberries and cola, and a finish that's almost sweet. However, there's a certain one-dimensionality. **86** *—S.H. (11/1/2007)*

SINE QUA NON

Sine Qua Non 2002 Whisperin' E Rhône White Blend (California) $72. 93 *—S.H. (6/1/2005)*

Sine Qua Non 1998 Alban Vineyard Syrah (Central Coast) $NA. 87 *—S.H. (6/1/2005)*

Sine Qua Non 1998 E-Raised Syrah (California) $75. 93 Editors' Choice *(11/1/2001)*

Sine Qua Non 1997 Impostor McCoy Syrah (California) $59. 94 *(6/1/2003)*

Sine Qua Non 1999 The Marauder Syrah (California) $75. 91 *(7/1/2002)*

SINEANN

Sineann 2005 Champoux Vineyard Cabernet Franc (Columbia Valley (OR)) $48. Lovers of Cab Franc should track this wine down; it's a perfect evocation of the grape. Ripe purple plum flavors are annotated with spice and dust; the tannins are ripe and muscular; the wine sits very comfortably in the mouth. Hints of coffee grounds and tobacco liven up the finish, and the core of sweet fruit just keeps on coming. **93** *—P.G. (11/15/2007)*

Sineann 2004 Champoux Vineyard Cabernet Franc (Columbia Valley (WA)) $42. 93 Editors' Choice *—P.G. (4/1/2006)*

Sineann 2005 Cabernet Sauvignon (Columbia Valley (OR)) $36. Fermented to a plus-size 15.4% alcohol, this rare wine from one of Washington's oldest and best Cabernet vineyards shows what a gifted winemaker can do with great fruit. The play of flavors, mixing red and purple fruits, toasted nuts, mocha, caramel, bark and earth, is exceptional. The detail is extraordinary for a wine with such high alcohol. The acids and tannins are seamless and fine, and the flavors extend into an unusual finish that suggests menthol and eucalyptus —not generally a character found in Champoux fruit. All in all it's a wonderful voyage, and one of a handful of essential Washington wines. **95** *—P.G. (11/15/2007)*

Sineann 2004 Cabernet Sauvignon (Columbia Valley (WA)) $30. 92 *—P.G. (12/31/2006)*

Sineann 2005 Baby Poux Vineyard Cabernet Sauvignon (Columbia Valley (WA)) $42. If anyone can perfectly evoke the ripe style of California Cabernet along with the structure of Washington state fruit, it's Peter Rosback of Sineann – conveniently located in Oregon. Why this iconoclastic winemaker does not just move to Washington is hard to figure; he obviously loves the grapes and knows exactly what to do with them. This Cabernet Sauvignon, from a relatively young block at the Champoux vineyard, has some heat and chewy tannins. But it should age well, and the tightly wound herb and tobacco and stone flavors that are now constrained will ultimately come out. **90** *—P.G. (12/31/2007)*

Sineann 2004 Baby Poux Cabernet Sauvignon (Columbia Valley (WA)) $42. 92 *—P.G. (4/1/2006)*

Sineann 2003 Baby Poux Cabernet Sauvignon (Columbia Valley (WA)) $42. 92 Cellar Selection *—P.G. (4/1/2005)*

Sineann 2001 Baby Poux Vineyard Cabernet Sauvignon (Columbia Valley (WA)) $27. 90 *—P.G. (12/31/2003)*

Sineann 2000 Block One Cabernet Sauvignon (Columbia Valley (WA)) $60. 93 Cellar Selection *—P.G. (12/31/2002)*

Sineann 2005 Block One Champoux Vineyard Cabernet Sauvignon (Columbia Valley (OR)) $72. Fermented to a plus-size 15.4% alcohol, this rare wine from one of Washington's oldest and best Cabernet vineyards shows what a gifted winemaker can do with great fruit. The play of flavors, mixing red and purple fruits, toasted nuts, mocha, caramel, bark and earth, is exceptional. The detail is extraordinary for a wine with such high alcohol. The acids and tannins are seamless and fine, and the flavors extend into an unusual finish that suggests menthol and eucalyptus – not generally a character found in Champoux fruit. All in all it's a wonderful voyage, and one of a handful of essential Washington wines. **95 Cellar Selection** *—P.G. (12/31/2007)*

Sineann 2001 McDuffee Vineyard Cabernet Sauvignon (Columbia Valley (OR)) $30. 89 *—P.G. (12/1/2003)*

Sineann 2000 McDuffee Vineyard Cabernet Sauvignon (Columbia Valley (OR)) $27. 91 *—P.G. (12/31/2002)*

Sineann 2006 Chardonnay (Oregon) $20. This is rich and creamy, retaining enough acid and wet stone character to bolster the lush, soft fruit. Papaya and peach are the dominant fruit flavors, but there is much more to this leesy, textural bottling. It smothers the palate in stone fruits but is neither fat nor heavy; quite a winemaking feat. **90 Editors' Choice** —*P.G. (11/15/2007)*

Sineann 2005 Chardonnay (Oregon) $18. No oak! Just a crisp, fruit-driven Chardonnay that delivers excellent complexity. Nice integration of apple, pear and peach flavors, leading to a firm and full-bodied wine that penetrates and lingers. Who knew that oakless Chardonnay could be this good? It's even got a nice lemony lift from the acids. **91** —*P.G. (1/3/2007)*

Sineann 2006 Celilo Vineyard Gewürztraminer (Columbia Gorge) $18. This stands well apart from Sineann's Oak Ridge bottling, trading in the creaminess for a more stand-up, acidic, stony texture. Stone fruits hold down the center and are uplifted with refreshing acids and a streak of licorice. That herbal note really carries it right through the lingering finish. **90 Editors' Choice** —*P.G. (11/15/2007)*

Sineann 2005 Celilo Vineyard Gewürztraminer (Columbia Gorge) $18. Pure pear and mineral, this is the fruitiest of the winery's trio of Gewürz. Intense, clean and focused, it's a pleasure wine, forward and with a suggestion of sweetness. **88** —*P.G. (1/3/2007)*

Sineann 2002 Celilo Vineyard Gewürztraminer (Columbia Valley (WA)) $18. 90 —*P.G. (12/31/2003)*

Sineann 2001 Celilo Vineyard Gewürztraminer (Columbia Valley (WA)) $18. 93 Editors' Choice —*P.G. (12/31/2002)*

Sineann 2006 Oak Ridge Vineyard Gewürztraminer (Columbia Valley (OR)) $18. So rich it's almost fat, this unctuous Gewürztraminer mingles massive floral rose petal flavors with a lightly soapy, caramel core. The fruit is soft and round and mixes up a wide variety of tropical flavors, mixed in with the oily, floral flavors of the grape. Creamy and lush, it's like a vendange tardive, only dry. **89** —*P.G. (11/15/2007)*

Sineann 2005 Oak Ridge Vineyard Gewürztraminer (Columbia Gorge) $18. Fragrant and varietal, this showers you with its pungent and penetrating perfume, then wraps the palate in a cascade of pear, pineapple and grapefruit. Lush and round, ripe and rich, it's a mouthful and a noseful, quite beautifully rendered. **93** —*P.G. (1/3/2007)*

Sineann 2002 Reed & Reynolds Gewürztraminer (Willamette Valley) $18. 91 Editors' Choice —*P.G. (12/1/2003)*

Sineann 2005 Resonance Vineyard Gewürztraminer (Willamette Valley) $18. This is the spicy Gewürz, with a bouquet of ginger, clove and mint wrapped into clean pear and stone fruits. There is excellent lift and balance, and together these three wines cover all the bases. **91** —*P.G. (1/3/2007)*

USA

Sineann 2005 Merlot (Columbia Valley (WA)) $36. This outstanding wine is a blend of 60% Merlot from Washington's Champoux vineyard and 40% from the Hillside vineyard in eastern Oregon. Beautifully integrated fruit flavors suggest pie cherry and ripe strawberry, with dusty herbs scattered throughout. The herbal notes are not at all bitter or tannic, so the wine has an elegance to it, and shows nicely developed and integrated flavors, with the muscular power that winemaker Peter Rosback knows how to coax from his grapes. **92** —*P.G. (12/31/2007)*

Sineann 2005 Merlot (Columbia Valley (OR)) $36. An outstanding wine. Beautifully integrated fruit flavors suggest cherry pie and ripe strawberry, with dusty herbs scattered throughout. The herbal notes are not at all bitter or tannic, so the wine has an elegance to it, and shows nicely developed and integrated flavors. **92** —*P.G. (11/15/2007)*

Sineann 2000 Merlot (Columbia Valley (OR)) $27. 94 Editors' Choice —*P.G. (12/31/2002)*

Sineann 2003 Hillside Merlot (Columbia Valley (OR)) $30. 91 —*P.G. (4/1/2005)*

Sineann 2004 Hillside Vineyard Merlot (Columbia Valley (WA)) $30. 91 —*P.G. (4/1/2006)*

Sineann 2001 Hillside Vineyard Merlot (Columbia Valley (OR)) $36. 91 —*P.G. (12/1/2003)*

Sineann 2006 Pinot Gris (Oregon) $18. Clean and varietal, this has crisp fruit-driven flavors of apple and pear. The winemaking is spot on, and keeps it fresh and forward, with everything in balance. This would be a terrific starter wine with soft cheeses as the appetizer. **87** —*P.G. (11/15/2007)*

Sineann 2005 Pinot Gris (Oregon) $18. Clean, ripe and rich, as are all of these wines, this shows fleshy pear highlighted with fresh cream. It's full-bodied, balanced and lush, with nice hints of cinnamon spice peaking out of the finish. **91** —*P.G. (1/3/2007)*

Sineann 2002 Pinot Gris (Oregon) $15. 89 —*P.G. (12/1/2003)*

Sineann 2001 Pinot Gris (Oregon) $15. 91 Best Buy —*P.G. (12/31/2002)*

Sineann 2006 Pinot Noir (Oregon) $36. Relatively soft, deliciously sweet, and nicely spiced up with pipe tobacco, herb and mint, this appealing blend is ready to go. It's a wine you can only call pretty and it finishes with a lovely, chocolate nougat streak. The fruit is ripe but not jammy, and perfectly slotted in around the barrel flavors. **90** —*P.G. (11/15/2007)*

Sineann 2005 Pinot Noir (Oregon) $30. This Oregon bottling, Sineann's compendium of many of its left-over barrels from the single-vineyard Pinots, is quite tart, with flavors of rhubarb and strawberry. It's a clean, modest wine, nicely balanced and detailed. The finish shows good length and doesn't fade. **88** —*P.G. (1/3/2007)*

Sineann 2004 Pinot Noir (Oregon) $30. 92 Editors' Choice —*P.G. (5/1/2006)*

Sineann 2003 Pinot Noir (Oregon) $30. 92 —*P.G. (12/15/2004)*

Sineann 2001 Pinot Noir (Oregon) $30. 88 —*P.G. (12/1/2003)*

Sineann 2005 Able Vineyard Pinot Noir (Columbia Gorge) $36. The winemaker calls this "our most delicate, most feminine Pinot Noir" and indeed it is a very pretty wine, with sweet fruit that sits right between pie cherry and cherry candy flavors. It's light in the manner of a simple Volnay, and like many of Sineann's '05 Pinots, may develop surprising complexity if given some years in the cellar. **89** —*P.G. (1/3/2007)*

Sineann 2005 Covey Ridge Vineyard Pinot Noir (Willamette Valley) $42. A classic Oregon style in a moderate year, with herb and leaf, beet and sour cherry. There is an earthy kick to the tannins, and a sniff of pot bud that continues through the palate; not unpleasantly. **89** —*P.G. (1/3/2007)*

Sineann 2003 Covey Ridge Pinot Noir (Willamette Valley) $42. 91 —*P.G. (12/15/2004)*

Sineann 2001 Covey Ridge Pinot Noir (Oregon) $42. 88 —*P.G. (12/1/2003)*

Sineann 2006 Lachini Vineyard Pinot Noir (Willamette Valley) $42. The barrel aging is still the defining element in this wine, adding layers of meaty fat to what appears to be very young fruit. Bright cranberry and cherry notes are set in firm acids. Well-integrated hints of herb and spice, bursts of sweet berry and dry, tea-flavored tannins sail through the finish. **90** —*P.G. (11/15/2007)*

Sineann 2005 Lachini Vineyard Pinot Noir (Willamette Valley) $42. Much lighter in '05, the Lachini is nonetheless ripened to a comfortable weight for Pinot Noir, rather than pushed into superripe jamminess. Perfectly balanced, it shows elegant flavors of sweet berry and tea-like tannins. **91** —*P.G. (1/3/2007)*

Sineann 2004 Lachini Vineyard Pinot Noir (Willamette Valley) $42. 93 —*P.G. (5/1/2006)*

Sineann 2005 Maresh Vineyard Pinot Noir (Willamette Valley) $42. This is the most concentrated and structured wine among 10 Pinots tasted from Sineann in this vintage. Still quite young, tart and juicy, it mixes strawberry, raspberry and plummy fruits, supported by firm, compact tannins. The impression of sappy, juicy, fresh-picked fruit continues with a finishing lift of spice. Excellent focus and concentration. **92** —*P.G. (1/3/2007)*

Sineann 2005 Phelps Creek Vineyard Pinot Noir (Columbia Gorge) $42. Always a top vineyard designate, the '05 Phelps shows good ripeness, firm acids and a rather soft and broad midpalate showcasing flavors of strawberry preserves. It's lightly spicy, still quite youthful, super clean and resonant right on through an extended, refreshing finish. **91** —*P.G. (1/3/2007)*

Sineann 2006 Phelps Vineyard Pinot Noir (Columbia Gorge) $42. This is a pungent, spicy wine, that smells like a rich bouquet of dried herbs. It's almost Provençal in its essence and the way the herbs are worked into the mix of tart and tangy red fruits. It's got some heat, which fires up the finish, but the tannins have been nicely smoothed out. **89** —*P.G. (11/15/2007)*

Sineann 2004 Phelps Creek Vineyard Pinot Noir (Columbia Gorge) $42. 93 Editors' Choice —*P.G. (5/1/2006)*

Sineann 2003 Phelps Creek Vineyard Pinot Noir (Columbia Gorge) $42. 93 Editors' Choice —*P.G. (12/15/2004)*

Sineann 2001 Reed & Reynolds Pinot Noir (Willamette Valley) $42. 90 —*P.G. (12/1/2003)*

Sineann 2000 Reed & Reynolds Vineyard Pinot Noir (Oregon) $54. 88 —*P.G. (12/31/2002)*

Sineann 2005 Resonance Vineyard Pinot Noir (Willamette Valley) $48. Biodynamically farmed grapes seem to provide an extra layer of texture, as the layers of ripe strawberry and cherry fruit spread across the palate. It hints at toast, espresso and cola while retaining its supple grace. Perhaps a bit less rich than in years past, but what a wonderfully elegant expression of the grape. **91** —*P.G. (1/3/2007)*

Sineann 2004 Resonance Vineyard Pinot Noir (Willamette Valley) $48. 93 —*P.G. (5/1/2006)*

Sineann 2003 Resonance Vineyard Pinot Noir (Willamette Valley) $42. 93 —*P.G. (12/15/2004)*

Sineann 2005 Schindler Vineyard Pinot Noir (Willamette Valley) $42. This Eola Hills Pinot is the lightest of the lineup, almost to the point of seeming thin. It is also the most herbal, and carries a whiff of blood, like raw meat. Pretty, delicate berry flavored fruit is laced with cinnamon, then turns rough in the tannic finish. **87** —*P.G. (1/3/2007)*

Sineann 2004 Schindler Vineyard Pinot Noir (Willamette Valley) $42. 90 —*P.G. (5/1/2006)*

Sineann 2005 Whistling Ridge Vineyard Pinot Noir (Willamette Valley) $42. This vineyard really shines in this vintage, sending up concentrated aromas of blackberry and raspberry fruit. It leads into a ripe, plump and gently rounded midpalate, with Burgundian balance. Sweet plum and cherry fruit, hints of cocoa, no overt oak and pleasingly soft tannins all contribute to this graceful wine. **90** —*P.G. (1/3/2007)*

Sineann 2004 Whistling Ridge Pinot Noir (Willamette Valley) $42. 89 —*P.G. (5/1/2006)*

Sineann 2003 Whistling Ridge Vineyard Pinot Noir (Columbia Valley (OR)) $36. 91 Cellar Selection —*P.G. (12/15/2004)*

Sineann 2005 Wyeast Vineyard Pinot Noir (Columbia Gorge) $42. This interesting wine carries scents of raisin, soy, cocoa and chocolate, and tastes lightly of pine needle and spice. Quite tart, the tannins seem to stand out at this point, with residual, dry flavors of green tea. This will benefit from some more bottle time. **88** —*P.G. (1/3/2007)*

Sineann 2004 Wyeast Vineyard Pinot Noir (Columbia Gorge) $42. 90 —*P.G. (5/1/2006)*

Sineann 2003 Wyeast Vineyard Pinot Noir (Columbia Gorge) $42. 90 —*P.G. (12/15/2004)*

Sineann 2005 Red Blend (Columbia Valley (OR)) $24. This red wine named simply Blend is a mix of Columbia Valley grapes. This is bigger and spicier than Sineann's Red Table Wine, with more concentration. The acids and tannins are in a standoff at the moment, but throw a steak into the mix and you'll have a party. **87** —*P.G. (11/15/2007)*

Sineann 2005 Blend Red Blend (Columbia Valley (WA)) $24. This red wine named simply Blend is – guess what! – a mix of Columbia valley grapes, including Syrah, Petite Sirah, Cabernet Sauvignon, Merlot, Zinfandel and Grenache. This is bigger and spicier than Sineann's other blend, called simple Red Table Wine, and shows more concentration. The acids and tannins are in a stand-off at the moment, but throw a steak into the mix and you'll have a party. **87** —*P.G. (12/31/2007)*

Sineann 2005 Red Table Wine Red Blend (Oregon) $16. This is a quintessential café red, with a lively, brambly potpourri of fruits and plenty of acid to juice it up. It's fresh and forward and ready to go right now. Nothing too fancy, but plenty of ripe flavor for the price. **87** —*P.G. (11/15/2007)*

Sineann 2003 Red Table Wine Red Blend (Oregon) $12. 87 Best Buy —*P.G. (4/1/2005)*

Sineann 2004 Red Wine Red Blend (Columbia Valley (WA)) $24. 90 —*P.G. (4/1/2006)*

Sineann 2002 Covey Ridge Vineyard Riesling (Willamette Valley) $18. 91 Editors' Choice —*P.G. (12/1/2003)*

Sineann 2006 Medici Vineyard Riesling (Willamette Valley) $18. This is done in a style that walks the line between Kabinett and Spatlese; it's just 11% alcohol but the fruit sweetness is largely hidden behind the tangy natural acids. It's got the mixed fruit flavors of peach, apricot, citrus and even a hint of tropical, along with the edgy definition of citrus peel that gives it a crisp finish. **88** —*P.G. (11/15/2007)*

Sineann 2002 Medici Vineyard Riesling (Willamette Valley) $15. 92 Best Buy —*P.G. (12/1/2003)*

Sineann 2006 Sauvignon Blanc (Columbia Valley (OR)) $20. Believe it or not, these are 30-year-old vines, from the Smith-Cerne vineyard, a real rarity here in the Pacific Northwest. The quality shines through; winemaker Peter Rosback has taken this fruit and shaken out every nuance and subtlety it possesses. It has the elegance, texture and complexity of Sancerre, with less of the rock. The herbaceous notes are restrained and the fruit is immaculate, but what is really impressive is the length of this wine, which seems as if it could age for a decade or more. **90 Editors' Choice** —*P.G. (11/15/2007)*

Sineann 2005 Kingfish Cuvée Sauvignon Blanc (Columbia Valley (OR)) $18. This is an unusual straw gold, a darker, rounder, riper version of Sauvignon Blanc than we are accustomed to seeing from the Northwest. Scented with honey, mint and vanilla tea, it is quite the opposite of the grassy, stony style of SB that I generally admire. But the winemaking is so polished, the wine so supple, toasty and flavorful, that it blows away all my objections. **90** —*P.G. (1/3/2007)*

Sineann 2005 Old Vine Zinfandel (Columbia Valley (WA)) $36. 93 —*P.G. (12/31/2006)*

Sineann 2004 Old Vine Zinfandel (Columbia Valley (OR)) $36. 93 —*P.G. (5/1/2006)*

Sineann 2003 Old Vine Zinfandel (Columbia Valley (OR)) $36. 93 —*P.G. (12/15/2004)*

Sineann 2000 Old Vine Zinfandel (Columbia Valley (OR)) $36. 92 —*P.G. (12/31/2002)*

Sineann 2005 The Pines Zinfandel (Columbia Valley (WA)) $27. 92 —*P.G. (12/31/2006)*

Sineann 2003 The Pines Zinfandel (Columbia Valley (OR)) $27. 90 —*P.G. (4/1/2005)*

SINGLE LEAF

Single Leaf 1999 Cabernet Franc (El Dorado) $16. 82 —*S.H. (9/1/2002)*

Single Leaf 1999 Zinfandel (El Dorado) $16. 85 —*S.H. (11/1/2002)*

Single Leaf NV Pammie's Cuvée Zinfandel (El Dorado County) $10. 82 —*S.H. (3/1/2004)*

SIQUEIRA

Siqueira 2002 Cabernet Sauvignon (Stags Leap District) $42. 92 —*S.H. (5/1/2005)*

Siqueira 2005 Chardonnay (Clarksburg) $14. Clarksburg is the Sacramento Delta region that's located in the hot inland, but benefits from fogs and breezes blowing in from the Golden Gate. This wine shows fresh acids that boost and cleanse the ripe tropical fruit, peach and apricot flavors. **86** —*S.H. (2/1/2007)*

SISKIYOU VINEYARDS

Siskiyou Vineyards 2000 La Cave Rouge Bordeaux Blend (Oregon) $15. 86 —*P.G. (8/1/2002)*

Siskiyou Vineyards 1998 Pinot Noir (Willamette Valley) $15. 86 —*M.S. (12/1/2000)*

Siskiyou Vineyards 1999 La Cave Blanche White Blend (Oregon) $10. 86 —*P.G. (8/1/2002)*

SIX PRONG

Six Prong 2001 Red Table Wine Red Blend (Columbia Valley (WA)) $10. 87 —*P.G. (1/1/2004)*

Six Prong 2003 Red Wine Red Blend (Columbia Valley (WA)) $13. 88 Best Buy —*P.G. (11/15/2005)*

SIX SIGMA

Six Sigma 2005 Sauvignon Blanc (Lake County) $20. 87 —*S.H. (12/31/2006)*

Six Sigma 2006 Michael's Vineyard Sauvignon Blanc (Lake County) $28. Lots of new French oak barrel fermentation and lees stirring went into the making of this wine, and it shows the yeasty richness and creamy texture of that expensive handling. Yet the underlying wine is just very good. It has very bright acidity, with slightly sweet flavors of spearmint chewing gum, lemons and limes. **87** —*S.H. (12/31/2007)*

Six Sigma 2006 Rooster Vineyard Sauvignon Blanc (Lake County) $20. Lots to like in this dry, crisp Sauvignon Blanc. It shows ripe grapefruit, peach, lemongrass, peppery spice and gooseberry flavors, but those sensitive to aggressively pungent scents will be turned off. **85** —*S.H. (12/31/2007)*

SJOEBLOM WINERY

Sjoeblom Winery 2001 Chauvignon Reserve Blanc de Noirs Cabernet Sauvignon (Napa Valley) $39. 89 —*S.H. (6/1/2006)*

Sjoeblom Winery 2000 Chauvignon Sparkling Rosé Cabernet Sauvignon (Napa Valley) $39. 90 —*J.M. (12/1/2003)*

SKETCHBOOK

Sketchbook 2000 Mendocino Collection Cabernet Sauvignon (Mendocino) $22. 87 —*S.H. (10/1/2003)*

Sketchbook 1997 Syrah (Mendocino) $20. 84 *(10/1/2001)*

Sketchbook 2001 Estate Syrah (Mendocino) $23. 84 —*S.H. (6/1/2004)*

SKEWIS

Skewis 2001 Bush Vineyard Pinot Noir (Russian River Valley) $42. A89 —*S.H. (12/15/2004)*

Skewis 2001 Demuth Vineyard Pinot Noir (Anderson Valley) $35. 86 —*S.H. (12/15/2004)*

Skewis 2001 Montgomery Vineyard Pinot Noir (Russian River Valley) $45. 90 —*S.H. (12/15/2004)*

Skewis 2001 Salzgeber Vineyard Pinot Noir (Russian River Valley) $40. 90 —*S.H. (12/15/2004)*

SKYHAWK LANE

Skyhawk Lane 2004 Three Cane Blend Bordeaux Blend (San Luis Obispo County) $46. Cabernet Sauvignon, Merlot and Cab Franc comprise the blend. The wine is dry and very forward in fruit, with black cherry, raspberry, and smoky, oaky vanilla flavors. It's delicious and a little one-dimensional, so drink now. **87** —*S.H. (9/1/2007)*

Skyhawk Lane 2004 Parrish Vineyards Cabernet Sauvignon (Paso Robles) $44. It's so rewarding to find a Cabernet this balanced from Paso, where ripeness is easy but elegance is hard. With a wealth of blackberry and cherry pie filling and mocha flavors finished with a coating of spicy oak, it's soft and gentle. **91** —*S.H. (4/1/2007)*

Skyhawk Lane 2004 Red Fusion Red Blend (San Luis Obispo County) $48. This is a blend of Zin, Syrah, Cab Sauvignon and Franc. It's simple, rustic and slightly sweet. This is a ridiculously high price to pay for what you get. **83** —*S.H. (4/1/2007)*

Skyhawk Lane 2004 Alamo Creek Vineyard Syrah (San Luis Obispo County) $44. I like the ripeness of the fruit, and the way the blackberry cola, coffee and spice flavors play against an edge of leathery, funky grilled beef. The tannins are powerful, so decant and drink it with rich, fatty meats and cheeses. **87** —*S.H. (4/1/2007)*

SKYLIGHT CELLARS

Skylight Cellars 2003 Syrah (Walla Walla (WA)) $26. Well done, tightly wound, showing tart berry fruit, racy acids, hints of toast, good length and a balanced, lightly spiced finish. A very promising debut. **88** —*P.G. (3/1/2007)*

SKYLITE

Skylite 2005 Syrah (Columbia Valley (WA)) $32. A blend of Minnick and Ash Hollow grapes, this is a punchy, high-toned take on Syrah. Particularly attractive are the bright raspberry flavors, peppered with, well, pepper! It's got the kind of verve that you find in a simple Grenache, and finishes light and tangy. **86** —*P.G. (12/31/2007)*

SLAUGHTERHOUSE CELLARS

Slaughterhouse Cellars 2004 Cabernet Sauvignon (Rutherford) $70. New smoky oak stars in this flashy young Cab. With 70% new French oak and 21 months of barrel aging, maybe there's a bit too much vanilla caramel, but it marries well with the enormously rich, ripe cherry-cassis fruit flavors. **90** —*S.H. (12/15/2007)*

Slaughterhouse Cellars 2003 Cabernet Sauvignon (Rutherford) $60. 91 Cellar Selection —*S.H. (12/15/2006)*

Slaughterhouse Cellars 2002 Cabernet Sauvignon (Rutherford) $60. 90 —*S.H. (12/15/2005)*

SLEIGHT OF HAND WINERY

Sleight of Hand Winery 2006 The Magician Gewürztraminer (Columbia Valley (WA)) $16. Though 100% Gewürz, the package plays down the grape in favor of catchy graphics and a hip moniker. It's a tasting-room style, rich and creamy, and a hint of sugar adds some roundness. **88** —*P.G. (12/1/2007)*

Sleight of Hand Winery NV Red Blend (Columbia Valley (WA)) $18. A non-vintage blend of 42% Cabernet Franc, 29% Cabernet Sauvignon and 29% Sangiovese, this is built upon strong, herbal tannins. The addition of the Sangiovese brings in fat, buttery oak flavors that linger through the finish. **87** —*P.G. (12/1/2007)*

Sleight of Hand Winery 2005 The Archimage Red Blend (Columbia Valley (WA)) $40. Toasty and tannic, it's a chewy, oaky wine with strong flavors of coffee, caramel and toast. The oak is the main flavor, but it's undeniably appealing. The fruit, spicy and tannic, features a green tea edge. **88** —*P.G. (12/1/2007)*

SLOAN

Sloan 2002 Red Wine Cabernet Blend (Rutherford) $245. 100 —*S.H. (9/1/2006)*

SMASHED GRAPES

Smashed Grapes 2004 Cabernet Sauvignon (California) $8. A bit on the rough and rustic side, but the wine is dry and balanced, and the fruit is pretty nice. It's a fair price for a full-bodied Cab, if that's what you're looking for. **83** —*S.H. (2/1/2007)*

Smashed Grapes 2004 Chardonnay (California) $8. There's a vegetal aroma and flavor throughout, like canned asparagus, that suggests a lack of ripeness, and detracts from the otherwise okay Chardonnay character of this dry wine. **82** —*S.H. (2/1/2007)*

Smashed Grapes 2004 Merlot (California) $8. Bone dry, crisp, a little earthy, with berry-cherry and coffee flavors, this is a good, sound everyday red wine, and this is a fair price. A juicy steak will pair nicely. **84 Best Buy** —*S.H. (2/1/2007)*

Smashed Grapes 2005 Pinot Grigio (California) $8. Thank goodness for good, cheap wines like this PG. It's completely dry, crisp in acidity and palate-stimulating in citrus and jasmine flavors, with a spicy finish. Try with Thai food. **84 Best Buy** —*S.H. (2/1/2007)*

Smashed Grapes 2004 Pinot Grigio (California) $10. 85 *(2/1/2006)*

SMASNE CELLARS

Smasne Cellars 2004 Estate Cabernet Sauvignon (Yakima Valley) $42. In keeping with their other estate wines, this pure, 100% varietal Cabernet from the Smasne Vineyard offers unblended and crisply defined varietal character. It's got plenty of cassis and cranberry fruit, compact and dense, and it tastes quite young still. The tannins are ripe and well-managed, but this is a wine that needs decanting or time in the bottle to fill out and show what's really in there. **90 Cellar Selection** —*P.G. (12/31/2007)*

Smasne Cellars 2003 Bunk House Red Blend (Columbia Valley (WA)) $50. Despite the extra bottle age, it's a very youthful, dense wine. The Malbec is battened down with spicy purple fruit flavors and compact tannins. The balance is acid-driven, and the presence of new oak is muted. Will the tannins soften before the fruit fades? It's worth socking a bottle or two away to find out. **90 Cellar Selection** —*P.G. (12/31/2007)*

Smasne Cellars 2005 Dry Riesling (Yakima Valley) $22. Scents of lemon polish, jasmine and honey-soaked apricots start this wine off with a surprise. It's rich, dense, concentrated and lush, almost fat, but balanced and packed with nuances. The finish carries on with honey, toasted almonds, flowers and tea. For a dry Riesling it shows remarkable concentration and lush fruit flavors. **91** —*P.G. (12/1/2007)*

Smasne Cellars 2005 Estate Syrah (Yakima Valley) $35. Well made, this is a sappy, snappy take on Syrah, with vivid wild berry fruit and lively acids. It snaps into focus right away, then slowly softens as it weaves through the palate, with mixed berries, rhubarb, plum and hints of citrus. The finish lasts a full minute, adding notes of black pepper as it fades. This is beautifully rendered and not overblown in any way, with the alcohol at just 13.5%. **91** —*P.G. (12/31/2007)*

SMITH & HOOK

Smith & Hook 2005 Grand Reserve Cabernet Blend (Central Coast) $25. Smith & Hook has tried hard to perfect their Cab, transferring fruit sourcing from Monterey to Paso Robles. As a result, the wines are riper, as evidenced by this fruity young Cab. The cherry and blackberry flavors are balanced by firm tannins and crisp acids, making it a versatile wine at the table. **88** —*S.H. (12/15/2007)*

Smith & Hook 1996 Baroness Reserve Cabernet Sauvignon (Santa Lucia Highlands) $40. 84 —*L.W. (12/31/1999)*

Smith & Hook 2003 Grand Reserve Cabernet Sauvignon (Santa Lucia Highlands) $25. 87 —*S.H. (11/1/2006)*

Smith & Hook 2002 Grand Reserve Cabernet Sauvignon (Santa Lucia Highlands) $25. 88 —*S.H. (6/1/2005)*

Smith & Hook 2001 Grande Reserve Cabernet Sauvignon (Santa Lucia Highlands) $20. 89 —*S.H. (10/3/2004)*

Smith & Hook 1997 Baroness Reserve Masterpiece E Chardonnay (Monterey County) $25. 85 —*L.H. (12/31/1999)*

SMITH WOOTON

Smith Wooton 1999 Cabernet Franc (Napa Valley) $40. 84 —*S.H. (12/1/2002)*

Smith Wooton 2002 Gallagher's Vineyard Cabernet Franc (Napa Valley) $32. 91 —*S.H. (11/1/2005)*

Smith Wooton 2001 Gallagher's Vineyard Cabernet Franc (Napa Valley) $32. 84 —*S.H. (7/1/2005)*

Smith Wooton 2003 Tanner Brothers Vineyard Syrah (Calaveras County) $28. 88 *(9/1/2005)*

SMITH-MADRONE

Smith-Madrone 2001 Cabernet Sauvignon (Napa Valley) $35. 89 —*S.H. (8/1/2005)*

Smith-Madrone 1997 Cabernet Sauvignon (Napa Valley) $35. 92 Editors' Choice —*S.H. (12/1/2001)*

Smith-Madrone 2002 Chardonnay (Napa Valley) $25. 88 —*S.H. (8/1/2005)*

Smith-Madrone 2000 Chardonnay (Napa Valley) $25. 91 —*S.H. (2/1/2003)*

Smith-Madrone 2006 Riesling (Spring Mountain) $22. Doesn't say "dry" on the label, like so many others do, but it really is basically dry, which allows the palate to savor the pure fruit of the grape and the beautifully crisp acids. This really is one of the most balanced Rieslings in California, with a slate and petrol edge to the green apple, pineapple, nectarine and wildflower flavors. If you like aging your whites, it should effortlessly glide through the next 10 years in a cool cellar. **92 Editors' Choice** —*S.H. (9/1/2007)*

Smith-Madrone 2001 Riesling (Napa Valley) $17. 90 —*S.H. (8/1/2003)*

Smith-Madrone 1999 Riesling (Napa Valley) $17. 87 —*S.H. (12/1/2001)*

SMOKING LOON

Smoking Loon 2005 Cabernet Sauvignon (California) $9. Offers plenty of real Cabernet character at an everyday price. The ripe, full-bodied flavors of blackberries, cherries, licorice and cocoa have a jammy edge. Finishes with a chocolate fudge richness. **84** —*S.H. (2/1/2007)*

Smoking Loon 2003 Cabernet Sauvignon (California) $9. 85 Best Buy —*S.H. (7/1/2005)*

Smoking Loon 2002 Cabernet Sauvignon (California) $9. 83 —*S.H. (5/1/2005)*

Smoking Loon 2005 Chardonnay (California) $9. 84 —*S.H. (12/1/2006)*

Smoking Loon 2003 Chardonnay (California) $9. 86 Best Buy —*S.H. (3/1/2005)*

Smoking Loon 2002 Chardonnay (California) $9. 85 —*S.H. (12/31/2003)*

Smoking Loon 2005 Merlot (California) $9. With its mint-accented cherry and blackberry flavors and raw tannins, this is a rustic sort of Merlot. It has the sharp, edgy mouthfeel of a country-style wine, but it's clean and fruity, and will do fine with anything that calls for a dry, full-bodied red. **84** —*S.H. (8/1/2007)*

Smoking Loon 2004 Merlot (California) $9. 86 Best Buy —*S.H. (5/1/2006)*

Smoking Loon 2002 Merlot (California) $9. 84 —*S.H. (5/1/2005)*

Smoking Loon 2001 Merlot (California) $10. 84 —*S.H. (12/1/2003)*

Smoking Loon 2005 Pinot Grigio (California) $9. There's a ton of fruity flavor packed into this inexpensive wine. Clean and crisp in acids, it bursts with ripe juicy peach, lime, kiwi, green apple, fig, spicy melon, papaya and honeysuckle flavors that finish with a honeyed richness. And that's just for starters. **85 Best Buy** —*S.H. (2/1/2007)*

Smoking Loon 2004 Pinot Noir (California) $9. 86 Best Buy —*S.H. (12/1/2005)*

Smoking Loon 2003 Pinot Noir (California) $9. 84 —*S.H. (12/15/2004)*

Smoking Loon 2002 Pinot Noir (California) $9. 84 Best Buy *(11/1/2004)*

Smoking Loon 2001 Pinot Noir (California) $9. 84 —*S.H. (7/1/2003)*

Smoking Loon 2005 Syrah (California) $9. On the sharp, bitter side, and despite a heavy coat of sweet toast, it struggles. The cherry flavors finish dry. **82** —*S.H. (8/1/2007)*

Smoking Loon 2004 Syrah (California) $9. 85 —*S.H. (5/1/2006)*

Smoking Loon 2003 Syrah (California) $9. 86 Best Buy *(9/1/2005)*

Smoking Loon 2002 Syrah (California) $9. 83 —*S.H. (6/1/2005)*

Smoking Loon 2005 Viognier (California) $9. 85 Best Buy —*S.H. (11/15/2006)*

Smoking Loon 2004 Viognier (California) $9. 84 —*S.H. (10/1/2005)*

Smoking Loon 2003 Viognier (California) $9. 86 Best Buy —*S.H. (10/1/2004)*

Smoking Loon 2000 Viognier (California) $10. 82 —*J.M. (12/15/2002)*

Smoking Loon 2005 Zinfandel (California) $9. This is the first Zin I can remember from the Loon. It's kind of on the rustic side, but rich in slightly sweet cherry and vanilla flavors with a drop of raspberry liqueur essence. High acidity makes it finish clean and bright. **84** —*S.H. (8/1/2007)*

SNAKE RIVER

Snake River 2002 Reserve Bordeaux Blend (Idaho) $26. This is Snake River's first reserve release and though it's a tad tannic now, it should age well. Spice, cherry, blackcurrant and violet on the nose unfold into flavors of meaty plum and oak. The Cabernet adds heft while Merlot, Cabernet Franc and Malbec add further character and color. Not terribly complex but an enjoyable wine. **83** —*S.K. (2/1/2007)*

Snake River 2002 Arena Valley Vineyard Cabernet Sauvignon (Idaho) $17. Bold and dark, this Cabernet from Idaho producer Snake River Winery has elements of black cherry, herbs and vanilla on the nose and on the palate and is smooth without being flabby. A bold-flavored wine with ample tannins and body mean this could age a little, too. **85** —*S.K. (2/1/2007)*

Snake River 2004 Arena Valley Vineyard Chardonnay (Idaho) $11. This will appeal to fans of lean and unoaked whites, but for a Chardonnay, it lacks dimension and balance. Lemon dominates the palate and the finish is fleeting. It's refreshing, though, making it an easy hot weather choice. **83** —*S.K. (7/1/2007)*

Snake River 2005 Arena Valley Vineyard White Riesling (Idaho) $10. A heavy dose of honey and apricots is the character of this 100% estate grown Riesling. On the palate, it's thick and semisweet, but the finish is relatively clean and long. A good choice for fans of the sweeter whites. **83** —*S.K. (7/1/2007)*

SNOB HILL WINERY

Snob Hill Winery 2002 Le Snoot Cabernet Sauvignon (North Coast) $11. 84 —*S.H. (12/31/2004)*

Snob Hill Winery 2002 Le Snoot Chardonnay (North Coast) $11. 84 —*S.H. (12/31/2004)*

Snob Hill Winery 2002 Merlot (North Coast) $11. 84 —*S.H. (12/31/2004)*

SNOQUALMIE

Snoqualmie 2005 Cabernet Sauvignon (Columbia Valley (WA)) $15. This delicious wine, made entirely from Cab Sauvignon grapes, displays clear varietal character and balance. The tart cherry fruit has been ripened appropriately, retaining some desirable herb and forest floor character. Further oak aging adds a bit more complexity. All in all, you get a sense that a talented hand is at the winemaking helm and getting the very most from these grapes. **86** —*P.G. (12/31/2007)*

Snoqualmie 2004 Reserve Cabernet Sauvignon (Columbia Valley (WA)) $23. This is showing an extraordinary amount of toasty oak in the nose, and once in the mouth it seems as if the oak and toast flavors overwhelm everything else. The fruit is very much on the light side, and can't begin to stand up to all the toast and butterscotch that is being tossed around. It's not bad, but it has not yet found its balance, and finishes with some lightly stemmy tannins. **84** —*P.G. (12/31/2007)*

Snoqualmie 2003 Reserve Cabernet Sauvignon (Columbia Valley (WA)) $23. 87 —*P.G. (8/1/2006)*

Snoqualmie 2002 Reserve Cabernet Sauvignon (Columbia Valley (WA)) $23. 87 —*P.G. (6/1/2005)*

Snoqualmie 2001 Reserve Cabernet Sauvignon (Columbia Valley (WA)) $23. 89 —*P.G. (5/1/2004)*

Snoqualmie 1997 Reserve Cabernet Sauvignon (Columbia Valley (WA)) $21. 86 —*P.G. (9/1/2000)*

Snoqualmie 2004 Rosebud Vineyard Cabernet Sauvignon (Columbia Valley (WA)) $15. 88 Best Buy —*P.G. (11/15/2006)*

Snoqualmie 2002 Rosebud Vineyard Cabernet Sauvignon (Columbia Valley (WA)) $15. 85 —*P.G. (12/15/2005)*

Snoqualmie 2001 Rosebud Vineyard Cabernet Sauvignon (Columbia Valley (WA)) $15. 88 Best Buy —*P.G. (12/15/2004)*

Snoqualmie 1999 Cabernet Sauvignon-Merlot (Columbia Valley (WA)) $11. 86 —*P.G. (9/1/2002)*

Snoqualmie 2003 Whistle Stop Red Cabernet Sauvignon-Merlot (Columbia Valley (WA)) $11. A blend of 70% Cabernet and 30% Merlot. It's got some muscle and depth along with the ripe, solid fruit flavors of pie cherry and black currant. The alcohol is just 13.5% and the varietal blend just perfect, offering tart, spicy fruit lightly speckled with dried herb, and finished with streaks of baker's chocolate. The wine chugs along gracefully without letup, a pleasure with food or without. **87 Best Buy** —*P.G. (5/1/2007)*

Snoqualmie 2006 Chardonnay (Columbia Valley (WA)) $11. The blend includes 5% Viognier, an interesting choice that brings in floral scents and provides counterweight to the ramped up oaky seasonings. It's a curious mix that doesn't quite knit together, but makes for a more complex wine than you would expect. There's some sweet spice in the finish. **87 Best Buy** —*P.G. (12/1/2007)*

Snoqualmie 2001 Chardonnay (Columbia Valley (WA)) $11. 88 Best Buy —*P.G. (5/1/2004)*

Snoqualmie 2000 Chardonnay (Columbia Valley (WA)) $11. 87 Best Buy —*P.G. (7/1/2002)*

Snoqualmie 1998 Chardonnay (Columbia Valley (WA)) $11. 85 —*P.G. (6/1/2000)*

Snoqualmie 2004 Chenin Blanc (Columbia Valley (WA)) $7. 86 Best Buy —*P.G. (6/1/2006)*

Snoqualmie 2001 Chenin Blanc (Columbia Valley (WA)) $7. 86 Best Buy —*M.S. (6/1/2003)*

Snoqualmie 2000 Chenin Blanc (Columbia Valley (WA)) $7. 84 —*S.H. (6/1/2002)*

Snoqualmie 2006 'Nearly Naked' Gewürztraminer (Columbia Valley (WA)) $11. From organically grown grapes, this off-dry Gewurztraminer shows a nice mix of orange blossom and varietal spice. Fruity and forward in the mouth, it carries through with ripe, sweet flavors of orange and lemon candy, with a hint of ginger spice. **87 Best Buy** —*P.G. (12/1/2007)*

Snoqualmie 2004 Merlot (Columbia Valley (WA)) $11. Sweet cherry and raspberry fruit with an herbal edge kicks off this rather tannic young wine. It shows exceptional depth and detail for a wine in this price range—baking chocolate, spicy clove, herb and smoke. Complex, acidic and well balanced, it is a very fine example of winemaker Joy Anderson's deft, light touch. **89 Best Buy** —*P.G. (5/1/2007)*

Snoqualmie 2003 Merlot (Columbia Valley (WA)) $11. 86 —*P.G. (12/31/2006)*

Snoqualmie 2003 Reserve Merlot (Columbia Valley (WA)) $23. Pure and classy, this is a bowl of cherries and raspberries in a wine glass. It's a bright, tart, vivid and delightful wine built solidly upon a round, sweet core of pretty fruit. Great balance and pleasing texture, with a nice citrus kiss on the finish. **90** —*P.G. (5/1/2007)*

Snoqualmie 2002 Reserve Merlot (Columbia Valley (WA)) $23. 87 —*P.G. (6/1/2005)*

Snoqualmie 2001 Reserve Merlot (Columbia Valley (WA)) $23. 89 —*P.G. (5/1/2004)*

Snoqualmie 2000 Reserve Merlot (Columbia Valley (WA)) $23. 88 —*P.G. (9/1/2004)*

Snoqualmie 1999 Reserve Merlot (Columbia Valley (WA)) $23. 86 —*P.G. (6/1/2002)*

Snoqualmie 1997 Reserve Merlot (Columbia Valley (WA)) $21. 84 —*P.G. (9/1/2000)*

Snoqualmie 2006 Naked Riesling (Columbia Valley (WA)) $11. A lovely effort, with round, spicy fruit and a pleasing lushness in the midpalate. Lemon tea and hints of sweet honey are backed with enough acid to give it plenty of grip. All in all, it's a very good Washington imitation of a Spatlëse. **89 Best Buy** —*P.G. (12/1/2007)*

Snoqualmie 2006 Winemaker's Select Riesling (Columbia Valley (WA)) $8. With full ripeness, density and concentration, this keeps its superb balance at just 10.8% alcohol and 5% residual sugar. The dynamic tension plays out beautifully, and doesn't veer into any sort of sugary slackness. This has the sort of weight and complexity you would expect in a $30 wine. **91 Best Buy** —*P.G. (12/1/2007)*

Snoqualmie 2005 Winemaker's Select Riesling (Columbia Valley (WA)) $11. 88 —*P.G. (8/1/2006)*

Snoqualmie 2004 Winemaker's Select Riesling (Columbia Valley (WA)) $7. 88 Best Buy —*P.G. (11/15/2005)*

Snoqualmie 2006 Sauvignon Blanc (Columbia Valley (WA)) $7. Though simple, this is a fresh, crisp, lightly herbal wine, with fruit flavors emphasizing melon and citrus. **85** —*P.G. (12/1/2007)*

Snoqualmie 2004 Sauvignon Blanc (Columbia Valley (WA)) $7. 87 Best Buy —*P.G. (6/1/2006)*

Snoqualmie 2001 Sauvignon Blanc (Columbia Valley (WA)) $7. 81 —*M.S. (6/1/2003)*

Snoqualmie 1998 Blanc Sémillon (Columbia Valley (WA)) $7. 83 —*P.G. (6/1/2000)*

Snoqualmie 2003 Syrah (Columbia Valley (WA)) $8. 88 Best Buy —*P.G. (11/15/2006)*

Snoqualmie 2001 Syrah (Columbia Valley (WA)) $11. 88 Best Buy —*P.G. (7/1/2004)*

Snoqualmie 2000 Syrah (Columbia Valley (WA)) $11. 88 —*P.G. (9/1/2002)*

Snoqualmie 1999 Syrah (Columbia Valley (WA)) $11 87 Best Buy —*P.G. (10/1/2001)*

Snoqualmie 2004 Reserve Syrah (Columbia Valley (WA)) $23. The 2004 vintage was a rough ride in Washington, and Ste. Michelle generously shared a lot of fruit from their vineyards that escaped the freeze. One senses that Snoqualmie drew the short straw, as these 2004 reserve wines are well below the quality that this outstanding value producer has shown in the past. This is not reserve quality by any stretch of the imagination; it's light, watery and vegetal. **83** —*P.G. (12/31/2007)*

Snoqualmie 2002 Reserve Syrah (Columbia Valley (WA)) $23. 91 Editors' Choice —*P.G. (6/1/2005)*

Snoqualmie 2001 Reserve Syrah (Columbia Valley (WA)) $23. 90 Editors' Choice —*P.G. (5/1/2004)*

SNOSRAP

Snosrap 2001 Cyrano Red Table Wine Bordeaux Blend (Carmel Valley) $24. 83 —*S.H. (8/1/2004)*

SNOWDEN

Snowden 2001 Cabernet Sauvignon (Napa Valley) $60. 91 —*J.M. (12/31/2004)*

Snowden 1998 Cabernet Sauvignon (Napa Valley) $60. 92 —*J.M. (11/15/2002)*

Snowden 2002 Estate Cabernet Sauvignon (Napa Valley) $50. 87 —*S.H. (3/1/2006)*

Snowden 2002 Lost Vineyard Cabernet Sauvignon (Napa Valley) $30. 87 —*S.H. (3/1/2006)*

Snowden 1997 Lost Vineyard Cabernet Sauvignon (Napa Valley) $30. 88 *(11/1/2000)*

SNOWS LAKE

Snows Lake 2004 Two Bordeaux Blend (Red Hills Lake County) $38. This is very, very tannic, making the mouthfeel astringent and sandpapery. That's the wine's only fault, because the Bordeaux-style fruit is gorgeous and so is acidity. Tannin management is the winemaker's challenge. **86** —*S.H. (11/1/2007)*

Snows Lake 2004 One Cabernet Sauvignon (Red Hills Lake County) $38. An admirable first effort from this winery on the high slopes of Lake County's Mount Konocti, but the winemaker has to figure out a way to rein in those tannins. The underlying wine is potentially great, with Bordeaux-like cassis, cedar, pencil lead and smoky oak flavors balanced by pure, crisp acids, but the tannins are raspingly dry. **86** —*S.H. (11/1/2007)*

SOBON ESTATE

Sobon Estate 2003 Cabernet Sauvignon (Amador County) $15. 91 Best Buy —*S.H. (10/1/2006)*

Sobon Estate 2001 Cabernet Sauvignon (Amador County) $15. 89 Best Buy —*S.H. (11/15/2003)*

Sobon Estate 2003 Rezerve Carignane (Shenandoah Valley (CA)) $24. 82 —*S.H. (7/1/2006)*

Sobon Estate 2002 Rezerve Carignane (Amador County) $24. 86 —*S.H. (10/1/2004)*

Sobon Estate NV Orange Muscat (Shenandoah Valley (CA)) $17. 85 —*S.H. (9/1/2004)*

Sobon Estate 2004 Rezerve Orange Muscat (Amador County) $15. 87 —*S.H. (8/1/2006)*

Sobon Estate 1999 Primitivo (Shenandoah Valley (CA)) $16. 83 —*S.H. (12/1/2002)*

Sobon Estate 1997 Primitivo (Shenandoah Valley (CA)) $18. 80 —*J.C. (10/1/1999)*

Sobon Estate 1998 Primitivo (Shenandoah Valley (CA)) $19. 84 —*S.H. (8/1/2001)*

Sobon Estate 1997 Rhône Red Blend (Shenandoah Valley (CA)) $18. 87 —*L.W. (2/1/2000)*

Sobon Estate 2006 Rezerve Rosé Blend (Amador County) $10. One of the lightest-colored wines of our tasting, this blend of Grenache, Syrah and Carignon is not light in flavor. It's a spicy, mouthwatering wine, with brisk acids and pleasant berry-cherry fruit. **86 Best Buy** —*S.H. (7/1/2007)*

Sobon Estate 2005 Rezerve Rosé Blend (Amador County) $10. 83 —*S.H. (12/1/2006)*

Sobon Estate 2004 Rezerve Rosé Blend (Amador County) $10. 86 Best Buy —*S.H. (12/15/2005)*

Sobon Estate 2002 Roussanne (Shenandoah Valley (CA)) $15. 85 —*S.H. (2/1/2004)*

Sobon Estate 2000 Roussanne (Shenandoah Valley (CA)) $15. 86 —*S.H. (12/15/2002)*

Sobon Estate 2002 Sangiovese (Amador County) $15. 85 —*S.H. (10/1/2004)*

Sobon Estate 1998 Sangiovese (Amador County) $13. 87 —*L.W. (10/1/1999)*

Sobon Estate 2005 Syrah (Amador County) $16. This is the kind of wine that goes with just about anything that goes with red. It's dry and completely balanced in acids and tannins, with a good mélange of cherries and mushroomy, earthy notes, and a silky, velvety mouthfeel. Really hard to find anything not to like. **88** —*S.H. (10/1/2007)*

Sobon Estate 2003 Syrah (Amador County) $14. 82 —*S.H. (7/1/2006)*

Sobon Estate 2001 Syrah (Shenandoah Valley (CA)) $15. 87 —*S.H. (12/1/2003)*

Sobon Estate 1999 Syrah (Shenandoah Valley (CA)) $15. 86 *(10/1/2001)*

Sobon Estate 1997 Syrah (Shenandoah Valley (CA)) $15. 87 —*J.C. (11/1/1999)*

Sobon Estate 2001 Rezerve Syrah (Shenandoah Valley (CA)) $24. 86 —*S.H. (12/1/2004)*

Sobon Estate 2006 Viognier (Amador County) $15. Here's a good, basic Viognier, showing the variety's exotic flair in an affordable package. It has tropical fruit, wildflower, honey and spice aromas and flavors, and is dryly balanced with crisp acids. **85** —*S.H. (11/1/2007)*

Sobon Estate 2005 Viognier (Amador County) $15. What Americans like about Viognier, namely an entire fruit stand in a bottle, this wine delivers. In alphabetical order, that would be apricots, apples, bananas (sauteed), guavas, nectarines, papayas, peaches and pineapples, for starters. That doesn't even count the spices and flowers. A wine of this size is enjoyable on its own. **87** —*S.H. (2/1/2007)*

Sobon Estate 2002 Viognier (Shenandoah Valley (CA)) $15. 86 —*S.H. (2/1/2004)*

Sobon Estate 2000 Viognier (Shenandoah Valley (CA)) $15. 83 —*S.H. (12/15/2002)*

Sobon Estate 2005 Zinfandel (Fiddletown) $20. Lovely mountain Zin, showing a briary, brambly quality to intensely flavored wild blackberries, blueberries and cherry liqueur. There also are tiers of peppery spices, licorice, chocolate mint and soy. Polished and dry, this fine, complex Zinfandel is drinking well now. **91** —*S.H. (10/1/2007)*

Sobon Estate 2003 Zinfandel (Fiddletown) $20. 82 —*S.H. (5/1/2006)*

Sobon Estate 2002 Zinfandel (Fiddletown) $18. 85 —*S.H. (9/1/2004)*

Sobon Estate 2001 Zinfandel (Fiddletown) $20. 84 —*S.H. (3/1/2004)*

Sobon Estate 1998 Zinfandel (Fiddletown) $18. 85 —*P.G. (3/1/2001)*

Sobon Estate 2005 Cougar Hill Zinfandel (Amador County) $16. Good, rich mountain Zin, marked by white peppery flavors of black and red currants. Finishes smooth and dry, with a firm grip of tannins. **88** —*S.H. (11/1/2007)*

Sobon Estate 2004 Cougar Hill Zinfandel (Amador County) $16. This is a good price for this wine, which has been boosted by Petite Sirah. It's full-bodied, balanced and rich in chocolate-covered cherries, blackberry and blueberry pie flavors, with a tart, spicy edge of tangerine rind. Complex and interesting, it changes in the glass as it warms. **88** —*S.H. (2/1/2007)*

Sobon Estate 2003 Cougar Hill Zinfandel (Amador County) $16. 89 —*S.H. (5/1/2006)*

Sobon Estate 2002 Cougar Hill Zinfandel (Shenandoah Valley (CA)) $17. 84 —*S.H. (4/1/2005)*

Sobon Estate 2001 Cougar Hill Zinfandel (Shenandoah Valley (CA)) $17. 89 *(11/1/2003)*

Sobon Estate 2000 Cougar Hill Zinfandel (Shenandoah Valley (CA)) $17. 88 —*S.H. (11/1/2002)*

Sobon Estate 1998 Cougar Hill Zinfandel (Shenandoah Valley (CA)) $16. 88 Editors' Choice —*S.H. (8/1/2001)*

Sobon Estate 2000 Fiddletown Zinfandel (Shenandoah Valley (CA)) $18. 86 —*S.H. (11/1/2002)*

Sobon Estate 2001 Lubenko Vineyard Zinfandel (Fiddletown) $18. 87 *(11/1/2003)*

Sobon Estate 2005 Old Vines Zinfandel (Amador County) $13. Gets the job done with simple, Zin-y flavors of wild berries, tobacco, spices and herbs, wrapped in firm tannins. A bit sharp on the finish, but fine as an inexpensive everyday red. **85** —*S.H. (10/1/2007)*

Sobon Estate 2004 Old Vines Zinfandel (Amador County) $13. 87 —*S.H. (5/1/2006)*

Sobon Estate 2004 Old Vines Zinfandel (Amador County) $13. 85 —*S.H. (10/1/2006)*

Sobon Estate 2002 Old Vines Zinfandel (Shenandoah Valley (CA)) $12. 91 Best Buy —*S.H. (11/15/2004)*

Sobon Estate 2001 Old Vines Zinfandel (Shenandoah Valley (CA)) $13. 88 *(11/1/2003)*

Sobon Estate 2000 Reserve Zinfandel (Shenandoah Valley (CA)) $24. 84 —*S.H. (11/1/2002)*

Sobon Estate 2002 Rezerve Zinfandel (Shenandoah Valley (CA)) $24. 88 —*S.H. (3/1/2005)*

Sobon Estate 2002 Rezerve Zinfandel (Shenandoah Valley (CA)) $24. 0 —*S.H. (10/1/2005)*

Sobon Estate 2001 Rezerve Zinfandel (Shenandoah Valley (CA)) $24. 90 *(11/1/2003)*

Sobon Estate 2004 Rezerve Zin Zinfandel (Amador County) $24. 90 —*S.H. (12/1/2006)*

Sobon Estate 2005 Rocky Top Zinfandel (Amador County) $18. Nice, smooth Zin, achieving a balance of ripeness and dryness. Shows the exuberance of Amador fruit, with blackberry, black cherry, licorice and mocha flavors that finish with a scour of briary tannins. **90** —*S.H. (11/1/2007)*

Sobon Estate 2004 Rocky Top Zinfandel (Amador County) $18. 82 —*S.H. (10/1/2006)*

Sobon Estate 2003 Rocky Top Zinfandel (Amador County) $18. 83 —*S.H. (10/1/2005)*

Sobon Estate 2002 Rocky Top Zinfandel (Shenandoah Valley (CA)) $16. 84 —*S.H. (9/1/2004)*

Sobon Estate 2001 Rocky Top Zinfandel (Shenandoah Valley (CA)) $16. 87 *(11/1/2003)*

Sobon Estate 2000 Rocky Top Zinfandel (Shenandoah Valley (CA)) $15. 91 Editors' Choice —*S.H. (11/1/2002)*

Sobon Estate 1998 Rocky Top Zinfandel (Shenandoah Valley (CA)) $15. 85 —*P.G. (3/1/2001)*

Sobon Estate 1997 Rocky Top Zinfandel (Shenandoah Valley (CA)) $15. 86 —*P.G. (11/15/1999)*

Sobon Estate 1997 Rocky Top Vineyards Zinfandel (Shenandoah Valley (CA)) $15. 90 —*L.W. (11/1/1999)*

Sobon Estate 1997 Vintner's Selection Zinfandel (Amador County) $12. 91 Best Buy —*L.W. (2/1/2000)*

Sobon Estate 2003 Zinfandel Port Zinfandel (Amador County) $15. 86 —*S.H. (12/1/2006)*

SOCKEYE

Sockeye 2002 Cabernet Sauvignon (Washington) $11. 87 Best Buy —*P.G. (11/15/2005)*

Sockeye 2004 Pinot Gris (California) $12. 84 —*S.H. (2/1/2006)*

Sockeye 2002 Syrah (Columbia Valley (WA)) $12. 84 *(9/1/2005)*

SOFIA

Sofia 2000 Blanc de Blancs Champagne Blend (California) $20. 83 *(12/1/2001)*

SOGNO

Sogno 2001 Reserve Cabernet Franc (El Dorado County) $22. 81 —*S.H. (11/15/2003)*

Sogno 2000 Giocchino Red Blend (El Dorado) $16. 82 —*S.H. (5/1/2002)*

Sogno 2000 Syrah (El Dorado) $15. 81 —*S.H. (9/1/2003)*

Sogno 2001 Zinfandel (El Dorado County) $14. 81 *(11/1/2003)*

Sogno 2001 Karma Vineyard Zinfandel (Amador County) $17. 82 *(11/1/2003)*

SOKOL BLOSSER

Sokol Blosser 2003 Pinot Gris (Willamette Valley) $21. 86 —*P.G. (11/15/2005)*

Sokol Blosser 2001 Pinot Gris (Willamette Valley) $18. 85 —*M.S. (8/1/2003)*

Sokol Blosser 2000 Pinot Gris (Willamette Valley) $19. 85 —*M.S. (12/31/2002)*

Sokol Blosser 2004 Pinot Noir (Dundee Hills) $29. Sokol Blosser's commitment to sustainable, near-biodynamic vineyard practices is yielding clear-cut results. This lovely effort has more detail, more well-defined nuances, than almost any other Oregon Pinot in this relatively modest price range. True Pinot character shines through, balanced elegantly on natural acid, with a tight core of spice, cola, mocha and mixed red fruits. Likeable but restrained now, it should age nicely over the next half decade or so. **90** —*P.G. (2/1/2007)*

Sokol Blosser 2003 Pinot Noir (Dundee Hills) $26. 87 —*P.G. (12/1/2006)*

Sokol Blosser 2002 Pinot Noir (Dundee Hills) $26. 88 —*P.G. (11/15/2005)*

Sokol Blosser 2000 Pinot Noir (Willamette Valley) $25. 87 —*P.G. (4/1/2003)*

Sokol Blosser 1999 Pinot Noir (Willamette Valley) $30. 85 *(10/1/2002)*

Sokol Blosser 1998 Pinot Noir (Willamette Valley) $28. 87 —*P.G. (4/1/2002)*

Sokol Blosser 2003 Estate Cuvée Pinot Noir (Dundee Hills) $28. 88 —*P.G. (9/1/2006)*

Sokol Blosser 2001 Old Vineyard Block Pinot Noir (Willamette Valley) $50. 90 —*P.G. (2/1/2005)*

Sokol Blosser 1998 Old Vineyard Block Pinot Noir (Willamette Valley) $65. 89 —*P.G. (4/1/2002)*

Sokol Blosser 2001 Twelve Row Block Pinot Noir (Willamette Valley) $66. 92 Cellar Selection —*P.G. (2/1/2005)*

Sokol Blosser 1998 Twelve Row Block Pinot Noir (Willamette Valley) $75. 89 —*P.G. (4/1/2002)*

Sokol Blosser 1999 Twelve Row Block Limited Production Pinot Noir (Willamette Valley) $65. 86 —*P.G. (4/1/2003)*

Sokol Blosser 2001 Watershed Block Pinot Noir (Willamette Valley) $50. 90 —*P.G. (2/1/2005)*

Sokol Blosser 1998 Watershed Block Pinot Noir (Willamette Valley) $65. 90 —*P.G. (4/1/2002)*

Sokol Blosser 1999 Watershed Block Limited Production Pinot Noir (Willamette Valley) $65. 87 —*P.G. (4/1/2003)*

Sokol Blosser NV Evolution 5th Edition White Blend (Oregon) $15. 86 —*P.G. (4/1/2002)*

Sokol Blosser NV Evolution 6th Edition White Blend (Oregon) $15. 86 —*M.S. (8/1/2003)*

SOLARIS

Solaris 2005 Cabernet Sauvignon (California) $10. Harsh, acidic and bitter, with a green, minty streak, this is an unrewarding Cabernet. **81** —*S.H. (9/1/2007)*

Solaris 2002 Reserve Cabernet Sauvignon (Napa Valley) $25. 87 *—S.H. (12/15/2005)*

Solaris 2000 Reserve Cabernet Sauvignon (Napa Valley) $25. 90 *S.H. (5/1/2005)*

Solaris 2002 Special Release Cabernet Sauvignon (Napa Valley) $15. 85 *—S.H. (3/1/2006)*

Solaris 2004 Chardonnay (Monterey) $12. 84 *—S.H. (11/15/2006)*

Solaris 2003 Chardonnay (North Coast) $13. Fruity and simple, with peach and citrus flavors that weaken on the finish. **83** *—S.H. (6/1/2005)*

Solaris 2005 Merlot (California) $10. Paso Robles, Monterey and Santa Barbara contributed the grapes to this everyday Merlot. It has pleasantly ripe cherry-berry flavors and smooth tannins. This is a good price for a good, dry Bordeaux-style red. **84** *—S.H. (9/1/2007)*

Solaris 2001 Merlot (Napa Valley) $16. 83 *—S.H. (6/1/2005)*

Solaris 2002 Special Release Merlot (Napa Valley) $15. 84 *—S.H. (3/1/2006)*

Solaris 2004 Pinot Noir (Carneros) $15. 81 *—S.H. (3/1/2006)*

Solaris 2003 Pinot Noir (Carneros) $13. 81 *—S.H. (6/1/2005)*

Solaris 2004 Zinfandel (Mendocino County) $14. 84 *—S.H. (11/15/2006)*

SOLEIL & TERROIR

Soleil & Terroir 1997 La Colline-Reserve Chardonnay (Arroyo Grande Valley) $30. 91 *—J.C. (3/1/2000)*

SOLÉNA

Soléna 2004 Pinot Gris (Oregon) $20. 92 *—P.G. (2/1/2006)*

Soléna 2003 Pinot Gris (Oregon) $18. 90 *—P.G. (8/1/2005)*

Soléna 2003 Grand Cuvée Pinot Noir (Willamette Valley) $25. 90 Editors' Choice *—P.G. (9/1/2006)*

SOLO ROSA

Solo Rosa 2002 Sangiovese (California) $15. 87 *—S.H. (3/1/2004)*

SONNET

Sonnet 2005 Amber Ridge Vineyard Pinot Noir (Russian River Valley) $40. This is one of your bigger, fatter, riper Russian River Pinots, with jammy, oak-accented cherry, raspberry, root beer and vanilla flavors that are very forward and lush. The wine is extremely soft, though, and could certainly use a boost of acidity for balance. Still, it sure is tasty. Drink now. **87** *—S.H. (10/1/2007)*

Sonnet 2005 Kruse Vineyard Pinot Noir (York Mountain) $40. There's lots of structure here. Acidity stars, making this brisk, and lifting the cherry, cola and oak flavors up and out. A dry, elegant young Pinot. **89** *—S.H. (10/1/2007)*

Sonnet 2003 Kruse Vineyard Pinot Noir (York Mountain) $40. 86 *—S.H. (8/1/2005)*

Sonnet 2005 Mun's Vineyard Pinot Noir (Santa Cruz Mountains) $40. Nice Pinot, with real elegance and complexity. Shows classic cool-climate balance, with crisp acidity and, from this long hangtime vintage, extremely ripe cola, root beer, raspberry jam, mocha and balsamic flavors, enriched with smoky oak. Best now for its opulent, youthful brilliance. **91** *—S.H. (10/1/2007)*

Sonnet 2005 Tondré's Grapefield Pinot Noir (Santa Lucia Highlands) $40. A simple, likeable wine. It's nice for the upfront cherry jam, raspberry, cola and vanilla flavors and easy, silky texture, but there's not much depth. Drink now. **85** *—S.H. (10/1/2007)*

SONOMA COAST VINEYARDS

Sonoma Coast Vineyards 2005 Chardonnay (Sonoma Coast) $50. A full-bodied, richly textured Chardonnay, with toasty, nutty notes accenting melon and pear flavors. Despite about 70% malolactic fermentation, this avoids buttery excess, instead coming across as toasted hazelnuts and whole grain. **90** *(11/1/2007)*

Sonoma Coast Vineyards 2004 Chardonnay (Sonoma Coast) $50. Toastier and more buttery than the 2005, with a touch of warmth to its flavors. Grilled nuts accent melon and ripe peach flavors, showing a greater degree of ripeness than the more refined 2005. Finishes with notes of toasted oak and coffee. **88** *(11/1/2007)*

Sonoma Coast Vineyards 2003 Chardonnay (Sonoma Coast) $45. This is one tough wine. It's all acidity, steel and minerals, and extreme dryness. with lots of new oak. The fruit veers toward toasted lemon zest. Winemaker Anthony Austin says he made this wine to age, which seems a safe bet. Best 2008–2010. **90** *—S.H. (7/1/2007)*

Sonoma Coast Vineyards 2004 Pinot Noir (Sonoma Coast) $57. A wine that blends fruit from seven vineyards and seven clones, this bears a family resemblance to the more expensive Balistreri Vineyard bottling in its tart, crisp profile, although there's some dark earth and cola notes layered over the pie cherry fruit. **90** *(11/1/2007)*

Sonoma Coast Vineyards 2003 Pinot Noir (Sonoma Coast) $60. 91 *(12/1/2006)*

Sonoma Coast Vineyards 2004 Balistreri Family Vineyard Freestone View Block Pinot Noir (Sonoma Coast) $100. The vineyard was closely planted in 1999 to a mix of Dijon clones and cropped at one ton per acre. The result in 2004 is a bright, tightly focused wine, filled with red berry fruit and cedary notes from its 20 months in barrel. Drink 2009–2015. **90** *(11/1/2007)*

Sonoma Coast Vineyards 2006 Hummingbird Hill Vineyards Sauvignon Blanc (Sonoma Coast) $30. An intriguing wine, fueled by contrasts. Tomato leaf and peppermint notes counter honeyed fruit; grapefruit balances figs and melons. Despite the hints of green leafiness, it's rich and rather full-bodied. Drink now, although it may prove to be a pleasant surprise in another year or two. **89** *(11/1/2007)*

Sonoma Coast Vineyards 2004 Syrah (Sonoma Coast) $40. Starts off showing mainly raspberry fruit, then moves on to mixed berries, accented by vanilla from 20 months in barrel. It's slightly syrupy in texture, ending with supple tannins and a bit of cracked pepper. **90** *(11/1/2007)*

SONOMA CREEK

Sonoma Creek 2005 Cabernet Sauvignon (Dry Creek Valley) $13. A little too soft and sweet to earn a higher score, this shows simple flavors of cherries, licorice and cola. **82** *—S.H. (11/1/2007)*

Sonoma Creek 2003 Cabernet Sauvignon (Sonoma County) $13. 84 *—S.H. (2/1/2006)*

Sonoma Creek 2005 Chardonnay (Sonoma County) $10. Pretty thin in fruit, which makes the bare-bones alcohol, acids and oak stick out. **83** *—S.H. (10/1/2007)*

Sonoma Creek 2004 Chardonnay (Sonoma County) $10. 84 *—S.H. (2/1/2006)*

Sonoma Creek 2003 Chardonnay (Sonoma County) $10. 82 *—S.H. (3/1/2006)*

Sonoma Creek 2005 Merlot (Dry Creek Valley) $13. Very dry and rather tannic, this Merlot strikes off in interesting directions. Along with the usual cherries and blackberries, it shows an array of dried-crushed herb aromas and flavors, such as thyme and sage. This increases balance and complexity, not to mention the wine's versatility at the table. **87** *—S.H. (11/15/2007)*

Sonoma Creek 2003 Merlot (Sonoma County) $13. 84 *—S.H. (2/1/2006)*

Sonoma Creek 2006 Pinot Noir (Sonoma County) $15. Not a very satisfying wine. Feels acidic and sharp in the mouth, with thin, minty flavors that only barely contain cherry fruit. But it's clean and silky. **83** *—S.H. (11/15/2007)*

Sonoma Creek 2005 Pinot Noir (Sonoma County) $13. 83 *—S.H. (12/15/2006)*

Sonoma Creek 2004 Pinot Noir (Sonoma County) $13. 85 *—S.H. (2/1/2006)*

Sonoma Creek 2000 Pinot Noir (Sonoma County) $9. 84 Best Buy *(10/1/2002)*

Sonoma Creek 2000 Pinot Noir (Carneros) $11. 86 Best Buy *(10/1/2002)*

Sonoma Creek 1998 Pinot Noir (Sonoma County) $15. 82 *—M.S. (12/15/2000)*

Sonoma Creek 1998 Duarte Old Vine Zinfandel (Contra Costa County) $15. 89 Best Buy *—P.G. (3/1/2001)*

SONOMA HILL

Sonoma Hill 2001 Cabernet Sauvignon (Sonoma County) $15. 84 *—S.H. (2/1/2004)*

Sonoma Hill 2002 Chardonnay (Sonoma County) $13. 83 *—S.H. (4/1/2004)*

Sonoma Hill 2001 Merlot (Sonoma County) $15. 85 *—S.H. (4/1/2004)*

Sonoma Hill 2002 Pinot Noir (Sonoma County) $12. 84 *(11/1/2004)*

SONOMA VINEYARDS

Sonoma Vineyards 2005 Chardonnay (Sonoma County) $15. Syrupy, with candied apricot flavors and a sugary finish. **82** *—S.H. (10/1/2007)*

Sonoma Vineyards 2003 Merlot (Sonoma County) $15. Still pretty tannic at nearly four years of age, this Merlot is also very dry, and it has a tart acidity. Structurally, it's a rustic wine, whose cherry-blackberry flavors have a weedy, minty, herbal edge. **83** *—S.H. (10/1/2007)*

SONOMA-CUTRER

Sonoma-Cutrer 1999 Founders Reserve Chardonnay (Sonoma Valley) $65. 93 *—S.H. (10/1/2003)*

Sonoma-Cutrer 1997 Les Pierres Chardonnay (Sonoma Valley) $30. 86 *(6/1/2000)*

Sonoma-Cutrer 1998 Russian River Ranches Chardonnay (Sonoma Coast) $18. 87 *(6/1/2000)*

Sonoma-Cutrer 1997 The Cutrer Chardonnay (Russian River Valley) $30. 89 *(6/1/2000)*

SONORA

Sonora 1998 Story Vineyard Old Vine Zinfandel (Amador County) $21. 84 *—P.G. (3/1/2001)*

Sonora 1997 Story Vineyard Zinfandel (Shenandoah Valley (CA)) $19. 86 *—P.G. (11/15/1999)*

Sonora 1998 TC Vineyard Old Vine Zinfandel (Amador County) $21. 84 *—P.G. (3/1/2001)*

Sonora 1997 TC Vineyard Old Vine Zinfandel (Amador County) $19. 86 *—P.G. (11/15/1999)*

SOOS CREEK

Soos Creek 2001 Artist's Series #1 Bordeaux Blend (Columbia Valley (WA)) $27. 86 *—P.G. (7/1/2004)*

Soos Creek 2003 Artist's Series #3 Red Wine Bordeaux Blend (Columbia Valley (WA)) $28. 93 *—P.G. (6/1/2006)*

Soos Creek 2004 Artist's Series #4 Bordeaux Blend (Columbia Valley (WA)) $30. The wine opens with dense, fragrant, supple scents of slate, cassis and mulberry. Slightly reductive, it's a wine that needs decanting. This is consistent with past vintages, nicely detailed with mineral and fine grained tannins resolving into flavors of lightly roasted coffee. **92** *—P.G. (5/1/2007)*

Soos Creek 2004 Sundance Bordeaux Blend (Columbia Valley (WA)) $23. Round and lush, the Sundance blend—half Cabernet Franc, 30% Merlot and 20% Cabernet Sauvignon—is made for early drinking. It shows appealing black cherry fruit, full and lively, and propped up with bright acids. The oak is generous and chocolaty, lingering through a smooth, silky finish. **89** *—P.G. (5/1/2007)*

Soos Creek 1999 Cabernet Sauvignon (Columbia Valley (WA)) $30. 92 *—P.G. (6/1/2002)*

Soos Creek 2003 Champoux Vineyard Cabernet Sauvignon (Columbia Valley (WA)) $30. 94 *—P.G. (6/1/2006)*

Soos Creek 1999 Champoux Vineyard Cabernet Sauvignon (Columbia Valley (WA)) $30. 91 *—P.G. (6/1/2002)*

Soos Creek 1998 Champoux Vineyard Cabernet Sauvignon (Columbia Valley (WA)) $30. 89 *—P.G. (10/1/2001)*

Soos Creek 2004 Ciel du Cheval Cabernet Sauvignon (Red Mountain) $35. Again winemaker Dave Larsen has made a classic Ciel du Cheval Cabernet, an austere mix of mineral and green tea flavors, hard and tight and densely compacted. The opening aromas hint at dried grass and wild berries, with a bracing minerality. This is a vintage (and a vineyard) that will certainly reward cellaring, for up to 20 years. The alcohol is a moderate 14.1%. **92** *—P.G. (5/1/2007)*

Soos Creek 2003 Ciel du Cheval Cabernet Sauvignon (Red Mountain) $33. 93 *—P.G. (6/1/2006)*

Soos Creek 1999 Reserve Cabernet Sauvignon (Columbia Valley (WA)) $36. 93 Editors' Choice *—P.G. (6/1/2002)*

Soos Creek 2004 Soleil Cabernet Sauvignon (Columbia Valley (WA)) $37. A 50-50 blend of two top vineyards—Ciel du Cheval and Champoux, this is Cabernet Sauvignon with 12% Cab Franc blended in. The nose is open and bursting with detail: whiffs of herb, spice, mineral, violets and cinnamon. Strawberry and cherry fruit is annotated with green tea, herb and soy. It's a chewy little devil, more herbal than funky, but fascinating and complex. **91** *—P.G. (5/1/2007)*

Soos Creek 2001 Merlot (Columbia Valley (WA)) $25. 91 *—P.G. (6/1/2006)*

Soos Creek NV Sundance Red Blend (Columbia Valley (WA)) $20. 90 *—P.G. (6/1/2002)*

SORENSON

Sorenson 2000 Cabernet Sauvignon (Napa Valley) $40. 90 *—J.M. (9/1/2003)*

SOTER

Soter 2002 Little Creek Cabernet Franc (Napa Valley) $75. 90 *—S.H. (4/1/2006)*

SOURCE NAPA

Source Napa 2003 Heritage Sites Red Wine Bordeaux Blend (Napa Valley) $38. Decent young Merlot-based Bordeaux blend, but the emphasis is on young. It's chunky in dry, numbing tannins at this point. Aging is iffy. There's some good fruit, but also a stubborn streak of green unripeness. Try after 2008. **84** *—S.H. (4/1/2007)*

Source Napa 2003 Paramount Red Wine Bordeaux Blend (Napa Valley) $75. This is the winery's Merlot-based Meritage blend. You might expect that to make it softer, but it's not. It's a hard, tannic wine, a little lean, but complex and dry. Not showing well now; decant or drink after 2008. **87** *—S.H. (4/1/2007)*

Source Napa 2003 Family Home Cabernet Sauvignon (Napa Valley) $60. This is a very young Cabernet, not really showing its stuff now, but it's pretty solid for the cellar. Dry and tannic, it shows a polished structure, and what it currently lacks in fruity oomph, it makes up for with a richly earthy elegance. Should develop well from 2007–2011. **89** *—S.H. (4/1/2007)*

SOUVERAIN

Souverain 2004 Cabernet Sauvignon (Alexander Valley) $22. An extremely nice wine, rich and balanced, that approximates Cabs costing far more. The flavors of blackberries, cherries and chocolate have an earthy edge of dried herbs and crushed spices, enhanced with smoky oak. Easy to find with 35,400 cases produced. **89** *—S.H. (12/15/2007)*

Souverain 2005 Merlot (Alexander Valley) $19. Not a success, with sweet-and-sour flavors. There's a vinegary edge to the sugared pineapples and tangerines. **81** *—S.H. (12/15/2007)*

SPANGLER VINEYARDS

Spangler Vineyards 2005 Cabernet Franc (Southern Oregon) $24. This is pure Cabernet Franc; tough and tannic, it is served up dry as a bone, the light plummy fruit a bit overwhelmed by the hard, chalky finish. **84** *—P.G. (7/1/2007)*

Spangler Vineyards 2004 Sundown Vineyard Cabernet Franc (Southern Oregon) $30. 86 *—P.G. (12/1/2006)*

Spangler Vineyards 2004 Reserve Cabernet Sauvignon (Southern Oregon) $30. Though it is mostly Cab Sauvignon, the blend also includes small percentages of Merlot, Cab Franc and, for unknown reasons, Pinot Noir. Labeled reserve, it has more grip, color and concentration than the winery's regular reds, but apart from generic red fruit and a lightly toasty barrel influence, there's nothing specific, flavorwise. **85** *—P.G. (7/1/2007)*

Spangler Vineyards 2006 Unoaked Chardonnay (Southern Oregon) $20. Light flavors of apple and pear come through in this unoaked Chardonnay. Just a splash of Semillon is blended in, but this is an instance where the unadorned fruit, though clean and presentable, lacks weight and varietal distinction. It's simple, light and a bit boring. **85** *—P.G. (7/1/2007)*

Spangler Vineyards 2005 Merlot (Southern Oregon) $20. Southern Oregon Merlot, it can be argued, should taste exactly like this—light and pretty cherry fruit, tart acids and lush, chocolaty tannins. For me the tannins way out-strip the fruit, which is delicate to the point of semi-invisibility. It's a pleasant wine, clean and true to its regional style. **84** *—P.G. (7/1/2007)*

Spangler Vineyards 2004 Reserve Merlot (Southern Oregon) $28. This unquestionably is a bigger, darker, more concentrated wine than Spangler's regular Merlot. But is it markedly better? I picked up a slightly roasted, slightly burned character to the fruit, and once again, tannins that are thick and chalky. Hints of chocolate and tobacco stretch out the finish a bit, although the fruit goes away quickly. **85** *—P.G. (7/1/2007)*

Spangler Vineyards 2004 Doerner Vineyard Pinot Noir (Southern Oregon) $18. 87 *—P.G. (12/1/2006)*

Spangler Vineyards 2006 Sauvignon Blanc (Southern Oregon) $17. There's a bit of Sémillon in the blend, but this comes through as a fresh and simple style of Sauvignon. Grapefruit, lime and a flash of pineapple give the fruit some dynamic interest, but it tails off quickly into a thin finish with a palate impression of sweetness, though the residual sugar is listed at zero. **86** *—P.G. (7/1/2007)*

Spangler Vineyards 2006 Sémillon (Southern Oregon) $15. The winery lists this as having just 12.1% alcohol but 2.5% residual sugar, and it tastes like it. If you think Sémillon is well-served by such sugary flavors, this is the wine for you. But it's not sweet enough to qualify for a dessert wine, so it's really stuck in an off-dry style. **83** *—P.G. (7/1/2007)*

Spangler Vineyards 2006 Viognier (Southern Oregon) $16. Though similar in style to the winery's 2005 Viognier, this edition lacks the complexity and aromatic detail. There's plenty of acid to cut through the 1.1% residual sugar, but something is lost in that equation. Rather than cutting through with Viognier's characteristic mix of floral, citrus and stone fruits, this just tastes like a basic white, peachy and slightly sweet. **84**—*P.G. (7/1/2007)*

Spangler Vineyards 2005 Viognier (Southern Oregon) $19. 88 *—P.G. (12/1/2006)*

SPANN VINEYARDS

Spann Vineyards 2004 Five Barrels Cabernet Sauvignon (Alexander Valley) $40. Soft and fruity, this is a nice drinking, somewhat complex Cab, with a lush texture framing flavors of chocolate-covered cherry candy, blackberry tea and cappuccino with a dash of Kahlúa. It's entirely ready now. **86** —*S.H. (7/1/2007)*

Spann Vineyards 2001 Mayacamas Range Five Barrels Cabernet Sauvignon (Sonoma Valley) $30. 87 —*S.H. (12/15/2004)*

Spann Vineyards 2004 Chardonnay-Viognier (Sonoma County) $20. 85 —*S.H. (12/1/2006)*

Spann Vineyards 2002 Chardonnay-Viognier (Sonoma County) $17. 88 —*J.M. (6/1/2004)*

Spann Vineyards 2001 Red Blend (Sonoma County) $18. 90 —*S.H. (12/15/2004)*

Spann Vineyards 2001 Mo Jo Red Blend (Russian River Valley) $30. 89 —*S.H. (12/15/2004)*

Spann Vineyards 2002 Mo Jo Ten Barrels Red Blend (Russian River Valley) $40. 86 —*S.H. (12/31/2006)*

Spann Vineyards 2003 Syrah (Russian River Valley) $25. This is fruity, dry and balanced. It's on the soft side, with black cherry, coffee, tobacco and leather flavors that finish with some dusty tannins. It's made for immediate consumption. **86** —*S.H. (7/1/2007)*

Spann Vineyards 2002 Syrah (Sonoma County) $20. 86 *(9/1/2005)*

Spann Vineyards 2005 Chardonnay-Viognier White Blend (Sonoma County) $20. Spann's bottling of these two varieties has been remarkably consistent, producing a delicious, easy wine with some real sophistication. It's filled with fruit, showing ripe apple sauce, pineapple, lime and vanilla flavors, brightened with crisp acidity. **86** —*S.H. (7/1/2007)*

Spann Vineyards 2003 Chardonnay-Viognier White Blend (Sonoma County) $18. 87 —*S.H. (11/1/2005)*

Spann Vineyards 2002 Mo Zin Zinfandel (Sonoma County) $18. 86 —*S.H. (10/1/2005)*

SPARROW LANE

Sparrow Lane 1999 Beatty Ranch Zinfandel (Napa Valley) $35. 88 —*J.M. (12/15/2001)*

SPELLETICH CELLARS

Spelletich Cellars 1998 Bodog Red Bordeaux Blend (Napa Valley) $25. 86 *(8/1/2001)*

Spelletich Cellars 1999 Cabernet Sauvignon (Napa Valley) $44. 84 —*S.H. (11/15/2002)*

Spelletich Cellars 1998 Cabernet Sauvignon (Napa Valley) $80. 90 —*S.H. (8/1/2001)*

Spelletich Cellars 1999 Heroncroft Vineyard-Keefur Ranch Chardonnay (Russian River Valley) $29. 86 *(8/1/2001)*

Spelletich Cellars 2000 Ochoa Chardonnay (Carneros) $29. 89 —*S.H. (12/15/2002)*

Spelletich Cellars 2000 Rustridge Chardonnay (Napa Valley) $24. 85 —*S.H. (12/15/2002)*

Spelletich Cellars 1999 Spotted Owl Chardonnay (Mount Veeder) $25. 90 *(8/1/2001)*

Spelletich Cellars 1999 Bodog Red Blend (Napa Valley) $27. 85 —*S.H. (9/1/2003)*

Spelletich Cellars 2001 Alviso Vineyard Zinfandel (Amador County) $24. 84 *(11/1/2003)*

Spelletich Cellars 2001 Tim and Edie's Vineyard Zinfandel (Shenandoah Valley (CA)) $23. 90 *(11/1/2003)*

SPENCER ROLOSON

Spencer Roloson 2001 Palaterra Red Blend (California) $16. 87 —*S.H. (11/15/2004)*

Spencer Roloson 1999 Palaterra Red Blend (California) $16. 85 —*S.H. (12/1/2002)*

Spencer Roloson 2002 Palaterra Red Wine Red Blend (California) $16. 86 —*S.H. (6/1/2005)*

Spencer Roloson 2000 Vin Gris Rosé Blend (California) $15. 82 —*J.M. (9/10/2002)*

Spencer Roloson 2002 Balyeat Vineyard Sauvignon Blanc (Chiles Valley) $24. 87 —*S.H. (12/1/2004)*

Spencer Roloson 2003 La Herradura Vineyard Syrah (Napa Valley) $38. 90 —*S.H. (3/1/2006)*

Spencer Roloson 2002 La Herradura Vineyard Syrah (Napa Valley) $35. 92 —*S.H. (6/1/2005)*

Spencer Roloson 1999 Sueno Syrah (Lodi) $28. 89 —*S.H. (12/1/2002)*

Spencer Roloson 2001 Sueno Vineyard Syrah (Lodi) $28. 90 —*S.H. (12/1/2004)*

Spencer Roloson 2001 Tempranillo (Clear Lake) $26. 87 —*S.H. (3/1/2004)*

Spencer Roloson 2002 Madder Lake Vineyard Tempranillo (Clear Lake) $25. 87 —*S.H. (6/1/2005)*

Spencer Roloson 2000 Viognier (Rutherford) $19. 86 —*S.H. (9/1/2002)*

Spencer Roloson 2004 Noble Vineyard Viognier (Knights Valley) $NA. 83 —*S.H. (3/1/2006)*

Spencer Roloson 2001 Skellenger Vineyards Viognier (Rutherford) $24. 90 —*S.H. (5/1/2003)*

Spencer Roloson 2003 Sueno Vineyard Viognier (Lodi) $26. 90 —*S.H. (6/1/2005)*

Spencer Roloson 2002 Sueno Vineyard Viognier (Lodi) $26. 90 —*S.H. (2/1/2004)*

Spencer Roloson 1999 Zinfandel (Chiles Valley) $30. 84 —*S.H. (11/1/2002)*

Spencer Roloson 1999 Zinfandel (Sonoma County) $25. 84 —*S.H. (11/1/2002)*

Spencer Roloson 2003 Madder Lake Vineyard Zinfandel (Clear Lake) $30. 83 —*S.H. (3/1/2006)*

SPIRIT RIDGE

Spirit Ridge 1998 Chardonnay (California) $7. 80 —*J.C. (7/1/2000)*

SPOTTSWOODE

Spottswoode 2003 Cabernet Sauvignon (St. Helena) $110. A sturdy young Cabernet showing great harmony and class. It's fresh in ripe tannins, very poised and balanced, with a great depth of cedary blackberry fruit. This is really classic Napa Cabernet, so elegant, and a great food wine. **92** —*S.H. (5/1/2007)*

Spottswoode 2002 Estate Cabernet Sauvignon (Napa Valley) $110. 92 Cellar Selection —*S.H. (3/1/2006)*

Spottswoode 2001 Estate Cabernet Sauvignon (Napa Valley) $90. 94 —*S.H. (3/1/2005)*

Spottswoode 1999 Spottswoode Estate Vineyard Cabernet Sauvignon (Napa Valley) $80. 88 —*S.H. (11/15/2002)*

Spottswoode 2005 Sauvignon Blanc (Napa Valley) $32. If you don't mind a little cat pee, you'll find some pretty aromas and flavors in this wine: figs, lemongrass, green apple, white peach, honeysuckle, spice. It's definitely on the sweet side, although crisp acidity helps balance it. **86** —*S.H. (5/1/2007)*

Spottswoode 2004 Sauvignon Blanc (Napa Valley) $32. 88 —*S.H. (3/1/2006)*

Spottswoode 2003 Sauvignon Blanc (Napa Valley) $32. 90 —*S.H. (3/1/2005)*

Spottswoode 2000 Sauvignon Blanc (Napa Valley) $25. 87 *(8/1/2002)*

SPRING MOUNTAIN

Spring Mountain 1997 Miravalle-La Perla-Chevalier Bordeaux Blend (Spring Mountain) $50. 89 *(11/1/2000)*

Spring Mountain 1997 Reserve Bordeaux Blend (Spring Mountain) $90. 92 *(11/1/2000)*

Spring Mountain 2002 Elivette Reserve Cabernet Blend (Napa Valley) $90. 92 —*S.H. (12/15/2006)*

Spring Mountain 2002 Estate Cabernet Sauvignon (Spring Mountain) $50. 92 —*S.H. (12/31/2005)*

Spring Mountain 2000 Elivette Cabernet Sauvignon-Merlot (Napa Valley) $90. 91 —*S.H. (4/1/2004)*

Spring Mountain 2000 Estate Cabernet Sauvignon-Merlot (Spring Mountain) $50. 92 —*S.H. (11/15/2003)*

Spring Mountain 2003 Pinot Noir (Spring Mountain) $50. 85 —*S.H. (2/1/2006)*

Spring Mountain 2001 Elivette Red Blend (Spring Mountain) $90. 91 —*J.C. (10/1/2004)*

Spring Mountain 1999 Reserve Red Wine Red Blend (Napa Valley) $50. 92 —*S.H. (12/31/2003)*

Spring Mountain 2004 Sauvignon Blanc (Spring Mountain) $28. 90 —*S.H. (5/1/2006)*

Spring Mountain 2003 Sauvignon Blanc (Spring Mountain) $28. 90 Editors' Choice —*S.H. (12/31/2005)*

Spring Mountain 2001 Sauvignon Blanc (Spring Mountain) $28. 84 —*S.H. (10/1/2003)*

Spring Mountain 1999 Syrah (Napa Valley) $NA. 89 —*S.H. (2/1/2004)*

Spring Mountain 2003 Co-Ferment Syrah (Spring Mountain) $50. 85 —*S.H. (2/1/2006)*

Spring Mountain 2003 Miravelle Syrah (Spring Mountain) $50. 91 Cellar Selection *—S.H. (2/1/2006)*

SPRING MOUNTAIN VINEYARD

Spring Mountain Vineyard 2001 Bordeaux Blend (Napa Valley) $50. 92 *(6/6/2005)*

Spring Mountain Vineyard 2003 Estate Cabernet Sauvignon (Napa Valley) $50. Tastes like it benefited from being held back for a while, because the tannins are beginning to melt, although they're still dusty and strong. The oak is strong, too, framing red stone fruit and cassis flavors. Fully dry, this mountain wine needs a little time. Give it at least until 2008, or decant for several hours. 90 *—S.H. (9/1/2007)*

Spring Mountain Vineyard 2005 Sauvignon Blanc (Napa Valley) $32. This bottling definitely needs a warmer vintage to fully ripen, because this '05 is aggressive in cat pee aromas. Everything else in the wine is good. 83 *—S.H. (9/1/2007)*

Spring Mountain Vineyard 2003 Sauvignon Blanc (Napa Valley) $28. 86 *(7/1/2005)*

Spring Mountain Vineyard 2004 Estate Syrah (Napa Valley) $50. This is serious Syrah. It shows mountain intensity, with potent cassis, licorice, grilled meat, cocoa and gingersnap cookie flavors, enhanced by all the loveliness that fine new oak contributes to a full-bodied red wine. The tannins are strong and thick, but of the sweetly ripe type. Just lovely. Drink now and for the next few years. 93 *—S.H. (9/1/2007)*

Spring Mountain Vineyard 2001 Estate Syrah (Napa Valley) $50. 88 *(9/1/2005)*

Spring Valley Vineyard 2003 Frederick Red Table Wine Bordeaux Blend (Walla Walla (WA)) $40. 92 *—P.G. (6/1/2006)*

SPRING VALLEY VINEYARD

Spring Valley Vineyard 2004 Uriah Bordeaux Blend (Walla Walla (WA)) $40. 93 *—P.G. (12/31/2006)*

Spring Valley Vineyard 2003 Uriah Red Table Wine Bordeaux Blend (Walla Walla (WA)) $40. 91 *—P.G. (6/1/2006)*

Spring Valley Vineyard 2003 Cabernet Franc (Walla Walla (WA)) $18. 90 *—P.G. (6/1/2006)*

Spring Valley Vineyard 2003 Derby Cabernet Sauvignon (Walla Walla (WA)) $42. 91 Editors' Choice *—P.G. (10/1/2006)*

Spring Valley Vineyard 2004 Nina Lee Syrah (Walla Walla (WA)) $50. 92 Editors' Choice *—P.G. (12/31/2006)*

Spring Valley Vineyard 2003 Nina Lee Syrah (Walla Walla (WA)) $40. 89 *—P.G. (6/1/2006)*

Spring Valley Vineyard 2002 Nina Lee Syrah (Walla Walla (WA)) $40. 85 *(9/1/2005)*

ST. AMANT

St. Amant 1999 Barbera (Lodi) $14. 88 *—S.H. (11/15/2001)*

St. Amant 1999 Syrah (California) $12. 86 *—S.H. (11/15/2001)*

St. Amant 1999 Reserve Syrah (Amador County) $18. 89 *—S.H. (11/15/2001)*

St. Amant 1999 Berghold Vineyard Viognier (Lodi) $12. 86 Best Buy *—S.H. (11/15/2001)*

ST. STALEY THOMAS

St. Staley Thomas 1997 Chardonnay (Russian River Valley) $13. 92 Best Buy *—L.W. (7/1/1999)*

ST. AMANT WINERY

St. Amant Winery 2001 Zinfandel (Amador County) $15. 87 *(11/1/2003)*

St. Amant Winery 2005 Marian's Vineyard Zinfandel (Lodi) $28. Either there's some residual sugar or the high alcohol, 15.8%, gives this wine a sweet taste, or both. Either way, it tastes like liquified raspberry, cherry and blackberry jam, with a squeeze of chocolate syrup. One third new oak adds caramel and butterscotch. 84 *—S.H. (12/15/2007)*

St. Amant Winery 2001 Marian's Vineyard Zinfandel (Lodi) $20. 87 *(11/1/2003)*

ST. CLAIR

St. Clair NV Riesling (New Mexico) $9. This Riesling has some pleasant pineapple and snappy fruit in the nose, but the flavors tend toward sappy and sweet. Could use a more delicate hand and lighter touch on the palate, but fans of sweeter styles will enjoy this. 81 *—S.K. (9/1/2007)*

St. Clair 2006 Rosé Blend (New Mexico) $9. Sweet scents of strawberry and a very subtle, bordering on watery, offering of flavors makes this rosé from New Mexico one with potential, but no staying power. What's there is too far toward syrupy. Needs balance. 82 *—S.K. (7/1/2007)*

ST. CLEMENT

St. Clement 2001 Oroppas Bordeaux Blend (Napa Valley) $50. 86 *—S.H. (2/1/2005)*

St. Clement 1999 Oroppas Bordeaux Blend (Napa Valley) $50. 88 *—J.M. (6/1/2002)*

St. Clement 2004 Cabernet Sauvignon (Napa Valley) $36. Soft, fruity and a little hot and peppery, this Cab shows ultraripe pie filling blackberry and cherry flavors that taste sugary on the finish. 83 *—S.H. (11/1/2007)*

St. Clement 2003 Cabernet Sauvignon (Napa Valley) $36. Not quite in the same league as the winery's Star Vineyard or Oroppas bottlings, but then, they cost a lot more. This one shows a mountain quality to the tight, firm tannins and intensely ripe core of blackberry fruit. Pretty good Cab, and should age well for 10 years. 90 *—S.H. (2/1/2007)*

St. Clement 2001 Cabernet Sauvignon (Napa Valley) $35. 89 *—S.H. (3/1/2005)*

St. Clement 2000 Cabernet Sauvignon (Napa Valley) $35. 87 *—S.H. (4/1/2004)*

St. Clement 1999 Cabernet Sauvignon (Napa Valley) $32. 87 *—S.H. (11/15/2002)*

St. Clement 1998 Cabernet Sauvignon (Howell Mountain) $35. 92 *—S.H. (6/1/2002)*

St. Clement 1998 Cabernet Sauvignon (Napa Valley) $35. 86 *—S.H. (6/1/2002)*

St. Clement 1997 Cabernet Sauvignon (Howell Mountain) $65. 92 *(11/1/2000)*

St. Clement 1997 Cabernet Sauvignon (Napa Valley) $35. 94 *(11/1/2000)*

St. Clement 1996 Cabernet Sauvignon (Howell Mountain) $50. 90 *—S.H. (9/1/2000)*

St. Clement 1996 Cabernet Sauvignon (Napa Valley) $30. 92 *(11/15/1999)*

St. Clement 1999 Howell Mountain Cabernet Sauvignon (Napa Valley) $70. 89 *(8/1/2003)*

St. Clement 2004 Oroppas Cabernet Sauvignon (Napa Valley) $55. Riper and certainly hotter than past vintages, this Oroppas, which is a Cab-Merlot blend, shows its very high alcohol in the raisins and prickly heat that dominate it. Decent in many respects, but not going anywhere, so drink up. 84 *—S.H. (6/1/2007)*

St. Clement 2003 Oroppas Cabernet Sauvignon (Napa Valley) $50. 91 Cellar Selection *—S.H. (12/1/2006)*

St. Clement 2002 Oroppas Cabernet Sauvignon (Napa Valley) $50. 88 *—S.H. (12/15/2005)*

St. Clement 2004 Star Vineyard Cabernet Sauvignon (Rutherford) $80. A first bottle was obviously off. A second was better, although still lacking the complexity you want at this price. It was a young Cab, dry and tannic, with a core of cassis and cherries. A few years in the cellar should soften it. 87 *—S.H. (12/15/2007)*

St. Clement 2003 Star Vineyard Cabernet Sauvignon (Rutherford) $80. 93 Cellar Selection *—S.H. (12/15/2006)*

St. Clement 2002 Star Vineyard Cabernet Sauvignon (Rutherford) $80. 85 *—S.H. (12/31/2005)*

St. Clement 2005 Chardonnay (Carneros) $17. Clean and dry, but too watery, like flat lemon juice with a drop of oak flavoring. What a disappointment. 82 *—S.H. (2/1/2007)*

St. Clement 2002 Chardonnay (Carneros) $16. 90 *—S.H. (3/1/2005)*

St. Clement 2001 Chardonnay (Napa Valley) $16. 87 *—S.H. (6/1/2004)*

St. Clement 1999 Chardonnay (Napa Valley) $16. 88 *—S.H. (11/15/2001)*

St. Clement 1999 Abbotts Vineyard Chardonnay (Carneros) $23. 86 *—S.H. (5/1/2002)*

St. Clement 1998 Abbotts Vineyard Chardonnay (Carneros) $20. 84 *(6/1/2000)*

St. Clement 2004 Merlot (Napa Valley) $28. Soft and fleshy, this is an easy, fruity Merlot that drinks well now. It has pleasant cherry, red currant and oak flavors, and is dry and spicy. 86 *—S.H. (11/1/2007)*

St. Clement 2002 Merlot (Napa Valley) $28. 82 *—S.H. (11/1/2006)*

St. Clement 2001 Merlot (Napa Valley) $28. 89 *—S.H. (9/1/2004)*

St. Clement 1999 Merlot (Napa Valley) $28. 92 *—S.H. (6/1/2002)*

St. Clement 1998 Merlot (Napa Valley) $26. 89 *—S.H. (12/1/2001)*

St. Clement 1997 Merlot (Napa Valley) $26. 89 *—S.H. (7/1/2000)*

St. Clement 1999 Petite Sirah (Napa Valley) $32. 90 *—S.H. (9/1/2002)*

St. Clement 2000 Oroppas Red Blend (Napa Valley) $50. 90 *—S.H. (11/15/2003)*

St. Clement 1998 Sauvignon Blanc (Napa Valley) $13. 88 —*S.H. (3/1/2000)*

St. Clement 2001 Sauvignon Blanc (Napa Valley) $13. 86 —*S.H. (10/1/2003)*

St. Clement 1999 Sauvignon Blanc (Napa Valley) $13. 84 —*S.H. (8/1/2001)*

ST. FRANCIS

St. Francis 2002 Claret Bordeaux Blend (Sonoma County) $20. At five years, the wine still retains some charm, but is showing its age. It's a little tired in structure, and the fruit is fading, turning dry and leathery. But there's cherries and cassis, with some complexity in the finish. Drink now. **87** —*S.H. (12/31/2007)*

St. Francis 2004 Cabernet Sauvignon (Sonoma County) $24. Softly tannic, this Cab is full-bodied and has some complexity. The black cassis and cherry flavors have layers of spice and smoky oak, with a fine, sweet finish that lingers. Drink now through 2010. **88** —*S.H. (12/31/2007)*

St. Francis 2003 Cabernet Sauvignon (Sonoma County) $21. Okay for everyday purposes, this Cab has well-ripened fruit flavors and an obvious coating of oak. It feels rustic, and finishes with a sugary swirl. **83** —*S.H. (5/1/2007)*

St. Francis 2002 Cabernet Sauvignon (Sonoma County) $18. 85 —*S.H. (6/1/2006)*

St. Francis 2001 Cabernet Sauvignon (Sonoma County) $20. 85 —*S.H. (10/1/2004)*

St. Francis 2000 Cabernet Sauvignon (Sonoma County) $16. 90 Editors' Choice —*S.H. (11/15/2003)*

St. Francis 1999 Cabernet Sauvignon (Sonoma County) $16. 85 —*S.H. (6/1/2002)*

St. Francis 1997 Kings Ridge Reserve Cabernet Sauvignon (Sonoma County) $85. 87 —*J.C. (6/1/2003)*

St. Francis 2001 Kings Ridge Vineyard Reserve Cabernet Sauvignon (Sonoma County) $NA. 91 *(11/15/2005)*

St. Francis 2001 Nuns Canyon Reserve Cabernet Sauvignon (Sonoma County) $28. 89 *(11/15/2005)*

St. Francis 1999 Nuns Canyon Reserve Cabernet Sauvignon (Sonoma Valley) $45. 92 —*S.H. (11/15/2003)*

St. Francis 1997 Reserve Cabernet Sauvignon (Sonoma Valley) $40. 90 *(11/1/2000)*

St. Francis 2005 Chardonnay (Sonoma County) $17. A little soft and frankly sweet, with a taste like old-fashioned cotton candy on top of the jellied LifeSaver fruit flavors. **83** —*S.H. (12/1/2007)*

St. Francis 2004 Chardonnay (Sonoma County) $12. 82 —*S.H. (10/1/2006)*

St. Francis 2003 Chardonnay (Sonoma County) $12. 85 *(11/15/2005)*

St. Francis 2001 Chardonnay (Sonoma County) $12. 87 Best Buy —*S.H. (9/1/2003)*

St. Francis 2000 Chardonnay (Sonoma County) $6. 84 —*S.H. (5/1/2002)*

St. Francis 1999 Chardonnay (Sonoma County) $13. 87 Best Buy —*S.H. (5/1/2001)*

St. Francis 2004 Behler Reserve Chardonnay (Sonoma County) $25. 85 —*S.H. (10/1/2006)*

St. Francis 2003 Behler Reserve Chardonnay (Sonoma Valley) $24. 85 —*S.H. (3/1/2006)*

St. Francis 2002 Behler Reserve Chardonnay (Sonoma County) $24. 87 *(11/15/2005)*

St. Francis 2001 Behler Reserve Chardonnay (Sonoma Valley) $24. 88 —*S.H. (12/15/2003)*

St. Francis 2000 Behler Vineyard Reserve Chardonnay (Sonoma Valley) $NA. 87 —*S.H. (2/1/2003)*

St. Francis 2000 Anthem Meritage (Sonoma Valley) $55. 91 —*S.H. (10/1/2004)*

St. Francis 1999 Anthem Meritage (Sonoma Valley) $65. 93 —*S.H. (10/1/2003)*

St. Francis 2003 Merlot (Sonoma County) $22. A Merlot with real elegance. This is fully dry, with firm, furry tannins, showing black cherry and currant flavors that are transforming into dried fruits and sweet leather. Could develop for a few more years. **87** —*S.H. (12/31/2007)*

St. Francis 1999 Merlot (Sonoma County) $24. 86 —*J.M. (6/1/2002)*

St. Francis 1998 Merlot (Solano County) $25. 86 —*S.H. (6/1/2001)*

St. Francis 1997 Merlot (Sonoma County) $20. 87 —*J.C. (7/1/2000)*

St. Francis 2001 Behler Reserve Merlot (Sonoma County) $28. 87 *(11/15/2005)*

St. Francis 1999 Behler Reserve Merlot (Sonoma Valley) $45. 90 —*S.H. (12/31/2003)*

St. Francis 1996 Reserve Merlot (Sonoma Valley) $39. 88 *(3/1/2000)*

St. Francis 2001 Port (Sonoma County) $25. 91 —*S.H. (12/1/2004)*

St. Francis 2001 Claret Red Blend (Sonoma County) $17. 85 —*S.H. (11/15/2004)*

St. Francis 2002 Red Blend (Sonoma County) $12. 84 —*S.H. (2/1/2006)*

St. Francis 2004 RED Red Blend (Sonoma County) $13. Soft and heavy, this Bordeaux-Zinfandel blend mixes overripe cherry syrup flavors with less ripe minty, green tastes. It finishes dry and harsh in acids and raw green tannins. **80** —*S.H. (11/15/2007)*

St. Francis 2002 Red Wine Red Blend (Sonoma County) $12. 84 —*S.H. (11/15/2006)*

St. Francis 2006 Rosé Blend (Sonoma County) $16. Simple and dry, with cherry cough drop and spice flavors. Tasted twice. **80** —*S.H. (12/31/2007)*

St. Francis 2004 Syrah (Sonoma County) $19. A good wine in many respects, but it has dry, astringent tannins that make it feel harsh and sticky. The cherry and blackberry flavors are ripe and somewhat medicinal. **83** —*S.H. (12/1/2007)*

St. Francis 2003 Syrah (Sonoma County) $20. 84 —*S.H. (11/1/2006)*

St. Francis 2002 Syrah (Sonoma County) $20. 82 *(9/1/2005)*

St. Francis 2001 Nuns Canyon Vineyard Syrah (Sonoma Valley) $35. 92 —*S.H. (12/1/2004)*

St. Francis 2004 Old Vines Zinfandel (Sonoma County) $22. With ripe cherry-berry and tobacco-spice flavors, this is a bit hot in alcohol and rustic in astringent tannins. But give it the right greasy food, such as barbecue ribs, and it will rise to the occasion. **83** —*S.H. (12/1/2007)*

St. Francis 2002 Old Vines Zinfandel (Sonoma County) $18. 85 —*S.H. (12/31/2005)*

St. Francis 2002 Old Vines Zinfandel (Sonoma Valley) $18. 85 *(11/15/2005)*

St. Francis 2001 Old Vines Zinfandel (Sonoma County) $22. 88 *(11/1/2003)*

St. Francis 2000 Old Vines Zinfandel (Sonoma County) $22. 86 —*S.H. (9/1/2003)*

St. Francis 1999 Old Vines Zinfandel (Sonoma County) $22. 88 —*S.H. (11/1/2002)*

St. Francis 1998 Old Vines Zinfandel (Sonoma County) $25. 91 —*P.G. (3/1/2001)*

St. Francis 1997 Old Vines Zinfandel (Sonoma County) $24. 90 —*P.G. (11/15/1999)*

St. Francis 2004 Pagani Vineyard Reserve Zinfandel (Sonoma Valley) $38. This is a Zin for lovers of big, ripe to overripe, tannic, high-alcohol interpretations of the variety. Made from very old vines, the flavors are mainly of raisins, with complexities of oak, balsam and peppery spices. **86** —*S.H. (12/31/2007)*

St. Francis 2002 Pagani Vineyard Reserve Zinfandel (Sonoma County) $46. 90 *(11/15/2005)*

St. Francis 2001 Pagani Vineyard Reserve Zinfandel (Sonoma Valley) $45. 90 *(11/1/2003)*

St. Francis 2001 Pagani Vineyard Reserve Zinfandel (Sonoma Valley) $45. 93 —*S.H. (11/15/2004)*

St. Francis 1999 Pagani Vineyard Reserve Zinfandel (Sonoma Valley) $44. 92 —*S.H. (9/1/2002)*

St. Francis 1998 Pagani Vineyard Reserve Zinfandel (Sonoma Valley) $40. 91 —*P.G. (3/1/2001)*

St. Francis 1997 Pagani Vineyard Reserve Zinfandel (Sonoma Valley) $39. 88 —*P.G. (11/15/1999)*

ST. GEORGE

St. George 2002 Cabernet Sauvignon (Sonoma County) $10. 84 —*S.H. (11/1/2005)*

St. George 2002 Barrel Reserve Cabernet Sauvignon (Sonoma County) $11. 86 Best Buy —*S.H. (9/1/2006)*

St. George 2003 Chardonnay (Sonoma County) $10. 82 —*S.H. (10/1/2005)*

St. George 2002 Chardonnay (California) $8. 82 —*S.H. (5/1/2005)*

St. George 2004 Barrel Reserve Chardonnay (Sonoma County) $11. 86 Best Buy —*S.H. (9/1/2006)*

St. George 2004 Barrel Reserve Chardonnay (Sonoma County) $10. 85 Best Buy —*S.H. (10/1/2006)*

St. George 2001 Barrel Reserve Chardonnay (Sonoma County) $9. 82 —*S.H. (11/1/2005)*

St. George 2004 Coastal Chardonnay (California) $8. 84 Best Buy *—S.H. (4/1/2006)*

St. George 2004 Barrel Reserve Merlot (Sonoma County) $11. 80 *—S.H. (9/1/2006)*

St. George Coastal 2003 Chardonnay (California) $6. 83 Best Buy *—S.H. (11/1/2005)*

ST. INNOCENT

St. Innocent 1998 Freedom Hill Vineyard Pinot Blanc (Willamette Valley) $14. 81 *—L.W. (12/31/1999)*

St. Innocent 1997 O'Connor Pinot Gris (Willamette Valley) $12. 86 *(8/1/1999)*

ST. SUPERY

St. Supery 1998 Bordeaux Blend (Napa Valley) $20. 90 *—L.W. (2/1/2000)*

St. Supery 2001 Élu Bordeaux Blend (Napa Valley) $60. 92 *—S.H. (3/1/2006)*

St. Supery 2002 Elu Red Wine Cabernet Blend (Napa Valley) $69. Elu is St. Supery's Napa Valley Bordeaux blend. Largely Cabernet Sauvignon, with a little Merlot and Petit Verdot, it is really a gorgeous wine. Hard to describe how smooth and rich it feels in the mouth. There's lots of dusty tannins, rich blackberry essence, cherry fruit and chocolate flavor, and sweet toasty oak. The wine is beautiful now, but it should glide along and improve for another 10 years. 94 *—S.H. (3/1/2007)*

St. Supery 2002 Cabernet Sauvignon (Napa Valley) $28. 88 *—S.H. (11/15/2006)*

St. Supery 1996 Cabernet Sauvignon (Napa Valley) $18. 88 *—L.W. (12/31/1999)*

St. Supery 2002 Limited Edition Dollarhide Cabernet Sauvignon (Napa Valley) $79. Lots to admire in this 100% Cabernet. The tannins are beautiful, gliding like silk and velvet across the palate and carrying ripe blackberry, cherry, spice and sweet oak flavors. Doesn't taste entirely dry; there is some sweetness on the finish, which might direct your pairing possibilities. 88 *—S.H. (3/1/2007)*

St. Supery 1999 Dollarhide Ranch Cabernet Sauvignon (Napa Valley) $70. 91 *—J.M. (6/1/2003)*

St. Supery 1997 Dollarhide Ranch Limited Edition Cabernet Sauvignon (Napa Valley) $70. 92 *(11/1/2000)*

St. Supery 2003 Limited Edition Estate Cabernet Sauvignon (Rutherford) $79. Made entirely from St. Supery's Rutherford estate, this is dry and fairly tannic, with an earthy, herbal edge. It's kind of chunky right now and not showing particularly well, almost rustic, but could fall into line in time. Try 2008 and beyond. 86 *—S.H. (3/1/2007)*

St. Supery 1999 Limited Edition Cabernet Sauvignon-Merlot (Rutherford) $60. 90 *—M.S. (11/15/2002)*

St. Supery 2004 Chardonnay (Napa Valley) $18. 87 *—S.H. (12/15/2006)*

St. Supery 2000 Chardonnay (Napa Valley) $19. 87 *—J.M. (2/1/2003)*

St. Supery 1998 Chardonnay (Napa Valley) $16. 90 *(6/1/2000)*

St. Supery 2005 Estate Oak Free Chardonnay (Napa Valley) $18. 87 *—S.H. (12/15/2006)*

St. Supery 2006 Oak Free Chardonnay (Napa Valley) $22. This is not the best example of unoaked Chard. Without any enriching barrel notes, the wine shows raw, thin fruit, citrusy and green. 83 *—S.H. (9/1/2007)*

St. Supery 2000 Élu Meritage (Napa Valley) $50. 91 *—S.H. (8/1/2005)*

St. Supery 1999 Final Blend Meritage (Napa Valley) $50. 89 *(7/1/2002)*

St. Supery 1998 Red Meritage (Napa Valley) $50. 88 *(7/1/2002)*

St. Supery 2000 White Meritage (Napa Valley) $22. 87 *(7/1/2002)*

St. Supery 2004 Merlot (Rutherford) $40. The talent at St. Supéry is evident in this lush, balanced Merlot. It has the famously ripe, forward fruit of a great Napa red, but shows the balance, harmony and complexity you expect when you fork over $40. Smooth and polished, this low-production red is gorgeous now, and should hold and soften for another eight years. Available exclusively from the winery. 92 *—S.H. (5/1/2007)*

St. Supery 2002 Merlot (Napa Valley) $24. On the raisiny sweet side, with a sweet-and-sour taste, this Merlot, from a hot vintage, has been held back for many years, apparently in the hopes it would improve. Unfortunately, it remains a stubbornly unrewarding wine. 83 *—S.H. (5/1/2007)*

St. Supery 1999 Merlot (Napa Valley) $21. 86 *(7/1/2002)*

St. Supery 2006 Moscato (California) $21. Crisp acidity fortunately balances this sweet dessert wine, with honeyed cherry, tangerine and apricot preserves, smoky meringue and vanilla fudge flavors. It's easy and delicious, and if there were an extra depth of fruity intensity, it would earn a near-perfect score. 87 *—S.H. (9/1/2007)*

St. Supery 2001 Sweet White Moscato (California) $15. 89 *(7/1/2002)*

St. Supery 2004 Sauvignon Blanc (Napa Valley) $20. 89 *(7/1/2005)*

St. Supery 2001 Sauvignon Blanc (Napa Valley) $15. 88 *(7/1/2002)*

St. Supery 2004 Dollarhide Limited Edition Sauvignon Blanc (Napa Valley) $32. 88 *(7/1/2005)*

St. Supery 2005 Estate Bottled Sauvignon Blanc (Napa Valley) $19. 85 *—S.H. (11/15/2006)*

St. Supery 2005 Limited Edition Dollarhide Sauvignon Blanc (Napa Valley) $35. 88 *—S.H. (11/15/2006)*

St. Supery 2002 Syrah (Napa Valley) $35. 84 *(9/1/2005)*

St. Supery 2005 Virtu White Blend (Napa Valley) $25. 88 *—S.H. (12/15/2006)*

St. Supery 2003 Virtu White Blend (Napa Valley) $25. 88 *—S.H. (10/1/2005)*

St. Supery 2004 Virtu White Blend (Napa Valley) $25. 92 Editors' Choice *—S.H. (3/1/2006)*

STAG HOLLOW

Stag Hollow 1998 Vendange Sélection Pinot Noir (Willamette Valley) $45. 83 *—M.S. (12/1/2000)*

STAG'S LEAP WINE CELLARS

Stag's Leap Wine Cellars 1998 Cask 23 Bordeaux Blend (Napa Valley) $150. 95 *—J.M. (6/1/2002)*

Stag's Leap Wine Cellars 2000 Cabernet Sauvignon (Napa Valley) $45. 91 *—S.H. (3/1/2003)*

Stag's Leap Wine Cellars 1999 Cabernet Sauvignon (Napa Valley) $45. 85 *—S.H. (11/15/2002)*

Stag's Leap Wine Cellars 2004 Artemis Cabernet Sauvignon (Napa Valley) $50. Artemis has been spotty over the years. The '04 is a good wine, showing many of the best qualities of Napa Cab. The blackberry and tobacco fruit is rich and dry, the oak is fine, and the tannic structure is deep enough to allow for midterm aging. Best now through 2010. 87 *—S.H. (6/1/2007)*

Stag's Leap Wine Cellars 2003 Artemis Cabernet Sauvignon (Napa Valley) $50. 84 *—S.H. (9/1/2006)*

Stag's Leap Wine Cellars 2002 Artemis Cabernet Sauvignon (Napa Valley) $48. 87 *—S.H. (5/1/2005)*

Stag's Leap Wine Cellars 2001 Artemis Cabernet Sauvignon (Napa Valley) $45. 91 *(2/1/2004)*

Stag's Leap Wine Cellars 2003 Cask 23 Cabernet Sauvignon (Napa Valley) $175. This is a good Cask 23, but it's by no means among the top ranks. Fairly tannic now, it shows oatmeal raisin cookie, blackberry, coffee, gingerbread and vanilla flavors. The tannins are wonderfully smooth, rich and intricate. It doesn't have the balance for longterm cellaring, so drink by 2009, if not earlier. 89 *—S.H. (6/1/2007)*

Stag's Leap Wine Cellars 2002 Cask 23 Cabernet Sauvignon (Napa Valley) $150. 90 Cellar Selection *—S.H. (4/1/2006)*

Stag's Leap Wine Cellars 2001 Cask 23 Cabernet Sauvignon (Napa Valley) $150. 96 Cellar Selection *—S.H. (2/1/2005)*

Stag's Leap Wine Cellars 2000 Cask 23 Cabernet Sauvignon (Napa Valley) $150. 93 Cellar Selection *(2/1/2004)*

Stag's Leap Wine Cellars 1999 Cask 23 Cabernet Sauvignon (Napa Valley) $150. 92 *—S.H. (2/1/2003)*

Stag's Leap Wine Cellars 2003 Fay Cabernet Sauvignon (Napa Valley) $80. This reminds me of the 2000; it's a little on the light side, but elegant. Feels dry and balanced in the mouth, with firm tannins and crisp, citrusy acidity. There is currant and cherry fruit, but it seems strangely diluted. Still, it could hold a surprise down the road. 88 *—S.H. (6/1/2007)*

Stag's Leap Wine Cellars 2002 Fay Cabernet Sauvignon (Napa Valley) $80. 90 Cellar Selection *—S.H. (4/1/2006)*

Stag's Leap Wine Cellars 2001 Fay Cabernet Sauvignon (Napa Valley) $75. 92 *—S.H. (2/1/2005)*

Stag's Leap Wine Cellars 2000 Fay Cabernet Sauvignon (Napa Valley) $75. 88 *(2/1/2004)*

Stag's Leap Wine Cellars 1999 Fay Vineyard Cabernet Sauvignon (Napa Valley) $75. 93 *—S.H. (2/1/2003)*

Stag's Leap Wine Cellars 1998 Fay Vineyard Cabernet Sauvignon (Napa Valley) $75. 93 *—S.H. (6/1/2002)*

Stag's Leap Wine Cellars 2003 S.L.V. Cabernet Sauvignon (Napa Valley) $110. Fruitier and softer than the tannic '02, this is probably a wine to open fairly early. It's rich and ripe in blackberry jam and milk chocolate flavors, with balancing acidity. The tannins are soft and sweet. This seems a little obvious, but in a deliciously Napa way. 88 *—S.H. (6/1/2007)*

Stag's Leap Wine Cellars 2002 S.L.V. Cabernet Sauvignon (Napa Valley) $110. 91 Cellar Selection *—S.H. (4/1/2006)*

Stag's Leap Wine Cellars 2001 S.L.V. Cabernet Sauvignon (Napa Valley) $100. 93 *—S.H. (2/1/2005)*

Stag's Leap Wine Cellars 1999 S.L.V. Cabernet Sauvignon (Napa Valley) $100. 91 *—S.H. (2/1/2003)*

Stag's Leap Wine Cellars 2000 S.L.V. Cabernet Sauvignon (Napa Valley) $100. 90 *(2/1/2004)*

Stag's Leap Wine Cellars 1998 S.L.V. Cabernet Sauvignon (Napa Valley) $100. 96 *—S.H. (6/1/2002)*

Stag's Leap Wine Cellars 1996 SLD Cabernet Sauvignon (Stags Leap District) $100. 93 *(12/31/1999)*

Stag's Leap Wine Cellars 2004 Chardonnay (Napa Valley) $32. 83 *—S.H. (10/1/2006)*

Stag's Leap Wine Cellars 2003 Chardonnay (Napa Valley) $29. 87 *—S.H. (7/1/2005)*

Stag's Leap Wine Cellars 2001 Chardonnay (Napa Valley) $29. 90 *—S.H. (5/1/2003)*

Stag's Leap Wine Cellars 1999 Chardonnay (Napa Valley) $30. 91 *(7/1/2001)*

Stag's Leap Wine Cellars 1998 Chardonnay (Napa Valley) $26. 89 *(6/1/2000)*

Stag's Leap Wine Cellars 2004 Arcadia Vineyard Chardonnay (Napa Valley) $45. 87 *—S.H. (10/1/2006)*

Stag's Leap Wine Cellars 2002 Arcadia Vineyard Chardonnay (Napa Valley) $45. 90 *—S.H. (12/15/2004)*

Stag's Leap Wine Cellars 2001 Arcadia Vineyard Chardonnay (Napa Valley) $45. 90 *—S.H. (4/1/2004)*

Stag's Leap Wine Cellars 1999 Arcadia Vineyard Chardonnay (Napa Valley) $45. 88 *(7/1/2001)*

Stag's Leap Wine Cellars 1998 Beckstoffer Ranch Chardonnay (Napa Valley) $40. 89 *—S.H. (11/15/2000)*

Stag's Leap Wine Cellars 2005 Karia Chardonnay (Napa Valley) $32. A new Chard from this producer. It shows typical Napa characteristics of dryness and a dried herb earthiness, in addition to the apple, pear, oak and lees flavors. The texture is great, brimming with crisp acidity, yet the wine would benefit from richer fruit. **85** *—S.H. (6/1/2007)*

Stag's Leap Wine Cellars 1997 Napa Valley Chardonnay (Napa Valley) $26. 90 *—S.H. (7/1/2000)*

Stag's Leap Wine Cellars 1998 Reserve Chardonnay (Napa Valley) $45. 89 *—S.H. (11/15/2000)*

Stag's Leap Wine Cellars 1998 Reserve Chardonnay (Napa Valley) $45. 92 *(7/1/2001)*

Stag's Leap Wine Cellars 2004 Merlot (Napa Valley) $42. Superior viticulture and winemaking has pulled this Merlot from the fire of a hot vintage and allowed it to be subtle and elegant. Although it's powerful upfront in cherry, chocolate, coffee and violet flavors, it's a balanced wine, with just enough Cab added to give it extra depth. **90** *—S.H. (6/1/2007)*

Stag's Leap Wine Cellars 2003 Merlot (Napa Valley) $42. 88 *—S.H. (10/1/2006)*

Stag's Leap Wine Cellars 2001 Merlot (Napa Valley) $40. 93 *—S.H. (12/15/2004)*

Stag's Leap Wine Cellars 2000 Merlot (Napa Valley) $40. 86 *(2/1/2004)*

Stag's Leap Wine Cellars 1999 Merlot (Napa Valley) $40. 92 *—S.H. (11/15/2002)*

Stag's Leap Wine Cellars 1997 Merlot (Napa Valley) $35. 93 *—S.H. (2/1/2001)*

Stag's Leap Wine Cellars 2003 Sauvignon Blanc (Napa Valley) $20. 88 *(7/1/2005)*

Stag's Leap Wine Cellars 2001 Sauvignon Blanc (Napa Valley) $20. 87 *—S.H. (2/1/2004)*

Stag's Leap Wine Cellars 1999 Sauvignon Blanc (Napa Valley) $20. 90 *—S.H. (5/1/2001)*

Stag's Leap Wine Cellars 2000 Rancho Chimiles Sauvignon Blanc (Napa Valley) $28. 87 *(8/1/2002)*

STAGLIN

Staglin 2002 Cabernet Sauvignon (Rutherford) $125. 97 Cellar Selection *—S.H. (12/31/2005)*

Staglin 2001 Cabernet Sauvignon (Rutherford) $110. 96 *—S.H. (10/1/2004)*

Staglin 2000 Cabernet Sauvignon (Rutherford) $100. 87 *—S.H. (2/1/2004)*

Staglin 1999 Cabernet Sauvignon (Rutherford) $85. 92 *(12/15/2002)*

Staglin 1997 Cabernet Sauvignon (Rutherford) $65. 92 *(11/1/2000)*

Staglin 2003 Estate Cabernet Sauvignon (Rutherford) $135. 94 Cellar Selection *—S.H. (12/31/2006)*

Staglin 2000 Salus Cabernet Sauvignon (Napa Valley) $50. 86 *—S.H. (4/1/2004)*

Staglin 1999 Salus Cabernet Sauvignon (Rutherford) $50. 88 *(12/15/2002)*

Staglin 2000 Chardonnay (Rutherford) $50. 90 *(12/15/2002)*

Staglin 1999 Chardonnay (Rutherford) $53. 91 *(7/1/2001)*

Staglin 2000 Salus Chardonnay (Rutherford) $35. 87 *(12/15/2002)*

Staglin 2000 Stagliano Sangiovese (Rutherford) $65. 89 *(12/15/2002)*

STAGS' LEAP WINERY

Stags' Leap Winery 2004 Cabernet Sauvignon (Napa Valley) $48. Good, rich Cab from this veteran producer, but falls shy of greatness. The power comes from the authority of the tannins and currant-cassis fruit, and there's elegance in the overall balance. Falls short, though, for an overripe raisiny edge in the finish. **87** *—S.H. (11/1/2007)*

Stags' Leap Winery 2002 Cabernet Sauvignon (Napa Valley) $45. 87 *—S.H. (12/15/2005)*

Stags' Leap Winery 2001 Cabernet Sauvignon (Napa Valley) $42. 84 *—S.H. (4/1/2005)*

Stags' Leap Winery 1999 Cabernet Sauvignon (Napa Valley) $40. 92 *—S.H. (3/1/2003)*

Stags' Leap Winery 1998 Cabernet Sauvignon (Napa Valley) $40. 86 *—S.H. (12/31/2001)*

Stags' Leap Winery 1997 Cabernet Sauvignon (Napa Valley) $35. 94 *(11/1/2000)*

Stags' Leap Winery 1997 Cabernet Sauvignon (Napa Valley) $35. 92 *(11/1/2000)*

Stags' Leap Winery 1996 Cabernet Sauvignon (Napa Valley) $32. 92 *(12/31/1999)*

Stags' Leap Winery 1999 Estate Grown Reserve Cabernet Sauvignon (Napa Valley) $65. 88 *—S.H. (11/15/2003)*

Stags' Leap Winery 2000 Estate Reserve Cabernet Sauvignon (Napa Valley) $65. 90 *—S.H. (5/1/2005)*

Stags' Leap Winery 2000 Napa Valley Cabernet Sauvignon (Napa Valley) $40. 95 Editors' Choice *—S.H. (11/15/2004)*

Stags' Leap Winery 2005 Chardonnay (Stags Leap District) $28. I wish there were more fruit in this wine, because it has the crisp, bold acidity that so many of today's Chards lack. But the fruit isn't there. You get a tease of citrus and peach, and then, poof, it's gone, disappearing into mere alcohol and wood. **83** *—S.H. (3/1/2007)*

Stags' Leap Winery 2004 Chardonnay (Napa Valley) $24. 88 *—S.H. (12/15/2005)*

Stags' Leap Winery 2002 Chardonnay (Napa Valley) $22. 87 *—S.H. (9/1/2004)*

Stags' Leap Winery 2001 Chardonnay (Napa Valley) $22. 91 Editors' Choice *—S.H. (5/1/2003)*

Stags' Leap Winery 2000 Chardonnay (Napa Valley) $29. 90 *(5/1/2002)*

Stags' Leap Winery 1998 Chardonnay (Napa Valley) $21. 85 *(6/1/2000)*

Stags' Leap Winery 2004 Merlot (Napa Valley) $31. The best thing about this wonderful Merlot is balance. The winemaker has modulated the blackberry and plum fruit with earthier notes that suggest balsamic, soy-splashed sautéed beef, Portobello mushrooms and coffee. The grippy tannins and acids add a welcome touch of bitterness to the finish. With charm in addition to complexity, this Merlot will drink well for five years. **91** *—S.H. (11/1/2007)*

Stags' Leap Winery 2003 Merlot (Napa Valley) $31. Here's the real deal in a sumptuous, elegant and complex Merlot, from a venerable Napa producer. Fully dry, this has deeply earthy, blackberry, rum and cola flavors that are wrapped in fine, ripely sweet tannins. It should gain bottle complexity over the next five years. **89** *—S.H. (3/1/2007)*

Stags' Leap Winery 2002 Merlot (Napa Valley) $31. 84 *—S.H. (12/15/2005)*

Stags' Leap Winery 2001 Merlot (Napa Valley) $31. 93 *—S.H. (12/15/2004)*

Stags' Leap Winery 2000 Merlot (Napa Valley) $40. 93 *—S.H. (5/1/2004)*

Stags' Leap Winery 1998 Merlot (Napa Valley) $31. 86 *—S.H. (6/1/2001)*

Stags' Leap Winery 1997 Merlot (Napa Valley) $30. 91 *(12/31/1999)*

Stags' Leap Winery 2000 Estate Grown Reserve Merlot (Napa Valley) $50. 91 *—S.H. (12/31/2003)*

Stags' Leap Winery 2001 Estate Reserve Merlot (Napa Valley) $50. 85 —*S.H. (5/1/2005)*

Stags' Leap Winery 2003 Petite Sirah (Napa Valley) $38. 92 Editors' Choice —*S.H. (12/1/2006)*

Stags' Leap Winery 2002 Petite Sirah (Napa Valley) $35. 90 Cellar Selection —*S.H. (12/15/2005)*

Stags' Leap Winery 2001 Petite Sirah (Napa Valley) $31. 91 —*S.H. (11/15/2004)*

Stags' Leap Winery 2000 Petite Sirah (Napa Valley) $31. 91 —*J.M. (8/1/2004)*

Stags' Leap Winery 1999 Petite Sirah (Napa Valley) $31. 93 —*S.H. (12/1/2002)*

Stags' Leap Winery 1998 Petite Sirah (Napa Valley) $32. 90 —*J.M. (5/1/2002)*

Stags' Leap Winery 1996 Petite Sirah (Napa Valley) $28. 93 —*S.H. (5/1/2000)*

Stags' Leap Winery 2000 Ne Cede Malis Red Blend (Napa Valley) $54. 92 —*S.H. (5/1/2005)*

Stags' Leap Winery 1999 Ne Cede Malis Red Wine Red Blend (Napa Valley) $50. 92 —*S.H. (12/31/2003)*

Stags' Leap Winery 1997 Ne Cede Malis Rhône Red Blend (Stags Leap District) $50. 89 —*J.M. (12/1/2001)*

Stags' Leap Winery 2001 Syrah (Napa Valley) $29. 90 —*S.H. (12/1/2004)*

Stags' Leap Winery 2000 Syrah (Napa Valley) $29. 86 —*J.M. (6/1/2003)*

Stags' Leap Winery 1998 Syrah (Napa Valley) $25. 89 *(11/1/2001)*

Stags' Leap Winery 2002 Viognier (Napa Valley) $25. 87 —*S.H. (11/15/2004)*

Stags' Leap Winery 2001 Viognier (Napa Valley) $25. 90 —*S.H. (5/1/2003)*

Stags' Leap Winery 1999 Viognier (Napa Valley) $25. 92 Editors' Choice —*J.M. (12/1/2001)*

STANDING STONE

Standing Stone 1999 Pinnacle Bordeaux Blend (Finger Lakes) $20. 84 *J.C. (1/1/2004)*

Standing Stone 1997 Cabernet Franc (Finger Lakes) $16. 86 —*J.C. (12/1/1999)*

Standing Stone 1999 Cabernet Franc (Finger Lakes) $16. 84 —*J.C. (1/1/2004)*

Standing Stone 2000 Gewürztraminer (Finger Lakes) $NA. 91 —*J.M. (12/11/2002)*

Standing Stone 2002 Estate Merlot (Finger Lakes) $20. 83 —*M.D. (8/1/2006)*

Standing Stone 1999 Pinot Noir (Finger Lakes) $17. 84 —*J.C. (3/1/2002)*

Standing Stone 2004 Riesling (Finger Lakes) $13. 84 —*M.D. (8/1/2006)*

Standing Stone 2002 Estate Bottled Riesling (Finger Lakes) $12. 89 Best Buy —*J.C. (8/1/2003)*

Standing Stone 2001 Ice Riesling (Finger Lakes) $32. 90 —*J.C. (8/1/2003)*

Standing Stone 2005 Vidal Ice Vidal Blanc (Finger Lakes) $25. With an elegance and minerality typical of Standing Stone wines, this Vidal Blanc sets a high standard for Finger Lakes dessert wines. Ripe but subtle aromas of apricot and honey lead to measured, lively layers of pineapple and nutty spice that are rich but balanced. The finish is long but also delicate, tingling on the palate. **88 Editors' Choice** —*S.K. (12/1/2007)*

STANGELAND

Stangeland 2000 Estate Reserve Pinot Noir (Willamette Valley) $39. 85 *(10/1/2002)*

Stangeland 1999 Estate Reserve Pinot Noir (Willamette Valley) $32. 89 *(10/1/2002)*

Stangeland 1999 Martha's Vineyard II Pinot Noir (Willamette Valley) $30. 84 *(10/1/2002)*

Stangeland 1999 Silver Leaf Vineyard Pinot Noir (Willamette Valley) $40. 88 *(10/1/2002)*

Stangeland 2000 Winemaker's Estate Reserve Pinot Noir (Willamette Valley) $59. 90 *(10/1/2002)*

Stangeland 1999 Winemakers Estate Reserve Pinot Noir (Willamette Valley) $40. 87 *(10/1/2002)*

STANTON

Stanton 2002 Cabernet Sauvignon (Oakville) $65. 86 —*S.H. (11/1/2005)*

Stanton 2001 Cabernet Sauvignon (Oakville) $65. 87 —*S.H. (10/1/2004)*

STAR LANE VINEYARD

Star Lane Vineyard 2005 Sauvignon Blanc (Santa Ynez Valley) $25. 87 —*S.H. (12/15/2006)*

Star Lane Vineyard 2003 Sauvignon Blanc (Santa Ynez Valley) $25. 87 *(7/1/2005)*

Star Lane Vineyard 2003 Syrah (Santa Ynez Valley) $35. 87 —*S.H. (12/31/2006)*

Star Lane Vineyard 2003 Syrah (Santa Ynez Valley) $35. 92 —*S.H. (12/15/2006)*

STARK

Stark 2004 Cuvée Julian Syrah (Russian River Valley) $35. Rustic and simple, with candied cherry, pomegranate and coffee flavors. On the border of dry and off-dry. Strong in tannins and acids. **83** —*S.H. (7/1/2007)*

Stark 2005 Damiano Vineyard Viognier (Sierra Foothills) $23. Shows off Viognier's exotic style. An opulent, dry wine bursting with honeysuckle, apricot jam and lime flavors, with a cinnamon spice finish. Brisk acidity makes it all clean and bright. **86** —*S.H. (7/1/2007)*

STARRY NIGHT

Starry Night 2002 Chardonnay (Russian River Valley) $17. 87 —*S.H. (12/15/2004)*

Starry Night 2002 Adara Rhône Red Blend (California) $14. 83 —*S.H. (12/15/2004)*

Starry Night 1999 Syrah (Lodi) $19. 91 —*S.H. (7/1/2002)*

Starry Night 2003 Zinfandel (Lodi) $16. 83 —*S.H. (12/1/2005)*

Starry Night 2001 Zinfandel (Lodi) $16. 85 *(11/1/2003)*

Starry Night 2001 Old Vine Zinfandel (Russian River Valley) $22. 88 *(11/1/2003)*

Starry Night 2002 Terre Vermeille Vineyard Zinfandel (Lake County) $18. 85 —*S.H. (12/15/2004)*

Starry Night 2001 Tom Feeney Ranch, Old Vine Zinfandel (Russian River Valley) $26. 90 —*J.M. (6/1/2004)*

Starry Night 2003 Wildotter Vineyard Zinfandel (Amador County) $18. 81 —*S.H. (12/1/2005)*

STATON HILLS

Staton Hills 1995 Cabernet Sauvignon (Columbia Valley (WA)) $17. 87 —*M.S. (9/1/1999)*

Staton Hills 1997 Chardonnay (Washington) $12. 82 —*P.G. (6/1/2000)*

STE. CHAPELLE

Ste. Chapelle 2000 Winemaker's Series Cabernet Sauvignon (Idaho) $10. 88 —*P.G. (9/1/2002)*

Ste. Chapelle NV Sparkling Brut Champagne Blend (Idaho) $8. 83 —*S.H. (12/1/2000)*

Ste. Chapelle NV Spumante Champagne Blend (Idaho) $8. 81 —*P.G. (6/1/2001)*

Ste. Chapelle 1999 Chardonnay (Idaho) $10. 84 —*P.G. (9/1/2002)*

Ste. Chapelle 2001 Soft Chenin Blanc (Idaho) $6. 86 —*P.G. (9/1/2002)*

Ste. Chapelle 2000 Fumé Blanc (Idaho) $10. 87 —*P.G. (9/1/2002)*

Ste. Chapelle 1998 Gewürztraminer (Idaho) $7. 81 —*J.C. (9/1/1999)*

Ste. Chapelle 2001 Dry Gewürztraminer (Idaho) $6. 88 Best Buy —*P.G. (9/1/2002)*

Ste. Chapelle 2001 Johannisberg Riesling (Idaho) $6. 88 Best Buy —*P.G. (9/1/2002)*

Ste. Chapelle 1998 Dry Johannisberg Riesling (Idaho) $7. 80 —*J.C. (9/1/1999)*

Ste. Chapelle 1997 Sally's Summit Vineyard Dry Johannisberg Riesling (Idaho) $10. 87 —*J.C. (9/1/1999)*

Ste. Chapelle 2001 Special Harvest Johannisberg Riesling (Idaho) $10. 90 Best Buy —*P.G. (9/1/2002)*

Ste. Chapelle 2000 Value Series Merlot (Idaho) $7. 87 Best Buy —*P.G. (9/1/2002)*

Ste. Chapelle 2000 Winemaker's Series Merlot (Idaho) $10. 88 —*P.G. (9/1/2002)*

Ste. Chapelle 1998 Riesling (Idaho) $6. 83 —*J.C. (9/1/1999)*

Ste. Chapelle 2001 Dry Riesling (Idaho) $6. 88 Best Buy —*P.G. (9/1/2002)*

Ste. Chapelle 1998 Special Harvest Riesling (Idaho) $8. 85 —*J.C. (9/1/1999)*

Ste. Chapelle 1996 Reserve Syrah (Idaho) $15. 90 —*M.G. (11/15/1999)*

Ste. Chapelle 2000 Winemaker's Series Syrah (Idaho) $10. 86 *—P.G. (9/1/2002)*

STE. MICHELLE

Ste. Michelle Wine Estates 2006 Nellie's Garden Dry Rosé Blend (Columbia Valley (WA)) $13. It's almost entirely Syrah, with very small amounts of Grenache, Viognier and Mourvèdre also included. Roughly 18% is barrel fermented and aged sur lie in neutral oak, adding richness to the mouthfeel. A pale cranberry color, this is bright and tart, with crisp acids and a finish that shows some of the white pepper of Syrah. **87** *—P.G. (7/1/2007)*

STEELE

Steele 2005 Cabernet Franc (Clear Lake) $16. Nice flavors, with cherry-pie filling, raspberry, root beer, gingerbread, smoke and vanilla spice flavors. But it's made in an exaggerated modern style, so soft and apparently sweet that it really fails to find balance. **83** *—S.H. (9/1/2007)*

Steele 2003 Cabernet Franc (Lake County) $18. 85 *—S.H. (12/15/2005)*

Steele 2006 Rosé Cabernet Franc (Lake County) $16. Heavy, sweet and cloying, with candied flavors of puréed cherries and vanilla. **80** *—S.H. (12/1/2007)*

Steele 2004 Cabernet Sauvignon (Red Hills Lake County) $32. One of the sweetest Cabs on the market, it's way too sugary, tasting like sweet plum and blackberry fruit juice with alcohol. **80** *—S.H. (12/31/2007)*

Steele 2002 Cabernet Sauvignon (Red Hills Lake County) $35. 87 *—S.H. (12/1/2006)*

Steele 2004 Bien Nacido Vineyard Chardonnay (Santa Barbara County) $28. 92 *—S.H. (12/15/2006)*

Steele 1998 Bien Nacido Vineyard Chardonnay (Santa Barbara) $30. 92 Best Buy *(7/1/2001)*

Steele 1997 Bien Nacido Vineyard Chardonnay (Santa Barbara County) $28. 94 *—L.W. (7/1/1999)*

Steele 1998 Cuvée Chardonnay (California) $18. 90 *(6/1/2000)*

Steele 2005 Du Pratt Vineyard Chardonnay (Mendocino Ridge) $28. There aren't many Chards from this hilly Mendocino area. This wine shows dryness and ripeness, with a stony minerality undergirding peach custard and pineapple tart flavors, enriched with a satisfying touch of smoky oak. **87** *—S.H. (9/1/2007)*

Steele 2004 Du Pratt Vineyard Chardonnay (Mendocino Ridge) $28. 92 *—S.H. (12/15/2006)*

Steele 1998 Du Pratt Vineyard Chardonnay (Mendocino) $30. 90 *(7/1/2001)*

Steele 1997 Du Pratt Vineyard (Late Harvest) Chardonnay (Mendocino) $30. 87 *—J.M. (6/1/2003)*

Steele 1997 Du Pratt Vineyard Chardonnay (Mendocino County) $27. 91 *—L.W. (7/1/1999)*

Steele 1998 Durell Vineyard Chardonnay (Carneros) $28. 87 *(6/1/2000)*

Steele 1997 Durell Vineyard Chardonnay (Carneros) $26. 92 *—L.W. (6/1/1999)*

Steele 1998 Goodchild Vineyard Chardonnay (Santa Barbara County) $30. 87 *(7/1/2001)*

Steele 1997 Goodchild Vineyard Chardonnay (Santa Barbara County) $24. 93 *—S.H. (2/1/2000)*

Steele 2004 Lolonis Vineyard Chardonnay (Mendocino County) $28. Jed Steele has fun working with vineyard-designated Chards from all over the place, but the Lolonis bottling has never been his best. This is an earthy, austere wine whose major influence is smoky, caramelized oak. **84** *—S.H. (4/1/2007)*

Steele 1998 Lolonis Vineyard Chardonnay (Mendocino) $32. 89 *(7/1/2001)*

Steele 1998 Lolonis Vineyard Chardonnay (Mendocino County) $28. 85 *(6/1/2000)*

Steele 1998 Parmalee-Hill Vineyard Chardonnay (Sonoma Valley) $26. 93 *—S.H. (2/1/2000)*

Steele 2001 Parmelee-Hill Vineyard Chardonnay (Sonoma Valley) $28. 83 *—S.H. (12/15/2005)*

Steele 1998 Parmelee-Hill Vineyard Chardonnay (Sonoma Valley) $30. 89 *(7/1/2001)*

Steele 1998 Sangiacomo Vineyard Chardonnay (Carneros) $30. 90 *(7/1/2001)*

Steele 1997 Sangiacomo Vineyard Chardonnay (Carneros) $24. 93 *—L.W. (6/1/1999)*

Steele 2004 Shooting Star Chardonnay (Santa Barbara County) $12. 83 *—S.H. (12/15/2005)*

Steele 1999 Fumé Blanc (Lake County) $16. 88 *(8/1/2002)*

Steele 1999 Clear Lake Merlot (Lake County) $26. 84 *—S.H. (12/1/2003)*

Steele 1997 Clear Lake Merlot (Lake County) $22. 86 *—J.C. (7/1/2000)*

Steele 2002 Pinot Blanc (Santa Barbara County) $16. 84 *—S.H. (12/1/2004)*

Steele 1998 Bien Nacido Vineyard Pinot Blanc (Santa Barbara County) $16. 84 *—L.W. (3/1/2000)*

Steele 2001 Pinot Noir (Anderson Valley) $22. 83 *—S.H. (12/1/2004)*

Steele 1997 Pinot Noir (Carneros) $19. 90 *(10/1/1999)*

Steele 2003 Bien Nacido Vineyard Pinot Noir (Santa Barbara County) $35. 90 *—S.H. (12/1/2006)*

Steele 2000 Bien Nacido Vineyard Pinot Noir (Santa Barbara County) $30. 84 *—S.H. (12/1/2004)*

Steele 1999 Bien Nacido Vineyard Pinot Noir (Santa Barbara County) $36. 87 *(10/1/2002)*

Steele 1999 Durell Vineyard Pinot Noir (Carneros) $28. 88 *(10/1/2002)*

Steele 2002 Goodchild Vineyard Pinot Noir (Santa Barbara County) $26. 92 *(11/1/2004)*

Steele 1999 Goodchild Vineyard Pinot Noir (Santa Barbara) $32. 88 *(10/1/2002)*

Steele 2001 Sangiacomo Vineyard Pinot Noir (Carneros) $30. 84 *—S.H. (12/1/2004)*

Steele 1999 Sangiacomo Vineyard Pinot Noir (Carneros) $32. 88 *(10/1/2002)*

Steele 2006 Shooting Star Riesling (Lake County) $14. Off-dry and easy to sip, with honeyed flavors of lemons, peaches, pineapples, wildflowers and spices that are balanced by crisp acidity. **86** *—S.H. (9/1/2007)*

Steele 1997 Syrah (Lake County) $16. 91 *—L.W. (5/1/2000)*

Steele 2003 Black Bubbles Syrah (Lake County) $16. Yes, it's sparkling Syrah, made famous by the Aussies. As dark as a red wine, it's so deliciously aromatic in cherry pie, chocolate fudge and caramel scents, it makes your mouth water. Once in that mouth, it has the dry effervescence of a sparkling wine, with the weight of, well, Syrah. A curiosity, but a good one. **90** *—S.H. (9/1/2007)*

Steele 2001 Clear Lake Syrah (Lake County) $16. 85 *(9/1/2005)*

Steele 2004 Parmalee-Hill Vineyard Syrah (Sonoma Valley) $28. Frankly sweet, as are so many Steele wines, this Syrah tastes like alcoholized cherry and blackberry jelly, with a chocolate fudge and caramelized finish. **81** *—S.H. (12/31/2007)*

Steele 2001 Parmelee-Hill Vineyard Syrah (Sonoma Valley) $22. 84 *(9/1/2005)*

Steele 2000 Parmalee-Hill Vineyard Syrah (Sonoma Valley) $22. 84 *—S.H. (12/1/2004)*

Steele 2002 Stymie Founder's Reserve Syrah (Lake County) $45. 82 *—S.H. (12/1/2006)*

Steele 2004 Syrah Port (Lake County) $11. With 7% residual sugar, tastes sweet and common, with chocolaty blackberry flavors that finish sharp. **84** *—S.H. (9/1/2007)*

Steele 2005 Writer's Block Syrah (Lake County) $15. From Jed Steele, up in Lake County, comes this slightly sweet, soft but pleasurable Syrah. It tastes like the fruit filling you get in a good cherry and blueberry pie, sprinkled with a dash of crème de cassis. **84** *—S.H. (11/15/2007)*

Steele 2004 Viognier (Lake County) $18. 84 *—S.H. (12/15/2005)*

Steele 2001 Viognier (Lake County) $18. 85 *—M.S. (5/1/2003)*

Steele 2002 Catfish Vineyard Zinfandel (Lake County) $21. 83 *—S.H. (12/31/2005)*

Steele 1998 Catfish Vineyard Zinfandel (Clear Lake) $19. 91 *—P.G. (3/1/2001)*

Steele 1998 Pacini Vineyard Zinfandel (Mendocino) $22. 89 *—P.G. (3/1/2001)*

Steele 1997 Pacini Vineyard Zinfandel (Mendocino County) $24. 85 *—J.C. (9/1/1999)*

Steele 2003 Shooting Star Zinfandel (Lake County) $12. 82 *—S.H. (12/31/2005)*

STEFAN DANIELS

Stefan Daniels 2001 Sauvignon Blanc (Redwood Valley) $15. 86 *—S.H. (12/31/2003)*

Stefan Daniels 1999 Terre Vermeille Vineyard Sauvignon Blanc (Lake County) $17. 88 *—S.H. (5/1/2001)*

Stefan Daniels 2000 Lockeford Syrah (Lodi) $15. 87 *—S.H. (3/1/2004)*

Stefan Daniels 1999 Lockeford Syrah (California) $20. 89 *(10/1/2001)*

STELLA MARIS

Stella Maris 2004 Red Blend (Columbia Valley (WA)) $28. There was no slippage for Stella in this second vintage; in fact, it's a clear step up from the 2003. 88% Merlot, 10% Cabernet Sauvignon and 2% Petit Verdot, this titillates with sweet raspberry fruit, leading into chocolate and cherry. It's a lively, delicious wine, that tops out at 14.5% alcohol. **90** *—P.G. (12/1/2007)*

Stella Maris 2003 Red Blend (Columbia Valley (WA)) $29. 88 *—P.G. (10/1/2006)*

Stella Maris 2002 Red Blend (Columbia Valley (WA)) $29. 87 *—P.G. (12/15/2005)*

STELTZNER

Steltzner 2001 Claret Bordeaux Blend (Napa Valley) $16. 84 *—S.H. (4/1/2004)*

Steltzner 2003 Claret Cabernet Blend (Napa Valley) $18. 90 *—S.H. (11/1/2006)*

Steltzner 1998 Cabernet Sauvignon (Napa Valley) $28. 90 *—S.H. (6/1/2002)*

Steltzner 1999 Merlot (Stags' Leap District) $26. 92 *—S.H. (6/1/2002)*

STEPHAN RIDGE

Stephan Ridge 2000 L'Adventure Estate Cuvée Red Blend (Paso Robles) $75. 92 Editors' Choice *—S.H. (11/15/2003)*

Stephan Ridge 2000 Syrah-Cabernet (Paso Robles) $25. 82 *—S.H. (3/1/2004)*

STEPHEN ROSS

Stephen Ross 2005 Chardonnay (Edna Valley) $22. Silky and crisp, with those long, penetrating Edna Valley flavors of ripe kiwis, Key lime pie and intense vanilla. Shows real elegance and flair, and this is a good price for the quality. **91** *—S.H. (9/1/2007)*

Stephen Ross 2004 Chardonnay (Edna Valley) $20. 89 *—S.H. (3/1/2006)*

Stephen Ross 2004 Bien Nacido Vineyard Chardonnay (Santa Maria Valley) $25. 90 *—S.H. (3/1/2006)*

Stephen Ross 2000 Edna Ranch Chardonnay (Edna Valley) $20. 85 *—S.H. (6/1/2003)*

Stephen Ross 2003 Thomann Station Petite Sirah (Napa Valley) $32. 90 *—S.H. (3/1/2006)*

Stephen Ross 2000 Thomann Station Petite Sirah (Napa Valley) $32. 88 *(4/1/2003)*

Stephen Ross 2004 Pinot Noir (Edna Valley) $28. 89 *—S.H. (12/1/2006)*

Stephen Ross 2003 Pinot Noir (Edna Valley) $28. 87 *—S.H. (3/1/2006)*

Stephen Ross 2002 Pinot Noir (Edna Valley) $28. 91 Editors' Choice *(11/1/2004)*

Stephen Ross 2000 Pinot Noir (Edna Valley) $28. 86 *(10/1/2002)*

Stephen Ross 2004 Aubaine Vineyards Pinot Noir (San Luis Obispo County) $40. 88 Cellar Selection *—S.H. (12/1/2006)*

Stephen Ross 2004 Bien Nacido Vineyard Pinot Noir (Santa Maria Valley) $35. 93 Cellar Selection *—S.H. (12/1/2006)*

Stephen Ross 2003 Bien Nacido Vineyard Pinot Noir (Santa Maria Valley) $35. 86 *—S.H. (3/1/2006)*

Stephen Ross 2002 Bien Nacido Vineyard Pinot Noir (Santa Maria Valley) $35. 87 *(11/1/2004)*

Stephen Ross 2000 Bien Nacido Vineyard Pinot Noir (Santa Maria Valley) $35. 89 *(10/1/2002)*

Stephen Ross 2000 Chamisal Vineyard Pinot Noir (Edna Valley) $40. 90 Editors' Choice *(10/1/2002)*

Stephen Ross 1999 Chamisal Vineyard Pinot Noir (Edna Valley) $24. 87 *—S.H. (12/15/2001)*

Stephen Ross 2000 Edna Ranch Pinot Noir (Edna Valley) $40. 86 *(10/1/2002)*

Stephen Ross 1999 Edna Ranch Pinot Noir (Edna Valley) $28. 89 *—S.H. (12/15/2001)*

Stephen Ross 2004 Stone Corral Vineyard Pinot Noir (Edna Valley) $45. 92 *—S.H. (12/1/2006)*

Stephen Ross 2003 Stone Corral Vineyard Pinot Noir (Edna Valley) $45. 87 *—S.H. (3/1/2006)*

Stephen Ross 2003 Dante Dusi Vineyard Zinfandel (Paso Robles) $24. 85 *—S.H. (3/1/2006)*

Stephen Ross 2001 Dante Dusi Vineyard Zinfandel (Paso Robles) $22. 90 Editors' Choice *(11/1/2003)*

Stephen Ross 2000 Dante Dusi Vineyard Zinfandel (Paso Robles) $22. 89 *—M.S. (9/1/2003)*

Stephen Ross 1999 Dusi Vineyard/Martini Vineyard Zinfandel (Paso Robles) $20. 85 *—S.H. (12/15/2001)*

Stephen Ross 2001 Monte Rosso Vineyard Zinfandel (Sonoma Valley) $28. 89 *(11/1/2003)*

Stephen Ross 1999 Monte Rosso Vineyard Zinfandel (Sonoma Valley) $28. 92 Editors' Choice *—S.H. (12/15/2001)*

STEPHEN VINCENT

Stephen Vincent 2003 Cabernet Sauvignon (California) $10. 84 *—S.H. (12/31/2005)*

Stephen Vincent 2003 Merlot (California) $10. 82 *—S.H. (12/31/2005)*

Stephen Vincent 2002 Crimson Rhône Red Blend (California) $9. 84 *—S.H. (12/31/2005)*

Stephen Vincent 2005 Sauvignon Blanc (California) $10. A nicely fruited, crisp wine that lots of people will like. But for me, it finishes way too sweet. Tastes like one or two teaspoons of white sugar were dissolved in the glass. **83** *—S.H. (5/1/2007)*

Stephen Vincent 2003 Sauvignon Blanc (Lake County) $9. 85 Best Buy *—S.H. (12/31/2005)*

Stephen Vincent 2002 Maxwell Vineyard Sauvignon Blanc (Lake County) $8. 87 Best Buy *—S.H. (11/15/2004)*

STEPHEN'S

Stephen's 2005 MacBride Vineyard Chardonnay (York Mountain) $28. Here's a minerally, acidic, very dry Chard with a firm structure. Slightly earthy, it has citrus fruit, smoky oak and spice flavors, with a wet stone, metallic tang in the finish. **87** *—S.H. (9/1/2007)*

Stephen's 2004 MacBride Vineyard Chardonnay (York Mountain) $24. 86 *—S.H. (5/1/2006)*

Stephen's 2004 Encell Vineyard Pinot Noir (San Luis Obispo County) $32. A little on the soft, heavy side, with weighty tannins framing ripe, almost overripe, cherry-berry flavors that finish with a raisiny taste. But the wine is dry and has a nice, silky mouthfeel. **84** *—S.H. (9/1/2007)*

Stephen's 2003 Encell Vineyard Pinot Noir (San Luis Obispo County) $24. 86 *—S.H. (5/1/2006)*

Stephen's 2003 William Cain Vineyard Pinot Noir (San Luis Obispo County) $18. 87 *—S.H. (5/1/2006)*

STEPHENSON CELLARS

Stephenson Cellars 2004 Cabernet Sauvignon (Washington) $32. This is pure Cab, from Wooded Island and Inland Desert vineyards. Sappy and tight, it opens with some notes of Band-Aid® and a very tart, astringent mouthfeel. There's good fruit here, but it's wrapped into a stiff and somewhat plastic base that doesn't feel as if it will go anywhere good. **86** *—P.G. (5/1/2007)*

Stephenson Cellars 2004 Merlot (Washington) $28. Just 100 cases were made by this boutique producer, with grapes from Wooded Island Vineyard. It is polished and classy, as usual with Stephenson. The fruit is perfectly showcased, with full, precise, lightly spicy flavors. Tannins are substantial, with no rough edges, no bitterness, nothing unripe and everything in balance. **88** *—P.G. (5/1/2007)*

Stephenson Cellars 2004 Syrah (Washington) $32. Tight and dense, this is a full-flavored, smoky and rich version of Syrah, with flavors that seem a bit cooked. The fruit is smooth, mature and showing a mix of berry, currant and plum flavors. Forward and softer than the reserve, it's a wine for near-term drinking. **88** *—P.G. (5/1/2007)*

Stephenson Cellars 2003 Syrah (Yakima Valley) $28. 94 *—P.G. (11/15/2006)*

Stephenson Cellars 2004 Reserve Syrah (Washington) $45. This is the winery's first (and only) wine to be given the 100% new oak treatment. Just 23 cases were made. The oak simply does not show; it might as well be stainless. The fruit is tight, citrusy, and slowly expands into a lovely, smooth expression of Syrah that seems to envelope the back palate with flavors of licorice, cotton candy, mint and bright berry. Intriguing and quite definitely cellar worthy. **92 Cellar Selection** *—P.G. (5/1/2007)*

STEPPE CELLARS

Steppe Cellars 2006 Gewürztraminer (Yakima Valley) $16. This is sugary sweet, light and hinting at honeysuckle, melon and tea. **84** *—P.G. (12/1/2007)*

Steppe Cellars 2005 Merlot (Yakima Valley) $23. This is a light, well-balanced Yakima Valley take on Merlot, with fresh strawberry and raspberry fruit flavors lightly dusted with chocolate. A pleasant quaffing wine for sure, but nothing substantial about it. **85** *—P.G. (12/31/2007)*

Steppe Cellars 2006 Dry Riesling (Yakima Valley) $16. Scents of stone and anise lead into pretty floral notes. Clean and racy, this comes across with a pleasing minerality. There's a good leesy texture to the midpalate. The only quibble is that it turns a little bit soft and soapy as it hits the finish. **87** *—P.G. (12/1/2007)*

Steppe Cellars 2005 Syrah (Yakima Valley) $19. This has the lift and berry-loaded kick of a young Côtes-de-Rhône, but without the texture or herbal detail. It's all up front, a mix of berries and vanilla wafer, sure to please if you don't look for too much beyond that. Serve it up with simple grilled foods. **85** *—P.G. (12/31/2007)*

STERLING

Sterling 2004 SVR Reserve Bordeaux Blend (Napa Valley) $50. Warm and soft, with hints of prune and cooked blackberries alongside touches of chocolate and tobacco, this blend of 62% Cabernet Sauvignon, 34% Merlot and 4% Petit Verdot is a plush, easy-drinking red. Like the Reserve Cabernet, it seems perfectly suited for near-term consumption with grilled steak. **88** *(12/1/2007)*

Sterling 2002 SVR Reserve Bordeaux Blend (Napa Valley) $50. 88 *(7/1/2006)*

Sterling 2003 Cabernet Sauvignon (Napa Valley) $25. 87 *—S.H. (11/1/2006)*

Sterling 2002 Cabernet Sauvignon (Napa Valley) $24. 85 *—S.H. (12/1/2005)*

Sterling 2000 Cabernet Sauvignon (Napa Valley) $24. 87 *—S.H. (12/31/2002)*

Sterling 2004 Diamond Mountain Ranch Vineyard Cabernet Sauvignon (Napa Valley) $65. The most structured of Sterling's recent releases and hence our favorite, the 2004 Diamond Mountain Ranch Cabernet boasts notes of cinnamon, cassis and clove, framed by firm tannins and finishing with a hint of anise. Drink 2008–2015. **91** *(12/1/2007)*

Sterling 1999 Diamond Mountain Ranch Vineyard Cabernet Sauvignon (Napa Valley) $40. 92 *(6/1/2002)*

Sterling 1998 Diamond Mountain Ranch Vineyard Cabernet Sauvignon (Napa Valley) $38. 92 Editors' Choice *(9/1/2001)*

Sterling 1997 Diamond Mountain Ranch Vineyard Cabernet Sauvignon (Napa Valley) $40. 93 *(11/1/2000)*

Sterling 2004 Reserve Cabernet Sauvignon (Napa Valley) $75. Not as rich or chewy as the Diamond Mountain Ranch bottling, Sterling's 2004 Reserve Cabernet is immediately accessible, offering aromas and flavors of cassis and dried spices and soft tannins. A good steak house red. **89** *(12/1/2007)*

Sterling 2002 Reserve Cabernet Sauvignon (Napa Valley) $75. 86 *(6/1/2006)*

Sterling 2001 Reserve Cabernet Sauvignon (Napa Valley) $75. 84 *—S.H. (2/1/2005)*

Sterling 2000 Reserve Cabernet Sauvignon (Napa Valley) $70. 86 *—S.H. (5/1/2004)*

Sterling 1999 Reserve Cabernet Sauvignon (Napa Valley) $70. 87 *—S.H. (8/1/2003)*

Sterling 1997 Reserve Cabernet Sauvignon (Napa Valley) $60. 90 *(11/1/2000)*

Sterling 2003 Vintner's Collection Cabernet Sauvignon (Central Coast) $15. 83 *—S.H. (12/1/2005)*

Sterling 2002 Vintner's Collection Cabernet Sauvignon (Central Coast) $15. 84 *—S.H. (7/1/2005)*

Sterling 2001 Vintner's Collection Cabernet Sauvignon (Central Coast) $13. 84 *—S.H. (11/15/2003)*

Sterling 2000 Vintner's Collection Cabernet Sauvignon (Central Coast) $13. 86 *—S.H. (4/1/2003)*

Sterling 2005 Chardonnay (Napa Valley) $16. Nice and creamy, with good varietal flavors of well-ripened peaches, pears, apricots and kumquats, enriched with a touch of smoky oak. Finishes with some real richness. **85** *—S.H. (7/1/2007)*

Sterling 2004 Chardonnay (Napa Valley) $17. 84 *—S.H. (3/1/2006)*

Sterling 2003 Chardonnay (Napa County) $17. 84 *—S.H. (3/1/2005)*

Sterling 2002 Chardonnay (North Coast) $17. 86 *—S.H. (12/15/2003)*

Sterling 2001 Chardonnay (North Coast) $17. 86 *—S.H. (12/15/2002)*

Sterling 1998 Chardonnay (North Coast) $17. 89 *(6/1/2000)*

Sterling 2002 Reserve Chardonnay (Napa Valley) $40. 84 *—S.H. (4/1/2005)*

Sterling 2001 Reserve Chardonnay (Napa Valley) $40. 91 *—S.H. (12/1/2003)*

Sterling 1999 Reserve Chardonnay (Napa Valley) $40. 90 *(7/1/2001)*

Sterling 2004 Vintner's Collection Chardonnay (Central Coast) $14. 84 *—S.H. (12/1/2005)*

Sterling 2001 Vintner's Collection Chardonnay (Central Coast) $13. 84 *—S.H. (6/1/2003)*

Sterling 2003 Vintner's Collection Chardonnay (Central Coast) $11. 84 *—S.H. (10/1/2004)*

Sterling 2002 Winery Lake Chardonnay (Carneros) $28. 88 *—S.H. (12/1/2004)*

Sterling 2000 Winery Lake Chardonnay (Carneros) $25. 88 *—S.H. (2/1/2003)*

Sterling 2001 Winery Lake Vineyard Chardonnay (Carneros) $25. 90 *—S.H. (12/1/2003)*

Sterling 1999 Winery Lake Vineyard Chardonnay (Carneros) $25. 89 *(9/1/2001)*

Sterling 1998 Winery Lake Vineyard Chardonnay (Carneros) $24. 87 *(6/1/2000)*

Sterling 2004 Merlot (Napa Valley) $22. A harshly tannic wine; while there's a good hit of cherries, it's so tannic that it will never soften out. **83** *—S.H. (12/1/2007)*

Sterling 2003 Merlot (Napa Valley) $22. 86 *—S.H. (12/1/2006)*

Sterling 2002 Merlot (Napa Valley) $22. 85 *—S.H. (12/1/2005)*

Sterling 2000 Merlot (Napa Valley) $22. 86 *—S.H. (12/31/2002)*

Sterling 1998 Merlot (Napa Valley) $23. 83 *—S.H. (6/1/2001)*

Sterling 1998 Diamond Mountain Ranch Merlot (Napa Valley) $33. 90 *(9/1/2001)*

Sterling 1997 Diamond Mountain Ranch Vineyard Merlot (Napa Valley) $30. 86 *—J.C. (7/1/2000)*

Sterling 2004 Reserve Merlot (Napa Valley) $65. The mouthfeel on this dry wine is as smoothly voluptuous as velvet, although there's also a thick dusting of tannins that are fairly astringent right now. I do not believe this is a cellar-worthy wine, because the fruit is just too thin to outlast the tannins. **85** *—S.H. (11/1/2007)*

Sterling 2002 Reserve Merlot (Napa Valley) $65. 87 *(6/1/2006)*

Sterling 2001 Reserve Merlot (Napa Valley) $65. 89 *—S.H. (4/1/2005)*

Sterling 2000 Reserve Merlot (Napa Valley) $65. 86 *—S.H. (5/1/2004)*

Sterling 1999 Reserve Merlot (Napa Valley) $70. 91 *—S.H. (8/1/2003)*

Sterling 1998 Reserve Merlot (Napa Valley) $71. 91 Cellar Selection *(9/1/2001)*

Sterling 2004 Three Palms Vineyard Merlot (Napa Valley) $75. Round, lush and a bit warm, this is a velvety-textured Merlot with fruit characters that border on dried black cherry and plum rather than fresh fruit. Mocha and tobacco notes chime in, adding welcome complexity. Drink now–2012. **89** *(12/1/2007)*

Sterling 2001 Three Palms Vineyard Merlot (Napa Valley) $55. 90 *—S.H. (8/1/2005)*

Sterling 1998 Three Palms Vineyard Merlot (Napa Valley) $56. 89 *(9/1/2001)*

Sterling 1997 Three Palms Vineyard Merlot (Napa Valley) $50. A **89** *—J.C. (7/1/2000)*

Sterling 2002 Vintner's Colleciton Merlot (Central Coast) $13. 85 *—S.H. (10/1/2004)*

Sterling 2003 Vintner's Collection Merlot (Central Coast) $15. 85 *—S.H. (12/1/2005)*

Sterling 2001 Vintner's Collection Merlot (Central Coast) $13. 85 *—S.H. (12/1/2003)*

Sterling 2000 Vintner's Collection Merlot (Central Coast) $13. 85 *—S.H. (4/1/2003)*

Sterling 1996 Winery Lake Merlot (Carneros) $35. 89 *—M.S. (3/1/2000)*

Sterling 1998 Winery Lake Vineyard Merlot (Carneros) $33. 88 *(9/1/2001)*

Sterling 2005 Pinot Grigio (Central Coast) $13. \85 *—S.H. (12/1/2006)*

Sterling 2003 Pinot Noir (Napa Valley) $19. 82 *—S.H. (10/1/2005)*

Sterling 2003 Vintner's Collection Pinot Noir (Central Coast) $13. 84 *—S.H. (7/1/2005)*

Sterling 2002 Vintner's Collection Pinot Noir (Central Coast) $13. 84 *—S.H. (4/1/2004)*

Sterling 2002 Winery Lake Pinot Noir (Carneros) $25. 85 *(11/1/2004)*

Sterling 2000 Winery Lake Pinot Noir (Napa Valley) $25. 88 *(10/1/2002)*

Sterling 1999 Winery Lake Pinot Noir (Carneros) $27. 88 *(9/1/2001)*

Sterling 2001 Winery Lake Vineyard Pinot Noir (Carneros) $25. 85 —*S.H. (2/1/2004)*

Sterling 1997 Winery Lake Vineyard Pinot Noir (Carneros) $21. 90 *(10/1/1999)*

Sterling 2001 SVR Red Blend (Napa Valley) $45. 87 —*S.H. (4/1/2005)*

Sterling 2005 Sauvignon Blanc (Napa Valley) $15. 85 —*S.H. (11/15/2006)*

Sterling 2004 Sauvignon Blanc (Napa Valley) $13. 83 —*S.H. (11/15/2005)*

Sterling 2003 Sauvignon Blanc (Napa Valley) $14. 83 —*S.H. (2/1/2005)*

Sterling 2002 Sauvignon Blanc (North Coast) $14. 86 —*S.H. (12/1/2003)*

Sterling 2005 Vintner's Collection Sauvignon Blanc (Central Coast) $11. 85 —*S.H. (12/1/2006)*

Sterling 2003 Vintner's Collection Sauvignon Blanc (Central Coast) $10. 84 —*S.H. (10/1/2004)*

Sterling 2003 Vintner's Collection Shiraz (Central Coast) $13. 84 —*S.H. (7/1/2005)*

Sterling 2002 Vintner's Collection Shiraz (Central Coast) $13. 86 *(9/1/2005)*

Sterling 2001 Vintner's Collection Shiraz (Central Coast) $13. 85 —*S.H. (12/15/2003)*

Sterling 2005 Vintner's Collection Zinfandel (Central Coast) $10. Supple and silky, it's a soft, gentle wine, but with plumped raisin flavors that taste sugary sweet side by side with a harshly green edge of chlorophyll, suggesting uneven ripening. **82** —*S.H. (9/1/2007)*

STERLING ALBERT

Sterling Albert 2004 Mt. Diablo Cabernet Sauvignon (Contra Costa County) $26. Softly tannic and a little rustic, yet the cherry, cassis and oak flavors are worth savoring. Will satisfy fans of dry, ripe Cabs now, but could develop nuances with four or five years in the bottle. **86** —*S.H. (6/1/2007)*

Sterling Albert 2004 Mt. Diablo Syrah (Contra Costa County) $23. Mt. Diablo is visible from San Francisco on a clear day. It's in Contra Costa County, the "opposite coast" from the City by the Bay, where the climate resembles southern Napa Valley. This Syrah is dry and finely structured, with a rich tannic structure shielding cherry, blackberry and mocha flavors. **87** —*S.H. (6/1/2007)*

STEVEN ANDRÉ

Steven André 2003 Merlot (Napa Valley) $19. 83 —*S.H. (10/1/2006)*

STEVEN BANNUS

Steven Bannus 2002 Reserve Pinot Noir (Central Coast) $8. 84 —*S.H. (11/1/2004)*

STEVEN KENT

Steven Kent 2002 Cabernet Sauvignon (Livermore Valley) $45. 90 —*S.H. (7/1/2006)*

Steven Kent 2000 Cabernet Sauvignon (Livermore Valley) $45. 92 —*S.H. (10/1/2003)*

Steven Kent 2001 Livermore Valley Cabernet Sauvignon (Livermore Valley) $45. 91 —*S.H. (8/1/2004)*

Steven Kent 2002 McGrail Vineyard Cabernet Sauvignon (Livermore Valley) $55. 91 —*S.H. (7/1/2006)*

Steven Kent 2001 Vincerre Cabernet Sauvignon-Barbera (Livermore Valley) $40. 85 —*S.H. (8/1/2004)*

Steven Kent 2000 Vincere Cabernet Sauvignon-Sangiovese (Livermore Valley) $40. 91 —*S.H. (5/1/2003)*

Steven Kent 1999 Folkendt Vineyard Merrillie Chardonnay (Livermore Valley) $36. 93 —*S.H. (12/15/2001)*

Steven Kent 2001 Merrillie Chardonnay (Livermore Valley) $23. 90 —*S.H. (8/1/2004)*

Steven Kent 2000 Merrillie Chardonnay (Livermore Valley) $36. 92 —*S.H. (12/15/2002)*

Steven Kent 2001 Song Bird Sangiovese (Livermore Valley) $32. 87 —*S.H. (9/1/2004)*

Steven Kent 2005 Ghielmetti Vineyard Sauvignon Blanc (Livermore Valley) $24. 87 —*S.H. (12/15/2006)*

Steven Kent 2001 Zin-Tonga Zinfandel (Livermore Valley) $32. 91 *(11/1/2003)*

STEVENOT

Stevenot 2006 Danza Blanca Albariño (Sierra Foothills) $10. I wish this wine were drier because it has polished citrus, floral and mineral flavors and a rich, pronounced acidity. But it's sugary throughout. **83** —*S.H. (10/1/2007)*

Stevenot 2004 Barbera (Sierra Foothills) $15. Barbera fans will find all the dry tannins, acidity and earthy fruity flavors they crave. A big, bold wine, with blackberry, coffee and dried herb flavors that will drink well against rich barbecue. **85** —*S.H. (4/1/2007)*

Stevenot 2001 Cabernet Franc (Calaveras County) $18. 85 —*S.H. (9/1/2004)*

Stevenot 2005 Cabernet Sauvignon (Sierra Foothills) $11. There's lots of richness in this full-bodied wine from the Sierra Foothills region. It's fruit-forward, with oak-influenced black currant, cherry and cocoa flavors that finish with elegance. **86 Best Buy** —*S.H. (11/15/2007)*

Stevenot 2004 Cabernet Sauvignon (Sierra Foothills) $10. Raw and sand-papery, a dry wine saved by some good blackberry fruit. **82** —*S.H. (4/1/2007)*

Stevenot 2001 Cabernet Sauvignon (Calaveras County) $12. 89 Best Buy —*S.H. (10/1/2005)*

Stevenot 2000 Gabriel Cabernet Sauvignon (Calaveras County) $25. 90 Editors' Choice —*S.H. (10/1/2005)*

Stevenot 2006 Chardonnay (Sierra Foothills) $11. Pretty basic Chard, with jammy apricot, pineapple and peach flavors. Has a rustic feel, but offers enough rich creamy fruit to satisfy. **83** —*S.H. (11/15/2007)*

Stevenot 2005 Chardonnay (Sierra Foothills) $10. A honeyed Chard that will please fruit fans for its powerful green-apple, pineapple, pear and vanilla-ginger flavors. Very nice for everyday drinking. **84** —*S.H. (7/1/2007)*

Stevenot 2001 Chardonnay (Calaveras County) $28. 86 —*S.H. (9/1/2004)*

Stevenot 2001 Chardonnay (Sierra Foothills) $14. 86 —*S.H. (2/1/2003)*

Stevenot 2002 Calaveras County Chardonnay (Calaveras County) $12. 84 —*S.H. (9/1/2004)*

Stevenot 2005 Gran Reserva Chardonnay (Calaveras County) $19. Easily the best Chard from Stevenot I've tasted, for the quality of the structure. The wine is very dry and crisp, with mineral, lime, pink grapefruit and dried herb flavors. A great food wine. **87** —*S.H. (11/1/2007)*

Stevenot 1997 Shaw Ranch Chardonnay (Calaveras County) $18. 86 *(6/1/2000)*

Stevenot 2003 Graciano (Calaveras County) $22. 86 —*S.H. (3/1/2005)*

Stevenot 2006 Gran Reserve Marsanne (Calaveras County) $25. High alcohol gives this a peppery heat, lots of wood makes it oaky, and the tropical fruit flavors are ripe and spicy. At tasting, this had not quite meshed together yet. Give it another six months. **85** —*S.H. (11/1/2007)*

Stevenot 2005 Merlot (Sierra Foothills) $11. A bit rustic, with jagged tannins and sweet-and-sour blackberry, red currant and mint flavors. Tannins make for an astringent finish. **83** —*S.H. (11/15/2007)*

Stevenot 2004 Merlot (Sierra Foothills) $10. Dry and tannic, with cherry, blackberry, plum and herb flavors. This is a good everyday full-bodied red wine, and versatile at the table. **84** —*S.H. (3/1/2007)*

Stevenot 2001 Merlot (Calaveras County) $12. 90 Best Buy —*S.H. (10/1/2005)*

Stevenot 1997 Merlot (Sierra Foothills) $13. 84 —*J.C. (7/1/2000)*

Stevenot 2002 Broll Mountain Vineyard Petite Sirah (Calaveras County) $22. 86 —*S.H. (10/1/2005)*

Stevenot 2006 Pinot Grigio (Sierra Foothills) $10. An easy, polished PG, with its flavorful burst of citrus, lemonflower, apricot, peach, fig, spice and vanilla flavors. Crisp and balanced, it makes you think of picnics, beach parties and warm summer nights. **87 Best Buy** —*S.H. (10/1/2007)*

Stevenot 2004 Gabriel Pinot Noir (Calaveras County) $28. This is an upscale bottling from the veteran winery, Stevenot. It's the best Foothills Pinot Noir I've had in a long time, and stands comparison with a fine coastal bottling, maybe a Russian River Valley. Dry and silky, it's complex in cherry, cola, pomegranate and plummy spice flavors, with good acids and soft, fuzzy tannins that make it instantly drinkable. **87** —*S.H. (5/1/2007)*

Stevenot 2004 Gran Reserve Pinot Noir (Calaveras County) $32. I haven't tasted many Pinot Noirs from the Sierra Foothills, but this wine shows some promise. The main drawback is excessive softness, which makes it flabby. On the upside are truly complex varietal flavors of cherries, cola and spice, and the variety's silky texture. **86** —*S.H. (11/1/2007)*

Stevenot 2005 Danza Roja Red Blend (California) $12. A Rhône-style blend of Garnacha (Grenache), Mourvèdre, Tempranillo, Syrah and Graciano, this pretty wine is soft and dry. It has an earthy, dried herb taste, with suggestions of cherries, and is rich and complex enough to serve with special foods. **87 Best Buy** —*S.H. (11/15/2007)*

Stevenot 2004 Danza Roja Red Blend (Sierra Foothills) $12. An unusual blend of Tempranillo, Grenache, Mourvèdre and Graciano, this has a raw edge of charred cherry pie filling, and is simple in structure. Not bad, just rustic. **83** —*S.H. (7/1/2007)*

USA

Stevenot 2005 Marsanne-Roussanne Rhône White Blend (Sierra Foothills) $12. A dry, fashionable white Rhône blend. There's a minerality to the tangerine, orange blossom, macadamia nut and vanilla flavors, and a refreshing cut of citrusy acidity, that make it superdrinkable. **87 Best Buy** *—S.H. (4/1/2007)*

Stevenot 2005 Rosado Rosé Blend (California) $10. This Tempranillo is bone-dry, high in acidity and kind of rustic; the kind of wine that doesn't show well in a tasting. But pair it with the right food, like bouillabaisse, and the right place, and you might love it. **84** *—S.H. (4/1/2007)*

Stevenot 2004 Syrah (Sierra Foothills) $13. Superfruity and jammy, with fresh cherry, raspberry and blackberry flavors that fill the mouth and finish long and peppery-spicy. Full-bodied and dry, with big, thick tannins, it's a nice wine for a char-broiled sirloin steak. **86** *—S.H. (8/1/2007)*

Stevenot 2002 Canterbury Vineyard Syrah (Calaveras County) $22. 85 *(9/1/2005)*

Stevenot 2001 Canterbury Vineyard Syrah (Calaveras County) $22. 84 *—S.H. (8/1/2004)*

Stevenot 1999 Canterbury Vineyard Syrah (Calaveras County) $16. 86 *(10/1/2001)*

Stevenot 2004 Tempranillo (Sierra Foothills) $13. A dry, country-style wine, rich in ripe red cherry jam flavors. Acidity is high, as it tends to be in this variety, but the tannins are soft and fine. Calls for some smoky, salty ham. **84** *—S.H. (7/1/2007)*

Stevenot 2001 Tempranillo (Calaveras County) $22. 86 *—S.H. (8/1/2004)*

Stevenot 1999 Tempranillo (Calaveras County) $18. 87 *—J.M. (5/1/2002)*

Stevenot 2004 Olivia Tempranillo (California) $12. 85 *—S.H. (10/1/2005)*

Stevenot 2006 Rosado Tempranillo (Sierra Foothills) $10. Made from Tempranillo, this is a really pleasant rosé that shows a balance rare in California. Totally dry, crisp and relatively low in alcohol, the wine manages to be long and deep in creamy, spicy cherry, raspberry and vanilla bean flavors. Great job. **87 Best Buy** *—S.H. (10/1/2007)*

Stevenot 2005 Verdelho (California) $10. One of the few California wineries to focus on this variety, Stevenot's efforts are really paying off. Marked by high acidity, the wine shows exotic pineapple, lemongrass, kiwi, white pepper and vanilla flavors, and is thoroughly dry. Try as an alternative to Sauvignon Blanc or Pinot Grigio. **88 Best Buy** *—S.H. (9/1/2007)*

USA

Stevenot 2003 Verdelho (California) $16. 86 *—S.H. (9/1/2004)*

Stevenot 2006 Persuasion Verdelho (California) $11. Stevenot has tinkered with Verdelho for years, and the work is paying off. This is a wonderful wine that fills a much needed niche in California whites. It's dry and crisp in the way of Sauvignon Blanc or Pinot Grigio, but incredibly rich in flavors of honeysuckle flowers, peaches, pineapples and vanilla cream, with a steely minerality that makes the finish bracing. Try as an alternative to Chardonnay. **89 Best Buy** *—S.H. (11/15/2007)*

Stevenot 2004 Silvaspoons Vineyard Verdelho (California) $16. 84 *—S.H. (10/1/2005)*

Stevenot 2001 Silvaspoons Vineyard Verdelho (California) $16. 87 *—S.H. (3/1/2005)*

Stevenot 2005 Zinfandel (Sierra Foothills) $12. Here's a lusty Zin made for grilled chicken, steak and ribs. With its rich tannins, heady alcohol and brawny blackberry, blueberry and cherry flavors, it will stand up well to spicy barbecue sauce. **86** *—S.H. (11/1/2007)*

Stevenot 1997 Zinfandel (Sierra Foothills) $13. 86 *—P.G. (11/15/1999)*

Stevenot 2001 Costello Vineyard Zinfandel (Sierra Foothills) $32. 80 *(11/1/2003)*

Stevenot 2005 Gran Reserve Zinfandel (Calaveras County) $45. This is the most expensive Stevenot Zin I've ever had. It's also the ripest and the best. It's the kind of Foothills Zin that rides on horseback into the mouth, puts up the Zin flag, and declares ownership. Juicy and fruit-driven, it showcases flamboyant blackberry, cassis, cherry, balsamic, soy, sweet leather and spice flavors and a tough, resilient layer of tannins. Cries out for rich meats and cheeses. **91** *—S.H. (11/1/2007)*

Stevenot 2000 Old Vine Zinfandel (Lodi) $17. 85 *—S.H. (2/1/2003)*

STEVENS

Stevens 2003 424 Red Wine Bordeaux Blend (Columbia Valley (WA)) $30. 90 *—P.G. (8/1/2006)*

Stevens 2002 Big Easy Cabernet Sauvignon (Columbia Valley (WA)) $27. 91 *—P.G. (8/1/2006)*

Stevens 2004 Reserve Cabernet Sauvignon (Yakima Valley) $42. Dark and dense, yet somehow soft and approachable, this 100% is once again loaded with rich black fruits. Everything is in balance, with a captivating tension strung between the fruit, acid and tannins. This is a wine you can't keep your lips off. **92** *—P.G. (12/1/2007)*

Stevens 2003 Reserve Cabernet Sauvignon (Columbia Valley (WA)) $NA. 92 *—P.G. (8/1/2006)*

Stevens 2004 Merlot (Yakima Valley) $28. Dark, meaty and substantial, beautifully proportioned, and loaded with grace notes of citrus and pineapple that set off the tart, spicy red fruits. Elegant, sophisticated winemaking that captures both power and subtlety in the bottle. **91** *—P.G. (12/1/2007)*

Stevens 2004 424 Red Blend (Yakima Valley) $30. This sleek, sexy blend is named for the winery's bond number (WA-424). This is immensely appealing. The fruit flavors are carefully layered in, with lots of blackberry and black cherry leading the way; the oak adds sweet spices, hints of cinnamon, cocoa and ground coffee. Lovely balance and palate presence. **91** *—P.G. (12/1/2007)*

Stevens 2005 Black Tongue Syrah (Yakima Valley) $32. Dineen fruit, in a singular vintage, equals spectacular Syrah. This has it all going on—rich, luscious flavors of berries and cherries, wrapped (soaked!) in chocolate, elevated with zippy acidity and smooth and creamy as fresh-churned butter. Seductive doesn't begin to cover it. You could take a bath in this stuff. Yum! **92** *—P.G. (12/1/2007)*

Stevens 2003 Black Tongue Syrah (Yakima Valley) $29. 89 *—P.G. (8/1/2006)*

STEVENSON-BARRIE

Stevenson-Barrie 1999 Shea Vineyard Pinot Noir (Willamette Valley) $35. 89 *—P.G. (11/1/2001)*

STEWART

Stewart 2003 Pinot Noir (Russian River Valley) $42. 92 *—S.H. (12/1/2006)*

STG

STG 2002 Cabernet Sauvignon (Dry Creek Valley) $15. 80 *—S.H. (12/1/2005)*

STG 2003 Chardonnay (Chalk Hill) $13. 82 *—S.H. (11/1/2005)*

STG 2002 Chardonnay (Chalk Hill) $14. 81 *—S.H. (10/1/2005)*

STG 2004 Merlot (Russian River Valley) $14. 86 *—S.H. (5/1/2006)*

STG 2003 Merlot (Russian River Valley) $14. 84 *—S.H. (10/1/2005)*

STG 2002 Zinfandel (Dry Creek Valley) $14. 81 *—S.H. (6/1/2006)*

STG 2001 Zinfandel (Dry Creek Valley) $15. 85 *—S.H. (10/1/2005)*

STILL WATERS

Still Waters 2004 Pinot Gris (Paso Robles) $18. 84 *—S.H. (2/1/2006)*

STILLMAN BROWN

Stillman Brown 2005 La Mort du Roi Hill of Graceland R.I.P. Rhône Red Blend (Paso Robles) $50. The latest vinous tribute to The King, this Syrah-Alicante blend is dark, soft, sweet, high in alcohol at 16.1% and oaky. Not my favorite kind of wine, but it is what it is. **84** *—S.H. (9/1/2007)*

STOLLER

Stoller 2002 Pinot Noir (Willamette Valley) $42. 85 *(11/1/2004)*

STOLPMAN

Stolpman 2000 Limestone Hill Cuvée Cabernet Blend (Santa Ynez Valley) $20. 87 *—S.H. (11/15/2003)*

Stolpman 2001 La Croce Red Blend (Santa Ynez Valley) $19. 91 *—S.H. (10/1/2003)*

Stolpman 2000 Rhône Ridge Cuvée Red Blend (Santa Ynez Valley) $15. 85 *—S.H. (12/31/2003)*

Stolpman 2002 Rosato Rosé Blend (Santa Ynez Valley) $NA. 86 *—S.H. (3/1/2004)*

Stolpman 2001 Angeli Sangiovese (Santa Ynez Valley) $42. 92 *—S.H. (10/1/2003)*

Stolpman 2001 Syrah (Santa Ynez Valley) $29. 90 *—S.H. (3/1/2004)*

Stolpman 2003 Estate Grown Syrah (Santa Ynez Valley) $25. 87 *(9/1/2005)*

Stolpman 2003 Hilltops Syrah (Santa Ynez Valley) $35. 90 Editors' Choice *(9/1/2005)*

STONE CREEK

Stone Creek 2005 Cabernet Sauvignon (Mendocino County) $9. Quite a good Cab for this everyday price. It's dry and smooth, with ripe flavors of blackberries, cherries, dark chocolate and oak. Easy to like because of the balance. **85 Best Buy** *—S.H. (11/15/2007)*

Stone Creek 2000 Special Selection Cabernet Sauvignon (California) $8. 83 *—S.H. (10/1/2004)*

Stone Creek 2005 Chardonnay (Mendocino County) $9. Stainless steel fermented and unoaked, this Chard is simple in structure, with peach, citrus and spice flavors and a dry finish. **84** *—S.H. (11/15/2007)*

Stone Creek 2004 Chardonnay (Mendocino County) $9. 80 —*S.H. (12/15/2006)*

Stone Creek 1998 Special Selection Chardonnay (California) $7. 80 —*J.C. (10/1/1999)*

Stone Creek 2004 Merlot (Mendocino County) $9. Pretty rich for the price, with deep blackberry, cherry, plum and chocolate flavors that finish very dry and smooth. **85 Best Buy** —*S.H. (11/15/2007)*

Stone Creek 2003 Merlot (Mendocino County) $9. 80 —*S.H. (12/15/2006)*

Stone Creek 2001 California Merlot (California) $8. 84 —*S.H. (9/1/2004)*

Stone Creek 1998 Special Selection Merlot (California) $8. 84 Best Buy *(6/1/2001)*

Stone Creek 2006 Sauvignon Blanc (Mendocino County) $9. Pretty good for the price, with real varietal character. Dryness and acidity bracket the citrus and pepper flavors, which are entirely unoaked, and the finish is tangy clean. **85 Best Buy** —*S.H. (11/15/2007)*

Stone Creek 1999 Chairman's Reserve Zinfandel (California) $17. 82 —*D.T. (3/1/2002)*

Stone Creek 2001 Special Selection Zinfandel (California) $8. 82 *(11/1/2003)*

Stone Creek 1998 Special Selection Zinfandel (California) $8. 85 Best Buy *(3/1/2001)*

STONE GARDEN

Stone Garden 2005 White Merlot (California) $8. 84 Best Buy —*S.H. (12/31/2006)*

Stone Garden 2005 Pinot Grigio (California) $8. 82 —*S.H. (12/31/2006)*

STONE WOLF

Stone Wolf 2001 Chardonnay (Willamette Valley) $10. 85 —*P.G. (12/31/2002)*

Stone Wolf 2001 Pinot Gris (Oregon) $10. 88 Best Buy —*P.G. (12/31/2002)*

STONECROFT

Stonecroft 1998 Reserve Pinot Noir (Willamette Valley) $30. 88 —*M.M. (12/1/2000)*

STONEGATE

Stonegate 2001 Cabernet Franc (Napa Valley) $22. 87 —*S.H. (7/1/2005)*

Stonegate 2001 Cabernet Sauvignon (Napa Valley) $25. 87 —*S.H. (8/1/2005)*

Stonegate 1999 Cabernet Sauvignon (Napa Valley) $40. 91 —*S.H. (6/1/2002)*

Stonegate 1998 Cabernet Sauvignon (Napa Valley) $29. 90 —*S.H. (12/1/2001)*

Stonegate 1997 Cabernet Sauvignon (Napa Valley) $25. 92 —*S.H. (2/1/2001)*

Stonegate 2001 Diamond Mountain Reserve Spaulding Vineyard Cabernet Sauvignon (Napa Valley) $50. 92 Cellar Selection —*S.H. (8/1/2005)*

Stonegate 1999 Diamond Mountain Reserve Spaulding Vineyard Cabernet Sauvignon (Diamond Mountain) $60. 91 —*S.H. (2/1/2003)*

Stonegate 2003 Spaulding Vineyard Reserve Cabernet Sauvignon (Diamond Mountain) $50. One of the more dependable bottlings from Napa, the '03 is a lovely wine. Rich and balanced, it offers intense cassis, cherry pie filling and coffee flavors, with a delicious overlay of new oak. The mountain tannins are firm and dusty, but very finely structured, ripe and sweet. Beautiful now, and should develop well for the next eight years or so. **93** —*S.H. (8/1/2007)*

Stonegate 1998 Estate Bottled Chardonnay (Napa Valley) $18. 84 *(6/1/2000)*

Stonegate 2001 Merlot (Napa Valley) $22. 87 —*S.H. (8/1/2005)*

Stonegate 2000 Merlot (Napa Valley) $22. 84 —*S.H. (12/15/2003)*

Stonegate 1999 Merlot (Napa Valley) $28. 91 —*S.H. (12/1/2001)*

Stonegate 1998 Merlot (Napa Valley) $22. 88 —*S.H. (2/1/2001)*

Stonegate 2003 Wappo Vineyard Reserve Petite Verdot (Napa Valley) $25. Normally used as a minor blending grape with Cabernet, Petit Verdot is difficult to make interesting by itself, and this one is no exception. Midnight black, raspingly dry and fiercely tannic, it has tobacco, cherry and oak flavors. Might someday evolve into something, but who knows. **84** —*S.H. (8/1/2007)*

Stonegate 2001 Petite Verdot (Napa Valley) $25. 87 —*S.H. (8/1/2005)*

Stonegate 2003 Sauvignon Blanc (Napa Valley) $14. 86 —*S.H. (8/1/2005)*

Stonegate 2000 Estate Bottled Sauvignon Blanc (Napa Valley) $16. 87 —*S.H. (11/15/2001)*

STONEHEDGE

Stonehedge 2000 Cabernet Sauvignon (California) $10. 83 —*S.H. (6/1/2002)*

Stonehedge 1999 Cabernet Sauvignon (Napa Valley) $30. 89 —*S.H. (6/1/2002)*

Stonehedge 2000 Chardonnay (California) $10. 82 —*S.H. (5/1/2002)*

Stonehedge 2000 Reserve Chardonnay (Monterey) $18. 84 —*S.H. (12/15/2002)*

Stonehedge 2000 Merlot (California) $10. 85 —*S.H. (6/1/2002)*

Stonehedge 2001 Petite Sirah (California) $10. 81 —*S.H. (9/1/2003)*

Stonehedge 2000 Reserve Petite Sirah (Mendocino) $35. 91 —*S.H. (9/1/2003)*

Stonehedge 2000 Pinot Noir (California) $10. 82 —*S.H. (2/1/2003)*

Stonehedge 2003 Sauvignon Blanc (California) $10. 84 —*S.H. (8/1/2005)*

Stonehedge 2001 Sauvignon Blanc (California) $10. 84 —*S.H. (3/1/2003)*

Stonehedge 2000 Sauvignon Blanc (California) $10. 84 —*S.H. (9/1/2002)*

Stonehedge 2000 Syrah (California) $10. 83 —*S.H. (9/1/2002)*

Stonehedge 1999 Syrah (California) $10. 86 *(10/1/2001)*

Stonehedge 2001 Zinfandel (California) $10. 82 —*J.M. (11/1/2003)*

Stonehedge 2000 Zinfandel (California) $10. 86 Best Buy —*S.H. (7/1/2002)*

Stonehedge 1999 Zinfandel (Napa Valley) $30. 86 —*S.H. (7/1/2002)*

Stonehedge 1997 Reserve Zinfandel (Napa Valley) $25. 88 —*P.G. (2/1/2001)*

STONESTREET

Stonestreet 1999 Legacy Bordeaux Blend (Alexander Valley) $67. 91 *(9/1/2003)*

Stonestreet 2000 Cabernet Sauvignon (Alexander Valley) $36. 88 *(9/1/2003)*

Stonestreet 1997 Cabernet Sauvignon (Sonoma County) $35. 86 *(11/1/2000)*

Stonestreet 2001 Christopher's Cabernet Sauvignon (Alexander Valley) $80. 93 Cellar Selection —*S.H. (7/1/2005)*

Stonestreet 1999 Christopher's Cabernet Cabernet Sauvignon (Alexander Valley) $80. 92 Cellar Selection *(9/1/2003)*

Stonestreet 1997 Christopher's Vineyard Cabernet Sauvignon (Sonoma County) $70. 90 *(11/1/2000)*

Stonestreet 2005 Chardonnay (Alexander Valley) $28. Pretty good Chard, not quite on a par with the winery's Upper Barn bottlings but close. The grapes come partially from the Upper Barn vineyard, but it's all mountain-grown, showing concentrated pear, pineapple and peach flavors, with a rich, tobacco herbaceousness. **87** —*S.H. (5/1/2007)*

Stonestreet 2001 Chardonnay (Sonoma County) $23. 86 *(9/1/2003)*

Stonestreet 1999 Block 66 Alexander Mountain Chardonnay (Alexander Valley) $34. 88 *(9/1/2003)*

Stonestreet 1998 Block Sixty-Six Chardonnay (Sonoma County) $30. 90 *(7/1/2001)*

Stonestreet 2001 Upper Barn Chardonnay (Alexander Valley) $40. 89 —*S.H. (7/1/2005)*

Stonestreet 2000 Upper Barn Chardonnay (Green Valley) $45. 90 *(9/1/2003)*

Stonestreet 1998 Upper Barn Chardonnay (Sonoma County) $40. 87 *(7/1/2001)*

Stonestreet 2003 Merlot (Alexander Valley) $23. The problem here is over-ripeness, a raisiny, pruny flavor that must have come from these mountain grapes baking under the summer sun during this hot vintage. Although the wine is fully dry and the tannins are sweetly ripe, that stewed taste is a bit of a turnoff. **83** —*S.H. (5/1/2007)*

Stonestreet 2000 Merlot (Sonoma County) $30. 87 *(9/1/2003)*

Stonestreet 2001 Upper Barn Sauvignon Blanc (Alexander Valley) $20. 88 *(7/1/2005)*

Stonestreet 2000 Upper Barn Sauvignon Blanc (Alexander Valley) $25. 88 *(9/1/2003)*

Stonestreet 1999 Upper Barn Vineyard Sauvignon Blanc (Alexander Valley) $23. 87 *(8/1/2002)*

STONY HILL

Stony Hill 2001 Chardonnay (Napa Valley) $27. 92 —*S.H. (5/1/2005)*

Stony Hill 2000 Chardonnay (Napa Valley) $27. 85 —*S.H. (2/1/2004)*

Stony Hill 1999 Chardonnay (Napa Valley) $27. 93 *—S.H. (5/1/2002)*

Stony Hill 1998 Chardonnay (Napa Valley) $NA. 90 *—S.H. (12/1/2001)*

Stony Hill 1997 Chardonnay (Napa Valley) $24. 93 *—S.H. (2/1/2000)*

Stony Hill 2002 Gewürztraminer (Napa Valley) $15. 84 *—S.H. (2/1/2004)*

Stony Hill 2001 Gewürztraminer (Napa Valley) $15. 88 *—S.H. (5/1/2005)*

Stony Hill 2000 Gewürztraminer (Napa Valley) $15. 88 *—S.H. (6/1/2002)*

Stony Hill 2000 Sémillon du Soleil Sémillon (Napa Valley) $15. 94 Editors' Choice *—S.H. (5/1/2005)*

Stony Hill 2002 White Riesling (Napa Valley) $15. 84 *—S.H. (2/1/2004)*

Stony Hill 2001 White Riesling (Napa Valley) $15. 86 *—S.H. (2/1/2005)*

Stony Hill 2000 White Riesling (Napa Valley) $15. 90 *—S.H. (6/1/2002)*

STONY RIDGE WINERY

Stony Ridge Winery 2001 Reserve Cabernet Sauvignon (Livermore Valley) $21. 82 *—S.H. (11/15/2003)*

Stony Ridge Winery 2000 Reserve Johannisberg Riesling (Monterey) $10. 88 Best Buy *—S.H. (12/31/2003)*

STORRS

Storrs 2004 Christie Vineyard Chardonnay (Santa Cruz Mountains) $26. 89 *—S.H. (3/1/2006)*

Storrs 2003 Christie Vineyard Chardonnay (Santa Cruz Mountains) $26. 86 *—S.H. (8/1/2005)*

Storrs 2002 Viento Vineyard Gewürztraminer (Monterey) $14. 85 *—S.H. (5/1/2005)*

Storrs 2001 Merlot (San Ysidro District) $24. 85 *—S.H. (8/1/2005)*

Storrs 2000 Rusty Ridge Petite Sirah (Santa Clara County) $22. 83 *(4/1/2003)*

Storrs 2001 Pinot Noir (Santa Cruz Mountains) $25. 91 *—S.H. (3/1/2006)*

Storrs 2003 Sauvignon Blanc (San Lucas) $16. 83 *—S.H. (5/1/2005)*

Storrs 2002 Riverview Vineyard White Riesling (Monterey) $14. 86 *—S.H. (5/1/2005)*

STORY

Story 2002 Picnic Hill Vineyard Old Vines Zinfandel (California) $30. 81 *—S.H. (3/1/2005)*

STORYBOOK MOUNTAIN

Storybook Mountain 2003 SEPS Estate Cabernet Sauvignon (Napa Valley) $65. The price suggests that the winery considers this an important Cabernet, and it may be, but it does require aging. It's fresh and young and tannicly aggressive right now, with direct blackberry, cherry and oak flavors, and not really showing all that well. But neither does young Bordeaux. My hunch is that it's a cellar bet. Try after 2007. **88** *—S.H. (5/1/2007)*

Storybook Mountain 2004 Antaeus Red Blend (Napa Valley) $40. This is a blend of Zinfandel, Cab, Merlot and Petit Verdot, but it's hard to like because it's so overripe and Port-y. Tastes like plumped raisins, with a hot finish. **82** *—S.H. (5/1/2007)*

Storybook Mountain 2001 Eastern Exposures Zinfandel (Napa Valley) $30. 88 *(11/1/2003)*

Storybook Mountain 2000 Eastern Exposures Zinfandel (Napa Valley) $35. 86 *—S.H. (11/1/2002)*

Storybook Mountain 1997 Eastern Exposures Zinfandel (Napa Valley) $25. 95 *—P.G. (11/15/1999)*

Storybook Mountain 2004 Eastern Exposures Napa Estate Zinfandel (Napa Valley) $40. What a beautiful job they did on this ripely soft, complex Zin. It resembles a nice Napa Cabernet with its rich, sweet tannins and upscale structure, yet is pure Zin in personality. Wild berries and cherries, milk chocolate, gingersnap cookies, and nearly every Asian spice you can name. **90** *—S.H. (5/1/2007)*

Storybook Mountain 2003 Estate Reserve Zinfandel (Napa Valley) $50. With a crunchy bite of tannins and acidity, this Zin drinks fresh and pert. Fully dry, it offers a rich array of blackberry, loganberry, cherry, mocha-choca and spicy flavors that finish dry and complex. It's Zins like this that have earned the winery its well-deserved reputation. **90** *—S.H. (5/1/2007)*

Storybook Mountain 1997 Estate Reserve Zinfandel (Napa Valley) $50. 90 *—P.G. (3/1/2001)*

Storybook Mountain 2001 Mayacamas Range Zinfandel (Napa Valley) $20. 87 *(11/1/2003)*

Storybook Mountain 2000 Mayacamas Range Zinfandel (Napa Valley) $25. 82 *—S.H. (11/1/2002)*

Storybook Mountain 1997 Mayacamas Range Zinfandel (Napa Valley) $20. 88 *—P.G. (11/15/1999)*

Storybook Mountain 1999 Reserve Zinfandel (Napa Valley) $45. 89 *—S.H. (11/1/2002)*

Storybook Mountain 2000 The First Hurrah Zinfandel (Atlas Peak) $25. 88 *—S.H. (11/1/2002)*

Storybook Mountain 1997 The Last Hurrah Zinfandel (Howell Mountain) $35. 92 *—S.H. (5/1/2000)*

STRANGELAND

Strangeland 2002 Pinot Noir (Willamette Valley) $20. 83 *(11/1/2004)*

Strangeland 2002 Stand Sure Vineyard Pinot Noir (Willamette Valley) $20. 84 *(11/1/2004)*

Strangeland 2002 Winemaker's Estate Reserve Pinot Noir (Willamette Valley) $60. 82 *(11/1/2004)*

STRATA

Strata 2001 Merlot (Napa Valley) $34. 92 *—S.H. (10/1/2005)*

STRATFORD

Stratford 1999 Syrah (California) $18. 84 *—S.H. (7/1/2002)*

STRATTON LUMMIS

Stratton Lummis 2003 Cabernet Sauvignon (Napa Valley) $25. Tastes kind of raw and common, with thinned-down cherry fruit and a sharp cut of acidity. All in all, it's an everyday Cab that's overpriced. **83** *—S.H. (4/1/2007)*

Stratton Lummis 2002 Cabernet Sauvignon (Napa Valley) $30. 82 *—S.H. (10/1/2005)*

Stratton Lummis 2005 Chardonnay (Carneros) $19. An interesting wine that marches to a different beat when it comes to today's buttery, ripe Chards. This one's austere and minerally, with a Meyer lemon drop taste, high acidity and a very dry finish. It's elegant and polished. **87** *—S.H. (4/1/2007)*

STRYKER SONOMA

Stryker Sonoma 2001 Syrah (Dry Creek Valley) $22. 83 *(9/1/2005)*

Stryker Sonoma 2000 Syrah (Sonoma County) $22. 83 *(9/1/2005)*

Stryker Sonoma 2002 Estate Syrah (Alexander Valley) $22. 85 *(9/1/2005)*

Stryker Sonoma 1999 Old Vine Estate Zinfandel (Alexander Valley) $25. 90 *—S.H. (9/1/2002)*

STUART CELLARS

Stuart Cellars 2004 Limited Estate Reserve Tatria Meritage Red Table Wine Bordeaux Blend (Temecula) $36. The grapes had no problem getting ripe, to judge by the flood of red cherry marmalade, cola and milk chocolate flavors. With its dryness and softness, the wine is delicious, if a little one-dimensional. **85** *—S.H. (6/1/2007)*

Stuart Cellars 2002 Limited Estate Reserve Tatria Meritage Cabernet Blend (Temecula) $36. 80 *—S.H. (4/1/2006)*

Stuart Cellars 2003 Vintner's Special Estate Reserve Cabernet Sauvignon (Temecula) $60. This is surely one of the better Temecula-grown Cabs out there. It's ripe and balanced, with a good array of varietal flavors. Cherry, red currant, cola, mocha and oaky spice flavors finish dry and smooth. Drink now. **87** *—S.H. (6/1/2007)*

Stuart Cellars 2005 Limited Bottling Viognier (California) $21. Smooth and polished, with toasty flavors of pineapple, pumpkin pie, cinnamon, gingersnap cookie, butterscotch and honey. The finish is crisp; very nice and rich. **90** *—S.H. (4/1/2007)*

Stuart Cellars 2003 Limited Bottling Viognier (California) $21. 84 *—S.H. (3/1/2006)*

Stuart Cellars 2004 Select Reserve Zinfandel (Temecula) $30. 80 *—S.H. (7/1/2006)*

Stuart Cellars 2003 Select Reserve Zinfandel (Temecula) $30. 85 *—S.H. (4/1/2006)*

Stuart Cellars 1998 Vintage Zinfandel (Temecula) $42. 95 *—S.H. (4/1/2002)*

STUBBS VINEYARD

Stubbs Vineyard 2002 Pinot Noir (Marin County) $24. 87 *(11/1/2004)*

Stubbs Vineyard 2004 Estate Grown Pinot Noir (Marin County) $36. 83 *—S.H. (12/1/2006)*

STUHLMULLER VINEYARDS

Stuhlmuller Vineyards 2002 Cabernet Sauvignon (Alexander Valley) $35. 83 *—S.H. (3/1/2006)*

Stuhlmuller Vineyards 1999 Cabernet Sauvignon (Alexander Valley) $35. 84 *—S.H. (12/15/2003)*

Stuhlmuller Vineyards 1998 Cabernet Sauvignon (Alexander Valley) $35. 85 *—S.H. (9/12/2002)*

Stuhlmuller Vineyards 2001 Estate Cabernet Sauvignon (Alexander Valley) $32. 90 *—S.H. (10/1/2005)*

Stuhlmuller Vineyards 2004 Chardonnay (Alexander Valley) $23. 87 *—S.H. (3/1/2006)*

Stuhlmuller Vineyards 2001 Chardonnay (Alexander Valley) $23. 88 *—S.H. (2/1/2004)*

Stuhlmuller Vineyards 1999 Chardonnay (Alexander Valley) $23. 88 *—J.M. (5/1/2002)*

Stuhlmuller Vineyards 2005 Estate Chardonnay (Alexander Valley) $23. If you're familiar with the lush, complex Chards from Robert Young, this will ring a bell. It's layered in ripe mango, guava, nectarine, peach and smoky, caramelized oak flavors, with an exotic taste of butter-sautéed bananas. All that flavor is nicely balanced by rich, lemony acidity. **92** *—S.H. (5/1/2007)*

Stuhlmuller Vineyards 2003 Estate Chardonnay (Alexander Valley) $23. 86 *—S.H. (10/1/2005)*

Stuhlmuller Vineyards 2000 Estate Bottled Chardonnay (Alexander Valley) $23. 84 *—S.H. (8/1/2003)*

Stuhlmuller Vineyards 2004 Reserve Chardonnay (Alexander Valley) $38. This is a dramatically structured Chardonnay, a finely balanced wine from Alexander Valley, which produces lush, exotic Chards. The warmth of the vintage has softened the acidity, and while it's not an ager, it's enormously complex. Papaya, mango, crystalized ginger candy and cinnamon spice flavors are long and deep, while extensive new oak adds luscious butterscotch and caramel notes. **94** *—S.H. (5/1/2007)*

SUBIO

Subio 2005 Dro Rosé Wine Rosé Blend (Mendocino) $15. Made from southern Rhône varieties, this wine has the crisp, silky charm of an inexpensive Provençal blush. The cherry, raspberry and vanilla flavors have earthier notes of dried herbs and spices. **84** *—S.H. (11/15/2007)*

SULA VINEYARDS

Sula Vineyards 2005 Shiraz (Napa-Sonoma) $12. 82 *—M.D. (12/15/2006)*

SULLIVAN

Sullivan 2000 Cabernet Sauvignon (Rutherford) $50. 85 *—S.H. (2/1/2004)*

Sullivan 1997 Cabernet Sauvignon (Rutherford) $45. 86 *(11/1/2000)*

Sullivan 2001 Estate Cabernet Sauvignon (Rutherford) $50. 93 *—S.H. (10/1/2004)*

Sullivan 2003 Estate Bottled Cabernet Sauvignon (Rutherford) $55. 89 *—S.H. (12/15/2006)*

Sullivan 2002 Estate Reserve Cabernet Sauvignon (Rutherford) $85. 93 Editors' Choice *—S.H. (12/15/2005)*

Sullivan 2004 Reserve Cabernet Sauvignon (Rutherford) $100. This displayed a medicinal aroma, and tasted like candied cherry cough medicine. That candied taste lingered into the finish, where the wine turned slightly harsh. **83** *—S.H. (12/15/2007)*

Sullivan 2004 Reserve Cabernet Sauvignon (Rutherford) $100. Made in an exotic style, almost bizarre, with cherry pie filling, candied ginger, red licorice and chocolate mint flavors that are not really Cabernet-like. The finish is dry and harsh in tannins. Tasted twice, with consistent results. **84** *—S.H. (12/15/2007)*

Sullivan 2003 Estate Merlot (Rutherford) $50. Too raisiny and hot for me, with stewed fruit flavors. The tannins are nice and ripe, but that cooked taste is a turnoff. Barbecued beef is your best bet. **83** *—S.H. (3/1/2007)*

Sullivan 2004 Red Ink Red Blend (Napa Valley) $25. I wanted to like this blend of Merlot, Syrah and Cabernet Sauvignon from Napa Valley, which has such nice tannins and oak. But for all its qualities, it has a jarring quality in the mouth, with unripe tannins and green fruit. **83** *—S.H. (4/1/2007)*

SULLIVAN BIRNEY

Sullivan Birney 2001 Chardonnay (Sonoma Mountain) $28. 91 *—S.H. (2/1/2004)*

Sullivan Birney 2002 Sonoma Coast Chardonnay (Sonoma Coast) $30. 88 *—S.H. (8/1/2004)*

Sullivan Birney 2002 Sonoma Mt. Chardonnay (Sonoma Mountain) $27. 88 *—S.H. (8/1/2004)*

Sullivan Birney 2002 Pinot Noir (Sonoma Coast) $28. 83 *(11/1/2004)*

Sullivan Birney 2002 Katherine Vineyard Pinot Noir (Sonoma Mountain) $34. 84 *(11/1/2004)*

Sullivan Birney 2001 Katherine Vineyard Pinot Noir (Sonoma Mountain) $30. 93 Editors' Choice *—S.H. (5/1/2004)*

SUMMERLAND

Summerland 2001 Cabernet Sauvignon (Santa Barbara County) $16. 82 *—S.H. (10/1/2004)*

Summerland 2002 Chardonnay (Santa Barbara County) $14. 84 *—S.H. (9/1/2004)*

Summerland 2002 Bien Nacido Vineyard Chardonnay (Santa Maria Valley) $22. 91 *—S.H. (9/1/2004)*

Summerland 2001 Merlot (Santa Barbara County) $16. 83 *—S.H. (12/15/2004)*

Summerland 2002 Pinot Noir (Central Coast) $18. 85 *(11/1/2004)*

Summerland 2002 Bien Nacido Vineyard Block T Pinot Noir (Santa Maria Valley) $30. 84 *(11/1/2004)*

Summerland 2002 Odyssey-Thurlestone Vineyard Pinot Noir (Edna Valley) $28. 86 *(11/1/2004)*

Summerland 2002 Syrah (Paso Robles) $16. 83 *—S.H. (12/1/2004)*

Summerland 2002 Highlands Vineyard Syrah (Santa Barbara County) $20. 88 *—S.H. (9/1/2004)*

SUMMERS

Summers 2004 Cabernet Sauvignon (Napa Valley) $46. Summers has been quietly perfecting Cabernet under the radar. The '04 continues a string of successful vintages. It's riper and more accessible than previous years, and rewards for expressive black currant flavors enhanced with lots of fine, smoky new oak. The tannins are so gentle, you can drink this wine now, but it should hold for a good six years. **91** *—S.H. (12/31/2007)*

Summers 2003 Cabernet Sauvignon (Napa Valley) $20. 87 *—S.H. (2/1/2006)*

Summers 2002 Cabernet Sauvignon (Napa Valley) $36. 87 *—S.H. (11/1/2005)*

Summers 2001 Cabernet Sauvignon (Napa Valley) $40. 90 *—S.H. (4/1/2004)*

Summers 2000 Cabernet Sauvignon (Napa Valley) $38. 93 Editors' Choice *—S.H. (11/15/2003)*

Summers 2003 Andriana's Cuvée Cabernet Sauvignon (Napa Valley) $20. 91 *—S.H. (5/1/2006)*

Summers 1999 Chevalier Noir Cabernet Sauvignon-Merlot (North Coast) $32. 87 *—S.H. (11/15/2002)*

Summers 2005 Villa Adriana Vineyard Charbono (Napa Valley) $28. Charbono makes a rustic, but long-lived, wine in California. Few specialize in it, but Summers does. The '05 is a big, black, inky wine, as tannic as Petite Sirah but earthier and softer. The flavors are of carob, blackberries and coffee. Totally dry. **85** *—S.H. (7/1/2007)*

Summers 2004 Villa Andriana Vineyard Charbono (Napa Valley) $28. 83 *—S.H. (11/15/2006)*

Summers 2000 Villa Andriano Vineyard Charbono (Napa Valley) $24. 84 *—S.H. (12/1/2002)*

Summers 2006 Chardonnay (Alexander Valley) $26. Shows the softness of Alexander Valley Chardonnay, and the delicious complexity that these wines can attain. Apricots, pineapples, peaches and Meyer lemons are the fruits, framed by vanilla and smoke from new oak, and finishing with a minerality that must come from the earth. **90** *—S.H. (12/31/2007)*

Summers 2005 Chardonnay (Alexander Valley) $24. 87 *—S.H. (12/1/2006)*

Summers 1999 Merlot (Knights Valley) $24. 85 *—S.H. (11/15/2002)*

Summers 1997 Merlot (Knights Valley) $25. 85 *—M.S. (7/1/2000)*

Summers 2004 Reserve Merlot (Knights Valley) $28. 85 *—S.H. (12/1/2006)*

Summers 2003 Reserve Merlot (Knights Valley) $30. 84 *—S.H. (11/1/2005)*

Summers 2000 Viognier (Monterey) $18. 90 Editors' Choice *—S.H. (12/15/2002)*

Summers 2005 Villa Andriana Vineyard Zinfandel (Napa Valley) $34. The vineyard is in Calistoga, the vines are fairly old, and you can taste the concentration that low yield has squeezed into the grapes. Blackberries, plums and blueberries are the fruit flavors, but there's a baked, raisiny taste, and the mouthfeel is hot and astringent in dry tannins. **83** *—S.H. (12/1/2007)*

Summers 2004 Villa Andriana Vineyard Zinfandel (Napa Valley) $34. 92 *—S.H. (11/1/2006)*

Summers 2003 Villa Adriana Vineyard Zinfandel (Napa Valley) $28. 88 *—S.H. (8/1/2005)*

Summers 2000 Villa Adriana Vineyard Zinfandel (Napa Valley) $24. 86 *—S.H. (11/1/2002)*

Summers 2001 Villa Andriana Vineyard Zinfandel (Napa Valley) $24. 90 *(11/1/2003)*

Summers 2002 Villa Andriana Vineyard Estate Zinfandel (Napa Valley) $28. 90 *—S.H. (6/1/2005)*

SUMMERWOOD

Summerwood 2001 Sentio III Bordeaux Blend (Central Coast) $50. 87 *—S.H. (12/31/2004)*

Summerwood 2001 Diosa Red Blend (Paso Robles) $50. 89 *—S.H. (12/31/2004)*

Summerwood 2002 SZG Red Blend (Paso Robles) $35. 89 *—S.H. (12/31/2004)*

Summerwood 2003 Diosa Rhône Red Blend (Paso Robles) $50. 91 *—S.H. (10/1/2005)*

Summerwood 2003 Diosa Blanc Rhône White Blend (Paso Robles) $40. 90 *—S.H. (10/1/2005)*

Summerwood 2002 Diosa Syrah (Paso Robles) $50. 86 *—S.H. (12/15/2004)*

Summerwood 2001 Lock Vineyard Syrah (Paso Robles) $40. 89 *—S.H. (12/31/2004)*

Summerwood 2001 Zinfandel (Paso Robles) $18. 84 *(11/1/2003)*

SUMMIT LAKE

Summit Lake 2000 Emily Kestrel Cabernet Sauvignon (Howell Mountain) $40. 88 *—S.H. (5/1/2005)*

Summit Lake 2001 Zinfandel (Howell Mountain) $20. 85 *—S.H. (5/1/2005)*

Summit Lake 2000 Zinfandel (Howell Mountain) $20. 84 *—J.M. (10/1/2004)*

Summit Lake 1999 Zinfandel (Howell Mountain) $22. 92 *—S.H. (9/1/2002)*

Summit Lake 2001 Clair Rileys Private Reserve Port Zinfandel (Howell Mountain) $85. 83 *—S.H. (5/1/2005)*

Summit Lake 1996 Howell Mountain Zinfandel (Napa Valley) $23. 85 *—P.G. (11/15/1999)*

SUNCÉ VINEYARD & WINERY

Suncé Vineyard & Winery 2000 Pl. Franicevic Stryker's Vineyard Cabernet Sauvignon (Clear Lake) $32. 84 *—S.H. (6/1/2004)*

Suncé Vineyard & Winery 2001 Pl. Franicevic Stryker's Vineyard Meritage Cabernet Sauvignon (Clear Lake) $40. 86 *—S.H. (6/1/2004)*

Suncé Vineyard & Winery 1999 Pl. Franicevic Pheasant Glen Vineyard Meritage (Dunnigan Hills) $58. 83 *—S.H. (6/1/2004)*

Suncé Vineyard & Winery 2000 Pl. Franicevic Stryker's Vineyard Meritage (Clear Lake) $65. 83 *—S.H. (6/1/2004)*

Suncé Vineyard & Winery 2000 Merlot (Monterey) $18. 90 *—S.H. (12/31/2003)*

Suncé Vineyard & Winery 2001 La Rochelle Vineyard Pinot Noir (Monterey) $18. 86 *—S.H. (12/1/2005)*

Suncé Vineyard & Winery 2000 Pl. Franicevic Karah's Hillside Vineyard Pinot Noir (Sonoma Coast) $28. 85 *—S.H. (6/1/2004)*

Suncé Vineyard & Winery 2001 Pl. Franicevic Piner Ranch Vineyard Pinot Noir (Russian River Valley) $32. 83 *—S.H. (6/1/2004)*

Suncé Vineyard & Winery 2001 Nova Vineyard Old Vines Zinfandel (Clear Lake) $25. 82 *—S.H. (6/1/2004)*

SUNSET

Sunset 1999 Zinfandel (Dry Creek Valley) $23. 85 *—S.H. (9/1/2002)*

SUNSTONE

Sunstone 2004 Eros Bordeaux Blend (Santa Ynez Valley) $50. From this congenial appellation comes this Merlot-based Bordeaux blend. It's rich and sturdy, with blackberry, oak, coffee, sage and dill flavors wrapped into fairly hard-edged tannins. Completely dry, it's best for a couple more years. **86** *—S.H. (8/1/2007)*

Sunstone 2003 Eros Bordeaux Blend (Santa Ynez Valley) $50. 90 *—S.H. (9/1/2006)*

Sunstone 1999 Eros Bordeaux Blend (Santa Ynez Valley) $36. 90 *—S.H. (2/1/2003)*

Sunstone 2003 Estate Cabernet Sauvignon (Santa Ynez Valley) $50. Soft and superripe, this Cab has jammy berry flavors, with an edge of green tannins. It's totally dry, and doesn't seem to have a future, so drink up. **84** *—S.H. (8/1/2007)*

Sunstone 2001 Chardonnay (Santa Barbara County) $18. 86 *—S.H. (12/15/2002)*

Sunstone 2000 Chardonnay (Santa Barbara County) $18. 86 *—S.H. (4/1/2002)*

Sunstone 2005 Reserve Chardonnay (Santa Barbara County) $36. This is ripe and heavy, with apricot jam and toast flavors. Might show more personality by autumn. **84** *—S.H. (8/1/2007)*

Sunstone 2000 Merlot (Santa Ynez Valley) $24. 85 *—S.H. (11/15/2002)*

Sunstone 1999 Merlot (Santa Barbara County) $24. 86 *—S.H. (4/1/2002)*

Sunstone 2003 Estate Merlot (Santa Ynez Valley) $36. 87 *—S.H. (11/15/2006)*

Sunstone 1999 Reserve Merlot (Santa Ynez Valley) $30. 88 *—S.H. (11/15/2002)*

Sunstone NV Rapsodie du Soleil Rhône Red Blend (Santa Barbara County) $40. A Rhônish blend of Syrah, Mourvèdre and Viognier, with some Merlot, this is a simple country wine, upfront in jammy cherry and blueberry flavors. **84** *—S.H. (8/1/2007)*

Sunstone 2005 Syrah Rosé Blend (Santa Ynez Valley) $26. 88 *—S.H. (11/1/2006)*

Sunstone 2000 Sauvignon Blanc (Santa Ynez Valley) $14. 85 *—S.H. (4/1/2002)*

Sunstone 2003 Syrah (Santa Barbara County) $32. 81 *—S.H. (11/15/2006)*

Sunstone 1999 Syrah (Santa Ynez Valley) $40. 90 *—S.H. (12/1/2002)*

Sunstone 2003 Estate Syrah (Santa Ynez Valley) $32. 86 *—S.H. (11/15/2006)*

Sunstone 2003 Reserve Syrah (Santa Ynez Valley) $42. 88 *—S.H. (12/1/2006)*

Sunstone 2000 Viognier (Santa Ynez Valley) $24. 85 *—S.H. (4/1/2002)*

SURH LUCHTEL

Surh Luchtel 2004 Cabernet Sauvignon (Napa Valley) $40. A blend of Atlas Peak and Howell Mountain, this elegant wine has all the qualities that make it classic Napa Cab. Balance is the key, with ripe, dusty tannins, sweet new oak, acidity and black currants poised in dry equilibrium. Drink now, as it's a bit on the thin side, fruitwise. **89** *—S.H. (9/1/2007)*

Surh Luchtel 2002 Cabernet Sauvignon (Napa Valley) $38. 88 *—S.H. (10/1/2005)*

Surh Luchtel 2001 Cabernet Sauvignon (Napa Valley) $35. 91 *—S.H. (10/1/2004)*

Surh Luchtel 1999 Cabernet Sauvignon (Napa Valley) $40. 92 *—S.H. (8/1/2003)*

Surh Luchtel 2004 Sacrashe Vineyard Cabernet Sauvignon (Napa Valley) $55. Sacrashe is a great vineyard, technically in Rutherford but really in the Vaca Mountains, 750 feet high east of the Silverado Trail. Its Cabernets always are balanced and intense. Surh Luchtel has produced an oaky Cab defined by tight tannins, and although they're of the sweet modern kind, this classic, balanced, black currant-rich wine is one you want to cellar for 5–8 years. **93 Cellar Selection** *—S.H. (9/1/2007)*

Surh Luchtel 2004 Stagecoach Vineyard Cabernet Sauvignon (Napa Valley) $60. This large vineyard, in the hills of eastern Napa, is source to many wineries, and now Surh Luchel dips into the pot. This is a very good wine, dry and classically structured, with thick but finely ground tannins and ripe flavors of black currants and new French oak. A touch of asperity in the finish warrants against aging. **90** *—S.H. (9/1/2007)*

Surh Luchtel 2001 Sacrashe Vineyard Cabernet Sauvignon (Napa Valley) $40. 93 Editors' Choice *—S.H. (10/1/2004)*

Surh Luchtel 1999 Mosaic Cabernet Sauvignon-Merlot (North Coast) $23. 86 *—S.H. (9/1/2002)*

Surh Luchtel 2001 Mosaique Meritage (Napa Valley) $25. 88 *—S.H. (10/1/2004)*

Surh Luchtel 2005 Garys' Vineyard Pinot Noir (Santa Lucia Highlands) $50. For the last several years Surh Luchtel has been tinkering to get this wine right. The '05 is their best yet, a dry, silky, light-bodied wine, with complex layers of cherry skin, rhubarb pie, root beer, rose petal and red licorice flavors, enhanced with toasted new oak. The winemaker seems to be striving to tame the aggressive character this vineyard can bring to Pinot, in favor of delicacy and elegance. He has largely succeeded. A wine to watch. **92** *—S.H. (9/1/2007)*

Surh Luchtel 2004 Garys' Vineyard Pinot Noir (Santa Lucia Highlands) $48. 88 *—S.H. (11/15/2006)*

Surh Luchtel 2003 Garys' Vineyard Pinot Noir (Santa Lucia Highlands) $42. 87 *—S.H. (10/1/2005)*

Surh Luchtel 2004 Page Nord Vineyard Syrah (Oak Knoll) $35. Smells like northern Rhône, with white pepper, blackberry, currant, sweet leather, fresh herb and oak aromas that are firm and complex. But once in the mouth, this Syrah turns distinctly Californian. It's soft and melted, with a milk chocolate edge to the blackberry jam flavors and a slightly sweet finish. **86** *—S.H. (10/1/2007)*

Surh Luchtel 2003 Page Nord Vineyard Syrah (Oak Knoll) $38. 89 —*S.H. (11/15/2006)*

Surh Luchtel 2002 Page Nord Vineyard Syrah (Napa Valley) $35. 90 Editors' Choice *(9/1/2005)*

Surh Luchtel 2004 Zinfandel (Napa Valley) $32. The alcohol is over the top; at nearly 16%, it shows both heat and sweetness. As tasty as the briary wild berry flavors are, the wine is just unbalanced. **82** —*S.H. (10/1/2007)*

Surh Luchtel 1999 Zinfandel (Napa Valley) $27. 85 —*S.H. (9/1/2002)*

SUTTER HOME

Sutter Home 2000 Family Vineyard Selection Cabernet Sauvignon (California) $12. 83 —*S.H. (10/1/2004)*

Sutter Home 2003 White Cabernet Sauvignon (California) $5. 84 Best Buy —*S.H. (11/15/2004)*

Sutter Home 2000 Chardonnay (California) $6. 87 —*P.G. (11/15/2001)*

Sutter Home 1999 Chardonnay (California) $6. 84 —*S.H. (2/1/2001)*

Sutter Home 1998 Chardonnay (California) $6. 85 Best Buy —*S.H. (11/1/1999)*

Sutter Home 2002 Family Vineyard Selection Chardonnay (California) $11. 84 —*S.H. (10/1/2004)*

Sutter Home 2000 Gewürztraminer (California) $6. 85 —*S.H. (11/15/2001)*

Sutter Home 1998 Rose Merlot (California) $7. 80 —*J.F. (8/1/2001)*

Sutter Home 2003 White Merlot (California) $5. 84 Best Buy —*S.H. (12/15/2004)*

Sutter Home 2000 Moscato (California) $5. 85 Best Buy —*S.H. (11/15/2001)*

Sutter Home 2004 Pinot Grigio (California) $5. 83 —*S.H. (2/1/2006)*

Sutter Home 2002 Pinot Grigio (California) $6. 84 Best Buy —*M.S. (12/1/2003)*

Sutter Home 1997 Pinot Noir (California) $6. 84 —*T.R. (11/15/1999)*

Sutter Home 1998 Sauvignon Blanc (California) $5. 87 Best Buy —*S.H. (2/1/2000)*

Sutter Home 1998 Shiraz (California) $6. 82 —*S.H. (2/1/2000)*

Sutter Home 2000 Zinfandel (California) $5. 83 *(11/15/2001)*

Sutter Home 1999 Zinfandel (California) $6. 83 —*S.H. (2/1/2001)*

Sutter Home 1997 Zinfandel (California) $6. 82 —*S.H. (2/1/2000)*

Sutter Home 2002 White Zinfandel (California) $7. 83 —*S.H. (9/1/2004)*

SWANSON

Swanson 2000 Alexis Bordeaux Blend (Napa Valley) $50. 87 —*S.H. (12/15/2003)*

Swanson 1996 Alexis Bordeaux Blend (Napa Valley) $35. 91 —*S.H. (6/1/1999)*

Swanson 1997 Cabernet Sauvignon (Napa Valley) $40. 91 *(11/1/2000)*

Swanson 1999 Alexis Cabernet Sauvignon-Syrah (Napa Valley) $35. 91 —*C.S. (11/15/2002)*

Swanson 2001 Alexis Red Table Wine Cabernet Sauvignon-Syrah (Oakville) $50. 95 Editors' Choice —*S.H. (11/15/2004)*

Swanson 2004 Merlot (Oakville) $34. Tannic and fruity, this young Merlot has upfront primary cherry, blackberry, plum and coffee flavors, and is very dry. It's balanced in every way, with a nice edge of oak, but those tannins dominate, and suggest rich meats and cheeses. **88** —*S.H. (11/1/2007)*

Swanson 2003 Merlot (Oakville) $32. 83 —*S.H. (12/31/2006)*

Swanson 2002 Merlot (Oakville) $30. 91 Editors' Choice —*S.H. (11/1/2005)*

Swanson 2001 Merlot (Oakville) $32. 91 —*S.H. (5/1/2005)*

Swanson 2000 Merlot (Napa Valley) $30. 85 —*S.H. (4/1/2004)*

Swanson 1999 Merlot (Napa Valley) $21. 87 —*D.T. (12/31/2002)*

Swanson 1997 Merlot (Napa Valley) $28. 88 —*J.C. (7/1/2000)*

Swanson 1996 Merlot (Napa Valley) $21. 93 *(11/15/1999)*

Swanson 2006 Pinot Grigio (Napa Valley) $21. Swanson deftly avoided green, unripe flavors in this cool vintage, although this wine flirts with them, offering a spearmint edge to the pineapple, peach, fig and honeysuckle flavors. It's really a delicious wine, dry and clean in acidity, with a long, racy finish. **90** —*S.H. (11/1/2007)*

Swanson 2005 Pinot Grigio (Napa Valley) $21. This is the kind of PG that makes the variety such a perfect all-purpose white. It's bone dry, with a great crunch of acidity that brightens slightly herbal grapefruit zest, white peach, Meyer lemon and wildflower flavors. Interestingly, the wine did not undergo malolactic, and while it was fermented in stainless steel, it was sur lies aged. **88 Editors' Choice** —*S.H. (8/1/2007)*

Swanson 2004 Pinot Grigio (Napa Valley) $20. 91 —*S.H. (2/1/2006)*

Swanson 2003 Pinot Grigio (Napa Valley) $20. 86 —*S.H. (5/1/2005)*

Swanson 1998 Pinot Grigio (Napa Valley) $18. 86 *(8/1/1999)*

Swanson 2003 Alexis Red Blend (Oakville) $64. This doesn't disappoint. It's a Cabernet-based blend, with Merlot and Syrah. The '03 is lushly soft but dry and rich, with ripe, velvety tannins framing intense blackberry, coffee, tobacco and spice flavors. Should hit its stride by the end of 2007, and glide down for a couple of years after. **90** —*S.H. (8/1/2007)*

Swanson 2002 Alexis Red Blend (Oakville) $55. 90 —*S.H. (11/1/2005)*

Swanson 1997 Alexis Red Table Wine Red Blend (Napa Valley) $45. 92 —*M.S. (9/1/2000)*

Swanson 1997 Sangiovese (Napa Valley) $24. 92 —*S.H. (11/1/1999)*

Swanson 1996 Late Harvest Sémillon (Napa Valley) $33. 88 —*J.C. (12/31/1999)*

Swanson 1998 Syrah (Napa Valley) $45. 89 *(11/1/2001)*

SWITCHBACK RIDGE

Switchback Ridge 1999 Cabernet Sauvignon (Napa Valley) $65.

Switchback Ridge 2000 Peterson Family Vineyard Merlot (Napa Valley) $48. 92 —*J.M. (8/1/2003)*

Switchback Ridge 1999 Peterson Family Vineyard Merlot (Napa Valley) $48. 92 —*J.M. (8/1/2003)*

Switchback Ridge 2000 Peterson Family Vineyard Petite Sirah (Napa Valley) $45. 91 *(4/1/2003)*

SYLVESTER

Sylvester 2004 Le Vigne di San Domenico Cabernet Franc (Paso Robles) $23. Decent everyday quality, but too hot and raw, although there's plenty of savory cherry fruit. The alcohol is a relatively modest 14.5%, but the wine leaves a burn on the finish. **84** —*S.H. (9/1/2007)*

Sylvester 2005 Kiara Private Reserve Cabernet Sauvignon (Paso Robles) $15. With its soft texture and dry, jammy blackberry, red currant and chocolate flavors, this is made in the modern, ripe style of Cabernet. Can't quite overcome its rustic tannins, but not bad for the price. **85** —*S.H. (11/15/2007)*

Sylvester 2005 Kiara Private Reserve Chardonnay (Paso Robles) $15. Not a bad Chard from this warm Central Coast region. It's a little rough around the edges, but is dry and creamy, with a nice mingling of fruit and oaky elements. **85** —*S.H. (9/1/2007)*

Sylvester 2005 Kiara Private Reserve Merlot (Paso Robles) $15. From down in Paso comes this soft, chocolaty Merlot. Acidity is deficient, but this kind of flavor goes a long way to saving the wine, which has the taste of perfectly ripe, crushed blackberries. **84** —*S.H. (9/1/2007)*

Sylvester 2003 Kiara Reserve Sangiovese Port Sangiovese (Paso Robles) $20. This extremely sweet wine has flavors of cherries, blackberries, raspberries, dark chocolate, coconut macaroon and vanilla custard, with rich tannins and a crisp spine of tangerine acidity. It's totally, decadently delicious. **94 Editors' Choice** —*S.H. (10/1/2007)*

Sylvester 2002 Syrah (Paso Robles) $14. 84 —*S.H. (12/1/2004)*

SYNCLINE

Syncline 2003 Late Harvest Chenin Blanc (Columbia Valley (WA)) $18. 92 —*P.G. (9/1/2004)*

Syncline 2003 Rosé Grenache (Columbia Valley (WA)) $13. 90 —*P.G. (9/1/2004)*

Syncline 2004 Cuvée Elena G-S-M (Columbia Valley (WA)) $35. This is the first bottling of what will be the winery's flagship Southern Rhône-inspired blend. It includes the first estate-grown fruit, and the rest from Alder Ridge. It has great concentration, and a tarry, jammy aspect that pushes the fruit into more richness and intensity. Complexity and ripeness shows right from the start, carrying through to a finish with citrusy, bright, cool-climate fruits. A captivating wine, with a forward and intriguing set of sauvage and tarry flavors; tremendous length. 122 cases produced. **93** —*P.G. (3/1/2007)*

Syncline 2002 Celilo Vineyard Pinot Noir (Washington) $20. 88 —*P.G. (11/1/2004)*

Syncline 2001 Subduction Red Blend (Columbia Valley (WA)) $14. 87 —*P.G. (9/1/2003)*

Syncline 2005 Subduction Rhône Red Blend (Columbia Valley (WA)) $18. The blend of this very appealing red includes Syrah, Grenache, Mourvèdre and Cinsault. Bright, forward, juicy fruit explodes from the glass; aromatic with dense, wild berry, cranberry and mineral. It's a Washington take on Cotes-du-Rhône, with all the bright spicy fruit, but less of the herb and garrigue flavor. It's a country wine, luscious and full, but not all that serious. **88** *—P.G. (3/1/2007)*

Syncline 2006 Rosé Blend (Columbia Valley (WA)) $17. Syncline consistently produces one of Washington's most interesting rosés. The blend, as usual, includes Grenache (68%), Mourvèdre (25%) and Cinsault (7%). Sourced from a diverse group of Columbia Valley vineyards, this is a lush, round and thoroughly delightful basket of tangy fruits: berries, citrus, rhubarb, white peach and more. It cleans the palate and fills the mouth with bracing, fresh flavors. **88** *—P.G. (7/1/2007)*

Syncline 2005 Alder Ridge Vineyard Roussanne (Horse Heaven Hills) $22. Juicy and ripe with rich scents of toasted almonds, Japanese pear and chamomile tea. The fruit hones in and focuses on pears and peaches, then shifts into lovely nutty flavors that liven up the mouthfeel and continue through an impressively persistent finish. 103 cases produced. **90** *—P.G. (3/1/2007)*

Syncline 2005 Syrah (Columbia Valley (WA)) $22. Aromatic and silky upon entry, this stylish Syrah brings dark berry fruit flavors laced with toast and smoked meats. It's saturated, bright and sappy, with fine-grained tannins that seem to spread the flavors fully across the palate. The finish is of medium length, expanding gradually as the wine airs, and adding vanilla and chocolate flavors. **90** *—P.G. (12/1/2007)*

Syncline 2004 Destiny Ridge Vineyard Syrah (Horse Heaven Hills) $28. This young fruit starts off with scents of huckleberries and violets, underscored with whiffs of clay and pepper. The minerality elevates it above the norm; the fruit is well-ripened but still tart and tight, acids are plentiful, and no new oak was used (or needed). This is impeccable winemaking, extracting every nuance from the grapes. 170 cases produced. **89** *—P.G. (3/1/2007)*

Syncline 2004 McKinley Springs Vineyard Syrah (Horse Heaven Hills) $30. The McKinley Springs Syrah has an intense, peppery, aromatic nose. Beyond the penetrating spice are layers of raspberry, black cherry, pepper and espresso, underscored with a musky chocolate. A finishing hint of orange zest (from a tiny bit of co-fermented Viognier) adds interest, and the finish lingers with sweet fruit right on through the end. This wine really pops. 438 cases produced. **91** *—P.G. (3/1/2007)*

Syncline 2004 Milbrandt Vineyards Syrah (Columbia Valley (WA)) $22. 93 *—P.G. (6/1/2006)*

Syncline 2002 Milbrandt Vineyards Syrah (Columbia Valley (WA)) $20. 89 *—P.G. (9/1/2004)*

Syncline 2001 Milbrandt Vineyards Syrah (Columbia Valley (WA)) $20. 90 *—P.G. (9/1/2003)*

Syncline 2002 Reserve Syrah (Columbia Valley (WA)) $30. 90 *—P.G. (9/1/2004)*

Syncline 2003 Reserve McKinley Springs Vineyard Syrah (Columbia Valley (WA)) $30. 89 *(9/1/2005)*

Syncline 2006 Viognier (Columbia Valley (WA)) $20. From Clifton and Coyote Canyon vines, this tastes of quinine, lime and citrus; it's sharp, fragrant and quite young. The finish falls off into hot, acidic, slightly bitter phenolics, but improves as it breathes. It's one of those gin and tonic-style Viogniers that pack plenty of flavor but turn a little harsh at the end. **87** *—P.G. (12/1/2007)*

Syncline 2005 Viognier (Columbia Valley (WA)) $20. It's 100% Viognier, a light blush/tawny color, and all neutral barrel fermented. Winemaker James Mantone calls Viognier "the white Pinot Noir" due to the difficulty of making it well, without bitterness or what he terms "muskiness." This is round and fruity, with scents of fig and peach and apricot, and the flavors follow. It sets a consistent note that it holds through a long, clean finish. **88** *—P.G. (3/1/2007)*

Syncline 2004 Viognier (Columbia Valley (WA)) $20. 89 *—P.G. (12/15/2005)*

Syncline 2003 Clifton Vineyard Viognier (Columbia Valley (WA)) $20. 88 *—P.G. (9/1/2004)*

SYZYGY

Syzygy 2004 Cabernet Sauvignon (Columbia Valley (WA)) $32. This is pure Cabernet from older vines, and has a meaty, herbal power to it. Streaks of tar and some lively cinnamon spice add life to the fruit, which is solid and earthy. I pick up black licorice, vanilla cream, and still more interesting flavors wrapped into the tannins, which seem dusty and smoky and a bit grainy. This has some real substance to it, and shows some of the herbal side of the grape. The best so far from Syzygy. **92** *—P.G. (12/1/2007)*

Syzygy 2003 Cabernet Sauvignon (Columbia Valley (WA)) $30. 89 *—P.G. (10/1/2006)*

Syzygy 2005 Red Blend (Columbia Valley (WA)) $22. A self-described "mad scientist wine" that blends 35% Syrah, 30% Cabernet Sauvignon, 23% Merlot and 12% Malbec, it turns out to be a smooth and flavorful, with some muscle and good berry flavors. The black raspberry, cherry and boysenberry come with plenty of sharp acid and spice; finishes with light chocolate. **88** *—P.G. (12/1/2007)*

Syzygy 2004 Red Blend (Columbia Valley (WA)) $20. 88 *—P.G. (10/1/2006)*

Syzygy 2003 Red Blend (Columbia Valley (WA)) $20. 88 *—P.G. (4/1/2006)*

Syzygy 2004 Syrah (Columbia Valley (WA)) $28. This may be the best Syrah yet from this promising young Walla Walla winery. It's sappy and full, spicy and textural, and the fruit is concentrated and lively, with a mix of grape, cherry and berry sweetness. A young, forward wine, it is showing the sort of bright and primary fruit flavors that can be so appealing, but it is also built to age and should improve over the next five or six years. **89** *—P.G. (3/1/2007)*

Syzygy 2003 Syrah (Walla Walla (WA)) $28. 87 *(9/1/2005)*

Syzygy 2003 Syrah (Walla Walla (WA)) $28. 88 *—P.G. (4/1/2006)*

TABLAS CREEK

Tablas Creek 1999 Reserve Cuvée Bordeaux Blend (Paso Robles) $35. 87 *—S.H. (11/15/2002)*

Tablas Creek 2000 Antithesis Chardonnay (Paso Robles) $35. 91 *—J.M. (5/1/2002)*

Tablas Creek 2005 Grenache Blanc (Paso Robles) $27. Tastes a little heavy and flowery, with fleshy, pulpy flavors of peaches, apricots and spicy mangoes. Needs more zesty tang to bring structure to the fruit. **84** *—S.H. (11/1/2007)*

Tablas Creek 2004 Grenache Blanc (Paso Robles) $27. 86 *—S.H. (6/1/2006)*

Tablas Creek 2000 Côtes de Tablas Grenache-Syrah (Paso Robles) $25. 89 *—S.H. (3/1/2004)*

Tablas Creek 2005 Mourvèdre (Paso Robles) $35. Mourvèdre has not been Tablas Creek's strong suit. The wine is soft and simple, with syrupy blackberry and chocolate-sweetened coffee flavors. Needs greater depth and complexity to succeed. **83** *—S.H. (11/1/2007)*

Tablas Creek 2003 Mourvèdre (Paso Robles) $32. 84 *—S.H. (10/1/2005)*

Tablas Creek 2002 Côtes de Tablas Red Blend (Paso Robles) $22. 85 *—S.H. (2/1/2005)*

Tablas Creek 2002 Esprit de Beaucastel Red Blend (Paso Robles) $40. 89 *—S.H. (2/1/2005)*

Tablas Creek 2005 Côtes de Tablas Rhône Red Blend (Paso Robles) $20. This is Côtes-du-Rhône, California style. A blend of Grenache, Mourvedre, Syrah and Counoise, it's a dry, rich, full-bodied red wine, flooded with easy-to-drink cherry, blackberry, blueberry and oak flavors, and a wealth of Provençal rosemary, lavender and thyme. Drink now for its soft, youthful purity. **88** *—S.H. (12/31/2007)*

Tablas Creek 2004 Cotes de Tablas Rhône Red Blend (Paso Robles) $20. A junior version of the winery's Esprit bottling, although this one's based on Grenache and is much richer and almost sweeter in cherry liqueur. It's a soft, simple wine, but beguiling. You might almost call it seductive. **87** *—S.H. (4/1/2007)*

Tablas Creek 2003 Côtes de Tablas Rhône Red Blend (Paso Robles) $20. 86 *—S.H. (10/1/2005)*

Tablas Creek 2001 Côtes de Tablas Rhône Red Blend (Paso Robles) $22. 89 *—S.H. (5/1/2004)*

Tablas Creek 2004 Esprit de Beaucastel Rhône Red Blend (Paso Robles) $45. The winery continues to make progress with this ambitious wine, a Rhône blend of Mourvèdre, Syrah, Grenache and Counoise. The challenge has always been to move beyond simple ripeness, which is easy to achieve, into true complexity. The '04 moves the ball forward, offering Provençal herb nuances to the cherries and cocoa. **90** *—S.H. (4/1/2007)*

Tablas Creek 2003 Esprit de Beaucastel Rhône Red Blend (Paso Robles) $40. 89 *—S.H. (10/1/2005)*

Tablas Creek 2000 Esprit de Beaucastel Rhône Red Blend (Paso Robles) $35. 91 *—S.H. (12/1/2003)*

Tablas Creek 1999 Petite Cuvée: Grenache, Syrah, Mourvèdre Rhône Red Blend (Paso Robles) $25. 88 *—J.M. (7/1/2002)*

Tablas Creek 2000 Rosé Rhône Red Blend (Paso Robles) $27. 90 *—S.H. (9/1/2003)*

Tablas Creek 2006 Côtes de Tablas Blanc Rhône White Blend (Paso Robles) $20. Côtes de Tablas is Tablas Creek's number two white, after their Esprit de Beaucastel. The '06 is a blend of Viognier, Marsanne, Grenache Blanc and Roussanne. It's a satisfying wine, somewhat sweet and simple in apricot, peach and pineapple flavors. **86** *—S.H. (12/31/2007)*

Tablas Creek 2005 Côtes de Tablas Blanc Rhône White Blend (Paso Robles) $20. This Roussanne, Marsanne and Grenache Blanc blend is dry and crisp in acidity, with flavors of baked papayas, guavas and nectarines, offset by high acidity. It doesn't possess the complexity of Esprit, but it's a nice, complex wine. **87** *—S.H. (4/1/2007)*

Tablas Creek 2002 Côtes de Tablas Blanc Rhône White Blend (Paso Robles) $22. 91 Editors' Choice —*S.H. (2/1/2004)*

Tablas Creek 2005 Esprit de Beaucastel Blanc Rhône White Blend (Paso Robles) $35. One of the more distinctive whites in California, this blend of Roussanne, Grenache Blanc and Picpoul Blanc is produced by a leading Rhône family from France. It will appeal to Chard lovers for its rich, oaky creaminess, but offers a completely different flavor profile of nectarines, apricots and wildflowers. **90** —*S.H. (4/1/2007)*

Tablas Creek 2003 Vin de Paille Rhône White Blend (Paso Robles) $65. 84 —*S.H. (10/1/2005)*

Tablas Creek 2006 Rosé Blend (Paso Robles) $25. Just delicious, a wine you can't stop drinking. The cherry-berry and spice flavors are full-bodied and dry, while the mouthfeel is just so pretty, all silk and crisp acidity. Drink this Mourvedre, Grenache and Counoise blend soon for its youthful beauty. **90** —*S.H. (7/1/2007)*

Tablas Creek 2005 Rosé Blend (Paso Robles) $27. 90 —*S.H. (11/1/2006)*

Tablas Creek 2004 Rosé Blend (Paso Robles) $25. 90 —*S.H. (10/1/2005)*

Tablas Creek 2003 Rosé Blend (Paso Robles) $27. 91 —*S.H. (3/1/2005)*

Tablas Creek 2002 Rosé Blend (Paso Robles) $26. 90 —*S.H. (3/1/2004)*

Tablas Creek 1999 Rosé Blend (Paso Robles) $27. 88 —*J.M. (12/1/2001)*

Tablas Creek 2005 Roussanne (Paso Robles) $27. Tablas Creek blows hot and cold with Roussanne, a tricky grape to get right. This one hits a double. It's dry, but a little too soft, with exotic flavors of white peach, guava, sautéed banana and buttered popcorn, and a candied finish of butterscotch LifeSavers. **86** —*S.H. (11/1/2007)*

Tablas Creek 2004 Roussanne (Paso Robles) $27. 84 —*S.H. (11/1/2006)*

Tablas Creek 2003 Roussanne (Paso Robles) $27. 86 —*S.H. (10/1/2005)*

Tablas Creek 2002 Roussanne (Paso Robles) $26. 90 —*S.H. (2/1/2004)*

Tablas Creek 2005 Syrah (Paso Robles) $35. Tablas Creek has struggled with Syrah and continues to do so. Ripeness isn't the problem, as the '05 shows, with powerful blackberry, raspberry and chocolate flavors. The challenge is structural. They need to build in an acid-tannin balance, and keep the finish dry. **85** —*S.H. (11/1/2007)*

Tablas Creek 2003 Syrah (Paso Robles) $32. 87 —*S.H. (10/1/2005)*

Tablas Creek 2000 Clos Blanc White Blend (Paso Robles) $35. 92 —*J.M. (9/1/2002)*

Tablas Creek 2003 Côtes de Tablas Blanc White Blend (Paso Robles) $22. 91 —*S.H. (2/1/2005)*

Tablas Creek 2003 Esprit de Beaucastel Blanc White Blend (Paso Robles) $35. 95 —*S.H. (2/1/2005)*

Tablas Creek 2002 Esprit de Beaucastel Blanc White Blend (Paso Robles) $35. 92 —*S.H. (5/1/2004)*

Tablas Creek 2001 Esprit de Beaucastel Blanc White Blend (Paso Robles) $35. 94 —*S.H. (12/1/2003)*

Tablas Creek 1998 Tablas Blanc White Blend (Paso Robles) $30. 90 —*S.H. (10/1/1999)*

Tablas Creek 1997 Tablas Blanc White Blend (Paso Robles) $30. 92 —*S.H. (10/1/1999)*

TABLE ROCK

Table Rock 1999 Merlot (Rogue Valley) $19. 85 —*C.S. (12/31/2002)*

Table Rock 1999 Pinot Noir (Rogue Valley) $16. 85 *(10/1/2002)*

TAFT STREET

Taft Street 1998 Chardonnay (Monterey County) $15. 87 *(6/1/2000)*

Taft Street 1998 Chardonnay (Russian River Valley) $15. 88 *(6/1/2000)*

Taft Street 2001 Chardonnay (Monterey County) $7. 87 Best Buy —*S.H. (11/15/2003)*

Taft Street 2003 Pinot Noir (Sonoma Coast) $15. 87 —*S.H. (12/15/2005)*

Taft Street 2004 Poplar Vineyard Sauvignon Blanc (Russian River Valley) $15. 88 —*S.H. (12/15/2005)*

Taft Street 1997 Zinfandel (Sonoma County) $12. 83 —*P.G. (11/15/1999)*

Taft Street 1998 Zinfandel (Dry Creek Valley) $NA. 87 —*P.G. (3/1/2001)*

Taft Street 2003 Old Vines Zinfandel (Russian River Valley) $20. 82 —*S.H. (12/15/2005)*

TAGARIS

Tagaris 1999 Chardonnay (Columbia Valley (WA)) $10. 83 —*P.G. (7/1/2002)*

Tagaris 2001 Johannisberg Riesling (Columbia Valley (WA)) $7. 88 —*P.G. (9/1/2002)*

Tagaris 2001 Reserve Johannisberg Riesling (Columbia Valley (WA)) $8. 88 —*P.G. (9/1/2002)*

TAHOE RIDGE

Tahoe Ridge 2005 Watts Vineyard Reserve Chardonnay (Lodi) $24. I like the low 13% alcohol on this Chard, and also the dryness. How many Chardonnays have both? What's not so pleasant is the heavy hand of overly toasted oak. **83** —*S.H. (12/1/2007)*

Tahoe Ridge 2004 Merlot (Lodi) $28. With its sugary, baked blackberry fruit, this Merlot is simply too soft and sweet, especially at this price. **81** —*S.H. (12/1/2007)*

TALBOTT

Talbott 2003 Cuvée Cynthia Chardonnay (Monterey County) $60. 95 Cellar Selection —*S.H. (12/31/2006)*

Talbott 2002 Cuvée Cynthia Chardonnay (Monterey County) $55. 95 Editors' Choice —*S.H. (12/31/2005)*

Talbott 1998 Cuvée Cynthia Chardonnay (Monterey) $45. 89 *(7/1/2001)*

Talbott 2003 Diamond T Estate Chardonnay (Monterey County) $65. Always an interesting wine, Talbott's '03 Diamond T is so distinctive, it's almost eccentric. The candied apricots and cinnamon flavors have a baked pie filling taste. With high acidity and a minerally edge, this Chard will develop nutty complexities over the next 3–5 years. **91** —*S.H. (12/1/2007)*

Talbott 2002 Diamond T Estate Chardonnay (Monterey) $65. 96 Editors' Choice —*S.H. (12/31/2006)*

Talbott 2001 Diamond T Estate Chardonnay (Monterey) $65. 87 —*S.H. (12/31/2005)*

Talbott 2000 Diamond T Estate Chardonnay (Monterey County) $65. 91 —*S.H. (12/1/2004)*

Talbott 1998 Diamond T Estate Chardonnay (Monterey) $55. 91 *(7/1/2001)*

Talbott 2003 Diamond T Estate Cuvée Audrey Chardonnay (Monterey) $75. The Audrey Cuvée brings extra richness to the regular Diamond T Estate Chard. It's an enormous wine that has honeyed sweetness. The flavors are of apricot jam, pineapple tart and lemon meringue, and new, smoky oak plays a prominant part. This Chard calls for careful pairing with food, since it's so rich, almost a dessert wine. **92** —*S.H. (12/15/2007)*

Talbott 2002 Diamond T Estate Cuvée Audrey Chardonnay (Monterey) $75. 96 Editors' Choice —*S.H. (7/1/2006)*

Talbott 2005 Kali Hart Vineyard Chardonnay (Monterey) $15. This is a letdown. Overtly sweet, with a flavor like canned apricot and peach syrup. A decent wine that will appeal to some. **83** —*S.H. (7/1/2007)*

Talbott 2003 Kali Hart Chardonnay (Monterey County) $13. 85 —*S.H. (6/1/2005)*

Talbott 2004 Sleepy Hollow Chardonnay (Santa Lucia Highlands) $42. Doesn't seem to have the elegant Burgundian quality of past vintages, and the main culprit is the flavor of apricot jam, which makes the wine a little heavy and suggests overripe fruit. Apricots are delicious, of course, but you don't want too much of that in a Chardonnay. **85** —*S.H. (5/1/2007)*

Talbott 2003 Sleepy Hollow Chardonnay (Santa Lucia Highlands) $42. 90 —*S.H. (12/15/2006)*

Talbott 2002 Sleepy Hollow Vineyard Chardonnay (Monterey County) $39. 90 —*S.H. (12/15/2005)*

Talbott 2001 Sleepy Hollow Chardonnay (Monterey County) $42. 93 —*S.H. (12/1/2004)*

Talbott 2000 Sleepy Hollow Chardonnay (Monterey County) $42. 93 —*S.H. (12/1/2003)*

Talbott 1999 Sleepy Hollow Chardonnay (Santa Lucia Highlands) $35. 89 —*S.H. (5/1/2003)*

Talbott 1998 Sleepy Hollow Chardonnay (Monterey) $35. 88 *(7/1/2001)*

Talbott 2005 Kali Hart Vineyard Pinot Noir (Monterey County) $20. Smells distinctly Port-y, with caramelized fruit scents, and tastes sharp and minty, with wintergreen and bitter cherryskin flavors. The finish is dry. **83** —*S.H. (7/1/2007)*

Talbott 2001 Logan Pinot Noir (Monterey) $18. 81 —*S.H. (10/1/2005)*

Talbott 2000 Sleepy Hollow Vineyard CASE Pinot Noir (Monterey County) $45. 87 —*S.H. (6/1/2005)*

Talbott 1999 Sleepy Hollow Vineyard CASE Pinot Noir (Monterey County) $42. 90 —*S.H. (3/1/2004)*

TALISMAN

Talisman 2001 Pinot Noir (Russian River Valley) $36. 89 —*J.M. (10/1/2004)*

Talisman 2001 Kathy's Cuvée Pinot Noir (Carneros) $40. 91 —*J.M. (10/1/2004)*

Talisman 2004 Red Dog Vineyard Pinot Noir (Sonoma Mountain) $46. This is the softest and sweetest of Talisman's three other '04 single-vineyard wines. The cherry cola, licorice, root beer and cinnamon spice flavors are indeed delicious, but the wine needs greater structural integrity, and is a little obvious in its appeal. Drink now. **86** —*S.H. (12/15/2007)*

Talisman 2004 Ted's Vineyard Pinot Noir (Russian River Valley) $42. You have to consider the vintage to understand this Pinot, which comes from prime, southern valley terroir. It was very hot, the earliest harvest ever, and it was difficult for vintners to achieve total balance. The '04 Ted's Vineyard is certainly forward in cherries, cola, spice and chocolate, and it has a nice, silky mouthfeel. But it lacks the acidic crispness that makes for balance. Drink now. **87** —*S.H. (12/15/2007)*

Talisman 2003 Ted's Vineyard Pinot Noir (Russian River Valley) $40. The facts look really good: low yields, modest alcohol, good acidity, the best clones, lots of new French oak and, of course, great grapes. It's rich, silky and complex, a gorgeous, raspberry-infused expression of Russian River. **93** —*S.H. (2/1/2007)*

Talisman 2004 Thorn Ridge Vineyard Pinot Noir (Sonoma Coast) $46. The vineyard is in a cool area of this sprawling appellation southwest of Sebastopol, but the heat of the vintage shows in the wine's relative softness and ripeness of fruit. The cherries, raspberries and dates are almost, but not quite, cooked, bringing to mind a Fig Newton cookie. Scores high on the deliciousness scale, but it's not a wine for the cellar. Drink now. **88** —*S.H. (12/15/2007)*

Talisman 2002 Truchard Vineyard Pinot Noir (Carneros) $38. 92 —*S.H. (12/15/2005)*

Talisman 2004 Wildcat Mountain Vineyard Pinot Noir (Carneros) $40. This is Steve MacRostie's vineyard, located in the far northwest of the appellation, practically in Sonoma Coast. Their '04 strikes me as a little heavy and obvious now, but that may be a function of its relative youth. The wine is dry and crisp, with jammy raspberry, cherry, cola and spice flavors. Could do interesting things in the next 3–5 years. **87** —*S.H. (12/15/2007)*

Talisman 2003 Wildcat Mountain Vineyard Pinot Noir (Carneros) $38. One doesn't think of Carneros in terms of mountains, but the appellation does slide onto the foothills of the Mayacamas. In fact the upper reaches catch the cold winds off San Francisco Bay more than the lowlands. You can taste the long hangtime cherries and raspberries, and crisp acids, in this deliciously silky, long-finishing Pinot. **93** —*S.H. (2/1/2007)*

TALLEY

Talley 2000 Chardonnay (Arroyo Grande Valley) $24. 89 —*S.H. (2/1/2003)*

Talley 1999 Chardonnay (Arroyo Grande Valley) $24. 93 *(12/31/2001)*

Talley 1998 Chardonnay (Arroyo Grande Valley) $22. 91 —*S.H. (2/1/2001)*

Talley 2005 Estate Chardonnay (Arroyo Grande Valley) $26. Clean and flinty-minerally, this is a light-bodied, delicate Chard whose appeal is in its elegance. Oak accents modest pineapple, pear and peach fruit. **86** —*S.H. (11/1/2007)*

Talley 2004 Estate Chardonnay (Arroyo Grande Valley) $26. 91 —*S.H. (6/1/2006)*

Talley 2005 Oliver's Vineyard Chardonnay (Edna Valley) $26. Shows classic Edna Valley acidity, upfront and zesty, that stimulates the palate and brightens the modest lime, kiwi and vanilla oak flavors. This is a pleasant, easy Chardonnay to drink now. **87** —*S.H. (11/1/2007)*

Talley 2004 Oliver's Vineyard Chardonnay (Edna Valley) $22. 87 —*S.H. (6/1/2006)*

Talley 2002 Oliver's Vineyard Chardonnay (Edna Valley) $20. 89 —*S.H. (6/1/2004)*

Talley 2000 Oliver's Vineyard Chardonnay (Edna Valley) $20. 90 —*S.H. (12/31/2001)*

Talley 1999 Oliver's Vineyard Chardonnay (Edna Valley) $20. 88 —*S.H. (2/1/2001)*

Talley 1998 Oliver's Vineyard Chardonnay (Edna Valley) $20. 86 *(6/1/2000)*

Talley 2004 Rincon Vineyard Chardonnay (Arroyo Grande Valley) $38. 92 Editors' Choice —*S.H. (12/1/2006)*

Talley 2003 Rincon Vineyard Chardonnay (Arroyo Grande Valley) $36. 92 —*S.H. (12/1/2005)*

Talley 2000 Rincon Vineyard Chardonnay (Arroyo Grande Valley) $35. 90 —*S.H. (2/1/2003)*

Talley 1997 Rincon Vineyard Chardonnay (Arroyo Grande Valley) $20. 88 —*S.H. (10/1/1999)*

Talley 2004 Rosemary's Vineyard Chardonnay (Arroyo Grande Valley) $45. 95 Editors' Choice —*S.H. (12/1/2006)*

Talley 2003 Rosemary's Vineyard Chardonnay (Arroyo Grande Valley) $44. 96 —*S.H. (7/1/2006)*

Talley 2000 Rosemary's Vineyard Chardonnay (Arroyo Grande Valley) $40. 91 —*S.H. (2/1/2003)*

Talley 1999 Rosemary's Vineyard Chardonnay (Arroyo Seco) $40. 89 *(7/1/2001)*

Talley 1997 Rosemary's Vineyard Chardonnay (Arroyo Grande Valley) $20. 90 —*S.H. (10/1/1999)*

Talley 2004 Pinot Noir (Arroyo Grande Valley) $32. 87 —*S.H. (12/1/2006)*

Talley 2003 Pinot Noir (Edna Valley) $28. 86 *S.H. (10/1/2006)*

Talley 2002 Pinot Noir (Arroyo Grande Valley) $30. 88 *(11/1/2004)*

Talley 2000 Pinot Noir (Arroyo Grande Valley) $28. 90 —*S.H. (2/1/2003)*

Talley 1998 Pinot Noir (Arroyo Grande Valley) $28. 86 *S.H. (2/1/2001)*

Talley 2005 Estate Pinot Noir (Arroyo Grande Valley) $34. This is Talley's basic appellation Pinot Noir, and it shares the elegance and balance this winery is known for, although the concentration of the single-vineyard bottlings isn't there. It's a pleasant wine, with dry flavors of cola, raspberries and vanilla and a rich, silky texture. **87** —*S.H. (11/1/2007)*

Talley 2001 Estate Pinot Noir (Arroyo Grande Valley) $28. 90 —*S.H. (6/1/2004)*

Talley 1997 Estate Pinot Noir (Arroyo Grande Valley) $28. 91 *(10/1/1999)*

Talley 2004 Rincon Vineyard Pinot Noir (Arroyo Grande Valley) $68. I don't think this is the greatest Rincon because the fruit was so ripe that it makes the resulting wine lose some finesse. Having said that, this is a delicious Pinot Noir. It's so juicy in cherry, raspberry, cola and root beer flavors, with a gorgeous edge of vanilla-infused oak, and a classically silky texture. As good as it is, it just misses greatness. **91** —*S.H. (6/1/2007)*

Talley 2003 Rincon Vineyard Pinot Noir (Arroyo Grande Valley) $50. 93 —*S.H. (12/31/2005)*

Talley 2002 Rincon Vineyard Pinot Noir (Arroyo Grande Valley) $48. 94 *(11/1/2004)*

Talley 2001 Rincon Vineyard Pinot Noir (Arroyo Grande Valley) $45. 92 —*S.H. (6/1/2004)*

Talley 2000 Rincon Vineyard Pinot Noir (Arroyo Grande Valley) $45. 92 —*S.H. (2/1/2003)*

Talley 1999 Rincon Vineyard Pinot Noir (Arroyo Grande Valley) $40. 92 —*S.H. (12/15/2001)*

Talley 2004 Rosemary's Vineyard Pinot Noir (Arroyo Grande Valley) $55. While not on a par with the previous vintages, this wine is silky and dry, replete in ripe cherry, raspberry, cola and mocha flavors. It finishes fully dry and long. Drink now. **89** —*S.H. (6/1/2007)*

Talley 2003 Rosemary's Vineyard Pinot Noir (Arroyo Grande Valley) $65. 94 Editors' Choice —*S.H. (11/1/2006)*

Talley 2002 Rosemary's Vineyard Pinot Noir (Arroyo Grande Valley) $62. 93 *(11/1/2004)*

Talley 2000 Rosemary's Vineyard Pinot Noir (Arroyo Grande Valley) $60. 92 Cellar Selection —*S.H. (7/1/2003)*

Talley 1999 Rosemary's Vineyard Pinot Noir (Arroyo Grande Valley) $60. 86 —*S.H. (7/1/2002)*

Talley 1997 Rosemary's Vineyard Pinot Noir (Arroyo Grande Valley) $45. 93 *(7/1/2003)*

Talley 2004 Stone Corral Vineyard Pinot Noir (Edna Valley) $45. This is the first Talley Pinot I've had from this vineyard, which is in Edna Valley. It shows young vine fruit, bright in cherries, raspberries and cola, with a deeper, earthier streak of dark chocolate and soy-splashed wild mushrooms. This is a wine to watch, as the vines gain age. **90** —*S.H. (6/1/2007)*

TALLULAH

Tallulah 2004 Syrah (Sonoma Coast) $28. 88—*S.H. (11/15/2006)*

Tallulah 2004 Bald Mountain Ranch Syrah (Mount Veeder) $40. 90 —*S.H. (11/15/2006)*

TALOMAS

Talomas 2000 Cabernet Sauvignon-Merlot (California) $14. 85 —*S.H. (8/1/2003)*

Talomas 2002 Basket Press Reserve Syrah (Central Coast) $30. 87 *(9/1/2005)*

Talomas 2001 Basket Press Reserve Syrah (Central Coast) $50. 91 —*S.H. (12/15/2004)*

TALTY VINEYARDS & WINERY

Talty Vineyards & Winery 2001 Zinfandel (Dry Creek Valley) $32. 88 *(11/1/2003)*

TALUS

Talus 2005 Cabernet Sauvignon (Lodi) $8. Talus is turning out to be the best buy king with wines like this juicy, appealing Cabernet. It shows Lodi-style ripeness, with a blast of blackberries and cherries, and also Lodi-style softness. Drink this simple Cab with anything calling for a full-bodied dry red. **84 Best Buy** *—S.H. (11/15/2007)*

Talus 2004 Cabernet Sauvignon (Lodi) $8. 83 *—S.H. (5/1/2006)*

Talus 2006 Chardonnay (California) $8. Sweet and simple, this Chard tastes like peach, pineapple and pear juice with a couple spoons of white sugar. **82** *—S.H. (11/15/2007)*

Talus 2004 Chardonnay (Lodi) $8. 84 Best Buy *—S.H. (7/1/2006)*

Talus 2003 Chardonnay (California) $8. 83 *—S.H. (2/1/2005)*

Talus 2001 Chardonnay (California) $NA. 84 *—S.H. (6/1/2003)*

Talus 2005 Merlot (Lodi) $8. Here's a very fruity wine just brimming with sun-ripened cherry, raspberry and blackberry flavors, with a kiss of smoky oak. It's nice, dry and balanced, and a good value for the money. **85 Best Buy** *—S.H. (11/15/2007)*

Talus 2004 Merlot (California) $8. 83 *—S.H. (12/15/2006)*

Talus 2003 Merlot (Lodi) $8. 85 Best Buy *—S.H. (11/15/2005)*

Talus 2002 Merlot (Lodi) $8. 83 *—S.H. (2/1/2005)*

Talus 2000 Merlot (California) $9. 84 *—S.H. (9/1/2003)*

Talus 2006 Pinot Grigio (California) $8. Pretty good everyday price, but too soft and sweet. The apricot, peach and pineapple flavors taste frankly sugared. **82** *—S.H. (11/15/2007)*

Talus 2004 Pinot Grigio (Lodi) $8. 82 *—S.H. (7/1/2005)*

Talus 2003 Pinot Grigio (California) $8. 83 *—S.H. (3/1/2005)*

Talus 2001 Pinot Grigio (California) $9. 85 *—S.H. (12/1/2003)*

Talus 2004 Pinot Noir (California) $8. 84 Best Buy *—S.H. (5/1/2006)*

Talus 2002 Pinot Noir (California) $8. 83 *—S.H. (2/1/2005)*

Talus 2000 Pinot Noir (California) $9. 84 Best Buy *(10/1/2002)*

Talus 1997 Red Blend (California) $9. 86 *(11/15/1999)*

Talus 2004 Shiraz (Lodi) $8. 84 Best Buy *—S.H. (6/1/2006)*

Talus 2003 Shiraz (Lodi) $8. 84 Best Buy *(9/1/2005)*

Talus 2002 Shiraz (Lodi) $8. 84 *—S.H. (2/1/2005)*

Talus 2000 Shiraz (California) $9. 83 *—S.H. (12/15/2003)*

Talus 1999 Shiraz (California) $8. 83 *(10/1/2001)*

Talus 2005 Zinfandel (Lodi) $8. A clean, fruity, affordable Zin to wash down burgers, pizza, and chicken. This one fits the bill, with pleasant raspberry, black cherry, gingerbread and licorice flavors that have the tannin-acid bite to cut through fatty oils and meats. **84 Best Buy** *—S.H. (11/15/2007)*

Talus 2003 Zinfandel (Lodi) $8. 85 Best Buy *—S.H. (10/1/2005)*

Talus 2002 Zinfandel (Lodi) $8. 84 *—S.H. (2/1/2005)*

Talus 2001 Zinfandel (Lodi) $8. 87 Best Buy *(11/1/2003)*

Talus 2000 Zinfandel (California) $9. 83 *—S.H. (3/1/2003)*

Talus 1998 Zinfandel (California) $8. 85 Best Buy *—P.G. (3/1/2001)*

TAMARACK CELLARS

Tamarack Cellars 2005 Cabernet Franc (Columbia Valley (WA)) $25. The fruit comes from Weinbau, DuBrul and Destiny Ridge. The Weinbau is old vine, and is the main component. This is a solid, meaty, deep purple and blue, with hints of smoked meat in the nose. Fruit flavors are tight, tart and run to the black cherry and blackberry flavors. Clearly varietal, with stiff tannins, a bit chalky, but plenty of varietal character and a long finish with streaks of coffee and light herb. This is winemaker Ron Coleman's favorite red, and he gives it plenty of TLC that shines through in the bottle. **90** *—P.G. (8/1/2007)*

Tamarack Cellars 2004 Cabernet Franc (Columbia Valley (WA)) $25. 87 *—P.G. (6/1/2006)*

Tamarack Cellars 2003 Cabernet Sauvignon (Columbia Valley (WA)) $32. 88 *—P.G. (6/1/2006)*

Tamarack Cellars 2001 Cabernet Sauvignon (Columbia Valley (WA)) $32. 88 *—P.G. (5/1/2004)*

Tamarack Cellars 1999 Cabernet Sauvignon (Columbia Valley (WA)) $34. 87 *—P.G. (12/31/2001)*

Tamarack Cellars 2004 Chardonnay (Columbia Valley (WA)) $18. 88 *—P.G. (6/1/2006)*

Tamarack Cellars 2002 Chardonnay (Columbia Valley (WA)) $18. 88 *—P.G. (5/1/2004)*

Tamarack Cellars 2005 Merlot (Columbia Valley (WA)) $28. Same vineyards as the '04, but a riper, deeper, denser vintage. This is good Washington Merlot, with muscle, extract and plenty of stuffing. Flavors run to the dark side, blue/black fruits, mineral, licorice, smoke. It's got the kind of mass that will stand up to all meats, and the balance to age over the next decade or so. Nicely built, still tight and chewy. **89** *—P.G. (8/1/2007)*

Tamarack Cellars 2004 Merlot (Columbia Valley (WA)) $28. 87 *—P.G. (6/1/2006)*

Tamarack Cellars 2001 Merlot (Columbia Valley (WA)) $28. 87 *—P.G. (5/1/2004)*

Tamarack Cellars 2000 Merlot (Columbia Valley (WA)) $28. 89 *—P.G. (9/1/2002)*

Tamarack Cellars 1999 Merlot (Columbia Valley (WA)) $28. 88 *—P.G. (12/31/2001)*

Tamarack Cellars 2001 Du Brul Vineyard Reserve Red Blend (Yakima Valley) $NA. 90 *—P.G. (5/1/2004)*

Tamarack Cellars 2004 Firehouse Red Red Blend (Columbia Valley (WA)) $20. 87 *—P.G. (6/1/2006)*

Tamarack Cellars 2005 Sangiovese (Columbia Valley (WA)) $25. This is all Sangiovese from Candy Mountain, and it's a fine followup to the 2004. At this young stage the barrel toast is front and center, although it's all second-fill barrels. The fruit shows a lot of spice, light plummy red flavor, and a bit of peppery herb. Simple, easy-drinking wine, without a lot of varietal presence. **86** *—P.G. (8/1/2007)*

Tamarack Cellars 2004 Sangiovese (Columbia Valley (WA)) $25. 87 *—P.G. (6/1/2006)*

Tamarack Cellars 2004 Syrah (Columbia Valley (WA)) $28. This shows the sappy, sweet, ripe character of the grape; fresh and forward and bursting with flavors of just-picked berries. It's nicely dusted with chocolate and has both power and precision. The oak is layered in beautifully, enhancing but not obliterating the fruit. This is a wine to drink young. **89** *—P.G. (8/1/2007)*

Tamarack Cellars 2003 Syrah (Columbia Valley (WA)) $28. 88 *—P.G. (6/1/2006)*

Tamarack Cellars 2002 Syrah (Columbia Valley (WA)) $28. 86 *(9/1/2005)*

TAMÁS ESTATES

Tamás Estates 2004 Barbera (Livermore Valley) $13. Barbera is not among my preferred wines, due to its hot, harsh rustic nature. But this is a good one, and while it keeps its dark, broodingly tannic nature, it offers a wealth of cherry pie filling and tobacco flavors that will marry well with roasted meats. **85** *—S.H. (5/1/2007)*

Tamás Estates 2004 Pinot Grigio (Monterey) $9. This is an enormously likeable wine, dry, crisply tart and citrusy in the way of PG, while a splash of Gewürztraminer adds richer notes of flowers and an oily hint of lychee. It's a very versatile food wine, and at this price, a great buy. **87 Best Buy** *—S.H. (5/1/2007)*

Tamás Estates 2004 Pinot Grigio (Monterey) $9. 83 *—S.H. (2/1/2006)*

Tamás Estates 2003 Pinot Grigio (Monterey) $9. 85 Best Buy *—S.H. (2/1/2006)*

Tamás Estates 1999 Pinot Grigio (Monterey County) $11. 84 *—S.H. (11/15/2001)*

Tamás Estates 2004 Sangiovese (Livermore Valley) $13. Tamas has always done a good job with Sangiovese, and that's because they don't try too hard. They're not attempting some kind of fancy Tuscan or super-Tuscan wine, just a dry, balanced red wine to have with great food. This is a true Chianti-style wine, with a splash of Barbera,offering a great deal of elegant pleasure at a great price. **88 Best Buy** *—S.H. (5/1/2007)*

Tamás Estates 2001 Sangiovese (Livermore Valley) $18. 90 Editors' Choice *—S.H. (12/1/2003)*

Tamás Estates 1996 Sangiovese (Livermore Valley) $11. 88 Best Buy *—S.H. (12/15/1999)*

Tamás Estates 2004 Zinfandel (Livermore Valley) $13. With 10% Barbera, this is a dark, gutsy wine, stuffed with coffee and plum flavors, but the sharpness and sweetness on the finish make it unbalanced. **82** *—S.H. (5/1/2007)*

Tamás Estates 1999 AVA's: San Francisco Bay/Livermore Valley Zinfandel (California) $12. 85 *—S.H. (9/1/2002)*

TAMAYO FAMILY

Tamayo Family 2005 Chardonnay (Oak Knoll) $20. There's an earthy taste to this Chard that brings to mind tobacco and dried sage, while the fruit veers towards apricots and peaches. Creamy oak adds the usual nuances to this dry, soft wine. **85** *—S.H. (4/1/2007)*

Tamayo Family 2004 Pinot Noir (Santa Lucia Highlands) $28. Big, dark and high in jammy cherry and blackberry extract and rich in tannins. Not showing much now, unless you're just into size, but should develop over the next six years, maybe longer. **87** —*S.H. (4/1/2007)*

Tamayo Family 2006 Sauvignon Blanc (Napa Valley) $16. The grapes were just short of perfectly ripe, leaving a touch of jalapeño to the more pleasant citrus and fig flavors. If you're sensitive to that, avoid. If not, this is a pleasantly dry, crisp white wine. **84** —*S.H. (11/1/2007)*

TAMBER BEY

Tamber Bey 2004 Cabernet Sauvignon (Oakville) $60. Very, very ripe, with blackberry flavors that veer into currants and almost into raisins. Yet the wine remains dry and balanced. The tannins are thick and sturdy, the acidity keen and sharp. Obviously youthful, this wine will benefit from short-term aging. Best after 2007. **87** —*S.H. (7/1/2007)*

Tamber Bey 2003 Cabernet Sauvignon (Oakville) $50. 93 Editors' Choice —*S.H. (8/1/2006)*

Tamber Bey 2002 Cabernet Sauvignon (Oakville) $50. 87 —*S.H. (11/1/2005)*

TANDEM

Tandem 2005 Kent Ritchie Vineyard Chardonnay (Russian River Valley) $42. I love this for its absolute dryness and crispness and minerally depth. There's something coldly metallic in the taste and mouthfeel, and to the extent there's fruit, it's of grapefruits and lime zest, with a flowery exoticness. Sur lies aging and toasty new oak have added richness and layers of subtle nuance. Strikes you for the sheer excellence of its balance. Enjoy now–2010. **93 Editors' Choice** —*S.H. (8/1/2007)*

Tandem 2005 Lorenzo Vineyard Chardonnay (Russian River Valley) $38. Notable for its dryness and minerally tang, this is a tight, young Chardonnay right now. The flavors veer toward grapefruits, with notes of passionfruit and honeysuckle. The wine has gone through malolactic, but it's still an acidic wine, almost lean, but elegant. Call it Chablisian. **88** —*S.H. (8/1/2007)*

Tandem 2004 Porter-Bass Vineyard Chardonnay (Russian River Valley) $48. The grapes got real ripe, to judge by the bright burst of yellow apricots and exotic passionfruits. At the same time, acidity is crisp and citrusy, and there's a pleasant yeasty character, like Champagne, or a nice fino Sherry. The wine finishes totally dry, leaving a palate impression of great elegance. Drink now through 2010. **90** —*S.H. (8/1/2007)*

Tandem 2002 Porter Bass Vineyards Chardonnay (Russian River Valley) $48. 92 —*S.H. (12/31/2004)*

Tandem 2002 Ritchie Vineyard Chardonnay (Sonoma Coast) $42. 90 —*S.H. (12/31/2004)*

Tandem 2004 Sangiacomo Vineyard Chardonnay (Sonoma Coast) $38. Showing the depth and nuance that mark great Chardonnay, this benefited from its chilly location in the Petaluma Gap in this hot vintage. The coolness allowed the grapes to achieve maximally ripe tropical fruit, nectarine and peach flavors, while preserving vital acidity. Extra dry and elegant, it's a Chard that can take up to six years of cellaring without missing a beat. **93 Editors' Choice** —*S.H. (8/1/2007)*

Tandem 2002 Sangiacomo Vineyard Chardonnay (Sonoma Coast) $38. 90 —*S.H. (12/31/2004)*

Tandem 2005 Auction Block Pinot Noir (Sonoma Coast) $54. This is a best-barrels blend whose proceeds go charity. The '05 is a blend of Silver Pines, Van der Kamp, Chris Lee and others, and it's gorgeous. Rewards for its high acid, silky feel, so light and airy, and for the intensity of cola, cherry, pomegranate, smoky vanilla cream and Asian spice flavors that last on the finish. Should pick up additional nuance for the next four years. **95 Editors' Choice** —*S.H. (8/1/2007)*

Tandem 2002 Auction Block Pinot Noir (Sonoma Coast) $60. 86 —*S.H. (11/1/2004)*

Tandem 2005 Chris Lee Vineyard Pinot Noir (Sonoma Valley) $60. Lovely, delicately silky, light-bodied and elegant, with charm and finesse. Some may find it lean in fruit, which emphasizes the acidity, but it's a connoisseur's Pinot Noir that gets better as it breathes. You have to understand complexity and subtlety in this variety to appreciate this bone dry, cherryskin-tart wine. Best now through 2010. **92** —*S.H. (8/1/2007)*

Tandem 2002 Halleck Vineyard Pinot Noir (Sonoma Coast) $54. 93 —*S.H. (11/1/2004)*

Tandem 2002 Keefer Ranch Pinot Noir (Green Valley) $38. 88 —*S.H. (11/1/2004)*

Tandem 2004 Sangiacomo Vineyards Pinot Noir (Sonoma Coast) $48. The grapes simply got too ripe, and the wine suffers from sugary-sweet cherry jam flavors with baked meringue, courtesy of well-charred oak. Those flavors are of course delicious, but the wine is direct and unageable. **85** —*S.H. (8/1/2007)*

Tandem 2002 Sangiacomo Pinot Noir (Sonoma Coast) $48. 92 —*S.H. (11/1/2004)*

Tandem 2005 Silver Pines Vineyard Pinot Noir (Sonoma Mountain) $54. Stunning. Combines the fleshy opulence of a sweetly youthful Pinot with the balanced tightness and acidity of a young, cellar-worthy one. No small feat! From a cool vintage in a cool appellation that's increasingly known for Pinot Noir, the wine is pale in color and delicate in the mouth, yet powerful in cherry cola and spice intensity. Gorgeous now, and should improve for six years before slowly bowing out. **94 Editors' Choice** —*S.H. (8/1/2007)*

Tandem 2003 Van der Kamp Vineyard Pinot Noir (Sonoma Mountain) $48. 91 —*S.H. (11/1/2005)*

Tandem 2002 Van der Kamp Vineyard Pinot Noir (Sonoma Mountain) $48. 88 —*S.H. (11/1/2004)*

Tandem 2005 Peloton Red Wine Red Blend (California) $25. There's no other blend of Carignan, Pinot Noir, Gewürz, Syrah and several other varieties, so far as I know. The wine is dry, with crisp acidity and deep cherry and raspberry flavors. It's not complicated, but it's fun. **87** —*S.H. (8/1/2007)*

Tandem 2001 Gabrielli Vineyard Sangiovese (Redwood Valley) $32. 87 —*S.H. (12/31/2004)*

Tandem 2004 Talmage Bench Aldine Vineyard Zinfandel (Mendocino County) $32. A little sweet and high in alcohol for my taste, this wine, which winemaker Greg La Follette calls "a fruit riot," indeed is explosive. Cherries, blueberries and black raspberries run rampant, with overtones of milk chocolate and coffee. On the plus side are rich, dusty tannins and good acidity, which lend structure. **85** —*S.H. (8/1/2007)*

TANGENT

Tangent 2006 Albariño (Edna Valley) $17. Think of this Albariño as a bone dry, high-acid version of Pinot Grigio. That's the personality of this likeable young wine. The citrus and spicy fig flavors are pleasing, but could use greater fruity concentration, as the wine is a bit watery. **85** —*S.H. (12/15/2007)*

Tangent 2005 Albariño (Edna Valley) $17. 90 Editors' Choice —*S.H. (12/1/2006)*

Tangent 2006 Pinot Blanc (Arroyo Grande Valley) $17. Tangent's been on a roll with dry white wines from the cool appellations of San Louis Obispo. Here's a Pinot Blanc that shows real varietal character. It's marked by peach, mango and white pepper flavors boosted by the high natural acidity of its appellation, and is frankly a luscious, absolutely dry wine. **90 Editors' Choice** —*S.H. (12/15/2007)*

Tangent 2005 Pinot Blanc (Arroyo Grande Valley) $17. 88 —*S.H. (12/1/2006)*

Tangent 2006 Paragon Vineyard Pinot Gris (Edna Valley) $17. The vineyard is in the cool Edna Valley, and in this cool vintage, this wine has lots of bright, crunchy acidity. It's also bone dry. The flavors, of lemon, lime and tangerine zest, are accented with vanilla, toasted coconut and pepper-cinnamon. Clean and vibrant, this is ideal as a cocktail wine, or try with butternut squash soup with cilantro and crème fraîche. **88** —*S.H. (12/15/2007)*

Tangent 2005 Paragon Vineyard Pinot Gris (Edna Valley) $17. 90 —*S.H. (12/1/2006)*

Tangent 2006 Paragon Vineyard Sauvignon Blanc (Edna Valley) $13. What a nice wine. It's so dry, acidically crisp, and so balanced, it puts many more expensive California Sauvignon Blancs to shame. There's no oak in this screwtopped wine, nothing to muck up the pure, fresh citrus and fig flavors. The winemaker has allowed high natural acidity to remain, which makes everything ultraclean and savory. **90 Best Buy** —*S.H. (11/15/2007)*

Tangent 2005 Paragon Vineyard Sauvignon Blanc (Edna Valley) $13. 86 —*S.H. (12/1/2006)*

Tangent 2006 Paragon Vineyard Viognier (Edna Valley) $20. This delicious wine captures the exotic side of Viognier's personality, with its lush array of tropical fruits, wildflowers and spices. Yet it's absolutely dry and very crisp in acidity, and not too high in alcohol, making it balanced and food-friendly. **88** —*S.H. (12/15/2007)*

Tangent 2006 Ecclestone White Blend (Central Coast) $20. A blend of six varieties, but it's not a simple wine made from the leftovers that some wineries use for blends. Instead, it's crisp and fruity, not as dry as Tangent's varietal wines, but rich in Muscat orange, Riesling flowers, Pinot Gris citrus, Viognier tropical fruit and Pinot Blanc peach. One percent Albariño seems to add to the acidity. **87** —*S.H. (12/15/2007)*

Tangent 2005 Ecclestone White Blend (San Luis Obispo County) $20. 87 —*S.H. (12/1/2006)*

TANTALUS

Tantalus 1998 Cabernet Sauvignon (Sonoma County) $28. 86 —*S.H. (12/1/2001)*

USA

Tantalus 1999 Sémillon (Russian River Valley) $14. 88 Best Buy *—S.H. (11/15/2001)*

TANTARA

Tantara 2004 Bien Nacido Vineyard Chardonnay (Santa Maria Valley) $33. 92 *—S.H. (8/1/2006)*

Tantara 2000 Bien Nacido Vineyard Chardonnay (Santa Maria Valley) $26. 90 *—S.H. (12/15/2002)*

Tantara 2000 Talley Vineyard Chardonnay (Arroyo Grande Valley) $30. 92 *—S.H. (12/15/2002)*

Tantara 2004 Pinot Noir (Santa Maria Valley) $30. 90 *—S.H. (12/31/2006)*

Tantara 2005 Ashley's Vineyard Pinot Noir (Santa Rita Hills) $45. Wow. This enormously aromatic wine explodes with the most inviting raspberry, cherry, gingerbread and cinnamon-spicebox notes. It tastes as rich as it smells, with rum punch, cola, tangerine, cherry and cinnamon stick flavors. For all the richness, the wine is dry and silkily complex. **91** *—S.H. (4/1/2007)*

Tantara 2000 Bien Nacido Vineyard Pinot Noir (Santa Maria Valley) $37. 86 *—S.H. (2/1/2003)*

Tantara 2004 Bien Nacido Vineyard Adobe Pinot Noir (Santa Maria Valley) $45. 89 *—S.H. (12/31/2006)*

Tantara 2004 Bien Nacido Vineyard Old Vine Pinot Noir (Santa Maria Valley) $45. 95 *—S.H. (12/31/2006)*

Tantara 2004 Brosseau Vineyard Pinot Noir (Chalone) $52. 90 *—S.H. (12/31/2006)*

Tantara 2004 Dierberg Vineyard Pinot Noir (Santa Maria Valley) $45. 90 *—S.H. (12/31/2006)*

Tantara 2000 Dierberg Vineyard Pinot Noir (Santa Maria Valley) $40. 89 *—S.H. (2/1/2003)*

Tantara 2004 Evelyn Pinot Noir (Santa Maria Valley) $80. 97 Editors' Choice *—S.H. (12/31/2006)*

Tantara 2004 Garys' Vineyard Pinot Noir (Santa Lucia Highlands) $52. 87 *—S.H. (12/31/2006)*

Tantara 2000 Garys' Vineyard Pinot Noir (Santa Lucia Highlands) $42. 91 *—S.H. (2/1/2003)*

Tantara 2004 La Colline Vineyard Pinot Noir (Arroyo Grande Valley) $45. 92 *—S.H. (12/31/2006)*

Tantara 2000 La Colline Vineyard Pinot Noir (Arroyo Grande Valley) $40. 89 *—S.H. (2/1/2003)*

Tantara 2004 Pisoni Vineyard Pinot Noir (Santa Lucia Highlands) $60. 94 Editors' Choice *—S.H. (12/31/2006)*

Tantara 2000 Pisoni Vineyard Pinot Noir (Santa Lucia Highlands) $54. 92 *—S.H. (2/1/2003)*

Tantara 2005 Rio Vista Vineyard Pinot Noir (Santa Rita Hills) $45. Made in the house style, an expressive, supple young wine of enormous fruit and early-drinking charm. Soft and silky, with barely noticable tannins, this has scads of raspberries, cherries, sweet pomegranates, tangerines and cola. Drink now–2010. **88** *—S.H. (4/1/2007)*

Tantara 2004 Rio Vista Vineyard Pinot Noir (Santa Rita Hills) $45. 87 *—S.H. (12/31/2006)*

Tantara 2005 Sanford & Benedict Vineyard Pinot Noir (Santa Rita Hills) $52. Dramatic young Pinot, immature and exuberant, showing huge, Dijon-inspired pure fruit flavors of cherry pie filling, tangerine zest, cola, cassis and charry, caramelized new oak. Tastes honeyed, almost sweet, but the tannins and acids keep things on track. Seems like one to drink early. **89** *—S.H. (4/1/2007)*

Tantara 2004 Silacci Vineyard Pinot Noir (Santa Lucia Highlands) $52. 92 *—S.H. (12/31/2006)*

Tantara 2004 Solomon Hills Vineyard Pinot Noir (Santa Maria Valley) $45. 87 *—S.H. (12/31/2006)*

Tantara 2003 Solomon Hills Vineyard Pinot Noir (Santa Maria Valley) $45. 83 *—S.H. (8/1/2006)*

TAPTEIL VINEYARD

Tapteil Vineyard 2002 Cabernet Sauvignon (Yakima Valley) $29. 89 *—P.G. (6/1/2006)*

TARA BELLA

Tara Bella 1999 Cabernet Sauvignon (Napa Valley) $60. 90 *—S.H. (11/15/2003)*

TARARA

Tarara 1997 Pinot Noir (Virginia) $15. 83 *—J.C. (8/1/1999)*

Tarara 1997 Vidal Blanc (Virginia) $13. 80 *—J.C. (8/1/1999)*

TARIUS

Tarius 1999 Pinot Noir (Santa Lucia Highlands) $36. 86 *(10/1/2002)*

Tarius 1999 Pinot Noir (Russian River Valley) $33. 86 *(10/1/2002)*

Tarius 1997 Pisoni Vineyard Pinot Noir (Santa Lucia Highlands) $39. 88 *(11/15/1999)*

Tarius 1998 Zinfandel (Mendocino) $23. 88 *—M.S. (10/1/2000)*

Tarius 1999 Aldine Vineyard Zinfandel (Mendocino) $29. 84 *—D.T. (3/1/2002)*

Tarius 1998 Aldine Vineyard Zinfandel (Mendocino) $29. 84 *—S.H. (5/1/2000)*

Tarius 1999 Korte Ranch Zinfandel (Napa Valley) $29. 88 *—D.T. (3/1/2002)*

TASSAJARA

Tassajara 2004 Ward Vineyard Pinot Noir (Contra Costa County) $20. This wine is sourced from Lafayette, a bedroom community of San Francisco, and you know what? It's pretty good. Dry and silky, it shows cherry, raspberry, root beer and smoky, oakspice flavors. I'm looking forward to tasting the '05. **87** *—S.H. (8/1/2007)*

Tassajara 2003 Syrah (Paso Robles) $22. This soft, ripe wine erupts with blackberry, raspberry, cherry jam and milk chocolate flavors. Gentle in tannins, it feels lush on the palate, immediately likeable for fruity richness and a complex overlay of smoky new oak. Drink now. **88** *—S.H. (8/1/2007)*

Tassajara 2002 Syrah (Paso Robles) $24. 87 *(9/1/2005)*

Tassajara 2003 Rousse Rouge Syrah (Paso Robles) $20. Softly gentle, this wine is easy to like for its wealth of pie filling blackberries, cherries, blueberries and milk chocolate. It's just this side of dry, with a honeyed finish of toasty oak and glycerine. Contains one quarter Grenache, with a drop of Zin. **87** *—S.H. (8/1/2007)*

TATE CREEK

Tate Creek 1999 Cabernet Sauvignon (California) $6. 82 *—S.H. (6/1/2002)*

Tate Creek 1999 Merlot (California) $6. 81 *—S.H. (6/1/2002)*

Tate Creek 1999 Syrah (California) $6. 84 *—S.H. (9/1/2002)*

TAYLOR

Taylor 2002 Chardonnay (Stags Leap District) $22. 90 *—S.H. (8/1/2004)*

Taylor 2003 Hillside Chardonnay (Stags Leap District) $34.85 *—S.H. (2/1/2006)*

Taylor 2002 Hillside Chardonnay (Stags Leap District) $34. 88 *—S.H. (8/1/2004)*

TAZ

Taz 2006 Chardonnay (Santa Barbara County) $20. Los Alamos is a Santa Barbara region that should have its own appellation, to judge by this and many other wines grown there. A cool place, it has given this Chardonnay brilliantly crisp acidity, while ripening the fruit to perfection. Apricots, peaches, pears and mangoes are the primary flavors, enhanced with rich, toasty oak. **92 Editors' Choice** *—S.H. (12/31/2007)*

Taz 2005 Chardonnay (Santa Barbara County) $20. Taz has been doing a pretty good job with Chard. I wish this wine were a little more controlled and drier. It's like an explosion in a fruit store, bombarding you with pineapples, guavas, nectarines, wild honey and little pieces of charry oak. But it sure is a ride. **86** *—S.H. (3/1/2007)*

Taz 2004 Chardonnay (Santa Barbara County) $20. 89 *—S.H. (3/1/2006)*

Taz 2003 Chardonnay (Santa Barbara County) $20. 87 *—S.H. (8/1/2005)*

Taz 2001 Merlot (Santa Barbara County) $20. 86 *(12/15/2004)*

Taz 2006 Pinot Gris (Santa Barbara County) $15. Semisweet and simple, this wine is a blend from the Los Alamos area and Santa Maria Valley. It has fine acidity, with jammy flavors of pineapples, peaches, nectarines and mangoes. **84** *—S.H. (11/15/2007)*

Taz 2005 Pinot Gris (Santa Barbara County) $15. Joins my short list for one of the most enjoyable PGs around, and what a nice price. There's a little oak, in the form of some older barrels, which adds a touch of soft creaminess, but mainly this is about fresh, ripe citrus, fig and green apple flavors and crisp, vital acidity. **88** *—S.H. (3/1/2007)*

Taz 2004 Pinot Gris (Santa Barbara County) $15. 86 *—S.H. (2/1/2006)*

Taz 2005 Pinot Noir (Santa Barbara County) $25. A little too soft and one-dimensional, but with enough polish and complexity that it rises to white-tablecloth status. The cherry, red raspberry, cola and carob flavors have a smoky oak edge. **86** *—S.H. (12/31/2007)*

Taz 2003 Pinot Gris (Santa Barbara County) $15. 87 *(11/15/2004)*

Taz 2003 Pinot Noir (Santa Barbara County) $25. 84 *—S.H. (12/31/2005)*

Taz 2002 Pinot Noir (Santa Barbara County) $25. 89 *(11/1/2004)*

Taz 2005 Cuyama River Pinot Noir (Santa Maria Valley) $28. The winery's Cuyama River Pinot typically is very ripe and full-bodied. The trick is to achieve elegance. Veteran Chuck Ortman tries hard here, wrestling the big, fruity cherry, raspberry, rhubarb pie, cola and mocha flavors to the ground, managing the alcohol, and keeping the finish dry, but the wine cannot be fully tamed. **87** *—S.H. (11/1/2007)*

Taz 2004 Cuyama River Pinot Noir (Santa Maria Valley) $28. 86 *—S.H. (12/1/2006)*

Taz 2003 Cuyama River Pinot Noir (Santa Maria Valley) $28. 88 *—S.H. (12/1/2005)*

Taz 2005 Fiddlestix Vineyard Pinot Noir (Santa Rita Hills) $35. This is a real success for Taz. The wine shows its pedigree both in regional terroir and the vineyard, which is large but well managed. Very dry and with a smooth, silky texture, this Dijon clone has forward flavors of cherries, blackberries, raspberries and cola. It shows the finesse and subtle power that have made cool, coastal California Pinot such a success. **92** *—S.H. (12/1/2007)*

Taz 2004 Fiddlestix Vineyard Pinot Noir (Santa Rita Hills) $35. 89 *—S.H. (11/15/2006)*

Taz 2003 Fiddlestix Vineyard Pinot Noir (Santa Rita Hills) $35. 86 *—S.H. (12/15/2005)*

Taz 2002 Fiddlestix Vineyard Pinot Noir (Santa Rita Hills) $35. 92 Editors' Choice *(11/1/2004)*

Taz 2003 Syrah (Santa Barbara County) $25. 87 *—S.H. (3/1/2006)*

Taz 2002 Syrah (Santa Barbara County) $25. 92 Editors' Choice *(11/1/2004)*

Taz 2005 Goat Rock Syrah (Santa Maria Valley) $28. The model for this 100% Syrah is clearly the Northern Rhône. The tannin-acid structure is there, and the wildly ripe, opulent blackberry fruit, but there's a touch of sweet-sour sharpness that lends a rustic touch to the finish. **86** *—S.H. (11/1/2007)*

Taz 2004 Goat Rock Syrah (Santa Maria Valley) $28. 92 *—S.H. (12/1/2006)*

Taz 2003 Goat Rock Syrah (Santa Maria Valley) $28. 92 Cellar Selection *—S.H. (12/1/2005)*

USA

TEADERMAN

Teaderman 2001 Cabernet Sauvignon (Oakville) $48. 90 Cellar Selection *—S.H. (11/1/2005)*

TEATOWN CELLARS

Teatown Cellars 2000 Chardonnay (Napa Valley) $30. 83 *—J.M. (5/1/2002)*

Teatown Cellars 2003 Merlot (Napa Valley) $22. 83 *—S.H. (3/1/2006)*

Teatown Cellars 2000 Merlot (Napa Valley) $20. 85 *—S.H. (2/1/2004)*

TEFFT CELLARS

Tefft Cellars 1999 Merlot (Yakima Valley) $15. 86 *—P.G. (9/1/2002)*

Tefft Cellars 1999 Estate Bottled Syrah (Yakima Valley) $20. 86 *(10/1/2001)*

TEN MILE

Ten Mile 2004 Proprietary Red Wine Red Blend (California) $11. 87 *—S.H. (12/15/2006)*

TENSLEY

Tensley 2001 Colson Canyon Vineyard Syrah (Santa Barbara County) $30. 89 *—S.H. (3/1/2004)*

Tensley 2001 Purimisa Mountain Vineyard Syrah (Santa Barbara County) $30. 87 *—S.H. (3/1/2004)*

Tensley 2001 Thompson Vineyard Syrah (Santa Barbara County) $30. 87 *—S.H. (3/1/2004)*

TERLATO

Terlato 2003 Angels' Peak Bordeaux Blend (Napa Valley) $50. 82 *—S.H. (12/31/2006)*

Terlato 2003 Episode Bordeaux Blend (Napa Valley) $125. Tannic and hard, with black currant, black cherry, pencil lead, cedar and spice flavors. This is a tight young wine now, but it shows promise. A blend of Cab and Merlot, it should open and improve over the next 6–8 years. **88** *—S.H. (6/1/2007)*

Terlato 2005 Chardonnay (Russian River Valley) $26. Proper rather than exciting, this Chard was made classic style, with 100% barrel fermentation, 100% malolactic fermentation and plenty of lees. It's creamy and smooth, with modest flavors of peaches, pineapples and green apples. **86** *—S.H. (12/15/2007)*

Terlato 2006 Pinot Grigio (Russian River Valley) $26. The fragrances of lemon blossoms and honeysuckle hit your nose as soon as you pop the cork on this seductive white wine. It's so flavorful, so long in fruit and exotic in spices, and finishes mercifully dry. Twenty percent of barrel fermentation adds the perfect touch of creaminess. **90 Editors' Choice** *—S.H. (12/15/2007)*

Terlato 2005 Pinot Grigio (Russian River Valley) $26. 87 *—S.H. (12/31/2006)*

Terlato 2004 Pinot Grigio (Russian River Valley) $24. 87 *—S.H. (2/1/2006)*

TERRA BLANCA

Terra Blanca 2001 Syrah (Red Mountain) $20. 88 *—P.G. (4/1/2005)*

Terra Blanca 1999 Syrah (Red Mountain) $20. 87 *(10/1/2001)*

Terra Blanca 2001 Block 8 Syrah (Red Mountain) $35. 85 *—P.G. (4/1/2005)*

Terra Blanca 1999 Block 8 Syrah (Washington) $28. 85 *(11/1/2001)*

Terra Blanca 2003 Viognier (Yakima Valley) $15. 83 *—P.G. (4/1/2005)*

TERRA D'ORO

Terra d'Oro 1997 Barbera (Amador County) $22. 88 *—S.H. (8/1/2001)*

Terra d'Oro 1999 Syrah (Amador County) $18. 88 *(10/1/2001)*

Terra d'Oro 2000 Deaver Vineyard Old Vine Zinfandel (Amador County) $24. 90 *—S.H. (9/1/2003)*

Terra d'Oro 1998 Deaver Vineyard Old Vine Zinfandel (Amador County) $22. 86 *—S.H. (8/1/2001)*

Terra d'Oro 2000 Home Vineyard Zinfandel (Amador County) $24. 90 *—S.H. (9/1/2003)*

Terra d'Oro 1999 Home Vineyard Zinfandel (Amador County) $12. 88 *—P.G. (3/1/2002)*

Terra d'Oro 1999 SHR Field Blend Zinfandel (Amador County) $12. 89 *—P.G. (3/1/2002)*

TERRA VALENTINE

Terra Valentine 2003 Cabernet Sauvignon (Spring Mountain) $35. What a roll this winery has been on. This '03 isn't their greatest effort, and it's not an ager, but it's absolutely delicious, a wine to drink now while the Cabs in your cellar snooze. Offers smooth, rich tannins framing classic cassis and oak flavors. **90** *—S.H. (4/1/2007)*

Terra Valentine 2002 Cabernet Sauvignon (Spring Mountain) $35. 90 Cellar Selection *—S.H. (4/1/2006)*

Terra Valentine 2000 Cabernet Sauvignon (Spring Mountain) $35. 90 *—S.H. (8/1/2003)*

Terra Valentine 1999 Cabernet Sauvignon (Spring Mountain) $35. 90 *—S.H. (2/1/2003)*

Terra Valentine 2003 Wurtele Vineyard Cabernet Sauvignon (Spring Mountain) $55. I have never had a Wurtele Cab that was anything less than classic, and this '03 is right up there. It's reminiscent of the 2000, a gorgeously structured, softly complex wine brimming with black currant, black cherry, cola and new oak flavors wrapped in near-perfect Napa tannins. Not a longterm ager, but lovely now–2010. **92** *—S.H. (4/1/2007)*

Terra Valentine 2002 Wurtele Vineyard Cabernet Sauvignon (Spring Mountain) $50. 96 Editors' Choice *—S.H. (4/1/2006)*

Terra Valentine 2000 Wurtele Vineyard Cabernet Sauvignon (Spring Mountain) $50. 92 *—J.M. (10/1/2003)*

Terra Valentine 1999 Wurtele Vineyard Cabernet Sauvignon (Spring Mountain) $50. 93 Editors' Choice *—S.H. (2/1/2003)*

Terra Valentine 2004 Wurtele Vineyard *Barrel Sample* Cabernet Sauvignon (Napa Valley) $NA. 93 *—S.H. (8/1/2004)*

Terra Valentine 2001 Wurtele Vineyard Reserve Cabernet Sauvignon (Spring Mountain) $50. 93 *—J.C. (10/1/2004)*

TERRE ROUGE

Terre Rouge 1999 Mourvèdre (Amador County) $20. 90 *—S.H. (7/1/2002)*

Terre Rouge 2000 Tete-a-Tete Red Blend (Sierra Foothills) $13. 85 *—S.H. (7/1/2002)*

Terre Rouge 1997 Rhône Red Blend (Sierra Foothills) $20. 84 *—S.H. (7/1/2002)*

Terre Rouge 2000 Vin Gris d'Amador Rosé Blend (Sierra Foothills) $12. 89 *—S.H. (9/10/2002)*

Terre Rouge 1999 Syrah (Sierra Foothills) $22. 93 *—S.H. (7/1/2002)*

Terre Rouge 2000 Les Côtes de L'Ouest Syrah (California) $15. 92 Best Buy *—S.H. (7/1/2002)*

Terre Rouge 1998 Sentinel Oak Vineyard Pyramid Bloc Syrah (Shenandoah Valley (CA)) $30. 89 *—S.H. (8/1/2001)*

Terre Rouge 1999 Sentinel Oak Vineyard Pyramid Block Syrah (Shenandoah Valley (CA)) $35. 94 *—S.H. (7/1/2002)*

Terre Rouge 1999 Enigma White Blend (Sierra Foothills) $18. 93 Editors' Choice *—S.H. (8/1/2001)*

TERRITORIAL

Territorial 2006 Pinot Gris (Willamette Valley) $16. This feels quite flat on the palate. The fruit is dull and feels almost rubbery. There is an artificial quality to it, and the wine quickly fades. **82** *—P.G. (11/15/2007)*

TERRY HOAGE

Terry Hoage 2004 The 46 Grenache and Syrah Rhône Red Blend (Paso Robles) $40. 88 *—S.H. (12/1/2006)*

Terry Hoage 2004 The Hedge Syrah (Paso Robles) $45. 89 *—S.H. (12/1/2006)*

TERTULIA CELLARS

Tertulia Cellars 2005 Syrah (Columbia Valley (WA)) $27. This excellent wine, co-fermented with 2% Viognier, shows a sinuous muscularity that gives the fruit supple definition. Scents of violets, sweet berry fruit, baking spices and hints of ginger all are wrapped into a smooth, almost velvety finish. This has grip and polish; it's a terrific first effort from this new winery. **91** *—P.G. (12/1/2007)*

Tertulia Cellars 2005 Les Collines Vineyard Syrah (Walla Walla (WA)) $29. The fruit is ripe and bright, with flavors of strawberry and raspberry preserves. New oak shows through with ground coffee and bitter chocolate. It's bright, spicy and lifted. **90** *—P.G. (12/1/2007)*

Tertulia Cellars 2006 Viognier (Columbia Valley (WA)) $18. Suffers from the common new winery kinds of faults. Overpriced for the competition; there are odd, off scents suggesting hay, honey, and yeast. It feels awkward on the palate, disjointed and incomplete. **84** *—P.G. (12/1/2007)*

TESSERA

Tessera 1997 Chardonnay (California) $10. 83 *—M.S. (10/1/1999)*

TESTAROSSA

Testarossa 1998 Chardonnay (Santa Maria Valley) $26. 88 *—S.H. (10/1/2000)*

Testarossa 2005 Bien Nacido Vineyard Chardonnay (Santa Maria Valley) $39. As ripe as any Chardonnay on earth, it's well-oaked and balanced in acidity. The pineapple, mango, papaya, passionfruit and smoky oak flavors, with a butter-sautéed, Cognac-splashed banana finish, will appeal to those who like their wines flamboyant. **89** *—S.H. (6/1/2007)*

Testarossa 2004 Bien Nacido Vineyard Chardonnay (Santa Maria Valley) $39. 90 *—S.H. (9/1/2006)*

Testarossa 2003 Bien Nacido Vineyard Chardonnay (Santa Maria Valley) $36. 91 *—S.H. (7/1/2005)*

Testarossa 2001 Bien Nacido VIneyard Chardonnay (Santa Lucia Highlands) $35. 87 *—S.H. (12/15/2003)*

Testarossa 2000 Bien Nacido Vineyard Chardonnay (Santa Maria Valley) $45. 90 *(10/1/2002)*

Testarossa 1999 Bien Nacido Vineyard Chardonnay (Santa Maria Valley) $32. 87 *(7/1/2001)*

Testarossa 2005 Brosseau Vineyard Chardonnay (Chalone) $39. A nice Chardonnay, delicious in tropical fruit, apricot and spice flavors boosted with crisp acidity, and well-oaked. Yet it's strangely one-dimensional. The fruit got so ripe that maybe it was stripped of complexity and nuance. **87** *—S.H. (6/1/2007)*

Testarossa 2004 Brosseau Vineyard Chardonnay (Chalone) $39. 92 *—S.H. (12/15/2006)*

Testarossa 2003 Brosseau Vineyard Chardonnay (Chalone) $36. 88 *—S.H. (10/1/2005)*

Testarossa 2006 Castello Chardonnay (Central Coast) $30. This is a blend of several vineyards, instead of the winery's usual single-vineyard Chards. It's been tastefully assembled, and displays good Central Coast acidity framing tropical fruit and oak flavors with a stony, minerally edge. **87** *—S.H. (12/31/2007)*

Testarossa 2005 Castello Chardonnay (Central Coast) $28. Puts all the pieces of the puzzle together, combining ripe tropical fruit, ample sweet oak and coastal acidity, but the picture is a little blurry. The wine is decadently ripe and obvious. **85** *—S.H. (6/1/2007)*

Testarossa 2004 Castello Chardonnay (Central Coast) $28. 88 *—S.H. (3/1/2006)*

Testarossa 2003 Castello Chardonnay (Central Coast) $26. 88 *—S.H. (7/1/2005)*

Testarossa 2002 Castello Chardonnay (Central Coast) $26. 90 *—S.H. (6/1/2004)*

Testarossa 2001 Castello Chardonnay (Santa Barbara) $26. 83 *—S.H. (10/1/2003)*

Testarossa 2000 Castello Chardonnay (Santa Barbara) $26. 91 *—S.H. (12/15/2002)*

Testarossa 2005 Diana's Reserve Chardonnay (California) $55. A statewide blend of the winemakers' favorite barrels from their multiple vineyard sites, the Diana's Reserve is easily Testarossa's best '05 Chardonnay. Blending seems to have ironed out the difficult spots, and made for a complete wine. Rich in fruit and oak, it shows all the hallmarks of great coastal California Chard. **92** *—S.H. (6/1/2007)*

Testarossa 2004 Diana's Reserve Chardonnay (California) $50. 94 Editors' Choice *—S.H. (12/15/2006)*

Testarossa 2003 Diana's Reserve Chardonnay (California) $50. 90 *—S.H. (11/15/2005)*

Testarossa 1997 George Troquato Signature Rese Chardonnay (California) $42. 92 *—S.H. (5/1/2000)*

Testarossa 2005 La Cruz Vineyard Chardonnay (Sonoma Coast) $39. The coolness of the site and the vintage has yielded a young, tart wine that fans of big, fat Chards might find lean and austere. But it's a grand wine for Burgundy lovers. Acidity is high, and there's a stony minerality undergirding the citrus, wildflower and smoky oak flavors. This is one of those rare Chards that needs some time to come around. Best 2008–2011. **93** *—S.H. (9/1/2007)*

Testarossa 2003 Michaud Vineyard Chardonnay (Chalone) $36. 87 *—S.H. (10/1/2005)*

Testarossa 2001 Michaud Vineyard Chardonnay (Chalone) $35. 92 *—S.H. (8/1/2003)*

Testarossa 2000 Michaud Vineyard Chardonnay (Chalone) $36. 93 *—S.H. (12/15/2002)*

Testarossa 1999 Michaud Vineyard Chardonnay (Chalone) $39. 92 *—S.H. (12/1/2001)*

Testarossa 2005 Rosella's Vineyard Chardonnay (Santa Lucia Highlands) $44. Front-loaded with fruit, this extraordinarily ripe Chard fortunately has the benefit of coastal acidity, without which it would be flat. Boosted by crispness, the pineapple, tangerine meringue, peach custard, banana cream pie and passionfruit flavors explode into a clean, spicy finish. **90** *—S.H. (6/1/2007)*

Testarossa 2004 Rosella's Vineyard Chardonnay (Santa Lucia Highlands) $39. 93 *—S.H. (3/1/2006)*

Testarossa 2003 Rosella's Vineyard Chardonnay (Santa Lucia Highlands) $36. 90 *—S.H. (7/1/2005)*

Testarossa 2001 Rosella's Vineyard Chardonnay (Santa Lucia Highlands) $35. 91 *—S.H. (8/1/2003)*

Testarossa 2005 Sanford & Benedict Vineyard Chardonnay (Santa Rita Hills) $39. I'm not sure what makes this Chard taste unbalanced, or maybe unready is a better word. All the pieces seem correct, especially the hedonistically ripe fruit, which spans the gamut from green apples and peaches to pineapples, guavas and nectarines. The oak is gorgeously creamy. Give it 2–4 years in the bottle, to let the parts knit together. **88** *—S.H. (4/1/2007)*

Testarossa 2004 Sanford & Benedict Vineyard Chardonnay (Santa Barbara County) $39. 91 *—S.H. (3/1/2006)*

Testarossa 2002 Signature Reserve Chardonnay (California) $44. 93 *—S.H. (6/1/2004)*

Testarossa 1999 Signature Reserve Chardonnay (California) $44. 93 Editors' Choice *—S.H. (12/15/2002)*

Testarossa 1998 Signature Reserve Chardonnay (California) $42. 91 *(7/1/2001)*

Testarossa 2005 Sleepy Hollow Vineyard Chardonnay (Santa Lucia Highlands) $39. This was a cool vintage, and while it had long hangtime, the grapes from this northwestern vineyard, in the coolest part of the appellation, struggled to ripen. The wine has high acidity and a minerally tang to the citrus, apples and kiwis. Toasty oak softens and enriches. Should gain bottle complexity over the next six years. **89** *—S.H. (6/1/2007)*

Testarossa 2004 Sleepy Hollow Vineyard Chardonnay (Santa Lucia Highlands) $39. 91 Cellar Selection *—S.H. (9/1/2006)*

Testarossa 2003 Sleepy Hollow Vineyard Chardonnay (Santa Lucia Highlands) $36. 86 *—S.H. (10/1/2005)*

Testarossa 2001 Sleepy Hollow Vineyard Chardonnay (Santa Lucia Highlands) $35. 93 Editors' Choice *—S.H. (8/1/2003)*

Testarossa 2000 Sleepy Hollow Vineyard Chardonnay (Santa Lucia Highlands) $34. 92 *—S.H. (12/15/2002)*

Testarossa 1999 Sleepy Hollow Vineyard Chardonnay (Santa Lucia Highlands) $32. 90 *—S.H. (12/1/2001)*

Testarossa 2002 Pinot Noir (Chalone) $49. 87 *(11/1/2004)*

Testarossa 2002 Bien Nacido Vineyard Pinot Noir (Santa Maria Valley) $49. 89 *(11/1/2004)*

Testarossa 2001 Bien Nacido Vineyard Pinot Noir (Santa Maria Valley) $50. 86 *—S.H. (7/1/2003)*

Testarossa 1999 Bien Nacido Vineyard Pinot Noir (Santa Maria Valley) $40. 91 *—S.H. (12/15/2001)*

Testarossa 2005 Bien Nacido Vineyard Elder Series Pinot Noir (Santa Maria Valley) $56. The "Elder Series" designation seems to refer to 30-year vines, which would make them among the first planted at this esteemed vineyard. I'm not sure that vine age shows in the resulting wine, though, which tastes young and fruity and immature. The keen acidity and grape-sappy, primary fruit cherry and raspberry flavors aren't yet integrated with the oak. But the wine shows enormous promise. Open after 2008, and through 2013. **91** *—S.H. (6/1/2007)*

Testarossa 2004 Bien Nacido Vineyard Elder Series Pinot Noir (Santa Maria Valley) $54. 92 *—S.H. (9/1/2006)*

Testarossa 2003 Bien Nacido Vineyard Elder Series Pinot Noir (Santa Lucia Highlands) $54. 90 *—S.H. (7/1/2005)*

Testarossa 2005 Brosseau Vineyard Pinot Noir (Chalone) $54. This Pinot shows the ripeness and richness that Testarossa is known for. Grape yields were evidently low, to judge by the concentration of cherries, raspberries, blackberries, cola, root beer and pomegranate flavors. Fully dry, the wine also is somewhat tight in tannins and acids. It should benefit from a few years in the cellar. **92** *—S.H. (12/1/2007)*

Testarossa 2004 Brosseau Vineyard Pinot Noir (Chalone) $54. 87 *—S.H. (12/15/2006)*

Testarossa 2003 Brosseau Vineyard Pinot Noir (Chalone) $54. 87 *—S.H. (11/15/2005)*

Testarossa 2005 Cuvée Niclaire Pinot Noir (California) $75. A best barrels blend of the winery's various vineyards, which are numerous throughout California, Niclaire shows a balance and elegance that prove Pinot doesn't have to come from a single vineyard to be great. The '05 is a delicious wine, soft and gentle and rich in flavor, yet dry and balanced. It fills the mouth with cherry pie, cassis, cola, Asian spice and smoky oak flavors that last long on the finish. This is a real crowd-pleaser, but it's not an ager. Drink now. **92** *—S.H. (9/1/2007)*

Testarossa 2004 Cuvée Niclaire Pinot Noir (California) $75. 88 *—S.H. (12/15/2006)*

Testarossa 2003 Cuvée Niclaire Pinot Noir (California) $75. 93 *—S.H. (11/15/2005)*

Testarossa 2002 Cuvée Niclaire Pinot Noir (California) $72. 89 *(11/1/2004)*

Testarossa 2000 Cuvée Niclaire Pinot Noir (Santa Lucia Highlands) $68. 91 *—S.H. (2/1/2003)*

Testarossa 1999 Cuvée Niclaire Pinot Noir (Santa Lucia Highlands) $68. 89 *(10/1/2002)*

Testarossa 1998 Cuvée Niclaire Reserve Pinot Noir (Santa Lucia Highlands) $60. 94 Cellar Selection *—S.H. (12/15/2001)*

Testarossa 1997 Cuvée Niclaire Reserve Pinot Noir (Santa Lucia Highlands) $50. 91 *(10/1/2000)*

Testarossa 2005 Fritschen Vineyard Pinot Noir (Russian River Valley) $54. You'll want to give this pretty Pinot some time in the bottle, to let it mellow out. Right now, it's a big-boned wine, with flamboyant raspberry, cherry and sassafras flavors of the pie filling kind, and a smoky, vanilla edge of oak. Despite the volume, the wine is dry and elegant, with a rich scour of cleansing acidity. Best after winter 2007. **92** *—S.H. (11/1/2007)*

Testarossa 2003 Fritschen Vineyard Pinot Noir (Russian River Valley) $54. 93 *—S.H. (10/1/2005)*

Testarossa 2005 Garys' Vineyard Pinot Noir (Santa Lucia Highlands) $59. Testarossa always does a good job at keeping Garys' Pinots, which can be outsized, tame. The '05 shows the vineyard's typicity in the big, ripe fruit and fullness of mouthfeel, yet stays elegant and polished. Cherries, black raspberries, sugared rosehip tea and sweetly smoky oak are the flavors, although the wine is fully dry on the finish. It will easily sustain some bottle age. Drink now–2010. **92** *—S.H. (9/1/2007)*

Testarossa 2004 Garys' Vineyard Pinot Noir (Santa Lucia Highlands) $54. 91 *—S.H. (12/15/2006)*

Testarossa 2003 Garys' Vineyard Pinot Noir (Santa Lucia Highlands) $54. 92 *—S.H. (10/1/2005)*

Testarossa 2002 Garys' Vineyard Pinot Noir (Santa Lucia Highlands) $55. 88 *(11/1/2004)*

Testarossa 2001 Garys' Vineyard Pinot Noir (Santa Lucia Highlands) $50. 89 *—S.H. (7/1/2003)*

Testarossa 2000 Garys' Vineyard Pinot Noir (Santa Lucia Highlands) $45. 91 *(10/1/2002)*

Testarossa 1999 Garys' Vineyard Pinot Noir (Santa Maria Valley) $40. 91 *—S.H. (12/15/2001)*

Testarossa 2005 Graham Family Vineyard Pinot Noir (Russian River Valley) $54. I've never tasted a Testarossa Pinot from this vineyard, and in fact this is only the second Russian River Pinot I've had from the winery, which favors Central and South Coast vineyards. Made from very young vines, the wine shows great promise. It's rich in primary fruit cherries, raspberries and spicy cola, with a Dijon-clone directness, and enormously balanced in acids and tannins. This is certainly a wine to follow. **92** *—S.H. (6/1/2007)*

Testarossa 2005 La Cruz Vineyard Pinot Noir (Sonoma Coast) $54. A good example of a fine, ripe coastal Pinot, with bright raspberry, cherry, cola and cinnamon spice flavors that finish dry and crisp. The silky mouthfeel, with its light, gentle dusting of tannins, is just what you want in a Pinot Noir. **89** *—S.H. (11/1/2007)*

Testarossa 2001 Michaud Vineyard Pinot Noir (Chalone) $50. 85 *—S.H. (7/1/2003)*

Testarossa 2005 Pallazzio Pinot Noir (Central Coast) $37. The winery's basic Central Coast blend is a good, rich Pinot with some complexity, and is fancy enough to serve with upscale food. It shows a fine balance of acidity, silkiness and oak-infused cherry-cola fruit. This is a nice by-the-glass red for restaurants. **88** *—S.H. (6/1/2007)*

Testarossa 2004 Palazzio Pinot Noir (Central Coast) $34. 87 *—S.H. (5/1/2006)*

Testarossa 2003 Palazzio Pinot Noir (Central Coast) $32. 88 *—S.H. (7/1/2005)*

Testarossa 2002 Palazzio Pinot Noir (Central Coast) $32. 90 *—S.H. (11/1/2004)*

Testarossa 2001 Palazzio Pinot Noir (Monterey) $32. 85 *—S.H. (7/1/2003)*

Testarossa 2000 Palazzio Pinot Noir (Monterey) $32. 91 *—S.H. (9/1/2003)*

Testarossa 2005 Pisoni Vineyard Pinot Noir (Santa Lucia Highlands) $65. This classic Pisoni has the translucent color and silky texture of a fine Pinot, but there's nothing delicate about the mouthfeel, which is explosive. Cherries, cola, pomegranates, rhubarb pie, coffee, herb tea, licorice, smoky oak—it all combines to provide an endlessly changing experience. This is a wine that should change in fascinating ways over the next 10 years. **94** *—S.H. (6/1/2007)*

Testarossa 2004 Pisoni Vineyard Pinot Noir (Santa Lucia Highlands) $54. 93 *—S.H. (12/15/2006)*

Testarossa 2003 Pisoni Vineyard Pinot Noir (Santa Lucia Highlands) $54. 92 Cellar Selection *—S.H. (11/15/2005)*

Testarossa 2002 Pisoni Vineyard Pinot Noir (Santa Lucia Highlands) $50. 91 *(11/1/2004)*

Testarossa 2000 Pisoni Vineyard Pinot Noir (Santa Lucia Highlands) $55. 92 *(10/1/2002)*

Testarossa 1999 Pisoni Vineyard Pinot Noir (Santa Lucia Highlands) $NA. 91 *—S.H. (9/1/2003)*

Testarossa 2005 Rosella's Vineyard Pinot Noir (Santa Lucia Highlands) $59. Not showing all that well at this point, with a baked or dried cherry flavor, and the toasty char from the oak. Plus, there's that burnt pie crust note. The wine also is young in acidity, with some tannins. I would give it some time, maybe four or five years, but no guarantees. **87** *—S.H. (6/1/2007)*

Testarossa 2004 Rosella's Vineyard Pinot Noir (Santa Lucia Highlands) $54. 91 *—S.H. (9/1/2006)*

Testarossa 2003 Rosella's Vineyard Pinot Noir (Santa Lucia Highlands) $54. 90 *—S.H. (10/1/2005)*

Testarossa 2002 Rosella's Vineyard Pinot Noir (Santa Lucia Highlands) $49. 89 *(11/1/2004)*

Testarossa 2001 Rosella's Vineyard Pinot Noir (Santa Lucia Highlands) $50. 88 *—S.H. (7/1/2003)*

Testarossa 2005 Sanford & Benedict Vineyard Pinot Noir (Santa Rita Hills) $56. This bottle is absolutely delicious now, with a silky texture that's so rich in cherries, raspberries, pomegranates, cola and all kinds of Asian spices, but will undoubtedly gain complexity with as long as eight years after release. **93** *—S.H. (4/1/2007)*

Testarossa 2004 Sanford & Benedict Vineyard Pinot Noir (Santa Barbara County) $54. 90 Cellar Selection *—S.H. (5/1/2006)*

Testarossa 2004 Schultze Family Vineyard Pinot Noir (Santa Cruz Mountains) $54. 91 Cellar Selection *—S.H. (12/15/2006)*

Testarossa 2005 Sleepy Hollow Vineyard Pinot Noir (Santa Lucia Highlands) $59. How effortless it was to get the grapes ripe in this long, dry vintage, when the weather so favored coastal Pinot Noir. This wine strikes the perfect balance of ripe, sweet cherry, raspberry, cola and pomegranate fruit balanced by fine acidity and tannins. The oak is just right.

Best now and for a year or two for its flamboyant, adolescent deliciousness. 92 —*S.H. (6/1/2007)*

Testarossa 2004 Sleepy Hollow Vineyard Pinot Noir (Santa Lucia Highlands) $54. 91 —*S.H. (9/1/2006)*

Testarossa 2003 Sleepy Hollow Vineyard Pinot Noir (Santa Lucia Highlands) $54. 89 —*S.H. (10/1/2005)*

Testarossa 2002 Sleepy Hollow Vineyard Pinot Noir (Santa Lucia Highlands) $49. 88 *(11/1/2004)*

Testarossa 2001 Sleepy Hollow Vineyard Pinot Noir (Santa Lucia Highlands) $50. 89 —*S.H. (7/1/2003)*

Testarossa 2000 Sleepy Hollow Vineyard Pinot Noir (Santa Lucia Highlands) $45. 90 *(10/1/2002)*

Testarossa 2005 Garys' Vineyard Syrah (Santa Lucia Highlands) $54. This is a big wine that's not ready now—it's too tannic. That gives it a lockdown, numbing quality that blocks a full appreciation of the fruit. But what fruit! Blackberries pure and simple, reduced to their quintessence. Such is the inherent integrity of this wine that it should effortlessly negotiate 4–6 years, gradually softening. 91 —*S.H. (12/1/2007)*

Testarossa 2003 Garys' Vineyard Syrah (Santa Lucia Highlands) $45. 90 —*S.H. (3/1/2006)*

Testarossa 2002 Garys' Vineyard Syrah (Santa Lucia Highlands) $42. 89 —*S.H. (7/1/2005)*

Testarossa 2000 Garys' Vineyard Syrah (Santa Lucia Highlands) $42. 90 —*S.H. (2/1/2003)*

Testarossa 1999 Garys' Vineyard Syrah (Santa Lucia Highlands) $42. 89 *(11/1/2001)*

Testarossa 2005 Subasio Syrah (California) $34. This is a blend of Sonoma, Santa Clara and Santa Barbara counties. The vineyards are not specified, but they're clearly of high quality, for the wine is balanced, elegant and delicious. It shows classic Syrah flavors of blackberries, cassis and chocolate, with a spicy edge of white pepper and cinnamon, and is just about as good as Testarossa's more expensive Syrahs. 90 —*S.H. (12/1/2007)*

Testarossa 2005 Thompson Vineyard Syrah (Santa Barbara County) $49. This is quite a luscious Syrah, soft, smooth, complex and layered, showing qualities of both warm and cool climates. From the cool end of the spectrum comes a lively acidity and not a trace of overripeness. The riper notes of blackberries, cassis, gingersnap cookie and licorice are delicious, enriched by smoky oak. Drink now and for a few years. 92 —*S.H. (12/1/2007)*

THE ACADEMY

The Academy 2000 Merlot (Applegate Valley) $20. 85 —*P.G. (8/1/2002)*

The Academy 2000 Pinot Noir (Applegate Valley) $16. 83 —*P.G. (12/31/2002)*

THE EYRIE VINEYARDS

The Eyrie Vineyards 1999 Estate Grown Chardonnay (Willamette Valley) $18. 87 —*P.G. (9/1/2003)*

The Eyrie Vineyards 1999 Reserve Chardonnay (Willamette Valley) $25. 88 —*P.G. (9/1/2003)*

The Eyrie Vineyards 2000 Pinot Gris (Willamette Valley) $15. 91 **Best Buy** —*P.G. (8/1/2003)*

The Eyrie Vineyards 2000 Estate Grown Pinot Noir (Willamette Valley) $25. 89 —*P.G. (4/1/2003)*

The Eyrie Vineyards 1999 Reserve Pinot Noir (Willamette Valley) $35. 91 —*P.G. (4/1/2003)*

THE FOUR GRACES

The Four Graces 2003 Pinot Gris (Willamette Valley) $20. 87 —*P.G. (2/1/2006)*

The Four Graces 2004 Estate Grown Reserve Pinot Noir (Dundee Hills) $35. Red fruits, light cranberry and refined tannins create a sense of stylish elegance. Impeccable balance and a light touch with the oak keep the wine lively and fresh through a medium-long finish. 89 —*P.G. (2/1/2007)*

THE GRAPES OF ROTH

The Grapes of Roth 2001 Merlot (Long Island) $50. Made from one of the best vintages ever on Long Island, and backed by Roman Roth, the winemaking talent behind Wolffer Estate, Shinn Estate and Roanoke. For the most part, it delivers with notes of exotic spice, spearmint and cherry in the nose, and a supple, smoked meat and herbal character whose parts come together with elegance. 86 —*S.K. (2/1/2007)*

THE GREY ROSE

The Grey Rose 2005 Pinot Pinot Rosé Blend (California) $13. 86 —*S.H. (11/15/2006)*

THE MAIDEN

The Maiden 2004 Bordeaux Blend (Napa Valley) $150. The '04 Maiden is very close to Harlan Estate in quality. The Maiden is a touch less elegant; but it is such a wholesome wine, so succulent in blackberry, cassis, licorice, and roasted cedar. The tannins are so regal—even the slight prickle of acidity works for polish. So beautiful now, it's hard to know when to suggest drinking it, but this should easily be a 10–15 year wine. 97 **Cellar Selection** —*S.H. (12/1/2007)*

The Maiden 2003 Cabernet Blend (Napa Valley) $110. This second label of Harlan Estate comes from the estate vineyard, and shares much in common with the main wine, which is a bit more focused and concentrated. The similarities include the briary, wild herb scents of sage and thyme that complex the ripe red cherry pie filling fruit, cocoa, cola and licorice. As with the main wine, the tannins here are gorgeous. This is a balanced, harmonious wine that combines power and elegance. 96 —*S.H. (2/1/2007)*

The Maiden 2002 Cabernet Blend (Napa Valley) $95. 94 —*S.H. (9/1/2006)*

The Maiden 2001 Cabernet Blend (Napa Valley) $95. 98 **Editors' Choice** —*S.H. (6/1/2005)*

THE MATRIARCH

The Matriarch 2003 Cabernet Blend (Napa Valley) $NA. This second label of BOND is so rich and opulent, it's hard to believe it's the least expensive of Harlan's stable. Masses of cherries, blackberries, chocolate and vanilla-caramel new oak, accented with mint and herbs, leading to a refined, smoothly tannic finish. Just delicious. 94 —*S.H. (2/1/2007)*

The Matriarch 2002 Cabernet Blend (Napa Valley) $80. 94 —*S.H. (9/1/2006)*

The Matriarch 2001 Cabernet Blend (Napa Valley) $75. 94 **Editors' Choice** —*S.H. (6/1/2005)*

THE ORGANIC WINE WORKS

The Organic Wine Works 2001 Proprietor's Reserve Cabernet Sauvignon (Mendocino County) $19. 85 —*S.H. (11/15/2003)*

The Organic Wine Works 2001 Proprietor's Reserve Merlot (Mendocino County) $19. 85 —*S.H. (2/1/2004)*

The Organic Wine Works 2001 Syrah (California) $12. 84 —*S.H. (2/1/2004)*

THE PRISONER

The Prisoner 2000 Red Blend (Napa Valley) $28. 90 —*J.M. (4/1/2003)*

THE SEVEN BROTHERS

The Seven Brothers 2001 Sauvignon Blanc (Clear Lake) $12. 87 —*J.M. (7/1/2003)*

The Seven Brothers 2001 Sauvignon Blanc (Clear Lake) $10. 80 —*J.M. (9/1/2004)*

THE SHOW

The Show 2005 Cabernet Sauvignon (California) $15. A blend of four coastal counties from Paso Robles to Dry Creek. It's ripe and soft and easy, with blackberry, chocolate, mint and vanilla flavors. 85 —*S.H. (7/1/2007)*

THE TERRACES

The Terraces 1997 Cabernet Sauvignon (Napa Valley) $60. 89 *(11/1/2000)*

The Terraces 1999 Cabernet Sauvignon (Napa Valley) $60. 90 *(8/1/2003)*

The Terraces 2001 Zinfandel (Napa Valley) $25. 87 *(11/1/2003)*

THE WHITE KNIGHT

The White Knight 2006 Sauvignon Blanc (Lodi) $14. Another successful release from Don Sebastiani & Sons, who seem to have no end of cleverly labeled, inexpensive wines of value. This Lodi entry is perfectly dry and beautifully crisp, with long, deep flavors of limes, Meyer lemons, savory figs and vanilla. 89 **Best Buy** —*S.H. (11/15/2007)*

The White Knight 2006 Viognier (Clarksburg) $14. I like this wine a lot, even though it doesn't have Viognier's typical exotic richness. Bone dry, with mouth-tingling acidity and low alcohol, it shows citrus, coconut macaroon, apricot and spice flavors that finish with real complexity. The cool vintage definitely was kind to this inland, Delta appellation. 88 —*S.H. (11/15/2007)*

The White Knight 2005 Viognier (Clarksburg) $16. 88 —*S.H. (12/1/2006)*

THE WILLIAMSBURG WINERY

The Williamsburg Winery 2004 Acte 12 Chardonnay (Virginia) $16. 81 —*M.D. (8/1/2006)*

The Williamsburg Winery 2005 Acte 12 of Sixteen Nineteen Chardonnay (Virginia) $16. There's some lift and citrus in the nose and a touch of vanilla on the palate, but in general, this Chardonnay is rather watery and lacks depth. 81 —*S.K. (5/1/2007)*

The Williamsburg Winery 2003 Acte 12 of Sixteen Nineteen Chardonnay (Virginia) $16. 86 *—J.C. (9/1/2005)*

The Williamsburg Winery 2004 John Adlum Chardonnay (Virginia) $11. 81 *—M.D. (8/1/2006)*

The Williamsburg Winery 2003 John Adlum Chardonnay (Virginia) $10. 85 Best Buy *—J.C. (9/1/2005)*

The Williamsburg Winery 2005 Vintage Reserve Chardonnay (Virginia) $28. A rich, toasty nose suggests depth and dimension in the glass, and on the palate, this 100% French oak-fermented Chard delivers most of what it advertises. Good fruit body and nice flavors of creamy spice. Lacks finish but good overall. Will pair well with grilled seafood and summer salads. **84** *—S.K. (7/1/2007)*

The Williamsburg Winery 2005 Susan Constant Red Syrah (Virginia) $8. A jammy, plummy character with a touch of spice makes this enjoyable on its own or paired with hearty dishes like ravioli or sausage. Soft but substantial, the wine has a smoky, lingering finish. **83** *—S.K. (10/1/2007)*

The Williamsburg Winery 2004 Late Harvest Vidal Blanc (Virginia) $24. 84 *—M.D. (8/1/2006)*

The Williamsburg Winery NV James River White Blend (Virginia) $8. 80 *—M.D. (8/1/2006)*

THIRTEEN

Thirteen 2003 Meritage Cabernet Blend (Napa Valley) $115. 92 *—S.H. (8/1/2006)*

THOMAS COYNE

Thomas Coyne 1996 Merlot (Sonoma County) $21. 91 *(11/15/1999)*

Thomas Coyne 1996 Contra Costa County Mourvèdre (Contra Costa County) $13. 88 *—S.H. (6/1/1999)*

Thomas Coyne 2000 Petite Sirah (California) $16. 82 *(4/1/2003)*

Thomas Coyne 1997 La Petite Quest Red Blend (California) $10. 87 Best Buy *—S.H. (10/1/1999)*

Thomas Coyne 1996 Quest Red Blend (California) $10. 86 *—S.H. (6/1/1999)*

Thomas Coyne 1997 Syrah (California) $13. 88 Best Buy *—S.H. (6/1/1999)*

Thomas Coyne 1998 Syrah (California) $12. 83 *—S.H. (7/1/2002)*

Thomas Coyne 1997 Viognier (California) $16. 87 *—S.H. (6/1/1999)*

Thomas Coyne 2000 Viognier (California) $15. 85 *—S.H. (11/15/2001)*

THOMAS FOGARTY

Thomas Fogarty 2003 Camel Hill Vineyard Lexington Meritage Bordeaux Blend (Santa Cruz Mountains) $45. You'll want to stick this Bordeaux blend in the cellar because right now the tannins dominate. There's a very rich vein of cherry, currant, cassis and new oak flavor, and the wine is totally dry, but those tannins give it a sticky astringency that obviously calls for time out. Give it a year or so, then try again. **87** *—S.H. (11/1/2007)*

Thomas Fogarty 2002 Camel Hill Vineyard Cabernet Franc (Santa Cruz Mountains) $48. 90 *—S.H. (5/1/2006)*

Thomas Fogarty 2001 Camel Hill Vineyard Cabernet Franc (Santa Cruz Mountains) $45. 91 *—S.H. (11/15/2004)*

Thomas Fogarty 2001 Cabernet Sauvignon (Santa Cruz Mountains) $55. 93 *—S.H. (10/1/2004)*

Thomas Fogarty 2001 Cabernet Sauvignon (Napa Valley) $55. 90 *—S.H. (10/1/2004)*

Thomas Fogarty 2000 Cabernet Sauvignon (Napa Valley) $50. 88 *—S.H. (11/15/2004)*

Thomas Fogarty 1999 Cabernet Sauvignon (Santa Cruz County) $45. 92 *—S.H. (10/1/2003)*

Thomas Fogarty 2002 Vallerga Vineyard Cabernet Sauvignon (Napa Valley) $59. 90 *—S.H. (9/1/2006)*

Thomas Fogarty 2003 Chardonnay (Santa Cruz Mountains) $25. 84 *—S.H. (2/1/2006)*

Thomas Fogarty 2002 Chardonnay (Santa Cruz Mountains) $24. 88 *—S.H. (2/1/2005)*

Thomas Fogarty 2001 Chardonnay (Santa Cruz Mountains) $23. 92 Editors' Choice *—S.H. (6/1/2004)*

Thomas Fogarty 1998 Chardonnay (Monterey County) $19. 88 *(6/1/2000)*

Thomas Fogarty 1997 Chardonnay (Santa Cruz Mountains) $20. 83 *(6/1/2000)*

Thomas Fogarty 2004 Albutom Vineyard Chardonnay (Santa Cruz Mountains) $45. Here's a wonderfully balanced Chardonnay. It's rich, ripe and oaky, with crisp cool-climate acidity boosting the pineapple and papaya fruit, but there's also a mineral, diesel note throughout that adds complexing interest and firmness. Should hold for five years. **92** *—S.H. (10/1/2007)*

Thomas Fogarty 2004 Camel Hill Vineyard Chardonnay (Santa Cruz Mountains) $45. Creamy and crisp, this Chard is ultra rich in fruit, with lemon drop, pineapple tart filling, crème brûlée and buttered toast flavors. Really delicious and complicated, it's from a vineyard on mountainous slopes in the heart of the Silicon Valley suburb of Los Gatos. **93** *—S.H. (10/1/2007)*

Thomas Fogarty 2004 Damiana Vineyard Chardonnay (Santa Cruz Mountains) $45. Absolutely delicious, first-rate Chard from this veteran producer. Shows the prettiest balance of all its parts, and just about as good as California Chard gets. Ripely opulent in tropical fruit, apricot and tangerine flavors and crisp in limey acids, the wine's 50% new oak adds luscious notes of buttercream, toast, smoke and vanilla. **95** *—S.H. (10/1/2007)*

Thomas Fogarty 2004 Estate Chardonnay (Santa Cruz Mountains) $27. Oaky and deeply flavored, with a wealth of passionfruit, mango and pineapple custard flavors, this Chard hails from a cool part of the mountains, but it's from a hot vintage. The combination of ripeness and acidity works well. **88** *—S.H. (2/1/2007)*

Thomas Fogarty 2003 Estate Reserve Chardonnay (Santa Cruz Mountains) $38. 90 *—S.H. (11/15/2006)*

Thomas Fogarty 1997 Estate Reserve Chardonnay (Santa Cruz Mountains) $30. 91 *(6/1/2000)*

Thomas Fogarty 2004 Portola Springs Vineyard Chardonnay (Santa Cruz Mountains) $45. There's a minerality to this Chard that makes it bracing, although it also shows the opulence of Fogarty's other '04s. A tang of gunmetal undergirds the tropical fruit and vanilla custard flavors that are wrapped into a creamy texture. Almost begs for shrimp, lobster, crab, the more richly prepared, the better. **92** *—S.H. (10/1/2007)*

Thomas Fogarty 2006 Skyline Chardonnay (California) $16. Named after the scenic highway that runs along the coastal mountains, this unoaked Chard is bone dry, crisp in acids, and lean. The flavors are of grapefruits and limes. A very elegant wine that appeals for its clean balance and zest. **86** *—S.H. (11/1/2007)*

Thomas Fogarty 2005 Gewürztraminer (Monterey) $17. Most of the grapes come from Ventana's vineyard in the Arroyo Seco, one of the most underestimated white grape terroirs in California. The vineyard's capacity for producing ripeness with acidity is amply shown in this dry, crisply fruity wine. Its dusty brown spice, white and yellow stone fruit and wildflower flavors are just delicious. **87** *—S.H. (2/1/2007)*

Thomas Fogarty 2004 Gewürztraminer (Monterey) $17. 87 *—S.H. (2/1/2006)*

Thomas Fogarty 2003 Gewürztraminer (Monterey) $16. 87 *—S.H. (12/1/2004)*

Thomas Fogarty 2002 Gewürztraminer (Monterey) $15. 86 *—S.H. (12/31/2003)*

Thomas Fogarty 2002 Gewürztraminer (Monterey) $15. 85 *—S.H. (2/1/2004)*

Thomas Fogarty 2001 Gewürztraminer (Monterey) $14. 87 *—S.H. (9/1/2003)*

Thomas Fogarty 2000 Gewürztraminer (Monterey) $14. 88 *—S.H. (11/15/2001)*

Thomas Fogarty 2002 Lexington Meritage (Santa Cruz Mountains) $45. 84 *—S.H. (7/1/2006)*

Thomas Fogarty 2001 Merlot (Santa Cruz Mountains) $32. 91 *—S.H. (10/1/2005)*

Thomas Fogarty 2000 Merlot (Santa Cruz Mountains) $30. 91 *—S.H. (12/15/2004)*

Thomas Fogarty 1999 Merlot (Santa Cruz Mountains) $28. 91 *—S.H. (10/1/2003)*

Thomas Fogarty 1998 Merlot (Santa Cruz Mountains) $30. 89 *—S.H. (11/15/2002)*

Thomas Fogarty 2002 Razorback Vineyard Merlot (Santa Cruz Mountains) $35. 86 *—S.H. (12/1/2006)*

Thomas Fogarty 2003 Razorback Vineyard Estate Merlot (Santa Cruz Mountains) $45. This is rich in cassis, cherry, coffee, tobacco and oak flavors, and is thoroughly dry. It's a little soft, in the way of California reds, and also a little aggressive in tannins at this time. Probably best now–2008, as the fruit fades. **87** *—S.H. (11/1/2007)*

Thomas Fogarty 2002 Pinot Noir (Santa Cruz Mountains) $30. 87 *—S.H. (2/1/2006)*

Thomas Fogarty 2001 Pinot Noir (Santa Cruz Mountains) $25. 87 *—S.H. (2/1/2005)*

USA

Thomas Fogarty 2000 Pinot Noir (Santa Cruz Mountains) $23. 91 Editors' Choice —*S.H. (6/1/2004)*

Thomas Fogarty 1999 Pinot Noir (Santa Cruz Mountains) $23. 88 *(10/1/2002)*

Thomas Fogarty 1998 Pinot Noir (Santa Cruz Mountains) $30. 86 —*S.H. (12/15/2001)*

Thomas Fogarty 2003 Estate Pinot Noir (Santa Cruz Mountains) $35. 86 —*S.H. (7/1/2006)*

Thomas Fogarty 2004 Estate Grown Pinot Noir (Santa Cruz Mountains) $45. A low-yield (one ton to the acre) mountain wine, tremendously complex and probably ageworthy. With concentrated cherry, black raspberry, cola and mocha flavors weighted by a deeper, earthier, mushroomy note and tons of Asian spice, it's entirely dry, with a beautiful tannin-acid balance. Drink now–2010. 94 Editors' Choice —*S.H. (2/1/2007)*

Thomas Fogarty 2001 Estate Reserve Pinot Noir (Santa Cruz Mountains) $45. 89 —*S.H. (12/1/2004)*

Thomas Fogarty 2004 Rapley Trail Vineyard Pinot Noir (Santa Cruz Mountains) $45. Beautiful; fully drinkable now for its soft, delicate structure and harmonious finish. Not a powerhouse, it shows nuanced varietal flavors of cherries, blackberries and cola, with elaborate oak shadings and a long, spicy finish. 90 —*S.H. (10/1/2007)*

Thomas Fogarty 2004 Rapley Trail Vineyard B Block Pinot Noir (Santa Cruz Mountains) $45. A very big Pinot, obviously chosen for its special designation due to the concentration of fruit. Almost Grenache-like in cherries, cassis, cocoa and glyceriney richness, it's a dry, silky wine whose elaborate oak finishings add opulence. Despite the Loire-like weight, it's a compelling Pinot that evolves as it warms in the glass, suggesting ageability. Drink now–2010. 93 —*S.H. (10/1/2007)*

Thomas Fogarty 2002 Rapley Trail Vineyard Block B Pinot Noir (Santa Cruz Mountains) $65. 83 *(11/1/2004)*

Thomas Fogarty 2004 Rapley Trail Vineyard M Block Pinot Noir (Santa Cruz Mountains) $45. This luscious Pinot is impressive now for the power of its black currant, cherry, raspberry, vanilla, cola and Provençal herb flavors, with their firm backbone of acidity. It's the kind of Pinot that dazzles from the first sip to the last, as it evolves in the glass. The tannins are sweet and gentle, but supportive enough to allow this gorgeous wine to age for 6–8 years. 95 —*S.H. (10/1/2007)*

Thomas Fogarty 2002 Rapley Trail Vineyard Block M Pinot Noir (Santa Cruz Mountains) $65. 86 *(11/1/2004)*

Thomas Fogarty 2004 Fat Buck Ridge Syrah (Santa Cruz Mountains) $52. The wine suffers from a cooked or baked quality that pushes the cassis into Port. Great vineyard, not so good vintage. 84 —*S.H. (11/1/2007)*

Thomas Fogarty 2003 Fat Buck Ridge Vineyard Syrah (Santa Cruz Mountains) $55. 93 Cellar Selection —*S.H. (10/1/2006)*

THOMAS MICHAEL

Thomas Michael 2002 Ledgewood Vineyard Syrah (Suisun Valley) $32. 86 *(9/1/2005)*

THORNTON

Thornton 1999 Cabernet Sauvignon-Merlot (South Coast) $13. 82 —*S.H. (9/1/2002)*

Thornton NV Champagne Blend (California) $11. 85 —*S.H. (12/1/1999)*

Thornton NV Brut Champagne Blend (California) $11. 86 —*S.H. (12/15/2000)*

Thornton 1996 Brut Reserve Champagne Blend (California) $21. 90 —*S.H. (12/1/2002)*

Thornton 1995 Brut Reserve Champagne Blend (California) $21. 90 —*S.H. (12/15/2000)*

Thornton 1992 Brut Reserve Champagne Blend (California) $17. 86 —*S.H. (12/1/1999)*

Thornton NV Brut Reserve Natural Champagne Blend (California) $35. 89 —*S.H. (12/1/2002)*

Thornton 1995 Brut Reserve Natural Champagne Blend (California) $35. 87 —*S.H. (12/15/2000)*

Thornton NV Cuvée de Frontignan Champagne Blend (California) $22. 85 —*S.H. (12/1/2002)*

Thornton NV Cuvée Rouge Champagne Blend (California) $11. 88 Best Buy —*S.H. (12/15/2000)*

Thornton NV Limited Release Blanc de Noir Champagne Blend (Temecula) $22. 86 —*S.H. (12/1/2002)*

Thornton NV Millennium Cuvée Champagne Blend (California) $21. 91 —*S.H. (12/15/2000)*

Thornton 2000 Dos Vinedos Cuvée Coastal Reserve Chardonnay (South Coast) $10. 87 —*S.H. (5/1/2002)*

Thornton 2000 Rosé Grenache (Cucamonga Valley) $14. 86 —*S.H. (9/1/2002)*

Thornton 2000 Miramonte Vineyards Pinot Blanc (South Coast) $10. 86 —*S.H. (9/1/2002)*

Thornton 1999 Côte Red Rhône Red Blend (South Coast) $NA. 82 —*S.H. (9/1/2002)*

Thornton 1999 Temecula Valley Sangiovese (South Coast) $12. 82 —*S.H. (5/1/2002)*

Thornton 2003 Syrah (Temecula) $22. 84 *(9/1/2005)*

Thornton 1999 Miramonte Vineyards Limited Bottling Syrah (South Coast) $15. 84 *(10/1/2001)*

Thornton 2000 Viognier (South Coast) $13. 84 —*S.H. (9/1/2002)*

Thornton NV Cuvée de Frontigan White Blend (California) $11. 86 —*S.H. (12/15/2000)*

THREE FAMILIES

Three Families 2003 Cabernet Sauvignon (Mendocino County) $16. Harsh and raw, this 100% Cab has some decent cherry-berry flavors. But it's tough in tannins, with a rustic finish that's not likely to age out. 82 —*S.H. (6/1/2007)*

Three Families 2002 Cabernet Sauvignon (Mendocino County) $16. 84 —*S.H. (5/1/2006)*

Three Families 2006 Chardonnay (Mendocino County) $12. Kind of weedy and green, with simple LifeSaver lemon candy flavors. The finish is dry and tart. 82 —*S.H. (11/15/2007)*

Three Families 2005 Chardonnay (Mendocino County) $12. 83 —*S.H. (11/1/2006)*

Three Families 2004 Chardonnay (Mendocino County) $12. 80 —*S.H. (12/15/2005)*

Three Families 2004 Merlot (Mendocino County) $14. This rustic wine has jellied blackberry and cherry flavors that finish a little sweet. 82 —*S.H. (11/15/2007)*

Three Families 2003 Merlot (Mendocino County) $14. 82 —*S.H. (11/1/2006)*

Three Families 2002 Merlot (Mendocino County) $14. 84 —*S.H. (5/1/2006)*

THREE RIVERS

Three Rivers 2003 Meritage White Wine Bordeaux White Blend (Columbia Valley (WA)) $19. 92 Editors' Choice —*P.G. (6/1/2005)*

Three Rivers 2004 Cabernet Sauvignon (Columbia Valley (WA)) $19. This is almost pure Cab, with the addition of just 2% Malbec. Solidly in the firm, muscular, polished style of winemaker Holly Turner, this is a substantial effort that will need to be decanted if you are going to drink it any time soon. Black cherry, cassis and blue plum are swathed in milk chocolate, but this is Cabernet with its sinews intact, showing streaks of herb, smoke and light pepper. I can't imagine a better companion to it than a good, rare steak. 90 —*P.G. (12/1/2007)*

Three Rivers 2003 Cabernet Sauvignon (Columbia Valley (WA)) $19. 89 —*P.G. (6/1/2006)*

Three Rivers 2002 Cabernet Sauvignon (Columbia Valley (WA)) $19. 89 —*P.G. (6/1/2005)*

Three Rivers 2001 Cabernet Sauvignon (Columbia Valley (WA)) $19. 85 —*P.G. (12/15/2004)*

Three Rivers 1999 Cabernet Sauvignon (Columbia Valley (WA)) $28. 88 —*P.G. (2/1/2002)*

Three Rivers 2003 Champoux Vineyard Cabernet Sauvignon (Columbia Valley (WA)) $50. 88 —*P.G. (6/1/2006)*

Three Rivers 2001 Champoux Vineyard Cabernet Sauvignon (Columbia Valley (WA)) $39. 91 —*P.G. (7/1/2004)*

Three Rivers 1999 Champoux Vineyard Cabernet Sauvignon (Columbia Valley (WA)) $40. 89 —*P.G. (2/1/2002)*

Three Rivers 2005 Chardonnay (Columbia Valley (WA)) $19. Spicy and brisk, this elegant Chardonnay delivers flavors of pear, melon and apple strudel. Barrel fermented in French oak (30% new), it tastes of lightly applied butter, toast and fresh baked brioche. Everything has been completely melded together. 90 —*P.G. (3/1/2007)*

Three Rivers 2004 Chardonnay (Columbia Valley (WA)) $17. 88 —*P.G. (6/1/2006)*

Three Rivers 2003 Chardonnay (Columbia Valley (WA)) $17. 89 —*P.G. (6/1/2005)*

Three Rivers 2002 Chardonnay (Columbia Valley (WA)) $17. 88 —*P.G. (12/15/2004)*

Three Rivers 2001 Chardonnay (Columbia Valley (WA)) $17. 88 —*P.G. (7/1/2004)*

Three Rivers 2000 Chardonnay (Columbia Valley (WA)) $24. 90 *—P.G. (9/1/2002)*

Three Rivers 1999 Chardonnay (Columbia Valley (WA)) $22. 87 *—P.G. (7/1/2002)*

Three Rivers 2001 Biscuit Ridge Vineyard Late Harvest Gewürztraminer (Walla Walla (WA)) $23. 92 *—P.G. (9/1/2002)*

Three Rivers 2005 Malbec (Columbia Valley (WA)) $25. A dark, firm, muscular wine, blended with 80% Malbec and 20% Cabernet Sauvignon. The grapes show flavors of the region – dark, spicy boysenberry fruit, wrapped in smoky tannins. Its excellent varietal character and concentration suggest that this wine has a potential cellar life of a decade or more. **89** *—P.G. (12/1/2007)*

Three Rivers 2005 Malbec-Merlot (Columbia Valley (WA)) $25. A 50–50 blend, this shows fruit flavors of plum and currant, hints of orange peel and citrus, and assertive, fairly stiff tannins. It's set up for steak, beef and grilled meats, which will work well with the tannins. I'd let it breathe for an hour or two to soften it up and bring out the fruit. **88** *—P.G. (12/1/2007)*

Three Rivers 2005 Meritage (Columbia Valley (WA)) $19. Roughly two thirds Sauvignon Blanc and one third Semillon, aged sur lie in French oak, this is one of the state's top white Meritage wines. It's immaculately fruity, with a lovely mix of pear, lime, citrus and apple. In the mouth it sails along with flavors both lively and fresh. **91** *—P.G. (3/1/2007)*

Three Rivers 2003 Meritage (Columbia Valley (WA)) $39. 91 *—P.G. (6/1/2006)*

Three Rivers 1999 Meritage (Columbia Valley (WA)) $45. 89 *—P.G. (2/1/2002)*

Three Rivers 2004 White Wine Meritage (Columbia Valley (WA)) $19. 89 *—P.G. (6/1/2006)*

Three Rivers 2004 Merlot (Columbia Valley (WA)) $19. This is a pretty Merlot, light and aromatic, and it has been handled well. The only off notes are some fairly tough, chewy tannins that overtake the elegant midpalate and don't quite fit the style. **87** *—P.G. (12/1/2007)*

Three Rivers 2003 Merlot (Columbia Valley (WA)) $19. 88 *—P.G. (6/1/2006)*

Three Rivers 2002 Merlot (Columbia Valley (WA)) $19. 90 *—P.G. (6/1/2005)*

Three Rivers 2001 Merlot (Columbia Valley (WA)) $19. 87 *—P.G. (7/1/2004)*

Three Rivers 2000 Merlot (Columbia Valley (WA)) $26. 90 *—P.G. (9/1/2002)*

Three Rivers 1999 Merlot (Columbia Valley (WA)) $28. 86 *—P.G. (6/1/2002)*

Three Rivers 2001 Reserve Merlot (Columbia Valley (WA)) $39. 88 *—P.G. (12/15/2004)*

Three Rivers 2000 Reserve Merlot (Columbia Valley (WA)) $37. 91 *—P.G. (9/1/2002)*

Three Rivers 2005 Red Blend (Columbia Valley (WA)) $13. A Cab/Merlot/Syrah blend, it's full-bodied and tastes of grapes and cherries. It has a firmly tannic spine that carries it solidly past the first impressions of pretty fruit and into more substantial territory. Complex and beautifully structured, the wine shows a good balance of herb, earth, clean fruit and ripe tannin. This is always a very consistent, well-made wine, though the blend and fruit sources change with each vintage. **88 Best Buy** *—P.G. (12/1/2007)*

Three Rivers 2003 MC2 Red Blend (Columbia Valley (WA)) $10. 87 Best Buy *—P.G. (6/1/2006)*

Three Rivers 2001 Meritage Red Wine Red Blend (Columbia Valley (WA)) $39. 91 *—P.G. (7/1/2004)*

Three Rivers 2004 River's Red Red Blend (Columbia Valley (WA)) $13. Once again the winery's cheap "mutt" wine red blend is a jewel; full-flavored and complex and beautifully structured with no obvious faults. It's half Merlot, 30% Cabernet Sauvignon, 14% Malbec and 5% Grenache—a great mix of spice and power. Throw it against a steak, a burger, any beef dish, and it will shine. **88 Best Buy** *—P.G. (3/1/2007)*

Three Rivers 2003 River's Red Red Blend (Columbia Valley (WA)) $15. 88 *—P.G. (6/1/2006)*

Three Rivers 2001 River's Red Table Wine Red Blend (Columbia Valley (WA)) $15. 86 *—P.G. (7/1/2004)*

Three Rivers 2006 Riesling (Yakima Valley) $19. This off-dry Riesling sources grapes from Willard Farms, outside of Prosser, in the heart of the Yakima Valley AVA. It's ripe and fruity with a pleasing mix of apricot, pear and Macintosh apple. The sweetness is carried well by the acids, and leaves an impression of light honey in the finish. **88** *—P.G. (12/1/2007)*

Three Rivers 1999 Sangiovese (Columbia Valley (WA)) $30. 84 *—C.S. (12/31/2002)*

Three Rivers 2003 Pepper Bridge Vineyard Sangiovese (Walla Walla (WA)) $39. 87 *—P.G. (6/1/2005)*

Three Rivers 2000 Pepper Bridge Vineyard Sangiovese (Walla Walla (WA)) $35. 87 *—P.G. (2/1/2002)*

Three Rivers 2002 Pepper Bridge Vineyards Sangiovese (Walla Walla (WA)) $39. 87 *—P.G. (7/1/2004)*

Three Rivers 2004 Syrah (Columbia Valley (WA)) $24. This is pure Syrah from a winemaker who makes a number of single-vineyard and blended Syrahs. This dark, sappy, seductive wine has you from the first sniff. Though the fruit is big and briary, winemaker Holly Turner manages to capture the polish and elegance of Washington Syrah in the way the flavors are sculpted together. Veins of tar, chocolate, smoke, black licorice, pepper and tobacco accent the young, tight fruit flavors. This wine definitely needs breathing time to show its stuff. **91** *—P.G. (12/1/2007)*

Three Rivers 2003 Syrah (Columbia Valley (WA)) $24. 91 *—P.G. (6/1/2006)*

Three Rivers 2003 Syrah (Columbia Valley (WA)) $24. 87 *(9/1/2005)*

Three Rivers 2002 Syrah (Columbia Valley (WA)) $24. 89 *—P.G. (6/1/2005)*

Three Rivers 2001 Syrah (Columbia Valley (WA)) $24. 88 *—P.G. (12/15/2004)*

Three Rivers 2000 Syrah (Columbia Valley (WA)) $32. 88 *P.G. (9/1/2002)*

Three Rivers 1999 Syrah (Columbia Valley (WA)) $28. 89 *—P.G. (6/1/2002)*

Three Rivers 2003 Ahler Vineyard Syrah (Walla Walla (WA)) $39. 85 *(9/1/2005)*

Three Rivers 2003 Ahler Vineyard Syrah (Columbia Valley (WA)) $39. 89 *—P.G. (6/1/2006)*

Three Rivers 2002 Ahler Vineyard Syrah (Walla Walla (WA)) $39. 88 *—P.G. (6/1/2005)*

Three Rivers 2004 Boushey Vineyard Syrah (Yakima Valley) $50. Young, tart, juicy and compact, this is quite flavorful and showing a good acid edge. I like the peppery finish and the clean, crisp definition; it's definitely a Yakima Valley style. Give it another couple of years to flesh out. **89** *—P.G. (3/1/2007)*

Three Rivers 2003 Boushey Vineyards Syrah (Yakima Valley) $39. 87 *(9/1/2005)*

Three Rivers 2001 Boushey Vineyards Syrah (Yakima Valley) $39. 90 *—P.G. (12/15/2004)*

Three Rivers 2000 Boushey Vineyard Syrah (Yakima Valley) $42. 91 *—P.G. (9/1/2002)*

Three Rivers 1999 Boushey Vineyard Syrah (Yakima Valley) $35. 90 Editors' Choice *(11/1/2001)*

Three Rivers 2002 Meritage White Wine White Blend (Columbia Valley (WA)) $19. 89 *—P.G. (7/1/2004)*

THREE SAINTS

Three Saints 2001 Cabernet Sauvignon (Santa Barbara County) $24. 90 *—S.H. (10/1/2004)*

Three Saints 2002 Chardonnay (Santa Maria Valley) $20. 88 *—S.H. (9/1/2004)*

Three Saints 2001 Merlot (Santa Ynez Valley) $24. 91 *—S.H. (9/1/2004)*

Three Saints 2002 Estate Grown Pinot Noir (Santa Maria Valley) $20. 88 *(11/1/2004)*

THREE THIEVES

Three Thieves 2002 Bandit 1 Liter Cabernet Sauvignon (California) $7. 86 Best Buy *—S.H. (11/15/2005)*

Three Thieves 2005 The Show Cabernet Sauvignon (California) $15. From Three Thieves, who are establishing a reputation for value, comes this Cab, a blend of four coastal counties from Paso Robles to Dry Creek. It's ripe, soft and easy, with blackberry, chocolate, mint and vanilla flavors. **85** *—S.H. (12/31/2007)*

Three Thieves 2004 Bandit 1 Liter Pinot Grigio (California) $7.]83 Best Buy *—S.H. (2/1/2006)*

Three Thieves 2004 Circle K Ranch Pinot Noir (California) $10. 84 Best Buy *—S.H. (12/31/2005)*

Three Thieves 2002 Zinfandel (California) $10. 87 *—J.M. (11/15/2003)*

THUMBPRINT CELLARS

Thumbprint Cellars 2002 Schneider Vineyard Cabernet Sauvignon (Alexander Valley) $35. 87 *—S.H. (11/1/2005)*

Thumbprint Cellars 2002 Schneider Vineyard Merlot (Dry Creek Valley) $30. 90 *—S.H. (11/1/2005)*

Thumbprint Cellars 2002 Schneider Vineyard Pinot Noir (Russian River Valley) $36. 92 Editors' Choice *—S.H. (11/1/2005)*

Thumbprint Cellars 2002 Threesome Red Blend (Alexander Valley) $35. 92 Editors' Choice —*S.H. (11/1/2005)*

Thumbprint Cellars 2001 C. Teldeschi Vineyard Zinfandel (Dry Creek Valley) $30. 87 *(11/1/2003)*

THUNDER MOUNTAIN

Thunder Mountain 1996 Bates Ranch Star Ruby Bordeaux Blend (Santa Cruz Mountains) $49. 86 —*J.C. (9/1/1999)*

Thunder Mountain 1996 Bate's Ranch Cabernet Sauvignon (Santa Cruz County) $39. 92 —*M.S. (7/1/1999)*

Thunder Mountain 1997 Bate's Ranch Cabernet Sauvignon (Santa Cruz Mountains) $48. 89 *(11/1/2000)*

Thunder Mountain 1997 Miller Vineyards 'Doc's' Cabernet Sauvignon (Cienega Valley) $48. 84 *(11/1/2000)*

Thunder Mountain 1997 Bald Mountain Vineyard Chardonnay (Santa Cruz Mountains) $29. 92 —*M.S. (7/1/1999)*

Thunder Mountain 1999 Beauregard Ranch Chardonnay (Santa Cruz Mountains) $43. 90 —*J.M. (12/15/2002)*

Thunder Mountain 1999 Ciardella Vineyard Chardonnay (Santa Cruz Mountains) $43. 87 —*J.C. (9/1/2002)*

Thunder Mountain 1997 Ciardella Vineyard Chardonnay (Santa Cruz Mountains) $29. 92 —*J.C. (7/1/1999)*

Thunder Mountain 1999 DeRose Vineyard Chardonnay (Cienega Valley) $34. 90 *(7/1/2001)*

Thunder Mountain 1998 DeRose Vineyard Chardonnay (Cienega Valley) $34. 90 *(10/1/2000)*

Thunder Mountain 1998 Merlot (Cienega Valley) $34. 88 —*J.C. (7/1/2000)*

Thunder Mountain 1999 Veranda Vineyards Pinot Noir (Santa Cruz Mountains) $48. 83 *(10/1/2002)*

THURSTON WOLFE

Thurston Wolfe 2004 Destiny Ridge Cabernet Sauvignon (Washington) $25. Destiny Ridge vineyard, in the Horse Heaven Hills, is one of Washington's most prolific and important new growers. Thurston Wolfe's Cab displays pretty raspberry flavors and somewhat chalky tannins. It's pure Cabernet, a good representation of the young vineyard. **87** —*P.G. (8/1/2007)*

Thurston Wolfe 2002 Destiny Ridge Cabernet Sauvignon (Columbia Valley (WA)) $25. 88 —*P.G. (6/1/2005)*

Thurston Wolfe 2005 Lemberger (Horse Heaven Hills) $15. This is classic stuff: ready for the grill, pizza, a picnic. The fruit is ripe and speckled with peppery spice, and the tannins are rough-sawn, like old timber. But the flavors are pure and honest; it's a wine you can glug down all night. **86** —*P.G. (8/1/2007)*

Thurston Wolfe 2001 Blue Franc Lemberger (Yakima Valley) $14. 86 —*P.G. (12/31/2003)*

Thurston Wolfe 2003 Horse Heaven Hills Lemberger (Columbia Valley (WA)) $14. 88 —*P.G. (6/1/2005)*

Thurston Wolfe 1998 Blue Franc Lemberger-Cabernet (Columbia Valley (WA)) $14. 86 —*P.G. (11/15/2000)*

Thurston Wolfe 2003 Sweet Rebecca Orange Muscat (Yakima Valley) $15. 93 —*P.G. (6/1/2005)*

Thurston Wolfe 2005 Zephyr Ridge Vineyard Petite Sirah (Horse Heaven Hills) $20. This is the fourth vintage for this rare Washington version of Petite Sirah, and the best yet. It doesn't have the sheer weight and bulk of California wines, but its firm acids, sweet tannins and ripe black cherry fruit add a stylish, almost elegant spin to the grape. **89** —*P.G. (8/1/2007)*

Thurston Wolfe 2002 Zephyr Ridge Vineyard Petite Sirah (Columbia Valley (WA)) $18. 88 —*P.G. (12/15/2004)*

Thurston Wolfe 2000 JTW Port (Columbia Valley (WA)) $17. 87 —*P.G. (12/1/2003)*

Thurston Wolfe 2003 JTW's Port (Washington) $20. 94 Editors' Choice —*P.G. (6/1/2005)*

Thurston Wolfe 2000 Blue Franc Red Blend (Columbia Valley (WA)) $13. 90 —*P.G. (9/1/2002)*

Thurston Wolfe 2005 Dr. Wolfe's Family Red Red Blend (Washington) $15. Primitivo makes up three fifths of the blend, Petite Sirah most of the rest. It's consistent with past vintages: dark, soft, and plummy. But in 2005 there was something special going on, and the decadently sweet black cherry fruit really sings here. **88** —*P.G. (8/1/2007)*

Thurston Wolfe 2002 Sangiovese (Columbia Valley (WA)) $20. 86 —*P.G. (12/1/2004)*

Thurston Wolfe 2000 Sangiovese (Columbia Valley (WA)) $20. 91 —*P.G. (9/1/2002)*

Thurston Wolfe 1998 Syrah (Columbia Valley (WA)) $20. 90 —*P.G. (9/1/2000)*

Thurston Wolfe 2001 Syrah (Columbia Valley (WA)) $18. 89 —*P.G. (12/31/2003)*

Thurston Wolfe 2000 Syrah (Columbia Valley (WA)) $18. 90 —*P.G. (9/1/2002)*

Thurston Wolfe 2005 Burgess Vineyard Syrah (Washington) $25. Scents of smoke, earth, citrus rind and a strong acidic foundation define this wine. It's a fine example of cooler-site Washington Syrah, with all the nuances that that brings to the wine. The alcohol hits 14.5%, but doesn't overwhelm the lighter side of the wine. It's genteel and stylish. **88** —*P.G. (8/1/2007)*

Thurston Wolfe 2003 PGV White Blend (Columbia Valley (WA)) $12. 86 —*P.G. (12/1/2004)*

Thurston Wolfe 2002 PGV White Blend (Columbia Valley (WA)) $12. 87 —*P.G. (12/31/2003)*

Thurston Wolfe 1999 Pinot Gris Viognier White Blend (Columbia Valley (WA)) $11. 87 —*P.G. (11/15/2000)*

Thurston Wolfe 2001 Pinot Gris-Viognier White Blend (Columbia Valley (WA)) $13. 86 —*P.G. (9/1/2002)*

Thurston Wolfe 2002 Zinfandel (Columbia Valley (WA)) $14. 87 —*P.G. (6/1/2005)*

Thurston Wolfe 2001 Zinfandel (Columbia Valley (WA)) $17. 88 —*P.G. (12/31/2003)*

Thurston Wolfe 2000 Burgess Vineyard Zinfandel (Columbia Valley (WA)) $20. 87 —*P.G. (9/1/2002)*

Thurston Wolfe 1998 Burgess Vineyard Zinfandel (Columbia Valley (WA)) $20. 87 —*P.G. (11/15/2000)*

Thurston Wolfe 2005 Howling Wolfe Zinfandel (Washington) $18. Plummy and ripe, this tannic, herbal take on Zinfandel is ready for near-term drinking. The red fruits mix berries, cherries and cranberry flavors, and there is plenty of chalky acid to prop it up. The alcohol is a moderate 14.5%. **87** —*P.G. (8/1/2007)*

TIN BARN

Tin Barn 2005 Sauvignon Blanc (Bennett Valley) $18. This is a white Bordeaux wannabe, barrel fermented and rich in citrus, fig, spicy melon and smoky flavors, but it's a little too soft and candied. **84** —*S.H. (12/15/2007)*

Tin Barn 2004 Sauvignon Blanc (Bennett Valley) $18. 82 —*S.H. (12/1/2005)*

Tin Barn 2001 Coryelle Fields Syrah (Sonoma Coast) $32. 90 —*J.C. (5/1/2004)*

Tin Barn 2002 Coryelle Fields Vineyard Syrah (Sonoma Coast) $32. 87 —*S.H. (4/1/2005)*

Tin Barn 2001 Zinfandel (Russian River Valley) $25. 88 —*J.M. (3/1/2004)*

Tin Barn 2004 Dalraddy Vineyard Zinfandel (Russian River Valley) $27. Despite some decent fruit, this Zin, from the Chiles Valley district is as dry and hot as a lit match, which makes the tannins feel really astringent. **82** —*S.H. (12/15/2007)*

Tin Barn 2004 Gilsson Vineyard Zinfandel (Russian River Valley) $27. They don't tell us what the residual sugar is, but the wine sure tastes sweet. Hot and simple, too, with a flabby texture. Not very good despite the fruit, especially at this price. **82** —*S.H. (12/15/2007)*

Tin Barn 2000 Jensen Lane Zinfandel (Russian River Valley) $24. 88 —*S.H. (11/1/2002)*

Tin Barn 2001 Jensen Lane Vineyard Zinfandel (Russian River Valley) $27. 87 *(11/1/2003)*

TIN HOUSE

Tin House 2004 Pinot Noir (Edna Valley) $32. 94 Editors' Choice —*S.H. (12/15/2006)*

Tin House 2003 Syrah (Edna Valley) $26. 86 —*S.H. (12/15/2006)*

TIN ROOF

Tin Roof 2005 Cabernet Sauvignon (California) $13. A nice glass of Cab for $13. It's bone dry, with a scour of sandpapery tannins, and hints of cherries, blackberries, plums, cola and cedar. Shows real class for a statewide-appellated Cab at this price. **86** —*S.H. (11/15/2007)*

Tin Roof 2006 Chardonnay (California) $13. Everyday Chard, a little on the sweet and soft side, but acceptable. The flavors are of canned peaches, apricots and pears. **83** —*S.H. (11/15/2007)*

Tin Roof 2003 Chardonnay (California) $9. 84 —*S.H. (3/1/2005)*

Tin Roof 2002 Chardonnay (Sonoma County) $9. 83 —*S.H. (6/1/2004)*

Tin Roof 2005 Merlot (California) $13. I found myself returning to this Merlot again and again, because it's such a good, gentle, easy sipper. It's a pleasure to drink one that's so nicely dry and balanced. Does a great job balancing ripe berry and stone fruits with earthy herbs and spices. Sommeliers and restaurateurs, scoop this one up while you can. **90 Best Buy** *—S.H. (11/15/2007)*

Tin Roof 2003 Rosé Pinot Noir (Russian River Valley) $9. 84 *—S.H. (12/15/2004)*

Tin Roof 2006 Sauvignon Blanc (California) $13. A little on the simple, green-grass side, with lemon and lime flavors that are slightly sweet. Fortunately, there's a good bite of acidity and a clean, spicy finish. **84** *—S.H. (11/15/2007)*

Tin Roof 2003 Sauvignon Blanc (North Coast) $9. 86 Best Buy *—S.H. (3/1/2005)*

Tin Roof 2002 Sauvignon Blanc (North Coast) $9. 84 *—S.H. (6/1/2004)*

Tin Roof 2005 Syrah-Cabernet (California) $13. Tin Roof's regular '05 Cab was pretty good, but this is overripe and raisiny, suggesting a problem with the Syrah. **83** *—S.H. (11/15/2007)*

Tin Roof 2002 Syrah-Cabernet (California) $9. 84 *—S.H. (12/15/2004)*

TITUS

Titus 2004 Cabernet Franc (Napa Valley) $34. Ripe and fruity, this is an elegant, easy to drink red with a dry to semisweet taste. It has a medium body and rich flavors of cherries, blueberries, mocha, toast and vanilla. **87** *—S.H. (2/1/2007)*

Titus 2003 Cabernet Sauvignon (Napa Valley) $39. 92 *—S.H. (8/1/2006)*

Titus 2002 Cabernet Sauvignon (Napa Valley) $39. 87 *—S.H. (10/1/2005)*

Titus 2001 Cabernet Sauvignon (Napa Valley) $39. 91 *—S.H. (10/1/2004)*

Titus 1999 Cabernet Sauvignon (Napa Valley) $36. 88 *—K.F. (8/1/2003)*

Titus 1997 Cabernet Sauvignon (Napa Valley) $32. 91 *(11/1/2000)*

Titus 2002 Reserve Cabernet Sauvignon (Napa Valley) $60. 91 *—S.H. (10/1/2005)*

Titus 2004 Petite Sirah (Napa Valley) $35. Not particularly likeable for its sharp acids and green, minty unripeness that simply emphasize the tannins. **82** *—S.H. (2/1/2007)*

Titus 2004 Zinfandel (Napa Valley) $25. Here's an everyday Zin, dry, tannic, a little rough in the sharp edgy mouthfeel, and with wild berry flavors. With a touch of Petite Sirah, it's a good wine to drink at your neighbor's barbecue to wash down burgers and such. **84** *—S.H. (2/1/2007)*

Titus 2003 Zinfandel (Napa Valley) $24. 87 *—S.H. (3/1/2006)*

Titus 2000 Zinfandel (Mendocino County) $24. 90 *—J.M. (9/1/2003)*

Titus 2000 Zinfandel (Napa Valley) $24. 88 *—J.M. (9/1/2003)*

USA

TOAD HALL

Toad Hall 2004 Bodacious Bordeaux Blend (Napa Valley) $40. This is Toad Hall's Meritage-style Bordeaux blend, 50-50 Cab and Merlot, and while it doesn't have much depth, it appeals instantly for a rich array of flavors. Cherries, blackberries, cassis, mocha, moo shu plum sauce—all of it slightly sweetened, but tannic enough to qualify as dry. Drink now for its youthful babyfat. **87** *—S.H. (12/1/2007)*

Toad Hall 2002 Bodacious Cabernet Blend (Napa Valley) $30. 82 *—S.H. (10/1/2005)*

Toad Hall 2003 Dijon Clones Pinot Noir (Carneros) $40. 86 *—S.H. (8/1/2005)*

Toad Hall 2005 Lavender Hill Vineyard Pinot Noir (Carneros) $40. This is dry wine, and properly silky, with earthy cola and cranberry-cherry flavors. It's also young and tight and a little hot, but it's not a wine to cellar. **85** *—S.H. (12/1/2007)*

Toad Hall 2003 Lavender Hill Vineyard Pinot Noir (Carneros) $25. 85 *S.H. (8/1/2005)*

Toad Hall 2002 Lavender Hill Vineyard Pinot Noir (Carneros) $22. 84 *—S.H. (2/1/2005)*

Toad Hall 2002 Lavender Hill Vineyard Pinot Noir (Carneros) $22. 88 *—S.H. (11/1/2004)*

Toad Hall 2003 Rod's Pride Goldie's Vines Pinot Noir (Russian River Valley) $45. 86 *—S.H. (12/31/2005)*

Toad Hall 1999 Bodacious Red Blend (Napa Valley) $30. 84 *—S.H. (2/1/2005)*

TOAD HOLLOW

Toad Hollow 2006 Eye of the Toad Dry Rosé Pinot Noir (Sonoma County) $10. Thin in flavor, with watery tea and cola flavors and a few drops of cherry essence, this wine has the benefit of extreme dryness and crisp acidity. Those latter qualities go a long way in making up for a lack of fruit, especially at this low price. **84** *—S.H. (7/1/2007)*

Toad Hollow 2001 Cacaphony Zinfandel (Paso Robles) $17. 84 *(11/1/2003)*

TOASTED HEAD

Toasted Head 1999 Meritage Bordeaux Blend (Dunnigan Hills) $25. 87 *—S.H. (11/15/2002)*

Toasted Head 2002 Cabernet Sauvignon (California) $17. 84 *—S.H. (8/1/2005)*

Toasted Head 2002 Cabernet Sauvignon (Alexander Valley) $18. 82 *—S.H. (10/1/2005)*

Toasted Head 2003 Chardonnay (Russian River Valley) $17. 85 *—S.H. (10/1/2005)*

Toasted Head 1999 Merlot (Dunnigan Hills) $18. 87 *—S.H. (6/1/2002)*

TOBIN JAMES

Tobin James 1999 Estate Private Reserve Stash Bordeaux Blend (Paso Robles) $38. 88 *—S.H. (12/31/2001)*

Tobin James 1997 Notorious Cabernet Franc (Paso Robles) $18. 90 Editors' Choice *—S.H. (5/1/2001)*

Tobin James 1999 James Gang Reserve Cabernet Sauvignon (Paso Robles) $28. 85 *—S.H. (12/31/2001)*

Tobin James 1999 Radiance Chardonnay (Paso Robles) $16. 84 *—S.H. (5/1/2001)*

Tobin James 1999 James Gang Reserve Merlot (Paso Robles) $45. 86 *—S.H. (12/31/2001)*

Tobin James 2000 James Gang Reserve Late Harvest Muscat (Paso Robles) $20. 90 *—S.H. (12/31/2001)*

Tobin James 2000 Ranchito Canyon Vineyard Petite Sirah (Paso Robles) $NA. 82 *(4/1/2003)*

Tobin James 1997 Ranchito Canyon Vineyard Petite Sirah (Paso Robles) $18. 88 *—S.H. (5/1/2001)*

Tobin James 1999 James Gang Reserve Primitivo (Paso Robles) $38. 84 *—S.H. (12/15/2001)*

Tobin James 1999 James Gang Reserve Refosco Red Blend (Paso Robles) $38. 87 *—S.H. (12/15/2001)*

Tobin James 2002 James Gang Reserve Syrah (Paso Robles) $28. 85 *(9/1/2005)*

Tobin James 1999 Rock-N-Roll Syrah (Paso Robles) $16. 83 *(10/1/2001)*

Tobin James 1998 James Gang Reserve Viognier (Paso Robles) $20. 87 *—S.H. (10/1/1999)*

Tobin James 2001 Ballistic Zinfandel (Paso Robles) $15. 85 *(11/1/2003)*

Tobin James 1999 Blue Moon Reserve Zinfandel (Paso Robles) $38. 87 *—S.H. (12/15/2001)*

Tobin James 1997 Blue Moon Reserve Zinfandel (Paso Robles) $35. 90 *—S.H. (5/1/2000)*

Tobin James 1997 Commemorative Zinfandel (Paso Robles) $30. 86 *—J.C. (5/1/2000)*

Tobin James 2001 Dusi Vineyard Zinfandel (Paso Robles) $28. 88 *(11/1/2003)*

Tobin James 1999 Dusi Vineyard Zinfandel (Paso Robles) $28. 87 *—S.H. (12/15/2001)*

Tobin James 2001 James Gang Reserve Zinfandel (Paso Robles) $28. 88 *(11/1/2003)*

Tobin James 1999 James Gang Reserve Zinfandel (Paso Robles) $28. 84 *—S.H. (12/15/2001)*

Tobin James 1998 James Gang Reserve Zinfandel (Paso Robles) $26. 87 *(3/1/2001)*

Tobin James 1997 James Gang Reserve Zinfandel (Paso Robles) $22. 86 *—J.C. (5/1/2000)*

TOLOSA

Tolosa 2004 1772 Edna Ranch Chardonnay (Edna Valley) $42. Here's a really good Chardonnay: Crisp, delicate and dry, it shows great acidity and brilliant fruit, saturating the palate with pineapple tart, Key lime pie, vanilla cream, crème brûlée and cinnamon spice flavors. Finishes with the deliciously creamy, yeasty complexities of lees aging. **94** *—S.H. (9/1/2007)*

Tolosa 2005 Edna Ranch Chardonnay (Edna Valley) $20. Shows classic Edna Valley Chardonnay structure and flavor, a brightly acidic, minerally wine with a great burst of Key lime pie, ripe kiwi, pineapple custard, honey and vanilla oak flavors. **87** *—S.H. (10/1/2007)*

Tolosa 2004 Edna Ranch Chardonnay (Edna Valley) $20. 91 *—S.H. (12/1/2006)*

Tolosa 2003 Edna Ranch Chardonnay (Edna Valley) $20. 92 Editors' Choice *—S.H. (11/1/2005)*

Tolosa 2001 Edna Ranch Chardonnay (Edna Valley) $20. 89 *—S.H. (9/1/2004)*

Tolosa 2006 Edna Ranch No-Oak Chardonnay (Edna Valley) $17. Just beautiful and oh, so refreshing. The cool vintage has resulted in a high-acid wine of enormous fruit, bursting with intense, classic Edna Valley flavors of limes, kiwis, Meyer lemons, honeysuckle and minerals. The vanilla spice and creamy smoke have got to come from the terroir, because the wine never saw a splinter of oak. **90 Editors' Choice** *—S.H. (12/15/2007)*

Tolosa 2004 Edna Ranch No-Oak Chardonnay (Edna Valley) $16. 90 Editors' Choice *—S.H. (11/1/2005)*

Tolosa 2006 Edna Ranch Pinot Gris (Edna Valley) $16. Here's a very dry, crisp and elegant PG, marked by its delicate flavors of citrus zest, flowers and minerals. It's really a clean, pure wine that shows off its cool-climate origins. **87** *—S.H. (10/1/2007)*

Tolosa 2005 1772 Barrel Select Pinot Noir (Edna Valley) $52. Shows the delicacy and finesse of the finest Pinot Noirs of this vintage, and is a solid expression of this always fine bottling, although lacking a shade of the opulence of the '04. With cola, cherry, licorice, pine, cinnamon and vanilla oak flavors, it's a complex, satisfying wine that will marry well with steak and grilled salmon. **90** *—S.H. (12/31/2007)*

Tolosa 2005 Edna Ranch Pinot Noir (Edna Valley) $30. Just delicious. It's so soft and silky, so easy to sip, and so seductive in lush cherry, cola, vanilla and spice flavors. Drink now for its youthful exuberance. **89** *—S.H. (12/15/2007)*

Tolosa 2003 Edna Ranch Pinot Noir (Edna Valley) $28. 91 *—S.H. (11/1/2006)*

Tolosa 2002 Edna Ranch Pinot Noir (Edna Valley) $25. 88 *—S.H. (11/1/2005)*

Tolosa 2000 Edna Ranch Pinot Noir (Edna Valley) $30. 88 *(10/1/2002)*

Tolosa 1998 Edna Ranch Pinot Noir (Edna Valley) $30. 89 *—M.S. (12/15/2000)*

Tolosa 2002 Edna Ranch 1772 Pinot Noir (Edna Valley) $52. 90 *—S.H. (11/1/2005)*

Tolosa 2001 Edna Ranch Reserve 1772 Pinot Noir (Edna Valley) $42. 92 *—S.H. (12/1/2004)*

Tolosa 2004 Heritage Blend Rhône Red Blend (Edna Valley) $38. 92 Editors' Choice *—S.H. (11/1/2006)*

Tolosa 2006 Edna Ranch Sauvignon Blanc (Edna Valley) $18. Ripeness was the issue in this cool vintage, and there's a touch of good old cat pee here. Not too much, but enough to make the wine unattractive despite the nice dryness. **84** *—S.H. (10/1/2007)*

Tolosa 2004 1772 Edna Ranch Syrah (Edna Valley) $46. Tolosa has been making seriously good Syrah for some years now. The quality shows not just in the ripeness, but in the acidity that gives the wine brightness and balance. This was a warm vintage, even in cool Edna Valley, and the wine shows extraordinarily powerful blackberry pie filling, cherry compote and chocolate flavors, but that high acidity really makes the fruit sing. **92** *—S.H. (9/1/2007)*

Tolosa 2003 Edna Ranch Syrah (Edna Valley) $20. 92 *—S.H. (7/1/2006)*

Tolosa 2002 Edna Ranch Syrah (Edna Valley) $20. 89 *—S.H. (12/1/2004)*

Tolosa 1999 Edna Ranch Syrah (Edna Valley) $28. 87 *(11/1/2001)*

Tolosa 2003 Edna Ranch 1772 Syrah (Edna Valley) $46. 90 *(9/1/2005)*

Tolosa 2006 Edna Ranch Viognier (Edna Valley) $20. Lean, dry and acidic, with minty, citrus and mineral flavors, this is more like an Albariño than Viognier, which is usually rich and opulent. It's actually quite a clean, zesty wine, but forewarned is forearmed. **85** *—S.H. (10/1/2007)*

TOM EDDY

Tom Eddy 1999 Cabernet Sauvignon (Napa Valley) $75. 88 *—S.H. (11/15/2004)*

Tom Eddy 2001 Dr. Crane Vineyard Cabernet Sauvignon (Napa Valley) $110. At nearly six years of age, this Cab tastes as fresh and tannic as a far younger wine. Those tannins remain firm and hard, and the blackberries and cherries still have a primary fruit taste. This likely will be one of those wines that takes a long time to show its stuff, but it's richly balanced and satisfying. Odds are this beautiful wine, from a veteran producer, will develop very well over the next 10 years. **93 Cellar Selection** *—S.H. (10/1/2007)*

TONDRÉ

Tondré 2004 Tondré Grapefield Pinot Noir (Santa Lucia Highlands) $43. As rich and complex in structure as you'd expect in a Pinot from this appellation. Wrapped into the silky structure are impressively ripe flavors of black cherries, cola, rhubarb pie and sweet oaky vanilla, balanced with a crisp tang of citrusy acids. Drink now for youthful freshness. **90** *—S.H. (10/1/2007)*

Tondré 2003 Tondré Grapefield Pinot Noir (Santa Lucia Highlands) $43. 90 *—S.H. (12/1/2006)*

TOPANGA

Topanga 2003 Celadon Esperanza Vineyard Grenache (Clarksburg) $20. 90 *—J.M. (10/1/2005)*

TOPEL

Topel 2001 Cabernet Sauvignon (Mendocino) $34. 89 *—S.H. (12/1/2005)*

Topel 1999 Cabernet Sauvignon (Mendocino) $45. 90 *—C.S. (5/1/2002)*

Topel 1997 Hidden Vineyard Reserve Cabernet Sauvignon (Mendocino) $45. 89 *(11/1/2000)*

Topel 2002 Cuvée Donnis Syrah (Monterey) $25. 85 *(9/1/2005)*

TOPOLOS

Topolos 1997 Old Vines Charbono (Napa Valley) $14. 87 *—J.C. (10/1/1999)*

Topolos 1997 Muscat L'Orange Orange Muscat (California) $9. 81 *—J.C. (12/31/1999)*

Topolos 1997 Dulce D'Oro White Blend (Russian River Valley) $18. 80 *—J.C. (12/31/1999)*

Topolos 1997 Pagani Ranch Zinfandel (Sonoma Valley) $30. 88 *—J.C. (5/1/2000)*

Topolos 1997 Piner Heights Zinfandel (Russian River Valley) $17. 82 *—M.S. (9/1/1999)*

Topolos 1997 Rossi Ranch Zinfandel (Sonoma Valley) $25. 86 *—J.C. (5/1/2000)*

TORII MOR

Torii Mor 2000 Olson Vineyard Chardonnay (Yamhill County) $25. 89 *—P.G. (9/1/2003)*

Torii Mor 2000 Pinot Blanc (Rogue Valley) $18. 87 *—P.G. (8/1/2002)*

Torii Mor 1998 Pinot Gris (Yamhill County) $15. 90 *—M.S. (11/15/1999)*

Torii Mor 2004 Pinot Gris (Willamette Valley) $16. 85 *—P.G. (2/1/2006)*

Torii Mor 2002 Pinot Gris (Oregon) $13. 88 *—P.G. (10/1/2004)*

Torii Mor 2000 Pinot Gris (Willamette Valley) $20. 87 *—P.G. (8/1/2002)*

Torii Mor 2004 Reserve Pinot Gris (Willamette Valley) $21. 86 *(2/1/2006)*

Torii Mor 2002 Reserve Pinot Gris (Oregon) $18. 86 *—P.G. (10/1/2004)*

Torii Mor 2005 Pinot Noir (Willamette Valley) $29. The black label Torii Mor Pinot is often as good, if not better, than the single-vineyard bottlings. Although the price keeps creeping higher, it's fair and this 2005 is an excellent rendition. It offers fruit flavors that are ripe but not sweet or jammy, nice details of herb and root, and suggestions of moist earth and black tea. If you believe in modest (13.5% here) levels of alcohol in your Pinots, this one should ring your bell. **89 Editors' Choice** *—P.G. (11/15/2007)*

Torii Mor 2004 Pinot Noir (Willamette Valley) $25. 89 *—P.G. (9/1/2006)*

Torii Mor 2002 Pinot Noir (Oregon) $17. 84 *(11/1/2004)*

Torii Mor 2001 Pinot Noir (Oregon) $17. 87 *—P.G. (10/1/2004)*

Torii Mor 2000 Pinot Noir (Oregon) $25. 84 *(10/1/2002)*

Torii Mor 1997 Pinot Noir (Oregon) $20. 87 *(11/15/1999)*

Torii Mor 2000 Amelia Rose Pinot Noir (Yamhill County) $42. 86 *(10/1/2002)*

Torii Mor 1999 Amelia Rose Cuvée Pinot Noir (Yamhill County) $45. 89 *—J.C. (11/1/2001)*

Torii Mor 2004 Anden Vineyard Pinot Noir (Polk County) $60. 90 *—P.G. (9/1/2006)*

Torii Mor 1999 Balcombe Vineyard Pinot Noir (Yamhill County) $50. 91 *—J.C. (11/1/2001)*

Torii Mor 1998 Balcombe Vineyard Pinot Noir (Willamette Valley) $38. 89 *—J.C. (12/1/2000)*

Torii Mor 2001 Deux Verres Pinot Noir (Willamette Valley) $40. 88 *—P.G. (10/1/2004)*

Torii Mor 2005 Deux Verres Reserve Pinot Noir (Willamette Valley) $45. This is a multi-vineyard blend, designated reserve because it is a barrel selection. It's got more pungent herb and slightly bitter spice than the less expensive black label Pinot, but otherwise is comparable in quality and flavor. Tart, austere, it mixes cranberry, pomegranate and sour cherry with firm acids and lots of herb. **88** *—P.G. (11/15/2007)*

Torii Mor 2004 Deux Verres Reserve Pinot Noir (Willamette Valley) $42. 89 *—P.G. (9/1/2006)*

Torii Mor 2005 Hawks View Vineyard Pinot Noir (Chehalem Mountain) $60. This is light and flavored with cranberry and hints of rhubarb. There's not much midpalate; once past the young fruit you go directly to tannins that are rather stemmy and hard. Maybe it needs more bottle age, but right now it's chewy and a bit on the sour side. **86** *—P.G. (11/15/2007)*

Torii Mor 2002 Hawks View Vineyard Pinot Noir (Washington County) $40. 87 *(11/1/2004)*

Torii Mor 2005 La Colina Vineyard Pinot Noir (Dundee Hills) $55. The juice is sharp and spicy, with some baking spice and cinnamon livening up the back of the palate. The fruit flavors suggest boysenberry and blackberry, set up against stiff acids and earthy tannins. Young and still a little rough around the edges, this distinctive bottling should be cellared for a few years and could go as long as a decade or more. **90 Cellar Selection** *—P.G. (11/15/2007)*

Torii Mor 2005 La Cuillère Member's Reserve Pinot Noir (Willamette Valley) $55. A blend of seven different vineyards, the name is French for spoon. This is a softer, less tannic wine than most of the other Torii Mor 2005s, but is not quite what you would call silky. Mixed red fruits, light scents suggesting flower as well as berry, and a feminine elegance characterize this Pinot. It's been carefully crafted to emphasize the subtle herbs and spices, without hiding behind the more obvious flavors of new oak. **90** *—P.G. (11/15/2007)*

Torii Mor 2005 Olson Vineyard Pinot Noir (Dundee Hills) $65. The vines were planted in 1972, making this one of the oldest vineyards in Oregon. Just a half ton an acre is brought in, 110 cases total. It's a pleasure to taste Oregon Pinot from vines this old; they have a certain grace and sensuous elegance that the young vines can't muster. Beautiful aromas are complex with mixed fruits, hints of mushroom and dried leaves. It's a silky, nicely defined wine that should age along Burgundian lines. **91 Cellar Selection** *—P.G. (11/15/2007)*

Torii Mor 2004 Olson Estate Vineyard Pinot Noir (Dundee Hills) $55. 90 *—P.G. (9/1/2006)*

Torii Mor 2002 Olson Vineyard Pinot Noir (Yamhill County) $42. 85 *(11/1/2004)*

Torii Mor 2001 Olson Vineyard Pinot Noir (Yamhill County) $40. 85 *—P.G. (10/1/2004)*

Torii Mor 1999 Olson Vineyard Pinot Noir (Yamhill County) $50. 90 *—J.C. (11/1/2001)*

Torii Mor 2000 Olson Vineyard East Slope Pinot Noir (Willamette Valley) $50. 87 *(10/1/2002)*

Torii Mor 2002 Reserve Deux Verres Pinot Noir (Willamette Valley) $35. 85 *(11/1/2004)*

Torii Mor 1999 Seven Springs Pinot Noir (Polk County) $50. 91 *—S.H. (8/1/2002)*

Torii Mor 2002 Seven Springs Vineyard Pinot Noir (Polk County) $40. 83 *(11/1/2004)*

Torii Mor 2000 Seven Springs Vineyard Pinot Noir (Oregon) $48. 90 *—P.G. (12/31/2002)*

Torii Mor 2004 Shea Vineyard Pinot Noir (Willamette Valley) $75. 87 *—P.G. (9/1/2006)*

Torii Mor 2002 Temperance Hill Vineyard Pinot Noir (Polk County) $40. 90 *(11/1/2004)*

Torii Mor 1999 Temperance Hill Vineyard Pinot Noir (Polk County) $50. 88 *(10/1/2002)*

Torii Mor 1998 Temperance Hill Vineyard Pinot Noir (Polk County) $40. 87 *—M.S. (12/1/2000)*

TORTOISE CREEK

Tortoise Creek 2004 Big Smile Pinot Noir (Central Coast) $14. 82 *—S.H. (12/31/2005)*

TOTT'S

Tott's NV Blanc de Noir Champagne Blend (California) $7. 80 *—S.H. (12/15/1999)*

Tott's NV Extra Dry Champagne Blend (California) $7. 82 *—S.H. (12/15/1999)*

Tott's NV Extra Dry Reserve Cuvée Champagne Blend (California) $7. 84 *—S.H. (12/1/2002)*

Tott's NV Reserve Cuvée Brut Champagne Blend (California) $11. 84 *—S.H. (12/1/2002)*

Tott's 2000 Reserve Cuvée Brut Champagne Blend (California) $7. 82 *—S.H. (12/15/1999)*

Tott's NV Brut Sparkling Blend (California) $7. 83 *—S.H. (12/31/2005)*

Tott's NV Extra Dry Sparkling Blend (California) $7. 83 *—S.H. (12/31/2005)*

TOWNSHEND

Townshend 2001 Reserve Bordeaux Blend (Columbia Valley (WA)) $34. It spends over 30 months in French and American oak, and emerges with more tannin, more density, but less bouquet and elegance than the other reds. Possibly a bit past its prime; it's a fine effort, just not the leap ahead in quality one would hope for, given the rest of the wines. This is 55% Cab, 30% Cab Franc, 15% Merlot. **88** *—P.G. (3/1/2007)*

Townshend 2000 Reserve Bordeaux Blend (Columbia Valley (WA)) $35. 88 *—P.G. (4/1/2006)*

Townshend 2001 Cabernet Franc (Columbia Valley (WA)) $24. Excellent varietal character and definition. This is the most firm and tannic of Townshend's lineup, an earthy, slightly chalky wine. The fruit is clean and well-delineated, with grace notes of coffee and coconut; just not quite as lingering as its siblings. **88** *—P.G. (3/1/2007)*

Townshend 2001 Cabernet Sauvignon (Columbia Valley (WA)) $29. Another fine effort in mid-life, this Cabernet shows fruit heading into maturity, with hints of prune, cooked cherry and raisin. You will also taste caramel, brown sugar, smoke, pepper—a three-ring circus of flavor, but always done in an elegant, balanced, food-friendly style. **90** *—P.G. (3/1/2007)*

Townshend 2000 Cabernet Sauvignon (Columbia Valley (WA)) $27. 89 *—P.G. (4/1/2006)*

Townshend 2004 Chenin Blanc (Columbia Valley (WA)) $10. This is Washington Chenin like you've never seen it—barrel fermented and concentrated like fruit candy. Unique and distinctive, bursting with floral scents and the honeyed sweetness of the grape, it's nonetheless a reasonably dry Chenin that clocks in at 13.4% alcohol. Wonderful long finish. **90 Best Buy** *—P.G. (3/1/2007)*

Townshend 2004 Chenin Blanc (Yakima Valley) $10. 90 Best Buy *—P.G. (6/1/2006)*

Townshend 2005 Lemberger (Yakima Valley) $15. If anyone can make converts to Lemberger, Washington's one-time answer to Zinfandel, it's talented winemaker Don Townshend. This bright, tangy, raspberry-laden wine comes across as a stable-mate to Grenache or a light Dry Creek Zin, but it really occupies a niche all its own. Barrel-aged and ripened to a moderate 13.5% alcohol, it screams out for pizza. **87** *—P.G. (12/31/2007)*

Townshend 2001 Merlot (Columbia Valley (WA)) $24. This is the current release, nicely aged and drinking like a mature, well-cellared wine. A bit of Cabernet and Cabernet Franc are blended in to beef it up, but it's Merlot that is the star here, with lovely mature flavors of dried cherry, dried plum and tobacco. Brilliant structure and surprising length. **89** *—P.G. (3/1/2007)*

Townshend 2004 Riesling (Yakima Valley) $10. 91 Best Buy *—P.G. (4/1/2006)*

Townshend 2003 Sangiovese (Columbia Valley (WA)) $19. Don Townshend has a gift for crafting wines of elegance. This feather-light Sangio is beautifully balanced, slightly floral, and blessed with good length. The fruit is almost ethereal, but not wimpy, attenuated or dull. It's like drinking air. **87** *—P.G. (3/1/2007)*

Townshend 2005 Sauvignon Blanc (Columbia Valley (WA)) $10. Fragrant, elegant to the point of delicate, with suggestions of mint, chervil, hay and fresh greens. Flavors favor fig, lemon wax; nothing aggressively herbaceous here, but the grape retains its varietal grassiness. Such length and delicacy in such an inexpensive wine. **90 Best Buy** *—P.G. (3/1/2007)*

Townshend 2003 Syrah (Columbia Valley (WA)) $19. Another stylish wine with a light touch. The flavors are airy, like whipped butter, but full and never tiring. Citrus and berry fill the palate, along with cracked pepper and dried leaf. A lovely, elegant Syrah. **89** *—P.G. (3/1/2007)*

Townshend 2002 Syrah (Columbia Valley (WA)) $20. 90 *—P.G. (4/1/2006)*

Townshend 2004 Viognier (Columbia Valley (WA)) $10. A showstopper! This intense wine sports an unusual mix of scents—wood, flower, fruit candy and menthol mint. There's a resinous quality that lifts the palate, and a honeyed toastiness wrapped into a wine of extraordinary concentration. **91** *—P.G. (3/1/2007)*

TRAVIESO

Travieso 2003 Watts Vineyard Compañero Ciego Syrah (Lodi) $27. 87 *—S.H. (12/1/2006)*

TREANA

Treana 2003 Red Blend (Paso Robles) $52. 87 *—S.H. (12/15/2006)*

Treana 2001 Red Blend (Central Coast) $52. 90 *—S.H. (7/1/2005)*

Treana 2000 Red Blend (Central Coast) $35. 88 *—S.H. (5/1/2004)*

Treana 1998 Red Blend (Central Coast) $35. 85 *—S.H. (8/1/2001)*

Treana 1999 Red Table Wine Red Blend (Central Coast) $35. 89 *—J.M. (9/1/2003)*

Treana 1997 Rhône Red Blend (Central Coast) $35. 88 *—S.H. (11/15/2000)*

Treana 2004 Mer Soleil Vineyard Rhône White Blend (Central Coast) $25. Drier, tarter and more minerally than usual, this elegant Viognier-Marsanne blend comes from a vineyard in the northern part of the Santa Lucia Highlands. Despite the warmth of the vintage, the wine is bone dry and quite acidic, but very complex in Meyer lemon zest, vanilla and honey flavors. **90** *—S.H. (10/1/2007)*

Treana 2001 Mer Soleil Vineyard Rhône White Blend (Central Coast) $25. 93 *—S.H. (7/1/2003)*

Treana 2000 Mer Soleil Vineyard Rhône White Blend (Central Coast) $25. 90 *—J.M. (9/1/2002)*

Treana 1999 Mer Soleil Vineyard Rhône White Blend (Central Coast) $25. 91 *—J.M. (9/1/2002)*

Treana 2003 Mer Soleil Vineyard Viognier-Marsanne Rhône White Blend (Central Coast) $25. 94 Editors' Choice *—S.H. (12/15/2006)*

Treana 2002 Austin Hope Roussanne (Central Coast) $39. 89 *—S.H. (2/1/2004)*

Treana 2002 Austin Hope Syrah (Paso Robles) $42. 92 *—S.H. (4/1/2005)*

Treana 2001 Austin Hope Syrah (Paso Robles) $49. 91 *—S.H. (12/1/2003)*

Treana 2000 Austin Hope Syrah (Paso Robles) $48. 89 *—S.H. (12/1/2003)*

Treana 2002 Mer Soleil Vineyard White Blend (Central Coast) $25. 90 *—S.H. (8/1/2005)*

Treana 1997 Mer Soleil Vineyard White Blend (Central Coast) $25. 86 *(10/1/1999)*

TRECINI

Trecini 2006 Vicini's Vineyard Rosé Merlot (Russian River Valley) $14. Rosés from Merlot often seem heavy to me, as the variety doesn't easily lend itself to blushdom. So it is here. On the other hand, the wine is rich and effusive in cherry, raspberry and vanilla flavors, and is nicely dry. **84** *—S.H. (7/1/2007)*

TREFETHEN

Trefethen 1997 Cabernet Sauvignon (Napa Valley) $30. 88 *(11/1/2000)*

Trefethen 2002 Estate Grown Cabernet Sauvignon (Oak Knoll) $45. 83 *—S.H. (11/1/2006)*

Trefethen 2001 Reserve Cabernet Sauvignon (Oak Knoll) $80. 86 *—S.H. (9/1/2006)*

Trefethen 1995 Reserve Cabernet Sauvignon (Napa Valley) $60. 90 *(3/1/2000)*

Trefethen 1998 Chardonnay (Napa Valley) $21. 87 *(10/1/2000)*

Trefethen 2004 Chardonnay (Oak Knoll) $30. 88 *—S.H. (11/1/2006)*

Trefethen 2000 Chardonnay (Napa Valley) $22. 87 *—S.H. (2/1/2003)*

Trefethen 1997 Estate Chardonnay (Napa Valley) $21. 86 *(6/1/2000)*

Trefethen 1995 Library Selection Chardonnay (Napa Valley) $37. 89 *(7/1/2001)*

Trefethen 2002 Estate Grown Merlot (Oak Knoll) $30. 83 *—S.H. (11/1/2006)*

Trefethen 2002 Riesling (Napa Valley) $15. 82 *—J.M. (8/1/2003)*

Trefethen 2005 Dry Riesling (Oak Knoll) $20. 90 Editors' Choice *—S.H. (11/1/2006)*

Trefethen 1999 Dry Riesling (Napa Valley) $15. 83 *(9/1/2000)*

Trefethen 1998 Dry Estate Bottled Riesling (Napa Valley) $14. 87 *—M.S. (11/15/1999)*

Trefethen 2001 Late Harvest Riesling (Napa Valley) $40. 92 *—J.M. (12/31/2003)*

TRELLIS

Trellis 1997 Cabernet Sauvignon (Sonoma County) $15. 83 *—S.H. (9/1/2000)*

Trellis 1999 Cabernet Sauvignon (Sonoma County) $19. 86 *—S.H. (6/1/2003)*

Trellis 2000 Alexander Valley Cabernet Sauvignon (Alexander Valley) $19. 87 *—S.H. (11/15/2004)*

Trellis 1997 Reserve Cabernet Sauvignon (Sonoma County) $39. 88 *—S.H. (12/15/2000)*

Trellis 1997 Chardonnay (Sonoma County) $11. 86 *—S.H. (11/1/1999)*

Trellis 2000 Chardonnay (Russian River Valley) $15. 85 *—S.H. (6/1/2003)*

Trellis 1998 Chardonnay (Russian River Valley) $11. 85 *—S.H. (10/1/2000)*

Trellis 2001 Clone #15 Chardonnay (Russian River Valley) $25. 89 *—S.H. (5/1/2003)*

Trellis 2002 Russian River Valley Chardonnay (Russian River Valley) $15. 84 *—S.H. (9/1/2004)*

Trellis 2000 Merlot (Alexander Valley) $17. 90 *—S.H. (9/1/2004)*

Trellis 1999 Merlot (Sonoma County) $17. 90 Editors' Choice *—S.H. (8/1/2003)*

Trellis 1997 Sauvignon Blanc (Sonoma County) $13. 88 *—S.H. (11/1/1999)*

Trellis 2002 Sauvignon Blanc (Dry Creek Valley) $13. 85 *—S.H. (9/1/2004)*

Trellis 1998 Special Selection Sauvignon Blanc (Sonoma County) $11. 84 *(9/1/2000)*

TRENTADUE

Trentadue 2003 La Storia Meritage Red Wine Bordeaux Blend (Alexander Valley) $45. 84 *—S.H. (12/15/2006)*

Trentadue 2004 Cabernet Sauvignon (Alexander Valley) $22. Dry and tannic, this Cab has flavors of cooked berries and cured tobacco. It's kind of old-fashioned. **84** *—S.H. (11/1/2007)*

Trentadue 2001 Cabernet Sauvignon (Sonoma County) $18. 89 *—S.H. (6/1/2004)*

Trentadue 2003 Geyservile Estate Cabernet Sauvignon (Alexander Valley) $22. 81 *—S.H. (12/15/2006)*

Trentadue 2000 La Storia Red Meritage (Alexander Valley) $45. 90 *—S.H. (5/1/2004)*

Trentadue 2003 Merlot (Alexander Valley) $18. 82 *—S.H. (12/15/2006)*

Trentadue 2001 Merlot (Alexander Valley) $16. 87 *—S.H. (6/1/2004)*

Trentadue 2004 Geyserville Estate Merlot (Alexander Valley) $18. Feels hot and heavy in the mouth, and although it's fully dry, there's a Port-y, cooked berry taste. **82** *—S.H. (11/1/2007)*

Trentadue 2004 Petite Sirah (North Coast) $18. 87 *—S.H. (12/31/2006)*

Trentadue 2002 Petite Sirah (Alexander Valley) $28. 89 *—S.H. (3/1/2005)*

Trentadue 2000 Petite Sirah (Dry Creek Valley) $20. 87 *(4/1/2003)*

Trentadue 2004 La Storia Cuvée 32 Red Blend (Alexander Valley) $32. Trentadue is building up a pretty good track record with this old-fashioned, field blend-style wine. Although the '04 isn't their best effort, it's dry and well-structured in acids and tannins, with a rich, earthy tang of tobacco and dried fruits. Mainly Sangiovese, Cab Sauvignon and Merlot. **86** *—S.H. (11/1/2007)*

Trentadue 2003 La Storia Cuvée 32 Red Wine Red Blend (Alexander Valley) $32. 88 *—S.H. (12/15/2006)*

Trentadue 2005 Old Patch Red Red Blend (Sonoma County) $14. This field-style blend of Petite Sirah, Carignane and Syrah is super-jammy, with jellied flavors of raspberries, cherries, blueberries, blackberries and loganberries. It's a fun, fairly complicated wine that finishes dry and tannic. **86** *—S.H. (11/1/2007)*

Trentadue 2004 Old Patch Red Red Blend (Sonoma County) $14. 85 *—S.H. (12/31/2006)*

Trentadue 2002 Old Patch Red Red Blend (North Coast) $16. 84 *—S.H. (5/1/2004)*

Trentadue 2001 Sangiovese (Alexander Valley) $16. 83 *—S.H. (5/1/2004)*

Trentadue 2000 La Storia Cuvée 32 Sangiovese (Alexander Valley) $32. 92 *—S.H. (5/1/2004)*

Trentadue 2005 Sauvignon Blanc (Dry Creek Valley) $14. 87 *—S.H. (12/15/2006)*

Trentadue 2003 Sauvignon Blanc (Dry Creek Valley) $14. 86 *—S.H. (2/1/2005)*

Trentadue 2000 Viognier (Dry Creek Valley) $18. 89 *—J.M. (12/15/2002)*

Trentadue 2002 Zinfandel (Dry Creek Valley) $18. 87 *—S.H. (3/1/2005)*

Trentadue 2001 Zinfandel (Dry Creek Valley) $14. 89 Best Buy *(11/1/2003)*

Trentadue 2004 La Storia Zinfandel (Alexander Valley) $28. 91 *—S.H. (12/15/2006)*

TRES SABORES

Tres Sabores 2004 Perspective Cabernet Sauvignon (Rutherford) $56. A very distinctive 100% Cab that some might even find controversial. It's ripe almost to the point of supermaturity, showing powerful currant and licorice flavors that are very well oaked. Finishes hard in tannins in its youth. Aims, with some success, at an extracted, modern or cult style. **88** *—S.H. (12/15/2007)*

Tres Sabores 2003 Perspective Cabernet Sauvignon (Rutherford) $48. 90 Cellar Selection *—S.H. (12/15/2006)*

Tres Sabores 2002 Perspective Cabernet Sauvignon (Rutherford) $45. 84 *—S.H. (12/15/2005)*

Tres Sabores 2001 Perspective Cabernet Sauvignon (Rutherford) $45. 89 —*S.H. (10/1/2004)*

Tres Sabores 2000 Karen Culler Zinfandel (Napa Valley) $30. 92 Editors' Choice —*J.M. (9/1/2003)*

Tres Sabores 2001 Ken Bernards Zinfandel (Rutherford) $38. 90 *(11/1/2003)*

Tres Sabores 2000 Ken Bernards Zinfandel (Napa Valley) $30. 93 Editors' Choice —*J.M. (9/1/2003)*

Tres Sabores 2001 Rudy Zuidema Zinfandel (Rutherford) $38. 90 *(11/1/2003)*

Tres Sabores 2000 Rudy Zuidema Zinfandel (Napa Valley) $30. 92 Editors' Choice —*J.M. (9/1/2003)*

TRESPASS

Trespass 2003 Cabernet Sauvignon (Napa Valley) $55. This is a wine that needed serious aeration. Although it started out mute and closed, it opened up to reveal polished cedar. mocha and black currant flavors, wrapped into creamy smooth tannins. A lovely young wine, it's good now, with decanting, but also should age for 8–10 years. **89** —*S.H. (5/1/2007)*

TREY MARIE

Trey Marie 1999 Trutina Cabernet Sauvignon-Merlot (Columbia Valley (WA)) $29. 87 —*D.T. (12/31/2002)*

Trey Marie 1998 Trutina Merlot-Cabernet Sauvignon (Columbia Valley (WA)) $30. 89 —*P.G. (6/1/2001)*

TRIA

Tria 1998 Pinot Noir (Carneros) $21. 86 —*S.H. (12/15/2001)*

Tria 1996 Syrah (Sonoma County) $20. 87 —*S.H. (10/1/1999)*

Tria 1997 Syrah (Monterey) $19. 86 —*S.H. (11/15/2001)*

Tria 1997 Viognier (Napa Valley) $14. 89 —*S.H. (10/1/1999)*

Tria 1998 Zinfandel (Dry Creek Valley) $18. 87 —*S.H. (11/15/2001)*

TRINCHERO

Trinchero 2004 Mario's Reserve Meritage Bordeaux Blend (Napa Valley) $45. Dry and tannic compared to today's lush, over-the-top Napa style, this Cabernet-based Bordeaux blend hearkens back to the old Inglenook and Martini Cabs, which were ready to drink on release, yet aged for a long time. It's a lovely wine, with rich cassis, pencil lead and cedar flavors that finish with complexity and elegance. Best now and for a good 10 years or more. **91 Cellar Selection** —*S.H. (10/1/2007)*

Trinchero 2000 Mario's Reserve Meritage Cabernet Blend (Napa Valley) $45. 92 —*S.H. (5/1/2003)*

Trinchero 2005 Cabernet Sauvignon (California) $12. This Cabernet is pretty simple and sugary-jammy. **82** —*S.H. (11/15/2007)*

Trinchero 2003 Chicken Ranch Reserve Cabernet Sauvignon (Rutherford) $30. 86 —*S.H. (12/31/2005)*

Trinchero 2001 Chicken Ranch Reserve Cabernet Sauvignon (Rutherford) $24. 89 —*S.H. (10/1/2004)*

Trinchero 2004 Chicken Ranch Vineyard Cabernet Sauvignon (Rutherford) $30. Made from 100% Cabernet, this wine is a bit light in fruit. It has cherry Lifesaver flavors that were thinned down with herbs, and is fairly tannic. Not an ageworthy blockbuster, but it shows the elegant structure of its appellation. **86** —*S.H. (12/15/2007)*

Trinchero 2002 Chicken Ranch Vineyard Cabernet Sauvignon (Rutherford) $25. 92 Editors' Choice —*S.H. (10/1/2005)*

Trinchero 2003 Family Selection Cabernet Sauvignon (California) $12. 85 *(4/1/2006)*

Trinchero 1999 Family Selection Cabernet Sauvignon (California) $12. 85 —*S.H. (2/1/2003)*

Trinchero 1998 Family Selection Cabernet Sauvignon (California) $14. 84 —*S.H. (11/15/2001)*

Trinchero 2003 Lewelling Vineyard Cabernet Sauvignon (Napa Valley) $50. Very oaky. So oaky, in fact, it's hard to get past all that woodsap and toasty char. Tannic, too. But for all the tannins and wood, the fruit just isn't strong enough. **83** —*S.H. (5/1/2007)*

Trinchero 2002 Lewelling Vineyard Cabernet Sauvignon (Napa Valley) $40. 89 *(4/1/2006)*

Trinchero 2001 Lewelling Vineyard Cabernet Sauvignon (Napa Valley) $45. 85 —*S.H. (10/1/2005)*

Trinchero 1999 Lewelling Vineyard Cabernet Sauvignon (Napa Valley) $38. 91 —*S.H. (6/1/2002)*

Trinchero 2003 Main Street Vineyard Cabernet Sauvignon (Napa Valley) $45. Ripely fruity in good Cabernet flavors, with blackberries and cherries spiced with toasty oak. This is a decent, classy wine. Drink now–2010. **86** —*S.H. (5/1/2007)*

Trinchero 2002 Main Street Vineyard Cabernet Sauvignon (Napa Valley) $40. 90 *(4/1/2006)*

Trinchero 2001 Main Street Vineyard Cabernet Sauvignon (St. Helena) $40. 84 —*S.H. (10/1/2005)*

Trinchero 1999 Mario's Reserve Cabernet Sauvignon (Napa Valley) $45. 91 —*S.H. (12/31/2002)*

Trinchero 1998 Mario's Reserve Cabernet Sauvignon (Napa Valley) $40. 90 —*S.H. (6/1/2002)*

Trinchero 1997 Proprietor's Series Cabernet Sauvignon (Napa Valley) $18. 88 —*S.H. (5/1/2001)*

Trinchero 2000 RSVP Lewelling Vineyard Cabernet Sauvignon (Napa Valley) $45. 90 —*S.H. (8/1/2003)*

Trinchero 2004 Stagecoach Vineyard Cabernet Sauvignon (Napa Valley) $50. Give this one some time to breathe, as it's a bit tight on opening. With a relatively modest 13.5% alcohol, it's not as ripe as some Napa Cabs, and it's also fairly tannic. There's an astringent, tea-like edge to the cassis and cherries. Finely structured and bone dry, this Cab should develop well over the next eight years. **90** —*S.H. (10/1/2007)*

Trinchero 1999 Family Selection Chardonnay (California) $12. 85 *(8/1/2001)*

Trinchero 2000 Mario's Reserve Chardonnay (Napa Valley) $30. 85 —*S.H. (12/1/2003)*

Trinchero 2000 Trinity Oaks Vineyard Chardonnay (California) $10. 85 —*S.H. (6/1/2003)*

Trinchero 2003 Mario's Reserve Meritage (Napa Valley) $40. 90 *(4/1/2006)*

Trinchero 2002 Mario's Reserve Meritage (Rutherford) $45. 85 —*S.H. (10/1/2005)*

Trinchero 2002 Chicken Ranch Vineyard Merlot (Rutherford) $25. 87 —*S.H. (10/1/2005)*

Trinchero 1999 Chicken Ranch Vineyard Merlot (Rutherford) $25. 89 —*S.H. (6/1/2002)*

Trinchero 2003 Day Break Block Merlot (Napa Valley) $25. 87 *(4/1/2006)*

Trinchero 2002 Family Selection Merlot (Monterey County) $10. 86 —*S.H. (10/1/2004)*

Trinchero 2000 Family Selection Merlot (California) $12. 86 —*S.H. (4/1/2003)*

Trinchero 1999 Family Selection Merlot (California) $12. 87 Best Buy —*J.M. (6/1/2002)*

Trinchero 1998 Family Selection Merlot (California) $12. 88 Best Buy *(8/1/2001)*

Trinchero 1998 Family Selection Merlot (California) $12. 88 *(8/1/2001)*

Trinchero 1999 Mee Vineyard Merlot (Rutherford) $28. 91 —*J.M. (6/1/2002)*

Trinchero 1998 Proprietor's Series Moscato (California) $12. 89 —*S.H. (5/1/2001)*

Trinchero 2003 Petite Verdot (St. Helena) $40. 88 Cellar Selection *(4/1/2006)*

Trinchero 2002 Pinot Noir (Napa Valley) $12. 88 *(11/1/2004)*

Trinchero 2004 Family Selection Pinot Noir (Napa Valley) $12. 84 —*S.H. (3/1/2006)*

Trinchero 2003 Family Selection Pinot Noir (Napa Valley) $10. 84 —*S.H. (10/1/2004)*

Trinchero 2004 Vista Montone Pinot Noir (Napa Valley) $25. 87 *(4/1/2006)*

Trinchero 2003 Vista Montone Pinot Noir (Napa Valley) $25. 85 —*S.H. (10/1/2005)*

Trinchero 2006 Family Riesling (Monterey County) $10. Acidity, the kind that makes the tastebuds bristle, is what makes this semi-sweet Riesling a success. Without it, the ripe apricot, pineapple, peach and honey flavors would be flat and simple. With it, the wine is bright and succulent. A sweet, sugar-glazed ham will be a match made in heaven. **86 Best Buy** —*S.H. (9/1/2007)*

Trinchero 2006 Sauvignon Blanc (Santa Barbara County) $10. Awkward and dry, with green citrus and vegetal flavors. **82** —*S.H. (11/15/2007)*

Trinchero 2000 Sauvignon Blanc (California) $12. 85 —*J.M. (9/1/2002)*

Trinchero 2005 Family Selection Sauvignon Blanc (Santa Barbara County) $12. 85 *(4/1/2006)*

Trinchero 2003 Family Selection Sauvignon Blanc (Napa Valley) $9. 85 Best Buy —*S.H. (10/1/2004)*

Trinchero 2001 Family Selection Sauvignon Blanc (California) $12. 84 —*S.H. (3/1/2003)*

Trinchero 1999 Mary's Vineyard Sauvignon Blanc (Napa Valley) $18. 87 *(8/1/2001)*

Trinchero 1998 Proprietor's Series Sauvignon Blanc (Monterey County) $14. 85 —*S.H. (5/1/2001)*

Trinchero 2005 Syrah (Monterey County) $12. Soft and syrupy, this simple Syrah has ripe cherry and raspberry jam flavors. **82** —*S.H. (11/15/2007)*

TRINITAS

Trinitas 2003 Old Vine Mataro (Contra Costa County) $25. 88 —*S.H. (11/15/2005)*

Trinitas 2003 Petite Sirah (Russian River Valley) $32. 90 —*S.H. (3/1/2006)*

Trinitas 2002 Petite Sirah (Russian River Valley) $32. 88 —*S.H. (12/15/2004)*

Trinitas 2003 Old Vine Petite Sirah (Lodi) $22. 83 —*S.H. (3/1/2006)*

Trinitas 2002 Old Vine Petite Sirah (Lodi) $22. 85 —*S.H. (12/15/2004)*

Trinitas 2004 Pinot Blanc (Russian River Valley) $20. 87 —*S.H. (11/15/2005)*

Trinitas 2003 Pinot Blanc (Russian River Valley) $20. 86 —*S.H. (12/15/2004)*

Trinitas 2003 Old Vine Cuvée Red Blend (Contra Costa County) $18. 86 —*S.H. (11/15/2005)*

Trinitas 2001 Zinfandel (Russian River Valley) $28. 89 *(11/1/2003)*

Trinitas 2002 Bigalow Vineyard Zinfandel (Contra Costa County) $28. 82 —*S.H. (12/15/2004)*

Trinitas 2002 Old Vine Zinfandel (Contra Costa County) $18. 85 —*S.H. (6/1/2004)*

TRINITY OAKS

Trinity Oaks 1998 Cabernet Sauvignon (California) $10. 86 *(8/1/2001)*

Trinity Oaks 1999 Chardonnay (California) $10. 85 Best Buy *(8/1/2001)*

Trinity Oaks 1998 Merlot (California) $10. 83 *(8/1/2001)*

Trinity Oaks 2004 Pinot Grigio (California) $5. 83 Best Buy —*S.H. (2/1/2006)*

Trinity Oaks 2002 Pinot Grigio (California) $8. 82 —*M.S. (12/1/2003)*

Trinity Oaks 2006 Riesling (California) $7. Soft, sweet and simple, with apricot, peach, citrus and honey flavors. Blended with 3% Gewürztraminer. **83** —*S.H. (9/1/2007)*

Trinity Oaks 1999 Zinfandel (California) $10. 87 Best Buy *(8/1/2001)*

TRIO

Trio 2003 Claret Red Wine Bordeaux Blend (Howell Mountain) $34. A Merlot-based Bordeaux blend, this stylish wine shows Howell Mountain's ability to craft a big, dense wine, but the tannins are soft and lush enough to drink now. Cab Sauvignon adds depth, while Cab Franc brings a cherry candy deliciousness. It's beautiful now, and should hang in there for 5–7 years. **91** —*S.H. (4/1/2007)*

TRIO VINTNERS

Trio Vintners 2006 Lewis Vineyards Riesling (Yakima Valley) $12. This is a lovely, orange blossom special. Sweet and tart, penetrating and long, with lovely peaches, apricots and oranges lighting it up. **89** —*P.G. (12/1/2007)*

Trio Vintners 2006 Trés Rosé Blend (Columbia Valley (WA)) $14. Bright and tasting of cherry LifeSavers and strawberry jam. The off-dry approach works here; it's got great texture, slight spritz and flavors well beyond simple sweet fruit. A 50/50 Mourvèdre/Sangiovese blend. Just 50 cases produced. **88** —*P.G. (12/1/2007)*

Trio Vintners 2005 Sangiovese (Wahluke Slope) $18. The color is very pretty, and the wine a bit tight. As it opens up it is surprisingly chewy, leafy and slightly hot at 14.1% alcohol. Perhaps from young vines? **85** —*P.G. (12/1/2007)*

Trio Vintners 2004 Boushey Vineyard Syrah (Yakima Valley) $24. This is young, peppery, tart and lively. Pleasing herbal textures lead into fruit laced with wild thyme. Clean and expressive, in a light, herbal style. **87** —*P.G. (12/1/2007)*

TROON VINEYARDS

Troon Vineyards 1999 Cabernet Sauvignon (Applegate Valley) $15. 85 —*P.G. (8/1/2002)*

Troon Vineyards 1999 Reserve Cabernet Sauvignon (Applegate Valley) $19. 85 —*P.G. (8/1/2002)*

Troon Vineyards 2002 Ltd. Reserve II Cabernet Sauvignon-Syrah (Applegate Valley) $25. 85 —*P.G. (9/1/2006)*

Troon Vineyards 2003 Estate Reserve Zinfandel (Applegate Valley) $60. 84 —*P.G. (9/1/2006)*

Troon Vineyards 2002 Estate Reserve Zinfandel (Applegate Valley) $100. 87 —*P.G. (9/1/2006)*

Troon Vineyards 1999 Reserve Zinfandel (Applegate Valley) $19. 86 —*P.G. (8/1/2002)*

TROU DE BONDE

Trou de Bonde 2004 Bien Nacido Vineyard Pinot Blanc (Santa Maria Valley) $18. 94 Editors' Choice —*S.H. (8/1/2006)*

TRUCHARD

Truchard 1998 Cabernet Sauvignon (Carneros) $38. 85 —*J.M. (6/1/2002)*

Truchard 1997 Cabernet Sauvignon (Carneros) $35.94 *(11/1/2000)*

Truchard 1996 Cabernet Sauvignon (Carneros) $32. 86 —*L.W. (12/31/1999)*

Truchard 1997 Reserve Cabernet Sauvignon (Carneros) $75. 91 —*J.M. (6/1/2002)*

Truchard 1995 Reserve Cabernet Sauvignon (Carneros) $55. 88 —*L.W. (12/31/1999)*

Truchard 2002 Chardonnay (Carneros) $28. 87 —*S.H. (8/1/2005)*

Truchard 2000 Chardonnay (Carneros) $30. 90 —*S.H. (5/1/2003)*

Truchard 1999 Chardonnay (Carneros) $30. 91 *(7/1/2001)*

Truchard 1998 Chardonnay (Carneros) $28. 90 *(6/1/2000)*

Truchard 2003 Merlot (Carneros) $28. Ripe to the point of raisiny, with sugary currant, cherry-pie filling and root beer flavors, this Merlot lacks balance. **83** —*S.H. (12/31/2007)*

Truchard 1998 Merlot (Carneros) $32. 88 —*J.M. (6/1/2002)*

Truchard 1996 Merlot (Carneros) $26. 92 —*L.W. (12/31/1999)*

Truchard 2004 Pinot Noir (Carneros) $28. Soft, silky and direct in its appeal, this has rich flavors of raspberries, cherries, cola, vanilla and woodspice. It's a good wine that would benefit from additional layers of complexity. **86** —*R.V. (12/31/2007)*

Truchard 2001 Pinot Noir (Carneros) $28. 85 —*S.H. (8/1/2005)*

Truchard 2000 Pinot Noir (Carneros) $32. 89 *(10/1/2002)*

Truchard 1999 Pinot Noir (Carneros) $32. 90 —*J.M. (5/1/2002)*

Truchard 2005 Roussanne (Carneros) $20. Packs plenty of powerful complexity into a dry wine that's a pretty good price. Made in full-Burgundian style, with barrel fermentation and lees aging, it's a rich, creamy wine packed with spicy tropical fruit and honeysuckle flavors. Try as an interesting alternative to an upscale Chardonnay. **91 Editors' Choice** —*R.V. (12/31/2007)*

Truchard 2002 Roussanne (Carneros) $25. 90 —*S.H. (8/1/2005)*

Truchard 2000 Roussanne (Carneros) $28. 91 —*J.M. (12/1/2001)*

Truchard 2002 Syrah (Carneros) $28. 93 Editors' Choice *(9/1/2005)*

Truchard 1997 Syrah (Carneros) $30. 89 —*S.H. (6/1/1999)*

Truchard 1999 Estate/Carneros Syrah (Carneros) $35. 88 *(11/1/2001)*

Truchard 1997 Zinfandel (Carneros) $20. 91 —*L.W. (9/1/1999)*

Truchard 2000 AVA's: Carneros/Napa Valley Zinfandel (California) $28. 88 —*S.H. (9/1/2002)*

TRUE EARTH

True Earth NV Cabernet Blend (Mendocino) $13. A mixture of Cabernet Sauvignon, Merlot and Petite Sirah, this has a funky smell, and tastes sweet and soft. **82** —*S.H. (11/1/2007)*

True Earth NV Chardonnay (Mendocino) $13. From certified organic grapes comes this clean, fruity Chard. There's little, if any oak; the fruit stars here, a burst of green apples, pears and spices, brightened with good acids. **85** —*S.H. (11/1/2007)*

TRUEBLOOD

Trueblood 2002 Cabernet Sauvignon (Napa Valley) $40. With hard, astringent tannins that give a dry scrubbing to the palate, this Cab isn't offering immediate pleasure, despite a core of ripe blackberry and cherry fruit. The question is, where's it going? **84** —*S.H. (12/1/2007)*

Trueblood 2004 Syrah (Napa Valley) $32. There's real richness in the fruit of this dry wine. It just explodes in blackberry, cassis, blueberry and cranberry flavor. The oak influence, while subtle, adds notes of toast. But be forewarned, the tannins are pretty strong. Great with lamb, grilled sirloin. **88** —*S.H. (12/1/2007)*

TRUSCOTT

Truscott 2005 Old Vine Zinfandel (Mendocino) $15. This is a label from Weibel. With 12% Syrah, it's a soft, simple wine, with spicy, candied flavors of cherries, raspberries and blackberries. Needs greater acidic structure, but okay for everyday fare. **83** *—S.H. (11/15/2007)*

TRUST CELLARS

Trust Cellars 2006 Rosé Cabernet Franc (Columbia Valley (WA)) $16. Inspired by Chinook and Amavi, who also make excellent rosés from Cab Franc, this is quite delicious, round and ripe with mixed cherry and apple fruit flavors. It's on the soft side, very accessible, with beautiful fruit and some delicate spice notes of cinnamon, sandalwood, hints of cotton candy. **89** *—P.G. (12/1/2007)*

Trust Cellars 2006 Riesling (Columbia Valley (WA)) $18. This soft, smooth entry coats the tongue with ripe flavors of peach and apricot. There are lovely highlights of mandarin orange and mixed citrus rind, and for a Riesling it is round and full, with the acid knocked back a bit. A lovely debut from this new Walla Walla winery. **88** *—P.G. (12/1/2007)*

Trust Cellars 2006 Icewine Sémillon (Columbia Valley (WA)) $40. Just 40 cases of half-bottles were produced. Tasting more like a late harvest than a true ice wine, this soft, lush and creamy wine bring lots of mashed banana flavors, very smooth and rich, with butter, caramel and butterscotch. The flavors compound and surround the palate in a luscious blanket of sweets. **90** *—P.G. (12/1/2007)*

Trust Cellars 2005 Syrah (Columbia Valley (WA)) $28. Though quite dark, spicy, smoky, fragrant and seductive, this is a very flavorful wine. Citrusy acids underscore flavors of grapefruit and orange, but the core of the wine is straightforward, pure and ripe berry. It's nice not to fight the fruit with oak; the aromatics are beautiful. **90** *—P.G. (12/1/2007)*

TSILLAN

Tsillan 2003 Syrah (Columbia Valley (WA)) $23. 84 *(9/1/2005)*

TUALATIN ESTATE

Tualatin Estate 1999 Estate Grown Chardonnay (Willamette Valley) $18. 86 *—M.S. (9/1/2003)*

TUALATIN ESTATE

Tualatin Estate 2001 Semi-Sparkling Muscat (Willamette Valley) $16. 86 *—S.H. (12/1/2002)*

Tualatin Estate 1999 Pinot Blanc (Oregon) $15. 88 Best Buy *—M.M. (11/1/2001)*

Tualatin Estate 1998 Pinot Blanc (Willamette Valley) $15. 86 *—L.W. (12/31/1999)*

Tualatin Estate 2001 Estate Grown Pinot Blanc (Willamette Valley) $11. 87 Best Buy *—P.G. (12/1/2003)*

Tualatin Estate 2000 Pinot Noir (Willamette Valley) $29. 85 *(10/1/2002)*

Tualatin Estate 1999 Pinot Noir (Willamette Valley) $24. 88 *—P.G. (4/1/2002)*

Tualatin Estate 1998 Pinot Noir (Willamette Valley) $24. 88 *—M.S. (12/1/2000)*

TUCKER

Tucker 2001 Gewürztraminer (Yakima Valley) $7. 86 *—P.G. (9/1/2002)*

Tucker 2001 Riesling (Yakima Valley) $8. 83 *—P.G. (9/1/2002)*

TUDOR WINES

Tudor Wines 2005 Pinot Noir (Santa Lucia Highlands) $40. Has a heavy, jellied taste that detracts from elegance. Hard to tell why, for the fruit certainly got ripe in cherries, cola and raspberries, and acidity is fine. Drink now. **85** *—S.H. (12/15/2007)*

Tudor Wines 2004 Pinot Noir (Santa Lucia Highlands) $40. Tudor does a good job interpreting Santa Lucia Pinot. This is a big, intensely fruity wine, bold and in-your-face with cherries, raspberries, cola and carob flavors, with the silky elegance that Pinot demands. It's a little obvious. But it's easy to imagine drinking this with a great steak in a fine restaurant. The wine shifts and changes as it warms in the glass. **90** *—S.H. (5/1/2007)*

Tudor Wines 2003 Pinot Noir (Santa Lucia Highlands) $35. 90 *—S.H. (12/1/2005)*

Tudor Wines 2000 Pinot Noir (Santa Lucia Highlands) $35. 90 *—S.H. (12/1/2003)*

Tudor Wines 2005 Tondré Reserve Pinot Noir (Santa Lucia Highlands) $59. This is not a particularly successful bottling. There's a minty edge to the flavor, and the thinness of fruit allows the alcohol to show as heat. On the plus side there is dryness and silkiness. **84** *—S.H. (12/15/2007)*

Tudor Wines 2000 Tondré Vineyard Pinot Noir (Santa Lucia Highlands) $25. 87 *—S.H. (12/1/2003)*

TULAROSA

Tularosa 2003 Shiraz (New Mexico) $12. 80 *—S.H. (3/1/2006)*

Tularosa 2004 Viognier (New Mexico) $14. 84 *—S.H. (3/1/2006)*

TULE BAY

Tule Bay 2002 Chardonnay (Mendocino County) $15. 84 *—S.H. (12/31/2003)*

Tule Bay 2000 Merlot (Mendocino County) $15. 84 *—S.H. (2/1/2004)*

TULIP HILL

Tulip Hill 2000 Cabernet Sauvignon (Napa Valley) $24. 84 *—S.H. (6/1/2004)*

Tulip Hill 2001 Mount Oso Vineyard Cabernet Sauvignon (California) $22. 82 *—S.H. (11/15/2004)*

Tulip Hill 2001 Mount Oso Vineyard Cabernet Sauvignon-Syrah (California) $28. 84 *—S.H. (10/1/2004)*

Tulip Hill 2001 Mount Oso Vineyard Chardonnay (California) $22. 82 *—S.H. (11/15/2004)*

Tulip Hill 2001 Mt. Oso Vineyard Merlot (California) $18. 90 Editors' Choice *—S.H. (5/1/2004)*

Tulip Hill 2002 Mount Oso Vineyard Mirage Merlot-Syrah (California) $24. 87 *—S.H. (10/1/2004)*

Tulip Hill 2001 Sauvignon Blanc (Lake County) $12. 80 *—J.M. (4/1/2004)*

Tulip Hill 2001 Mt. Oso Vineyard Syrah (California) $16. 85 *—S.H. (5/1/2004)*

Tulip Hill 2001 Old Vine Zinfandel (Lake County) $18. 84 *—J.M. (4/1/2004)*

TURLEY

Turley 2000 Estate Petite Sirah (Napa Valley) $60. 83 *(4/1/2003)*

Turley 2003 Hayne Vineyard Petite Sirah (Napa Valley) $80. 94 Cellar Selection *—S.H. (12/1/2006)*

Turley 2001 Old Vines Zinfandel (California) $25. 91 *(11/1/2003)*

Turley 2000 Tofanelli Vineyard Zinfandel (Napa Valley) $32. 92 *—J.M. (9/1/2003)*

TURNBULL

Turnbull 2003 Cabernet Sauvignon (Napa Valley) $40. 92 *—S.H. (10/1/2006)*

Turnbull 2002 Cabernet Sauvignon (Oakville) $40. 86 *—S.H. (8/1/2005)*

Turnbull 2003 Merlot (Oakville) $30. 91 *—S.H. (10/1/2006)*

Turnbull 2001 Petite Sirah (Oakville) $35. 87 *(4/1/2003)*

Turnbull 2003 Old Bull Red Wine Red Blend (Napa Valley) $20. 91 Editors' Choice *—S.H. (10/1/2006)*

Turnbull 1997 Sangiovese (Oakville) $20. 88 *—S.H. (12/15/1999)*

Turnbull 2004 Sauvignon Blanc (Oakville) $16. 88 *—S.H. (12/15/2005)*

Turnbull 2000 Sauvignon Blanc (Oakville) $16. 86 *(8/1/2002)*

Turnbull 1998 Syrah (Oakville) $25. 86 *(11/1/2001)*

Turnbull 2000 Estate Grown Viognier (Oakville) $25. 88 *—J.M. (12/15/2002)*

TURNER ROAD

Turner Road 2004 Cabernet Sauvignon (Paso Robles) $11. 83 *—S.H. (12/15/2006)*

Turner Road 2003 Cabernet Sauvignon (Paso Robles) $11. 84 *—S.H. (6/1/2005)*

Turner Road 2002 Cabernet Sauvignon (Paso Robles) $11. 84 *—S.H. (6/1/2005)*

Turner Road 2005 Chardonnay (Central Coast) $11. 83 *—S.H. (12/1/2006)*

Turner Road 2003 Chardonnay (Central Coast) $11. 84 *—S.H. (6/1/2005)*

Turner Road 2004 Merlot (Central Coast) $11. 85 *—S.H. (12/15/2006)*

Turner Road 2005 Appellation Series Merlot (Central Coast) $11. It's Merlots like this that keep the variety so popular in America. At an affordable price, it gives upfront cherry-berry, chocolate and spice flavors, in a rich, soft texture. **84** *—S.H. (3/1/2007)*

Turner Road 2005 Pinot Grigio (Lodi) $11. 81 *—S.H. (12/1/2006)*

Turner Road 2003 Shiraz (Lodi) $11. 85 Best Buy *—S.H. (6/1/2005)*

Turner Road 2002 Shiraz (Lodi) $11. 84 *—S.H. (6/1/2005)*

Turner Road 2004 Appellation Series Shiraz (Lodi) $11. Tastes raw and sharp, like a young wine just out of the fermenter, with those fresh fruity acids still unresolved. On the other hand the wine is fully dry, and the fruit is ripe and luscious. **83** *—S.H. (2/1/2007)*

TURNING LEAF

Turning Leaf 2004 Reserve Cabernet Sauvignon (California) $8. 84 Best Buy *—S.H. (11/15/2006)*

Turning Leaf 2004 Reserve Chardonnay (California) $8. 84 *—S.H. (4/1/2006)*

Turning Leaf 2002 Reserve Chardonnay (California) $12. 84 *—S.H. (12/1/2004)*

Turning Leaf 2003 Sonoma Reserve Chardonnay (Sonoma County) $12. 87 Best Buy *—S.H. (12/15/2005)*

Turning Leaf 2004 Reserve Merlot (California) $8. Juicy and deep in blackberry, cherry and cola flavors, with smooth, polished tannins. It's a very nice wine with real charm. **85 Best Buy** *—S.H. (3/1/2007)*

Turning Leaf 1997 Reserve Merlot (Sonoma County) $10. 82 *—J.C. (7/1/2000)*

Turning Leaf 2004 Reserve Pinot Grigio (California) $8. 85 Best Buy *—S.H. (3/1/2006)*

Turning Leaf 2002 Coastal Reserve Pinot Noir (North Coast) $10. 83 *—S.H. (11/1/2004)*

Turning Leaf 1999 Coastal Reserve Pinot Noir (North Coast) $NA. 87 *—P.G. (11/15/2001)*

Turning Leaf 2003 Sonoma Reserve Pinot Noir (Sonoma County) $11. 83 *—S.H. (10/1/2005)*

Turning Leaf 2001 Reserve Riesling (Monterey) $7. 80 *—J.M. (8/1/2003)*

Turning Leaf 2002 Vineyards Riesling (Monterey County) $9. 84 *—S.H. (12/1/2004)*

Turning Leaf 2003 Sauvignon Blanc (California) $9. 83 *—S.H. (12/1/2004)*

Turning Leaf 1999 Shiraz (California) $8. 83 *(10/1/2001)*

Turning Leaf 2003 Syrah (California) $8. 85 Best Buy *(9/1/2005)*

TUSK 'N RED

Tusk 'n Red 2004 Red Blend (Mendocino County) $12. They dropped the price and upped the quality this year on this dry, field-style blend of Syrah, Zin, Sangiovese, Petite Sirah and Grenache. With its earthy, leather and wild berry flavors and fine, gritty tannins, it's a good match for a grilled steak. **86** *—S.H. (11/1/2007)*

Tusk 'n Red 2003 Red Blend (Mendocino County) $15. 83 *—S.H. (12/31/2005)*

TWIN FIN

Twin Fin 2004 Cabernet Sauvignon (California) $10. Made mostly from San Lucas and Hames Valley fruit, from warm southern Salinas Valley, this is a dry, ripe Cab with some polished blackberry and coffee fruit. **83** *—S.H. (4/1/2007)*

Twin Fin 2003 Cabernet Sauvignon (California) $10. 86 Best Buy *—S.H. (12/31/2005)*

Twin Fin 2002 Cabernet Sauvignon (California) $10. 85 Best Buy *—S.H. (10/1/2005)*

Twin Fin 2005 Chardonnay (California) $10. Good everyday Chard here, nothing fancy, but it shows true varietal character at a good price. Full of peaches and cream, toasty oak, and a spicy finish. **84** *—S.H. (4/1/2007)*

Twin Fin 2004 Chardonnay (California) $10. 86 Best Buy *—S.H. (10/1/2005)*

Twin Fin 2003 Merlot (California) $10. 85 Best Buy *—S.H. (12/15/2005)*

Twin Fin 2002 Merlot (California) $10. 85 Best Buy *—S.H. (10/1/2005)*

Twin Fin 2005 Pinot Grigio (California) $10. A great value in popular PG, this stainless steel fermented wine contains 5% Gewürztraminer from Monterey. It's tartly acidic and fruity, and the Gewürz gives a lemon flower and spice brightness. Nice with Chinese chicken salad, or a salad with pears. **85 Best Buy** *—S.H. (4/1/2007)*

Twin Fin 2004 Pinot Grigio (California) $10. 85 Best Buy *—S.H. (7/1/2005)*

Twin Fin 2004 Pinot Noir (California) $10. 82 *—S.H. (12/31/2005)*

Twin Fin 2003 Pinot Noir (California) $10. 85 Best Buy *—S.H. (10/1/2005)*

Twin Fin 2006 Sunset Rosé Sangiovese (California) $10. Made from Sangiovese, this blush straddles the line between simple and flawed. It's soft, sweet and simple, with sugary cherry-berry flavors. **83** *—S.H. (7/1/2007)*

Twin Fin 2003 Shiraz (California) $10. 86 Best Buy *—S.H. (12/15/2005)*

Twin Fin 2002 Shiraz (California) $10. 82 *(9/1/2005)*

TWISTED CHARD

Twisted Chard 2005 New Vine Chardonnay (California) $8. A nice, crisp Chard, with perky acidity boosting flavors of apples, peaches, limes, pineapples, vanilla and buttered toast. Easy to like, and not a bad price for a wine of this quality. From Delicato. **86 Best Buy** *—S.H. (11/15/2007)*

TWISTED LOT

Twisted Lot 2005 Merlot (California) $8. Here's a generic, country-style red wine, not particularly varietal, but dry, fruity and balanced. It has pretty flavors of cherries, raspberries and cocoa, with the vanilla and toast of oak. **84 Best Buy** *—S.H. (11/15/2007)*

TWISTED OAK

Twisted Oak 2004 Grenache (Sierra Foothills) $24. 84 *—S.H. (12/1/2006)*

Twisted Oak 2002 Grenache (Sierra Foothills) $20. 85 *—S.H. (9/1/2004)*

Twisted Oak 2004 The Spaniard Red Blend (Calaveras County) $45. 91 *S.H. (12/1/2006)*

Twisted Oak 2002 The Spaniard Red Blend (Calaveras County) $35. 92 *—S.H. (11/15/2005)*

Twisted Oak 2004 *%#&@! Rhône Red Blend (Sierra Foothills) $32. 85 *—S.H. (12/1/2006)*

Twisted Oak 2003 *%#&@! Rhône Red Blend (Sierra Foothills) $32. 90 *—S.H. (11/15/2005)*

Twisted Oak 2002 *%#&@! Rhône Red Blend (Sierra Foothills) $28. 86 *—S.H. (12/1/2004)*

Twisted Oak 2003 Syrah (Calaveras County) $24. 86 *—S.H. (12/1/2006)*

Twisted Oak 2001 Syrah (Sierra Foothills) $26. 84 *—S.H. (9/1/2004)*

Twisted Oak 2003 Tanner Syrah (Calaveras County) $28. 87 *(9/1/2005)*

Twisted Oak 2002 Tanner Vineyard Syrah (Calaveras County) $22. 90 *—S.H. (2/1/2005)*

Twisted Oak 2004 Tempranillo (Calaveras County) $22. 86 *—S.H. (12/1/2006)*

Twisted Oak 2002 Tempranillo (Calaveras County) $22. 85 *—S.H. (9/1/2004)*

Twisted Oak 2005 Silvaspoons Vineyard Verdelho (Lodi) $16. 85 *—S.H. (12/1/2006)*

Twisted Oak 2004 Silvaspoons Vineyard Verdelho (Lodi) $16. 88 *—S.H. (11/15/2005)*

Twisted Oak 2005 Viognier (Calaveras County) $20. 86 *—S.H. (12/1/2006)*

Twisted Oak 2003 Viognier (Calaveras County) $18. 91 *—S.H. (2/1/2005)*

TWISTED PIG

Twisted Pig 2006 Pinot Grigio (California) $8. A cool vintage resulted in good acids in this polished PG, which shows long hangtime flavors of fresh fruits, berries and spices. It's a savory wine, dry, clean and easy to like. **85 Best Buy** *—S.H. (11/15/2007)*

TWISTED ZIN

Twisted Zin 2005 Old Vine Zinfandel (California) $8. So fresh and young, it tastes like it was just scooped out of the fermenting vat. Bursts with zingy raspberry, cherry, toast and cinnamon spice flavors, with fine crisp acidity for balance. **84 Best Buy** *—S.H. (11/15/2007)*

TWO ANGELS

Two Angels 2005 Petite Sirah (High Valley) $26. Port-y, and has that rustically thick, soft, syrupy cherry flavor often referred to as medicinal. **82** *—S.H. (4/1/2007)*

Two Angels 2003 Petite Sirah (Lake County) $24. 90 *—S.H. (12/1/2005)*

Two Angels 2004 Shannon Ridge Vineyard Petite Sirah (Lake County) $30. 90 *—S.H. (3/1/2006)*

Two Angels 2006 Sauvignon Blanc (High Valley) $15. Like a breath of springtime in the California hills. Hints of new green grass, acacia blossom, clover honey and buttercup lead to notes of cassis in this bone dry, crisply acidic wine, which shows how beautifully Lake County deals with Sauvignon Blanc. **91 Best Buy** *—S.H. (9/1/2007)*

Two Angels 2005 Sauvignon Blanc (High Valley) $15. 89 Best Buy *—S.H. (10/1/2006)*

Two Angels 2004 Shannon Ridge Sauvignon Blanc (Lake County) $15. 86 *—S.H. (10/1/2005)*

Two Angels 2005 Syrah (High Valley) $26. Somewhat harsh and tannicly acidic. The wine is fruity but a bit tough. **81** *—S.H. (4/1/2007)*

Two Angels 2003 Shannon Ridge Syrah (Lake County) $25. 82 *(9/1/2005)*

TWO MOUNTAIN

Two Mountain 2002 Cabernet Sauvignon (Yakima Valley) $25. 85 *—P.G. (6/1/2006)*

Two Mountain 2002 Merlot (Yakima Valley) $20. 86 *—P.G. (6/1/2006)*

TWO TONE FARM

Two Tone Farm 2002 Chardonnay (Napa Valley) $13. 88 Best Buy *—S.H. (3/1/2005)*

Two Tone Farm 2001 Merlot (Napa Valley) $16. 87 *—S.H. (3/1/2005)*

TWO WIVES

Two Wives 2006 Pink Red Table Wine Rosé Blend (Napa Valley) $15. This is certainly full-bodied for a rosé. It's a soft, thick wine, with cherry and blackberry Lifesaver flavors and something stewed and caramelly, like licorice. Finishes a little off-dry. Mostly Merlot, with a drop of Syrah. **84** *—S.H. (11/15/2007)*

Two Wives 2006 Sauvignon Blanc (Napa Valley) $16. There's a thin line between attractive gooseberry and hay aromas, and more severe pungency. This wine is strong in the latter. **81** *—S.H. (12/1/2007)*

TWOMEY

Twomey 2003 Merlot (Napa Valley) $65. Lots to like in this four-year-old Merlot. It's fully dry and not too fruity, with rich blackberry, sage, anise and oak flavors that are complex and long. On the minus side, the wine is too soft, lacking the vital acidity and tannins needed for structure. **86** *—S.H. (12/1/2007)*

TY CATON

Ty Caton 2001 Cabernet Sauvignon (Sonoma Valley) $24. 86 *—S.H. (12/31/2004)*

Ty Caton 2003 Merlot (Dry Creek Valley) $29. 83 *—S.H. (4/1/2006)*

Ty Caton 2001 Merlot (Sonoma County) $24. 89 *—S.H. (12/31/2004)*

Ty Caton 2004 Caton Vineyard Petite Sirah (Sonoma Valley) $35. Comes down on the soft, earthy side, with an herb and tobacco edge to the cherry-berry fruit. There's some heat in the finish, but overall, the wine wears its high alcohol tolerably well. **83** *—S.H. (11/1/2007)*

Ty Caton 2003 Tytanium Red Blend (Sonoma Valley) $39. 86 *—S.H. (5/1/2006)*

Ty Caton 2004 Caton Vineyard Syrah (Sonoma Valley) $25. Lots of polished, ripe blackberry, cherry, mocha and spicy flavors in this dry, rather tannic wine. It shows good structure and balance. Best now. **86** *—S.H. (11/1/2007)*

Ty Caton 2002 Ty Caton Vineyards Syrah (Sonoma Valley) $19. 88 *—S.H. (12/15/2004)*

Ty Caton 2006 Caton Vineyard Rosé Syrah (Sonoma Valley) $18. The wine is very young and fresh, with that Beaujolais-like vinous taste of cherries and spices. Fully dry, it's a fun wine that will please folks who claim not to like red wines. **84** *—S.H. (7/1/2007)*

Ty Caton 2003 Zinfandel (Sonoma County) $24. 83 *—S.H. (2/1/2006)*

USA

TYRUS EVAN

Tyrus Evan 2003 Del Rio Claret Bordeaux Blend (Southern Oregon) $36. Ken Wright creates a powerful, ripe and somewhat alcoholic red blend in this hot vintage. It feels a bit manipulated—the chalky tannins have been softened up and made more accessible—but the soft cherry fruit stands out and gives a warm, silky impression in the mouth. **88** *—P.G. (4/1/2007)*

Tyrus Evan 2003 Walla Walla Claret Bordeaux Blend (Walla Walla (OR)) $36. Ken Wright sources this fruit from the Pepper Bridge and Seven Hills vineyards, crafting a pleasant Bordeaux blend that shows the softer side of the valley's fruit. Clean and forward, the mixed flavors of plum and berry are right up front, but the relative weightlessness of the finish suggests that these are from some of the younger vines. **86** *—P.G. (4/1/2007)*

TYEE

Tyee 1997 Pinot Blanc (Willamette Valley) $12. 83 *—D.T. (11/1/2001)*

Tyee 1996 Pinot Blanc (Willamette Valley) $12. 86 *—L.W. (12/31/1999)*

UNIONVILLE VINEYARDS

Unionville Vineyards 2004 Hunter's Red Reserve Bordeaux Blend (New Jersey) $25. This Bordeaux blend from New Jersey has appropriate aromas and flavors of dark berry, cedar, tobacco and spice, but it lacks the dimension and muscularity that makes this type of blend memorable. Still, it's a pretty wine and will pair well with numerous meat and fowl dishes. **82** *—S.K. (12/1/2007)*

Unionville Vineyards 2005 Chardonnay (New Jersey) $20. A good effort from New Jersey's Unionville, this delicate Chard offers harmonious flavors of tropical fruit and flowers, with a touch of spice to add complexity. Balanced acid keeps the wine clean and light. **84** *—S.K. (10/1/2007)*

UNITED WE STAND

United We Stand 2003 Reserve Chardonnay (California) $10. 82 *—S.H. (3/1/2005)*

United We Stand 2003 Reserve Merlot (California) $10. 80 *—S.H. (3/1/2005)*

UNKNOWN BOTTLING

Unknown Bottling 1983 Pinot Noir (Santa Ynez Valley) $NA. 81 *—S.H. (6/1/2005)*

UNTI

Unti 2003 Barbera (Dry Creek Valley) $24. 87 *—S.H. (11/1/2005)*

Unti 2003 Grenache (Dry Creek Valley) $26. 92 Editors' Choice *—S.H. (11/1/2005)*

Unti 2004 Rosé Grenache (Dry Creek Valley) $16. 88 *—S.H. (8/1/2005)*

Unti 2003 Segromigno Red Blend (Dry Creek Valley) $15. 89 Editors' Choice *—S.H. (11/1/2005)*

Unti 2006 Rosé Blend (Dry Creek Valley) $18. Unti specializes in Rhône-style wines from their Dry Creek vineyard. The reds are pretty good, and so is this rosé, made from Grenache and Mourvedre. It's completely dry, and despite a delicate mouthfeel, delivers plenty of berry, cherry and spice flavor. For such a light-bodied wine, it has surprising complexity. **90** *—S.H. (7/1/2007)*

Unti 2003 Sangiovese (Dry Creek Valley) $30. 89 *—S.H. (11/1/2005)*

Unti 2002 Syrah (Dry Creek Valley) $24. 87 *(9/1/2005)*

Unti 2002 Benchland Syrah (Dry Creek Valley) $30. 88 *(9/1/2005)*

Unti 2002 Zinfandel (Dry Creek Valley) $22. 93 Editors' Choice *—S.H. (11/1/2005)*

UPLAND

Upland 2006 Gewürztraminer (Yakima Valley) $14. This is a little gem, perfectly capturing the mix of flower, body powder, citrus and stone that only Gewürztraminer can evoke. Graceful and elegant, it spreads evenly across the palate and slides down the back of the throat. The residual sugar—1.8%—puts it squarely in the Alsatian camp. **90 Best Buy** *—P.G. (12/1/2007)*

URSA

Ursa 2002 Merlot (Santa Clara Valley) $16. 84 *—S.H. (8/1/2004)*

Ursa 2003 Petite Sirah (Paso Robles) $22. 88 *—S.H. (10/1/2006)*

Ursa 2003 Petite Sirah (Sierra Foothills) $22. 93 Editors' Choice *—S.H. (10/1/2006)*

Ursa 2002 Petite Sirah (Paso Robles) $22. 88 *—S.H. (8/1/2004)*

Ursa 2002 Petite Sirah (Lodi) $16. 86 *—S.H. (8/1/2004)*

Ursa 2003 Vineyard Blend Petite Sirah (California) $16. 89 *—S.H. (10/1/2006)*

USED AUTOMOBILE PARTS

Used Automobile Parts 2002 Red Table Wine Bordeaux Blend (Napa Valley) $50. 92 *—S.H. (9/1/2006)*

UVADA

Uvada 2002 Merlot (Oakville) $30. Uvada is flying under the radar but worthy of your attention at this price-quality ratio. The '02 Merlot, mainly from Beckstoffer Vineyard X, has been held back longer than most, allowing it to soften and fatten. It's fully ready now, showing blackberry, cassis, chocolate and vanilla oak flavors that finish dry and firm in ripe, sweet tannins. The 15% Cabernet Sauvignon adds needed structure. **92 Editors' Choice** *—S.H. (10/1/2007)*

Uvada 2001 Merlot (Oakville) $28. 91 Editors' Choice *—S.H. (10/1/2005)*

V. SATTUI

V. Sattui 2002 Cabernet Sauvignon (Napa Valley) $29. 90 *—S.H. (12/1/2005)*

V. Sattui 2000 Cabernet Sauvignon (Napa Valley) $21. 84 *—S.H. (12/15/2003)*

V. Sattui 2000 Cabernet Sauvignon (Sonoma County) $16. 84 *—S.H. (12/15/2003)*

V. Sattui 1999 Cabernet Sauvignon (Napa Valley) $21. 87 *—S.H. (11/15/2002)*

V. Sattui 1999 Morisoli Cabernet Sauvignon (Napa Valley) $32. 87 *—S.H. (11/15/2002)*

V. Sattui 2000 Morisoli Vineyard Cabernet Sauvignon (Napa Valley) $35. 92 *—S.H. (12/31/2003)*

V. Sattui 1999 Preston Cabernet Sauvignon (Napa Valley) $32. 87 *—S.H. (11/15/2002)*

V. Sattui 2000 Preston Vineyard Cabernet Sauvignon (Napa Valley) $33. 90 *—S.H. (12/31/2003)*

V. Sattui 1999 Suzanne's Cabernet Sauvignon (Napa Valley) $25. 87 *—S.H. (11/15/2002)*

V. Sattui 2000 Suzanne's Vineyard Cabernet Sauvignon (Napa Valley) $25. 91 Editors' Choice *—S.H. (12/31/2003)*

V. Sattui 2000 Carsi Chardonnay (Napa Valley) $21. 84 *—S.H. (12/15/2002)*

V. Sattui 1999 Carsi Vineyard Chardonnay (Napa Valley) $20. 84 *—J.M. (5/1/2002)*

V. Sattui 2001 Carsi Vineyard Old Vine Chardonnay (Napa Valley) $25. 89 *—S.H. (8/1/2003)*

V. Sattui 2001 Sattui Family Chardonnay (Napa Valley) $15. 84 *—S.H. (8/1/2003)*

V. Sattui 2001 Rouge Gamay (California) $15. 83 *—S.H. (12/1/2002)*

V. Sattui 2001 Dry Johannisberg Riesling (Napa Valley) $15. 86 *—S.H. (9/1/2003)*

V. Sattui 2001 Off-Dry Johannisberg Riesling (Napa Valley) $15. 85 *—S.H. (9/1/2003)*

V. Sattui 2000 Merlot (Napa Valley) $24. 84 *—S.H. (12/1/2003)*

V. Sattui 1999 Merlot (Napa Valley) $24. 90 *—S.H. (11/15/2002)*

V. Sattui 2001 Muscat (California) $16. 89 *—S.H. (12/1/2002)*

V. Sattui NV Angelica Muscat (California) $22. 88 *—S.H. (12/1/2002)*

V. Sattui 2001 Hendry Ranch Pinot Noir (Carneros) $35. 84 *—S.H. (7/1/2003)*

V. Sattui 2003 Henry Ranch Pinot Noir (Carneros) $NA. 82 *—S.H. (12/1/2005)*

V. Sattui 2000 Cuvée Rouge Red Blend (Napa Valley) $20. 83 *—S.H. (12/1/2003)*

V. Sattui 1999 Sattui Family Red Red Blend (California) $13. 86 *—S.H. (5/1/2002)*

V. Sattui 2000 Beatty Ranch Zinfandel (Howell Mountain) $27. 91 *—S.H. (12/1/2002)*

V. Sattui 2005 Crow Ridge Vineyard Zinfandel (Russian River Valley) $29. Superripe, almost sweet, this has good acidity and firm, fuzzy tannins that help balance the jammy cherry, raspberry and cola flavors. Good with a slightly sweet barbecue sauce on ribs and chicken. **86** *—S.H. (12/31/2007)*

V. Sattui 2000 Duarte Vineyard Ancient Vine Zinfandel (Contra Costa County) $35. 86 *—S.H. (12/1/2002)*

V. Sattui 2000 Duarte Vineyard Old Vine Zinfandel (Contra Costa County) $22. 90 *—S.H. (12/1/2002)*

V. Sattui 2005 Eaglepoint Ranch Zinfandel (Mendocino County) $29. Eaglepoint red wines are big and powerful, seldom less than fully ripe and usually with a good boost of alcohol. So it is with this hearty, tannic Zin. Its blackberry and mulberry flavors are almost Port-like, except that the wine is dry. **86** *—S.H. (12/31/2007)*

V. Sattui NV Madeira Zinfandel (California) $29. 90 *—S.H. (12/1/2002)*

V. Sattui 2005 Pilgrim Vineyard Zinfandel (Lodi) $26. Soft and superripe, with flavors of red currants and dried orange peel. Although the wine is fully dry, there's something Port-y about it. **83** *—S.H. (12/31/2007)*

V. Sattui 2005 Quaglia Vineyard Zinfandel (Napa Valley) $33. You can taste the warm sunshine in the spicy berry flavors of this Zin. It comes right up to the edge of overripe, with suggestions of bitter raisins, then pulls back to let the cassis and cherry liqueur shine through. **87** *—S.H. (12/31/2007)*

V. Sattui 1999 Quaglia Vineyard Zinfandel (Napa Valley) $24. 84 *—S.H. (12/1/2002)*

V. Sattui 2005 Ramazzotti Vineyard Zinfandel (Dry Creek Valley) $29. A rich, balanced Zin that shows the variety's brambly side. Tastes like freshly picked wild blackberries and raspberries, crushed into wine and seasoned with white pepper, cinnamon and a drop of balsamic. **89** *—S.H. (12/31/2007)*

V. Sattui 2000 Suzanne's Vineyard Zinfandel (Napa Valley) $20. 86 *—S.H. (9/1/2003)*

V. Sattui 1999 Suzanne's Vineyard Zinfandel (Napa Valley) $20. 86 *—S.H. (12/1/2002)*

VA PIANO

Va Piano 2004 Cabernet Sauvignon (Columbia Valley (WA)) $38. Pure Cabernet, from Lewis and Cold Creek. Flavors are fresh and clean with sappy, tart berry flavors. Aromatic notes from the barrel add toasted coconut and mocha. Firm acids buoy the fruit, while retaining a pleasing roundness in the midpalate. This is still quite young with pure, sweet cherry fruit and a slight rawness to the tannins. It should continue to improve in bottle for some years. **90** *—P.G. (5/1/2007)*

Va Piano 2005 Syrah (Columbia & Walla Walla Valleys) $38. Smooth, luscious, dense and brilliant—the color is saturated and superbright—this silky wine has kept the tannins supple and ripe. It captures the essence of young, fresh, spicy Syrah, unadulterated or modified with other grapes. This is tight, firm, sappy, young and a bit relentless in a tough, confident style. Flavors of cranberry and wild raspberry run rampant, with plenty of acid to keep it clean and penetrating. **91** *—P.G. (12/1/2007)*

Va Piano 2003 Syrah (Columbia & Walla Walla Valleys) $38. 88 *—P.G. (6/1/2006)*

VACHE

Vache 2000 Cabernet Sauvignon (Cienega Valley) $37. 84 *—S.H. (5/1/2005)*

Vache 2002 Chardonnay (Cienega Valley) $37. 82 *—S.H. (12/1/2005)*

Vache 2001 Chardonnay (Cienega Valley) $37. 83 *—S.H. (4/1/2005)*

Vache 2002 Pinot Noir (Cienega Valley) $37. 81 *—S.H. (12/1/2005)*

Vache 2001 Pinot Noir (Cienega Valley) $37. 82 *—S.H. (4/1/2005)*

VALDEZ

Valdez 2005 Sauvignon Blanc (Sonoma County) $23. 85 *—S.H. (12/31/2006)*

Valdez 2004 Lancel Creek Reserve Zinfandel (Russian River Valley) $35. 93 *—S.H. (12/31/2006)*

Valdez 2004 Rockpile Road Vineyard Zinfandel (Rockpile) $38. 92 *—S.H. (12/31/2006)*

VALENTINE

Valentine 1999 Echo Valley Cabernet Sauvignon (Mendocino County) $27. 84 *—S.H. (11/15/2002)*

VALLEY OF THE MOON

Valley of the Moon 2003 Cuvée de la Luna Bordeaux Blend (Sonoma County) $30. A Bordeaux blend, and a nice one at that, with layers of berry and herb flavors. Shows great structure, with dusty oak tannins and juicy acidity, and while the fruit could be more concentrated, the wine finishes with elegant style. **87** *—S.H. (11/1/2007)*

Valley of the Moon 2002 Cuvée de la Luna Bordeaux Blend (Sonoma County) $30. This Bordeaux blend is pretty good, showing polished berry, cherry and earth flavors with a dry edge of coffee and tobacco. It's still fresh in tannins, even at this age, but is unlikely to develop. Drink now. **85** *—S.H. (2/1/2007)*

Valley of the Moon 1999 Cuvée de la Luna Cabernet Blend (Sonoma County) $28. 91 *—S.H. (5/1/2003)*

Valley of the Moon 2001 Cuvée de la Luna Cabernet Blend (Sonoma County) $30. 91 *—S.H. (11/15/2005)*

Valley of the Moon 2004 Cabernet Sauvignon (Sonoma County) $20. This is what Valley of the Moon does so well—make a varietally true wine with some complexity, and offer it at a mid-priced range. This is not an ager, but it's balanced and elegant, with modulated blackberry, cassis, cherry and oak flavors that finish dry, tannic and spicy. **87** *—S.H. (12/1/2007)*

Valley of the Moon 2003 Cabernet Sauvignon (Sonoma County) $20. Valley of the Moon's Cabernets are always solid and pleasing, and often good values for their price point. The '03 satisfies for its ripe cherry, blackberry and chocolate fruit, lush, smooth tannins and polished softness that carries through the finish. **86** *—S.H. (5/1/2007)*

Valley of the Moon 2002 Cabernet Sauvignon (Sonoma County) $20. 85 *—S.H. (10/1/2006)*

Valley of the Moon 2001 Cabernet Sauvignon (Sonoma County) $20. 84 *—S.H. (11/15/2005)*

Valley of the Moon 2000 Cabernet Sauvignon (Sonoma County) $20. 85 *—S.H. (11/15/2004)*

Valley of the Moon 1998 Cabernet Sauvignon (Sonoma Valley) $20. 86 *—J.M. (6/1/2002)*

Valley of the Moon 1999 Sophomore Sensation Cabernet Sauvignon (Sonoma County) $20. 88 *—S.H. (11/15/2003)*

Valley of the Moon 2006 Chardonnay (Sonoma County) $16. Here's a county-appellated Chardonnay that shows how the art of blending can produce a really nice Chardonnay at a fair price. It shows bracing, cool-climate acidity and is quite dry, with a rich spicing of oak that gives a vanilla-cream smokiness to the peach and pineapple fruit. **87** *—S.H. (12/15/2007)*

Valley of the Moon 2005 Chardonnay (Sonoma County) $16. 88 *—S.H. (12/15/2006)*

Valley of the Moon 2004 Chardonnay (Sonoma County) $16. 84 *—S.H. (12/31/2005)*

Valley of the Moon 2003 Chardonnay (Sonoma County) $15. 86 *—S.H. (6/1/2005)*

Valley of the Moon 2002 Chardonnay (Sonoma County) $15. 90 Editors' Choice —*S.H. (12/15/2003)*

Valley of the Moon 2001 Chardonnay (Sonoma County) $15. 87 —*S.H. (12/15/2002)*

Valley of the Moon 2000 Chardonnay (Sonoma County) $14. 87 —*J.M. (5/1/2002)*

Valley of the Moon 1999 Chardonnay (Sonoma County) $18. 86 —*S.H. (8/1/2001)*

Valley of the Moon 1998 Chardonnay (Sonoma County) $17. 86 *(6/1/2000)*

Valley of the Moon 1998 Cuvée de la Luna Meritage (Sonoma County) $25. 89 —*J.M. (5/1/2002)*

Valley of the Moon 2000 Cuvée de la Luna Meritage (Sonoma County) $25. 90 —*S.H. (6/1/2004)*

Valley of the Moon 2006 Pinot Blanc (Sonoma County) $16. This is the kind of wine that will be wildly popular as a cocktail sipper. It has the fruit, spice and oaky vanilla to appeal to almost all palates, yet is dry and crisp in acidity, leaving behind a clean, fruity finish. **87** —*S.H. (12/15/2007)*

Valley of the Moon 2005 Pinot Blanc (Sonoma County) $16. 88 —*S.H. (12/15/2006)*

Valley of the Moon 2004 Pinot Blanc (Sonoma County) $16. 87 —*S.H. (12/31/2005)*

Valley of the Moon 2003 Pinot Blanc (Sonoma County) $15. 85 —*S.H. (5/1/2005)*

Valley of the Moon 2002 Pinot Blanc (Sonoma Valley) $15. 87 —*S.H. (2/1/2004)*

Valley of the Moon 2001 Pinot Blanc (Sonoma County) $15. 87 —*J.M. (12/15/2002)*

Valley of the Moon 2000 Pinot Blanc (Sonoma County) $15. 87 —*S.H. (11/15/2001)*

Valley of the Moon 1999 Pinot Blanc (Sonoma County) $15. 88 —*S.H. (2/1/2001)*

Valley of the Moon 1998 Pinot Blanc (Sonoma County) $20. 80 —*L.W. (3/1/2000)*

Valley of the Moon 2005 Pinot Noir (Carneros) $20. Easy does it with this clean, fruity Pinot, which is made for immediate drinking. It's light and silky, with pleasant cherry, rhubarb, rosehip tea and cola flavors, and finishes very dry and spicy. **85** —*S.H. (5/1/2007)*

Valley of the Moon 2004 Pinot Noir (Carneros) $20. 85 —*S.H. (7/1/2006)*

Valley of the Moon 2003 Pinot Noir (Carneros) $20. 85 —*S.H. (11/15/2005)*

Valley of the Moon 2002 Pinot Noir (Carneros) $20. 88 —*S.H. (3/1/2005)*

Valley of the Moon 2001 Pinot Noir (Carneros) $20. 90 Editors' Choice —*S.H. (12/1/2003)*

Valley of the Moon 2000 Pinot Noir (Sonoma County) $20. 87 *(10/1/2002)*

Valley of the Moon 2004 Sangiovese (Sonoma County) $16. Dry to the point of astringent, this is a tannic, acidic wine with cherry flavors. It really needs olive oil, hard cheese and rich meats to break it down. **83** —*S.H. (4/1/2007)*

Valley of the Moon 2003 Sangiovese (Sonoma County) $16. 86 —*S.H. (11/15/2006)*

Valley of the Moon 2002 Sangiovese (Sonoma County) $16. 86 —*S.H. (10/1/2005)*

Valley of the Moon 2001 Sangiovese (Sonoma County) $15. 85 —*S.H. (10/1/2004)*

Valley of the Moon 2000 Sangiovese (Sonoma County) $15. 89 —*S.H. (12/1/2003)*

Valley of the Moon 1999 Sangiovese (Sonoma County) $15. 86 —*S.H. (12/1/2002)*

Valley of the Moon 1998 Sangiovese (Sonoma County) $16. 90 —*S.H. (7/1/2002)*

Valley of the Moon 2006 Rosato di Sangiovese (Sonoma County) $14. Sangiovese doesn't do well in California as a dry table wine but it makes a pretty good rosé. The grape's naturally high acidity frames its classic cherry flavors, which are deliciously clean and pure in this steel-fermented wine. Best of all, the wine is relatively low in alcohol and dry. Try this polished rosé with sushi. **88** —*S.H. (11/15/2007)*

Valley of the Moon 2005 Rosato di Sangiovese Sangiovese (Sonoma County) $14. Soft, simple and sugary, with jellied cherry and raspberry flavors and a LifeSaver candy finish. **83** —*S.H. (7/1/2007)*

Valley of the Moon 2005 Rosato di Sangiovese (Sonoma County) $16. 84 —*S.H. (12/1/2006)*

Valley of the Moon 2004 Syrah (Sonoma County) $16. There's value for the money in this smooth wine. It smacks of cherries, not the darker, deeper fruits of Syrah, but it does have a complex leathery, meaty edge. The tannin-acid balance is just right, and leads to a simple, fruity finish. **86** —*S.H. (12/31/2007)*

Valley of the Moon 2003 Syrah (Sonoma County) $16. 87 —*S.H. (12/31/2006)*

Valley of the Moon 2002 Syrah (Sonoma County) $16. 84 —*S.H. (5/1/2006)*

Valley of the Moon 2001 Syrah (Sonoma County) $15. 88 —*S.H. (12/15/2004)*

Valley of the Moon 2000 Syrah (Sonoma County) $15. 84 —*S.H. (12/1/2003)*

Valley of the Moon 1999 Syrah (Sonoma County) $15. 85 —*J.M. (12/1/2002)*

Valley of the Moon 1998 Syrah (Sonoma County) $17. 88 Editors' Choice *(10/1/2001)*

Valley of the Moon 2005 Zinfandel (Sonoma County) $16. Comes down on the hot, rustic side, with pruny, raisiny flavors. But it's dry, with a certain liqueury lusciousness. If you like that baked cherry, roasted blackberry quality, it's for you. **84** —*S.H. (11/1/2007)*

Valley of the Moon 2003 Zinfandel (Sonoma County) $16. 82 —*S.H. (5/1/2006)*

Valley of the Moon 2002 Zinfandel (Sonoma County) $15. 85 —*S.H. (5/1/2005)*

Valley of the Moon 2001 Zinfandel (Sonoma County) $15. 87 *(11/1/2003)*

Valley of the Moon 1998 Zinfandel (Sonoma County) $15. 88 Best Buy —*S.H. (11/15/2001)*

Valley of the Moon 1997 Zinfandel (Sonoma Valley) $15. 88 Best Buy —*S.H. (12/1/2000)*

VALLEY VIEW VINEYARD

Valley View Vineyard 2000 Anna Maria Chardonnay (Oregon) $15. 87 —*P.G. (8/1/2002)*

Valley View Vineyard 1999 Anna Maria Chardonnay (Rogue Valley) $22. 8 —*P.G. (2/1/2002)*

Valley View Vineyard 1999 Meritage (Rogue Valley) $40. 88 —*P.G. (4/1/2002)*

Valley View Vineyard 1998 Anna Maria Merlot (Oregon) $18. 85 —*P.G. (8/1/2002)*

Valley View Vineyard 1999 Anna Maria Old Stage Vineyard Merlot (Rogue Valley) $22. 87 —*P.G. (8/1/2002)*

Valley View Vineyard 1999 Anna Maria Quail Run Merlot (Rogue Valley) $30. 87 —*P.G. (8/1/2002)*

Valley View Vineyard 1999 Anna Maria Pinot Gris (Rogue Valley) $12. 86 —*P.G. (8/1/2002)*

Valley View Vineyard 1999 Anna Maria Syrah (Applegate Valley) $30. 87 —*P.G. (8/1/2002)*

VAN ASPEREN

Van Asperen 1995 Cabernet Sauvignon (Napa Valley) $18. 88 —*L.W. (7/1/1999)*

Van Asperen 1997 Krupp Vineyard Cabernet Sauvignon (Atlas Peak) $50. 89 —*J.C. (6/1/2003)*

Van Asperen 1997 Zinfandel (Napa Valley) $18. 90 *(5/1/2000)*

Van Asperen 1997 Zinfandel (Napa Valley) $18. 87 —*P.G. (3/1/2001)*

VAN DER HEYDEN

Van Der Heyden 2000 Chardonnay (Napa Valley) $18. 85 —*S.H. (12/1/2003)*

VAN DUZER

Van Duzer 2000 Chardonnay (Willamette Valley) $15. 88 —*P.G. (2/1/2002)*

Van Duzer 2002 Pinot Gris (Willamette Valley) $13. 87 —*P.G. (12/1/2003)*

Van Duzer 2003 Estate Pinot Gris (Willamette Valley) $14. 86 —*P.G. (1/1/2004)*

Van Duzer 2001 Pinot Noir (Willamette Valley) $19. 84 —*P.G. (12/1/2003)*

Van Duzer 2002 Dijon Blocks Pinot Noir (Willamette Valley) $33. 85 *(11/1/2004)*

Van Duzer 2002 Estate Pinot Noir (Willamette Valley) $22. 86 *(11/1/2004)*

Van Duzer 2002 Flagpole Block Pinot Noir (Willamette Valley) $33. 87 *(11/1/2004)*

Van Duzer 2002 Homestead Block Pinot Noir (Willamette Valley) $33. 86 *(11/1/2004)*

VAN ROEKEL

Van Roekel 2000 Viognier (Temecula) $13. 84 —*S.H. (4/1/2002)*

VAN RUITEN

Van Ruiten 2002 Cabernet Sauvignon (Lodi) $15. 80 —*S.H. (7/1/2006)*

Van Ruiten 2004 Pinot Gris (Lodi) $12. 81 —*S.H. (2/1/2006)*

Van Ruiten 2003 Cab-Shiraz Red Blend (Lodi) $15. 81 —*S.H. (7/1/2006)*

Van Ruiten 2003 Late Harvest Zinfandel (Lodi) $26. 80 —*S.H. (7/1/2006)*

Van Ruiten 2004 Old Vine Zinfandel (Lodi) $18. Rich in the flavors of blackberry, cherry, raspberry and blueberry, this dry wine has a rustic texture. Even though the official alcohol is 14.5%, it tastes a little prickly. **86** —*S.H. (12/15/2007)*

VAN RUITEN-TAYLOR

Van Ruiten-Taylor 1999 Chardonnay (Lodi) $10. 84 —*S.H. (11/15/2001)*

VARNER

Varner 2001 Amphitheater Block Chardonnay (Santa Cruz Mountains) $30. 91 —*S.H. (6/1/2003)*

Varner 2001 Bee Block Chardonnay (Santa Cruz Mountains) $32. 92 —*S.H. (5/1/2003)*

Varner 2001 Home Vineyard Chardonnay (Santa Cruz Mountains) $34. 90 —*S.H. (5/1/2003)*

Varner 2000 Spring Ridge Vineyard Amphitheater Block Chardonnay (Santa Cruz County) $30. 87 —*S.H. (5/1/2002)*

Varner 2000 Spring Ridge Vineyard Bee Block Chardonnay (Santa Cruz County) $32. 92 —*S.H. (5/1/2002)*

VAROZZA

Varozza 2002 Cabernet Sauvignon (St. Helena) $45. A good followup to the '01, the '02 is a soft, dense, chocolaty Cab, a bit one-dimensional. It offers a solid array of ripe blackberries and smoky oak, with a melted fudge opulence. **87** —*S.H. (5/1/2007)*

Varozza 2001 Cabernet Sauvignon (St. Helena) $45. 89 —*S.H. (8/1/2006)*

VELOCITY

Velocity 2002 Red Wine Red Blend (Rogue Valley) $30. 88 —*P.G. (2/1/2005)*

VENEZIA

Venezia 1996 Meola Vineyards Cabernet Sauvignon (Sonoma County) $14. 87 —*J.C. (9/1/1999)*

Venezia 1997 Regusci Vineyard Chardonnay (Napa Valley) $20. 83 —*J.C. (10/1/1999)*

Venezia 1996 Regusci Vineyard Chardonnay (Napa Valley) $20. 83 —*M.S. (6/1/1999)*

Venezia 1996 Alegria Vineyard Sangiovese (Russian River Valley) $23. 83 —*J.C. (10/1/1999)*

Venezia 1997 Nuovo Mondo Sangiovese (Sonoma County) $24. 87 —*S.H. (10/1/1999)*

Venezia 1996 Van Noy Vineyard Sangiovese (Russian River Valley) $22. 86 —*J.C. (10/1/1999)*

Venezia 1997 Sonoma Moment Viognier (Sonoma County) $20. 82 —*J.C. (10/1/1999)*

VENGE

Venge 2000 Family Reserve Cabernet Sauvignon (Oakville) $95. 90 —*S.H. (11/1/2005)*

Venge 1999 Merlot (Oakville) $46. 93 —*J.M. (4/1/2003)*

Venge 2001 Family Reserve Merlot (Oakville) $46. 91 Cellar Selection —*S.H. (11/1/2005)*

Venge 1997 Reserve Merlot (Napa Valley) $35. 94 —*S.H. (3/1/2000)*

Venge 2000 Scout's Honor Red Blend (Napa Valley) $30. 89 —*J.M. (11/15/2003)*

Venge 2000 Penny Lane Vineyard Sangiovese (Napa Valley) $30. 90 —*J.M. (2/1/2003)*

Venge 2003 Syrah (Napa Valley) $32. 84 *(9/1/2005)*

Venge 2002 Family Reserve Syrah (California) $32. 84 *(9/1/2005)*

VENTANA

Ventana 2003 Cabernet Sauvignon (Arroyo Seco) $18. I have often praised Arroyo Seco as a great home to whites and Burgundians, but Cab-friendly, it's not. This is a soft, sweet, simple wine with medicinal cherry flavors. **82** —*S.H. (5/1/2007)*

Ventana 2001 Cabernet Sauvignon (Arroyo Seco) $18. 84 —*S.H. (10/1/2004)*

Ventana 2000 Cabernet Sauvignon (Arroyo Seco) $18. 85 —*S.H. (4/1/2003)*

Ventana 2000 Due Amici Cabernet Sauvignon-Sangiovese (Arroyo Seco) $18. 87 —*S.H. (2/1/2003)*

Ventana 1997 Chardonnay (Monterey County) $13. 86 —*S.H. (2/1/2000)*

Ventana 1999 Chardonnay (Arroyo Seco) $14. 86 —*S.H. (12/31/2001)*

Ventana 2005 Gold Stripe Chardonnay (Arroyo Seco) $18. Crisp and zesty, this Chard has very bright, pure flavors of tangerines, limes, pineapples and vanilla-caramel oak. High acidity balances the honeyed sweetness. **87** —*S.H. (5/1/2007)*

Ventana 2001 Gold Stripe Chardonnay (Arroyo Seco) $16. 86 —*S.H. (12/1/2003)*

Ventana 2000 Gold Stripe Chardonnay (Arroyo Seco) $14. 86 —*S.H. (9/1/2002)*

Ventana 1999 Reserve Chardonnay (Arroyo Seco) $20. 87 —*S.H. (9/1/2002)*

Ventana 2000 Dry Chenin Blanc (Monterey) $12. 85 —*S.H. (9/1/2002)*

Ventana 2005 Gewürztraminer (Arroyo Seco) $17. 86 —*S.H. (12/15/2006)*

Ventana 2004 Gewürztraminer (Arroyo Seco) $16. 87 —*S.H. (12/1/2005)*

Ventana 2001 Gewürztraminer (Arroyo Seco) $12. 88 —*S.H. (9/1/2003)*

Ventana 2004 The Lady Grenache (Arroyo Seco) $28. 85 —*S.H. (12/15/2006)*

Ventana 2001 Merlot (Arroyo Seco) $18. 87 —*S.H. (9/1/2004)*

Ventana 2000 Merlot (Arroyo Seco) $18. 85 —*S.H. (4/1/2003)*

Ventana 1998 Merlot (Monterey) $16. 89 —*S.H. (2/1/2001)*

Ventana 1999 Muscat d'Orange Muscat (Monterey) $12. 87 —*S.H. (9/1/2002)*

Ventana 2005 Orange Muscat (Arroyo Seco) $18. Shows the brilliant acidity that the Arroyo Seco coaxes from almost every white wine, but unfortunately the tangerine flavors are way too thin, and the wine isn't even all that sweet. Given more concentration, this would be a fabulous dessert wine. **84** —*S.H. (9/1/2007)*

Ventana 2000 Pinot Blanc (Arroyo Seco) $16. 87 —*S.H. (9/1/2003)*

Ventana 1999 Pinot Blanc (Monterey) $14. 87 —*S.H. (2/1/2001)*

Ventana 2004 Pinot Noir (Arroyo Seco) $34. Raw in acids, with modest cherry flavors and more unripe ones of wintergreen, this Pinot at least is clean and silky. But it's seriously overpriced. **83** —*S.H. (5/1/2007)*

Ventana 2001 Pinot Noir (Arroyo Seco) $24. 87 —*S.H. (12/1/2004)*

Ventana 2003 Due Amici Red Blend (Arroyo Seco) $28. 90 —*S.H. (12/15/2006)*

Ventana 2003 Beaugravier Red Wine Rhône Red Blend (Arroyo Seco) $28. A blend of Syrah and Grenache that's simple, soft and sweet. It has sugary flavors of orange tea and raspberry jam. **82** —*S.H. (9/1/2007)*

Ventana 2005 Dry Rosado Rosé Blend (Arroyo Seco) $14. Cherries, cherries, cherries! So good and pure. That's from the Grenache, while Syrah lends weight. Dry, silky and crisp from the acidity that characterizes all Arroyo Seco wines, this is the kind of blush that's turning consumers on to rosé wines. **87** —*S.H. (5/1/2007)*

Ventana 2005 Riesling (Arroyo Seco) $16. 85 —*S.H. (12/15/2006)*

Ventana 2001 Riesling (Arroyo Seco) $12. 87 —*S.H. (9/1/2003)*

Ventana 2005 Sauvignon Blanc (Arroyo Seco) $16. The weather didn't cooperate in fully ripening the grapes this cool vintage, so you'll find some cat pee flavors and Marlborough-style gooseberry, juniper and grapefruit. But such is the acidity and cleanliness that this single-vineyard wine packs plenty of interest and power. **86** —*S.H. (5/1/2007)*

Ventana 2002 Sauvignon Blanc (Arroyo Seco) $14. 89 —*S.H. (9/1/2004)*

Ventana 1997 Sauvignon Blanc (Monterey County) $9. 88 Best Buy —*S.H. (2/1/2000)*

Ventana 2003 Syrah (Arroyo Seco) $18. Sweet and simple, with plenty of ripe cherry and chocolate flavor. I'd be surprised if there's not residual sugar, given the fairly moderate alcohol of 13.2%. **83** —*S.H. (9/1/2007)*

Ventana 2001 Syrah (Arroyo Seco) $18. 90 —*S.H. (9/1/2004)*

Ventana 2000 Syrah (Arroyo Seco) $18. 88 —*S.H. (2/1/2003)*

Ventana 1999 Syrah (Arroyo Seco) $20. 85 —*S.H. (9/1/2002)*

Ventana 1997 Syrah (Monterey County) $18. 88 —*L.W. (2/1/2000)*

VENUS

Venus 1998 Cervina Zinfandel (Sonoma County) $22. 85 —*P.G. (3/1/2001)*

Venus 1999 Eve Zinfandel (Sonoma County) $22. 87 —*D.T. (3/1/2002)*

VERAISON

Veraison 2003 Stagecoach Vineyard Synchrony Bordeaux Blend (Napa Valley) $65. Kudos to the winery for holding back this Cab Franc, Cab Sauvignon, Merlot and Malbec blend until it's had time to turn gently soft and velvety. It's at its peak now, showing a bouquet of blackberries, cherries, raspberries and cedar. **87** *—S.H. (12/15/2007)*

Veraison 2004 Stagecoach Vineyard Cabernet Sauvignon (Napa Valley) $55. Lots of richness in this smooth, complex Cab. It shows real quality in the depth of blackberry and spice fruit and the balance of ripe, sweet tannins and acidity. Elegant; probably at its best now and for a year or two. **89** *—S.H. (12/15/2007)*

Veraison 2004 Krupp Vineyard Merlot (Atlas Peak) $50. There aren't many Merlots coming off Atlas Peak, but there should be, to judge by this rich, dense, complex wine. It's enormously packed in black cherry, red currant, blueberry, milk chocolate and spicy licorice flavors that go on and on into the finish. Fortunately, the structure is great, providing a firm architecture of tannins and acids. **91** *—S.H. (12/15/2007)*

VERDAD

Verdad 2006 Rosé Blend (Arroyo Grande Valley) $14. A blend of Grenache and Mourvèdre, this light-colored blush shows the bright acidity and purity of the appellation, but it's really too thin, flavorwise. The bitter cherry flavors are really watery. **83** *—S.H. (7/1/2007)*

VERITÉ

Verité 1998 Cabernet Sauvignon-Merlot (Sonoma-Napa) $150. 93 Cellar Selection *(12/1/2001)*

Verité 2000 Le Desir Meritage (Sonoma County) $100. 86 *—S.H. (11/15/2003)*

Verité 1999 La Muse Merlot-Cabernet Sauvignon (Sonoma County) $100. 87 *—S.H. (11/15/2003)*

Verité 1999 La Joie Red Blend (Sonoma County) $100. 90 *—S.H. (11/15/2003)*

Verité 1998 La Joie Red Blend (Sonoma County) $100. 85 *—S.H. (8/29/2003)*

VERSANT VINEYARDS

Versant Vineyards 2001 Cabernet Sauvignon (Napa Valley) $70. 92 *—J.M. (6/1/2004)*

VERSO

Verso 2003 Cabernet Sauvignon (Grand Valley) $30. 82 *—M.D. (8/1/2006)*

VIA FIRENZE

Via Firenze 1995 Charbono (Napa Valley) $14. 86 *—M.S. (6/1/1999)*

Via Firenze 1995 Dolcetto (Napa Valley) $15. 85 *—M.S. (6/1/1999)*

Via Firenze 1994 Nobella Red Blend (Napa Valley) $18. 87 *—M.S. (6/1/1999)*

VIADER

Viader 2002 Cabernet Blend (Napa Valley) $85. 87 *—S.H. (11/1/2005)*

Viader 2002 V Cabernet Blend (Napa Valley) $100. 90 *—S.H. (11/1/2005)*

Viader 1999 Red Blend (Napa Valley) $75. 92 *—J.M. (6/1/2002)*

Viader 2005 DARE Dry Rosé Blend (Napa Valley) $15. Made from Cab Sauvignon and Franc, this new wine from Viader is dark and dry, and just too full-bodied for a blush. It's almost as heavy as a table red, with blackberry and cherry marmalade flavors. Viader's rosé challenge is to lighten up and not try to make such a serious statement. **85** *—S.H. (7/1/2007)*

Viader 2002 Syrah (Napa Valley) $65. 85 *(9/1/2005)*

Viader 2001 Syrah (Napa Valley) $65. 92 *—S.H. (12/15/2004)*

Viader 2003 DARE Tempranillo (Napa Valley) $41. 83 *—S.H. (11/1/2005)*

VIANO

Viano 2001 Reserve Selection Old Vines Zinfandel Port (Contra Costa County) $11. 82 *—S.H. (12/15/2005)*

Viano 2000 Reserve Selection Zinfandel (Lodi) $9. 81 *—S.H. (12/15/2005)*

VIANSA

Viansa 2002 Athena Dolcetto (California) $19. 84 *—S.H. (9/1/2004)*

Viansa 2001 Piccolo Sangiovese (Sonoma Valley) $25. 84 *—S.H. (9/1/2004)*

VICTOR HUGO

Victor Hugo 2004 Opulence Bordeaux Blend (Paso Robles) $24. This Bordeaux blend is very dry and tannic, with cherry and blackberry flavors and a scouring, prickly mouthfeel. Okay, but not going anywhere. **84** *—S.H. (8/1/2007)*

Victor Hugo 2004 Petite Sirah (Paso Robles) $18. Thick in the mouth, and soft, this superripe wine has just enough tannic structure to keep it from being pure syrup. It's slightly sweet in Port-y berry and pepper flavors. **83** *—S.H. (7/1/2007)*

Victor Hugo 2000 Petite Sirah (Paso Robles) $18. 86 *(4/1/2003)*

Victor Hugo 2005 Rosé Syrah (Paso Robles) $14. Dark, rustic and kind of medicinal, this wine has the benefit of dryness. The flavors are of slightly stewed cherries. **83** *—S.H. (7/1/2007)*

Victor Hugo 2000 Syrah (Paso Robles) $20. 86 *—S.H. (12/1/2002)*

Victor Hugo 2001 Zinfandel (Paso Robles) $16. 81 *(11/1/2003)*

Victor Hugo 2005 Estate Bottled Zinfandel (Paso Robles) $18. Port-sweet, with high acidity, high alcohol and some tough tannins. The flavors are of cherries, raspberries and blueberries. This is the house style. **84** *—S.H. (8/1/2007)*

VIENTO

Viento 1999 Nocturne Muscat Canelli (Columbia Valley (WA)) $25. 92 *—P.G. (6/1/2005)*

VIERRA VINEYARDS

Vierra Vineyards 2002 Claret Bordeaux Blend (Walla Walla (WA)) $20. 88 *—P.G. (7/1/2004)*

Vierra Vineyards 2002 Syrah (Walla Walla (WA)) $22. 87 *—P.G. (7/1/2004)*

VIEUX - OS

Vieux - Os 2002 Ira Carter Vineyard Zinfandel (Napa Valley) $36. 90 *—J.M. (10/1/2004)*

VIDAL VINEYARDS

Vidal Vineyards 2003 Cabernet Sauvignon (Napa Valley) $55. An inaugural vintage from an estate vineyard, and one to watch despite some structural weakness. Feels a bit rough and jagged around the edges, with a greenness to the tannins and acids. Yet it feels like there's potential, given a better vintage and careful vineyard management to limit yields. **87** *—S.H. (10/1/2007)*

VIE WINERY

Vie Winery 2005 L'Imaginaire Grenache (Santa Barbara County) $39. Not a whole lot going on in this soft, simple wine. The cherry, raspberry and root beer flavors are ultraripe, with a liqueured quality, and the finish is semisweet. **84** *—S.H. (12/1/2007)*

Vie Winery 2005 L'Intruse Mourvèdre (Santa Barbara County) $39. Made from a warmer inland area, and blended with some Syrah and Grenache, this is a soft, fruity wine that offers immediate pleasure. It floods the mouth with blackberry, cherry, chocolate, leather and coffee flavors that finish in a sprinkling of cinnamon, white pepper and nutmeg. **87** *—S.H. (12/1/2007)*

Vie Winery 2005 L'Etranger Zinfandel Blend Red Blend (Sonoma County) $39. The grapes represent an interesting span, coming from Carneros, Dry Creek Valley and even some from Mendocino's Eaglepoint Ranch. The blend is Zin, with Syrah and Petite Syrah. The flavors are a wild medley of LifeSaver candies, and the finish is too sweet. **84** *—S.H. (12/1/2007)*

Vie Winery 2004 Last Leg Cuvee Red Blend (North Coast) $38. In an era of extravagant, extracted reds that overwhelm food, this is elegantly sophisticated and complex. Bone dry, it has a rich earthiness and balance that's almost Bordeaux-like. A blend of Syrah, Zin and Petite Sirah. **92 Editors' Choice** *—S.H. (2/1/2007)*

Vie Winery 2006 Belle-Amie Rosé Blend (Santa Barbara County) $18. Tastes overtly sweet, with sugary raspberry and cherry candy flavors. It's a tasty country wine, but not really dry. Mourvèdre, Grenache and Syrah. **84** *—S.H. (12/15/2007)*

Vie Winery 2005 Belle-Amie Rosé Blend (Santa Barbara County) $18. Tastes overtly sweet, with sugary raspberry and cherry candy flavors. It's a tasty country wine, but not really dry. Mourvèdre, Grenache and Syrah. **84** *—S.H. (12/1/2007)*

Vie Winery 2005 Las Madres Vineyard Syrah (Carneros) $39. Very nice, complex Syrah, soft and a little melted in structure, but with such luscious fruit, you have to like it. The ripe blackberry, raspberry and blueberry liqueur flavors have a rich edge of anisette-dipped biscotti. Drink now through 2009. **89** *—S.H. (12/1/2007)*

Vie Winery 2004 Las Madres Vineyard Syrah (Carneros) $38. There's a rusticity here, a sharpness of texture, that interferes with the otherwise delicious blackberry, plum, coffee, balsamic, soy and spice flavors. Texture is so important in a wine like this. Disregard it, and no amount of ripeness can compensate. **84** *—S.H. (2/1/2007)*

Vie Winery 2005 Les Amours Syrah (Santa Barbara County) $45. Soft and fairly one-dimensional, this Syrah has the taste of perfectly ripened blackberries and black raspberries, crushed and seasoned with cocoa, white pepper and powerded anise. It has 20% Mourvèdre, which seems to bring a slight gaminess. **86** —*S.H. (12/1/2007)*

Vie Winery 2005 Beatty Ranch Vineyard Zinfandel (Howell Mountain) $39. The fault with this enormous Zin is that despite a hefty 15.6% alcohol, it still tastes as sweet as a ruby Port. Fifty percent new oak only contributes caramel to what should properly be labeled a dessert wine. **82** —*S.H. (12/1/2007)*

Vie Winery 2004 Beatty Ranch Vineyard Zinfandel (Howell Mountain) $38. The 15.9% alcohol is the price you pay for dryness. The wine shows a nice Howell Mountain quality in the hugely ripe fruit and perfectly sculpted tannins that feel so lush and smooth in the mouth. It's beautiful, in its way, but that alcohol is really challenging. **85** —*S.H. (3/1/2007)*

VIGIL

Vigil 1997 Solari Vineyard Cabernet Franc (Napa Valley) $25. 86 —*L.W. (9/1/1999)*

Vigil 1997 Terra Vin Reserve Red Blend (Napa Valley) $22. 92 —*L.W. (11/1/1999)*

Vigil 1998 Zinfandel (Napa Valley) $24. 90 —*S.H. (9/1/2000)*

Vigil 1998 Marissa Vineyard Zinfandel (California) $16. 85 —*P.G. (3/1/2001)*

Vigil 1998 Mohr-Fry Ranch Zinfandel (California) $18. 89 —*S.H. (9/1/2000)*

Vigil 1998 Tres Condados Zinfandel (California) $14. 87 —*P.G. (3/1/2001)*

Vigil 1997 Tres Condados Zinfandel (California) $14. 88 Best Buy —*S.H. (9/1/2000)*

VILLA CREEK

Villa Creek 2002 James Berry Vineyard Garnacha (Paso Robles) $24. 90 —*S.H. (12/31/2004)*

Villa Creek 2002 Avenger Red Blend (Paso Robles) $24. 91 —*S.H. (12/31/2004)*

Villa Creek 2002 James Berry Vineyard High Road Red Blend (Paso Robles) $40. 92 —*S.H. (12/31/2004)*

Villa Creek 2002 Mas de Maha Red Blend (Central Coast) $24. n85 —*S.H. (12/31/2004)*

Villa Creek 2001 Avenger Rhône Red Blend (Paso Robles) $20. 94 —*S.H. (3/1/2004)*

VILLA HELENA

Villa Helena 2001 Viognier (Napa Valley) $16. 84 —*S.H. (12/15/2002)*

VILLA MT. EDEN

Villa Mt. Eden 1997 Coastal Cabernet Sauvignon (California) $10. 80 —*S.H. (7/1/2000)*

Villa Mt. Eden 2004 Grand Reserve Cabernet Sauvignon (Napa Valley) $15. A little harsh and green, with a hard grip of tannins, this Cab shows minty flavors of cherries, blackberries and mocha, with a coating of smoky oak. **84** —*S.H. (11/15/2007)*

Villa Mt. Eden 2003 Grand Reserve Cabernet Sauvignon (Napa Valley) $15. Not a grand success, but a decently ripe, dry Cab with some raw, green edges. Blackberry jam, coffee, herbs and a touch of oak. **83** —*S.H. (4/1/2007)*

Villa Mt. Eden 2002 Grand Reserve Cabernet Sauvignon (Napa Valley) $15. 81 —*S.H. (12/31/2005)*

Villa Mt. Eden 1998 Grand Reserve Cabernet Sauvignon (Napa Valley) $20. 84 —*S.H. (11/15/2001)*

Villa Mt. Eden 1996 Grand Reserve Cabernet Sauvignon (Napa Valley) $20. 91 *(2/1/2000)*

Villa Mt. Eden 2001 Grande Reserve Tall Trees Vineyard Cabernet Sauvignon (Napa Valley) $15. 85 —*S.H. (10/1/2004)*

Villa Mt. Eden 1998 Signature Cabernet Sauvignon (Napa Valley) $54. 87 —*S.H. (12/1/2001)*

Villa Mt. Eden 1997 Chardonnay (California) $10. 87 Best Buy —*S.H. (2/1/2000)*

Villa Mt. Eden 2002 Chardonnay (California) $10. 83 —*S.H. (10/1/2005)*

Villa Mt. Eden 2005 Bien Nacido Vineyard Grand Reserve Chardonnay (Santa Maria Valley) $15. Not a real success for this often good bottling, spoiled by a taste of burnt wood. The oak doesn't taste quite natural; like something synthetic, almost medicinal. **82** —*S.H. (6/1/2007)*

Villa Mt. Eden 2004 Bien Nacido Vineyard Grand Reserve Chardonnay (Santa Maria Valley) $15. 84 —*S.H. (12/31/2005)*

Villa Mt. Eden 2003 Bien Nacido Vineyard Grand Reserve Chardonnay (Santa Maria Valley) $15. 88 —*S.H. (5/1/2005)*

Villa Mt. Eden 2002 Bien Nacido Vineyard Grand Reserve Chardonnay (Santa Maria Valley) $15. 90 Best Buy —*S.H. (6/1/2004)*

Villa Mt. Eden 1998 Bien Nacido Vineyard Grand Reserve Chardonnay (Santa Maria Valley) $17. 87 —*S.H. (11/15/2000)*

Villa Mt. Eden 2001 Bien Nacido Vineyard Signature Chardonnay (Santa Maria Valley) $32. 92 —*S.H. (12/1/2005)*

Villa Mt. Eden 1999 Bien Nacido Vineyard Signature Chardonnay (Santa Maria Valley) $32. 90 —*S.H. (12/1/2001)*

Villa Mt. Eden 1999 Coastal Chardonnay (Monterey County) $10. 84 —*S.H. (11/15/2001)*

Villa Mt. Eden 2000 Grand Reserve Chardonnay (Santa Maria Valley) $14. 87 —*S.H. (2/1/2003)*

Villa Mt. Eden 1999 Grand Reserve Chardonnay (Santa Maria Valley) $17. 88 —*S.H. (11/15/2001)*

Villa Mt. Eden 1997 Grand Reserve Bien Nacido Vineyard Chardonnay (Santa Maria Valley) $18. 89 *(6/1/2000)*

Villa Mt. Eden 1997 Coastal Merlot (California) $10. 88 Best Buy —*J.C. (3/1/2000)*

Villa Mt. Eden 1997 Pinot Noir (California) $12. 87 Best Buy *(5/1/2000)*

Villa Mt. Eden 2005 Bien Nacido Vineyard Grand Reserve Pinot Noir (Santa Maria Valley) $25. Other than a sugary sweetness, this wine shows all the hallmarks of a very nice Pinot Noir from this famed vineyard. The raspberry, cherry and vanilla flavors are accented by dusty spices, and the texture is silky. But the wine just doesn't taste dry. **84** —*S.H. (12/15/2007)*

Villa Mt. Eden 1997 Bien Nacido Vineyard Grand Res Pinot Noir (Santa Maria Valley) $20. 86 *(10/1/1999)*

Villa Mt. Eden 2003 Bien Nacido Vineyard Grand Reserve Pinot Noir (Santa Maria Valley) $22. 85 —*S.H. (12/31/2005)*

Villa Mt. Eden 1998 Bien Nacido Vineyard Grand Reserve Pinot Noir (Santa Maria Valley) $20. 89 —*S.H. (12/15/2000)*

Villa Mt. Eden 2000 Coastal Pinot Noir (California) $10. 84 Best Buy *(10/1/2002)*

Villa Mt. Eden 1999 Coastal Pinot Noir (California) $10. 85 —*J.C. (11/15/2001)*

Villa Mt. Eden 2002 Grand Reserve Pinot Noir (Russian River Valley) $22. 87 —*S.H. (11/1/2004)*

Villa Mt. Eden 2000 Grand Reserve Pinot Noir (Sonoma County) $22. 89 Editors' Choice *(10/1/2002)*

Villa Mt. Eden 1999 Grand Reserve Pinot Noir (Santa Maria Valley) $21. 92 Best Buy —*S.H. (12/15/2001)*

Villa Mt. Eden 2004 Grand Reserve Bien Nacido Vineyard Pinot Noir (Santa Maria Valley) $19. 89 —*S.H. (12/15/2006)*

Villa Mt. Eden 1999 Coastal Sauvignon Blanc (Central Coast) $10. 85 —*S.H. (11/15/2000)*

Villa Mt. Eden 1998 Syrah (California) $10. 84 *(5/1/2000)*

Villa Mt. Eden 1999 Coastal Syrah (California) $10. 84 *(10/1/2001)*

Villa Mt. Eden 1998 Grand Reserve Syrah (California) $21. 88 *(11/1/2001)*

Villa Mt. Eden 1999 Fox Creek Vineyard Grand Reserve Zinfandel (Sierra Foothills) $21. 91 —*S.H. (12/15/2001)*

Villa Mt. Eden 2003 Grand Reserve Antique Vines Zinfandel (Napa-Amador) $16. 90 —*S.H. (12/15/2006)*

Villa Mt. Eden 2001 Grand Reserve Fox Creek Vineyard Zinfandel (Sierra Foothills) $22. 85 —*S.H. (12/15/2004)*

Villa Mt. Eden 2002 Grand Reserve Mead Ranch Vineyard Zinfandel (Napa Valley) $22. 92 Editors' Choice —*S.H. (12/1/2005)*

Villa Mt. Eden 2001 Grand Reserve Mead Ranch Vineyard Zinfandel (Napa Valley) $22. 90 Editors' Choice —*S.H. (10/1/2005)*

Villa Mt. Eden 1995 Grand Reserve Monte Rosso Vine Zinfandel (Sonoma Valley) $20. 92 —*S.H. (9/1/1999)*

Villa Mt. Eden 2001 Grand Reserve Monte Rosso Vineyard Zinfandel (Sonoma Valley) $24. 86 —*S.H. (12/1/2005)*

Villa Mt. Eden 1999 Mead Ranch Vineyard Grand Reserve Zinfandel (Napa Valley) $21. 90 —*S.H. (12/15/2001)*

Villa Mt. Eden 1997 Monte Rosso Vineyard Grand Res Zinfandel (Sonoma Valley) $21. 85 —*J.C. (5/1/2000)*

Villa Mt. Eden 1998 Monte Rosso Vineyard Grand Reserve Zinfandel (Sonoma Valley) $21. 90 Editors' Choice —*P.G. (3/1/2001)*

Villa Mt. Eden 1999 Monte Rosso Vineyard Grand Reserve Zinfandel (Sonoma Valley) $21. 88 —*S.H. (12/15/2001)*

Villa Mt. Eden 1999 Old Vines Zinfandel (Napa Valley) $10. 87 —*S.H. (12/9/2002)*

VILLA SPALLA

Villa Spalla 2002 Tuscia Red Blend (Amador County-Oregon) $36. 83 —*S.H. (12/31/2005)*

VILLICANA

Villicana 2000 Cabernet Sauvignon (Paso Robles) $25. 84 —*J.M. (4/1/2004)*

Villicana 2001 Merlot (Paso Robles) $30. 87 —*J.M. (4/1/2004)*

VIN DE MANIES

Vin de Manies 2003 Cabernet Sauvignon (Napa Valley) $45. 89 —*S.H. (12/15/2006)*

Vin de Manies 2003 Reserve Cabernet Sauvignon (Napa Valley) $75. 90 —*S.H. (12/15/2006)*

VIN DU LAC

Vin du Lac 2004 Barrel Select Cabernet Franc (Columbia Valley (WA)) $28. A jammy, ripe red wine the sort of wine that sticks out in a large crowd and wins medals (which it has done, quite successfully) and it is certainly well made in a big, ripe, tannic style. But it is right on the edge of pushing it too far at 14.8% alcohol. 87 —*P.G. (3/1/2007)*

Vin du Lac 2003 Barrel Select Cabernet Sauvignon (Yakima Valley) $28. Licorice and sweet grape flavors dominate; the fruits remain sweet, primary flavors, like blueberry compote. The blend is a four-grape Bordeaux mix, lacking only Merlot, and it was given 21 months in almost entirely new French oak, hence the strong licorice note. It could merit a higher score with additional bottle age. 88 —*P.G. (3/1/2007)*

Vin du Lac 2003 Barrel Select Merlot (Columbia Valley (WA)) $28. The best of the winery's reds; it's thick and round, soft and luscious. A warm, forward, delicious wine, ripe and structured. Three quarters Merlot, with the rest split evenly between Malbec and Cab Franc. 88 —*P.G. (3/1/2007)*

Vin du Lac 2006 Grisant! Pinot Gris (Columbia Valley (WA)) $15. This is generic white wine, with hints of light pear flavor but nothing else. 84 —*P.G. (12/1/2007)*

Vin du Lac 2005 LEHM Dry Riesling (Columbia Valley (WA)) $21. Very good, succulent and juicy with bright, bold flavors of citrus and tangerine. This has especially fine weight for a bone dry Riesling, and it's quite fresh and flavorful, rather than simply austere. 89 —*P.G. (3/1/2007)*

Vin du Lac 2005 Les Amis Riesling-Muscat (Columbia Valley (WA)) $11. This tasting room blend is soft, fruity and quite light. 84 —*P.G. (12/1/2007)*

Vin du Lac 2005 Savvy! Blanc Sauvignon Blanc (Columbia Valley (WA)) $11. Unusually sweet for Sauvignon Blanc at 1.6% residual sugar. It doesn't have enough stuffing to compensate. 82 —*P.G. (12/1/2007)*

Vin du Lac 2004 Barrel Select Syrah (Columbia Valley (WA)) $26. Somehow this seems tilted a bit too much toward the flavors of oak, perhaps because half of the barrels were new American. The scent and flavor of concentrated licorice is overwhelming, submerging the rather light flavors of the Syrah, and giving this a feeling of being a one-trick (and one note) pony. 86 —*P.G. (3/1/2007)*

Vin du Lac 2006 'Vie!' Viognier-Roussanne (Columbia Valley (WA)) $15. This is a very light, thin, spicy wine, pleasant but undistinguished. 83 —*P.G. (12/1/2007)*

VINA ROBLES

Vina Robles 2003 Cabernet Sauvignon (Paso Robles) $14. Kudos to Vina Robles for holding this inexpensive Cab back for so long, presumably to let it develop in the bottle. It's a nice, polished wine, soft in tannins and acids, with polished cherry, blackberry and spicy plum flavors that finish dry and smooth. 86 —*S.H. (11/15/2007)*

Vina Robles 2002 Cabernet Sauvignon (Paso Robles) $19. 84 —*S.H. (12/31/2005)*

Vina Robles 2001 Estate Cabernet Sauvignon (Paso Robles) $19. 87 —*S.H. (8/1/2004)*

Vina Robles 2004 Jardine Petite Sirah (Paso Robles) $26. Classic warm country Petite Sirah, this is soft, dense and full-bodied, almost heavy in dark stone fruit, coffee, unsweetened chocolate, moo shu sauce, soy and spicy, peppery flavors. A bit of a brute in its youth, it should hold well for 10 years. 87 —*S.H. (4/1/2007)*

Vina Robles 2003 Jardine Petite Sirah (Paso Robles) $26. 92 Editors' Choice —*S.H. (7/1/2006)*

Vina Robles 2002 Jardine Petite Sirah (Paso Robles) $26. 82 —*S.H. (10/1/2005)*

Vina Robles 2001 Jardine Vineyard Petite Sirah (Paso Robles) $22. 86 —*S.H. (8/1/2004)*

Vina Robles 2005 Huerhuero Red Red Blend (Paso Robles) $14. A blend of Syrah, the Portuguese variety, Touriga, and Tannat, the grape of Madiran, this is a dry, young red. Acidity and tannins star, giving balance to the cherry, red currant and spice flavors. Drink this simple, enjoyable wine now. 84 —*S.H. (11/15/2007)*

Vina Robles 2004 Signature Red Blend (Paso Robles) $34. An unusual blend of Petit Verdot and Syrah, this shows a green peppercorn streak to the modest cherry fruit flavors. Medium-bodied, very dry and pretty tannic, could use more richness and depth, especially at this price. 85 —*S.H. (4/1/2007)*

Vina Robles 2003 Signature Red Blend (Paso Robles) $29. 87 —*S.H. (12/31/2005)*

Vina Robles 2002 Signature Red Blend (Paso Robles) $28. 86 —*S.H. (4/1/2005)*

Vina Robles 2006 Roseum Huerhuero Rosé Blend (Paso Robles) $13. Not much going on in this thin, simple wine. It's dry and crisp, with slight cherry flavors. 82 —*S.H. (7/1/2007)*

Vina Robles 2006 Jardine Sauvignon Blanc (Paso Robles) $14. Sweet and simple, with lemon LifeSaver candy, ripe pear and sugared vanilla flavors. The low alcohol, just 13%, seems to come at the cost of a pronounced sugary taste. 83 —*S.H. (10/1/2007)*

Vina Robles 2001 Jardine Vineyard Sauvignon Blanc (Paso Robles) $14. 86 —*S.H. (8/1/2004)*

Vina Robles 2001 Estate Syrah (Paso Robles) $18. 86 *(9/1/2005)*

Vina Robles 2000 Estate Syrah (Paso Robles) $19. 84 —*S.H. (8/1/2004)*

Vina Robles 2001 Huerhuero Vineyard Syrah (Paso Robles) $24. 84 *(9/1/2005)*

Vina Robles 2005 Roseum Syrah (Paso Robles) $13. 84 —*S.H. (7/1/2006)*

Vina Robles 2004 Roseum Syrah (Paso Robles) $13. 84 —*S.H. (11/15/2005)*

Vina Robles 2004 Westside Zinfandel (Paso Robles) $26. With low, soft acidity, rich tannins and extraordinarily ripe fruit, drink now for its vibrant youthfulness. It floods the mouth with blackberry jam, melted chocolate candy and licorice. Perfect with barbecue. 86 —*S.H. (4/1/2007)*

Vina Robles 2003 Westside Zinfandel (Paso Robles) $24. 82 —*S.H. (12/31/2005)*

Vina Robles 2002 Westside Zinfandel (Paso Robles) $24. 87 —*S.H. (10/1/2005)*

Vina Robles 2001 Westside Zinfandel (Paso Robles) $24. 91 —*S.H. (8/1/2004)*

VINAVERA

Vinavera 2005 Dry Rosé Blend (Napa Valley) $15. A blend of Syrah and Grenache, this is from giant Diageo. It's a pretty good wine, nice and dry, and while it's a little soft, it shows control in the herbs and earthiness that balance the fruit. The all-important mouthfeel is silky and delicate. 86 —*S.H. (7/1/2007)*

VINE CLIFF

Vine Cliff 2004 Cabernet Sauvignon (Napa Valley) $55. Here's the latest in a string of great Cabs from Vine Cliff. It shows the full ripeness of the vintage, with a rich array of blackberry, cassis, cherry, chocolate and caramel flavors. But it wisely preserves structure with fine acidity and a complex tannic architecture. Should develop well over the next 10 years. 92 —*S.H. (12/1/2007)*

Vine Cliff 2004 Cabernet Sauvignon (Oakville) $75. Vine Cliff is in the serious Cabernet business, crafting Cabs that aim for early drinkability but long ageability. The '04 is a success. It may lack the extra edge for profundity, but is delicious now for its oaky flavors of black currants, cassis, plums and mocha. Yet such are the tannins and acids that it should easily negotiate the next 10 years, if not longer. 91 —*S.H. (10/1/2007)*

Vine Cliff 2003 Cabernet Sauvignon (Napa Valley) $49. 92 —*S.H. (11/1/2006)*

Vine Cliff 2003 Cabernet Sauvignon (Oakville) $65. 93 —*S.H. (9/1/2006)*

Vine Cliff 2002 Cabernet Sauvignon (Oakville) $75. 86 —*S.H. (12/15/2005)*

Vine Cliff 2002 Cabernet Sauvignon (Napa Valley) $45. 95 Editors' Choice —*S.H. (11/1/2005)*

Vine Cliff 2001 Cabernet Sauvignon (Napa Valley) $45. 92 —*S.H. (6/1/2004)*

Vine Cliff 2001 Cabernet Sauvignon (Oakville) $75. 91 —*S.H. (10/1/2004)*

Vine Cliff 1998 Cabernet Sauvignon (Oakville) $75. 83 —*D.T. (6/1/2002)*

Vine Cliff 2004 16 Rows Cabernet Sauvignon (Oakville) $150. They raised the price on this limited bottling, and it's a delicious wine, but not on par with recent vintages. There's extreme ripeness, which yields almost dessert-quality blackberry and cherry fruit; sweet, soft, complex tannins and high oak. But the '04 tastes less dry and more simply structured than its predecessors. 89 —*S.H. (12/1/2007)*

Vine Cliff 2003 16 Rows Cabernet Sauvignon (Oakville) $135. This is Vine Cliff's highest designation Cab, and it just keeps getting better and better. It's a very serious wine. Shows its Oakville origins in the ripe blackberry and currant flavors, extraordinary balance and elegant power, but the tannins are fairly tough at this time. It's nothing that decanting and good beef can't handle, but this dense, complex wine should soften and improve over the next decade. **95 Editors' Choice** —*S.H. (2/1/2007)*

Vine Cliff 2002 16 Rows Cabernet Sauvignon (Oakville) $125. 91 Cellar Selection —*S.H. (12/15/2005)*

Vine Cliff 1996 Oakville Estate Cabernet Sauvignon (Napa Valley) $45. 91 *(3/1/2000)*

Vine Cliff 2004 Pickett Road Cabernet Sauvignon (Napa Valley) $150. This is certainly dramatic in structure, akin to a young Pauillac from Bordeaux, with concentrated currant, cherry, pencil lead and cedar flavors wrapped into youthfully hard tannins. It needs time, and should soften with increased complexity by 2009. Could reward with even longer cellaring, but '04 was not a great vintage. **93** —*S.H. (12/15/2007)*

Vine Cliff 2001 Private Stock 16 Rows Cabernet Sauvignon (Oakville) $125. 92 Cellar Selection —*S.H. (10/1/2004)*

Vine Cliff 2005 Chardonnay (Carneros) $34. Vine Ciff has become one of the most successful producers of Chardonnay in Napa Valley. The reason why, besides sourcing great grapes, is balance. Everything works in this wine, which is a mélange of rich tropical fruit, crisp acidity, a creamy texture, and sweet wood tannins. **92** —*S.H. (10/1/2007)*

Vine Cliff 2004 Chardonnay (Carneros) $34. 93 —*S.H. (11/1/2006)*

Vine Cliff 2003 Chardonnay (Carneros) $34. 94 Editors' Choice —*S.H. (11/1/2005)*

Vine Cliff 2002 Chardonnay (Napa Valley) $25. 90 —*S.H. (11/15/2004)*

Vine Cliff 1998 Chardonnay (Napa Valley) $34. 90 *(7/1/2001)*

Vine Cliff 1997 Chardonnay (Napa Valley) $34. 87 *(10/1/2000)*

Vine Cliff 2003 Bien Nacido Vineyard Chardonnay (Santa Maria Valley) $34. 90 —*S.H. (12/31/2005)*

Vine Cliff 2002 Bien Nacido Vineyard Chardonnay (Santa Maria Valley) $39. 87 —*S.H. (12/1/2004)*

Vine Cliff 2000 Bien Nacido Vineyard Chardonnay (Santa Maria Valley) $39. 94 Editors' Choice —*S.H. (2/1/2003)*

Vine Cliff 2004 Proprietress Reserve Chardonnay (Carneros) $55. This Chard, Vine Cliff's reserve, is actually less immediately rich and opulent than the regular, released last Spring, which was a very elaborate wine. This one may not be ready to drink quite yet. It's tight and spicy, with a leesy, minerally streak and lots of oak. Hold through 2007, then drink for a few more years. **92** —*S.H. (2/1/2007)*

Vine Cliff 2002 Proprietress Reserve Chardonnay (Carneros) $50. 94 —*S.H. (12/1/2004)*

Vine Cliff 1997 Merlot (Napa Valley) $35. 87 —*J.C. (7/1/2000)*

Vine Cliff 2002 Merlot (Napa Valley) $30. 89 —*S.H. (11/1/2006)*

Vine Cliff 2001 Merlot (Napa Valley) $30. 92 —*S.H. (12/15/2004)*

VINEYARD 29

Vineyard 29 2003 Cabernet Sauvignon (St. Helena) $195. Yes, it's a lot of money for a bottle of wine, and yes, it's stunning. From the famous Philippe Melka, this 100% Cab pours inky black, and smells dramatically oaked. No surprise that it's 100% new French barrels. But the underlying wine is massive in blackberry, cherry, mocha, lavender and thyme, just gigantically proportioned, and easily able to handle all that wood. Beautiful now, it's a keeper. Drink now–2018. **95 Cellar Selection** —*S.H. (5/1/2007)*

Vineyard 29 1999 Cabernet Sauvignon (Napa Valley) $160. 95 Cellar Selection —*C.S. (12/31/2002)*

VINEYARD 48

Vineyard 48 2004 Vignetta Bordeaux Blend (North Fork of Long Island) $25. There's a weakness to this wine that is tough to get beyond—its spice and cranberry aromas and plummy flavors swimming in a watery structure. What's there is good, it's just too muted to fully enjoy. **81** —*S.K. (2/1/2007)*

Vineyard 48 2004 Cabernet Franc (North Fork of Long Island) $28. 87 —*M.D. (8/1/2006)*

Vineyard 48 2005 Chardonnay (North Fork of Long Island) $16. Citrus mingles with toast. The lively acidity and a tendency toward the lean and flinty means this could use a touch of balance and roundness, but the flavors of apple and peach are appealing and flavorful. **84** —*S.K. (7/1/2007)*

Vineyard 48 2005 Reserve Chardonnay (North Fork of Long Island) $30. Vanilla and oak on the nose lead this opulently colored wine from Long Island's Vineyard 48, and on the palate, apple and vanilla mingle. It's a touch sweet for a Chardonnay but the oak is tempered with a zing of acidity that saves the day. Overall, good fruit flavors and mouthfeel. **85** —*S.K. (7/1/2007)*

Vineyard 48 2004 Reserve Chardonnay (North Fork of Long Island) $30. An aromatic, floral, and slightly spicy nose is followed by fresh pear and apple on the palate and a touch of oak to ground the fruit and create a nice balance. The initial impression here is pleasing but overall, the wine is somewhat one-dimensional and lean on flavor nuances. Would still pair well with food; think fresh seafood. **84** —*S.K. (2/1/2007)*

Vineyard 48 2004 Reserve Merlot (North Fork of Long Island) $35. A spicy aroma with wafts of clove and fruit entice, but there's little depth beyond. There's a thinness to the mouthfeel and the flavors are overoaked, but the wine is easy to drink if you are not expecting much more than the basics. The finish is short and lean. **82** —*S.K. (2/1/2007)*

Vineyard 48 2005 Riesling (North Fork of Long Island) $17. Sweet flavors of apples, pears and peaches are balanced with a lively acidity in this playful wine. This is not for fans of dry Riesling—it's a little too voluptuous for that—but if you like whites that are a little more decadent, this is a tasty bet. It's an accessible wine and not too complicated, but easy to like. **85** —*S.K. (7/1/2007)*

Vineyard 48 2005 Sauvignon Blanc (North Fork of Long Island) $15. Grassy, citric flavors on this fresh Sauvignon Blanc give it a tight edge, but give it a little time in the glass and the wine opens up into a rounder, more layered sip. Good acidity keeps the wine light on the palate. Serve with seafood. **85** —*S.K. (10/1/2007)*

VINEYARD 7&8

Vineyard 7&8 2004 7 Cabernet Sauvignon (Spring Mountain) $90. Spring Mountain Cabs typically are hard in youth but not this one, to which all the techniques of early drinkability seem to have been applied. The tannins are here, bigtime, but so finely grained you can drink the wine tonight. Flavorwise, there's nothing unusual about the ripe cassis and oak flavors; what's distinctive about this Cab is its dignified balance and finesse. Drink now through 2014. **92** —*S.H. (12/1/2007)*

Vineyard 7&8 2002 Vineyard 7 Reserve Cabernet Sauvignon (Spring Mountain) $85. 92 Cellar Selection —*S.H. (12/31/2006)*

Vineyard 7&8 2001 Vineyard 7 Reserve Cabernet Sauvignon (Spring Mountain) $75. 90 —*S.H. (8/1/2005)*

Vineyard 7&8 2004 8 Chardonnay (Spring Mountain) $50. This Chard's acid-laden minerality dominates, tasting of cold metal and wet flint, with undertones of pineapple liqueur, and the finish is dry and oaky. Elegant, it's a Chard to drink with buttery lobster. Should develop interestingly, over the next eight years. **92** —*S.H. (12/1/2007)*

Vineyard 7&8 2003 Vineyard 8 Reserve Chardonnay (Spring Mountain) $50. 93 Cellar Selection —*S.H. (12/31/2006)*

Vineyard 7&8 2001 Vineyard 8 Reserve Chardonnay (Spring Mountain) $45. 92 —*S.H. (8/1/2005)*

VINEYARD OF PASTERICK

Vineyard of Pasterick 2002 Syrah (Dry Creek Valley) $35. A dry, elegant Syrah. It starts with aromas of crushed black peppercorns, blackberries and oak, with a slightly animal, leathery note, then turns rich and soft in the mouth. Drink now, while the fruit is forward enough to balance the sticky tannins. **90** —*S.H. (10/1/2007)*

VINO BELLO

Vino Bello 2003 Bordeaux Style Meola Vineyards Bordeaux Blend (Alexander Valley) $30. Overripe and Port-y, this smells and tastes like raisins, not currants, and finishes with dry, astringent tannins. **82** —*S.H. (11/1/2007)*

Vino Bello 2004 Meolo Vineyards Merlot (Alexander Valley) $30. There are several things wrong here, although there's lots to like. On the plus side is lush, ripe blackberry, cherry and oak flavor. On the minus is a Port-y smell and rustic, slightly green tannins that make the finish astringent. **84** —*S.H. (11/1/2007)*

VINO CON BRIO

Vino Con Brio 2004 Pinot Grigio (Lodi) $16. 90 —*S.H. (5/1/2006)*

Vino Con Brio 2003 Pinot Grigio (Lodi) $16. 83 —*S.H. (5/1/2005)*

Vino Con Brio 2001 Pinotage (Lodi) $20. 81 —*S.H. (5/1/2005)*

Vino Con Brio 2000 Pinotage (Lodi) $20. 82 —*S.H. (8/1/2003)*

Vino Con Brio 2004 Estate Pinotage (Lodi) $20. Dark, thick, soft and juicy, an amazingly flavorful wine with a depth of exotic flavors. Blackberry liqueur, dark chocolate, cherry jam, violet flower, charred beef bones and peppery spice flavors swirl together into a complex finish. But it's a tannic wine that needs time. Best after 2008. **88** —*S.H. (4/1/2007)*

Vino Con Brio 2003 Vibrante Red Wine Red Blend (Lodi) $16. Country-style and rustic, with ripe to over-ripe blackberry flavors veering into raisins, this Syrah-based Rhône blend has a chocolate fudge, off-dry finish. **83** —*S.H. (4/1/2007)*

Vino Con Brio 2002 Vibrante Red Blend (Lodi) $16. 80 *—S.H. (6/1/2006)*

Vino Con Brio 2006 Passione Rosé Rosé Blend (Lodi) $14. This blend of Sangiovese and Petite Sirah is on the heavy side, and the cherry-berry and vanilla flavors have a sugary sweetness, only partly offset by acidity. That makes it a decent, country-style rosé wine, but you have to love that low, low alcohol. **84** *—S.H. (7/1/2007)*

Vino Con Brio 2002 Goehring Vineyard Sangiovese (Lodi) $16. 84 *—S.H. (6/1/2006)*

Vino Con Brio 2001 Goehring Vineyard Sangiovese (Lodi) $16. 81 *—S.H. (5/1/2005)*

Vino Con Brio 2002 McQueen Vineyard Syrah (Lodi) $16. 80 *—S.H. (5/1/2006)*

Vino Con Brio 2001 McQueen Vineyard Syrah (Lodi) $16. 84 *—S.H. (5/1/2005)*

Vino Con Brio 2005 Late Harvest Viognier (Lodi) $30. Shows that attractive apricot liqueur aroma that many late harvest whites have, and turns richly fruity and sweet in the mouth, with Bosc pear, wildflower honey, smoky caramel and vanilla flavors, wrapped in an unctuous texture. Crisp acidity balances and cleans. **91** *—S.H. (4/1/2007)*

Vino Con Brio 2002 Ripken Vineyard Viognier (Lodi) $17. 83 *—S.H. (3/1/2006)*

Vino Con Brio 2001 Ripken Vineyard Viognier (Lodi) $17. 85 *—S.H. (6/1/2003)*

Vino Con Brio 2001 Matzin Estate Old Vine Zinfandel (Lodi) $21. 90 *—S.H. (5/1/2005)*

Vino Con Brio 2004 Matzin Old Vine Zinfandel (Lodi) $24. Fans of big, thick, chocolaty and slightly sweet Zins will love this one. It has the softly tannic structure of hot country reds, with a luscious depth of blackberries, and the rustic nature of a wine made for barbecue. **87** *—S.H. (4/1/2007)*

Vino Con Brio 2003 Matzin Old Vine Zinfandel (Lodi) $21. 83 *—S.H. (6/1/2006)*

Vino Con Brio 1999 Matzin Old Vines Zinfandel (Lodi) $21. 85 *—S.H. (3/1/2004)*

VINO NOCETO

Vino Noceto 2003 Sangiovese (Shenandoah Valley (CA)) $16. 87 *—S.H. (3/1/2006)*

Vino Noceto 2002 Riserva Sangiovese (Shenandoah Valley (CA)) $24. 90 *—S.H. (3/1/2006)*

VINOCE

Vinoce 2000 Bordeaux Blend (Mount Veeder) $60. 93 Editors' Choice *—J.M. (10/1/2003)*

Vinoce 1999 Bordeaux Blend (Mount Veeder) $60. 92 *—J.M. (2/1/2003)*

Vinoce 2001 Sauvignon Blanc (Rutherford) $18. 88 *—J.M. (7/1/2003)*

VINUM CELLARS

Vinum Cellars 2004 The Scrapper Cabernet Franc (El Dorado County) $30. Smells better than it tastes. Opens with sun-bright aromas of cherries, violets and vanilla-infused smoky oak, but turns sharp in the finish, a deficiency that might age out. Give it a year or two. **84** *—S.H. (8/1/2007)*

Vinum Cellars 2003 The Scrapper Cabernet Franc (El Dorado) $30. 93 Editors' Choice *—S.H. (10/1/2006)*

Vinum Cellars 2006 Rosé It's Okay! Cabernet Sauvignon (Napa Valley) $11. Here's a 100% Cabernet Sauvignon, and it shows the difficulty of making this Bordeaux grape into a rosé. It just can't overcome a heavy, soft mouth-filling fullness, even though it's dry. **84** *—S.H. (7/1/2007)*

Vinum Cellars 2005 Rosé It's Okay! Cabernet Sauvignon (Napa Valley) $10. 85 Best Buy *—S.H. (10/1/2006)*

Vinum Cellars 2004 Slow Lane Cabernet Sauvignon (Napa Valley) $27. If this Cab was a few bucks cheaper, it would be a pretty good buy. The fruit is ripe and rich in blackberries and currants, the tannins are sturdy, and the finish is dry. Drink now. **85** *—S.H. (8/1/2007)*

Vinum Cellars 2003 Slow Lane Cab Cabernet Sauvignon (Napa Valley) $27. 82 *—S.H. (4/1/2006)*

Vinum Cellars 2006 CNW Chard-No-Way Chenin Blanc (Clarksburg) $11. Very dry, very acidic and very citrusy-flowery. Clarksburg has been making a reputation for Chenin for many years, and this wine confirms it, for it's quite elegant and polished. **87 Best Buy** *—S.H. (11/15/2007)*

Vinum Cellars 2005 Chard No Way Chenin Blanc (Clarksburg) $10. 85 Best Buy *—S.H. (10/1/2006)*

Vinum Cellars 2000 CNW Wilson Vineyards Chenin Blanc (Clarksburg) $10. 86 *(11/15/2001)*

Vinum Cellars 2003 CNW Cuvée-Wilson Vineyards Chenin Blanc (Clarksburg) $10. 85 Best Buy *—S.H. (7/1/2005)*

Vinum Cellars 2004 Late Harvest Gewürztraminer (San Benito County) $20. 91 *—S.H. (4/1/2006)*

Vinum Cellars 2000 Vista Verde Vineyard Late Harvest Gewürztraminer (San Benito County) $20. 91 *—J.M. (12/1/2002)*

Vinum Cellars 2004 Pets Petite Sirah (Clarksburg) $14. 84 *—S.H. (4/1/2006)*

Vinum Cellars 2000 Pets Wilson Vineyards Petite Sirah (Clarksburg) $13. 80 *(4/1/2003)*

Vinum Cellars 2003 Red Dirt Red Red Blend (El Dorado) $30. 87 *—S.H. (4/1/2006)*

Vinum Cellars 2004 Red Dirt Red Rhône Red Blend (El Dorado County) $30. 84 *—S.H. (12/31/2006)*

Vinum Cellars 2002 Vista Verde Vineyard Syrah (San Benito County) $22. 84 *(9/1/2005)*

Vinum Cellars 1999 Vista Verde Vineyard Syrah (San Benito County) $20. 85 *(10/1/2001)*

Vinum Cellars 2004 Vista Verde Vineyard Viognier (San Benito County) $25. 85 *—S.H. (4/1/2006)*

Vinum Cellars 2003 Vista Verde Vineyard Viognier (San Benito County) $22. 85 *—S.H. (8/1/2005)*

Vinum Cellars 2000 Vista Verde Vineyard Viognier (San Benito County) $20. 90 *—J.M. (9/1/2002)*

Vinum Cellars 2005 Vista Verde Vineyard Vio Viognier (San Benito County) $25. 90 *—S.H. (12/31/2006)*

Vinum Cellars 2002 Elephantus Blanc White Blend (California) $15. 84 *—S.H. (8/1/2005)*

Vinum Cellars 1998 Pointe Blanc White Blend (California) $15. 86 *—J.C. (9/1/2000)*

Vinum Cellars 2004 White Elephant White Blend (California) $15. 90 Best Buy *—S.H. (4/1/2006)*

VIRGIN

Virgin 2001 Sauvignon Blanc (Central Coast) $11. 85 *—S.H. (12/31/2003)*

VISION CELLARS

Vision Cellars 2000 Pinot Noir (Sonoma County) $39. 90 *—S.H. (5/1/2004)*

VITA LUCE

Vita Luce 2002 Syrah (Paso Robles) $36. 87 *(9/1/2005)*

VIVÁC WINERY

Vivác Winery 2004 V. Single Vineyard Cabernet Sauvignon (New Mexico) $21. Earth and spice on the nose are intriguing but slightly rustic on this Cab, aged in French Oak for 18 months and grown in the northern region of the state. The flavors are edgy and slightly thin, though the oak imparts a nice spicy base. **82** *—S.K. (7/1/2007)*

Vivác Winery 2004 V. Single Vineyard Merlot (New Mexico) $24. Good fruit, substantial, meaty spices and a long finish recommend this. The nose is a little edgy and there's a bit of elbow to the tannins, but overall, good flavors and finish. **83** *—S.K. (7/1/2007)*

Vivác Winery 2005 Diavolo Red Blend (New Mexico) $28. Mocha and spice on the nose lead into soft but structured flavors of berry, spice and tobacco in this red blend from New Mexico. It's integrated and interesting, but more of a simple, everyday sip than a collectible selection. Pair with red meat dishes. **83** *—S.K. (12/1/2007)*

Vivác Winery 2005 Divino Red Blend (New Mexico) $22. This unique red blend from New Mexico has a nose of candied spice and a smooth but structured character of red berry, spice and a touch of sweetness. It's not terribly complex but the flavors are good and the overall impression appealing. **84** *—S.K. (12/1/2007)*

VIVIANO

Viviano 1997 Noble Cepage Bordeaux Blend (Texas) $32. 90 *—S.H. (5/1/2001)*

VIXEN

Vixen 2005 Virtuoso Cabernet Franc (Santa Barbara County) $29. Pale in color, soft and flat in the mouth, this wine has a vegetal edge to the stewed cherry flavors. **81** *—S.H. (12/31/2007)*

Vixen NV The Villain Red Blend (Santa Barbara County) $29. This bistro-style red is dry and lusty in cherry, tobacco and spice flavors. The winery has not revealed what varieties are in it, but it tastes like a juicy, old-fashioned field blend, and will go well with a range of fare. **87** *—S.H. (12/31/2007)*

Vixen 2004 The Villain Red Blend (Santa Barbara County) $29. 85 *—S.H. (12/31/2006)*

Vixen 2005 Vacaras Rhône Red Blend (Santa Barbara County) $35. This is a southern Rhône-style blend of Grenache, Cinsault, Counoise and Mourvèdre. It's rustic, with sweet-and-sour flavors of cherries, pineapples and rice vinegar. **83** *—S.H. (12/31/2007)*

Vixen 2006 V Cuvée Rhône White Blend (Santa Barbara County) $32. This is a white Rhône blend of Grenache Blanc and Roussanne, and it shows exuberant fruit and a nice, spicy richness. The flavors of apricots, pears and pineapples have a caramelized, honeyed finish. **87** *—S.H. (12/31/2007)*

Vixen 2005 V Cuvée Rhône White Blend (Santa Barbara County) $32. 91 *—S.H. (12/31/2006)*

Vixen 2005 Vivant Rose Rosé Blend (Santa Ynez Valley) $22. 85 *—S.H. (12/31/2006)*

Vixen 2005 Harmony Syrah (Santa Barbara County) $45. Fruity, tannic and sharp in acids, this Syrah has stewed cherry, blackberry and pineapple flavors that taste like they were lightly sugared, then baked into a pie. Drink now. **84** *—S.H. (12/31/2007)*

Vixen 2004 Harmony Syrah (Santa Barbara County) $45. 90 *—S.H. (12/31/2006)*

Vixen 2006 Vivant Syrah Rosé Syrah (Santa Barbara County) $20. Starts with a harsh smell of burnt jam, then turns simple, soft and slightly sweet in jellied cherry flavors. **80** *—S.H. (12/31/2007)*

Vixen 2006 Viognier (Santa Barbara County) $29. Shows the flamboyant side of Viognier, with superripe, jammy flavors of peach, apricot, spicy mango and honeysuckle flower; a voluptuous wine if ever there was one. It's not really dry, but has good acidity. **86** *—S.H. (12/31/2007)*

Vixen 2005 Viognier (Santa Barbara County) $29. 90 *—S.H. (12/31/2006)*

VJB

VJB 2005 Barbera (Mendocino) $34. Made in an old-fashioned way, this is the kind of wine the immigrants probably drank. It's soft, fruity-raisiny and simple, with enough tannins and acids to combat tomato sauce and garlic. **84** *—S.H. (12/15/2007)*

VJB 2004 Barbera (Mendocino County) $34. 90 *—S.H. (12/1/2006)*

VJB 2003 Barbera (Mendocino) $30. 83 *—S.H. (3/1/2006)*

VJB 2004 Danté Cabernet Sauvignon (Sonoma Valley) $28. Overripe, tannic and sweet like cherry cough drops, this blend of 85% Cabernet Sauvignon and 15% Sangiovese leaves a lot to be desired. **82** *—S.H. (10/1/2007)*

VJB 2003 Dante Cabernet Sauvignon (Sonoma Valley) $40. 85 *—S.H. (9/1/2006)*

VJB 2002 Dante Cabernet Sauvignon (Sonoma County) $36. 91 *—S.H. (11/15/2005)*

VJB 2000 Dante Cabernet Sauvignon (Sonoma County) $24. 86 *—S.H. (11/15/2003)*

VJB 1999 Dante Cabernet Sauvignon (Sonoma County) $23. 89 *—S.H. (11/15/2002)*

VJB 2004 Gregory Vineyard Cabernet Sauvignon (Sonoma Valley) $36. Open tonight and enjoy for its immediate pleasures. Soft and expressive, it shows a wealth of cherry, blackberry, raspberry, cola, licorice, cedar and vanilla-spice flavors that are wrapped into rich, finely ground tannins. Nice with a grilled steak. **88** *—S.H. (10/1/2007)*

VJB 2003 V Cabernet Sauvignon (Sonoma Valley) $40. Nice and lush. The flavors of cherry, cassis, anise, milk chocolate and cinnamon spice are just delicious, and there's a good texture, too. Ripe, firm tannins girdle the wine, and just-enough acidity keeps it from tasting candied. Drink now for its youthful babyfat. **88** *—S.H. (10/1/2007)*

VJB 2000 V Cabernet Sauvignon (Sonoma County) $35. 87 *—S.H. (11/15/2003)*

VJB 2001 V Private Reserve Cabernet Sauvignon (Sonoma County) $40. 89 *—S.H. (11/15/2005)*

VJB NV Baci di Famiglia Chardonnay Port 375mL Chardonnay (Sonoma Valley) $28. 84 *—S.H. (10/1/2006)*

VJB 2005 Garbiella Ranch Chardonnay (Sonoma Valley) $14. Soft and sweet, although there's a lot going on, tastewise. Flavors of pineapples, peaches, pears and vanilla are wrapped into an oaky, creamy package. But the wine would benefit from more acidity and less sweetness. **84** *—S.H. (10/1/2007)*

VJB 2000 Gabriella Ranch Chardonnay (Sonoma Valley) $11. 84 *—S.H. (12/15/2002)*

VJB 2005 Montepulciano (Sonoma Valley) $32. Brings to mind the old jug wines, with its tannic dryness and earthy berry flavors. Those were the kind of wines that happily washed down anything that called for a red. So is this, although it's a lot pricier. **87** *—S.H. (12/15/2007)*

VJB 2005 Sangiovese (Sonoma Valley) $32. Rustic and acidic, this is dry, with cherry flavors. The harshness will benefit from decanting, but it's not an ager. **82** *—S.H. (12/15/2007)*

VJB 2005 Syrah (El Dorado County) $28. Too sweet and Port-y. This mountain-grown Syrah has rich cherry-berry flavors and smooth tannins, but seems to have some residual sugar that makes it taste more like a dessert wine than a table wine. **83** *—S.H. (12/15/2007)*

VJB 2003 Syrah (Dry Creek Valley) $28. 85 *—S.H. (2/1/2006)*

VJB 2002 Syrah (Alexander Valley) $28. 87 *(9/1/2005)*

VJB 2005 Tocai Friulano (Mendocino County) $18. The best thing about this fine young white wine is the acidity. It's high and crisp and bracing, and makes the peach pie, honeysuckle and vanilla wafer flavors come alive. There's a honeyed sweetness, but that wonderful acidity balances it nicely. **86** *—S.H. (10/1/2007)*

VJB 2004 Zinfandel (El Dorado County) $24. High alcohol makes this wine a little hot and sweet, and there may be some residual sugar, but it works in this Foothills Zin, of which this is a classic expression. With some rugged tannins and soft, low acidity, it shows expressive red and black berries, milk chocolate, root beer, gingerbread and peppery spices, with a sweet overlay of oak. Drink now. **87** *—S.H. (10/1/2007)*

VJB 2003 Zinfandel (El Dorado County) $26. 84 *—S.H. (2/1/2006)*

VJB 2000 Zinfandel (Sonoma County) $23. 82 *—S.H. (12/1/2002)*

VOLKER EISELE

Volker Eisele 2002 Terzetto Bordeaux Blend (Napa Valley) $75. 87 *—S.H. (12/1/2005)*

Volker Eisele 2001 Terzetto Bordeaux Blend (Napa Valley) $75. 94 *—S.H. (10/1/2004)*

Volker Eisele 2006 Gemini White Wine Bordeaux White Blend (Napa Valley) $25. From Chiles Valley, this blend of 71% Semillon and 29% Sauvignon Blanc is one of the best wines of its type of the vintage. Cofermented and barrel aged in 15% new French oak, it shows extraordinary richness, and savory flavors of green and yellow tree fruits, green tea, cashew, Asian spices and gingery vanilla. It even has some dusty tannins that make for grip and structure. The finish is absolutely dry. **93 Editors' Choice** *—S.H. (12/1/2007)*

Volker Eisele 2003 Terzetto Red Wine Cabernet Blend (Napa Valley) $75. 88 *—S.H. (12/31/2006)*

Volker Eisele 2002 Cabernet Sauvignon (Napa Valley) $38. 88 *—S.H. (12/1/2005)*

Volker Eisele 2001 Cabernet Sauvignon (Napa Valley) $38. 92 *—S.H. (10/1/2004)*

Volker Eisele 1999 Cabernet Sauvignon (Napa Valley) $40. 92 *—J.M. (2/1/2003)*

Volker Eisele 1998 Cabernet Sauvignon (Napa Valley) $35. 91 *—J.M. (12/1/2001)*

Volker Eisele 2003 Estate Cabernet Sauvignon (Napa Valley) $40. 92 Editors' Choice *—S.H. (12/31/2006)*

Volker Eisele 2004 Family Estate Cabernet Sauvignon (Napa Valley) $40. This is just a little too soft, sweet and ripe, although it retains the classic structure and elegance you demand from the venerable name Eisele. The flavor of sugared crushed blackberries, cherries and caramelly vanilla suggest drinking now. **87** *—S.H. (12/1/2007)*

Volker Eisele 2005 Gemini White Blend (Napa Valley) $25. 87 *—S.H. (12/31/2006)*

Volker Eisele 2004 Gemini White Blend (Napa Valley) $25. 90 *—S.H. (12/1/2005)*

Volker Eisele 2003 Gemini White Blend (Napa Valley) $25. 86 *—S.H. (2/1/2005)*

VON STRASSER

Von Strasser 2001 Sori Bricco Vineyard Bordeaux Blend (Diamond Mountain) $60. 91 *—S.H. (2/1/2005)*

Von Strasser 1997 Cabernet Sauvignon (Diamond Mountain) $50. 92 *(11/1/2000)*

Von Strasser 2001 Cabernet Sauvignon (Diamond Mountain) $50. 88 *—S.H. (2/1/2005)*

Von Strasser 2000 Cabernet Sauvignon (Diamond Mountain) $45. 89 *(8/1/2003)*

Von Strasser 1999 Diamond Mountain Cabernet Sauvignon (Napa Valley) $50. 91 *—J.M. (6/1/2002)*

Von Strasser 2001 Estate Vineyards Cabernet Sauvignon (Diamond Mountain) $60. 87 *—S.H. (2/1/2005)*

Von Strasser 2002 Estate Vineyards Cabernet Sauvignon (Diamond Mountain) $70. 90 Cellar Selection *—S.H. (8/1/2006)*

Von Strasser 2000 Estate Vineyards Cabernet Sauvignon (Diamond Mountain) $70. 91 *(8/1/2003)*

Von Strasser 2002 Post Vineyard Cabernet Sauvignon (Diamond Mountain) $75. 92 Cellar Selection *—S.H. (9/1/2006)*

Von Strasser 2001 Post Vineyard Cabernet Sauvignon (Diamond Mountain) $60. 91 *—S.H. (2/1/2005)*

Von Strasser 1997 Chardonnay (Diamond Mountain) $36. 89 *—M.S. (10/1/1999)*

Von Strasser 2000 Aurora Vineyard Chardonnay (Diamond Mountain) $40. 87 *—S.H. (2/1/2003)*

Von Strasser 2000 Rainin Vineyard Chardonnay (Diamond Mountain) $40. 87 *—S.H. (2/1/2004)*

Von Strasser 1999 Rainin Vineyard Chardonnay (Diamond Mountain) $45. 94 *—J.M. (5/1/2002)*

Von Strasser 2002 Reserve Red Blend (Diamond Mountain) $100. 97 Cellar Selection *—S.H. (9/1/2006)*

Von Strasser 2001 Reserve Red Blend (Diamond Mountain) $100. 93 *—S.H. (2/1/2005)*

Von Strasser 2002 Sori Bricco Vineyard Red Blend (Diamond Mountain) $70. 92 Cellar Selection *—S.H. (8/1/2006)*

Von Strasser 2000 Sori Bricco Vineyard Red Blend (Diamond Mountain) $65. 90 *(8/1/2003)*

Von Strasser 1999 Sori Bricco Vineyards Red Blend (Diamond Mountain) $60. 90 *—S.H. (11/15/2002)*

Von Strasser 2001 Monhoff Vineyard Zinfandel (Diamond Mountain) $40. 90 *(11/1/2003)*

Von Strasser 2000 Monhoff Vineyard Zinfandel (Diamond Mountain) $40. 88 *(8/1/2003)*

VOSS

Voss 1997 Merlot (Rutherford) $20. 84 *—J.C. (3/1/2000)*

Voss 2006 Sauvignon Blanc (Rutherford) $20. It's rare to get a white wine from Cabernet-centric Rutherford, but Voss does a good job with this dry, crisp, low-alcohol Sauvignon Blanc. You can taste the coolness of the vintage in the tangy acidity and the gooseberry-accented citrus, fig and white pepper flavors. 90 Editors' Choice *—S.H. (12/15/2007)*

Voss 2005 Sauvignon Blanc (Rutherford) $19. 89 *—S.H. (12/15/2006)*

Voss 2003 Sauvignon Blanc (Napa Valley) $19. 90 *—S.H. (10/1/2005)*

Voss 2001 Sauvignon Blanc (Napa Valley) $18. 88 *—S.H. (9/1/2003)*

Voss 2000 Sauvignon Blanc (Napa Valley) $18. 88 *(8/1/2002)*

Voss 1998 Sauvignon Blanc (Napa Valley) $15. 86 *(3/1/2000)*

Voss 1997 Botrytis Sauvignon Blanc (Napa Valley) $NA. 86 *—J.C. (12/31/1999)*

Voss 1996 Shiraz (Oakville) $24. 92 *—M.S. (3/1/2000)*

Voss 1999 Shiraz (Napa Valley) $25. 90 *(11/1/2001)*

Voss 2003 Syrah (Napa Valley) $20. A little tannic right now, which limits immediate pleasure, but I have a strong hunch the wine will develop for five years. Alternatively, decanting will help. The wine has a solid core of blackberry fruit that's almost jammy. Interestingly, the winemaker added small amounts of Petit Verdot and Viognier, which boost depth and brightness. 89 *—S.H. (3/1/2007)*

Voss 2001 Syrah (Napa Valley) $20. 87 *(9/1/2005)*

Voss 2001 Ocala Syrah (Napa Valley) $45. 88 *(9/1/2005)*

Voss 2005 Viognier (Carneros) $26. A most interesting and complex Viognier. The strong, brisk acidity really strikes you, and is unusual for this variety, which is usually soft. Then the flavors hit, showy but elegant, an array of crushed citrus zest, white peach yogurt, apricot, vanilla and dusty spices. Try this racy wine as an alternative to Chardonnay. 90 *—S.H. (3/1/2007)*

Voss 2003 Viognier (Carneros) $25. 85 *—S.H. (10/1/2005)*

Voss 2000 Botrytis White Blend (Napa Valley) $25. 95 *—S.H. (12/1/2002)*

W.H. SMITH

W.H. Smith 2005 Bronze Label Cabernet Sauvignon (Howell Mountain) $42. Starting out as a very tannic, closed wine, this is one for the cellar. The question is how long. It's a big, dry, ripe Cab, with extracted blackberry, blueberry and cedar flavors, and while it should soften over the next five years, it doesn't have the stuffing for the long haul. 89 *—S.H. (12/15/2007)*

W.H. Smith 2005 Purple Label Cabernet Sauvignon (Howell Mountain) $54. Bill Smith is better known for his Pinot Noirs, but he founded La Jota and knows a thing or two about Howell Mountain Cabs. This is a big, dry, tannic mountain wine, virtually undrinkable now for its hard astringency. However, it's a fine cellar candidate. Brims with ripe blackberries and cherries that just need time. Should begin to open in 2008, and develop for another eight years or so. 93 Cellar Selection *—S.H. (12/15/2007)*

W.H. Smith 2006 Pinot Noir (Sonoma Coast) $28. Smith's basic regional Pinot is a very fine wine. It shows the elegant combination of power and subtlety that mark a fine Pinot Noir, and the alcohol level is low. Dry and crisp, the flavors are of cola, raspberries, rosehip tea, licorice and spice. Drink now. 89 *—S.H. (12/15/2007)*

W.H. Smith 2004 Pinot Noir (Sonoma Coast) $28. 91 *—S.H. (10/1/2006)*

W.H. Smith 2002 Pinot Noir (Sonoma Coast) $24. 91 Editors' Choice *—S.H. (11/1/2004)*

W.H. Smith 2006 Marimar Estate Vineyard Pinot Noir (Sonoma Coast) $48. Raspberries, cherries, cola, tea, rhubarb pie, licorice, vanilla and sweet leather flavors flood the mouth, wrapped in a delicately silky, complex texture, and the finish goes on and on in oak-inspired fruit and Asian spices. Compellingly delicious; drinks now and through 2009. 93 *—S.H. (12/15/2007)*

W.H. Smith 2006 Maritime Pinot Noir (Sonoma Coast) $54. Shows the precision and control of Smith's previous Maritime Pinot, marked by a tense, exciting structure. Crisp acids and fine, dusty tannins dance with earthy cherry and cola fruit, herbs and oak to create a complex, tremendously rewarding palate experience. Best now through 2010. 93 *—S.H. (12/15/2007)*

W.H. Smith 2005 Maritime Vineyard Pinot Noir (Sonoma Coast) $52. The first thoughts on this wine are how young it is, and how much potential it shows. The immaturity lies in the primary fruit, acidic character, like a big gulp of fruity cola. But the wine's awesome future is in its vast complexity and balance, and the way it dominates the palate and lasts and lasts. A blend of several vineyards, it's high in acidity, with massive cherry, pomegranate, rhubarb preserve, licorice, earthy mushroom and cedar flavors. So balanced and dry, so elegant and powerful, so silky and complex, it is quite simply a very great Pinot Noir, and an early indication that the vintage on the far Sonoma Coast may be the greatest ever. Tasted twice. 98 Editors' Choice *—S.H. (5/1/2007)*

W.H. Smith 2002 Maritime Ridge Pinot Noir (Sonoma Coast) $45. 92 *—S.H. (11/1/2004)*

W.H. Smith 2006 Umino Vineyard Pinot Noir (Sonoma Coast) $48. Good and dry, with a fine oak edge to the fruit and a delicately silky structure, but there's just too much of a cooked or taste, especially in the finish. It's like the cherries were plumped, diluting the flavors, and even though alcohol is low, it tastes hot. 86 *—S.H. (12/15/2007)*

WAGNER

Wagner 2000 Estate Bottled Ice Wine Riesling (Finger Lakes) $30. 84 *—J.C. (8/1/2003)*

Wagner 2002 Fermented Dry Riesling (Finger Lakes) $10. 84 *—J.C. (8/1/2003)*

Wagner 2006 Ice Riesling (Finger Lakes) $23. This zesty icewine, with its lemon, spice and mineral backbone, offers a light and playful take on the dessert wine coveted by so many worldwide. Delicate and not overly sweet, this shows some restraint and subtlety, lending it to food pairing and solo sipping. 89 *—S.K. (12/1/2007)*

Wagner 1998 Ice Wine Riesling (Finger Lakes) $18. 89 *—J.C. (3/1/2001)*

Wagner 2006 Ice Vidal Blanc (Finger Lakes) $22. With its aromas of citrus and honey and its exuberant flavors of tropical fruit and toasted spice, this is both pretty and playful. Sweet but full of finesse, the wine has floral element that adds to its allure. 87 *—S.K. (12/1/2007)*

Wagner 1998 Ice Wine Vidal Blanc (Finger Lakes) $18. 81 *—J.C. (3/1/2001)*

Wagner 1998 Ice Wine Vignoles (Finger Lakes) $18. 87 *—J.C. (3/1/2001)*

Wagner 1999 Late Harvest Vignoles (Finger Lakes) $15. 86 *—J.C. (3/1/2001)*

WALLA WALLA

Walla Walla 2003 Sagemoor Vineyard Cuvée Bordeaux Blend (Columbia Valley (WA)) $40. 89 *—P.G. (6/1/2006)*

Walla Walla 2002 Cabernet Franc (Walla Walla (WA)) $25. 89 *—P.G. (12/15/2005)*

Walla Walla 2004 Cabernet Sauvignon (Columbia Valley (WA)) $35. In this unusually difficult vintage, the winery sourced some of its fruit from Cold Creek, some from Goose Ridge, some from Sagemoor. The flavors are on the light side, almost thin, not progressing much past the watermelon and strawberry stage. In a flight of meatier wines, this one seemed rather insubstantial, and definitely not up to the winery's usual standards. 86 *—P.G. (3/1/2007)*

Walla Walla 2003 Cabernet Sauvignon (Walla Walla (WA)) $35. 89 *—P.G. (6/1/2006)*

Walla Walla 2002 Cabernet Sauvignon (Columbia Valley (WA)) $35. 92 —*P.G. (12/15/2005)*

Walla Walla 1999 Cabernet Sauvignon (Columbia Valley (WA)) $35. 92 Editors' Choice —*P.G. (6/1/2002)*

Walla Walla 2004 Sagemoor Vineyard Cabernet Sauvignon (Columbia Valley (WA)) $40. I found decent overall weight and structure in this vineyard designate, and good, supporting acids under a wash of chocolate and butterscotch. Even so, the fruit is submerged, and much of the detail is lost, or at least missing. The finish shows a bit of heat, and the wine never quite comes into focus. 87 —*P.G. (3/1/2007)*

Walla Walla 2003 Vineyard Select Cabernet Sauvignon (Walla Walla (WA)) $45. 92 —*P.G. (6/1/2006)*

Walla Walla 1997 Windrow Vineyard Cabernet Sauvignon (Washington) $32. 90 —*M.S. (4/1/2000)*

Walla Walla Village 2004 Merlot (Columbia Valley (WA)) $22. This well-made Merlot is smooth and chocolaty in a style reminiscent of Walla Walla Vintners. I pick up some mint in the finish; overall it's a broad, smooth, medium-bodied, forward style that is very appealing and ready to enjoy right now. 88 —*P.G. (3/1/2007)*

Walla Walla 2003 Merlot (Walla Walla (WA)) $28. 88 —*P.G. (12/15/2005)*

Walla Walla 2000 Merlot (Walla Walla (WA)) $25. 91 —*P.G. (9/1/2002)*

Walla Walla 2003 Cordon Grove Vineyard Cuvée Red Blend (Yakima Valley) $28. 90 —*P.G. (12/15/2005)*

WALTER DACON

Walter Dacon 2005 Sangiovese (Red Mountain) $28. A pure Sangiovese, it shows the lighter colors of the grape, and offers quite soft, round fruit flavors of plum and ripe strawberry. Full-bodied (for Sangio) and almost lush, it's a user-friendly style that de-emphasizes the grape's natural acidity and ripens it to almost 15% alcohol. There's not a lot of detail here, just round, sweet fruit. 87 —*P.G. (12/1/2007)*

Walter Dacon 2003 C'est Beaux Syrah (Columbia Valley (WA)) $35. 88 —*P.G. (6/1/2006)*

Walter Dacon 2003 C'est Belle Syrah (Columbia Valley (WA)) $28. 89 —*P.G. (6/1/2006)*

Walter Dacon 2003 C'est Magnifique Syrah (Columbia Valley (WA)) $38. 88 —*P.G. (6/1/2006)*

Walter Dacon 2005 C'est Syrah Beaux Syrah (Columbia Valley (WA)) $35. The Beaux is Walter Dacon's American-oaked Syrah (then why the French name?). It is the lightest, most feminine of the trio of Dacon Syrahs, yet also the most aromatic and interesting. There are notes of flower and leaf not found in the other wines, perhaps because the barrels were used with more restraint. I like the violets-and-chocolate imprint it leaves in the back of the mouth. 90 —*P.G. (12/1/2007)*

Walter Dacon 2003 C'est Syrah Beaux Syrah (Columbia Valley (WA)) $35. 88 *(9/1/2005)*

Walter Dacon 2005 C'est Syrah Belle Syrah (Columbia Valley (WA)) $28. This is the winery's French-oaked Syrah, thick and smoky, with a balanced mix of red and black fruits, nicely retained acids, and layers of creamy oak. The alcohol hits 14.6% but the wine remains smooth and supple. Barrel flavors expand into a lingering finish with butterscotch, mocha and spice. 90 —*P.G. (12/1/2007)*

Walter Dacon 2003 C'est Syrah Belle Syrah (Columbia Valley (WA)) $28. 85 *(9/1/2005)*

Walter Dacon 2005 C'est Syrah Magnifique Syrah (Columbia Valley (WA)) $38. The Magnifique is a barrel selection from the French oak-aged side of the winery. It's 100% Syrah and packed with blackberry, black cherry and streaks of citrus. It's very well balanced, complete and firm; the wine should age nicely for another decade at least. 91 —*P.G. (12/1/2007)*

Walter Dacon 2003 C'est Syrah Magnifique Syrah (Yakima Valley) $38. 87 *(9/1/2005)*

Walter Dacon 2004 C'est Beaux Syrah (Columbia Valley (WA)) $35. 89 —*P.G. (11/15/2006)*

Walter Dacon 2004 C'est Belle Syrah (Columbia Valley (WA)) $28. 90 —*P.G. (11/15/2006)*

Walter Dacon 2004 C'est Syrah Magnifique Syrah (Columbia Valley (WA)) $38. 91 —*P.G. (11/15/2006)*

Walter Dacon 2006 Viognier (Yakima Valley) $20. This is quite delicious, bright and tasting of fresh-squeezed oranges and tangerines. Fruity, forward and lush, it's really quite charming. The aromas convey light hints of rose petals, jasmine and honey; the fruit an intriguing mix of ripe pear, papaya and apricot. 90 —*P.G. (12/1/2007)*

WALTZING BEAR

Waltzing Bear 2003 Cargasacchi Jalama Vineyard Pinot Noir (Santa Barbara County) $42. 90 —*S.H. (8/1/2006)*

Waltzing Bear 2003 Garys' Vineyard Pinot Noir (Santa Lucia Highlands) $45. 89 —*S.H. (8/1/2006)*

Waltzing Bear 2003 Rancho Ontiveros Vineyard Pinot Noir (Santa Maria Valley) $42. 91 —*S.H. (8/1/2006)*

Waltzing Bear 2003 Solomon Hills Vineyard Pinot Noir (Santa Maria Valley) $45. 85 —*S.H. (8/1/2006)*

WASHINGTON HILLS

Washington Hills 1999 Cabernet Sauvignon (Columbia Valley (WA)) $10. 84 —*P.G. (6/1/2002)*

Washington Hills 2000 Fumé Blanc (Yakima Valley) $7. 86 Best Buy —*P.G. (6/1/2002)*

Washington Hills 1999 Merlot (Columbia Valley (WA)) $10. 84 —*P.G. (6/1/2002)*

Washington Hills 2001 Dry Riesling (Columbia Valley (WA)) $7. 88 Best Buy —*P.G. (12/31/2002)*

Washington Hills 2000 Sémillon-Chardonnay (Columbia Valley (WA)) $7. 87 Best Buy —*P.G. (6/1/2002)*

Washington Hills 2002 Shiraz (Columbia Valley (WA)) $9. 85 Best Buy *(9/1/2005)*

Washington Hills 2000 Syrah (Yakima Valley) $17. 83 —*P.G. (6/1/2002)*

Washington Hills 1999 Syrah (Columbia Valley (WA)) $14. 83 *(10/1/2001)*

WATERBROOK

Waterbrook 1998 Red Mountain Meritage Bordeaux Blend (Columbia Valley (WA)) $36. 89 —*P.G. (6/1/2001)*

Waterbrook 2004 Cabernet Sauvignon (Columbia Valley (WA)) $22. More tannic and substantial than the Merlot, this shows cool-climate flavors that bring out citrus, pepper and some lightly green tannins. It's a medium-bodied wine shows its varietal character, opens up for near term drinking but has the guts and structure to sock away for up to a decade. 89 —*P.G. (8/1/2007)*

Waterbrook 2003 Cabernet Sauvignon (Columbia Valley (WA)) $21. 90 —*P.G. (4/1/2006)*

Waterbrook 2002 Cabernet Sauvignon (Columbia Valley (WA)) $24. 86 —*P.G. (11/15/2004)*

Waterbrook 1997 Cabernet Sauvignon (Columbia Valley (WA)) $22. 90*(6/1/2000)*

Waterbrook 2005 Chardonnay (Columbia Valley (WA)) $13. Oaky, supple and structured, this sturdy Chardonnay is built upon clean green apple fruit and nicely layered toasty oak. It's the same formula as before: one third new French oak, one third malolactic, and nicely expresses open, fruit-driven, barrel-enhanced flavors with crisp citrus fruit. 88 Best Buy —*P.G. (8/1/2007)*

Waterbrook 2004 Chardonnay (Columbia Valley (WA)) $12. 88 Best Buy —*P.G. (4/1/2006)*

Waterbrook 2001 Chardonnay (Columbia Valley (WA)) $10. 89 —*P.G. (9/1/2002)*

Waterbrook 1998 Chardonnay (Columbia Valley (WA)) $9. 85 —*P.G. (6/1/2000)*

Waterbrook 2004 Merlot (Columbia Valley (WA)) $20. This is a perfect melding of fruit, barrel and tannin. The mix of tangy black cherry, wild blackberry, smoke, fig and herbal structure leads into a seductive, lingering finish with cocoa, coffee and spice. 89 —*P.G. (8/1/2007)*

Waterbrook 2003 Merlot (Columbia Valley (WA)) $19. 88 —*P.G. (4/1/2006)*

Waterbrook 2002 Merlot (Columbia Valley (WA)) $20. 87 —*P.G. (11/15/2004)*

Waterbrook 1997 Merlot (Columbia Valley (WA)) $20. 89 —*P.G. (6/1/2000)*

Waterbrook 2005 Mélange Red Blend (Columbia Valley (WA)) $15. Merlot, Cabernet, Cab Franc, Sangiovese and Syrah all pour into this graceful and accommodating blend, particularly ripe and fruity in the excellent 2005 vintage. It puts the mixed red fruits up front, lays back on the oak, and makes itself flexible enough for anything from a picnic to a poulet. 86 —*P.G. (8/1/2007)*

Waterbrook 2004 Mélange Red Blend (Columbia Valley (WA)) $14. 87 —*P.G. (4/1/2006)*

Waterbrook 1999 Mélange Red Blend (Columbia Valley (WA)) $15. 86 —*P.G. (6/1/2001)*

Waterbrook 2000 Ciel du Cheval Vineyard Sangiovese (Red Mountain) $28. 90 —*P.G. (9/1/2002)*

Waterbrook 2006 Rosé Sangiovese (Columbia Valley (WA)) $12. This light rosé is scented with rosewater, melon and strawberry. Finished dry and nicely structured. 86 —*P.G. (12/1/2007)*

Waterbrook 2006 Sauvignon Blanc (Columbia Valley (WA)) $12. Waterbrook offers up a clean, palate-refreshing style of Sauvignon Blanc, with fruit flavors of melon and mixed fruits. **86 Best Buy** —*P.G. (12/1/2007)*

Waterbrook 2005 Sauvignon Blanc (Columbia Valley (WA)) $14. This wine fits the winery style like a comfy old shoe. It feels good, smells good and wears well. There is a nod to the grassy quality of the grape, but it's smoothed over with toasty cracker flavors and thicker seams of fig, melon and pear. **88** —*P.G. (8/1/2007)*

Waterbrook 2004 Sauvignon Blanc (Columbia Valley (WA)) $12. 89 —*P.G. (4/1/2006)*

Waterbrook 2001 Sauvignon Blanc (Columbia Valley (WA)) $14. 88 —*P.G. (9/1/2002)*

Waterbrook 1998 Sauvignon Blanc (Columbia Valley (WA)) $8. 89 Best Buy *(6/1/2000)*

Waterbrook 2000 Klipsun Vineyard Sauvignon Blanc (Red Mountain) $9. 88 —*P.G. (11/15/2001)*

Waterbrook 1999 Klipsun Vineyard Sauvignon Blanc (Columbia Valley (WA)) $8. 90 Best Buy —*P.G. (6/1/2001)*

Waterbrook 2005 Syrah (Columbia Valley (WA)) $20. The addition of 5% Grenache and 4% Viognier—roughly the same as last year's excellent wine—enhances this fruity, forward, well-built Syrah. It's a light, open and attractive style; fragrant, varietal and effusively fruity. Don't look for power or mass here; it's all up front. This is quite delicious. **88** —*P.G. (8/1/2007)*

Waterbrook 2004 Syrah (Columbia Valley (WA)) $21. 88 —*P.G. (4/1/2006)*

Waterbrook 2002 Syrah (Columbia Valley (WA)) $20. 86 —*P.G. (11/15/2004)*

Waterbrook 2004 Viognier (Columbia Valley (WA)) $17. 91 —*P.G. (4/1/2006)*

Waterbrook 2001 Viognier (Columbia Valley (WA)) $20. 90 —*P.G. (9/1/2002)*

WATERMILL

Watermill 2005 Cabernet Sauvignon (Columbia Valley (OR)) $30. Supple and lightly toasty, this is an easy-drinking wine that seems more like a Merlot than a Cab. There's an herbal side, some green tea, light spice and broad, strawberry/cherry fruit. It's very pleasant in a lighter style. **87** —*P.G. (11/15/2007)*

Watermill 2005 Chances R Red Blend (Columbia Valley (OR)) $20. This is a decent effort, three quarters Merlot, front-loaded with berry/ cherry fruit and some lumbery oak. Though very drinkable, it quickly falls away; there seems to be no back end to it. **86** —*P.G. (11/15/2007)*

Watermill 2005 Syrah (Walla Walla (OR)) $32. This shows why Walla Walla has such a fine reputation for Syrah. There's definition, cut and grace to this wine; it's got style. The fruit is tart and bracing, set against steely mineral and composted earth. It hints at other, more Rhône-ish flavors also, and it's a wine that you want to cellar to see where it goes. This is definitely the star of the show among Watermill's debut releases. **89** —*P.G. (11/15/2007)*

WATERS

Waters 2004 Interlude Red Bordeaux Blend (Columbia Valley (WA)) $25. 91 —*P.G. (6/1/2006)*

Waters 2003 Cabernet Sauvignon (Walla Walla (WA)) $38. 88 —*P.G. (6/1/2006)*

Waters 2005 Syrah (Columbia Valley (WA)) $25. This is a thoroughly delicious wine, pure-blooded Syrah from three vineyards. It puts bright, clean raspberry fruit right up front, then layers in a hint of bramble and earth against a foundation of firm, fine-grained tannins. It's authoritative, substantial, straightforward and absolutely tongue-riveting, a brilliant combination of finesse, tension and balance. **90** —*P.G. (8/1/2007)*

Waters 2005 Pepper Bridge Vineyard Syrah (Walla Walla (WA)) $40. This completes the 2005 Syrah quartet for Waters Syrahs. Very well made, both soft upon entry and substantial in midpalate, this mixes berries and cassis, accented with bourbon barrel, coffee grounds and smoke. If there is a complaint, it's that it's been pushed to 14.6% alcohol, and suffers somewhat as a result from a hot finish. **88** —*P.G. (12/1/2007)*

WATERS CREST

Waters Crest 2004 Compania Rosso Bordeaux Blend (North Fork of Long Island) $45. Made of 80% Merlot, 10% Cabernet Franc, 6% Cabernet Sauvignon and 4% Malbec, this blend from Long Island's Waters Crest is somewhat complex, with an herbal, peppery nose and tastes of cherry, plum and oak. The nose is robust but on the palate, the wine feels a little watered down and thin. **83** —*S.K. (2/1/2007)*

Waters Crest 2004 Cabernet Franc (North Fork of Long Island) $30. Made with 100% Cabernet Franc, this wine has an herbaceous, earthy nose and jaunty plum and cherry flavors. It's a bit bracing on the palate and the fruit initially overrides the herbal notes beneath, giving it a flavorful yet one-dimensional character. The nose implies more depth—leaving you wanting more. **83** —*S.K. (2/1/2007)*

Waters Crest 2004 Private Reserve Cabernet Franc (North Fork of Long Island) $39. Some nice aromas of bright red fruit and spice but the flavors are thin and charred and the feel and finish tannic. The regular 2004 Cab Franc is actually preferable. **81** —*S.K. (2/1/2007)*

Waters Crest 2004 Chardonnay (North Fork of Long Island) $16. 80 —*M.D. (8/1/2006)*

Waters Crest 2004 Private Reserve Chardonnay (North Fork of Long Island) $25. 81 —*J.C. (3/1/2006)*

Waters Crest 2004 Merlot (North Fork of Long Island) $20. There's a depth and meatiness to the nose on this wine, with its black cherry, plum, clove and peppercorn aromas. But the wall of blockbuster tannins that hit the palate next make it difficult to discern any of the qualities beyond, and makes it too tight and chalky for what should be a softer, more integrated variety. May improve with age, once the edge drops off. **83** —*S.K. (2/1/2007)*

Waters Crest 2004 Private Reserve Merlot (North Fork of Long Island) $35. 89 —*M.D. (12/1/2006)*

Waters Crest 2005 Rosé Table Wine Rosé Blend (North Fork of Long Island) $15. Watery and supersubtle flavors fail to impress with this rosé. What's there is good—strawberry, fresh fruit—but it's buried in the mix. **81** —*S.K. (7/1/2007)*

WATERSTONE

Waterstone 2004 Cabernet Sauvignon (Napa Valley) $24. Very ripe, with sun-enriched blackberry, cherry and mocha flavors, and rich in sweet, dusty tannins. The finish on this polished, gentle Cab is a little sweet and oaky. Drink now. **86** —*S.H. (12/31/2007)*

Waterstone 2003 Cabernet Sauvignon (Napa Valley) $24. 82 —*S.H. (5/1/2006)*

Waterstone 2002 Cabernet Sauvignon (Napa Valley) $20. 85 —*S.H. (6/1/2005)*

Waterstone 2001 Cabernet Sauvignon (Napa Valley) $20. 87 —*S.H. (10/1/2004)*

Waterstone 2003 Reserve Cabernet Sauvignon (Napa Valley) $75. This is the best Waterstone Cab in years. A barrel selection, the wine is beautifully ripe and shows great Napa tannins. It's also sharper and more acidic than many of the cults, making it more companionable at the dinner table. Should drink well over the next five years. **89** —*S.H. (3/1/2007)*

Waterstone 2005 Chardonnay (Carneros) $18. With its polished acidity and herb-infused tropical fruit flavors, this is an especially nice Chard to have with food. It's thoroughly dry and very clean, with enough oak to provide an extra layer of vanilla cream and buttered toast. **87** —*S.H. (2/1/2007)*

Waterstone 2004 Chardonnay (Carneros) $18. 89 —*S.H. (5/1/2006)*

Waterstone 2002 Chardonnay (Carneros) $18. 86 —*S.H. (12/31/2004)*

Waterstone 2004 Pinot Noir (Carneros) $20. Simple and easy, a textbook correct Pinot with good varietal character. It's dry and silky, with cola, rhubarb, coffee, cherry and oak flavors that finish with tons of oriental spices. **85** —*S.H. (2/1/2007)*

Waterstone 2003 Pinot Noir (Carneros) $20. 85 —*S.H. (7/1/2006)*

Waterstone 2002 Pinot Noir (Carneros) $18. 84 —*S.H. (10/1/2005)*

Waterstone 2001 Pinot Noir (Carneros) $18. 86 —*S.H. (10/1/2004)*

Waterstone 2002 Sauvignon Blanc (Napa Valley) $12. 83 —*S.H. (10/1/2004)*

Waterstone 2005 Syrah (Napa Valley) $22. This Syrah was grown in Carneros in the cool, long '05 vintage, which may explain its minty sharpness, despite the low case production level. You'll find enough cherry fruit and new French oak to make it fairly rich, but that sharp green tang remains. **84** —*S.H. (12/31/2007)*

WATTLE CREEK

Wattle Creek 2004 Cabernet Sauvignon (Alexander Valley) $50. Wattle Creek has done a good job with Cabernet over the years, and here's another one. I don't think '04 was their best vintage, as the wine is a little raisiny, despite an official alcohol of only 14.1%. But it shows a classy structure, polished dryness and a good depth of varietal black currant fruit, accented with new oak. Probably best now and for a few years. **87** —*S.H. (12/15/2007)*

Wattle Creek 2003 Cabernet Sauvignon (Alexander Valley) $50. There's tons of ripe fruit in this totally dry Cab, which has a drop of Malbec. It has a full-bodied, weighty feel, a blackberry jam density, and is fairly tannic, although the tannins are of the sweet kind. A little forward and obvious now, the wine should develop bottle complexity over the next years. **88** —*S.H. (7/1/2007)*

USA

Wattle Creek 2002 Cabernet Sauvignon (Alexander Valley) $50. 88 —*S.H. (9/1/2006)*

Wattle Creek 1997 Cabernet Sauvignon (Sonoma County) $50. 90 *(11/1/2000)*

Wattle Creek 1995 Cabernet Sauvignon (Sonoma County) $50. 90 *(6/1/2001)*

Wattle Creek 2000 Alexander Valley Cabernet Sauvignon (Alexander Valley) $47. 89 —*S.H. (8/1/2004)*

Wattle Creek 2005 Chardonnay (Mendocino County) $26. It has very crisp acids and those kiwi and lime flavors that mark cool-climate Chards. Oak and lees aging add richer, creamier notes. 86 —*S.H. (12/15/2007)*

Wattle Creek 2004 Chardonnay (Mendocino County) $26. 85 —*S.H. (11/15/2006)*

Wattle Creek 2000 Chardonnay (Alexander Valley) $25. 88 —*J.M. (12/15/2002)*

Wattle Creek 1999 Chardonnay (Sonoma County) $30. 87 *(6/1/2001)*

Wattle Creek 2001 Alexander Valley Chardonnay (Alexander Valley) $24. 84 —*S.H. (8/1/2004)*

Wattle Creek 2005 Pinot Noir (Yorkville Highlands) $35. This complex Pinot has the soft, silky texture you want in the variety, with delicious cherry-raspberry flavors and a spicy finish. The alcohol is moderate, making it easy to drink. 89 —*S.H. (12/15/2007)*

Wattle Creek 2004 The Triple Play Rhône Red Blend (Yorkville Highlands) $28. A little simple, but likeable for its complex array of berry-cherry fruit with leather, balsamic, coffee and mushroom nuances. Would benefit from a better structure, as it's on the soft side. Mainly Syrah, with Petite Sirah and Viognier. 84 —*S.H. (12/15/2007)*

Wattle Creek 2003 The Triple Play Red Wine Blend Rhône Red Blend (Yorkville Highlands) $28. 87 —*S.H. (12/31/2006)*

Wattle Creek 2006 Rosé Rosé Blend (Yorkville Highlands) $15. Made from Syrah, Cabernet and Petite Sirah, this heavy, somewhat flat rosé has the weight of those varieties normally used in red wine. The flavors are of cooked or stewed black raspberries, cherries, licorice and nougat. 83 —*S.H. (11/15/2007)*

Wattle Creek 2006 Sauvignon Blanc (Mendocino County) $17. Only 4% of this wine was barrel fermented in new oak. The majority was stainless-steel fermented. But that little bit of oak adds a subtle smoky richness to the brilliant fruit, which is a blast of tart gooseberries and Meyer lemons. Totally dry, with relatively low alcohol of only 13.3%, this is really great Sauvignon Blanc. **90 Editors' Choice** —*S.H. (12/15/2007)*

Wattle Creek 2005 Sauvignon Blanc (Mendocino) $17. 82 —*S.H. (12/31/2006)*

Wattle Creek 2004 Sauvignon Blanc (Mendocino) $15. 86 —*S.H. (12/1/2005)*

Wattle Creek 2003 Sauvignon Blanc (Mendocino) $18. 88 —*S.H. (8/1/2004)*

Wattle Creek 2001 Sauvignon Blanc (Mendocino County) $18. 89 *(8/1/2002)*

Wattle Creek 1999 Sauvignon Blanc (Sonoma County) $20. 87 *(6/1/2001)*

Wattle Creek 2003 Shiraz (Alexander Valley) $28. The winery seems to be calling this Shiraz, not Syrah, because of the wine's direct simplicity, in the Aussie style. It's a soft, fruity wine, bigtime in cherries and blackberries, made to be immediately drinkable. 86 —*S.H. (12/15/2007)*

Wattle Creek 2001 Shiraz (Alexander Valley) $25. 84 *(9/1/2005)*

Wattle Creek 1998 Shiraz (Sonoma County) $39. 89 *(6/1/2001)*

Wattle Creek 2000 Alexander Valley Shiraz (Alexander Valley) $35. 85 —*S.H. (8/1/2004)*

Wattle Creek 2005 Viognier (Alexander Valley) $31. 87 —*S.H. (12/31/2006)*

Wattle Creek 2000 Viognier (Alexander Valley) $25. 85 —*M.S. (3/1/2003)*

Wattle Creek 1999 Viognier (Sonoma County) $24. 88 *(6/1/2001)*

Wattle Creek 2002 Alexander Valley Viognier (Alexander Valley) $24. 89 —*S.H. (8/1/2004)*

WATTS

Watts 2003 Dos Amores Bordeaux Blend (Lodi) $26. Soft and sweet-sour in oranges and cherries, this blend of Cabernets leaves a lot to be desired. It'll be okay with simple fare, like a ham sandwich with lots of mayo. 81 —*S.H. (7/1/2007)*

Watts 2005 Casa Azul Vineyard Chardonnay (Lodi) $12. On the dull, soft side, this earthy Chard has modest pineapple, apricot and peaches and cream flavors. It's an okay wine for easy fare. 83 —*S.H. (7/1/2007)*

Watts 2004 Los Robles Vineyard Dolcetto (Lodi) $16. This is a country wine, rustic in texture, with slightly sweet berry and spice flavors. It's strong in acidity and tannins, but there's a certain charm. 85 —*S.H. (7/1/2007)*

Watts 2004 Montepulciano Red Blend (Lodi) $31. A pretty good country-style red, with pleasant cherry and tobacco flavors and nice acidity and tannins. The acidity will help it negotiate cheese, olive oil and red meats. 86 —*S.H. (7/1/2007)*

Watts 2003 Los Robles Vineyard Reserve Syrah (Lodi) $17. Rustic, with wintergreen and cherry flavors and a dry finish. The acidity is its biggest problem, making the wine overly sharp. Drink now. 83 —*S.H. (8/1/2007)*

Watts 2005 Los Robles Vineyard Syrah Rosado Syrah (Lodi) $12. Awkward, with its semisweet cherry flavors and low acidity, which makes it somewhat cloying. Okay for picnics and stuff, if you're not stuffy. 82 —*S.H. (7/1/2007)*

Watts 1999 Old Vine Zinfandel (Lodi) $14. **90 Best Buy** —*S.H. (9/1/2002)*

Watts 2003 Pescador Vineyard Zinfandel (Lodi) $15. The wine is tannicly dry and exuberant in raisin-tinged blackberries, with a rustic mouthfeel. Good for everyday fare, like pizza, lasagna or burgers. 84 —*S.H. (8/1/2007)*

WAUGH CELLARS

Waugh Cellars 2002 Cabernet Sauvignon (Napa Valley) $45. 85 —*S.H. (4/1/2006)*

Waugh Cellars 2005 Indindoli Vineyard Chardonnay (Russian River Valley) $30. 88 —*S.H. (12/31/2006)*

Waugh Cellars 2004 Indindoli Vineyard Chardonnay (Russian River Valley) $30. 89 —*S.H. (7/1/2006)*

Waugh Cellars 2003 Indindoli Vineyard Chardonnay (Russian River Valley) $28. 83 —*S.H. (2/1/2005)*

Waugh Cellars 2002 Indindoli Vineyard Chardonnay (Russian River Valley) $28. 86 —*S.H. (12/1/2003)*

Waugh Cellars 2004 Indindoli Vineyard Reserve Chardonnay (Russian River Valley) $40. 91 —*S.H. (7/1/2006)*

Waugh Cellars 2003 Susy's Cuvée Sauvignon Blanc (Napa Valley) $20. 85 —*S.H. (2/1/2005)*

Waugh Cellars 2002 Susy's Cuvée Sauvignon Blanc (Napa Valley) $24. 86 —*S.H. (12/15/2003)*

Waugh Cellars 2001 Susy's Cuvée Sauvignon Blanc (Napa Valley) $18. 86 *(8/1/2002)*

Waugh Cellars 2004 Zinfandel (Dry Creek Valley) $38. 83 —*S.H. (12/31/2006)*

Waugh Cellars 2003 Zinfandel (Dry Creek Valley) $38. 85 —*S.H. (5/1/2006)*

Waugh Cellars 2002 Zinfandel (Dry Creek Valley) $35. 82 —*S.H. (2/1/2005)*

Waugh Cellars 2001 Zinfandel (Sonoma) $28. 83 *(11/1/2003)*

WEDELL CELLARS

Wedell Cellars 1999 Chardonnay (Edna Valley) $24. 86 —*S.H. (6/1/2003)*

Wedell Cellars 2002 Hillside Vineyard Chardonnay (Edna Valley) $45. 95 —*S.H. (7/1/2006)*

Wedell Cellars 2004 Pinot Noir (Santa Rita Hills) $50. Wedell is a pioneer in the Santa Rita Hills, now known as Santa Rita due to objections by the Chileans. With this juicy wine, which is their lower-priced, regional bottling, they certify their presence. It's dry, racy and absolutely delicious, rich in superripe cherry pie, cola, mocha and vanilla oak flavors that finish clean and crisp. Drink now. 92 —*S.H. (2/1/2007)*

Wedell Cellars 2003 Pinot Noir (Arroyo Grande Valley) $60. **94 Editors' Choice** —*S.H. (11/1/2006)*

Wedell Cellars 2000 Pinot Noir (Edna Valley) $30. 85 —*S.H. (7/1/2003)*

Wedell Cellars 2002 Hillside Vineyard Pinot Noir (Edna Valley) $95. 93 —*S.H. (11/1/2006)*

Wedell Cellars 2000 Hillside Vineyard Pinot Noir (Edna Valley) $90. 92 —*S.H. (7/1/2003)*

Wedell Cellars 2001 Viognier (Edna Valley) $21. 90 —*S.H. (5/1/2003)*

WEDGE MOUNTAIN

Wedge Mountain 2003 Dry White Riesling (Columbia Valley (WA)) $14. 88 —*P.G. (12/15/2004)*

WEINSTOCK CELLARS

Weinstock Cellars 2001 Cellar Select Cabernet Sauvignon (Napa Valley) $20. 83 —*S.H. (8/1/2005)*

Weinstock Cellars 1997 Chardonnay (California) $11. 86 *(4/1/2001)*

Weinstock Cellars 2003 Cellar Select Chardonnay (Sonoma County) $14. 88 *—S.H. (5/1/2006)*

Weinstock Cellars 2001 Cellar Select Chardonnay (Sonoma County) $15. 85 *—S.H. (8/1/2005)*

Weinstock Cellars 2004 Cellar Select Sauvignon Blanc (Central Coast) $14. 84 *—S.H. (5/1/2006)*

Weinstock Cellars 2004 Cellar Select Zinfandel (Lodi) $16. Dry, tannic and well-structured, this wine erupts with white pepper aromas and flavors. Then the fruit kicks in, all blackberry jam, leather, espresso, bitter chocolate and toasted cedar wood. It's different from the usual Lodi Zin, taking it to a higher plane of elegance and sophistication. **90 Editors' Choice** *—S.H. (8/1/2007)*

Weinstock Cellars 2002 Cellar Select Zinfandel (Lodi) $18. 85 *—S.H. (8/1/2005)*

WEISINGER'S OF ASHLAND

Weisinger's of Ashland 2000 Petite Pompadour Bordeaux Blend (Rogue Valley) $27. 85 *—M.S. (8/1/2003)*

Weisinger's of Ashland 1999 Petite Pompadour Bordeaux Blend (Rogue Valley) $25. 85 *—P.G. (4/1/2002)*

Weisinger's of Ashland 1999 Pompadour Vineyard Cabernet Franc (Rogue Valley) $25. 84 *—P.G. (8/1/2002)*

Weisinger's of Ashland 1999 Chardonnay (Rogue Valley) $15. 87 *—P.G. (2/1/2002)*

Weisinger's of Ashland 1999 Gewürztraminer (Rogue Valley) $15. 85 *—P.G. (8/1/2002)*

Weisinger's of Ashland 1997 Merlot (Rogue Valley) $19. 83 *—P.G. (6/1/2000)*

Weisinger's of Ashland 1999 Pompadour Vineyard Merlot (Rogue Valley) $20. 85 *—P.G. (8/1/2002)*

Weisinger's of Ashland NV Mescolare Lot 12 Red Blend (Rogue Valley) $19. 83 *—M.S. (8/1/2003)*

Weisinger's of Ashland NV Mescolare Red Wine Red Blend (Oregon) $18. 84 *—P.G. (8/1/2002)*

Weisinger's of Ashland 1999 50% CH / 50% SEM Sémillon-Chardonnay (Rogue Valley) $15. 84 *—P.G. (8/1/2002)*

WELLINGTON

Wellington 2005 Noir de Noirs Alicante Bouschet (Sonoma Valley) $25. One of the darkest pours of the year, this is inky black in color with a dense, molten mouthfeel. Completely dry, it shows dark flavors of coffee, plums, violets, unsweetened bitter chocolate. Desperately needs long decanting, or aging for a decade. **87** *—S.H. (4/1/2007)*

Wellington 2004 Noir de Noirs Alicante Bouschet (Sonoma Valley) $25. 87 *—S.H. (3/1/2006)*

Wellington 2003 Old Vines Noir de Noirs Alicante Bouschet (Sonoma Valley) $25. 92 *—S.H. (6/1/2005)*

Wellington 2004 Victory Reserve Bordeaux Blend (Sonoma County) $40. This Cab-based Bordeaux blend drinks harsh and somewhat medicinal. It has peppery flavors of cherries, blackberries, mint and herbs, and the tannins are a little on the green side. **84** *—S.H. (12/1/2007)*

Wellington 2001 Cabernet Sauvignon (Sonoma Valley) $20. 85 *—S.H. (5/1/2005)*

Wellington 2000 Cabernet Sauvignon (Sonoma Valley) $25. 86 *—S.H. (12/15/2003)*

Wellington 2003 Handal-Denier Cabernet Sauvignon (Dry Creek Valley) $28. Kind of soft and collapsed, but dry, with earthy cherry and blackberry flavors, this Cab hails from the cooler west side of the valley. It has a good edge of tannins. **85** *—S.H. (11/1/2007)*

Wellington 2001 Hulen Vineyard Cabernet Sauvignon (Dry Creek Valley) $28. 88 *—S.H. (6/1/2005)*

Wellington 2000 Hulen Vineyard Cabernet Sauvignon (Dry Creek Valley) $28. 86 *—S.H. (12/15/2003)*

Wellington 2003 Karren Vineyard Cabernet Sauvignon (Sonoma Mountain) $30. A toughly tannic 100% Cab that is virtually undrinkable without cellaring. It locks the palate down into numbness, but the fundamentals are promising. With its deep, rich core of blackberry fruit and balanced structure, it should easily negotiate the next 10 years. **90** *—S.H. (4/1/2007)*

Wellington 2003 Mohrhardt Ridge Cabernet Sauvignon (Sonoma County) $22. Here's a wine with the polished features of a nice Saint-Julien. Opens with refined aromas of cedar and cassis, then turns complex in the mouth, with cherry, raspberry, spice and oak flavors. Feels too soft for cellaring, though. **86** *—S.H. (11/1/2007)*

USA

Wellington 2001 Mohrhardt Ridge Cabernet Sauvignon (Sonoma County) $22. 90 *—S.H. (5/1/2005)*

Wellington 1999 Mohrhardt Ridge Cabernet Sauvignon (Sonoma County) $22. 87 *—S.H. (8/1/2003)*

Wellington 1997 Mohrhardt Ridge Vineyard Cabernet Sauvignon (Sonoma County) $18. 88 *(9/1/2000)*

Wellington 2000 Mohrhardt Vineyard Cabernet Sauvignon (Sonoma County) $22. 92 Editors' Choice *—S.H. (11/15/2003)*

Wellington 2005 Chardonnay (Sonoma Valley) $18. Decent everyday Chard, with peachy, pineapply fruit and a creamy texture. The finish is spicy. **84** *—S.H. (4/1/2007)*

Wellington 2003 Chardonnay (Sonoma Valley) $16. 84 *—S.H. (3/1/2006)*

Wellington 2002 Chardonnay (Sonoma County) $16. 84 *—S.H. (5/1/2005)*

Wellington 2001 Chardonnay (Sonoma County) $16. 87 *—S.H. (6/1/2004)*

Wellington 2000 Chardonnay (Sonoma Valley) $17. 86 *—S.H. (6/1/2003)*

Wellington 2001 Reserve Chardonnay (Russian River Valley) $26. 89 *—S.H. (6/1/2004)*

Wellington 2005 Marsanne (Sonoma Valley) $18. This is a straightforward wine with a certain resemblance to Sauvignon Blanc for its dry crispness and grassy, citrus flavors. But there's a richer streak of apricots, wildflowers and tangerines and a Chardonnay-like creaminess, that lends complexity and appeal. **87** *—S.H. (11/1/2007)*

Wellington 2000 Estate Grown Marsanne (Sonoma County) $20. 83 *—S.H. (6/1/2003)*

Wellington 1997 Merlot (Sonoma County) $18. 88 *—L.W. (12/31/1999)*

Wellington 2002 Merlot (Sonoma Valley) $18. 85 *—S.H. (3/1/2006)*

Wellington 2003 Estate Merlot (Sonoma Valley) $18. There's a sharp, minty smell and taste in this as well as hard tannins and cutting acidity, all of which hint at less-than-ripe grapes. The wine is fully dry, but lacks the sensuality you want in Merlot. **82** *—S.H. (12/15/2007)*

Wellington 2001 Estate Merlot (Sonoma Valley) $18. 86 *—S.H. (5/1/2005)*

Wellington 2001 Old Vines Port (Sonoma Valley) $14. 82 *—S.H. (6/1/2005)*

Wellington 1997 Côtes de Sonoma Old Vines Red Blend (Sonoma Valley) $18. 88 *—S.H. (6/1/1999)*

Wellington 2001 Reserve Victory Red Blend (Sonoma County) $32. 86 *—S.H. (5/1/2005)*

Wellington 2005 Roussanne (Russian River Valley) $18. A bit on the simple side, this wine has floral, fruity flavors and a creamy smooth finish. It's clean, with good acidity. **84** *—S.H. (4/1/2007)*

Wellington 2002 Roussanne (Sonoma County) $18. 84 *—S.H. (5/1/2005)*

Wellington 2001 Roussanne (Russian River Valley) $20. 83 *—S.H. (6/1/2003)*

Wellington 1998 Sauvignon Blanc (Sonoma Mountain) $14. 87 *—L.W. (3/1/2000)*

Wellington 2003 Sauvignon Blanc (Sonoma Valley) $14. 84 *—S.H. (6/1/2005)*

Wellington 2001 Sauvignon Blanc (Sonoma Mountain) $14. 84 *—S.H. (7/1/2003)*

Wellington 1997 Syrah (Russian River Valley) $17. 86 *—S.H. (6/1/1999)*

Wellington 2002 Syrah (Sonoma Valley) $18. 85 *—S.H. (3/1/2006)*

Wellington 2000 Syrah (Sonoma County) $20. 85 *—S.H. (12/15/2003)*

Wellington 2004 England Crest Syrah (Sonoma Valley) $18. This wine is harsh in texture, with a green stem, puckery mouthfeel that frames unripe herb and mint flavors barely suggesting cherries. **81** *—S.H. (12/15/2007)*

Wellington 2002 Reserve Syrah (Sonoma Valley) $28. 90 *—S.H. (3/1/2006)*

Wellington 1997 Viognier (Sonoma County) $18. 87 *—S.H. (6/1/1999)*

Wellington 2001 Timbervine Ranch Viognier (Russian River Valley) $20. 82 *—S.H. (6/1/2003)*

Wellington 1998 Zinfandel (Russian River Valley) $16. 88 *—S.H. (5/1/2000)*

Wellington 1997 Zinfandel (Russian River Valley) $16. 87 *—L.W. (2/1/2000)*

Wellington 2001 Zinfandel (Sonoma County) $18. 89 *(11/1/2003)*

Wellington 2000 Zinfandel (Sonoma Valley) $22. 84 *—S.H. (9/1/2003)*

Wellington 2003 100 Year Old Vines Zinfandel (Sonoma Valley) $30. 89 *—S.H. (3/1/2006)*

Wellington 2004 Meeks Hilltop Zinfandel (Sonoma Valley) $24. It's a big glass of wild berry fruit, with ample tannins and a touch of raisins in the finish that will play nicely against barbecue sauce. **86** *—S.H. (4/1/2007)*

WENTE

Wente 2004 Cabernet Sauvignon (Livermore Valley) $12. 86 *—S.H. (12/31/2006)*

Wente 2001 Cabernet Sauvignon (Livermore Valley) $14. 87 *—S.H. (12/31/2004)*

Wente 2000 Cabernet Sauvignon (Livermore Valley) $13. 83 *—S.H. (12/31/2003)*

Wente 1997 Cabernet Sauvignon (Livermore Valley) $11. 88 Best Buy *—S.H. (12/15/2000)*

Wente 2004 Charles Wetmore Reserve Cabernet Sauvignon (Livermore Valley) $22. Opens with the jammy, primary fruit aromas of a wine fresh out of the fermenter, then turns acidic and fruity, with grapy blackberry and cherry flavors. This is obviously a young wine that needs bottle age. Should come into its own sometime in 2007. **86** *—S.H. (5/1/2007)*

Wente 2000 Charles Wetmore Reserve Cabernet Sauvignon (Livermore Valley) $27. 84 *—S.H. (3/1/2004)*

Wente 1999 Charles Wetmore Reserve Cabernet Sauvignon (Livermore Valley) $24. 86 *—S.H. (3/1/2003)*

Wente 1998 Charles Wetmore Reserve Cabernet Sauvignon (Livermore Valley) $24. 91 Editors' Choice *—S.H. (12/1/2001)*

Wente 1997 Charles Wetmore Reserve Cabernet Sauvignon (Livermore Valley) $25. 92 *—S.H. (12/15/2000)*

Wente 1996 Charles Wetmore Reserve Cabernet Sauvignon (Livermore Valley) $20. 89 *(1/1/2000)*

Wente 2002 The Nth Degree Cabernet Sauvignon (Livermore Valley) $50. 88 *—S.H. (11/1/2005)*

Wente 2001 Wetmore Reserve Cabernet Sauvignon (Livermore Valley) $25. 89 *—S.H. (12/31/2004)*

Wente 1997 Chardonnay (Central Coast) $10. 88 Best Buy *(1/1/2000)*

Wente 2005 Chardonnay (Livermore Valley) $13. Shows lots of sophistication at a good price. Brimming with ripe peach and mango fruit, there's a richer streak of butter-sautéed banana, finishing with caramelized honey. The wine is quite dry, even minerally, and modest in alcohol, only 13.5%. **88 Best Buy** *—S.H. (4/1/2007)*

Wente 2004 Chardonnay (Livermore Valley) $12. 86 *—S.H. (12/31/2006)*

Wente 2001 Chardonnay (San Francisco Bay) $8. 86 *—S.H. (12/15/2003)*

Wente 2004 Riva Ranch Reserve Chardonnay (Arroyo Seco) $16. 89 Editors' Choice *—S.H. (12/31/2006)*

Wente 2001 Riva Ranch Reserve Chardonnay (Arroyo Seco) $17. 88 *—S.H. (8/1/2003)*

Wente 2000 Riva Ranch Reserve Chardonnay (Arroyo Seco) $15. 92 Best Buy *—S.H. (12/15/2002)*

Wente 1999 Riva Ranch Reserve Chardonnay (Arroyo Seco) $15. 89 Best Buy *—S.H. (12/31/2001)*

Wente 1998 Riva Ranch Reserve Chardonnay (Arroyo Seco) $15. 85 *(6/1/2000)*

Wente 1997 Riva Ranch Reserve Chardonnay (Arroyo Seco) $14. 88 *(1/1/2000)*

Wente 2005 Small Lot Chardonnay (Arroyo Seco) $30. 87 *—S.H. (4/1/2007)*

Wente 2003 The Nth Degree Chardonnay (Livermore Valley) $35. 86 *—S.H. (11/1/2005)*

Wente 2005 Small Lot Grenache (Livermore Valley) $30. Kind of rustic, with black and red cherry pie filling flavors tarted up with espresso and a concentrated, red wine reduction richness. The rusticity comes from the edgy tannins and sweetness that make the wine a little medicinal. **84** *S.H. (4/1/2007)*

Wente 1997 Merlot (Central Coast) $10. 83 *(1/1/2000)*

Wente 2004 Merlot (Arroyo Seco) $12. 82 *—S.H. (12/31/2006)*

Wente 2001 Merlot (Central Coast) $12. 85 *—S.H. (2/1/2004)*

Wente 1999 Crane Ridge Merlot (San Francisco Bay-Livermore Valley) $15. 91 Best Buy *—S.H. (11/15/2001)*

Wente 2003 Crane Ridge Reserve Merlot (Livermore Valley) $18. 80 *—S.H. (12/31/2006)*

Wente 1997 Crane Ridge Reserve Merlot (Livermore Valley) $16. 87 *(1/1/2000)*

Wente 2001 Crane Ridge Vineyard Reserve Merlot (Livermore Valley) $18. 85 *—S.H. (2/1/2004)*

Wente 2004 Reliz Creek Reserve Pinot Noir (Arroyo Seco) $19. Light-bodied and elegant, this polished wine has pretty cola, cherry, pomegranate and licorice flavors, and finishes very dry. High acidity, and while it's not an ager or particularly complex, it's lovely and clean. **86** *—S.H. (4/1/2007)*

Wente 2000 Reliz Creek Reserve Pinot Noir (Arroyo Seco) $17. 88 *—S.H. (2/1/2003)*

Wente 1996 Reliz Creek Reseve Pinot Noir (Arroyo Seco) $15. 85 *(1/1/2000)*

Wente 2005 Riesling (Monterey) $9. 82 *—S.H. (12/31/2006)*

Wente 2006 Riverbank Riesling (Arroyo Seco) $12. Made very much in a German style, with low alcohol (by California standards), very high acidity and residual sugar of 2%. Shows well-ripened apricot, pineapple, peach, honeysuckle, vanilla meringue and Asian spice flavors. **86** *—S.H. (9/1/2007)*

Wente 2004 Sauvignon Blanc (Livermore Valley) $9. 83 *—S.H. (12/31/2006)*

Wente 1999 Sauvignon Blanc (Central Coast) $8. 86 Best Buy *—S.H. (11/15/2001)*

Wente 2003 Vineyard Selection Sauvignon Blanc (Livermore Valley) $9. 86 Best Buy *—S.H. (10/1/2005)*

Wente 2002 Vineyard Selection Sauvignon Blanc (Livermore Valley) $9. 85 Best Buy *—S.H. (10/1/2005)*

Wente 2002 The Nth Degree Shiraz (Livermore Valley) $45. 87 *—S.H. (9/1/2005)*

Wente 2004 Syrah (Livermore Valley) $12. 82 *—S.H. (12/31/2006)*

Wente 2002 Syrah (Livermore Valley) $12. 84 *(9/1/2005)*

Wente 2003 Smith Bench Reserve Zinfandel (Livermore Valley) $18. Lots of ripe wild berry fruit, a streak of wintergreen and white pepper, lush tannins, crisp acids and dry. That pretty much describes this elegant, complex Zinfandel. Some might find the mint unripe, but I think it adds an extra layer of interest. **87** *—S.H. (2/1/2007)*

WESTBROOK WINE FARM

Westbrook Wine Farm 2006 Uber Rhenish Dry Riesling (Madera) $17. Here's a real success in a variety that's always struggling for acceptance. If more Rieslings were like this, more Americans would drink it. Very dry, as the name states, and crisp, it has complex, subtle flavors of citrus fruits, apricots and pine needles. Try as an alternative to Sauvignon Blanc. **90 Editors' Choice** *—S.H. (9/1/2007)*

WESTERLY VINEYARDS

Westerly Vineyards 2002 Sauvignon Blanc (Santa Ynez Valley) $20. 86 *(7/1/2005)*

WESTOVER VINEYARDS

Westover Vineyards 2002 Palomares Vineyards Reserve Chardonnay (San Francisco Bay) $15. 84 *—S.H. (3/1/2004)*

Westover Vineyards 2000 Beyer's Ranch Vineyard Zinfandel (Livermore Valley) $15. 83 *—S.H. (3/1/2004)*

WESTPORT RIVERS

Westport Rivers 1999 Estate Classic Chardonnay (Southeastern New England) $18. 86 *—J.C. (1/1/2004)*

WESTREY

Westrey 2002 Pinot Noir (Willamette Valley) $19. 86 *(11/1/2004)*

Westrey 2002 Abbey Ridge Vineyard Pinot Noir (Willamette Valley) $32. 89 *(11/1/2004)*

Westrey 1999 Croft-Bailey Pinot Noir (Willamette Valley) $22. 86 *—S.H. (8/1/2002)*

Westrey 2002 Reserve Pinot Noir (Willamette Valley) $29. 86 *(11/1/2004)*

Westrey 2002 Shea Vineyard Pinot Noir (Willamette Valley) $32. 85 *(11/1/2004)*

Westrey 1999 Temperance Hill Pinot Noir (Willamette Valley) $22. 87 *—S.H. (8/1/2002)*

WHALER

Whaler 1999 Flagship Shiraz (Mendocino) $28. 87 *—S.H. (12/1/2002)*

Whaler 1999 Flagship Zinfandel (Mendocino) $NA. 84 *—S.H. (11/1/2002)*

WHETSTONE

Whetstone 2002 Hirsch Vineyard Pinot Noir (Sonoma Coast) $38. 89 *(11/1/2004)*

Whetstone 2002 Savoy Vineyard Pinot Noir (Anderson Valley) $46. 84 *(11/1/2004)*

WHIDBEY ISLAND WINERY

Whidbey Island Winery 2003 Madeleine Angevine (Puget Sound) $12. 87 Best Buy *—P.G. (6/1/2006)*

Whidbey Island Winery 2000 Madeleine Angevine (Puget Sound) $11. 84 —*P.G. (2/1/2002)*

Whidbey Island Winery 2002 Composition Red Wine Bordeaux Blend (Yakima Valley) $19. 87 —*P.G. (6/1/2006)*

Whidbey Island Winery 2004 Cabernet Franc (Yakima Valley) $18. 88 —*P.G. (6/1/2006)*

Whidbey Island Winery 1999 Merlot (Yakima Valley) $15. 85 —*P.G. (2/1/2002)*

Whidbey Island Winery 2003 Pinot Grigio (Yakima Valley) $13. 87 —*P.G. (2/1/2006)*

Whidbey Island Winery 2000 Pinot Gris (Columbia Valley (WA)) $13. 84 —*P.G. (2/1/2002)*

Whidbey Island Winery 2004 Sangiovese (Yakima Valley) $17. 88 —*P.G. (6/1/2006)*

Whidbey Island Winery 2004 Siegerrebe (Puget Sound) $12. 88 Best Buy —*P.G. (6/1/2006)*

Whidbey Island Winery 2002 Syrah (Yakima Valley) $19. 90 Editors' Choice *(9/1/2005)*

Whidbey Island Winery 1999 Syrah (Yakima Valley) $20. 84 *(10/1/2001)*

Whidbey Island Winery 2003 Viognier (Yakima Valley) $15. 82 —*P.G. (6/1/2006)*

WHITCRAFT

Whitcraft 2004 Bien Nacido Vineyard Barrel Select Chardonnay (Santa Maria Valley) $NA. 81 —*S.H. (8/1/2006)*

Whitcraft 2000 French Camp Vineyard Lagrein (San Luis Obispo County) $20. 89 Editors' Choice —*S.H. (8/1/2003)*

WHITE BARN

White Barn 1992 La Romanee Pisoni Pinot Noir (Santa Lucia Highlands) $NA. 88 —*S.H. (6/1/2005)*

WHITE CRANE WINERY

White Crane Winery 2001 Folkendt Vineyard Cabernet Sauvignon (Livermore Valley) $48. 83 —*S.H. (11/15/2003)*

WHITE HAWK

White Hawk 2001 Syrah (Santa Maria Valley) $20. 92 Editors' Choice *(9/1/2005)*

White Hawk 2000 Syrah (Santa Maria Valley) $30. 90 —*J.M. (4/1/2004)*

White Hawk 2001 Estate Syrah (Santa Maria Valley) $25. 87 —*S.H. (12/1/2004)*

WHITE HERON

White Heron 2003 Piper Frenchman Hill Vineyard Chardonnay (Columbia Valley (WA)) $10. 87 Best Buy —*P.G. (10/1/2006)*

White Heron 2002 Roussanne (Columbia Valley (WA)) $15. 88 —*P.G. (11/15/2004)*

White Heron 2004 Mariposa Vineyard Roussanne (Columbia Valley (WA)) $15. 86 —*P.G. (10/1/2006)*

WHITE OAK

White Oak 2004 Reserve Bordeaux Blend (Alexander Valley) $50. A blend of the two Cabernets and Merlot, it's dry and elegant, with new oak flavors framing blackberry, plum, herb, cedar and spice flavors. Decant now, or cellar for up to eight years to let the tannins mellow. 90 —*S.H. (6/1/2007)*

White Oak 2003 Cabernet Sauvignon (Napa Valley) $26. 86 —*S.H. (12/1/2006)*

White Oak 2002 Cabernet Sauvignon (Napa Valley) $26. 91 Editors' Choice —*S.H. (3/1/2006)*

White Oak 2000 Cabernet Sauvignon (Napa Valley) $18. 84 —*S.H. (6/1/2003)*

White Oak 2004 25th Anniversary Cabernet Sauvignon (Napa Valley) $27. Firm and young now, almost hard in tannins, with a rich core of blackberry, cherry and dark chocolate fruit, this is one to cellar for a while. With a drop of Merlot, it's a rich, dry wine, with classic Napa structure. Best a few years after 2008. 88 —*S.H. (6/1/2007)*

White Oak 1999 Maripose Cabernet Sauvignon (Napa Valley) $22. 83 —*S.H. (9/12/2002)*

White Oak 2005 Chardonnay (Russian River Valley) $20. They put all the bells and whistles into this wine, from new oak to sur lie aging. It shows in the creamy depth, yet the wine has an herbaceous, green peppercorn edge. It wants to be fruitier and richer than it is. 84 —*S.H. (6/1/2007)*

White Oak 2004 Chardonnay (Russian River Valley) $20. 88 —*S.H. (7/1/2006)*

White Oak 2002 Chardonnay (Russian River Valley) $20. 90 Editors' Choice —*S.H. (6/1/2004)*

White Oak 2001 Chardonnay (Russian River Valley) $20. 86 —*S.H. (12/31/2003)*

White Oak 2000 Chardonnay (Russian River Valley) $16. 90 —*S.H. (12/15/2002)*

White Oak 1999 Chardonnay (Russian River Valley) $17. 90 —*S.H. (5/1/2002)*

White Oak 2000 Myers Limited Reserve Chardonnay (Russian River Valley) $22. 88 —*S.H. (6/1/2003)*

White Oak 2002 Merlot (Napa Valley) $24. 86 —*S.H. (3/1/2006)*

White Oak 2001 Merlot (Napa Valley) $24. 90 —*S.H. (6/1/2004)*

White Oak 2000 Merlot (Napa Valley) $24. 82 —*S.H. (11/15/2002)*

White Oak 2000 Merlot (Alexander Valley) $28. 91 —*S.H. (11/15/2002)*

White Oak 1999 Merlot (Sonoma County) $25. 90 —*S.H. (9/1/2002)*

White Oak 2006 Sauvignon Blanc (Russian River Valley) $15. My bottle was still fermenting—a bad sign—but by the time the wine is in widespread distribution, that may die down. If it does, what you'll find is a very dry, crisp wine, with pleasant flavors of lemongrass and lime. The spritz lowers the score. 83 —*S.H. (11/15/2007)*

White Oak 2005 Sauvignon Blanc (Russian River Valley) $15. 85 —*S.H. (10/1/2006)*

White Oak 2004 Sauvignon Blanc (Russian River Valley) $15. 88 —*S.H. (12/1/2005)*

White Oak 2003 Sauvignon Blanc (Russian River Valley) $14. 87 —*S.H. (12/31/2004)*

White Oak 2002 Sauvignon Blanc (Napa Valley) $13. 87 —*S.H. (12/1/2003)*

White Oak 2001 Sauvignon Blanc (Napa Valley) $18. 84 —*S.H. (9/1/2003)*

White Oak 2001 20th Vintage Sauvignon Blanc Sauvignon Blanc (North Coast) $12. 83 —*S.H. (9/1/2003)*

White Oak 2001 Pantianna Ranch Sauvignon Musqué (Mendocino) $25. 84 —*S.H. (9/1/2003)*

White Oak 2003 Syrah (Napa Valley) $25. White Oak's Syrahs have been okay over the years—clean, dry wines that have some charm. What they lack is richness, as evidenced again by this '03. At four years of age, its tannins stick out because the cherry-berry fruit is too thin to balance them, giving it an astringent feel. 85 —*S.H. (8/1/2007)*

White Oak 2002 Syrah (Napa Valley) $25. 87 —*S.H. (12/31/2004)*

White Oak 2001 Syrah (Napa Valley) $24. 86 —*S.H. (2/1/2004)*

White Oak 2000 Zinfandel (Alexander Valley) $24. 88 —*S.H. (11/1/2002)*

White Oak 1999 Pourroy Zinfandel (Alexander Valley) $25. 89 —*S.H. (11/1/2002)*

WHITE ROSE

White Rose 2002 Pinot Noir (Yamhill County) $65. 87 —*P.G. (2/1/2005)*

White Rose 2004 Quiotee's Lair Pinot Noir (Dundee Hills) $45. Quiotee's Lair is named for one of winemaker Greg Sander's children. A special selection from the estate vineyard, planted in 1980, it is a low-yield (one ton per acre), own-rooted, Pommard clone pinot of exceptional power. Oaky, leathery, earthy flavors with a potent resinous scent recall a certain illicit weed. Finally, the wine slides into a finish loaded with chocolate, coffee and butterscotch. There's nothing subtle here, but plenty to like. 91 —*P.G. (2/1/2007)*

WHITE ROSE ESTATE

White Rose Estate 2002 White Rose Vineyard Pinot Noir (Yamhill County) $65. 89 *(11/1/2004)*

WHITE TRUCK

White Truck 2005 Chardonnay (California) $13. 85 —*S.H. (11/15/2006)*

White Truck 2004 White Blend (California) $9. 85 Best Buy —*S.H. (12/31/2005)*

White Truck 2005 White Wine (California) $11. 81 —*S.H. (12/31/2006)*

WHITEHALL LANE

Whitehall Lane 2004 Cabernet Sauvignon (Napa Valley) $40. For 40 bucks, this is a sumptuous, lush young wine that offers all the fancy fruit and oak you expect from an upscale Napa Cab. 91 —*S.H. (12/1/2007)*

Whitehall Lane 2003 Cabernet Sauvignon (Napa Valley) $40. 88 —*S.H. (11/15/2006)*

Whitehall Lane 2001 Cabernet Sauvignon (Napa Valley) $21. 85 —*S.H. (10/1/2004)*

Whitehall Lane 2001 Cabernet Sauvignon (Napa Valley) $40. 93 Editors' Choice *—S.H. (10/1/2004)*

Whitehall Lane 1997 Cabernet Sauvignon (Napa Valley) $28. 87 *—L.W. (12/31/1999)*

Whitehall Lane 2003 Leonardini Vineyard Cabernet Sauvignon (Napa Valley) $100. 90 *—S.H. (12/15/2006)*

Whitehall Lane 1997 Leonardini Vineyard Cabernet Sauvignon (Napa Valley) $75. 90 *(11/1/2000)*

Whitehall Lane 2003 Reserve Cabernet Sauvignon (Napa Valley) $75. 89 *—S.H. (12/15/2006)*

Whitehall Lane 2002 Reserve Cabernet Sauvignon (Napa Valley) $75. 87 *—S.H. (12/1/2005)*

Whitehall Lane 2001 Reserve Cabernet Sauvignon (Napa Valley) $70. 95 Cellar Selection *—S.H. (4/1/2005)*

Whitehall Lane 1997 Reserve Cabernet Sauvignon (Napa Valley) $60. 90 *(11/1/2000)*

Whitehall Lane 1998 Chardonnay (Carneros) $20. 89 *(6/1/2000)*

Whitehall Lane 1997 Chardonnay (Napa Valley) $16. 91 *—S.H. (2/1/2000)*

Whitehall Lane 2004 Merlot (Napa Valley) $28. Pretty nice Merlot, soft and sensual, like Merlot is supposed to be, and wonderfully ripe in blackberry, cherry, blueberry, plum, chocolate, cedar, vanilla and spice flavors. A pretty complex wine that finishes long and smooth. Drink now. **90** *—S.H. (12/1/2007)*

Whitehall Lane 2003 Merlot (Napa Valley) $26. 88 *—S.H. (11/15/2006)*

Whitehall Lane 2001 Merlot (Napa Valley) $26. 93 *—S.H. (12/15/2004)*

Whitehall Lane 1997 Merlot (Napa Valley) $24. 87 *—L.W. (12/31/1999)*

Whitehall Lane 2006 Sauvignon Blanc (Napa Valley) $16. In Napa Valley, unless Sauvignon Blanc gets fully ripe, those gooseberries veer toward cat pee and mint. But there's just enough pink grapefruit and honey flavors to save the day for this dry, crisp wine. **85** *—S.H. (12/1/2007)*

Whitehall Lane 2005 Sauvignon Blanc (Napa Valley) $15. 85 *—S.H. (11/15/2006)*

Whitehall Lane 2004 Sauvignon Blanc (Napa Valley) $15. 86 *—S.H. (12/1/2005)*

Whitehall Lane 2003 Sauvignon Blanc (Napa Valley) $15. 87 *—S.H. (12/15/2004)*

Whitehall Lane 2000 Sauvignon Blanc (Napa Valley) $15. 87 *(8/1/2002)*

Whitehall Lane 1998 Sauvignon Blanc (Rutherford) $15. 90 *—S.H. (2/1/2000)*

WHITFORD

Whitford 2003 Haynes Vineyard Chardonnay (Napa Valley) $20. 86 *—S.H. (11/1/2006)*

Whitford 2002 Haynes Vineyard Chardonnay (Napa Valley) $20. 85 *—S.H. (10/1/2005)*

Whitford 2001 Haynes Vineyard Chardonnay (Napa Valley) $19. 91 Editors' Choice *—S.H. (12/1/2003)*

Whitford 2000 Haynes Vineyard Old Vines Chardonnay (Napa Valley) $25. 92 *—S.H. (12/1/2003)*

Whitford 2002 Haynes Vineyard Pinot Noir (Napa Valley) $23. 88 *—S.H. (10/1/2005)*

Whitford 2001 Pinot Noir (Napa Valley) $22. 85 *—S.H. (2/1/2004)*

Whitford 2003 Haynes Vineyard Syrah (Napa Valley) $25. 89 *—S.H. (11/15/2006)*

Whitford 2002 Haynes Vineyard Syrah (Napa Valley) $25. 85 *(9/1/2005)*

WHITMAN CELLARS

Whitman Cellars 2004 Cabernet Sauvignon (Columbia Valley (WA)) $36. This is a dark, smoky wine, with aromas of cooked fruit and smoke. It's a style that is popular and valid, but not to my personal taste. The wine is open and shows plenty of ripe fruit, the tannins are managed well, and the acids provide some much-needed support. This wine is designed for drink-now enjoyment. **86** *—P.G. (12/1/2007)*

Whitman Cellars 2003 Cabernet Sauvignon (Walla Walla (WA)) $36. This is a supple, oaky and forward wine, with little that suggests true Cabernet character. Rather, it is friendly, fruity, simple and straightforward, generic and pleasant with a spicy lift to the finish. **85** *—P.G. (5/1/2007)*

Whitman Cellars 2002 Cabernet Sauvignon (Walla Walla (WA)) $36. 85 *—P.G. (12/15/2005)*

Whitman Cellars 2001 Cabernet Sauvignon (Walla Walla (WA)) $36. 88 *—P.G. (5/1/2004)*

Whitman Cellars 1999 Seven Hills Cabernet Sauvignon (Walla Walla (WA)) $40. 86 *—P.G. (6/1/2002)*

Whitman Cellars 2004 Merlot (Columbia Valley (WA)) $32. The nose is volatile and pruney, the color dark, almost Port-like. The wine is very soft and flat. The fruit seems waxy and dead, lightly pruney but also a bit green; it tastes as though half the grapes were underripe and half were raisined. **84** *—P.G. (12/1/2007)*

Whitman Cellars 2003 Merlot (Walla Walla (WA)) $32. This is pleasant drinking, with its soft, chalky, rather lightweight fruit, depending upon the barrels to provide added flavors of coffee, toast and chocolate. But in this rather standard Bordeaux blend there isn't much to hang your hat on besides the oak, and the finish is a bit hot and chalky. **86** *—P.G. (3/1/2007)*

Whitman Cellars 2002 Merlot (Walla Walla (WA)) $32. 85 *—P.G. (12/15/2005)*

Whitman Cellars 2001 Merlot (Walla Walla (WA)) $32. 86 *—P.G. (5/1/2004)*

Whitman Cellars 1999 Seven Hills Merlot (Walla Walla (WA)) $32. 85 *—P.G. (6/1/2002)*

Whitman Cellars 2003 Narcissa Red Blend (Walla Walla (WA)) $24. This is soft, pretty and ready to drink. The light fruit is wrapped in toasty new oak, accented with cinnamon and mocha. A bit of spice keeps it interesting, but it comes across as a generic red, with pretty oak. **85** *—P.G. (5/1/2007)*

Whitman Cellars 2002 Narcissa Red Blend (Walla Walla (WA)) $24. 86 *—P.G. (12/15/2005)*

Whitman Cellars 2001 Narcissa Red Red Blend (Walla Walla (WA)) $24. 87 *—P.G. (5/1/2004)*

Whitman Cellars 2002 Syrah (Walla Walla (WA)) $28. 88 *—P.G. (12/15/2004)*

Whitman Cellars 2006 Viognier (Columbia Valley (WA)) $19. Scents of beeswax and lemon tea open into a pretty, lemon drop flavor set. Winemaker Steve Lessard has softened the sometimes bitter phenolics of the grape, so the fruit flavors, though not quite tropical, are ripe and smooth as they open up. Hints of pineapple, lemon and grapefruit mingle to create a user-friendly, approachable wine. **88** *—P.G. (12/1/2007)*

Whitman Cellars 2005 Viognier (Walla Walla (WA)) $19. From the Cougar Hills vineyard, this soft, fruity Viognier is done in a Chardonnay style. The fruit is tropical and broad, and there is a strong toasty, nutty finish to it, from the aging in new French oak. It's a friendly, approachable style, though not necessarily one that showcases the unique qualities of Viognier. **85** *—P.G. (5/1/2007)*

Whitman Cellars 2003 Viognier (Walla Walla (WA)) $19. 87 *—P.G. (12/15/2004)*

WIDGEON HILLS

Widgeon Hills 2002 HRP Ranch Area 51 Syrah (Yakima Valley) $22. 86 *(9/1/2005)*

WIENS CELLARS

Wiens Cellars 2001 Zinfandel (Lodi) $14. 86 *(11/1/2003)*

WILD BUNCH

Wild Bunch 2003 Red Wine Red Blend (California) $10. 86 Best Buy *—S.H. (12/31/2005)*

Wild Bunch 2004 White Wine White Blend (California) $10. 85 Best Buy *—S.H. (12/31/2005)*

WILD COYOTE

Wild Coyote 2001 Lisenshes Zinfandel (Paso Robles) $14. 84 *(11/1/2003)*

WILD HORSE

Wild Horse 2000 Blaufränkisch (Paso Robles) $NA. 85 *—S.H. (9/1/2003)*

Wild Horse 1997 Cabernet Sauvignon (Paso Robles) $19. 85 *—S.H. (2/1/2000)*

Wild Horse 2002 Cabernet Sauvignon (Paso Robles) $20. 88 *(10/1/2005)*

Wild Horse 1999 Cabernet Sauvignon (Paso Robles) $20. 83 *—S.H. (11/15/2002)*

Wild Horse 2005 Chardonnay (Central Coast) $17. As always, a nice, easy-drinking Chard with plenty of Central Coast character. The cool, long hangtime has given very ripe fruit, while preserving vital acidity. The winemaker brings a deft touch of oak. **85** *—S.H. (9/1/2007)*

Wild Horse 2004 Chardonnay (Central Coast) $18. 86 *(10/1/2005)*

Wild Horse 2004 Chardonnay (Central Coast) $20. 82 *—S.H. (11/15/2006)*

Wild Horse 2003 Chardonnay (Central Coast) $16. 84 *—S.H. (5/1/2005)*

Wild Horse 2002 Chardonnay (Central Coast) $16. 84 *—S.H. (4/1/2004)*

Wild Horse 2000 Chardonnay (Central Coast) $16. 87 *—S.H. (12/15/2002)*

Wild Horse 1998 Chardonnay (Central Coast) $16. 87 *—S.H. (11/15/1999)*

Wild Horse 2003 Merlot (Paso Robles) $20. 87 *(10/1/2005)*

Wild Horse 2002 Merlot (Paso Robles) $20. 83 *—S.H. (5/1/2005)*

Wild Horse 2001 Merlot (Paso Robles) $18. 89 *—S.H. (4/1/2004)*

Wild Horse 1997 Merlot (Paso Robles) $18. 83 *—S.H. (12/31/1999)*

Wild Horse 1999 Merlot (Paso Robles) $18. 87 *—S.H. (9/1/2003)*

Wild Horse 1998 Pinot Blanc (Monterey County) $14. 90 Best Buy *—S.H. (3/1/2000)*

Wild Horse 2005 Pinot Noir (Central Coast) $25. Wild Horse captures the essence of Central Coast Pinot. The wine isn't especially complex or ageable, but defines the fruit and acid balance of the region. Cherries, black raspberries, root beer and spiced rum punch are the flavors, and the wine is silky and dry. **87** *—S.H. (9/1/2007)*

Wild Horse 2003 Pinot Noir (Central Coast) $23. 85 *(10/1/2005)*

Wild Horse 2000 Pinot Noir (Central Coast) $20. 86 *(10/1/2002)*

Wild Horse 1997 Pinot Noir (Central Coast) $20. 87 *—J.C. (5/1/2000)*

Wild Horse 2004 Cheval Sauvage Pinot Noir (Santa Barbara County) $65. The sourcing is Bien Nacido and the old Ashley's, two of the best vineyards in the county. The pedigree shows in the wine's balance and harmony, while the warm vintage is evident in the pie filling fruit and spice flavors and a touch of funk. Probably at its best now and in the next few years. **89** *—S.H. (12/1/2007)*

Wild Horse 2004 Unbridled Solomon Hills Vineyard Pinot Noir (Santa Maria Valley) $45. 92 *—S.H. (8/1/2006)*

Wild Horse 1998 Roussanne (Paso Robles) $18. 90 *—S.H. (10/1/1999)*

Wild Horse 2002 Syrah (Paso Robles) $18. 88 *(10/1/2005)*

Wild Horse 2001 Syrah (Paso Robles) $18. 87 *—S.H. (12/1/2004)*

Wild Horse 2002 James Berry Vineyard Syrah (Paso Robles) $38. 90 *(10/1/2005)*

Wild Horse 2004 Viognier (Central Coast) $18. 87 *(10/1/2005)*

Wild Horse 2003 Viognier (Central Coast) $18. 84 *—S.H. (5/1/2005)*

Wild Horse 2002 Viognier (Central Coast) $16. 85 *—S.H. (11/15/2004)*

Wild Horse 1998 Viognier (Central Coast) $24. 87 *—S.H. (10/1/1999)*

Wild Horse 2001 Zinfandel (Paso Robles) $16. 85 *(11/1/2003)*

Wild Horse 1997 Zinfandel (Paso Robles) $14. 85 *—J.C. (2/1/2000)*

WILD OAK BY ST. FRANCIS

Wild Oak by St. Francis 2005 Chardonnay (Sonoma County) $25. So oaky, it tastes like a toothpick; this is all caramel, butterscotch and toast. **83** *—S.H. (11/1/2007)*

Wild Oak by St. Francis 2004 Syrah (Sonoma County) $30. Although this is pretty tannic, with a sandpapery grip that finishes with astringency, it's fancy and layered. Waves of blackberries, cassis, coffee, cherries, leather and pepper-cinnamon spices wash over the palate, leaving the impression of importance. Still, it's not an ager. Best now and for a couple of years. **87** *—S.H. (12/1/2007)*

WILDHURST

Wildhurst 2002 Reserve Cabernet Sauvignon (Lake County) $16. 87 *—S.H. (11/15/2004)*

Wildhurst 1997 Chardonnay (Clear Lake) $11. 85 *—M.S. (10/1/1999)*

Wildhurst 1999 Chardonnay (Lake County) $14. 83 *—S.H. (8/1/2001)*

Wildhurst 1997 Private Reserve Chardonnay (Sonoma County) $18. 80 *(6/1/2000)*

Wildhurst 2005 Reserve Chardonnay (Lake County) $14. Very ripe, with enormous peach, tropical fruit and apple flavors, and nicely dry and crisp. But it tastes very oaky, like toothpicks, actually, with in-your-face toasty, vanilla and honeysweet woodsap flavors that the beautiful fruit doesn't even need. **83** *—S.H. (3/1/2007)*

Wildhurst 2003 Reserve Chardonnay (Lake County) $14. 86 *—S.H. (12/15/2004)*

Wildhurst 2002 Reserve Merlot (Lake County) $16. 87 *—S.H. (12/15/2004)*

Wildhurst 2004 Sauvignon Blanc (Lake County) $11. 88 Best Buy *—S.H. (10/1/2005)*

Wildhurst 2001 Sauvignon Blanc (Clear Lake) $11. 86 *—S.H. (7/1/2003)*

Wildhurst 2000 Sauvignon Blanc (Clear Lake) $11. 84 *—S.H. (11/15/2001)*

Wildhurst 2005 Reserve Sauvignon Blanc (Lake County) $11. Wildhurst has been producing one of the best SBs at this price point in California, and this one continues the beat. It's dry and acidic, with zesty citrus, gooseberry, fig and melon flavors that finish in a swirl of rich, crushed brown spices. **87 Best Buy** *—S.H. (3/1/2007)*

Wildhurst 2004 Reserve Sauvignon Blanc (Lake County) $11. 86 Best Buy *—S.H. (10/1/2005)*

Wildhurst 2002 Reserve Syrah (Lake County) $16. 84 *—S.H. (12/15/2004)*

Wildhurst 1998 Catfish Vineyard Zinfandel (Clear Lake) $14. 88 *—P.G. (3/1/2001)*

WILDWOOD

Wildwood 2003 Jackson's Vineyard Cabernet Sauvignon (San Luis Obispo County) $35. SLO has always struggled with this variety, but Wildwood seems to be getting the knack for Cabernet. Tastes like the grapes were grown in a warm area and yields were carefully limited: the flavors of blackberries plums and mocha are rich. The challenge is to improve structure, and particularly tannins, in a wine of this price. **86** *—S.H. (10/1/2007)*

Wildwood 2002 Jackson's Vineyard Cabernet Sauvignon (San Luis Obispo County) $35. 87 *—S.H. (11/1/2006)*

Wildwood 2001 Syrah (San Luis Obispo) $35. 86 *—S.H. (12/1/2004)*

Wildwood 2003 Gina's Vineyard Syrah (San Luis Obispo) $28. Kind of on the sweet, sugary side, but not so much that it gives you a toothache. The flavors of blackberry jam, cherry and raspberry pie filling and vanilla fudge could only have come from a hot climate vineyard. **83** *—S.H. (11/1/2007)*

Wildwood 2002 Gina's Vineyard Syrah (San Luis Obispo County) $28. 85 *—S.H. (11/1/2006)*

Wildwood 2003 Sheri's Vineyard Syrah (San Luis Obispo) $28. Too soft and sugary to earn a better score, this Syrah's cherry-blackberry and carob flavors taste sweet. The wine needs greater acid-tannin balance. **82** *—S.H. (11/1/2007)*

Wildwood 2002 Sheri's Vineyard Syrah (San Luis Obispo County) $28. 85 *—S.H. (11/1/2006)*

WILLAKENZIE

WillaKenzie 1999 Estelle Chardonnay (Willamette Valley) $25. 89 *—P.G. (8/1/2002)*

WillaKenzie 1998 Gamay (Oregon) $16. 87 *—P.G. (9/1/2000)*

WillaKenzie 2006 Pinot Blanc (Willamette Valley) $18. Almost always a guaranteed winner from WillaKenzie, this latest Pinot Blanc comes across as a peppery, spicy, bright and challenging white wine, without the lush fruit of Pinot Gris or the comforting oak cloak of Chardonnay. But you get crisply defined apple flavors, nuanced with a spicy burn reminiscent of daikon. Done entirely in stainless and fermented whole cluster, this merits the comparison to an Alsatian style. **88** *—P.G. (11/15/2007)*

WillaKenzie 2005 Pinot Blanc (Willamette Valley) $19. 90 *—P.G. (12/1/2006)*

WillaKenzie 2004 Pinot Blanc (Willamette Valley) $18. 87 *—P.G. (11/15/2005)*

WillaKenzie 1998 Pinot Blanc (Willamette Valley) $16. 90 *—P.G. (9/1/2000)*

WillaKenzie 1997 Pinot Grigio (Willamette Valley) $15. 87 *(8/1/1999)*

WillaKenzie 2005 Pinot Gris (Willamette Valley) $19. 91 Editors' Choice *—P.G. (12/1/2006)*

WillaKenzie 2004 Pinot Gris (Willamette Valley) $18. 90 *—P.G. (11/15/2005)*

WillaKenzie 2001 Pinot Gris (Oregon) $20. 92 Editors' Choice *—P.G. (8/1/2002)*

WillaKenzie 2000 Pinot Gris (Oregon) $18. 90 *—P.G. (2/1/2002)*

WillaKenzie 1999 Pinot Gris (Oregon) $16. 90 *—P.G. (9/1/2000)*

WillaKenzie 1997 Pinot Gris (Willamette Valley) $15. 87 *(8/1/1999)*

WillaKenzie 1998 Pinot Meunier (Oregon) $20. 88 *(9/1/2000)*

WillaKenzie 2005 Pinot Noir (Willamette Valley) $23. Estate-grown, high-density vines supply the juice for this entry-level wine from this outstanding Oregon producer. It's supple and juicy, with bright fruit flavors that mix berries, cherries and even a hint of Concord grape. This has some of the velvety texture of more expensive wines, and beyond the fruit there are hints of earth, soy and leather that add interesting details to the finish. **87** *—P.G. (11/15/2007)*

WillaKenzie 2004 Pinot Noir (Willamette Valley) $23. 87 *—P.G. (9/1/2006)*

WillaKenzie 1998 Pinot Noir (Oregon) $22. 87 *—P.G. (9/1/2000)*

WillaKenzie 2004 Aliette Pinot Noir (Willamette Valley) $36. The Aliette bottling is the prettiest of the entire flight from WillaKenzie. Softly scented with floral and spice, it is also from the oldest vines, planted in 1992. It's an elegant wine that actually fits the claim to be Burgundian in style (does anyone in Oregon not claim to be Burgundian?). The finish is nicely nuanced with cinnamon, saffron and sandalwood. **89** *—P.G. (11/15/2007)*

WillaKenzie 2003 Aliette Pinot Noir (Willamette Valley) $36. 90 *—P.G. (9/1/2006)*

WillaKenzie 2002 Aliette Pinot Noir (Willamette Valley) $36. 86 *(11/1/2004)*

WillaKenzie 2004 Emery Pinot Noir (Willamette Valley) $45. It is forward and textural, almost spritzy, with a lively mouthfeel and flavors of cola, tomato leaf and herb. More old Oregon in style, it is nonetheless concentrated and balanced, albeit brawny and rough around the edges. Lots of flavor for those who like their Pinot to take a little walk on the wild side. **89** *—P.G. (11/15/2007)*

WillaKenzie 2003 Emery Pinot Noir (Willamette Valley) $45. 89 *—P.G. (9/1/2006)*

WillaKenzie 2004 Kiana Pinot Noir (Willamette Valley) $45. The Kiana bottling, named for the owners' granddaughter, is made with Dijon clones planted in 1996 and 1997. Initially quite tight and unyielding, it first opens into flavors of leaf, herb and green tea. Tucked neatly into the midpalate is a core of good red strawberry/cherry fruit. The tannins are earthy but not rough; everything here is balanced and well-managed; the alcohol a moderate 14.3%. **88** *—P.G. (11/15/2007)*

WillaKenzie 2003 Kiana Pinot Noir (Willamette Valley) $45. 90 *—P.G. (9/1/2006)*

WillaKenzie 2002 Kiana Pinot Noir (Willamette Valley) $45. 85 *(11/1/2004)*

WillaKenzie 2000 Kiana Pinot Noir (Willamette Valley) $35. 88 *(10/1/2002)*

WillaKenzie 2004 Pierre Léon Pinot Noir (Willamette Valley) $36. This is, in some respects, the most approachable of WillaKenzie's six estate Pinots, a selection of clones from various plots among the 68 acres. It is the earthiest, as far as the finish is concerned, but also brings smooth, pretty cherry and red fruit flavors right at the start. Elegant, young and lightly accented with cedar and anise, this can be enjoyed immediately or cellared for a few more years. **89** *—P.G. (11/15/2007)*

WillaKenzie 2003 Pierre Léon Pinot Noir (Willamette Valley) $36. 89 *—P.G. (9/1/2006)*

WillaKenzie 2002 Pierre Leon Vineyard Pinot Noir (Willamette Valley) $36. 88 *(11/1/2004)*

WillaKenzie 1999 Pierre Leon Pinot Noir (Willamette Valley) $35. 88 *(10/1/2002)*

WillaKenzie 2004 Terres Basses Pinot Noir (Willamette Valley) $55. This is outstanding Pinot, from a vineyard yielding a miserly one ton per acre. Unfined and unfiltered, this dark, deeply flavored wine offers scents and tastes of cut tobacco wrapped into rich blueberry fruit. Long and complex, it rewards your attention with notes of bitter chocolate and citrus rind as it winds through a lingering finish. **91** *—P.G. (11/15/2007)*

WillaKenzie 2003 Terres Basses Pinot Noir (Willamette Valley) $55. 91 *—P.G. (9/1/2006)*

WillaKenzie 2004 Triple Black Slopes Pinot Noir (Willamette Valley) $55. The name refers to the vineyard's unusually steep slopes. The reward for farming such difficult terrain, the owners believe, is complexity, character and concentration. That is certainly the case in 2004, as this is the most dense and focused of the six WillaKenzie releases. It's built upon a solid foundation of black cherry fruit, but elevated with herb, acid and a feathery touch to the tannins. Despite its exceptional heft, the wine manages to feel elegant. **91** *—P.G. (11/15/2007)*

WillaKenzie 2003 Triple Black Slopes Pinot Noir (Willamette Valley) $55. 91 *—P.G. (9/1/2006)*

WILLAMETTE VALLEY VINEYARDS

Willamette Valley Vineyards 2000 Chardonnay (Willamette Valley) $10. 88 Best Buy *—P.G. (12/1/2003)*

Willamette Valley Vineyards 2004 Dijon Clone Chardonnay (Willamette Valley) $17. This is not the estate bottling, but it is also from Dijon clones, and almost as good. A solid effort, it sports clean, ripe fruit and zippy acids. There is less of the buttery softness of the estate Chardonnay, but plenty of crisp green apple, Japanese pear and even a smattering of papaya. Fine value. **89** *—P.G. (4/1/2007)*

Willamette Valley Vineyards 2003 Estate Vineyard Chardonnay (Willamette Valley) $22. A fine effort, rich, soft and buttery. The smooth, lush flavors—a mix of apple, white peach and buttered nuts—are elevated by crisp acids. The Dijon clones and extra bottle time have produced a Chardonnay that is at the top of its form, and outshines most of the California competition in this price range. **90** *—P.G. (4/1/2007)*

Willamette Valley Vineyards 1999 Estate Vineyard Chardonnay (Willamette Valley) $22. 83 *—M.S. (8/1/2003)*

Willamette Valley Vineyards 2000 Late Harvest Ehrenfelser (Willamette Valley) $20. 88 *—J.M. (12/1/2002)*

Willamette Valley Vineyards 2002 Gewürztraminer (Willamette Valley) $12. 88 Best Buy *—P.G. (12/1/2003)*

Willamette Valley Vineyards 2006 Pinot Gris (Willamette Valley) $16. Crisp, authoritative, dry and racy. The fruit mixes apple and pear, then heads off into a finish that is underscored with mineral and light fennel. Very fresh and refreshing, beautifully rendered. **90** *—P.G. (7/1/2007)*

Willamette Valley Vineyards 2005 Pinot Gris (Oregon) $16. 85 *—P.G. (9/1/2006)*

Willamette Valley Vineyards 2004 Pinot Gris (Oregon) $15. 89 *—P.G. (8/1/2005)*

Willamette Valley Vineyards 2002 Pinot Gris (Oregon) $13. 89 Best Buy *—P.G. (12/1/2003)*

Willamette Valley Vineyards 2001 Pinot Gris (Willamette Valley) $13. 82 *—M.S. (8/1/2003)*

Willamette Valley Vineyards 2000 Pinot Gris (Willamette Valley) $14. 86 *—P.G. (4/1/2002)*

Willamette Valley Vineyards 2000 Founder's Reserve Pinot Gris (Willamette Valley) $18. 88 *—P.G. (4/1/2002)*

Willamette Valley Vineyards 2001 Founders' Reserve Pinot Gris (Willamette Valley) $18. 81 *—M.S. (12/31/2002)*

Willamette Valley Vineyards 2005 Pinot Noir (Willamette Valley) $25. The vintage delivers the goods—a pretty nose scented with red fruits, earth and spice, and an elegant structure that lays gently on the palate. It's ripe but laid back, with the alcohol a sensible, food-friendly 13.5%, and the wine true to varietal, with persistent flavors of cola and berry dusted with cinnamon. **88** *—P.G. (4/1/2007)*

Willamette Valley Vineyards 2004 Pinot Noir (Oregon) $19. 86 *—P.G. (9/1/2006)*

Willamette Valley Vineyards 2003 Pinot Noir (Willamette Valley) $19. 87 *—P.G. (9/1/2006)*

Willamette Valley Vineyards 1999 Pinot Noir (Oregon) $17. 84 *(10/1/2002)*

Willamette Valley Vineyards 2000 Barrel Select Pinot Noir (Willamette Valley) $15. 87 *—M.S. (9/1/2003)*

Willamette Valley Vineyards 2005 Estate Pinot Noir (Willamette Valley) $40. More austere and resinous than the regular 2005 bottling, the estate Pinot Noir is also tighter. It has green, leafy flavors and tannins that taste of tea, but there is complexity in the mixed tart red fruits and an underlying minerality that promises more development in the bottle. Decant or give it another few years in the cellar. **89** *—P.G. (4/1/2007)*

Willamette Valley Vineyards 2004 Estate Pinot Noir (Oregon) $28. 87 *—P.G. (9/1/2006)*

Willamette Valley Vineyards 2003 Estate Pinot Noir (Willamette Valley) $28. 87 *—P.G. (9/1/2006)*

Willamette Valley Vineyards 2002 Estate Pinot Noir (Willamette Valley) $30. 84 *(11/1/2004)*

Willamette Valley Vineyards 2000 Estate Vineyard Pinot Noir (Willamette Valley) $31. 84 *(10/1/2002)*

Willamette Valley Vineyards 1999 Estate Vineyard Pinot Noir (Willamette Valley) $45. 85 *—P.G. (4/1/2002)*

Willamette Valley Vineyards 1999 Founders' Reserve Pinot Noir (Oregon) $27. 85 *(10/1/2002)*

Willamette Valley Vineyards 2002 Freedom Hill Vineyard Pinot Noir (Willamette Valley) $45. 85 *(11/1/2004)*

Willamette Valley Vineyards 1999 Freedom Hill Vineyard Pinot Noir (Oregon) $45. 87 *—P.G. (4/1/2002)*

Willamette Valley Vineyards 1998 Freedom Hill Vineyard Pinot Noir (Willamette Valley) $44. 91 *—M.M. (11/1/2001)*

Willamette Valley Vineyards 2000 Hoodview Vineyard Pinot Noir (Willamette Valley) $31. 88 *(10/1/2002)*

Willamette Valley Vineyards 1999 Hoodview Vineyard Pinot Noir (Oregon) $45. 86 *—P.G. (4/1/2002)*

Willamette Valley Vineyards 2002 Joe Dobbes Signature Cuvée Pinot Noir (Willamette Valley) $50. 84 *(11/1/2004)*

Willamette Valley Vineyards 2000 Joe Dobbes Signature Cuvée Pinot Noir (Willamette Valley) $42. 88 *(10/1/2002)*

Willamette Valley Vineyards 1999 Joe Dobbes Signature Cuvée Pinot Noir (Willamette Valley) $60. 91 Cellar Selection *—P.G. (4/1/2002)*

Willamette Valley Vineyards 2000 Karina Vineyard Pinot Noir (Willamette Valley) $31. 83 *(10/1/2002)*

Willamette Valley Vineyards 1999 Karina Vineyard Pinot Noir (Willamette Valley) $45. 90 *—P.G. (4/1/2002)*

Willamette Valley Vineyards 2002 Mt. Hood Pinot Noir (Willamette Valley) $45. 83 *(11/1/2004)*

Willamette Valley Vineyards 1998 O'Connor Vineyard Pinot Noir (Willamette Valley) $39. 88 *—M.S. (9/1/2003)*

Willamette Valley Vineyards 2006 Whole Clister Fermented Pinot Noir (Willamette Valley) $18. The fruit jumps out and says, "Drink me now." This is a no-frills, unpretentious party-style of Pinot, but unlike most of the cheap California stuff it has some weight behind its fruit. Pleasing black cherry and blackberry flavors are right up front, with sturdy tannins providing a solid foundation. **86** *—P.G. (7/1/2007)*

Willamette Valley Vineyards 2001 Whole Cluster Pinot Noir (Oregon) $17. 87 Best Buy *—P.G. (4/1/2003)*

Willamette Valley Vineyards 2000 Whole Cluster Pinot Noir (Oregon) $12. 86 Best Buy *(10/1/2002)*

Willamette Valley Vineyards 2005 Whole Cluster Fermented Pinot Noir (Oregon) $18. 86 *—P.G. (9/1/2006)*

Willamette Valley Vineyards 2004 Whole Cluster Fermented Pinot Noir (Oregon) $18. 85 *—P.G. (8/1/2005)*

Willamette Valley Vineyards 2006 Riesling (Oregon) $12. This winery offers very solid wines at consumer-friendly prices, and the Riesling is no exception. Full-flavored with melon, apple and pear fruit, it is sweet, clean and refreshing, and for the price, there is no better Riesling in Oregon. **87 Best Buy** *—P.G. (11/15/2007)*

Willamette Valley Vineyards 2001 Riesling (Oregon) $8. 88 *—P.G. (8/1/2003)*

Willamette Valley Vineyards 2002 Founders' Reserve Sauvignon Blanc (Oregon) $16. 90 *—P.G. (12/1/2003)*

Willamette Valley Vineyards 2001 Viognier (Rogue Valley) $28. 87 *—P.G. (12/1/2003)*

WILLIAM HARRISON

William Harrison 2002 Estate Cabernet Sauvignon (Rutherford) $45. 86 *—S.H. (12/15/2005)*

WILLIAM HILL ESTATE

William Hill Estate 2004 Cabernet Sauvignon (Napa Valley) $27. A medium-weight, silky-textured Cabernet Sauvignon, this is immediately approachable. Standard cassis fruit flavors take on a touch of leafyness or herb, while there's a touch of warmth to the finish. Drink now–2010. **86** *(8/1/2007)*

William Hill Estate 1997 Cabernet Sauvignon (Napa Valley) $20. 86 *(3/1/2000)*

William Hill Estate 1996 Cabernet Sauvignon (Napa Valley) $16. 88 *(11/1/1999)*

William Hill Estate 1996 Cabernet Sauvignon (Napa Valley) $16. 88 *(11/1/1999)*

William Hill Estate 1995 Cabernet Sauvignon (Napa Valley) $16. 90 Best Buy *—S.H. (6/1/1999)*

William Hill Estate 2003 Cabernet Sauvignon (Napa Valley) $20. 85 *—S.H. (10/1/2006)*

William Hill Estate 2001 Cabernet Sauvignon (Napa Valley) $22. 89 *—S.H. (10/1/2004)*

William Hill Estate 2000 Cabernet Sauvignon (Napa Valley) $22. 90 *—S.H. (8/1/2003)*

William Hill Estate 1999 Cabernet Sauvignon (Napa Valley) $22. 86 *—S.H. (9/12/2002)*

William Hill Estate 1998 Cabernet Sauvignon (Napa Valley) $22. 87 *—S.H. (2/1/2001)*

William Hill Estate 2004 Reserve Cabernet Sauvignon (Napa Valley) $52. Already in the bottle, this is set for a September release. Right now, it's a bit ruggedly tannic, although the flavors are spot on. Chocolate, plum and cassis notes are tinged with just enough cinnamon spice to add complexity. Best from 2009–2014. **87** *(8/1/2007)*

William Hill Estate 2003 Reserve Cabernet Sauvignon (Napa Valley) $36. 91 Cellar Selection *—S.H. (9/1/2006)*

William Hill Estate 2002 Reserve Cabernet Sauvignon (Napa Valley) $36. 91 *—S.H. (8/3/2006)*

William Hill Estate 2001 Reserve Cabernet Sauvignon (Napa Valley) $36. 92 *—S.H. (11/15/2005)*

William Hill Estate 1999 Reserve Cabernet Sauvignon (Napa Valley) $38. 90 *—S.H. (11/15/2003)*

William Hill Estate 1998 Reserve Cabernet Sauvignon (Napa Valley) $38. 85 *—S.H. (11/15/2002)*

William Hill Estate 1996 Reserve Cabernet Sauvignon (Napa Valley) $35. 88 *—S.H. (7/1/2000)*

William Hill Estate 1995 Reserve Cabernet Sauvignon (Napa Valley) $27. 91 *(11/1/1999)*

William Hill Estate 1995 Reserve Cabernet Sauvignon (Napa Valley) $27. 91 *(11/1/1999)*

William Hill Estate 2005 Chardonnay (Napa Valley) $20. Sourced primarily from the estate's Carneros vineyards, this is entirely barrel-fermented in French oak. Yet the oak provides gentle accents rather than an outsized coating. Pineapple fruit is lightly touched with hints of vanilla and butter, turning crisp and lemony on the finish. **86** *(8/1/2007)*

William Hill Estate 2004 Chardonnay (Napa Valley) $20. 85 *—S.H. (10/1/2006)*

William Hill Estate 2003 Chardonnay (Napa Valley) $13. 85 *—S.H. (11/15/2005)*

William Hill Estate 2002 Chardonnay (Napa Valley) $15. 89 *—S.H. (10/1/2004)*

William Hill Estate 2001 Chardonnay (Napa Valley) $15. 85 *—S.H. (6/1/2003)*

William Hill Estate 2000 Chardonnay (Napa Valley) $15. 88 *—J.M. (5/1/2002)*

William Hill Estate 1998 Chardonnay (Napa Valley) $15. 86 *(6/1/2000)*

William Hill Estate 1997 Chardonnay (Napa Valley) $14. 88 Best Buy *(11/1/1999)*

William Hill Estate 2005 Reserve Chardonnay (Napa Valley) $26. The reserve Chardonnay is primarily taken from Atlas Peak, but like the regular Chardonnay is entirely barrel-fermented. Hints of butter, marshmallow and spice on the nose give way to flavors of citrus custard and melon on the palate. Finishes with some spicy oak notes. **87** *(8/1/2007)*

William Hill Estate 2004 Reserve Chardonnay (Napa Valley) $26. 89 *—S.H. (10/1/2006)*

William Hill Estate 2003 Reserve Chardonnay (Napa Valley) $20. 88 *—S.H. (12/31/2005)*

William Hill Estate 2001 Reserve Chardonnay (Napa Valley) $21. 84 *—S.H. (12/31/2004)*

William Hill Estate 2000 Reserve Chardonnay (Napa Valley) $23. 90 *—S.H. (12/15/2002)*

William Hill Estate 1998 Reserve Chardonnay (Napa Valley) $22. 88 *(6/1/2000)*

William Hill Estate 1997 Reserve Chardonnay (Napa Valley) $20. 90 *(11/1/1999)*

William Hill Estate 1996 Merlot (Napa Valley) $18. 89 *(11/1/1999)*

William Hill Estate 2003 Merlot (Napa Valley) $23. 88 *—S.H. (12/15/2006)*

William Hill Estate 2001 Merlot (Napa Valley) $22. 91 *—S.H. (10/1/2005)*

William Hill Estate 2000 Merlot (Napa Valley) $21. 87 *—S.H. (2/1/2004)*

William Hill Estate 1999 Merlot (Napa Valley) $21. 84 *—S.H. (6/1/2002)*

William Hill Estate 1998 Merlot (Napa Valley) $22. 83 *—S.H. (8/1/2001)*

William Hill Estate 1999 Chardonnay (Napa Valley) $15. 84 *—S.H. (2/1/2001)*

WILLIAM ROAN

William Roan 2002 Shiraz (North Coast) $12. 83 *—S.H. (6/1/2005)*

WILLIAMS SELYEM

Williams Selyem 2005 Chardonnay (Russian River Valley) $35. What great structure you get in this quintessentially food-friendly wine. Absolutely dry, it shows a crisp mineralityF to the pear, pineapple, toasted meringue and sweet, charry oak flavors, and the finish is amazingly deep and long. This is really an impressive Chardonnay. **92 Editors' Choice** *—S.H. (8/1/2007)*

Williams Selyem 2004 Chardonnay (Russian River Valley) $35. 93 Editors' Choice *—S.H. (11/1/2006)*

Williams Selyem 2004 Allen Vineyard Chardonnay (Russian River Valley) $48. This is one of the best Chardonnays I've had recently. It's a tremendously ripe wine, exploding with apricot nectar, peach custard, quince, butterscotch, buttered toast and spice flavors. There's even a spine of minerality. But what really makes it so special is the acidity. This is just a tremendous Chard, totally addictive, and it's best now in its flamboyant youth. **96 Editors' Choice** *—S.H. (3/1/2007)*

Williams Selyem 2001 Allen Vineyard Chardonnay (Russian River Valley) $48. 94 *—S.H. (2/1/2004)*

Williams Selyem 2004 Hawk Hill Vineyard Chardonnay (Russian River Valley) $46. This is my least favorite of Bob Cabral's three current Chards, although it's still very good. It has an overripe quality, a stewed peach and boiled apricot taste, with some golden currants on the finish. **89** *—S.H. (3/1/2007)*

Williams Selyem 2003 Hawk Hill Vineyard Chardonnay (Russian River Valley) $46. 87 *—S.H. (3/1/2006)*

Williams Selyem 2001 Hawk Hill Vineyard Chardonnay (Russian River Valley) $44. 95 Editors' Choice *—S.H. (2/1/2004)*

Williams Selyem 2000 Hawk Hill Vineyard Chardonnay (Russian River Valley) $44. 92 *—J.M. (2/1/2003)*

Williams Selyem 2003 Heintz Vineyard Chardonnay (Russian River Valley) $44. 87 *—S.H. (3/1/2006)*

Williams Selyem 2001 Heintz Vineyard Chardonnay (Russian River Valley) $40. 94 *—S.H. (2/1/2004)*

Williams Selyem 2000 Heintz Vineyard Chardonnay (Russian River Valley) $40. 93 *—J.M. (2/1/2003)*

Williams Selyem 2000 Hirsch Vineyard Chardonnay (Sonoma Coast) $42. 95 Editors' Choice *—J.M. (2/1/2003)*

Williams Selyem 2003 Vista Verde Vineyard Late Harvest Gewürztraminer (San Benito County) $35. 91 *—S.H. (11/1/2005)*

Williams Selyem 2001 Vista Verde Vineyard Late Harvest Gewürztraminer (San Benito County) $32. 86 *—S.H. (5/1/2004)*

Williams Selyem 2000 Vista Verde Vineyard Late Harvest Gewürztraminer (San Benito County) $32. 93 *—J.M. (9/1/2003)*

Williams Selyem 2000 Windsor Oaks Vineyard Late Harvest Muscat Canelli (Russian River Valley) $32. 93 *—J.M. (7/1/2003)*

Williams Selyem 2003 Weir Vineyard Pinot Nero (Yorkville Highlands) $49. 86 *—S.H. (3/1/2006)*

Williams Selyem 2005 Pinot Noir (Central Coast) $31. Light and elegant, this polished Pinot is for early drinking. Bone dry and crisply acidic, the wine has the silky delicacy of the variety, with cherry, raspberry, tea, rose petal, cola and woodspice flavors, and a slightly astringent finish of finely ground tannins. 90 *—S.H. (8/1/2007)*

Williams Selyem 2005 Pinot Noir (Russian River Valley) $42. This is one of the winery's ripest, softest current Pinot releases. It's dry, but a bit heavy in mouthfeel, with a slightly stewed quality to the cherry and berry flavors. It also has some dry, astringent tannins in the finish. Could evolve over the next five years, but the overall quality is not likely to improve. 86 *—S.H. (8/1/2007)*

Williams Selyem 2005 Pinot Noir (Sonoma County) $34. Lots of true Pinot character in this dry, elegant wine, which contains mainly Russian River fruit. Made for early drinking, it has complex cherry, root beer, pomegranate, herb tea and spice flavors, wrapped into a delicately silky texture. 89 *—S.H. (8/1/2007)*

Williams Selyem 2005 Pinot Noir (Sonoma Coast) $39. Similar to the winery's '05 Russian River bottling in the ripeness of the fruit and tannins, but somehow fresher, although it's still a big, full-bodied Pinot Noir. Maybe it's the acidity that makes the framboise and cherry flavors come alive. Deeper notes of Portobello mushrooms and balsamic suggest moderate aging possibilities. Drink now through 2009. 91 *—S.H. (8/1/2007)*

Williams Selyem 2004 Pinot Noir (Central Coast) $39. 89 *—S.H. (11/15/2006)*

Williams Selyem 2004 Pinot Noir (Sonoma Coast) $39. 90 *—S.H. (11/1/2006)*

Williams Selyem 2004 Pinot Noir (Sonoma County) $32. 88 *—S.H. (11/1/2006)*

Williams Selyem 2004 Pinot Noir (Russian River Valley) $35. 89 *—S.H. (11/1/2006)*

Williams Selyem 2003 Pinot Noir (Central Coast) $29. 88 *—S.H. (11/1/2005)*

Williams Selyem 2003 Pinot Noir (Russian River Valley) $42. 92 *—S.H. (11/1/2005)*

Williams Selyem 2003 Pinot Noir (Sonoma Coast) $38. 87 *—S.H. (11/1/2005)*

Williams Selyem 2003 Pinot Noir (Sonoma County) $32. 90 *—S.H. (11/1/2005)*

Williams Selyem 2002 Pinot Noir (Central Coast) $29. 87 *(11/1/2004)*

Williams Selyem 2002 Pinot Noir (Russian River Valley) $39. 87 *(11/1/2004)*

Williams Selyem 2002 Pinot Noir (Sonoma Coast) $35. 86 *(11/1/2004)*

Williams Selyem 2002 Pinot Noir (Sonoma County) $29. 88 *(11/1/2004)*

Williams Selyem 2000 Pinot Noir (Central Coast) $27. 91 Editors' Choice *—J.M. (7/1/2003)*

Williams Selyem 2000 Pinot Noir (Sonoma Coast) $34. 88 *—J.M. (2/1/2003)*

Williams Selyem 2000 Pinot Noir (Russian River Valley) $39. 87 *—S.H. (2/1/2003)*

Williams Selyem 2004 Allen Vineyard Pinot Noir (Russian River Valley) $75. Not showing a lot right now, a closed, muted Pinot that doesn't want to give it up quite yet. Feels soft in the mouth, with some dusty tannins. You have to chew on the wine to find the blackberries and cherries, but they're there. We know that this is a wine that ages well, so stick it away for five years. 89 *—S.H. (3/1/2007)*

Williams Selyem 2003 Allen Vineyard Pinot Noir (Russian River Valley) $75. 92 *—S.H. (6/1/2005)*

Williams Selyem 2003 Allen Vineyard Pinot Noir (Russian River Valley) $75. 91 *—S.H. (3/1/2006)*

Williams Selyem 2002 Allen Vineyard Pinot Noir (Russian River Valley) $72. 85 *(11/1/2004)*

Williams Selyem 2001 Allen Vineyard Pinot Noir (Russian River Valley) $69. 93 *—S.H. (5/1/2004)*

Williams Selyem 2000 Allen Vineyard Pinot Noir (Russian River Valley) $NA. 92 *—S.H. (6/1/2005)*

Williams Selyem 2000 Allen Vineyard Pinot Noir (Russian River Valley) $68. 92 *(10/1/2002)*

Williams Selyem 1995 Allen Vineyard Pinot Noir (Russian River Valley) $NA. 84 *—S.H. (6/1/2005)*

Williams Selyem 2004 Bucher Vineyard Pinot Noir (Russian River Valley) $49. Young and closed now, this is a terrific Pinot, stuffed with major league blackberry, cherry and cola fruit, and so balanced and rich. The tannins are there, the acidity, the bigtime oak, and it all comes together in a complex finish. Fine now, if you decant for a few hours, or hold for 10 years. 91 *—S.H. (3/1/2007)*

Williams Selyem 2003 Bucher Vineyard Pinot Noir (Russian River Valley) $49. 91 *—S.H. (3/1/2006)*

Williams Selyem 2004 Coastlands Vineyard Pinot Noir (Sonoma Coast) $69. This has never been my favorite Williams Selyem Pinot, but this is Bob Cabral's best effort to date. Part of the reason, I think, is because 2004 was a warm vintage, and those coastal grapes need heat. The wine brims with cherries, cola, black raspberries, yet maintains that luscious coastal acidity. The mouthfeel is gorgeously silky and delicate. But it's young and immature now. Best 2007—2010. 92 *—S.H. (3/1/2007)*

Williams Selyem 2003 Coastlands Vineyard Pinot Noir (Sonoma Coast) $62. 87 *—S.H. (3/1/2006)*

Williams Selyem 2002 Coastlands Vineyard Pinot Noir (Sonoma Coast) $59. 88 *(11/1/2004)*

Williams Selyem 2001 Coastlands Vineyard Pinot Noir (Sonoma Coast) $59. 87 *—S.H. (5/1/2004)*

Williams Selyem 1999 Coastlands Vineyard Pinot Noir (Sonoma Coast) $52. 86 *—S.H. (2/1/2003)*

Williams Selyem 2004 Ferrington Vineyard Pinot Noir (Anderson Valley) $59. A bit hot, sweet and soft for my taste, this Pinot seems deficient in acidity, perhaps the result of the hot vintage. It has pie filling flavors of black cherries, black raspberries, cola and pomegranates. Doesn't seem like an ager, but it's pretty fancy now with a good steak. 87 *—S.H. (3/1/2007)*

Williams Selyem 2003 Ferrington Vineyard Pinot Noir (Anderson Valley) $59. 89 *—S.H. (3/1/2006)*

Williams Selyem 2002 Ferrington Vineyard Pinot Noir (Anderson Valley) $59. 84 *(11/1/2004)*

Williams Selyem 2001 Ferrington Vineyard Pinot Noir (Anderson Valley) $57. 89 *—S.H. (5/1/2004)*

Williams Selyem 2004 Flax Vineyard Pinot Noir (Russian River Valley) $54. This is really a fabulous Pinot Noir that is absolutely Grand Cru. It's balanced, but what's hard to describe is how the wine can be silky and airy, yet dense and complex. The fruit is amazingly ripe, a detonation of cherries, cola, raspberries, pomegranates and coffee, with new oaky layers of caramel, toast and vanilla, but it all comes together in a seamless, elegant, complex experience that's a joy to savor. Terrific now. Should hit its peak in 2007–2009, and hold for a decade. 96 Editors' Choice *—S.H. (3/1/2007)*

Williams Selyem 2003 Flax Vineyard Pinot Noir (Russian River Valley) $54. 92 *—S.H. (3/1/2006)*

Williams Selyem 2002 Flax Vineyard Pinot Noir (Russian River Valley) $49. 90 *(11/1/2004)*

Williams Selyem 2001 Flax Vineyard Pinot Noir (Russian River Valley) $46. 94 Editors' Choice *—S.H. (5/1/2004)*

Williams Selyem 2004 Heintz Vineyard Pinot Noir (Russian River Valley) $44. There's so much fruitsap richness and toasty sweet oak on this Chard, it's almost like a food group of its own. Just tremendous in ripe apricot jam, peach pie, and hazelnut-infused vanilla cream eclair flavors. That sounds sweet, but the wine is wonderfully dry. It's also richly balanced in acids. 95 *—S.H. (3/1/2007)*

Williams Selyem 2004 Hirsch Vineyard Pinot Noir (Sonoma Coast) $69. The most notable feature of this wine, the thing that really distinguishes it from the other Pinots in Bob Cabral's stable, is acidity. It just sings and zings. Meanwhile the fruity flavor from this hot vintage is enormous. Blackberries, cherries, mocha, molasses, the list goes on. Delicious now, this will improve for four years, and hold for another six. **94** —*S.H. (3/1/2007)*

Williams Selyem 2001 Hirsch Vineyard Pinot Noir (Sonoma Coast) $59. 92 —*S.H. (5/1/2004)*

Williams Selyem 2000 Hirsch Vineyard Pinot Noir (Sonoma Coast) $57. 93 Editors' Choice *(10/1/2002)*

Williams Selyem 1997 Olivet Lane Pinot Noir (Russian River Valley) $45. 90 *(10/1/1999)*

Williams Selyem 2004 Peay Vineyard Pinot Noir (Sonoma Coast) $49. The acidity is there, and the tannins. Both together make the wine young, immature, gritty, but they enable the wine to age. There's a terrific core of cherries, rhubarb, cola and pomegranates. It's a big Pinot, dry and gutsy, yet never loses its silky, lightly tannic expressiveness. You could drink it now with a few hours decanting, but it's best left alone for five or six years. **91** —*S.H. (3/1/2007)*

Williams Selyem 2003 Peay Vineyard Pinot Noir (Sonoma Coast) $49. 92 —*S.H. (3/1/2006)*

Williams Selyem 2004 Precious Mountain Vineyard Pinot Noir (Sonoma Coast) $85. This is always one of Williams Selyems' best Pinots, and the '04 is a fabulous wine. The grapes got real ripe up there in the coastal mountains, producing complex blackberry, cherry, cola, rhubarb, pomegranate and spice flavors, but the cool nights preserved vital acidity, and that makes for a rich balance. The wine never gives up its basically silky, elegant mouthfeel. So savory and delicious now, it's hard to pass up, but this wine should improve for six years. **96 Editors' Choice** —*S.H. (3/1/2007)*

Williams Selyem 2003 Precious Mountain Vineyard Pinot Noir (Sonoma Coast) $85. 93 —*S.H. (3/1/2006)*

Williams Selyem 2002 Precious Mountain Vineyard Pinot Noir (Sonoma Coast) $80. 87 *(11/1/2004)*

Williams Selyem 2001 Precious Mountain Vineyard Pinot Noir (Sonoma Coast) $80. 93 —*S.H. (5/1/2004)*

Williams Selyem 1999 Precious Mountain Pinot Noir (Sonoma Coast) $80. 89 *(10/1/2002)*

Williams Selyem 2004 Rochioli Riverblock Pinot Noir (Russian River Valley) $72. This is the least of the Riverblocks in the last five years. It's soft and obvious. Was that because of the heat? The wine lacks vital acidity, and the cherry, raspberry and pomegranate flavors are a little cooked or stewed. Drink now. **85** —*S.H. (3/1/2007)*

Williams Selyem 2003 Rochioli Riverblock Vineyard Pinot Noir (Russian River Valley) $72. 92 —*S.H. (3/1/2006)*

Williams Selyem 2002 Rochioli Riverblock Vineyard Pinot Noir (Russian River Valley) $69. 93 *(11/1/2004)*

Williams Selyem 2001 Rochioli Riverblock Vineyard Pinot Noir (Russian River Valley) $64. 93 —*S.H. (5/1/2004)*

Williams Selyem 2000 Rochioli Riverblock Vineyard Pinot Noir (Russian River Valley) $64. 92 —*J.M. (7/1/2003)*

Williams Selyem 1999 Rochioli Riverblock Pinot Noir (Russian River Valley) $60. 88 *(10/1/2002)*

Williams Selyem 2004 Vista Verde Vineyard Pinot Noir (San Benito County) $49. Vista Verde hasn't been my favorite Williams Selyem Pinot over the years. The '03 was a real disappointment. The '04 is better, a firmly structured wine, with tannins and acids that support ripe black cherry and cola fruit. It's a bit rustic, but has the stuffing to improve for a few years. **87** —*S.H. (3/1/2007)*

Williams Selyem 2003 Vista Verde Vineyard Pinot Noir (San Benito County) $49. 85 —*S.H. (3/1/2006)*

Williams Selyem 2002 Vista Verde Vineyard Pinot Noir (San Benito County) $49. 90 *(11/1/2004)*

Williams Selyem 2001 Vista Verde Vineyard Pinot Noir (San Benito County) $46. 88 —*S.H. (5/1/2004)*

Williams Selyem 2000 Vista Verde Vineyard Pinot Noir (San Benito County) $32. 90 —*J.M. (7/1/2003)*

Williams Selyem 2004 Weir Vineyard Pinot Noir (Yorkville Highlands) $54. This is the best Weir yet from Williams Selyem. It's not in the league of their great Sonoma County bottlings, but is a rich wine capable of aging. It's tannic and acidic for a Pinot, but never loses its silky quality, and is deeply flavored in black cherries, raspberries, cola and pomegranate. Drink now—2010. **89** —*S.H. (3/1/2007)*

Williams Selyem 2002 Weir Vineyard Pinot Noir (Yorkville Highlands) $49. 86 *(11/1/2004)*

Williams Selyem 2001 Weir Vineyard Pinot Noir (Yorkville Highlands) $48. 86 —*S.H. (5/1/2004)*

Williams Selyem 2000 Weir Vineyard Pinot Noir (Yorkville Highlands) $48. 87 —*S.H. (2/1/2003)*

Williams Selyem 2005 Westside Road Neighbors Pinot Noir (Russian River Valley) $65. I love the delicate complexity of this Pinot, which is a blend of five vineyards along this famous wine trail. If you want to understand RRV Pinot, and particularly from the stretch they call the Middle Reach, study this wine. Dry, crisp and silky, it shows beautifully ripened cherry, raspberry, cola, pomegranate and spicy-herbal flavors, perfectly integrated with smoky oak, and the brilliant acid-tannin balance of a great vintage. **93** —*S.H. (8/1/2007)*

Williams Selyem 2004 Westside Road Neighbors Pinot Noir (Russian River Valley) $62. 88 —*S.H. (11/1/2006)*

Williams Selyem 2003 Westside Road Neighbors Pinot Noir (Russian River Valley) $62. 93 —*S.H. (11/1/2005)*

Williams Selyem 2002 Westside Road Neighbors Pinot Noir (Russian River Valley) $59. 87 *(11/1/2004)*

Williams Selyem 2001 Mistral Vineyard Port (Central Coast) $35. 93 Editors' Choice —*S.H. (3/1/2006)*

Williams Selyem 2001 Zinfandel (Russian River Valley) $25. 90 *(11/1/2003)*

Williams Selyem 2000 Zinfandel (Russian River Valley) $25. 92 Editors' Choice —*J.M. (2/1/2003)*

Williams Selyem 2005 Bacigalupi Vineyard Zinfandel (Russian River Valley) $45. Enormously ripe berries characterize this wine; it explodes with wild raspberries, cherries, blackberries and dark chocolate, with a peppery, minty finish. But it's young and vigorous in rich, dense tannins, suggesting ageability. Best now, with decanting, and for several years. **91** —*S.H. (9/1/2007)*

Williams Selyem 2004 Bacigalupi Vineyard Zinfandel (Russian River Valley) $45. 91 —*S.H. (11/1/2006)*

Williams Selyem 2003 Bacigalupi Vineyard Zinfandel (Russian River Valley) $42. 80 —*S.H. (11/1/2005)*

Williams Selyem 2005 Feeney Vineyard Zinfandel (Russian River Valley) $45. Big, raw and frankly not really showing its best now, this young Zin needs time in the bottle. It has everything that it takes for 2–3 years aging, at least. Aromas and flavors of crushed pepper, fennel seed and cardamom spice up the blackberry, roasted coffee and bitter chocolate flavors, while the tannins are hefty, but negotiable. **91** —*S.H. (9/1/2007)*

Williams Selyem 2004 Feeney Vineyard Zinfandel (Russian River Valley) $45. 90 —*S.H. (11/1/2006)*

Williams Selyem 2003 Feeney Vineyard Zinfandel (Russian River Valley) $42. 83 —*S.H. (11/1/2005)*

Williams Selyem 2002 Feeney Vineyard Zinfandel (Russian River Valley) $38. 91 —*S.H. (10/1/2004)*

Williams Selyem 2004 Forchini Vineyard Zinfandel (Russian River Valley) $45. Port-y, hot and raisiny, the nicest aspect is dryness. After that, it's hard to find much to praise. **82** —*S.H. (3/1/2007)*

Williams Selyem 2003 Forchini Vineyard Zinfandel (Russian River Valley) $42. 92 —*S.H. (3/1/2006)*

Williams Selyem 2001 Forchini Vineyard North Flats Zinfandel (Russian River Valley) $32. 90 *(11/1/2003)*

WILLIAMSON

Williamson 2003 Amourette Chardonnay (Dry Creek Valley) $28. 84 —*S.H. (12/1/2005)*

Williamson 2002 Amour Merlot (Dry Creek Valley) $38. 87 —*S.H. (12/1/2005)*

WILLIS HALL

Willis Hall 2003 Stone Tree Reserve Syrah (Columbia Valley (WA)) $35. 86 *(9/1/2005)*

WILLOW CREST

Willow Crest 2001 Black Muscat (Yakima Valley) $8. 88 —*P.G. (9/1/2002)*

Willow Crest 1999 Cabernet Franc (Yakima Valley) $15. 88 —*P.G. (6/1/2002)*

Willow Crest 2005 Chenin Blanc (Yakima Valley) $10. 87 —*P.G. (12/31/2006)*

Willow Crest 2003 Merlot (Yakima Valley) $16. 88 —*P.G. (12/31/2006)*

Willow Crest 2000 Mourvèdre (Yakima Valley) $20. 87 —*P.G. (6/1/2002)*

Willow Crest 2005 Pinot Gris (Yakima Valley) $10. 88 —*P.G. (12/31/2006)*

Willow Crest 2000 Pinot Gris (Yakima Valley) $8. 87 Best Buy —*P.G. (6/1/2002)*

Willow Crest 2004 XIII Red Blend (Yamhill County) $28. In a Champagne bottle, this new wine is one part each of Grenache, Mourvèdre and Syrah, with a splash (4%) of Viognier. It tries to emulate a Châteauneuf-du-Pape, but mostly tastes like a young, ripe, mutt red, with a tannic, iron spine and tangy red fruits. 88 —*P.G. (2/1/2007)*

Willow Crest 2003 Collina Bella Red Blend (Yakima Valley) $24. 87 —*P.G. (12/31/2006)*

Willow Crest 2003 Syrah (Yakima Valley) $16. 89 —*P.G. (12/31/2006)*

Willow Crest 1999 Syrah (Yakima Valley) $18. 88 —*P.G. (6/1/2002)*

Willow Crest 1998 Sparkling Syrah Syrah (Yakima Valley) $15. 84 —*M.M. (12/1/2001)*

Willow Crest 2005 Viognier (Yakima Valley) $12. 86 —*P.G. (12/31/2006)*

WILLOWBROOK CELLARS

WillowBrook Cellars 2002 Owl Ridge Vineyard Chardonnay (Russian River Valley) $28. 82 —*S.H. (12/1/2004)*

WillowBrook Cellars 2001 Owl Ridge Vineyards Chardonnay (Russian River Valley) $28. 88 —*S.H. (7/1/2003)*

WillowBrook Cellars 2004 Dutton Morelli Vineyard Pinot Noir (Russian River Valley) $42. 82 —*S.H. (12/1/2006)*

WillowBrook Cellars 2005 Estate Grown Pinot Noir (Russian River Valley) $34. There's a one-dimensional, candied feeling to this Pinot. It has cola, green mint jelly and raspberry jam flavors. Drink now. 84 —*S.H. (12/15/2007)*

WillowBrook Cellars 2004 Estate Grown Pinot Noir (Russian River Valley) $34. Not a success. The wine has a rustic feeling, and is so soft, it makes the cola and cherry flavors taste syrupy. Lacks life and vivacity. 82 —*S.H. (9/1/2007)*

WillowBrook Cellars 2005 Kastania Vineyard Pinot Noir (Sonoma Coast) $48. This single-vineyard Pinot doesn't have the firm dryness you expect of a Pinot Noir from this appellation, but instead collapses in sugary, simple raspberry and cherry jelly flavors. Regains a point or two for silkiness. 84 —*S.H. (12/15/2007)*

WillowBrook Cellars 2005 Morelli Lane Pinot Noir (Russian River Valley) $42. The vineyard has been the source of great Pinots from the likes of Dutton-Goldfield and Sebastopol, but Willowbrook's bottling is a disappointment. It's simple and sweet, with cola and candied Lifesaver flavors. 83 —*S.H. (12/15/2007)*

WillowBrook Cellars 2002 Owl Ridge Vineyard Pinot Noir (Russian River Valley) $34. 84 *(11/1/2004)*

WILRIDGE

Wilridge 2002 Cabernet Sauvignon (Red Mountain) $29. 81 —*P.G. (12/31/2006)*

Wilridge 1998 Klipsun Vineyards Cabernet Sauvignon (Yakima Valley) $29. 90 —*P.G. (6/1/2001)*

Wilridge 2003 Merlot (Columbia Valley (WA)) $19. 87 —*P.G. (12/31/2006)*

Wilridge 2002 Merlot (Red Mountain) $29. 82 —*P.G. (12/31/2006)*

Wilridge 1998 Klipsun Vineyard Merlot (Yakima Valley) $29. 86 —*P.G. (6/1/2001)*

Wilridge 2000 Klipsun Vineyards Merlot (Red Mountain) $NA. 86 —*P.G. (9/1/2004)*

Wilridge 1997 Klipsun Vineyards Merlot (Yakima Valley) $29. 91 —*M.S. (4/1/2000)*

Wilridge 1998 Spring Valley Vineyards Merlot (Walla Walla (WA)) $29. 90 —*P.G. (6/1/2002)*

Wilridge NV Di Klipsun Nebbiolo (Red Mountain) $19. 91 —*P.G. (6/1/2002)*

Wilridge 2004 Klipsun Nebbiolo (Red Mountain) $24. 87 —*P.G. (12/31/2006)*85 —*P.G. (12/31/2006)*

Wilridge 2004 Rattlesnake Hills Syrah (Washington) $29. 88 —*P.G. (12/31/2006)*

WILSON

Wilson 2002 Sydney Vineyard Reserve Cabernet Sauvignon (Dry Creek Valley) $44. Classic Dry Creek Cab, with its tobacco-accented, slightly rough-hewn edge and dry, balanced flavors of wild blackberries, loganberries, coffee and fresh sweet herbs. Really a nice wine that's so different from Napa, and seems perfect for grilled meats, game and poultry. 90 —*S.H. (5/1/2007)*

Wilson 1999 Sydney Vineyard Cabernet Sauvignon (Dry Creek Valley) $28. 87 —*S.H. (11/15/2003)*

Wilson 2000 Chenin Blanc (Clarksburg) $11. 85 —*S.H. (5/1/2003)*

Wilson 2001 Isabella Late Harvest Chenin Blanc (Clarksburg) $16. 86 —*J.M. (12/1/2002)*

Wilson 1999 Sydney Vineyard Merlot (Dry Creek Valley) $24. 84 —*S.H. (12/1/2003)*

Wilson 2001 Petite Sirah (Clarksburg) $10. 82 *(4/1/2003)*

Wilson 1999 Petite Sirah (California) $10. 84 *(4/1/2003)*

Wilson 2004 Carl's Vineyard Zinfandel (Dry Creek Valley) $26. From a 1,700-foot vineyard high above the valley comes this compellingly delicious Zinfandel. A word of caution: The alcohol is 16.6%. But the wine isn't at all hot, and high alcohol is the price you pay for the lush, ripe fruitiness achieved in this scorching vintage. Brims with cherries, blackberries, raspberries, chocolate and spice, finishing long and dry. 92 —*S.H. (5/1/2007)*

Wilson 2000 Carl's Vineyard Zinfandel (Dry Creek Valley) $25. 84 —*S.H. (9/1/2003)*

Wilson 2004 Reserve Zinfandel (Dry Creek Valley) $38. Dry Creek Zins can be rustic, but not this one, which is closer in style to cult Napa Cabernet in the lush, soft, appealing mouthfeel and ripe flavors. It's enormously high in alcohol, (16.8%) but feels smooth, soft and polished, with raspberry-infused chocolate truffle flavors and Zin's zesty dusting of spicebox. Absolutely delicious. 93 —*S.H. (5/1/2007)*

Wilson 2001 Reserve Zinfandel (Dry Creek Valley) $38. 86 —*S.H. (3/1/2004)*

Wilson 2005 Sawyer Vineyard Zinfandel (Dry Creek Valley) $32. Way too hot and alcoholic, almost Port-like, this is the victim of excessive alcohol (15.8%) that makes it burn like a chili pepper. It also tastes weirdly sweet, which is probably the result of the alcohol, although it may have a little residual sugar. 82 —*S.H. (11/1/2007)*

Wilson 2005 Tori Vineyard Zinfandel (Dry Creek Valley) $32. The problem with this Zin is heat, as in 16.1% alcohol. While the wine is fully dry, that alcoholic burn districts from the otherwise tasty wild berry and spice flavors and smooth tannins. 84 —*S.H. (11/1/2007)*

WINCHESTER

Winchester 2000 Syrah (Paso Robles) $30. 91 —*S.H. (12/1/2002)*

WINDEMERE

Windemere 2003 Chardonnay (Edna Valley) $12. 84 —*S.H. (10/1/2006)*

Windemere 1997 Cathy MacGregor Vineyard Signature Chardonnay (Edna Valley) $32. 87 *(6/1/2000)*

Windemere 2002 MacGregor Vineyard Pinot Noir (Edna Valley) $18. 83 —*S.H. (10/1/2006)*

Windemere 2005 Windemere Pinot Noir (Edna Valley) $19. Soft and simple, with thinned-down cherry and cola flavors. Not much going on. 82 —*S.H. (10/1/2007)*

Windemere 2004 Windemere Pinot Noir (Edna Valley) $19. Kind of raw and thin, with tart acids and some cherry, cola, oak and herb flavors. Overpriced. 83 —*S.H. (10/1/2007)*

WINDMILL

Windmill 2003 Syrah (Lodi) $12. 84 *(9/1/2005)*

Windmill 2005 Old Vine Zinfandel (Lodi) $12. 85 —*S.H. (12/15/2006)*

Windmill 2001 Old Vine Zinfandel (Lodi) $10. 86 —*J.M. (11/15/2003)*

Windsor 1999 Private Reserve Cabernet Sauvignon (Mendocino) $17. 86 —*S.H. (11/15/2002)*

Windsor 2000 Chardonnay (Sonoma County) $17. 88 —*S.H. (6/1/2003)*

WINDSOR

Windsor 1997 Barrel-Fermented Private Reserve Chardonnay (Russian River Valley) $17. 83 *(6/1/2000)*

Windsor 1997 Preston Ranch Private Reserve Chardonnay (Russian River Valley) $15. 88 *(6/1/2000)*

Windsor 2000 Middle Ridge Vineyard Private Reserve Fumé Blanc (Mendocino County) $13. 86 —*S.H. (12/15/2001)*

Windsor 1997 Toni Stockhausen Signature Series Meritage (Sonoma County) $23. 89 —*S.H. (12/1/2001)*

Windsor 1999 40th Anniversary Reserve Merlot (Dry Creek Valley) $40. 84 *(11/15/2002)*

Windsor 1996 Shelton Signature Series Merlot (Sonoma County) $25. 83 —*J.C. (7/1/2000)*

Windsor 1998 Signature Series Merlot (Sonoma County) $25. 86 —*S.H. (6/1/2001)*

Windsor 1997 Stockhausen Signature Series Merlot (Sonoma County) $25. 87 —*S.H. (12/1/2001)*

Windsor 1998 Toni Stockhausen Signature Series Merlot (Sonoma County) $25. =87 —*S.H. (12/1/2001)*

Windsor 2000 Murphy Ranch Late Harvest Muscat Canelli (Alexander Valley) $15. 86 *—S.H. (12/31/2001)*

Windsor 1999 Petite Sirah (Mendocino County) $13. 83 *(4/1/2003)*

Windsor 2000 Pinot Noir (Sonoma County) $19. 84 *(10/1/2002)*

Windsor 1999 Private Reserve Pinot Noir (Sonoma County) $17. 85 *(10/1/2002)*

Windsor 1999 Signature Series Pinot Noir (Sonoma County) $19. 86 *(10/1/2002)*

Windsor 2000 Private Reserve Sémillon (Mendocino) $15. 86 *—S.H. (12/15/2001)*

Windsor 1998 Private Reserve Syrah (Sonoma County) $16. 87 *(10/1/2001)*

Windsor 1997 Zinfandel (Sonoma County) $18. 86 *—P.G. (3/1/2001)*

Windsor 1997 Old Vines Wild Thing Zinfandel (Mendocino County) $16. 89 *—P.G. (11/15/1999)*

Windsor 1997 Private Reserve Zinfandel (Mendocino) $15. 85 *—P.G. (3/1/2001)*

Windsor 2001 Signature Series Zinfandel (Mendocino County) $15. 86 *(11/1/2003)*

Windsor 1999 Toni Stockhausen Signature Series Zinfandel (Mendocino County) $17. 90 Best Buy *—S.H. (12/15/2001)*

WINDWALKER

Windwalker 1999 Reserve Chardonnay (El Dorado) $18. 85 *—S.H. (5/1/2002)*

WINDWARD VINEYARD

Windward Vineyard 2000 Monopole Pinot Noir (Paso Robles) $30. 85 *(10/1/2002)*

Windward Vineyard 1999 Monopole Pinot Noir (Paso Robles) $30. 85 *(10/1/2002)*

WINDY OAKS

Windy Oaks 1999 Pinot Noir (Santa Cruz County) $39. 86 *—S.H. (12/1/2003)*

Windy Oaks 2002 Schultze Family Vineyard Estate Blend Pinot Noir (Santa Cruz Mountains) $18. 87 *—S.H. (11/1/2005)*

Windy Oaks 2001 Schultze Family Vineyard Estate Reserve Pinot Noir (Santa Cruz Mountains) $36. 91 Editors' Choice *—S.H. (11/1/2005)*

WINDY POINT

Windy Point 2004 Exclamation Point! Bordeaux Blend (Yakima Valley) $19. A blend of 60% Cab Franc and 40% Merlot, this pleasant, screwcapped red is all estate grown and produced. It's a good, quaffable red, smooth and flavorful. It comes across as generic, in that it shows no specific identity, relating to grapes or terroir, that marks it as distinct from the myriad other red blends in the market. Just 220 cases produced. 86 *—P.G. (5/1/2007)*

Windy Point 2003 Estate Cabernet Franc (Yakima Valley) $18. 88 *—P.G. (4/1/2006)*

Windy Point 2004 Reserve Cabernet Franc (Yakima Valley) $29. Extremely tight, compact and tart, this remained acidic and lean even after 24 hours of breathing time. Hints of pickle barrel don't add much pleasure to the tannins, and the wine simply refuses to come out of its shell at this point in time. I'm sure the winemaker tasted something in these barrels that seemed like reserve, but I can't find it. 85 *—P.G. (5/1/2007)*

Windy Point 2002 Merlot (Yakima Valley) $15. 87 *—P.G. (11/15/2005)*

Windy Point 2003 !Exclamation Point! Red Blend (Yakima Valley) $15. 88 *—P.G. (4/1/2006)*

Windy Point 2004 Estate Syrah (Yakima Valley) $20. This pure, estate-grown Syrah is marked with grapefruit rind and citrus—sure signs of cool-climate Washington Syrah. Despite its healthy (14.8%) alcohol, it lacks sweet fruit. In fact it's a bit of a sourball, grainy, herbal and tannic. There's plenty of color and varietal pepper, but it's a bit too heavy with acid and tannin. 85 *—P.G. (5/1/2007)*

WINDY RIDGE

Windy Ridge 2005 Cabernet Sauvignon (Central Coast) $12. The wine is certainly ripe, with jellied cherry and blackberry flavors. But the balance is off, and the finish is too sweet in this soft, simple wine. 82 *—S.H. (11/15/2007)*

WINE BLOCK

Wine Block 2002 Cabernet Sauvignon (California) $10. 86 Best Buy *—S.H. (12/1/2005)*

Wine Block 2004 Chardonnay (California) $10. 84 Best Buy *—S.H. (12/1/2005)*

Wine Block 2002 Merlot (California) $10. 86 Best Buy *—S.H. (12/1/2005)*

WINE BY JOE

Wine by Joe 2004 Pinot Gris (Oregon) $13. 85 *—P.G. (2/1/2006)*

WINEGLASS CELLARS

Wineglass Cellars 1998 Rich Harvest Red Wine Bordeaux Blend (Yakima Valley) $50. 91 *—P.G. (6/1/2001)*

Wineglass Cellars 2000 Cabernet Sauvignon (Yakima Valley) $20. 87 *—P.G. (9/1/2004)*

Wineglass Cellars 1999 Cabernet Sauvignon (Yakima Valley) $21. 88 *—P.G. (9/1/2004)*

Wineglass Cellars 1999 Cabernet Sauvignon (Yakima Valley) $21. 88 *—P.G. (9/1/2004)*

Wineglass Cellars 1998 Cabernet Sauvignon (Yakima Valley) $25. 90 *—P.G. (6/1/2001)*

Wineglass Cellars 2000 Elerding Vineyard Cabernet Sauvignon (Yakima Valley) $45. 89 *—P.G. (9/1/2004)*

Wineglass Cellars 2000 Elerding Vineyard Cabernet Sauvignon (Yakima Valley) $45. 87 *—P.G. (9/1/2004)*

Wineglass Cellars 1999 Elerding Vineyard Cabernet Sauvignon (Yakima Valley) $45. 92 *—P.G. (6/1/2002)*

Wineglass Cellars 1998 Elerding Vineyard Cabernet Sauvignon (Yakima Valley) $40. 92 *—P.G. (6/1/2001)*

Wineglass Cellars 2000 Reserve Cabernet Sauvignon (Yakima Valley) $28. 90 *—P.G. (9/1/2004)*

Wineglass Cellars 1999 Reserve Cabernet Sauvignon (Yakima Valley) $35. 86 *—P.G. (6/1/2002)*

Wineglass Cellars 2003 Chardonnay (Yakima Valley) $13. 85 *—P.G. (9/1/2004)*

Wineglass Cellars 2001 Chardonnay (Yakima Valley) $13. 87 *—P.G. (9/1/2004)*

Wineglass Cellars 1999 Chardonnay (Yakima Valley) $13. 88 Best Buy *—P.G. (6/1/2001)*

Wineglass Cellars 2006 In The Buff Chardonnay (Columbia Valley (WA)) $15. Light and pleasant, but not up to the richness of the sensational 2005. This has light flavors suggestive of pineapple, cracker and a hint of mint. It's pleasant drinking, but generic. 85 *—P.G. (12/1/2007)*

Wineglass Cellars 2005 In The Buff Chardonnay (Columbia Valley (WA)) $13. 89 Best Buy *—P.G. (10/1/2006)*

Wineglass Cellars 2001 Reserve Chardonnay (Yakima Valley) $16. 87 *—P.G. (9/1/2004)*

Wineglass Cellars 2001 Merlot (Yakima Valley) $22. 88 *—P.G. (9/1/2004)*

Wineglass Cellars 2000 Merlot (Yakima Valley) $22. 86 *—P.G. (9/1/2004)*

Wineglass Cellars 1999 Merlot (Yakima Valley) $22. 90 *—P.G. (2/1/2002)*

Wineglass Cellars 1998 Merlot (Yakima Valley) $20. 92 Editors' Choice *—P.G. (6/1/2001)*

Wineglass Cellars 1998 DuBrul Vineyard Merlot (Yakima Valley) $30. 91 *—P.G. (6/1/2001)*

Wineglass Cellars 2000 Reserve Merlot (Yakima Valley) $35. 87 *—P.G. (9/1/2004)*

Wineglass Cellars 1999 Reserve Merlot (Yakima Valley) $35. 88 *—P.G. (6/1/2002)*

Wineglass Cellars NV Capizimo Red Red Blend (America) $15. 84 *—P.G. (2/1/2004)*

Wineglass Cellars 2000 Rich Harvest Red Blend (Yakima Valley) $50. 89 *—P.G. (9/1/2004)*

Wineglass Cellars 1999 Rich Harvest Red Blend (Yakima Valley) $50. 88 *—P.G. (6/1/2002)*

Wineglass Cellars 2003 Sangiovese (Yakima Valley) $18. 88 *—P.G. (6/1/2006)*

Wineglass Cellars 2002 Boushey Vineyard Syrah (Yakima Valley) $23. 91 *—P.G. (6/1/2006)*

Wineglass Cellars NV Batch 00 Zinfandel (America) $19. 86 *—P.G. (1/1/2004)*

WINES OF CARMEL

Wines of Carmel 2001 Carmel Chardonnay (Monterey County) $23. 85 *—S.H. (2/1/2004)*

WINESMITH

WineSmith 2002 Student Vineyard Faux Chablis Chardonnay (Napa Valley) $30. 84 *—S.H. (11/1/2005)*

WING CANYON

Wing Canyon 2000 Cabernet Sauvignon (Mount Veeder) $25. 87 *—S.H. (5/1/2005)*

WINGS

Wings 2003 Cabernet Sauvignon (Napa Valley) $60. 91 *—S.H. (12/31/2006)*

WINTER'S HILL

Winter's Hill 2000 Pinot Gris (Willamette Valley) $12. 87 *—P.G. (2/1/2002)*

Winter's Hill 2004 Pinot Noir (Dundee Hills) $28. Firm and well-defined, this moderately-priced Pinot blends its lightly spicy, tart red fruit with annotations of mocha/cola, spice and toast. It does not push to be massive or jammy, but nicely expresses itself at appropriate (14.3%) levels of alcohol and with just a light dusting of new oak seasoning. **88** *—P.G. (2/1/2007)*

Winter's Hill 2002 Pinot Noir (Willamette Valley) $20. 82 *(11/1/2004)*

Winter's Hill 2000 Pinot Noir (Willamette Valley) $25. 88 *—P.G. (12/1/2003)*

Winter's Hill 1999 Pinot Noir (Willamette Valley) $25. 85 *—P.G. (12/31/2001)*

Winter's Hill 2002 Reserve Pinot Noir (Willamette Valley) $29. 85 *(11/1/2004)*

WITNESS TREE

Witness Tree 2005 Pinot Noir (Willamette Valley) $27. Very clean and pretty, showcasing lovely varietal flavors of cherries and berries. There's a well-managed earthy component, with suggestions of forest floor and organic matter, and the tannins are ripe and fine. A very fine bottle for the price. **90** *—P.G. (7/1/2007)*

Witness Tree 2000 Estate Pinot Noir (Willamette Valley) $20. 83 *(10/1/2002)*

Witness Tree 1997 Estate Pinot Noir (Willamette Valley) $34. 85 *(11/15/1999)*

Witness Tree 2000 Vintage Select Pinot Noir (Willamette Valley) $40. 89 *(10/1/2002)*

Witness Tree 1997 Vintage Select Pinot Noir (Willamette Valley) $18. 90 Best Buy *(11/15/1999)*

WOLFF

Wolff 2005 Estate Old Vines Chardonnay (Edna Valley) $19. Very dry and acidic, this elegant Chard has a tangy minerality that undergirds the lime, kiwi and mango flavors. It's a bone dry wine, perfect for roasted salmon, chicken or pork with a tropical fruit, green onion and cilantro salsa topping. **88** *—S.H. (11/1/2007)*

Wolff 2004 Old Vines Chardonnay (Edna Valley) $19. 88 *—S.H. (7/1/2006)*

Wolff 2003 Old Vines Chardonnay (Edna Valley) $19. 87 *—S.H. (11/15/2005)*

Wolff 2002 Old Vines Chardonnay (Edna Valley) $19. 90 *—S.H. (9/1/2004)*

Wolff 2001 Old Vines Chardonnay (Edna Valley) $19. 90 Editors' Choice *—S.H. (5/1/2003)*

Wolff 2004 Estate Grown Petite Sirah (Edna Valley) $19. 92 Cellar Selection *—S.H. (7/1/2006)*

Wolff 2001 Dijon Clones Selection Pinot Noir (Edna Valley) $25. 87 *—S.H. (7/1/2003)*

Wolff 2005 Dijon Clones Selection Pinot Noir (Edna Valley) $24. Wolff has struggled with this bottling, which never seems quite ripe despite low production. The wine is clean and delicate, but characterized by high acidity and lean, green minty flavors that just barely suggest cherries. **84** *—S.H. (11/1/2007)*

Wolff 2004 Dijon Clones Selection Pinot Noir (Edna Valley) $24. Lots of rich fruit in this wine, which is riper and fuller-bodied than most Edna Valley Pinots. Seems like they left the fruit to hang for a long time in this hot vintage, resulting in blackberry and cherry flavors that are big, soft and dry. Flavorful, but lacks the silky delicacy you want in Pinot Noir. **84** *—S.H. (2/1/2007)*

Wolff 2003 Estate Dijon Clones Selection Pinot Noir (Edna Valley) $25. 88 *—S.H. (8/1/2006)*

Wolff 2005 Syrah (Edna Valley) $19. What a great aroma! Promises real Northern Rhône complexity, with white pepper-accented blackberries and currants and luscious smoky oak. All the more tragic when the wine turns sugary sweet instead of dry in the mouth. **83** *—S.H. (11/1/2007)*

Wolff 2002 Syrah (Edna Valley) $19. 87 *—S.H. (9/1/2004)*

Wolff 2001 Syrah (Edna Valley) $18. 88 *—S.H. (6/1/2003)*

Wolff 2003 Wolff Vineyards Syrah (Edna Valley) $20. 84 *—S.H. (11/15/2005)*

WÖLFFER

Wölffer 2003 Cabernet Franc (The Hamptons, Long Island) $40. 84 *—M.D. (8/1/2006)*

Wölffer 1998 Cabernet Franc (The Hamptons, Long Island) $25. 88 *—J.C. (4/1/2001)*

Wölffer 1997 Brut Champagne Blend (The Hamptons, Long Island) $27. 90 Editors' Choice *—J.M. (12/1/2002)*

Wölffer 1995 Brut Champagne Blend (The Hamptons, Long Island) $30. 87 *—J.C. (4/1/2001)*

Wölffer 2000 Cuvée Christian Brut Champagne Blend (The Hamptons, Long Island) $29. 84 *—J.C. (12/31/2004)*

Wölffer 2001 Estate Selection Chardonnay (The Hamptons, Long Island) $27. 84 *—J.C. (3/1/2006)*

Wölffer 2000 Estate Selection Chardonnay (The Hamptons, Long Island) $27. 84 *—J.C. (10/2/2004)*

Wölffer 1998 Estate Selection Chardonnay (The Hamptons, Long Island) $27. 89 *—J.C. (4/1/2001)*

Wölffer 2003 Late Harvest Chardonnay (Long Island) $35. 87 *—J.C. (10/2/2004)*

Wölffer 2000 Late Harvest Chardonnay (The Hamptons, Long Island) $35. 88 *—J.M. (7/1/2002)*

Wölffer 2003 Reserve Chardonnay (The Hamptons, Long Island) $20. This deep golden Chardonnay from respected Long Island producer Wölffer Estate offers a pleasing combination of bright, tropical fruit flavors and toasted oak. There's a slightly lean edge to the wine but overall, it's versatile and well-integrated. **84** *—S.K. (5/1/2007)*

Wölffer 2002 Reserve Chardonnay (The Hamptons, Long Island) $20. Still young-looking, with a touch of green to the pale yellow color, this wine offers white fruit aromas in addition to burnt popcorn. The oak is more subdued in the mouth, where toasty flavors play a secondary role to white fruits and citrus. **84** *—M.D. (8/1/2006)*

Wölffer 1999 Reserve Chardonnay (The Hamptons, Long Island) $19. 83 *—J.C. (1/1/2004)*

Wölffer 1998 Reserve Chardonnay (The Hamptons, Long Island) $18. 87 *—J.C. (4/1/2001)*

Wölffer 1998 Merlot (The Hamptons, Long Island) $20. 87 *—J.C. (4/1/2001)*

Wölffer 2002 Estate Selection Merlot (The Hamptons, Long Island) $35. Wölffer Merlots are similar in style: high acidity and mild tannins on a light- to medium-bodied frame. This vintage has aromas of red berry, earth, spice, and dill, while the palate is similar, but with a burnt character and dill playing a leading role. **84** *—M.D. (12/1/2006)*

Wölffer 2001 Estate Selection Merlot (The Hamptons, Long Island) $35. 85 *—J.C. (3/1/2006)*

Wölffer 2000 Estate Selection Merlot (The Hamptons, Long Island) $35. 85 *—J.C. (10/2/2004)*

Wölffer 1999 Estate Selection Merlot (The Hamptons, Long Island) $33. 88 *—J.M. (1/1/2003)*

Wölffer 1998 Estate Selection Merlot (The Hamptons, Long Island) $30. 89 *—J.C. (4/1/2001)*

Wölffer 2000 La Ferme Martin Merlot (The Hamptons, Long Island) $14. 83 *—J.C. (10/2/2004)*

Wölffer 2003 Reserve Merlot (The Hamptons, Long Island) $22. 83 *—M.D. (12/1/2006)*

Wölffer 2002 Reserve Merlot (The Hamptons, Long Island) $22. 87 *—M.D. (8/1/2006)*

Wölffer 2001 Reserve Merlot (Long Island) $22. 86 *—J.C. (10/2/2004)*

Wölffer 2005 Pinot Gris (Long Island) $24. Elegant, fruity and light on the palate with a mineral edge, this wine is another success from Wölffer. A perfect summer wine with a substantial finish, it offers tingle on the tongue alongside ripe fruit flavors. Unique and likeable. **85** *—S.K. (7/1/2007)*

Wölffer 2004 Pinot Gris (Long Island) $22. 81 *—J.C. (2/1/2006)*

Wölffer 2004 Pinot Noir (The Hamptons, Long Island) $50. 82 *—M.D. (12/1/2006)*

Wölffer 2002 Pinot Noir (The Hamptons, Long Island) $50. 88 *(11/1/2004)*

Wölffer 2005 Rosé Blend (The Hamptons, Long Island) $14. Aromas of peach, rose petals and citrus greet the nose with this popular, fun rose from Wolffer. It's fruit-driven, dry and zingy and would pair deliciously with lobster or a mild cheese. Perhaps just a touch too much acidity overrides the delicate fruit flavors but overall this is an elegant and accessible rose. 85 —*S.K. (2/1/2007)*

Wölffer 2002 Rosé Blend (The Hamptons, Long Island) $NA. 83 —*J.C. (7/1/2003)*

Wölffer 1999 Rosé Blend (Long Island) $11. 84 —*J.C. (4/1/2001)*

Wölffer 2001 Estate Bottled Rosé Blend (The Hamptons, Long Island) $11. 81 —*J.M. (1/1/2003)*

Wölffer 2006 Rosé Rosé Blend (The Hamptons, Long Island) $14. This poised salmon-amber rosé blend is a refreshing alternative to the old-school sweet rose of the past. The nose exudes peaches, apricots and cherries while on the palate, the wine is largely dry and balanced with a minerally, lime finish. That's not to say the wine lacks complexity; it's weightier on the tongue than many of the flirtier rosés and may be a touch ponderous for fans of tingling styles. A balance between crispness and complexity means it will pair well with diverse dishes and make a wonderful bridge wine from flavor to flavor. Think salmon, summer salads and grilled herb chicken. 86 —*S.K. (7/1/2007)*

Wölffer 1998 Cuvée Christian Brut Sparkling Blend (The Hamptons, Long Island) $27. 86 —*M.S. (6/1/2003)*

WOOD FAMILY VINEYARDS

Wood Family Vineyards 2001 Quail Creek Cabernet Sauvignon (Livermore Valley) $24. 87 —*S.H. (11/15/2003)*

WOODBRIDGE

Woodbridge 1997 Barbera (Lodi) $12. 88 Best Buy —*S.H. (11/15/2001)*

Woodbridge 1997 Cabernet Sauvignon (California) $8. 83 —*S.H. (2/1/2000)*

Woodbridge 2002 Cabernet Sauvignon (California) $8. 83 —*S.H. (7/1/2005)*

Woodbridge 2000 Cabernet Sauvignon (California) $8. 82 —*S.H. (12/31/2002)*

Woodbridge 1998 Cabernet Sauvignon (California) $8. 82 —*S.H. (5/1/2001)*

Woodbridge 2001 California Cabernet Sauvignon (California) $8. 82 —*S.H. (10/1/2004)*

Woodbridge 2001 Red Dirt Ridge Cabernet Sauvignon (Lodi) $11. 84 —*S.H. (10/1/2004)*

Woodbridge 2000 Red Dirt Ridge (PT) Cabernet Sauvignon (Lodi) $11. 84 *(11/15/2003)*

Woodbridge 1999 Twin Oaks Cabernet Sauvignon (California) $12. 85 —*S.H. (12/31/2002)*

Woodbridge 1998 Chardonnay (California) $8. 85 Best Buy —*S.H. (11/15/1999)*

Woodbridge 2003 Chardonnay (California) $8. 83 —*S.H. (7/1/2005)*

Woodbridge 2000 Chardonnay (California) $9. 83 —*S.H. (9/1/2002)*

Woodbridge 1999 Chardonnay (California) $9. 83 —*S.H. (5/1/2001)*

Woodbridge 2001 Barrel-Aged Chardonnay (California) $8. 83 —*S.H. (8/1/2003)*

Woodbridge 2002 California Chardonnay (California) $8. 83 —*S.H. (9/1/2004)*

Woodbridge 2002 Ghost Oak Chardonnay (California) $11. 85 —*S.H. (11/15/2004)*

Woodbridge 2001 Select Vineyard Series Ghost Oak (PT) Chardonnay (California) $11. 84 *(11/15/2003)*

Woodbridge 2002 Select Vineyard Series Ghost Oak Chardonnay (California) $11. 84 —*S.H. (12/15/2004)*

Woodbridge 2003 Johannisberg Riesling (California) $7. 84 Best Buy —*S.H. (12/1/2004)*

Woodbridge 2002 Johannisberg Riesling (California) $7. 83 —*J.M. (8/1/2003)*

Woodbridge 1997 Merlot (California) $8. 80 —*L.W. (12/31/1999)*

Woodbridge 2002 Merlot (California) $8. 83 —*S.H. (7/1/2005)*

Woodbridge 2000 Merlot (California) $9. 83 —*S.H. (12/31/2002)*

Woodbridge 1999 Merlot (California) $8. 84 Best Buy —*S.H. (11/15/2001)*

Woodbridge 1998 Merlot (California) $8. 83 —*S.H. (9/1/2003)*

Woodbridge 2001 California Merlot (California) $8. 83 —*S.H. (9/1/2004)*

Woodbridge 2000 Clay Hollow (PT) Merlot (California) $11. 84 *(11/15/2003)*

Woodbridge 2001 Select Vineyard Series Clay Hollow Merlot (Lodi) $11. 86 Best Buy —*S.H. (12/15/2004)*

Woodbridge 1998 Winemaker's Selection Muscat (California) $12. 89 Best Buy —*S.H. (12/1/2003)*

Woodbridge 2003 Pinot Grigio (California) $8. 83 —*S.H. (12/15/2004)*

Woodbridge 2002 Pinot Grigio (California) $8. 83 —*S.H. (12/1/2003)*

Woodbridge 2000 Pinot Grigio (California) $8. 84 —*S.H. (11/15/2001)*

Woodbridge 1997 Portacinco Port (Lodi) $20. 88 Editors' Choice —*S.H. (7/1/2005)*

Woodbridge 1995 Portacinco Port (Lodi) $20. 91 —*S.H. (8/1/2004)*

Woodbridge 1994 Portacinco Port (California) $20. 90 —*S.H. (12/31/2000)*

Woodbridge 2002 Sauvignon Blanc (California) $6. 84 —*S.H. (9/1/2004)*

Woodbridge 2001 Sauvignon Blanc (California) $6. 84 Best Buy —*S.H. (7/1/2003)*

Woodbridge 2000 Sauvignon Blanc (California) $7. 83 —*S.H. (10/1/2003)*

Woodbridge 1999 Sauvignon Blanc (California) $7. 83 —*S.H. (11/15/2000)*

Woodbridge 2001 Syrah (California) $9. 83 —*S.H. (12/15/2004)*

Woodbridge 2000 Syrah (California) $9. 88 Best Buy —*S.H. (12/1/2002)*

Woodbridge 1999 Syrah (California) $8. 83 *(10/1/2001)*

Woodbridge 1997 Zinfandel (California) $7. 82 —*S.H. (2/1/2000)*

Woodbridge 2002 Zinfandel (California) $8. 83 —*S.H. (12/15/2004)*

Woodbridge 2001 Zinfandel (California) $7. 82 *(11/1/2003)*

Woodbridge 2000 Zinfandel (California) $7. 85 Best Buy —*S.H. (12/1/2002)*

Woodbridge 1999 Zinfandel (California) $6. 84 —*S.H. (9/12/2002)*

Woodbridge 2001 Select Vineyard Series Fish Net Creek Zinfandel (Lodi) $11. 85 —*S.H. (9/1/2004)*

Woodbridge 2000 Select Vineyard Series-Old Vine-Fish Net Creek Zinfandel (Lodi) $11. 86 *(11/15/2003)*

Woodbridge 2003 White Zinfandel (California) $5. 83 Best Buy —*S.H. (12/15/2004)*

Woodbridge 2002 White Zinfandel Zinfandel (California) $5. 84 —*S.H. (3/1/2004)*

WOODBRIDGE BY ROBERT MONDAVI

Woodbridge by Robert Mondavi 2005 Cabernet Sauvignon (California) $9. A little sharp and pricked throughout, but the dryness, smooth, oaky tannins and ripe blackberries and cherries make this wine balanced and savory. Pretty good value in a dry, everyday Cab. 84 —*S.H. (11/15/2007)*

Woodbridge by Robert Mondavi 2006 Chardonnay (California) $9. This shows real varietal character with spicy peaches-and-cream flavors and a nice vein of smoky oak, and a honeyed, crisp finish. 85 Best Buy —*S.H. (11/15/2007)*

Woodbridge by Robert Mondavi 2005 Pinot Grigio (California) $8. Made in a very dry, very crisp style, making it different from the run-of-the-mill, slightly sweet PGs, and that makes it a really nice wine. With rich citrus, fig, melon and spice flavors, it's a great cocktail sipper, and will go with a wide variety of food. Easy to find, with 300,000 cases produced. 88 Best Buy —*S.H. (6/1/2007)*

Woodbridge by Robert Mondavi 2004 Pinot Grigio (California) $8. 85 Best Buy *(2/1/2006)*

Woodbridge by Robert Mondavi 2005 Sauvignon Blanc (California) $6. This is one of the best buys out there for a dry white wine. At this price, you should stock up by the case. With its lemon, lime, tart green apple and honeydew melon flavors, and the crisp acidity that makes it so clean and tangy, it's just a great sipper. 88 Best Buy —*S.H. (6/1/2007)*

Woodbridge by Robert Mondavi 2003 Sauvignon Blanc (California) $6. 82 —*S.H. (8/1/2005)*

Woodbridge by Robert Mondavi 2005 Shiraz (California) $9. A little too sharp and acidic, with jammy cherry and blackberry flavors that finish dry. It straddles that line between likeable and a turnoff because it's so tart. 82 —*S.H. (6/1/2007)*

Woodbridge by Robert Mondavi 2005 Zinfandel (California) $6. This tastes so fresh and sharp, it's almost still fermenting. Really too green and harsh to recommend. 82 —*S.H. (6/1/2007)*

WOODEN VALLEY

Wooden Valley 1999 Suisun Valley Cabernet Sauvignon (Solano County) $12. 86 —*S.H. (11/15/2003)*

Wooden Valley 2002 Pinot Noir (Suisun Valley) $10. 83 *(11/1/2004)*

WOODENHEAD

Woodenhead 2000 Elk Prairie Pinot Noir (California) $42. 85 *(10/1/2002)*

Woodenhead 2005 Morning Dew Ranch Pinot Noir (Anderson Valley) $50. Youth characterizes this fresh wine, with crisp, citrusy acidity and firm tannins. The flavors are of cranberries, pomegranates, rhubarb and cola, with a thoroughly dry finish. Very much in the mode of a good, cool-area RRV Pinot Noir. **87** *—S.H. (11/1/2007)*

Woodenhead 2004 Wiley Vineyard Pinot Noir (Anderson Valley) $46. Rich and juicy in cherry, cranberry, red currant, licorice and oaky vanilla flavors, but finishes a bit hot in alcohol, with a sweet, caramelized finish. **85** *—S.H. (11/1/2007)*

Woodenhead 2001 Braccialini Vineyards Zinfandel (Alexander Valley) $30. 86 *(11/1/2003)*

Woodenhead 2001 Martinelli Road Vineyard Old Vine Zinfandel (Russian River Valley) $30. 87 *(11/1/2003)*

WOODINVILLE WINE CELLARS

Woodinville Wine Cellars 2004 Ausonius Bordeaux Blend (Columbia Valley (WA)) $35. This young Bordeaux blend is almost impenetrable; tight, compact, dark and chewy. It sports all the tar, smoke, earth and soy flavors you could ever wish for, in a massive, grainy, thick style. To its credit, it's not monolithic and certainly not unbalanced; it just needs more time to soften up a bit. **91** *—P.G. (3/1/2007)*

Woodinville Wine Cellars 2003 Ausonius Bordeaux Blend (Columbia Valley (WA)) $35. 89 *—P.G. (4/1/2006)*

Woodinville Wine Cellars 2003 Merlot (Yakima Valley) $25. 88 *—P.G. (4/1/2006)*

Woodinville Wine Cellars 2004 Little Bear Creek Red Blend (Columbia Valley (WA)) $20. Solid, with full-bodied, muscular fruit. There's also plenty of big wine stuff—tar, tea and cracker—in this substantial blend of Syrah, Merlot, Cab Franc and Cabernet. A very drinkable bottle, packed with black cherry and clove. This is what a secondary wine, taken from the lesser barrels of its big brother, should taste like. **89** *—P.G. (3/1/2007)*

Woodinville Wine Cellars 2004 O.M.O. Red Blend (Columbia Valley (WA)) $30. Plenty of deep color, thick tannin and dark streaks of smoke and tar make this a stand-up steakhouse wine. The fruit does have an herbal edge but it is lingering, complex and interesting. Think of it as the vinous equivalent of a cello-viola sonata—dark and mysteriously intertwined. **89** *—P.G. (12/1/2007)*

Woodinville Wine Cellars 2006 Sauvignon Blanc (Columbia Valley (WA)) $18. This lively, 100% Sauvignon Blanc sports fresh flavors of grapefruit, lemon meringue and quinine—much like a cool-climate Viognier. Racy and fresh, it was mostly stainless-steel fermented, and is young enough to capture a bit of spritz in the mouthfeel. **89** *—P.G. (12/1/2007)*

Woodinville Wine Cellars 2005 Artz Vineyard Sauvignon Blanc (Red Mountain) $17. 87 *—P.G. (8/1/2006)*

Woodinville Wine Cellars 2004 Syrah (Columbia Valley (WA)) $28. Dense with cherry fruit, yet shows the pleasing lift of citrusy grapefruit. Oozes power, and packed with flavor. 200 cases made. **90** *—P.G. (3/1/2007)*

Woodinville Wine Cellars 2003 Syrah (Washington) $28. 89 *—P.G. (4/1/2006)*

WOODINVILLE WINE COMPANY

Woodinville Wine Company 2001 Red Wine Bordeaux Blend (Washington) $32. 88 *—P.G. (11/15/2004)*

Woodinville Wine Company 2002 Syrah (Washington) $28. 87 *—P.G. (11/15/2004)*

WOODWARD CANYON

Woodward Canyon 2003 Charbonneau Bordeaux Blend (Walla Walla (WA)) $50. This is a very distinctive, flavorful red Bordeaux blend—soft and spicy with unusual accents of grass and caramel. The flavors persist, the caramel streak gaining strength as it rolls through the palate, but always behind it is the taste of grain. Truly a unique red wine. **90** *—P.G. (3/1/2007)*

Woodward Canyon 2003 Estate Red Bordeaux Blend (Walla Walla (WA)) $55. 89 *—P.G. (11/15/2006)*

Woodward Canyon 2001 Estate Red Bordeaux Blend (Walla Walla (WA)) $55. 93 *—P.G. (9/1/2004)*

Woodward Canyon 2000 Estate Red Bordeaux Blend (Walla Walla (WA)) $55. 91 *—P.G. (9/1/2003)*

Woodward Canyon 2005 Cabernet Sauvignon (Walla Walla (WA)) $39. Despite its youth, this is a complete and satisfying wine. Woodward Canyon reds virtually always develop well in bottle, and so you can assume that this will continue to improve. At the moment it is tightly wound, firmly built, a complex weave of purple fruit and tobacco leaf, leading into white chocolaty tannins. **91** *—P.G. (8/1/2007)*

Woodward Canyon 1998 Cabernet Sauvignon (Walla Walla (WA)) $45. 93 *—P.G. (6/1/2001)*

Woodward Canyon 2001 Artist Series Cabernet Sauvignon (Columbia Valley (WA)) $42. 91 *—P.G. (7/1/2004)*

Woodward Canyon 2000 Artist Series Cabernet Sauvignon (Washington) $42. 92 *—P.G. (9/1/2003)*

Woodward Canyon 2003 Artist Series #12 Cabernet Sauvignon (Columbia Valley (WA)) $44. 91 *—P.G. (11/15/2006)*

Woodward Canyon 2004 Artist Series #13 Cabernet Sauvignon (Columbia Valley (WA)) $44. This Bordeaux blend has a surprisingly broad aspect, with very young fruit that opens up and then sits on the midpalate. It's much more open and expressive than the last few vintages. At first it seems dumbed down on the finish, but it slowly opens, and re-tasted on the second day it has filled out with muscle and verve. **91** *—P.G. (12/1/2007)*

Woodward Canyon 1998 Artist Series #7 Cabernet Sauvignon (Washington) $37. 93 *—P.G. (11/15/2000)*

Woodward Canyon 1999 Artist Series #8 Cabernet Sauvignon (Washington) $43. 92 Editors' Choice *—C.S. (12/31/2002)*

Woodward Canyon 1999 Klipsun Vineyard Cabernet Sauvignon (Columbia Valley (WA)) $45. 89 *—P.G. (6/1/2002)*

Woodward Canyon 2004 Old Vines Cabernet Sauvignon (Columbia Valley (WA)) $75. This is 95.5% Cabernet and 4.5% Petit Verdot—a new twist. The wine is almost pure black, and made in a super-sappy, rich, ripe, dense and saturated style—the currently fashionable mode. Thick, chocolaty and young, it tastes great, juicy and sappy, making this a real impact wine. Though powerful and raw, it is irresistibly vibrant and packed with gorgeous fruit. **94** *—P.G. (12/1/2007)*

Woodward Canyon 2001 Old Vines Cabernet Sauvignon (Columbia Valley (WA)) $67. 93 Cellar Selection *—P.G. (9/1/2004)*

Woodward Canyon 2000 Old Vines Cabernet Sauvignon (Columbia Valley (WA)) $67. 92 *—P.G. (9/1/2003)*

Woodward Canyon 1999 Old Vines Cabernet Sauvignon (Columbia Valley (WA)) $60. 91 Editors' Choice *—P.G. (6/1/2002)*

Woodward Canyon 1998 Old Vines Cabernet Sauvignon (Columbia Valley (WA)) $60. 94 Cellar Selection *—P.G. (6/1/2001)*

Woodward Canyon 2000 Charbonneau Red Cabernet Sauvignon-Merlot (Walla Walla (WA)) $50. 89 *—P.G. (9/1/2003)*

Woodward Canyon 2006 Chardonnay (Washington) $36. This is classic Washington Chardonnay, from the winery that first put it on the national map. It's beautifully built upon ripe apple, pineapple and kiwi fruit, with proportionate acid and lovely, lightly toasty oak. The alcohol is 14.3%, and the wine strikes a perfect note of weight and density, without being fat or fatiguing. **92** *—P.G. (12/1/2007)*

Woodward Canyon 2005 Chardonnay (Washington) $36. Inviting scents of buttered toast lead into a fruit-filled mèlange of Japanese pear, fresh pineapple, crisp citrus and green apple. Nicely balanced and proportioned, it is structured for aging over the next five or six years. **89** *—P.G. (3/1/2007)*

Woodward Canyon 2004 Chardonnay (Columbia Valley (WA)) $36. 88 *—P.G. (10/1/2006)*

Woodward Canyon 2002 Chardonnay (Columbia Valley (WA)) $33. 91 *—P.G. (7/1/2004)*

Woodward Canyon 2001 Chardonnay (Columbia Valley (WA)) $32. 89 *—P.G. (9/1/2003)*

Woodward Canyon 2000 Chardonnay (Columbia Valley (WA)) $33. 88 *—P.G. (7/1/2002)*

Woodward Canyon 1999 Chardonnay (Columbia Valley (WA)) $28. 90 *—P.G. (11/15/2000)*

Woodward Canyon 1998 Unfined/Unfiltered Estate Chardonnay (Walla Walla (WA)) $40. 93 *—P.G. (6/1/2001)*

Woodward Canyon 2006 Dolcetto (Washington) $19. Spectacular blueberry aromatics enliven this fruit-driven wine. The extraction is right up to the edge of being too much, but sits just perfectly in the mouth. A deep, saturated garnet color with scents of berry and sweet, musky Concord accents. It's solid in the mouth, tannic with a slightly chewy edge to the tannins. **88** *—P.G. (12/1/2007)*

Woodward Canyon 2005 Merlot (Columbia Valley (WA)) $39. Still young and tasting somewhat like a barrel sample, it has some fermentation flavors of ripe banana, chewy tannins, and a core of wood, earth and black cherry. It still needs to be softened up a bit; it has some hard, chewy edges, and is definitely a wine that should be decanted. Retasted on the second day it's still chewy and tight. **88** *—P.G. (12/1/2007)*

Woodward Canyon 2003 Merlot (Columbia Valley (WA)) $39. 89 *—P.G. (10/1/2006)*

Woodward Canyon 2000 Merlot (Walla Walla (WA)) $45. 92 Editors' Choice *—P.G. (9/1/2002)*

Woodward Canyon 2000 Merlot (Columbia Valley (WA)) $38. 88 *—P.G. (9/1/2002)*

Woodward Canyon 1999 Merlot (Columbia Valley (WA)) $38. 89 *—P.G. (6/1/2001)*

Woodward Canyon 1999 Charbonneau Merlot-Cabernet Sauvignon (Walla Walla (WA)) $50. 87 *—P.G. (6/1/2002)*

Woodward Canyon 1998 Charbonneau Red Blend (Walla Walla (WA)) $50. 92 *—P.G. (6/1/2001)*

Woodward Canyon 2003 Old Vines Dedication Series #23 Red Blend (Columbia Valley (WA)) $75. 93 *—P.G. (10/1/2006)*

Woodward Canyon 2005 Dry Riesling (Columbia Valley (WA)) $25. Once again Woodward Canyon has crafted a dense and powerful dry Riesling from DuBrul vineyard grapes. It strikes me as Australian in style, the perfect pairing of New World fruit and an almost austere minerality. Lingering notes of sweet grapefruit, orange, tangerine and lemon rind carry into a lush finish that keeps adding new flavors—ginger, apple, honey graham and more. **93** *—P.G. (3/1/2007)*

Woodward Canyon 2002 Dry White Riesling (Columbia Valley (WA)) $22. 89 *—P.G. (5/1/2004)*

Woodward Canyon 2001 Dry White Riesling (Columbia Valley (WA)) $22. 88 *—P.G. (9/1/2002)*

Woodward Canyon 2004 Syrah (Columbia Valley (WA)) $39. Champoux and DuBrul vineyards supplied the excellent fruit, roughly half each. This is Washington Syrah at its most dark, dense and deeply extracted. Beautifully structured, this exceptional wine is laced with roasted, toasty streaks of espresso and smoke. The fruit is substantial and more than up to the job of balancing the barrel flavors; you can't really tell what flavors come from which. Long, polished and powerful, this is quite seductive and delicious. **92** *—P.G. (3/1/2007)*

Woodward Canyon 2005 Sauvignon Blanc (Walla Walla (WA)) $24. 87 *—P.G. (10/1/2006)*

Woodward Canyon 2003 Estate Sauvignon Blanc (Walla Walla (WA)) $24. 81 *(7/1/2005)*

Woodward Canyon 2001 Charbonneau Blanc Sémillon-Sauvignon Blanc (Walla Walla (WA)) $28. 90 *—P.G. (9/1/2003)*

Woodward Canyon 2002 Syrah (Columbia Valley (WA)) $34. 86 *(9/1/2005)*

Woodward Canyon 2000 Charbonneau White Blend (Walla Walla (WA)) $28. 90 *—P.G. (6/1/2002)*

Woodward Canyon 1999 Charbonneau Blanc White Blend (Walla Walla (WA)) $28. 90 *—P.G. (6/1/2001)*

WOOLDRIDGE CREEK

Wooldridge Creek 1998 Cabernet Sauvignon (Applegate Valley) $18. 84 *—P.G. (8/1/2002)*

Wooldridge Creek 1999 Merlot (Applegate Valley) $16. 85 *—P.G. (8/1/2002)*

Wooldridge Creek 1999 IL Carrino Rosso Red Wine Red Blend (Applegate Valley) $15. 85 *—P.G. (8/1/2002)*

Wooldridge Creek 1999 Syrah (Applegate Valley) $16. 84 *—P.G. (8/1/2002)*

Wooldridge Creek 2000 Viognier (Rogue Valley) $16. 85 *—P.G. (8/1/2002)*

Wooldridge Creek 1999 Viognier (Rogue Valley) $20. 83 *—P.G. (4/1/2002)*

WORK

Work 2006 Sauvignon Blanc (Napa Valley) $25. With a touch of green bell pepper, this also shows riper citrus, fig and melon flavors that finish in a swirl of tangy spice. No oak, but sur lie aging gives it creamy complexities. **86** *—S.H. (11/1/2007)*

Work 2003 Sauvignon Blanc (Napa Valley) $23. 89 *—S.H. (12/15/2004)*

Work 2002 Sauvignon Blanc (Napa Valley) $23. 89 *—S.H. (12/1/2003)*

Work 2001 Sauvignon Blanc (Napa Valley) $23. 91 *—S.H. (9/1/2003)*

Work 2005 Work Vineyard Sauvignon Blanc (Napa Valley) $25. 90 *—S.H. (11/1/2006)*

WORKHORSE

Workhorse 2000 Syrah (Dry Creek Valley) $15. 82 *—S.H. (3/1/2004)*

Workhorse 2002 Zinfandel (Dry Creek Valley) $15. 83 *—S.H. (3/1/2004)*

WORTHY

Worthy 2002 Sophia's Cuvée Red Blend (Napa Valley) $29. 88 *—S.H. (10/1/2005)*

WRITER'S BLOCK

Writer's Block 2005 Cabernet Franc (Lake County) $16. From Steele, although it's hard to tell why they don't say so on the label. It's one of those country-style wines you either like or don't, extremely soft, semi-sweet and simple, and full of superripe fruit, with a dollop of new French oak. **83** *—S.H. (9/1/2007)*

Writer's Block 2006 Grenache (Lake County) $15. Very soft and fairly diluted in raspberry, cherry, mocha and vanilla flavors, this Grenache also is sweet. From Steele. **82** *—S.H. (11/15/2007)*

Writer's Block 2005 Petite Sirah (Lake County) $16. Rustic and sweet on the finish, with jellied blackberry, cherry, licorice, cola and Asian spice flavors. Gains a point or two for its smooth, rich tannins. Drink now. **84** *—S.H. (12/31/2007)*

Writer's Block 2006 Roussanne (Lake County) $16. Somewhere in all the sugar there is a crisp, subtlely fruity Roussanne, with citrus, pear and wildflower flavors. But the sweetness buries everything else. **83** *—S.H. (12/31/2007)*

Writer's Block 2002 Syrah (Lake County) $14. 81 *(9/1/2005)*

Writer's Block 2005 Writer's Block Zinfandel (Lake County) $15. If you like semisweet, medicinal-tasting Zins, you'll love this one. It tastes like melted blackberry jam. From Steele. **81** *—S.H. (11/15/2007)*

WYNELAND ESTATES

Wyneland Estates 2002 Proprietor's Reserve Alicante Bouschet (Lodi) $26. 87 *—S.H. (12/31/2005)*

WYVERN

Wyvern 1998 Cabernet Sauvignon (Yakima Valley) $25. 90 *—S.H. (6/1/2002)*

Wyvern 2000 Syrah (Columbia Valley (WA)) $25. 90 *—S.H. (6/1/2002)*

X

X 2004 Cabernet Sauvignon (California) $19. Largely from Lake County, with a splash of Napa, this wine exhibits ripe blackberry and cherry jam fruit. It's dry and balanced, with a sweet chocolaty veneer of oak. There's a nice acid-tannin balance. **85** *—S.H. (2/1/2007)*

X 2002 Cabernet Sauvignon (Napa Valley) $22. 85 *—S.H. (10/1/2005)*

X 2001 Cabernet Sauvignon (California) $15. 84 *—S.H. (2/1/2004)*

X 2000 Cabernet Sauvignon (Napa Valley) $20. 81 *—S.H. (11/15/2002)*

X 2002 Napa-Sonoma-San Luis Obispo Cabernet Sauvignon (Napa-Sonoma) $19. 87 *—S.H. (3/1/2005)*

X 2005 Chardonnay (Carneros) $19. Superrich in pineapple pie-filling fruit flavors, this Chard is on the sweet, honeyed side. But crisp Carneros acidity gives it needed balance. Oak adds caramel and vanilla richness. **84** *—S.H. (12/15/2007)*

X 2004 Chardonnay (Carneros) $19. Well-ripened, a balanced Chard showing plenty of upfront fruit flavor and an opulent layer of toasty oak. Peaches and cream, tropical fruit and vanilla custard flavors lead to a spicy, slightly astringent finish. **85** *—S.H. (2/1/2007)*

X 2002 Chardonnay (Carneros) $19. 84 *—S.H. (3/1/2005)*

X 2002 Chardonnay (Carneros) $19. 84 *—S.H. (10/1/2004)*

X 2000 Chardonnay (Russian River Valley) $15. 90 Best Buy *—S.H. (12/31/2003)*

X 2004 Truchard Vineyard Chardonnay (Carneros) $20. 84 *—S.H. (8/1/2006)*

X 2003 Two Rivers Vineyard Chardonnay (Yountville) $17. 82 *—S.H. (10/1/2005)*

X 2004 Merlot (Napa Valley) $25. Merlot hasn't been X's strong variety. This wine is dry and sharp and not quite ripe, with green, minty flavors despite the hot vintage. The lack of ripeness makes it finish sharp and tannic. **83** *—S.H. (7/1/2007)*

X 2002 Merlot (Napa Valley) $25. 86 *—S.H. (8/1/2005)*

X 2005 Petite Sirah (Paso Robles) $25. This is a heavy, bitterly tannic young wine that shows ripe blackberry and coffee flavors and spices. The raw astringency makes it tough now, fit only for greasy foods like barbecued ribs. It should age well for a long time, but will never quite overcome its rustic profile. **85** *—S.H. (12/31/2007)*

X 2004 Petite Sirah (Paso Robles) $22. The grapes got cooked under the heat waves that relentlessly struck the vintage, and this wine is rather unbalanced and kind of flat. It has earthy, dried herb flavors, with a bit of wild berry, along with substantial tannins and brusque, green acids. **82** *—S.H. (2/1/2007)*

X 2003 Petite Sirah (Paso Robles) $22. 87 *—S.H. (3/1/2006)*

X 2000 Petite Sirah (Paso Robles) $19. 83 *—S.H. (12/1/2002)*

X 2004 Truchard Vineyard Pinot Noir (Carneros) $25. 87 *—S.H. (12/1/2006)*

X 2003 Truchard Vineyard Pinot Noir (Carneros) $22. 88 *—S.H. (10/1/2005)*

X 2005 Red X Red Blend (California) $14. A leftover blend of various varieties, this is a dry, soft, rustic wine for everyday drinking with ordinary fare. The cherry-berry flavors have a raisined edge. **83** —*S.H. (11/15/2007)*

X 2003 Red X Red Blend (California) $13. 82 —*S.H. (12/1/2005)*

X 2002 Red X Red Blend (California) $13. 84 —*S.H. (4/1/2005)*

X 2004 Red X Winemaker's Blend Red Blend (California) $14. A blend of Cabernet Sauvignon, Syrah, Merlot and Petite Sirah, this wine, from Lake County, Paso Robles and Napa, shows how ripe grapes get in California. It just bursts with berries and cherries and chocolate, and is dry, with smooth tannins. What a versatile and inexpensive red wine. **85** —*S.H. (2/1/2007)*

X 2003 Syrahtica Red Blend (California) $14. 84 —*S.H. (5/1/2006)*

X 2002 Syrahtica Red Blend (California) $14. 84 —*S.H. (5/1/2005)*

X 2002 Sauvignon Blanc (Lake County) $15. 89 —*S.H. (12/15/2003)*

X 2006 ES Vineyard Sauvignon Blanc (Lake County) $17. Another super Sauvignon Blanc that shows how well Lake County does with this variety. It's all about the citrus, fig and spicy melon flavors and the juicy acidity, which makes the wine so fresh and clean. Made from the Musqué clone. **87** —*S.H. (12/15/2007)*

X 2005 ES Vineyard Sauvignon Blanc (Lake County) $17. 84 —*S.H. (12/15/2006)*

X 2004 ES Vineyard Sauvignon Blanc (Lake County) $17. 85 —*S.H. (12/1/2005)*

X 2003 Eutenier Sylar Vineyard Sauvignon Blanc (Lake County) $17. 84 —*S.H. (3/1/2005)*

X 2005 Syrahtica Syrah (California) $15. Simple and fruity, this Syrah tastes like cherry and blackberry jam. Crisp acids and tannins provide needed balance. **82** —*S.H. (11/15/2007)*

X 2005 Nova Vineyard Zinfandel (Lake County) $20. No doubt this is Zinfandel, with its wealth of wild, brambly-fresh berry fruit that seems like it was just picked. Blackberries, loganberries and raspberries, with an earthy edge of coffee and peppery tobacco, mingle together in this totally dry, crisp young wine. Drink now for its exuberance. **88** —*S.H. (7/1/2007)*

X 2003 Nova Vineyard Zinfandel (Lake County) $20. 82 —*S.H. (10/1/2006)*

XYZIN

XYZin 2002 Sandy Lane Vineyard Zinfandel (Contra Costa County) $29. 85 —*S.H. (11/1/2005)*

YAKIMA CELLARS

Yakima Cellars 2002 Elephant Mountain Vineyard Syrah (Yakima Valley) $20. 87 *(9/1/2005)*

YAMHILL COUNTY VINEYARDS

Yamhill County Vineyards 1999 Pinot Noir (Willamette Valley) $20. 80 *(10/1/2002)*

YAMHILL VALLEY

Yamhill Valley 1998 Pinot Blanc (Oregon) $14. 85 —*L.W. (12/31/1999)*

Yamhill Valley 1998 Pinot Noir (Willamette Valley) $28. 87 —*P.G. (9/1/2000)*

Yamhill Valley 1999 Reserve Pinot Noir (Willamette Valley) $30. 87 *(10/1/2002)*

Yamhill Valley 1998 Reserve Pinot Noir (Willamette Valley) $48. 89 —*S.H. (8/1/2002)*

YELLOW HAWK CELLAR

Yellow Hawk Cellar 2005 Barbera (Columbia Valley (WA)) $17. Leathery aromas are followed with clear indications of brett on the palate. The wine tastes leathery and slightly bitter; the pretty strawberry fruit is mostly masked as well. Tight, hard and a bit hot. **84** —*P.G. (12/1/2007)*

Yellow Hawk Cellar 2004 Barbera (Columbia Valley (WA)) $17. 84 —*P.G. (6/1/2006)*

Yellow Hawk Cellar 2001 Muscat Canelli (Columbia Valley (WA)) $12. 89 —*P.G. (9/1/2002)*

Yellow Hawk Cellar 2003 Mescolanza di Rosso Riserva Red Blend (Columbia Valley (WA)) $28. This wine doesn't have much going on. It's dried out, chalky in the mouth, stemmy and bitter with green tannins. The fruit is dried out and there is a scent of brett as well. **82** —*P.G. (12/1/2007)*

Yellow Hawk Cellar 2004 Sangiovese (Columbia Valley (WA)) $19. Good vineyard sources—Ranch at the End, Chandler Reach and Willow Crest—but the bitter, leathery flavors impact all these wines. Here it's less intrusive than in the Barbera, but it still fouls the finish with bacterial funk. Somewhere in here is some pretty cherry fruit. **84** —*P.G. (12/1/2007)*

Yellow Hawk Cellar 2003 Sangiovese (Walla Walla (WA)) $19. 82 —*P.G. (6/1/2006)*

YN

YN 2000 White Blend (California) $4. 83 —*S.H. (6/1/2002)*

YOAKIM BRIDGE

Yoakim Bridge 2002 Syrah (Dry Creek Valley) $34. 91 —*S.H. (11/1/2005)*

Yoakim Bridge 2002 Zinfandel (Dry Creek Valley) $30. 88 —*S.H. (11/1/2005)*

Yoakim Bridge 2001 Zinfandel (Dry Creek Valley) $26. 87 *(11/1/2003)*

Yoakim Bridge 1999 Zinfandel (Dry Creek Valley) $25. 90 —*S.H. (12/15/2001)*

YORK MOUNTAIN WINERY

York Mountain Winery 2006 Albariño (Edna Valley) $16. Shows the qualities that are making this Spanish variety so popular. Bone dry, crisp in acidity, low in alcohol and palate-stimulating, this oak-free wine bursts with rich lemongrass, pineapple and peach flavors. That acidity makes it clean and vibrant and terrifically versatile at the table. **87** —*S.H. (12/15/2007)*

York Mountain Winery 2003 Albariño (Edna Valley) $17. 87 —*S.H. (7/1/2006)*

York Mountain Winery 2005 Chardonnay (Edna Valley) $16. The underlying wine here is so good in fruity flavor and zesty acidity, you have to wonder why the winery piled so much new oak on top. The Chard is dominated by caramel, vanilla cream and butterscotch. **84** —*S.H. (12/15/2007)*

York Mountain Winery 2003 Unfiltered Chardonnay (Edna Valley) $25. 88 —*S.H. (7/1/2006)*

York Mountain Winery 2001 Merlot (Napa Valley) $26. 85 —*S.H. (10/1/2004)*

York Mountain Winery 2003 Pinot Noir (Edna Valley) $25. 88 —*S.H. (7/1/2006)*

York Mountain Winery 2003 Pinot Noir (San Luis Obispo County) $15. 86 —*S.H. (7/1/2006)*

York Mountain Winery 2002 Pinot Noir (Paso Robles) $25. 84 —*S.H. (2/1/2005)*

York Mountain Winery 2001 Pinot Noir (San Luis Obispo County) $15. 84 —*S.H. (2/1/2005)*

York Mountain Winery 2001 Pinot Noir (Edna Valley) $25. 84 —*S.H. (2/1/2005)*

York Mountain Winery 2005 Jack Ranch Pinot Noir (Edna Valley) $18. The Jack Ranch has been source to very good Syrahs and Chardonnays from several wineries, but York Mountain's Pinot Noirs haven't been as successful. This wine is a little hot and jammy, with simple cherry, fig and vanilla flavors. **84** —*S.H. (12/15/2007)*

York Mountain Winery 2003 Jack Ranch Pinot Noir (Edna Valley) $25. 82 —*S.H. (7/1/2006)*

York Mountain Winery 2000 Stephen's Pinot Noir (San Luis Obispo County) $28. 83 —*S.H. (7/1/2003)*

York Mountain Winery 2003 Jack Ranch Syrah (Edna Valley) $22. 85 —*S.H. (4/1/2006)*

York Mountain Winery 2003 Jack Ranch Clone 174 Syrah (Edna Valley) $18. 90 —*S.H. (4/1/2006)*

York Mountain Winery 2003 Jack Ranch Clone 383 Syrah (Edna Valley) $18. 88 —*S.H. (4/1/2006)*

York Mountain Winery 2003 Jack Ranch Clone 877 Syrah (Edna Valley) $18. 90 —*S.H. (4/1/2006)*

York Mountain Winery 2006 Viognier (Paso Robles) $16. You'll find a crisp, acidic structure in this dry wine. It shows peach, apricot and spice flavors, with a touch of smoky oak. Good with Asian food, or as an apéritif. **85** —*S.H. (12/15/2007)*

York Mountain Winery 2004 Viognier (Paso Robles) $25. 88 —*S.H. (8/1/2006)*

YORKVILLE CELLARS

Yorkville Cellars 1997 Richard the Lion-Heart Bordeaux Blend (Mendocino County) $25. 90 —*S.H. (6/1/2002)*

Yorkville Cellars 2001 Cabernet Franc (Yorkville Highlands) $19. 83 —*S.H. (3/1/2005)*

Yorkville Cellars 1998 Cabernet Franc (Mendocino) $17. 84 —*S.H. (5/1/2002)*

Yorkville Cellars 1997 Cabernet Franc (Yorkville Highlands) $17. 87 —*S.H. (9/1/2002)*

Yorkville Cellars 1999 Cabernet Sauvignon (Yorkville Highlands) $19. 85 —*S.H. (5/1/2003)*

Yorkville Cellars 1997 Cabernet Sauvignon (Mendocino) $19. 91 *—S.H. (6/1/2002)*

Yorkville Cellars 2001 Rennie Vineyard Cabernet Sauvignon (Yorkville Highlands) $22. 88 *—S.H. (10/1/2004)*

Yorkville Cellars 1998 Malbec (Mendocino) $17. 87 *—S.H. (5/1/2002)*

Yorkville Cellars 1997 Malbec (Yorkville Highlands) $17. 89 *—S.H. (9/1/2002)*

Yorkville Cellars 2003 Rennie Vineyard Malbec (Yorkville Highlands) $20. 82 *—S.H. (10/1/2006)*

Yorkville Cellars 1999 Merlot (Yorkville Highlands) $18. 85 *—S.H. (8/1/2003)*

Yorkville Cellars 1997 Merlot (Mendocino) $18. 85 *—S.H. (6/1/2002)*

Yorkville Cellars 2002 Rennie Vineyard Merlot (Yorkville Highlands) $20. 84 *—S.H. (8/1/2006)*

Yorkville Cellars 2001 Rennie Vineyard Merlot (Yorkville Highlands) $22. 85 *—S.H. (12/15/2004)*

Yorkville Cellars 1998 Petite Verdot (Mendocino County) $17. 84 *—S.H. (5/1/2002)*

Yorkville Cellars 1997 Petite Verdot (Yorkville Highlands) $17. 86 *—S.H. (9/1/2002)*

Yorkville Cellars 2001 Sauvignon Blanc (Yorkville Highlands) $13. 88 *—S.H. (9/1/2003)*

Yorkville Cellars 1999 Sauvignon Blanc (Mendocino) $12. 85 *—S.H. (5/1/2002)*

Yorkville Cellars 1999 Eleanor of Aquitaine Sauvignon Blanc (Mendocino) $17. 84 *—S.H. (5/1/2002)*

Yorkville Cellars 1999 Sémillon (Mendocino) $13. 84 *—S.H. (5/1/2002)*

Yorkville Cellars 2004 Randle Hill Vineyard Sémillon (Yorkville Highlands) $18. 90 Editors' Choice *—S.H. (7/1/2006)*

Z-52

Z-52 2004 Agnes' Vineyard Zinfandel (Lodi) $16. I've never had a Zin from this vineyard that wasn't rustic and tannic. The '04 is in that tradition. The official alcohol is only 14.3%, but it feels hot and Port-y, with flavors of raisins and stewed berries, although it is fully dry. **82** *—S.H. (10/1/2007)*

Z-52 2002 Agnes' Vineyard Old Vines Zinfandel (Lodi) $16. 84 *—S.H. (12/1/2005)*

Z-52 2001 Agnes' Vineyard Old Vines Zinfandel (Lodi) $16. 84 *—S.H. (12/15/2004)*

Z-52 2004 Clockspring Vineyard Old Vine Zinfandel (Amador County) $20. I'm not a huge Zinfandel fan, but this is a good one that shows the best qualities of Amador Zin. Dry and lusty, it shows delicious flavors of wild berries and thyme, with a touch of sweet oak, and the ripe, savory tannins that come from a perfectly warm vintage. **87** *—S.H. (10/1/2007)*

Z-52 2003 Clockspring Vineyard Old Vines Zinfandel (Amador County) $20. 88 *—S.H. (12/1/2005)*

Z-52 2001 Clockspring Vineyard Old Vines Zinfandel (Lodi) $20. 86 *—S.H. (12/15/2004)*

Zaca Mesa 1998 Chardonnay (Santa Barbara County) $15. 88 *(6/1/2000)*

ZACA MESA

Zaca Mesa 2000 Zaca Vineyards Chardonnay (Santa Barbara) $15. 87 *—S.H. (5/1/2003)*

Zaca Mesa 1997 Zaca Vineyards Chardonnay (Santa Barbara County) $13. 85 *—S.H. (7/1/1999)*

Zaca Mesa 1999 Chapel Vineyard Mourvèdre (Santa Barbara County) $15. 88 *—J.M. (7/1/2002)*

Zaca Mesa 2001 Z-Gris Red Blend (Santa Ynez Valley) $9. 85 *—S.H. (9/1/2003)*

Zaca Mesa 2004 Z Cuvee Red Wine Rhône Red Blend (Santa Ynez Valley) $18. A Châteauneuf-style blend of Grenache, Mourvèdre, Syrah and Cinsault, coopered in some new French oak, this is a richly drinkable red wine. Soft and dry, it shows complex cherry, berry and spice flavors and an intricate structure, and will play beautifully against a grilled steak. **87** *—S.H. (7/1/2007)*

Zaca Mesa 2003 Z Cuvée Rhône Red Blend (Santa Ynez Valley) $18. 83 *—S.H. (11/15/2006)*

Zaca Mesa 2002 Z Cuvée Rhône Red Blend (Santa Ynez Valley) $15. 88 *—S.H. (12/1/2005)*

Zaca Mesa 2000 Z Cuvée Rhône Red Blend (Santa Barbara County) $16. 87 *—S.H. (11/15/2002)*

Zaca Mesa 1997 Z Cuvée Rhône Red Blend (Santa Barbara County) $17. 90 *—S.H. (10/1/1999)*

Zaca Mesa 2000 Z Gris Rhône Red Blend (Santa Barbara County) $9. 82 *—J.F. (8/1/2001)*

Zaca Mesa 2004 Z Three Red Wine Rhône Red Blend (Santa Ynez Valley) $40. A southern Rhône blend of Syrah, Mourvèdre and Grenache, this wine is stylish and elegant, with a smooth, silky texture. But it's just a little too sugary sweet to earn a higher score, with the blackberry and cherry fruit having a jellied, candied edge. **86** *—S.H. (12/1/2007)*

Zaca Mesa 2003 Z Three Red Wine Rhône Red Blend (Santa Ynez Valley) $40. 92 Editors' Choice *—S.H. (12/1/2006)*

Zaca Mesa 1998 Z-Gris Rhône Red Blend (Santa Barbara County) $8. 89 Best Buy *—S.H. (10/1/1999)*

Zaca Mesa 2006 Z Gris Dry Rosé Wine Rosé Blend (Santa Ynez Valley) $15. Mainly Grenache, with a drop of Cinsault, this is a really nice rosé. Give it a few moments for the sulfur to blow off, and it's a rich, full-bodied, dry blush wine, upfront in red cherry pie, raspberry sorbet and white peppery-spice flavors. **86** *—S.H. (7/1/2007)*

Zaca Mesa 2005 Roussanne (Santa Ynez Valley) $25. On the one-dimensional side, but rewarding for a wealthy array of citrus and floral flavors, in a dry, crisp and fairly oaky wine. Shows an elegance that suggests rosemary chicken with a rich, buttery polenta. **86** *—S.H. (7/1/2007)*

Zaca Mesa 1998 Roussanne (Santa Barbara County) $16. 87 *—M.S. (8/1/2000)*

Zaca Mesa 2004 Estate Roussanne (Santa Ynez Valley) $25. 87 *—S.H. (5/1/2006)*

Zaca Mesa 2003 Estate Roussanne (Santa Ynez Valley) $25. 82 *—S.H. (10/1/2005)*

Zaca Mesa 1997 Zaca Vineyards Roussanne (Santa Barbara County) $16. 86 *—S.H. (6/1/1999)*

Zaca Mesa 2003 Syrah (Santa Ynez Valley) $22. Good, rich Syrah, dry and tannic, although the tannins are finely ground and easily negotiable now. Satisfies for deep blackberry, cherry, cocoa and oak flavors, with extra points for its upscale, fancy quality. But it's a little thin for aging. Drink now. **87** *—S.H. (9/1/2007)*

Zaca Mesa 2002 Syrah (Santa Ynez Valley) $20. 86 *(9/1/2005)*

Zaca Mesa 2000 Syrah (Santa Ynez Valley) $20. 90 Editors' Choice *—S.H. (6/1/2003)*

Zaca Mesa 2003 Black Bear Block Syrah (Santa Ynez Valley) $50. 91 *—S.H. (12/15/2006)*

Zaca Mesa 2002 Black Bear Block Syrah (Santa Ynez Valley) $50. 87 *(9/1/2005)*

Zaca Mesa 2001 Black Bear Block Syrah (Santa Ynez Valley) $50. 92 *—S.H. (8/1/2005)*

Zaca Mesa 1999 Black Bear Block Syrah (Santa Ynez Valley) $45. 92 *—S.H. (2/1/2003)*

Zaca Mesa 1996 Black Bear Block Syrah (Santa Barbara County) $20. 88 *—M.S. (2/1/2000)*

Zaca Mesa 2002 Eight Barrel Syrah (Santa Ynez Valley) $35. 85 *(9/1/2005)*

Zaca Mesa 2002 Estate Syrah (Santa Ynez Valley) $20. 91 Editors' Choice *—S.H. (10/1/2006)*

Zaca Mesa 2001 Estate Bottled Syrah (Santa Ynez Valley) $20. 86 *—S.H. (8/1/2005)*

Zaca Mesa 2001 The Mesa O & N Syrah (Santa Ynez Valley) $40. 92 *—S.H. (8/1/2005)*

Zaca Mesa 1999 Zaca Vineyards Syrah (Santa Barbara County) $20. 85 *(10/1/2001)*

Zaca Mesa 2004 Viognier (Santa Ynez Valley) $15. 87 *—S.H. (12/31/2005)*

Zaca Mesa 2001 Viognier (Santa Ynez Valley) $14. 84 *—S.H. (12/15/2002)*

Zaca Mesa 2005 Estate Viognier (Santa Ynez Valley) $17. 90 *—S.H. (11/15/2006)*

Zaca Mesa 2003 Estate Viognier (Santa Ynez Valley) $15. 85 *—S.H. (10/1/2005)*

Zaca Mesa 2000 Zaca Vineyards Viognier (Santa Barbara) $15. 89 *—J.M. (12/15/2002)*

ZAHTILA

Zahtila 2003 Cabernet Sauvignon (Napa Valley) $33. 88 *—S.H. (12/1/2006)*

Zahtila 2002 Cabernet Sauvignon (Napa Valley) $33. 86 *—S.H. (12/1/2005)*

Zahtila 2001 Cabernet Sauvignon (Napa Valley) $27. 90 *—S.H. (10/1/2004)*

Zahtila 2000 Beckstoffer Georges III Cabernet Sauvignon (Rutherford) $40. 86 *—S.H. (2/1/2004)*

Zahtila 2003 Beckstoffer Vineyard Georges III Cabernet Sauvignon (Rutherford) $48. 93 —*S.H. (12/1/2006)*

Zahtila 2002 Beckstoffer Vineyard Georges III Cabernet Sauvignon (Rutherford) $48. 90 —*S.H. (12/1/2005)*

Zahtila 2001 Beckstoffer Vineyard Georges III Cabernet Sauvignon (Rutherford) $48. 93 —*S.H. (10/1/2004)*

Zahtila 2005 Chardonnay (Napa Valley) $18. 87 —*S.H. (12/1/2006)*

ZD

ZD 2004 Cabernet Sauvignon (Napa Valley) $50. This is one of those Cabs that's so ripe, it's almost sweet, although it stops just short of sugariness. It's a soft, pleasant wine, with all sorts of cherry and cassis flavors, but it doesn't seem quite worth the hefty price. 85 —*S.H. (5/1/2007)*

ZD 1996 Cabernet Sauvignon (Napa Valley) $38. 87 —*M.S. (7/1/2000)*

ZD 2002 Cabernet Sauvignon (Napa Valley) $42. 86 —*S.H. (8/1/2005)*

ZD 2001 Cabernet Sauvignon (Napa Valley) $40. 91 —*S.H. (10/1/2004)*

ZD 1999 Cabernet Sauvignon (Napa Valley) $42. 88 *(3/1/2003)*

ZD 2001 Reserve Cabernet Sauvignon (Napa Valley) $115. 85 —*S.H. (8/1/2005)*

ZD 1999 Reserve Cabernet Sauvignon (Napa Valley) $100. 91 *(3/1/2003)*

ZD 2005 Chardonnay (California) $33. The wine's a blend of top Chard growing regions, but it's a little thin in flavor, with watered-down apricot and peach flavors. 84 —*S.H. (12/1/2007)*

ZD 2001 Chardonnay (California) $30. 87 *(3/1/2003)*

ZD 2005 Reserve Chardonnay (Napa Valley) $55. Big, bold and a little obvious, this Chard's main feature is oak, and plenty of it. Smoky and charry, the wine also has big fruit, along the lines of apricot jam, peach cobbler and pineapples. Don't drink it too cold. 87 —*S.H. (8/1/2007)*

ZD 2002 Reserve Chardonnay (Napa Valley) $48. 87 —*S.H. (8/1/2005)*

ZD 2000 Reserve Chardonnay (Napa Valley) $48. 89 *(3/1/2003)*

ZD 1998 Reserve Chardonnay (Napa Valley) $48. 92 *(7/1/2001)*

ZD 2005 Pinot Noir (Carneros) $33. Fairly direct and villages-style, this red wine shows good varietal character, with a light, delicately silky texture and dry flavors of cherries and cola. It's not a big wine, but it's elegant, and doesn't disappoint. 85 —*S.H. (12/1/2007)*

ZD 2002 Pinot Noir (Carneros) $30. 88 *(11/1/2004)*

ZD 2000 Pinot Noir (Carneros) $34. 88 *(10/1/2002)*

ZD 2005 Reserve Pinot Noir (Carneros) $60. This has a lean, stalky green character. Yes, there are cherries and plenty of oak, but that minty acidic thing dominates. 84 —*S.H. (8/1/2007)*

ZD 2002 Reserve Pinot Noir (Carneros) $48. 87 *(11/1/2004)*

ZD 2001 Reserve Pinot Noir (Carneros) $48. 87 —*S.H. (12/1/2004)*

ZD NV Abacus IV Red Blend (Napa Valley) $300. 93 *(3/1/2003)*

ZD 2006 Rosa Lee Sauvignon Blanc (Napa Valley) $20. Fresh, clean and frankly delicious, this Sauvignon Blanc, which doesn't seem to have any wood on it, tastes like a romp through an orchard. Peaches, grapefruits, Meyer lemons, kiwis, sweet limes and apricots begin to suggest the fruitiness. Best of all are the dryness and acidity, which make the wine so balanced. 88 —*S.H. (12/15/2007)*

ZEALEAR

Zealear 2001 Reprise Cabernet Sauvignon (Napa Valley) $40. 85 —*S.H. (5/1/2005)*

Zealear 2002 Bolero Syrah (California) $20. 85 —*S.H. (5/1/2005)*

Zealear 2001 Fusion Zinfandel (Sonoma County) $25. 83 —*S.H. (5/1/2005)*

ZEFINA

Zefina 2003 Serience Red Blend (Columbia Valley (WA)) $30. This unusual wine mixes Syrah, Grenache, Mourvèdre, Counoise and Cinsault—not gonna find that in California! It's got a great spicy edge to it, along with chocolatey tannins and acids that suggest a lick of grapefruit—the Washington Syrah signature. It's a very appealing red blend, great for tossing into any party mix, unpretentious, rich and flavorful. 87 —*P.G. (5/1/2007)*

Zefina 2001 Serience Red Wine Red Blend (Columbia Valley (WA)) $35. 87 —*P.G. (1/1/2004)*

Zefina 2004 Serience Rhône White Blend (Columbia Valley (WA)) $20. This 50/50 Viognier/Roussanne blend brings sharp, crisp, acid-driven flavors to your mouth. It's a confident mix of pineapple, tropical fruit, melon and citrus with a sharp tang to the finish. Though it feels a little hot when sipped alone, it's got the stuffing to be an intriguing accompaniment to certain foods, such as spicy Asian shellfish and seafood. 87 —*P.G. (5/1/2007)*

Zefina 2002 Serience White Wine White Blend (Columbia Valley (WA)) $20. 88 —*P.G. (1/1/2004)*

Zefina 2003 Zinfandel (Columbia Valley (WA)) $25. Quite ripe, roasted and lush; this is Zinfandel at its most full and rich, to the point of tasting like a confectionary dessert. If you like flavors of cooked berries, powdered sugar and baking spices, this is the wine for you. 86 —*P.G. (5/1/2007)*

Zefina 2001 Zinfandel (Columbia Valley (WA)) $25. 88 —*P.G. (1/1/2004)*

ZENAIDA CELLARS

Zenaida Cellars 2000 Pinot Noir (Paso Robles) $20. 83 —*S.H. (7/1/2003)*

Zenaida Cellars 2001 Sangiovese (Paso Robles) $21. 81 —*S.H. (9/1/2003)*

Zenaida Cellars 2000 Syrah (Paso Robles) $24. 84 —*S.H. (12/15/2003)*

Zenaida Cellars 1999 Syrah (Paso Robles) $20. 91 —*S.H. (11/15/2001)*

Zenaida Cellars 2001 Estate Zinfandel (Paso Robles) $24. 85 *(11/1/2003)*

ZERBA CELLARS

Zerba Cellars 2005 Cabernet Sauvignon (Walla Walla (WA)) $30. This spicy Bordeaux blend has barrel flavors of cinnamon toast, coffee and caramel that run rampant over the fruit. Raspberry and cherry candy flavors hit you midpalate, and with a little more time in bottle this has every chance of turning out to be a much smoother and more polished wine than it is currently showing. 87 —*P.G. (12/31/2007)*

Zerba Cellars 2004 Merlot (Columbia Valley (WA)) $28. This is clean and juicy, with tart red berry flavors and light cinnamon toast. Supple and approachable, it's a good effort in a difficult year, when the estate vineyard was shut down by the freeze. 89 —*P.G. (3/1/2007)*

Zerba Cellars 2004 Wild Z Red Blend (Columbia Valley (WA)) $19. Previously called "Wild Thing" and now dubbed "Wild Z," this all-purpose red again features a grinning zebra on the label—an anagram for Zerba. The Columbia Valley blend of Cab, Merlot, Cab Franc, sangiovese and Grenache is a true mutt wine. Don't look for focus or terroir here, but you will find pleasant, mature, well-rounded fruit-driven flavor. 85 —*P.G. (3/1/2007)*

Zerba Cellars 2005 Syrah (Columbia Valley (WA)) $28. This is the third vintage for Zerba Syrah, and they have struck a consistent note, with spicy fruit suggesting fresh-picked strawberries, wrapped in slightly pickley barrel flavors. Supple and well-defined, it is a light wine that needs a little more time to smooth out the wood. 86 —*P.G. (12/31/2007)*

Zerba Cellars 2004 Syrah (Columbia Valley (WA)) $28. Following the excellent '03 Syrah, this young, tightly wound effort, from Yakima Valley (Minick Farms) fruit, frames its tangy strawberry preserve flavors in spicy American oak. Solid craftsmanship, nothing showy. It has a moderately concentrated black cherry midpalate and continues along a seamless path to a satisfying finish. 88 —*P.G. (3/1/2007)*

Zerba Cellars 2006 Viognier (Columbia Valley (WA)) $18. An interesting blend that incorporates 12% Sémillon with the Viognier. The Bordeaux grape adds weight and smoothes out the Viognier, which tends to be hot and sharp. What you end up with is a slightly buttery white blend that could go well with a variety of spicy dishes. 86 —*P.G. (12/31/2007)*

ZIG ZAG

Zig Zag 2004 Zinfandel (Mendocino County) $18. Not a great success. The wine is harsh in texture, with a raw, jagged mouthfeel, and the flavors are unbalanced. You get semisweet raisins one second, then green, unripe minty ones. It does have the benefit of dryness. 82 —*S.H. (3/1/2007)*

ZINA HYDE CUNNINGHAM

Zina Hyde Cunningham 2005 Pinot Noir (Anderson Valley) $40. A rich burst of red berry and red tree fruit flavors fills the mouth, enriched with toasty, spicy oak shadings. Likeable for its crisply balanced texture and long, smooth finish. Drink now through 2009. 87 —*S.H. (11/1/2007)*

Zina Hyde Cunningham 2005 Reserve Pinot Noir (Anderson Valley) $50. Made in a leaner, more elegant style that emphasizes restraint, the '05 Reserve has a mineral and rhubarb tartness, and is very dry. Could use a little more ripeness, but is very sleek and streamlined. Probably at its best now. 88 —*S.H. (11/1/2007)*

ZINGARO

Zingaro 2000 Zinfandel (Mendocino) $13. 84 —*S.H. (9/1/2003)*

Zingaro 1999 Reserve Zinfandel (Mendocino) $18. 87 —*S.H. (5/1/2002)*

ZUCCA

Zucca 2003 Tesoro Red Wine Red Blend (Sierra Foothills) $15. 83 —*S.H. (2/1/2005)*

Zucca 2002 Syrah (Calaveras County) $20. 82 —*S.H. (2/1/2005)*

Glossary

Acidity: A naturally occurring component of every wine; the level of perceived sharpness; a key element to a wine's longevity; a leading determinant of balance.

Ageworthy: Wines whose general characteristics make it likely that they will improve with age.

Alcohol: The end product of fermentation; technically ethyl alcohol resulting from the interaction of natural grape sugars and yeast; generally above 12.5 percent in dry table wines.

Alsace: A highly regarded wine region in eastern France renowned for dry and sweet wines made from Riesling, Gewürztraminer, Pinot Blanc, Pinot Gris, and others.

Amarone: A succulent higher-alcohol red wine hailing from the Veneto region in northern Italy; made primarily from Corvina grapes dried on racks before pressing.

AOC: *Appellation d'Origine Contrôlée*, a French term for a denominated, governed wine region, such as Margaux or Nuits-St.-Georges.

Aroma: A scent that's a component of the bouquet or nose; i.e. cherry is an aromatic component of a fruity bouquet.

AVA: American Viticultural Area; a denominated American wine region approved by the Bureau of Alcohol, Tobacco, and Firearms.

Bacchus: The Roman god of wine, known as Dionysus in ancient Greece; a hybrid white grape from Germany.

Balance: The level of harmony between acidity, tannins, fruit, oak, and other elements in a wine; a perceived quality that is more individual than scientific.

Barrel Fermented: A process by which wine (usually white) is fermented in oak barrels rather than in stainless steel tanks; a richer, creamier, oakier style of wine.

Barrique: French for "barrel," generally a barrel of 225 liters.

Beaujolais: A juicy, flavorful red wine made from Gamay grapes grown in the region of the same name.

Beaujolais Nouveau: The first Beaujolais wine of the harvest; its annual release date is the third Thursday in November.

Blanc de Blancs: The name for Champagne made entirely from Chardonnay grapes.

Blanc de Noirs: The name for Champagne made entirely from red grapes, either Pinot Noir or Pinot Meunier, or both.

Blend: The process whereby two or more grape varieties are combined after separate fermentation; common blends include Côtes de Rhône and red and white Bordeaux.

Blush: A wine made from red grapes but which appears pink or salmon in color because the grape skins were removed from the fermenting juice before more color could be imparted; more commonly referred to as Rosé.

Bodega: Spanish for winery; literally "room where barrels are stored."

Body: The impression of weight on one's palate; "light," "medium," and "full" are common body qualifiers.

Bordeaux: A city on the Garonne River in southwest France; a large wine-producing region with more than a dozen subregions; a red wine made mostly from Cabernet Sauvignon, Merlot, and Cabernet Franc; a white wine made from Sauvignon Blanc and Sémillon.

Botrytis Cinerea: (also Noble Rot) A beneficial mold that causes grapes to shrivel and sugars to concentrate, resulting in sweet, unctuous wines; common botrytis wines include Sauternes, Tokay, and German Beerenauslese.

Bouquet: The sum of a wine's aromas; how a wine smells as a whole; a key determinant of quality.

Breathe: The process of letting a wine open up via the introduction of air.

Brettanomyces: An undesirable yeast that reeks of sweaty saddle scents.

Brix: A scale used to measure the level of sugar in unfermented grapes. Multiplying brix by 0.55 will yield a wine's future alcohol level.

Brut: A French term used to describe the driest Champagnes.

Burgundy: A prominent French wine region stretching from Chablis in the north to Lyons in the south; Pinot Noir is the grape for red Burgundy, Chardonnay for white.

Cabernet Franc: A red grape common to Bordeaux; characteristics include an herbal, leafy flavor and a soft, fleshy texture.

Cabernet Sauvignon: A powerful, tannic red grape of noble heritage; the base grape for many red Bordeaux and most of the best red wines from California, Washington, Chile, and South Africa; capable of aging for decades.

Cap: Grape solids like pits, skins, and stems that rise to the top of a tank during fermentation; what gives red wines color, tannins, and weight.

Carbonic Maceration: A wine-making process in which whole grapes are sealed in a fermenter with carbon dioxide and left to ferment without yeast and grape crushing.

Cava: Spanish for "cellar," but also a Spanish sparkling wine made in the traditional Champagne style from Xarello, Macabeo, and Parellada grapes.

Chablis: A town and wine region east of Paris known for steely, minerally Chardonnay.

Champagne: A denominated region northeast of Paris in which Chardonnay, Pinot Noir, and Pinot Meunier grapes are made into sparkling wine.

Chaptalization: The process of adding sugar to fermenting grapes in order to increase alcohol.

Chardonnay: Arguably the best and most widely planted white wine grape in the world.

Château: French for "castle;" an estate with its own vineyards.

Chenin Blanc: A white grape common in the Loire Valley of France.

Chianti: A scenic, hilly section of Tuscany known for fruity red wines made mostly from Sangiovese grapes.

Claret: An English name for red Bordeaux.

Clos: Pronounced "Cloh," this French word once applied only to vineyards surrounded by walls.

Color: A key determinant of a wine's age and quality; white wines grow darker in color as they age while red wines turn brownish orange.

Cooperative: A winery owned jointly by multiple grape growers.

Corked: A wine with musty, mushroomy aromas and flavors resulting from a cork tainted by TCA (trichloroanisol).

Crianza: A Spanish term for a red wine that has been aged in oak barrels for at least one year.

Cru: A French term for ranking a wine's inherent quality, i.e. Cru Bourgeois, Cru Classé, Premier Cru, and Grand Cru.

Decant: The process of transferring wine from a bottle to another holding vessel. The purpose is generally to aerate a young wine or to separate an older wine from any sediment.

Denominación de Origen: Spanish for appellation of origin; like the French AOC or Italian DOC.

Denominazione di Origine Controllata: Italian for a controlled wine region; similar to the French AOC or Spanish DO.

Disgorge: The process by which final sediments are removed from traditionally made sparkling wines prior to the adding of the dosage.

Dosage: A sweetened spirit added at the very end to Champagne and other traditionally made sparkling wines. It determines whether a wine is brut, extra dry, dry, or semisweet.

Douro: A river in Portugal as well as the wine region famous for producing Port wines.

Dry: A wine containing no more than 0.2 percent unfermented sugar.

Earthy: A term used to describe aromas and flavors that have a certain soil-like quality.

Enology: The science of wine production; an enologist is a professional winemaker; an enophile is someone who enjoys wine.

Fermentation: The process by which sugar is transformed into alcohol; how grape juice interacts with yeast to become wine.

Filtration: The process by which wine is clarified before bottling.

Fining: Part of the clarification process whereby elements are added to the wine, i.e. egg whites, in order to capture solids prior to filtration.

Fortified Wine: A wine in which brandy is introduced during fermentation; sugars and sweetness are high due to the suspended fermentation.

Fumé Blanc: A name created by Robert Mondavi to describe dry Sauvignon Blanc.

Gamay: A red grape exceedingly popular in the Beaujolais region of France.

Gewürztraminer: A sweet and spicy white grape popular in eastern France, Germany, Austria, northern Italy, and California.

Graft: A vineyard technique in which the bud-producing part of a grapevine is attached to an existing root.

Gran Reserva: A Spanish term used for wines that are aged in wood and bottles for at least five years prior to release.

Grand Cru: French for "great growth;" the very best vineyards.

Green: A term used to describe underripe, vegetal flavors in a wine.

Grenache: A hearty, productive red grape popular in southern France as well as in Spain, where it is called Garnacha.

Grüner Veltliner: A white grape popular in Austria that makes lean, fruity, racy wines.

Haut: A French word meaning "high." It applies to quality as well as altitude.

Hectare: A metric measure equal to 10,000 square meters or 2.47 acres.

Hectoliter: A metric measure equal to 100 liters or 26.4 gallons.

Herbaceous: An aroma or flavor similar to green; often an indication of underripe grapes or fruit grown in a cool climate.

Hollow: A term used to describe a wine that doesn't have depth or body.

Hybrid: The genetic crossing of two or more grape types; common hybrids include Müller-Thurgau and Bacchus.

Ice Wine: From the German *eiswein,* this is a wine made from frozen grapes; Germany, Austria, and Canada are leading ice wine producers.

Jeroboam: An oversized bottle equal to six regular 750 ml bottles.

Kabinett: A German term for a wine of quality; usually the driest of Germany's best Rieslings.

Kosher: A wine made according to strict Jewish rules under rabbinical supervision.

Labrusca: Grape types native to North America, such as Concord and Catawba.

Late Harvest: A term used to describe dessert wines made from grapes left on the vines for an extra long period, often until botrytis has set in.

Lees: Heavy sediment left in the barrel by fermenting wines; a combination of spent yeast cells and grape solids.

Legs: A term used to describe how wine sticks to the inside of a wineglass after drinking or swirling.

Library Wines: Wines kept by the bottler as a reference of previous wines bottled.

Loire: A river in central France as well as a wine region famous for Chenin Blanc, Sauvignon Blanc, and Cabernet Franc.

Maceration: The process of allowing grape juice and skins to ferment together, thereby imparting color, tannins, and aromas.

Madeira: A fortified wine that has been made on a Portuguese island off the coast of Morocco since the fifteenth century.

Maderized: Stemming from the word Madeira, this term means oxidization in a hot environment.

Magnum: A bottle equal to two regular 750 ml bottles.

Malbec: A hearty red grape of French origin now exceedingly popular in Argentina.

Malolactic Fermentation: A secondary fermentation, often occurring in barrels, whereby harsher malic acid is converted into creamier lactic acid.

Médoc: A section of Bordeaux on the west bank of the Gironde Estuary known for great red wines; Margaux, St. Estèphe, and Pauillac are three leading AOCs in the Médoc.

Merlot: A lauded red grape popular in Bordeaux and throughout the world; large amounts of Merlot exist in Italy, the United States, South America, and elsewhere.

Must: Crushed grapes about to go or going through fermentation.

Nebbiolo: A red grape popular in the Piedmont region of northwest Italy; the grape that yields both Barolo and Barbaresco.

Négociant: A French term for a person or company that buys wines from others and then labels it under his or her own name; stems from the French word for "shipper."

Noble Rot: *see* Botrytis Cinerea.

Nose: Synonymous with "bouquet;" the sum of a wine's aromas.

Oaky: A term used to describe woody aromas and flavors; butter, popcorn, and toast notes are found in "oaky" wines.

Organic: Grapes grown without the aid of chemical-based fertilizers, pesticides, or herbicides.

Oxidized: A wine that is no longer fresh because it was exposed to too much air.

pH: An indication of a wine's acidity expressed by how much hydrogen is in it.

Phylloxera: A voracious vine louse that over time has destroyed vineyards in Europe and California.

Piedmont: An area in northwest Italy known for Barolo, Barbaresco, Barbera, Dolcetto, and Moscato.

Pinot Blanc: A white grape popular in Alsace, Germany, and elsewhere.

Pinot Gris: Also called Pinot Grigio, this is a grayish-purple grape that yields a white wine with a refreshing character.

Pinot Noir: The prime red grape of Burgundy, Champagne, and Oregon.

Pinotage: A hybrid between Pinot Noir and Cinsault that's grown almost exclusively in South Africa.

Plonk: A derogatory name for cheap, poor-tasting wine.

Pomace: The mass of skins, pits, and stems left over after fermentation; used to make grappa in Italy and marc in France.

Port: A sweet, fortified wine made in the Douro Valley of Portugal and aged in the coastal town of Vila Nova de Gaia; variations include Vintage, Tawny, Late Bottled Vintage, Ruby, White, and others.

Premier Cru: French for "first growth;" a high-quality vineyard but one not as good as Grand Cru.

Press: The process by which grape juice is extracted prior to fermentation; a machine that extracts juice from grapes.

Primeur (en): A French term for wine sold while it is still in the barrels; known as "futures" in English-speaking countries.

Pruning: The annual vineyard chore of trimming back plants from the previous harvest.

Racking: The process of moving wine from barrel to barrel, while leaving sediment behind.

Reserva: A Spanish term for a red wine that has spent at least three years in barrels and bottles before release.

Reserve: A largely American term indicating a wine of higher quality; it has no legal meaning.

Rhône: A river in southwest France surrounded by villages producing wines mostly from Syrah; the name of the wine-producing valley in France.

Riddling: The process of rotating Champagne bottles in order to shift sediment toward the cork.

Riesling: Along with Chardonnay, one of the top white grapes in the world; most popular in Germany, Alsace, and Austria.

Rioja: A well-known region in Spain known for traditional red wines made from the Tempranillo grape.

Rosé: French for "pink," used to describe a category of refreshing wines that are pink in color but are made from red grapes.

Sancerre: An area in the Loire Valley known mostly for wines made from Sauvignon Blanc.